PUBLIC LIBRARY CORE COLLECTION:

NONFICTION

SIXTEENTH EDITION

CORE COLLECTION SERIES

Formerly
STANDARD CATALOG SERIES

MARIA HUGGER, MLIS, GENERAL EDITOR

CHILDREN'S CORE COLLECTION
MIDDLE AND JUNIOR HIGH CORE COLLECTION
SENIOR HIGH CORE COLLECTION
FICTION CORE COLLECTION
GRAPHIC NOVELS CORE COLLECTION
YOUNG ADULT FICTION CORE COLLECTION

PUBLIC LIBRARY CORE COLLECTION: NONFICTION

**Collection Development Recommendations
by Librarians for Librarians**

SIXTEENTH EDITION

Former title:

Public Library Catalog

EDITED BY

Neal Wyatt, MSLS

Kendal Spires, MLIS

AND

Gabriela Toth, MLIS

H. W. Wilson
A Division of EBSCO Information Services
Ipswich, Massachusetts
2017
GREY HOUSE PUBLISHING

ISBN 978-1-68217-071-7
ebook ISBN: 978-0-8242-1462-3

Abridged Dewey Decimal Classification and Relative Index, Edition 15 is © 2004-2012 OCLC Online Computer Library Center, Inc. Used with Permission. DDC, Dewey, Dewey Decimal Classification, and WebDewey are registered trademarks of OCLC.

Public Library Core Collection, 2017, published by Grey House Publishing, Inc., Amenia, NY, under exclusive license from EBSCO Information Systems, Inc.

A catalog record for this title is available from the Library of Congress.

PRINTED IN CANADA

CONTENTS

Preface   vii

Acknowledgments   ix

Directions for Use   xi

Outline of Classification   xv

Part 1. Classified Collection   1

Part 2. Author, Title, and Subject Index   1933

CONTENTS

Preface ... vii

Acknowledgements ... ix

Directions for Use ... xi

Outline of Classification ... xv

Part 1. Classified Collection ... 1

Part 2. Author, Title, and Subject Index ... 1983

PREFACE

PUBLIC LIBRARY CORE COLLECTION: NONFICTION is a curated list of collection development recommendations created by librarians for librarians for any kind of library serving general adult populations. It is derived from the NONFICTION CORE COLLECTION database from EBSCOhost, updated weekly.

What's new in this edition?

The 16th edition of PUBLIC LIBRARY CORE COLLECTION: NONFICTION provides almost 12,000 reference and nonfiction titles. A star (★) at the start of an entry indicates that a book is a "most highly recommended" title. These titles constitute a shortlist of the essential books in a given category or on a given subject. There are often a number of recommended titles on a single subject and the star designation helps a user who wants only one or two. This edition includes 1,700 titles at the Most Highly Recommended level and over 10,000 at the Core Collection level.

Each new edition of PUBLIC LIBRARY CORE COLLECTION: NONFICTION is a mixture of the old and the new. Older titles, some in updated versions, are included if they remain the best titles in their field. Newer titles reflect new topics of interest and new interpretations of traditional knowledge. This edition features general revisions to most subject areas, significant additions in STEM and graphic novel titles, and weeding in the 600s and 700s.

History

The first of several installments of the "Standard Catalog" for the general library was published in 1918. It was called STANDARD CATALOG: SOCIOLOGY SECTION. Additional installments were issued over the next fourteen years, covering Biography; Fiction; Fine Arts; History and Travel; Science and Useful Arts; Literature and Philology; and Philosophy, Religion and General Works. Finally, a fully integrated first edition of the STANDARD CATALOG FOR PUBLIC LIBRARIES was assembled and published in 1934. The contents were displayed in classified order, according to the Dewey Decimal Classification. The name was changed to PUBLIC LIBRARY CATALOG with the publication of the fifth edition in 1969 and then to PUBLIC LIBRARY CORE COLLECTION: NONFICTION with the thirteenth edition in 2008. The collection subsequently evolved, along with the other Core Collections, into an online resource called WilsonWeb. EBSCO Information Services acquired H.W. Wilson in July 2011, and the collections became EBSCOhost databases in January 2012. Despite many changes over the last 100 years, the 16th edition of PUBLIC LIBRARY CORE COLLECTION: NONFICTION remains a premier collection development tool for adult nonfiction recommendations.

Although a Fiction Section was issued in 1923, followed by supplements in 1928 and 1931, fiction was omitted from the first edition of the complete Catalog in 1934. A new expanded edition of the Fiction Section was published as FICTION CATALOG in 1942. In its preface that Catalog was referred to as "a companion volume to the Standard Catalog for Public Libraries." This complementary relationship has continued to the present. PUBLIC LIBRARY CORE COLLECTION: NONFICTION has always listed works of literary criticism and literary history and books about literary technique.

Scope and Purpose

This volume lists nonfiction books published in the United States or published in other countries and distributed in the United States. It excludes non-print materials, periodicals, non-English items (with the exception of dictionaries), and works of an ephemeral nature. All books were in print at the time of listing. Original paperback editions are included. Entries for hardcover editions provide information about the availability of paperback reprints where possible. This volume comprises over 12,000 book titles with multiple subject access.

The Core Collection is intended to serve the needs of public and undergraduate libraries and stand as a basic or "opening day" collection. The newer titles help in identifying areas in a collection that can be updated or strengthened. Retention of useful material from the previous edition enables the librarian to make informed decisions about weeding a collection. With its classified arrangement, complete bibliographical data, and descriptive and critical annotations, the Core Collection provides useful information for the acquisitions librarian, the reference librarian, and the cataloger. Entries provide information about the availability of electronic versions of books listed.

The Database

In 2017 EBSCO renamed PUBLIC LIBRARY CORE COLLECTION: NONFICTION with the broader term NONFICTION CORE COLLECTION, which brings it in line with the other database names, makes it less cumbersome, and signifies suitability for a variety of library types. Although the title of this edition is different from the database from which it is excerpted, this volume is a derivation—the top two recommendation levels—of the NONFICTION CORE COLLECTION from EBSCOhost, not a separate and distinct set of book recommendations. For more information or for a free trial, contact your EBSCO sales rep or visit https://www.ebscohost.com/public/core-collections

Preparation

Books included in this edition were selected by experienced librarians representing public library systems and academic libraries across the United States who also act as a committee of advisors on library policy and trends. The names of participating librarians and their affiliations are listed in the Acknowledgments. EBSCO invites feedback from Core Collections customers at corecollections@ebsco.com.

Organization

The Core Collection is organized into two parts: the Classified Collection and an Author, Title, and Subject Index.

Part 1. Classified Collection. This is arranged according to the Dewey Decimal Classification. Within classes, arrangement is by main entry, with complete bibliographical and cataloging information given for each book. The classified arrangement, along with the descriptive and critical annotations, provides a useful guide to book selection. Entries include such information as price and ISBN to facilitate acquisitions.

Part 2. Author, Title, and Subject Index. This is a comprehensive key to the Classified List with entries for authors, titles, and subjects.

ACKNOWLEDGMENTS

H. W. Wilson and EBSCO Information Services express special gratitude to the following librarians who both advised the company in editorial matters and assisted in the selection of titles for this Core Collection:

Advisory Board

James E. Bobick
Author and Consultant
Pittsburgh, Pennsylvania

Gail de Vos
University of Alberta
Edmonton, Alberta, Canada

Brian Flota
Humanities Librarian
James Madison University
Harrisonburg, Virginia

Leigh Anne Focareta
Adult Nonfiction Selector
Carnegie Library of Pittsburgh
Pittsburgh, Pennsylvania

Mary Griffin
Omaha Public Library
Omaha, Nebraska

Steven Jablonski
Skokie Public Library
Skokie, Illinois

John J. Meier
Science Librarian
Penn State University
University Park, Pennsylvania

Liza Oldham
Instructional Librarian
Phillips Academy, Oliver
Wendell Holmes Library
Andover, Massachusetts

Mary Rasner
Library Consultant
Melrose, Massachusetts

Rebecca Vargha
Head, School of Information
and Library Science Library
University of North Carolina
Chapel Hill, North Carolina

DIRECTIONS FOR USE OF THE CORE COLLECTION

USES OF THE COLLECTION

PUBLIC LIBRARY CORE COLLECTION: NONFICTION is designed to serve a number of purposes:

As an aid in purchasing. The Core Collection is designed to assist in the selection and ordering of titles. Annotations are provided for each title along with information concerning the publisher, ISBN, price, and availability. Since Part 1, Classified Collection, is arranged according to the Dewey Decimal Classification, the Core Collection may be used to identify parts of the library collection that should be updated or strengthened. In evaluating the suitability of a work each library will want to consider the special character of the community it serves.

As an aid to the reader's advisor. The work of the reader's advisor is furthered by the information about sequels and companion volumes and the descriptive and critical annotations in the Classified Collection, and by the subject access in the Index.

As an aid in verification of information. For this purpose full bibliographical data are provided in the Classified Collection. Entries also include recommended subject headings based on *Sears List of Subject Headings* and a suggested classification derived from the *Abridged Dewey Decimal Classification and Relative Index*. Notes describe editions available, awards, publication history, and other titles in the series.

As an aid in collection maintenance. Information about titles available on a subject facilitates decisions to rebind, replace, or discard items. If a book has been deleted from the Core Collection in this edition because it is no longer in print, that deletion is not intended as a sign that the book is no longer valuable or that it should necessarily be weeded from the collection.

As an instructional aid. The Core Collection is useful in courses that deal with literature and book selection for public libraries.

ORGANIZATION

The Core Collection consists of two parts: a Classified Collection, and an Author, Title, and Subject Index.

Part 1. Classified Collection

The Classified Collection is arranged with nonfiction books first, classified according to the Dewey Decimal Classification in numerical order from 000 to 999. Individual biographies are classed at 92 and precede the 920s (collective biography). The information supplied for each book includes bibliographic description, suggested subject headings, an annotation, and frequently, an evaluation from a notable source.

An Outline of Classification, which serves as a table of contents for the Classified Collection, is reproduced following this section. It should be noted that many topics can be classified in more than one discipline. If a particular title is not found where it might be expected, the Index should be consulted to determine if it is classified elsewhere.

Within classes, works are arranged alphabetically under main entry, usually the author. Works of individual biography are arranged alphabetically under the biography's subject.

Each listing consists of a full bibliographical description. Prices, which are always subject to change, have been obtained from the publisher, when available, and are as current as possible. Entries include recommended subject headings derived from the *Sears List of Subject Headings*, a suggested classification number from the *Abridged Dewey Decimal Classification and Relative Index*, a brief description of the contents, and, whenever possible, an evaluation from a quoted source. The following is an example of a typical entry and a description of its components:

Roach, Mary, 1959-
★ **Stiff**; the curious lives of human cadavers.
Norton 2003 303 p il $23.95; pa $13.95   **611**
1. Dead 2. Dissection 3. Human experimentation in medicine
ISBN 0-393-05093-9; 0-393-32482-6 pa
                    LC 2002-152908
The author "explains how surgeons and doctors use cadavers donated for research purposes to help the living, and also examines potential new variations on how we bury the dead." Libr J
"For those who are interested in the fields of medicine or forensics and are aware of some of the procedures, this book makes excellent reading." SLJ
Includes bibliographical references

The star at the beginning of the entry indicates that this is a "most highly recommended" title. The name of the author, Mary Roach, is given in conformity with *Anglo-American Cataloguing Rules*, 2nd edition, 2002 revision. The title of the book is *Stiff: the curious lives of human cadavers*. The book was published by Norton in 2003.

The book has 303 pages and contains illustrations. It is published in hardcover and paperback, and sells for $23.95 and $13.95, respectively. (Prices given were current when the Collection went to press.)

At the end of the last line of type in the body entry is 611 in boldface type. This is the classification number or category derived from the fifteenth edition of the *Abridged Dewey Decimal Classification*.

The numbered terms "1. Dead 2. Dissection 3. Human experimentation in medicine" are recommended subject headings for this book based on *Sears List of Subject Headings*.

The ISBN (International Standard Book Number) is included to facilitate ordering. The Library of Congress control number is provided when available.

Following are three notes supplying additional information about the book. The first is a description of the book's content, in this case, an excerpt from *Library Journal*. The second is a critical note from *School Library Journal*. Such annotations are useful in evaluating books for selection and in determining which of several books on the same subject is best suited for the individual reader. The final note describes special features, such as a bibliography, if applicable. Notes are also made to describe sequels and companion volumes, editions available, awards, and publication history.

Part 2. Author, Title, and Subject Index

The Index is a single alphabetical list of all the books entered in the Core Collection. Each book is entered under author; title (if distinctive); and subject. The classification number, displayed in boldface type, is the key to the location of the main entry for the book in the Classified Collection.

Appropriate added entries are made for joint authors and editors. "See" references are made from forms of names or subjects that are not used as headings. "See also" references are made to related or more specific headings.

The following are examples of Index entries for the book cited above:

Author	**Roach, Mary, 1959-**	
	Stiff	**611**
Title	**Stiff.** Roach, M.	**611**
Subject	**DEAD**	
	Roach, M. Stiff.	**611**

Standards Used

Anglo-American Cataloguing Rules, 2nd ed., 2002 revision, 2005 update. Chicago: American Library Association, 2005.

Bristow, Barbara A. and Christi Showman Farrar, eds. *Sears List of Subject Headings.* 21st ed. Ipswich, MA: The H. W. Wilson Company, 2014.

Dewey, Melvil. *Abridged Dewey Decimal Classification and Relative Index*. 15th ed. Edited by Joan S. Mitchell, et al. Dublin, Ohio: OCLC, 2012.

OUTLINE OF CLASSIFICATION

Reproduced below is the Second Summary of the Dewey Decimal Classification. * As Part 1 of this Core Collection is arranged according to this classification, the outline will serve as a table of contents for it. Please note, however, that the inclusion of this outline is not to be considered a substitute for consulting the Dewey Decimal Classification itself.

000 Computer science, knowledge & systems
010   Bibliographies
020   Library & information sciences
030   Encyclopedias & books of facts
040   [Unassigned]
050   Magazines, journals & serials
060   Associations, organizations & museums
070   News media, journalism & publishing
080   Quotations
090   Manuscripts & rare books

100 Philosophy
110   Metaphysics
120   Epistemology
130   Parapsychology & occultism
140   Philosophical schools of thought
150   Psychology
160   Logic
170   Ethics
180   Ancient, medieval & eastern philosophy
190   Modern western philosophy

200 Religion
210   Philosophy & theory of religion
220   The Bible
230   Christianity & Christian theology
240   Christian practice & observance
250   Christian pastoral practice & religious orders
260   Christian organization, social work & worship
270   History of Christianity
280   Christian denominations
290   Other religions

300 Social sciences, sociology & anthropology
310   Statistics
320   Political science
330   Economics
340   Law
350   Public administration & military science
360   Social problems & social services
370   Education
380   Commerce, communications & transportation
390   Customs, etiquette & folklore

400 Language
410   Linguistics
420   English & Old English languages
430   German & related languages
440   French & related languages
450   Italian, Romanian & related languages
460   Spanish & Portuguese languages
470   Latin & Italic languages
480   Classical & modern Greek languages
490   Other languages

500 Science
510   Mathematics
520   Astronomy
530   Physics
540   Chemistry
550   Earth sciences & geology
560   Fossils & prehistoric life
570   Life sciences; biology
580   Plants (Botany)
590   Animals (Zoology)

600 Technology
610   Medicine & health
620   Engineering
630   Agriculture
640   Home & family management
650   Management & public relations
660   Chemical engineering
670   Manufacturing
680   Manufacture for specific uses
690   Building & construction

700 Arts
710   Landscaping & area planning
720   Architecture
730   Sculpture, ceramics & metalwork
740   Drawing & decorative arts
750   Painting
760   Graphic arts
770   Photography & computer art
780   Music
790   Sports, games & entertainment

800 Literature, rhetoric & criticism
810   American literature in English
820   English & Old English literatures
830   German & related literatures
840   French & related literatures
850   Italian, Romanian & related literatures
860   Spanish & Portuguese literatures
870   Latin & Italian literatures
880   Classical & modern Greek literatures
890   Other literatures

900 History
910   Geography & travel
920   Biography & genealogy
930   History of ancient world (to ca. 499)
940   History of Europe
950   History of Asia
960   History of Africa
        History of North America
980   History of South America
990   History of other areas

* Reproduced from Edition 15 of the Abridged Dewey Decimal Classification and Relative Index, published in 2012, by permission of OCLC Online Computer Library Center, Inc., owner of copyright.

PUBLIC LIBRARY CORE COLLECTION: NONFICTION
SIXTEENTH EDITION
CLASSIFIED COLLECTION

000 COMPUTER SCIENCE, KNOWLEDGE & SYSTEMS

001.1 Intellectual life

Levine, Lawrence W.

The **opening** of the American mind; canons, culture, and history. Beacon Press 1996 xxiv, 212p hardcover o.p. pa $18 **001.1**

1. Higher education 2. Multiculturalism 3. United States -- Intellectual life

ISBN 0-8070-3119-4 pa

LC 96-33866

"Levine's presentation is eloquent, eminently reasonable, and gratifyingly optimistic." Booklist

Includes bibliographical references

001.2 Scholarship and learning

Lima, Manuel

The **book** of trees; visualizing branches of knowledge. Manuel Lima. Princeton Architectural Press 2014 208 p. illustrations (chiefly color) (alkaline paper) $29.95 **001.2**

1. Charts, diagrams, etc. 2. Statistics -- Graphic methods 3. Graphic methods -- History 4. Knowledge, Theory of -- History 5. Visual communication -- History 6. Learning and scholarship -- History 7. Trees -- Symbolic aspects -- History 8. Communication in learning and scholarship -- History

ISBN 1616892188; 9781616892180

LC 2013026128

In this book, "Manuel Lima examines the . . . history of the tree diagram, from its roots in the illuminated manuscripts of medieval monasteries to its current resurgence as an elegant means of visualization. Lima presents two hundred intricately detailed tree diagram illustrations on a remarkable variety of subjects--from some of the earliest known examples from ancient Mesopotamia to the manuscripts of medieval monasteries to contributions by leading contemporary designers." (Publisher's note)

"Sure to appeal to a diverse group of readers, the book beautifully combines art and science, as well as ancient and contemporary worldviews." Pub Wkly

Includes bibliographical references and index

001.4 Research; statistical methods

Feldman, Burton

The **Nobel** Prize; a history of genius, controversy, and prestige. Arcade Pub. 2000 489p il $29.95; pa $15.95 **001.4**

1. Nobel Prizes

ISBN 1-55970-537-X; 1-55970-592-2 pa

LC 00-42002

The author provides a "history of the prizes awarded in the sciences, literature, social sciences, and humankind's . . . peace efforts. This is the first comprehensive critical history of the prizes to appear, and it's very good." Libr J

Includes bibliographical references

MacLeod, Don

How to find out anything; from extreme Google searches to scouring government documents, a guide to uncovering anything about everyone and everything. Don MacLeod. 1st ed. Prentice Hall Press 2012 x, 256 p.p (pbk.) $20 **001.4**

1. Research 2. Internet searching 3. Information resources 4. Research -- Methodology 5. Electronic information resources 6. Electronic information resource searching

ISBN 0735204675; 9780735204676

LC 2012010974

In this book, "researcher Don MacLeod explains how to find what you're looking for quickly, efficiently, and accurately--and how to avoid the most common mistakes of the Google Age. . . . [The author] shows you how to unveil nearly anything about anyone. From top CEO's salaries to police records, . . . researching for a term paper or digging up dirt on an ex, the advice in this book arms you with the sleuthing skills to tackle any mystery." (Publisher's note)

Tufte, Edward R., 1942-

The **visual** display of quantitative information; 2nd ed; Graphics Press 2001 197p il $40 **001.4**

1. Statistics -- Graphic methods

ISBN 0-9613921-4-2

LC 2001-271866

First published 1983

This book focuses "on statistical graphics, charts, tables. Theory and practice in the design of data graphics, 250 illustrations of the best (and a few of the worst) statistical graphics, with . . . analysis of how to display data for precise, effective, quick analysis." Publisher's note

001.9   Controversial knowledge

Bullard, Thomas E.

The **myth** and mystery of UFOs. University Press of Kansas 2010 417p il $35   **001.9**
1. Unidentified flying objects
ISBN 978-0-7006-1729-6; 0-7006-1729-9

LC 2010-26289

"Bullard is well known in the UFO community because he leaves the door open that there may be some basis in reality behind UFO stories while also contending that the UFO field is fertile ground for rumor and legend. His bibliography is impressive, and the book is a full account of UFO sightings and the development of 'Ufology.' He concludes that there is enough evidence to suggest that UFOs deserve a place in academic inquiry, with more scientific research needed. . . . Those interested in the UFO phenomenon will find tons of interesting material to ponder and a different way of looking at it." Libr J

Includes bibliographical references

Shermer, Michael

Why people believe weird things; pseudoscience, superstition, and other confusions of our time. foreword by Stephen Jay Gould. rev and expanded; Freeman, W.H. 2002 xxvi, 349p il pa $16   **001.9**
1. Science 2. Parapsychology 3. Belief and doubt
ISBN 0-8050-7089-3

LC 2002-68784

First published 1997

The author "explores the very human reasons people find otherworldly phenomena, conspiracy theories, and cults so appealing. In . . . [the] chapter, 'Why Smart People Believe in Weird Things' he takes on science luminaries like physicist Frank Tippler and others, who hide their spiritual beliefs behind the trappings of science." Publisher's note

Includes bibliographical references

001.94   Mysteries

Krulos, Tea

Monster hunters; on the trail with ghost hunters, bigfooters, ufologists, and other paranormal investigators. by Tea Krulos. Chicago Review Press, Inc. 2015 320 p. illustrations (some color) (paperback) $16.95   **001.94**
1. Monsters 2. Supernatural -- Miscellanea 3. Parapsychology -- Miscellanea
ISBN 1613749813; 9781613749814

LC 2015002299

In this book, journalist Tea Krulos "spent over a year traveling nationwide to meet individuals who have made it their life's passion to hunt down evidence of entities that they believe exist, but that others might shrug off as nothing more than myths, fairytales, or overactive imaginations." (Publisher's note)

"This work is bound to be fascinating to those already interested in these fields and even to readers who are seeking an easy way to learn about people who work in these specialized areas. Recommended for public libraries." LJ

Includes bibliographical references and index

001.942   Unidentified flying objects (UFOs)

Mezrich, Ben

The **37th** parallel; The Secret Truth Behind America's UFO Highway. Ben Mezrich. Atria Books 2016 272 p. illustrations, maps (ebook) $19.99; (hardback) $26   **001.942**
1. Conspiracies 2. Parapsychology 3. Unidentified flying objects 4. Parapsychology -- Southwestern States 5. Unidentified flying objects -- Southwestern States
ISBN 9781501135545; 9781501135521

LC 2016021639

This book, by Ben Mezrich, "tells the true story of a computer programmer who tracks paranormal events along a 3,000-mile stretch through the heart of America and is drawn deeper and deeper into a vast conspiracy. . . . So begins an extraordinary and fascinating journey from El Paso and Rush, Colorado, to a mysterious space studies company and MUFON, from Roswell and Area 51 to the Pentagon and beyond." (Publisher's note)

"Mezrich probably won't sway the skeptical, but fans of Art Bell and company will find all the affirmation they need." Kirkus

001.944   Monsters and related phenomena

Kaplan, Matt

Medusa's gaze and vampire's bite; the science of monsters. Matt Kaplan. Scribner 2012 244 p. (hardcover : alk. paper) $26   **001.944**
1. Zombies 2. Monsters 3. Vampires 4. Anthropology 5. Cyclopes (Greek mythology) 6. Monsters -- History 7. Animals, Mythical -- History 8. Dangerous animals -- Folklore -- History
ISBN 1451667981; 9781451667981; 9781451667998; 9781451668001

LC 2012016553

In this book, journalist "[Matt] Kaplan sheds light on why people fear monsters, from the Calydonian Boar depicted on ancient Greek friezes to the creatures of films like Alien and Jurassic Park. He uses science and anthropology to make educated guesses about how figures like cyclopes, zombies, vampires, and dragons worked their way into humanity's collective imagination." (Library Journal)

Prothero, Donald R., 1954-

Abominable science! origins of the Yeti, Nessie, and other famous cryptids. Daniel Loxton and Donald R. Prothero. Columbia University Press 2013 432 p. (cloth : alk. paper) $29.95   **001.944**
1. Cryptozoology 2. Pseudoscience 3. Mythical animals 4. Animals, Mythical
ISBN 0231153201; 9780231153201

LC 2013008424

In this book, "after examining the nature of science and pseudoscience and their relation to cryptozoology, [Daniel] Loxton and [Donald R.] Prothero take on Bigfoot; the Yeti . . .; the Loch Ness monster . . . [and] the Congo dinosaur. They conclude with an analysis of the psychology behind the persistent belief in paranormal phenomena . . . and consider . .

. the challenge it poses to clear and critical thinking in our increasingly complex world." (Publisher's note)

Includes bibliographical references and index

002 The book

Basbanes, Nicholas A.

Patience & fortitude; a roving chronicle of book people, book places, and book culture. HarperCollins Pubs. 2001 636p il hardcover o.p. pa $19.95 **002**

1. Libraries 2. Book collecting 3. Books and reading

ISBN 0-06-019695-5; 0-06-051446-9 pa

LC 2001-16935

"Basbanes's fund of stories will delight readers who value books for more than just a good story, have a yen for second-hand books plucked from dusty shops or look to book catalogs for suspense and excitement." Publ Wkly

Includes bibliographical references

Buzbee, Lewis

The **yellow**-lighted bookshop; a memoir, a history. Graywolf Press 2006 216p $17 **002**

1. Booksellers and bookselling

ISBN 1-55597-450-3

LC 2005-938151

This "is a tribute to those who crave the cozy confines of a bookshop." Booklist

Darnton, Robert

The **case** for books; past, present, and future. PublicAffairs 2009 218p il $23.95 **002**

1. Books and reading -- History

ISBN 978-1-58648-826-0

"These essays bring balance and a refreshing perspective to the nervous predictions over the future of print." Libr J

Includes bibliographical references

002.07 Education, research, related topics

Lansky, Aaron

Outwitting history; the amazing adventures of a man who rescued a million Yiddish books. Algonquin Books of Chapel Hill 2004 316p **002.07**

1. Book collecting 2. Yiddish language 3. National Yiddish Book Center

ISBN 1-56512-429-4

LC 2004-51587

"The book is a testimony to [Lansky's] love of Judaism and literature and his desire to make a difference in the world." Publ Wkly

Includes bibliographical references

002.075 Book collecting

Occhipinti, Lisa

Novel living; collecting, decorating, and crafting with books. Lisa Occhipinti. STC Craft/A Melanie

Falick Book 2014 143 p. illustrations (some color) $24.95 **002.075**

1. Books 2. Interior design

ISBN 1617690872; 9781617690877

LC 2014930834

In this book, "artist Lisa Occhipinti celebrates her love for physical books by presenting us with her unique ideas for collecting and displaying them, for conserving and preserving them, and for crafting with them. Guided by Occhipinti's artful eye, you'll be inspired to build and display collections based on your personal passions and to use books for crafting, either by deconstructing or by copying favorite elements." (Publisher's note)

"An elegant layout and excellent instructions pay appropriate homage to many of our best friends." Booklist

002.09 The book—History, geographic treatment, biography

Houston, Keith

The **Book**; A Cover-to-Cover Exploration of the Most Powerful Object of Our Time. by Keith Houston. W W Norton & Co Inc 2016 448 p. illustrations (some color) $29.95 **002.09**

1. Books and reading -- History

ISBN 0393244792; 9780393244793

In this book, author "Keith Houston reveals that the paper, ink, thread, glue, and board from which a book is made tell as rich a story as the words on its pages—of civilizations, empires, human ingenuity, and madness. In an invitingly tactile history of this 2,000-year-old medium, Houston follows the development of writing, printing, the art of illustrations, and binding to show how we have moved from cuneiform tablets and papyrus scrolls to the hardcovers and paperbacks of today." (Publisher's note)

"Pulling together aspects of archaeology, history, literature, and biography, the author reveals the facts, conjecture, and educated guesses experts have made about how and when the first modern tome came to be, which is surprisingly difficult to pin down." LJ

Includes bibliographical references (pages 339-401) and index.

003 Systems

Domingos, Pedro

The **master** algorithm; how the quest for the ultimate learning machine will remake our world. Pedro Domingos. Basic Books, a member of the Perseus Books Group 2015 352 p. illustrations (hardcover) $29.99 **003**

1. Algorithms 2. Mathematics 3. Artificial intelligence 4. Cognitive science -- Mathematics 5. Artificial intelligence -- Philosophy 6. Artificial intelligence -- Social aspects 7. Knowledge representation (Information theory)

ISBN 0465065708; 9780465065707

LC 2015007615

In this book, author Pedro Domingos "lifts the veil for the first time to give us a peek inside the learning machines that power Google, Amazon, and your smartphone. He charts a course through machine learnings five major schools of thought, showing how they turn ideas from neuroscience, evolution, psychology, physics, and statistics into algorithms ready to serve you. Step by step, he assembles a blueprint for the future universal learner the Master Algorithm." (Publisher's note)

"Skeptics may dismiss Domingos' vision as hopelessly utopian, and libertarians may brand it as dangerously intrusive. But no one will find it boring. An exhilarating venture into groundbreaking computer science." Booklist

Taleb, Nassim Nicholas

The **black** swan; the impact of the highly improbable. [by] Nassim Nicholas Taleb. 2nd ed; Random House Trade Paperbacks 2010 xxxiii, 444p il pa $17 **003**

1. Forecasting
ISBN 0-8129-7381-X; 978-0-8129-7381-5
LC 2010-292618

First published 2007

Examines the role of the unexpected, discussing why improbable events are not anticipated or understood properly, and how humans rationalize the black swan phenomenon to make it appear less random.

The author "is really a philosopher in a businessman's clothing and his irreverent writing style, with its frequent first-person asides and tangential musings that go on for pages, actually helps make heavy intellectual discussions more accessible." Risk Management

Includes bibliographical references

004 Computer science; computer programming, programs, data; special computer methods

Dyson, George

Turing's cathedral; the origins of the digital universe. George Dyson. Pantheon Books 2012 xxii, 401 p.p (hardback) $29.95 **004**

1. Symbolic logic 2. Computers -- History 3. Mathematics -- History 4. Computer science -- History 5. Turing, Alan Mathison, 1912-1954 6. Turing machines 7. Computable functions 8. Random access memory
ISBN 9780375422775
LC 2011030265

In this book, "science historian George Dyson shines light on the critical period when computers came into being. He begins with British mathematician Alan Turing's . . . 1936 description of a machine designed to resolve a problem in mathematical logic. . . . Dyson focuses on US efforts, when . . . a group of engineers, scientists and mathematicians, gathered together by Hungarian-American polymath John von Neumann . . . bent their minds to the making of the IAS machine." (New Scientist)

Includes bibliographical references and index

Isaacson, Walter

★ The **innovators**; how a group of inventors, hackers, geniuses, and geeks created the digital revolution. Walter Isaacson. Simon & Schuster 2014 560 p. illustrations (hardback) $35 **004**

1. Computer scientists 2. Internet -- History 3. Computers -- History 4. Computer science -- History
ISBN 147670869X; 9781476708690; 9781476708706
LC 2014021391

Los Angeles Times Book Prize Finalist: History (2014)

This book, by Walter Isaacson, is the "story of the people who created the computer and the Internet. . . . [He] begins with Ada Lovelace, Lord Byron's daughter, who pioneered computer programming in the 1840s. He explores the fascinating personalities that created our current digital revolution, such as Vannevar Bush, Alan Turing, John von Neumann, J.C.R. Licklider, Doug Engelbart, Robert Noyce, Bill Gates, Steve Wozniak, Steve Jobs, Tim Berners-Lee, and Larry Page." (Publisher's note)

"Although full biographies of the individuals profiled here have been written in spades, Isaacson manages to bring together the entire universe of computing, from the first digitized loom to the web, presented in a very accessible manner that often reads like a thriller." Booklist

Markoff, John

What the dormouse said-- how the sixties counterculture shaped the personal computer industry. Viking Penguin 2005 xxiii, 310p il $25.95; pa $16 **004**

1. Counter culture 2. Computers and civilization 3. Computers -- History
ISBN 0-670-03382-0; 0-14-303676-9 pa
LC 2004-61181

"This book is a rare treat and a must-read for everyone who has had the pleasure of using the mysterious friend called the PC." Choice

Includes bibliographical references

Pogue, David

Pogue's basics; essential tips and shortcuts (that no one bothers to tell you) for simplifying the technology in your life. David Pogue. Flatiron Books 2014 368 p. illustrations (some color) (paperback) $19.99 **004**

1. Internet -- Miscellanea 2. Electronic apparatus and appliances -- Miscellanea 3. Technology -- Miscellanea 4. Computer science -- Miscellanea 5. Online social networks -- Miscellanea
ISBN 125005348X; 9781250053480
LC 2014032515

This book, by David Pogue, presents tips for working with technology. "When it comes to technology, . . . somehow, you're just supposed to know how to use your phone, tablet, computer, camera, Web browser, e-mail, and social networks. . . . Tech expert David Pogue comes to the rescue with . . . a book that . . . collects every essential technique for making your gadgets seem easier, faster, and less of a hassle." (Publisher's note)

Vamosi, Robert

When gadgets betray us; the dark side of our infatuation with new technologies. Basic Books 2011 222p **004**

1. Computer crimes 2. Computer security 3. Electronic apparatus and appliances 4. Software failures 5. Computers -- Health aspects 6. Computers -- Social aspects

ISBN 978-0-465-01958-8

LC 2010-43829

"The book is about hardware hacking and new kinds of identity fraud." (Publisher's note) Index.

"Read this, and you'll never again ignore the default security settings on accounts or your devices again. Gadget geeks and lay readers would benefit from Vamosi's information." Libr J

Includes bibliographical references

White, Ron, 1944-

How Computers Work; the evolution of technology. by Ron White; illustrated by Tim Downs. 10th ed Que 2014 432 p. color illustrations pbk $39.99 **004**

1. Personal computers

ISBN 9780789749840; 078974984X

First published 1993 by Ziff-Davis Press. Frequently revised

An "illustrated guide to the world of PCs and technology. In this . . . edition, you'll find detailed information not just about every last component of hardware found inside your PC, but also . . . . explanations about home networking, the Internet, PC security, and even how cell phone networks operate." (Publisher's note)

004.1 General works on specific types of computers

Johnson, George

A shortcut through time; the path to a quantum computer. Knopf 2003 204p il hardcover o.p. pa $13 **004.1**

1. Computers 2. Quantum theory

ISBN 0-375-41193-3; 0-375-72618-7 pa

LC 2002-73013

"Johnson has presented the fascinating science of quantum computing and its future development in a down-to-earth style." Libr J

Includes bibliographical references

004.16 Personal computers

Mueller, Scott M.

Upgrading and repairing PCs; Scott M. Mueller. 22nd edition Que 2015 1162 p. illustrations hbk $59.99 **004.16**

1. Personal computers

ISBN 9780789756107; 0789756102

"Scott Mueller delivers practical answers about PC processors, mother-boards, buses, BIOSes, memory, SSD and HDD storage, video, audio, networks, Internet connectivity, power, and much more. You'll find the industry's best coverage of diagnostics, testing, and repair--plus cutting-edge discussions of improving PC performance via overclocking and other techniques." (Publisher's note)

004.67 Wide-area networks

Arora, Pankaj

To the cloud; cloud powering an enterprise. Pankaj Arora, Raj Biyani, Salil Dave. McGraw Hill 2012 xx, 119 p.p ill. $30 **004.67**

1. Cloud computing 2. Business planning 3. Web services 4. Information technology -- Management 5. Business enterprises -- Data processing

ISBN 007179221X; 9780071792219

LC 2011277377

This book looks at cloud computing. This guide "lays out a four-step framework, leveraging the experience and best practices of Microsoft's own IT group. The book delivers end-to-end business and technology guidance, describing how to analyze application portfolios to identify good cloud candidates, choose the right cloud models, consider architecture and security, and understand how shifting operations to the cloud affects budgeting and staffing." (Publisher's note)

Includes bibliographical references and index

Boyd, Danah

It's complicated; the social lives of networked teens. Danah Boyd. Yale University Press 2014 296 p. (clothbound : alk. paper) $25 **004.67**

1. Teenagers 2. Internet and teenagers 3. Online social networks 4. Information technology -- Social aspects 5. Teenagers -- Social life and customs -- 21st century

ISBN 0300166311; 9780300166316

LC 2013031950

Author Danah Boyd "uncovers some of the major myths regarding teens' use of social media. She explores tropes about identity, privacy, safety, danger, and bullying. Ultimately, Boyd argues that society fails young people when paternalism and protectionism hinder teenagers' ability to become informed, thoughtful, and engaged citizens through their online interactions. Yet despite an environment of rampant fear-mongering, Boyd finds that teens often find ways to engage and to develop a sense of identity." (Publisher's note)

"This groundbreaking survey of the online social habits and realities of American teens, based on extensive fieldwork, also serves as an important corrective to numerous persistent, widely held notions about young people, public life, and the Internet...Boyd discusses bullying, media literacy, and social inequality; debunks the pervasiveness of online predation; addresses problematic assumptions behind the term digital native; defends Wikipedia as a great educational tool that makes transparent the evolution of knowledge; and astutely points out that the technology may be new, but teens, as always, simply want to socialize, be known, spend time with friends, and participate in public life... Exciting, challenging, and liberating; this title is essential reading for adults with any interest in or control over teens." (Library Journal)

Includes bibliographical references and index

Dunckley, Victoria L.

Reset your child's brain; a four-week plan to end meltdowns, raise grades, and boost social skills by reversing the effects of electronic screen-time. Victoria L. Dunckley. New World Library 2015 384 p. illustrations (paperback) $18.95   **004.67**
1. Parenting 2. Child psychology 3. Children -- Conduct of life 4. Internet and children 5. Electronics -- Social aspects 6. Problem children -- Behavior modification 7. Video games and children -- Health aspects 8. Behavior disorders in children -- Prevention
ISBN 1608682846; 9781608682843
LC 2014046885

In this book "based on emerging scientific research and extensive clinical experience, integrative child psychiatrist Dr. Victoria Dunckley has pioneered a four-week program to treat the frequent underlying cause, Electronic Screen Syndrome (ESS). Dunckley provides hope for parents who feel that their child has been misdiagnosed or inappropriately medicated, by presenting an alternative explanation for their child's difficulties and a concrete plan for treating them." (Publisher's note)

"Decreasing childhood use of electronics often results in better behavior, but whether that's because parent and child find new ways of communicating and spending time together or because the electronics are creating long-term damage is still up for debate." LJ

Includes bibliographical references and index

Lessig, Lawrence

The **future** of ideas; the fate of the commons in a connected world. Random House 2001 352p hardcover o.p. pa $15   **004.67**
1. Internet 2. Copyright 3. Information society
ISBN 0-375-72644-6 pa
LC 2001-31968

"Some of Lessig's sweeping proposals are sure to spark a lively debate, but his well-reasoned, clearly written argument is powerful." Publ Wkly

Moreno, Megan

Sex, drugs 'n Facebook; a parents' toolkit for promoting healthy Internet use. by Megan A. Moreno. Hunter House Inc. 2013 268 p. (trade paper) $17.95   **004.67**
1. Social media 2. Internet and teenagers 3. Parenting 4. Online etiquette
ISBN 0897936590; 9780897936590; 9780897936606
LC 2012048533

In this book, author Megan Moreno presents "a guide to help [parents] teach your kids about balance and boundaries in their internet and media use and the skills they need to thrive online. This guide provides a clear toolkit for teaching our young people how to avoid the dangers of the internet while taking advantage of its full potential." (Publisher's note)

Includes bibliographical references and index

Naughton, John

From Gutenberg to Zuckerberg; Disruptive Innovation in the Age of the Internet. John Naughton. Quercus 2014 352 p. illustrations (hardcover) $24.95   **004.67**
1. Internet 2. Technological innovations
ISBN 1623650623; 9781623650629; 9781623650636
LC 2013937747

This book, by John Naughton, "is a . . . history of one of the most central, and yet most taken-for-granted, features of modern life: the internet. Once a technological novelty and now the very plumbing of the Information Age, the internet is something we have learned to take largely for granted. So, how exactly has our society become so dependent upon a utility it barely understands? And what does it say about us that this is so?" (Publisher's note)

"This is a solid overview of Internet technology for those who use it but who don't feel that they comprehend it. Experts might not find much new information here, but the author's observations and analysis will give any reader a better grasp of the web's big picture." LJ

Obee, Jennifer

Social networking; the ultimate teen guide. Jenna Obee. Scarecrow Press 2012 258 p.   **004.67**
1. Social networking 2. Internet and teenagers 3. Online social networks
ISBN 0810881209; 9780810881204; 9780810881211
LC 2011049875

This book by Jennifer Obee "helps young adults make the most of their online experience, giving them a complete understanding of social networking while also addressing online safety. . . . Author Jennifer Obee helps teens navigate through the challenging intricacies of social networks, covering such topics as: Facebook . . . Youtube . . . [and] Twitter." The book includes "quotes from teenagers about their favorite sites and personal stories." (Publisher's note)

Includes bibliographical references and index

Peters, Justin

The **Idealist**; Aaron Swartz and the Rise of Free Culture on the Internet. Justin Peters. Simon & Schuster 2016 352 p. $28   **004.67**
1. Internet 2. Open access publishing
ISBN 1476767726; 9781476767727
LC 2015044638

This book, by Justin Peters, presents a "history of the Internet free culture movement and its larger effects on society--and the life and shocking suicide of Aaron Swartz, a founding developer of Reddit and Creative Commons. [It] situates Swartz in the context of other 'data moralists' past and present, from lexicographer Noah Webster to ebook pioneer Michael Hart to NSA whistleblower Edward Snowden. In the process, the book explores the history of copyright statutes and the public domain." (Publisher's note)

"Swartz's writings and Peters' historically grounded and deeply involving biography illuminate the roots of today's thorny quandaries." Booklist

Includes bibliographical references (pages 309-317) and index.

Sales, Nancy Jo

★ American girls; social media and the secret lives of teenagers. Nancy Jo Sales. Alfred A. Knopf 2016 416 p. (hardcover) $26.95   **004.67**

    1. Social media 2. Teenage girls 3. Internet and teenagers

    ISBN 9780385353922; 9780385353939

                       LC 2016931806

For this book author Nancy Jo Sales "crisscrossed the country, speaking to more than two hundred girls, ages thirteen to nineteen, and documenting a massive change in the way girls are growing up. 'American Girls' provides a disturbing portrait of the end of childhood as we know it and of the inexorable and ubiquitous experience of a new kind of adolescence—one dominated by new social and sexual norms." (Publisher's note)

"Sales takes a broader view than simply being the scold of technology; she spoke with teens who point out the empowerment possibilities of a smartphone: being able to document injustices as they happen and broadcast them to the world. For parents with young daughters, this book is an ice-cold, important wake-up call." Kirkus

Stryker, Cole

Hacking the Future; Privacy, Identity, and Anonymity on the Web. Cole Stryker. Penguin Group USA 2012 255 p. (hardcover) $25.95   **004.67**

    1. Right of privacy 2. Internet -- Social aspects

    ISBN 1590209745; 9781590209745

This book, by Cole Stryker, offers "a broad look at how anonymity influences politics, activism, religion, and art. Stryker presents a strong defense of anonymity and explores some of the tools and organizations relating to this issue, especially as it has evolved with the ubiquity of the Internet." (Publisher's note)

"A multilayered and well-reasoned retort against all those who would seek to erase anonymity from the Web... The author explores the rich history of anonymity in politics, literature and culture, while also debunking the notion that only troublemakers fear revealing their identities to the world... One of the most well-informed examinations of the Internet available today." Kirkus

005   Computer programming, programs, data

Campbell-Kelly, Martin

From airline reservations to Sonic the Hedgehog; a history of the software industry. MIT Press 2003 372p il (History of computing) $42.50; pa $16.95   **005**

    1. Computer software industry

    ISBN 0-262-03303-8; 0-262-53262-X pa

                       LC 2002-75351

The author presents a "history of the software industry from the 1950s to 1995. Dividing the business into three sectors (software contracting, corporate software precuts, and mass-market software products), he examines the key products and players in each. . . . The result is a well-rounded look at the software industry from a business perspective." Libr J

Includes bibliographical references

Davis, Mark

Digital assassination; protecting your reputation, brand, or business against online attacks. by Richard Torrenzano and Mark Davis. 1st ed. St. Martin's Press 2011 viii, 289 p.p (hardcover) $25.99   **005**

    1. Reputation 2. Public opinion 3. Internet -- Security measures

    ISBN 0312617917; 9780312617912

                       LC 2011025849

In this book, authors [Richard] Torrenzano . . . and [Mark] Davis . . . discuss how various Internet tools are being used by digital maligners to harm reputations and perform character assassinations. The authors explain how anyone can tap into social media . . . to mount an electronic onslaught, severely altering the digital reputation of a person or a company. They argue that the dark side of human behavior, not technology, is the driving factor behind this phenomenon." (Library Journal)

Includes bibliographical references and index.

005.7   Data in computer systems

O'Neil, Cathy

Weapons of math destruction; How Big Data Increases Inequality and Threatens Democracy. Cathy O'Neil. Crown Publishers 2016 272 p. (hardcover) $26   **005.7**

    1. Big data 2. Democracy -- United States 3. United States -- Social conditions 4. Big data -- Social aspects -- United States 5. Big data -- Political aspects -- United States 6. United States -- Social conditions -- 21st century 7. Social indicators -- Mathematical models -- Moral and ethical aspects

    ISBN 9780553418811; 9780553418835

                       LC 2016003900

In this book, author Cathy O'Neil "sounds an alarm on the mathematical models that pervade modern life—and threaten to rip apart our social fabric. . . . Tracing the arc of a person's life, O'Neil exposes the black box models that shape our future, both as individuals and as a society. These 'weapons of math destruction' score teachers and students, sort résumés, grant (or deny) loans, evaluate workers, target voters, set parole, and monitor our health." (Publisher's note)

Includes bibliographical references (pages 219-252) and index

005.8   Data security

Olson, Parmy

We are Anonymous; inside the hacker world of Lulzsec, Anonymous, and the global cyber insurgency. Parmy Olson. Little, Brown and Co. 2012 xi, 498 p.p $26.99   **005.8**

    1. Hacktivism 2. Lulzsec (Group) 3. Computer hackers 4. Anonymous (Group)

    ISBN 0316213543; 9780316213547

                       LC 2012936919

This book by Parmy Olson presents an "account of the hacker collective Anonymous and its splinter group, Lulz-

Sec. . . . A nebulous group of hackers and Internet activists . . . [Anonymous] not only took down the Scientology website, but went on to attack other targets, including the anti-gay Westboro Baptist Church and the Tunisian government. . . . [LulzSec] attacked companies just for the sake of publicly embarrassing them for laughs." (Kirkus Reviews)

Includes bibliographical references and index.

006.3   Artificial intelligence

Baker, Stephen
Final Jeopardy; man vs. machine and the quest to know everything. Houghton Mifflin Harcourt 2011 268p $24   **006.3**
1. Database management 2. Artificial intelligence 3. Watson (Computer) 4. Jeopardy (Television program) 5. Natural language processing (Computer science)
ISBN 978-0-547-48316-0; 0-547-48316-3
LC 2010051653

"In February 2011, the world watched as a computer named Watson handily beat the two greatest Jeopardy champions of all time. The contest was reminiscent of when IBM's Deep Blue defeated chess grandmaster Garry Kasparov, but Jeopardy was a much more difficult game for a computer to master. Although Baker . . . reviews the match in his last chapter, his primary focus here is on the compelling story of Watson's creation and education. . . . This is a thought-provoking view of one of IBM's major contributions to the computing field." Libr J

Includes bibliographical references

Bostrom, Nick, 1973-
Superintelligence;   paths, dangers, strategies. Nick Bostrom. Oxford University Press 2014 352 p. (hardback) $29.95   **006.3**
1. Theory of knowledge 2. Artificial intelligence 3. Cognitive science 4. Artificial intelligence -- Philosophy
ISBN 0199678111; 9780199678112
LC 2013955152

This book, by Nick Bostrom, asks "[w]hat happens when machines surpass humans in general intelligence? Will artificial agents save or destroy us? . . . The human brain has some capabilities that the brains of other animals lack. . . . If machine brains surpassed human brains in general intelligence, then this new superintelligence could become extremely powerful - possibly beyond our control. . . . But we have one advantage: we get to make the first move." (Publisher's note)

Bostrom "delivers a comprehensive outline of the philosophical foundations of the nature of intelligence and the difficulty not only in agreeing on a suitable definition of that concept but in living with the possibly dire consequences of that concept." Choice

Includes bibliographical references and index

Zarkadakis, George
In   Our Own Image;   Savior or Destroyer? the History and Future of Artificial Intelligence. George

Zarkadakis. W W Norton & Co Inc 2016 384 p. $27.95   **006.3**
1. Artificial intelligence 2. Human-computer interaction
ISBN 1605989649; 9781605989648

In this book, author George Zarkadakis "explores the history and future, as well as the societal and ethical implications, of Artificial Intelligence as we approach the cusp of a fourth industrial revolution. . . . He traces AI's origins in ancient myth, through literary classics like Frankenstein, to today's sci-fi blockbusters, arguing that a fascination with AI is hardwired into the human psyche." (Publisher's note)

"A delightfully lucid combination of the history, philosophy, and science behind thinking machines." Kirkus

Includes bibliographical references (pages [322]-347) and index.

006.7   Multimedia systems

Bilton, Nick
Hatching Twitter; a true story of money, power, friendship, and betrayal. Nick Bilton. Portfolio Hardcover Portfolio/Penguin 2013 304 p. illustrations (hardback) $28.95   **006.7**
1. Twitter (Web site) 2. Twitter 3. Twitter (Firm) 4. Internet industry -- United States 5. Online social networks -- United States 6. Businesspeople -- United States -- Biography
ISBN 1591846013; 9781591846017
LC 2013037924

This book examines "Twitter's contentious origins in the techie subculture of San Francisco." Author Nick Bilton "reconstructed this history from interviews and the digital trails . . . of his four principals: blogger, founder and chief investor Evan 'Ev' Williams and his friends and employees Noah Glass, Christopher 'Biz' Stone and Jack Dorsey. Each contributed an important share in the invention of the platform that . . . would revolutionize the way the world communicates and interrelates." (Kirkus Reviews)

Krug, Steve
★ Don't make me think, revisited; a common sense approach to Web usability. Steve Krug. New Riders 2014 xi, 200 p.p ill (some col) (pbk.) $45   **006.7**
1. Web sites -- Design 2. Web site development
ISBN 9780321965516; 0321965515
LC 2014397947

Previous ed.: 2006

This revised book on web design, by Steve Krug, is a "guide to help . . . understand the principles of intuitive navigation and information design . . . . with updated examples and a new chapter on mobile usability." (Publisher's note)

Includes bibliographical references and index

Solomon, Laura
The librarian's nitty-gritty guide to social media; Laura Solomon. ALA Editions, an imprint of the American Library Association 2013 224 p. $52   **006.7**
1. Librarians 2. Social media 3. Online social networks

-- Library applications
ISBN 0838911609; 9780838911600
LC 2012027302

Here, Laura Solomon offers a guide for the use of social media by libraries. The book "provides case studies of libraries that have excelled with their marketing efforts." She offers an "analysis of what success is and how to measure it to gain support from stakeholders." Also provided are "detailed sample postings that not only give suggestions for libraries to model but also examine unsuccessful posts and explain what makes them less than desirable." (Library Journal)

Includes bibliographical references and index

Stone, Biz

Things a little bird told me; confessions of the creative mind. Biz Stone. Grand Central Publishing 2014 240 p. illustrations (hardback) $26   **006.7**
1. Businesspeople 2. Internet industry 3. Twitter (Web site) 4. Success in business 5. Twitter 6. Online social networks -- United States 7. Entrepreneurship -- United States -- Anecdotes
ISBN 1455528714; 9781455528714
LC 2013047280

In this book, Biz Stone "discusses the power of creativity and how to harness it, through stories from his remarkable life and career. . . . Biz tells fascinating, pivotal, and personal stories from his early life and his careers at Google and Twitter, sharing his knowledge about the nature and importance of ingenuity today. . . . Biz also addresses failure, the value of vulnerability, ambition, and corporate culture." (Publisher's note)

"Readers will enjoy the tales of the ups and downs of Silicon Valley among major players, from Google to Apple to Facebook, as well as the insightful advice that can be applied to any career or enterprise." Booklist

Tortorella, Neil

Starting your career as a freelance web designer. Allworth Press 2011 251p il pa $19.95   **006.7**
1. Vocational guidance 2. Web sites -- Design
ISBN 978-1-58115-859-5
LC 2011019292

"This is not a book about how to design websites; it is about managing the financial, legal, and business realities of being a freelance web designer. . . . Part One deals with the fundamentals of being a freelancer, including analyzing one's abilities and talents, formulating a business plan, understanding taxes and insurance, and finding trusted business advisers. In Part Two, Tortorella discusses the necessary proficiencies of the portfolio, proposals, project management, and marketing. . . . Tortorella's contribution is the nuts-and-bolts handbook for success in the field of freelance web design and will find a ready audience with the fledgling right-brain designer or the college student considering web design as a career." Libr J

Includes bibliographical references

Wellman, Barry

Networked; the new social operating system. Lee Rainie and Barry Wellman. MIT Press 2012 xiii, 358 p.p ill.   **006.7**
1. Online social networks 2. Interpersonal relations 3.

Internet -- Social aspects 4. Social networks
ISBN 0262017199; 9780262017190
LC 2011038146

This book "outline[s] the 'triple revolution'" in human communication: "the rise of social networking, the capacity of the Internet to empower individuals, and the always-on connectivity of mobile devices." The authors "examine how the move to networked individualism has expanded personal relationships . . . . transformed work into less hierarchical, more team-driven enterprises; encouraged individuals to create and share content; and changed the way people obtain information." (Publisher's note)

Includes bibliographical references and index.

011   Bibliographies and catalogs

American reference books annual 2016; edited by Juneal M. Chenoweth. Libraries Unlimited 2016 616 p. Volume 47 $140   **011**
1. Reference books -- Bibliography 2. Libraries -- Collection development
ISBN 1440847010; 9781440847011

Cumulative indexes available 1990-1994; 2000-2004; 2005-2009

Annual. First published 1970

"Each issue covers the reference book output (including reprints) of the previous year (i.e., the 1970 volume covers 1969 publications). Offers descriptive and evaluative notes (many of them signed by contributors), with references to selected reviews. Limited to titles in English. Classed arrangement; author-subject-title index." Guide to Ref Books. 11th edition

Ellington, Elisabeth

A **year** of reading; a month-by-month guide to classics and crowd-pleasers for you and your book group. by H. Elisabeth Ellington and Jane Freimiller. Sourcebooks 2002 314p pa $14.95   **011**
1. Best books 2. Books and reading
ISBN 1-57071-935-7
LC 2002-6926

"Five titles designated as crowd pleasers, classics, challenges, memoirs, or potluck options are provided for each month. . . . There are brief descriptions of each book, thought-provoking discussion questions, information about the authors, video and Internet resources, and lists of related readings. Literary discussion groups will welcome this invaluable resource." Booklist

Guide to reference; essential general reference and library science sources. Jo Bell Whitlatch and Susan E. Searing, Editors. ALA Editions, An imprint of the American Library Association 2014 xiv, 230 p.p (paperback : alk. paper) $65   **011**
1. Reference services (Libraries) 2. Reference books -- Bibliography 3. Reference sources -- Bibliography
ISBN 083891232X; 9780838912324
LC 2014013098

This book, edited by Jo Bell Whitlatch and Susan E. Searing, "collects . . . sources of general reference and library science information. Encompassing internet resources, digital image collections, and print resources, it includes the full section on LIS Resources from the Guide to Reference database. . . . Organized by topic and thoroughly indexed, this guide makes it a snap to find the right sources." (Publisher's note)

Includes bibliographical references and indexes

Guide to reference books; edited by Robert Balay; associate editor, Vee Friesner Carrington; with special editorial assistance by Murray S. Martin. 11th ed; American Lib. Assn. 1996 xxvii, 2020p $275   **011**
1. Reference books 2. Reference books -- Bibliography
ISBN 0-8389-0669-9

LC 95-26322

First published 1902

Nearly 16,000 entries provide details on general reference works and on reference books in the humanities, social and behavioral sciences, history and area studies, and science, technology, and medicine. Electronic resources are included

Includes bibliographical references

O'Gorman, Jack
Reference Sources for Small and Medium-Sized Libraries; Jack O'Gorman, editor. Amer Library Assn 2014 289 p. $129   **011**
1. Book selection 2. Reference books -- Bibliography
3. Reference books
ISBN 0838912125; 9780838912126

LC 200740026

"Focusing on new reference sources published since 2008 and reference titles that have retained their relevance, this new edition brings [author Jack] O'Gorman's complete and authoritative guide to the best reference sources for small and medium-sized academic and public libraries fully up to date. About 40 percent of the content is new to this edition." (Publisher's note)

Pearl, Nancy
Book lust; recommended reading for every mood, moment, and reason. Sasquatch Books 2003 287p pa $16.95   **011**
1. Best books 2. Books and reading
ISBN 1-57061-381-8

LC 2003-45796

Pearl's "recommendations are arranged under an alphabetical, subjective, but certainly comprehensive system of categories, which range from 'Academic Mysteries' to 'World War II Nonfiction' and from 'First Novels' to 'Three-Hanky Readers.' Within each category, Pearl's commentaries are concise and sound. A book difficult to put down and easy to be guided by." Booklist

★ **Recommended** reference books for small and medium-sized libraries and media centers, Vol. 34; volume 34 Shannon Graff Hysell, associate editor. Libraries Unlimited 2014 301 p. $75 **011**
1. Reference books 2. Reference books -- Reviews 3. Reference books -- Bibliography
ISBN 9781610695510
Annual. First published 1981

"This volume presents the top 550 reviews from the latest edition of American Reference Books Annual (ARBA) to give collection development librarians working in small to medium-sized libraries the best information for choosing new titles for their libraries. Overviewing the breadth of reference products (both print and online) that became available in 2013, all of the titles . . . have price points that will appeal to libraries on a budget." (Publisher's note)

Includes "books, e-books, free websites, and pay sites. These are broken down into major subject headings and minor ones within the major." VOYA

Saricks, Joyce G.
Read on--audiobooks; reading lists for every taste. Libraries Unlimited 2011 145p (Read on series) pa $30   **011**
1. Audiobooks -- Catalogs 2. Libraries -- Special collections -- Audiobooks
ISBN 978-1-59158-804-7 pa; 978-1-59158-807-8 ebook

LC 2010051372

"More than 300 selections, fiction and nonfiction, are grouped into five chapters according to their primary appeal: language (including voice), mood, story, characters, or setting. Within each category, titles are listed by shared themes, such as full-cast readings or armchair travel. . . . All libraries that circulate audiobooks should shelve this guide alongside." Booklist

Includes bibliographical references

011.6   General bibliographies and catalogs of works for young people and people with disabilities; for specific types of libraries

Rosow, La Vergne
★ **Accessing** the classics; great reads for adults, teens, and English language learners. Libraries Unlimited 2006 301p pa $40   **011.6**
1. Best books 2. Reading -- Remedial teaching
ISBN 1-56308-891-6; 978-1-56308-891-9

LC 2005-30838

"The intended audience is wide-ranging and includes anyone who wishes to foster language and literacy skills. Essential reading." Booklist

Includes bibliographical references

Safford, Barbara Ripp
Guide to reference materials for school library media centers; 6th ed; Libraries Unlimited 2010 236p $60   **011.6**
1. Instructional materials centers 2. School libraries -- Catalogs 3. Reference books -- Bibliography
ISBN 978-1-59158-277-9; 1-59158-277-6

LC 2009-51190

First edition by Christine Gehrt Wynar published 1973 with title: Guide to reference books for school media centers

"This volume has been updated to include web-based reference offerings as well as listings of older sources, provided that their content is still valid. . . . This title profiles resources recommended for use by school librarians for collection management, readers' advisory, teaching, general reference materials, the social sciences and humanities, and science and technology. This volume is an excellent starting point for new school librarians, as well as for those who are building a library from scratch." SLJ

Includes bibliographical references

011.62 Works for young people

Martin, William Patrick

Wonderfully wordless; the 500 most recommended graphic novels and picture books. William Patrick Martin. Rowman & Littlefield 2015 334 p. (hardcover : alk. paper) $38   011.62

1. Graphic novels -- Bibliography 2. Best books 3. Picture books -- Bibliography 4. Picture books for children -- Bibliography

ISBN 9781442254770

LC 2015019482

Written by William Patrick Martin, "'Wonderfully Wordless: The 500 Most Recommended Graphic Novels and Picture Books' is the first comprehensive best book guide to wordless picture books. . . . It is an indispensable resource for parents and teachers who love graphic storytelling or who recognize the value of these exceptional books in working with different types of students, particularly preschool, English as a Second Language (ESL), and special needs, and creative writers." (Publisher's note)

"No dark corner is left unexplored, illuminating a far greater array of choices than any reader might have guessed." Booklist

Includes bibliographical references

016 Bibliographies and catalogs of works on specific subjects

Adamson, Lynda G.

Notable women in American history; a guide to recommended biographies and autobiographies. Greenwood Press 1999 450p $52.95   016

1. Reference books 2. Women -- Biography -- Dictionaries

ISBN 0-313-29584-0

LC 98-55350

Companion volume to Notable women in world history

This volume "concentrates on women who made contributions to U.S. history from the colonial period through 1998. The 500 women covered were born in America or became naturalized citizens; had a full-length biography or autobiography published since 1970; and, in the case of twentieth-century actors, authors, and poets, have been recognized by their peers." Booklist

Notable women in world history; a guide to recommended biographies and autobiographies. Greenwood Press 1998 401p $52.95   016

1. Reference books 2. Women -- Biography -- Dictionaries

ISBN 0-313-29818-1

LC 97-33136

"The entries are arranged alphabetically by last name with appropriate cross-references for alternative designations. Each contains the woman's name, key dates, occupation or avocation, and birthplace. A short biographical sketch about parents, education, general achievement, and recognition or awards follows. Women of all time periods are included. . . . Because it includes only those born outside the U.S., it complements sources on American women. Notable Women in World History is a useful addition to academic, public, and high-school libraries. It would be especially useful for women's studies collections." Booklist

All music guide to classical music; the definitive guide to classical music. edited by Chris Woodstra, Gerald Brennan, Allen Schrott. Backbeat Books 2005 1607p $34.95   016

1. Music -- Discography

ISBN 0-87930-865-6

LC 2005-23988

"The 1500 A-to-Z entries include established composers, performers, and ensembles of every style and era. . . . The final 25 pages are devoted to one-page discussions of form in classical music, historical periods (ten divisions), and genres such as ballet, film music, and opera. . . . This is an excellent resource for both classical novices and aficionados. There is simply no other single volume on the market as inclusive." Libr J

Alpert, Abby, 1961-

Read on-- graphic novels; reading lists for every taste. Abby Alpert. Libraries Unlimited 2012 xxi, 177 p.p (acid-free paper) $40   016

1. Best books 2. Graphic novels -- Bibliography 3. Readers' advisory services -- United States 4. Public libraries -- United States -- Book lists 5. Libraries -- Special collections -- Graphic novels

ISBN 1591588251; 1610691555; 9781591588252; 9781610691550

LC 2011039792

This book on graphic novels by Abby Alpert, part of the Read On series, offers "more than 500 original annotations organized within 70 thematic lists. The broad selection of titles is further categorized by key appeal elements, including story, character, setting, language, and mood, providing unique access points that allow discovery of interests to transcend subject headings in catalogs." (Publisher's note)

"This accessible guide is equally effective for collection building, readers' advisory, or individual perusal, and most public collections will find it perceptive and helpful. Recommended." Booklist

American foreign relations since 1600; a guide to the literature. Robert L. Beisner, editor. 2nd ed; ABC-CLIO 2003 2v set $255   016

1. Reference books 2. United States -- Foreign relations -- Bibliography

ISBN 1-57607-080-8

LC 2003-8684

First published 1983 under the editorship of Richard Dean Burns with title: Guide to American foreign relations since 1700

"The arrangement is essentially chronological, with the first of 32 chapters covering reference works and bibliographies and the second chapter, overviews and synthesis. Individual chapter editors . . . include journal articles, essays in collections, and dissertations. . . . Each chapter begins with a brief statement of the editor's selection criteria. Works in related specialties are listed for their influence on foreign relations, including Native American relations, gender and ethnic issues, and religious groups. . . . This is an excellent book; imaginative users will find ways to apply these listings to a wide variety of projects." Libr J

Includes bibliographical references

Barsanti, Chris

The **science** fiction movie guide; the universe of film from Alien to Zardoz. by Chris Barsanti. Visible Ink Press 2014 500 p. illustrations (pbk. : alk. paper) $19.95 **016**

1. Science fiction films -- Catalogs
ISBN 1578595037; 9781578595037

LC 2014017822

This book, by Chris Barsanti, "covers the broad and widening range of science-fiction movies. From the trashy to the epic, from the classics to today's blockbusters, this cinefile's guidebook reviews nearly 1,000 of the biggest, baddest, and brightest from every age and genre of cinematic and TV science fiction." (Publisher's note)

"A great book for science fiction cinephiles and novices alike, this is a must for those interested in updating their film guidebook collections." Choice

Includes bibliographical referencfes

The **basic** business library; core resources and services. edited by Eric Forte and Michael R. Oppenheim. Libraries Unlimited 2012 xi, 227 p.p $50 **016**

1. Business libraries 2. Business -- Bibliography 3. Business -- Information services 4. Business libraries -- United States 5. Business -- Computer network resources 6. Business -- Reference books -- Bibliography 7. Business information services -- United States
ISBN 1598846116; 1598846124; 9781598846119; 9781598846126

LC 2011037666

This book, edited by Eric Forte and Michael R. Oppenheim, "is a modern sourcebook of core resources for the business library and the business information consumers and researchers it serves. This up-to-date guide also discusses strategies for acquiring and building the business collection in a Web 2.0/3.0 world and recommended approaches to providing reference service for business research." (Publisher's note)

"This is a valuable resource for small and medium-sized public libraries and an essential purchase for libraries that do not have an experienced business librarian or material selector on staff." Booklist

Includes bibliographical references and index

A **basic** music library; essential scores and sound recordings. compiled by the Music Library Association; Daniel F. Boomhower, editor; Edward Komara, Amanda Maple, and Liza Vick, associate editors. American Library Association 2013 752 p. (alk. paper) $258 **016**

1. Music libraries 2. Music -- Bibliography 3. Libraries -- Collection development 4. Music libraries -- Collection development
ISBN 0838910394; 9780838910399

LC 2013020223

This book, edited by Daniel F. Boomhower, Edward Komara, Amanda Maple, and Liza Vick on behalf of the Music Library Association, "constitutes the most authoritative music collection resource available. Completely revised and reorganized, this . . . reference is divided into" the three classical, popular, and world music genres. (Publisher's note)

Includes bibliographical references and index

Bleiler, Richard

★ **Reference** and research guide to mystery and detective fiction; [by] Richard J. Bleiler. 2nd ed; Libraries Unlimited 2003 828p (Reference sources in the humanities series) $78 **016**

1. Reference books 2. Mystery fiction -- Bibliography
ISBN 1-56308-924-6

LC 2003-58905

First published 1999 with title: Reference guide to mystery and detective fiction

"Separate chapters cover sources as diverse as maps and atlases, writers' associations and awards, character indexes, calendars, and quotations in addition to guides, encyclopedias, and dictionaries." Choice

Includes bibliographical references

Bosman, Ellen

Gay, lesbian, bisexual, and transgendered literature; a genre guide. [by] Ellen Bosman and John P. Bradford; edited by Robert B. Marks Ridinger. Libraries Unlimited 2008 422p (Genreflecting advisory series) $60 **016**

1. Homosexuality in literature
ISBN 978-1-59158-194-9; 1-59158-194-X

LC 2007-49022

"This addition to the Genreflecting Advisory Series fills a gap, focusing on popular literature with gay, lesbian, bisexual, and transgendered characters, themes, or authors. The first three chapters provide an excellent introduction and history of GLBT literature along with a discussion of collection develop-ment and readers'-advisory issues . . . An excellent tool for readers' advisory, as well as an outstanding reference on an important type of literature, this guide is highly recommended for public and academic libraries with GLBT collections." Booklist

Includes bibliographical references

Bouricius, Ann

The **romance** readers' advisory; the librarian's guide to love in the stacks. American Lib. Assn. 2000 107p pa $56 **016**

1. Reference books 2. Love stories -- Bibliography 3. Love stories -- History and criticism
ISBN 0-8389-0779-2

LC 99-57295

The author provides "information about the highly popular romance genre and its diverse subgenres; addresses key issues regarding the establishment of a romance collection; and, in a series of reading lists, recommends outstanding romances of all flavors for avid fans and new converts." Booklist

Burgess, Michael

Reference guide to science fiction, fantasy, and horror; [by] Michael Burgess, Lisa R. Bartle. 2nd ed; Libraries Unlimited 2002 605p (Reference sources in the humanities series) $75   **016**

1. Reference books 2. Science fiction -- Bibliography
ISBN 1-56308-548-8

LC 2002-151707

First published 1992

A guide to "amateur and professional reference materials in the related fields of science fiction, fantasy, and horror. . . . The book is divided into 32 sections . . . including 'Encyclopedias and Dictionaries,' 'Magazine and Anthology Indexes,' 'Subject Bibliographies,' 'Character Dictionaries and Author Cyclopedias,' and 'Film and Television Catalogs.' . . . Complete bibliographic citations are followed by literature and readable annotations that vary from a brief note to three or four lengthy paragraphs. The annotations consist of description and succinct analysis of the strengths and weaknesses of each item. . . . 'Major On-Line Resources,' is a particularly valuable examination of 20 Web sites." Booklist

Includes bibliographical references

Burt, Daniel S.

The **biography** book; a reader's guide to nonfiction, fictional, and film biographies of the 500 most fascinating individuals of all time. Oryx Press 2001 629p $83.95   **016**

1. Reference books 2. Biography -- Bibliography
ISBN 1-57356-256-4

LC 00-10116

This "book provides annotated bibliographies of works on international historical figures. Entries are arranged alphabetically by person and begin with a paragraph on the individual's life and significance. Each entry contains a birth and death date, and recommended autobiographical and biographical studies. Primary sources include letters, memoirs, diaries, interviews, etc. Biographical novels, fictional portraits, films, documentaries, and theatrical performances are also identified. . . . A wonderful resource for students, biography lovers, and librarians." SLJ

Includes bibliographical references

Clark, Craig A.

Read on...sports; reading lists for every taste. Craig Clark, Richard T. Fox. Libraries Unlimited 2014 xv, 165 p.p (Read on series) (pbk.) $40   **016**

1. Books and reading 2. Sports -- Bibliography
ISBN 1610693574; 9781610693578

LC 2013034587

This library reference book, by Craig Clark and Richard T. Fox, "features reading lists of sports-oriented titles written by talented authors that are cataloged by character, story, setting, mood, and language. The lists are perfect for advising readers, creating thematic reading lists for library websites, and as plans for those who enjoy reading about athletic pursuits." (Publisher's note)

"This book would be useful for readers' advisory in libraries and will appeal to sports fans, so consider a copy in your circulating collection as well." Booklist

De Richemond, Jeanette

The **Medical** Library Association guide to finding out about heart disease; the best print and electronic resources. Jeanette de Richemond, Terry Paula Hoffman. Neal-Schuman, an imprint of the American Library Association 2013 468 p. (alk. paper) $88   **016**

1. Heart diseases 2. Reference books 3. Diet in disease -- Bibliography 4. Heart -- Diseases -- Bibliography 5. Diet in disease -- Computer network resources 6. Heart -- Diseases -- Computer network resources 7. Cardiovascular system -- Diseases -- Bibliography 8. Cardiovascular system -- Diseases -- Computer network resources
ISBN 1555707505; 9781555707507

LC 2013011592

"'The Medical Library Association Guide to Finding Out About Heart Disease' does the organizing for you and offers evaluated print and online resources to help you develop a collection or research your personal medical options. This . . . reference incorporates important data and key concepts about risk factors and symptoms of heart disease." (Publisher's note)

Includes bibliographical references and index

Dilevko, Juris

Contemporary world fiction; a guide to literature in translation. Juris Dilevko, Keren Dali, and Glenda Garbutt. Libraries Unlimited 2011 xxvi, 526 p.p $85   **016**

1. Translating and interpreting 2. Fiction -- 21st century
ISBN 1591583535; 9781591583530

LC 2010052517

In this book, by Juris Dilevko, Keren Dali, and Glenda Garbutt, "provides an overview of the tremendous range and scope of translated world fiction available in English. . . . Within the guide, approximately 1,000 contemporary non-English-language fiction titles are fully annotated and thousands of others are listed. Organization is primarily by language, . . . but also by country and culture." (Publisher's note)

"Highly recommended for the casual reader wishing to discover international contemporary fiction and for students of literature." LJ

Includes bibliographical references and indexes

Ernsthausen, David G.

★ **Strauss's** handbook of business information; a guide for librarians, students, and researchers. Rita W. Moss and David G. Ernsthausen. 2nd ed; Libraries Unlimited 2012 xix, 399 p.p il (acid-free paper) $100   **016**

1. Business 2. Reference books 3. Business -- Databases -- Handbooks, manuals, etc 4. Government publications -- United States -- Handbooks, manuals, etc 5. Business -- Reference books -- Bibliography -- Handbooks, manuals, etc 6. Business -- Electronic

information resources -- Handbooks, manuals, etc
7. Business information services -- United States --
Handbooks, manuals, etc
ISBN 1598848070; 1610692365; 9781598848076;
9781610692366

LC 2011041547

First edition by Diane Wheeler Strauss published 1988
with title: Handbook of business information

This business information handbook by Diane Wheeler
Straus "is divided into two main parts. The first seven chapters cover business information according to the formats
in which it is made available. The second part of the book
covers specific topics within the area of business. Included
are chapters on marketing; money, credit, and banking; and
the many aspects of investment ranging from stocks through
bonds, mutual funds, and futures and options." (Publisher's note)

This edition "first covers 'formats': directories, periodicals, loose-leaf services, government information services,
and electronic sources. References are then organized by
'fields': banking, marketing, accounting, stocks and bonds,
etc. Graphics include screen shots of e-sources." Libr J

Includes bibliographical references and indexes.

Flora illustrata; great works on botany, horticulture,
and garden design in the luesther t. mertz library.
[edited by] Susan M. Fraser, Vanessa Bezemer
Sellers. Yale University Press 2014 320 p. illustrations, maps, portraits (alk. paper) $50 **016**
1. Botanical illustration 2. Plants -- Collection and
preservation
ISBN 0300196628; 9780300196627

LC 2014931108

This book, edited by Susan M. Fraser and Vanessa Bezemer Sellers, examines "exceedingly rare books, stunning
botanical artworks, handwritten manuscripts, Renaissance
herbals, nursery catalogs, explorers' notebooks, and more"
from the LuEsther T. Mertz Library of The New York Botanical Garden. (Publisher's note)

"A wonderful title for the botanist and layperson—anyone who appreciates the aesthetic beauty of books, plants,
and gardens." LJ

Fonseca, Anthony J.
Hooked on horror III; a guide to reading interests. [by] Anthony J. Fonseca and June Michele Pulliam. Libraries Unlimited 2009 xxiii, 515p (Genreflecting advisory series) $62 **016**
1. Horror films 2. Reference books 3. Horror fiction
-- Bibliography
ISBN 978-1-59158-540-4

LC 2008-45518

First published 1999 with title: Hooked on horror

This book "provides annotations of horror books published between 2003 and 2008, including collections, anthologies, and series." Voice Youth Advocates

Includes bibliographical references

Frolund, Tina
Genrefied classics; a guide to reading interests in
classical literature. Libraries Unlimited 2007 xxiv,
365p (Genreflecting advisory series) $45 **016**
1. Reference books 2. Fiction -- Bibliography
ISBN 1-59158-172-9; 978-1-59158-172-7

LC 2006-33740

"By identifying the genre characteristics of more than
400 classic fiction works, and organizing titles according to
these features, this guide helps readers find the type of books
they enjoy." Publisher's note

Includes bibliographical references

Read on...history; reading lists for every taste.
Tina Frolund. Libraries Unlimited 2013 xiv, 195 p.p
(Read on series) (pbk.) $30 **016**
1. Best books 2. History -- Bibliography 3. United
States -- History -- Bibliography 4. Readers' advisory
services -- United States 5. Public libraries -- United
States -- Book lists
ISBN 1610690346; 9781610690348

LC 2013029492

"This invaluable resource offers reading lists of contemporary and classic non-fiction history books and historical fiction, covering all time periods throughout the world,
and including practically all manner of human endeavors. .
. . Organized by appeal characteristics, this book will help
readers zero in on the history books they will like best."
(Publisher's note)

Guide to Reference in Business and Economics;
Steven W. Sowards, Elisabeth Leonard, editors.
Amer Library Assn 2014 375 p. $65 **016**
1. Business -- Bibliography 2. Economics --
Bibliography 3. Reference books -- Bibliography
ISBN 0838912346; 9780838912348

This book, edited by Steven W. Sowards and Elisabeth
Leonard, "focusing on print and electronic sources that are
key to business and economics reference, . . . is a must-have
[bibliography] for every reference desk. . . . This book will
help connect librarians and researchers to the most relevant
sources of information on business and economics." (Publisher's note)

Herald, Diana Tixier
Fluent in fantasy; the next generation. [by] Diana Tixier Herald and Bonnie Kunzel. Libraries Unlimited 2008 312p (Genreflecting advisory series)
$52 **016**
1. Reference books 2. Fantasy fiction -- Bibliography
ISBN 978-1-59158-198-7; 1-59158-198-2

LC 2007-28840

First published 1999

"More than 2,000 titles are arranged by author in 14
thematic chapters, including 'Epic Fantasy,' 'Arthurian Legend,' and 'Time Travel Romance.' . . . An essential collection
development and readers'-advisory tool." Booklist

Includes bibliographical references

★ **Genreflecting**; a guide to popular reading interests. edited by Wayne A. Wiegand. Libraries Un-

limited 2013 622 p. (Genreflecting advisory series) (Hardcopy : acid-free paper) $75   **016**
  1. Reference books 2. Books and reading 3. Reading interests 4. Fiction -- Bibliography 5. Fiction genres -- Bibliography 6. English fiction -- Stories, plots, etc 7. American fiction -- Stories, plots, etc 8. Popular literature -- Stories, plots, etc
  ISBN 9781598848403; 1598848402
                                        LC 2012051480
  First published 1982 under the authorship of Betty Rosenberg
  This book for librarians on popular reading interests features "chapters devoted to each major genre with an overview of the genre's characteristics and appeal elements followed by definitions of popular subgenres, lists of benchmark titles, reader favorites, book-group selections, and resources for further investigation. Parts I and 2 focus on readers'-advisory services in the public library for the novice. . . , The chapters on the genres, found in part 3, are the series' stock-in-trade." (Booklist)
  Includes bibliographical references

  ★ **Strictly** science fiction; a guide to reading interests. [by] Diana Tixier Herald, Bonnie Kunzel. Libraries Unlimited 2002 xxii, 297p (Genreflecting advisory series) $55   **016**
  1. Reference books 2. Science fiction -- Bibliography 3. Science fiction -- History and criticism
  ISBN 1-56308-893-2
                                        LC 2002-3186
  "Good indexing, by author, title, subject, and character name, along with chapters devoted to books written for children and young adults and genre-blended books (such as science fiction/ romance or science fiction/mystery), sets this reference apart." Libr J
  Includes bibliographical references

Hollands, Neil
  Read on . . . fantasy fiction; reading lists for every taste. Libraries Unlimited 2007 210p (Read on series) pa $30   **016**
  1. Reference books 2. Fantasy fiction -- Bibliography
  ISBN 978-1-59158-330-1; 1-59158-330-6
                                        LC 2007-7841
  "Librarians who do readers advisory for teens or adults will wonder how they ever got along without this funny, opinionated, wide-angle guide." SLJ

Honig, Megan
  Urban grit; a guide to street lit. Megan Honig. Libraries Unlimited 2010 xxiv, 251 p.p $55   **016**
  1. Fiction in libraries 2. Urban fiction, American -- Bibliography 3. Readers' advisory services -- United States 4. Urban fiction, American -- Stories, plots, etc
  ISBN 159158857X; 9781591588573
                                        LC 2010041099
  In this book, by Megan Honig, "more than 400 entries appear in eleven chapters, each focusing on a different subgenre of street lit. The author has organized titles by popular subgenres and themes, such as prison life and urban erotica, to help librarians more easily identify read-alikes." (Publisher's note)

"Recommended for professional reading shelves as well as for researchers who will find value in Honig's defining the genre. This should be the definitive choice on the subject, with Andrew Ratner's practical teaching and classroom guide Street Lit: Teaching and Reading Fiction in Urban Schools as a good complement." LJ
  Includes bibliographical references and index

Hooper, Brad
  Read on....historical fiction; reading lists for every taste. by Brad Hooper. Libraries Unlimited 2006 xii, 152 p.p $40   **016**
  1. Best books 2. Historical fiction -- Bibliography 3. Historical fiction
  ISBN 1591582393; 9781591582397
                                        LC 2006003711
  In this book by Brad Hooper, part of the Read On series, "Hundreds of popular historical fiction titles are described and categorized according to their underlying appeal features, and under topics and themes you'll never find in the library catalog--women with true grit, greatest war stories, royalty rules, quick reads, humor, and many others." (Publisher's note)
  This is definitely an unusual, thoughtful book that will be a useful addition to most professional and reference collections. Recommended." Library Media Connection
  Includes bibliographical references and index

Husband, Janet
  Sequels; an annotated guide to novels in series. [by] Janet G. Husband & Jonathan F. Husband. 4th ed; American Library Association 2009 782p pa $95   **016**
  1. Reference books 2. Fiction -- Bibliography
  ISBN 978-0-8389-0967-6
                                        LC 2009-16426
  First published 1982
  "A selective, annotated list of the best, most enduring, and most popular novels in series. Short stories and children's books are excluded; classics, mysteries, and science fiction are included. Each work is listed in the best current edition, in the preferred order for reading. Arranged by author, with a title and subject index." Ref Sources for Small & Medium-sized Libr. 5th edition
  Includes bibliographical references

Johnson, Sarah L.
  Historical fiction II; a guide to the genre. Libraries Unlimited 2009 738p (Genreflecting advisory series) $65   **016**
  1. Reference books 2. Historical fiction -- Bibliography
  ISBN 978-1-59158-624-1
                                        LC 2008-45537
  "Johnson has updated her outstanding Historical Fiction: A Guide to the Genre (2005) by covering historical fiction from 2004 through mid-2008 and adding such new features as ISBNs for each book and keyword descriptors after each annotation. . . . This volume continues rather than replaces the earlier work, adding more than 2,700 new titles." Booklist
  Includes bibliographical references

Kallio, Jamie

Read on ... speculative fiction for teens; reading lists for every taste. Jamie Kallio. Libraries Unlimited 2012 126 p. (Read on series) (pbk.) $40   **016**
1. Fantasy fiction 2. Science fiction 3. Dystopian fiction 4. Apocalyptic fiction 5. Fiction in libraries -- United States 6. Young adults' libraries -- Book lists 7. Fantasy fiction, English -- Bibliography 8. Fantasy fiction, American -- Bibliography 9. Readers' advisory services -- United States 10. Speculative fiction, English -- Bibliography 11. Young adult fiction, English -- Bibliography 12. Speculative fiction, American -- Bibliography 13. Young adult fiction, American -- Bibliography 14. Teenagers -- Books and reading -- United States
ISBN 1598846531; 9781598846539

LC 2012014172

This book on speculative fiction for teens, by Jamie Kallio, "features popular, contemporary themes ranging from vampire love and ghost stories to epic fantasy and out-of-this-world science fiction. Each of the five chapters caters to a specific area of interest-- story, character, setting, mood, and language-- and within the chapter, numerous lists of novels are organized by topic, with the best titles highlighted." (Publisher's note)

"The summaries are well written, and the selection of books is very broad. The one missing feature that would be helpful is an indicator of which books are for older teens and which are for the junior high crowd. Nevertheless, this is a terrific book to have by the stacks or at the front desk of any school library, or in classrooms where the students are asking what to read next." VOYA

Includes bibliographical references and index
Speculative fiction for teens

Ladd, Dana L.

The **Medical** Library Association guide to finding out about diabetes; the best print and electronic resources. Dana L. Ladd and Alyssa Altshuler. Neal-Schuman, an imprint of the American Library Association 2012 336 p. (alk. paper) $80   **016**
1. Diabetes 2. Diabetes -- Bibliography 3. Diabetes -- Computer network resources -- Directories
ISBN 1555708900; 9781555708900

LC 2012028333

This book, by Dana L. Ladd and Alyssa Altshuler, "provides . . . background on key diabetes concepts, encompassing reliable print and electronic resources, including hard-to-find periodicals and audiovisual sources. Each chapter in this guide presents an overview and description as well as an annotated list of multi-format resources on topics including Types 1 and 2 and gestational diabetes, diet, clinical trials, and support sources, and legal and insurance issues." (Publisher's note)

"This basic, plainly written bibliography is a must for any collection expected to provide current resources on diabetes to health-care students, medical professionals, or patients and their families." LJ

Includes bibliographical references and index
Guide to finding out about diabetes

Martinez, Sara E.

Latino literature; A guide to reading interests. edited by Sara E. Martinez; foreword by Connie Van Fleet. Libraries Unlimited 2009 xxii, 364 p.p $60   **016**
1. American literature (Spanish) 2. American literature -- Latino authors 3. Reference books 4. Hispanic American literature (Spanish) 5. American literature -- Hispanic American authors 6. American literature -- Hispanic American authors/Bibliography
ISBN 159158292X; 9781591582922

LC 2009026355

"Focusing on popular works by Latino authors, i.e. U.S. authors of Latino heritage; and authors from Latin American countries or Spain," this book, edited by Sara E. Martinez, "organizes and describes approximately 750 titles by genre, subgenre and theme. . . . Complete bibliographic information is provided for each title, along with a concise plot summary, a subject list, award information, a brief quote from the book, and a list of similar reads." (Publisher's note)

"This well-written book is an essential resource for public and high-school libraries, especially if they serve Latino populations." Booklist

Includes bibliographical references and indexes

Montgomery, Denise L.

Ottemiller's index to plays in collections; an author and title index to plays appearing in collections published since 1900. Scarecrow Press, Inc. 2011 xlix, 781 p.p   **016**
1. Drama -- Indexes
ISBN 9780810877207; 9780810877214

LC 2010053010

"Returning after some 20 years, this volume (7th ed., 1988) remains the classic index to plays in collections and anthologies... Plays are indexed by title, author, and anthology title. Montgomery adds more than 2,300 new authors and 3,593 new plays, expanding the work's focus to include works from 103 countries and making works by women and LGBT authors more discoverable." Choice

Morris, Vanessa Irvin

The **readers'** advisory guide to street literature; Vanessa Irvin Morris; foreword by Teri Woods. American Library Association 2012 xxiii, 138 p.p ill. (alk. paper) $48.00   **016**
1. Readers' advisory services 2. Urban fiction -- Bibliography 3. Urban fiction -- History and criticism 4. Fiction in libraries 5. Street life -- Fiction -- Bibliography 6. Urban fiction, American -- Bibliography 7. Readers' advisory services -- United States 8. Young adult fiction, American -- Bibliography 9. Urban fiction, American -- History and criticism
ISBN 0838911102; 9780838911105

LC 2011029685

In this book, author Vanessa Irvin "Morris presents a[n] . . . overview of the genre [of street literature]. From exploring the genre's roots . . . to articulating the appeal of the books, this . . . volume covers unique . . . material. For example, there is an entire chapter on teen-friendly street lit as well as material on collection development. Appendixes include a list of publishers and unannotated book lists." (Booklist)

Includes bibliographical references (p. 113-130) and index

Niebuhr, Gary Warren

Caught up in crime; a reader's guide to crime fiction and nonfiction. [compiled by] Gary Warren Niebuhr. Libraries Unlimited 2009 xviii, 304 p.p $60 **016**

1. Crime 2. Organized crime 3. White collar crimes 4. Crime writing 5. Criminal investigation
ISBN 1591584280; 9781591584285

LC 2009008733

In this book, "librarian Gary Warren Niebuhr organizes and describes more than 600 crime titles according to popular reading tastes. . . . Books are arranged in three broad categories' professional criminals,' 'caught up in crime,' and 'criminal detectives.' Within these chapters, titles are organized in sections on the mob, serial killers, white-collar crime, criminals on the run, victims, cops-gone-bad, rogues, and more." (Publisher's note)

"The only challenge that readers or readers' advisors face when confronted with so many excellent choices is deciding where to begin reading. Whether you're after capers, serial-killer tales, white-collar crime, mobsters, dirty cops or lawyers, criminals on the lam, amateur criminals, or any other kind of crime tale, this work is recommended as a thoughtful starting point." Booklist

Make mine a mystery II; a reader's guide to mystery and detective fiction. Gary Warren Niebuhr. Libraries Unlimited 2011 xiv, 292 p.p (acid-free paper) $60 **016**

1. Mystery fiction 2. Detective and mystery stories -- Bibliography 3. Detective and mystery stories -- Stories, plots, etc
ISBN 1598845896; 9781598845891

LC 2011017226

This book, by Gary Warren Niebuhr, "examines works by prominent established authors and includes books from new writers not in the previous edition. Organizing some 700 titles in popular mystery series, the books within are divided into the broader types-- amateur, public, and private detective. Each of the selections within these groups is further categorized by the type of protagonist: classic, eccentric, lone wolf, police, lawyer, and so on." (Publisher's note)

"The authors included give a good representation of popular writers today. The bibliographies have also been updated. This is an excellent companion to the original volume and an essential readers' advisory tool." Booklist

Includes bibliographical references and indexes

Pearl, Nancy

Now read this; a guide to mainstream fiction, 1978-1998. [by] Nancy Pearl, with the assistance of Martha Knappe and Chris Higashi; foreword by Joyce S. Saricks. Libraries Unlimited 1999 432p $65 **016**

1. Best books 2. Reference books 3. Fiction --

Bibliography
ISBN 1-56308-659-X

LC 99-15280

Annotated list of 1000 books categorized by setting, story, characterization, or language

Includes bibliographical references

Now read this II; a guide to mainstream fiction, 1990-2001. Libraries Unlimited 2002 300p il $55 **016**

1. Best books 2. Reference books 3. Fiction -- Bibliography
ISBN 1-56308-867-3

LC 2002-274079

This is an annotated list of 500 books categorized by setting, story, characterization, or language. "New features include a YA designation for selected titles, a section on fiction trends, and two appendixes, one on genre bridges (books that share elements with genre fiction) and one on book groups. Like others in the Genreflecting series, this work is a truly useful tool." Booklist

★ **Now** read this III; a guide to mainstream fiction. [by] Nancy Pearl and Sarah Statz Cords. Libraries Unlimited 2010 xxiii, 405p $60 **016**

1. Best books 2. Reference books 3. Fiction -- Bibliography
ISBN 978-1-59158-570-1

LC 2009-49898

An annotated list of over 500 books categorized by setting, story, characterization, or language. "This volume covers books published since 2002, with heavy emphasis on the last three years. Appendixes provide bridges to other genres, book award information, further resources, and advice for book groups, and everything is thoroughly indexed by author, title, and subject." Booklist

Includes bibliographical references

Perrault, Anna H.

Information resources in the humanities and the arts; by Anna H. Perrault, Elizabeth S. Aversa, Sonia Ramirez Wohlmuth, Cynthia Miller. Libraries Unlimited, an imprint of ABC-CLIO, LLC 2013 xvii, 461 p.p (Libraries Unlimited library and information science text series) (paperback) $65 **016**

1. Humanities 2. Reference books 3. Arts -- Bibliography 4. Humanities -- Bibliography 5. Arts -- Reference books -- Bibliography 6. Arts -- Electronic information resources 7. Arts -- Information services -- Directories 8. Humanities -- Reference books -- Bibliography 9. Humanities -- Electronic information resources 10. Humanities -- Information services -- Directories
ISBN 159884833X; 9781598848328; 9781598848335

LC 2012028606

This book "introduces new librarians to the breadth of humanities collections, experienced librarians to nature of humanities scholarship, and the scholars themselves to a wealth of information they might otherwise have missed. This new version . . . has been refreshed to account for the myriad of digital resources that have rewritten the rules of the reference and research world, and been expanded to include significantly increased coverage of world literature and languages." (Publisher's note)

Includes bibliographical references and indexes

Printed sources; a guide to published genealogical records. edited by Kory L. Meyerink. Ancestry 1998 840p $49.95 **016**
1. Reference books 2. Genealogy -- Bibliography 3. United States -- History -- Bibliography
ISBN 0-916489-70-1

LC 98-10852

The book opens with an "introductory chapter that highlights categories of research, the evaluation of records, interlibrary loan, and even the Dewey Decimal system. Editor Meyerink then divides the book into four sections encompassing background information (how-to-books, atlases), finding aids, printed original records, and compiled records (family histories, periodicals)." Libr J

Quillen, C. L.

Read on... romance; reading lists for every taste. C.L. Quillen and Ilene N. Lefkowitz. Libraries Unlimited 2014 xii, 136 p.p (paperback) $40 **016**
1. Best books 2. Love stories -- Bibliography 3. Books and reading 4. Reading interests 5. Love stories -- History and criticism
ISBN 1610694007; 9781610694001

LC 2014005515

Written by C. L. Quillen and Ilene N. Lefkowitz, "This book helps adult and teen readers quickly find the books they love to read, identifies other titles with shared qualities for more reading suggestions, and provides librarians with carefully reviewed read-alike lists that they can use with confidence. Featuring romance novels published from 2000 to the present day, this . . . guide offers you hundreds of reading suggestions." (Publisher's note)

"Keep this slimmer, solid resource on the shelf next to Kristen Ramsdell's Romance Fiction: A Guide to the Genre (2012)." Booklist

Includes bibliographical references and index

Ramsdell, Kristin

Romance fiction; a guide to the genre. Kristin Ramsdell. Libraries Unlimited 2012 xxii, 719 p.p (hardcopy : acid-free paper) $55 **016**
1. Romances 2. Book selection 3. Romance literature 4. Love stories -- Bibliography 5. Love stories -- History and criticism
ISBN 159158177X; 9781591581772; 9781610692359
LC 2011045879

Author Kristin Ramsdell explains in the preface that "this volume is actually the second edition of her 'Happily Ever After: A Guide to Reading Interests in Romance Fiction', published . . . in 1987. . . . [The book discusses] the definition and appeal of romance and contain[s] general information about advising readers and building collections, [while also looking at] subgenres of romance, from contemporary to ethnic/multicultural." (Booklist)

Includes bibliographical references and indexes.

Reisner, Rosalind

Read on-- life stories; reading lists for every taste. Rosalind Reisner. Libraries Unlimited 2009 xv, 175 p.p $40 **016**
1. Biography 2. Autobiographies
ISBN 1591587662; 9781591587668

LC 2009023222

This book, by Rosalind Reisner, "offers brief descriptions of nearly 450 published memoirs, from classics. . . to recent bestsellers. . . . Titles are grouped together by their appeal to readers, and there is something for everyone: humorous memoirs, thrilling adventure stories, chatty celebrity reminiscences, cathartic dramas of family dysfunction, fascinating career retrospectives, and insightful stories of family and personal lives in many eras and places." (Publisher's note)

"With both a detailed table of contents and an excellent index, this is a must-have tool for public libraries." Booklist

Includes bibliographical references and index.

Riechel, Rosemarie

Easy information sources for ESL, adult learners, & new readers. Neal-Schuman Publishers 2009 285p pa $65 **016**
1. Libraries -- Special collections 2. English as a second language -- Bibliography 3. High interest-low vocabulary books -- Bibliography
ISBN 978-1-55570-650-0; 1-55570-650-9

LC 2008-40028

"This work is aimed at educators and librarians working with adults whose English is poor. Advice on ways to use children's nonfiction for adults; reference interview strategies; book selection, placement, and utilization; collection development; and readers' advisory enables this work to not only suggest sources but also offer new ways of serving this growing and diverse population." Booklist

Includes bibliographical references

Roche, Rick

Read on-- biography; reading lists for every taste. Rick Roche. Libraries Unlimited 2012 xvi, 163 p.p (hardcover) $30 **016**
1. Autobiography 2. Book selection 3. Biography -- Bibliography 4. Autobiography -- Bibliography
ISBN 1610691792; 9781610691796; 1598847015; 9781598847017

LC 2011046293

In this book, author Rick Roche "focuses on life stories written in the third person, with subjects ranging from individuals who lived in ancient times to the present-day, hailed from myriad nations, and gained fame in diverse fields. The contents are organized in order to facilitate identification of read-alikes and easy selection of titles according to appeal features such as character, story, language, setting, and mood.

Includes bibliographical references and indexes.

Scales, Pat R.

★ **Books** under fire; a hit list of banned and challenged children's books. Pat Scales. ALA Editions,

an imprint of the American Library Association 2015 xvi, 208 p.p illustrations (pbk.) $47 **016**
1. Books -- Censorship 2. Children -- Books and reading -- United States 3. School libraries -- Censorship -- United States 4. Challenged books -- United States -- Bibliography 5. Prohibited books -- United States -- Bibliography 6. Children's literature -- Censorship -- United States
ISBN 0838911099; 9780838911099

LC 2014023945

This book on banned and challenged books, by Pat R. Scales, "covers both children's and young adult books. The main section profiles 34 books (and series such as 'Harry Potter' and 'Captain Underpants') that have recently been challenged for library or curriculum suitability in the US... . Each entry includes a . . . synopsis, quotations from some reviews, details of known challenges, awards/accolades, and a 'Further Reading' section." (Choice)

Includes bibliographical references and index

Torres-Roman, Steven A.

Read on-- science fiction; reading lists for every taste. Steven A. Torres-Roman. Libraries Unlimited 2010 xxi, 252 p.p (pbk : acid-free paper) $40 **016**
1. Science fiction -- Bibliography 2. Fiction in libraries -- United States 3. Science fiction, English -- Bibliography 4. Science fiction, American -- Bibliography 5. Readers' advisory services -- United States 6. Public libraries -- United States -- Book lists
ISBN 1591587697; 9781591587699

LC 2010024075

This book, by Steven A. Torres-Roman, "is for new science fiction readers looking for a place to start exploring the genre, as well as for long-time fans who want to delve in deeper. The guide covers a broad spectrum of science fiction titles, organizing books into lists designed to appeal to a variety of reading tastes.... The book spans the genre's time stream, including classics . . . as well as the latest bestsellers." (Publisher's note)

Includes bibliographical references and index

Trott, Barry

Read on . . . crime fiction; reading lists for every taste. Libraries Unlimited 2008 146p (Read on series) pa $30 **016**
1. Reference books 2. Mystery fiction -- Bibliography
ISBN 978-1-59158-373-8.

LC 2007-33858

The author organizes recommended crime fiction titles by "five 'appeal characteristics' commonly employed by RA professionals: story, character, setting, mood, and language. Under these broad categories, he offers an assortment of creatively titled reading lists ('Serf and Turf: Medieval Mysteries') that illustrate aspects of one of the appeal factors. Arrows designate one title per list selected as a good starting point for that category.... Both readers' advisors and crime-fiction fans will find all sorts of inventive ways to use this book, including, of course, compiling their own lists of titles or categories that should have been represented." Booklist

Vnuk, Rebecca

Read on-- women's fiction; reading lists for every taste. Rebecca Vnuk. Libraries Unlimited 2009 126 p. $40 **016**
1. Women -- Fiction 2. American fiction -- Women authors
ISBN 1591586348; 9781591586340

LC 2009012315

This book, by Rebecca Vnuk, "offers new reading paths for women's fiction lovers. the organization and approach are based on various appeal factors of the genre, rather than on the formal genres and subgenres adhered to by other guides. Use these lists to advise readers; to create thematic reading lists for library websites, flyers, and newsletters; and as checklists or reading plans for those who enjoy women's fiction." (Publisher's note)

"The work also includes a combined index of titles and authors. Like others in the Read On ... series, this book complements more formal genre guides and is intended to be used by readers as well as readers' advisors." Booklist

Includes bibliographical references and index

Women's fiction; a guide to popular reading interests. Rebecca Vnuk and Nanette Donohue. Libraries Unlimited, an imprint of ABC-CLIO, LLC 2013 xv, 233 p.p (Genreflecting advisory series) (hardback : acid-free paper) $55 **016**
1. Women -- Fiction 2. American fiction -- Women authors 3. Women -- Fiction -- Bibliography 4. Fiction in libraries -- United States 5. Readers' advisory services -- United States 6. Women -- Books and reading -- United States 7. Public libraries -- United States -- Book lists 8. American fiction -- 20th century -- Bibliography 9. American fiction -- 21st century -- Bibliography 10. American fiction -- Women authors -- Bibliography
ISBN 1598849204; 9781598849202

LC 2013023685

This book on women's fiction is part of the Libraries Unlimited Genreflecting Advisory series. "Nine chapters gather titles under such categories as 'Grande Dames of Women's Fiction,' 'Gentle Reads,' 'Chick Lit and Beyond,' and 'Multicultural Women's Fiction.' Each chapter begins with a brief explanation of the subgenre or classificadon; for each title presented within each chapter, a two-to- three-sentence annotation highlights plot, theme, and characters." (Booklist)

Includes bibliographical references and indexes

016.6   Bibliographies of technology (Applied sciences)

Covert, Jack

★ The **100** best business books of all time; what they say, why they matter, and how they can help you. [by] Jack Covert and Todd Sattersten. Portfolio 2009 335p il $25.95 **016.6**
1. Best books 2. Business -- Bibliography
ISBN 978-1-59184-240-8

LC 2008-36664

"Covert and Sattersten operate 800-CEO-READ, a specialty business-book retailer. Out of the countless business books they have read every year for a quarter century, they have culled 100 of the best and presented them in review format. . . . This list and the fine reviews are proof positive that business books can offer a rich treasure of stories and inspiration." Booklist

Includes bibliographical references

Introduction to reference sources in the health sciences; edited by Jeffrey T. Huber and Susan Swogger. ALA Neal-Schuman 2014 468 p. (Medical Library Association Guides) $118 **016.6**
1. Medicine -- Bibliography 2. Medicine -- Information services 3. Medicine -- Reference books -- Bibliography
ISBN 0838911846; 9780838911846

LC 2014004660

This book for medical librarians "lists classic and up-to-the-minute print and electronic resources in the health sciences, helping librarians find the answers that library users seek. Included are electronic versions of traditionally print reference sources, trustworthy electronic-only resources, and resources that library users can access from home or on the go through freely available websites or via library licenses." (Publisher's note)

"As with any reference work, particularly one that relies heavily on online materials, some of the resources mentioned likely will become outdated over time. Nevertheless, the larger context in which these resources are often presented should slow the inevitable decline in relevance." Choice

Includes bibliographical references and index

Stoeger, Melissa Brackney

Food lit; a reader's guide to epicurean nonfiction. Melissa Brackney Stoeger. Libraries Unlimited 2013 xx, 350 p.p (Real stories) (hardback) $60   **016.6**
1. Food in literature 2. Food -- Bibliography
ISBN 1598847066; 9781598847062

LC 2012038052

This book, by Melissa Brackney Stoeger, "provides a much-needed resource for librarians assisting adult readers interested in the topic of food. . . . Containing annotations of hundreds of nonfiction titles about food that are arranged into genre and subject interest categories for easy reference, the book addresses a diversity of reading experiences by covering everything from foodie memoirs and histories of food to extreme cuisine and food exposés." (Publisher's note)

"The hundreds of annotations alone make any librarian's job much, much easier, but Stoeger's inclusion of appendix materials from famous cooks and their books, food blogs, feature films and documentaries, fiction featuring food, and food-writing awards makes this an outstanding reference tool for any public library collection." Booklist

Includes bibliographical references and indexes

020   Library and information sciences

The **21st**-century black librarian in America; issues and challenges. edited by Andrew P. Jackson (Sekou Molefi Baako), Julius Jefferson Jr., Akilah

Nosakhere. Scarecrow Press 2012 xxii, 277 p.p (hardcover) $80   **020**
1. Library science 2. African American librarians 3. African Americans and libraries
ISBN 0810882450; 9780810882454

LC 2011042051

BCALA Literary Award: Outstanding Contribution to Publishing Citation (2013)

This book is a "collection of 48 essays by Black librarians and library supporters [that] identifies racism as one of many challenges of the new century." Topics covered include "poorly equipped school libraries and the need to preserve the school library, a call to action to all librarians to make the shift to new and innovative models of public education, . . . racism in the history of library and information science, and challenges that have plagued librarianship for decades." (Publisher's note)

Includes bibliographical references and index.

ALA glossary of library and information science; edited by Michael Levine-Clark and Toni M. Carter. ALA Editions 2013 viii, 280 p.p (pbk. : alk. paper) $55   **020**
1. Library science -- Dictionaries 2. Information science -- Dictionaries
ISBN 0838911110; 9780838911112

LC 2012010060

This book, edited by Michael Levine-Clark and Toni M. Carter, "presents a thorough yet concise guide to the specific words that describe the materials, processes and systems relevant to the field of librarianship. Written by a panel of experts from across the LIS world, . . . [this edition is] updated to include the latest technology- and internet-related terms." (Publisher's note)

Includes bibliographical references (pages 277-280)

★ **Core** technology competencies for librarians and library staff; a LITA guide. Susan M. Thompson, editor. Neal-Schuman Publishers 2009 248p il pa $65   **020**
1. Library education 2. Information technology 3. Technological innovations 4. Librarians -- In-service training
ISBN 978-1-55570-660-9

LC 2008-46174

In this book, "a coterie of experts identify competencies for technology specialists and describe several competency implementation programs. Useful for everyone from the systems librarian to the 'lone information technology librarian.'" Am Libr

Includes bibliographical references

Defending professionalism; a resource for librarians, information specialists, knowledge managers, and archivists. Bill Crowley, editor. Libraries Unlimited, an imprint of ABC-CLIO, LLC 2012 235 p. (paperback) $50.00   **020**
1. Librarians 2. Professional ethics 3. Information scientists 4. Library education 5. Libraries and society 6. Archivists -- Training of 7. Knowledge workers -- Training of 8. Archivists -- Professional ethics 9. Librarians -- Professional ethics 10. Information

scientists -- Training of 11. Knowledge workers -- Professional ethics 12. Information scientists -- Professional ethics

ISBN 1598848690; 9781598848694

LC 2012006410

This book, edited by Bill Crowley, offers "arguments and approaches for combating library and information deprofessionalization. . . . Composed of 14 chapters written by contemporary practitioners," the book "provides managers, funding authorities, educators, and practitioners with practical, political, and theoretical reasons why it is in their self-interest to employ professionally educated personnel." (Publisher's note)

Includes bibliographical references and index

Gleick, James

The **information**. Pantheon Books 2011 526p il $29.95 **020**

1. Information science

ISBN 978-0-375-42372-7; 0-375-42372-9

LC 2010-23221

"As he traces the evolution of intertwined ideas, [Gleick] provides vivid portraits of [Claude] Shannon and other pioneers of our Information Age, including Charles Babbage, whose unbuilt 19th-century 'Analytical Engine' anticipated modern computers, and Alan Turing, whose machines helped the Allies crack German codes during World War II." Wall Street J

Includes bibliographical references

Johnson, Marilyn

★ **This** book is overdue! how librarians and cybrarians can save us all. Harper 2010 272p $24.99 **020**

1. Librarians 2. Library science

ISBN 978-0-06-143160-9; 0-06-143160-5

LC 2010-07860

"In an information age full of Google-powered searches, free-by-Bittorrent media downloads and Wiki-powered knowledge databases, the librarian may seem like an antiquated concept. . . . [The author] is here to reverse that notion with a topical, witty study of the vital ways modern librarians uphold their traditional roles as educators, archivists, and curators of a community legacy. . . . Johnson's wry report is a must-read for anyone who's used a library in the past quarter century." Publ Wkly

Includes bibliographical references

Kroski, Ellusa

Web 2.0 for librarians and information professionals. Neal-Schuman Publishers 2008 209p il pa $75 **020**

1. Web 2.0 2. Web 2.0 -- Library applications

ISBN 978-1-55570-614-2; 1-55570-614-2

LC 2007-43249

"Whether you are just beginning the journey in the transformation of the Web or want to begin implementing this exciting tool in your library, this outstanding resource will take the mystery out of these concepts and be an excellent addition to your reference section." Libr Media Connect

Includes glossary and bibliographical references

Lankes, R. David

The **atlas** of new librarianship. MIT Press; Association of College & Research Libraries 2011 408p il $55 **020**

1. Library science 2. Libraries and community 3. Librarianship

ISBN 978-0-262-01509-7

LC 2010-22788

The author initiates a "conversation about librarianship and its future. He builds this conversation using an atlas, or topical mapping, to engage librarians in exploring their profession, their mission, and their future. . . . Grounding the atlas in the why of librarianship, Lankes argues that libraries serve not only as repositories providing access to information but as fertile ground for actively using collections, resources, and information to create knowledge and foster learning via ongoing conversations with our communities. He invites librarians to expand librarianship beyond the support of information seeking, access, and literacy and toward participation in and co-ownership of a community's knowledge-creation processes. . . . Essential for all librarians." Libr J

Includes bibliographical references.

Library mashups; exploring new ways to deliver library data. edited by Nicole C. Engard. Information Today, Inc. 2009 334p il map pa $39.50 **020**

1. Internet resources 2. Web sites -- Design

ISBN 978-1-57387-372-7

LC 2009-25999

"Editor Engard assembles 21 articles from 25 international contributors to focus on mashups within the library environment. Readers with little knowledge of mashups will find chapters such as 'What Is a Mashup?' and 'Behind the Scenes: Some Technical Details on Mashups' especially helpful. Other portions of this book cover topics such as mashups in library Web sites, mashups of catalog data, and mashups and media (e.g., photos)." Booklist

Includes bibliographical references

What Do I Read Next? A Reader's Guide to Current Genre Fiction. Gale Cengage Learning. Gale / Cengage Learning 2012 738 p. (hardcover) $254 **020**

1. Book selection 2. Books and reading

ISBN 1414461372; 9781414461373

This volume is a book selection guide. It uses similarities in various books to help "readers to independently choose titles of interest published in the last year. Each entry describes a separate book, listing everything readers need to know to make selections. Arranged by author within six genre sections, detailed entries provide" information about the title, publisher, series, and temporal and geographical setting. (Publisher's note)

Woodward, Jeannette

The **transformed** library; e-books, expertise, and evolution. Jeannette Woodward. ALA Editions, an imprint of the American Library Association 2013 131 p. $55 **020**

1. Libraries 2. Technological innovations 3. Libraries

and society 4. Libraries -- Forecasting 5. Libraries and the Internet 6. Library science -- Philosophy 7. Libraries -- Aims and objectives 8. Libraries -- Information technology 9. Libraries and electronic publishing 10. Librarians -- Effect of technological innovations on
ISBN 0838911641; 9780838911648

LC 2012023767

In this book, Jeannette Woodward considers: are "librarians and libraries facing oblivion as some prognosticators claim? Woodward outlines the technological forces that have coalesced to 'threaten' the future of libraries including financial constraints, digital books, ebook-publisher approaches to libraries, outsourcing, downsizing library space, and librarians' reaction to perceived threats." (Library Journal)

Includes bibliographical references and index

020.9 History, geographic treatment, biography

Wright, Alex

Cataloging the world; Paul Otlet and the birth of the information age. Alex Wright. Oxford University Press 2014 360 p. (acid-free paper) $27.95 **020.9**
1. Bibliographers -- Biography 2. Bibliographic control -- History 3. Documentation 4. Mundaneum -- History 5. Universal bibliography 6. Classification -- Books 7. World Wide Web -- History 8. Information organization -- History 9. Bibliographers -- Belgium -- Biography
ISBN 0199931410; 9780199931415

LC 2013035233

"In 'Cataloging the World,' Alex Wright introduces us to a figure who stands out in the long line of thinkers and idealists who devoted themselves to the task. Beginning in the late nineteenth century, Paul Otlet, a librarian by training, worked at expanding the potential of the catalog card, the world's first information chip." (Publisher's note)

"Wright ends his illuminating story in the present, where Otlet's thoughts about the connection of information to knowledge, and knowledge to insight, are still urgent." Kirkus

Includes bibliographical references and index

021.2 Relationships with the community

The **artist's** library; a field guide. edited by Laura C. Damon-Moore and Erinn P. Batykefer. Coffee House Press 2014 220 p. illustrations (Books in action) $23.95 **021.2**
1. Libraries and community 2. Creation (Literary, artistic, etc.) 3. Arts -- Library resources 4. Libraries -- Social aspects 5. Library users -- Case studies 6. Libraries -- Cultural programs 7. Libraries -- Problems, exercises, etc 8. Creation (Literary, artistic, etc.) -- Case studies
ISBN 1566893534; 9781566893534

LC 2013035168

This book, edited by Laura C. Damon-Moore and Erinn P. Batykefer, "offers the idea that an artist is any person who uses creative tools to make new things, and the guidance and resources to make libraries of all sizes and shapes come alive

as spaces for art-making and cultural engagement. Case studies included in the book range from the crafty . . . to the community-minded . . . to documentary . . . to the technically complex." (Publisher's note)

"Librarians who wish to make their library the connecting point between artists and the community should purchase. Perfect for brainstorming planning guides, this book is a permission slip to have fun at the library." LJ

Brookover, Sophie

Pop goes the library; using pop culture to connect with your whole community. [by] Sophie Brookover and Elizabeth Burns. Information Today, Inc. 2008 298p il pa $39.50 **021.2**
1. Libraries and community 2. Libraries -- Special collections -- Popular culture
ISBN 978-1-57387-336-9

LC 2008-19509

"This work defines how popular culture can contribute to any library. . . . The authors explore what popular culture is and, more importantly, what it is not. Also examined are what it means to create a popular-culture collection and how to use popular culture to generate staff and public support. . . . This book is required reading." Booklist

Includes bibliographical references

Hill, Chrystie

Inside, outside, and online; building your library community. foreword by Steven Cohen. American Library Association 2009 175p pa $48 **021.2**
1. Libraries and community 2. Library administration 3. Libraries -- Evaluation
ISBN 978-0-8389-0987-4; 0-8389-0987-6

LC 2008-52520

In this "how-to manual, author Hill makes a . . . case for community building as an essential form of service in public libraries, both for their survival and relevance and also for the needs of those Americans who find themselves 'bowling alone.' She outlines five steps in the process she recommends public libraries follow to build communities: assess, deliver, engage, iterate, and sustain." Booklist

Includes bibliographical references

Librarians as community partners; an outreach handbook. edited by Carol Smallwood. American Library Association 2010 204p pa $55 **021.2**
1. Cultural programs 2. Libraries and community 3. Libraries -- Public relations
ISBN 978-0-8389-1006-1

LC 2009-20359

"Thirty-seven public, school, and academic librarians here share 'how we did outreach good' and produce a joyful collection. . . . Beyond a bounty of ideas are practical suggestions and examples that can be used for the library to approach organizations, groups, and governmental entities for grant applications. While the creative is foremost, the financial and efficient are also addressed with the essential details of who did what, how it was funded, and the nature of follow-up. . . . Even the smallest library with a handful of staff could benefit from this book." Libr J

Includes bibliographical references

021.7   Promotion of libraries, archives, information centers

Imhoff, Kathleen R.

Library contests; a how-to-do-it manual. [by] Kathleen R.T. Imhoff, Ruthie Maslin. Neal-Schuman Publishers 2007 182p il pa $55   **021.7**

1. Contests 2. Libraries and community 3. Advertising -- Libraries 4. Libraries -- Public relations
ISBN 1-55570-559-6 pa; 978-1-55570-559-6 pa
LC 2006-33177

"This comprehensive book covers planning, implementing, and evaluating contests of all kinds, for all kinds of libraries. It addresses setting budgets and schedules, choosing prizes and judges, establishing rules, promoting the contest, and evaluating it once it is over. The final chapter details four tried-and-true programs various libraries have held." (School Library Journal)

Marketing your library; tips and tools that work. edited by Carol Smallwood, Vera Gubnitskaia and Kerol Harrod; foreword by Michael Germano. McFarland & Company, Inc., Publishers 2012 ix, 221 p.p ill. (softcover : acid-free paper) $55.00   **021.7**

1. Libraries -- Marketing 2. Libraries -- Public relations
ISBN 0786465433; 9780786465439
LC 2012004460

This book, edited by Carol Smallwood, Vera Gubnitskaia, and Kerol Harrod, presents "how-to case studies from practicing public, school, academic, and special librarians" intended to help librarians "improve brand management, campaign organization, community outreach, media interaction, social media, and event planning and implementation." (Publisher's note)

Includes bibliographical references and index

Phillips, Susan P.

Great displays for your library step by step. McFarland & Co. 2008 234p il pa $45   **021.7**

1. Libraries -- Exhibitions
ISBN 978-0-7864-3164-9; 0-7864-3164-4
LC 2007-47450

This book "offers practical advice on utilizing everyday materials to create lively but economical presentations on all sorts of topics including authors, world cultures, traditions, natural habitats and book genres. Each of 46 featured displays includes a brief introduction to the subject; an explanation of the genesis of the idea; specifics regarding the information included and its source; step-by-step instructions for assembly; and ideas on how to customize the display to any available space." (Publisher's note)

Schall, Lucy

Teen talkback with interactive booktalks! Lucy Schall. Libraries Unlimited, an imprint of ABC-CLIO, LLC 2013 xviii, 305 p.p (hardcopy) $45   **021.7**

1. Reading 2. Book talks 3. Young adult literature 4. Young adults' libraries 5. Fiction genres -- Bibliography 6. Reading promotion -- United States 7. Teenagers --

Books and reading -- United States
ISBN 1610692896; 9781610692892
LC 2013000241

This book, by Lucy Schall, "is . . . a resource, supplying ready-to-use, interactive booktalks and curriculum connections for more than 100 recently published young adult books. This . . . book is . . . [a] tool for motivating teens to read. It shows how to make booktalks interactive and get teens participating in the presentation, rather than passively listening. Book selections include titles published from 2008 to 2012 organized in seven categories." (Publisher's note)

"Although mostly fiction, there are some nonfiction choices included and the balance of newer titles is respectable. Due to the plethora of topics, detail in descriptions, and variety of related works listed, librarians will be able to locate books for the pickiest of readers." Lib Med Con

Includes bibliographical references and index

Thenell, Jan

The **library's** crisis communications planner; a PR guide for handling every emergency. American Library Association 2004 77p il pa $25   **021.7**

1. Libraries -- Public relations
ISBN 0-8389-0870-5
LC 2004-10891

Offering "advice, firsthand experience, scenarios, and guidelines for communicating effectively before, during, and after a crisis or crisis-producing events, ... [the author's] guide is a ready-made workshop on how to establish and maintain relationships with the media, including how to write a press release, how to keep all staff informed and aware of what to do when an emergency occurs, and how to make sure library board members and other community stakeholders are notified and/or involved. Whether or not you have a public relations office or officer, this slim volume is a must for your professional shelf." Libr J

Includes bibliographical references

022   Administration of physical plant

Petroski, Henry

The **book** on the bookshelf. Knopf 1999 290p $26   **022**

1. Books 2. Libraries 3. Bookbinding
ISBN 0-375-40649-2
LC 99-14336

The author discusses the formatting and housing of books throughout history

"The charm of this book lies in the way that it helps us take a fresh look at an old, long-familiar object. . . . This survey of the subject is probably definitive." Christ Sci Monit

Includes bibliographical references

023   Personnel management (Human resource management)

Giesecke, Joan

★ **Fundamentals** of library supervision; [by] Joan Giesecke and Beth McNeil. 2nd ed.; American

Library Association 2010 189p il (ALA fundamentals series) pa $55 **023**

1. Personnel management 2. Libraries -- Administration
ISBN 978-0-8389-1016-0

LC 2009-28890

First published 2005

"The authors give advice on how to build relationships with bosses, peers, and reports; establish good communication skills; create a healthy work climate; motivate others; and build a team. . . . Each chapter includes a succinct bibliography, allowing the new manager to continue his or her education—especially useful for more complex topics like project management." Libr J

Includes bibliographical references

Stanley, Mary J.

Managing library employees; a how-to-do-it manual. Neal-Schuman Publishers 2008 247p il (How-to-do-it manuals for libraries) pa $59.95 **023**

1. Personnel management 2. Libraries -- Handbooks, manuals, etc.
ISBN 978-1-55570-628-9; 1-55570-628-2

LC 2007-51961

"Oriented to librarians who do not have a human resources department in the library, Managing Library Employees is for the nonexpert trying to come to terms with managing a library's largest expenditure and asset—its employees. The chapters are divided into subtopics posed as questions. . . . The chapters also provide information on writing an effective job description, designing a disciplinary procedure, and identifying potential issues that might lead to a lawsuit. . . . This useful guide for everyday situations should be on any library director or manager's professional reference shelf." Booklist

Includes bibliographical references

Tucker, Dennis C.

Crash course in library supervision; meeting the key players. [by] Dennis C. Tucker and Shelley Elizabeth Mosley. Libraries Unlimited 2008 139p il (Crash course series) pa $30 **023**

1. Libraries -- Administration
ISBN 978-1-59158-564-0; 1-59158-564-3

LC 2007-30131

This book "covers the basics for new public library administrators, with an emphasis on interpersonal relations. . . . The book should prove valuable to all new library administrators." Booklist

Includes bibliographical references

025 Operations of libraries, archives, information centers

Bolan, Kimberly

Technology made simple; an improvement guide for small and medium libraries. [by] Kimberly Bolan and Robert Cullin. American Library Association 2007 213p il $40 **025**

1. Information technology 2. Libraries -- Automation
ISBN 0-8389-0920-5; 978-0-8389-0920-1

LC 2006-13191

The authors present an "overview of basic public library technologies. . . . Using examples from a plethora of small- and medium-sized libraries to illustrate how such specific issues as self-check, hiring for attitude, tech policies, staff and public training, and formal planning can be approached as doable and nonthreatening to the non-specialist, this guide is an excellent demonstration of how order can make big issues approachable. . . . Libraries should purchase it for their staff collections but also make reading and implementing various suggestions part of their work plans." Voice Youth Advocates

Includes bibliographical references

Burke, John J., 1875-1936

Neal-Schuman library technology companion; a basic guide for library staff. [by] John J. Burke. 3rd ed.; Neal-Schuman Publishers 2009 279p il **025**

1. Information technology 2. Technological innovations 3. Libraries -- Automation
ISBN 978-1-55570-676-0

LC 2009-23646

First published 2001

"Separated into five parts, the work begins with a discussion of the basics, followed by descriptions of the tools, such as computers and networks. Next addressed are how to put technology to work and how to build and maintain the technology environment. The final chapter talks about future trends. . . . [This is] a valuable reference manual for practicing librarians and textbook for a library-school course. The work addresses all aspects of librarianship and technology—teaching, security, databases, social networking, and more." Booklist

Includes bibliographical references

Cohn, John M.

The **complete** library technology planner; a guidebook with sample technology plans and RFPs on CD-ROM. [by] John M. Cohn and Ann L. Kelsey; with a foreword by Keith Michael Fiels. Neal-Schuman Publishers 2010 xxiv, 163p il pa $99.95 **025**

1. Information technology 2. Planning, Library 3. Libraries -- Automation 4. Automation of library processes -- Handbooks, manuals, etc.
ISBN 978-1-55570-681-4; 1-55570-681-9

LC 2009-41008

"This book provides a comprehensive wealth of information for libraries in need of creating or updating a technology plan. Whether your goal is to introduce an integrated library system (ILS) or transfer from an existing system to a new one, Cohn and Kelsey make clear the strategic planning process involved and provide the tools needed to create a plan, including how to meet funding requirements, implement the plan, and evaluate its success. The accompanying CD-ROM contains 38 sample technology plans and requests for proposals (RFPs) that have been collected from 32 different libraries." Libr J

Includes bibliographical references

Kovacs, Diane K.

The **Kovacs** guide to electronic library collection development; essential core subject collections, selection criteria, and guidelines. 2nd ed; Neal-Schuman Publishers 2009 xxiii, 303p il pa $150   **025**

1. Digital libraries
ISBN 978-1-55570-664-7; 1-55570-664-9
LC 2009-27772

First published 2004; written by Diane K. Kovacs and Kara L. Robinson

"Chapters cover general collection guidelines and licensing basics; especially useful are individual sections citing specific Web sites for e-collection sources in ready reference, business, medicine, biology, engineering, physical and earth sciences, and the social sciences and humanities. Kovacs . . . is a very diligent researcher, and her latest title again offers librarians much useful information. " Booklist

Includes bibliographical references

More technology for the rest of us; a second primer on computing for the non-IT librarian. Nancy Courtney, editor. Libraries Unlimited 2010 172p il pa $50   **025**

1. Digital libraries. 2. Digital preservation. 3. Libraries and the Internet. 4. Libraries -- Information technology. 5. Libraries -- Technological innovations.
ISBN 978-1-59158-939-6 pa; 1-59158-939-8 pa; 978-1-59158-941-9 ebook; 1-59158-941-X ebook
LC 2009051166

Continuation of Technology for the rest of us (2005)

"11 chapters provide readings on technology topics of interest to today's librarian. Each chapter, authored by a different practicing librarian, describes how the specific technology works and addresses its current and potential use in the library. . . . This book is a one-stop resource for gaining a basic overview of topics such as Web services, digital data preservation and curation, cloud computing, learning management systems, content management systems, metadata repurposing using XSLT, and more." Booklist

Includes bibliographical references

Pearl, Nancy

More book lust; recommended reading for every mood, moment, and reason. Sasquatch Books 2005 286p pa $16.95   **025**

1. Best books 2. Books and reading
ISBN 1-57061-435-0
LC 2004-66292

Sequel to: Book lust (2003)

The author presents a list of "books she or someone else really enjoyed reading, presented in more than 100 lists covering a delightful range of topics, from the biographical or geographical (Winston Churchill, Africa) to favorite writers categorized as 'too good to miss'. . . . If you're clueless about what to read next, you'll find something to pique your interest here." Publ Wkly

Includes bibliographical references

Pulliam, June Michele

Read on . . . horror fiction; [by] June Michele Pulliam and Anthony J. Fonseca. Libraries Unlimited 2006 xvii, 182 p (Read on series)   **025**

1. Reference books 2. Horror tales -- Bibliography. 3. Fiction in libraries -- United States. 4. Horror tales, American -- Bibliography. 5. Readers' advisory services -- United States. 6. Public libraries -- United States -- Book lists.
ISBN 1-59158-176-1; 978-1-59158-176-5 (pbk. : alk. paper)
LC 2006012719

"Pulliam and Fonseca have taken 350 popular horror titles from the last decade and divided them by their appeal factors. The authors point out that some readers may prefer books that are plot driven, while others want books that emphasize characters, while still others are interested in the mood of the book, and these factors are not found in the library catalog. Five chapters analyze the appeal factors of story, mood, setting, character, and language, with each chapter further subdivided into various themes--complex plots, plot twists, intense endings, gross stories, home-alone frights, wilderness horror, and psychic detectives, to name just a few." (Publisher's note)

Includes bibliographical references and index.

025.04 Information storage and retrieval systems

Bell, Suzanne S.

Librarian's guide to online searching; cultivating database skills for research and instruction. Suzanne S. Bell. 4th edition Libraries Unlimitied 2015 xvii, 320 p.p illustrations $55   **025.04**

1. Internet searching 2. Librarians -- Training of
ISBN 161069998X; 9781610699983
LC 2014038457

"In its fourth edition, this work still serves as the best how-to on online searching for library degree students and those new to the profession. Bell . . . provides an updated version that includes a more thorough discussion on Google Scholar, and offers fresh discussions on discovery services and video tutorials. . . . Bell discusses the gamut of database basics, starting with database construction, moving to specialized databases by broad subject area and search strategies, and ending with advice on effectively working to engage the audience during instruction." LJ

Includes bibliographical references (pages 299-309) and index

Dornfest, Rael

Google hacks; [by] Rael Dornfest, Paul Bausch, and Tara Calishain. 3rd ed.; O'Reilly 2006 xxxii, 510p il $24.99   **025.04**

1. Google (Web site) 2. Internet searching
ISBN 0-596-52706-3; 978-0-596-52706-8
LC 2006-285771

First published 2003 under the authorship of Tara Calishain and Rael Dornfest

This guide to the search engine Google gives instructions on how to use such tools as Google Earth, Google Maps,

Google Blog Search, Video Search, and Music Search, as well as different ways of using Google products, such as using Google to keep track of new blog posts and building customized Google maps.

Includes bibliographical references

Gale directory of databases. Gale Res. 2008 2v in 4 parts set $585   **025.04**
> 1. Reference books 2. Information systems -- Directories
>
> ISBN 978-0-7876-9755-6; 0-7876-9755-9
>
> Annual. First published 1993. Formed by the merger of Directory of online databases, Directory of portable databases, and Computer-readable databases
>
> "Descriptive entries include such details as producer name and contact information, summary of content, database language, geographic coverage, year first available, time span, updating, availability, rates, and more." Publisher's note

McClure, Charles R.
★ **Public** libraries and internet service roles; measuring and maximizing Internet services. [by] Charles R. McClure and Paul T. Jaeger. American Library Association 2009 112p il map $65 **025.04**
> 1. Internet 2. Public libraries 3. Libraries and the Internet 4. Internet -- Public libraries 5. Librarianship -- Social aspects 6. Public libraries -- Social aspects 7. Public libraries -- Aims and objectives
>
> ISBN 978-0-8389-3576-7; 0-8389-3576-1
>
> LC 2008-26622
>
> The authors "summarize the existing research on the meanings of social roles and expectations of public libraries and the results of studies detailing those roles and expectations in relation to the Internet. . . . Their book raises our awareness of some very critical issues and is required reading for anyone who cares about public libraries." Booklist
>
> Includes bibliographical references

Pariser, Eli
The **filter** bubble; what the Internet is hiding from you. Penguin Press 2011 294p $25.95 **025.04**
> 1. Internet 2. World Wide Web 3. Information systems 4. Semantic Web 5. Invisible Web 6. Internet -- Censorship 7. Information organization
>
> ISBN 978-1-59420-300-8; 1-59420-300-8
>
> LC 2011010403
>
> The author examines "the personalization of search-engine results. . . . He is most concerned with its political and social implications, and particularly with what he believes to be its high toll on serendipitous discovery." (N Y Times Book Rev) Index.
>
> "The distinction between citizen and consumer forms the core of [this book] . . . . Are we consumers whose role in society is primarily to purchase and use products, or are we citizens who make informed decisions in an attempt to make life better for ourselves and the world? The Internet, as Eli Pariser convincingly argues in the book, is hurtling toward a consumer model, existing primarily to sell people stuff at the expense of everything else. Pariser is focused on the 'personalization' model, as well as the 'filter bubble' that the gives the book its name. The biggest companies on

the Internet, specifically Google and Facebook, are changing the Internet to match users' specific interests, habits, and purchasing preferences, often without us even knowing we're getting personalized content. Pariser isn't simply a disgruntled anticapitalist, though—he lays out the societal and cognitive reasons this particular form of personalization is threatening, using anecdotes, data, philosophy, and social as well as cognitive psychology." A V Club

Includes bibliographical references

Seife, Charles
Virtual unreality; just because the Internet told you, how do you know it's true? Charles Seife. Viking 2014 256 p. $26.95   **025.04**
> 1. Internet 2. Information literacy 3. Information resources 4. Internet literacy 5. Internet -- Safety measures 6. Internet fraud -- Prevention 7. Computer network resources -- Evaluation 8. Electronic information resource literacy
>
> ISBN 0670026085; 9780670026081
>
> LC 2013047849
>
> This book, by Charles Seife, "explains how to separate fact from fantasy in the digital world. . . . Digital information is a powerful tool that spreads unbelievably rapidly . . ., even when that information is actually a lie. . . . Charles Seife uses the skepticism, wit, and sharp facility for analysis . . . to take us deep into the Internet information jungle and cut a path through the trickery, fakery, and cyber skullduggery that the online world enables." (Publisher's note)
>
> "Intense and incisive, Seife's exposé of potent tricks on the mesmerizing, overpowering Internet makes us very wary about anything that cannot be verified with our own eyes." Pub Wkly
>
> Includes bibliographical references and index

025.042   Search and retrieval

Devine, Jane
Going beyond Google again; strategies for using and teaching the Invisible Web. Jane Devine and Francine Egger-Sider. Amer Library Assn Neal-Schuman, an imprint of the American Library Assn 2013 160 p. illustrations (paperback) $72 **025.042**
> 1. Internet in education 2. Internet searching -- Study and teaching 3. Invisible Web 4. Database searching 5. Internet searching 6. Invisible Web -- Study and teaching
>
> ISBN 1555708986; 9781555708986
>
> LC 2013010867
>
> This book is a follow-up volume to book "Going Beyond Google" by Jane Devine and Francine Egger-Sider, "which placed teaching the Invisible Web into information literacy programs. [This volume] expands on the teaching foundation laid in the first book and continues to document the Invisible Web's existence and evolution, and suggests ways of teaching students to use it." (Publisher's note)
>
> "Chapter summaries and extensive citations make this an attractive choice for students. It should also be of interest to librarians and anyone interested in optimizing their research resources and strategies." LJ
>
> Includes bibliographical references and index

Hock, Randolph

The **Extreme** Searcher's Internet Handbook; A Guide for the Serious Searcher. by Randolph Hock. 3rd ed.; Information Today, Inc. 2013 xxi, 315 p.p ill.; (paperback) $24.95 **025.042**
   1. Internet research 2. Internet searching 3. Web search engines
ISBN 1937290026; 9781937290023
                 LC 2012039960
  This book by Randolph Hock presents a "guide for anyone who conducts research on the internet—including librarians, teachers, students, business professionals, and writers. This fully revised handbook details what users must know to take full advantage of internet search tools and resources. From the latest online tools to the new and enhanced services offered by standbys such as Google, the major search engines and their myriad of possibilities are thoroughly discussed." (Publisher's note)

025.06   Information storage and retrieval systems devoted to specific subjects

Guide to reference in medicine and health; Christa Modschiedler and Denise Bennett, editors. ALA Editions, an imprint of the American Library Association 2014 xviii, 468 p.p (print : alk. paper) $75 **025.06**
   1. Medicine -- Bibliography 2. Reference books -- Bibliography 3. Medicine -- Information services 4. Medicine -- Reference books -- Bibliography 5. Reference Books, Medical -- Resource Guides
ISBN 0838912214; 9780838912218
                 LC 2014005002
  This book, edited by Christa Modschiedler and Denise Bennett, "provides an annotated list of print and electronic biomedical and health-related reference sources, including internet resources and digital image collections. . . . Entries are selected and annotated by an editorial team of top reference librarians and are used internationally as a go-to source for identifying information as well as training reference professionals." (Publisher's note)
  Includes bibliographical references and indexes
  Reference in medicine and health

025.1   Administration

The **frugal** librarian; thriving in tough economic times. edited by Carol Smallwood. American Library Association 2011 277p il **025.1**
   1. Library finance 2. Libraries and community 3. Libraries -- United States
ISBN 0-8389-1075-0; 978-0-8389-1075-7
                 LC 2010034317
  "The thirty-four chapters in Smallwood's collection address a myriad of issues faced by libraries and librarians when times get tough and money is tight. Written by practicing librarians from academic, public, and school libraries, the concise essays are easy to read, sometimes personal, and highly practical. Each chapter can stand alone, so the volume can serve as a reference tool for a librarian needing specific help; or the entire volume can be perused from start to finish." (VOYA)
  Includes bibliographical references

Gerding, Stephanie K.

Winning grants; a how-to-do-it manual for librarians with multimedia tutorials and grant development tools. [by] Pamela H. MacKellar and Stephanie K. Gerding. Neal-Schuman Publishers 2010 xxi, 242p il (How-to-do-it manuals for librarians) **025.1**
   1. Fund raising 2. Grants-in-aid
ISBN 978-1-55570-700-2
                 LC 2010017965
  First published 2006 with title: Grants for libraries
  "This great all-around resource should be a staple for those just entering the challenging world of grant seeking and for the well-rounded library collection." Libr J
  Includes bibliographical references

Johnson, Doug

★ The **indispensable** librarian; surviving and thriving in school libraries in the information age. Doug Johnson; illustrations by Brady Johnson. Linworth, an imprint of ABC-CLIO, LLC 2013 xix, 207 p.p illustrations (pbk.) $40 **025.1**
   1. Librarians 2. School libraries 3. School librarians -- United States 4. School libraries -- United States -- Administration
ISBN 161069239X; 9781610692397
                 LC 2012051394
  This book, by Doug A. Johnson, "defines and clarifies the role of the school library media specialist in a technologically enhanced school, providing relevant examples and useful advice on a variety of topics; and underscores the importance of strong management skills, especially regarding collaborative planning and communications. The book is written especially for K-12 school librarians, both new and experienced, and is also suitable for pre-service librarians as a textbook." (Publisher's note)
  "Johnson offers both theory and practical suggestions on ways to embed [librarians] and [their] jobs into the fabric of a school's culture and curriculum." Lib Med Con
  Includes bibliographical references and index

Landau, Herbert B.

The **small** public library survival guide; thriving on less. American Library Association 2008 159p pa $42 **025.1**
   1. Library finance 2. Public libraries 3. Libraries and community
ISBN 978-0-8389-3575-0; 0-8389-3575-3
                 LC 2008-7425
  This "volume covers many topics of interest to staff in small public libraries. Written in a conversational, accessible style, information is presented in short chapters with relevant examples and sample documents. . . . Covering topics from low-budget programming to building 'noncash support from the community,' this text has something for almost everyone involved in the operations of a small public library. . . . Easy and enjoyable to read." Voice Youth Advocates
  Includes bibliographical references

Larson, Jeanette C.

★ The **public** library policy writer; a guidebook with model policies on CD-ROM. [by] Jeanette C. Larson and Herman L. Totten. Neal-Schuman Publishers 2008 xxi, 280p $75　　　　　**025.1**
1. Public libraries 2. Libraries -- Administration
ISBN 978-1-55570-603-6; 1-55570-603-7
LC 2008-17622

"This guidebook is written mainly for small to medium-sized library directors who need to analyze current policies, revise or update those still in use, and develop new ones. The book is organized by administrative and service areas such as employment practices, staff and patron conduct, use of materials, collection development, and access to facilities... . This practical tool should be useful to administrators, staff, and library boards." Booklist

Includes bibliographical references

Laughlin, Sara

The **quality** library; a guide to staff-driven improvement, better efficiency, and happier customers. [by] Sara Laughlin and Ray W. Wilson. American Library Association 2008 144p il pa $55　　　**025.1**
1. Customer services 2. Management 3. Planning, Library 4. Library administration 5. Libraries -- Management 6. Total quality management 7. Libraries -- Administration
ISBN 0-8389-0952-3; 978-0-8389-0952-2
LC 2007-30710

"Building on an earlier publication, The Library's Continuous Improvement Fieldbook: 29 Ready-to-Use Tools . . . Laughlin and Wilson have created a manual for administrators and employees who want to improve their libraries by improving their processes. . . . This can be a useful guide for libraries whose governing bodies are looking for business-like solutions and for managers who want to heed input from those who do the job." Booklist

Includes bibliographical references

MacKellar, Pamela H.

Writing successful technology grant proposals; a LITA guide. Pamela H. MacKellar. Neal-Schuman Publishers, Inc. 2012 xviii, 227 p.p (alk. paper) $70.00　　　　　**025.1**
1. Information technology 2. Libraries -- Administration 3. Proposal writing for grants 4. Proposal writing for grants -- United States 5. Libraries -- Automation -- United States -- Finance 6. Proposal writing in library science -- United States 7. Libraries -- Information technology -- United States -- Finance
ISBN 1555707637; 9781555707637
LC 2011046318

This book, by Pamela H. MacKellar, offers instruction on grant writing. "[H]ow can you write a successful grant proposal? . . . This comprehensive book on grants for libraries focuses on technology, . . . specific sources and resources for technology grants, . . . and technology project success stories so you get real life examples of how others like you made their libraries stronger through technology grants." (Publisher's note)

Includes bibliographical references and index

Managing Electronic Resources; a LITA Guide. Edited by Ryan O. Weir. ALA TechSource, an imprint of the American Library Assoc. 2012 xii, 179 p.p (pbk.) $65　　　　　**025.1**
1. Digital libraries 2. Libraries -- Collection development 3. Electronic reference services (Libraries) 4. Electronic information resources -- Management 5. Libraries -- Special collections -- Electronic information resources
ISBN 155570767X; 9781555707675
LC 2012015102

In this book, Ryan O. Weir presents a "guide to developing and maintaining electronic library collections. Topics include evaluation, selection, and cataloging of electronic resources; strategies for contract negotiation; how to gather and interpret data about electronic resource use; . . . and staffing for electronic collections, as well as projections about how electronic resources will continue to evolve and impact libraries in the future." (Voice of Youth Advocates)

Includes bibliographical references and index

Mosley, Pixey Anne

The **challenge** of library management; leading with emotional engagement. by Wyoma vanDuinkerken and Pixey Anne Mosley. American Library Association 2011 169 p. $52　　　**025.1**
1. Personnel management 2. Libraries -- Administration 3. Leadership 4. Library administration 5. Organizational change -- Management 6. Library administration -- Problems, exercises, etc
ISBN 0838911021; 9780838911020
LC 2011011349

This book, by Wyoma vanDuinkerken and Pixey Anne Moseley, is designed to show library managers how to "engage library staff in the process and encourage their active participation, navigate successfully through common types of change, such as space planning, departmental reorganization, and changes in work responsibilities, [and] draw on concepts from psychology, communication, empowerment, planning, and evaluation to minimize friction." (Publisher's note)

"The information they provide mostly concerns dealing with employees in order to ensure an effective and successful change initiative in a library setting...While the authors tailor the advice to librarians by using example specific to libraries, the advice could be applied to any organizational setting. All in all, the suggestions contained here are helpful when planning change in a library. Each chapter concludes with a list of key ideas to keep in mind and questions for reflection." (VOYA)

Includes bibliographical references (p. 155-163) and index

Our new public, a changing clientele; bewildering issues or new challenges for managing libraries? edited by James R. Kennedy, Lisa Vardaman, and Gerard B. McCabe. Libraries Unlimited 2008 305p (Libraries Unlimited library management collection) $45　　　　　**025.1**
1. Libraries and students 2. Libraries -- Administration
ISBN 978-1-59158-407-0
LC 2007-35907

"Several chapters in this . . . title discuss the milennials—children of the baby boomers—and digital natives and how they have already had an impact on library service. . . . Each chapter offers practical advice based on experiences, and each includes a list of references. Library managers and those aspiring to be managers will find help in providing services for a younger demographic." Booklist

Includes bibliographical references

Smith, G. Stevenson

Cost control for nonprofits in crisis; G. Stevenson Smith. American Library Association 2011 viii, 133 p.p ill. (pbk.: alk. paper) $75.00   **025.1**
1. Finance 2. Financial crises 3. Nonprofit organizations 4. Libraries -- Cost control 5. Libraries -- Cost effectiveness 6. Library finance -- United States 7. Nonprofit organizations -- Cost control 8. Library administration -- Decision making 9. Nonprofit organizations -- Cost effectiveness 10. Nonprofit organizations -- United States -- Finance 11. Nonprofit organizations -- Management -- Decision making
ISBN 083891098X; 9780838910986

LC 2011025285

Author G. Stevenson Smith's book provides financial advice and tips. "Libraries, like many other cultural institutions such as museums, art councils, and theater groups, are looking for answers to the pressing problem of financial stability, and ultimately survival . . . [Smith's book] helps managers and directors tackle the harsh realities before them . . . [He] offers [t]echniques for determining the most cost-effective methods of providing services to clients and patrons of nonprofit cultural institutions." (Publisher's note)

Includes bibliographical references and index

025.17   Administration of collections of special materials

★ **No** shelf required; e-books in libraries. edited by Sue Polanka. American Library Association 2011 182p pa $65   **025.17**
1. Electronic books
ISBN 978-0-83891-054-2

LC 2010-14045

"Following a chapter on e-book history are chapters discussing e-books and students' learning; e-books in school, public, and academic libraries; and e-book acquisitions and management. . . . An essential guide to a topic of high importance." Booklist

Includes bibliographical references

025.2   Acquisitions and collection development

Alabaster, Carol

Developing an outstanding core collection; a guide for libraries. 2nd ed; American Library Association 2010 191p il pa $60   **025.2**
1. Best books 2. Reference books 3. Libraries -- Collection development 4. Public libraries -- Collection

development
ISBN 978-0-8389-1040-5

LC 2009-40342

First published 2002

The author suggests "that the general public needs materials beyond current best-sellers and ready-reference works; that those materials should be high-quality, enduring pieces; and that librarians are the best persons to decide what constitutes appropriate core collections for their communities. . . . [She also] addresses the technological changes that drastically affect reading habits and our ability to satisfy the needs of 'the people's university.', . . . [This book is] required reading for all those charged with the task of adult collection development." Booklist

Includes bibliographical references

Baker, Nicholson

Double fold; libraries and the assault on paper. Random House 2001 370p il hardcover o.p. pa $14   **025.2**
1. Paper 2. Libraries -- Special collections 3. Library resources -- Conservation and restoration
ISBN 0-375-72621-7 pa

LC 00-59171

Baker criticizes libraries for discarding books, magazines and newspapers and disputes the arguments for doing so "that libraries are running out of space, and that paper, because of its acid content, is rapidly turning to dust. . . . What the Library of Congress spends in a year on microfilming would, (according to Baker), buy a storage facility 'the size of a Home Depot, which would hold a century of newsprint.' . . . Librarians, he says, 'have lied to us shamelessly about the extent of paper's fragility, and they continue to lie about it.'" N Y Times Book Rev

Includes bibliographical references

Bartlett, Wendy K.

Floating collections; a collection development model for long-term success. Wendy K. Bartlett. Libraries Unlimited, an imprint of ABC-CLIO, LLC 2014 xix, 128 p.p (pbk.: acid-free paper) $55 **025.2**
1. Libraries -- Collection development 2. Public libraries -- Collection development -- United States 3. Cooperative collection development (Libraries) -- United States
ISBN 1598847430; 9781598847437

LC 2013033820

This book, by Wendy K. Bartlett, is "about floating and floating collections. . . . Not only does this book help librarians to decide rationally if, how, and when to float, it also outlines a how-to process for maximum success based on the real-world experience of many systems and identifies ways to maximize the advantages of a floating collection. In addition, the author addresses common collection concerns and outlines workable solutions for problematic issues that can arise." (Publisher's note)

"Chapters include tips on how to approach the practice with staff, how to ready facilities and collections, and, most importantly, how to manage new collections. Also offered are practical evaluations, FAQs, and a list of larger systems in the United States that offer floating collections." SLJ

Includes bibliographical references and index

Brenner, Robin E.

★ **Understanding** manga and anime. Libraries Unlimited 2007 335p il pa $40   **025.2**

1. Anime 2. Manga -- Study and teaching 3. Libraries -- Collection development 4. Libraries -- Special collections -- Graphic novels

ISBN 978-1-59158-332-5; 1-59158-332-2

LC 2007-9773

The author "provides thorough explanations of manga and anime vocabulary, potential censorship issues because of cultural disparities, and typical Manga conventions. . . . No professional collection could possibly be complete without this all-inclusive and exceptional work." Voice Youth Advocates

Building and managing e-book collections; a how-to-do-it manual for librarians. edited by Richard Kaplan. Neal-Schuman 2012 xv, 197 p.p (pbk. : alk. paper) $75   **025.2**

1. Libraries -- Collection development 2. Libraries and electronic publishing 3. Libraries -- Special Collections -- Electronic books

ISBN 1555707769; 9781555707767

LC 2012018143

This book on library collections of e-books, edited by Richard B. Kaplan, focuses on "collection development issues, including the selection process and development policies, the use of approval plans, patron-driven acquisition, and practical solutions for creating your e-book collection policies. Chapters on budgeting and licensing cover ownership versus leasing models . . . on digital rights management, and strategies for success in retention, access, and budgeting." (Publisher's note)

"This title features a wealth of useful information . . . the concepts and issues covered are applicable to all libraries. This book provides a solid snapshot of the current best practices in the world of e-book collecting." CHOICE

Includes bibliographical references and index

Charles, John A.

The **mystery** readers' advisory; the librarian's clues to murder and mayhem. [by] John Charles, Joanna Morrison, [and] Candace Clark. American Library Association 2002 227p (ALA readers' advisory series) pa $45   **025.2**

1. Reference books 2. Reference services (Libraries) 3. Mystery fiction -- Bibliography

ISBN 0-8389-0811-X; 978-0-8389-0811-2

LC 01-45083

"Covering everything a librarian would need to know to successfully build and promote a mystery collection, the authors include chapters on weeding and marketing the collection, with a great section on how to do a readers' advisory interview. . . . The text is peppered with authors and titles to know and plenty of plot teasers to fill your reading list. There are thorough discussions of the different subgenres, from police procedural to romantic suspense and other genre blends. . . . The lists of mystery periodicals, reference sources, and Web sites are well-rounded and up-to-date." Voice Youth Advocates

Includes bibliographical references

Disher, Wayne

Crash Course in Collection Development; Wayne Disher. Libraries Unlimited 2014 139 p. (paperback) $45   **025.2**

1. Libraries -- Collection development 2. Collection development -- Handbooks, manuals, etc.

ISBN 1610698134; 9781610698139

LC 2014018813

This book, by Wayne Disher, is a handbook on collection development "covering everything from community analysis through developing collection policies. Librarians will learn how to use reviews to acquire materials as well as to help weed the collection, how to market the collection to patrons, and how to handle censorship issues when collections are challenged." (Publisher's note)

"Disher, a seasoned practitioner and part-time instructor in San Jose State University's School of Library and Information Science, speaks primarily to public library staff with little, if any, experience in collection development. Short on theory but long on practicality, the book provides the reader with basic definitions and step-by-step outlines... Recommended for all public library collections." Booklist

Evans, G. Edward

Collection management basics; G. Edward Evans and Margaret Zarnosky Saponaro. Libraries Unlimited 2012 xvi, 343 p.p (Library and information science text series) (paperback : acid-free paper) $48   **025.2**

1. Libraries -- Special collections 2. Libraries -- Collection development 3. Collection development (Libraries) 4. Libraries -- Special collections -- Electronic information resources

ISBN 159884864X; 9781598848632; 9781598848649

LC 2012008872

This book, by G. Edward Evans and Margaret Zarnosky Saponaro, "cover[s] all aspects of collection development and management, including subjects such as needs assessment, policies, selection process theory and practice, protection, legal issues, censorship, and intellectual freedom. The book represents a total restructuring of the previous work, and reflects changes brought on by new technology and the up-and-down economy." (Publisher's note)

Includes bibliographical references and index

Foerstel, Herbert N.

★ **Banned** in the U.S.A; a reference guide to book censorship in schools and public libraries. rev and expanded ed; Greenwood Press 2002 xxvii, 296p $54.95   **025.2**

1. Censorship 2. Books -- Censorship 3. Libraries -- Censorship 4. Censorship -- United States 5. Book selection -- United States 6. Textbooks -- Censorship -- United States 7. Public schools -- Censorship -- United States 8. Public libraries -- Censorship -- United States 9. Public libraries -- Book selection -- United States

ISBN 0-313-31166-8

LC 2001-55620

First published 1994

"Librarians and teachers need this book, but patrons who want to better understand the threats to their First Amendment rights should be led to it as well." SLJ

Includes bibliographical references

Gallaway, Beth

★ **Game** on! gaming at the library. Neal-Schuman Publishers 2009 306p il pa $55　**025.2**

1. Video games 2. Video games and children 3. Video games and teenagers 4. Multimedia library services 5. Electronic games -- Collections 6. Libraries -- Special collections

ISBN 1-55570-595-2; 978-1-55570-595-4

LC 2009-14110

"An essential guide for any librarian who plans on embracing the video-game phenomenon, or at the very least, understanding it. . . . [The chapters] are well organized and contain an abundance of practical information. The sections on selection, collection, and circulation of video games include relevant advice on policy, cataloging, marketing, storage, and displays. . . . The annotated list of video games for a core collection is wonderful for selection purposes." SLJ

Includes bibliographical references

Goldsmith, Francisca

The **readers'** advisory guide to graphic novels. American Library Association 2010 124p (ALA readers' advisory series) pa $45　**025.2**

1. Graphic novels -- Bibliography 2. Libraries -- Special collections -- Graphic novels

ISBN 978-0-8389-1008-5; 0-8389-1008-4

LC 2009-25239

"After dispelling the two main myths that ghettoize graphic novels—they are just for adolescents and they are far less complex than texts without pictures—Goldsmith emphasizes that GNs are a format and not a genre. She suggests active and passive ways to offer readers' advisory (RA) from face-to-face encounters with patrons to book displays and book groups and offers guidance on helping established GN readers to find new titles they might enjoy. . . . All in all it is a valuable and quite readable resource that belongs in every library's professional collection." Voice Youth Advocates

Includes glossary and bibliographical references

Graphic novels beyond the basics; insights and issues for libraries. Martha Cornog and Timothy Perper, editors. Libraries Unlimited 2009 xxx, 281p il pa $45　**025.2**

1. Graphic novels -- History and criticism 2. Comic books, strips, etc. -- History and criticism 3. Libraries -- Special collections -- Graphic novels

ISBN 978-1-59158-478-0; 1-59158-478-7

LC 2009-16189

Editors Cornog and Perper have collected essays by experts Robin Brenner, Francisca Goldsmith, Trina Robbins, Michael R. Lavin, Gilles Poitras, Lorena O'English, Michael Niederhausen, Erin Byrne, and Cornog herself, all about graphic novels in libraries. Topics covered range from the appeal of superheroes to manga, the appeal of comics to women and girls, anime, independent comics, dealing with challenges to the material, and more. Appendices provide resource information on African American-interest

graphic novels, Latino-Interest graphic novels, LGBT-interest graphic novels, religious-themed graphic novels, a bibliography of books about graphic novels in libraries, and online resources.

"Whether you are serious about the genre, interested in the history, or looking for ammunition, this book should be on your shelf. The wealth of knowledge and research that went into these essays is impressive, and reading this book will put you on the road to becoming an expert." Libr Media Connect

Includes bibliographical references

★ **Intellectual** Freedom Manual; Trina Magi, Martin Garnar, Office for Intellectual Freedom of the American Library Association. 9th Edition American Library Association 2015 434 p. $70　**025.2**

1. Freedom of information -- United States -- Handbooks, manuals, etc. 2. Libraries -- Censorship -- United States -- Handbooks, manuals, etc.

ISBN 0838912923; 9780838912928

This book by Trina Magi, Martin Garnar, and the Office for Intellectual Freedom "is more than just an invaluable compendium of guiding principles and policies. It s also an indispensable resource for day-to-day guidance on maintaining free and equal access to information for all people. Fortifying and emboldening professionals and students from across the library spectrum, this manual includes . . , 34 ALA policy statements and documents [and] explanations of legal points." (Publisher's note)

Johnson, Peggy

Developing and managing electronic collections; the essentials. Peggy Johnson. ALA Editions, an imprint of the American Library Association 2013 ix, 186 p.p illustrations (paper) $65　**025.2**

1. Libraries -- Collection development 2. Libraries and electronic publishing 3. Electronic reference services (Libraries) 4. Libraries -- Special Collections -- Electronic books 5. Electronic information resources -- Management 6. Libraries and electronic publishing -- United States 7. Libraries -- Special collections -- Electronic information resources

ISBN 0838911900; 9780838911907

LC 2013005038

This book, by Peggy Johnson, discusses the "complex issues associated with developing and managing electronic collections [in libraries]." The book discusses "the evolving world of acquisition options, licenses, and contracts [as well as] budgeting and financial considerations, with guidance on how to collaborate across library organizational lines to acquire and manage e-content more efficiently." (Publisher's note)

"This short volume is a must-read for librarians who are just starting to explore how electronic collections will affect their libraries, and it would be a solid choice for most librarians currently working with electronic collections." Booklist

Includes bibliographical references and index

Fundamentals of Collection Development and Management; Peggy Johnson. Amer Library Assn 2014 554 p. $77   **025.2**
1. Libraries -- Administration 2. Libraries -- Collection development 3. Collection development (Libraries) 4. Collection development -- Administration
ISBN 0838911919; 9780838911914

LC 2008019989

This book, by Peggy Johnson, "addresses the art in controlling and updating your library's collection. Each chapter offers complete coverage of one aspect of collection development, including suggestions for further reading and a narrative case study exploring the issue. Johnson also integrates electronic resources throughout the book." (Publisher's note)

Laguardia, Cheryl

Marketing your library's electronic resources; a how-to-do-it manual. Marie R. Kennedy, Cheryl LaGuardia. Neal-Schuman, an imprint of the American Library Association 2013 177 p. (How-to-do-it manuals) $60   **025.2**
1. Library resources 2. Libraries -- Collection development 3. Libraries -- Special Collections -- Electronic books 4. Libraries -- Marketing 5. Electronic information resources -- Marketing 6. Libraries -- United States -- Marketing -- Case studies 7. Libraries -- Special collections -- Electronic information resources
ISBN 1555708897; 9781555708894

LC 2012028267

This book, by Marie R. Kennedy and Cheryl LaGuardia, "guides readers through every step of developing, implementing, and evaluating plans to market [a library's] e-resources in an approachable and user-friendly way.... Their book includes four complete programs from both public and academic libraries [and] a step-by-step organization guide, with a variety of feedback and assessment forms which can be used as models." (Publisher's note)

"Every library needs to know how to educate its patrons about these resources, and this book provides a well-organized, uncomplicated plan for doing so." VOYA

Includes bibliographical references and index

Lewis, Linda K.

The **complete** guide to acquisitions management; Frances C. Wilkinson, Linda K. Lewis, and Rebecca L. Lubas. Libraries Unlimited, An Imprint of ABC-CLIO, LLC 2015 xiv, 200 p.p (pbk : alk. paper) $60   **025.2**
1. Library education 2. Libraries -- Acquisitions 3. Acquisitions (Libraries) -- United States
ISBN 1610697138; 9781610697132

LC 2015007852

This book, by Frances C. Wilkinson, Linda K. Lewis, and Rebecca L. Lubas, part of the publisher's "Library and Information Science Text" series, "provides both library students and practitioners with a thorough understanding of procedural and philosophical approaches in acquisitions

management. [It] incorporates thoroughly updated information that reflects today's fast-changing world of acquisitions management and addresses the changing landscape of publishing overall." (Publisher's note)

"This is an excellent introductory text for novice acquisitions librarians and students as well as a helpful reference for the more experienced." LJ

Includes bibliographical references and index

Pinnell-Stephens, June

★ **Protecting** intellectual freedom in your public library; scenarios from the front lines. June Pinnell-Stephens for the Office for Intellectual Freedom. American Library Association 2012 xi, 148 p.p (pbk. : alk. paper) $50.00   **025.2**
1. Censorship 2. Library science 3. Public libraries 4. Intellectual freedom 5. Intellectual freedom -- United States 6. Public libraries -- Censorship -- United States 7. Public libraries -- Censorship -- United States -- Case studies
ISBN 0838935834; 9780838935835

LC 2011029691

This book, by June Pinnell-Stephens, offers a guide to intellectual freedom concerns and rights as relating to public library administration. "When confronted with challenges like censorship and policy disputes, public librarians and paraprofessionals need reliable how-to guidance.... [T]his book provides ... analysis of how IF plays out in the world of public libraries ... and advice on how to effectively handle intellectual freedom challenges." (Publisher's note)

Includes bibliographical references and index.

Rethinking collection development and management; Becky Albitz, Christine Avery, and Diane Zabel, editors. Libraries Unlimited 2014 xiv, 394 p.p (pbk. : acid-free paper) $60   **025.2**
1. Libraries -- Acquisitions 2. Libraries -- Collection development 3. Acquisitions (Libraries) 4. Collection management (Libraries) 5. Collection development (Libraries) 6. Library materials -- Conservation and restoration
ISBN 1610693051; 9781610693059

LC 2013038447

"This collection of thought-provoking essays ... covers theory, research, and best practices in collection development, examining how it has evolved, identifying how some librarians are creatively responding to these changes, and predicting what is coming next." (Publisher's note)

Includes bibliographical references and index

Serchay, David S.

The **librarian's** guide to graphic novels for adults. Neal-Schuman Publishers 2010 320p il $65   **025.2**
1. Graphic novels -- Collections 2. Graphic novels -- Administration 3. Libraries -- Special collections -- Graphic novels
ISBN 978-1-55570-662-3

LC 2009-41011

"This book will inspire librarians—and others—with little knowledge of graphic novels (GNs) for adults to pick one up and see what all the buzz is about. Serchay puts forth a complete guide that will enable any librarian, whether a GN novice or seasoned fan, to establish a brand-new collection, fully understanding what GNs are, where to purchase them, how to catalog them, and how to review, promote, and maintain the new collection." Libr J

Includes bibliographical references

Singer, Carol A.

Fundamentals of Managing Reference Collections; Carol A. Singer. American Library Association 2012 xii, 167 p.p (pbk.) $60 **025.2**
1. Reference books 2. Libraries -- Special collections 3. Electronic reference services (Libraries) 4. Reference books -- United States 5. Electronic reference sources -- United States 6. Libraries -- Special collections -- Reference sources 7. Collection management (Libraries) -- United States -- Case studies
ISBN 0838911536; 9780838911532
LC 2011044446

Author Carol A. "Singer's book offers information and insight on best practices for reference collection management, no matter the size, and shows why managing without a plan is a recipe for clutter and confusion." Singer discusses "the importance of collection development policies, and how to effectively involve others in the decision-making process," in addition to "new insights into selecting reference materials" and "strategies for collection maintenance." (Publisher's note)

Includes bibliographical references and index

Vnuk, Rebecca

The **weeding** handbook; a shelf-by-shelf guide. Rebecca Vnuk. ALA Editions, an imprint of the American Library Association 2015 196 p. (pbk. : alk. paper) $45 **025.2**
1. Libraries -- Collection development 2. Public libraries -- Collection development -- United States 3. Discarding of books, periodicals, etc. -- Handbooks, manuals, etc 4. Collection development (Libraries) -- United States -- Policy statements
ISBN 9780838913277
LC 2015008707

This guidebook, by Rebecca Vnuk, focuses on "weeding" libraries. "A library is an ever-changing organism; when done the right way, weeding helps a library thrive by focusing its resources on those parts of the collection that are the most useful to its users. Her handbook takes the guesswork out of this delicate but necessary process, giving public and school library staff the knowledge and the confidence to effectively weed any collection, of any size." (Publisher's note)

"Vnuk's clear writing and motivating tone will give confidence to reluctant weeders, resulting in a worthy purchase for all public libraries." LJ

Includes bibliographical references and index

White, Andrew C.

★ **E-metrics** for library and information professionals; how to use data for managing and evaluating electronic resource collections. Neal-Schuman Publishers 2006 249p il pa $75 **025.2**
1. Digital libraries
ISBN 1-55570-514-6
LC 2004-54678

"Designed to introduce readers to e-metrics ('the measurements of the use and activity of networked information'), this book is made up of 10 chapters that are divided among three major sections. Part 1 supplies a definition of e-metrics, explores their use in libraries, and discusses vendor-supplied electronic data reports. Part 2 explains why libraries need e-metrics, focusing on how they can be used for public relations, collection management, and library administration. Part 3 offers ways that libraries can build local e-metrics. Chapters cover the capturing and processing of statistics, infrastructure and technical requirements, and staffing needs. With its coherent structure, well-articulated language, and illustrative material (tables, figures, and examples), this book has much to recommend it." Booklist

Includes bibliographical references

025.3 Bibliographic analysis and control

Maxwell, Robert L.

FRBR; a guide for the perplexed. American Library Association 2008 151p il pa $50 **025.3**
1. FRBR (Conceptual model)
ISBN 978-0-8389-0950-8; 0-8389-0950-7
LC 2007-27845

This book explains "Functional Requirements for Bibliographic Records (FRBR), an evolving conceptual model developed to assist users in navigating library catalogs to find the information they want and need. Maxwell . . . explains and illustrates the FRBR model, details why the document and model are important for the future of information organization, and explains what a catalog based on FRBR principles might look like. He also briefly illustrates the use of Functional Requirements for Authority Data (FRAD)." Booklist

Includes bibliographical references

Maxwell's handbook for RDA, resource description & access; explaining and illustrating RDA: resource description and access using MARC21. Robert L. Maxwell. ALA Editions, an imprint of the American Library Association 2013 x, 900 p.p (pbk. : alk. paper) $98 **025.3**
1. Cataloging 2. Resource description and access -- Handbooks, manuals, etc. 3. Resource description & access -- Handbooks, manuals, etc 4. Descriptive cataloging -- Standards -- Handbooks, manuals, etc
ISBN 0838911722; 9780838911723
LC 2013035124

In this book, "cataloging expert Robert Maxwell brings his trademark practical commentary to bear on the new, unified cataloging standard. Designed to interpret and explain RDA: Resource Description and Access, this handbook illustrates and applies the new cataloging rules in the MARC21 environment for every type of information format." (Publisher's note)

"Through full and numerous cataloging examples, the author covers FRBR (functional requirements for bibliographic records) basics and how to record the attributes for entities such as manifestations, items, persons, corporate bodies, places, expressions, and works. The examples are not limited to just the print format but also include electronic materials, music, series, and maps." LJ

Includes bibliographical references and index

Mitchell, Anne M.

★ **Cataloging** and organizing digital resources; a how-to-do-it manual for librarians. Neal-Schuman Publishers 2005 219p il (How-to-do-it manuals for librarians) pa $75   **025.3**
1. Cataloging 2. Reference books 3. Digital libraries 4. Information systems
ISBN 1-55570-521-9

LC 2005-903

This "volume addresses the ways a library can manage electronic collections. The goal is to provide an overview of management concerns and issues regarding bibliographic control in an online environment and to suggest tools that are available. The 10 chapters address such topics as development of digital libraries, organization of work flow, alternatives to cataloging, cataloging rules and records, online monographs and serials, integration of resources, and trends. Each chapter offers an introduction; guidelines, instructions, or strategies; and a summary and references. The writing is clear, with plentiful examples that include figures and titles." Booklist

Oliver, Chris

★ **Introducing** RDA; a guide to the basics. Chris Oliver. American Library Association 2010 vii, 117 p.p ill. (paperback) $45   **025.3**
1. Cataloging 2. Resource description and access -- Handbooks, manuals, etc. 3. Cataloging -- Standards 4. Anglo-American cataloguing rules 5. Descriptive cataloging -- Standards
ISBN 083893594X; 9780838935941

LC 2010021719

This book looks at Resource Description and Access (RDA), the cataloging standard that's replacing Anglo-American Cataloguing Rules (AACR). "Through numerous examples, [Chris] Oliver compares and contrasts RDA and AACR. He also discusses RDA background and its connection to the Functional Requirements for Bibliographic Records (FRBR) and Functional Requirements for Authority Data (FRAD) models and international standards." (Library Journal)

This is "a useful guide that provides a clear explanation of what RDA is all about. . . . Highly recommended for novice and experienced catalogers." Libr J

Includes bibliographical references (p. 105-109) and index.

025.4   Subject analysis and control

Dewey, Melvil

★ **Dewey** decimal classification and relative index; devised by Melvil Dewey. ed 22; OCLC 2003 4v set $375   **025.4**
1. Dewey Decimal Classification
ISBN 0-910608-70-9

LC 2003-50872

First published anonymously in 1876

★ **Sears** List of Subject Headings; Barbara A. Bristow, editor; Christi Showman Farrar, associate editor. 21st edition Grey House Publishing/H.W. Wilson 2014 946 pp. (hardcover) $165.00 **025.4**
1. Cataloging 2. Library science 3. Subject headings
ISBN 9781619251908

LC 2013498263

This book, edited by Barbara A. Bristow and Christi Showman Farrar, presents the frameworks for the Sears List of Subject Headings cataloging system. "This resource lists subject headings used by small and medium-sized libraries, with patterns, examples, and notes on usage. The subject headings are listed alphabetically and aligned with the Dewey Decimal Classification system and include a list of canceled and replacement headings, as well as a discussion of the theoretical foundations of the list and the general principles of subject cataloging." (Book News)

025.5   Services for users

Berard, G. Lynn

Science and technology resources; a guide for information professionals and researchers. James E. Bobick and G. Lynn Berard. Libraries Unlimited 2011 xiii, 285 p.p illustrations (Library and information science text series) (paperback) $60   **025.5**
1. Technology 2. Science -- Bibliography 3. Science -- Bibliography -- Methodology 4. Technology -- Bibliography -- Methodology 5. Technical literature -- Bibliography -- Methodology 6. Scientific literature -- Bibliography -- Methodology 7. Science and technology libraries -- Reference services
ISBN 159158793X; 1591587948; 1591588014; 9781591587934; 9781591587941; 9781591588016

LC 2011000461

This science and technology resource, by James E. Bobick and G. Lynn Berard, "begins with an overview of the nature of sci-tech literature, the information-seeking behavior of scientists and engineers, and an examination of the research cycle. . . . This practical guide will be invaluable to librarians, information specialists, engineering and science professionals, and students interested in acquiring a practical knowledge of science and technology resources." (Publisher's note)

"Database descriptions contain annotations, but the listings for websites, dictionaries, handbooks, and other materials do not. A timely resource to add to reference collections and to the library science curriculum." Booklist

Includes bibliographical references and index

Buker, Derek M.

The **science**-fiction and fantasy readers' advisory; the librarian's guide to cyborgs, aliens, and sorcerers. American Lib. Assn. 2002 230p (ALA readers' advisory series) pa $50 **025.5**

1. Reference books 2. Reference services (Libraries) 3. Fantasy fiction -- Bibliography 4. Science fiction -- Bibliography

ISBN 0-8389-0831-4; 978-0-8389-0831-0

LC 2002-1494

A "well-organized, humorous guide to providing readers' advisory to customers wanting science fiction or fantasy recommendations. . . . The book is divided into two parts, one dealing with science fiction and one with fantasy, and further divides these genres into their many subgenres, providing short annotated lists of recommended titles as well as longer lists without annotations. . . . What this guide does best is demonstrate the wide scope of science fiction and fantasy literature; it gives many suggestions and recommendations across this broad range." SLJ

Includes bibliographical references

Cords, Sarah Statz

The **real** story; a guide to nonfiction reading interests. edited by Robert Burgin. Libraries Unlimited 2006 xxxii, 460p (Genreflecting advisory series) $55 **025.5**

1. Books and reading 2. Reference services (Libraries)

ISBN 1-59158-283-0

LC 2006-3712

The author "describes more than 555 popular nonfiction titles published over the last 15 years, along with classic titles such as Truman Capote's In Cold Blood. . . . Cords has identified 11 broad categories based on subjects, genres, and appeal factors. Among the categories are 'Biography,' 'Travel,' 'True Adventure,' and 'True Crime.' . . . A must-read for any librarian who recommends popular reading titles, it belongs at the reference and readers'-advisory desks of most libraries." Booklist

Includes bibliographical references

Evans, G. Edward

Introduction to library public services; [by] G. Edward Evans and Thomas L. Carter. 7th ed; Libraries Unlimited 2009 401p il (Library and information science text series) $65; pa $50 **025.5**

1. Library services 2. Library circulation 3. Reference services (Libraries)

ISBN 978-1-59158-596-1; 978-1-59158-595-4 pa

LC 2008-37445

First published 1972 under the authorship of Marty Bloomberg with title: Introduction to public services for library technicians

"Each chapter covers the role, purpose, and philosophy related to major functional areas of public service, including points to ponder, forms and flowcharts, review questions and suggested readings." Publisher's note

Ford, Charlotte

Crash course in reference. Libraries Unlimited 2008 143p il (Crash course) **025.5**

1. Reference books 2. Reference services (Libraries) 3. Reference services -- Handbooks, manuals, etc.

ISBN 978-1-59158-463-6

LC 2007-52948

"A basic explanation of reference services for those with little formal LIS training working in small rural libraries or others who have been working in other areas and wish to brush up on their skills, this author provides an introduction to reference services including search strategies." Publisher's note

Includes bibliographical references

Hernon, Peter

Assessing service quality; satisfying the expectations of library customers. [by] Peter Hernon + Ellen Altman. 2nd ed; American Library Association 2010 206p il pa $65 **025.5**

1. Library services 2. Libraries -- Public relations

ISBN 978-0-8389-1021-4; 0-8389-1021-1

LC 2009-40332

First published 1998

The authors "concentrate on how to assess service quality and customer satisfaction. Here they suggest . . . ways to think about library services, clarify the distinction between service quality and customer satisfaction, present strategies for developing a customer service plan, identify procedures to measure service quality and satisfaction, and . . . challenge conventional thinking about these powerful principles. . . . Kudos to these authors for providing an essential resource for librarians who understand that folks who walk into their libraries are not patrons but customers." Libr J

Includes bibliographical references

Jerrard, Jane

★ **Crisis** in employment; a librarian's guide to helping job seekers. foreword by Denise Davis. American Library Association 2009 66p il pa $40 **025.5**

1. Unemployment 2. Libraries and community 3. Reference services (Libraries) 4. Vocational guidance -- Information services

ISBN 978-0-8389-1013-9

LC 2009-16684

This "special report provides suggestions for providing low-cost assistance to job-seeking unemployed library users. With examples from various public libraries, the report offers advice for planning, how to get the most out of resources at hand, dealing with the need for additional computers, suggestions for community partnerships, and how to best assist users who need to become computer literate for a successful job search." Libr J

Includes bibliographical references

Kern, M. Kathleen

★ **Virtual** reference best practices; tailoring services to your library. American Library Association 2009 148p il pa $50   **025.5**
1. Reference services (Libraries)
ISBN 978-0-8389-0975-1

LC 2008-15379

The author "offers advice and assistance for libraries considering VR. . . . Kern's guidebook includes useful forms and exercises for every aspect of the VR process from a market assessment of the library's community served to an evaluation of the service. . . . Even those [libraries] which already offer virtual reference will find assistance and suggestions to improve their services." Voice Youth Advocates

Includes bibliographical references

Moyer, Jessica E.

The **readers'** advisory handbook; edited by Jessica E. Moyer and Kaite Mediatore Stover. American Library Association 2010 220p (ALA readers' advisory series) pa $55   **025.5**
1. Best books 2. Reference services (Libraries)
ISBN 978-0-8389-1042-9

LC 2009-45793

"This great generalist title offers guidelines not only on readers' advisory (RA) but on related matters of collection development and marketing books to different reading audiences. . . . [The authors] gather information and instruction from 15 contributing public and school librarians on self-education, managing and improving groups of selectors, making quick but thorough evaluations of different types of materials, writing reviews, and working with book groups as well as other kinds of programming." Libr J

Includes bibliographical references

Research-based readers' advisory; with contributions by Amanda Blau and others. American Library Association 2008 278p (ALA readers' advisory series) pa $50   **025.5**
1. Reference services (Libraries)
ISBN 978-0-8389-0959-1; 0-8389-0959-0

LC 2007-49421

"Following a survey of the current state of RA, 11 chapters cover topics such as 'Nonfiction Readers and Nonfiction Advisory,' 'Romance and Genre Readers,' and 'Tools for Readers' Advisory.' Each chapter begins with a 'Research View,' in which Moyer summarizes the latest literature. Following the 'Research View' is a 'Librarian's View,' in which an impressive array of contributors talk about practical applications." Booklist

Includes bibliographical references

Mulac, Carolyn M.

Fundamentals of reference; Carolyn M. Mulac. American Library Association 2012 xii., 131 p.p (pbk. : alk. paper) $52   **025.5**
1. Reference services (Libraries) 2. Reference books -- Bibliography 3. Electronic reference services (Libraries) 4. Reference sources -- Bibliography 5. Internet in library reference services 6. Reference services (Libraries) -- United States
ISBN 0838910874; 9780838910870

LC 2012010058

Author Carolyn M. Mulac's book offers an "introduction to reference sources and services for a variety of readers, from library staff members who are asked to work in the reference department to managers and others who wish to familiarize themselves with this important area of librarianship." Mulac "presents an overview of the basic tools and techniques of reference work, including" reference services and reference sources. (Publisher's note)

Includes bibliographical references and index

Nilsen, Kirsti

Conducting the reference interview; a how-to-do-it manual for librarians. [by] Catherine Sheldrick Ross, Kirsti Nilsen, and Marie L. Radford. 2nd ed; Neal-Schuman Publishers Inc. 2009 290p il (How-to-do-it manuals for librarians) pa $75   **025.5**
1. Reference services (Libraries) 2. Reference interview 3. Reference services -- Automation 4. Electronic reference services (Libraries)
ISBN 978-1-55570-655-5

LC 2009-17660

First published 2002

This book aims to teach librarians how "to understand the needs of public, academic and special library users across any virtual setting—email, text messaging, social networking websites—as well as in traditional and face-to-face models of communication." Publisher's note

Includes bibliographical references

Orr, Cynthia

★ **Crash** course in readers' advisory; Cynthia Orr. Libraries Unlimited 2015 125 p. (paperback) $45   **025.5**
1. Library services 2. Readers' advisory services
ISBN 1610698258; 9781610698252

LC 2014027064

This book on library services, by Cynthia Orr, "is built around understanding books, reading, and readers and will quickly show you how to identify reading preferences and advise patrons effectively. You'll learn about multiple RA approaches, such as genre, appeal features, and reading interests and about essential tools that can help with RA. Plus, you'll discover tips to help you keep up with this ever-changing field." (Publisher's note)

Includes bibliographical references and index

Reference reborn; breathing new life into public services librarianship. Diane Zabel, editor; preface by Linda C. Smith. Libraries Unlimited 2010 xx, 401 p.p illustrations $65   **025.5**
1. Library science 2. Library education 3. Reference services (Libraries) 4. Internet in library reference services 5. Electronic reference services (Libraries) 6. Public services (Libraries) -- United States 7. Reference services (Libraries) -- United States
ISBN 1591588286; 9781591588283

LC 2010041105

This book, edited by Diane Zabel, "is a collection of over two dozen essays on developments and trends in reference and public services librarianship, highlighting some of the best thinking on reference services, outreach initiatives, the migration from print to e-reference collections, staffing 21st century libraries, library school curriculum, and more." (Publisher's note)

"Essential for public service librarians—academic and public, both veterans and new to the profession—and for students or potential students in information science. Highly recommended." LJ

Includes bibliographical references and index

Saricks, Joyce G.

★ The **readers'** advisory guide to genre fiction; 2nd ed; American Library Association 2009 352p (ALA readers' advisory series) pa $65   **025.5**
1. Reference services (Libraries) 2. Fiction -- Bibliography
ISBN 978-0-8389-0989-8
                                          LC 2008-51029

First published 2001

"Each section includes three or four specific genres . . . and features a definition and introduction to the genre, the characteristics of the genre's appeal, suggested authors and titles, and other practical information. Well-crafted back matter add to the ease of navigation. This very readable text employs a playful tone that reflects Saricks's love of her work and will inspire readers to use RA techniques in a variety of ways. [This is] a useful tool for both new library employees and established practitioners." Voice Youth Advocates

Includes bibliographical references

★ **Readers'** advisory service in the public library; 3rd ed; American Library Association 2005 211p il pa $38   **025.5**
1. Public libraries 2. Reference services (Libraries)
ISBN 0-8389-0897-7
                                          LC 2004-29271

First published 1989

In this guide to readers' advisory, "online tools for identifying and evaluating titles to suggest to today's new adult leisure readers are described, in addition to . . . tried-and-true print sources. The value of personal reading suggestions from staff and patrons is addressed. Topics for discussion and techniques for marketing good reading material are offered. . . . A priority for all libraries involved in readers' advisory." Booklist

Includes bibliographical references

Spratford, Becky Siegel

The **horror** readers' advisory; the librarian's guide to vampires, killer tomatoes, and haunted houses. [by] Becky Siegel Spratford [and] Tammy Hennigh Clausen. American Library Association 2004 161p il (ALA readers' advisory series) pa $36 **025.5**
1. Reference services (Libraries) 2. Horror fiction -- History and criticism
ISBN 0-8389-0871-3
                                          LC 2003-25530

This is a "guide to horror fiction, explaining its appeal and advising on how librarians unfamiliar with the genre can broaden their own knowledge and build a viable collec-

tion. The text briefly outlines the characteristics of the main categories, or subgenres, including the usual monsters and occult creatures; extreme suspense of all types; hauntings and possession; and a section on classic works of horror, along with tips for interviewing readers of each subgenre. . . . [This] small, helpful book will be a boon to readers' advisors needing fresh meat for horror fans." Libr J

Includes bibliographical references

Virtual reference service; from competencies to assessment. edited by R. David Lankes . . . [et al.] Neal-Schuman Publishers 2008 206p il (Virtual reference desk series) $75   **025.5**
1. Reference services (Libraries)
ISBN 978-1-55570-528-2
                                          LC 2007-24104

"Featuring essays from the 2005 7th Annual Virtual Reference Desk Conference, this book focuses on the evolving aspects of virtual reference theory, research, and practice. . . . The topics explored include the implementation and expansion of virtual reference programs, and the training and assessment that is necessary to ensure the success of these services. . . . This is a valuable resource for library practitioners involved with reference services." Am Ref Books Annu, 2008

Includes bibliographical references

Wichman, Emily T.

Librarian's guide to passive programming; easy and affordable activities for all ages. Emily T. Wichman. Libraries Unlimited Inc. 2012 xvii, 152 p.p ill. (pbk. : acid-free paper) $40   **025.5**
1. Librarians 2. Library finance 3. Library services 4. Libraries -- Activity programs -- United States
ISBN 159884895X; 9781598848953; 9781598848960
                                          LC 2011045419

In her book, author Emily T. Wichman discusses library budget cuts, and how "librarians are seeking new ways to stretch their programming dollars and maximize staff resources. Passive programming allows libraries to inexpensively showcase their services while inviting visitors of all ages to enjoy the value that libraries bring to the community." (Publisher's note)

Includes bibliographical references and index.

Wyatt, Neal

The **readers'** advisory guide to nonfiction. American Library Association 2007 318p (ALA reader's advisory series) pa $48   **025.5**
1. Public libraries 2. Reference services (Libraries)
ISBN 978-0-8389-0936-2; 0-8389-0936-1
                                          LC 2006-102318

Wyatt "focuses on eight popular categories: history, true crime, true adventure, science, memoir, food/cooking, travel, and sports. Within each, she explains the scope, popularity, style, major authors and works, and the subject's position in readers' advisory interviews. Wyatt addresses who is reading nonfiction and why, while providing RAs with the tools and language to incorporate nonfiction into discussions that point readers to what to read next. . . . [This] guide includes nonfiction bibliography, key authors, benchmark books with annotations, and core collections." Publisher's note

Includes bibliographical references

025.7   Physical preparation for storage and use

Lavender, Kenneth

★ **Book** repair; a how-to-do-it manual. Kenneth Lavender. 2nd ed; Neal-Schuman Publishers Inc. 2011 xiv, 265 p.p il (How-to-do-it manuals for libraries) (alk. paper) $80   **025.7**

1. Librarians 2. Paperback books 3. Bookbinding -- Repairing -- Handbooks, manuals, etc 4. Books -- Conservation and restoration -- Handbooks, manuals, etc
ISBN 1555707475; 1555707483; 9781555707477; 9781555707484

LC 2011022636

First published 1992

Author Kenneth Lavender provides a "step-by-step manual . . . on basic book repair techniques and sound preservation practices . . . [which] offers illustrated sections on cleaning, mending, hinge and spine repair, strengthening paperbacks, and more. . . . A full discussion of when and how to make repairs is provided, as is a discussion of alternative conservation practices that will enable each librarian to develop procedures appropriate to his or her library." (Publisher's note)

"Covering both basic book repair techniques and . . . conservation practices, this . . . manual offers illustrated sections on cleaning, mending, hinge and spine repair, strengthening paperbacks, [etc.]. . . . Chapters cover: wet and water-damaged books; mold and mildew; repair of book linings and pamphlet bindings; using acid-free materials to repair damaged books; lining paper objects; affordable repair tools and supplies. . . . A full discussion of when and how to make repairs, and alternative conservation practices that enable each librarian to develop procedures appropriate to his or her library are also provided." Publisher's note

Includes bibliographical references and index.

Schechter, Abraham A.

Basic book repair methods; illustrated by the author. Libraries Unlimited 1999 102p il pa $37 **025.7**

1. Books -- Conservation and restoration
ISBN 1-56308-700-6

LC 98-50950

Photographs accompany step-by-step instructions for common preservation techniques, from the cleaning of pages and their readhesion, to case reattachment and rebacking.

Includes bibliographical references

025.8   Maintenance and preservation of collections

Halsted, Deborah D.

★ **Disaster** planning; a how-to-do-it manual for librarians with planning templates on CD-ROM.

Neal-Schuman Publishers 2005 xx, 247p il (How-to-do-it manuals for librarians) pa $85   **025.8**

1. Disaster relief 2. Accidents -- Prevention 3. Library resources -- Conservation and restoration
ISBN 1-55570-486-7

LC 2003-65152

"Step-by-step instructions discuss creating a working disaster team, establishing a communications strategy, identifying relief and recovery agencies, developing response plans, and examining issues of cutting-edge library security. . . . This valuable resource is an important addition to most professional collections." Booklist

Includes bibliographical references

Hammer, Joshua

The **bad-**ass librarians of Timbuktu; and their race to save the world's most precious manuscripts. Joshua Hammer. Simon & Schuster 2016 288 p. (hardcover) $26   **025.8**

1. Librarians 2. Islamic literature 3. Cultural property -- Protection 4. Librarians -- Mali -- Tombouctou 5. Cultural property -- Protection -- Mali 6. Manuscripts, Arabic -- Mali -- Tombouctou 7. Centre de documentation et de recherches 'Ahmed Baba.' 8. Islamic learning and scholarship -- Mali -- Tombouctou 9. Libraries -- Destruction and pillage -- Mali -- Tombouctou 10. Mali -- History -- Tuareg Rebellion, 2012- -- Destruction and pillage
ISBN 9781476777405; 9781476777412; 9781476777436

LC 2015030396

In this book, by Joshua Hammer, "To save precious centuries-old Arabic texts from Al Qaeda, a band of librarians in Timbuktu pulls off a brazen heist. . . . In the 1980s, a young adventurer and collector for a government library, Abdel Kader Haidara, . . . track[ed] down and salvag[ed] tens of thousands of ancient Islamic and secular manuscripts. . . . [This book] tells the incredible story of how Haidara . . . later became one of the world's greatest and most brazen smugglers." (Publisher's note)

"Hammer's clearly written and engaging chronicle of the achievements of Timbuktu, the risks presented to this area, and the portraits of several brave and dedicated individuals brings to light an important and unfamiliar story." LJ

Includes bibliographical references and index.

Kahn, Miriam B.

Disaster response and planning for libraries; Miriam B. Kahn. 2nd ed; American Library Association 2012 158 p. bibl il (paperback) $60.00 **025.8**

1. Libraries -- Safety measures 2. Disaster response and recovery 3. Library resources -- Conservation and restoration 4. Libraries -- Safety measures -- Planning 5. Library materials -- Conservation and restoration 6. Library materials -- Conservation and restoration -- Planning
ISBN 083891151X; 9780838911518

LC 2011043703

This book by Miriam B. Kahn presents a "step-by-step, how-to guide for preparing and responding to all types of library disasters." It includes "guidance for creating protocols and response plans tailored to your own institution . . .

pointers for handling . . . library materials when damaged . . . information on preparing for technology recovery . . . [and] reproducible checklists and forms." (Publisher's note)

Includes bibliographical references (pages 143-154) and index

026 Specific kinds of institutions

Baker, Jennifer S., 1953-

The **readers'** advisory guide to historical fiction; Jennifer S. Baker. ALA Editions, an imprint of the American Library Association 2015 176 p. (print : alk. paper) $48 **026**

1. Best books 2. Historical fiction 3. Historical fiction -- Bibliography 4. Fiction in libraries -- United States 5. Readers' advisory services -- United States 6. Libraries -- United States -- Special collections -- Historical fiction
ISBN 083891165X; 9780838911655

LC 2014018024

Written by Jennifer S. Baker, "this guide provides an overview of historical fiction's roots, highlighting foundational classics, as well as covering the latest and most popular authors and titles; explores the genre in terms of its scope, style, and appeal; [and] includes lists of recommendations, with a compendium of print and web-based resources." (Publisher's note)

"Although not as hefty as Sarah L. Johnson's Historical Fiction II, this volume strikes the perfect balance of thoroughness and accessibility. RA enthusiasts will be thrilled to add this book to their arsenal." LJ

Includes bibliographical references and indexes

★ **Directory** of special libraries and information centers; a guide to more than 35,000 special libraries, research libraries, information centers, archives, and data centers maintained by government agencies . . . Matthew Miskelly, content project editor. Thompson/Gale 3v **026**

1. Reference books 2. Special libraries -- Directories
Annual. First published 1963. Volume one is kept up to date by mid-year supplementary volume (v3)

"Volume 1, in three parts, provides . . . contact and descriptive information on more than 35,800 subject-specific resource collections maintained by various government agencies, businesses, publishers, educational and nonprofit organizations, and associations around the world. . . . Volume 2, Geographic and Personnel Indexes, provides access to profiled libraries by geographic region, as well as by the professional staff that are cited in each listing." Publisher's note

027 General libraries, archives, information centers

Butler, Patricia M.

Joint libraries; models that work. Claire B. Gunnels, Susan E. Green, and Patricia M. Butler. American Library Association 2012 220 p. $60.00 **027**

1. Public libraries 2. Academic libraries 3. Library

cooperation 4. Joint-use libraries -- United States
ISBN 0838911382; 9780838911389

LC 2011044057

This book provides a "look at joint library models, including the determining factors that lead to increased success and issues that may lead to project failures. This title includes a brief discussion of the history behind school library joint partnerships; however, the authors primarily focus on joint academic/public libraries, giving concrete examples from their own experiences as well as information from examples of multi-use libraries across the country." (Voice of Youth Advocates)

Includes bibliographical references and index.

Johnson, Alex

Improbable libraries; a visual journey to the world's most unusual libraries. Alex Johnson. University of Chicago Press 2015 240 p. color illustrations (cloth : alk. paper) $27.50 **027**

1. Library architecture 2. Libraries -- Pictorial works 3. Curiosities and wonders 4. Libraries -- Miscellanea 5. Library architecture -- Miscellanea 6. Library architecture -- Pictorial works
ISBN 022626369X; 9780226263694

LC 2014035714

This book, by Alex Johnson, "showcases a wide range of unforgettable, never-before-seen images and interviews with librarians who are overcoming geographic, economic, and political difficulties to bring the written word to an eager audience. Alex Johnson charts the changing face of library architecture, as temporary pop-ups rub shoulders with monumental brick-and-mortar structures, and many libraries expand their mission to function as true community centers." (Publisher's note)

"This delightful book will give bibliophiles everywhere ideas for how to exhibit their collection as well as add some destinations to their bucket list. A great option for the children's room, too." LJ

Includes bibliographical references

Ryback, Timothy W.

Hitler's private library; the books that shaped his life. Alfred A. Knopf 2008 xx, 278p il map $25.95 **027**

1. Heads of state 2. Nazi leaders 3. Germany -- History -- 1933-1945
ISBN 978-1-4000-4204-3; 1-4000-4204-6

LC 2008-22010

"Thanks to [Ryback's] imaginative research—and his willingness to investigate a very creepy subject—we come closer to one of the most elusive men ever to shape world history." New Repub

Includes bibliographical references

027.4   Public libraries

Matthews, Joseph R.

Scorecards for results; a guide for developing a library balanced scorecard. Libraries Unlimited 2008 112p pa $45   **027.4**
   1. Public libraries 2. Libraries -- Administration
   ISBN 978-1-59158-698-2
            LC 2008-3689

"A balanced scorecard (BSC) is 'a process and culture for choosing, using, and revising measures' to help libraries focus on the success of their mission. . . . [The author] has developed a BSC workbook for public libraries. . . . Individual chapters here detail the six steps in developing and using a balanced scorecard, with sample vision statements, strategic themes, and performance measures." Libr J
   Includes bibliographical references

McCook, Kathleen de la Peña

   ★ **Introduction** to public librarianship. Neal-Schuman Publishers 2004 406p il   **027.4**
   1. Public libraries 2. Public librarianship 3. Public libraries -- United States
   ISBN 1-55570-475-1
            LC 2004-46012

"The book is a necessary addition to all professional collections, not to collect dust, but to become respectfully dog-eared and coffee-stained through repeated use." Florida Libraries
   Includes bibliographical references

027.5   Government libraries

Conaway, James

America's library; the story of the Library of Congress, 1800-2000. foreword by James Billington; introduction by Edmund Morris. Yale Univ. Press 2000 226p il $48   **027.5**
   1. Library of Congress
   ISBN 978-0-300-08308-8; 0-300-08308-4
            LC 99-58751

This history of the Library of Congress is organized "around that tiny, hardy band of men and women who have used both political acumen and intellectual vision to build the library's collections and establish those services that make the LC library to both Congress and nation. Richly supplemented with photographs, this history reaches out to touch all who love libraries." Booklist
   Includes bibliographical references

027.6   Libraries for special groups and organizations

Moller, Sharon Chickering

Library service to Spanish speaking patrons; a practical guide. Libraries Unlimited 2001 207p pa $30   **027.6**
   1. Public libraries 2. Libraries and Hispanic Americans
   ISBN 1-56308-719-7
            LC 00-45090

"Intended to stimulate discussion among library service planners and to offer counsel to service providers, this book should become required reading in any jurisdiction with an underserved Latino population." Voice Youth Advocates
   Includes bibliographical references

027.62   Libraries for specific age groups

Braafladt, Keith

Technology and literacy; 21st century library programming for children and teens. by Jennifer Nelson and Keith Braafladt. American Library Association 2012 129 p. (alk. paper) $50.00   **027.62**
   1. Library services 2. Literacy programs 3. Literature and technology 4. Children's libraries -- Activity programs 5. Scratch (Computer program language) 6. Computer literacy -- Study and teaching 7. Technological literacy -- Study and teaching 8. Young adults' libraries -- Activity programs
   ISBN 0838911080; 9780838911082
            LC 2011035104

This book by Jennifer Nelson presents a "guide for creating and implementing technology-based programming in public libraries. . . . Beginning chapters explain and present a plan for offering such programs, providing steps on how to execute them. . . . The author explains the value of this type of programming and the process involved with adoption, and covers planning, gathering support from both administration and staff, marketing . . . managing time, etc." (School Library Journal)
   Includes bibliographical references and index.

Brown, Amy

Let's start the music; programming for primary grades. Amy Brown. ALA Editions, an imprint of the American Library Association 2013 184 p. $45   **027.62**
   1. Music -- Study and teaching 2. Children's libraries -- Activity programs 3. Music -- Instruction and study -- United States 4. School libraries -- Activity programs -- United States
   ISBN 0838911668; 9780838911662
            LC 2013010871

In this book, author Amy Brown "explores several benefits of integrating music into story and literacy programs, then outlines simple strategies for all children's staff to feature more music and instruments in their events. Brown shares 13 themed programs, ranging from sing-alongs and animals to fairy tales and food, and each theme includes an extensive list of books, songs, an activity, and an instrument craft." (School Library Journal)

Includes bibliographical references and index

Del Negro, Janice M.

Folktales aloud; practical advice for playful storytelling. Janice M. Del Negro. American Library Association 2014 212 p. (alk. paper) $47   **027.62**
1. Fairy tales 2. Storytelling 3. Children's libraries -- Activity programs 4. Elementary school libraries -- Activity programs
ISBN 0838911358; 9780838911358

LC 2013028036

This book, by Janice M. Del Negro, "aims to show that storytelling is still vital in librarianship and throughout the greater community. . . . The text provides useful information for novice and seasoned storytellers alike while engaging the reader with its conversational tone. The chapters are broken down by audience age . . . and include information about audience needs and wants, stories, and resource information." (Booklist)

"Folktales are an integral part of children's literature and are the basis for many classic books librarians use daily in their work. These much loved tales are also the backbone of the art of storytelling...Del Negro leads novice tellers through the nuances of successful storytelling...Advice is offered in a very practical way on how to approach this group and suggestions are made as to how to grab and hold their interest with pacing, movement and suspense. If you have even a passing interest in the art of storytelling, this guide is not to be missed." SLJ

Includes bibliographical references and index

Eagle, MK

★ **Answering** teens' tough questions; a YALSA guide. mk Eagle. Neal-Schuman, an imprint of the American Library Association 2012 x, 125 p.p $49.95   **027.62**
1. Librarians 2. Library services 3. Teenagers -- Attitudes 4. Teenagers -- United States -- Attitudes 5. Libraries and teenagers -- United States 6. Young adults' libraries -- United States 7. Teenagers -- Services for -- United States 8. Teenagers -- United States -- Social conditions 9. Young adult services librarians -- United States -- Attitudes
ISBN 1555707947; 9781555707941

LC 2012015104

Author mk Eagle presents a book that "offers any librarian a quick primer on talking with young adults about the tough and often controversial topics of sex, drugs, alcohol, and violence." It provides "quick overviews on the issues themselves as well as tips for navigating these waters with teens. . . . . Chapters include sex, sexuality, homelessness, tattoos and piercings, dating violence, abuse, drugs and alcohol, emotional and mental health, and the juvenile justice system." (Publisher's note)

Includes bibliographical references and index

Fiore, Carole D.

★ **Fiore's** summer library reading program handbook. Neal-Schuman Publishers 2005 xxiii, 312p pa $65   **027.62**
1. Books and reading 2. Children's libraries
ISBN 1-55570-513-8

LC 2004-31104

"This research-laden handbook . . . serves as a 'comprehensive program-planning and implementation tool' for public libraries seeking to revamp, revise, or develop a summer library reading program. . . . This is an invaluable resource, both for its concrete guidance and its abstract exploration of the meaning of summer library programs." Bull Cent Child Books

Includes bibliographical references

Flowers, Sarah

Evaluating teen services and programs; Sarah Flowers. Neal-Schuman, an imprint of the American Library Association 2012 xv, 119 p.p (pbk.) $49.95   **027.62**
1. Library services 2. Young adults' libraries 3. Libraries -- United States 4. Libraries and teenagers -- United States 5. Young adults' libraries -- Evaluation -- United States
ISBN 1555707939; 9781555707934

LC 2012015105

Author Sarah Flowers presents "a guide that provides basic information to help teen/youth services librarians, library directors, library school students studying teen services, and middle/high school librarians examine all aspects of their teen programs and services to determine where improvement is needed. Find out what you need to develop goals and objectives for evaluation, and learn how to collect the data that will give you a realistic picture of your library's strengths and weaknesses." (Publisher's note)

Includes bibliographical references and index

Ghoting, Saroj Nadkarni

STEP into storytime; using storytime effective practice to strengthen the development of newborns to five-year-olds. Saroj Nadkarni Ghoting and Kathy Fling Klatt. ALA Editions, an imprint of the American Library Association 2014 368 p. illustrations $59   **027.62**
1. Storytelling 2. Early childhood education 3. Children's libraries -- Activity programs 4. Storytelling -- United States 5. Libraries and preschool children -- United States 6. Children's libraries -- Activity programs -- United States
ISBN 0838912222; 9780838912225

LC 2014004162

This book, by Saroj Nadkarni Ghoting and Kathy Fling Klatt, focuses on "Story Time Effective Practice (STEP). . . . [It] is an approach that articulates the link between child development theory and storytimes. This important resource shows how presenters can use STEP to craft a storytime that is effective for mixed-age groups and adheres to best practices for emotional, social, physical, and cognitive support." (Publisher's note)

"It is a rare volume that could serve as both pleasure reading or as a textbook, but STEP into Storytime walks that fine line...The majority of children's librarians have studied childhood development and early literacy best practices; consider this book required reading to keep this knowledge fresh while reminding us of the importance—and delightful fun—of our work." Booklist

Includes bibliographical references and index

Pattee, Amy S.

Developing library collections for today's young adults; Amy S. Pattee. The Scarecrow Press, Inc. 2013 267 p. (cloth) $55 **027.62**

1. Multimedia 2. Library services 3. Young adults' libraries 4. Libraries -- Special collections 5. Libraries and teenagers -- United States 6. Multimedia library services -- United States

ISBN 0810887347; 9780810887343

LC 2013018596

This book, by Amy S. Pattee, "features policies that deal expressly with materials that respect the intellectual freedom of young library patrons. It emphasizes the importance of everything from needs assessment to collection development, encouraging librarians to consider informational, recreational, and curricular needs and interests as the library staff select material on behalf of young adults." (Publisher's note)

"The book's greatest asset is that it manages to be extremely specific and thorough without becoming overwhelming." VOYA

Includes bibliographical references and index

Sweeney, Jennifer

Literacy; a way out for at-risk youth. Jennifer Sweeney. Libraries Unlimited 2012 xx, 133 pagesp (pbk. : acid-free paper) $40.00 **027.62**

1. Literacy 2. Prison librarians 3. Juvenile delinquents -- Books and reading 4. Prison libraries -- United States 5. Literacy programs -- United States 6. Juvenile corrections -- United States 7. Libraries and prisons -- United States 8. Literacy -- Social aspects -- United States 9. Juvenile delinquents -- Education -- United States 10. Libraries and juvenile delinquents -- United States 11. Problem youth -- Books and reading -- United States 12. Juvenile delinquents -- Rehabilitation -- United States 13. Juvenile delinquents -- Books and reading -- United States

ISBN 9781598846744; 9781598846751; 1598846744

LC 2011042804

This looks at corrections librarianship, focusing on juvenile institutions. The book "provides librarians in juvenile detention facilities with tools to face their unique challenges, such as collaborating with corrections staff and encouraging youth to maintain their connection to the library after release." (Barnes and Noble)

Includes bibliographical references and index.

Vaillancourt, Renee J.

Bare bones young adult services; tips for public library generalists. American Lib. Assn. 2000 142p il pa $33 **027.62**

1. Public libraries 2. Young adults' libraries 3.

Libraries and students

ISBN 0-8389-3497-8

LC 99-35643

The author "provides guidelines for forming Teen Advisory Boards and focus groups, dealing with unruly adolescent patrons, providing homework support, as well as some basic programming ideas. She also discusses collection development and suggests resources that specialize in reviewing teen-level materials." SLJ

Includes bibliographical references

028 Reading and use of other information media

Basbanes, Nicholas A.

★ **Every** book its reader; the power of the printed word to stir the world. HarperCollins 2005 360p il $29.95; pa $15.95 **028**

1. Best books 2. Books and reading

ISBN 0-06-059323-7; 978-0-06-059323-0; 0-06-059324-5 pa; 978-0-06-059324-7 pa

LC 2005-46164

The author "focuses on peoples' reading habits and on the books they have read, both obscure and renowned, as well as on the importance of particular books in specific contexts. Basbanes begins by interviewing some of the best-read people alive, among them David McCullough, Harold Bloom, Helen Vendler, and Elaine Pagels; he also mentions a wide variety of contemporary and historical personages. The loosely related stories are often inspirational, making this an engrossing read." Libr J

Includes bibliographical references

The **CIA** World Factbook. Skyhorse Publishing various pagings maps **028**

1. Almanacs 2. Geopolitics 3. Population -- Statistics

Annual

This book "offers complete and up-to-date information on the world's nations. This comprehensive guide is packed with data on the politics, populations, military expenditures, and economics." (Publisher's note)

Dirda, Michael

Book by book; notes on reading and life. Henry Holt 2006 170p $17 **028**

1. Best books 2. Books and reading

ISBN 978-0-8050-7877-0; 0-8050-7877-0

LC 2005-55451

The author "writes a guide to reading and its life lessons ranging widely and pithily through the universal themes of learning, school, work, love, childhood and spiritual guidance. Dirda's message is simple: if reading is to be life enhancing, we need to focus our attention on books that are rewarding. . . . For those who enjoy books about reading, and for all those seeking to encourage others to read, Dirda's brief yet suggestive book will inspire." Publ Wkly

Browsings; A Year of Reading, Collecting, and Living With Books. by Michael Dirda. W W Norton & Co Inc. 2015 336 p. (hardcover) $24.95 **028**
1. Authors 2. Authorship 3. Books and reading
ISBN 9781605988443; 1605988448

This book, by Michael Dirda, "collects fifty of his witty and wide-ranging reflections on literary journalism, book collecting, and the writers he loves. Reaching from the classics to the post-moderns, his allusions dance from Samuel Johnson, Ralph Waldo Emerson and M. F. K. Fisher to Marilynne Robinson, Hunter S. Thompson, and David Foster Wallace." (Publisher's note)

"This joy-filled, reflective collection makes perfect bedside reading... Literate but never snobby, this collection of essays surely will entertain and enlighten book lovers of all stripes." Booklist

Hooper, Brad
The **short** story readers' advisory; a guide for librarians. American Lib. Assn. 2000 135p pa $32 **028**
1. Short stories -- History and criticism
ISBN 0-8389-0782-2
LC 99-85751

This work contains over 200 critical essays covering short story authors past and present. A step-by-step guide on how to interview readers in order to match their tastes with appropriate stories is included.
Includes bibliographical references

Maatta, Stephanie L.
A **few** good books; using contemporary readers' advisory strategies to connect readers with books. Neal-Schuman Publishers 2010 xix, 387p pa $69.95 **028**
1. Reference services (Libraries) 2. Books and reading -- History
ISBN 978-1-55570-669-2; 1-55570-669-X
LC 2009-40999

"This comprehensive and up-to-date guide is a treasure trove of practical advice and resources that will help make the RA experience even more effective and enjoyable." Libr J
Includes bibliographical references

Mendelsund, Peter
What we see when we read; a phenomenology, with illustrations. Peter Mendelsund. Vintage Contemporaries 2014 448 p. illustrations (Vintage original) (paperback) $16.95 **028**
1. Phenomenology 2. Visual literacy 3. Books and reading 4. Visual perception in literature
ISBN 0804171637; 9780804171632
LC 2014007896

This book, by Peter Mendelsund, is an "exploration into the phenomenology of reading-- how we visualize images from reading works of literature. . . . The collection of fragmented images on a page-- a graceful ear there, a stray curl, a hat positioned just so-- and other clues and signifiers helps

us to create an image of a character. But in fact our sense that we know a character intimately has little to do with our ability to concretely picture our beloved-- or reviled-- literary figures." (Publisher's note)

"This work was written for those who enjoy fully the creative experience of reading, and who read about reading." LJ

Ross, Catherine Sheldrick
★ The **pleasures** of reading; a booklover's alphabet. Catherine Sheldrick Ross. Libraries Unlimited, An imprint of ABC-CLIO, LLC 2014 270 p. (paperback) $45 **028**
1. Books and reading 2. Libraries and community 3. Reading interests 4. Reading -- Social aspects
ISBN 159158695X; 9781591586951
LC 2014008161

In this book, author Catherine Sheldrick Ross "takes a new look at pleasure reading through 30 thought-provoking essays based on themes arranged from A to Z. . . . Drawing on her own research as well as other published sources, Ross comments on the significance of each theme, provides examples of the phenomenon, and develops the topic chronologically, through further examples, or through reversals." (Publisher's note)

"Librarians who work with RA will not find much new information but will have their experiences validated. Those new to RA will receive a thorough introduction." LJ
Includes bibliographical references and index

★ **Reading** matters; what the research reveals about reading, libraries, and community. by Catherine Sheldrick Ross, Lynne E.F. McKechnie, and Paulette M. Rothbauer. Libraries Unlimited 2006 p. cm. **028**
1. Books and reading. 2. Reading interests. 3. Reading promotion. 4. Popular literature. 5. Libraries and community. 6. Reading -- Social aspects. 7. Public services (Libraries)
ISBN 1-59158-066-8 (pbk. : alk. paper)
LC 2005030839
Includes bibliographical references and index..

028.1   Reviews

Naidoo, Jamie Campbell
★ **Rainbow** family collections; selecting and using children's books with lesbian, gay, bisexual, transgender, and queer content. Jamie Campbell Naidoo. Libraries Unlimited, an imprint of ABC-CLIO, LLC 2012 xvii, 260 p.p ill. (hardback) $50 **028.1**
1. Libraries and sexual minorities 2. Sexual minorities in literature 3. Libraries and sexual minorities -- United States 4. Libraries -- Special collections -- Sexual minorities 5. Sexual minorities -- Juvenile literature -- Bibliography 6. Children's libraries -- Collection development -- United States 7. Children's libraries -- Services to minorities -- United States 8. Children of sexual minority parents -- Books and reading -- United

States
ISBN 1598849603; 9781598849608
LC 2012008362

This book by Jamie Campbell Naidoo "highlight[s] titles for children from infancy to age 11" featuring lesbian, gay, bisexual, transgender, and queer content. It "supplies a synopsis of the title's content, lists awards it has received, cites professional reviews, and provides suggestions for librarians considering acquisition. The book also provides a brief historical overview of LGBTQ children's literature along with the major book awards for this genre." (Publisher's note)

Includes bibliographical references and index

Szymborska, Wislawa

Nonrequired reading; prose pieces. translated from the Polish by Clare Cavanagh. Harcourt 2002 233p $24 **028.1**
1. Books and reading
ISBN 0-15-100660-1
LC 2002-2440

"The skillful simplicity and lyric quality of these essays make them distinctive. With her poet's gift for compression, Szymborska captures large concepts and brilliantly reduces them to pithy, two-page essays." Libr J

Includes bibliographical references

028.5 Reading and use of other information media by young people

Allyn, Pam

What to read when; the books and stories to read with your child, and all the best times to read them. Avery 2009 318p pa $16.95 **028.5**
1. Children -- Books and reading
ISBN 978-1-58333-334-1
LC 2008-54501

The author "provides many ways to promote a love of reading to children and offers top-ten lists of reasons to read to kids that incorporate practical, easy-to-use tips to encourage literacy from a young age. . . . This is an indispensable guide to choosing age-appropriate books for children. Allyn provides a list of more than 300 titles on 50 themes including such issues as adoption, feelings about school, sharing, and coping with illness. This valuable resource for children's librarians, educators, and parents is highly recommended." Libr J

The **Cambridge** guide to children's books in English; [edited by] Victor Watson; advisory editors, Elizabeth L. Keyser, Juliet Partridge, Morag Styles. Cambridge Univ. Press 2001 814p il $75 **028.5**
1. Reference books 2. Children's literature -- Encyclopedias
ISBN 0-521-55064-5
LC 00-65163

This reference provides an "overview of historic and contemporary children's books published in English. The entries include authors, illustrators, and significant works primarily from Britain, the US, Canada, Australia, New Zealand, India, and Africa. . . . Major themes, such as fairy tales,

fantasy, folktales, legends, mythology, and young adult fiction, are covered as well as less-expected entries on topics such as bias, the bush, disability, ecology, and nudity in children's books. Nonbook media are also covered by entries on animated cartoons, comics, superheroes, and television for children." Choice

Includes bibliographical references

Helbig, Alethea

Dictionary of American young adult fiction, 1997-2001; books of recognized merit. {by} Alethea K. Helbig and Agnes Regan Perkins. Greenwood Press 2004 xxii, 558p $75 **028.5**
1. Best books 2. Reference books 3. Youth -- Books and reading 4. Young adult literature -- Dictionaries 5. Young adult literature -- Bio-bibliography
ISBN 0-313-32430-1
LC 2003-56804

"The 290 books included {in this volume} have been recognized by one or more of the following: Alex Award, ALA Best Books for Young Adults, Booklist, NYPL, and the Michael L. Printz Award. Approximately 60 of the listed books are adult books considered appropriate for young adults by the award committees. The 741 entries, which include books, their authors, major characters, and settings, are listed alphabetically and range in length from a couple of paragraphs to a bit more than a page. Book entries describe plot, themes, and characters, as well as relevant literary awards, while author entries consist of a brief biography and bibliography. . . . {The information is collected} usefully for selectors of young adult fiction, reader's advisers, teachers, and libraries supporting young adult fiction teaching." Libr J

Includes bibliographical references

Keane, Nancy J.

101 great, ready-to-use book lists for teens; Nancy J. Keane. Libraries Unlimited, an imprint of ABC-CLIO, LLC 2012 xiv, 263 p.p (paperback) $40; (ebook) $40 **028.5**
1. Book selection 2. Books and reading 3. Young adult literature -- Bibliography 4. High school libraries -- Book lists 5. Young adults' libraries -- Book lists 6. Teenagers -- Books and reading -- United States
ISBN 1610691342; 9781610691345; 9781610691352
LC 2011051428

This book offers a "compilation of YA [Young Adult] materials . . . published prior to August 2011. The book is divided . . . into themed lists such as 'Genres,' 'Readalikes,' and 'Teaching Literary Elements.' The themes . . . include . . . topics such as 'Romance,' 'Autism & Asperger's Syndrome,' 'Different Belief Systems,' and 'Crossing the Border.' Each entry includes the title, author, publisher, publication date, page numbers, an annotation, Lexile level when available, and interest level by grade or age range." (School Library Journal)

"This is a useful resource for new librarians and may also be helpful to seasoned librarians. The emphasis is on books published within the last ten years, but some older titles are included." Lib Med Con

Includes bibliographical references and index

030 General encyclopedic works

The **World** Almanac and Book of Facts 2015; edited by Sarah Janssen. Simon & Schuster 2014 1008 p. illustrations $13.99 **030**
1. Almanacs 2. Geography 3. Popular culture
ISBN 1600571905; 9781600571909
Annual. First published 1868. Publisher varies

"The World Almanac and Book of Facts is America's top-selling reference book of all time, with more than 82 million copies sold. Published annually since 1868, this compendium of information is the authoritative source for all your entertainment, reference, and learning needs. The 2015 edition of The World Almanac [edited by Sarah Janssen] reviews the events of 2014 and will be your go-to source for any questions on any topic." (Publisher's note)

"This is the most comprehensive and well-known of almanacs. . . . Contains a chronology of the year's events, consumer information, historical anniversaries, annual climatological data, and forecasts. Color section has flags and maps. Includes detailed index." N Y Public Libr Book of How & Where to Look It Up

031 General encyclopedic works in specific languages and language families

Guinness world records 2015; by Guinness World Records. St. Martin's Press 2014 255 p. ill. (some col.) $28.95 **031**
1. World records 2. World records -- Periodicals 3. Curiosities and wonders -- Periodicals
ISBN 1908843632; 9781908843630
Published annually

This 2015 edition of the Guinness World Records book "presents thousands of new and updated records. . . . [It] showcases the very best of the most recent world records, with new subjects as diverse as castles, 3D printing, the search for alien life and the latest developments in AI and robotics. Plus, the Flashback features offer a look back at the archives to bring you the best of the classic and iconic records from the past 60 years." (Publisher's note)

Jacobs, A. J.
The **know-it-all**; one man's humble quest to become the smartest person in the world. Simon & Schuster 2004 386p $25 **031**
1. Encyclopaedia Britannica
ISBN 0-7432-5060-5
LC 2004-48233

This "book stems from the author's herculean effort to read every volume of the majestic Encyclopaedia Britannica. . . . Jacobs turns his quest for intellectual enlightenment into alphabetically ordered, humorous ruminations on all persons and events of his life. . . . Plenty of good fun pours out of this prose." Booklist
Includes bibliographical references

Lih, Andrew
The **Wikipedia** revolution; how a bunch of nobodies created the world's greatest encyclopedia. Hyperion 2009 246p il map $24.99 **031**
1. User generated content 2. Electronic encyclopedias
ISBN 978-1-4013-0371-6
LC 2008-51137

"Wikipedia is a revolutionary phenomenon, changing fundamentally the landscape of networked collaboration, e-learning, and, as librarians know all too well, mediated information provision. Depicted here is a Wikipedia insider's narrative of the development of Wikipedia. . . . [Lih] characterizes this revolution as only partly technological. The real revolution is social-an apt point when one considers the philosophical underpinnings of this resource, the articles' neutral point of view, while remaining a free resource anyone can use and distribute." Libr J
Includes bibliographical references

The **World** Book Encyclopedia. World Book, Inc 22 v col ill, col maps **031**
1. Reference books 2. Encyclopedias and dictionaries
New editions published yearly; revised frequently

"A 22-volume, highly illustrated, A-Z general encyclopedia for all ages, featuring sections on how to use World Book, other research aids, pronunciation key, a student guide to better writing, speaking, and research skills, and comprehensive index." (Publisher's note)

031.02 Books of miscellaneous facts

Famous first facts, international edition; a record of first happenings, discoveries, and inventions in world history. {edited by} Steven Anzovin & Janet Podell. Wilson, H.W. 2000 837p $140 **031.02**
1. Reference books 2. Encyclopedias and dictionaries
ISBN 0-8242-0958-3
LC 99-86869

This work "contains more than 5000 firsts from hundreds of countries and ranging in time from 3.5 billion years ago (the age of the oldest continental land discovered) to 2001 (the scheduled date of completion of the first building over 1500 feet tall). . . . {It} groups related entries under broad subject categories (arranged alphabetically) and subcategories. Within each category or sub-category, entries are arranged chronologically." Publisher's note

The **New** York Public Library desk reference; 4th ed; Hyperion 2002 999p il maps $34.95 **031.02**
1. Reference books 2. Encyclopedias and dictionaries
ISBN 0-7868-6846-5
LC 2002-27480

First published 1989 by Webster's New World
Divided into chapters, this reference features charts, tables, lists, and illustrations providing information in such categories as signs and symbols, mathematics and science basics, the arts, grammar and punctuation, etiquette, personal finance, first aid, and household tips.
Includes bibliographical references

051 General serial publications in specific languages and language families

Meyerowitz, Rick

✓ **Drunk** stoned brilliant dead; the writers and artists who made the National Lampoon insanely great. Abrams 2010 319p il $40 **051**

1. Satire 2. American wit and humor 3. National lampoon (Periodical)

ISBN 978-0-8109-8848-4; 0-8109-8848-8

This is the "first Lampoon book that celebrates the wild, eye-intoxicating diversity of its illustrations, photography, cartoons, comic strips, graphics—parodies of everything from matchbooks to Marvel Comics to modern art. In toto this volume is a testament to the dazzling design expertise of its formative art directors, Michael Gross and David Kaestle. Rick Meyerowitz, a charter member of the Lampoon crew . . ., has in effect edited a magnificent 320-page issue of the magazine that reprints much of its finest work. And in brief, funny, and for once malice-free memoirs from its principals, the collection evokes the sparkling camaraderie that drove it. If you grew up with the Lampoon, this book is a trip down memory lane like no other; if not, it will demonstrate that the much-maligned 70s could produce humor that has never been surpassed." Vanity Fair

060.4 Special topics of general organizations

American Institute of Parliamentarians standard code of parliamentary procedure; [by American Institute of Parliamentarians] McGraw-Hill 2012 x, 326 p.p (alk. paper) $19 **060.4**

1. Parliamentary practice

ISBN 0071778640; 9780071778640

LC 2011048926

This book, by American Institute of Parliamentarians, "for more than 60 years, . . . (formerly, the Sturgis Standard Code) has been helping meeting organizers and participants ensure fairness and justice on a consistent basis. This updated edition provides important new motions and protocols pertaining to electronic meetings, discipline, and finance and audit committees." (Publisher's note)

Includes bibliographical references and index

Encyclopedia of Associations; An Associations Unlimited Reference. 53 edition Gale / Cengage Learning 2014 3700 p. 3v $1084 **060.4**

1. Associations 2. Encyclopedias and dictionaries

ISBN 1414477988; 9781414477985

Annual

This book, edited by Tara E. Atterberry, offers a "comprehensive source for detailed information on nonprofit American membership organizations of national scope. Every entry offers a wealth of valuable data, typically including the organization's complete name, address and phone number together with the primary official's name and title; . . . founding date, purpose, activities and dues; . . . and more." (Publisher's note)

Robert, Henry M.

Robert's rules of order newly revised; Henry M. Robert III, Daniel H. Honemann, and Thomas J. Balch; with the assistance of Daniel E. Seabold and Shmuel Gerber. 11th ed Da Capo Press 2011 lii, 716 p.p $18.95 **060.4**

1. Parliamentary practice 2. Life skills -- Handbooks, manuals, etc.

ISBN 030682020X; 9780306820205; 9780306820212

LC 2011932260

"'Robert's Rules of Order' is the book on parliamentary procedure for parliamentarians and anyone involved in an organization, association, club, or group. . . . The eleventh edition has been thoroughly revised to address common inquiries and incorporate new rules, interpretations, and procedures made necessary by the evolution of parliamentary procedure, including new material relating to electronic communication and 'electronic meetings.'" (Publisher's note)

Robert's rules of order, newly revised, in brief; updated in accord with the eleventh edition of the complete manual. Henry M. Robert III ... [et al.] Da Capo Press 2011 vii, 197 p.p (alk. paper) $7.50 **060.4**

1. Parliamentary practice 2. Life skills -- Handbooks, manuals, etc.

ISBN 0306820196; 9780306820199

LC 2011932261

"'Robert's Rules of Order, Newly Revised, In Brief' was first published in 2005 to meet the need for a simple and short book on parliamentary procedure. This second edition of 'In Brief' is now updated and revised to match the new full edition of 'Robert's Rules of Order, Newly Revised,' also published this year. . . . This concise, user-friendly edition takes readers through the rules most often needed at meetings." (Publisher's note)

Webster's New World Robert's rules of order; simplified and applied. by Robert McConnell Productions. 3rd ed Houghton Mifflin Harcourt 2014 xxii, 388p $11.95 **060.4**

1. Parliamentary practice

ISBN 0764563998; 9780544236035

This book, by Robert McConnell Productions, is the "revised and updated edition of the clearest, most useful guide to parliamentary procedure. . . . Among its helpful features are sample scripts to help figure out what to say while conducting meetings, hands-on examples to show how the rules are applied, and timesaving tips to help make meetings more efficient." (Publisher's note)

"Organized so users can find what they need quickly and easily, this revised edition includes an entire new chapter on proper procedure for conducting homeowners' associations." Publisher's note

061 General organizations

The **Foundation** directory; compiled by The Foundation Center. Foundation Center 2730p **061**

1. Reference books 2. Endowments -- Directories

Annual. First published 1960 by Russell Sage. Replaces American foundations and their fields

"Provides detailed information concerning independent, corporate, community, and private foundations with assets of at least $2 million or annual giving of at least $200,000. Geographical arrangement. Entries give date founded; names of officers, contact, and donors; foundation type; financial data; fields of interest; types of support; limitations; application information; and number of staff. Six indexes: Donors, officers, and trustees; Geographic; Types of support; Subject; Foundations new to edition; Foundations name index." Guide to Ref Books. 11th edition

069   Museology (Museum science)

Conniff, Richard

House of Lost Worlds; Dinosaurs, Dynasties, and the Story of Life on Earth. Richard Conniff. Yale University Press 2016 352 p. illustrations (some color) (hardcover) $35   **069**
1. Natural history 2. Museums -- History
ISBN 9780300211634; 0300211635

This book, by Richard Conniff, "tells the story of how one museum changed ideas about dinosaurs, dynasties, and even the story of life on earth. . . . Delving into the [Yale Peabody Museum of Natural History's] storied and colorful past, award-winning author Richard Conniff introduces a cast of bold explorers, roughneck bone hunters, and visionary scientists." (Publisher's note)

"Colored, boxed sections highlighting people and events and over 100 illustrations and photos provide a pleasant coffee table-book feel, and 23 pages of footnotes attest to Conniff's exhaustive research." Kirkus

Includes bibliographical references (pages 293-316) and index.

Museums of the World; by De Gruyter Saur. De Gruyter Saur 2014 1553 p. $694.38   **069**
1. Museums
ISBN 3110337940; 9783110337945
First published 1973. Periodically revised.

This book "covers in its 18th edition about 55,000 museums in 202 countries, listed hierarchically by country and place, and within places, alphabetically by name. . . . A typical entry contains the following details: name of the museum, address, telephone number, fax, eMail address and URL, museum type, year of foundation, name of the director and museum staff, special collections and equipment, number of the entry." (Publisher's note)

070   Documentary media, educational media, news media; journalism; publishing

Brokaw, Tom

A **long** way from home; growing up in the American heartland. Random House 2002 272p $24.95; pa $12.95   **070**
1. Journalists 2. Television news anchors
ISBN 0-375-50763-9; 0-375-75935-2 pa
LC 2002-31865

"Peppered with photographs . . . this tribute to an idyllic childhood should please Brokaw's loyal fans." Publ Wkly

Cronkite, Walter, 1916-2009

A **reporter's** life. Knopf 1997 384p il $26.95; pa $15   **070**
1. Radio reporters 2. Television news anchors
ISBN 0-394-57879-1; 0-345-41103-X pa
LC 96-21053

Cronkite's "memoir is a short course on the flow of events in the second half of this century—events the world knows more about because of Walter Cronkite's work, and some of which might not have happened without it." N Y Times Book Rev

Knight, Robert M., 1948-

Journalistic writing; building the skills, honing the craft. Robert M. Knight. Marion Street Press 2010 315 p. $29.95   **070**
1. Authorship 2. Journalism 3. Journalism -- Authorship
ISBN 1933338385; 1936863626; 9781933338385; 9781936863624
LC 2010012080

This book, by Robert M. Knight, "is the definitive handbook for aspiring journalists. Offering budding writers suggestions on how to improve their skills—even when faced with a tight deadline—this guide also reviews many elements essential to the occupation such as utilizing strong nouns and verbs, paring down adjectives and adverbs, describing with concrete detail, and avoiding clichés and the passive voice." (Publisher's note)

Includes bibliographical references (p. 301-305) and index

Kovach, Bill

Blur; how to know what's true in the age of information overload. [by] Bill Kovach and Tom Rosenstiel. Bloomsbury 2010 227p $26   **070**
1. Journalism -- Objectivity
ISBN 978-1-59691-565-7
LC 2010-19766

"Kovach and Rosenstiel combine journalism and civics in this valuable and insightful resource to help Americans adapt to an era that demands that readers become their own editors and news aggregators." Booklist

Includes bibliographical references

O'Faolain, Nuala

Are you somebody; the accidental memoir of a Dublin woman. Holt & Co. 1998 215p hardcover o.p. pa $13   **070**
1. Authors 2. Novelists 3. Columnists 4. Memoirists
ISBN 0-8050-5664-4 pa
LC 97-29725

First published 1996 in Ireland

This is a "moving and painfully honest memoir." Libr J

★ **Reporting** Iraq; an oral history of the war by the journalists who covered it. edited by Mike Hoyt, John Palattella, and the staff of the Columbia

Journalism Review. Melville House 2007 191p il pa $21.95 **070**

1. Reporters and reporting 2. Iraq War, 2003- -- Personal narratives

ISBN 978-1-93363-334-3; 1-93363-334-4

"44 reporters casually and directly discuss all angles of the War in Iraq, including their own shock, fear and incomprehension, in this compilation of interviews conducted by The Columbia Journalism Review. . . . This vital, breathtaking collection may be the closest contemporary reporting gets to cutting through the fog of war." Publ Wkly

Schorr, Daniel

Staying tuned; a life in journalism. Pocket Bks. 2001 354p il hardcover o.p. pa $14 **070**

1. Television reporters 2. Political commentators

ISBN 0-671-02088-9 pa

LC 2001-21014

Schorr tells of his life as a reporter for CBS, CNN and National Public Radio.

"Schorr's memoir is as much an inside look at the famous world figures of the latter half of the twentieth century as it is the story of one man's life and career." Booklist

Thompson, Hunter S., 1937-2005

★ **Fear** and loathing in America; the brutal odyssey of an outlaw journalist, 1968-1976. foreword by David Halberstam; edited by Douglas Brinkley. Simon & Schuster 2000 xxv, 756p il $30; pa $15 **070**

1. Authors 2. Novelists 3. Journalists 4. Satirists 5. Columnists 6. Nonfiction writers

ISBN 0-684-87315-X; 0-684-87316-8 pa

LC 00-47012

"During the period covered in this collection, Thompson was a vital, deliriously erratic force in journalism, covering the turbulent 1968 Democratic National Convention in Chicago, the 1968 election of Richard M. Nixon, the 1972 campaign, Watergate, the falls of Nixon and Saigon." N Y Times Book Rev

070.1 Documentary media, educational media, news media

Weller, Sheila

The **News** Sorority; Diane Sawyer, Katie Couric, Christiane Amanpour and the (Ongoing, Imperfect, Complicated) Triumph of Women in TV News. by Sheila Weller. Penguin Group USA 2014 448 p. illustrations $29.95 **070.1**

1. Women journalists

ISBN 1594204276; 9781594204272

LC 2014009725

This book, by Sheila Weller, tells the story of how "Diane Sawyer, Katie Couric, and Christiane Amanpour . . . broke into the newsroom's once impenetrable 'boys' club.' . . . . Drawing on exclusive interviews with their colleagues and intimates from childhood on, . . . [it] crafts a lively and exhilarating narrative that reveals the hard struggles and inner strengths that shaped these women and powered their success." (Publisher's note)

"News junkies and fans will love all of the insider details on the media and the lives of these women." LJ

Wenger, Debora Halpern

Advancing the story; broadcast journalism in a multimedia world. [by] Debora Halpern Wenger and Deborah Potter. 2nd ed.; CQ Press 2011 xxxi, 380p il pa $36.95 **070.1**

1. Broadcast journalism

ISBN 978-1-60871-714-9

LC 2010049469

First published 2008

"While stressing basics of good journalism with emphasis on attention to detail, [the] authors explain how technology has changed the approach to content preparation among those invested in the Internet and integrated technology." Journalism and Mass Communication Educator [review of 2008 edition]

Includes bibliographical references

070.4 Journalism

Buell, Hal

Moments; Pulitzer Prize-winning photographs: a visual chronicle of our time. text by Hal Buell; introduction by David Halberstam. Hachette Books 2015 336 p. illustrations (some color) $24.99 **070.4**

1. Photojournalism 2. Pulitzer Prizes 3. Pulitzer prizes 4. Photojournalism -- United States -- Awards

ISBN 1631910086; 9781631910081

This book presents a "complete collection of more than 600 Pulitzer Prize-winning photographs, from the first awards in 1942 through the 2015 honors. Organized by year, the photographs . . . create a poignant visual chronicle of our times. The images here, many of which are seared into our collective consciousness, include raising the flag at Iwo Jima, a young Vietnamese girl fleeing her village, her body burned by napalm, and the collapse of the World Trade towers." (Publisher's note)

Includes index

Cronkite, Walter, 1916-2009

Cronkite's war; his World War II letters home. Walter Cronkite IV and Maurice Isserman. National Geographic Society 2013 xxxiv, 318 p.p ill., map (hardcover) $28 **070.4**

1. Letters 2. World War, 1939-1945 -- Journalists 3. Love-letters -- United States 4. United Press International -- Biography 5. World War, 1939-1945 -- Campaigns -- Europe 6. World War, 1939-1945 -- Personal narratives 7. World War, 1939-1945 -- Aerial operations, American 8. War correspondents -- United States -- Correspondence 9. World War, 1939-1945 -- Journalists -- Correspondence 10. World War, 1939-1945 -- England -- London -- Anecdotes

ISBN 1426210191; 9781426210198

LC 2012045334

This book presents a selection of letters that journalist Walter Cronkite sent to his wife Betsy in Kansas City while he was in London, England reporting on World War II.

These letters, "which barely mention any dangers the journalist faced, are mostly from England in the period 1943-45. They detail the daily routines of a journalist in wartime: arranging meetings, writing stories under deadline, dealing with military censors, struggling to travel anywhere, shortages and rationing of everything." (Library Journal)

Includes bibliographical references (pages 313-314) and index.

Friedlander, Edward Jay

Feature writing for newspapers and magazines; the pursuit of excellence. [by] Edward Jay Friedlander, John Lee. 6th ed.; Pearson/A&B 2008 334p pa $86.80   **070.4**
1. Journalism
ISBN 0-205-48466-2; 978-0-205-48466-9
LC 2007-20885
First published 1988
Through suggestions and examples this guide for the novice writer provides tips from Pulitzer Prize-winning journalists and other magazine and newspaper feature writers.

Fuller, Jack, 1946-2016

What is happening to news; the information explosion and the crisis in journalism. The University of Chicago Press 2010 214p $25   **070.4**
1. Journalism 2. Information society 3. Journalistic ethics
ISBN 0-226-26898-5; 978-0-226-26898-9; 978-0-226-26899-6 ebook
LC 2009039090
"This worthy addition to the journalism bookshelf will stand the test of time." Choice
Includes bibliographical references

Hargreaves, Ian

Journalism; a very short introduction. Ian Hargreaves. 2nd edition Oxford University Press 2014 153 p. illustrations, map pbk $11.95   **070.4**
1. Journalism 2. Mass media
ISBN 0199686874; 9780199686872
LC 2014937968
First published as Journalism: truth or dare, 2003
Includes bibliographical references (p. 147-148) and index
In this book, author Ian Hargreaves "examines the world of contemporary journalism. He considers how technology has impacted the way major international events are reported, examines the development of online entertainment journalism, and chronicles the impact of the international financial crisis on the industry. . . . [M]ajor issues related to reportage, warfare, celebrity culture, privacy, and technology worldwide are closely examined." (Publisher's note)

Ross, Lillian

Reporting always; writing for The New Yorker. Lillian Ross; foreword by David Remnick. Scribner 2015 320 p. illustrations (hardback) $27   **070.4**
1. Journalism 2. Women journalists
ISBN 1501116002; 9781501116001; 9781501116018
LC 2015013297

This book "collects a wide range of [author] Lillian Ross's New Yorker articles and 'Talk of the Town' pieces spanning sixty years, bringing readers into Robin Williams's living room; Harry Winston's office; the afterschool hangouts of Manhattan private-school children; the hotel rooms of Ernest Hemingway, John Huston, and Charlie Chaplin; onto the tennis court with John McEnroe; and into the lives of many other famous and not-so-famous characters." (Publisher's note)
"Readable and rewarding and, though more than a touch old-fashioned, full of exemplary reporting." Kirkus

Spillman, Rob

All Tomorrow's Parties; Rob Spillman. Grove Press 2016 400 p. $25   **070.4**
1. Arts 2. Berlin (Germany)
ISBN 0802124836; 9780802124838
In this memoir, author Rob Spillman tells how "after an unsettled youth moving between divorced parents in disparate cities, Spillman would eventually find his way into the literary world of New York City, only to abandon it to return to Berlin just months after the Wall came down. Twenty-five and newly married, Spillman and his wife . . . moved to the anarchic streets of East Berlin in search of the bohemian lifestyle of their idols. But Spillman soon discovered he was chasing . . . a place, or person, to call home." (Publisher's note)
"Musically and culturally astute, this well-structured book is a delightful coming-of-age story couched within a travel narrative that deftly evokes one of the major historical moments of the 20th century. A richly detailed and always engaging memoir on artistic discovery." Kirkus

Tobin, James

Reporting America at war; an oral history. compiled by Michelle Ferrari with commentary by James Tobin. Hyperion 2003 241p il $23.95   **070.4**
1. War 2. Reporters and reporting
ISBN 1-401-30072-3
LC 2003-49966
"Beginning with Edward R. Morrow's live reports during the London blitz and ending with an epilogue on the second war in Iraq, this oral history contains transcripts of interviews with 11 top correspondents. Murrow is one of three deceased reporters included (the others are Martha Gellhorn and Homer Bigart), along with Walter Cronkite, Andy Rooney, Frank Gibney, Malcolm Browne, David Halberstam, Morley Safer, Ward Just, Gloria Emerson, Chris Hedges and Christiane Amanpour. . . . Tobin's introductions and transitional and informational interpolations within the transcripts hold this informative volume together." Publ Wkly
Includes bibliographical references

Tobin, James E.

Ernie Pyle's war; America's eyewitness to World War II. Free Press 1997 312p il pa $15   **070.4**
1. Journalists 2. World War, 1939-1945 3. Biography, Individual
ISBN 0-684-83642-4; 0-7432-8476-3 pa; 978-0-7432-8476-9 pa
LC 97-6165

This is a biography of the World War II correspondent who "followed the troops from North Africa to Italy to Normandy and then across the Pacific to Okinawa, where he was killed." (Choice) Index.

"Living and working among the troops he so vividly chronicled, Pyle offered a unique insider's perspective of the harsh reality experienced by the common soldier during World War II. . . . A respectful and insightful biography of a giant among journalists." Booklist

Includes bibliographical references

070.444   Journalism--Miscellaneous information, advice, amusement

Havrilesky, Heather

How to be a person in the world; ask Polly's guide through the paradoxes of modern life. Heather Havrilesky. Doubleday 2016 272 p. illustrations (hardcover) $24.95   **070.444**
1. Self-realization 2. Self-actualization (Psychology)
ISBN 9780385540391

LC 2015023592

This book, by Heather Havrilesky, offers "a collection of brand new, impassioned, and inspiring letters by the author of the popular advice column Ask Polly, featured weekly on 'New York Magazine''s The Cut. Should you quit your day job to follow your dreams? How do you rein in an overbearing mother? Will you ever stop dating wishy-washy, noncommittal guys? Should you put off having a baby for your career?" (Publisher's note)

"Funny, frank advice for people searching for solutions to a myriad of relationship issues." Kirkus

070.449   Journalism—Specific subjects

Lascher, Bill

Eve of a Hundred Midnights; The Star-crossed Love Story of Two Wwii Correspondents and Their Epic Escape Across the Pacific. by Bill Lascher. HarperCollins 2016 288 p. illustrations $26.99 **070.449**
1. Journalists 2. Married people 3. World War, 1939-1945 -- Journalists
ISBN 0062375202; 9780062375209

LC 2015046489

This book, by Bill Lascher, is the "true story of two married journalists on an island-hopping run for their lives across the Pacific after the Fall of Manila during World War II. . . . The couple had worked in China as members of a tight community of foreign correspondents with close ties to Chinese leaders; if captured by invading Japanese troops, they were certain to be executed." (Publisher's note)

"From interviews and archival documents, Lascher creates a seamless narrative of daring and dedication." Kirkus

Includes bibliographical references (pages 382-398) and index.

Ryan, Bob

Scribe; my life in sports. Bob Ryan. Bloomsbury Press 2014 336 p. 16 plates; color illustrations (alk. paper) $27   **070.449**
1. Sports journalism 2. Reporters and reporting 3. Sportswriters -- United States -- Biography
ISBN 1620405067; 9781620405062

LC 2014012348

In this memoir, author Bob Ryan discusses his career in sports journalism. "As a young man, he became sports editor of his high school paper-and at age twenty-three, a year into his Boston Globe experience, he was handed the Boston Celtics beat. 'Scribe' reveals the people behind the stories, as only Bob Ryan can, from the NBA to eleven Olympics to his surprising favorite sport to cover-golf-and much more." (Publisher's note)

"This thoroughly engaging book is recommended to all sports enthusiasts, especially readers interested in Boston-area teams." LJ

070.5   Publishing

★ **American** book trade directory. Information Today various pagings   **070.5**
1. Book industry 2. Book collecting 3. Reference books 4. Publishers and publishing -- Directories

Annual. First published 1915 by Bowker with title: American book trade manual

"Includes lists of booksellers, wholesalers, and publishers in the United States, with related information on the book trade in Canada, the United Kingdom, and Ireland. Bookstores are arranged under state and city with speciality of each noted. Separate lists include exporters, importers, and dealers in foreign books. Index of retailers and wholesalers in the United States and Canada." Ref Sources for Small & Medium-sized LIbr. 6th edition

Germano, William P.

Getting it published; a guide for scholars and anyone else serious about serious books. William Germano. 3rd edition University of Chicago Press 2016 253 p. pbk $20   **070.5**
1. Authors and publishers 2. Publishers and publishing
ISBN 022628140X; 9780226281407

LC 2015038629

"Today there are more ways to publish than ever, more challenges to traditional publishing, and more room for confusion among authors trying to understand their options. This extensively revised third edition brings Germano's classic up to date, charting a path across today's publishing landscape while showing why book publication rightly remains the highest aspiration for authors with big ideas and consequential arguments." (Publisher's note)

Includes bibliographical references and index

Guide to literary agents. Writer's Digest Bks.   **070.5**
1. Authors and publishers -- Directories

Annual. Supersedes in part Guide to literary agents & art/photo reps

"An invaluable tool for writers in search of an agent, this guide is indexed by agency, agent, format, subject, and geographic location. Submission procedures, fees, contracts and what to ask a prospective agent are covered." Libr J

Herman, Jeff

Jeff Herman's guide to book publishers, editors, & literary agents. Writer Bks. **070.5**
1. Authors and publishers 2. Publishers and publishing
Annual. First published 1992 by Prima Pub. with title: Insider's guide to book editors, publishers, and literary agents. Variant title: Writer's guide to book editors, publishers, and literary agents

Herman provides "portraits of more than 100 agents plus tips on writing query letters and nonfiction book proposals, dealing with rejections, ghostwriting, and self-publishing. With an excellent glossary and sample author-agent and collaboration agreements." Libr J

Literary market place. Bowker 2v $399 **070.5**
1. Reference books 2. Publishers and publishing -- Directories
Annual. First published 1940. In 1972 absorbed Names & numbers. Subtitle varies

"Directory of U.S. and Canadian book publishers and related businesses such as book clubs, literary agents, translators, and manufacturers. Gives names of executives and addresses, telephone numbers, and fields of specialization for each publishing company." N Y Public Libr Book of How & Where to Look It Up

Nasaw, David

The **chief**: the life of William Randolph Hearst. Houghton Mifflin 2000 687p il $35; pa $16 **070.5**
1. Newspaper editors 2. Newspaper executives
ISBN 0-395-82759-0; 0-618-15446-9 pa
LC 99-462122
"Few publishers have loomed as large in their lifetimes, or cast as long a shadow after death, as William Randolph Hearst. . . . Nasaw's judicious and comprehensive biography sensibly seeks to understand its subject, not to judge him." New Yorker

Includes bibliographical references

No shelf required 2; use and management of electronic books. edited by Sue Polanka. American Library Association 2012 xiv, 254 p.p ill. (alk. paper) $65 **070.5**
1. Electronic books 2. Library resources 3. Electronic publishing 4. Libraries and electronic publishing 5. Libraries -- Special collections -- Electronic books
ISBN 0838911455; 9780838911457
LC 2011040497
This book "brings together a variety of professionals to share their expertise about e-books with librarians and publishers. Providing forward-thinking ideas while remaining grounded in practical information that can be implemented in all kinds of libraries, the topics explored include an introduction to e-books . . . and an overview of their history and development . . . e-book technology . . . why e-books are good for learning, and how librarians can market them." (Publisher's note)

Includes bibliographical references and index

Pettegree, Andrew

The **book** in the Renaissance. Yale University Press 2010 421p il $40 **070.5**
1. Printing 2. Renaissance 3. Book industry 4. Reformation -- Europe 5. Europe -- History -- 1492-1789 6. Books -- Europe -- History -- 1400-1600 7. Printing -- Europe -- History -- 16th century 8. Book industries and trade -- Europe -- History -- 16th century
ISBN 978-0-300-11009-8; 0-300-11009-X
LC 2009-26513
The author's "treatment is both thorough and engaging, ably situating the social, economic, and historical within the stories of individuals involved." Libr J

Includes bibliographical references

Publishers, distributors & wholesalers of the United States. Bowker 2v **070.5**
1. Reference books 2. Publishers and publishing -- Directories
Annual. First published 1979 with title: Publishers and distributors of the United States

This directory provides information on "more than 150,000 U.S. publishers, wholesalers, distributors, software firms, audiocassette producers, museum and association imprints, and trade organizations that publish." Publisher's note

Seaver, Richard

The **tender** hour of twilight; Paris in the '50s, New York in the '60s: a memoir of publishing's golden age. Richard Seaver; edited by Jeannette Seaver. Farrar, Straus and Giroux 2012 xxi, 457 p.p (alk. paper) $35 **070.5**
1. Translators -- United States -- Biography 2. Book editors -- United States -- Biography 3. Publishers and publishing -- United States -- Biography
ISBN 0374273782; 9780374273781
LC 2011024951
"[T]he first part of . . . [Richard Seaver's] memoir is about Paris in the Fifties and the adventure of publishing [Samuel] Beckett among others, [while] the second part is about Grove Press in New York, where he became one of the early editors of an enterprise financed and led by Barney Rosset. It's a story of Grove's long battles with censorship, with which Seaver was closely involved. . . . [One] censorship problem was encountered with Henry Miller's 'Tropic of Cancer,' about which Rosset had written an essay and which was banned in almost every country in the world. . . . [In addition,] Seaver's memoir testifies to Beckett's patience in dealing with collaborators, even if he held them to the highest standards." (New York Review of Books)

Shepard, Stephen B.

Deadlines and disruption; the turbulent road from print to digital. by Stephen Shepard. McGraw-Hill 2012 304 p. (hardback) $28 **070.5**
1. Journalism 2. Online journalism 3. Journalism -- Technological innovations 4. Newspaper publishing -- Technological innovations
ISBN 0071802649; 9780071802642
LC 2012016577
This book is "[Stephen B.] Shepard's story of his life in print journalism, and a . . . look at the way journalism is

evolving due to electronic media, social networking, and the ability of anyone with a computer and an opinion to make him- or herself heard. Is journalism dying? Not according to Shepard. It's changing, yes, but in some respects it's also improving." (Booklist)

Suber, Peter

Open access; Peter Suber. MIT Press 2012 xii, 242 p.p (paperback) $12.95   **070.5**
1. Open access publishing
ISBN 0262517639; 9780262517638

LC 2011038297

This book, by Peter Suber, is part of the "MIT Press Essential Knowledge" series. "The Internet lets us share perfect copies of our work with a worldwide audience at virtually no cost. . . . In this concise introduction, . . . Suber tells us what open access is and isn't, how it benefits authors and readers of research, how we pay for it, how it avoids copyright problems, how it has moved from the periphery to the mainstream, and what its future may hold." Publisher's note

Includes bibliographical references (p. [177]-221) and index

070.92   Biography regardless of area, region, place

Brinkley-Rogers, Paul

Please Enjoy Your Happiness; Paul Brinkley-Rogers. Simon & Schuster 2016 368 p. (hardcover) $25   **070.92**
1. World War, 1939-1945 -- Personal narratives
ISBN 1501151258; 9781501151255

LC 2016017224

This memoir, by Paul Brinkley-Rogers, tells the story "of his haunting love affair with a mysterious older Japanese woman in 1959. Paul was a sailor aboard the USS Shangri-La that long-ago summer when he met Kaji Yukiko in the seaport of Yokosuka. A fierce intellectual, Yukiko shared her astonishing knowledge of literature, film, and poetry with Paul and encouraged, even demanded, that he use his gifts to become the writer he is today." (Publisher's note)

"Brinkley-Rogers' young innocence is poignant, and the picture he paints of times past, Japanese culture, and the making of a writer is memorable." Booklist

071   Geographic treatment of journalism and newspapers

Baker, Nicholson

The **World** on Sunday; graphic art in Joseph Pulitzer's newspaper (1898-1911) [by] Nicholson Baker and Margaret Brentano. Bulfinch Press 2005 131p il $50   **071**
1. New York world (Newspaper)
ISBN 0-8212-6193-2

LC 2005-00224

This book collects 85 examples of graphic art from the Sunday edition of the New York World

This volume "offers a kaleidoscopic tour through an ebullient moment in American history when the country was emerging from the shadowy gaslight age and bursting into the glare of the modern. It is a big, lush, coffee-table-size book suffused with gaiety and the optimism of an age blissfully unaware of darknesses soon to come. . . . The World on Sunday is the result of a heroic piece of cultural preservation." N Y Rev Books

Burns, Eric

Infamous scribblers; the founding fathers and the rowdy beginnings of American journalism. Public Affairs 2006 467p hardcover o.p. pa $15.95 **071**
1. Journalism 2. Newspapers -- United States
ISBN 978-1-58648-334-0; 1-58648-334-X; 978-1-58648-428-6 pa; 1-58648-428-1 pa

LC 2005-53542

"From the sniping feuds among Boston's first papers to sex scandals involving Alexander Hamilton and Thomas Jefferson, the snappy patter gives clear indication of how much Burns . . . relishes telling his story." Publ Wkly

Includes bibliographical references

Campbell, W. Joseph

Getting it wrong; ten of the greatest misreported stories in American journalism. University of California Press 2010 269p il $60; pa $24.95   **071**
1. Journalistic ethics 2. Journalism -- Objectivity
ISBN 0-520-25566-6; 0-520-26209-3 pa; 978-0-520-25566-1; 978-0-520-26209-6 pa

LC 2009047705

This "provocative book provides a wealth of case studies in the complexity of journalism and history. It reinforces the truism that journalists, authors and book reviewers alike should all be more skeptical—and definitely more humble." Am Journalism Rev

Includes bibliographical references

Carpini, Michael X. Delli

After broadcast news; media regimes, democracy, and the new information environment. Bruce A. Williams, Michael X. Delli Carpini. Cambridge University Press 2011 xii, 361 p.p (paperback) $32.99   **071**
1. Mass media 2. Online journalism 3. Broadcast journalism 4. Democracy -- United States 5. Press and politics -- United States 6. Mass media -- Political aspects -- United States 7. Popular culture -- Political aspects -- United States 8. Broadcast journalism -- Political aspects -- United States
ISBN 0521279836; 9780521279833; 9781107010314

LC 2011009191

This book posits that the "new media environment has challenged the role of professional journalists as the primary source of politically relevant information" and "puts this challenge into historical context, arguing that it is the latest of several critical moments, driven by economic, political, cultural, and technological changes, in which the relationship among citizens, political elites, and the media has been contested." (Publisher's note)

Includes bibliographical references and index.

Kovach, Bill

The **elements** of journalism; Bill Kovach and Tom Rosenstiel. Three Rivers Press 2014 332 p. (pbk.) $15   **071**
1. Journalistic ethics 2. Journalism -- United States
ISBN 0804136785; 9780804136785
LC 2013049716

This book on journalism, by Bill Kovach and Tom Rosenstiel, is "[r]evised and updated with a new preface and material on the rise of social media, the challenges facing printed news, and how journalism can fulfill its purpose in the digital age." (Publisher's note)

"Kovach and Rosenstiel have issued a clarion call to their colleagues, and they hope that all journalists, editors and owners of news organizations will incorporate the principles of the profession as they've outlined them into their everyday work. However, the authors offer no specific suggestions as to how to enact these principles in a wide-reaching or systematic manner." Pub Wkly

Includes bibliographical references and index

Michaeli, Ethan

The **defender**; how the legendary black newspaper changed America : from the age of the Pullman porters to the age of Obama. Ethan Michaeli. Houghton Mifflin Harcourt 2016 656 p. (hardback) $32   **071**
1. Chicago (Ill.) -- History 2. African American newspapers 3. Newspapers -- United States 4. African Americans -- Chicago (Ill.) 5. Chicago defender -- History 6. African Americans -- Illinois -- Chicago -- Newspapers 7. African American press -- Illinois -- Chicago -- History 8. African American newspapers -- Illinois -- Chicago -- History
ISBN 0547560699; 9780547560694
LC 2015017437

This book, by Ethan Michaeli, presents the history of the newspaper the "Chicago Defender." "Drawing on dozens of interviews and extensive archival research, . . . Michaeli constructs a revelatory narrative of race in America and brings to life the reporters who braved lynch mobs and policemen's clubs to do their jobs, from the age of Teddy Roosevelt to the age of Barack Obama." (Publisher's note)

"Engagingly written and copiously sourced, Michaeli's stimulating read treating central personalities and an iconic institution offers general readers and scholars alike a focused look back at 20th-century battles against America's pervasive racism." LJ

The **New** new journalism; conversations with America's best nonfiction writers on their craft. [edited and with an introduction by] Robert S. Boynton. Vintage Books 2005 xxxiv, 456p pa $13.95 **071**
1. Journalism
ISBN 1-400-03356-X
LC 2004-57161

The author "offers interviews with 19 writers who detail how and why they produce their work. . . . A fascinating book that makes the reader want to go out and get every book the writers have written as well as those mentioned as sources of inspiration." Booklist

Includes bibliographical references

Ostertag, Bob

People's movements, people's press; the journalism of social justice movements. Beacon Press 2006 232p il $23.95   **071**
1. Social movements 2. Alternative press
ISBN 0-8070-6164-6; 978-0-8070-6164-0
LC 2005-31735

"Readers interested in the intersection of the media and social movements will appreciate this insightful book." Booklist

Includes bibliographical references

Written into history; Pulitzer Prize reporting of the twentieth century from the New York times. edited and with an introduction by Anthony Lewis. Times Bks. 2001 xxv, 355p hardcover o.p. pa $17   **071**
1. Journalism 2. Pulitzer Prizes
ISBN 0-8050-6849-X; 0-8050-7178-4 pa
LC 2001-35555

"For anyone interested in recent history or journalism at its best, this book will prove worthwhile." Publ Wkly

080   General collections

Adler, Mortimer J.

How to think about the great ideas; from the great books of Western civilization. {by} Mortimer J. Adler; edited by Max Weismann. Open Court 2000 xxiv, 530p pa $24.95 **080**
1. Great books of the Western world
ISBN 0-8126-9412-0
LC 99-45251

This volume contains the transcripts of 52 half-hour segments of Adler's 1953-1954 television program The great ideas

"The book showcases Adler's ideas about all the big categories—truth, beauty, freedom, love, sex, art, justice, rationality, humankind's nature, Darwinism, government." Publ Wkly

081   General collections in specific languages and language families

McPhee, John A.

Irons in the fire; {by} John McPhee. Farrar, Straus & Giroux 1997 215p $22; pa $14   **081**
ISBN 0-374-17726-0; 0-374-52545-5 pa
LC 96-32358

"John McPhee's essays are proof that the kind of journalism that can effortlessly put a topic into perfect perspective will never go out of style." N Y Times Book Rev

Pauling, Linus C.

Linus Pauling in his own words; selections from his writings, speeches, and interviews. edited by Barbara Marinacci; introduction by Linus Pauling.

Simon & Schuster 1995 320p hardcover o.p. pa
$20 **081**
1. Chemists 2. College teachers 3. Writers on science
4. Nobel laureates for peace 5. Nobel laureates for
chemistry
ISBN 0-6848-1387-4 ps

LC 95-31123

This book "attempts to follow the life and career of Dr.
Pauling through his own writings, interspersed with narrative by the editor. The book succeeds wonderfully. Linus
Pauling is unique among modern scientists, both for winning two Nobel Prizes and for his political and social views.
Through his writings, the breadth and depth of his work become clear to the reader." Sci Books Films

Includes bibliographical references

082 General collections in English

Oxford dictionary of quotations; edited by Elizabeth
Knowles. Oxford University Press 2014 xxvii,
1126 p.p $50 **082**
1. Quotations 2. Quotations, English -- Dictionaries 3.
Quotations -- Translations into English
ISBN 0199668701; 9780199668700

LC 2014930368

This book, edited by Elizabeth Knowles, offers a dictionary of quotations. "Drawing on Oxford's unrivalled dictionary research program and unique language monitoring, over
700 new quotations have been added to this eighth edition
from authors ranging from St Joan of Arc and Coco Chanel
to Albrecht Durer and Thomas Jefferson." (Publisher's note)

Dictionary of quotations

★ The **Yale** book of quotations; edited by Fred R.
Shapiro; foreword by Joseph Epstein. Yale University Press 2006 1104p $50 **082**
1. Quotations
ISBN 978-0-300-10798-2; 0-300-10798-6

LC 2006-12317

The more than 12,000 "range over literature, history,
popular culture, sports, computers, science, politics, law, and
the social sciences, and although American quotations are
emphasized, the book's scope is global. The authors represented are as diverse as William Shakespeare, John Lennon,
Jack Dempsey, both Presidents Bush, J.K. Rowling, Rita
Mae Brown, Confucius, Warren Buffet, and Deng Xiaoping.
The entries are arranged by author, then chronologically and
alphabetically by source title within the same year. A significant effort was made to trace the first published occurrence
of a quotation, and whenever possible the wording is taken
from the original source. . . . Electronic products such as the
Times Digital Archive, JSTOR, Proquest Historical Newspapers and American Periodical Series, LexisNexis, News-
paperarchive.com, Questia, Eighteenth Century Collections
Online, and Literature Online were all used." Libr J

098 Prohibited works, forgeries, hoaxes

Bosmajian, Haig A.
★ **Burning** books; [by] Haig Bosmajian. Mc-
Farland 2006 233p $39.95 **098**
1. Book burning
ISBN 0-7864-2208-4; 978-0-7864-2208-1

LC 2005-35201

"This work provides a detailed account of book burning worldwide over the past 2000 years. The book burners
are identified, along with the works they deliberately set
aflame." Publisher's note

Includes bibliographical references

100 PHILOSOPHY

100 Philosophy, parapsychology and occultism, psychology

Blackburn, Simon, 1944-
Think: a compelling introduction to philosophy.
Oxford Univ. Press 1999 312p $25 **100**
1. Philosophy
ISBN 0-19-210024-6

LC 00-265266

The author explores such areas as knowledge, mind, free
will, identity, God, goodness and justice. "His method is to
introduce what other philosophers—primarily Plato, Descartes, Locke, Berkeley, Leibniz, Hume, and Kant—have
had to say about these themes. . . . Readers new to the subject
could very well be captivated." Libr J

Includes bibliographical references

Ferry, Luc
A **brief** history of thought; Luc Ferry; translated
by Theo Cuffe. HarperPerennial 2012 304p. **100**
1. Philosophy 2. Christianity 3. Postmodernism 4.
Existentialism
ISBN 9780062074249

This book "offers a thematic introduction to continental
philosophy constructed around the biggest questions: how
can we lead a meaningful life knowing that we will die but
without the consolation of religion? . . . The author's episodic treatment starts with the Stoic concept of man as a
fragment of a harmonious cosmos, moves on to Descartes,
Rousseau, and Kant and their establishment of philosophy
based on reason and individual freedom, climaxes with
Nietzsche's demolition of modernist certitudes-a stance
he finds both thrilling and unsatisfying--and ponders the
abiding need to embrace a world we must ultimately lose."
(Publishers Weekly)

Gutting, Gary
What philosophy can do; Gary Gutting. W
W Norton & Co Inc 2015 320 p. (hardcover)
$27.95 **100**
1. Philosophy 2. Social conditions
ISBN 0393242277; 9780393242270

LC 2015013783

In this book, author Gary Gutting presents his "approach to some of the most divisive [philosophical] issues on the table today. He scrutinizes our relationship to work and freedom in capitalism; our modern understanding of happiness and the good life; the value of liberal arts education and the humanities; the role of science and politics in shaping public policy today; and the value of art and popular culture." (Publisher's note)

"While Gutting applies complex philosophical and logical principles in his essays, he does so in an accessible way. The range of essays makes this work appealing to anyone with an interest in philosophy." LJ

Includes bibliographical references and index

Russell, Bertrand

★ The **problems** of philosophy. Hackett Pub. Co 1990 167p (Hackett classics) $27.95; pa $8.95 **100**
1. Philosophy
ISBN 978-0-87220-099-9; 0-87220-099-X; 978-0-87220-098-2 pa; 0-87220-098-1 pa

LC 90-81389

First published 1912 by Holt
The author discusses: appearance and reality, matter, idealism, theories of knowledge, universals, intuition, and truth

"The work is concise, free from technical terms and perfectly clear to the general reader with no prior knowledge of the subject." Booklist

Includes bibliographical references

103 Dictionaries, encyclopedias, concordances of philosophy

Blackburn, Simon, 1944-

The **Oxford** dictionary of philosophy; 2nd ed.; Oxford University Press 2005 407p il $45   **103**
1. Reference books 2. Philosophy -- Dictionaries
ISBN 0-19-861014-9; 978-0-19-861014-4

LC 2006-271895

First published 1994
This dictionary "contains over 2,500 entries, including biographies of nearly 500 influential philosophers. The dictionary provides . . . coverage of not only Western philosophical traditions, but also themes from Chinese, Indian, Islamic, and Jewish philosophy." Publisher's note

Includes bibliographical references

★ The **Cambridge** dictionary of philosophy; edited by Robert Audi. 2nd ed; Cambridge Univ. Press 1999 xxxv, 1001p il hardcover o.p. pa $32.99   **103**
1. Reference books 2. Philosophy -- Dictionaries
ISBN 0-521-63136-X; 0-521-63722-8 pa

LC 99-12920

First published 1995
This work contains some 4,400 entries including 50 on major contemporary philosophers. Wide coverage of Western philosophy as well as non-Western and non-European philosophers is included. The rapidly growing fields of philosophy of mind and applied ethics are also covered

★ The **Oxford** companion to philosophy; edited by Ted Honderich. 2nd ed., new ed; Oxford University Press 2005 1056p il $60   **103**
1. Reference books 2. Philosophy -- Encyclopedias
ISBN 0-19-926479-1

LC 2005-275452

First published 1995
"Including more than 2200 alphabetically arranged entries from nearly 300 contributors, . . . [this book] provides an encyclopedic view of philosophy's past and present, its ideas, disputes (the editor himself contributes an article on unlikely philosophical propositions), and key figures, living and dead. . . . This title makes an excellent companion for standard multivolume subject encyclopedias." SLJ

Includes bibliographical references

109 History and collected biography

Durant, William James

★ The **story** of philosophy; the lives and opinions of the great philosophers. by Will Durant. [2nd ed]; Simon & Schuster 1933 412p hardcover o.p. pa $15   **109**
1. Philosophy -- History
ISBN 0-671-69500-2; 0-671-20159-X pa

First published 1926
A selective account of western thinkers from Socrates and Kant to Schopenhauer and Dewey.

Includes bibliographical references

Russell, Bertrand

A **history** of Western philosophy; and its connection with political and social circumstances from the earliest times to the present day. Simon & Schuster 1945 xxiii, 895p hardcover o.p. pa $25   **109**
1. Rome -- Civilization 2. Philosophy -- History 3. Sparta (Extinct city) 4. Greece -- Civilization
ISBN 0-671-31400-9; 0-671-20158-1 pa

Originally designed and partly delivered as lectures at the Barnes Foundation in Pennsylvania

"My purpose is to exhibit philosophy as an integral part of social and political life; not as the isolated speculations of remarkable individuals." Preface

Solomon, Robert C.

A **passion** for wisdom; a very brief history of philosophy. {by} Robert C. Solomon, Kathleen M. Higgins. Oxford Univ. Press 1997 137p hardcover o.p. pa $12.95   **109**
1. Philosophy -- History
ISBN 0-19-511209-1 pa

LC 96-42034

The authors "provide a multicultural account of philosophical thought and developments across nearly 4000 years. The volume is necessarily simplified but not simplistic, and the thoughts themselves are given precedent over the biographies of the thinkers." SLJ

Includes bibliographical references

World philosophers and their works; editor, John K. Roth; managing editor, Christina J. Moose; project editor, Rowena Wildin. Salem Press 2000 3v il set $331   **109**
1. Philosophers
ISBN 0-89356-878-3

LC 99-55143

The editor "presents substantial entries that for 226 philosophers give brief biographies, justify the inclusion of each thinker, list their most important works, analyze their lifework, and locate them within the context of philosophy." Choice

Includes bibliographical references

111   Ontology

Barrow, John D.
The **book** of nothing; vacuums, voids, and the latest ideas about the origins of the universe. Pantheon Bks. 2001 361p il hardcover o.p. pa $15 **111**
1. Zero (The number) 2. Science -- History
ISBN 0-375-72609-8 pa

LC 00-58894

This volume traces the concept of nothing "from a Babylonian place holder, a Mayan decoration in the empty space where no number fell and an Indian dot signifying all the current aspects of zero, to one of the most essential elements in mathematics, physics and cosmology." Publ Wkly

The **infinite** book; a short guide to the boundless, timeless, and endless. Pantheon Books 2005 328p il $26   **111**
1. Infinite
ISBN 0-375-42227-7

LC 2004-60206

First published 2004 in the United Kingdom

The author "approaches the subject [of infinity] from the viewpoints of mathematics, physics, and scientific cosmology and also delves into philosophers' and theologians' reflections concerning infinity. . . . Well suited to a general audience, this book requires no specialized knowledge of mathematics or science." Libr J

Includes bibliographical references

Eco, Umberto
History of beauty; translated by Alastair McEwen. Rizzoli Int. Pubs. 2004 438p il $40   **111**
1. Aesthetics 2. Arts -- Philosophy
ISBN 0-8478-2646-5

Published in the United Kingdom with title: On beauty: a history of a western idea

The editor "traces the protean subject of beauty in art, literature, philosophy, the mass media, and other humanities from ancient times to the present, setting forth various Western cultural aesthetic ideals ranging from ancient Greek to modern American. . . . This is not a quick, one-time coffeetable read but a nearly flawless presentation of the history of a fascinating and elusive idea that will delight and enlighten general readers as well as scholars." Libr J

Includes bibliographical references

Heidegger, Martin
★ **Being** and time; translated by John Macquarrie & Edward Robinson. Harper & Row 1962 589p hardcover o.p. pa $19.99   **111**
1. Ontology 2. Phenomenology
ISBN 0-06-063850-8; 0-06-157559-3 pa
Original German edition, 1927

"All of Heidegger's work revolves around the essential inquiry: what is the nature of being? In his most important book, . . . he distinguishes between two types of being: human existence (Dasein) and nonhuman presence (Vorhandensein)." Reader's Ency. 4th edition

Includes bibliographical references

On ugliness; edited by Umberto Eco; translated by Alastair McEwen. Rizzoli 2007 455p il $45 **111**
1. Aesthetics 2. Arts -- Philosophy
ISBN 978-0-8478-2986-6; 0-8478-2986-3

LC 2007-930249

In this "collection of images and written excerpts from ancient times to the present, all woven together with a provocative commentary and translated by Alastair McEwen, . . . [the editor] asks: Is repulsiveness, too, in the eye of the beholder? And what do we learn about that beholder when we delve into his aversions? Selecting stark visual images of gore, deformity, moral turpitude and malice, and quotations from sources ranging from Plato to radical feminists, Eco unfurls a taxonomy of ugliness. As gross-out contests go, it's both absorbing and highbrow." N Y Times Book Rev

Includes bibliographical references

Watson, Lyall
Dark nature; a natural history of evil. HarperCollins Pubs. 1996 318p hardcover o.p. pa $19 **111**
1. Human beings 2. Good and evil 3. Biology -- Philosophy
ISBN 0-06-092790-9 pa

LC 96-1663

First published 1995 in the United Kingdom

The author "ranges through philosophy, psychology, anthropology, history, ecology and especially biology. . . . Watson believes that aggression is in our genes and examines such phenomena as war, rape and murder as manifestations of that aggression. But while he firmly believes that humans are made up of both good and evil and that natural selection is completely amoral, he is sanguine about humans as the world's first ethical animals with the capability of making moral decisions." Publ Wkly

Includes bibliographical references

111.85   Beauty

Whitefield-Madrano, Autumn
Face value; the hidden ways that beauty shapes women's lives. Autumn Whitefield-Madrano. Simon & Schuster 2016 288 p. (hardcover) $25   **111.85**
1. Aesthetics 2. Body image 3. Self-perception 4. Personal appearance 5. Women -- Psychology 6. Body image in women 7. Appearance (Philosophy) 8. Self-perception in women 9. Aesthetics -- Social aspects 10. Beauty, Personal -- Social aspects 11. Feminine beauty

(Aesthetics) -- Social aspects
ISBN 9781476754000; 9781476754048

LC 2015038730

In this book, "journalist Autumn Whitefield-Madrano thoughtfully examines the relationship between appearance and science, social media, sex, friendship, language, and advertising to show how beauty actually affects us day to day. Through meticulous research and interviews with dozens of women across all walks of life, she reveals surprising findings." (Publisher's note)

"This is a valuable addition to contemporary feminist writing, providing much-needed perspective to a pervasive issue that young women and staunch feminists will glean much from, whether they agree with the author's findings or not." LJ

Includes bibliographical references (pages 233-266) and index.

113   Cosmology (Philosophy of nature)

Holt, Jim

Why does the world exist? an existential detective story. Jim Holt. 1st ed. Liveright Pub. Corp. 2012 vi, 309 p.p ill. (hardcover) $27.95   **113**
1. Cosmology
ISBN 0871404095; 9780871404091; 9780871403599

LC 2012015177

It was the author's intent to answer the question "'why is there something rather than nothing?'" Author Jim Holt explores "the claims of evolutionary biology, neuropsychology, theoretical physics, natural religion theology, contemporary mysticism, and militant atheism. . . . He interviews several philosophers and scientists currently engaged in answering the question." (Library Journal)

Includes bibliographical references and index.

Teilhard de Chardin, Pierre

★ The **phenomenon** of man; with an introduction by Julian Huxley. Harper & Row 1959 318p hardcover o.p. pa $14.95   **113**
1. Universe 2. Evolution 3. Human beings
ISBN 0-06-090495-X pa
Original French edition, 1955; this translation by Bernard Wall

The author integrates scientific findings with the tenets of Christian faith in this study of human evolution and destiny

Wilson, Edward O.

★ **In** search of nature. Island Press 1996 214p il $22; pa $15   **113**
1. Human beings 2. Sociobiology 3. Human ecology 4. Philosophy of nature 5. Biological diversity
ISBN 1-55963-215-1; 1-55963-216-X pa

LC 96-11226

"Concerned people of all ages should enjoy the reasoning provided by the dedicated scientific writing presented in this attractive book." Sci Books Films
Includes bibliographical references

121   Epistemology (Theory of knowledge)

Blackburn, Simon, 1944-

★ **Truth**; a guide. Simon Blackburn. Oxford University Press 2005 xxi, 238p $25   **121**
1. Truth
ISBN 0-19-516824-0

LC 2004-19800

This book "traverses a broad terrain, exploring many points of the map of human knowledge and thinkers of all stripes." N Y Times Book Rev
Includes bibliographical references

Dennett, Daniel Clement, 1942-

Intuition Pumps and Other Tools for Thinking; Daniel C. Dennett. W W Norton & Co Inc 2013 512 p. $28.95   **121**
1. Thought experiments 2. Thought and thinking 3. Philosophy -- Miscellanea 4. Thought and thinking -- Miscellanea
ISBN 0393082067; 9780393082067

LC 2013000930

In this book, "opening with . . . [a] tutorial on argumentative strategies from reductio ad absurdum to Occam's Razor to rhetorical questions, [Daniel C.] Dennett expounds his ideas through a series of 'intuition pumps,' his term for the hypothetical scenarios philosophers contrive to explore difficult concepts." These include "conceiving of the body as a robotic survival vehicle for the genes, or the brain as a clueless man trapped in a sealed chamber." (Publishers Weekly)
Includes bibliographical references and index

Hecht, Jennifer Michael

Doubt: a history; the great doubters and their legacy of innovation, from Socrates and Jesus to Thomas Jefferson and Emily Dickinson. HarperSanFrancisco 2003 xxi, 551p il $27.95; pa $16.95   **121**
1. Belief and doubt
ISBN 0-06-009772-8; 0-06-009795-7 pa

LC 2004-266061

The author's "brief but splendid study of the great Renaissance skeptic Montaigne is alone worth the price of the book. Hecht's warm prose, lucid insights, and impeccable research combine for a lively, thoughtful, and first-rate study of a neglected idea." Libr J

Locke, John

An **essay** concerning human understanding; edited by Roger Woolhouse. Penguin Books 1997 xxvii, 784p pa $17   **121**
1. Theory of knowledge 2. Thought and thinking
ISBN 0-14-043482-8

LC 98-175907

This essay first published 1690, deals "with the nature and scope of human knowledge. Its basic premise is the empirical origin of ideas, which can be described as the raw material with which the mind works. Locke's essay contributed greatly to the growth of 18th-century empiricism." Reader's Ency, 4th edition
Includes bibliographical references

Sartre, Jean Paul

★ **Truth** and existence; original text established and annotated by Arlette Elkaïm-Sartre; translated by Adrian van den Hoven; edited and with an introduction by Ronald Aronson. University of Chicago Press 1992 xlix, 94p hardcover o.p. pa $11   **121**
1. Theory of knowledge
ISBN 0-226-73523-0 pa

LC 92-5889

Written in 1948; original French edition, 1989

This book "presents Sartre's ontology of truth in terms of his characteristic key moral questions of freedom, action, and bad faith. Here is Sartre the existentialist at his most original and most provocative." Univ Press Books for Public and Second Sch Libr

Includes bibliographical references

Wilson, Edward O.

Consilience; the unity of knowledge. Knopf 1998 332p $27.50; pa $15   **121**
1. Philosophy 2. Theory of knowledge 3. Science -- Philosophy
ISBN 0-679-45077-7; 0-679-76867-X pa

LC 97-2816

The author's "extraordinarily clear, evocative imagery and elegant sentences make us see how a consilient world of knowledge might look. . . . Wilson's book of faith in the dream of reason and objective knowledge is a tour de force." Publ Wkly

Includes bibliographical references

128 Humankind

Bloom, Howard

The **Lucifer** principle; a scientific expedition into the forces of history. Atlantic Monthly Press 1995 466p hardcover o.p. pa $16   **128**
1. Culture 2. Evolution 3. Human beings 4. Good and evil 5. Modern civilization 6. History -- Philosophy
ISBN 0-87113-664-3 pa

LC 94-11464

"A disturbing book, but its broad generalities wear down the sharp edges of its arguments, leaving something that becomes food for thought rather than reason to despair." Booklist

Includes bibliographical references

Cannadine, David, 1950-

The **undivided** past; humanity beyond our differences. by David Cannadine. 1st ed. Alfred A. Knopf 2013 352 p. (hardcover) $26.95   **128**
1. Sociology 2. Human behavior 3. World history
ISBN 0307269078; 9780307269072

LC 2012029278

This book is David Cannadine's "examination of the fundamental ways in which humanity divides itself. While these all stem from an innate 'us vs. them' mentality, Cannadine takes the investigation a step further, looking at how we think of ourselves in terms of religion, class, nation, race, gender, and civilization. . . . He points out that . . . a wide variety of factors can create numerous factions and differences within any grouping." (Publishers Weekly)

Includes bibliographical references and index

Chittister, Joan

Between the Dark and the Daylight; Embracing the Contradictions of Life. Joan Chittister. Random House Inc 2015 176 p. (hardcover) $20   **128**
1. Quality of life 2. Self-realization
ISBN 9780804140942; 0804140944

This book, by Joan Chittister, "explores the concerns of modern life, of the overworked mind and hurting heart. These are the paradoxical--and often frustrating--moments when our lives feel at odds with everything around us. Only by embracing the contradictions, Chittister contends, may we live well amid stress, withstand emotional storms, and satisfy our yearnings for something transcendent and real." (Publisher's note)

"Chittister's beautifully crafted short reflections are salve for the soul and an antidote to the apathy, depression, and obsession with material goods that beset so many." Pub Wkly

Christian, Brian

The **most** human human; what talking with computers teaches us about what it means to be alive. Doubleday 2011 303p $27.95; ebook $13.99 **128**
1. Human beings 2. Artificial intelligence
ISBN 978-0-385-53306-5; 978-0-385-53307-2 ebook

LC 2010-48572

"In a fast-paced, witty, and thoroughly winning style, Christian documents his experience in the 2009 Turing Test, a competition in which judges engage in five-minute instant-message conversations with unidentified partners, and must then decide whether each interlocutor was a human or a machine. . . . This fabulous book demonstrates that we are capable of experiencing and sharing far deeper thoughts than even the best computers—and that too often we fail to achieve the highest level of humanness." Publ Wkly

Frayn, Michael

The **human** touch; our part in the creation of a universe. Metropolitan Books 2007 505p $32.50   **128**
1. Cosmology 2. Science -- Philosophy
ISBN 978-0-8050-8148-0; 0-8050-8148-8

LC 2006-48204

First published 2006 in the United Kingdom

"Beginning with a description of the continual 'traffic' between humans and the universe, Frayn shapes a cohesive introduction to philosophy that includes elements of science, determinism, physics, mathematics, psychology, linguistics, and epistemology." Libr J

Includes bibliographical references

Irvine, William Braxton

On desire; why we want what we want. [by] William B. Irvine. Oxford University Press 2005 322p $24   **128**
1. Desire
ISBN 0-19-518862-4

LC 2005-05938

The author "explains how desire–really a multitude of desires, uninvited and unannounced–manifests itself, how it can be identified and parsed, and how it can be mastered in a way that offers the best chance at self-fulfillment. He uses modern psychology to delineate desire but then shows how the world's great religions–here mainly Christianity and Buddhism, but also Hinduism, Islam, and Judaism–address this phenomenon. He advocates no particular approach, admitting instead that different tacks probably work for different people. And he never lets the reader think that mastering desire will be easy. This is that rare book that should appeal to a wide range of readers without necessarily trying to do so." Booklist

Louv, Richard, 1949-

The **nature** principle; human restoration and the end of nature-deficit disorder. Algonquin Books of Chapel Hill 2011 317p $24.95 **128**
1. Nature 2. Environmental influence on humans 3. Nature -- Psychological aspects
ISBN 9781565125810; 1565125819
LC 2011-3626

This book argues for the importance of fulfilling the "need to be outdoors" for adults. Author Richard Louv "believes that seven nature-based precepts can reshape our lives, including balancing technology with nature; achieving a mind/body/nature connection; incorporating biophilic design in our homes, communities and workplaces; and giving natural history more importance. . . . He affirms and expands on how nature is essential for our mental and physical health--and our very souls." (Christian Century)

An "exploration of nature's significance in our lives and what role it will play in the future. . . . [Louv discusses] seven precepts of natural power, introducing such concepts as the 'purposeful place,' where natural history is as highly valued as human history. While the author comes across as a bit self-obsessed and the book is written to suburban and urban audiences, his writing style is clear and raises many valid points. . . . Louv heartily exhorts readers to become more engaged in the world around them, as citizen naturalists out to discover their own bioregions. Taking time to find and create an everyday Eden is not only beneficial to the individual, but to the community as a whole." Kirkus
Includes bibliographical references and index.

★ The **Oxford** companion to the mind; edited by Richard L. Gregory. 2nd ed; Oxford University Press 2005 1004p il $75 **128**
1. Reference books 2. Psychology -- Dictionaries
ISBN 0-19-866224-6
LC 2004-275127
First published 1987
This book "contains over 1000 alphabetically arranged entries on all aspects of the mind, including topics in neurophysiology, communication, psychology, and philosophy, as well as people relevant to the field." Libr J

Terkel, Studs, 1912-2008

Will the circle be unbroken? reflections on death, rebirth, and a hunger for faith. New Press (NY) 2001 xxiv, 407p $25.95 **128**
1. Death 2. Faith
ISBN 1-56584-692-3
"Terkel talks to 60 people about their encounters with death. His subjects range from emergency room doctors and paramedics to public figures such as author Kurt Vonnegut and guitarist Doc Watson. A stirring celebration of life and exploration of death." Booklist

Trachtenberg, Peter

The **book** of calamities; five questions about suffering and its meaning. Little, Brown 2008 450p $23.99 **128**
1. Suffering
ISBN 978-0-316-15879-4; 0-316-15879-8
LC 2008-13351
This book "succeeds because it asks the right questions, calls on the experience of articulate witnesses and—through skillful narrative and trenchant observation—beguiles the reader into facing heartbreaking reality." Publ Wkly
Includes bibliographical references

Wilson, Edward O., 1929-

The **Meaning** of Human Existence; by Edward O. Wilson. W.W. Norton & Co Inc. 2014 207 p. $23.95 **128**
1. Human beings 2. Meaning (Philosophy)
ISBN 0871401002; 9780871401007
LC 2014016707
In this book, author Edward O. Wilson, "bridges science and philosophy to create a twenty-first-century treatise on human existence. Once criticized for his over-reliance on genetics, Wilson unfurls here his most expansive and advanced theories on human behavior, recognizing that, even though the human and the spider evolved similarly, the poet's sonnet is wholly different from the spider's web." (Publisher's note)
"Wilson's suggested solutions to our paradoxical predicaments are firmly rooted in science and finely crafted with tonic common sense, unusual directness, and no small measure of valor." Booklist

130 Parapsychology and occultism

Dolnick, Barrie

Luck; understanding luck and improving the odds. [by] Barrie Dolnick and Anthony H. Davidson. Harmony Books 2007 236p $19.95 **130**
1. Chance 2. Superstition
ISBN 978-0-307-34750-3; 0-307-34750-8
LC 2007-13235
This "mini reference examines the concept of luck throughout history as observed by a variety of religious sects and practiced in many cultures. The authors help readers develop a personal-luck profile and detail how to apply astrology, numerology, and even herbology toward increasing the odds in one's favor. A practical section on gambling advises

readers how to play cards, dice, or the roulette wheel with caution." Libr J

Includes bibliographical references

Goodman, Linda

Linda Goodman's star signs; the secret codes of the universe: forgotten rainbows and forgotten melodies of ancient wisdom. St. Martin's Press 1987 xli, 477p il hardcover o.p. pa $17.95   **130**
1. Astrology 2. Occultism 3. Parapsychology 4. New Age movement
ISBN 0-312-19203-7 pa

LC 87-28375

"Goodman explains numerology, lexigrams (secret codes of words, names, and titles), the power of sound, and the power of color. . . . Along with explanations of karma and other modes of spiritual growth, she interweaves her own experiences with avatars and gurus, as well as common folk who are on their own spiritual path." Booklist

131 Parapsychological and occult methods for achieving well-being, happiness, success

Dale, Cyndi

Llewellyn's complete book of chakras; your definitive source of energy center knowledge for health, happiness, and spiritual evolution. Cyndi Dale. Llewellyn Worldwide, Ltd 2015 1056 p. (paperback) $39.99   **131**
1. Chakras
ISBN 9780738739625

LC 2015026134

This book, by Cyndi Dale, part of the "Llewellyn's Complete Book Series," presents a comprehensive overview of the Indian system of Chakras. "This definitive encyclopedia explores the science, history, practices, and structures of subtle energy systems, with chakras as the center point. . . . It features full-color illustrations, plus a wealth of exercises that you can use to immediately experience chakra healing and clearing." (Publisher's note)

"This is not a beginner's book (though Dale includes a "pocket guide" to orient new students), but it truly lives up to its "complete book" moniker; if it's related to chakras, it's in here." Pub Wkly

Includes bibliographical references and index

Mildon, Emma

The **soul** searcher's handbook; a modern girl's guide to the new-age world. Emma Mildon. Beyond Words 2015 272 p. illustrations $18.99   **131**
1. Women 2. Occultism 3. Spiritual life
ISBN 9781582705248

LC 2015018843

This book, by Emma Mildon, "offers easy tips, tricks, and how-tos for incorporating everything from dreamology and astrology to mysticism and alternative healing into your everyday life. . . . Your destiny, gifted to you at birth, is waiting. So plug into the universe, dig your toes into the soil of Mother Earth, and open your soul to your full potential." (Publisher's note)

"One of the best New Age texts without being preachy." LJ

Includes bibliographical references

133.1   Apparitions

Aykroyd, Peter

A **history** of ghosts; the true story of seances, mediums, ghosts, and ghostbusters. by Peter H. Aykroyd; with Angela Narth; foreword by Dan Aykroyd. Rodale 2009 237p il $25.99   **133.1**
1. Ghosts 2. Spiritualism
ISBN 978-1-60529-875-7; 1-60529-875-1

LC 2009-18360

The author's "grandfather was a spiritualist; he believed the human personality survives after bodily death, and practiced regular communication with ghosts—much of which he documented in journals. Aykroyd broadens the discussion with historical figures like Sir Arthur Conan Doyle, creator of Sherlock Holmes, who joined the Society of Psychical Research three weeks after his father's death. . . . This is a smart consideration of the paranormal and a curious artifact of the Aykroyd legacy." Publ Wkly

Includes bibliographical references

Dickey, Colin

Ghostland; An American History in Haunted Places. Colin Dickey. Penguin Group USA 2016 336 p. (ebook) $65; (hardcover) $27   **133.1**
1. Ghosts 2. Supernatural 3. Haunted houses -- United States
ISBN 1101980192; 9781101980217; 9781101980194

LC 2016044006

This book by Colin Dickey takes readers "on a journey across the continental United States to decode and unpack the American history repressed in our most famous haunted places. Some have established reputations as 'the most haunted mansion in America,' or 'the most haunted prison'; others, like the haunted Indian burial grounds in West Virginia, evoke memories from the past our collective nation tries to forget." (Publisher's note)

"His book is a fascinating, measured assessment of phenomena more often exploited for sensationalism." Pub Wkly

Includes bibliographical references (pages 289-308) and index.

Guiley, Rosemary Ellen

★ The **encyclopedia** of ghosts and spirits; foreword by Troy Taylor. 3rd ed; Facts on File 2007 564p il $75   **133.1**
1. Reference books 2. Ghosts -- Encyclopedias
ISBN 978-0-8160-6737-4; 0-8160-6737-6

LC 2006-103302

First published 1992

This work examines famous hauntings, historical personages and happenings, and various legends and myths about ghosts and spirits throughout the world. Recent events, new findings about old myths and updated information on major figures in the field are covered.

"Believers and skeptics alike seeking information on various phenomena will find this book useful." Booklist

Includes bibliographical references

Norman, Michael

Haunted America; {by} Michael Norman and Beth Scott. TOR Bks. 1994 411p maps hardcover o.p. pa $7.99 **133.1**

1. Ghosts

ISBN 0-8125-5054-4 pa

LC 94-28984

"This collection of chilling tales of the supernatural includes at least one story from each state and from the English-speaking Canadian provinces. The stories recount sightings of ghostly apparitions and mysterious happenings, and their history and evolution is documented." Libr J

Includes bibliographical references

Ramsland, Katherine M., 1953-

Ghost; investigating the other side. {by} Katherine Ramsland. St. Martin's Press 2001 322p il $25.95; pa $6.99 **133.1**

1. Ghosts

ISBN 0-312-26164-0; 0-312-98373-5 pa

LC 2001-41725

"Although prepared to dismiss many so-called paranormal occurrences in favor of natural explanations, {the author} nevertheless encounters, experiences, and investigates a variety of inexplicable visual, photographic, and verbal manifestations. Both skeptics and believers will be intrigued by this first-person exploration of ghostly visitations." Booklist

Includes bibliographical references

133.3   Divinatory arts

Crispin, Jessa

★ The **creative** tarot; a modern guide to an inspired life. Jessa Crispin. Touchstone 2016 352 p. illustrations (some color) $22 **133.3**

1. Tarot 2. Creative ability 3. Creative ability -- Miscellanea

ISBN 9781501120237

LC 2015038927

This book, by Jessa Crispin, "is a unique guidebook that reimagines tarot cards and the ways they can boost the creative process. . . . Thought to be esoteric and mystical, tarot cards are approachable and endlessly helpful to overcoming creative blocks. Crispin offers spiritual readings of the cards, practical information for the uninspired artist, and a wealth of fascinating anecdotes about famous artists including Virginia Woolf, Rembrandt, and David Bowie, and how they found inspiration." (Publisher's note)

"Even readers with no previous interest in the tarot will be intrigued and delighted by Crispin's ardently researched, spirited, creative, and inspiring elucidation." Booklist

133.4   Demonology and witchcraft

Adler, Margot

Drawing down the moon; witches, Druids, goddess-worshippers, and other pagans in America. [Rev and updated ed]; Penguin Books 2006 646p il pa $18 **133.4**

1. Paganism 2. Witchcraft

ISBN 0-14-303819-2; 978-0-14-303819-1

LC 2006-43786

First published 1979 by Viking

A survey of goddess worship and witchcraft movements discussing their basic philosophies and practices

"Despite its clear anti-Judaic and anti-Christian bias, this book is recommended for general and college audiences interested in religion, the occult, and modern social phenomena." Choice {review of 1979 edition}

Includes bibliographical references

Carlson, Laurie M.

A **fever** in Salem; a new interpretation of the New England witch trials. Dee, I.R. 1999 197p hardcover o.p. pa $14.95 **133.4**

1. Witchcraft 2. Salem (Mass.) -- History

ISBN 1-56663-253-6; 1-56663-309-5 pa

LC 99-27520

"Carlson's compelling narrative begs for assessment by medical experts. A valuable purchase for libraries seeking more than a basic summary of the witch trials." Libr J

Includes bibliographical references

Guiley, Rosemary Ellen

The **encyclopedia** of demons and demonology; foreword by John Zaffis. Facts On File 2009 302p il $82.50; pa $24.95 **133.4**

1. Reference books 2. Demonology -- Encyclopedias

ISBN 978-0-8160-7314-6; 0-8160-7314-7; 978-0-8160-7315-3 pa; 0-8160-7315-5 pa

LC 2008-52488

"This encyclopedia delineates beliefs about demons and demonology. The text emerges from an exploration of the darker aspects of folklore, myths, culture, and religion, covering major issues, people, and events in a historical and phenomenological perspective. Its over 400 A-to-Z entries cover topics such as demons in different cultures and religious traditions, possession, exorcism, and demon types. . . . Clear, concise, and balanced, this will attract a range of non-scholarly audiences, especially those interested in the occult, paranormal, folklore, myths, and religion. A solid addition to public libraries." Libr J

Includes bibliographical references

The **encyclopedia** of witches, witchcraft, and Wicca; 3rd ed; Facts On File 2008 436p il $85; pa $24.95 **133.4**

1. Reference books 2. Witchcraft -- Encyclopedias

ISBN 978-0-8160-7103-6; 0-8160-7103-9; 978-0-8160-7104-3 pa; 0-8160-7104-7 pa

LC 2008-8917

First published 1989 with title: The encyclopedia of witches and witchcraft

"Spanning centuries and continents, the book defines 480 of witchcraft's and wizardry's major historical events, figures, tools, sites, symbols, and abstract terms. The highly engaging, alphabetically organized entries run several paragraphs in length and deftly clarify a term's etymology as well as its spiritual, historical, or spell-making significance." Libr J

Includes bibliographical references

Hutton, Ronald

The **triumph** of the moon; a history of modern pagan witchcraft. Oxford Univ. Press 1999 486p $55.50; pa $17.95   **133.4**
1. Witchcraft 2. Neopaganism
ISBN 0-19-820744-1; 0-19-285449-6 pa
LC 99-31586

This "history of paganism in 19th- and 20th-century Britain centers on Wicca, the system of witchcraft Gerald B. Gardner introduced to a startled public in the 1950s. . . . Hutton's exceptional work is by far the most scholarly, comprehensive and judicious analysis of the subject yet published." Publ Wkly

Includes bibliographical references

Karlsen, Carol F.

★ The **devil** in the shape of a woman; witchcraft in colonial New England. Norton 1987 360p hardcover o.p. pa $16.95   **133.4**
1. Witchcraft 2. New England -- History -- 1600-1775, Colonial period
ISBN 0-393-02478-4; 0-393-31759-5 pa
LC 87-16615

The author presents a "social history of witchcraft in Puritan New England (1620-1725). She unearths detailed evidence which demonstrates that prosecuted and accused witches generally were older, married women who had violated the religious and/or economic Puritan social hierarchy. . . . A well-written, provocative addition to the . . . scholarship on New England witchcraft." Libr J

Includes bibliographical references

Levack, Brian P.

The **Devil** within; possession and exorcism in the Christian West. by Brian Levack. Yale University Press 2013 360 p. (cl : alk. paper) $35   **133.4**
1. Exorcism 2. Europe -- Religion 3. Demoniac possession 4. Exorcism -- Europe -- History 5. Demoniac possession -- Europe -- History
ISBN 0300114729; 9780300114720
LC 2012042933

This book "focuses on possession and exorcism in the Reformation period, but also reaches back to the fifteenth century and forward to our own times. . . . Challenging the commonly held belief that possession signals physical or mental illness, the author argues that demoniacs and exorcists--consciously or not--are following their various religious cultures, and their performances can only be understood in those contexts." (Publisher's note)

"In this riveting, readable study, Levack . . . offers readers a comprehensive view of reports of demon possession and efforts to rid victims of it." Pub Wkly

The **Penguin** Book of Witches; edited by Katherine Howe. Penguin Group USA 2014 320 p. $17   **133.4**
1. Witchcraft 2. History -- Sources
ISBN 014310618X; 9780143106180

This book, edited by Katherine Howe, explores the history of witchcraft. "From a manual for witch hunters written by King James himself in 1597, to court documents from the Salem witch trials of 1692, to newspaper coverage of a woman stoned to death on the streets of Philadelphia while the Continental Congress met, . . . [this book] is a treasury of historical accounts of accused witches that sheds light on the reality behind the legends." (Publisher's note)

"Recent titles such as Lois Martin's The History of Witchcraft (2010) provide an accessible, albeit brief, overview of a well-covered phenomenon. The antiquated writing style of some of the original documents in Howe's collection is challenging, however, this superbly edited and annotated work provides in-depth material for those interested in the origins of witchcraft persecution in America." LJ

Robisheaux, Thomas

The **last** witch of Langenburg; murder in a German village. [by] Thomas Robisheaux. W. W. Norton & Co. 2009 427p il map   **133.4**
1. Homicide 2. Witchcraft 3. Murder -- Germany -- History 4. Germany -- History -- 1517-1740 5. Witchcraft -- Germany -- History
ISBN 0-393-06551-0; 9780393065510
LC 2008-43052

This "account of one of Europe's last witch panics draws on court documents, eyewitness testimonies, and an early autopsy report to chronicle the 1672 trial of Anna Schmeig and her family, who were accused of sorcery when a neighbor girl died after eating one of Anna's butter cakes." (Publisher's note) Bibliography. Index.

The author "gives us the story of one of the last witch hunts in Europe. In 1672, in a German village, a young woman who had just given birth to her second child died after eating a Shrovetide cake made by her neighbor. Stories of witches poisoning innocents were common in the Franconia region. The neighbor was arrested, and the entire family charged with witchcraft. You can't beat a witch hunt for drama. Every childhood nightmare is called to mind—the dark forest on the edge of town, the inaccessibility of God and, worse, our own friends and family. Forget memoir; this is nonfiction." Seattle Times

Includes bibliographical references

133.5   Astrology

Goodman, Linda

Linda Goodman's sun signs. Taplinger 1968 xxiii, 549p $29.95   **133.5**
1. Zodiac 2. Astrology
ISBN 0-8008-4900-0

The author tells how to identify and deal with people according to their astrological signs

"This book is part astrology, part psychology, and always entertaining." Libr J

Lewis, James R.

★ The **astrology** book; the encyclopedia of heavenly influences. 2nd ed; Visible Ink Press 2003 928p il pa $24.95 **133.5**
1. Reference books 2. Astrology -- Encyclopedias
ISBN 1-57859-144-9

First published 1994 by Gale Res. with title: The astrology encyclopedia

"Although aimed at the believer, Lewis' work may be confidently consulted by the skeptic seeking basic information about astrology." Booklist

Miller, Susan

Planets and possibilities; explore the worlds beyond your sun sign. Warner Bks. 2001 418p il $30; pa $15.95 **133.5**
1. Astrology
ISBN 0-446-52434-4; 0-446-67806-6 pa

The author provides "character analysis of each sign. The cosmic gifts, relationship trends, financial tendencies, and career tendencies associated with each sign are all described in detail. The mythology of each sign is included as well, nicely rounding out the book." Libr J

Snodgrass, Mary Ellen

Signs of the zodiac; a reference guide to historical, mythological, and cultural associations. illustrated by Raymond Miller Barrett, Jr. Greenwood Press 1997 243p il $46.95 **133.5**
1. Zodiac 2. Astrology
ISBN 0-313-30276-6

LC 97-5598

"After brief descriptions of zodiacal variants from other parts of the world, plus chapters on the historical foundations of astrology and its pervasiveness in the arts and sciences, Snodgrass treats each sign to a full workover: major stars in each, mythological background and symbology, commonly accepted character traits of those born under its influence, and thumbnail biographies of select prominent people who exemplify those traits." SLJ

Includes bibliographical references

133.6 Palmistry

Reid, Lori

The **art** of hand reading. DK Pub. 1996 120p il hardcover o.p. pa $15 **133.6**
1. Palmistry
ISBN 0-7894-4837-8 pa

LC 96-15506

This volume uses color photographs of hands and handprints to analyze all the significant lines, mounts, and markings on hands. It shows how the different areas of the palm reveal the balance between instinctive desires and powers of intellect and reason

133.8 Psychic phenomena

Bader, Christopher D.

Paranormal America; ghost encounters, UFO sightings, Bigfoot hunts, and other curiosities in religion and culture. [by] Christopher D. Bader, F. Carson Mencken, and Joseph O. Baker. New York University Press 2010 264p il $70; pa $20 **133.8**
1. Parapsychology 2. Curiosities and wonders
ISBN 978-0-8147-9134-9; 978-0-8147-9135-6 pa; 978-0-8147-8642-0 ebook

LC 2010-16525

Authors "Christopher D. Bader, F. Carson Mencken, and Joseph O. Baker take their readers on a . . . journey into 'the world of people who devote themselves to the "quest"' for contact with angels, aliens, and other unusual beings. . . . To flesh out the findings of the 2005 Baylor Religion Survey, a national random sample of American religious beliefs (two of the authors were principle investigators), and to understand who is attracted to paranormal beliefs, Bader, Mencken, and Baker accompany bigfoot hunters into the woods and listen to stories about alien abductions and ghostly apparitions. . . . By drawing on both the Baylor survey and qualitative research, these three sociologists conclude that 'the paranormal is normal' and challenge the stereotype that those drawn to the paranormal come from the margins of society." (Journal of American History)

The authors "examine America's belief in paranormal phenomena inside and outside of mainstream religion—from UFOs and Bigfoot to speaking in tongues and guardian angels. They look at how belief affects lives, examining common stereotypes faced by believers and considering whether belief in a mainstream religion makes one likely to ascribe to more otherworldly occurrences. . . . While this academic work showcases an astounding amount of research, the quick pacing and engaging language keep it from being a dry report of BRS findings. It is accessible to any reader with an interest in the convergence of paranormal beliefs and religion." Libr J

Includes bibliographical references

Clegg, Brian

Extra Sensory; The Science and Pseudoscience of Telepathy and Other Powers of the Mind. Brian Clegg. St. Martin's Press 2013 320 p. (hardcover) $25.99 **133.8**
1. Parapsychology 2. Extrasensory perception
ISBN 1250019060; 9781250019066

LC 2013004038

This book, by Brian Clegg, "look[s] at the untapped abilities of human beings, from ESP to Telekenesis and other real life sciences that are currently being studied today. . . . Is there any solid evidence to back up these talents, or are they nothing more than fantasy? . . . By looking at possible physical mechanisms for ESP and taking in the best scientific evidence, the reader can discover if this is all wishful thinking and deception, or a fascinating reality." (Publisher's note)

Sheldrake, Rupert

Dogs that know when their owners are coming home; and other unexplained powers of animals. Crown 1999 352p il hardcover o.p. pa $14 **133.8**

1. Pets 2. Extrasensory perception
ISBN 0-609-80533-9 pa

LC 99-25439

"The author reports the results of five years of extensive research as he followed up on anecdotal accounts from pet owners on the homing abilities of lost pets, animals that show premonitions of earthquakes or epileptic seizures, and the fact that animals anticipate the arrival home of their owners." Booklist

Includes bibliographical references

The **sense** of being stared at; and other aspects of the extended mind. Crown 2003 369p il hardcover o.p. pa $13.95 **133.8**

1. Extrasensory perception
ISBN 1-4000-5129-0 pa

LC 2002-9943

"A most unusual book—fascinating, scientifically sound, and fun to read—it posits that ESP and 'other aspects of the extended mind' are not paranormal but natural functions. Every library should make room on its shelves for this one." Libr J

Includes bibliographical references

133.9   Spiritualism

Blum, Deborah

Ghost hunters; William James and the search for scientific proof of life after death. Penguin Press 2006 370p $25.95; pa $15 **133.9**

1. Philosophers 2. Spiritualism 3. Psychologists 4. Parapsychology 5. Writers on science
ISBN 1-59420-090-4; 978-1-59420-090-8; 0-14-303895-8 pa; 978-0-14-303895-5 pa

LC 2006-44948

In this book, the author examines the Victorian era conflict between science and religion "by reviewing the history of the British Society for Psychical Research and its U.S. counterpart, the American Society for Psychical Research, both of which aimed to find scientific proof of the existence of the supernatural. . . . Her clearly written presentation of the history, frauds, and personalities involved in this unique slice of Victorian life is recommended for all history of science collections." Libr J

Includes bibliographical references

Moody, Raymond A.

★ Life after life; the investigation of a phenomenon--survival of bodily death. [by] Raymond A. Moody, Jr.; with a new preface by Melvin Morse and a foreword by Elizabeth Kübler-Ross. HarperSanFrancisco 2001 xxviii, 175p pa $14 **133.9**

1. Death 2. Future life 3. Near-death experiences
ISBN 0-06-251739-2

LC 00-46156

First published 1975 by MBB Inc.

The author "investigates more than one hundred case studies of people who experienced 'clinical death' and were subsequently revived." Publisher's note

Roach, Mary, 1959-

★ Spook; science tackles the afterlife. Norton 2005 311p il **133.9**

1. Future life 2. Religion and science 3. Soul 4. Death
ISBN 0393059626

LC 2005-14450

The author investigates a range of theories and beliefs about the soul's migration after death.

"Roach perfectly balances her skepticism and her boundless curiosity with a sincere desire to know. . . . She is an original who can enliven any subject with wit, keen reporting and a sly intelligence." Publ Wkly

Includes bibliographical references

141   Idealism and related systems and doctrines

★ The **essential** transcendentalists; edited and introduced by Richard G. Geldard. J.P. Tarcher/Penguin 2005 265p pa $15.95 **141**

1. Transcendentalism
ISBN 1-58542-434-X

LC 2005-44016

This study "is divided into three main sections. . . . The first is 'Primary Texts,' with selections from the writings of Sampson Reed, James Marsh, Amos Alcott (father of Louisa May), and Ralph Waldo Emerson. The second, 'Individual Voices,' introduces selections from Frederic Hedge, Margaret Fuller, and Henry David Thoreau. The last is 'The Transcendental Heritage,' which features the works of Walt Whitman, Emily Dickinson, Wallace Stevens, Loren Eiseley, and Annie Dillard. This is a highly informed, elegantly written, fascinating story told through commentary, historical overview, and selections from classic works. It belongs in all libraries." Libr J

Includes bibliographical references

142   Critical philosophy

Bakewell, Sarah

★ At the Existentialist Cafe; Freedom, Being, and Apricot Cocktails With Jean-paul Sartre, Simone De Beauvoir, Albert Camus, Martin Heidegger, Maurice Merleau-ponty and Others. by Sarah Bakewell. Other Press 2016 439 p. illustrations (hbk.) $25 **142**

1. Paris (France) -- Intellectual life 2. Existentialism 3. Philosophers -- France -- Biography 4. Philosophy, Modern -- 20th century Philosophy -- France -- History -- 20th century
ISBN 9781590514887; 1590514882

This book, by Sarah Bakewell, is an "account of one of the twentieth century's major intellectual movements and the revolutionary thinkers who came to shape it. . . . They are the young Jean-Paul Sartre, Simone de Beauvoir, and longtime friend Raymond Aron, a fellow philosopher who raves to them about a new conceptual framework from Berlin called Phenomenology." (Publisher's note)

"A fresh, invigorating look into complex minds and a unique time and place." Kirkus

Includes bibliographical references (pages 403-420) and index

Barrett, William

★ **Irrational** man; a study in existential philosophy. Doubleday 1958 278p hardcover o.p. pa $12.95   **142**

1. Existentialism

ISBN 0-385-03138-6 pa

This discussion of existentialism traces its origins and analyzes the contributions of chief exponents of existentialist thought—Nietzsche, Kierkegaard, Heidegger and Sartre

Existentialism from Dostoevsky to Sartre; rev and expanded; New Am. Lib. 1975 384p pa $15.95   **142**

1. Existentialism

ISBN 0-452-00930-8

First published 1956 by World Pub.

This book contains selections from the basic writings of Dostoevsky, Kierkegaard, Nietzsche, Rilke, Ortega y Gasset, Jaspers, Heidegger, Sartre and Camus.

Sartre, Jean Paul

★ **Being** and nothingness; an essay on phenomenological ontology. translated and with an introduction by Hazel E. Barnes. Philosophical Lib. 1956 638p   **142**

1. Existentialism

Original French edition, 1943

This is "Sartre's major attempt to systematize his theoretical analysis of the human condition and human consciousness which underlies 'Existentialism.'" Reader's Ency. 4th edition

Existentialism and human emotions. Philosophical Library: Distributed to the Book trade by Citadel Press 1957 96p pa $9.95   **142**

1. Existentialism

ISBN 0-8065-0902-3 pa

"Sartre refutes the idea that existentialism drains meaning from human life, by claiming that the philosophy instead gives man total freedom to achieve his own significance." (Publisher's note)

146   Naturalism and related systems and doctrines

Dennett, Daniel Clement

Darwin's dangerous idea; evolution and the meanings of life. {by} Daniel C. Dennett. Simon & Schuster 1995 586p il hardcover o.p. pa $16   **146**

1. Authors 2. Evolution 3. Geologists 4. Mathematicians 5. Natural selection 6. Paleontologists 7. College teachers 8. Writers on science

ISBN 0-684-82471-X pa

LC 94-49158

"Current controversies associated with the origin of life, sociobiology, punctuated equilibrium, the evolution of culture and language, and evolutionary ethics are investigated rigorously within the context of Darwinian science and philosophy. Dennett challenges the ideas of several imminent scientists, including Roger Penrose and Stephen Jay Gould, who, Dennett asserts, tend to limit the power or implications of Darwin's dangerous ideas." Libr J

Includes bibliographical references

150   Psychology

Colman, Andrew M.

★ **A dictionary** of psychology; 2nd ed; Oxford University Press 2006 861p il $45; pa $17.95 **150**

1. Reference books 2. Psychology -- Dictionaries

ISBN 978-0-19-280632-1; 0-19-280632-7; 978-0-19-861035-9 pa; 0-19-861035-1 pa

LC 2005-31810

First published 2001

"This work defines the most common as well as the most important issues facing psychology today.... [The book features] over 11,000 cross-referenced entries, covering everything from anxiety and cognitive impairment to hypolexia (another name for dyslexia) and postpartum depression.... For professionals and students of psychology, this is a good place to start their research." SLJ

Includes bibliographical references

Cordon, Luis A.

★ **Popular** psychology; an encyclopedia. Greenwood Press 2005 274p il $75   **150**

1. Reference books 2. Psychology -- Encyclopedias

ISBN 0-313-32457-3

LC 2004-17426

This book "provides a concise guide for anyone seeking to understand the true scientific nature of psychology." Libr Media Connect

Includes bibliographical references

Glasser, William

Choice theory; a new psychology of personal freedom. HarperCollins Pubs. 1998 340p il $24; pa $13.95   **150**

1. Psychology

ISBN 0-06-019109-0; 0-06-093014-4 pa

LC 97-36025

"Choice theory helps its users avoid confrontation and ask pertinent questions. It sees conscious or unconscious desire for external control as the main problem in the four major personal relationships: husband-wife, parent-child, teacher-student, and manager-worker.... Combining choice theory and reality therapy in his practice, Glasser has been able to shorten the durations of his treatment programs substantially. As he presents them here, his theories and approaches can be applied in education and business as well as for self-help." Booklist

Kubler-Ross, Elisabeth

The **wheel** of life; a memoir of living and dying.
Scribner 1997 286p il hardcover o.p. pa $13   **150**
1. Psychiatrists 2. College teachers 3. Writers on
medicine
ISBN 0-684-84631-4 pa

LC 97-6435

In this autobiography "Kübler-Ross describes her grow-
ing-up years in Switzerland as one of a set of triplet sisters,
her fight to become a doctor, and later, the even stronger opposition she met when she began her research on death and
dying. Despite the weightiness inherent in working with and
writing about mortality, the book has a light, almost airy feel
to it, which goes along with the author's central theme that
death is merely a transformation." Booklist

150.19   Systems, schools, viewpoints

Bettelheim, Bruno

Freud and man's soul. Knopf 1983 111p hardcover o.p. pa $9   **150.19**
1. Psychoanalysis 2. Psychoanalysts 3. Writers on
medicine
ISBN 0-394-71036-3 pa

LC 82-47809

The author argues that Freud was a great humanist and that mistranslation of his work has lead American
psychoanalysis astray

Freud, Sigmund

★ The **basic** writings of Sigmund Freud; translated and edited by A.A. Brill. Modern Lib. 1995
973p $24.95   **150.19**
1. Dreams 2. Psychoanalysis
ISBN 0-679-60166-X

LC 95-13411

A reissue of the 1938 edition

Includes Psychopathology of Everyday Life, The Inter-
pretation of Dreams, Three Contributions to the Theory of
Sex, Wit and Its Relation to the Unconscious, Totem and
Taboo, and The History of the Psychoanalytic Movement.

★ The **Freud** reader; edited by Peter Gay. Norton 1989 832p hardcover o.p. pa $21.95   **150.19**
1. Psychoanalysis
ISBN 0-393-31403-0 pa

LC 89-2949

This "work includes some 50 of Freud's texts, organized
chronologically with headnotes. The selections range from
case studies and theoretical discussions about dreams, anxiety and anal eroticism to essays on lay analysis and religion
as humankind's obsessional neurosis." Libr J

Includes bibliographical references

Fromm, Erich

On being human; foreword by Rainer Funk. Continuum 1994 180p hardcover o.p. pa $29.95 **150.19**
1. Humanism 2. Psychoanalysis 3. Social psychology
ISBN 0-8264-0576-2; 0-8264-1005-7 pa

LC 93-9243

This volume includes the author's writings on humanism, social psychology, and psychoanalysis from the 1960s,
based on Fromm's lectures, works written for specific occasions, and manuscripts intended as books.

Includes bibliographical references

Gay, Peter

A **Godless** Jew; Freud, atheism, and the making of psychoanalysis. Yale Univ. Press 1987 182p
hardcover o.p. pa $17   **150.19**
1. Atheism 2. Psychoanalysis 3. Psychoanalysts 4.
Writers on medicine
ISBN 0-300-04008-3; 0-300-04608-1 pa

LC 87-8267

The author "reviews the various claims for the Jewishness of psychoanalysis and finds them to be wholly without
merit. Paradoxically, he argues that Freud's position as an
outsider—an atheist and Jew—enabled him to pierce the taboo topics of sexuality and the unconscious which led to his
momentous discoveries." Publ Wkly

Includes bibliographical references

Hayman, Ronald

A **life** of Jung. Norton 2001 xxi, 522p il hardcover o.p. pa $18.95   **150.19**
1. Psychiatrists 2. Psychologists 3. Writers on
medicine
ISBN 0-393-32322-6 pa

LC 00-54802

First published 1999 in the United Kingdom

"One of the many strengths of this candid and discerning
biography is that Hayman enlists . . . provocative, alarming
material to build a careful, nuanced portrait of his subject
that neither excuses nor excoriates his actions and words."
Publ Wkly

Includes bibliographical references

Judith, Anodea

Eastern body, Western mind; psychology and
the chakra system as a path to the self. Anodea Judith. Celestial Arts 2004 xii, 488 p.p illustrations
$18.99   **150.19**
1. Self 2. Psychology 3. Chakras -- Miscellanea
ISBN 1587612259; 9781587612251

LC 2004010256

Author "Anodea Judith brought a fresh approach to the
yoga-based Eastern chakra system, adapting it to the Western framework of Jungian psychology, somatic therapy,
childhood developmental theory, and metaphysics. This
groundbreaking work in transpersonal psychology has been
revised and redesigned for a more accessible presentation.
Arranged schematically, the book uses the inherent structure of the chakra system as a map upon which to chart our
Western understanding of individual development." (Publisher's note)

Includes bibliographical references (p. 465-474)
and index

Jung, C. G.

★ The **basic** writings of C. G. Jung; edited with an introduction by Violet Staub de Laszlo. Modern Lib. 1993 xxxiii, 691p $21.95   **150.19**
1. Psychoanalysis
ISBN 0-679-60071-X
                                                        LC 93-17801

This is a reissue of the 1959 edition

This volume contains excerpts from Symbols of transformation, On the nature of the psyche, Relations between the ego and the unconscious, Psychological types, Psychology of the transference, and Psychology and religion. It also includes Archetypes of the collective unconscious, Psychological aspects of the mother archetype, On the nature of dreams, On the psychogenesis of schizophrenia, Introduction to the religious and psychological problems of alchemy, and Marriage as a psychological relationship.

Includes bibliographical references

The **essential** Jung; selected and introduced by Anthony Storr. Princeton Univ. Press 1983 447p hardcover o.p. pa $18.95   **150.19**
1. Psychoanalysis
ISBN 0-691-02935-0 pa
                                                        LC 82-61441

Storr's "selections from Jung's writings are lucid and accessible; linked by skillful explanatory passages, they provide both interested laypersons and students with a perspective on Jung." Libr J

Includes bibliographical references

★ **Man** and his symbols; {by} Carl G. Jung {et al.} Doubleday 1964 320p il $30; pa $7.99 **150.19**
1. Self 2. Dreams 3. Symbolism 4. Psychology 5. Art -- Psychology
ISBN 0-385-05221-9; 0-440-35183-9 pa

"The basic ideas of Jungian psychology are presented in popular language in six essays by Dr. Jung and {four} of his pupils; these are correlated to dreams and symbols and are shown in their archetypal relationships to ancient myths, present-day thought and art." Libr J

Includes bibliographical references

Memories, dreams, reflections; recorded and edited by Aniela Jaffé; translated from the German by Richard and Clara Winston. rev ed; Vintage Bks. 1989 430p pa $14   **150.19**
1. Psychiatrists 2. Psychologists 3. Writers on medicine
ISBN 0-679-72395-1
                                                        LC 88-37040

First published 1963 by Pantheon Bks.

"This volume of recollections reveals the intellectual and spiritual development of an eminent Swiss psychologist and psychiatrist while only touching upon the outward events of his long and productive life. . . . An important,

firsthand document for readers who wish to understand this seminal writer and thinker." Booklist

Includes bibliographical references

The **portable** Jung; edited with an introduction by Joseph Campbell; translated by R. F. C. Hull. Viking 1971 xli, 659p hardcover o.p. pa $17 **150.19**
1. Psychoanalysis
ISBN 0-14-015070-6 pa

A collection of writings spanning the career of the pioneering psychoanalyst. Includes a chronology and bibliography.

May, Rollo

★ The **discovery** of being; writings in existential psychology. Norton 1983 192p hardcover o.p.   **150.19**
1. Psychotherapy 2. Existentialism
                                                        LC 83-4282

The author "provides the reader with principles of his existential psychotherapy; delineates his view of the cultural-historical context that gave rise to both psychoanalysis and existentialism; and sets forth what he considers to be the contributions to therapy of an existential approach." Choice

Includes bibliographical references

Rogers, Carl R.

A **way** of being. Houghton Mifflin 1980 395p hardcover o.p. pa $15   **150.19**
1. Humanism 2. Psychology
ISBN 0-395-75530-1 pa
                                                        LC 80-20275

"This is a book rich in theoretical insights and experiential sharing, and full of invigorating optimism." Libr J

Includes bibliographical references

Skinner, B. F.

★ **About** behaviorism. Knopf 1974 256p hardcover o.p. pa $12   **150.19**
1. Behaviorism
ISBN 0-394-71618-3 pa

The author defines, analyzes and defends the science of behaviorism with chapters exploring the causes of behavior, operant behavior, verbal behavior, thinking, causes and reasons, knowledge, emotion and self

Includes bibliographical references

152.1 Sensory perception

Ackerman, Diane, 1948-

A **natural** history of the senses. Random House 1990 331p hardcover o.p. pa $14.95   **152.1**
1. Senses and sensation
ISBN 0-394-57335-8; 978-0-679-73566-3 pa; 0-679-73566-6 pa
                                                        LC 89-43416

"Ackerman celebrates the senses by examining their biological bases and the various and bizarre ways we have come to indulge them. Her catalog of the senses is itself a sensuous journey, with prose rich in imagery and rhythm. Ackerman's book is a provocative and entertaining treat whose details will bestir the reader's imagination." Libr J

Includes bibliographic references

Herz, Rachel S.

The **scent** of desire; discovering our enigmatic sense of smell. [by] Rachel Herz. William Morrow 2007 xxi, 266p $24.95; pa $13.95 **152.1**

1. Smell

ISBN 978-0-06-082537-9; 0-06-082537-5; 978-0-06-082538-6 pa; 0-06-082538-3 pa

LC 2007-33563

"This is one of those all-too-rare books that is involving, well written, and solidly grounded in research." Libr J

Includes bibliographical references

152.14 Visual perception

Herman, Amy E.

Visual intelligence; sharpen your perception, change your life. Amy E. Herman. Houghton Mifflin Harcourt 2016 336 p. illustrations (chiefly color) (hardcover) $28 **152.14**

1. Visual literacy 2. Visual perception

ISBN 9780544381056

LC 2015037245

This book, by Amy E. Herman, is a "guide to seeing–and communicating–more clearly. . . . By showing people how to look closely at images, she helps them hone their 'visual intelligence,' a set of skills we all possess but few of us know how to use properly." (Publisher's note)

"Sharp and original, this book should alter how readers look at the world." Kirkus

Includes bibliographical references and index

Hoffman, Donald D.

Visual intelligence; how we create what we see. Norton 1998 294p il hardcover o.p. pa $17.95 **152.14**

1. Vision 2. Perception

ISBN 0-393-31967-9 pa

LC 98-6181

This book offers "wit, insight and charm. . . . An outstanding example of creative popular science." Publ Wkly

Includes bibliographical references

152.3 Movements and motor functions

Provine, Robert R.

Curious behavior; yawning, laughing, hiccupping, and beyond. Robert R. Provine. Harvard University Press 2012 288 p. (alk. paper) $24.95 **152.3**

1. Hiccups 2. Sneezing 3. Human body 4. Human behavior 5. Human biology 6. Neuropsychology 7. Evolutionary psychology

ISBN 0674048512; 9780674048515

LC 2012007754

This book by author Robert R. Provine is "about many instinctive behaviors. . . which science has overlooked.

Provine 'redresses historic debts' by focusing on such bodily behaviors as 'Farting and Belching.' Tickling, for example, may tap into a neural mechanism for distinguishing ourselves from others. . . . Contagious yawns--affecting 55% of those watching yawn videos--may reflect how our brains replicate observed behavior to create empathy." (Publishers Weekly)

Includes bibliographical references.

152.4 Emotions

Ackerman, Diane, 1948-

A **natural** history of love. Random House 1994 xxiii, 358p hardcover o.p. pa $14 **152.4**

1. Love 2. Sexual behavior

ISBN 0-679-76183-7 pa

LC 94-171385

Companion volume to A natural history of the senses

"Ackerman sets out on her exploration by reviewing the lessons provided across time by such lovers as Antony and Cleopatra, Orpheus and Eurydice, Dido and Aeneas, Abelard and Heloise and Romeo and Juliet. During this journey, she explores the neurophysiology of love. . . . With dazzling poetic charm and insight, she uses history, literature, science, psychology, and personal experience as tools to illuminate the vigor and vehemence of the thrilling, devastating, and comforting phenomenon of love." Libr J

Bloom, Paul

How pleasure works; the new science of why we like what we like. W. W. Norton 2010 280p il $26.95 **152.4**

1. Pleasure

ISBN 0-393-06632-0; 978-0-393-06632-6

LC 2010-05803

Refuting the "explanation of pleasure as a simple sensory response, Bloom . . . [argues] that pleasure is grounded in our beliefs about the deeper nature or essence of a given thing." (Publisher's note) Index.

Bloom "presents essentialism as a weighty determinant of our pleasures. . . . [He] probes the history of sentimental objects, the contact and context that give them meaning; how we hope that qualities of the things we eat will pervade us; the ways in which we are attracted to the process of making art and storytelling; and the strange case of giving and receiving pain. A heartening, well-developed argument." Kirkus

Includes bibliographical references

Clark, Taylor

Nerve; poise under pressure, serenity under stress, and the brave new science of fear and cool. Little, Brown and Company 2011 310p $25.99; ebook $12.99 **152.4**

1. Fear 2. Anxiety

ISBN 978-0-316-04289-5; 978-0-316-12686-1 ebook

LC 2010-38835

"A compassionate psychological page-turner." Kirkus

Includes bibliographical references

Damasio, Antonio R.

Looking for Spinoza; joy, sorrow, and the feeling rain. {by} Antonio Damasio. Harcourt 2003 355p il $28; pa $15 **152.4**
1. Authors 2. Emotions 3. Philosophers 4. Essayists 5. Writers on religion
ISBN 0-15-100557-5; 0-15-602871-9 pa
LC 2002-11347

This is a "discussion of the difference between emotions (of the body) and feelings (of the mind), various sites in the brain that trigger these states, and the . . . synthesis of the homeostatic process, memory, sensory input, imagination, and foresight that links the unconscious to consciousness and feelings to reasoning." Booklist
Includes bibliographical references

Fromm, Erich

★ The **art** of loving; Centennial ed; Continuum 2000 130p $18.95 **152.4**
1. Love
ISBN 0-8264-1260-2
LC 00-21030

A reissue of the title first published 1956
"An astonishingly simple presentation of an abstract subject." Booklist

Gardner, Daniel

The **science** of fear; why we fear the things we shouldn't-- and put ourselves in greater danger. Dutton 2008 339p $24.95 **152.4**
1. Fear
ISBN 978-0-525-95062-2; 0-525-95062-1
LC 2008-03024

Gardner "analyses everything from the media's predilection for irrational scare stories to the cynical use of fear by politicians pushing a particular agenda. . . . [He] never falls into the trap of becoming frustrated and embittered by the waste and needless worry that he is documenting. A personal anecdote about an unwise foray into a Nigerian slum in search of a stolen wallet disposes of the idea that the author is immune to the foibles he describes. What could easily have been a catalogue of misgovernance and stupidity instead becomes a cheery corrective to modern paranoia." Economist
Includes bibliographical references

Gilligan, Carol

★ The **birth** of pleasure. Knopf 2002 253p $24; pa $13 **152.4**
1. Love 2. Interpersonal relations
ISBN 0-679-44037-2; 0-679-75943-3 pa
LC 2001-50329

Gilligan's "mastery of literary sources and her intelligent but nonacademic writing style make this an enjoyable, challenging work." Publ Wkly
Includes bibliographical references

Goleman, Daniel

★ **Emotional** intelligence; 10th anniversary ed.; Bantam Books 2006 xxiv, 358p il $29; pa $18 **152.4**
1. Emotions 2. Marriage 3. Medicine 4. Intellect

5. Parenting 6. Temperament 7. Industrial relations 8. Emotionally disturbed children 9. Education -- Curricula
ISBN 978-0-553-80491-1; 0-553-80491-X; 978-0-553-38371-3 pa; 0-553-38371-X pa
LC 2006-283929

First published 1995
The author explains "how to develop our emotional intelligence in ways that can improve our relationships, our parenting, our classrooms, and our workplaces. Goleman assures us that our temperaments may be determined by neurochemistry, but they can be altered." Booklist
Includes bibliographical references

Jamison, Kay R.

Exuberance; the passion for life. by Kay Redfield Jamison. Knopf 2004 405p il $24.95 **152.4**
1. Happiness
ISBN 0-375-40144-X
LC 2004-46561

The author "examines the contagious nature of exuberance, which she defines as 'a psychological state characterized by high mood and high energy,' offering diverse examples that range from John Muir and FDR to Mary Poppins and Peter Pan. Having in mind the simply put idea that 'those who are exuberant act,' the author details the energetic efforts of scientists, naturalists, politicians and even her meteorologist father." Publ Wkly
Includes bibliographical references

Jeffers, Susan J.

Feel the fear--and do it anyway; [by] Susan Jeffers. Ballantine Books 2007 214p il pa $13.95 **152.4**
1. Fear
ISBN 978-0-345-48742-1
LC 2007-271292

First published 1987 by Harcourt Brace Jovanovich
"By mixing positive thinking with situational exercises that examine basic fear responses, psychologist Jeffers shows that fear is what you make of it and that in most cases it is unfounded." Libr J
Includes bibliographical references

Lenoir, Frédéric

Happiness; a philosopher's guide. Frédéric Lenoir; translated by Andrew Brown. Melville House 2015 208 p. black and white illustrations (hardcover) $23.95 **152.4**
1. Happiness 2. Philosophy
ISBN 1612194397; 9781612194394
LC 2014040205

This book, edited by Frédéric Lenoir, translated by Andrew Brown, "examines how history's greatest philosophers and religious figures have answered life's most fundamental question: What is happiness and how do I achieve it? From the ancient Greeks . . . to the Buddha, Jesus, and Muhammad; from Voltaire . . . and Schopenhauer to Kant, Freud, and even modern neuroscientists--Lenoir considers the idea that true and lasting happiness is indeed possible." (Publisher's note)
"Throughout the book, Lenoir writes economically, devoting only enough words to particular thoughts and ap-

proaches as are necessary to stir questions in the minds of readers. A brief though well-considered guide to a wide range of the many schools of thought regarding contentment, joy and happiness." Kirkus

Includes bibliographical references

Lerner, Harriet Goldhor

★ The **dance** of anger; a woman's guide to changing the patterns of intimate relationships. [by] Harriet Lerner. Perennial Currents 2005 239p il pa $13.95   **152.4**

    1. Anger 2. Women -- Psychology
    ISBN 0-06-074104-X

                       LC 2004-60074

First published 1985

The author examines the ways women express anger, as well as how women's anger is viewed by society and throughout history.

Includes bibliographical references

Levy, Alexander

The **orphaned** adult; understanding and coping with grief and change after the death of our parents. Perseus Bks. 1999 190p hardcover o.p. pa $15.95   **152.4**

    1. Death 2. Bereavement 3. Loss (Psychology)
    ISBN 0-7382-0361-0 pa

                       LC 99-64773

"Incorporating his own personal experience with the accounts of others who have lost their parents, psychologist Levy examines this profound life-changing event with compassion and understanding." Libr J

Lewis, Thomas

★ A **general** theory of love; [by] Thomas Lewis, Fari Amini, Richard Lannon. Random House 2000 274p il hardcover o.p. pa $13   **152.4**

    1. Love
    ISBN 0-375-70922-3 pa

                       LC 99-49930

The authors "aim to help physicians treat patients by showing how the many and varied aspects of love, including the lack and the warping of it, affect patients' problems and strengths and by discussing what must, therefore, be involved in treating patients." Booklist

Includes bibliographical references

Nettle, Daniel

Happiness; the science behind your smile. Oxford University Press 2005 216p il $21; pa $13.95   **152.4**

    1. Happiness
    ISBN 0-19-280558-4; 978-0-19-280558-4; 0-19-280559-2 pa; 978-0-19-280559-1 pa

                       LC 2004-30585

"With absolute clarity and admirable brevity, Nettle explores the pursuit of happiness and, happily, makes good sense of it all." Publ Wkly

Includes bibliographical references

Orloff, Judith

Emotional freedom; liberate yourself from negative emotions and transform your life. Harmony Books 2009 401p $24.95   **152.4**

    1. Emotions 2. Self-realization
    ISBN 978-0-307-33818-1

                       LC 2008-21482

"In Part 1, Orloff presents four components of emotion—biology, energy, spirituality, and psychology—and provides a 20-question assessment to highlight individuals' strengths and weaknesses. . . . Orloff divides Part 2 into seven chapters, each devoted to a difficult negative emotion. Throughout, Orloff details how one can use the four components of emotion to transform negative emotions into positive ones and become a more centered and emotionally healthy person. . . . This well-written book is full of good advice for anyone who wants to take more control of his or her emotional life." Libr J

Ronson, Jon

So you've been publicly shamed; a journey through the world of public humiliation. Jon Ronson. Riverhead Hardcover 2015 304 p. illustrations (hardback) $27.95   **152.4**

    1. Shame 2. Interpersonal relations 3. Social control
    ISBN 9781594487132; 1594487138

                       LC 2014038382

This book reports on how "for the past three years, [author] Jon Ronson has been immersing himself in the world of modern-day public shaming--meeting famous shamees, shamers, and bystanders who have been impacted." This book is "a radically empathetic book about public shaming, and about shaming as a form of social control." (Publisher's note)

"With confidence, verve, and empathy, Ronson skillfully informs and engages the reader without excusing those caught up in the shame game. As he stresses, we are the ones wielding this incredible power over others' lives, often with no regard for the lasting consequences of our actions." Booklist

Rosenblatt, Roger

The **book** of love; improvisations on a crazy little thing. by Roger Rosenblatt. HarperCollins 2015 177 p. $22.99   **152.4**

    1. Love 2. Marriage 3. Interpersonal relations
    ISBN 0062349422; 9780062349422

In this book, "Roger Rosenblatt looks at love in all its themes and variations--romantic love, courtship, marriage, battle, heartbreak, fury, confusion, melancholy, beauty, delirium, ecstasy; love of lovers, family, friends, of country, of work, writing, solitude, of art; love of nature; love of life itself. . . . Rosenblatt intersperses thoughts about love with fictional vignettes." (Publisher's note)

"True to its subtitle, this is a collection of "improvisations," meandering in a way that allows readers to pick it up and begin from any page in this tiny, precious book." LJ

Saviuc, Luminita D.

15 things you should give up to be happy; an inspiring guide to discovering effortless joy. Lumi-

nita D. Saviuc; foreword by Vishen Lakhiani. Perigee Books 2016 208 p. (paperback) $16 **152.4**
1. Happiness 2. Conduct of life 3. Self-help techniques
ISBN 9780399172823

LC 2015032168

This book, by Luminita D. Saviuc, offers "a simple and counterintuitive approach to finding true joy. . . . When . . . Luminita Saviuc posted a list of things to let go in order to be happy, she had no idea that it would go viral. . . . Based on that inspiring post, this heartfelt book gives readers permission to give up--that is, to let go of the bad habits that are holding them back from achieving authentic happiness and living their best lives." (Publisher's note)

"Therapeutic, compassionate prodding for those who feel like they're unable to move forward." Library Journal

Fifteen things you should give up to be happy

Tavris, Carol

Anger; the misunderstood emotion. rev ed; Simon & Schuster 1989 383p pa $14 **152.4**
1. Anger
ISBN 0-671-67523-0

LC 89-33129

First published 1983

The author contends that anger is a complex, socially learned response that is not necessarily cathartic

Includes bibliographical references

Waal, F. B. M. de (Frans B. M.), 1948-

The **age** of empathy; nature's lessons for a kinder society. with drawings by the author. Harmony Books 2009 291p il **152.4**
1. Empathy 2. Animal behavior
ISBN 0-307-40776-4; 978-0-307-40776-4

The author "examines what he calls the behavioral 'glue' of primate societies: empathy, sympathy, a sense of fair play, and trust. In tracing the origins and evolution of empathy, de Waal points out that our ability to take another's perspective is an automatic impulse with a long evolutionary history in the mammalian line. . . . This insightful work . . . will appeal to a wide variety of general readers interested in the links between human evolution and animal behavior." Libr J

Includes bibliographical references

153   Conscious mental processes and intelligence

Damasio, Antonio R.

The **feeling** of what happens; body and emotion in the making of consciousness. Harcourt Brace & Co. 1999 386p il $28; pa $15 **153**
1. Emotions 2. Consciousness
ISBN 0-15-100369-6; 0-15-601075-5 pa

LC 99-26357

The author contends "that consciousness arises from our ability to map relations between the self and others through our emotions. This bold attempt to mend the classical breach between emotion and reason is all the more compelling for its poetic expression." Publ Wkly

Includes bibliographical references

Eagleman, David

Incognito; the brains behind the mind. Pantheon 2011 290p il $26.95 **153**
1. Brain 2. Subconsciousness
ISBN 978-0-307-37733-3

LC 2010053184

"Eagleman's main theme is that what one calls 'me,' the conscious mind, is only the tip of the iceberg, and that most of the interesting and important things the brain does are inaccessible to the brain's 'owner.' . . . What Eagleman does is explain the idea to the neophyte through discussion of dozens of fascinating, engaging examples. . . . Eagleman's prose is vivid and, more important, accessible." Choice

Includes bibliographical references

Edelman, Shimon

★ The **happiness** of pursuit; what neuroscience can teach us about the good life. Shimon Edelman. Basic Books 2012 x, 237 p.p **153**
1. Happiness 2. Perception 3. Psychology 4. Thought and thinking 5. Ego 6. Self 7. Thinking 8. Cognition 9. Mind-Body Relations, Metaphysical
ISBN 0465022243; 9780465022243

LC 2011039326

This book by psychologist Shimon Edelman "offers a fundamental understanding of pleasure and joy via the brain. Using the concept of the mind as a computing device, he unpacks how the human brain is highly active, involved in patterned networks, and constantly learning from experience. As our brains predict the future through pursuit of experience, we are rewarded both in real time and in the long run. Essentially, as Edelman discovers, it's the journey, rather than the destination, that matters." (Publisher's note)

Includes bibliographical references and index.

Hallinan, Joseph T.

Why we make mistakes; how we look without seeing, forget things in seconds, and are all pretty sure we are way above average. Broadway Books 2009 283p $24.95 **153**
1. Errors 2. Failure (Psychology)
ISBN 978-0-7679-2805-2; 0-7679-2805-9

LC 2008-30818

"Hallinan examines 13 pitfalls that make us vulnerable to mistakes: 'we look but don't always see,' 'we like things tidy' and 'we don't constrain ourselves' among them. Each chapter takes on a different drawback, packing in an impressive range of intriguing and practical real-world examples. . . . He also looks at the serious consequences of multitasking and data overload on what is at best a two or three-track mind." Publ Wkly

Includes bibliographical references

Hofstadter, Douglas R.

I am a strange loop. Basic Books 2007 412p il $26.95 **153**
1. Self 2. Consciousness
ISBN 978-0-465-03078-1; 0-465-03078-5

The author's model of self is neither "spiritual—he's not a religious man—nor is it locked into the cold neurological materialism of cellular mechanics. . . . [The book] scales some lofty conceptual heights, but it remains very personal, and it's deeply colored by the facts of Hofstadter's later life." Time

Includes bibliographical references

Kandel, Eric R.

★ **In** search of memory; the emergence of a new science of mind. W. W. Norton & Company 2006 510p il $29.95   **153**

1. Memory 2. Nervous system 3. Neuroscientists 4. College teachers 5. Nobel laureates for physiology or medicine

ISBN 0-393-05863-8; 978-0-393-05863-5

LC 2005-28565

The author "recounts his own revolutionary research in establishing the molecular chemistry of short-term memory and the cellular dynamics of long-term memory, highlighting particularly the potential of his findings for the treatment of Alzheimer's and other mental disorders. But even as he outlines the biomechanics of memory, Kandel shares his personal reminiscences of the years during which he unraveled those mysteries. . . . An autobiography of exceptional substance." Booklist

Includes bibliographical references

Lewis, Michael

★ The **Undoing** Project; A Friendship That Changed Our Minds. by Michael Lewis. W W Norton & Co Inc 2016 320 p. $28.95   **153**

1. Cognitive therapy 2. Cognitive psychology

ISBN 0393254593; 9780393254594

This book, by Michael Lewis, tells "how a Nobel Prize–winning theory of the mind altered our perception of reality. . . . Israeli psychologists Daniel Kahneman and Amos Tversky wrote a series of . . . studies undoing our assumptions about the decision-making process. . . . Their work created the field of behavioral economics, revolutionized Big Data studies, advanced evidence-based medicine, [and] led to a new approach to government regulation." (Publisher's note)

Medina, John, 1956-

Brain rules; 12 principles for surviving and thriving at work, home, and school. John Medina. 2nd ed. Pear Press 2014 288 p. illustrations pbk $15.95   **153**

1. Brain 2. Perception 3. Senses and sensation 4. Human information processing

ISBN 9780983263371

"Dr. John Medina, a molecular biologist, shares his lifelong interest in how the brain sciences might influence the way we teach our children and the way we work. In each chapter, he describes a brain rule--what scientists know for sure about how our brains work--and then offers transformative ideas for our daily lives." Publisher's note

Pinker, Steven

How the mind works. Norton 1997 660p il hardcover o.p. pa $18.95   **153**

1. Brain 2. Emotions 3. Evolution 4. Intellect 5. Reasoning 6. Psychology 7. Natural selection

ISBN 978-0-393-33477-7 pa

LC 97-1855

Pinker "has a gift for making enormously complicated mechanisms—and human foibles—accessible." Publ Wkly

Includes bibliographical references

Rosenbaum, David A., 1952-

It's a jungle in there; how competition and cooperation in the brain shape the mind. David A. Rosenbaum. Oxford University Press 2014 272 p. ill. $29.95   **153**

1. Cognitive psychology 2. Competition (Psychology) 3. Brain 4. Neuropsychology

ISBN 0199829772; 9780199829774

LC 2013028959

In this book, author David A. Rosenbaum "argues that the overarching theory of biology, Darwin's theory, should be the overarching theory of cognitive psychology, the science of mental functioning. He explores this new and intriguing idea by showing how neural elements compete and cooperate in a kind of inner jungle, where only the fittest survive. Competition within your brain does as much to shape who you are as the physical and figurative competition you face externally." (Publisher's note)

"Tying the vicissitudes of psychology to any one principle, even loosely, is bold, but Rosenbaum's careful prose will ignite thoughtful debate." Pub Wkly

Includes bibliographical references and index

Sagan, Carl

The **dragons** of Eden; speculations on the evolution of human intelligence. Random House 1977 263p il hardcover o.p. pa $7.50   **153**

1. Brain 2. Genetics 3. Intellect

ISBN 0-345-34629-7 pa

LC 76-53472

In this study of human intellect "Sagan is principally preoccupied with the neocortex, with its left hemisphere, responsible for language and logic, a right hemisphere in charge of intuition and spatial dimension, and a corpus callosum that mediates and synthesizes the two." Atl Mon

Includes bibliographical references

Schulz, Kathryn

Being wrong; adventures in the margin of error. Ecco 2010 405p il $26.99; pa $20.99   **153**

1. Errors 2. Decision making 3. Error 4. Expertise 5. Fallibility 6. Errors -- Psychological aspects

ISBN 0-06-117604-4; 0-06-199793-5 pa; 978-0-06-117604-3; 978-0-06-199793-8 pa

Schulz explores"why we find it so gratifying to be right and so maddening to be mistaken, and how this attitude toward error corrodes relationships—whether between family members, colleagues, neighbors, or nations. Along the way, she takes us on a . . . tour of human fallibility, from wrongful convictions to no-fault divorce; medical mistakes to misadventures at sea; failed prophecies to false memories; 'I told you so!' to 'Mistakes were made.' Drawing on thinkers such as Augustine, Darwin, Freud, Gertrude Stein, Alan Greenspan, and Groucho Marx, she proposes a new way of looking at wrongness. In this view, error is both a given and a gift—one that can transform our worldviews, our relationships, and ourselves." (Publisher's note) Index.

The author discusses "how we make mistakes, how we behave when we find we have been wrong, and how our errors change us. . . . Schulz writes with such lucidity and wit that her philosophical enquiry becomes a page-turner." Publ Wkly

Includes bibliographical references

153.1 Memory and learning

Carey, Benedict

How we learn; the surprising truth about when, where, and why it happens. Benedict Carey. Random House 2014 338 p. illustrations $27 **153.1**
1. Psychology of learning 2. Learning 3. Learning, Psychology of
ISBN 0812993888; 9780812993882
LC 2013049850

In this book, "science reporter Benedict Carey sifts through decades of education research and landmark studies to uncover the truth about how our brains absorb and retain information. What he discovers is that, from the moment we are born, we are all learning quickly, efficiently, and automatically; but in our zeal to systematize the process we have ignored valuable, naturally enjoyable learning tools like forgetting, sleeping, and daydreaming." (Publisher's note)

"A totally fascinating look at learning, with helpful insights for students and any reader interested in learning everything from a new language to flying to playing chess." Booklist

Foer, Joshua

Moonwalking with Einstein; the art and science of remembering everything. Penguin Press 2011 307p $26.95 **153.1**
1. Memory 2. Memory disorders -- Treatment
ISBN 978-1-59420-229-2
LC 2010-30265

"Mr. Foer writes in these pages with fresh enthusiasm. His narrative is smart and funny and . . . it's informed by a humanism that enables its author to place the mysteries of the brain within a larger philosophical and cultural context." N Y Times (Late N Y Ed)

Includes bibliographical references

Fogler, Janet

Improving your memory; how to remember what you're starting to forget. Janet Fogler and Lynn Stern. Johns Hopkins University Press 2014 168 p. (pbk. : alk. paper) $18.95 **153.1**
1. Memory 2. Mnemonics 3. Memory in old age 4. Memory -- Age factors
ISBN 1421415704; 9781421415703
LC 2014008681

This book, by Janet Fogler and Lynn Stern, "have completely updated their friendly and usable guide to memory improvement techniques. Recognizing that people worry something is wrong with them when they forget things, Fogler and Stern suggest that the antidote to worry is taking positive actions to help us remember what we want to remember." (Publisher's note)

Goldman, Bob

Brain fitness; anti-aging strategies for achieving super mind power. {by} Robert M. Goldman with Ronald Klatz and Lisa Berger. Doubleday 1999 333p il hardcover o.p. pa $14.95 **153.1**
1. Aging 2. Sleep 3. Memory 4. Stress (Physiology)
ISBN 0-385-48869-6 pa
LC 98-18785

This is an "exploration of techniques—mental workouts, memory training, physical exercises, and nutrition and dietary supplements—that readers can use to maximize their concentration, memory, imagination, energy, intelligence, and creativity while decreasing fatigue and stress and preventing Alzheimer's disease and other brain diseases." Libr J

Includes bibliographical references

Malone, Michael S.

The guardian of all things; the epic story of human memory. Michael S. Malone. St. Martin's Press 2012 xii, 290 p.p (hardcover) $25.99 **153.1**
1. Memory 2. Civilization 3. Technology and civilization 4. Civilization -- History
ISBN 0312620314; 9780312620318; 9781250014924
LC 2012010246

This book by Michael S. Malone is an "exploration of the history of memory and human civilization. . . . [The book] is a sweeping scientific history that takes us on a 10,000-year-old journey replete with incredible ideas, inventions, and transformations. From cave drawings to oral histories to libraries to the internet, 'The Guardian of All Things' is the history of how humans have relentlessly pursued new ways to preserve and manage memory, both within the human brain and as a series of inventions external to it." (Publisher's note)

Includes bibliographical references and index.

Pink, Daniel H.

Drive; the surprising truth about what motivates us. Daniel H. Pink. Riverhead Books, a member of Penguin Group (USA) 2009 xii, 242 p.p illustrations $26.95 **153.1**
1. Psychology 2. Motivation (Psychology)
ISBN 1594488843; 9781594488849
LC 2009040651

Author Daniel H. Pink "exposes the mismatch between what science knows and what business does--and how that affects every aspect of our lives. He demonstrates that while the old-fashioned carrot-and-stick approach worked successfully in the 20th century, it's precisely the wrong way to motivate people for today's challenges." (Publisher's note)

"The author presents an integral addition to a growing body of literature that argues for a radical shift in how businesses operate in a world dominated by technology, and soon to be led by a generation that doesn't necessarily equate money with happiness.Important reading for frustrated but open-minded business leaders struggling to connect with stressed-out workers." Kirkus

Includes bibliographical references (p. [221]-229) and index

Schacter, Daniel L.

✓ **Searching** for memory; the brain, the mind, and the past. Basic Bks. 1996 398p il hardcover o.p. pa $17.50   **153.1**
   1. Brain 2. Memory
   ISBN 0-465-07552-5 pa

                    LC 96-19521

"This is an excellent book on an important topic: it is exceptionally well written; its examples of defects in memory are fascinating, as are the theories based on them; and its arguments are illustrated with opposite pictures, reproduced from works by many modern artists, and passages from novels." N Y Times Book Rev

   Includes bibliographical references

✓ The **seven** sins of memory; how the mind forgets and remembers. Houghton Mifflin 2001 272p il hardcover o.p.   **153.1**
   1. Memory 2. Memory disorders 3. Recollection (Psychology)
   ISBN 0-618-04019-6; 0-618-21919-6 pa

                    LC 00-53885

Schacter discusses "the 'different ways in which memory can get us into trouble.' . . . We forget things over time (transience). We often forget where we put our house keys because we were preoccupied with something else (absent-mindedness). We can't remember someone's name (blocking). We mistake an idealized version of our past for a real recollection (misattribution) or claim an 'implanted' memory as our own when it has been suggested by someone else (suggestibility). Our memories are often . . . influenced by our current beliefs (bias). In some cases, we obsessively remember traumatic or painful events that we'd much rather forget (persistence)." (N Y Times Book Rev) Index.

   The author discusses "the curious processes of memory by classifying its malfunctions into seven categories: transience, absent-mindedness, blocking, misattribution, suggestibility, bias, and persistence. Schacter illustrates each of these 'sins' with examples of routine misfortunes common to all." Libr J

   Includes bibliographical references

153.3   Imagination, imagery, creativity

Bloomston, Carrie

The **little** spark; 30 ways to ignite your creativity. Carrie Bloomston. Stash Books 2014 128 p, illustrations (soft cover) $19.95   **153.3**
   1. Creative ability 2. Creation (Literary, artistic, etc.) 3. Inspiration
   ISBN 1607059606; 9781607059608

                    LC 2014009342

This book, by Carrie Bloomston, explores and seeks to foster creativity. "Do you look at yourself now and wonder if the spark has gone out? Ignite that inner fire with the 30 engaging exercises, fun activities, inspirational images, and motivating ideas in this book. Learn what your Little Spark of creative passion looks like, how to capture it, and how to make room for it in your life." (Publisher's note)

   "Bloomston also offers her own personal anecdotes, as well as stories and tips from numerous others; the extensive list of contributors includes designers, artists and business owners.A sparkling blueprint for stimulating creativity." Kirkus

Csikszentmihalyi, Mihaly

✓ **Creativity**; flow and the psychology of discovery and invention. HarperCollins Pubs. 1996 456p hardcover o.p. pa $15   **153.3**
   1. Creative ability 2. Creative thinking
   ISBN 0-06-092820-4 pa

                    LC 96-4116

"Utilizing the interviews garnered from 91 respondents (ranging from philosopher Mortimer Adler to biologist Edward O. Wilson to politician Eugene McCarthy), the author . . . demonstrates the processes that these acknowledged creative thinkers and doers go through and the characteristics that make them stand out. . . . Csikszentmihalyi also deals with creativity and aging and ways to enhance one's own personal creativity." Libr J

   Includes bibliographical references

Gawain, Shakti

✓ ★ **Creative** visualization; use the power of your imagination to create what you want in your life. 30th anniversary ed.; Nataraj Pub./New World Library 2008 175p $25; pa $12.95   **153.3**
   1. Imagination 2. Self-realization
   ISBN 978-1-577-31636-7; 1-577-31636-3; 978-1-577-31229-1 pa; 1-577-31229-5 pa

                    LC 2008-14400

   First published 1978 by Whatever Pub.

   "The author asserts that people can achieve an ideal existence simply through mental visualization." Libr J

   Includes bibliographical references

Gilbert, Elizabeth, 1969-

★ **Big** magic; creative living beyond fear. Elizabeth Gilbert. Riverhead Books 2015 288 p. (hardback) $24.95   **153.3**
   1. Conduct of life 2. Creation (Literary, artistic, etc.) 3. Courage 4. Confidence 5. Inspiration 6. Creative ability 7. Magical thinking
   ISBN 9781594634710

                    LC 2015010717

In this book, by Elizabeth Gilbert, "digs deep into her own generative process to share her wisdom and unique perspective about creativity. With profound empathy and radiant generosity, she offers potent insights into the mysterious nature of inspiration. She asks us to embrace our curiosity and let go of needless suffering." (Publisher's note)

   "Gilbert serves as an enthusiastic coach for readers who want more out of life. Highly recommended." Library Journal

Grant, Adam

Originals; how non-conformists move the world. Grant Adam; foreword by Sheryl Sandberg. Penguin Group USA 2016 336 p. illustrations (hardback) $27   **153.3**
   1. Entrepreneurship 2. Creative thinking 3.

Organizational change
ISBN 9780525429562; 0525429565

LC 2015041287

This book, by Grant Adam, "addresses the challenge of improving the world, but now from the perspective of becoming original: choosing to champion novel ideas and values that go against the grain, battle conformity, and buck outdated traditions. How can we originate new ideas, policies, and practices without risking it all?" (Publisher's note)

"No matter whether the reader is an original or a wannabe, this book is enjoyable and full of useful information." LJ

May, Rollo
The **courage** to create. Norton 1975 143p hardcover o.p. pa $11.95   **153.3**
     1. Courage 2. Consciousness 3. Creative ability
     ISBN 0-393-31106-6 pa
     The author argues that creativity is an act of encounter and draws on examples from literature, art, and psychoanalysis
     Includes bibliographical references

153.35   Creativity

Harford, Tim
Messy; The Power of Disorder to Transform Our Lives. Tim Harford. Penguin Group USA 2016 304 p. (hardcover) $28; (ebook) $65   **153.35**
     1. Chaos (Science) 2. Creative ability
     ISBN 9781594634796; 9780698408906; 1594634793

LC 2016026363

This book by Tim Harford "celebrates the benefits that messiness has in our lives: why it's important, why we resist it, and why we should embrace it instead. Using research from neuroscience, psychology, social science, as well as captivating examples of real people doing extraordinary things, Harford explains that the human qualities we value –creativity, responsiveness, resilience–are integral to the disorder, confusion, and disarray that produce them." (Publisher's note)

"Weaving together lessons from history, art, technology, and social and scientific research, Harford's theories have many potential benefits for individuals and businesses seeking to remain on the creative cutting edge, as well as profound implications for society." Pub Wkly

Includes bibliographical references and index.

153.4   Thought, thinking, reasoning, intuition, value, judgment

Berdik, Chris
Mind over mind; the surprising power of placebos, expectations, and assumptions. Chris Berdik. Current Hardcover 2012 272 p. (hardback) $26.95   **153.4**
     1. Perception 2. Mind and body 3. Expectation (Psychology) 4. Cognitive psychology 5. Thought and thinking
     ISBN 1591845092; 9781591845096

LC 2012019144

This book, by Chris Berdik, "offers a . . . look at the frontiers of expectations research, revealing how our brains work in the future tense and how our assumptions . . . bend reality. We learn how placebo calories can fill us up, . . . how fake surgery can sometimes work better than real surgery, and how imaginary power can be corrupting. . . . Their influence seems based on illusion, even trickery, but they can create their own reality, for good or for ill." (Publisher's note)

Includes bibliographical references and index

Brotherton, Rob
Suspicious Minds; Why We Believe Conspiracy Theories. by Rob Brotherton. St. Martin's Press 2015 304 p. illustrations $27   **153.4**
     1. Psychology 2. Conspiracies
     ISBN 1472915615; 9781472915610

This book, by Rob Brotherton, focuses on "the psychology of believing in conspiracy theories. . . . We instinctively see events in the world in terms of human motives and intentions, leading us to discount the role of chance and unintended consequences, and we look for some hidden hand behind catastrophic events. These psychological quirks can lead us to suspect a conspiracy where none exists." (Publisher's note)

"Clearly written and with liberal use of humor and numerous examples from scholarly research, this title provides a valuable look at why conspiracy theories abound and why we should continually assess our thinking." Library Journal

Dobelli, Rolf
The **art** of thinking clearly; Rolf Dobelli; translated by Nicky Griffin. HarperBusiness 2013 384 p. (hardcover) $25.99   **153.4**
     1. Decision making 2. Thought and thinking 3. Cognition 4. Reasoning (Psychology) 5. Errors -- Psychological aspects
     ISBN 0062219707; 9780062219688

LC 2013003934

This book, by Rolf Dobelli, is a "look at human psychology and reasoning--essential reading for anyone who wants to avoid 'cognitive errors' and make better choices in all aspects of their lives. . . . [It offers] examples of cognitive biases, simple errors we all make in our day-to-day thinking. But by knowing what they are and how to spot them, we can avoid them and make better decisions." (Publisher's note)

Gladwell, Malcolm
Blink: the power of thinking without thinking. Little, Brown and Co 2005 277p il $25.95   **153.4**
     1. Intuition 2. Decision making
     ISBN 0-316-17232-4

LC 2004-13916

Gladwell "has a dazzling ability to find commonality in disparate fields of study. . . . Each case study is satisfying, and Gladwell imparts his own evident pleasure in delving into a wide range of fields and seeking an underlying truth." Publ Wkly

Includes bibliographical references

Herbert, Wray

On second thought; outsmarting your mind's hard-wired habits. Crown Publishers 2010 289p $25 **153.4**

1. Thought and thinking

ISBN 0-307-46163-7; 978-0-307-46163-6

LC 2010-03073

"The brain is like a dual processor, [Herbert] argues—one part is logical, deliberate, and cautious, while the other is much older and primitive. The latter is the heuristic brain—fast, impressionistic, and sometimes irrational. After years of evolution, the brain has become hardwired with mental shortcuts that help us quickly navigate our daily lives. However, they can also distort our thinking and lead to poor decision making. . . . Heuristics are neither good nor bad—the trick, Herbert says, is in recognizing when to question an instant response." Libr J

Kahneman, Daniel, 1934-

Thinking, fast and slow; Daniel Kahneman. Farrar, Straus and Giroux 2011 499p. ill. **153.4**

1. Intuition 2. Reasoning 3. Decision making 4. Thought and thinking

ISBN 0374275637; 9780374275631

LC 2011027143

In this book, author Daniel Kahneman examines "the mind and explains the two systems that drive the way we think. System 1 is fast, intuitive, and emotional; System 2 is slower, more deliberative, and more logical. Kahneman exposes the . . . capabilities--and also the faults and biases--of fast thinking, and reveals the pervasive influence of intuitive impressions on our thoughts and behavior." (Publisher's note)

Includes bibliographical references (p. 447-481) and index.

Konnikova, Maria, 1987-

Mastermind; how to think like Sherlock Holmes. Maria Konnikova. Viking Adult 2013 273 p. (hardback) $26.95 **153.4**

1. Perception 2. Logic 3. Reasoning

ISBN 0670026573; 9780670026579

LC 2012035455

In this book, psychologist Maria Konnikova "examines [fictional character Sherlock] Holmes's powers of perception and problem solving through the lens of her discipline. The book is part literary analysis and part self-help guide, teaching readers how to sharpen the ways they observe the world, store and retrieve memories, and make decisions." (Scientific American)

Levitin, Daniel J.

★ A field guide to lies; critical thinking in the information age. Daniel J. Levitin. Dutton 2016 304 p. (hardcover) $28 **153.4**

1. Critical thinking 2. Information science 3. Truthfulness and falsehood 4. Reasoning 5. Fallacies (Logic)

ISBN 9780525955221; 0525955224

LC 2016007356

This book, by Daniel J. Levitin, asks "how do we distinguish misinformation, pseudo-facts, distortions, and out-right lies from reliable information? Levitin groups his field guide into two categories--statistical information and faulty arguments--ultimately showing how science is the bedrock of critical thinking." (Publisher's note)

"Levitin (The Organized Mind) equips readers with tools to combat misinformation—bad data, false facts, distortions, and their ilk—in this useful primer on the importance of critical thinking in daily life. . . . In all three sections Levitin explores material that has often been written about elsewhere, but the book still serves its purpose as a valuable primer on critical thinking that convincingly illustrates the prevalence of misinformation in everyday life." PW

Includes bibliographical references and index

Manage your day-to-day; build your routine, find your focus, and sharpen your creative mind. by Jocelyn K. Glei. Amazon Pub 2013 253 p. $14.95 **153.4**

1. Work ethic 2. Work-life balance

ISBN 1477800670; 9781477800676

This book, by Jocelyn K. Glei, "will give you a toolkit for tackling the new challenges of a 24/7, always-on workplace. Featuring contributions from: Dan Ariely, Leo Babauta, Scott Belsky, Lori Deschene, Aaron Dignan, Erin Rooney Doland, Seth Godin, Todd Henry, Christian Jarrett, Scott McDowell, Mark McGuinness, Cal Newport, Steven Pressfield, Gretchen Rubin, Stefan Sagmeister, Elizabeth G. Saunders, Tony Schwartz, Tiffany Shlain, Linda Stone, and James Victore." (Publisher's note)

Mudd, Philip

The **Head** Game; A Spy's Guide to High-stakes Risk Management and Decision Making. by Philip Mudd. W W Norton & Co Inc 2015 288 p. $26.95 **153.4**

1. Management 2. Decision making

ISBN 0871407884; 9780871407887

LC 2015006002

This book, by Philip Mudd, "gives us the definitive guidebook for how to approach complex decisions today. Filled with logical yet counterintuitive answers to ordinary and extraordinary problems . . . Mudd's 'HEAD' (High Efficiency Analytic Decision-making) methodology provides readers with a battle-tested set of guiding principles that promise to bring order to even the most chaotic problems, all in five practical steps." (Publisher's note)

"How do you make decisions when the stakes are really, really high? The former deputy director of the CIA's Counterterrorist Center and the FBI's National Security Branch, currently director of enterprise risk at SouthernSun asset management, should know." LJ

Nisbett, Richard E.

Mindware; tools for smart thinking. Richard E. Nisbett. Farrar, Straus & Giroux 2015 336 p. illustrations (hardcover) $27 **153.4**

1. Problem solving 2. Critical thinking 3. Thought and thinking 4. Reasoning

ISBN 0374112673; 9780374112677

LC 2015005007

In this book, author Richard E. Nisbett explores how "scientific and philosophical concepts can change the way we solve problems by helping us to think more effectively about our behavior and our world. . . . Nisbett has made a . . . career of studying and teaching . . . the law of large numbers, statistical regression, cost-benefit analysis, sunk costs and opportunity costs, and causation and correlation, probing the best methods for teaching others how to use them effectively in their daily lives." (Publisher's note)

"Nisbett's goal is to help us look at problems and choices in new ways, to attack them from new analytic angles, to find clarity out of chaos. No psychological self-help book succeeds completely, but this one comes close." Booklist

Includes bibliographical references and index

Shermer, Michael

The **believing** brain; from ghosts and gods to politics and conspiracies--how we construct beliefs and reinforce them as truths. Times Books 2011 385p il $28 **153.4**
1. Belief and doubt 2. Theory of knowledge 3. Knowledge, Theory of 4. Cognitive neuroscience
ISBN 9780805091250; 0805091254

LC 2010-30706

This book discusses the science of the human brain in relation to belief formation. "[T]he book is clearly less about the examples than about the theory Shermer uses to explain them all. . . . Shermer's theory looks like this: The human mind is inherently a 'belief engine'; we perceive endless bits of information, and we must posit beliefs as ways of organizing and making sense of them. . . . Having found a possible explanation, we then seek confirming evidence and deepenings of the patterns and agents we believe we have discerned. The result, Shermer claims, is that we live much of the time in 'belief-dependent realism,' which is to say that our beliefs are shaping what we see in the world, rather than the world shaping our beliefs. . . . Shermer also believes in a dividing line between benign or helpful beliefs and malignant ones (like religion)." (Commonweal)

"A timely, reasoned reflection on the nature of belief, offering a levelheaded corrective to the divisiveness of extreme partisanship." Kirkus

Includes bibliographical references and index.

Trivers, Robert

The **folly** of fools; the logic of deceit and self-deception in human life. Robert Trivers. Basic Books 2011 xvi, 397 p.p $28 **153.4**
1. Deception 2. Evolution 3. Psychology 4. Self-deception 5. Deception -- Social aspects 6. Deception -- Psychological aspects
ISBN 0465027555; 9780465027552; 9780465028054

LC 2011028453

The author "argues that self-deception evolved in the service of deceit--the better to fool others. We do it for biological reasons--in order to help us survive and procreate. From viruses mimicking host behavior to humans misremembering (sometimes intentionally) the details of a quarrel, science has proven that the deceptive one can always outwit the masses. But we undertake this deception at our own peril." (Publisher's note)

Includes bibliographical references (p. 355-383) and index

Watts, Duncan J.

Everything is obvious; once you know the answer. Crown Business 2011 335p il $26 **153.4**
1. Reasoning 2. Thought and thinking 3. Common sense
ISBN 978-0-385-53168-9; 0-385-53168-0

LC 2010031550

The author posits "that common sense is a shockingly unreliable guide to truth and yet we rely on it virtually to the exclusion of other methods of reasoning. Mr. Watts, a former sociology professor and physicist who is now a researcher for Yahoo, has written a fascinating book that ranges through psychology, economics, marketing and the science of social networks. He is especially interested in the mistakes we make when we reason about how people influence one another—such as our tendency to think of groups in terms of representative or important members rather than as whole entities. . . . The enterprise of prediction-making is another casualty of the limits of common sense. Mr. Watts suggests that the entire field of business strategy suffers from a delusion that the future can be forecast with enough numerical precision to enable accurate planning. One solution he endorses is a systematic process of imagining detailed alternative narratives of the future." Wall Street J

Includes bibliographical references

153.6 Communication

McMillan, Ron

Crucial conversations; tools for talking when stakes are high. Kerry Patterson, Joseph Grenny, Ron McMillan, and Al Switzler. McGraw-Hill 2011 244 p. $32 **153.6**
1. Communication 2. Interpersonal relations 3. Interpersonal communication
ISBN 0071775307; 9780071775304

LC 20021129

2nd edition.

This book, by Kerry Patterson, Joseph Grenny, Ron McMillan, and Al Switzler, "exploded onto the scene ten years ago and revolutionized the way people communicate when stakes are high, opinions vary, and emotions run strong. . . . Now, the authors have revised their bestselling classic to provide even more ways to help you take the lead in any tough conversation." (Publisher's note)

"Being an efficient advocate for the self and others depends on the ability to participate effectively in difficult and critical discussions. Readers will appreciate how Patterson's techniques apply both to interpersonal relationships and when acting in the interests of another." LJ

Includes bibliographical references and index

Pease, Allan

The **definitive** book of body language; [by] Allan & Barbara Pease. Bantam Books 2006 386p il $23 **153.6**
1. Nonverbal communication
ISBN 0-553-80472-3; 978-0-553-80472-0

LC 2006-42657

"The book is amply and wittily illustrated with celebrity photographs. . . . This is a fascinating book." N Y Times Book Rev

Includes bibliographical references

153.7 Perceptual processes

Beilock, Sian

How the body knows its mind; the unseen influence of your physical environment on your thoughts and feelings. Sian Beilock. Atria Books 2015 288 p. (hardback) $26   **153.7**
1. Mind and body 2. Thought and thinking
ISBN 1451626681; 9781451626681; 9781451626698
LC 2014007653

Author Sian Beilock offers a "new understanding of the mind-body connection and its profound impact on everything from advertising to romance. From the tricks used by advertisers to the ways body language can improve your memory, Beilock explains a wealth of fascinating interconnections between mind and body and how mastering them can make us happier, safer, and more successful." (Publisher's note)

"A must-read for those who want to understand and embrace a greater connection between body and brain." LJ

Includes bibliographical references and index

Chabris, Christopher

The **invisible** gorilla; and other ways our intuitions deceive us. [by] Christopher Chabris and Daniel Simons. Crown 2010 306p $27; pa $14 **153.7**
1. Memory 2. Perception 3. Thought and thinking
ISBN 978-0-307-45965-7; 0-307-45965-9; 978-0-307-45966-4 pa; 0-307-45966-7 pa
LC 2009-45325

The authors "won a 2004 Ig Nobel Prize for their widely reported 'gorilla experiment,' which showed that when people focus on one thing, it's easy to overlook other things—even a woman in a gorilla suit. . . . [In this book,] they explore this habit of 'inattentional blindness' and other common ways in which we distort our perception of reality. Their readable book offers surprising insights into just how clueless we are about how our minds work and how we experience the world." Kirkus

Includes bibliographical references

Ellard, Colin

★ **You** are here; why we can find our way to the moon but get lost in the mall. Doubleday 2009 328p il map $25   **153.7**
1. Direction sense 2. Space perception
ISBN 978-0-385-52806-1; 0-385-52806-X
LC 2009-07822

Ellard argues that in the modern age the human sense of navigation and direction has diminished greatly.

"If you're looking for an eye-opening, if somewhat embarrassing, book to help understand why you keep getting lost when you know you shouldn't and what you can do about it well, here you are." Booklist

Includes bibliographical references

Goleman, Daniel

Focus; the hidden driver of excellence. Daniel Goleman. Harper 2013 320 p. $28.99   **153.7**
1. Attention 2. Self-control 3. Thought and thinking
ISBN 0062114867; 9780062114860
LC 2013007290

Author Daniel Goleman's book "delves into the science of attention in all its varieties, presenting a long overdue discussion of this little-noticed and under-rated mental asset. In an era of unstoppable distractions, Goleman persuasively argues that now more than ever we must learn to sharpen focus if we are to survive in a complex world." (Publisher's note)

Greenspan, Stanley I.

The **first** idea; how symbols, language, and intelligence evolved from our early primate ancestors to modern humans. [by] Stanley I. Greenspan, Stuart G. Shanker. 1st Da Capo Press ed; Da Capo Press 2004 504p $25   **153.7**
1. Evolution 2. Theory of knowledge
ISBN 0-7382-0680-6
LC 2004-10658

"This book should appeal most to readers working in psychology and child development, but its revolutionary ideas no doubt will lead to lively and well-publicized debates." Publ Wkly

Includes bibliographical references

Parr, Ben

Captivology; the science of capturing people's attention. Ben Parr. HarperOne 2015 256 p. (hardback) $27.99   **153.7**
1. Attention 2. Marketing
ISBN 0062324195; 9780062324191
LC 2014035615

This book, by Ben Parr, "presents a new understanding of attention--how it works, why it matters, and how we leverage psychological triggers to draw and retain attention for our passions, projects, and ideas. Parr combines the latest research on attention with interviews with more than fifty scientists and visionaries . . . who have successfully brought their ideas, projects, companies, and products to the forefront of cultural consciousness." (Publisher's note)

Zimbardo, Philip G.

The **time** paradox; the new psychology of time that will change your life. [by] Philip Zimbardo and John Boyd. Free Press 2008 358p il $27 **153.7**
1. Time perception
ISBN 978-1-4165-4198-1; 1-4165-4198-5
LC 2008-2149

This is an "investigation of how attitudes toward time affect every aspect of human life. The authors help readers determine their personal time zone before revealing how to 'reclaim yesterday, enjoy today, and master tomorrow.' Balance never seemed so attainable." Libr J

Includes bibliographical references

153.8 Will (Volition)

Akst, Daniel

We have met the enemy; self-control in an age of excess. Penguin Press 2011 303p $26.95   **153.8**

1. Self-control 2. Supply and demand
ISBN 978-1-59420-281-0

LC 2010-28525

"Akst combines the disciplines of history, philosophy, psychology, economics, and literature in examining this phenomenon and inspires readers to view self-control in a positive light. Essential for all people concerned with their own overindulgences and with the future of society in general." Libr J

Includes bibliographical references

Cialdini, Robert B.

★ **Influence**: the psychology of persuasion; Rev. ed.; 1st Collins business essentials ed; Collins 2007 320p il pa $17.95   **153.8**

1. Persuasion (Psychology)
ISBN 0-06-124189-X; 978-0-06-124189-5
First published 1984

The author "explains the psychology of why people say 'yes'—and how to apply these understandings." Publisher's note

Includes bibliographical references

Dennett, Daniel Clement

Freedom evolves; {by} Daniel C. Dennett. Viking 2003 347p il $24.95; pa $17   **153.8**

1. Decision making 2. Free will and determinism
ISBN 0-670-03186-0; 0-14-200384-0 pa

LC 2002-28085

"Drawing on evolutionary biology, neuroscience, economic game theory, philosophy and Richard Dawkins's meme, the author argues that there is indeed such a thing as free will, but it 'is not a preexisting feature of our existence, like the law of gravity.' . . . This book comprises a kind of toolbox of intellectual exercises favoring cultural evolution, the idea that culture, morality and freedom are as much a result of evolution by natural selection as our physical and genetic attributes. Yet genetic determinism, he argues, does not imply inevitability, as his critics may claim, nor does it cancel out the soul. . . . Dennett clearly relishes pushing other scientists' buttons. Though natural selection itself is still a subject of controversy, the author . . . most certainly is in the vanguard of the philosophy of science." Publ Wkly

Includes bibliographical references

Dutton, Kevin

Split-second persuasion; the ancient art and new science of changing minds. Houghton Mifflin Harcourt 2011 296p il $26   **153.8**

1. Persuasion (Psychology)
ISBN 978-0-15-101279-4

LC 2010-5739

First published 2010 in the United Kingdom

"This is a well-researched, wide-ranging treatise on the psychology of persuasion. The first section reviews research from an impressive variety of disciplines, from neuroscience to the biological and social sciences. The second sec-

tion focuses on the author's main theme—split-second persuasion—a powerful 'superstrain' of persuasion that occurs quickly. Written for a less-experienced audience, the book is clear and nontechnical." Choice

Includes bibliographical references

Iyengar, Sheena

The **art** of choosing. Twelve 2010 329p il $25.99   **153.8**

1. Decision making 2. Choice (Psychology)
ISBN 978-0-446-50410-2; 0-446-50410-6

LC 2009-37664

"In 'The Art of Choosing,' a broad and fascinating survey of current research on the subject, Iyengar stitches together personal anecdotes, examples from popular culture, and scientific evidence to explain the complex calculus that goes into our everyday choices, from picking our favorite soda to choosing our medical insurance. She also writes about the ways in which her blindness — Iyengar lost her sight as a teenager — has given her a unique perspective on the subject." Salon

Lehrer, Jonah

How we decide. Houghton Mifflin Harcourt 2009 302p $25   **153.8**

1. Decision making
ISBN 978-0-618-62011-1; 0-618-62011-7

LC 2008036769

"Lehrer is a delight to read, and this is a fascinating book that will help everyone better understand themselves and their decision making." Publ Wkly

Includes bibliographical references

Levine, Robert

The **power** of persuasion; how we're bought and sold. Wiley 2003 278p hardcover o.p. pa $14.95   **153.8**

1. Interpersonal relations 2. Persuasion (Psychology)
ISBN 0-471-26634-5; 0-471-76317-9 pa

LC 2002-9952

The author "opens by demonstrating that all of us . . . can be persuaded under the right circumstances. He goes on to study financial manipulation and the use of the sense of obligation . . . and then proceeds to a nuts-and-bolts analysis of salesmanship by describing what he learned and did (and had done to him) as an automobile salesman. . . . Inevitably, he moves to cults, the Moonies and the ultimate persuasion horror story, Jonestown." Publ Wkly

Includes bibliographical references

McKeown, Greg

Essentialism; the disciplined pursuit of less. Greg McKeown. Crown Business 2014 272 p. illustrations hbk $23   **153.8**

1. Decision making 2. Choice (Psychology) 3. Essentialism (Philosophy)
ISBN 0804137382; 9780804137386

LC 2013038729

"Punctuated with zippy, thoughtful one-liners, this guide to doing 'less but better' offers strategies for determining what is truly necessary, and shedding what is not. Too many people fall for the having-it-all myth, and would benefit from shifting from a non-essentialist mindset (unable to distinguish and parse out the truly important) to an essentialist one (capable of identifying the goal), contends McKeown. Instead of attempting to achieve everything, readers need to figure out how to do the 'right thing the right way at the right time.'" (Pub Wkly)

Includes bibliographical references and index

Partnoy, Frank

Wait; the art and science of delay. Frank Partnoy. PublicAffairs 2012 xii, 290 p.p   **153.8**

1. Patience 2. Decision making 3. Thought and thinking 4. Procrastination

ISBN 1610390040; 9781610390040; 9781610390057

LC 2012010970

In this book, Frank Partnoy "weaves together findings from hundreds of scientific studies and interviews with wide-ranging experts to craft a picture of effective decision-making that runs counter to our . . . fast-paced world. Even as technology exerts new pressures to speed up our lives, it turns out that the choices we make . . . benefit profoundly from delay. As this . . . book reveals, taking control of time and slowing down our responses yields better results in almost every arena of life." (Publisher's note)

Includes bibliographical references and index.

Vanderbilt, Tom

You may also like; taste in an age of endless choice. by Tom Vanderbilt. Alfred A. Knopf 2016 320 p. (hardcover) $26.95   **153.8**

1. Consumers 2. Aesthetics 3. Choice (Psychology) 4. Consumers' preferences 5. Aesthetics -- Psychological aspects

ISBN 9780307948595; 9780307958242

LC 2015026997

This book, by Tom Vanderbilt, is "an enlightening and illuminating look at why we like the things we like, why we hate the things we hate, and what our preferences reveal about us. . . . Vanderbilt stalks the elusive beast of taste, probing research in psychology, marketing, and neuroscience to answer myriad complex and fascinating questions." (Publisher's note)

"Essential for readers who are interested in getting a glimpse of the decision-making process at influential online media companies, as well as those who are interested in the processes that govern individual preferences and taste making." LJ

Includes bibliographical references

153.9   Intelligence and aptitudes

Beilock, Sian L.

Choke; what the secrets of the brain reveal about getting it right when you have to. Free Press 2010 294p il $26; ebook $12.99   **153.9**

1. Success 2. Failure (Psychology)

ISBN 978-1-4165-9617-2; 978-1-4391-0962-5 ebook

LC 2010-10595

"A star golfer misses a critical putt; a brilliant student fails to ace a test; a savvy salesperson blows a key presentation. Each of these people has suffered the same bump in

mental processing: They have just choked under pressure. . . . By studying how the brain works when we are doing our best — and when we choke — Beilock has formulated practical ideas about how to overcome performance lapses at critical moments." Science Daily

Bloom, Harold

Genius; a mosaic of one hundred exemplary creative minds. Warner Bks. 2002 814p il $35.95; pa $19.95   **153.9**

1. Genius 2. Authors 3. Literature -- History and criticism

ISBN 0-446-52717-3; 0-446-69129-1 pa

LC 2002-16808

"Although the book is a delight to read, its real value lies in the author's ability to provoke the reader into thinking about literature, genius, and related topics. No similar work discusses literary genius in this way or covers this many writers." Libr J

Includes bibliographical references

Brogaard, Berit

The **superhuman** mind; free the genius in your brain. Berit Brogaard, PhD, and Kristian Marlow, MA. Hudson Street Press 2015 288 p. illustrations $25.95   **153.9**

1. Intellect 2. Psychology 3. Self-perception 4. Self-actualization (Psychology)

ISBN 1594633681; 9781594633683

LC 2014041967

This book by Berit Brogaard and Kristian Marlow "takes us inside the lives and brains of geniuses, savants, virtuosos, and a wide variety of ordinary people who have acquired truly extraordinary talents, one way or another. Delving into the neurological underpinnings of these abilities, the authors even reveal how we can acquire some of them ourselves--from perfect pitch and lightning fast math skills to supercharged creativity." (Publisher's note)

"An enjoyable book, but don't expect to make a major contribution to world civilization as a direct result of reading it." LJ

Includes bibliographical references and index

Ericsson, Anders

Peak; secrets from the new science of expertise. Anders Ericsson and Robert Pool. Houghton Mifflin Harcourt 2016 336 p. (hardcover) $28   **153.9**

1. Ability 2. Psychology of learning 3. Expertise 4. Performance -- Psychological aspects

ISBN 9780544456235; 9780544809703

LC 2015042796

This book, by Anders Ericsson and Robert Pool, offers "a powerful new approach to mastering almost any skill. . . . Expert performance guru Anders Ericsson has made a career studying chess champions, violin virtuosos, star athletes, and memory mavens. . . . [It] condenses three decades of original research to introduce an incredibly powerful approach to learning that is fundamentally different from the way people traditionally think about acquiring a skill." (Publisher's note)

"Throughout, the authors encourage dreaming big, even when conventional wisdom might dictate otherwise. This is an empowering, encouraging work that will challenge readers to reach for excellence." Pub Wkly

Includes bibliographical references and index

Gould, Stephen Jay

The **mismeasure** of man; rev & expanded ed; Norton 1996 444p il hardcover o.p. pa $15.95 **153.9**
1. Intelligence tests 2. Ability -- Testing
ISBN 0-393-31425-1 pa

LC 95-44442

First published 1981

The author examines the history of various scientific methods used to measure intelligence. He demonstrates how the research was used to perpetuate the myth of the intellectual superiority of the white male

Includes bibliographical references

Kurzweil, Ray, 1948-

★ The **singularity** is near; when humans transcend biology. [by] Ray Kurzweil. Viking 2005 652p il $29.95; pa $18 **153.9**
1. Robots 2. Genetics 3. Evolution 4. Nanotechnology
ISBN 0-670-03384-7; 0-14-303788-9 pa

LC 2004-61231

The book provides an "argument that a sudden acceleration in the growth of knowledge is about to make immortality technologically feasible. . . . A part of the argument concerns the transformation the human body will undergo as a result of the explosive increase of knowledge he believes is imminent. Nanotechnology will enable the design of nanobots . . . that will 'have myriad roles within the human body, including reversing human aging (to the extent that this task will not already have been completed through biotechnology, such as genetic engineering).' . . . But this will still not be immortality, and perfecting the human body is a phase in a much larger transformation. . . . 'Ultimately, the entire universe will become saturated with our intelligence.'" (New York Review of Books)

"Anyone can grasp Mr. Kurzweil's main idea: that mankind's technological knowledge has been snowballing, with dizzying prospects for the future. The basics are clearly expressed. But for those more knowledgeable and inquisitive, the author argues his case in fascinating detail." N Y Times (Late N Y Ed)

Includes bibliographical references

Murdoch, Stephen

IQ; a smart history of a failed idea. J. Wiley and Sons 2007 269p $24.95 **153.9**
1. Intelligence tests
ISBN 978-0-471-69977-4; 0-471-69977-2

LC 2006-32488

The author "traces now ubiquitous but still controversial attempts to measure intelligence to its origins in the late 19th and early 20th centuries. . . . This is a thoughtful overview and a welcome reminder of the dangers of relying on such standardized tests." Publ Wkly

Includes bibliographical references

154.2   The subconscious

Kandel, Eric R., 1929-

The **age** of insight; the quest to understand the unconscious in art, mind, and brain : from Vienna 1900 to the present. Eric R. Kandel. Random House 2011 636 p. **154.2**
1. Intellect 2. Perception 3. Subconsciousness 4. Art -- Psychological aspects 5. Subconsciousness in art
ISBN 9781400068715; 9781588369307

LC 2011025274

This book examines "the interplay among art, psychology and brain science." It focuses on "Austrian artists Gustav Klimt, Oskar Kokoschka and Egon Schiele, each of whom was profoundly influenced by Sigmund Freud and by the emerging scientific approach to medicine in their day. Kandel describes the psychological and biological insights reflected in their paintings, as well as the neuroscience behind how the beholder perceives the paintings." (Scientific American)

Mlodinow, Leonard

Subliminal; how your unconscious mind rules your behavior. Leonard Mlodinow. Pantheon Books 2012 viii, 260 p.p ill. (hardcover) $25.95 **154.2**
1. Human behavior 2. Decision making 3. Subconsciousness 4. Applied psychology
ISBN 9780307378217; 0307378217

LC 2011048098

In this book about the unconscious, physicist Leonard "Mlodinow runs through study after study and some . . . real-life examples to reveal how subliminal processing controls our sensory systems, creates and distorts memories and guides our intuitions about people. . . . He is pragmatic about how completely it leads us astray and the near-impossibility of overriding it, but he . . . acknowledg[es] how lost he would be without it." (New Scientist)

Includes bibliographical references and index

Tallis, Frank

Hidden minds; a history of the unconscious. Arcade Pub. 2002 194p $25.95 **154.2**
1. Subconsciousness
ISBN 1-55970-643-0

LC 2002-74566

"Highly readable and possessing a surprising degree of depth, this book manages to be both entertaining and informative." Libr J

Includes bibliographical references

Vedantam, Shankar

The **hidden** brain; how our unconscious minds elect presidents, control markets, wage wars, and save our lives. Spiegel & Grau 2009 270p $26; pa $16 **154.2**
1. Perception 2. Subconsciousness 3. Motivation (Psychology)
ISBN 978-0-385-52521-3; 0-385-52521-4; 978-0-385-52522-0 pa; 0-385-52522-2 pa

LC 2009-19717

"A tour into dark realms of the psyche by a personable guide." Kirkus

Includes bibliographical references

154.6   Sleep phenomena

Freud, Sigmund

★ **Interpretation** of dreams; translated by Joyce Crick; edited with an introduction by Ritchie Robinson. Oxford University Press 2008 514p il (Oxford world's classics) pa $14.95   **154.6**

    1. Dreams 2. Psychoanalysis

    ISBN 978-0-19-953758-7; 0-19-953758-5

    Original German edition, 1900; first English translation published 1913

    Groundbreaking analysis of dreams as manifestations of suppressed unconscious desires

Lewis, James R.

★ The **dream** encyclopedia; [by] James R. Lewis and Evelyn Dorothy Oliver. 2nd ed.; Visible Ink Press 2009 xxi, 410p il pa $24.95   **154.6**

    1. Reference books 2. Dreams -- Encyclopedias

    ISBN 978-1-57859-216-6

                         LC 2009-5132

    First published 1995 by Gale Res.

    This "reference examines more than 250 dream-related topics, from art to history to science, including how factors such as self-healing, ESP, literature, religion, sex, cognition and memory, and medical conditions can all have an effect on dreams. Dream symbolism and interpretation is examined in historical, cultural, and psychological detail." Publisher's note

    Includes bibliographical references

155   Differential and developmental psychology

Bailey, Rebecca Anne

    Easy to love, difficult to discipline; the 7 basic skills for turning conflict into cooperation. {by} Becky A. Bailey. Morrow 2000 285p hardcover o.p. pa $12.95   **155**

    1. Parenting 2. Child rearing

    ISBN 0-06-000775-3 pa

                         LC 99-44313

    "Bailey contends that the difficult but rewarding task of guiding children's behavior starts only when parents are able to discipline themselves and become models of self-control. . . . Bailey's underlying message is positive and hopeful, supported with humorous anecdotes and helpful solutions." Publ Wkly

    Includes bibliographical references

Kagan, Jerome

    The **human** spark; the science of human development. Jerome Kagan. Basic Books 2013 352 p. (hardcover) $28.99   **155**

    1. Psychology 2. Child development 3. Child psychology

    ISBN 0465029825; 9780465029822

                       LC 2012047558

    In this book, developmental psychologist Jerome Kagan points out that "a great deal of what we 'know' about human development isn't firmly anchored in empirical science.

He aims to correct that by encouraging readers to question received knowledge . . . and he does so by presenting [a] . . . discussion of the epistemology of psychology, alongside . . . critiques of the methodologies used in psychological research and the social applications of misinterpreted findings." (Publishers Weekly)

    Includes bibliographical references and index

155.2   Individual psychology

Bluestein, Jane

    The **perfection** deception; why striving to be perfect is sabotaging your relationships, making you sick, and holding your happiness hostage. Jane Bluestein. HCI 2015 312 p. charts (paperback) $15.95   **155.2**

    1. Psychology 2. Self-help techniques 3. Perfectionism (Personality trait)

    ISBN 0757318258; 9780757318252

                       LC 2015027944

    In this book, Dr. Jane Bluestein "exposes the truth: perfectionism is actually a mask for a fear of making mistakes, a desperate need to avoid negative judgments and rejection. . . . Through personal interviews and the latest research, she explores how our culture fuels the dysfunction, how perfectionism develops, and how it can hurt our physical, mental, and social well-being. Further, she provides practical strategies for moving toward authenticity and wholeness.." (Publisher's note)

    "An excellent and full description of the problems of perfectionism that helps readers alter their self-conceptions." LJ

    Includes bibliographical references and index

Cain, Susan

    Quiet; the power of introverts in a world that can't stop talking. Susan Cain. Crown Publishers 2012 x, 333 p.p   **155.2**

    1. Interpersonal relations 2. Introversion and extroversion 3. Introverts

    ISBN 9780307352149; 9780307452207

                       LC 2010053204

    It was the author's intent to discuss "the one-third to one-half of the population who are introverts. She defines the term broadly, including 'solitude-seeking' and 'contemplative,' but also 'sensitive,' 'humble,' and 'risk-averse,' Such individuals, she claims . . . are "'disproportionately represented among the ranks of the spectacularly creative.' Yet the American school and workplace make it difficult for those who draw strength from solitary musing by overemphasizing teamwork. . . . She notes [that] introverts can negotiate as well as, or better than, alpha males and females because they can take a firm stand 'without inflaming [their] counterpart's ego.' Cain provides tips to parents and teachers of children who are introverted or seem socially awkward and isolated. She suggests, for instance, exposing them gradually to new experiences that are otherwise overstimulating." (Publishers Weekly)

    Includes bibliographical references (p. [277]-323) and index

Crawford, Matthew B.

The **World** Beyond Your Head; On Becoming an Individual in an Age of Distraction. Farrar Straus & Giroux 2015 320 p. $26 **155.2**
1. Psychology 2. Thought and thinking
ISBN 0374292981; 9780374292980
LC 2015933043

Author Matthew B. Crawford "investigates the challenge of mastering one's own mind. [He] makes sense of an astonishing array of common experience, from the frustrations of airport security to the rise of the hipster. With implications for the way we raise our children, the design of public spaces, and democracy itself, this is a book of urgent relevance to contemporary life." (Publisher's note)

"This illuminating work will appeal to students of philosophy and sociology, as well as fans of good cultural analysis." LJ

Csikszentmihalyi, Mihaly

★ **Flow**: the psychology of optimal experience. Harper Perennial 2008 303p pa $14.95 **155.2**
1. Attention 2. Happiness 3. Applied psychology
ISBN 978-0-06-133920-2; 0-06-133920-2
First published 1990

This book offers a discussion of "'flow,' a field of behavioral science examining connections between satisfaction and daily activities. [According to the author], a flow state ensues when one is engaged in self-controlled, goal-related, meaningful actions. . . . This thoroughly researched study is an intriguing look at the age-old problem of the pursuit of happiness and how, through conscious effort, we may more easily attain it." Libr J

Dimitrius, Jo-Ellan

Reading people; how to understand people and predict their behavior--anytime, anyplace. {by} Jo-Ellan Dimitrius and Mark Mazzarella. Random House 1998 281p hardcover o.p. pa $14.95 **155.2**
1. Personality 2. Nonverbal communication
ISBN 0-345-42587-1 pa
LC 98-4934

"Dimitrius shares the people-reading techniques she developed over 15 years as a jury consultant. In so doing, she provides a wealth of tips and strategies for ferreting out people's real viewpoints, motives and character traits." Publ Wkly

Ehrenreich, Barbara

★ **Bright**-sided; how the relentless promotion of positive thinking has undermined America. Metropolitan Books/Henry Holt and Co. 2009 235p $23 **155.2**
1. Success 2. Optimism 3. Happiness 4. Self-confidence
ISBN 978-0-8050-8749-9; 0-8050-8749-4
LC 2009-23588

"The author's tough-minded and convincing broadside raises troubling questions about many aspects of contemporary American life. . . . Bright, incisive, provocative thinking." Kirkus

Includes bibliographical references

Gladwell, Malcolm, 1963-

David and Goliath; underdogs, misfits, and the art of battling giants. Malcolm Gladwell. Little, Brown & Co. 2013 304 p. illustrations (hardcover) $29 **155.2**
1. Success 2. Self-help techniques 3. Opportunity 4. Motivation (Psychology) 5. Struggle -- Psychological aspects
ISBN 9780316204361; 0316204366; 9780316239851
LC 2013941807

In this book, author Malcolm Gladwell "examines and challenges our concepts of 'advantage' and 'disadvantage' in a way that may seem intuitive to some and surprising to others. Beginning with the classic tale of David and Goliath and moving through history with figures such as Lawrence of Arabia and Martin Luther King Jr., Gladwell shows how, time and again, players labeled 'underdog' use that status to their advantage and prevail through the elements of cunning and surprise." (Booklist)

"Gladwell rewards readers with moving stories, surprising insights and consistently provocative ideas." Kirkus

Includes bibliographical references and index

Goldsmith, Marshall

Triggers; creating behavior that lasts-- becoming the person you want to be. by Marshall Goldsmith and Mark Reiter. Random House Inc 2015 244 p. illustrations $27 **155.2**
1. Human behavior 2. Behavior modification
ISBN 0804141231; 9780804141239

In this book, authors Marshall Goldsmith and Mark Reiter examine "the environmental and psychological triggers that can derail us at work and in life. . . . These triggers are constant and relentless and omnipresent. . . . So often the environment seems to be outside our control. Even if that is true, as Goldsmith points out, we have a choice in how we respond." (Publisher's note)

Greitens, Eric, 1974-

Resilience; hard-won wisdom for living a better life. Eric Greitens. Houghton Mifflin Harcourt 2015 320 p. (hardback) $26 **155.2**
1. Life skills 2. Self-help techniques 3. Resilience (Personality trait)
ISBN 054432398X; 9780544323988
LC 2014035279

In this book, Navy SEAL Eric Greitens "offer[s] a masterpiece of warrior wisdom that will change your life. . . . There is a path through pain to wisdom, through suffering to strength, and through fear to courage if we have the virtue of resilience. . . . [Greitens] explains how we can build purpose, confront pain, practice compassion, develop a vocation, find a mentor, create happiness, and much more." (Publisher's note)

"Based on the practices he suggests to build compassion, confront pain and create happiness, readers can move beyond their fears and create creative, energized lives rich in wisdom and filled with friendships and mentorships. Robust, heart-to-heart lessons for moving beyond obstacles to create a better life." Kirkus

Harris, Judith Rich

No two alike; human nature and human individuality. W.W. Norton & Co. 2006 322p il $26.95 **155.2**
1. Personality 2. Individuality
ISBN 0-393-05948-0

LC 2005-25837

"Harris makes behavioral genetics and evolutionary psychology enjoyable and accessible to general readers as well as scholars." Libr J

Includes bibliographical references

Helgoe, Laurie A.

Introvert power; why your inner life is your hidden strength. [by] Laurie Helgoe. Sourcebooks 2008 xxiv, 256p il pa $15.95 **155.2**
1. Introversion and extroversion
ISBN 978-1-4022-1117-1; 1-4022-1117-1

LC 2008-4967

Shows readers how to use introversion not as a weakness but as a source of power.

"The author's voice is vivid and engaging, and she skillfully draws real-life examples of awkward scenarios introverts find themselves in when forced to play a role in society or the workplace. Readers will find much insight, as well as a comforting sense of being understood and validated." Publ Wkly

Includes bibliographical references

Hood, Bruce

The self illusion; how the social brain creates identity. Bruce Hood. Oxford University Press 2012 xvii, 349 p.p ill. (trade : alk. paper) $29.95 **155.2**
1. Self 2. Brain 3. Theory of knowledge 4. Cognition
ISBN 019989759X; 9780199897599

LC 2011047151

This book presents an "account of . . . developments in psychology and neuroscience that are helping to substantiate theories of selfhood positing that there is no concrete identity at the core of our being, and that our sense of self is an illusion spun from narratives we construct about our lives." It "explor[es] subjects such as free will, the unconscious, [and] the role of (false) memories in building identity." (New Scientist)

Includes bibliographical references (p. 297-341) and index.

Keltner, Dacher

Born to be good; the science of a meaningful life. W. W. Norton & Co. 2009 336p il $25.95 **155.2**
1. Altruism 2. Cooperation 3. Helping behavior 4. Interpersonal relations
ISBN 978-0-393-06512-1

LC 2008-42492

"A landmark book in the science of emotion and its implications for ethics and human universals, this is essential for all libraries." Libr J

Includes bibliographical references

Mischel, Walter

The marshmallow test; mastering self-control. Walter Mischel. Little, Brown & Co. 2014 336 p. illustrations (paperback) $16.99 **155.2**
1. Self-control 2. Applied psychology
ISBN 0316230863; 9780316230865; 9780316230872; 9780316336192

LC 2014018058

In this book, by Walter Mischel, the "designer of the famous Marshmallow Test, explains what self-control is and how to master it. . . . [The author] explains how self-control can be mastered and applied to challenges in everyday life-- from weight control to quitting smoking, overcoming heartbreak, making major decisions, and planning for retirement . . . , with profound implications for the choices we make in parenting, education, public policy and self-care." (Publisher's note)

Includes bibliographical references (pages 283-316) and index

Myers, Isabel Briggs

Gifts differing; understanding personality type. [by] Isabel Briggs Myers with Peter B. Myers. Davies-Black Pub 1995 228p il pa $16.95 **155.2**
1. Personality
ISBN 0-89106-074-X

LC 95-4184

First published 1980 by Consulting Psychologists Press
This is a guide to the 16 personality types distinguished in the Myers-Briggs Type Indicator.
Includes bibliographical references

Pinker, Steven

The blank slate; the denial of human nature in modern intellectual life. Viking 2002 509p $27.95; pa $16 **155.2**
1. Nature and nurture
ISBN 0-670-03151-8; 0-14-2003344 pa

LC 2002-22719

The author "attacks the notion that an infant's mind is a blank slate, arguing instead that human beings have an inherited universal structure shaped by the demands made upon the species for survival, albeit with plenty of room for cultural and individual variation." Publ Wkly

Includes bibliographical references

Rudder, Christian

Dataclysm; our life in numbers. Christian Rudder. Crown Publishers 2014 368 p. illustrations, maps (hardback) $28 **155.2**
1. Social media 2. Human behavior 3. Big data 4. Behavioral assessment
ISBN 0385347375; 9780385347372; 9780385347396

LC 2014007364

Los Angeles Times Book Prizes Finalist: Science and Technology (2014)

In this book, author Christian Rudder "explains how Facebook 'likes' can predict, with surprising accuracy, a person's sexual orientation and even intelligence; how attractive women receive exponentially more interview requests; and why you must have haters to be hot. He charts the rise and fall of America's most reviled word through Google

Search and examines the new dynamics of collaborative rage on Twitter. He shows how people express themselves, both privately and publicly." (Publisher's note)

"Demographers, entrepreneurs, students of history and sociology, and ordinary citizens alike will find plenty of provocations and, yes, much data in Rudder's well-argued, revealing pages." Kirkus

Includes bibliographical references (pages 249-281) and index

Seligman, Martin E. P.

★ **Learned** optimism; how to change your mind and your life. Vintage Books 2006 319p pa $14.95   **155.2**
  1. Self-perception 2. Adjustment (Psychology)
  ISBN 1-4000-7839-3; 978-1-4000-7839-4
                                                          LC 2006-277713
  First published 1991
  Seligman "has written a lively, very accessible book. . . . Presented for lay readers, this book can be highly recommended to professionals as well for its lucid and informative introduction to cognitive therapy and its approach to issues of mood and depression." Libr J
  Includes bibliographical references

Shenk, David

The **genius** in all of us; why everything you've been told about genetics, talent, and IQ is wrong. Doubleday 2010 302p il $26.95   **155.2**
  1. Ability 2. Heredity 3. Intellect
  ISBN 978-0-385-52365-3; 0-385-52365-3
                                                          LC 2009-18376
  Shenk "tells engaging stories, lucidly explains complex research and offers fresh insights into the nature of exceptional performance. . . . [This is] deeply interesting and important book." N Y Times Book Rev
  Includes bibliographical references

Triandis, Harry C.

Fooling ourselves; self-deception in politics, religion, and terrorism. Harry C. Triandis. Praeger Publishers 2009 xxvi, 246p (alk. paper) $49.95 **155.2**
  1. Deception 2. Psychology 3. Social psychology 4. Psychology of religion
  ISBN 9780313364389; 0313364389
                                                          LC 2008033679
  In this book, author Harry C. "Triandis shows how and why self-deception takes place, and its subtle and profound effects on our everyday lives. Self-deception occurs because we often see the world the way we would like it to be, rather than the way it is. Our brains so long for things the way we want them, we might not even be aware we are fooling ourselves. . . . Across cultures and around the world, self-deception is a phenomenon that has subtle and profound effects on everyday life, explains Triandis, . . . former president of the International Association of Cross-Cultural Psychology. In this work, he not only explains how and why self-deceptions occur in three areas - politics, religion, and terrorism - but also how to recognize and reduce the frequency of fooling ourselves." (Publisher's note)

  Includes bibliographical references (p. [209]-235) and indexes.

Weber, Robert J.

The **created** self; reinventing body, persona, spirit. Norton 2000 350p il hardcover o.p. pa $14.95   **155.2**
  1. Self 2. Psychology
  ISBN 0-393-32121-5 pa
                                                          LC 99-37480
  The author contends that "having a self enables the individual to pursue creative endeavors, which though often adaptive from an evolutionary standpoint, actually extend beyond what can be explained in terms of biological, reproductive aims. Using the model of the self developed by William James . . . Weber attempts to show that the self is a constantly developing, 'unitary system', consisting of bodily awareness, persona and spirit, over which the individual has control." Publ Wkly
  Includes bibliographical references

Young-Eisendrath, Polly

The **self**-esteem trap; raising confident and compassionate kids in an age of self-importance. Little, Brown 2008 248p $25.99   **155.2**
  1. Self-esteem 2. Child psychology
  ISBN 978-0-316-01311-6; 0-316-01311-0
                                                          LC 2008-2224
  The author argues that "those born between 1970 and 2000 (Gen Me-ers) . . . are a vastly discontented group who find their lives unsatisfying and feel entitled to success owing to an overestimation of what the world will bring. She views this as a cultural problem begun in the 1980s when the collapse of the traditional parental hierarchy coincided with a hyperfocus on self-esteem. . . . This is well written, accessible, soundly researched, and beautifully insightful." Libr J
  Includes bibliographical references

155.3 Sex psychology; psychology of people by gender or sex, by sexual orientation

Eldredge, Niles

★ **Why** we do it; rethinking sex and the selfish gene. Norton 2004 269p il $24.95   **155.3**
  1. Evolution 2. Sociobiology 3. Sex (Biology)
  ISBN 0-393-05082-3
                                                          LC 2003-27564
  "This book, while written for the lay reader, is appropriate for a scientific audience as well. It could be used as supplementary reading in college courses in animal behavior." Sci Books & Films

Gottman, John

The **man's** guide to women; scientifically proven secrets from the "love lab" about what women really want. John Gottman, PhD, Julie Schwartz Gottman, PhD, Douglas Abrams, Rachel Carlton Abrams, MD, with Lara Love Hardin. Rodale 2015 224 p. illustrations (trade hardcover) $22.99   **155.3**
  1. Women -- Psychology 2. Man-woman relationship
  3. Sex -- Psychological aspects 4. Sex (Psychology)
  5. Sexual attraction 6. Man-woman relationships --

Psychological aspects
ISBN 9781623361846

LC 2015041297

This book, by John Gottman, Julie Schwartz Gottman, Douglas Abrams, and Rachel Carlton Abrams, is a "definitive guide for men, providing answers on everything from how to approach a woman and build a connection with her to how to truly satisfy her in bed and know when the relationship is on the right track. [It] is a must-have playbook for how to play—and win—the game of love." (Publisher's note)

"This should be required reading for men who are both baffled by and interested in women." Pub Wkly

Includes bibliographical references and index

Lerner, Harriet Goldhor

The **dance** of deception; pretending and truth-telling in women's lives. HarperCollins Pubs. 1993 254p hardcover o.p.   **155.3**
1. Truthfulness and falsehood 2. Women -- Psychology
LC 92-53376

"Patriarchal culture teaches women to pretend and sometimes deceive, Lerner says, and in her study of the role this dissembling plays in women's lives, she shows how 'pretending reflects deep prohibitions, real and imagined, against a more direct and forthright assertion of self.' . . . She acknowledges that truth telling is not easy, yet her discussion of the many ways women lie and how lying affects them clearly shows the benefits of honesty and makes her prescription appealing." Booklist

Includes bibliographical references

Pincott, J.

Do gentlemen really prefer blondes? bodies, behavior and brains: the science behind sex, love, and attraction. [by] Jena Pincott. Delacorte Press 2008 351p il $20   **155.3**
1. Dating (Social customs) 2. Sexual behavior
ISBN 978-0-385-34215-5; 0-385-34215-2
LC 2008-23933

The author "argues that desire is strongly rooted in evolutionary biases and consults a variety of studies . . . to reveal the extent to which hormones dictate human behavior." Publ Wkly

Includes bibliographical references

155.333   Differential and developmental psychology--Women

Huston, Therese

How women decide; what's true, what's not, and what strategies spark the best choices. Therese Huston. Houghton Mifflin Harcourt 2016 384 p. (hardcover) $28   **155.333**
1. Businesswomen 2. Decision making 3. Women -- Psychology 4. Decision making -- Sex differences 5. Decision making -- Psychological aspects
ISBN 9780544416093

LC 2015037243

In this book, by Therese Huston, "from confidence gaps to power poses, leaning in to calling bias out, bossypants to girl bosses, women have been hearing a lot of advice lately. Most of this aims at greater success, but very little focuses on a key set of skills that ensures such success—making the wisest, strongest decisions." (Publisher's note)

"Useful, practical strategies based on informed analysis." Kirkus

Includes bibliographical references

155.4   Psychology of specific ages

Brazelton, T. Berry

The **irreducible** needs of children; what every child must have to grow, learn, and flourish. {by} T. Berry Brazelton, Stanley I. Greenspan. Perseus Bks. 2000 xx, 228p hardcover o.p. pa $14   **155.4**
1. Child rearing 2. Child psychology 3. Child development
ISBN 0-7382-0516-8 pa

LC 2001-2290

This is "a practical, well-organized volume, of value to parents, physicians, teachers, sociologists, and others who wish to improve children's lives locally and globally." Booklist

Includes bibliographical references

★ **To** listen to a child; understanding the normal problems of growing up. photographs by B.A. King. Addison-Wesley 1984 184p il hardcover o.p.   **155.4**
1. Sleep 2. Asthma 3. Child psychology 4. Child development 5. Parent-child relationship 6. Emotionally disturbed children 7. Children -- Health and hygiene
LC 84-6174

"Brazelton's sensible, authoritative, clear approach provides parents with the kinds of information they need to relax over the long pull, and to understand and cope with day-to-day difficulties." Publ Wkly

Elkind, David

★ The **power** of play; how spontaneous, imaginative activities lead to happier, healthier children. Da Capo Lifelong 2007 240p $24   **155.4**
1. Play
ISBN 0-7382-1053-6; 978-0-7382-1053-7
LC 2006-35592

"Prescribing the trinity of play, love, and work, . . . [the author] shows how the integration of these elements at various stages of development, from infancy to adolescence, leads to happier, well-adjusted individuals with a greater potential for academic success. Elkind will connect with parents when he reveals that 'Toys R Not Us' and argues that less is more; that children should use toys for inspiration, not distraction." Libr J

Includes bibliographical references

Gopnik, Alison

The **gardener** and the carpenter; What the New Science of Child Development Tells Us About the Relationship Between Parents and Children. Alison Gopnik. Farrar, Straus & Giroux 2016 320 p. illustrations (hardback) $26   **155.4**
1. Parenting 2. Child psychology 3. Child development 4. Developmental psychology
ISBN 9780374229702

LC 2015048667

In this book, "developmental psychologist and philosopher Alison Gopnik argues that the familiar twenty-first-century picture of parents and children is profoundly wrong. . . . Drawing on the study of human evolution and her own cutting-edge scientific research into how children learn, Gopnik shows that although caring for children is profoundly important, it is not a matter of shaping them to turn out a particular way." (Publisher's note)

"A highly thoughtful and entertaining treatment of a subject that merits serious consideration." Kirkus

Includes bibliographical references and index

The **scientist** in the crib; minds, brains, and how children learn. [by] Alison Gopnik, Andrew N. Meltzoff, Patricia K. Kuhl. Morrow 1999 279p hardcover o.p. pa $14   **155.4**
1. Child development 2. Psychology of learning
ISBN 0-688-17788-3 pa

LC 99-24247

The authors examine "how children learn to understand and use language, control their emotions and arouse the emotions of others, and establish relationships. . . . Prospective and actual parents stand to learn much that may be helpful to them and their children from this lively book." Booklist

Includes bibliographical references

Linn, Susan

The **case** for make believe; saving play in a commercialized world. New Press 2008 258p $24.95   **155.4**
1. Play 2. Imagination 3. Advertising and children
ISBN 978-1-56584-970-9; 1-56584-970-1

LC 2007-42435

"Puppeteer and therapist Linn draws on years of work at Boston Children's Hospital to make a thoughtful case for creative play. She distinguishes between children who are familiar with concepts of imagination and make-believe versus those who know only how to play with manufactured toys linked to media campaigns or within the constructs of rule-driven environments. . . . None of this will be news to most parents, but Linn seeks to discover what it means for children to no longer spend time pretending to be someone or somewhere else. Her research is comprehensive, her firsthand knowledge is impressive, and her examples are damning in their conclusions." Booklist

Includes bibliographical references

Louv, Richard

Last child in the woods; saving our children from nature-deficit disorder. Algonquin Books of Chapel Hill 2005 323p $24.95   **155.4**
1. Child psychology 2. Environmental influence on humans
ISBN 1-56512-391-3

LC 2004-66034

"Louv's book is a call to action, full of warnings—but also full of ideas for change." Publ Wkly

Includes bibliographical references

Piaget, Jean

★ The **moral** judgment of the child; {translated by Marjorie Gabain} Free Press 1948 418p hardcover o.p. pa $15   **155.4**
1. Ethics 2. Human behavior 3. Child psychology
ISBN 0-684-83330-1 pa
Original French edition, 1932

Piaget studies, not the moral behavior of children, but their ideas about right and wrong, the rules of a game, adult authority, and cooperation and justice

Tuck, Shonna

Getting from me to we; how to help young children fit in and make friends. Shonna L. Tuck, M.A., SLP. Woodbine House Inc. 2015 220 p. (pbk. : alk. paper) $24.95   **155.4**
1. Friendship 2. Child development 3. Adjustment (Psychology) 4. Adjustment (Psychology) in children
ISBN 9781606132692

LC 2015023676

This book, by Shonna L. Tuck, "helps parents understand the roots of [children's social] problems, which take hold at a very young age, and give their kids the foundational skills necessary to form connections and friendships. The book explains how parents can teach their children social observing skills at an early stage in their development." (Publisher's note)

"This book joins Ross W. Greene's The Explosive Child as a helpful tool to aid those who love and work with children with social issues." LJ

Includes bibliographical references and index

White, Burton L.

The **new** first three years of life; 20th anniversary ed; Fireside Bks. 1995 384p il pa $14 **155.4**
1. Child psychology 2. Infants -- Development
ISBN 0-684-80419-0

LC 95-18297

First published 1975 with title: The first three years of life

"White describes the seven developmental phases of the first three years of life. He provides parents with a comprehensive treasury of techniques for enhancing development and establishing discipline that are refreshingly straight-forward and based on real-world experience." Publ Wkly

155.433   Differential and developmental psychology--Girls

Tassler, Nina

What I Told My Daughter; Lessons from Leaders on Raising the Next Generation of Empowered Women. by Nina Tassler. Pocket Books 2016 320 p. $25   **155.433**

1. Mother-daughter relationship

ISBN 1476734674; 9781476734675

In this book, "entertainment executive Nina Tassler has brought together a powerful, diverse group of women—from Madeleine Albright to Ruth Bader Ginsburg, from Dr. Susan Love to Whoopi Goldberg—to reflect on the best advice and counsel they have given their daughters either by example, throughout their lives, or in character-building, teachable moments between parent and child." (Publisher's note)

155.44   Children by status and relationships

Wright, Lawrence

Twins; and what they tell us about who we are. Wiley 1997 202p $22.95; pa $14.95   **155.44**

1. Twins

ISBN 0-471-25220-4; 0-471-29644-9 pa

LC 97-38827

"Wright does an admirable job of sorting through the differing research in a well-reasoned, clearheaded manner." Publ Wkly

Includes bibliographical references

155.45   Exceptional children; children by social and economic levels, by ethnic or national group

Stephens, Kimberly

The Prodigy's Cousin; The Family Link Between Autism and Extraordinary Talent. by Joanne Ruthsatz and Kimberly Stephens. Penguin Group USA 2016 288 p. $28   **155.45**

1. Autism 2. Genius 3. Child psychology 4. Autistic children

ISBN 1617230189; 9781617230189

LC 2015048520

In this book, authors Joanne Ruthsatz and Kimberly Stephens "propose a startling possibility: What if the abilities of child prodigies stem from a genetic link with autism? And could prodigies—children who have many of the strengths of autism but few of the challenges—be the key to a long-awaited autism breakthrough? . . . Ruthsatz and Stephens narrate the poignant stories of the children they have studied." (Publisher's note)

"People with an interest in autism or prodigies will be intrigued by the interesting hypothesis posed by this psychologist-journalist duo, who provide a lovely epilogue about what their young prodigies are doing today." Booklist

Includes bibliographical references and index.

Winner, Ellen

Gifted children; myths and realities. Basic Bks. 1996 449p il hardcover o.p. pa $21   **155.45**

1. Gifted children

ISBN 0-465-01759-2 pa

LC 95-49279

This study considers the following questions "are gifted children gifted in all subject areas? Are artistically gifted children gifted or talented? Does giftedness depend on IQ? What role do environment and biology play in giftedness? Are gifted children psychological and social misfits? In her analyses, Winner cites and explains a broad range of recent research, including extensive notes and references with each chapter. She then offers her recommendations for dealing with gifted children in America's educational systems." Libr J

155.5   Psychology of young people twelve to twenty

Siegel, Daniel J.

Brainstorm; the power and purpose of the teenage brain. Daniel J. Siegel, M.D. Jeremy P. Tarcher/Penguin 2013 336 p. ill $27.95   **155.5**

1. Adolescent psychology 2. Brain 3. Cognition in adolescence

ISBN 158542935X; 9781585429356

LC 2013029724

This book, by Daniel J. Siegel, "illuminates how brain development impacts teenagers' behavior and relationships. Drawing on important new research in the field of interpersonal neurobiology, he explores exciting ways in which understanding how the teenage brain functions can help parents make what is in fact an incredibly positive period of growth, change, and experimentation in their children's lives less lonely and distressing on both sides of the generational divide." (Publisher's note)

"Smart advice . . . on providing the most supportive and brain-healthy environment during the tumultuous years of adolescence." Kirkus

155.6   Psychology of adults

Ackerman, Diane, 1948-

Deep play; illustrations by Peter Sis. Random House 1999 235p il hardcover o.p. pa $13   **155.6**

1. Play -- Psychological aspects

ISBN 0-679-77135-2 pa

LC 98-35067

The author contends that "deep play, 'ecstatic' play, transcends practical concerns and grants us passage to the sacred and the holy. Art is deep play, so is religion, the contemplation of nature, and playing sports; in short, pursuits that are all-consuming and inspire feelings of awe and a profound sense of connection with the universe. By turns anecdotal and philosophic, Ackerman vividly recounts her own 'deep play' experiences." Booklist

Includes bibliographical references

Engel, Beverly

The **nice** girl syndrome; stop being manipulated and abused--and start standing up for yourself. John Wiley & Sons 2008 245p $24.95 **155.6**

1. Self-esteem 2. Conduct of life 3. Self-confidence 4. Women -- Psychology

ISBN 978-0-470-17938-3; 0-470-17938-4

LC 2008-8382

The author argues "that while society superficially rewards nice girls, they suffer deeply in their intimate and work relationships by losing personal power and parading inauthentic selves. . . . Most useful for its thorough treatment for how 'nice girls' are socialized and for Engel's concise antidote (the four 'Power C's': confidence, competence, conviction and courage) this book will challenge, entertain and empower its readers." Publ Wkly

Includes bibliographical references

Friday, Nancy

My mother/my self; the daughter's search for identity. Delta Trade Paperbacks 1997 425p pa $17 **155.6**

1. Mothers 2. Mother-daughter relationship 3. Women -- Psychology

ISBN 0-385-32015-9; 978-0-385-32015-3

LC 98-115632

First published 1977 by Delacorte Press

The author explores the psychological aspects of the mother-daughter relationship.

Includes bibliographical references

Lerner, Harriet Goldhor

The **dance** of intimacy; a woman's guide to courageous acts of change in key relationships. Harper & Row 1989 255p hardcover o.p. pa $14 **155.6**

1. Interpersonal relations 2. Women -- Psychology

ISBN 0-06-091646-X pa

LC 88-45519

The author explains "how to operate more effectively in key relationships—whether it be with a distant or unfaithful spouse, a depressed sister, a difficult mother, an alcoholic father, an uncommitted lover, a dying parent, or a family member that we have written off." Publisher's note

Includes bibliographical references

Levinson, Daniel J.

The **seasons** of a man's life; by Daniel J. Levinson {et al.} Knopf 1978 363p hardcover o.p. pa $15 **155.6**

1. Middle age 2. Men -- Psychology

ISBN 0-394-533901-0 pa

LC 77-20978

The Levinson theory divides a man's "life cycle into five overlapping eras. . . . Each era is marked by periods of stability during which life structures are built. These stable

periods alternate with transition periods during which life structures change." Saturday Rev

Includes bibliographical references

The **seasons** of a woman's life; in collaboration with Judy D. Levinson. Knopf 1996 438p hardcover o.p. pa $23 **155.6**

1. Middle age 2. Women -- Psychology

ISBN 0-345-31174-4 pa

LC 95-20893

"This work asks whether there is a human life cycle and a process of adult growth similar to the process of child development, and how gender affects the lives of individual women and women in general. The Levinson team interviewed 15 homemakers, 15 women with corporate-financial careers, and 15 women with academic careers. Their stories are the core of Levinson's book." Booklist

Includes bibliographical references

155.67 People in late adulthood

Cameron, Julia B., 1948-

It's never too late to begin again; discovering creativity and meaning at midlife and beyond. Julia Cameron, Emma Lively. TarcherPerigee 2016 304 p. (paperback) $17 **155.67**

1. Middle age 2. Creative ability 3. Aging

ISBN 9780399174216

LC 2015050216

In this book, by Julia Cameron and Emma Lively, the authors "turns [their] eye to a segment of the population that, ironically, while they have more time to be creative, are often reluctant or intimidated by the creative process. Cameron shows readers that retirement can, in fact, be the most rich, fulfilling, and creative time of their lives." (Publisher's note)

"Organized into a 12-week program designed to help individuals define and re-create their lives in middle age and beyond, Cameron's guide offers useful assigned tasks (warning: these include fill-in writing exercises), making this a must-read for all hoping to enhance their creativity in all aspects of life." Booklist

Includes bibliographical references and index

155.7 Evolutionary psychology

Clark, William R.

Are we hardwired? the role of genes in human behavior. by William R. Clark & Michael Grunstein. Oxford Univ. Press 2000 322p il hardcover o.p. pa $24.95 **155.7**

1. Behavior genetics

ISBN 0-19-513826-0; 978-0-19-517800-5 pa; 0-19-517800-9 pa

LC 99-54699

The authors offer an "overview of the current evidence supporting genetic causes for general behavioral tendencies, such as aggression, consumption, sexual preferences, and, most controversial, intelligence. Case studies of identical twins separated as infants provide some of the most compelling proofs." Libr J

Includes bibliographical references

Dunbar, Robin

Human evolution; Our Brains and Behavior. Robin Dunbar. Oxford University Press 2016 432 p. (hardback) $29.95   **155.7**

1. Evolutionary psychology
ISBN 9780190616786

LC 2016009401

In this book, author "Robin Dunbar appeals to the human aspects of every reader, as subjects of mating, friendship, and community are discussed from an evolutionary psychology perspective. With a table of contents ranging from prehistoric times to modern days, [it] focuses on an aspect of evolution that has typically been overshadowed by the archaeological record: the biological, neurological, and genetic changes that occurred with each 'transition' in the evolutionary narrative." (Publisher's note)

"Readers who pay attention and do not skim the many graphs, tables, and statistics will discover a rich trove of discoveries on how primitive primates became modern humans." Kirkus

Includes bibliographical references and index

Maestripieri, Dario

Games primates play; an undercover investigation of the evolution and economics of human relationships. Dario Maestripieri. Basic Books 2012 xviii, 302 p.p (hardcover : alk. paper) : $27.99 **155.7**

1. Evolution 2. Interpersonal relations 3. Behavior evolution 4. Control (Psychology) 5. Primates -- Behavior 6. Dominance (Psychology)
ISBN 046502078X; 9780465020782

LC 2011045523

In this book, "[Dario] Maestripieri argues that human behaviour, like our anatomy, can be explained by looking at our biology. Natural selection strongly shaped our social behaviour, and the same pressures faced by our ancestors would also have influenced our closest living relatives--other primates. . . . In economic terms, he argues that we choose mates who enhance our material interests--but only so long as the benefits outweigh the costs." (New Scientist)

Includes bibliographical references (p. 277-295) and index

Ridley, Matt

The **agile** gene; how nature turns on nurture. Perennial 2004 326p pa $13.99   **155.7**

1. Genetics 2. Nature and nurture
ISBN 978-0-06-000679-2; 0-06-000679-X

First published 2003 with title: Nature via nurture

"In February 2001 it was announced that the human genome contains not 100,000 genes, as originally postulated, but only 30,000. This . . . revision led some scientists to conclude that there are simply not enough human genes to account for all the different ways people behave: we must be made by nurture, not nature. . . . [Ridley argues that] nurture depends on genes, too, and genes need nurture. Genes not only predetermine the broad structure of the brain, they also absorb formative experiences, react to social cues, and even

run memory. They are consequences as well as causes of the will." Publisher's note

Includes bibliographical references

155.8   Ethnopsychology and national psychology

Levi-Strauss, Claude

★ The **savage** mind. University of Chicago Press 1966 290p il (Nature of human society series) hardcover o.p. pa $18   **155.8**

1. Anthropology 2. Ethnopsychology
ISBN 0-226-47484-4 pa

Original French edition, 1962

"An anthropological study of the nature of thought, concepts and systems as they occur in various cultures." Chicago Public Libr

Includes bibliographical references

155.9   Environmental psychology

Aiken, Mary

The **cyber** effect; A Pioneering Cyberpsychologist Explains How Human Behavior Changes Online. Mary Aiken. Spiegel & Grau 2016 400 p. (ebook) $65; (hardback) $28   **155.9**

1. Internet 2. Human behavior 3. Social psychology 4. Interpersonal relations 5. Internet users -- Psychology 6. Interpersonal relations -- Psychological aspects
ISBN 9780812997866; 9780812997859

LC 2016007455

This book, by Mary Aiken, is an "exploration of how cyberspace is changing the way we think, feel, and behave. . . . Aiken covers a wide range of subjects from the impact of screens on the developing child to the explosion of teen sexting, and the acceleration of compulsive and addictive behaviors online (gaming, shopping, pornography). She examines the escalation of cyberchondria (anxiety produced by self-diagnosing online), cyberstalking, and organized cybercrime in the Deep Web." (Publisher's note)

"Aiken provides a thoughtful approach to the attractions, distractions, and pitfalls of our digital culture." Kirkus

Includes bibliographical references (pages 337-370) and index.

Benson, Herbert

★ The **relaxation** response; by Herbert Benson, with Miriam Z. Klipper. Updated & expanded [ed.]; Quill 2001 liv, 179p il pa $13.99   **155.9**

1. Rest 2. Stress (Physiology) 3. Stress (Psychology)
ISBN 0-380-81595-8

LC 2003-269877

First published 1975 by Morrow

This guide to relieving stress is "recommended for patients suffering from heart conditions, hypertension, chronic pain, and other ailments. A classic." Libr J

Includes bibliographical references

Bettencourt, Megan Feldman

Triumph of the heart; forgiveness in an unforgiving world. Megan Feldman Bettencourt. Avery 2015 288 p. (hardback) $25.95 **155.9**
1. Forgiveness
ISBN 1594632634; 9781594632631
LC 2014048570

This book, by Megan Feldman Bettencourt, explores the concept of forgiveness "from both a scientific perspective and a human one. She draws on cutting-edge research showing that forgiveness can provide a range of health benefits, from relieving depression to decreasing high blood pressure. She examines situations as mundane as road rage, as painful as cheating spouses, and as unthinkable as war crimes." (Publisher's note)

"This compelling investigation into an important subject may well inspire readers to give the concept of forgiveness a bigger place in their lives." Pub Wkly

Includes bibliographical references and index

Doka, Kenneth J.

Grief is a journey; finding your path through loss. Dr. Kenneth J. Doka. Atria Books 2016 304 p. (hardback) $26 **155.9**
1. Grief 2. Bereavement 3. Loss (Psychology) 4. Death
ISBN 9781476771489; 1476771480
LC 2015014071

This book, by Kenneth J. Doka, "explores a new, compassionate way to grieve, explaining that grief is not an illness to get over but an individual and ongoing journey. . . . In doing so, he helps us realize that our experiences following a death are far more individual and much less predictable than the conventional 'five stages' model would have us believe." (Publisher's note)

"Well supported by footnotes, this is a useful and reassuring resource." Pub Wkly

Includes bibliographical references and index

Dresser, Norine

Saying goodbye to someone you love; your journey through end-of-life and grief. [by] Norine Dresser, Fredda Wasserman. DemosHealth Pub. 2010 210p pa $16.95 **155.9**
1. Death 2. Bereavement
ISBN 978-1-932603-85-9
LC 2010-2096

The authors "draw from their experience as hospice workers to illustrate how people have brought up the subject of death with the dying, made end-of-life decisions, and planned (or not held) a funeral service. Dresser and Wasserman not only offer comfort and companionship but provide practical suggestions for conversation starters, ideas for memorials, and a whole section on handling the grief of children. Essential for anyone experiencing end-of-life issues." Libr J

Includes bibliographical references

Edelman, Hope

Motherless daughters; the legacy of loss. 2nd ed; Da Capo Press 2006 pa $15.95 **155.9**
1. Bereavement 2. Loss (Psychology) 3. Mother-

daughter relationship
ISBN 978-0-7382-1026-1
LC 2005-33840

First published 1994 by Addison-Wesley

"Writing of her own experiences of losing her mother when she was 17, and the grief of hundreds of women she interviewed who lost their mothers through death, abandonment or another form of separation . . . Edelman marshals a wealth of anecdotal evidence, supplemented with psychological research about bereavement, that indicates that one's longing for a mother never disappears." Publ Wkly

Includes bibliographical references

Motherless mothers; how mother loss shapes the parents we become. HarperCollins 2006 xxxiii, 410p hardcover o.p. pa $14.95 **155.9**
1. Parenting 2. Bereavement 3. Loss (Psychology) 4. Mother-daughter relationship
ISBN 0-06-053246-7 pa; 978-0-06-053246-8 pa
LC 2005-52812

Edelman "presents emotionally charged concepts in clear, memorable terms (e.g., reaching the 'neon number' of a mother's age of death) to encourage frank, cathartic discussion." Publ Wkly

Includes bibliographical references

Emswiler, Mary Ann

Guiding your child through grief; {by} Mary Ann Emswiler and James P. Emswiler. Bantam Bks. 2000 286p il pa $13.95 **155.9**
1. Death 2. Bereavement 3. Child rearing
ISBN 0-553-38025-7
LC 00-23645

"Thoroughly researched and bolstered with the wisdom of bereavement experts nationwide, this fine guide does those working through the loss of loved ones an enormous service. It should rank amongst the first line of defense and support for those facing a death in the family." Publ Wkly

Includes bibliographical references

Enayati, Amanda

Seeking serenity; the 10 new rules for health and happiness in the age of anxiety. Amanda Enayati. NAL Hardcover 2015 272 p. illustrations (hardback) $25.95 **155.9**
1. Health 2. Anxiety 3. Happiness 4. Well-being 5. Inner peace 6. Mental health 7. Stress management 8. Stress (Psychology)
ISBN 0451471512; 9780451471512
LC 2014029563

In this book, author "Amanda Enayati challenges our long-held assumptions about stress, painting a groundbreaking picture that separates myth from reality when it comes to what is commonly referred to as the plague of modern life. Weaving together stories, research from science, history, philosophy and diverse faiths, and everyday exercises, she crafts a fascinating tale that begins with the behind-the-scenes machinations of corporate villains and ends in the power of our stories to shape our realities." (Publisher's note)

"Enayati's work, while not earth-shattering, provides a positive, inexpensive avenue to inner peace." LJ

Gilbert, Sandra M.

★ **Death's** door; modern dying and the ways we grieve. Norton 2006 580p il $29.95; pa $17.95   **155.9**

1. Death 2. Bereavement

ISBN 0-393-05131-5; 978-0-393-05131-5; 0-393-32969-0 pa; 978-0-393-32969-8 pa

LC 2004-65430

"Those who have experienced the death of a loved one will recognize themselves in this meticulously researched, comprehensively organized, and exceptionally caring examination of society's attitudes about mortality and mourning." Booklist

Includes bibliographical references

Gonzales, Laurence, 1947-

Surviving survival; the art and science of resilience. Laurence Gonzales. W.W. Norton 2012 272 p. (hardcover) $26.95   **155.9**

1. Psychology 2. Brain -- Physiology 3. Adjustment (Psychology) 4. Resourcefulness 5. Resilience (Personality trait) 6. Disasters -- Psychological aspects

ISBN 0393083187; 9780393083187

LC 2012015592

This book examines "the mental processes that enable us to cope with the trauma that often sets in during and after a challenge to our survival. . . . [Laurence] Gonzales narrates . . . tales, not all of them elective; his survivors are those who have suffered war and terrorism as well as falls off mountains and into choppy surf." The book includes "explanations of the science behind . . . how the amygdala works. . . . One characteristic of success, writes Gonzales, is the ability to step outside oneself to help others." (Kirkus Reviews)

Includes bibliographical references and index

Gosling, Sam

Snoop; what your stuff says about you. Basic Books 2008 263p il map $25   **155.9**

1. Materialism 2. Social psychology

ISBN 978-0-465-02781-1; 0-465-02781-4

LC 2007-52071

"Unlike many current books on behaviour, Snoop does not contain a single brain scan or discussion of neural activity. Instead, it adopts a shamelessly social approach, focusing on how people behave in the real world rather than in a brain scanner, and presents explanations at the level of individual personalities and social interactions. It works, not least because it has the huge advantage of being exclusively concerned with the one topic that most people find endlessly fascinating: themselves." New Sci

Includes bibliographical references

Greenfield, Susan, 1950-

Mind change; how digital technologies are leaving their mark on our brains. Susan Greenfield. Random House Inc 2015 368 p. illustration (hardback) $28   **155.9**

1. Information technology 2. Technology -- Psychological aspects 3. Cognition 4. Information technology -- Social aspects 5. Information technology

-- Psychological aspects

ISBN 0812993829; 9780812993820

LC 2014020059

In this book, author Susan Greenfield "explores whether incessant exposure to social media sites, search engines, and videogames is capable of rewiring our brains, and whether the minds of people born before and after the advent of the Internet differ. Stressing the impact on Digital Natives--those who've never known a world without the Internet--Greenfield exposes how neuronal networking may be affected by unprecedented bombardments of audiovisual stimuli." (Publisher's note)

"While Greenfield is cautious about making definitive statements, she is determined to persuade readers to think about how all our texting, e-mailing, and social networking may be affecting our very brains. Although densely written at times, Mind Change is exceedingly well organized and hits the right balance between academic and provocative. There is no question about the need for us to think more deeply about this topic." Booklist

Karr-Morse, Robin

Scared sick; Robin Karr-Morse with Meredith S. Wiley. Basic Books 2012 xvii, 301p   **155.9**

1. Mothers 2. Diseases 3. Parenting 4. Child psychology 5. Child development 6. Psychic trauma

ISBN 9780465013548; 9780465028122

LC 2011029405

This book presents an "investigation of the importance of attachment between baby and caretaker—usually the mother—in setting the path to physical and mental health. . . . [The authors] write that without that bond, there is danger that a baby will be stressed, triggering the hypothalamus-pituitary-adrenal axis and flooding the baby's developing nervous system with flight-or-fight hormones. The baby, unable to flee or fight, may succumb to trauma, defined as being frozen in fear. Such trauma is the root of being 'scared sick': suffering ills that may not appear until later in life. Among many others, these can include autism, Alzheimer's, addiction, ADHD, schizophrenia, PTSD, suicide, chronic pain, obesity, heart disease, diabetes and cancer." (Kirkus)

Includes bibliographical references and index.

Kingma, Daphne Rose

The **ten** things to do when your life falls apart; an emotional and spiritual handbook. New World Library 2010 xxiv, 214p pa $14.95   **155.9**

1. Suffering 2. Adjustment (Psychology)

ISBN 978-1-57731-698-5

LC 2010-1049

The author "writes for readers whose lives are being wrenched apart by sudden job loss, the death of a loved one, financial ruin, or a dire medical diagnosis. When any of these things happens, either separately or simultaneously, Kingma offers a list of ten ways whereby readers can eventually learn that their difficulties have meaning and purpose. . . . For those lost in the turbulence of life, Kingma offers a genuine hand through." Libr J

Kubler-Ross, Elisabeth

★ **On** children and death. Macmillan 1983 279p hardcover o.p. pa $12 **155.9**
1. Death 2. Child psychology
ISBN 0-684-83939-3 pa

LC 83-11252

A look at how one copes with a child's death by disease, accident or murder
Includes bibliographical references

★ **On** death and dying. Scribner Classics 1997 286p il $23; pa $13 **155.9**
1. Death 2. Terminal care
ISBN 0-684-84223-8; 0-684-83938-5 pa

LC 97-177294

A reissue of the title first published 1969 by Macmillan
A look at the psychological, sociological and theological issues faced by the terminally ill and their caregivers
Includes bibliographical references

Louv, Richard, 1949-

Vitamin N; the essential guide to a nature-rich life. Richard Louv. Algonquin Books of Chapel Hill 2016 304 p. illustrations (paperback) $15.95 **155.9**
1. Nature 2. Outdoor recreation 3. Nature study 4. Family recreation 5. Nature -- Psychological aspects
ISBN 9781616205782; 1616205784

LC 2015031470

This book, by Richard Louv, "is a complete prescription for connecting with the power and joy of the natural world right now, with 500 activities for children and adults, dozens of inspiring and thought-provoking essays, scores of informational websites, [and] down-to-earth advice." (Publisher's note)

"Louv has become a national leader in advocating for kids to connect with nature. His macrovision of ecological health speaks beyond the benefits of youngsters getting dirty." LJ

Includes bibliographical references (pages 243-251) and index.

Padgett, Jason

Struck by genius; how a brain injury made me a mathematical marvel. Jason Padgett, Maureen Ann Seaberg. Houghton Mifflin Harcourt 2014 256 p. colored illustrations (hardback) $27 **155.9**
1. Autobiographies 2. Savants (Savant syndrome) 3. Brain -- Wounds and injuries 4. Psychic trauma
ISBN 0544045602; 9780544045606

LC 2013041065

"In September 2002, author Padgett was brutally mugged as he exited a Tacoma karaoke bar. The hospital medical exam revealed a profound brain concussion, and Padgett was treated and released. The next day, the author began to experience a keen ability to understand high levels of math and physics, as well as grasp developed skills for drawing complex geometric shapes that he started to see in everything. Padgett's diagnosis was acquired savant syndrome, a condition that had formerly been diagnosed in only 30 other individuals.." (Library Journal)

A "beautiful, inspiring and intimate account of Padgett's struggles and breakthroughs. An exquisite insider's look into the mysteries of consciousness." Kirkus
Includes bibliographical references and index

Ripley, Amanda

The **unthinkable**; who survives when disaster strikes and why. Crown Publishers 2008 xx, 266p il $24.95 **155.9**
1. Disasters 2. Disaster relief 3. Survival skills
ISBN 978-0-307-35289-7

LC 2007-40315

Ripley "offers an elementary discussion of disaster and survival, drawing on both survivors' personal accounts and scientific studies that reveal how the human brain functions under duress. She shows how individuals and groups react when such disasters as shipwrecks, fires, terrorist attacks, and tsunamis occur, detailing the traits survivors demonstrate that help them respond effectively. . . . Offering tips on how we can boost our odds, her self-help approach to survival will attract readers." Libr J
Includes bibliographical references

Sife, Wallace

The **loss** of a pet; 3rd ed; Howell Book House 2005 260p il pa $14.99 **155.9**
1. Pets 2. Death 3. Bereavement
ISBN 0-7645-7930-4

LC 2005-12603

First published 1993
The author "addresses the pet owner whose grief at a pet's death is largely misunderstood or even ridiculed by friends, associates and society in general. . . . Sife is to be commended for offering information that is not only compassionate but concise, wide-ranging and, above all, practical." Publ Wkly {review of 1993 edition}

Wickersham, Joan

The **suicide** index; putting my father's death in order. Harcourt 2008 316p $25; pa $14.95 **155.9**
1. Suicide 2. Father-daughter relationship
ISBN 978-0-1510-1490-3; 0-1510-1490-6; 978-0-1560-3380-0 pa; 0-1560-3380-1 pa

LC 2007-29299

"Wickersham's memoir unravels the twisted branches of family ties in the aftermath of her father's suicide as she attempts to answer the question, Why did he do it? . . . Wickersham's effort is worth the read. . . . This book is beautifully written and haunts the reader long after it's closed. Recommended." Libr J

Zimbardo, Philip

The **Lucifer** effect; understanding how good people turn evil. [by] Philip Zimbardo. Random House 2007 xx, 551p il $27.95 **155.9**
1. Good and evil 2. Social psychology 3. Good and evil -- Psychological aspects
ISBN 1-4000-6411-2; 978-1-4000-6411-3

LC 2006-50388

The author "masterminded the famous Stanford Prison Experiment, in which college students randomly assigned to be guards or inmates found themselves enacting sadistic abuse or abject submissiveness. In this penetrating investigation, he revisits . . . the SPE study and applies it to historical examples of injustice and atrocity, especially the Abu Ghraib outrages by the U.S. military. . . . Combining a dense but readable and often engrossing exposition of social psychology research with an impassioned moral seriousness, Zimbardo challenges readers to look beyond glib denunciations of evil-doers and ponder our collective responsibility for the world's ills." Publ Wkly

Includes bibliographical references

155.94   Influence of community and housing

Warnick, Melody

This Is Where You Belong; The Art and Science of Loving the Place You Live. by Melody Warnick. Penguin Group USA 2016 320 p. (hardcover) $26   **155.94**
1. Moving 2. Social integration 3. United States -- Social life and customs
ISBN 9780525429128; 0525429123

LC 2016017846

In this book, journalist Melody Warnick "embarks on a project to discover what it takes to love where you live. . . . She dives into the body of research around place attachment—the deep sense of connection that binds some of us to our cities and increases our physical and emotional well-being—then travels to towns across America to see it in action. Inspired by a growing movement of placemaking, she examines what its practitioners are doing to create likeable locales." (Publisher's note)

"Warnick shifts between sharing her stories and the results of her extensive research, crafting an enjoyable book for anyone who cherishes their hometown as well as for those who don't and would like to do so." LJ

Includes bibliographical references (pages 261-298) and index.

156   Comparative psychology

Fouts, Roger

Next of kin; what chimpanzees have taught me about who we are. {by} Roger Fouts with Stephen Tukel Mills; introduction by Jane Goodall. Morrow 1997 420p il hardcover o.p. pa $14   **156**
1. Chimpanzees 2. Animal communication
ISBN 0-380-72822-2 pa

LC 97-15144

This is an account of a study known as Project Washoe where a female chimpanzee was taught American Sign Language

"What makes this book an exceptional popularization of scientific research is the authors' ability to charm with a fascinating story while also teaching why the story is so fascinating." Booklist

Includes bibliographical references

Miller, Peter

The **smart** swarm; how understanding flocks, schools, and colonies can make us better at communicating, decision making, and getting things done. Avery 2010 xx, 283p $26   **156**
1. Human behavior 2. Animal behavior 3. Decision making
ISBN 978-1-58333-390-7

LC 2009-48619

The author "examines hives, mounds, colonies, and swarms, whose complex systems of engagement and collective decision making have catalyzed innovations in engineering and can suggest solutions to such problems as climate change. . . . Miller informs, engages, entertains, and even surprises in this thought-provoking study of problem making and problem solving, and through the comparison of human and insect scenarios, shows how social cues and signals can either bring about social cooperation or destruction." Publ Wkly

Includes bibliographical references

Peterson, Dale

The **moral** lives of animals. Bloomsbury Press 2010 342p   **156**
1. Ethics 2. Animal behavior 3. Animal intelligence 4. Moral motivation 5. Animal psychology
ISBN 978-1-59691-424-7

LC 2010024662

Peterson "examines the moral behavior observed in animals and argues that human beings are not the only species to live by the principles of cooperation, kindness, and empathy." (Publisher's note) Bibliography. Index.

The author "develops his thoughts on how morality evolved in mammals, including humans. He initially concentrates on where morality comes from, covering basic concepts, linguistic bias, definitions of morality, and a theory of morality's structure. Rules of morality follow with topics such as authority, violence, sex, possession, and communication. . . . Although written for a general audience, this book challenges readers to absorb new information in an area unfamiliar to most. It is definitely worth the effort and is highly recommended for high school-age readers and up." Libr J

Includes bibliographical references

Suddendorf, Thomas

The **gap**; the science of what separates us from other animals. Thomas Suddendorf. Basic Books 2013 368 p. (hardcover) $29.99   **156**
1. Human beings 2. Comparative psychology 3. Psychology 4. Psychology, Comparative
ISBN 0465030149; 9780465030149

LC 2013017538

Author Thomas Suddendorf "provides a definitive account of the mental qualities that separate humans from other animals. Drawing on . . . research on apes, children, and human evolution, he surveys the abilities most often cited as uniquely human--language, intelligence, morality, culture, theory of mind--and finds that two traits account for most of the ways in which our minds appear so distinct: [the] ability to imagine . . .and our insatiable drive to link our minds together." (Publisher's note)

"A reader-friendly examination of the great gap that exists between human beings and the rest of the animal world and an explanation of how our minds came to be unique." Kirkus

Includes bibliographical references and index

Waal, Frans de

Our inner ape; a leading primatologist explains why we are who we are. photographs by the author. Riverhead Books 2005 274p il $24.95 **156**

1. Human behavior 2. Comparative psychology 3. Primates -- Behavior

ISBN 1-57322-312-3

LC 2005-42768

"Readers might be surprised at how much these apes and their stories resonate with their own lives, and may well be left with an urge to spend a few hours watching primates themselves at the local zoo." Publ Wkly

Includes bibliographical references

158 Applied psychology

Achor, Shawn

Before happiness; the 5 hidden keys to achieving success, spreading happiness, and sustaining positive change. by Shawn Achor. Crown Business 2013 256 p. (hc : alk. paper) $26 **158**

1. Happiness 2. Change (Psychology) 3. Success 4. Positive psychology

ISBN 0770436730; 9780770436735

LC 2013022564

In this book, "a happiness researcher investigates why some people can embrace positivity while others are mired in pessimism. Expanding on the theories he presented in 'The Happiness Advantage' . . . [Shawn] Achor now turns his attention to the question of how people learn to accept the possibility of happiness. . . . Happiness . . . is not the same as blind optimism but rather the ability to focus on the positive aspects of a situation while not becoming overwhelmed by the challenges." (Kirkus Reviews)

Includes bibliographical references and index

Bloomfield, Harold H.

Making peace with your past; the six essential steps to enjoying a great future. {by} Harold H. Bloomfield with Philip Goldberg. HarperCollins Pubs. 2000 269p hardcover o.p. pa $13 **158**

1. Self-realization 2. Applied psychology

ISBN 0-06-093314-3 pa

LC 99-89719

The author "addresses the syndrome Freud called 'repetition compulsion'—humans' tendency to re-create what they have not worked through. . . . With revealing exercises, Bloomfield shows readers how to rediscover 'the passion to live {their} highest destiny.'" Libr J

Includes bibliographical references

Brown, Brene

Rising strong; Brené Brown. Spiegel & Grau 2015 336 p. (hardback) $27 **158**

1. Courage 2. Resilience (Personality trait) 3. Self-actualization (Psychology)

ISBN 0812995821; 9780812995824

LC 2015010832

In this book author Brene Brown "has listened as a range of people--from leaders in Fortune 500 companies and the military to artists, couples in long-term relationships, teachers, and parents--shared their stories of being brave, falling, and getting back up. They recognize the power of emotion and they're not afraid to lean in to discomfort." (Publisher's note)

"An innovative one-two-three-punch approach to self-help and healing from an author who has helped count less readers change their lives." Kirkus

Burns, David D.

Feeling good; the new mood therapy. preface by Aaron T. Beck. Rev and updated; Avon Bks. 1999 xxxii, 706p il pa $15 **158**

1. Psychotherapy 2. Depression (Psychology)

ISBN 0-380-73176-2

LC 99-461798

First published 1980

"The author . . . writes simply, clearly, and without any jargon; better yet, he has a sense of compassion and a sense of humor, and is aware of his own limitations." Libr J {review of 1980 edition}

Includes bibliographical references

Canfield, Jack

The **success** principles; how to get from where you are to where you want to be. by Jack Canfield with Janet Switzer. HarperCollins Publishers 2005 xxxiii, 473p il $24.95 **158**

1. Success

ISBN 0-06-059488-8

LC 2004-54259

A self-improvement guide for business professionals, teachers, students, parents, or anyone interested in promoting themselves within today's success-oriented culture shares sixty-four principles on how to reach desired goals

The author "has an easy style and talks directly to readers, responding to potential 'what ifs' and 'buts' with encouragement and sound advice. The book's layout is superb—small paragraphs are punctuated by italicized quotes, questions for self-study, and several appropriate cartoons." Libr J

Includes bibliographical references

Carnegie, Dale

★ **How** to win friends and influence people; editorial consultant, Dorothy Carnegie, editorial assistance, Arthur R. Pell. Pocket Books 1982 276p pa $6.99 **158**

1. Success 2. Applied psychology

ISBN 0-671-72365-0; 978-0-671-72365-1

LC 94-176452

First published 1936 by Simon & Schuster

An examination of the psychology of business and social success.

"This grandfather of all people-skills books was first published in 1937. It was an overnight hit, eventually selling 15 million copies. . . . [It] emphasizes fundamental techniques for handling people without making them feel manipulated. . . . Carnegie illustrates his points with anecdotes of historical figures, leaders of the business world, and everyday folks." Joan Price [This text refers to an out of print or unavailable edition of this title.]

Includes bibliographical references

Covey, Stephen R.

★ The **7** habits of highly effective people; restoring the character ethic. [Rev. ed.]; Free Press 2004 372p il $26; pa $15.95   **158**
1. Success 2. Conduct of life
ISBN 0-7432-7245-5; 0-7432-6951-9 pa

LC 2004-57494

First published 1989

The author describes seven habits designed to help people solve personal and professional problems.

The **8th** habit; from effectiveness to greatness. Free Press 2004 408p il $26   **158**
1. Success 2. Self-realization
ISBN 0-684-84665-9

LC 2004-56371

"Though conceived for individuals, Covey's book will be of tremendous importance to organizations and businesses." Libr J

Includes bibliographical references

First things first; to live, to love, to learn, to leave a legacy. {by} Stephen R. Covey, A. Roger Merrill, Rebecca R. Merrill. Simon & Schuster 1994 360p il hardcover o.p. pa $14   **158**
1. Conduct of life 2. Time management
ISBN 0-684-80203-1 pa

LC 94-2305

The authors "offer a 'principle-centered' approach to time management that emphasizes what 'represents our vision, values, principles, mission, conscience, direction—what we feel is important and how we lead our lives.' The authors argue that central to our lives are 'four needs and capacities—to live, to love, to learn, to leave a legacy.' The ideas here are not only clearly explained but are reinforced by scenarios from the authors' lives and self-directed activities for the reader." Libr J

Includes bibliographical references

Duhigg, Charles

Smarter faster better; the secrets of productivity in life and business. Charles Duhigg. Random House Inc 2016 400 p. illustrations $28   **158**
1. Performance 2. Decision making 3. Self-help techniques 4. Motivation (Psychology) 5. Organizational behavior 6. Success 7. Mental efficiency
ISBN 9780812993394

LC 2015034214

This book, by journalist Charles Duhigg, is "a groundbreaking exploration of the science of productivity, one that can help anyone learn to succeed with less stress and struggle, and to get more done without sacrificing what we care about most—to become smarter, faster, and better at everything we do." (Publisher's note)

"Duhigg shows an uncanny ability to find just the right exciting example of productivity-boosting methods, leaving readers to nod in recognition that they might act in the same way to improve their lives and work." Kirkus

Includes bibliographical references and index

Dyer, Wayne W.

★ The **power** of intention; learning to co-create your world your way. Hay House 2004 259p $24.95; pa $14.95   **158**
1. Intentionalism
ISBN 1-401-90215-4; 1-401-90216-2 pa

LC 2003-14622

The author argues that "there are seven faces, or energy fields, of intention: creativity, kindness, love, beauty, expansion, abundance and receptivity. Drawing on a variety of spiritual traditions and gurus, Dyer . . . describes how to surmount the barriers that may get in the way of connecting to this power, such as negative thinking, relying on the opinion of others or retaining a controlling ego." Publ Wkly

Foster, Rick

How we choose to be happy; the 9 choices of extremely happy people--their secrets, their stories. Rev; Berkley Publishing Group 2004 xxi, 228p pa $14.95   **158**
1. Happiness
ISBN 978-0-399-52990-0; 0-399-52990-X

First published 1999

The authors "interviewed happy people from all walks of life, from the United States to Eastern Europe. The resulting personal stories, writing exercises, and quotes together inform and instruct the reader in the nine principles discovered by the authors in their travels." Libr J

Gilbert, Daniel

★ **Stumbling** on happiness; [by] Daniel Gilbert. Alfred A. Knopf 2006 277p il   **158**
1. Happiness
ISBN 1-4000-4266-6; 1-4000-7742-7 pa; 978-1-4000-4266-1; 978-1-4000-7742-7 pa

LC 2005044459

This book argues that "events that we anticipate will give us joy make us less happy than we think; things that fill us with dread will make us less unhappy, for less long, than we anticipate." (N Y Times Book Rev) Index.

"The book is a sly, irresistible romp down, or through, memory lane—past, present, and future. It is not only wildly entertaining but also hilarious . . . and yet full of startling insight, imaginative conclusions, and even bits of wisdom." Booklist

Includes bibliographical references

Goleman, Daniel

★ **Social** intelligence; the new science of human relationships. Bantam Books 2006 403p il $28; pa $14 **158**

1. Emotions 2. Intellect

ISBN 0-553-80352-2; 978-0-553-80352-5; 0-553-38449-X pa; 978-0-553-38449-9 pa

LC 2006-45971

The author "argues for a new social model of intelligence drawn from the emerging field of social neuroscience. . . . Goleman illuminates new theories about attachment, bonding, and the making and remaking of memory as he examines how our brains are wired for altruism, compassion, concern and rapport." Publ Wkly

Includes bibliographical references

Hay, Louise L.

You can heal your life. Hay House 1987 226p pa $14.95 **158**

1. Mind and body 2. Health self-care 3. Self-realization 4. Holistic medicine

ISBN 0-937611-01-8

LC 88-200391

First published 1984

The author's "key message in this . . . work is: 'If we are willing to do the mental work, almost anything can be healed.' Louise explains how limiting beliefs and ideas are often the cause of illness." Publisher's note

Includes bibliographical references

Klauser, Henriette Anne

Write it down, make it happen; knowing what you want--and getting it! Scribner 2000 250p hardcover o.p. pa $12 **158**

1. Applied psychology

ISBN 0-684-85002-8 pa

LC 99-43551

The author "instructs her readers to write down their most extravagant wishes and, merely by the act of recording them, make them come true. . . . Her technique is intended to clarify goals, increase self-confidence, and dispel self-doubt, and she describes how it has dramatically improved her life and the lives of her friends and acquaintances." Libr J

Includes bibliographical references

Langshur, Eric

Start here; master the lifelong habit of wellbeing. by Eric Langshur and Nate Klemp. North Star Way 2016 320 p. illustrations (hardback) $26 **158**

1. Well-being 2. Stress management 3. Self-help techniques 4. Happiness 5. Satisfaction 6. Mental health

ISBN 1501129082; 9781501129087

LC 2015043325

This book, by Eric Langshur and Nate Klemp, "is the manual for anyone seeking to achieve emotional fitness. Combining ancient wisdom with modern neuroscience from the world's leading experts, LIFE XT is a groundbreaking training program to master the art of wellbeing. The program teaches practices proven to rewire the brain for increased focus, engagement, and resilience to stress." (Publisher's note)

"Personal anecdotes add interest to the nuts-and-bolts format. Other books have touched on these same principles, but this book does an especially good job, walking readers step-by-step through the practices, presenting achievable goals, and encouraging readers to take charge of their emotional lives." Booklist

Includes bibliographical references and index

May, Rollo

★ **Freedom** and destiny. Norton 1981 275p hardcover o.p. pa $14 **158**

1. Fate and fatalism 2. Applied psychology 3. Free will and determinism

ISBN 0-393-31842-7 pa

LC 81-4009

This book examines "the continuing tension in our lives between the possibilities freedom offers and the various limitations imposed upon us by our particular fate or destiny." America

Includes bibliographical references

McGraw, Phillip C.

Life strategies; doing what works, doing what matters. Hyperion 1999 282p il $21.95; pa $13.95 **158**

1. Success

ISBN 0-7868-6548-2; 0-7868-8459-2 pa

LC 98-46748

"McGraw claims that people in dire situations have serious problems, including denial and choosing initial assumptions without testing them for accuracy. To create a life strategy that works, McGraw lays out his ten 'Life Laws' along with checklists and 18 assignments." Libr J

Michels, Barry, 1954-

The **tools**; transform your problems into courage, confidence, and creativity. Phil Stutz and Barry Michels. 1st ed. Spiegel & Grau 2012 271 p. ill. (alk. paper) $25 **158**

1. Applied psychology 2. Change (Psychology) 3. Self-help techniques 4. Self-actualization (Psychology)

ISBN 067964444X; 9780679644446; 9780679644453

LC 2011044717

In this book, "psychiatrist [Phil] Stutz and psychotherapist [Barry] Michels promote a rapid and streamlined method of self-improvement. Michels . . . teaches readers to end procrastination and negativity by tapping into higher forces. . . . [T]he authors' techniques are designed to access intense intrapersonal areas. The 'Inner Authority' tool, for example, involves imagining the Jungian Shadow to reach greater self-expression." (Publishers Weekly)

Miller, Caroline Adams

★ **Creating** your best life; the ultimate life list guide. [by] Caroline Adams Miller and Dr. Michael B. Frisch. Sterling Pub. 2009 276p il $19.95; pa $14.95 **158**

1. Success 2. Happiness

ISBN 978-1-4027-6259-8; 1-4027-6259-3; 978-1-4027-7998-5 pa; 1-4027-7998-4 pa

LC 2010-275766

"Instead of making New Year's resolutions, it may be more beneficial to assemble a goal-setting list. So believe positive psychologist/life coach Miller and clinical psychologist Frisch . . . who have put together dozens of interactive exercises and assessments to guide readers in self-discovery and life-list creation. Whether or not readers follow through with every assignment, they will undoubtedly be inspired to think about goals and live more consciously and productively." Libr J

Includes bibliographical references

Peck, M. Scott

Further along the road less traveled; the unending journey toward spiritual growth: the edited lectures. Simon & Schuster 1993 255p hardcover o.p. pa $14   **158**

1. Spiritual life 2. Self-realization 3. Applied psychology
ISBN 0-684-84723-X pa

LC 93-31322

The author "discusses 'growing up'—becoming self-aware, working through cycles of blame and toward wholesale forgiveness—and then the self-examination we each must undergo in order to groom ourselves for the most important step of all: the search for God." Booklist

★ The **road** less traveled; a new psychology of love, traditional values, and spiritual growth. 25th anniversary ed; Simon & Schuster 2002 315p $22.95   **158**

1. Love 2. Applied psychology
ISBN 0-7432-3825-7

LC 2002-75858

A reissue of the title first published 1978

This book attempts to bring together "psychology and religion. It is divided into four areas—discipline, love, religion and growth, and grace—and within each Peck tackles the . . . struggle between stagnation and progress which goes on in all of us throughout our lives." Libr J

The **road** less traveled and beyond; spiritual growth in an age of anxiety. Simon & Schuster 1997 314p $23; pa $14   **158**

1. Self-realization 2. Applied psychology
ISBN 0-684-81314-9; 0-684-83561-4 pa

LC 96-43391

In this volume Peck "continues his journey through the existential conflicts and baffling paradoxes on the meandering road of personal development. . . . Through copious detailed references from his previous books, he allows readers unfamiliar with them to understand and enjoy the present work, which completes his Road trilogy." Publ Wkly

Prager, Dennis

Happiness is a serious problem; a human nature repair manual. ReganBooks 1998 179p hardcover o.p. pa $13   **158**

1. Happiness
ISBN 0-06-098735-1 pa

LC 97-35404

The author "uses the pursuit of happiness as a central motif but generally instructs in the modern art of self-im-

provement. The 31 short chapters . . . are cogent, complete, and preach a nonreligious yet morally guided moderation that should appeal across a wide range of patron groups." Libr J

Robbins, Tony

Unlimited power; the new science of personal achievement. [by] Anthony Robbins. 1st Fireside ed.; Simon & Schuster 1997 425p il pa $15   **158**

1. Success 2. Applied psychology
ISBN 0-684-84577-6

LC 97-35403

First published 1986

The author offers advice and techniques for achieving personal and professional success using neurolinguistic programming (NLP).

Rowling, J. K., 1965-

Very good lives; the fringe benefits of failure and the importance of imagination. J.K. Rowling. Little, Brown & Co. 2015 80 p. illustrations $15   **158**

1. Imagination 2. Commencements 3. Failure (Psychology)
ISBN 0316369152; 9780316369152

LC 2014959607

In this book, which reproduces her 2008 commencement speech at Harvard University, author J.K. Rowling "asks the profound and provocative questions: How can we embrace failure? And how can we use our imagination to better both ourselves and others? Drawing from stories of her own postgraduate years, the world famous author addresses some of life's most important questions." (Publisher's note)

"Though she's best known for a few Latin taglines by way of magical spells, Rowling makes neat connections between the challenges of modern life and the tutelary examples of Seneca, Plutarch, and the other ancients. While she discounts the ennobling aspects of poverty and misery, it's also clear that her education provided her with some steel to face those hardships. The author's quiet praise of liberal education forms one theme. A second, the importance of the imagination, is perhaps the more expected one, but Rowling takes a nicely unsettling detour by recounting her time spent working for Amnesty International and witnessing how monstrous people can be." Kirkus

Salzberg, Sharon

Real happiness; learn the power of meditation: a 28-day program. Workman Publishing 2011 208p pa $14.99   **158**

1. Meditation
ISBN 978-0-7611-5925-4

LC 2010-52087

The author "provides a 28-day program for incorporating meditation into one's life. Written for beginners, the book explains breathing and sitting techniques, the science behind the practice, and 12 guided meditations. Interspersed throughout are FAQs from Salzberg's students regarding their difficulties with the practice. The accompanying CD includes nine meditations to guide readers through breathing, walking, emotional, and loving-kindness exercises. This is one of the best guides for anyone interested in exploring meditation or mindfulness." Libr J

Includes bibliographical references

Schwartz, David Joseph

★ The **magic** of thinking big; 1st Fireside ed.; Simon & Schuster 1987 192p pa $14.95   **158**

1. Success

ISBN 0-671-64678-8

LC 87-8516

First published 1959 by Prentice-Hall

In this motivational book, the author presents a "program for getting the most out of your job, your marriage and family life, and your community." Publisher's note

Siegel, Bernie S.

Prescriptions for living; inspirational lessons for a joyful, loving life. HarperCollins Pubs. 1998 xxiv, 210p hardcover o.p. pa $14   **158**

1. Spiritual life 2. Self-realization

ISBN 0-06-092936-7 pa

LC 98-39059

"Among the topics Siegel covers are how to find peace of mind; how to love, encourage, and forgive other people as well as yourself; and how to thrive in bad times and survive the good times. For those ready to be uplifted by the soothing repetition of time-tested homilies, Siegel delivers the goods." Booklist

Stone, Douglas

Difficult conversations; how to discuss what matters most. {by} Douglas Stone, Bruce Patton, Sheila Heen. Viking 1999 xxi, 250p il hardcover o.p. pa $14   **158**

1. Communication 2. Interpersonal relations

ISBN 0-14-028852-X pa

LC 98-33346

The authors "blend a daunting array of disciplines into highly readable and practical advice." Booklist

Sugar, Lisa

Power your happy; Work Hard, Play Nice & Build Your Dream Life. Lisa Sugar. Dutton, a member of Penguin Random House LLC 2016 256 p. illustrations (hardcover) $25   **158**

1. Success 2. Happiness 3. Self-realization 4. Success in business

ISBN 9781101985069

LC 2016020264

In this book author Lisa Sugar, founder of POPSUGAR, "shares her personal and business story. [Sugar] knows that creating your dream job requires hard work, patience, and experience. She'll give advice, in big and small ways, about exactly how to do that, from starting a company to ditching a relationship that isn't working to becoming a fabulous boss." (Publisher's note)

"While the advice is often lighthearted ("eating ice cream" is frequently prescribed as a quick fix), readers will discover substantial guidance that is easy to implement on everything from networking to interviewing to parenting." LJ

Tolle, Eckhart

A **new** earth; awakening to your life's purpose. Dutton/Penguin Group 2005 315p $24.95   **158**

1. Spiritual life 2. Self-realization

ISBN 978-0-525-94802-5; 0-525-94802-3

LC 2005-23358

"According to Tolle, . . . humans are on the verge of creating a new world by a personal transformation that shifts our attention away from our ever-expanding egos." Publ Wkly

Includes bibliographical references

The **power** of now; a guide to spiritual enlightenment. New World Library 1999 193p $22.95; pa $14   **158**

1. Spiritual life 2. Self-realization

ISBN 978-1-57731-152-2; 1-57731-152-3; 978-1-57731-480-6 pa; 1-57731-480-8 pa

LC 99-42366

First published 1997 in Canada

"The author describes his transition from despair to self-realization soon after his 29th birthday. Tolle took another ten years to understand this transformation, during which time he evolved a philosophy that has parallels in Buddhism, relaxation techniques, and meditation theory. . . In The Power of Now he shows readers how to recognize themselves as the creators of their own pain, and how to have a pain-free existence by living fully in the present." Publisher's note

Ury, William

Getting past no; negotiating with difficult people. {by} William L. Ury. Bantam Bks. 1991 161p hardcover o.p. pa $14.95   **158**

1. Negotiation

ISBN 0-553-37131-2 pa

LC 91-10101

"Ury presents a five-step agenda to deal successfully with opponents, be they unruly teenagers, labor leaders, terrorists or international politicians. Strategies focus on self-discipline, or tactics for defusing the adversary's attacks, and suggestions for developing options designed to lead to a mutually satisfactory agreement." Publ Wkly

Includes bibliographical references

Viscott, David S.

Emotional resilience; simple truths for dealing with the unfinished business of your past. by David Viscott. Harmony Bks. 1996 358p il hardcover o.p. pa $15   **158**

1. Human behavior 2. Attitude (Psychology)

ISBN 0-517-88825-4 pa

LC 96-407

The author outlines his 10 step self help program. "His method, which includes truth telling, acceptance of self and others, letting go of the past and of false expectations, and taking responsibility for one's life, is for those trapped in emotionally confining situations, whether personal relationships, educational impasses, or financial situations." Booklist

Yate, Martin

Knock 'em dead 2015; the ultimate job search guide. by Martin Yate. Adams Media Corp 2014 384 p. $16.99   **158**

1. Job hunting 2. Job interviews 3. Resumes (Employment)

ISBN 1440579059; 9781440579059

LC 2001242089

In this book on job searching, author Martin Yate "shares his proven, unique, and ever-evolving tactics for professional success. You'll learn how to create resumes that get results, maximize social networks to quadruple your interviews, turn those job interviews into job offers, [and] negotiate the best salary and benefits package." (Publisher's note)

158.1   Personal improvement and analysis

André, Christophe

Looking at Mindfulness; 25 Ways to Live in the Moment Through Art. by Christophe Andre. Penguin Group USA 2015 304 p. color illustrations $27.95   **158.1**

1. Mind and body 2. Art appreciation

ISBN 0399175636; 9780399175633

In this book, author Christophe Andre "guides readers through the art of mindfulness beginning with art itself. Beautifully illustrated in color throughout, André curates a collection of classic and esoteric works, from Rembrandt to Hopper to Magritte, providing a lucid commentary on the inner workings of each painting-- as he describes the dynamic on the canvas, he turns to the reader's own reactions, exploring the connection between what we see and what we feel." (Publisher's note)

"A fascinating book, suitable for those who are interested in art or the discipline of mindfulness." LJ

Cardillo, Joseph

Body intelligence; harness your body's energies for your best life. Joseph Cardillo. Atria Books 2015 272 p. (hardback) $24   **158.1**

1. Self-improvement 2. Self-realization 3. Mind and body 4. Self-actualization (Psychology)

ISBN 1582705186; 9781582705187

LC 2015015373

Author Joseph Cardillo "combines Western science, technology, psychology, and holistic medicine to show that we must first balance the body's energies before we can enhance the mind. Based on cutting-edge ideas, this perennial guide teaches us to tap into our energetic "sweet spot" and identify specific steps we must take to remove energy blocks. Packed with exercises, self-tests, and step-by-step instructions, [it] provides all the interactive tools for beginners and experienced energy-balancing practitioners alike." (Publisher's note)

"Although Cardillo's reasoning can be complex, his practical suggestions will be useful for all those wanting to tap into surrounding energy forces to correct their emotional and physical balance and fine-tune their minds." Booklist

Cuddy, Amy

Presence; bringing your boldest self to your biggest challenges. Amy Cuddy. Little, Brown & Co. 2015 352 p. illustrations (hardcover) $28   **158.1**

1. Self-perception 2. Self-realization

ISBN 0316256579; 9780316256575; 9780316305624; 9780316387804

LC 2015952382

In this book author Amy Cuddy suggests "we don't need to embark on a grand spiritual quest or complete an inner transformation to harness the power of presence. Instead, we need to nudge ourselves, moment by moment, by tweaking our body language, behavior, and mind-set in our day-to-day lives. 'Presence' is filled with stories of individuals who learned how to flourish during the stressful moments that once terrified them." (Publisher's note)

"Given the popularity of Cuddy's TED Talk, one would expect that this book will be in demand, and readers will not be disappointed." LJ

Duckworth, Angela

Grit; the power of passion and perseverance. Angela Duckworth. Scribner 2016 352 p. illustrations (hardback) $28   **158.1**

1. Perseverance 2. Success in business 3. Academic achievement 4. Success 5. Diligence 6. Perseverance (Ethics) 7. Expectation (Psychology)

ISBN 9781501111105; 9781501111112

LC 2015042880

In this book, author Angela Duckworth "shows anyone striving to succeed—be it parents, students, educators, athletes, or business people—that the secret to outstanding achievement is not talent but a special blend of passion and persistence she calls 'grit.' . . . She takes readers into the field to visit cadets struggling through their first days at West Point, teachers working in some of the toughest schools, and young finalists in the National Spelling Bee." (Publisher's note)

"Not your grandpa's self-help book, but Duckworth's text is oddly encouraging, exhorting us to do better by trying harder, and a pleasure to read." Kirkus

Includes bibliographical references and index

Duhigg, Charles

★ The **power** of habit; by Charles Duhigg. Random House 2012 xx, 371 p.p   **158.1**

1. Habit 2. Business planning 3. Change (Psychology) 4. Habit -- Social aspects

ISBN 9780679603856; 9781400069286

LC 2011029545

In this book, "science writer Charles Duhigg explores the reasons why we find it so hard to change ingrained behaviour. . . . [H]abits usually start with a simple sensory cue . . . which sets up a craving in the brain's reward centres. This yearning overrides the regions involved in self-control. . . . From nail-biting to alcoholism, Duhigg offers . . . insights into the triggers that set people on a downward spiral, and proven ways to fight those urges. . . . Habitual behaviours can propagate through an organisation or society, he argues, offering convincing anecdotes that cover everything from the success of Starbucks to the civil rights movement. . . . [Duhigg examines the] way advertising hijacks your

brain's reward centres to set off a new, irresistible habit."
(New Scientist)

Includes bibliographical references and index

Harris, Dan

★ **10%** happier; how I tamed the voice in my head, reduced stress without losing my edge, and found self-help that actually works--a true story. Dan Harris. It Books 2014 256 p. (hardback) $25.99   **158.1**

1. Buddhism 2. Meditation 3. Mind and body 4. Stress management

ISBN 0062265423; 9780062265425; 9780062265432
LC 2013043037

News anchor Dan Harris "embarks on an . . . odyssey through the strange worlds of spirituality and self-help, and discovers a way to get happier. . . . After having a nationally televised panic attack on Good Morning America, . . . Harris knew he had to make some changes. . . . After learning about research that suggests meditation can do everything from lower your blood pressure to essentially rewire your brain, Harris . . . us[ed] it for increased calm, focus, and happiness." (Publisher's note)

Heller, Rick

Secular meditation; 32 practices for cultivating inner peace, compassion, and joy : a guide from the humanist community at Harvard. Rick Heller. New World Library 2015 287 p. (paperback) $15.95   **158.1**

1. Happiness 2. Meditation 3. Relaxation 4. Secularism -- 21st century 5. Meditation -- Psychological aspects

ISBN 1608683699; 9781608683697
LC 2015027201

In this book, by Rick Heller, "step-by-step instructions, personal stories, and provocative questions teach empathy for others, stress reduction, and the kind of in-the-moment living that fosters appreciation for life and resilience in the face of adversity. Heller simplifies what is often found mysterious, describing and providing detailed instructions for 32 different practices, ensuring that anyone can find the right one." (Publisher's note)

"This book is an ideal guide for those who want to study meditation and mindfulness but are put off by the focus on Buddhism or religion in general." LJ

Includes bibliographical references and index

Manson, Mark

The **subtle** art of not giving a fu*k; a counterintuitive approach to living a good life. Mark Manson. HarperOne 2016 224 p. (hardback) $24.99; (ebook) $23.99   **158.1**

1. Conduct of life 2. Self-realization 3. Self-help techniques

ISBN 0062457713; 9780062457714; 9780062457738
LC 2016011724

This book, by Mark Manson, is a "generation-defining self-help guide. . . . Manson makes the argument, backed both by academic research and well-timed poop jokes, that improving our lives hinges not on our ability to turn lemons into lemonade, but on learning to stomach lemons better." (Publisher's note)

"This book, full of counterintuitive suggestions that often make great sense, is a pleasure to read and worthy of re-reading. A good yardstick by which self-improvement books should be measured." Kirkus

Roth, Bernard

The **Achievement** Habit; Stop Wishing, Start Doing, and Take Command of Your Life. Bernard Roth. HarperCollins 2015 288 p. illustrations $27.99   **158.1**

1. Self-confidence 2. Self-realization 3. Thought and thinking

ISBN 0062356100; 9780062356109
LC 2015303295

This book by Bernard Roth presents a "primer to the basic elements of design theory, based on the premise that 'achievement can be learned.' Tenets include 'making the familiar unfamiliar,' individual responsibility, and reframing questions in order to find solutions. To illustrate the last principle's importance, Roth describes some D.school success stories, including presenting MRI testing to child patients as an 'adventure.'" (Publishers Weekly)

"Roth's excellent advice on how to overcome obstacles and triumph should be of interest to readers college age and up." LJ

Rubin, Gretchen

Better than before; Mastering the Habits of Our Everyday Lives. Gretchen Rubin. Crown 2015 320 p. illustrations (hardback) $26   **158.1**

1. Habit 2. Change (Psychology)

ISBN 0385348614; 9780385348614; 9780385348638
LC 2014031703

In this book, author Gretchen Rubin explains that "[h]abits are the invisible architecture of everyday life. It takes work to make a habit, but once that habit is set, we can harness the energy of habits to build happier, stronger, more productive lives. . . . Rubin uses herself as guinea pig, tests her theories on family and friends, and answers readers' most pressing questions." (Publisher's note)

Readers looking to keep those New Year's resolutions should consider consulting Rubin's suggested reading section for more robust data. The airy, conversational writing style makes this a quick but not terribly substantial read." Kirkus

Tippett, Krista

Becoming Wise; An Inquiry into the Mystery and Art of Living. Krista Tippett. Penguin Group USA 2016 304 p. $28   **158.1**

1. Life 2. Meaning (Philosophy)

ISBN 1594206805; 9781594206801

This book, by Krista Tippett, " offers a grounded and fiercely hopeful vision of humanity for this century--of personal growth but also renewed public life and human spiritual evolution. It insists on the possibility of a common life for this century marked by resilience and redemption, with beauty as a core moral value and civility and love as muscular practice. The book is a master class in living, curated by Tippett and accompanied by a delightfully ecumenical dream team of teaching faculty." (Publisher's note)

"A hopeful consideration of the human potential for enlightenment." Kirkus

Vincent, Isabel

Dinner with Edward; the story of a remarkable friendship. Isabel Vincent. Algonquin Books of Chapel Hill 2016 224 p. $23.95   **158.1**
1. Widowers 2. Friendship 3. New York (N.Y.) -- Biography 4. Self-actualization (Psychology) 5. Friendship -- Psychological aspects 6. Dinners and dining -- New York (State) -- New York 7. Women authors, American -- New York (State) -- New York -- Biography
ISBN 9781616204228; 1616204222

LC 2015034310

Author Isabel Vincent presents this memoir "about sorrow and joy, love and nourishment. As Edward and Isabel meet weekly for . . . dinners that Edward prepares, he shares so much more than his recipes. Edward is teaching Isabel the luxury of slowing down and taking the time to think through everything she does, to deconstruct her own life, cutting it back to the bone and examining the guts, no matter how messy that proves to be." (Publisher's note)

"Delightfully combining the warmheartedness of Tuesdays with Morrie with the sensual splendor of Julie and Julia, this is a memoir to treasure." Booklist

Viorst, Judith

Imperfect control; our lifelong struggles with power and surrender. Simon & Schuster 1998 446p hardcover o.p. pa $14   **158.1**
1. Psychology
ISBN 0-684-84814-7 pa

LC 97-37302

"Referring to the works of social scientists, psychologists, and philosophers as well as literary examples and personal experiences, Viorst shows how issues of power and surrender confront and affect us throughout our lives. . . . Her book is very readable, with traces of the author's special brand of humor woven throughout." Libr J

Includes bibliographical references

Wax, Ruby

Sane new world; a user's guide to the normal-crazy mind. Ruby Wax. Perigee Trade 2014 247 p. illustrations (paperback) $16   **158.1**
1. Mental health 2. Cognitive therapy 3. Mind and body 4. Mindfulness-based cognitive therapy
ISBN 039917060X; 9780399170607

LC 2014016530

In this book, Ruby Wax, "comedian, writer and mental health advocate--shows us just how our minds can send us mad as our internal critics play on a permanent loop tape. . . . Ruby knows those voices well. She has been on a tough but ultimately enlightening journey that has taken her from battling depression to achieving a Masters Degree from Oxford University in Mindfulness-based Cognitive Therapy." (Publisher's note)

"Wax's unconventional approach may inspire others to seek help in coping with mental illness." LJ

158.12   Personal improvement and analysis through meditation

Wellings, Nigel

Why can't I meditate? how to get your mindfulness practice on track. Nigel Wellings. TarcherPerigee 2016 384 p. (paperback) $16   **158.12**
1. Meditation 2. Mindfulness (Psychology)
ISBN 9781101983270

LC 2016007917

This book, by Nigel Wellings, is a "guide . . . on how to get the most out of meditation--and make the practice a permanent part of your daily life. . . . Full of practical ways to help our mindfulness practice flourish, it also features guidance from a wide spectrum of secular and Buddhist mindfulness teachers, and personal accounts by new meditators on what they find difficult and what helps them overcome those blocks." (Publisher's note)

"The instructions are clear, easy to follow, and kind, offering readers a path forward while leaving plenty of room for them to decide what works best. New students of mediation would be hard-pressed to find a more patient teacher." Booklist

Includes bibliographical references and index

158.2   Interpersonal relations

Bright, Deb

The truth doesn't have to hurt; how to use criticism to strengthen relationships, improve performance, and promote change. Deb Bright. American Management Association 2015 256 p. illustrations (pbk.) $17.95   **158.2**
1. Change (Psychology) 2. Feedback (Psychology) 3. Interpersonal relations 4. Performance 5. Criticism, Personal
ISBN 0814434819; 9780814434819

LC 2014020765

This book, by Deborah Bright, offers advice on utilizing criticism positively. "Executives, managers, team leaders--anyone who needs to temper praise with a dose of reality--will learn to: deliver the truth and have it taken as helpful; create an atmosphere of acceptance; avoid mistakes that sabotage an exchange; and control how they receive criticism so they benefit--even if it's badly presented." (Publisher's note)

"A useful book for almost anyone, giving helpful insight into ways to deliver (and receive) criticism so that it can do good, not harm. Recommended for all libraries." LJ

Fontes, Lisa Aronson

Invisible chains; overcoming coercive control in your intimate relationship. Lisa Aronson Fontes. The Guilford Press 2015 220 p. (paperback) $14.95   **158.2**
1. Domestic violence 2. Interpersonal relations 3. Intimidation 4. Control (Psychology) 5. Dominance (Psychology) 6. Intimate partner violence
ISBN 1462520243; 9781462520244; 9781462520350

LC 2014048835

This book, by Lisa Aronson Fontes, asks "what happens when [male] attentiveness becomes domination? In some relationships, the desire to control leads to jealousy, threats, micromanaging--even physical violence. If you or someone you care about are trapped in a web of coercive control, this book provides answers, hope, and a way out." (Publisher's note)

"Excellent for people who are under someone's coercive control or know someone who might be. The book is also recommended for those who have the opportunity to help victims in their work such as therapists, lawyers, and police officers." LJ

Includes bibliographical references and index

Goodman, Ellen

I know just what you mean; the power of friendship in women's lives. {by} Ellen Goodman, Patricia O'Brien. Simon & Schuster 2000 300p il $25; pa $14   **158.2**
1. Friendship 2. Women -- Psychology
ISBN 0-684-84287-4; 0-7432-0171-X pa
LC 00-24859
"Heavy on insight and light on psychological jargon, this book is an intelligent, observant read." Publ Wkly

Grant, Adam

Give and take; a revolutionary approach to success. Adam M. Grant. Viking 2013 320 p. $27.95   **158.2**
1. Success 2. Social networking 3. Success in business 4. Interpersonal relations
ISBN 0670026557; 9780670026555
LC 2012039995
This book, by Adam M. Grant, focuses on the topic of success. Grant "shows how one of America's best networkers developed his connections, why the creative genius behind one of the most popular shows in television history toiled for years in anonymity, how a basketball executive responsible for multiple draft busts transformed his franchise into a winner, and how we could have anticipated Enron's demise four years before the company collapsed." (Publisher's note)

Includes bibliographical references and index

Karlins, Marvin

The **like** switch; an ex-FBI agent's guide to influencing, attracting, and winning people over. Jack Schafer, Marvin Karlins. Simon & Schuster 2015 288 p. illustrations (A Touchstone book) (pbk.) $19.99   **158.2**
1. Personality 2. Influence (Psychology) 3. Friendship 4. Interpersonal relations 5. Interpersonal attraction
ISBN 1476754489; 9781476754482
LC 2014009121
This book by Jack Schafer, with Marvin Karlins, presents "proven strategies on how to instantly read people and influence how they perceive you, so you can easily turn on the like switch. He presents these techniques for how you can influence, attract, and win people over. Learn how to think and react like your favorite TV investigators from Criminal Minds or CSI as Dr. Schafer shows you how to improve your LQ (Likeability Quotient)." (Publisher's note)

"The author's approach to observing human nature should prove practical and useful in a variety of situations, from romantic meetings to interviewing criminals. A unique and pragmatic tome." Pub Wkly

Miller, Donald

Scary close; dropping the act and finding true intimacy. Donald Miller. Thomas Nelson 2015 256 p. $19.99   **158.2**
1. Intimacy (Psychology) 2. Interpersonal relations
ISBN 078521318X; 9780785213185
LC 2014945329
This book, by Donald Miller, is "about the risk involved in choosing to impress fewer people and connect with more, about the freedom that comes when we stop acting and start loving. It is a story about knocking down old walls to create a healthy mind, a strong family, and a satisfying career. And it all feels like a conversation with the best kind of friend: smart, funny, true, important." (Publisher's note)

"Older, married readers might chuckle at the author's description of Betsy as near perfect, but younger readers will relate to the frankly expressed concerns about pressure to fit in, difficulties in the dating scene, and hard lessons learned, some with the help of counseling." Pub Wkly

Rollag, Keith

What to do when you're new; how to be confident, comfortable, and successful in new situations. Keith Rollag. AMACOM--American Management Association 2015 240 p. (pbk.) $17.95   **158.2**
1. Success 2. Self-confidence 3. Interpersonal relations
ISBN 9780814434895
LC 2015011043
This book, by Keith Rollag, "opens your eyes to the necessary skills and teaches you how to: Overcome fears, make great first impressions, talk to strangers with ease, get up to speed quickly, connect with people wherever you go. Blending stories and insights with simple techniques and exercises, this one-of-a-kind guide will get you out of your comfort zone and trying new things in no time." (Publisher's note)

"Key points are highlighted in this well-organized, comprehensive book." LJ

Includes bibliographical references and index

Waxman, Jamye

How to break up with anyone; letting go of friends, family, and everyone in-between. Jamye Waxman. Seal Press 2015 240 p. (paperback) $16   **158.2**
1. Conflict management 2. Breaking up (Interpersonal relations) 3. Friendship 4. Self-actualization (Psychology)
ISBN 9781580055970
LC 2015019613
In this book, by Jamye Waxman, a "relationship expert . . . has written a much-needed guide to every step of a nonromantic breakup. Drawing from her own experiences, Jamye provides strategies for disengaging from a friend, family member, community, or even former version of oneself, addressing both practical and emotional concerns." (Publisher's note)

"Sound guidance for those involved in toxic relationships and looking for a way out." LJ

160　Philosophical logic

Copi, Irving M.

★ **Introduction** to logic; [by] Irving M. Copi, Carl Cohen. 13th ed; Pearson/Prentice-Hall 2008 670p il $104 **160**

1. Logic

ISBN 978-0-13-614139-6; 0-13-614139-0

LC 2007-41752

First published 1953. Periodically revised

This introduction to logic covers language, fallacies, definitions, categories, arguments, deduction, probability and other areas of logical inquiry such as thought and reasoning

Includes bibliographical references

169　Analogy

Hofstadter, Douglas

√ **Surfaces** and essences; Analogy As the Fuel and Fire of Thinking. Douglas Hofstadter, Emmanuel Sander. Basic Books 2013 608 p. (hardcover) $35 **169**

1. Analogy 2. Thought and thinking

ISBN 0465018475; 9780465018475

LC 2013932688

This book, by Douglas Hofstadter and Emmanuel Sander, "put[s] forth a highly novel perspective on cognition. We are constantly faced with a swirling and intermingling multitude of ill-defined situations. Our brain's job is to try to make sense of this unpredictable, swarming chaos of stimuli. How does it do so? The ceaseless hail of input triggers analogies galore, helping us to pinpoint the essence of what is going on." (Publisher's note)

170　Ethics (Moral philosophy)

Aristotle

★ **Nicomachean** ethics; translation (with historical introduction) by Christopher Rowe; philosophical introduction and commentary by Sarah Broadie. Oxford University Press 2002 468p pa $29.95 **170**

1. Ethics

ISBN 978-0-19-875271-4; 0-19-875271-7

LC 2002-283430

According to Aristotle's ethical treatises, "happiness is the goal of life. Pleasure, fame, and wealth, however, will not bring one the highest happiness, which is achieved only through the contemplation of philosophic truth, because it exercises man's peculiar virtue, the rational principle." Reader's Ency. 3d edition

Includes bibliographical references

Brooks, David Benjamin, 1961-

/ The **Road** to Character; The Humble Journey to an Excellent Life. David Brooks. Random House Inc 2015 320 p. $28 **170**

1. Character 2. Personality

ISBN 081299325X; 9780812993257

LC 2015001791

In this book author David Brooks "focuses on the deeper values that should inform our lives. Responding to what he calls the culture of the Big Me, which emphasizes external success, Brooks challenges us, and himself, to rebalance the scales between our 'résumé virtues'--achieving wealth, fame, and status--and our 'eulogy virtues,' those that exist at the core of our being: kindness, bravery, honesty, or faithfulness, focusing on what kind of relationships we have formed." (Publisher's note)

"Although Brooks goes after the selfie generation, he does so in a fairly nuanced way, noting that it was really the World War II Greatest Generation who started the ball rolling. He is careful to emphasize that no one—even those he profiles—is anywhere near flawless. The author's sincere sermon—at times analytical, at times hortatory—remains a hopeful one." Kirkus

Coles, Robert

/ ★ **Lives** of moral leadership. Random House 2000 247p hardcover o.p. pa $13.95 **170**

1. Ethics 2. Leadership 3. Conduct of life

ISBN 0-375-75835-6 pa

LC 00-27858

Drawing on interviews he conducted over the past four decades with public and private figures, Coles reflects on the meaning of moral leadership in the United States

Comte-Sponville, Andre

√ A **small** treatise on the great virtues; the uses of philosophy in everyday life. translated by Catherine Temerson. Metropolitan Bks. 2001 352p $27.50; pa $16 **170**

1. Ethics

ISBN 0-8050-4555-4; 0-8050-4556-2 pa

LC 2001-30299

Original French edition, 1995

"His subject demands a sober seriousness, but Comte-Sponville still manages to avoid taking himself too seriously: humility makes it into his litany of virtues, as does humor. A laudable renewal of the ancient quest for ethical wisdom." Booklist

Includes bibliographical references

Edelman, Marian Wright

The **measure** of our success; a letter to my children and yours. HarperPerennial 1993 97p pa $10 **170**

1. Ethics 2. Child rearing 3. Human behavior 4. United States -- Moral conditions

ISBN 0-06-097546-6; 978-0-06-097546-3

LC 92-54846

First published 1992 by Beacon Press

The author presents her "beliefs on child rearing and moral values. . . . She includes a personal letter to her three sons, who were born into a family with a shared African

American and Jewish heritage, and offers 25 lessons, or 'road maps', for life." Libr J

★ **Ethics**; edited by John K. Roth. Rev. ed.; Salem Press 2005 3v set $331 **170**
1. Reference books 2. Ethics -- Encyclopedias
ISBN 1-58765-170-X
LC 2004-21797
First published 1994
For a fuller review, see: Booklist, June 1 & 15, 2005
The aim of this set is "to provide accessible entry points for those grappling with ethical issues and concerns. The 1000-plus articles cover people, events, organizations, trends, and issues. . . . This well-organized, highly useful work will be popular with researchers and general readers." SLJ
Includes bibliographical references

Gottlieb, Daniel
Learning from the heart; lessons on living, loving, and listening. Sterling Pub. 2008 170p $17.95 **170**
1. Conduct of life
ISBN 978-1-4027-4999-5; 1-4027-4999-6
LC 2007-35100
"Having rebuilt his life after an accident that left him a quadriplegic in his thirties, . . . [the author] here shares his observations on what makes us human. . . . An uplifting book abounding with encouragement for daily living; recommended for public libraries." Libr J

Greene, Joshua
Moral tribes; emotion, reason, and the gap between us and them. by Joshua D. Greene. Penguin Press 2013 432 p. $29.95 **170**
1. Ethics 2. Emotions 3. Social psychology 4. Civilization
ISBN 1594202605; 9781594202605
LC 2013007775
In this book, "[Joshua] Greene, a philosopher and scientist, draws on research in psychology and neuroscience to explore the roots of morality, particularly the tragedy of commonsense morality, when people of different races, religions, ethnic groups, and nationalities share the same sense of morality but apply it from different perspectives in whose differences lie the roots of conflict. Us-versus-them conflicts date back to tribal life." (Booklist)
Includes bibliographical references (pages 388-403) and index

Haidt, Jonathan
The **happiness** hypothesis; finding modern truth in ancient wisdom. Basic Books 2005 297p il $26; pa $15.95 **170**
1. Happiness
ISBN 978-0-465-02801-6; 0-465-02801-2; 978-0-465-02802-3 pa; 0-465-02802-0 pa
LC 2005-21163
"Using the wisdom culled from the world's greatest civilizations as a foundation, social psychologist Haidt comes to terms with 10 Great Ideas, viewing them through a contemporary filter to learn which of their lessons may

still apply to modern lives. . . . Fascinating stuff, accessibly expressed." Booklist
Includes bibliographical references

Kubler-Ross, Elisabeth
★ **Life** lessons; two experts on death and dying teach us about the mysteries of life and living. [by] Elisabeth Kübler-Ross and David Kessler. Scribner 2000 224p $24; pa $13 **170**
1. Death 2. Conduct of life
ISBN 0-684-87074-6; 0-684-87075-4 pa
LC 00-57387
"As in each of their previous individual works, the authors provide useful and accessible information." Libr J

McCullough, David, Jr.
You Are Not Special; And Other Encouragements. David G. McCullough. HarperCollins 2014 352 p. illustrations $21.99 **170**
1. Commencements 2. High school students
ISBN 006225734X; 9780062257345
"In 'You Are (Not) Special,' [author David] McCullough elaborates on his now-famous speech exploring how, for what purpose, and for whose sake, we're raising our kids. With wry, affectionate humor, McCullough takes on hovering parents, ineffectual schools, professional college prep, electronic distractions, club sports, and generally the manifestations, and the applications and consequences of privilege." (Publisher's note)
"The author tackles big issues, such as gender and race, with searching sincerity, open-heartedness, and a deft, light touch." Kirkus

Reader's Digest Association
Everyday greatness; inspiration for a meaningful life. insights and commentary by Steven R. Covey; compiled by David K. Hatch. Rutledge Hill Press 2006 445p $24.99 **170**
1. Conduct of life
ISBN 978-1-4016-0241-3; 1-4016-0241-X
LC 2006-19786
"The stories, which the authors have gleaned from Reader's Digest, illustrate 21 principles such as integrity, gratitude, respect, and perseverance. Covey provides commentary, reflections, and further insights on how readers can apply each principle to their own lives in today's world. Truly inspiring." Libr J
Includes bibliographical references

This I believe; the personal philosophies of remarkable men and women. edited by Jay Allison and Dan Gediman, with John Gregory and Viki Merrick; photographs by Nubar Alexanian. H. Holt 2006 xxi, 281p il $23 **170**
1. Conduct of life 2. Belief and doubt
ISBN 0-8050-8087-2; 978-0-8050-8087-2
LC 2006-43522
This collection of essays from a popular radio series "draws transcripts from both the original series and its newer version, including some remarkable statements from the likes of dancer/choreographer Martha Graham, autistic aca-

demic Temple Grandin, writer and physicist Alan Lightman, novelist and social critic Thomas Mann, economic historian Arnold Toynbee, and feminist writer Rebecca West. Astonishing to hear and astonishing to read and reread, this work is a wonderful addition to any library." Libr J

This I believe II; more personal philosophies of remarkable men and women. edited by Jay Allison and Dan Gediman; with John Gregory and Viki Merrick; additional editing by Emily Botein . . . [et al.] Henry Holt 2008 268p $23 **170**

1. Conduct of life 2. Belief and doubt

ISBN 978-0-8050-8768-0; 0-8050-8768-0

LC 2008-10110

"Many [of these essays] will leave you breathless. And those that don't astonish may simply humble you." Christ Sci Monit

Tutu, Desmond, 1931-

Made for goodness; and why this makes all the difference. [by] Desmond M. Tutu and Mpho A. Tutu; edited by Douglas C. Abrams. HarperOne 2010 206p $25.99 **170**

1. Good and evil 2. Religious life 3. Conduct of life 4. Christian life

ISBN 978-0-06-170659-2

LC 2010-3774

In this book, the South African archbishop and his daughter, an Anglican priest, present their spiritual vision of hope for humanity.

"The book is founded on the broad notion that we are created with the freedom to choose good or evil but also incline fundamentally to the good. . . . A crucially important book from the Nobel Peace Prize winner; a witness to our tumultuous times." Libr J

Wolfe, Alan

Moral freedom; the impossible idea that defines the way we live now. Norton 2001 256p hardcover o.p. pa $14.95 **170**

1. Ethics 2. Values 3. Public opinion 4. United States -- Moral conditions

ISBN 0-393-04843-8; 0-393-32302-1 pa

LC 00-51969

"Wolfe here discusses the results of a national public opinion poll he helped design on American beliefs about values, which he supplemented with detailed interviews of people from eight different U.S. communities. These ranged widely, from the Castro district of San Francisco to San Antonio." Libr J

Includes bibliographical references

170.44 Normative ethics

Egan, Kerry

On living; Kerry Egan. Riverhead Books 2016 224 p. (hardback) $24 **170.44**

1. Life 2. Death 3. Spiritual life 4. Terminally ill 5.

Conduct of life 6. Church work with the terminally ill

ISBN 9781594634819

LC 2016026365

This book, by Kerry Egan, is "a book about living. . . . An emergency procedure during the birth of her first child left her physically whole but emotionally and spiritually adrift. Her work as a hospice chaplain healed her. . . . Each of her patients taught her something—how to find courage in the face of fear or the strength to make amends; how to be profoundly compassionate and fiercely empathetic; how to see the world in grays instead of black and white." (Publisher's note)

"As the title suggests, this is not just a book about dying. It's one that will inspire readers to make the most of every day." Pub Wkly

171 Ethical systems

Rand, Ayn

★ The **virtue** of selfishness; a new concept of egoism. with additional articles by Nathaniel Branden. Centennial ed; Signet/New American Library 2005 173p pa $7.99 **171**

1. Egoism 2. Objectivism (Philosophy)

ISBN 0-451-16393-1

First published 1964

The author "sets forth the moral principles of Objectivism, the philosophy that holds man's life—the life proper to a rational being—as the standard of moral values and regards altruism as incompatible with man's nature, with the creative requirements of his survival, and with a free society." Publisher's note

172 Applied ethics

Sandel, Michael J., 1953-

Justice; what's the right thing to do? Farrar, Straus & Giroux 2009 308p $25; pa $15 **172**

1. Ethics 2. Values 3. Justice

ISBN 0-374-18065-2; 0-374-53250-8 pa; 978-0-374-18065-2; 978-0-374-53250-5 pa

LC 2009-25438

This book is based on a course the author teaches at Harvard University. It is a companion to a series on public television. Sandel examines various philosophical approaches to justice and seeks to show how they relate to contemporary political debates on such issues as same-sex marriage, reparations for slavery, surrogate motherhood and immigration reform. Index.

"The author has a talent for making the difficult—Kant's 'categorical imperative' or Rawls's 'difference principle'— readily comprehensible, and his relentless, though never oppressive, reason shines throughout the narrative. Sparkling commentary from the professor we all wish we had." Kirkus

Includes bibliographical references

174 Occupational ethics

Callahan, David

The **cheating** culture; why more Americans are doing wrong to get ahead. Harcourt 2004 353p $26; pa $14 **174**

1. Social ethics 2. Business ethics

ISBN 0-15-101018-8; 0-15-603005-5 pa

LC 2003-15529

"If all business school students could be required to read one book, this should be it." Choice

Includes bibliographical references

Conway, Erik M.

Merchants of doubt; how a handful of scientists obscured the truth on issues from tobacco smoke to global warming. [by] Naomi Oreskes and Erik M. Conway. Bloomsbury Press 2010 355p $27 **174**

1. Science -- Ethical aspects

ISBN 978-1-59691-610-4; 1-59691-610-9

LC 2009-43183

"A well-documented, pulls-no-punches account of how science works and how political motives can hijack the process by which scientific information is disseminated to the public." Kirkus

Includes bibliographical references

Covey, Stephen M. R.

★ **Smart** trust; creating prosperity, energy and joy in a low-trust world. Stephen M.R. Covey and Greg Link; with Rebecca R. Merrill. Free Press 2012 xxiii, 296 p.p $27 **174**

1. Trust 2. Ethics 3. Business ethics 4. Organizational behavior 5. Leadership -- Moral and ethical aspects

ISBN 1451651457; 9781451651454; 9781451651478

LC 2011039458

It was the authors' intent to demonstrate that "the biggest impediment to global economic health is not the economics of the financial crisis but the loss of trust the crisis caused. . . . The authors make the case for the importance of trust and then teach readers how to trust in an untrustworthy world: by coupling the universal innate propensity to trust with a high level of critical analysis." (Library Journal)

Includes bibliographical references and index

Gentile, Mary C.

Giving voice to values; how to speak your mind when you know what's right. Yale University Press 2010 xliv, 273p $26 **174**

1. Values 2. Leadership 3. Business ethics

ISBN 978-0-300-16118-2

LC 2010011905

Gentile "offers a powerful action-oriented manifesto for living with integrity, fighting for one's convictions, and building a more ethical workplace." Publ Wkly

Includes bibliographical references

Mackey, John, 1954-

Conscious capitalism; liberating the heroic spirit of business. John Mackey & Raj Sisodia. Harvard Business Review Press 2013 344 p. (hardcover) $27 **174**

1. Capitalism -- Ethical aspects 2. Social responsibility of business 3. Social values 4. Business ethics 5. Capitalism -- Moral and ethical aspects 6. Corporations -- Moral and ethical aspects

ISBN 1422144208; 9781422144206

LC 2012025305

"In this book, Whole Foods Market cofounder John Mackey and professor and Conscious Capitalism, Inc. cofounder Raj Sisodia argue for the inherent good of both business and capitalism. Featuring some of today's best-known companies, they illustrate how these two forces can--and do--work most powerfully to create value for all stakeholders: including customers, employees, suppliers, investors, society, and the environment." (Publisher's note)

Includes bibliographical references

174.2 Medical and health professions

Dreger, Alice

Galileo's middle finger; heretics, activists, and the search for justice in science. Alice Dreger. Penguin Press 2015 352 p. (hardback) $27.95 **174.2**

1. Heresy 2. Science and civilization 3. Science -- Ethical aspects 4. Heresy in science 5. Science -- Political aspects 6. Scientists -- Professional ethics 7. Science -- Moral and ethical aspects

ISBN 1594206082; 9781594206085

LC 2014036659

This book "begins with [author Alice] Dreger's own research into the treatment of people born intersex (once called hermaphrodites). Realization of the shocking surgical and ethical abuses conducted in the name of 'normalizing' intersex childre's gender identities moved Dreger to become an internationally recognized patient rights activist." (Publisher's note)

"A crusader in the mold of muckrackers from a century ago, Dreger doesn't try to hide her politics or her agenda. Instead she advocates for change intelligently and passionately. Highly recommended for those interested in academic freedom, controversial issues in academia, and intersex and gender issues." LJ

Includes bibliographical references and index

Elliott, Carl

White coat, black hat; adventures on the dark side of medicine. Beacon Press 2010 224p $24.95 **174.2**

1. Drug industry 2. Medical ethics 3. Medicine -- United States 4. Medical ethics -- United States 5. Drugs -- Effectiveness -- Evaluation 6. Conflict of interests -- United States 7. Pharmaceutical industry -- United States

ISBN 978-0-8070-6142-8

LC 201006119

The author argues that "over the past twenty-five years, the practice of medicine has been subverted by the business of medicine, sacrificing old-style doctoring to fit the values of consumer capitalism. In this . . . narrative, physician and moral philosopher Carl Elliott traces the evolutionary path of this new direction in health care." (Publisher's note) Index.

Elliott "examines the part played by the pharmaceutical industry in constructing 'a medical system in which deception is often not just tolerated but rewarded.' While some abuses—including the use of subjects to test drugs without informed consent—are not new, these practices continue despite the existence of regulatory institutional-review boards set up by Congress, because these too have now become profit centers. Elliott writes that pharmaceutical companies hire PR specialists who not only supply educational materials to promote products, they also train medical professionals to be 'opinion leaders' and even write papers in their name." Kirkus

Includes bibliographical references

Tucker, Todd

★ The **great** starvation experiment; the heroic men who starved so that millions could live. Free Press 2006 270p il $26   **174.2**

1. Starvation 2. Human experimentation in medicine 3. Centenarians 4. Physiologists 5. College teachers
ISBN 0-7432-7030-4; 978-0-7432-7030-4

LC 2006-278255

"As WWII neared an end, 36 idealistic conscientious objectors, members of the Civilian Public Service, volunteered to be systematically starved. The project, headed by Dr. Ancel Keys, was designed to develop an understanding of the physiology and psychology of starvation and to provide strategies to manage the mass starvation that might follow the war's end in Europe. Tucker . . . provides a fascinating and moving history of the experiment, centering on the lives and experiences of the volunteers and the formidable obstacles they overcame." Publ Wkly

Includes bibliographical references and index

Washington, Harriet A.

★ **Medical** apartheid; the dark history of medical experimentation on Black Americans from colonial times to the present. Doubleday 2006 501p il hardcover o.p. pa $17   **174.2**

1. Human experimentation in medicine 2. African Americans -- Health and hygiene
ISBN 0-385-50993-6; 978-0-385-50993-0; 0-7679-1547-X pa; 978-0-7679-1547-2 pa

LC 2005-51873

The author offers a "history of medical experimentation on and mistreatment of black Americans in this stunning work, which is both broad in scope and well documented." Booklist

Includes bibliographical references

176   Ethics of sex and reproduction

Freitas, Donna

The **end** of sex; how hookup culture is leaving a generation unhappy, sexually unfulfilled, and confused about intimacy. Donna Freitas. Basic Books 2013 240 p. (pbk. : alk. paper) $25.99   **176**

1. Sex -- Psychological aspects 2. College students -- Sexual behavior 3. Sexual ethics 4. Intimacy (Psychology) 5. Dating (Social customs) 6. Youth --

Sexual behavior
ISBN 0465002153; 9780465002153

LC 2012042226

This book is an "attack on the casual-sex culture at American universities, which is marked not by free love, but by pressure to have as much sex with as little emotional connection as possible (and often while drunk). Through interviews and demographic surveys, [Donna] Freitas constructs an anthropological survey on what hooking up and dating (or its absence) look like on campuses today. She lays out convincing arguments against this harmful kind of sexual culture." (Publishers Weekly)

Includes bibliographical references

Stock, Gregory

Redesigning humans; our inevitable genetic future. Houghton Mifflin 2002 277p $24; pa $14 **176**

1. Genetics 2. Genetic engineering 3. Reproductive technology
ISBN 0-618-06026-X; 0-618-34083-1 pa

LC 2001-51890

The author gives an "overview of the new biotechnology that will allow scientists to delay aging and to insert genes that enhance physical and cognitive performance, combat disease or improve looks into embryos. Stock thoughtfully weighs the ethical dilemmas such advances present, arguing that the real threat is not frivolous abuse of technology but the fact that we don't know the long-term effects of these genetic changes." Publ Wkly

Includes bibliographical references and index

Wilmut, Ian

★ **After** Dolly; the uses and misuses of human cloning. Norton 2006 335p il $24.95; pa $15.95   **176**

1. Cloning 2. Reproductive technology
ISBN 0-393-06066-7; 978-0-393-06066-9; 0-393-33026-5 pa; 978-0-393-33026-7 pa

LC 2006-2030

In this "account of the program that eventuated in Dolly, . . . [Wilmut] covers a variety of the social, medical, and scientific implications of cloning. . . . Wilmut, aided by science writer Highfield, well explains potentially confusing issues, in the end making a strong enough case to convince us that Dolly neither lived nor died in vain." Booklist

Includes bibliographical references

177   Ethics of social relations

Ariely, Dan

The **honest** truth about dishonesty; how we lie to everyone---especially ourselves. Dan Ariely. 1st ed. Harper 2012 xiii, 285 p.p (hardback) $26.99   **177**

1. Honesty 2. Deception 3. Truthfulness and falsehood
ISBN 0062183591; 9780062183590; 9780062183613

LC 2012015990

This book "explains the psychological and economic factors that drive people to lie and cheat." Author Dan Ariely "explores the rational cost-benefit forces that propel dishonesty, such as the amount of money to be gained, the probability of being caught, and conflicts of interest. To illustrate his argument, Ariely cites examples ranging from the Enron scandal to Ponzi schemes to owning fake designer bags." (Library Journal)

Includes bibliographical references (pages 267-273) and index.

Armstrong, Karen, 1944-

Twelve steps to a compassionate life. Alfred A. Knopf 2010 222p $22.95; ebook $11.99　　**177**
　　1. Compassion 2. Twelve-step programs 3. Ethics 4. Sympathy 5. Conduct of life
　　ISBN 978-0-307-59559-1; 978-0-307-59563-8 ebook
　　　　　　　　　　　　　　　　LC 2010-36870
The author of A History of God, Islam, and Buddha sets out a program that is intended to lead readers "toward a more compassionate life. The twelve steps Armstrong suggests begin with 'Imagine a World of Compassion' and close with 'Love Your Enemies.' In between, she takes up self-love, mindfulness, suffering, sympathetic joy, the limits of our knowledge of others, and 'concern for everybody.' She suggests concrete ways of putting compassion into action in our everyday lives." (Publisher's note)

"Armstrong weaves together the teachings of diverse religions in a graceful, approachable manner. A commendable effort well-executed." Kirkus

Includes bibliographical references

Campbell, Jeremy

The **liar's** tale; a history of falsehood. Norton 2001 363p $26.95; pa $15.95　　**177**
　　1. Truthfulness and falsehood
　　ISBN 0-393-02559-4; 0-393-32361-7 pa
　　　　　　　　　　　　　　　　LC 2001-30286
"This challenging romp through the underbelly of intellectual history . . . is fascinating and troublesome." NY Times Book Rev

Includes bibliographical references

★ **Count** on me; tales of sisterhoods and fierce friendships. by Las Comadres para las Americas. Atria Books 2012 272 p. $16.00　　**177**
　　1. Essays 2. Hispanic American women 3. Female friendship -- Fiction 4. Social networks -- America 5. Female friendship -- America 6. Las Comadres para las Americas 7. Social networks -- United States 8. Female friendship -- United States 9. Hispanic American women -- Biography 10. Hispanic American women -- Social conditions 11. Hispanic American women -- Social life and customs
　　ISBN 1451642016; 9781451642018
　　　　　　　　　　　　　　　　LC 2012015552
This book is "[a]n anthology celebrating sisterhood and the special bonds that connect Latinas from diverse backgrounds. . . . The stories in this collection [nearly] all deal with the topic of female friendship . . . . Several of the pieces deal with the relationship between a Latina author and a cherished teacher who became a lifelong 'comadre,' a Spanish word to describe complex relationships between women." (Kirkus)

179　Other ethical norms

Baur, Gene

Farm Sanctuary; changing hearts and minds about animals and food. Simon & Schuster 2008 286p il $25　　**179**
　　1. Animal welfare 2. Livestock industry
　　ISBN 978-0-7432-9158-3; 0-7432-9158-1
　　　　　　　　　　　　　　　　LC 2008-297873
A founder of an organization dedicated to promoting the compassionate treatment of animals and combating factory farming addresses the ethics of breeding animals for food, exposing inhumane practices utilized by typical food-production companies.

"Baur's report is not for the faint of heart, but it is critical reading for anyone willing to ask about the origin of their food, and readers are rewarded with tales of animals who have been saved, and the surprising things that have been learned about farm animals from close observation of their habits. A life-altering read." Booklist

Includes bibliographical references

Beers, Diane L.

★ **For** the prevention of cruelty; the history and legacy of animal rights activism in the United States. Swallow Press/Ohio University Press 2006 312p il $34.95; $19.95　　**179**
　　1. Animal rights movement
　　ISBN 0-8040-1086-2; 978-0-8040-1086-3; 0-8040-1087-0 pa; 978-0-8040-1087-0 pa
　　　　　　　　　　　　　　　　LC 2006-4294
This "study of the animal advocacy movement in the U.S. since the ASPCA's founding in 1866 fills a glaring historical gap with exceptional style, accuracy and insight." Publ Wkly

Includes bibliographical references

Coetzee, J. M.

The **lives** of animals; {by} J.M. Coetzee; {reflections by} Marjorie Garber {et al.}; edited and introduced by Amy Gutmann. Princeton Univ. Press 1999 127p (University Center for Human Values series) $29.95; pa $13.95　　**179**
　　1. Animal rights 2. Animal welfare
　　ISBN 0-691-00443-9; 0-691-07089-X pa
　　　　　　　　　　　　　　　　LC 98-39591
"This hybrid collection of fiction and essays is a provocative version of Socratic philosophy. It begins with a story about a Doris Lessing-like author who visits her conflicted son and his antagonistic wife while lecturing at the university where they teach. The mother's hobbyhorse, that Animals R Us, embarrasses the academic couple, and her suggestion that they are like Nazis because they eat meat infuriates them. Other distinguished academics carry on this dialogue in playful fiction and sober commentary, in which the most eloquent part may be the descriptions of communication with animals." New Yorker

Includes bibliographical references

Greek, C. Ray

Sacred cows and golden geese; the human cost of experiments on animals. {by} C. Ray Greek and Jean Swingle Greek; foreword by Jane Goodall. Continuum 2000 256p $24.95; pa $18.95   **179**

1. Animal experimentation

ISBN 0-8264-1226-2; 0-8264-1402-8 pa

LC 99-57157

This "covers the history of animal experimentation, legislation that promulgates it, the real cost to humans, and alternatives. It is a well-written, if disturbing, book." Libr J

Includes bibliographical references (p. {227}-251) and index

Hall, Stephen S.

Wisdom; from philosophy to neuroscience. Alfred A. Knopf 2010 333p $27.95   **179**

1. Decision making 2. Neuropsychology

ISBN 978-0-307-26910-2; 0-307-26910-2

LC 2009-27438

"Those searching for easy tips on achieving wisdom will not find them here, but diligent readers will be rewarded. A steady stream of insights into the psychology and neurological mechanisms of wise decision-makingand the researchers uncovering them." Kirkus

Magill, R. Jay

Sincerity; how a moral ideal born five hundred years ago inspired religious wars, modern art, hipster chic, and the curious notion that we all have something to say (no matter how dull) R. Jay Magill, Jr. W. W. Norton & Co. Inc. 2012 272 p. (hardcover) $25.95   **179**

1. Catholic Church 2. Christian heresies 3. Doctrinal theology 4. Sincerity

ISBN 0393080986; 9780393080988

LC 2012010360

Author R. Jay Magill "examines sincerity from a variety of perspectives--religious, philosophical, political, sociological, artistic--as Western culture has alternately feared sincerity, embraced it, or denied the very possibility of it. . . . Sincerity and irony, rather than polar opposites, are complementary correctives, with the latter exposing the hypocrisies within professions of the former. The author . . . traces the early equation of sincerity with heresy as a challenge to the dogmatic authority of the Catholic Church." (Kirkus Reviews)

Includes bibliographical references and index.

McCain, John S.

Why courage matters; the way to a braver life. [by] John McCain with Mark Salter. Random House 2004 209p il $16.95   **179**

1. Courage

ISBN 1-400-06030-3

LC 2003-58626

Senator McCain tells his favorite stories of courage. "In offering anecdotes of individuals whose actions embody the rarity of true courage, his well-drawn examples range from Navajo leaders to Colorado River explorers to Jewish freedom fighter Hannah Senesh and Burmese dissident and Nobel Peace Prize-recipient Aung San Suu Kyi. He reflects on the wellsprings of courage, defining it as conscious self-sacrifice 'for the sake of others or to uphold a virtue,' encompassing actions that may be spurred by honor, outrage, a sense of duty, one's conscience, or moral obligation." SLJ

Santi, Jenny

The giving way to happiness; stories and science behind the transformative power of giving. Jenny Santi; foreword by Deepak Chopra. Tarcher 2015 352 p. (hardback) $25.95   **179**

1. Happiness 2. Generosity 3. Self-realization 4. Self-actualization (Psychology)

ISBN 9780399175497

LC 2015027341

In this book, author Jenny Santi "overturns conventional thinking about what it takes to be happy by revealing how giving to others—whether in the form of money, expertise, time, or love—has helped people from all walks of life find purpose and joy. Drawing on the wisdom of great thinkers past and present, as well as cutting-edge scientific research, Santi makes an eloquent and passionate case that oftentimes the answers to the problems that haunt us." (Publisher's note)

"Both of these inspiring books will prompt readers to consider and act on making the world a better place." LJ

Includes bibliographical references and index

Shevelow, Kathryn

For the love of animals; the rise of the animal protection movement. Henry Holt and Co. 2008 352p il $27.50   **179**

1. Animal rights movement

ISBN 978-0-8050-8090-2; 0-8050-8090-2

LC 2007-47353

The author "documents the history of animal cruelty and the slow, controversial and much maligned rise of the animal protection movement in 17th and 18th-century England. . . . This is a fascinating, often disturbing and frequently funny book, a must read for anyone concerned with the treatment of animals and a call to action for the next generation of animal rights activists." Publ Wkly

Includes bibliographical references

Tillich, Paul

★ The courage to be; with an introduction by Peter J. Gomes. 2nd ed; Yale Univ. Press 2000 197p (Yale Nota bene) pa $12.95   **179**

1. Anxiety 2. Courage 3. Ontology 4. Existentialism

ISBN 0-300-08471-4

LC 00-102364

First published 1952

The author offers advice on how to conquer the anxiety caused by the loss of meaning in one's life

Tutu, Desmond, 1931-

The book of forgiving; the fourfold path for healing ourselves and our world. Desmond Tutu and

Mpho A. Tutu; edited by Douglas C. Abrams. HarperOne 2014 240 p. ill $25.99 **179**

1. Forgiveness 2. Reconciliation

ISBN 0062203568; 9780062203564; 9780062203571

LC 2013033890

In this book, Desmond Tutu and his daughter Mpho "lay out the simple but profound truths about the significance of forgiveness, how it works, why everyone needs to know how to grant it and receive it, and why granting forgiveness is the greatest gift we can give to ourselves when we have been wronged." (Publisher's note)

"The book is almost entirely practical in focus, geared toward helping people come to grips with issues of anger, grief and loss. It includes meditations, rituals and journal exercises after each chapter." Kirkus

Includes bibliographical references

Wise, Steven M.

★ **Drawing** the line; science and the case for animal rights. Perseus Bks. 2002 322p $26; pa $18 **179**

1. Animal rights

ISBN 0-7382-0340-8; 0-7382-0810-8 pa

Wise "sets out to determine whether animals ranging from dolphins to his family dog . . . have mental abilities meriting {legal} protection. . . . The key to granting any of them rights, Wise argues, is whether they possess 'practical autonomy'—desires and the ability to act to satisfy them." Christ Sci Monit

Includes bibliographical references

179.7 Respect and disrespect for human life

Durkheim, Emile

★ **Suicide,** a study in sociology; translated by John A. Spaulding and George Simpson; edited with an introduction by George Simpson. Free Press 1951 405p maps hardcover o.p. pa $18.95 **179.7**

1. Suicide

ISBN 0-684-83632-7 pa

Original French edition, 1897

Durkheim's "Suicide is a major sociological classic, one that is still read today, not so much for its data, which are limited and out-of-date, but for the brilliance of his analysis of suicide rates and other data that had been initially obtained for administrative rather than scientific purposes." Reader's Adviser

Includes bibliographical references

Humphry, Derek

★ **Final** exit; the practicalities of self-deliverance and assisted suicide for the dying. 3rd ed; Delta Trade Paperbacks 2002 xxviii, 220p pa $13.95 **179.7**

1. Suicide 2. Right to die

ISBN 0-385-33653-5

LC 2002-19403

First published 1991 by Hemlock Society

This offers information about how to commit suicide for the terminally ill and about the legality and ethics of assisted suicide and euthanasia

Includes bibliographical references

Kiernan, Stephen P.

★ **Last** rights; rescuing the end of life from the medical system. St. Martin's Press 2006 301p $25.95 **179.7**

1. Death 2. Terminal care

ISBN 978-0-312-34224-1; 0-312-34224-1

LC 2006-47449

"Anyone who has stood helplessly by as physicians insisted that a battery of tests and interventions could prolong the life of a loved one, only to see those expensive efforts fail, is certain to be moved by Kiernan's presentation." Booklist

Includes bibliographical references

Marcus, Eric

Why suicide? answers to 200 of the most frequently asked questions about suicide, attempted suicide, and assisted suicide. HarperSanFrancisco 1996 240p pa $14 **179.7**

1. Suicide

ISBN 0-06-251166-1

LC 95-33431

The author's "questions range from 'Does everyone have thoughts of suicide?' to 'What are the arguments against legalizing doctor-assisted suicide?' His responses reflect not only a knowledgeable and well-informed consideration of suicidology but also empathetic treatment. The typical response aims to educate by giving factual information and/or practical advice as well as to console by providing personal stories from suicide survivors." Libr J

Includes bibliographical references

Peck, M. Scott

Denial of the soul; spiritual and medical perspectives on euthanasia and mortality. Harmony Bks. 1997 242p hardcover o.p. pa $19 **179.7**

1. Death 2. Suicide 3. Euthanasia 4. Right to die 5. Medical ethics

ISBN 0-609-80134-1 pa

LC 97-157271

"Peck is a wonderful writer, engaging, intelligent, and full of stories from his long psychiatric practice; as usual, he takes on big issues with seriousness, sensitivity, and balance." Libr J

Includes bibliographical references

Wanzer, Sidney H.

★ **To** die well; your right to comfort, calm, and choice in the last days of life. Da Capo 2007 209p $24; pa $15 **179.7**

1. Euthanasia 2. Right to die 3. Terminal care -- Ethical aspects

ISBN 0-7382-1083-8; 978-0-7382-1083-4; 0-7382-1163-X pa; 978-0-7382-1163-3 pa

The authors present "what individuals can do to achieve a peaceful death for themselves and their loved ones. Using a combination of patient stories and their own expert discussions, the authors describe the legal rights of terminally ill patients to end their medical care. They also address the controversial issue of hastening the death of terminally ill patients. . . . More useful than the many other recent books on death and dying, this influential volume should be on the shelves of every public and university library." Libr J

Wiesenthal, Simon

★ The **sunflower**; on the possibilities and limits of forgiveness. [by] Simon Wiesenthal; with a symposium edited by Harry James Cargas and Bonny V. Fetterman. rev and expanded ed, 2nd pa. ed; Schocken Books 1998 289p pa $14   **179.7**
  1. Forgiveness 2. Holocaust, 1933-1945 -- Personal narratives
  ISBN 0-8052-1060-1
                 LC 99-198049
  Original French edition, 1969
  "The responses to the author's question are as varied as their authors. The mystery of evil and atonement remain, and the reader is left challenged on these most basic issues of meaning in human life." Publ Wkly

Yount, Lisa

★ **Right** to die and euthanasia; rev ed; Facts on File 2007 312p il (Library in a book) $45   **179.7**
  1. Euthanasia 2. Right to die
  ISBN 978-0-8160-6275-1
                 LC 2006-33424
  First published 2000 with title: Physician-assisted suicide and euthanasia
  This reference source contains an overview of the subjects, a chronology of significant events (including the Terri Schiavo case), biographical information on important figures, a glossary of terms, and an annotated bibliography.
  Includes glossary and bibliographical references

180 History, geographic treatment, biography

Gottlieb, Anthony

The **dream** of reason; a history of western philosophy from the Greeks to the Renaissance. Norton 2000 468p $27.95; pa $17.95   **180**
  1. Philosophy -- History
  ISBN 0-393-04951-5; 0-393-32365-X pa
                 LC 00-49012
  "This eloquent book offers a lively chronicle of the evolution of Western philosophy." Publ Wkly
  Includes bibliographical references and index

181 Eastern philosophy

Buber, Martin

★ **I** and thou; translated by Ronald Gregor Smith. Scribner 2000 126p $22; pa $11   **181**
  1. God 2. Ontology 3. Jewish philosophy
  ISBN 0-7432-0133-7; 0-7432-0133-7 pa
  Original German edition, 1923; first published in English 1958
  In this book, the author "conceived the individual as in permanent relationship with all forms of life, finding his fulfillment in the reciprocity of the relationship—the 'Thou' being God." Reader's Adviser

Confucius

★ The **Analects**; [by] Confucius; translated by Arthur Waley; with an introduction by Sarah Allan. Knopf 2000 xxxi, 257p $19   **181**
  1. Chinese ethics 2. Chinese philosophy
  ISBN 0-375-41204-2
                 LC 00-53460
  This translation first published 1938 in the United Kingdom
  "One of the Chinese 'Four Books.' A brief, unsystematic collection of fragmentary writings attributed to Confucius and his school. . . . It is one of the most influential works in the history of Chinese thought." Reader's Ency
  Includes bibliographical references

Pacheco, Rebecca

Do your om thing; bending yoga tradition to fit your modern life. Rebecca Pacheco. HarperWave 2015 288 p. $26.99   **181**
  1. Yoga 2. Health 3. Well-being 4. Spirituality 5. Spiritual life
  ISBN 006227337X; 9780062273376
               LC 2014044390
  This book by Rebecca Pacheco "explores the traditional practice of yoga, from the eight limbs of the ancient path to the five koshas and the seven chakras of the yoga body. Pacheco translates these ancient texts for modern readers and puts them into the context of our everyday lives. Complete with a practical overview of the many different styles of yoga, simple poses, and sequences for daily balance." (Publisher's note)
  "She taps into the lessons of ancient sages, discusses ethics as well as principles, and offers practical suggestions on how to apply these teachings in 'How You Can Do It' and 'Doing Your Om Thing' sections found at the end of each chapter. Her gift is her ability to weave traditional yoga wisdom into everyday life and to make the principles so accessible and nonthreatening that even beginning students can be enlightened without feeling overwhelmed." Booklist
  Includes bibliographical references

183 Sophistic, Socratic, related Greek philosophies

Kreeft, Peter

★ **Philosophy** 101 by Socrates; an introduction to philosophy via Plato's apology : forty things philosophy is according to history's first and wisest philosopher. by Peter Kreeft. St. Augustines Press 2012 149 p. $12   **183**
  1. Teaching 2. Philosophers 3. History -- Philosophy 4. Philosophy -- Introductions
  ISBN 0898709253; 158731830X; 9781587318306
               LC 2001098029
  Author Peter "Kreeft uses the dialogues of Socrates in this book to help the reader grow in that love of wisdom. He says that no master of the art of philosophizing has ever been

more simple, clear, and accessible to beginners as Socrates. He focuses on Plato's dialogues, the Apology of Socrates, as a model partner for the reader to dialogue with. Kreeft calls it 'the Magna Carta of philosophy,' a timeless classic that is 'a portable classroom.'" (Publisher's note)

Stone, I. F. (Isidor Feinstein), 1907-1989
The **trial** of Socrates. Anchor Bks. 1989 282p pa $14.95 **183**
    1. Philosophers
    ISBN 0-385-26032-6; 978-0-385-26032-9
    First published 1988 by Little, Brown
    The author attempts "to show that Athens was totally committed to free speech and did not normally place any check on it, and, therefore, that the trial of Socrates was a singular aberration which might be explicable, if finally not justifiable." Commentary
    Includes bibliographical references

Waterfield, Robin
Why Socrates died; dispelling the myths. W. W. Norton & Co. 2009 253p il map $27.95 **183**
    1. Trials 2. Hellenism 3. Philosophers 4. Philosophy, Ancient
    ISBN 978-0-393-06527-5
                   LC 2009-4317
    This "account of the trial and execution of the philosopher draws on Greek sources to separate truth from myth, . . . [arguing for] Socrates' character as a deeply moral thinker whose convictions strongly contrasted those of his former student, Alcibiades." (Publishers note)
    The author "sets out to explain why Socrates died: he discusses his trial, but also offers an informed and well-written account of classical Athenian history." Times Higher Ed
    Includes bibliographical references

184 Platonic philosophy

Hare, R. M.
Plato. Oxford Univ. Press 1982 82p (Past masters series) hardcover o.p. pa $9.95 **184**
    1. Authors 2. Philosophers 3. Essayists
    ISBN 0-19-287585-X pa
                   LC 83-159441
    The author examines the chief Platonic concepts in their political and intellectual contexts
    Includes bibliographical references

185 Aristotelian philosophy

Adler, Mortimer J.
Aristotle for everybody; difficult thought made easy. Macmillan 1978 206p hardcover o.p. pa $13 **185**
    1. Philosophers 2. Writers on science
    ISBN 0-684-83823-0 pa
                   LC 78-853

Adler traces "in the simplest language and with occasional modern analogues, the logic and growth of Aristotle's basic doctrines." Publ Wkly
    Includes bibliographical references

Shields, Christopher John
Aristotle; Christopher Shields. Routledge, Taylor & Francis Group 2014 xviii, 505 pagesp (Routledge philosophers) (hardback : alk. paper) $160; (pbk. : alk. paper) $32.95 **185**
    1. Values 2. Virtue 3. Philosophers 4. Ancient philosophy
    ISBN 9780415622486; 9780415622493
                 LC 2013021013
    This book, by Christopher John Shields, "introduces the whole of Aristotle's philosophy, showing . . . . much of his thinking on the nature of the soul and the mind, ethics, politics, and the arts. Beginning with a brief biography, Shields carefully explains the fundamental elements of Aristotle's thought. . . . Subsequently he discusses Aristotle's metaphysics, the theory of categories, logical theory, and his conception of the human being as a composite of soul and body." (Publisher's note)
    Includes bibliographical references and index

187 Epicurean philosophy

Lucretius Carus, Titus
On the nature of things: De rerum natura; [by] Lucretius; edited and translated by Anthony M. Esolen. Johns Hopkins Univ. Press 1995 296p pa $25 **187**
    1. Poetry -- By individual authors
    ISBN 978-0-8018-5055-4; 0-8018-5055-X
                 LC 94-25165
    "Writing in the waning days of the Roman Republic—as Rome's politics grew individualistic and treacherous, its high-life wanton, its piety introspective and morbid—Lucretius sets forth a rational and materialistic view of the world which offers a retreat into a quiet community of wisdom and friendship." Publisher's note

188 Stoic philosophy

Marcus Aurelius
★ **Meditations**; a new translation, with an introduction, by Gregory Hays. Modern Lib. 2002 lvii, 191p $19.95 **188**
    1. Ethics 2. Stoics
    ISBN 0-679-64260-9
                 LC 2001-57947
    "An emperor and Stoic philosopher records his thoughts as he struggles for composure and order in the face of national disaster." Good Read

189 Medieval western philosophy

Davies, Brian

The **thought** of Thomas Aquinas. Oxford Univ. Press 1992 391p hardcover o.p. pa $44.95   **189**

1. Saints 2. Theologians 3. Doctrinal theology
ISBN 0-19-826753-3 pa

LC 91-35671

"Davies aims to cover the whole programme of the Summa in 370 pages. This necessarily means that, though his writing is admirably clear and never cryptic, much of what he says is extremely concise, and some topics get less airing than others." Times Lit Suppl

Includes bibliographical references

The **Renaissance** philosophy of man; {by} Petrarca {and others}; selections in translation, edited by Ernst Cassirer, Paul Oskar Kristeller, John Herman Randall, Jr. University of Chicago Press 1948 405p hardcover o.p. pa $17.50   **189**

1. Poets 2. Authors 3. Philosophers 4. Medieval philosophy 5. Writers on science
ISBN 0-226-09604-1 pa

This book provides English translations from selected writings of six early Italian Renaissance philosophers from about the middle of the fourteenth century to the end of the sixteenth. Francesco Petrarca, Lorenzo Valla, Marsilio Ficino, Giovanni Pico della Mirandola, Pietro Pomponazzi, and Juan Luis Vives are represented. An introduction accompanies each of the translations

Includes bibliographical references

Rubenstein, Richard E.

Aristotle's children; how Christians, Muslims, and Jews rediscovered ancient wisdom and illuminated the Dark Ages. Harcourt 2003 368p $27 **189**

1. Philosophers 2. Medieval philosophy 3. Writers on science
ISBN 0-15-100720-9

LC 2003-6582

"Although the book purports to trace Aristotle's influence on Christianity, Islam and Judaism, it devotes more attention to Christianity. Even so, Rubenstein's lively prose, his lucid insights and his crystal-clear historical analyses make this a first-rate study in the history of ideas." Publ Wkly

Includes bibliographical references

Thomas, Aquinas, Saint, 1225?-1274

Selected writings; edited and translated with an introduction and notes by Ralph McInerny. Penguin Bks. 1998 xxxviii, 841p pa $14.95   **189**

ISBN 0-14-043632-4

Arranged chronologically, this collection of theological and philosophical writings brings together sermons, commentaries, responses to criticism and lengthy extracts from the Summa theologia.

Includes bibliographical references

190 Modern western and other noneastern philosophy

The **Columbia** history of Western philosophy; edited by Richard H. Popkin. Columbia Univ. Press 1999 xxvi, 836p $64.50   **190**

1. Philosophy -- History
ISBN 0-231-10128-7

LC 98-15219

"This survey's coverage of medieval Islamic, Jewish, and Christian philosophy is particularly strong." Choice

Includes bibliographical references

Gay, Peter

The **rise** of modern paganism. Norton 1995 xviii, 555, xvp (The Enlightenment: an interpretation) pa $19.95   **190**

1. Enlightenment 2. Modern philosophy 3. Europe -- Intellectual life
ISBN 0-393-31302-6

First published 1966 by Knopf

Voume one of a two volume series examining the ideas, experiences and impact of leading Enlightenment figures in 18th century Europe and America.

Includes bibliographical references

The **science** of freedom. Norton 1996 xx, 705, xviiip (The Enlightenment: an interpretation) pa $19.95   **190**

1. Enlightenment 2. Modern philosophy 3. Europe -- Intellectual life
ISBN 0-393-31366-2

First published 1969

Volume two of a two-volume series examining the ideas, experiences and impact of leading Enlightenment figures in 18th century Europe and America.

Gottlieb, Anthony

★ The **dream** of enlightenment; the rise of modern philosophy. Anthony Gottlieb. Liveright Publishing Corporation, a division of W. W. Norton & Co. Inc. 2016 384 p. (hardcover) $27.95   **190**

1. Modern philosophy
ISBN 9780871404435

LC 2016015063

In this book, author Anthony Gottlieb "navigates a . . . great explosion of thought, taking us to northern Europe in the wake of its wars of religion and the rise of Galilean science. In a relatively short period—from the early 1640s to the eve of the French Revolution—Descartes, Hobbes, Spinoza, Locke, Leibniz, and Hume all made their mark. [This book] tells their story and that of the birth of modern philosophy." (Publisher's note)

"A former executive editor of the Economist who has held visiting fellowships at Harvard University and All Souls College, Oxford, Gottlieb won raves for The Dream of Reason, a history of philosophy from the Greeks to the Renaissance. Finally, after 16 years, we have the sequel, which focuses on the key philosophers Descartes, Hobbes, Spinoza, Locke, Leibniz, Hume, and Rousseau, who rethought thinking itself as Galilean science challenged previously held assumptions and religious beliefs. Accessibly written philosophical studies can be surprisingly popular as evidenced by the current success of Sarah Bakewell's At the Existentialist Café. Don't miss." LJ

Includes bibliographical references and index

Himmelfarb, Gertrude

The **moral** imagination; from Edmund Burke to Lionel Trilling. Ivan R. Dee 2006 259p $26 **190**
1. Modern philosophy 2. Political science
ISBN 1-56663-624-8

LC 2005-19838

The author "specializes in Victorian Britain and profiles some of its leading writers and statesmen, along with philosophical forerunners and descendants, to probe the complexities of two centuries of conservative thought. . . . Himmelfarb's stylish blend of literary criticism and intellectual history yields a stimulating reappraisal of a multifaceted and influential worldview." Publ Wkly

Includes bibliographical references

The **roads** to modernity; the British, French, and American enlightenments. Knopf 2004 284p $25 **190**
1. Enlightenment 2. Europe -- Intellectual life 3. United States -- Intellectual life
ISBN 1-400-04236-4

LC 2003-60576

"This is a book with important ideological implications that deserves to be read and debated across the political spectrum." Publ Wkly

Includes bibliographical references

Magee, Bryan

The **story** of philosophy. DK Pub. 1998 240p il hardcover o.p. pa $20 **190**
1. Philosophy
ISBN 0-7894-3511-X; 0-7894-7994-X pa

LC 98-3780

"Writing with a clear and lively style, Magee provides an excellent introduction to the topic." SLJ

Includes bibliographical references

Miller, Jim

Examined lives; [by] James Miller. Farrar, Straus and Giroux 2011 422p ill. $28 **190**
1. Biography 2. Philosophers 3. Conduct of life 4. Biography, Collective 5. Philosophers -- Biography 6. Philosophy -- Psychological aspects
ISBN 978-0-374-15085-3

LC 201014385

This book, a "New York Times" Notable Book for 2011, looks at the lives of "12 philosophers: Socrates, Plato, Diogenes the Cynic, . . . Aristotle, Seneca, Augustine, Montaigne, Descartes, Rousseau, Kant, Emerson and Nietzsche. In each case, he explores the life selectively, looking for 'crux' points and investigating how ideas of the philosophical life have changed. Few readers will be astounded to learn that philosophers make as much of a mess of their lives as anyone else. But [James] Miller . . . shows us philosophers becoming ever more inclined to reflect on these failings, and

suggests that this makes their lives more rather than less studying." (N Y Times)

Includes bibliographical references

Nadler, Steven M.

The **best** of all possible worlds; a story of philosophers, God, and evil. [by] Steven Nadler. Farrar, Straus and Giroux 2008 300p $25 **190**
1. God 2. Theologians 3. Philosophers 4. Good and evil 5. Mathematicians 6. Modern philosophy 7. Essayists
ISBN 978-0-374-22998-6; 0-374-22998-8

LC 2008-29143

This book "is written simply and clearly, without condescension, flashiness or oversimplification. But it's a demanding book nonetheless, and you need to pay attention. You'll be amply rewarded if you do." Washington Post Book World

Includes bibliographical references

The **Oxford** history of Western philosophy; edited by Anthony Kenny. Oxford Univ. Press 1994 407p il maps hardcover o.p. pa $15 **190**
1. Philosophy -- History
ISBN 0-19-824278-6; 0-19-289329-7 pa

LC 94-9858

"The illustrations have been wisely chosen to show the constant play between art and idea. Some familiarity with analytic philosophy would be useful to gain the most from the text, but this is a significant addition to the literature." Libr J

Includes bibliographical references

Sedgwick, Peter

★ **Descartes** to Derrida; an introduction to European philosophy. Blackwell 2001 310p $76.95; pa $33.95 **190**
1. Modern philosophy
ISBN 0-631-20142-4; 0-631-20143-2 pa

LC 00-57917

"This book should take a place as one of the key texts in humanities programs throughout the English-speaking world." Choice

Includes bibliographical references

191 Philosophy of United States and Canada

Kaag, John

American philosophy; A Love Story. John Kaag. FSG 2016 272 p. (cloth) $26 **191**
1. Pragmatism 2. Rare books 3. Philosophers 4. American philosophy 5. Philosophy, American -- Miscellanea
ISBN 9780374154486

LC 2016001908

In this book, "John Kaag--a disillusioned philosopher at sea in his marriage and career--stumbles upon a treasure trove of rare books on an old estate in the hinterlands of New Hampshire that once belonged to the Harvard philosopher William Ernest Hocking. . . . As he begins to catalog and preserve these priceless books, Kaag rediscovers the very tenets of American philosophy--self-reliance, pragmatism, the transcendent--and sees them in a twenty-first-century context." (Publisher's note)

" Kaag's lively prose, acute self-examination, unfolding romance, and instructive history of philosophy as a discipline make for a surprisingly absorbing book." Kirkus

Includes bibliographical references and index

Rand, Ayn

The **voice** of reason; essays in objectivist thought; edited and with an introduction by Leonard Peikoff; and with additional essays by Leonard Peikoff and Peter Schwartz. New Am. Lib. 1989 353p hardcover o.p. pa $18   **191**

1. American philosophy 2. Objectivism (Philosophy)
ISBN 0-45-300634-5; 0-45-201046-2 pa

LC 88-18192

The late author opposed liberalism and championed "capitalism, self-interest, and objective reality against collectivism, altruism, and mysticism. . . . These lectures, newspaper columns, and magazine articles are entirely characteristic of her—surprisingly emotional and dogmatic for a professed rationalist. Additional essays by editor Peikoff and disciple Peter Schwartz are of a piece." Booklist

Includes bibliographical references

Romano, Carlin

America the philosophical; Carlin Romano. Knopf 2012 672 p.   **191**

1. American philosophy 2. Philosophy -- Social aspects 3. Popular culture -- United States 4. United States -- Intellectual life 5. Philosophy -- United States
ISBN 0679434704; 9780679434702

LC 2011034753

This book offers a "diagnosis of the condition of philosophical thinking in America today. . . . [Carlin Romano] realizes that philosophy has traditionally been the ballpark for white men to play in, so he . . . add[s] to the team some prominent women, African Americans, Native Americans, gays and others. But he begins with the famous white men (William James, George Santayana, John Dewey et al.) and looks at key figures later on--John Rawls and Richard Rorty among them." (Kirkus)

Includes bibliographical references (p. [611]-639) and index

192   Philosophy of British Isles

Edmonds, David

Wittgenstein's poker; the story of a ten-minute argument between two great philosophers. {by} David Edmonds and John Eidinow. Ecco Press 2001 340p il $24; pa $13.95   **192**

1. Philosophers 2. Logicians 3. Nonfiction writers
ISBN 0-06-621244-8; 0-06-093664-9 pa

LC 2002-276301

"On the Cambridge University campus in 1946, two of the twentieth-century's most notable philosophers, Ludwig Wittgenstein and Karl Popper, squared off in an intense 10-minute clash rumored to have culminated with Wittgenstein brandishing a red-hot poker. The authors explain what the fight was about and how it reflects the develop-

ment of philosophy. Ivory-tower drama at its crackling best." Booklist

Includes bibliographical references (p. {317}-327) and index

193   Philosophy of Germany and Austria

Hegel, Georg Wilhelm Friedrich

★ The **philosophy** of Hegel; edited with an introduction by Carl J. Friedrich. Modern Lib. 1954 552p pa $10.75   **193**

1. Philosophy
ISBN 0-07-553655-2 pa

Contents: The philosophy of history; The history of philosophy; The science of logic; Philosophy of right and law, or natural law and political science outlines; Lectures on aesthetics; The phenomenology of the spirit (1807); Political essays; Bibliography

Heidegger, Martin

Basic writings; from Being and time (1927) to The task of thinking (1964) edited, with general introduction and introductions to each selection by David Farrell Krell. rev and expanded ed; HarperSanFrancisco 1993 452p pa $17.95   **193**

1. Philosophy
ISBN 0-06-063763-3

LC 91-58187

This anthology first published 1977 by Harper & Row

Includes bibliographical references

Kant, Immanuel

★ **Basic** writings of Kant; edited and with an introduction by Allen W. Wood. Modern Lib. 2001 xxv, 478p pa $15.95   **193**

1. Philosophy
ISBN 0-375-75733-3

LC 2001-18303

First Modern Library edition published 1949 with title: The philosophy of Kant

This volume presents the essential works of the philosopher including "selected excerpts from his most frequently taught essays and book-length publications, including 'Critique of Pure Reason, Critique of Judgment,' and 'Eternal Peace.'" Publisher's note

★ **Critique** of pure reason; translated by Marcus Weigelt. Rev ed; Penguin 2003 lxxvi, 708p (Penguin classics) pa $20   **193**

1. Reason 2. Theory of knowledge
ISBN 978-0-14-044747-7; 0-14-044747-4

Original German edition, 1781

In this philosophical work Kant "attempted to define the possibility and limits of our knowledge. He denied that we can ever know how the world 'really' is. However, he tried to show that science nevertheless has a sort of universal validity, insofar as it consists of sense experience, which comes from the world, coupled with the mind, which orders this sense experience according to the 'categories of the understanding' and the intuitions of space and time." Reader's Ency. 4th edition

Nietzsche, Friedrich Wilhelm

★ **Basic** writings of Nietzsche; introduction by Peter Gay; translated and edited, with commentaries, by Walter Kaufmann. Modern Lib. 2000 xxiv, 862p pa $14.95 **193**
    1. Philosophy
    ISBN 0-679-78339-3
                 LC 00-64578
First Modern Library edition published 1968
"Gathers the complete texts of five of Nietzsche's most important works, from his first book to his last: The Birth of Tragedy, Beyond Good and Evil; On the Genealogy of Morals; The Case of Wagner; and Ecce Homo. . . . Included also are seventy-five aphorisms, selections from Nietzsche's correspondence, and variants from drafts for Ecce Homo." Publisher's note

The **portable** Nietzsche; selected and translated, with an introduction, prefaces, and notes, by Walter Kaufmann. Viking 1954 687p hardcover o.p. pa $17 **193**
    1. Philosophy
    ISBN 0-14-015062-5 pa
Includes the complete texts of Thus spake Zarathustra, Twilight of the idols, The antichrist, and Nietzsche contra Wagner. Selections from other works, notes and letters complete the volume

★ **Thus** spoke Zarathustra; a book for everyone and nobody. [by] Friedrich Nietzsche; translated with an introduction and notes by Graham Parkes. Oxford University Press 2005 xliii, **335p** (Oxford world's classics) pa $14.95 **193**
    ISBN 0-19-280583-5
             LC 2005-19431
Written between 1883-1892
A philosophical narrative in which Nietzsche "transforms the ancient Persian philosopher Zarathustra . . . into a mouthpiece for his own views. Nietzsche develops his doctrine of the 'Ubermensch' in a prophetic, quasi-biblical style. Nietzsche's Zarathustra announces the death of God, and preaches a new 'faithfulness to the earth,' which includes a new respect for the body . . . and attentiveness to this world rather than the next. He also attacks pity and virtue as weapons of weakness." Reader's Ency. 4th edition
Includes bibliographical references

The **will** to power; a new translation by Walter Kaufmann and R. J. Hollingdale; edited with commentary by Walter Kaufmann; with facsimiles of the original manuscript. Random House 1967 xxxii, 576p hardcover o.p. pa $16 **193**
    1. Nihilism 2. Values
    ISBN 0-394-70437-1 pa
"Represents a selection from Nietzsche's notebooks to find out what he wrote on nihilism, art, morality, religion, and the theory of knowledge, among others." (Publisher's note)

Safranski, Rudiger

Nietzsche; a philosophical biography. translated by Shelley Frisch. Norton 2001 409p $29.95; pa $18.95 **193**
    1. Authors 2. Philosophers 3. Essayists
    ISBN 0-393-05008-4; 0-393-32380-3 pa
            LC 2001-52130
"With brilliant insights and impressive scholarship, Safranski . . . here makes a major contribution to understanding and appreciating the lasting significance of Friedrich Nietzsche." Libr J
Includes bibliographical references

Sherratt, Yvonne

Hitler's philosophers; Yvonne Sherratt. Yale University Press 2012 328 p. (hardcover) $35 **193**
    1. Political philosophy 2. Philosophers -- Germany 3. Philosophy, German -- 20th century 4. Philosophers -- Germany -- History -- 20th century
    ISBN 0300151934; 9780300151930
            LC 2012026930
This book, by Yvonne Sherratt, explores the philosophical policy of Adolf Hitler. The author presents "evidence back to the 1920s of Hitler's vulgarization of noble thinkers of the past. . . . She reveals how philosophers of the 1930s eagerly collaborated to lend the Nazi regime a cloak of respectability. . . . And while these eminent men sanctioned slaughter, Semitic thinkers like Walter Benjamin and opponents like Kurt Huber were hunted down or murdered." (Publisher's note)

Solomon, Robert C.

What Nietzsche really said; {by} Robert C. Solomon and Kathleen M. Higgins. Schocken Bks. 2000 263p hardcover o.p. pa $13 **193**
    1. Authors 2. Philosophers 3. Essayists
    ISBN 0-8052-1094-6 pa
            LC 99-33796
The authors offer an "overview of Friedrich Nietzsche's life, thought, and influence. . . . Particularly helpful are their brief annotations of Nietzsche's 14 books and short analyses of the thinkers who influenced him." Libr J
Includes bibliographical references

196 Philosophy of Spain and Portugal

Ortega y Gasset, Jose

What is philosophy? translated from the Spanish by Mildred Adams. Norton 1961 252p hardcover o.p. pa $10.95 **196**
    1. Philosophy
    ISBN 0-393-00126-1 pa
This volume by the influential Spanish philosopher, essayist and critic "consists of a series of lectures begun in 1929 at the University of Madrid. Interrupted when the University was closed as a result of political troubles, they were resumed in a Madrid theatre. Part of the lectures had been given earlier in Buenos Aires." N Y Times Book Rev

200 RELIGION

200 Religion

Ahlstrom, Sydney E.

A **religious** history of the American people; Sydney E. Ahlstrom. Yale University Press 2004 xxiv, 1192 p.p $45 **200**
1. United States -- Religion 2. United States -- Church history
ISBN 0300100124; 9780300100129

LC 2003116918

This book, by Sydney E. Ahlstrom, "winner of the 1973 National Book Award in Philosophy and Religion and Christian Century's choice as the Religious Book of the Decade (1979), is now issued with a new chapter by noted religious historian David Hall, who carries the story of American religious history forward to the present day." (Publisher's note)

Includes bibliographical references (p. 1119-1162) and index

Armstrong, Karen

A **history** of God; the 4000 year quest of Judaism, Christianity, and Islam. Knopf 1993 xxiii, 460p maps hardcover o.p. pa $15.95 **200**
1. God 2. Islam 3. Judaism 4. Christianity
ISBN 0-345-38456-3 pa

LC 92-38318

This is a study of ideas and experiences of God in Judaism, Christianity and Islam from Abraham to the twentieth century

"Public librarians should be aware that conservative readers may be offended by this book, and even religious scholars may find Armstrong's rather one-sided 'death of God' optimism about humanity a bit passé. Otherwise, this is an excellent and informative book." Libr J

Bowker, John

World religions; contributing consultants: David Bowker [et al.] DK Pub. 1997 200p il maps $35; pa $16.95 **200**
1. Religion 2. Religions
ISBN 0-7894-1439-2; 0-7566-1772-3 pa

LC 96-38277

Each chapter begins with an "introduction and is followed by one-or-two page sections that explain the basic tenets of the faith, symbols, events, people, buildings, works of art, and the differences and similarities to other religions. Hinduism, Buddhism, Judaism, Christianity, and Islam are included as are Jainism, Sikhism, Chinese and Japanese religions, and Native religions." SLJ

Chittister, Joan

The **gift** of years; growing older gracefully. BlueBridge 2008 222p $19.95 **200**
1. Elderly 2. Aging -- Religious aspects
ISBN 978-1-933346-10-6; 1-933346-10-8

LC 2008-00332

"This collection of inspirational reflections, 'not meant to be read in one sitting, or even in order, but one topic at a time,' abounds in gentle insights and arresting aphorisms." Publ Wkly

Includes bibliographical references

Dawkins, Richard

★ The **God** delusion. Houghton Mifflin Co. 2006 406p $27; pa $15.95 **200**
1. God 2. Atheism 3. Religion
ISBN 978-0-618-68000-9; 0-618-68000-4; 978-0-618-91824-9 pa; 0-618-91824-8 pa

LC 2006-15506

"Both fans of Dawkins and his many opponents will want to read this book." Libr J

Includes bibliographical references

De Botton, Alain, 1969-

Religion for atheists; Alain de Botton. Pantheon Books 2012 320p. ill. **200**
1. Atheism 2. Religious life 3. Conduct of life 4. Religion -- Philosophy 5. Atheists
ISBN 9780307379108

LC 2011021286

It was the author's intent to demonstrate "that the supernatural claims of religion are entirely false--but that it still has some very important things to teach the secular world." The author "suggests . . . that we look to religion for insights into how to, among other concerns, build a sense of community, make our relationships last, overcome feelings of envy and inadequacy, inspire travel and reconnect with the natural world." (Publisher's note)

The **encyclopedia** of cults, sects, and new religions; {edited by} James R. Lewis. 2nd ed; Prometheus Bks. 2002 951p il $180 **200**
1. Cults 2. Reference books 3. Sects -- Encyclopedias 4. United States -- Religion -- Encyclopedias
ISBN 1-57392-888-7

LC 2002-19180

First published 1998

This reference contains "information on approximately 1,000 religious groups, ranging from small churches with less than a hundred members (Chishti Order of America) to organizations such as the Assemblies of God that number in the millions. Most entries are relatively short. The more controversial religions, as well as religious groups that have had a high profile lately, receive more lengthy treatments. Also included are entries on broader religious movements such as the New Age and the Charismatic Movement. . . . Each article outlines the history of the group, its founders and leaders, its main teachings, and an approximate number of followers or congregations. The explanations are clearly written, interesting and understandable, without too much scholarly jargon." Booklist

Includes bibliographical references

★ **Encyclopedia** of religion; Lindsay Jones, editor in chief. 2nd ed; Macmillan Reference USA 2005 15v il set $1295 **200**
1. Reference books 2. Religions -- Encyclopedias
ISBN 0-02-865733-0

LC 2004-17052

First published 1987 in 16 volumes

"Treats theoretical (e.g., doctrines, myths, theologies, ethics), practical (e.g., cults, sacraments, meditations), and sociological (e.g., religious groups, ecclesiastical forms) aspects of religion; includes extensive coverage of non-Western religions. Signed articles by some 1,400 contributors worldwide end with bibliographies. Many composite entries treat two or more related topics. . . . Has quickly become the standard work." Guide to Ref Books. 11th edition [review of 1993 edition]

Includes bibliographical references

★ **Encyclopedia** of religious rites, rituals, and festivals; Frank A. Salamone, editor. Routledge 2004 487p il (Routledge encyclopedias of religion and society) $150 **200**
1. Reference books 2. Rites and ceremonies 3. Religions -- Encyclopedias
ISBN 0-415-94180-6

LC 2003-20389

"The entries can be understood by readers unfamiliar with the topics covered, but the work is suitable for all levels of scholars." Choice

Includes bibliographical references

Hexham, Irving
Understanding world religions. Zondervan 2011 512p il map $39.99; ebook $30.99 **200**
1. Religions
ISBN 978-0-310-25944-2; 0-310-25944-4; 978-0-310-31448-6 ebook; 0-310-31448-8 ebook

LC 2010013103

This "world religions text explores various religions under the broad categories of African Religions, the Yogic Traditions (including Buddhism), and the Abrahamic traditions." Publisher's note

Includes bibliographical references

Hitchens, Christopher
God is not great; how religion poisons everything. Twelve 2007 307p $24.99 **200**
1. Atheism 2. Religion
ISBN 978-0-44657-980-3; 0-44657-980-7

LC 2006-23039

In this work Hitchens catalogs "the major arguments against religion, which he deems a pernicious force. First, he writes, faith misrepresents the origin of the cosmos as well as that of humanity; second, it fosters servility, solipsism, and sexual repression; and, third, it is based on wishful thinking. Hitchens spares no targets in this manifesto, criticizing both Western and Eastern faiths." Libr J

Includes bibliographical references

Hutchison, William R.
Religious pluralism in America; the contentious history of a founding ideal. Yale University Press 2003 262p $32.50; pa $18 **200**
1. United States -- Religion
ISBN 0-300-09813-8; 0-300-10516-9 pa

LC 2002-151893

The author "illuminates the cultural transformations that enabled twentieth-century Americans to embrace belatedly the religious diversity that emerged in the nineteenth-

century influx of Catholic and Jewish immigrants and in the rise of new American-born faiths such as Mormonism and Transcendentalism. . . . Though he acknowledges the concerns of critics worried about the moral balkanization of a society lacking shared religious premises, Hutchison hails America's new religious pluralism as a great achievement. A balanced and informative narrative." Booklist

Includes bibliographical references

Minois, Georges
The **atheist's** Bible; the most dangerous book that never existed. Georges Minois; translated by Lys Ann Weiss. The University of Chicago Press 2012 249 p. map (cloth : alk. paper) $30 **200**
1. Atheism -- History 2. De tribus impostoribus 3. Rationalism -- History
ISBN 0226530299; 9780226530291

LC 2012011212

This book by Georges Minois, translated by Lys Ann Weiss, explains that "in 1239, Pope Gregory IX accused Frederick II, the Holy Roman Emperor, of . . . [writing] a supremely blasphemous book--'De tribus impostoribus,' or the 'Treatise of the Three Impostors'--in which Frederick denounced Moses, Jesus, and Muhammad as impostors. . . . Minois tracks the course of the book from its origins in 1239 to its most salient episodes in the seventeenth and eighteenth centuries." (Publisher's note)

Includes bibliographical references and index

National Geographic concise history of world religions; an illustrated time line. edited by Tim Cooke. National Geographic 2011 352 p. col. ill. (hardcover) $40.00 **200**
1. Ethics 2. World history 3. Religious institutions 4. Religions -- Encyclopedias 5. Religion -- History -- Chronology 6. Religions 7. Religion and ethics 8. Religions -- History
ISBN 1426206984; 9781426206986

LC 2011276808

This book "continues the 'Concise History' series with [a] . . . take on major religions and lesser-known faiths of all times and nations." It offers a "global perspective on the history of faith in the Americas, Europe, Asia and Oceania, and Africa and the Middle East. . . . 50 feature essays explore in detail the origins, development and influence of faith." (Publisher's Note)

Includes bibliographical references (p. 343-344) and index

Prothero, Stephen R.
God is not one; the eight rival religions that run the world--and why their differences matter. [by] Stephen Prothero. HarperOne 2010 388p $26.99; ebook $9.99 **200**
1. Religions
ISBN 978-0-06-157127-5; 0-06-157127-X; 978-0-06-199120-2 ebook; 0-06-199120-1 ebook

LC 2009053372

Prothero argues that each of the major world religions have different worldviews and approaches to spiritual questions. The book contains chapters on Islam (the way of submission); Christianity (the way of salvation); Confucianism (the way of propriety); Hinduism (the way of devotion); Buddhism (the way of awakening); Yoruba religion (the way of connection); Judaism (the way of exile and return); Daoism (the way of flourishing); Atheism (the way of reason).

"Provocative, thoughtful, fiercely intelligent and, for both believing and nonbelieving, formal and informal students of religion, a must-read." Booklist

Includes bibliographical references

Religious literacy; what every American needs to know--and doesn't. [by] Stephen Prothero. HarperSanFrancisco 2007 296p $24.95   **200**
1. Religions
ISBN 978-0-06-084670-1; 0-06-084670-4
LC 2006-41310
"In this book, the author combines a lively history of the rise and fall of American religious literacy with a set of proposed remedies based on his hope that 'the Fall into religious ignorance is reversible.' He also includes a useful multicultural glossary of religious definitions and allusions, in which religious illiterates can find the prodigal son, the promised land, the Quakers and the Koran." Washington Post Book World

Includes bibliographical references

Turner, Alice K.
The **history** of hell. Harcourt Brace & Co. 1993 275p il hardcover o.p. pa $22   **200**
1. Hell
ISBN 0-15-600137-3 pa
LC 93-9909
"Belief in a hell or some sort of afterlife has been intrinsic to the religions of the world ever since the first stories were shared aloud and incised in clay tablets. Turner's richly illustrated history surveys the myriad forms hell has taken in the West from Sumer to Rome and beyond." Booklist

Weber, Eugen
Apocalypses; prophesies, cults, and millennial beliefs through the ages. [by] Eugen Weber. Harvard Univ. Press 1999 294p $27.50; pa $16.95   **200**
1. Millennium 2. End of the world
ISBN 0-674-04080-5; 0-674-00395-0 pa
LC 99-18001
"Weber traces millennial beliefs as professed through the ages. From ancient and pre-Christian times to the present day, humankind has had an unshakable belief that the end is at hand. . . . Weber has an excellent grasp of his subject, an accessible style, and an understated sense of humor." Booklist

Includes bibliographical references

Williams, Juan
This far by faith; stories from the African-American religious experience. [by] Juan Williams and Quinton Dixie. Morrow 2003 326p il hardcover o.p. pa $15.95   **200**
1. African Americans -- History 2. African Americans -- Religion
ISBN 0-06-018863-4; 0-06-093424-7 pa
LC 2002-71884

"Brief topical articles and captioned illustrations supplement the main text, creating a balanced, readable, and nuanced introduction to the power of faith to sustain the African American community." Libr J

200.1 Systems, scientific principles, psychology of religion

Barrett, Justin L.
Born believers; the science of children's religious belief. Justin L. Barrett. Free Press 2012 x, 302 p.p   **200.1**
1. Belief and doubt 2. Child psychology 3. Faith -- Psychology 4. Children -- Religious life 5. God 6. Psychology, Religious
ISBN 1439196540; 9781439196540
LC 2011039581
In this book, "the author looks at cross-cultural studies of children conducted by experts in the 'cognitive science of religion.' The studies indicate that, from an early age, humans know the difference between inanimate objects and 'agents'--people or forces that can move or make things move. As they develop, children are prone to see agents as powerful forces unlike humans. By four or five, kids see a purpose, not only in objects, but also in creatures, rocks, rivers and mountains. . . . In the second part of the book, the author indicts atheism by arguing that if one accepts natural selection then one cannot reject the natural religion of childhood--it must have survival value." (Kirkus)

Includes bibliographical references and index

200.8 Groups of people

Circling faith; Southern women on spirituality. edited by Wendy Reed and Jennifer Horne. University of Alabama Press 2012 xiv, 230 p.p (trade cloth) $29.95   **200.8**
1. Women -- Religious life -- Southern states 2. Spirituality 3. Women authors -- Religious life 4. Southern women -- Religious life
ISBN 0817317678; 0817357017; 0817386084; 9780817317676; 9780817357016; 9780817386085
LC 2011034803
This book, edited by Wendy Reed and Jennifer Horne, "is a collection of essays by southern women that encompasses spirituality and the experience of winding through the religiously charged environment of the American South. . . . These essays showcase the large spectrum of spirituality that abides in the South, as well as the equally large spectrum of individual women who hold these faiths." (Publisher's note)

200.9 History, geographic treatment, biography

Almond, Gabriel Abraham
★ **Strong** religion; the rise of fundamentalisms around the world. {by} Gabriel A. Almond, R. Scott

Appleby, and Emmanuel Sivan. University of Chicago Press 2003 281p il $49; pa $19 **200.9**
1. Religious fundamentalism
ISBN 0-226-01497-5; 0-226-01498-3 pa
LC 2002-13665
This "may be the single most cogent sociohistorical analysis of the modern religious phenomenon called fundamentalism. . . . This foundational work is essential for academic and major public libraries." Libr J
Includes bibliographical references

Armstrong, Karen
★ The **battle** for God; fundamentalism in Judaism, Christianity, and Islam. Knopf 2000 442p $29.95; pa $15.95 **200.9**
1. Judaism 2. Islamic fundamentalism 3. Christian fundamentalism 4. Religious fundamentalism 5. Israel -- History
ISBN 0-679-43597-2; 0-345-39169-1 pa
LC 99-34022
This is a "study of fundamentalism among Jews (in Israel), Christians (American Protestants), and Muslims (Sunni Egyptians and Shiite Iranians). Armstrong argues that all strains of fundamentalism, despite their differences, are fearful defenses against modernity. . . . The author is sympathetic to the human need for spiritual meaning, but she points out that the intellectual flaws of fundamentalist beliefs are customarily accompanied by paranoia, anger, and aggression—which, in turn, frequently betray the message of the faith." New Yorker
Includes bibliographical references

★ The **great** transformation; the beginning of our religious traditions. Knopf 2006 469p il map $30 **200.9**
1. Religion -- History
ISBN 0-375-41317-0
LC 2005-47536
"This could very possibly be one of the greatest intellectual histories ever written." Libr J
Includes bibliographical references

Believer, beware; first person dispatches from the margins of faith. selected by Jeff Sharlet, Peter Manseau, and the editors of Killing the Buddha. Beacon Press 2009 263p pa $16 **200.9**
1. Faith 2. United States -- Religion
ISBN 978-0-8070-7739-9; 0-8070-7739-9
LC 2008-47403
"The editors are among the smart, candid, and insightful authors whose personal narratives form the book's 35 brief chapters. The selections represent a wide range of experiences from cheating on bar mitzvah prep to discovering hunger as spiritual food in a Ramadan fast, from sabotaging Bible camp to stumbling upon barbershop theology. Contributions reflect the scope of religious diversity, including orthodox Judaism, Roman Catholicism, Islam, Zen Buddhism and even a meditation on agnosticism. Some are funny, others heartbreaking, and some are simply revelatory." Publ Wkly
Includes bibliographical references

★ The **Cambridge** illustrated history of religions; edited by John Bowker. Cambridge Univ. Press 2002 336p il (Cambridge illustrated history) $40 **200.9**
1. Religions
ISBN 0-521-81037-X
LC 2001-37866
"The major religions get thoroughgoing treatment, with short introductions also given to the Zoroastrianism; the religions of Greece, Rome, Egypt, and Mesopotamia; aboriginal religions; and new religious movements. . . . Christianity receives a separate chapter as well as substantial treatment in chapters on Chinese, Korean, and Japanese religions. . . . This volume presents a large amount of information in an engaging way, offering much scholarly insight for the lay reader." Libr J
Includes bibliographical references

Controversial New Religions; edited by James R. Lewis and Jesper Aa. Petersen. 2nd Edition Oxford University Press 2014 480 p. pa. $35 **200.9**
ISBN 9780199315314
LC 2013049363
"This volume collects papers on those specific New Religious Movements (NRMS) that have generated the most scholarly attention. With few exceptions, these organizations are also the controversial groups that have attracted the attention of the mass media, often because they have been involved in, or accused of, violent or anti-social activities. Among the movements . . . profiled are such groups as the Branch Davidians, Heaven's Gate, Aum Shinrikyo, Solar Temple, Scientology, and Falun Gong." (Publisher's note)

★ **Eastern** religions; origins, beliefs, practices, holy texts, sacred places. general editor, Michael D. Coogan; [contributors] Vasudha Narayanan . . . [et al.] Oxford University Press 2005 552p il $35; pa $19.95 **200.9**
1. Shinto 2. Taoism 3. Buddhism 4. Hinduism 5. Confucianism 6. East Asia -- Religion 7. South Asia -- Religion
ISBN 0-19-522190-7; 978-0-19-522190-9; 0-19-522191-5 pa; 978-0-19-522191-6 pa
LC 2004-30376
This is an introduction "to major South Asian and East Asian religious traditions. Four expert authors introduce Hinduism, Buddhism, Taoism, Confucianism, and Shinto. To aid comparison, each article has parallel sections on origins and historical development, aspects of the divine, sacred texts, sacred persons, ethical principles, sacred space, sacred time, death and the afterlife, and society and religion. The clear, crisp prose avoids academic jargon without losing the complexity and richness of the traditions being examined." Libr J
Includes bibliographical references

Leon, Luis D.
Religion and American cultures; an encyclopedia of traditions, diversity, and popular expressions. Gary Laderman and Luis León, editors; foreword

by Amanda Porterfield. ABC-CLIO 2003 3v set
$285   **200.9**
    1. Reference books 2. United States -- Religion --
Encyclopedias
    ISBN 1-57607-238-X

LC 2003-8644

"This resource explores the various ways Americans approach religion. Its first volume features chapters on ethnic groups and sectarian beliefs, the second comprises essay entries on distinct practices, and the third collects primary documents. Cotton Mather, Shirley MacLaine, and Elijah Muhammad are represented, along with such pivotal documents as The Maryland TolerationAct and the American Indian Religious Freedom Act." Libr J
    Includes bibliographical references

Melton, J. Gordon
    ★ **Melton's** encyclopedia of American religions; [by] J. Gordon Melton; James Beverley, associate editor; Constance Jones, assistant editor; Pamela S. Nadell, assistant editor; foreword by Rodney Stark. 8th ed.; Gale, Cengage Learning 2009 xxvi, 1386p il map $380   **200.9**
    1. Reference books 2. Sects -- Encyclopedias 3. United States -- Religion -- Encyclopedias
    ISBN 978-0-7876-9696-2

LC 2008-37465

    First published 1978 by McGrath Publishing Company with title: Encyclopedia of American religions
    This encyclopedia features "coverage on more than 2,300 North American religious groups in the U.S. and Canada—from Adventists to Zen Buddhists. Information on these groups is presented in two . . . sections. These sections contain essays and directory listings that describe the historical development of religious families and give . . . information about each group within those families, including, when available, rubrics for membership figures, educational facilities and periodicals." Publisher's note
    Includes bibliographical references

200.973   Religion--United States

Ozment, Katherine
    Grace without God; The Search for Meaning, Purpose, and Belonging in a Secular Age. Katherine Ozment, Harper Wave. HarperCollins Publishers 2016 320 p. (hardcover) $25.99   **200.973**
    1. Spiritual life 2. United States -- Religion 3. Religion 4. Spirituality 5. Spiritual biography
    ISBN 9780062305114

LC 2016004086

    This book, by Katherine Ozment, is an "exploration of secular America. . . . Ozment takes readers on a quest to understand the trends and ramifications of a nation in flight from organized religion. . . . Most Americans are raised in a religious tradition, but in recent decades many have begun to leave religion. . . . So how do the nonreligious fill the need for ritual, story, community, . . . purpose and meaning without . . . religion?"

"Ozment successfully writes an informative and relatable discussion on the changing landscape of religion, society, and identity." LJ
    Includes bibliographical references and index

Schmidt, Leigh Eric
    The **religious** history of America; The Heart of the American Story from Colonial Times to Today. by Edwin S. Gaustad and Leigh E. Schmidt. Rev ed; HarperSanFrancisco 2002 x, 454 p.p illustrations $18.99   **200.973**
    1. United States -- Religion 2. United States -- Church history
    ISBN 0060630566; 9780060630560

LC 2002190208

    This book on American religious history, by Edwin S. Gaustad and Leigh E. Schmidt, is a "fully revised, updated, and expanded version. . . . [It] expands its scope, increasing the emphasis on pluralism, religious practices, and spiritual seeking, as well as the direct connection of religion to social and political struggle. . . . [It also has] a new emphasis on African-American and Native American religious life, Eastern religions, and the recent boom in spirituality." (Publisher's note)
    "The overall result is a well-balanced enhancement of an excellent work." LJ
    Includes bibliographical references (p. 433-435) and index

201   Specific aspects of religion

Armstrong, Karen, 1944-
    ★ **Fields** of Blood; Religion and the History of Violence. by Karen Armstrong. Random House Inc 2014 496 p. $30   **201**
    1. Violence -- Religious aspects
    ISBN 0307957047; 9780307957047
    This book, by Karen Armstrong, is an "exploration of religion and the history of human violence. . . . While many historians have looked at violence in connection with particular religious manifestations (jihad in Islam or Christianity's Crusades), Armstrong looks at each faith--not only Christianity and Islam, but also Buddhism, Hinduism, Confucianism, Daoism, and Judaism--in its totality over time." (Publisher's note)
    Includes bibliographic references, notes, and index

Barr, Stephen M.
    ★ **Modern** physics and ancient faith. University of Notre Dame Press 2003 312p il hardcover o.p. pa $18   **201**
    1. Physics 2. Religion and science
    ISBN 0-268-03471-0; 978-0-268-02198-6 pa; 0-268-02198-8 pa

LC 2002-151565

    The author "argues that the great discoveries of modern physics are more compatible with the central teachings of Christianity and Judaism about God, the cosmos, and the human soul than with the atheistic viewpoint of scientific materialism." Publ Wkly
    Includes bibliographical references

Campbell, Joseph

Creative mythology. Arkana 1991 730p (The masks of God) pa $18 **201**

1. Mythology in literature
ISBN 978-0-14-019440-1; 0-14-019440-1
First published 1968 by Viking

"This volume explores the whole inner story of modern culture since the Dark Ages, treating modern man's unique position as the creator of his own mythology." Publisher's note

Includes bibliographical references

Occidental mythology. Arkana 1991 564p (The masks of God) pa $18 **201**

1. Mythology
ISBN 978-0-14-019441-8; 0-14-019441-X
First published 1964 by Viking

"A systematic . . . comparison of the themes that underlie the art, worship, and literature of the Western world." Publisher's note

Includes bibliographical references

Oriental mythology. Arkana 1991 561p (The masks of God) pa $18 **201**

1. Oriental mythology
ISBN 978-0-14-019442-5; 0-14-019442-8
First published 1962 by Viking

"An exploration of Eastern mythology as it developed into the distinctive religions of Egypt, India, China, and Japan." Publisher's note

Includes bibliographical references

★ The **power** of myth; [by] Joseph Campbell, with Bill Moyers; Betty Sue Flowers, editor. Doubleday 1988 231p il hardcover o.p. pa $29.95 **201**

1. Mythology 2. Religious art 3. Spiritual life
ISBN 0-385-24773-7; 0-385-24774-5

LC 88-4218

This companion to a public television series records conversations between Campbell and Bill Moyers. Campbell reflects on themes and symbols from world religions and mythologies and explores their relevance for his own spiritual journey.

"Campbell is the hero on his own voyage of discovery. This well-bound book on lovely paper with helpful illustrations from art is highly recommended for all libraries." Choice

Primitive mythology. Arkana 1991 504p (The masks of God) pa $18 **201**

1. Mythology
ISBN 978-0-14-019443-2; 0-14-019443-6
First published 1959 by Viking

The author "discusses the primitive roots of mythology, examining them in light of . . . discoveries in archaeology, anthropology, and psychology." Publisher's note

Includes bibliographical references

Frank, Adam

The **constant** fire; beyond the science vs. religion debate. University of California Press 2009 288p $24.95 **201**

1. Religion and science
ISBN 978-0-520-25412-1; 0-520-25412-0

LC 2008-25402

"An elegant reimagining of the relationship between science and spirituality. . . . Challenges the assumption that science and religion are implacable foes." Chron Higher Educ

Includes bibliographical references (p. 269-281) and index

Haidt, Jonathan

The **righteous** mind; why good people are divided by politics and religion. Jonathan Haidt. Pantheon Books 2012 419 p. $28.95 **201**

1. Social values 2. Social psychology 3. Political psychology 4. Psychology of religion 5. Ethics -- Psychological aspects 6. Ethics 7. Psychology, Religious
ISBN 9780307377906

LC 2011032036

"The core of the book [by Jonathan Haidt] is an attempt at a Darwinian explanation of morality, contending that moral behavior emerges from a natural process of competition among human groups. . . . A part of 'The Righteous Mind' is a . . . critique of . . . [a] primitive type of rationalism. . . . Much of his book is an attempt to apply the findings of evolutionary psychology to the political gridlock that . . . exists in the United States." (New Republic)

Includes bibliographical references and index

The **History** of science and religion in the western tradition; an encyclopedia. Gary B. Ferngren, general editor; Edward J. Larson, Darrel W. Amundsen, co-editors; Anne-Marie E. Nakhla, assistant editor. Garland 2000 xxi, 586p (Garland reference library of the humanities) $195 **201**

1. Religion and science
ISBN 0-8153-1656-9

LC 00-25153

This is a collection of articles "grouped under ten headings covering everything from the relationship of science and religion to the approaches taken by specific religious traditions, from alchemy to chemistry to materialism to spiritualism. Ferngren . . . and his coeditors take the stand that the historical relationship between science and religion follows a complex model rather than the popularly understood model of unalterable conflict. The result is a work, well worth reading through or browsing, that is filled with respect for the roles and methodologies of both religion and science." Libr J

Includes bibliographical references and index

Jordan, Michael

Dictionary of gods and goddesses; 2nd ed; Facts on File 2004 402p il (Facts on File library of religion and mythology) $45 **201**

1. Reference books 2. Gods and goddesses --

Dictionaries
ISBN 0-8160-5923-3

LC 2004-13028

First published 1993

The author's "alphabetical list includes gods and goddesses from a variety of religions. Each entry provides a brief description with cross-references where appropriate; some supply translations of the names. Longer entries include origin, dates of observance, synonyms, geographic location of the cult center, art references by type (e.g., stone carvings), and literary sources. . . . This [is] a usable, well-written resource for short descriptions of cross-cultural deities." Choice

Includes bibliographical references

Karabell, Zachary

Peace be upon you; the story of Muslim, Christian, and Jewish coexistence. Random House 2007 343p map $26.95 **201**
1. Interfaith relations 2. Christianity and other religions 3. Islam -- Relations 4. Judaism -- Relations
ISBN 978-1-4000-4368-2; 1-4000-4368-9

LC 2006-31501

"This outstanding book . . . combines in a single volume centuries of interaction among the three great monotheistic religions." Choice

Includes bibliographical references (p. 317-326)

Kimball, Charles

When religion becomes lethal; the explosive mix of politics and religion in Judaism, Christianity, and Islam. Jossey-Bass 2011 254p $27.95; ebook $14.99 **201**
1. Islam and politics 2. Religion and politics 3. Religious fundamentalism 4. Christianity and politics 5. Judaism and politics
ISBN 978-0-470-58190-2; 0-470-58190-5; 978-1-1180-3056-1 ebook

LC 2010052515

The author "begins with a careful overview of how, in sacred text and history, religion and politics interact in Judaism, Christianity, and Islam. He then examines the constructive and destructive ways adherents of the faiths have interpreted and acted on their traditions in the public square, focusing specifically on Israel, the U.S., Iraq, and Iran." Sojourners

Includes bibliographical references (p. 229-232)

Leeming, David Adams

★ The **Oxford** companion to world mythology. Oxford University Press 2006 xxxvii, 469p $65 **201**
1. Reference books 2. Mythology -- Dictionaries
ISBN 0-19-515669-2

LC 2005-14216

"This volume presents approximately 2,000 concise entries in dictionary format. Leeming, . . . in an attempt to be 'inclusive and reasonably comprehensive,' ranges far outside the Western tradition to cover figures and folklore from Africa, Asia, and the Americas, as well as from the sacred narratives of religions. . . . Approximately 100 black-and-white illustrations, along with a few color plates, provide examples of artistic renderings of various myths. .

. . This work should find a place in any general reference collection." Choice

Includes bibliographical references

Niebuhr, Gustav

Beyond tolerance; searching for interfaith understanding in America. Viking 2008 xxxviii, 218p $25.95 **201**
1. Religious tolerance 2. Interfaith relations
ISBN 978-0-670-01956-4; 0-670-01956-9

LC 2007-40479

"Niebuhr brings his reporter's eye for detail to this work, which he populates with people and organizations who strive to find religious meaning in our diverse lives. This is no dry, academic exposition. Written for a general audience, it is also valuable for scholars wishing to see an America many might have thought was calcifying into an insular continent, worshipping hard gods or God." Libr J

Includes bibliographical references (p. 208-212)

Nussbaum, Martha Craven, 1947-

★ The **new** religious intolerance; overcoming the politics of fear in an anxious age. Martha C. Nussbaum. Belknap Press of Harvard University Press 2012 xiii, 285 p.p (hbk. : alk. paper) $26.95 **201**
1. Freedom of religion 2. Religious tolerance 3. Islamophobia -- United States 4. Religious discrimination 5. Fear -- Religious aspects
ISBN 0674065905; 9780674065901

LC 2011051712

In this book Martha C. Nussbaum "enters the debate on anti-Muslim discrimination. . . . She invites us to examine disputes about women's use of the burka and the construction of an Islamic-initiated 'multifaith community center' near New York's Ground Zero. The author's argument for tolerant accommodation falls within the 'Socratic and Christian/Kantian' commitment to live an examined life in relations with religious minorities." (Library Journal)

Includes bibliographical references (p. 247-267) and index

Stark, Rodney

For the glory of God; how monotheism led to reformations, science, witch-hunts, and the end of slavery. Princeton Univ. Press 2003 488p il $45; pa $18.95 **201**
1. Slavery 2. Monotheism 3. Witchcraft 4. Reformation 5. Religion and science
ISBN 0-691-11436-6; 0-691-11950-3 pa

LC 2002-31746

A "provocative volume—lucid and tightly reasoned." Booklist

Includes bibliographical references and index

201.65   Religion and science

Sacks, Jonathan, 1948-

★ The **great** partnership; science, religion, and the search for meaning. Jonathan Sacks. Schocken Books 2011 x, 370 p.p $28.95   **201.65**
1. Faith 2. Religion and science
ISBN 0805243011; 9780805243017

LC 2012006601

In this book Jonathan Sacks "argues not only that science and religion are compatible, but that they complement each other--and that the world needs both. . . . [According to Sacks,] Science teaches us where we come from. Religion explains to us why we are here. Science is the search for explanation. Religion is the search for meaning. We need scientific explanation to understand nature. We need meaning to understand human behavior." (Publisher's note)

Includes bibliographical references

202   Doctrines

Anderson, Herbert

The **divine** art of dying; How to Live Well While Dying. Karen Speerstra + Herbert Anderson; foreword by Ira Byock, MD. Divine Arts. 2014 268 p. $18.95   **202**
1. Death 2. Death -- Religious aspects
ISBN 1611250234; 9781611250237

LC 2013047709

This book, by Karen Speerstra and Herbert Anderson, "explores the unique moment when seriously ill people choose to turn toward death. Combining personal stories with solid research on palliative and hospice care, it provides a well-integrated look at the spiritual dimensions of living fully when death is near." (Publisher's note)

"A valuable resource; this books brims with wisdom and grace." Pub Wkly

203   Public worship and other practices

★ **How** to be a perfect stranger; the essential religious etiquette handbook. edited by Stuart M. Matlins & Arthur J. Magida. 5th ed.; SkyLight Paths Pub. 2011 402p (Perfect stranger series) pa $19.99   **203**
1. Etiquette 2. Rites and ceremonies
ISBN 978-1-59473-294-2

LC 2010-31668

First published 1996-1997 in two volumes by Jewish Lights Pub.

This guide "provides brief overviews of many religions: services, life-cycle events, home celebrations. It explains rituals so that those unfamiliar with them will know what to expect, how to dress, whether to bring a gift, and so on. It also has a glossary, explains various religious calendars, and lists religious festivals." Booklist

204   Religious experience, life, practice

Coles, Robert

★ The **spiritual** life of children. Houghton Mifflin 1990 358p il hardcover o.p. pa $14   **204**
1. Children -- Religious life
ISBN 0-395-59923-7 pa

LC 90-40097

"One of the delights of his presentation is the combination of the children's searching comments and the struggle the author makes to hear beyond his own conceptions." J Youth Serv Libr

Includes bibliographical references

Wathey, John C.

The **illusion** of God's presence; the biological origins of spiritual longing. John C. Wathey. Prometheus Books 2016 445 p. (hardcover) $28   **204**
1. God 2. Faith 3. Religion and science 4. Experience (Religion) 5. Biology -- Religious aspects -- Christianity
ISBN 1633880745; 9781633880740

LC 2015030319

In this book, "starting with a vivid narrative account of the life-threatening hike that triggered his own mystical experience, biologist John Wathey takes the reader on a scientific journey to find the sources of religious feeling and the illusion of God's presence. His book delves into the biological origins of this compelling feeling, attributing it to innate neural circuitry that evolved to promote the mother-child bond." (Publisher's note)

Includes bibliographical references and index

208   Sources

Three Testaments; Torah, Gospel, and Quran. edited by Brian Arthur Brown, foreword by Amir Hussain. Rowman & Littlefield Pub Inc 2014 (paperback) $29.95   **208**
1. Islam -- Relations 2. Judaism -- Relations 3. Christianity and other religions
ISBN 1442214937; 9781442214927; 9781442214934; 9781442214941

This book "brings together for the first time the text of the Torah, the New Testament, and the Quran, along with commentaries from notable religion scholars, to help readers explore the connections, as well as the points of departure, of the three Abrahamic traditions." (Publisher's note)

209   Sects and reform movements

★ **Belief** beyond boundaries; Wicca, Celtic spirituality and the new age. edited by Joanne Pearson. Ashgate 2002 339p il maps (Religion today) $94.95; pa $29.95   **209**
1. Cults
ISBN 0-7546-0744-5; 0-7546-0820-4 pa

LC 2001-53654

"Though somewhat academic in tone, this is a solid overview of several New Age spiritual movements." Libr J

Includes bibliographical references

210   Philosophy and theory of religion

Gutting, Gary

Talking God; Philosophers on Belief. by Gary Gutting. W W Norton & Co Inc 2016 240 p. (ebook) $50; (pbk.) $16.95 **210**

1. Religion -- Philosophy 2. Philosophy and religion 3. Religions

ISBN 9780393352825; 9780393352818

LC 2016023255

This book, by Gary Gutting, "offers new perspectives on religion, including the challenge to believers from evolution, cutting-edge physics and cosmology; arguments both for and against atheism; and meditations on the value of secular humanism and faith in the modern world. Experts offer insights on Islam, Buddhism, and Hinduism, as well as Judaism and Christianity." (Publisher's note)

"An exceptional introduction to the philosophical questions surrounding God and atheism." Kirkus

Huxley, Aldous

★ The **perennial** philosophy. Harper & Row 1945 312p hardcover o.p. pa $14 **210**

1. Philosophy and religion 2. Religion -- Philosophy

ISBN 0-06-057058-X pa

An anthology of and commentary on Chinese, Latin, Greek, Catholic and Protestant mysticism

Includes bibliographical references

James, William

★ The **varieties** of religious experience; a study in human nature. introduction by Reinhold Niebuhr. Simon & Schuster 2004 398p pa $15 **210**

1. Mysticism 2. Conversion 3. Psychology 4. New Thought 5. Religious life 6. Spiritual healing 7. Religion -- Philosophy

ISBN 978-0-7432-5787-9; 0-7432-5787-1

LC 2004-42870

First published 1902 by Longman

"Based on material James had collected on the psychology and philosophy of religion for lectures at the University of Edinburgh in 1901 and 1902. The varieties of religious experience contains numerous descriptions of religious states of consciousness, which James presented from a pragmatic point of view." HarperCollins Reader's Ency of Am Lit. 2nd edition

Includes bibliographical references

211   Concepts of God

Armstrong, Karen

The **case** for God. Knopf 2009 406p $27.95 **211**

1. God 2. Apologetics 3. Christian life 4. Religious

life

ISBN 978-0-307-26918-8

LC 2009-14044

"'Magisterial' is the adjective of choice to describe Armstrong's work; her usual confident sweep across times and cultures rises above the 'answer-the-atheists' tired angle to make a passionate footnoted argument for the human need for a God." Publ Wkly

Includes bibliographical references

Berlinerblau, Jacques

How to be secular; a call to arms for religious freedom. Jacques Berlinerblau. Houghton Mifflin Harcourt 2012 xxix, 306 p.p $26.00 **211**

1. Humanism 2. Freedom of religion 3. Christianity -- United States 4. United States -- Religion 5. Secularism -- United States 6. Church and state -- United States 7. Freedom of religion -- United States

ISBN 0547473346; 9780547473345

LC 2012014226

Author Jacques Berlinerblau looks at secularism. "Arguing that the revival of religion in the United States since the 1970s has led to the ascent of the Christian Right and the crackup of secularism, the author cites examples of ways in which traditional boundaries have been breached, including the creation of the White House Office of Faith-based and Neighborhood Partnerships and frequent threats by elected officials to establish Christianity as the national religion." (Kirkus)

Includes bibliographical references (p. [212]-290) and index

Hazleton, Lesley, 1945-

Agnostic; a spirited manifesto. Lesley Hazleton. Riverhead 2016 224 p. (print) $26 **211**

1. Religion 2. Agnosticism

ISBN 1594634130; 9781594634130

LC 2016006449

Author Lesley Hazleton "gives voice to the case for agnosticism, breaks it free of its stereotypes as watered-down atheism or amorphous 'seeking,' and celebrates it as a reasoned, revealing, and sustaining stance toward life. Stepping over the lines imposed by rigid conviction, she draws on philosophy, theology, psychology, science, and more to explore, with curiosity and passion, the vital role of mystery in a deceptively information-rich world." (Publisher's note)

"This engaging and highly accessible read will satisfy those who puzzle over the idea of infinity, question theological "truth" or what death means for the mind and body, and who wish to delve deeper into our belief system." Library Journal

Niose, David

Nonbeliever nation; the rise of secular Americans. David Niose. Palgrave Macmillan 2012 262 p. (hardcover) $27 **211**

1. Secularism -- United States 2. Religion and politics -- United States

ISBN 023033895X; 9780230338951

LC 2011049323

This book, by David Niose, explores trends in non-religious observance in the United States. "Nearly one in five

Americans are nonbelievers . . . and they are flexing their muscles like never before. . . . From gay marriage to education policy to contentious church-state battles . . . [the author] shows how . . . secular Americans . . . are mobilizing and forming groups all over the country . . . to challenge the exaltation of religion in American politics and public life." (Publisher's note)

Zuckerman, Phil
Living the Secular Life; New Answers to Old Questions. Phil Zuckerman. Penguin Group USA Penguin Press 2014 288 p. $25.95   **211**
   1. United States -- Religion 2. Secularism -- United States 3. United States -- United States
   ISBN 1594205086; 9781594205088
                    LC 2014009785
   This book by Phil Zuckerman, "reveals that, despite opinions to the contrary, nonreligious Americans possess a unique moral code that allows them to effectively navigate the complexities of modern life. Spiritual self-reliance, clear-eyed pragmatism, and an abiding faith in the Golden Rule to adjudicate moral decisions: these common principles are shared across secular society." (Publisher's note)
   "Highly recommended for all readers, both religious and nonreligious, seeking a more accurate understanding of this ever-growing segment of the American population." LJ
   Includes bibliographical references and index

212 Existence of God, ways of knowing God, attributes of God

Overman, Dean L.
A **case** for the existence of God. Rowman & Littlefield 2008 xxxii, 229p $24.95   **212**
   1. God 2. Religion and science
   ISBN 978-0-7425-6312-4; 0-7425-6312-X
                    LC 2008-21731
   "Drawing on modern cosmology and information theory, Overman exposes fallacies that have infested skeptics' thinking since Hume and Kant. Clearer reasoning establishes an astonishing harmony between quantum physics and religious orthodoxy, so providing a credible defense for free will and moral judgment. Still, readers looking for certainty will not find it here: Overman acknowledges that the believer must make a leap of faith. . . . The intensely personal character of spiritual conversion emerges in the lives of the nine remarkable believers—including St. Augustine and Pascal, Dostoyevsky and Weil—whose testimonies resonate with passionate conviction. A book for readers willing to wrestle with the largest questions." Booklist
   Includes bibliographical references

215 Science and religion

Ecklund, Elaine Howard
Science vs. religion; what scientists really think. Oxford University Press 2010 228p $27.95   **215**
   1. Religion and science 2. Scientists -- Attitudes 3.

Universities and colleges -- United States -- Faculty
   ISBN 978-0-19-539298-2; 0-19-539298-1
                    LC 2009-34731
   Ecklund's "outstanding research, articulately presented, and judicious recommendations make this a valuable work for all who care about the subject of science and religion." Libr J
   Includes bibliographical references

220.3 Encyclopedias and topical dictionaries

Eerdmans dictionary of the Bible; David Noel Freedman, editor-in-chief; Allen C. Myers, associate editor; Astrid B. Beck, managing editor. Eerdmans 2000 xxxiii, 1425p il maps $45 **220.3**
   1. Reference books 2. Bible (as subject) -- Dictionaries
   ISBN 0-8028-2400-5
                    LC 00-56124
   "Up-to-date, comprehensive, and well written, the EDB is highly recommended." Libr J
   Includes bibliographical references

The HarperCollins Bible dictionary; Mark Allan Powell, general editior; with the Society of Bible Literature. 3rd edition HarperCollins 2011 xxiii, 1142 p.p illustrations, maps hbk $47.99 **220.3**
   1. Bible -- Dictionaries
   ISBN 0061469068; 9780061469060
                    LC 2010007897
   First published 1985 with title: Harper's Bible Dictionary
   "This volume usefully aids readers in understanding the Bible, while avoiding polemics and personal theories. It incorporates contributions from a wide spectrum of confessional and ideological positions. Updates include entries for all the deuterocanonical books, and their citation where relevant; entries on all the fauna/flora in the Bible; entries on important theological terms and words used in the Bible in a significant way; and entries treating the phenomena of everyday life in the biblical world." (Choice Reviews)
   Includes bibliographical references and index

Oxford University Press
The **Oxford** companion to the Bible; edited by Bruce M. Metzger, Michael D. Coogan. Oxford Univ. Press 1993 xxi, 874p il map $70 **220.3**
   1. Reference books 2. Bible (as subject) -- Dictionaries
   ISBN 0-19-504645-5
                    LC 93-19315
   "The many contributors read as a veritable who's who among biblical scholars. Although this companion is not meant to be an exhaustive reference, it is a highly reliable guide." Booklist

Zondervan illustrated Bible dictionary; [edited by] J.D. Douglas and Merrill C. Tenney; revised by Moises Silva. Zondervan 2011 1571 p. col. ill., maps $29.99 **220.3**
   1. Bible -- Dictionaries
   ISBN 9780310229834
                    LC 2010034210

This reference book "provides a visual . . . journey for anyone interested in learning more about the world of the Bible. Through the articles, sidebars, charts, maps, and full-color images included in this volume, the text of the Old and New Testaments [is enhanced]. . . . As a condensation of the Zondervan Pictorial Encyclopedia of the Bible, the information contained within this reference work is . . . biblically sound. The material is based completely on the NIV [New International Version] and cross-referenced to the King James Version, and it contains over 7,200 entries, 500 full-color photographs, charts, and illustrations, 75 full-color maps, and a Scripture index." (Publisher's note)

Includes bibliographical references.

220.5 Modern versions and translations

★ The **Bible**: Authorized King James Version; with an introduction and notes by Robert Carroll and Stephen Prickett. Oxford University Press 2008 lxxiv, 1039, 248, 445p il map (Oxford world's classics) pa $18.95 **220.5**
ISBN 978-0-19-953594-1
LC 2008-273825
This Oxford World's Classics version first published 1997
The authorized or King James Version originally published 1611.
Includes bibliographical references

Cruden, Alexander
★ **Cruden's** Complete concordance; with index to proper names and their meanings. edited by A.D. Adams, C.H. Irwin, S.A. Waters. Zondervan Pub. House 1968 803p (Zondervan classic reference series) $24.99; pa $8.99 **220.5**
1. Bible -- Concordances
ISBN 0-310-22920-0; 0-310-48971-7 pa
First edition 1737. Frequently revised
"The special value of this title is that Cruden provides an index to the Apocrypha. Note that some reprints of the work omit the Apocrypha in the concordance." Ref Sources for Small & Medium-sized Libr. 5th edition

Ferrell, Lori Anne
The **Bible** and the people. Yale University Press 2008 273p il map $32.50 **220.5**
1. Bible -- History
ISBN 978-0-300-11424-9
LC 2008-26769
"The Christian Bible is not only a physical object but also a delivery system for spiritual and secular ideas, according to cultural historian Ferrell. . . . Examining the English Bible collection at the Huntington Library, Ferrell discusses these Bibles' historical, political, and social impact on Christian belief and practice in Great Britain and America from the Middle Ages to the present. . . . Written for a general audience, this is an engaging and accessible overview of the history of the English Bible." Libr J
Includes bibliographical references

★ The **New** American Bible; translated from the original languages with critical use of all the ancient sources including the revised Psalms and the revised New Testament. authorized by the Board of Trustees of the Confraternity of Christian Doctrine and approved by the Administrative Committee Board of the National Conference of Catholic Bishops and the United States Catholic Conference. Oxford University Press 2006 xxiii, 1514p $39.99 **220.5**
ISBN 978-0-19-528904-6; 0-19-528904-8
First published 1970 by Kenedy
"Roman Catholic version based on modern English translations; replaces the Douay edition." N Y Public Libr Book of How & Where to Look It Up

★ The **new** Jerusalem Bible; [general editor: Henry Wansbrough] Doubleday 1985 2108p map $45; pa $29.95 **220.5**
ISBN 0-385-14264-1; 978-0-385-14264-9; 0-385-24833-4 pa; 978-0-385-24833-4 pa
LC 85-16070
First published in this format 1966 with title: The Jerusalem Bible
"Derives from the French version edited at the Dominican Ecole Biblique de Jerusalem and known as 'La Bible de Jerusalem.' The introductions and notes are 'a direct translation from the French, though revised and brought up to date in some places' but translation of the Biblical text goes back to the original languages." Guide to Ref Books. 11th edition

The **Oxford** study Bible; Revised English Bible with the Apocrypha. edited by M. Jack Suggs, Katharine Doob Sakenfeld, James R. Mueller. Oxford University Press 1992 xxviii, 199, 1597p map hardcover o.p. pa $34.99 **220.5**
ISBN 0-19-529001-1; 0-19-529000-3 pa
LC 92-137886
A revised edition of The new English Bible, published 1970
An annotated version of the Revised English Bible.
"This volume combines a cultural guide to the biblical world and an annotated Bible. Its notes feature the reflections of Protestant, Roman Catholic, and Jewish scholars." Publisher's note

Strong, James
The **strongest** Strong's exhaustive concordance of the Bible; 21st century ed, fully rev and corrected by John R. Kohlenberger III and James A. Swanson; Zondervan 2001 1742p maps $34.99 **220.5**
1. Bible -- Concordances
ISBN 0-310-23343-7
LC 2001-26577
A version of Strong's exhaustive concordance of the Bible originally published 1894
"Kohlenberger has teamed with James A. Swanson to produce a volume that cross-indexes a . . . database with exhaustive Hebrew and Greek dictionaries and adds Nave's Topical Bible Reference System (essentially a Bible dictionary with subjects, persons, places, and biblical books in al-

phabetic order). .... Charts plot the chronology of events in the Old and New Testament, miracles and parables of Jesus, and messianic prophecies. There is a harmony (parallels) of gospel stories, lists of biblical kings, weights and measures, Old Testament feasts, sacred days, sacrifices, and the major social concerns of the Mosaic Covenant. There is also a chart of the Hebrew Calendar. The work is based on the King James Version of the Bible and is generally conservative." Am Ref Books Annu, 2003

220.6   Interpretation and criticism (Exegesis)

Bowker, John

The **complete** Bible handbook; an illustrated companion. DK Pub. 1998 544p il maps $39.95; pa $25   **220.6**

1. Bible -- Commentaries

ISBN 0-7894-3568-3; 0-7894-8154-5 pa

LC 98-4478

In this volume "every book of the Bible (including Jewish Apocrypha) has its own entry, and there are supplementary entries on specific stories, theological concerns, history (Routes of the Exodus), or background (Gods and Goddesses of the Ancient Near East). In his introduction, Bowker presents a well-balanced summary of the Bible as a piece of literature and as scripture in our time and in history. . . . One of the book's strengths is its abundance of pictures." Voice Youth Advocates

Includes bibliographical references

Manser, Martin H.

Critical companion to the Bible; a literary reference. [by] Martin H. Manser; associate editors, David Barratt, Pieter J. Lalleman, Julius Steinberg. Facts On File, Inc. 2009 488p il (Facts on File library of world literature) $75   **220.6**

1. Bible as literature 2. Bible -- Criticism

ISBN 978-0-8160-7065-7

LC 2008-29257

"This reference provides an excellent introduction to not only just the literary but also the theological studies of the Bible through the ages." Booklist

Includes bibliographical references

Wray, T. J.

What the Bible really tells us; the essential guide to biblical literacy. Rowman & Littlefield Publishers 2011 249p $24.95; ebook $23.99   **220.6**

1. Bible -- Criticism

ISBN 978-0-7425-6253-0; 978-1-4422-1293-0 ebook

LC 2011011778

"Wray devotes a couple of introductory chapters to the biblical world and the tools and methods scholars use in their exegetical work. But her intention is to get people reading the Bible, not to offer an academic, verse-by-verse commentary. Subsequent chapters, therefore, explore what the Bible says about such issues as wealth, heaven, hell, sex, and the environment, dispelling many commonly held assumptions and pointing out where disagreements in interpretation lie

along the way. Wray succeeds in sharing the wisdom of the Bible by making it accessible, interesting, and fun." Booklist

Includes bibliographical references

220.8   Nonreligious subjects treated in Bible

Murphy, Cullen

The **Word** according to Eve; women and the Bible in ancient times and our own. Houghton Mifflin 1998 302p $24; pa $14   **220.8**

1. Feminism 2. Women in the Bible 3. Bible -- Criticism

ISBN 0-395-70113-9; 0-618-00192-1 pa

LC 98-18015

This is an examination of feminist Biblical scholarship. Murphy "divides his study into Old Testament scholarship and New Testament and early church history." N Y Times Book Rev

Includes bibliographical references

220.9   Geography, history, chronology, persons of Bible lands in Bible times

Currie, Robin

The **letter** and the scroll; what archaeology tells us about the Bible. [by] Robin Currie and Stephen Hyslop. National Geographic 2009 335p il map $40   **220.9**

1. Bible (as subject) -- Antiquities

ISBN 978-1-4262-0514-9

LC 2009-8572

"This gorgeous book . . . covering the people and events of the Bible, placed into their archaeological context, will delight and inform those who are interested in the Bible from a religious, cultural, or historical perspective. . . . [The book] investigates a variety of topics—such as cities, languages, luxury goods, wars, taxes, writings, and ancient art—through artifacts and archaeological evidence to provide an extensive background for the reader." Libr J

Includes bibliographical references

Curtis, Adrian

Oxford Bible atlas; edited by Adrian Curtis. 4th ed.; Oxford University Press 2007 229p il map $35   **220.9**

1. Reference books 2. Bible -- Geography

ISBN 0-19-100158-9; 978-0-19-100158-1

First published 1962

This atlas includes "81 full-color illustrations as well as 27 maps—e.g., of Jerusalem and the Holy Land, the Middle East and the eastern Mediterranean lands—all with terrain modeling. The text is divided into four main sections: 'The Setting,' 'The Hebrew Bible,' 'The New Testament,' and 'Archaeology in Bible Lands.' . . . [This is] a handsome background resource for Bible study." Libr J

Includes bibliographical references

Kee, Howard Clark

The **Cambridge** companion to the Bible; Bruce Chilton, general editor; Howard Clark Kee . . . [et al.] 2nd ed; Cambridge University Press 2008 724p il $100; pa $34.99   **220.9**
1. Bible -- History of Biblical events
ISBN 978-0-521-86997-3; 978-0-521-69140-6 pa
LC 2008-270190

First published 1997

"This is an excellent, single-volume resource for serious students of the Bible. . . . The text is generally accessible; extensive maps and illustrations add to its popular appeal." Booklist [review of 1997 edition]
Includes bibliographical references

The **Oxford** history of the biblical world; edited by Michael D. Coogan. Oxford Univ. Press 1998 643p il maps $60; pa $19.95   **220.9**
1. Ancient civilization 2. Bible -- History of biblical events
ISBN 0-19-508707-0; 0-19-513937-2 pa
LC 98-16042

"Organized chronologically, the essays explore the many cultures of ancient Canaan, Israel, Judea, and Palestine from 10,000 B.C.E. to the rise of Islam in the seventh century C.E. Illustrations, maps, charts, chronologies, and bibliographies enhance the uniformly well-written essays. But the strengths of the work are its currency and breadth of coverage and perspective." Libr J
Includes bibliographical references

Tischler, Nancy M.

Men and women of the Bible; a readers guide. Greenwood Press 2002 267p il $59.95   **220.9**
1. Bible -- Biography
ISBN 0-313-31714-3
LC 2002-75347

This resource provides "information on 100 biblical characters and their cultural significance in Western civilization. . . . Entries are arranged alphabetically from Aaron to Zephaniah, concisely written, and adhere to a uniform pattern. Subjects are listed by name with the addition of etymological information. A synopsis of the relevant biblical story follows, utilizing the King James version of the Bible. . . . The author also includes information on each person as a character in later works, including Western literature, legend, and painting." Booklist
Includes bibliographical references

221   Old Testament (Tanakh)

The **Jewish** Bible. The Jewish Publication Society 2008 291p il map (JPS guide) pa $22   **221**
1. Bible -- O.T. -- Introductions
ISBN 978-0-8276-0851-1; 0-8276-0851-9
LC 2008-10794

"One in a series of concise reference books on different aspects of Judaism, this includes a history of the Jewish scriptures, translations through the centuries, how to read the Bible, summaries of each book, and an extensive glossary." Univ Press Books for Public and Second Sch Libr, 2009
Includes bibliographical references

Kugel, James L.

How to read the Bible; a guide to scripture, then and now. Free Press 2007 819p il map $35   **221**
1. Bible -- O.T. -- Criticism
ISBN 978-0-7432-3586-0; 0-7432-3586-X
LC 2007-23466

"Kugel has written a wonderful book, one that lays bare the worlds both of modern biblical scholarship and of ancient biblical interpretation with wit and erudition." Commentary
Includes bibliographical references

★ **Tanakh**; a new translation of the Holy Scriptures according to the traditional Hebrew text. Jewish Publ. Soc. 1985 xxvi, 1624p $35; pa $22   **221**
ISBN 0-8276-0252-9; 0-8276-0366-5 pa
LC 85-10006

This volume represents a "collaboration between rabbis from the Orthodox, Conservative, and Reform branches of Judaism, and scholars in Semitic languages and biblical studies. The translators relied on the Hebrew tenth-century Masoretic text that is Judaism's standard. The Torah, Prophets, and Writings are here in a single volume." Publisher's note

Telushkin, Joseph

Biblical literacy; the most important people, events, and ideas of the Hebrew Bible. Morrow 1997 xxviii, 628p $29.95   **221**
1. Jewish ethics 2. Bible -- O.T. -- Criticism
ISBN 0-688-14297-4
LC 97-6645

"Biblical truths that many a reader may have glossed over before stand out, thanks to this superb book, and, more important, misunderstandings are cleared up and previously mistranslated words correctly rendered." Booklist
Includes bibliographical references

222   Historical books of Old Testament

The **contemporary** Torah; a gender-sensitive adaptation of the JPS translation. revising editor, David E.S. Stein; consulting editors, Adele Berlin, Ellen Frankel, and Carol L. Meyers. Jewish Publication Society 2006 xlii, 412p $28   **222**
ISBN 0-8276-0796-2; 978-0-8276-0796-5
LC 2006-40608

A modern adaptation of the Jewish Publication Society's translation of the Torah. "In places where the ancient audience probably would not have construed gender as pertinent to the text's plain sense, the editors changed words into gender-neutral terms; where gender was probably understood to be at stake, they left the text as originally translated, or even introduced gendered language where none existed before. They made these changes regardless of whether words referred to God, angels, or human beings." Publisher's note

★ The **five** books of Moses; a translation with commentary. {by} Robert Alter. Norton 2004 xlviii, 1064p map $39.95 **222**
ISBN 0-393-01955-1

LC 2004-14067

In "this new translation of the first five books of the Bible {Alter} . . . seeks to reproduce as faithfully as possible in standard English the nuances, literary devices, and metaphors of the original Hebrew text. In doing so, he aims to show where many modern translations (including the King James Bible) have failed to represent the original Hebrew's varied nuances. In his commentary, found in the introductions to each book and on many individual verses, Alter expounds the theological meaning of the text's narrative in its larger biblical context." Libr J

Includes bibliographical references

Kass, Leon

The **beginning** of wisdom; reading Genesis. {by} Leon R. Kass. Free Press 2003 576p $35 **222**
1. Bible -- O.T. -- Genesis -- Criticism
ISBN 0-7432-4299-8

LC 2002-45593

The author "sees Genesis as a text that offers wisdom about the nature of man and how we ought to live, while it also calls for interpretation, reflection, and judgment. . . . Kass presents many enlightening insights, the result of his attempts to understand the text on its own terms and relating it to contemporary concerns, especially tradition and parenthood. While not everyone will agree with his interpretations, which tend to be conservative, Kass offers much to be pondered by thoughtful readers, both academics and, especially, educated laypeople." Libr J

Includes bibliographical references

Moyers, Bill

Genesis: a living conversation. Doubleday 1996 361p il hardcover o.p. pa $22.95 **222**
1. Bible -- O.T. -- Genesis -- Criticism
ISBN 0-385-49043-7 pa

LC 96-15318

Companion volume to the PBS series led by Bill Moyers in which writers and religious thinkers discussed episodes from the first book of the Bible. Among the participants are Burton Visotzky, a rabbi who initiated the conversations which gave rise to the series, "Elaine Pagels, Karen Armstrong, . . . John Barth, and Oscar Hijuelos. The book is divided by biblical tale (Adam and Eve, Cain and Abel, the blinding of Isaac) with five or six of the participants discussing the moral, literary, and personal meanings of the stories." Booklist

★ The **Torah**: the five books of Moses; a new translation of the Holy Scriptures according to the Masoretic text; first section. Jewish Publication Society 1963 393p $20; pa $15 **222**
ISBN 0-8276-0015-1; 0-8276-0680-X pa

This "translation of Genesis, Exodus, Leviticus, Numbers, and Deuteronomy was prepared . . . to present a version of the Bible that takes into account modern insights and knowledge of ancient times. . . . Of chief value to persons of the Jewish religion but of interest to Bible scholars of any religion." Booklist

223 Poetic books of Old Testament

Kushner, Harold S., 1935-

The **book** of Job; when bad things happened to a good person. Harold S. Kushner. Nextbook : Schocken 2012 201 p. $24 **223**
1. God 2. Suffering -- Religious aspects 3. Bible. O.T. Job -- Commentaries 4. Suffering -- Religious aspects -- Judaism
ISBN 0805242929; 9780805242928

LC 2011051531

This book by Harold S. Kushner presents a "guide to that most fascinating of biblical texts, the book of Job, and what it can teach us about living in a troubled world. Kushner examines the questions raised by Job's experience, questions that have challenged wisdom seekers and worshippers for centuries. What kind of God permits such bad things to happen to good people? Why does God test loyal followers? Can a truly good God be all-powerful?" (Publisher's note)

225 New Testament

Borg, Marcus J., 1942-2015

Evolution of the Word; reading the New Testament in the order it was written. Marcus J. Borg. 1st ed. HarperOne 2012 viii, 608 p.p $29.99 **225**
1. Bible. New Testament 2. Bible. N.T. -- Chronology 3. Bible. N.T. -- Criticism, interpretation, etc
ISBN 9780062082121; 0062082108; 9780062082107

LC 2012001947

This New Testament with commentary, edited by Marcus J. Borg, changes "the order of the New Testament, . . . putting the books in . . . the order in which they were written. By doing so, [he] allows us to read these documents in their historical context. . . . Borg offers . . . introductions for each book so that as we read through these biblical documents . . . we see afresh what concerns and pressures shaped this movement as it evolved into a new religion." (Publisher's note)

Includes bibliographical references

Brown, Raymond Edward

An **introduction** to the New Testament; by Raymond E. Brown. Yale University Press 1997 xxxviii, 878p map (Anchor Bible reference library) $55 **225**
1. Bible -- N.T. -- Criticism
ISBN 978-0-300-14016-3; 0-300-14016-9

A reissue of the title first published 1997 by Doubleday

Brown's book "culminates his life's work and synthesizes the best of his generation's historical-critical scholarship clearly and cogently for beginners and advanced students alike." N Y Times Book Rev

225.9 Geography, history, chronology, persons of New Testament lands in New Testament times

Murphy-O'Connor, J.

Paul; a critical life. {by} Jerome Murphy-O'Connor. Clarendon Press 1996 416p maps hardcover o.p. pa $21   **225.9**
1. Saints 2. Apostles 3. Writers on religion
ISBN 01-9-285342-2 pa

LC 95-49173

"This is likely to become the standard work on Paul's life for the next generation and is warmly recommended as such." Choice

Includes bibliographical references

Ruden, Sarah

Paul among the people; the Apostle reinterpreted and reimagined in his own time. Pantheon Books 2010 214p $25; ebook $25   **225.9**
1. Saints 2. Apostles 3. Writers on religion 4. Bible -- N.T. -- Epistles of Paul -- Criticism
ISBN 978-0-375-42501-1; 978-0-307-37902-3 ebook

LC 2009-20969

"In 'reimagining' Paul with the aid of her intimate knowledge of classical literature, Ruden hasn't only helped us to better understand him and his message in the context of his time (as indispensable as that service is). She has also brought Paul to us, to our time. . . . In an uncanny way, her book is animated by the apostle's style: his urgency, his argumentative agility, his bluntness, his exasperation, his vision of great felicity." Natl Rev

Includes bibliographical references

226 Gospels and Acts

Bonhoeffer, Dietrich

The **cost** of discipleship; containing material not previously translated. rev and unabridged ed; Macmillan 1959 hardcover o.p. pa $12   **226**
1. Sermon on the mount 2. Bible -- N.T. -- Gospels -- Criticism
ISBN 0-684-81500-1 pa

Original German edition, 1937. This edition translated by R. H. Fuller with some revision by Irmgard Booth

The first part of the book "is an exposition of the conception of discipleship that is to be found in the Synoptic Gospels, together with an interpretation of the Sermon on the Mount. The second part consists of Bonhoeffer's attempt to show how the terminology used by the evangelists has been translated into the language of the Church of the Apostle Paul." Magill. Masterpieces of Christ Lit in Summary Form

Kloppenborg, John S.

Q, the earliest Gospel; an introduction to the original stories and sayings of Jesus. Westminster John Knox Press 2008 170p il pa $19.95   **226**
1. Q hypothesis (Synoptics criticism)
ISBN 978-0-664-23222-1; 0-664-23222-1

LC 2008-8394

The author is an "authority on the Q Gospel, a 'sayings gospel' that is thought to be a source (from the German Quelle for source) for the Gospels of Matthew and Luke. No copy of Q has been found, but scholars have recreated it through analysis of the three synoptic Gospels, looking for common elements and focusing on the sayings of Jesus. This book is a succinct introduction to Q, addressing questions about its composition and importance. . . . A complete reconstruction of Q is included as well as notes and a bibliography." Libr J

226.2 Specific Gospels

Spong, John Shelby

Biblical literalism; a gentile heresy: a journey into a new Christianity through the doorway of Matthew's gospel. John Shelby Spong. HarperOne 2016 416 p. (hardcover) $26.99   **226.2**
1. Bible 2. Judaism 3. Bible. Matthew -- Criticism, interpretation, etc
ISBN 9780062362308; 9780062362315; 0062362313

LC 2015018099

This book, by John Shelby Spong, "explores the Bible's literary and liturgical roots—its grounding in Jewish culture, symbols, icons, and storytelling tradition—to explain how the events of Jesus' life, including the virgin birth, the miracles, the details of the passion story, and the resurrection and ascension, would have been understood by both the Jewish authors of the various gospels and by the Jewish audiences for which they were originally written." (Publisher's note)

"A worthwhile read for the progressive layperson concerned with living out one's faith and applying the Bible as a touchstone." Library Journal

226.3 Mark

Bible/N.T./Gospels

The **three** Gospels; {by} Reynolds Price. Scribner 1996 288p $23; pa $13   **226.3**
ISBN 0-684-80336-4; 0-684-83281-X pa

LC 95-39948

"Although there is so much to appreciate in these commentaries and in the translated texts, the best part of the book . . . is left to last: Price's own joyously written account of Jesus' life." Booklist

226.8 Parables

Short stories by Jesus; the enigmatic parables of a controversial rabbi. Amy-Jill Levine. HarperOne 2014 320 p. $25.99   **226.8**
ISBN 0061561010; 9780061561016; 9780061561030

LC 2014012012

In this book, author Amy-Jill Levine "interweaves history and spiritual analysis to explore Jesus' most popular teaching parables, exposing their misinterpretations and making them lively and relevant for modern readers. . . . With this revitalized understanding, she interprets these moving stories for the contemporary reader, showing how the parables are not just about Jesus, but are also about us." (Publisher's note)

227 Epistles

Borg, Marcus J.
The first Paul; reclaiming the radical visionary behind the Church's conservative icon. [by] Marcus J. Borg, John Dominic Crossan. HarperOne 2009 230p $24.99; pa $13.99 **227**
  1. Saints 2. Apostles 3. Writers on religion 4. Bible -- N.T. -- Epistles of Paul -- Criticism
  ISBN 978-0-06-143072-5; 0-06-143072-2; 978-0-06-143073-2 pa; 0-06-143073-0 pa
                  LC 2009-004881
  "The great epistolary apostle is revealed as neither anti-Semitic, anti-sex, nor misogynist, but a preacher of social and political equality." Booklist
  Includes bibliographical references

229 Apocrypha, pseudepigrapha, intertestamental works

Bible/O.T./Apocrypha
★ The Apocrypha; new revised standard version. Cambridge University Press 1993 262p pa $14.99 **229**
  ISBN 978-0-521-50776-9; 0-521-50776-6
  "These books form part of the sacred literature of the Alexandrian Jews. . . . Some of them form an historical link between the Old and New Testament, others have a linguistic value in connexion with the Hellenistic phraseology of the latter. The narratives of Apocrypha are partly historical records, and partly allegorical." Oxford Univ. Press

Pagels, Elaine H.
★ Beyond belief; the secret Gospel of Thomas. {by} Elaine Pagels. Random House 2003 241p $26.95 **229**
  1. Christianity 2. Gospel of Thomas 3. Bible -- N.T. -- John -- Criticism
  ISBN 0-375-50156-8
                  LC 2002-36840
  "Even those who possess only a nodding acquaintance with Gnostic writings will find themselves stimulated by the author's arguments and perhaps transformed by her conclusions. A fresh and exciting work of theology and spirituality." Booklist
  Includes bibliographical references

230 Christianity

Christian reconstruction; R.J. Rushdoony and American religious conservatism. Michael J. McVicar. University of North Carolina Press 2015 326 p. **230**
  1. Dominion theology 2. United States -- Church

history 3. Christian conservatism -- United States 4. Conservatism -- Religious aspects -- Christianity
  ISBN 9781469622743
                  LC 2014035500
  This book is a "critical history of Christian Reconstruction and its founder and champion, theologian and activist Rousas John Rushdoony (1916-2001). Drawing on exclusive access to Rushdoony's personal papers and extensive correspondence, [author] Michael J. McVicar demonstrates the considerable role Reconstructionism played in the development of the radical Christian Right and an American theocratic agenda." (Publisher's note)
  Includes bibliographical references and index

Edman, Elizabeth M., 1962-
Queer virtue; what LGBTQ people know about life and love and how it can revitalize Christianity. The Reverend Elizabeth M. Edman. Beacon Press 2016 216 p. (hardcover : alk. paper) $25.95 **230**
  1. Christianity 2. Queer theory 3. Queer theology 4. Sex -- Religious aspects -- Christianity
  ISBN 0807061344; 9780807061343
                  LC 2015027701
  In this book, by Elizabeth M. Edman, the author, "an openly lesbian Episcopal priest and professional advocate for LGBTQ justice, . . . posits that Christianity, at its scriptural core, incessantly challenges its adherents to rupture false binaries, to 'queer' lines that pit people against one another. . . . Edman proposes that queer experience be celebrated as inherently valuable, ethically virtuous, and illuminating the sacred." (Publisher's note)
  "An intellectual and provocative perspective challenging Christians and others to reconsider the confines of spiritual interconnection, harmony, and progressive inclusion in modern religion." Kirkus
  Includes bibliographical references

Holifield, E. Brooks
★ Theology in America; Christian thought from the age of the Puritans to the Civil War. Yale University Press 2003 617p hardcover o.p. pa $23 **230**
  1. Doctrinal theology
  ISBN 0-300-09574-0; 978-0-300-10765-4 pa; 0-300-10765-X pa
                  LC 2003-42289
  "In this majestic achievement, Holifield . . . provides a first-rate, richly evocative and unrivaled history of theology in America. . . . This masterfully narrated, splendid book will become the definitive study of the development of American theology." Publ Wkly
  Includes bibliographical references

Kung, Hans
Great Christian thinkers. Continuum 1994 235p hardcover o.p. pa $19.95 **230**
  1. Saints 2. Bishops 3. Apostles 4. Theology 5. Theologians 6. Philosophers 7. Social reformers 8. Religious leaders 9. Writers on religion
  ISBN 0-8264-0848-6 pa
                  LC 94-883
  The author "attempts a new approach to the introduction-to-theology genre by critically tracing the developing

thought of key, usually 'paradigm-shifting,' theologians (Paul, Origen, Augustine, Aquinas, Luther, Schleiermacher, and Karl Barth) in relation to their social, intellectual, and religious environment. He explores the significance of their life and work for the Christian world in an interesting, quite understandable manner." Libr J

Includes bibliographical references

Lewis, C. S.

★ **Mere** Christianity; a revised and amplified edition, with a new introduction, of the three books, Broadcast talks, Christian behaviour, and Beyond personality. HarperSanFrancisco 2001 xx, 227p $19.95; pa $10   **230**
   1. Christian philosophy
   ISBN 0-06-065288-5; 0-06-065292-6 pa
                    LC 00-49862

First published 1952
   This omnibus edition includes most of C. S. Lewis' writings on Christian theology and moral philosophy
   Includes bibliographical references

Moore, Russell

Onward; engaging the culture without losing the gospel. Russell D. Moore. B & H Books 2015 224 p. $24.99   **230**
   1. Culture 2. Christianity
   ISBN 1433686171; 9781433686177
   Author Russell D. Moore suggests "as the culture changes all around us, it is no longer possible to pretend that we are a Moral Majority. That may be bad news for America, but it can be good news for the church. What's needed now, in shifting times, is neither a doubling-down on the status quo nor a pullback into isolation. Instead, we need a church that speaks to social and political issues with a bigger vision in mind: that of the gospel of Jesus Christ." (Publisher's note)
   "Mainline Christian readers will wonder whether this is old wine in new bottles, but Moore may be pointing the way for a new guard, as the Christian Right ages and loses key cultural battles. This important book is sure to provoke interesting discussions among many different kinds of Christians." Pub Wkly

Oxford companion to Christian thought; edited by Adrian Hastings {et al.} Oxford Univ. Press 2000 xxviii, 777p $75   **230**
   1. Reference books 2. Theology -- Dictionaries
   ISBN 0-19-860024-0
                    LC 2001-267818

This volume focuses "on the movement of ideas among Christians. The articles (more than 500) by 268 scholars (mostly British) range in length from half a column . . . to seven pages. . . . They broadly cover the themes . . . persons . . . places . . . and historical periods . . . that characterize Christian thought." Choice

Includes bibliographical references

Teilhard de Chardin, Pierre

★ The **divine** milieu; an essay on the interior life. Harper & Row 1960 144p hardcover o.p. pa $14   **230**
   1. Christian philosophy
   ISBN 978-0-06-093725-6 pa; 0-06-093725-4 pa
   Original French edition, 1957
   In this book Father de Chardin describes his spiritual philosophy

231   Christian doctrinal theology

Bass, Diana Butler

Grounded; finding God in the world--a spiritual revolution. Diana Butler Bass. HarperOne 2015 336 p. (hardcover) $26.99   **231**
   1. God -- Christianity 2. Christianity -- Spiritual life 3. God (Christianity) 4. Christianity -- 21st century 5. Spirituality -- Christianity
   ISBN 0062328549; 9780062328540; 9780062328564
                    LC 2015018071

This book, by Diana Butler Bass, argues "that what appears to be a decline [in religion] actually signals a major transformation in how people understand and experience God. The distant God of conventional religion has given way to a more intimate sense of the sacred that is with us in the world. This shift . . . is at the heart of a spiritual revolution that surrounds us–and that is challenging not only religious institutions but political and social ones as well." (Publisher's note)
   "It's a deeply theological book, but also a practical one; a book that causes one to ponder the spiritual implications of farmers' markets in altogether new ways." Booklist

Cairns, Scott

The **end** of suffering; finding purpose in pain. Paraclete Press 2009 126p pa $15.99   **231**
   1. Suffering
   ISBN 978-1-55725-563-1; 1-55725-563-6
                    LC 2009-18728

The author "offers a profoundly touching and deeply considered treatment of the notion of suffering, especially grief, in a Christian's life. For Cairns, suffering is not about the presence of evil; instead, it provides occasions where God can be known more intimately. . . . Eloquent in its simplicity, Cairns's brief book is a superb treatment of the thorny issues of suffering and grief." Libr J

Includes bibliographical references

231.7   Relation to the world

Lewis, C. S.

Miracles; a preliminary study. HarperSanFrancisco 2001 294p pa $13.95   **231.7**
   1. Miracles
   ISBN 0-06-065301-9; 978-0-06-065301-9
                    LC 00-49863

First published 1947 by Macmillan

"Mr. Lewis casts his net fairly wide and, under the guise of a book on miracles, offers a rational justification both of theism and of doctrinal Christianity." Times Lit Suppl

McKnight, Scot

Kingdom conspiracy; returning to the radical mission of the local church. Scot McKnight. Brazos Press 2014 304 p. (pbk.) $21.99 **231.7**
1. Church 2. Church work 3. Pastoral theology 4. Kingdom of God 5. Mission of the church
ISBN 1587433605; 9781587433603
LC 2014015580

This book, by Scot McKnight, "defines the biblical concept of kingdom, offering a thorough corrective and vision for the contemporary church. The most important articulation of kingdom was that of Jesus, who contended that the kingdom was in some sense present and in some sense in the future. . . . McKnight explains that kingdom mission is local church mission and that the present-day fetish with influencing society, culture, and politics distracts us from the mission of God." (Publisher's note)

"This is a must-read for church leaders today." Pub Wkly
Includes bibliographical references and index

Panagore, Peter Baldwin

Heaven Is Beautiful; How Dying Taught Me That Death Is Just the Beginning. Peter Baldwin Panagore. Red Wheel/Weiser 2015 256 p. illustrations $16.95 **231.7**
1. Spiritual life 2. Near-death experiences
ISBN 1571747346; 9781571747341

In this book, author Peter Baldwin Panagore "combines the thrills of a wilderness adventure with the awe inspiring elements of a paranormal novel. In March of 1980, ... Panagore went ice climbing on the world-famous Lower Weeping Wall . . . Alberta, Canada. He died on the side of that mountain. He experienced hell, forgiveness, and unconditional love. Heaven was beautiful. Panagores near death experience (NDE) changed his life and resulted in an intense spiritual journey." (Publisher's note)

"Readers who have a fascination with near-death experiences and mysticism will be drawn into Panagore's remembrances of dying on the side of that mountain and the unexplainable feelings he encountered, and may find comfort in his assurance that death is not to be feared." Pub Wkly

Winner, Lauren F.

Wearing God; clothing, laughter, fire, and other overlooked ways of meeting God. Lauren F. Winner. HarperOne 2015 304 p. (hardcover) $24.99 **231.7**
1. Christian life 2. Spiritual life 3. Image of God 4. Spirituality -- Christianity 5. Spiritual life -- Christianity 6. Christian women -- Religious life
ISBN 006176812X; 9780061768125; 9780061768132
LC 2015001455

In this book, author Lauren F. Winner presents "this exploration of little known--and, so, little used--biblical metaphors for God, metaphors which can open new doorways for our lives and spiritualities. . . . Lauren Winner gathers a number of lesser-known tropes, reflecting on how they work biblically and culturally, and reveals how they can deepen our spiritual lives." (Publisher's note)

"Winner's honest, charming reflections stir the imagination and invite the reader to explore not just the metaphors she has chosen, but the treasure trove the Bible provides. Prayers and quotations promote further contemplation." Pub Wkly
Includes bibliographical references and index

Wintz, Jack

Will I see my dog in heaven? God's saving love for the whole family of creation. Paraclete Press 2009 153p pa $14.99 **231.7**
1. Future life 2. Animals -- Religious aspects
ISBN 978-1-55725-568-6
LC 2009-259

The author, a Franciscan friar, argues that "God's promise of a new creation at the end of time extends to the animal companions we have known and loved in this life. . . . Strongly recommended." Libr J
Includes bibliographical references

Woodward, Kenneth L.

The **book** of miracles; the meaning of the miracle stories in Christianity, Judaism, Buddhism, Hinduism, Islam. Simon & Schuster 2000 429p hardcover o.p. pa $16 **231.7**
1. Miracles
ISBN 0-7432-0029-2 pa
LC 99-88083

"A great resource for studies in comparative religions and interfaith dialog." Libr J
Includes bibliographical references

232 Jesus Christ and his family

Blum, Edward J.

★ The **color** of Christ; the Son of God and the saga of race in America. Edward J. Blum and Paul Harvey. University of North Carolina Press 2012 340 p. ill. $32.5 **232**
1. Racism 2. African Americans -- Religion 3. United States -- Church history 4. Racism -- United States 5. Indians of North America -- Religion 6. Racism -- Religious aspects -- Christianity
ISBN 0807835722; 9780807835722
LC 2012004088

This book, by Edward J. Blum and Paul Harvey, discusses Christianity and racism in the U.S., discussing "how, in a country founded by Puritans who destroyed depictions of Jesus, Americans came to believe in the whiteness of Christ. Some envisioned a white Christ who would sanctify the exploitation of Native Americans and African Americans and bless imperial expansion. Many others gazed at a messiah, not necessarily white, who was willing and able to confront white supremacy." (Publisher's note)

Includes bibliographical references (p. [283]-325) and index

Gordon, Mary

Reading Jesus; a writer's encounter with the Gospels. Pantheon Books 2009 205p $24.95   **232**

1. Bible -- N.T. -- Gospels -- Criticism

ISBN 978-0-375-42457-1

LC 2009-04975

Gordon "examines her faith by closely reading, in a kind of literary lectio divina (sacred reading), the four Christian gospels that recount the life of Christ. The accounts by evangelists Matthew, Mark, Luke and John of the life of Jesus have a common subject and amazingly different treatments. Gordon tackles the power and puzzle of the Christian gospels with measure and imagination, providing welcome relief for those left cold by scholarly or fundamentalist parsing." Publ Wkly

232.9   Family and life of Jesus

Benedict XVI, Pope, 1927-

Jesus of Nazareth. part two; Holy week, from the entrance into Jerusalem to the Resurrection. by Joseph Ratzinger, Pope Benedict XVI. Ignatius Press 2011 362p $24.95   **232.9**

1. Holy Week 2. Biography, Individual 3. Bible -- N.T. -- Gospels -- Criticism 4. Bible -- N.T. -- Gospels -- Criticism, interpretation, etc.

ISBN 978-1-58617-500-9; 1-58617-500-9

This is "the second volume in [the author's] 'Jesus of Nazareth' series. . . . [This book] is a worthy contribution to the field not only because it was written by a pope, but also because it combines solid scholarship with deep spirituality. As such it joins the Jesus of history to the Christ of faith in an accessible narrative. This volume explores the drama of Holy Week. . . . The focus is on the meaning of the events, with a strong reiteration of recent church teaching against imputing guilt for Jesus' death to the Jews of that time or now." Publ Wkly

Fredriksen, Paula

Jesus of Nazareth, King of the Jews; a Jewish life and the emergence of Christianity. Knopf 1999 327p hardcover o.p. pa $14   **232.9**

ISBN 0-679-76746-0 pa

LC 99-31054

"To Fredriksen, Jesus was an observant Jew immersed in a context bounded by Galilee and Jerusalem. He was crucified as an imperial Roman deterrent to unruly inhabitants of a region prone to rebellion, and the emergence of Christianity is a work of creative theological reinterpretation as much as of historical memory." Booklist

Includes bibliographical references

Girzone, Joseph F.

A portrait of Jesus. Doubleday 1998 179p il hardcover o.p. pa $11.95   **232.9**

1. Christian life

ISBN 0-385-48477-1 pa

LC 98-15618

"This is popular liberal Catholic theology, more filled with forgiveness and fellowship than shaming and hierarchy.

Many a non-Catholic and even non-Christian may embrace it, too." Booklist

Meier, John P.

A marginal Jew; rethinking the historical Jesus. Doubleday 1991 3v maps (Anchor Bible reference library) v1 $45; v2 $42.50; v3 $45   **232.9**

ISBN 0-385-26425-9 v1; 0-385-46992-6 v2; 0-385-46993-4 v3

LC 91-10538

The first three volumes in a projected series of four devoted to an examination of the historical Jesus and his Jewish environment

The author "summarizes the first two volumes of A Marginal Jew and forecasts the next while meticulously documenting his understanding of the relations between the historical Jesus, his historical companions, and his historical competitors—Pharisees, Sadduccees, Essenes, and others. . . . The only thing common about Meier's project is fascination with the character of Jesus. Those who share that will find this dense, academic work worth their effort." Booklist {review of volume 3}

Includes bibliographical references

Pelikan, Jaroslav Jan

The illustrated Jesus through the centuries. Yale Univ. Press 1997 254p il $25   **232.9**

ISBN 0-300-07268-6

LC 97-7360

Companion volume to Mary through the centuries

In this revision of Jesus through the centuries (1985) the author "has abridged the text and turns to illustrations to convey his interpretations. . . . Very beautiful and very appealing for the general reader, this edition by no means replaces the scholarship and documentation of the first; those notations and references are missing in the illustrated edition. However, the illustrations enhance this interesting and insightful text." Libr J

Wilson, A. N.

Jesus. Norton 1992 269p $22.95   **232.9**

ISBN 0-393-03087-3

LC 92-37046

The author attempts to understand Jesus as a historical figure and ethical teacher within the context of first-century Judaism

Includes bibliographical references

232.91   Mary, mother of Jesus

Pelikan, Jaroslav Jan

Mary through the centuries; her place in the history of culture. Yale Univ. Press 1996 267p il $40; pa $14.95   **232.91**

1. Saints

ISBN 0-300-06951-0; 0-300-07661-4 pa

LC 96-24726

Companion volume to The illustrated Jesus through the centuries

"Although volumes have been written about the Virgin Mary from a wide variety of perspectives, it is rare to find a scholarly work that is easily accessible to the general, educated reader." Choice

Includes bibliographical references

233 Humankind

Jacobs, Alan

Original sin; a cultural history. HarperOne 2008 286p $24.95; pa $14.99   **233**

1. Sin

ISBN 978-0-06-078340-2; 0-06-078340-0; 978-0-06-087257-1 pa; 0-06-087257-8 pa

LC 2008-06582

This is "a playful, wide-ranging, erudite meditation on the nagging question of whether human beings enter the world predisposed to evil and sinfulness. . . . Original Sin has a great deal to offer both the general reader and those already well versed in this most controversial of theological arenas." America

Includes bibliographical references

Kierkegaard, Søren, 1813-1855

The **concept** of anxiety; a simple psychologically oriented deliberation in view of the dogmatic problem of hereditary sin. Soren Kierkegaard; edited and translated with introduction and notes by Alastair Hannay. Liveright Publishing Corporation 2014 288 p. (hardcover) $27.95   **233**

1. Sin 2. Anxiety 3. Psychology of religion 4. Psychology, Religious 5. Anxiety -- Religious aspects -- Christianity

ISBN 0871407191; 9780871407191

LC 2013037399

In this book, author Soren Kierkegaard "describes the nature and forms of anxiety, placing the domain of anxiety within the mental-emotional states of human existence that precede the qualitative leap of faith to the spiritual state of Christianity. It is through anxiety that the self becomes aware of its dialectical relation between the finite and the infinite, the temporal and the eternal." (Publisher's note)

"Almost as valuable as the translation is Hannay's introduction in which he provides the background necessary to grapple with Kierkegaard and a heartfelt argument for the value of studying this fountainhead of existentialism in general and Anxiety in particular." LJ

Includes bibliographical references

234 Salvation and grace

Strobel, Lee

The **Case** for Grace; A Journalist Explores the Evidence of Transformed Lives. Lee Strobel. Harpercollins Christian Pub 2015 240 p. $22.99   **234**

1. God 2. Grace (Theology)

ISBN 0310259177; 9780310259176

Author Lee Strobel "draws upon his own journey from atheism to Christianity to explore the depth and breadth of God's redeeming love for spiritually wayward people. He travels thousands of miles to capture the inspiring stories of

everyday people whose values have been radically changed and who have discovered the 'how' and 'why' behind God's amazing grace." (Publisher's note)

"This eloquent and honest book should appeal to those who have found grace, as well as those seeking it." Pub Wkly

234.5 Repentance and forgiveness

A **call** to mercy; Mother Teresa; edited and with a preface and introduction by Brian Kolodiejchuk, MC. Image 2016 xx, 364 p.p (ebook) $65; (hardcover) $25   **234.5**

1. Corporal works of mercy 2. Spiritual works of mercy 3. Catholic Church -- Doctrines 4. Mercy

ISBN 0451498208; 9780451498212; 9780451498205

LC 2016288106

This book "offers Mother Teresa's profound yet accessible wisdom on how we can show mercy and compassion in our day-to-day lives. . . . Compiled and edited by Brian Kolodiejckuk, M.C., the postulator of Mother Teresa's cause for sainthood, [the book] . . . discusses such topics as: the need for us to visit the sick and the imprisoned, the importance of honoring the dead and informing the ignorant, [and] the necessity to . . . forgive willingly, [among others]." (Publisher's note)

"These reflections, stories, and testimonials will challenge and inspire readers to bear witness to a venerable spiritual legacy." Pub Wkly

Includes bibliographical references (pages 333-364)

235 Spiritual beings

McCarthy, David Matzko

Sharing God's Good Company; A Theology of the Communion of Saints. David Matzko McCarthy. W.B. Eerdmans Pub. Co. 2012 viii, 174 p.p (pbk. : alk. paper) $28   **235**

1. Christian saints 2. Christian saints -- Biography -- History and criticism

ISBN 080286709X; 9780802867094

LC 2011049265

This book by David Matzko McCarthy "explores the role and significance of the saints in Christians' lives today. While examining the lives of specific saints like Martin de Porres, Thérèse de Lisieux, and Mother Teresa, McCarthy especially focuses on such topics as the veneration of martyrs, realism and hagiography, science and miracles, images and pilgrimage, and why the saints continue to captivate Christians and inspire devotion." (Publisher's note)

Includes bibliographical references and index.

Pagels, Elaine H.

The **origin** of Satan; {by} Elaine Pagels. Random House 1995 214p hardcover o.p. pa $12 **235**

1. Devil 2. Bible -- N.T. -- Gospels -- Criticism

ISBN 0-679-73118-0 pa

LC 95-7983

Pagels "shows herself to be a masterful guide through the risk-laden complexities of biblical studies." Publ Wkly

Includes bibliographical references

Woodward, Kenneth L.

Making saints; how the Catholic Church determines who becomes a saint, who doesn't, and why. Simon & Schuster 1990 461p il hardcover o.p. pa $21.50   **235**

1. Catholic Church 2. Christian saints

ISBN 0-684-81530-3 pa

LC 90-10117

A study of the politics and procedures of the modern process of canonization in the Roman Catholic church

This is "the most comprehensive, critical and up-to-date look at saint making so far written." N Y Times Book Rev

Includes bibliographical references

Wray, T. J.

The **birth** of Satan; tracing the devil's biblical roots. [by] T.J. Wray, Gregory Mobley. Palgrave Macmillan 2005 211p $24.95   **235**

1. Devil

ISBN 1-4039-6933-7

LC 2005-43046

The authors find Satan's "origins in a biblical character and in early Jewish and Christian writings outside of the scriptures. They try to understand why we as a species strive to feel fearful, why being frightened—vicariously, at least—is so appealing. . . . A thoughtful, informative examination." Booklist

Includes bibliographical references

236 Eschatology

Brown, Samuel Morris

In heaven as it is on earth; Samuel Morris Brown. Oxford University Press 2012 xii, 392 p illustrations   **236**

1. Death 2. Church of Jesus Christ of Latter-day Saints -- History

ISBN 9780199793570

LC 2011002848

'This book examines Mormonism "through the lens of founder Joseph Smith's profound preoccupation with the specter of death. Revisiting historical documents and scripture from this . . . perspective, Brown offers . . . insight into the origin and meaning of some of Mormonism's earliest beliefs and practices. The world of early Mormonism was besieged by death--infant mortality, violence, and disease were rampant. A prolonged battle with typhoid fever, punctuated by painful surgeries including a threatened leg amputation, and the sudden loss of his beloved brother Alvin cast a long shadow over Smith's own life. Smith embraced and was deeply influenced by the culture of 'holy dying'--with its emphasis on deathbed salvation, melodramatic bereavement, and belief in the Providential nature of untimely death--that sought to cope with the widespread mortality of the period." (Publisher's note)

Includes bibliographical references and index

Eire, Carlos M. N.

A **very** brief history of eternity; [by] Carlos Eire. Princeton University Press 2010 268p il $24.95; ebook $24.95   **236**

1. Eternity 2. Western civilization

ISBN 978-0-691-13357-7; 978-1-4008-3187-6 ebook

LC 2009-22951

The author's "skill at engaging readers conceals the rigorous, thoughtful research and methodology that went into this volume. . . . This thought-provoking book is sure to be a classic." Choice

Includes bibliographical references

Miller, Lisa

Heaven; our enduring fascination with the afterlife. Harper 2010 331p $25.99   **236**

1. Heaven 2. United States -- Religion

ISBN 978-0-06-055475-0; 0-06-055475-4

LC 2009-26063

In this "sweeping historical and literary geography of heaven . . . [Miller] talks to priests, a Dominican monk, Muslim clerics, rabbis, and professors (and even visits a psychic, who channels a balding Ed Asner look-alike — no one she knows, though she racks her brain). She doesn't ignore pop culture, either, touching on everything from The Lovely Bones to the hugely popular Left Behind series. . . . But once she has finished reporting and researching, Miller's book loses its hard journalistic edge and becomes something else: a memoir. Her own qualms about faith have danced around the edges of the story, but finally they come front and center. What Miller ultimately concludes may surprise you. It certainly surprised her." Entertainment Wkly

Spong, John Shelby

Eternal life; a new vision: beyond religion, beyond theism, beyond heaven and hell. Harper One 2009 xx, 268p $24.99   **236**

1. Death 2. Eternity 3. Future life

ISBN 978-0-06-076206-3

LC 2008-51443

This book "offers new insights into religion's big questions about life and death, making an invaluable contribution to both religious scholarship and faithful exploration." Publ Wkly

Includes bibliographical references

Wright, N. T.

Surprised by hope; rethinking heaven, the resurrection, and the mission of the church. HarperOne 2008 332p $24.95   **236**

1. Hope 2. Eschatology 3. Future life

ISBN 978-0-06-155182-6; 0-06-155182-1

"Readers will need a Bible handy to appreciate this work fully, as Wright prefers to cite rather than print Scripture. His prose, deep but not murky, is lightened by glints of humor. For any library serving patrons who are willing to think a bit about religion." Libr J

Includes bibliographical references

239   Apologetics and polemics

De civitate Dei./English

Concerning the city of God against the pagans; [by] St. Augustine; translated by Henry Bettenson; with a new introduction by G.R. Evans. Penguin Books 2003 lxxi, 1097p (Penguin classics) pa $16   **239**

1. Apologetics

ISBN 978-0-14-044894-8; 0-14-044894-2

LC 2004-269353

This translation first published 1972

"Written as an eloquent defence of the faith at a time when the Roman Empire was on the brink of collapse, it examines the ancient pagan religions of Rome, the arguments of the Greek philosophers and the revelations of the Bible. Pointing the way forward to a citizenship that transcends worldly politics and will last for eternity, City of God represents a dramatic turning point in the unfolding of Christian doctrine. The new introduction by Gill Evans examines the text in the light of contemporary Greek and Roman thought and political change." Publisher's note

Includes bibliographical references

Keller, Timothy J.

The **reason** for God; belief in an age of skepticism. Dutton 2008 293p $24.95   **239**

1. Faith 2. Skepticism 3. Apologetics

ISBN 978-0-525-95049-3; 0-525-95049-4

LC 2007-43745

"Using literature, philosophy, and pop culture, the author gives . . . reasons for a strong belief in God. . . . [The author] presents a religious view without being overly critical of the secular side presented in other books. . . . This book presents a valid, well-written, and well-researched argument." Libr J

241   Christian ethics

Chapman, Gary D.

Love as a way of life; seven keys to transforming every aspect of your life. [by] Gary Chapman. Doubleday 2008 239p $19.95; pa $13.95   **241**

1. Love -- Religious aspects 2. Interpersonal relations -- Religious aspects

ISBN 978-0-385-51858-1; 0-385-51858-7; 978-1-4000-7259-0 pa; 1-4000-7259-X pa

LC 2007-50546

"All self-help books run the risk of cliché, but Chapman manages to make tried-and-true material feel fresh through carefully chosen examples from his pastoral counseling practice and his own life. . . . Although Christian faith provides the scaffolding for his program and a concluding chapter makes the need for God's help explicit, Chapman's judicious counsel can be implemented by people of many religious traditions." Publ Wkly

Includes bibliographical references

Davis, Will

Enough; finding more by living with less. Will Davis, Jr. Revell 2012 232 p. (pbk.) $13.99   **241**

1. Christian life 2. Conduct of life 3. Simplicity -- Religious aspects -- Christianity 4. Contentment -- Religious aspects -- Christianity

ISBN 0800720024; 9780800720025

LC 2012003547

This Christian book, by Will Davis Jr., "challenges readers to discover the peace that comes through contentment with what we have and compassion for those in need. Through . . . statistics, scriptural insight, and real-life stories, Davis gently leads readers to consider living with less in order to do more for the kingdom." (Publisher's note)

Includes bibliographical references (p. 231-232)

Price, Reynolds

A **serious** way of wondering; the ethics of Jesus imagined. Scribner 2003 146p hardcover o.p. pa $14.95   **241**

1. Christian ethics

ISBN 0-7432-3008-6; 0-7432-3009-4 pa

LC 2003-41506

"In three . . . apocryphal gospel stories, Price's Jesus engages in conversations about homosexuality, suicide and the plight of women in male-dominated societies. . . . Elegant and passionate, Price's provocative parables provide no simple answers to the saccharine question 'What would Jesus do?' Rather, they compel us to imagine creatively our engagements with Jesus' teachings and the impact of those teachings on our lives." Publ Wkly

Includes bibliographical references

241.68   Christian ethics--Consumption

Becker, Josh, 1958-

The **more** of less; finding the life you want under everything you own. Joshua Becker. WaterBrook Press 2016 230 p. (hardback) $17.99   **241.68**

1. Consumers 2. Simplicity 3. Quality of life 4. Simplicity -- Religious aspects -- Christianity 5. Consumption (Economics) -- Religious aspects -- Christianity

ISBN 1601427964; 9781601427960

LC 2015042586

This book, by Joshua Becker, focuses on non-consumption and minimalism. The book seeks to help "recognize the life-giving benefits of owning less, realize how all the stuff you own is keeping you from pursuing your dreams, craft a personal, practical approach to decluttering your home and life, experience the joys of generosity, [and] learn why the best part of minimalism isn't a clean house, it's a full life." (Publisher's note)

"With action plans, lists, and appeals to the reader's quiet nature, Becker successfully presents a well-rounded argument that a journey toward minimalism is possible and even enjoyable." Pub Wkly

Includes bibliographical references (pages 223-230).

242   Devotional literature

Augustine, Saint 354-430

Confessions; translated with an introduction and notes by Henry Chadwick. Oxford University Press 1998 xxviii, 311p (Oxford world's classics) pa $7.95   **242**

ISBN 978-0-19-283372-3; 0-19-283372-3

"These confessions were written at the end of the fourth century by the most distinguished of the Latin fathers as a revelation of his spiritual experience. They have been a source of religious inspiration through the centuries." Pratt Alcove

Includes bibliographical references

King, Martin Luther, Jr., 1929-1968

Thou, dear God; Martin Luther King, Jr.; foreword by the Julius R. Scruggs; edited and introduced by Lewis V. Baldwin. Beacon Press 2012 245 p.   **242**

1. Prayers

ISBN 9780807086032

LC 2011031431

This book "is the first and only collection of sixty-eight prayers by Martin Luther King, Jr. Arranged thematically in six parts--with prayers for spiritual guidance, special occasions, times of adversity, times of trial, uncertain times, and social justice--Baptist minister and King scholar Lewis Baldwin introduces the book and each section with short essays. Included are both personal and public prayers King recited as a seminarian, graduate student, preacher, pastor, and, finally, civil rights leader, along with a special section that reveals the biblical sources that most inspired King. Collectively they illustrate how King turned to private prayer for his own spiritual fulfillment and to public prayer as a way to move, inspire, and reaffirm a quest for peace and social justice." (Publisher's note)

Includes bibliographical references (p. 239-245).

The **little** flowers of St. Francis of Assisi; written by Ugolino di Monte Santa Maria; edited by and adapted from a translation by W. Heywood; with a new preface by Madeleine L'Engle. Vintage Books 1998 xxxviii, 120p (Vintage spiritual classics) pa $13   **242**

1. Saints 2. Writers on religion

ISBN 978-0-375-70020-0; 0-375-70020-X

LC 97-48815

This translation first published 1906 in the United Kingdom

These "simple anecdotes exemplify St. Francis' love of nature, man and of God." Bookman's Manual

Includes bibliographical references

Thomas, a Kempis, 1380-1471

The **imitation** of Christ; {by} Thomas à Kempis. Vintage Books 1998 xliii, 242p pa $12.95   **242**

ISBN 978-0-375-70018-7; 0-375-70018-8

This devotional classic originally written in Latin in the 15th century "traces in four books the gradual progress of the soul to Christian perfection, its detachment from the

world, and its union with God." Oxford Companion to Engl Lit. Concise edition

248   Christian experience, practice, life

Brizendine, Judy

Stunned by grief; remapping your life when loss changes everything. BennettKnepp Publishing 2011 274p il pa $18.95   **248**

1. Bereavement 2. Loss (Psychology) 3. Spiritual healing 4. Adjustment (Psychology)

ISBN 978-0-9831688-1-2

"A former market analyst and interior designer, . . . [the author] found her world turned upside down when her husband died. She uses her own experience combined with the advice of psychologists, grief counselors, the Bible, and fellow mourners to provide a sort of roadmap for the unwelcome journey of grief. In bite-size pieces, she covers the progression of grief, the intrinsic anger and guilt felt in the process, and the possibility of dealing with and planning a new future. . . . This book will comfort and support anyone new to grief and will serve as a companion in times of loneliness. Realistic, practical, and highly recommended." Libr J

Includes bibliographical references

Evans, Rachel Held

Searching for Sunday; loving, leaving, and finding the church. Rachel Held Evans. Thomas Nelson 2015 288 p. $16.99   **248**

1. Christian life

ISBN 0718022122; 9780718022129

LC 2014956181

This book, by Rachel Held Evans, is an "ode to the past and hopeful gaze into the future of what it means to be a part of the Church. . . . Centered around seven sacraments, Evans' quest takes readers through a liturgical year with stories about baptism, communion, confirmation, confession, marriage, vocation, and death that are funny, heartbreaking, and sharply honest." (Publisher's note)

"Elegantly structured and thoughtfully written, Evans's approach to church through the metaphors of the sacraments should please many reading groups and individual seekers." LJ

Lamott, Anne

Small victories; spotting improbable moments of grace. Anne Lamott. Riverhead Books, a member of Penguin Group (USA) 2014 304 p. (hardback) $22.95   **248**

1. Hope 2. Christianity -- Spiritual life 3. Joy 4. Grace 5. Spiritual life 6. Christian biography -- United States 7. Life -- Religious aspects -- Christianity 8. Novelists, American -- 20th century -- Biography

ISBN 1594486298; 9781594486296

LC 2014026967

This book, by Anne Lamott, is a "collection of new and selected essays on hope, joy, and grace. . . . Our victories over hardship and pain may seem small, . . . but they change us-- our perceptions, our perspectives, and our lives. Lamott writes of forgiveness, restoration, and transformation, how we can turn toward love even in the most hopeless situations, how we find the joy in getting lost and our amazement in finally being found." (Publisher's note)

"Whether attending a service where the ashes of the departed stuck to her fingers as she attempted to throw them overboard, hiking the trails of Muir Woods with a woman who knew she was dying ("The worst possible thing you can do when you're down in the dumps, tweaking, vaporous with victimized self-righteousness, or bored, is to take a walk with dying friends"), or demonstrating against the wars started by George W. Bush in a peace march through the streets of San Francisco, Lamott confronts each situation with humor and rectitude and shows readers how she found something redeeming in each one. Sage advice on finding beauty and happiness in life despite bad circumstances." Kirkus

Spotting improbable moments of grace

Lewis, C. S.
Letters to Malcolm: chiefly on prayer. 1964 124p hardcover o.p. pa $13   **248**
1. Prayer 2. Christian life
ISBN 978-0-15-602766-3

The author's "reflections on prayer are here set down in the form of thoughtful and engaging letters to his friend Malcolm." Cincinnati Public Libr

★ The **Screwtape** letters; with, Screwtape proposes a toast. HarperSanFrancisco 2001 209p $22.95; pa $11.95   **248**
1. Satire 2. Christian life
ISBN 0-06-065289-6; 0-06-065293-4 pa
            LC 00-49860
The Screwtape letters first published 1943 by Macmillan; this combined edition first published 1961 by Macmillan

"A popular work on Christian moral and theological problems. . . . . It is in the form of a series of letters in which a devil, Screwtape, advises his nephew, Wormwood, on how to deal with his human 'patients.'" Reader's Ency. 4th edition

Lucado, Max
Fearless; imagine your life without fear. Thomas Nelson 2009 221p $24.99   **248**
1. Fear -- Religious aspects
ISBN 978-0-8499-2139-1
            LC 2009-707
The author offers a faith-based primer on how to live without fear.

"Skillful as a surgeon, . . . [Lucado] discerns and identifies the cancer of fear that touches every human being, and with like precision speaks healing words that cut right the heart. While there exists no fast fix or simple cure for the fear-bound individual, Lucado's tempered counsel and faith-driven remedies will offer day-by-day spiritual medicine of the most potent kind." Publ Wkly

Includes bibliographical references

Peale, Norman Vincent
★ The **power** of positive living. Fawcett Columbine 1996 224p pa $13.95   **248**
1. Success 2. Applied psychology 3. Pastoral

psychology
ISBN 0-449-91166-7; 978-0-449-91166-2
            LC 96096721
First published 1952 by Prentice-Hall

In this volume "Peale strings together dozens of personal success stories ('success' is always materialistic) that make readers feel good. Believing (in yourself, others, values, God) is all-important, and the stories of wealthy business executives who made it on their own grab center stage." Libr J

Zondervan dictionary of Christian spirituality; Glen G. Scorgie, general editor; consulting editors: Simon Chan, Gordon T. Smith, James D. Smith III. Zondervan 2011 852p $39.99   **248**
1. Reference books 2. Christianity -- Dictionaries
ISBN 978-0-310-29066-7
            LC 2010037314
"The first section presents six to seven-page entries on topics such as spiritual theology, human personhood, education and spiritual formation, and liturgical spirituality. Also included are articles describing the history of Christian spirituality from 100 C.E. to the present. Each article is followed by a bibliography and a further-reading list. The second section is a dictionary with entries on a broad variety of subjects: biblical figures, popes, mystics, saints, philosophers, spiritual leaders, and educators, as well as concepts and areas of concern including poverty, humanism, suffering, vows, the Kingdom of God, and peace." Libr J

Includes bibliographical references

248.2   Religious experience

Armstrong, Karen
Visions of God; four medieval mystics and their writings. Bantam Bks. 1994 228p pa $19   **248.2**
1. Authors 2. Hermits 3. Mysticism 4. Mystics 5. Writers on religion
ISBN 0-553-35199-0
            LC 94-20217
"The collection is eminently readable and should serve to make these important sources more accessible to a general audience. The selections are arranged chronologically, but Armstrong's reflections also place them in a 'developmental sequence.'" Booklist

Includes bibliographical references

Downing, David C.
Into the region of awe; mysticism in C. S. Lewis. InterVarsity Press 2005 207p $17   **248.2**
1. Authors 2. Mysticism 3. Novelists 4. Theologians 5. Essayists 6. Satirists 7. Literary critics 8. Children's authors
ISBN 0-8308-3284-X; 978-0-8308-3284-2
            LC 2004-29844
This is a "book on the writer/thinker's complex attitudes toward mysticism and mystical experience. Downing is keenly responsible in his approach to Lewis's biography and background and candid about Lewis's reservations about mysticism in his own theology; the author's affection for his

subject ably informs this sensitive reading of Lewis's life and writings." Libr J

Includes bibliographical references

248.3   Worship

Lucado, Max

Before amen; the power of a simple prayer. Max Lucado. Thomas Nelson 2014 192 p. $19.99 **248.3**

> 1. Prayer 2. Christian life 3. Devotional literature 4. Prayer -- Christianity
> ISBN 0849948487; 9780849948480

> LC 2014007855

In this Christian devotional book, by Max Lucado, "joins readers on a journey to the very heart of biblical prayer, offering hope for doubts and confidence even for prayer wimps. Distilling prayers in the Bible down to one pocket-sized prayer, Max reminds readers that prayer is not a privilege for the pious nor the art of a chosen few. Prayer is simply a heartfelt conversation between God and his child." (Publisher's note)

"The concept that there is power in a simple prayer normally wouldn't take a whole book to convey, but Lucado (You'll Get Through This), a prolific author with 92 million books in print, succeeds in getting readers to approach communication with God in a whole new way." Pub Wkly

Includes bibliographical references

248.4   Christian life and practice

Carter, Jimmy

Sources of strength; meditations on scripture for a living faith. Times Bks. 1997 252p hardcover o.p. pa $14.99   **248.4**

> 1. Christian life 2. Bible -- Meditations
> ISBN 0-8129-3236-6 pa

> LC 97-27501

Companion volume to Living faith

This "is a collection of 52 brief Bible lessons—one for each week of the year—written by former president Jimmy Carter. All were used in adult Sunday school classes he taught himself. Carter's lessons are open-minded and socially progressive while remaining unapologetically conservative and Christian theologically. . . . The lessons are grouped in nine categories, such as 'What We Believe' and 'Christians in the World,' but each lesson stands well on its own." Libr J

Chittister, Joan

Following the path; the search for a life of passion, purpose, and joy. Image 2012 188 p. $18.00   **248.4**

> 1. Self-help techniques
> ISBN 030795398X; 9780307953988

This book considers "the questions 'What am I supposed to do with my life?' and 'How do I know when I've found my purpose?' [which] can seem endless and overwhelming. . . . [Author] Sister Joan [Chittister] brings the insights of her years of teaching and contemplation to bear on this issue."

She examin[es] . . . spiritual calling and gifts, change and discernment." (Publisher's note)

This book "is meant to give someone in the process of making a life decision at any age—in early adulthood, at the point of middle-age change and later, when we find ourselves at the crossroads without a name—some ideas against which to pit their own minds, their own circumstances." (Author's note)

Girzone, Joseph F.

Never alone; a personal way to God. Doubleday 1994 115p il hardcover o.p. pa $10.95   **248.4**

> 1. Spiritual life
> ISBN 0-3854-7683-3 pa

> LC 93-38725

Girzone's "empathy for the loneliness and insecurity of being human guides readers toward a more satisfying religious experience than that provided by organized religions, which he continues to criticize for not sufficiently following the living message of Jesus' life." Booklist

Heim, Tami

@stickyjesus; how to live out your faith online. Toni Birdsong, Tami Heim. Abingdon Press 2012 224 p.   **248.4**

> 1. Christian life 2. Computer literacy 3. Online social networks 4. Internet -- Social aspects 5. Christian life -- Meditations
> ISBN 1426741898; 9781426741890

> LC 2011044377

This book instructs Christian readers in incorporating technology, computers, and the Internet into their faith. The book "is a fusion of discipleship, faith sharing, marketing, and a Get Started 101 on Twitter, Facebook and blogging. '@stickyJesus' . . . challenges Christ followers to regain [their] God-given dominion on earth, which includes the Internet. With knowledge, skills, and Holy Spirit guidance, [the authors] encourage believers to dig in and learn how to navigate this online world. . . . The book also includes personal testimonies. . . . These are real people and ministries (about a dozen) making a difference because they walk, talk and connect differently online." (Publisher's Note)

Includes bibliographical references.

Jakes, T. D., 1957-

Destiny; step into your purpose. T.D. Jakes. Faith Words 2015 272 p. (hardcover) $25   **248.4**

> 1. Self-realization 2. Fate and fatalism 3. Vocation -- Christianity 4. Fate and fatalism -- Religious aspects -- Christianity 5. Self-actualization (Psychology) -- Religious aspects -- Christianity
> ISBN 1455553972; 9781455553976; 9781455589630

> LC 2015017111

This inspirational self-help book, by T. D. Jakes, encourages readers to embrace their self-confidence and sense of having a destiny. "Life offers more when destiny is our focus! Our divine purpose maneuvers us past challenges, pains, and shortcuts and even what appears on the surface to be failure. On deeper reflection, we understand them as catalysts that shift us toward authentic self-identity, greater exposure, and bold life adventures." (Publisher's note)

"Readers will specifically learn how to prioritize wisely; decide what works best for their unique gifts and talents; protect the undervalued commodity of time; push past failure; and find the courage to actively pursue their destinies. Jakes's passion for life and colloquial style translate effortlessly from screen to page. This book of hard-nosed spiritual advice is an uplifting rally cry for self-determination." Pub Wkly

Instinct; the power to unleash your inborn drive. T.D. Jakes. Faith Words 2014 271 p. (hardcover) $25   **248.4**
1. Spiritual life 2. Self-help techniques 3. Instinct 4. Christian life
ISBN 1455554049; 9781455554041
LC 2014007406

In this book, author T. D. Jakes "outlines how to rediscover your natural aptitudes and re-claim the wisdom of your past experiences." He claims that "Knowing when to close a deal, when to take a risk, and when to listen to your heart will become possible when you're in touch with the instincts that God gave you." (Publisher's note)

"This positive book encourages readers to get in touch with their instincts, trust them, and rely on them." Pub Wkly

Martin, James
The **Jesuit** guide to almost everything; a spirituality for real life. HarperOne 2010 420p il $26.99; ebook $11.99   **248.4**
1. Saints 2. Priests 3. Spiritual life 4. Catholic Church 5. Religious leaders 6. Writers on religion
ISBN 978-0-06-143268-2; 978-0-06-198140-1 ebook
LC 2009030505

"In this digestible account of all things Jesuit, James Martin, S.J., encapsulates the uniquely Ignatian concept of spirituality. Translating the essence of the Jesuit philosophy into layman's terms, he uses both traditional stories and personal anecdotes to vividly illustrate the Jesuit approach to God, friendship, social justice, decision-making, prayer, simplicity, obedience, and self-actualization. Martin's engaging, intimate tone will appeal to anyone interested in understanding the history, the efficacy, and the universality of the Jesuit mission and way of life." Booklist

Includes bibliographical references

Meyer, Joyce
Seize the day; living on purpose and making every day count. Joyce Meyer. Faith Words 2016 234 p. (hardcover) $24   **248.4**
1. Christian life 2. Older persons -- Religious life
ISBN 145555989X; 9781455559893; 9781455559923
LC 2016015536

This book, by Joyce Meyer, "shares a purposeful approach to everyday living, helping readers claim the good things God has in store for them each day. Today is no ordinary day. You may perform simple routines, feel uninspired, or lack the excitement of hope. But today could be the most important one of your life--depending on how you choose to spend it." (Publisher's note)

"Meyer advocates seizing control of one's schedule to focus on life's purpose, but also recommends being flex-

ible, finding a system that fits one's style, and taking time to laugh." Pub Wkly

Nouwen, Henri
Discernment; reading the signs of daily life. Henri J. M. Nouwen, with Michael J. Christensen and Rebecca J. Laird. HarperOne 2013 xxix, 223 p.p (hc) $25.99   **248.4**
1. Theology 2. Christian life 3. Christian ethics 4. Discernment (Christian theology)
ISBN 9780061686153; 0061686158; 9780061686160
LC 2013004593

This book "features the wisdom that spiritual leader and counselor Henri J. M. Nouwen brought to the essential question asked by every Christian and seeker: What should I do with my life? Nouwen emphasizes listening to the Word of God--in our hearts, in the Bible, in the community of faith, and in the voice of the poor as a way to discern God's plan." (Publisher's note)

Includes bibliographical references

Osteen, Joel, 1963-
The **power** of I am; two words that will change your life today. Joel Osteen. Faith Words 2015 269 p. (hardcover) $26   **248.4**
1. Self-realization 2. Motivation (Psychology) 3. Affirmations 4. Self-talk -- Religious aspects -- Christianity 5. Self-confidence -- Religious aspects -- Christianity
ISBN 0892969962; 9780892969968; 9781455536207
LC 2015025973

Author Joel Osteen attempts to "help you discover your unique abilities and advantages to lead a more productive and happier life. His insights and encouragement are illustrated with many amazing stories of people who turned their lives around by focusing on the positive power of this principle. You can choose to rise to a new level and invite God's goodness by focusing on these two words: I AM!" (Publisher's note)

"Directing believers to look beyond their own needs and wants, Osteen advances his message to a higher plane, advocating a life of reaching out and sharing your blessings." Publisher's Weekly

Riess, Jana
Flunking sainthood; a year of breaking the Sabbath, forgetting to pray, and still loving my neighbor. Paraclete Press 2011 179p pa $16.99   **248.4**
1. Success 2. Christian life 3. Spiritual life 4. Failure (Psychology)
ISBN 978-1-55725-660-7
LC 2011022595

The author "intended to devote an entire year ('a yearlong experiment') to mastering 12 different spiritual challenges, including praying at fixed times during the day, exhibiting gratitude, observing the Sabbath, practicing hospitality according to the rules set by St. Benedict, abstaining from eating meat, and amply demonstrating her generosity. But nothing turned out as planned. ... Although her spiritual quest falls far short, she can still proffer spiritual lessons.

Anyone who has failed to live up to expectations, which means most everyone, will love this book." Booklist

Includes bibliographical references

Smith, Myquillyn

The **nesting** place; your home doesn't have to be perfect to be beautiful. Myquillyn Smith. Zondervan 2014 199 p. color illustrations (hardcover) $19.99 **248.4**

1. Apartments 2. Interior design 3. Home economics 4. Rental housing 5. Home -- Religious aspects -- Christianity

ISBN 0310337909; 9780310337904

LC 2013034145

"Popular blogger and self-taught decorator Myquillyn Smith (The Nester) is all about

embracing reality--especially when it comes to decorating a home bursting with boys, pets, and all the unpredictable messes of life. In 'The Nesting Place,' Myquillyn shares the secrets of decorating for real people--and it has nothing to do with creating a flawless look to wow your guests. It has everything to do with embracing the natural imperfection and chaos of daily living." (Publisher's note)

248.8 Guides to Christian life for specific groups of people

Billings, J. Todd

Rejoicing in lament; wrestling with incurable cancer and life in Christ. J. Todd Billings. Brazos Press 2015 224 p. (pbk.) $18.99 **248.8**

1. Christianity -- Doctrines 2. Suffering -- Religious aspects 3. Cancer patients -- Religious life 4. Cancer -- Patients -- Religious life 5. Cancer -- Religious aspects -- Christianity 6. Suffering -- Religious aspects -- Christianity

ISBN 1587433583; 9781587433580

LC 2014040099

This book, by J. Todd Billings, "shares . . . [the author's] journey, struggle, and reflections on providence, lament, and life in Christ in light of his illness, moving beyond pat answers toward hope in God's promises. Theologically robust yet eminently practical, it engages the open questions, areas of mystery, and times of disorientation in the Christian life." (Publisher's note)

"His poignant insight into the role of lament in faithful Christian living makes this a work of both astute scholarship and powerful testimony." Pub Wkly

Includes bibliographical references and index

Hendey, Lisa M.

A **book** of saints for Catholic moms; 52 companions for your heart, mind, body, and soul. Lisa M. Hendey. Ave Maria Press 2011 xiv, 334 p.p ill. **248.8**

1. Prayers 2. Catholics 3. Motherhood 4. Christian saints 5. Devotional exercises 6. Mothers -- Prayers and devotions 7. Catholic Church -- Prayers and

devotions 8. Christian saints -- Prayers and devotions

ISBN 1594712735; 9781594712739

LC 2011025284

In this book, Lisa M. Hende "familiarizes readers with saints—one for each week of the year—who are relevant to nearly every aspect of a Catholic mother's life, divided into categories of heart, mind, body and soul. She offers related Scripture verses for the week as well as practical suggestions and activities. . . . [The book covers] topics such as 'overflowing mounds of dirty laundry' or serious issues such as mental illness and single parenthood. . . . Hendey . . . details the saints' trials and triumphs that . . . people struggle with the same intrinsic issues today. Although many of the individual saints are patrons to various groups or issues . . . Hendey . . . relat[es] each saint's legacy to common dilemmas faced by mothers." (Our Sunday Visitor)

252 Texts of sermons

American sermons; the pilgrims to Martin Luther King, Jr. Library of Am. 1999 939p $40 **252**

1. Sermons

ISBN 1-88301-165-5

LC 98-34295

"To peruse this work is to become reacquainted with the literary eloquence of our distant and recent past and to observe what has happened to rhetoric itself over the centuries." N Y Times Book Rev

Includes bibliographical references

King, Martin Luther, Jr., 1929-1968

★ **Strength** to love; foreword by Coretta Scott King. Fortress 2010 168p il pa $20 **252**

1. Sermons

ISBN 978-0-8006-9740-2

First published 1963 by Harper & Row

A collection of sermons addressing social injustice and racism.

Includes bibliographical references

253 Pastoral office and work (Pastoral theology)

McKibben, Bill

Eaarth; making a life on a tough new planet. Times Books 2010 253p $24 **253**

1. Environmental degradation 2. Human influence on nature 3. Greenhouse effect 4. Climate -- Environmental aspects

ISBN 978-0-8050-9056-7; 0-8050-9056-8

LC 2009-30040

The author "demonstrates how global warming has already occurred and is irreversible. He describes a new 'Eaarth,' where the cumulative effects of the release of carbon dioxide in the atmosphere have already changed the planet. . . . McKibben envisions a future in which humanity transitions from unfettered growth and a dependence on external markets for sustenance and fossil-fuel-driven energy, to smaller, self-contained communities, growing food locally and generating sustainable distributed electricity. An absolute must-read." Kirkus

Includes bibliographical references

Pattison, John

Slow church; cultivating community in the patient way of Jesus. C. Christopher Smith, John Pattison. InterVarsity Press 2014 247 p. (pbk. : alk. paper) $16 **253**

1. Church 2. Religion and sociology 3. Communities -- Religious aspects -- Christianity
ISBN 0830841148; 9780830841141

LC 2014011067

In this book, authors C.Christopher Smith and John Pattison suggests we "leave franchise faith behind and enter into the ecology, economy and ethics of the kingdom of God, where people know each other well and love one another as Christ loved the church." (Publisher's note)

"Though primarily focused upon church communities, the ideas presented here may appeal to other types of religious or intentional communities. Individuals who are attempting to bring their own lives into line with their ethics and values will also find help." Pub Wkly

Includes bibliographical references

255 Religious congregations and orders

Norris, Kathleen

The **cloister** walk. Riverhead Bks. 1996 384p hardcover o.p. pa $12.95 **255**

1. Spiritual life 2. Monasticism and religious orders 3. Catholic Church -- Liturgy
ISBN 1-57322-584-3 pa

LC 96-863

Companion volume to Dakota: a spiritual geography (1993)

The author relates her experiences as a lay oblate at St. John's Abbey, a Benedictine monastery in Collegeville, Minnesota. The narrative is arranged chronologically according to the rhythm of the Catholic liturgical calendar

"Kathleen Norris knows about faith. She also knows a lot about doubt. . . . As a married Protestant woman, Norris appears to be an improbable candidate to live in a community of celibate men. Yet as she 'walks' with the Benedictine monks, spending days in continual reading, prayer, and singing, she gains new perspectives on their life and her own." Christ Sci Monit

261.2 Christianity and other systems of belief

Kertzer, David I.

The **Popes** against the Jews; the Vatican's role in the rise of modern anti-semitism. Knopf 2001 355p $27.95; pa $15 **261.2**

1. Antisemitism 2. Catholic Church -- Relations -- Judaism
ISBN 0-375-40623-9; 0-375-70605-4 pa

LC 2001-33728

"This is a devastating indictment, and fair-minded critics will find flaws in Kertzer's methodology and sweeping con-

clusions. Nevertheless, he has opened a window that should be opened." Booklist

Includes bibliographical references

261.5 Christianity and secular disciplines

Barbour, Ian G.

When science meets religion; enemies, strangers, or partners? HarperSanFrancisco 2000 205p pa $16.95 **261.5**

1. Religion and science
ISBN 0-06-060381-X

LC 99-55579

The author "guides readers through a four-fold typology of the science/religion relationship—Conflict, Independence, Dialogue and Integration. . . . Barbour's own sympathies are markedly on the side of dialogue and integration, but he makes an unusually sucessful effort to represent other perspectives in a fair light." Publ Wkly

Includes bibliographical references

Grant, Edward

★ **Science** and religion, 400 B.C. to A.D. 1550; from Aristotle to Copernicus. Greenwood Press 2004 xxvi, 307p il (Greenwood guides to science and religion) $67.95 **261.5**

1. Religion and science
ISBN 0-313-32858-7

LC 2004-17429

"With this new book, grounded in five decades of active scholarship, Edward Grant provides a synthetic account of the relationship between science and religion from Greek antiquity to the beginnings of the Scientific Revolution. Intended as an introduction for the general reader, the book successfully argues its central point–namely, that contrary to popular belief today, the medieval Church promoted scientific thought, which in turn profoundly influenced theological understanding. . . . Grant's book, along with the eight primary documents it provides, is an introduction students and teachers will welcome." Journal of the History of Science in Society

Includes bibliographical references

Olson, Richard

★ **Science** and religion, 1450-1900; from Copernicus to Darwin. [by] Richard G. Olson. Greenwood Press 2004 292p il (Greenwood guides to science and religion) $65 **261.5**

1. Religion and science
ISBN 0-313-32694-0

LC 2004-47501

The issues discussed "should be especially helpful to those who are interested in the historical background to current science-religion issues being debated in the United States." Sci Books Films

Includes bibliographical references

261.8   Christianity and socioeconomic problems

Chu, Jeff, 1977-
Does Jesus Really Love Me? A Gay Christian's Pilgrimage in Search of God in America. by Jeff Chu. HarperCollins 2013 368 p. $26.99   **261.8**
1. Gay men 2. Christianity 3. Homosexuality -- United States 4. Christian gays -- United States 5. Homosexuality -- Religious aspects -- Christianity
ISBN 0062049739; 9780062049735
LC 2013464818
Lambda Literary Awards Finalist (2014)

This book, by Jeff Chu, "is part memoir and part investigative analysis that explores the explosive and confusing intersection of faith, politics, and sexuality in Christian America. . . . From Brooklyn to Nashville to California, from Westboro Baptist Church and their 'God Hates Fags' protest signs, to the pioneering Episcopalian bishop Mary Glasspool--who proclaims a message of liberation and divine love, Chu captures spiritual snapshots of Christian America." (Publisher's note)

"[T]he book brings complexity and humanity to a discourse often lacking in both." Pub Wkly

D'Antonio, Michael
★ **Mortal** Sins; Sex, Crime, and the Era of Catholic Scandal. Michael D'Antonio. St. Martin's Press 2013 416 p. $26.99   **261.8**
1. Child sexual abuse by clergy 2. Catholic Church -- Clergy -- Sexual behavior 3. Catholic Church -- Discipline 4. Catholic Church -- United States
ISBN 0312594895; 9780312594893
LC 2013003725
This book presents a "history of the Catholic Church's 'most severe crisis since the Reformation': the revelations of endemic sexual abuse of minors by priests in the United States and Europe. . . . In 1984, American priest Thomas Doyle learned of a lawsuit brought by parents of a victim, and was deeply troubled. . . . Along with plaintiffs' attorney Jeffrey Anderson, Doyle and a few others worked tirelessly to get the church, the media, and the public to pay attention." (Publishers Weekly)

Lehmann, Chris
The **money** cult; Capitalism, Christianity, and the Unmaking of the American Dream. Chris Lehmann. Melville House 2016 403 p. (hardback) $28.95   **261.8**
1. Capitalism 2. Christianity and economics 3. Wealth -- Religious aspects -- Christianity 4. Capitalism -- United States -- History 5. Christianity -- United States -- History 6. Capitalism -- Religious aspects -- Christianity 7. Christianity -- Economic aspects -- United States -- History
ISBN 9781612195087
LC 2016001439
In this book, author Chris Lehmann "reveals how America's religious leaders became less worried about sin and the afterlife and more concerned with the material world, until the social gospel was overtaken by the gospel of wealth. Showing how American Christianity came to accommodate—and eventually embrace—the pursuit of profit, as well

as the inescapability of economic inequality, [it is a wide-ranging . . . book." (Publisher's note)

"This book is unlikely to embarrass believers into a social conscience or different political allegiance, but Lehmann does reveal the modern evangelical right as deeply faithful to an American economic model—one focused on industrial production—that no longer exists." Pub Wkly

Includes bibliographical references and index.

Martin, William C.
With God on our side; the rise of the religious right in America. {by} William Martin. Broadway Bks. 1996 418p il $27.50; pa $15   **261.8**
1. Conservatism 2. Religion and politics 3. Religious fundamentalism 4. Christianity and politics 5. Evangelists 6. Inspirational writers 7. Christian Coalition (Organization)
ISBN 0-553-06745-1; 0-553-06749-4 pa
LC 96-2919
"Unlike some companion volumes to television documentaries, Martin's well-written, superbly organized work stands on its own. . . . {It} is required reading for anyone seeking to understand the rise of the Religious Right. . . . Nothing has been published that can match Martin's book in sweep and substance." Christ Century

Includes bibliographical references

262   Ecclesiology

Chaves, Mark
Ordaining women; culture and conflict in religious organizations. Harvard Univ. Press 1997 237p hardcover o.p. pa $18.50   **262**
1. Christian sociology 2. Ordination of women 3. Women in Christianity 4. United States -- Church history
ISBN 0-674-64146-9 pa
LC 97-12518
The author provides a "study of the 19th- and 20th-century ordination policies and practices of many Christian groups in the United States, including the Roman Catholic Church." Libr J

Includes bibliographical references

264   Public worship

Episcopal Church
★ The **Book** of common prayer and administration of the sacraments and other rites and ceremonies of the church; together with the Psalter or Psalms of David according to the use of the Episcopal Church. Church Hymnal Corp, Seabury Press 1979 1001p pew ed., black $19   **264**
ISBN 0-89869-081-1
LC 81-204603
The official liturgy of the Episcopal Church.

Lucatero, Heliodoro

★ The **living** Mass; changes to the Roman missal and how we worship. Liguori 2011 64p il pa $4.99 **264**

1. Catholic Church -- Liturgy
ISBN 978-0-7648-2007-6

This book seeks to answer questions about the changes made to the Roman Missal "as well as to give some insight into the history of the development of the Roman Missal from early Church times, through the Middle Ages, through the different Church councils, and up to the present day. A comparison of each change features old and new text side-by-side with the changes highlighted in bold type." Publisher's note

Includes bibliographical references

270 History, geographic treatment, biography of Christianity; Church history; Christian denominations and sects

The **Bloomsbury** Guide to Christian Spirituality. Bloomsbury Academic 2012 356 p. $49.95 **270**

1. Spiritual life 2. Christianity -- Encyclopedias
ISBN 1441184848; 9781441184849

This book is a "single-volume orientation to Christian spirituality. . . . Topics are . . . inclusive (sources, traditions, practices, dialogue with other faiths, contemporary issues). Three indexes (biblical citations, names, subjects) enable rapid searches through the text. The 30-plus contributors include world-class scholars Bernard McGinn, Richard Rohr, Benedicta Ward, and coeditor [Richard] Woods." (Choice)

Jenkins, Philip

The **new** faces of Christianity; believing the Bible in the global south. Oxford University Press 2006 252p $26 **270**

1. Forecasting 2. Christianity
ISBN 978-0-19-530065-9; 0-19-530065-3
LC 2006-15490

Jenkins explores the growth of Christianity in Africa, Asia and Latin America.

"Those interested in religious trends across the globe, the Muslim-Christian friction, and world politics will benefit from this resource." Libr J

Includes bibliographical references

MacCulloch, Diarmaid

★ **Christianity**; the first three thousand years. Viking 2010 1161p il map $45 **270**

1. Church history
ISBN 978-0-670-02126-0; 0-670-02126-1
LC 2009-40184

First published 2009 in the United Kingdom

"It is difficult to imagine a more comprehensive and surprisingly accessible volume on the subject than MacCulloch's. . . . Want a refresher on the rise of the papacy? It is here. On Charlemagne and Carolingians? That is here, too. On the Fourth Crusade and its aftermath? Look no farther." N Y Times Book Rev

Includes bibliographical references

Tickle, Phyllis, 1934-2015

The **great** emergence; how Christianity is changing and why. Baker Books 2008 172p il $17.99 **270**

1. Christianity
ISBN 0-8010-1313-5; 978-0-8010-1313-3
LC 2008-21706

"This is a must-read for anyone seeking to understand the face and future of Christianity." Publ Wkly

Includes bibliographical references

270.1 Historical periods

Riley, Gregory J.

The **river** of God; a new history of Christian origins. HarperSanFrancisco 2001 252p hardcover o.p. pa $14.95 **270.1**

1. Church history -- 30-600, Early church
ISBN 0-06-066979-9; 0-06-066980-2 pa
LC 2001-16888

"This volume will become one of the most important books on the subject." Libr J

Includes bibliographical references

Voices of early Christianity; documents from the origins of Christianity. Kevin W. Kaatz, editor. Greenwood 2013 xxii, 277 p.p (Voices of an era) (hardcopy : alk. paper) $100 **270.1**

1. Christianity 2. Religion -- History 3. Women in Christianity 4. Church history -- Primitive and early church, ca. 30-600 -- Sources
ISBN 1598849522; 9781598849523
LC 2012041162

The "editor's intention with this book is to teach about early Christianity using primary-source documents, with the title also offering a treatise on how to evaluate and think critically about primary sources." Topics include "'Early Christian Life,' 'The Church,' 'Early Christian Women,' 'Conflicts of the Early Church,' 'Persecution,' and 'Church and Politics.'" (Library Journal)

Includes bibliographical references (pages 255-264) and index

270.2 Period of ecumenical councils, 325-787

Brown, Peter

Through the eye of a needle; wealth, the fall of Rome, and the making of Christianity in the West, 350-550 AD. Peter Brown. Princeton University Press 2012 759 p. **270.2**

1. Rome -- History 2. Church history -- 30-600, Early church 3. Wealth -- Religious aspects -- Christianity 4. Rome -- History -- Empire, 284-476 5. Wealth -- Religious aspects -- Christianity -- History 6. Church history -- Primitive and early church, ca. 30-600
ISBN 069115290X; 9780691152905
LC 2011045697

This book, by Peter Brown, is a history "of the vexing problem of wealth in Christianity in the waning days of the Roman Empire. . . . Peter Brown examines the rise of the church through the lens of money and the challenges it posed to an institution that espoused the virtue of poverty and called avarice the root of all evil, ... challeng[ing] the widely held notion that Christianity's growing wealth sapped Rome of its ability to resist the barbarian invasions." (Publisher's note)

Includes bibliographical references and index

Wills, Garry

Saint Augustine. Viking 1999 xx, 152p (Penguin lives series) $19.95   **270.2**
1. Saints 2. Bishops 3. Theologians 4. Philosophers 5. Writers on religion
ISBN 0-670-88610-6

LC 98-50317

Wills begins "by addressing centuries of misconceptions. Though his admiration for the saint is occasionally tainted by defensiveness, his account of Augustine's search for a faith and a philosophy engages our sympathy. He also conveys the turbulence of the era, when the Roman Empire was beleaguered by barbarians and the Catholic Church by heretics, and shows how Augustine's responses to the troubles of his time have shaped Christianity down to our own." New Yorker

Includes bibliographical references

270.6 Period of Reformation and Counter-Reformation, 1517-1648

MacCulloch, Diarmaid

The Reformation; a house divided. Viking 2004 xxiv, 792p il map $34.95; pa $18   **270.6**
1. Reformation
ISBN 0-670-03296-4; 0-14-303538-X pa

LC 2003-61607

First published 2003 in the United Kingdom

The author "has produced the definitive survey for this generation. ... This well-written book is a joy to read, with new facts and interpretations on nearly every page." Libr J

Includes bibliographical references

271 Religious congregations and orders in church history

Butcher, Carmen Acevedo

Man of blessing; a life of St. Benedict. Paraclete Press 2006 180p map $21.95   **271**
1. Monks 2. Saints 3. Writers on religion
ISBN 1-55725-485-0; 978-1-55725-485-6

LC 2005-35827

This is the "story of the life of St. Benedict of Nursia, who founded Western monasticism in the sixth century and later became the patron saint of Europe. ... The book's readability will make it easy for patrons to escape into late Roman culture and find peace in a monastic simplicity." Libr J

Includes bibliographical references

Haag, Michael

The Tragedy of the Templars; The Rise and Fall of the Crusader States. Michael Haag. HarperCollins 2013 384 p. $16.99   **271**
1. Crusades 2. Templars -- History
ISBN 0062059750; 9780062059758

In this book, Michael Haag provides an "account of the Crusades, including the history of the Crusader states--known as Outremer--established by the Franks after the First Crusade. He ... examines the Crusades from both the Christian and Muslim perspectives, drawing from contemporary chronicles, church records, and correspondence by Templars. Haag covers the motivations for the Crusades, why both Muslims and Christians wanted control of the Holy Land, and how the Templars were established." (Library Journal)

Merton, Thomas

Intimate Merton; his life from his journals. edited by Patrick Hart and Jonathan Montaldo. HarperSanFrancisco 1999 374p il hardcover o.p. pa $16   **271**
1. Monks 2. Poets 3. Authors 4. Nonfiction writers 5. Writers on religion
ISBN 0-06-251629-9 pa

LC 99-33239

"This is a one-volume condensation of Merton's journals, which have been published over the last few years; its seven chapters correspond to the seven volumes of Merton's complete journals. ... {The editors} have maintained all of Merton's central themes—including controversial ones, like the relationship with the nurse identified as 'M.' and Merton's doubts about his vocation." Libr J

Spink, Kathryn

Mother Teresa; a complete authorized biography. HarperSanFrancisco 1997 306p il hardcover o.p. pa $15.95   **271**
1. Nuns 2. Missionaries 3. Missions -- India 4. Missionaries of Charity 5. Nobel laureates for peace
ISBN 0-06-251553-5 pa

LC 97-41349

"Spink's biography benefits from her own 18-year involvement with the work of the Missionaries of Charity Order as well as from the intimate relationship she developed over the years with Mother Teresa. ... A final chapter in the book provides glimpses of Mother Teresa's affection for Princess Diana, a brief description of Mother Teresa's funeral and a short account of the election of Sister Nirmal as her successor." Publ Wkly

272 Persecutions in general church history

Kamen, Henry

The Spanish Inquisition; a historical revision. Yale Univ. Press 1998 369p il $45; pa $14.80 **272**
1. Inquisition 2. Antisemitism 3. Jews -- Spain 4. Spain -- History
ISBN 0-300-07522-7; 0-300-07880-3 pa

LC 97-32451

First published 1965 in the United Kingdom; first United States edition 1966 by New Am. Lib.

In this revision of his 1965 study, the author "restates his original argument. . . . He reaffirms his contention that an all-powerful, torture-mad Inquisition is largely a 19th-century myth. In its place he portrays a poor, understaffed institution whose scattered tribunals had only a limited reach and whose methods were more humane than those of most secular courts. . . . As for the Inquisition's much-vaunted role as Big Brother and its responsibility for intellectual decline, Kamen rejects this hypothesis out of hand. . . . {He} also dismisses the notion that the Inquisition enjoyed widespread popular support." N Y Times Book Rev

Includes bibliographical references

Perez, Joseph

★ The **Spanish** Inquisition; a history. trans. by Janet Lloyd. Yale University Press 2005 248p $26; pa $17   **272**

1. Inquisition 2. Spain -- History
ISBN 0-300-10790-0; 0-300-11982-8 pa
LC 2004-114614

The author "tells the history of the Spanish Inquisition from its medieval beginnings to its nineteenth-century ending. . . . He explores the inner workings of its councils, and shows how its officers, inquisitors, and leaders lived and worked." Univ Press Books for Public and Second Sch Libr, 2006

Includes bibliographical references

275.1   Christianity--China

Liao Yiwu

God is red; the secret story of how Christianity survived and flourished in Communist China. Liao Yiwu; translated by Wen Huang. HarperOne 2011 231 p. $25.99   **275.1**

1. Persecution 2. Communism -- China 3. Christianity -- China 4. China -- Church history -- 21st century 5. China -- Church history -- 20th century 6. Communism and Christianity -- China -- History -- 20th century 7. Communism and Christianity -- China -- History -- 21st century
ISBN 0062078461; 9780062078469; 9780062078483
LC 2010051154

"The author examines Christianity, which survived under China's Cultural Revolution despite attempts to eradicate it as a 'lackey of the imperialists.' . . . In an attempt to understand why a foreign religion gained such popularity, Liao interviews a wide range of Chinese Christians, from an elderly nun who witnessed both the closing and eventual reopening of her church by the Communist regime, to a missionary doctor treating impoverished villagers in lieu of working in a government-run hospital, to a dying tailor who finds meaning in his recent conversion to the faith. . . . Will appeal to both Christian and secular readers interested in the cultural realities of China's Great Leap Forward." Kirkus

277   Christianity in North America

Boyle, Gregory J.

Tattoos on the heart; the power of boundless compassion. [by] Gregory Boyle. Free Press 2010 217p $25; pa $14; ebook $11.99   **277**

1. Church work 2. Christian life
ISBN 978-1-4391-5302-4; 1-4391-5302-7; 978-1-4391-5315-4 pa; 1-4391-5315-9 pa; 978-1-4391-7177-6 ebook; 1-4391-7177-7 ebook
LC 2009-32970

"Jesuit priest Boyle recounts his two decades of working with 'homies' in Los Angeles County, which contains 1,100 gangs with nearly 86,000 members. Boyle's Homeboy Industries is the largest gang intervention program in the country, offering job training, tattoo removal, and employment to members of enemy gangs." Publ Wkly

Dochuk, Darren

From Bible belt to sunbelt; plain-folk religion, grassroots politics, and the rise of evangelical conservatism. W.W. Norton 2011 520p il   **277**

1. Conservatism 2. Evangelicalism 3. California 4. Evangelicalism -- Southern California 5. Christianity and politics -- Evangelicalism 6. California -- Church history -- 20th century 7. Conservatism -- Religious aspects -- Christianity -- History -- 20th century
ISBN 0393066827; 9780393066821
LC 2010032740

"A five-decade history of the evangelical movement in southern California [argues that] . . . the influx of migrants from the Bible Belt during the Great Depression ultimately led to the rise of the New Right and modern conservatism in the late twentieth century." (Publisher's note) Bibliography. Index.

"Well-written and documented, a supremely helpful guide in sorting out how we arrived at that odd state of affairs." Kirkus

Includes bibliographical references and index

Marty, Martin E.

Pilgrims in their own land; 500 years of religion in America. Penguin Books 1985 500p il pa $18   **277**

1. United States -- Religion 2. United States -- Church history
ISBN 0-14-008268-9; 978-0-14-008268-5
LC 85-3596

First published 1984 by Little, Brown

This book examines "the force of religion in the United States since colonial times. Marty considers not only the religious beliefs and rituals brought to America by the various European settlers, but also those of native Americans. The clashes between Protestant, Catholic, Judaic, and other religious groups are perceived in light of their influence upon the development of this nation up to the present." Booklist

Includes bibliographical references

Yancey, Philip

Vanishing grace; whatever happened to the good news? Philip Yancey. Zondervan 2014 304 p. (hardcover) $22.99 **277**

1. Christianity -- United States 2. United States -- Church history 3. Witness bearing (Christianity) 4. Christianity and culture -- United States 5. Christianity -- United States -- Public opinion

ISBN 0310339324; 9780310339328

LC 2014010695

"In this important and compelling new book, a New York Times best-selling author explores what may have contributed to hostility toward Christians, especially Evangelicals, and offers illuminating stories of how faith can be expressed in ways that disarm even the most cynical critics." Publisher's Note

"The world is thirsty for truth that can make a difference, and the author believes that Christians are capable of influencing culture, despite its embrace of atheism and fuzzy New Age philosophy, by adopting a 'show' rather than 'tell' method for reaching out to those in need. A section comparing points of view for the world's major religions particularly helps give perspective." Pub Wkly

277.3 Christianity—United States

Sutton, Matthew Avery

American apocalypse; a history of modern evangelicalism. Matthew Avery Sutton. Belknap Press 2014 480 p. illustrations (alk. paper) $35 **277.3**

1. United States -- Religion 2. Evangelicalism -- United States 3. Evangelicalism -- History 4. United States -- Church history -- 20th century

ISBN 0674048369; 9780674048362

LC 2014014034

Author "Matthew Avery Sutton draws on extensive archival research to document the ways an initially obscure network of charismatic preachers and their followers reshaped American religion, at home and abroad, for over a century. [He] shows how a group of radical Protestants, anticipating the end of the world, paradoxically transformed it." (Publisher's note)

"The result is so seamless a history that readers may wonder whether he engages in overstatement at times. Factual errors, such as stating the U.S. pummeled Iraq with Scud missiles during the first Gulf War (Scuds were never part of the U.S. arsenal), or that Reverend Billy Graham is dead (as of this writing, he is not), don't help. Despite these caveats, this remains an important story, and it is exceedingly well told." Booklist

Includes bibliographical references and index

280 Denominations and sects of Christian church

Atwood, Craig D.

★ **Handbook** of denominations in the United States; [by] Craig D. Atwood, Frank S. Mead, Samuel S. Hill. 13th ed.; Abingdon Press 2010 416p il $24 **280**

1. Sects 2. United States -- Religion

ISBN 978-1-4267-0048-4; 1-4267-0048-2

LC 2010-07092

First published 1951. Periodically revised

"History and present structure of Christian religious bodies in the United States. Reports on doctrines of different churches. Includes bibliography and index." NY Public Libr Book of How & Where to Look It Up

Includes bibliographical references

281.9 Orthodox churches

Mathewes-Green, Frederica

Welcome to the Orthodox Church; an introduction to Eastern Christianity. Frederica Mathewes-Green. Paraclete Press 2015 xviii, 361 p.p (paperback) $19.99 **281.9**

1. Christian life 2. Orthodox Eastern Church

ISBN 1557259216; 9781557259219

LC 2014041905

This book, by Frederica Mathewes-Green, "provides a comprehensive introduction to [Eastern] Orthodoxy, but with a twist: readers learn by making a series of visits to a fictitious church, and get to know the faith as new Christians did for most of history, by immersion. Mathewes-Green provides commentary and explanations on everything from how to 'venerate' an icon, the Orthodox understanding of the atonement, to the Lenten significance of tofu." (Publisher's note)

Includes bibliographical references and index

282 Roman Catholic Church

Allen, John L., 1965-

The **Catholic** church; what everyone needs to know. by John L. Allen. Oxford University Press 2013 298 p. (What Everyone Needs to Know) $16.95 **282**

1. Catholic Church -- History 2. Catholic Church -- Doctrines 3. Theology, Doctrinal -- Popular works

ISBN 0199975108; 9780199975105; 9780199975112

LC 2012038594

In this book, author John L. Allen, Jr, "one of the world's leading authorities on the Vatican, offers an authoritative and accessible guide to the past, present, and future of the Church. The Catholic Church remains by far the largest branch of the worldwide Christian family, and is growing at a remarkable clip. Yet the Church has also been rocked by a series of scandals related to the sexual abuse of minors by clergy, and, even more devastating, the cover-up by the Church hierarchy." (Publisher's note)

Betrayal; the crisis in the Catholic Church. by the Investigative Staff of the Boston Globe. Little, Brown & Co. 2015 304 p. illustrations $16.99 **282**

1. Catholic Church 2. Child sexual abuse 3. Child

sexual abuse by clergy
ISBN 0316271535; 9780316271530

LC 2015951503

This book, by the Investigative Staff of the Boston Globe, presents "the devastating revelations that triggered a crisis within the Catholic Church. Here is the truth about the scores of abusive priests who preyed upon innocent children and the cabal of senior Church officials who covered up their crimes." (Publisher's note)

Includes bibliographical references (p. 251-263) and index

Buckley, William F.

Nearer, my God; an autobiography of faith. Harcourt Brace & Co. 1998 xx, 313p il pa $14 **282**
1. Authors 2. Novelists 3. Columnists 4. Magazine editors
ISBN 0-15-600618-9

LC 98-16194

First published 1997 by Doubleday

"As we might expect, Nearer My God is rich in anecdote, witty, and animated by what Buckley refers to as his 'polemical inclinations.'. . . But what gives it unity as a book, and not just a loose collection of pieces bound in cloth, is the warmth and the depth of Buckley's faith, at once complex and many-sided." Christ Today

Buttiglione, Rocco

Karol Wojtyla; the thought of the man who became Pope John Paul II. translated by Paolo Guietti and Francesca Murphy. Eerdmans 1997 384p $35 **282**
1. Popes
ISBN 0-8028-3848-0

LC 97-23188

Original Italian edition, 1982

The author traces the Pope's "intellectual development, offering a critique of his literary works and a detailed analysis of how he was influenced by Thomism and phenomenology, which he sought to reconcile while emphasizing individual freedom of conscience. . . . Recommended for general collections for its broad sweep complementary to other biographies on the pope." Libr J

Duffy, Eamon

Saints & sinners; a history of the popes. 3rd ed.; Yale Nota Bene/Yale University Press 2006 474p il pa $22 **282**
1. Papacy 2. Catholic Church -- History
ISBN 978-0-300-11597-0

First published 1997

This illustrated volume is a companion piece to a six-part television series of the same name. The book offers an overview of the 2,000-year history of the papacy.

Includes bibliographical references

Francis, Pope, 1936-

★ The **church** of mercy; a vision for the Church. Pope Francis. Loyola Press 2014 200 p. (hardcover) $22.95 **282**
1. Popes 2. Catholic Church
ISBN 9780829441680; 9780829441697;

9780829441703

LC 2014934036

This book, "[c]ollected from Pope Francis's speeches, homilies, and papers presented during the first year of his papacy, . . . is the first Vatican-authorized book detailing his vision for the Catholic Church. From how to be citizens of the world to answering God's call for evangelization, Pope Francis's deep wisdom reminds us that the Church must move beyond its own walls and joyfully bring God's mercy wherever suffering, division, or injustice exists." (Publisher's note)

"Refreshingly humane, focusing on people rather than institutions. Admirers of Francis and students of church history alike will find this a useful introduction to the pontiff's thought." Kirkus

Includes bibliographical references

Walking with Jesus; a way forward for the church. Pope Francis. Loyola Press 2015 160 p. (hardcover) $22.95 **282**
1. Christianity
ISBN 0829442480; 9780829442489; 9780829442496; 9780829442540

LC 2015930346

In this book, Pope Francis "urges us to make Jesus central in our individual lives and in the collective life of the Church--to walk toward him, and ultimately to walk with him at all times and in all places. Each chapter of this Vatican-authorized book helps us put one foot in front of the other as we move ever closer to God and to our neighbors through the sacraments, prayer, evangelization, the gifts of the Spirit, and service to others." (Publisher's note)

"Perhaps no one has as much potential to buoy the human spirit through his words as Francis, whose life and public speeches are closely watched by so many. The book's foreword is by Archbishop Blase J. Cupich of Chicago, the pope's first major U.S. appointment." Pub Wkly

Guiley, Rosemary Ellen

The **encyclopedia** of saints. Facts on File 2001 419p il $82.50; pa $24.95 **282**
1. Reference books 2. Christian saints -- Dictionaries
ISBN 0-8160-4133-4; 0-8160-4134-2 pa

LC 00-69176

This volume offers "accounts of the lives and experiences of more than 400 principal saints, from early martyrs such as Lucy of Syracuse to recently canonized saints such as Katherine Drexel. Entries provide a biographical overview, a record of the saint's religious journeys and mystical experiences, a discussion of personal philosophies and important theological influences, as well as his or her patronage, feast days and popular role within the Church." Publisher's note

The **HarperCollins** encyclopedia of Catholicism; general editor, Richard P. McBrien; associate editors, Harold W. Attridge {et al.} HarperSanFrancisco 1995 xxxviii, 1349p il maps $47.50 **282**
1. Reference books 2. Catholic Church -- Encyclopedias
ISBN 0-06-065338-8

LC 94-39972

"This encyclopedic dictionary contains 4700 entries by 277 experts. . . . Broad-ranging topics in Catholic theology, history, culture, art, canon law, literature, etc., are replete with cross references, photos, maps, tables, diagrams, and charts." Libr J

John Paul II, Pope, 1920-2005

   Crossing the threshold of hope; edited by Vittorio Messori. Knopf 1994 244p hardcover o.p. pa $15   **282**
   1. Faith 2. Apologetics 3. Christian life 4. Catholic Church
   ISBN 0-679-76561-1 pa
                       LC 94-78675
   In this book the Pope responds to written questions by an Italian Catholic journalist originally planned for a television interview which never took place. The questions addressed include: what is the papacy?; when and how should one pray?; is there proof of God's existence?; is Jesus the Son of God?; why is there so much evil in the world?; why does God tolerate suffering?; is only Rome right?; and what are human rights?
   "This is a book to be read for insights, perspectives, connections, formulations that spark meditation and enrich our understanding." Commonweal

Maxwell-Stuart, P. G.

   Chronicle of the popes; the reign-by-reign record of the papacy from St. Peter to the present. Thames & Hudson 1997 240p il maps $34.95   **282**
   1. Papacy 2. Catholic Church -- History
   ISBN 0-500-01798-0
                       LC 97-60230
   This survey examines the lives and deeds of the 264 popes from St. Peter to John Paul II
   This history of the papacy "provides a good selection of illustrations with a lightweight text." N Y Times Book Rev
   Includes bibliographical references

★ **New** Catholic encyclopedia; prepared by an editorial staff at the Catholic University of America. 2nd ed; Gale Group 2003 15v il maps set $1,981   **282**
   1. Reference books 2. Catholic Church -- Encyclopedias
   ISBN 978-0-7876-4004-0; 0-7876-4004-2
                    LC 2002-924
   First published 1967 as an update to the Catholic encyclopedia. Kept up-to-date-by yearly supplements
   This encyclopedia "covers the history of the eastern churches, the churches of the Protestant Reformation, and other ecclesial communities as well as the Christian roots based in ancient Israel and Judaism. No comprehensive resource on Catholicism can be complete without touching on other world religions as well, including Islam, Buddhism, and Hinduism. This resource provides entries not only on the doctrine, organization, and history of the church, but also on the people, institutions, and social changes that have affected the church over the years. Arranged alphabetically, the entries run in length from half a page to several pages in length. All entries provide the name of the contributor and a bibliography. Cross-references to related articles are located throughout the work. Adding to the usefulness of the set are more than 3,000 black-and-white photographs, maps,

and charts that complement the scholarly articles." Am Ref Books Annu, 2003

Our Sunday Visitor Catholic almanac. Our Sunday Visitor   **282**
   1. Almanacs 2. Catholic Church -- Directories
   Annual. First published 1904. Title varies
   "Includes much miscellaneous information, e.g., annual survey of news, ecclesiastical calendar, glossary of terms in Catholic use, the Catholic church in various countries of the world, statistics, directory of information, etc." Guide to Ref Books. 11th edition

Politi, Marco

   Pope Francis among the wolves; the inside story of a revolution. Marco Politi; translated by William McCuaig. Columbia University Press 2015 288 p. (cloth : alk. paper) $27.95   **282**
   1. Catholic Church 2. Catholic Church -- History -- 21st century
   ISBN 9780231174145
                  LC 2014046193
   This book, by Marco Politi, translated by William McCuaig, "takes us deep inside the power struggle roiling the Roman Curia and the Catholic Church worldwide, beginning with Benedict XVI . . . and intensifying with the contested and unexpected election of . . . Francis. Politi's account balances the perspectives of Pope Francis's supporters, Benedict's sympathizers, and those disappointed members of the Catholic laity who feel alienated by the institution." (Publisher's note)
   "This book is well translated and accessible to a wide audience of Francis's admirers and opponents, both inside and outside of the Catholic Church." LJ
   Includes bibliographical references and index

Wills, Garry, 1934-

   The **Future** of the Catholic Church With Pope Francis; Garry Wills. Penguin Group USA 2015 320 p. 24 cm $27.95   **282**
   1. Catholic Church
   ISBN 0525426965; 9780525426967
                  LC 2014038534
   This book, by Garry Wills, "argues that changes have been the evidence of life in the Catholic Church. It has often changed, sometimes with bad consequences, more often with good. . . . In this . . . study, . . . [the author] gives seven examples of deep and serious changes that have taken place (or are taking place) within the last century. None of them was effected by the pope all by himself." (Publisher's note)
   "Highly recommended for all interested in a fact-based study of the church's evolution." LJ

282.092   Roman Catholic Church--Biography

Shriver, Mark

   Pilgrimage; My Search for the Real Pope Francis. by Mark K. Shriver. Random House Inc 2016 304 p. $28   **282.092**
   1. Popes -- Biography 2. Catholic Church -- Clergy

-- Biography

ISBN 0812998022; 9780812998023

LC 2016022799

This book by Mark K. Shriver "retraces [Pope] Francis's personal journey, revealing the origins of his open, unpretentious style and explaining how it revitalized Shriver's own faith and renewed his commitment to the Church. To help us understand how Jorge Mario Bergoglio became Pope Francis, Shriver travels to Bergoglio's native Argentina to meet with the people who knew him as a child, as a young Jesuit priest, and as a reformist bishop." (Publisher's note)

"In this excellent book, Shriver takes readers on a pilgrimage to numerous significant people and places in the life of Pope Francis." Pub Wkly

Includes bibliographical references.

284.1 Lutheran churches

Bolz-Weber, Nadia

Accidental saints; finding God in all the wrong people. Nadia Bolz-Weber. Convergent Books 2015 224 p. $23   **284.1**

1. Christianity 2. Christian biography 3. House for All Sinners and Saints (Denver, Colo.) -- Biography

ISBN 1601427557; 9781601427557

LC 2015012506

This memoir, by Nadia Bolz-Weber, "invites readers into a surprising encounter with what she calls 'a religious but not-so-spiritual life.' Tattooed, angry and profane, this former standup comic turned pastor stubbornly, sometimes hilariously, resists the God she feels called to serve. But God keeps showing up in the least likely of people--a church-loving agnostic, a drag queen, a felonious Bishop and a gun-toting member of the NRA." (Publisher's note)

"Recommended for readers who enjoyed Bolz-Weber's previous books or authors such as Anne Lamott and Brian McClaren. An entertaining, reality-based alternative to the polished "professional Christian" memoir." LJ

287 Methodist churches; churches related to Methodism

Tomkins, Stephen

★ **John** Wesley; a biography. Eerdmans 2003 208p pa $20   **287**

1. Theologians 2. Methodist Church 3. Evangelists 4. Writers on religion

ISBN 0-8028-2499-4

LC 2003-54328

In this biography of the founder of the Methodist religion "Tomkins presents a keenly engaging portrait of a great man full of contradictoriness. Wesley insisted he was loyal to the Church of England yet consented to his followers setting up establishments and engaging in practices that flouted Anglican authority. . . . He altered the face of Christianity in the West by inspiring modern evangelicalism and Pentecostalism. A fascinating figure, fascinatingly limned." Booklist

Includes bibliographical references

289 Other denominations and sects

Stein, Stephen J.

The **Shaker** experience in America; a history of the United Society of Believers. Yale Univ. Press 1992 xx, 554p il $65; pa $21   **289**

1. Shakers

ISBN 0-300-05139-5; 0-300-05933-7 pa

LC 91-30836

A historical look at the evolution of Shakerism focusing on the movement's cultural values, religion and artifacts

Includes bibliographical references

289.3 Latter-Day Saints (Mormons)

Beam, Alex

American crucifixion; the murder of Joseph Smith and the fate of the Mormon church. Alex Beam. PublicAffairs 2014 352 p. illustrations, maps (hardcover) $26.99   **289.3**

1. Mormons 2. Church of Jesus Christ of Latter-day Saints -- History

ISBN 1610393139; 9781610393133; 9781610393140

LC 2014004063

This book, by Alex Beam, focuses on "founding prophet of Mormonism, Joseph Smith. . . . Beam tells how Smith went from charismatic leader to public enemy: How his most seismic revelation--the doctrine of polygamy--created a rift among his people; how that schism turned to violence; and how, ultimately, Smith could not escape the consequences of his ambition and pride . . . Smith's brutal assassination propelled the Mormons to colonize the American West." (Publisher's note)

"Beam offers a captivating saga of Smith's rise and fall and of a colorful cast of characters who contributed to the internal politics and rivalries that led to Smith's death and drove the Mormons forward to their destiny." Booklist

Includes bibliographical references and index

Book of Mormon

★ The **Book** of Mormon; another testament of Jesus Christ. [translated by Joseph Smith, Jr.] Doubleday 2004 586p $24.95   **289.3**

1. Mormons 2. Church of Jesus Christ of Latter-day Saints

ISBN 0-385-51316-X

LC 2004-51982

First published 1830

"Based on golden plates which Joseph Smith claimed were revealed to him, and which he unearthed from Cumorah Hill, New York, this book is roughly similar in structure to the Bible. . . . Emphasized are the doctrines of pre-existence, perfection, the afterlife, and Christ's second coming." Haydn. Thesaurus of Book Dig

Bushman, Richard L.

Joseph Smith and the beginnings of Mormonism. University of Ill. Press 1984 262p maps hardcover o.p. pa $16.95   **289.3**

1. Church of Jesus Christ of Latter-day Saints 2.

Mormon leaders
ISBN 0-252-06012-1 pa

LC 84-2451

The author surveys the historical background of the Mormon church with particular emphasis on the spiritual growth of its founder, Joseph Smith

"Resulting from many years of careful research and reflections, this book will stand for decades as a major contribution in the field." Choice

Includes bibliographical references

Mormonism; a very short introduction. [by] Richard Lyman Bushman. Oxford University Press 2008 130p il (Very short introductions) pa $11.95 **289.3**
1. Church of Jesus Christ of Latter-day Saints
ISBN 978-0-19-531030-6

LC 2007-44444

This is an "outstanding, reliable overview of Mormon history and beliefs." Libr J

Includes bibliographical references (p. 121-123)

Givens, Terryl

By the hand of Mormon; the American scripture that launched a new world religion. [by] Terryl L. Givens. Oxford Univ. Press 2002 230p il maps hardcover o.p. pa $16.95 **289.3**
1. Book of Mormon
ISBN 0-19-513818-X; 0-19-516888-7 pa

LC 2001-53118

The author "investigates the history and theology of the Book of Mormon, which he calls 'perhaps the most religiously influential, hotly contested, and, in the secular press at least, intellectually under-investigated book in America.' Givens persuasively demonstrates how the Book of Mormon was trumpeted by early Latter-day Saints more for the fact of its existence . . . than for its content per se." Publ Wkly

Includes bibliographical references

Gutjahr, Paul C.

The **Book** of Mormon; a biography. Paul C. Gutjahr. Princeton University Press 2012 xix, 255 p.p **289.3**
1. Mormons 2. Sacred books 3. Church of Jesus of Latter-day Saints -- History 4. Book of Mormon -- History 5. Book of Mormon -- Criticism, interpretation, etc
ISBN 9780691144801

LC 2011044063

This book presents a history of the Book of Mormon. "[Paul C.] Gutjahr recounts the life of Joseph Smith, whose status as the prophet of the Church of Jesus Christ of Latter-Day Saints rests upon his claim that he translated the Book of Mormon from ancient gold plates delivered to him by an angel. . . . Undeterred by skeptics' allegations of fraud, a small army of missionaries have made the book a powerful proselytizing tool, attracting millions . . . to their faith." (Booklist)

Includes bibliographical references (pages 209-246) and index

Hardy, Grant

★ **Understanding** the Book of Mormon; a reader's guide. Oxford University Press 2010 336p $29.95 **289.3**
1. Book of Mormon -- Criticism
ISBN 978-0-19-973170-1

LC 2009-26675

In this analysis of the Book of Mormon's narrative structure, the author describes the work's "characters, events, and ideas, as he explores the story and its messages. He identifies the book's literary techniques, such as characterization, embedded documents, allusions, and parallel narratives." Publisher's note

Includes bibliographical references

Turner, John G.

★ **Brigham** Young, pioneer prophet; John G. Turner. The Belknap Press of Harvard University Press 2012 500 p. (alk. paper) $35.00 **289.3**
1. Biography 2. Religious life 3. Church of Jesus Christ of Latter-day Saints -- Presidents -- Biography
ISBN 0674049675; 9780674049673

LC 2012015555

Author John G. Turner tells the story of "Brigham Young, [who] was Joseph Smith's lieutenant in spreading the newly coined doctrine of Mormonism and his successor on Smith's murder." Turner chronicles "Young's rise in the early hierarchy. . . . The author looks at the various strains of Protestantism, 'ecstatic' and otherwise, that fed into early Mormonism, drawing particularly on Methodism in the British Isles, where Young worked as one of the church's first missionaries." (Kirkus Reviews)

Includes bibliographical references and index

289.5 Church of Christ, Scientist (Christian Science)

Eddy, Mary Baker

★ **Science** and health, with key to the Scriptures; Trustees under the will of Mary Baker G. Eddy. Christian Science Pub. Soc. 2000 pa $9.95 **289.5**
1. Christian Science
ISBN 978-0-87952-259-9; 0-87952-259-3
First published 1875

This work is the foundation of the Christian Science religion, setting forth Mrs. Baker's interpretations of the Holy Scriptures and the method of healing. It has not been revised since her death in 1910.

Schoepflin, Rennie B.

Christian Science on trial; religious healing in America. Johns Hopkins Univ. Press 2002 301p il (Medicine, science, and religion in historical context) $39.95 **289.5**
1. Christian Science
ISBN 0-8018-7057-7

LC 2001-8512

"A historical examination of Christian Science's evolution during the late 19th and early 20th centuries and the faith's struggle for existence and respectability in the midst of organized American medicine's efforts to curtail its influence." Libr J

Includes bibliographical references and index

289.6   Society of Friends (Quakers)

Hamm, Thomas D.

★ The **Quakers** in America. Columbia Univ. Press 2003 293p il (Columbia contemporary American religion series) $48.50; pa $27   **289.6**

1. Society of Friends

ISBN 0-231-12362-0; 0-231-12363-9 pa

LC 2002-41422

The author provides an "introduction to Quaker origins abroad, their influences on American politics and culture, as well as their beliefs and traditions as they are played out on American soil. Though this is a serious history with a glossary, chronology, and 40 pages of notes, cartoons and anecdotes leaven the text. For both public and academic libraries." Libr J

Includes bibliographical references

289.7   Mennonite churches

Hostetler, John A.

Amish society; 4th ed; Johns Hopkins Univ. Press 1993 435p il maps hardcover o.p. pa $20   **289.7**

1. Amish

ISBN 0-8018-4441-X; 0-8018-4442-8

LC 92-19304

First published 1963

This book discusses the sectarian origins of the Amish, immigration history, family and community life, population trends, farming practices, technological innovations, education, medicine and the effects of government regulation.

Includes bibliographical references

Kraybill, Donald B.

Concise encyclopedia of Amish, Brethren, Hutterites, and Mennonites; Donald B. Kraybill. Johns Hopkins University Press 2010 302p ill., maps   **289.7**

1. Amish 2. Mennonites 3. Hutterian Brethren

ISBN 9780801896576; 0801896576

LC 2009046015

In this book author "[Donald B.] Kraybill [provides an] . . . overview of the beliefs and cultural practices of Amish, Brethren, Hutterites, and Mennonites in North America. Found throughout Canada, Central America in Mexico, and the United States, these religious communities include more than 200 different groups with 800,000 members in 17 countries. Through 340 short entries, Kraybill offers readers information on a wide range of topics related to religious views and social practices. With . . . consideration of how these diverse communities are related, this compact reference provides a . . . synopsis of these groups in the twenty-first century." (Publisher's note)

Includes bibliographical references   (p. 259-285)

and index.

★ **On** the backroad to heaven; Old Order Hutterites, Mennonites, Amish, and Brethren. {by} Donald B. Kraybill, Carl F. Bowman. Johns Hopkins Univ. Press 2001 330p il maps (Center books in Anabaptist studies) $57; pa $16.95   **289.7**

1. Amish 2. Mennonites 3. Hutterian Brethren

ISBN 0-8018-6565-4; 0-8018-7089-5 pa

LC 00-10406

"This look at the history, similarities and differences between four groups of Old Order faithful in North America—Hutterites, Mennonites, Amish and Brethren—is fascinating. . . . A book that, in one volume, tackles history, sociology and future trends—and does it well." Christ Century

Includes bibliographical references

The **riddle** of Amish culture; rev ed; Johns Hopkins Univ. Press 2001 397p il maps (Center books in Anabaptist studies) $65; pa $16.95   **289.7**

1. Amish

ISBN 0-8018-6771-1; 0-8018-6772-X pa

LC 00-13054

First published 1989

The author examines the history and culture of the Amish, discussing such topics as the social structure of Amish society, rites of redemption and purification, recreation and social gatherings, work, technology, public relations, and social change

Includes bibliographical references and index

Mackall, Joe

Plain secrets; an outsider among the Amish. Beacon Press 2007 xxxiv, 208p $24.95; pa $13 **289.7**

1. Amish

ISBN 0-80701-064-2; 978-0-80701-064-8; 0-80701-065-0 pa; 978-0-80701-065-5 pa

LC 2007-924329

"This is a loving portrait, warts and all, of an often-misunderstood people." Booklist

Includes bibliographical references

292   Classical religion (Greek and Roman religion)

Graves, Robert

★ The **Greek** myths; Combined ed; Penguin Books 1992 782p pa $19.95   **292**

1. Classical mythology

ISBN 0-14-017199-1

First published 1955

A collection of the author's interpretations of Greek myths based on anthropological and archaeological findings

★ The **Oxford** dictionary of classical myth and religion; edited by Simon Price and Emily Kearns. Oxford University Press 2003 599p maps $39.95; pa $17.95   **292**

1. Reference books 2. Classical mythology --

Dictionaries
ISBN 0-19-280288-7; 0-19-280289-5 pa

LC 2004-298013

"Instead of separating mythology and Judeo-Christian religion into separate references, this work covers all religious life in the ancient Greco-Roman world. The result is a generally accessible and academically current compendium of information on gods and holy beings, religious practices, festivals, sacred sites, myths, authors, and texts of the period. The reader will find not only Athena and Zeus but also Jesus Christ and St. Augustine, Mani and Zoroaster." Libr J

294   Religions of Indic origin

Dalrymple, William

Nine lives; in search of the sacred in modern India. A.A. Knopf 2010 275p il map $26.95   **294**

1. India -- Religion
ISBN 978-0-307-27282-9; 0-307-27282-6

LC 2010-06362

First published 2009 in the United Kingdom

"Throughout the book, Dalrymple showcases his knowledge of the breadth of India and his fearless willingness to penetrate its sometimes unsavory nooks and crannies, rendering this a truly heartfelt work for readers craving a deeper connection to India and its rich spiritual heritage. A remarkable feat of journalism." Kirkus

Includes bibliographical references

Iyengar, B. K. S.

Light on life; the yoga journey to wholeness, inner peace, and ultimate freedom. [by] B.K.S. Iyengar, with John J. Evans and Douglas Abrams. Rodale 2005 xxii, 282p il $24.95; pa $15.95   **294**

1. Yoga
ISBN 1-59486-248-6; 978-1-59486-248-9; 1-59486-524-8 pa

LC 2005-15700

The author "expounds the philosophy of yoga—its metaphysics, of which yoga poses, or asanas, represent the physical component. . . . Not the book with which to begin the yoga journey, it is highly recommended for those advanced on the path and interested in learning from a master of flexibility and wisdom." Publ Wkly

294.3   Buddhism

Armstrong, Karen

Buddha. Viking 2001 xxix, 205p map (Penguin lives series) hardcover o.p. pa $13   **294.3**

1. Philosophers 2. Buddhist leaders
ISBN 0-670-89193-2; 0-14-303436-7 pa

LC 00-43808

"Armstrong interprets the mythologized story of the Buddha's abandonment of his life of comfort and privilege; commitment to practicing advanced forms of yoga and nearly fatal asceticism; enlightenment beneath a bodhi tree; and 45 years of wandering and teaching until his death in 483.

And as she does so, she lucidly explains his revelations and influence." Booklist

Includes bibliographical references

Chödrön, Pema

How to meditate; a practical guide to making friends with your mind. Pema Chodron. Sounds True 2013 viii, 175 p.p $19.95   **294.3**

1. Buddhism 2. Meditation
ISBN 1604079339; 9781604079333

LC 2012046126

In this book, by Pema Chödrön, the author, an "American-born Tibetan Buddhist nun . . . , explores in-depth what she considers the essentials for an evolving practice [of meditation] that helps you live in a wholehearted way. . . . Meditation, Pema explains, gives us a golden key to address this yearning. This comprehensive guide shows readers how to honestly meet and openly relate with the mind to embrace the fullness of our experience." (Publisher's note)

"At all times Chodron is careful not to overwhelm readers or make meditation feel like an Everest expedition, and she features her own practice as an example of challenges and successes." LJ

Dalai Lama XIV, 1935-

★ **How** to be compassionate; a handbook for creating inner peace and a happier world. [by] His Holiness the Dalai Lama; translated from oral teachings and edited by Jeffrey Hopkins. Atria Books 2011 xi, 147 p.p $14   **294.3**

1. Buddhism 2. Compassion 3. Religious life
ISBN 1451623917; 9781451623901; 9781451623925

LC 2011281813

In this book, the Tibetan Buddhist spiritual leader the Dalai Lama demonstrates that "the surest path to true happiness lies in being intimately concerned with the welfare of others," or "in compassion." (Publisher's note) The author "works . . . from the Buddhist places (awareness, nonattachment) to speak to general readers about habits that make for unhappiness (anger, for one) and the attitudes that increase contentment." (Library Journal)

"Light on politics and even lighter on the more abstruse points of Tibetan Buddhism, this is a fine and accessible book for the everyday reader." Libr J

Includes bibliographical references (p. [145]-147)

Violence and compassion; {by} the Dalai Lama and Jean-Claude Carrière. Doubleday 1996 248p hardcover o.p. pa $11.50   **294.3**

1. Buddhism
ISBN 0-385-50144-7 pa

LC 95-30694

"This is a rich and invigorating volume, full of ponderable wisdom." Booklist

Emet, Joseph

Finding the blue sky; A Mindful Approach to Choosing Happiness Here and Now. Joseph Emet. TarcherPerigee, an imprint of Penguin Random House, LLC 2016 208 p. (ebook) $48; $16 **294.3**

1. Buddhism 2. Happiness 3. Spiritual life 4. Spiritual

life -- Buddhism 5. Happiness -- Religious aspects -- Buddhism
ISBN 9781101992364; 9780143109631

LC 2016022074

This book, by Joseph Emet, "explores the intersection between Positive Psychology--the study of what makes people happy--and the ancient wisdom of Buddhism. . . . As Joseph explains in this work, the blue sky of happiness is found just beyond the grey clouds of sadness, everyday concerns, stress, or anxiety." (Publisher's note)

"While Emet's teaching of mindfulness is fairly basic for those already familiar with the subject, his approach through positive psychology is fresh and welcome; the newcomer will find a fount of compassionate wisdom to begin the work of personal growth." Pub Wkly

Includes bibliographical references

Greenblat, Musho Rodney Alan

Dharma Delight; a visionary post pop comic guide to Buddhism and Zen. Rodney Allan Greenblat. Tuttle Pub 2016 128 p. color illustrations (paperback) $16.95   **294.3**
1. Buddhism 2. Zen Buddhism
ISBN 0804845263; 9780804845267

This book, by Rodney Allan Greenblat, "illustrates how seeking the path of compassion and acceptance can be as zany and exuberant as it is profound. It is a happy exploration of Buddhist Enlightenment--what it is, where to seek it--and how to recognize the perfection in ourselves." (Publisher's note)

"The relatively brief text invites rereading, and those readers who truly want to learn more will do so. Thoughtful older teens and adults seeking a spiritual outlet may find much to enjoy here. Though the format is graphic-novel-like, this would be just as at home in the religion section." Booklist

Includes bibliographical references.

Johnson, Tim

Tragedy in crimson; how the Dalai Lama conquered the world but lost the battle with China. Nation Books 2011 333p map pa $26.99   **294.3**
1. Buddhist leaders 2. Political leaders 3. Nobel laureates for peace 4. China -- Politics and government 5. Tibet (China) -- Description and travel
ISBN 978-1-56858-601-4

LC 2010-37497

"A current, objective, basic primer on the Free Tibet movement and the Dalai Lama was sorely needed, and . . . [the author] has provided exactly that." Natl Rev

Includes bibliographical references

Keown, Damien

★ A **dictionary** of Buddhism; contributors, Stephen Hodge, Charles Jones, Paoli Tinti. Oxford Univ. Press 2003 357p il maps hardcover o.p. pa $15.95   **294.3**
1. Buddhism
ISBN 0-19-860560-9; 978-0-19-280062-6 pa; 0-19-280062-0 pa

LC 2003-276701

"The entries are short . . . but such accessibility is the very reason why this should be on the bookshelf of every student of Buddhism." Publ Wkly

Kerouac, Jack

Some of the dharma. Viking 1997 419p hardcover o.p. pa $20   **294.3**
1. Buddhism
ISBN 0-14-028707-8 pa

LC 97-12870

"Begun in December 1951 as a notebook for his Buddhist studies, this work records Kerouac's reactions to a variety of Buddhist texts. Over the course of five years, it grew to include poems, prayers, dialogs, meditations, and notes on his reading, as well as commentary on family, friends, and meaningful concerns in his life. . . . Long anticipated by Kerouac scholars, this major work belongs in all literature collections." Libr J

Nichtern, Ethan

The **road** home; a contemporary exploration of the Buddhist path. Ethan Nichtern; foreword by Sharon Salzberg. North Point Press 2015 288 p. (hardback) $25   **294.3**
1. Buddhism 2. Meditation 3. Meditation -- Buddhism
ISBN 0374251932; 9780374251932

LC 2014030912

In this book, by Ethan Nichtern, the author, "drawing from contemporary research on meditation and mindfulness and his experience as a Buddhist teacher and practitioner, . . . describes in fresh and deeply resonant terms the basic existential experience that gives rise to spiritual seeking--and also to its potentially dangerous counterpart, spiritual materialism." (Publisher's note)

"Valuable for readers looking for an introduction to Buddhist teachings as they relate to meditation practice or for those searching for ways to live their lives in the here and now." LJ

Olson, Carl

1993 **Historical** dictionary of Buddhism. Scarecrow Press 2009 xxix, 327p il map (Historical dictionaries of religions, philosophies, and movements) $105; ebook $105   **294.3**
1. Reference books 2. Buddhism -- Dictionaries
ISBN 978-0-8108-5771-1; 0-8108-5771-5; 978-0-8108-6317-0 ebook; 0-8108-6317-0 ebook

LC 2009-7383

First published 1993 under the authorship of Charles S. Prebish

This dictionary covers "Buddhist concepts, significant figures, movements, schools, places, activities, and periods. . . . [It also features] a chronology, an introductory essay, a bibliography, and over 700 cross-referenced dictionary entries." Publisher's note

Includes bibliographical references

Rinzler, Lodro

The **Buddha** walks into a bar; a guide to life for a new generation. Lodro Rinzler. Shambhala 2012 211 p. pbk. : alk. paper $14.95   **294.3**
1. Buddhism 2. Spiritual life 3. Spiritual life --

Buddhism
ISBN 1590309375; 9781590309377

LC 2011014498

This book, by Lodro Rinzler, offers an "introduction to Buddhism for anyone who wants to ride the waves of life with mindfulness and compassion. You'll learn how to use meditation techniques to work with your own mind, how to manage the pervasive 'Incredible Hulk Syndrome,' how to relax into your life despite external pressures, and ultimately how you can start to bring light to a dark world." (Publisher's note)

"A fine beginning resource for younger adults ready to try the approaches of Buddhism; this is Eastern spirituality for the Harry Potter generation." LJ

Includes bibliographical references (p. 210-211)

Siff, Jason

Thoughts are not the enemy; an innovative approach to meditation practice. Jason Siff. Shambhala 2014 224 p. (paperback) $16.95   **294.3**
1. Meditation 2. Meditation -- Buddhism
ISBN 1611800439; 9781611800432

LC 2013046153

In this book, author Jason Siff offers a "new approach to meditation. . . . In most forms of meditation, the meditator is instructed to let go of thoughts as they arise. . . . [Siff argues,] if we allow thoughts to arise and become mindful of the thoughts themselves, we gain tranquillity and insight just as in other methods without having to reject our natural mental processes." (Publisher's note)

"Though Siff emphasizes open and unstructured exploration, some instructions veer toward technical, which may leave inexperienced meditators behind. Meditation scenarios, in which he presents fictionalized accounts of practitioners using different methods, often serve as awkward detours in this otherwise excellent work. Unafraid to go against the grain, Siff teaches readers how to adequately approach conceptual thought, the everyday state of existence, in all of its messiness." Pub Wkly

Includes bibliographical references and index

Sogyal

The **Tibetan** book of living and dying; edited by Patrick Gaffney and Andrew Harvey. rev and updated ed; HarperSanFrancisco 2002 441p il $28.95; pa $17.95   **294.3**
1. Death 2. Buddhism
ISBN 0-06-250793-1; 0-06-250834-2 pa

LC 2002-523084

First published 1992

The author "is well qualified to pass on his tradition. He does this beautifully, in limpid prose free of the scholastic list making that deadens many Tibetan Buddhist primers." N Y Times Book Rev {review of 1992 edition}

Includes bibliographical references

Sutin, Lawrence

★ **All** is change; the two-thousand year journey of Buddhism to the West. Little, Brown 2006 403p il $25.99   **294.3**
1. Buddhism
ISBN 978-0-316-74156-9; 0-316-74156-6

LC 2006-40824

"Greeks and Buddhists in India found common metaphysical ground 2,000 years ago, and Sutin also documents parallels between Buddist and Gnostic teachings in this vital study of a remarkable spiritual migration." Booklist

Includes bibliographical references

Suzuki, Daisetz Teitaro

★ **Manual** of Zen Buddhism. Grove Press 1960 192p il pa $13   **294.3**
1. Buddhist art 2. Zen Buddhism
ISBN 0-8021-3065-8

Fisrt published 1950 in the United Kingdom

In this volume, D. T. Suzuki has brought together some of Zen Buddhism's original sources. Included are the sutras or sermons of the Buddha: the gathas or hymns; the philosophical puzzles known as koan; and the dharanis or invocations to expel evil spirits. In addition to the written selections there are reproductions of Buddhist drawings and paintings, including religious statues found in Zen temples

Thondup, Tulku

Enlightened journey; Buddhist practice as daily life. edited by Harold Talbott. Shambhala Publs. 1995 268p pa $16.95   **294.3**
1. Buddhism
ISBN 1-57062-021-0

LC 94-36154

This is an "exposition on one of the more important sects of Tibetan Buddhism. As such, it comprises 15 talks and articles by Thondup, {a} leader and teacher of the Nyingma school of Tibetan Buddhism. His purpose here is to show how daily life can become the basis of Buddhist spiritual training, and each talk is an introduction to various aspects of Buddhism, covering such topics as meditation as a means to arouse compassion and the importance of suffering to reach enlightenment." Libr J

Includes bibliographical references

Thurman, Robert A. F.

Why the Dalai Lama matters; his act of truth as the solution for China, Tibet, and the world. [by] Robert Thurman. Beyond Words Pub. 2008 xxiv, 231p il map $23   **294.3**
1. Buddhism 2. Tibet (China) 3. Buddhist leaders 4. Political leaders 5. Nobel laureates for peace
ISBN 978-1-58270-220-9; 1-58270-220-9

LC 2008-8529

The author presents an "introduction to Buddhism and the Tibetan concept of the Dalai Lama before focusing on the current 'living embodiment of the Buddha'—a man born as Tenzin Gyatso—the 14th Dalai Lama. Thurman sympathetically renders his lifelong friend as a 'simple Buddhist monk,' a teacher, philosopher, scientist and the political representative of the Tibetan people. . . . The book concludes with a five-step plan to broker peace between Tibet

and China—an agenda simultaneously pragmatic and idealistic, demonstrating truly the talent and power of faith."
Publ Wkly

Includes bibliographical references

Watts, Alan

The **way** of Zen. Vintage Books 1999 236p il pa $13.95   **294.3**
1. Zen Buddhism
ISBN 0-375-70510-4
First published 1957 by Pantheon Bks.

This is an historical and cultural survey of Zen, tracing its origins in Indian and Chinese thought. The author describes the Zen way of living and its techniques for overcoming the mind's conflict between symbolic thought and actual experience.

Includes bibliographical references

294.5 Hinduism

Calasso, Roberto

Ardor;   Roberto Calasso; translated from the Italian by Richard Dixon. Farrar Straus & Giroux 2014 432 p. illustrations (some color) (hardback) $35   **294.5**
1. Vedas 2. Hinduism 3. Vedas -- Criticism, interpretation, etc
ISBN 0374182310; 9780374182311
LC 2013044345

This book by Roberto Calasso "explores the ancient texts known as the Vedas. Often at odds with modern thought, these texts illuminate the nature of consciousness more than anybody else has managed up to now. Following the 'hundred paths of the Śatapatha Brāhmaṇa, an impressive exegesis of Vedic ritual, 'Ardor' indicates that it may be possible to reach what is closest to us by passing through that which is most remote." (Publisher's note)

"Richard Dixon's supple and elegant translation brings Calasso's poetic meditations to life. Readers will return again and again for wisdom and insight." Pub Wkly

Davis, Richard H.

The **Bhagavad** Gita; a biography. Richard H. Davis. Princeton University Press 2014 256 p. illustrations (Lives of great religious books) (hardback) $24.95   **294.5**
1. Hinduism 2. Sacred books 3. Bhagavadgītā -- History 4. Bhagavadgītā -- Criticism, interpretation, etc
ISBN 0691139962; 9780691139968
LC 2014023890

This book, by Richard H. Davis, part of the "Lives of great religious books" series, "tells the story of [the Bhagavad Gita,] . . . from its origins in ancient India to its reception today as a spiritual classic that has been translated into more than seventy-five languages. . . . [The author] highlights the place of this legendary dialogue in classical Indian culture, and then examines how it has lived on in diverse settings and contexts." (Publisher's note)

"Davis neatly organizes a great deal of material, and he presents it in utterly accessible prose." Choice

Includes bibliographical references and index

Doniger, Wendy

On Hinduism; Wendy Doniger. Oxford University Press, USA 2014 680 p. (hardback : alk. paper) $39.95   **294.5**
1. Hinduism
ISBN 0199360073; 9780199360079
LC 2013038952

Includes bibliographical references (pages 627-648) and index

This book of essays, by Wendy Doniger, is about Hinduism. "The essays contemplate the nature of Hinduism; Hindu concepts of divinity; attitudes concerning gender, control, and desire; the question of reality and illusion; and the impermanent and the eternal in the two great Sanskrit epics, the 'Ramayana' and the 'Mahabharata.' . . . Doniger concludes with . . . autobiographical essays in which she reflects on . . . the influence of Hinduism on her own philosophy of life." (Publisher's note)

"This book assumes some basic knowledge of the subject, but [Doniger's] writing is clear and direct and will be intelligible to readers unacquainted with the technicalities of Hindu doctrine and literature." LJ

Goldberg, Philip

American Veda; from Emerson and the Beatles to yoga and meditation: how Indian spirituality changed the West. Doubleday Religion 2010 398p il ebook $26; $26   **294.5**
1. Yoga 2. Vedanta 3. Hinduism 4. United States -- Religion
ISBN 978-0-307-71961-4 ebook; 978-0-385-52134-5
LC 2010-11040

"From meditating movie stars, scandalous gurus, and psychedelic drugs to genuine spiritual breakthroughs and devotion to helping others, Goldberg's history of 'American Veda' takes measure of a powerful, if underappreciated, force." Booklist

Includes bibliographical references

Mahabharata/Bhagavadgita

★ **Bhagavad** Gita; a new translation. [translated by] Stephen Mitchell. Harmony Bks. 2000 223p hardcover o.p. pa $13.95   **294.5**
ISBN 0-609-60550-X; 0-609-81034-0 pa
LC 00-28286

"An eighteen-part discussion between the god Krishna, an avatar of Vishnu appearing as a charioteer, and Arjuna, a warrior about to enter battle, on the nature and meaning of life. Sometimes called the New Testament of Hinduism, it is an interpolation in the great Hindu epic the Mahabharata." Reader's Ency. 4th edition

294.6 Sikhism

Singh, Patwant

The **Sikhs**. Knopf 2000 276p il hardcover o.p. pa $14   **294.6**
1. Sikhs
ISBN 0-375-40728-6; 0-385-50206-0 pa
LC 99-31807

The author "traces Sikh history from its origins in the 15th century through Indira Gandhi's 1984 storming of the Golden Temple. . . . Sikhs, he argues, have for centuries been an embattled people because their culture and religion defy the predominant religions in the region, as well as the Indian caste system with its ruling elite." Publ Wkly

Includes bibliographical references

296 Judaism

Bronfman, Edgar M., 1929-2013

Why be Jewish? a testament. Edgar M. Bronfman. Twelve 2016 256 p. (hardback) $26 **296**
1. Judaism 2. Jews -- Identity 3. Jewish way of life 4. Judaism -- Essence, genius, nature
ISBN 9781455562886; 9781455562893; 9781478961024

LC 2015039135

In this book, author Edgar M. Bronfman "walks readers through the major tenets and ideas in Jewish life. . . . Bronfman shares . . . insights gleaned from his own personal journey and makes a compelling case for the meaning and transcendence of a secular Judaism that is still steeped in deep moral values, authentic Jewish texts, and a focus on deed over creed or dogma." (Publisher's note)

"Excellent for nontheistic and unaffiliated readers, Jewish or not, who want to better understand this religion." LJ

Includes bibliographical references and index

The **Cambridge** history of Judaism; v2 edited by W.D. Davies [and] Louis Finkelstein; assistant editor, John Sturdy. Cambridge Univ. Press 1990 738p v2 il maps $205 **296**
1. Judaism -- History
ISBN 0-521-21929-9

This "second volume in the four-volume Cambridge History of Judaism deals with Judaism's encounter with Hellenism under Alexander the Great and his successors, the efforts of Jews led by the Maccabees to counter this influence and to establish their own state and the resulting Jewish ideologies and literary activities. The 18 chapters treat the archaeology of Hellenistic Palestine, languages, the interpenetration of Judaism and Hellenism in the pre-Maccabean period, the Hasmonean revolt and dynasty, the matrix of apocalyptic and the Samaritans, as well as various writings and historical movements." America

Includes bibliographical references

Encyclopaedia Judaica; Fred Skolnik, editor-in-chief; Michael Berenbaum, executive editor. 2nd ed; Macmillan Reference USA in association with the Keter Pub. House 2007 22v il map **296**
1. Jews 2. Judaism 3. Reference books 4. Judaism -- Encyclopedias
ISBN 0-02-865928-7; 978-0-02-865928-2

LC 2006020426

First published 1972 in 16 volumes

ALA RUSA Dartmouth Medal (2007)

This "is a welcome addition to reference collections. By documenting the modern Jewish experience while retaining links with its rich past, it provides users with information about all aspects of Jewish religion and culture." Booklist

Includes bibliographical references

Freedman, Samuel G.

Jew vs. Jew; the struggle for the soul of American Jewry. Simon & Schuster 2000 397p $26; pa $14 **296**
1. Judaism 2. Jews -- United States
ISBN 0-684-85944-0; 0-684-85945-9 pa

LC 00-33907

The author "describes the paradoxical situation faced by today's American Jews, living in a country where religious freedom has yielded unreconcilable devisiveness. . . . This is a helpful guide for anyone seeking an understanding of intra-Jewish conflicts in contemporary America." Libr J

Includes bibliographical references

The **New** encyclopedia of Judaism; editor-in-chief, Geoffrey Wigoder; coeditors, Fred Skolnik & Shmuel Himelstein. New York Univ. Press 2002 856p il $79.95 **296**
1. Reference books 2. Judaism -- Dictionaries
ISBN 0-8147-9388-6

LC 2002-16614

First published 1989 with title: The Encyclopedia of Judaism

This reference "seeks to present a balanced picture, offering current thinking among scholars in Reform, Conservative, and Orthodox movements and a roster of contributors hailing from Israel, England, and the United States. While the scholarship is solid, the material is readily accessible to a popular audience, and the work is magnificently illustrated." Libr J

Includes bibliographical references

The **Oxford** dictionary of the Jewish religion; editor in chief, Adele Berlin. 2nd ed. Oxford University Press 2011 xxiv, 934 p.p (hardcover) $195 **296**
1. Judaism -- Dictionaries 2. Judaism -- Encyclopedias
ISBN 0199730040; 9780199730049; 9780199759279

LC 2010035774

This book, by Maxine Grossman, edited by Adele Berlin, presents an updated, second edition of its original 1997 publication. It "focuses on recent and changing rituals in the Jewish community. . . . Nearly 200 internationally renowned scholars have created a new edition that incorporates updated bibliographies, biographies of 20th-century individuals who have shaped the recent thought and history of Judaism, and an index with alternate spellings of Hebrew terms." (Publisher's note)

Includes bibliographical references and index.

Reader's guide to Judaism; editor, Michael Terry. Fitzroy Dearborn Pubs. 2000 718p (Reader's guide) $135 **296**
1. Reference books 2. Judaism -- Encyclopedias
ISBN 1-57958-139-0

LC 2001-274119

This "work covers over 400 topics, including interfaith relations, historical periods, philosophical and mystical movements, important figures, and more. Preceding each essay is a bibliography of five to ten English-language titles. . . . Written by librarians and scholars . . . these 1000 to 2000-word essays include a descriptive and often analytical overview of each book. . . . This is an excellent tool for building Judaica collections in public and academic libraries." Libr J

Includes bibliographical references

Robinson, George

Essential Judaism; a complete guide to beliefs, customs and rituals. Pocket Bks. 2000 xxi, 644p hardcover o.p. pa $20   **296**

1. Judaism

ISBN 0-671-03480-4; 0-671-03481-2 pa

LC 99-55288

This book "attempts to provide the essentials of Judaism for novices, outsiders and those who, like Robinson, rediscovered their heritage as adults. It's an excellent introductory resource, vast but accessibly organized." Publ Wkly

Includes bibliographical references

Sarna, Jonathan D.

★ **American** Judaism; a history. Yale University Press 2004 xx, 490p il $35   **296**

1. Judaism 2. Jews -- United States

ISBN 0-300-10197-X

LC 2003-14464

"This comprehensive and insightful study of the American Jewish experience is much more than just a record of events. It is an account of how people shaped events: establishing and maintaining communities, responding to challenges, and working for change. It is compelling reading for Jews and non-Jews alike." Booklist

Includes bibliographical references

296.09   History, geographic treatment, biography

The **Cambridge** history of Judaism; v3 edited by William Horbury, John Sturdy and W.D. Davies. Cambridge Univ. Press 1999 1254p v3 il maps $190   **296.09**

1. Judaism -- History

ISBN 0-521-24377-7

This third volume of a four-volume history "contains thirty-two essays on aspects of Judaism in the early Roman period, primarily the period between Pompey and Vespasian but often ranging into the rabbinic period." J Relig

Includes bibliographical references

Cole, Peter

★ **Sacred** trash; [by] Adina Hoffman & Peter Cole. Nextbook : Schocken 2011 283p. ill., ports.   **296.09**

1. Manuscripts 2. Jews -- History 3. Cultural property 4. Cairo Genizah 5. Judaism -- History -- Sources

ISBN 978-0-8052-4258-4; 0-8052-4258-9

LC 201016751

Sophie Brody Award (2012)

This is an account of the discovery, about 120 years ago, of a cache of documents in the storeroom of a synagogue in Cairo. The cache, referred to as a geniza, includes "letters, wills, bills of lading, prayers, marriage contracts and writs of divorce, Bibles, money orders, court depositions, business inventories, leases, magic charms and receipts." (N Y Times Book Rev)

Includes bibliographical references.

296.1   Sources

Abegg, Martin G.

The **Dead** Sea scrolls; a new translation. [by] Michael O. Wise, Martin G. Abegg Jr., and Edward M. Cook. Rev ed; HarperSanFrancisco 2005 662p pa $24.95   **296.1**

ISBN 0-06-076662-X

LC 2005-46285

First published 1996

"An engaging necessity for updating Dead Sea Scrolls collections." Booklist

Includes bibliographical references

The **Encyclopedia** of the Dead Sea scrolls; {edited by} Lawrence H. Schiffman and James C. VanderKam. Oxford Univ. Press 2000 2v set $295   **296.1**

1. Dead Sea scrolls

ISBN 0-19-508450-0

LC 99-55300

"In addition to individual texts, coverage extends to the archeological sites themselves; important historical figures (Moses) and groups (Essenes, Pharisees) as they are represented in the scrolls; scholars important to Dead Sea scroll research . . . and methods employed both to date and to preserve these ancient documents." Booklist

Freedman, Harry

The **Talmud**; A Biography - Banned, Censored and Burned. the Book They Couldn't Suppress. St. Martin's Press 2014 256 p. $26   **296.1**

1. Jewish diaspora 2. Talmud -- Biography

ISBN 1472905946; 9781472905949

LC 2015376128

In this book, "Jewish scholar Harry Freedman tells the . . . story of an ancient classic, the legal and mystical pillar of Judaism and recounts the story of a book which, in many ways, parallels the history of the Jewish people. . . . Freedman traces the spiraling paths of the Jewish diaspora and explores the story of the Talmud's early origins in Babylon, its role during the Enlightenment and its influence over traditional Judaism." (Publisher's note)

"Freedman (independent scholar) makes clear that this is no academic volume; his goal is to make the Talmud's story interesting and perhaps even inspiring to the unacquainted reader." Choice

Golb, Norman

Who wrote the Dead Sea scrolls? the search for the secret of Qumran. Scribner 1995 446p il maps hardcover o.p. pa $22 **296.1**

1. Dead Sea scrolls 2. Judaism -- History
ISBN 0-684-80692-4 pa

LC 94-23295

"This is an archival book that should be considered for any collection dealing with the Dead Sea Scrolls. It is well written and can be read by the interested person as well as by the professional scholar." Choice

Includes bibliographical references

Schiffman, Lawrence H.

Reclaiming the Dead Sea scrolls; the history of Judaism, the background of Christianity, the lost library of Qumran. with a foreword by Chaim Potok. Jewish Publ. Soc. 1994 xxvii, 529p il maps **296.1**

1. Dead Sea scrolls 2. Judaism -- History

LC 94-26489

Schiffman provides a "description and evaluation of the scrolls, the archeology of Qumran (the site near the Dead Sea from which the scrolls originated), the history and nature of the Jewish community that lived at Qumran and the setting of the scrolls in Jewish history and thought from the second century B.C. through the first century A.D." N Y Times Book Rev

Includes bibliographical references

296.3 Theology, ethics, views of social issues

Epstein, Lawrence J.

The **basic** beliefs of Judaism; a twenty-first-century guide to a timeless tradition. Lawrence J. Epstein. Jason Aronson 2013 203 p. (cloth : alk. paper) $35 **296.3**

1. Judaism 2. Jews -- Social life and customs 3. Jewish way of life
ISBN 0765709694; 9780765709691; 9780765709707
LC 2013015985

In this book, Lawrence J. Epstein "culls from nearly 3,000 years of Jewish moral, ethical, and philosophical thought to present an overview of fundamentals for an educated, 21st-century audience. In ten chapters, he discusses themes such as the mystery of God, the suffering of the innocent, and ethical foundations for a good life, from a broad array of Jewish perspectives." (Choice: Current Reviews for Academic Libraries)

Includes bibliographical references and index

Kushner, Harold S.

★ **When** bad things happen to good people; with a new preface by the author. 20th anniversary ed; Schocken Bks. 2001 202p $21 **296.3**

1. Suffering 2. Providence and government of God
ISBN 0-8052-4193-0

LC 2001-531062

A reissue of the title first published 1981

"A bright and happy infant, Rabbi Kushner's first-born son gradually succumbed to progeria, 'rapid aging': he nev-

er grew beyond three feet tall, looked like a hairless, wizened old man, and died in his teens. This book is his father's attempt to make sense out of his son's fate, his own pain, and the pain of others enduring undeserved misfortunes." Libr J

Telushkin, Joseph

Jewish wisdom; ethical, spiritual, and historical lessons from the great works and thinkers. {by} Rabbi Joseph Telushkin. Morrow 1994 xxiv, 663p $26 **296.3**

1. Judaism 2. Jewish ethics
ISBN 0-688-12958-7

LC 94-9186

"Organized by subject, this is a collection of teachings and quotations from the Talmud, the Bible, rabbinical commentaries, and ancient and modern religious and secular writings. Writers include Elie Wiesel, Isaac Bashevis Singer, Hebrew poet Hayim Bialik, Cynthia Ozick, Emile Zola, Albert Einstein, Bruno Bettelheim, Gertrude Stein, Irving Howe, and Maimonides. . . . Jews—and even non-Jews—will find the book a treasure." Booklist

Includes bibliographical references

296.4 Traditions, rites, public services

Ashton, Dianne

Hanukkah in America; a history. by Dianne Ashton. New York University Press 2013 368 p. illustrations (The Goldstein-Goren series in American Jewish history) (cl : alk. paper) $29.95 **296.4**

1. Hanukkah 2. Jews -- United States 3. Hanukkah -- United States 4. Judaism -- United States -- History -- 21st century
ISBN 0814707394; 9780814707395

LC 2013014009

In this history of Hanukkah in the U.S. author Diane Ashton argues that the holiday "has been a vehicle for asserting solidarity among a never-large American minority and establishing that minority's credentials as faithful Americans as well as faithful Jews. Further, Ashton asserts, Hanukkah has always played a role in response to the successive challenges American Jews have faced over the course of the last century and a half." (Booklist)

"... Ashton demonstrates how such influences shaped a minor holiday into what today is perhaps the signal celebration of the American Jewish year. Through engaging and exacting detail, she treats her readers to an inside look at the evolving American Jewish psyche, as it is played out in American homes and synagogue celebrations. In so doing, she articulates an important point toward understanding religion in general: Hanukkah has evolved so as to narrate the story of the Maccabees in ways that meet the distinctive needs of successive generations of Jews." Choice

Includes bibliographical references and index

Axelrod, Matt

Your guide to the Jewish holidays; from shofar to Seder. cantor Matt Axelrod. Jason Aronson 2013 214 p. (cloth : alk. paper) $30 **296.4**
1. Jewish holidays 2. Fasts and feasts -- Judaism
ISBN 0765709899; 9780765709899; 9780765709905
LC 2013033886

This book, by cantor Matt Axelrod, "takes a . . . look at the 11 most important Jewish holidays. Instead of simply explaining that Jews are obligated to observe in a certain way because of a biblical text, Axelrod shows where each holiday, along with its rituals, came from in a historical context. He provides a humorous retelling of the biblical passages relating to the holiday, explorations of rituals associated with each holiday, and descriptions of traditional foods." (Publisher's note)

Bolsta, Hyla Shifra

The **illuminated** Kaddish; interpretations of the Mourner's Prayer. paintings, calligraphy, and interpretations by Hyla Shifra Bolsta. KTAV Pub. House, Inc. 2012 108 p. col. ill. $27.50 **296.4**
1. Prayer 2. Judaism -- Customs and practices 3. Illumination of books and manuscripts 4. Kaddish 5. Judaism -- Liturgy -- Texts 6. Jewish illumination of books and manuscripts
ISBN 1602801916; 9781602801912
LC 2011033483

This book from author and illustrator Hyla Bolsta is an illuminated version of the Kaddish, "a prayer recited as part of the funeral rites of a Jewish believer." Here, "she connects the words throughout by a motif of leaves and branches from the tree of life." The prayer "is a kind of perennial puzzle . . . . Why praise God, in the words of Ezekiel, rather than mourn the death? Bolsta's scholarship, insights, and art suggest some answers." (Library Journal)

Includes bibliographical references

Eisenberg, Ronald L.

★ The **JPS** guide to Jewish traditions; [by] Ron Eisenberg. The Jewish Publication Society 2004 xxiii, 806p $40 **296.4**
1. Reference books 2. Judaism -- Encyclopedias
ISBN 0-8276-0760-1
LC 2004-6399

This "work covers the major elements of Jewish life, including life-cycle events (birth, bar and bat mitzvah, marriage, divorce, parenting, and death), the Sabbath and holidays, the synagogue, prayer, and the Bible and Jewish literature. . . . The author has done a masterful job in distilling the major beliefs and practices of a 3,000-year-old religion into lively and informative prose and in creating an accessible, essential reference work." Booklist

Includes bibliographical references

Goldman, Ari L.

Being Jewish; the spiritual and cultural practice of Judaism today. Simon & Schuster 2000 286p $25 **296.4**
1. Jewish holidays 2. Judaism -- Customs and practices
ISBN 0-684-82389-6
LC 00-44047

"An excellent resource." Booklist
Includes bibliographical references

★ **New** American Haggadah; edited by Jonathan Safran Foer; with a new translation by Nathan Englander; designed by Oded Ezer; commentaries by Nathaniel Deutsch ("House of Study") ... [et al.]; timeline created by Mia Sara Bruch. Little, Brown & Co. 2012 149 p. ill. $29.99 **296.4**
1. Seder 2. Prayers 3. Jews -- History 4. Rites and ceremonies 5. Haggadah 6. Haggadot -- Texts 7. Seder -- Liturgy -- Texts 8. Judaism -- Liturgy -- Texts
ISBN 0316069868; 9780316069861
LC 2011040637

Author Jonathan Foer retells a major story in Jewish history. "Read each year around the seder table, the Haggadah recounts through prayer, song, and ritual the extraordinary story of Exodus, when Moses led the Israelites out of slavery in Egypt to wander the desert for forty years before reaching the Promised Land. . . . [This prayer book includes] commentary by major Jewish writers and thinkers [including] Jeffrey Goldberg, Lemony Snicket, Rebecca Newberger Goldstein, and Nathaniel Deutsch." (Publisher's note)

Shulevitz, Judith

The **Sabbath** world; glimpses of a different order of time. Random House 2010 246p $26 **296.4**
1. Sabbath 2. Rest -- Religious aspects 3. Time -- Religious aspects
ISBN 978-1-4000-6200-3; 1-4000-6200-4
LC 2009-26417

"In personal terms, and without sanctimony, [the author] explores the history of the Sabbath, its philosophical foundations, its consolations, its purposes, and, in doing so, writes a swift, penetrating book intent on shattering the habits of mindless workaholism and the inability to recognize the blessings of rest, reflection, spirit, and family." New Yorker

Wagner, Jordan Lee

The **synagogue** survival kit; A Guide to Understanding Jewish Religious Services. Jordan Lee Wagner. Jason Aronson 1997 xvi, 347 p.p illustrations $35 **296.4**
1. Synagogues 2. Siddur 3. Prayer -- Judaism 4. Judaism -- Liturgy 5. Synagogue etiquette 8. Judaism -- Customs and practices
ISBN 0765709686; 1568219679; 9780765709684; 9781568219677
LC 96039695

This book, by Jordan Lee Wagner, "offers introductions and instructions for all aspects of the synagogue experience. No matter what kind of synagogue you attend, the roadmap is the same. Some synagogues may read certain prayers in English translation rather than the original Hebrew or replace some traditional prayers with newer versions, but the service will still touch on the same topics in the same order for the same reasons." (Publisher's note)

"Extensive notes follow each chapter, and a cross-reference to selections in the most commonly used prayer books fleshes out this carefully crafted primer, which is perfect for

Jews rediscovering their own traditions, Jews by choice and others who wish to participate in Jewish events." Pub Wkly

Includes bibliographical references and index

Wieseltier, Leon

Kaddish. Knopf 1998 588p $27.50; pa $16 **296.4**

1. Funeral rites and ceremonies 2. Kaddish 3. Judaism -- Customs and practices

ISBN 0-375-40389-2; 0-375-70362-4 pa

LC 98-15881

"When his father died in 1996 . . . Wieseltier began to observe the Jewish rituals of the traditional year of mourning. His own mourning led him to an in-depth study of the history and meaning of Kaddish in Judaism. Wieseltier provides a work of history, philosophy and spiritual memoir that demonstrates how the practice of religion meets the needs of a troubled soul." Publ Wkly

296.7   Religious experience, life, practice

Davidson, Sara

The **December** Project; an extraordinary Rabbi and a skeptical seeker confront life's greatest mystery. Sara Davidson. HarperOne 2014 224 p. **296.7**

1. Death 2. Rabbis 3. Skepticism 4. Self-actualization (Psychology) -- Religious aspects -- Judaism

ISBN 9780062281746; 9780062281753; 0062281755

LC 2013020725

National Jewish Book Award Finalist: Contemporary Jewish Life and Practice (2014)

"Author Sara Davidson met every Friday with 89-year-old Rabbi Zalman Shachter-Shalomi, the iconic founder of the Jewish Renewal movement. This is Davidson's memoir of what they learned and how they changed. Interspersed with their talks are sketches from Reb Zalman's extraordinary life. Together they created strategies to deal with pain and memory loss, and found tools to cultivate simplicity, fearlessness, and joy." (Publisher's note)

"Both a kind of biography of Zalman and a moving manual on dying, this book should reach far beyond a Jewish or aging readership." LJ

Diamant, Anita

Pitching my tent; on marriage, motherhood, friendship, and other leaps of faith. Scribner 2003 223p hardcover o.p. pa $15 **296.7**

1. Jewish women

ISBN 0-7432-4616-0; 0-7432-4617-9 pa

LC 2003-45440

"This collection of short essays, culled primarily from the Boston Globe Sunday Magazine and then reworked, . . . [are] organized around such themes as love and marriage, child rearing, friendship and living a religious life. . . . The book's strength lies in its woman-to-woman conversational tone, especially in the opening section about married life and its dark side. . . . These morsels will make a tasty snack for Diamant's admirers." Publ Wkly

Isaacs, Ronald H.

★ **Kosher** living; it's more than just the food. [by] Ron Isaacs. Jossey-Bass 2005 xlvii, 286p $22.95 **296.7**

1. Judaism -- Customs and practices

ISBN 0-7879-7642-3

LC 2004-26727

"The book not only covers the expected Jewish topics— circumcision, marriage, prayer, Shabbat, synagogue behavior and more—but also . . . [items] such as employer-employee relations, shopping and even war. . . . This resource offers timeless wisdom through a contemporary lens." Publ Wkly

Includes bibliographical references

Kushner, Harold S.

How good do we have to be? a new understanding of guilt and forgiveness. Little, Brown 1996 181p hardcover o.p. pa $11.95 **296.7**

1. Guilt 2. Good and evil 3. Bible -- O.T. -- Genesis -- Criticism

ISBN 0-316-51933-2 pa

LC 95-25350

"This is one psychological self-help book that deserves the popularity it is likely to achieve." Booklist

Who needs God; [by] Harold Kushner. Fireside 2002 212p pa $14 **296.7**

1. God -- Judaism

ISBN 0-7432-3477-4

First published 1989 by Summit Bks.

The author "believes that 'human life has meaning . . . but only in religious terms.' According to this crucial realization, it is religion that connects us to God and community." Libr J

Levy, Naomi

To begin again; a journey toward comfort, strength, and faith in difficult times. Knopf 1998 267p hardcover o.p. pa $12.95 **296.7**

1. Bereavement 2. Judaism -- Customs and practices

ISBN 0-345-41383-0 pa

LC 98-16024

"A wise and practical guide for readers of any religious persuasion." Libr J

Reuben, Steven Carr

★ **Becoming** Jewish; the challenges, rewards, and paths to conversion. [by] Steven Carr Reuben and Jennifer S. Hanin; [foreword by Bab Saget] Rowman & Littlefield Publishers 2011 256p $22.95; ebook $22.95 **296.7**

1. Conversion 2. Converts to Judaism

ISBN 978-1-4422-0848-3; 978-1-4422-0849-0 ebook

LC 2011014083

"The authors explain such details as finding the right denomination, choosing a rabbi, selecting a Hebrew name, and the need to learn Hebrew. They also discuss Jewish culture and beliefs, holidays, and traditions. Chapters on telling family and friends about the decision to convert, raising Jewish children, kabbalah, anti-Semitism, and Israel help those converting understand important issues. . . . Written in a casual, friendly style with good humor and warmth, this accessible guide will help anyone considering conversion to Judaism." Booklist

297 Islam, Babism, Bahai Faith

Armstrong, Karen
★ **Islam**; a short history. Modern Lib. 2000
xxxiv, 222p maps $19.95; pa $11.95   **297**
1. Islam
ISBN 0-679-64040-1; 0-8129-6618-X pa
LC 00-25285
This history of the Islamic faith focuses on the religion's attitude toward politics
The author "does an admirable job of presenting Islamic history from an objective, unbiased point of view." Libr J
Includes bibliographical references

Muhammad; a prophet for our time. Atlas Books/HarperCollins Publishers 2006 249p map (Eminent lives) $21.95; pa $14.95   **297**
1. Islam 2. Prophets 3. Islamic leaders 4. Writers on religion
ISBN 0-06-059897-2; 978-0-06-059897-6; 0-06-115577-2 pa; 978-0-06-115577-2 pa
LC 2006-45864
First published 1991 in the United Kingdom with subtitle: A Western attempt to understand Islam; Original American edition published 1992 with subtitle: A biography of the prophet
This is a biography of the founder of Islam.
"Readers of these pages cannot escape the genius of Muhammad and his aim for peace and compassion among nations and among Muslims themselves. . . . Recommended for all libraries." Libr J
Includes bibliographical references

Aslan, Reza
★ **No** god but God; the origins, evolution, and future of Islam. Random House 2005 xxiv, 310p $25.95; pa $14.95   **297**
1. Islam
ISBN 1-4000-6213-6; 0-8129-7189-2 pa
LC 2004-54053
"Beginning with an exploration of the religious climate in the years before the Prophet's Revelation, Aslan traces the story of Islam from the Prophet's life and the so-called golden age of the first four caliphs all the way through European colonization and subsequent independence. . . . This is an excellent overview that doubles as an impassioned call to reform." Booklist
Includes bibliographical references

Bawer, Bruce
Surrender; appeasing Islam, sacrificing freedom. Doubleday 2009 321p $24.95   **297**
1. Freedom of speech 2. Islam -- Relations
ISBN 978-0-385-52398-1; 0-385-52398-X
LC 2008-35743

"Bawer files a hefty brief of case reports on Muslim campaigns against free speech, primarily in western Europe but also in Canada and the U.S. Official infatuation with political correctness (PC), the determination that no one ever be offended, and multiculturalism, the dogma that all cultural perspectives are equally and universally valid, undergird what Bawer believes amounts to a surrender of Western liberal traditions. What may seal the fate of free speech, he argues, are the apparent inabilities of Western ruling elites to be offended by Muslims rioting, threatening by fatwa, and murdering non-Muslims . . . and to assert the priority of Western liberal values in the West. . . . Sublimely literate and rational, Bawer is no crank, however angry he gets." Booklist
Includes bibliographical references

Ben Jelloun, Tahar
Islam explained. New Press (NY) 2002 120p hardcover o.p. pa $13.95   **297**
1. Islam
ISBN 1-56584-781-4; 1-56584-897-7 pa
LC 2002-30500
"Cast in the form of an extended conversation between Ben Jelloun and his young daughter. . . . Father and child discuss the history of Islam, what it means to be a Muslim today, the challenges facing the Islamic world, and terrorism. . . . Its openness and emotional honesty, particularly when discussing the tragedy of 9/11, make it a valuable addition to a growing public discourse. As an introduction to the religion, it is spotty, but as a liberal Muslim voice of reconciliation, heartbreak, and compassion, it is priceless." Booklist

Campo, Juan Eduardo
Encyclopedia of Islam; [by] Juan E. Campo. Facts On File 2008 750p il map (Encyclopedia of world religions) $85   **297**
1. Reference books 2. Islam -- Encyclopedias
ISBN 978-0-8160-5454-1; 0-8160-5454-1
LC 2008-5621
"In about 600 A-to-Z entries, this encyclopedic guide explores the terms, concepts, personalities, historical events, and institutions that helped shape the history of this religion and the way it is practiced today." Publisher's note
Includes bibliographical references

Ernst, Carl W.
Following Muhammad; rethinking Islam in the contemporary world. University of North Carolina Press 2003 244p il (Islamic civilization & Muslim networks) $24.95; pa $16.95   **297**
1. Islam
ISBN 0-8078-2837-8; 0-8078-5577-4 pa
LC 2003-11162
The author "informs readers of the roles played by colonialism, Christian missionary efforts, and Western conceptions of just what 'religion' is, all in relation to American conceptions of Islam." Libr J
Includes bibliographical references

Esposito, John L., 1940-

Islam; the straight path. Rev. 3rd ed., updated with new epilogue; Oxford University Press 2005 304p map pa $39.95   **297**

1. Islam

ISBN 0-19-518266-9

    LC 2004-61688

First published 1988

This "survey text introduces the faith, belief, and practice of Islam from its earliest origins up to its contemporary resurgence." Publisher's note

Includes bibliographical references

What everyone needs to know about Islam. Oxford Univ. Press 2002 204p $18.95   **297**

1. Islam

ISBN 0-19-515713-3

    LC 2002-8387

In question-and-answer format the author presents information on a variety of aspects of Islam. The "format allows readers to skip ahead to areas that interest them, including hot-button issues such as 'Why are Muslims so violent?' or 'Why do Muslim women wear veils and long garments?' In his answers, which are anywhere from a paragraph to several pages long, Esposito elegantly educates the reader through what the Qur'an says, how Muslims are influenced by their local cultures, and how the unique politics of Islamic countries affects Muslims' views." Publ Wkly

Includes bibliographical references

Fuller, Graham E., 1937-

A **world** without Islam. Little, Brown and Co. 2010 328p $25.99   **297**

1. East and West 2. Islamic civilization 3. Islam -- History 4. Islam -- Relations

ISBN 978-0-316-04119-5; 978-0-316-07201-4 ebook

    LC 2009-54078

"A cogent argument demonstrating that a knowledgeable awareness of the rich dynamics that drive societies will better help diffuse tensions." Kirkus

Includes bibliographical references

Gardell, Mattias

In the name of Elijah Muhammad; Louis Farrakhan and the Nation of Islam. Duke Univ. Press 1996 482p (C. Eric Lincoln series on the black experience) $59.95; pa $23.95   **297**

1. Black Muslims 2. Black Muslim leaders 3. Civil rights activists

ISBN 0-8223-1852-0; 0-8223-1845-8 pa

    LC 96-22666

"Some will appreciate the author's brief critical airing of claims of pre-Columbian Africans in America and accounts of Muslims and the slave trade, but he is at his best when focusing on the leaders and on the changing theology of the Nation of Islam (NOI) and similar African American groups in the 20th-century US. The book is balanced and well researched." Choice

Includes bibliographical references

Glassé, Cyril

The **new** encyclopedia of Islam; Cyril Glassé. Rowman & Littlefield Pub Inc 2013 736 p. ill., maps $95   **297**

1. Islam 2. Muslims

ISBN 1442223480; 9781442223486

This book, by Cyril Glassé, "revised, updated, and re-designed in a fresh larger-format, with more than 1,500 entries . . . [is] a single-volume work that encompasses the beliefs, practices, history, and culture of the Islamic world. . . . In this expanded new edition, with an extensive chronology, Cyril Glasse provides a . . . study of one of the world's great religions." (Publisher's note)

"This beautifully illustrated and clearly written book provides a myriad of facts and insights about Islam that many readers--novices and scholars alike--will find informative, interesting, and enlightening." Choice

Gordon, Matthew

Understanding Islam; origins, beliefs, practices, holy texts, sacred places. [by] Matthew S. Gordon. Sterling Pub. Co. 2010 112p pa $9.95   **297**

1. Islam

ISBN 978-1-90748-616-6

    LC 2010-2376

First published 2001 by Facts on File

This "exploration of Islam's history, beliefs, and practices . . . [addresses] issues such as political Islam, Islam and Israel, and Islamic fundamentalism." Publisher's note

Includes bibliographical references

Grieve, Paul

★ A **brief** guide to Islam; history, faith and politics: the complete introduction. Carroll & Graf 2006 433p il map pa $13.95   **297**

1. Islam

ISBN 0-7867-1804-8; 978-0-7867-1804-7

    LC 2006-282191

"If you read only one book about Islam this year, this should be it." Publ Wkly

Griswold, Eliza

The **tenth** parallel; dispatches from the fault line between Christianity and Islam. Farrar, Straus and Giroux 2010 317p il map $27; ebook $12.99 **297**

1. Christianity and other religions 2. Islam -- Relations -- Christianity

ISBN 978-0-374-27318-7; 0-374-27318-9; 978-1-4299-7966-5 ebook; 1-4299-7966-6 ebook

    LC 2010-1480

This "is a beautifully written book, full of arresting stories woven around a provocative issue—whether fundamentalism leads to violence—which Griswold investigates through individual lives rather than caricatures or abstractions." N Y Times Book Rev

Includes bibliographical references

Hazleton, Lesley

After the prophet; the epic story of the Shia-Sunni split in Islam. Doubleday 2009 239p map $26.95 **297**

1. Shi'ah 2. Sunnis 3. Prophets 4. Imams 5. Caliphs 6. Islamic leaders 7. Islam -- History 8. Writers on religion 9. Spouses of prominent persons

ISBN 978-0-385-52393-6

LC 2009-6498

"In June 632, the founder of Islam died without having clearly designated a successor. It seemed obvious to some that Muhammad's first cousin, Ali, who occupied the place of a son in the prophet's circle, would assume leadership. But Aisha, Muhammad's favorite, youngest, and most forceful wife, favored her father, and others backed Muhammad's greatest warrior. Ali would succeed, but not until 25 years later. Thus began the turmoil that eventuated in the bisection of Muslims into Sunni and Shia and that Hazleton describes in a new masterpiece of a kind of history seldom seen these days, in which the telling of a complicated, eventful story takes precedence over constant quotation of documents and squabbling with other historians." Booklist

Includes bibliographical references

Islam in der Gegenwart./English.

★ Islam in the world today; a handbook of politics, religion, culture, and society. edited by Werner Ende and Udo Steinbach. Cornell University Press 2010 1114p il $85 **297**

1. Islamic civilization 2. Islam -- History

ISBN 978-0-8014-4571-2

LC 2009-39910

First published 1989 in Germany

This is "one of the most authoritative works on Islam in the modern world. . . . The volume is divided into three parts; the first is a historical overview of the Islamic world from its beginnings in the seventh century to the present, including a description of the different sects and movements of Islam and their influence in the world today. The second, and most extensive, section discusses the political role of Islam in the modern world, Islamic economics, social systems, and law. . . . The final section describes Islamic culture and civilization, including art, literature, and architecture, and their intersection with the West." Libr J

Includes bibliographical references

Johnson, Ian

A mosque in Munich; Nazis, the CIA, and the Muslim brotherhood in the West. Houghton Mifflin Harcourt 2010 318p $27 **297**

1. Mosques 2. Cold war 3. Islam and politics 4. Islamic fundamentalism 5. Cold War 6. Munich (Germany) 7. Mosques -- Germany 8. Islamic Brotherhood 9. Islamic fundamentalism -- Germany 10. United States -- Central Intelligence Agency

ISBN 978-0-15-101418-7; 0-15-101418-3

LC 2009-35285

"Mr. Johnson brings to life a previously overlooked episode in the Muslim Brotherhood's story and thus in the story of Islamism as a whole: How a radical European beachhead came to be established in Munich. It should be said that the story takes some confusing turns; even alert readers may

find themselves flipping to the list of characters at the back of the book, or to the index, to help them follow the narrative. But many of the details are astonishing and the larger implications for our own time disturbing." Wall Street J

Includes bibliographical references

Karsh, Efraim

Islamic imperialism; a history. Yale University Press 2006 276p map $30 **297**

1. Jihad 2. Imperialism 3. Islam and politics

ISBN 0-300-10603-3

LC 2005-34836

The author "surveys for a general audience the region's Islamic political past. Parallel to his narrative, Karsh frequently contrasts the universalistic proclamations of Islam with cycles of imperial consolidation and fragmentation. After recounting the Prophet Muhammad's religio-political establishment of Islam, and the discord about his legacy that continues today, Karsh narrates the battles over Muhammad's caliphate that eventuated in the Umayyad and Abbasid Empires. Karsh's commentary often looks forward to contemporary ideologues of Islam who ransack history to justify grievances. . . . An informative foundation for further exploration of Islamic history." Libr J

Kepel, Gilles

Jihad; the trail of political Islam. translated by Anthony F. Roberts. Harvard Univ. Press 2002 454p $33.95; pa $15.95 **297**

1. Islam and politics

ISBN 0-674-00877-4; 0-674-01090-6 pa

LC 2002-17181

Original French edition, 2000

"Kepel argues that the terrorism seen today throughout the world results from the failure of Islamic fundamentalism and not its success. . . . Fascinating despite its copious detail." Booklist

Kugle, Scott Siraj al-Haqq

Living out Islam; voices of gay, lesbian, and transgender Muslims. Scott Siraj al-Haqq Kugle. NYU Press 2014 x, 265 p.p (hardback) $85 **297**

1. Homosexuality 2. Islam -- Customs and practices 3. Homosexuality -- Religious aspects -- Islam

ISBN 0814744486; 9780814744482; 9781479894673

LC 2013023734

Stonewall Book Award: Nonfiction (2015)

This book "documents the rarely-heard voices of Muslims who live in secular democratic countries and who are gay, lesbian, and transgender. It weaves original interviews with Muslim activists into a compelling composite picture which showcases the importance of the solidarity of support groups in the effort to change social relationships and achieve justice." (Publisher's note)

Includes bibliographical references and index

Lewis, Bernard

★ The crisis of Islam; holy war and unholy terror. Modern Library 2003 xxxii, 184p map hardcover o.p. pa $13.95 **297**

1. Islam and politics 2. Islamic fundamentalism 3.

Terrorism -- Religious aspects
ISBN 0-679-64281-1; 0-8129-6785-2 pa
LC 2002-45219

"Written in an easily accessible style, this analysis provides a digestible overview for Westerners still asking why." Booklist

Includes bibliographical references

The **Many** faces of Islam; perspectives on a resurgent civilization. Nissim Rejwan {editor} University Press of Fla. 2000 282p $55 **297**
1. Islam 2. Islamic countries -- Politics and government
ISBN 0-8130-1807-2
LC 00-32587

The editor offers "perspectives on modern Islamic culture and religious practice. Seeking to dispel the perception that Islamic fundamentalism and extremism represent Islam in its entirety, Rejwan surveys the issues and provides numerous excerpts from modern writers and scholars, Muslim and non-Muslim, summarizing the many problems and dilemmas facing contemporary Muslims." Univ. Press Books for Public and Second Sch Libr, 2001

Nasr, Seyyed Hossein
Islam: religion, history, and civilization. HarperSanFrancisco 2002 xx, 198p pa $12.95 **297**
1. Islam 2. Islamic civilization
ISBN 0-06-050714-4
LC 2002-32810

This introduction to the world of Islam explores the following topics: What is Islam?; The doctrines and beliefs of Islam; Islamic practices and institutions; The history of Islam; Schools of Islamic thought; Islam in the contemporary world; Islam and other religions; The spiritual and religious significance of Islam

"Provides compelling analysis of contemporary Islam and its conflicts without overwhelming the reader with information." Booklist

Includes bibliographical references

Nasr, Vali
★ The **Shia** revival; how conflicts within Islam will shape the future. Norton 2006 287p map $25.95 **297**
1. Shi'ah 2. Islam and politics
ISBN 0-393-06211-2; 978-0-393-06211-3
LC 2006-12361

"So enlightening and perspective altering that no one concerned about the Middle East should miss reading it." Booklist

Includes bibliographical references

★ The **Oxford** dictionary of Islam; John L. Esposito, editor in chief. Oxford Univ. Press 2003 359p hardcover o.p. pa $18.95 **297**
1. Reference books 2. Islam -- Dictionaries
ISBN 0-19-512558-4; 0-19-512559-2 pa
LC 2002-30261

"This is an excellent resource for ready-reference collections in any library." Libr J

Includes bibliographical references

The **Oxford** history of Islam; {edited by} John Esposito. Oxford Univ. Press 1999 749p il map $49.95 **297**
1. Islam
ISBN 0-19-510799-3
LC 99-13219

"Contributors treat, among other things, Muslim history, law, and society; art and architecture; and regional differences. Chapters on the 'Globalization of Islam' and 'Contemporary Islam' are particularly relevant to current events. . . . An ideal one-volume source." Libr J

Includes bibliographical references

Power, Carla
If the oceans were ink; an unlikely friendship and a journey to the heart of the Quran. Carla Power. Henry Holt & Co. 2015 352 p. (hardcover) $19 **297**
1. Islam 2. Friendship 3. Interfaith relations 4. Islam -- Appreciation 5. Islamophobia -- Europe 6. Islam -- Public opinion 7. Muslim converts -- Biography 8. Islam -- Essence, genius, nature
ISBN 0805098194; 9780805098198; 9780805098242
LC 2014017543

National Book Award Finalist: Nonfiction (2015)
Pulitzer Prize Finalist: General Nonfiction (2016)

This book, by Carla Power, offers the author's story of how she "and her longtime friend Sheikh Mohammad Akram Nadwi found a way to confront ugly stereotypes and persistent misperceptions that were cleaving their communities. . . . Both knew that a close look at the Quran would reveal a faith that preached peace and not mass murder; respect for women and not oppression. And so they embarked on a yearlong journey through the controversial text." (Publisher's note)

"Power's narrative offers an accessible and enlightening route into a topic fraught with misunderstanding." Pub Wkly

Includes bibliographical references and index

Renard, John
The **handy** Islam answer book; John Renard. Visible Ink Press 2015 435 p. illustrations, maps (paperback) $21.95 **297**
1. Islam
ISBN 157859510X; 9781578595105
LC 2014033780

This book, by John Renard, "provides detailed descriptions of the history, beliefs, symbols, rituals, observations, customs, leaders, and organization of the world's second largest religion. [The author] . . . explains the significance of the Five Pillars, Muhammad, various sects, the Qur'an, Islamic law, and much more." (Publisher's note)

"This very well-written and captivating resource explains Islam using an accessible and balanced approach and rectifies the more egregious misconceptions about the religion that are often popularly cited. A strong choice for anyone of high school age and above who wishes to know about Islam and for those who provide ready reference." LJ

Zafar, Harris, 1979-

Demystifying Islam; tackling the tough questions. Harris Zafar. Rowman & Littlefied 2014 218 p. map (cloth : alk. paper) $35 **297**
1. Islamophobia 2. Islam -- Relations 3. Islam 4. Islam -- Doctrines
ISBN 1442223278; 9781442223271; 9781442223288
LC 2014004827

This book, by Harris Zafar, asks questions such as "What really is Shariah law? How is a Muslim to understand Jihad? Does Islam oppose Western values such as free speech or freedom of religion? What place do women have according to Islam? . . . Author Harris Zafar . . . is forthright about issues where Muslims disagree, and he digs into history through vast research and scholarship to track the origins of differing beliefs." (Publisher's note)

"This book is less of a spiritual introduction than it is a cultural one, and an excellent starting point for people navigating interfaith relationships or working to improve understanding and representation in organizations and public discussion." Pub Wkly

Includes bibliographical referencees and index

297.09 Islam--History, geographic treatment, biography

Abdul Rauf, Feisal, 1948-

Moving the mountain; beyond ground zero to a new vision of Islam in America. Feisal Abdul Rauf. Free Press 2012 xiv, 225 p.p (hardcover) $24 **297.09**
1. Islamic law 2. Religious tolerance 3. Muslims -- United States 4. Islam -- United States
ISBN 1451656009; 9781451656008
LC 2011050797

Author Feisal Abdul Rauf "offers a . . . comparative study of the 'People of the Book,' focusing partly on the similarities between the three Abrahamic faiths. . . . Rauf delves into the 'bogeyman' of Shariah law, comparing it to the U.S. Constitution." He also discusses "Islam since 9/11" and his time as "imam of the al-Farah Mosque in New York City." (Kirkus Reviews)

Includes bibliographical references

Nasr, Amir Ahmad

My Isl@m; how fundamentalism stole my mind--and doubt freed my soul. Amir Ahmad Nasr. St. Martin's Press 2013 304 p. **297.09**
1. Belief and doubt 2. Internet and religion 3. Islamic fundamentalism 4. Muslims -- Malaysia -- Biography
ISBN 9781250016485; 9781250016799
LC 2013004044

The author, "a Sudanese blogger . . . blends memoir with political thought and activism in his book, a distillation of his last few years blogging about Islam and the Muslim world. [Amir Ahmad] Nasr, who grew up in Qatar and Malaysia, recounts his early religious education. . . . . The book . . . follows his journey out of a simplistic understanding of Islam, through rationalism and semi-atheism, towards a conversion to Sufism, the mystical school of Islam." (Publishers Weekly)

297.092 Islam--Biography

All-American; 45 American men on being Muslim. edited by Wajahat Ali & Zahra T. Suratwala; foreword by Congressman Keith Ellison. White Cloud Press 2012 xiv, 256 p.p ill. (pbk.) $16.95 **297.092**
1. Muslims -- United States 2. Muslim men -- United States 3. Muslim men -- United States -- Biography
ISBN 1935952595; 9781935952596
LC 2012014744

"In this second book in the 'I Speak For Myself' series," edited by Wajahat Ali, "American Muslim men speak out on their lives and how their Muslim beliefs play out in private and on the public stage. Contributors include high profile figures in the American Muslim community, representing a new generation that is making a profound impact inside and outside the Muslim world." (Publisher's note)

Smith, Jane Idleman

Islam in America; {by} Jane I. Smith. Columbia Univ. Press 1999 251p il (Columbia contemporary American religion series) $60; pa $20.50 **297.092**
1. Islam
ISBN 0-231-10966-0; 0-231-10967-9 pa
LC 98-31943

The author discusses "the basic tenets of the Muslim faith, surveys the history of Islam in this country, and profiles the lifestyles, religious practices, and worldviews of American Muslims. Sections of the book cover the role of women in American Islam, raising and educating children, the use of products acceptable to Muslims, appropriate dress and behavior, concerns about prejudice and unfair treatment, and other issues related to life in {America}." Univ Press Books for Public and Second Sch Libr, 2001

Includes bibliographical references

297.1 Islam

★ The **meaning** of the glorious Koran; an explanatory translation by Marmaduke Pickthall; with an introduction by William Montgomery Watt. A.A. Knopf 1992 xxiv, 693p il $22 **297.1**
1. Qur'an
ISBN 0-679-41736-2; 978-0-679-41736-1
LC 92-52928

This translation first published 1930

"The sacred scripture of Islam, regarded by Muslims as the Word of God, and except in sura I.—which is a prayer to God—and some few passages in which Muhammad or the angels speak in the first person, the speaker throughout is God." Ency Britannica

The **Qur'an**; English translation and parallel Arabic text. translated, with an introduction and notes, by M.A.S. Abdel Haleem. Oxford University

Press 2010 xxxix, 624 p.p maps (hardcover)
$45 **297.1**
1. Qur'an
ISBN 019957071X; 9780199570713
LC 2010281328
This book, by M. A. S. Abdel Haleem, offers an English translation of the Qur'an with Arab text presented in parallel. "This translation is written in contemporary language . . ., set page-for-page against the most widespread traditional calligraphic Arabic text. . . . Furthermore, Haleem includes notes that explain geographical, historical, and personal allusions as well as an index in which Qur'anic material is arranged into topics for easy reference." (Publisher's note)
"Because the Koran stresses its Arabic nature, devout Muslims believe that only an Arabic version is the actual Koran and insist that its translation cannot be more than an approximate interpretation. . . Yet anyone wishing to understand Islamic civilization and global affairs may find this Koran very useful. . . . Highly recommended." LJ
Includes bibliographical references and index

The **Qur'an**: an encyclopedia; edited by Oliver Leaman. Taylor & Francis Group 2006 xxvii, 771p $280; pa $45 **297.1**
1. Reference books 2. Koran -- Encyclopedias
ISBN 0-415-32639-7; 978-0-415-32639-1; 0-415-77529-9 pa; 978-0-415-32639-1 pa
"The objective of this encyclopedia is to fill a gap between general introductions and more technical works and provide the non-specialist with a resource covering all aspects of the text and its reception." Booklist
Includes bibliographical references

Wagner, Walter H.
Opening the Qur'an; introducing Islam's holy book. University of Notre Dame Press 2008 547p $45 **297.1**
1. Qu'ran -- Criticism
ISBN 978-0-268-04415-2; 0-268-04415-5
LC 2008-27221
This "work makes an important contribution to the contemporary Muslim-Christian conversation." Catholic Hist Rev
Includes bibliographical references

297.2 Islamic doctrinal theology ('Aqā'id and Kalām); Islam and secular disciplines; Islam and other systems of belief

Harris, Sam, 1967-
Islam and the future of tolerance; a dialogue. Sam Harris, Maajid Nawaz. Harvard University Press 2015 138 p. (alk. paper) $17.95 **297.2**
1. Islam 2. Religious tolerance 3. Dialogue -- Religious aspects 4. Toleration -- Religious aspects -- Islam
ISBN 9780674088702; 0674088700
LC 2015009535
In this book, authors "Sam Harris and Maajid Nawaz invite [readers] to join an urgently needed conversation: Is Islam a religion of peace or war? Is it amenable to re-

form? Why do so many Muslims seem drawn to extremism? What do words like Islamism, jihadism, and fundamentalism mean in today's world? Harris and Nawaz demonstrate how two people with very different views can find common ground." (Publisher's note)
"Those interested in a deferential and detailed dialogue about human rights, Islam, jihadism, and pluralism will find this book both enlightening and engaging." Pub Wkly
Includes bibliographical references

297.4 Sufism (Islamic mysticism)

Ernst, Carl W.
The **Shambhala** guide to Sufism. Shambhala Publs. 1997 xxi, 264p il pa $18.95 **297.4**
1. Sufism
ISBN 1-57062-180-2
LC 97-10189
This guide to Sufism "covers its beginnings, its basic philosophies, and its place in Islam." Libr J
Includes bibliographical references

297.6 Islamic leaders and organization

Hazleton, Lesley, 1945-
The **First** Muslim; The Story of Muhammad. Lesley Hazleton. Riverhead Hardcover 2013 320 p. map (hardcover) $27.95 **297.6**
1. Islam -- History
ISBN 1594487286; 9781594487286
LC 2012038501
This book, by Lesley Hazleton, offers a biography of the Prophet Muhammad. "Muhammad's was a life of almost unparalleled historical importance; yet for all the iconic power of his name, the intensely dramatic story of the prophet of Islam is not well known. . . . Hazleton's account follows the arc of Muhammad's rise from powerlessness to power, from anonymity to renown, from insignificance to lasting significance." (Publisher's note)
Includes bibliographical references (p. [299]-310) and index.

297.8 Islamic sects and reform movements

Evanzz, Karl
The **messenger**: the rise and fall of Elijah Muhammad. Pantheon Bks. 1999 667p hardcover o.p. pa $18 **297.8**
1. Black Muslim leaders 2. Civil rights activists
ISBN 0-679-77406-8 pa
LC 99-11826
A "critical biography of one of America's leading black nationalists of the 20th century. One of the founders of the Nation of Islam (NOI), Muhammad helped convert thousands of African Americans to the religion popularly known as the Black Muslims. Evanzz concludes that Muhammad was essentially a con man who used his considerable powers of persuasion to get rich and seduce women. Especially

fascinating is Evanzz's extensive use of FBI files to make his case." Libr J

Includes bibliographical references

Levinsohn, Florence Hamlish

Looking for Farrakhan. Dee, I.R. 1997 305p $25 **297.8**
1. Black Muslims 2. Black Muslim leaders
ISBN 1-56663-157-2

LC 97-11335

Levinsohn's "biography, which reflects on the black experience and how it changed young Eugene Walcott into Louis Farrakhan, leader of the Nation of Islam, attempts to make sense of this prominent figure in American politics." Libr J

299   Religions not provided for elsewhere

★ The **Gnostic** Bible; edited by Willis Barnstone and Marvin Meyer. Rev. ed.; Shambhala 2009 881p pa $29.95 **299**
1. Gnosticism
ISBN 978-1-59030-631-4; 1-59030-631-7

LC 2008-36431

First published 2003

"The book provides Gnostic texts from their Jewish origins, into early Christianities, on into the medieval world. Though it concentrates on the early Jewish-Christian matrix of early Gnosticism, the collection . . . manifests the breadth and depth of Gnostic variations in neo-Platonist, Manichean, Mandean, Islam, and Cathar movements." Choice

Includes bibliographical references

Mar, Alex

Witches of America; Alex Mar. Sarah Crichton Books 2015 288 p. (hardcover) $26 **299**
1. Paganism 2. Occultism 3. Wicca -- United States 4. Neopaganism -- United States
ISBN 0374291373; 9780374291372

LC 2015010897

This book follows author Alex Mar "on her immersive five-year trip into the occult, charting modern Paganism from its roots in 1950s England to its current American mecca in the San Francisco Bay Area; from a gathering of more than a thousand witches in the Illinois woods to the New Orleans branch of one of the world's most influential magical societies. Along the way she takes part in dozens of rituals and becomes involved with a wild array of characters." (Publisher's note)

A top-notch read for pagans and open-minded seekers curious about the fascinating beginnings of American witchcraft and some of the various directions its form is taking." Library Journal

Pagels, Elaine H.

★ The **Gnostic** Gospels; by Elaine Pagels. Random House 1979 xxxvi, 182p hardcover o.p. pa $12 **299**
1. Gnosticism
ISBN 0-679-72453-2 pa

LC 79-4764

An examination of the origins of early Christianity based on Gnostic texts rediscovered in the 20th century.

Pagels "writes for the layman, which is refreshing, and she does so lucidly, which is a challenge, especially when 'gnosticism' was regarded by its own adherents to be for the initiated only." Christ Sci Monit

Includes bibliographical references

Reitman, Janet

★ **Inside** Scientology. Houghton Mifflin Harcourt 2011 xx, 444p $28 **299**
1. Scientology 2. United States -- Religion
ISBN 978-0-618-88302-8; 0-618-88302-9

LC 2010-49837

An expose "culled from hundreds of interviews with active Scientologists and defectors alike. Reitman brings an almost clinical detachment to the religion's story, from its birth in the sci-fi imagination of founder L. Ron Hubbard to its current Hollywood heyday. Her revelations—including abuse allegations against church leader David Miscavige and details about the organization's aggressive courtship of Tom Cruise—come with impressive backup." Entertaiment Wkly

Includes bibliographical references

Wilkinson, Richard H.

★ The **complete** gods and goddesses of ancient Egypt. Thames & Hudson 2003 256p il $39.95 **299**
1. Egyptian mythology 2. Gods and goddesses 3. Egypt -- Religion
ISBN 0-500-05120-8

LC 2002-110321

"Wilkinson's gorgeously illustrated book adds new dimension to popular literature on ancient Egypt. . . . And once readers open the book to look at the pictures, they well may stay to read the well-organized, comprehensive, clearly written text." Booklist

Includes bibliographical references

Wright, Lawrence, 1947-

★ **Going** Clear; Scientology, Hollywood, and the Prison of Belief. Lawrence Wright. Random House Inc 2013 xiii, 430 p.p ill. $28.95 **299**
1. Cults 2. Scientology 3. Scientology. 4. Scientology --Doctrines.
ISBN 0307700666; 9780307700667

LC 2012532009

National Book Award: Nonfiction Finalist (2013)

This book from Pulitzer Prize winner Lawrence Wright looks at the Church of Scientology. It begins "with the life of L. Ron Hubbard, a manic-depressive, wannabe naval hero, sci-fi writer and self-styled shaman" whose book "Dianetics" "laid the groundwork for a 'religion' where 'thetans' (souls) are stymied by 'engrams,' self-destructive suggestive impulses lodged in the brain." The Church's connections to the U.S. entertainment industry and its behavior toward outsiders are examined. (Kirkus Reviews)

Includes bibliographical references (p. [373]-418) and index.

299.5   Religions of East and Southeast Asian origin

I ching

★ The **classic** of changes; a new translation of the I Ching as interpreted by Wang Bi. translated by Richard John Lynn. Columbia Univ. Press 1994 602p (Translations from the Asian classics) $27.95; pa $17.95   **299.5**

1. Divination
ISBN 0-231-08294-0; 0-231-08295-9 pa

LC 93-43999

"Most available editions of the I Ching are based on the James Legge translation, a work produced over 140 years ago and characterized by romanticized and idiomatic Victorian English. Although not more accurate or revealing than the Legge, this new translation is welcome because of its crisp usage of modern-day English." Libr J

Lao-tzu

★ **Tao** te ching; the new translation from Tao te ching: the definitive edition. translation by Jonathan Star. Jeremy P. Tarcher/Penguin 2008 103p pa $10   **299.5**

ISBN 978-1-58542-618-8

LC 2007-44948

This translation first published 2001 with title: Tao te ching: the definitive edition

"Chinese Taoist text attributed to Lao Tzu, supposedly an elder contemporary of Confucius (551?-479 BC). . . . A brief work in eighty-one-paragraphs in both verse and prose, it probably dates from the 4th or 3rd century BC, although some believe it may be as early as the 6th century BC. Because of its concise, poetic language, its meaning is subject to many interpretations. It is generally agreed that it is both a mystical book about union with the absolute, and a political handbook on how to rule and survive in chaotic times." Reader's Ency. 4th edition

Yang Lihui

★ **Handbook** of Chinese mythology; [by] Lihui Yang and Deming An, with Jessica Anderson Turner. ABC-CLIO 2005 293p il (Handbooks of world mythology) $75   **299.5**

1. Asian mythology
ISBN 1-57607-806-X

LC 2005-13851

"This volume provides useful information to the reader. The authors' credibility and in-depth scholarship offer a rare opportunity to experience Chinese mythology through Chinese eyes." Booklist

Includes bibliographical references

299.6   Religions originating among Black Africans and people of Black African descent

Chevannes, Barry

Rastafari: roots and ideology. Syracuse Univ. Press 1994 298p (Utopianism and communitarianism) hardcover o.p. pa $19.95   **299.6**

1. Rastafari movement 2. Jamaica -- Religion
ISBN 0-8156-0296-0 pa

LC 94-18608

"Vital for students of African American religions and Caribbean religions, but also of interest to anthropologists, sociologists, and historians." Choice

Includes bibliographical references

★ The **Encyclopedia** of African and African-American religions; Stephen D. Glazier, editor. Routledge 2000 xx, 452p il maps $150   **299.6**

1. Reference books 2. Blacks -- Religion 3. African Americans -- Religion -- Encyclopedias
ISBN 0-415-92245-3

LC 00-59136

"This encyclopedia is a good starting point for understanding the complex interrelationships among African, African American, and European religious beliefs, practices, and traditions in a global context." Libr J

299.7   Religions of North American native origin

Castaneda, Carlos

The **teachings** of Don Juan; a Yaqui way of knowledge. University of Calif. Press 1968 196p $32.50; pa $16.95   **299.7**

1. Mystics 2. Yaqui Indians -- Religion
ISBN 0-520-21755-1; 0-520-21757-8 pa

"This book is the record of a young anthropologist's experiences as the apprentice of a [Yaqui] Indian sorcerer. Over a period of four years, Mr. Castaneda paid intermittant visits to Don Juan, first in Arizona, then in Sonora, Mexico." N Y Times Book Rev

Other titles about Don Juan are:
The active side of infinity (1999)
The art of dreaming (1993)
The eagle's gift (1981)
The fire from within (1984)
Journey to Ixtlan (1972)
Magical passes (1998)
The power of silence (1987)
The second ring of power (1977)
A separate reality (1971)
Tales of power (1974)

Emrys, Barbara

The **Toltec** art of life and death; a story of discovery. Don Miguel Ruiz and Barbara Emrys. HarperElixir 2015 416 p. (hardback) $25.99   **299.7**

1. Near-death experiences 2. Spiritual biography
ISBN 0062390929; 9780062390929; 9780062390936; 9780062423559

LC 2015009856

This book, by Don Miguel Ruiz and Barbara Emrys, responds to how, "in 2002, Don Miguel Ruiz suffered a near fatal heart attack that left him in a nine-weeks-long coma. The spiritual journey he undertook while suspended between this world and the next forms the heart of . . . . [the book.] As his body lies unconscious, Ruiz's spirit encounters the people, ideas, and events that have shaped him, illuminating the eternal struggle between life . . . and death." (Publisher's note)

"Readers might find it difficult to follow Ruiz's winding road to the truth, but will come away from this book with a deeper understanding of life's complexities." Publisher's Weekly

Nabokov, Peter

Where the lightning strikes; the lives of American Indian sacred places. Viking 2005 350p hardcover o.p. pa $17   **299.7**
1. Sacred space 2. Native Americans -- Religion
ISBN 0-670-03432-0; 0-14-303881-8 pa
LC 2005-42227

The author presents "16 'biographies of place,' each of a habitat illustrating the bond between North American Indian cultures and their environment perpetuated by myths, legends, and rituals. . . . The author's careful documentation of unbroken reverence for these sacred places powerfully illuminates Native American attachment to the earth itself." Booklist

Includes bibliographical references

Popol vuh

Popol vuh; the Mayan book of the dawn of life. translated by Dennis Tedlock; with commentary based on the ancient knowledge of the modern Quiché Maya. rev ed; Simon & Schuster 1996 388p il maps pa $15   **299.7**
1. Mayas -- Religion 2. Native Americans -- Religion
ISBN 0-684-81845-0
LC 95-46822

A modern translation of the 16th century Mayan holy book

"Tedlock's translation splendidly combines scholarship, imagination, and literary sensitivity. His photographs (derived from field work in Guatemala) vividly illustrate the text, and the notes (based on his collaboration with a contemporary Quiché shaman) fascinate and inform." Libr J

Includes bibliographical references

299.93   New Age religions

Williamson, Marianne

Tears to triumph; The Spiritual Journey from Suffering to Enlightenment. Marianne Williamson. HarperOne 2016 240 p. (hardcover) $25.99 **299.93**
1. Suffering -- Religious aspects
ISBN 9780062205445; 9780062441591
LC 2016011730

In this book, author Marianne Williamson "argues that our desire to avoid pain is actually detrimental to our lives, disconnecting us from our deepest emotions and preventing true healing and spiritual transcendence. . . . In refusing to

acknowledge our suffering, we actually prolong it and deny ourselves the opportunity for profound wisdom—ultimately limiting our personal growth and opportunity for enlightenment." (Publisher's note)

"Those who are searching for a spiritual, not religious answer to the aspects of hurt and hardship will find it here." LJ

300   SOCIAL SCIENCES, SOCIOLOGY & ANTHROPOLOGY

300   Social sciences

Calhoun, Craig J.

★ **Dictionary** of the social sciences; edited by Craig Calhoun. Oxford Univ. Press 2002 563p $75   **300**
1. Reference books 2. Social sciences -- Dictionaries
ISBN 0-19-512371-9
LC 00-68151

This dictionary provides "definitions of key terms, offering entries that also discuss the intellectual issues behind the terms' usage. The entries cover all the social sciences except for law, education, and public administration. . . . Some 275 biographies are included." Libr J

Includes bibliographical references

Rosenblatt, Roger

★ **Kayak** morning; Roger Rosenblatt. Ecco 2012 160p.   **300**
1. Grief 2. Autobiographies 3. Kayaks and kayaking
ISBN 9780062084033

In this memoir, the author questions "why [he] cannot come to terms with his grief [over the death of his 38-year-old daughter] two and a half years later. As [Roger] Rosenblatt, a writer and professor of English and writing at Stony Brook University, takes up kayaking near his home in Quogue on Long Island, he begins to contemplate his connection to nature and his place in it by observing the sea. The kayak becomes a metaphorical conveyance as he floats from one topic to the next . . . everything from life versus death to personal memories and classical literature. . . . The piece . . . combines short vignettes, poetic verses, snippets of conversations and meaningful quotations." (Publishers Weekly)

301   Sociology and anthropology

Best, Joel

Stat-spotting; a field guide to identifying dubious data. University of California Press 2008 132p il $19.95   **301**
1. Statistics
ISBN 978-0-520-25746-7; 0-520-25746-4
LC 2008-17175

This "is an easily digestible guide to understanding how simple miscalculations, botched translations and inappropriate graphics misled the American public. This concise book helps readers understand how politicians and the media twist statistics to match the goals of their agenda. Author Joel Best describes how things like bloating figures by misplacing a decimal point or using enlarged graphics to visually distract readers from analyzing the data objectively. If you want a better understanding of the reality behind those charts and graphs you see in books, on television and in the media then you need to read this book." Univ Press Books for Public and Second Sch Libr, 2009

Includes bibliographical references

Lefebvre, Henri, 1901-1991

Critique of everyday life; Henri Lefebvre, translated by John Moore and Gregory Elliott. Random House Inc. 2014 912 p. (paperback) $44.95   **301**
1. Marxism 2. Modern philosophy
ISBN 9781781683170; 9781781683187; 1781683174

This book, by Henri Lefebvre, translated by John Moore and Gregory Elliott, "written at the birth of post-war consumerism, . . . was a philosophical inspiration for the 1968 student revolution in France and is considered to be the founding text of all that we know as cultural studies, as well as a major influence on the fields of contemporary philosophy, geography, sociology, architecture, political theory and urbanism." (Publisher's note)

Morris, Aldon D.

The **scholar** denied; W.E.B. Du Bois and the birth of modern sociology. Aldon D. Morris. University of California Press 2015 320 p. 8 plates; illustrations (cloth : alk. paper) $29.95   **301**
1. Sociology -- History 2. Sociologists -- United States 3. Sociology -- United States -- History
ISBN 0520276353; 0520286766; 9780520276352; 9780520286764

LC 2014042410

This book, by Aldon D. Morris, seeks "to help rewrite the history of sociology and to acknowledge the primacy of W. E. B. Du Bois's work in the founding of the discipline. Calling into question the prevailing narrative of how sociology developed, Morris, a major scholar of social movements, probes the way in which the history of the discipline has traditionally given credit." (Publisher's note)

"Morris's provocative exposé of how economic and political power elevates the ideas, images, and intellectuals America publicly embraces. A must-read for anyone interested in American sociology and/or the U.S. marketplace of ideas." Library Journal

Includes bibliographical references and index

Required reading; sociology's most influential books. edited by Dan Clawson. University of Mass. Press 1998 221p hardcover o.p. pa $17.95   **301**
1. Best books 2. Reference books 3. Sociology -- Bibliography
ISBN 1-55849-153-8 pa

LC 98-11944

This volume "identifies and discusses 17 of the 'most influential' books in sociology written during the last 25 years. . . . The power of this book lies in reconsiderations by eminent sociologists of important titles in light of a quar-

ter of a century's worth of political, social, and economic change." Libr J

Includes bibliographical references

World of sociology; Joseph M. Palmisano, editor. Gale Group 2001 2v il set $160   **301**
1. Reference books 2. Sociology -- Encyclopedias
ISBN 0-7876-4965-1

LC 00-48399

This is a "subject-specific guide to concepts, theories, discoveries, pioneers, issues and ethical questions associated with sociology. It includes approximately 1,000-1,500 alphabetically arranged topical essays, definitions and biographies." Publisher's note

Includes bibliographical references

302 Specific topics in sociology and anthropology

Gladwell, Malcolm, 1963-

Outliers; the story of success. Little, Brown and Co. 2008 309p $27.99   **302**
1. Success
ISBN 978-0-316-01792-3; 0-316-01792-2

LC 2008-32824

Gladwell's "subject is success—an 'outlier' is a super-achiever, like Bill Gates or the four Beatles, and Gladwell wants to know what sets these titans apart. It's not mere talent, he insists, offering up instead one thrilling, exquisitely unfurled counterargument after another. . . . There are both brilliant yarns and life lessons here: Outliers is riveting science, self-help, and entertainment, all in one book." Entertainment Wkly

Includes bibliographical references

The **tipping** point; how little things can make a big difference. Malcolm Gladwell. Little, Brown 2000 viii, 279 p $27.99   **302**
1. Causation 2. Social psychology 3. Contagion (Social psychology)
ISBN 0316316962; 9780316316965

LC 99047576

It was the author's intent to demonstrate "that ideas, products, messages and behaviors 'spread just like viruses do.' . . . [Malcolm Gladwell] follows the growth of 'word-of-mouth epidemics' triggered with the help of three pivotal types. These are Connectors, sociable personalities who bring people together; Mavens, who like to pass along knowledge; and Salesmen, adept at persuading the unenlightened. (Paul Revere, for example, was a Maven and a Connector). . . . [The book] offers a smorgasbord of . . . snippets summarizing research on topics such as conversational patterns, infants' crib talk, judging other people's character, cheating habits in schoolchildren, memory sharing among families or couples, and the dehumanizing effects of prisons." (Publishers Weekly)

Includes bibliographical references and index.

Lieberman, Matthew D., 1970-

Social; why our brains are wired to connect. Matthew D. Lieberman. Crown Publishers 2013 384 p. $26 **302**

1. Neurosciences 2. Social networking 3. Social psychology 4. Cognitive psychology 5. Social networks 6. Social interaction 7. Cognitive neuroscience

ISBN 0307889092; 9780307889096; 9780307889119

LC 2013006226

LA Times Book Prize Finalist: Science & Technology (2013)

This book, by Matthew D. Lieberman, "shows readers how their brains may be wired . . . to harmonize and connect with others, rather than simply to act in their own interests. With the help of new functional MRI technology, Lieberman . . . investigat[es] how our perceptions of others affect our cognition and, even more elementally, how social interaction and its absence can produce the same mental responses as physical pain and pleasure." (Publishers Weekly)

"A fascinating explanation of why 'a broken heart can feel as painful as a broken leg' and social recognition is frequently prized above money." Kirkus

Wright, Jennifer

It Ended Badly; Thirteen of the Worst Breakups in History. Jennifer Wright. Henry Holt & Co. 2015 256 p. illustrations $21 **302**

1. Marriage 2. Interpersonal relations 3. Breaking up (Interpersonal relations)

ISBN 1627792864; 9781627792868

LC 2015004347

In this book author Jennifer Wright "digs deep into the archives to bring these thirteen terrible breakups to life. [She] guides [readers] through the worst of the worst in historically bad breakups. In the throes of heartbreak, Emperor Nero had just about everyone he ever loved . . . put to death. Oscar Wilde's lover . . . abandoned him when faced with being cut off financially. And poor volatile Caroline Lamb sent Lord Byron one hell of a torch letter." (Publisher's note)

"Wright's ability to blend historical facts with humor will make this book attractive to readers looking for a delightful page-turner, as well as those who enjoy the dynamic people who have been peppered throughout history." LJ

302.1   General topics of social interaction

Kaufman, Sarah L.

The art of grace; on moving well through life. Sarah L. Kaufman. W W Norton & Co Inc 2015 336 p. illustrations (hardcover) $24.95; (ebook) $40 **302.1**

1. Aesthetics 2. Manners and customs 3. Grace (Aesthetics)

ISBN 9780393243956; 9780393243963

LC 2015028036

In this book, author "Sarah L. Kaufman sifts the graceful from the graceless, celebrating heart-catching moments of physical elegance in sports, movies, dance, fashion, and music; rare sightings of celebrity grace; the secrets of gracious hosts; and grace found unexpectedly, in the kitchen

of a high-end restaurant and among strippers in a basement bar." (Publisher's note)

"Kaufman reminds us that even in a world where most eyes are locked on smart phones, there are still people who really listen, think before they speak, and move gracefully. It's up to us to notice and emulate their techniques." Booklist

Includes bibliographical references and index

302.13   Social choice

Berger, Jonah

Invisible Influence; The Hidden Forces That Shape Behavior. by Jonah Berger. Simon & Schuster 2016 288 p. illustrations (hardcover) $26.99 **302.13**

1. Decision making 2. Social sciences 3. Influence (Psychology)

ISBN 9781476759692; 1476759693

This book, by Jonah Berger, "explores the subtle, secret influences that affect the decisions we make—from what we buy, to the careers we choose, to what we eat. . . . Berger integrates research and thinking from business, psychology, and social science to focus on the subtle, invisible influences behind our choices as individuals. By understanding how social influence works, we can decide when to resist and when to embrace it." (Publisher's note)

"Berger's unique knowledge will appeal to readers from many backgrounds, especially individuals interested in making better decisions." LJ

Includes bibliographical references and index.

302.2   Communication

Biedermann, Hans

★ Dictionary of symbolism; cultural icons and the meanings behind them. translated by James Hulbert. Meridan Book 1994 465p il pa $25 **302.2**

1. Reference books 2. Signs and symbols

ISBN 0-452-01118-3

LC 93-30616

Original German edition, 1989

This dictionary "incorporates symbols that originated in Asia, Africa, Europe and the 'New World'. There are almost 600 entries from mythology, fairy tale, psychology, religion, and sociology, plus historical and legendary figures. With 2000 black-and-white illustrations, the book is highly attractive. The symbols are accompanied by thorough interpretations based on various sources." SLJ

Includes bibliographical references

McLuhan, Marshall

The global village; transformations in world life and media in the 21st century. [by] Marshall McLuhan and Bruce R. Powers. Oxford Univ. Press 1989 220p il (Communication and society) hardcover o.p. pa $14.95 **302.2**

1. Mass media 2. Technology and civilization

ISBN 0-19-507910-8 pa

LC 88-22718

This book "was written, according to Powers, between 1974 and 1980 . . . and 'put together' between 1976 and 1984. McLuhan's thesis has always been that electronic technologies have been altering and reconstituting people in ways they don't understand and causing them to lose their private identities. This book probes the same theme from different angles, but with the same McLuhanesque all-over-the-place reasoning." Libr J

Includes bibliographical references

Tannen, Deborah

You just don't understand; women and men in conversation. Quill 2001 342p pa $13.95   **302.2**

1. Conversation 2. Sex differences (Psychology)

ISBN 978-0-06-095962-3; 0-06-095962-2

First published 1990 by Morrow

"Aside from the vivid examples and lively prose, what makes this book particularly engaging is that the author makes linguistics . . . interesting and usable." N Y Times Book Rev

Includes bibliographical references

302.23   Media (Means of communication)

Bartlett, Jamie

The **Dark** Net; Jamie Bartlett. William Heinemann 2014 320 p. $27.95   **302.23**

1. Internet 2. Internet industry

ISBN 0434023159; 1612194893; 9780434023158; 9781612194899

LC 2015013287

This book by Jamie Bartlett, presents an "examination of the internet today, and of its most innovative and dangerous subcultures: trolls and pornographers, drug dealers and hackers, political extremists and computer scientists, Bitcoin programmers and self-harmers, libertarians and vigilantes." (Publisher's note)

"A provocative excursion to the darker side of human nature set free by the anonymous and unregulated boundaries of cyberspace." Kirkus

Clark, Lynn Schofield

The **parent** app; understanding families in the digital age. Lynn Schofield Clark. Oxford University Press 2013 xx, 299 p.p (alk. paper) $29.95 **302.23**

1. Digital media and families 2. Parent and child 3. Internet and families 4. Internet -- Social aspects

ISBN 0199899614; 9780199899616

LC 2012006687

This book by Lynn Schofield Clark provides families with "strategies for coping with the dilemmas of digital and mobile media in modern life. . . . Clark set about interviewing scores of mothers and fathers, identifying not only their various approaches, but how they differ according to family income. Clark tackles a host of issues, such as family communication, online predators, cyber bullying, sexting, gamer drop-outs, helicopter parenting, . . . and much more." (Publisher's note)

Includes bibliographical references (p. 275-291) and index

Durham, M. Gigi

The **Lolita** effect; the media sexualization of young girls and what we can do about it. [by] M. Gigi Durham, Ph.D. Overlook Press 2008 320p $24.95; pa $14.95   **302.23**

1. Body image 2. Mass media 3. Girls -- Sexual behavior 4. United States -- Social conditions

ISBN 978-1-5902-00636; 1-5902-0063-2; 978-1-5902-0215-9 pa; 1-5902-0215-5 pa

In this "exploration of the media's exploitation of girls, Durham exposes the links between destructive teenage self-images and the popular, highly sexed, and negative representations of girls in magazines, television programs, and movies. . . . [Her] provocative and erudite study of the demeaning way society views girls serves to both alarm and educate; consider it required reading for parents and their daughters." Booklist

Includes bibliographical references

Gladstone, Brooke

★ The **influencing** machine; Brooke Gladstone on the media. illustrated by Josh Neufeld; with additional penciling by Randy Jones and Susann Ferris-Jones. W. W. Norton 2011 xxii, 170p ill. (chiefly col.) (hbk.) $23.95; (hbk.) $16.95   **302.23**

1. Journalism 2. Mass media 3. Broadcast journalism 4. Comic books, strips, etc. 5. Graphic novels 6. Journalism -- Graphic novels 7. Broadcast journalism -- Graphic novels

ISBN 0393077799; 9780393077797

LC 2011009820

This work of graphic nonfiction explores the "history of media's influence. . . . [F]rom the 'Acta Diurna' posted in ancient Rome to the outcries over President Adams's Alien and Sedition Acts and McCarthy's Red Scare, [Brooke] Gladstone traces not only the birth of the press, but also its various muzzles. The press will not always stay silent, as she illustrates with Daniel Ellsberg and the Pentagon Papers. . . . Yet government opacity still abounds, and Gladstone pointedly wonders if secrecy really makes us safer. . . . Gladstone points to seven key biases that cognizant media consumers should worry about: commercial, bad news, status quo, access, visual, narrative, and fairness. These dovetail . . . into a . . . discussion of war journalism." (Publishers Weekly)

"Gladstone's is an indispensible guide to our ever-evolving media landscape that's brought vividly to life." Publ Wkly

Includes bibliographical references (p. 163-170).

Gonzalez, Juan, 1969-

News for all the people; Juan Gonzalez and Joseph Torres. Verso 2011 432p $29.95   **302.23**

1. Mass media 2. United States -- Race relations

ISBN 978-1-84467-687-3

This book "provide[s] a history of the development of 'the American system of news,' with emphasis on the government's role . . . and . . . construct[s] an account of the struggle across the 'fundamental fault-line' of race and ethnicity that shaped both mainstream and dissident media. . . . The stories of Hispanic, Native-American, African-American, and Asian-American journalists risking lives and well-being to raise their voices, constitute the true heart of this book. Some of the pioneers' names are reasonably familiar, . . . [b]ut there are dozens of others rescued from obscurity, ranging from Joaquín de Lisa and Joseph Antonio Boniquet, founders in 1809 of 'El Mensajero' of New Orleans, to Ruben Salazar of Los Angeles, assassinated while covering a riot in 1970." (Columbia Journalism Review)

Includes bibliographical references

Harris, Michael

The **End** of absence; reclaiming what we've lost in a world of constant connection. Michael Harris. Current 2014 256 p. (hardback) $26.95 **302.23**
1. Information society 2. Information technology -- Social aspects 3. Internet -- Social aspects 4. Technology -- Social aspects
ISBN 1591846935; 9781591846932
LC 2014009772

In this book, author "Michael Harris argues that amid all the changes we're experiencing, the most interesting is the one that future generations will find hardest to grasp. That is the end of absence--the loss of lack. The daydreaming silences in our lives are filled; the burning solitudes are extinguished. There's no true 'free time' when you carry a smartphone. Today's rarest commodity is the chance to be alone with your own thoughts." (Publisher's note)

"Harris' core argument regarding the values of technological disengagement feels valid, and his prose is graceful, but as a social narrative, the book becomes repetitive and less focused as it proceeds. A thoughtful addition to the bookshelf addressing the unintended consequences of a wired world." Kirkus

Includes bibliographical references and index

Iyer, Pico

The **Art** of Stillness; Adventures in Going Nowhere. by Pico Iyer. Simon & Schuster 2014 96 p. color illustrations $14.99 **302.23**
1. Spiritual life 2. Conduct of life
ISBN 1476784728; 9781476784724
LC 2014498836

This book, by Pico Iyer, "considers the unexpected adventure of staying put and reveals a counterintuitive truth: The more ways we have to connect, the more we seem desperate to unplug. . . . . Iyer investigate[s] the lives of people who have made a life seeking stillness: from Matthieu Ricard, a Frenchman with a PhD in molecular biology who left a promising scientific career to become a Tibetan monk, to revered singer-songwriter Leonard Cohen." (Publisher's note)

"Rather than reading it quickly and filing it, readers will likely slow down to meet its pace and might continue carrying it around as a reminder." Kirkus

Jones, Gerard

Killing monsters; why children need fantasy, super heroes, and make-believe violence. foreword by Lynn Ponton. Basic Bks. 2002 261p $25; pa $15 **302.23**
1. Fantasy 2. Children 3. Violence 4. Mass media
ISBN 0-465-03695-3; 0-465-03696-1 pa
LC 2001-52667

"Although not an academic, the author has done his homework. He presents his case convincingly, and the concluding notes provide support." SLJ

Includes bibliographical references (p. 233-250) and index

Keen, Andrew

The **Internet** Is Not the Answer; Andrew Keen. Atlantic Monthly Press 2015 256 p. $25 **302.23**
1. Internet 2. Internet industry 3. Technological innovations
ISBN 0802123139; 9780802123138

In this book, author Andrew Keen "traces the technological and economic history of the internet from its founding in the 1960s through the rise of the big data companies to the increasing attempts to monetize almost every human activity, and investigates how the internet is reconfiguring our world--often at great cost." (Library Journal)

"A must-read for technophiles and business leaders, or those curious about technology's societal effects." LJ

McChesney, Robert Waterman, 1952-

Digital disconnect; how capitalism is turning the Internet against democracy. Robert W. McChesney. The New Press 2013 320 p. (hardcover) $27.95 **302.23**
1. Democracy 2. Capitalism 3. Internet -- Political aspects
ISBN 1595588671; 9781595588678
LC 2012035748

This book, by Robert W. McChesney, "address[es] the relationship between economic power and the digital world. . . . McChesney . . . argues that the sharp decline in the enforcement of antitrust violations, the increase in patents on digital technology . . . and other policies have made the internet a place of numbing commercialism. . . . Robert McChesney . . . urg[es] us to reclaim the democratizing potential of the digital revolution while we still can." (Publisher's note)

Includes bibliographical references and index

McLuhan, Marshall, 1911-1980

Understanding media; the extensions of man. by Marshall McLuhan; edited by W. Terrence Gordon. Critical ed.; Gingko Press 2003 611p ill.; **302.23**
1. Mass media 2. Mass media -- United States -- History
ISBN 1584230738
LC 2003012174

"Terms and phrases such as "the global village" and "the medium is the message" are ow part of the lexicon, and McLuhan's theories continue to challenge our sensibilities and our assumptions about how and what we communicate." (Publisher's Note)

Includes bibliographical references (p. 569-574) and index..

Palfrey, John

Born digital; understanding the first generation of digital natives. [by] John Palfrey and Urs Gasser. Basic Books 2008 375p $25.95 **302.23**
1. Information society 2. Internet and children 3. Information technology 4. Internet and teenagers 5.

Internet -- Social aspects
ISBN 9780465005154

LC 2008-21538

The authors "document the myriad ways downloading, text-messaging, Massively Multiplayer Online Games-playing, YouTube-watching youth are transforming society. Energetic, expert, and forward-looking, the authors serve as envoys between the generations, addressing issues that worry parents and educators, from privacy and safety concerns to the quality of digital information, the psychological and physical effects of information overload and excessive on-line time, and legal and ethical issues, all the while stressing the need for digital literacy and critical thinking." Booklist

Includes bibliographical references

Postman, Neil

Amusing ourselves to death; public discourse in the age of show business. Viking 1985 184p hard-cover o.p. pa $14   **302.23**

1. Mass media 2. Television broadcasting 3. United States -- Civilization
ISBN 0-14-009438-5 pa

LC 85-5335

The author argues that the constant exposure to television has contributed to a decline in America's intellectual life.

"A sustained, withering and thought-provoking attack on television and what it is doing to us." Publ Wkly

Includes bibliographical references

Standage, Tom

Writing on the wall; Social Media - the First 2,000 Years. Tom Standage. St. Martin's Press 2013 288 p. illustrations $26   **302.23**

1. Social media -- History 2. Social networking -- History
ISBN 1620402831; 9781620402832

In this book, author Tom Standage "draws comparisons between modern social media and the forms of communication and information dissemination used over 2,000 years to show how, in fact, 'History retweets itself.' Examples include ancient Roman graffiti that bears a strong resemblance to a Facebook status update . . . and Martin Luther's 95 theses, perhaps the first document to go viral." (Publishers Weekly)

"Standage offers historical perspective on such concerns about evolving social media as faddishness, coarsening of discourse, distraction from serious work, and erosion of social skills." Booklist

Includes bibliographical references and index

Thompson, David C.

The **reputation** economy; how to optimize your digital footprint in a world where your reputation is your most valuable asset. Michael Fertik, David C. Thompson. Crown Business 2015 256 p. (hard-back) $25   **302.23**

1. Reputation 2. Technology 3. Public relations 4. Success in business 5. Internet in publicity 6. Online social networks 7. Online identities -- Social aspects
ISBN 0385347596; 9780385347594; 9780804139236

LC 2014038611

In this book, authors Michael Fertik and David C. Thompson "will draw on the insider tools, insights, re-

search, and secrets that has make Reputation.com the leading reputation management firm, to show how to capitalize on the trends the Reputation Economy will trigger to improve your professional, financial, and even social prospects." (Publisher's note)

Turkle, Sherry

Reclaiming Conversation; The Power of Talk in a Digital Age. by Sherry Turkle. Penguin Group USA 2015 448 p. (ebook) $32.50; $27.95   **302.23**

1. Conversation
ISBN 9781101617397; 1594205558; 9781594205552

This book, by Sherry Turkle, "investigates how a flight from conversation undermines our relationships, creativity, and productivity—and why reclaiming face-to-face conversation can help us regain lost ground. . . . Based on five years of research and interviews in homes, schools, and the workplace, Turkle argues that we have come to a better understanding of where our technology can and cannot take us and that the time is right to reclaim conversation." (Publisher's note)

"A timely wake-up call urging us to cherish the intimacy of direct, unscripted communication." Kirkus

Includes bibliographical references (pages 367-416) and index.

Zuckerman, Ethan

Rewire; digital cosmopolitans in the age of connection. Ethan Zuckerman. W W Norton & Co Inc 2013 288 p. (hardcover) $26.95   **302.23**

1. Internet 2. Cosmopolitanism 3. Internet -- Social aspects 4. Social media
ISBN 0393082830; 9780393082838

LC 2013007124

This book is a reflection "on what it means to be a citizen of the world in the Internet age," where Ethan Zuckerman "declares that, far from aspiring to full engagement with others around the world, we seek to connect with people who share our values, nationality, gender, and race. . . . He argues that we all possess the capacity to build networks that 'rewire' our world with a better sense of interdependence." (Publishers Weekly)

Includes bibliographical references and index

302.3   Social interaction within groups

Fisher, Helen, 1942-

Anatomy of Love; A Natural History of Mating, Marriage, and Why We Stray. by Helen Fisher. W W Norton & Co Inc 2016 400 p. illustrations, charts $26.95   **302.3**

1. Sex 2. Marriage 3. Natural history 4. Man-woman relationship
ISBN 0393285227; 9780393285222

LC 2015037510

In this book, anthropologist Helen Fisher presents a " four-million-year history of the human species. She demystifies much about romance and pairing that we tend to believe is willfull or just plain careless. She offers new explanations for why men and women fall in love, marry, and divorce, and discusses the future of sex in a way that will surprise you." (Publisher's note)

"This work remains a solid introduction to the nature of sex and relationships, albeit cursory in depth of coverage. Highly recommended to readers interested in human sexuality." LJ

Junger, Sebastian, 1962-

Tribe; On Homecoming and Belonging. by Sebastian Junger. Grand Central Pub 2016 160 p. $22   **302.3**
   1. Tribes
   ISBN 1455566381; 9781455566389

                         LC 2016013022

This book, by Sebastian Junger, "explores what we can learn from tribal societies about loyalty, belonging, and the eternal human quest for meaning. It explains the irony that-for many veterans as well as civilians-war feels better than peace, adversity can turn out to be a blessing, and disasters are sometimes remembered more fondly than weddings or tropical vacations." (Publisher's note)

"Junger uses every word in this slim volume to make a passionate, compelling case for a more egalitarian society." Booklist

Includes bibliographical references (pages 139-168).

O'Connor, Rory

Friends, followers, and the future; how social media are changing politics, threatening big brands, and killing traditional media. Rory O'Connor. City Lights Books 2012 285 p. (pbk.) $15.95   **302.3**
   1. Mass media 2. Communication 3. Social networking 4. Social media 5. Social media -- Economic aspects 6. Social media -- Political aspects
   ISBN 0872865568; 9780872865563

                         LC 2012005506

This book, by Rory O'Connor, offers "a look at how social media are transforming our world. . . . O'Connor explains the trends and explores what tech visionaries, media makers, political advisers, and businesspeople are saying about the meteoric rise of the various social networks of friends and followers, and what they bode for our future." (Publisher's note)

Sciolino, Elaine

La seduction; how the French play the game of life. Times Books/Henry Holt 2011 338p il   **302.3**
   1. Seduction 2. Sex customs -- France -- History 3. France -- Social life and customs
   ISBN 0-8050-9115-7; 9780805091151

                         LC 2010049572

According to the author, "seduction plays a crucial role in how the French relate to one another—not just in romantic relationships but also in how they conduct business, enjoy food and drink, define style, engage in intellectual debate, elect politicians, and project power around the world. While sexual repartee and conquest remain at the heart of seduction, for the French seduction has become a philosophy of life, even an ideology, that can confuse outsiders. In [this book, Sciolino looks at] . . . how seduction works in all areas, analyzing its limits as well as its power." (Publisher's note)

The author "deals with the subtle and cultural ways seduction shapes all aspects of French life. She takes a broad approach and writes less about the sexual associations of the word and more about the pleasure game the French play in order to 'attract or influence, to win over, even if just for fun.' Ms. Sciolino's pedigree as a commentator on things French is first class. She was a student in France in 1969 and returned to live and work there as a correspondent for Newsweek, then later as the Bureau Chief of The New York Times in Paris, and now as a correspondent for the paper. She finds French life permeated with the seduction factor, and in a journalistic fashion looks at it in an array of fields, including politics, foreign affairs, literature, history, film, advertising, beauty, scent, fashion, entertaining, food and wine, and sex, and makes her mostly French victims unveil some rules and secrets." Daily Beast

Includes bibliographical references

302.34   Social interaction in primary groups

Bazelon, Emily, 1971-

★ **Sticks** and stones; defeating the culture of bullying and rediscovering the power of character and empathy. by Emily Bazelon. Random House 2013 viii, 386 p.p ill. (hardcover) $27   **302.34**
   1. Bullies 2. Adolescence 3. Social media 4. Bullying 5. Bullying in schools 6. Bullying -- Prevention 7. Bullying in schools -- Prevention
   ISBN 0812992806; 9780679644002; 9780812992809

                         LC 2012022773

This book, by Emily Bazelon, discusses teen culture in the U.S., focusing on bullying. "Being a teenager has never been easy, but in recent years, with the rise of the Internet and social media, it has become exponentially more challenging. . . . Bazelon defines what bullying is and, just as important, what it is not. She explores when intervention is essential and when kids should be given the freedom to fend for themselves. She also dispels persistent myths." (Publisher's note)

"While less prescriptive than other books on the topic, very useful FAQs are included, as are resource lists for readers. Masterfully written, Bazelon's book will increase understanding, awareness, and action." Pub Wkly

Includes bibliographical references and index

Kowalski, Robin M.

Cyberbullying; bullying in the digital age. Robin M. Kowalski, Susan P. Limber, and Patricia W. Agatston. Wiley-Blackwell 2012 xi, 282 p.p (pbk.) $24.95   **302.34**
   1. Social media 2. Cyberbullying 3. School children 4. Computers and children 5. Bullying
   ISBN 1444334816; 9781444334814; 9781444334807

                         LC 2011046026

In this book, "psychologists explore the reality of cyberbullies. . . . Advances in social media, email, instant messaging, and cell phones . . . have moved bullying from a schoolyard fear to a constant threat. The second edition of "Cyberbullying' offers the most current information on this constantly-evolving issue and outlines the unique concerns and challenges it raises for children, parents, and educators." (Publisher's note)

Includes bibliographical references and index

Strauss, Susan L.

★ **Sexual** harassment and bullying; a guide to keeping kids safe and holding schools accountable. Susan L. Strauss. Rowman & Littlefield Publishers 2012 290 p. (cloth : alk. paper) $34.95   **302.34**
1. Bullies 2. Social media 3. Sexual harassment 4. Bullying 5. Bullying -- Prevention 6. Sexual harassment in education 7. Sexual harassment -- Prevention
ISBN 1442201622; 9781442201620

LC 2011031731

In this book, "[Susan L.] Strauss draws on her experiences as consultant, former high-school teacher, and parent of a child who was sexually harassed to advise parents, teachers, and other adults on how to protect children" from bullying and harassment. She gives definitions of bullying and harassment, "offers a particular focus on the kind of harassment of gay, bisexual, and transgendered students," and examines "how social media . . . have ramped up bullying and harassment." (Booklist)

Includes bibliographical references and index.

Whitson, Signe

8 keys to end bullying; strategies for parents & schools. Signe Whitson; foreword by Babette Rothschild. W.W. Norton & Co Inc. 2014 240 p. (8 keys to mental health series) (pbk.) $19.95   **302.34**
1. Bullies 2. Classroom management 3. Bullying -- Prevention 4. Aggressiveness in children 5. Bullying in schools -- Prevention
ISBN 0393709280; 9780393709285

LC 2014001241

This book by Signe Whitson discusses how "social media bullying . . . has given the widespread problem a new dimension. While no magic cure-all exists, adults can learn . . . techniques that can make a huge difference in the lives of kids. In 8 core strategies, this book lays them out, from establishing meaningful connections with kids to creating a positive school climate, addressing cyberbullying, building social emotional competence, . . . and much more." (Publisher's note)

"Complete with example scenarios, exercises for readers, and sample responses, the author does a convincing job of helping adults feel empowered to address this important issue." LJ

Includes bibliographical references and index

302.5   Relation of individual to society

Olds, Jacqueline

The **lonely** American; drifting apart in the twenty-first century. [by] Jacqueline Olds and Richard S. Schwartz. Beacon Press 2008 228p $24.95 **302.5**
1. Loneliness 2. Loneliness -- United States 3. Social isolation -- United States
ISBN 978-0-8070-0034-2; 0-8070-0034-5

LC 2008-19339

The authors "paint a tragic picture of a nation of individual units—families, couples and, increasingly, single people—that have all but ceased to function as a society. While the authors focus largely on the psychological impact of all this isolation, they also explain its physical toll on Americans and their world. Not only is social isolation an indicator for substance abuse, violent crime and early death, it is also linked to greater consumption of consumer goods. . . . In keeping with their profession as psychoanalysts, Olds and Schwartz maintain a kind and caring tone throughout The Lonely American, neither scolding nor scoffing at the nation of individuals Americans have become" PopMatters

Includes bibliographical references and index.

303.3   Coordination and control

Century, Douglas

Making a difference; stories of vision and courage from America's leaders. Chesley "Sully" Sullenberger, with Douglas Century. 1st ed. HarperCollins 2012 x, 318 p.p (hbk.) $26.99   **303.3**
1. Leadership 2. Leadership -- United States -- Case studies
ISBN 0061924709; 9780061924705; 9780061924712; 9780062101365; 9780062128317

LC 2011045074

Author Chesley Sullenberger tells his own story and the story of "first officer Jeff Skiles . . . [as] advocates and champions for aviation safety and the profession of airline pilots. . . . [He also looks at] three-time World Series-winning baseball manager Tony La Russa; Admiral Thad Allen, who brought innovative methods . . . to deal . . . with the aftermath of Hurricane Katrina; Gene Kranz, the NASA Flight Director who . . . brought Apollo 13 and its crew safely home; and Michelle Rhee, who was brought in to overhaul the Washington, D.C., school system." (Kirkus Reviews)

Corning, Peter

The **fair** society; [by] Peter Corning. University of Chicago Press 2011 237p $27.50   **303.3**
1. Fairness 2. Basic needs 3. Social ethics 4. Social policy 5. Social justice 6. Social contract
ISBN 978-0-226-11627-3; 0-226-11627-1

LC 2010021771

It was the author's intent to demonstrate "that human nature has evolved in such a way as to create a natural revulsion to [unfair situations] . . . He recounts various evolutionary arguments for the notion that our hunter-gatherer ancestors possessed a deep sense of fairness and developed 'a pattern of egalitarian sharing' in which 'dominance behaviors were actively resisted by coalitions of other group members.' . . .Corning endeavors to show that the capitalist system as currently practiced in the United States and elsewhere is manifestly unfair. . . . he proposes a new type of society founded on a biosocial contract, which he describes as a 'truly voluntary bargain among various (empowered) stakeholders over how the benefits and obligations in a society are to be apportioned among the members' that is 'grounded in our growing understanding of human nature and the basic purpose of a human society.'"(American Scientist)

"Corning argues that both capitalism and socialism fail the fairness test—both in theory and in practice—and he calls for a new social contract based on three complementary fairness principles: equality in relation to our basic needs, equity (or merit) in relation to our personal efforts and accomplishments, and reciprocity—an obligation for everyone to contribute a fair share in return for the benefits they receive from society. Corning also proposes a set of transformative economic and political reforms that would move us toward the ideal of what he terms a Fair Society, including full employment and a 'basic needs guarantee' for all of our people, a shift in our economic system toward stakeholder (versus shareholder) capitalism, a strong effort to promote cooperative, not-for-profit community development and, not least, a lifelong community service ethic that would include a year or two of national service for all who are able to do so." Politics and Life Sciences

Includes bibliographical references

Huxley, Aldous

★ **Brave** new world revisited. Harper & Row 1958 147p hardcover o.p. pa $11.95　　**303.3**
1. Culture 2. Propaganda 3. Brainwashing 4. Totalitarianism
ISBN 0-06-089852-6 pa

In response to his 1932 novel Brave new world "Huxley reconsiders his prophecies and fears that some of these may be coming true much sooner than he thought." Oxford Companion to Engl Lit. 5th edition

Kellerman, Barbara

The **end** of leadership. Harper Business 2012 256 p. $27.99　　**303.3**
1. Leadership 2. Social change
ISBN 0062069160; 9780062069160

Here, Barbara Kellerman "details vast societal changes that have demeaned and downgraded leaders and altered the relationship between leaders and followers. The Internet and other advances in communication technology brought more information, encouraged greater self-expression and expanded connection. With information available instantly to everyone, followers (citizens, employees, stockholders) learned of their leaders' faults and began questioning their authority." (Kirkus)

Nader, Ralph

Told you so; the big book of weekly columns. by Ralph Nader. Seven Stories Press 2013 xv, 520 p.p (pbk.) $29.95　　**303.3**
1. Social problems 2. United States -- Social conditions 3. Social justice -- United States 4. Corporate power -- United States 5. United States -- Social policy -- 21st century 6. United States -- Economic policy -- 21st century 7. United States -- Social conditions -- 21st century 8. United States -- Politics and government -- 21st century
ISBN 1609804740; 9781609804749
　　　　　　　　　　　　　　LC 2013001625
Author Ralph Nader "presents a panoramic portrait of the problems confronting our society and provides examples of the many actions an organized citizenry could and should take to create a more just and environmentally sustainable

world. Drawing on decades of experience, Nader's columns document the consequences of concentrated corporate power; threats to our food, water and air; the corrosive effect of commercialism on our children; the dismantling of worker rights; and the attacks on our civil rights." (Publisher's note)

Includes index

Naím, Moisés, 1952-

The **end** of power; from boardrooms to battlefields and churches to states, why being in charge isn't what it used to be. Moisés Naím. Basic Books, a member of the Perseus Books Group 2013 xiii, 306 p.p (hardcover) $27.99　　**303.3**
1. Power (Social sciences) 2. Organization
ISBN 0465031560; 9780465031566
　　　　　　　　　　　　　　LC 2012049642
This book, by Moises Naim, explores "the struggle between once-dominant megaplayers and the new micropowers challenging them in every field of human endeavor. . . . Naim . . . covers the seismic changes underway in business, religion, education, within families, and in all matters of war and peace. . . . Those in power retain it by erecting powerful barriers . . . [and] insurgent forces dismantle those barriers more quickly and easily than ever." (Publisher's note)

Includes bibliographical references and index

Rosenberg, Tina

Join the club; how peer pressure can transform the world. W.W. Norton & Company 2011 xxiv, 402p $25.95　　**303.3**
1. Peer pressure 2. Social change 3. Social groups
ISBN 978-0-393-06858-0
　　　　　　　　　　　　　　LC 2010-52146
"A solid, sweeping examination of peer pressure as a force for social change." Kirkus

Includes bibliographical references

Surowiecki, James

The **wisdom** of crowds; why the many are smarter than the few and how collective wisdom shapes business, economies, societies and nations. Doubleday 2004 xxi, 296p $24.95; pa $14　　**303.3**
1. Crowds 2. Social psychology 3. Intellect 4. Consensus (Social sciences)
ISBN 0-385-50386-5; 0-385-72170-6 pa
　　　　　　　　　　　　　　LC 2003-70095

The author argues that "large groups of people are smarter than an elite few, no matter how brilliant: better at solving problems, fostering innovation, coming to wise decisions, even predicting the future." (Publisher's note)

The author "analyzes the concept of collective wisdom and applies it to various areas of the social sciences, including economics and politics. . . . This work is an intriguing study of collective intelligence and how it works in contemporary society." Libr J

Includes bibliographical references

Taibbi, Matt, 1970-

The **divide**; American injustice in the age of the wealth gap. Matt Taibbi; illustrations by Molly Crabapple. Spiegel & Grau 2014 448 p. illustrations (hardback) $27   **303.3**

1. Equality 2. Social policy -- United States 3. Administration of criminal justice -- United States 4. Poor -- United States 5. Rich people -- United States 6. Social justice -- United States 7. Income distribution -- United States

ISBN 081299342X; 9780812993424

LC 2013024907

Taibbi "takes readers on a galvanizing journey through both sides of our new system of justice--the fun-house-mirror worlds of the untouchably wealthy and the criminalized poor. . . . Through . . . accounts of the high-stakes capers of the wealthy and nightmare stories of regular people caught in the Divide's punishing logic, Taibbi lays bare one of the greatest challenges we face in contemporary American life." (Publisher's note)

"Taibbi's chapters are high-definition photographs contrasting the ways we pursue small-time corruption and essentially reward high-level versions of the same thing. [He mixes] case studies, interviews and anecdotes with comprehensive research on his topics." Kirkus

Includes bibliographical references and index

Wills, Garry

Certain trumpets; the call of leaders. Simon & Schuster 1994 336p il hardcover o.p. pa $16 **303.3**

1. Leadership 2. Power (Social sciences) 3. Leadership -- Case studies. 4. Social participation -- Case studies. 5. Power (Social sciences) -- Case studies.

ISBN 0-671-65702-X; 978-0-684-80138-4 pa; 0-684-80138-8 pa

LC 94-6526

The author "has chosen 16 figures who exemplify a distinctive leadership type—for example, military (Napoleon), charismatic (King David), saintly (Catholic worker activist Dorothy Day). Each leader is contrasted with an 'anti-type' who, in Wills's judgment, failed to capitalize on strengths similar to those of his or her successful counterpart. . . . Wills pairs Martha Graham with Madonna, Socrates with Ludwig Wittgenstein, Eleanor Roosevelt with Nancy Reagan in a wise, witty, entertaining look at the psychology of leaders and their followers." Publ Wkly

Includes bibliographical references

303.4   Social change

Baker, Stephen

The **numerati**. Houghton Mifflin Co. 2008 244p $26   **303.4**

1. Data processing 2. Mathematical models

ISBN 978-0-618-78460-8; 0-618-78460-8

LC 2008-17830

The author "spotlights a new breed of entrepreneurial mathematicians (the numerati) engaged in harnessing the avalanche of private data individuals provide when they use a credit card, donate to a cause, surf the Internet—or even make a phone call. . . . An intriguing but disquieting look at a not too distant future when our thoughts will remain private, but computers will disclose our tastes, opinions, habits

and quirks to curious parties, not all of whom have our best interests at heart." Publ Wkly

Includes bibliographical references

Barash, David P.

Homo mysterious; evolutionary puzzles of human nature. David P. Barash. Oxford University Press 2012 329 p. (hardback : alk. paper) $27.95   **303.4**

1. Evolution 2. Human beings 3. Sociobiology 4. Sex (Biology) 5. Human evolution 6. Social evolution 7. Evolution (Biology)

ISBN 0199751943; 9780199751945

LC 2011044302

This book, by David P. Barash, examines "evolutionary questions about the human condition . . . [such as] why do women have orgasms; why does menopause exist; why do men have shorter average life spans than women; what's the evolutionary reason for homosexuality, the arts, and religion. . . . He shows how tentative scientific explanations are and the critical role hypothesis testing plays in our understanding of the world." (Publishers Weekly)

Includes bibliographical references and index.

Carr, Nicholas G., 1959-

The **big** switch; rewiring the world, from Edison to Google. W. W. Norton & Company 2008 278p $25.95; pa $16.95   **303.4**

1. Internet 2. Information technology 3. Technological innovations 4. Computers and civilization

ISBN 0-393-06228-7; 0-393-33394-9 pa; 978-0-393-06228-1; 978-0-393-33394-7 pa

LC 2007-38084

The author "examines the future of the Internet, which he says may one day completely replace the desktop PC as all computing services are delivered over the Net as a utility, the Internet morphing into one giant 'World Wide Computer.'" Booklist

Includes bibliographical references

Diamond, Jared M.

★ **Guns,** germs, and steel; the fates of human societies. [by] Jared Diamond. Norton 2005 518p il map $24.95   **303.4**

1. Ethnology 2. Food supply 3. Social change 4. Technology and civilization 5. Environmental influence on humans

ISBN 0-393-06131-0; 978-0-393-06131-4

LC 2005-284261

First published 1997

"This book poses a simple but profound question about the distribution of wealth and power in the modern world: 'Why weren't Native Americans, Africans, and Aboriginal Australians the ones who decimated, subjugated, or exterminated Europeans and Asians?'. . . To explore the discrepancies in technological and cultural development he looks not at peoples but at places, and at the natural resources available to different indigenous populations since 11,000 B.C. The scope and the explanatory power of this book are astounding." New Yorker [review of 1997 edition]

Includes bibliographical references

Ferris, Timothy

The **science** of liberty; democracy, reason and the laws of nature. Harper 2010 368p $26.99 **303.4**
1. Democracy 2. Science and civilization 3. Science -- History
ISBN 978-0-06-078150-7; 0-06-078150-5
LC 2009-27505

The author "argues that science and the rise of 'science societies' are the fundamental drivers of liberty and democracy. . . . Ferris traces the dual scientific and democratic revolutions from their Renaissance, Enlightenment, and early modern origins to the titanic twentieth-century battles between the liberal democracies and their fascist and communist rivals. Ferris also explores the scientific orientation of the United States' founders, such as Thomas Jefferson and Benjamin Franklin, and its relevance to their constitutional thinking and their noble 'experiment' of a new nation. The Science of Liberty is sweeping and provocative, even if many may still doubt that science can extinguish prejudices, parochialisms, and illiberal impulses." Foreign Affairs

Includes bibliographical references

Gore, Albert, 1948-

The **future**; six drivers of global change. Al Gore. Random House 2013 xxxi, 558 p.p (hardback) $30 **303.4**
1. Forecasting 2. Climate change 3. World history -- 21st century 4. Globalization 5. Social change 6. Technological innovations 7. Global environmental change 8. Economic history -- 21st century
ISBN 0812992946; 9780812992946
LC 2012039890

This book, by Al Gore, offers an "assessment of six critical drivers of global change in the decades to come. . . . Al Gore surveys . . . ever-increasing economic globalization . . . , worldwide digital communications, . . . the balance of global political, economic, and military power . . . , unsustainable growth in consumption, pollution flows, and depletion of the planet's strategic resources . . . , [and] genomic, biotechnology, neuroscience, and life sciences revolutions." (Publisher's note)

"Gore's strengths lie in his passion for the subject and in his ability to take the long view by putting current events and trends in historical context," PubWkly

Includes bibliographical references (pages 379-387) and index

Heath, Chip

Switch; how to change things when change is hard. [by] Chip Heath and Dan Heath. Broadway Books 2010 305p $26; pa $15.95; ebook $11.99 **303.4**
1. Change (Psychology)
ISBN 978-0-385-52875-7; 978-0-307-74235-3 pa; 978-0-307-59016-9 ebook
LC 2009-27814

This book "offers many insights about human behavior and psychology that marketing professionals, communications experts, and public-policy makes might all appreciate." Futurist

Includes bibliographical references

Hessler, Peter

Country driving; a journey through China from farm to factory. Harper 2010 438p map $27.99 **303.4**
1. Highway transportation 2. Journalists 3. China -- Description and travel 4. Transportation, Automotive -- China
ISBN 0-06-180409-6; 978-0-06-180409-0
LC 2009-27502

In 2001, Peter Hessler, the Beijing correspondent for The New Yorker, acquired his Chinese driver's license. For the next seven years, he traveled the country, tracking how the automobile and improved roads were transforming China. . . . Country Driving begins with Hessler's 7,000-mile trip across northern China, following the Great Wall, from the East China Sea to the Tibetan plateau. He investigates a historically important rural region being abandoned, as young people migrate to jobs in the southeast. Next Hessler spends six years in Sancha, a small farming village in the mountains north of Beijing, which changes dramatically after the local road is paved and the capital's auto boom brings new tourism. Finally, he turns his attention to urban China, researching development . . . in Lishui, a small southeastern city where officials hope that a new government-built expressway will transform a farm region into a major industrial center. (Publisher's note)

"Full of exotic detail, solid reporting, and ironic observation, Country Driving offers a personal snapshot of the world's second superpower hurtling through the 21st century." Boston Globe

Includes bibliographical references

Ladd, Brian

Autophobia; love and hate in the automotive age. University of Chicago Press 2008 227p il $22.50 **303.4**
1. Automobiles 2. Environmental degradation 3. Automobiles -- Social aspects 4. Transportation, Automotive -- United States
ISBN 0-226-46741-4; 978-0-226-46741-2
LC 2008-14520

This is "a look at the car and its critics." (N Y Times Book Rev) Index.

Ladd "documents a century of expanding U.S. reliance on vehicles powered by oil, most of which has to be imported. He frames his analysis in familiar concepts: the automotive industry as employer, urban migration from cities by families relying on automobiles for transportation, traffic/congestion/roadways, and damage to the environment from burning fossil fuels. . . . [The author shows] how the car is completely woven into the fabric of our cultural and economic history. As such, he writes, we have accepted the dark side of the automobile—pollution, congestion, high energy costs, and accidental loss of life—in exchange for personal mobility." Libr J

Includes bibliographical references

Lanier, Jaron

★ **You** are not a gadget; a manifesto. Alfred A. Knopf 2010 209p $24.95 **303.4**
1. Information technology 2. Technological innovations 3. Technology and civilization 4. Web sites -- Design

5. Digital media -- Social aspects 6. Information technology -- Social aspects 7. Technological innovations -- Social aspects

ISBN 0-307-26964-7; 978-0-307-26964-5

LC 2009-20298

The author, an artist and computer scientist, offers an examination of the way the World Wide Web "is transforming our lives. . . . [He maintains that] the web's first designers made crucial choices (such as making one's presence anonymous) that have had enormous—and often unintended—consequences. What's more, these designs quickly became 'locked in,' a permanent part of the web's very structure. Lanier discusses the technical and cultural problems that [he believes] can grow out of poorly considered digital design and warns that our financial markets and sites like Wikipedia, Facebook, and Twitter are elevating the 'wisdom' of mobs and computer algorithms over the intelligence and judgment of individuals. . . . [Lanier argues that] a new humanistic technology is necessary." (Publisher's note)

"In the nineteen-eighties, Lanier belonged to what he calls a 'merry band' of Internet pioneers who believed that the digital revolution would mean a groundswell of creativity. But, he argues in this manifesto, around the turn of this century the dream was hijacked by 'digital Maoists,' who value the crowd above the individual. Their influence, he writes, has led to an online culture of mashups, 'pervasive anonymity' (which encourages bullying and moblike behavior), open access (so that individual ownership is devalued or lost), and social-networking sites that reduce 'the deep meaning of personhood.' He fears that these characteristics are perilously close to 'lock-in': becoming permanent features of the Web. Lanier's detractors have accused him of Ludditism, but his argument will make intuitive sense to anyone concerned with questions of propriety, responsibility, and authenticity." New Yorker

Linden, Eugene

The **ragged** edge of the world; encounters at the frontier where modernity, wildlands, and indigenous peoples meet. Viking 2011 260p $26.95   **303.4**

1. Ethnology

ISBN 978-0-670-02251-9

LC 2010043578

"Traveling to the rain forests of Borneo and to the Amazon, the Antarctic, and Africa, Linden provides firsthand accounts of cargo cults in New Guinea, practices of Pygmy tribes in Africa, and conservation efforts in Cuba—some of which show positive responses to deforestation and loss of habitat for wildlife, while others reveal the downward spiral to extinction for rain forests and many animal species. He highlights cultural extinction as much as environmental devastation to habitats. . . . Linden provides an original look at globalization and its impact on various cultures and species throughout the world. Anyone interested in global environmental issues will find this book informative." Libr J

Otto, Shawn

Fool me twice; fighting the assault on science in America. [by] Shawn Lawrence Otto. Rodale 2011 376p $25.99   **303.4**

1. Learning and scholarship 2. Science -- United States 3. Science -- Study and teaching 4. United States --

Intellectual life

ISBN 978-1-60529-217-5; 1-60529-217-6

LC 2011033902

The author "explores the devaluation of science in America. His exhaustively researched text explains the three-pronged attack on science: how right-wing Christian fervor discredits evolution; how post-modernism and cultural sensitivity makes people believe that objective truth doesn't exist; and how corporations discredit scientists in order to further economic agendas. . . . The accessible book will inform scientists about what has happened to their field, provide an overview for laypeople, and allow educators to equip themselves to address these issues for the next generation and reverse this troubling trend." Publ Wkly

Includes bibliographical references

Pagel, Mark

Wired for culture; origins of the human social mind. Mark Pagel. W. W. Norton & Company 2012 416 p.   **303.4**

1. Culture 2. Evolution 3. Social change 4. Social sciences 5. Language and languages 6. Human evolution 7. Social evolution 8. Evolution (Biology) 9. Evolutionary genetics

ISBN 0393065871; 9780393065879

LC 2011044465

This book "frames cultural development in the language of Richard Dawkins's selfish gene theory. . . . Dawkins . . . coined the term 'meme' as the cultural analogue of a gene. [Mark] Pagel . . . [argues that m]emes . . . have built vehicles around themselves made up of groups of people. . . . [He] explores the implications of the emerging consensus across . . . religion, the arts and economics, . . . consciousness, deception, conflict and the very idea of truth." (New Scientist)

Includes bibliographical references and index

Pipher, Mary

The **green** boat; reviving ourselves in our capsized culture. Mary Pipher. Riverhead Books 2013 240 p. $16   **303.4**

1. Environmental movement 2. Culture shock 3. Adjustment (Psychology) 4. Social change -- Psychological aspects 5. Social problems -- Psychological aspects

ISBN 1594485852; 9781594485855

LC 2012043406

Here, Mary Pipher offers an "approach to acknowledging the global environmental crisis." She "explains, the overwhelming amount of information about the desperate state of our planet leads to stress, avoiding discussion, willful ignorance, and outright denial. . . . Piper distinguishes between 'distractionable intelligence,' which makes us feel helpless, and 'actionable intelligence,' which combines information with suggestions for addressing problems." (Publishers Weekly)

★ The **Radical** reader; a documentary history of the American radical tradition. edited by Timothy Patrick McCarthy and John McMillian; foreword

by Eric Foner. New Press 2003 688p $65; lib bdg $21.95 **303.4**
1. Radicalism
ISBN 1-56584-827-6; 1-56584-682-6 lib bdg
LC 2002-41051

"By bringing many hard-to-find documents under one cover, this anthology will excite readers in discussing why radicals from all walks of life have made progressive ideals meaningful to Americans. Recommended for college, high school, and public libraries." Libr J

Includes bibliographical references

Shirky, Clay

Cognitive surplus; creativity and generosity in a connected age. Penguin Press 2010 242p $25.95 **303.4**
1. Social networking 2. Information society 3. Social media 4. Mass media -- Social aspects
ISBN 1-59420-253-2; 978-1-59420-253-7
LC 2009-53882

This is an "inquiry into what we might join together to do instead if we weren't watching TV." (N Y Times Book Rev) Index.

Shirky "argues that new technology is making it possible for people to collaborate in ways that have the potential to change society. By 'cognitive surplus,' the author refers to the free time of the world's educated citizenry, which amounts to more than one trillion hours per year. . . . [He] discusses the many factors that have given rise to social media and suggests the conditions that will best allow voluntary groups to take advantage of the world's aggregate free time to benefit society. . . . [Shirky] may be overly optimistic about the possible benefits of social media, but he makes clear their growing global importance. An informed look at the social impact of the Internet." Kirkus

Includes bibliographical references

Solnit, Rebecca

A **paradise** built in hell; the extraordinary communities that arise in disasters. Viking 2009 353p $27.95 **303.4**
1. Disasters
ISBN 978-0-670-02107-9; 0-670-02107-5
LC 2009-04101

"An engaging book, full of fascinating detail, 'Paradise' especially deserves a close reading by political leaders at every level, as well as the news media who cover disasters." Christ Sci Monit

Includes bibliographical references

Tapscott, Don, 1947-

Macrowikinomics; rebooting business and the world. [by] Don Tapscott and Anthony D. Williams. Portfolio/Penguin 2010 424p $27.95 **303.4**
1. Information technology 2. Online social networks 3. Technological innovations
ISBN 978-1-59184-356-6
LC 2010023338

The authors "present a new framework for understanding social and economic innovations applicable to the spectrum of industries under which people utilize emerging Web applications to foster a more economically, socially, and ecologically sustainable world. . . . [This book] addresses an important issue and is good preparation for an epoch of staggering technological leaps." Choice

Includes bibliographical references

Toffler, Alvin

★ **Future** shock. Bantam Books 1990 561p pa $7.99 **303.4**
1. Family 2. Children 3. Democracy 4. Education 5. Social change 6. Adaptation (Biology) 7. Interpersonal relations 8. Technology and civilization 9. Modern civilization -- 1950-
ISBN 978-0-553-27737-1; 0-553-27737-5
First published 1970 by Random House

According to the author, "future shock is 'the dizzying disorientation brought on by the premature arrival of the future.' . . . Toffler outlines some interesting strategies for survival, writing in a clear popular style." Publ Wkly

Includes bibliographical references

Turkle, Sherry

Alone together. Basic Books 2011 360p $28.95 **303.4**
1. Information technology 2. Interpersonal relations 3. Human-computer interaction 4. Information technology -- Social aspects
ISBN 978-0-465-01021-9; 0-465-01021-0
LC 2010-30614

This book "is the third in a trilogy, part of a project [author Sherry Turkle] . . . has been working on since she joined MIT in 1976 and noticed that the people there were using the language of psychology to talk about their machines. . . . Turkle picks out the contradictions of the networked life that everyone has now come to take for granted, but adolescents especially: the desire for attention and the desire to hide, constantly online but dreading the exposure of a phone call. . . . Turkle argues that people risk impairing the quality of their thought and communication by so often resorting to media designed only for short, simplified messages." (London Review of Books)

"Turkle argues that people are increasingly functioning without face-to-face contact. For all the talk of convenience and connection derived from texting, e-mailing, and social networking, Turkle reaffirms that what humans still instinctively need is each other, and she encounters dissatisfaction and alienation among users. . . . Turkle's prescient book makes a strong case that what was meant to be a way to facilitate communications has pushed people closer to their machines and further away from each other." Publ Wkly

Includes bibliographical references

303.48 Causes of change

Burrough, Bryan

Days of Rage; America's Radical Underground, the FBI, and the First Age of Terror. Bryan Burrough. Penguin Group USA 2015 464 p. 16 plates; illustrations $29.95 **303.48**
1. Revolutionaries 2. United States -- Civilization --

1970- 3. United States. Federal Bureau of Investigation
ISBN 1594204292; 9781594204296

LC 2014036663

This book by Bryan Burrough presents an "account of
the decade-long battle between the FBI and the homegrown
revolutionary movements of the 1970s. [It] is filled with
revelations and fresh details about the major revolutionaries
and their connections and about the FBI and its desperate efforts to make the bombings stop. The result is a mesmerizing
book that takes us into the hearts and minds of homegrown
terrorists and federal agents." (Publisher's note)

"The author's history is thoroughgoing and fascinating,
though with a couple of curious notes—e.g., the likening
of the Weathermen et al. to the Nazi Werewolf guerrillas
'who briefly attempted to resist Allied forces after the end
of World War II.' A superb chronicle, long—but no longer
than needed—and detailed, that sheds light on how the war
on terror is being waged today." Kirkus

Encyclopedia of mathematics and society; Sarah
J. Greenwald, Jill E. Thomley, [editors] Salem
Press 2012 3 v. (xxxi, 1191 p.)p   **303.48**
1. Mathematics -- History 2. Mathematics --
Encyclopedias 3. Mathematics -- Social aspects
ISBN 1587658445; 1587658453; 1587658461;
158765847X; 9781587658440; 9781587658457;
9781587658464; 9781587658471

LC 2011021856

This encyclopedia of mathematics "focus[es] on how the
basic concepts of figures relate to everyday life. As the editors phrase it, the purpose of these compact volumes is to
'weave multilayered connections between society, history,
people, applications, and mathematics.' . . . [T]opics covered
include 'Cooking,' 'Earthquakes,' 'Mathematics and Religion,' and 'Skydiving.' While some purely mathematical
principles are discussed, they are always placed in relation to
the larger context of human affairs, such as in the essay 'Algebra in Society.' Pieces open with boldface headword(s), a
classification of the subject matter, and a one-line summary
of the material to follow. A short bibliography and cross-
references follow." (Libr J)

Includes bibliographical references and index

Freeberg, Ernest

The **Age** of Edison; Electric Light and the Invention of Modern America. Ernest Freeberg. Penguin Group USA 2013 368 p. ill. (hardcover)
$27.95   **303.48**
1. Technological innovations -- History 2. Electric
lighting -- United States -- History 3. Technological
innovations -- United States -- History 4. Technological
innovations -- Social aspects -- United States -- History
ISBN 1594204268; 9781594204265

LC 2012039513

This book, by Ernest Freeberg, discusses the social impact of the invention of electricity, as part of the "Penguin
History of American Life" series. It "places the story of
Edison's invention in the context of a technological revolution that transformed America and Europe. . . . Edison and
his fellow inventors emerged from a culture shaped by . . .
a lively popular press that took an interest in science and

technology, and an American patent system that encouraged
innovation." (Publisher's note)

Includes bibliographical references (pages 317-341)
and index

Guest, Robert

Borderless economics; Chinese sea turtles, Indian fridges, and the new fruits of global capitalism.
Robert Guest. Palgrave Macmillan 2011 256 p.
$27.00   **303.48**
1. Wealth 2. Economics 3. Business networks 4.
Diffusion of innovations 5. Immigrants -- United States
6. Globalization -- Economic aspects
ISBN 0230113826; 9780230113824

LC 2011022135

This book offers a "survey of the global impact of the
215 million people who live outside their countries of origin." Author Robert Guest "contends that the three percent
(and growing) part of the world's population that is migrating is disproportionately contributing to the creation of international wealth, both in the sense of financial assets and the
development of new technological and economic capabilities." (Kirkus)

Includes bibliographical references and index.

Hedges, Chris

Wages of rebellion; by Chris Hedges. Nation
Books 2015 304 p. (hardback) $26.99   **303.48**
1. Revolutions 2. Social movements 3. Protest
movements 4. Revolutions -- Social aspects
ISBN 1568589662; 9781568589664

LC 2014044940

In this book, author Chris Hedges "investigates what
social and psychological factors cause revolution, rebellion, and resistance. Drawing on an ambitious overview of
prominent philosophers, historians, and literary figures he
shows not only the harbingers of a coming crisis but also the
nascent seeds of rebellion. Hedges' message is clear: popular
uprisings in the United States and around the world are inevitable in the face of environmental destruction and wealth
polarization." (Publisher's note)

"People tend to either love or hate Hedges, but librarians
in public, academic, and relevant special libraries will want
this book because, even if the revolution isn't about to happen, Hedges's voice is an important one." LJ

Includes bibliographical references and index

Heffernan, Virginia

Magic and Loss; The Internet as Art. by Virginia Heffernan. Simon & Schuster 2016 272 p.
$26   **303.48**
1. Internet
ISBN 1439191700; 9781439191705

In this book, author Virginia Heffernan "reveals the logic
and aesthetics behind the Internet. Since its inception, the
Internet has morphed from merely an extension of traditional media into its own full-fledged civilization. It is among
mankind's great masterpieces—a massive work of art. . . .
Heffernan presents an original and far-reaching analysis of
what the Internet is and does." (Publisher's note)

"A thoroughly engrossing examination of the Internet's
past, present, and future." Kirkus

Johnson, Clay

The **information** diet; Clay A. Johnson. 1st ed. O'Reilly Media 2012 ix, 150p.p   **303.48**
   1. Conduct of life 2. Information society
   ISBN 9781449304683; 1449304680
                       LC 2011410787

This book examines how humans have "become gluttons for texts, instant messages, emails, RSS feeds, downloads, videos, status updates, and tweets. We're all battling a storm of distractions, buffeted with notifications and tempted by tasty tidbits of information. And just as too much junk food can lead to obesity, too much junk information can lead to cluelessness. 'The Information Diet' shows you how to thrive in this information glut--what to look for, what to avoid, and how to be selective. In the process, author Clay Johnson explains the role information has played throughout history, and why following his prescribed diet is essential for everyone who strives to be smart, productive, and sane." (Publisher's note)

Includes bibliographical references.

Johnson, Steven, 1968-

Future perfect; the case for progress in a networked age. Steven Johnson. Riverhead Books 2012 xxxvii, 231 p.p (alk. paper) $26.95   **303.48**
   1. Progress 2. Social change 3. Information networks 4. Technology and civilization 5. Information technology -- Social aspects 6. Social networks
   ISBN 1594488207; 9781594488207
                       LC 2012026086

This book by Steven Johnson "makes the case that a new model of political change is on the rise, transforming everything from local governments to classrooms, from protest movements to health care . . . -- influenced by the success and interconnectedness of the Internet, but not dependent on high-tech solutions. . . . Johnson explores this new vision of progress through a series of . . . narratives: from the 'miracle on the Hudson' to the planning of the French railway system." (Publisher's note)

Includes bibliographical references and index

Kotler, Steven, 1967-

Abundance; the future is better than you think. Peter H. Diamandis and Steven Kotler. Simon & Schuster 2012 p. cm.   **303.48**
   1. Population 2. Food supply 3. Natural resources 4. Technological forecasting 5. Technology -- Social aspects 6. Technological innovations -- Forecasting
   ISBN 1451614217; 9781451614213
                      LC 2011039926

"Diamandis, a tech-entrepreneur turned philanthropist, and journalist Kolter . . . contend that widespread pessimism about the future is due in part to our cognitive biases and the effects of mass media. Bad news sells newspapers, while good news escapes our attention or remains hidden in statistics. This engaging book is a needed corrective, a whirlwind tour of the latest developments in health care, agriculture, energy, and other fields as well as an introduction to thinkers and innovators such as Daniel Kahneman, Ray Kurzweil, and Craig Venter." (Choice)

Kunstler, James Howard

Too much magic; wishful thinking, technology, and the fate of the nation. James Howard Kunstler. Atlantic Monthly Press 2012 245 p. (hardcover) $25.00   **303.48**
   1. Technological innovations 2. Technology and civilization 3. United States -- Economic conditions
   ISBN 080212030X; 9780802120304

In this book, James Howard Kunstler "recount[s] the evidence supporting his predictions about our radically altered future. . . . The dangerously stressed systems that underpin the society we've known since World War II -- 'agriculture, commerce, manufacturing, transport, finance, the oil-gas-coal industry, the electric grid' -- are too large, too complex and too expensive to sustain any longer." (Kirkus Reviews)

Moreno, Jonathan D.

The **body** politic; Jonathan D. Moreno. Bellevue Literary Press 2011 207p.   **303.48**
   1. Science 2. Abortion 3. Eugenics 4. United States 5. Stem cell research
   ISBN 9781934137383 pa; 1934137383 pa
                       LC 2011026354

In this book, a "Kirkus Reviews" Best Book of the Year, the author uses the term "'biopolitics,' popularized by [philosopher] Michel Foucault . . . to describe historical and current debates over issues ranging from abortion and health care to stem cells and genetically modified organisms. . . . [He] unpacks . . . distrust of technology, on both the political right and left. . . . Both extremes place 'human dignity' as central to their trepidation toward technology, but they have starkly contrasting ideas of what such a concept embodies. The far-left greens fear the effects of technology on social justice, while the neoconservatives are more concerned with technology as a source of alienation from what makes us truly human. . . . Ultimately, Moreno shows that the disarming features of modern biology reflect those of all science as a human endeavor." (washingtonindependentreveiwof-books.com)

Includes bibliographical references and index.

Morozov, Evgeny

The **net** delusion; Evgeny Morozov. Public Affairs 2011 xvii, 409 p.p   **303.48**
   1. Democracy 2. Freedom of information 3. Internet -- Political aspects 4. Iran -- Politics and government 5. Internet -- Social aspects
   ISBN 978-1-58648-874-1; 1-58648-874-0
                       LC 2010039066

This book challenges "[t]he idea that the internet was fomenting revolution and promoting democracy in Iran . . . [and the] belief that communications technology, and the internet in particular, is inherently pro-democratic. In this gleefully iconoclastic book, Evgeny Morozov takes a stand against this "cyber-utopian" view, arguing that the internet can be just as effective at sustaining authoritarian regimes. By assuming that the internet is always pro-democratic, he says, Western policymakers are operating with a 'voluntary intellectual handicap' that makes it harder rather than easier to promote democracy. . . . He starts with the events in Iran, which illustrate his argument in microcosm. . . . Mr Morozov catalogues many similar examples of the internet being used with similarly pacifying consequences today, as authoritarian regimes make an implicit deal with their populations: help yourselves to pirated films, silly video clips and online pornography, but stay away from politics." (Economist)

Includes bibliographical references and index.

Razsa, Maple

Bastards of Utopia; Living Radical Politics After Socialism. by Maple Razsa. Indiana University Press 2015 296 p. $30 **303.48**

  1. Protest movements 2. Yugoslavia -- History

ISBN 0253015839; 0253015863; 9780253015839; 9780253015860

                    LC 2014044169

This book, by Maple Razsa, "the companion to a feature documentary film of the same name, explores the experiences and political imagination of young radical activists in the former Yugoslavia, participants in what they call alterglobalization or 'globalization from below.' . . . Razsa follows individual activists from the transnational protests against globalization of the early 2000s through the Occupy encampments." (Publisher's note)

Ridley, Matt

The **evolution** of everything; how new ideas emerge. Matt Ridley. Harper, an imprint of HarperCollinsPublishers 2015 360 p. (hardcover) $28.99 **303.48**

  1. Evolution 2. Thought and thinking 3. Civilization, Modern 4. Diffusion of innovations 5. Technology and civilization

ISBN 9780062296009; 9780062296016

                    LC 2015026886

This book by Matt Ridley "is about bottom-up order and its enemy, the top-down twitch--the endless fascination human beings have for design rather than evolution, for direction rather than emergence. Drawing on anecdotes from science, economics, history, politics and philosophy, Matt Ridley's wide-ranging, highly opinionated opus demolishes conventional assumptions that major scientific and social imperatives are dictated by those on high, whether in government, business, academia, or morality." (Publisher's note)

"All along, Ridley shows how hard it has been for even the most definite evolutionists to fully abandon the notion of a guiding intelligence, whether divine or human. Yet that is what the hard evidence to the effect that good things come by undirected means that Ridley adduces in every chapter compels us all to do." Booklist

Includes bibliographical references (pages 323-341) and index

Rushkoff, Douglas

Present Shock; When Everything Happens Now. Douglas Rushkoff. Penguin Group USA 2013 vii, 296 p.p (hardcover) $26.95 **303.48**

  1. Conduct of life 2. Mass media -- Social aspects 3. Information technology -- Social aspects 4. Technology -- Philosophy 5. Technology -- Social aspects

ISBN 1591844762; 9781591844761

                    LC 2012039915

This book, by Douglas Rushkoff, explains how 21st-century society has "created technologies that would help

connect us faster, gather news, map the planet, compile knowledge, and connect with anyone, at anytime. . . . . And the dissonance between our digital selves and our analog bodies has thrown us into a new state of anxiety: present shock." (Publisher's note)

Includes bibliographical references and index

Steiner-Adair, Catherine

The **Big** Disconnect; Protecting Childhood and Family Relationships in the Digital Age. HarperCollins 2013 384 p. $26.99 **303.48**

  1. Parenting 2. Parent-child relationship 3. Internet -- Social aspects

ISBN 0062082426; 9780062082428

"Parents text relentlessly or worship the computer screen, while children learn more from social media than from school. The result? Distorted family dynamics and children unable to develop sustaining relationships. Advice from a clinical psychologist." (Library Journal)

Tenner, Edward

Our own devices; How Technology Remakes Humanity. Alfred A. Knopf 2004 336p hardcover o.p. pa $14.95; pa $18 **303.48**

  1. Technological innovations 2. Technology and civilization

ISBN 0-375-70707-7 pa; 9780375707070

                    LC 2002-40694

"For a work that covers such a broad topic, this book is a page-turner, largely due to its clear prose and the author's approach to the material. While not lavishly illustrated, there seems to be a picture every time one is needed to illustrate the technology being discussed." SLJ

Includes bibliographical references

Thompson, Clive

Smarter Than You Think; How Technology Is Changing Our Minds for the Better. Clive Thompson. Penguin Group USA 2013 352 p. $27.95 **303.48**

  1. Internet -- Social aspects 2. Technological innovations -- Social aspects 3. Social media 4. Thought and thinking 5. Internet -- Psychological aspects 6. Information technology -- Social aspects 7. Information technology -- Psychological aspects

ISBN 1594204454; 9781594204456

                    LC 2013017155

In this book "about the advent of technology and its influence on humans, journalist [Clive] Thompson . . . admits that we often allow ourselves to be used by facets of new technologies and that we must exercise caution to avoid this; yet, he demonstrates, digital tools can have a huge positive impact on us, for they provide us with infinite memory, the ability to discover connections . . . previously unknown to us, and new and abundant avenues for communication and publishing." (Publishers Weekly)

Includes bibliographical references and index

Venter, J. Craig, 1946-

Life at the Speed of Light; From the Double Helix to the Dawn of Digital Life. by J. Craig Venter. Penguin Group USA 2013 240 p. $26.95 **303.48**

  1. Biology 2. Genomes 3. Genomics 4. Artificial life

5. Biology -- Philosophy 6. Science -- Social aspects
ISBN 0670025402; 9780670025404

LC 2013017049

In this book author J. Craig Venter "presents a fascinating and authoritative study of [synthetic genomics]—detailing its origins, current challenges and controversies, and projected effects on our lives. This scientific frontier provides an opportunity to ponder anew the age-old question 'What is life?' and examine what we really mean by 'playing God.'" (Publisher's note)

Includes bibliographical references and index

Weinberger, David

Too big to know; rethinking knowledge now that the facts aren't the facts, experts are everywhere, and the smartest person in the room is the room. David Weinberger. Basic Books 2011 xiv, 231 p.p (alk. paper) $25.99   **303.48**

1. Internet 2. Theory of knowledge 3. Information technology 4. Knowledge, Sociology of 5. Internet -- Social aspects 6. Information technology -- Social aspects
ISBN 0465021425; 9780465021420; 9780465028139

LC 2011034727

It was the author's intent to demonstrate "that the collaborative, hyperlinked, instant nature of the Internet has fundamentally altered the way humans relate with knowledge. . . . The democratizing of knowledge is not without its dangers. Bad information has equal access to the common well with good information, and is just as viral. But crowdsourced and refereed resources like Wikipedia give [David] Weinberger hope." (Kirkus Reviews)

Includes bibliographical references (p. 199-218) and index.

Young, Ralph

Dissent; the history of an American idea. Ralph Young. New York University Press 2015 640 p. illustrations (cl : alk. paper) $39.95   **303.48**

1. United States -- History 2. Dissenters -- United States 3. Dissenters -- United States -- History 4. United States -- Politics and government 5. Social reformers -- United States -- History 6. Protest movements -- United States -- History 7. United States -- Social conditions -- Sources
ISBN 147980665X; 9781479806652

LC 2014040999

This book, by Ralph Young, "examines the key role dissent has played in shaping the United States. It focuses on those who, from colonial days to the present, dissented against the ruling paradigm of their time: from the Puritan Anne Hutchinson and Native American chief Powhatan in the seventeenth century, to the Occupy and Tea Party movements in the twenty-first century." (Publisher's note)

Includes bibliographical references and index

303.482   Contact between cultures

Foer, Franklin

How soccer explains the world; an unlikely theory of globalization. by Franklin Foer. HarperCollins 2004 261p (ebook) $13.99   **303.482**

ISBN 0-06-621234-0; 9780061864704; 9780061978050

This book, by Franklin Foer, "is a unique and . . . illuminating look at soccer, the world's most popular sport, as a lens through which to view the pressing issues of our age, from the clash of civilizations to the global economy." (Publisher's note)

"Though the globalism thread sometimes disappears, the author is unfailingly interesting. Lively and provocative-even for those who just don't get what FIFA is all about." Kirkus

Includes bibliographical references and index.

303.483   Development of science and technology

Carr, Nicholas G., 1959-

Utopia is creepy; And Other Provocations. Nicholas Carr. W W Norton & Co Inc 2016 384 p. (hardcover) $26.95   **303.483**

1. Social sciences 2. Technology and civilization
ISBN 9780393254549

LC 2016018920

This book, by Nicholas Carr, "offers an alternative history of the digital age, chronicling its roller-coaster crazes and crashes, its blind triumphs, and its unintended consequences. . . . Carr offers searching assessments of the future of work, the fate of reading, and the rise of artificial intelligence, challenging us to see our world anew." (Publisher's note)

"A collection that reminds us that critical thinking is the best way to view the mixed blessings of rampant technology." Kirkus

Colvile, Robert

The Great Acceleration; How the World is Getting Faster, Faster. by Robert Colvile. St. Martin's Press 2016 400 p. $28   **303.483**

1. Speed 2. Social change 3. Quality of life
ISBN 163286455X; 9781632864550

In this book, author Robert Colvile "inspects the various ways in which the pace of life in our society is increasing and examines the evolutionary science behind our rapidly accelerating need for change, as well as why it's unlikely we'll be able to slow down . . . or even want to. Exploring theories surrounding the effect of this speed on our minds and bodies, Colvile reveals how . . . living in a faster age might be beneficial for us, both physically and mentally." (Publisher's note)

"Anyone worried about our increasingly frenetic lives will find food for thought" Booklist

Includes bibliographical references (pages 329-374) and an index.

303.49 Social forecasts

Kaku, Michio

Physics of the future; how science will shape human destiny and our daily lives by the year 2100. Doubleday 2011 389p il $28.95; ebook $12.99 **303.49**

1. Science 2. Forecasting 3. Science -- Social aspects 4. Science -- History -- 21st century

ISBN 978-0-385-53080-4; 978-0-385-53081-1 ebook

LC 2010-26569

"The book's lively, user-friendly style should appeal equally to fans of science fiction and popular science." Booklist

Includes bibliographical references

303.6 Conflict and conflict resolution

Camus, Albert

The **rebel**; an essay on man in revolt. with a foreword by Sir Herbert Read; a revised and complete translation of L'homme révolté by Anthony Bower. Vintage Bks. 1991 306p pa $12 **303.6**

1. Authors 2. Nihilism 3. Novelists 4. Revolutions 5. Philosophers 6. Essayists 7. Memoirists 8. Revolutionaries 9. Short story writers 10. Writers on politics 11. Political and social philosophers

ISBN 0-679-73384-1

LC 91-50022

Original French edition, 1951; this translation first published 1956 by Knopf

The author describes how the theories of philosophers have been used with disastrous effect by political leaders from the French Revolution through the nihilist revolutions of Russia and the governments of Lenin, Hitler and Stalin. The conclusion calls for a return to a political philosophy having as its aim the happiness and development of living human beings

Carr, Caleb

The **lessons** of terror; a history of warfare against civilians: why it has always failed and why it will fail again. Random House 2002 272p hardcover o.p. pa $12.95 **303.6**

1. Terrorism

ISBN 0-375-76074-1 pa

LC 2002-280604

The author argues "that terrorism must be viewed in terms of 'military history, rather than political science or sociology,' and that the refusal to label terrorists as soldiers, rather than criminals, is a mistake. . . . This often fascinating, accessible tome skillfully contends that the terrorizing of civilians has a long and controversial history but, as an inferior method, is prone to failure." Publ Wkly

Includes bibliographical references

Dershowitz, Alan M.

Why terrorism works; understanding the threat, responding to the challenge. Yale Univ. Press 2002 271p $24.95; pa $16 **303.6**

1. Terrorism

ISBN 0-300-09766-2; 0-300-10153-8 pa

LC 2002-6387

The author "argues forcefully that the attacks of September 11 were largely of our own doing—the international community, Dershowitz says, repeatedly rewards terrorists with appeasement and legitimization, refusing to take the necessary steps to curtail attacks. . . . These penetrating arguments force readers to consider how we got to September 11, how far we are willing to pursue terrorists and how much freedom we are willing to give up for our security." Publ Wkly

Includes bibliographical references

Morris, Ian

War! What is it good for? conflict and the progress of civilization from primates to robots. Ian Morris. Farrar Straus & Giroux 2014 512 p. illustrations, maps (hardback) $30 **303.6**

1. War 2. Military history 3. War and civilization 4. War and society

ISBN 0374286000; 9780374286002

LC 2013038722

This book, by Ian Morris, "tells the gruesome . . . story of fifteen thousand years of war, going beyond the battles and brutality to reveal what war has really done to and for the world. . . . War, and war alone, has created bigger, more complex societies, ruled by governments that have stamped out internal violence. Strangely enough, killing has made the world safer, and the safety it has produced has allowed people to make the world richer too." (Publisher's note)

"A profoundly uncomfortable but provocative argument that 'productive war' promotes greater safety, a decrease in violence and economic growth." Kirkus

Includes bibliographical references and index

Sontag, Susan

Regarding the pain of others. Farrar, Straus & Giroux 2003 131p hardcover o.p. pa $12 **303.6**

1. Violence 2. Atrocities 3. Photojournalism 4. War photography 5. Documentary photography

ISBN 978-0-312-42219-6

LC 2002-192527

Companion volume to On photography (1977)

"All libraries, regardless of type, size, or demographics, should own this book." Libr J

304 Factors affecting social behavior

Davies, William

The **happiness** industry; how the government and big business sold us well-being. William Davies. Verso 2015 320 p. (hardcover : U.K. : alkaline paper) $26.95 **304**

1. Happiness 2. Capitalism 3. Social psychology 4. Happiness -- Social aspects 5. Marketing -- Social

aspects 6. Capitalism -- Social aspects 7. Well-being -- Social aspects 8. Well-being -- Economic aspects 9. Neoliberalism -- Social aspects 10. Well-being -- Political aspects 11. Economics -- Psychological aspects 12. Well-being -- Social aspects -- Great Britain
ISBN 1781688451; 9781781688458

LC 2014041594

This book by William Davies is a "guide to the marketization of modern life. Davies shows that the science of happiness is less a science than an extension of hyper-capitalism. Davies shows how this philosophy, first pronounced by Jeremy Bentham in the 1780s, has dominated the political debates that have delivered neoliberalism." (Publisher's note)

Includes bibliographical references and index

304.2   Human ecology

Cerveny, Randall S.

Weather's greatest mysteries solved! [by] Randy Cerveny. Prometheus Books 2009 328p il map $26.98   **304.2**
1. Climate
ISBN 978-1-59102-720-1; 1-59102-720-9

LC 2009-04493

The author discusses "the investigative process, theories, and the techniques of weather and climate research. Presenting the issues as unsolved mysteries, he engages readers and explains how science is conducted. Each short chapter contains a fictional vignette personalizing a weather or climate-related mystery." Choice

Includes bibliographical references

Diamond, Jared M.

★ **Collapse**: how societies choose to fail or succeed. Viking 2005 575p il $29.95; pa $17 **304.2**
1. Social change 2. Environmental policy
ISBN 0-670-03337-5; 0-14-303655-6 pa

LC 2004-57152

The author "examines storied examples of human economic and social collapse, and even extinction, including Easter Island, classical Mayan civilization and the Greenland Norse. He explores patterns of population growth, overfarming, overgrazing and overhunting, often abetted by drought, cold, rigid social mores and warfare, that lead inexorably to vicious circles of deforestation, erosion and starvation prompted by the disappearance of plant and animal food sources. . . . Readers will find his book an enthralling, and disturbing, reminder of the indissoluble links that bind humans to nature." Publ Wkly

Includes bibliographical references

Flannery, Tim, 1956-

An **explorer's** notebook; essays on life, history and climate. Tim Flannery. Atlantic Monthly Press 2014 284 p. illustrations (hardcover) $26   **304.2**
1. Essays 2. Scientists 3. Human ecology 4. Human beings -- Effect of climate on 5. Human beings -- Effect of environment on
ISBN 9780802122315; 0802122310
Includes bibliographical references

"With its selection of . . . essays and articles written over the past 25 years, 'An Explorer's Notebook' charts the evolution of a young scientist doing fieldwork in remote locations to the major thinker who has changed the way we think about global warming. In over thirty pieces, [author Tim] Flannery writes about his journeys in the jungles of New Guinea and Indonesia, about the extraordinary people he met and the species he discovered." (Publisher's note)

"Flannery offers readers insight into his extraordinary career through selected essays he wrote about his own work as well as about the books that have shaped his thinking." Kirkus

Gilding, Paul

The **great** disruption; why the climate crisis will bring on the end of shopping and the birth of a new world. Bloomsbury Press 2011 292p $25   **304.2**
1. Human ecology 2. Social change 3. Economic development
ISBN 978-1-60819-223-6

LC 2010-35843

"Gilding's confidence in our ability to transform disaster into a 'happiness economy' may astonish readers, but the book provides a refreshing, provocative alternative to the recent spate of gloom-and-doom climate-change studies." Publ Wkly

Includes bibliographical references

Hertsgaard, Mark

Hot; living through the next fifty years on earth. Houghton Mifflin Harcourt 2011 339p $25   **304.2**
1. Greenhouse effect 2. Climate -- Environmental aspects
ISBN 978-0-618-82612-4; 0-618-82612-2

LC 2010-12416

"The author notes that we have entered the 'second era of global warming.' Even if greenhouse-gas emissions ceased today, the consequences would continue for hundreds of years. Consequently, the author persuasively argues that we need to begin adapting to those changes, which does not mean that mitigating global warming is no longer important; in fact, it grows more urgent every day. . . . Starkly clear and of utmost importance. " Kirkus

Includes bibliographical references

Jensen, Derrick

What we leave behind; [by] Derrick Jensen and Aric McBay. Seven Stories Press 2009 453p pa $24.95   **304.2**
1. Pollution 2. Refuse and refuse disposal
ISBN 978-1-58322-867-8

LC 2008-47287

Jensen and McBay argue that "the global industrial system . . . produces massive amounts of unsustainable and toxic wastes. . . . The authors focus on some of these harmful products, discuss reasons why our culture produces so much waste, and explain why individual action is insufficient to solve our enormous problems. . . . This compelling book has a refreshing style, at once very personal and very passionate. It is also thorough, with historical, scientific, statistical, and anecdotal evidence filtered through a lot of anger and some quirky humor." Libr J

Includes bibliographical references

McPhee, John, 1931-

The **control** of nature. Farrar, Straus & Giroux 1989 272p $17.95; pa $12   **304.2**

1. Environmental protection 2. Human influence on nature 3. Human ecology 4. Environmental influence on humans

ISBN 0-374-12890-1; 0-374-52259-6 pa

LC 89-1052

The three essays which make up this book first appeared in the New Yorker. They describe "efforts to pit human ingenuity against the might of Mother Nature . . . in the lower Mississippi Valley, on the volcanic islands of Iceland, and in the canyons of Los Angeles's San Gabriel mountains. In each case, {McPhee argues}, people risk their lives and incur colossal expense to live in places where geology and weather say they have no business to be." (Libr J)

Owen, David, 1955-

Green metropolis; why living smaller, living closer, and driving less are the keys to sustainability. Riverhead Books 2009 357p $25.95   **304.2**

1. Human ecology 2. Urban ecology 3. Sustainable architecture 4. Green technology 5. Urban ecology -- Social aspects

ISBN 1-59448-882-7; 978-1-59448-882-5

LC 2009-17116

Owen argues "that Manhattan, Hong Kong and large, old European cities are inherently greener than less densely populated places because a higher percentage of their inhabitants walk, bike and use mass transit than drive; they share infrastructure and civic services more efficiently; they live in smaller spaces and use less energy to heat their homes." (N Y Times Book Rev) Index.

This is "a compelling analysis of the world's environmental predicament that upends orthodox opinion and points the way to practical solutions." Publ Wkly

Includes bibliographical references

Smith, Laurence C.

The **world** in 2050; four forces shaping civilization's northern future. Dutton 2010 322p il map $26.95   **304.2**

1. Forecasting 2. Climate -- Environmental aspects

ISBN 978-0-525-95181-0

LC 2010-29553

"Smith demonstrates the breadth of geography and emerges as a champion of the discipline. His engaging style and understandable prose will appeal to a wide range of readers interested in social and environmental sciences." Libr J

Includes bibliographical references

Weintraub, Robert

No better friend; one man, one dog, and their extraordinary story of courage and survival in wwii. by Robert Weintraub. Little, Brown & Co. 2015 400 p. 8 plates; illustrations, maps $28   **304.2**

1. Human-animal relationship 2. World War, 1939-

1945 -- Prisoners and prisons

ISBN 0316337064; 9780316337069

LC 2015932606

This book, by Robert Weintraub, is a "tale of survival and friendship between a man and a dog in war. Flight technician Frank Williams and Judy, a purebred pointer, met in the most unlikely of places: a World War II internment camp in the Pacific. Judy was a fiercely loyal dog, with a keen sense for who was friend and who was foe, and the pair's relationship deepened throughout their captivity." (Publisher's note)

"By mutual trust and aid, dog and man survived several brutal Japanese camps together, braving hunger, sadistic guards, snakes, and tigers. Weintraub's research on the prisoners' experiences in the camps is remarkable as he narrates Judy and Frank's heroic tale." Kirkus

Weisman, Alan

Countdown; Our Last, Best Hope for a Future on Earth? Alan Weisman. Little, Brown and Co. 2013 528 p. $28   **304.2**

1. Population 2. Sustainability 3. Overpopulation 4. Population ecology 5. Nature -- Effect of human beings on

ISBN 0316097756; 9780316097758

LC 2013017113

In this book, author Alan Weisman "visits an extraordinary range of the world's cultures, religions, nationalities, tribes, and political systems to learn what in their beliefs, histories, liturgies, or current circumstances might suggest that sometimes it's in their own best interest to limit their growth. [He] reveals what may be the fastest, most acceptable, practical, and affordable way of returning our planet and our presence on it to balance." (Publisher's note)

"Provocative and sobering, this vividly reported book raises profound concerns about our future." Pub Wkly

Includes bibliographical references (pages 442-496) and index

The **world** without us. Thomas Dunne Books/ St. Martin's Press 2007 324p il pbk $18; hbk $24.95   **304.2**

1. Human influence on nature 2. Material culture 3. Human-plant relationships 4. Human-animal relationships 5. Nature -- Effect of human beings on

ISBN 978-0-312-34729-1; 0312427905; 0-312-34729-4

LC 2007-11565

Weisman speculates on what would become of the Earth if the human population disappeared.

"Weisman is a thoroughly engaging and clarion writer fueled by curiosity and determined to cast light rather than spread despair. His superbly well researched and skillfully crafted stop-you-in-your-tracks report stresses the underappreciated fact that humankind's actions create a ripple effect across the web of life." Booklist

Includes bibliographical references

Wohlforth, Charles

The **fate** of nature; rediscovering our ability to rescue the earth. Thomas Dunne Books/St. Martin's Press 2010 434p map $27.99 **304.2**
1. Human ecology 2. Environmental protection 3. Conservation of natural resources 4. Human ecology -- Alaska 5. Natural history -- Alaska 6. Alaska -- Environmental conditions 7. Conservation of natural resources -- Alaska
ISBN 0-312-37737-1; 978-0-312-37737-3
LC 2009-45779

The author "examines humanity's emotional and spiritual relationship with the physical world." (Sci Books Films) Index.

The author "considers the consequences of Captain John Cook's hasty visit to the gulf in 1778, the Russian conquest of coastal Alaska, . . . the crash of the herring fisheries, and the cruel fates of the region's indigenous peoples. But Wohlforth believes that our 'consuming nature' is balanced by the impulse to understand and cherish the living world, which is borne out in his compelling profiles of whale biologist Eva Saulitis; Geerat Vermeij, a blind evolutionary scientist who discovered an arms race among crustaceans; and various environmental heroes. . . . By analyzing competition and evolution, culture and economics, habits of living and of mind, science and suffering, Wohlforth brings a truly ecological perspective to the global debate over how to protect the biosphere." Booklist

Includes bibliographical references

Worster, Donald

Shrinking the Earth; The Rise and Decline of American Abundance. by Donald Worster (Author) Oxford University Press 2016 280 p. ill. (some color), color maps $27.95 **304.2**
1. Human ecology 2. Human influence on nature 3. United States -- History -- 20th century
ISBN 019984495X; 9780199844951
LC 2016301463

In this book, environmental historian Donald Worster "takes a global view in his examination of the ways in which complex issues of worldwide abundance and scarcity have shaped American society and behavior over three centuries. Looking at the limits nature imposes on human ambitions, he questions whether America today is in the midst of a shift from a culture of abundance to a culture of limits and whether American consumption has become reliant on the global South." (Publisher's note)

"A bracing, intelligent survey of wealth become immiseration, essential for students of environmental history." Kirkus

Includes bibliographical references (pages 227-252) and index.

304.5 Genetic factors

Taylor, Shelley E.

The **tending** instinct; how nurturing is essential for who we are and how we live. Times Bks. 2002 290p $25; pa $16 **304.5**
1. Sociobiology 2. Stress (Psychology) 3. Sex

differences (Psychology)
ISBN 0-8050-6837-6; 0-8050-7289-6 pa
LC 2002-19879

The author "launched a series of innovative experiments that led her to believe that humans are biologically wired to nurture. She thus devised no less than a whole new psychology of women, presented in this accessible and well-grounded work." Libr J

Includes bibliographical references

304.6 Population

Encyclopedia of the U.S. Census; from the constitution to the American community survey. editors, Margo J. Anderson, Constance F. Citro, and Joseph J. Salvo. 2nd ed. CQ Press 2013 456 p. Hardcover $195 **304.6**
1. United States -- Census -- Encyclopedias
ISBN 9781608710256
LC 2011036339

"The Encyclopedia of the U.S. Census, Second Edition" updates and expands a critically-acclaimed resource for the history, politics, content, procedures and uses of the decennial census of the American population. The new edition highlights changes in the Census Bureau's data collection and dissemination practices for the 2010 enumeration, including the use of a short-form questionnaire for the actual population count, and the release in late 2010 of the American Community Survey (ACS) 5-year data set based on rolling samples of the U.S. population and gathered using the long-form questionnaire. The second edition also comprehensively covers the fallout from the 2000 census and recent issues affecting the administration of the 2010 count." (Publisher's Note)

The alphabetically arranged articles "explain the history, methodology, and results of U.S. censuses since 1790... Maps, tables, and charts show how the composition of the population has changed, where the center of population has moved over time, and how the address lists and census tracts are developed." Booklist

Includes bibliographical references and index

Hitchens, Christopher, 1949-2011

★ **Mortality**; Christopher Hitchens. 1st ed. Twelve 2012 160 p. (hardcover) $22.99; (paperback) $14.99; (ebook) $21.80 **304.6**
1. Terminally ill 2. Cancer patients 3. Cancer -- Chemotherapy 4. Death 5. Mortality 6. Authors, American -- Biography 7. Terminally ill -- United States -- Biography 8. Cancer -- Patients -- United States -- Biography
ISBN 1455502758; 9781455502752; 9781455523474; 9781742695198
LC 2012014024

This memoir chronicles the decline of cultural critic Christopher Hitchens during the later stages of esophageal cancer. Here, he "shares his thoughts about his suffering, the etiquette of illness and wellness, and religion." He talks about the battle metaphors doctors and friends use to describe his illness and his feelings about the loss of his voice from the treatment. (Publishers Weekly)

Peake, Riley

Mapping Census 2010; the geography of American change. Riley Peake. Esri Press 2012 1 atlas (xiv, 90 p.)p col. maps (pbk.) $18.95   **304.6**
1. United States -- Census 2. United States -- Population 3. United States -- Census, 23rd, 2010 -- Maps 4. United States -- Population -- Statistics -- Maps 5. Minorities -- United States -- Population -- Statistics -- Maps
ISBN 1589483197; 9781589483194

LC 2012288678

Author Riley Peake's book "is an atlas of the American people--who we are, and where we are. Using the latest census data and geographic information system (GIS) technology, this atlas examines how our unique population is moving and changing. These large, full-color maps illustrate population density, age, and racial and ethnic composition with clarity." (Publisher's note)

Includes bibliographical references

305   Groups of people

Azam Zanganeh, Lila

My sister, guard your veil; my brother guard, your eyes; uncensored Iranian voices. Lila Azam Zanganeh, editor. Beacon Press 2006 132p il pa $12   **305**
1. Women -- Iran 2. Iran -- Social conditions
ISBN 0-8070-0463-4; 978-0-8070-0463-0

LC 2005-27496

This "volume features frank interviews with an array of reputable Iranians intellectuals, artists, and writers, some of whom live in exile. Their compelling personal experiences, views, and opinions answer some persistent questions about the lives of ordinary people in Iran and challenge established myths and stereotypes. . . . This volume opens a window on the irrepressible talents, aspirations, and energy of Iranians both at home and abroad, despite their adverse conditions" MultiCult Rev

Baldwin, Neil

★ **Henry** Ford and the Jews; the mass production of hate. PublicAffairs 2001 416p il $27.50; pa $16   **305**
1. Antisemitism 2. Philanthropists 3. Automobile industry 4. Automobile executives 5. Jews -- United States
ISBN 1-891620-52-5; 1-58648-163-0 pa

LC 2001-41679

"The strength of this biography lies in context: by emphasizing Ford's background, influences and the world around the auto manufacturer, Baldwin . . . brings a fresh approach to what has long been known about one of America's most famous anti-Semites." Publ Wkly

Includes bibliographical references

Bergner, Daniel

★ **What** Do Women Want? Adventures in the Science of Female Desire. Daniel Burgner. HarperCollins 2013 224 p. (hardcover) $25.99   **305**
1. Women -- Sexual behavior 2. Sex -- Psychological

aspects
ISBN 0061906085; 9780061906084

This book, by Daniel Bergner, "disseminates the latest scientific research and paints an unprecedented portrait of female lust: the triggers, the fantasies, the mind-body connection (and disconnection), the reasons behind the loss of libido, and, most revelatory, that this loss is not inevitable. . . . While debunking the myths popularized by evolutionary psychology, Bergner also looks at the future of female sexuality." (Publisher's note)

"Stylishly written and cogently organized, making it easy and rewarding for lay readers to understand and appreciate some fairly complex science." Kirkus

Gates, Henry Louis

The **African**-American century; how Black Americans have shaped our country. {by} Henry Louis Gates, Jr. and Cornel West. Free Press 2000 414p il hardcover o.p. pa $16   **305**
1. African Americans -- Biography 2. African Americans -- Intellectual life
ISBN 0-684-86414-2; 0-684-86415-0 pa

LC 00-63596

"Gates and West have listed and written biographies of their choices of the 100 most important and influential [African Americans] of the . . . twentieth century. In their opinion the subjects that they have selected have made significant impacts and contributions to American society. . . . The entries are arranged by decade and by the person's period of prominence in society, 1900-1909 through 1990-1999. Profiles include Madame C.J. Walker, Langston Hughes, Carter G. Woodson, Paul Robeson, Thurgood Marshall, and Colin Powell." MultiCult Rev

Includes bibliographical references

Reef, Catherine

Working in America. Facts On File 2007 xxviii, 484p il map (American experience) $80   **305**
1. Labor -- United States
ISBN 978-0-8160-6239-3; 0-8160-6239-0

LC 2006-31191

First published 2000

"Each chapter begins with a . . . narrative that chronicles the experience of workers in the United States—from factory workers, cowboys, seamstresses, and newsboys to truck drivers, migrant farm workers, computer programmers, and genetic engineers. Chronologies of important events follow, along with eyewitness testimonies on the experience of working in a wide range of professions and trades—from Thomas Jefferson, Malcolm X, Samuel Gompers, Charlotte Perkins Gilman, Jesse Jackson, Cesar Chavez, and Jane Addams, as well as a wide range of American workers." Publisher's note

Includes bibliographical references

305.23 Young people

Canada, Geoffrey

Fist, stick, knife, gun; a personal history of violence in America. Beacon Press 1995 179p pa $13 **305.23**

1. Children 2. Violence 3. New York (N.Y.) -- Social conditions

ISBN 0-8070-0422-7; 978-0-8070-0423-4 pa; 0-8070-0423-5 pa

LC 94-41357

"This is a graphic adaptation of famous activist and educator Canada's work of the same name. It explores his Bronx, NY, childhood and foray into increasingly violent activity. The use of violence as self-protection in a rough neighborhood and the introduction of guns into the mix make for a profound reflection on inner-city violence." (Library Journal)

"A more powerful depiction of the tragic life of urban children and a more compelling plea to end 'America's war against itself' cannot be imagined." Publ Wkly

Clinton, Hillary Rodham, 1947-

It takes a village; and other lessons children teach us. Hillary Rodham Clinton. Simon & Schuster 2006 xviii, 331 p.p illustrations (ebook) $13.99; $26 **305.23**

1. Parenting 2. Child welfare 3. Child development 4. Family -- United States 5. Presidents' spouses -- United States 6. Parenting -- United States 7. Child welfare -- United States 8. Child development -- United States 9. Presidents' spouses -- Family relationships -- United States -- Case studies

ISBN 9781416574644; 1416540644; 9781416540649

LC 2007297957

This book, by Hillary Rodham Clinton, "reflects on how our village has changed over the last decade—from the impact of the Internet to new research in early child development and education. She discusses issues of increasing concern—security, the environment, the national debt—and looks at where we have made progress and where there is still work to be done." (Publisher's note)

Coles, Robert

Children of crisis; selections from the Pulitzer Prize-winning five-volume Children of crisis series; with a new introduction by the author. Little, Brown 2003 714p il pa $22.95 **305.23**

1. Children with social disabilities 2. Children -- United States

ISBN 9780316151023

LC 2003-47522

These are selections of Coles' social study of "African American children caught in the throes of the South's racial integration; the young children of impoverished sharecroppers, migrant workers, and mountaineers in Appalachia; children whose families were transformed by the migration from South to North, from rural to urban communities; Latino, Native American, and Eskimo children in the poorest communities of the American West; the children of America's wealthiest families, wrestling with the burden of their own privilege." Publisher's note

Konner, Melvin

The **evolution** of childhood. Belknap Press of Harvard University Press 2010 943p $39.95 **305.23**

1. Children 2. Evolution 3. Child development 4. Emotions in children 5. Human evolution 6. Children -- Anthropometry

ISBN 978-0-674-04566-8; 0-674-04566-1

LC 2009050775

It was the author's intent "to describe 'the foundations of psychosocial growth' in an evolutionary context. A goal of the book is to provide the basis for understanding the modification of that biological heritage in interaction with the environment. . . . [Melvin] Konner's focus is on how 'the laws and facts of biology underlie normally developing social behavior' . . . . [The book] is divided into five broad sections: evolution (focused on the phylogenetic origins of childhood), maturation (the genetic, physiological, and anatomical bases of psychosocial growth), socialization ('the evolving social context of ontogeny'), enculturation (the transmission and evolution of culture), and a conclusion. Between each of the first four major parts of the book, there is a transition essay." (Current Anthropology)

This book "explores the biological evolution of human behavior and specifically the behavior of children. Melvin Konner . . . weaves a compelling web of theories and studies across a remarkable array of disciplines, from experimental genetics to ethnology. He ranges back to the earliest, egg-laying mammals, discusses topics as seemingly modern as cross-gender identity conflicts, and draws on scientific work examining all manner of species with which humans share distinct characteristics. . . . To read this book is to be in the company of a helpful and hopeful teacher who is eager to share what he's found." Atl Mon

Includes bibliographical references

Kozol, Jonathan

Ordinary resurrections; children in the years of hope. Harper Perennial 2001 388p pa $14 **305.23**

1. Children 2. Bronx (New York, N.Y.) -- Social conditions

ISBN 978-0-06-095645-5; 0-06-095645-3

First published 2000 by Crown

"Kozol tells of his continued visits with the children who attend the afterschool program at St. Ann's Episcopal Church in the racially segregated, impoverished South Bronx." SLJ

Includes bibliographical references

Mintz, Steven

★ **Huck's** raft; a history of American childhood. Belknap Press of Harvard University Press 2004 445p il $29.95 **305.23**

1. Children -- United States

ISBN 0-674-01508-8

LC 2004-42220

The author "revisits the treatment of children from the Puritan era up to the edge of the millennium, . . . showing that we have alternately vilified our offspring . . . and glorified them. . . . In addition, the roles children have assumed in the workforce have fluctuated with the needs of the era—economic expansion led to harsh child labor, while its aftermath, prosperity, led to an interest in child welfare. .

. . Mintz's thorough yet accessibly written study delves into the external forces that have shaped the lives of our young while also probing the internal developments in their collective consciousness." Libr J

Includes bibliographical references

Orenstein, Peggy

Cinderella ate my daughter; dispatches from the frontlines of the new girlie-girl culture. HarperCollins 2011 244p $25.99   **305.23**

1. Mother-daughter relationship 2. Femininity 3. Girls -- Psychology 4. Mothers and daughters

ISBN 0061711527; 9780061711527

LC 2010-28724

Orenstein examines aspects and manifestations of sexualized girlhood such as child beauty pageants and Disney Princess dolls. Bibliography. Index.

The author "finds today's pink and princess-obsessed girl culture grating when it threatens to lure her own young daughter, Daisy. In her quest to determine whether princess mania is merely a passing phase or a more sinister marketing plot with long-term negative impact, Orenstein travels to Disneyland, American Girl Place, the American International Toy Fair; visits a children's beauty pageant; attends a Miley Cyrus concert; tools around the Internet; and interviews parents, historians, psychologists, marketers, and others. . . . With insight and biting humor, the author explores her own conflicting feelings as a mother as she protects her offspring and probes the roots and tendrils of the girlie-girl movement." Publ Wkly

Includes bibliographical references

Shachtman, Tom

★ **Rumspringa**; to be or not to be Amish. North Point Press 2006 286p hardcover o.p. pa $16 **305.23**

1. Amish 2. Teenagers -- Religious life

ISBN 0-86547-687-X; 978-0-86547-687-5; 0-86547-742-6 pa; 978-0-86547-742-1 pa

LC 2006-4329

"Rumspringa is Tom Shachtman's celebrated look at a little-known Amish coming-of-age ritual, the rumspringa--the period of "running around" that begins for their youth at age sixteen. During this time, Amish youth are allowed to live outside the bounds of their faith, experimenting with alcohol, premarital sex, revealing clothes, telephones, drugs, and wild parties. By allowing such broad freedoms, their parents hope they will learn enough to help them make the most important decision of their lives--whether to be baptized as Christians, join the church, and forever give up worldly ways, or to remain in the world." (Publisher's note)

"Shachtman is like a maestro, masterfully conducting an orchestra of history, anthropology, psychology, sociology, and journalism together in a harmonious and evocative symphony of all things Amish." Christ Sci Monit

Includes bibliographical references

Simmons, Rachel

★ **Odd** girl out; the hidden culture of aggression in girls. Revised and updated Harcourt 2011 296p pa $15   **305.23**

1. Girls 2. Aggressiveness (Psychology) 3. Girls --

Psychology 4. Aggressiveness in children

ISBN 9780547520193

LC 2001-6864

"In this updated edition, educator and bullying expert Rachel Simmons gives girls, parents, and educators proven and innovative strategies for navigating social dynamics in person and online, as well as brand new classroom initiatives and step-by-step parental suggestions for dealing with conventional bullying. With up-to-the-minute research and real-life stories, Odd Girl Out continues to be the definitive resource on the most pressing social issues facing girls today." (Publisher's note)

"Why are girls inclined to relational rather than physical aggression? Simmons contends that girls are socialized into a psychological double bind. They are told that they must be good, nice and quiet and that they should value close and intimate relationships. . . . According to Simmons, girls fear that an expression of conflict will damage their relationships. . . . Trapped in a constraining, stereotypical gender role, some girls craft ways of expressing their anger covertly. . . . Odd Girl Out explores this grim side of girlhood with {stories} . . . about girls hurting other girls." (Women's Rev Books) Index.

Includes bibliographical references

Tanenbaum, Leora

I Am Not a Slut; Slut-shaming in the Age of the Internet. Leora Tanenbaum. HarperCollins 2015 416 p. $15.99   **305.23**

1. Shame 2. Internet -- Social aspects 3. Stereotype (Social psychology)

ISBN 006228259X; 9780062282590

In this book by Leora Tanenbaum, "as the Internet's omnipresence continues to realign attitudes regarding what constitutes appropriate behavioral standards, the author revisits former arguments on issues of female empowerment and verbal sexual harassment, refreshing her research with new interviews with girls on the frontlines of name-calling and bullying. She updates readers on what has changed on the name-calling landscape, noting that the term 'slut' has 'metastasized' outward throughout our culture". (Kirkus Reviews)

"This brilliant, thoughtful, and compelling investigation of young womanhood commands the reader's attention from beginning to end." Booklist

305.235   Young people twelve to twenty

Connolly, Daniel

The **Book** of Isaias; A Child of Hispanic Immigrants Seeks His Own America. by Daniel Connolly. St. Martin's Press 2016 272 p. $26.99   **305.235**

1. Children of immigrants -- Education

ISBN 1250083060; 9781250083067

In this book, by Daniel Connolly, "a bright 18-year-old Hispanic student named Isaias Ramos sets out on the journey to college. Isaias, who passed a prestigious national calculus test as a junior and leads the quiz bowl team, is the hope of Kingsbury High in Memphis. . . . Isaias also doubts the value of college and says he might go to work in his family's painting business after high school, despite his academic potential. Is Isaias making a rational choice?" (Publisher's note)

"Connolly unearths the human element behind one of today's most debated issues, asking expert and everyday readers alike to consider how the immigrant experience is affecting one of the fastest-growing youth populations in the nation." Pub Wkly

Damour, Lisa

Untangled; guiding teenage girls through the seven transitions into adulthood. Lisa Damour. Ballantine Books 2016 352 p. hbk $27 **305.235**

1. Adolescence 2. Teenage girls 3. Adulthood 4. Adolescent psychology 5. Teenage girls -- Psychology
ISBN 9780553393057; 0553393057

LC 2015040046

"Damour offers a hopeful, helpful new way for parents to talk about--and with--teenage girls. Raising a teenage girl doesn't have to be the proverbial roller-coaster ride or feel like a 'tangled mess,' she asserts. There is a predictable pattern to teenage development, and parents can learn how to understand and support their daughters. Damour identifies seven distinct, sequential 'strands,' one per chapter, from middle school through high school: parting with childhood; joining a new tribe; harnessing emotions; contending with adult authority; planning for the future; entering the romantic world; and caring for herself." (Publishers Weekly)

Includes bibliographical references and index

Flanagan, Caitlin

Girl land; Caitlin Flanagan. Little, Brown and Co. 2012 209 p. **305.235**

1. Girls 2. Adolescence 3. American essays 4. Teenage girls -- Psychology 5. Teenage girls -- United States
ISBN 9780316065986

LC 2011024934

The book discusses "[t]he transition from girl to woman [which according to the author] is an experience that has changed radically over the generations: everything from how a girl learns about her period to how she expects to be treated by boys and men. Girls today observe these passages very differently, and yet the landmarks themselves have remained remarkably constant-proof, [Caitlin] Flanagan believes, of their significance. In a world where protections of girls' privacy and personal freedom seem to disappear every day, the ultimate challenge modern parents face is finding a way to defend both." (Publisher's note)

Includes bibliographical references

Hine, Thomas

The **rise** and fall of the American teenager. Bard 1999 322p $24; pa $14; prebind $23.99 **305.235**

1. Teenagers 2. Adolescence
ISBN 0-380-97358-8; 0-380-72853-2 pa; 9781439573587

LC 99-24381

In this social history Hine "writes about ways the culture has affected what teenage has meant for youth and how youth have been perceived, as in World War II when teenagers readily took on roles supporting the war effort. Interesting, enjoyable, and multifaceted, Hine's work defies

pigeonholing by covering anthropology, psychology, communications, and sociology." Libr J

Includes bibliographical references

305.24   Adults

Sheehy, Gail

New passages; mapping your life across time. Random House 1995 xxv, 498p hardcover o.p. pa $15.95 **305.24**

1. Aging 2. Adulthood 3. Middle age 4. Socialization 5. United States -- Social conditions
ISBN 0-345-40445-9 pa

LC 94-43996

Companion volume to Passages (1976)

This work is "grounded in the economic and psychological realities that make adult life so complex today. The major themes of this book are accurate and important." N Y Times Book Rev

Includes bibliographical references

305.242   People in early adulthood

Burge, Kimberly

The **born** frees; writing with the girls of Gugulethu. Kimberly Burge. W.W. Norton & Co. Inc. 2015 384 p. (hardcover) $26.95 **305.242**

1. Creative writing 2. Women -- South Africa 3. Youth -- South Africa 4. South Africa -- Social life and customs 5. Post-apartheid era -- South Africa 6. Young women -- South Africa -- Social conditions 7. Creative writing (Study and teaching) -- South Africa
ISBN 0393239160; 9780393239164

LC 2015010037

In this book, by Kimberly Burge, a "creative writing group unites and inspires girls of the first South African generation 'born free.' Born into post-apartheid South Africa, the young women of the townships around Cape Town still face daunting challenges. . . . Yet, as . . . Burge discovered when she set up a writing group in the township of Gugulethu, the spirit of these girls outshines their circumstances." (Publisher's note)

"Incredible and inspiring, this account belongs in every library and on every bookshelf." LJ

Includes bibliographical references

305.26   People in late adulthood

Carter, Jimmy

The **virtues** of aging. Ballantine Pub. Group 1998 140p (Library of contemporary thought) hardcover o.p. pa $11.95 **305.26**

1. Aging
ISBN 0-345-42826-9; 0-345-42592-8 pa

LC 98-25298

"At age 56, Jimmy Carter 'involuntarily retired' when he was defeated for a second term as president by Ronald Reagan in 1980. . . . Carter sketches how he and Rosalynn created new careers and new lives for themselves—as authors, educators, and senior family members and as a couple growing old together. He adds statistics about the aging population, makes suggestions for healthy living, and defines successful aging." Libr J

Jacoby, Susan

Never say die; the myth and marketing of the new old age. Pantheon Books 2011 332p $27.95 **305.26**

1. Aging 2. Elderly 3. Old age 4. Aged -- United States

ISBN 978-0-307-37794-4; 0-307-37794-6

LC 2010-17123

In this book, author "Susan Jacoby turns an . . . eye on the marketers of longevity--pharmaceutical companies, lifestyle gurus, and scientific businessmen who suggest that there will soon be a 'cure' for the 'disease' of aging. She separates wishful hype from realistic hope. . . . Finally, Jacoby raises the fundamental question of whether living longer is a desirable thing unless it means living better, and she considers the profound moral and ethical concerns raised by increasing longevity." (Publisher's note)

Includes bibliographical references

Lawrence-Lightfoot, Sara

The **third** chapter; passion, risk, and adventure in the 25 years after 50. Farrar, Straus and Giroux 2009 260p $25 **305.26**

1. Aging 2. Old age 3. Elderly -- United States

ISBN 978-0-374-27549-5; 0-374-27549-1

LC 2008-29147

"New opportunities for creativity and self-fulfillment await men and women between the ages of 50 and 75. . . . [The author] coins the term 'Third Chapter' to describe the rich possibilities as illustrated in her extended interviews with 40 well-educated, affluent Americans. Founding her thesis on classic formulations of life-stage development, particularly that of Erik Erikson, the author offers a wide range of models for people who feel burned out, restless or dissatisfied with their lives, describing how each of her subjects became 'a different person.' . . . Readers feeling that something is missing from their lives, that there is something more they can contribute, will find this book a helpful guide." Publ Wkly

Includes bibliographical references

Pillemer, Karl A.

30 lessons for living; tried and true advice from the wisest Americans. [by] Karl Pillemer. Hudson Street Press 2011 271p $25.95 **305.26**

1. Aging 2. Old age 3. Happiness 4. Conduct of life 5. Elderly -- United States

ISBN 978-1-59463-084-2

LC 2011017113

"Who better to teach lessons on living . . . than the thousands of Americans over the age of 65 who have successfully navigated the territories of marriage, career, money, and aging? By conducting innumerable interviews, Pillemer found that their advice upends contemporary wisdom: they suggest marrying a person like oneself, choosing a career for intrinsic rewards, and spending more time with one's children. The author skillfully weaves a prevailing theme (e.g.,

parenting, aging fearlessly) with self-disclosing statements from interviewees to create a compelling, inspirational book. One of the best of its kind. " Libr J

Includes bibliographical references

305.31 Men

Bly, Robert

★ **Iron** John; a book about men. DaCapo Press 2004 268p pa $15 **305.31**

1. Men -- Psychology

ISBN 0-306-81376-9

LC 2004-56137

First published 1990 by Addison-Wesley

"Drawing vitally upon such diverse sources as ancient mythology, classic literature (including his own poetry), anthropology, psychology, and even the responses of the real-life men who have participated in his seminars ('gatherings'), Bly staunchly redefines male identity, emphasizing the importance of what he calls 'warrior energy' and all its positive implications." Booklist

Includes bibliographical references.

Vaillant, George E.

Triumphs of experience; the men of the Harvard Grant Study. George E. Vaillant. Belknap Press of Harvard University Press 2012 457 p. (alk. paper) $27.95 **305.31**

1. Aging 2. Elderly men 3. Longitudinal studies 4. Men -- United States -- Longitudinal studies 5. Aging -- Social aspects -- United States -- Longitudinal studies 6. Aging -- Psychological aspects -- United States -- Longitudinal studies

ISBN 0674059824; 9780674059825

LC 2012028519

This book, by George E. Vaillant, profiles "the longest longitudinal study of human development ever undertaken. . . . Begun in 1938, the Grant Study of Adult Development charted the physical and emotional health of over 200 men, starting with their undergraduate days. . . . Now George Vaillant follows the men into their nineties, documenting for the first time what it is like to flourish far beyond conventional retirement." (Publisher's note)

Includes bibliographical references and index

305.38 Specific groups of men

McCall, Nathan

Makes me wanna holler; a young black man in America. Random House 1994 404p hardcover o.p. pa $14.95 **305.38**

1. Journalists 2. Essayists 3. Memoirists 4. African Americans -- Biography

ISBN 0-679-74070-8 pa

LC 93-30654

The author relates the "story of his rise from poverty to success as a journalist at the Washington Post. He uses graphic language, blunt descriptions, honest expression, introspection, and careful observation to describe his early years in Portsmouth, Virginia, as a young black male, the recipient of a 12-year prison sentence for armed robbery, whose life was dangerously out of control. Insensitivity, alienation, racial hatred, drugs (especially crack), guns, rape, robbery, the black American as an endangered species—McCall covers it all in a depressing yet spellbinding documentary." Libr J

305.4 Women

Beauvoir, Simone de

★ The **second** sex; translated and edited by H. M. Parshley; with an introduction by Margaret Crosland. Knopf 1993 lv, 786p $23; pa $17 **305.4**
1. Women
ISBN 0-679-42016-9; 0-679-72451-6 pa

LC 92-54303

Original French edition, 1949; this translation first published 1953

This "thorough analysis of women's secondary status in society, became a classic of feminist literature." Reader's Ency. 3d edition

Collins, Gail

America's women; four hundred years of dolls, drudges, helpmates, and heroines. Morrow 2003 556p il $27.95; pa $15.95 **305.4**
1. Women -- United States -- History
ISBN 0-06-018510-4; 0-06-122722-6 pa

LC 2003-51011

This is a history of American women from colonial times to the present

"Collins elegantly and eruditely celebrates the hard-won victories, overwhelming obstacles, and selfless contributions of a captivating array of influential women." Booklist
Includes bibliographical references

When everything changed; the amazing journey of American women from 1960 to the present. Little, Brown and Co. 2009 471p il $27.99 **305.4**
1. Women -- United States -- History
ISBN 978-0-316-05954-1; 0-316-05954-4

LC 2008-54933

"Collins can be deadly serious and great fun to read at the same time. A revelatory book for readers of both sexes, and sure to become required reading for any American women's-studies course." Kirkus
Includes bibliographical references

The **essential** feminist reader; edited and with an introduction by Estelle B. Freedman. Modern Library 2007 472p pa $17.95 **305.4**
1. Feminism
ISBN 0-8129-7460-3; 978-0-8129-7460-7

This collection of writings by feminist authors "features primary source material from around the globe, including short works of fiction and drama, political manifestos, and the work of less well-known writers." Publisher's note
Includes bibliographical references

Friedan, Betty

★ The **feminine** mystique; with a new introduction. Norton 1997 xlviii, 452p hardcover o.p. pa $15.95 **305.4**
1. Feminism 2. Women -- United States
ISBN 0-393-32257-2 pa

LC 97-8877

A reissue of the title first published 1963
An "analysis of the dilemma facing the educated American woman; the post-war emphasis on the feminine image of the role as wife and mother has caused the American woman to lose her identity, says the author." Cincinnati Public Libr
Includes bibliographical references

Grunwald, Lisa

★ **Women's** letters; America from the Revolutionary War to the present. edited by Lisa Grunwald & Stephen J. Adler. Dial Press 2005 824p il hardcover o.p. pa $18; pa $18 **305.4**
1. Women -- United States -- History -- Sources
ISBN 9780385335560; 0-385-33553-9; 0-385-33556-3 pa

LC 2005-41446

"Historical events of the last three centuries come alive through these women's singular correspondences—often their only form of public expression. In 1775, Rachel Revere tries to send financial aid to her husband, Paul, in a note that is confiscated by the British; First Lady Dolley Madison tells her sister about rescuing George Washington's portrait during the War of 1812; one week after JFK's assassination, Jacqueline Kennedy pens a heartfelt letter to Nikita Khrushchev; and on September 12, 2001, a schoolgirl writes a note of thanks to a New York City firefighter, asking him, "Were you afraid?" (Publisher's note)

"This collection of more than 400 entries begins with a letter written by Abigail Grant, accusing her husband of cowardice in battle, and ends with an e-mail by Wall Street Journal correspondent Farnaz Fassihi on the stark state of affairs in war-torn Iraq. In between, a wide variety of compelling subjects is covered. . . . The letters are accompanied by information about the topics included, biographical details about the author and the recipient, and other interesting facts." SLJ
Includes bibliographical references

No small courage; a history of women in the United States. edited by Nancy Cott. Oxford Univ. Press 2000 646p il maps hardcover o.p. pa $21.95 **305.4**
1. Women -- United States -- History
ISBN 0-19-513946-1; 978-0-19-517323-9 pa; 0-19-517323-6 pa

LC 00-21130

"By examining the flow of American history as it has affected women {the authors} illuminate aspects of the past that have often been neglected." Booklist
Includes bibliographical references

Rodriguez, Deborah

Kabul Beauty School; an American woman goes behind the veil. Random House 2007 275p $24.95; pa $14.95   **305.4**

1. Beauty shops 2. Women -- Afghanistan 3. Kabul Beauty School (Afghanistan)
ISBN 978-1-4000-6559-2; 1-4000-6559-3; 978-0-8129-7673-1 pa; 0-8129-7673-8 pa

LC 2006-50384

"Rodriguez's experiences will delight readers as she recounts such tales as two friends acting as 'parents' and negotiating a dowry for her marriage to an Afghan man or her students puzzling over a donation of a carton of thongs. Most of all, they will share her admiration for Afghan women's survival and triumph in chaotic times." SLJ

Schnall, Marianne

What will it take to make a woman president? conversations about women, leadership, and power. by Marianne Schnall. Seal Press 2013 384 p. $17   **305.4**

1. Women politicians 2. Gender and politics 3. Presidential candidates -- United States 4. Women -- United States -- Interviews 5. Politicians -- United States -- Attitudes 6. Women political activists -- United States 7. Women presidential candidates -- United States
ISBN 158005496X; 9781580054966

LC 2013031218

Amelia Bloomer Project (2014)

This book, by Marianne Schnall, "features interviews with politicians, public officials, thought leaders, writers, artists, and activists in an attempt to discover the obstacles that have held women back and what needs to change in order to elect a woman into the White House. With insights and personal anecdotes . . . , this book addresses timely, provocative issues involving women, politics, and power." (Publisher's note)

"Through far-ranging conversations, Schnall gained insight into factors contributing to the country's failure to elect a woman to its highest office and sought advice as to how we can not only better prepare for the next presidential election but create a world in which today's young women feel empowered to break out of stereotypical roles. The good news is that there is universal agreement among those profiled that the country will, indeed, elect a woman president. The more disconcerting message is that there is still much work to do in order to achieve true gender parity." (Booklist)

Sigerman, Harriet

The **Columbia** documentary history of American women since 1941; edited by Harriet Sigerman. Columbia University Press 2003 690p $94; pa $34.50   **305.4**

1. Feminism 2. Women's rights 3. Women -- United States -- History -- Sources
ISBN 0-231-11698-5; 0-231-11699-3 pa

LC 2002-41395

This collection of public and private primary sources includes such topics as employment opportunities, "the ideas and changes brought about by the women's movement, the challenges to and defense of reproductive rights, the back-lash against feminism in the name of family values, and new visions for women's lives in the twenty-first century." Publisher's note

Includes bibliographical references

Ulrich, Laurel

Well-behaved women seldom make history; [by] Laurel Thatcher Ulrich. Alfred A. Knopf 2007 xxxiv, 284p il $24   **305.4**

1. Poets 2. Authors 3. Feminism 4. Novelists 5. Suffragists 6. Women in literature 7. Essayists 8. Biographers 9. Women -- History 10. Short story writers
ISBN 978-1-4000-4159-6; 1-4000-4159-6

LC 2006-100581

This book "is by no means jargon-ridden or academic in tone. Ulrich's style is plain and direct, agreeable but without frills, and she moves efficiently right along. The book is a pleasure to read." Washington Post Book World

Includes bibliographical references

Wolf, Naomi

The **beauty** myth; how images of beauty are used against women. Perennial 2002 348p pa $14.95   **305.4**

1. Women 2. Gender role 3. Personal appearance 4. Sex role
ISBN 0-06-051218-0

LC 2002-72516

First published 1991 by Morrow

The author "presents a provocative and persuasive account of the pervasiveness of the beauty ideal in all facets of Western culture." Libr J

Includes bibliographical references

Xinran

Message from an unknown Chinese mother; stories of loss and love. translated from Chinese by Nicky Harman. Scribner 2011 xxvii, 239p $25; ebook $11.99   **305.4**

1. Mothers 2. Children -- China 3. China -- Social conditions
ISBN 978-1-4516-1089-5; 978-1-4516-1095-6 ebook

First published 2010 in the United Kingdom

The author "collects the heartbreaking stories of Chinese women forced to give up their baby girls because of the one-child-only policy or feudal traditions that prefer boys, in an oral history written for those abandoned daughters. . . . This is a brutally honest book written for those relinquished children, so that they will know how much their birth mothers loved them and how—in the words of one mother who gave up her daughter—'they paid for that love with an endless stream of bitter tears.'" Publ Wkly

Zeitz, Joshua

Flapper; a madcap story of sex, style, celebrity, and the women who made America modern. Crown Publishers 2006 338p il $24.95   **305.4**

1. Women -- United States 2. Popular culture -- United States 3. United States -- History -- 1919-1933
ISBN 1-4000-8053-3; 978-1-4000-8053-3

LC 2005-24297

"An essential exploration of the women Zeitz deems 'the first thoroughly modern American[s].'" Booklist

Includes bibliographical references

305.409   Biography

Fuller, Alexandra, 1969-

Leaving Before the Rains Come; Alexandra Fuller. Penguin Press 2015 258 p. map (hardcover) $26.95   **305.409**

1. Divorced women 2. Africans -- United States 3. Women -- Biography 4. Zambia -- Biography 5. Wyoming -- Biography 6. Intercountry marriage 7. Zimbabwe -- Biography 8. Divorced women -- Biography

ISBN 1594205868; 9781594205866

LC 2014036654

This memoir tells how, "a child of the Rhodesian wars and daughter of two deeply complicated parents, [author] Alexandra Fuller is no stranger to pain. But the disintegration of Fuller's own marriage leaves her shattered. Looking to pick up the pieces of her life, she finally confronts the tough questions about her past, about the American man she married, and about the family she left behind in Africa." (Publisher's note)

"Although her batty and unhinged relatives emerge more vividly than her taciturn husband, Fuller's talent as a storyteller makes this memoir sing." Kirkus

305.42   Social role and status of women

Adichie, Chimamanda Ngozi, 1977-

We Should All Be Feminists; by Chimamanda Ngozi Adichie. Random House Inc 2015 64 p. $7.95   **305.42**

1. Women 2. Feminism 3. Women's rights
ISBN 110191176X; 9781101911761

In this book, author Chimamanda Ngozi Adichie "offers readers a unique definition of feminism for the twenty-first century, one rooted in inclusion and awareness. Drawing extensively on her own experiences and her deep understanding of the often masked realities of sexual politics, here is one remarkable author's exploration of what it means to be a woman now—and an of-the-moment rallying cry for why we should all be feminists." (Publisher's note)

"An eloquent, stirring must-read for budding and reluctant feminists." SLJ

Armstrong, Jennifer Keishin

Sexy feminism; a girl's guide to love, success, and style. Jennifer Keishin Armstrong and Heather Wood Rudúlph. Mariner Books 2013 xxii, 228 p.p (paperback) $15.95   **305.42**

1. Feminism 2. Self-realization 3. Women -- Social conditions 4. Success 5. Self-realization in women
ISBN 0547738307; 9780547738307

LC 2012040351

This book, by Jennifer Keishin Armstrong and Heather Wood Rudulph, discusses feminism in the 21st century. "For

many young women the radicalism of the Second Wave is unappealing, and the . . . Third Wave feels out of date. . . . [This book offers] an inclusive, approachable kind of feminism--miniskirts, lip gloss, and waxing permitted. Covering a range of topics from body issues and workplace gender politics to fashion, dating, and sex." (Publisher's note)

Includes bibliographical references (p. [217]-228).

Brownmiller, Susan

In our time; memoir of a revolution. Dial Press (NY) 1999 360p hardcover o.p. pa $15.95 **305.42**

1. Feminism 2. Women's movement
ISBN 0-385-31831-6 pa

LC 99-39344

This book focuses on the women's movement between 1967 and 1977.

"A riveting blend of eyewitness accounts and keen analysis, this is history at its most vital and a stirring testament to our ability to come together to combat social injustice, no matter how deeply entrenched it has become." Booklist

Coontz, Stephanie

A **strange** stirring; the Feminine mystique and American women at the dawn of the 1960s. Stephanie Coontz. Basic Books 2011 xxiii, 222 p.p (hc : alk. paper) $25.95   **305.42**

1. Authors 2. Feminism 3. Feminism -- United States -- History -- 20th century 4. Women -- United States -- Social conditions -- 20th century
ISBN 0465002005; 9780465002009

LC 2010022163

The book "documents the circumstances of middle-class American women in the early 1960s and the impact of Betty Friedan's The Feminine Mystique (1963). Stephanie Coontz makes it clear that although Friedan, and many observers since, have exaggerated the book's role in launching the second wave of the feminist movement, thousands of women were profoundly affected by it. . . . [Stephanie] Coontz begins with a stark look at the circumstances facing women in the early 1960s, including legal discrimination and widely held cultural beliefs about women's nature and proper role. . . . The book ends with a chapter on the circumstances of women today. Despite the gains of the feminist movement, gender expectations still limit women's possibilities." (Journal of American History)

Includes bibliographical references (p. 191-208) and index

Nordberg, Jenny

★ **The** **underground** girls of Kabul; in search of a hidden resistance in Afghanistan. Jenny Nordberg. Crown Publishers 2014 288 p. hbk $25   **305.42**

1. Gender role 2. Women -- Afghanistan 3. Afghanistan -- Social conditions 4. Girls -- Afghanistan 5. Gender Identity -- Afghanistan 6. Male impersonators -- Afghanistan
ISBN 0307952495; 9780307952493

LC 2014000295

Author Jenny Nordberg presents this book on the Afghan custom of "bacha posh . . . a third kind of child--a girl temporarily raised as a boy and presented as such to the outside world. Nordberg, the reporter who broke the story of this phenomenon for the New York Times, constructs a powerful and moving account of those secretly living on the other side of a deeply segregated society where women have almost no rights and little freedom. " (Publisher's note)

"Nordberg's subtle, sympathetic reportage makes this one of the most convincing portraits of Afghan culture in print; through a small breach in the wall of gender apartheid, she reveals the harsh ironies of a system that so devalues women that it forces them to become men." Pub Wkly

Includes bibliographical references and index

Rosin, Hanna

The **end** of men; and the rise of women. Hanna Rosin. Riverhead Books 2012 310 p. (hbk.) $27.95   **305.42**

1. Women -- History 2. Man-woman relationship 3. Feminism 4. Women -- Social conditions -- 21st century 5. Women -- Economic conditions -- 21st century
ISBN 1594488045; 9781594488047

LC 2012018005

This book by Hanna Rosin is a "portrait of women, men, and power in a transformed world. Men have been the dominant sex since, well, the dawn of mankind. . . . [But] this unprecedented moment, by almost every measure, women are no longer gaining on men: They have pulled decisively ahead. Rosin reveals how this new state of affairs is radically shifting the power dynamics between men and women at every level of society, with profound implications for marriage, sex, children, work, and more." (Publisher's note)

Includes bibliographical references and index.

Spar, Debora L.

Wonder Women; Sex, Power, and the Quest for Perfection. Sarah Crichton Books 2013 320 p. $27   **305.42**

1. Feminism 2. Women -- Social conditions
ISBN 0374298750; 9780374298753

This book "addresses the state of feminism and suggests that, despite historic gains in education, the workforce, and equal rights, American women suffer under 'an excruciating set of mutually exclusive expectations' resulting, paradoxically, from the proliferation of options that feminism made possible." Debora L. Spar "traces how the movement's 'expansive and revolutionary' political goals have evolved into a set of 'vast and towering expectations' that trouble women at every stage of their lives." (Publishers Weekly)

Steinem, Gloria

Moving beyond words. Simon & Schuster 1994 319p hardcover o.p. pa $19.95   **305.42**

1. Feminism
ISBN 0-671-51052-5 pa

LC 94-4839

"Ms. Steinem's enduring contribution to the women's movement has been her ability to popularize feminist issues to a wide and often wary audience." N Y Times Book Rev

Includes bibliographical references

Outrageous acts and everyday rebellions; 2nd ed; Holt & Co. 1995 xxii, 406p pa $17   **305.42**

1. Feminism
ISBN 0-8050-4202-4

LC 95-31711

First published 1983

In addition to material addressing specific feminist issues, this collection includes personal accounts of political leaders and noted women.

Includes bibliographical references

The **unfinished** revolution; voices from the global fight for women's rights. edited by Minky Worden. Seven Stories Press 2012 xviii, 361 p.p col. ill. (paperback) $25.95   **305.42**

1. Human rights 2. Women's rights
ISBN 1609803876; 9781609803872

LC 2011052738

This book edited by Minky Worden is a collection of "essays assessing the progress of worldwide rights for women and girls since the UN's human rights conferences in the 1990s. The ongoing global struggle consists of three distinct spheres: economic issues (human trafficking, property rights); violence against women and their health rights (including genital mutilation); and harmful traditions (religious clothing restraints, so-called honor crimes)." (Booklist)

Includes bibliographical references and index

Valenti, Jessica, 1978-

Full Frontal Feminism; A Young Woman's Guide to Why Feminism Matters. Jessica Valenti. Pgw 2014 279 p. illustrations $17   **305.42**

1. Feminism 2. Women's movement 3. Women -- Social conditions
ISBN 1580055613; 9781580055611

LC 200638573

This book, by Jessica Valenti, is an updated "guide to the issues that matter to today's young women. . . . With new openers from Valenti in every chapter, the book covers a range of topics, including pop culture, health, reproductive rights, violence, education, relationships, and more." (Publisher's note)

"These are lessons we already know; little in this book will prove useful to most women. Most public libraries will want the Siegel book; a few may want Valenti's." LJ

Wolf, Naomi

Vagina; A New Biography. Naomi Wolf. HarperCollins 2012 xii, 381 p., [8] p. of platesp ill. $27.99   **305.42**

1. Vagina 2. Femininity 3. Nervous system 4. Reproductive system 5. Women -- Sexual behavior
ISBN 0061989169; 9780061989162

LC 2012454997

This book by Naomi Wolf "explores the effect of new neurobiological discoveries on our understanding of female sexuality. When the author began noticing . . . diminished sexual response at age 46, she visited a gynecologist, who diagnosed her with an impacted pelvic nerve. . . . Wolf set out to document the mind-body link with the goal of informing women of the crucial role that neurology plays not only in their sex lives, but also in . . . their creativity and sense of well-being." (Kirkus Reviews)

Includes bibliographical references (p. [335]-365) and index.

305.48   Specific groups of women

Mah, Adeline Yen

Falling leaves; a true story of an unwanted Chinese daughter. Wiley 1998 278p il $22.95 **305.48**
1. Physicians 2. China -- Social life and customs
ISBN 0-471-24742-1

LC 97-40144

First published 1997 in the United Kingdom with title: Falling leaves return to their roots

"Although the focus of this memoir is the author's struggle to be loved by a family that treated her cruelly, it is more notable for its portrait of the domestic affairs of an immensely wealthy, Westernized Chinese family in Shanghai as the city evolved under the harsh strictures of Mao and Deng. . . . In recounting this painful tale, Yen Mah's unadorned prose is powerful, her insights keen and her portrait of her family devastating." Publ Wkly

Scroggins, Deborah

Wanted women; faith, lies, and the war on terror : the lives of Ayaan Hirsi Ali and Aafia Siddiqui. by Deborah Scroggins. Harper 2011 p. cm.   **305.48**
1. Feminism 2. Terrorism 3. Muslim women 4. Women political activists 5. Muslim women -- Social conditions 6. Muslim women -- Political activity
ISBN 9780060898977

LC 2011022153

This book explores the topics of "militant Islam, Muslim women's rights, and the war on terror--brought into focus through two lives on opposite sides: activist Ayaan Hirsi Ali and religious extremist Aafia Siddiqui. . . . Ayaan Hirsi Ali, a Somali-born former member of the Dutch Parliament and the author of the international bestseller 'Infidel,' was raised as a Muslim fundamentalist in Kenya. A feminist, political analyst, writer, and fierce critic of her former religion, she champions the West in what she insists must be a war against Islam. . . . Aafia Siddiqui, a native of Pakistan, moved to the United States to pursue a doctorate in neuroscience. A decade later, she returned to Pakistan, where her involvement with al-Qaeda, including her marriage to one of the 9/11 plotters, led the CIA to regard her as one of the most dangerous terrorists in the world." (Publisher's note)

305.5   People by social and economic levels

Bageant, Joe

Deer hunting with Jesus; dispatches from America's class war. Crown Publishers 2007 273. **305.5**
1. Social classes -- United States. 2. United States --

Social conditions -- 1980-
ISBN 978-0-307-33936-2

LC 2007-01343

"Returning after 30 years to the 'dirt-poor' neighborhoods of his native Winchester, VA, Bageant examines the lives of the working poor using the stories of his friends and neighbors. Through these bleak tales, he paints a picture of a permanent underclass exploited by the Right and forgotten or even disdained, by the Left." (Library Journal)

Boo, Katherine

★ **Behind** the beautiful forevers; Katherine Boo. Random House 2012 xxii, 256 p.p   **305.5**
1. Poverty 2. Bombay (India) 3. Political corruption 4. Creative nonfiction 5. Urban poor -- India -- Bombay 6. Urban poor -- India -- Mumbai
ISBN 1400067553; 9780679645504; 9781400067558

LC 2011019555

This book examines "the stark lives of the inhabitants of Annawadi, a slum across from Mumbai's Sahar Airport, to reveal the . . . inequality and urban poverty still endemic in India's democracy. Using recorded and videotaped conversations, interviews, documents, and the assistance of interlocutors, [Katherine] Boo profiles the lives of some of the slum dwellers from November 2007 to March 2011. . . . [Boo] claims she witnessed most of the events described in the book." (Library Journal)

Brooks, David, 1961-

The **social** animal; the hidden sources of love, character, and achievement. Random House 2011 424p $27; ebook $13.99   **305.5**
1. Character 2. Social status 3. Elite (Social sciences)
ISBN 978-1-4000-6760-2; 1-4000-6760-X; 978-0-679-60393-1 ebook; 0-679-60393-X ebook

LC 2010045785

"Brooks offers fictional characters Harold and Erica to illustrate how humans communicate, are educated, and succeed—or don't. Synthesizing research on human unconsciousness, Brooks meshes sociology, psychology, and economics to show how character is formed and how we strive for happiness and success. . . . [The author] offers a new look at the assumptions we make about life and a close, deep examination of the failure of social and economic policies that do not take into account the complexities of human behavior, treating us as if we were totally rational and guided by our thoughts rather than some combination of intellect and emotion." Booklist

Includes bibliographical references

Ehrenreich, Barbara

★ **Nickel** and dimed; on (not) getting by in America. Metropolitan Bks. 2001 221p hardcover o.p. pa $15   **305.5**
1. Poverty 2. Minimum wage 3. Labor -- United States
ISBN 0-8050-6388-9; 0-8050-8838-5 pa

LC 00-52514

"No real answers to the problem but a compelling sketch of its reality and pervasiveness." Libr J

Epstein, Joseph, 1937-

Snobbery; The American Version. Houghton Mifflin 2002 274p $25; pa $14   **305.5**

1. Snobs and snobbishness 2. Social status -- United States 3. Snobs and snobbishness -- United States

ISBN 0-395-94417-1; 0-618-34073-4 pa

LC 2001-51623

Epstein tracks the evolution of intellectual and cultural snobbery in the United States. He suggests that the traditional snobbery associated with the class system has given way in recent decades to a more complex phenomenon based on taste. Index.

"Every bracing page is a mirror in which readers can't help but recognize themselves, and each offers a quotable quip . . . and much to think about." Booklist

Includes bibliographical references

Freeland, Chrystia

Plutocrats; the rise of the new global super-rich and the fall of everyone else. Chrystia Freeland. Penguin Press 2012 xv, 330 p.p $27.95   **305.5**

1. Rich 2. Elite (Social sciences) 3. Power (Social sciences) 4. Poor 5. Rich people -- Conduct of life

ISBN 1594204098; 9781594204098

LC 2012015119

This book, by Chrystia Freeland, offers an "examination of wealth disparity, income inequality, and the new global elite. . . . In the last few decades what it means to be rich has changed dramatically. . . . The wealthiest 0.1 percent . . . are outpacing the rest of us at break-neck speed. . . . [The book] demonstrates how social upheavals generated by the first Gilded Age may pale in comparison to what is in store for us." (Publisher's note)

Includes bibliographical references and index

Hayes, Christopher

Twilight of the elites; America after meritocracy. Christopher Hayes. Crown Publishers 2012 292 p.   **305.5**

1. Equality 2. Leadership 3. Elite (Social sciences) 4. United States -- Politics and government -- 21st century 5. Power (Social sciences) 6. Corporate power -- United States 7. Business and politics -- United States 8. Elite (Social sciences) -- United States 9. United States -- Social conditions -- 21st century 10. United States -- Economic conditions -- 21st century

ISBN 9780307720450; 9780307720474

LC 2012002435

This book looks at the meritocracy and income inequality in the U.S. since the 1960s. Combining "political analysis, . . . social commentary, . . . and . . . historical understanding, 'Twilight of Elites' describes how the society we have come to inhabit -- utterly forgiving at the top and relentlessly punitive at the bottom -- produces leaders who are out of touch with the people they have been trusted to govern." (Publisher's note)

Includes bibliographical references and index.

Hedges, Chris

Days of destruction, days of revolt; Chris Hedges and Joe Sacco. Nation Books 2012 xv, 302 p.p ill. (hardback) $28   **305.5**

1. Camden (N.J.) 2. Social conflict 3. Poor -- United States 4. Pine Ridge Indian Reservation (S.D.) 5. Mines and mineral resources -- United States 6. Crime -- United States 7. Social classes -- United States 8. United States -- Social conditions -- 20th century

ISBN 1568586434; 9781568586434; 9781568587103

LC 2012004701

This book by Chris Hedges and Joe Sacco examines the impact of capitalism in America's society through a "tour of some of the worst places in America: the Pine Ridge reservation in South Dakota, which paces the nation in drug abuse, alcoholism, and teen suicide rates; Camden, NJ, one of the country's poorest and most dangerous cities; Welch, WV, where coal companies have relentlessly mined both human and natural resources; and Immokalee, FL, where migrant farm workers toil in virtual slavery." (Columbia Journalism Review)

Includes bibliographical references (p. 287-291) and index

Jadhav, Narendra

★ Untouchables; my family's triumphant journey out of the caste system in modern India. Scribner 2005 307p $26   **305.5**

1. Caste 2. India -- Social conditions

ISBN 0-7432-7079-7

LC 2005-44166

Original Indian edition, 1993; first published in English 2003 by Viking with title: Outcaste, a memoir

"This moving story of perseverance from a sector of India rarely represented to American readers will be a standard text on Indian and Dalit themes for years to come." Libr J

Laskas, Jeanne Marie, 1958-

★ Hidden America; from coal miners to cowboys, an extraordinary exploration of the unseen people who make this country work. Jeanne Marie Laskas. Penguin Group USA 2012 318 p.   **305.5**

1. Cheerleading 2. Migrant labor 3. Coal mines and mining 4. Subculture -- United States 5. United States -- Description and travel 6. United States -- Social conditions -- 1980- 7. Working class -- United States -- Biography 8. Manual work -- Social aspects -- United States 9. United States -- Social life and customs -- 1971- 10. Working class -- United States -- Social conditions 11. Working class -- United States -- Social life and customs

ISBN 0399159002; 9780399159008

LC 2012025457

Author Jeanne Marie Laskas presents a book "about the people who make our lives run every day--and yet we barely think of them. Laskas spent weeks in an Ohio coal mine and on an Alaskan oil rig; in a Maine migrant labor camp, a Texas beef ranch, the air traffic control tower at New York's LaGuardia Airport, a California landfill, an Arizona gun shop, the cab of a long-haul truck in Iowa, and the stadium of the Cincinnati Ben-Gals cheerleaders." (Publisher's note)

LeBlanc, Adrian Nicole

★ **Random** family; love, drugs, trouble, and coming of age in the Bronx. Scribner 2003 408p $25 **305.5**

1. Poor -- New York (N.Y.) 2. Youth -- New York (N.Y.) 3. Bronx (New York, N.Y.) -- Social conditions

ISBN 0-684-86387-1

LC 2002-26673

"A painstaking feat of reporting and empathy that resulted from 10 years of hanging out with a hard-pressed, loosely defined family in the Bronx." N Y Times Book Rev

Painter, Nell Irvin

★ **Sojourner** Truth; a life, a symbol. Norton 1996 370p il hardcover o.p. pa $15.95 **305.5**

1. Feminism 2. Abolitionists 3. Memoirists 4. African American women -- Biography

ISBN 0-393-02739-2; 0-393-31708-0 pa

LC 95-47595

"Painter persuasively offers us the real woman behind the myth." Publ Wkly

Includes bibliographical references

Smith, Douglas

Former people; the final days of the Russian aristocracy. Douglas Smith. 1st ed. Farrar, Straus and Giroux 2012 xvii, 464 pages, 32 unnumbered pages of platesp illustrations, maps (hardcover : alk. paper) $30.00 **305.5**

1. Communism 2. Russia -- History 3. Nobility -- Russia 4. Aristocracy (Social class) -- Soviet Union 5. Aristocracy (Social class) -- Russia -- History -- 20th century

ISBN 0374157618; 9780374157616

LC 2012003819

This book "examines the . . . 'fate of the nobility in the decades following the Russian Revolution,' when they were sometimes given the Orwellian title 'former people.' The author of several books on Russia . . . , [Douglas] Smith focuses on three generations of two families: the Sheremetsevs of St. Petersburg and the Golitsyns of Moscow." (Publishers Weekly)

Includes bibliographical references (pages 416-435) and index.

Stiglitz, Joseph E., 1943-

★ The **price** of inequality; how today's divided society endangers our future. Joseph E. Stiglitz. W.W. Norton & Co. 2012 xxxi, 414 p,p (hbk.) $27.95 **305.5**

1. Wealth 2. Finance -- United States 3. Equality -- United States 4. Global Financial Crisis, 2008-2009 5. United States -- Social conditions -- 21st century 6. United States -- Economic conditions -- 21st century 7. Income distribution -- Social aspects -- United States

ISBN 0393088693; 9780393088694

LC 2012014811

In this book, author Joseph E. Stiglitz "insists that increasing inequality in the United States stems from a breakdown of the country's political and economic systems." Stiglitz suggests that "inequality is a by-product of the ability to exploit consumers through monopoly power. . . . He shows that the consequences include a monopolistic redistribution

powerful enough to have caused massive distortions in the U.S. financial system." (Kirkus Reviews)

Includes bibliographical references and index.

Veblen, Thorstein

★ The **theory** of the leisure class; edited with an introduction and notes by Martha Banta. Oxford University Press 2007 (Oxford world's classics) pa $15.95 **305.5**

1. Social classes

ISBN 978-0-19-280684-0; 0-19-280684-X

LC 2007-8544

First published 1899 by Macmillan

In this economic treatise, "Veblen held that the feudal subdivision of classes had continued into modern times, the lords employing themselves uselessly . . . while the lower classes labored at industrial pursuits to support the whole of society. The leisure class, Veblen said, justifies itself solely by practicing 'conspicuous leisure and conspicuous consumption'; he defined waste as any activity not contributing to material productivity." Benet Reader's Ency. 4th edition

305.8   Ethnic and national groups

★ The **African** American almanac; Christopher A. Brooks, editor; foreword by Benjamin Jealous. 11th ed; Gale Cengage Learning 2011 1601p il map $297 **305.8**

1. Reference books 2. African Americans

ISBN 978-1-4144-4547-2

First edition under the editorship of Harry A. Ploski published 1967 by Bellwether with title: The Negro almanac. Periodically revised. Editors vary

"Reference covering the cultural and political history of Black Americans. Includes generous amount of statistical information and biographies of Black Americans, both historical and contemporary." N Y Public Libr. Book of How & Where to Look It Up

Bayoumi, Moustafa

How does it feel to be a problem? being young and Arab in America. Penguin Press 2008 290p pa $15; $24.95 **305.8**

1. Arab American youth 2. Young men -- Psychology 3. Young men -- United States 4. Race awareness -- United States 5. United States -- Race relations 6. Arab Americans -- Ethnic identity 7. Arab Americans -- Social conditions 8. Brooklyn (New York, N.Y.) -- Ethnic relations

ISBN 978-0-14-311541-0 pa; 978-1-59420-176-9

LC 2007-49272

This book is based on interviews with seven young Arab Americans who live in Brooklyn. It "evaluates their daily encounters with such factors as prejudice, the Christian faith, and their relationships with friends and family members in the Middle East." (Publisher's note)

The author "wondered how younger generations of Arab Americans were faring in a post-9/11 U.S. against the backdrop of fear and suspicion. By focusing on the lives of seven young people living in Brooklyn, Bayoumi offers a revealing portrait of life for people who are often scrutinized but seldom heard from." Booklist

Includes bibliographical references

Berlin, Ira

The **making** of African America; the four great migrations. Viking 2010 304p $27.95   **305.8**
1. Slave trade 2. Internal migration 3. African Americans -- History 4. Slave trade -- United States 5. African Americans -- Migrations -- History 6. United States -- Immigration and emigration 7. Migration, Internal -- United States -- History 8. United States -- Emigration and immigration -- History
ISBN 978-0-670-02137-6; 0-670-02137-7

LC 2009-28366

"This . . . book proposes a new framework for African American history. Breaking with what he calls the 'master narrative' that frames the subject as an ongoing struggle for freedom and equality, Ira Berlin argues that the experience of relocation and the formation of new communities in new contexts have been pivotal in the making and remaking of African American society. . . . Based on secondary sources, this . . . book briskly narrates four hundred years of history, highlighting the 'four great migrations.' . . . 'The Making of African America' aims to show how migrations reorganized culture and social life. Each of his four major relocations yields a new African America." (Journal of American History)

"Berlin's neat synthesis offers the sharp insights and provocative commentary of one of the foremost historians of black America. Essential for library collections, general readers, and scholars of African American history." Libr J

Includes bibliographical references

Bishop, Bill

The **big** sort; why the clustering of like-minded America is tearing us apart. with Robert G. Cushing. Houghton Mifflin 2008 370p il map $25   **305.8**
1. Minorities 2. Minorities -- United States 3. Regionalism -- United States 4. Segregation -- United States 5. Regionalism -- Political aspects 6. Social conflict -- United States 7. Political culture -- United States 8. United States -- Social conditions 9. Group identity -- Political aspects 10. United States -- Social conditions -- 1980- 11. United States -- Politics and government -- 1989-
ISBN 0-618-68935-4; 978-0-618-68935-4

LC 2007-43907

This volume originated in a series of articles written by journalist Bill Bishop and sociologist Robert Cushing, contending that "Americans have been sorting themselves over the past three decades into . . . homogeneous communities, not by region or by red state or blue state, but by city and even neighborhood." (Publisher's note) Index.

"Bishop's argument is meticulously researched—surveys and polls proliferate—and his reach is broad. . . . [The] portrait of our 'post materialistic' society will . . . generate chatter [and] the idea is catchy." Publ Wkly

Includes bibliographical references

Biss, Eula

Notes from no man's land; American essays. Graywolf Press 2009 230p   **305.8**
1. Poets 2. Authors 3. Essayists 4. Group identity -- United States 5. United States -- Race relations 6. United States -- Description and travel
ISBN 1-55597-518-6; 978-1-55597-518-0

LC 20080935599

"In a book that begins with a series of lynchings and ends with a series of apologies, Eula Biss explores race in America. Her response to the topic is informed by the experiences chronicled in these essays--teaching in a Harlem school on the morning of 9/11, reporting for an African American newspaper in San Diego, watching the aftermath of Katrina from a college town in Iowa, and settling in Chicago's most diverse neighborhood." (Publisher's note)

"These essays are about many things, but the theme of race runs through them all. They are not 'about' race, however, not in the way essays are usually 'about' something. Instead of presenting her opening gambits and using the body of the essay to support her initial points, Biss finds her jumping-off point and examines her observations and experiences. Although her juxtapositions are occasionally forced, it is impossible to remain unmoved by Biss's work." Libr J

Blackmon, Douglas A.

Slavery by another name; the re-enslavement of Black people in America from the Civil War to World War II. Doubleday 2008 466p il $29.95; pa $16.95   **305.8**
1. Slavery -- United States 2. United States -- Race relations 3. African Americans -- Civil rights
ISBN 978-0-385-50625-0; 0-385-50625-2; 978-0-385-72270-4 pa; 0-385-72270-2 pa

LC 2007-34500

The author "gives a groundbreaking and disturbing account of a sordid chapter in American history—the lease (essentially the sale) of convicts to commercial interests between the end of the 19th century and well into the 20th. . . . [The] book reveals in devastating detail the legal and commercial forces that created this neoslavery along with deeply moving and totally appalling personal testimonies of survivors." Publ Wkly

Includes bibliographical references (p. 444-459)

Chesler, Phyllis

The **new** anti-semitism; the current crisis and what we must do about it. Jossey-Bass 2003 307p $24.95; pa $15.95   **305.8**
1. Antisemitism 2. Israel-Arab conflicts
ISBN 0-7879-6851-X; 0-7879-7803-5 pa

LC 2003-6448

The author "addresses what she sees as a re-emergence of virulent anti-Jewish hatred cloaked in 'political correctness,' closely linked to anti-American attitudes, sustained by many liberal feminists, intellectuals and Jewish leftists, acted upon by Islamic terrorists and jihadists, and fueled by a 'demonization of Jews' in the media. One of the main thrusts of Chesler's argument is that in our contemporary world anti-Zionism is nearly inseparable from anti-Semitism, and that while there are valid criticisms to be made of Israeli policies—for instance, she sees the West Bank settlements as an impediment to peace—many of these critiques are, she contends, rooted in a profound and socially accepted anti-Semitism." Publ Wkly

Includes bibliographical references

Coates, Ta-Nehisi, 1975-

★ **Between** the World and Me; Ta-Nehisi Coates. Random House Inc. 2015 176 p. illustrations (hardback) $24.00   305.8

   1. United States -- Race relations 2. African Americans -- Social conditions

   ISBN 0812993543; 9780812993547

LC 2015008120

   National Book Critics Circle Award Finalist: Criticism (2015)

   NAACP Image Award: Outstanding Literary Work- Biography/Autobiography (2016)

   Pulitzer Prize Finalist: General Nonfiction (2016)

   Alex Award (2016)

   National Book Award: Nonfiction (2015)

   Kirkus Prize: Nonfiction (2015)

   This book, by Ta-Nehisi Coates, argues "Americans have built an empire on the idea of 'race,' a falsehood that damages us all but falls most heavily on the bodies of black women and men--bodies exploited through slavery and segregation, and, today, threatened, locked up, and murdered out of all proportion. What is it like to inhabit a black body and find a way to live within it? And how can we all honestly reckon with this fraught history and free ourselves from its burden?" (Publisher's note)

   "In this brief book, which takes the form of a letter to the author's teenage son, Coates . . . comes to grips with what it means to be black in America today. . . . There is awesome beauty in the power of his prose and vital truth on every page." Booklist

Curtis, Edward E., 1970-

Muslims in America; a short history. Oxford University Press 2009 144p il (Religion in American life) pa $12.95   305.8

   1. Muslims 2. Ethnic relations 3. Islam -- History 4. Muslims -- United States 5. Islam -- United States -- History 6. Muslims -- United States -- History 7. United States -- Religious life and customs

   ISBN 978-0-19-536756-0

LC 2008-47566

   The author "has authored a fine and succinct history that spans centuries. . . . Although geared toward non-Muslims, American Muslims would also learn a great deal from reading about their own history. . . . [Readers] will undoubtedly be intrigued by Curtis's compelling little read." Publ Wkly

   Includes bibliographical references

Diner, Hasia R.

A **time** for gathering; the second migration, 1820-1880. Johns Hopkins Univ. Press 1992 313p il (Jewish people in America) hardcover o.p. pa $20.95   305.8

   1. Jews -- United States -- History

   ISBN 0-8018-4344-8; 0-8018-5121-1 pa

LC 91-45368

This second volume in a five-volume history of American Jewry focuses on the German-speaking Jewish immigrants who came to the United States in the nineteenth century.

   Includes bibliographical references

Du Bois, W. E. B.

★ The **souls** of Black folk; edited with an introduction and notes by Brent Hayes Edwards. Oxford University Press 2007 xxxvi, 223p il (Oxford world's classics) pa $12.95   305.8

   1. African Americans

   ISBN 978-0-19-280678-9; 0-19-280678-5

LC 2006-35193

   First published 1903 by McClurg

   "A collection of fifteen essays and sketches by W.E.B. Du Bois. In it he describes the lives of African American farmers, sketches the role of music in their churches, details the history of the Freedman's Bureau, discusses the career of Booker T. Washington, and advocates a commitment to higher education for the most talented African American youth." Benet's Reader's Ency of Am Lit

   Includes bibliographical references

Dyson, Michael Eric

The **Black** presidency; Barack Obama and the politics of race in America. Michael Eric Dyson. Houghton Mifflin Harcourt 2016 346 p. (hardcover) $27   305.8

   1. Racism 2. United States -- Race relations 3. African Americans -- Politics and government 4. United States -- Politics and government -- 2009- 5. Race -- Political aspects -- United States 6. Racism -- Political aspects -- United States 7. United States -- Race relations -- Political aspects 8. African Americans -- Politics and government -- 21st century

   ISBN 9780544387669; 9780544811805

LC 2015037026

   This book, by Michael Eric Dyson, "explores the powerful, surprising way the politics of race have shaped Barack Obama's identity and groundbreaking presidency. How has President Obama dealt publicly with race—as the national traumas of Tamir Rice, Trayvon Martin, Michael Brown, Eric Garner, Freddie Gray, and Walter Scott have played out during his tenure? What can we learn from Obama's major race speeches about his approach to racial conflict and the black criticism it provokes?" (Publisher's note)

   "Dyson succeeds admirably in creating a base line for future interpretations of this historic presidency. His well-written book thoroughly illuminates the challenges facing a black man elected to govern a society that is far from post-racial." Kirkus

   Includes bibliographical references (pages 282-333) and index.

Everett, Daniel Leonard

Don't sleep, there are snakes; life and language in the Amazonian jungle. [by] Daniel L. Everett. Pantheon Books 2008 283p il $26.95   305.8

   1. Pirahã Indians 2. Amazon River valley -- Languages

   ISBN 978-0-375-42502-8; 0-375-42502-0

LC 2008-16306

The author "has crafted a fascinating account of his 30 years of linguistics work among the Pirahã (pronounced pee-da-HAN) Indians, a tribal group living along the Maici and Marmelos Rivers in a remote area of western Brazil. . . . With a clear, detail-rich writing style, Everett provides evocative ethnographic descriptions of Pirahã life and culture as well as perceptive linguistic analysis." Libr J

Includes bibliographical references

Family affair; what It means to be African American today. [edited by] Gil L. Robertson IV. Bolden 2009 407p pa $16　　　**305.8**

1. African Americans -- Race identity
ISBN 978-1932841-35-0; 1-932841-35-0

LC 2008-45716

"This thoughtful collection of short essays, addressing a wide range of issues and emotions facing African Americans, should become a well-thumbed nightstand fixture." Publ Wkly

Franklin, John Hope

★ **From** slavery to freedom; a history of African Americans. [by] John Hope Franklin, Evelyn Higginbotham. 9th ed.; McGraw-Hill 2010 xxv, 710p il map $100.63　　　**305.8**

1. Slavery -- United States 2. African Americans -- History
ISBN 978-0-07-296378-6; 0-07-296378-6

LC 2009-42935

First published 1947

A survey of African-Americans history from slavery to the present.

Includes bibliographical references

★ **Freedom** on my mind; the Columbia documentary history of the African American experience. Manning Marable, general editor; Nishani Frazier and John McMillian, assistant editors. Columbia University Press 2003 734p $80　　　**305.8**

1. African Americans -- History -- Sources
ISBN 0-231-10890-7

LC 2003-51605

This "anthology features the works of noteworthy figures of African American history and culture . . . and provides a tapestry of personal correspondence, excerpts from slave narratives and autobiographies, leaflets, speeches, oral histories and interviews, political manifestos, song lyrics, and important statements of black institutions and organizations. . . . A necessary text of readings for both introductory and advanced African American studies courses." Choice

Includes bibliographical references

Gates, Henry Louis

In search of our roots; how 19 extraordinary African Americans reclaimed their past. Crown Publishers 2008 438p il map $27.50　　　**305.8**

1. Genealogy 2. African Americans
ISBN 978-0-307-38240-5

LC 2008-11860

"Bright, inquisitive take on the multifarious murky stories and relationships that make up the history of a dispossessed people." Kirkus

Includes bibliographical references

Life upon these shores; looking at African American history, 1513-2008. Knopf 2011 487p il $50　　　**305.8**

1. African Americans -- History 2. United States -- Civilization
ISBN 978-0-307-59342-9

LC 2011014277

"With nearly 900 illustrations (formal portraits, news photos, historic lithographs, broadsides, flyers, posters, newspaper clippings, advertisements) complemented by a succinct but informing text, Harvard professor Gates (Black in Latin America) provides a visual sojourn through African-American history, a generally upbeat march from Juan Garrido, accompanying Cortés in 1519, to Barack Obama taking the presidential oath in 2008. Gathered in this chronologically arranged compendium, with its focus on the accomplishments and moments of achievement in the African-American community, is a wealth of materials about the historical, political, social, literary, and scientific events influencing American social and political culture." Publ Wkly

Includes bibliographical references

Gibbon, Piers

Tribe; endangered peoples around the world. [by] Piers Gibbon with Jane Houston. Firefly Books 2010 192p il $45　　　**305.8**

1. Ethnology 2. Acculturation
ISBN 978-1-55407-742-7; 1-55407-742-7

LC 2011-380573

Presents the cultures, beliefs, and societal patterns of over two hundred indigenous peoples and describes their degrees of integration with other societies and the integrity of their indigenous identities. Contains some images of nudity.

This is "a wonderful compendium of diversity and a useful platform for thought, providing an opportunity to pose questions to ourselves. . . . It reminds us that there is so much that we still don't know, so much more to the world than we see in our homes and high streets; that the world is wondrous and precious and has an innate value that must be both defended and empowered if it is to survive." Geographical

Includes bibliographical references

Griffin, John Howard

★ **Black** like me; the definitive Griffin estate edition, corrected from original manuscripts. foreword by Studs Terkel; with historic photographs by Don Rutledge; and an afterword by Robert Bonazzi. 2nd Wings Press ed., with index; Wings Press 2006 243p il $29.95　　　**305.8**

1. Prejudices 2. African Americans -- Southern States
ISBN 978-0-930324-73-5

First published 1961 by Houghton Mifflin

The author, "who is white, a Catholic, and a Texan, conceived and carried out the unusual notion of blackening his skin with a newly developed pigment drug and traveling through the Deep South as a Negro. This book, part of which appeared in the Negro magazine Sepia, is a journal account of that experience." New Yorker

Includes bibliographical references

Hahn, Steven

A **nation** under our feet; Black political struggles in the rural South, from slavery to the great migration. Steven Hahn. Belknap Press of Harvard University Press 2003 610p il $35; pa $18.95   **305.8**

1. Southern States -- Race relations 2. African Americans -- Political activity

ISBN 0-674-01169-4; 0-674-01765-X pa
                                LC 2003-45326

This book "is one of the most important works in American social history to appear in recent years." Nation

Includes bibliographical references

Hendrickson, Paul

Sons of Mississippi; a story of race and its legacy. Knopf 2003 343p il map $26; pa $15   **305.8**

1. Police brutality 2. Mississippi -- Race relations 3. African Americans -- Mississippi

ISBN 0-375-40461-9; 0-375-70425-6 pa
                                LC 2002-29857

"The number of telling quotes, interviews with friends and family, primary and secondary sources, allusions to art and history, and gut reactions Hendrickson offers are what really make the book. . . . He repeatedly comes up with electric interview material, and deftly places these men within the defining events of their times, when 'a 100-year-old way of life was cracking beneath them.'" Publ Wkly

Includes bibliographical references

Hill, Anita, 1956-

Reimagining equality; stories of gender, race, and finding home. Beacon Press 2011 xxiv, 195p $25.95   **305.8**

1. African American women 2. African Americans -- Housing 3. Houses -- Buying and selling 4. African Americans -- Social conditions

ISBN 978-0-8070-1437-0
                                LC 2011020232

The author "addresses the prime mortgage debacle, specifically how 'owning a home, and thus acquiring this piece of the American Dream has become increasingly difficult for people of color and single women,' and presents an indictment of subprime and predatory lending." Publ Wkly

Includes bibliographical references

Johnson, Walter

River of dark dreams; slavery and empire in the cotton kingdom. Walter Johnson. The Belknap Press of Harvard University Press 2013 560 p. (hardcover) $35   **305.8**

1. Cotton manufacture 2. Slavery -- United States 3. Mississippi River Valley -- History 4. Slavery -- Mississippi River Valley -- History -- 19th century 5. Mississippi River Valley -- Commerce -- History -- 19th century 6. Cotton growing -- Mississippi River Valley -- History -- 19th century 7. Mississippi River Valley

-- Race relations -- History -- 19th century

ISBN 0674045556; 9780674045552
                                LC 2012030065

This book, by Walter Johnson, explores how "when Jefferson acquired the Louisiana Territory, he envisioned an 'empire for liberty' populated by self-sufficient white farmers . . . , [but] was transformed instead into a booming capitalist economy . . . , dependent on the coerced labor of slaves. [The book] places the Cotton Kingdom at the center of worldwide webs of exchange and exploitation that extended across oceans and drove an insatiable hunger for new lands." (Publisher's note)

Includes bibliographical references and index

Jones, Jacqueline

A **dreadful** deceit; the myth of race from the colonial era to Obama's America. Jacqueline Jones. Basic Books 2013 400 p. (hardback) $29.99 **305.8**

1. African Americans 2. United States -- Race relations -- History 3. Race -- Philosophy 4. African Americans -- Biography 5. Race awareness -- United States -- History 6. African Americans -- Race identity -- History

ISBN 0465036708; 9780465036707
                                LC 2013031130

"In 'A Dreadful Deceit,' . . . historian Jacqueline Jones traces the lives of [six] African Americans to illustrate the strange history of 'race' in America. In truth, Jones shows, race does not exist, and the very factors that we think of as determining it--a person's heritage or skin color--are mere pretexts for the brutalization of powerless people by the powerful." (Publisher's note)

Includes bibliographical references and index

Kendi, Ibram X.

★ **Stamped** from the beginning; the definitive history of racist ideas in America. Ibram X. Kendi. Nation Books 2016 592 p. (hardcover) $32.99 **305.8**

1. Racism -- History 2. United States -- Race relations 3. Racism -- United States -- History

ISBN 1568584636; 9781568584638
                                LC 2015033671

National Book Award: Nonfiction (2016)

In this book, author Ibram X. Kendi chronicles "the entire story of anti-Black racist ideas. . . . [He] uses the life stories of five major American intellectuals to offer a window into the contentious debates between assimilationists and segregationists and between racists and antiracists. From Puritan minister Cotton Mather to Thomas Jefferson, from fiery abolitionist William Lloyd Garrison to brilliant scholar W.E.B. Du Bois to legendary anti-prison activist Angela Davis." (Publisher's note)

"Kendi's provocative egalitarian argument combines prodigious reading and research with keen insights into the manipulative power of racist ideologies that suppress the recognition of diversity." LJ

Includes bibliographical references and index

Lehr, Dick

★ The **Birth** of a Nation; how a legendary director and a crusading editor reignited America's

Civil War. Dick Lehr. PublicAffairs 2014 368 p.
illustrations (hardcover : alk. paper) $26.99 **305.8**
1. United States -- Race relations 2. Motion pictures
-- United States 3. Birth of a nation (Motion picture) 4.
United States -- History -- Civil War, 1861-1865
ISBN 1586489879; 9781586489878

LC 2014029679

This book, by Dick Lehr, focuses on the 1915 film "The
Birth of a Nation," by D. W. Griffith and the efforts to censor
it. The film "dramatized the Civil War and Reconstruction in
a post-Confederate South. . . . [It] included actors in blackface, heroic portraits of Knights of the Ku Klux Klan, and .
. . [f]reed slaves were portrayed as villainous. . . . Monroe
Trotter's titanic crusade to have the film censored became
a blueprint for dissent during the 1950s and 1960s." (Publisher's note)

"The book culminates, as expected, with the highly publicized battle in Boston over the censorship of Griffith's film.
However, the larger story for the reader is Lehr's fascinating
portrait of simmering American racial tensions moving into
the early 20th century, and his spotlight on men and women
who, intentionally or not, helped galvanize painful and necessary conversations about civil rights, race relations, and
the power of mass media for decades to come." LJ
Includes bibliographical references and index

Letters from Black America; edited by Pamela
Newkirk. Farrar, Straus, and Giroux 2009 372p
il $30 **305.8**
1. African Americans -- Social conditions 2. American
letters -- African American authors
ISBN 978-0-374-10109-1; 0-374-10109-4

LC 2008-41265

"This anthology features the writings of individuals who
range from highly celebrated to barely literate and presents
stories that are of vital historical importance and touchingly
personal. Newkirk divides the letters by topic—covering
family, courtship and romance, politics and social justice,
education and scholarship, war, art and culture, and the African diaspora—and offers concise introductions to each. . . .
While this unique collection of letters represents a frank depiction of the black experience, the great achievement is that
these writings often go far beyond race and class to simply
tell the story of the human experience in America." Libr J
Includes bibliographical references

Lukas, J. Anthony
Common ground; a turbulent decade in the lives
of three American families. Knopf 1985 659p il
maps hardcover o.p. pa $18 **305.8**
1. School integration 2. Busing (School integration) 3.
Boston (Mass.) -- Race relations
ISBN 0-394-74616-3 pa

LC 85-127

"By focusing on three families—one of them welfare
black, one upper-middle-class white and one working-class
Irish—a veteran journalist recreates the school-busing struggles of Boston in the 1970s, and delineates . . . the moral
complexities of caste and class in America." Newsday

Malek, Alia
A **country** called Amreeka; Arab roots, Ameri-
can stories. Free Press 2009 305p il $25 **305.8**
1. Immigrants -- United States 2. Arab Americans --
Social conditions
ISBN 978-1-4165-8972-3

LC 2008-55091

"In this superb snapshot of the Americans of Arab-
speaking descent, individuals with roots in Jordan, Yemen,
the Palestinian territories and Lebanon share their stories
and demonstrate the extent to which, even as they play football, work assembly lines and hold public office, they remain
shut out of the national narrative. With a remarkable ability
to capture her subjects' voices, . . . [the author] sketches illuminating responses to her question: 'What does American
history look and feel like in the eyes and skin of Arab Americans?'" Publ Wkly
Includes bibliographical references

McWhorter, John H.
Losing the race; self-sabotage in Black America.
[with a new afterword by the author] Perennial 2001
299p pa $13.95 **305.8**
1. African Americans -- Education 2. African
Americans -- Social conditions
ISBN 978-0-06-093593-1; 0-06-093593-6

LC 2001-24092

First published 2000 by Free Press

McWhorter discusses what he sees as "a cult of anti-
intellectualism 'that has infected black America. . . . He
concluded [black students] were held back by three defeat-
ist thought patterns': the Cult of Victimology, which leads
blacks to blame their problems on racism; the Cult of Sepa-
ratism, which makes blacks think that whatever whites do,
they should do the opposite; and the Cult of Anti-Intellectualism, which holds that scholastic excellence is a white
thing." Time
Includes bibliographical references

Monterrey, Manuel
Americanos; Latino life in the United States.
[by] Edward James Olmos, Lea Ybarra, Manuel Monterrey; preface by Edward James Olmos; introduction
by Carlos Fuentes. Little, Brown 1999 176p il $39;
pa $25 **305.8**
1. Latinos (U.S.) 2. Hispanic Americans
ISBN 0-316-64914-7; 0-316-64909-0 pa

LC 98-51930

This work includes essays, poetry, and commentary in
English and Spanish by such authors as Carlos Fuentes and
Maya Angelou and over 200 photographs of Latin Ameri-
cans from many parts of the United States.

"This is a beautiful, vibrant . . . book; it may also be
one of the more socially important books to appear in some
time." Booklist

Murray, Charles, 1943-
Coming apart; Charles Murray. Crown Forum
2012 407 p. **305.8**
1. Equality 2. Upper class 3. Working class 4. Social
conflict 5. Social classes -- United States 6. Social
mobility -- United States 7. United States -- Social

conditions -- 1980- 8. Whites -- United States -- Social conditions 9. United States -- Economic conditions -- 1945- 10. Whites -- United States -- Economic conditions 11. United States -- Social conditions -- 1960-1980

ISBN 0307453421; 9780307453426; 9780307453440

LC 2011501987

This book argues "that a new upper class and a new lower class have diverged so far in core behaviors and values that they barely recognize their underlying American kinship." It argues that "[t]he top and bottom of white America increasingly live in different cultures, . . . with the powerful upper class living in enclaves surrounded by their own kind, ignorant about life in mainstream America, and the lower class suffering from erosions of family and community life." (Publisher's note)

"Though it provides much to argue with, the book is a timely investigation into a worsening class divide no one can afford to ignore." (Publishers Weekly)

Includes bibliographical references and index

Nelson, Jimmy

Before they pass away; Jimmy Nelson; text, Mark Blaisse. teNeues Verlag 2013 423 p. chiefly color illustrations (hardcover : alk. paper) $150 **305.8**
1. Indigenous peoples 2. Indigenous peoples -- Portraits 3. Indigenous peoples -- Pictorial works
ISBN 3832797599; 9783832797591

LC 2013940504

This book, by Jimmy Nelson, "showcases tribal cultures around the world. With globalization, these societies are to be prized for their distinctive lifestyles, art and traditions. They live in close harmony with nature, now a rarity in our modern era. . . . Nelson not only presents us with . . . images of customs and artifacts, but also offers insightful portraits of people who are the guardians of a culture that they--and we--hope will be passed on to future generations in all its glory." (Publisher's note)

Packard, Jerrold M.

American nightmare; the history of Jim Crow. St. Martin's Press 2002 291p $24.95; pa $14.95 **305.8**
1. African Americans -- Segregation 2. Southern States -- Race relations
ISBN 0-312-26122-5; 0-312-30241-X pa

LC 2001-41960

"American Nightmare examines and explains Jim Crow from its beginnings to its end: how it came into being, how it was lived, how it was justified, and how, at long last, it was overcome only a few short decades ago. Most importantly, this book reveals how a nation founded on principles of equality and freedom came to enact as law a pervasive system of inequality and virtual slavery." (Publisher's Note)

"This is a clear, concise, historical narrative of a draconian reality." Publ Wkly

Includes bibliographical references (p. {275}-280) and index

Painter, Nell Irvin

The **history** of White people. W.W. Norton 2010 496p il map $27.95 **305.8**
1. Whites 2. United States -- Race relations
ISBN 978-0-393-04934-3; 0-393-04934-5

LC 2009-34515

The author "examines the history of 'whiteness' as a racial category and rhetorical weapon: who is considered to be 'white,' who is not, what such distinctions mean, and how notions of whiteness have morphed over time in response to shifting demographics, aesthetic tastes, and political exigencies. . . . Painter's narrative succeeds as an engaging and sophisticated intellectual history, as well as an eloquent reminder of the fluidity (and perhaps futility) of racial categories." Booklist

Includes bibliographical references

Phillips, Patrick

★ **Blood** at the root; A Racial Cleansing in America. Patrick Phillips. W W Norton & Co Inc 2016 320 p. illustrations (hardcover) $26.95 **305.8**
1. Racism -- Georgia 2. Race discrimination 3. United States -- Race relations -- History 4. Forsyth County (Ga.) -- Race relations -- History
ISBN 9780393293012

LC 2016018237

This book by Patrick Phillips tells "Forsyth's tragic story in vivid detail and traces its long history of racial violence all the way back to antebellum Georgia. Recalling his own childhood in the 1970s and '80s, Phillips sheds light on the communal crimes of his hometown and the violent means by which locals kept Forsyth 'all white' well into the 1990s." (Publisher's note)

"This is a gripping, timely, and important examination of American racism, and Phillips tells it with rare clarity and power." Pub Wkly

Includes bibliographical references and index

Prentice, Claire

The **lost** tribe of Coney Island; headhunters, Luna Park, and the man who pulled off the spectacle of the century. Claire Prentice. New Harvest 2014 416 p. illustrations, maps (hardcover) $26 **305.8**
1. Exhibitions 2. Igorot (Philippine people) 3. Exploitation 4. Igorot (Philippine people) -- United States
ISBN 054426228X; 9780544262287

LC 2014011690

This book, by Claire Prentice, "unearths the incredible true story of the Igorrotes, a group of 'headhunting, dog eating' tribespeople brought to America from the Philippines by the opportunistic showman Truman K. Hunt. At Luna Park, the g-string-clad Filipinos performed native dances and rituals before a wide-eyed public in a mocked-up tribal village." (Publisher's note)

"Without scholarly pretensions, Prentice has crafted an entertaining popular account likely to appeal to fans of true crime and social history." LJ

Includes bibliographical references(pages 363-370) and index

Reed, Ishmael

Another day at the front; dispatches from the race war. Basic Bks. 2002 xliv, 189p $24; pa $14.95   **305.8**

1. Racism 2. United States -- Race relations 3. African Americans -- Civil rights

ISBN 0-465-06891-X; 0-465-06892-8 pa

LC 2002-10563

The author "gathers a series of original and revamped essays from recent years on a variety of topics, from the Confederate flag to NPR, with the underlying theme that African Americans have been living in a police state for the past 300 years. These brief essays, written in Reed's lively hit-and-run style, are certainly provocative, particularly as he jabs at many well-known critics both black and white." Libr J

Roberts, Dorothy

Fatal invention; how science, politics, and big business re-create race in the twenty-first century. New Press 2011 388p $29.95   **305.8**

1. Race 2. Physical anthropology 3. Genomics 4. Human population genetics

ISBN 9781595584953; 1595584951

LC 2011012830

In this book, "legal scholar and social critic Dorothy Roberts argues that America is once again at the brink of a virulent outbreak of classifying population by race. By searching for differences at the molecular level, a new race-based science is obscuring racism in our society and legitimizing state brutality against communities of color at a time when America claims to be post-racial." (Publisher's note)

The author "examines the development and contemporary consequences of 'race as a political system,' bringing science, law, commerce, and race ideologies, virtual thickets of controversy, under one canopy. . . . Roberts is consistently lucid. Her book is alarming but not alarmist, controversial but evidential, impassioned but rational." Publ Wkly

Includes bibliographical references and index.

Robinson, Eugene

Disintegration; the splintering of Black America. Doubleday 2010 254p $24.95   **305.8**

1. United States -- Race relations 2. African Americans -- Race identity 3. United States -- Social conditions 4. African Americans -- Social conditions 5. African Americans -- Economic conditions

ISBN 978-0-385-52654-8; 0-385-52654-7

LC 2010-20405

"This book will have great appeal to African Americans and others concerned about issues of race and equality." Libr J

Includes bibliographical references

Sabar, Ariel

My father's paradise; a son's search for his Jewish past in Kurdish Iraq. Algonquin Books of Chapel Hill 2008 332p il map $25.95   **305.8**

1. Sephardim 2. Linguists 3. Jews -- Iraq 4. College teachers

ISBN 978-1-56512-490-5; 1-56512-490-1

LC 2008-24811

Sabar writes about his father's early life as a Sephardic Jew in Iraq and his father's authorship of a dictionary of Neo-Aramaic.

This "is an engaging account of a wonderful, enlightening journey, a voyage with the power to move readers deeply even as it stretches across differences of culture, family, and memory." Christ Sci Monit

Includes bibliographical references

Sharfstein, Daniel J.

The **invisible** line; three American families and the secret journey from black to white. Penguin Press 2011 396p il $27.95   **305.8**

1. Race awareness 2. Racially mixed people 3. Race awareness -- United States 4. United States -- Race relations 5. Racially mixed people -- United States 6. Race -- Social aspects -- United States 7. Miscegenation -- United States -- History

ISBN 978-1-59420-282-7; 1-59420-282-6

LC 2010-29647

"This popular history makes vivid use of primary documents to reconstruct the sagas of three families who crossed the color line from black to white. They negotiated this transition by means of legal challenges and such racial categories as 'Melungeons' and 'Black Dutch,' or simply by staying quiet when neighbors made assumptions based on cues of class and complexion. . . . This is an important reconsideration of the porousness of racial categories . . . and also a powerful evocation of the peril and insecurity that blacks faced both before and after the Civil War." New Yorker

Includes bibliographical references

Sokol, Jason

★ **There** goes my everything; white Southerners in the age of civil rights, 1945-1975. Knopf 2006 433p il $27.95   **305.8**

1. African Americans -- Civil rights 2. Southern States -- Race relations

ISBN 0-307-26356-8; 978-0-307-26356-8

LC 2005-44488

"This chronicle of the destruction of the white Southern hierarchy belongs in all libraries, public and academic." Libr J

Includes bibliographical references

Thompson, Tracy

★ The **new** mind of the South; an unconventional portrait for the twenty-first century. Tracy Thompson. 1st Simon & Schuster hc. ed. Simon & Schuster 2013 263 p. (hardcover) $26   **305.8**

1. Group identity 2. Southern States -- Civilization 3. Group identity -- Southern States 4. Southern States -- Race relations 5. Southern States -- Civilization -- 21st century

ISBN 1439158037; 9781439158036; 9781439160138

LC 2012021581

This book, by Tracy Thompson, explores the culture of the American South. "Thompson spent years traveling through the region and discovered a South both amazingly similar and radically different from the land she knew as a child. . . . Drawing on mountains of data, interviews, and a whole new set of historic archives, Thompson upends stereotypes and fallacies to reveal the true heart of the South today--a region still misunderstood by outsiders and even by its own people." (Publisher's note)

Includes bibliographical references and index

Thorpe, Helen

Just like us; the true story of four Mexican girls coming of age in America. Scribner 2009 387p $27.99 **305.8**

1. Mexican Americans 2. Hispanic American women 3. Unauthorized immigrants 4. Illegal aliens

ISBN 978-1-4165-3893-6

LC 2009-22722

"Thorpe does a masterful job of exploring issues of class, race, and culture in the American amalgam through the lives of four young Mexican women." Booklist

Those who forget the past; the question of anti-Semitism. edited and with an introduction by Ron Rosenbaum; afterword by Cynthia Ozick. Random House Trade Paperbacks 2004 lxix, 649p pa $16.95 **305.8**

1. Antisemitism

ISBN 0-8129-7203-1

LC 2003-65542

"This is an important and vital contribution to efforts to comprehend what is new and what is the same in this ancient virus of ignorance and hatred." Booklist

Includes bibliographical references

Wilson, Jennifer

Running away to home; our family's journey to Croatia in search of who we are, where we came from, and what really matters. St. Martin's Press 2011 320p il $25.99; ebook $12.99 **305.8**

1. Croatia -- Description and travel 2. Croatia -- Social life and customs

ISBN 978-0-312-59895-2; 978-1-4299-8908-4 ebook

LC 2011024841

"Travel writer Wilson, her architect husband, and their two small children spent a family sabbatical in Mrkopalj, Croatia, an unlikely destination for most folks but the birthplace of Wilson's great-grandparents. Wilson and family arrived in the village speaking little Croatian but soon became part of the community. She relates how they explored the area, tracked down distant relatives, and became immersed in the traditions of daily life. . . . This thoughtful, amusing tale reads like a novel and will have wide appeal." Libr J

Woodward, C. Vann

The **strange** career of Jim Crow; 3rd rev ed; Oxford Univ. Press 1974 233p hardcover o.p. pa $17.95 **305.8**

1. African Americans -- Segregation

ISBN 0-19-514690-5 pa

First published 1955

An account of segregation in the South which analyzes events from 1877 to the Nixon administration.

Includes bibliographical references

Zeskind, Leonard

Blood and politics; the history of the white nationalist movement from the margins to the mainstream. Farrar, Straus and Giroux 2009 xxiv, 645p $37.50 **305.8**

1. Racism 2. White supremacy movements 3. Nationalism -- United States 4. United States -- Race relations 5. United States -- Politics and government -- 1945-

ISBN 0-374-10903-6; 978-0-374-10903-5

LC 2008-46131

"Zeskind's rigorously researched and eloquent book is a definitive history of white nationalism and contains alarming warnings for a resurgence in racist politics." Publ Wkly

Includes bibliographical references

305.868   Spanish Americans

Morales, Ed

Living in Spanglish; the search for a new Latino identity in America. St. Martin's Press 2002 310p $25.95; pa $14.95 **305.868**

1. Latinos (U.S.) 2. Racially mixed people 3. Hispanic Americans 4. United States -- Ethnic relations

ISBN 0-312-26232-9; 0-312-31000-5 pa

LC 2001-48867

"To the author, Spanglish isn't just . . . {an} increasingly common linguistic mélange. . . . It is the breakdown of the either/or of a black/white worldview through the inevitable mingling of race and culture. . . . The author meditates on his own coming to terms with Latino identity as well as positing the larger point that 'We have spent the last several centuries preparing for our role as the first wholly postmodern culture.'. . . His ideas are provocative and engaging." Booklist

305.892   Semites

Goldhagen, Daniel Jonah

The **Devil** That Never Dies; The Rise and Threat of Global Antisemitism. Daniel Jonah Goldhagen. Little, Brown and Co. 2013 432 p. $30 **305.892**

1. Antisemitism 2. Globalization -- Social aspects 3. Antisemitism -- History -- 20th century 4. Antisemitism -- History -- 21st century

ISBN 031609787X; 9780316097871

LC 2013941806

In this book, by Daniel Jonah Goldhagen, "reveals the unprecedented, global form of [antisemitism]; its strategic use by states; its powerful appeal to individuals and groups; and how technology has fueled the flames that had been smoldering prior to the millennium." (Publisher's note)

"Goldhagen . . . comes out swinging in this frontal assault on anti-Semitism and its practitioners . . . . A frightening photograph of a mutable demon so many fail to recognize and continue to embrace." Kirkus

Includes bibliographical references (pages 460-472) and index

Nirenberg, David

Anti-Judaism; the Western tradition. David Nirenberg. W. W. Norton & Company 2013 624 p. (hardcover) $35   **305.892**
1. Judaism 2. Philosophy 3. Jewish philosophy 4. Jewish civilization 5. Antisemitism -- Europe -- History 6. Europe, Western -- Ethnic relations 7. Civilization, Western -- Jewish influences
ISBN 0393058247; 9780393058246

LC 2012031082

This book is a "history tracing how the engagement with 'Jewish questions' have shaped 3,000 years of Western thought. [David] Nirenberg . . . fashions a . . . study of how writers and thinkers from Jesus to Marx to Edward Said have recycled ideas about Jews and Jewishness in creating their own constructions of reality." (Kirkus)

Includes bibliographical references and index

Vincent, Leah

Cut me loose; sin and salvation after my ultra-Orthodox girlhood. by Leah Vincent. Nan A. Talese/Doubleday 2014 viii, 228 p.p (alk. paper) $25.95   **305.892**
1. Jewish women 2. Jewish women -- New York (State) -- New York -- Biography 3. Ultra-Orthodox Jews -- New York (State) -- New York -- Biography
ISBN 038553809X; 9780385538091

LC 2013016764

This book, by Leah Vincent, is a "memoir about a young woman's self-destructive spiral after being cast out by her ultra-Orthodox Jewish family. . . . Sent to live on her own in New York City, adrift and unprepared for the freedoms of secular life, Leah's desperate loneliness coupled with her stubborn loyalty to the dogma of her past pulled her into a vicious cycle of promiscuity and self-harm." (Publisher's note)

Wasserstein, Bernard

On the eve; the Jews of Europe before the Second World War. Bernard Wasserstein. Simon & Schuster 2012 xxi, 552 p.p   **305.892**
1. Antisemitism 2. Jews -- Europe 3. Jews -- History 4. Jews -- Social conditions 5. World War, 1939-1945 -- Causes 6. Jews -- Europe -- History -- 20th century 7. Jews -- Persecutions -- Europe -- History -- 20th century
ISBN 1416594272; 9781416594277; 9781416594284; 9781439101698

LC 2011020529

This book by Bernard Wasserstein "presents a[n] . . . interpretation of the collapse of European Jewish civilization even before the Nazi onslaught." Wasserstein "focuses not on the anti-Semites but on the Jews . . . refut[ing] the common misconception that they were unaware of the gathering forces of their enemies. . . . It explores their hopes, anxieties, and ambitions, their family ties, social relations, and intellectual creativity." (Publisher's note)

Includes bibliographical references and index.

305.896   Africans and people of African descent

Badkhen, Anna, 1976-

Walking With Abel; Journeys With the Nomads of the African Savannah. by Anna Badkhen. Penguin Group USA 2015 320 p. illustrations $27.95   **305.896**
1. Africa 2. Nomads
ISBN 1594632480; 9781594632488

LC 2015004476

In this book, journalist Anna Badkhen "embeds herself with a family of Fulani cowboys-- nomadic herders in Mali's Sahel grasslands-- as they embark on their annual migration across the savanna. It[s a cycle that connects the Fulani to their past even as their present is increasingly under threat-- from Islamic militants, climate change, and the ever-encroaching urbanization that lures away their young." (Publisher's note)

"Readers with hectic lives may find the pace a bit slow, but the poetry in Badkhen's prose demands that readers slow down and savor her gentle, elegant story." Kirkus

Du Bois, W. E. B.

The Oxford W. E. B. Du Bois reader; edited by Eric J. Sundquist. Oxford Univ. Press 1996 680p pa $34.95   **305.896**
1. African Americans 2. United States -- Race relations
ISBN 0-19-509178-7

LC 95-21307

This reader covers Du Bois's "writing career, from the 1890s through the early 1960s. The volume selects key essays and longer works that portray the range of Du Bois's thought on such subjects as African American culture, the politics and sociology of American race relations, art and music, black leadership, gender and women's rights, Pan-Africanism and anti-colonialism, and Communism in the U.S. and abroad." Publisher's note

Includes bibliographical references

The Fire This Time; A New Generation Speaks About Race. edited by Jesmyn Ward. Simon & Schuster 2016 288 p. $26   **305.896**
1. Racism 2. African Americans 3. United States -- Race relations
ISBN 1501126342; 9781501126345

LC 2016005371

This book, by Jesmyn Ward, is a "collection of essays and poems about race. . . . In light of recent tragedies and widespread protests across the nation, The Progressive magazine republished one of its most famous pieces: James Baldwin's 1962 'Letter to My Nephew.' . . . Ward knows that Baldwin's words ring as true as ever today. In response, she has gathered short essays, memoir, and a few essential poems to engage the question of race in the United States." (Publisher's note)

"Ward's remarkable achievement is the gift of freshly minted perspectives on a tale that may seem old and twice-told. Readers in search of conversations about race in America should start here." Pub Wkly

Gates, Henry Louis

The **future** of the race; by Henry Louis Gates, Jr. and Cornel West. Knopf 1996 196p hardcover o.p. pa $12.95   **305.896**

1. Authors 2. Novelists 3. Historians 4. Editors 5. Essayists 6. Sociologists 7. Nonfiction writers 8. Civil rights activists 9. United States -- Race relations 10. African Americans -- Intellectual life 11. African Americans -- Social conditions

ISBN 0-679-44405-X; 0-679-76378-3 pa

LC 96-14450

"Gates and West explore the challenge of W.E.B. Du-Bois's famous essay 'The Talented Tenth' and consider the future of African American society in light of it. . . . The authors examine the responsibility of the successful and talented black middle and upper classes to uplift the impoverished. . . . The text includes DuBois's 'The Talented Tenth' and, reprinted for the first time, his 1948 critique of it." Libr J

Includes bibliographical references

Kelly, Joseph

America's longest siege; Charleston, slavery, and the slow march toward Civil War. by Joseph Kelly. Overlook Duckworth 2013 384 p. ill., maps (hardcover) $28.95   **305.896**

1. Slavery -- United States 2. Charleston (S.C.) -- History -- Siege, 1863 3. Charleston (S.C.) -- History -- 1775-1865 4. Charleston (S.C.) -- Race relations -- History 5. Slaves -- South Carolina -- Charleston -- History 6. Slavery -- South Carolina -- Charleston -- History 7. African Americans -- South Carolina -- Charleston -- Social conditions

ISBN 159020719X; 9781590207192

LC 2013015841

In this book, Joseph Kelly "examines the great ideological dispute [around slavery] that underpinned the Civil War by focusing on [Charleston, South Carolina's] long-running internal conflict regarding its moral distaste for and economic addiction to slave labor (Charleston was a major port for incoming slaves)." Kelly "traces the development of the town's views on slavery while simultaneously relating attempts to break down or bulwark the institution." (Publishers Weekly)

Includes bibliographical references and index.

King, Gilbert, 1962-

★ **Devil** in the grove; Thurgood Marshall, the Groveland Boys, and the dawn of a new America. Gilbert King. Harper 2012 x, 434 p.p ill.   **305.896**

1. Civil rights 2. Florida -- Race relations 3. United States -- History -- 1945-1953 4. Rape -- Florida -- Groveland 5. African Americans -- Civil rights 6. Groveland (Fla.) -- Race relations 7. National Association for the Advancement of Colored People 8. Discrimination in criminal justice administration -- Florida -- Groveland

ISBN 9780061792267; 9780061792281; 9780062097712

LC 2011033757

Pulitzer Prize: General Nonfiction (2013)

This book presents an "account of Thurgood Marshall's role as a prominent civil rights attorney in challenging racist 'justice' in the South. . . . Principally . . . the 1949 arrest and unjust prosecution of four young black men, designated 'the Groveland Boys.' In this case, Marshall and the NAACP pursued every legal remedy to save the lives of these young men falsely accused of rape by a white woman, whose preposterous story went unquestioned by authorities. At great personal risk, Marshall tenaciously challenged the hegemony of McCall, eventually bringing to an end the racist reign of terror in Lake County and drawing it and its underlying mentality to national attention." (Libr J)

Includes bibliographical references (p. [413]-416) and index.

Raboteau, Emily

Searching for Zion; The Quest for Home in the African Diaspora. by Emily Raboteau. Atlantic Monthly Press 2013 320 p. $25   **305.896**

1. Home 2. Blacks

ISBN 0802120032; 9780802120038

This book by Emily Raboteau focuses on "black communities that left home in search of a Promised Land. . . . On her ten-year journey back in time and around the globe, through the Bush years and into the age of Obama, Raboteau wanders to Jamaica, Ethiopia, Ghana, and the American South to explore the complex and contradictory perspectives of Black Zionists." (Publisher's note)

★ **Remembering** Jim Crow; African Americans tell about life in the segregated South. edited by William H. Chafe [et al.] New Press (NY) 2001 xxxv, 346p il $55; pa $16.95   **305.896**

1. African Americans -- Segregation 2. Southern States -- Race relations 3. African Americans -- Southern States

ISBN 1-56584-697-4; 1-56584-778-4 pa

LC 2001-31224

Companion volume to Remembering slavery

This work offers "views into the thoughts, activities, and anxieties of black Americans. . . . Included are two one-hour CDs of the radio documentary produced by American Radio Works, a transcript of the audio program, 50 rare segregation-era photographs, biographical information, and suggestions for further reading. This [is a] superb primary source." Libr J

Includes bibliographical references

Scott, Rebecca J.

Freedom papers; an Atlantic odyssey in the age of emancipation. Rebecca J. Scott and Jean M. Hébrard. Harvard University Press 2012 259 p.   **305.896**

1. Freedom 2. Slavery 3. Biography 4. Blacks -- Atlantic Ocean Region -- Social conditions 5. Creoles -- Atlantic Ocean Region -- Social conditions

ISBN 0674047745; 9780674047747

LC 2011038130

This book, by Rebecca J. Scott and Jean M. Hébrard, received the 2012 Albert J. Beveridge Award and the 2012 James A. Rawley Prize in Atlantic History. The book "follows the Tinchants as each generation tries to use the power and legitimacy of documents to help secure freedom and respect. The strategies they used to overcome the constraints of slavery, war, and colonialism suggest the contours of the lives of people of color across the Atlantic world during this turbulent epoch." (Publisher's note)

Includes bibliographical references and index

305.897   North American native peoples

Burns, Mike
★ The **only** one living to tell; the autobiography of a Yavapai Indian. Mike Burns; edited by Gregory McNamee. University of Arizona Press 2012 179 p. (pbk. : alk. paper) $17.95   **305.897**
   1. Yavapai Indians -- History   2. Yavapai Indians -- Biography
   ISBN 0816501203; 9780816501205
LC 2011046513
This book is an autobiography of Mike Burns edited by Gregory McNamee. "Mike Burns--born Hoomothya--was around eight years old in 1872 when the US military murdered his family and as many as seventy-six other Yavapai men, women, and children in the Skeleton Cave Massacre in Arizona. One of only a few young survivors, he was adopted by an army captain and ended up serving as a scout in the US army and adventuring in the West." (Publisher's note)
Includes bibliographical references.

Fenn, Elizabeth A. (Elizabeth Anne), 1959-
Encounters at the heart of the world; a history of the mandan people. Elizabeth A. Fenn. Hill and Wang, a division of Farrar, Straus and Giroux 2014 480 p. illustrations, maps (hardback) $35   **305.897**
   1. Mandan Indians 2. Native Americans -- History
   ISBN 0809042398; 9780809042395
LC 2013032994
Pulitzer Prize: History (2015)
This book, by Elizabeth A. Fenn, tells the "history of the tribe that once thrived on the upper Missouri River in present-day North Dakota. . . . Peaking at a population of 12,000 by 1500, and still a vital presence when Lewis and Clark visited in 1804, the Mandans were besieged by a 'daunting succession of challenges,' including Norway rats that decimated their corn stores, two waves of smallpox, whooping cough, and cholera, reducing their numbers to 300 by 1838." (Booklist)
"A nonpolemical, engaging study of a once-thriving Indian nation of the American heartland whose origins and demise tell us much about ourselves." Kirkus
Includes bibliographical references and index

Wohlforth, Charles
The **whale** and the supercomputer; on the northern front of climate change. 1st ed; North Point Press 2004 322p $25; pa $14   **305.897**
   1. Inuit 2. Climate 3. Arctic regions
   ISBN 0-86547-659-4; 0-86547-714-0 pa
LC 2003-19448
"While the book's main focus is on climate change in the Arctic, . . . [the author includes] discussions of the worldview of the Inupiat in contrast to that of Western scientists, the conflict between rural and urban culture, the philosophy

of science, and the machinations surrounding funding for science. Wohlforth writes beautifully, managing to wax philosophical while providing detailed notes for those skeptical of the points he makes." Sci Books Films
Includes bibliographical references

305.9   People by occupation and miscellaneous social statuses; people with disabilities and illnesses, gifted people

Martinez, Ruben
★ The **new** Americans; photographs by Joseph Rodríguez. New Press 2004 251p il $25   **305.9**
   1. United States -- Immigration and emigration
   ISBN 1-565-84792-X
LC 2003-70621
"Masterfully evoking such diverse settings as a Palestinian wedding in Chicago, a raucous ball game in Guatemala City and a torpid migrant trailer camp in California, Martínez's writing is clear-eyed and incisive—and sometimes heartbreaking and hilarious." Publ Wkly
Includes bibliographical references

Nugent, Benjamin
American nerd; the story of my people. Scribner 2008 224p $20   **305.9**
   1. Gifted children 2. Creative ability 3. Popular culture -- United States
   ISBN 978-0-7432-8801-9; 0-7432-8801-7
A study of the nerd in American popular culture and throughout history discussed in such contexts as the rise of online gaming, the science fiction club, ethnicity, Asperger's syndrome, autism, and high school and college debating.
"In a lighthearted, often laugh-out-loud manner, Nugent challenges us to reexamine our long-held belief of what it means to be a nerd and to reposition the nerd as, if not an American hero, at least an American antihero. Great fun and remarkably insightful between the laughs." Booklist

Pipher, Mary Bray
The **middle** of everywhere; the world's refugees come to our town. {by} Mary Pipher. Harcourt 2002 xxv, 390p $25; pa $14; $23.95   **305.9**
   1. Refugees
   ISBN 0-15-100600-8; 0-15-602737-2 pa; 9781439560235
LC 2001-5863
"In cities all over the country, refugees arrive daily. Lost Boys from Sudan, survivors from Kosovo, families fleeing Afghanistan and Vietnam: they come with nothing but the desire to experience the American dream. Their endurance in the face of tragedy and their ability to hold on to the virtues of family, love, and joy are a lesson for Americans. Their stories will make you laugh and weep--and give you a deeper understanding of the wider world in which we live. The Middle of Everywhere moves beyond the headlines into the homes of refugees from around the world. Working as a cultural broker, teacher, and therapist, Mary Pipher has once again opened our eyes--and our hearts--to those with whom we share the future." (Publisher's Note)

The author "writes in rich, empathetic language and with a keen, observant eye for detail and nuance." Publ Wkly

Includes bibliographical references

Shannon, Lisa

A **thousand** sisters; my journey into the worst place on earth to be a woman. [by] Lisa J. Shannon; foreword by Zainab Salbi. Seal Press 2010 335p il $24.95 **305.9**

    1. Women -- Congo (Republic)

    ISBN 978-1-58005-296-2

                    LC 2009-25391

"Shannon presents images of the uncensored horror stories that, to many Congolese, have become regrettably routine: Congo's vile colonial history and the Rwandan genocide spillover that has caused the murders of more than five million Congolese people; children forced to kill and rape in their own communities; daily child deaths from easily curable illnesses; grisly murders of men and children in front of their wives and mothers; families burned alive inside their homes; women who must choose between rape and watching their children starve. . . . Juxtaposing brutality with beauty, Shannon's direct prose is a stirring reminder that these horrors are real and ongoing. An alarming and inspiring message that will hopefully spur much-needed action." Kirkus

Includes bibliographical references

Stephenson, Michael

The **last** full measure; how soldiers die in battle. Michael Stephenson. Crown Publishers 2012 xvi, 464 p.p $28.00; $28.00 **305.9**

    1. Ordnance 2. Soldiers 3. Weapons -- History 4. Military art and science -- History 5. Military history 6. Battle casualties -- History

    ISBN 0307395847; 0307952770; 9780307395849; 9780307952776

                    LC 2011005874

In this book, "[Michael] Stephenson . . . provides . . . descriptions of the ways in which soldiers have died in battle throughout history. Arranged chronologically, the book begins with analyses of ancient weapons and armor, and the deaths and destruction they caused, and then proceeds through history to discuss modern warfare. The physical and psychological effects of weapons are constant themes." (Library Journal)

Includes bibliographical references (p. [441]-452) and index

306   Culture and institutions

Calcaterra, Regina

Girl Unbroken; a sister's harrowing story of survival from the streets of Long Island to the farms of Idaho. Regina Calcaterra. HarperCollins 2016 416 p. (paperback) $15.99 **306**

    1. Adult child abuse victims

    ISBN 9780062412584; 0062412582

In this book, by Regina Calcaterra, the author "pairs with her youngest sister Rosie to tell Rosie's harrowing, yet ultimately triumphant, story of childhood abuse and survival. They were five kids with five different fathers and

an alcoholic mother who left them to fend for themselves for weeks at a time. Yet through it all they had each other." (Publisher's note)

"As engrossing as Etched in Sand, this book is a testament to Maloney's remarkable resilience and a moving tribute to the unbreakable bond of love she shared with her siblings. Courageous and emotionally intense." Kirkus

De Grazia, Victoria

Irresistible empire; America's advance through twentieth-century Europe. Belknap Press of Harvard University Press 2005 586p il $29.95 **306**

    1. Consumption (Economics) 2. Europe -- Foreign relations -- United States 3. United States -- Foreign relations -- Europe

    ISBN 0-674-01672-6

                    LC 2004-59943

The author "contends that U.S. companies—and consumerism—have been making inroads in Europe for the past hundred years. She argues that an early, and major, U.S. innovation treated foreign territories as extensions of domestic markets. . . . De Grazia writes clearly, giving an uncommon perspective on the ways and means by which the U.S. and Europe drew close after WWII." Publ Wkly

Includes bibliographical references

Mead, Margaret

★ **Coming** of age in Samoa; a psychological study of primitive youth for Western civilisation. foreword by Franz Boas. Morrow 1928 297p il hardcover o.p. pa $14 **306**

    1. Adolescence 2. Sex differences (Psychology) 3. Samoan Islands -- Social life and customs

    ISBN 0-688-05033-6 pa

    An anthropological study of adolescent Samoan girls

Pickett, Kate

The **spirit** level; why greater equality makes societies stronger. Richard Wilkinson and Kate Pickett. Bloomsbury Press 2010 xv, 330 p.p il (hardcover : alk. paper) $28 **306**

    1. Equality 2. Social policy 3. Social classes 4. Quality of life 5. Social mobility

    ISBN 1608193411; 9781608193417; 9781608190362; 1608190366

                    LC 2009030428

First published in Great Britain by Allen Lane, 2009

It was the authors' intent to "rank the quality of life in twenty-three countries, mainly European, but with Singapore, Israel, and the United States also on the list. To evaluate the well-being of each society, Richard Wilkinson and Kate Pickett use indices ranging from obesity and incarceration rates to teenage births and the feelings people have about their fellow countrymen. They then relate these variables to how income is distributed in each society. . . . Linking social indicators to economic disparities, the authors conclude that 'reducing inequality is the best way of improving the quality of the social environment.'" (New York Review of Books)

The authors "make an eloquent case that the income gap between a nation's richest and poorest is the most powerful indicator of a functioning and healthy society. . . . Felicitous

prose and fascinating findings make this essential reading."
Publ Wkly

Includes bibliographical references (p. 27-1297)
and index.

Pomerantsev, Peter

Nothing is true and everything is possible; the
surreal heart of the new Russia. Peter Pomerantsev.
PublicAffairs 2014 256 p. (hardcover) $25.99 **306**
1. Russia 2. Social problems 3. Political corruption 4.
Corruption -- Russia (Federation) 5. Interviews -- Russia
(Federation) 6. Social change -- Russia (Federation) 7.
Social problems -- Russia (Federation) 8. Power (Social
sciences) -- Russia (Federation) 9. Russia (Federation)
-- Social conditions -- 1991- 10. Russia (Federation) --
Economic conditions -- 1991- 11. Russia (Federation)
-- History -- 1991- -- Biography 12. Authoritarianism
-- Social aspects -- Russia (Federation)
ISBN 1610394550; 9781610394550

LC 2014018638

In this book "when British producer Peter Pomerantsev
plunges into the booming Russian TV industry, he gains access to every nook and corrupt cranny of the country. As the
Putin regime becomes more aggressive, Pomerantsev finds
himself drawn further into the system. [He recounts his]
voyage into a country spinning from decadence into madness." (Publisher's note)

Shadid, Anthony

★ **House** of stone; a memoir of home, family,
and a lost Middle East. Anthony Shadid. Houghton
Mifflin Harcourt 2012 xviii, 311 p.p (hardback)
$26   **306**
1. Family life 2. Arab Americans 3. Houses
-- Remodeling 4. Families -- Lebanon 5. Home --
Lebanon -- History 6. Middle East -- Social conditions
7. Lebanon -- Emigration and immigration -- Social
aspects
ISBN 0547134665; 9780547134666

LC 2011036906

National Book Awards Finalist (2012)

This memoir offers the following: "an Arab-American
story of immigrant roots; an evocation of Lebanon and its
anguished history; a lament for a vanishing Middle East; an
exploration of the meaning of home. . . . The story of [the]
. . . effort [of rebuilding a house in Marjayoun, Lebanon,]
forms the frame of the book, with each stage of building in-
tercut by tales of [Anthony] Shadid's globe-straddling family across four generations." (New York Review of Books)

Talbot, David

Season of the witch; enchantment, terror, and
deliverance in the City of Love. David Talbot. Free
Press 2012 xvii, 452 p.p   **306**
1. Counter culture 2. Social problems 3. San Francisco
(Calif.) -- History 4. Political culture -- San Francisco
(Calif.) 5. San Francisco (Calif.) -- Biography 6. San
Francisco (Calif.) -- History -- 20th century 7. San
Francisco (Calif.) -- Social conditions -- 20th century 8.
San Francisco (Calif.) -- Social life and customs -- 20th
century 9. Social change -- California -- San Francisco
-- History -- 20th century 10. Counterculture --

California -- San Francisco -- History -- 20th century 11.
Social problems -- California -- San Francisco -- History
-- 20th century 12. Culture conflict -- California -- San
Francisco -- History -- 20th century 13. Political culture
-- California -- San Francisco -- History -- 20th century
14. City and town life -- California -- San Francisco --
History -- 20th century
ISBN 1439108218; 9781439108215

LC 2011032082

In this book, author David Talbot "recounts the . . . story
of San Francisco in the turbulent years between 1967 and
1982. . . . The cool gray city of love was the epicenter of the
1960s cultural revolution. But by the early 1970s, San Francisco's ecstatic experiment came crashing down from its
starry heights. The city was rocked by savage murder sprees,
mysterious terror campaigns, political assassinations, street
riots, and finally a terrifying sexual epidemic. . . . David Talbot takes us deep into the riveting story of his city's ascent,
decline, and heroic recovery. He draws intimate portraits of
San Francisco's legendary demons and saviors. . . . He reveals how the city emerged from the trials of this period with
a new brand of 'San Francisco values.'" (Publisher's note)

Includes bibliographical references, discography, filmographies, and index.

Underhill, Paco

The call of the mall; a walking tour through the
crossroads of our shopping culture. Simon & Schuster 2004 227p hardcover o.p. pa $14   **306**
1. Consumers 2. Consumption (Economics) 3.
Shopping centers and malls
ISBN 0-7432-3591-6; 0-7432-3592-4 pa

LC 2003-64960

The author takes readers on a "tour of a typical Saturday
at a large, regional mall. He examines the routes there, the
shopping center itself, the stores, food, entertainment, ambi-
ence. and the customers. He shows why the mall is the way
it is and how it could be improved. He provides insight into
how the stores are arranged, how they display merchandise.
and the different ways that men and women respond to this
environment." SLJ

Victorian house

Inside the Victorian home; a portrait of domestic
life in Victorian England. W.W. Norton 2004 xxviii,
499p il $34.95   **306**
1. Great Britain -- History -- 19th century 2. Great
Britain -- Social life and customs
ISBN 0-393-05209-5

LC 2003-27693

First published 2003 in the United Kingdom with title:
The Victorian house

"Room by room, Flanders walks us through the typical home of upper-middle-class Britain, explaining its use,
its décor, the habits of occupants, and more. The result is
a genteel yet absorbing and thoroughly researched book. .
. . Fearsomely entertaining and yet a wonderful addition to
academic literature, this book is sure to become a classic."
Libr J

Includes bibliographical references

Wann, David

The **new** normal; an agenda for responsible living. St. Martin's Griffin 2011 274p il pa $14.99 **306**
1. Lifestyles 2. Social values 3. Conduct of life 4. Quality of life
ISBN 978-0-312-57543-4

LC 2010-37913

"Wann pulls from the disciplines of biology, anthropology, history, and psychology to make his case that the current paradigm of bigger and more is not working. He proposes the 'Era of Emerging Restoration,' in which healthy families, communities, and ecosystems are the best measures of wealth. . . . This is one of the best approaches to promoting a sustainable world." Libr J

Includes bibliographical references

306.2 Cultural institutions

Freeman, Joanne B.

Affairs of honor; national politics in the new republic. Yale Univ. Press 2001 xxiv, 376p $29.95; pa $16.95 **306.2**
1. United States -- Politics and government -- 1783-1865
ISBN 0-300-08877-9; 0-300-09755-7 pa

LC 2001-915

"Freeman's prose is lively, and she balances entertaining narrative with sharp analysis." Publ Wkly

Includes bibliographical references (p. 347-364) and index

Goldwag, Arthur

The **new** hate; a history of fear and loathing on the populist right. Arthur Goldwag. Pantheon Books 2012 368 p. $27.95 **306.2**
1. Conspiracies 2. Radicalism -- United States 3. Conservatism -- United States -- History 4. United States -- Politics and government 5. United States -- Ethnic relations -- History 6. Politics and culture -- United States 7. Right-wing extremists -- United States 8. Hate groups -- Political aspects -- United States 9. Conspiracy theories -- Political aspects -- United States
ISBN 0307379698; 9780307379696

LC 2011028589

The author "[Arthur] Goldwag . . . delivers an . . . history of organized hate groups and their role in U.S. politics. Less about prejudice than America's 'relentless quest for scapegoats,' he traces the American conspiratorial tradition from colonial times--where the Puritans feared Jesuit conspiracies as much as Indian ambushes--to the present, covering the movements and vitriolic commentary against the Masons, Catholics, Jews, Communists, and Muslims. . . . Goldwag combines his research with contemporary analysis to explain what conspiracy theories all have in common and to show how the new hate is the same as the old, though it's now 'hiding in plain sight.'" (Publishers Wkly)

Includes bibliographical references and index

Maddow, Rachel, 1973-

Drift; the unmooring of American military power. Rachel Maddow. Crown 2012 275 p. **306.2**
1. Military policy -- United States 2. United States

-- Military history 3. National security -- United States 4. United States -- Foreign relations 5. United States -- Politics and government -- 2001- 6. Militarism -- United States 7. United States -- Military policy 8. Political culture -- United States 9. United States -- Foreign relations -- 1989- 10. United States -- Politics and government -- 1989- 11. United States -- Armed Forces -- Appropriations and expenditures
ISBN 9780307460981; 9780307461001

LC 2012000998

The author "examines how the country has lost control of its national-security policy. The author holds Dick Cheney . . . responsible, . . . associating . . . [him] with the presidential prerogative of war-making powers. . . . American forces are now accompanied by . . . private contractors who perform functions that used to be reserved to the military, without either accountability or military control. . . . She grounds her argument in the Founding Fathers' debates about going to war." (Kirkus Reviews)

Includes bibliographical references and index

Sehat, David

The **Jefferson** rule; why we think the founding fathers have all the answers. David Sehat. Simon & Schuster 2015 320 p. (hardcover : alk. paper) $27 **306.2**
1. Political philosophy 2. Founding Fathers of the United States 3. United States -- Politics and government 4. Persuasion (Rhetoric) 5. Political culture -- United States 6. Collective memory -- Political aspects -- United States
ISBN 1476779775; 9781476779775; 9781476779782

LC 2014034708

This book, by David Sehat, "describes how liberals, conservatives, secessionists, unionists, civil rights leaders, radicals, and libertarians have sought out the Founding Fathers to defend their policies. [The author begins] . . . with the debate between Thomas Jefferson and Alexander Hamilton over the future of the nation, and continuing through the Civil War, the New Deal, the Reagan Revolution, and Obama and the Tea Party." (Publisher's note)

Includes bibliographical references and index

Wilentz, Sean

The **Politicians** and the Egalitarians; The Hidden History of American Politics. by Sean Wilentz. W W Norton & Co Inc 2016 400 p. $28.95 **306.2**
1. Political parties 2. United States -- Politics and government
ISBN 0393285022; 9780393285024

LC 2016009662

This book, by Sean Wilentz, "reminds us of the commanding role party politics has played in America's enduring struggle against economic inequality. . . . First, America is built on an egalitarian tradition. . . . Second, partisanship is a permanent fixture in America. . . . With these two insights . . . Wilentz offers a crystal-clear portrait of American history, told through politicians and egalitarians including Thomas Paine, Abraham Lincoln, and W. E. B. Du Bois." (Publisher's note)

"In other hands, this would seem silly and lacking force; in Wilentz's, it's authoritative and telling. The result is wonderfully readable and the best kind of serious, sharp argumentation from one of the leading historians of the United States." Pub Wkly

Includes bibliographical references and index.

306.3   Economic institutions

Annis, Barbara

Work with me; the 8 blind spots between men and women in business. Barbara Annis and John Gray, Palgrave Macmillan 2013 272 p. (hardcover) $27   306.3

1. Gender role 2. Work environment 3. Business communication 4. Men -- Attitudes 5. Women -- Attitudes 6. Interpersonal relations 7. Communication in organizations 8. Sex discrimination in employment 9. Sex role in the work environment
ISBN 023034190X; 9780230341906

LC 2012044297

This book, by Barbara Annis and John Gray, seeks "to resolve the most stressful and confusing challenges facing men and women at work. Annis and Gray reveal . . . the Eight Gender Blind Spots, the false assumptions and opinions men and women have of each other, and in many ways, believe of themselves. Through research, science, and stories, Annis and Gray expose the blind spots that cause our misunderstandings, miscommunications, mistrust, resentment, and frustrations at work." (Publisher's note)

Baptist, Edward E.

★ The **half** has never been told; slavery and the making of American capitalism. Edward E. Baptist. Basic Books 2014 528 p. illustrations, maps (hardcover) $35   306.3

1. Capitalism 2. Slavery -- United States 3. Slavery -- Economic aspects 4. African Americans -- Social conditions
ISBN 046500296X; 9780465044702; 9780465002962

LC 2014012546

"As historian Edward Baptist reveals in 'The Half Has Never Been Told,' the expansion of slavery in the first eight decades after American independence drove the evolution and modernization of the United States. . . . Until the Civil War, Baptist explains, the most important American economic innovations were ways to make slavery ever more profitable. Through forced migration and torture, slave owners extracted continual increases in efficiency from enslaved African Americans." (Publisher's note)

"Through an incredible amount of detail and the use of an array of primary sources, the author argues that the South's use of slave labor in cotton production was the primary factor in the United States becoming a leading modern industrial nation." LJ

Includes bibliographical references and index

Davis, David Brion, 1927-

★ The **problem** of slavery in the age of emancipation; by David Brion Davis. Knopf 2014 448 p. (hardback) $30   306.3

1. Slavery -- History 2. Slaves -- Emancipation 3. Antislavery movements 4. Free African Americans 5.

American Colonization Society
ISBN 0307269094; 9780307269096

LC 2013032893

National Book Critics Circle Award: General Nonfiction (2014)

Author David Brion Davis "offers . . . insights into what slavery and emancipation meant to Americans. He explores how the Haitian Revolution respectively terrified and inspired white and black Americans, hovering over the antislavery debates like a bloodstained ghost, and he offers a surprising analysis of the complex and misunderstood significance of colonization. Davis presents the age of emancipation as a model for reform." (Publisher's note)

"This is a well-researched and broad historical and global analysis of the complex motives and actions on all fronts, highlighting the transcontinental tension between efforts by white society to dehumanize and the fight by freedmen and slaves for freedom, full humanity, and citizenship." Booklist

Includes bibliographical references and index

Dewitt, David

Precious Cargo; How Foods from the Americas Changed the World. by David DeWitt. Counterpoint 2014 256 p. illustrations (chiefly color) $28   306.3

1. Food -- History
ISBN 1619023091; 9781619023093

IACP Cookbook Award Winner: Culinary History (2015)

This book, by David DeWitt, "tells the fascinating story of how western hemisphere foods conquered the globe and saved it from not only mass starvation, but culinary as well. Focusing heavily American foods—specifically the lowly crops that became commodities, plus one gobbling protein source, the turkey—Dewitt describes how these foreign and often suspect temptations were transported around the world, transforming cuisines and the very fabric of life on the planet." (Publisher's note)

"Both public and academic libraries will find this a welcome addition to sociological, anthropological, and culinary collections." LJ

DeWolf, Thomas Norman

Gather at the table; the healing journey of a daughter of slavery and a son of the slave trade. Thomas Norman DeWolf and Sharon Leslie Morgan; foreword by Joy Angela DeGruy. Beacon Press 2012 xvii, 212 p.p (hbk. : alk. paper) $25.95   306.3

1. Slavery -- United States 2. United States -- Race relations 3. Slavery -- United States -- History
ISBN 0807014419; 9780807014417

LC 2012009318

In this book by Thomas Norman DeWolf and Sharon Morgan "two people--a black woman and a white man--confront the legacy of slavery and racism head-on. . . . [DeWolf and Morgan] visit[ed] ancestral towns, courthouses, cemeteries, plantations, antebellum mansions, and historic sites. They spent time with one another's families and friends and engaged in deep conversations about how the lingering trauma of slavery shaped their lives." (Publisher's note)

Includes bibliographical references (p. 210-212)

Levs, Josh

All in; how our work-first culture fails Dads, families, and businesses--and how we can fix it together. Josh Levs. HarperOne 2015 272 p. (hardcover) $25.99 **306.3**

1. Work and family 2. Father-child relationship 3. Families -- United States 4. Parental leave -- United States 5. Work and family -- United States 6. Father and child -- United States

ISBN 0062349619; 9780062349613; 9780062349620
LC 2014042031

This book, by Josh Levs, "explores the changing face of fatherhood and what it means for our individual lives, families, workplaces, and society. . . . Stay-at-home dads are increasingly common, and growing numbers of men are working part-time or flextime schedules to spend more time with their children. . . . Dads today are . . . 'all in' and--like mothers--they are struggling with work-life balance and doing it all." (Publisher's note)

"Lev's thoughtful plea for men and women to work together is more persuasive, providing a useful guide for those looking to effect change in their own workplaces and communities." PW

Includes bibliographical references

Nathans, Sydney

To free a family; Sydney Nathans. Harvard University Press 2012 330 p. [20] p of plates, ill, maps **306.3**

1. Family 2. Fugitive slaves 3. United States -- History -- 1783-1865 4. Cambridge (Mass.) -- Biography 5. Orange County (N.C.) -- Biography 6. Fugitive slaves -- Northeastern States -- Biography 7. Women slaves -- North Carolina -- Orange County -- Biography 8. African American women -- Massachusetts -- Cambridge -- Biography 9. Family reunions -- Massachusetts -- Cambridge -- History -- 19th century

ISBN 9780674062122
LC 2011023122

This book "tells the . . . story of Mary Walker, who in August 1848 fled her owner for refuge in the North and spent the next seventeen years trying to recover her family. . . . This story is anchored in two . . . collections of letters and diaries, that of her former North Carolina slaveholders and that of the northern family--Susan and Peter Lesley--who protected and employed her." (Publisher's note)

Includes bibliographical references and index

Postma, Johannes

The Atlantic slave trade. Greenwood Press 2003 xxii, 177p map (Greenwood guides to historic events, 1500-1900) $45 **306.3**

1. Slave trade

ISBN 0-313-31862-X
LC 2002-35338

The author "covers the entire Atlantic slave trade era, from the 1400s to the final abolition of chattel slavery in the New World in 1888. The focus is on Africa and the entire New World. While he describes the many horrors of the Middle Passage, he also examines how the slave trade contributed to the development of the modern international economy. The last chapters discuss the efforts to abolish the slave trade and its legacy." SLJ

Includes bibliographical references

Reséndez, Andrés

The other slavery; the uncovered story of Indian enslavement in America. Andrés Reséndez. Houghton Mifflin Harcourt 2016 448 p. (hardcover) $30 **306.3**

1. Slave trade 2. Native Americans 3. Slavery -- History 4. Native Americans -- United States 5. Slavery -- North America -- History 6. Slavery -- United States -- History 7. Slave trade -- North America -- History 8. Slave trade -- United States -- History

ISBN 9780547640983
LC 2015037557

National Book Award Finalist: Nonfiction (2016)

This book, by Andrés Reséndez, presents "the sweeping story of the enslavement of tens of thousands of Indians across America, from the time of the conquistadors up to the early 20th century. . . . New evidence, including testimonies of courageous priests, rapacious merchants, Indian captives, and Anglo colonists, sheds light too on Indian enslavement of other Indians." (Publisher's note)

"This eye-opening exposure of the abuse of the indigenous peoples of America is staggering; that the mistreatment continued into the 20th century is beyond disturbing." Kirkus

Includes bibliographical references and index

Williams, Heather Andrea

Help me to find my people; the African American search for family lost in slavery. by Heather Andrea Williams. University of North Carolina Press 2012 251 p. ill. (cloth : alk. paper) $30 **306.3**

1. Archives 2. Family reunions 3. Slave narratives 4. African American families -- History 5. Slavery -- Social aspects -- United States -- History 6. Slaves -- Family relationships -- United States -- History

ISBN 0807835544; 9780807835548
LC 2011050216

Author "Heather Andrea Williams uses slave narratives, letters, interviews, public records, and diaries to guide readers back to devastating moments of family separation during slavery when people were sold away from parents, siblings, spouses, and children. . . . [She tells the] stories of separation and the long, usually unsuccessful journeys toward reunification. . . . Williams follows those who were separated, chronicles their searches, and documents the rare experience of reunion." (Publisher's note)

Includes bibliographical references (p. [225]-233) and index

306.362 Slavery

Warren, Wendy

New England Bound; slavery and colonization in early America. Wendy Warren. Liveright Publishing

Corporation 2016 352 p. illustrations, map (hardcover) $29.95 **306.362**
1. Slavery -- History 2. United States -- History
ISBN 9780871406729; 0871406721

LC 2016007276

This book, by Wendy Warren, "links the growth of the northern colonies to the Atlantic slave trade, demonstrating how New England's economy derived its vitality from the profusion of slave-trading ships coursing through its ports. Warren documents how Indians were systematically sold into slavery in the West Indies and reveals how colonial families like the Winthrops were motivated not only by religious freedom but also by their slave-trading investments." (Publisher's note)

"For students of early American history, this is an eye-opening book about Puritans and Anglicans who disapproved of slavery but accepted it as a normal part of life and reaped its profits." Kirkus

Includes bibliographical references and index.

306.4   Specific aspects of culture

Amidon, Stephen

Something like the gods; a cultural history of the athlete from Achilles to Lebron. Stephen Amidon. St. Martin's Press 2012 240 p. (hardback) $24.99 **306.4**
1. Athletes 2. Gladiators 3. Olympic athletes 4. Knights and knighthood 5. Athletes -- History 6. Sports -- Social aspects -- History
ISBN 1609611233; 9781609611231

LC 2012002365

In this book, Stephen Amidon examines the history of athletes and their perceived prowess. "From the shamanistic athletic rituals of Paleolithic hunters to the exploits of today's millionaire sports superstars, athletes have fascinated and transfixed us for centuries. . . . Amidon explores this universalist nature of the athlete, including the godlike efforts of the Greek warriors of the ancient Olympics; the tragic heroics of the Roman gladiator; and the romantic image of the jousting knight errant to the civilized amateur ideal of the Victorian era." (Kirkus Reviews)

Burr, Ty

Gods like us; on movie stardom and modern fame. Ty Burr. Pantheon 2012 448 p. (hardback) $28.95 **306.4**
1. Motion pictures -- History and criticism 2. Fame -- Social aspects -- United States 3. Popular culture -- United States -- History
ISBN 0307377660; 9780307377661

LC 2012000618

This book is a "history of stardom from the early days of silent film through the contemporary world of YouTube. [Ty] Burr . . . traces the rise of Hollywood legends, television stars, and musicians ranging from Mary Pickford, Lucille Ball, and Marlon Brando to Tom Cruise and Michael Jackson. He analyzes their roles both onscreen and off, their symbolic significance, and how they have inspired both the adoration and the envy of their audiences." (Library Journal)

Includes bibliographical references and index.

Ekirch, A. Roger, 1950-

★ **At** day's close; night in times past. Norton 2005 447p il $25.95 **306.4**
1. Night 2. Social history 3. Night -- Social aspects
ISBN 0-393-05089-0

LC 2005-2784

This is a social history of night before the industrial age. Index.

"This history finds Ekirch reminding us of how preindustrial Westerners lived during the nocturnal hours, when most were plunged into almost total darkness. . . . A rich weave of citation and archival evidence, Ekirch's narrative is rooted in the material realities of the past, evoking a bygone world of extreme physicality and preindustrial survival stratagems." Publ Wkly

Includes bibliographical references

Fadiman, Anne

★ **The spirit** catches you and you fall down; a Hmong child, her American doctors, and the collision of two cultures. Anne Fadiman. Farrar, Straus & Giroux 1997 xi, 339p $25; (pbk.) $15 **306.4**
1. Epilepsy 2. Medical care 3. Culture conflict 4. Hmong (Asian people) 5. Epilepsy in children 6. Hmong Americans -- Medicine 7. Intercultural communication 8. Hmong American children -- Medical care -- California 9. Transcultural medical care -- California -- Case studies
ISBN 0374267812; 9780374533403

LC 97005175

Los Angeles Times Book Prizes: Current Interest (1997), National Book Critics Circle Award: General Nonfiction (1997)

This book presents an "anthropological exploration of the Hmong population in Merced County, California. Following the case of Lia (a Hmong child with a progressive and unpredictable form of epilepsy), Fadiman maps out the controversies raised by the collision between Western medicine and holistic healing traditions of Hmong immigrants. Unable to enter the Laotian forest to find herbs for Lia that will 'fix her spirit,' her family becomes resigned to the Merced County emergency system, which has little understanding of Hmong animist traditions. [Anne] Fadiman reveals the rigidity and weaknesses of these two ethnographically separated cultures." (Library Journal)

Includes bibliographical references (p. [311]-324) and index.

Leonard, Annie

The story of stuff; how our obsession with stuff is trashing the planet, our communities, and our health--and a vision for change. [by] Annie Leonard with Ariane Conrad. Free Press 2010 xxxiv, 317p il $26 **306.4**
1. Material culture 2. Consumption (Economics)
ISBN 978-1-4391-2566-3

LC 2009-42207

"Leonard explains that our consumer goods undergo extraction, production, distribution, consumption, and disposal processes that are trashing the planet, diminishing our resources, exploiting workers, and contributing to high levels of disease and death. She advocates an international cooperative effort to develop domestic and international policies and laws that will reverse our planet's ecological decline and leave a sustainable world for future generations." LJ

McGonigal, Jane

Reality is broken; why games make us better and how they can change the world. Jane McGonigal. Penguin Press 2011 388 p. $16.00 **306.4**

1. Video games 2. Computer games 3. Simulation games 4. Educational games 5. Computers and civilization 6. Computer games -- Social aspects
ISBN 0143120611; 1594202850; 9780143120612; 9781594202858

LC 2010029619

In this book, author Jane McGonigal offers a vision of "how we can harness the power of games to boost global happiness. . . . [Why] should games be used for escapist entertainment alone? . . . [The author] shows how we can leverage the power of games to fix what is wrong with the real world--from social problems . . . to global issues-- . . . and introduces us to cutting-edge games that are already changing the business, education, and nonprofit worlds." (Publisher's note)

Includes bibliographical references.

Pollan, Michael, 1955-

The **botany** of desire; Michael Pollan. Random House 2001 xxv, 271 p.p $24.95; pa $13.95 **306.4**

1. Apples 2. Tulips 3. Potatoes 4. Marijuana 5. Economic botany 6. Human-plant relationships
ISBN 0-375-50129-0; 0-375-76039-3 pa; 9780375760396; 9780375501296

LC 00066479

In this book, author "Michael Pollan . . . demonstrates how people and domesticated plants have formed a similarly reciprocal relationship. He . . . links four fundamental human desires--sweetness, beauty, intoxication, and control--with the plants that satisfy them: the apple, the tulip, marijuana, and the potato. In telling the stories of four familiar species, Pollan illustrates how the plants have evolved to satisfy humankind's most basic yearnings. And just as we've benefited from these plants, we have also done well by them. So who is really domesticating whom?" (Publisher's note)

"Pollan intertwines history, anecdote, and revelation as he investigates the connection between four plants that have thrived under human care—apples, tulips, marijuana, and potatoes—and the four human desires they satisfy in return: sweetness, beauty, intoxication, and control. . . . Pollan's dynamic, intelligent, and intrepid parsing of the wondrous dialogue between plants and humans is positively paradigm-altering." Booklist

Includes bibliographical references and index.

Robinson, Jo

Eating on the wild side; the missing link to optimum health. Jo Robinson; illustrations by Andie Styner. Little Brown & Co 2013 416 p. ill. $16 **306.4**

1. Nutrition 2. Natural foods
ISBN 0316227935; 9780316227933; 9780316227940

LC 2013934815

IACP Cookbook Award (2014)

This book, by Jo Robinson. discusses how "ever since farmers first planted seeds . . . , humans have been destroying the nutritional value of their fruits and vegetables. Unwittingly, we've been selecting plants that are high in starch and sugar and low in vitamins, minerals, fiber, and antioxidants." Robinson "reveals the solution--choosing modern varieties that approach the nutritional content of wild plants but that also please the modern palate." (Publisher's note)

Rose, Frank

The **art** of immersion; how the digital generation is remaking Hollywood, Madison Avenue, and the way we tell stories. W.W. Norton & Co. 2011 354p $26.95 **306.4**

1. Internet marketing 2. Internet entertainment 3. Internet -- Social aspects
ISBN 978-0-393-07601-1

LC 2010-38676

The author "theorizes that we are encountering a profound shift in the way we play, consume, and communicate. He explains that our experiences with television, movies, games, and advertisements are becoming increasingly more immersive and consumer-driven. . . . This engrossing study of how new media is reshaping the entertainment, advertising, and communication industries is an essential read for professionals in the fields of digital communications, marketing, and advertising, as well as for fans of gaming and pop culture." Libr J

Includes bibliographical references

Simons, Eric

The **Secret** Lives of Sports Fans; Eric Simons. Penguin Group USA 2013 320 p. (hardcover) $26.95 **306.4**

1. Social psychology 2. Sports spectators
ISBN 1590208641; 9781590208649

This book, by Eric Simons, explores how "sports fandom is either an aspect of a person's fundamental identity, or completely incomprehensible to those who aren't fans at all. What is happening in our brains and bodies when we feel strong emotion while watching a game? How do sports fans resemble political junkies, and why do we form such a strong attachment to a sports team?" (Publisher's note)

Trumble, Angus

The **finger**; a handbook. Farrar, Straus and Giroux 2010 300p il $28 **306.4**

1. Fingers
ISBN 978-0-374-15498-1; 0-374-15498-8

LC 2009-42220

On the whole, The Finger is a deft, enjoyable and often provocative investigation into some overlooked and interrelated aspects of human experience. Washington Post

Includes bibliographical references

306.44   Language

Dorren, Gaston

Lingo; Around Europe in Sixty Languages. Gaston Dorren. Atlantic Monthly Press 2015 303 p. illustrations, maps $25   **306.44**

1. Europe 2. Language and languages
ISBN 0802124070; 9780802124074

This book, by Gaston Dorren, brings the "reader on a whirlwind tour of sixty European languages and dialects, sharing quirky moments from their histories and exploring their commonalities and differences. Most European languages are descended from a single ancestor, a language not unlike Sanskrit known as Proto-Indo-European (or PIE for short), but the continent's ever-changing borders and cultures have given rise to a linguistic and cultural diversity." (Publisher's note)

"This intriguing, thoughtful book will delight those who love words; it is also a round, solid education in the vastness of the world's citizens' ability and desire to express themselves, intended, Dorren states, 'as an amuse-bouche.' Amusing, too!" Booklist

Includes bibliographical references and index.

Lepore, Jill

A is for American; letters and other characters in the newly United States. Knopf 2002 241p il $25; pa $13   **306.44**

1. Slaves 2. Artists 3. Painters 4. Inventors 5. Architects 6. Americanisms 7. Sociolinguistics 8. Artisans 9. Essayists 10. Metalworkers 11. Indian leaders 12. Lexicographers 13. Writers on law 14. Teachers of the deaf 15. Telecommunications executives 16. English language -- Social aspects
ISBN 0-375-40449-X; 0-375-70408-6 pa
LC 2001-38057

"Each man's story delivers a wealth of irony along with valuable history. . . . Some familiar accounts, some not well known, but all told with a fresh eye to their national significance." Booklist

Includes bibliographical references

306.46   Cultural institutions--Technology

Cukier, Kenneth

Big data; a revolution that will transform how we live, work, and think. Viktor Mayer-Schönberger and Kenneth Cukier. Houghton Mifflin Harcourt 2013 242 p. (hardcover) $27   **306.46**

1. Data processing 2. Information resources 3. Internet -- Social aspects 4. Social change 5. Big data -- Social aspects 6. Technological innovations -- Social aspects 7. Electronic information resources -- Social aspects
ISBN 0544002695; 9780544002692
LC 2012538859

This book, by Viktor Mayer-Schönberger and Kenneth Cukier, discusses Big Data "and the dramatic impact it will have on the economy, science, and society at large. . . . 'Big data' refers to our . . . ability to crunch vast collections of information, analyze it instantly, and draw sometimes profoundly surprising conclusions from it. This emerging sci-

ence can translate myriad phenomena . . . into searchable form, and uses our increasing computing power to unearth epiphanies." (Publisher's note)

Includes bibliographical references (p. [217]-226) and index.

306.7   Sexual relations

Bader, Michael J.

Arousal, the secret logic of sexual fantasies. Thomas Dunne Bks./St. Martin's Press 2002 293p $23.95; pa $14.95   **306.7**

1. Sexual behavior
ISBN 0-312-26933-1; 0-312-30242-8 pa
LC 2001-51290

"Bader covers how arousal works, how fantasies assist in arousal, the role of fantasies in therapy, and the social meaning of fantasies. Throughout, he gives numerous case studies, examples, and sensible and compassionate conjectures about particular fantasies and the fantasizing process. Bader is a clear, graceful writer, and he makes his points with rare facility in a way useful to both lay people and therapeutic professionals." Libr J

Includes bibliographical references

Barash, David P.

The **myth** of monogamy; fidelity and infidelity in animals and people. [by] David P. Barash, Judith Eve Lipton. Freeman, W.H. 2001 227p $24.95; pa $15   **306.7**

1. Adultery 2. Marriage 3. Sexual behavior
ISBN 0-7167-4004-4; 0-8050-7136-9 pa

This is "guaranteed to entertain and may even pique thoughtful readers' interests." Sci Books Films

Includes bibliographical references

Bergner, Daniel

The **other** side of desire; four journeys into the far realms of lust and longing. Ecco 2009 208p $24.95   **306.7**

1. Compulsive behavior 2. Sexual behavior
ISBN 978-0-06-088556-4; 0-06-088556-4

The author "approaches deviance with a reporter's notepad. He selects four areas: foot fetishism, sadomasochism, pedophilia, and an obsession for amputees. In each case, he finds and follows a devotee. In the process, Bergner does what science cannot: He illuminates peculiar longings. His method is at first descriptive and finally poetic. The message of the book is in the interplay among personal narratives that prove alternately bizarre and mundane." Slate

Berkowitz, Eric

The **boundaries** of desire; bad laws, good sex, and changing identities. Eric Berkowitz. Counterpoint 2015 468 p. (hardback) $28   **306.7**

1. Sex 2. Sex -- Social aspects 3. Sex customs -- History
ISBN 9781619025295
LC 2015005123

This book, by Eric Berkowitz, "traces the fast-moving bloodsport of sex law over the past century, and challenges our most cherished notions about family, power, gender, and identity. Starting when courts censored birth control information as pornography and let men rape their wives, and continuing through the 'sexual revolution' and into the present day, . . . Berkowitz shows how the law has remained out of synch with the convulsive changes in sexual morality." (Publisher's note)

"A bracing look at the often-strange relationship between sexuality and the legal system over six tumultuous decades." Booklist

Includes bibliographical references (pages 343-458) and index.

Kipnis, Laura

How to become a scandal; adventures in bad behavior. Metropolitan Books 2010 209p il $24 **306.7**
1. Scandals 2. Celebrities 3. Conduct of life 4. Deviant behavior
ISBN 978-0-8050-8979-0; 0-8050-8979-9
LC 2010-05036

The author "picks through the mortifying carnage of other people's lives, exploring why we both relish and condemn bad behavior. Divided in two parts, 'Downfalls' and 'Uproars,' this slight and easy-to-digest book covers four major popular-culture scandals of the last two decades. These include those of love-crazed, diaper-wearing astronaut Lisa Nowak; the dishonorable judge Sol Wachtler; whistle-blower Linda Tripp; and the 'overimaginative,' so-called memoirist James Frey. . . . Light and fun." Kirkus

Includes bibliographical references

Longing to tell; Black women talk about sexuality and intimacy. {compiled by} Tricia Rose. Farrar, Straus & Giroux 2003 415p $25; pa $15 **306.7**
1. African American women 2. Women -- Sexual behavior
ISBN 0-374-19061-5; 0-312-42372-1 pa
LC 2002-32541

"By letting the women speak for themselves and following the histories with a passionate afterword, Rose provides a collection that is as compelling as it is sorely needed." Publ Wkly

Includes bibliographical references

McConnachie, James

The **book** of love; the story of the Kamasutra. Metropolitan Books 2008 267p il $27.50; pa $17 **306.7**
1. Kamasutra 2. Sexual behavior
ISBN 978-0-8050-8818-2; 0-8050-8818-0; 978-0-8050-9019-2 pa; 0-8050-9019-3 pa
LC 2007-47172

"In an impressively researched, charming volume, McConnachie traces the Kamasutra's history from its creation by the third-century sage Vatsyayana as a guide to the good life for urbane dandies. . . . Since not a single posture is described, consider it G-rated." Booklist

Includes bibliographical references

Orenstein, Peggy

Girls and Sex; Navigating the Complicated New Landscape. by Peggy Orenstein. HarperCollins 2016 320 p. $26.99 **306.7**
1. Young women 2. Teenage girls 3. Sex -- Psychological aspects 4. Teenagers -- Sexual behavior
ISBN 0062209728; 9780062209726

In this book, by Peggy Orenstein, "A generation gap has emerged between parents and their girls. Even in this age . . . the mothers and fathers of tomorrow's women have little idea what their daughters are up to sexually. . . . Drawing on in-depth interviews with over seventy young women and a wide range of psychologists, academics, and experts, . . . Orenstein goes where most others fear to tread." (Publisher's note)

"Ample, valuable information on the way young women in America perceive and react to their sexual environment." Kirkus

Includes bibliographical references (pages 239-290) and index.

Shlain, Leonard

Sex, time, and power; how women's sexuality shaped human evolution. Viking 2003 xx, 420p il $25.95; pa $16 **306.7**
1. Evolution 2. Women -- Sexual behavior
ISBN 0-670-03233-6; 0-14-200467-7 pa
LC 2002-41186

The author "takes an evolutionary approach to solving the conundrums of misogyny and patriarchy, guiding his . . . readers through . . . speculations about the purpose of such seemingly impractical, even dangerous traits as bipedalism, menstruation, the perils of childbirth, and the helplessness of infants. . . . Lucid and compelling, Shlain asks startling and crucial questions about human nature and presents truly imaginative and mind-stretching answers." Booklist

Includes bibliographical references

Sugar in my bowl; real women write about real sex. edited by Erica Jong. Ecco 2011 238p il $21.99; ebook $9.99 **306.7**
1. Sex 2. Sexual behavior 3. Women -- Sexual behavior
ISBN 9780061875762; 0061875767; 9780062092205 ebook; 0062092200 ebook
LC 2011012689

In this book, "poet, novelist, and essayist . . . Erica Jong . . . offers us a provocative collection of essays about sex from some of the most respected female authors writing today." Contributors to the book, including "Gail Collins, Eve Ensler, Daphne Merken, Anne Roiphe, Liz Smith, Naomi Wolf, and Jennifer Weiner . . . speak openly about female desire--what provokes it and what satisfies it." (Publisher's note)

A "frank collection of personal essays, short fiction and cartoons celebrating female desire. The approaches to the still-taboo topic of feminine sexuality—at least, for women writers seeking approbation from the literary establishment—are, as Jong notes, 'as varied as sexuality itself' and as exuberantly diverse as the contributors themselves. They range from such emerging talents as Elisa Albert and J.A.K. Andres to such luminaries as Rebecca Walker, Eve Ensler, Susan Cheever, Anne Roiphe and Fay Weldon, and represent a multiethnic, multigenerational swath of some of the finest women writers in the United States. Most of the pieces deal with the perennial themes of sexual coming-of-age, social and religious sexual hang-ups and lusty obsessions for male bodies (as well as female ones). Some deal with lesser-discussed—but no less important—subjects like procreative sex and eroticism in old age. Still others fearlessly explore fetishism, childhood masturbation, kink, [and] sexual addiction." Kirkus

Wolf, Naomi

Promiscuities; the secret struggle for womanhood. Random House 1997 xxx, 286p hardcover o.p. pa $15   **306.7**
1. Girls -- Sexual behavior 2. Women -- Sexual behavior
ISBN 0-449-90764-3 pa

LC 96-46724

"Wolf offers some astute and eminently realizable suggestions for a new approach to sexual education, even healing." Booklist

Includes bibliographical references

Yes means yes! visions of female sexual power & a world without rape. [by] Jaclyn Friedman & Jessica Valenti [editors]; foreword by Margaret Cho. Seal Press 2008 361p pa $16.95   **306.7**
1. Rape 2. Sexism 3. Gender role 4. Sex role 5. Women -- Sexual behavior
ISBN 978-1-58005-257-3; 1-58005-257-6

LC 2008-20989

The editors "present an extraordinary, eye-opening essay collection that focuses on the importance of sexual identity and ownership in the struggle against rape in the U.S., as well as a number of related issues, including sexual pleasure, self-esteem and the mixed societal messages that turn 'nice guys' bad." Publ Wkly

Includes bibliographical references

306.74   Prostitution

Moran, Rachel

Paid for; my journey through prostitution. Rachel Moran. Gill & Macmillan 2013 295 p. $15.95   **306.74**
1. Homelessness 2. Women -- Ireland 3. Juvenile prostitution 4. Sex -- Psychological aspects 5. Prostitution -- Ireland 6. Prostitutes -- Ireland -- Dublin -- Biography
ISBN 9780393351972; 0717156028; 9780717156023

LC 2013412048

In this memoir, author Rachel Moran was "Born into a troubled family [and left] home at the age of fourteen. Being homeless, she was driven into prostitution to survive. . . . She describes the exploitation she and others endured on the streets and in the brothels. Moran also speaks to the psychological damage inherent to prostitution and the inevitable estrangement from one's body. At twenty-two, Moran escaped the sex trade." (Publisher's note)

"Moran's thoughtful, highly readable, and provocative treatise shines a necessary light on a dark and underdiscussed topic." Kirkus

Includes bibliographical references.

306.76   Sexual orientation, transgenderism, intersexuality

Beachy, Robert

Gay Berlin; birthplace of a modern identity. by Robert Beachy. Alfred A. Knopf 2014 336 p. (hardback) $27.95   **306.76**
1. Gay men 2. Homosexuality 3. Germany -- History 4. Gay culture -- Germany -- Berlin 5. Homosexuality -- Germany -- Berlin 6. Gender identity -- Germany -- Berlin 7. Gay men -- Germany -- Berlin -- Identity
ISBN 0307272109; 9780307272102

LC 2014004986

Stonewall Honor Book - Nonfiction (2015)

"Berlin, before the turn of the twentieth century, became a place where scholars, activists, and medical professionals could explore and begin to educate both themselves and Europe about new and emerging sexual identities. . . . Chapter by chapter [author Robert] Beachy's scholarship illuminates forgotten firsts, including the life and work of Dr. Magnus Hirschfeld, first to claim (in 1896) that same-sex desire is an immutable, biologically determined characteristic." (Publisher's note)

Bingham, Emily

Irrepressible; the Jazz Age life of Henrietta Bingham. Emily Bingham. Farrar, Straus & Giroux 2015 384 p. illustrations (hardcover) $28   **306.76**
1. Alcoholics 2. Bisexuality 3. Upper class -- Biography 4. Louisville Region (Ky.) -- Biography 5. Lesbians -- United States -- Biography 6. Socialites -- United States -- Biography 7. Bisexual women -- United States -- Biography 8. Women alcoholics -- United States -- Biography 9. Women analysands -- United States -- Biography 10. Upper class women -- United States -- Biography
ISBN 0809094649; 9780809094646

LC 2014039375

Lambda Literary Award: Bisexual Nonfiction (2016)

This book, by Emily Bingham, is a biography of Henrietta Bingham. "Raised like a princess in one of the most powerful families in the American South, Henrietta Bingham was offered the helm of a publishing empire. Instead, she ripped through the Jazz Age like an F. Scott Fitzgerald character: intoxicating and intoxicated, selfish and shameless, seductive and brilliant, endearing and often terribly troubled." (Publisher's note)

"A fascinating glimpse into Southern LGBT history and another angle on the exploits of the Bloomsbury Group." LJ

Includes bibliographical references and index

Blank, Hanne

Straight; the surprisingly short history of heterosexuality. Hanne Blank. Beacon Press 2012 xxvii, 228 p.p (hardcover : acid-free paper) $26.95 **306.76**
1. Homosexuality -- History 2. Heterosexuality -- History
ISBN 0807044431; 9780807044438

LC 2011031432

In this book, Hanne Blank "sets out to explore the changing views of marriage, heterosexuality, and conceptions of biological sex itself over the past 150 years, systematically exploring the history from scientific, philosophical, and sociological perspectives. . . . She argues that although sexual contact between men and women has existed since time immemorial, the word and idea of heterosexuality as an identity is a relatively recent invention." (Library Journal)

Includes bibliographical references and index

Bronski, Michael

★ A **queer** history of the United States. Beacon Press 2011 xx, 287p $27.95 **306.76**

1. Homosexuality -- United States -- History

ISBN 978-0-8070-4439-1

LC 2010-50225

"This enthralling history spans 500 years of evolving perspectives on sexuality in America—from the European setters' violent responses to the more fluid gender roles of Native Americans to how the birth control pill, which separated sex from reproduction, contributed to the cause of LGBT liberation. . . . A savvy political, legal, literary (and even fashion) history, Bronski's narrative is as intellectually rigorous as it is entertaining." Publ Wkly

Carter, David

Stonewall; David Carter. Griffin 2010 336 p. ill., maps $17.99 **306.76**

1. Gay men 2. Lesbians 3. Gay rights 4. Gay liberation movement 5. Greenwich Village (New York, N.Y.) -- History 6. Stonewall Riots, New York, N.Y., 1969

ISBN 9780312671938

"In 1969, a series of riots over police action against The Stonewall Inn, a gay bar in New York City's Greenwich Village, changed the longtime landscape of the homosexual in society literally overnight. Since then the event itself has become the stuff of legend, with relatively little hard information available on the riots themselves. Now, based on hundreds of interviews, an exhaustive search of public and previously sealed files, and over a decade of intensive research into the history." (Publisher's note)

"Not only the definitive examination of the riots but an absorbing history of pre-Stonewall America, and how the oppression and pent-up rage of those years finally ignited on a hot New York night." Boston Globe

Duberman, Martin B., 1930-

The **Martin** Duberman reader; the essential historical, biographical, and autobiographical writings. Martin Duberman. The New Press 2013 384 p. (paperback) $21.95 **306.76**

1. LGBT people 2. United States -- Social conditions 3. United States -- History 4. Gays -- United States -- History 5. Gay rights -- United States -- History 6. United States -- Politics and government

ISBN 1595586792; 9781595586797

LC 2012041856

This book, by Martin Duberman, offers a reader featuring essays and autobiographical writings of the LGBT scholar. "For the past fifty years, prize-winning historian Martin Duberman's groundbreaking writings have established him as one of our preeminent public intellectuals. Founder of the first graduate program in LGBT studies in the country, . . . Duberman is also an equally gifted playwright and essayist." (Publisher's note)

Eisner, Shiri

Bi; notes for a bisexual revolution. Shiri Eisner. Seal Press 2013 345 p. $16 **306.76**

1. Sex 2. Bisexuality

ISBN 1580054749; 9781580054744

LC 2012047200

Lambda Literary Awards Finalist (2014)

This book, by Shiri Eisner, offers a "comprehensive look at bisexual politics—from the issues surrounding biphobia/monosexism, feminism, and transgenderism to the practice of labeling those who identify as bi as either 'too bisexual' . . . or 'not bisexual enough'. . . . In this . . . book, feminist bisexual and genderqueer activist Shiri Eisner takes readers on a journey through the many aspects of the meanings and politics of bisexuality." (Publisher's note)

Faderman, Lillian, 1940-

The **gay** revolution; the story of the struggle. Lillian Faderman. Simon & Schuster 2015 512 p. 16 plates; illustrations (hardcover : alk. paper) $35 **306.76**

1. Gay men 2. Lesbians 3. Same-sex marriage 4. Gay rights -- United States 5. Gays and lesbians in the military 6. Gays -- United States -- History 7. Gay rights -- United States -- History 8. Gay liberation movement -- United States -- History

ISBN 1451694113; 9781451694116; 9781451694123

LC 2015007285

Stonewall Honor Book in Non-Fiction (2016)

This book, by Lillian Faderman, presents the "story of the modern struggle for gay, lesbian, and trans rights--from the 1950s to the present--based on . . . interviews with politicians, military figures, legal activists, and members of the entire LGBT community who face these challenges every day." (Publisher's note)

"Throughout this engaging and extremely well-documented book, Faderman clearly shows that for the LGBT community, equality is not a completed goal. Yet the ideal of fully integrated citizenship is closer to becoming reality than ever before. Inspiring and necessary reading for all Americans interested in social justice." Kirkus

Includes bibliographical references and index

Hirshman, Linda

Victory; the triumphant gay revolution. Linda Hirshman. Harper 2012 464 p. $27.99 **306.76**

1. Civil rights 2. LGBT people -- Legal status, laws, etc. 3. Gays -- Legal status, laws, etc. -- United States 4. United States -- Social conditions -- 21st century 5. Gay liberation movement -- United States -- History

ISBN 0061965502; 9780061965500

LC 2012406399

This book, by Linda Hirshman discusses the "triumph of the gay-rights movement. Drawing on previous histories and more than 100 interviews, the author shows how the movement has been successful over the years in countering bigoted notions. . . . Hirshman . . . [presents] discussions of court cases and their attendant legal issues, and on occasion she offers perceptive comparisons between the gay-rights movement and other, concurrent movements for equality." (Kirkus Reviews)

Includes bibliographical references (p. [357]-423)

and index

Jacques, Juliet

Trans; A Memoir. Juliet Jacques. Random House Inc 2015 320 p. (hbk.) $26.95; (pbk.) $24.95   **306.76**

1. Sex 2. Transgender people
ISBN 1784781649; 9781784781675; 9781784781644; 1784781673

This memoir by Juliet Jacques is an "exploration of debates that comprise trans politics, issues which promise to redefine our understanding of what it means to be alive. In July 2012, aged thirty, Juliet Jacques underwent sex reassignment surgery—a process she chronicled with unflinching honesty in a serialised national newspaper column. Trans tells of her life to the present moment." (Publisher's note)

Mock, Janet

Redefining Realness; My Path to Womanhood, Identity, Love & So Much More. by Janet Mock. Atria Books 2014 288 p. (hardback) $24.99 **306.76**

1. Self-realization 2. Transgender people 3. Identity (Psychology) 4. Racially mixed people 5. Self-actualization (Psychology) -- Case studies 6. Gender identity -- United States -- Case studies 7. Transgender people -- United States -- Biography 8. Racially mixed people -- United States -- Biography
ISBN 1476709122; 9781476709123

LC 2013047625

Stonewall Honor Book - Nonfiction (2015)

This memoir follows author Janet Mock's "quest for identity, from an early, unwavering conviction about her gender to a turbulent adolescence in Honolulu that saw her transitioning during the tender years of high school, self-medicating with hormones at fifteen, and flying across the world alone for sex reassignment surgery at just eighteen. . . . Mock uses her own experience to impart vital insight about the unique challenges and vulnerabilities of trans youth." (Publisher's note)

Nutt, Amy Ellis

Becoming Nicole; the transformation of an American family. Amy Ellis Nutt. Random House Inc 2015 304 p. (hardback) $27   **306.76**

1. Family 2. Transgender people 3. Transgender teenagers 4. Families -- United States 5. Transgender youth -- United States 6. Transgender people -- United States
ISBN 0812995414; 9780812995411

LC 2015031162

Stonewall Honor Book in Non-Fiction (2016)

"The inspiring true story of a transgender girl, her identical twin brother, and an ordinary American family's extraordinary journey to understand, nurture, and celebrate the right to be different--from the Pulitzer Prize-winning science reporter for The Washington Post." (Publisher's note)

"This poignant account of a transgender girl's transition offers a heartfelt snapshot of a family whose only objective is to protect their daughter. Tackling the subject from a biological, social, and psychological viewpoint, Pulitzer-winning reporter Nutt (Shadows Bright as Glass) weaves complex elements of what being transgender means into a compelling

narrative about a young woman who has identified as female since early childhood. . . . Writing in a very journalistic tone, Nutt succeeds in placing Nicole's individual story within the more general narrative of transgender rights in the United States and humanizes the issues currently at play." Pub Wkly

Includes bibliographical references

Parkinson, R. B.

A little gay history; desire and diversity across the world. Richard Parkinson; with contributions by Kate Smith and Max Carocci. Columbia University Press 2013 128 p. col. ill., map (pbk. : alk. paper) $19.95   **306.76**

1. Art 2. Homosexuality -- History
ISBN 023116663X; 9780231166638

LC 2013001699

Stonewall Book Awards: Nonfiction Honor Book (2014)

Author R.B. Parkinson presents answers to questions such as "When was the first chat line between men established? Who was the first 'lesbian'? Were ancient Greek men who had sex with each other necessarily 'gay' and what did Shakespeare think about crossdressing? . . . through close readings of art objects from the British Museum's far-ranging collection." (Publisher's note)

"This little gay history is a little terrific book. . . . Parkinson . . . explore[s] the subject of homosexual desire throughout history; he discusses artistic movements, ordinary material culture, facades of conventional life, warrior traditions, legal persecutions, and definitions of the sacred." (Library Journal)

Includes bibliographical references

Robb, Graham

★ Strangers: homosexual love in the nineteenth century. W.W. Norton 2004 341p il $26.95; pa $15.95   **306.76**

1. Homosexuality
ISBN 0-393-02038-X; 0-393-32649-7 pa

LC 2003-66239

The author "has produced a brilliant work of social archaeology. . . . In excavating the long-buried lives of our gay great-great-granduncles and lesbian great-great-grandaunts, Robb has done more than make a major historical contribution. He has, as it were, provided their distant nieces and nephews, gay and straight, with a family tree that we have never had before." N Y Times Book Rev

Savage, Dan, 1964-

American Savage; insights, slights, and fights on faith, sex, love, and politics. by Dan Savage. Dutton 2013 320 p. (hardcover) $26.95   **306.76**

1. Sex 2. LGBT people 3. Gays -- United States 4. Gay men -- United States -- Biography
ISBN 0525954104; 9780525954101

LC 2013001374

This book by sex columnist and gay rights advocate Dan Savage presents a "collection of 17 new essays. . . . Savage introduces readers to his son's coming out as straight . . . . Sexual mores such as debates over monogamy and the closeted are grappled with. He also takes on conservative opponents . . . his Roman Catholic upbringing and his mother." (Library Journal)

Schwartz, John

Oddly normal; one family's struggle to help their teenage son come to terms with his sexuality. John Schwartz. 1st ed. Gotham Books 2012 xiv, 290 p.p ill. (hardcover) $26 **306.76**

1. Gay teenagers 2. Parents of gays 3. Families 4. Parent and teenager

ISBN 1592407285; 9781592407286

LC 2012014369

This book by John Schwartz is a "memoir by the father of a gay teen. . . . After mustering the courage to come out to his classmates, [Shwartz's] thirteen-year-old son, Joe, was in the hospital following a failed suicide attempt. . . . 'Oddly Normal' is Schwartz's . . . attempt to address his family's own struggles within a culture that is changing fast, but not fast enough to help gay kids like Joe." (Publisher's note)

Smith, Rachelle Lee

Speaking Out; Queer Youth in Focus. Rachelle Lee Smith. Independent Pub Group 2014 128 p. 7 plates; color photographs (paperback) $14.95 **306.76**

1. LGBT youth 2. Documentary photography

ISBN 1629630411; 9781629630410

This book by Rachelle Lee Smith, is "a photographic essay that explores a wide spectrum of experiences told from the perspective of a diverse group of young people, ages 14-24, identifying as queer (lesbian, gay, bisexual, transgender, or questioning). . . . [It] presents portraits without judgment or stereotype by eliminating environmental influence with a stark white backdrop." (Publisher's note)

"A salutary addition to the growing body of LGBTQ literature." Booklist

Trans bodies, trans selves; a resource for the transgender community. edited by Laura Erickson-Schroth. Oxford University Press, USA 2014 672 p. illustrations (paperback) $41.95 **306.76**

1. Transgender people 2. Gender identity

ISBN 9780199325351

LC 2014007921

This book, edited by Laura Erickson-Schroth, is "a comprehensive, reader-friendly guide for transgender people, with each chapter written by transgender or genderqueer authors. . . . Each chapter takes the reader through an important transgender issue, such as race, religion, employment, medical and surgical transition, mental health topics, relationships, sexuality, parenthood, arts and culture, and many more." (Publisher's note)

"A glossary and biographical information for each contributor round out this much-needed and well-done workbook, suitable for all types of libraries." Booklist

306.77   Sexual and related practices

Solomon, John

DSK; the scandal that brought down Dominique Strauss-Kahn. John Solomon. Thomas Dunne Books 2012 xi, 274 p.p (hardback) $25.99 **306.77**

1. Scandals 2. Sex crimes 3. Statesmen -- France -- Biography 4. Statesmen -- France 5. LAW -- Criminal

Law -- General 6. Sex scandals -- New York State -- New York

ISBN 1250012635; 9781250012630; 9781250012647

LC 2012009436

This book, by John Solomon, about the 2011 sex scandal surrounding French politician Dominique Strauss-Kahn "grew out of . . . an interview with Ms. [Nafi] Diallo published . . . shortly before the prosecutors dropped the case. His book [asserts that] . . . the prosecutors first rushed too quickly to judgment against Mr. Strauss-Kahn. . . . But when they then found that Ms. Diallo had told lies about her past in Guinea, . . . they rushed too fast in the other direction." (Economist)

"This is a fascinating examination of the roles of politics, race, class, social status, and egos in one of the decade's most sensational criminal cases." Booklist

306.8   Marriage and family

Because I said so; 33 mothers write about children, sex, men, aging, faith, race, and themselves. from the editors of Mothers who think Camille, Peri, & Kate Moses. HarperCollins 2005 xxi, 372p $24.95; pa $13.95 **306.8**

1. Mothers

ISBN 0-06-059878-6; 0-06-059879-4 pa

LC 2004-62007

"Women will appreciate the humor and candor, and men will gain insight into the stunning challenges of motherhood." Booklist

Includes bibliographical references

Brower, Sam

Prophet's prey; my seven-year investigation into Warren Jeffs and the Fundamentalist Church of Latter-Day Saints. [preface by Jon Krakauer] Bloomsbury USA 2011 323p il $27 **306.8**

1. Polygamy 2. Mormon fundamentalism 3. Fundamentalist Church of Latter-day Saints 4. Mormon leaders

ISBN 1-60819-275-X; 978-1-60819-275-5

"Private investigator Brower gives readers a firsthand look at the investigation that brought down prophet Warren Jeffs and the cultlike Fundamentalist Church of Jesus Christ of Latter Day Saints. . . . This compelling story of one man's crusade against a pedophile prophet will appeal to readers of current events and religious history as well as to crime fans." Libr J

Garner, Abigail

★ **Families** like mine; children of gay parents tell it like it is. HarperCollins 2004 256p hardcover o.p. pa $13.95 **306.8**

1. Gay parents 2. Parent-child relationship

ISBN 0-06-052757-9; 0-06-052758-7 pa

LC 2003-56975

This book "should quickly become a mainstay resource for many family service agencies and public libraries serving LGBT patrons." Booklist

Includes bibliographical references

Maybe baby; 28 writers tell the truth about skepticism, infertility, baby lust, childlessness, ambivalence, and how they made the biggest decisions of their lives. edited by Lori Leibovich; foreword by Anne Lamott. HarperCollins 2006 266p $24.95; pa $13.95   **306.8**

1. Parenting 2. Pregnancy 3. Childlessness
ISBN 0-06-073781-6; 978-0-06-073781-8; 0-06-073782-4 pa; 978-0-06-073782-5 pa

LC 2005-52686

"This work, an outgrowth of a Salon.com series that ran in 2003, considers one of modern life's great issues: parenthood. Divided into three sections ('No,' 'Maybe,' and 'Yes'), the 28 essays personalize the choices found in broader society today. . . . These superbly written essays are recommended for all libraries, especially gender studies and sociology collections." Libr J

Ray, Barbara E.

Not quite adults; why 20-somethings are choosing a slower path to adulthood, and why it's good for everyone. [by] Rick Settersten and Barbara E. Ray. 1st ed. Delacorte Press 2010 xxiii, 239 p.p (paperback) $15.00   **306.8**

1. Adulthood 2. Youth -- Education 3. Youth -- Employment 4. Youth -- United States
ISBN 0553807404; 9780440339793; 9780553807400

LC 2010027109

This authors of this book "document the many ways that touch points of adulthood . . . are happening years later for people currently in their twenties and thirties than for their parents and grandparents" as well as "the vast disparity of resources and opportunities . . . between 'swimmers,' as the authors term college-educated youth with strong family support and wide social networks, and 'treaders,' a larger group of young people suffering chronic, generational resource deficits." (Library Journal)

"Drawing on eight years of data and more than 500 interviews with young people between 18 and 34, Richard Settersten and Barbara Ray dismantle the common belief that this generation has been coddled into laziness. Rather, these young adults have come of age at a particularly merciless moment. . . . 'Not Quite Adults' offers a valuable portrait of the diverging destinies of young people today." Economist
Includes bibliographical references

Warner, Judith

★ **Perfect** madness; motherhood in the age of anxiety. Riverhead Books 2005 327p $23.95; pa $15   **306.8**

1. Mothers 2. Dual-career families
ISBN 1-573-22304-2; 1-594-48170-9 pa

LC 2004-56615

"Writing from the perspective of her first few years of motherhood spent in France and her subsequent return to the U.S., Warner ponders the cultural factors driving the madness of pursuing perfect motherhood and the toll it is taking on American women." Booklist
Includes bibliographical references

306.81   Marriage and marital status

Klinenberg, Eric

Going solo; the extraordinary rise and surprising appeal of living alone. Eric Klinenberg. Penguin Press 2012 273 p.   **306.81**

1. Housing 2. Social psychology 3. Youth -- United States 4. Single people -- United States 5. Living alone -- United States 6. Single people -- United States -- Psychology
ISBN 9781594203220

LC 2011031522

This book explores why more than 50 percent of American adults are single--and why the usually prefer to live that way. . . . The author examines both ends of the age spectrum in an attempt to understand the social implication of this trend. He finds that among relatively affluent young adults in the 25-to-34 age bracket, living solo is seen as a rite of passage into adulthood--a period allowing more sexual freedom, a chance to explore relationships without commitment and a major focus on career building. A similar increase in solitary living is becoming the norm among the elderly. . . . [Eric] Klinenberg suggests that public support is needed to provide affordable, urban assisted-living facilities in which the elderly can maintain their independence for as long as possible. (Kirkus)
Includes bibliographical references and index

Roiphe, Anne Richardson

Married; a fine predicament. {by} Anne Roiphe. Basic Bks. 2002 285p $25; pa $14.95   **306.81**

1. Marriage
ISBN 0-465-07066-3; 0-465-07067-1 pa

LC 2002-3506

The author writes "about how marriage and women's lives have changed since the 1950s, and about constants in human nature and the beleaguered but not yet improved upon institution of marriage. . . . Roiphe's rumination is a bit indulgent and soft with hearsay, yet it is timely, clever, candid, generous, and free of sentiment or trivialization." Booklist

306.84   Types of marriage and relationships

Cleves, Rachel Hope

Charity and Sylvia; a same-sex marriage in early America. Rachel Hope Cleves. Oxford University Press 2014 296 p. $29.95   **306.84**

1. Same-sex marriage 2. Same-sex marriage -- United States -- To 1865
ISBN 0199335427; 9780199335428

LC 2013050416

Stonewall Honor Book: Nonfiction (2015)

"Born in 1777, Charity Bryant was raised in Massachusetts. A brilliant and strong-willed woman with a clear attraction for her own sex, Charity found herself banished from her family home at age twenty. . . . At age twenty-nine, still defiantly single, Charity visited friends in Weybridge, Vermont. There she met a pious and studious young woman named Sylvia Drake. . . . In 1809, they moved into their own home together, and over the years, came to be recognized, essentially, as a married couple. Revered by their community, Charity and Sylvia operated a tailor shop employing many local women, served as guiding lights within their church, and participated in raising their many nieces and nephews." (Publisher's note)

"This volume provides an exhaustive and valuable look into a relatively unknown lesbian relationship in Colonial America, proving that Puritans could be accepting in their own way of 'marriages' between women." LJ

Includes bibliographical references and index

Sheff, Elisabeth

Stories from the Polycule; Real Life in Polyamorous Families. by Dr. Elisabeth Sheff; illustrated by Tikva Wolf. Itasca Books 2015 288 p. illustrations (ebook) $7.99; $17.99   **306.84**
    1. Polygamy
    ISBN 9780991399789; 0991399773; 9780991399772

This book, by Dr. Elisabeth Sheff, with illustrations by Tikva Wolf, is "an anthology of work from people living in polyamorous families of all configurations." (Publisher's note)

"Readers engaged in or curious about polyamorous families will find plenty to ponder in this eclectic and enlightening collection." Pub Wkly

306.85   Family

Barry, Dave, 1947-

You can date boys when you're forty; Dave Barry on parenting and other topics he knows very little about. Dave Barry. G.P. Putnam's Sons 2014 240 p. illustrations (hardback) $26.95   **306.85**
    1. Family life 2. Wit and humor 3. Parenting -- Humor 4. Family -- Humor
    ISBN 0399165940; 9780399165948

                      LC 2013037714

This book, by humorist Dave Barry "includes nine never-before-published essays. . . Though not only about parenting (Viagra commercials, horseback riding, cremation and grammar are just a few of the topics addressed), Barry . . . [focuses on] describing his role as the 65-year-old dad of a 13-year-old daughter." (Publishers Weekly)

"A mishmash, but even those who don't have children and have never lived in Miami or searched for a Wi-Fi connection in the Israeli desert will appreciate Barry's light-hearted absurdity." Kirkus

Carbone, June

Marriage markets; how inequality is remaking the American family. June Carbone and Naomi Cahn. Oxford University Press, USA 2014 272 p. illustrations (hardback) $29.95   **306.85**
    1. Family -- Economic aspects 2. United States -- Economic conditions 3. Equality -- United States 4. Social classes -- United States 5. Domestic relations -- United States 7. Families -- Economic aspects -- United States 6. Marriage -- Economic aspects -- United States 7. Working class -- Economic aspects -- United States
    ISBN 0199916586; 9780199916580

                      LC 2013045704

In this book, authors "June Carbone and Naomi Cahn examine how macroeconomic forces are transforming our most intimate and important spheres, and how working class and lower income families have paid the highest price. Why is this so? The book provides the answer: greater economic inequality has profoundly changed marriage markets, the way men and women match up when they search for a life partner." (Publisher's note)

"This book is a methodical and skillful discussion of how the American family has changed and what needs to happen to rescue it. Social scientists, family advocates, and policymakers will find it thought provoking." LJ

Hochschild, Arlie Russell

The **outsourced** self; intimate life in market times. Arlie Russell Hochschild. Metropolitan Books 2012 300 p. ill.   **306.85**
    1. Sociology 2. Outsourcing 3. Free enterprise 4. Family -- Economic aspects 5. Families -- Economic aspects -- United States -- History 6. Interpersonal relations and culture -- United States -- History
    ISBN 080508889X; 9780805088892

                      LC 2011044135

In this book, "sociologist [Arlie Russell] Hochschild . . . compares Turner, Maine--the self-sufficient farming village where she spent summers as a child--with the global marketplace, where" outsourcing is common. Some of "Hochschild's . . . chapters center on surrogate motherhood. . . . Hochschild makes the . . . observation that many pressing for a greater expansion of the free market, gutting of regulations, and cuts in social services are the same people who call for stronger family values, perhaps unaware of the way the market distorts them." (Publishers Weekly)

Includes bibliographical references and index.

Winik, Marion

The **lunch**-box chronicles; notes from the parenting underground. Pantheon Bks. 1998 229p hardcover o.p. pa $15   **306.85**
    1. Parenting 2. Single parent family
    ISBN 0-375-70170-2 pa

                      LC 97-26753

"Winik brings together in winning fashion her decidedly nonmainstream attitude, laugh-out-loud humor, and refreshing candor." Booklist

306.87   Intrafamily relationships

Duron, Lori

Raising my rainbow; adventures in raising a slightly effeminate, possibly gay,totally fabulous son. Lori Duron. Crown Trade 2013 224 p. $15 **306.87**
    1. LGBT youth 2. Gender role 3. Parent-child relationship 4. Child rearing 5. Child psychology
    ISBN 0770437729; 9780770437725

                      LC 2012042444

Stonewall Book Award: Israel Fishman Non-Fiction Award (2014)

This book, by Lori Duron, is the author's "account of her and her family's adventures of distress and happiness raising a gender-creative son. . . . C.J. is gender variant or gender nonconforming. . . . whatever the term, Lori has a boy who likes girl stuff. . . . He floats on the gender-variation spectrum from super-macho-masculine on the left all the way to super-girly-feminine on the right." (Publisher's note)

"In Duron's story, parents will find support for a 'love them, not change them' style of parenting, optimism about the outcomes for their gender-creative children, sympathy for the difficulties of parenting, and an affirmation of the appropriateness and necessity for fierce advocacy." Pub Wkly

Tannen, Deborah

I only say this because I love you; how the way we talk can make or break family relationships throughout our lives. Random House 2001 xxvii, 336p hardcover o.p. pa $15.95   **306.87**
1. Family 2. Communication
ISBN 0-345-40752-0 pa

LC 00-68851

"With lively prose and genuine concern for people, Tannen brings linguistic concepts—metamessage, re-framing, indirect request—to bear on dozens of situations to help lay readers strenghten family ties." Libr J

Includes bibliographical references

306.872   Spousal relationship

Yalom, Marilyn

A history of the wife. HarperCollins Pubs. 2001 441p il hardcover o.p. pa $14.95   **306.872**
1. Marriage 2. Women -- History
ISBN 0-06-093156-6 pa

LC 00-58153

Yalom "has apparently written the first truly comprehensive history of the Western female spousal experience; indeed, there are precious few long views of either marriage or the family to which this book can be compared." Libr J

306.874   Parent-child relationship

Block, Shira

When Your Parent Moves in; Every Adult Child's Guide to Living With an Aging Parent. [by] David Horgan and Shira Block. 1st ed. Adams Media Corp 2009 xxi, 233 p.p (paperback) $12.95 **306.874**
1. Aging parents 2. Shared housing 3. Parent-child relationship
ISBN 1605500127; 9781605500126

This book on deciding whether and how to share one's home with an aging parent is focused on "help[ing] readers make the best possible decision for their individual situations. . . . Chapter 1 offers an overview of the signals that a parent might need a change in lifestyle and living arrangements. . . . Each subsequent chapter deals with a specific issue. The chapters present two scenarios that illustrate the challenges faced when dealing with this issue." (Adaptation & Aging)

Chua, Amy

Battle hymn of the tiger mother. Penguin Press 2011 237p il   **306.874**
1. Lawyers 2. Mothers 3. Parenting 4. Child rearing 5. Memoirists 6. Law teachers 7. College teachers 8. Biography, Individual 9. Mothers and daughters 10. Chinese American families
ISBN 9781594202841; 1594202842; 9780143120582

LC 2010029623

It was the author's "stated intent . . . to present the differences between Western and Chinese parenting styles by sharing experiences with her own children.....As the daughter of Chinese immigrants, she is poised to contrast the two disparate styles, even as she points out that being a 'Chinese Mother' . . . is more a state of mind than a genetic trait. . . . She insists that Western children are no happier than Chinese ones." (Booklist)

Includes bibliographical references

Cusk, Rachel

A life's work; on becoming a mother. Picador 2002 213p $22; pa $13   **306.874**
1. Mothers 2. Parenting 3. Motherhood
ISBN 0-312-26987-0; 0-312-31130-3 pa

LC 2001-54894

First published 2001 in the United Kingdom
The author discusses childbirth and motherhood.

"This is not a happy guide; instead, it is a penetrating, sometimes joyful and amusing, sometimes frightening and disturbing look at pregnancy and motherhood." Booklist

DeGarmo, John

The foster parenting manual; a practical guide to creating a loving, safe and stable home. John DeGarmo; foreword by Mary Perdue. Jessica Kingsley Publishers 2013 160 p. $17.95   **306.874**
1. Parenting 2. Foster children 3. Foster home care 4. Foster parents
ISBN 184905956X; 9781849059565

LC 2013012292

This book, by John Degarmo, "is a comprehensive guide offering proven, friendly advice for novice and experienced parents alike. . . . He describes what to expect from the process, how to access help and how to ensure the best care for your child. He tackles thorny issues such as children's use of the Internet and social media, managing contact with birth parents and how to support your child at school." (Publisher's note)

"DeGarmo includes both big-picture ideas about child development and nuts-and-bolts considerations for fostering, such as how often a caseworker must visit a home, what foster families are reimbursed for, and what training is required." LJ

Includes bibliographical references (page 142-154) and index

Gallagher, Shaun

Experimenting with babies; 50 amazing science projects you can perform on your kid. by Shaun Gallagher. Perigee Book 2013 224 p. (pbk.) $16   **306.874**
1. Infants 2. Science -- Experiments 3. Parent and

child
ISBN 0399162461; 9780399162466
LC 2013021018

This book, by Shaun Gallagher, "shows you how to re-create landmark scientific studies on cognitive, motor, language, and behavioral development—using your [infant] as the research subject. Simple [and] engaging, . . . each project sheds light on how your baby is acquiring new skills--everything from recognizing faces, voices, and shapes to understanding new words, learning to walk, and even distinguishing between right and wrong." (Publisher's note)

"This is a unique work that presents an enjoyable and intelligent look at child development." LJ

Includes bibliographical references

Greene, Ross W.

Raising human beings; Creating a Collaborative Partnership with Your Child. Ross W. Greene, Ph.D. Scribner 2016 304 p. (hardcover : alk. paper) $26   **306.874**
1. Parenting 2. Child rearing 3. Parent-child relationship 4. Parent and child
ISBN 9781476723747; 9781476723761
LC 2016021664

This book by Ross W. Greene "explains how to cultivate a better parent-child relationship while also nurturing empathy, honesty, resilience, and independence. . . . Parents have an important task: figure out who their child is--his or her skills . . . beliefs, values, . . . goals and direction. . . . Greene offers . . . guide for raising kids in a way that enhances relationships, improves communication, and helps kids learn how to resolve disagreements without conflict." (Publisher's note)

"This book is a game-changer for parents, teachers, and other caregivers of children. Its advice is reasonable and empathetic, and readers will feel ready to start creating a better relationship with the children in their lives." Pub Wkly

Hodgman, George

Bettyville; a memoir. George Hodgman. Viking Adult 2015 288 p. (hardback) $27.95   **306.874**
1. Gay men 2. Aging parents 3. Parent-adult child relationship 4. Mothers and sons -- United States 5. Aging parents -- Care -- United States 6. Caregivers -- United States -- Biography 7. Sons -- Family relationships -- United States 8. Gay men -- Family relationships -- United States 9. Adult children of aging parents -- United States -- Biography
ISBN 9780525427209
LC 2014038536

National Book Critics Circle Award Finalist: Autobiography (2015)

In this memoir, by George Hodgman, the author "leaves Manhattan for his hometown of Paris, Missouri, he finds himself . . . in a head-on collision with his aging mother, Betty, a woman of wit and will. . . . He can't bring himself to force her from the home both treasure . . . , and, behind the dusty antiques, a rarely acknowledged conflict: Betty, who speaks her mind but cannot quite reveal her heart, has never really accepted the fact that her son is gay." (Publisher's note)

"A tender, resolute look at a place, literal and figurative, baby boomers might find themselves." Booklist

Holroyd, Michael

A **book** of secrets; Michael Holroyd. Farrar, Straus and Giroux 2011 xiv, 258p.p ill.   **306.874**
1. Essays 2. Biography 3. Illegitimacy 4. Gifted women 5. Women -- Biography 6. Biography, Collective
ISBN 0-374-11558-3; 978-0-374-11558-6 0-374-11558-3
LC 2011003839

In this book, author "[Michael] Holroyd brings a company of unknown women into the light. From Alice Keppel, the mistress of both the second Lord Grimthorpe and the Prince of Wales; to Eve Fairfax, a muse of Auguste Rodin; to the novelist Violet Trefusis, the lover of Vita Sackville-West--these women are always on the periphery of the respectable world. Also on the margins is the . . . biographer, who on occasion turns an . . . eye upon himself as part of his investigations in the maze of biography." (Publisher's note)

Includes bibliographical references and index.

Khetarpal, Roma

The **perfect** parent; 5 tools for using your inner perfection to connect with your kids. Roma Khetarpal; [edited by] Jordan. Greenleaf Book Group Press 2014 224 p. illustrations $15.95   **306.874**
1. Parenting 2. Parent-child relationship
ISBN 1626341036; 9781626341036
LC 2014931325

This parenting guidebook, by Roma Khetarpal, "leads you through five communication tools designed to help parents strengthen their bond with their kids and handle the doubt, guilt, worry, and fear that often accompany the challenges of raising children. Along the way, . . . [the author] shares helpful, humorous real-life stories taken from the popular parenting classes she's taught for years." (Publisher's note)

"Complete with affirmation reminders and "quick take-aways" at the end of each chapter, Khetarpal's work has some wise words for finding joy amid the chaos and keeping relationships the primary focus of our daily interactions. Enthusiastically recommended." LJ

Leap, Jorja

Project Fatherhood; a story of courage and healing in one of America's toughest communities. Jorja Leap. Beacon Press 2015 256 p. (hardback) $24.95   **306.874**
1. Fathers 2. Parenting 3. Parenting -- California -- Los Angeles 4. Fatherhood -- California -- Los Angeles 5. Father and child -- California -- Los Angeles
ISBN 0807014524; 9780807014523
LC 2014043792

This book by Jorja Leap "follows the lives of the men as they struggle with the pain of their own losses, the chronic pressures of poverty and unemployment, and the unquenchable desire to do better and provide more for the next generation. Although the group begins as a forum for them to discuss issues relating to their roles as parents, it slowly grows to mean much more: it becomes a place where they can share jokes and traumatic experiences, joys and sorrows." (Publisher's note)

"Leap observes and captures, in the members' own words, the group's development and its members' four years of progress toward healing their families and, perhaps, their community." Pub Wkly

Lythcott-Haims, Julie

How to raise an adult; break free of the overparenting trap and prepare your kid for success. Julie Lythcott-Haims. Henry Holt & Co. 2015 368 p. illustrations (hardback) $27   306.874

1. Parenting 2. Parent-child relationship
ISBN 1627791779; 9781627791779

LC 2014044394

This book by Julie Lythcott-Haims "draws on research . . . and on her own insights as a mother and as a student dean to highlight the ways in which overparenting harms children, their stressed-out parents, and society at large. While empathizing with the parental hopes and, especially, fears that lead to overhelping, Lythcott-Haims offers practical alternative strategies that underline the importance of allowing children to make their own mistakes." (Publisher's note)

"Well-presented, solid facts that address the many detriments of helicopter parenting." Kirkus

Includes bibliographical references

McConville, Brigid

On Becoming a Mother; Welcoming Your New Baby and Your New Life With Wisdom from Around the World. Brigid McConville. Pgw 2014 304 p. illustrations $16.99   306.874

1. Infants 2. Mother-child relationship
ISBN 1780743890; 9781780743899
Includes index

This book by Brigid McConville discusses mothering practices around the world. "From the Mexican rebozo used to rock the belly and ease back pain during pregnancy to the Bengali practice of taking off a woman's bangles to help her visualize a speedy labor, . . . from the proverbs printed on the kangas used to carry East African newborns to the Japanese ritual where Sumo wrestlers are asked to make infants cry." (Publisher's note)

"The American baby shower, Islamic naming ceremonies, and first birthdays in Korea sit comfortably next to each other in this global celebration of motherhood." Pub Wkly

Newman, Katherine S., 1953-

The accordion family; boomerang kids, anxious parents, and the private toll of global competition. Katherine S. Newman. Beacon Press 2012 xxiii, 261 p.p charts $25.95   306.874

1. Parent-child relationship 2. Globalization -- Economic aspects 3. Adult children living with parents 4. Parent and adult child 5. Competition, International 6. Adult children -- Family relationships
ISBN 0807007439; 9780807007433

LC 2011027846

This book "examines the proliferation of 'accordion families,' in which children continue to live with their parents late into their 20s and 30s. . . . [Katherine] Newman's inquiry takes her around the world to examine how family structures are responding to societal changes. She examines how high unemployment rates, the rise of short-term employment, staggered birth rates, longer life expectancies, and the high cost of living have affected the younger generation's transition to adulthood." (Publishers Weekly)

Includes bibliographical references and index

Pipher, Mary Bray

Another country; navigating the emotional terrain of our elders. [by] Mary Pipher. Riverhead Bks. 1999 xx, 328p hardcover o.p. pa $13.95   306.874

1. Aging parents 2. Parent-child relationship
ISBN 1-57322-784-6 pa

LC 98-31877

The author is interested in studying "the aging process in order to promote meaningful connections between the generations and more cultural support for pursuing them. . . . Pipher describes strategies for dealing with illness, physical decline, the death of a husband or wife and the emotional problems that arise for both the elderly and their families. . . . One of the strengths of this excellent study is that Pipher includes examples of troubled as well as rewarding marital and parent/child relationships." Publ Wkly

Rosswood, Eric

Journey to Same-sex Parenthood; Firsthand Advice, Tips and Stories from Lesbian and Gay Couples. Eric Rosswood: foreword by Melissa Gilbert; introduction by Charlie Condou; epilogue by Gabriel Blau. New Horizon Press 2016 240 p. (paperback) $15.95   306.874

1. Adoption 2. Parenthood 3. Gay couples
ISBN 9780882825144; 0882825143

LC 2015913633

This book, by Eric Rosswood, "guides and helps prospective LGBT parents to explore . . . , five popular options [of parenting]: Adoption, Foster Care, Assisted Reproduction, Surrogacy and Co-Parenting. Each section includes a description of the specific family-building approach, followed by personal stories from same-sex couples and individuals who have chosen and gone through that particular journey." (Publisher's note)

"This supportive and helpful volume is full of warmth, encouragement, and advice, and it's a good place for prospective parents to start." Pub Wkly

Sandler, Lauren

One and only; the freedom of having an only child, and the joy of being one. Lauren Sandler. Simon & Schuster 2013 224 p. $24.99   306.874

1. Parenting 2. Only child 3. Families 4. Family size
ISBN 1451626959; 9781451626957

LC 2013000707

Author Lauren Sandler, an only child, considers only children. "Though she says this is not a memoir, her personal story is woven throughout, beginning with her mother's decision to have one child and ending with the author's apparent decision not to have a second child . . . The focus of the book, however, is on dissecting the research surrounding the myth of the lonely, selfish, maladjusted only child." (Publishers Weekly)

Includes bibliographical references

Senior, Jennifer

All Joy and No Fun; The Paradox of Modern Parenthood. by Jennifer Senior. HarperCollins 2014 320 p. hbk $26.99 **306.874**

1. Happiness 2. Parenting 3. Gender role 4. Home economics

ISBN 0062072226; 9780062072221

LC 2013498720

In this book, author Jennifer Senior "argues that changes in the last half century have radically altered the roles of today's mothers and fathers. . . . Recruiting from a wide variety of sources--in history, sociology, economics, psychology, philosophy, and anthropology--she dissects both the timeless strains of parenting and the ones that are brand new, and then brings her research to life in the homes of ordinary parents around the country." (Publisher's note)

"Full of fascinating ideas and information about the family structure and its history, this work is sure to be of strong interest to parents, in particular, as they look for meaning beyond the day to day." LJ

Includes bibliographical references and index

When I first held you; 22 critically acclaimed writers talk about the triumphs, challenges, and transformative experience of fatherhood. edited by Brian Gresko; introduction by Darin Strauss. Berkley Books 2014 304 p. $15 **306.874**

1. Fatherhood 2. Authors -- Family life 3. Fathers

ISBN 0425269248; 9780425269244

LC 2013050514

In this book, edited by Brian Gresko, "22 of today's masterful writers get straight to the heart of modern fatherhood. . . . From making that ultimate decision to have a kid to making it through the birth to tangling with a toddler mid-tantrum, and eventually letting a teen loose in the world, these fathers explore every facet of fatherhood and show how being a father changed the way they saw the world--and themselves." (Publisher's note)

"This impressive collection deeply probes both the exterior and interior changes that come with fatherhood." Pub Wkly

306.88   Alteration of family arrangements

Aikman, Becky

Saturday night widows; the adventures of six friends remaking their lives. Becky Aikman. Crown 2013 337 p. $26 **306.88**

1. Widows 2. Self-help groups 3. Widowhood

ISBN 0307590437; 9780307590435

LC 2012021057

This book, by Becky Aikman, profiles "six marriages, six heartbreaks, [and] one shared beginning. . . . In this . . . memoir, she explores surprising new discoveries about how people experience grief and transcend loss and, following her own remarriage, forms a group with five other young widows to test these unconventional ideas. Together, these friends summon the humor, resilience, and striving spirit essential for anyone overcoming adversity." (Publisher's note)

306.89   Separation and divorce

Moffett, Kay

Not your mother's divorce; a practical, girlfriend-to-girlfriend guide to surviving the end of an early marriage. [by] Kay Moffett and Sarah Touborg. Broadway Bks. 2003 259p pa $12.95 **306.89**

1. Divorce

ISBN 0-7679-1350-7

LC 2003-58531

The authors "help young divorcées tackle both legal and emotional problems. . . . Overwhelming issues like mutual photographs, wedding rings, and family, as well as legal console, mediators, and even Internet divorce, are discussed with authority and sensitivity. The authors realize that each person is different and comes out her relationship with a different set of circumstances, so they also provide many personal stories—including their own." Libr J

Wallerstein, Judith S.

The **unexpected** legacy of divorce; a 25 year landmark study. by Judith Wallerstein, Julia Lewis and Sandy Blakeslee. Hyperion 2000 xxxv, 347p o.p.; pbk $16.99 **306.89**

1. Divorce 2. Children of divorced parents

ISBN 0-7868-6394-3; 9780786886166

LC 00-35071

The author follows her two studies "on the effects of divorce on children (Surviving the Breakup, 1980; Second Chances, 1989) with this third study of 93 adults whom she first interviewed as children 25 years ago. Her findings are presented through five very readable case studies interwoven with other data." Libr J

Includes bibliographical references

306.9   Institutions pertaining to death

Lovejoy, Bess

Rest in pieces; the curious fates of famous corpses. Bess Lovejoy. Simon & Schuster 2013 xviii, 329 p.p ill. (hardcover) $22 **306.9**

1. Dead -- Miscellanea 2. Celebrities -- Biography 3. Celebrities -- Death -- Miscellanea 4. Celebrities -- Biography -- Miscellanea

ISBN 1451654987; 9781451654981

LC 2012034706

This book, by Bess Lovejoy, discusses how "the famous deceased have been stolen, burned, sold, pickled, frozen, stuffed, impersonated, and even filed away in a lawyer's office. . . . From Mozart to Hitler, [the book] . . . connects the lives of the famous dead to the hilarious and horrifying adventures of their corpses, and traces the evolution of cultural attitudes toward death." (Publisher's note)

Includes bibliographical references and index

Schechter, Harold

The **whole** death catalog; a lively guide to the bitter end. Ballantine Books 2009 304p il pa $18   **306.9**

1. Death

ISBN 978-0-345-49964-6

LC 2009-13779

The author "offers readers a scholarly yet wildly hilarious romp through the cultural history of death and dying. It is not only rollicking entertainment but also provides a wealth of practical and historical information about death." Libr J

Includes bibliographical references

307   Communities

Wilkerson, Isabel

★ The **warmth** of other suns; the epic story of America's great migration. Random House 2010 622p $30; ebook $30   **307**

1. Internal migration 2. African Americans -- History 3. African Americans -- Migrations -- History -- 20th century 4. Migration, Internal -- United States -- History -- 20th century 5. Rural-urban migration -- United States -- History -- 20th century

ISBN 978-0-679-44432-9; 0-679-44432-7; 978-0-679-60407-5 ebook; 0-679-60407-3 ebook

LC 2009-49753

This book focuses on "the Great Migration (1910-1970)--the six-million-strong African American flights from the U.S. South." Author Isabel Wilkerson "seeks to tell the 'larger emotional truths' of the Migration in such ways that spotlight 'people's interior lives and motivations.' . . . Wilkerson contends that this movement was more than a demographic shift, but an action of then-unparalleled collective black agency: [I]t was the first big step the nation's servant class ever took without asking.'" (Contemporary Sociology)

An "account of the Great Migration, the 55-year stretch (1915–70) during which 6 million black Americans fled the Jim Crow South. Wilkerson, a Pulitzer Prize-winning journalist, uses the journeys of three of them—a Mississippi sharecropper, a Louisiana doctor, and a Florida laborer—to etch an indelible and compulsively readable portrait of race, class, and politics in 20th-century America. History is rarely distilled so finely." Entertainment Wkly

Includes bibliographical references

307.1   Planning and development

Binelli, Mark

Detroit City is the place to be; the afterlife of an American metropolis. Mark Binelli. Metropolitan Books 2012 318 p. (hardback) $28   **307.1**

1. Detroit (Mich.) 2. City planning -- Michigan -- Detroit 3. Cities and towns -- Michigan -- Detroit

ISBN 0805092293; 9780805092295

LC 2012016123

This book by Mark Binelli describes how the 21st century economic crisis in Detroit, Michigan, "has managed to

do the unthinkable: turn the end of days into a laboratory for the future. Urban planners, land speculators, neopastoral agriculturalists, and utopian environmentalists--all have been drawn to Detroit's baroquely decaying, nothing-left-to-lose frontier. . . . We glimpse a longshot future Detroit that . . . could be the boldest reimagining of a post-industrial city in our new century." (Publisher's note)

307.24   Movement from rural to urban communities

Saunders, Doug

Arrival city; Doug Saunders. Pantheon Books 2010 356p. ill.   **307.24**

1. Urbanization 2. Globalization 3. Internal migration 4. Cities and towns -- Growth

ISBN 9780375425493

LC 2010029651

In this book, the author examines "global urbanization. He concentrates on the slums and satellite communities that act as portals from villages to cities and, in turn, revitalize village economies. . . . Citing the statistical relationship between urbanization and falling poverty rates, as well as historical precedents like Paris, . . . Saunders insists urban migration means improvement overall, and that the arrival city serves as a springboard for the integration of new populations. While the picture of urbanization veers from gloomier forecasts by analysts like Mike Davis (Planet of Slums), it does so by eschewing direct questioning of the global economic system driving much of this migration." (Publishers Weekly)

Includes bibliographical references (p. 325-343) and index.

307.7   Specific kinds of communities

Grandin, Greg

Fordlandia; the rise and fall of Henry Ford's forgotten jungle city. Metropolitan Books 2009 416p il map   **307.7**

1. Plantations 2. Philanthropists 3. Ford Motor Co. 4. Automobile executives 5. Planned communities -- Brazil 6. Fordlandia Plantation (Brazil)

ISBN 0-8050-8236-0; 978-0-8050-8236-4

LC 2008049642

National Book Award Finalists (2009)

This is an account of Henry Ford's attempt to recreate small-town America in the . . . Amazon. In 1927, Ford . . . bought a tract of land twice the size of Delaware in the Brazilian Amazon. . . . Ford's early success in imposing time clocks and square dances on the jungle soon collapsed, as indigenous workers . . . turned the place into a . . . tropical boomtown. (Publisher's note) Index.

Grandin's account is an epic tale of a clash between cultures, values, man, and nature. Booklist

Includes bibliographical references

Green, Hardy

The **company** town; the industrial Edens and Satanic mills that shaped the American economy. Basic Books 2010 248p il $26.95 **307.7**

1. Cities and towns 2. Industrial relations 3. Industries -- United States 4. Industries -- United States -- History 5. Company towns -- United States -- History 6. Industrial relations -- United States -- History

ISBN 978-0-465-01826-0

LC 2010-13434

"The book provides a valuable perspective on a well-worn history, detailing the heinous, lofty, and occasionally absurd ways companies have tried to shape their workers' lives beyond factory walls." Publ Wkly

Includes bibliographical references

Mumford, Lewis

The **city** in history; its origins, its transformation, and its prospects. Harcourt Brace & World 1961 657p il hardcover o.p. pa $29 **307.7**

1. City and town life 2. Civilization -- History 3. Cities and towns -- History

ISBN 0-15-618035-9 pa

More than a history of the forms and functions of the city throughout the ages, this is a portrait of the development of man as a religious, a political, an economic, a cultural, and a sexual being

Includes bibliographical references

The **culture** of cities. Greenwood Press 1981 586p il lib bdg $57.95 **307.7**

1. City planning 2. Cities and towns 3. Regional planning

ISBN 0-313-22746-2

LC 80-23130

First published 1938 by Harcourt Brace & Co.

Traces the growth of cities from medieval times to the twentieth century

Includes bibliographical references

Wilson, David Sloan

The **neighborhood** project; using evolution to improve my city, one block at a time. Little, Brown and Company 2011 432p $25.99; ebook $12.99 **307.7**

1. Cities and towns -- Growth 2. Cities and towns -- Civic improvement

ISBN 978-0-316-03767-9; 978-0-316-17525-8 ebook

LC 2011002752

"Although the book meanders—Wilson gives a vivid, in-depth description of several scientific studies, and offers a biography for each scientist he cites—the tangents are mostly pleasurable and provide more evidence for how lives, like ideas, intersect in fascinating ways." Publ Wkly

Includes bibliographical references

307.76 Urban communities

Duany, Andrés, 1949-

Suburban nation; the rise of sprawl and the decline of the American dream. [by] Andres Duany, Elizabeth Plater-Zyberk and Jeff Speck. 10th anniversary ed. North Point Press 2010 xxiv, 294 p.p ill., maps $20 **307.76**

1. Suburbs 2. Urbanization 3. City planning 4. Urban renewal 5. Suburbs -- United States 6. Urban policy -- United States 7. Urbanization -- United States 8. Urban renewal -- United States 9. Community development, Urban -- United States

ISBN 0865477507; 9780865477506

LC 2011292714

Originally published 2000

"In this culmination of a 20-year crusade against suburban sprawl, the husband-and-wife architectural firm of Duany and Plater-Zyberk (DPZ) presents its manifesto for city planning. Armed with studies and statistics, the authors fault unchecked suburban growth for sapping vitality from urban centers, depleting natural resources, and breeding an alienated, enslaved automobile citizenry. Their solution is to reconsider pre-World War II methods of mixed-use planning and pedestrian-centered, environmentally sensitive design." (Library Journal)

Includes bibliographical references (p. 273-280) and index

Smith, P. D.

★ **City**; a guidebook for the urban age. P.D. Smith. Bloomsbury 2012 383 p. **307.76**

1. Civilization 2. Urban sociology 3. Cities and towns -- History 4. City and town life -- History 5. City life -- History 6. Cities and towns -- History 7. Sociology, Urban -- History

ISBN 1608196763; 9781608196760

LC 2011051430

This book is an "illustrated guide to 7,000 years of urban life for an age when more than half of the world's population lives in cities. From the earliest Sumerian city of Eridu to the wired eco-cities of the future, [P.D.] Smith embarks on a multicentury tour highlighting urban history, customs, infrastructure, architecture, language, markets, crime, parks, cemeteries, transportation, food, and leisure activities across cultures. He . . . provid[es] panoramic yet focused views of a particular subject, such as . . . . the development of language from cuneiform script to 16th-century street speech and its effect on cockney, to the new London dialect of the 21st-century, Jafaican." (Publishers Weekly)

Includes bibliographical references and index

Winkless, Laurie

Science and the City; The Mechanics Behind the Metropolis. Laurie Winkless. St. Martin's Press 2016 304 p. illustrations (ebook) $66; (hardcover) $27 **307.76**

1. Cities and towns 2. Technological innovations 3. Technology and civilization

ISBN 9781472913227; 1472913213; 9781472913210

This book by physicist Laurie Winkless guides readers "through the technology of everyday city life: how new approaches to building materials help to construct the tallest skyscrapers in Dubai, how New Yorkers use light to treat their drinking water, how Tokyo commuters' footsteps power gates in train stations. . . . [It uncovers] the science and engineering that shapes our cities, . . . [and] how technology will help us meet the challenges of a soaring world population." (Publisher's note)

"Where necessary, Winkless includes diagrams of scientific processes, but this is mainly a packed-with-detail, textual work that will be a hit with both young adult and adult patrons curious about what makes cities tick." Booklist

Includes bibliographical references (pages 271-280) and index.

310   Collections of general statistics

★ The **Europa** world year book 2014; 55th ed. Europa Publications 2014 2v   **310**
1. Statistics 2. Reference books 3. Political science
Annual. First published 1959 with title: The Europa year book

"The best annual directory of the nations of the world. For each country it includes demographic and economic statistics, and facts about constitution and government, political parties, press, trade and industry, publishers, etc. Also incorporates a substantive section with listings and information about international organizations." Ref Sources for Small & Medium-sized Libr. 6th edition

★ The **statesman's** yearbook; the politics, cultures, and economies of the world. Palgrave Macmillan illustrations, maps   **310**
1. Political science
Annual. First published 1864

"Descriptive and statistical information about international organizations and countries of the world-brief history, area, political status, economy, etc." N Y Public Libr. Ref Books for Child Collect. 2nd edition
Includes bibliographical references

Vital Statistics of the United States 2014; Births, Life Expectancy, Deaths, and Selected Health Data. edited by Shana Hertz Hattis. Rowman & Littlefield Publishers, Inc. 2014 442 p. $121 **310**
1. Vital statistics
ISBN 1598887041; 9781598887044

This sixth edition of editor Shana Hertz-Hattis' collection of U.S. vital statistics "supplies 230 updated tables and charts. More than half the content comprises birth and mortality data, but the largest section is the health statistics chapter, which contains 93 tables. A new chapter features 11 marriage statistics tables. . . . Coverage is current as of 2011, and many tables contain historical data." (Choice: Current Reviews for Academic Libraries)

"This is a core title that is ideal for ready-reference collections. It should be close at hand to answer such basic questions as, 'Has cigarette smoking increased or declined over the past 20 years?' Highly recommended for purchase by both public and academic libraries." LJ

317.3   Statistics (Collections)--United States

★ **Proquest** Statistical Abstract of the United States 2015. Bernan Press 2015 1050 p. ill., maps hc $179   **317.3**
1. United States -- Statistics
ISBN 1598887297; 9781598887297

This book of statistical information on the United States has been "published annually by the Federal Government since 1878. . . . Librarians value the Statistical Abstract as both an answer book and a guide to statistical sources. As a carefully selected collection of statistics on the social, political, and economic conditions of the United States, it is a snapshot of America and its people." (Publisher's note)
Includes bibliographical references and index

The **who**, what, and where of America; understanding the American Community Survey. edited by Deirdre A. Gaquin. Rowman & Littlefield Pub Inc 2014 400 p. illustrations $115   **317.3**
1. United States -- Census 2. Cities and towns -- United States 3. Cities and towns -- United States -- Statistics
ISBN 1598887092; 9781598887099

LC 2012455070

This book, edited by Deirdre A. Gaquin and Gwenavere W. Dunn, "uses the 2010–2012 ACS data to present a concise resource of information that tells a story about America--its population, levels of education, types of employment and housing, and patterns of migration and transportation in one, convenient volume." (Publisher's note)

"This would be a useful resource for libraries that find themselves in need of population information." Booklist

320   Political science (Politics and government)

Aristotle
Politics. Oxford University Press 1998 480p (Oxford world's classics) pa $12.95   **320**
1. Political science
ISBN 978-0-19-283393-8

"Discussion of public affairs by the most eminent of the Greek philosophers in terms applicable to many of the problems of modern political science." Pratt Alcove

Bawer, Bruce
The **victims'** revolution; the rise of identity studies and the closing of the liberal mind. Bruce Bawer. Broadside Books 2012 378 p.   **320**
1. Humanities 2. Group identity 3. Learning and scholarship 4. United States -- Intellectual life 5. Identity politics -- United States 6. Group identity -- Political aspects -- United States
ISBN 0061807370; 9780061807374

LC 2012032311

This book, by Bruce Bawer, offers a "critique of the identity-based revolution that has transformed American campuses." In "the 1960s and '70s, . . . a new generation of scholar-activists rejected traditional humanism in favor of a radical ideology that denied esthetic merit and objective truth. . . . Bawer concludes that . . . these programs ha[ve] impoverished our thought [and] confused our politics . . . with politically correct mush." (Publisher's note)

Includes bibliographical references and index

Brookhiser, Richard

What would the Founders do? our questions, their answers. Basic Books 2006 261p $26   **320**
1. Statesmen -- United States 2. Presidents -- United States 3. United States -- Politics and government -- 2001-

ISBN 0-465-00819-4; 978-0-465-00819-3

The author "uses the Founders' written and oral statements to imagine their thoughts concerning contemporary issues ranging from stem cells and terrorism to censorship and gay marriage. The short answers he gives for each question can be serious or witty and are often infused with interesting historical facts." Libr J

Includes bibliographical references

Edwards, Mickey

The **parties** versus the people; how to turn Republicans and Democrats into Americans. Mickey Edwards. Yale University Press 2012 xxiii, 208 p.p (hardcover) $25   **320**
1. Democratic Party (U.S.) 2. Republican Party (U.S.) 3. United States -- Politics and government 4. Democracy -- United States 5. Political parties -- United States 6. Two-party systems -- United States 7. Divided government -- United States 8. Polarization (Social sciences) -- United States

ISBN 0300184565; 9780300184563

LC 2012013008

This book, by Mickey Edwards, "identifies exactly how [the American] . . . political and governing systems reward intransigence, discourage compromise, and undermine our democracy. He then describes exactly what must be done to banish the negative effects of partisan warfare from our political system. . . . He offers graphic examples of how this problem has intensified and reveals how political battles have become nothing more than conflicts between party machines." (Publisher's note)

Includes bibliographical references (p. 187-192) and index.

Fukuyama, Francis

The **origins** of political order; from prehuman times to the French Revolution. Farrar, Straus and Giroux 2011 585p $35   **320**
1. Democracy 2. State, The 3. Comparative government

ISBN 978-0-374-22734-0; 0-374-22734-9

LC 2010-38534

"Political theorist Fukuyama presents nothing less than a unified theory of state formation, a comparative study of how tribally organized societies in various parts of the world and various moments in history have transformed into societies with political systems and institutions and, in some cases, political accountability. Drawing upon a diverse range of sources--sociobiology and anthropology as well as macroeconomics and legal history--and paying particular attention to political development in Asia, Fukuyama describes a somewhat evolutionary mechanism wherein political systems develop in response to certain societal conditions and

become institutionalized because of, among other things, their ability to adapt." (Booklist)

Includes bibliographical references

Kaplan, Robert D.

Warrior politics; why leadership demands a pagan ethos. Random House 2002 xxii, 198p $22.95; pa $12   **320**
1. Leadership 2. Political ethics 3. International relations

ISBN 0-375-50563-6; 0-375-72627-6 pa

LC 2001-31862

"This is a provocative, smart and polemical work that will stimulate lively discussion." Publ Wkly

Includes bibliographical references

Paine, Thomas

★ **Rights** of man; and, Common sense. Knopf 1994 lii, 306p $19   **320**
1. Political science 2. France -- History -- 1789-1799, Revolution 3. United States -- Politics and government -- 1775-1783, Revolution

ISBN 0-679-43314-7

LC 94-5989

This volume combines Rights of man with Common sense which was "published anonymously at Philadelphia (Jan. 10, 1776). . . . Over 100,000 copies were sold by the end of March, and it is generally considered the most important literary influence on the movement for independence." Oxford Companion to Am Lit. 5th edition

Includes bibliographical references

320.01   Philosophy and theory

The **politics** book; Big ideas simply explained. edited by Rebecca Warren and Kate Johnsen; illustrated by James Graham. 1st American ed. DK Pub. 2013 352 p. ill. (some col.) (Big ideas simply explained) (hardcover) $25.00   **320.01**
1. Political philosophy

ISBN 1465402144; 9781465402141

LC 2012533724

This book, part of the Big Ideas Simply Explained series, looks at political philosophy. "More than 100 political philosophers, among them Confucius, Plato, Machiavelli, Mary Wollstonecraft, Karl Marx, Ito Hirobumi, Emiliano Zapata, Jomo Kenyatta, and Mao Zedong, are covered in seven chronological sections ranging from 'Ancient Political Thought' to 'Postwar Politics.'" (Library Journal)

Ryan, Alan

On politics; a history of political thought from Herodotus to the present. Alan Ryan. W. W. Norton & Co. 2012 1114 p. (hardcover) $75   **320.01**
1. Political science 2. Political philosophy 3. Political scientists -- History 4. Political science -- Philosophy -- History

ISBN 1846147794; 9780871404657; 9781846147791

LC 2012012351

This is a two-volume work that looks at the "history of political theory." The first volume covers writings "from Herodotus through Aristotle, the ancient Roman theorists of law, St. Augustine and the medievals, right up to Machiavelli." The second volume "covers the turn of the 17th century to the present. Starting with Thomas Hobbes, whom Ryan regards as the father of our modern conceptions of politics, the book ranges through Locke, Rousseau, Hegel, and Marx." (Publishers Weekly)

Includes bibliographical references and index

320.092 Biography

Judt, Tony

Thinking the twentieth century; Tony Judt, with Timothy Snyder. Penguin 2012 414 p.	**320.092**
1. Historians 2. Jews -- History 3. Political science 4. Philosophy -- History 5. United States -- Politics and government -- 20th century 6. College teachers 7. Nonfiction writers 8. History -- Philosophy
ISBN 9781594203237

LC 2011031473

"The book is a history of twentieth-century thought. It begins with . . . [author Tony Judt's] reflections on Jewish idealism and Jewish suffering in Europe and ends with a devastating account of the failure of American politics in the post-cold war world. It is also an intellectual autobiography. . . . [Topics include] the argument . . . for a one-state solution in Israel . . . [and] Friedrich Hayek's ideas about economics and state planning." (New York Review of Books)

Includes bibliographical references

Love, Reggie

Power forward; my presidential education. Reggie Love. Simon & Schuster 2015 224 p. 16 plates; illustrations (hardback) $26	**320.092**
1. Presidents -- United States -- Staff 2. Presidents -- United States -- Staff -- Biography 3. United States -- Politics and government -- 2009- 4. United States -- Politics and government -- 2001-2009
ISBN 1476763348; 9781476763347; 9781476763354
LC 2014040838

NAACP Image Award Nominee: Outstanding Literary Work- Biography/Autobiography (2016)

In this memoir, author Reggie Love describes his time "as 'body man' to [Barack] Obama during his first presidential campaign, . . . [and] as President Obama's personal aide during that momentous first term. Keeping the President company at every major turning point of his historic first campaign and administration, . . . Love learned how persistence and passion can lead not only to success, but to a broader concept of adulthood." (Publisher's note)

"Though Love admits to his share of mistakes, both he and the president he served emerge from this memoir as admirable and likable." Kirkus

320.1 The state

Cicero, Marcus Tullius

The **republic;** and, The laws; [by] Cicero; translated by Niall Rudd; with an introduction and notes by Jonathan Powell and Niall Rudd. Oxford University Press 1998 xliii, 242p (Oxford world's classics) pa $12.95	**320.1**
1. State, The 2. Political science 3. Rome -- History
ISBN 978-0-19-283236-8; 0-19-283236-0

LC 97-23394

"Cicero's The Republic is an impassioned plea for responsible government written just before the civil war that ended the Roman Republic in a dialogue following Plato. Drawing on Greek political theory, the work embodies the mature reflections of a Roman ex-consul on the nature of political organization, on justice in society, and on the qualities needed in a statesman. Its sequel, The Laws , expounds the influential doctrine of Natural Law, which applies to all mankind, and sets out an ideal code for a reformed Roman Republic, already half in the realm of utopia." Publisher's note

Includes bibliographical references

Fukuyama, Francis, 1952-

★ **Political** Order and Political Decay; From the Industrial Revolution to the Globalization of Democracy. Francis Fukuyama. Farrar Straus & Giroux 2014 752 p. illustrations hbk $35	**320.1**
1. Democracy 2. Comparative government 3. Globalization 4. Order -- History 5. State, The -- History
ISBN 0374227357; 9780374227357

LC 2014016973

"The distinction between strong and accountable government is seen as a driver of history in this second volume of . . . [Francis Fukuyama's] study of politics and the state. Following up 'The Origins of Political Order,' Stanford scholar Fukuyama surveys political developments of the past 250 years, from the French Revolution to the Arab Spring, focusing on the often clashing imperatives of democratic accountability, rule of law, and effective governmental administration." (Publishers Weekly)

A "compelling historical overview of a useful template for the retooling of institutions in the modern state. . . . Systematic, thorough and even hopeful fodder for reform-minded political observers." Kirkus

Includes bibliographical references and index

Hobbes, Thomas

★ **Leviathan;** edited with an introduction and notes by J.C.A. Gaskin. Oxford University Press 2008 lv, 508p (Oxford world's classics) pa $9.95	**320.1**
1. State, The 2. Political science
ISBN 978-0-19-953728-0
First published 1651

"A treatise on the origin and ends of government. . . . This work, a defense of secular monarchy, written while the Puritan Commonwealth ruled England, contains Hobbes's famous theory of the sovereign state." Benet's Reader's Ency. 4th edition

Machiavelli, Niccolo

★ The **prince**. Knopf 1992 xxxi, 190p (Everyman's library) $16 **320.1**
1. Political ethics 2. Political science
ISBN 0-679-41044-9

LC 91-53225

Written in 1513
"A handbook of advice on the acquisition, use, and maintenance of political power, dedicated to Lorenzo de Medici." Haydn. Thesaurus of Book Dig

Rousseau, Jean-Jacques

★ The **social** contract; translated by Maurice Cranston. Penguin Books 2006 167p pa $10 **320.1**
1. Political science
ISBN 978-0-14-303749-1; 0-14-303749-8

LC 2006-43772

First published 1762
"A treatise on the origins and organization of government and the rights of citizens. Rousseau's thesis states that, since no man has any natural authority over another, the social contract, freely entered into, creates natural reciprocal obligations between citizens." Benet's Reader's Ency. 4th edition
Includes bibliographical references

320.4 Structure and functions of government

Han, Lori Cox

Handbook to American democracy; Lori Cox Han and Tomislav Han. Facts On File 2011 224 p. **320.4**
1. United States -- History 2. Democracy -- United States -- History 3. United States -- Politics and government 4. United States -- Politics and government -- Handbooks, manuals, etc
ISBN 0816078548; 9780816078547

LC 2011005185

The authors "address the foundations of American democracy and the three branches of American government. The books introduce offices, history, and issues in eight chapters each (e.g., 'The Founding Fathers and the American Revolution,' 'How Congress Is Organized,' and 'Vice Presidents, Presidential Advisers, and America's First Ladies'). The material is complemented by black-and-white photos and sidebars on legal cases, laws and legislation, statistics, maps, biographies of major figures such as Henry VIII, and other primary materials, and chapters close with a summary. . . . [The volumes] each include an individual glossary, index, selected bibliography, and table of contents." (Libr J)
Includes bibliographical references and index

320.5 Political ideologies

Allitt, Patrick

★ The **conservatives**; ideas and personalities throughout American history. Yale University Press 2009 325p $35 **320.5**
1. Conservatism 2. United States -- Politics and

government
ISBN 978-0-300-11894-0; 0-300-11894-5

LC 2008-42559

"From present-day questions of taxation and big government, Allitt traces conservative principles to the earliest days of the republic. . . . Cutting across the stereotypes of present-day conservatism, this nuanced, thoughtful history should educate the unaffiliated and help the disillusioned recover." Publ Wkly
Includes bibliographical references

Brown, Archie

★ The **rise** and fall of communism. Ecco 2009 720p il map $35.99 **320.5**
1. Communism
ISBN 0-06-113879-7; 978-0-06-113879-9

Brown has crafted a readable and judicious account of Communist history, from its theoretical beginnings in 19th-century Europe to its practical collapse at the end of the 1980s, that is both controversial and commonsensical. . . . Given the immense sweep of time, ideology and geography he strives to cover in 600-odd pages, as Brown observes, almost every one of his chapters could be a book on its own. The Rise and Fall of Communism is a work of considerable delicacy and nuance. Salon
Includes bibliographical references

Ezekiel, Raphael S.

The **racist** mind; portraits of American Neo-Nazis and Klansmen. Viking 1995 xxxv, 330p hardcover o.p. pa $20 **320.5**
1. Racism 2. Ku Klux Klan 3. White supremacy movements 4. White Aryan Resistance 5. United States -- Race relations
ISBN 0-14-023449-7 pa

LC 94-45177

"White supremacy groups are examined in this brutally honest portrait of hate and fear, based on personal interviews and interactions. A disturbingly provocative look at the frightening ignorance existing in the 1990s." Booklist
Includes bibliographical references

Potter, Will

Green is the new red. City Lights Books 2011 301 p. **320.5**
1. Ecoterrorism 2. Political activists 3. Environmental movement
ISBN 9780872865389

LC 2010053209

It was the author's intent to demonstrate that "the U.S. government is using post-9/11 anti-terrorism resources to target environmentalists and animal rights activists. . . . Tracing funds from animal-exploiting corporations to Congress and the passing of the big business-friendly Animal Enterprise Terrorism Act, Potter reports on an increased usage of the terrorism enhancement in court cases. . . . [Will] Potter warns of the crumbling of the 'legal wall separating "terrorist" from "dissident" or "undesirable" and concludes his account with a call to action and a decry of the injustice that results in the "terrorist" label being put on those who threaten American corporate interests." (Publishers weekly)
Includes bibliographical references and index.

320.51   Liberalism

Brennan, Jason

Libertarianism; what everyone needs to know. by Jason Brennan. Oxford University Press 2012 xvi, 213 p.p (hardback) $74; (pbk.) $16.95 **320.51**

1. Libertarianism 2. Republican Party (U.S.) 3. Libertarianism -- United States 4. United States -- Politics and government

ISBN 0199933898; 019993391X; 9780199933891; 9780199933914

LC 2012020049

Author Jason Brennan "offers a nuanced portrait of libertarianism, proceeding through a series of questions to illuminate the essential elements of libertarianism and the problems the philosophy addresses, including such topics as the Value of Liberty, Human Nature and Ethics, Economic Liberty, Civil Rights, Social Justice and the Poor, Government and Democracy, and Contemporary Politics." (Publisher's note)

Includes bibliographical references (p. [191]-198) and index

Carville, James

★ **It's** the middle class, stupid! James Carville and Stan Greenberg. Blue Rider Press 2012 321 p. $26.95 **320.51**

1. Middle class 2. Equality -- United States 3. United States -- Social conditions 4. Politics, Practical -- United States 5. United States -- Politics and government -- 2009- 6. United States -- Politics and government -- 2001-2009

ISBN 0399160396; 9780399160394

LC 2012018191

In this book, "[James] Carville . . . and [Stan] Greenberg offer a plea to save America's floundering middle class. . . . The authors outline a grim cycle of 'institutionalize inequality,' declining wages, reduced benefits, and skyrocketing higher education prices, all of which that are blocking middle class children from top educations and, later on, career benefits." (Publishers Weekly)

Includes bibliographical references.

320.52   Conservatism

Hochschild, Arlie Russell

Strangers in their own land; Anger and Mourning on the American Right. Arlie Russell Hochschild. New Press, The 2016 288 p. illustrations (ebook) $27.99; (hardback) $27.95 **320.52**

1. Political psychology 2. Liberalism -- United States 3. Conservatism -- United States 4. Liberalism -- United States -- History -- 21st century 5. Conservatism -- United States -- History -- 21st century

ISBN 9781620972267; 9781620972250

LC 2016017892

National Book Award Finalist: Nonfiction (2016)

In this book author Arlie Russell Hochschild "embarks on a . . . journey from her liberal hometown of Berkeley, California, deep into Louisiana bayou country—a stronghold of the conservative right. As she gets to know people who strongly oppose many of the ideas she . . . champions, Hochschild . . . warms to the people she meets. . . . People whose concerns are actually ones that all Americans share: the desire for community, the embrace of family, and hopes for their children." (Publisher's note)

"A well-told chronicle of an ambitious sociological project of significant current importance." Kirkus

Includes bibliographical references (pages 317-338) and index.

Mayer, Jane

Dark money; the hidden history of the billionaires behind the rise of the radical right. Jane Mayer. Doubleday 2016 464 p. chart (hardcover) $29.95 **320.52**

1. Journalists 2. Rich -- United States 3. United States -- Politics and government

ISBN 9780385535595; 9780385535601

LC 2015957180

Author "Jane Mayer spent five years conducting hundreds of interviews--including with several sources within the network--and scoured public records, private papers, and court proceedings in reporting this book. . . . She traces the byzantine trail of the billions of dollars spent by the network and provides vivid portraits of the colorful figures behind the new American oligarchy." (Publisher's note)

Includes bibliographical references (pages 381-425) and index.

320.54   Nationalism, regionalism, internationalism

Avineri, Shlomo

Herzl's vision; Theodor Herzl and the foundation of the Jewish state. Shlomo Avineri. BlueBridge / United Tribes Media Inc. 2014 304 p. illustrations $22.95 **320.54**

1. Zionism

ISBN 1933346981; 9781933346984

LC 2014948524

National Jewish Book Award Finalist: History (2014)

This book, by Shlomo Avineri, is a biography of the Swiss Zionist Theodor Herzl. The author portrays "Herzl's intellectual and spiritual odyssey from a private and marginal individual into a Jewish political leader and shows how it was the political crisis of the Austro-Hungarian Habsburg Empire, torn apart by contending national movements, which convinced Herzl of the need for a Jewish polity." (Publisher's note)

320.6   Policy making

Collins, Gail

As Texas goes; how the Lone Star State hijacked the American agenda. Gail Collins. Liveright Pub. Corporation 2012 267 p. **320.6**

1. Texas -- History 2. Social policy -- Texas 3. Economic policy -- Texas 4. Texas -- Politics and government 5.

Texas -- Politics and government -- 1951-
ISBN 0871404079; 9780871404077

LC 2012007794

This book is a "study of Texas's government and its discontents. New York Times columnist [Gail] Collins . . . argues . . . [that Texas] is a disastrous model of public policy that inspired the Republican Party's national platform: a rickety economic boom based on insecure, poverty-level jobs and massive state incentives to corporations; financial deregulation that led to banking meltdowns; a raft of ill-advised education nostrums." (Publishers Weekly)

Includes bibliographical references and index

320.9 Political situation and conditions

Perry, Alex

The **Rift**; A New Africa Breaks Free. Alex Perry. Little, Brown & Co. 2015 448 p. 16 plates; illustrations; maps $30 **320.9**

1. Africa -- Social conditions 2. Africa -- Description and travel
ISBN 0316333778; 9780316333771

LC 2015946918

This book by Alex Perry takes a "look at how the world gets Africa wrong, and how a resurgent Africa is forcing it to think again. Perry traveled the continent for most of a decade, meeting with entrepreneurs and warlords, professors and cocaine smugglers, presidents and jihadis. Beginning with a devastating investigation into a largely unreported war crime-in 2011, when the US and the major aid agencies helped cause a famine in which 250,000 Somalis died-he finds Africa at a moment of furious self-assertion." (Publisher's note)

"This in-depth, investigative report will intrigue readers concerned with U.S. policy and its impact on African nations." Library Journal

321.8 Democratic government

Cartledge, Paul

Democracy; a life. Paul Cartledge. Oxford University Press 2016 416 p. illustrations (hardback) $29.95 **321.8**

1. Political science 2. Democracy -- History 3. Greece -- Politics and government 4. Democracy -- Greece -- History -- To 1500 5. Greece -- Politics and government -- To 146 B.C
ISBN 9780190494322; 9780199837458; 9780199837465

LC 2015034058

This book, by Paul Cartledge, "surveys the emergence and development of Greek politics, the invention of political theory, and-intimately connected to the latter- the birth of democracy, first at Athens in c. 500 bce and then at its greatest flourishing in the Greek world 150 years later. Cartledge then traces the decline of genuinely democratic Greek institutions at the hands of the Macedonians and-subsequently and decisively-the Romans." (Publisher's note)

"No library should be without this wonderful book, in which Cartledge has abundantly shared his love and knowledge of ancient Greece with us." Kirkus

Includes bibliographical references and index

Dobson, William J.

The **dictator's** learning curve; inside the global battle for democracy. by William J. Dobson. Doubleday 2012 341p. $28.95 **321.8**

1. Democracy 2. Dictators 3. Dictatorship 4. Democratization
ISBN 0385533357; 9780385533355

LC 2011050286

This book presents a "study of how heavy-handed repression by authoritarian regimes has given way to more subtle forms of control. Despite some reassuring advances in democracy over the last 40 years. . . . [William J.] Dobson sees a pernicious, no-less-repressive shift in the tactics of autocrats still hanging on. . . . Dobson travels around the globe, from Malaysia to Venezuela, chronicling his encounters with both camps." (Kirkus Reviews)

Includes bibliographical references and index

321.9 Authoritarian government

Arendt, Hannah

★ **Origins** of totalitarianism; new ed with added prefaces; Harcourt Brace Jovanovich 1973 xliii, 527p pa $19 **321.9**

1. Imperialism 2. Antisemitism 3. Totalitarianism
ISBN 0-15-670153-7

First published 1951 in the United Kingdom with title: The burden of our time

In this book, the author documents her "belief that Nazism and Communism had their roots in the anti-Semitism and imperialism of the 19th century." Benet's Reader's Ency. 4th edition

Includes bibliographical references

Paxton, Robert O.

★ The **anatomy** of fascism; [by] Robert Paxton. Knopf 2004 321p $26; pa $15 **321.9**

1. Fascism
ISBN 1-4000-4094-9; 1-4000-3391-8 pa

LC 2004-100489

"While there are countless studies on fascism, readers will be hard pressed to find anything more in-depth from a scholar with Paxton's credentials." Libr J

Includes bibliographical references

322 Relation of the state to organized groups and their members

Kertzer, David I., 1948-

The **Pope** and Mussolini; the secret history of Pius XI and the rise of Fascism in Europe. David I. Kertzer. Random House 2014 576 p. illustrations, maps hbk $32 **322**

1. Church and state -- Italy -- History 2. Fascism and

the Catholic Church -- Italy
ISBN 0812993462; 9780812993462

LC 2013019402

Pulitzer Prize: Biography or Autobiography (2015)

"'The Pope and Mussolini' tells the story of two men who came to power in 1922, and together changed the course of twentieth-century history.... Pius XI and 'Il Duce' had many things in common. They shared a distrust of democracy and a visceral hatred of Communism.... In a challenge to the conventional history of this period ... [author David I.] Kertzer shows how Pius XI played a crucial role in making Mussolini's dictatorship possible and keeping him in power." (Publisher's note)

"Kertzer unravels the relationship between two of 20th-century Europe's most important political figures and does so in an accessible style that makes for a fast-paced must-read." Pub Wkly

Includes bibliographical references and index

Kruse, Kevin M.

One nation under God; how corporate America invented Christian America. Kevin M. Kruse. Basic Books 2015 448 p. (hardback : alkaline paper) $29.99   **322**

1. New Deal, 1933-1939 2. Church and state -- United States 3. Christianity and politics -- United States 4. New Deal, 1933-1939 -- Public opinion 5. United States -- Religion -- 20th century 6. United States -- Politics and government -- 1933-1945 7. United States -- Politics and government -- 1945-1989 8. Conservatism -- United States -- History -- 20th century 9. Social conflict -- United States -- History -- 20th century 10. Church and state -- United States -- History -- 20th century 11. Political culture -- United States -- History -- 20th century 12. Christianity and politics -- United States -- History -- 20th century 13. Corporations -- Political activity -- United States -- History -- 20th century
ISBN 0465049494; 9780465049493

LC 2014035883

In this book, "historian Kevin M. Kruse reveals that the idea of 'Christian America' is an invention--and a relatively recent one at that. As Kruse argues, the belief that America is fundamentally and formally a Christian nation originated in the 1930s when businessmen enlisted religious activists in their fight against FDR's New Deal." (Publisher's note)

"In a book for readers from both parties, Kruse ably demonstrates how the simple ornamental mottoes 'under God' and 'In God We Trust,' as well as the fight to define America as Christian, were parts of a clever business plan."

Includes bibliographical references and index

Preston, Andrew

Sword of the spirit, shield of faith; religion in American war and diplomacy. by Andrew Preston. Alfred A. Knopf 2012 815 p.   **322**

1. Protestantism 2. Military policy -- United States 3. United States -- Foreign relations 4. Religion and politics -- United States 5. International relations -- Religious aspects 6. United States -- Military policy -- Religious aspects 7. United States -- Foreign relations -- Religious aspects 8. United States -- History, Military --

Religious aspects 9. Religion and international relations -- United States -- History
ISBN 9781400043231

LC 2011035138

It was the author's intention to provide an "examination of the consistent application of the founding religious principles to American foreign policy, from the colonists' sense of a Protestant exceptionalism to President Obama's 'Good Niebuhr Policy.' ... [Author Andrew] Preston explores this fascinating paradox of a nation founded on freedom of religion yet exhibiting, in its relations with the wider world, a profound belief in a Judeo-Christian sense of 'exceptional virtue.'" (Kirkus Reviews)

Includes bibliographical references and index

Rothkopf, David

Power, Inc. the epic rivalry between big business and government--and the reckoning that lies ahead. David Rothkopf. Farrar, Straus and Giroux 2011 436 p.   **322**

1. Capitalism 2. Industrial policy 3. Economics -- History 4. Business and politics 5. Big business 6. Capitalism -- Political aspects
ISBN 9780374151287

LC 2011036672

In this book, "[David] Rothkopf ... uses ... examples ... to show the massive influence big business wields in our world and claims that our current economic struggles are not new but, rather, have their roots in history. The rivalry between public and private power has existed for centuries, and, Rothkopf argues, must be managed to achieve a balance that will work for the future. He examines the watershed years of 1288, 1648, 1776, and 1848 to illustrate the common threads of this struggle through history. Whether it is the Treaty of Westphalia, the Industrial Revolution, or the fall of communism, Rothkopf puts an economic spin on historic events and times of change. (Libr J)

Includes bibliographical references and index

Tobin, Jacqueline

★ **From** Midnight to Dawn; the last tracks of the underground railroad. [by] Jacqueline Tobin with Hettie Jones. Doubleday 2006 272p il hardcover o.p. pa $14   **322**

1. Abolitionists 2. Underground railroad 3. Slavery -- United States
ISBN 978-0-385-51431-6; 0-385-51431-X; 978-1-4000-7936-0 pa; 1-4000-7936-5 pa

LC 2006-46304

"There's an enlightening portrait of Josiah Henson (the model for Stowe's Uncle Tom) as a political activist, a fascinating look at the pioneering journalist and early feminist Mary Ann Shadd and an intriguing section on the deep 'Canadian connection to Harpers Ferry,' as John Brown meets with the fugitives in Chatham. Accessible and fluidly written, the book will appeal to general readers." Publ Wkly

Includes bibliographical references

322.4   Political action groups

Chalmers, David Mark

Hooded Americanism: the history of the Ku Klux Klan; 3rd ed; Duke Univ. Press 1987 477p il hardcover o.p.   pa $24.95   **322.4**
    1. Ku Klux Klan
    ISBN 0-8223-0772-3 pa

LC 86-29133

First published 1965 by Doubleday; this is a reissue of the 1981 edition published by Watts

This book recounts the history of the Klan. It describes the sociological and psychological forces behind the Klan, and sets forth its dogmas

"The book is written in a breezy, journalistic style. . . . Especially instructive and sobering is Chalmers' account of the role of the Klan in politics." J Am Hist

Includes bibliographical references

Conner, Claire

Wrapped in the flag; a personal history of America's radical right. Claire Conner. Beacon Press 2013 264 p. (alk. paper) $25.95   **322.4**
    1. Conservatism 2. John Birch Society 3. United States -- Politics and government -- 1945-1989 4. Right-wing extremists -- United States -- History -- 20th century 5. Right and left (Political science) -- United States -- History -- 20th century
    ISBN 080707750X; 9780807077504

LC 2012049353

This book provides an insider's view of the John Birch Society (JBS), "the most radical right-wing organization of the Cold War era." It "describes the seeming paranoia and questionable logic of the most devoted JBS members. [Claire] Conner provides . . . descriptions of many of the eccentric JBS leaders, including founder Robert Welch. . . . She describes her evolution from a fervently pro-life organizer to a somewhat disillusioned woman who is more" pro-choice. (Library Journal)

Includes bibliographical references and index

Esposito, John L.

Unholy war; terror in the name of Islam. Oxford Univ. Press 2002 196p hardcover o.p. pa $15.95   **322.4**
    1. Islam and politics 2. Terrorism -- Religious aspects 3. United States -- Foreign opinion
    ISBN 0-19-515435-5; 0-19-516886-0 pa

LC 2001-58009

The author "explains the teachings of Islam—the Quran, the example of the Prophet, Islamic law—about jihad or holy war, the use of violence, and terrorism. He chronicles the rise of extremist groups and examines their frightening worldview and tactics." Publisher's note

Includes bibliographical references

Gandhi, Mahatma, 1869-1948

★ **Gandhi** on non-violence; selected texts from Mohandas K. Gandhi's Non-violence in peace and war. edited with an introduction by Thomas Merton; preface by Mark Kurlansky. New Directions 2007 101p pa $13.95   **322.4**
    1. Passive resistance 2. India -- Politics and government
    ISBN 978-0-8112-1686-9

LC 2007-32262

First published 1965

In an introductory essay Merton "considers Gandhi's ideas, not in relation to their Indian context, but in terms of their applicability to all men's lives. Brief quotations from Gandhi's writings make up most of the book." Asia: a Guide to Paperbacks

Includes bibliographical references

Ronson, Jon

Them: adventures with extremists.   Simon & Schuster 2002 330p $24; pa $13   **322.4**
    1. Radicalism 2. Conspiracies
    ISBN 0-7432-2707-7; 0-7432-3321-2 pa

LC 2001-47411

First published 2001 in the United Kingdom

This book "is at times funny, other times unsettling, but always astonishing. So difficult to accept are Ronson's narratives that any conclusions must be left up to the reader." Booklist

Toobin, Jeffrey

★ **American** Heiress; The Wild Saga of the Kidnapping, Crimes and Trial of Patty Hearst. Jeffrey Toobin. Random House Inc 2016 368 p. illustrations, portraits $28.95   **322.4**
    1. Kidnapping
    ISBN 0385536712; 9780385536714

LC 2016016625

In this book, author Jeffrey Toobin shows how "the saga of Patty Hearst highlighted a decade in which America seemed to be suffering a collective nervous breakdown. Based on more than a hundred interviews and thousands of previously secret documents, [it] thrillingly recounts the craziness of the times. Toobin portrays the lunacy of the half-baked radicals of the SLA and the toxic mix of sex, politics, and violence that swept up Patty Hearst and re-creates her melodramatic trial." (Publisher's note)

"His thorough research, careful parsing of all the evidence, and superior prose make the book read like a summertime thriller." Pub Wkly

Includes bibliographical references (pages [345]-351) and index.

323   Civil and political rights

Arsenault, Raymond

★ **Freedom** riders; 1961 and the struggle for racial justice. Oxford University Press 2006 690p il map (Pivotal moments in American history) $32.50   **323**
    1. Congress of Racial Equality 2. Segregation in transportation 3. African Americans -- Segregation 4. African Americans -- Civil rights 5. Southern States -- Race relations 6. Civil rights -- Constitutional history 7. Civil rights movements -- Southern States

8. Civil rights workers -- Southern states -- History 9. African Americans -- Segregation -- Southern States 10. Civil rights activists -- Southern States -- History 11. Segregation in transportation -- Southern States -- History 12. Civil rights workers -- United States -- History -- 20th century 13. African Americans -- Civil rights -- Southern States -- History -- 20th century
ISBN 0-19-513674-8; 978-0-19-513674-6
LC 2005-18108

This is a history of the "six months [in 1961] in which black and white volunteers descended on the South to challenge segregated travel." N Y Times (Late N Y Ed)
Includes bibliographical references

Cleaver, Eldridge

Target zero; a life in writing. edited by Kathleen Cleaver; foreword by Henry Louis Gates, Jr.; afterword by Cecil Brown. Palgrave Macmillan 2005 xxvi, 336p $27.95; pa $16.95   **323**
1. Dissenters 2. Memoirists 3. Civil rights activists
ISBN 978-1-4039-6237-9; 1-4039-6237-5; 978-1-4039-7657-4 pa; 1-4039-7657-0 pa
LC 2005-51252

"The book's four parts chart Cleaver's life trhough his essays, short stories, letters, interviews, and poems, many previously unpublished. . . . This well-crafted reader . . . is a rich experience." Choice
Includes bibliographical references

Dershowitz, Alan M.

★ **Rights** from wrongs; a secular theory of the origins of rights. Basic Books 2004 261p $24 **323**
1. Civil rights 2. Human rights
ISBN 0-465-01713-4
LC 2004-20006

The author "asserts that human rights derive from the world's experience with 'wrongs,' i.e., injustice. Only after seeing genocide, for example, did the notion develop that this was a violation of human rights. Dershowitz . . . has a rare ability to develop complex ideas in readable prose. . . . Whether conservative or liberal, absolutist or relativist, readers will find areas of disagreement, but most will concur that a talented and creative legal mind is at work." Publ Wkly
Includes bibliographical references

Dyson, Michael Eric

I may not get there with you: the true Martin Luther King, Jr. Free Press 2000 404p $25; pa $15   **323**
1. Clergy 2. Nonfiction writers 3. Civil rights activists 4. Nobel laureates for peace 5. African Americans -- Biography 6. African Americans -- Civil rights
ISBN 0-684-86776-1; 0-684-83037-X pa
LC 99-40478

Dyson "believes that the ministry fostered King's rhetorical gifts but also encouraged his authoritarian personality. We learn much about his flaws, and about conflict, dissent, and generational differences within the black community, as Dyson insists that King, properly understood, remains a controversial figure." New Yorker
Includes bibliographical references

Hartman, Saidiya V.

★ **Lose** your mother; a journey along the Atlantic slave route. [by] Saidiya Hartman. Farrar, Straus and Giroux 2007 270p il $25; pa $14   **323**
1. Slave trade 2. Ghana -- Description and travel
ISBN 978-0-374-27082-7; 0-374-27082-1; 978-0-374-53115-7 pa; 0-374-53115-3 pa
LC 2006-29407

This "is a groundbreaking book for its ability to combine autobiography, history, and politics in an unprecedented style. . . . Hartman's book is not just to be read by historians of slavery or the Atlantic World, but by all of those who desire to write of the past." Rev Am Hist
Includes bibliographical references

King, Martin Luther, Jr., 1929-1968

The **autobiography** of Martin Luther King, Jr; edited by Clayborne Carson. Warner Bks. 1998 400p il $25; pa $15.95   **323**
1. Clergy 2. Nonfiction writers 3. Civil rights activists 4. Nobel laureates for peace 5. African Americans -- Biography 6. African Americans -- Civil rights
ISBN 0-446-52412-3; 0-446-67650-0 pa
LC 98-35704

"Carson, director of Martin Luther King Jr. Papers Project, brings together selections from King's writings, speeches, and recordings to create this fascinating 'autobiography' of the famed civil rights leader and Nobel Peace Prize winner. The writings trace King's struggles with religion, philosophy, and the racial politics of the U.S." Booklist
Includes bibliographical references

Kotz, Nick

★ **Judgment** days; Lyndon Baines Johnson, Martin Luther King, Jr., and the laws that changed America. Houghton Mifflin 2005 522p $26 **323**
1. Clergy 2. Presidents 3. Vice-presidents 4. Senators 5. Nonfiction writers 6. Members of Congress 7. Civil rights activists 8. Civil Rights Act of 1964 9. Nobel laureates for peace 10. Voting Rights Act of 1965 11. United States -- Race relations 12. United States -- Politics and government -- 1961-1974
ISBN 0-618-08825-3
LC 2004-59852

This is a "narrative of how President Johnson and King temporarily overcame their mutual suspicion to battle successfully for the Civil Rights Acts of 1964 and 1968 and the 1965 Voting Rights Act. . . . This book is an informed political investigation of these two civil rights warriors and the cause for which they fought and, in King's case, died." Libr J

The **radical** King; Martin Luther King, Jr.; edited and introduced by Cornel West. Beacon Press 2014 320 p. illustrations (hardcover : alk. paper) $26.95   **323**
ISBN 9780807012826
LC 2014022515

Featuring works by Martin Luther King, Jr., "Arranged thematically in four parts, 'The Radical King' includes twenty-three selections, curated and introduced by Dr. Cornel West, that illustrate King's revolutionary vision, underscoring his identification with the poor, his unapologetic opposition to the Vietnam War, and his crusade against global imperialism." (Publisher's note)

"This volume features a popularly referenced spiritual giant too seldom recognized in his true dimensions. Readers looking to discover the 'real' Martin Luther King Jr., revolutionary Christianity, social justice, or the state of contemporary America will enjoy West's provocative and pithy work as it calls on King to speak again about America, the world, and 'where we go from here.'" LJ

Includes bibliographical references and index

Schulz, William F.

In our own best interest; how defending human rights benefits us all. foreword by Mary Robinson. Beacon Press 2001 235p $25; pa $15   **323**

1. Human rights

ISBN 0-8070-0226-7; 0-8070-0227-5 pa

LC 2001-392

According to the author, "defending human rights pays off not only in terms of justice, but also in ways that can include greater economic growth, a more protected environment, better public health, and a generally less violent world." America

Includes bibliographical references

Shipler, David K.

The **rights** of the people; how our search for safety invades our liberties. Alfred A. Knopf 2011 366p $27.95; ebook $13.99   **323**

1. Civil rights 2. Law enforcement 3. Rule of law -- United States 4. Civil rights -- United States

ISBN 978-1-4000-4362-0; 978-0-307-59550-8 ebook

LC 2010-34255

The book "offers provocative real-life accounts of how privacy has been sacrificed in the modern era. The outlines of some of the stories he tells are familiar, such as the arrest of Brandon Mayfield, a Muslim lawyer in Portland, Oregon, whose fingerprint the FBI erroneously 'matched' to fingerprints from the Madrid train bombing in 2004. . . . [David K.] Shipler's goal is not to reformulate legal doctrine but to show us, through the experience of Americans subject to intrusive police tactics, where existing doctrine has left us; we live in a world where a federal judge can resignedly say, as Shipler quotes US District Judge Paul Friedman, 'I don't think that there's much left of the Fourth Amendment in criminal law.' As Shipler . . . illustrates, the dual wars on drugs and terror have brought us to this point. Time and again, constitutional law has bent to the imperatives of the state in conflict." (New York Review of Books)

"Identifying five periods in American history when the Bill of Rights has been under particular assault, Shipler . . . argues that we are in the middle of a sixth, a post-9/11 era in which our liberties are once again endangered . . . A timely call for vigilance, for insisting on the protections the Framers provided against an always overreaching government." Kirkus

Includes bibliographical references

Sugrue, Thomas J.

Sweet land of liberty; the forgotten struggle for civil rights in the North. Random House 2008 xxviii, 688p il $35   **323**

1. United States -- Race relations 2. African Americans -- Civil rights 3. African American civil rights workers 4. Northeastern States -- Race relations 5. Civil rights movements -- Northeastern States 6. United States -- Race relations -- History -- 20th century 7. African Americans -- Civil rights -- History -- 20th century 8. Civil rights workers -- United States -- History -- 20th century 9. Civil rights movements -- United States -- History -- 20th century

ISBN 0-679-64303-6; 978-0-679-64303-6

LC 2008-2081

This is a an account of the civil rights movement in the North from the 1920s to the present. Index.

The author "shows that black exclusion, poverty, and racial violence permeated America on both sides of the Mason-Dixon Line. . . . This splendid read brims with insights broadening and deepening understanding of the black-white mold of modern America. Highly recommended and essential for collections on U.S. history, social movements, race relations, or civil rights." Libr J

Includes bibliographical references

323.1   Civil and political rights of nondominant groups

Boyd, Herb

★ **We** shall overcome; a living history of the civil rights struggle told in words, pictures and the voices of the participants. Sourcebooks 2004 272p il $45   **323.1**

1. African Americans -- Civil rights

ISBN 1-402-20213-X

LC 2004-12509

"Through text, images, and actual recordings (found on 2 CDs), Boyd . . . presents some of the major events in the Civil Rights Movement, including the murder of Emmett Till, the march on Washington, and the life and death of Martin Luther King Jr." Libr J

Includes bibliographical references

Euchner, Charles

Nobody turn me around; a people's history of the 1963 march on Washington. Beacon Press 2010 226p $26.95   **323.1**

1. Civil rights demonstrations 2. Washington (D.C.) 3. African Americans -- Civil rights

ISBN 978-0-8070-0059-5

LC 2009-46943

Draws on the oral histories of more than one hundred participants to provide a behind-the-scenes look at the historic 1963 March on Washington that culminated in Martin Luther King Jr.'s "I Have a Dream" speech.

"A sweeping, comprehensive look at a pivotal march in American history." Booklist

Includes bibliographical references

The **Eyes** on the prize civil rights reader; documents, speeches, and firsthand accounts from the black freedom struggle, 1954-1990. general editors, Clayborne Carson {et al.} Penguin Bks. 1991 764p pa $18 **323.1**
1. United States -- Race relations 2. African Americans -- Civil rights
ISBN 0-14-015403-5

LC 91-9507

First published 1987 with title: Eyes on the prize: America's civil rights years, a reader and guide

"An anthology of primary material important in the historiography of this country's civil rights movement. . . . Not simply for reference use, this compilation makes provocative cover-to-cover reading and is extremely worthy of consideration by every library." Booklist

Includes bibliographical references

Greenhaw, Wayne
Fighting the devil in Dixie; how civil rights activists took on the Ku Klux Klan in Alabama. Lawrence Hill Books 2011 316p il $26.95 **323.1**
1. Ku Klux Klan (1915-) 2. Alabama -- Race relations 3. African Americans -- Civil rights
ISBN 978-1-56976-345-2

LC 2010-30114

"The author skillfully weaves a rich historical tapestry from his deeply engaged, firsthand observations. Impressively captures stark, stunning history in the making." Kirkus
Includes bibliographical references

Halberstam, David
★ The **children**. Fawcett Books 1999 783p il pa $18.95 **323.1**
1. Clergy 2. Mayors 3. Educators 4. Physicians 5. Psychiatrists 6. Songwriters 7. College teachers 8. Social activists 9. Members of Congress 10. School administrators 11. Civil rights activists 12. Local government officials 13. United States -- Race relations 14. African Americans -- Civil rights
ISBN 978-0-449-00439-5; 0-449-00439-2
First published 1998 by Random House
This is a "recreation of the early days of the civil rights movement. . . . The author focuses on a small group of young African Americans who attended the Reverend James Lawson's workshop for nonviolent demonstrators in Nashville in 1959, then went on to play active roles in the movement. . . . A masterful achievement in reporting, research and understanding." Publ Wkly

Includes bibliographical references

Hoxie, Frederick E.
This Indian country; American Indian political activists and the place they made. Frederick E. Hoxie. Penguin Press 2012 467 p. $32.95 **323.1**
1. Native Americans -- History 2. Native American political activists 3. Native Americans -- Politics and government 4. United States -- Race relations 5. United States -- Politics and government 6. Political activists -- United States -- History
ISBN 1594203652; 9781594203657

LC 2012009287

This book by Frederick E. Hoxie "profiles eight Native American lawyers, lobbyists, writers, and politicians who 'chose to oppose the oppressions of the United States with words and ideas rather than violence.'" These include 'mid-19th-century leader William Potter Ross . . . who negotiated with the Union Pacific Railroad over its claims to tribal lands . . . and writer Vine Deloria Jr., who . . . argued that U.S. policies should forward Indian self-governance." (Publishers Weekly)
Includes bibliographical references and index.

Joseph, Peniel E.
★ **Waiting** 'til the midnight hour; a narrative history of Black power in America. Henry Holt and Co. 2006 399p il hardcover o.p. pa $17 **323.1**
1. Black power 2. African Americans -- Civil rights
ISBN 978-0-8050-7539-7; 0-8050-7539-9; 978-0-8050-8335-4 pa; 0-8050-8335-9 pa

LC 2005-46765

"Rather than simply detailing the history of radical organizations, Joseph . . . also profiles several famous leaders and uses their stories to spearhead a discussion of the intellectual and practical history of Black Power as a political movement. . . . Enthusiastically recommended for public and academic libraries." Libr J
Includes bibliographical references

Kantrowitz, Stephen
More than freedom; fighting for black citizenship in a white republic, 1829-1889. Stephen Kantrowitz. Penguin Press 2012 514 p. **323.1**
1. Abolitionists 2. Slaves -- Emancipation 3. Reconstruction (1865-1876) 4. African Americans -- Civil rights 5. United States -- History -- 1861-1865, Civil War 6. Boston Region (Mass.) -- Race relations -- History -- 19th century 7. African Americans -- Civil rights -- Massachusetts -- Boston Region -- History -- 19th century
ISBN 1594203423; 9781594203428

LC 2011044724

This book by Stephen Kantrowitz provides a "narrative account of the long struggle of Northern activists-both black and white, famous and obscure-to establish African Americans as free citizens, from abolitionism through the Civil War, Reconstruction, and its demise. . . . [Kantrowitz] chronicles this epic struggle through the lived experiences of black and white activists in and around Boston. . . . [T]heir goals and achievements went far beyond emancipation." (Publisher's note)
Includes bibliographical references (p. [442]-499) and index

Katznelson, Ira
★ **When** affirmative action was white; an untold history of racial inequality in twentieth-century America. W.W. Norton 2005 238p pa $16.95; $25.95 **323.1**
1. Race discrimination 2. Affirmative action programs 3. African Americans -- Economic conditions
ISBN 9780393328516; 0-393-05213-3

LC 2004-24359

"Katznelson offers a penetrating . . . analysis, supported by vivid examples and statistics." N Y Times Book Rev

Includes bibliographical references

Kelley, Kitty

Let Freedom Ring; Stanley Tretick's Iconic Images of the March on Washington. Kitty Kelly. St. Martin's Press 2013 176 p. $24.99   323.1

1. Civil rights demonstrations -- United States -- Pictorial works 2. March on Washington for Jobs and Freedom (1963 : Washington, D.C.) 3. Documentary photography 4. Photographers -- United States 5. African Americans -- Civil rights -- History -- 20th century -- Pictorial works 6. March on Washington for Jobs and Freedom (1963 : Washington, D.C.) -- Pictorial works 7. Civil rights demonstrations -- Washington (D.C.) -- History -- 20th century -- Pictorial works

ISBN 1250021464; 9781250021465

LC 2013009956

This book presents photographs of the 1963 "March on Washington to urge passage of the civil rights bill." It includes "never-before-published photographs of the historic march as well as the events that led up to it. [Photographer Stanley] Tretick . . . documents the rising hopes and tensions as blacks and whites pressed for equity and obstructionists fought their efforts. . . . [Kitty] Kelley provides narrative background and context." (Booklist)

Includes bibliographical references and index

King, Martin Luther, Jr., 1929-1968

★ A **testament** of hope; the essential writings of Martin Luther King, Jr. edited by James Melvin Washington. Harper & Row 1986 xxvi, 676p hardcover o.p. pa $23.95   323.1

1. United States -- Race relations 2. African Americans -- Civil rights

ISBN 0-06-250931-4; 0-06-064691-8 pa

LC 85-45370

"King's most important writings are gathered together in one source. The arrangement is topical: philosophy, sermons and public addresses, essays, interviews and excerpts of his books. The material within each of these categories is arranged chronologically. Included are Dr. King's writings on nonviolence, integration and politics." SLJ

Includes bibliographical references

Where do we go from here; chaos or community? [by] Martin Luther King, Jr.; [foreword by Coretta Scott King; introduction by Vincent Harding] Beacon Press 2010 xxiv, 223p (King legacy series) $24.95; pa $14   323.1

1. Racism 2. United States -- Race relations 3. African Americans -- Civil rights

ISBN 978-0-8070-0076-2; 978-0-8070-0067-0 pa

LC 2009035950

First published 1967 by Harper & Row

The author reaffirms his belief in the power of nonviolence to achieve full citizenship for black people in America

and defines his attitude toward the Black Power movement and the white backlash.

Includes bibliographical references

Why we can't wait; [by] Martin Luther King, Jr. Harper & Row 1964 178p il hardcover o.p. pa $6.95   323.1

1. African Americans -- Civil rights 2. Birmingham (Ala.) -- Race relations

ISBN 0-06-012395-8; 0-451-52753-4 pa

The author first reviews the background of the 1963 civil rights demands. He then describes the strategy of the Birmingham campaign and outlines future action

Lewis, Andrew B.

The **shadows** of youth; the remarkable journey of the civil rights generation. Hill and Wang 2009 356p $28   323.1

1. Political activists 2. African Americans -- Biography 3. United States -- Race relations 4. African Americans -- Civil rights 5. Student Nonviolent Coordinating Committee

ISBN 978-0-8090-8598-9; 0-8090-8598-4

LC 2009-9980

The author "offers an engaging look at some of the major figures in the budding civil rights movement: John Lewis, son of a poor tenant cotton farmer; Marion Barry, ambitious son of poor southern parents; Diane Nash, from a middle-class Chicago family; Stokely Carmichael, who learned black culture from his Caribbean roots and politics from a leftist friend; and Julian Bond, born of black privilege. Lewis chronicles the coming together of these young people, and others, in the formation of the Student Nonviolent Coordinating Committee." Booklist

Includes bibliographical references (p. 329-335)

McGuire, Danielle L.

At the dark end of the street; Black women, rape, and resistance: a new history of the civil rights movement, from Rosa Parks to the rise of Black Power. Alfred A. Knopf 2010 324p il $27.95; e-book $27.95   323.1

1. Rape 2. African American women 3. African Americans -- Civil rights 4. Southern States -- Race relations 5. African American women -- Violence against 6. Rape -- Political aspects -- Southern States 7. Southern States -- Race relations -- History -- 20th century 8. African American women -- Civil rights -- History -- 20th century 9. Civil rights movements -- Southern States -- History -- 20th century

ISBN 978-0-307-26906-5; 978-0-307-59447-1 e-book

LC 2010-12072

"McGuire restores to memory the courageous black women who dared seek legal remedy, when black women and their families faced particular hazards for doing so. McGuire brings the reader through a dark time via a painful but somehow gratifying passage in this compelling, carefully documented work." Publ Wkly

Includes bibliographical references and index

★ **Reporting** civil rights. Library of Am. 2003 2v
ea $40 **323.1**
1. Journalism 2. United States -- Race relations 3.
African Americans -- Civil rights
ISBN 1-931082-28-6 v1; 1-931082-29-4 v2

LC 2002-27459

"From A. Philip Randolph's defiant call in 1941 for African Americans to march on Washington to Alice Walker in 1973, Reporting Civil Rights presents firsthand accounts of the revolutionary events that overthrew segregation in the United States. This two-volume anthology brings together for the first time nearly 200 newspaper and magazine reports and book excerpts, and features 151 writers, including James Baldwin, Robert Penn Warren, David Halberstam, Lillian Smith, Gordon Parks, Murray Kempton, Ted Poston, Claude Sitton, and Anne Moody. A newly researched chronology of the movement, a 32-page insert of rare journalist photographs, and original biographical profiles are included in each volume." (Publisher's note)

"An important anthology for readers interested in the history of the civil rights movement." Booklist

Rieder, Jonathan

Gospel of freedom; Martin Luther King, Jr.'s letter from Birmingham Jail and the struggle that changed a nation. Jonathan Rieder. St. Martin's Press 2013 240 p. illustrations $25 **323.1**
1. Nonviolence 2. African Americans -- Civil rights 3. Birmingham (Ala.) -- Race relations 4. African Americans -- Civil rights -- Alabama -- Birmingham 5. Civil disobedience -- Alabama -- Birmingham -- History -- 20th century 6. Civil rights movements -- Alabama -- Birmingham -- History -- 20th century
ISBN 1620400588; 9781620400586

LC 2012044387

This book, by Jonathan Rieder, focuses on "[t]he letter that Martin Luther King Jr. penned from a Birmingham, Alabama, jail 50 years ago. . . . The letter was King's impassioned response to eight white Birmingham clergymen who had appealed to him for moderation. Here Rieder first discusses the events that led to King's arrest, then addresses the letter's importance during the civil rights struggle." (Library Journal)

"Rieder's trenchant comments approach the letter on historical and literary grounds but also as a way to better understand the often elusive King. Several chapters offer a close analysis of the letter, while later chapters trace the impact it had on subsequent events." Booklist

Includes bibliographical references and index

Sokol, Jason

All eyes are upon us; race and politics from Boston to Brooklyn. Jason Sokol. Basic Books 2014 416 p. illustrations (hardback) $32 **323.1**
1. Race relations 2. African Americans -- Civil rights 3. Progressivism (United States politics) 4. Northeastern States -- Politics and government 5. Racism -- Political aspects -- Northeastern States -- History 6. African Americans -- Segregation -- Northeastern States -- History 7. Northeastern States -- Race relations -- Political aspects -- History 8. African Americans -- Civil rights -- Northeastern States -- History -- 20th century 9.

African Americans -- Civil rights -- Northeastern States -- History -- 21st century
ISBN 046502226X; 9780465022267

LC 2014023616

This book by Jason Sokol "exposes the troubled truth about the North's racial integration. The Northern states could point to the Southern states' ongoing practices of Jim Crow legislation, white supremacist violence and suppression of voting rights with righteous disgust, but the author shows how, in unsubtle and pernicious ways, the North, too, was 'at war with itself.'" (Kirkus Reviews)

"Sokol provides some of the participants' previously unavailable recollections, based on interviews conducted for this history. Ultimately, the book provides a much-needed reminder of the difficult battles discrimination's enemies faced, even in the heart of what was supposed to be an already color-blind society." Choice

Includes bibliographical references and index

Sullivan, Patricia

Lift every voice; the NAACP and the making of the Civil Rights Movement. New Press 2009 514p il $26.95 **323.1**
1. United States -- Race relations 2. African Americans -- Civil rights 3. Civil rights -- United States -- History -- 20th century 4. National Association for the Advancement of Colored People 5. United States -- Race relations -- History -- 20th century 6. African Americans -- Civil rights -- History -- 20th century 7. National Association for the Advancement of Colored People -- History
ISBN 978-1-59558-446-5

LC 2009-9473

This is an "examination of the NAACP's growth and influence, from its inception in 1909 to the present." Index.

The author "delivers a solidly researched examination of the organization's growth and influence, leaving us with a vital account of 100 years of foundational civil rights activism." Publ Wkly

Includes bibliographical references

Voices in our blood; America's best on the civil rights movement. edited by Jon Meacham. Random House 2001 561p hardcover o.p. pa $16.95 **323.1**
1. United States -- Race relations 2. African Americans -- Civil rights
ISBN 0-375-75881-X pa

LC 00-41474

A "collection of acclaimed 'voices' narrating the environment, origin, and progress of the Civil Rights movement, as told by reporters, artists, novelists, historians, and authors such as Maya Angelou, Eudora Welty, James Baldwin, Richard Wright, Willie Morris, Robert Penn Warren, Alice Walker, Murray Kempton, E. B. White, William Faulkner, Ralph Ellison, and Rebecca West." Libr J

Wallace, Anthony F. C.

The **long** bitter trail; Andrew Jackson and the Indians. consulting editor, Eric Foner. Hill & Wang

1993 143p maps (Critical issue series) hardcover o.p. pa $11 **323.1**

1. Generals 2. Presidents 3. Native Americans -- Government relations

ISBN 0-8090-1552-8 pa

LC 92-32609

A "retelling of the story of the Trail of Tears. This refers to the forced removal in the 1830s of thousands of Indians, particularly the Cherokee and the Choctaw, from the American east to west of the Mississippi River. The author expands his focus to examine the relocation of numerous Indian groups. Central to the story is Andrew Jackson, who assumed the presidency confronted with a government divided over the question of Indian removal and who soon became one of its major proponents." Publ Wkly

Watson, Bruce

Freedom summer; the savage season that made Mississippi burn and made America a democracy. Viking 2010 369p il $27.95 **323.1**

1. African Americans -- Suffrage 2. Mississippi -- Race relations 3. African Americans -- Civil rights 4. Student Nonviolent Coordinating Committee

ISBN 978-0-670-02170-3

LC 2009-47211

This book "combines a political overview of the Mississippi civil rights struggle in the summer of 1964 with more than 50 personal accounts from those who were there, both the famous (including Sidney Poitier, Pete Seeger, John Lewis, Stokely Carmichael) and the lesser known, including the more than 200 volunteer students from the North who lived and worked with local residents and taught in the Freedom Schools in converted shacks and church basements. . . . The personal interviews, some from people telling their stories for the first time, make gripping drama, as they recount the standoffs, the struggle for voter registration, the reign of terror that encompassed church burnings and murders." Booklist

Includes bibliographical references

Williams, Juan

Eyes on the prize: America's civil rights years, 1954-1965; [by] Juan Williams with the Eyes on the prize production team; introduction by Julian Bond. Viking 1987 300p il hardcover o.p. pa $20 **323.1**

1. United States -- Race relations 2. African Americans -- Civil rights

ISBN 0-670-81412-1; 0-14-009653-1 pa

LC 86-40271

"Highly recommended both as a socio-historical document and as a heartfelt, poignant remembrance of a movement and its activists." Booklist

Includes bibliographical references

323.4   Specific civil rights; limitation and suspension of civil rights

Conroy, John

Unspeakable acts, ordinary people; the dynamics of torture. University of California Press 2001 304p pa $19.95 **323.4**

1. Torture 2. Persecution 3. Police brutality 4. Israel 5. Northern Ireland

ISBN 0-520-23039-6

LC 2001-33218

First published 2000 by Knopf

The author "interviews torturers, torture victims, and government officials from such diverse locations as Israel, Northern Ireland, and a Chicago police interrogation room, focusing on how torture is performed and why." Booklist

Includes bibliographical references

McCoy, Alfred W.

★ A **question** of torture; CIA interrogation from the Cold War to the War on Terror. Metropolitan Books 2006 290p il (The American empire project) $25; pa $15 **323.4**

1. Torture 2. Intelligence service -- United States 3. United States -- Central Intelligence Agency

ISBN 978-0-8050-8041-4; 0-8050-8041-4; 978-0-8050-8248-7 pa; 0-8050-8248-4 pa

LC 2005-51124

The author "shows how, since 1950, the CIA and various nations have augmented traditional physical torture with psychological abuse techniques of 'sensory disorientation' and 'self-inflicted pain,' which he documents with some gruesome first-person accounts by victims and with stories of doctors who conducted horrific experiments." Libr J

Includes bibliographical references

323.44   Freedom of action (Liberty)

Angwin, Julia

Dragnet nation; a quest for privacy, security, and freedom in a world of relentless surveillance. Julia Angwin. Times Books, Henry Holt & Co. 2014 304 p. (hardcover) $28 **323.44**

1. Right of privacy 2. Electronic surveillance 3. Civil rights 4. Privacy, Right of 5. National security -- Moral and ethical aspects 6. Information technology -- Moral and ethical aspects

ISBN 0805098070; 9780805098075

LC 2013042041

In this book "Julia Angwin reports from the front lines of America's surveillance economy, offering a revelatory and unsettling look at how the government, private companies, and even criminals use technology to indiscriminately sweep up vast amounts of our personal data." (Publisher's note)

"A solid work for both privacy freaks and anyone seeking tips on such matters as how to strengthen passwords (make them longer and avoid simple dictionary words)." Kirkus

Includes bibliographical references and index

Fischer, David Hackett

Liberty and freedom. Oxford University Press 2004 851p il (America, a cultural history) $50   **323.44**

1. Freedom 2. American national characteristics 3. Liberty -- History 4. United States -- History 5. National characteristics, American

ISBN 0-19-516253-6

LC 2004-5197

"This book studies American ideas of liberty and freedom as visions of an open society, through the symbols they have inspired from the Revolutionary era through 9/11." (Publisher's note) Index.

This "beautifully illustrated book shifts subtly from a rich graphic survey, incorporating painting, flags and sculpture, to a broader chronicle of the many ways Americans have articulated their most cherished ideals." Publ Wkly

Includes bibliographical references

Foner, Eric

The story of American freedom. Norton 1998 422p il hardcover o.p. pa $16.95   **323.44**

1. Freedom 2. Cold war 3. Conservatism 4. Labor movement 5. Slavery -- United States 6. United States -- History 7. Women -- Social conditions 8. African Americans -- Civil rights 9. United States -- Economic conditions -- 1933-1945

ISBN 0-393-31962-8 pa

LC 98-3290

"The book's strongest claim to distinction lies . . . in its succinct, information-packed, wonderfully readable account of the twists and turns in 20th-century American history." N Y Times Book Rev

Includes bibliographical references

Shipler, David K.

Freedom of speech; mightier than the sword. David K. Shipler. Alfred A. Knopf 2015 352 p. (hardback) $28.95   **323.44**

1. Freedom of speech -- United States 2. Constitutional law -- United States 3. United States. Constitution. 1st Amendment

ISBN 0307957322; 9780307947611; 9780307957320; 9781101874691

LC 2014032127

This book presents author David K. Shipler's "investigations of the cultural limits on both expression and the willingness to listen build to expose troubling instabilities in the very foundations of our democracy. Focusing on recent free speech controversies across the nation, Shipler maps a rapidly shifting topography of political and cultural norms." (Publisher's note)

"This book addresses a timely subject and is written by someone with a deep interest in the controversies and difficulties surrounding freedom of speech. Recommended for large public libraries, academic libraries, law schools and law students, political science students, and informed lay readers." LJ

Includes bibliographical references and index

Stone, Geoffrey R.

★ Perilous times; free speech in wartime from the Sedition Act of 1798 to the war on terrorism. Norton 2004 xx, 730p il $35   **323.44**

1. Freedom of speech

ISBN 0-393-05880-8

LC 2004-17871

The author "delivers rich material in an engaging, character-based narrative. Stone offers deep insight into rhetorical history and the men and women who made it—resisters like Clement Vallandingham, Emma Goldman, Fred Korematsu and Daniel Ellsberg; presidents faced with wartime dilemmas; and the prosecutors, defenders and Supreme Court justices who shaped our understanding of the First Amendment today." Publ Wkly

Includes bibliographical references

324   The political process

Larson, Edward J.

A magnificent catastrophe; the tumultuous election of 1800, America's first presidential campaign. Free Press 2007 335p il $27   **324**

1. Statesmen 2. Architects 3. Presidents 4. Vice-presidents 5. Essayists 6. Secretaries of the treasury 7. Presidents -- United States -- Election -- 1800 8. United States -- Politics and government -- 1783-1809

ISBN 978-0-7432-9316-7; 0-7432-9316-9

LC 2007-16017

The author "recreates the dramatic presidential race of 1800, which, Larson says, stamped American democracy with its distinctive partisan character as Republicans and Federalists battled for the presidency. . . . [This is] an invaluable study of a crucial chapter in the lives of the founding fathers—and of the nation." Publ Wkly

Includes bibliographical references

Schoen, Douglas E.

The power of the vote; electing presidents, overthrowing dictators, and promoting democracy around the world. William Morrow 2007 396p pa $25.95   **324**

1. Democratic Party (U.S.) 2. Political consultants 3. United States -- Politics and government

ISBN 978-0-06-123188-9; 0-06-123188-6

LC 2006-52877

The author presents an account of his work as a politcal strategist.

Includes bibliographical references

Traister, Rebecca

Big girls don't cry; the election that changed everything for American women. Free Press 2010 336p $26   **324**

1. Mayors 2. Lawyers 3. Feminism 4. Governors 5. Senators 6. Secretaries of state 7. Spouses of presidents 8. Hospital administrators 9. Presidential candidates 10. Women -- Political activity 11. Women in politics -- United States 12. Presidents -- United

States -- Election -- 2008
ISBN 978-1-4391-5028-3; 1-4391-5028-1

LC 2010-09631

This is "a passionate, visionary and very personal account of the cultural ferment that accompanied the election of '08." N Y Times Book Rev

Includes bibliographical references

324.1   International party organizations, auxiliaries, activities

Lichtblau, Eric

The **Nazis** next door; how America became a safe haven for Hitler's men. Eric Lichtblau. Houghton Mifflin Harcourt 2014 288 p. 8 plates; illustrations (hardback) $28   **324.1**
1. Cold war 2. American espionage 3. National socialists 4. Cold War 5. Espionage, American -- History -- 20th century 6. United States -- Foreign relations -- 1945-1989 7. Nazis -- United States -- History -- 20th century 8. Refugees -- United States -- History -- 20th century 9. United States -- Politics and government -- 1945-1989 10. War criminals -- United States -- History -- 20th century 11. Anti-communist movements -- United States -- History -- 20th century 12. United States. Central Intelligence Agency -- History -- 20th century 13. United States. Federal Bureau of Investigation -- History -- 20th century
ISBN 0547669194; 9780547669199

LC 2014023543

Written by Eric Lichtblau, this book describes how "thousands of Nazis--from concentration camp guards to high-level officers in the Third Reich--came to the United States after World War II and quietly settled into new lives. They had little trouble getting in. . . . The CIA, the FBI, and the military all put Hitler's minions to work as spies, intelligence assets, and leading scientists and engineers, whitewashing their histories." (Publisher's note)

"An essential read for all those interested in World War II, the Cold War, and 20th-century history." LJ

Includes bibliographical references and index

324.2   Political parties

McGerr, Michael E.

A **fierce** discontent; the rise and fall of the Progressive movement in America, 1870-1920. [by] Michael McGerr. Oxford University Press 2005 395p pa $19.95   **324.2**
1. Progressivism (United States politics)
ISBN 978-0-19-518365-8; 0-19-518365-7

LC 2004-30592

First published 2003 by the Free Press

The author "examines the social, cultural and political currents of a movement that, through its early successes and ultimate failure, has defined today's 'disappointing' political climate. . . . In three parts, McGerr illuminates the origins of Progressive thought, the movement's meteoric ascent in American life and its descent into 'the Red scare, race riots, strikes and inflation,' positing that the Progressive vision of

remaking America in its own middle-class image eventually sparked a backlash that persists to this day. . . . Simply put, this is history at its best." Publ Wkly

Includes bibliographical references

McGregor, Richard

The **Party**; the secret world of China's communist rulers. Harper 2010 302p il map   **324.2**
1. Communism -- China 2. Communist Party (China) 3. Economic policy -- China 4. China -- Politics and government
ISBN 9780061708770; 9780061998089

McGregor "examines China's Communist Party, with a focus on the large role it has played in the nation's competition with the United States." (Publisher's note) Index.

"An astute, well-crafted work that should be enormously useful in understanding China's role in the world." Kirkus

Includes bibliographical references

324.273   Parties founded or in existence after 1945

Gould, Lewis L.

★ **Grand** Old Party; a history of the Republicans. Random House 2003 597p il $35   **324.273**
1. Republican Party (U.S.)
ISBN 0-375-50741-8

LC 2003-46604

This is an "account of the Grand Old Party that spans its earliest days under Abraham Lincoln to its conservative bent today. Much of the book documents the shifts of its platform. . . . Gould also discusses the leadership qualities, farsighted policies, conservative federal spending, and willingness to provide social programs at the cost of future generations of four Republican presidents—Lincoln, Theodore Roosevelt, Eisenhower, and Reagan." Libr J

Includes bibliographical references

Lofgren, Mike

The **party** is over; how Republicans went crazy, Democrats became useless, and the middle class got shafted. Mike Lofgren. Viking 2012 p. cm. **324.273**
1. Democratic Party (U.S.) 2. Republican Party (U.S.) 3. United States -- Politics and government 4. Democratic Party (U.S.) -- History -- 20th century 5. Democratic Party (U.S.) -- History -- 21st century 6. Republican Party (U.S. : 1854-) -- History -- 20th century 7. Republican Party (U.S. : 1854-) -- History -- 21st century 8. Political parties -- United States -- History -- 20th century 9. Political parties -- United States -- History -- 21st century
ISBN 9780670026265

LC 2012014990

This New York Times bestselling book, by Mike Lofgren, criticizes 21st-century American politics. "There was a time, not so very long ago, when perfectly rational people ran the Republican Party. So how did the party of Lincoln become the party of lunatics? That is what this book aims to answer. Fear not, the [Democrats] come in for their share of tough talk--they are zombies, a party of the living dead." (Publisher's note)

Includes bibliographical references and index

324.6 Election systems and procedures; suffrage

Berman, Ari

★ **Give** us the ballot; the modern struggle for voting rights in America. Ari Berman. Farrar, Straus & Giroux 2015 384 p. (hardback) $27 **324.6**
1. Suffrage 2. Minorities -- Suffrage -- United States 3. United States. Voting Rights Act of 1965 4. Suffrage -- United States -- History -- 20th century 5. Suffrage -- United States -- History -- 21st century
ISBN 0374158274; 9780374158279; 9780374711498
LC 2015004989
National Book Critics Circle Award Finalist: Nonfiction (2015)

This book, by Ari Berman, focuses on "the Voting Rights Act (VRA) [of] 1965. . . . The act enfranchised millions of Americans and is widely regarded as the crowning achievement of the civil rights movement. And yet, fifty years later, we are still fighting heated battles over race, representation, and political power, with lawmakers devising new strategies to keep minorities out of the voting booth and with the Supreme Court declaring a key part of the Voting Rights Act unconstitutional." (Publisher's note)

"General readers will appreciate the panoramic survey of the cases in which the VRA has been challenged and defended in federal and state courts and legislatures, and the fair inclusion of voices from both sides of the arguments. A timely and needed addition to the voting rights debate." LJ

Includes bibliographical references (pages 315-351) and index

Congressional Quarterly, Inc.

★ **Presidential** elections 1789-2008. CQ Press 2010 295p il map pa $65 **324.6**
1. Presidents -- United States -- Election
ISBN 978-1-60426-541-5
LC 2009-40267
First published 1995 with title: Presidential elections, 1789-1992

This book offers information about the electoral college, electoral votes and popular votes in each presidential election, voter turnout, primary returns, and Democratic and Republican Party conventions.

Includes bibliographical references

Dudden, Faye E.

Fighting chance; the struggle over woman suffrage and Black suffrage in Reconstruction America. Oxford University Press 2011 287p il $34.95 **324.6**
1. Reconstruction (1865-1876) 2. Women -- Suffrage 3. African Americans -- Suffrage
ISBN 978-0-19-977263-6; 0-19-977263-0
LC 2010053188
"Likely to be a classic study, it is recommended for all readers in American studies and Reconstruction history." Libr J

Includes bibliographical references

Waldman, Michael

The **Fight** to Vote; by Michael Waldman. Simon & Schuster 2016 288 p. $28 **324.6**
1. Suffrage 2. United States -- Politics and government
ISBN 1501116487; 9781501116483
LC 2015030899

In this book, author Michael Waldman "takes a succinct and comprehensive look at a crucial American struggle: the drive to define and defend government based on 'the consent of the governed.' From the beginning, and at every step along the way, as Americans sought to right to vote, others have fought to stop them. This is the first book to trace the full story from the founders' debates to today's challenges." (Publisher's note)

"Waldman urges citizens to find a way to celebrate democracy and reinvigorate political engagement for all. A timely contribution to the discussion of a crucial issue." Kirkus

Includes bibliographical references (pages 285-353) and index

324.7 Conduct of election campaigns

Roberts, Robert North

Campaigning for president in America, 1788-2016; Scott John Hammond, Robert North Roberts, and Valerie A. Sulfaro. Greenwood 2016 xxxv, 954 p.p (hardback) $68 **324.7**
1. Presidents -- United States -- Election -- History 2. Presidential candidates -- United States -- History 3. Political campaigns -- United States -- History
ISBN 1440848904; 9781440848889; 9781440848902; 9781440850790
LC 2015046107
This book by Scott John Hammond, Robert North Roberts, and Valerie A. Sulfaro offers "readers insight into the major issues and events surrounding American presidential elections across more than two centuries, from the earliest years of the Republic through the campaigns of the 21st century. . . . [It] presents a chronological account of presidential campaigns that showcases the key personalities, issues, and campaign themes as they emerged in American political history." (Publisher's note)

"Both the topical and historical sections of this consistently objective and analytical encyclopedia-cum-history will reward readers who want to understand recurring and one-off phenomena in electoral history." Booklist

Includes bibliographical references (pages 881-898) and index

Vogel, Kenneth P.

Big money; 2.5 billion dollars, one suspicious vehicle, and a pimp-on the trail of the ultra-rich hijacking American politics. Kenneth P. Vogel. PublicAffairs 2014 304 p. (hardback) $27.99 **324.7**
1. Economic policy -- United States 2. United States -- Politics and government 3. Campaign funds -- United States 4. Citizens United -- Trials, litigation, etc 5. United States. Congress -- Elections -- Finance 6. Presidents -- United States -- Election -- Finance 7.

Campaign funds -- Law and legislation -- United States
ISBN 1610393384; 9781610393386

LC 2014004954

This book by Kenneth P. Vogel is a "tour of a new political world dramatically reordered by ever-larger flows of cash. From the casino magnate Sheldon Adelson to the bubbling nouveau cowboy Foster Friess; from the Texas trial lawyer couple, Amber and Steve Mostyn, to the micromanaging Hollywood executive Jeffrey Katzenberg--the multimillionaires and billionaires are swaggering up to the tables for the hottest new game in politics." (Publisher's note)

Includes bibliographical references and index

324.9 History and geographic treatment of elections

Halperin, Mark

★ **Double** Down; Game Change 2012. Mark Halperin, John Heilemann. Penguin Group USA 2013 499 p. ill. (hardback) $29.95 **324.9**
1. Presidents -- United States -- Election -- 2012 2. Presidential candidates -- United States 3. United States -- Politics and government -- 2009- 4. Political campaigns -- United States -- History -- 21st century
ISBN 1594204403; 9781594204401

LC 2013431166

This book by Mark Halperin and John Heileman chronicles the 2012 U.S. Presidential election. "Their focus is always on the candidates with the most buzz among not just voters, but the Washington, D.C., cognoscenti." Candidates profiled include Barack Obama, Mitt Romney, Jon Huntsman, Newt Gingrich, and Chris Christie. (Kirkus Reviews)

"The well-connected authors have worked their sources thoroughly to give readers a warts-and-all look at what went on behind the scenes." Booklist

Karabell, Zachary

The **last** campaign; how Harry Truman won the 1948 election. Knopf 2000 308p hardcover o.p. pa $14 **324.9**
1. Governors 2. Presidents 3. Vice-presidents 4. Senators 5. District attorneys 6. Presidential candidates 7. Presidents -- United States -- Election -- 1948
ISBN 0-375-70077-3 pa

LC 99-28567

This is an account of the presidential campaign which pitted Truman against Dewey.

"The author is strongest discussing the impact of the press, polls, and radio and describing the importance of the convention, which was then 'a mix of high politics, low politics and entertainment.'" Libr J

Includes bibliographical references

Morris, Roy

Fraud of the century; Rutherford B. Hayes, Samuel Tilden, and the stolen election of 1876. {by} Roy Morris, Jr. Simon & Schuster 2003 311p il hardcover o.p. pa $14 **324.9**
1. Lawyers 2. Generals 3. Governors 4. Presidents 5. Political corruption 6. Political leaders 7. Presidential

candidates 8. Presidents -- United States -- Election
ISBN 0-7432-2386-1; 978-0-7432-5552-3; 0-7432-5552-6 pa

LC 2002-36507

"Morris has an eye for detail and a lively writing style that make this highly detailed, first-rate work of history read more like a whodunnit than a historical examination." Libr J

Includes bibliographical references (p. 287-296) and index

Popkin, Samuel L.

The **candidate**; what it takes to win, and hold the White House. Samuel L. Popkin. Oxford University Press 2012 viii, 350 p.p (hardcover) $27.95 **324.9**
1. Presidents -- United States -- Election 2. Presidential candidates -- United States 3. Presidents -- United States -- Election -- History 4. Presidential candidates -- United States -- History 5. Presidential candidates -- United States -- Case studies
ISBN 9780199922079

LC 2012006845

In this book, Samuel L. Popkin "analyzes what it takes to win [a political] campaign. . . . Based on detailed analyses of the winners--and losers--of the last 60 years of presidential campaigns, Popkin explains how challengers get to the White House, how incumbents stay there for a second term, and how successors hold power for their party." (Publisher's note)

Includes bibliographical references and index

325 International migration and colonization

Cannato, Vincent J.

American passage; the history of Ellis Island. [by] Vincent J. Cannato. Harper 2009 487p il $27.99 **325**
1. Immigrants -- United States 2. Ellis Island (N.J. and N.Y.) 3. Ellis Island Immigration Station 4. Immigrants -- United States -- History 5. United States -- Immigration and emigration 6. United States -- Emigration and immigration -- History
ISBN 978-0-06-074273-7; 0-06-074273-9

LC 2008-52245

"The author reaches back to the island's beginnings in the early 19th century, when, then named Gibbet Island, it served as a venue for hanging convicted pirates. Cannato then chronicles the many different people—immigrants, immigration officials, politicians and others—who made Ellis Island what it was in the early 20th century. . . . Ambitious in scope and rooted in solid storytelling." Kirkus

Includes bibliographical references

Handlin, Oscar

The **uprooted**; 2nd ed; Little, Brown 1973 333p hardcover o.p. pa $18.99 **325**
1. Acculturation 2. United States -- Immigration and emigration
ISBN 0-316-34313-7 pa

First published 1951

This account of the American immigrant experience and the acculturation process describes employment, religion, ghetto life, benevolent societies, boss politics, family life, and social alienation

Truax, Eileen

Dreamers; an immigrant generation's fight for their American dream. Eileen Truax. Beacon Press 2015 224 p. (paperback) $15   325

    1. Unauthorized immigrants 2. Immigrants -- United States 3. Illegal aliens -- Education (Higher) -- United States 4. Illegal alien children -- Government policy -- United States 5. United States -- Emigration and immigration -- Social aspects 6. Children of illegal aliens -- Education -- Law and legislation -- United States

    ISBN 9780807030332; 0807030333

                    LC 2014031771

This book by Eileen Truax describes how, "in the face of congressional inertia and furious opposition from some, the DREAM Act has yet to be passed. But recently, this young generation has begun organizing, and with their rallying cry 'Undocumented, Unapologetic, and Unafraid' they are the newest face of the human rights movement." (Publisher's note)

"Immigration buffs and ethnic studies aficionados will not be disappointed. Truax's informative, engaging read provides a new perspective on this country's ongoing immigration debate." LJ

Includes bibliographical references

Urrea, Luis Alberto

★ **The devil's** highway; a true story. Luis Alberto Urrea. Little, Brown 2004 xii, 239p (pbk.) $13.99   325

    1. Unauthorized immigrants 2. Mexico -- Immigration and emigration 3. United States -- Immigration and emigration 4. Illegal aliens -- Crimes against -- Mexican-American Border Region

    ISBN 9780316746717; 9780316010801

                    LC 2003058930

"In May 2001, 26 Mexican men scrambled across the border and into an area of the Arizona desert known as the Devil's Highway. Only 12 made it safely across. . . . In artful yet uncomplicated prose, Urrea captivatingly tells how a dozen men squeezed by to safety, and how 14 others whom the media labeled the Yuma 14 did not. But while many point to the group's smugglers (known as coyotes) as the prime villains of the tragedy, Urrea unloads on, in the words of one Mexican consul, 'the politics of stupidity that rules both sides of the border.'" (Publishers Weekly)

Yans-McLaughlin, Virginia

Ellis Island and the peopling of America; the official guide. [by] Virginia Yans-McLaughlin and Marjorie Lightman, with the Statue of Liberty-Ellis Island Foundation. New Press (NY) 1997 209p il maps pa $19.95; $28.95   325

    1. Ellis Island Immigration Station 2. United States -- Immigration and emigration

    ISBN 1-56584-364-9; 9781439504628

                    LC 96-54713

Photographs, time lines, charts and historical documents from the Ellis Island Museum accompany a text that places immigration policy in its historical context.

326   Slavery and emancipation

Berlin, Ira

Generations of captivity; a history of African-American slaves. Belknap Press 2003 374p maps $29.95; pa $16.95   326

    1. Slavery -- United States

    ISBN 0-674-01061-2; 0-674-01624-6 pa

                    LC 2002-28142

"Berlin has given us a moving, insightful account of slavery in the United States. Readers will not soon forget the story he has told, nor should they." N Y Times Book Rev

Includes bibliographical references

Blight, David W.

A slave no more; two men who escaped to freedom: including their own narratives of emancipation. Harcourt 2007 307p il map   326

    1. Slaves 2. Diarists 3. Slavery -- United States 4. African Americans -- Biography

    ISBN 978-0-15-101232-9; 0-15-101232-6

                    LC 2007-14467

"Required reading for scholars or even casual students, this signal [sic] contribution is essential for any collection on slavery, emancipation, or African American or U.S. history and literature." Libr J

Includes bibliographical references

Douglass, Frederick, 1818-1895

★ **Frederick** Douglass: selected speeches and writings; edited by Philip S. Foner; abridged and adapted by Yuval Taylor. Hill Bks. 1999 789p hardcover o.p. pa $32.95   326

    1. Speeches, addresses, etc., American 2. African Americans -- Civil rights -- History -- 19th century 3. Slaves -- United States -- Social conditions -- 19th century 4. Antislavery movements -- United States -- History -- 19th century

    ISBN 1-55652-352-1 pa

                    LC 99-23180

Based on Foner's five-volume The life and writings of Frederick Douglass (1950-1975), this volume "covers Douglass' speeches and writings over a 54-year period. The breadth and depth of his focus and concerns reflected in more than 2,000 speeches, editorials, articles, and letters provide a wellspring of knowledge about the man and his intellect." Booklist

Includes bibliographical references

Hochschild, Adam

★ **Bury** the chains; prophets, slaves, and rebels in the first human rights crusade. Houghton Mifflin 2005 468p il $26.95   326

    1. Slavery

    ISBN 0-618-10469-0

                    LC 2004-54091

The author "brings drama and incredible research to this thrilling look at the little-celebrated abolition movement in Britain and its reverberations throughout modern democracies." Booklist

Includes bibliographical references

Horton, James Oliver

★ **Slavery** and the making of America; [by] James Oliver Horton [and] Lois E. Horton. Oxford University Press 2004 254p il maps $35; pa $18.95 **326**

1. Slavery -- United States 2. African Americans -- History

ISBN 0-19-517903-X; 0-19-530451-9 pa

LC 2004-13617

"The oft-told tale is made fresh through up-to-date slavery scholarship, the extensive use of slave narratives and archival photos and, especially, a focus on individual experience." Publ Wkly

Johnson, Walter

Soul by soul; life inside the antebellum slave market. Harvard Univ. Press 1999 283p il $28.50; pa $15.95 **326**

1. Slave trade 2. Slavery -- United States 3. New Orleans (La.) -- Race relations

ISBN 0-674-82148-3; 0-674-00539-2 pa

LC 99-46696

This is an examination of the antebellum slave market. "Using slave narratives, court records, planters' letters, and more, Johnson enters the slave pens and showrooms of the New Orleans slave market to observe how slavery turned men and women into merchandise and how slaves resisted such efforts to steal their humanity." Libr J

Includes bibliographical references

Jordan, Don

White cargo; the forgotten history of Britain's white slaves in America. [by] Don Jordan and Michael Walsh. New York University Press 2008 320p il map hardcover o.p. pa $20 **326**

1. Contract labor 2. Slavery -- History 3. Great Britain -- Social conditions 4. United States -- History -- 1600-1775, Colonial period

ISBN 978-0-8147-4272-3; 0-8147-4296-3; 978-0-8147-4296-9 pa; 0-8147-4296-3 pa

LC 2007-37976

First published 2007 in the United Kingdom

This "is a colorful series of portraits of villains and victims, exploiters and exploited, rendered with bemused outrage." Choice

Includes bibliographical references

Rediker, Marcus

★ The **Amistad** rebellion; an Atlantic odyssey of slavery and freedom. Marcus Rediker. Viking 2012 288 p. $27.95 **326**

1. Slave trade 2. Slave revolts 3. Slavery -- United States 4. Amistad (Schooner) 5. Slave trade -- America -- History 6. Slave insurrections -- United States 7. Antislavery movements -- United States 8. Sierra Leoneans -- United States -- History -- 19th century

ISBN 0670025046; 9780670025046

LC 2012014810

In this book, Marcus Rediker "reframes the story [of the Spanish slave schooner Armistad] to show how a small group of courageous men fought and won an epic battle against Spanish and American slaveholders and their governments. He reaches back to Africa to find the rebels' roots, narrates their cataclysmic transatlantic journey, and unfolds a prison story . . . featuring . . . portraits of the Africans, their captors, and their abolitionist allies." (Publisher's note)

Includes bibliographical references and index

Remembering slavery; African Americans talk about their personal experiences of slavery and emancipation. edited by Ira Berlin, Marc Favreau, and Steven F. Miller. New Press (NY) 1998 355p hardcover o.p. pa $16.95 **326**

1. Slavery -- United States 2. African Americans -- History -- Sources

ISBN 1-56584-587-0 pa

This "book-and-tapes collection of slave narratives, drawn from slave narratives and audio recordings of former slaves collected by the Federal Writers' Project (FWP) during the 1930s and 1940s (some of which have been remastered and included in two 60-minute cassettes with the book), brings slavery to life as few recent books have done." Libr J

Includes bibliographical references

White, Shane

★ The **sounds** of slavery; discovering African American history through songs, sermons, and speech. [by] Shane White and Graham White. Beacon Press 2005 xxii, 241p hardcover o.p. pa $17 **326**

1. Plantation life 2. Slavery -- United States 3. African Americans -- History

ISBN 0-8070-5026-1; 0-8070-5027-X pa

LC 2004-21447

"Drawing on WPA interviews with former slaves, slave narratives, and other historical documents from the 1700s through the 1850s, the authors provide the context for the field calls, work songs, sermons, and other sounds and utterances of slaves on American plantations. The authors also focus on recollections of the wails of slaves being whipped, the barking of hounds hunting down runaways, and the keening of women losing their children to the slave block. The combination of the CD and the book brings vibrancy and texture to a complex history that has been long neglected." Booklist

Includes discography and bibliographical references

Wills, Garry

'**Negro** president' Jefferson and the slave power. Houghton Mifflin 2003 274p il $25; pa $14 **326**

1. Architects 2. Presidents 3. Vice-presidents 4. Essayists 5. Slavery -- United States 6. United States -- Politics and government -- 1783-1865

ISBN 0-618-34398-9; 0-618-48537-6 pa

LC 2003-56710

"Wills makes a valuable contribution to our understanding of Jefferson and the new American nation." Choice

Includes bibliographical references

326.8 Emancipation

Berlin, Ira

The **long** emancipation; the demise of slavery in the United States. Ira Berlin. Harvard University Press 2015 240 p. (The Nathan I. Huggins lectures) (alk. paper) $22.95; (ebook) $28.95   **326.8**

1. Slaves -- Emancipation -- United States 2. African American abolitionists -- History 3. Antislavery movements -- United States -- History

ISBN 9780674286085; 9780674495487

LC 2015005604

In this book, author Ira Berlin "draws upon decades of study to offer a framework for understanding slavery's demise in the United States. Freedom was not achieved in a moment, and emancipation was not an occasion but a near-century-long process—a shifting but persistent struggle that involved thousands of men and women." (Publisher's note)

"This summary analysis of emancipation should be on the shelves of all public library history and social science collections." Booklist

Includes bibliographical references and index

327 International relations

Burk, Kathleen

Old world, new world; Great Britain and America from the beginning. Atlantic Monthly Press 2008 830p il map $35   **327**

1. Great Britain -- Foreign relations -- United States 2. United States -- Foreign relations -- Great Britain

ISBN 978-0-87113-971-9

First published 2007 in the United Kingdom

This is "the most reliable, lucidly narrated and generous history of the mutual entanglement of Britain and America we are likely to have for some time." Times Lit Suppl

Includes bibliographical references

Crist, David

★ The **twilight** war; the secret history of America's thirty-year conflict with Iran. David Crist. Penguin Press 2012 638 p., [16] p. of platesp ill., maps $36.00   **327**

1. Iran -- History -- 1979- 2. Iran -- Politics and government 3. United States -- Foreign relations -- Iran 4. United States -- Politics and government -- 1945- 5. Espionage, Iranian -- History 6. Espionage, American -- History 7. Iran -- Foreign relations -- United States 8. United States. Central Intelligence Agency 9. Iran -- Military relations -- United States 10. United States -- Foreign relations -- 1989- 11. United States -- Military relations -- Iran 12. United States -- Foreign relations -- 1981-1989

ISBN 1594203415; 9781594203411

LC 2011050573

This book by David Crist presents an "account of American-Iranian hostilities since the 1979 revolution. . . . Crist makes the case that the United States is already enmeshed in a hidden war with Iran that has raged unacknowledged for decades. This shadow war is characterized by espionage, assassination plots, and frequent eruptions of open hostilities, and exacerbated by egregious missteps and blunders by both sides." (Publishers Weekly)

Includes bibliographical references (p. [576]-623) and index

Feingold, Russ, 1953-

While America sleeps; Russ Feingold. Crown Publishers 2011 viii, 304 p col. ill., maps   **327**

1. International relations 2. United States -- Foreign relations 3. September 11 terrorist attacks, 2001 4. United States -- Politics and government 5. September 11 Terrorist Attacks, 2001 -- Influence 6. Political culture -- United States -- History -- 21st century 7. Progressivism (United States politics) -- History -- 21st century 8. Terrorism -- Government policy -- United States -- History -- 21st century

ISBN 9780307952523; 9780307952547

LC 2011051735

In this book, former U.S. Senator Russ "Feingold revisits the U.S. reaction in the wake of the [September 2001 terrorist] attacks, which set off an 'unfortunate trend' in soured international relations that is only presently being arrested under President Obama. While Feingold graciously allows former President Bush accolades for his initial words of resolve and restraint after 9/11, he grew increasingly alarmed by the hysterical fear gripping Washington, and cast the lone vote against the Patriot Act. . . . In the post-9/11 Risk game, as he calls it, Feingold urged the government not to lose sight of other important strategic spots like Yemen, Indonesia and Somalia. . . . [H]e first urged the troop withdrawal from Iraq in 2005. . . . He has been a vocal proponent for 'restoring the rule of law' to the presidency and of Obama's health-care legislation." (Kirkus)

Includes bibliographical references and index

Gaddis, John Lewis, 1941-

George F. Kennan; An American Life. John Lewis Gaddis. Penguin Press 2011 xi, 784p.p 16 p. of plates   **327**

1. Cold war 2. Diplomats 3. Historians 4. World Politics -- 1945-1989 5. Cold War -- Diplomatic history 6. United States -- Foreign Relations 7. Ambassadors -- United States -- Biography

ISBN 1594203121; 9781594203121

LC 2011021786

Pulitzer Prize: Biography or Autobiography (2012)

National Book Critics Circle Award: Biography (2011)

The book presents a biography of U.S. statesman George F. Kennan, which the author composed using "Kennan's . . . diary, . . . the 300-plus boxes of other papers by Kennan now open for research at Princeton, . . . interviews with the former diplomat and his associates, . . . [and] family papers still in the possession of Kennan's daughter." The author "sides largely with Kennan's critics . . . in the heated debate over Kennan's advocacy in 1957-1958 for US 'disengagement' from the cold war in Europe." (New York Review of Books)

Includes bibliographical references and index.

Gates, Robert Michael, 1943-

From the shadows; the ultimate insider's story of five presidents and how they won the Cold War. Simon & Schuster 1996 604p il hardcover o.p. pa $16   **327**

1. Cold war 2. Cold War 3. Soviet Union -- Foreign relations -- United States 4. United States -- Foreign relations -- Soviet Union

ISBN 0-684-83497-9 pa

LC 95-51704

This book on U.S. politics during the Cold War details author Robert Gates' "career in the Central Intelligence Agency, where he rose from his entry-level job as a Soviet analyst in 1969 to become director in 1991 lays out his insider's view of the agency's role in the collapse of the Soviet Union. He defends himself against charges that his CIA overestimated Soviet military power and the threat it posed." (Commonweal)

This is an "often entertaining, frequently self-serving but always thoughtful account of the United States' long effort to contain the Soviet Union." N Y Times Book Rev

Includes bibliographical references

Herring, George C., 1936-

From colony to superpower; U.S. foreign relations since 1776. Oxford University Press 2008 1035p il map (Oxford history of the United States) $35; pa. $24.95   **327**

1. United States -- Foreign relations

ISBN 978-0-19-507822-0; 0-19-507822-5; 9780199765539

LC 2008-07996

The author "recaptures a quarter-millennium of American foreign policy with fluidity and felicity." N Y Times Book Rev

Includes bibliographical references (p. 965-995)

Jacques, Martin

When China rules the world; the end of the western world and the birth of a new global order. Penguin Press 2009 xxv, 550p il map $29.95   **327**

1. Globalization 2. Forecasting 3. China -- History 4. China -- Foreign relations 5. China -- Economic conditions 6. China -- Foreign economic relations

ISBN 1-59420-185-4; 978-1-59420-185-1

LC 2009-27298

The author contends "that we are moving into an era of contested modernity. The central player in this new world will be China. . . . Although clearly influenced by the west, its extraordinary size and history mean that it will remain highly distinct, and as it exercises its rapidly growing power it will change much more than the world's geopolitics. The nation-state as we understand it will no longer be globally dominant, and the Westphalian state-system will be transformed; ideas of race will be redrawn." (Publisher's note)

This "comprehensive and richly detailed analysis will be an indispensable resource for anyone who wants to understand contemporary China." New Statesman

Includes bibliographical references

Kaplan, Robert D., 1952-

Monsoon; the Indian Ocean and the future of American power. Random House 2010 366p map $28   **327**

1. National security -- United States 2. Indian Ocean region -- Strategic aspects 3. National security -- Indian Ocean region 4. Indian Ocean region -- Foreign relations -- United States 5. United States -- Foreign relations -- Indian Ocean region

ISBN 1-4000-6746-4; 978-1-4000-6746-6

LC 2009-49752

This is an "examination of the Indian Ocean region and the countries known as 'Monsoon Asia.'" (Publisher's note) Glossary. Index.

"The book's political and economic focus and forecasts are smart and brim with apercus on the intersection of power, politics, and resource consumption (especially water), and give full weight to the impact of colonialism. An ambitious and prescient study equally at ease analyzing the work of the Indian poet Rabindranath Tagore, the finer points of the Indian state of Gujarat's flirtation with fascism, and the economic impact of the Asian tsunami on Indonesia." Publ Wkly

Includes bibliographical references

Kinzer, Stephen

All the Shah's men; an American coup and the roots of Middle East terror. John Wiley & Sons 2003 258p il map hardcover o.p. pa $14.95   **327**

1. Prime ministers 2. Iran -- Politics and government 3. United States -- Foreign relations -- Iran

ISBN 0-471-26517-9; 0-471-67878-3 pa

LC 2003-9968

"This comprehensive . . . account of the nationalization of the Anglo-Iranian Oil Company under the leadership of Mohammad Mossadegh in 1951 . . . is a valuable and informative work." Choice

Includes bibliographical references

Kissinger, Henry, 1923-

World Order; Henry Kissinger. Penguin Group USA Penguin Press 2014 384 p. maps $36   **327**

1. World politics 2. International relations 3. Geopolitics 4. Security, International 5. World politics -- 21st century

ISBN 1594206147; 9781594206146

LC 2014028152

Author Henry Kissinger offers "a deep meditation on the roots of international harmony and global disorder. Drawing on his experience as one of the foremost statesmen of the modern era . . . . Kissinger now reveals his analysis of the ultimate challenge for the twenty-first century: how to build a shared international order in a world of divergent historical perspectives, violent conflict, proliferating technology, and ideological extremism." (Publisher's note)

"Critics are unlikely to find much interest in this volume as it largely summarizes Kissinger's thinking, but students and historians of political science may appreciate his suggestion that both realism and idealism are necessary in modern times." LJ

Includes bibliographical references (pages 379-403) and index

Moynihan, Daniel Patrick

On the law of nations. Harvard Univ. Press 1990 211p $37; pa $10.95 **327**

1. International law 2. United States -- Foreign relations

ISBN 0-674-63575-2; 0-674-63576-0 pa

LC 90-33227

"In the seven essays in this volume, Moynihan traces U.S. attitudes toward international law from the American Revolution to the current administration, and he makes a powerful argument for a return to the conventions of international behavior set out by Woodrow Wilson and the United Nations." Libr J

Toumani, Meline

There was and there was not; a journey through hate and possibility in Turkey, Armenia, and beyond. Meline Toumani. Metropolitan Books/Henry Holt and Company 2014 304 p. map (hardback) $28 **327**

1. Ethnicity 2. Social change 3. Armenian Americans 4. Turkey -- Foreign relations 5. Armenian massacres, 1915-1923 6. Social change -- Turkey 7. Armenia -- Relations -- Turkey 8. Turkey -- Relations -- Armenia 9. Turkey -- Social conditions -- 1960- 10. Armenian Americans -- Ethnic identity 11. Armenian massacres, 1915-1923 -- Influence 12. Genocide -- Armenia -- Psychological aspects

ISBN 0805097627; 9780805097627

LC 2014018362

In this memoir, "young Armenian-American . . . Meline Toumani grew up in a close-knit Armenian community in New Jersey where Turkish restaurants were shunned and products made in Turkey were boycotted. The source of this enmity was the Armenian genocide of 1915 at the hands of the Ottoman Turkish government, and Turkey's refusal to acknowledge it. . . . Frustrated by her community's all-consuming campaigns for genocide recognition, Toumani . . . moves to Istanbul." (Publisher's note)

"This remarkable memoir serves as a moving examination of the complex forces of ethnicity, nationality and history that shape one's sense of self and foster, threaten or fray the fragile tapestry of community." Kirkus

Tuchman, Barbara Wertheim

★ Stilwell and the American experience in China, 1911-45; [by] Barbara W. Tuchman. Grove Press 2001 621p map pa $20 **327**

1. Generals 2. Presidents 3. Sino-Japanese Conflict, 1937-1945 4. World War, 1939-1945 -- China 5. China -- Foreign relations -- United States 6. United States -- Foreign relations -- China

ISBN 0-8021-3852-7; 978-0-8021-3852-1

LC 2001-40154

First published 1970 by Macmillian

Using the career of General "Vinegar Joe" Stilwell as a vehicle, this is a history of America's relations with China from the end of the Manchu Empire to the rise of Mao Tse-tung.

Includes bibliographical references

Westad, Odd Arne

Restless empire; China and the world since 1750. Odd Arne Westad. Basic Books 2012 ix, 515 p.p maps **327**

1. China -- Foreign relations -- History 2. China -- Foreign relations -- 1949- 3. China -- Foreign relations -- 1644-1912 4. China -- Foreign relations -- 1912-1949

ISBN 0465019331; 9780465019335; 9780465029365

LC 2012021635

This book by Odd Arne Westad "traces China's complex foreign affairs over the past 250 years, identifying the forces that will determine the country's path in the decades to come. . . . Since the height of the Qing Empire in the eighteenth century, China's interactions--and confrontations--with foreign powers have caused its worldview to fluctuate wildly between extremes of dominance and subjugation, emulation and defiance." (Publisher's note)

Includes bibliographical references (p. 479-499) and index

327.1 Foreign policy and specific topics in international relations

Brzezinski, Zbigniew, 1928-

Strategic vision; America and the crisis of global power. Zbigniew Brzezinski. Basic Books 2012 viii, 208 p.p (hbk.) $26 **327.1**

1. Economic development 2. World politics -- 1991- 3. Balance of power -- Forecasting 4. World politics -- 21st century -- Forecasting 5. Geopolitics -- History -- 21st century -- Forecasting 6. International relations -- History -- 21st century -- Forecasting 7. United States -- Foreign relations -- 21st century -- Forecasting

ISBN 046502954X; 0465029558; 9780465029549; 9780465029556

LC 2011033312

This book, by Zbigniew Brzezinski, "argues that without an America that is economically vital, socially appealing, responsibly powerful, and capable of sustaining an intelligent foreign engagement, the geopolitical prospects for the West could become increasingly grave. The ongoing changes in the distribution of global power and mounting global strife make it all the more essential that America does not retreat into an ignorant garrison-state mentality or wallow in cultural hedonism." (Publisher's note)

"Jimmy Carter's national security advisor offers an astute, elegant appraisal of the waning of America's "global appeal" and the severe consequences of the shifting of power from West to East." Kirkus

Includes bibliographical references (p. 195-196) and index

Schlesinger, Arthur M. (Arthur Meier), 1917-2007

★ War and the American presidency; [by] Arthur M. Schlesinger, Jr. W. W. Norton 2004 160p **327.1**

1. Iraq War, 2003-2011 2. Governors 3. Presidents 4. Iraq War, 2003 5. Iraq War, 2003- 6. Baseball executives 7. Children of presidents 8. Democracy -- United States 9. Energy industry executives 10. United States -- Foreign relations 11. War and emergency

powers -- United States

ISBN 0393060020; 0393327698

LC 200409872

This book by Arthur M. Schlesinger Jr. "offers a 21st-century . . . examination of the revolution in foreign policy that defines the US response to the terrorist attacks of 2001. Schlesinger places the Bush Doctrine and the war against Iraq in historical context, tracing the evolution of presidential power and US national security doctrine from the early presidencies to the Bush presidency." (Choice: Current Reviews for Academic Libraries)

This book "explores the war in Iraq, the presidency, and the future of democracy." Publisher's note

327.12   Espionage and subversion

Andrew, Christopher M.

Defend the realm; the authorized history of MI5. [by] Christopher Andrew. Alfred A. Knopf 2009 xxii, 1032p il $40   **327.12**

1. Great Britain -- MI5 2. Intelligence service -- Great Britain

ISBN 978-0-307-26363-6; 0-307-26363-0

LC 2009-25463

"This unique publication is definitive and fascinating. Definitive because, after decades of ill-informed or partial accounts this book fully defines and describes its subject; no future writer can ignore it. Fascinating because the fluent clarity of Andrew's narrative, his eye for colourful individual detail and the sheer interest of his subjects. . . . This book is essential reading for anyone with even the slightest interest in intelligence in the modern period." Spectator

Includes bibliographical references

Bamford, James

The **shadow** factory; the ultra-secret NSA from 9/11 to the eavesdropping on America. Doubleday 2008 395p $27.95   **327.12**

1. Intelligence service 2. Electronic surveillance 3. United States -- National Security Agency 4. United States -- Politics and government -- 2001-

ISBN 978-0-385-52132-1; 0-385-52132-4

LC 2008-26448

The book is "full of technical details and insider politics for those who follow such things, but Bamford's overarching theme is the grand scale of the threat to privacy." San Francisco Chron

Includes bibliographical references

Dorril, Stephen

MI6; inside the covert world of Her Majesty's secret intelligence service. Free Press 2000 907p $40; pa $22   **327.12**

1. Great Britain -- MI6 2. Intelligence service -- Great Britain

ISBN 0-7432-0379-8; 0-7432-1778-0 pa

LC 00-29385

This study of the British secret intelligence service "focuses on the years since World War II, when MI6 was dedicated to winning the cold war. . . . The book is invalu-able for readers who want to separate spy fact from spy fiction." Booklist

Garton-Ash, Timothy

The **file**; a personal history. Random House 1997 262p hardcover o.p. pa $14   **327.12**

1. Authors 2. Essayists 3. Historians 4. Nonfiction writers 5. Secret service -- Germany (East) 6. Intelligence service -- Germany (East) 7. Germany (East) -- Ministerium für Staatssicherheit

ISBN 0-679-77785-7 pa

"For much of 1980, while working on a doctorate in history, Garton Ash lived in East Berlin. . . . He became an object of interest to East Germany's . . . secret police known by the acronym Stasi. In The File, Garton Ash, now 42, tries to reconstruct that year . . . by comparing his private notes from the period with what he found in Stasi's newly opened records. Going further, he located and interviewed some of the informers and bureaucrats who had spied on him." (Time)

"The author went to Berlin to study in 1978 and soon came under the scrutiny of the Stasi, the notorious East German secret police. In 1993, Garton Ash had the opportunity to examine the secret file kept on him. Comparing the file reports with his private diary of the time, he finds distortions, fabrications, and surprising omissions in the file. . . . This work makes an important contribution to the literature of the new Europe." Libr J

Greenwald, Glenn, 1967-

★ **No** place to hide; Edward Snowden, the NSA, and the U.S. surveillance state. Glenn Greenwald. Henry Holt & Co. 2014 320 p. illustrations (hardcover) $27   **327.12**

1. Whistle blowing 2. Intelligence service -- United States

ISBN 162779073X; 9781627790734; 9781627790741

LC 2014932888

This book tells how "In May 2013, [author] Glenn Greenwald set out for Hong Kong to meet an anonymous source who claimed to have astonishing evidence of pervasive government spying. . . . That source turned out to be the 29-year-old NSA contractor Edward Snowden, and his revelations about the agency's widespread, systemic overreach proved to be some of the most explosive and consequential news in recent history." (Publisher's note)

"In his analysis, the author breaks down the dense NSA subject matter and uses excerpts and slides from the documents to illustrate his points, making this work readable for even those unfamiliar with the technical concepts." LJ

Includes bibliographical references and index

Gup, Ted

Book of honor; covert lives and classified deaths at the CIA. Doubleday 2000 390p il hardcover o.p. pa $15   **327.12**

1. Spies 2. United States -- Central Intelligence Agency

ISBN 0-385-49541-2 pa

LC 99-89017

This exposé "reveals the names—and personal stories—of some three dozen CIA agents who died in the line of duty and whose identities have been kept secret—sometimes for decades. . . . Gup's sleuthing is a remarkable coup, full of high-level intrigue, cover-ups and drama." Publ Wkly

Hayes, Paddy

Queen of Spies; Daphne Park, Britain's Cold War Spy Master. by Paddy Hayes. Overlook Press 2016 336 p. illustrations, portraits (ebook) $50; $29.95   **327.12**
1. Intelligence service -- Great Britain
ISBN 9781468313253; 1468312685; 9781468312683
LC 2015039895

This book, by Paddy Hayes, "recounts the . . . story of the evolution of the British Secret Intelligence Service (SIS) from World War II to the Cold War through the eyes of Daphne Park, one of its outstanding and most unusual operatives. He provides the reader with one of the most intimate narratives yet of how the modern SIS actually went about its business, . . . and shows how Park was able to rise through the ranks of a field that had been comprised almost entirely of men." (Publisher's note)

"She was forthright and obdurate, and she had an infectious sense of humor. Most importantly, she personified the qualities required: loyalty, respect, tradition, and absolute secrecy. As exciting as any good spy thriller—but it's all true." Kirkus

Includes bibliographical references and index.

Haynes, John Earl

Spies; the rise and fall of the KGB in America. [by] John Earl Haynes, Harvey Klehr, and Alexander Vassiliev; with translations by Philip Redko and Steven Shabad. Yale University Press 2009 liii, 650p il $35; pa $24   **327.12**
1. Spies 2. Russian espionage 3. KGB
ISBN 978-0-300-12390-6; 0-300-12390-6; 978-0-300-16438-1 pa; 0-300-16438-6 pa
LC 2008-45628

This history of Soviet espionage in the United States "offers a remarkable portrait of the KGB's efforts—drawn largely from the KGB's own files. This achievement is possible only because Alexander Vassiliev, a former KGB agent, was allowed extensive access to the raw espionage files for two years in the mid-1990s. . . . Spies is chockablock with poignant individual tales." Newsweek

Includes bibliographical references

Venona; decoding Soviet espionage in America. [by] John Earl Haynes and Harvey Klehr. Yale Univ. Press 1999 487p $35; pa $14.95   **327.12**
1. Lawyers 2. Diplomats 3. Russian espionage 4. Communist Party (U.S.) 5. Communism -- United States
ISBN 0-300-07771-8; 0-300-08462-5 pa
LC 98-51464

"The Venona Project, a U.S. secret revealed only in 1995, decrypted Soviet intelligence's wartime cable traffic. . . . The authors systematically recount Venona's references to approximately 350 Soviet spies in U.S. government and industry—some of them highly placed, most notoriously Alger Hiss. . . . Venona may open a fundamental revision of U.S. history." Booklist

Hemming, Henry

The **ingenious** Mr. Pyke; inventor, fugitive, spy. Henry Hemming. PublicAffairs 2015 512 p. illustrations (hardcover) $26.99   **327.12**
1. Inventors
ISBN 1610395778; 9781610395779; 9781610395786
LC 2014952648

This book presents a biography of Geoffrey Pyke, who "audaciously planned to enter Germany in 1914 to get the scoop as a war correspondent for the British newspaper Daily Chronicle. He successfully sneaked in, was imprisoned, escaped with a spy, and had a heart attack, but made it back to England . . . While Pyke did not graduate from college, this never hindered his copious writing and inventing; his creations caught the imagination of Winston Churchill and the British military." (Library Journal)

"Those fond of biographies and 20th-century European war tales told in a modern vein will enjoy this book." LJ

Herrington, Stuart A.

Traitors among us; inside the spy catcher's world. Harcourt 2000 409p il pa $14   **327.12**
1. Spies 2. Soldiers 3. Russian espionage 4. Berlin (Germany) 5. Intelligence service -- United States
ISBN 0-15-601117-4
LC 00-38893

First published 1999 by Presidio Press

"Herrington, former head of the U.S. Army Counterintelligence Unit . . . offers a fascinating view of life as a spy catcher in West Berlin during the height of the Cold War. His description of the search for and capture of Clyde Conrad and James Hall . . . (who for 13 years handed over America's secret war plans to the Soviets) surpasses any spy fiction." Libr J

Hoffman, David E., 1953-

The **Billion** Dollar Spy; A True Story of Cold War Espionage and Betrayal. by David E. Hoffman. Random House Inc 2015 352 p. illustrations, map $28.95   **327.12**
1. Cold war 2. Espionage 3. Soviet Union 4. Intelligence service
ISBN 0385537603; 9780385537605
LC 2015003370

In this book, by David E. Hoffman, "it was the height of the Cold War, and a dangerous time to be stationed in the Soviet Union. One evening, while the chief of the CIA's Moscow station was filling his gas tank, a stranger approached and dropped a note into the car. The chief, suspicious of a KGB trap, ignored the overture. But the man had made up his mind. . . . In the years that followed, that man, Adolf Tolkachev, became one of the most valuable spies ever for the U.S." (Publisher's note)

"Hoffman ably navigates the many strands of this complex espionage story. An intricate, mesmerizing portrayal of the KGB-CIA spy culture." Kirkus

Includes bibliographical references (pages 267-297) and index.

Laird, Thomas

Into Tibet; the CIA's first atomic spy and his secret expedition to Lhasa. Grove Press 2002 364p il $26; pa $15   **327.12**

1. American espionage 2. Tibet (China) 3. China -- Foreign relations -- United States 4. United States -- Foreign relations -- China

ISBN 0-8021-1714-7; 0-8021-3999-X pa

LC 2001-58459

The author "traces the story of two CIA agents, Douglas Mackiernan and Frank Bessac, sent on an intelligence expedition to Tibet in 1949-1950. . . . Focusing on the heart-stopping details of the expedition itself, Laird gives the now familiar story of callous CIA manipulation an absorbing twist." Publ Wkly

Includes bibliographical references

Macintyre, Ben, 1963-

A Spy Among Friends; Kim Philby and the Great Betrayal. Ben Macintyre. Crown Publishers 2014 384 p. illustrations, portraits $27   **327.12**

1. Spies 2. Betrayal 3. Spies -- Great Britain -- Biography 4. Espionage, Soviet -- Great Britain -- History

ISBN 0804136637; 9780804136631

LC 2014003296

This book by Ben MacIntyre describes how "even as the web of suspicion closed around him, and [spy Kim] Philby was driven to greater lies to protect his cover, his two friends never abandoned him--until it was too late. The stunning truth of his betrayal would have devastating consequences on the two men who thought they knew him best, and on the intelligence services he left crippled in his wake." (Publisher's note)

"A tale of espionage, alcoholism, bad manners and the chivalrous code of spies--the real world of James Bond, that is, as played out by clerks and not superheroes." Kirkus

Includes bibliographical references (pages 309-359) and index

Richelson, Jeffrey

The wizards of Langley; inside the CIA's Directorate of Science and Technology. {by} Jeffrey T. Richelson. Westview Press 2001 386p il hardcover o.p. pa $17   **327.12**

1. United States -- Central Intelligence Agency -- Directorate of Science and Technology

ISBN 0-8133-4059-4 pa

The author "provides a richly detailed account of the agency's work." Libr J

Weiner, Tim

★ Legacy of ashes; the history of the CIA. Tim Weiner. Doubleday 2007 702p ill. (pbk.) $17.95; o.p.; o.p.   **327.12**

1. United States -- History -- 1945- 2. Intelligence service -- United States 3. United States. Central Intelligence Agency

ISBN 9780307389008; 9780385514453; 038551445X

LC 2007004077

Los Angeles Times Book Prizes: History (2007); National Book Awards: Nonfiction (2007)

This book is a "chronicle of the [U.S.] Central Intelligence Agency . . . [and] C.I.A. incompetence. . . . The author has . . . studied the archival record, teased out newly declassified primary documents and done numerous interviews to glean as much as can be publicly known about the agency's history. Some of the most damning criticism of the C.I.A.'s past performance in this book comes . . . from ex-officials and long-secret authorized accounts by C.I.A. historians. . . . [Author Tim] Weiner argues that a bad C.I.A. track record has encouraged many of . . . [the U.S.'s] gravest contemporary problems: Iran, Iraq, Afghanistan, terrorism." (New York Times)

This book "takes the CIA from its creation after World War II, through its battles in the cold war and the war on terror, to its . . . [circumstances] after 9/11." Publisher's note

Includes bibliographical references and index.

Weinstein, Allen

The haunted wood; Soviet espionage in America--the Stalin era. {by} Allen Weinstein, Alexander Vassiliev. Random House 1999 xxviii, 402p il hardcover o.p. pa $23   **327.12**

1. Spies 2. Russian espionage 3. United States -- History -- 1933-1945

ISBN 0-375-75536-5 pa

LC 98-11801

"This is a relentlessly powerful book and an eye-opener for all readers." Libr J

Includes bibliographical references

Wise, David

Spy: the inside story of how the FBI's Robert Hanssen betrayed America. Random House 2002 309p $24.95; pa $13.95   **327.12**

1. Spies 2. Espionage 3. FBI agents 4. United States -- Federal Bureau of Investigation

ISBN 0-375-50745-0; 0-375-75894-1 pa

LC 2002-31867

"A relentless reporter and true expert on the world of spying, Wise recounts Hanssen's story and the hunt to catch him in precise, if sometimes overwhelming detail." N Y Times Book Rev

327.2 Diplomacy

Grandin, Greg

Kissinger's Shadow; The Long Reach of America's Most Controversial Statesman. by Greg Grandin (Author) Henry Holt & Co. 2015 288 p. $28 **327.2**

1. Military policy -- United States 2. United States -- Foreign relations

ISBN 1627794492; 9781627794497

LC 2015003553

This book, written by Greg Grandin, "reveals how Richard Nixon's top foreign policy advisor . . . was helping to revive a militarized version of American exceptionalism centered on an imperial presidency. Believing that reality could be bent to his will . . . and vowing that past mistakes should never hinder future bold action, [Henry] Kissinger anticipated, even enabled, the ascendance of the neoconservative idealists who took America into crippling wars in Afghanistan and Iraq." (Publisher's note)

"Grandin will win no friends among Kissinger supporters, yet this book will find its audience among political scientists, historians, and informed readers attempting to assess the statesman's complex legacy." LJ

Includes bibliographical references (pages 231-259) and index.

Kissinger, Henry

Diplomacy. Simon & Schuster 1994 912p il maps hardcover o.p. pa $22   **327.2**
1. Actors 2. Princes 3. Cold war 4. Emperors 5. Generals 6. Diplomacy 7. Governors 8. Statesmen 9. Historians 10. Presidents 11. Heads of state 12. Prime ministers 13. Vice-presidents 14. World War, 1914-1918 15. Vietnam War, 1961-1975 16. People with disabilities 17. Senators 18. Memoirists 19. Nazi leaders 20. Philatelists 21. Cabinet members 22. Communist leaders 23. Political leaders 24. College presidents 25. Nonfiction writers 26. Members of Congress 27. Members of Parliament 28. Nobel laureates for peace 29. Nobel laureates for literature 30. World War, 1939-1945 -- Children 31. United States -- Foreign relations
ISBN 0-671-51099-1 pa
LC 93-44001

"This is an important contribution to the theoretical literature on foreign affairs and will also serve quite ably as a one-volume synthesis of modern diplomatic history. All libraries should have this impressive book." Libr J

Includes bibliographical references

327.73 Foreign relations--United States

Bass, Gary Jonathan, 1969-

The **Blood** telegram; Nixon, Kissinger, and a forgotten genocide. by Gary J. Bass. Alfred A. Knopf 2013 528 p. $30   **327.73**
1. Bangladesh 2. Nixon, Richard M. (Richard Milhous), 1913-1994 3. Genocide -- Bangladesh 4. United States -- Foreign relations -- 1969-1974 5. South Asia -- Foreign relations -- United States 6. United States -- Foreign relations -- South Asia 7. Bangladesh -- History -- Revolution, 1971 -- Atrocities
ISBN 0307700208; 9780307700209
LC 2013014788

This book by Gary J. Bass examines the"humanitarian crisis that propelled the creation of Bangladesh." Particular focus is given to how "[Richard] Nixon's deep distrust of India--which he viewed as an ungovernable cauldron of Soviet-leaning liberals, lefties and hippies--and his longtime support of the military in Pakistan disastrously steered his and [Henry] Kissinger's resolve not to stay the hand of Gen. Agha Mohammad Yahya Khan against a dissenting East Pakistan in March 1971." (Kirkus Reviews)

Includes bibliographical references and index

Bernstein, Richard, 1944-

China 1945; Mao's revolution and America's fateful choice. Richard Bernstein. Alfred A.

Knopf 2014 464 p. illustrations, maps (hardcover) $30   **327.73**
1. China -- History -- 1912-1949 2. China -- Foreign relations -- United States 3. Taiwan -- History -- 1945- 4. China -- History -- Republic, 1912-1949 5. United States -- Foreign relations -- China
ISBN 0307595889; 9780307595881; 9780307743213
LC 2014003598

This book by Richard Bernstein "examines the first episode in which American power and good intentions came face-to-face with a powerful Asian revolutionary movement, and challenges familiar assumptions about the origins of modern Sino-American relations." (Publisher's note)

"This thoroughly researched and well-argued work is highly recommended for those interested in Sino-American relations during the World War II and Cold War periods. The inclusion of stories from individuals impacted by these events adds to the book's value. Readers interested in China's World War II experience should also consider Rana Mitter's Forgotten Ally." LJ

Includes bibliographical references and index

Bordewich, Fergus M.

The **First** Congress; How James Madison, George Washington, and a Group of Extraordinary Men Invented the Government. by Fergus M. Bordewich. Simon & Schuster 2016 448 p. 8 plates; illustrations $30   **327.73**
1. United States -- Politics and government -- 1783-1809
ISBN 1451691939; 9781451691931
LC 2015017286

This book, by Fergus M. Bordewich, is about "the most productive Congress in US history, the First Federal Congress of 1789–1791. . . . The Constitution was a broad set of principles. It was left to the members of the First Congress and President George Washington to create the machinery that would make the government work. Fortunately, James Madison, John Adams, Alexander Hamilton, and others less well known today, rose to the occasion." (Publisher's note)

"This engaging and accessible book sheds new light on the meaning of constitutionality. It will fit into any collection." LJ

Haass, Richard N., 1951-

Foreign policy begins at home; the case for putting America's house in order. by Richard Haass. Basic Books 2013 viii, 195 p.p (hardcover) $25.99   **327.73**
1. Economic policy -- United States 2. United States -- Foreign relations 3. World politics 4. International relations 5. Security, International 6. United States -- Politics and government
ISBN 0465057985; 9780465057986
LC 2012049203

Here, Richard N. Haass focuses on "domestic economic policy as the foundation of U.S. power. He notes the current national budget debates, which, he says, result from systemic changes in the U.S. economy and in international geoeconomic realities that impact our national security." He explores the post-Cold War world, the effects of 9/11 and the 2008 global financial crisis, and discusses a "more discriminating and pragmatic foreign policy that is supported by a more disciplined domestic policy." (Library Journal)

Includes bibliographical references (pages 169-183) and index.

Hersh, Seymour, 1937-

The **killing** of Osama Bin Laden; Seymour M. Hersh. Verso Books 2016 144 p. (hardback : alk. paper) $19.95   **327.73**
1. Syria 2. United States -- Foreign relations 3. United States -- Military policy 4. United States -- Foreign relations -- 2009-
ISBN 9781784784362

LC 2016002833

This book, by Seymour M. Hersh, is an "investigation of White House lies about the assassination of Osama bin Laden. . . . At the same time, the full story of the United States' involvement in the Syrian civil war has been kept behind a diplomatic curtain, concealed by doublespeak. It is a policy of obfuscation that has compelled the White House to turn a blind eye to Turkey's involvement in supporting ISIS and its predecessors in Syria." (Publisher's note)

"The Pulitzer Prize winner builds on his reputation as an iconic investigative journalist, skewering the conventional wisdom about the death of Osama bin Laden." Kirkus

Leverett, Flynt

Going to Tehran; why the United States must come to terms with the Islamic Republic of Iran. Flynt Leverett and Hillary Mann Leverett. Henry Holt & Co 2013 496 p. (hardback) $32   **327.73**
1. Nuclear weapons 2. Iran -- Foreign relations -- United States 3. United States -- Foreign relations -- Iran 4. United States -- Foreign relations -- 2001-
ISBN 0805094199; 9780805094190

LC 2012036700

This book offers an "analysis of the Islamic Republic's policies, intentions, and capabilities," focusing particularly on Iran's developing nuclear capabilities. The authors "call for a reset in relations and substantial engagement rather than saber-rattling and sanctions" and "accuse the American government of 'shameless duplicity.'" (Publishers Weekly)

Morris, Seymour

Supreme Commander; MacArthur's Triumph in Japan. by Seymour Morris Jr. HarperCollins 2014 368 p. illustrations $26.99   **327.73**
1. World War, 1939-1945 -- Peace 2. Japan -- History -- 1945-1952, Allied occupation
ISBN 0062287931; 9780062287939

LC 2013498721

Includes bibliographical references and index

In this book, author Seymour Morris Jr. "combines political history, military biography, and business management to tell the story of General Douglas MacArthur's tremendous success in rebuilding Japan after World War II. . . . As the uniquely titled Supreme Commander for the Allied Powers, he was charged with transforming a defeated, militarist empire into a beacon of peace and democracy." (Publisher's note)

"A well-crafted history of an underappreciated aspect of MacArthur's career." LJ

Nasr, Vali

The **dispensable** nation; American foreign policy in retreat. Vali Nasr. Doubleday 2013 336 p. $28.95   **327.73**
1. Political science 2. United States -- Foreign relations 3. Middle East -- Foreign relations -- United States 4. United States -- Foreign relations -- Middle East 5. Islamic countries -- Foreign relations -- United States 6. United States -- Foreign relations -- Islamic countries
ISBN 038553647X; 9780385536479

LC 2012043100

In this book, author Vali Nasr "questions America's . . . choice to engage less and matter less in the world. Nasr makes a compelling case that behind specific flawed decisions lurked a desire by the White House to pivot away from the complex problems of the Muslim world. Drawing on his . . . expertise in Middle East affairs and firsthand experience in diplomacy, Nasr demonstrates why turning our backs is dangerous and, what's more, sells short American power." (Publisher's note)

Includes bibliographical references (pages 259-283) and index

Rice, Condoleezza, 1954-

No higher honor; A Memoir of My Years in Washington. Condoleezza Rice. Random House Inc. 2011 xviii, 766 p.p illustrations, maps $35 **327.73**
1. Israel-Arab conflicts 2. September 11 terrorist attacks, 2001 3. United States -- Politics and government 4. War on Terrorism, 2001-2009 5. Stateswomen -- United States -- Biography 6. United States. Dept. of State -- Biography 7. National Security Council (U.S.) -- Biography 8. Cabinet officers -- United States -- Biography 9. United States -- Foreign relations -- 2001-2009 10. Women cabinet officers -- United States -- Biography
ISBN 030758786X; 9780307587862; 9780307952479

LC 2011534059

Author Condoleezza Rice "takes the reader into secret negotiating rooms where the fates of Israel, the Palestinian Authority, and Lebanon often hung in the balance, and it draws back the curtain on how frighteningly close all-out war loomed . . . [in response to] the September 11, 2001, terrorist attacks . . . [and] in clashes involving Pakistan-India and Russia-Georgia, and in East Africa." (Publisher's note)

Ross, Dennis, B., 1948-

Doomed to succeed; the U.S.-Israel relationship from Truman to Obama. Dennis Ross. Farrar, Straus & Giroux 2015 496 p. (hardcover) $30   **327.73**
1. Presidents -- United States 2. United States -- Foreign relations -- Israel 3. United States -- Politics and government -- 1945- 4. United States -- Foreign relations -- 1989- 5. Israel -- Foreign relations -- United States 6. United States -- Foreign relations -- 1945-1989
ISBN 0374141460; 9780374141462

LC 2015010959

This book, by Dennis Ross, discusses the Israeli-U.S. diplomatic relationship since World War II. The author "takes us through every administration from [Harry] Truman to [Barack] Obama, throwing into dramatic relief each president's attitudes toward Israel and the region, the often tumultuous debates between key advisers, and the events that drove the policies and at times led to a shift in approach." (Publisher's note)

"Ross provides a learned, wise template for understanding the long-term relationship between two countries tethered to one another out of shared self-inter e st and geopolitical necessity and yet with sometimes-conflicting senses of the way forward." Kirkus

Includes index

The **WikiLeaks** files; the world according to US empire. by WikiLeaks, with an introduction by Julian Assange. Verso 2015 624 p. (ebook) $29.95   **327.73**

1. Government information 2. WikiLeaks (Organization) 3. Leaks (Disclosure of information) 4. United States -- Foreign relations 5. Official secrets -- United States 6. Government information -- United States 7. United States -- Foreign relations -- 2009- 8. United States -- Foreign relations -- 2001-2009 9. Leaks (Disclosure of information) -- United States
ISBN 9781781688755; 9781781689448; 9781784782719; 9781781689448

LC 2015017220

This book by WikiLeaks "exposes the machinations of the United States as it imposes a new form of imperialism on the world, one founded on tactics from torture to military action, to trade deals and 'soft power,' in the perpetual pursuit of expanding influence. The book also includes an introduction by Julian Assange examining the ongoing debates about freedom of information, international surveillance, and justice." (Publisher's note)

"The insights from researchers provide an excellent resource and solid foundation for further research by scholars or lay readers." Pub Wkly

Includes bibliographical references (pages 546-588) and index.

328   The legislative process

Barone, Michael

The **almanac** of American politics 2012; Michael Barone, Chuck McCutcheon. University of Chicago Press 2011 xviii, 1838 p.p (hardcover) $110; (paperback) $85.00   **328**

1. Almanacs 2. United States -- Politics and government -- 2001-
ISBN 0226038076; 0226038084; 9780226038070; 9780226038087

LC 2011929193

This book, by Michael Barone and Chuck McCutcheon, is a 2012 edition almanac on U.S. politics. It "includes profiles of every member of Congress and every governor. It offers in-depth and completely up-to-date narrative profiles of all 50 states and 435 House districts, covering everything from economics to history to, of course, politics." (Publisher's note)

Congressional Quarterly, Inc.

★ **Congress** A to Z; 5th ed.; CQ Press 2008 xxxiv, 704p il map (CQ's American government A to Z series) $85   **328**

1. Reference books 2. United States -- Congress
ISBN 978-0-87289-558-4

LC 2008-11284

First published 1988

This work provides information on the structure and work of Congress in some 340 alphabetical entries.

Includes bibliographical references

Kaiser, Robert Greeley

So damn much money; the triumph of lobbying and the corrosion of American government. [by] Robert G. Kaiser. Knopf 2009 398p il $27.95 **328**

1. Lobbying 2. Political corruption 3. Lobbyists 4. United States -- Congress
ISBN 978-0-307-26654-5; 0-307-26654-0

LC 2008-33862

"Lobbying, Kaiser writes, is a business of 'huge numbers and vague standards,' forever reorienting itself in an effort to skate just inside the limits of legality. Kaiser follows the career of Gerald S. J. Cassidy, a kid from a poor family who became a lawyer for migrant workers, an aide to George McGovern, and, latterly, a lobbyist for universities, cranberries, defense contractors, and Taiwan. Cassidy pioneered the use of earmarks, fought to save the Seawolf submarine, and took congressmen to N.C.A.A. Final Four games. . . . Kaiser's account dwells less on blatant corruption than on what is perfectly, depressingly legal." New Yorker

Includes bibliographical references

Remini, Robert Vincent

Daniel Webster; the man and his time. {by} Robert V. Remini. Norton 1997 796p il $26; pa $14   **328**

1. Lawyers 2. Statesmen 3. Secretaries of state 4. United States -- Politics and government -- 1815-1861
ISBN 0-393-04552-8; 0-375-72715-9 pa

LC 97-24371

This work explores the life and times of the influential politician and statesman of antebellum America

"Remini tends to exaggerate Webster's personal peccadilloes, but it cannot be said that he underestimates his subject's importance to American political culture. For Remini, Webster's muscular nationalism, embroidered with Lincoln's democratic eloquence, provided the foundation for a strong and enduring union." Choice

Includes bibliographical references

Robert C. Byrd Center for Legislative Studies

Congress investigates; a critical and documentary history. edited by Roger A. Bruns, David L. Hostetter, Raymond W. Smock; Robert C. Byrd Center for Legislative Studies. Rev. ed; Facts on File 2011 2v il (Facts on File library of American history) set $195   **328**

1. Reference books 2. Governmental investigations --

United States
ISBN 978-0-8160-7679-6; 978-1-4381-3545-8 ebook
LC 2010020268

First published 1975

The editors "have gathered here information on congressional investigations from the Colonial period to the 21st century. The entries, written by U.S. historians and archivists, each offer an overview, chronology, documents, excerpts from congressional committee reports and testimony, and a bibliography; many also include black-and-white illustrations, photographs, or political cartoons. They cover well-known events such as the Teapot Dome scandal, the burning of Washington in 1814, the Hurricane Katrina inquiry of 2005–06, and several lesser-known happenings—General St. Clair's defeat of 1792–93 and the Pujo Committee on the 'Money Trust,' for example. . . . This well-researched and richly detailed resource provides an excellent overview of major congressional investigations and will be a quality addition to a high school, public, or undergraduate academic library." Libr J

Includes bibliographical references

328.73   Legislative process--United States

Bai, Matt

All the truth is out; the week politics went tabloid. Matt Bai. Alfred A. Knopf 2014 288 p. illustrations (hardback) $26.95   **328.73**
1. Scandals 2. Public opinion 3. Presidential candidates -- United States 4. Legislators -- United States -- Biography 5. United States. Congress. Senate -- Biography 6. Scandals -- United States -- History -- 20th century 7. Public opinion -- United States -- History -- 20th century 8. Press and politics -- United States -- History -- 20th century 9. Tabloid newspapers -- United States -- History -- 20th century 10. Character -- Political aspects -- United States -- History -- 20th century 11. Mass media -- Political aspects -- United States -- History -- 20th century 12. Presidential candidates -- Press coverage -- United States -- History -- 20th century
ISBN 0307273385; 9780307273383; 9780307474681
LC 2014001033

In this book, political correspondent Matt Bai "offers a poignant, highly original, and news-making reappraisal of [Gary] Hart's fall from grace (and overlooked political legacy) as he makes the compelling case that this was the moment when the paradigm shifted-private lives became public, news became entertainment, and politics became the stuff of Page Six." (Publisher's note)

"The author takes inspiration from Richard Ben Cramer, whose What It Takes (1992) is often considered the best book about any presidential campaign. Here Bai shows he is Cramer's worthy successor—his important cautionary tale will resonate with journalists and members of the media as well as with political players and readers of current history." LJ

Baker, Richard A.

The American Senate; an insider's history. Neil MacNeil and Richard A. Baker. Oxford University Press, Inc. 2013 472 p. (hardcover) $29.95 **328.73**
1. United States. Congress. Senate -- History
ISBN 0195367618; 9780195367614
LC 2012046807

This book by Richard A. Baker and Neil MacNeil "explore[s] the [U.S.] Senate's historical evolution with one eye on persistent structural pressures and the other on recent transformations. Here, for example, are the Senate's struggles with the presidency--from George Washington's first, disastrous visit . . . through now-forgotten conflicts with Presidents Garfield and Cleveland, to current war powers disputes. The authors also explore the Senate's potent investigative power." (Publisher's note)

Includes bibliographical references and index.

Spieler, Matthew

The U.S. House of Representatives; the fundamentals of American government. Matthew Spieler. Thomas Dunne Books/St. Martin's Press 2015 192 p. (hardback) $22.99   **328.73**
1. United States. Congress. House
ISBN 9781250040367; 9781466835641
LC 2015028828

This book, by Matthew Spieler, part of the Fundamentals of American Government civics series, "carefully examines and explains exactly how the House of Representatives operates. From its voting procedure to historic beginnings and modern day issues, there is no area of this governmental body left un-revealed." (Publisher's note)

"A concise civics handbook that focuses a spotlight on the House's design and where its leadership does not measure up." Kirkus

Includes bibliographical references and index.

330   Economics

Acemoglu, Daron

Why nations fail; the origins of power, prosperity and poverty. Daron Acemoglu and James A. Robinson. Crown Publishers 2012 529 p. ill., map $30   **330**
1. Nations 2. Economic conditions 3. Poverty -- Developing countries 4. Economics -- Political aspects 5. Revolutions -- Economic aspects 6. Developing countries -- Social policy 7. Economic history -- Political aspects 8. Developing countries -- Economic policy 9. Economic development -- Developing countries
ISBN 0307719219; 9780307719218
LC 2011023538

This book attempts to answer the question "'Why Nations Fail.' . . . [The authors] favour . . . an approach rooted solely in institutional economics, which studies the impact of political environments on economic outcomes. . . . They offer [the following] . . . diagnosis: some governments get it wrong on purpose. . . . Inclusive institutions protect individual rights and encourage investment and effort. Where inclusive governments emerge, great wealth follows." (Economist)

"The authors make what could be a weighty topic both engaging and accessible. It will appeal not only to students of economics and political science but also to anyone looking to gain insight into the current state of our global economy, its origins, and the kind of transformations that might level the playing field." LJ

Includes bibliographical references (p. [465]-509) and index

Adler, Moshe

Economics for the rest of us; debunking the science that makes life dismal. New Press 2009 217p il $24.95; ebook $24.95   **330**

1. Income 2. Economics 3. Salaries, wages, etc.
ISBN 978-1-59558-101-3; 978-1-59558-527-1 ebook
LC 2009-24968

"Only occasionally relying on graphs or tables, Adler provides an accessible summary of quite complex debates in economic theory." Choice

Includes bibliographical references

Chang, Ha-Joon

Economics; The User's Guide. Ha-Joon Chang. St. Martin's Press 2014 384 p. illustration $30 **330**

1. Finance 2. Economics
ISBN 1620408120; 9781620408124
LC 2014498623

In this book author Ha-Joon Chang "explains how the global economy actually works--in real-world terms. Writing with irreverent wit, a deep knowledge of history, and a disregard for conventional economic pieties, Chang offers insights that will never be found in the textbooks." (Publisher's note)

"A solid choice for those who want to learn more about economics without feeling like they are back in the classroom." LJ

Dubner, Stephen J., 1963-

★ **Freakonomics**; a rogue economist explores the hidden side of everything. [by] Steven D. Levitt and Stephen J. Dubner. William Morrow 2005 242p hardcover o.p. pa $15.99   **330**

1. Economics 2. Economics -- Sociological aspects 3. Economics -- Psychological aspects
ISBN 0-06-073132-X; 0-06-073133-8 pa
LC 2004-65478

The authors "evaluate intriguing questions such as 'What do Schoolteachers and Sumo Wrestlers Have in Common?' 'How is the Ku Klux Klan Like a Group of Real Estate Agents?' 'Where Have All the Criminals Gone?' and 'What Makes a Perfect Parent?' . . . This excellent, readable book will enlighten many library patrons." Booklist

Includes bibliographical references

Encyclopedia of Business Information Sources; edited by Virgil L. Burton. Gale / Cengage Learning 2013 1210 p. (paperback) $657   **330**

1. Businesspeople 2. Business -- Encyclopedias
ISBN 1414478119; 9781414478111

The 23rd edition of this book, edited by Virgil L. Burton, offers "a bibliographic guide to citations covering over 1,100 subjects of interest to business personnel." It "includes

abstracts and indexes, almanacs and yearbooks, bibliographies, online databases, research centers and institutes and much more." (Publisher's note)

Ferguson, Niall

★ The **ascent** of money; a financial history of the world. Penguin Press 2008 441p $29.95 **330**

1. Money 2. International finance 3. Economics -- History
ISBN 978-1-59420-192-9; 1-59420-192-7

The author "presents the history of money within these contexts: the rise of money and the history of credit, and the histories of the bond market, the stock market, insurance, the real-estate market, and international finance. There is an ease to his prose that leaves this complicated subject interesting to and approachable by any general reader." Booklist

Includes bibliographical references

Levitt, Steven D.

Superfreakonomics; global cooling, patriotic prostitutes, and why suicide bombers should buy life insurance. [by] Steven D. Levitt & Stephen J. Dubner. William Morrow 2009 270p $29.99; pa $15.99; ebook $9.99   **330**

1. Economics
ISBN 978-0-06-088957-9; 0-06-088957-8; 978-0-06-088958-6 pa; 0-06-088958-6 pa; 978-0-06-195993-6 ebook; 0-06-195993-6 ebook
LC 2009035852

Sequel to Freakonomics (2005)

The authors "assert that the unifying principle in the various topics they address is people responding to incentives in ways that are not necessarily predictable or manifest. Major themes are explored using a wide range of examples, e.g., life and death issues, terrorism, altruism, medical care, crime, and the environment. . . . Levitt and Dubner succeed in applying economic analysis to timely topics with stimulation, wit, and humor. Best of all, their book will appeal to a broad segment of the population." Choice

Includes bibliographical references

Mezrich, Ben

Once Upon a Time in Russia; The Rise of the Oligarchs. by Ben Mezrich. Pocket Books 2015 288 p. $28   **330**

1. Businessmen 2. Russia -- History -- 1991- 3. Russia -- History -- 1953-1991
ISBN 1476771898; 9781476771892
LC 2015295889

This book, by Ben Mezrich, "is the untold true story of the larger-than-life billionaire oligarchs who surfed the waves of privatization to reap riches after the fall of the Soviet regime: 'Godfather of the Kremlin' Boris Berezovsky, a former mathematician whose first entrepreneurial venture was running an automobile reselling business, and Roman Abramovich, his dashing young protégé who built a multi-billion-dollar empire of oil and aluminum." (Publisher's note)

"Mezrich's ability to tell a true (and well-documented) story, in a way that makes it look and feel like the most involving of narratives, is nearly unparalleled. He is one of the few writers whose name on a piece of nonfiction guarantees not only quality but also interest, no matter the subject, and this fine book is one more example of just how talented a storyteller he is." Booklist

Oxford University Press

The **Oxford** encyclopedia of economic history; Joel Mokyr, editor in chief. Oxford University Press 2003 5v set $695 **330**
 1. Reference books 2. Economic history -- Encyclopedias
 ISBN 0-19-510507-9
 LC 2003-8992

This encyclopedia includes "over 900 contributions from 800 scholars to explore key concepts of economics, firms and individuals, institutions, countries, and cities. Although scholarly in tone, this volume is an excellent starting point for those wishing to trace ideas and industries across chronological boundaries." Libr J

Includes bibliographical references and index

Sowell, Thomas

Basic economics; a common sense guide to the economy. 4th ed.; Basic Books 2011 689p $39.95 **330**
 1. Economics
 ISBN 978-0-465-02252-6
 First published 2000

Thomas Sowell explains the principles of economics in plain jargon for the general public, answering questions like: Why are homeless people sleeping on the sidewalks of New York in the winter, when the abandoned apartment buildings have four times as many dwelling units as there are homeless people in the city? Why did Russians have to import food to feed people in Moscow, when Russia itself had vast amounts of some of the richest farmland in Europe?

"Sowell's volume does a fantastic job in cultivating the reader's 'economic imagination.'" Choice

Taylor, Timothy

The **instant** economist; Timothy Taylor. Plume 2012 x, 260p.p ill. pa $16 **330**
 1. Economics
 ISBN 978-0-452-29752-4
 LC 2011033416

This book provides an introduction to "[e]conomics [which] isn't just about numbers: It's about politics, psychology, history, and so much more. We are all economists-when we work, save for the future, invest, pay taxes, and buy our groceries. Yet many of us feel lost when the subject arises. . . . Timothy Taylor tackles all the key questions and hot topics of both microeconomics and macroeconomics, including: Why do budget deficits matter? What exactly does the Federal Reserve do? Does globalization take jobs away from American workers? Why is health insurance so costly?" (Publisher's note)

Includes bibliographical references

330.01 Philosophy and theory

Roth, Alvin E., 1951-

Who gets what--and why; the new economics of matchmaking and market design. Alvin E. Roth. Eamon Dolan/Houghton Mifflin Harcourt 2015 272 p. (ebook) $15.95; (hardback) $28 **330.01**
 1. Markets 2. Economics 3. Game theory 4. Matching theory
 ISBN 9780544288393; 9780544291133
 LC 2015010771

This book, by Alvin E. Roth, "guides us through the jungles of modern life, pointing to the many markets that are hidden in plain view all around us. . . . Most of the study of economics deals with commodity markets, where the price of a good connects sellers and buyers. But what about other kinds of 'goods' like a spot in the Yale freshman class or a position at Google?" (Publisher's note)

"An exciting practical approach to economics that enables both individuals and institutions to achieve their goals without running afoul of the profit motive." Kirkus

Includes bibliographical references (pages 233-246) and index.

Thaler, Richard H., 1945-

Misbehaving; the making of behavioral economics. Richard H. Thaler. W W Norton & Co Inc 2015 432 p. illustrations (hardcover : alk. paper) $27.95 **330.01**
 1. Human behavior 2. Economics -- Psychological aspects
 ISBN 0393080943; 9780393080940
 LC 2015004600

In this book, by Richard H. Thaler, "coupling recent discoveries in human psychology with a practical understanding of incentives and market behavior, . . . [the author] enlightens readers about how to make smarter decisions in an increasingly mystifying world. He reveals how behavioral economic analysis opens up new ways to look at everything from household finance to assigning faculty offices in a new building, to TV game shows, the NFL draft, and businesses like Uber." (Publisher's note)

"Misbehaving chronicles Thaler's participation in the development of behavioral economics, describes how it happened, and details some of what he and his colleagues learned along the way. This challenging book is written in an understandable manner and contains valuable insight for those interested in economics, psychology, other social sciences, public policy, and business." Booklist

Includes bibliographical references and index

330.1 Systems, schools, theories

Appleby, Joyce

The **relentless** revolution; a history of capitalism. [by] Joyce Appleby. W.W. Norton 2010 494p $29.95 **330.1**
 1. Capitalism 2. Economic conditions 3. Economic history 4. Capitalism -- History
 ISBN 978-0-393-06894-8; 0-393-06894-3
 LC 2009-35676

"Whether masterfully discussing the significance of agricultural progress that made capitalism possible, or touching lightly on the impact of Amazon and e-mail, Appleby offers consistently illuminating commentary. A useful introduction to a vast, complex topic." Kirkus

Includes bibliographical references

Heilbroner, Robert L.

★ The **worldly** philosophers; the lives, times, and ideas of the great economic thinkers. Rev. 7th ed.; Simon & Schuster 1999 365p pa $16   **330.1**
1. Authors 2. Utopias 3. Economics 4. Capitalism 5. Economists 6. Depressions 7. Imperialism 8. Journalists 9. Social critics 10. Nonfiction writers 11. Patrons of the arts 12. Writers on politics 13. Political and social philosophers
ISBN 0-684-86214-X

LC 99-14050

First published 1953

The author traces the story of economics and the great economists from Adam Smith, Malthus, Ricardo, the Utopians, Marx, Veblen and Keynes to those working with the problems of our contemporary world

Includes bibliographical references

Keynes, John Maynard

★ The **general** theory of employment, interest and money. Harcourt Brace & Co. 1936 403p hardcover o.p. pa $15   **330.1**
1. Money 2. Economics 3. Interest (Economics)
ISBN 0-15-634711-3 pa

This work "revolutionized economic theory by showing how unemployment could occur 'involuntarily'. For 30 years after the Second World War governments of western nations pursued 'Keynesian' full-employment policies." Oxford Companion to Engl Lit. 5th edition

Lanchester, John

How to Speak Money; What the Money People Say--and What It Really Means. John Lanchester. W W Norton & Co Inc 2014 288 p. illustrations $26.95   **330.1**
1. Economics 2. Personal finance 3. Economics -- Terminology
ISBN 0393243370; 9780393243376

LC 2014028529

In this book, John Lanchester "reveals how the world of finance really works: from the terms and conditions of your personal checking account to the evasions of bankers appearing in front of Congress. As Lanchester writes, we need to understand what the money people are talking about so that those who speak the language don't just write the rules for themselves." (Publisher's note)

"This entertaining, informative, useful reference, written in a lively style, is suitable for both practitioners and newcomers to the subject of economics." Choice

Includes bibliographical references and index

Marx, Karl

★ **Capital**: an abridged edition; edited with an introduction and notes by David McLellan. Oxford

University Press 2008 xxxii, 499p (Oxford world's classics) pa $16.95   **330.1**
1. Capital 2. Economics
ISBN 978-0-19-953570-5

LC 2008-274361

Abridged edition first published 1995

This abridged edition of Marx's three-volume "denunciation of mid-Victorian capitalist society . . . offers virtually all of Volume 1, which Marx himself published in 1867; excerpts from a . . . translation of 'The Result of the Immediate Process Production'; and a selection of key chapters from Volume 3, which Engels published in 1895." Publisher's note

Patel, Raj

The **value** of nothing; how to reshape market society and redefine democracy. Picador 2010 250p pa $14   **330.1**
1. Democracy 2. Economic policy 3. Free enterprise
ISBN 978-0-312-42924-9

LC 2009-41546

The author "lays bare the social, political, and environmental damage caused by free markets and the commoditization of every facet of any market society. . . . Patel debunks the myth that markets are the perfect form of social organization, effectively arguing that the tyranny they exert can and must be replaced by strategies benefiting all humanity and ensuring our very survival. This work is written calmly and sensibly enough that it could change some readers' minds, although it will leave free-market apologists spluttering. Highly recommended." Libr J

Includes bibliographical references

Sandel, Michael J., 1953-

What money can't buy; the moral limits of markets. Michael J. Sandel. Farrar Straus & Giroux 2012 244 p.   **330.1**
1. Capitalism 2. Business ethics 3. Free enterprise 4. Economics -- Philosophy
ISBN 0374203032; 9780374203030

LC 2011052182

In this book author Michael J. Sandel "takes on . . . the . . . ethical questions . . . Is there something wrong with a world in which everything is for sale? If so, how can we prevent market values from reaching into spheres of life where they don't belong? What are the moral limits of markets? In recent decades, market values have crowded out nonmarket norms in almost every aspect of life—medicine, education, government, law, art, sports, even family life and personal relations. Without quite realizing it, Sandel argues, we have drifted from having a market economy to being a market society. . . . What is the proper role of markets in a democratic society—and how can we protect the moral and civic goods that markets don't honor and that money can't buy?" (Publisher's note)

Includes bibliographical references and index

Smith, Adam

★ The **wealth** of nations; introduction by Robert Reich; edited, with notes, marginal summary, and enlarged index by Edwin Cannan. Modern Library 2000 xxvi, 1154p pa $15.95 **330.1**

1. Economics

ISBN 0-679-78336-9; 978-0-679-78336-7

LC 00-64573

First published 1776

This treatise "is the first comprehensive treatment of the whole subject of political economy, and is remarkable for its breadth of view. . . . In it, the author presents an attack on the mercantile system, and an advocacy of freedom of commerce and industry." Oxford Companion to Engl Lit. 6th edition

Includes bibliographical references

330.12 Systems

Burgin, Angus

The **great** persuasion; reinventing free markets since the Depression. Angus Burgin. Harvard University Press 2012 303 p. (hardcover) $29.95 **330.12**

1. Free enterprise 2. Economic policy -- United States -- History 3. United States -- Economic conditions -- 20th century 4. Capitalism 5. Economic policy

ISBN 0674058135; 9780674058132

LC 2012015061

This book, by Angus Burgin, explores the history of free market capitalism in the U.S. It "traces the evolution of postwar economic thought. . . . Conservatives often point to Friedrich Hayek as the most influential defender of the free market. By examining the work of such organizations as the Mont Pèlerin Society, . . . Burgin reveals that Hayek and his colleagues were deeply conflicted about many of the enduring problems of capitalism." (Publisher's note)

Includes bibliographical references and index

McMillan, John

Reinventing the bazaar; a natural history of markets. Norton 2002 278p $25.95; pa $15.95 **330.12**

1. Capitalism

ISBN 0-393-05021-1; 0-393-32371-4 pa

LC 2002-521

The author "examines how markets in ancient times evolved and shows how countries experimented with markets, some successfully and some not. . . . He takes a refreshingly commonsense approach to his subject, doesn't talk down to his readers, and refrains from excessive economic jargon." Libr J

Includes bibliographical references

Soto, Hernando de

The **mystery** of capital; why captitalism triumphs in the West and fails everywhere else. Basic Bks. 2000 276p il $27.50; pa $17 **330.12**

1. Capitalism

ISBN 0-465-01614-6; 0-465-01615-4 pa

LC 00-34301

The author contends that "the poor do not really 'own' the property they work, because they are not registered as owning it, and because of this, they cannot turn it into capital. . . . The market is restricted and the growth of wealth retarded. His solution is simple: give the poor title to the property they own de facto, and their countries will become capital rich." N Y Times Book Rev

330.122 Free enterprise economy

King, Mervyn A., 1948-

The **End** of Alchemy; Money, Banking, and the Future of the Global Economy. by Mervyn King. W W Norton & Co Inc 2016 368 p. $28.95 **330.122**

1. Money 2. Economics 3. Banks and banking

ISBN 0393247023; 9780393247022

LC 2015048306

In this book, author Mervyn King "offers us an essential work about the history and future of money and banking, the keys to modern finance. . . . Common paper became as precious as gold, and risky long-term loans were transformed into safe short-term bank deposits. As King argues, this is financial alchemy—the creation of extraordinary financial powers that defy reality and common sense." (Publisher's note)

"King (former governor, Bank of England; Alan Greenspan Professor of Economics, New York Univ.) provides a terrific analysis of what went wrong in the global financial system and with economics in general." LJ

Includes bibliographical references and index.

330.9 Economic situation and conditions

Bartiromo, Maria

The **weekend** that changed Wall Street; an eyewitness account. [by] Maria Bartiromo, with Catherine Whitney. Portfolio Penguin 2010 232p $26.95 **330.9**

1. Bank failures 2. Global Financial Crisis, 2008-2009

ISBN 978-1-59184-351-1

LC 2010026892

"Bartiromo lays out the facts of the Lehman Brothers downfall using both her own account and those of the most powerful people on Wall Street. . . . The most fascinating aspects of . . . [this book] were not so much the details of the collapse . . . but the book's early focus on the lavish lives of those involved in the Wall Street game; Bartiromo details the parties they threw, the apartments they owned that resembled art galleries and the confidence they exuded, which came across not only in their business conversations, but also in the casual talks between the author and her trusting subjects." Risk Management

Includes bibliographical references

The **best** business writing 2013; edited by Dean Starkman, Martha M. Hamilton, Ryan Chittum, and Felix Salmon. Columbia University Press 2013 568 p. (Columbia Journalism Review books) (pbk. : alk. paper) $18.95 **330.9**

1. Journalism 2. Business writing 3. Business 4. Businesspeople 5. Business enterprises -- Corrupt practices

ISBN 0231160755; 9780231160759

LC 2012047913

This book, edited by Dean Starkman, Martha M. Hamilton, Ryan Chittum, and Felix Salmon, is a collection of the "most engaging or rigorous business writing" of 2013. It "showcases content from diverse sources, including newspapers, magazines, and blogs." Several articles "scrutinize the recent economic downturn." (Publishers Weekly)

De Graaf, John

What's the economy for, anyway? why it's time to stop chasing growth and start pursuing happiness. [by] John de Graaf and David K. Batker; foreword by James Gustave Speth. Bloomsbury Press 2011 292p il $25   **330.9**

    1. Happiness 2. Economic development 3. United States -- Economic conditions

    ISBN 978-1-60819-510-7; 1-60819-510-4

                     LC 2011017438

De Graaf and Batker "examine new ways to think about economic processes, specifically as they relate to human happiness and well-being. The authors show that the indicators of performance developed during World War II—the 'Gross National Product'—have become both obscurantist and counterproductive. They argue that human purposes and needs ought to provide the basis for much more broadly based measures of performance, which would consider what is the greatest good and benefit for the greatest number of people over the longest period of time. . . . An entertaining presentation of important ideas and information about how lives could be improved." Kirkus

Includes bibliographical references

The **economists'** voice 2.0; the financial crisis, health care reform, and more. editors, Aaron S. Edlin, Joseph E. Stiglitz; coeditors, Bradford DeLong ... [et al]. Columbia University Press 2012 viii, 270 p.p ill. (cloth : alk. paper) $27.95   **330.9**

    1. Medical policy -- United States 2. Economic policy -- United States 3. United States -- Economic conditions 4. Economics -- United States 5. United States -- Economic policy -- 2009- 6. United States -- Economic conditions -- 2009-

    ISBN 0231160143; 9780231160148

                     LC 2011047626

"This collection," edited by Aaron S. Edlin and Joseph E. Stiglitz, "contains thirty-two essays written by academics, economists, presidential advisors, legal specialists, researchers, consultants, and policy makers. They tackle the plain economics and architecture of health care reform, its implications for society and the future of the health insurance industry, and the value of the health insurance subsidies and exchanges built into the law." (Publisher's note)

Includes bibliographical references and index.

Epping, Randy Charles

The **21st** century economy; a beginner's guide: with 101 easy-to-learn tools for surviving and thriving in the new global marketplace. Vintage Books 2009 316p pa $14.95   **330.9**

    1. Globalization 2. Economic conditions 3. International trade 4. International finance

    ISBN 978-0-307-38790-5

                     LC 2008-41554

This is an "explanation of the workings of our modern economy and hundreds of terms, such as subprime debt, CDO, IMF, money supply, and discount rate. . . . [The author] is able to explain the global economy in language that most readers will find both understandable and interesting." Libr J

Friedman, Jeffrey

Engineering the financial crisis; systemic risk and the failure of regulation. Jeffrey Friedman and Wladimir Kraus. University of Pennsylvania Press 2011 x, 212 p.p   **330.9**

    1. Cooperative banks 2. Banks and banking -- United States 3. Global Financial Crisis, 2008-2009 4. Basel II (2004) 5. Basel Accord (1988) 6. Economics -- Political aspects 7. Bank capital -- Law and legislation 8. Banks and banking -- Risk management 9. Financial crises -- United States -- History -- 21st century

    ISBN 0812243579; 9780812243574

                     LC 2011024456

Author Jeffrey Friedman discusses "the Basel Accords, a set of international standards for banking supervision and regulation . . . [The book looks at the] role that bank capital requirements and other government regulations played in the recent financial crisis . . . [The author argues] that by encouraging banks to invest in highly rated mortgage-backed bonds, the Basel Accords created an overconcentration of risk in the banking industry." (Publisher's note)

Includes bibliographical references (p. [175]-200) and index

Huffington, Arianna

Third World America; how our politicians are abandoning the middle class and betraying the American dream. Crown Publishers 2010 276p $23.99; ebook $9.99   **330.9**

    1. Social policy -- United States 2. Economic policy -- United States 3. United States -- Politics and government -- 2001-

    ISBN 978-0-307-71982-9; 978-0-307-71997-3 ebook

                     LC 2010-26871

The author "argues that overspending on war at the expense of domestic issues and the alarming decline of the middle class are troubling signals that the U.S. is losing its economic, political, and social stability—a stability that has always been maintained by the middle class. . . . An engaging analysis of troubling economic and political trends." Booklist

Krugman, Paul R., 1953-

    ★ **End** this depression now! Paul Krugman. W.W. Norton & Co. 2012 xii, 259 p.p ill. $24.95   **330.9**

    1. Recessions 2. Unemployment 3. Economic policy -- United States 4. United States -- Economic conditions 5. United States -- Economic policy -- 21st century 6. Recessions -- United States -- History -- 21st century 7. Unemployment -- United States -- History -- 21st century 8. Financial crises -- United States -- History -- 21st century

    ISBN 0393088774; 9780393088779.

                     LC 2012009067

This book, by Nobel Prize-winning economist Paul Krugman, discusses the U.S. Great Recession of 2008 and following. It asks why "'nations rich in resources, talent, and knowledge--all the ingredients for prosperity and a decent standard of living for all--remain in a state of intense pain.' . . . How did we get stuck in what now can only be called a depression? And above all, how do we free ourselves?" (Publisher's note)

"Krugman's forceful jargon-free criticisms and solutions directed at a general audience are a thoughtful contribution to both economic and political discourse in this election year. Highly recommended for a broad readership." LJ

Lanchester, John

★ **I.O.U.** why everyone owes everyone and no one can pay. Simon & Schuster 2010 260p $25   330.9

1. Economic conditions 2. International finance 3. Global Financial Crisis, 2008-2009

ISBN 978-1-4391-6984-1; 1-4391-6984-5

LC 2009-36465

This book is "equal parts history, economic primer, and social commentary—that manages to be, by turns, acidic, frightening, and sharply funny." Entertainment Wkly

Includes bibliographical references

Lewis, Michael

The **big** short; inside the doomsday machine. W.W. Norton 2010 266p   330.9

1. Financial crises 2. Global Financial Crisis, 2008-2009 3. Financial crises -- United States 4. United States -- Economic conditions 5. United States -- Economic conditions -- 2001-2009

ISBN 0-393-07223-1; 0-393-33882-7 pa; 978-0-393-07223-5; 978-0-393-33882-9 pa

LC 201004804

This is a study of the financial crisis that began in 2008. Michael Lewis, the author of Liar's Poker (1989) contends that "the roots of the meltdown of 2008 can be found in the 1980s, . . . when complex financial products like mortgage derivatives were developed." (N Y Times (Late N Y Ed))

"'The Big Short' manages to give us the truest picture yet of what went wrong on Wall Street—and why. At times, it reads like a morality play, at other times like a modern-day farce. But as with any good play, its value lies in the way it reveals character and motive and explores the cultural context in which the plot unfolds." Washington Post

Liveris, Andrew

Make it in America; the case for re-inventing the economy. Wiley 2011 xxi, 208p il $24.95; ebook $16.99   330.9

1. Manufactures 2. Economic forecasting 3. Industrial policy -- United States 4. United States -- Economic conditions

ISBN 978-0-470-93022-9; 0-470-93022-5; 9781118019405 ebook

LC 2010045654

The author "calls for a national strategy to revive manufacturing. We need manufacturing jobs, he says, if we are to keep a growing population busy and start paying off our debts to the rest of the world." Wall Street J

Includes bibliographical references

Madrick, Jeffrey G.

Age of greed; the triumph of finance and the decline of America, 1970 to the present. [by] Jeff Madrick. Alfred A. Knopf 2011 464p il $30; ebook $14.99   330.9

1. Wealth 2. Financial crises 3. Capitalists and financiers 4. Wealth -- Moral and ethical aspects 5. Financial crises -- United States -- History 6. United States -- Economic policy -- 2001-2009 7. United States -- Economic policy -- 20th century 8. United States -- Politics and government -- 20th century 9. United States -- Politics and government -- 21st century

ISBN 978-1-4000-4171-8; 978-0-307-59671-0 ebook

LC 2011003399

This book "is a fascinating and deeply disturbing tale of hypocrisy, corruption, and insatiable greed. But more than that, it's a much-needed reminder of just how we got into the mess we're in—a reminder that is greatly needed when we are still being told that greed is good." New York Rev Books

Includes bibliographical references

Martínez, Rubén

Desert America; boom and bust in the new Old West. Rubén Martínez. Metropolitan Books/ Henry Holt and Company 2012 333 p. $28.00   330.9

1. Poverty 2. West (U.S.) 3. Drugs and crime 4. Immigrants -- United States 5. New Mexico -- Race relations 6. New Mexico -- Social conditions -- 21st century 7. New Mexico -- Economic conditions -- 21st century

ISBN 0805079777; 9780805079777

LC 2011040587

"In this first-person report . . . [Rubén] Martínez . . . sojourns in the more remote regions of the Southwest . . . and finds the front line of a battle over the American past and future. . . . Martínez does his best to immerse himself in a largely Latino community that is extremely aware of outsiders, weighing the stark realities of his neighbors' lives while musing on disparities and dislocations teaching back hundreds of years." (Publishers Weekly)

McLean, Bethany

All the devils are here; the hidden history of the financial crisis. [by] Bethany McLean and Joe Nocera. Portfolio/Penguin 2010 380p il $32.95 330.9

1. Mortgages 2. International finance 3. Global Financial Crisis, 2008-2009 4. Mortgage-backed securities 5. Financial crises -- United States

ISBN 978-1-59184-363-4; 1-59184-363-4

LC 2010-32893

This is an "account of the late financial meltdown, when, in the words of one analyst, 'we went from a collective belief in soundness to a collective belief in insolvency.' . . . Hard-hitting reporting and fluent writing bring the utter devastation of the Great Recession to life." Kirkus

Includes bibliographical references

Paulson, Henry M.

★ **On** the brink; inside the race to stop the collapse of the global financial system. Business Plus 2010 478p il $28.99   **330.9**

1. Global Financial Crisis, 2008-2009 2. Economic policy -- United States
ISBN 978-0-446-56193-8; 0-446-56193-2

LC 2009-939043

"This is the ultimate insider's account of the crisis, and, owing to its evenhanded tone and penetrating insights into government actions, it will also remain an important contribution to the historical record of the crisis, essential reading for everyone interested in knowing what happened." Libr J

Perino, Michael A.

The **hellhound** of Wall Street; how Ferdinand Pecora's investigation of the Great Crash forever changed American finance. [by] Michael Perino. Penguin Press 2010 341p il $27.95   **330.9**

1. Judges 2. Lawyers 3. Stock exchanges 4. Financial crises 5. Stock market crash, 1929 6. Regulatory agency officials
ISBN 978-1-59420-272-8

LC 2010-19157

The author "recounts the 1933 investigation into Wall Street abuses by the Senate Committee on Banking and Currency, focusing on the 10-day interrogation by chief counsel Ferdinand Pecora of executives of National City Bank (precursor to Citigroup). . . . Perino's book is a trenchant, entertaining study of the New Deal's heroic beginnings, one with obvious relevance to latter-day efforts to rein in Wall Street's excesses." Publ Wkly

Includes bibliographical references

Piscione, Deborah Perry

Secrets of Silicon Valley; what everyone else can learn from the innovation capital of the world. Deborah Perry Piscione. Palgrave Macmillan 2013 256 p. (hardcover) $27   **330.9**

1. High technology industry 2. Santa Clara Valley (Santa Clara County, Calif.) -- Economic conditions 3. Technological innovations -- California -- Santa Clara County 4. High technology industries -- California -- Santa Clara County
ISBN 0230342116; 9780230342118

LC 2012038481

This book, by Deborah Perry Piscione, explores the economics of Silicon Valley. "While the global economy languishes, one place just keeps growing . . . : Silicon Valley. . . . Piscione takes us inside this vibrant ecosystem where meritocracy rules the day. She explores Silicon Valley's exceptionally risk-tolerant culture, and why it thrives despite the many laws that make California one of the worst states in the union for business." (Publisher's note)

Rajan, Raghuram G., 1963-

Fault lines; how hidden fractures still threaten the world economy. Princeton University Press 2010 260p   **330.9**

1. Global Financial Crisis, 2008-2009 2. Economic history -- 21st century 3. United States -- Social

conditions 4. United States -- Economic conditions 5. Income distribution -- United States -- History 6. United States -- Social conditions -- 21st century 7. United States -- Economic conditions -- 21st century
ISBN 9780691146836; 9780691152639; 9781400834211

LC 2010-6031

Some have blamed global financial crisis of 2008-2009 on "bankers who took irrational risks and left the rest of us to foot the bill. . . . Rajan argues that serious flaws in the economy are also to blame, and warns that a potentially more devastating crisis awaits us if they aren't fixed. Rajan [aims to] show how the individual choices that collectively brought about the economic meltdown—made by bankers, government officials, and ordinary homeowners—were rational responses to a flawed global financial order in which the incentives to take on risk are . . . out of step with the dangers those risks pose. He traces [what he views as] the deepening fault lines in a world overly dependent on the indebted American consumer to power global economic growth and stave off global downturns. He [argues that] . . . America's growing inequality and thin social safety net create tremendous political pressure to encourage easy credit and keep job creation robust, no matter what the consequences to the economy's long-term health; and . . . [that] the U.S. financial sector, with its skewed incentives, is the critical but unstable link between an overstimulated America and an underconsuming world. . . . . He outlines the hard choices [he believes] we need to make to ensure a more stable world economy and restore lasting prosperity." (Publisher's note) Bibliography. Index.

The author "explains the financial market panic of 2008 and argues that the weaknesses or fault lines in the world economy that led to financial collapse and recession persist. . . . Economists who can challenge their peers while remaining accessible to the general reader are rare, but Rajan belongs to this elite group. No short summary can do justice to this well-written, insightful, and nuanced study." Choice

Includes bibliographical references

Reich, Robert B.

Aftershock; the next economy and America's future. Alfred A. Knopf 2010 174p il $25; ebook $11.99   **330.9**

1. United States -- Economic policy 2. United States -- Social conditions 3. United States -- Economic conditions 4. United States -- Social conditions -- Forecasting
ISBN 978-0-307-59281-1; 0-307-59281-2; 978-0-307-59452-5 ebook

LC 2010-04134

Reich "argues that America will not have a sustained economic recovery until the middle class has more buying power. In this call for reform, the author writes that the increasing concentration of wealth among a small percentage of Americans was the main culprit in the destabilization of the U.S. economy in 2008. . . . Lucid and cogent." Kirkus

Includes bibliographical references

Sachs, Jeffrey, 1954-

The **price** of civilization; reawakening American virtue and prosperity. Random House 2011 324p il $27; ebook $12.99 **330.9**

1. Economic policy -- United States 2. United States -- Economic policy -- 2009- 3. Environmental responsibility -- United States 4. United States -- Economic conditions -- 2009- 5. Social responsibility of business -- United States 6. United States -- Economic conditions -- 21st century 7. United States -- Politics and government -- 21st century

ISBN 9781400068418; 140006841X; 9780679605027 ebook; 0679605029 ebook

LC 2011014631

The author "explores the economic, political, social, and psychological roots of the U.S.'s 30-year journey 'from decades of consensus and high achievement to an era of deep division and growing crisis.' He indicts America's elites for abandoning social responsibility, politicians for giving up on solving problems, the media for distraction and hyper-commercialization, and citizens for surrendering to that distraction. He urges mindfulness, clear goals for political reform, and significant tax changes, and he suggests that the millennial generation will lead the way to a restoration of the nation's highest aspirations" Booklist

Includes bibliographical references (p. [277]-307) and index.

Sorkin, Andrew Ross

★ **Too** big to fail; the inside story of how Wall Street and Washington fought to save the financial system from crisis--and themselves. Viking 2009 xx, 600p il $32.95; pa $18 **330.9**

1. Financial crises 2. Global Financial Crisis, 2008-2009

ISBN 978-0-670-02125-3; 0-670-02125-3; 978-0-14-311824-4 pa; 0-14-311824-2 pa

LC 2009-36494

This is an account of the recent financial crisis.

"Sorkin boasts of the hours spent interviewing, emailing, inspecting telephone call logs, billing time sheets and even expense reports [for this book], and his reward is the fullest and most convincing account of the Lehman debacle. Conversations are reconstructed, and an air of authenticity created by the accumulation of thousands of small facts." Times Lit Suppl

Includes bibliographical references

330.91 Areas, regions, places in general

Sharma, Ruchir

★ **Breakout** nations; in pursuit of the next economic miracles. Ruchir Sharma. W.W. Norton & Co. 2012 x, 292 p.p $26.95 **330.91**

1. Economic development 2. Economic forecasting 3. Developing countries -- Economic conditions 4. Economic history -- 21st century

ISBN 0393080269; 9780393080261

LC 2012005810

This book, by Ruchir Sharma, examines how "[a]fter a decade of rapid growth, the world's most celebrated emerg-

ing markets are poised to slow down. . . . To identify the economic stars of the future we should abandon the habit of extrapolating from the recent past and lumping wildly diverse countries together. . . . What emerges is a clear picture of the shifting balance of global economic power and how it plays out for emerging nations and for the West." (Publisher's note)

Includes bibliographical references and index.

330.973 Economic conditions--United States

Barlett, Donald L.

The **betrayal** of the American dream; Donald L. Barlett and James B. Steele. 1st ed. PublicAffairs 2012 xxi, 289 p.p ill. (hardcover) $26.99; (ebook) $26.99 **330.973**

1. Middle class -- United States 2. Economic policy -- United States 3. United States -- Economic conditions 4. United States -- Economic policy -- 2009- 5. United States -- Economic conditions -- 2009- 6. Middle class -- United States -- Economic conditions -- 21st century 7. Working class -- United States -- Economic conditions -- 21st century

ISBN 1586489690; 9781586489694; 9781586489700

LC 2012012879

In this book, authors Donald L. Barlett and James B. Steele "maintain that the deficit is less the result of government programs than plummeting tax revenue from the rich. . . . The authors' solutions include: Revise the tax code so corporations and the rich pay more than the middle class instead of less, discard the clueless ideology of free trade . . . re-regulate disastrously unregulated areas, and enforce current laws equally instead of giving the influential a free pass." (Kirkus Reviews)

Includes bibliographical references and index.

Blinder, Alan S.

After the music stopped; the financial crisis, the response, and the work ahead. Alan S. Blinder. Penguin Press 2013 xix, 476 p.p ill. (hardcover) $29.95 **330.973**

1. Global Financial Crisis, 2008-2009 2. United States -- Economic conditions 3. Finance -- United States 4. Financial crises -- United States 5. United States -- Economic policy -- 2009- 6. United States -- Economic conditions -- 2009-

ISBN 1594205302; 9781594205309

LC 2012031025

In this book, "[Alan S.] Blinder, a corporate executive and former vice chairman of the Federal Reserve, sets out to tell the American people what happened during the financial crisis of 2007-09. He explains the events that are still reverberating in the U.S. and globally and will challenge public policy for years." (Booklist)

Includes bibliographical references (p. [455]-462) and index.

Ferguson, Charles

Predator nation; corporate criminals, political corruption, and the hijacking of America. Charles

Ferguson. Crown Business 2012 vii, 369 p.p ill. $27.00   **330.973**
1. Securities fraud 2. Elite (Social sciences) 3. Wall Street (New York, N.Y.) 4. Manufacturing industries -- United States 5. Equality -- United States 6. United States -- Economic policy 7. Financial crises -- United States 8. Banks and banking -- United States 9. Global Financial Crisis, 2008-2009 10. United States -- Politics and government 11. United States -- Economic conditions -- 2009-
ISBN 030795255X; 9780307952554
LC 2011052366

In this book, "author Charles H. Ferguson . . . explains how a predator elite took over the country, step by step, and he exposes the networks of academic, financial, and political influence, in all recent administrations, that prepared the predators' path to conquest." Topics include the decline of the manufacturing industry, fraud in the finance industry, and income inequality in the U.S. (Publisher's note)

Includes bibliographical references (p. 333-349) and index

Lind, Michael, 1962-
Land of promise; an economic history of the United States. by Michael Lind. Broadside Books 2012 586 p. (hardback) $29.99   **330.973**
1. United States -- History 2. Technological innovations -- History 3. United States -- Economic conditions
ISBN 0061834807; 9780061834806; 9780061834813
LC 2011047794

Author Michael Lind presents an "account of how a weak collection of former British colonies became an industrial, financial, and military colossus. From the eighteenth to the twenty-first centuries, the American economy has been transformed by wave after wave of emerging technology: the steam engine, electricity, the internal combustion engine, computer technology." Lind "demonstrates that Americans, since the earliest days of the republic, have reinvented the American economy--and have the power to do so again." (Publisher's note)

McCraw, Thomas K., 1940-2012
★ The **founders** and finance; how Hamilton, Gallatin, and other immigrants forged a new economy. Thomas K. McCraw. Belknap Press of Harvard University Press 2012 485 p. (hardcover) $35 **330.973**
1. Fiscal policy -- United States -- History 2. United States -- Economic policy 3. United States -- History -- 1783-1865 4. Finance, Public -- United States -- History 5. Monetary policy -- United States -- History 6. United States. Dept. of the Treasury -- History 7. United States -- History -- Revolution, 1775-1783 8. United States -- Politics and government -- 1783-1865
ISBN 0674066928; 9780674066922
LC 2012014006

This book, by Thomas K. McCraw, shows how "analyzes the skills and worldliness of Alexander Hamilton . . . , Albert Gallatin . . . , and other immigrant founders who guided the [United States] to prosperity. . . . Innovations designed by Hamilton, Gallatin, and other immigrants enabled the United States to control its debts, to pay for the Louisiana

Purchase of 1803, and . . . preserve[] the nation's hard-won independence from Britain." (Publisher's note)

"McCraw is a talented storyteller. His highly readable and fascinating work portrays the brilliance of Hamilton and Gallatin against the difficulty of their time and is strongly recommended to all readers interested in American and financial history." LJ

Includes bibliographical references and index

Reich, Robert B.
Saving capitalism; for the many, not the few. Robert B. Reich. Alfred A. Knopf 2015 304 p. illustrations (hardcover : alk. paper) $26.95 **330.973**
1. Capitalism 2. Economic policy -- United States 3. Business and politics -- United States 4. Capitalism -- United States 5. Income distribution -- United States 6. Democracy -- Economic aspects -- United States
ISBN 9780345806222; 9780385350570
LC 2015001873

In this book, author Robert B. Reich exposes "one of the most pernicious obstructions to progress today: the enduring myth of the 'free market' when, behind the curtain, it is the powerful alliances between Washington and Wall Street that control the invisible hand. . . . Reich shows that the truly critical choice ahead is between a market organized for broad-based prosperity and one designed to deliver ever more gains to the top." (Publisher's note)

"Reich's overriding message is that we don't have to put up with things as they are. It's a useful and necessary one, if not likely to sway the powers that be to become more generous of their own volition." Kirkus

Includes bibliographical references and index

Stone, James M.
Five easy theses; common-sense solutions to America's greatest economic challenges. James M. Stone. Houghton Mifflin Harcourt 2016 288 p. (hardcover) $26   **330.973**
1. Social policy -- United States 2. Economic policy -- United States 3. United States -- Social conditions 4. United States -- Economic conditions -- 2009- 5. United States -- Social policy -- 1993- 6. United States -- Economic policy -- 2009- 7. United States -- Social conditions -- 1980-
ISBN 9780544749009
LC 2015037880

In this book, author James M. Stone "presents specific, common-sense solutions to a handful of our most pressing challenges, showing how simple it would be to shore up Social Security, rein in an out-of-control financial sector, reduce inequality, and make healthcare and education better and more affordable." (Publisher's note)

"In a presidential election year, Stone does a wonderful job summarizing these critical topics clearly for a wide readership" LJ

Includes bibliographical references and index.

331 Economics of labor, finance, land, energy

Crawford, Matthew B.

Shop class as soulcraft; an inquiry into the value of work. Penguin Press 2009 246p il $25.95 **331**

1. Work

ISBN 978-1-59420-223-0

LC 2009-1789

The author "extols the value of making and fixing things in this masterful paean to what he calls 'manual competence,' the ability to work with one's hands. . . . With wit and humor, the author deftly mixes the details of his own experience as a tradesman and then proprietor of a motorcycle repair shop with more philosophical considerations." Publ Wkly

Includes bibliographical references

De Botton, Alain, 1969-

The pleasures and sorrows of work. Pantheon Books 2009 326p il $26 **331**

1. Work 2. Labor 3. Work -- Social aspects

ISBN 978-0-375-42444-1

LC 2008-46060

In this study of the workplace, the author visits "the under-charted worlds of the office, the factory, the fishing fleet and the logistics centre. . . . [He discusses such questions about work as]: Why do we do it? What makes it pleasurable? What is its meaning? And why do we daily exhaust not only ourselves but also the planet?" (Publisher's note)

"De Botton's sprightly mix of reportage and rumination expands beyond the workplace to investigate the broader meaning of life." Publ Wkly

Lichtenstein, Nelson

State of the Union: a century of American labor. Princeton Univ. Press 2002 336p il (Politics and society in twentieth-century America) hardcover o.p. pa $18.95 **331**

1. Labor unions 2. Labor -- United States

ISBN 0-691-11654-7 pa

LC 2001-36863

The author "analyzes the history of the labor movement from the 1930's to the present in the context of U.S. economics, politics, and democracy and from this he formulates ideas about where labor may find opportunities in this new century." Libr J

Includes bibliographical references

Murolo, Priscilla

From the folks who brought you the weekend; a short, illustrated history of labor in the United States. {by} Priscilla Murolo and A.B. Chitty; illustrations by Joe Sacco. New Press (NY) 2001 xx, 364p hardcover o.p. pa $17.95 **331**

1. Working class 2. Labor movement 3. Labor -- United States

ISBN 1-56584-776-8 pa

LC 2001-30978

"Brandishing little-known facts, the authors reshape common views of social history." Publ Wkly

Includes bibliographical references

Murray, R. Emmett

★ The lexicon of labor; more than 500 key terms, biographical sketches, and historical insights concerning labor in America. Rev. and updated ed.; New Press 2010 235p pa $16.95 **331**

1. Reference books 2. Labor -- United States -- Dictionaries

ISBN 978-1-59558-226-3

LC 2010-8276

First published 1998

This is an "encyclopedia of 500 entries for terms, concepts, people, legislation, places, and events in U.S. labor history." Booklist

Includes bibliographical references

331.1 Labor force and market

Damp, Dennis V.

★ The book of U.S. government jobs; where they are, what's available, and how to complete a Federal resume. 11th ed.; Bookhaven Press 2011 308p il pa $27.95 **331.1**

1. Civil service -- United States

ISBN 978-0-943641-29-4

LC 2011903343

First published 1986

This is "an essential guide to securing well-paying federal positions. [Its] . . . 11 chapters offer highly detailed instruction on where to locate and how to apply for federal jobs. Featuring tips for interview and exam performance, the accessible text presents instructive narratives and helpful sidebar hints. . . . Other chapters clarify the qualifications necessary for securing positions with the police, the postal service, and the homeland security administration." Libr J

Includes bibliographical references

Johnson, Jean

Where did the jobs go-- and how do we get them back? your guided tour to America's employment crisis. Scott Bittle and Jean Johnson. WilliamMorrow 2012 xix, 342 p.p (paperback) $16.99 **331.1**

1. Employment 2. Unemployment 3. United States -- Economic conditions 4. Employment (Economic theory) 5. Unemployment -- United States 6. Unemployment -- Government policy -- United States

ISBN 0061715662; 9780061715662

LC 2012371737

This book by Scott Bittle and Jean Johnson presents a "discussion and study guide on unemployment. . . . The authors provide a[n] . . . analysis of the many problems caused by the unemployment crisis, as well as possible solutions. . . . The authors . . . provide a[n] . . . historical discussion of the 1930s Depression and FDR's WPA program, as well as estimates of the financial costs of possible solutions and the ramifications for other sectors of American society." (Kirkus Reviews)

Includes bibliographical references (p. [302]-342)

Taylor, Nick

★ **American**-made; the enduring legacy of the WPA: when FDR put the nation to work. Bantam Books 2008 630p il $27   **331.1**

1. New Deal, 1933-1939 2. United States -- Works Progress Administration

ISBN 978-0-553-80235-1; 0-553-80235-6

LC 2007-34563

"Lavishly illustrated, the book also has a list of New Deal organizations, a partial list of construction projects, a New Deal chronology, and endnotes. It will be a boon to all 20th-century history collections." Libr J

Includes bibliographical references

Woodward, Bob, 1943-

Maestro: Greenspan's Fed and the American boom. Simon & Schuster 2000 270p il $25; pa $14   **331.1**

1. Economists 2. Bankers 3. Government officials 4. Presidential advisers 5. Regulatory agency officials 6. Monetary policy -- United States 7. Board of Governors of the Federal Reserve System 8. Federal Reserve System (U.S.) -- Board of Governors 9. Monetary policy -- United States -- History -- 20th century

ISBN 0-7432-0412-3; 0-7432-0562-6 pa

LC 00-52627

Woodward discusses the influence exerted over the American economy by the chairman of the Federal Reserve Board, Alan Greenspan. Index.

"In a surprisingly short book, Woodward lucidly explains the axes of intellectual and political disagreement over monetary policy, productivity growth, irrational exuberance and more, shedding new light on major conflicts of the Greenspan era and demystifying this most political of ostensibly technical institutions." N Y Times Book Rev

Includes bibliographical references

331.2   Conditions of employment

Jayaraman, Saru

Forked; a new standard for American dining. Saru Jayaraman. Oxford University Press 2016 240 p. illustrations (hardcover) $24.95   **331.2**

1. Restaurants 2. Salaries, wages, etc.

ISBN 9780199380473; 0199380473

LC 2015033657

This book, by Saru Jayaraman, "is an enlightening examination of what we don't talk about when we talk about restaurants. . . . [The author] offers an insider's view of the highest--and lowest--scoring restaurants for worker pay and benefits in each sector of the restaurant industry, and with it, a new way of thinking about how and where we eat." (Publisher's note)

"A revealing exposé of the realities of restaurant work that makes a strong case for reform." Kirkus

Includes bibliographical references and index.

Lowenstein, Roger

While America aged; how pension debts ruined General Motors, stopped the NYC subways, bank-

rupted San Diego, and loom as the next financial crisis. Penguin Press 2008 274p $25.95   **331.2**

1. Pensions 2. Retirement income

ISBN 978-1-594-20167-7; 1-59420-167-6

LC 2007-42508

"A chilling anatomy of one bad decision followed by another—and another." Kirkus

Includes bibliographical references

Schultz, Ellen

Retirement heist; how companies plunder and profit from the nest eggs of American workers. [by] Ellen E. Schultz. Portfolio/Penguin 2011 245p $26.95   **331.2**

1. Pensions 2. Corporations 3. Life insurance

ISBN 978-1-59184-333-7; 1-59184-333-2

LC 2011015064

"Readers are no stranger to the grumblings of their corporate overlords: Pensions are untenable; health-care costs too high; retiree benefits hurt competitiveness. But according to . . . Schultz, employee pensions actually make money for corporations, and the funds diverted from them help feather the beds of multimillionaire executives. She exposes all this and more in a rapid-fire narrative. Individual stories of retired men and women (some with more than 40 years of service) robbed of their nest eggs put a human face on the proceedings. . . . Essential reading for anyone who works for a living." Kirkus

Includes bibliographical references

Shulman, Beth

The **betrayal** of work; how low-wage jobs fail 30 million Americans and their families. New Press (NY) 2003 255p $25.95   **331.2**

1. Work 2. Minimum wage 3. Labor -- United States 4. United States -- Economic conditions

ISBN 1-56584-733-4

LC 2003-43413

The author "analyzes one of the downsides of the 'new economy': the large number of American jobs that pay poverty-level wages, have few or no benefits, and create child-care nightmares." Libr J

Includes bibliographical references

Terkel, Studs, 1912-2008

Working; people talk about what they do all day and how they feel about what they do. The New Press 1997 589p pa $16.95   **331.2**

1. Work 2. Labor -- United States 3. United States -- Social conditions

ISBN 978-1-56584-342-4; 1-56584-342-8

First published 1974 by Pantheon Bks.

Based on interviews, this study describes the working lives and feelings of people engaged in occupations ranging from interstate truck driver to stockbroker to bookbinder to corporation president.

This "is not a dry, academic treatise but a sensitive portrayal of the experience of working, with all its pain, tension, frustrations, and occasional satisfactions." Best Sellers

331.25 Other conditions of employment

Chertavian, Gerald.

A **Year** Up; how a pioneering program that teaches young adults real skills for real jobs-- with real success. Gerald Chertavian. Viking 2012 viii, 358 p.p **331.25**
1. Mentoring 2. Youth -- Employment 3. Year Up (Organization) 4. Internship programs -- United States 5. Occupational training -- United States 6. Internship programs -- New York (State) 7. Young adults -- Employment -- United States 8. Poor youth -- Employment -- New York (State) 9. Poor youth -- Education, Higher -- New York (State) 10. Young adults -- Vocational education -- United States 11. Poor youth -- Vocational education -- New York (State)
ISBN 9780670023776
LC 2012000606

This book is an "account of the origins and growth of Year Up, a groundbreaking employment program. Year Up founder and [chief executive officer] [Gerald] Chertavian debuts with this memoir about his nationwide program, which is aimed at 'closing the ever-widening Opportunity Divide in this country.'" (Kirkus)

331.3 Labor force by personal attributes

Fideler, Elizabeth F.

Men still at work; professionals over sixty and on the job. Elizabeth F. Fideler. Rowman & Littlefield Pub Inc. 2014 232 p. (cloth : alk. paper) $36 **331.3**
1. Age and employment 2. Elderly men -- Employment 3. Retirement age -- United States 4. Age and employment -- United States 5. Professional employees -- United States 6. Older men -- Employment -- United States
ISBN 1442222751; 9781442222755
LC 2013040402

This book, by Elizabeth F. Fideler, "explores the reasons why many men are continuing to work well beyond the traditional retirement age. In today's challenging economy, they are the second-fastest growing group of workers (just behind older women). Filled with profiles of older working men, . . . [it] explores thorny issues such as masculinity and the 'need to provide,' as well as economic issues, job satisfaction, and more." (Publisher's note)

"Overall, an engaging, accessible overview of what the future holds for many younger men who will undoubtedly work into their 60s ... and beyond." Choice

Includes bibliographical references and index

Levine, Marvin J.

Children for hire; the perils of child labor in the United States. Praeger Pubs. 2003 233p $49.95 **331.3**
1. Child labor 2. Youth -- Employment 3. Teenagers -- Employment
ISBN 1-56720-433-3
LC 2002-29767

The author defines the problem of child labor and "analyzes the working conditions of people under 18, the legal context for their employment and exploitation, and the impact of such labor upon the education and development of America's young people. An important work about a hidden social problem." Libr J

Includes bibliographical references and index

331.4 Women workers

Berebitsky, Julie

Sex and the office; a history of gender, power, and desire. Julie Berebitsky. Yale University Press 2012 x, 359 p.p (cloth : alk. paper) $38 **331.4**
1. Sexual harassment 2. Sex in the workplace 3. Women employees -- United States -- History 4. Sex role -- United States -- History -- 20th century 5. Women -- Employment -- United States -- History -- 20th century
ISBN 0300118996; 9780300118995
LC 2011026337

This book by Julie Berebitsky "explores how Americans' attitudes toward sexuality and gender in the office have changed since the 1860s. . . . Berebitsky recounts the actual experiences of female and male office workers; draws on archival sources . . . and explores how popular sources--including cartoons, advertisements, advice guides, and a wide array of fictional accounts--have represented wanted and unwelcome romantic and sexual advances." (Publisher's note)

Includes bibliographical references and index

Bohnet, Iris

What works; gender equality by design. Iris Bohnet. The Belknap Press of Harvard University Press 2016 400 p. illustrations (alk. paper) $26.95 **331.4**
1. Gender role 2. Organizational behavior 3. Sex discrimination in employment 4. Gender mainstreaming
ISBN 9780674089037
LC 2015039199

In this book, by Iris Bohnet, "Gender equality is a moral and a business imperative. But unconscious bias holds us back, and de-biasing people's minds has proven to be difficult and expensive. Diversity training programs have had limited success, and individual effort alone often invites backlash. Behavioral design offers a new solution. By de-biasing organizations instead of individuals, we can make smart changes that have big impacts." (Publisher's note)

Includes bibliographical references and index

Chang, Leslie T.

Factory girls; from village to city in a changing China. Spiegel & Grau 2008 420p map $26; pa $16 **331.4**
1. Migrant labor 2. Manufacturing industries 3. Women -- China
ISBN 978-0-385-52017-1; 0-385-52017-4; 978-0-385-52018-8 pa; 0-385-52018-2 pa
LC 2008-12880

This "is an exceptionally vivid and compassionate depiction of the day-to-day dramas, and the fears and aspirations, of the real people who are powering China's economic boom." N Y Times Book Rev

Includes bibliographical references

Featherstone, Liza

Selling women short; the landmark battle for workers' rights at Wal-Mart. Basic Bks. 2004 282p $25 **331.4**

1. Sex discrimination 2. Wal-Mart Stores, Inc.
ISBN 0-465-02315-0

LC 2004-10298

Using an "investigation of the class action suit Dukes v. Wal-Mart Stores, Inc. and . . . interviews with female workers, Featherstone indicts Wal-Mart for low wages, discriminatory policies and sexist practices. . . . This is a clearly written and compelling book." Publ Wkly

Includes bibliographical references

Fideler, Elizabeth F.

Women still at work; professionals over sixty and on the job. Elizabeth S. Fideler. Rowman & Littlefield Publishers 2012 vii, 209 p.p (cloth : alk. paper) $37.50; (ebook) $36.99 **331.4**

1. Age and employment 2. Elderly women -- Employment 3. Age and employment -- United States 4. Older women -- Employment -- United States
ISBN 144221550X; 9781442215504; 9781442215528

LC 2012017802

In this book on older women in the workforce, Elizabeth F. Fideler "tells the everyday stories of hard-working women and the reasons they're still on the job, with a focus on women in the professional workforce. . . . Their stories showcase some of the key themes women choose to stay at work -- including job satisfaction, diminishing retirement savings, the need to support children or parents longer in life, exercising the hard-won right to work, and more." (Publisher's note)

Includes bibliographical references

Kessler-Harris, Alice

★ **Out** to work; a history of wage-earning women in the United States. 20th anniversary ed; Oxford Univ. Press 2003 414p il pa $19.95 **331.4**

1. Women -- Employment -- History
ISBN 0-19-515709-5

LC 2003-267644

First published 1982

"This work remains a landmark in the field of analyzing the history of women's work in the United States from Colonial times to the Reagan era." Libr J

Includes bibliographical references

Povich, Lynn

★ The **good** girls revolt; how the women of Newsweek sued their bosses and changed the workplace. Lynn Povich. PublicAffairs 2012 xx, 249 p.p (hardcover) $25.99 **331.4**

1. Sexism 2. Women journalists 3. Sex discrimination in employment 4. Sex discrimination -- Law and legislation 5. Newsweek 6. Women journalists -- United States 7. Sex discrimination in employment -- United States 8. Sex role in the work environment

-- United States
ISBN 161039173X; 9781610391733; 9781610391740

LC 2012006936

Amelia Bloomer Project (2014)

This book by Lynn Povich explains how, in 1970, "forty-six 'Newsweek' women charged the magazine with discrimination in hiring and promotion. It was the first female class action lawsuit--the first by women journalists--and it inspired other women in the media to quickly follow suit. . . . 'The Good Girls Revolt' also explores why changes in the law didn't solve everything. Through the lives of young female journalists at Newsweek today, Lynn Povich shows what has--and hasn't--changed in the workplace." (Publisher's note)

Includes bibliographical references and index.

Ryckman, Pamela

Stiletto network; inside the women's power circles that are changing the face of business. Pamela Ryckman. American Management Association 2013 256 p. (hardcover) $22.95 **331.4**

1. Women executives 2. Women -- Social conditions 3. Businesswomen 4. Business networks 5. Strategic alliances 6. Women in the professions
ISBN 0814432530; 9780814432532

LC 2012051563

This book by Pamela Ryckman looks at the "female heads of industry [who] are the forerunners of a radical shift in power. It's about what happens when bright, extraordinary women, from captains of industry to aspiring entrepreneurs, come together to celebrate and unwind, debate and compare notes. It's about how they mine their collective intelligence to realize their dreams or champion a cause, . . . how they join forces to ensure each woman gets what she needs." (Publisher's note)

331.5 Workers by personal attributes other than age

Browne, John

The **Glass** Closet; Why Coming Out Is Good Business. John Browne. HarperCollins Publishers 2014 240 p. $27.99 **331.5**

1. LGBT people 2. Businesspeople 3. Autobiographies
ISBN 0062316974; 9780062316974

1st U.S. edition

"Part memoir and part social criticism, 'The Glass Closet' addresses the issue of homophobia that still pervades corporations around the world and underscores the immense challenges faced by LGBT employees. . . . In 'The Glass Closet,' Lord John Browne . . . seeks to unsettle business leaders by exposing the culture of homophobia that remains rampant in corporations around the world, and which prevents employees from showing their authentic selves." (Publisher's note)

"Brown's rhetoric is businesslike and a little dry but also to the point, supported by research, and culturally significant. He has taken pains to provide strikingly honest personal narratives and uses them to put a face on the problems at hand." Booklist

Includes bibliographical references (p. 203-234)

and index

331.6 Workers by ethnic and national origin

Bacon, David

Illegal people; how globalization creates migration and criminalizes immigrants. Beacon Press 2008 261p $25.95; pa $18 **331.6**
1. Labor policy 2. Globalization 3. Migrant labor 4. Unauthorized immigrants 5. Illegal aliens
ISBN 978-0-8070-4226-7; 978-0-8070-4230-4 pa
LC 2008-15394

The author "follows the lives of undocumented workers at the Westin Suite Hotel in California and a Smithfield meatpacking plant in North Carolina, who travel back and forth from Mexico to the U.S. He examines the economic and social forces in both countries that lure workers to a market where they can earn higher wages but are vulnerable to exploitation. . . . A fascinating look at trade and immigration policies and the people directly affected by them." Booklist
Includes bibliographical references

Breslin, Jimmy

The **short** sweet dream of Eduardo Gutierrez. Crown 2002 213p hardcover o.p. pa $12 **331.6**
1. Construction workers
ISBN 1-400-04682-3 pa
LC 2001-47283

"A true-life account of an illegal Mexican immigrant who died on a New York construction site, and of the dreary lives and modest ambitions common to Mexicans in this country." N Y Times Book Rev

331.7 Labor by industry and occupation

Bureau of Labor Statistics

Occupational outlook handbook. U.S. Dept. of Labor Bureau of Labor Statistics il **331.7**
1. Occupations 2. Reference books 3. Vocational guidance
Biennial. First published 1949.

"Gives information on employment trends and outlook in more than 800 occupations. Indicates nature of work, qualifications, earnings and working conditions, how to enter, where to go for more information, etc." Guide to Ref Books. 11th edition

Ferguson Publishing

The **top** 100; the fastest growing careers for the 21st century. 5th ed.; Ferguson 2011 388p $75; pa $19.95 **331.7**
1. Occupations 2. Vocational guidance
ISBN 978-0-8160-8367-1; 0-8160-8367-3; 978-0-8160-8359-6 pa; 0-8160-8359-2 pa; 978-1-4381-3767-4 ebook; 1-4381-3767-2 ebook
LC 2011004455
First published 1998

This book provides information "on jobs projected to experience the fastest growth, the greatest opportunity, and the best earnings through 2018, according to statistics from the U.S. Department of Labor. . . . Each job article describes the job duties; required education, training, and skills; expected earnings; and . . . more." Publisher's note

Fisher, James Terence

On the Irish waterfront; the crusader, the movie, and the soul of the port of New York. [by] James T. Fisher. Cornell University Press 2009 370p il map (Cushwa Center studies of Catholicism in Twentieth-century America) $29.95 **331.7**
1. Stevedores 2. Irish Americans 3. Catholic Church -- Missions 4. New York Harbor (N.Y. and N.J.) 5. On the waterfront (Motion picture)
ISBN 978-0-8014-4804-1; 0-8014-4804-2
LC 2009-13058

The author presents a "history of the New York-New Jersey waterfront depicted in Elia Kazan's Oscar-winning 1954 film, On the Waterfront. Fischer's impeccable research delves into the real-life stories behind the characters, particularly Pete Corridan, the crusading Catholic priest who tried to reform the longshoremen's union and the recently deceased Bud Schulberg, who adapted Malcolm Johnson's 1949 Pulitzer Prize-winning 'Crime on the Waterfront' newspaper series for the screen. . . . This engaging narrative is essential reading for both labor historians and cinema buffs, plus anyone studying the waterfront, working-class and immigrant history, anticommunism, blacklisting, and the House Un-American Activities Committee." Libr J
Includes bibliographical references

J.G. Ferguson Publishing Company

★ **Encyclopedia** of careers and vocational guidance; 15th ed.; Ferguson 2010 5v il set $249.95 **331.7**
1. Reference books 2. Occupations -- Encyclopedias 3. Vocational guidance -- Encyclopedias
ISBN 978-0-8160-8313-8; 0-8160-8313-4
LC 2010-17724
First published 1967

"These five volumes contain more than 700 . . . [articles] on careers in nearly 100 industries. Each three to five-page entry provides a concise and engaging profile of fields like accounting, animal care, computers, the environment, publishing, sales, and the visual arts. Included in each job entry are an overview, a history, a description, requirements, employers, advancement, earnings, work environment, outlook, and more." Libr J [review of 2008 edition]
Includes bibliographical references

Nagle, Robin

Picking up; on the streets and behind the trucks with the sanitation workers of New York City. Robin Nagle. Farrar, Straus and Giroux 2013 x, 280 p., [8] p. of platesp ill., map (hardcover) $28 **331.7**
1. Municipal officials and employees 2. Refuse and refuse disposal -- New York (N.Y.) 3. Sanitation workers -- New York (State) -- New York
ISBN 0689825528; 9780374299293
LC 2012028941
In this book, "Robin Nagle introduces us to the men and women of New York City's Department of Sanitation and

makes clear why this small army of uniformed workers is the most important labor force on the streets. Seeking to understand every aspect of the Department's mission, Nagle accompanied crews on their routes, questioned supervisors and commissioners, and listened to story after story about blizzards, hazardous wastes, and the insults of everyday New Yorkers." (Publisher's note)

Includes bibliographical references and index

331.702   Choice of vocation

McKenna, Amy

Nontraditional careers for women and men; more than 30 great jobs for women and men with apprenticeships through phds. by Andrew Morkes and Amy McKenna. College & Career Press 2012 280 p. $19.95   **331.702**
1. Occupations 2. Professions 3. Vocational guidance 4. Men -- Employment -- United States -- Juvenile literature 5. Vocational guidance -- United States -- Juvenile literature 6. Women -- Employment -- United States -- Juvenile literature
ISBN 0974525197; 9780974525198

LC 2011046915

This book about nontraditional employment with an emphasis on gender "is chock-full of career articles encompassing a wide variety of fields. Each career article includes salary information, skills needed, minimum education level, employment outlook, information about the career, certification and licensing information, tips for getting a job in this career, and industry resources." (Voice of Youth Advocates)

331.8   Labor unions, labor-management bargaining and disputes

Dray, Philip

There is power in a union; the epic story of labor in America. Doubleday 2010 772p il $35; ebook $35   **331.8**
1. Labor movement 2. Industrialization 3. Labor unions -- United States 4. United States -- Social conditions 5. Labor unions -- United States -- History 6. Labor movement -- United States -- History 7. Industrialization -- United States -- History
ISBN 978-0-385-52629-6; 0-385-52629-6; 978-0-385-53360-7 ebook

LC 201002357

This is a "narrative history of American labor. . . . From the textile mills of Lowell, Massachusetts . . . to the triumph of unions in the twentieth century and their waning influence today, the contest between labor and capital for their share of American bounty has shaped our national experience. Philip Dray's ambition is to show us the vital accomplishments of organized labor in that time and illuminate its central role in our social, political, economic, and cultural evolution." (Publisher's note) Bibliography. Index.

The author "follows organized labor from the struggles of early 19th-century female textile workers to the present-day retreat of organized labor following the failed 1981 air traffic controllers' strike. . . . Packed with vivid characters and dramatic scenes, Dray's fine recap of a neglected but vital tradition has much to say about labor's current straits." Publ Wkly

Includes bibliographical references

Dubofsky, Melvyn

★ **Labor** in America; a history. [by] Melvyn Dubofsky, Foster Rhea Dulles. 7th ed; Harlan Davidson 2005 472p il pa $34.95   **331.8**
1. Labor unions 2. Working class 3. Labor -- United States
ISBN 978-0-88295-998-6; 0-88295-998-0

LC 2003-13265

First published 1949 by Crowell under the authorship of Foster Rhea Dulles. Periodically revised

A study of the social and political impact of the American labor movement since colonial times

Includes bibliographical references

★ **Historical** encyclopedia of American labor; edited by Robert Weir and James P. Hanlan. Greenwood Press 2003 2v set $175   **331.8**
1. Reference books 2. Labor movement -- Encyclopedias 3. Labor -- United States -- Encyclopedias
ISBN 0-313-31840-9

LC 2003-52847

This "encyclopedia includes approximately 400 entries designed for the general researcher, students, and lay readers interested in learning more about such topics as unions, union leaders, union history, important laws and court cases, and labor terminology. An appendix contains excerpts from over 50 primary documents." Libr J

Includes bibliographical references

Shaw, Randy

Beyond the fields; Cesar Chavez, the UFW, and the struggle for justice in the 21st century. University of California Press 2008 347p il   **331.8**
1. Social action 2. Agricultural laborers 3. Labor leaders 4. United Farm Workers of America 5. Social justice -- United States 6. Social action -- United States -- History -- 20th century
ISBN 0520251075; 0520268040; 9780520251076; 9780520268043

LC 2008-31252

This book explores the impact of César Chávez and the United Farm Workers "on 21st-century social justice movements. Beyond the Fields [aims to show] . . . how Chávez and the UFW's imprint can be found in the modern reshaping of the American labor movement, the building of Latino political power, the transformation of Los Angeles and California politics, the fight for environmental justice, and the . . . movement for immigrant rights. [According to the author], many of the ideas, tactics, and strategies that Chávez and the UFW initiated or revived—including the boycott, the fast, clergy-labor partnerships and door-to-door voter outreach— are now so commonplace that their roots in the farmworkers' movement [are] forgotten. . . . UFW volunteers and staff were dedicated to furthering economic justice, and many devoted their post-UFW lives to working for social change." (Publisher's note) Index.

"Shaw's book is the product of extensive research, and it's invaluable for anyone interested in the evolution of unionization over the past forty years." Washington Monthly

Includes bibliographical references and index

★ **St.** James encyclopedia of labor history worldwide; major events in labor history and their impact. with introductions by Willie Thompson and Daniel Nelson; Neil Schlager, editor; produced by Schlager Groups. St. James Press 2003 2v set $260 **331.8**
1. Reference books 2. Labor movement -- Encyclopedias
ISBN 1-558-62542-9
LC 2003-294
"This reference promises to fill an important niche for larger public and academic libraries." Libr J

Stepan-Norris, Judith
Left out; Reds and America's industrial unions. [by] Judith Stepan-Norris, Maurice Zeitlin. Cambridge Univ. Press 2002 375p $75; pa $27 **331.8**
1. Labor -- United States 2. Labor unions -- United States
ISBN 0-521-79212-6; 0-521-79840-X pa
LC 2001-37655
"In 1947, ten 'Communist-dominated unions' were expelled from the CIO. The mythology that developed is that these unions sacrificed the interests of the American worker to the foreign policy dictates of the Statlin-era Soviet Union. The authors, both sociologists, use statistical analysis of contracts to argue that these unions actually had the most democracy, the most pro-labor contracts, and the best track record in fighting for gender and racial equality in the labor movement." Libr J

Includes bibliographical references

Zieger, Robert H.
American workers, American unions; the twentieth century. {by} Robert H. Zieger & Gilbert J. Gall. 3rd ed; Johns Hopkins Univ. Press 2002 292p (The American moment) pa $17.95 **331.8**
1. Labor unions 2. Labor -- United States
ISBN 0-8018-7078-X
LC 2002-3250
First published 1986
"This standard work of American labor history from the Gilded Age onward has been updated to almost the present, with the last paragraph discussing September 11. Zieger's strength lies in his striving for a balanced survey." Libr J

Includes bibliographical references

331.88 Labor unions (Trade unions)

Gorn, Elliott J.
Mother Jones; the most dangerous woman in America. Hill & Wang 2001 408p il hardcover o.p. pa $14 **331.88**
1. Centenarians 2. Labor leaders
ISBN 0-8090-7094-4 pa
LC 00-44997

This is a biography of union organizer and labor leader Mary Harris Jones, known more popularly as Mother Jones

Gorn "has successfully separated fact from myth . . . situating Jones's story within a wider cultural frame." Publ Wkly

Includes bibliographical references

Labor rising; the past and future of working people in America. edited by Richard A. Greenwald, Daniel Katz. New Press, The 2012 318 p. (paperback) $20.95 **331.88**
1. Working class 2. Labor economics 3. Labor movement -- History 4. Working class -- United States -- History 5. Labor movement -- United States -- History
ISBN 1595585184; 9781595585189
LC 2012001464
Editors Daniel Katz and Richard A. Greenwald present a "volume [that] provides readers with an understanding of the history that is directly relevant to the economic and political crises working people face today, and points the way to a revitalized twenty-first-century labor movement. With original contributions from leading labor historians, social critics, and activists," the book "makes crucial connections between the past and present, and then looks forward, asking how we might imagine a different future for all Americans." (Publisher's note)

332 Financial economics

Gasparino, Charles
The **sellout**; how three decades of Wall Street greed and government mismanagement destroyed the global financial system. Harper Business 2009 553p $27.99 **332**
1. Wall Street (New York, N.Y.) 2. Global Financial Crisis, 2008-2009
ISBN 978-0-06-169716-6; 0-06-169716-8
LC 2009-28097
"Of all the books documenting the financial crisis . . . The Sellout tells it better than most. Filled with very little of the boring, complex financial jargon that comprises many books of the genre, this tome makes for a surprisingly entertaining and easy read." Risk Management

Includes bibliographical references

Mayer, Robert
Quick cash; the story of the loan shark. Northern Illinois University Press 2010 293p $35 **332**
1. Loans 2. Usury
ISBN 978-0-8758-0430-9; 0-8758-0430-6
LC 2010014718
This book "traces high-interest lending from the late 19th century through the latest financial crisis. While the book focuses on Chicago, it does reference lending practices throughout the South and New York City. Chapters delve into the social issues of the early 20th century that created a market for these high-interest loans, the various government policies that tried to regulate the lenders, and the legal and economic changes that gave rise to the current methods of payday lending since the 1980s. . . . [The author] has created an original and multidisciplinary look at subprime lending in

the United States that is accessible to a wide variety of readers, including students and professionals." Libr J

Includes bibliographical references

Piketty, Thomas, 1971-

Capital in the twenty-first century; Thomas Piketty; translated by Arthur Goldhammer. The Belknap Press of Harvard University Press 2014 696 p. illustrations (alk. paper) $39.95   **332**

1. Equality 2. Economic forecasting 3. Economic development -- History 4. Wealth 5. Capital 6. Labor economics 7. Income distribution

ISBN 067443000X; 9780674430006

LC 2013036024

"In 'Capital in the Twenty-First Century,' Thomas Piketty analyzes a unique collection of data from twenty countries, ranging as far back as the eighteenth century, to uncover key economic and social patterns. . . . Piketty shows that modern economic growth and the diffusion of knowledge have allowed us to avoid inequalities on the apocalyptic scale predicted by Karl Marx. . . . Political action has curbed dangerous inequalities in the past, Piketty says, and may do so again." (Publisher's note)

Shows "that plain language can be put to work explaining the most complex of ideas, foremost among them the fact that economic inequality is at an all-time high--and is only bound to grow worse." Kirkus

Includes bibliographical references and index

332.024   Personal finance

Armstrong, Frank

The retirement challenge--will you sink or swim? a complete, do-it-yourself toolkit to navigate your financial future. FT Press 2009 266p il pa $21.99   **332.024**

1. Retirement 2. Personal finance

ISBN 0-13-236132-9; 978-0-13-236132-3

LC 2008-29134

"With a companion web site (www.sink-swim.com), this planning guide takes readers through the steps: determining retirement age, setting up retirement funds, forecasting financial needs, and much, much more." Libr J

Bradford, Stacey L.

The Wall Street Journal: financial guidebook for new parents. Three Rivers Press 2009 196p il pa $14.95   **332.024**

1. Parents 2. Personal finance

ISBN 978-0-307-40707-8; 0-307-40707-1

LC 2008-50657

The author "presents a relevant and witty overview of the awesome task facing new parents—affording their kids. She covers all the major issues, including child tax credits, the Family and Medical Leave Act of 1993, flexible spending accounts, and 529 plans; even wills, trusts, and disability insurance are considered." Libr J

D'Agnese, Joseph

The money book for freelancers, part-time, and the self-employed; the only personal finance system for people with not-so-regular jobs. [by] Joseph D'Agnese & Denise Kiernan. Three Rivers Press 2010 306p il pa $15   **332.024**

1. Self-employed 2. Personal finance

ISBN 978-0-307-45366-2; 0-307-45366-9

LC 2009-31596

"The authors describe how one can maximize financial security without compromising success by addressing debts, taxes, emergency funds, and retirement savings using their 'Freelance Finance System.' They preach commonsense ideas such as accountability and restraint but also describe plenty of clever ways to make one's money go further. . . . Developed from the personal experiences of the authors, this book is fun and relevant. . . . Recommended for anyone who is self-employed now or is facing a new work-life situation." Libr J

Economides, Annette, 1961-

The moneysmart family system; teaching financial independence to children of every age. Steve Economides, Annette Economides. Thomas Nelson 2012 272 p. $16.99   **332.024**

1. Child rearing 2. Personal finance 3. Household budgets 4. Families -- Economic aspects 5. Children -- Finance, Personal

ISBN 1400202841; 9781400202843

LC 2012941594

This book, by Steve and Annette Economides, teaches how to "raise financially responsible kids of any age in a society filled with consumerism." The "Economides raised their five kids while spending 77 percent less than the USDA predicted. And the money they did spend was also used to train their children to become financially independent." Their "system will show you how to teach your children to manage money and have a good attitude while they're learning." (Publisher''s note)

Hirshman, Susan L.

Does this make my assets look fat? a woman's guide to finding financial empowerment and success. St. Martin's Press 2010 302p il $24.99; ebook $11.99   **332.024**

1. Investments 2. Personal finance 3. Women -- United States

ISBN 978-0-312-38553-8; 0-312-38553-6; 978-1-4299-5006-0 ebook; 1-4299-5006-4 ebook

LC 2010-21668

"Comparing getting one's financial house in order to dieting, Hirshman . . . presents chapters on assessing personal finance fitness and gives comprehensive definitions and explanations of, as well as practical suggestions on, various investment strategies." Libr J

Jason, Julie

✓ ★ The **AARP** Retirement Survival Guide; how to make smart financial decisions in good times and bad. Sterling Pub. Co. 2009 340p pa $14.95 **332.024**

1. Pensions 2. Personal finance 3. Retirement income
ISBN 978-1-4027-4341-2

LC 2008-20577

This guide to retirement "includes a solid grounding in the basics (such as the infamous What's your number? discussion), careful outlines of how to approach retirement income products as well as the stock market, and approaches to taxes and to potential advisors." Booklist

Includes bibliographical references

Kessel, Brent

✓ **It's** not about the money; unlock your money type to achieve spiritual and financial abundance. Harper-One 2008 xxi, 299p il $24.95; pa $14.99 **332.024**

1. Money 2. Self-perception 3. Personal finance 4. Applied psychology
ISBN 978-0-06-123406-4; 978-0-06-123405-7 pa

LC 2007-18380

The author "offers 'holistic financial advice' in this Buddhist-influenced . . . [book] promising both a better financial strategy and greater fulfillment and happiness. . . . Readers interested in an Eastern-influenced approach will find useful advice on how to think about money, as well as insight into what makes us tick." Publ Wkly

Includes bibliographical references

Kiyosaki, Robert T., 1947-

Why "A" Students Work for "C" Students and Why "B" Students Work for the Government; Rich Dad's Guide to Financial Education for Parents. Robert T. Kiyosaki. Perseus Distribution Services 2013 453 p. (paperback) $16.95 **332.024**

1. Creative ability 2. Education -- Aims and objectives
ISBN 1612680763; 9781612680767

In this book, Robert T. Kiyosaki "expands on his belief that the school system was created to churn out . . . 'A Students' who read well, memorize well and test well . . . and not the creative thinkers . . . who grow up to be the innovators and creators of new ideas, businesses, applications and products. The book urges parents . . . to . . . focus, instead, on concepts, ideas, and helping their child find their true genius, their special gift." (Publisher's note)

Kobliner, Beth

Get a financial life; personal finance in your twenties and thirties. Beth Kobliner. 3rd ed. Simon & Schuster 2009 336 p. $16 **332.024**

1. Debt 2. Money 3. Housing 4. Personal finance 5. Finance, Personal 6. Young adults -- Finance, Personal
ISBN 0743264363; 9780743264365

LC 2008046645

Author Beth Kobliner "focuses exclusively on what you need to know when you're just starting to pay serious attention to money matters. . . . [The book offers] solutions and cutting edge tools in this brave new world of financial madness. . . . [It] covers everything a young person needs to know to get on the path to long-lasting financial security . .

. from debt and housing issues to banking, investing, taxes, and insurance." (bethkobliner.com)

Includes bibliographical references and index

Lieber, Ron

✓ The **Opposite** of Spoiled; Raising Kids Who Are Grounded, Generous, and Smart About Money. Ron Lieber. HarperCollins 2015 256 p. $26.99 **332.024**

1. Parenting 2. Personal finance
ISBN 0062247018; 9780062247018

LC 2014035600

This book, by Ron Lieber, "delivers a . . . manifesto that explains how talking openly to children about money can help parents raise modest, patient, grounded young adults who are financially wise beyond their years. . . . It identifies a set of traits and virtues that embody the opposite of spoiled, and shares how to embrace the topic of money to help parents raise kids who are more generous and less materialistic." (Publisher's note)

"Humble stories of kids raising money for Down syndrome research or creating kit bags to give to people living on the street offer inspiration for those who do have money to spend it wisely in the world and to teach their children to do the same. Sound advice on managing family finances but only if you have sufficient finances to manage." Kirkus

McNaughton, Deborah

The **essential** credit repair handbook; [a quick and handy guide for anyone who wants to get and stay out of debt] Career Press 2011 224p pa $14.99 **332.024**

1. Debt 2. Consumer credit 3. Personal finance
ISBN 978-1-60163-160-2 pa; 1-60163-160-X pa; 978-1-60163-666-9 ebook; 1-60163-666-0 ebook

LC 2011010730

This book discusses "how to: dispute late payments, charge-offs, and collection accounts; rebuild your life after a bankruptcy, foreclosure, or short sale; re-establish your credit in spite of a bad credit report; set new financial goals; [and] understand the latest credit card laws and regulations. . . . [This is a] guide for people who are getting over bankruptcy, foreclosure, short sale, or any financial hardship affecting their credit and are looking to rebuild or re-establish their credit." Publisher's note

Includes bibliographical references

Miller, Mark

The **hard** times guide to retirement security; practical strategies for money, work, and living. Wiley 2010 223p il pa $16.95; ebook $11.99 **332.024**

1. Retirement income
ISBN 978-1-57660-362-8 pa; 978-0-470-90834-1 ebook

LC 2010-14478

This guide to retirement after the financial crisis touches upon "issues such as insuring against the risk of outliving your assets, recalibrating damaged retirement portfolios, managing the risk of health-care expenses in retirement, and career strategies for workers who are 50 years old and up." Publisher's note

Orman, Suze

The **money** class; learn to create your new American dream. Spiegel & Grau 2011 281p $26; ebook $13.99   **332.024**

1. Wealth 2. Personal finance

ISBN 978-1-4000-6973-6; 978-0-679-60470-9 ebook

LC 2011-1394

"Organized into nine 'classes,' with each class/chapter further divided into related lessons, . . . [this book is] upbeat and no-nonsense, offering lessons on family matters, homeownership, saving for college, emergencies, retirement, and more. Orman firmly guides readers when dealing with parenting issues or underwater mortgages. . . . After finishing Orman's book, and completing her exercises, readers will have a very clear sense of how they can achieve what she has rechristened the 'New American Dream.'" Publ Wkly

Pepper, Carol

The **seven** pearls of financial wisdom; a woman's guide to enjoying wealth and power. Carol Pepper and Camilla Webster. 1st ed. St. Martin's Press 2012 viii, 338 p.p (hardcover) $25.99; (paperback) $19.99   **332.024**

1. Businesswomen 2. Life cycle, Human 3. Women -- Personal finance 4. New business enterprises 5. Women -- Finance, Personal 6. Investments -- Psychological aspects

ISBN 0312641664; 1250008328; 9780312641665; 9781250008329; 9781250035486

LC 2012010250

"The goal of wealth-management adviser [Carol] Pepper and financial journalist [Camilla] Webster is to assist with common issues that arise in women's financial lives and to turn those issues into assets. . . . They discuss romance, children, crises ranging from health problems to natural disasters, leadership, wealth accrual, leaving a legacy, and mapping out a path to financial security. . . . Women are encouraged to start their own businesses, invest wisely . . . and live well." (Library Journal)

Includes bibliographical references and index.

Pond, Jonathan D.

Grow your money! 101 easy tips to plan, save, and invest. Collins 2008 xlv, 352p $26.95 **332.024**

1. Investments 2. Public finance 3. Retirement income

ISBN 978-0-06-112140-1; 0-06-112140-1

LC 2007-24071

The author offers "investment and financial definitions, debt-management strategies, retirement and home-ownership considerations, tax tips, and more, enabling lay readers to understand these seemingly daunting and complex issues." Libr J

Quinn, Jane Bryant

Making the most of your money now; the classic bestseller. Completely rev. for the new economy; Simon & Schuster hardcover ed.; Simon & Schuster 2010 1242p $35   **332.024**

1. Investments 2. Personal finance

ISBN 978-0-7432-6996-4; 0-7432-6996-9

LC 2009-32610

First published 1991 with title: Making the most of your money

This guide includes information about investing, buying a home, life and health insurance, retirement planning, checklists for life changes, finding a financial advisor, and financing college.

"This is an excellent primer, especially for those new to managing their money." Libr J

Schwab-Pomerantz, Carrie

It pays to talk; how to have the essential conversations with your family about money and investing. [by] Carrie Schwab-Pomerantz and Charles R. Schwab. Crown Business 2003 386p il hardcover o.p. pa $14   **332.024**

1. Investments 2. Personal finance

ISBN 0-609-61028-7; 1-4000-4960-1 pa

LC 2002-5994

The authors "share their insights on money, investing and the conversations that need to accompany these. Their focus is on the importance of conducting different lifestage conversations (e.g., how to financially approach being single, getting married, raising children, helping parents); and this . . . primer provides one-stop shopping for the many phases of financial understanding and planning. . . . This educational volume provides a useful framework that a family can refer to when approaching those often difficult but necessary conversations about finances." Publ Wkly

Includes bibliographical references

Solin, Daniel R.

The **smartest** retirement book you'll ever read. Penguin Group 2009 255p $21.95   **332.024**

1. Investments 2. Personal finance 3. Retirement income

ISBN 978-0-399-53520-8

LC 2009014075

The author "offers short chapters on a variety of retirement subjects, each concluding with a pithy summarization. . . [It is] clearly written and easy to understand, tackling such topics as stocks, bonds, annuities, pensions, and cash withdrawal strategies." Libr J

Includes bibliographical references

Tobias, Andrew P.

★ The **only** investment guide you'll ever need; [by] Andrew Tobias. Completely updated and rev.; Houghton Mifflin Harcourt 2011 306p il pa $14.95   **332.024**

1. Investments 2. Personal finance

ISBN 978-0-547-44725-4

LC 2010-41533

First published 1978

This book offers advice on such topics as personal investments, tax strategies, life insurance, stock market trading, college funds, real estate, and inheritance.

Includes bibliographical references

Velshi, Ali

How to speak money; the language and knowledge you need now. Ali Velshi and Christine Romans. John Wiley & Sons 2012 xviii, 190 p.p   **332.024**
1. Money 2. Personal finance 3. Economics -- Terminology 4. Finance, Personal
ISBN 9781118114957

LC 2011033518

In this book about personal finance, "[a]uthors and CNN financial experts Ali Velshi and Christine Romans speak the global language of money. . . . Speaking money affects every area of your life. It's more than simply your savings or the investments you may have. It involves the way you think about money, the way you teach your children about it, and the way you were taught about it yourself. It's about the way you spend it, save it, invest it, use it, need it and want it. The book will . . . [cover] the male and female spending and investing disparity, . . . emerging international economies, . . . [the] hurdle of student debt, . . . [and explain] how to plan appropriately for retirement." (Publisher's note)

Includes bibliographical references (p. 179-180) and index

Walsh, Peter

Lighten up; love what you have, have what you need, be happier with less. Free Press 2011 288p $26; pa $15; ebook $12.99   **332.024**
1. Happiness 2. Conduct of life 3. Personal finance
ISBN 978-1-4391-5514-1; 978-1-4391-5515-8 pa; 978-1-4391-6008-4 ebook

LC 2010030244

The author "coaches readers in dealing with psychological clutter tied to money and finances so they can live thrifty lives that are also liberating, pleasurable, and rewarding. . . . At the crux of this book are three audits designed to instigate life changes: a financial audit combined with assessments of the physical junk filling our homes and the emotional junk causing tension in our lives. Throughout, Walsh challenges readers to face not just the physical clutter overwhelming their homes but also the psychological underpinnings to their habits and attitudes, to confront family members, and to establish tough boundaries within the limits of their family's means. . . . Motivated readers will find plenty of helpful tips to jump-start their self-transformations." Publ Wkly

Weltman, Barbara

★ J.K. Lasser's guide for tough times; tax and financial solutions to see you through. John Wiley 2009 224p pa $18.95   **332.024**
1. Taxation 2. Income tax 3. Investments 4. Personal finance
ISBN 978-0-470-40232-0; 0-470-40232-6

LC 2008-32269

"Besides tax and financial advice for coping with a down economy, Weltman examines steps being taken by the federal government (mortgage relief, stimulus packages) to ease the recession." Libr J

Yeager, Jeff

The cheapskate next door; the surprising secrets of Americans living happily below their means.

Broadway Books 2010 231p pa $12.99; ebook $12.99   **332.024**
1. Personal finance
ISBN 978-0-7679-3132-8 pa; 978-0-307-59247-7 ebook

LC 2009-42287

"The amazing fact about this book is that in addition to his instructions making perfect sense, like no other book of its kind, this one can be read simply for the humor of the author's prose." Booklist

332.1   Banks

Ahamed, Liaquat

Lords of finance; the bankers who broke the world. Penguin Press 2009 564p il $32.95   **332.1**
1. Capitalists and financiers
ISBN 978-1-59420-182-0

LC 2008-44512

"A grand, sweeping narrative of immense scope and power." N Y Times Book Rev

Includes bibliographical references

Farrell, Greg

Crash of the titans; greed, hubris, the fall of Merrill Lynch, and the near-collapse of Bank of America. Crown Business 2010 471p $27; pa $17; ebook $12.99   **332.1**
1. Bank failures 2. Corporate mergers and acquisitions 3. Bank of America NA 4. Merrill Lynch & Co., Inc.
ISBN 978-0-307-71786-3; 978-0-307-71787-0 pa; 978-0-307-71788-7 ebook

LC 2010485623

This is an account of the decline of Merrill Lynch & Co. and Bank of America Corp. The author claims that "at the moment they should have been minding their balance sheets, . . . many of the financial industry's masters of the universe were preoccupied with their bonuses, expense accounts, and office renovations." Businessweek

Includes bibliographical references

Johnson, Simon

13 bankers; the Wall Street takeover and the next financial meltdown. [by] Simon Johnson and James Kwak. Pantheon Books 2010 304p il $26.95; pa $15.95; ebook $11.99   **332.1**
1. Bank failures 2. Financial crises 3. Finance -- United States 4. Banks and banking -- United States
ISBN 978-0-307-37905-4; 0-307-37905-1; 978-0-307-47660-9 pa; 0-307-47660-X pa; 978-0-307-37922-1 ebook

LC 2010-00168

Johnson and Kwak examine not only how Wall Street's ideology, wealth, and political power among policy makers in Washington led to the financial debacle of 2008, but also what the lessons learned portend for the future.

"The book is a thoughtful, stimulating read on a topic of much ongoing debate and concern." Choice

Includes bibliographical references

Lefevre, John

Straight to Hell; true tales of deviance, debauchery, and billion-dollar deals. John LeFevre. Atlantic Monthly Press 2015 288 p. (hardback) $26 **332.1**
1. Banks and banking -- Corrupt practices
ISBN 0802123309; 9780802123305; 9781611855548
LC 2015460485

This book, by John LeFevre, is "an unapologetic . . . account of a career as a globe-conquering investment banker spanning New York, London, and Hong Kong. . . . [The author] pulls back the curtain on a world that is both hated and envied, taking readers from the trading floors and roadshows to private planes and after-hours overindulgence." (Publisher's note)

"This will appeal readily to heterosexual males with an inflated sense of entitlement and a mental age below 30, particularly those working in large corporations." LJ

Lowenstein, Roger

America's Bank; The Epic Struggle to Create the Federal Reserve. by Roger Lowenstein. Penguin Group USA 2015 368 p. illustrations $29.95 **332.1**
1. Federal Reserve banks 2. Banks and banking -- United States
ISBN 1594205493; 9781594205491

This book, by Roger Lowenstein, "illuminates the tumultuous era and remarkable personalities that spurred the unlikely birth of America's modern central bank, the Federal Reserve. Today, the Fed is the bedrock of the financial landscape, yet the fight to create it was so protracted and divisive that it seems a small miracle that it was ever established." (Publisher's note)

"Readers seeking a comprehensive history of the Federal Reserve from its conception to modern times will find this work especially appealing." LJ

Meltzer, Allan H.

★ A **history** of the Federal Reserve; v1 with a foreword by Alan Greenspan. University of Chicago Press 2002 800p v1 $75; pa $25 **332.1**
1. Federal Reserve banks 2. Federal Reserve System (U.S.) -- Board of Governors
ISBN 0-226-51999-6; 0-226-52000-5 pa
LC 2002-72007

The author "provides a definitive history of the U.S. Federal Reserve from its founding in 1913 to its establishment as a separate, independent entity in 1951. Using meeting minutes, correspondence, and internal Federal Reserve documents, he traces the reasons behind Federal Reserves policy decisions, highlights the impact that individuals and events had on the Fed, and examines the Fed's influence on international affairs. . . . This well-written and thoroughgoing account is recommended for academic, business, and public libraries." Libr J

Includes bibliographical references

Overtveldt, Johan van

Bernanke's test; Ben Bernanke, Alan Greenspan, and the drama of the central banker. Agate 2009 287p il $26 **332.1**
1. Economists 2. Bankers 3. Government officials 4. Presidential advisers 5. Regulatory agency officials 6.

Economic policy -- United States 7. Monetary policy -- United States 8. Banks and banking -- United States 9. Federal Reserve System (U.S.) -- Board of Governors
ISBN 978-1-932841-37-4; 1-932841-37-7
LC 2008-45741

"Anyone who wants to understand the role of the Fed in the current crisis will find this an accessible primer." Publ Wkly

Includes bibliographical references

Parks, Tim

Medici money; banking, metaphysics, and art in fifteenth-century Florence. W. W. Norton & Co. 2005 273p il map (Enterprise) $22.95 **332.1**
1. Banks and banking 2. Bankers 3. Political leaders 4. Florence (Italy) -- History
ISBN 0-393-05827-1
LC 2004-30516

"The general reader will learn from this book a great deal about the era, and those who bestrode it, without getting bogged down in excessive scholarly detail." Natl Rev

Includes bibliographical references

Rockefeller, David

Memoirs. Random House 2002 517p $35; pa $17.95 **332.1**
1. Philanthropists 2. Bankers 3. Chase Manhattan Bank, N.A.
ISBN 0-679-40588-7; 0-8129-6973-1 pa
LC 2002-24800

"Rockefeller's style is restrained and self-deprecating; the account of his attempts to modernize and globalize Chase makes for excellent business history, and his sketch of his complicated relationship with his brother is especially convincing." New Yorker

Wessel, David

★ **In** Fed we trust; Ben Bernanke's war on the great panic. Crown Business 2009 323 p. (hbk.) $26.99 **332.1**
1. Economists 2. Banks and banking 3. Global Financial Crisis, 2008-2009 4. Government officials 5. Regulatory agency officials 6. Federal Reserve System (U.S.) 7. Monetary policy -- United States 8. Financial crises -- United States 9. Federal Reserve System (U.S.) -- Board of Governors
ISBN 9780307459688; 0307459683
LC 2009-289789

This book reviews events of 2008 as the U. S. government attempted to stave off financial panic. Under the leadership of Ben Bernanke, the Federal Reserve "spearheaded the biggest government intervention in more than half a century. . . . [Wessel discusses questions such as]: What did Bernanke and his team at the Fed know—and what took them by surprise? Which of their actions stretched—or even ripped through—the Fed's legal authority? . . . What were they thinking at pivotal moments during the race to sell Bear Stearns, the unsuccessful quest to save Lehman Brothers, and the virtual nationalization of AIG, Fannie Mae, and Freddie Mac? . . . How well did Bernanke, former treasury secretary Hank Paulson, and then New York Fed president

Tim Geithner perform under intense pressure?" (Publisher's note)

The author "has written a gripping blow-by-blow account of how the top brass at the Federal Reserve and Treasury flailed against financial collapse. . . . [The story] is a thrilling one, deftly told by a veteran journalist with access to those involved. Mr Wessel has an eye for enlivening detail, . . . and he has a knack for making finance accessible to the layman without boring the specialist." Economist

Includes bibliographical references

332.3   Credit and loan institutions

Grind, Kirsten

The **lost** bank; the story of Washington Mutual--the biggest bank failure in American history. Kirsten Grind. Simon & Schuster 2012 389 p.   **332.3**

1. Bank failures 2. Financial crises 3. Washington Mutual, Inc. 4. Savings and loan associations 5. Banks and banking -- United States 6. Washington Mutual, Inc 7. Bank failures -- United States -- History 8. Banks and banking -- Washington (State) -- Seattle -- History 9. Savings and loan association failures -- United States -- History 10. Savings and loan associations -- Washington (State) -- Seattle -- History

ISBN 1451617925; 9781451617924; 9781451617931; 9781451617948

LC 2011048587

In this book, "reporter [Kirsten] Grind chronicles the rise of Washington Mutual from a sleepy Seattle-based thrift to America's biggest savings and loan bank, its reckless plunge into the can't-lose subprime mortgage market, and its 2008 failure. . . . [The book includes] personalities like Kerry Killinger, WaMu's . . . CEO, and Jamie Dimon, the . . . JPMorgan leader who swallowed WaMu, . . . [as well as the] WaMu salespeople. . . . Grind pens a . . . guide to the delusions and frauds powering the debacle, from Fed chief Alan Greenspan's . . . economic forecasts down to the falsified documents that put people with no income, assets, or perhaps even pulses into mortgages they could never repay." (Publishers Weekly)

Includes bibliographical references.

332.4   Money

Rickards, James

Currency wars; the making of the next global crisis. Portfolio/Penguin 2011 288p $26.95   **332.4**

1. Monetary policy 2. Financial crises 3. Foreign exchange

ISBN 978-1-59184-449-5

LC 2011026906

The author "tells us we are in a new currency war that could destroy faith in the U.S. dollar; he examines that war through the lens of economic policy, national security, and historical precedent. As a national security issue, he tells a fascinating story of his involvement with the Pentagon and other agencies in designing and participating in a war game using currencies and capital markets, instead of ships and planes, to gain early warning of attacks on the U.S. dollar.

. . . He presents a compelling case for his views and offers thought-provoking information for library patrons. This is a must-read book." Booklist

Includes bibliographical references

332.6   Investment

Bernstein, William

The **four** pillars of investing; lessons for building a winning portfolio. [by] William J. Bernstein. McGraw Hill 2010 331p il $30   **332.6**

1. Investments

ISBN 978-0-07-174705-9

First published 2002

The author discusses "the four pillars—the theory of investing, the history of investing, the psychology of investing, and the business of investing. . . . Using humor, Bernstein advises readers to employ sound tenets of investing to manage risk while building a foundation of assests for the long term." Libr J

Includes bibliographical references

The **investor's** manifesto; preparing for prosperity, Armageddon, and everything in between. [by] William J. Bernstein. Wiley 2010 xxii, 201p il $24.95; ebook $24.95   **332.6**

1. Stocks 2. Securities 3. Investments

ISBN 978-0-470-50514-4; 978-0-470-55807-2 ebook

LC 2009-20116

"Touching on lessons from the dot.com and 2008 market sell-offs, . . . [the author] discusses market and investor psychology, asset allocation, the unpredictability of returns, how to keep costs low, and, ultimately, how to avoid dying poor." Libr J

Includes bibliographical references

Boeckh, J. Anthony

The **great** reflation; how investors can profit from the new world of money. John Wiley & Sons 2010 xxii, 314p il $34.95   **332.6**

1. Investments 2. Business cycles 3. Financial crises 4. Personal finance

ISBN 978-0-470-53877-7

LC 2009-54227

"After laying out the post-2008 state of the U.S. economy and the inflation/deflation dangers as the Federal Reserve attempts to stimulate activity in the shadow of massive debt deleveraging, economist Boeckh then presents various investing scenarios." Libr J

Includes bibliographical references

Bogle, John C., 1929-

The **clash** of the cultures; investment vs. speculation. John C. Bogle. John Wiley & Sons 2012 xxv, 353 p.p ill. (hardcover) $29.95; (ebook) $29.95; (ebook) $40.00   **332.6**

1. Investments 2. Speculation 3. Mutual funds 4. Capital gains

ISBN 9781118122778; 9781118224748 pdf;

9781118414378

LC 2012026770

This book, by John C. Bogle, explores how "speculation has come to dominate investment. . . . Over the course of his sixty-year career in the mutual fund industry, Vanguard Group founder John C. Bogle has witnessed . . . the prudent, value-adding culture of long-term investment . . . crowded out by an aggressive, value-destroying culture of short-term speculation. . . . [This book] urges a return to the common sense principles of long-term investing." (Publisher's note)

Includes bibliographical references and index.

Buffett, Mary

Warren Buffett and the art of stock arbitrage; proven strategies for arbitrage and other special investment situations. [by] Mary Buffett & David Clark. Scribner 2010 153p $25; ebook $11.99 **332.6**

1. Investments 2. Financiers

ISBN 978-1-4391-9882-7; 978-1-4516-0645-4 ebook

LC 2011280299

Analyzes Buffett's techniques for arbitrage and special situations investing and offers step-by-step instructions on how to take advantage of such events as spin-offs, liquidations, recapitalizations, and tender offers.

"The writing is concise and straightforward, the examples are current and clear, and there are simple formulas on how to determine risk in both arbitrage and valuing liquidations." Libr J

Includes glossary

Cohan, William D.

Money and power; how Goldman Sachs came to rule the world. Doubleday 2011 658p $30.50; ebook $14.99 **332.6**

1. Securities 2. Investments 3. Banks and banking 4. Goldman Sachs & Co. 5. Goldman Sachs Group, Inc.

ISBN 978-0-385-52384-4; 978-0-385-53497-0 ebook

This is a history of the New York-based banking and investment firm from its founding in 1869 to the present.

"The book offers the best analysis yet of Goldman's increasingly tangled web of conflicts. . . . The writing is crisp and the research meticulous, drawing on reams of documents made publicly available by congressional committees and the Financial Crisis Inquiry Commission." Economist

Includes bibliographical references

Cortese, Amy

Locavesting; the revolution in local investing and how to profit from it. John Wiley 2011 252p $22.95; ebook $10.99 **332.6**

1. Investments 2. Small business 3. Community development

ISBN 978-0-470-91138-9; 978-1-1180-8578-3 ebook

LC 2011005647

"With the recent crash of the financial markets, many investors are looking for new places to put their money. At the same time, many small businesses are finding it ever more difficult to get credit. Cortese . . . covers this current confluence, providing examples of how investing in local small businesses can be beneficial to all parties. . . . Various types of funding methods are discussed, including cooperatives, credit unions, local stock exchanges, community de-

velopment funds, public venture capital, and raising money through social networking. . . . Timely and easy to read, this is a nice introduction to something many of us have never considered. A good choice for public libraries and fruitful reading for small businesses and investors." Libr J

Includes bibliographical references

Cramer, James J.

Confessions of a street addict. Simon & Schuster 2002 339p $26; pa $14 **332.6**

1. Stocks 2. Wall Street (New York, N.Y.)

ISBN 0-7432-2487-6; 0-7432-2488-4 pa

LC 2002-22902

The author "recounts his turbulent dual career as hedge fund manager and media pundit. . . . This is a lively, informative portrait of the highest levels of finance and media in the last decade." Publ Wkly

Downes, John

★ Finance and investment handbook; [by] John Downes, Jordan Elliot Goodman. 8th ed.; Barron's Educational Series 2010 1152p il $39.99 **332.6**

1. Investments 2. Personal finance

ISBN 978-0-7641-6269-5; 0-7641-6269-1

LC 2010-31548

First published 1986 with title: Barron's finance & investment handbook. Periodically revised

This "volume presents a financial dictionary with definitions of more than 5,000 terms, an analysis of . . . investment opportunities, guidelines for non-experts on what to look for when reading corporate reports and financial news sources, . . . [a] directory of hundreds of publicly traded corporations in the United States and Canada, and a directory listing the names and addresses of brokerage houses, mutual funds families, banks, . . . information on federal and state regulators, and other major financial institutions." Publisher's note

Includes bibliographical references

Fox, Justin

★ The myth of the rational market; a history of risk, reward, and delusion on Wall Street. Harper Business 2009 382p $27.99; pa $16.99 **332.6**

1. Economics 2. Wall Street (New York, N.Y.) 3. Economics -- History 4. Economics -- Psychological aspects 5. Rational expectations (Economic theory)

ISBN 0-06-059899-9; 0-06-059903-0 pa; 978-0-06-059899-0; 978-0-06-059903-4 pa

LC 2008-52718

This book chronicles "the rise and fall of the efficient market theory. . . . The theory holds that the market is always right, and that the decisions of millions of rational investors, all acting on information to outsmart one another, always provide the best judge of a stock's value." (Publisher's note) Index.

"A must-read for anyone interested in the markets, our economy or government, this dense but spellbinding work brings modern finance and economics to life." Publ Wkly

Includes bibliographical references

Hagstrom, Robert G., 1956-

The **Warren** Buffett Way; Robert G. Hagstrom. 3rd edition Wiley 2013 281 p. hbk $29.95 **332.6**
1. Investments 2. Capitalists and financiers
ISBN 1118503252; 9781118503256
LC 2013023887
First published 1994
"Warren Buffett is the most famous investor of all time and one of today's most admired business leaders. He became a billionaire and investment sage by looking at companies as businesses rather than prices on a stock screen. . . . The new edition updates readers on the latest investments by Buffett. And, more importantly, it draws on the new field of behavioral finance to explain how investors can overcome the common obstacles that prevent them from investing like Buffett." (Publisher's note)

Hudson, Michael

The **monster**; how a gang of predatory lenders and Wall Street bankers fleeced America--and spawned a global crisis. [by] Michael W. Hudson. Times Books 2010 365p $26; ebook $12.99 **332.6**
1. Mortgages 2. Global Financial Crisis, 2008-2009 3. Banks and banking -- Corrupt practices
ISBN 978-0-8050-9046-8; 978-1-4299-4004-7 ebook
LC 2010-3223
The author "exposes the source of the so-called toxic subprime mortgages that led to the 2008 financial crisis. He picks his way through a warren of mortgage brokers and lending companies that sat just outside banking regulations in the years following the savings and loan crisis. The book concentrates on the practices of mortgage lenders FAMCO and Ameriquest Mortgage, at one point the largest U.S. subprime lender. . . . This is essential reading for anyone concerned with the mortgage crisis." Libr J
Includes bibliographical references

Kelly, Kate

Street fighters; the last 72 hours of Bear Stearns, the toughest firm on Wall Street. Portfolio 2009 247p hardcover o.p. pa $16 **332.6**
1. Investments 2. Wall Street (New York, N.Y.) 3. Bear, Stearns & Co. Inc.
ISBN 978-1-5918-4273-6; 1-5918-4273-5; 978-1-5918-4318-4 pa; 1-5918-4318-9 pa
LC 2009-07694
This is an account of the collapse of the Bear Stearns investment bank in March 2008.
"Enlivened by graphic descriptions of executive disarray and cameo profiles of scrambling financiers as they come to appreciate the magnitude of the disaster they unleashed . . . this riveting account puts the ensuing worldwide financial crises in stark perspective." Publ Wkly
Includes bibliographical references

Lewis, Michael

Flash boys; a Wall Street revolt. Michael Lewis. W.W. Norton & Co Inc. 2014 288 p. (hardcover : alk. paper) $27.95 **332.6**
1. Financial services industry 2. Wall Street (New York, N.Y.) 3. Business -- Corrupt practices 4. Stockbrokers -- United States 5. Finance -- United States -- History

-- 21st century
ISBN 0393244660; 9780393244663
LC 2014003208
Written by Michael Lewis, "'Flash Boys' is about a small group of Wall Street guys who figure out that the U.S. stock market has been rigged for the benefit of insiders and that, post-financial crisis, the markets have become not more free but less, and more controlled by the big Wall Street banks. Working at different firms, they come to this realization separately; but after they discover one another, the flash boys band together and set out to reform the financial markets." (Publisher's note)
An "engrossing true-life morality play that unmasks the devil in the details of high finance." Pub Wkly
Includes bibliographical references and index

Lowenstein, Roger

The **end** of Wall Street. Penguin Press 2010 xxv, 339p $27.95 **332.6**
1. Wall Street (New York, N.Y.) 2. Global Financial Crisis, 2008-2009
ISBN 978-1-59420-239-1; 1-59420-239-7
LC 2009-50864
Lowenstein "examines the past three years of economic collapse, chronicling actions and inactions from dozens of villains and a few heroes. . . . [He] identifies more than 100 key players, almost all of them middle-aged white males from Wall Street, private mortgage companies, law firms, federal government agencies and the U.S. Congress. The narrative consistently demonstrates how almost all of those who could have halted the coming recession by employing common sense instead decided that the housing market would never collapse." Kirkus
Includes bibliographical references

Lutnick, Howard

On top of the world; Cantor Fitzgerald and 9/11: a story of loss and renewal. {by} Howard Lutnick and Tom Barbash. HarperCollins Pubs. 2002 282p il $25.95; pa $14.95 **332.6**
1. September 11 terrorist attacks, 2001 2. Cantor Fitzgerald LP 3. World Trade Center (New York, N.Y.)
ISBN 0-06-051029-3; 0-06-051030-7 pa
LC 2002-27550

The bond-trading firm Cantor Fitzgerald lost 658 employees on September 11, 2001. "'On Top of the World' sets out to tell the story of Cantor Fitzgerald's tragedy, and its survival, largely from its chairman's point of view; the book is interspersed with . . . passages in {Howard} Lutnick's own voice." N Y Times Book Rev

Mahar, Maggie

★ **Bull!**: a history of the boom, 1982-1999; what drove the breakneck market--and what every investor needs to know about financial cycles. HarperBusiness 2003 xxii, 486p il $27.95; pa $16.95 **332.6**
1. Business cycles 2. Wall Street (New York, N.Y.)
ISBN 0-06-056413-X; 0-06-056414-8 pa
LC 2003-51131
This is a "history of the 1982-99 bull market in U.S. stocks. {The author} explains that this bull market got its initial impetus from both the undervaluation of equities

during the 1970s and the end of the Cold War. . . . Mahar concludes by summarizing how investors who haven't seen a bear market for 17 years might plan their investing strategies. Mahar takes complicated topics and explains them clearly for the average reader. Her exceptional book is most highly recommended to even the smallest public or academic library." Libr J

Includes bibliographical references

Malkiel, Burton Gordon, 1932-

★ A **random** walk down Wall Street; the time-tested strategy for successful investing. [by] Burton G. Malkiel. Rev. ed.; W.W. Norton & Co. 2011 445p il $29.95   332.6

1. Stocks 2. Investments
ISBN 978-0-393-08143-5

LC 2010-41866

First published 1973

The author argues "that it is extremely rare for an individual investor to consistently beat the stock-market averages. Investors are better off buying and holding an index fund than attempting to buy and sell individual securities or actively managed mutual funds. . . . This readable investment guide for individuals offers information on the full range of new investment products available, the results of current research by academics and other marketplace professionals, and a section on investment strategies for retired investors or those anticipating retirement. This excellent book offers important information for individual investors and is a valuable resource for library patrons." Booklist

McGee, Suzanne

Chasing Goldman Sachs; how the masters of the universe melted Wall Street down--and why they'll take us to the brink again. Crown Publishers 2010 398p $27; ebook $13.99   332.6

1. Banks and banking 2. Global Financial Crisis, 2008-2009 3. Goldman Sachs & Co.
ISBN 978-0-307-46011-0; 0-307-46011-8; 978-0-307-46012-7 ebook

LC 2009-53440

This " is an exceptionally lucid, well-written account of how and why the financial system broke down." Washington Post

Includes bibliographical references

Tengler, Nancy

The **women's** guide to successful investing; achieving financial security and realizing your goals. Nancy Tengler. Palgrave Macmillan 2014 210 p. illustrations (hardback) $28   332.6

1. Investments 2. Women -- Personal finance 3. Stocks -- Prices 4. Women -- Finance, Personal
ISBN 1137403349; 9781137403346

LC 2014005402

In this book, wealth advisor Nancy Tengler "delivers advice about building a rational, reliable investment portfolio. Investing, she writes, is not gambling. And it's not rocket science. In fact, the value-based approaches employed by the most successful investors will resonate with women who manage their own finances and households. Filled with fascinating case studies and engaging, personal stories of

financial management, Tengler entertains as she educates." (Publisher's note)

Tett, Gillian

Fool's gold; how the bold dream of a small tribe at J.P. Morgan was corrupted by Wall Street greed and unleashed a catastrophe. Free Press 2009 293p $26; pa $16   332.6

1. Investments 2. Wall Street (New York, N.Y.)
ISBN 978-1-4165-9857-2; 1-4165-9857-X; 978-1-4391-0013-4 pa; 1-4391-0013-6 pa

LC 2009-5127

Traces the relationship between a team of JP Morgan banking gurus and the current financial crisis, documenting their invention of a bold variety of allegedly risk-free investments that sparked a frenzy in the banking world and may have directly contributed to the market crash.

Tett "deploys a remarkable sense of pacing, generating real suspense over rapidly inflating debt on bank balance sheets; by the time Lehman Brothers fails, the book has become a bonafide page-turner. . . . Tett's explosive, illuminating narrative is the one to read for anyone confused by the present financial mess." Publ Wkly

Includes bibliographical references

332.601   Philosophy and theory

Dreman, David

Contrarian investment strategies; the psychological edge. David Dreman. Free Press 2012 viii, 481 p.p $30   332.601

1. Profit 2. Stocks 3. Stock exchanges 4. Investment analysis 5. Investments -- Psychological aspects
ISBN 0743297962; 9780743297967

LC 2011023716

Author David Dreman discusses "new findings in psychology that explain why the stock market is inescapably given to bubbles, panics, and periods of high volatility. He also shows how we can use these findings to reliably profit from market errors, crash-proof our portfolios, and earn market-beating long-term returns. . . . [The book] shows why the 'best' stocks are consistently overvalued while the so-called worst, contrarian stocks are undervalued, and [Dreman] lays out his proven and simple rules for avoiding the pitfalls and spotting the bargains." (Publisher's note)

Includes bibliographical references and index.

332.63   Specific forms of investment

Shiller, Robert J., 1946-

Irrational exuberance; Robert J. Shiller. Princeton University Press 2015 392 p. illustrations (hardcover : alk. paper) $29.95   332.63

1. Economics 2. Financial crises 3. Capitalists and financiers 4. Risk 5. Stocks -- United States 6. Dow Jones industrial average 7. Stock exchanges -- United States 8. Stocks -- Prices -- United States 9. Real

property -- Prices -- United States
ISBN 0691166269; 9780691166261

LC 2014036705

This book by "Robert Shiller, who warned of both the tech and housing bubbles, now cautions that signs of irrational exuberance among investors have only increased since the 2008-9 financial crisis. It shows how investor euphoria can drive asset prices up to dizzying and unsustainable heights, and how, at other times, investor discouragement can push prices down to very low levels." (Publisher's note)

Includes bibliographical references and index

Siegel, Jeremy J.

Stocks for the long run; the definitive guide to financial market returns & long-term investment strategies. Jeremy J. Siegel. Fifth edition McGraw-Hill Education 2014 422 p illustrations $40   **332.63**
1. Stocks 2. Rate of return
ISBN 9780071800518; 0071800514

LC 2013037218

First published 1994 by Irwin

This book, by Jeremy J. Siegel, "answers all the important questions of today: How did the crisis alter the financial markets and the future of stock returns? What are the sources of long-term economic growth? How does the Fed really impact investing decisions? Should you hedge against currency instability?" (Publisher's note)

"New material encompasses the causes and consequences of the 2008-09 financial crises. . . . The writing is so lucid that lay investors can readily comprehend the concepts." Choice

Includes bibliographical references and index

Weatherall, James Owen

The **physics** of Wall Street; a brief history of predicting the unpredictable. James Owen Weatherall. Houghton Mifflin Harcourt 2013 304 p. $27 **332.63**
1. Finance 2. Physics 3. Securities -- United States 4. Wall Street (New York, N.Y.)
ISBN 0547317271; 9780547317274

LC 2012017323

In this book, professor "[James Owen] Weatherall looks at the role played by physicists and their ideas in financial markets, and argues . . . that their contributions should be more widely used and recognized. Himself a physicist, philosopher, and mathematician, Weatherall suggests that the profession's essential contribution to finance is to develop models of how financial markets operate using insights from science." (Publishers Weekly)

Includes bibliographical references and index

332.64   Exchange of securities and commodities; speculation

Schwed, Fred

Where are the customers' yachts? or, A good hard look at Wall Street. illustrated by Peter Arno. John Wiley & Sons 2006 170 p. illustrations $21.95   **332.64**
1. Stocks 2. Investments 3. Wall Street (New York,

N.Y.)
ISBN 0471770892; 9780471770893

LC 2005043670

This book on the finance industry "was written by Fred Schwed Jr., who went to work on Wall Street in 1927 after being kicked out of Princeton. His job gave him a front-row seat to watch the last three years of what he calls the 'incredible' 1920s, including the 1929 crash. During his 15 years as a broker and financial journalist, Schwed became an astute observer of the absurdities of the securities industry." (Kiplinger's Personal Finance Magazine)

332.67   Investments in specific industries, in specific kinds of enterprise, by specific kinds of investors; international investment; investment guides

Nolan, Peter

Is China buying the world? Peter Nolan. Polity 2012 147 p. $19.95   **332.67**
1. International competition 2. China -- Economic conditions -- 1970-
ISBN 0745660789; 9780745660783

This book by Peter Nolan "probes behind the media rhetoric and shows that the idea that China is buying the world is a myth. . . . Giant firms from high income countries with leading technologies and brands have greatly increased their investments in developing countries, with China at the forefront. . . . By contrast, Chinese firms have a negligible presence in the high-income countries." (Publisher's note)

332.7   Credit

Acharya, Viral V.

Guaranteed to fail; Fannie Mae, Freddie Mac, and the debacle of mortgage finance. [by] Viral V. Acharya [et al.] Princeton University Press 2011 232p il $24.95; ebook $24.95   **332.7**
1. Housing 2. Mortgages 3. Financial crises 4. Business failures 5. Fannie Mae 6. Federal Home Loan Mortgage Corporation
ISBN 978-0-691-15078-9; 978-1-4008-3809-7 ebook

LC 2011000247

"The authors of Guaranteed to Fail are specialists in applied financial and housing economics. They believe in the necessity of choosing among three options: should Fannie Mae and Freddie Mac exist? Should there be a private-public partnership of mortgage guarantees? Should government end housing subsidies? . . . The authors argue that overextension in housing came from the private sector, Congress, and government-sponsored enterprises." Choice

Includes bibliographical references

Atwood, Margaret, 1939-

Payback; debt and the shadow side of wealth. House of Anansi Press 2008 230p (CBC Massey lectures)   **332.7**
1. Debt 2. Wealth 3. Debt in literature 4. Debt --

Social aspects 5. Debt -- Moral and ethical aspects
ISBN 978-0-88784-800-1

This volume collects novelist Margaret Atwood's Massey Lectures, originally broadcast on the CBC. She investigates the "subject of debt, exploring debt as an ancient and central motif in religion, literature, and the structure of human societies." (Publisher's note) Bibliography. Index.

"Delivered with . . . [Atwood's] trademark wit and imagination, this is a meditation that challenges conventional thinking on one of the most morally pressing issues we face." Booklist

Includes bibliographical references

Halpern, Jake

Bad paper; chasing debt from wall Street to the underworld. Jake Halpern. Farrar Straus & Giroux 2014 256 p. (hardback) $25   **332.7**
1. Consumer credit 2. Collecting of accounts 3. Finance, Personal 4. Collection agencies
ISBN 0374108234; 9780374108236

LC 2014013576

This book, by Jake Halpern, explores why "the Federal Trade Commission receives more complaints about rogue debt collecting than about any activity besides identity theft. . . . It tells the story of Aaron Siegel, a former banking executive, and Brandon Wilson, a former armed robber, who become partners and go in quest of 'paper'-- the uncollected debts that are sold off by banks for pennies on the dollar." (Publisher's note)

"Colorful and chilling, this work is an important peek into the dark corner of consumer finance and recommended for all consumers and true crime aficionados." LJ

Howard, Timothy

The **mortgage** wars; inside Fannie Mae, big-money politics, and the collapse of the American dream. Timothy Howard. McGraw-Hill 2013 304 p. (hardback) $30   **332.7**
1. Mortgages 2. Housing -- United States -- History 3. Federal National Mortgage Association 4. Mortgage loans -- United States 5. Subprime mortgage loans -- United States 6. Mortgage banks -- United States -- History
ISBN 0071821090; 9780071821094

LC 2013033450

In this book "former Fannie Mae CFO [Timothy] Howard lays bare . . . how the agency was undermined, and its executive leadership framed, by a confederation of political opponents. . . . His . . . account traces behind-the-scenes activity beginning around 1998. He describes a bipartisan league of free market ideologues, political hatchet men operating as financial regulators, and major business and corporate interests eager to privatize Fannie Mae's mortgage business for their own benefits." (Kirkus Reviews)

Leonard, Robin

★ **Credit** repair; make a plan, improve your credit, avoid scams. Robin Leonard, J.D.; updated by Attorney Amy Loftsgordon. 12th edition Nolo 2015 394 p. pbk $24.99   **332.7**
1. Consumer credit
ISBN 9781413321548; 1413321542

LC 2014043496

First published 1996. Periodically revised
Includes bibliographical references

This book offers advice on assessing your debt situation, avoiding overspending, handling existing debts, cleaning your credit file, how credit reports are used, and building and maintaining good credit.

Morgenson, Gretchen

Reckless endangerment; how outsized ambition, greed, and corruption led to economic armageddon. [by] Gretchen Morgenson, Joshua Rosner. Times Books 2011 331p il $30; ebook $12.99   **332.7**
1. Mortgages 2. Financial crises 3. Global Financial Crisis, 2008-2009 4. Fannie Mae 5. Subprime mortgage loans 6. Financial crises -- United States -- 21st century
ISBN 978-0-8050-9120-5; 978-1-4299-6577-4 ebook

LC 2010047594

"A sobering account of some sordid recent history that's so clear and detailed that pros and novices will find its account rich and informative, and deeply depressing." Publ Wkly

333   Economics of land and energy

Clover, Charles

The **end** of the line; how overfishing is changing the world and what we eat. New Press 2006 386p $26.95   **333**
1. Commercial fishing
ISBN 978-1-59558-109-9; 1-59558-109-X

LC 2006-12058

First published 2004 in the United Kingdom

"Clover's hard-hitting approach will probably anger some, but his argument that we will soon run out of fish unless we take drastic measures . . . is persuasive." Publ Wkly

Includes bibliographical references

Renewable energy; sustainable concepts for the energy change. edited by Roland Wengenmayr and Thomas Bührke, translated by William D. Brewer. Wiley-VCH 2013 vi, 164 p.p $44.95   **333**
1. Energy policy 2. Energy development 3. Renewable energy resources 4. Renewable energy sources
ISBN 3527411879; 9783527411870

LC 2012540474

This book, edited by Roland Wengenmayr and Thomas Bührke, examines "changes in terms of energy sources. The increasing number of wind power plants, solar collectors and photovoltaic installations demonstrates perceptibly that many innovations for tapping renewable energy sources have matured: very few other technologies have developed so dynamically in the past years. Nearly all the chapters were written by professionals in the respective fields." (Publisher's note)

Includes bibliographical references and index

333.3   Private ownership of land

Haden, Jeff

★ The **complete** dictionary of real estate terms explained simply; what smart investors need to know. Atlantic Pub. Group 2006 286p pa $21.95   **333.3**

1. Reference books 2. Real estate -- Dictionaries

ISBN 978-0-910627-01-6; 0-910627-01-0

LC 2006-29746

"A licensed real estate broker defines over 2400 terms for potential home buyers and sellers." Libr J

Includes bibliographical references

Irwin, Robert

Tips & traps for negotiating real estate; 3rd ed.; McGraw-Hill 2010 246p (Tips & traps series) pa $17; ebook $17   **333.3**

1. Negotiation 2. Real estate business 3. Real estate investment 4. Houses -- Buying and selling

ISBN 978-0-07-175040-0 pa; 978-0-07-175088-2 ebook

LC 2010029971

First published 1995

This guide to negotiating real estate transactions covers "getting a better price in a down market; negotiating a quick sale; dealing with reluctant lenders; keeping the upper hand when buying a foreclosed property; [and] talking a seller into financing your purchase." Publisher's note

Linklater, Andro

Owning the earth; the transforming history of land ownership. by Andro Linklater. Bloomsbury USA 2013 496 p. illustrations, maps (alk. paper) $30   **333.3**

1. Feudalism 2. Land tenure 3. Landlord and tenant 4. Land tenure -- History

ISBN 1620402890; 9781620402894

LC 2013011970

In this book, author Andro Linklater "focuses on the history of land ownership as driving human activity from the earliest ages and being the key to the creation of democracy. . . . Evolving from the collision of crown and chief barons that resulted in the Magna Carta, the impetus for owning land gained steam in the 1500s in England with the land revolution, which displaced subsistence farming via the feudal system in favor of a few rich owners profiting from the buying of land and increasing yields." (Kirkus Reviews)

"Many aspire to land ownership, taking the concept--that individuals may obtain a sliver of our planet as their own--for granted. Linklater's global study looks at land ownership--feudal, private, communal--through the lens of history and politics, rather than as merely a matter for economic study. The results are enlightening for our understanding not only of the past but of our future." (Library Journal)

Includes bibliographical references and index

333.7   Natural resources and energy

Duncan, Dayton

The **national** parks; America's best idea: an illustrated history. with a preface by Ken Burns; picture research by Susanna Steisel and Aileen Silverstone. Alfred A. Knopf 2009 403p il map $50 **333.7**

1. Nature conservation 2. United States -- Local history 3. National parks and reserves -- United States 4. United States -- National Park Service -- History

ISBN 978-0-307-26896-9

LC 2009-20880

The author delves "into the history of the park idea, from the first sighting by white men in 1851 of the valley that would become Yosemite and the creation of the world's first national park at Yellowstone in 1872, through the most recent additions to a system that now encompasses nearly four hundred sites and 84 million acres." Publisher's note

Includes bibliographical references

Encyclopedia of global resources; editor, Craig W. Allin. Salem Press 2010 4v il map set $395   **333.7**

1. Reference books 2. Natural resources -- Encyclopedias

ISBN 978-1-58765-644-6; 1-58765-644-2

LC 2010-1984

First published 1998 with title: Natural resources

"This four-volume set provides a wide variety of perspectives about Earth's natural resources and explains the interrelationships among resource exploitation, environmentalism, geology, and biology. Allin . . . presents 576 articles on resources such as oil and tar sands, nations from Argentina to Zimbabwe, government laws and conventions, and historical events. . . . [This encyclopedia] offers real value and sheds important light on where we derive our mineral and biological resources, how they are processed, what they are used for, and how they fit into the global economy." Libr J

Includes bibliographical references

Goleman, Daniel

Ecological intelligence; how knowing the hidden impacts of what we buy can change everything. Doubleday 2009 276p $26   **333.7**

1. Consumers 2. Industries 3. Environmental protection

ISBN 0-385-52782-9; 978-0-385-52782-8

LC 2008-41811

"Brimming with intriguing, useful, and galvanizing information, this is an exceptionally sharp, innovative, and realistic approach to raising the demand for environmentally safe merchandise." Booklist

Miller, Char

Gifford Pinchot and the making of modern environmentalism. Island Press (Washington, D.C.) 2001 458p il $28   **333.7**

1. Governors 2. Conservationists 3. Foresters

ISBN 1-55963-822-2

LC 2001-5665

"Charismatic, progressive, and controversial, Gifford Pinchot (1865-1946) established and directed the Forest Service under Theodore Roosevelt, lobbied hard for responsible logging practices, expressed prescient warnings about pollution, and called for sustainable energy. Miller's animated biography portrays Pinchot in all his fervor, and environmentalism in all its complexity." Booklist

Includes bibliographical references and index

Park, Chris

A **dictionary** of environment and conservation; by Chris Park. 2nd ed. Oxford University Press 2013 484 p. (Oxford paperback reference) (paperback) $21.95   **333.7**
1. Environment 2. Conservation of natural resources 3. Environmental sciences -- Dictionaries 4. Conservation of natural resources -- Dictionaries
ISBN 0199641668; 9780199641666
LC 2008006450

This book by Michael Allaby and Chris Park "provides over 9,000 alphabetically arranged entries on scientific and social aspects of the environment, including concise and authoritative information on key thinkers, treaties, movements, organizations, concepts, and theories. For the second edition, Allaby has added over 700 new entries, including 'aerial plankton,' 'cyclone collector,' 'oasis,' and 'supertramp.'" (Publisher's note)

"The second edition of this user-friendly title is updated with 800 new entries, expanding the work to more than 500 pages...Students will appreciate having access to this information in one convenient source. This affordable title is recommended for public and academic libraries." (Booklist)

Speth, James Gustave

The **bridge** at the end of the world; capitalism, the environment, and crossing from crisis to sustainability. Yale University Press 2008 295p il $28   **333.7**
1. Capitalism 2. Environmental policy
ISBN 978-0-300-13611-1; 0-300-13611-0
LC 2007-43584

This book "is a superb synthesis of the great economic questions of our time: how to reconcile markets with environmental sustainability; efficiency with equality; and trade and global openness with socially defensible standards of living." Am Prospect

Includes bibliographical references

333.72   Conservation and protection

★ **American** earth; environmental writing since Thoreau. edited by Bill McKibben; foreword by Al Gore. Literary Classics of the United States 2008 1047p il (Library of America) $40 **333.72**
1. Nature conservation 2. Environmental movement 3. Environmental protection 4. Literature -- Collections
ISBN 978-1-59853-020-9; 1-59853-020-8
LC 2007-940683

This book "can be read as a survey of the literature of American environmentalism, but above all, it should be enjoyed for the sheer beauty of the writing." Publ Wkly

Includes bibliographical references

Beavan, Colin

No impact man; the adventures of a guilty liberal who attempts to save the planet, and the discoveries he makes about himself and our way of life in the process. Farrar, Straus, and Giroux 2009 274p $25; pa $15   **333.72**
1. Environmental protection
ISBN 978-0-374-22288-8; 0-374-22288-6; 978-0-312-42983-6 pa; 0-312-42983-5 pa
LC 2009-10188

"An inspiring, persuasive argument that individuals are not helpless in the battle against environmental degradation and global warming." Kirkus

Includes bibliographical references

Brinkley, Douglas

The **quiet** world; saving Alaska's wilderness kingdom, 1879-1960. Harper 2011 576p il map $29.99; ebook $23.99   **333.72**
1. Nature conservation 2. Environmental protection 3. Natural history -- Alaska
ISBN 978-0-06-200596-0; 978-0-06-203533-2 ebook

This book "brims over with information and insight, passion and insistence and some carelessness. In fact, it's a bit like Alaska itself: large, formidable, raw and ultimately unforgettable." Washington Post

Includes bibliographical references

Green volunteers; the world guide to voluntary work in nature conservation. editor, Fabio Ausenda. 7th ed; Green Volunteers; distributed by Universe Pub 2009 255p (We care guides) pa $16.95   **333.72**
1. Reference books 2. Volunteer work -- Directories 3. Nature conservation -- Directories
ISBN 978-88-89060-14-8; 88-89060-14-X
LC 2008-943207

First published 1999. Frequently revised

This book "lists over 200 projects worldwide for those who want to experience active conservation work as a volunteer. Projects are in a variety of habitats and countries, lasting from one week to one year or more. Projects involve volunteer work in wildlife rehabilitation centers, national parks, and protected areas, and general conservation work with a variety of animal species." Publisher's note

McDaniel, Carl N.

Wisdom for a livable planet; the visionary work of Terri Swearingen, Dave Foreman, Wes Jackson, Helena Norberg-Hodge, Werner Fornos, Herman Daly, Stephen Schneider, and David Orr. Trinity University Press 2005 277p hardcover o.p. pa $17.95   **333.72**
1. Environmental sciences
ISBN 1-595-34008-4; 1-595-34009-2 pa
LC 2004-19081

The author personalizes "critical environmental issues via profiles of eight 'visionaries' agitating for a more livable planet. . . . His subjects are prominent in the areas of hazardous waste incineration, biodiversity, sustainable agriculture, appropriate technology, population control, rational economic planning, climate concerns and environmental education. . . . The stories of these eight ecological warriors are profoundly appealing in that they show the diverse ways that people can commit to a common cause." Publ Wkly

Includes bibliographical references

McKibben, Bill

★ The **Bill** McKibben reader; pieces from an active life. Henry Holt 2008 442p pa $18 333.72

1. Environmental protection

ISBN 978-0-8050-7627-1 pa; 0-8050-7627-1 pa

LC 2007-39609

This is a "collection of essays gleaned from books and periodicals published between 1982 and 2007. Most of the 44 essays come from a diverse array of magazines, including The New Yorker, Mother Jones, Outside, Gourmet, and Christian Century. . . . Essays are loosely divided into categories that include consumerism, activism, the changing planet, the meaning of community, and the sufficiency of nature. . . . Readers new to McKibben will be entertained, informed, and perhaps even inspired to make the positive changes that McKibben desires for the world." Libr J

333.73   Land

Biggers, Jeff

Reckoning at Eagle Creek; the secret legacy of coal in the heartland. Nation Books 2010 300p il $26.95 333.73

1. Coal mines and mining 2. Shawnee National Forest region (Ill.)

ISBN 978-1-56858-421-8; 1-56858-421-0

LC 2009-32686

Biggers "takes a look at coal and its role in the history of southern Illinois as well as its human and environmental costs. Biggers also tells a personal story as he chronicles the saga of his family's strip-mined homestead in an area that one day would be a part of the Shawnee National Forest. . . . A lot of history is presented here in a personal style by a cultural historian with a keen eye. A valuable read for followers of environmental history." Libr J

Includes bibliographical references

333.79   Energy

Barnham, Keith

The **Burning** Answer; The Solar Revolution: a Quest for Sustainable Power. by Keith Barnham. W.W. Norton & Co. Inc. 2015 400 p. illustrations $27.95 333.79

1. Solar energy

ISBN 160598776X; 9781605987767

In this book, author Keith Barnham "uncovers the connections between physics and politics that have resulted in our dependence on a high-carbon lifestyle, which only a solar revolution can now overcome. . . . While everyone is aware of solar energy, people are still not paying enough attention, and so as well as explaining the science behind it, Barnham takes his subject forward to advise on what

we should be doing to utilize this amazing energy source." (Publisher's note)

"The author makes some big claims about the viability (and necessity) of solar energy, and while he seems oblivious to the strength of NIMBYism (Not In My Backyard), many readers will be inclined to agree with him. He persuades not with charts and graphs but with the power of his storytelling and his passion for science." LJ

Ferguson, Charles D.

Nuclear energy; what everyone needs to know. Charles D. Ferguson. Oxford University Press 2011 xvii, 222 p.p (What everyone needs to know) (hardback) $74 333.79

1. Nuclear energy 2. Nuclear power plants

ISBN 0199759456; 9780199759453; 9780199759460

LC 2010044449

In this book, "Charles D. Ferguson provides an authoritative account of the key facts about nuclear energy. What is the origin of nuclear energy? What countries use commercial nuclear power, and how much electricity do they obtain from it? How can future nuclear power plants be made safer? What can countries do to protect their nuclear facilities from military attacks? How hazardous is radioactive waste? Is nuclear energy a renewable energy source?" (Publisher's note)

"This compelling assembly of historical and scientific information deftly steps through the essential discoveries, definitions, and theory that led to the development of nuclear reactors and nuclear bombs. . . . [F]ollowing chapters . . . cover safety, climate change, nuclear proliferation concerns, security, and the politically charged options for disposal of radioactive waste." Choice

Includes bibliographical references and index

Helm, Dieter

The **carbon** crunch; how we're getting climate change wrong--and how to fix it. Dieter Helm. Yale University Press 2012 xiii, 273 p.p (hardcover) $35 333.79

1. Energy policy 2. Climate change 3. Renewable energy resources 4. Energy conservation 5. Renewable energy sources 6. Greenhouse gas mitigation 7. Climatic changes -- Prevention

ISBN 0300186592; 9780300186598

LC 2012017386

In this book Dieter Helm examines the economics of climate change regulation policies, finding fault in "their basic design. They have caused people to focus on the most expensive ways of mitigating climate change, rather than the cheapest, imposing high cost for little gain. . . . The heart of Mr Helm's book is an examination of the economics of renewable energy" and wind energy in particular. (Economist)

Includes bibliographical references and index

Koerth-Baker, Maggie

Before the lights go out; conquering the energy crisis before it conquers us. Maggie Koerth-Baker. John Wiley & Sons 2012 xii, 290 p.p $27.95 333.79

1. Solar energy 2. Biomass energy 3. Climate change 4. Energy policy -- United States 5. Energy consumption -- United States 6. Energy development -- United States 7. Energy conservation -- United States

8. Renewable energy sources -- United States
ISBN 0470876255; 9780470876251

LC 2011043334

Author Maggie KoerthBaker tells "how our energy systems really work today, and what we'll have to do to keep them working in the years to come. . . . [She discusses] climate change, [solar farms,] and conversion efficiency. . . . [KoerthBaker provides information on the future of] economics and social incentives [and how they] will be the things that build our new world." (maggiekb.com)

Includes bibliographical references and index.

Levi, Michael

Power surge; energy, opportunity, and the battle for America's future. by Michael Levi. Oxford University Press 2013 260 p. (hardback : alk. paper) $27.95　　　**333.79**

1. Energy resources 2. Energy policy -- United States 3. Renewable energy -- United States 4. Energy industries -- United States
ISBN 0199986169; 9780199986163

LC 2012043264

In this book, author Michael Levi "takes on the big claims made by both sides in the fight over American energy, showing what the changes underway mean for the United States and the world. Both unfolding revolutions in American energy offer big opportunities for the country to strengthen its economy, bolster its security, and protect the environment. Levi shows how to seize those with a new strategy that blends the best of old and new energy while avoiding the real dangers." (Publisher's note)

"Readers seeking to understand America's energy policies and prospects will welcome this even-handed, smart, and accessible book on a topic of incomparable economic importance." Pub Wkly

Includes bibliographical references and index

McGraw, Seamus

The end of country. Random House 2011 245p $26; ebook $13.99　　　**333.79**

1. Energy policy 2. Energy resources 3. Pennsylvania
ISBN 978-1-4000-6853-1; 978-0-679-60431-0 ebook

LC 2010035972

"In 2006, in a hardscrabble part of Pennsylvania that had long lost its allure as a farming and industrial area, geologists began investigating the Marcellus Shale. It turned out to be the richest deposit of natural gas ever discovered anywhere. When his widowed mother was approached about permitting natural-gas exploration on their farm, journalist McGraw had to weigh their need for money against the future prospects of the farmland. Chronicling the impact of the find on his mother and her neighbors, McGraw's research led to this impressively detailed, highly engaging look at issues of energy policy, economics, and sociology that arose when a bucolic town was suddenly faced with the 'traveling circus' of energy exploration. . . . A completely engaging look at how energy policy affected a quiet, rural town." Booklist

Muller, Richard A., 1944-

Energy for future presidents; the science behind the headlines. Richard A. Muller. W. W. Norton 2012 xvii, 350 p.p ill., maps (hardcover) $26.95　　**333.79**

1. Energy resources 2. Energy development 3. Energy policy -- United States 4. Technology and state 5. Energy policy -- Social aspects 6. Power resources -- Social aspects
ISBN 0393081613; 9780393081619

LC 2012015586

This book, by Richard A. Muller, discusses U.S. energy policy. "The near-meltdown of Fukushima, the upheavals in the Middle East, the BP oil rig explosion, and the looming reality of global warming have reminded . . . all U.S. citizens that nothing has more impact on our lives than the supply of and demand for energy. Its procurement dominates our economy and foreign policy. . . . But the 'energy question' is more confusing, contentious, and complicated than ever before." (Publisher's note)

Includes bibliographical references and index

Newton, David E.

World energy crisis; a reference handbook. David E. Newton. ABC-CLIO 2013 xviii, 334 p.p ill. (Contemporary world issues. Science, technology, and medicine) (hardcover) $58　　**333.79**

1. Energy policy 2. Energy consumption 3. Energy conservation 4. Energy security 5. Energy industries 6. Energy development
ISBN 1610691474; 9781610691475; 9781610691482

LC 2012016975

This book, by David E. Newton, is part of the "Contemporary World Issues" reference series. It "provides a thorough investigation of . . . our current global energy situation, and what actions should be taken to prevent a crippling fuel-supply catastrophe in the future. The book presents a historical background for current energy problems that discusses the supply and consumption of various forms of energy at different periods of history." (Publisher's note)

Includes bibliographical references (p. 269-305) and index

Yergin, Daniel

The quest; energy, security and the remaking of the modern world. Penguin Press 2011 804p il map $37.95　　　**333.79**

1. Energy policy 2. Globalization 3. Energy resources 4. Money -- Political aspects 5. Power resources -- Political aspects
ISBN 978-1-59420-283-4; 1-59420-283-4

LC 2011013100

This book "combines four books. The first . . . provides global history of oil, natural gas, and nuclear power from 1991 to 2011. . . . The second part of 'The Quest' traces a path from the discovery of climate change as an esoteric interest of a few scientists in the nineteenth century to the introduction of 'new climate change policies . . . intended to make a profound transformation of the energy foundations that support the world economy.' . . . 'The Quest's third part looks at nuclear and renewable alternatives to fossil fuels. . . . When Yergin looks to the future in his fourth book, he asks how the economic benefits from an average megawatt of power can be increased while at the same time reducing its negative effects on the environment and health." (New York Review of Books)

This book "is a masterly piece of work and, as a comprehensive guide to the world's great energy needs and dilemmas, it will be hard to beat." Economist

Includes bibliographical references

333.793   Secondary forms of energy

Couch, Julianne

Traveling the power line; from the Mojave Desert to the Bay of Fundy. Julianne Couch. University of Nebraska Press 2013 xx, 214 p.p (Our sustainable future) (paperback) $19.95   **333.793**
1. Electric power 2. Power resources -- United States 3. Electric power plants -- United States
ISBN 0803245068; 9780803245068

LC 2012035997

In this book, journalist Julianne Couch "chronicles her visits to nine electrical power stations across the country, examining the pros and cons of the fuel sources used at each site." She looks at sources including "wind, water, geothermal, solar and nuclear power. Between 2008 and 2010, Couch traveled . . . to talk to 'scientists, engineers, policy advocates, environmental activists, industry experts and the folks who work in or live around various sites of energy production.'" (Kirkus)

Includes bibliographical references (pages 213-216).

333.794   Renewable energy resources

Pernick, Ron

Clean Tech Nation; How the U.S. Can Lead in the New Global Economy. Ron Pernick. HarperCollins 2012 320 p. $29.99   **333.794**
1. Economic development 2. Sustainable development 3. Technological innovations 4. Economic policy -- United States
ISBN 0062088440; 9780062088444

This book, by Ron Pernick and Clint Wilder, discusses how "the United States risks losing out on the most critical opportunity for job creation and global economic leadership in the 21st century. . . . If the U.S. is to remain dominant, as it has in the earlier high-tech and Internet revolutions, it needs to supercharge efforts at every level--in federal, state, and city governments, and in schools, small businesses, and large companies." (Publisher's note)

333.8   Subsurface resources

Goodstein, David L.

Out of gas; the end of the age of oil. {by} David Goodstein. Norton 2004 140p il $21.95; pa $13.95   **333.8**
1. Petroleum
ISBN 0-393-05857-3; 0-393-32647-0 pa

LC 2003-10376

"Goodstein's predictions are based on a sophisticated understanding of physics and thermodynamics, and on a simple observation about natural resources." N Y Times Book Rev

Includes bibliographical references and index

Wilber, Tom

Under the surface; fracking, fortunes and the fate of the Marcellus Shale. Tom Wilber. Cornell University Press 2012 272 p. (cloth : alk. paper) $27.95   **333.8**
1. Natural gas 2. Shale gas industry 3. Hydraulic fracturing 4. Marcellus Shale 5. Shale gas industry -- Pennsylvania 6. Hydraulic fracturing -- Pennsylvania 7. Shale gas industry -- New York (State) 8. Hydraulic fracturing -- New York (State)
ISBN 0801450160; 9780801450167

LC 2011047166

This book by Tom Wilber is a "journalistic overview of shale gas development and the controversies surrounding it. . . . [Wilber] gives a voice to all constituencies, including farmers and landowners tempted by the prospects of wealth but wary of the consequences, policymakers struggling with divisive issues, and activists coordinating campaigns based on their visions of economic salvation and environmental ruin." (Publisher's note)

Includes bibliographical references and index.

333.91   Water and lands adjoining bodies of water

Dean, Cornelia

Against the tide; the battle for America's beaches. Columbia Univ. Press 1999 279p il $60; pa $18.95   **333.91**
1. Coasts 2. Beaches 3. Seashore ecology
ISBN 0-231-08418-8; 0-231-08419-6 pa

LC 98-50755

Dean discusses the ecology of American beaches and contends that they are threatened by coastal development and erosion

"This thoroughly researched and thoughtful book is destined to become a classic of environmental science writing." Libr J

Includes bibliographical references

Fishman, Charles

The **big** thirst; Charles Fishman. Free Press 2011 388p. ebook $12.99; $26.99   **333.91**
1. Water supply 2. Infrastructure (Economics) 3. Water resources development
ISBN 978-1-4391-2493-2 ebook; 978-1-4391-0207-7

LC 2010033989

This is a "lively and invaluable assessment of the current politics, economics, and culture of water. Lyrical in his descriptions of the beauty and wonder of water, Fishman is rigorous when explaining that the water we have now is all the water we will ever have and that our 'golden age' of 'abundant, safe, and cheap' water may soon end, thanks to deteriorating infrastructure (7 billion gallons leak out of our water systems every day), rising urban populations, and climate change." Booklist

Includes bibliographical references and index.

Harden, Blaine

A **river** lost; the life and death of the Columbia. Norton 1996 271p maps $25; pa $14.95   **333.91**
1. Columbia River
ISBN 0-393-03936-6; 0-393-31690-4 pa

LC 95-38618

In this look at the development of Columbia River region, the author "examines the changes—sociological, environmental, economic and aesthetic—that the taming of this great river wrought. His wonderful account touches on the destruction of Native American cultures dependent on the river and its salmon, and on the near extinction of the salmon themselves. Also fairly portrayed are the people and industries currently dependent on both the managed river and massive government subsidies." Publ Wkly

Includes bibliographical references

Rothfeder, Jeffrey

Every drop for sale; our desperate battle over water in a world about to run out. Tarcher/Putnam 2001 205p hardcover o.p. pa $14.95   **333.91**
1. Water supply
ISBN 1-58542-114-6; 978-1-58542-367-5 pa;
1-58542-367-X pa

LC 2001-27903

"Like the drip of water on stone, Rothfeder's steady exposition of horrors will wear down any reader's doubts that water is the next flashpoint of global politics, human rights and health issues." Publ Wkly

Includes bibliographical references

Ward, Diane Raines

Water wars; drought, flood, folly, and the politics of thirst. Riverhead Bks. 2002 280p $24.95; pa $14   **333.91**
1. Water rights 2. Water supply 3. Hydraulic engineering
ISBN 1-57322-229-1; 1-57322-995-4 pa

LC 2002-21301

"Ward writes with the sensibilities and concerns of an environmentalist. But unexpectedly, delightfully, she's an environmentalist who loves the scale, ingenuity and power of engineering." N Y Times Book Rev

Includes bibliographical references

333.95   Biological resources

Barrow, Mark V.

Nature's ghosts; confronting extinction from the age of Jefferson to the age of ecology. [by] Mark V. Barrow, Jr. University of Chicago Press 2009 497p il $35   **333.95**
1. Biologists 2. Extinct animals 3. Endangered species 4. Wildlife conservation 5. Extinction (Biology) 6. Endangered species -- Law and legislation 7. Wildlife

conservation -- United States -- History
ISBN 978-0-226-03814-8; 0-226-03814-9

LC 2008-49085

The author "retraces the history of the earliest European and North American naturalists, from those who refused to believe that species comprising a perfect, stable world could go extinct, to the acceptance of extinction at the hands of humans and the legal mechanisms created to halt it. . . . Professionals in ecology, conservation biology, and wildlife management and readers interested in natural history will find this book hard to put down." Choice

Includes bibliographical references

Chadwick, Douglas H.

The **company** we keep; America's endangered species. {by} Douglas H. Chadwick and Joel Sartore. National Geographic Soc. 1996 157p il hardcover o.p. pa $16   **333.95**
1. Endangered species 2. Wildlife conservation 3. Environmental policy -- United States
ISBN 0-7922-7132-7 pa

LC 96-18874

"The book is not built solely around the photographs. But the pictures are collectively a good storyteller. They're well-edited, and accompanied by maps and charts that help explain how man is threatening many species." Christ Sci Monit

Includes bibliographical references

Cousteau, Jacques Yves

The **human,** the orchid, and the octopus; exploring and conserving our natural world. [by] Jacques Cousteau and Susan Schiefelbein. Bloomsbury 2007 305p hardcover o.p. pa $16   **333.95**
1. Oceanography 2. Nature conservation 3. Human influence on nature
ISBN 978-1-59691-417-9; 1-59691-417-3; 978-1-59691-418-6 pa; 1-59691-418-1 pa

LC 2007-18824

Original French edition, 1997

"Cousteau's reverence for life's miracles . . . shines through in this eloquent testimony on the importance of pursuing higher ideals, particularly the preservation of the oceans and the natural world for future generations." Publ Wkly

Includes bibliographical references

Ellis, Richard

Tuna; a love story. Alfred A. Knopf 2008 334p il $27.95; pa $16   **333.95**
1. Tuna 2. Commercial fishing 3. Endangered species
ISBN 978-0-307-26715-3; 0-307-26715-6; 978-0-307-38710-3 pa; 0-307-38710-0 pa

LC 2007-52253

"Ellis loves this fish. His rapt description of the physiology that makes tunas one of the fastest things in the ocean . . . lends emotional urgency to his account of the collapsing tuna fishery." Orion

Includes bibliographical references

Fraser, Caroline

  Rewilding the world; dispatches from the conservation revolution. Metropolitan Books 2009 400p map $28.50   **333.95**
    1. Ecology 2. Endangered species 3. Wildlife conservation
    ISBN 978-0-8050-7826-8; 0-8050-7826-6
                                                    LC 2009-32989
  "Heavily researched with endnotes for those looking for more information, this truly is an essential read for conservationists, biologists, and anyone interested in the natural world." Libr J
    Includes bibliographical references

Goodall, Jane

  ★ The **ten** trusts; what we must do to care for the animals we love. {by} Jane Goodall and Marc Bekoff. HarperSanFrancisco 2002 xx, 200p hardcover o.p. pa $14.95   **333.95**
    1. Animal rights 2. Animal welfare 3. Wildlife conservation 4. Human influence on nature
    ISBN 0-06-251757-0; 0-06-055611-0 pa
                                                    LC 2002-68717
  "An accessible, compelling, and important exposé." Booklist
    Includes bibliographical references

Greenberg, Paul

  American catch; the fight for our local seafood. Paul Greenberg. The Penguin Press 2014 320 p. $26.95   **333.95**
    1. Seafood industry -- United States 2. Commercial fishing -- United States 3. Fish trade 4. Local foods -- United States 5. Fishes -- Conservation -- United States
    ISBN 1594204489; 9781594204487
                                                    LC 2014005395
  In this book, author Paul Greenberg tells "the surprising story of why Americans stopped eating from their own waters. In 2005, the United States imported five billion pounds of seafood, nearly double what we imported twenty years earlier. . . . During that same period, our seafood exports quadrupled. 'American Catch' examines New York oysters, Gulf shrimp, and Alaskan salmon to reveal how it came to be that 91 percent of the seafood Americans eat is foreign." (Publisher's note)
    Includes bibliographical references and index

  Four fish; the future of the last wild food. Penguin Press 2010 284p $25.95   **333.95**
    1. Tuna 2. Salmon 3. Codfish 4. Bass (Fish) 5. Fish culture 6. Commercial fishing
    ISBN 978-1-59420-256-8
                                                    LC 2010-1276
  "The narrative is grounded in common sense and anchored by first-rate, on-scene reporting from the Yukon and Mekong Rivers, Lake Bardawil in the Sinai Peninsula and the waters off the coasts of Long Island, Greece, Hawaii and the Shetland Islands. Hugely informative, sincere and infectiously curious and enthusiastic." Kirkus
    Includes bibliographical references

Hoekstra, Jonathan M.

  The **atlas** of global conservation; changes, challenges and opportunities to make a difference. [by] Jonathan Hoekstra ... [et al.]; edited by Jennifer L. Molnar. University of California Press 2010 234p il map $49.95   **333.95**
    1. Atlases 2. Globalization 3. Reference books 4. Environmental protection 5. Conservation of natural resources
    ISBN 978-0-520-26256-0
                                                    LC 2009-23617
  "Focusing primarily on biomes and ecosystems, this valuable atlas promotes a deeper understanding of the challenges involved in preserving and maintaining these habitats and resources. Basically an analysis of the current state of the globe, the book highlights conservation challenges through chapters on habitats, species distributions, deforestation, global warming, coastal development, and pollution. . . . The book is unique and well done." Voice Youth Advocates
    Includes bibliographical references

Horwitz, Joshua

  War of the Whales; A True Story. by Joshua Horwitz. Simon & Schuster 2014 448 p. ill. (some col.), col. map $28   **333.95**
    1. Whales 2. Military research 3. United States. Navy
    ISBN 1451645015; 9781451645019
  This book, by Joshua Horwitz, "is the gripping tale of a crusading attorney who stumbles on one of the US Navy's best-kept secrets: a submarine detection system that floods entire ocean basins with high-intensity sound--and drives whales onto beaches. As Joel Reynolds launches a legal fight to expose and challenge the Navy program, marine biologist Ken Balcomb witnesses a mysterious mass stranding of whales near his research station in the Bahamas." (Publisher's note)
  "Based on years of interviews and research, Horwitz delivers a powerful, engrossing narrative that raises serious questions about the unchecked use of secrecy by the military to advance its institutional power." Kirkus

Kurlansky, Mark

  Cod; a biography of the fish that changed the world. Penguin Bks. 1998 294p il pa $14 **333.95**
    1. Codfish 2. Commercial fishing 3. Cooking -- Fish
    ISBN 0-14-027501-0
                                                    LC 97-12165
  First published 1997 by Walker & Co.
  Kurlansky discusses the history of commercial cod fishing and the plight of the Atlantic fish and fisheries today as the cod faces extinction.
  This book offers "maximum readability, plenty of handsome illustrations, and a 40-page appendix of superlatively annotated recipes." Booklist
    Includes bibliographical references

Lebbin, Daniel J.

  The **American** Bird Conservancy guide to bird conservation; [by] Daniel J. Lebbin, Michael J. Parr, and George H. Fenwick; with a foreword by Jonathan

Franzen. University of Chicago Press 2010 446p il map $45; ebook $27   **333.95**
1. Wildlife conservation 2. Birds -- United States
ISBN 978-0-226-64727-2; 0-226-64727-7; 978-0-226-6472-6 ebook

LC 2010007646

The authors survey "the comprehensive status of bird conservation in the Americas, primarily focusing on North America. . . . 'WatchList Birds' provides accounts for 212 US birds—priority species for conservation—with a color plate, map, and text sections on distribution, threats, conservation, and action. 'Habitats' gives an overview of 12 major North American habitats (tundra, wetlands, grasslands, etc.) and includes several prime site descriptions within each, accompanied by the same features as the 'WatchList' accounts. The third major section, 'Threats,' includes sections such as 'Habitat Loss,' 'Pollution and Toxics,' and 'Climate Change,' and describes problems, solutions, and actions. . . . A beautiful production visually, the book is inviting as well as an unprecedented, rewarding conservation reference source." Choice

Includes glossary and bibliographical references

McNamee, Thomas
The **return** of the wolf to Yellowstone. Holt & Co. 1997 354p il maps hardcover o.p. pa $15   **333.95**
1. Wolves 2. Endangered species 3. Yellowstone National Park
ISBN 0-8050-5792-7 pa

LC 96-39702

"An advocate for the reintroduction of the gray wolf to Yellowstone National Park, McNamee kept careful watch over the legal wrangling that accompanied this controversial endeavor, the challenges of its execution, and the complex questions it has raised, then recorded the entire story in this vivid day-by-day chronicle." Booklist

Includes bibliographical references

Mooallem, Jon
Wild ones; a sometimes dismaying, weirdly reassuring story about looking at people looking at animals in America. Jon Mooallem. The Penguin Press 2013 339 p. (hardcover) $27.95   **333.95**
1. Ecology 2. Human-animal relationship 3. Endangered species -- United States 4. Wildlife conservation -- United States 5. Endangered species -- United States -- Psychological aspects
ISBN 159420442X; 9781594204425

LC 2012047006

In this book, the "plights of polar bears, Lange's metalmark butterflies and whooping cranes frame [a] discussion of humankind's relations with the animal kingdom, the environment and itself." Author Jon Mooallem "contrasts the perilous circumstances threatening some species with the conflicts that arise among sentiment, commerce and environmental science." (Kirkus Reviews)

Includes bibliographical references and index

Orenstein, Ronald
Ivory, horn and blood; behind the elephant and rhinoceros poaching crisis. Ronald Orenstein. Firefly Books 2013 216 p. color illustrations $29.95 **333.95**
1. Ivory 2. Poaching 3. Elephants 4. Rhinoceros 5. Ivory industry -- Corrupt practices 6. Rhinoceroses -- Effect of poaching on 7. African elephant -- Effect of poaching on 8. Asiatic elephant -- Effect of poaching on 9. Rhinoceros horn industry -- Corrupt practices
ISBN 1770852271; 9781770852273

LC 2013427986

This book, by Ronald Orenstein, describes how "today a new ivory crisis has arisen, fuelled by internal wars in Africa and a growing market in the Far East. . . . Bands of militia have crossed from one side of Africa to the other, slaughtering elephants with automatic weapons. A market surge in Vietnam and elsewhere has led to a growing criminal onslaught against the world's rhinoceroses. The situation, for both elephants and rhinos, is dire." (Publisher's note)

"Orenstein brings his considerable expertise to bear on this complex catastrophe, presenting all sides of some of the most polarizing issues." LJ

Includes bibliographical references (pages [194]-211) and index

Owens, Delia
The **eye** of the elephant; an epic adventure in the African wilderness. [by] Delia and Mark Owens. Houghton Mifflin 1992 305p il hardcover o.p. pa $16   **333.95**
1. Elephants 2. Wildlife conservation 3. Endangered species 4. North Luangwa National Park (Zambia)
ISBN 0-395-42381-3; 0-395-68090-5 pa

LC 92-17691

This is an account of the authors' experiences attempting to stop elephant poaching in North Luangwa National Park in Zambia. Index.

This "is a provocative, disturbing, and eminently readable work." Nat Hist

Includes bibliographic references

Followed by Secrets of the savanna

★ **Sustaining** life; how human health depends on biodiversity. edited by Eric Chivian and Aaron Bernstein; Center for Health and the Global Environment Harvard Medical School; foreword by Edward O. Wilson; prologue by Kofi Annan. Oxford University Press 2008 542p il map $34.95   **333.95**
1. Environmental health 2. Biological diversity
ISBN 978-0-19-517509-7; 0-19-517509-3

LC 2007-20609

"A collaborative survey of biodiversity issues written and/or reviewed for accuracy by more than 100 scientists, this volume is motivated by its UN sponsors' sense of the world populace's indifference to the consequences of environmental degradation. Conceiving that implicating human health with the health of other species may enlist its concern, the authors collectively warn that present extinction rates are abnormally high. Seven categories of endangered species stand in as portents of the dire effects to ecosystems when extinction occurs. . . . Abundantly illustrated, this is a valuable, urgent resource suited to any general-interest library." Booklist

Includes bibliographical references (p. 445-514)

Wilson, Edward O.

The **diversity** of life. Harvard Univ. Press 1992 424p il maps (Questions of science) $31.50 **333.95**
1. Ecology 2. Nature conservation
ISBN 0-674-21298-3

LC 92-9018

"Identifying five natural events that have disrupted evolution and global diversity (climatic changes, meteorite strikes), Wilson maintains that the present sixth great extinction is being caused by human neglect and ignorance. This important book is highly recommended." Libr J

Includes bibliographical references

★ The **future** of life. Knopf 2002 xxiv, 229p il $22; pa $13 **333.95**
1. Endangered species 2. Nature conservation
ISBN 0-679-45078-5; 0-679-76811-4 pa

LC 2001-38316

Wilson "proposes that there is yet time to avoid a grand planetary environmental crash provided we get serious, acknowledge a duty of stewardship and recognize an emotional affiliation . . . with other kinds of life." NY Times Book Rev

A **window** on eternity; A Biologist's Walk Through Gorongosa National Park. Edward O. Wilson; photographs by Piotr Naskrecki. Simon & Schuster 2014 228 p. col illustrations, color maps (hardback) $30 **333.95**
1. Ecology 2. Mozambique 3. Biodiversity 4. Nature conservation 5. Biodiversity -- Mozambique -- Parque Nacional da Gorongosa 6. Parque Nacional da Gorongosa (Mozambique) -- Pictorial works 7. Natural history -- Mozambique -- Parque Nacional da Gorongosa 8. Nature conservation -- Mozambique -- Parque Nacional da Gorongosa 9. Restoration ecology -- Mozambique -- Parque Nacional da Gorongosa 10. Parque Nacional da Gorongosa (Mozambique) -- Description and travel 11. Parque Nacional da Gorongosa (Mozambique) -- Environmental conditions
ISBN 1476747415; 9781476747415

LC 2013032607

In this book, author Edward O. Wilson presents a book of "prose and . . . photography about . . . Gorongosa National Park in Mozambique. . . . Wilson takes readers to the summit of Mount Gorongosa, sacred to the local people and the park's vital watershed. From the forests of the mountain he brings us to the deep gorges on the edge of the Rift Valley, previously unexplored by biologists, to search for new species and assess their ancient origins." (Publisher's note)

"Wilson . . . presents a lyrical ode to biodiversity within the framework of a memoir of his work in Mozambique's Gorongosa National Park, helping to rebuild it from the loss of nearly all of its megafauna as it was neglected, repurposed as a battleground, and destroyed by poachers during the 16-year civil war." Pub Wkly

335   Socialism and related systems

Avrich, Karen

Sasha and Emma; the anarchist odyssey of Alexander Berkman and Emma Goldman. Paul Avrich and Karen Avrich. Belknap Press of Harvard University Press 2012 x, 490 p.p (hbk. : alk. paper) $35 **335**
1. Anarchism and anarchists 2. Anarchism -- United States -- History 3. Anarchists -- United States -- Biography
ISBN 0674065980; 9780674065987

LC 2012008659

This book, by Paul and Karen Avrich, is a biography of the anarchists, terrorists and political extremists Emma Goldman and Alexander Berkman. "Berkman shocked the country in 1892 with . . . the failed assassination of the industrialist Henry Clay Frick. . . . Through an attempted prison breakout, multiple bombing plots, and a dramatic deportation from America, these two unrelenting activists insisted on the improbable ideal of a socially just, self-governing utopia." (Publisher's note)

Includes bibliographical references and index

Butterworth, Alex

The **world** that never was; a true story of dreamers, schemers, anarchists and secret agents. Pantheon Books 2010 482p il ebook $30.00; $30.00 **335**
1. Anarchism and anarchists 2. Anarchism -- History
ISBN 9780307379030; 9780375425110

LC 2009-48115

Butterworth "presents a history of anarchism from the 1871 Paris Commune to the 1905 Russian Revolution through stories of violent revolutionaries, the secret police who tracked them, and famous figures who played lesser-known roles." (Publisher's note) Index.

"A narrative taut with intrigue and freighted with contemporary significance." Booklist

Includes bibliographical references

Rudahl, Sharon

A **dangerous** woman; the graphic biography of Emma Goldman. The New Press 2007 115p il $17.95 **335**
1. Graphic novels 2. Biographical graphic novels 3. Essayists 4. Anarchists 5. Memoirists 6. Writers on politics 7. Family planning advocates 8. Anarchism and anarchists -- Graphic novels
ISBN 978-1-59558-064-1

LC 2007-15415

Emma Goldman was a revolutionary activist, speaker, writer, and feminist and anarchist. An immigrant to the U.S., she spoke out against inhumane working conditions, taught contraception, and opposed conscription for World War I. She founded the Free Speech League (a precursor to the ACLU), and the magazine Mother Earth. When she was deported to Russia just after the Bolshevik Revolution, she became disillusioned with the authoritarianism she found there, and she ended up supporting the fight against fascism in the Spanish Civil War. Rudahl based her graphic novel on Goldman's autobiography. The book includes nudity, sexual situations, and some violence.

335.4   Marxian systems

Marx, Karl

★ The **Communist** manifesto; [by] Karl Marx and Friedrich Engels; with an introduction and notes by Gareth Stedman Jones. Penguin Books 2002 287p pa $7   **335.4**

1. Communism

ISBN 0-14-044757-1

First published 1848

This document "analyzes history in terms of class conflict, predicts the imminent overthrow of the ruling bourgeoisie by the oppressed proletariat, and envisions a resulting classless society in which personal property would be abolished. The 'Manifesto' calls upon the proletariat of the world to unite and strengthen itself for this final revolution." Benet's Reader's Ency 4th edition

Includes bibliographical references

Pipes, Richard

★ **Communism**: a history. Modern Lib. 2001 175p hardcover o.p. pa $10.95   **335.4**

1. Communism

ISBN 0-679-64050-9; 0-8129-6864-6 pa

LC 2001-275458

"As a brief, polemical diatribe . . . this short account of communism should provoke and instruct." Libr J

Includes bibliographical references

Priestland, David

The **red** flag; a history of communism. Grove Press 2009 xxvii, 675p il $30   **335.4**

1. Communism

ISBN 978-0-8021-1924-7

"Starting with the origins of communist ideology in the French Revolution, . . . [this book] presents an interesting analysis of Marx's thinking as being shaped as much by Romanticism as by the Enlightenment. Priestland also examines communist governments and movements in Africa, Asia, Europe and Latin America as well as the Soviet Union, and discusses the Nazi-Soviet pact as well as Stalin's ban on anti-fascist activity in Europe, concluding with a level-headed account of the communist collapse." New Statesman

Includes bibliographical references

Wheen, Francis

Karl Marx; a life. Norton 2000 431p il $27.95; pa $14.95   **335.4**

1. Communism 2. Writers on politics 3. Political and social philosophers

ISBN 0-393-04923-X; 0-393-32157-6 pa

LC 99-87466

First published 1999 in the United Kingdom

"Following Marx from his childhood in Trier, Germany, through his exile in London, Wheen . . . takes readers from hovel to grand house, from the International Working Man's Association to Capital, from obscurity to notoriety and back again." Publ Wkly

Includes bibliographical references

336.2   Taxes

Burman, Leonard, 1953-

Taxes in America; what everyone needs to know. Leonard E. Burman, Joel Slemrod. Oxford University Press 2013 280 p. (pbk. : alk. paper) $16.95 **336.2**

1. Taxation -- United States

ISBN 0199890269; 9780199890262; 9780199890279

LC 2012026106

In this book, Leonard E. Burman and Joel Slemrod provide an "explanation of how . . . [the U.S.] tax system works, how it affects people and businesses, and how it might be improved. They address such questions as how to recognize Fool's Gold tax reform plans. How much more tax could the IRS collect with better enforcement? How do tax burdens vary around the world? Why do corporations pay so little tax, even though they earn trillions of dollars every year?" (Publisher's note)

Includes bibliographical references and index

★ **J.K.** Lasser's your income tax; prepared by the J.K. Lasser Tax Institute. Wiley il   **336.2**

1. Income tax

Annual. First published by Simon & Schuster. Began publication with 1936 issue. Title varies. Early issues prepared by J.K. Lasser

This "guide offers line-by-line instructions on filling out tax forms and what to do to prepare throught the year." Libr J

336.3   Public debt and expenditures

Johnson, Simon

White House burning; the founding fathers, our national debt, and why it matters to you. Simon Johnson, James Kwak. 1st ed. Pantheon Books 2012 352 p. ill. $26.95   **336.3**

1. Public debts -- United States 2. Deficit financing -- United States 3. United States -- Appropriations and expenditures 4. Debts, Public -- United States 5. Budget deficit -- United States 6. Government spending policy -- United States

ISBN 0307906965; 9780307906960

LC 2012000435

In this book, "[Simon] Johnson (Entrepreneurship and Management/MIT) and [James] Kwak (Univ. of Connecticut School of Law) . . . explain how the [U.S.] national debt began to grow, why it is willfully misrepresented by politicians and misunderstood by much of the citizenry and whether it is ever likely to cripple the richest nation in the world. . . . The authors . . . [also offer a] demonstration of the fallacy of likening government debt to the debt of an individual family." (Kirkus Reviews)

Includes bibliographical references (p. [241]-324) and index.

Kleinbard, Edward D.

We are better than this; how government should spend our money. Edward D. Kleinbard. Oxford

University Press 2015 544 p. illustrations (hard-back) $29.95 **336.3**

1. Public finance 2. United States -- Appropriations and expenditures 3. Fiscal policy -- United States 4. Finance, Public -- United States 5. Government spending policy -- United States

ISBN 019933224X; 9780199332243

LC 2014024466

This book "fundamentally reframes budget debates in the United States. Author Edward D. Kleinbard explains how the public's preoccupation with tax policy alone has obscured any understanding of government's ability to complement the private sector through investment and insurance programs that enhance the general welfare and prosperity of our society at large." (Publisher's note)

Includes bibliographical references and index

Lane, Carl

A **Nation** Wholly Free; The Elimination of the National Debt in the Age of Jackson. by Carl Lane. Westholme Pub Llc 2014 256 p. 6 plates; illustrations $28 **336.3**

1. South Carolina -- History 2. Public debts -- United States 3. Banks and banking -- United States

ISBN 1594162093; 9781594162091

This book, by Carl Lane, "shows that the great and disparate issues that confronted [U.S. President Andrew] Jackson, such as internal improvements, the 'war' against the Second Bank of the United States, and the crisis surrounding South Carolina's refusal to pay federal tariffs, become unified when debt freedom is understood as a core element of Jacksonian Democracy." (Publisher's note)

"Lane brings life to the dry topics of debt, tariffs, taxes, and banks, and he's not above calling participants to account when he thinks criticism is warranted. His only error is holding figures of the past to today's standards. Otherwise, this is first-rate history rendered with unusual clarity and verve." Pub Wkly

337 International economics

Friedman, Thomas L.

The **Lexus** and the olive tree; Updated and expanded ed; Farrar, Straus, Giroux 2000 xxi, 469p $30 **337**

1. Free trade 2. Business and politics 3. International economic relations 4. United States -- Foreign economic relations

ISBN 978-0-374-18552-7; 0-374-18552-2

LC 00-29411

First published 1999

Friedman "explains, with anecdotes as well as analyses, what the instant electronic global economy is and what it may take to live there." N Y Times Book Rev

Stiglitz, Joseph E.

Globalization and its discontents. Norton 2002 xxii, 282p $24.95; pa $15.95 **337**

1. Globalization 2. International finance 3. International economic relations 4. International Monetary Fund 5.

Developing countries -- Economic conditions

ISBN 0-393-05124-2; 0-393-32439-7 pa

LC 2002-23148

"This smart, provocative study contributes significantly to the ongoing globalization debate." Publ Wkly

Includes bibliographical references

Zizek, Slavoj

First as tragedy, then as farce. Verso 2009 157p pa $12.95 **337**

1. Communism 2. Capitalism 3. Globalization

ISBN 978-1-84467-428-2

"An earnest and timely challenge, Zizek's critique of capitalism and repositioning of communist thought is both insightful and well-reasoned, and guaranteed to rile readers across the political and theoretical spectrum." Publ Wkly

Includes bibliographical references

338 Production

Clark, Taylor

Starbucked; a double tall tale of caffeine, commerce, and culture. Little, Brown 2007 297p $25.99 **338**

1. Coffeehouses 2. Coffee industry 3. Starbucks Corporation

ISBN 978-0-316-01348-2; 0-316-01348-X

LC 2007-13074

This "is a breezily written business yarn with plenty of big-picture punch." Christ Sci Monit

Includes bibliographical references

Cook, John

Our noise; the story of Merge Records, the indie label that got big and stayed small. [by] John Cook with Mac McCaughan and Laura Ballance. Algonquin Books of Chapel Hill 2009 289p il pa $18.95 **338**

1. Rock music -- History and criticism 2. Merge Records (Chapel Hill, N.C.: Firm)

ISBN 978-1-56512-624-4; 1-56512-624-6

LC 2009-12495

This is "an oral history of Merge Records, featuring interviews from its founders (McCaughan and Ballance), its numerous signees (featuring members of Lambchop, Spoon, the Arcade Fire, and more), and various admirers and business partners (like Dischord Records founder/Fugazi frontman Ian MacKaye). Author John Cook alternates his chapters between recounting the history of the Merge label and then profiling one particular band. . . . For still being in the game after putting out two decades worth of classic albums . . . , it's obvious that Merge—with its success and its struggles—is still wanting nothing more than to make some peers of its own. In our rushed digital age of today, there's something profoundly sweet about such a simple sentiment." PopMatters

Cox, Hank H.

American drive; how manufacturing will save our country. Richard E. Dauch with Hank H. Cox.

St. Martin's Press 2012 xii, 334 p.p ill. (chiefly
col.)   **338**
1. Banks and banking 2. Automobile industry 3.
United States -- Economic conditions 4. Job creation --
United States 5. Industrial management -- United States
ISBN 9781250010827; 9781250010834

LC 2012028235

Author Richard E. "Dauch narrates the story of AAM
[American Axle and Manufacturing] against the backdrop
of his nearly fifty years in the auto industry, from . . . foreign competition, government bailouts, battles with unions,
and the recent Great Recession . . . [He provides] lessons on
leadership, advanced product technology, communication,
negotiation, and making profits in the most difficult times
. . . [The book] transcends the auto industry and draws a
blueprint for job creation, manufacturing competitiveness,
economic growth, and excellence in America." (Amazon)

★ **Encyclopedia** of American business; general
editor, W. Davis Folsom; associate editor, Stacia
N. VanDyne. Rev. ed.; Facts On File 2011 2v
(Facts on File library of American history) set
$150   **338**
1. Reference books 2. Business -- Encyclopedias
ISBN 978-0-8160-8112-7

LC 2010-28372

First published 2004

"Five general areas of business are covered: accounting, banking, finance, marketing, and management. This
encyclopedia focuses on the terms, concepts, and associations that one is most likely to encounter in business." Publisher's note

Includes bibliographical references

Schwantes, Carlos A.

The **West** the railroads made; [by] Carlos A.
Schwantes, James P. Ronda. University of Washington Press in association with Washington State Historical Society and the John 2008 xx, 229p il map
$39.95   **338**
1. West (U.S.) -- History 2. Railroads -- United States
ISBN 978-0-295-98769-9

LC 2007-29363

"Sprinkled throughout with marvelous reproductions of
photos, maps, artwork and railroad memorabilia, this book
highlights a fascinating era in our history. . . . A stunning
work using well chosen archival resources to tell the story."
Univ Press Books for Public and Second Sch Libr, 2009

Includes bibliographical references

338.1 Specific kinds of industries

Ackerman-Leist, Philip

Rebuilding the foodshed; how to create local,
sustainable, and secure food systems. Philip Ackerman-Leist. Post Carbon Institute Chelsea Green Pub.
2013 360 p. (A community resilience guide) (paperback) $19.95   **338.1**
1. Local foods 2. Agriculture -- Government policy 3.

Food supply 4. Food security
ISBN 1603584234; 9781603584234; 9781603584241

LC 2012043955

This book is about food policy. Farmer and professor
Philip Ackerman-Leist "ruminates his way through the conundrums and possibilities of local food, demonstrating how
words and their definitions can shed light on and transform
our understanding of the rapidly evolving, often confusing,
emotion-fraught questions of what people eat, where the
food comes from, who has access to what, and how the answers to these questions affect the lives of eaters and growers." (Publishers Weekly)

Includes bibliographical references and index

Astyk, Sharon

A **nation** of farmers; defeating the food crisis on American soil. [by] Sharon Astyk & Aaron
Newton. New Society Publishers 2009 392p il pa
$19.95   **338.1**
1. Food relief 2. Food supply
ISBN 978-0-86571-623-0

LC 2009-483077

The authors "argue that it is both possible and necessary to stop the harm caused by industrial agriculture. They
show how the food crisis is tied to the energy crisis, global
warming, and resource depletion and conclude that worldwide food shortages are imminent. . . . This outstanding and
well-written compendium of insights and recommendations,
of fervent idealism and practical solutions, is highly recommended." Libr J

Includes bibliographical references

Bittman, Mark, 1950-

A **bone** to pick; the good and bad news about
food, along with wisdom, insights, and advice on
diets, food safety, GMOs policy, farming, and more.
Mark Bittman. Clarkson Potter 2015 272 p. (hard-
back) $26   **338.1**
1. Diet 2. Food industry -- United States 3. Diet --
United States 4. Nutrition policy -- Untied States 5.
Agriculture and state -- United States 6. Food industry
and trade -- United States
ISBN 0804186545; 9780804186544

LC 2014044874

This book, by Mark Bittman, collects the author's "most
memorable and thought-provoking columns . . . into a single
volume. . . . As abundant and safe as the American food supply appears to be, the state of our health reveals the presence
of staggering deficiencies in both the system that produces
food and the forces that regulate it. Bittman leaves no issue
unexamined: agricultural practices, government legislation,
fad diets, and corporate greed." (Publisher's note)

"The author's keen analysis of the weakness of the
Food and Drug Administration and its failures regarding
food safety proves especially informative and enraging.
Bittman successfully links a sound food system not just to
the tastes of foodies (a word the author dislikes), but also
to larger public health issues. An intelligent rallying cry for
anyone seeking a safe and healthy food supply, and all that
entails." Kirkus

Faruqi, Sonia

Project Animal Farm; An Accidental Journey into the Secret World of Farming and the Truth About Our Food. Sonia Faruqi. W.W. Norton & Co. Inc. 2015 336 p. illustrations $27.95; (ebook) $59.95 **338.1**
  1. Food industry 2. Animal welfare 3. Livestock industry
  ISBN 1605987980; 9781605987989; 9781504609326
  LC 2015490657

This book by Sonia Faruqi offers a "look at what truly happens behind farm doors. . . . Over the course of living with farmers, hitchhiking with strangers, and risking her life, she developed surprising insights and solutions—both about the food industry and herself. . . . Sonia takes readers on an unforgettable adventure from top-secret egg warehouses in Canada to dairy feedlots in the United States, from farm offices in Mexico to lush pastures in Belize." (Publisher's note)

"Not for the fainthearted, but a good wake-up call for those concerned with decent treatment of animals and healthy food on the table." Kirkus

Includes bibliographical references (pages 357-390).

Hamilton, Lisa M.

Deeply rooted; unconventional farmers in the age of agribusiness. Counterpoint 2009 313p $25 **338.1**
  1. Farmers
  ISBN 978-1-5937-6180-6; 1-5937-6180-5
  LC 2008-50526

Hamilton "profiles farmers and ranchers who believe that 'agriculture is not an industry' but, rather, 'a fundamental act that determines whether we as a society will live or die.'. . . Hamilton's in-depth portraits of independent farmers offer invaluable perspectives on American agriculture, past and present, while offering hope for a life-sustaining future." Booklist

Includes bibliographical references

Hesterman, Oran B.

Fair food; growing a healthy, sustainable food system for all. PublicAffairs 2011 302p il $24.99; ebook $9.99 **338.1**
  1. Food supply 2. Food industry 3. Sustainable agriculture
  ISBN 978-1-61039-006-4; 978-1-61039-007-1 ebook
  LC 2010-53129

Hesterman "writes that our food system is broken and will not be able to continue supporting the world population for much longer. The author's deft explanation of our current cultivation and consumption of food should have families moving away from their supermarket aisles and into farmers' markets and community-supported agriculture programs. Hesterman urges much-needed change on the federal level, as well. . . . Guides and resources are included to help the average consumer source food locally, and the author also includes a breakdown of federal legislation and how it should be amended. A thorough, inspiring guide on how to restructure the food system for a long and healthy future, for consumers and legislators alike." Kirkus

Includes bibliographical references

Hewitt, Ben

The town that food saved; how one community found vitality in local food. Rodale 2009 234p $24.99 **338.1**
  1. Food supply 2. Food industry 3. Entrepreneurship 4. Sustainable agriculture
  ISBN 978-1-60529-686-9; 1-60529-686-4
  LC 2009-34294

"Adroitly balancing professional neutrality with personal commitment, Hewitt engagingly examines this paradigm shift in the way a community feeds its citizens." Booklist

Peacock, Kathy Wilson

★ Food security; Kathy Wilson Peacock; foreword by Mary K. Hendrickson. Facts On File 2011 344 p. (acid-free paper) $45.00 **338.1**
  1. Scarcity 2. Nutrition 3. Food supply 4. Food security -- Juvenile literature 5. Food -- Safety measures -- Juvenile literature
  ISBN 0816082030; 9780816082032
  LC 2011018414

This reference book "examines problems related to the amount, accessibility, and nutritional quality of the human food supply. Set up by a foreword by rural sociologist Mary Hendrickson, this topically arranged volume features three sections: a substantial introduction to global food security, with comprehensive case studies from representative countries (Bangladesh, China, the Democratic Republic of Congo, Haiti, the U.S., and Yemen); primary source documents; and research tools. The introduction defines food security and elucidates related topics such as global food supplies, causes and effects of food shortfalls, the potential effects of climate change and the global water crisis on food production, international history of food insecurity, and counter-strategies." (Booklist)

Includes bibliographical references and index.

Stuart, Andrea

Sugar in the Blood; A Family's Story of Slavery and Empire. Andrea Stuart. Knopf 2013 xix, 353 p.p ill., maps, geneal. tables $27.95 **338.1**
  1. Stuart family 2. Slavery -- History 3. Barbados -- History 4. Slavery -- Barbados -- History 5. Sugar trade -- Barbados -- History 6. Sugarcane industry -- Barbados -- History
  ISBN 0307272834; 9780307272836
  LC 2012034259

This book, by Andrea Stuart, is a family history and overview of slavery and the sugar industry. "In the late 1630s, . . . George Ashby . . . fell into the life of a sugar plantation owner by mere chance, but by the time he harvested his first crop, a revolution was fully under way. . . . Stuart uses her own family story--from the seventeenth century through the present--as the pivot for this . . . tale of migration, settlement, survival, slavery and the making of the Americas." (Publisher's note)

Includes bibliographical references (p. [335]-341) and index

338.2 Extraction of minerals

Burgis, Tom

The **looting** machine; warlords, oligarchs, corporations, smugglers, and the theft of Africa's wealth. Tom Burgis. PublicAffairs 2015 352 p. illustrations, map (hardcover) $27.99 **338.2**

1. Natural resources 2. International relations 3. Africa -- Social conditions 4. Africa -- Politics and government
ISBN 1610394399; 9781610394390; 9781610394406
LC 2015930296

In this book, "Tom Burgis exposes the truth about the African development miracle. . . . As global demand for Africa's resources rises, a handful of Africans are becoming legitimately rich but the vast majority, like the continent as a whole, is being fleeced. Outsiders tend to think of Africa as a great drain of philanthropy. But look more closely at the resource industry and the relationship between Africa and the rest of the world looks rather different." (Publisher's note)

"Essential for understanding the colonial Africa of the past and, even more so, the diverse Africa of today." LJ

Burrough, Bryan

The **big** rich; the rise and fall of the greatest Texas oil fortunes. Penguin Press 2009 466p il $29.95; pa $16 **338.2**

1. Petroleum industry
ISBN 978-1-59420-199-8; 1-59420-199-4; 978-0-14-311682-0 pa; 0-14-311682-7 pa
LC 2008-27043

"Full of schadenfreude and speculation—and solid, timely history too." Kirkus

Includes bibliographical references

House, Silas

Something's rising; Appalachians fighting mountaintop removal. [by] Silas House and Jason Howard; foreword by Lee Smith. University Press of Kentucky 2009 xiv, 306 p.p $27.95 **338.2**

1. Landscape protection 2. Coal mines and mining 3. Appalachian region 4. Mountaintop mining 5. Environmentalism -- Appalachian Region, Southern 6. Appalachian Region, Southern -- Environmental conditions 7. Celebrities -- Appalachian Region, Southern -- Interviews 8. Landscape protection -- Appalachian Region, Southern -- Citizen participation 9. Mountaintop removal mining -- Environmental aspects -- Appalachian Region, Southern
ISBN 978-0-8131-2546-6; 0813125464; 9780813125466
LC 2008049846

The authors focus on "the long-growing mining crisis in Central Appalachia. Twelve Appalachians—among them a college student, former union organizers, community activists and the octogenarian 'mother of folk,' Jean Ritchey—provide firsthand accounts of a disappearing way of life, a vital ecology in rapid decline, an industry that refuses to take responsibility for the devastation it causes (blowing the tops off mountains is only the latest, most destructive technique), and a nation too hooked on cheap energy to help. . . . This important collection illuminates the ongoing betrayal of the American mining town." Publ Wkly

Includes bibliographical references (p. [287]-290) and index

LeCain, Timothy J.

Mass destruction; the men and giant mines that wired America and scarred the planet. Rutgers University Press 2009 273p il map $26.95 **338.2**

1. Mining engineering 2. Copper mines and mining 3. Mining engineers 4. Copper industry and trade -- History 5. Copper mines and mining -- Western States 6. Copper mines and mining -- Environmental aspects
ISBN 978-0-8135-4529-5; 0-8135-4529-3
LC 2008-35434

The author writes "about the history, the engineering challenges, the successes of production and resulting consumption, and the environmental consequences of open-pit copper mining, mainly in the first half of the 20th century. . . . This book provokes serious second thoughts about the future of the exploitation of nature's bounty, and it should appeal to a wide audience." Choice

Includes bibliographical references and index

Maass, Peter

Crude world; the violent twilight of oil. Alfred A. Knopf 2009 276p il $27 **338.2**

1. Petroleum industry
ISBN 978-1-4000-4169-5
LC 2009-12303

"An absorbing, relentlessly discouraging account of the disastrous effect of oil wealth on nearly everyone." Kirkus

Includes bibliographical references (p. 233-62)

Margonelli, Lisa

Oil on the brain; adventures from the pump to the pipeline. Doubleday 2007 324p hardcover o.p. pa $14.95 **338.2**

1. Petroleum industry
ISBN 0-385-51145-0; 978-0-385-51145-2; 0-7679-1697-2 pa; 978-0-7679-1697-4 pa
LC 2006-20789

Margonelli examines how oil travels from petroleum fields to neighborhood gas stations.

The author "adds something fresh to the discussion by eschewing the popular (but dreary) doomsday angle in favor of an 'adventures in . . .' approach. . . . By giving voice to the people who are the links in the global oil chain, Margonelli invites us to leapfrog all the rhetoric, dry statistics, and dire pronouncements about oil in order to truly understand it." Fast Company

Includes bibliographical references

Yergin, Daniel

★ The **prize**; the epic quest for oil, money & power. Free Press 2008 908p il map pa $22 **338.2**

1. World politics 2. Petroleum industry
ISBN 978-1-4391-1012-6; 1-4391-1012-3
LC 2009-291302

First published 1991

This is a "history of the oil industry, from the first oil well ever drilled (near Titusville, Pennsylvania, in 1859) to the Iraqi invasion of Kuwait. It recalls advances in technology, innovations in salesmanship, and wars and truces among corporations and nations." New Yorker

Includes bibliographical references

Zuckerman, Gregory

The **frackers**; the outrageous inside story of the new billionaire wildcatters. Gregory Zuckerman. Portfolio Penguin 2013 416 p. (hardback) $29.95 **338.2**

1. Energy resources 2. Shale gas industry 3. Hydraulic fracturing 4. Businesspeople -- United States -- Biography 5. Energy industries -- United States -- Biography 6. Petroleum industry and trade -- United States -- Biography

ISBN 1591846455; 9781591846451

LC 2013037926

This book explores "one of America's biggest economic and scientific revolutions of recent decades: the tapping of abundant oil and natural gas reserves within our own borders using a technique called fracking. . . . Focusing on a half dozen 'wildcatters,' the ones who seek out potential drilling sites, Zuckerman takes us through their decades long drought while they refined the techniques of horizontal hydraulic drilling." (Publishers Weekly)

"[S]hows us the beneficial side of fracking and the potentially environmentally disastrous side, and lets us find our own ground to stand on. A lively, exciting, and definitely thought-provoking book." Booklist

Includes bibliographical references

338.3   Other extractive industries

Hilborn, Ray

Overfishing; what everyone needs to know. Ray Hilborn with Ulrike Hilborn. Oxford University Press 2012 xviii, 150 p.p (pbk. : alk. paper) $16.95 **338.3**

1. Overfishing 2. Commercial fishing 3. Sustainable fisheries 4. Fisheries -- Environmental aspects

ISBN 0199798141; 9780199798131; 9780199798148

LC 2011031308

This book by Ray and Ulrike Hilborn provides an "explanation of the broad issues associated with overfishing. Guiding readers through the scientific, political, economic, and ethical issues associated with harvesting fish from the ocean, it will provide answers to questions about which fisheries are sustainably managed and which are not. Overall, the authors present a hopeful view of the future of fisheries." (Publisher's note)

Includes bibliographical references (p. [131]-139) and index

338.4   Secondary industries and services

2015 songwriter's market; Where & How to Market Your Songs. edited by James Duncan. F & W Media Inc 2014 331 p. illustrations $29.99 **338.4**

1. Music -- Publishing 2. Songwriters and songwriting

ISBN 1599638428; 9781599638423

LC 78648269

This book, edited by James Duncan, "provide[s] songwriters and performing artists with the most complete and up-to-date information needed to place songs with music publishers, find record companies and producers, obtain representation with managers, and more. This comprehensive guide gives you the tools and first-hand knowledge you need to launch your songwriting career right now!" (Publisher's note)

Almond, Steve

★ **Candyfreak**: a journey through the chocolate underbelly of America. Algonquin Books of Chapel Hill 2004 266p $21.95 **338.4**

1. Candy 2. Authors 3. Chocolate 4. Humorists 5. Journalists 6. Short story writers

ISBN 1-56512-421-9

LC 2003-70801

The author tells how candy "shaped his childhood and continues to define his life in ways large and small. . . . Once hundreds of American confectioners delivered regional favorites to consumers, but now the big three of candy—Hershey, Mars, and Nestlé—control the market. To find out what happened to those candies of yesteryear, Almond talks to candy collectors and historians and visits a few of the remaining independent candy companies. . . . Flavored with the author's amusingly tart sense of humor, Candyfreak is an intriguing chronicle of the passions that candy inspires and the pleasures it offers." Libr J

Includes bibliographical references

Becker, Elizabeth

Overbooked; the exploding business of travel and tourism. Elizabeth Becker. Simon & Schuster 2013 464 p. (hardback) $28 **338.4**

1. Travel 2. Cultural tourism 3. Tourism 4. TRAVEL -- General 5. Tourism -- Political aspects 6. Tourism -- Cross cultural studies 7. Tourism -- Moral and ethical aspects

ISBN 1439160996; 9781439160992; 9781439161005

LC 2012032848

In this book, Elizabeth Becker explores the growing global tourism industry. She "travels widely, experiencing and analyzing 'the stealth industry of the twenty-first century,' which is proliferating across regions, cultures, and ecosystems, and developing in specialized niches like 'sex tourism,' 'dark tourism,' and 'heritage tourism.'" (Publishers Weekly)

Beckert, Sven

Empire of cotton; a global history. Sven Beckert. Alfred A. Knopf 2014 704 p. illustrations, maps (hardback) $35 **338.4**

1. Textile industry 2. Cotton manufacture 3. Slaves 4. Textile workers 5. Labor -- History 6. Capitalism -- History 7. Cotton trade -- History 8. Slavery -- Economic aspects 9. Cotton textile industry -- History 10. Cotton plantation workers -- History

ISBN 0375414142; 9780375414145

LC 2014009320

Pulitzer Prize Finalist: History (2015)

This book by Sven Beckert "tells the story of how, in a remarkably brief period, European entrepreneurs and powerful statesmen recast the world's most significant manu-facturing industry, combining imperial expansion and slave labor with new machines and wage workers to change the world. . . . The empire of cotton was, from the beginning, a fulcrum of constant global struggle between slaves and planters, merchants and statesmen, workers and factory owners." (Publisher's note)

"Both chronologically and geographically, this is a wide-ranging saga that examines the role of nation-states, politi-cians, entrepreneurs, and laborers on every continent. This is not a pretty story, since Beckert shows that this empire often depended upon coercion and violence for its growth and maintenance. This is a highly detailed, provocative work that combines history, economics, and sociology in an effort to show how cotton shaped the modern world." Booklist

Burhans, Dirk E.

Crunch! a history of the great American potato chip. [by] Dirk Burhans. University of Wisconsin Press 2008 203p il $26.95   338.4
  1. Potato chips
  ISBN 978-0-299-22770-8
                                    LC 2008-11962

"A wonderfully readable history that spans popular cul-ture, local history, agriculture, economics, business and bi-ography. Pass the chips please!" Univ Press Books for Pub-lic and Second Sch Libr, 2009

Includes bibliographical references

Callahan, Daniel

Taming the beloved beast; how medical tech-nology costs are destroying our health care system. Princeton University Press 2009 267p $29.95 338.4
  1. Medical technology 2. Medical care -- Costs
  ISBN 978-0-691-14236-4; 0-691-14236-X
                                    LC 2009-1503

According to Callahan, . . . Americans want universal health care but are divided over how to obtain it. While bringing insightful ethical, social, political, and economic perspectives to this timely, well-documented discourse of the ballooning costs of American health care and Medi-care, Callahan concentrates on the growing costs of medical technology, which, along with uncontrolled governmental health-care spending, threaten to drag this country into fi-nancial crisis. Libr J

Includes bibliographical references and index

Diaz, Tom

The last gun; how changes in the gun industry are killing Americans and what it will take to stop it. Tom Diaz. The New Press 2013 319 p. (hardcover) $26.95   338.4
  1. Firearms industry -- United States 2. Firearms ownership -- United States 3. Gun control -- United States 4. Firearms industry and trade -- United States 5. Firearms -- Law and legislation -- United States
  ISBN 1595588302; 9781595588302
                                    LC 2012047230

This book, by Tom Diaz, explores gun control in the U.S. "By any account, gun violence in the United States has reached epidemic proportions. . . . Tom Diaz presents a chilling, up-to-date survey of the changed landscape of gun

manufacturing and marketing. [The book] explores how the gun industry and the nature of gun violence have changed . . . [and arguing] that now is the time for a renewed political effort to attack gun violence at its source--the guns them-selves." (Publisher's note)

Includes bibliographical references (pages 255-319).

Fine, Doug

Too high to fail; cannabis and the new green economic revolution. Doug Fine. Gotham Books 2012 xlv, 314 p.p (hardcover) $28.00; (paperback) $16.00   338.4
  1. Marijuana industry 2. Marijuana -- Economic aspects
  ISBN 1592407099; 9781592407095; 9781592407613
                                    LC 2012014437

It was author "[Doug] Fine's intention . . . to track one cloned female cannabis plant, later named Lucille, from the farmer who tended her to the first patient who inhaled her smoke. Along the way, the author explores the intertwined history of humans and cannabis, as well as potential future benefits of cannabis, including biofuel, textiles, foodstuffs, farming and substantial economic boosts for cash-strapped communities." (Kirkus Reviews)

Goldstone, Lawrence

Drive! Henry Ford, George Selden, and the Race to Invent the Auto Age. Lawrence Goldstone. Bal-lantine Books 2016 384 p. $28   338.4
  1. Automobile industry 2. Automobiles -- Design and construction
  ISBN 0553394185; 9780553394184
                                    LC 2016002581

Author Lawrence Goldstone "tells the fascinating story of how the internal combustion engine, a 'theory looking for an application,' evolved into an innovation that would change history. Debunking many long-held myths along the way, Drive! shows that the creation of the automobile was not the work of one man, but very much a global effort. Long before anyone had heard of Henry Ford, men with names like Benz, Peugeot, Renault, and Daimler were building and marketing the world's first cars." (Publisher's note)

"A splendid dissection of the Selden/Ford patent face-off and its place in automotive historiography, this work will be enjoyed by business, legal, transportation, social, and intel-lectual historians; general readers; and all libraries." LJ

Includes bibliographical references and index.

Lewis, Michael D., 1960-

The new new thing; a Silicon Valley story. Nor-ton 1999 268p $25.95   338.4
  1. Computer software industry 2. Computer software executives 3. Businessmen -- United States -- Biography 4. Computer software industry -- United States -- History
  ISBN 0-393-04813-6
                                    LC 99-43412

This is an account of the career of James H. Clark, "the former chairman of Silicon Graphics, who went on to start Netscape. . . . {Healtheon is} the firm he founded in 1996 to Internetize the health-care industry." (Newsweek)

This "is a splendid, entirely satisfying book, intelligent and fun and revealing and troubling in the correct proportions, resolutely skeptical but not at all cynical, brimming with fabulous scenes as well as sharp analysis." NY Times Book Rev

Martinez, Antonio Garcia

Chaos Monkeys; Obscene Fortune and Random Failure in Silicon Valley. by Antonio Garcia Martinez. HarperCollins 2016 528 p. $29.99   **338.4**
    1. Privacy 2. Internet 3. Marketing 4. Social media
    ISBN 0062458191; 9780062458193

This book, by Antonio Garcia Martinez, "unravels the chaotic evolution of social media and online marketing and reveals how it is invading our lives and shaping our future. Weighing in on everything from startups and credit derivatives to Big Brother and data tracking, social media monetization and digital 'privacy,' García Martínez shares his scathing observations and outrageous antics, taking us on a humorous, subversive tour of the fascinatingly insular tech industry." (Publisher's note)

McMillan, Tracie

★ The **American** way of eating; undercover at Walmart, Applebee's, farm fields, and the dinner table. Tracie McMillan. Scribner 2012 x, 319 p.p $25   **338.4**
    1. Poverty 2. American cooking 3. Agriculture -- United States 4. Food industry -- United States 5. Cooking, American 6. Food supply -- United States 7. Food industry and trade -- United States 8. Food habits -- Economic aspects -- United States
    ISBN 1439171955; 9781439171950; 9781439171974
                                LC 2012372266

This book by journalist Tracie McMillan discusses the economics of the food industry of the United States. "[S]he watched the debate about America's meals unfold, one that urges us to pay food's true cost—which is to say, pay more. So in 2009 McMillan embarked on a[n] . . . undercover journey to see what it takes to eat well in America. For nearly a year, she worked, ate, and lived alongside the working poor to examine how Americans eat when price matters." (Publisher's note)

"Full of personal stories of the daily struggle to put food of any kind on the table in today's economy, McMillan's book will force readers to question their own methods of purchasing and preparing food." Kirkus

Includes bibliographical references (p. 255-318)

McNish, Jacquie

Losing the signal; the untold story behind the extraordinary rise and spectacular fall of Blackberry. Jacquie McNish, Sean Silcoff. Flatiron Books 2015 279 p. (hardback) $27.99   **338.4**
    1. Smartphones 2. BlackBerry Limited 3. BlackBerry (Smartphone)
    ISBN 1250060176; 9781250060174
                                LC 2015012152

This book, by Jacquie McNish and Sean Silcoff, "is a riveting story of a company that toppled global giants before succumbing to the ruthlessly competitive forces of Silicon Valley. This is not a conventional tale of modern business failure by fraud and greed. The rise and fall of BlackBerry

reveals the dangerous speed at which innovators race along the information superhighway." (Publisher's note)

Includes bibliographical references and index

Mitford, Jessica

★ The **American** way of death revisited. Knopf 1998 296p hardcover o.p. pa $14   **338.4**
    1. Cremation 2. Undertakers and undertaking 3. Funeral rites and ceremonies
    ISBN 0-679-77186-7 pa
                                LC 97-49349

First published 1963 by Simon & Schuster with title: The American way of death

"Very interesting, informative, and easy to read, this book is written with wit, solid information, and refreshing bluntness." Libr J

Noonan, Meg Lukens

The **coat** route; craft, luxury, and obsession on the trail of a $50,000 coat. Meg Lukens Noonan. Spiegel & Grau 2013 272 p. (alk. paper) $27 **338.4**
    1. Luxuries 2. Men's clothing 3. Luxury 4. Custom-made clothing
    ISBN 1400069939; 9781400069934
                                LC 2012042994

In this book, Meg Lukens Noonan follows the making of a $50,000 overcoat. The "journey begins in the Peruvian mountains with the elusive . . . vicuna (the animal that provides the fleece for the coat), and is followed by stops in Florence, to meet the creator of the coat's silk lining—enigmatic menswear designer Stefano Ricci; Yorkshire, where a textile mill spins vicuna fleece into yarn that Gary Eastwood's Pennine Weavers turns into cloth; and Birmingham, for hand-carved buffalo horn buttons." (Publishers Weekly)

Includes bibliographical references and index

Petersen, Melody

Our daily meds; how the pharmaceutical companies transformed themselves into slick marketing machines and hooked the nation on prescription drugs. Farrar, Straus and Giroux 2008 432p $26   **338.4**
    1. Drug industry
    ISBN 978-0-374-22827-9; 0-374-22827-2
                                LC 2008-2097

The author shows how corporate salesmanship has triumphed over science inside the biggest pharmaceutical companies and, in turn, how this promotion driven industry has taken over the practice of medicine and is changing American life.

"Petersen takes readers beyond glossy advertising and celebrity endorsements to glimpse the alarming dark side of the American pharmaceutical industry." Libr J

Includes bibliographical references (p. 409-412)

Rudacille, Deborah

Roots of steel; the boom and bust of an American mill town. Pantheon Books 2010 290p $27   **338.4**
    1. Steel industry 2. Maryland -- History 3. United States -- Economic conditions
    ISBN 9780375423680; 978-0-375-42368-0
                                LC 2009020962

"Rudacille has delivered a book that would do Studs Terkel proud, partaking of his oral-historical approach to the past at turns, imbued with his pro-labor spirit throughout. Required reading for activists and for those wondering where things went wrong for America's working people." Kirkus

Includes bibliographical references

Suisman, David

Selling sounds; the commercial revolution in American music. Harvard University Press 2009 356p il $29.95   **338.4**

1. Music industry 2. Music -- United States 3. Music trade -- United States 4. Music -- United States -- History and criticism

ISBN 0-674-03337-X; 978-0-674-03337-5

LC 2008-55620

"Suisman investigates the early decades of the popular music industry, from 1880 to 1930." (Nation) Index.

"A fascinating, well-written, richly detailed story of how music became a commodity in America. . . . [Suisman's] scholarship is amazingly wide-ranging." Washington Times

Includes bibliographical references

Tobbell, Dominique A.

Pills, power, and policy; the struggle for drug reform in Cold War America and its consequences. Dominique A. Tobbell. University of California Press 2012 xv, 294 p.p (pbk. : alk. paper) $26.95   **338.4**

1. Drugs 2. Industrial policy 3. Industrial relations -- United States 4. History, 20th Century -- United States 5. Drug Industry -- history -- United States 6. Economics, Pharmaceutical -- United States 7. Drugs -- Research -- United States -- History -- 20th century 8. Pharmaceutical industry -- United States -- History -- 20th century

ISBN 0520271130; 0520271149; 9780520271135; 9780520271142

LC 2011014878

This book "offers a . . . history of how the American drug industry and key sectors of the medical profession came to be allies against pharmaceutical reform. It details the political strategies they have used to influence public opinion, shape legislative reform, and define the regulatory environment of prescription drugs." (Amazon.com)

Includes bibliographical references and index.

Vlasic, Bill

Once upon a car; the fall and resurrection of America's big three auto makers--GM, Ford, and Chrysler. William Morrow 2011 394p   **338.4**

1. Automobile industry 2. Chrysler Corp. 3. Ford Motor Co. 4. General Motors Corp.

ISBN 978-0-06-184562-8; 978-0-06-204222-4 ebook

LC 2011020572

The author "examines the perfect storm of overseas competition, economic downturn, rising gas prices, union pressures, legacy costs, and lumbering bureaucracy that brought the U.S. auto industry to its knees. He takes us into the boardrooms and inside the heads of such people as Rick Wagoner, former GM CEO, who was ousted by Steve Rattner; Obama's 'car czar,' Bill Ford Jr., great-grandson of Henry Ford and chairman of Ford Motor Company; and

billionaire financier Kirk Kerkorian, who at different times held 10-percent stakes in both GM and Ford. This is an engrossing look at big business in crisis, forever changed but never willing to give up." Booklist

Includes bibliographical references

Washington, Harriet A.

Deadly monopolies; the shocking corporate takeover of life itself, and the consequences for your health and our medical future. Doubleday 2011 433p il $28.95; ebook $14.99   **338.4**

1. Drug industry 2. Medical ethics 3. Drugs -- Marketing

ISBN 978-0-385-52892-4; 978-0-385-53405-5 ebook

LC 2011013033

"Extensively documented with minimal scientific jargon, this book is recommended for any reader interested in the future of our health system." Libr J

Includes bibliographical references

338.5   General production economics

Galbraith, John Kenneth

★ The **great** crash, 1929; with a new introduction by the author; foreword by James K. Galbraith. Houghton Mifflin Co. 2009 206p pa $14.95 **338.5**

1. Great Depression, 1929-1939 2. United States -- Economic conditions -- 1919-1933

ISBN 978-0-547-24816-5

First published 1955

Beginning with the bull market of Coolidge and Hoover and continuing through the stock market crash, the author analyzes its causes and speculates about the chances of another crash.

Includes bibliographical references

Panic; the story of modern financial insanity. [edited by] Michael Lewis. W. W. Norton & Company 2009 391p il $27.95; pa $18.95   **338.5**

1. Financial crises

ISBN 978-0-393-06514-5; 978-0-393-33798-3 pa

LC 2008-39523

The editor "has compiled an anthology of articles related to five major financial crises in recent decades: the 1987 stock market crash, the Russian default, the Asian currency crisis, the Internet bubble and . . . the subprime mortgage collapse (the final article included is from January 2008). For each crisis, Lewis offers articles from journals, books, transcripts, and newspapers, all written immediately before, during, or after the event. . . . Timely and highly readable, this work includes in one accessible source two decades' worth of some of the best writing on the various crises and panics." Libr J

Reinhart, Carmen M., 1955-

This time is different; eight centuries of financial folly. [by] Carmen M. Reinhart, Kenneth S. Rogoff. Princeton University Press 2009 xlv, 463p il $35   **338.5**

1. Fiscal policy 2. Business cycles 3. Financial crises

4. International finance
ISBN 978-0-691-14216-6; 0-691-14216-5
LC 2009-22616

The authors "have compiled an impressive database, which covers eight centuries of government debt defaults from around the world. They have also collected statistics on inflation rates from every country where information is available and on banking crises and international capital flows over the past couple of centuries. This lengthy historical study gives what they call a 'panoramic view' of the unending cycle of boom and bust, showing how claims that 'this time is different' are invariably proven wrong. . . . [This] is an important addition to the literature of financial history." Wall Street J

Includes bibliographical references (p. 400-433)

Shafir, Eldar
Scarcity; why having too little means so much. Sendhil Mullainathan and Eldar Shafir. Times Books, Henry Holt and Company 2013 304 p. $28   **338.5**
1. Scarcity 2. Decision making 3. Supply and demand
ISBN 0805092641; 9780805092646
LC 2013004167

In this book, authors Sendhil Mullainathan and Eldar Shafir "discuss how scarcity affects our daily lives, recounting anecdotes of their own foibles and making . . . connections that bring this research alive. Their book provides a new way of understanding why the poor stay poor and the busy stay busy, and it reveals not only how scarcity leads us astray but also how individuals and organizations can better manage scarcity for greater satisfaction and success." (Publisher's note)

Includes bibliographical references and index

The **value** of a dollar; prices and incomes in the United States, 1860-2009. [edited] by Scott Derks. 4th ed; Grey House Pub. 2009 690p il $155   **338.5**
1. Prices 2. Reference books 3. Salaries, wages, etc. 4. Cost and standard of living
ISBN 978-1-59237-403-8
First published 1994

"Both great-grandparents and serious students in historical research will benefit from this book. It will be an especially valuable study to students of American history, economics, and even mathematics." Libr J

Includes bibliographical references

The **value** of a dollar: colonial era to the Civil War, 1600-1865; [edited by] Scott Derks and Tony Smith. Grey House Pub. 2005 436p il $155   **338.5**
1. Prices 2. Reference books 3. Salaries, wages, etc. 4. Cost and standard of living
ISBN 1-59237-094-2; 978-1-59237-094-8
LC 2006-275331

"This source is an engaging statistical summary that looks at the history of the American people through the eyes of everyday workers and consumers. The 265 years it covers are presented in six chronological chapters: '1600-1749: The Development of the Colonies,' '1750-1774: The Run up to the War of American Independence,' and so on, ending with

the close of the Civil War in 1865. . . . [This book] will find a happy audience among students, researchers, and general browsers. It offers a fascinating and detailed look at early American history from the viewpoint of everyday people trying to make ends meet." Booklist

Includes bibliographical references

338.7 Business enterprises

Abrams, John
Companies we keep; employee ownership and the business of community and place. foreword by William Greider. 2nd ed.; Chelsea Green Pub. Co. 2008 333p il pa $17.95   **338.7**
1. Management 2. Business ethics 3. Employee ownership
ISBN 978-1-60358-000-7
LC 2008-25075

First published 2005 with title: Company we keep

The author posits a "business model based on community, goodwill, craftsmanship, and not-so-big growth, outlining the steps he took to help his own firm become a 'more democratic, more responsible, more permanent kind of company.'" Libr J

Includes bibliographical references

Angwin, Julia
Stealing MySpace; the battle to control the most popular website in America. Random House 2009 371p il $27   **338.7**
1. MySpace (Web site) 2. Electronic commerce
ISBN 978-1-4000-6694-0; 1-4000-6694-8
LC 2008-23504

"This engrossing look at how MySpace became a media powerhouse will find a solid audience of business history, technology and entrepreneurship readers." Publ Wkly

Includes bibliographical references

Arden, Lynie
★ The **work**-at-home sourcebook; 10th ed.; Live Oak Pubns 2009 400p il pa $19.95   **338.7**
1. Home-based business
ISBN 978-0-911781-20-5
First published 1987. Frequently revised

"Each entry in this helpful listing of firms that hire freelancers and franchises that can be home-based includes contact information and advice on how to get one's foot in the door. The book also features directories of marketplaces for handicrafts and online certification programs." Libr J

Auletta, Ken
Googled; the end of the world as we know it. Penguin Press 2009 384p $27.95   **338.7**
1. Internet industry 2. Internet searching 3. Web search engines 4. Computer scientists 5. Social responsibility of business 6. Google, Inc. 7. Internet executives 8. Information technology executives
ISBN 978-1-594-20235-3
LC 2009-24770

The author's "thorough reporting and declarative writing provide a crisp, informative read. . . . Auletta displays the skill of a responsible journalist in both researching and crafting this snapshot of today's technological landscape. " Christ Sci Monit

Includes bibliographical references

Bissonnette, Zac

The **great** Beanie Baby bubble; mass delusion and the dark side of cute. Zac Bissonnette. Portfolio 2015 272 p. illustrations (some color) (hardback) $26.95 **338.7**

1. Fads 2. Teddy bears 3. Ty, Inc. -- History 4. Toy industry -- United States -- History 5. Beanie Babies (Trademark) -- Collectors and collecting -- History
ISBN 9781591846024

LC 2014038639

This book, by Zac Bissonnette, "delivers the never-before-told story of the plush animal craze that became the tulip mania of the 1990s. . . . Beanie Babies were ten percent of eBay's sales in its early days, with an average selling price of $30--six times the retail price. . . . The end of the craze was swift and devastating, with 'rare' Beanie Babies deemed worthless as quickly as they'd once been deemed priceless." (Publisher's note)

"Equally heartwarming and heartbreaking, this accessible work will captivate fans of the TV series Mr. Selfridge and Brad Stone's The Everything Store, as well as sociology buffs, pop culture enthusiasts, and anyone who has worked in retail." LJ

Includes bibliographical references and index

Breen, Bill

Brick by brick; by David C. Robertson and Bill Breen. 1st ed. Crown Business 2013 xii, 305 p.p (hardcover) $26.00 **338.7**

1. LEGO toys 2. Toy industry 3. LEGO toys -- History 4. LEGO koncernen (Denmark) 5. Toy industry -- Denmark -- Management
ISBN 030795160X; 9780307951601

LC 2013004798

This book, written by David Robertson and Bill Breen, examines toy manufacturer LEGO. "it spotlights the company's disciplined approach to harnessing creativity and recounts one of the most remarkable business transformations in recent memory." It "reveals how LEGO failed to keep pace with the revolutionary changes in kids' lives and began sliding into irrelevance. It took a new LEGO management team–faced with the growing rage for electronic toys, few barriers to entry, and ultra-demanding consumers to . . . transform LEGO." (Publisher's note)

Brenner, Joel Glenn

The **emperors** of chocolate; inside the secret world of Hershey and Mars. Random House 1999 366p il hardcover o.p. pa $14.95 **338.7**

1. Chocolate 2. Mars, Inc. 3. Hershey Foods Corp. 4. Food industry executives
ISBN 0-7679-0457-5 pa

LC 98-21610

"Brenner examines the candy industry, focusing on the rivalry between Hershey and Mars. Milton Hersey was and Forrest Mars is highly secretive and eccentric, and they both

amassed huge fortunes. A wonderful inside look at successful businessmen." Booklist

Includes bibliographical references

Brinkley, Douglas

★ **Wheels** for the world; Henry Ford, his company, and a century of progress, 1903-2003. Viking 2003 xxii, 858p il $34.95; pa $18 **338.7**

1. Philanthropists 2. Automobile industry 3. Ford Motor Co. 4. Automobile executives
ISBN 0-670-03181-X; 0-14-200439-1 pa

LC 2003-33066

"Car lovers will appreciate this amazing account of the birth of the automobile industry, including funny anecdotes about the trusty Model T, the evolution of the V-8 engine, the artistic design of the Thunderbird, sophistication of the Lincoln Continental, and popularity of the Mustang." Booklist

Includes bibliographical references

Bruck, Connie

When Hollywood had a king; the reign of Lew Wasserman, who leveraged talent into power and influence. Random House 2003 512p il hardcover o.p. pa $16.95 **338.7**

1. MCA Inc. 2. Talent agents 3. Motion picture executives
ISBN 0-375-50168-1; 978-0-8129-7217-7 pa; 0-8129-7217-1 pa

LC 2003-41418

"Those who are interested in comprehensive details about the inner workings of the entertainment industry—its history, business, customs, people, and gossip—will find this a fascinating read and a solid resource." Libr J

Includes bibliographical references

Burrows, Peter

Backfire: Carly Fiorina's high-stakes battle for the soul of Hewlett-Packard. Wiley 2003 296p il $27.95 **338.7**

1. Computer industry 2. Hewlett-Packard Co. 3. Compaq Computer Corporation 4. Computer industry executives 5. Telecommunications executives
ISBN 0-471-26765-1

LC 2002-156443

This is an account "of the bitter boardroom fight that erupted after Hewlett-Packard announced plans to merge with Compaq in the late summer of 2001 . . . [with a focus on] the charismatic Carleton S. Fiorina, who became one of the highest-ranking women in American business in 1999 when she was tapped as the first outside chief executive of the Hewlett-Packard company. . . . [This] is a riveting, colorful, fast-paced account of the Compaq battle." N Y Times Book Rev

Includes bibliographical references

Casnocha, Ben

My start-up life; what a (very) young CEO learned on his journey through Silicon Valley. Ben Casnocha; foreword by Marc Benioff. Jossey-Bass 2007 xiv, 189 p.p (cloth) $24.95 **338.7**

1. Entrepreneurship 2. New business enterprises 3.

Computer software industry 4. Comcate (Firm) 5. Entrepreneurship -- United States 6. Computer software industry -- United States 7. Internet software industry -- United States 8. New business enterprises -- United States -- Management
ISBN 0787996130; 9780787996130

LC 2007007866

"Ben Casnocha discovered he was an entrepreneur at age 12 and hasn't slowed down since. In this . . . instructive book, Ben dissects the entrepreneurship 'gene,' explaining that everyone has inherited it if they have an idea to make the world a better place. In Casnocha's case, he found a better way for city governments to communicate with constituents on the Web. Six years later, Comcate has dozens of municipal clients, a growing staff, and a record of excellence. This book is the story of his start-up, but also a conversation with his mentors, clients and fellow entrepreneurs about how to make a business idea work and how to have the time of your life trying." (Publisher's note)

Includes bibliographical references (p. 185-188).

Cohen, Rich

The **fish** that ate the whale; the life and times of America's banana king. Rich Cohen. Farrar, Straus and Giroux 2012 xiii, 270 p.p   **338.7**
1. Biography 2. Businessmen 3. Business and politics 4. United Fruit Company -- Biography 5. Banana trade -- Louisiana -- New Orleans -- History 6. Jewish businesspeople -- Louisiana -- New Orleans -- Biography
ISBN 0374299277; 9780374299279

LC 2011041207

This biography describes the life of the 20th-century American fruit businessman Samuel Zemurray. "He worked as . . . a banana hauler, a dockside hustler, and a plantation owner. He battled and conquered the United Fruit Company, becoming a symbol of the best and worst of the United States. . . . Starting with nothing but a cart of freckled bananas, he built a sprawling empire . . . connected to the birth of modern American diplomacy, public relations, business, and war." (Publisher's note)

Includes bibliographical references.

Coll, Steve, 1958-

★ **Private** empire; ExxonMobil and American power. Steve Coll. Penguin Press 2012 685 p. $36.00   **338.7**
1. Global warming 2. Petroleum industry 3. Iraq War, 2003-2011 4. Corporate mergers and acquisitions 5. Exxon Corporation 6. Exxon Mobil Corporation 7. Big business -- United States 8. Corporate power -- United States 9. Petroleum industry and trade -- Political aspects -- United States
ISBN 1594203350; 9781594203350

LC 2011044722

In this book "two-time Pulitzer winner [Steve] Coll . . . demonstrates how the merger of Exxon and Mobil has allowed the company to wield more power and wealth than even the American government, in the manner of John D. Rockefeller. . . . The Exxon-Mobil merger in 1999 created a global behemoth and also provoked small wars at drilling spots where the poor and disenfranchised deeply resented

the foreign workers on native soil and disrupted the extraction by violence and insurgency." (Kirkus Reviews)

Includes bibliographical references (p. [659]-664) and index

Denton, Sally

The **Profiteers**; Bechtel and the Men Who Built the World. by Sally Denton. Simon & Schuster 2016 448 p. illustrations (some color) $30   **338.7**
1. Corporations 2. Hoover Dam (Ariz. and Nev.) 3. Family-owned business enterprises
ISBN 1476706468; 9781476706467

LC 2015510596

In this book, by Sally Denton, "The tale of the Bechtel family dynasty is a classic American business story. It begins with Warren A. 'Dad' Bechtel, who led a consortium that constructed the Hoover Dam. From that auspicious start, the family and its eponymous company would go on to 'build the world,' from the construction of airports in Hong Kong and Doha, to pipelines and tunnels in Alaska and Europe, to mining and energy operations around the globe." (Publisher's note)

"However readers view the company, Denton's extensively researched work informs readers about the firm's maintenance as a privately held concern during its growth into a huge, multinational enterprise." Booklist

Includes bibliographical references (pages 317-408) and index.

Elmore, Bartow J.

Citizen Coke; the making of Coca-Cola capitalism. Bartow J. Elmore. W W Norton & Co Inc 2015 304 p. 9 plates; illustrations (hardcover) $27.95   **338.7**
1. Coca-Cola Company 2. Soft drink industry 3. Sustainable development 4. Social responsibility of business 5. Soft drink industry -- United States
ISBN 0393241122; 9780393241129

LC 2014022329

This book, by Bartow J. Elmore, is a "history of how Coke's insatiable thirst for natural resources shaped the company and reshaped the globe. How did Coca-Cola build a global empire by selling a low-price concoction of mostly sugar, water, and caffeine? The easy answer is advertising, but the real formula to Coke's success was its strategy, from the start, to offload costs and risks onto suppliers, franchisees, and the government." (Publisher's note)

"Without a doubt, Coke has been a good public citizen that stimulates economies and improves lives, writes the author, but the costs to taxpayers—for recycling systems, public pipes and subsidized farms—and the environment call into question how such unsustainable practices can continue in an age of scarcity. A superb, quietly devastating environmental and business history." Kirkus

Includes bibliographical references and index

Genoways, Ted

The **chain**; farm factory. Ted Genoways. Harper 2014 320 p. illustrations $26.99   **338.7**
1. Food industry 2. Meat industry 3. Occupational health and safety 4. Factory farms 5. Industrial safety 6. Hormel Foods Corporation 7. Food processing

plants -- United States 8. Meat industry and trade --
United States
ISBN 006228875X; 9780062288752

LC 2014019018

James Beard Foundation Award Nominee: Writing and
Literature (2015)

This book, by Ted Genoways, is a "work of investigative
journalism that explores the runaway growth of the American meatpacking industry and its dangerous consequences.
. . . Genoways uses the story of Hormel Foods and soaring
recession-era demand for its most famous product, Spam, to
probe the state of the meatpacking industry, including the
expansion of agribusiness and the effects of immigrant labor
on Middle America." (Publisher's note)

"Readers curious about meatpacking and agriculture as
well as the social, economic, and environmental impacts of
the food industry will find Genoways's nonfiction debut a
valuable and stimulating read." LJ

Includes bibliographical references

Harris, Blake J.
  Console wars; Sega, Nintendo, and the battle that
defined a generation. Blake J. Harris. It Books 2014
576 p. (hardback) $22.99   **338.7**
  1. Video games 2. Video games -- History 3. Video
games industry -- History 4. Electronic games industry
-- History
  ISBN 0062276719; 9780062276698; 9780062276704

LC 2013050668

This book, by Blake J. Harris, is a "behind-the-scenes
business thriller that chronicles how Sega . . . took on the
juggernaut Nintendo and revolutionized the video game
industry. In 1990, Nintendo had a virtual monopoly on the
video game industry. Sega, on the other hand, was just a faltering arcade company with big aspirations and even bigger
personalities. But that would all change with the arrival of
Tom Kalinske." (Publisher's note)

"Harris defines the players immediately, honing in on
their most notable characteristics, and puts the reader in the
thick of the meetings and deal-making with a confidence
stemming from hundreds of interviews." Booklist

Kealing, Bob
  Tupperware, unsealed; Brownie Wise, Earl
Tupper, and the home party pioneers. University
Press of Florida 2008 250p il $28   **338.7**
  1. Containers 2. Sales personnel 3. Tupperware Corp.
  4. Household products industry executives
  ISBN 0-8130-3227-X; 978-0-8130-3227-6

LC 2007-47539

The author "explores the origins of the Tupperware
industry as seen through the insightful genius of Brownie
Wise, the impetus behind the home party craze that catapulted Tupperware revenues into the millions. . . . This work
proves to be a valuable contribution to the growing body
of literature that focuses on the individual contributions of
women to US business and industry." Choice

Includes bibliographical references

Kirkpatrick, David
  The **Facebook** effect; the inside story of the
company that is connecting the world. Simon &
Schuster 2010 372p il $26   **338.7**
  1. Internet industry 2. Social networking 3. Online
social networks 4. Facebook Inc. 5. Internet executives
  6. Internet -- Social aspects
  ISBN 978-1-4391-0211-4; 1-4391-0211-2

LC 2009-51983

The author was encouraged by Mark Zuckerberg, the
founder and chief executive of Facebook.com, to write this
book and was granted extensive access to him and his associates. Their cooperation has resulted in a mostly sympa-
theticat times, gushingly laudatoryaccount of the company,
though Mr. Kirkpatrick does not shy away from dissecting its missteps and successive disputes over privacy. He
gives the reader a detailed understanding of how the company grew from a 2004 Harvard dorm-room project into the
world's second-most-visited site after Google. N Y Times
(Late NY Ed)

Includes bibliographical references

Knoedelseder, William
  Bitter brew; the rise and fall of Anheuser-Busch
and America's kings of beer. William Knoedelseder.
HarperBusiness 2012 396 p. $27.99   **338.7**
  1. Anheuser-Busch, inc. -- History 2. Beer industry --
United States -- History 3. Brewing industry -- United
States -- History
  ISBN 0062009265; 9780062009265

LC 2012026942

This book by William Knoedelseder is a history of the
Anheuser-Busch beer company. It is a "saga of one of the
wealthiest, longest-lasting, and most colorful family dynasties in the history of American commerce--a cautionary tale
about prosperity, profligacy, hubris, and the blessings and
dark consequences of success. . . . [The] narrative captures
the Busch saga through five generations. At the same time,
it weaves a broader story of American progress and decline
over the past 150 years." (Publisher's note)

Krass, Peter
  Carnegie. Wiley 2002 612p il $35; pa
$19.95   **338.7**
  1. Philanthropists 2. Metal industry executives
  ISBN 0-471-38630-8; 0-471-46883-5 pa

LC 2002-10162

"From bobbin boy in a cotton mill to one of American
history's most famous characters, Carnegie's life was one of
contradictions. In his lifetime, Carnegie gave away a staggering $350 million, setting a standard for social conscience.
Krass used original sources such as letters, diaries, and other
writings by primary and peripheral characters in Carnegie's
life to penetrate the public persona and show the man who
crusaded for universal literacy and world peace." Booklist

Includes bibliographical references

Kurlansky, Mark, 1948-
  Birdseye; the adventures of a curious man. Mark
Kurlansky. Doubleday 2012 251 p.   **338.7**
  1. Businessmen 2. Frozen foods 3. Inventors
-- Biography 4. Food industry -- United States 5.

Inventors -- United States -- Biography 6. Businessmen -- United States -- Biography 7. Frozen foods industry -- United States -- History

ISBN 0385527055; 9780385527057; 9780385535885

LC 2011044891

This book explains that "[t]here was far more to American inventor Clarence Birdseye (1886-1956) than met the eye; he was slight and cheerful but restlessly curious. He was drawn into a life of travel to remote parts of the continent in search of adventure and new experiences. He invented tools and processes, notably that which enabled quick freezing of foodstuffs and revolutionized culinary habits. Birdseye launched not just the frozen-vegetable company that bears his now-famous name but an entire industry. [Mark] Kurlansky, whose past works include the popular histories 'Salt' and 'Cod,' paints a complete picture of Birdseye's unusual career and accomplishments." (Libr J)

Includes bibliographical references and index

Lashinsky, Adam

Inside Apple; how America's most admired-and secretive-company really works. Adam Lashinsky. Business Plus 2012 223 p. $26.99   **338.7**
1. Business planning 2. Apple Computer, Inc 3. Corporate culture -- United States 4. Success in business -- United States 5. Computer industry -- United States -- Management

ISBN 145551215X; 9781455512157

LC 2011044773

In this book, "[Adam] Lashinsky . . . investigates the core of Apple before, during, and after the reign of the late Steve Jobs, not only to discover how the company works and if its success can be replicated, but also to speculate about Apple's future." He "outlines salient factors that concurrently contribute to Apple's success and deviate from standard business practice." (Publishers Weekly)

Levy, Steven

In the plex; how Google thinks, works, and shapes our lives. Simon & Schuster 2011 424p $26; ebook $12.99   **338.7**
1. Google (Web site) 2. Google, Inc.

ISBN 978-1-4165-9658-5; 1-4165-9658-5; 978-1-4165-9671-4 ebook; 1-4165-9671-2 ebook

LC 2010049964

The author presents a behind-the-scenes story of the Internet search engine company Google.

This is "the most comprehensive, intelligent and readable analysis of Google to date. Levy is particularly good on how those behind Google think and work. . . . [This work] teems with original insight into Google's most controversial affairs." New Sci

Includes bibliographical references

Lutz, Bob, 1932-

Car guys vs. bean counters; the battle for the soul of American business. [by] Bob Lutz. Portfolio/Penguin 2011 241p il $26.95   **338.7**
1. Automobile industry 2. Automobile executives 3. Corporate turnarounds 4. General Motors Corp. -- Bankruptcy 5. Automobile industry and trade -- United

States -- Finance

ISBN 978-1-59184-400-6; 1-59184-400-2

LC 2011010720

The author "describes how he was pulled out of retirement to turn around a bankrupt General Motors in 2008, recounting how he transitioned the company away from office politics and penny pinching." Publisher's note

Macy, Beth

Factory man; how one furniture maker battled offshoring, stayed local - and helped save an american town. Beth Macy. Little, Brown and Co. 2014 464 p. illustrations (hardcover) $28   **338.7**
1. Outsourcing 2. Furniture making 3. American furniture

ISBN 0316231436; 9780316231411; 9780316231435; 9780316231565

LC 2014937343

"With over $500 million a year in sales, the Bassett Furniture Company was once the world's biggest wood furniture manufacturer. . . . But beginning in the 1980s, the Bassett company suffered from an influx of cheap Asian furniture as the first wave of imports struck, and ultimately moved nearly all its production to Asia. Only one man fought back: John Bassett III, a shrewd and determined third-generation factory man who used grit, tenacity, and will to compete against China and ultimately save his family's company." (Publisher's note)

"Macy's down-to-earth writing style and abundance of personal stories from manufacturing's beleaguered front lines make her work a stirring critique of globalization." Booklist

Includes bibliographical references (pages [415]-442) and index

Magner, Mike

Poisoned legacy; the human cost of BP's rise to power. Mike Magner. St. Martin's Press 2011 432 p. $18   **338.7**
1. Oil wells -- Blowouts 2. Oil spills -- Environmental aspects 3. Petroleum industry -- Ethical aspects 4. Offshore oil well drilling -- Safety measures 5. British Petroleum Company 6. Petroleum refineries -- Accidents -- United States 7. Petroleum workers -- Health and hygiene -- United States 8. Petroleum industry and trade -- Moral and ethical aspects

ISBN 9780312554941

LC 2010054461

In this book, an "exposé of the British oil giant," BP, "gives a comprehensive rundown of the [2010] Gulf oil well explosion and leak, and of the rushed scheduling, substandard engineering, skipped tests, and faulty equipment that precipitated that disaster. That's just the capstone of [Mike Magner's] detailed account of BP's misadventures in North America, which include a 2005 explosion at the company's Texas refinery that killed 15 people, a 200,000-gallon leak from a corroded Alaskan oil pipeline, a steady drip of workplace accidents, fatalities, and pollution violations and a drumbeat of callow apologies, lawsuits, fines, and criminal probes." (Publishers Wkly)

Includes bibliographical references (p. [381]-398) and index

Maxfield, Katherine

Starting up Silicon Valley; how ROLM became a cultural icon and fortune 500 company. Katherine Maxfield. Greenleaf Book Group Emerald Book Co. 2014 368 p. color illustrations $21.95 **338.7**

1. Technology 2. New business enterprises 3. ROLM Corporation -- History 4. Corporate culture -- California -- Santa Clara County 5. Success in business -- California -- Santa Clara County 6. Santa Clara Valley (Santa Clara County, Calif.) -- History 7. Computer industry -- California -- Santa Clara County -- History 8. Technological innovations -- California -- Santa Clara County -- History

ISBN 1937110621; 9781937110628

LC 2013955281

Author Katherine Maxfield "draws from materials collected by the Silicon Valley Historical Association, newspaper and magazine articles, and interviews with the founders and former employees of ROLM to write a corporate history unusual in its candor. Readers don't need to know the difference between a PBX and a CBX--although they'll know after reading this book--to appreciate the intense emotions and exuberant personalities Maxfield portrays." (Publisher's note)

"Few authors have Maxfield's knack for describing both the forest and the trees, which makes her history of ROLM a worthy model for other histories of Silicon Valley companies.Corporate history with enough drama for a movie." Kirkus

Includes bibliographical references and index

Mazzeo, Tilar J.

The **secret** of Chanel No. 5; the intimate history of the world's most famous perfume. Harper 2010 281p il $25.99 **338.7**

1. Perfumes 2. Fashion designers 3. Perfumers 4. Chanel (Firm) 5. Cosmetics industry executives

ISBN 978-0-06-179101-7; 0-06-179101-6

LC 2010-15284

This "'unauthorized biography of a scent' unearths the roots of the creation and fame of Coco Chanel's famous perfume. . . . Mazzeo's lush prose covers relevant aspects of Coco Chanel's life, from the stark beauty of the orphanage where she was raised to the glamour and luxury of her adulthood, to the scents that wove through her life and shaped the development of her signature perfume. However, the book never bogs down in the details—despite the extensive research showcased in the bibliography—and a smooth pacing keeps it moving along at a fast clip." Libr J

Includes bibliographical references

Micklethwait, John

The **company**; a short history of a revolutionary idea. [by] John Micklethwait and Adrian Wooldridge. Modern Library 2003 xxiii, 227p (Modern Library chronicles) hardcover o.p. pa $14.95 **338.7**

1. Corporations 2. Business enterprises

ISBN 0-679-64249-8; 0-8129-7287-2 pa

LC 2002-26429

In this history of the joint-stock company, Micklethwait and Wooldridge "trace its progress from Assyrian partnership agreements through the 16th- and 17th-century Europe-

an 'charter companies' that opened trade with distant parts of the world, to today's multinationals. The authors' breadth of knowledge is impressive. They infuse their engaging prose with a wide range of cultural, historical and literary references, with quotes from poets to presidents. . . . Moreover, the authors argue that for all the change companies have engendered over time, their force has been for an aggregate good." Publ Wkly

Includes bibliographical references

Nalebuff, Barry, 1958-

Mission in a bottle; the honest guide to doing business differently--and succeeding. by Seth Goldman and Barry J. Naelbuff and illustrated by Sungyoon Choi. Crown Business 2013 288 p. $23 **338.7**

1. Entrepreneurship 2. Business enterprises 3. Graphic novels 4. Iced tea -- United States -- Comic books, strips, etc 5. Tea trade -- United States -- Comic books, strips, etc 6. Honest Tea (Firm) -- History -- Comic books, strips, etc 7. Soft drink industry -- United States -- Comic books, strips, etc

ISBN 0770437494; 9780770437497

LC 2013004799

Authors Seth Goldman and Barry Nalebuff, "cofounders of Honest Tea tell the engaging story of how they created and built a mission-driven business, offering a wealth of insights and advice to entrepreneurs, would-be entrepreneurs, and millions of Honest Tea drinkers about the challenges and hurdles of creating a successful business--and the importance of perseverance and creative problem-solving." (Publisher's note)

"[T]his candid portrait of leveraging resources to build a business from the ground up is a useful and cleverly conceptualized read." Pub Wkly

Orbanes, Philip

The **game** makers; the story of Parker Brothers from Tiddledy Winks to Trivial Pursuit. {by} Philip E. Orbanes. Harvard Business School Press 2003 272p il $29.95 **338.7**

1. Parker Brothers (Firm)

ISBN 1-591-39269-1

LC 2003-10768

This is a study of the Parker Brothers, who developed such games as Monopoly, Clue and Risk. The author contends that the games "reflect the American world view of the 20th century. Life is a ruthless struggle in which there are many losers, but it takes place within a framework of unbendable and fairminded rules." Economist

Includes bibliographical references

Saxon, A. H.

P. T. Barnum: the legend and the man. Columbia Univ. Press 1989 437p il hardcover o.p. pa $22.50 **338.7**

1. Circus executives

ISBN 0-231-05687-7 pa

LC 89-982

"Working primarily from Barnum's letters, business papers, family members' and associates' diaries, and legal documents, Saxon has pieced together a picture of the legendary circus owner. Saxon's detailed coverage of Barnum's life . . . is rich with anecdotes yet scholarly enough to please any researcher. Saxon succeeds admirably in capturing the essence of Barnum." Booklist

Includes bibliographical references

Stross, Randall

Planet Google; how one company's all-encompassing vision is transforming our lives. [by] Randall Stross. Free Press 2008 275p $26   338.7

1. Google (Web site) 2. Internet searching 3. Google, Inc. 4. Internet industry 5. Web search engines 6. Information organization

ISBN 1-41654-691-X; 978-1-41654-691-7

LC 2008-18788

New York Times columnist Randall Stross examines the internet search engine Google and the company that developed it. He contends that Google is "becoming as dominant a force on the Web as Microsoft became on the PC. . . . The more offerings Google adds, and the more ubiquitous a presence it becomes, [Stross argues], the more dependent its users become on its services and the more information they contribute to its . . . collection of data." (Publisher's note) Index.

This is "an outstanding business history of Google from its humble beginnings through the dot-com era to current times." Libr J

Includes bibliographical references (p. 201-257)

Vaidhyanathan, Siva

The Googlization of everything; (and why we should worry) University of California Press 2011 265p $26.95; ebook $22   338.7

1. Google (Web site) 2. Internet industry 3. Google, Inc. 4. Internet -- Social aspects

ISBN 978-0-520-25882-2; 978-0-520-94869-3 ebook

LC 2010-27772

The author "shows how Google's methods of capturing, storing and filtering information are often elitist and increasingly invasive. . . . Citing some of the company's most controversial headlines, from the toddler who was captured naked in his grandmother's garden with Google Street View to the settlement between Google and the Author's Guild over copyrights, the author unmasks the monster behind the friendly interface with the suspense of a horror novel. An urgent reminder to look more closely at dangers that lurk in plain sight. " Kirkus

Includes bibliographical references

338.8 Combinations

Bown, Stephen R.

Merchant kings; when companies ruled the world, 1600-1900. [by] Stephen Bown. Thomas Dunne Books 2010 314p il map $26.99   338.8

1. Merchants 2. Multinational corporations 3. Europe -- Commerce

ISBN 978-0-312-61611-3

LC 2010-34783

The author "has produced a magnificent description of the six great companies, and their leaders, that dominated

the 'Heroic Age of Commerce.' Bown demonstrates how the corporations served as stalking horses for kings and parliaments while enriching shareholders and the powerful managers themselves. . . . Bown presents a fascinating look at the men who exploited resources and native peoples while laying the foundations of empires." Publ Wkly

Includes bibliographical references

MacIntosh, Julie

Dethroning the king; the hostile takeover of Anheuser-Busch, an American icon. Wiley 2010 408p il $27.95   338.8

1. Corporate mergers and acquisitions 2. Anheuser-Busch, Inc. 3. Beverage industry executives

ISBN 978-0-470-59270-0

LC 2010-32279

"In a narrative that reads as fast as any fiction thriller, . . . MacIntosh details the 2008 takeover of the iconic Anheuser-Busch brewing company by Belgian corporation InBev, focusing particularly on the company's importance to the St. Louis region; its management, or lack thereof, by the Busch family (particularly the August Busches III and IV); and the broader unsettled economic climate of 2008." Libr J

Includes bibliographical references

338.9 Economic development and growth

Sachs, Jeffrey, 1954-

The age of sustainable development; Jeffrey D. Sachs. Columbia University Press 2015 544 p. illustrations, maps, portraits (pbk. : alk. paper) $34.95   338.9

1. Sustainable development 2. Economic development -- Environmental aspects

ISBN 0231173156; 9780231173148; 9780231173155

LC 2014034070

In this book, Jeffrey D. Sachs "argues that it's time for humankind to reconcile its needs with those of the planet, in this sprawling manifesto. He surveys the great dilemma facing civilization: how to ensure broadly inclusive economic growth, especially in the poorest countries, without destroying the natural environment and deranging the climate on which survival depends." (Publishers Weekly)

"Overall, Sachs's book provides a basic but ambitious argument: to reverse current unsustainable trends, global warming must be mitigated, extreme poverty must end, gender imbalance must be corrected, and access to basic health care and education must be granted to all." Choice

Includes bibliographical references and index

Speth, James Gustave, 1942-

★ America the possible; manifesto for a new economy. James Gustave Speth. Yale University Press 2012 249 p. (hardback) $30.00   338.9

1. Economics 2. Democracy -- United States 3. United States -- Politics and government 4. Social justice -- United States 5. United States -- Economic policy 6. Environmental policy -- United States 7. Progressivism (United States politics)

ISBN 0300180764; 9780300180763

LC 2012012170

The book, by author James Gustave Speth, "spells out the specific changes that are needed to move toward a new political economy--one in which the true priority is to sustain people and planet. Supported by a . . . "theory of change" that explains how system change can come to America, the book also presents a vision of political, social, and economic life in a renewed America. . . . In short, this is a book about the American future and the strong possibility that we . . . have it in ourselves to use our freedom and our democracy in powerful ways to create . . . a reborn America." (Publisher's note)

Includes bibliographical references and index

339.2 Distribution of income and wealth

Garson, Barbara

Down the up escalator; how the 99 percent live in the Great Recession. Barbara Garson. Doubleday 2013 288 p. (hardcover) $26.95; (electronic) $80.85 **339.2**

1. Employment 2. Global Financial Crisis, 2008-2009 3. United States -- Economic conditions 4. Equality -- United States -- History -- 21st century 5. Income distribution -- United States -- History -- 21st century
ISBN 0385532741; 9780385532747; 9780385532754
LC 2012020359

This book, by Barbara Garson, explores how "the Great Recession has thrown huge economic challenges at almost all Americans save the super-affluent few. . . . Garson has interviewed an economically and geographically wide variety of Americans to show the painful waste in all this loss and insecurity, and describe how individuals are coping." (Publisher's note)

Milanović, Branko

The **haves** and the have-nots; a short and idiosyncratic history of global inequality. Basic Books 2010 258p il map $27.95 **339.2**

1. Wealth 2. Poverty 3. Wealth -- History 4. Poverty -- History 5. Income distribution
ISBN 0-465-01974-9; 978-0-465-01974-8
LC 2010-29295

The first essay in this book discusses "how economists think about income inequality within a country—in particular, how it is measured, and how it is related to a country's overall economic health. . . . In his second and third essays, Milanovic switches to . . . inequality around the world." (N Y Times Book Rev) Index.

"Students, practitioners, and anyone interested in economics and the issue of inequality would enjoy this." Libr J

Includes bibliographical references

Noah, Timothy

The **great** divergence; America's growing inequality crisis and what we can do about it. Timothy Noah. Bloomsbury 2012 264 p. **339.2**

1. Wealth 2. Poverty 3. Equality 4. Economic policy -- United States 5. United States -- Economic conditions 6. Wealth -- United States 7. Poverty -- United States 8. Equality -- United States 9. United States -- Economic

policy 10. Income distribution -- United States
ISBN 9781608196333
LC 2011048447

This book examines the "political dimensions of the outrageous disparity in incomes that has developed since 1979. . . . [Timothy] Noah discusses the rise and fall of the trade-union movement and demonstrates that turning points in that movement were also turning points in the growth of income inequality. . . . Noah also calls out financial deregulation as a major offender, and he lists measures that he believes can help the situation." (Kirkus Reviews)

Piketty, Thomas, 1971-

The **economics** of inequality; Thomas Piketty; translated by Arthur Goldhammer. Belknap Press of Harvard University Press 2015 160 p. illustrations (alk. paper) $22.95 **339.2**

1. Income 2. Equality 3. Economics 4. Income distribution 5. Equality -- Economic aspects
ISBN 0674504801; 9780674504806
LC 2015008813

This book, by Thomas Piketty, is "an introduction to the conceptual and factual background necessary for interpreting changes in economic inequality over time. . . . Piketty begins by explaining how inequality evolves and how economists measure it. In subsequent chapters, he explores variances in income and ownership of capital and the variety of policies used to reduce these gaps." (Publisher's note)

"Most readers will be better served by Capital in the Twenty-First Century, leaving students and economists as the likeliest audience for this title." LJ

Includes bibliographical references and index

Ridley, Matt

The **rational** optimist; how prosperity evolves. Fourth Estate, Harper 2010 438p il $26.99 **339.2**

1. Reason 2. Wealth 3. Optimism
ISBN 978-0-06-145205-5
LC 2010-4907

The author posits that as long as civilization engages in exchange and specialization, we will be able to reinvent ourselves and responsibly use earthly resources ad infinitum. . . . Ridley puts current perceptions about violence, wealth, and the environment into historical perspective, reaching back thousands of years to advocate global free trade, smaller government, and the use of fossil fuels. He confidently takes on the experts, from modern sociologists who fret over the current level of violence in the world to environmentalists who disdain genetically modified crops. An ambitious and sunny paean to human ingenuity, this is an argument for why ambitious optimism is morally mandatory. Publ Wkly

Includes bibliographical references

339.4 Factors affecting income and wealth

Banerjee, Abhijit V.

Poor economics; a radical rethinking of the way to fight global poverty. [by] Abhijit V. Banerjee and Esther Duflo. PublicAffairs 2011 303p $26.99 **339.4**

1. Poverty 2. Foreign aid 3. Poverty -- Prevention 4.

Economic assistance -- Developing countries
ISBN 9781586487980; 1586487981

LC 2010-50938

This book "draws on a variety of evidence, not limiting itself to the results of randomised trials, as if they are the only route to truth. And the authors' interest is not confined to 'what works', but also to how and why it works. Indeed, Ms Duflo and Mr Banerjee, perhaps more than some of their disciples, are able theorists as well as thoroughgoing empiricists." Economist

Includes bibliographical references

Cohen, Lizabeth
A **consumer's** republic; the politics of mass consumption in postwar America. Knopf 2003 567p il $35; pa $16.95 **339.4**
1. Consumers 2. Consumption (Economics) 3. United States -- Social conditions
ISBN 0-375-40750-2; 0-375-70737-9 pa

LC 2002-141599

"Without question, this is a difficult, demanding, and dense book—but it is also a greatly significant contribution to business literature. . . . Cohen submits a copiously researched, brilliantly conceived, and ultimately quite instructive study of American economics since the Depression." Booklist

Includes bibliographical references

Desmond, Matthew, ca. 1970-
Evicted; poverty and profit in the American city. Matthew Desmond. Crown 2016 432 p. (ebook) $20; (hardback) $28 **339.4**
1. Profit -- United States 2. Poverty -- United States 3. Eviction -- United States 4. Cities and towns -- United States 5. Low-income housing -- United States
ISBN 9780553447446; 9780553447439; 9780553447453

LC 2015027374

This book by Matthew Desmond describes "Sherrena Tarver, a former schoolteacher turned inner-city entrepreneur, and Tobin Charney, who runs one of the worst trailer parks in Milwaukee. They loathe some of their tenants and are fond of others, but as Sherrena puts it, 'Love don't pay the bills.' She moves to evict Arleen and her boys a few days before Christmas." (Publisher's note)

"This stunning, remarkable book—a scholar's 21st-century How the Other Half Lives—demands a wide audience." Kirkus

Includes bibliographical references (pages 343-405) and index.

Gerth, Karl
As China goes, so goes the world; how Chinese consumers are transforming everything. Hill and Wang 2010 258p il $26; ebook $12.99 **339.4**
1. Consumers 2. Consumption (Economics) 3. China -- Economic conditions
ISBN 978-0-8090-3429-1; 978-1-4299-6246-9 ebook

LC 2010-12647

"Nuanced, balanced and accessible—essential reading for anyone trying to make sense of China today." Kirkus

Includes bibliographical references

Miller, Geoffrey F.
Spent; sex, evolution, and consumer behavior. [by] Geoffrey Miller. Viking 2009 374p $26.95 **339.4**
1. Consumers 2. Consumption (Economics)
ISBN 978-0-670-02062-1; 0-670-02062-1

LC 2008-51554

"Since evolutionary psychology seeks to examine how natural selection acts on psychological and mental traits, Miller applies this knowledge to help us understand what actually motivates us to buy. He pokes fun at popular culture and at the things we buy and flaunt to inflate our self-esteem and try to make ourselves more attractive. Personality research can inform the study of consumer behavior, and Miller shows us how having a better understanding of our own personalities will help us avoid the pitfalls of runaway consumerism." Libr J

Includes bibliographical references

Novogratz, Jacqueline
The **blue** sweater; bridging the gap between rich and poor in an interconnected world. Jacqueline Novogratz. Rodale Distrib. to the trade by Macmillan 2009 x, 262 p.p $15.99 **339.4**
1. Globalization 2. Poverty -- Developing countries 3. Philanthropists -- Personal narratives 4. Domestic economic assistance -- Developing countries 5. Poverty 6. Charities 7. Microfinance 8. Economic assistance
ISBN 1594869154 (hardcover); 9781594869150 (hardcover)

LC 2008043621

This book, "[p]art coming-of-age story, part blueprint for effecting real change, . . . explores what it means to create meaningful solutions to global poverty and release human potential in an interconnected world. For [author] Jacqueline Novogratz it all started back home in Alexandria, Virginia, with the blue sweater . . . she outgrew . . . and gave . . . to Goodwill. Eleven years later in Africa, she spotted a young boy wearing that very sweater, with her name still on the tag inside. . . . Novogratz relates her experiences over two decades, first in Africa and later in India and Pakistan. She began as a banker and philanthropist, and now works as a venture capitalist, trying to effect real change in countries where the average citizen lives on less than $4 a day." (Publisher's note)

Rivlin, Gary
Broke, USA; from pawnshops to Poverty, Inc.: how the working poor became big business. Harper 2010 358p $26.99 **339.4**
1. Poor -- United States 2. United States -- Economic conditions
ISBN 978-0-06-173321-5

LC 2010-2874

"A timely, important, and deeply disturbing look at the cycle of debt of the nation's most vulnerable." Publ Wkly

Includes bibliographical references

Roberts, James A.

Shiny objects; why we spend money we don't have in search of happiness we can't buy. James A. Roberts. HarperOne 2011 368 p. $25.99   **339.4**

1. Consumers 2. American dream 3. Consumption (Economics) -- United States 4. American Dream 5. Materialism -- United States

ISBN 0062093606; 9780062093608

LC 2010005086

In this book James A. Roberts "studies why Americans believe and behave as if possessions will induce, increase, and enhance happiness -- when, as studies show, materialism 'negatively correlate[s]' with well-being. He examines the psychological underpinnings of our desire to purchase -- even beyond our means. . . . Roberts offers a history of American consumerism, drawing parallels between different eras." (Publishers Weekly)

Includes bibliographical references.

Shaefer, H. Luke

$2.00 a Day; Living on Almost Nothing in America. Kathryn J. Edin; H. Luke Shaefer. Houghton Mifflin Harcourt 2015 240 p. (hardback) $28 **339.4**

1. Poverty -- United States 2. Income gap -- United States 3. United States -- Social conditions

ISBN 0544303180; 9780544303188

LC 2015004337

This book by Kathryn J. Edin and H. Luke Shaefer describes how "American families in urban and rural areas, across all races and family structures, are living on wages so low they can barely sustain themselves. Focusing on families in the inner cities of Chicago and Cleveland; the small Appalachian town of Johnson City, Tennessee; and the small rural towns of Jefferson and Percy, Mississippi, the authors highlight the day-to-day struggle of families living well below the poverty line." (Booklist)

"An eye-opening account of the lives ensnared in the new poverty cycle." Kirkus

Includes bibliographical references (pages 179-199) and index.

Waldfogel, Joel

Scroogenomics; why you shouldn't buy presents for the holidays. Princeton University Press 2009 173p $9.95   **339.4**

1. Gifts 2. Consumption (Economics)

ISBN 9780691142647

LC 2009-6177

The author "assesses holiday gift giving through the lens of economic tenets such as opportunity costs and deadweight loss. The result is a short but engaging manifesto on the inefficiency of the tradition, concluding with several solutions to increase satisfaction for both givers and receivers." Libr J

Includes bibliographical references

339.5 Macroeconomic policy

Conway, Ed

The Summit; Bretton Woods, 1944: J. M. Keynes and the Reshaping of the Global Economy. Ed Con-

way. W W Norton & Co Inc 2015 480 p. 16 plates; illustrations $28.95   **339.5**

1. Monetary policy 2. International finance

ISBN 160598681X; 9781605986814

This book, by Ed Conway, discusses the history of the 1944 Bretton Woods meeting, the "most colorful and important economic summit in history-- held during the height of World War II. . . . Countries from around the world . . . agreed to overhaul the structure of the international monetary system. Against all odds, they were successful. The system they set up presided over the longest, strongest and most stable period of growth the world economy has ever seen." (Publisher's note)

"This is a gripping story for both general readers and scholars interested in World War II, the Cold War, and domestic and international political economy. The author knows how to write for those who are less informed about economics while telling the history of the turbulent conference through its leading characters and updating its legacy today. An essential purchase on this topic." LJ

Steil, Benn

The battle of Bretton Woods; John Maynard Keynes, Harry Dexter White, and the making of a new world order. Benn Steil. Princeton University Press 2013 472 p. (hardcover) $29.95   **339.5**

1. Economic conditions 2. World War, 1939-1945 3. Monetary policy -- History -- 20th century 4. International finance -- History -- 20th century

ISBN 0691149097; 9780691149097

LC 2012035709

Author Benn Steil, the director of international economics at the Council on Foreign Relations, "revisits the 1944 conference that created 'the new global monetary architecture' for the postwar world. As the American Army entered Rome and the Russians drove the Nazis out of Minsk, delegates from 44 Allied nations gathered in Bretton Woods, N.H., to hammer out the ground rules for international economic equilibrium following the defeat of the Axis powers." (Kirkus Reviews)

Includes bibliographical references and index

340 Law

Black's law dictionary; Bryan A. Garner, editor in chief. 10th edition Thomson Reuters 2014 2016 p. deluxe $140; hbk $81.95   **340**

1. Law -- United States -- Dictionaries

ISBN 9780314621306; 031462130X; 9780314613004; 0314613005

LC 2015372206

First published 1891 with title: A dictionary of law. (7th edition 1999) Periodically revised to bring terms up to date

"Contains more than 50,000 terms, earliest usage dates for nearly all terms, pronunciation guidance, Latin maxims, and more." (Publisher's note)

Feinman, Jay M.

★ **Law** 101; 3rd ed.; Oxford University Press 2010 363p $27.95   **340**

1. Law -- United States
ISBN 978-0-19-539513-6

LC 2010-487303

First published 2000

This book "covers the main subjects taught in the first year of law school. Readers are introduced to every aspect of the legal system, from constitutional law and the litigation process to tort law, contract law, property law, and criminal law." Publisher's note

Legal systems of the world; a political, social, and cultural encyclopedia. edited by Herbert M. Kritzer. ABC-CLIO 2002 4v il maps set $385   **340**

1. Reference books 2. Law -- Encyclopedias
ISBN 1-57607-231-2

LC 2002-2659

"Written by an international team of more than 350 legal scholars, the more than 400 signed entries cover legal systems of countries from around the world, Australia, and the provinces of Canada; transnational systems (International Court of Justice); general systems (Islamlic law, indigenous, and folk legal systems); and key concepts. Each country profile includes a map with an inset of its location on the globe, general information about the country, its history, diagrams of its court structure, the evolution of its legal framework, its current structure, staffing or how judges are appointed, any specialized judicial bodies (i.e. military court), and the impact that the legal system has had on the country. Articles conclude with references and a bibliography. Academic and public libraries will find this source invaluable for comparative studies in legal and judicial systems."—"The Best of the Best Reference Sources." Am Libr

Includes bibliographical references

Nolo (Firm)

★ **Nolo's** encyclopedia of everyday law; answers to your most frequently asked legal questions. by Shae Irving & Nolo editors. 8th ed.; Nolo 2011 494p pa $34.99   **340**

1. Law -- United States
ISBN 978-1-4133-1321-5 pa; 1-4133-1321-3 pa; 978-1-4133-1347-5 ebook; 1-4133-1347-7 ebook

LC 2010-31328

First published as a replacement of Nolo's everyday law book. Frequently revised

This offers answers to frequently asked legal questions about such topics as credit and debt, workplace rights, wills, divorce, bankruptcy, social security, tenant's rights, child custody and visitation, patents and trademarks, travel, partnerships, healthcare directives and powers of attorney.

Includes bibliographical references

Tamanaha, Brian Z.

Failing law schools; Brian Z. Tamanaha. The University of Chicago Press 2012 xvi, 235 p.p (cloth) $25.00   **340**

1. Debt 2. Law schools 3. Lawyers -- United States 4. American Bar Association 5. Law schools -- United States -- Finance 6. Law -- Study and teaching -- United States
ISBN 0226923614; 0226923622; 9780226923611; 9780226923628

LC 2012006829

In this book, Brian Z. Tamanaha "argues that ABA [American Bar Association] accreditation was established to keep out poor and immigrant students, 'U.S. News' doesn't verify schools' self-reported numbers, most professors have little or no experience practicing law, and schools artificially inflate the employment numbers of their graduates. The result is that too many schools produce impossibly indebted graduates who can't find work and, when they do, make legal services unaffordable." (Library Journal)

Tucker, Virginia

Finding the answers to legal questions; a how-to-do-it manual. [by] Virginia Tucker and Marc Lampson. Neal-Schuman Publishers 2011 274p (How-to-do-it manuals for libraries) pa $75   **340**

1. Law -- Research
ISBN 978-1-55570-718-7

LC 2010-36421

"Comprehensive and easily understood by the non-lawyer, this book would be a useful addition to the reference collections of public libraries." Catholic Library World

Includes bibliographical references

341.23   United Nations

Annan, Kofi A. (Kofi Atta), 1938-

Interventions; a life in war and peace. Kofi Annan with Nader Mousavizadeh. Penguin Press 2012 xiv, 383 p.p $36   **341.23**

1. Diplomats 2. World politics -- 1989- 3. United Nations -- Biography 4. Statesmen -- Ghana -- Biography
ISBN 1594204209; 9781594204203

LC 2012008173

In this memoir, "with the assistance of . . . [Nader] Mousavizadeh . . . , former United Nations Secretary-General [Kofi] Annan discusses the major benchmarks of his life and career. The author, born in 1934, passes briefly over his education and early career at the World Health Organization and U.N., where he worked until his retirement in 2006, and moves rapidly into his main topic: the transformation of U.N. Peacekeeping Operations since the late 1980s and early '90s." (Kirkus Reviews)

Fasulo, Linda M.

★ An **insider's** guide to the UN; [by] Linda Fasulo. 2nd ed; Yale University Press 2009 262p il pa $17   **341.23**

1. United Nations
ISBN 978-0-300-14197-9; 0-300-14197-1

LC 2008-52231

First published 2003

This "guide to the United Nations surveys the world body's programs and activities, and covers key issues including human rights, climate change, counterterrorism, nu-

clear proliferation, peacekeeping, and UN reform. It also offers guidelines for setting up a Model UN." Publisher's note
Includes bibliographical references

Mires, Charlene

Capital of the world; the race to host the United Nations. Charlene Mires. New York University Press 2013 320 p. (hardcover) $29.95   **341.23**
1. United Nations 2. United States -- History 3. United Nations -- Headquarters 4. New York (N.Y.) -- Buildings, structures, etc
ISBN 0814707947; 9780814707944
LC 2012035350

In this book, Pulitzer Prize winner Charlene Mires "investigates a largely unexamined aspect of the birth of the United Nations: the attempt by many U.S. cities during the closing days of World War II to persuade it to base its headquarters in their respective communities. Mires has tracked down . . . archival sources and forgotten newspaper accounts, uncovering a . . . chronicle involving countless American politicians, foreign diplomats, and community promoters who participated." (Library Journal)
Includes bibliographical references and index

Moore, John Allphin

★ **Encyclopedia** of the United Nations; [by] John Allphin Moore, Jr., Jerry Pubantz. 2nd ed.; Facts On File 2008 2v il (Facts on File library of world history) set $125   **341.23**
1. United Nations 2. Reference books 3. International relations -- Encyclopedias
ISBN 978-0-8160-6913-2
LC 2007-29559

First published 2002
This set features entries on "the United Nations's institutions, procedures, policies, specialized agencies, historic personalities, initiatives, and involvement in world affairs. . . . The appendixes contain important UN documents, such as the Charter of the United Nations, the Universal Declaration of Human Rights, the Statute of the International Court of Justice, and the recent Security Council Resolution." Publisher's note
Includes bibliographical references

Osmanczyk, Edmund Jan

Encyclopedia of the United Nations and international agreements; [by] Jan Edmund Osmancyzk; edited and revised by Anthony Mango. 3rd ed; Routledge 2002 4v set $550   **341.23**
1. United Nations 2. Reference books 3. International relations -- Encyclopedias
ISBN 0-415-93920-8
LC 2002-10761

Original Polish edition, 1975; first English language edition 1985
"An alphabetically arranged treasure trove of information on the United Nations, its specialized agencies, and many intergovernmental and non-governmental organizations. This especially valuable resource for smaller collections includes the full or partial texts of some 3,000 international agreements, conventions, and treaties as well as definitions of political, economic, military, geographical, and

diplomatic terms. Analytical and agreements-conventions-treaties indexes." Ref Sources for Small & Medium-sized Libr. 6th edition [entry for 1990 edition]
Includes bibliographical references and index

341.5   Disputes and conflicts between states

Bass, Gary Jonathan, 1969-

★ **Freedom's** battle; the origins of humanitarian intervention. Alfred A. Knopf 2008 509p $35   **341.5**
1. Humanitarian intervention
ISBN 978-0-307-26648-4; 0-307-26648-6
LC 2007-52252

This "history of nineteenth-century campaigns to stop atrocities in Greece, Syria, and Bulgaria is a corrective to the idea that humanitarian interventions are a product of the 'dreamy interlude' between 1989 and 9/11. The compelling narrative, rich with accounts of parliamentary debate and battlefield confrontation, presents a world of familiar political and military concerns, from the pressure of nonstop media coverage to the importance of a clear exit strategy. Bass's thesis that humanitarianism long preceded the crises of Bosnia and Rwanda is persuasive." New Yorker
Includes bibliographical references

341.69   War crimes

Rashke, Richard

★ **Useful** Enemies; John Demanjuk and America's Open-Door Policy for Nazi War Criminals. Delphinium 2013 621 p. $29.95   **341.69**
1. War criminals 2. United States -- Immigration and emigration
ISBN 1883285518; 9781883285517

This book looks at John Demjanjuk, convicted of Nazi war crimes in 2011. Richard Rashke "uses Demjanjuk's story to explore the troubling implications of U.S. immigration patterns after WWII; the author contends that the United States knowingly accepted Nazis while simultaneously denying entry to Holocaust survivors, a trend motivated by a political agenda concerned with monitoring Europe in the postwar period and during the cold war." (Publishers Weekly)

342   Branches of law; laws, regulations, cases; law of specific jurisdictions, areas, socioeconomic regions

Amar, Akhil Reed

★ **America's** constitution; a biography. Random House 2005 657p il $29.95; pa $16.95   **342**
1. Constitutional history -- United States
ISBN 1-400-06262-4; 0-8129-7272-4 pa
LC 2004-61464

"Only rarely do you find a book that embodies scholarship at its most solid and invigorating; this is such a book." Publ Wkly
Includes bibliographical references

The **annotated** U.S. Constitution and Declaration of Independence; edited by Jack N. Rakove. Belknap Press 2009 354p il $24.95 **342**
1. United States -- Constitution 2. Constitutional law -- United States 3. Constitutional history -- United States 4. United States -- Declaration of Independence 5. United States -- Constitution -- 1st-10th amendments
ISBN 0-674-03606-9; 978-0-674-03606-2
LC 2009-22907

This is an explication of the Declaration of Independence, the Bill of Rights, and the Constitution. Bibliography.

The author "presents both the Declaration and the Constitution with carefully laid out annotation that's accessible to general readers as well as high school and college students. His extended introduction provides a readable and instructive analysis of how the writing of the Constitution progressed, especially on matters concerning representation, executive power, and creation of the amendments. His annotations often rely upon contemporary usage and meaning from the time of the Declaration of Independence and Constitution . . . and he compares such usage to other documents of the time." Libr J

Includes bibliographical references

Beeman, Richard
★ **Plain,** honest men; the making of the American Constitution. [by] Richard Beeman. Random House 2009 514p il $30 **342**
1. Constitutional history -- United States 2. United States -- Constitutional Convention (1787)
ISBN 978-1-4000-6570-7; 1-4000-6570-4
LC 2008-28841

"Masterfully told American history for the scholar and general reader alike." Kirkus

Includes bibliographical references

Berkin, Carol
A **brilliant** solution; inventing the American Constitution. Harcourt 2002 310p $26; pa $14 **342**
1. Constitutional history -- United States 2. United States -- Constitutional Convention (1787) 3. United States -- Politics and government -- 1783-1809
ISBN 0-15-100948-1; 0-15-602872-7 pa
LC 2002-5648

This history of the 1787 Constitutional Convention "emphasizes the importance of the delegates' anxieties, showing how they insinuated themselves into some of the compromises, such as the equality of the states in the Senate. Shrewd at integrating biographical detail on the delegates into their debates, Berkin fares well in comparison with previous historians on the topic." Booklist

Bezanson, Randall P.
How free can the press be? University of Illinois Press 2003 258p (History of communication) $34.95 **342**
1. Freedom of speech
ISBN 0-252-02866-X
LC 2003-2148

The author "ponders the contradictions of a free press in this study of nine historical court cases involving free speech. He critically explores the thorny issues surrounding

freedom of the press and the press's use of First Amendment protections. Drawing on selected Supreme Court and lower court cases to illustrate his argument, Bezanson articulates important legal questions pertaining to First Amendment rights." Libr J

Includes bibliographical references

Bray, Ilona M.
★ **U.S.** Immigration Made Easy; Ilona Bray, J.D.; updated by Attorney Richard Link. 18th edition Nolo 2017 688 p. $44.99 **342**
1. Immigration law -- United States 2. United States -- Immigration and emigration
ISBN 1413323677; 9781413323672

First published 1989 by Sheridan Chandler Co. under the authorship of Martha S. Siegel and Laurence A. Canter. Periodically revised

This guide "discusses immigration paperwork, green cards, and other types of temporary visas and when to involve a lawyer." Libr J

"Thoroughly updated and revised, this edition covers the latest changes in immigration law, including expansion of the new 'provisional waiver of unlawful presence' to family members of lawful permanent residents living in the U.S.), the latest average processing times, and much more." (Publisher's note)

Breyer, Stephen G.
Active liberty; interpreting our democratic Constitution. [by] Stephen Breyer. Knopf 2005 161p $21 **342**
1. United States -- Supreme Court 2. Constitutional law -- United States
ISBN 0-307-26313-4
LC 2005-44242

The Supreme Court Justice presents his view on the Constitution of the United States.

"This will be essential reading at a possibly watershed moment for the Supreme Court." Publ Wkly

Includes bibliographical references

★ The **Constitution** of the United States of America; analysis and interpretation : analysis of cases decided by the Supreme Court of the United States to June 28, 2012. prepared by the Congressional Research Service, Library of Congress; Kenneth R. Thomas, editor-in-chief; Larry M. Eig, managing editor; Henry Cohen, George Costello, contributing editors. Centennial edition U.S. Government Printing Office 2013 2789 p. hbk $290 **342**
1. Constitutional law -- United States
ISBN 0160917352; 9780160917356

"Sometimes known by its short title, the Constitution Annotated provides commentary on every article, section, and clause of the basic instrument, as well as the amendments, with citations to selected United States Supreme Court decisions construing these provisions." Introd to U.S. Govt Info Sources. 5th edition

Davis, Thomas J.

Plessy v. Ferguson; Thomas J. Davis. Greenwood 2012 xx, 238 p.p (Landmarks of the American mosaic) (hardcover) $58   **342**

1. Segregation 2. United States -- Race relations -- History 3. Segregation -- Law and legislation -- United States -- History 4. Segregation in transportation -- Law and legislation -- Louisiana -- History

ISBN 0313391874; 9780313391873

              LC 2012011735

This book, by Thomas J. Davis, discusses the U.S. Supreme Court case Plessy v. Ferguson as part of the "Landmarks of the American Mosaic" series. "Contrary to popular misconceptions, Plessy v. Ferguson was not a simple case of black vs. white separation, but rather a challenging and complex protest for U.S. law to fully accept mixed ancestry and multiculturalism." (Publisher's note)

Includes bibliographical references (p. 219-222) and index.

The **Debate** on the Constitution; Federalist and Anti-federalist speeches, articles, and letters during the struggle over ratification. Library of Am. 1993 2v ea $35   **342**

1. Constitutional history -- United States 2. United States -- Politics and government -- 1783-1809

ISBN 0-940450-42-9; 0-940450-64-X

              LC 92-25449

In addition to the documents themselves, these volumes contain "brief biographical notes on the various speakers and writers, a chronology of key events in American independence and the establishment of the new governmental system, notes on contemporary state constitutions, and notes explicating the text of the reprinted documents." Christ Sci Monit

★ **Encyclopedia** of the First Amendment; edited by John R. Vile, David L. Hudson Jr., David Schultz. CQ Press 2009 2v il set $275   **342**

1. Reference books 2. United States -- Constitution -- 1st-10th amendments -- Encyclopedias

ISBN 978-0-87289-311-5; 0-87289-311-1

              LC 2008-36077

This "is an excellent resource for anyone who wants to learn more about broadcast regulation, the establishment of religion clause, students' rights, or a myriad of other topics involving the First Amendment and its political, cultural, and legal significance." Booklist

Includes bibliographical references

★ The **Federalist**; edited, with introduction and notes, by Jacob E. Cooke. Wesleyan Univ. Press 1982 xxx, 672p pa $27.95   **342**

1. United States -- Constitution

ISBN 0-8195-6077-4

              LC 82-2815

A reissue of the 1961 edition

"From 27 Oct. 1787 to 2 April 1788, 77 essays were published in the semi-weekly 'Independent Journal' of New York, entitled 'The Federalist,' and signed first 'A Citizen of New York' then 'Publius.' Eight more were added when they were collected in book form {in 1789}. . . . They were

so acute and massively learned in their exposition of the true intent of the Constitution, that even the courts have accepted them as authoritative comments in doubtful cases; and they are held by all the civilized world as among the noblest storehouses of political philosophy in existence. A classic textbook of political science." Ency Americana

Ford, Richard T.

Rights gone wrong; Richard Thompson Ford. Farrar, Straus and Giroux 2011 272p.   **342**

1. Racism 2. Civil rights 3. Discrimination 4. United States -- Social conditions

ISBN 9780374250355

              LC 2011010705

It was the author's intent to demonstrate "that both the progressive left and the colorblind right are guilty of the same error: defining discrimination too abstractly and condemning it too categorically, with similarly perverse results. According to Ford, the urge to condemn discrimination in all its forms . . . has led people on the left and the right to reject 'reasonable, prudent and innocent distinctions.' It has also led activists, judges and government officials to concentrate on eliminating even trivial forms of discrimination at the expense of more effective means to social justice, like expanding economic opportunities for the poor." (N Y Times)

Includes bibliographical references and index.

Hennessey, Jonathan

The **United** States Constitution; a graphic adaptation. written by Jonathan Hennessey; art by Aaron McConnell. Hill and Wang 2008 149p il $35; pa $16.95   **342**

1. Graphic novels 2. United States -- Constitution -- Graphic novels 3. Constitutional history -- United States -- Graphic novels

ISBN 978-0-8090-9487-5; 0-8090-9487-8; 978-0-8090-9470-7 pa; 0-8090-9470-3 pa

              LC 2008-17927

The author and illustrator go "through the entire U. S. Constitution, article by article, amendment by amendment, explaining their meaning and implications—in comics format. Avoiding the didactic, the book succeeds in being both consistently entertaining and illuminating." Publ Wkly

Includes bibliographical references

Lewis, Loida Nicolas

How to Get a Green Card; Ilona Bray, J.D. & Loida Nicolas Lewis, J.D.; updated by Attorney Kristina Gasson. 12 edition Nolo 2016 402 p. pbk $39.99   **342**

1. Noncitizens -- United States 2. United States -- Immigration and emigration

ISBN 1413322557; 9781413322552

First published 1993. Periodically revised

This guide covers different ways to get a green card, alternatives to a green card, fiancé and fiancée visas, visa lotteries, applying for refugee status and political asylum, and immigration applications.

Maddex, Robert L.

The **U.S.** Constitution A to Z; 2nd ed.; CQ Press 2008 xxix, 736p il map (CQ's American government A to Z series) $85 **342**
1. Reference books 2. Constitutional law -- United States -- Encyclopedias 3. Constitutional history -- United States -- Encyclopedias
ISBN 978-0-87289-764-9

LC 2008-21902

First published 2002

"Maddex offers over 200 articles about issues (abortion, gun control), legal concepts (due process, privacy), landmark cases (Roe v. Wade, Brown v. Board of Education) and people (John Adams, Thurgood Marshall) related to the Constitution. . . . The unique feature of this work is its collection of source materials. . . . It is an excellent, concise reference." Choice [review of 2002 edition]
Includes bibliographical references

Madison, James

★ The **Constitutional** Convention; a narrative history from the notes of James Madison. [edited by] Edward J. Larson and Michael P. Winship. Modern Library 2005 229p pa $13.95 **342**
1. Constitutional history -- United States 2. United States -- Constitutional Convention (1787) 3. United States -- Politics and government -- Sources
ISBN 0-8129-7517-0

LC 2005-41649

"This book tells the convention's turbulent story in Madison's own words, drawn from the notes he took at the scene and giving us a daily blow-by-blow. . . . [The editors] steer readers through the fierce debates with helpful explanations and editorial asides, as well as a cogent epilogue, making this primary source far more than a tidy civics lesson." Publ Wkly
Includes bibliographical references

Maier, Pauline, 1938-2013

Ratification; the people debate the Constitution, 1787-1788. Simon & Schuster 2010 589p il map $30 **342**
1. Constitutional history -- United States
ISBN 978-0-684-86854-7; 0-684-86854-7

LC 2010-27709

In this book on the ratification of the U.S. Constitution, Pauline Maier explores "dynamics within the individual state ratification conventions" with a focus on "how the structure of debate within the individual state conventions affected the final votes in each state. Rather than demonstrate the inevitability of the Constitution's triumph, Maier . . . shows how remarkable the Federalist victory was." (Reviews in American History)

"On Sept. 17, 1787, the convention that had been sitting in Philadelphia for four months to design a new form of government for the United States adjourned, offering its handiwork to the nation. Almost a year later, on Sept. 13, 1788, Congress declared that the Constitution had been duly ratified, and prescribed the rules for the first presidential election the following year. . . . [This] book shows how America got from the first date to the second—and ultimately to to-

day, since we still live with the same document, however modified." N Y Times Book Rev
Includes bibliographical references

Meyerson, Michael

Liberty's blueprint; how Madison and Hamilton wrote the Federalist Papers, defined the constitution, and made democracy safe for the world. [by] Michael I. Myerson. Basic Books 2008 309p $26.95 **342**
1. Constitutional law -- United States 2. Constitutional history -- United States
ISBN 978-0-465-00264-1; 0-465-00264-1

LC 2007-35376

"This fine book is the fullest and most insightful account we have of the collaboration between Alexander Hamilton and James Madison." J Am Hist
Includes bibliographical references

Noonan, John Thomas

Narrowing the nation's power: the Supreme Court sides with the states; {by} John T. Noonan, Jr. University of Calif. Press 2002 203p $34.95; pa $14.95 **342**
1. State governments 2. United States -- Supreme Court
ISBN 0-520-23574-6; 0-520-24068-5 pa

LC 2002-19473

"In this highly recommended work, the author convincingly sounds the alarm." Libr J
Includes bibliographical references

Nussbaum, Martha Craven

Liberty of conscience; in defense of America's tradition of religious equality. [by] Martha Nussbaum. Basic Books 2008 406p $28.95 **342**
1. Freedom of religion
ISBN 978-0-465-05164-9; 0-465-05164-2

LC 2007-38176

This "is a historical and conceptual study of the American tradition of religious freedom." (Publisher's note) Index.

The author "plumbs the historical, political, philosophical, and legal debates surrounding religious freedom." Booklist

The **Oxford** guide to United States Supreme Court decisions; edited by Kermit L. Hall, James W. Ely, Jr. 2nd ed.; Oxford University Press 2009 499p $35 **342**
1. Reference books 2. United States -- Supreme Court 3. Constitutional law -- United States
ISBN 978-0-19-537939-6

LC 2008-23763

First published 1999

The editors "assemble the scholarship of 161 field specialists, who summarize the Supreme Court's 440 most significant cases. Scholar-signed, multiparagraph entries are alphabetized by case name, include argued and decided dates, and detail vote divisions. The book closes with a glossary, an appendix containing the complete Constitution, a chronology of justices since 1789, and a list of presidential appointments. An outstanding single-volume reference." Libr J

Includes bibliographical references

Rabban, David M.

Free speech in its forgotten years. Cambridge Univ. Press 1997 404p il (Cambridge historical studies in American law and society) $60; pa $22   **342**

1. Freedom of speech 2. Constitutional law -- United States

ISBN 0-521-62013-9; 0-521-65537-4 pa

LC 97-15281

The author "focuses on free speech issues between the Civil War and World War I. Through an impressive marshaling of controversies, cases, and litigants, he persuasively argues that libertarian radicalism and the Free Speech League . . . deserve much of the credit for pushing valuable First Amendment issues to the forefront of American social, political, and legal circles. . . . This enlightening work fills a void in First Amendment civil liberties studies." Libr J

Includes bibliographical references

Rehnquist, William H.

All the laws but one; civil liberties in wartime. Knopf 1998 254p il $27.50; pa $14   **342**

1. Civil rights 2. World War, 1914-1918 3. World War, 1939-1945 4. National security -- United States 5. United States -- History -- 1861-1865, Civil War 6. Japanese Americans -- Evacuation and relocation, 1942-1945

ISBN 0-679-44661-3; 0-679-76732-0 pa

LC 98-12641

This is "Supreme Court Chief Justice Rehnquist's narrative of the conflict between civil liberties and military necessity. . . . Fully two-thirds of the book covers Civil War issues. . . . One chapter discusses World War I espionage and draft resistance cases; three, the World War II internment of Japanese Americans and the imposition of martial law in Hawaii. . . . Far from a complete survey of wartime civil liberties—reviewing only cases that reached the Supreme Court before 1950—this is nonetheless both enlightening and entertaining." Booklist

Includes bibliographical references

Schultz, David A.

Encyclopedia of the United States Constitution; [by] David Schultz. Facts On File 2009 2v il (Facts on File library of American history) set $150   **342**

1. Reference books 2. Constitutional law -- United States -- Encyclopedias

ISBN 978-0-8160-6763-3; 0-8160-6763-5

LC 2008-23349

"This reference source can help high-school students, the general public, and other interested parties comprehend the fundamental concepts, evolutionary character, and historic people and events that have shaped the [Constitution.] . . . The alphabetically arranged entries cover terms, events, people, landmark cases, and issues that help explain the Constitution's history. The appendix provides the Declaration of Independence, the Articles of Confederation, the Constitution, and the Bill of Rights as well as 'Other Amendments

to the Constitution,' a 'U.S. Constitution Time Line,' and instructions on locating court cases." Booklist

Includes bibliographical references

Simon, James F.

What kind of nation; Thomas Jefferson, John Marshall, and the epic struggle to create a United States. Simon & Schuster 2002 348p $27.50; pa $14   **342**

1. Architects 2. Presidents 3. Executive power 4. Vice-presidents 5. Essayists 6. Biographers 7. Writers on law 8. Secretaries of state 9. Supreme Court justices 10. United States -- Supreme Court 11. Constitutional history -- United States 12. United States -- Politics and government -- 1783-1809

ISBN 0-684-84870-8; 0-684-84871-6 pa

LC 2001-55027

"Simon's enlivening account proves that writing about constitutional law needn't be the dry preserve of academics." Booklist

Includes bibliographical references

Strebeigh, Fred

Equal; women reshape American law. W.W. Norton 2009 582p $35   **342**

1. Trials 2. Women's rights 3. Women -- Law and legislation

ISBN 978-0-393-06555-8; 0-393-06555-3

LC 2008-44463

"This book generates a genuine appreciation for the legal entrepreneurs who fought long and hard to make possible the careers of many a professional woman." Wilson Quarterly

Includes bibliographical references

Vile, John R.

The **Constitutional** Convention of 1787; a comprehensive encyclopedia of America's founding. ABC-CLIO 2005 2v il set $185   **342**

1. Reference books 2. Constitutional law -- United States -- Encyclopedias 3. Constitutional history -- United States -- Encyclopedias

ISBN 1-85109-669-8

LC 2005-24214

This "resource covers the people, events, committees, ideology, and documents related to the drafting of the Constitution." SLJ

Includes bibliographical references

Encyclopedia of constitutional amendments, proposed amendments, and amending issues, 1789-2010; 3rd ed.; ABC-CLIO 2010 2v set $165   **342**

1. Reference books 2. Constitutional law -- United States -- Encyclopedias 3. Constitutional history -- United States -- Encyclopedias

ISBN 978-1-59884-316-3; 1-59884-316-8; 978-1-59884-317-0 ebook; 1-59884-317-6 ebook

LC 2010-2113

First published 1996, covering 1789-1995

The author "discusses the Constitution, its 27 ratified amendments, and the approximately 11,700 amendments proposed within the titular time frame to present 'a unique window into American history and politics.' The alphabetical format and detailed index make information access a breeze, and the six appendixes provide a reprint of the Constitution along with charts of the number of proposals by decade, key events, and names of individuals submitting the proposals." Libr J

Includes bibliographical references

Waldman, Steven

Founding faith; providence, politics, and the birth of religious freedom in America. Random House 2008 277p $26 **342**

1. Freedom of religion 2. United States -- Religion 3. Freedom of religion -- United States 4. United States -- Religion -- History 5. Founding Fathers of the United States -- Religious life

ISBN 1400064376; 9781400064373

LC 2007-21710

Walman examines the religious attitude of various founding fathers, focusing particularly on Benjamin Franklin, John Adams, George Wshington, Thomas Jefferson, and James Madison. He argues that "our nation's Founders forged a new approach to religious liberty, a revolutionary formula that promoted faith by leaving it alone. . . . [Waldman contends that] neither side in the culture war has accurately depicted the true origins of the First Amendment." (Publisher's note) Index.

This "is an excellent book about an important subject: the inescapable—but manageable—intersection of religious belief and public life. With a grasp of history and an understanding of the exigencies of the moment, Waldman finds a middle ground between those who think of the Founders as apostles in powdered wigs and those who assert, equally inaccurately, that the Founders believed religion had no place in politics." Newsweek

Includes bibliographical references

Weiner, Mark Stuart

Black trials; citizenship from the beginnings of slavery to the end of caste. [by] Mark S. Weiner. Alfred A. Knopf 2004 421p $26.95; pa $16.95 **342**

1. Trials 2. African Americans -- Civil rights

ISBN 0-375-40981-5; 0-375-70884-7 pa

LC 2004-40860

The author "examines how court proceedings involving black people—and whites trying to assist them—have served as windows onto race relations and the power of whites over blacks in the U.S. from its earliest days. . . . This book is the best of its kind—a serious, deeply felt reflection on the weight of history on contemporary affairs." Publ Wkly

Includes bibliographical references

Wexler, Jay

Holy hullabaloos; a road trip to the battlegrounds of the church/state wars. Beacon Press 2009 251p pa $20 **342**

1. Freedom of religion 2. Church and state 3. Religious minorities 4. Church and state -- United States

ISBN 0-8070-0044-2; 978-0-8070-0044-1

LC 2008-47405

"This is a rare treat, a combination of thoughtful analysis and quirky humor that illuminates an issue that rarely elicits

a laugh—and that is central to the American body politic." Publ Wkly

Includes bibliographical references

Wise, Steven M.

Though the heavens may fall; the landmark trial that led to the end of human slavery. Da Capo Press 2005 282p il $25; pa $17.95 **342**

1. Slaves 2. Trials 3. Slavery

ISBN 0-7382-0695-4; 0-306-81450-1 pa

LC 2004-25346

The author "has an eye for evocative detail and an interest in the trappings and procedures of an 18th-century courtroom that do as much to engage the reader as the drama of the trials themselves." N Y Times Book Rev

Includes bibliographical references

342.73 Constitutional law--United States

Carpenter, Dale

Flagrant conduct; the story of Lawrence v. Texas: how a bedroom arrest decriminalized gay Americans. Dale Carpenter. W. W. Norton & Company 2012 xv, 345 p.p **342.73**

1. Gay rights -- United States 2. United States. Supreme Court 3. Right of privacy -- United States 4. Gay men -- Legal status, laws, etc. 5. Homosexuality -- Law and legislation -- Texas 6. Trials (Sodomy) -- Texas 7. Texas -- Trials, litigation, etc. 8. Gays -- Legal status, laws, etc. -- United States 9. Homosexuality -- Law and legislation -- Texas -- Criminal provisions

ISBN 0393062082; 9780393062083

LC 2011047245

"The 2003 landmark Lawrence v. Texas Supreme Court case established the right of homosexuals to engage in private sexual conduct. After setting the sociopolitical and legal scene, [Dale] Carpenter . . . describes the 1998 arrest of John Lawrence and Tyron Garner and the ensuing events as gay rights groups in Houston grasped the potential of the case as a national test. Chapters introduce participants, describe the so-called crime, compare differing accounts of the arrest, follow court events, and explain the stakes. Carpenter . . . discuss[es] legal strategies and Supreme Court arguments, and the elite lawyers and strategists of the defense team . . . in stark contrast to the ill-prepared Harris County district attorney." (Libr J)

Includes bibliographical references and index

Davis, Lennard J.

Enabling acts; the hidden story of how the Americans with Disabilities Act gave the largest US minority its rights. Lennard Davis. Beacon Press 2015 296 p. illustrations (hardback) $26.95 **342.73**

1. Legislation -- United States 2. People with disabilities -- Legal status, laws, etc. 3. United States. Americans with Disabilities Act of 1990 4. People with disabilities -- Services for -- United States 5. People with disabilities -- United States -- Social conditions 6. People with disabilities -- Legal status, laws, etc. -- United States 7. Discrimination against people with

disabilities -- Law and legislation -- United States
ISBN 9780807071564

LC 2014046510

This book on the Americans with Disabilities Act (ADA) by Lennard J. Davis delivers a behind-the-scenes narrative "of how a band of leftist Berkeley hippies managed to make an alliance with upper-crust, conservative Republicans to bring about a truly bipartisan bill. . . . From inside the offices of newly formed disability groups to secret breakfast meetings . . . , here we meet countless unsung characters, including political heavyweights and disability advocates." (Publisher's note)

"A lively and well-researched legal saga suited to general readers interested in current events and disability issues." LJ

Includes bibliographical references and index

Healy, Thomas

The **great** dissent; how Oliver Wendell Holmes changed his mind and changed the history of free speech in America. by Thomas Healy. Henry Holt and Company 2013 336 p. $28   342.73
1. Freedom of speech 2. United States. Constitution. 1st-10th amendments 3. Freedom of speech -- United States 4. Trials (Anarchy) -- New York (State) -- New York -- History -- 20th century
ISBN 0805094563; 9780805094565

LC 2012047539

Author Thomas Healy examines U.S. Supreme Court Justice Oliver Wendell Holmes' "1919 the court opinion that solidified free speech rights in American political doctrine. Holmes' change of heart has long been pondered by legal scholars and historians. Drawing on newly uncovered letters and memos, legal scholar Healy recounts Holmes' long, slow process of advocating for free speech at a time of great national turmoil." (Booklist)

Includes bibliographical references and index

Paulsen, Michael Stokes

The **Constitution**; an introduction. Michael Stokes Paulsen and Luke Paulsen. Basic Books, a member of the Perseus Books Group 2015 368 p. portraits (hardback) $29.99   342.73
1. Constitutional history 2. United States. Constitution 3. Constitutional law -- United States 4. Constitutional history -- United States
ISBN 0465053726; 9780465053711; 9780465053728

LC 2014041943

"Beginning with the Constitution's birth in 1787, [author Michael Stokes] Paulsen and [Luke] Paulsen offer a grand tour of its provisions, principles, and interpretation, introducing readers to the characters and controversies that have shaped the Constitution in the 200-plus years since its creation. Along the way, the authors provide correctives to the shallow myths and partial truths that pervade so much popular treatment of the Constitution." (Publisher's note)

"This is a highly accessible and scholarly but lively look at the nation's guiding document." Booklist

Includes bibliographical references and index

Purdum, Todd S., 1959-

An **idea** whose time has come; two presidents, two parties, and the battle for the Civil Rights Act of 1964. Todd S. Purdum. Henry Holt & Co 2014 416 p. 8 plates; illustrations (hardback) $30   342.73
1. Civil Rights Act of 1964 2. Civil rights -- United States 3. United States -- Politics and government -- 1961-1974 4. United States. Civil Rights Act of 1964 5. United States -- Politics and government -- 1961-1963 6. United States -- Politics and government -- 1963-1969 7. Civil rights -- United States -- History -- 20th century
ISBN 0805096728; 9780805096729

LC 2013038545

In this book, "Todd S. Purdum tells the story of the Civil Rights Act of 1964, recreating the legislative maneuvering and the larger-than-life characters who made its passage possible. . . . Purdum shows how these all-too-human figures managed, in just over a year, to create a bill that prompted the longest filibuster in the history of the U.S. Senate yet was ultimately adopted with overwhelming bipartisan support." (Publisher's note)

"Those battling the neo-Confederates and nullificationists of today will want this book to see how it's done. Readers with an interest in American history and the American promise will find it a must-read as well." Kirkus

Includes bibliographical references and index

Raphael, Ray

Constitutional myths; what we get wrong and how to get it right. by Ray Raphael. The New Press 2013 xiii, 316 p.p (hardcover) $26.95   342.73
1. United States. Constitution 2. Founding Fathers of the United States 3. Constitutional history -- United States 4. United States -- History -- 1783-1815 5. Constitutional history -- United States -- 18th century
ISBN 1595588329; 9781595588326

LC 2012041849

This book on the U.S. Constitution is "more concerned with contextualizing the Founder Fathers than in interpreting them. One by one, [Ray] Raphael . . . addresses some of the more pervasive interpretations of the Constitution and the men who crafted it. . . .Through careful analysis of the 1787 Constitutional Convention, Raphael demonstrates that nothing about the Constitution is as simple as contemporary discourse makes it seem." (Publishers Weekly)

Includes bibliographical references and index.

Richards, Leonard L.

Who freed the slaves? the fight over the Thirteenth Amendment. Leonard L. Richards. University of Chicago Press 2015 320 p. illustrations, portraits (cloth : alk. paper) $30   342.73
1. Slavery -- United States 2. Slaves -- Emancipation -- United States 3. United States. Constitution. 13th Amendment -- History 4. Slaves -- Emancipation -- United States -- History -- 19th century 5. United States. President (1861-1865 : Lincoln). Emancipation Proclamation 6. Slavery -- Law and legislation -- United States -- History -- 19th century
ISBN 022617820X; 9780226178202

LC 2014023200

In this book, historian Leonard L. Richards "tells the little-known story of the battle over the Thirteenth Amendment, and of James Ashley, the unsung Ohio congressman who proposed the amendment and steered it to passage. Taking readers to the floor of Congress and the back rooms where deals were made, Richards brings to life the messy process of legislation—a process made all the more complicated by the bloody war and the deep-rooted fear of black emancipation." (Publisher's note)

"It... provides a perceptive explanation as to how and why the promise of the 13th Amendment as an instrument for civil rights never came to fruition. In doing so, it reminds us that freedom is not a given; principled, pragmatic, and persistent advocates must work to realize and secure it." LJ

Includes bibliographical references and index

Risen, Clay

The **bill** of the century; the epic battle for the Civil Rights Act. Clay Risen. Bloomsbury Press 2014 320 p. illustrations (hardback) $28   **342.73**
    1. United States. Civil Rights Act of 1964 2. Civil rights -- United States -- History
    ISBN 1608198243; 9781608198245

LC 2014004662

"Clay Risen shows [that] the battle for the Civil Rights Act was a . . . broad, epic struggle, a sweeping tale of unceasing grassroots activism, ringing speeches, backroom deal-making and finally, hand-to-hand legislative combat. The larger-than-life cast of characters ranges from Senate lions like Mike Mansfield and Strom Thurmond to NAACP lobbyist Charles Mitchell, called 'the 101st senator' for his Capitol Hill clout, and industrialist J. Irwin Miller, who helped mobilize a powerful religious coalition for the bill." (Publisher's note)

"A work of high academic quality written with a journalist's flair for telling a tale." Choice

Includes bibliographical references and index

Tribe, Laurence H., 1941-

Uncertain justice; the Roberts court and the constitution. Laurence Tribe, Joshua Matz. Henry Holt & Co. 2014 416 p. (hardback) $32   **342.73**
    1. Roberts, John G., 1955- 2. United States. Supreme Court 3. Constitutional law -- United States 4. Constitutional law -- Social aspects -- United States
    ISBN 0805099093; 9780805099096

LC 2014002845

This book, by Laurence Tribe and Joshua Matz, argues that "the Roberts Court is shaking the foundation of our nation's laws. . . . Tribe . . . and Matz dig deeply into the court's recent rulings, stepping beyond tired debates over judicial 'activism' to draw out hidden meanings and silent battles. The undercurrents they reveal suggest a strikingly different vision for the future of our country, one that is sure to be hotly debated." (Publisher's note)

"A well-researched, unsettling investigation of recent trends in the nation's highest court." Kirkus

Includes bibliographical references and index

Urofsky, Melvin I.

Dissent and the Supreme Court; Its Role in the Court's History and the Nation's Constitutional Dialogue. Melvin I. Urofsky. Pantheon Books 2015 544 p. illustrations (hard cover : alk. paper) $35 **342.73**
    1. United States. Constitution 2. United States.

Supreme Court 3. Judicial opinion -- United States 4. Constitutional law -- United States 5. Dissenting opinions -- United States 6. Government, Resistance to -- United States 7. Dissenters -- Legal status, laws, etc. -- United States
    ISBN 9780307379405; 9781101870631

LC 2014048245

This book, by Melvin I. Urofsky, "looks at the role of dissent in the Supreme Court and the meaning of the Constitution through the greatest and longest lasting public-policy debate in the country's history, among members of the Supreme Court, between the Court and the other branches of government, and between the Court and the people of the United States." (Publisher's note)

"This is an insightful look at dissents as dialogues between the justices that reflect broader dialogues among citizens on the controversial issues of our time." Kirkus

Includes bibliographical references (pages 429-488) and index.

343   Military, defense, public property, public finance, tax, commerce (trade), industrial law

Benedict, Jeff

Little pink house; a true story of defiance and courage. Grand Central Publishing 2009 397p il $26.99   **343**
    1. Nurses 2. Eminent domain
    ISBN 978-0-446-50862-9; 0-446-50862-4

LC 2008-17650

"Benedict has pieced together a fascinating narrative, using e-mail messages, planning documents, interviews and personal diaries to produce a sordid account of ruthless local politicians working hand-in-medical-glove with big business to drive hardworking Americans from their homes." N Y Times Book Rev

Fishman, Stephen

Working for yourself; law & taxes for independent contractors, freelancers & consultants. 8th ed.; Nolo 2011 360p pa $39.99   **343**
    1. Self-employed
    ISBN 978-1-4133-1331-4 pa; 978-1-4133-1357-4 ebook

LC 2010-38423

First published 1997 with title: Wage slave no more. Frequently revised

"There's a good chance having a side business will mean being an independent contractor, a freelancer, or a consultant. This thorough and well-organized volume will guide individuals through the legal and tax issues that come with the territory. From deciding on legal structures to drafting contracts to collecting payment from deadbeat clients, this is excellent information." Libr J

Includes bibliographical references

Witt, John Fabian

Lincoln's code; the laws of war in American history. John Fabian Witt. Free Press 2012 viii, 498 p., [16] p.p ill. (hbk.) $32   **343**
    1. Law 2. War 3. United States -- History -- 1861-

1865, Civil War 4. War -- United States -- History 5. War (International law) -- History 6. Military law -- United States -- History 7. United States -- History -- Civil War, 1861-1865 8. War and emergency legislation -- United States -- History

ISBN 1416569839; 9781416569831

LC 2012006187

This book by author John Fabian Witt "reviews the background of U.S. laws of war. Witt . . . examines the laws of war in the 18th and 19th centuries from the French and Indian Wars to the Spanish American War. The focus is on the Civil War, where an entirely new rulebook on the laws of war was drafted by Franz Lieber and approved by President Lincoln." (Library Journal)

Includes bibliographical references (p. 401-470) and index

344   Labor, social service, education, cultural law

Ball, Howard, 1937-

At liberty to die; the battle for death with dignity in America. Howard Ball. New York University Press 2012 ix, 229 p.p (alk. paper) $30.00   **344**
1. Euthanasia 2. Brain death 3. Right to die -- Law and legislation 4. Euthanasia -- Law and legislation -- United States 5. Right to die -- Law and legislation -- United States 6. Assisted suicide -- Law and legislation -- United States

ISBN 081474527X; 0814769756; 0814791042; 9780814745274; 9780814769751; 9780814791042

LC 2011052258

In this book, political scientist Howard Ball offers a "legal history of the right to die in America. He starts with the case of Nancy Cruzan, who was left in a persistent vegetative state after a car accident, and the Supreme Court's ruling that the state had the right to require 'clear and convincing evidence' of Cruzan's intentions before removing her from life support. He then traces battles to legalize physician-assisted death (PAD) in Oregon, Washington State, Montana, Vermont, and Hawaii." (Library Journal)

Includes bibliographical references and index.

Barrett, Paul M.

Law of the jungle; the $19 billion brawl over oil, indians, and the fate of the rainforest. by Paul M. Barrett. Crown Publishers 2014 viii, 290 p.p map (hbk.) $26   **344**
1. Trials 2. Petroleum industry 3. Chevron Corporation -- Trials, litigation, etc 4. Liability for oil pollution damages -- Ecuador 5. Environmental lawyers -- United States -- Biography

ISBN 9780770436360; 0770436366; 9780770436346; 077043634X

LC 2013038226

This book by Paul M. Barrett describes how "Steven Donziger, a self-styled social activist and Harvard educated lawyer, signed on to a budding class action lawsuit against multinational Texaco (which later merged with Chevron to become the third-largest corporation in America). The suit sought reparations for the Ecuadorian peasants and tribes

people whose lives were affected by decades of oil production near their villages and fields." (Publisher's note)

"Although legal jargon appears often here, Barrett's prose is far from tedious in telling a story that is almost Shakespearean in scope, featuring a flawed protagonist with good intentions but tragically overreaching ambitions." Booklist

Includes bibliographical references (pages 277-280) and index.

Cohen, Adam

Imbeciles; The Supreme Court, American Eugenics, and the Sterilization of Carrie Buck. Adam Cohen. Penguin Group USA 2016 416 p. $28   **344**
1. United States. Supreme Court 2. Sterilization (Birth control)

ISBN 1594204187; 9781594204180

LC 2015044207

This book by Adam Cohen tells of "one of the darkest moments in the American legal tradition: the Supreme Court's decision to champion eugenic sterilization for the greater good of the country. In 1927, when the nation was caught up in eugenic fervor, the justices allowed Virginia to sterilize Carrie Buck, a perfectly normal young woman, for being an 'imbecile.'" (Publisher's note)

"A shocking tale about science and law gone horribly wrong, an almost forgotten case that deserves to be ranked with Dred Scott, Plessy, and Korematsu as among the Supreme Court's worst decisions." Kirkus

Green, Lisa

On Your Case; A Comprehensive, Compassionate (And Only Slightly Bossy) Legal Guide for Every Stage of a Woman's Life. Lisa Green. HarperCollins 2015 320 p. $26.99   **344**
1. Law 2. Women -- Law and legislation

ISBN 0062307991; 9780062307996

LC 2015372846

This book, by Lisa Green, "offers . . . a witty, direct and empowering legal guide for women, filled with accessible information they can employ to understand and respond to common legal issues throughout their lives, from dating, marriage, and kids to jobs, retirement, aging parents, and wills." (Publisher's note)

"Green's confident voice resonates like a smart, funny girlfriend giving solid counsel over a glass of wine. It's personal, practical, and backed up with plenty of legal reality. This book will appeal to women with legal troubles and to those hoping to avoid them." LJ

Hull, N. E. H.

★ Roe v. Wade; the abortion rights controversy in American history. [by] N.E.H. Hull and Peter Charles Hoffer. 2nd ed., rev. & expanded.; University Press of Kansas 2010 370p (Landmark law cases & American society) $39.95; pa $19.95   **344**
1. Roe v. Wade 2. District attorneys 3. Pro-choice activists 4. Abortion -- Law and legislation

ISBN 978-0-7006-1753-1; 0-7006-1753-1; 978-0-7006-1754-8 pa; 0-7006-1754-X pa

LC 2010-21294

First published 2001

Thsi book "highlights the abortion issue's historical background; highlights Roe v. Wade's core issues, essential personalities, and key precedents; tracks the case's path through the courts; clarifies the jurisprudence behind the court's ruling in Roe; and gauges its impact on American society and subsequent challenges to it in Webster v. Reproductive Services (1989) and Casey v. Planned Parenthood (1992). . . . [It includes] chapters covering abortion politics and legal battles in the post-9/11 era." Publisher's note

Includes bibliographical references

James, Vaughn E.

The **Alzheimer's** advisor; a caregiver's guide to dealing with the tough legal and practical issues. AMACOM - American Management Association 2009 300p pa $19.95   **344**
1. Caregivers 2. Alzheimer's disease 3. Medicine -- Law and legislation
ISBN 978-0-8144-0924-4; 0-8144-0924-5

LC 2008-20258

The author "deals with the often overlooked but difficult legal and financial responsibilities associated with caring for elders with memory loss and/or dementia." Libr J

Includes bibliographical references

Lombardo, Paul A.

Three generations, no imbeciles; eugenics, the Supreme Court, and Buck v. Bell. Johns Hopkins University Press 2008 365p il   **344**
1. Eugenics 2. Sterilization (Birth control) 3. People with mental disabilities 4. Buck v. Bell 5. Forced sterilization 6. Constitutional history 7. Sterilization, Eugenic 8. Constitutional law -- United States 9. United States -- Supreme Court -- History 10. Insanity -- Jurisprudence -- United States 11. Eugenics -- United States -- History -- 20th century
ISBN 0-8018-9010-1; 978-0-8018-9010-9

LC 2008-6546

This book examines the case of Buck v. Bell, covering the events of the trial and the 1927 Supreme Court decision that upheld Virginia's 1924 Eugenical Sterilization Act, which called for compulsory sterilization of the "feebleminded". Index.

The author "traces a seminal 1927 Supreme Court case arising from the attempt by authorities in Virginia to force the sterilization of a woman believed to be mentally and socially 'insufficient.'" Libr J

Includes bibliographical references

Matthews, Joseph L.

★ **Social** security, Medicare & government pensions; get the most out of your retirement & medical benefits. with Dorothy Matthews Berman. 16th ed.; Nolo 2011 482p pa $29.99   **344**
1. Medicare 2. Pensions 3. Social security
ISBN 978-1-4133-1327-7 pa; 1-4133-1327-2 pa; 978-1-4133-1353-6 ebook; 1-4133-1353-1 ebook

LC 2010-38404

First published 1983 with title: Sourcebook for older Americans. Frequently revised

This guide discusses such topics as how to claim social security benefits, social security disability, civil service and veterans benefits, and Medicare procedures.

Nather, David

★ The **new** health care system; everything you need to know. Thomas Dunne Books 2010 230p pa $12.99   **344**
1. Medicaid 2. Medicare 3. Health insurance 4. Medical care -- Government policy
ISBN 978-0-312-64934-0

In this "primer on health-care reform, . . . Nather explains how insurance works, what the big changes are, and when everything will happen. It's a conversational guide that tells readers how to sign up for Medicare, and what to do if they're uninsured, or if they work for a small business versus a large company. . . . Nather's book, which includes a useful glossary, provides an excellent snapshot of how the post-reform health-care system should work as it stands now." Booklist

Nourse, Victoria F.

In reckless hands; Skinner v. Oklahoma and the near-triumph of American eugenics. W.W. Norton & Company 2008 240p il map $24.95   **344**
1. Thieves 2. Eugenics 3. Prisoners 4. Sterilization (Birth control) 5. Sterilization, Eugenic 6. Constitutional law -- United States 7. Eugenics -- United States -- History -- 20th century
ISBN 978-0-393-06529-9; 0-393-06529-4

LC 2008-13140

The author "provides a legal history of the Supreme Court case that served to increase the recognition of individual rights, although it fell short of ending the practice and debate of eugenics in the US. . . . This book deserves attention from those interested in the history and politics of the legal system." Choice

Includes bibliographical references

Sack, Steven Mitchell

The **employee** rights handbook; effective legal strategies to protect your job from interview to pink slip. 3rd ed., rev. & enlarged ed.; Legal Strategies Publications 2010 620p $39.95   **344**
1. Employee rights 2. Labor -- Law and legislation
ISBN 978-0-9636306-7-4

LC 2010-926886

First published 1990 by Facts on File

The author "advises readers on topics from avoiding prehiring abuses and protecting on-the-job rights through postemployment litigation and finding and hiring a lawyer. . . . Readers looking for an all-in-one employee legal primer or layperson's quick reference should find this a useful tool." Libr J

Steingold, Fred S.

The **employer's** legal handbook; manage your employees & workplace effectively. Fred S. Steingold. 13th edition Nolo 2017 496 p. pbk $49.99 **344**
1. Labor -- Law and legislation
ISBN 9781413323993; 1413323995

"This guide for employers discusses "how to comply with the most recent workplace laws and regulations, run a safe and fair workplace and avoid lawsuits." Publisher's note

345 Criminal law

Bogira, Steve

Courtroom 302; a year behind the scenes in an American criminal courthouse. Knopf 2005 404p hardcover o.p. pa $16 **345**

1. Courts 2. Administration of criminal justice
ISBN 0-679-43252-3; 0-679-75206-4 pa

LC 2004-57636

Bogira provides "a balanced view of the realities of the day-to-day, assembly-line grind that marks so much of the process from arrest to final disposition. . . . The brilliance of Bogira's insights will lead many to hope that he will follow this debut with proposals to cure the many ills he has diagnosed." Publ Wkly

Includes bibliographical references

Boyle, Kevin

Arc of justice; a saga of race, rights, and murder in the Jazz Age. Holt & Co. 2004 415p il $26; pa $15 **345**

1. Physicians 2. Trials (Homicide) 3. Lawyers 4. Memoirists 5. Writers on law 6. Trials (Murder) 7. State legislators 8. African Americans -- Civil rights 9. Detroit (Mich.) -- Race relations 10. African Americans -- Michigan -- Detroit 11. African Americans -- Civil rights -- History -- 20th century
ISBN 0-8050-7145-8; 0-8050-7933-5 pa

LC 2004-47352

In 1925, Dr. Ossian Sweet, an African American, moved into an all-white neighborhood in Detroit with his wife, Gladys. Mobs attacked his home. He and his friends fired on the attackers in self-defense and a white man was killed. "The Sweets and the nine other men there that night were charged with first-degree murder. The case was a significant moment in the early civil rights movement. . . . {This is an} account of the incident and trial. . . . {Clarence Darrow} joined the defense team three months after the end of the Scopes trial." (N Y Times (Late N Y Ed)) Bibliography. Index.

Boyle "has brilliantly rescued from obscurity a fascinating chapter in American history that had profound implications for the rise of the Civil Rights movement." Publ Wkly

Includes bibliographical references

Colmez, Coralie

Math on trial; how numbers get used and abused in the courtroom. Leila Schneps and Coralie Colmez. Basic Books 2013 xi, 256 p.p ill., ports. (hardcover) $26.99 **345**

1. Mathematics 2. Judicial error 3. Forensic sciences 4. Forensic statistics
ISBN 0465032923; 9780465032921

LC 2012040624

In this book, "Leila Schneps and Coralie Colmez describe ten trials spanning from the nineteenth century to today, in which mathematical arguments were used--and disastrously misused--as evidence. . . . Offering a fresh angle

on cases from the nineteenth-century Dreyfus affair to the murder trial of Dutch nurse Lucia de Berk, Schneps and Colmez show how the improper application of mathematical concepts can mean the difference between walking free and life in prison." (Publisher's note)

Includes bibliographical references and index.

Feige, David

Indefensible; one lawyer's journey into the inferno of American justice. Little, Brown and Co. 2006 276p $24.95 **345**

1. Lawyers 2. Administration of criminal justice 3. Writers on law
ISBN 978-0-316-15623-3; 0-316-15623-X

LC 2006-1283

The author "takes us through a typically harrowing day as a public defender, dealing with arbitrary judges and clients who are often victims of the judicial system. . . . Feige skillfully shares his wisdom and his humanity and sheds light on a justice system that too often works irrationally." Publ Wkly

Hoffer, Peter Charles

The Salem witchcraft trials; a legal history. University Press of Kan. 1997 165p (Landmark law cases & American society) hardcover o.p. pa $12.95 **345**

1. Trials 2. Salem (Mass.) -- History
ISBN 0-7006-0858-3; 0-7006-0859-1 pa

LC 97-19986

"Hoffer discusses the legal nature of the charges of witchcraft, the evidential and procedural characteristics of the trials of the accused, and the roles and attitudes of the ministers and magistrates who controlled the proceedings. . . . Hoffer offers little that is new in terms of interpretation, but he presents it well and in a manner easily grasped by the general reader." Choice

Includes bibliographical references

Kadri, Sadakat

The trial; a history, from Socrates to O. J. Simpson. Random House 2005 459p il $29.95 **345**

1. Trials
ISBN 0-375-50550-4

LC 2005-42925

This "history of the trial from ancient times to the present provides . . . [a] history of the various forms and purposes of trials throughout Western civilization. . . . The result is a magnificent book suitable for all sorts of people, from inquisitive high school students to blue-chip lawyers." Choice

Includes bibliographical references

Lewis, Anthony

Gideon's trumpet. Random House 1964 262p hardcover o.p. pa $12.95 **345**

1. Law -- United States 2. United States -- Supreme Court
ISBN 0-679-72312-9 pa

An account of the case of a Florida man convicted of burglary which brought about a historic decision of the Supreme Court decreeing that in all states a defendant is entitled to counsel.

Includes bibliographical references

Lipstadt, Deborah E.

The **Eichmann** trial. Nextbook/Schocken 2011 237p (Jewish encounters) $24.95 **345**
1. War criminals 2. War crime trials 3. Nazi leaders 4. Holocaust, 1933-1945 5. Holocaust, Jewish (1939-1945)

ISBN 978-0-8052-4260-7; 0-8052-4260-0

LC 2010-28620

"Lipstadt has done a great service by untethering the trial from [Hannah] Arendt's polarizing presence, recovering the event as a gripping legal drama, as well as a hinge moment in Israel's history and in the world's delayed awakening to the magnitude of the Holocaust." N Y Times Book Rev

Includes bibliographical references

Malcolm, Janet

Iphigenia in Forest Hills; anatomy of a murder trial. Yale University Press 2011 155p $25 **345**
1. Dentists 2. Trials (Homicide) 3. Murderers 4. Internists 5. Murder victims 6. Trials (Murder) -- Queens (New York, N.Y.)

ISBN 978-0-300-16746-7; 0-300-16746-6

LC 2010-35851

"Malcolm's book chronicles the fate of Mazoltuv Borukhova, a 35-year-old doctor and a member of the Bukharan Jewish sect who stands accused of hiring an assassin to kill her ex-husband, Daniel Malakov. On the morning of Oct. 28, 2007, Malakov was shot to death in a park in Queens, N.Y., in front of his and Borukhova's 4-year-old daughter. . . Malcolm shows us what happens when the abstract ideals of the law are applied, as they always are, by human beings. We meet one judge who, acting out of incompetence or malice, makes an inexplicable and terrible child-custody decision. Another proves less interested in serving justice than in wrapping up proceedings in time for his Caribbean vacation. A lawyer who, on the stand, appears to be 'intelligent and well-spoken' turns out to be both negligent and delusional. . . . All told, it's such a damning portrait of American jurisprudence that Malcolm scarcely need editorialize. As lawyers would say, res ipsa loquitur: the thing speaks for itself." Boston Globe

Newton, Michael A.

Enemy of the state; the trial and execution of Saddam Hussein. [by] Michael A. Newton & Michael P. Scharf. St. Martin's Press 2008 305p il $26.95 **345**
1. Trials 2. Presidents

ISBN 978-0-312-38556-9; 0-312-38556-0

LC 2008-21087

The authors "provided judicial assistance to the trial of Saddam Hussein and other Ba'athists, including training of judicial personnel, writing rules for the Iraqi Tribunal, and observing the nine-month trial proceedings. Here, they write of their experiences and provide perspective on the trial, which began in October 2005, including gavel-to-gavel coverage of the proceedings. . . . Their insiders' account is directed toward general adult audiences and will effectively

aid them in understanding this crucial phase as Iraq struggles toward its future." Libr J

Includes bibliographical references

Rabinowitz, Dorothy

★ **No** crueler tyrannies; accusation, false witness, and other terrors of our times. Simon & Schuster 2003 239p (A Wall Street Journal book) $25; pa $13 **345**
1. Trials 2. Child sexual abuse

ISBN 0-7432-2834-0; 0-7432-2840-5 pa

LC 2002-44670

This book "reexamines high-profile cases of the 1980s and 1990s involving mass sexual abuse. Demonstrating that overzealous prosecutors and indifferent courts led to the prosecution of many innocents, Rabinowitz provides . . . analyses of the major cases, especially those that involved child-care workers. . . . This gripping, well-written book about social injustice and public hysteria is recommended for social science and law collections." Libr J

Sands, Philippe

East West Street; on the origins of genocide and crimes against humanity. Philippe Sands. Alfred A. Knopf 2016 448 p. illustrations, maps (hardcover) $32.50 **345**
1. Lawyers 2. Genocide 3. War crimes

ISBN 9780385350716; 9780385350723; 0385350716

LC 2016933268

This book, by Philippe Sands, "looks at the personal and intellectual evolution of [Rafael Lemkin and Hersch Lauterpacht,] the two men who simultaneously originated the ideas of 'genocide' and 'crimes against humanity.' And the author writes of a third man, Hans Frank, Hitler's personal lawyer. Sands . . . writes of how all three men came together, in October 1945 in Nuremberg." (Publisher's note)

"Readers interested in history, political science, and/or religion shouldn't miss this compelling work with unforgettable characters." LJ

Includes bibliographical references (pages 381-409) and index.

Schiff, Stacy, 1961-

★ The **Witches**; Salem, 1692. Stacy Schiff. Little, Brown & Co. 2015 512 p. 16 plates; color illustrations (hardcover) $32 **345**
1. Salem witch trials 2. Salem (Mass.) -- History

ISBN 9780316200608; 0316200603

LC 2015939026

This book, by Stacy Schiff, "unpacks the mystery of the Salem Witch Trials. It began in 1692, over an exceptionally raw Massachusetts winter, when a minister's daughter began to scream and convulse. It ended less than a year later, but not before 19 men and women had been hanged and an elderly man crushed to death. . . . In curious ways, the trials would shape the future republic." (Publisher's note)

"This fully documented narrative, if a bit exhausting and disorganized, will find a welcome audience among readers of witchcraft or colonial histories as well as Schiff's legion of fans." LJ

Spence, Gerry

The **smoking** gun; day by day through a shocking murder trial with Gerry Spence: a true story. Scribner 2003 435p hardcover o.p. pa $7.99   **345**
1. Trials (Homicide)
ISBN 0-7432-4696-9; 978-0-7434-7052-0; 0-7434-7052-4

LC 2003-42722

"This disquieting book shows that the facts don't speak for themselves, innocence is rarely presumed and justice is far from a first priority in America's courtrooms. Spence is a gifted storyteller and his rhetorical skills are mesmerizing. The blizzards of argument and counterargument that would be tedious reading in less talented hands are neatly incorporated into this thrilling account of injustice barely averted." Publ Wkly

Strang, Dean A.

Worse than the devil; anarchists, Clarence Darrow, and justice in a time of terror. Dean A. Strang. The University of Wisconsin Press 2013 xviii, 268 p.p ill., map (paperback) $26.95   **345**
1. Trials 2. Judicial error 3. Anarchism and anarchists 4. Milwaukee (Wis.) -- History -- 20th century 5. Bay View (Milwaukee, Wis.) -- History -- 20th century 6. Anarchists -- Wisconsin -- Milwaukee -- History -- 20th century 7. Trials (Riots) -- Wisconsin -- Milwaukee -- History -- 20th century 8. Italian Americans -- Wisconsin -- Milwaukee -- History -- 20th century 9. Judicial corruption -- Wisconsin -- Milwaukee -- History -- 20th century
ISBN 0299293947; 9780299293932; 9780299293949

LC 2012032689

This book, by Dean A. Strang, profiles how "in 1917 a bomb exploded in . . . Milwaukee. . . . Those responsible never were apprehended, but . . . all assumed that the perpetrators were Italian. Days later, eleven alleged Italian anarchists went to trial on unrelated charges involving a fracas that had occurred two months before. Against the backdrop of World War I . . . and . . . a prevailing hatred and fear of radical immigrants, the Italians had an unfair trial." (Publisher's note)

Includes bibliographical references and index

Temkin, Moshik, 1971-

The **Sacco-**Vanzetti Affair; America on trial. Yale University Press 2009 316p il $35   **345**
1. Trials (Homicide) 2. Sacco-Vanzetti case 3. Sacco-Vanzetti Trial, Dedham, Mass., 1921 4. Sacco-Vanzetti trial, Dedham (Mass.), 1921 5. Trials (Murder) -- Massachusetts -- Dedham 6. United States -- Foreign public opinion, European -- History
ISBN 978-0-300-12484-2; 0-300-12484-8

LC 2008-45606

This "study of the trial and appeals of these two condemned murderers and of the life and times of the country, which feared foreign contamination, surpasses all prior analyses of this subject in terms of scope, erudition, and objectivity. . . . This book discusses many fascinating elements of controversy, not least the long-term views held by Sacco and Vanzetti's defenders and accusers and how their participation in the search for justice was perceived by their peers." Libr J

Includes bibliographical references

Turow, Scott

★ **Ultimate** punishment; a lawyer's reflections on dealing with the death penalty. Farrar, Straus and Giroux 2003 164p $18   **345**
1. Capital punishment
ISBN 0-374-12873-1

LC 2003-7873

"In 2000 Governor George Ryan of Illinois declared a moratorium on executions. . . . Ryan established a commission to study the state's capital punishment system and propose reforms. In 2002 the commission issued its report. . . . Among the people Ryan appointed to the commission was Scott Turow, a . . . novelist and practicing attorney, with experience in death penalty cases. He was, at the time of his appointment, a self-described 'agnostic' on capital punishment. Ultimate Punishment is Turow's account of his struggle to resolve for himself the question, Should we retain the death penalty?" Christ Century

Includes bibliographical references

Walsh, John Evangelist

Moonlight; Abraham Lincoln and the Almanac trial. St. Martin's Press 2000 166p il $22.95   **345**
1. Trials 2. Lawyers 3. Presidents 4. State legislators 5. Members of Congress
ISBN 0-312-22922-4

LC 99-59606

This is "the story of how Abraham Lincoln secured the acquittal of murder suspect William 'Duff' Armstrong, the son of an old New Salem friend, by making use of an almanac to discredit a witness's description of the position of the moon on the night in question." Libr J

Includes bibliographical references

Watson, Bruce

★ **Sacco** and Vanzetti; the men, the murders and the judgment of mankind. Viking 2007 433p il $25.95; pa $16   **345**
1. Trials (Homicide) 2. Sacco-Vanzetti case 3. Anarchists
ISBN 978-0-670-06353-6; 0-670-06353-3; 978-0-14-3114284 pa; 0-14-311428-X pa

LC 2006-103092

The author "has written a well-researched page-turner. Highly recommended." Libr J

Includes bibliographical references

345.73   Criminal justice--United States

Beloof, Douglas E.

Victims' rights; a documentary and reference guide. Douglas E. Beloof. Greenwood 2012 xi, 313 p.p (hbk. : alk. paper) $100.00   **345.73**
1. Victims of crimes 2. Victims of crimes -- Legal status, laws, etc. 3. Victims of crimes -- Legal status,

laws, etc. -- United States
ISBN 0313393451; 9780313393457; 9780313393464
LC 2011043292

This book by Douglas E. Beloof "traces the origins, evolution, and results of the victims' rights movement. It puts victims' rights in a legal, historical, and contemporary context, and . . . collects important victims' rights documents in a single volume." It "bring[s] together dozens of varied documents such as presidential task force reports and recommendations, Supreme Court cases, state constitutions, human rights reports, critical articles, and political documents." (Publisher's note)

Includes bibliographical references and index.

Garrett, Brandon L.

Too big to jail; how prosecutors compromise with corporations. Brandon L. Garrett. Belknap Press 2014 384 p. illustrations (hardcover : alk. paper) $29.95 **345.73**
1. Corporation law 2. Administration of criminal justice -- United States 3. Prosecution -- United States 4. Tort liability of corporations -- United States 5. Corporations -- Corrupt practices -- United States 6. Corporation law -- United States -- Criminal provisions 7. Criminal liability of juristic persons -- United States 8. Corporate governance -- Law and legislation -- United States
ISBN 0674368312; 9780674368316
LC 2014013351

Author Brandon L. Garrett "takes readers into a complex, compromised world of backroom deals, for an unprecedented look at what happens when criminal charges are brought against a major company in the United States. Presenting detailed data from more than a decade of federal cases, . . . Garrett reveals a pattern of negotiation and settlement in which prosecutors demand admissions of wrongdoing, impose penalties, and require structural reforms." (Publisher's note)

"A well-written, detailed exposé for all audiences." LJ
Includes bibliographical references and index

Houppert, Karen

Chasing Gideon; the elusive quest for poor people's justice. Karen Houppert. The New Press 2013 288 p. (hardcover) $26.95 **345.73**
1. Legal aid 2. Right to counsel 3. Right to counsel -- United States
ISBN 1595588698; 9781595588692
LC 2012047464

This book, by Karen Houppert, profiles public defense in U.S. law. "On March 18, 1963, . . . the U.S. Supreme Court unanimously ruled in Gideon v. Wainright that all defendants facing significant jail time have the constitutional right to a free attorney if they cannot afford their own. . . . [The] book . . . chronicles the stories of people in all parts of the country who have relied on Gideon's promise." (Publisher's note)

Includes bibliographical references.

Mandery, Evan J.

A wild justice; the death and resurrection of capital punishment in America. Evan J. Mandery.

W W Norton & Co Inc 2013 496 p. (hardcover) $29.95 **345.73**
1. Capital punishment -- United States 2. Constitutional law -- United States 3. Capital punishment -- United States. -- History -- 20th century
ISBN 0393239586; 9780393239584
LC 2013010126

In this book, Evan J. Mandery "traces the building momentum within the country and the court to question the legality of a punishment the Founding Fathers took for granted", the death penalty. He starts with "when the Supreme Court declined to accept the appeal of a 1963 rape case, [and] Justice Arthur Goldberg published an unusual dissent questioning the constitutionality of the death penalty." (Kirkus Reviews)

Includes bibliographical references and index

Smith, Clive Stafford

The **injustice** system; a murder in Miami and a trial gone wrong. Clive Stafford Smith. Viking 2012 xi, 352 p.p $27.95 **345.73**
1. Trials (Homicide) 2. Capital punishment -- United States 3. Administration of criminal justice -- United States 4. Trials (Murder) -- Florida
ISBN 0670023701; 9780670023707
LC 2012019068

This book presents an "account of a questionable 1989 death penalty case by the lawyer who tried to get it overturned. By the time [Clive Stafford] Smith . . . became involved in the case of Kris Maharaj . . . [he] had been convicted and sentenced to death in Miami for the murder of a former business partner and his son. . . . In the author's view, the case is a glaring, but by no means unique, example of massive flaws in the American criminal justice system." (Kirkus Reviews)

Includes bibliographical references and index

Toobin, Jeffrey

The **run** of his life; the people v. O.J. Simpson. {by} Jeffrey Toobin. Random House 1996 466p $25/Can$35; $16 **345.73**
1. Football players 2. Trials (Homicide) 3. Sportscasters
ISBN 0-679-44170-0; 9780812988543
LC 96-210907

"The definitive account of the O. J. Simpson trial, The Run of His Life is a prodigious feat of reporting that could have been written only by the foremost legal journalist of our time. First published less than a year after the infamous verdict, Jeffrey Toobin's nonfiction masterpiece tells the whole story, from the murders of Nicole Brown Simpson and Ronald Goldman to the ruthless gamesmanship behind the scenes of "the trial of the century." Rich in character, as propulsive as a legal thriller, this enduring narrative continues to shock and fascinate with its candid depiction of the human drama that upended American life." (Publisher's note)

346 Private law

American Bar Association

★ The **American** Bar Association legal guide for small business; everything you need to know about small business, from start-up to employment to financing and selling. 2nd ed.; Random House Reference 2010 472p pa $16.99   **346**

1. Small business

ISBN 978-0-375-72303-2; 0-375-72303-X

LC 2009-49394

First published 2000

Topics covered "include legal forms of operating businesses, buying an existing business or a franchise, hiring and firing employees, managing temps and independent contractors, dealing with contracts and scams, taxes of all types, and, finally, closing, selling, or bequeathing the business." Libr J [review of 2000 edition]

Baldwin, Peter

The **copyright** wars; three centuries of trans-Atlantic battle. Peter Baldwin. Princeton University Press 2014 552 p. (alk. paper) $35   **346**

1. Copyright 2. Right of property 3. Intellectual property 4. Copyright -- Europe -- History 5. Copyright -- United States -- History

ISBN 0691161828; 9780691161822

LC 2013049603

In this book, author "Peter Baldwin explains why the copyright wars have always been driven by a fundamental tension. Should copyright assure authors and rights holders lasting claims, much like conventional property rights, as in Continental Europe? Or should copyright be primarily concerned with giving consumers cheap and easy access to a shared culture, as in Britain and America? 'The Copyright Wars' describes how the Continental approach triumphed." (Publisher's note)

"This book will be of interest to readers in comparative law and history as it includes discussions of both policy and national history." Choice

Includes bibliographical references and index

Butler, Rebecca P.

★ **Copyright** for teachers & librarians in the 21st century. Neal-Schuman Publishers 2011 274p il pa $70   **346**

1. Copyright 2. Fair use (Copyright)

ISBN 978-1-55570-738-5

LC 2011012600

First published 2004 with title: Copyright for teachers and librarians

"Library educator Rebecca Butler explains fair use, public domain, documentation and licenses, permissions, violations and penalties, policies and ethics codes, citations, creation and ownership, how to register copyrights, and gives tips for staying out of trouble." Publisher's note

Includes bibliographical references

Dickey, Lisa

Then comes marriage; United States v. Windsor and the defeat of DOMA. Roberta Kaplan with Lisa Dickey; Foreword by Edie Windsor. W W Norton & Co Inc 2015 336 p. 8 plates; illustrations (hardcover) $27.95   **346**

1. Same-sex marriage -- United States 2. Marriage law -- United States 3. United States. Defense of Marriage Act 4. Gay couples -- Legal status, laws, etc. -- United

States 5. Same-sex marriage -- Law and legislation -- United States

ISBN 0393248674; 9780393248678

LC 2015023636

This book, by Roberta Kaplan with Lisa Dickey, presents the author's "story of her defeat of the Defense of Marriage Act (DOMA) before the Supreme Court. . . . In this . . . account . . . , Kaplan describes meeting Windsor and their journey together to defeat DOMA. She shares the behind-the-scenes highs and lows, the excitement and the worries, and provides intriguing insights into her historic argument before the Supreme Court." (Publisher's note)

"Readers with an interest in constitutional law and Supreme Court politics, as well as the road to marriage equality, will find this account deliciously gripping." Library Journal

Elias, Stephen

Chapter 13 bankruptcy; keep your property & repay debts over time. [by] Stephen Elias & Robin Leonard. 10th ed.; Nolo 2010 486p il pa $39.99   **346**

1. Bankruptcy

ISBN 978-1-4133-1069-6; 1-4133-1069-9

LC 2009-21416

First published 1995. Periodically revised

Answers questions about bankruptcy that range from how to face the reality of being in debt and possible alternatives to filing procedures and strategies for rebuilding credit after the process is complete.

The **foreclosure** survival guide; keep your house or walk away with money in your pocket. attorneys Stephen Elias and Amy Loftsgordon; with bankruptcy updates by attorney Leon Bayer. 5th edition Nolo 2015 346 p. pbk $24.99   **346**

1. Foreclosure

ISBN 1413321844; 9781413321845

LC 2015009962

First published 2008. Frequently revised

"Elias explains how foreclosure works, what options there may be for keeping a home when in default, and what to do when that is not possible. He includes instruction on negotiating a workout with a lender as well as chapters on how to use bankruptcy to avoid foreclosure. . . . Straightforward and timely." Libr J

Includes bibliographical references and index

Encyclopedia of crime and punishment; edited by David Levinson. Sage Publs. 2002 4v set $600   **346**

1. Reference books 2. Administration of criminal justice 3. Crime -- Encyclopedias

ISBN 0-7619-2258-X

LC 2002-1220

"The 439 signed entries cover 13 major themes: crimes and related behaviors, law and justice, policing, forensics, corrections, victimology, punishment, social and cultural context, international aspects, concepts and theories, research methods and information, organizations and institutions, and special populations. . . . {This is} easy to understand and useful for beginning research in the field of criminal justice." Booklist

Includes bibliographical references

Fishman, Stephen

The **public** domain; how to find & use copyright-free writings, music, art & more. 5th ed.; Nolo 2010 462p il map pa $39.99 **346**

1. Copyright

ISBN 978-1-4133-1205-8; 1-4133-1205-5

LC 2009-39940

First published 2001. Frequently revised

This book offers "information about finding copyright-free writings, music, art, photography, software, maps, databases, videos, and more." Publisher's note

Leonard, Robin

★ **Solve** your money troubles; Strategies to get out of debt and stay that way. Robin Leonard; updated by Amy Loftsgordon. 15th edition Nolo 2015 375 p. pbk $24.99 **346**

1. Credit 2. Debtor and creditor

ISBN 1413321704; 9781413321708

First published 1991 with title: Money troubles. Frequently revised

This guide offers advice on how to manage debts, including how to create a budget, negotiate with creditors, and rebuild your credit.

Includes bibliographical references

Lessig, Lawrence

Remix; making art and commerce thrive in the hybrid economy. Penguin Press 2008 xxii, 327p $25.95 **346**

1. Copyright

ISBN 978-1-59420-172-1

LC 2008-32392

As Lessig "sees it, if intellectual-property law is left as it is an entire generation will be criminalized. He argues that the ways in which young people break copyright laws help them to become the sort of people we want them to be—creative and collaborative. Kids today are simply not going to give up downloading music and using copyrighted material in YouTube videos: they belong to a culture for which 'remix' is 'the essential art.' Lessig's proposals for revising copyright are compelling, because they rethink intellectual-property rights without abandoning them." New Yorker

Includes bibliographical references

McGinty, Brian

Lincoln's Greatest Case; The River, the Bridge, and the Making of America. Brian McGinty. W W Norton & Co Inc 2015 320 p. illustrations, maps $26.95 **346**

1. Trials 2. Bridges

ISBN 0871407841; 9780871407849

LC 2014036938

This book, by Brian McGinty, examines the 1850s "case ... Hurd et al. v. The Railroad Bridge Company. In the early hours of May 6, 1856, the steamboat Effie Afton barreled into a pillar of the Rock Island Bridge--the first railroad bridge ever to span the Mississippi River. McGinty . . . animates this legal cauldron of the late 1850s, which turned out to be the most consequential trial in [Abraham] Lincoln's nearly quarter century as a lawyer." (Publisher's note)

"McGinty's book gives us the best accounting of Lincoln, the lawyer, to date. Highly recommended." LJ

Pakroo, Peri

★ The **small** business start-up kit; by Peri H. Pakroo; edited by Marcia Stewart. 6th ed.; Nolo 2010 352p pa $29.99 **346**

1. Commercial law 2. Small business 3. Business enterprises

ISBN 978-1-4133-1099-3; 1-4133-1099-0

LC 2009-37822

First published 2000. Frequently revised

"In addition to covering essential legal basics, . . . [the author] advises on picking a business name and the best location, drafting and using contracts, managing business finances using technology, choosing the right business structure, and reaching customers using social media. . . . The CD-ROM includes contact information for state agencies that deal with businesses and taxes." Libr J

Pascoe, Peggy

What comes naturally; miscegenation law and the making of race in America. Oxford University Press 2009 404p il map **346**

1. Interracial marriage 2. Racially mixed people 3. United States -- Race relations 4. Miscegenation -- United States -- History 5. Interracial marriage -- United States -- History 6. Racially mixed people -- Legal status, laws, etc. -- United States

ISBN 0-19-509463-8; 978-0-19-509463-3

LC 2008-18035

"Peggy Pascoe's book, 'What Comes Naturally,' has won five major book awards--two from the American Historical Association, two from the Organization of American Historians, and one from the Law and Society Association; it was also a finalist for another from the American Studies Association. . . . It . . . [examines] laws banning interracial marriage in the United States, . . . informed by sociological, anthropological, and feminist theories of race-making, the state, law, and the intersections of race, class, and gender." (Contemporary Sociology)

"This compelling history of the United States miscegenation law demonstrates its centrality to maintaining white supremacy in the century following the Civil War. Pascoe, broadening her focus beyond black-white relations, considers Western states' prohibition of marriage between whites and American Indians, Chinese, Japanese, and Filipinos, as well as blacks. She weaves a fascinating story out of significant court cases." New Yorker

Includes bibliographical references and index

Pressman, David

Patent it yourself; your step-by-step guide to filing at the U.S. Patent Office. 14th ed.; Nolo 2009 596p il pa $49.99 **346**

1. Patents 2. Inventions

ISBN 978-1-4133-1058-0; 1-4133-1058-3

LC 2009-11888

First published 1979. Periodically revised

This guide for the amateur inventor covers patent searching, filing and infringement.

Includes bibliographical references

Stim, Richard

Contracts; the essential business desk reference. Nolo 2011 477p (Nolo's quick reference series) pa $39.99; ebook $39.99   **346**

1. Contracts 2. Reference books

ISBN 978-1-4133-1281-2 pa; 1-4133-1281-0 pa; 978-1-4133-1289-8 ebook; 1-4133-1289-6 ebook

LC 2010-21161

The author "helps laypeople navigate the sometimes murky waters of contractual agreements. Stim dedicates sections to writing different types of contracts, a dictionary of terms found in contracts and similar legal documents, and how to enforce these agreements once they're made. The bulk of the book is an alphabetized list of terms related to legal words and concepts. There is also a well-thought-out section on statutes of limitations on contract claims by state as well as contract sample documents scattered throughout." Libr J

★ **Patent,** copyright & trademark; 11th ed.; Nolo 2010 636p il pa $44.99   **346**

1. Patents 2. Copyright 3. Trademarks

ISBN 978-1-4133-1200-3; 1-4133-1200-4

LC 2009-48208

First published 1996. Periodically revised

The author explains concepts, issues, and terms concerning intellectual property, discusses trade secrets, copyright, patent, and trademark law, and provides sample forms.

Includes bibliographical references

346.01   Persons and domestic relations

American Civil Liberties Union

★ The **rights** of women; the authoritative ACLU guide to women's rights. [by] Lenora M. Lapidus, Emily J. Martin, and Namita Luthra. 4th ed.; New York University 2009 412p (American Civil Liberties Union handbook) $75; pa $19   **346.01**

1. Women's rights 2. Women -- Law and legislation

ISBN 978-0-8147-5230-2; 0-8147-5230-6; 978-0-8147-5229-6 pa; 0-8147-5229-2 pa

LC 2008-47033

First published 1973 by Sunrise Books/Dutton

Topics covered include "employment, education, housing, and public accommodations. This handbook also examines the specific issues of trafficking, violence against women, welfare reform, and reproductive freedom." Publisher's note

Includes bibliographical references

Doskow, Emily

★ **Nolo's** essential guide to divorce; 3rd ed.; Nolo 2010 496p il pa $24.99   **346.01**

1. Divorce -- Law and legislation

ISBN 978-1-4133-1255-3; 1-4133-1255-1

LC 2010-8698

First published 2006

The author "covers the before, during, and after of divorce, counseling readers on the types of divorces, how to make decisions about living arrangements and the division of property, and how custody decisions are made. She advocates minimizing conflict but includes sections on domestic violence and kidnapping if the worst happens. Appendixes contain state-to-state grounds for divorce and financial inventory forms." Libr J

Hertz, Frederick

A **legal** guide for lesbian and gay couples; Frederick Hertz and Emily Doskow. 18th edition Nolo 2016 pbk $34.99   **346.01**

1. Gay couples -- Legal status, laws, etc.

ISBN 9781413322798; 1413322794

LC 2016019762

First published 1980 by Addison-Wesley under the authorship of Hayden Curry and Denis Clifford

This handbook addresses "legal issues with which gay and lesbian couples are certain to contend . . . [including] advice for GLBT parents and prospective parents. Moreover, it addresses other legal considerations such as finanical arrangements. Indispensable for gay and lesbian readers, as well as for attorneys who may lack familiarity in this area." Libr J

Includes bibliographical references

Sember, Brette McWhorter

★ **Seniors'** rights; your legal guide to living life to the fullest. Sphinx Pub 2004 243p pa $19.95   **346.01**

1. Elderly -- Law and legislation

ISBN 1-572-48386-5

LC 2004-10704

"The author endeavors to help seniors understand their rights involving medical care, bank accounts, retirement accounts, housing, and discrimination. . . . The first step to protecting your rights, as she indicates, is understanding them, and this book will help seniors achieve that goal." Booklist

Woodhouse, Violet

★ **Divorce** & money; how to make the best financial decisions during divorce. with Dale Fetherling. 10th ed.; Nolo 2011 511p pa $34.99 **346.01**

1. Divorce -- Law and legislation

ISBN 978-1-4133-1314-7 pa; 1-4133-1314-0 pa; 978-1-4133-1337-6 ebook; 1-4133-1337-X ebook

LC 2010-31198

First published 1991. Periodically revised

A guide to financial problems that arise as a result of divorce proceedings.

Includes bibliographical references

346.04 Property

Crews, Kenneth D.

Copyright law for librarians and educators; creative strategies and practical solutions. with contributions from Dwayne K. Buttler . . . [et al.] 2nd ed; American Library Association 2012 xii, 192 p.p ill. (alk. paper) $57   **346.04**

1. Copyright   2. Sound recordings   3. Fair use (Copyright)   4. Copyright -- United States   5. Fair use (Copyright) -- United States   6. Teachers -- United States -- Handbooks, manuals, etc   7. Librarians -- United States -- Handbooks, manuals, etc

ISBN 0838910920; 9780838910924

LC 2011027604

First published 2000 with title: Copyright essentials for librarians and educators

Author Kenneth D. Crews' book "allows readers to get up to speed on current interpretations of the Digital Millennium Copyright Act from a librarian-educator viewpoint." It also "draws on cutting-edge case law in 18 discrete areas of copyright, including specialized and controversial music and sound recording issues. [This guide offers] information professionals . . . the tools they need to take control of their rights and responsibilities as copyright owners and users." (Publisher's note)

The author "addresses 18 areas of copyright in 5 parts. He begins with the scope of protectable works as well as works without copyright protection. Next, he discusses the rights of ownership, including duration and exceptions. He then explains fair use and its related guidelines. Part 4 focuses on the TEACH Act, Section 108, and responsibilities and liabilities. Lastly, Crews examines special issues such as the Digital Millennium Copyright Act." Booklist

Includes bibliographical references and index.

Elias, Stephen

★ **Trademark**; legal care for your business & product name. by Stephen Elias & Richard Stim. 9th ed.; Nolo 2010 448p il pa $39.99   **346.04**

1. Trademarks

ISBN 978-1-4133-1256-0; 1-4133-1256-X

LC 2010-9267

First published 1992. Periodically revised

The authors explain "how to: choose a distinctive name or logo that others can't copy; search for other marks that might conflict with your own; register your mark with the U.S. Patent and Trademark Office; protect your marks from unauthorized use by others; resolve trademark disputes outside the courtroom; [and] create an Internet presence with an eye on trademark law." Publisher's note

Fishman, Stephen

★ The **copyright** handbook; what every writer needs to know. Stephen Fishman. 12th edition Nolo 2014 458 p. pbk $49.99   **346.04**

1. Copyright

ISBN 9781413320480; 1413320481

First published 1991. Frequently revised

"Designed as a practical handbook for writers and publishers. Includes a list of legal aid groups and sample forms." Guide to Ref Books. 11th edition

Includes bibliographical references

Hyde, Lewis, 1945-

Common as air; revolution, art, and ownership. Farrar, Straus and Giroux 2010 306p $26   **346.04**

1. Arts   2. Culture   3. Patents   4. Copyright   5. Intellectual property   6. Information commons

ISBN 0-374-22313-0; 978-0-374-22313-7

LC 2010-02388

Hyde argues against "efforts to close off sectors of knowledge so as to exploit them for private profit." (N Y Times Book Rev) Index.

This is "an eloquent and erudite plea for protecting our cultural patrimony from appropriation by commercial interests." N Y Times Book Rev

Includes bibliographical references

Hylton, Keith N.

Laws of creation; property rights in the world of ideas. by Ronald A. Cass and Keith N. Hylton. Harvard University Press 2013 275 p. $55   **346.04**

1. Copyright   2. Intellectual property

ISBN 9780674066458; 0674066456

LC 2012011488

In this book authors Ronald A. Cass and Keith N. Hylton "look closely at the [intellectual property] doctrines that have been developed over many years in patent, copyright, trademark, and trade secret law. Over time, the authors show, a set of rules has emerged that supports wealth-creating innovation while generally avoiding overly expansive, growth-retarding licensing regimes." (Publisher's note)

Includes bibliographical references and index

Jameson, Marni

Downsizing the family home; what to save, what to let go. Marni Jameson. Sterling Pub Co Inc 2016 237 p. illustrations $16.95   **346.04**

1. Moving   2. Personal belongings

ISBN 1454916338; 9781454916338

LC 2015510856

This book, by Marni Jameson, focuses on the "emotional journey of downsizing your or your aging parents' home. Jameson sensitively guides readers through the process, from opening that first closet, to sorting through a lifetime's worth of possessions, to selling the homestead itself. Using her own personal journey as a basis, she helps you figure out a strategy and create a mindset to accomplish the task quickly, respectfully, rewardingly--and, in the best of situations, even memorably." (Publisher's note)

"The common-sense advice and practical information here will be of interest to persons facing downsizing or needing to get rid of stuff they no longer use." LJ

Includes bibliographical references (pages 228-229) and index.

Portman, Janet

★ **Every** tenant's legal guide; by Janet Portman and Marcia Stewart. 6th ed.; Nolo 2009 445p il pa $34.99 **346.04**
1. Landlord and tenant
ISBN 978-1-4133-1015-3; 1-4133-1015-X

LC 2009-4832

First published 1997. Frequently revised

This guide explains how to find and inspect a home, negotiate clauses in a lease or rental agreement, understand rules on rent increases and late rent, get repairs and maintenance, protect privacy rights, fight discrimination, deal with environmental hazards, security deposits, evictions and legal procedures.

Stewart, Marcia

★ **Every** landlord's legal guide; by Marcia Stewart and Ralph Warner & Janet Portman. 10th ed.; Nolo 2010 462p pa $44.99 **346.04**
1. Landlord and tenant
ISBN 978-1-4133-1197-6; 1-4133-1197-0

LC 2009-39934

First published 1996. Frequently revised

This guide covers how to "screen and choosing tenants; prepare leases and rental agreements; collect and returning deposits; avoid discrimination charges; keep up with repairs and maintenance; hire the right property manager; minimize your liability; [and] deal with problem tenants." Publisher's note

346.05 Inheritance, succession, fiduciary trusts, trustees

Clifford, Denis

★ **Make** your own living trust; 10th ed.; Nolo 2011 338p pa $39.99 **346.05**
1. Estate planning 2. Inheritance and succession
ISBN 978-1-4133-1316-1 pa; 1-4133-1316-7 pa; 978-1-4133-1344-4 ebook; 1-4133-1344-2 ebook

LC 2010-38422

First published 1993. Periodically revised

"Explains what trusts are, how they work, and who should use them. The CD provides a basic living trust, basic shared living trust, and AB living trust, plus other key forms." Publisher's note

★ **Plan** your estate; 10th ed; Nolo 2010 539p pa $44.99 **346.05**
1. Estate planning
ISBN 978-1-4133-1201-0

First published 1989. Periodically revised

This guide covers basic estate planning, probate avoidance, living wills, federal estate and gift taxes, trusts, durable powers of attorney, and more.

346.07 Commercial law

Elias, Stephen

★ **How** to file for Chapter 7 bankruptcy; by Stephen Elias, Albin Renauer, & Robin Leonard. 16th ed.; Nolo 2009 555p il pa $39.99 **346.07**
1. Bankruptcy
ISBN 978-1-4133-1060-3; 1-4133-1060-5

LC 2009-21419

First published 1989. Periodically revised. Variant title: How to file for bankruptcy

This guide offers advice on such topics as personal debt, property liability, asset protection, rebuilding credit, and filling out and filing forms.

Includes bibliographical references

346.73 Private law—United States

Becker, Jo

★ **Forcing** the spring; inside the fight for marriage equality. Jo Becker. The Penguin Press 2014 480 p. illustrations (hardback) $29.95 **346.73**
1. United States. Supreme Court 2. Same-sex marriage -- United States 3. California. Proposition 8 (2008) 4. Locus standi -- United States -- Cases 5. United States. Defense of Marriage Act 6. Same-sex marriage -- Law and legislation -- United States -- Cases
ISBN 1594204446; 9781594204449

LC 2014005342

Written by Jo Becker, this book offers an "account of five remarkable years in American civil rights history: when the United States experienced a tectonic shift on the issue of marriage equality. Beginning with the historical legal challenge of California's ban on same-sex marriage, Becker expands the scope to encompass all aspects of this momentous struggle, offering a . . . behind-the-scenes narrative." (Publisher's note)

"Becker's chronicle of a legal battle reveals deeper changes in the cultural and political landscape of a nation grappling with old prejudices and changing public opinion that continue to resonate." Booklist

Includes bibliographical references and index

Decherney, Peter

Hollywood's copyright wars; from Edison to the internet. Peter Decherney. Columbia University Press 2012 287 p. (cloth : alk. paper) $34.50 **346.73**
1. Copyright 2. Motion picture industry 3. Television supplies industry 4. Copyright -- Motion pictures -- United States -- History 5. Copyright -- Broadcasting rights -- United States -- History
ISBN 0231159463; 9780231159463

LC 2011041745

This book by Peter Decherney "follows the struggle of the film, television, and digital media industries to influence and adapt to copyright law . . . beginning with Thomas Edison's aggressive patent and copyright disputes and concluding with recent lawsuits against YouTube and Universal. Decherney shows that the history of intellectual property in Hollywood has not always mirrored the evolution of the law.

Many landmark decisions have barely changed the industry's behavior." (Publisher's note)

Includes bibliographical references and index

Gasaway, Laura N., 1945-

Copyright questions and answers for information professionals; from the columns of Against the Grain. by Laura N. Gasaway. Purdue University Press 2013 xiii, 284 p.p (paperback) $24.95; (ebook) $11.99; (ebook) $11.99   **346.73**

1. Copyright 2. Fair use (Copyright) 3. Intellectual property 4. Copyright -- United States 5. Fair use (Copyright) -- United States 6. Photocopying -- Fair use(Copyright) -- United States
ISBN 1557536392; 9781557536396; 9781612492537 pdf; 9781612492544

LC 2012032276

Laura N. Gasaway's "book begins with a basic primer on copyright. Then each topical chapter (e.g., Licensing, Performance and Displays, Digitization, etc.) presents a short introduction to the issues involved, followed by related questions and answers. The author includes reference to the applicable section of the copyright law as well as to other laws dealing with the subject. All in all, there are answers to well over 300 questions concerning copyright, fair use, and related issues." (Library Journal)

Kaiser, Robert G.

Act of Congress; how America's essential institution works, and how it doesn't. Robert G. Kaiser. 1st ed. Alfred A. Knopf 2013 xxvi, 417 p.p (hardcover) $27.95   **346.73**

1. United States. Congress 2. United States. Dodd-Frank Wall Street Reform and Consumer Protection Act 3. Global Financial Crisis, 2008-2009 4. Financial services industry -- Law and legislation -- United States
ISBN 030770016X; 9780307700162

LC 2012038245

In this book, journalist Robert G. Kaiser "chronicles the journey of the Dodd-Frank act, a complex package of banking and market regulations passed in 2011 that few voters paid attention to. . . . While the bill was moving through Congress, Kaiser had access to lawmakers of both parties and their staffs, executive-branch officials, and lobbyists; he finds the drama in arcane parliamentary procedure and paints . . . fly-on-the-wall scenes of legislative sausage making." (Publishers Weekly)

Includes bibliographical references (pages 391-400) and index.

Legal rights; the guide for deaf and hard of hearing people. National Association of the Deaf. Gallaudet University Press 2015 304 p. (pbk. : alk. paper) $34.95   **346.73**

1. Deaf -- Legal status, laws, etc. -- United States 2. Hearing impaired -- Legal status, laws, etc. -- United States
ISBN 9781563686443; 9781563686450

LC 2015005783

This book by the National Association of the Deaf "describes those statutes that prohibit discrimination against deaf and hard of hearing people, and any others with physi-

cal challenges. . . . The new edition describes the core legislation and laws and their critical importance since their inception: The Rehabilitation Act of 1973, the Individuals with Disabilities Education Act (IDEA), and the Americans with Disabilities Act (ADA)." (Publisher's note)

"Highly recommended for those with hearing impairments and their loved ones, along with students and practitioners of law, education, medicine, and politics. A necessity for all public library collections." LJ

Includes bibliographical references and index.

Leamer, Laurence

The **price** of justice; a true story of two lawyers' epic battle against corruption and greed in coal country. Laurence Leamer. Times Books 2013 xii, 432 p.p (hardcover) $30.00   **346.73**

1. Fair trial -- United States 2. Judges -- Recusal -- United States 3. Massey Energy (Firm) -- Trials, litigation, etc 4. Coal trade -- Corrupt practices -- West Virginia
ISBN 9780805094718

LC 2012041537

"Not content to dominate the coal-mining industry through Massey Energy and the West Virginia judicial system that indirectly supported it, CEO Don Blankenship ferociously punished anyone who dared to challenge that dominance. So, in 1998, when attorneys Bruce Stanley and Dave Fawcett went after Massey on behalf of their client, a small mining company, they set off a 14-year-long struggle that eventually took them to the U.S. Supreme Court to argue against corporate corruption of the judicial system." (Booklist)

Includes bibliographical references and index.

Yoshino, Kenji

Speak now; marriage equality on trial. Kenji Yoshino. Crown 2015 336 p.   **346.73**

1. Same-sex marriage 2. Gay couples -- Legal status, laws, etc. 3. California. Proposition 8 (2008) 4. United States. Defense of Marriage Act 5. Gay couples -- Legal status, laws, etc. -- United States -- Cases 6. Same-sex marriage -- Law and legislation -- United States -- Cases
ISBN 9780385348805; 9780385348812; 9780385348829

LC 2014042967

Stonewall Book Awards: Israel Fishman Non-Fiction Award (2016)

"'Speak Now' tells the story of a watershed trial that unfolded over twelve tense days in California in 2010. . . . In telling the story of Hollingsworth v. Perry, the groundbreaking federal lawsuit against Proposition 8, Kenji Yoshino has also written a paean to the vanishing civil trial--an oasis of rationality in what is often a decidedly uncivil debate." (Publisher's note)

"This is the well-told story of one of the most important civil trials in recent American history, Hollingsworth v. Perry, the 12-day trial challenging the constitutionality of California's Proposition 8. Because this case was tried in federal court, most of America was aware that it might end up being argued before the US Supreme Court. Yoshino (New York Univ. School of Law) takes the reader behind the scenes of both sides of this civil trial. . . . Well beyond its outcome, however, this case is all about why trials can be crucial to the American system of justice." Choice

347 Procedure and courts

Breyer, Stephen G., 1938-

Making our democracy work; a judge's view. [by] Stephen Breyer. Alfred A. Knopf 2010 270p il $26.95 **347**

1. United States -- Supreme Court 2. Judicial review -- United States 3. Separation of powers -- United States 4. United States -- Politics and government 5. Judicial review -- United States -- History 6. Political questions and judicial power -- United States

ISBN 0-307-26991-4; 978-0-307-26991-1

LC 2010-16839

"Why does the public accept the Court's decisions as legitimate and follow them, even when those decisions are highly unpopular? What must the Court do to maintain the public's faith? How can the Court help make . . . democracy work? These are the questions that Justice Stephen Breyer [examines]." (Publisher's note) Index.

"A sitting Justice explains how the Supreme Court won the public trust and what it must do to keep it. Employing a succession of cases from Marbury v. Madison to Bush v. Gore, Breyer . . . offers a short, highly accessible course on the evolution of judicial review, the doctrine permitting the Court to invalidate laws conflicting with the Constitution. . . . Speaking out without talking down, Breyer renders a signal service to his fellow citizens." Kirkus

Includes bibliographical references

Faigman, David L.

Laboratory of justice; the Supreme Court's 200-year struggle to integrate science and the law. Times Books, Henry Holt 2004 417p $27.50; pa $17 **347**

1. Science -- Governmental policy 2. United States -- Supreme Court 3. Constitutional law -- United States

ISBN 0-8050-7274-8; 0-8050-7845-2 pa

LC 2003-57049

"This insightful and accessible study throws light on how new ways of understanding the world produce new readings of our Constitution." Publ Wkly

Includes bibliographical references

Finkelman, Paul

★ **Landmark** decisions of the United States Supreme Court; [by] Paul Finkelman, Melvin I. Urofsky. 2nd ed.; CQ Press 2008 791p il $250 **347**

1. United States -- Supreme Court 2. Constitutional law -- United States

ISBN 978-0-87289-409-9

LC 2007-42588

First published 2003

This "provides the historical context and constitutional perspective of more than 1,000 of the most important Supreme Court cases." Publisher's note

Includes bibliographical references

Friedman, Barry

The **will** of the people; how public opinion has influenced the Supreme Court and shaped the meaning of the Constitution. Farrar, Straus and Giroux 2009 614p **347**

1. Public opinion 2. United States -- Supreme Court 3. Public opinion -- United States 4. United States -- Supreme Court -- Public opinion 5. Judicial process -- United States -- Public opinion

ISBN 0374220344; 0374532370 pa; 9780374220341; 9780374532376 pa

LC 2008054247

This is an account of the relationship between popular opinion and the Supreme Court from the Declaration of Independence to the end of the Rehnquist court in 2005. (Publisher's note) Index.

This book is a thought-provoking and authoritative history of the Supreme Court's relationship to popular opinion. . . . Friedman's contribution to [the] discussion is the breadth and detail of his historical canvas, and it's a significant one. N Y Times Book Rev

Includes bibliographical references

★ **Great** American trials; Edward W. Knappman, editor; Stephen G. Christianson and Lisa Paddock, consulting legal editors. 2nd ed; Gale Group 2002 2v il set $170 **347**

1. Trials

ISBN 0-7876-4901-5

First published 1994

Featuring approximately 360 trials from the 1800s to the present, entries "cover the principals involved, the crime charged, the verdict and sentence, and the significance and impact of each trial." Publisher's note

Includes bibliographical references

Leiter, Richard A.

Landmark Supreme Court cases; the most influential decisions of the Supreme Court of the United States. [by] Gary Hartman, Roy M. Mersky, [and] Cindy Tate Slavinski. Facts on File 2004 594p (Facts on File library of American history) $70; pa $21.95 **347**

1. Law -- United States 2. United States -- Supreme Court

ISBN 0-8160-2452-9; 0-8160-6923-9 pa

LC 2003-57776

This is "an excellent source for beginning researchers. . . . The discussion of the case's significance and its implications will be useful for students." SLJ

Includes bibliographical references

Marshall, Thurgood

Thurgood Marshall; his speeches, writings, arguments, opinions, and reminiscences. edited by Mark Tushnet; foreword by Randall Kennedy. Hill Bks. 2001 xxvi, 548p (Library of Black America) $40; pa $24.95 **347**

1. Lawyers 2. Solicitors general 3. Civil rights activists 4. Supreme Court justices 5. African Americans -- Biography 6. United States -- Supreme Court 7.

African Americans -- Civil rights
ISBN 1-55652-385-8; 1-55652-386-6 pa
LC 2001-16793

"In a career ranging from his trial and appellate work for the NAACP to his tenure as an associate justice of the Court, Marshall wrought revolutionary changes in U.S. law and politics, and this collection of his legal briefs, writings, speeches, and judicial opinions, plus a never-before-published oral interview, gives us a superior analysis of the advocate, the democrat, the dissenter, and the unflagging fighter for equality." Libr J

Includes bibliographical references

O'Brien, David M.

Storm center; the Supreme Court in American politics. 8th ed; W.W. Norton 2008 xx, 458p il pa $29.85 **347**

1. United States -- Supreme Court
ISBN 978-0-393-93218-8; 0-393-93218-4
LC 2008-7373

First published 1986. Periodically revised

The author discusses "the day-to-day workings of the Court justices and their law clerks, how cases are accepted for hearing, what negotiations and compromises go on, how case opinions get written—and what happens to American society when two conservative presidents, Reagan and Bush, appoint the majority of justices." Publisher's note

Includes bibliographical references

★ The **Oxford** companion to the Supreme Court of the United States; editor in chief, Kermit L. Hall; editors, James W. Ely, Jr., Joel B. Grossman. 2nd ed.; Oxford University Press 2005 xxv, 1239p il $65 **347**

1. Reference books 2. United States -- Supreme Court
ISBN 0-19-517661-8
LC 2004-29463

First published 1992

This encyclopedia includes over 1200 articles "on all aspects of the court's history, justices, operations, and cases. Over 300 experts contributed the entries, which vary in length; some have bibliographic references. The organization . . . [includes] alphabetical entries, portraits of the justices, cross-references, and indexes by both case name and topic." Choice

Shesol, Jeff

★ **Supreme** power; Franklin Roosevelt vs. the Supreme Court. W. W. Norton & Co. 2010 644p il $27.95 **347**

1. Governors 2. Presidents 3. People with disabilities 4. Philatelists 5. United States -- Supreme Court 6. United States -- Politics and government -- 20th century 7. Political questions and judicial power -- United States -- History
ISBN 978-0-393-06474-2; 0-393-06474-3
LC 2009-46365

The book examines the interaction between U.S. President Franklin Delano Roosevelt and the Supreme Court. "FDR took up the idea of expanding the number of justices on the Court. This was the famous 'court-packing plan.' The story of the plan and the . . . political battle over it . . . [is]

told . . . by Jeff Shesol in his . . . [book] 'Supreme Power.' Shesol looks at the battle through the eyes of all the major players--FDR and his advisers, the congressional leadership that was handed the unappealing job of putting the plan into effect, the congressional opposition, the many politicians and interest groups that organized over the plan, and the justices themselves." (New York Review of Books)

This "is an impressive and engaging book—an excellent work of narrative history. It is deeply researched and beautifully written. Even readers who already know the outcome will find it hard not to feel the suspense that surrounded the battle, so successfully does Shesol recreate the atmosphere of this great controversy." N Y Times Book Rev

Includes bibliographical references

Smith, Jean Edward

John Marshall; definer of a nation. Holt & Co. 1996 736p il hardcover o.p. pa $22 **347**

1. Biographers 2. Writers on law 3. Secretaries of state 4. Supreme Court justices 5. United States -- Supreme Court
ISBN 0-8050-5510-X pa
LC 96-15072

"Mr. Smith's splendid biography deserves a large readership mostly because it has recovered Marshall the man." N Y Times Book Rev

Includes bibliographical references

Toobin, Jeffrey R.

★ The **nine**; inside the secret world of the Supreme Court. [by] Jeffrey Toobin. Doubleday 2007 369p il $27.95 **347**

1. United States -- Supreme Court
ISBN 978-0-385-51640-2
LC 2007-20287

"Beautifully written, this is an essential purchase for all libraries interested in the contemporary Supreme Court." Libr J

Includes bibliographical references

Warner, Ralph E.

★ **Everybody's** guide to small claims court; by Ralph Warner. 13th ed.; Nolo 2010 480p pa $29.99 **347**

1. Small claims court
ISBN 978-1-4133-1102-0; 1-4133-1102-4
LC 2009-41947

First published 1980 by Addison-Wesley. Periodically revised

Presents resources and step-by-step instructions for defending one's case in small claims court, and discusses specific kinds of cases, such as motor vehicle repair and purchase, vehicle accident, and landlord-tenant cases.

347.73   Civil procedure and courts of the United States

Coyle, Marcia

★ The **Roberts** court; the struggle for the constitution. Marcia Coyle. Simon & Schuster 2013 352 p. (hardcover) $28   **347.73**
1. Roberts, John G., 1955- 2. United States. Constitution 3. United States. Supreme Court 4. United States. Supreme Court -- History -- 21st century 5. Political questions and judicial power -- United States -- History -- 21st century
ISBN 1451627513; 9781451627510; 9781451627527; 9781451627534

LC 2012051637

In this book, author Marcia Coycle "reveals the fault lines in the conservative-dominated [U.S. Supreme] Court led by Chief Justice John Roberts Jr." It "captures four landmark decisions--concerning health care, money in elections, guns at home, and race in schools. Her analysis shows how dedicated conservative lawyers and groups are strategizing to find cases and crafting them to bring up the judicial road to the Supreme Court with an eye on a receptive conservative majority." (Publisher's note)

Includes bibliographical references and index

Gibson, Larry S.

Young Thurgood; the making of a Supreme Court Justice. by Larry S. Gibson. Prometheus Books 2012 413 p. (cloth : alk. paper) $28 **347.73**
1. Judges -- United States -- Biography 2. United States. Supreme Court -- History 3. United States. Supreme Court -- Officials and employees
ISBN 1616145714; 9781616145712

LC 2012027517

This book by Larry S. Gibson is a biography of U.S. Supreme Court Justice Thurgood Marshall. "He transformed the nation's legal landscape by challenging the racial segregation that had relegated millions to second-class citizenship. . . . Marshall's personality, attitudes, priorities, and work habits had crystallized during earlier years in Maryland. . . . [This book] is the first close examination of the formative period in Marshall's life." (Publisher's note)

Includes bibliographical references and index.

Haygood, Wil

★ **Showdown**; Thurgood Marshall and the Supreme Court nomination that changed America. by Wil Haygood. Alfred A. Knopf 2015 416 p. illustrations, portraits (hardcover) $32.50   **347.73**
1. Judges 2. United States. Supreme Court 3. Judges -- Selection and appointment -- United States -- History -- 20th century 4. United States. Supreme Court -- Officials and employees -- Selection and appointment -- History -- 20th century
ISBN 0307957195; 9780307957191

LC 2014044440

NAACP Image Award Nominee: Outstanding Literary Work- Nonfiction (2016)

Haygood "examines the confirmation battle over the first African-American nominated to the Supreme Court. During the summer of 1967, Thurgood Marshall (1908-1993)

appeared for an unprecedented fifth day before the Senate Judiciary Committee. This confrontation between arguably the most consequential appellate attorney ever and the 'Old Bulls' who dominated the interrogating panel is both the spine of Haygood's narrative and the occasion for a number of ancillary stories that lend blood and guts to the superficial civilities of a Senate hearing." (Kirkus Reviews)

"The behind-the-scenes look at the hard-fought battle that Lyndon Johnson and his supporters waged on Marshall's behalf creates suspense, even though readers will already know of their ultimate success." Pub Wkly

Includes bibliographical references and index

Hirshman, Linda

Sisters in law; how Sandra Day O'Connor and Ruth Bader Ginsburg went to the Supreme Court and changed the world. Linda Hirshman. HarperCollins 2015 416 p. illustrations $28.99; (ebook) $15.99   **347.73**
1. Women judges 2. United States. Supreme Court 3. Judges -- United States -- Biography 4. Women judges -- United States -- Biography
ISBN 9780062238467; 9780062238481

LC 2015002577

This book, by Linda Hirshman, "tells the fascinating story of the intertwined lives of Sandra Day O'Connor and Ruth Bader Ginsburg, the first and second women to serve as Supreme Court justices. The relationship between Sandra Day O'Connor and Ruth Bader Ginsburg—Republican and Democrat, Christian and Jew, western rancher's daughter and Brooklyn girl—transcends party, religion, region, and culture." (Publisher's note)

"Hirshman's conversational style and deep analysis of several precedent-setting constitutional cases should appeal to both casual and professional readers." Pub Wkly

Includes bibliographical references and index

Jost, Kenneth

★ The **Supreme** Court A to Z; Kenneth Jost. 5th ed. CQ Press 2012 xvii, 668 p.p ill. (hardcover : alk. paper) $125.00   **347.73**
1. United States. Supreme Court -- Biography 2. United States. Supreme Court -- Encyclopedias
ISBN 1608717445; 9781608717446

LC 2012000642

This book by Kenneth Jost "offers . . . information about the Supreme Court, including its history, traditions, organization, dynamics, and personalities. The entries in The Supreme Court A to Z are arranged alphabetically and are . . . cross-referenced to related information. This volume also has a detailed index, reference materials on Supreme Court nominations, a seat chart of the justices, the U.S. Constitution, online sources of decisions, and a bibliography." (Publisher's note)

Includes bibliographical references (p. 617-630) and index.

Justices of the United States Supreme Court; their lives and major opinions. edited by Leon Friedman & Fred L. Israel. Facts On File 2013 1600 p. (hbk. alk. paper) $375   **347.73**
1. Judges -- Biography 2. Judges -- United States

-- Biography 3. United States. Supreme Court --
Biography
ISBN 0816070156; 9780816070152

LC 2009021252

This book by Leon Friedman and Fred L. Israel "examines the biographical facts of each Supreme Court justice's life, including his or her background in the law, the paths that led each one to the Supreme Court, and each justice's major decisions, as well as how these decisions reveal an underlying legal philosophy. All entries and their corresponding bibliographies have been thoroughly updated in this revised four-volume set." (Publisher's note)

Includes bibliographical references and index

Mersky, Roy M.

Landmark Supreme Court cases; the most influential decisions of the Supreme Court of the United States. Richard A. Leiter, Roy M. Mersky. 2nd ed. Facts on File 2012 3 v., xx, 1224 p.p (hardbound : alk. paper) $250.00 **347.73**
1. Civil rights 2. Freedom of speech 3. Freedom of the press 4. United States. Supreme Court 5. Law -- United States -- Cases
ISBN 9780816069576; 0816069573

LC 2010048195

Authors Richard A. Leiter and Roy M. Mersky's book discusses landmark U.S. Supreme Court "cases on such issues as freedom of speech, freedom of the press, civil rights, labor unions, abortion, antitrust and competition, due process, search and seizure, executive privilege, and more. Organized chronologically by issue, each entry includes the case title and legal citation, year of decision, key issue, historical background, legal arguments, decision (majority and dissenting opinions), aftermath and significance, related cases, and recommended reading." (Publisher's note)

"The authors describe some 350 influential US Supreme Court decisions. Arranged by subjects such as abortion and taxation, the . . . entries include an abstract of the decision, . . . the case's history, summary of the arguments, the salient issues involved, its significance, related cases, and recommended readings including law journal articles." Choice

Includes bibliographical references and index.

O'Connor, Sandra Day, 1930-

★ Out of order; stories from the history of the Supreme Court. Sandra Day O'Connor. 1st ed. Random House Inc. 2013 xviii, 233 p.p ill. (hardcover) $26; (ebook) $78.00 **347.73**
1. Courts -- History 2. United States. Supreme Court 3. Law -- United States -- History 4. United States. Supreme Court -- History 5. United States. Supreme Court -- Anecdotes 6. Courts of last resort -- United States -- History 7. Courts of last resort -- United States -- Anecdotes
ISBN 0812993926; 9780812993929; 9780812993936

LC 2012025708

This book, by Sandra Day O'Connor, "the first woman to sit on the United States Supreme Court, . . . [discusses] the history and evolution of the highest court in the land. . . . [This book] sheds light on the centuries of change and upheaval that transformed the Supreme Court from its un-

certain beginnings into the . . . institution that thrives and endures today." (Publisher's note)

Includes bibliographical references and index

The **Supreme** Court justices; illustrated biographies, 1789-2012. edited by Clare Cushman, the Supreme Court Historical Society; foreword by Chief Justice John G. Roberts, Jr. 3rd ed. CQ Press, an imprint of SAGE Publications 2013 xx, 562 p.p ill., ports. (hardcover) $135 **347.73**
1. Judges -- Biography 2. Judges -- United States -- Biography 3. United States. Supreme Court -- History 4. United States. Supreme Court -- Officials and employees -- Biography
ISBN 1608718328; 9781608718320

LC 2012031502

This book, edited by Clare Cushman, is "a single-volume reference profiling every Supreme Court justice from John Jay through Elena Kagan. An original essay on each justice paints a . . . picture of his or her individuality as shaped by family, education, pre-Court career, and the times in which he or she lived. Each biographical essay also presents the major issues on which the justice presided. Essays are arranged in the order of the justices' appointments." (Publisher's note)

"Written by leading constitutional scholars, the well-researched essays are arranged in chronological order of the justices' appointment to the Court. The volume includes a revised bibliography organized by individual justices, and a thorough index. . . . Recommended." Choice

Includes bibliographical references (pages 516-538) and index.

Toobin, Jeffrey

The **oath**; the Obama White House and the Supreme Court. Jeffrey Toobin. Doubleday 2012 viii, 325 p.p $28.95 **347.73**
1. Roberts, John G., 1955- 2. United States. Supreme Court 3. United States -- Politics and government -- 2009- 4. Constitutional history -- United States 5. United States. Supreme Court -- History -- 21st century 6. Political questions and judicial power -- United States -- History -- 21st century
ISBN 0385527209; 9780385527200

LC 2012029205

This book by Jeffrey Toobin offers an "account of the current struggle over constitutional interpretation." It "interweaves three topics: the leading cases that illustrate the ambition of the [John] Roberts Court; the four appointments since 2006 ([John] Roberts, Samuel Alito, Sonia Sotomayor, and Elena Kagan) that have turned the court into an institution . . . divided between five committed Republicans and four committed Democrats; and . . . sketches of all the justices, including the three recent retirees (Sandra Day O'Connor, David Souter, and John Paul Stevens)." (Bookforum)

Includes bibliographical references and index.

Tushnet, Mark

In the balance; law and politics on the Roberts Court. Mark Tushnet. W W Norton & Co Inc 2013 352 p. (hardcover) $28.95 **347.73**
1. Judicial power 2. Roberts, John G., 1955- 3. United

States. Supreme Court 4. Judges -- United States 5.
Law -- Political aspects -- United States 6. Political
questions and judicial power -- United States
ISBN 0393073440; 9780393073447

LC 2013012744

In this book, "constitutional law expert Mark Tushnet
clarifies the lines of conflict and what is at stake on the Supreme Court as it hangs 'in the balance' between its conservatives and its liberals." He "cover[s] the legal philosophies
that have informed decisions on major cases such as the
Affordable Care Act, the political structures behind Court
appointments, and the face-off between John Roberts and
Elena Kagan for intellectual dominance of the Court." (Publisher's note)

Includes bibliographical references and index

348   Laws, regulations, cases

★ **Major** acts of Congress; Brian K. Landsberg,
editor in chief. Macmillan Reference USA 2004
3v il set $290   **348**
1. Reference books 2. Law -- United States --
Encyclopedias
ISBN 0-02-865749-7

LC 2003-18747

This "will be a top-tier reference work for students and
laypersons researching federal legislation." Booklist

Includes bibliographical references

Stathis, Stephen W.

Landmark legislation, 1774-2002; major U.S.
acts and treaties. {by} Stephen Stathis. CQ Press
2003 22, 429p $130   **348**
1. Legislation 2. Legislation -- United States
ISBN 1-56802-781-8

LC 2003-3531

"This well-organized volume will allow users to quickly
find a description of important legislation and determine
where they can locate the full text. . . . This will be a useful
source for academic and public libraries." Booklist

Includes bibliographical references

★ **U.S.** laws, acts, and treaties; edited by Timothy L.
Hall. Salem Press 2003 3v (Magill's choice) set
$188   **348**
1. Law -- United States 2. United States -- Foreign
relations -- Treaties
ISBN 1-58765-098-3

LC 2002-156063

This "is a collection of 433 major U.S. acts of Congress and U.S. treaties covering the time period from 1776
through 2002, beginning with the Declaration of Independence and ending with the Homeland Security Act. . . . The
essays, chronically arranged and varying in length from 500
to 2,000 words, cover the historical origins and main provisions of each law or treaty. . . . This set presents a good
coverage of landmark laws and treaties in a concise, easy-to-
read, and easy-to-use work. It is geared toward high-school
and undergraduate students but would also make a useful
and functional reference tool for public libraries." Booklist

Includes bibliographical references

349   Law of specific jurisdictions, areas, socioeconomic regions, regional intergovernmental organizations

Clark, David Scott

The **Oxford** companion to American law; editor
in chief, Kermit L. Hall; editors, David S. Clark {et
al.} Oxford Univ. Press 2002 xxvi, 912p $75   **349**
1. Law -- United States
ISBN 0-19-508878-6

LC 2002-284010

The alphabetically arranged "entries consider how law,
legal institutions, and court decisions are related to social
demands and legal responses. . . . The volume also includes
standard legal terms and key legal concepts, such as verdicts
and venues, as well as biographical statements about leading
individuals in the legal profession. . . . With a substantial
breadth of information and analysis, this volume is accessible to every reader. All libraries will find it an invaluable
reference source." Libr J

Includes bibliographical references

Friedman, Lawrence Meir

American law in the 20th century; {by} Lawrence M. Friedman. Yale Univ. Press 2002 722p
$38   **349**
1. Law -- United States
ISBN 0-300-09137-0

LC 2001-3332

The author "examines the American legal system as an
integral part of the larger society, both reflecting and causing changes therein. By adopting such a focus, the author
makes his book accessible to readers who are not legal
scholars." Booklist

Includes bibliographical references

★ **Gale** encyclopedia of American law; 3rd ed.;
Gale/Cengage Learning 2011 14v il map set
$1604   **349**
1. Reference books 2. Law -- United States --
Encyclopedias
ISBN 978-1-4144-3684-5; 1-4144-3684-X; 978-1-
4144-4302-7 ebook; 1-4144-4302-1 ebook

LC 2010-45527

First published 1983-1985 with title: The Guide to
American law. Previous edition published with title: West's
encyclopedia of American law

Explains legal terms and concepts in everyday language,
covering a wide variety of persons, entities, and events that
have shaped the U.S. legal system and influenced public perceptions of it.

Includes bibliographical references

★ **Gale** encyclopedia of everyday law; Jeffrey Wilson, editor. 2nd ed.; Thomson Gale 2006 2v set
$325   **349**
1. Law -- United States
ISBN 1-4144-0353-4

LC 2006-10071

First published 2003

This encyclopedia includes "descriptions of each issue's
historical background, covering important statutes and cas-

es; profiles of various U.S. laws and regulations; details of how laws and regulations vary from state to state, and; bibliographies, including print and Web resources and lists of relevant organizations." Publisher's note

Includes bibliographical references

★ **National** survey of state laws; Richard A. Leiter, editor. 6th ed; Thomson Gale 2008 808p $140 **349**

1. Law -- United States
ISBN 978-0-7876-9874-4; 0-7876-9874-1
Irregular. First published 1993

Summarizes state laws on 50 subjects, divided into general legal categories: business and consumer, criminal, education, employment, family, general civil, real estate, and tax.

351 Public administration

Kettl, Donald F.

The **next** government of the United States; why our institutions fail us and how to fix them. W. W. Norton & Co. 2009 288p il $25.95 **351**

1. Administrative agencies 2. United States -- Politics and government -- 2001-
ISBN 978-0-393-05112-4; 0-393-05112-9
LC 2008-38584

"Kettl's cogent and unbiased analysis of the failure of government institutions posits that current challenges, whether in health care or disaster response, have outgrown the capacity of monolithic government agencies, even while the size of government continues to swell. . . . He presents a balanced and unpartisan analysis of the Hurricane Katrina debacle, examining human error and generations of poor decision making as well as the intricacies of federalism and the organizational complexity of government institutions." Publ Wkly

Includes bibliographical references

352.13 Administration of subordinate jurisdictions

★ The **book** of the states; [compiled by] the Council of State Governments. 2010 ed; Council of State Governments 2010 627p il map $125 **352.13**

1. State governments
ISBN 978-0-87292-7667
Biennial, 1935-2001, Annual from 2002. Began publication 1935

"In addition to general articles on various aspects of state government, this source provides many statistical and directory data, the principal state officials, and such information as the nickname, motto, flower, bird, song, and tree of each state." Ref Sources for Small & Medium-sized Libr. 6th edition

★ **Counties** USA; a directory of United States counties. Darren L. Smith, managing editor. Omnigraphics 2006 840p il map $149 **352.13**

1. Reference books 2. County government 3. United States -- Statistics
ISBN 978-0-7808-0821-8
First published 1997

This is "an excellent choice, offering multiple uses as a country directory, demographic source, and gazetteer." Choice [review of 2003 edition]

352.23 Chief executives

Encyclopedia of the U.S. presidency; a historical reference. edited by Nancy Beck Young. Facts On File 2013 6 v., 2500 p.p ill., maps (hardcover) $550 **352.23**

1. Presidents -- United States -- Encyclopedias 2. Presidents -- United States -- Encyclopedias, Juvenile 3. Presidents -- United States -- History -- Encyclopedias, Juvenile 4. United States -- Politics and government -- Encyclopedias, Juvenile
ISBN 0816067449; 9780816067442
LC 2010020746

This six-volume set looks at the American presidency. The "opening volume includes 19 thematic essays dealing with various topics surrounding the history of the presidency including 'Origins of the Presidency,' 'Presidency and the Politics of Race,' and 'The Presidency and Popular Culture.' The ensuing volumes follow a chronological arrangement of individually signed entries covering from Washington to Obama." (Library Journal)

Includes bibliographical references and index

Fellow citizens; the Penguin book of U.S. presidential inaugural addresses. edited with an introduction and commentaries by Robert V. Remini and Terry Golway. Penguin Books 2008 476p $16 **352.23**

1. American speeches 2. Presidents -- United States -- Inaugural addresses
ISBN 978-0-14-311453-6; 0-14-311453-0
LC 2008-19970

"Two distinguished historians round up every presidential inaugural address and preface it with commentary on the rhetoric and historical context of the discourse. . . . Reflecting the major events of American history, as well as a rhetorical evolution from prolixity to brevity, this . . . is a great resource." Booklist

Includes bibliographical references

Guide to the presidency and the executive branch; Michael Nelson, editor. 5th ed. CQ Press 2013 2 v. (xix, 2141 p.)p ill. (cloth : alk. paper) $425 **352.23**

1. Political science 2. Presidents -- United States
ISBN 9781608719068
LC 2012023291

This two-volume guide is a source "for researchers seeking an understanding of those who have occupied the

White House and on the institution of the U.S. presidency." Its chapters "explain the structure, powers, and operations of the office and the president's relationship with Congress and the Supreme Court." In this fifth edition, there is "coverage of the George W. Bush presidency, the 2008 election, and the first 3 years of the presidency of Barack Obama." (Publisher's note)

Includes bibliographical references and index

My fellow citizens; the inaugural addresses of the presidents of the United States, 1789-2009. with an introduction by Arthur M. Schlesinger, Jr. and commentary by Fred L. Israel. Facts On File 2010 428p (Facts on File library of American history) $45   **352.23**
1. Presidents -- United States -- Inaugural addresses
ISBN 978-0-8160-8253-7; 0-8160-8253-7
                           LC 2009-32184

First published 2007

"Features the original text of all 56 inaugural speeches, each with an explanatory essay." Publisher's note

Owen, Roger

The **rise** and fall of Arab presidents for life; Roger Owen. Harvard University Press 2012 xi, 248 p.p (alk. paper) $24.95   **352.23**
1. Dictators 2. Presidents -- Middle East 3. Middle East -- Politics and government 4. Monarchy -- Middle East 5. Monarchy -- Arab countries 6. Authoritarianism -- Middle East 7. Middle East -- Kings and rulers 8. Arab countries -- Kings and rulers 9. Authoritarianism -- Arab countries 10. Presidents -- Middle East -- History 11. Presidents -- Arab countries -- History 12. Middle East -- Politics and government -- 1945- 13. Arab countries -- Politics and government -- 1945-
ISBN 0674065832; 9780674065833
                         LC 2011045764

This book, by Roger Owen, examines the political history of Arab political regimes in the 20th century. "Monarchical presidential regimes in the Arab world looked as though they would last indefinitely--until events in Tunisia and Egypt made clear their time was up. This . . . book [seeks] to lay bare the dynamics of a governmental system that largely defined the Arab Middle East in the twentieth century, and the popular opposition they engendered." (Publisher's note)

Includes bibliographical references (p. 217-226) and index

Raphael, Ray

Mr. president; how and why the founders created a chief executive. by Ray Raphael. Alfred A. Knopf 2012 324 p.   **352.23**
1. Executive power -- United States 2. Founding Fathers of the United States 3. Presidents -- United States -- Biography 4. Constitutional conventions -- United States 5. United States -- Politics and government -- 1783-1809 6. Presidents -- United States -- History -- 18th century
ISBN 9780307595270
                         LC 2011033471

This book presents a "biography of the Constitutional Convention and the herculean task faced by the representa-

tives. The author paints a picture of heroes--Edmund Randolph, George Mason, James Wilson and James Madison, among others--noting that the founders developed a government presupposing that George Washington would be the first chief executive. . . . . In order to show how their views evolved as they toiled, Raphael explores the founders' writings in chronological order." (Kirkus Reviews)

Includes bibliographical references (p. [289]-309) and index

State of the union; presidential rhetoric from Woodrow Wilson to George W. Bush. CQ Press 2007 1185p il $140   **352.23**
1. American speeches 2. Presidents -- United States -- Messages 3. Presidents -- United States -- Inaugural addresses 4. United States -- Politics and government -- Sources
ISBN 978-0-87289-433-4; 0-87289-433-9
                         LC 2006-35973

"This volume includes over 100 full-text addresses delivered by Presidents from 1913 to 2006 and comes complete with prefatory notes for context." Libr J

Includes bibliographical references

Witcover, Jules

America's vice presidents; from irrelevance to power. Jules Witcover. Smithsonian Institution Press 2014 592 p. illustrations $34.95   **352.23**
1. Vice-presidents -- United States 2. United States -- Politics and government 3. Vice-Presidents -- United States -- History 4. Vice-Presidents -- United States -- Biography
ISBN 1588344711; 9781588344717
                         LC 2014004242

This book by Jules Witcover is an "examination of the vice presidency throughout American history. Witcover chronicles each of the 47 vice presidents, including their personal biographies and their achievements--or lack thereof--during their vice presidential tenures." (Publisher's note)

"The essays included here are well-rounded, concise perspectives of the vice president's time in office, and in many cases, his pursuits after leaving that position. Adults and motivated high school students could pick and choose from among the entries or read straight through for an inside view of an oft-overlooked position." Library Jorunal

Includes bibliographical references

352.3   Executive management

Moynihan, Daniel Patrick

Secrecy; the American experience. {by} Daniel Patrick Moynihan; introduction by Richard Gid Powers. Yale Univ. Press 1998 262p il $38; pa $16   **352.3**
1. Executive power 2. National security -- United States
ISBN 0-300-07756-4; 0-300-08079-4 pa
                         LC 98-8144

"Using his background as chairman of the bipartisan Commission on Protecting and Reducing Government Secrecy, Moynihan provides a fascinating account of the development of secrecy as a mode of regulation for the U.S.

government since World War I: how it was born, how world events shaped it, how it has adversely affected momentous political decisions—dropping the bomb on Hiroshima, the Bay of Pigs fiasco, the Iran-contra affair—and how it has eluded efforts to curtail or end it." America

Includes bibliographical references

352.4 Financial administration and budgets

Kramer, Mattea
★ A **people's** guide to the federal budget; National Priorities Project; written by Mattea Kramer ... [et al.]; foreword by Barbara Ehrenreich; afterword by Josh Silver. Interlink Books 2012 219 p. (pbk.) $15.00 **352.4**
1. Budget -- United States 2. United States. Congress 3. United States -- Appropriations and expenditures 4. Fiscal policy -- United States 5. Budget deficits -- United States 6. Government spending policy -- United States
ISBN 1566568870; 9781566568876
LC 2012007930

This book focuses on U.S. fiscal policy, government spending, and the federal budget. It "addresses such issues as discretionary and mandatory spending; how the federal government creates a budget; where the money comes from and goes; and the federal debt. . . . Other important priorities include construction of roads and highways, law enforcement, and veterans' assistance." (Booklist)

Includes bibliographical references.

353 Specific fields of public administration

Gentry, Curt
J. Edgar Hoover; the man and the secrets. Norton 1991 846p il hardcover o.p. pa $17.95 **353**
1. FBI officials 2. United States -- Federal Bureau of Investigation
ISBN 0-393-32128-2 pa
LC 90-30576

The author "has based his account of Hoover on more than 300 interviews and on access to previously classified FBI documents. . . . Gentry paints a portrait of Hoover as the 'indispensable man,' with many provocative revelations about his political dealings." Libr J

Includes bibliographical references

353.4 Public administration of justice

Stevenson, Bryan
★ **Just** Mercy; a story of justice and redemption. Bryan Stevenson. First edition Random House Inc 2014 336 p. $28 **353.4**
1. Lawyers 2. Administration of criminal justice 3. Social reformers
ISBN 0812994523; 9780812994520
LC 2014430900
Carnegie Medal: Nonfiction (2015)

Los Angeles Times Book Prize Finalist: Current Interest (2014)

"Bryan Stevenson was a young lawyer when he founded the Equal Justice Initiative, a legal practice dedicated to defending those most desperate and in need: the poor, the wrongly condemned, and women and children trapped in the farthest reaches of our criminal justice system. One of his first cases was that of Walter McMillian, a young man who was sentenced to die for a notorious murder he insisted he didn't commit." (Publisher's note)

"Stevenson details changes in victims' rights, incarceration of juveniles, death penalty reforms, inflexible sentencing laws, and the continued practices of injustice that see too many juveniles, minorities, and mentally ill people imprisoned in a frenzy of mass incarceration in the U.S. A passionate account of the ways our nation thwarts justice and inhumanely punishes the poor and disadvantaged." Booklist

Includes bibliographical references

353.9 Public administration of safety, sanitation, waste control

Hilts, Philip J.
★ **Protecting** America's health; the FDA, business, and one hundred years of regulation. University of North Carolina Press 2004 394p pa $19.95 **353.9**
1. Drug industry 2. Food adulteration and inspection 3. Food -- Law and legislation 4. United States -- Food and Drug Administration
ISBN 978-0-8078-5582-9; 0-8078-5582-0
First published 2003 by Knopf
"This fascinating look at the inside story reveals how disastrous unfettered capitalism would be without reasonable regulation." Booklist
Includes bibliographical references

355 Military science

★ **Amazons** to fighter pilots; a biographical dictionary of military women. Reina Pennington, editor; foreword by Gerhard Weinberg. Greenwood Press 2003 2v il set $175 **355**
1. Reference books 2. Women soldiers -- Biography -- Dictionaries
ISBN 0-313-29197-7
LC 2002-44777

"This peerless work, situated at the nexus of military history and women's studies, is an essential companion to more male-biased biographical resources." Choice

Includes bibliographical references

Arnold, James R.
Jungle of snakes; a century of counterinsurgency warfare from the Philippines to Iraq. Bloomsbury Press 2009 291p map $28 **355**
1. Military history 2. Counterinsurgency
ISBN 978-1-59691-503-9; 1-59691-503-X
LC 2008-54018

The author "studies past insurgency responses to help clarify the U.S. efforts in Iraq. The author investigates four counterinsurgencies that either proved successful in putting down rebellion—the United States in the Philippines following war with Spain in 1898; the British response to the Malayan Emergency in 1948—or disastrous—the French invasion of Algeria in 1830; the U.S. quagmire in Vietnam—and offers lessons to be drawn from them. . . . A reasonably argued work that delivers needed insight and historical precedent to the current war debate." Kirkus

Includes bibliographical references

Axelrod, Alan

★ The **encyclopedia** of the American armed forces. Facts on File 2005 2v il (Facts on File library of American history) set $175 **355**

1. Reference books 2. United States -- Armed forces -- Encyclopedias
ISBN 0-8160-4700-6

LC 2004-20549

"The four sections each document a major branch of the United States military: Army, Navy, Marine Corps, and Air Force. Each branch has an initial list of entries, a list of branch-specific abbreviations and acronyms, and a short bibliography." Choice

Includes bibliographical references

Bacevich, Andrew J., 1947-

Washington rules; America's path to permanent war. [by] Andrew J. Bacevich. Metropolitan Books 2010 286p $25 **355**

1. Military policy -- United States 2. United States -- Foreign relations 3. United States -- Military policy -- Decision making 4. United States -- Foreign relations -- Decision making
ISBN 978-0-8050-9141-0; 0-8050-9141-6

LC 2010-06302

"From Harry S. Truman's presidency to today, Bacevich argues, Americans have trumpeted the credo that they alone must 'lead, save, liberate and ultimately transform the world.'" (N Y Times Book Rev) Index.

"The U.S. spends more on the military than the entire rest of the world combined and maintains 300,000 troops abroad in an 'empire of bases,' all part of a credo of global leadership and a consensus that the U.S. must maintain a state of semiwar. . . . [The author offers an] analysis of the assumptions behind the credo of global leadership and eternal military vigilance that has become increasingly expensive and unsustainable." Booklist

Includes bibliographical references

Belfiore, Michael

★ The **department** of mad scientists; how DARPA is remaking our world, from the Internet to artificial limbs. Smithsonian Books/Harper 2009 xxiii, 295p $26.99; ebook $12.99 **355**

1. Science -- Governmental policy 2. United States -- Advanced Research Projects Agency
ISBN 978-0-06-157793-2; 0-06-157793-6; 978-0-06-195937-0 ebook; 0-06-195937-5 ebook

LC 2009-18015

"Founded by Eisenhower in response to Sputnik and the Soviet space program, DARPA [Defense Advanced Research Projects Agency] mixes military officers with sneaker-wearing scientists, seeking paradigm-shifting ideas in varied fields—from energy, robotics, and rockets to peopleless operating rooms, driverless cars, and planes that can fly halfway around the world in just hours. DARPA gave birth to the Internet, GPS, and mind-controlled robotic arms. . . . Michael Belfiore was given unprecedented access to write this first-ever popular account of DARPA." Bookmarks

Includes bibliographical references

The **Book** of war; edited by John Keegan. Viking 1999 492p hardcover o.p. pa $17 **355**

1. Military history
ISBN 0-14-029655-7 pa

LC 99-42660

This is an "anthology of eyewitness and participant writing covering 25 centuries, from Thucydides' history of the Peloponnesian War to a small-unit engagement between British and Iraqi infantry in the Persian Gulf war." N Y Times Book Rev

Includes bibliographical references

Boot, Max

★ **War** made new; technology, warfare, and the course of history, 1500 to today. Gotham Books 2006 624p il map $24.95 **355**

1. Military history 2. Military art and science
ISBN 978-1-592-40222-9; 1-592-40222-4

LC 2006-15518

"Throughout, Boot provides a vivid and engaging mix of historical narrative and analysis, showing the bloody real-world results of abstract decisionmaking about the nature and degree of a country's military preparedness. His twelve case studies, stretching from the defeat of the Spanish Armada to the current situation in Iraq, point to a variety of disparate lessons but some themes that are surprisingly constant over time and space." Commentary

Buckley, Gail Lumet

★ **American** patriots; the story of Blacks in the military from the Revolution to Desert Storm. [by] Gail Buckley. Random House 2001 xxiv, 534p il hardcover o.p. pa $15.95 **355**

1. African American soldiers 2. United States -- Race relations 3. United States -- Military history
ISBN 0-375-50279-3; 0-375-76009-1 pa

LC 00-51825

This is an account "of blacks in the U.S. military, both at home and abroad, from the 1770s to the 1990s. . . . This readable, spirited story deserves a place in every U.S. history collection, as well as in the black or military collections." Libr J

Includes bibliographical references

Carroll, James

House of war; the Pentagon and the disastrous rise of American power. Houghton Mifflin Co. 2006 657p il $30 **355**

1. Military policy -- United States 2. United States --

Dept. of Defense 3. Pentagon (Arlington, Va.: Building)
ISBN 0-618-18780-4; 978-0-618-18780-5
LC 2005-24014

"Chronicling the ascent of America's military establishment from 1943 to the aftermath of 9/11, Carroll uses the Pentagon as a metaphor for a U.S. political culture that values military power over human rights and seeks to project U.S. influence and values abroad by force, if necessary, whether invited by other countries or not. . . . Certain to be a widely read and discussed book, this is worthy of space on the shelves of all libraries." Libr J
Includes bibliographical references

Clausewitz, Carl von

★ On war; {by} Carl von Clausewitz; edited and translated by Michael Howard and Peter Paret; introductory essays by Peter Paret, Michael Howard and Bernard Brodie; with commentary by Bernard Brodie. Princeton Univ. Press 1976 717p $95; pa $26.95 **355**
1. War 2. Military art and science
ISBN 0-691-05657-9; 0-691-01854-5 pa
Original German edition, 1833

"Drawing on the experiences of Frederick the Great and Napoleon, Clausewitz tried to analyze the workings of military genius by isolating the factors that decide success in war. His conclusions have remained generally applicable, and since his work contains a minimum of technical discussion, it has retained a wide appeal." Ency Britannica

Cohen, Eliot A.

Conquered into liberty. Free Press 2011 405p il map $30; ebook $14.99 **355**
1. New York (State) -- History 2. United States -- Military history 3. United States -- History -- 1755-1763, French and Indian War
ISBN 978-0-7432-4990-4; 978-1-4516-2733-6 ebook
LC 2011023717

It was the author's intent to demonstrate "that there is more to the American military heritage than the U.S.'s conventional war-fighting and its European antecedents. We should expand the concept of 'American' to include pre-revolutionary times, and so include nearly 200 years of frontier fighting . . . In . . . [an] examination of 18th-century warfare along the northeastern seaboard . . . Cohen sees two less-appreciated sources for the way Americans currently fight. First was the birth of a unique strain of raiding, ambushing, subversion, living off the land, ad hoc alliance-building with indigenous peoples, long-range reconnaissance, and patrolling behind enemy lines. Second, writes Cohen, was the very fact that these non-traditional tactics were rooted in the distinctiveness of colonial society. . . . Cohen believes that this legacy endures". (National Review)

This is "an engaging account of the wars fought on the 'Great Warpath.' These were the trails, especially around Lakes George and Champlain, which marked a kind of western border for early settlers. The author recounts the eight major battles in those successive campaigns. He includes two naval battles: Plattsburgh, during the War of 1812, and Valcour Island in 1776, both of which he presents as decisive but underrated contributions to securing the young republic

from foreign threat. . . . A delightful-to-read piece of American history." Kirkus
Includes bibliographical references

Daalder, Ivo H.

In the shadow of the Oval Office; profiles of the national security advisers and the presidents they served: from JFK to George W. Bush. [by] Ivo H. Daalder and I.M. Destler. Simon & Schuster 2009 386p $27 **355**
1. National security -- United States 2. Presidents -- United States -- Staff 3. United States -- Special Assistant to the President for National Security Affairs
ISBN 978-1-416-55319-9; 1-416-55319-3
LC 2008-40699

"A revealing, unsettling look at how our presidents receive advice on foreign policy." Kirkus
Includes bibliographical references

De Pauw, Linda Grant

Battle cries and lullabies; women in war from prehistory to the present. University of Okla. Press 1998 395p il hardcover o.p. pa $21.95 **355**
1. Women soldiers 2. Military history 3. Women -- History
ISBN 0-8061-3288-4 pa
LC 98-21219

"Though the book never directly states its larger claims, the wealth of evidence it provides renders the controversy over women in combat almost quaint—their presence on and near the battlefield is ancient, inescapable and irreversible." Publ Wkly
Includes bibliographical references

Dictionary of wars; George Childs Kohn, editor. 3rd ed.; Facts on File 2006 692p il (Facts on File library of world history) $85; pa $22.95 **355**
1. Reference books 2. Military history -- Dictionaries
ISBN 0-8160-6577-2; 978-0-8160-6577-6; 0-8160-6578-0 pa; 978-0-8160-6578-3 pa
LC 2005-58936

First published 1986

"Entries include the dates of events and a brief summary of their causes, effects, and consequences. The straightforward writing style emphasizes basic facts rather than arguments justifying or opposing each conflict. This, along with the occasional cross-references and helpful and complete general and geographic indexes, makes the encyclopedia accessible to most students." SLJ

Dower, John W., 1938-

Cultures of war; Pearl Harbor, Hiroshima, 9-11, Iraq. New Press 2010 596p il $29.95 **355**
1. Iraq War, 2003-2011 2. War and civilization 3. World War, 1939-1945 4. September 11 terrorist attacks, 2001 5. Iraq War, 2003- 6. Military policy -- United States 7. United States -- Military policy 8. War and society -- United States 9. United States -- History, Military -- 20th century 10. United States -- History, Military -- 21st century
ISBN 978-0-393-06150-5; 0-393-06150-7
LC 2010-20395

The author "draws astute ironies between Pearl Harbor and 9/11 in terms of the overweening arrogance of military superpowers. The author moves back and forth between these two definitive eras in history, providing a brilliant examination of the willful self-delusion and selective reasoning involved in the highest levels of decision making—from Japan's spectacularly ill-advised bombing of Pearl Harbor to the Bush Administration's bundling of 'weapons of mass destruction' and Osama bin Laden as justification for invasion of Iraq. . . . An unrelenting, incisive, masterly comparative study." Kirkus

Includes bibliographical references and index.

★ **Encyclopedia** of American military history; Spencer C. Tucker, general editor; associate editors David Coffey, John C. Fredriksen, Justin D. Murphy. Facts on File 2003 3v il maps set $225   **355**
1. Reference books 2. United States -- Military history -- Encyclopedias
ISBN 0-8160-4355-8

LC 2002-29658

"More than 1,200 entries cover military leaders, wars, campaigns, battles, events, famous soldiers, military branches, key technological developments, overviews of weapons systems, and more. It covers the period from the colonial wars to the present, and gives special attention to the minorities and women who have contributed significantly to American military success." Publisher's note

Includes bibliographical references

The **encyclopedia** of Middle East wars; the United States in the Persian Gulf, Afghanistan, and Iraq conflicts. Spencer C. Tucker, editor; Priscilla Mary Roberts, editor, documents volume; foreword by Anthony C. Zinni. ABC-CLIO 2010 1887p 5v il map set $495   **355**
1. Reference books 2. Iraq War, 2003- -- Encyclopedias 3. Afghan War, 2001- -- Encyclopedias 4. Persian Gulf War, 1991 -- Encyclopedias 5. Middle East -- Military history -- Encyclopedias
ISBN 978-1-85109-947-4; 978-1-85109-948-1 ebook

LC 2010-33812

"An essential resource for anyone seeking detailed information and in-depth reading on U.S. actions and involvement in the Middle East region during the last 15 years." Libr J

Includes bibliographical references

France, John

Perilous glory; the rise of western military power. John France. Yale University Press 2011 ix, 448 p.p ill., maps $35   **355**
1. War -- History 2. War and civilization 3. Military art and science -- History 4. Military history
ISBN 0300120745; 9780300120745

LC 2011006437

In this book, "[John] France acknowledges the significance of democracy . . . and technology in the nineteenth-century transformation of warfare . . . [but] argues . . . that the resulting rise of the 'Western' style of warfare to international significance was largely fortuitous, coinciding with the decline and stagnation of the Ottomans and the Mughals, inheritors of the previously dominant form of steppe warfare that had emerged from Eurasia in antiquity." (Times Literary Supplement)

Fredriksen, John C.

American military leaders; from colonial times to the present. ABC-CLIO 1999 2v il set $175 **355**
1. Soldiers -- United States 2. United States -- Military history
ISBN 1-57607-001-8

LC 99-27929

"Prominent men and women of the military are the scope of this reference work. Coverage includes the most famous of leaders such as Grant, Patton, and Schwarzkopf; but what makes the source so outstanding is its inclusion of forgotten leaders such as Native American Stand Watie, aviator Jackie Cochran, and army educator Alden Partridge. Biographies range from two to three pages, concluding with a bibliography. Photographs and illustrations are included, and both a subject index and a list of leaders organized by their military titles can be found at the end of volume two." Am Libr

Includes bibliographical references

Gordin, Michael D.

Red cloud at dawn; Truman, Stalin, and the end of the atomic monopoly. Farrar, Straus and Giroux 2009 402p il map $27   **355**
1. Arms race 2. Presidents 3. Heads of state 4. Nuclear weapons 5. Vice-presidents 6. Senators 7. Communist leaders 8. Political leaders 9. Nuclear weapons -- History 10. World politics -- 1945-1955 11. Arms race -- History -- 20th century 12. Soviet Union -- Foreign relations -- 1945-1991 13. United States -- Foreign relations -- 1945-1953 14. Soviet Union -- Foreign relations -- United States 15. United States -- Foreign relations -- Soviet Union
ISBN 0-374-25682-9; 978-0-374-25682-1

LC 2009-01424

Gordin examines the years from 1945 to 1949 "in which only the United States possessed atomic weapons." (N Y Times Book Rev) Index.

The author "brings considerable scholarship to the subject of how the Soviets succeeded in building an atomic bomb. He weaves an impressively wide range of sources, including new material from ex-Soviet and western archives, into a brilliant narrative about the intelligence war." Hist Today

Includes bibliographical references

Hagedorn, Ann

The **invisible** soldiers; how America outsourced our security. Ann Hagedorn. Simon & Schuster 2014 352 p. $28   **355**
1. Private military companies 2. National security -- United States 3. United States -- Military policy 4. United States -- Politics and government
ISBN 1416598804; 9781416598800

LC 2014015007

This book, by Ann Hagedorn, is "about the privatization of America's national security. . . . [P]rivate military and security companies (PMSCs) . . . are a bona-fide industry, an indispensable part of American foreign and military policy. PMSCs assist US forces in combat operations and replace them after the military withdraws from combat zones; they guard our embassies; they play key roles in US counterterrorism strategies; and Homeland Security depends on them." (Publisher's note)

"A brisk, disturbing account that adds to the sense that liberties taken in the war on terror have created long-term liabilities for American society." Kirkus

Includes bibliographical references and index

Hanson, Victor Davis

The **father** of us all; war and history, ancient and modern. Bloomsbury 2010 259p $25   355
   1. War 2. Military history
   ISBN 978-1-60819-165-9; 1-60819-165-6
                                          LC 2009-41714

"This anthology brings together 13 of Hanson's essays and reviews, revised and re-edited. They have appeared over the past decade in periodicals from the American Spectator to the New York Times. Hanson's introductory generalization that war is a human enterprise that seems inseparable from the human condition structures such subjects as an eloquent answer to the question 'Why Study War?', a defense of the historicity of the film 300, about the Persian Wars, in a masterpiece of envelope pushing, and a comprehensive and dazzling analysis of why America fights as she does. . . . The pieces are well written, sometimes elegantly so, and closely reasoned." Publ Wkly

Includes bibliographical references

The **soul** of battle; from ancient times to the present day, how three great liberators vanquished tyranny. Anchor Books 2001 480p pa $16.95 355
   1. Generals 2. Military history 3. Memoirists 4. Army officers 5. Secretaries of war
   ISBN 0-385-72059-9; 978-0-385-72059-5
                                          LC 00-63979
First published 1999 by Free Press

"Hanson narrates the success of three military campaigns-Epaminondas defeat of the Spartans in the fourth century B.C., Sherman's march through Georgia and the Carolinas during the Civil War, and Patton's race into Germany at the head of the Third Army in 1944-45. . . . In Hanson's view, the individual traits of spontaneity and creativity that are nourished in a free society are assets, not hindrances, in warfare." Booklist

Includes bibliographical references

Hastings, Max

Warriors; portraits from the battlefield. Knopf 2006 xxiii, 354p il maps $27.50   355
   1. Soldiers 2. Military history
   ISBN 1-4000-4441-3; 978-1-4000-4441-2
                                          LC 2005-44302

The author "selects memoirs and biographies about 15 combatants (one of them a woman) and distills accounts of their lives and trenchant observations about their personalities. . . . Filled with poignant psychological insight, Hastings' remarkable sketches will provoke greater-than-average demand from the military affairs readership." Booklist

Includes bibliographical references

Jacobsen, Annie

The **Pentagon's** Brain; An Uncensored History of DARPA, America's Top-secret Military Research Agency. by Annie Jacobsen. Little, Brown & Co. 2015 560 p. 16 plates; illustrations $30   355
   1. United States. Dept. of Defense 2. United States -- Politics and government
   ISBN 0316371769; 9780316371766
                                          LC 2015304581
Pulitzer Prize Finalist: History (2016)

This book, by Annie Jacobsen, is the "definitive history of DARPA, the Defense Advanced Research Project Agency. . . . Jacobsen draws on inside sources, exclusive interviews, private documents, and declassified memos to paint a picture of DARPA, or 'the Pentagon's brain,' from its Cold War inception in 1958 to the present." (Publisher's note)

"This engrossing, conversation-starting read is highly recommended for policymakers, historians, scientists, and others who study technology's implications. It will complement Jonathon Moreno's Mind Wars and Sarah Bridger's Scientists at War." LJ

Karpin, Michael I.

The **bomb** in the basement; how Israel went nuclear and what that means for the world. [by] Michael Karpin. Simon & Schuster 2006 404p il map $26; pa $15   355
   1. Nuclear weapons 2. Israel -- Military history
   ISBN 0-7432-6594-7; 978-0-7432-6594-2; 0-7432-6595-5 pa; 978-0-7432-6595-9 pa
                                          LC 2005-51689

"For all those interested in understanding how Israel's idealistic origins dovetail with its hawkish position in the game of nuclear deterrence and fraught relationship with other countries in the Middle East, this well-researched study is a must-read." Publ Wkly

Includes bibliographical references

Kindsvatter, Peter S.

American soldiers; ground combat in the World Wars, Korea, and Vietnam. foreword by Russell F. Weigley. University Press of Kan. 2003 432p il (Modern war studies) $34.95   355
   1. Soldiers -- United States 2. United States -- Marine Corps 3. United States -- Army -- Infantry 4. United States -- Military history
   ISBN 0-7006-1229-7
                                          LC 2002-12957

"Mining twentieth-century foot soldiers' memoirs and novels, Kindsvatter integrates this literature of personal experience into a generalized assessment of what combat was like and how men reacted to it. . . . Kindsvatter's illuminating work is about coping with . . . fear at the foxhole level, and it . . . powerfully conveys the psychology and military sociology of combat in the draft-era armies." Booklist

Includes bibliographical references

Langewiesche, William

The **atomic** bazaar; the rise of the nuclear poor. Farrar, Straus and Giroux 2007 179p map $22 **355**

1. Arms control 2. Nuclear weapons

ISBN 978-0-374-10678-2; 0-374-10678-9

LC 2006-102539

"Langewiesche's bracing expose of nuclear criminality blasts away the ubiquitous misinformation usually attendant on this alarming subject." Booklist

Lipsky, David

Absolutely American; four years at West Point. Houghton Mifflin 2003 317p il $25 **355**

1. United States Military Academy

ISBN 0-618-09542-X

LC 2002-191339

"The book must have been extremely hard to organize. And yet it reads with a novelistic flow. . . . It turns out that how teenagers get turned into leaders is not a simple story, but it is wonderfully told in this book." N Y Times Book Rev

Magill's guide to military history; editor, John Powell; managing editor, Christina J. Moose; project editor, Rowena Wildin. Salem Press 2001 5v il set $473 **355**

1. Reference books 2. Military history -- Dictionaries

ISBN 0-89356-014-6

LC 00-66072

This "is a worldwide, illustrated, alphabetical survey of war, weapons, battles, civilizations, people and their place in military history, ancient times to the 21st century. Its 1,518 entries and over 300 thorough essays with keywords in bold-face are all indexed by category in volume 5." Choice

Includes bibliographical references

Nicholson, Alexander

Fighting to serve; behind the scenes in the war to repeal "don't ask, don't tell" Alexander Nicholson. Chicago Review Press 2012 288 p. $26.95 **355**

1. Military policy -- United States 2. Don't ask, don't tell (Military policy) 3. LGBT people -- Legal status, laws, etc. 4. Nicholson, Alexander 5. Servicemembers United (United States) 6. United States. Army -- Gays -- Biography 7. Gay military personnel -- United States -- Biography 8. Gay rights -- United States -- History -- 21st century 9. Gay military personnel -- Government policy -- United States 10. Homosexuality -- Political aspects -- United States -- History -- 21st century

ISBN 1613743726; 9781613743720

LC 2012021821

This book "provides an . . . account of the road to repeal the 'Don't Ask, Don't Tell' (DADT) law prohibiting the open service of" LGBT "military members." Author Alexander Nicholson "offer[s] commentary on a range of incidents: being personally forced out of the army by the DADT policy; meeting and persuading former chairman of the Joint Chiefs of Staff, Gen. John Shalikashvili, of the cause's benefits . . . leading and speaking at rallies; and coordinating directly with the White House." (Publishers Weekly)

Rhodes, Richard

Arsenals of folly; the making of the nuclear arms race. Alfred A. Knopf 2007 386p il $28.95 **355**

1. Arms race 2. Nuclear weapons

ISBN 978-0-375-41413-8; 0-375-41413-4

LC 2007-17613

"This historical record, drawing upon many firsthand accounts and interviews, details pivotal events in world history and should be necessary reading for anyone interested in 20th-century history." Libr J

Includes bibliographical references

Rose, Gideon

How wars end; why we always fight the last battle: a history of American intervention from World War I to Afghanistan. Simon & Schuster 2010 413p $27 **355**

1. War 2. War -- Termination 3. Disengagement (Military science) 4. Military policy -- United States 5. United States -- Military policy 6. United States -- Military history 7. Military planning -- United States 8. United States -- History, Military -- 20th century 9. United States -- History, Military -- 21st century

ISBN 978-1-4165-9053-8; 1-4165-9053-6

LC 2010-34817

"Surveying the settlements of America's wars since WWI, Rose analyzes reasons for the manner and substance of their conclusions. . . . Public spirited and accessible, Rose's presentation should impress anyone hoping for better management of war and peace by Washington." Booklist

Includes bibliographical references

Ruggero, Ed

Duty first; West Point and the making of American leaders. HarperCollins Pubs, 2001 342p il $27.50; pa $14.95 **355**

1. Leadership 2. United States Military Academy

ISBN 0-06-019317-4; 0-06-093133-7 pa

LC 00-59775

In this report about the contemporary West Point experience, the author "tries to explain precisely what makes the United States Military Academy, better known as West Point, a breeding ground for future leaders." Publ Wkly

Singer, P. W.

Wired for war; the robotics revolution and conflict in the twenty-first century. Penguin Press 2009 499p il $29.95 **355**

1. Robots 2. Military weapons 3. Military art and science

ISBN 978-1-59420-198-1; 1-59420-198-6

This is "a vivid picture of the current controversies and dazzling possibilities of war in the digital age." Kirkus

Includes bibliographical references

Sites, Kevin

The **things** they cannot say; stories soldiers won't tell you about what they've seen, done or failed to do in war. Kevin Sites. HarperCollins 2013 336 p. $15.99 **355**

1. Soldiers -- Psychology 2. Afghan War, 2001- --

Personal narratives 3. Iraq War, 2003-2011 -- Personal narratives

ISBN 0061990523; 9780061990526

In this book author Kevin Sites asks soldiers, "many of whom Sites first met while in Afghanistan and Iraq, . . . difficult questions. . . . One struggles to recover from a head injury he believes has stolen his ability to love; another attempts to make amends for the killing of an innocent man; yet another finds respect for the enemy fighter who tried to kill him. Sites also shares the unsettling narrative of his own failures during war--including his complicity in a murder." (Publisher' note)

Sun-tzu

★ The **illustrated** art of war; [by] Sun Tzu; the definitive English translation by Samuel B. Griffith. Oxford University Press 2005 272p il map $29.95　**355**

1. Military art and science

ISBN 0-19-518999-X; 978-0-19-518999-5

LC 2005-10651

An illustrated version of The art of war, a military treatise written in China during the 6th century BC discussing different military tactics and strategies.

Includes bibliographical references

Sutherland, Jonathan

★ **African** Americans at war; an encyclopedia. [by] Jonathan D. Sutherland. ABC-CLIO 2004 2v set $185　**355**

1. Reference books 2. African American soldiers 3. United States -- Armed forces -- Encyclopedias 4. African Americans -- Biography -- Encyclopedias

ISBN 1-57607-746-2

LC 2003-21501

"There are more than 250 [alphabetically arranged] entries conveying biographical, thematic, and conceptual information. Well-known leaders (Colin Powell), groups (Buffalo Soldiers), specific units [and battles] . . . have their own entries. . . . This is a superb resource for any . . . library looking to enrich its history, military or African American studies collections." Booklist

★ **Voices** of war; stories of service from the home front and the front lines. edited by Tom Wiener. National Geographic Society 2004 336p il $30; pa $6.95　**355**

1. Veterans 2. United States -- Military history 3. United States -- Armed forces -- Military life

ISBN 0-7922-7838-0; 0-7922-4204-1 pa

LC 2004-49986

This book showcases "the oral histories collected by the Veteran's History Project, the Library of Congress's nationwide effort to collect and preserve the stories not only of war veterans, but also of those who served in support of the frontline troops. . . . The personal accounts cover the major conflicts of the 20th century, from World War I to the Persian Gulf War, and include letters, diaries, and journals. The chapters are nicely arranged to show the commonalities of military experience, e.g., basic training, daily life, combat, the home front, and returning home." Libr J

★ **War**: from ancient Egypt to Iraq; editorial consultant, Saul David. DK 2009 512p il $50　**355**

1. Reference books 2. War -- Encyclopedias 3. Military history -- Encyclopedias

ISBN 978-0-7566-5572-3

LC 2010-278612

"From the Punic wars to the Crusades to the wars of the league of Cognac and modern conflicts like those in the former Yugoslavia, War is an outstanding catalog of conflict. Each of the seven chapters . . . opens with a time line and is peppered with sidebars of military superlatives such as youngest commanders, famous female warriors, and even landmark war movies. . . . An essential reference title for all libraries." Libr J

355.009　History, geographic treatment, biography

Brands, H. W.

★ The **man** who saved the union; Ulysses Grant in war and peace. H. W. Brands. Doubleday 2012 736 p. $35.00　**355.009**

1. Civil rights 2. Presidents -- United States 3. Generals -- United States -- Biography

ISBN 0385532415; 9780385532419

LC 2011043795

This book offers a biography of U.S. President Ulysses S. Grant. Here, "Pulitzer [prize] finalist [H. W.] Brands . . . treats Grant's entire life, showing its full arc. He breaks with earlier interpretations . . . , concluding that Grant did the best he could in trying circumstances, particularly in the area of civil and minority rights." (Library Journal)

Keegan, John

Fields of battle; the wars for North America. Knopf 1996 348p il maps hardcover o.p. pa $15　**355.009**

1. North America -- Military history

ISBN 0-679-42413-X; 0-679-74664-1 pa

LC 96-154385

First published 1995 in the United Kingdom with title: Warpaths: travels of a military historian in North America

The author "demonstrates how North America's geography has influenced its history: how its mountain chains and river systems have determined where people fought, and fought repeatedly. For example, the defenses that Cornwallis built at Yorktown to deter American forces were improved and reused by the Confederates almost a century later. Keegan's tour of the continent skips the Mexican War, and his book is atypically discursive. For Americans, the charm is the familiarity of its sites—Brooklyn, Pittsburgh, Laramie, and other home towns." New Yorker

★ **New** York at war; Steven H. Jaffe. Basic Books 2012 p. cm.　**355.009**

1. War 2. New York (N.Y.) -- History, Military

ISBN 9780465029709; 9780465036424

LC 2012000454

In this book "historian Steven H. Jaffe offers a . . . history of New York City" from a local, military perspective. "Beginning with an Indian attack on one of Henry Hudson's crewmen (who in 1609 became the first recorded fatality of an act of war in the region's history), Jaffe describes, in turn, each of the city's encounters with war over the past four centuries. . . . [including] how New York became hugely powerful . . . during the Civil War . . . during the build-up to World War I . . . during World War II, and in the atomic era." The book's scope discusses the impact of military and ethnic conflicts in the city "stretching from the colonial era to 9/11 and beyond." (Publisher's note)

Includes bibliographical references

Reader's guide to military history; edited by Charles Messenger. Fitzroy Dearborn Pubs. 2001 xxxvi, 948p $135 **355.009**
1. Military history
ISBN 1-57958-241-9

LC 2002-275907

Topics covered "include land, sea, and air services; conflicts; types of warfare; military theory; prominent military leaders; and national armed services. . . . {This} is a unique, well-designed reference tool." Booklist

Includes bibliographical references

Ricks, Thomas E.
★ The **generals**; American military command from World War II to today. Thomas E. Ricks. Penguin Press 2012 576 p. **355.009**
1. Generals 2. Command of troops 3. United States -- Military history 4. Generals -- United States -- History -- 20th century 5. Command of troops -- History -- 20th century -- Case studies 6. United States -- History, Military -- 20th century -- Case studies
ISBN 1594204047; 9781594204043

LC 2012015110

This book, by Thomas E. Ricks, presents an overview of U.S. military leadership since 1945. "History has been kind to the American generals of World War II--Marshall, Eisenhower, Patton, and Bradley--and less kind to the generals of the wars that followed. . . . Thomas E. Ricks sets out to explain why that is. . . . [W]e meet great leaders and suspect ones, generals who rose to the occasion and those who failed themselves and their soldiers." (Publisher's note)

Includes bibliographical references and index

Wheelan, Joseph
★ **Terrible** swift sword; the life of General Philip H. Sheridan. Joseph Wheelan. Da Capo Press 2012 387 p. (hardcover : alk. paper) $26 **355.009**
1. Native Americans -- History 2. United States -- History -- 1861-1865, Civil War -- Campaigns 3. Native Americans -- Wars 4. United States. Army -- Biography 5. Generals -- United States -- Biography 6. United States -- History -- Civil War, 1861-1865 -- Campaigns
ISBN 0306820277; 9780306820274; 9780306821097

LC 2012018587

This book, by Joseph Wheelan, is a biography of the Civil War general Philip H. Sheridan. "Sheridan is the least known of the triumvirate of generals most responsible for winning the Civil War. . . . It was General Sheridan who introduced scorched-earth warfare to the South. . . . After the war, Sheridan ruthlessly suppressed the raiding Plains Indians much as he had the Confederates, . . . but he also

defended reservation Indians from corrupt agents and contractors." (Publisher's note)

Includes bibliographical references and index

355.02   War and warfare

Gentile, Gian P.
Wrong turn; America's deadly embrace of counterinsurgency. Colonel Gian Gentile. The New Press 2013 208 p. (hardback) $24.95 **355.02**
1. Counterinsurgency 2. Iraq War, 2003-2011 3. Counterinsurgency -- Case studies 4. Counterinsurgency -- Iraq -- History -- 21st century 5. Counterinsurgency -- Malaya -- History -- 20th century 6. Counterinsurgency -- Government policy -- United States 7. Counterinsurgency -- Vietnam -- History -- 20th century 8. Counterinsurgency -- Afghanistan -- History -- 21st century
ISBN 1595588744; 9781595588746

LC 2012049114

In this book about the U.S. Iraq war, Gian Gentile "argues that the U.S. military's appropriation of COIN [counterinsurgency], a strategy with a long and fraught history, as the author explains, was a dangerously misguided attempt 'to refight the Vietnam War—but this time in Iraq.' COIN, in Gentile's estimation, is little more than 'a recipe for perpetual war.'" (Publishers Weekly)

Includes bibliographical references and index

Hedges, Chris
War is a force that gives us meaning. PublicAffairs 2002 211p $23 **355.02**
1. War
ISBN 1-58648-049-9

LC 2002-68136

"This should be required reading in this post-9/11 world." Libr J

Includes bibliographical references

Scahill, Jeremy, 1974-
Dirty wars; the world is a battlefield. Jeremy Scahill. Nation Books 2013 680 p. (hbk.) $29.99 **355.02**
1. Military intelligence 2. Terrorism -- Prevention 3. Military art and science 4. United States -- History, Military -- 21st century 5. United States -- Military policy -- History -- 21st century 6. Targeted killing -- United States -- History -- 21st century 7. United States -- Military policy -- Moral and ethical aspects 8. Intelligence service -- United States -- History -- 21st century 9. Special operations (Military science) -- United States -- History -- 21st century 10. Terrorism -- Prevention -- United States -- Government policy -- History -- 21st century
ISBN 156858671X; 9781568586717

LC 2012051769

In this book, author Jeremy Scahill "questions the legality and command methods of the ongoing war against al-Qaida. Focusing on the career of Anwar al Awlaki, an American citizen and reported al-Qaida leader killed by a drone in Yemen, and the evolution of special forces-led global strikes, the author seeks to establish his case that Barack Obama's military policies are best seen as a continuation of the policies of George W. Bush." (Kirkus Reviews)

Includes bibliographical references (pages 531-613) and index

Wilson, Ward

Five myths about nuclear weapons; Ward Wilson. Houghton Mifflin Harcourt 2013 208 p. $22 **355.02**

1. Arms control 2. Nuclear warfare 3. Nuclear weapons 4. Strategy 5. Nuclear weapons -- Psychological aspects
ISBN 054785787X; 9780547857879

LC 2012017322

This book, by Ward Wilson, offers a "rethinking of the power and purpose of nuclear weapons--and a call for radical action. Nuclear weapons have always been a serious but seemingly insoluble problem: while they're obviously dangerous, they are also, apparently, necessary. This . . . study shows why five central arguments promoting nuclear weapons are, in essence, myths." (Publisher's note)

"This slim, persuasively argued, tightly written book provides much food for thought." Booklist

355.07   Military research and development

Roach, Mary, 1959-

Grunt; The Curious Science of Humans at War. Mary Roach. W W Norton & Co Inc 2016 256 p. illustrations $26.95 **355.07**

1. War 2. Soldiers -- Psychology
ISBN 0393245446; 9780393245448

LC 2016008754

This book, by Mary Roach, examines "the science behind some of a soldier's most challenging adversaries--panic, exhaustion, heat, noise--and introduces us to the scientists who seek to conquer them. Roach samples caffeinated meat, sniffs an archival sample of a World War II stink bomb, and stays up all night with the crew tending the missiles on the nuclear submarine USS Tennessee." (Publisher's note)

"Roach's book is not for the squeamish or those who envision war as a glorious enterprise; it is a captivating look at the lengths scientists go to in order to reduce the horrors of war." Pub Wkly

Includes bibliographical references (pages [277]-285).

355.1   Military life and customs

Hickman, Joseph

Murder at Camp Delta; a staff sergeant's pursuit of the truth about Guantanamo Bay. Joseph Hickman. Simon & Schuster 2014 240 p. (hardcover : alk. paper) $28 **355.1**

1. Civil rights 2. Prisoners of war 3. Guantanamo Bay Detention Camp 4. War on Terrorism, 2001-2009 5. Guantánamo Bay Detention Camp 6. United States. Marine Corps -- Officers 7. Reporters and reporting -- United States 8. Prisoners -- Civil rights -- United States 9. Political prisoners -- Cuba -- Guantánamo Bay Naval Base 10. Detention of unlawful combatants --

Cuba -- Guantánamo Bay Naval Base
ISBN 9781451650792; 9781451650808

LC 2014012099

This book by Joseph Hickman presents an "account of abuse and secrecy at the Guantánamo Bay military prison. . . . Although Hickman suspected that many detainees were potentially dangerous jihadi, he was disturbed by the unprovoked harassment and abuse handed out by the guards. His unease climaxed in June 2006, when, on his supervisory watch, three inmates died mysteriously." The book recounts Hickman's participation in "a six-year investigation" of the deaths. (Kirkus Reviews)

"Some readers will see this book as a traitorous attack on patriots protecting the United States from fanatics by any means, while others will view it as confirmation from a veteran that an out-of-control government and individuals went way beyond the law—and gained nothing but trouble from it." LJ

Scott, Jeff

Raising children in the military; Cheryl Lawhorne-Scott, Don Philpott, and Jeff Scott. Rowman & Littlefield 2014 224 p. (Military life) (cloth : alk. paper) $36 **355.1**

1. Children of military personnel 2. Military personnel -- United States 3. Child rearing -- United States -- Handbooks, manuals, etc 4. United States -- Armed Forces -- Military life -- Handbooks, manuals, etc 5. Children of military personnel -- United States -- Handbooks, manuals, etc 6. Families of military personnel -- United States -- Handbooks, manuals, etc
ISBN 1442227486; 9781442227484

LC 2013046688

This book by Cheryl Lawhorne-Scott, Don Philpott, and Jeff Scott, part of the Military Life series, describes how "[m]ilitary life places unique demands on military families with children including frequent moves, disruptions in schooling, family separation, health care issues, loss of friends. . . . It also covers other critical issues such as wellness, family solidarity, benefits, insurance and problems such as addiction and domestic violence." (Publisher's note)

"This is a helpful guide aimed at the special challenges of military families." Booklist

355.3   Organization and personnel of military forces

Geraghty, Tony

Soldiers of fortune; a history of the mercenary in modern warfare. Pegasus Books 2009 392p il $27.95 **355.3**

1. Mercenary soldiers
ISBN 978-1-60598-048-5; 1-60598-048-X

"Covering the 1960s to the present, with revealing interviews, Geraghty looks at the virtues and failings of the world's second-oldest profession. . . . This serious study should find its way to most readers of military history." Libr J

Includes bibliographical references

Harris, Shane

@WAR; the rise of the military-Internet complex. Shane Harris. Houghton Mifflin Harcourt 2014 304 p. (hardcover) $27   **355.3**

1. War 2. Technology 3. Military art and science 4. Information warfare -- United States 5. United States. National Security Agency 6. Cyberterrorism -- Prevention -- Government policy 7. Computer crimes -- Prevention -- Government policy 8. Cyberspace -- Security measures -- Government policy 9. United States. Strategic Command (2002-). Cyber Command
ISBN 0544251792; 9780544251793

LC 2014016741

Author "Shane Harris delves into the frontlines of America's new cyber war. As recent revelations have shown, government agencies are joining with tech giants like Google and Facebook to collect vast amounts of information. The military has also formed a new alliance with tech and finance companies to patrol cyberspace, and Harris offers a deeper glimpse into this partnership than we have ever seen before." (Publisher's note)

Includes bibliographical references and index

Lawhorne-Scott, Cheryl

★ Military mental health care; a guide for service members, veterans, families, and community. Cheryl Lawhorne and Don Philpott. Rowman & Littlefield Publishers, Inc. 2012 240 p. (Military life) (cloth : alk. paper) $34.95   **355.3**

1. Mental health services 2. Military personnel -- Health and hygiene 3. Psychology, Military -- Handbooks, manuals, etc 4. Veterans' families -- United States -- Handbooks, manuals, etc 5. Soldiers -- Mental health -- United States -- Handbooks, manuals, etc 6. Veterans -- Mental health -- United States -- Handbooks, manuals, etc
ISBN 1442220937; 9781442220935; 9781442220942

LC 2012034879

This book is a "reference guide on mental health for returning veterans. Chapters cover problems (e.g., PTSD, head injuries), symptoms (e.g., stress, anger, depression), social issues (e.g., suicide, homelessness, family relationships), resilience, and wellness. Self-help sections include bulleted lists, suggested websites, and resources from the Veterans Administration and other service agencies." (Library Journal)

Includes bibliographical references and index

Paglen, Trevor, 1974-

Blank spots on the map; the dark geography of the Pentagon's secret world. Dutton/Penguin Group 2009 324p il map   **355.3**

1. Military bases 2. Intelligence service -- United States
ISBN 9780525951018

LC 2008042862

The author "explores the clandestine activities of the U.S. military and the CIA, giving readers a thorough and provocative tour of places that officially do not exist. Paglen has a brisk reporting style and is an engaging storyteller. His journey into what he calls the 'black world' of classified lo-

cations—from research facilities to secret prisons—this time takes him across the country and around the world." Libr J

Includes bibliographical references

355.4   Military operations

Kilcullen, David

The accidental guerrilla; fighting small wars in the midst of a big one. Oxford University Press 2009 xxviii, 346p il map $27.95   **355.4**

1. Guerrilla warfare 2. War on terrorism
ISBN 978-0-19-536834-5

LC 2008-54870

This "excellent book has an anthropologist's sense of social dynamics and a reporter's eye for telling detail. . . . [The author's] account of how the Americans use soft and hard power to pacify parts of eastern Afghanistan . . . should be compulsory reading in military academies on both sides of the Atlantic." Economist

Includes bibliographical references

355.5   Military training

Man, John

Ninja; 1,000 years of the shadow warrior. John Man. William Morrow 2013 304 p. (hardcover) $25.99   **355.5**

1. Ninja 2. Ninjutsu 3. Ninja -- History 4. Ninjutsu -- History
ISBN 0062222023; 9780062222022

LC 2012031912

This book, by John Man, offers a popular history "of the Japanese stealth assassins. . . . [The book] is a . . . blend of mythology, anthropology, travelogue, and history of the legendary shadow warriors. Spies, assassins, saboteurs, and secret agents, Ninja have become the subject of countless legends that continue to enthrall us in modern movies, video games, and comics--and their arts are still practiced in our time by dedicated acolytes who study the ancient techniques." (Publisher's note)

Includes bibliographical references and index

355.6   Military administration

Vogel, Steve

The Pentagon; a history: the untold story of the wartime race to build the Pentagon--and to restore it sixty years later. Random House 2007 xxv, 626p il map $32.95   **355.6**

1. Public buildings -- United States 2. United States -- Dept. of Defense 3. Pentagon (Arlington, Va.; Building)
ISBN 978-1-4000-6303-1; 1-4000-6303-5

LC 2006-50873

Vogel's "work recounts the construction of one of the world's most iconic buildings—the Pentagon. But more compelling by far, he relates the human stories underlying this huge construction effort. . . . All this would of itself be enough to warrant a book but Vogel plunges on to an appropriate second story: the terrorist assault of 9/11 and the Pentagon's subsequent resurrection. This section of the book, due perhaps to the proximity of the event, is all the more compelling." New York Post

Includes bibliographical references

355.8 Military equipment and supplies (Material)

Baggott, J. E.

The **first** war of physics; the secret history of the atom bomb, 1939-1949. [by] Jim Baggott. Pegasus Books 2010 576p il $35   **355.8**
1. Atomic bomb
ISBN 978-1-60598-084-3; 1-60598-084-6
First published 2009 in the United Kingdom with title: Atomic

"Baggott contributes a novel perspective to the story, looking at the Anglo-American, German, and Soviet atomic programs, and as such provides a broad thematic history." Libr J

Includes bibliographical references

Levy, Joel

Fifty Weapons That Changed the Course of History; Joel Levy. Firefly Books Ltd 2014 224 p. illustrations (some color) $29.95   **355.8**
1. Weapons 2. Military history
ISBN 1770854266; 9781770854260
Author Joel Levy presents this "guide to the arms and armaments that have had the greatest impact on the development of human civilization. Like the other titles in this series, the book organizes the weapons into brief illustrated chapters. The stories span human history, from our hunter-gatherer ancestors who devised the spear and the wheel, which brought about the war chariot, to gunpowder, which democratized warfare and has been the basis for almost every weapon used in war from that point on." (Publisher's note)

"The format, layout, and liveliness of the text enhance its readability. A list of further reading, useful websites, and an accurate index further the volume's usefulness. With its modest price, this book is recommended for a wide range of public, school, and academic libraries." Booklist

Light, Michael

100 suns, 1945-1962. Knopf 2003 208p il $49.95   **355.8**
1. Nuclear weapons -- Pictorial works
ISBN 1-4000-4113-9

LC 2003-106275
"The 'suns' Light presents to readers in this . . . photography collection are manmade: aboveground atomic detonations captured on film both in the Nevada desert and at sea, terrifyingly beautiful images that remind readers of the apocalyptic might of nuclear weapons." Booklist

Includes bibliographical references

Pollack, Kenneth M.

Unthinkable; Iran, the Bomb, and American Strategy. Kenneth M. Pollack. Simon & Schuster 2013 560 p. illustration, maps $30   **355.8**
1. Nuclear weapons 2. Iran -- Foreign relations -- United States 3. United States -- Foreign relations -- Iran 4. Nuclear weapons -- Iran 5. Nuclear nonproliferation -- Iran 6. Iran -- Politics and government -- 21st century 7. Nuclear arms control -- Government policy -- United States
ISBN 1476733929; 9781476733920

LC 2013431171
In this book on U.S. relations with Iran, author Kenneth Pollack "clearly states his preference for containment but not before thoroughly exploring the pros and cons of a military attack (including one by Israel) and not without conceding the dangers of the policy he recommends. As the Cold War demonstrated, the path of nuclear deterrence and containment is a difficult slog, but this choice . . . . is likely less bad than the alternative." (Kirkus Reviews)

Includes bibliographical references (pages 429-512) and index

Preston, Diana

Before the fallout; from Marie Curie to Hiroshima. Walker 2005 438p il $27   **355.8**
1. Atomic bomb
ISBN 0-8027-1445-5

LC 2004-61953
"Avidly researched and gracefully constructed, Preston's revelatory history is rich in telling moments, powerful personalities, intense confrontations, and indelible images of the devastation delivered by nuclear weapons, our Damoclean sword." Booklist

Includes bibliographical references

356 Specific kinds of military forces and warfare

Carney, John T.

No room for error; the covert operations of America's special tactics units from Iran to Afghanistan, {by} John T. Carney Jr. and Benjamin F. Schemmer. Ballantine Books 2003 334p il map $25.95   **356**
1. Military art and science 2. United States -- Army -- Special Forces
ISBN 0-345-45333-6

LC 2002-28158
The author's "dramatic tales place special operations history in perspective, particularly as the war in Afghanistan has been led by special forces units." Publ Wkly

Includes bibliographical references

Couch, Dick

Sua sponte; the forging of a modern American Ranger. Dick Couch. Berkley Books 2012 364 p.   **356**
1. Commando troops 2. United States. Army 3. Special forces (Military science) -- United States 4. United States. Army. Ranger Regiment, 75th 5. United States.

Army -- Commando troops -- Training of 6. United States. Army. Ranger Regiment, 75th -- Recruiting, enlistment, etc

ISBN 0425247589; 9780425247587

LC 2011038693

This book, by Dick Couch, profiles the U.S. Army Rangers. "They stand alone, even among our other Special Operations forces, as the most active brigade-sized force in the current Global War on Terrorism. . . . Granted . . . access to the training of this highly-restricted component of America's Special Operations Forces in a time of war, . . . Couch tells the personal story of the young men who begin this difficult and dangerous journey to become a Ranger." (Publisher's note)

Halevi, Yossi Klein

Like dreamers; the story of the Israeli paratroopers who reunited Jerusalem and divided a nation. Yossi Klein Halevi. HarperCollins Publishers 2013 608 p. (hardcover : alk. paper) $35   **356**

1. Israel -- History 2. Israel-Arab War, 1967 3. Arab-Israeli conflict -- 1967-1973 4. Arab-Israeli conflict -- 1973-1993 5. Israel -- Parachute troops -- Biography 6. Israel. Tseva haganah le-Yiśra'el -- Parachute troops -- History -- 20th century 7. Israel. Tseva haganah le-Yiśra'el. Hel-ha-tsanhanim -- History -- 20th century

ISBN 0060545763; 9780060545765; 9780060545772; 9780062274823

LC 2013018850

National Jewish Book Awards: Jewish Book of the Year (2013)

In this book, author Yossi Klein Halevi, "interweaves the stories of a group of 1967 paratroopers who reunited Jerusalem, tracing the history of Israel and the divergent ideologies shaping it from the Six-Day War to the present. Following the lives of seven young members from the 55th Paratroopers Reserve Brigade . . . Halevi reveals how this band of brothers played pivotal roles in shaping Israel's destiny long after their historic victory." (Publisher's note)

Includes bibliographical references

Haney, Eric L.

★ Inside Delta Force; the story of America's elite counterterrorist unit. Delacorte Press 2002 324p il hardcover o.p. pa $14   **356**

1. United States -- Army -- Delta Force

ISBN 0-385-33603-9; 0-385-33936-4 pa

LC 2001-58408

The author relates his "experiences during the formation and early operations of 1st Special Forces Operational Detachment-Delta. . . . He served three times in Beirut guarding the American ambassador, participated in the invasion of Grenada, served in several Central American countries and narrowly escaped death during the abortive rescue attempt of the American hostages in Iran. . . . Readers of other special forces memoirs will find this one distinctive for Haney's attention to interservice rivalries . . . that he believes compromised several missions, as well as for Haney's nuanced, often disgusted descriptions of the human cost of war." Publ Wkly

Mazzetti, Mark

The **way** of the knife; the CIA, a secret army, and a war at the ends of the Earth. Mark Mazzetti. The Penguin Press 2013 400 p. $29.95   **356**

1. Terrorism 2. Military policy -- United States 3. United States. Dept. of Defense 4. Interagency coordination -- United States 5. United States. Central Intelligence Agency 6. United States -- Military policy -- Decision making 7. National security -- United States -- Decision making

ISBN 1594204802; 9781594204807

LC 2013006820

In this book, "Pulitzer Prize-winning New York Times national security correspondent [Mark] Mazzetti demonstrates in . . . detail how the new-style warfare approved by both George W. Bush and Barack Obama has led to controversial assassinations by the U.S. government and blowback yielding new terrorists determined to harm American citizens." (Kirkus Reviews)

Includes bibliographical references and index

357   Mounted forces and warfare

Cotterell, Arthur

Chariot; from chariot to tank, the astounding rise and fall of the world's first war machine. Overlook Press 2005 344p il map $29.95   **357**

1. Military art and science

ISBN 1-58567-667-5

LC 2004-65980

"This work is a welcome addition to a collection specializing in military history or ancient history but will appeal to general readers as well because the writing is accessible despite the plethora of detail." Libr J

Includes bibliographical references

358   Air and other specialized forces and warfare; engineering and related services

Engelberg, Stephen

Germs; America's secret war against biological weapons. Judith Miller, Stephen Engelberg, William Broad. Simon & Schuster 2001 382p $27; pa $14   **358**

1. Biological warfare

ISBN 0-684-87158-0; 0-684-87159-9 pa

LC 2001-42690

Three reporters survey the history of biological weapons and recount incidents of their use by terrorist groups. They explain why advances in biology and the spread of germ weapons poses grave risks as countries such as Iran, Iraq and North Korea continually engage in research

Includes bibliographical references

Guillemin, Jeanne

★ **Biological** weapons; from the invention of state-sponsored programs to contemporary bioterrorism. Columbia University Press 2005 258p $75; pa $22.95 **358**

1. Biological warfare
ISBN 0-231-12942-4; 0-231-12943-2 pa
LC 2004-51911

This is a "history of biological weaponry, beginning with the British, American and Japanese programs that predate WWII. . . . Admirably free of finger-pointing, shrillness and Luddite tendencies, the book ranks high as a historical introduction to the subject and a handbook on contemporary remedies." Publ Wkly

Includes bibliographical references

Lockwood, Jeffrey A.

Six-legged soldiers; using insects as weapons of war. Oxford University Press 2009 xx, 377p il $27.95 **358**

1. Biological warfare 2. Insects as carriers of disease
ISBN 978-0-19-533305-3; 0-19-533305-5
LC 2008-6935

"Both science and military history buffs will learn much from Lockwood." Publ Wkly

Includes bibliographical references (p. 315-322)

Tucker, Jonathan B.

★ **War** of nerves; chemical warfare from World War I to al-Qaeda. Pantheon Books 2006 479p il $30; pa $17.95 **358**

1. Chemical warfare
ISBN 0-375-42229-3; 978-0-375-42229-4; 1-4000-3233-4 pa; 978-1-4000-3233-4 pa
LC 2005-50053

This "book makes a sobering case for a less poisonous world." N Y Times Book Rev

Includes bibliographical references

Weapons of mass destruction; an encyclopedia of worldwide policy, technology, and history. Eric A. Croddy and James J. Wirtz, editors. ABC-CLIO 2004 2v il set $185 **358**

1. Nuclear weapons 2. Chemical warfare 3. Biological warfare
ISBN 1-85109-490-3
LC 2004-24651

"No other reference source covers such a wide array of topics related to WMD. It will dispel many myths but will also draw attention to the lethal consequences of WMD." Booklist

Includes bibliographical references

358.4 Air forces and warfare

Jacobsen, Annie

Area 51; an uncensored history of America's top secret military base. Little, Brown 2011 523p il map $27.99 **358.4**

1. Area 51 (Nev.)
ISBN 978-0-316-13294-7; 0-316-13294-2

"Seventy-five miles north of Las Vegas sits a land parcel in the middle of the desert. Called Area 51, the parcel is just outside of the abandoned Nevada Test and Training Range, where more than 100 atmospheric bomb tests were conducted in the 1950s. Officially, the U.S. government has never acknowledged the existence of Area 51. Unofficially, it has become a place associated with conspiracy theories, alien landings and tiny spaceships. Journalist Annie Jacobsen . . . [reveals] that the site has remained classified for many years — not because of aliens or spaceships, but because the government once used the site for top-secret nuclear testing and weapons development. . . Jacobsen details how several agencies — including the Atomic Energy Commission, the Department of Defense and the CIA — once used the site to conduct controversial and secretive research on aircraft and pilot-related projects." NPR

Includes bibliographical references

Wildsmith, Snow

Joining the United States Air Force; a handbook. Snow Wildsmith. McFarland & Co. 2012 x, 229 p.p (Joining the military) (pbk. : alk. paper) $25 **358.4**

1. Employment 2. United States -- Armed forces 3. Military personnel -- United States 4. United States. Air Force -- Vocational guidance
ISBN 0786447583; 9780786447589
LC 2012010677

Author Snow Wildsmith presents a book on the U.S. Air Force. "This book is for the teenager or young adult who is interested in enlisting in the United States Air Force. It will walk him or her through the enlistment and recruit training process: making the decision to join the military, talking to recruiters, getting qualified, preparing for and learning what to expect at basic recruit training." (Publisher's note)

Includes bibliographical references and index

359 Sea forces and warfare

Crowley, Roger

Empires of the sea; the siege of Malta, the battle of Lepanto, and the contest for the center of the world. Random House 2008 336p il map $30; pa $16 **359**

1. Naval battles 2. Christianity and other religions 3. Europe -- Naval history 4. Islam -- Relations -- Christianity
ISBN 978-1-4000-6624-7; 1-4000-6624-7; 978-0-8129-7764-6 pa; 0-8129-7764-5 pa
LC 2007-33794

This book "is well-crafted narrative history in the best sense of the word, lucid, colorful, and beautifully written. . . . Crowley draws on a wealth of sources reflecting a multiplicity of viewpoints and the results are convincing." Journal of Military History

Includes bibliographical references

Grant, R. G.

Battle at sea; 3,000 years of naval warfare. written by R.G. Grant. DK Pub. 2008 360p il map $40 **359**

1. Naval history 2. Naval art and science
ISBN 978-0-7566-3973-0
LC 2008-10019

"This oversized book . . . is perhaps the most comprehensive one-volume history of war at sea, covering engagements large and small, from 1200 B.C.E. to the present day. . . . Highly recommended." Libr J

★ **Naval** warfare; an international encyclopedia. edited by Spencer C. Tucker; associate editors, John Fredriksen {et al.}; introduction by James C. Bradford. ABC-CLIO 2002 3v il maps set $295 **359**
1. Reference books 2. Naval art and science -- Encyclopedias
ISBN 1-57607-219-3
LC 2002-4401

This set "explores the history of combat at sea, from ancient Greek galleys to the sophisticated ships of the U.S. Sixth Fleet. More than 1500 signed entries . . . describe the three key eras: Age of Galley Warfare, Age of Sail, and Age of Steam or Modern Era. . . . Each new development is examined in painstaking detail." Libr J
Includes bibliographical references

Toll, Ian W.
★ **Six** frigates; the epic history of the founding of the U.S. Navy. Norton 2006 560p il map $27.95 **359**
1. United States -- Navy
ISBN 978-0-393-05847-5; 0-393-05847-6
LC 2006-20769

This is "a must-read for fans of naval history and the early American Republic." Publ Wkly
Includes bibliographical references

359.9 Specialized combat forces; engineering and related services

Couch, Dick
The **warrior** elite; the forging of Seal Class 228. photographs by Cliff Hollenbeck. Crown 2001 319p il hardcover o.p. pa $14.95 **359.9**
1. United States -- Navy -- Sea Air Land Team
ISBN 1-4000-4695-5 pa
LC 2001-28368

This is an account of the Basic Underwater Demolition course, (BUD) training for the U.S. Navy Sea Air Land Team (SEALs)
This book "is unique. Couch, a Vietnam-era SEAL and retired naval reserve captain was given the most complete access possible. . . . On view is much serious thought by serious thinkers on the making of warriors at the dawn of the twenty-first century." Booklist

Parrish, Thomas
★ The **submarine**; a history. Viking 2004 576p il $29.95; pa $16 **359.9**
1. Submarines
ISBN 0-670-03313-8; 0-14-303519-3 pa
LC 2003-70515

"This brilliant, dramatic account of submarines and the men who sailed in them is a required acquisition for every military history collection." Choice
Includes bibliographical references

359.984 Special warfare services

Henican, Ellis
Worth dying for; a Navy Seal's call to a nation. Rorke Denver and Ellis Henican. Howard Books, an imprint of Simon & Schuster, Inc. 2016 230 p. (hardcover) $24 **359.984**
1. Heroes and heroines 2. Military policy -- United States 3. Military personnel -- United States 4. Terrorism -- Prevention 5. United States. Navy. SEALs 6. War on Terrorism, 2001-2009 7. United States. Navy -- Commando troops
ISBN 1501124110; 9781501124112; 9781501125683
LC 2015034024

In this book, by Rorke Denver and Ellis Henican, "tackles the questions that have emerged about America's past decade at war—from what makes a hero to why we fight and what it does to us. Heroes are not always the guys who jump on grenades. Sometimes, they are the snipers who decide to hold their fire, the wounded operators who find fresh ways to contribute, or the wives who keep the families together back home." (Publisher's note)

361.2 Social action

Rieff, David
A **bed** for the night; humanitarianism in crisis. Simon & Schuster 2002 367p $26; pa $15 **361.2**
1. International agencies 2. War relief 3. Humanitarianism 4. International relief
ISBN 0-684-80977-X; 0-7432-5211-X pa
LC 2002-29432

This book argues that "humanitarian organizations trying to bring relief in an ever more violent and dangerous world are often betrayed and misused, and have increasingly lost sight of their purpose." (Publisher's note) Index.
Readers "will come away from this passionate, eloquent argument with a distinctly clearer understanding of the complex moral issues facing humanitarian aid in a world filled with brutality and suffering." Publ Wkly
Includes bibliographical references

361.7 Private action

Addams, Jane
Twenty years at Hull-House. **361.7**
1. Authors 2. Philanthropists 3. Hull House (Chicago, Ill.) 4. Essayists 5. Pacifists 6. Social welfare leaders 7. Nobel laureates for peace 8. Chicago (Ill.) -- Social conditions
ISBN 9780486457499
"This classic of the reform era is actually an autobiography of the woman who practically founded social ser-

vice work in this country. . . . It tells her life story, but the greater part of it is devoted to the setting up of Chicago's Hull House, the first settlement house in the United States." Guide to Read in Am Hist

Budd, Ken

The **voluntourist**; a six-country tale of love, loss, fatherhood, fate, and singing Bon Jovi in Bethlehem, Ken Budd. 1st ed. William Morrow 2012 451 p. ill. (acid-free paper) $15.99   **361.7**
    1. Social action 2. Volunteer work 3. Self-realization 4. Voluntarism 5. Social service 6. Parents -- Death 7. Adult children -- Psychology
    ISBN 006194646X; 9780061946462
                      LC 2011032000
  "In this . . . memoir, [Ken] Budd . . . records how he changes 'emotionally, physically, spiritually' as he travels to work with 'people with real problems and different perspectives.' Budd begins his journey in New Orleans . . . then moves on to . . . rural Costa Rica. But these two experiences become the genesis of a broader project -- the heart of his memoir -- to make four more trips in nine months, volunteering in Asia, South America, the Middle East, and Africa." (Publishers Weekly)

Zunz, Olivier

Philanthropy in America; a history. Olivier Zunz. Princeton University Press 2012 x, 381 p.p $29.95   **361.7**
    1. Charities 2. Philanthropy -- History 3. Philanthropy -- United States 4. Humanitarianism -- History 5. Charities -- United States -- History 6. Endowments -- United States -- History 7. Nonprofit organizations -- United States -- History
    ISBN 0691128367; 9780691128368 (hardcover : alk. paper)
                      LC 2011017479
  This book "trace[s]the evolution of American philanthropy over the past 150 years and its contribution to democracy and civil society." It "focus[es] . . . on the extent to which foundations and other grantmaking programs have been involved in shaping national affairs and public policy. . . . Zunz explains the transformation of charitable giving from individual acts of financial relief to the formidable efforts of institutions to influence education, health, and welfare policies." (Nation)
  Includes bibliographical references and index

362   Specific social problems and services

Manguso, Sarah

The **two** kinds of decay. Farrar, Straus and Giroux 2008 184p $22; pa $14   **362**
    1. Poets 2. Authors 3. Editors 4. Guillain-Barré syndrome
    ISBN 978-0-374-28012-3; 0-374-28012-6; 978-0-312-42844-0 pa; 0-312-42844-8 pa
                      LC 2008-1766
  "What makes this lightning-quick book extraordinary is not just Manguso's deadpan delivery of often unthinkable details, nor her poet's struggle with the damaging metaphors

of disease, but the compassion she acquires as she comes to understand her pain in relation to the pain of others." Publ Wkly

362.1   People with illnesses and disabilities

Blumenthal, David

The **heart** of power; health and politics in the Oval Office. [by] David Blumenthal and James A. Morone. University of California Press 2009 484p il $26.95   **362.1**
    1. Medical care -- Government policy 2. Presidents -- United States -- Health
    ISBN 978-0-520-26030-6; 0-520-26030-9
                      LC 2008-54361
  "More than an excellent primer on American health policy, the book offers a thorough, incisive look at the presidency as an institution and the men who have occupied the office." Publ Wkly
  Includes bibliographical references

Chase, Marilyn

The **Barbary** plague; the Black Death in Victorian San Francisco. Random House 2003 276p map $25.95; pa $13.95   **362.1**
    1. Plague 2. San Francisco (Calif.)
    ISBN 0-375-50496-6; 0-375-75708-2 pa
                      LC 2002-68102
  This is "a pleasure to read, full of people, dramatic situations, individual foibles and collective hard work. I closed the book wishing it had been longer." N Y Times Book Rev

Crosby, Molly Caldwell

Asleep; the forgotten epidemic that remains one of medicine's greatest mysteries. Berkley Books 2010 291p il $24.95   **362.1**
    1. Epidemics 2. Encephalitis
    ISBN 978-0-425-22570-7; 0-425-22570-4
                      LC 2009-34928
  "Crosby is a fine storyteller, peppering her case studies with facts about the history of neurology and details about 1910s New York. She also provides fully realized portraits of not only her case studies' patients, but also the brilliant doctors who treated them. . . . A capable, readable account of a medical mystery." Kirkus
  Includes bibliographical references

Encyclopedia of public health; edited by Lester Breslow. Macmillan Ref. USA 2001 4v set $475   **362.1**
    1. Reference books 2. Public health -- Encyclopedias
    ISBN 0-02-865354-8
                      LC 2001-31501
  "Information on more than 900 programs, services, organizations, health behaviors, and the prevalence, epidemiology, and costs of communicable diseases. Although the work focuses on the United States, there are also references to worldwide problems." Libr J

Farley, Tom

Saving Gotham; a billionaire mayor, activist doctors, and the fight for eight million lives. Tom Farley. W W Norton & Co Inc 2015 304 p. (ebook) $50; (hardcover) $27.95 **362.1**

1. Public health 2. Health Policy -- New York City -- Personal Narratives 3. Environmental Health -- New York City -- Personal Narratives 4. Public Health -- methods -- New York City -- Personal Narratives 5. Preventive Health Services -- New York City -- Personal Narratives 6. Chronic Disease -- prevention & control -- New York City -- Personal Narratives

ISBN 9780393248807; 9780393071245

LC 2015022457

In this book, by Tom Farley, "in 2002, a dynamic doctor named Thomas Frieden became health commissioner of New York City. With support from the new mayor, billionaire Michael Bloomberg, Frieden and his health department team prohibited smoking in bars, outlawed trans fats in restaurants, and attempted to cap the size of sodas, among other groundbreaking actions. The initiatives drew heated criticism, but they worked." (Publisher's note)

"An inspiring story in which the author demonstrates unequivocally that public health policy can not only save lives; it can change the way we view the landscape of food." Kirkus

Includes bibliographical references and index

Garrett, Laurie

Betrayal of trust; the collapse of global public health. Hyperion 2000 754p il $30; pa $16.95 **362.1**

1. Medical care 2. Public health

ISBN 0-7868-6522-9; 0-7868-8440-1 pa

LC 00-33425

This book examines contemporary "health systems in the former Soviet Union, India, central Africa, and the United States." N Y Times Book Rev

Gruber, Jonathan, 1965-

Health care reform; what it is, why it's necessary, how it works. Jonathan Gruber, with HP Newquist; illustrated by Nathan Schreiber. Hill and Wang 2011 151 p. **362.1**

1. Medical care 2. Access to health care 3. Medical care -- Costs 4. Medical policy -- United States 5. Health care reform -- United States 6. Medical care -- United States

ISBN 0809053977; 0809094622; 9780809053971; 9780809094622

LC 2011020495

This book is "[a] cartoon-driven examination of what's wrong with the American way of health care--and why the legislative reform of 2010 was necessary." (Kirkus) "It delivers information . . . through an earnest but informal lecture by a cartoon version of an expert--in this case [Jonathan] Gruber, an MIT economics professor who helped craft Massachusetts's successful health care reform plan as well as the Affordable Care Act, which has been the subject of so much confusion and deliberate misinformation. He begins the presentation by confronting a small group of people with the enormous medical bills they could receive after medical treatment, then moves from the individual to the national level to show that our present system is unfair and unsustainable." (Publishers Wkly)

Hoffman, Beatrix

Health care for some; rights and rationing in the United States since 1930. Beatrix Hoffman. University of Chicago Press 2012 xxxv, 319 p.p (cloth : alkaline paper) $30 **362.1**

1. Access to health care 2. Medical care -- Costs 3. Health care reform -- United States 4. Right to health -- United States -- History 5. Health care rationing -- United States -- History 6. Health services accessibility -- United States -- History

ISBN 0226348032; 9780226348032

LC 2012000338

Author Beatrix Rebecca Hoffman looks at "America's long tradition of unequal access to health care. . . . Hoffman argues that two main features have characterized the US health system: a refusal to adopt a right to care and a particularly American type of rationing." The book "shows that the haphazard way the US system allocates medical services--using income, race, region, insurance coverage, and many other factors--is a disorganized, illogical, and powerful form of rationing." (Publisher's note)

Includes bibliographical references and index.

Hurley, Dan

Diabetes rising; how a rare disease became a modern pandemic, and what to do about it. foreword by Zachary T. Bloomgarden. Kaplan Pub. 2010 xxiii, 312p $26.95 **362.1**

1. Diabetes

ISBN 978-1-60714-458-8

LC 2009-29382

The author, "diagnosed at age 18 with type 1 diabetes, recounts the 3500-year history of the disease, its possible causes, and the latest promising treatments and cures with a professional writer's skills and a patient's passion. . . . [This is] a compelling layperson's overview of diabetes research, enlivened by multiple interviews with scientists in the field. Diabetics and those who love them will find this a fascinating and hope-filled read." Libr J

Includes bibliographical references

Kaufman, Sharon R.

--And a time to die; how American hospitals shape the end of life. Scribner 2005 400p $28 **362.1**

1. Death 2. Terminal care -- Ethical aspects

ISBN 0-7432-6476-2

LC 2004-52530

The author "reveals the dilemmas of hospital death in America today: the shift to patients' control of decision making despite the doctors' greater knowledge; the ethics and practical effects of resuscitation versus pain relief; the complexities of assessing 'quality of life' while guessing at the desires of an unconscious patient. . . . This deeply probing study lays bare the cultural and institutional assumptions and rhetoric that frame our search for 'a good death.'" Publ Wkly

Includes bibliographical references

Keene, Nancy

Your Child in the Hospital; A Practical Guide for Parents. Nancy Keene & Rachel Prentice. Childhood Cancer Guides 2015 176 p. $14.95 **362.1**
    1. Children -- Medical care 2. Parent-child relationship 3. Parent and child 4. Children -- Hospital care 5. Sick children -- Psychology
    ISBN 1941089992; 9781941089996

                  LC 99019134

Author Nancy Keene offers "tips and home-grown wisdom that will make any visit to the hospital easier. It explains how cope with procedures, plan for surgery, communicate with doctors and nurses, and deal with insurance companies. Woven throughout the text are dozens of practical and encouraging stories from parents who have been through the experience of having a child in the hospital." (Publisher's note)

"The brevity of information, while somewhat dry in presentation, may be just what the doctor ordered for the concerned or uninitiated parent. Libraries would serve their communities well by having this title available in its newest edition." LJ

Includes bibliographical references (p. 155-157)

Kessler, Lauren

Dancing with Rose; finding life in the land of Alzheimer's. Viking 2007 260p $24.95 **362.1**
    1. Caregivers 2. Alzheimer's disease
    ISBN 0-670-03859-8; 978-0-670-03859-6

                LC 2006-35699

"Invaluable intelligence, especially for anyone considering a residential facility for a loved one." Booklist

Khan, Ali S.

The **next** pandemic; On the Front Lines Against Humankind's Gravest Dangers. Ali S. Khan with William Patrick. PublicAffairs 2016 288 p. illustrations (hardcover) $26.99 **362.1**
    1. Disasters 2. Epidemics 3. Disease management 4. Internationality 5. Disease Outbreaks
    ISBN 9781610395915

                LC 2016001718

This book, by Ali S. Khan with William Patrick, offers an "account of the fight to contain the world's deadliest diseases—and the panic and corruption that make them worse. Throughout history, humankind's biggest killers have been infectious diseases: the Black Death, the Spanish Flu, and AIDS alone account for over one hundred million deaths. We ignore this reality most of the time, but when a new threat . . . seems imminent, we send our best . . . doctors to contain it." (Publisher's note)

"The details are sometimes disturbing, but Khan writes with verve, clarity, and a touch of humor." Kirkus

Includes bibliographical references and index

Monette, Paul

Borrowed time; an AIDS memoir. Harcourt Brace Jovanovich 1988 342p $22; pa $13 **362.1**
    1. AIDS (Disease)
    ISBN 0-15-113598-3; 0-15-600581-6 pa

                LC 88-7215

"The memoir transcends the particulars of the AIDS epidemic to stand as an eloquent testimonial to the power of love and the devastation of loss." Publ Wkly

Orbach, Susie

Bodies. Picador 2009 216p (Big ideas/small books) pa $14 **362.1**
    1. Body image
    ISBN 978-0-312-42720-7; 0-312-42720-4

                LC 2008-50352

The author "delves into the touchy subject of commercial exploitation of 'the body' and explores how modern culture is eroding individual appreciation of the unaltered human form. She uses specific case studies from her own practice to show the long-term effects that can result from body dissatisfaction. . . . Orbach's timely analysis is a key addition to the growing discussion of what is becoming a national trend, the favoring of delusion over reality, a troubling tendency that is threatening to steadily encompass all facets of American life." Booklist

Includes bibliographical references

Reid, T. R.

The **healing** of America; a global quest for better, cheaper, and fairer health care. Penguin Press 2009 277p il $25.95 **362.1**
    1. Medical care -- Government policy
    ISBN 9781594202346

                LC 2009-9555

"Reid's concise—and surprisingly humorous—study is recommended to anyone following the ongoing debate over health-care reform." Libr J

Includes bibliographical references

Shah, Sonia

The **body** hunters; testing new drugs on the world's poorest patients. New Press 2006 242p $24.95 **362.1**
    1. Drug industry 2. Medical ethics 3. Developing countries
    ISBN 1-56584-912-4; 978-1-56584-912-9

                LC 2005-58394

The author "uncovers a series of recent unethical drug trials conducted on impoverished and sick people in the developing world. . . . Meticulously researched and packed with documentary evidence, Shah's tautly argued study will provoke much needed public debate about this disturbing facet of globalization." Publ Wkly

Includes bibliographical references

Shilts, Randy

★ **And** the band played on; politics, people, and the AIDS epidemic. 20th anniversary ed.; St Martin's Griffin 2007 630p pa $17.95 **362.1**
    1. AIDS (Disease)
    ISBN 978-0-312-37463-1
    First published 1987

The author traces the history of the AIDS epidemic in the United States.

"Shilts successfully weaves comprehensive investigative reporting and commercial page-turner pacing, politi-

cal intrigue and personal tragedy into a landmark work."
Publ Wkly

Includes bibliographical references

Silver, Daniel B.

Refuge in hell; how Berlin's Jewish hospital out-
lasted the Nazis. Houghton Mifflin 2003 xxii, 311p
$24　　　　　　　　　　　　　　　　　**362.1**

1. Jews -- Germany 2. Holocaust, 1933-1945 3.
Jüdisches Krankenhaus (Berlin, Germany)

ISBN 0-618-25144-8

LC 2003-47896

"This enlightening work is essential for public and academic libraries." Libr J

Includes bibliographical references

Smith, Tom

A **balanced** life; 9 strategies for coping with
the mental health problems of a loved one. Hazelden
2008 147p pa $14.95　　　　　　　　　　　　**362.1**

1. Mentally ill

ISBN 978-1-59285-662-6

LC 2008-18794

"Through extensive research and his own experience
with his daughter's mental illness and subsequent suicide, .
. . [the author] suggests nine strategies for coping, including
helping loved ones find and continue to take their medication, urging them to maintain a supportive relationship with
a therapist, and recognizing the warning signs. . . . Smith
provides empathetic information that has the potential to
buoy people up." Libr J

Includes bibliographical references

Sommer, Alfred

Getting what we deserve; health and medical
care in America. Johns Hopkins University Press
2009 133p il map $21.95　　　　　　　　　**362.1**

1. Social medicine 2. Public health -- United States 3.
Medical care -- Government policy

ISBN 978-0-8018-9387-2; 0-8018-9387-9

LC 2009-6039

"Opposing what we've been led to believe about the
health-care situation in the United States, . . . [the author]
posits that there's less complexity than meets the eye and
that solutions are possible. . . . First illustrating how much
improvement there was in life expectancy in the 20th century even before the advent of antibiotics and advanced
technology, he proceeds to emphasize the importance of
environment—e.g., hygiene, pollution, smoking—in creating public health problems and the relatively simple steps
to improvement. . . . Sommer keeps it short and clear, with
plenty of understandable graphs and charts. His common-
sense points will interest consumers trying to understand the
ongoing debate as well as policymakers." Libr J

Includes bibliographical references

Starr, Paul

Remedy and reaction; the peculiar American
struggle over health care reform. Yale University
Press 2011 324p $28.50　　　　　　　　　　**362.1**

1. Health insurance 2. Medical care -- Government

policy

ISBN 978-0-300-17109-9

LC 2011019577

The author "recounts the long and largely unsuccessful
fight to provide all Americans with health care. . . . Starr
shows how the window of opportunity for health-care reform has opened several times in the last 100 years and how
each time it has been slammed shut by powerful interests
including the American Medical Association, big insurance
companies, and the conservative politicians they support. . .
. This is a must-read in order to understand why health-care
reform has been and continues to be so difficult to achieve
in America." Libr J

Includes bibliographical references

Steinberg, Jonny

Sizwe's test; a young man's journey through Africa's AIDS epidemic. Simon & Schuster 2008 349p
il $26　　　　　　　　　　　　　　　　　**362.1**

1. AIDS (Disease) 2. South Africa

ISBN 978-1-4165-5269-7; 1-4165-5269-3

LC 2007-29672

The author "becomes intertwined with his subject, but
balances critical distance and compassion with gleanings
from his own psychological barriers to HIV testing that
further deepen the concern and understanding he accords to
Sizwe's story." Publ Wkly

Includes bibliographical references

Torrey, E. Fuller (Edwin Fuller), 1937-

The **insanity** offense; how America's failure to
treat the seriously mentally ill endangers its citizens.
W.W. Norton 2008 265p il　　　　　　　　**362.1**

1. Mentally ill -- Institutional care

ISBN 0-393-06658-4; 978-0-393-06658-6

LC 2008-2697

"Released en masse from institutions beginning in the
1960s, the most severely ill are most likely to become homeless, incarcerated, victimized, and/or violent. Torrey details
how civil liberties suits have prevented such people from
being involuntarily institutionalized, leaving them a danger
both to themselves and to others. . . . Chilling and well documented, this text has many no-nonsense solutions to protect
the mentally ill themselves as well as society as a whole."
Publ Wkly

Includes bibliographical references

362.106　Management

Friedman, Leonard H.

101 careers in healthcare management; by Leonard H. Friedman, Anthony R. Kovner. Springer Pub.
Co. 2013 xix, 332 p.p ill. (paperback) $25.00;
(eBook) $25.00　　　　　　　　　　　　**362.106**

1. Vocational guidance 2. Medical personnel --
Employment 3. Career Choice -- United States 4.
Health Services Administration -- United States

ISBN 082619334X; 9780826193346; 9780826193353
pdf

LC 2012033692

This book by Leonard H. Friedman and Anthony R. Kovner is a "resource describing the many career opportunities in healthcare management. The book begins with general chapters providing an overview of the field of healthcare management, information on educational requirements, and advice on finding a job in the field. Following chapters outline specific job titles and feature many real-life examples." (Choice)

362.109   History, geographic treatment, biography

Atlas, Scott W.

In excellent health; setting the record straight on America's health care and charting a path for future reform. Scott W. Atlas, MD. Hoover Institution Press, Stanford University 2011 xxiv, 359 p.p (cloth : alk. paper) $24.95   **362.109**
1. Technological innovations 2. Medical care -- United States 3. Health insurance -- United States 4. Health care reform -- United States
ISBN 0817914447; 9780817914448

LC 2011037058

In this book, "[Scott W.] Atlas admits that U.S. health care faces serious challenges . . . , [but] he asserts that we have made remarkable advances in the past 60 years" and that "we lead the world in" developing medical innovations. "He argues for substantive tax reforms, an overhaul of private insurance, and the 'minimization of the role of government as direct insurer' as essential." (Library Journal)
Includes bibliographical references and index.

Brawley, Otis Webb

How we do harm; Otis Webb Brawley with Paul Goldberg. St. Martin's Press 2012 256p.   **362.109**
1. Medical care 2. Access to health care 3. Medical policy -- United States 4. Medical care -- United States 5. Health care reform -- United States
ISBN 9780312672973

LC 2011035843

'In this book, Dr. Otis Webb Brawley, M.D., explores "how medicine is really practiced in America. Brawley tells of doctors who select treatment based on payment they will receive, rather than on demonstrated scientific results; hospitals and pharmaceutical companies that seek out patients to treat even if they are not actually ill (but as long as their insurance will pay); a public primed to swallow the latest pill, no matter the cost; and rising healthcare costs for unnecessary—and often unproven—treatments that we all pay for. Brawley calls for rational healthcare, healthcare drawn from results-based, scientifically justifiable treatments, and not just the peddling of hot new drugs." (Publisher's note)

362.11   Services of specific kinds of institutions

Cosgrove, Toby

The Cleveland Clinic way; lessons in excellence from one of the world's leading health care organizations. by Toby Cosgrove, MD., President and CEO of Cleveland Clinic. McGraw-Hill Education 2014 xvi, 222 p.p (alk. paper) $30   **362.11**
1. Medical care 2. Health facilities 3. Integrative medicine 4. Cleveland Clinic Foundation 5. Integrative medicine -- United States -- Ohio 6. Health facilities -- Standards -- United States -- Ohio
ISBN 0071827242; 9780071827249

LC 2013038181

This book, by Dr. Toby Cosgrove, "is a blueprint for fixing what's wrong with healthcare. . . . It's all happening at Cleveland Clinic, one of the most innovative, forward-looking medical institutions in the nation. . . . Cosgrove . . . reveals how the Clinic works so well and argues persuasively for why it should be the model for the nation. He details how Cleveland Clinic focuses on the eight key trends that are shaping the future of medicine." (Publisher's note)
Includes bibliographical references and index

Fink, Sheri

★ Five days at memorial; life and death in a storm-ravaged hospital. Sheri Fink. Crown Publishers 2013 432 p. $27   **362.11**
1. Hospitals 2. Disaster relief 3. Hurricane Katrina, 2005 4. Memorial Medical Center (New Orleans, La.) 5. Disaster medicine -- Louisiana -- New Orleans -- Case studies 6. Disaster hospitals -- Louisiana -- New Orleans -- Case studies 7. Forensic pathology -- Louisiana -- New Orleans -- Case studies 8. Health facilities -- Louisiana -- Administration -- Case studies
ISBN 0307718964; 9780307718969

LC 2013019693

Andrew Carnegie Medal for Excellence in Nonfiction Shortlist (2014)

"Fink reconstructs 5 days at Memorial Medical Center and draws the reader into the lives of those who struggled mightily to survive and to maintain life amid chaos. After Katrina struck and the floodwaters rose, the power failed, and the heat climbed, exhausted caregivers chose to designate certain patients last for rescue. Months later, several health professionals faced criminal allegations that they deliberately injected numerous patients with drugs to hasten their deaths." (Publisher's note)

Fink draws those few days in the hospital's life with a fine, lively pen, providing stunningly framed vignettes of activities in the hospital and sharp pocket profiles of many of the characters. She gives measured consideration to such explosive issues as class and race discrimination in medicine, end-of-life care, medical rationing and euthanasia, and she presents the injection of some patients with a cocktail of drugs to reduce their breathing in such a manner that readers will be able to fully fashion their own opinions... (Kirkus)
Includes bibliographical references and index

Manheimer, Eric

Twelve patients; life and death at Bellevue Hospital. Eric Manheimer. Grand Central Pub. 2012 vii, 355 p.p (regular) $26.99   **362.11**
1. Patients 2. Hospitals 3. Cancer patients 4. Physicians -- Biography 5. Bellevue Hospital 6. Hospital care -- New York (State) -- New York -- Case studies 7. Hospital patients -- New York (State) -- New

York -- Case studies
ISBN 1455503886; 9781455503889

LC 2012005513

This book presents "a memoir from the Medical Director of Bellevue Hospital that uses the plights of twelve very different patients -- from dignitaries at the nearby UN . . . to illegal immigrants, and Wall Street tycoons -- to illustrate larger societal issues. . . . As the book unfolds, the narrator is diagnosed with cancer, and he is forced to wrestle with the end of his own life even as he struggles to save the lives of others." (Publisher's note)

362.17 Specific services

Gawande, Atul

★ **Being** mortal; medicine and what matters in the end. Atul Gawande. Henry Holt & Co. 2014 288 p. illustrations (hardcover) $26   **362.17**
1. Hospices 2. Terminal care 3. Elderly -- Medical care 4. Prognosis 5. Quality of life 6. Attitude to death 7. Aging -- Physiology
ISBN 0805095152; 9780805095159

LC 2014017442

Los Angeles Times Book Prize Finalist: Current Interest (2014)

"In 'Being Mortal,' . . . author Atul Gawande . . . addresses his profession's ultimate limitation, arguing that quality of life is the desired goal for patients and families. Gawande offers examples of freer, more socially fulfilling models for assisting the infirm and dependent elderly, and he explores the varieties of hospice care to demonstrate that a person's last weeks or months may be rich and dignified." (Publisher's note)

"A sensitive, intelligent and heartfelt examination of the processes of aging and dying." Kirkus

Includes bibliographical references

Robbins, Alexandra

The **nurses**; a year of secrets, drama, and miracles with the heroes of the hospital. Alexandra Robbins. Workman Publishing 2015 368 p. (alk. paper) $24.95   **362.17**
1. Nurses 2. Nursing 3. Emergency medicine 4. Nursing Care -- United States -- Popular Works 5. Nursing Care -- United States -- Personal Narratives 6. Nurse-Patient Relations -- United States -- Popular Works 7. Nursing Staff, Hospital -- United States -- Popular Works 8. Nursing Service, Hospital -- United States -- Popular Works 9. Physician-Nurse Relations -- United States -- Popular Works 10. Nurse-Patient Relations -- United States -- Personal Narratives 11. Nursing Staff, Hospital -- United States -- Personal Narratives 12. Nursing Service, Hospital -- United States -- Personal Narratives 13. Physician-Nurse Relations -- United States -- Personal Narratives
ISBN 0761171711; 9780761171713

LC 2015011380

In this book, Alexandra Robbins "trains her sights on the adrenaline-infused world of emergency nursing, offering a disturbing snapshot of the barriers imposed on healthcare providers by colleagues, myopic bosses, and a changing healthcare system. She follows four ER nurses at four hospitals where patients range from the wealthy and privileged to the down and out, aiming to represent the varied perspectives of America's 3.5 million nurses." (Publishers Weekly)

"Robbins works in lots of fascinating facts as she argues for improved working conditions for nurses, citing research that shows how much that benefits patients. An educational, sometimes alarming read for anyone interested in learning behind-the-scenes details about hospital life." Booklist

Includes bibliographical references and index

362.19 Services to patients with specific conditions

Taylor, Jill Bolte

My stroke of insight; a brain scientist's personal journey. Jill Bolte Taylor. Plume 2009 206 p. illustrations $16   **362.19**
1. Stroke patients 2. Neuroanatomy 3. Biography, Individual 4. Brain -- Hemorrhage -- Patients
ISBN 0452295548; 9780452295544

LC 2008271243

This book, by Jill Bolte Taylor, "chronicles how a brain scientist's own stroke led to enlightenment. . . . On December 10, 1996, Jill Bolte Taylor, a thirty-seven- year-old Harvard-trained brain scientist experienced a massive stroke in the left hemisphere of her brain. . . . For Taylor, her stroke . . . taught her that by 'stepping to the right' of our left brains, we can uncover feelings of well-being that are often sidelined by 'brain chatter.'" (Publisher's note)

362.196 Specific conditions

Baroni, Bill

Fat kid got fit; Bill Baroni with Damon DiMarco; with a foreword by Howard Eisenson. Lyons Press 2012 x, 245p.p   **362.196**
1. Weight loss 2. Autobiography 3. Physical fitness 4. Overweight persons -- New Jersey -- Biography
ISBN 9780762770472

LC 2011028047

This book tells the story of "Bill Baroni [who] was just twenty years old, [when] he was convinced he was dying. He thought he was having a heart attack because it felt like he had an elephant sitting on his chest. It turned out to be only indigestion, but more than that, it was the wake up call he needed to save his life. Bill weighed 320 pounds and was hooked on junk food. He set about to change his life forever. . . . He lost his weight using common sense. It took dedication, and even some gumption. But it worked! He lost 120 pounds and, more importantly, he has kept it off! He has maintained a healthy 185 pounds for fifteen years. At 65, he is trim, handsome, and healthy." (Publisher's note)

"[Baroni] traces his own path and, with humor and style, passes the information he learned along to readers. This can work for anyone." (Libr J)

Includes bibliographical references (p. 241-245).

Brzezinski, Mika, 1967-

Obsessed; America's Food Addiction -- And My Own. Perseus Books Group 2013 256 p. $26 **362.196**

1. Eating habits 2. Eating disorders

ISBN 1602861765; 9781602861763

This book by Mika Brzezinski looks at eating habits in the U.S. As a television host for "Morning Joe," she "admonish[es] viewers about the importance of proper diet and exercise. Few would suspect that her vehemence stems from a personal addiction to junk food and binge eating that has plagued her all her life and that her ironclad willpower actually border on an unhealthy obsession to stay thin at any cost." (Booklist)

Cody, Joshua

[Sic] W.W. Norton 2011 266 p. **362.196**

1. Autobiographies 2. Cancer patients

ISBN 9780393081060

LC 2011026035

In this book "Joshua Cody, a . . . young composer, was about to receive his PhD when he was diagnosed with an aggressive cancer. Facing a bone-marrow transplant and full radiation, he charts his struggle: the fury, the tendency to self-destruction, and the ruthless grasping for life and sensation; the encounter with a strange woman on Canal Street that leads to sex at his apartment; the detailed morphine fantasy complete with a bride called Valentina while, in reality, hospital staff are pinning him to his bed." (Publisher's note)

Includes bibliographical references.

Forrest, Emma

Your voice in my head; a memoir. Other Press 2011 215 p. **362.196**

1. Authors 2. Bulimia 3. Novelists 4. Journalists 5. Self-mutilation 6. Screenwriters 7. Biography, Individual

ISBN 1590514467; 9781590514467; 978-1-59051-446-7; 1-59051-446-7

LC 201030930

This book presents a memoir by writer Emma Forrest which details a period in her life in which, despite "the support of her parents . . . as well as a precocious career in journalism and a first novel . . . already on the way, she became a bulimic and an obsessive cutter, and soon began walking 'hand in hand with the thought of suicide.' She also had a knack for acquiring terrible boyfriends whose bad behavior inspired her to hurt herself more, and who sometimes aided and abetted the abuse." Particular focus is given to "the therapist who ultimately changed her life, a man she refers to as Dr. R. . . . [and his] unexpected death." Also included are "letters from Dr. R.'s other patients . . . [and] a sermon by her rabbi." (N Y Times)

Geiger, Chris

The **Cancer** Survivors' Club; A Collection of Inspirational and Uplifting Stories. Chris Geiger. Oneworld Publication 2015 272 p. $15.99 **362.196**

1. Cancer patients 2. Cancer -- Chemotherapy

ISBN 1780747268; 9781780747262

This book by author Chris Geiger " brings together firsthand accounts of ordinary people who have beaten cancer.

They are old and young, their diagnoses common and rare, their courses of treatment long and short, but all are survivors. In these honest, unflinching and deeply personal stories, they write about the most difficult times in their lives, telling us how they found a strength and determination that they never knew they possessed." (Publisher's note)

"An inspiring compilation for anyone struggling with cancer. Readers will find comfort and even a few laughs in the pages. A note: this book is from the UK; the survivors refer to the nation's National Health Service, and the list of cancer-related websites and blogs is mostly from the UK." LJ

Iweala, Uzodinma

Our kind of people; a continent's burden, a country's hope. by Uzodinma Iweala. 1st ed. HarperCollins 2012 228 p. (hardback) $24.99 **362.196**

1. Health 2. Nigeria 3. Epidemics 4. AIDS (Disease) -- Social aspects -- Nigeria 5. HIV infections -- Social aspects -- Nigeria

ISBN 0061284904; 9780061284908

LC 2011047861

Author Uzodinma "Iweala embarks on a . . . journey through his native Nigeria, meeting individuals and communities that are struggling daily to understand both the impact and meaning of HIV/AIDS. He speaks with people from all walks of life--the ill and the healthy, doctors, nurses, truck drivers, sex workers, shopkeepers, students, parents, and children. Their testimonies are . . . [a] personal exploration of life, love, and connection in the face of disease, and an incisive critique of our existing ideas of health and happiness." (Publisher's note)

Leavitt, Sarah

Tangles; A Story About Alzheimer's, My Mother, and Me. Sarah Leavitt. Skyhorse Pub. 2012 127 p. ill., port. (paperback) $14.95 **362.196**

1. Family life 2. Autobiographies 3. Alzheimer's disease

ISBN 1616086394; 9781616086398

"In this . . . graphic memoir, Sarah Leavitt reveals how Alzheimer's disease transformed her mother Midge -- and her family -- forever. . . . Sarah shares her family's journey . . . managing to find moments of happiness. Midge, a Harvard-educated intellectual, struggles to comprehend the simplest words; Sarah's father Rob slowly adapts to his new role as full-time caretaker . . . Sarah and her sister Hannah argue, laugh, and grieve together." (Publisher's note)

Stratton, Stephen E.

The **encyclopedia** of HIV and AIDS; Stephen E. Stratton, Evelyn J. Fisher; foreword by Edward A. Morales. 3rd ed. Facts On File 2012 414 p. (hardcover) $75 **362.196**

1. AIDS (Disease) 2. HIV infections 3. Reference books 4. AIDS (Disease) -- Dictionaries

ISBN 0816077231; 9780816077236

LC 2011017597

First published 1998 with title: The AIDS dictionary

This book is the third edition of an encyclopedia of HIV and AIDS. "Coverage includes definitions of AIDS and HIV; information on medications used to treat the conditions-

-including side effects, dosage, and drug interactions; and related medical conditions. Further research is supported by the inclusion of a bibliography for each essay. The appendixes include frequently used abbreviations, lists of online resources, and U.S. and global HIV and AIDS statistics." (Library Journal)

This volume includes "entries covering the basic biological, medical, financial, legal, political, and social issues and terms associated with HIV and AIDS. Entries explain symptoms and treatments, opportunistic infections, prevention strategies, and much more. Appendixes include HIV/AIDS associations, education centers, clinical trials, hotlines, publications, and additional material." Publisher's note

Includes bibliographical references and index.

Weldon, Michele

Escape Points; A Memoir. by Michele Weldon. Chicago Review Press 2015 272 p. (ebook) $21.99; $26.95   **362.196**
1. Mothers 2. Single parents 3. Divorced people 4. Women journalists
ISBN 9781613733554; 1613733526; 9781613733523
       LC 2015008965

In this memoir, "journalist Michele Weldon provides a potent antidote to the harried single mom stereotype. . . . Untethered from a seemingly idyllic life with a handsome but abusive attorney husband, Weldon relates the challenges and triumphs of the years that followed her divorce as she maneuvers through a complicated life of long daily commutes, radiation treatments, [and] supporting [her three] boys." (Publisher's note)

"Weldon pins life to the mat in this valiant, passionate, purposeful memoir." Kirkus

Zimmer, Carl

A planet of viruses; Carl Zimmer. University of Chicago Press 2011 x, 109p.p col. ill.   **362.196**
1. Viruses
ISBN 9780226983356 pa; 0226983358 pa; 9780226983363; 9780226983332
       LC 2010036742

"This . . . book explores the hidden world of viruses. . . . Here Carl Zimmer, popular science writer and author of Discover magazine's award-winning blog The Loom, presents the latest research on how viruses hold sway over our lives and our biosphere, how viruses helped give rise to the first life-forms, how viruses are producing new diseases, how we can harness viruses for our own ends, and how viruses will continue to control our fate for years to come. In this . . . tour of the frontiers of biology, . . . we learn that some treatments for the common cold do more harm than good; that the world's oceans are home to an astonishing number of viruses; and that the evolution of HIV is now in overdrive, spawning more mutated strains than we care to imagine." (Publisher's note)

Includes bibliographical references (p. 97-101) and index.

362.2   People with mental illness and disabilities

Schüll, Natasha Dow

Addiction by design; machine gambling in Las Vegas. Natasha Dow Schüll. Princeton University Press 2012 xi, 442 p.p (hardcover) $35   **362.2**
1. Las Vegas (Nev.) 2. Compulsive gambling 3. Casinos -- Nevada -- Las Vegas 4. Gambling -- Nevada -- Las Vegas 5. Compulsive gambling -- Nevada -- Las Vegas 6. Gambling -- Equipment and supplies -- Nevada -- Las Vegas
ISBN 0691127557; 9780691127552
       LC 2012004339

In this book, Natasha Dow Schüll looks at problem gambling. "She begins by tracing the spectacular growth of machine gambling over the last several decades to where it now stands as the dominant gambling form in the US. Applying an anthropological perspective, the author focuses especially on the Las Vegas gambling industry." (Choice)

Includes bibliographical references (p. 385-423) and index

362.28   Suicide

✓ Ackerman, Diane, 1948-

A slender thread. Random House 1997 305p hardcover o.p. pa $14   **362.28**
1. Suicide 2. Crisis centers 3. Hotlines (Telephone counseling)
ISBN 0-679-77133-6 pa
       LC 96-8721

This is an account of the author's work as a volunteer counselor at a suicide-prevention and crisis center in a New York college town

"In a narrative that is lush with her signature gift for metaphor and delight in the senses and taut with the drama of her often frightening negotiations with people in the throes of every imaginable form of crisis, Ackerman illuminates the bewildering workings of the resilient human psyche." Booklist

362.29   Substance abuse

Clegg, Bill

Ninety days; a memoir of recovery. Bill Clegg. Little, Brown and Co. 2012 194 p.   **362.29**
1. New York (N.Y.) 2. Drug addicts -- Rehabilitation 3. Literary agents -- Personal narratives 4. Recovering addicts -- Personal narratives 5. Drug addicts -- United States -- Biography 6. Literary agents -- United States -- Biography
ISBN 9780316122528
       LC 2011032542

"In this . . . memoir, a follow-up to Portrait of an Addict as a Young Man, literary agent and author [Bill] Clegg describes his struggle to stay clean. Returning to New York City after a stint in rehab, Clegg faces the ruin he's made of his life: his literary agency has closed, his lover has moved on, and he faces mounting debts with no income to speak of. Making matters worse, in spite of the many meetings Clegg attends, he's helplessly drawn to vice. Many organizations dealing with substance abuse emphasize 90 days sober as a real signpost toward recovery. Clegg discovers that reaching that signpost is going to take him a lot longer than three months." (Publishers Weekly)

Courtwright, David T.

Forces of habit; drugs and the making of the modern world. Harvard Univ. Press 2001 277p $24.95; pa $16.95 **362.29**

    1. Drug abuse 2. Psychotropic drugs

    ISBN 0-674-00458-2; 0-674-01003-5 pa

                  LC 00-61466

"Reasoned and informative, Courtwright's book is a cogent source of dispassionate information on drugs and their role in society." Booklist

    Includes bibliographical references

Dahl, Linda

Loving Our Addicted Daughters Back to Life; A Guidebook for Parents. Linda Dahl. Central Recovery Press 2015 200 p. $16.95 **362.29**

    1. Parenting 2. Drug addicts 3. Drug abuse counseling

    ISBN 1937612856; 9781937612856

This book, by Linda Dahl, offers "the latest information on gender-specific treatment of addiction and recovery . . . for parents seeking direction to help their daughters. Step-by-step guidelines present tools for recognizing substance abuse in young women; communicating with them and their care providers; dealing with relapse and long-term recovery; and managing parental shame, guilt, fear, anger, and loving detachment." (Publisher's note)

"This book's down-to-earth style is for parents or any reader seeking facts and guidance. The female focus is atypical and makes this an essential addition to the literature." LJ

Feiling, Tom

Cocaine nation; how the white trade took over the world. Pegasus Books 2010 350p $27.95 **362.29**

    1. Cocaine 2. Drug traffic

    ISBN 978-1-60598-101-7; 1-60598-101-X

First published 2009 in the United Kingdom with title: The candy machine

"Studying the cultivation, distribution, and use of cocaine, . . , [the author] probes the drug's meteoric rise in sales and traces traffic from Colombian coca fields to Miami, Kingston, Tijuana, London, and New York. He follows consumers, traders, producers, police officers, doctors, and custom officials. . . . Packed with facts and figures, this is a well-researched survey of the subject." Publ Wkly

    Includes bibliographical references

Fletcher, Anne M.

Inside rehab; the surprising truth about addiction treatment : and how to get help that works. Anne M. Fletcher. Penguin Group USA 2013 448 p. $27.95 **362.29**

    1. Substance abuse 2. Drug abuse -- Treatment 3. Drug addicts -- Rehabilitation 4. Addicts -- Rehabilitation 5. Substance abuse -- Treatment

    ISBN 0670025224; 9780670025220

                  LC 2012037030

This book is an "overview of modern treatment methods for substance abuse." Anne M. Fletcher "conducted interviews with patients and the administrators and staff of addiction programs, visiting more than a dozen such programs (both residential and outpatient). The author challenges the notion that an addict is powerless to overcome an addiction on his or her own or with minimal professional counseling." (Kirkus)

    Includes bibliographical references and index

Hart, Carl

High Price; A Neuroscientist's Journey of Self-discovery That Challenges Everything You Know About Drugs and Society. Carl Hart. HarperCollins 2013 352 p. $26.99 **362.29**

    1. Scientists 2. Drug education

    ISBN 0062015885; 9780062015884

In this book, "combining memoir, popular science, and public policy" author Carl Hart "lambasts current drug laws as draconian and repressive, arguing that they're based more on assumptions about race and class than on a real understanding of the physiological and societal effects of drugs. . . . Central to his work is the idea that addiction is actually a combination of physiological and social factors, and the use of drugs does not itself lead to violence and crime." (Publishers Weekly)

"An eye-opening, absorbing, complex story of scientific achievement in the face of overwhelming odds." Kirkus

Larsen, Laura

Drug abuse sourcebook; basic consumer health information about the abuse of cocaine, club drugs, marijuana, inhalants, heroin, hallucinogens, and other illicit substances . . . edited by Laura Larsen. Omnigraphics, Inc. 2014 xx, 636 p.p (hardcover : acid-free paper) $95 **362.29**

    1. Drug abuse 2. Drug abuse -- Treatment -- Handbooks, manuals, etc 3. Drug abuse -- Prevention -- Handbooks, manuals, etc 4. Drug addiction -- Treatment -- Handbooks, manuals, etc

    ISBN 9780780813076; 0780813073

                  LC 2013037324

This book, edited by Laura Larsen, "provides basic consumer health information about the abuse of illegal drugs and misuse of prescription and over-the-counter medications, along with facts about prevention, treatment, and recovery. Includes index, glossary of related terms and directory of resources." (Publisher's note)

    Includes bibliographical references and index

Proctor, Robert N.

Golden holocaust; origins of the cigarette catastrophe and the case for abolition. Robert N. Proctor. University of California Press 2011 x, 737 p.p ill. (cloth : alk. paper) $49.95 **362.29**

    1. Cigarettes 2. Tobacco habit 3. Smoking cessation programs 4. Tobacco use -- Health aspects 5. Smoking -- Psychological aspects 6. History, 20th Century -- United States 7. Smoking -- psychology -- United States 8. Persuasive Communication -- United States 9. Smoking -- adverse effects -- United States 10. Tobacco Industry -- history -- United States 11. Tobacco industry

-- United States -- History
ISBN 0520270169; 9780520270169

LC 2011003825

Author Robert N. Proctor discusses the cigarette, "the deadliest artifact in the history of human civilization . . . [and] how the cigarette came to be the most widely-used drug on the planet, with six trillion sticks sold per year . . . [He looks at] tobacco manufacturers conspiring to block the recognition of tobacco-cancer hazards, even as they ensnare legions of scientists and politicians in a web of denial." (Publisher's note)

Includes bibliographical references and index

Quinones, Sam

Dreamland; the true tale of America's opiate epidemic. by Sam Quinones. Bloomsbury Press 2014 384 p. maps (alk. paper) $28   **362.29**

1. Narcotics 2. Drug abuse 3. Heroin abuse 4. American dream 5. Drug traffic -- Mexico 6. American Dream 7. Narcotics -- United States 8. Oxycodone -- United States 9. Heroin abuse -- United States 10. Drug addiction -- United States
ISBN 1620402505; 9781620402504

LC 2014025398

National Book Critics Circle Award Finalist: Nonfiction (2015)

This book, by Sam Quinones, "delves into the heart of America's obsession with opiates like heroin, morphine, and OxyContin. He looks at how aggressive marketing and irresponsible business tactics led to the widespread use of addictive prescription painkillers (especially OxyContin) and how Mexican drug cartels introduced black tar heroin into small towns and vulnerable areas around the U.S." (Publishers Weekly)

"Journalist Quinones weaves an extraordinary story, including the personal journeys of the addicted, the drug traffickers, law enforcement, and scores of families affected by the scourge, as he details the social, economic, and political forces that eventually destroyed communities in the American heartland and continues to have a resounding impact." Booklist

Includes bibliographical references and index

Reding, Nick

Methland; the death and life of an American small town. Bloomsbury 2009 255p $25   **362.29**

1. Methamphetamine 2. Iowa 3. Methamphetamine abuse
ISBN 1-59691-650-8; 978-1-59691-650-0

LC 2008-45398

This is an account of the effect of crystal methamphetamine on "the community of Oelwein, Iowa (pop. 6,159), a once-thriving farming and railroad community." (Publisher's note)

The author traces "rise of meth use across the Midwest, focusing on Oelwein, an Iowa railroad town (pop. 6,772) that by 2005 had been 'destroyed' by the drug. . . . An important report on an extremely dangerous drug and the consequences of addiction." Kirkus

Includes bibliographical references

Ruta, Domenica

With or without you; a memoir. Domenica Ruta. Spiegel & Grau 2013 224 p. $25   **362.29**

1. Substance abuse 2. Children of drug addicts 3. Drug addicts -- Massachusetts -- Biography 4. Children of drug addicts -- Massachusetts -- Biography
ISBN 0812993241; 9780679645023; 9780812993240

LC 2012017991

This book is Domenica Ruta's memoir of her relationship with "her drug-dealer, addict mother. . . . Ruta holds nothing back as she . . . portrays her childhood in Massachusetts, whether she's writing about school events at her Catholic school, her mother's ascent as a millionaire and subsequent loss of money due to drug use, or the sexual abuse at the hands of . . . one of her mother's friends." (Kirkus Reviews)

Streatfeild, Dominic

Cocaine; an unauthorized biography. Thomas Dunne Bks./St. Martin's Press 2002 510p il $27.95; pa $15   **362.29**

1. Cocaine 2. Drug abuse 3. Drug traffic
ISBN 0-312-28624-4; 0-312-42226-1 pa

First published 2001 in the United Kingdom

"Thorough, engrossing, balanced, and entertaining, it is important social history in palatable form." Booklist

Includes bibliographical references

362.292   Alcohol

Bowman, Dana

Bottled; A Mom's Guide to Early Recovery. Dana Bowman. Central Recovery Press 2015 264 p. $16.95   **362.292**

1. Alcoholism 2. Motherhood
ISBN 193761297X; 9781937612979

This memoir by Dana Bowman "explains the perils moms face with drinking and chronicles the author's path to recovery, from hitting bottom to the months of early sobriety--a blur of pain and chaos--to her now (in)frequent moments of peace. [It] offers practical suggestions on how to be a sober, present-in-the-moment mom, one day at a time, and provides much needed levity on an issue too often treated with deadly seriousness." (Publisher's note)

"This memoir filled with hope and humor is as good as Ann Dowsett Johnston's Drink: The Intimate Relationship Between Women and Alcohol but much lighter." Library Journal

Dorris, Michael

The **broken** cord; with a foreword by Louise Erdrich. Harper & Row 1989 300p il hardcover o.p. pa $14   **362.292**

1. Alcoholism 2. Native Americans 3. Father-son relationship
ISBN 0-06-016071-3; 0-06-091682-6 pa

LC 88-45893

"The alarming statistics and consequences of fetal alcohol syndrome are skillfully interwoven with the human story of one of its victims in 'The Broken Cord.' Mr. Dorris's prose is clear and affecting." N Y Times Book Rev

Includes bibliographical references

Glaser, Gabrielle

Her best-kept secret; why women drink -- and how they can regain control. Gabrielle Glaser. Simon & Schuster 2013 256 p. $24   **362.292**

1. Alcoholism 2. Women -- Alcohol use 3. Women -- Alcohol use -- United States 4. Women alcoholics -- Rehabilitation -- United States

ISBN 1439184380; 9781439184387

LC 2013001088

This book by Gabrielle Glaser looks at U.S. women's alcohol consumption. She "traces the increasingly besotted history of women's relationship with alcohol (focusing mostly on middle-class women), but . . . argues against the efficacy of Alcoholics Anonymous (AA) for women. Rather than guiding women down a healing path of humility and acceptance, AA and its Twelve Steps, Glaser argues, have failed to protect women from predatory men, thereby consigning many" women to failure. (Publishers Weekly)

Includes bibliographical references

Johnston, Ann Dowsett

Drink; the intimate relationship between women and alcohol. by Ann Dowsett Johnston. HarperWave 2013 320 p. (hardback) $27.99   **362.292**

1. Alcoholism 2. Women -- Alcohol use 3. Women alcoholics

ISBN 0062241796; 9780062241795

LC 2013026103

In this book, author "Anne Dowsett Johnston combines in-depth research with her own personal story of recovery, and delivers a[n] . . . examination of a shocking yet little recognized epidemic threatening society today: the precipitous rise in risky drinking among women and girls." (Publisher's note)

Includes bibliographical references

362.4 People with physical disabilities

Nielsen, Kim E.

A disability history of the United States; Kim E. Nielsen. Beacon Press 2012 272 p. (alk. paper) $26.95   **362.4**

1. Autonomy (Psychology) 2. United States -- History 3. People with disabilities -- Legal status, laws, etc. 4. Sociology of disability -- United States -- History 5. People with disabilities -- United States -- History 6. People with disabilities -- Legal status, laws, etc. -- United States -- History

ISBN 0807022020; 9780807022023

LC 2012014236

This book "seeks to define the pivotal role of people with disabilities in [the U.S.'s] past and their contribution to our laws, policy, economics, popular culture, and our collective identity. Disability, with its presumed need for dependency, challenges the American ideal of independence and autonomy. [Kim E.] Nielsen uses various concepts of disability and

dependency that go to 'the heart of both human and American experience.'" (Publisher's Weekly)

Includes bibliographical references and index.

Sacks, Oliver W.

Seeing voices; a journey into the world of the deaf. [by] Oliver Sacks. Vintage Books 2000 222p il pa $13.95   **362.4**

1. Deaf 2. Sign language 3. Gallaudet University

ISBN 0-375-70407-8

LC 00-42340

First published 1989 by University of California Press

"With his philosopher's penchant for profound discovery and his neurologist's knowledge of biology and the brain, Sacks offers provocative connections and acute observations about the nature of language and culture." Booklist

Includes bibliographical references

Solomon, Andrew

★ Far from the tree; parents, children and the search for identity. Andrew Solomon. Scribner 2012 962 p. (hbk. : alk. paper) $37.50   **362.4**

1. Parenting 2. Family life 3. Exceptional children 4. Slow learning children 5. Identity (Psychology) -- United States 6. Parents of exceptional children -- United States 7. Exceptional children -- United States -- Psychology 8. Parents of children with disabilities -- United States 9. Children with disabilities -- United States -- Psychology 10. Parent and child -- United States -- Psychological aspects

ISBN 0743236718; 9780743236713; 9780743236720; 9781439183106; 9781442356108; 9781442357433

LC 2012020878

In this book, Andrew Solomon "writes about families coping with deafness, dwarfism, Down syndrome, autism, schizophrenia, multiple severe disabilities, with children who are prodigies, who are conceived in rape, who become criminals, who are transgender. . . . All parenting turns on a crucial question: to what extent parents should accept their children for who they are, and to what extent they should help them become their best selves." (Publisher's note)

Includes bibliographical references (p. 831-906) and index.

Witter, Bret

Until Tuesday; a wounded warrior and the golden retriever who saved him. [by] Luis Carlos Montalvan with Bret Witter. Hyperion 2011 272p illustrations hardcover $23   **362.4**

1. Veterans 2. Army officers

ISBN 9781401324292

LC 2010051147

"A highly decorated captain in the U.S. Army, Luis Montalvan never backed down from a challenge during his two tours of duty in Iraq. After returning home from combat, however, the pressures of his physical wounds, traumatic brain injury, and crippling post-traumatic stress disorder began to take their toll. . . . Then Luis met Tuesday, a beautiful and sensitive golden retriever trained to assist the disabled. Tuesday had lived amongst prisoners and at a home for troubled boys, blessing many lives; he could turn on lights, open doors, and sense the onset of anxiety and flashbacks.

But because of a unique training situation and sensitive nature, he found it difficult to trust in or connect with a human being--until Luis." (Publisher's note)

"Montalvan's mixture of memoir, military history, and pet story results in an urgently important tale." Booklist

362.5 Poor people

Kozol, Jonathan

Rachel and her children; homeless families in America. Three Rivers Press 2006 303p pa $13.95 **362.5**

1. Homeless persons

ISBN 0-307-34589-0

LC 2007-281899

A reissue of the title first published 1988

"While the individual stories that Kozol tells so affectingly point out the vivid realities of urban poverty, the book also supplies statistics that detail the more abstract-and inhuman-attitudes that contemporary society assumes when attempting to deal with its victims." Booklist

Includes bibliographical references

Tirado, Linda

Hand to mouth; living in bootstrap America. Linda Tirado. G.P. Putnam's Sons, a member of Penguin Group (USA) 2014 224 p. (hardback) $25.95 **362.5**

1. Poor -- United States 2. Poverty -- United States 3. Social classes -- United States

ISBN 9780399171987

LC 2014023347

This book, by Linda Tirado, "articulates not only what it is to be working poor in America (yes, you can be poor and live in a house and have a job, even two), but what poverty is truly like—on all levels. Frankly and boldly, Tirado discusses openly how she went from lower-middle class, to sometimes middle class, to poor and everything in between, and in doing so reveals why 'poor people don't always behave the way middle-class America thinks they should.'" (Publisher's note)

"Outspoken and vindictive, Tirado embodies the cyclical vortex of today's struggle to survive." Kirkus

Vollmann, William T.

★ **Poor** people. Ecco 2007 314p il $29.95; pa $16.95 **362.5**

1. Poor 2. Poverty

ISBN 0-06-087882-7; 978-0-06-087882-5; 0-06-087884-3 pa; 978-0-06-087884-9 pa

LC 2006-48547

The author "brings to bear his keen powers of observation on the world around him and, not incidentally, on himself; he is unabashed about allowing his emotional reactions to inform his thoughts about what it means to be poor. This remarkable book is sui generis and should be in all collections." Libr J

362.6 People in late adulthood

Delehanty, Hugh

Caring for your parents; the complete AARP guide. [by] Hugh Delehanty & Elinor Ginzler; foreword by Mary Pipher. Rev. and expanded ed.; Sterling Pub. 2008 xvii, 238p il pa $12.95 **362.6**

1. Aging parents 2. Elderly -- Care

ISBN 1-4027-5857-X; 978-1-4027-5857-7

LC 2008-277441

First published 2005

The authors "provide information on everything from the first difficult conversations with parents about their changing situation to coping with terminal illness and death. The book has a wealth of data on long-distance caregiving, financial matters, community-based and professional case management, Medicare, and age-related physical changes." Libr J

Includes bibliographical references

Hogan, Paul Ross

Stages of senior care; your step-by-step guide to making the best decisions. by Paul Hogan and Lori Hogan. McGraw-Hill 2009 292p il pa $18.95 **362.6**

1. Aging parents 2. Elderly -- Care

ISBN 978-0-07-162109-0

LC 2009-20572

This is "a helpful guide for families choosing among home care-giving and other assisted-living options for aging or ailing parents." Publ Wkly

Includes bibliographical references

362.7 Young people

Caughman, Susan

You can adopt; an Adoptive Families guide. [by] Susan Caughman and Isolde Motley; with the editors and readers of Adoptive Families magazine. Ballantine Books 2009 296p il pa $16 **362.7**

1. Adoption

ISBN 978-0-345-50401-2; 0-345-50401-1

LC 2009-20252

"This thorough and honest resource stands out among other books on the topic in both its comprehensiveness and the authors' candor in discussing potentially controversial adoption-related issues. Domestic or international adoption? An infant or an older child? A sibling group? What about adopting transracially? These questions and many more are addressed here via a straightforward text interspersed with firsthand, sometimes wrenching accounts by adoptive parents, birth parents, and adoptees themselves." Booklist

Includes bibliographical references

Gammage, Jeff

China ghosts; my daughter's journey to America, my passage to fatherhood. William Morrow 2007 255p il $25.95 **362.7**

1. Adoption

ISBN 978-0-06-124029-4; 0-06-124029-X

LC 2007-61204

"A father's account of going to China with his wife to adopt their first and second daughters. . . . Gammage, a staff writer for the Philadelphia Inquirer, had been happily married without children for many years, although he knew his wife really wanted children. By the time they discovered they couldn't have biological children, the best option was adopting from China. While there were tensions over their first daughter's medical problems (an infected scalp injury), both adoptions went reasonably smoothly. Back home, Gammage wrestled with his mixed feelings about the birth parents and his burden of good fortune, that guilty knowledge that his own happiness came from someone else's misfortune. Realizing that his own relationship to China was being shaped by the process of raising two Chinese girls, he ends this upbeat memoir by wondering about the impact of this new wave of immigrants on the future of Sino-American relations." Publ Wkly

Groza, Victor

Adopting older children; a practical guide to adopting and parenting children over age four. Stephanie Bosco-Ruggiero, Gloria Russo-Wassell, Victor Graza. New Horizon Press 2014 240 p. $15.95 **362.7**
  1. Adoption 2. Parenting
  ISBN 0882824821; 9780882824826
                     LC 2014938451

This book by Stephanie Bosco-Ruggiero, Gloria Russo Wassell, and Victor Groza "addresses the most significant challenges surrounding older-child adoption (both domestically and internationally), including mental health, behavioral, and educational concerns. This thorough guide enumerates the issues an older adopted child faces and provides a comprehensive overview of problems and how adopting parents can successfully deal with them, including critical information about developmental issues." (Publisher's note)

An appendix of online resources—websites, video interviews, documentaries, etc.—rounds out this helpful, if far from comprehensive, addition to the literature on adoption." Publisher's Weekly

Kozol, Jonathan

Amazing grace; the lives of children and the conscience of a nation. HarperPerennial 1996 284p pa $14.95
                    362.7
  1. Inner cities 2. Children with social disabilities 3. Poor -- New York (N.Y.)
  ISBN 0-06-097697-7; 978-0-06-097697-2
  First published 1995 by Crown
  Kozol's "powerfully understated report takes us inside rat-infested homes that are freezing in winter, overcrowded schools, dysfunctional clinics, soup kitchens. . . . While his narrative offers no specific solutions, it forcefully drives home his conviction: a civilized nation cannot allow this situation to continue." Publ Wkly
  Includes bibliographical references

Fire in the ashes; twenty-five years among the poorest children in America. Jonathan Kozol. 1st ed. Crown Publishers 2012 x, 368 p.p $27 **362.7**
  1. Poor -- United States 2. Poor children -- United States 3. Children -- United States -- Social conditions 4. Child welfare -- United States 5. Poor families --

United States
  ISBN 1400052467; 9781400052462
                  LC 2012005183
  In this book, author Jonathan Kozol profiles "a group of inner-city children he has known for many years, . . . as they grow into adulthood. . . . Jonathan tells the stories of young men and women who have come of age in one of the most destitute communities of the United States. Some of them never do recover from the battering they undergo in their early years, but many more battle back with fierce . . . determination to overcome the formidable obstacles they face." (Publisher's note)
  Includes bibliographical references and index.

Leach, Penelope

Child care today; getting it right for everyone. Alfred A. Knopf 2009 350p $25.95 **362.7**
  1. Child care
  ISBN 978-1-4000-4256-2
                  LC 2008-38373
  The author "evaluates the state of child care in the Western world in the context of caring for children (as opposed to rearing children). . . . There's no doubt Child Care Today will become the bible on the subject. Stock up." Booklist
  Includes bibliographical references

Tough, Paul

Whatever it takes; Geoffrey Canada's quest to change Harlem and America. Houghton Mifflin Co. 2008 296p il map **362.7**
  1. Poverty -- Prevention 2. Organization officials 3. Social welfare leaders 4. Poor -- Social conditions 5. Education -- United States 6. African American children -- Education 7. Harlem (New York, N.Y.) -- Economic conditions
  ISBN 0-618-56989-8; 978-0-618-56989-2
                  LC 2008-13303
  This is an account of Geoffrey Canada's creation of "the Harlem Children's Zone, a ninety-seven-block . . . [area] in central Harlem where he is testing new . . . ideas about poverty in America." (Publisher's note) Index.
  "Tough profiles educational visionary Geoffrey Canada, whose Harlem Children's Zone—currently serving more than 7,000 children and encompassing 97 city blocks—represents an audacious effort to end poverty within underserved communities. . . . This book gives readers a solid look at the problems facing poor communities and their reformers, as well as good cause to be optimistic about the future." Publ Wkly
  Includes bibliographical references

362.73 Institutional and related services

Beam, Cris

★ **To** the end of June; the intimate life of American foster care. Cris Beam. Houghton Mifflin Harcourt 2013 336 p. $26 **362.73**
  1. Foster home care 2. United States -- Social conditions 3. Foster home care -- United States
  ISBN 0151014124; 9780151014125
                  LC 2013001331

This book looks at the foster care system in the U.S. "Following the lives of foster children, meeting their natural and foster parents, and interviewing experts, [Cris] Beam developed a broad overview. Intended to be a temporary arrangement, foster care frequently fails to lead either to resolution of the biological parents' problems and restoration of the birth family or to the children's permanent adoption into a new home." (Kirkus Reviews)

Includes bibliographical references

Bernstein, Nina

The **lost** children of Wilder; the epic struggle to change foster care. Pantheon Bks. 2001 482p hardcover o.p. pa $15   **362.73**

1. Child welfare 2. Foster home care

ISBN 0-679-75834-8 pa

LC 00-57456

"Bernstein explores the genesis and aftermath of the landmark 1973 legal case filed by young ACLU attorney Marcia Lowry against the New York State foster-care system. Known as Wilder for its 14-year-old African-American plaintiff, Shirley 'Pinky' Wilder, the suit claimed Jewish and Catholic child welfare services had a lock on foster care funding and placements. . . . This viscerally powerful history of institutionalized child abuse and the criminalization of poverty, of civil rights and social change, is compelling and essential reading." Publ Wkly

Includes bibliographical references

362.734   Adoption

Aronson, Jane

Carried in Our Hearts; The Gift of Adoption: Inspiring Stories of Families Created Across Continents. Penguin Group USA 2013 336 p. $25.95   **362.734**

ISBN 0399161058; 9780399161056

"...There is a wealth of information—and hope—here for people looking at possibilities for international adoption, and there is certainly no better advocate on the long journey than the upbeat, passionate Aronson." PubWkly

Joyce, Kathryn

★ The **child** catchers; rescue, trafficking, and the new gospel of adoption. Kathryn Joyce. PublicAffairs 2013 352 p. (hardback) $26.99   **362.734**

1. Adoption 2. Evangelicalism -- United States 3. Abortion -- Religious aspects -- Christianity 4. Adoption -- Religious aspects -- Christianity

ISBN 1586489429; 9781586489427; 9781586489434

LC 2012044316

This book "examines the rise of adoption as a practice and cause among American evangelical communities . . . . The more than 150 million so-termed orphans and vulnerable children worldwide frequently have living family members . . . capable of raising them, circumstances . . . lost in the mix of aggressive agencies, inadequate regulation, vulnerable families lacking understanding of the concept of adoption as permanent, and adoptive families with emotional and financial resources invested." (Library Journal)

Includes bibliographical references and index

Sweeney, Julia

If it's not one thing, it's your mother; Julia Sweeney. Free Press 2013 256 p. (hardcover) $26   **362.734**

1. Working mothers 2. Adopted children 3. Parenting -- California 4. Motherhood -- California 5. Adopted children -- California

ISBN 145167404X; 9781451674040; 9781451674057

LC 2012049503

This book is comedian Julia Sweeney's "memoir on adopting and raising a family." She writes about "her childhood, finding a suitable nanny during her daughter's childhood, her failed relationships and life as a working mother . . . . Her thoughts swirled around the complexities of educating her daughter about human anatomy and sex." (Kirkus)

362.74   Specific kinds of young people

Phelps, Carissa

Runaway girl; escaping life on the streets, one helping hand at a time. Carissa Phelps with Larkin Warren. Viking 2012 311 p. $19.99   **362.74**

1. Runaway children 2. Juvenile prostitution 3. Prostitution -- California 4. Runaway children -- California -- Biography

ISBN 1561636150; 9780670023721

LC 2011038441

In this memoir, Carissa Phelps discusses "her loveless, troubled childhood." After running away from a state group home at age 12, "she meets crack-addicted Natara, a prostitute, and Icey, a pimp, a pair who promise to take care of her." Eventually, "she lands in the Youth Authority detention center. There, she meets her first mentor, counselor Ron Jenkins. Slowly and with setbacks, Phelps rebuilds her life and graduates from high school thanks to the perseverance of a teacher." (Publishers Weekly)

Includes bibliographical references.

362.786   Young people by sexual orientation

Berg, Ryan

No house to call my home; Love, Family, and Other Transgressions. Ryan Berg. Nation Books 2015 320 p. (hardback) $25.99; (ebook) $9.99 **362.786**

1. LGBT youth -- New York (State) -- New York 2. Gay teenagers -- Counseling of -- New York (State) -- New York 3. Residence counselors -- New York (State) -- New York 4. Group homes for youth -- New York (State) -- New York 5. Gay teenagers -- Services for -- New York (State) -- New York 6. Sexual minority youth -- Services for -- New York (State) -- New York 7. Sexual minority youth -- Counseling of -- New York (State) -- New York

ISBN 9781568585093; 9781568585109

LC 2015011424

This book by Ryan Berg focuses "on the lives and loves of eight unforgettable youth. . . [and] traces their efforts to break away from dangerous sex work and cycles of drug and alcohol abuse.... From Bella's fervent desire for stability to

Christina's . . . dreams of stardom to Benny's . . . efforts to find someone to love him, Berg uncovers the real lives behind the harrowing statistics: over 4,000 youth are homeless in New York City—43 percent of them identify as LGBTQ." (Publisher's note)

"Through their compelling stories, Berg looks at inequalities suffered by LGBTQ youth in housing, public safety, health care, prison, immigration, employment, poverty, and homelessness." Booklist

Includes bibliographical references and index

362.82 Families

Dalpiaz, Christina M.
Breaking free, starting over; parenting in the aftermath of family violence. Praeger 2004 232p $39.95   **362.82**
1. Parenting 2. Domestic violence
ISBN 0-275-98167-3
LC 2003-62436

This guide provides "techniques for reparenting children who've been exposed to domestic violence. Lacking a safe haven, many of these children exhibit significant behavior, communication, and self-management problems." Libr J

Includes bibliographical references and index

Denham, Wes
Arrested; what to do when your loved one's in jail. Chicago Review Press 2010 263p il pa $16.95   **362.82**
1. Prisoners
ISBN 978-1-55652-834-7; 1-55652-834-5
LC 2009-42270

This book is an "extended checklist for those coping with the incarceration of a family member or significant friend, from the time the phone rings with news of the arrest onward. Denham shares the jargon, procedures, tricks, and traps in his coverage of jail visits, bail, public defenders, jail medical care, and legal and jail costs, and he outlines a decision-making process that considers the well-being of the entire family. . . .Hard-hitting, blunt, and practical, this book is packed with inside knowledge of the jail experience. It's a necessary purchase for criminal justice collections in public libraries." Libr J

Includes bibliographical references

Domestic violence sourcebook; edited by Joyce Brennfleck Shannon. 3rd ed.; Omnigraphics 2009 665p il (Health reference series) $84   **362.82**
1. Reference books 2. Domestic violence
ISBN 978-0-7808-1038-9; 0-7808-1038-4
LC 2009-4386

First published 2000 under the editorship of Helene Henderson with title: Domestic violence & child abuse sourcebook

"Provides basic consumer health information about the physical, mental, and social effects of violence against intimate partners, children, teens, parents, and the elderly, along with prevention and intervention strategies." Publisher's note

Includes bibliographical references

Fessler, Ann
The **girls** who went away; the hidden history of women who surrendered children for adoption in the decades before Roe v. Wade. Penguin Press 2006 354p hardcover o.p. pa $16   **362.82**
1. Adoption
ISBN 1-59420-094-7; 0-14-303897-4 pa
LC 2005-58179

"These knowing oral histories are an emotional boon for birth mothers and adoptees struggling to make sense of troubled pasts." Publ Wkly

Includes bibliographical references

Marshall, Samantha
Reunited; an investigative genealogist unlocks some of life's greatest family mysteries. Pamela Slaton; with Samantha Marshall. St. Martin's Griffin 2012 248 p. (trade pbk.) $14.99   **362.82**
1. Adoption 2. Genealogy 3. Adoptees -- United States -- Identification -- Case studies 4. Birthparents -- United States -- Identification -- Case studies
ISBN 0312617321; 9780312617325; 9781250012135
LC 2012004630

This book shares the experience of investigative genealogist Pamela Slaton. An "adopted child herself, the author's sleuthing career began 15 years ago when her husband hired an investigator to locate her birth mother. Although she was raised by a loving adoptive family, Slaton had always wondered about her roots. . . . The author tells about finding her own extended birth family and the touching stories of some of the clients she has helped." (Kirkus Reviews)

Weiss, Elaine
Family & friends' guide to domestic violence; how to listen, talk, and take action, when someone you care about is being abused. Volcano Press 2003 143p pa $17.95   **362.82**
1. Domestic violence
ISBN 1-88424-422-X
LC 2003-4642

This is a "guide for family and friends, with practical tips for communicating with a likely victim of abuse, including how to broach the subject." Libr J

Includes bibliographical references

Surviving domestic violence; voices of women who broke free. Volcano Press 2004 214p pa $17.95   **362.82**
1. Domestic violence
ISBN 1-88424-427-0
LC 2003-27829

First published 2000 by Agreka Bks.

The author tells the "stories of 12 survivors, ranging in age and socioeconomic circumstances. She concludes each case study with a reflective commentary that emphasizes the strength and courage of these women." Libr J

Includes bibliographical references

362.83　Women

Kristof, Nicholas D., 1959-

★ **Half** the sky; turning oppression to opportunity for women worldwide. [by] Nicholas D. Kristof and Sheryl WuDunn. Alfred A. Knopf 2009 xxii, 294p il $27.95; ebook $15.95; pa $15.95　**362.83**
1. Women's rights 2. Women -- Developing countries 3. Women's rights -- Developing countries 4. Women -- Crimes against -- Developing countries 5. Women -- Developing countries -- Social conditions
ISBN 9780307267146; 9780307273154; 9780307387097

LC 2009-12270

Kristof and WuDunn address what they consider to be "our era's most pervasive human rights violation: the oppression of women in the developing world. They show that a little help can transform the lives of women and girls abroad and that the key to economic progress lies in unleashing women's potential." (Publisher's note) Index.

This book "is a call to arms, a call for help, a call for contributions, but also a call for volunteers. It asks us to open our eyes to this enormous humanitarian issue. It does so with exquisitely crafted prose and sensationally interesting material." Washington Post Book World

Includes bibliographical references

Sered, Susan Starr

Can't catch a break; gender, jail, drugs and the limits of personal responsibility. Susan Starr Sered and Maureen Norton-Hawk. University of California Press 2014 216 p. (Paper) $29.95　**362.83**
1. Boston (Mass.) 2. Responsibility 3. Women -- Social conditions 4. Responsibility -- Social aspects -- Massachusetts -- Boston 5. Abused women -- Massachusetts -- Boston -- Social conditions 6. Female offenders -- Massachusetts -- Boston -- Social conditions 7. Women drug addicts -- Massachusetts -- Boston -- Social conditions
ISBN 0520282787; 0520282795; 9780520282780; 9780520282797

LC 2014011744

This book, by Susan Starr Sered and Maureen Norton-Hawk, "based on five years of fieldwork in Boston, . . . documents the day-to-day lives of forty women as they struggle to survive sexual abuse, violent communities, ineffective social and therapeutic programs, discriminatory local and federal policies, criminalization, incarceration, and a broad cultural consensus that views suffering as a consequence of personal flaws and bad choices." (Publisher's note)

"In the study's most original chapter, the authors argue that the therapeutic and mental health services available to the incarcerated and formerly incarcerated, rather than directing attention to how society has stacked the deck against marginal women and suggesting political solutions, teach that people's problems are the result of their own unhealed trauma. This compelling and important book deserves to be widely read." Pub Wkly

Includes bibliographical references and index

362.84　Ethnic and national groups

Youngstedt, Scott M.

★ **Surviving** with dignity; Hausa communities of Niamey, Niger. by Scott M. Youngstedt. Lexington Books 2012 xv, 226 p.p ill., map (hbk. : alk. paper) $65　**362.84**
1. Niger 2. Internal migration 3. Rural-urban migration -- Niger 4. Hausa (African people) -- Niger -- Niamey -- Social conditions 5. Hausa (African people) -- Niger -- Niamey -- Economic conditions
ISBN 0739173502; 9780739173503; 9780739173510

LC 2012040502

This book, by Scott M. Youngstedt, "explores three key interconnected themes—structural violence, suffering, and surviving with dignity—through examining the lived experiences of first and second-generation migrant Hausa men in Niamey over the past two decades in the current neoliberal moment. The central goal of the book is to explain the material (migration and informal economy work) and symbolic (meaning-making) strategies that Hausa individuals and communities have deployed in their struggles . . . to survive with dignity." (Publisher's note)

Includes bibliographical references (p. [213]-223) and index

362.86　Veterans of military service

Bannerman, Stacy

Homefront 911; how families of veterans are wounded by our wars. Stacy Bannerman. Arcade Publishing 2015 304 p. (hardcover : alkaline paper) $24.99　**362.86**
1. Afghan War, 2001- 2. Iraq War, 2003-2011 3. Veterans -- United States 4. Civil-military relations -- United States 5. Veterans -- Services for -- United States 6. Veterans -- Mental health -- United States 7. Afghan War, 2001- -- Veterans -- United States 8. Families of military personnel -- United States 9. Iraq War, 2003-2011 -- Veterans -- United States 10. Veterans -- Family relationships -- United States 11. Families of military personnel -- Services for -- United States 12. Families of military personnel -- Mental health -- United States
ISBN 9781628725698

LC 2015019123

This book, by Stacy Bannerman, "provides an insider's view of how more than a decade of war has contributed to the emerging crisis we are experiencing in today's military and veteran families as they battle with overwhelmed VA offices, a public they feel doesn't understand their sacrifices, and a nation that still isn't fully prepared to help those who have given so much." (Publisher's note)

"An activist, Bannerman has set up programs for women, drafted legislation, and testified before congressional committees. Here, she takes her message to a broader public in a disturbing cry for help." Kirkus

Includes bibliographical references (pages 270-282).

Finkel, David

★ **Thank** You for Your Service; by David Finkel. Farrar, Straus and Giroux 2013 272 p. $27 **362.86**

1. Veterans -- Employment 2. Veterans -- United States 3. Iraq War, 2003-2011 -- Psychological aspects 4. Post-traumatic stress disorder -- United States 5. Iraq War, 2003-2011 -- Veterans -- United States

ISBN 0374180660; 9780374180669

LC 2013021990

In this book, author David Finkel "has embedded with some of the men of the 2-16 [Infantry Battalion]--but this time he has done it . . . after their deployments have ended. He is with them in their most intimate, painful, and hopeful moments as they try to recover, and in doing so, he creates a . . . portrait of what life after war is like." (Publisher's note)

"It is impossible not to be moved, outraged, and saddened by these stories, and Finkel's deeply personal brand of narrative journalism is both heartbreaking and gut-wrenching in its unflinching honesty." Booklist

Includes bibliographical references and index

362.88 Victims of crimes and war

Crompton, Vicki

Saving beauty from the beast; how to protect your daughter from an unhealthy relationship. by Vicki Crompton and Ellen Zelda Kessner. Little, Brown 2003 259p il $22.95; pa $13.95 **362.88**

1. Parenting 2. Abused women

ISBN 0-316-09058-1; 0-316-73552-3 pa

LC 2002-19153

This book "illuminates the problems of dangerous relationships by describing their characteristics, mapping out warning signs of abuse and offering sound advice for parents seeking to empower their daughters. The authors interviewed psychologists, counselors and girls who have had violent boyfriends; the girls' stories, as well as first-person accounts from parents and abusive boyfriends, are woven throughout the text. . . . This book serves as both fervent friend and practical coach to parents whose daughters may be facing abuse." Publ Wkly

Includes bibliographical references

Feinberg, Kenneth R.

What is life worth? the unprecedented effort to compensate the victims of 9/11. Public Affairs 2005 xxv, 213p $24 **362.88**

1. September 11 terrorist attacks, 2001

ISBN 1-58648-323-4

LC 2005-47699

"Feinberg's willingness to put himself into the book makes what could have been an alternately dry and self-serving case study crackle with care, frustration, intellectual energy and good writing." Publ Wkly

Kushner, David

Alligator candy; a memoir. David Kushner. Simon & Schuster 2016 256 p. (hardcover) $26 **362.88**

1. Brothers 2. Homicide 3. Children of anthropologists -- Biography 4. Murder victims -- Florida -- Tampa

-- Biography 5. Murder victims' families -- Florida -- Tampa -- Biography

ISBN 9781451682533; 9781451682601; 9781451682632

LC 2015022792

This memoir, by David Kushner, "is the story of [his brother] Jon's murder at the hands of two sadistic drifters and everything that happened after. [It] isn't only the chronicle of Jon's death, it is also the story of how parenting in America changed, casting light on the transition between two generations of children—one raised on freedom, the other on fear. Jon's death was one of the first in what turned out to be a rash of child abductions and murders that dominated headlines for much of the 1970s and 80s." (Publisher's note)

"This emotional account invites readers to journey down a path that at first is in the shade but eventually wanders through strands of sunlight. You will hold those close to you tight after reading. For fans of true crime, books about getting past tragedy, and memoirs." Library Journal

Nelson, Maggie

The **red** parts; Autobiography of a Trial. Maggie Nelson. Graywolf Press 2016 201 p. illustrations (alk. paper) $16 **362.88**

1. Evidence 2. Trials (Homicide) 3. Cold cases (Criminal investigation)

ISBN 9781555977368

LC 2015953598

In this memoir, "in 2004, Maggie Nelson was looking forward to the publication of her book Jane: A Murder, . . . about the life and death of her aunt, who had been murdered thirty-five years before. The case remained unsolved, but Jane was assumed to have been the victim of an infamous serial killer. . . . Then, one November afternoon, Nelson received a call from her mother, who announced that the case had been reopened; a new suspect would be arrested and tried." (Publisher's note)

Surviving sexual violence; a guide to recovery and empowerment. edited by Thema Bryant-Davis. Rowman & Littlefield Publishers 2011 ix, 372 p.p (cloth : alk. paper) $49.95; (electronic) $49.95 **362.88**

1. Rape 2. Sex crimes 3. Sexual harassment 4. Sexual abuse victims -- Psychology 5. Sexual abuse victims -- Rehabilitation

ISBN 144220639X; 9781442206397; 9781442206410

LC 2011013937

Author Thema Bryant-Davis's "book outlines and describes the impact of particular types of sexual violation . . . [including] childhood sexual abuse, sexual assault during adulthood, marital rape, sexual harassment, sex trafficking, or sexual violence within the military. . . . [Readers] are introduced to various pathways to surviving sexual violence and moving forward. . . . Survivors can make use of the particular approaches, which include mind-body practices, counseling, group therapies, self-defense training, and others." (Publisher's note)

Includes bibliographical references and index.

362.883   Rape

Krakauer, Jon, 1954-

Missoula; by Jon Krakauer. Doubleday 2015 384 p. (hardcover : alk. paper) $28.95   **362.883**
1. Date rape 2. Trials (Rape) 3. Missoula (Mont.) 4. Rape -- Montana -- Missoula 5. Rape victims -- Montana -- Missoula 6. Trials (Rape) -- Montana -- Missoula
ISBN 0385538731; 9780385538732

LC 2015002686

This book "follows a rash of rapes at the University of Montana in Missoula from 2010 to 2012." Author Jon Krakauer "sticks with two cases in particular through agonizing courtroom dramas, spotlighting the two obstacles to justice. The first is haphazard investigation, made worse by . . . callousness and suspicion about the motives of women making rape allegations. . . . The second is the counterintuitive behavior of traumatized victims, which often undermines their claims." (Kirkus Reviews)

"Krakauer has done considerable research into acquaintance rape, and his recounting of trials, both legal and university proceedings, is riveting. His focus on quoting from testimony means that it is harder for readers to understand the motivations of someone like Kirsten Pabst, a former prosecutor who became a lawyer for an accused football player; an interview with her could have been useful. A raw and difficult but necessary read." Kirkus

Includes bibliographical references and index

Ream, Anne K.

Lived through this; listening to the stories of sexual-violence survivors. Anne K. Ream; with photographs by Patricia Evans. Beacon Press 2014 216 p. illustrations (hardcover : alk. paper) $24.95 **362.883**
1. Sex crimes 2. Rape victims 3. Sex crimes -- Case studies 4. Sexual abuse victims -- Case studies
ISBN 0807033367; 9780807033364

LC 2013045411

This book, by Anne K. Ream, is about "rape and sexual violence survivors. . . . In these pages we are introduced to . . . the women of Atenco, Mexico, victims of rape and political torture who are speaking out about gender-based violence in Latin America; Beth Adubato, a woman who was raped by a popular athlete; . . . and Jenny and Steve Bush, a rape survivor and her father who are working together to share Jenny's testimony of surviving rape at the hands of a veteran." (Publisher's note)

"Ream's prose is approachable, making the book a useful introductory primer for anyone studying sexual violence. The helpful inclusion of statistics at the end, which puts quantitative weight behind these individual stories, enhances the book's educational value." Pub Wkly

Includes bibliographical references

Sebold, Alice

Lucky. Back Bay Books 2002 246p pa $11.95   **362.883**
1. Rape
ISBN 0-316-09619-9
First published 1999 by Scribner

When the author "was a college freshman at Syracuse University, she was attacked and raped on the last night of school. . . . Sebold launches her memoir headlong into the rape itself, laying out its visceral physical as well as mental violence, and from there spins a narrative of her life before and after the incident, weaving memories of parental alcoholism together with her post-rape addiction to heroin. In the midst of each wrenching episode, from the initial attack to the ensuing courtroom drama, Sebold's wit is as powerful as her searing candor." Publ Wkly

363.1   Public safety programs

Genetically modified foods; debating biotechnology. edited by Michael Ruse, David Castle. Prometheus Bks. 2002 355p il (Contemporary issues series) $20   **363.1**
1. Farm produce 2. Food -- Biotechnology
ISBN 1-57392-996-4

LC 2002-70510

In this collection of essays the first section focuses on "the history and the science of genetically modified foods. The next section focuses on the morality of modifying organisms for human use. . . . Succeeding sections include articles discussing religious attitudes toward genetically modified food, legal issues involving patenting and environmental damage, risk assessment, and possible environmental threats and benefits." Publisher's note

Includes bibliographical references

Nestle, Marion

Pet food politics; the Chihuahua in the coal mine. University of California Press 2008 219p il $18.95   **363.1**
1. Product recall 2. Pets -- Food
ISBN 978-0-520-25781-8; 0-520-25781-2

LC 2008-3995

This book "provides a vivid and detailed account of the [contaminated pet food] affair and its aftermath. The book . . . deserves a wider readership." Economist

Includes bibliographical references

Pringle, Peter

★ **Food,** inc; Mendel to Monsanto--the promises and perils of the biotech harvest. Simon & Schuster 2003 239p hardcover o.p. pa $13   **363.1**
1. Farm produce 2. Food -- Biotechnology
ISBN 0-7432-2611-9; 0-7432-6763-X pa

LC 2003-42823

"This is a book to satisfy curiosity and engender concern, and any of its chapters would provide an excellent subject for discussion groups." SLJ

Puleo, Stephen

Dark tide; the great Boston molasses flood of 1919. Beacon Press 2003 263p il $23   **363.1**
1. Industrial accidents 2. Boston (Mass.) -- History
ISBN 0-8070-5020-2

LC 2003-10433

"On January 15, 1919, a fifty-foot tall steel tank filled with 2.3 million gallons of molasses collapsed on Boston's waterfront, disgorging its contents as a fifteen-foot high wave of molasses that briefly traveled at thirty-five miles per hour. The Great Boston Molasses Flood claimed the lives of twenty-one people and scores of animals, injured 150, and caused widespread destruction. Tracing the era from the tank's construction in 1915 through the multiyear lawsuit that followed the tragedy, Dark Tide uses the drama of the flood to examine the sweeping changes brought about by World War I, Prohibition, the Anarchist movement, the Red Scare, Immigration, and the role of big business in society." Univ Press Books 2004

Includes bibliographical references

Wilson, Bee

Swindled; the dark history of food fraud, from poisoned candy to counterfeit coffee. Princeton University Press 2008 384p il map $26.95 **363.1**
1. Food industry 2. Food contamination
ISBN 978-0-691-13820-6

LC 2008-9688

"In this day and age of tainted milk, pet food and genetically altered food, Bee Wilson has given us an immensely readable history from the 1820's to the 21st century. Timely and purposeful, this book should bring many people to the whole foods world." Univ Press Books for Public and Second Sch Libr, 2009

Includes bibliographical references (351-361)

363.11   Occupational and industrial hazards

Galuszka, Peter A.

Thunder on the Mountain; Death at Massey and the Dirty Secrets Behind Big Coal. Peter A. Galuszka. St. Martin's Press 2012 xvii, 283 p., [8] p. of plates p ill. (hardcover) $25.99 **363.11**
1. Coal mines and mining 2. Massey Energy (Firm) 3. Coal trade -- Appalachian Region 4. Coal mines and mining -- Appalachian Region
ISBN 1250000211; 9781250000217

LC 2012028241

This book by journalist Peter A. Galuszka focuses on the U.S. coal industry. He examines a "central dichotomy: the geographical and cultural isolation of the Appalachian people, perpetuated by inaccurate and condescending popular conceptions, has fostered a big-profit environment for Big Coal even as the region remains impoverished." (Publishers Weekly)

Tobar, Héctor

★ Deep down dark; the untold stories of 33 men buried in a Chilean mine, and the miracle that set them free. Hector Tobar. Fararr, Straus & Giroux 2014 320 p. illustrations (cloth) $26 **363.11**
1. Chile 2. Rescue work 3. Gold mines and mining 4. Copper mines and mining 5. San José Mine Accident, Chile, 2010
ISBN 0374280606; 9780374280604

LC 2014008385

Los Angeles Times Book Prize Finalist: Current Interest (2014)

This book, by Hector Tobar, focuses on "the San José mine [collapse] outside of Copiapó, Chile, in August 2010, [which] trapped thirty-three miners beneath thousands of feet of rock for a record-breaking sixty-nine days. . . . . Even while still buried, they all agreed that if by some miracle any of them escaped alive, they would share their story only collectively." (Publisher's note)

"Rich in local color, this is a sensitive, suspenseful rendering of a legendary story." Pub Wkly

363.12   Transportation hazards

Gonzales, Laurence, 1947-

Flight 232; A Story of Disaster and Survival. Laurence Gonzales. W.W. Norton & Co Inc. 2014 432 p. illustrations (some color) $27.95 **363.12**
1. Journalism 2. Aircraft accidents
ISBN 0393240029; 9780393240023

LC 2014005238

"United Airlines Flight 232 wallowed drunkenly over the bluffs northwest of Sioux City. The plane slammed onto the runway and burst into a vast fireball. . . . Drawing on interviews with hundreds of survivors, crew, and airport and rescue personnel, [author] Laurence Gonzales, a commercial pilot himself, captures, minute by minute, the harrowing journey of pilots flying a plane with no controls and flight attendants keeping their calm in the face of certain death." (Publisher's note)

"Gonzalez presents an absorbing account of the delicate machinery of flight—and the titanic forces it must withstand—and of the investigation that traced the disaster to a tiny flaw therein." Pub Wkly

Includes bibliographical references and index

363.14   Hazards in sports and recreation

Chowdhury, Bernie

The last dive; a father and son's fatal descent into the ocean's depths. Bernie Chowdhury. HarperCollins 2000 xi, 356 p.p illustrations (some color) (ebook) $14.99; $25 **363.14**
1. Shipwrecks 2. Scuba diving 3. Shipwrecks -- Atlantic Coast (U.S.) 4. Scuba diving -- Accidents -- Atlantic Coast (U.S.)
ISBN 9780062196828; 0060194626; 9780060194628

LC 00033426

In this book, author Bernie Chowdhury "recounts the (eventually) fatal adventures of the Rouses, a father-and-son pair of divers who met their match eight years ago in the wreck of a German U-boat that lies under 230 feet of water off the coast of New Jersey. The Rouses practiced a sport called technical diving, in which divers seek depths as great as 1,000 feet using elaborate equipment and multiple air tanks." (N Y Times Book Rev)

"A sorrowful education in diving history and technique, in the psychology of the adventurer, and in the dominion of death." Kirkus

363.17   Hazardous materials

Brown, Kate

Plutopia; nuclear families, atomic cities, and the great Soviet and American plutonium disasters. Kate Brown. Oxford University Press 2013 416 p. (acid-free paper) $27.95   **363.17**

1. Cold war 2. Arms race 3. Plutonium 4. Working class families -- Russia (Federation) -- Ozërsk (Cheliabinskaia oblast) -- History -- 20th century 5. Plutonium industry -- Accidents -- Russia (Federation) -- Ozërsk (Cheliabinskaia oblast) -- History -- 20th century 6. Plutonium industry -- Social aspects -- Russia (Federation) -- Ozërsk (Cheliabinskaia oblast) -- History -- 20th century 7. Richland (Wash.) -- History -- 20th century 8. Industrial safety -- Government policy -- Soviet Union -- Case studies 9. Industrial safety -- Government policy -- United States -- Case studies 10. Working class families -- Washington (State) -- Richland -- History -- 20th century 11. Plutonium industry -- Accidents -- Washington (State) -- Richland -- History -- 20th century 12. Plutonium industry -- Social aspects -- Washington (State) -- Richland -- History -- 20th century 13. Ozërsk (Cheliabinskaia oblast, Russia) -- History -- 20th century

ISBN 0199855765; 9780199855766

LC 2012041758

This book, written by Kate Brown, "draws on official records and dozens of interviews to tell the extraordinary stories of Richland, Washington and Ozersk, Russia-the first two cities in the world to produce plutonium. An untold . . . piece of Cold War history, Plutopia invites readers to consider the nuclear footprint left by the arms race and the enormous price of paying for it." (Publisher's note)

Includes bibliographical references and index

Iversen, Kristen

★ **Full** body burden; growing up in the nuclear shadow of Rocky Flats. Kristen Iversen. Crown Publishers 2012 400 p. ill. $25.00   **363.17**

1. Nuclear weapons 2. Women journalists 3. Rocky Flats Plant (U.S.) 4. Rocky Flats Plant (U.S.) -- History 5. Plutonium -- Health aspects -- Colorado 6. Jefferson County (Colorado) -- Biography 7. Rocky Flats Plant (U.S.) -- Health aspects 8. Radioactive waste sites -- Cleanup -- Colorado 9. Rocky Flats Plant (U.S.) -- Environmental aspects 10. Nuclear weapons plants -- Health aspects -- Colorado 11. Radioactive pollution -- Colorado -- Jefferson County

ISBN 030795563X; 9780307955630

LC 2011045902

This book is about "[t]he Rocky Flats nuclear weapons plant near Denver [that] began production in 1953; within four years, the plutonium factory had its first major accident, the first of many. In fact, by the end of its forty-year run, the plant would gain notoriety as 'the most contaminated site in America.' Kristen [Iversen], the author , . . , grew up in the radioactive shadow of this secret facility and she witnessed at close quarters the disastrous effects of its activities." Here, "she combines . . . personal experiences and . . . investigative reporting to expose [the U.S.] government's betrayal of its responsibility to its citizens." (Barnes & Noble)

Includes bibliographical references and index

Lyman, Edwin

Fukushima; the story of a nuclear disaster. David Lochbaum, Edwin Lyman, Susan Q. Stranahan, and The Union of Concerned Scientists. The New Press 2014 320 p. illustrations, maps (hc. : alk. paper) $27.95   **363.17**

1. Tsunamis 2. Nuclear reactors 3. Fukushima Nuclear Accident, Fukushima, Japan, 2011 4. Fukushima Nuclear Disaster, Japan, 2011 5. Nuclear power plants -- Accidents -- Japan -- Fukushima-ken

ISBN 1595589082; 9781595589088

LC 2013035284

Authors David Lochbaum, Edwin Lyman, and Susan Q. Stranahan present an "account of the Fukushima disaster. [It] combines a fast-paced . . . account of the tsunami and the nuclear emergency it created with an explanation of the science and technology behind the meltdown as it unfolded in real time." (Publisher's note)

Includes bibliographical references and index

Schlosser, Eric, 1959-

★ **Command** and control; nuclear weapons, the Damascus Accident, and the illusion of safety. Eric Schlosser. The Penguin Press 2013 640 p. $36   **363.17**

1. Nuclear weapons -- United States -- History 2. Nuclear weapons -- Accidents -- United States -- History 3. Titan (Missile) -- History 4. Nuclear weapons -- Accidents -- Arkansas -- History 5. Nuclear weapons -- United States -- Safety measures 6. Nuclear weapons -- Government policy -- United States 7. United States. Air Force. Strategic Air Command. Strategic Missile Wing, 308th

ISBN 1594202273; 9781594202278

LC 2013017151

This book "interweaves the minute-by-minute story of an accident at a nuclear missile silo in rural Arkansas with a historical narrative that spans more than fifty years. It depicts the urgent effort by American scientists, policymakers, and military officers to ensure that nuclear weapons can't be stolen, sabotaged, used without permission, or detonated inadvertently." (Publisher's note)

Includes bibliographical references and index

363.2   Police services

Bell, Suzanne

Encyclopedia of forensic science; foreword by Barry A.J. Fisher; preface by Robert C. Shaler. rev ed; Facts on File 2008 402p il (Facts on File science library) $85   **363.2**

1. Reference books 2. Forensic sciences -- Encyclopedias

ISBN 978-0-8160-6799-2; 0-8160-6799-6

LC 2008-5862

First published 2003

"In addition to explaining the science of forensics, Bell . . . reviews various disciplines related to forensic science, among them entomology, odontology, and psychology. Other entries cover professional organizations, government agencies, famous names in the field of forensics, evidence, and legal issues. . . . With its clear language and brief entries [this] volume will provide readers with a nuts-and-bolts understanding of the real world of forensic science." Booklist [review of 2003 edition]

Includes bibliographical references

Englert, Rod

Blood secrets; a forensic expert reveals how blood spatter tells the crime scene's story. [by] Rod Englert, with Kathy Passero; foreword by Ann Rule. Thomas Dunne Books 2010 286p il $25.99; ebook $12.99 **363.2**

1. Blood 2. Forensic sciences 3. Criminal investigation
ISBN 978-0-312-56400-1; 0-312-56400-7; 978-1-4299-2921-9 ebook; 1-4299-2921-9 ebook
LC 2009-40294

"Englert deftly balances real-life examples and detailed scientific analysis, giving readers a richer understanding of this developing avenue of forensic science." Publ Wkly

Includes bibliographical references

Geary, Rick

J. Edgar Hoover; a graphic biography. Hill and Wang 2008 102p il $16.95 **363.2**

1. Graphic novels 2. Biographical graphic novels 3. FBI officials 4. United States -- Federal Bureau of Investigation -- Graphic novels
ISBN 978-0-8090-9503-2; 0-8090-9503-3
LC 2007-25193

Rick Geary has written a biography of J. Edgar Hoover, who served in the federal government for 55 years and under eight presidents, most notably as director of the Federal Bureau of Investigation. He was appointed to that position on May 10, 1924. Geary covers Hoover's sometimes controversial career, including his refusal to involve the FBI directly into investigations of crimes against civil rights workers and the 1963 bombing in Birmingham, Alabama, and the bureau's investigation of Martin Luther King, Jr. He tastefully discusses Hoover's undercover sexual life.

"As solid, thrilling and informative a guide to the life of the America's most powerful authoritarian as one could ask for." Kirkus

Neme, Laurel A.

Animal investigators; how the world's first wildlife forensics lab is solving crimes and saving endangered species. foreword by Richard Leakey. Scribner 2009 230p il $25 **363.2**

1. Poaching 2. Forensic sciences 3. Wild animal trade 4. Endangered species 5. Wildlife conservation 6. U.S. Fish and Wildlife Service -- Forensics Laboratory
ISBN 978-1-4165-5056-3; 1-4165-5056-9
LC 2008-56004

"Illegal wildlife trafficking is worth an estimated $20 billion a year. That makes it the third most lucrative criminal activity, coming in just behind drug and human trafficking and, incredibly, ahead of arms smuggling. . . . Animal

Investigators documents this black market in unflinching and often depressing detail. But the book is more than just a journey into the criminal underworld, a litany of dismal statistics or a roll-call of cowardly, greedy intermediaries. Instead, Laurel A. Neme centres her book on a more inspiring place: the US Fish and Wildlife Service Forensics Lab in Ashland, Oregon, the world's only laboratory dedicated to solving crimes against wildlife." New Sci

Includes bibliographical references

Stillman, Deanne

Desert reckoning; a town sheriff, a Mojave hermit, and the biggest manhunt in modern California history. Deanne Stillman. Nation Books 2012 308 p. (hbk.) $26 **363.2**

1. California -- History 2. Criminal investigation 3. Mojave Desert (Calif.) 4. Criminal investigation -- California -- Mojave Desert -- Case studies
ISBN 1568586086; 1568586914; 9781568586083; 9781568586915
LC 2012004961

This book by author Deanne Stillman features "a brilliant, paranoid, drug-abusing hermit and a former surfer-turned-law enforcement officer, and the subsequent seven-day manhunt . . . Stillman explores . . . the broken families and failed strivings of her two protagonists: hermit Donald Kueck and the murdered sheriff, Steve Sorenson. . . . . The details of the manhunt for Kueck are interspersed with Stillman's imaginings about his seven days on the run, with the desert sometimes becoming the main character." (Publishers Weekly)

Includes bibliographical references and index.

Wagner, E. J.

The **science** of Sherlock Holmes; from Baskerville Hall to the Valley of Fear, the real forensics behind the great detective's greatest cases. Wiley 2006 244p il $24.95; pa $16.95 **363.2**

1. Forensic sciences 2. Criminal investigation 3. Holmes, Sherlock (Fictitious character)
ISBN 0-471-64879-5; 978-0-471-64879-6; 0-470-12823-2 pa; 978-0-470-12823-7 pa
LC 2005-22236

The author discusses forensic science in Arthur Conan Doyle's stories of the 'consulting detective' Sherlock Holmes. She compares Holmes's investigative techniques to those used in actual cases such as the killing of Lizzie Borden's parents in 1892, the 1902 murder of Joseph Browne Elwell, and the disappearance of Dr. George Parkman in 1849.

This book "will intrigue readers with incredible stories and amazing tales from the early days of forensic science." Christ Sci Monit

Includes bibliographical references

363.25   Detection of crime (Criminal investigation)

Halber, Deborah

The **skeleton** crew; how amateur sleuths are solving America's coldest cases. Deborah Halber. Simon & Schuster 2014 304 p. (hardcover) $25   **363.25**
1. Private investigators 2. Cold cases (Criminal investigation) 3. Criminal investigation -- United States
ISBN 1451657587; 9781451657586; 9781451657593
LC 2013034949

This book, by Deborah Halber, "provides an entree into the gritty and tumultuous world of Sherlock Holmes-wannabes who race to beat out law enforcement--and one another--at matching missing persons with unidentified remains. In America today, upwards of forty thousand people are dead and unaccounted for. These murder, suicide, and accident victims, separated from their names, are being adopted by the bizarre online world of amateur sleuths." (Publisher's note)

"The author paints a colorful picture of armchair investigators pursuing their first 'solves' amid the conflicting motivations of their peers and of various law enforcement agencies." LJ

Includes bibliographical references

Lance, Peter

Deal With the Devil; The FBI's Secret Thirty-Year Relationship with a Mafia Killer. by Peter Lance. William Morrow 2013 672 p. (hardcover) $29.99   **363.25**
1. Mafia 2. Criminal investigation -- United States
ISBN 0061455342; 9780061455346

In this book, author Peter Lance draws on three decades of once secret FBI files—and exclusive new interviews—to tell the . . . story of Gregory Scarpa Sr., aka "The Grim Reaper;" a Mafia capo, who "stopped counting" after 50 murders, while secretly betraying the Colombo crime family as a Top Echelon Criminal Informant for the Bureau. Lance draws on thousands of pages of court transcripts, interviews and declassified FBI files, to trace Scarpa's . . . relationship with the Bureau starting in 1960." (Publisher's note)

McCrery, Nigel

Silent witnesses; the often gruesome but always fascinating history of forensic science. by Nigel McCrery. Chicago Review Press, Inc. 2014 288 p. illustrations (some color) (paperback) $16.95 **363.25**
1. Forensic sciences 2. Criminal investigation 3. Forensic sciences -- History 4. Forensic sciences -- Case studies 5. Criminal investigation -- Case studies
ISBN 1613730020; 9781613730027
LC 2014006713

This book, by Nigel McCrery, "provides an account of all the major areas of forensic science from around the world over the past two centuries. The book weaves dramatic narrative and scientific principles together in a way that allows readers to figure out crimes along with the experts." (Publisher's note)

"Where McCrery really shines is in his storytelling, which is no surprise given his background as a successful crime novelist. While certain technical portions may be dif-

ficult for some readers, true-crime enthusiasts will find the payoff worth the effort." Kirkus

Weiner, Tim

Enemies; the history of the FBI at war. Tim Weiner. 1st ed. Random House 2011 537 p. (alk. paper) $30   **363.25**
1. National security -- United States 2. Intelligence service -- United States 3. United States -- History -- 20th century 4. Espionage -- United States -- History -- 20th century 5. United States. Federal Bureau of Investigation -- History -- 20th century
ISBN 9780679643890; 9781400067480
LC 2011005353

This book "delivers a . . . history of what has been, in effect, America's secret police. The history of the FBI is easily divided into two periods: the J. Edgar Hoover period and after. In 1924, before he was 30, Hoover took over a tiny, tawdry Bureau and built it into a fearsome empire he ruled as a personal fiefdom until his death in 1972. . . . Weiner focuses on the FBI's activities investigating and attempting to prevent subversion and terrorism." (Kirkus Reviews)

Includes bibliographical references and index

Wilber, Del Quentin

A **good** month for murder; the inside story of a homicide squad. Del Quentin Wilber. Henry Holt & Co. 2016 288 p. map (hardback) $30   **363.25**
1. Homicide 2. Detectives 3. Washington (D.C.) 4. Criminal investigation -- United States 5. Homicides -- Washington Metropolitan Area 6. Criminal investigation -- Washington Metropolitan Area
ISBN 9780805098815
LC 2015036515

This book, by Del Quentin Wilber, "tells the inside story of how a homicide squad---a dedicated, colorful team of detectives—does its almost impossible job. Twelve homicides, three police-involved shootings and the furious hunt for an especially brutal killer--February 2013 was a good month for murder in suburban Washington, D.C." (Publisher's note)

"A fascinating report written in a relentless, real-life noir tone." Booklist

363.28   Services of special kinds of security and law enforcement agencies

Carr, Matthew, 1953-2011

Fortress Europe; dispatches from a gated continent. Matthew Carr. New Press 2012 xiii, 279 p.p (hbk. : alk. paper) : $27.95   **363.28**
1. Border patrols 2. Unauthorized immigrants 3. Europe -- Immigration and emigration 4. Borderlands -- Europe 5. Border crossing -- Europe 6. Illegal aliens -- Europe -- Social conditions 7. Illegal aliens -- Government policy -- Europe 8. Border security -- Government policy -- Europe 9. Europe -- Emigration and immigration -- Government policy
ISBN 1595586857; 9781595586858
LC 2012012225

This book presents an "exposé of European immigration policy and its devastating effects" focusing on "the 'contradictory character' of the 1985 Schengen Agreement, which opened borders between 25 European states. . . . The grimly ironic result for undocumented immigrants, refugees, and victims of human trafficking has been people 'drowning in the Mediterranean, shot trying to cross border fences, mutilating themselves in detention centers, or reduced to destitution'." (Publishers Weekly)

Includes bibliographical references (p. [255]-266) and index

Crooks, Peter

The **setup**; a true story of dirty cops, soccer moms, and reality TV. by Pete Crooks. BenBella Books, Inc. 2014 311 p. illustrations (trade cloth : alk. paper) $24.95 **363.28**
1. Police corruption 2. Private investigators 3. Criminal investigation 4. Police corruption -- California 5. Private investigators -- California 6. Reality television programs -- California 7. Criminal investigation -- Corrupt practices -- California 8. Women private investigators -- Press coverage -- California
ISBN 1940363314; 9781940363318

LC 2014027929

In this book, "the pitch went like this: Chris Butler, a retired cop, ran a private investigator firm in Concord, California. His business had a fascinating angle—his firm was staffed entirely by soccer moms. . . . When this story came across Pete Crooks's desk when he was working at Diablo magazine in 2010, he was instantly hooked. . . . But after [a] ride-along . . . Crooks started to realize something didn't seem right." (Publisher's note)

Includes bibliographical references and index

Hill, Clint

Five presidents; my extraordinary journey with Eisenhower, Kennedy, Johnson, Nixon, and Ford. Clint Hill with Lisa McCubbin. Gallery Books 2016 464 p. illustrations (some color) $28 **363.28**
1. Secret service -- United States 2. Presidents -- United States -- Staff 3. Presidents -- Protection -- United States 4. United States. Secret Service -- Officials and employees -- Biography
ISBN 9781476794136; 9781476794143

LC 2015050618

In this book, "Secret Service agent Clint Hill brings history . . . to life as he reflects on his seventeen years protecting . . . Presidents Dwight D. Eisenhower, John F. Kennedy, Lyndon B. Johnson, Richard M. Nixon, and Gerald R. Ford, seeing them through a long, tumultuous era—the Cold War; the Cuban Missile Crisis; the assassinations of John F. Kennedy, Martin Luther King, Jr., and Robert F. Kennedy; the Vietnam War; Watergate." (Publisher's note)

"An eloquently written travelog through midcentury America from the periphery of political power." LJ

Mackay, James A.

Allan Pinkerton; the first private eye. {by} James Mackay. Wiley 1997 256p il $35 **363.28**
1. Private investigators 2. Pinkerton's National Detective Agency
ISBN 0-471-19415-8

LC 97-21271

"Though Pinkerton started the first U.S. detective agency after successfully uncovering a counterfeit ring, little was known about him. The author does an excellent job of tracing Pinkerton's early life and his arrival in the United States from Scotland. Then he examines better-known aspects of Pinkerton's career—his part in Lincoln's train ride through Baltimore, investigation of the Confederate spy Rose Greenhow, and association with Gen. George McClellan, his mentor and hero." Libr J

Includes bibliographical references

Miller, Todd

Border patrol nation; dispatches from the front lines of homeland security. Todd Miller. City Lights Publishers 2014 256 p. ill., maps (City lights open media) (pbk.) $16.95 **363.28**
1. Border patrols 2. Immigration law -- United States 3. United States. Immigration Border Patrol -- History 4. Mexican-American Border Region -- Economic conditions
ISBN 0872866319; 9780872866317

LC 2013043754

In this book, author "Todd Miller sounds an alarm as he chronicles the changing landscape. Traveling the country--and beyond--to speak with the people most involved with and impacted by the Border Patrol, he combines these firsthand encounters with careful research to expose a vast and booming industry for high-end technology, weapons, surveillance, and prisons." (Publisher's note)

An "alarming story of U.S. Border Patrol and Homeland Security's ever-widening reach into the lives of American citizens and legal immigrants as well as the undocumented." Pub Wkly

Includes bibliographical references and index. (p. 326-343) and index

363.283 Secret police

Goodavage, Maria

Secret Service Dogs; The Heroes Who Protect the President of the United States. by Maria Goodavage. Penguin Group USA 2016 304 p. $28 **363.283**
1. Service dogs 2. Secret service -- United States
ISBN 1101984732; 9781101984734

LC 2016025219

This book, by Maria Goodavage, "immerses readers into the heart of this elite world of canine teams who protect first families, popes, and presidential candidates: the selection of dogs and handlers, their year-round training, their missions around the world, and, most important, the bond—the glue that holds the teams together and can mean the difference between finding bombs and terrorists or letting them slip by." (Publisher's note)

363.3   Other aspects of public safety

Maclean, John N.

Fire and ashes; on the front lines of American wildfire. Holt & Co. 2003 238p il map $25; pa $14   **363.3**

1. Wildfires

ISBN 0-8050-7212-8; 0-8050-7591-7 pa

LC 2002-38704

"This work tells of two infernos: a 1999 conflagration in Nevada and a 1953 case of arboreal arson in California that took 15 lives when the fire exhibited unexpected behavior... . Careful in analysis, Maclean turns visceral when imparting the sudden terror of life-ending flames, or, as for a survivor of the 1949 Mann Gulch disaster whom he visits, a life-searing whirlwind. A solid choice that will be in demand, particularly during the West's summer fire season." Booklist

363.31   Censorship

Simon, Joel

The new censorship; inside the global battle for media freedom. Joel Simon. Columbia University Press 2014 248 p. (Columbia journalism review books) (cloth : alk. paper) $27.95   **363.31**

1. Censorship 2. Journalism 3. Freedom of the press 4. Journalists -- Violence against 5. Censorship -- History -- 21st century 6. Press and politics -- History -- 21st century 7. Freedom of the press -- History -- 21st century 8. Journalism -- Political aspects -- History -- 21st century

ISBN 023116064X; 9780231160643

LC 2014012961

This book, by Joel Simon, part of the "Columbia Journalism Review Books" series, "warns that we can no longer assume that our global information ecosystem is stable, protected, and robust. Journalists are increasingly vulnerable to attack by authoritarian governments, militants, criminals, and terrorists, who all seek to use technology, political pressure, and violence to set the global information agenda." (Publisher's note)

"Most moving are Simon's wrenching stories of the ordeals journalists have suffered, from kidnappings through imprisonment through death. Simon's assessment of what it means to be a journalist and his call to action at book's end are moving and practical. A must-read." Booklist

Includes bibliographical references and index

363.32   Social conflict

Allison, Graham T.

Nuclear terrorism; the ultimate preventable catastrophe. [by] Graham Allison. Times Books\Henry Holt 2004 263p il $24   **363.32**

1. Terrorism 2. Nuclear warfare

ISBN 0-8050-7651-4

LC 2004-47427

"Allison's comprehensive but accessible treatment of this vital subject is a major contribution to public understanding." N Y Times Book Rev

Includes bibliographical references

Anderson, Sean

Historical dictionary of terrorism; [by] Sean K. Anderson, with Stephen Sloan. 3rd ed; Scarecrow Press 2009 lxxvi, 800p (Historical dictionaries of war, revolution, and civil unrest) $115   **363.32**

1. Reference books 2. Terrorism -- Dictionaries

ISBN 978-0-8108-5764-3; 0-8108-5764-2

LC 2009-3226

First published 1995

"The dictionary encompasses individuals, groups, events, doctrines, and concepts such as Power law, which is the mathematical relation between the numbers and intensity of events. . . . . This is an accurate, objective, and clearly written resource that will be useful in public and academic libraries." Booklist

Includes bibliographical references (p. 713-798)

Aust, Stefan

Baader-Meinhof; the inside story of the R.A.F. translated from the German by Anthea Bell. Rev ed; Oxford University Press 2009 xxi, 457p il $29.95   **363.32**

1. Terrorism 2. Red Army Faction

ISBN 978-0-19-537275-5; 0-19-537275-1

LC 2008-49401

Original German edition, 1985

"The quintessential radical leftist terrorist group, founded in 1970 and eventually known as the Red Army Faction, Baader-Meinhof was responsible for 34 deaths in Germany over a 30-year period. . . . Exhaustively detailing the group's exploits from 1970 until the prison suicides of the leaders in 1977, Aust offers fascinating insights into both the spectacular and the mundane aspects of life in a terrorist cadre." Libr J

Baker, Stewart A.

Skating on stilts; why we aren't stopping tomorrow's terrorism. Hoover Institution Press 2010 370p $19.95   **363.32**

1. Terrorism 2. Right of privacy 3. United States -- Foreign relations 4. United States -- Dept. of Homeland Security

ISBN 978-0-8179-1154-6

LC 2010-20763

Baker "makes a persuasive case against the privacy absolutists." Los Angeles Times

Includes bibliographical references

Bobbitt, Philip

Terror and consent; the wars for the twenty-first century. Alfred A. Knopf 2008 672p il $35 **363.32**

1. Terrorism 2. United States -- Foreign relations

ISBN 1-4000-4243-7; 978-1-4000-4243-2

LC 2007-34194

The author examines "the relationship between the emergent constitutional order and the emergence of modern 'market state terrorism,' which, mirroring the market state and availing itself of the same technological advances, may be lethal enough to pose an existential threat to the very possibility of government by consent of the governed." Booklist

Includes bibliographical references

Dickey, Christopher

Securing the city; inside America's best counterterror force--the NYPD. Simon & Schuster 2009 321p $26 **363.32**

1. Terrorism 2. Police -- New York (N.Y.) 3. New York (N.Y.) -- Police Dept.

ISBN 978-1-4165-5240-6; 1-4165-5240-5

LC 2008-43085

"Vivid and thought-provoking. . . . The general reader can enjoy a book that has the pace and drama of a thriller, and for the specialist, . . . there is much to ponder." Economist

Includes bibliographical references

Elshtain, Jean Bethke

Just war against terror; the burden of American power in a violent world. Basic Books 2003 240p $23; pa $14 **363.32**

1. Terrorism 2. War on terrorism

ISBN 0-465-01910-2; 0-465-01911-0 pa

LC 2002-154549

"While this volume is not a radical departure from the abundance of post-September 11 books, it presents well the moral case for U.S. military engagement in the world and gives credence to those who advocate the use of force as a response to terrorism." Publ Wkly

Includes bibliographical references

Encyclopedia of terrorism; Peter Chalk, editor. ABC-CLIO 2013 xviii, 871 p.p ill. (hardcopy) $205; (ebook) $205.00 **363.32**

1. Terrorism -- Encyclopedias

ISBN 0313308950; 9780313308956; 9780313385353

LC 2012016710

This book, edited by Peter Chalk, "provides comprehensive coverage of the events, individuals, groups, incidents, and trends in terrorism in the modern era. [It] . . . presents . . . information on developments since the watershed events of September 11, 2001, providing readers with an invaluable reference tool for understanding major developments that have occurred in domestic and international terrorism." (Publisher's note)

Includes bibliographical references and index

Harris, Shane

The watchers; the rise of America's surveillance state. Penguin Press 2010 418p il $27.95; pa $17 **363.32**

1. Terrorism 2. National security -- United States 3. Intelligence service -- United States

ISBN 978-1-59420-245-2; 978-0-14-311890-9 pa

LC 2009-37205

The author examines the development of domestic surveillance programs in the United States intended to prevent terrorist attacks.

"A sharply written, wise analysis of the complex mashup of electronic sleuthing, law, policy and culture." Kirkus

Includes bibliographical references

Herridge, Catherine

The **next** wave; on the hunt for al Qaeda's American recruits. Crown Forum 2011 258p il $25 **363.32**

1. Terrorists 2. Islamic fundamentalism 3. Al Qaida (Organization) 4. Muslims -- United States 5. Terrorism -- Religious aspects

ISBN 978-0-307-88525-8; 0-307-88525-9

LC 2010-53585

A "report on a new generation of terrorists and the American-born Islamic cleric Anwar al-Awlaki, who has inspired many of them to commit violent acts. Now believed to be in Yemen, al-Awlaki was targeted for killing by the U.S. government in 2010. He is linked to three of the 9/11 hijackers, the massacre at Foot Hood, the attempted Christmas Day 2009 bombing and the cargo printer plot in October 2010. Drawing on documents and interviews, the author shows how the charismatic al-Awlaki has become a leading al-Qaeda propagandist, using the Internet to recruit alienated American youths, many newly arrived in America, to join the terrorist cause. . . . A sobering view of why the 9/11 nightmare continues a decade later." Kirkus

Includes bibliographical references

Merriman, John M.

The **dynamite** club; how a bombing in fin-de-siecle Paris ignited the age of modern terror. Houghton Mifflin Co. 2009 259p il map $26 **363.32**

1. Bombings 2. Terrorism 3. Anarchism and anarchists 4. Anarchists 5. Paris (France) -- History

ISBN 978-0-618-55598-7; 0-618-55598-6

LC 2008-49470

"Because he neither makes excuses for anyone nor takes simplistic ideological swipes, Merriman is a solid guide through these dark back lanes of European history." Houston Chron

Includes bibliographical references

Pedahzur, Ami

The **Israeli** secret services and the struggle against terrorism. Columbia University Press 2009 215p il $27.50 **363.32**

1. Terrorism 2. Secret service -- Israel 3. Intelligence service -- Israel

ISBN 978-0-231-14042-3; 0-231-14042-8

LC 2008-25949

"Dividing the potential responses to terrorism into four categories (defensive, reconciliatory, criminal justice and war), the author tracks the development of an Israeli war model and demonstrates that rather than sending terrorists running, the approach leads to an escalating cycle of terrorism, citing many examples in which Israels elimination of threats has created the impetus for more violence. . . . While Pedahzurs style leans toward the dryly academic, his insights are so well reasoned and relevant that the pages almost turn themselves." Publ Wkly

Includes bibliographical references

363.325 Terrorism

Bergen, Peter L.

Manhunt; the ten-year search for Bin Laden from 9/11 to Abbottabad. Peter L. Bergen. 1st ed. Crown Publishers 2012 xxi, 359 p.p col. ill., maps $26   **363.325**

1. Terrorists 2. Special forces (Military science) -- United States 3. Qaida (Organization) 4. Terrorists -- Saudi Arabia 5. War on Terrorism, 2001-2009 6. Fugitives from justice -- United States 7. Terrorism -- United States -- Prevention 8. Special operations (Military science) -- United States

ISBN 0307955575; 9780307955579

LC 2012004258

This book provides an "account of the . . . effort to track and kill the al-Qaeda leader. . . . Only in 2010 did the monitoring of a Kuwaiti courier's cellphone use suggest ties to bin Laden, and they followed his car to the compound in the quiet Pakistani town of Abbottabad, where he actually lived with bin Laden's extended family. . . . Bergen . . . delineates the U.S. government decision-making process in pursuing the Special Operations infiltration of the compound, despite the lack of certainty that bin Laden was actually there." (Kirkus Reviews)

Includes bibliographical references and index

Graff, Garrett M.

The **threat** matrix; Garrett M. Graff. 1st ed. Little, Brown and Company 2011 666 p. ill.   **363.325**

1. Terrorism -- Prevention 2. National security -- United States 3. United States. Federal Bureau of Investigation 4. War on Terrorism, 2001-2009 5. Intelligence service -- United States 6. Terrorism -- United States -- Prevention

ISBN 9780316068611

LC 2010053237

In this book, author Garrett M. "Graff shows how . . . [Former FBI Director Louis Freeh's] leadership slowed intelligence operations preceding 9/11 and in what ways the agency still suffers from his tenure. Graff . . . track[s] the ways that the FBI adapted as terrorism changed. He takes seriously even ridiculous threats, such as an absurd letter penned by a Filipino teenager and the realization that the FBI lacked a file on the Japanese cult that released sarin gas in Tokyo even though they were listed in the Manhattan phone book. Some episodes . . . [include a] discussion of the events behind a July 2001 memo's theory that terrorists were in the U.S. training at civil aviation facilities. Graff's focus, though it covers a time span from J. Edgar Hoover's death to the present day, rests particularly on the massive intelligence failures in the 10 years preceding 9/11, and after." (Publishers Weekly)

Includes bibliographical references (p. 638-646) and index

Johnsen, Gregory D.

The **last** refuge; Yemen, al-Qaeda, and America's war in Arabia. Gregory D. Johnsen. W.W. Norton & Co. 2013 p. cm.   **363.325**

1. Yemen 2. Qaida (Organization) 3. War on Terrorism, 2001-2009 4. Terrorism -- Yemen (Republic) 5. United States -- Military policy 6. Terrorism -- Persian Gulf Region -- Prevention

ISBN 9780393082425

LC 2012027875

In this book on Yemen, Gregory D. Johnson presents an "analysis of how a nation that had been a success story in the U.S. effort to defeat al-Qaeda and stabilize the region has been the site for resurgence instead. He examines the historical factors that have contributed to the buildup of al-Qaeda in Yemen as young men were recruited by the government, Yemeni tribes, and mosques in a concerted effort to turn the war in Afghanistan into a broader jihad." (Booklist)

Includes bibliographical references and index

Kaplan, Fred, 1937-

Dark territory; the secret history of cyber war. Fred Kaplan. Simon & Schuster 2016 352 p. (ebook) $20.99; (hardback) $28   **363.325**

1. Cyberterrorism -- Prevention -- United States -- History

ISBN 9781476763279; 9781476763255; 9781476763262

LC 2015027335

In this book, author Fred "Kaplan probes the inner corridors of the National Security Agency, the beyond-top-secret cyber units in the Pentagon, the 'information warfare' squads of the military services, and the national security debates in the White House, to tell this never-before-told story of the officers, policymakers, scientists, and spies who devised this new form of warfare and who have been planning . . . these wars for decades." (Publisher's note)

"An important, disturbing, and gripping history arguing convincingly that, as of 2015, no defense exists against a resourceful cyberattack." Kirkus

Includes bibliographical references and index

Levy, Adrian

The **siege**; 68 hours inside the Taj Hotel. Cathy Scott-Clark and Adrian Levy. Penguin Books 2013 318 p. chiefly col. ill., maps $28   **363.325**

1. Terrorism 2. India -- History -- 21st century 3. Taj Mahal Palace Hotel 4. Victims of terrorism -- India -- Mumbai 5. Mumbai Terrorist Attacks, Mumbai, India, 2008

ISBN 0143123750; 9780143123750

LC 2013031108

In this book, authors Cathy Scott-Clark and Adrian Levy, present an "account of the 2008 terrorist attacks in Mumbai . . . with a deep understanding of the region and its politics. On the night of November 26, Lashkar-e-Toiba terrorists attacked targets throughout the city, including the Taj Mahal Palace Hotel, one of the world's most exclusive luxury hotels." (Publisher's note)

"A great read that gives readers a better understanding of a terrorist attack from many points of view." Kirkus

McDermott, Terry

The **hunt** for KSM; inside the pursuit and takedown of the real 9/11 mastermind, Khalid Sheikh Mohammed. Terry McDermott and Josh Meyer. Little, Brown and Co. 2012 350 p.   **363.325**

1. Terrorists 2. September 11 terrorist attacks, 2001

3. Terrorism -- Prevention -- United States 4. Qaida (Organization) 5. Terrorists -- Islamic countries 6. September 11 Terrorist Attacks, 2001 7. Terrorism -- United States -- Prevention
ISBN 9780316186599

LC 2011041533

This book follows "[t]he cat-and-mouse game between American investigators and Khalid Sheikh Mohammed, architect of the 9/11 attacks and other terrorist spectaculars. . . . Journalists [Terry] McDermott . . . and [Josh] Meyer (the L.A. Times's chief terrorism reporter) present a police procedural starring an FBI agent, Frank Pellegrino, Port Authority detective Matt Besheer, and the inter-agency anti-terrorism experts who tracked KSM and his confederates for a decade before his 2003 capture. . . . The authors" . . . profile of Khalid Sheikh Mohammed depicts a resourceful, charismatic man . . . and paints a . . . portrait of the workaday terrorist life of fund-raising, recruitment, bomb-rigging, and general plotting, all carried out while dodging a global manhunt." (Publishers Weekly)

Includes bibliographical references

Molotch, Harvey

Against security; how we go wrong at airports, subways, and other sites of ambiguous danger. Harvey Molotch. Princeton University Press 2012 xv, 260 p.p ill., maps (hardcover) $35.00 **363.325**
1. Fear 2. Security (Psychology) 3. Offenses against public safety 4. National security -- United States 5. Transportation -- Security measures -- United States 6. Terrorism -- Prevention -- Government policy -- United States
ISBN 069115581X; 9780691155814

LC 2012012128

In this book, Harvey Molotch "profiles the workings of our anxieties and fears and how they can be exploited by authorities who have an interest in stoking them. The author is concerned with the complex systems that permit us to feel safe in public places. He traces a path from public toilet facilities through subways and airports to the reconstruction of ground zero before taking on the catastrophic effects of nature in the hurricane damage and flooding of New Orleans in 2005." (Kirkus)

Includes bibliographical references and index

Morell, Michael J.

The great war of our time; an insider's account of the CIA's fight against al Qa'ida. Michael Morell with Bill Harlow. Twelve 2015 384 p. illustrations (hardback) $28 **363.325**
1. Terrorism -- Prevention 2. United States. Central Intelligence Agency 3. Qaida (Organization) 4. War on Terrorism, 2001-2009 5. Terrorism -- United States -- Prevention 6. United States. Central Intelligence Agency -- Officials and employees -- Biography
ISBN 1455585661; 9781455585663

LC 2014049799

In this book, author Michael Morrell "offer[s] an unblinking and insightful assessment of CIA's counterterrorism successes and failures of the past twenty years and, perhaps most important, shows readers that the threat of terrorism did not die with Bin Ladin in Abbottabad. Morell describes how efforts to throw off the shackles of oppression have too often resulted in broken nation states unable or unwilling to join the fight against terrorism." (Publisher's note)

"Recently retired as the CIA's deputy director, Morell was the only person with President Bush on 9/11 and President Obama when Osama Bin Laden was killed. No wonder 60 Minutes calls him "the most important spook you have never heard of." Here he goes inside the CIA to reveal its operations during the war on terror." LJ

Powell, Jonathan

Terrorists at the table; why negotiating is the only way to peace. by Jonathan Powell. Palgrave Macmillan Trade 2015 336 p. (hardback) $30 **363.325**
1. Terrorism 2. Negotiation 3. Conflict management 4. Terrorism -- Government policy
ISBN 1250069882; 9781250069887

LC 2014047030

In this book, author Jonathan Powell argues "we will never end armed conflict. . . . Powell draws on his own experiences negotiating peace in Northern Ireland and talks to all the major players from the last thirty years--terrorists, Presidents, secret agents and intermediaries--exposing the subterranean world of secret exchanges between governments and armed groups to give us the inside account of negotiations on the front line." (Publisher's note)

"Powell's compelling argument on a touchy topic makes one consider that without attempting to engage in negotiations, a resolution cannot be reached." LJ

Russell, Jenna

Long mile home; Boston under attack, the city's courageous recovery, and the epic hunt for justice. Scott Helman and Jenna Russell, reporters for the Boston Globe. Penguin Group 2014 352 p. ill. (chiefly col.), col map (hardcover) $27.95 **363.325**
1. Bombings 2. Boston Marathon 3. Terrorism -- United States 4. Boston Marathon Bombing, Boston, Mass., 2013 5. Terrorism -- Massachusetts -- Boston -- Case studies
ISBN 0525954481; 9780525954484

LC 2014000091

This book, by Scott Helman and Jenna Russell, is about "the Boston Marathon bombing and subsequent manhunt for the Tsarnaev brothers. [It tells] the . . . story of the tragic, surreal, and ultimately inspiring week of April 15, 2013: the preparations of the bombers; the glory of the race; the . . . emergency response to the explosions; the massive deployment of city, state, and federal law enforcement personnel; and the . . . world's emotional and humanitarian response." (Publisher's note)

"Despite the multitude of sources drawn upon, the writing is seamless and riveting. . . . Sensitive in its treatment and thrilling in its pace and immediacy." LJ

Includes bibliographical references and index

Sadler, Anthony

The 15:17 to Paris; the true story of a terrorist, a train, and three American heroes. Anthony Sadler, Alek Skarlatos, Spencer Stone, with Jeffrey E. Stern.

PublicAffairs 2016 245 p. map (hardback) $25.99; (ebook) $15.99   **363.325**

1. Railroad travel 2. Terrorism -- Prevention 3. Americans -- Foreign countries 4. Heroes -- United States -- Biography 5. Soldiers -- United States -- Biography 6. Railroad trains -- Belgium -- History -- 21st century 7. Terrorism -- Prevention -- European Union countries -- History -- 21st century

ISBN 1610397339; 9781610397339; 9781610397346

LC 2016015296

In this book, by Anthony Sadler, Alek Skarlatos, and Spencer Stone, with Jeffrey E. Stern, "on August 21, 2015, Ayoub El-Khazzani boarded train #9364 in Brussels, bound for Paris. . . . Another major ISIS attack was about to begin. . . . [But] near tragedy [was] averted by three young men who found the heroic unity and strength inside themselves at the moment when they, and 500 other innocent travelers, needed it most." (Publisher's note)

Includes bibliographical references and index.

Seierstad, Åsne

One of Us; The Story of Anders Breivik and the Massacre in Norway. by Asne Seierstad, Sarah Death (translator) Farrar, Straus & Giroux 2015 544 p. $28   **363.325**

1. Domestic terrorism -- Norway

ISBN 0374277893; 9780374277895

LC 2015932749

This book, by Asne Seierstad, translated by Sarah Death, provides "a harrowing and thorough account of the [July 22, 2011 terrorism] massacre that upended Norway, and the trial that helped put the country back together. . . . [The book] is at once a psychological study of violent extremism, a dramatic true crime procedural, and a compassionate inquiry into how a privileged society copes with homegrown evil." (Publisher's note)

"A powerful read that sociologists, historians, and political science students alike will find very informative." LJ

Theoharis, Athan G.

Abuse of power; Athan G. Theoharis. Temple University Press 2011 xvi, 212p (hbk: alk. paper) $29.95   **363.325**

1. Wiretapping 2. Intelligence service 3. Electronic surveillance 4. Cold War 5. September 11 Terrorist Attacks, 2001

ISBN 9781439906644; 9781439906651; 9781439906668

LC 2010042416

In this book, "[Athan G.] Theoharis continues his investigation of U.S. government surveillance and historicizes the 9/11 response. Criticizing the U.S. government's secret activities and policies during periods of 'unprecedented crisis,' he recounts how presidents and FBI officials exploited concerns about foreign-based internal security threats. Drawing on information sequestered until recently in FBI records, Theoharis shows how these secret activities in the World War II and Cold War eras expanded FBI surveillance powers and, in the process, eroded civil liberties without substantially advancing legitimate security interests. . . . [T]his . . . book speaks to the costs and consequences of still-secret post-9/11 surveillance programs and counterintelligence failures [and]

. . . makes the case that the abusive surveillance policies of the Cold War years were repeated in the government's responses to the September 11 attacks." (Publisher's note)

Willman, David

The **mirage** man; David Willman. Bantam Books 2011 xiii, 448p ill.   **363.325**

1. Bioterrorism 2. Iraq War, 2003-2011 3. Governmental investigations -- United States

ISBN 9780553807752; 9780345530219

LC 2011006232

This book "offers . . . [an] account of the . . . FBI investigation into the 'anthrax attacks' as the [George W.] Bush administration strove to use the public panic to strengthen their case to go to war, while the culprit was, in all likelihood, a military microbiologist named Bruce Ivins. . . . [It] traces Ivins's unhappy life, how he endured childhood abuse and privation to become a successful scientist only to find his life unraveling as a result of his . . . obsessions and fixations with women. . . . [David] Willman pivots to focus on the flawed investigation . . . and how . . . Ivins benefited both financially and professionally from the public paranoia about anthrax as his research into an anthrax vaccine became a national priority." (Publishers Weekly)

Includes bibliographical references and index

Wright, Lawrence, 1947-

★ The **terror** years; from al-Qaeda to the Islamic State. Lawrence Wright. Knopf 2016 400 p. (hardback) $28.95   **363.325**

1. Terrorism 2. Terrorists 3. Qaida (Organization) 4. United States -- Foreign relations 5. Middle East -- Politics and government 6. IS (Organization) 7. Terrorism -- Middle East 8. Middle East -- History -- 1979- 9. Terrorism -- Religious aspects -- Islam 10. Terrorism -- United States -- Prevention 11. Middle East -- Politics and government -- 1945-

ISBN 9780385352055

LC 2015046064

In this book, journalist Lawrence Wright "recalls the path that terror in the Middle East has taken, from the rise of al-Qaeda in the 1990s to the recent beheadings of reporters and aid workers by ISIS. . . . The American response is covered in profiles of two FBI agents and the head of the intelligence community. The book ends with a devastating piece about the capture and slaying by ISIS of four American journalists and aid workers, and our government's failed response." (Publisher's note)

"The research that Wright did for the 10 essays contained in his latest work, all of which first appeared in the magazine, also contributed to Wright's deeper insight into the jihadist mindset, including its latest embodiment in ISIS. In "The Man behind Bin Laden" Wright recounts his return to Egypt, where he taught English decades earlier, to investigate the background of Bin Laden's sidekick Ayman al-Zawahiri, describing a country embroiled in post-9/11 political turmoil. . . . Other pieces on Saudi Arabia, ISIS violence, and Israel round out a brilliant volume that is a must-read for anyone looking for greater illumination of the baffling world of religious extremism." Booklist

363.33 Control of firearms

Giffords, Gabrielle D. (Gabrielle Dee), 1970-
Enough; Our Fight to Keep America Safe from Gun Violence. Gabrielle Giffords and Mark Kelly; with Harry Jaffe. Simon & Schuster 2015 256 p. $25   **363.33**
1. Gun control 2. Firearms ownership -- United States 3. Violence -- United States 4. Gun control -- United States 5. Firearms -- Law and legislation 6. United States. Constitution. 2nd Amendment
ISBN 1476750076; 9781476750071

LC 2013497343

In this book, by Gabrielle Giffords and Mark Kelly, with Harry Jaffe, the authors "share their impassioned argument for responsible gun ownership. . . . As gun owners and strong supporters of the Second Amendment, Gabby and Mark offer a bold but sensible path forward, preserving the right to own guns for collection, recreation, and protection while taking common-sense actions to prevent the next Tucson, Aurora, or Newtown." (Publisher's note)

"Lay readers and political science students who want to understand the emotional debate surrounding gun ownership and current efforts to limit access to lethal weapons will appreciate the balanced discussion of the issues facing those who intend to change current firearms legislation." LJ

Guns in American society; an encyclopedia of history, politics, culture, and the law. Gregg Lee Carter, editor. ABC-CLIO 2012 3 v. lxx, 1096 p.p ill.   **363.33**
1. Weapons 2. Law -- United States 3. Violence -- Encyclopedias 4. Gun control -- United States -- Encyclopedias 5. Violent crimes -- United States -- Encyclopedias 6. Social movements -- United States -- Encyclopedias 7. Firearms -- Social aspects -- United States -- Encyclopedias 8. Firearms -- Law and legislation -- United States -- Encyclopedias
ISBN 0313386706; 0313386714; 9780313386701; 9780313386718

LC 2011043435

In this book, editor Gregg Lee Carter focuses on the following questions: Is "the high rate of violence in the United States linked to the prevalence of guns--or to a lack of social homogeneity and economic inequality? Should there be support for stricter or more lenient gun control? Should people carry concealed weapons for personal protection? . . . The encyclopedia . . . [offers] the latest thinking and research in the fields of criminology, history, law, medicine, politics, and sociology, [while] providing objective information." (Publisher's note)

Includes bibliographical references and index

363.34 Disasters

Cross, Kim
What Stands in a Storm; Three Days in the Worst Superstorm to Hit the South's Tornado Alley. Kim Cross. Pocket Books 2015 320 p. illustration $25   **363.34**
1. Storms 2. Tornadoes 3. Natural disasters -- United States
ISBN 1476763062; 9781476763064

LC 2014035817

In this book by Kim Cross "immersive reporting and dramatic storytelling set you right in the middle of the horrific superstorm of April 2011, a weather event that killed 348 people. Cross weaves together the heart-wrenching stories of several characters--including three college students, a celebrity weatherman, and a team of hard-hit rescuers--to create a nail-biting chronicle in the Tornado Alley of America." (Publisher's note)

"Though topographical media and photographs aren't included, Cross journalistically illustrates the storm's unrelenting fury, heartbreaking aftermath and organized recovery efforts through dramatic firsthand stories, putting a human face on a tragic chain of events that claimed a devastating 348 casualties in 72 hours. The author also includes an 'In Memoriam' section that lists the 'Alabamians who lost their lives and the people who face a world without them.' Armchair storm chase r s' will find much to savor in this grippingly detailed, real-time chronicle of nature gone awry." Kirkus

De Villiers, Marq
The end; natural disasters, manmade catastrophes, and the future of human survival. Thomas Dunne Books/St. Martin's Press 2008 362p il $26.95   **363.34**
1. Human ecology 2. Disaster relief 3. Natural disasters
ISBN 978-0-312-36569-1; 0-312-36569-1

LC 2008-39096

Published in Canada with title: Dangerous world

The author presents an analysis of humanity's role in catastrophic natural disasters to consider whether or not such threats are increasing and how they can be managed.

"This book effectively summarizes the latest scientific thought on disasters, and de Villiers's entrancing prose will hook even the most reluctant reader." Libr J

Includes bibliographical references

Ehrlich, Gretel
Facing the wave; a journey in the wake of the tsunami. Gretel Ehrlich. Pantheon Books 2012 240 p. $25   **363.34**
1. Tsunamis 2. Sendai Earthquake, Japan, 2011 3. Fukushima Nuclear Accident, Fukushima, Japan, 2011 4. Tohoku Earthquake and Tsunami, Japan, 2011 5. Tsunami damage -- Japan -- Tōhoku Region 6. Tsunami relief -- Japan -- Tōhoku Region 7. Disaster victims -- Japan -- Tōhoku Region
ISBN 0307907317; 9780307907318

LC 2012020400

In this book, Gretel Ehrlich, winner of PEN New England's Henry David Thoreau Prize, "explains how a fascination with Japanese art and poetry drove her to Japan's devastated Tohoku coast after last year's tsunami." (Library Journal) Ehrlich "made several visits to Japan in the months after the shattering earthquake and tsunami" and tried to make sense of the event by "recording accounts by traumatized survivors and [sharing] her own . . . on-the-ground observations." (Kirkus)

Includes bibliographical references

Halberstam, David

  Firehouse. Hyperion 2002 201p $22.95; pa $14   363.34

  1. Fire fighters 2. World Trade Center terrorist attack, 2001 3. New York (N.Y.) -- Fire Dept.

  ISBN 1-4013-0005-7; 0-7868-8851-2 pa

  "A journalist's homage to firefighters, their values, their culture and their courage during the martyrdom imposed on the New York Fire Department by the catastrophe of the attack on the World Trade Center." N Y Times Bk Rev

Katz, Jonathan M.

  The **big** truck that went by; how the world came to save Haiti and left behind a disaster. Jonathan Katz. Palgrave Macmillan 2013 306 p. ill., maps hbk $26   363.34

  1. Humanitarian intervention 2. Haiti Earthquake, Haiti, 2010 3. Disaster response and recovery 4. Haiti 5. Disaster relief -- Haiti 6. Earthquake relief -- Haiti

  ISBN 023034187X; 9780230341876

                                                          LC 2012037217

  This book by Jonathan M. Katz is "about the January 2010 earthquake and its aftermath. . . . Katz, a former AP correspondent, was the only full-time American reporter stationed in Haiti when the quake hit; he stayed for more than a year thereafter, reporting on the charitable aftershocks--as small donations were mishandled by NGOs, as big donations never materialized, and as the world gradually lost interest and left Haiti to fend for itself." (Columbia Journalism Review)

  "The author reports how promised aid funds didn't arrive and NGO relief funds were misspent, while Haitians, presumed to be corrupt, were shut out of involvement in relief efforts. . . . An eye-opening, trailblazing exposé." Kirkus

  Includes bibliographical references and index

Pilkey, Orrin H., 1934-

  The **rising** sea; [by] Orrin H. Pilkey and Rob Young. Island Press/Shearwater Books 2009 203p il map $25.95   363.34

  1. Ocean 2. Coasts 3. Sea level 4. Coast changes 5. Greenhouse effect

  ISBN 978-1-59726-191-3; 1-59726-191-2

                                                          LC 2009-06152

  "This book's title represents the most obvious effect of global warming: the incursion of ocean water onto land due to thermal expansion and, more ominously, the melting of mountain glaciers and polar ice sheets. This phenomenon is often dismissed as inconsequential (or even denied), but as the authors convincingly demonstrate with stories of distress at vulnerable locations (e.g., the Maldives), it is already ravaging coastlines directly and indirectly, helped by human intrusion. . . . This book offers a wealth of opportunities for further reading. Its greatest strength is the cogent, well-organized, layman-friendly narrative that makes up each chapter." Sci Books Films

  Includes bibliographical references

Smith, Dennis

  Report from ground zero; the story of the rescue efforts at the World Trade Center. Viking 2002 366p il maps $24.95; pa $14   363.34

  1. Fire fighters 2. World Trade Center terrorist attack, 2001 3. New York (N.Y.) -- Fire Dept.

  ISBN 0-670-03116-X; 0-452-28395-7 pa

                                                          LC 2002-19840

  Based on his personal observations and interviews with other rescue workers, the author describes the efforts of the New York City Fire Department to rescue survivors of the September 11 attack on the World Trade Center

Tougias, Mike

  Ten hours until dawn; the true story of heroism and tragedy aboard the Can Do. [by] Michael Tougias. St. Martins Press 2005 322p il map $24.95 363.34

  1. Blizzards 2. Shipwrecks 3. Rescue work

  ISBN 0-312-33435-4

  The author "delivers a well-researched, vividly written tale of brave men overwhelmed by the awesome forces of nature." Publ Wkly

Welky, David

  The **thousand**-year flood; the Ohio-Mississippi disaster of 1937. University of Chicago Press 2011 355p il $27.50   363.34

  1. Disaster relief 2. New Deal, 1933-1939 3. Floods -- Mississippi River 4. Floods -- Ohio River valley 5. United States -- Politics and government -- 1933-1945

  ISBN 978-0-226-88716-6; 0-226-88716-2; 978-0-226-88718-0 ebook

                                                          LC 2011014875

  "Vividly written and carefully documented, . . . [this book] masterfully brings a turning point in American history back to life." Wilson Quarterly

  Includes bibliographical references

Zebrowski, Ernest

  Category 5; the story of Camille, lessons unlearned from America's most violent hurricane. [by] Ernest Zebrowski & Judith A. Howard. University of Michigan Press 2005 276p il map $27.95 363.34

  1. Hurricanes 2. Gulf Coast (U.S.)

  ISBN 0-472-11525-1

                                                          LC 2005-28583

  "Partly a narrative and partly a pondering of how people and authorities prepare for predictable risk, the work focuses on the areas devastated by the maelstrom: Plaquemines Parish, Louisiana; Mississippi's Gulf Coast; and faraway Nelson County, Virginia. . . . The authors sound a pessimistic note about society's short-term memory in their sobering, able history of Camille." Booklist

  Includes bibliographical references

Zeilinga de Boer, Jelle

  Earthquakes in human history; the far-reaching effects of seismic disruptions. [by] Jelle Zeilinga de

Boer and Donald Theodore Sanders. Princeton University Press 2005 278p il maps $24.95 **363.34**
1. Earthquakes
ISBN 0-691-05070-8

LC 2004-40122

The authors provide "facts and insights on geologic processes and the effects of . . . natural disasters on the course of human history. Narratives on especially impactful earthquakes include events in the Holy Land, Ancient Greece, England, Portugal, Missouri, San Francisco, Japan, Peru and Chile, and Nicaragua. The influence of the earthquakes on religion, politics, economy, wars, and literature is portrayed in fascinating prose, embellished with carefully selected photos, drawings, and maps." Choice
Includes bibliographical references

363.37   Fire hazards

Dickman, Kyle
On the burning edge; a fateful fire and the men who fought it. by Kyle Dickman. Random House Inc 2015 277 p. color illustrations, maps $26 **363.37**
1. Wildfires 2. Fire fighters
ISBN 0553392123; 9780553392128

This book, by Kyle Dickman, "is the definitive account of the Yarnell Hill Fire. On June 28, 2013, a single bolt of lightning sparked an inferno that devoured more than eight thousand acres in northern Arizona. Twenty elite firefighters—the Granite Mountain Hotshots—walked together into the blaze, tools in their hands and emergency fire shelters on their hips. Only one of them walked out." (Publisher's note)

363.4   Controversies related to public morals and customs

McGirr, Lisa
The war on alcohol; prohibition and the rise of the American state. Lisa McGirr. W W Norton & Co Inc 2015 352 p. 8 plates; illustrations (hardcover) $27.95 **363.4**
1. Prohibition 2. United States -- History -- 20th century
ISBN 0393066959; 9780393066951

LC 2015028038

This book, by Lisa McGirr, presents an alternative analysis of prohibition in U.S. history. "Prohibition was the seedbed for a pivotal expansion of the federal government, the genesis of our contemporary penal state. . . . [The author] uncovers patterns of enforcement still familiar today: the war on alcohol was waged disproportionately in African American, immigrant, and poor white communities." (Publisher's note)

"McGirr's new perspective on Prohibition is recommended for all readers interested in American history." LJ
Includes bibliographical references and index

Okrent, Daniel, 1948-
Last call; the rise and fall of Prohibition, 1920-1933. Scribner 2010 468p $30 **363.4**
1. Prohibition 2. Drinking of alcoholic beverages 3.

United States -- History -- 20th century 4. Prohibition -- United States -- History -- 20th century 5. Drinking of alcoholic beverages -- United States -- History -- 20th century
ISBN 978-0-7432-7702-0; 0-7432-7702-3

LC 2009-51127

"Okrent's style is bracing and wry, his research is vast and impressive and his insight is penetrating. Intoxicating." Kirkus
Includes bibliographical references

Watman, Max
Chasing the white dog; an amateur outlaw's adventures in moonshine. Simon & Schuster 2010 292p $25 **363.4**
1. Liquors 2. Distillation
ISBN 978-1-4165-7178-0; 1-4165-7178-7

LC 2009-24657

"No matter where the chase takes him, from policing a lobster pot full of boiling molasses to getting schnockered at a conference for hobby distillers, Watman is a hands-on, no-holds-barred participant. He gamely learns to race cars to absorb the moonshine/NASCAR culture, and sits through the trial of a group of large-scale bootleggers in a multistate investigation. He profiles local color like Daytona 500 winner Junior Johnson, onetime moonshiner, famous for inventing the 'bootleg turn' to outrun the feds; and 'whitecollar' distillers like George Stranahan in Colorado." PopMatters

363.45   Drug traffic

Ainslie, Ricardo C.
The fight to save Juárez; life in the heart of Mexico's drug war. by Ricardo C. Ainslie. 1st ed. University of Texas Press 2013 xii, 282 p.p ill. (paperback) $25 **363.45**
1. Ciudad Juarez (Mexico) 2. Drug traffic -- Mexico 3. Law enforcement -- Mexico 4. Drug control -- Mexico -- Ciudad Juárez 5. Drug traffic -- Mexico -- Ciudad Juárez 6. Violent crime -- Mexico -- Ciudad Juárez
ISBN 9780292738904

LC 2012035822

This book, by Ricardo C. Ainslie, discusses the Mexican drug war. "The city of Juárez is ground zero for the drug war that is raging across Mexico and has claimed close to 60,000 lives since 2007. . . . [The book] takes us into the heart of Mexico's bloodiest city through the lives of four people who experienced the drug war from very different perspectives--Mayor José Reyes Ferriz, a mid-level cartel player's mistress, a human rights activist, and a photojournalist." (Publisher's note)
Includes bibliographical references and index.

Gibler, John
To die in Mexico; dispatches from inside the drug war. City Lights Books 2011 218p (Open media) pa $15.95 **363.45**
1. Drug traffic 2. Crime -- Mexico
ISBN 978-0-87286-517-4; 0-87286-517-7

LC 2011-02970

The author "recounts an endless litany of violence that has exploded during the tenures of Carlos Salinas, Ernesto Zedillo, Vicente Fox and, especially, Felipe Calderon. The various drug cartels—the Gulf cartel, the Zetas, the Sinaloa Cartel, among others—have only grown stronger over the years. . . . Hence, drugs are big business, especially for the banks, who launder the spectacular profits. The corruption of organized crime has infiltrated every segment of Mexican society, as Gibler demonstrates here, visiting prisons and civic groups, who express an utter sense of hopelessness and despair. However, the author has found fighting spirits, such as young murdered men's mothers who show up bravely and demand a police reckoning; and the journalists mourning their murdered fellow colleagues at El Diario de Juarez. Gibler argues passionately to undercut this 'case study in failure.' . . . With legality, both U.S. and Mexican society could address real issues of substance abuse through education and public-health initiatives." Kirkus

Includes bibliographical references

Schou, Nicholas

Orange sunshine; the Brotherhood of Eternal Love and its quest to spread peace, love, and acid to the world. Thomas Dunne Books 2010 306p il $24.99   **363.45**

1. Drug traffic 2. Dissenters 3. Narcotics dealers 4. Brotherhood of Eternal Love

ISBN 978-0-312-55183-4; 0-312-55183-5

LC 2009-40284

"Blue Cheer. Window Pane. Orange Sunshine. Maui Wowie. These were the brand names of the psychedelic counterculture of the 1960s and '70s, a culture led by the Brotherhood of Eternal Love. Chances are, if a brand of acid, pot or hashish was known to stoners, it first made its way into the underground market via the Brotherhood. Originally a marijuana-dealing motorcycle gang of toughs, the Brotherhood had a mass religious experience with LSD in 1965-they believed they'd found a lysergic shortcut to God. They resolved, under the charismatic leadership of John 'the Farmer' Griggs, whom Timothy Leary called 'the holiest man ever to live in this country,' to become apostles of acid with a mission to turn on the entire world. . . . A fascinating read for any audience and essential history for anyone interested in the roots of psychedelia." Kirkus

Includes bibliographical references

363.46   Abortion

Palmer, Louis J.

Encyclopedia of abortion in the United States; [by] Louis J. Palmer, Jr. and Xueyan Z. Palmer. 2nd ed.; McFarland & Co. 2009 624p il $150   **363.46**

1. Reference books 2. Abortion -- Encyclopedias

ISBN 978-0-7864-3838-9; 0-7864-3838-X

LC 2008-31047

First published 2002

"Ranging in length from a single paragraph to several pages, the A-to-Z entries define noteworthy events, significant figures, state and federal legislation, prochoice and prolife organizations, case specifics, abortion methods, and contraceptive devices. . . . This balanced, unblinking, and comprehensive subject reference makes complex legal details accessible to the lay reader." Libr J

Includes bibliographical references

Pollitt, Katha, 1949-

Pro; Reclaiming Abortion As Good for Society. Katha Pollitt. St. Martin's Press 2014 256 p. $25   **363.46**

1. Abortion 2. Pro-life movement

ISBN 0312620543; 9780312620547

LC 2014017553

"In this . . . book, Katha Pollitt reframes abortion as a common part of a woman's reproductive life, one that should be accepted as a moral right with positive social implications. In 'Pro,' Pollitt takes on the personhood argument, reaffirms the priority of a woman's life and health, and discusses why terminating a pregnancy can be a force for good for women, families, and society." (Publisher's note)

"Although the 'muddled middle' may not welcome the ascription, pro-choice advocates will find Pollitt's summation helpful in recruitment." LJ

Press, Eyal

Absolute convictions; my father, a city, and the conflict that divided America. Henry Holt and Co. 2006 292p il map hardcover o.p. pa $15   **363.46**

1. Abortion 2. Gynecologists 3. Pro-life movement 4. Abortion providers

ISBN 0-8050-7731-6; 978-0-312-42657-6 pa; 0-312-42657-7 pa

LC 2005-34064

The author "manages the extraordinary feat of bringing light to a political issue that for far too long has generated nothing but blistering heat." N Y Times Book Rev

Includes bibliographical references

Reagan, Leslie J.

When abortion was a crime; women, medicine, and law in the United States, 1867-1973. University of Calif. Press 1997 387p il hardcover o.p. pa $19.95   **363.46**

1. Abortion 2. Women -- United States

ISBN 0-520-21657-1 pa

LC 96-22568

This is a history of abortion in the United States from its criminalization between 1860 and 1880 to Roe v. Wade in 1973

"Important and original, vigorously written even down to the footnotes, {this book} manages with apparent ease to combine serious scholarship . . . and broad appeal." Atl Mon

Includes bibliographical references

363.5   Housing

Loewen, James W.

Sundown towns; a hidden dimension of American racism. New Press 2005 562p il $29.95 **363.5**

1. Discrimination in housing 2. United States -- Race

relations 3. African Americans -- Segregation
ISBN 1-56584-887-X

LC 2005-43855

"This book is sure to become a landmark in several fields and a sure bet among Loewen's many fans." Publ Wkly
Includes bibliographical references

Satter, Beryl

Family properties; race, real estate, and the exploitation of Black urban America. Metropolitan Books 2009 495p il $30   363.5
1. Lawyers 2. Discrimination in housing 3. Social activists 4. African Americans -- Chicago (Ill.)
ISBN 978-0-8050-7676-9; 0-8050-7676-X

LC 2008-33005

The author "leaps from the particulars of one man's story to become a panoramic retelling of the Chicago real-estate wars during a period when, after the postwar migration of Southern blacks, that city was the most segregated in the North." N Y Times (Late N Y Ed)
Includes bibliographical references

363.6   Public utilities and related services

Farabee, Charles R.

National park ranger; an American icon. {by} Charles R. "Butch" Farabee Jr. Roberts Rinehart Publishers 2003 180p il pa $18.95   363.6
1. United States -- National Park Service 2. National parks and reserves -- United States
ISBN 1-570-98392-5

LC 2003-1022

"In this study of the vocation of park ranger since Maryland's park caretakers in 1696 to the present day, former ranger Farabee not only explores a ranger's role but also touches on the establishment of the National Park Service, the introduction of women rangers, and early resource management. Readers will enjoy the abundance of archival photographs, ranger profiles, and numerous other features." Libr J
Includes bibliographical references

Heacox, Kim

National Geographic the national parks; an illustrated history. Kim Heacox. National Geographic 2015 367 p. color illustrations (hardcover : alk. paper) $50   363.6
1. National parks and reserves -- United States -- History
ISBN 1426215592; 9781426215599

LC 2015014107

This book is a "celebration of the 100th anniversary of the National Park Service. [It] collects the very best of National Geographic's photographs, combined with an expertly told history: from the multi-hued layers of the Grand Canyon to the verdigris flame of the Statue of Liberty, this book presents a breathtaking panorama of the National Parks. With the stories behind the first female park ranger, a decidedly amateur scuba expedition that unearthed a submerged Civil War treasure trove, and so much more, Heacox takes readers on a VIP tour of America's rich natural and cultural heritage." (Publisher's note)

"Gorgeous in every way, and essential for travel and history shelves." LJ

363.7   Environmental problems

Berners-Lee, Mike

How bad are bananas? the carbon footprint of everything. Greystone Books 2011 232p il pa $16.95   363.7
1. Carbon 2. Greenhouse effect
ISBN 978-1-55365-831-3 pa; 978-1-55365-832-0 ebook
First published 2010 in the United Kingdom
Discusses the carbon footprint—the carbon emissions used to manufacture and transport—of everyday items, including paper bags and imported produce, and provides information to help build carbon considerations into everyday purchases.
"A book like this risks being preachy or overly serious, but Berners-Lee approaches his topics with humor and curiosity. He rarely advocates radical change. Rather, he gives readers information." Christ Sci Monit
Includes bibliographical references

Bloom, Jonathan

American wasteland; how America throws away nearly half of its food (and what we can do about it) Da Capo Press 2010 360p il $26   363.7
1. Salvage 2. Food supply 3. Food industry 4. Waste (Economics)
ISBN 978-0-7382-1364-4

LC 2010-15075

"An eye-opening account of what used to be considered a sin—the willful waste of perfectly edible food. . . . An urgent, necessary book." Kirkus
Includes bibliographical references

Braasch, Gary

Earth under fire; how global warming is changing the world. Updated ed; University of California Press 2009 xxx, 267p il pa $24.95   363.7
1. Greenhouse effect 2. Climate -- Environmental aspects
ISBN 978-0-520-26025-2
First published 2007
"What sets Earth Under Fire apart from other books on the same topic are the inspiring photographs. These images are an effective tool that helps the reader understand what the implications of climate change are—for people, for other organisms, and for entire ecosystems." Sci Books Films
Includes bibliographical references

Busch, Akiko

The incidental steward; reflections on citizen science. Akiko Busch; illustrations by Debby Cotter Kaspari. Yale University Press 2013 256 p. (hardcover) $25   363.7
1. Wildlife conservation 2. Environmental protection 3. Wildlife conservation -- Hudson River Valley (N.Y. and N.J.) 4. Environmental monitoring -- Hudson River

Valley (N.Y. and N.J.)
ISBN 0300178794; 9780300178791

LC 2012040301

This book, by Akiko Busch, illustrated by Debby Cotter Kaspari, "highlights factors that distinguish twenty-first-century citizen scientists from traditional amateur naturalists: a greater sense of urgency, helpful new technologies, and the expanded possibilities of crowdsourcing. . . . While not a primer on the prescribed protocols of citizen science, the book combines vivid natural history, a deep sense of place, and reflection about our changing world." (Publisher's note)

Includes bibliographical references and index

Carson, Rachel, 1907-1964

★ **Silent** spring; introduction by Linda Lear; afterword by Edward O. Wilson. 40th anniversary ed; Houghton Mifflin 2002 378p il   **363.7**

1. Pesticides and wildlife 2. Pesticides -- Environmental aspects

ISBN 0-618-24906-0 pa; 0-618-25305-X
First published 1962

In The silent spring, Carson "contended that the indiscriminate use of weed killers and insecticides constituted a hazard to wildlife and to human beings. Her provocative work inspired many subsequent environmental studies." Reader's Ency. 4th edition

Flannery, Tim F.

The **weather** makers; how man is changing the climate and what it means for life on Earth. [by] Tim Flannery. Atlantic Monthly Press 2006 357p il maps hardcover o.p. pa $15   **363.7**

1. Climate 2. Greenhouse effect

ISBN 0-8711-3935-9; 0-8021-4292-3 pa

LC 2005-52350

"This work is distinctive in its marriage of science to an act-now attitude and should energize environmentally minded readers." Booklist

Includes bibliographical references (p. 289-297)

Freudenburg, William R.

Blowout in the Gulf; the BP oil spill disaster and the future of energy in America. [by] William R. Freudenburg and Robert Gramling. MIT Press 2010 254p il $18.95   **363.7**

1. Oil spills 2. Drilling platforms 3. Offshore oil well drilling 4. British Petroleum Co. plc

ISBN 978-0-262-01583-7

LC 2010-937510

The authors "set the deadly BP blowout within a technologically precise history of oil in America, from the first primitively constructed well on land to the development of offshore rigs, explaining that the Deepwater Horizon was actually a technical marvel—if only its operation hadn't been compromised. . . . Science, commerce, and the politics of oil are all newly illuminated here, accompanied by invaluable explanations of the risks of offshore drilling and a pragmatic look at the energy conundrums we now face." Booklist

Includes bibliographical references

Friedman, Thomas L.

Hot, flat, and crowded; why we need a green revolution--and how it can renew America. Farrar, Straus & Giroux 2008 438p il $27.95   **363.7**

1. Energy resources 2. Environmental movement 3. Climate -- Environmental aspects 4. Environmental policy -- United States

ISBN 978-0-374-16685-4; 0-374-16685-4

LC 2008-930589

"Friedman's big, passionate, and solidly specific ecological primer, social manifesto, and realistic plan for a green revolution aimed at restoring America's greatness and securing a sustainable future should serve as a playbook for innovators and civic leaders." Booklist

Gates, Alexander E.

Encyclopedia of pollution; [by] Alexander E. Gates and Robert P. Blauvelt. Facts on File 2011 2v il map (Facts on File science library) set $170 **363.7**

1. Pollution 2. Reference books 3. Pollution -- Encyclopedias

ISBN 978-0-8160-7002-2

LC 2009048190

"Broad topics encompass all aspects of pollutants, including properties, production, uses, environmental release and fate, regulations, and adverse health effects in response to exposure. Summary entries on general subjects, such as water pollution, provide topical overviews. Case studies of pollution events supply instructive background information." Booklist

Includes bibliographical references

George, Rose

The **big** necessity; the unmentionable world of human waste and why it matters. Metropolitan Books 2008 288p il $26   **363.7**

1. Sanitation 2. Sewage disposal

ISBN 978-0-8050-8271-5; 0-8050-8271-9

LC 2008-29999

The author "breaks the embarrassed silence over the economic, political, social and environmental problems of human waste disposal. . . . From the depths of the world's oldest surviving urban sewers in to Japan's robo-toilet revolution, George leads an intrepid, erudite and entertaining journey through the public consequences of this most private behavior." Publ Wkly

Includes bibliographical references

Gessner, David

All the Wild That Remains; Edward Abbey, Wallace Stegner, and the American West. David Gessner. W W Norton & Co Inc 2015 320 p. illustrations $26.95   **363.7**

1. West (U.S.)

ISBN 0393089991; 9780393089998

LC 2014036995

In this book about writers Edward Abbey and Wallace Stegner, author " David Gessner follows the ghosts of these two remarkable writer-environmentalists from Stegner's birthplace in Saskatchewan to the site of Abbey's pilgrimages to Arches National Park in Utah, braiding their stories and asking how they speak to the lives of all those who care about the West." (Publisher's note)

"Highly recommended for everyone interested in literature, environmentalism, and the American West." LJ

Gore, Al

★ An **inconvenient** truth; the planetary emergency of global warming and what we can do about it. Rodale 2006 325p il map pa $23.95   **363.7**

1. Human ecology 2. Environmental protection 3. Greenhouse effect 4. Environmental policy -- United States

ISBN 978-1-59486-567-1; 1-59486-567-1

LC 2006-926537

"Gore has put together a coherent account of a complex topic that Americans desperately need to understand. . . . By telling the story of climate change with striking clarity . . . Al Gore may have done for global warming what [Rachel Carson's] Silent Spring [1962] did for pesticides." N Y Rev Books

Our choice; a plan to solve the climate crisis. Rodale 2009 414p il map pa $26.99   **363.7**

1. Human ecology 2. Environmental policy 3. Environmental protection 4. Greenhouse effect

ISBN 978-1-59486-734-7; 1-59486-734-8

LC 2009-38291

The former vice president addresses key environmental issues while profiling and evaluating possible solutions.

This "is an inviting and momentous compendium of environmental discovery . . . that addresses one of the greatest threats our species has encountered with intelligence, knowledge, wisdom, and faith in human empowerment. This is a book that should be displayed and talked about everywhere." Booklist

Hansen, James E.

Storms of my grandchildren; the truth about the coming climate catastrophe and our last chance to save humanity. [by] James Hansen; illustrations by Makiko Sato. Bloomsbury USA 2009 304p il $25   **363.7**

1. Environmental influence on humans 2. Greenhouse effect 3. Climate -- Environmental aspects

ISBN 978-1-60819-200-7

LC 2009-44553

"Rich in invaluable insights into the geopolitics as well as the geophysics of climate change, Hansen's guaranteed-to-be-controversial manifesto is the most comprehensible, realistic, and courageous call to prevent climate change yet. It belongs in every library." Booklist

Includes bibliographical references

Humes, Edward

Eco Barons; the dreamers, schemers and millionaires who are saving our planet. Ecco 2009 367p $25.99   **363.7**

1. Conservationists 2. Environmentalists

ISBN 978-0-06-135029-0; 0-06-135029-X

"The millionaires of the subtitle are Doug Tompkins, who put Esprit clothing profits to work protecting Argentina's Patagonia; Roxanne Quimby, who used Burt's Bees

cosmetics earnings to purchase vast wild lands in Maine; and Ted Turner, whose CNN fortune allowed him to become America's single largest landowner, with 15 immense ranches managed for native species. Others featured in the book get the job done through sheer tenacity. . . . Although too fast-paced for much nuance, this book is full of captivating facts and well-told tales of environmentalism's human side." Libr J

Jacobs, Chip

Smogtown; the lung-burning history of pollution in Los Angeles. [by] Chip Jacobs & William J. Kelly. Overlook Press 2008 384p il $26.95   **363.7**

1. Air pollution 2. Los Angeles (Calif.)

ISBN 978-1-58567-860-0

"This friendly, accessible history should appeal to any American environmentalist." Publ Wkly

Includes bibliographical references

Jones, Van

The **green**-collar economy; how one solution can fix our two biggest problems. with Ariane Conrad. HarperOne 2008 237p $25.95; pa $14.99   **363.7**

1. Environmental protection 2. Social policy -- United States 3. Environmental policy -- United States

ISBN 978-0-06-165075-8; 0-06-165075-7; 978-0-06-165076-5 pa; 0-06-165076-5 pa

The author "argues that developing a sustainable energy industry in America would lessen our dependency on non-renewable and foreign energy sources, as well as provide local and well-paid employment. With a resource list to help individuals become involved." Libr J

Includes bibliographical references

Keizer, Garret

The **unwanted** sound of everything we want; a book about noise. PublicAffairs 2010 385p $27.95   **363.7**

1. Noise 2. Sound 3. Noise -- Psychological aspects 4. Sound -- Psychological aspects

ISBN 1586485520; 9781586485528

LC 2010-05391

This book presents an "argument about the politics of sound. [Garret] Keizer acknowledges the subjective dimension of noise, which is sometimes defined as unwanted sound. What I deem noise may not be bothersome to someone else, and what bothers me in one context could be acceptable to me in another." Keizer offers an "analysis of power and inequality, noting the disproportionate effect of noise on people on the margins. . . . In response, he argues for a renewed human community of civility and sustainability." (Christian Century)

This "book explores the unforeseen (and sometimes unwanted) side effects of our inventive natures. We usually use the word noise as a pejorative, a term denoting unwanted sound: somebody's loud music, a blaring car alarm, the din from a nearby airport. But, as Keizer points out, noise is often—perhaps even usually—a product of human achievement, invention, or ambition. In broad terms, you can't have civilization without noise. . . . An enlightening look at an issue most of us ignore." Booklist

Includes bibliographical references

Kirby, David

Animal factory; the looming threat of industrial pig, dairy, and poultry farms to humans and the environment. St. Martin's Press 2010 492p $26.99 **363.7**

1. Livestock industry 2. Agriculture -- Environmental aspects

ISBN 0-312-38058-5; 978-0-312-38058-8

"Thanks to Kirby's extraordinary journalism, we have the most relatable, irrefutable, and unforgettable testimony yet to the hazards of industrial animal farming." Booklist

Kolbert, Elizabeth

★ Field notes from a catastrophe; man, nature, and climate change. Bloomsbury Pub. 2006 210p il map hardcover o.p. pa $14.95 **363.7**

1. Climate 2. Greenhouse effect

ISBN 1-59691-125-5; 978-1-59691-125-3; 1-59691-130-1 pa; 978-1-59691-130-7 pa

LC 2005-30972

"On the burgeoning shelf of cautionary but occasionally alarmist books warning about the consequences of dramatic climate change, Kolbert's calmly persuasive reporting stands out for its sobering clarity." Publ Wkly

Includes bibliographical references

McKibben, Bill, 1960-

Oil and Honey; The Education of an Unlikely Activist. Bill McKibben. Times Books 2013 272 p. $26 **363.7**

1. Beekeeping 2. Environmentalists 3. Environmental movement 4. Environmentalism -- United States 5. Beekeepers -- United States -- Biography 6. Climatic changes -- Environmental aspects 7. Environmentalists -- United States -- Biography 8. Petroleum industry and trade -- Environmental aspects 9. Petroleum industry and trade -- Political aspects -- United States

ISBN 0805092846; 9780805092844

LC 2013010995

This book is a memoir by environmental activist Bill McKibben. "McKibben intersperses his accounts of his intense and wide-ranging efforts as an environmental activist with his sometimes-humbling experiences as a novice beekeeper, learning from [farmer Kirk] Webster the art and science of raising bees and making honey." (Kirkus Reviews)

Mooney, Chris

Storm world; hurricanes, politics, and the battle over global warming. Harcourt 2007 392p il map $26 **363.7**

1. Hurricanes 2. Greenhouse effect

ISBN 978-0-15-101287-9; 0-15-101287-3

LC 2007-09742

"This is certainly one of the most thought-provoking and accessible accounts of climate change to appear since Katrina." Booklist

Includes bibliographical references

Moore, Charles

Plastic ocean; how a sea captain's chance discovery launched a determined quest to save the oceans.
[by] Capt. Charles Moore with Cassandra Phillips. Avery 2011 358p il map $26 **363.7**

1. Plastics 2. Marine pollution

ISBN 978-1-58333-424-9; 1-58333-424-6

LC 2011034559

"The author is an impassioned, fiercely inquisitive writer, detailing the many unorthodox ways he's managed to get these issues into the news and in peer-reviewed science journals. . . . Fast-paced and electrifying, Moore's story is 'gonzo science' at its best." Kirkus

Includes bibliographical references

Pooley, Eric

The climate war; true believers, power brokers, and the fight to save the earth. Hyperion 2010 481p $27.99 **363.7**

1. Environmental policy 2. Climate -- Environmental aspects

ISBN 978-1-4013-2326-4

LC 2010-12422

This "is a fascinating, well-researched, behind-the-scenes account of the political twists and turns and efforts of corporate bosses and climate activists. Pooley . . . puts a human face on the topic and writes a gripping account— whether one reads it cover to cover or consults individual chapters in any order." Choice

Includes bibliographical references

Rogers, Heather

Gone tomorrow; the hidden life of garbage. New Press 2005 288p il $23.95 **363.7**

1. Refuse and refuse disposal

ISBN 1-56584-879-9

LC 2005-41562

The author "analyzes the contents of America's garbage and its disposal while also revealing the corporate strategies behind the disposable-goods explosion and assessing the ecological toll of our consumer habits." Booklist

Includes bibliographical references

Royte, Elizabeth

Garbage land; on the secret trail of trash. Little, Brown 2005 311p hardcover o.p. pa $14.99 **363.7**

1. Refuse and refuse disposal

ISBN 0-316-73826-3; 0-316-15461-X pa

LC 2004-24732

"There's little waste in Royte's winning words. . . . Seldom has garbage been handled with such care." Christ Sci Monit

Includes bibliographical references

Shulman, Seth

Cooler smarter; practical steps for low-carbon living : expert advice from the Union of Concerned Scientists. Seth Shulman ... [et al.] Island Press 2012 321 p. (pbk.) $21.95 **363.7**

1. Fuel 2. Environmental health 3. Transportation -- Environmental aspects 4. Sustainable living -- United States 5. Environmental protection -- United States -- Citizen participation

ISBN 161091192X; 9781610911924

LC 2012008656

In the book, the Union of Concerned Scientists discusses "proven strategies to cut carbon, with chapters on transportation, home energy use, diet, personal consumption, as well as how best to influence your workplace, your community, and elected officials. The book explains how to make the biggest impact and when not to sweat the small stuff. It also turns many eco-myths on their head, like the importance of locally produced food or the superiority of all hybrid cars." (Publisher's note)

Stager, Curt

Deep future; Curt Stager. Thomas Dunne Books 2011 284p ill.   **363.7**
    1. Global warming 2. Geological time 3. Historical geology 4. Climate -- Research
    ISBN 9780312614621; 9780312614638
                                    LC 2010040381

This book, a 'Kirkus Reviews' Best Nonfiction of 2011 title, presents an "exploration of the impact of climate change over geological time. [Curt] Stager takes the long view of global climate change . . . [and] examines both moderate and extreme scenarios. . . . A key point is that humanity has the ability to moderate the release of carbon, shaping the long-range impact on climate. While we are already past the point where significant global warming can be prevented, the author points out that cutting carbon now preserves some for a future era when its release could help prevent another ice age -- a global disaster every bit as threatening to the human race as warming." (Kirkus)

Includes bibliographical references (p. 243-270) and index.

Walker, Gabrielle

The **hot** topic; what we can do about global warming. [by] Gabrielle Walker and Sir David King. Harcourt 2008 276p il map pa $14   **363.7**
    1. Greenhouse effect
    ISBN 978-0-15-603318-3
                                    LC 2007-45080

"This is the best overview of global warming that this reviewer has read. . . . What is most valuable about this book is that the text clearly explains to lay readers a very complex and highly controversial topic." Libr J

Includes bibliographical references

Watts, Jonathan

When a billion Chinese jump; how China will save mankind--or destroy it. Scribner 2010 435p map pa $17; ebook $9.99   **363.7**
    1. China -- Economic conditions 2. Environmental policy -- China 3. China -- Politics and government
    ISBN 978-1-4165-8076-8 pa; 1-4165-8076-X pa; 978-1-4391-4193-9 ebook; 1-4391-4193-2 ebook
                                    LC 2010-29901

"Watts' comprehensive, revealing study is eye-opening, not only for the way it illuminates how China's population growth and rapid modernization affect the environment, but also for its exposure of the way Western waste contributes to the problem." Booklist

Includes bibliographical references

363.72   Sanitation

Fagin, Dan

★ **Toms** River; a small town, a cancer cluster, and the epic quest to expose pollution's hidden consequences. Dan Fagin. Bantam Books 2013 560 p. $28   **363.72**
    1. Rivers 2. Pollution 3. Industrial waste 4. Cancer -- Toms River Region 5. Water quality -- New Jersey -- Toms River Watershed 6. Toms River Watershed (N.J.) -- Environmental conditions 7. Groundwater -- Pollution -- Health aspects -- Toms River Region 8. Drinking water -- Contamination -- Health aspects -- Toms River Region
    ISBN 055380653X; 9780345538611; 9780553806533
                                    LC 2012017030

Pulitzer Prize: General Nonfiction (2014)

This book by Dan Fagin "recounts the sixty-year saga of rampant pollution and inadequate oversight that made Toms River [New Jersey] a cautionary example for fast-growing industrial towns from South Jersey to South China. He tells the stories of the pioneering scientists and physicians who first identified pollutants as a cause of cancer, and brings to life the everyday heroes in Toms River who struggled for justice." (Publisher's note)

Includes bibliographical references and index

363.73   Pollution

Blackwell, Andrew

★ **Visit** sunny Chernobyl; and other adventures in the world's most polluted places. Andrew Blackwell. Rodale 2012 xiii, 306 p.p maps (hardcover) $25.99   **363.73**
    1. Pollution 2. Ecotourism 3. Environmental degradation 4. Tourism -- Environmental aspects
    ISBN 1605294454; 9781605294452
                                    LC 2011053229

"[I]n 'Visit Sunny Chernobyl,' Andrew Blackwell embraces a different kind of travel, taking a jaunt through the most gruesomely polluted places on Earth. . . . From the hidden bars and convenience stores of a radioactive wilderness to the sacred but reeking waters of India, 'Visit Sunny Chernobyl' fuses . . . first-person reporting with satire and analysis, making the case that it's time to start appreciating our planet as it is--not as we wish it would be." (Publisher's note)

Jenkins, McKay

Poison spring; the secret history of pollution and the EPA. by E.G. Vallianatos with McKay Jenkins. Bloomsbury Press 2013 304 p. (alk, paper) $28   **363.73**
    1. Political corruption 2. United States. Environmental Protection Agency 3. Corporate power -- United States 4. Pollution -- Research -- United States 5. Environmental responsibility -- United States
    ISBN 1608199142; 9781608199143
                                    LC 2013041923

"For twenty-five years [author] E.G. Vallianatos saw the EPA from the inside, with rising dismay over how pressure from politicians and threats from huge corporations were turning it from the public's watchdog into a 'polluter's protection agency.' Based on his own experience . . . and hundreds of documents Vallianatos collected inside the EPA, 'Poison Spring' [co-authored by McKay Jenkins] reveals how the agency has continually reinforced the chemical-industrial complex." (Publisher's note)

"The authors tout healthier living through small, non-toxic family farms while delivering an alarming, comprehensive account of a 'fatally compromised' EPA mission crippled by bad enforcement practices and numerous corrupting influences." Pub Wkly

Includes bibliographical references and index

363.738 Pollutants

Climate change; an encyclopedia of science and history. Brian C. Black, general editor; David M. Hassenzahl, Jennie C. Stephens, Gary Weisel, and Nancy Gift, associate editors. ABC-CLIO, LLC 2013 xx, 1774 p.p ill. (hardcover) $399 **363.738**
1. Climate change 2. Global warming 3. Climatic changes -- History -- Encyclopedias 4. Climatic changes -- Research -- Encyclopedias
ISBN 1598847619; 9781598847611

LC 2012034673

This book afford a "historical overview of the topic" of climate change. "The volume provides a foundational understanding of climate change for students, policymakers, and the general public. . . . More than 100 subject experts contributed more than 225 articles, typically several pages in length, to the compilation. The articles examine the potential effects of climate change on both human and natural systems; many contain climate change mitigation" strategies. (Booklist)

Includes bibliographical references (pages 1651-1693) and index.

Encyclopedia of global warming & climate change; general editor, S. George Philander. SAGE Publications, Inc. 2012 3 v.,1641 p. 3v il (cloth) $375 **363.738**
1. Climate change 2. Encyclopedias and dictionaries 3. Global warming -- Encyclopedias 4. Climatic changes -- Encyclopedias
ISBN 1412992613; 9781412992619

LC 2012002545

This encyclopedia has "40 new articles . . . and extensive revision" and "offers students and . . . 'laymen' close looks at recent developments. The set also examines broad historical, scientific, national, geographical, political, and thematic pictures of climate change's mechanisms, effects, and controversies." (School Library Journal)

"The set includes more than 750 articles addressing major topics related to global warming and climate change ranging geographically from the North Pole to the South Pole and thematically from social effects to scientific causes. Coverage encompasses the science and history of climate change, the polarizing controversies over climate-change

theories, the role of societies, the industrial and economic factors, and the sociological aspects of climate change. . . . This valuable resource provides an excellent historical overview and framework of this topic and serves as a general resource for geography, oceanography, biology, climatology, history, and many other subjects." Libr J

Includes bibliographical references and index

The **global** warming reader; A Century of Writing About Climate Change. Penguin Books 2012 421 p. (paperback) $18.00 **363.738**
1. Climate change 2. Global warming 3. Environmental sciences 4. Human influence on nature
ISBN 0143121898; 9780143121893

This book, edited by Bill McKibben, "brings together the essential voices on global warming, from its 19th-century discovery to the present. . . . [The book] provides more than thirty-five answers . . . from more than one hundred years of engagement with the topic. Here is Elizabeth Kolbert's groundbreaking essay 'The Darkening Sea,' . . . NASA scientist James Hansen's testimony before the U.S. Congress, and clarion calls for action by Al Gore, Arundhati Roy, Naomi Klein, and many others." (Publisher's note)

Guzman, Andrew T.
Overheated; The Human Cost of Climate Change. Andrew T. Guzman. Oxford University Press 2013 280 p. (hardcover) $29.95 **363.738**
1. Human ecology 2. Climate change 3. Climatic changes -- Social aspects 4. Climatic changes -- Economic aspects 5. Climatic changes -- Effect of human beings on
ISBN 0199933871; 9780199933877

LC 2012047000

This book, by Andrew T. Guzman, discusses the political aspects surrounding climate change. "Guzman takes climate change out of the realm of scientific abstraction to explore its real-world consequences. . . . He takes as his starting point a fairly optimistic outcome in the range predicted by scientists. . . . Even this modest rise would lead to catastrophic . . . problems. . . . He shows in vivid detail how climate change is already playing out in the real world." (Publisher's note)

Includes bibliographical references and index

Klein, Naomi
This changes everything; capitalism vs. the climate. Naomi Klein. Simon & Schuster 2014 576 p. (hardback) $30 **363.738**
1. Capitalism 2. Climate change 3. Environmental policy 4. Environmental economics 5. Climatic changes -- Economic aspects 6. Environmental policy -- Economic aspects 7. Global environmental change -- Economic aspects
ISBN 1451697384; 9781451697384

LC 2014013864

Los Angeles Times Book Prize Finalist: Science and Technology (2014)

In this book, author "Naomi Klein argues that climate change isn't just another issue to be neatly filed between taxes and health care. It's an alarm that calls us to fix an economic system that is already failing us in many ways. Klein . . . builds the case for how massively reducing our greenhouse emissions is our best chance to simultaneously reduce gaping inequalities, re-imagine our broken democracies, and rebuild our gutted local economies." (Publisher's note)

"In part, Klein's narrative is a personal story about her own awakening to and increasing engagement with the climate issue. But this always-interesting polemic is built mostly on her interviews with experts, environmentalists and activists and her colorful on-site reporting from various international meetings and conferences." Kirkus

Includes bibliographical references and index

Lerner, Steve
Sacrifice zones; the front lines of toxic chemical exposure in the United States. Steve Lerner; foreword by Phil Brown. MIT Press 2010 xiv, 346p (hardcover : alk. paper) 29.95   363.738
1. Pollution 2. United States 3. Chemical spills 4. Hazardous wastes 5. Hazardous waste sites 6. Pollution -- United States -- Case studies 7. Hazardous waste sites -- United States -- Case studies 8. Environmental toxicology -- United States -- Case studies 9. Chemical spills -- Health aspects -- United States -- Case studies 10. Hazardous substances -- Health aspects -- United States -- Case studies
ISBN 0262014408; 9780262014403
          LC 2009051289
In this book, author "Steve Lerner tells the stories of twelve communities, from Brooklyn to Pensacola, that rose up to fight the industries and military bases causing disproportionately high levels of chemical pollution. He calls these low-income neighborhoods 'sacrifice zones'—repurposing a Cold War term coined by U.S. government officials to designate areas contaminated with radioactive pollutants during the manufacture of nuclear weapons. And he argues that residents of a new generation of sacrifice zones, tainted with chemical pollutants, need additional regulatory protections." (Publisher's note)
Includes bibliographical references (p. [315]-337) and index

McGraw, Seamus
Betting the farm on a drought; stories from the front lines of climate change. Seamus McGraw. University of Texas Press 2015 192 p. illustrations (hardback) $24.95   363.738
1. Climate change 2. United States -- Environmental conditions 3. Climatic changes -- United States -- Popular works
ISBN 9780292756618; 0292756615
          LC 2014027613
Author Seamus McGraw presents this "book that lays out the whole story of climate change—the science, the math, and . . . the human stories of people fighting both the climate and their own deeply held beliefs. McGraw takes us on a trip along America's culturally fractured back roads and listens to farmers and ranchers and fishermen, many of them people who are not ideologically, politically, or in some cases even religiously inclined to believe in man-made global climate change." (Publisher's note)
"Effectively blending story, science, and context, this engaging, readable book will be invaluable for those study-

ing or working on issues associated with climate change, especially those with a social science or policy focus." Choice
Includes bibliographical references and index

Stewart, Ben
Don't trust, don't fear, don't beg; the extraordinary story of the Arctic 30. Ben Stewart. The New Press 2015 336 p. illustrations, map (hardback : alk. paper) $26.95   363.738
1. Political prisoners -- Russia 2. Protest movements -- Arctic regions 3. Arctic Sunrise (Ship) 4. Greenpeace International 5. Protest movements -- Arctic Regions 6. Environmental protection -- Arctic regions 7. Political prisoners -- Russia (Federation) 8. Offshore gas industry -- Environmental aspects -- Arctic regions 9. Offshore oil industry -- Environmental aspects -- Arctic regions 10. Petroleum industry and trade -- Environmental aspects -- Arctic Regions
ISBN 9781620971093; 1620971097
          LC 2015008418
This book, by Ben Stewart, describes how "in 2013 thirty men and women from eighteen countries--the crew of Greenpeace's Arctic Sunrise--decide to . . . protest the drilling in the Arctic. . . . But their protest is met with brutal force as [Russian leader Vladimir] Putin's commandos seize the Arctic Sunrise. Held under armed guard by masked men, they are charged with piracy and face fifteen years in Russia's nightmarish prison system." (Publisher's note)
"A well-written, faced-paced narrative with real human spark—essential." LJ

Terry, Beth
Plastic-free; how I kicked the plastic habit and you can too. Beth Terry. Skyhorse Pub. 2012 viii, 344 p.p (alk. paper) $19.95   363.738
1. Pollution 2. Recycling 3. Environmental health 4. Plastic scrap -- Environmental aspects 5. Plastic waste -- Environmental aspects
ISBN 1616086246; 9781616086244
          LC 2012002817
In this book, author Beth "Terry provides personal anecdotes, stats about the environmental and health problems related to plastic, and personal solutions and tips on how to limit your plastic footprint. Terry includes . . . lists and charts for easy reference, ways to get involved in larger community actions, and profiles of individuals . . . who have gone beyond personal solutions to create a change on a larger scale." (Publisher's note)
Includes bibliographical references.

363.739   Pollution of specific environments

Kelly, William J.
The People's Republic of Chemicals; William J. Kelly and Chip Jacobs. Rare Bird Books 2014 280 p. map $24.95   363.739
1. Climate change 2. Environmental policy -- China
ISBN 1940207258; 9781940207254
In this book authors "William J. Kelly and Chip Jacobs follow up their acclaimed Smogtown with a provocative examination of China's ecological calamity already imper-

ling a warming planet. Kelly and Jacobs describe China's ancient love affair with coal, Bill Clinton's blunders cutting free-trade deals, . . . Communist Party manipulation of eco-statistics, the horror of cancer villages, the deception of the 2008 Beijing Olympics, and spellbinding peasant revolts." (Publisher's note)

"A powerful warning that "a growing cloud of toxin s aloft [are] swirling in the winds around the world" and recirculating the pollution we hoped to shed." Kirkus

363.8 Food supply

Soussan, Michael
  Backstabbing for beginners; my crash course in international diplomacy. Nation Books 2008 332p il $25.95 **363.8**
  1. United Nations -- Office of Iraq Programme -- Oil-for-Food Programme
  ISBN 978-1-56858-397-6; 1-56858-397-4
  LC 2008-31698

"Soussan brings provocative wit, a keen eye for detail and a knack for revealing anecdotes to this important account of the rampant greed, hypocrisy and cynicism festering behind the United Nations' humanitarian credo." Publ Wkly
  Includes bibliographical references

Stuart, Tristram
  Waste; uncovering the global food scandal. W.W. Norton & Co. 2009 xxii, 451p il $27.95 **363.8**
  1. Recycling 2. Food industry 3. Waste minimization
  ISBN 978-0-393-06836-8

The author "shows how we could have much more food overnight simply by not tossing away so much of it. This simple concept ingeniously unites many food scandals that often do not get the attention they deserve: the mould that destroys a third or more of Third World harvests; . . . [and] the millions of tonnes of edible food wasted by modern food processing and 'sell-by' dates. . . . Usefully, Stuart offers examples of what we could be doing better, from processing technologies to offal sausages." New Sci
  Includes bibliographical references

363.9 Population problems

Bruinius, Harry
  Better for all the world; the secret history of forced sterilization and America's quest for racial purity. Knopf 2006 401p il hardcover o.p. pa $16.95; ebook $16.95 **363.9**
  1. Eugenics 2. Sterilization (Birth control)
  ISBN 0-375-41371-5; 0-375-71305-0 pa; 978-0-307-42496-9 ebook
  LC 2005-44150

"Bruinius' account of one of America's dirty little secrets is . . . a real page-turner." Booklist
  Includes bibliographical references

May, Elaine Tyler, 1947-
  America and the pill; a history of promise, peril, and liberation. Basic Books 2010 214p $25.95 **363.9**
  1. Birth control 2. Oral contraceptives 3. Women -- Social conditions 4. Oral contraceptives -- Social aspects 5. Birth control -- United States -- History 6. Women -- United States -- Social conditions -- 20th century
  ISBN 978-0-465-01152-0
  LC 2009-46957

The author describes "the now extravagant-seeming hopes and fears the pill first elicited, how the pill became a symbol of the 1960s sexual revolution without demonstrably affecting it, how feminists used the pill to push for an analogue for men as part of their gender-egalitarian agenda, and how reaction to the pill's ill effects on many women contributed to the late-twentieth-century dissipation of respect for professional and institutional authority. . . . Understanding that the book is fundamentally, nonargumentatively pro-pill, one couldn't ask for a better short history of its subject." Booklist
  Includes bibliographical references and index

Overdevelopment, Overpopulation, Overshoot; Edited by Tom Butler. Goff Books 2015 330 p. chiefly color illustrations $50 **363.9**
  1. Overpopulation 2. Community development
  ISBN 1939621232; 9781939621238

This book, edited by Tom Butler, presents a "series of photo essays illuminating the depth of the damage that human numbers and behavior have caused to the Earth—and which threatens humanity's future. [It answers] why is the demographic explosion and its effects ignored by policymakers and the media? Why do important people within the global environmental movement itself avoid the great challenges of the population issue?" (Publisher's note)

"This accessible work ought to make readers uncomfortable: it tells us there are too many people now and that there are soon to be many more, and our collective activities, including industrial agriculture and feedlots, are degrading our only home." LJ

Tone, Andrea
  Devices and desires; a history of contraceptives in America. Hill & Wang 2001 366p hardcover o.p. pa $15 **363.9**
  1. Birth control
  ISBN 0-8090-3817-X; 0-8090-3816-1 pa
  LC 00-50547

"Part 1 examines the 'contraceptive entrepreneurs' who practiced what was for many years an illegal trade, regulated by no one. In part 2, 'From Smut to Science,' Tone considers the development of relatively reliable contraceptive techniques, . . . part 3, 'The Medicalization of Contraceptives,' covers birth control pills, Norplant, and intrauterine devices." Booklist

364   Criminology

Nash, Jay Robert

The **great** pictorial history of world crime. History 2004 2v il set $249   **364**

1. Reference books 2. Crime -- Encyclopedias
ISBN 1-928831-20-6

LC 2004-100992

"Each of these topical sections opens with a general overview and then explores individual crimes in chronological order. As befits the title, there are thousands of black-and-white photographs and illustrations and although their quality varies they are, by and large, helpful and interesting. . . . [This is] the most comprehensive true crime book available." SLJ

Rosen, Fred

The **historical** atlas of American crime. Facts on File 2005 xx, 296p il map (Facts on File crime library) $75; pa $24.95   **364**

1. Crime -- United States
ISBN 0-8160-4841-X; 0-8160-4842-8 pa

LC 2004-11346

The author "brings a fresh point of view to American crime by placing it within the larger context of American history; at the same time he observes multiple disciplines (e.g., history, economics, literature) through the lens of crime." Choice

Includes bibliographical references

Slater, Dan

Wolf Boys; two American teenagers and Mexico's most dangerous drug cartel. Dan Slater. Simon & Schuster 2016 352 p. (hardcover) $26.95   **364**

1. Drug traffic -- Mexico 2. Organized crime -- Mexico
ISBN 1501126547; 9781501126543

This book, by Dan Slater, offers "the story of two American teens recruited as killers for a Mexican cartel, and their pursuit by a Mexican-American detective who realizes the War on Drugs is unwinnable. What's it like to be an employee of a global drug-trafficking organization? And how does a fifteen-year-old American boy go from star quarterback to trained assassin, surging up the cartel corporate ladder?" (Publisher's note)

"Engrossing and readable yet nightmarish vision of a hyperviolent and corporatized narcotics industry, seducing a new generation with minimal alternatives." Kirkus

Zuckoff, Mitchell

Ponzi's scheme; the true story of a financial legend. Random House 2005 390p il $25.95; pa $14.95   **364**

1. Swindlers
ISBN 1-400-06039-7; 0-8129-6836-0 pa

LC 2004-46770

The author "chronicles Ponzi's mercurial rise and fall as he conjured up one get-rich-quick scheme after another. . . . Zuckoff provides not only a definitive portrait of Ponzi's life but also insights into immigrant life and the social world of early 20th-century Boston." Publ Wkly

Includes bibliographical references

364.1   Criminal offenses

Anderson, Devery S.

Emmett Till; the murder that shocked the world and propelled the civil rights movement. by Devery S. Anderson; foreword by Julian Bond. University Press of Mississippi 2015 560 p. illustrations (cloth : alk. paper) $45   **364.1**

1. Lynching 2. Hate crimes 3. Racism -- History 4. Trials (Homicide) 5. African Americans -- History 6. Hate crimes -- Mississippi 7. Mississippi -- Race relations 8. Trials (Murder) -- Mississippi -- Sumner 9. Racism -- Mississippi -- History -- 20th century 10. African Americans -- Crimes against -- Mississippi 11. Lynching -- Mississippi -- History -- 20th century 12. United States -- Race relations -- History -- 20th century
ISBN 9781496802842

LC 2015005681

This book, by Devery S. Anderson, "offers the first truly comprehensive account of the 1955 murder and its aftermath. It tells the story of Emmett Till, the fourteen-year-old African American boy from Chicago brutally lynched for a harmless flirtation at a country store in the Mississippi Delta. His death and the acquittal of his killers by an all-white jury set off a firestorm of protests that reverberated all over the world and spurred on the civil rights movement." (Publisher's note)

"At times, Anderson's devotion to detail can bury the reader, but historians will welcome his commitment to the story. It will become the go-to reference for scholars and those who teach the Till case in classrooms." Choice

Includes bibliographical references and index

Emmett Till, the murder that shocked the world and propelled the civil rights movement

Atwood, Roger

Stealing history; tomb raiders, smugglers, and the looting of the ancient world. St. Martin's Press 2004 337p il map hardcover o.p. pa $15.95 **364.1**

1. Art thefts 2. Antiquities -- Collection and preservation
ISBN 0-312-32406-5; 0-312-32407-3 pa

LC 2004-50862

The author's "ability to bring a story dramatically to life and his keen interest in stemming the illegal antiquities trade makes this an important book for anyone interested in archeology, preservation or the potentially tangled provenance of works they love." Publ Wkly

Includes bibliographical references

Bergreen, Laurence

Capone; the man and the era. Simon & Schuster 1994 701p il hardcover o.p. pa $19   **364.1**

1. Mobsters 2. Bootleggers
ISBN 0-684-82447-7 pa

LC 94-5941

"Mr. Bergreen has written a book objective and rigorous enough to meet scholarly standards, yet colorful enough to engross the general reader." N Y Times Book Rev

Includes bibliographical references

Bugliosi, Vincent

★ **Helter** skelter; the true story of the Manson murders. {by} Vincent Bugliosi with Curt Gentry. 25th anniversary ed; Norton 1994 528p il $25; pa $13.95   **364.1**
   1. Homicide 2. Prisoners 3. Murderers
   ISBN 0-393-08700-X; 0-393-32223-8 pa
                                                LC 94-20957
   A reissue of the title published 1974
   "This book by the prosecutor at the Tate-LaBianca murder trial tells the inside story of the Manson Family murders, the investigations, and the trial." Libr J

Burns, Sarah

The **Central** Park Five. Alfred A. Knopf 2011 240p il map $25.95   **364.1**
   1. Rape 2. False accusation 3. Victims of crimes 4. Administration of criminal justice 5. Rape victims 6. Investment bankers 7. Crime -- New York (N.Y.) 8. Criminal justice, Administration of -- New York (N.Y.)
   ISBN 978-0-307-26614-9; 0-307-26614-1
                                                LC 2010039661
   This book recounts "the public frenzy surrounding the April 19, 1989, attack on Trisha Meili in Central Park. The 28-year-old investment banker was out for a run when she was . . . raped, beaten and left for dead. The assault, pinned on a group of black and Hispanic boys aged 13 to 16 who'd been misbehaving in the park that night, incited media diatribes about civic decay. . . . [C]ourt cases found five of the boys guilty in 1990. Then, in 2002, convicted rapist and murderer Matias Reyes confessed to the attack and the five convictions were overturned. [Sarah] Burns's deconstruction of how justice was hijacked is part police procedural, part courtroom drama, part cultural critique . . . Burns . . . reveals how 'winning the case trumped investigating the evidence.'" Particular focus is given to "media and public resistance to Reyes's confession: so entrenched was the 'wilding' narrative that many refused to give it up." (Maclean's)
   "An important cultural document, and unquestionably worth reading. . . . Burns's gripping tale may serve as an allegory for some of the most pressing criminal justice issues of our time." N Y Times Book Rev
   Includes bibliographical references

Capote, Truman

★ **In** cold blood; a true account of a multiple murder and its consequences. Random House 2002 343p $22; pa $13   **364.1**
   1. Homicide 2. Murderers
   ISBN 0-375-50790-6; 0-679-74558-0 pa
                                                LC 2002-282920
   A reissue of the title first published 1966
   "Truman Capote called his account of the 1959 murder of a Kansas farm family a nonfiction novel. Using information he collected through interviews with townspeople and the killers, Capote created a vivid portrait of the criminals and graphically described the crime, the criminals' escape to Mexico, capture, trial, appeals, and hanging." HarperCollins Reader's Ency of Am Lit. 2nd edition

Carney, Scott

The **red** market; on the trail of the world's organ brokers, bone thieves, blood farmers, and child traffickers. William Morrow 2011 254p il $25.99 **364.1**
   1. Procurement of organs, tissues, etc.
   ISBN 978-0-06-193646-3; 0-06-193646-4
                                                LC 2010-47807
   "The 'red market' of Scott Carney's lucid and alarming book refers to the various medical activities through which the human body can generate a profit: surrogate motherhood, organ transplantation, drug testing, baby selling and blood farming, to mention just a few items on Mr. Carney's disturbing list. The buyers of red-market goods are usually well-to-do Westerners, while the sellers tend to come from developing countries. A surprisingly large number of the sellers are women, and many appear to be forced into the business. Middlemen, beyond taking large profits, encourage the trade by assuring buyers that the transaction is conducted ethically. . . . [This] is not an abstract philosophical meditation or an ethnographic treatise, though it has elements of both. It is a work of investigative journalism, written by an experienced health reporter who lived in India for more than 10 years. Mr. Carney knows how to tell a story and digs deeply." Wall Street J
   Includes bibliographical references

Chayes, Sarah

Thieves of state; why corruption threatens global security. Sarah Chayes. W W Norton & Co Inc 2015 272 p. illustrations (hardcover) $26.95   **364.1**
   1. Political corruption 2. International security 3. Political corruption -- Case studies 4. Security, International -- Case studies
   ISBN 0393239462; 9780393239461
                                                LC 2014031700
   Los Angeles Times Book Prize: Current Interest (2015)
   In this book on corruption, author Sarah Chayes "reveals that canonical political thinkers such as John Locke and [Niccolo] Machiavelli, as well as the great medieval Islamic statesman Nizam al-Mulk, all named corruption as a threat to the realm. In . . . [an] argument connecting the Protestant Reformation to the Arab Spring, [it] presents a powerful new way to understand global extremism." (Publisher's note)
   "From ancient tales of avaricious rulers to modern headlines of greedy politicians, Chayes offers insightful analysis of how government corruption invites instability and insurgency and why we will never see peace in some of the world's hot spots until we address that corruption." Booklist
   Includes bibliographical references and index

Cullen, Kevin

Whitey Bulger; America's most wanted gangster and the manhunt that brought him to justice. Kevin Cullen and Shelley Murphy. 1st ed. W W Norton & Co Inc 2013 viii, 478 p., 16 unnumbered pages of platesp (hardcover) $26.95   **364.1**
   1. Fugitives from justice 2. Organized crime -- United States 3. Gangsters -- Massachusetts -- Boston -- Biography 4. Fugitives from justice -- United States -- Biography 5. Organized crime -- Massachusetts --

Boston -- Case studies
ISBN 0393087727; 9780393087727
LC 2012050752

This book, by Kevin Cullen and Shelley Murphy, "follows the astonishing career and epic manhunt for Whitey Bulger. . . . Raised in a South Boston housing project, James 'Whitey' Bulger became the most wanted fugitive of his generation. . . . Reporters Kevin Cullen and Shelley Murphy follow Whitey's extraordinary criminal career--from teenage thievery to bank robberies to the building of his underworld empire and a string of brutal murders." (Publisher's note)

Includes bibliographical references (pages 431-464) and index.

Dash, Mike

The **first** family; terror, extortion, revenge, murder, and the birth of the American mafia. Random House 2009 375p il map $27 **364.1**
1. Mafia 2. Organized crime 3. Mobsters 4. Mafia -- History 5. Biography, Individual 6. Mafia -- United States -- History 7. Organized crime -- United States -- History
ISBN 978-1-4000-6722-0
LC 2009-5681

This "history of the birth of the Italian mafia in America traces the life of Giuseppe Morello, describing his rise from poverty in rural Sicily to one of the nation's most influential underworld crime heads, in a portrait that also evaluates the contributions of Morello's brothers, police officer Joseph Petrosino, and secret service agent William Flynn." (Publisher's note) Index.

"Essential for students of organized crime in America. Murder and mayhem buffs will enjoy it too." Kirkus

Includes bibliographical references (p. 350-357)

Dolnick, Edward

The **rescue** artist; a true story of art, thieves, and the hunt for a missing masterpiece. HarperCollins Publishers 2005 270p il $25.95; pa $14.95 **364.1**
1. Artists 2. Painters 3. Art thefts
ISBN 0-06-053117-7; 978-0-06-053117-1; 0-06-053118-5 pa; 978-0-06053118-8 pa
LC 2004-62060

This is an "account of the 1994 theft of one of the world's most famous paintings, The Scream. . . . This is a tightly woven, fast-paced story." SLJ

Includes bibliographical references

Douglas, John E.

The **cases** that haunt us; from Jack the Ripper to JonBenet Ramsey, the FBI's legendary mindhunter sheds light on the mysteries that won't go away. [by] John Douglas, Mark Olshaker. Pocket Books 2001 487p il pa $7.99 **364.1**
1. Homicide 2. Criminal psychology
ISBN 978-0-671-01706-4; 0-671-01706-3
First published 2000 by Scribner

The authors discuss "eight controversial cases that include the Lindbergh baby kidnapping, the Boston Strangler, the Zodiac Killer, and the JonBenet Ramsey killing." Libr J

Dray, Philip

At the hands of persons unknown; the lynching of Black America. Random House 2002 528p il hardcover o.p. pa $14.95 **364.1**
1. Lynching 2. Southern States -- Race relations 3. African Americans -- Southern States
ISBN 0-375-75445-8 pa
LC 2001-40366

"Dray balances moral indignation with a sound understanding of history and politics. The result is vital, hard-hitting cultural history." Publ Wkly

Includes bibliographical references

Fisher, Kenneth L.

How to smell a rat; the five signs of financial fraud. [by] Ken Fisher with Lara Hoffmans. Wiley 2009 209p (Fisher investments series) $24.95 **364.1**
1. Fraud 2. Investments 3. Swindlers and swindling
ISBN 978-0-470-52653-8
LC 2009-21631

"With five straightforward rules that would have saved any investor from Bernie Madoff, . . . [Fisher] gives readers a secure plan for fraudproof investing, worthwhile for novices and sophisticated financiers alike. . . . Much more than what to avoid, Fisher's concise guide should be highly illuminating and confidence-building for anyone with a bank account." Publ Wkly

Includes bibliographical references

Geary, Rick

The **Lindbergh** child; America's hero and the crime of the century. written and illustrated by Rick Geary. NBM/ComicsLit 2008 un il map (Treasury of XXth century murder) pa $15.95 **364.1**
1. Generals 2. Air pilots 3. Graphic novels 4. Mystery graphic novels 5. Memoirists 6. Air force officers 7. Homicide -- Graphic novels 8. Kidnapping -- Graphic novels
ISBN 978-1-56163-529-0

Charles Lindbergh was an American hero following his solo crossing of the Atlantic in an airplane. He married into a wealthy family, he and his wife had a baby, they were building their dream home. Then, one night, the baby was abducted from the house. Geary's account retraces all the highly publicized events, ransom notes (false and otherwise), as well as the string of colorful characters who all claimed they could help but instead snookered the Lindberghs. While Bruno Hauptmann was arrested, tried, convicted, and executed, there remain many questions about what really happened. Geary brings them up for readers to consider.

"A good example of the origins of modern forensics, crime-scene investigation, and celebrity hysteria, this work is an excellent choice for most collections." SLJ

Glenny, Misha

McMafia; a journey through the global criminal underworld. Alfred A. Knopf 2008 375p il map $27.95 **364.1**
1. Organized crime
ISBN 978-1-4000-4411-5; 1-4000-4411-1
LC 2007-30522

"Readers yearning for a deeper understanding of the real-life, international counterparts to The Sopranos need look no further than Glenny's engrossing study." Publ Wkly

Includes bibliographical references

Goldhagen, Daniel Jonah

Worse than war; genocide, eliminationism, and the ongoing assault on humanity. [by] Daniel Jonah Goldhagen. PublicAffairs 2009 658p il   **364.1**

1. Racism 2. Genocide 3. Prejudices 4. Mass murder 5. Racism -- Psychological aspects 6. Genocide -- Psychological aspects

ISBN 1-58648-769-8; 978-1-58648-769-0

LC 2009-28035

This is an investigation into the phenomenon of genocide and mass killing—explaining why genocides begin, are sustained, and end; why societies support them and why they happen so frequently; and how the international community should and can successfully stop them.

The author "convincingly disparages bureaucratic 'banality of evil' explanations of genocide and spotlights the ideologies of leaders who exploit ordinary citizens' hate-filled beliefs to instigate mass murder. It's not easy reading, but Goldhagen's vehemence and the sheer weight of horrors that he recounts move one's conscience." Publ Wkly

Includes bibliographical references

Guinn, Jeff

Go down together; the true, untold story of Bonnie and Clyde. Simon & Schuster 2009 467p il $27   **364.1**

1. Criminals 2. Outlaws 3. Murderers 4. Biography, Individual

ISBN 1-4165-5706-7; 978-1-4165-5706-7

LC 2008-53342

In this true crime book by Jeff Guinn, "Clyde Barrow, a scrawny kid in poverty-stricken West Dallas in the late 1920s, stole chickens before moving on to cars, following in the footsteps of his older brother, Buck. In 1930, he met 19-year-old Bonnie Parker, and during the next four years Clyde, Bonnie and the ever-revolving members of the Barrow Gang robbed banks and armories all over the South, murdering at least seven people." (Publishers Weekly)

"As Guinn relates, Bonnie and Clyde didn't commit many of the acts—particularly the murders—they were accused of. Their crime spree only lasted from spring 1932 to May 1934. But in the worst of the Depression, Americans ate up accounts of the Barrow exploits as a form of entertainment. The gang fed the newspapers terrific stuff, including the staged photo of Bonnie holding a gun and smoking a cigar. For folks living hardscrabble lives, the fact that the gang robbed the same bankers who were foreclosing on their farms made the exploits of Bonnie and Clyde even sweeter. Guinn succeeds marvelously in recreating the spirit of the times, the desperation of unemployment and financial ruin." PopMatters

Includes bibliographical references

Ifill, Sherrilyn A.

On the courthouse lawn; confronting the legacy of lynching in the twenty-first century. Beacon Press 2007 xx, 204p il $25.95; pa $16   **364.1**

1. Lynching 2. Reconciliation 3. United States -- Race relations 4. Lynching -- United States -- History

ISBN 978-0-8070-0987-1; 0-8070-0987-3; 978-0-8070-0988-8 pa; 0-8070-0988-1 pa

LC 2006-16618

The author explores the continued effects of lynching. Ifill contends that "the lynchings implicated average white citizens, some of whom actively participated in the violence while many others witnessed the lynchings but did nothing to stop them. Ifill observes that this history of complicity has become embedded in the social and cultural fabric of local communities, who either supported, condoned, or ignored the violence. She . . . [presents] ideas to help communities heal. . . . Ifill argues that reconciliation and reparation efforts must also be locally based in order to bring both black and white Americans together in an efficacious dialogue." (Publisher's note) Index.

"An intriguing, immodest proposal that itself warrants discussion—and action." Kirkus

Includes bibliographical references

James, Bill, 1949-

Popular crime; reflections on the celebration of violence. Scribner 2011 482p il   **364.1**

1. Crime 2. Homicide 3. Crime -- United States -- History

ISBN 1416552731; 9781416552734

LC 2010-36180

This "book is primarily a history of the murders that have obsessed American newspaper readers since Dec. 22, 1799, when the body of a young Manhattan woman named Elma Sands was found floating in a well at what is now 89 Greene Street. Between . . . accounts of Lizzie Borden, the Boston Strangler and the Zodiac killer, Mr. James offers proposals for penal and judicial reform, theories about the cultural significance of crime stories and brief book reviews." (N Y Times (Late N Y Ed)) Index.

This is a "very entertaining book, and it will instigate arguments even as it scores many important points. . . . James's layman status is a big part of this book's bracing charm. And his real point is more universal. He loves crime books and wants you to love them, too, and not just because they're a good way to pass the time in a motel room or airport. He wants you to take them seriously, as he does, and consider the ways they reflect and reshape the culture, what they say about our justice system and our very concept of justice." Washington Post Book World

Javers, Eamon

Broker, trader, lawyer, spy; inside the secret world of corporate espionage. Harper 2010 306p $26.99; ebook $11.99   **364.1**

1. Espionage 2. Business intelligence

ISBN 978-0-06-169720-3; 978-0-06-196938-6 ebook

LC 2009031010

"Javers traces spying activity, which began in Washington, D.C., in 1790, when the city became the capital, through the Civil War, when Allan Pinkerton was chasing Confederate spies, to Allen Dulles and the CIA developing drugs to enhance interrogations and in 2002 capturing traitor Robert Hanssen. The author also offers a fascinating explanation of the role of spies in today's world economy with hundreds of firms globally in the corporate espionage business using as operatives alumni from the FBI, CIA, Secret Service, British M15 and Russian KGB, and military intelligence officers. . . . This is a must-read, excellent book." Booklist

Includes bibliographical references

Jimenez, Stephen

The **Book** of Matt; Hidden Truths About the Murder of Matthew Shepard. Stephen Jimenez. Steerforth Press 2013 viii, 360 p.p $26; $16 **364.1**
1. Homicide 2. Drug traffic 3. Mass media and gays -- United States 4. Gays -- Crimes against -- United States 5. Mass media -- United States -- Influence 6. Hate crimes -- United States -- Public opinion 7. Mass media and public opinion -- United States
ISBN 1586422146; 9781586422141; 9781586422264
LC 2013431178

Author Stephen Jiminez presents his story of "determination to ascertain why Matthew Shepard--a gay University of Wyoming student--was viciously killed in 1998. Jimenez makes a strong case that the unappreciated lesson of the Shepard murder is one about the dangers of methamphetamine. Shepard and his killer, Aaron McKinney, were not strangers after all. In fact Aaron McKinney was a bisexual, who had had sex with Shepard. And both were dealers of methamphetamine." (Amazon)

"In claiming that Shepard was killed because of drugs, and the 'gay panic' story was offered as a cover and heavily pushed by media and politicians as part of a larger agenda, Jimenez completely changes the meaning and impact of Shepard's death." Pub Wkly

Includes bibliographical references (pages 355-357)

Keefe, Patrick Radden

The **snakehead**; an epic tale of the Chinatown underworld and the American dream. Doubleday 2009 414p map **364.1**
1. Smuggling 2. Unauthorized immigrants 3. Smugglers 4. Businesspeople 5. Illegal aliens 6. Illegal aliens -- United States 7. Human trafficking -- United States 8. China -- Emigration and immigration 9. United States -- Emigration and immigration 10. United States -- Immigration and emigration
ISBN 0-307-27927-8 pa; 0-385-52130-8; 978-0-307-27927-9 pa; 978-0-385-52130-7
LC 2008-50049

This book tells the story of human smuggling and trafficking among Fujianese immigrants to the United States. It focuses on Cheng Chui Ping, a Chinese immigrant who came to New York in the early 1980s. Her path to the American "dream began with an underground bank . . . run out of a noodle shop. . . . She became known as Sister Ping and built a global people-smuggling conglomerate that stretched from China's Fujian province to Africa, Europe, and South America, relying on one of Chinatown's . . . gangs to protect her power and profits. Sister Ping's empire came to light in 1993, when [the Golden Venture], a ship loaded with 300 near-starving immigrants ran aground off Queens. It took . .

. nearly ten years to untangle the criminal network and home in on its mastermind." (Publisher's note) Index.

"This is one of the freshest accounts of modern-day migration I've read, one filled with moral ambiguity, one that doesn't pretend to have the answers, one that . . . feels like essential reading." Washington Post Book World

Includes bibliographical references

Lebsock, Suzanne

A **murder** in Virginia; Southern justice on trial. Norton 2003 442p il $26.95; pa $15.95 **364.1**
1. Trials (Homicide) 2. Virginia 3. Southern States -- Race relations
ISBN 0-393-04201-4; 0-393-32606-3 pa
LC 2002-15946

"On a warm afternoon in June 1895, a 56-year-old white woman was brutally murdered in Lunenburg County, VA. Despite the absence of any truly incriminating eyewitness testimony or physical evidence, four blacks—three women and one man—were arrested and tried for the murder. Lebsock . . . recreates the subsequent trials, introducing the defendants, their prosecutors, and the witnesses and placing the proceedings within the context of the black and white communities and deteriorating conditions for African Americans in the post-Reconstruction South. Here historical narrative is every bit as intriguing as fictional mystery but more edifying for the information it gives its readers concerning race relations and criminal justice in the latter part of the 19th century." Libr J

Includes bibliographical references

Lehr, Dick

The **fence**; a police cover-up along Boston's racial divide. Harper 2009 383p il map $25.99; pa $14.99 **364.1**
1. Police brutality 2. Police corruption 3. Boston (Mass.) -- Race relations
ISBN 978-0-06-078098-2; 0-06-078098-3; 978-0-06-078099-9 pa; 0-06-078099-1 pa

The author "details one of the most controversial cases in the annals of the Boston Police Department, involving a brutal assault on a black plainclothes officer by his fellow cops and the resulting 1998 civil rights trial against the police force. Not only does Lehr paint the racial and political turbulence of Boston at the time, but he explores the cultural backgrounds of the black officer, Michael Cox; his attacker and fellow officer, Kenny Conley; and Robert 'Smut' Brown, a drug dealer involved in the killing that started it all. . . . Jolting, nightmarish and potent, this true cop yarn bests any bogus reality show or overblown tabloid tale with its hardboiled spin." Publ Wkly

Includes bibliographical references

Levitt, Len

NYPD confidential; power and corruption in the country's greatest police force. Thomas Dunne Books 2009 304p $25.99 **364.1**
1. Police corruption 2. Police -- New York (N.Y.) 3. New York (N.Y.) -- Police Dept.
ISBN 978-0-312-38032-8; 0-312-38032-1
LC 2009-7602

"Using the administrations of recent New York City police commissioners Raymond W. Kelly (twice), William J. Bratton, Howard Safir, and Bernard Kerick as a frame, Levitt . . . pries into the inner workings of the NYPD. Levitt spins a fascinating tale of politics, rivalries, infighting, counterterrorism, and corruption inside the police department of America's largest city." Libr J

Includes bibliographical references

Longman, Jere

Among the heroes; United Flight 93 and the passengers and crew who fought back. HarperCollins Pubs. 2002 288p il $24.95; pa $13.95　　**364.1**
1. Hijacking of airplanes　2. September 11 terrorist attacks, 2001

ISBN 0-06-009908-9; 0-06-009909-7 pa
LC 2002-68530

This is an account of the United Airlines flight which was hijacked on September 11, 2001 and crashed in Pennsylvania before reaching its intended target

This book "gives us an incredibly detailed and personal tale of that horrific episode." Booklist

Includes bibliographical references

Mallon, Thomas

Mrs. Paine's garage and the murder of John F. Kennedy. Pantheon Bks. 2002 211p $22; pa $13　　**364.1**
1. Homemakers　2. Presidents　3. Senators　4. Murderers　5. Members of Congress　6. Spouses of prominent persons

ISBN 0-375-42117-3; 0-15-602755-0 pa
LC 2001-36157

"A journalistic inquiry into Ruth Paine, the woman who welcomed Marina Oswald—and sometimes her husband, Lee—into her suburban Dallas home in 1963; it offers a new theory about the antecedents of the assassination." N Y Times Book Rev

Matthews, Joe

Bringing Adam home; the abduction that changed America. [by] Les Standiford with Detective Sergeant Joe Matthews. Ecco 2011 291p il map　　**364.1**
1. Children　2. Homicide　3. Kidnapping　4. Kidnap victims　5. Murder victims

ISBN 0-06-198390-X; 978-0-06-198390-0
LC 2010-43572

"This is the ultimate cold case—tragic, high-profile, and, finally, successfully solved. Six-year-old Adam Walsh was abducted from a crowded Sears store in Hollywood, Florida, in 1981. Later, he was murdered and decapitated. Identifying Adam's killer took 25 years. His parents turned into tireless advocates for missing and abused children; Adam's father, John Walsh, moved from a sales job to being the executive producer and host of America's Most Wanted. This forceful account . . . gives readers the ultimate insider's account of the grueling search for Adam's killer and for the evidence to convict him. While many true-crime books claim to shine a light on society by examining one particular case, this account actually does." Booklist

McGinniss, Joe

★ **Fatal** vision. New American Library 1989 684p il pa $7.99　　**364.1**
1. Homicide　2. Surgeons　3. Murderers
ISBN 978-0-451-16566-4; 0-451-16566-7
First published 1983 by Putnam

"This is a wisely observant, well-written, and understated book." Harpers

Includes bibliographical references

Murakami, Haruki

Underground; translated from the Japanese by Alfred Birnbaum and Philip Gabriel. Vintage Bks. 2001 366p map pa $14　　**364.1**
1. Terrorism　2. Aum Shinrikyo
ISBN 0-375-72580-6
LC 00-69310

"On March 20, 1995, followers of the religious cult Aum Shinrikyo unleashed lethal sarin gas into cars of the Tokyo subway system. Many died, many more were injured. This is {Murakami's} . . . account of this episode." Publ Wkly

Olsen, Jack

I: the creation of a serial killer. St. Martin's Press 2002 365p il $24.95; pa $6.99　　**364.1**
1. Homicide　2. Murderers
ISBN 0-312-24198-4; 0-312-98384-0 pa
LC 2001-58892

"A truly horrifying account of a serial killer, told with shocking candor." Booklist

Pepper, William F.

An **act** of state; the execution of Martin Luther King. Norton 2003 334p il map $25　　**364.1**
1. Clergy　2. Conspiracies　3. Nonfiction writers　4. Civil rights activists　5. Nobel laureates for peace
ISBN 1-85984-695-5
Companion volume to Orders to kill (1995)

This book continues the author's examination of the life and death of Martin Luther King Jr.

"Forget everything you think you know, Pepper insists. James Earl Ray did not pull the trigger. . . . Pepper gradually introduces the vast cast of characters in a dizzying murder conspiracy that winds from a Memphis bar through the shadows of organized crime to the far reaches of national government. He carefully maps each player's place and role in the tangled web and doggedly tries to stick to a straightforward narrative. . . . Pepper attempts nothing less than a rewrite of history, and a spurring of further investigation." Publ Wkly

Includes bibliographical references

Queen, William

Under and alone; the true story of the undercover agent who infiltrated America's most violent outlaw motorcycle gang. Random House 2005 270p il $24.95　　**364.1**
1. Gangs
ISBN 1-400-06084-2
LC 2004-51176

"The strength and white-hot intensity of the writing make this read like a movie, and Hollywood is certain to take note." Publ Wkly

Raab, Selwyn

Five families; the rise, decline, and resurgence of America's most powerful Mafia empires. Thomas Dunne Books 2005 765p il $29.95   **364.1**

1. Mafia 2. Organized crime

ISBN 0-312-30094-8

LC 2005-48416

"With vivid characterizations of a cavalcade of thugs, Raab's account is the most lively and informative Mafia history in years." Booklist

Includes bibliographical references

Rule, Ann

--and never let her go; Thomas Capano, the deadly seducer. Pocket Star Books 2000 680p il pa $7.99   **364.1**

1. Lawyers 2. Homicide 3. Secretaries 4. Missing persons 5. Trials (Homicide) 6. Murderers 7. Murder victims 8. District attorneys 9. State government employees

ISBN 0-671-86871-3; 978-0-671-86871-0

First published 1999 by Simon & Schuster

"In June 1996, Anne Marie Fahey, a 30-year-old secretary to the governor of Delaware, disappeared and was reported missing by her family. In the weeks that followed, a charming, successful, and well-connected attorney, Tom Capano, was charged with her murder. Rule . . . tells the riveting story of the three-year secret affair between Fahey and Capano and a cruel obsession that led to murder." Booklist

Saviano, Roberto

Gomorrah; translated from the Italian by Virginia Jewiss. Farrar, Straus & Giroux 2007 301p map $25   **364.1**

1. Organized crime 2. Italy

ISBN 978-0-374-16527-7; 0-374-16527-0

LC 2007-31004

Original Italian edition, 2006

This "is an eyepopping, hair-raising, stomach-turning book. The mob has never looked so bad—or read so well." Christ Sci Monit

Selby, Scott Andrew

Flawless; inside the largest diamond heist in history. by Scott Andrew Selby and Greg Campbell. Sterling Pub. Co. 2010 319p il map $24.95   **364.1**

1. Theft 2. Diamonds

ISBN 978-1-4027-6651-0

LC 2009-40766

The authors "provide an engrossing nonfiction thriller with a truly improbable story at its center, but they also provide a colorful look at the shadowy world of the diamond trade—how they're graded, sold, secured and stolen." Kirkus

Includes bibliographical references

Sifakis, Carl

The **mafia** encyclopedia; 3rd ed; Facts on File 2005 510p il (Facts on File crime library) $65; pa $21.95   **364.1**

1. Reference books 2. Mafia -- Dictionaries

ISBN 0-8160-5694-3; 0-8160-5695-1 pa

LC 2004-58487

First published 1987

"Sifakis provides detailed, informed, and colorful information." Libr J

Smith, Jennie Erin

Stolen world; a tale of reptiles, smugglers and skulduggery. Crown 2011 322p il $25; ebook $25   **364.1**

1. Reptiles 2. Smuggling 3. Rare animals 4. Wild animal trade 5. Rare reptiles 6. Animal dealers 7. Wildlife smuggling 8. Wild animal trade -- Corrupt practices

ISBN 978-0-307-38147-7; 0-307-38147-1; 978-0-307-72026-9 ebook; 0-307-72026-8 ebook

LC 2010-9548

"Smith's affection for these unsavory people gives the book an intriguing moral ambiguity (which might make some environmentalists cringe), but the subculture's brazen shenanigans make for a convoluted, fascinating tale." Publ Wkly

Stewart, James B.

Blind eye; how the medical establishment let a doctor get away with murder. Simon & Schuster 1999 334p il hardcover o.p. pa $14   **364.1**

1. Homicide 2. Physicians 3. Murderers

ISBN 0-684-86563-7 pa

LC 99-37044

This is "not only a fascinating look at a psychopath masquerading as a healer but also a disturbing exposé of the system that fails to protect the public." Libr J

Watkins, D.

The **Cook** Up; A Crack Rock Memoir. by D. Watkins. Grand Central Publishing 2016 272 p. $26   **364.1**

1. Drug traffic 2. Baltimore (Md.)

ISBN 1455588636; 9781455588633

This memoir, by D. Watkins, is a "look inside the Baltimore drug trade. . . . D. was certain he would escape the life of drugs, decadence, and violence that had surrounded him since birth. But when his brother Devin is shot-only days after D. receives notice that he's been accepted into Georgetown University-the plans for his life are exploded, and he takes up the mantel of his brother's crack empire." (Publisher's note)

"Watkins, whose essays often appear in Salon and the New York Times, is a powerful writer, and he uses short chapters to heighten the quick-strike effect of his words, which often land like a punch in the stomach. The treatment of women in the drug subculture, as it is described here, will disturb many readers, but there's no doubting that Watkins is the real deal." Booklist

Welch, Craig

Shell games; rogues, smugglers, and the hunt for nature's bounty. William Morrow 2010 274p il map $25.99   **364.1**

1. Poaching 2. Smuggling 3. Puget Sound region (Wash.)

ISBN 978-0-06-153713-4; 0-06-153713-6

LC 2009-38980

"Welch covers the wildlife crime beat in Puget Sound, where shellfish poachers wreak havoc on the region's once bountiful, now imperiled marine ecosystem. Writing with the sizzle of a mystery novelist, Welch portrays a complex, driven, and irresistible cast of real-life characters, from fish cops Ed Volz and Kevin Harrington to Doug Tobin, a larger-than-life Native American fisherman. . . . Welch's utterly compelling true tale of black-market trade in endangered ocean wildlife is astounding and infuriating." Booklist

Includes bibliographical references

Wittman, Robert

Priceless; how I went undercover to rescue the world's stolen treasures. [by] Robert K. Wittman with John Shiffman. Crown Publishers 2010 324p il $25; ebook $25   **364.1**

1. Art thefts 2. Criminal investigation

ISBN 978-0-307-46147-6; 978-0-307-46149-0 ebook

LC 2009-49083

This "book has the excitement of an espionage novel. It's suspenseful, thought provoking, and funny." ARTnews

364.106   Organized crime

Grillo, Ioan

Gangster Warlords; Drug Dollars, Killing Fields, and the New Politics of Latin America. Ioan Grillo. St. Martin's Press 2016 384 p. color illustrations $28   **364.106**

1. Gangs 2. Drug traffic 3. Latin America -- Politics and government

ISBN 162040379X; 9781620403792

LC 2015021253

Author Ioan Grillo presents this "definitive account of the crime wars now wracking Central and South America and the Caribbean, regions largely abandoned by the U.S. after the Cold War. Moving between militia-controlled ghettos and the halls of top policy-makers, Grillo provides a disturbing new understanding of a war that has spiraled out of control." (Publisher's note)

"A striking exploration of the horrors of mass violence in the Western Hemisphere, with the author offering hope that radical policies could provide positive change." Kirkus

Includes bibliographical references and index.

Reavill, Gil

Mafia summit; J. Edgar Hoover, the Kennedy Brothers, and the meeting that unmasked the mob. Gil Reavill. Thomas Dunne Books 2012 320 p. (hbk.) $26.99   **364.106**

1. Mafia 2. Mafia -- United States 3. Organized crime

-- United States

ISBN 0312657757; 9780312657758; 9781250021106

LC 2012038009

Author Gil Reavill presents a book on the Mafia in the U.S. "For years, FBI director J. Edgar Hoover had adamantly denied the existence of the Mafia, but young Robert Kennedy immediately recognized the shattering importance of the Appalachian summit. As attorney general when his brother JFK became president, Bobby embarked on a campaign to break the spine of the mob, engaging in a furious turf battle with the powerful Hoover." Reavill details "mob killings, the early days of the heroin trade, and the crusade to loosen the hold of organized crime." (Publisher's note)

Includes bibliographical references

Seligman, Scott D.

Tong wars; the untold story of vice, money, and murder in New York's Chinatown. Scott D. Seligman. Penguin Group USA 2016 368 p. illustrations (hardcover) $29   **364.106**

1. Gangs 2. Chinese -- United States 3. Crime -- New York (N.Y.) 4. New York (N.Y.) -- History 5. Chinatown (New York, NY) -- History -- 20th century 6. Crime -- New York (State) -- New York -- History -- 20th century 7. Chinese American criminals -- New York (State) -- New York--History--20th century 8. Chinese American gangs -- New York (State) -- New York -- History -- 20th century

ISBN 9780399562273; 0399562273

LC 2016029498

This book, by Scott D. Seligman, is the "true story of money, murder, gambling, prostitution, and opium: the Chinese gang wars that engulfed New York's Chinatown from the 1890s through the 1930s. . . . The city government was already corrupt from top to bottom, so once one tong began taxing the gambling dens and paying off the authorities, a rival, jealously eyeing its lucrative franchise, co-opted a local reformist group to help eliminate it." (Publisher's note)

"The depth of this research is remarkable—the product of uncovering and analyzing accounts in old newspapers, census and court records, and material in the National Archives—and his results are delivered compellingly. A story about immigrants and their suffering that needed to be told." Booklist

Includes bibliographical references and index.

364.134   Offenses against administration of justice

Brannan, Karen

The Family Tree; A Kinship Lynching in Jim Crow Georgia. Pocket Books 2016 320 p. ill., maps, genealogical table $26   **364.134**

1. Racism 2. Lynching 3. Family secrets

ISBN 1476717184; 9781476717180

LC 2015043375

"Harris County, Georgia, 1912. A white man, the beloved nephew of the county sheriff, is shot dead on the porch of a black woman. Days after the sheriff is sworn into office, he allows the lynching of a woman and three men, all African American. Now, in a personal account like no other, the great-granddaughter of that sheriff, Karen Branan, digs deep into the past to deliver a shattering historical memoir a century after that gruesome day." (Publisher's note)

"A ghastly, dizzying descent into the coldblooded clannishness of the Southern racist mindset."

Includes bibliographical references and index.

Leamer, Laurence

The **Lynching**; The Epic Courtroom Battle That Brought Down the Klan. by Laurence Leamer. HarperCollins 2016 384 p. illustrations $27.99 **364.134**
1. Lynching 2. Ku Klux Klan 3. United States -- Race relations
ISBN 0062458345; 9780062458346

LC 2016022037

This book, by Laurence Leamer, "chronicles the . . . true story of a brutal race-based killing in 1981 and subsequent trials that undid one of the most pernicious organizations in American history—the Ku Klux Klan. . . . In addition to telling a gripping and consequential story, . . . Leamer chronicles the KKK and its activities in the second half the twentieth century, and illuminates its lingering effect on race relations in America today." (Publisher's note)

"The writing is solid, the research (especially the interviews) imposing, the case important, and the book's unquestionable hero, Dees, emerges powerfully." Booklist

Includes bibliographical references (pages 355-358) and index.

364.15   Offenses against the person

Citron, Danielle Keats

Hate crimes in cyberspace; Danielle Keats Citron. Harvard University Press 2014 352 p. (alk. paper) $29.95 **364.15**
1. Internet 2. Hate crimes 3. Cyberbullying 4. Cyberstalking 5. Computer crimes
ISBN 0674368290; 9780674368293

LC 2014008325

In this book author "Danielle Keats Citron exposes the startling extent of personal cyber-attacks and proposes practical, lawful ways to prevent and punish online harassment. A refutation of those who claim that these attacks are legal, or at least impossible to stop, Hate Crimes in Cyberspace reveals the serious emotional, professional, and financial harms incurred by victims." (Publisher's note)

"Bearing in mind the protection for free speech, Citron proposes new tools of law that would apply to both harassers and to website operators and employers." Choice

Includes bibliographical references and index

Cohan, William D.

★ The **price** of silence; the Duke lacrosse scandal, the power of the elite, and the corruption of our great universities. Willam D. Cohan. Scribner 2014 672 p. (hardcover : alk. paper) $35 **364.15**
1. Rape 2. College sports 3. Duke University 4. Lacrosse players 5. Malicious accusation 6. Prosecution -- Corrupt practices
ISBN 1451681798; 9781451681796; 9781451681802

LC 2013043923

This book, by Willam D. Cohan, presents an account of the "Duke lacrosse team scandal that reveals the pressures faced by America's elite colleges and universities and pulls back the curtain . . . on the larger issues of sexual misconduct, underage drinking, and bad-boy behavior. . . . What transpired at Duke followed upon the university's . . . effort to compete directly with the Ivy League for the best students and with its Division I rivals for supremacy in selected sports." (Publisher's note)

"Cohan explores the usual disconnects that occur in high-profile crime cases between what is reported by the press, chronicled in official records, and perceived as public opinion and what really happened. A gripping account of a sensational case." Booklist

Includes bibliographical references and index.

Connors, Joanna

I Will Find You; A Reporter Investigates the Life of the Man Who Raped Her, a memoir. by Joanna Connors (Author) Atlantic Monthly Press 2016 272 p. $25 **364.15**
1. Rape victims 2. Women journalists 3. Women -- Biography 4. Crime -- United States 5. Violence against women
ISBN 0802122604; 9780802122605

This book is a memoir by newspaper reporter and rape victim Joanna Connors. "Once her assailant was caught and sentenced, Joanna never spoke of the trauma again, until 21 years later. . . . Connors embarked on a journey to find out who [her attacker] was. . . . What she discovers stretches beyond one violent man's story and back into her own, interweaving a narrative about strength and survival with one about rape culture and violence in America." (Publisher's note)

"The author insightfully reflects on the idea that the greatest monster anyone, including victims of violent crime, must face is the monster within. A courageous and unsettlingly forthright memoir of overcoming trauma." Kirkus

Foxman, Abraham H., 1940-

Viral hate; containing its spread on the Internet. Abraham H. Foxman and Christopher Wolf. Palgrave Macmillan 2013 256 p. (alk. paper) $27 **364.15**
1. Hate speech 2. Internet -- Social aspects 3. Online hate speech 4. Hate crimes -- Prevention 5. Internet -- Moral and ethical aspects
ISBN 0230342175; 9780230342170

LC 2012047877

Here, the authors explore "the increasingly volatile subject of Internet hate speech and cyberbullying, a 'serious illness' with lethal ramifications. The authors support this statement in chapters . . . defining various types of noxious online rhetoric and the most recognizable extremist groups spreading it through Internet social portals and artistic media." (Kirkus Reviews)

Includes bibliographical references

Garcia Marquez, Gabriel

News of a kidnapping; translated from the Spanish by Edith Grossman. Knopf 1997 291p $25   **364.15**

1. Hostages 2. Kidnapping 3. Drug traffic
ISBN 0-375-40051-6

LC 97-5445

The author discusses kidnappings in Colombia orchestrated by "Pablo Escobar, once head of the Medellín drug cartel. . . . The writer's respondents are mainly the survivors of a group of prominent residents of Bogotá whom the drug lord held hostage during 1990 and 1991." Time

Hatch, Thom

The **Last** Outlaws; The lives and legends of Butch Cassidy and the Sundance Kid. by Thom Hatch. New American Library 2013 xii, 350 p.p ill., maps (The last outlaws) (hardcover) $26.95 **364.15**

1. West (U.S.) -- Biography 2. Outlaws -- West (U.S.) -- Biography
ISBN 0451239199; 9780451239198

LC 2012031697

This book, by Thom Hatch, presents a biography of "Butch Cassidy and the Sundance Kid--as leaders of the Wild Bunch, they planned and executed the most daring bank and train robberies of the day. . . . For several years at the end of the 1890s, the two friends, along with a revolving cast who made up their band of thieves, eluded local law enforcement and bounty hunters, all while stealing from the rich bankers and eastern railroad corporations who exploited western land." (Publisher's note)

Koerner, Brendan I.

The **skies** belong to us; love and terror in the golden age of hijacking. Brendan I. Koerner. Crown Publishers 2013 336 p. illustrations $26   **364.15**

1. Hijacking of airplanes 2. Hijacking of aircraft -- United States -- Case studies
ISBN 0307886107; 9780307886101

LC 2012043203

This book on the history of airplane hijacking "follows the strange and romantic exploits of Willie Roger Holder and Cathy Kerkow, lovers and radicals who became international celebrities when they hijacked Western Airlines Flight 701 in June 1972, demanding a ransom and the release of Angela Davis. Their escape to Algiers and their subsequent adoption by French radicals contributed to the cachet of hijacking." (Library Journal)

"A riveting, highly readable tale of terror in the skies." Kirkus

Includes bibliographical references and index

Larson, Erik

★ The **devil** in the white city; murder, magic, and madness at the fair that changed America. Erik Larson. Crown 2003 xi, 447p ill., maps $25.95 **364.15**

1. Homicide 2. Murderers 3. World's Columbian Exposition (1893: Chicago, Ill.)
ISBN 0609608444; 9780609608449

LC 20020154046

International Horror Guild Awards: Best Nonfiction (2003); Edgar Allan Poe Awards: Best Fact Crime (2004)

This nonfiction 'tale of Chicago Worlds' Fair of 1893 focuses primarily on two men: Daniel H. Burnham, the architect who was the driving force behind the fair, and Henry H. Holmes, a sadistic serial killer working under the cover of the busy fair. . . Burnham and his partner, John Root, the leading architects in Chicago, were tapped for the job, and they in turn called on Frederick Law Olmstead, Louis Sullivan, and Richard M. Hunt to help them build the world's greatest fair. . . . Unbeknownst to any of them, Holmes, a charismatic, handsome doctor, had arrived in the city and built a complex with apartments, a drugstore, and a vault, which he used to trap his victims until they suffocated." (Booklist)

This is an account of how "H.H. Holmes (born Herman Webster Mudgett) dispatched somewhere between 27 and 200 people, mostly single young women, in the churning new metropolis of Chicago; many of the murders occurred during (and exploited) the city's finest moment, the World's Fair of 1893. Larson's breathtaking new history is a novelistic yet wholly factual account of the fair and the mass murderer who lurked within it." Publ Wkly

Includes bibliographical references (p. [423]-429) and index.

McConnell, David

American honor killings; desire and rage among men. David McConnell. Akashic Books 2013 256 p. (trade pbk. original) $15.95   **364.15**

1. Homicide 2. Hate crimes 3. Crime -- United States 4. Murder -- United States -- Case studies 5. Murderers -- United States -- Case studies 6. Victims of crimes -- United States -- Case studies
ISBN 1617751324; 9781617751325; 9781617751530

LC 2012939273

Stonewall Book Award: Israel Fishman Non-Fiction Award

Author David McConnell presents a "look at the subculture of violent crime [and] shows how fluid terms like 'gay' and 'straight' can actually be. The author's case studies reflect an intensive investigation into the economic and cultural backgrounds of a wide variety of extremist cultures, research that involved interviews with law enforcement officials, families of victims and the convicted criminals themselves." (Kirkus)

"With no clear answers, but some very intriguing questions, these vignettes of masculine pride and rage will appeal to those interested in gender politics and gay studies as well as true crime fans." LJ

Schiller, Lawrence

Perfect murder, perfect town. HarperCollins Pubs. 1999 621p hardcover o.p. pa $7.99 **364.15**

1. Children 2. Homicide 3. Homemakers 4. Murder victims 5. Beauty contest winners 6. Computer industry executives 7. Parents of murdered children 8. Boulder (Colo.) -- Police Dept.
ISBN 0-06-109696-2 pa

LC 99-207248

Schiller argues that the "Boulder Police Department bungled the investigation, in large part out of ego and inexperience." N Y Times Book Rev

Sexual violence and abuse; an encyclopedia of prevention, impacts, and recovery. edited by Judy L. Postmus. ABC-CLIO, LLC 2013 2 v.(xxxii, 841 p.)p (hardcover) $189; (ebook) $189.00 **364.15**
1. Sex crimes 2. Sexual harassment 3. Sex crimes -- Prevention
ISBN 1598847554; 9781598847550; 9781598847567 pdf

LC 2012018355

This book, by Judy L. Postmus, provides a "resource on sexual violence and abuse for students, practitioners, and general readers. . . . The two-volume work contains 264 fully cross-referenced entries in alphabetical order, starting with abortion and ending with yoga therapy. The bibliography [also] provides important books, articles, online resources, and videos on a wide range of topics." (Publisher's note)

Includes bibliographical references and index.

Stiles, T. J.
Jesse James; last rebel of the Civil War. Knopf 2002 510p il maps $27.50; pa $16 **364.15**
1. Thieves 2. Outlaws
ISBN 0-375-40583-6; 0-375-70558-9 pa

LC 2002-25493

"This is a well-written and often surprising reinterpretation of the life of a legendary and enigmatic figure." Booklist
Includes bibliographical references

The **Ultimate** Jack the Ripper companion; an illustrated encyclopedia. {compiled by} Stewart P. Evans & Keith Skinner. Carroll & Graf Pubs. 2000 692p il $35; pa $16 **364.15**
1. Homicide 2. Murderers
ISBN 0-7867-0768-2; 0-7867-0926-X pa

LC 00-711560

Published in the United Kingdom with title: Ultimate Jack the Ripper sourcebook

This is a collection of primary and secondary source material pertaining to the Whitechapel murders

"This volume is undoubtedly the single largest resource on this case ever published." Libr J
Includes bibliographical references

Worrall, Simon
The **poet** and the murderer; a true story of literary crime and the art of forgery. Dutton 2002 270p il $23.95; pa $14 **364.15**
1. Forgery 2. Homicide 3. Forgers 4. Murderers
ISBN 0-525-94596-2; 0-452-28402-3 pa

LC 2001-53878

"In 1997, Sotheby's unveiled what experts believed was a newly discovered poem, 'That God Cannot Be Understood,' by Emily Dickinson. A few weeks later, the . . . discovery was revealed a forgery by a man who had already convincingly forged documents by more than 100 literary and historical figures, including Daniel Boone and Betsy Ross. This book examines the psychology of . . . forger and murderer (he killed two people who threatened his unmasking) Mark Hofmann." Booklist

364.152 Homicide

Appignanesi, Lisa
Trials of passion; crimes in the name of love and madness. Lisa Appignanesi. W W Norton & Co Inc 2015 434 p. illustrations $28.95 **364.152**
1. Love 2. Crime 3. Emotions 4. Crimes of passion -- Case studies
ISBN 1605988146; 9781605988146

LC 2014450096

Author Lisa Appignanesi "brings to life some sensational trials between 1870 and 1914, a period when the psychiatric professions were consolidating their hold on our understanding of what is human. Appignanesi teases out the vagaries of passion and the clashes between the law and the clinic as they stumble towards a (sometimes reviled) collaboration." (Publisher's note)

"An endlessly fascinating account of the history of insanity pleas that will find an audience with social history fans as well as enthusiasts of true crime." LJ

Includes bibliographical references (pages 399-416) and index

Blum, Howard
American lightning; terror, mystery, moviemaking, and the crime of the century. Crown Publishers 2008 339p il $24.95 **364.152**
1. Bombings 2. Terrorism
ISBN 978-0-307-34694-0

LC 2008-2974

"Blum's prose is tight, his speculations unfailingly sound and his research extensive—all adding up to an absorbing and masterful true crime narrative." Publ Wkly
Includes bibliographical references

Bowden, Charles
Murder city; Ciudad Juarez and the global economy's new killing fields. photographs by Julian Cardona. Nation Books 2010 320p il $27.50 **364.152**
1. Homicide 2. Drug traffic 3. Ciudad Juarez (Mexico)
ISBN 978-1-56858-449-2; 1-56858-449-0

LC 2010-01716

"Bowden uses his tremendous talents to tell a haunting, darkly poetic story of a city's horrifying descent into madness and anarchy. A potent book that readers won't soon forget, and a warning of what can come of an insatiable market that knows no borders." Kirkus

Braude, Joseph
The **honored** dead; Joseph Braude. 1st ed. Spiegel & Grau 2011 xvi, 318p.p **364.152**
1. Arabs 2. Morocco 3. Homicide 4. Friendship 5. Journalism
ISBN 9780385527033; 0385527039; 9780679604327 ebook

LC 2010046496

This book recounts the author's experiences as a journalist with "'embed-style access' to a police precinct in Casablanca, [Morocco]. . . . The Judiciary Police, an FBI-like agency, were . . . proud of their low crime rate compared to the United States, although bedeviled by a pesky sect of Islamist militants. . . . The particular murder that fascinated the author during this period involved a 41-year-old home-less Berber man, Ibrahim Dey, who was beaten to death in a warehouse where he had been sleeping for five years—ostensibly for theft. Dey was well liked and considered a majdub, or someone who brings fortune to others, and his best friend, Muhammad Bari, whom Braude befriended, swore to vindicate the suspicious murder." (Kirkus)

Brown, Ethan

Shake the devil off; a true story of the murder that rocked New Orleans. Henry Holt and Co. 2009 286p il $25   **364.152**
1. Homicide 2. Soldiers 3. Murderers 4. Bartenders 5. New Orleans (La.)
ISBN 978-0-8050-8893-9; 0-8050-8893-8
LC 2009-06698
Drawing the parallel between Katrina's aftermath and Bowen's unraveling psyche, Brown creates a riveting portrait of a gruesome crime while detailing the heart of a city in distress. A grim murder-suicide story delivered with skill and verve. Kirkus

Includes bibliographical references

Bryan, Patricia L.

Midnight assassin; a murder in America's heartland. [by] Patricia L. Bryan & Thomas Wolf. Algonquin Books of Chapel Hill 2005 278p $23.95 **364.152**
1. Farmers 2. Homemakers 3. Trials (Homicide)
ISBN 1-565-12306-9
LC 2004-59782
Bryan and Wolf offer "not only an interesting trial drama but also a look into social attitudes of rural America at the beginning of the 20th century, especially toward women." Libr J

Includes bibliographical references

Burke, Timothy M.

The **Paradiso** files; Boston's unknown serial killer. Steerforth Press 2008 346p il $24.95 **364.152**
1. Homicide 2. Murderers 3. Sex offenders
ISBN 978-1-58642-140-3; 1-58642-137-9
LC 2007-42576
"Burke tells a compelling story, with chilling accounts of Paradiso's crimes gleaned from victims' accounts and evidence that never made it to court. . . . The story transcends Boston with an insider's view of the criminal justice system." Boston Globe

Buruma, Ian

Murder in Amsterdam; the death of Theo van Gogh and the limits of tolerance. Penguin Press 2006 278p $24.95   **364.152**
1. Ethnic relations 2. Netherlands 3. Television producers 4. Motion picture directors
ISBN 1-59420-108-0; 978-1-59420-108-0
LC 2006-43606
This is a "shrewd, subtly argued inquiry into the tensions and resentments underlying two of the most shocking events in the recent history of the Netherlands." N Y Times (Late N Y Ed)

Includes bibliographical references

Chaudry, Rabia

Adnan's Story; The Search for Truth and Justice After Serial. Rabia Chaudry. St. Martin's Press 2016 416 p. facsimilies $26.99   **364.152**
1. Homicide 2. Criminals 3. Criminal investigation -- United States
ISBN 1250087104; 9781250087102
LC 2016024062
This book by Rabia Chaudry focuses on the case of Adnan Syed, who "was convicted and sentenced to life plus thirty years for the murder of his ex-girlfriend Hae Min Lee. . . . In this . . . narrative, . . . Chaudry presents new key evidence that she maintains dismantles the State's case: a potential new suspect, forensics indicating Hae was killed and kept somewhere for almost half a day, and documentation withheld by the State." (Publisher's note)

"Any murder is a tragedy, but a young, potentially innocent suspect sentenced to life in prison after a cursory, slipshod investigation full of cultural bias—and defended by an inept attorney—only magnifies the travesty. For Serial and true-crime fans, this book is a page-turner perfect for a quiet weekend." Kirkus

Collins, Paul

Duel With the Devil; The True Story of How Alexander Hamilton and Aaron Burr Teamed Up to Take on America's First Sensational Murder Mystery. by Paul Collins. Random House Inc 2013 viii, 289 p.p map (hardcover) $26.00   **364.152**
1. Trials (Homicide)
ISBN 0307956458; 9780307956453
LC 2013371593
This book, written by Paul Collins, is the "true account of a . . . turn-of-the-19th century murder and the trial that ensued—a showdown in which iconic political rivals Alexander Hamilton and Aaron Burr joined forces to make sure justice was done. Still our nation's longest running 'cold case,' the mystery of Elma Sands finally comes to a close with this book, which delivers the first substantial break in the case in over 200 years." (Publisher's note)

The **murder** of the century; Paul Collins. Crown 2011 viii, 325p ill.   **364.152**
1. Homicide 2. Journalism 3. Newspapers -- United States
ISBN 9780307592200; 0307592200
LC 2011009390
This book discusses "a sensational 1897 murder case that fascinated the public as it played out across the front pages of the New York City's leading newspapers: Joseph Pulitzer's 'New York World' and William Randolph Hearst's 'New York Journal.' After a group of children discovered the ghastly severed trunk of William Guldensuppe, a Turkish bath-house attendant, the rival news organs spared no expense to ferret out the culprits, eventually tracking the purchase of an oilcloth used to wrap the torso to Mrs. Augusta Nack, a German immigrant midwife and rumored back-room abortionist. Guldensuppe had been Nack's lover before being replaced by Martin Thorn, a hotheaded barber. Things failed to progress smoothly." (Kirkus)

Includes bibliographical references and index.

Colquhoun, Kate

Did she kill him? a Victorian tale of deception, adultery, and arsenic. Kate Colquhoun. Overlook Press 2014 432 p. illustrations (hardback) $27.95   **364.152**
     1. Trials (Homicide) 2. Murder -- England -- Case studies 3. Poisoning -- England -- Case studies
     ISBN 146830934X; 9781468309348
               LC 2014034054

This book, by Kate Colquhoun, explores how "in the summer of 1889, young Southern belle Florence Maybrick stood trial for the alleged arsenic poisoning of her much older husband, Liverpool cotton merchant James Maybrick. . . . The case cracked the varnish of Victorian respectability, shocking and exciting the public in equal measure as they clambered to read the latest revelations of Florence's past and glimpse her likeness in Madame Tussaud's." (Publisher's note)

"Award-nominated Colquhoun (Murder in the First-Class Carriage, 2011—a Victorian whodunit as well) employs again her fine storytelling sense, eye for detail, and impeccable research to ensure that contemporary readers will snap up this tale of treachery, deceit, love gone awry, poison, and 'the slipperiness of truth.'" Booklist

Includes bibliographical references (pages 351-361) and index

Cullen, Dave

Columbine. Twelve 2009 417p $26.99 **364.152**
     1. School shootings 2. Columbine High School (Littleton, Colo.)
     ISBN 978-0-446-54693-5; 0-446-54693-3
               LC 2008-31441

This is an account of the shootings at Columbine High School in 1999.

This book "is an excellent work of media criticism, showing how legends become truths through continual citation; a sensitive guide to the patterns of public grief . . . and, at the end of the day, a fine example of old-fashioned journalism." N Y Times Book Rev

Includes bibliographical references

Epstein, Edward Jay

The **annals** of unsolved crime; by Edward Jay Epstein. Melville House 2013 347 p. (hardcover) $26   **364.152**
     1. Cold cases (Criminal investigation) 2. Criminal investigation 3. Assassination -- History 4. Assassination -- Investigation
     ISBN 1612190480; 9781612190488
               LC 2012049984

This book by Edward Jay Epstein presents "case studies of 35 controversial crimes. Several involve conspiracy theories, e.g., JFK's assassination and the Dominique Strauss-Kahn case. He includes well-known historical cases (e.g., Jack the Ripper, the Lindbergh baby kidnapping) . . . and media-sensation cases such as those of Amanda Knox, O.J. Simpson, and JonBenet Ramsey. . . . After describing each case, he outlines theories, and offers his opinion on the most likely solution." (Library Journal)

Includes bibliographical references (pages [335]-338) and index

Flanders, Judith

★ The **invention** of murder; how the Victorians revelled in death and detection and created modern crime. by Judith Flanders. Thomas Dunne Books 2013 576 p. il (hardcover) $26.99   **364.152**
     1. Homicide 2. Detectives -- Fiction 3. Great Britain -- History -- Victoria, 1837-1901 4. Murder -- Great Britain -- History -- 19th century
     ISBN 1250024870; 9781250024879
               LC 2013010535

This book by Judith Flanders is an "exploration of murder in the nineteenth century, [which] examines some of the most gripping cases that captivated the Victorians and gave rise to the first detective fiction. Flanders retells the gruesome stories of many different types of murder, both famous and obscure. Through these stories of murder—from the brutal to the pathetic—Flanders builds a rich and multi-faceted portrait of Victorian society." (Publisher's note)

Graeber, Charles

The **good** nurse; America's most prolific serial killer, the hospitals that allowed him to thrive, and the detectives who brought him to justice. Charles Graeber. 1st ed. Twelve 2013 320 p. (hardcover) $26.99   **364.152**
     1. Serial killers 2. Nurses -- United States -- Biography 3. Serial murderers -- United States -- Biography
     ISBN 0446505293; 9780446505291
               LC 2012041982

This book, by Charles Graeber, profiles the serial murderer and registered nurse "Charlie Cullen. . . . Implicated in the deaths of as many as 300 patients, he was also perhaps the most prolific serial killer in American history. . . . Graeber's portrait of Cullen depicts a surprisingly intelligent and complicated young man whose promising career was overwhelmed by his compulsion to kill, and whose shy demeanor masked a twisted interior life hidden even to his family and friends." (Publisher's note)

Includes bibliographical references

Guinn, Jeff

★ **Manson**; the life and times of Charles Manson. Jeff Guinn. Simon & Schuster 2013 512 p. $27.50   **364.152**
     1. Criminals -- United States -- Biography 2. Murderers -- United States -- Biography
     ISBN 1451645163; 9781451645163
               LC 2012050176

This book by Jeff Guinn "reexamines the life of Charles Manson, interviewing Manson's sister and cousin, who have not previously spoken out, and gleaning new information from childhood friends, cellmates, and Manson Family members. Guinn argues that while Manson spouted incoherent race-war rhetoric, the killings were in fact related to his failed ambitions to be a rock star." (Library Journal)

Includes bibliographical references and index

Hakkakiyan, Ru'ya

Assassins of the Turquoise Palace. Grove Press 2011 322p   **364.152**
     1. Assassination 2. Trials (Homicide) 3. Political

crimes and offenses 4. Iran -- Politics and government
ISBN 0-8021-1911-5; 978-0-8021-1911-7

A "look at the September 17, 1992, terror killing of four Kurdish exiles who were holding a meeting in a small restaurant in Berlin. This crime resulted in a massive German investigation and an equally massive four-year trial that ended with guilty verdicts for the accused and, more importantly, a condemnation of Iran's leaders as the instigators of the murder plot." (Publishers Weekly)

Includes bibliographical references

Hempel, Sandra

The **inheritor's** powder; a tale of arsenic, murder, and the new forensic science. by Sandra Hempel. W W Norton & Co Inc 2013 288 p. (hardcover) $25.95   **364.152**

1. Arsenic 2. Forensic sciences 3. Poisons and poisoning 4. Forensic toxicology 5. Murder -- Great Britain -- History -- 19th century 6. Poisoning -- Great Britain -- History -- 19th century 7. Toxicology -- Great Britain -- History -- 19th century 8. Arsenic -- Toxicology -- Great Britain -- History -- 19th century
ISBN 0393239713; 9780393239713

LC 2013024989

Author Sandra Hempel presents a "look at how the science of poison detection developed. Hempel focuses on a different dilemma for the Victorian medical profession: how to successfully determine when poison is the cause of death. In 1833 the strange death of farmer George Bodle and the investigation of his family members, with whom he lived, frames the history of scientists' struggles to develop foolproof tests for the presence, in the victims' digestive tracts, of arsenic." (Publishers Weekly)

"An unexpected verdict and its aftermath make this a satisfying murder mystery in the grand tradition." Kirkus

Includes bibliographical references and index

Kirn, Walter

Blood will out; the true story of a murder, a mystery, and a masquerade. Walter Kirn. First edition Liveright Publishing Corporation 2014 272 p. (hardcover) $25.95   **364.152**

1. Murderers -- United States -- Case studies 2. Impostors and imposture -- United States -- Case studies
ISBN 0871404516; 9780871404510

LC 2013046327

This book, by Walter Kirn, is the true story of Clark Rockefeller, an "eccentric son of privilege who ultimately would be unmasked as a brazen serial impostor, child kidnapper, and brutal murderer. . . . As Kirn uncovers the truth about his friend, a psychopath masquerading as a gentleman, he also confronts hard truths about himself. Why, as a writer of fiction, was he susceptible to the deception of a sinister fantasist whose crimes, Kirn learns, were based on books and movies?" (Publisher's note)

"Kirn's reflecting, musing, and personal dealings add a killer punch to this true-crime memoir." Booklist

Kolker, Robert

Lost Girls; An Unsolved American Mystery. by Robert Kolker. HarperCollins 2013 xiv, 399 p.p (hardcover) $25.99   **364.152**

1. Crime 2. Prostitution 3. Serial murders 4. Computer crimes
ISBN 006218363X; 9780062183637

LC 2013021815

This book from Robert Kolker looks at the murder of five prostitutes in Oak Beach, Long Island. He "probes the 21st-century innovations that facilitated these crimes, which launched a media blitz." A major focus of the book is the author's attention to "the girls' back stories and to the efforts of their families and friends to bring the killer to justice." (Kirkus Reviews)

Kraybill, Donald B.

Amish grace; how forgiveness transcended tragedy. [by] Donald B. Kraybill, Steven M. Nolt, [and] David L. Weaver-Zercher. Jossey-Bass 2007 237p $24.95   **364.152**

1. Amish 2. Forgiveness 3. Amish -- Doctrines 4. West Nickel Mines Amish School (Pa.) 5. Amish School Shooting, Nickel Mines, Pa., 2006 6. Forgiveness -- Religious aspects -- Christianity
ISBN 978-0-7879-9761-8; 0-7879-9761-7

This book explains "Amish reaction to the horrific Nickel Mines shootings. . . . This anguished and devastating account of a national tragedy and a hopeful, life-affirming lesson in how to live is itself a marvel of grace." Booklist

Includes bibliographical references

Larson, Erik

Thunderstruck. Crown Publishers 2006 463p il map $25.95   **364.152**

1. Radio 2. Homicide 3. Inventors 4. Murderers 5. Electrical engineers 6. Homeopathic physicians 7. Nobel laureates for physics
ISBN 1-4000-8066-5; 978-1-4000-8066-3

LC 2006-11908

This book "alternates the story of Marconi's quest for the first wireless transatlantic communication amid scientific jealousies and controversies with the tale of [Dr. Hawley Harvey Crippen,] a mild-mannered murderer caught as a result of the invention. . . . A thrilling read." SLJ

Includes bibliographical references

Leovy, Jill

★ **Ghettoside**; a true story of murder in America. Jill Leovy. 1st edition Spiegel & Grau 2015 336 p. hbk $28   **364.152**

1. Homicide 2. Detectives 3. Los Angeles (Calif.) 4. United States -- Social conditions 5. Murder -- United States
ISBN 0385529988; 9780385529983

LC 2013046367

National Book Critics Circle Award Finalist: Nonfiction (2015); NAACP Image Award Nominee: Outstanding Literary Work- Nonfiction (2016)

In this book, author Jill Leovy "uses the senseless murder of a policeman's progeny as a jumping-off point to investigate broader issues. Leovy's big-picture thesis is . . .

that the gang violence in [Los Angeles] is the result of the local police simply not doing their jobs. On a microcosmic level, the author follows the lives of two LAPD officers, John Skaggs and Wally Tennelle, the former investigating the murder of the latter's son." (Kirkus Reviews)

"Readers may come for Leovy's detective story; they will stay for her lucid social critique." Pub Wkly

Includes bibliographical references and index

Liebman, James S.

The **wrong** Carlos; anatomy of a wrongful execution. James S. Liebman, Shawn Crowley, Andrew Markquart, Lauren Rosenberg, Lauren Gallo White, and Daniel Zharkovsky. Columbia University Press 2014 464 p. illustrations (pbk. : alk. paper) $27.95 **364.152**

1. Judicial error 2. Trials (Homicide) 3. Capital punishment -- United States 4. Judicial error -- Texas 5. Trials (Murder) -- Texas 6. Capital punishment -- Texas
ISBN 0231167237; 9780231167222; 9780231167239; 9780231536684

LC 2013044147

This book focuses on the history of a wrongful execution. "In 1989, Texas executed Carlos DeLuna, a poor Hispanic man with childlike intelligence, for the murder of Wanda Lopez, a convenience store clerk. His execution passed unnoticed for years until a team of Columbia Law School faculty and students almost accidentally chose to investigate his case and found that DeLuna almost certainly was innocent." (Publisher's note)

"A masterpiece of its type and a disturbing true crime account." LJ

Includes bibliographical references and index

Mann, William J.

Tinseltown; Murder, Morphine, and Madness at the Dawn of Hollywood. by William J. Mann. Harper, an imprint of HarperCollins Publishers 2014 xi, 463 p.p illustrations $27.99 **364.152**

1. Motion picture industry -- History 2. Motion picture producers and directors -- United States 3. Murder -- Investigation -- California -- Los Angeles -- Case studies 4. Motion picture producers and directors -- Crimes against -- United States 5. Cold cases (Criminal investigation) -- California -- Los Angeles -- Case studies
ISBN 0062242164; 9780062242167

LC 2015410477

Edgar Award: Best Fact Crime (2015)

This book, by William J. Mann, is the "true tale of ambition, scandal, intrigue, murder, and the creation of the modern film industry. By 1920, the movies had suddenly become America's new favorite pastime. . . . Yet Hollywood's glittering ascendency was threatened by a string of headline-grabbing tragedies—including the murder of William Desmond Taylor, the popular president of the Motion Picture Directors Association, a legendary crime that has remained unsolved until now." (Publisher's note)

"Fans of historical true crime and those who enjoy Old Hollywood gossip will like this title, which could spur the curious to further research of the Taylor case." LJ

Includes bibliographical references (pages 429-463)

Morris, Errol, 1948-

A **wilderness** of error; the trials of Jeffrey MacDonald. Errol Morris; illustrations by Niko Skourti. Penguin Press 2012 xviii, 524 p.p ill. $29.95 **364.152**

1. Administration of criminal justice 2. Murder -- North Carolina -- Case studies 3. Murderers -- United States -- Case studies
ISBN 1594203431; 9781594203435

LC 2012017906

This book by Errol Morris is about the murder trials of Jeffrey MacDonald "that led to the conviction and imprisonment for life of this man for butchering his wife and two young daughters. . . . It shows us that almost everything we have been told about the case is deeply unreliable, and crucial elements of the case against MacDonald simply are not true. . . . Along the way Morris poses bracing questions about the nature of proof, criminal justice, and the media." (Publisher's note)

Includes bibliographical references and index

Parry, Richard Lloyd

People who eat darkness; the true story of a young woman who vanished from the streets of Tokyo and the evil that swallowed her up. Richard Lloyd Parry. Farrar, Straus and Giroux 2012 454 p. **364.152**

1. Homicide 2. Trials (Homicide) 3. Victims of crimes 4. Murder -- Investigation -- Japan -- Tokyo 5. Young women -- Crimes against -- Japan -- Tokyo
ISBN 9780224079174 Jonathan Cape; 0224079174 Jonathan Cape; 0374230595 Farrar, Straus and Giroux; 9780374230593 Farrar, Straus and Giroux

LC 2011047019

This true crime book by Richard Lloyd Parry tells the story of how "Lucie Blackman--tall, blond, twenty-one years old--stepped out into the vastness of Tokyo in the summer of 2000, and disappeared forever. The following winter, her dismembered remains were found buried in a seaside cave. . . . [The author], an award-winning foreign correspondent, covered Lucie's disappearance and followed the massive search for her, the long investigation, and the even longer trial." (Publisher's note)

Includes bibliographical references.

Presley, James

The **Phantom** Killer; Unlocking the Mystery of the Texarkana Serial Murders: the Story of a Town in Terror. W.W. Norton & Co. Inc. 2014 400 p. 16 plates; illustrations $27.95 **364.152**

1. Homicide 2. Texas -- History 3. Cold cases (Criminal investigation)
ISBN 1605986429; 9781605986425

LC 2015452738

In this book, "the salacious and scandalous murders of a series of couples on Texarkana's 'lovers lanes' in seemingly idyllic post-WWII America created a media maelstrom and cast a pall of fear over an entire region. What is even more surprising is that the case has remained cold for decades. Combining archival research and investigative journalism, . . . James Presley reveals evidence that provides crucial keys to unlocking this decades-old puzzle." (Publisher's note)

"A thoroughgoing but occasionally plodding story that awaits a better writer. For now, though, this is the best available account of a crime that, though a cold case, still has people talking." Kirkus

Rule, Ann

Too late to say goodbye; a true story of murder and betrayal. Free Press 2007 456p il $26 **364.152**

1. Homicide 2. Homemakers 3. Murder victims

ISBN 978-0-7432-3852-6; 0-7432-3852-4

LC 2007-9168

"Rule's meticulous 2½ years of research provides a cinematically satisfying look into how police in two jurisdictions worked together to prove Corbin was a serial murderer of women who tried to leave him." USA Today

Safran, John

God'll Cut You Down; The Tangled Tale of a White Supremacist, a Black Hustler, a Murder, and How I Lost a Year in Mississippi. Penguin Group USA 2014 368 p. $27.95   **364.152**

1. Homicide 2. Southern States -- Race relations

ISBN 1594633355; 9781594633355

LC 2014017207

Author John Safran presents a true "story about race, money, sex, and power in the modern American South from an outsider's point of view. White supremacist .... Richard Barrett was brutally murdered in Mississippi in 2010 by a young black man named Vincent McGee. Maybe it was a dispute over money rather than race--or, maybe and intriguingly, over sex." (Publisher's note)

"Safran discovers that the truth behind the crime is driven as much by sex, money, and power as it is by race. Safran's account is at turns hilarious and often bizarre as he riffs on his perspective as an outsider mixing into a complex environment and failing to understand all manner of nuances." Booklist

Schechter, Harold

Psycho USA; famous american killers you never heard of. Harold Schechter. Ballantine Books 2012 xiii, 396 p.p   **364.152**

1. Homicide 2. Serial Killers -- History 3. Murder -- United States -- Case studies 4. Murderers -- United States -- Biography

ISBN 0345524470; 9780345524478; 9780345524485

LC 2012004990

This book by Harold Schechter focuses on "a bevy of all-but-forgotten homicidal fiends studding the bloody margins of U.S. history. . . . Spurred by profit, passion, paranoia, or perverse pleasure, these killers -- the Witch of Staten Island, the Smutty Nose Butcher, the Bluebeard of Quiet Dell, and many others -- span three centuries and a host of harrowing murder methods." (Publisher's note)

Includes bibliographical references and index

Sides, Hampton

★ Hellhound on his trail; the stalking of Martin Luther King, Jr., and the international hunt for his assassin. Doubleday 2010 459p il $28.95   **364.152**

1. Clergy 2. Murderers 3. Nonfiction writers 4. Civil rights activists 5. Nobel laureates for peace

ISBN 978-0-385-52392-9; 0-385-52392-0

LC 2009-43659

"Sides begins with Ray's escape from a maximum security prison in Missouri the prior April. In short, crisp chapters, Sides then cuts back and forth between Ray's movements during the ensuing year and King's increasing challenges during the same period, as a fraying civil rights movement struggled to transform hard-won legal equality into economic justice. Along the way, we're treated to vignettes featuring J. Edgar Hoover's vicious antiKing smear tactics; George Wallace's race-driven politics of hate during the 1968 presidential campaign; and an embittered Lyndon Johnson's estrangement from King over the ongoing war in Vietnam. None of this is new, but Sides ensures that it's still compulsively readable." Milwaukee Journal Sentinel

Includes bibliographical references

Siegel, Barry

Manifest injustice; the true story of a convicted murderer and the lawyers who want him freed. by Barry Siegel. 1st ed. Henry Holt and Co. 2012 xiv, 384 p.p (hardcover) $28   **364.152**

1. Miscarriage of justice 2. Macumber, William, 1935- -- Trials, litigation, etc. 3. Judicial error 4. Arizona Justice Project 5. Trials (Murder) -- Arizona -- Maricopa County

ISBN 0805094156; 9780805094152

LC 2012028986

In this book, Pulitzer Prize-winning journalist Barry Siegel "describes the efforts of the Arizona Justice Project to free Bill Macumber, who has spent 38 years in prison for a double murder he denies committing. In 1962, a young couple was shot on a lovers lane in Maricopa County, AZ. There were no credible leads at the time, but a decade later Carol Macumber, a clerk in the sheriff's office, claimed that her ex-husband [Bill] was the murderer." (Library Journal)

Includes bibliographical references (p. [365]-371) and index.

Singular, Stephen

The Spiral Notebook; The Aurora Theater Shooter and the Epidemic of Mass Violence Committed by American Youth. by Stephen Singular and Joyce Singular. Counterpoint 2015 304 p. $26   **364.152**

1. School shootings 2. Youth -- United States

ISBN 1619025345; 9781619025349

This book, by Stephen and Joyce Singular, "investigates why America keeps producing twenty-something mass killers. . . . While following the legal proceedings in the Aurora shooting, [it] is full of interviews with Generation Z, a group dogged by big pharma and anti-depressants and ADHD drugs, by a doomsday/apocalyptic mentality present since birth, and by an entertainment industry that has turned violence into parlor games." (Publisher's note)

"Tragic, gripping, and authentic, this book deserves a wide audience." Kirkus

Starr, Douglas

The killer of little shepherds; a true crime story and the birth of forensic science. A.A. Knopf 2010 300p il $26.95   **364.152**

1. Homicide 2. Physicians 3. Forensic sciences 4. Trials (Homicide) 5. Murderers 6. Criminologists 7.

Law enforcement officials
ISBN 978-0-307-26619-4; 0-307-26619-2

LC 2010-14930

This book is "like an episode of CSI: 19th-Century France. As he prowled the countryside, Joseph Vacher preyed on young shepherds, ultimately slaughtering four times as many people as Jack the Ripper. How the bumbling French authorities finally pieced together the evidence — while learning to study bodies and crime scenes for clues and to compare details about the killings — represents, Starr says, nothing less than the birth of forensic science. In gripping, almost novelistic chapters, he alternates between Vacher and Alexandre Lacassagne, the criminologist who helped crack the case." Entertainment Wkly

Includes bibliographical references

Stashower, Daniel

The **beautiful** cigar girl; Mary Rogers, Edgar Allan Poe, and the invention of murder. Dutton 2006 326p il $25.95 **364.152**

1. Poets 2. Authors 3. Homicide 4. Essayists 5. Murder victims 6. Short story writers
ISBN 0-525-94981-X; 978-0-525-94981-7

LC 2006-19335

The author "tells the story of New York City cigar store clerk Mary Rogers, whose violent death in 1841 brought on a frenzy of sensational newspaper stories and prompted the interest of Edgar Allan Poe. . . . [He] details how the mystery surrounding Rogers's murder became the inspiration for Poe's story 'The Mystery of Marie Rogêt.' . . . Well researched and accessible, here is a gripping story that is hard to put down." Libr J

Includes bibliographical references

Summerscale, Kate

The **suspicions** of Mr. Whicher; a shocking murder and the undoing of a great Victorian detective. Walker & Company 2008 360p il map $24.95 **364.152**

1. Homicide 2. Detectives 3. London (England)
ISBN 978-0-8027-1535-7; 0-8027-1535-4

LC 2008-00247

This is the story of Inspector Jonathan Whicher of Scotland Yard, who investigated the 1860 murder of three-year-old Francis Saville Kent in the village of Road, Wiltshire.

The author's "clean writing makes . . . [this book] so dynamic that she can't be accused of 'freezing' the past—instead, she has done a masterly job of reviving it, with all its curiosities and contradictions. But, most strikingly, she has created an enthralling mystery by overlaying the fictional tools of misdirection and suspense onto a nonfiction narrative." Am Scholar

Includes bibliographical references

Swanson, James L.

Manhunt; the 12-day chase for Lincoln's killer. William Morrow 2006 448p il $26.95 **364.152**

1. Actors 2. Lawyers 3. Presidents 4. Murderers 5. State legislators 6. Members of Congress
ISBN 0-06-051849-9

LC 2005-44911

While this book "belongs in the history section . . . it's as gripping a page-turner as anything you'll find on the mystery shelf." Entertainment Weekly

Includes bibliographical references

Urschel, Joe

The **Year** of Fear; Machine Gun Kelly and the Manhunt That Changed the Nation. by Joe Urschel. St. Martin's Press 2015 304 p. $26.99 **364.152**

1. Gangsters 2. Great Depression, 1929-1939
ISBN 1250020794; 9781250020796

LC 2015022093

In this book by Joe Urschel "it's 1933 and Prohibition has given rise to the American gangster. . . . Gangster George 'Machine Gun' Kelly and his wife, Kathryn, are some of the most celebrated criminals of the Great Depression. With gin-running operations facing extinction and bank vaults with dwindling stores of cash, Kelly sets his sights on the easy-money racket of kidnapping. His target: rich oilman, Charles Urschel." (Publisher's note)

"Many true-crime books claim to shine a light on their chosen eras. This one is the real deal." Booklist

Includes bibliographical references (pages [271]-274) and index.

Zacharias, Karen Spears

A **silence** of mockingbirds; the memoir of a murder. by Karen Spears Zacharias. MacAdam/Cage Pub. 2012 322 p. (hardcover) $25.00 **364.152**

1. Homicide 2. Child abuse 3. Autobiographies 4. Murder -- Oregon -- Case studies
ISBN 159692375X; 9781596923751

LC 2012000748

This book is a true crime story by Karen Spears Zacharias. Zacharias "never anticipated that she would become . . . involved in a high-profile murder. But when she reconnects with . . . Sarah, . . . Karen discovers that something unspeakable has happened to Sarah's daughter, Karly. . . . Karen pieces together what happened to Karly through court documents, investigators' interviews, and interviews with friends, family, law enforcement officials, and key witnesses." (Publisher's note)

"Journalist Zacharias presents a searing account of child abuse and murder, bringing to life a tragedy with which she is intimately familiar...A harrowing cautionary tale that will touch fans of Ann Rule's chilling works." LJ

364.16 Offenses against property

Crosby, Molly Caldwell

The **great** pearl heist; London's greatest jewel thief and Scotland Yard's hunt for the world's most valuable necklace. by Molly Caldwell Crosby. Berkely Books 2012 304 p. (alk. paper) $25.95 **364.16**

1. Jewelry theft -- History 2. Great Britain -- History -- 20th century 3. Criminal investigation -- Great Britain -- History 4. Jewelry theft -- England -- Case studies 5. Robbery investigation -- England -- London -- Case studies 6. Burglary investigation -- England -- London -- Case studies 7. Receiving stolen goods

-- England -- London -- Case studies
ISBN 0425252809; 9780425252802

LC 2012008261

This book by Molly Caldwell Crosby presents "a World War I-era true-crime tale about the theft of the world's most valuable necklace. . . . The setting is the underworld of London's Hatton Garden jewelry district in the days before the war, and the object of desire is a pink pearl necklace. . . . Criminal mastermind Joseph Grizzard . . . had his eye on the necklace, and he concocted a plan to intercept it as it traveled by mail between two dealers." (Kirkus Reviews)

Includes bibliographical references and index.

Krebs, Brian

Spam nation; the inside story of organized cybercrime--from global epidemic to your front door. Brian Krebs. Sourcebooks, Inc. 2014 256 p. $24.99 **364.16**

1. Fraud 2. Internet 3. Computer crimes 4. Phishing 5. Spam (Electronic mail) 6. Internet fraud -- United States 7. Computer crimes -- United States 8. Organized crime -- United States

ISBN 1402295618; 9781402295614

LC 2014023007

This book, by Brian Krebs, "unmasks the criminal masterminds driving some of the biggest spam and hacker operations targeting Americans and their bank accounts. Tracing the rise, fall, and alarming resurrection of the digital mafia behind the two largest spam pharmacies--and countless viruses, phishing, and spyware attacks--[the author] . . . delivers the first definitive narrative of the global spam problem and its threat to consumers everywhere." (Publisher's note)

"For lay readers, an effectively revealing closing chapter offers tips on how anyone can safeguard their personal online information from hacker infiltration. An eye-opening, immensely distressing exposé on the current state of organized cyberspammers." Kirkus

Mitnick, Kevin D. (Kevin David), 1963-

Ghost in the wires; my adventures as the world's most wanted hacker. by Kevin Mitnick, with William L. Simon. Little, Brown and Company 2011 xiv, 413 p.p ill. $25.99 **364.16**

1. Thieves 2. Computer hackers 3. Computer crimes -- United States 4. Computer security -- United States 5. Computer hackers -- United States -- Biography 6. Information superhighway -- Security measures -- United States

ISBN 0316037702; 9780316037709

LC 2010043461

In this book, computer hacker Kevin Mitnick "recounts his epic illegal computer hacks of Sun Microsystems, Digital Equipment Corporation, and any number of cellphone makers; his exploits triggered a manhunt that made headlines. He insists he did it not for money but for the transgressive thrill of looking at big, secret computer programs." (Publishers Weekly)

Posner, Gerald

God's Bankers; A History of Money and Power at the Vatican. By Gerald Posner. Simon & Schuster 2015 728 p. 16 plates; illustrations $30 **364.16**

1. Vatican City 2. Church finance 3. Political corruption 4. Catholic Church -- Finance 5. Banks and banking -- Vatican City 6. Catholic Church -- Corrupt practices 7. Catholic Church -- History -- 20th century 8. Catholic Church -- History -- 21st century 9. Catholic Church -- Controversial literature 10. Istituto per le opere di religione -- Corrupt practices

ISBN 1416576576; 9781416576570

LC 2014021061

Author Gerald Posner offers an "exposé of the money and the cardinals-turned-financiers at the heart of the Vatican . . .marked by poisoned business titans, murdered prosecutors, mysterious deaths of private investigators, and questionable suicides; . . . and a set of moral and political circumstances that clarify not only the church's aims and ambitions, but reflect the larger dilemmas of the world's more recent history." (Publisher's note)

"The destruction of documents, stonewalling by prelates, and closed Vatican archives made Posner's work harder, necessitating conjectures. This sad tale is known in its outlines, but Posner provides much more detail." Choice

Potter, Maximillian

Shadows in the vineyard; the true story of a plot to poison the world's greatest wine. Maximillian Potter. Grand Central Publishing 2014 304 p. (hardback) $27 **364.16**

1. Crime 2. Wine and wine making -- France 3. Crime -- France -- Burgundy -- Case studies 4. Wineries -- France -- Burgundy -- Case studies 5. Viticulture -- France -- Burgundy -- Case studies 6. Grapes -- France -- Burgundy -- Herbicide injuries -- Case studies

ISBN 1455516104; 9781455516100

LC 2014015787

In this book, by Maximillian Potter, the author "uncovers a fascinating plot to destroy the vines of La Romanée-Conti, Burgundy's finest and most expensive wine. . . . [The author] takes us deep into a captivating world full of . . . small-town French politics . . . and a local culture defined by the twinned veins of excess and vitality and the deep reverent attention to the land that runs through it." (Publisher's note)

"Digressions on the wine market and various viticultural techniques, as well as profiles of the police officers and the criminal they pursued, give the story depth and context. Even the most devout teetotaler will have a hard time putting this one down." Pub Wkly

364.163 Fraud

Konnikova, Maria, 1987-

The **Confidence** Game; Why We Fall for It--Every Time. by Maria Konnikova. Penguin Group USA 2016 352 p. (ebook) $65; $28 **364.163**

1. Deception 2. Ponzi schemes 3. Swindlers and swindling

ISBN 9780698170995; 0525427414; 9780525427414

LC 2015041266

"From multimillion-dollar Ponzi schemes to small-time frauds, [author Maria] Konnikova pulls together a selection of fascinating stories to demonstrate what all cons share in common, drawing on scientific, dramatic, and psychological perspectives. . . . 'The Confidence Game' asks not only why we believe con artists, but also examines the very act of believing and how our sense of truth can be manipulated by those around us." (Publisher's note)

"With meticulous research and a facility for storytelling, Konnikova makes this intriguing topic absolutely riveting." Kirkus

Includes bibliographical references and index.

364.3 Offenders

Benforado, Adam

Unfair; the new science of criminal injustice. Adam Benforado. Crown Publishers 2015 400 p. (hardback) $26 **364.3**

1. Discrimination 2. Criminal psychology 3. Administration of criminal justice 4. Criminal justice, Administration of -- Psychological aspects 5. Discrimination in criminal justice administration -- Psychological aspects

ISBN 0770437761; 9780770437763; 9780770437787

LC 2014041693

This book, by Adam Benforado, argues "our system of justice is fundamentally broken. . . . Even if the system operated exactly as it was designed to, we would still end up with wrongful convictions, trampled rights, and unequal treatment. This is because the roots of injustice lie not inside the dark hearts of racist police officers or dishonest prosecutors, but within the minds of each and every one of us." (Publisher's note)

"A stimulating critique of today's criminal justice system with applications to recent cases in Ferguson, MO, and elsewhere, this authoritative and accessible book is suited to a general audience and students." LJ

Paradis, Cheryl

The **measure** of madness; inside the disturbed and disturbing criminal mind. Citadel Press 2010 272p pa $16.95 **364.3**

1. Forensic sciences 2. Criminal psychology

ISBN 978-0-8065-3105-2

LC 2010-924994

The author "has spent more than two decades evaluating mentally ill and violent individuals and giving expert testimony in court. Here she details criminal cases in which the prosecution or defense asked her to establish whether defendants were competent to stand trial, or to vet such psychiatric defenses as insanity and extreme emotional disturbance. The cases, all tried in New York City, are fascinating, unsettling and often horrifying. . . . The author also discusses the psycho-legal issues of cases involving juveniles and abused wives. . . . A welcome inside account." Kirkus

Includes bibliographical references

Rhodes, Richard

Why they kill; the discoveries of a maverick criminologist. Knopf 1999 371p $26.95; pa $14 **364.3**

1. Violence 2. Criminals 3. Criminal psychology 4. College teachers

ISBN 0-375-40249-7; 0-375-70248-2 pa

LC 99-18920

The author discusses the history of violence and the work of social scientist Lonnie H. Athens. "Athens interviewed prisoners in maximum security prisons in Iowa, California and elsewhere, predominantly men. . . . His hope was to bypass inmates' typical narratives and get to what they actually thought and felt when they assaulted or raped or killed." N Y Times Book Rev

Includes bibliographical references

364.4 Prevention of crime and delinquency

Stuntz, William J.

The **collapse** of American criminal justice. Belknap Press of Harvard University Press 2011 413p il $35 **364.4**

1. Crime prevention 2. Administration of criminal justice 3. United States -- Race relations 4. African Americans -- Civil rights

ISBN 978-0-674-05175-1; 0-674-05175-0

LC 2011006905

This is "a fascinating, passionate, compassionate, often brilliant book. Flawless? No. But it's a work that deserves to have a significant influence on American criminal-justice thinkers from across the political spectrum." Natl Rev

Includes bibliographical references

364.66 Capital punishment

Echols, Damien

★ **Life** after death; Damien Echols. Blue Rider Press 2012 399 p. **364.66**

1. Prisons 2. False imprisonment -- United States 3. Prisoners -- United States -- Biography 4. Death row inmates -- United States -- Biography

ISBN 0399160205; 9780399160202

LC 2012026115

Author Damien Echols, "sentenced to death . . . for the murders of three eight-year-old boys in Arkansas, [and] known worldwide as a symbol of wrongful conviction and imprisonment, . . . shares his story in full -- from abuse by prison guards and wardens, to portraits of fellow inmates and deplorable living conditions, to the incredible reserves of patience, spirituality, and perseverance that kept him alive and sane while incarcerated for nearly two decades." (Publisher's note)

Harrington, Joel F.

The **faithful** executioner; life and death, honor and shame in the turbulent sixteenth century. Joel F.

Harrington. Farrar Straus & Giroux 2013 320 p.
(hardcover) $28   **364.66**
1. Executions and executioners 2. Crime -- Germany
-- Nuremberg -- History 3. Criminal procedure --
Germany -- Nuremberg -- History 4. Executions and
executioners -- Germany -- Nuremberg -- Biography
ISBN 0809049929; 9780809049929

LC 2012029017

This book, by Joel F. Harrington, "takes us deep inside
the alien world and thinking of Meister Frantz Schmidt of
Nuremberg, who, during forty-five years as a professional
executioner, personally put to death 394 individuals and tortured, flogged, or disfigured many hundreds more. But the
picture that emerges of Schmidt from his personal papers
is not that of a monster. Could a man who routinely practiced such cruelty also be insightful, compassionate--even
progressive?" (Publisher's note)

Heard, Alex

The **eyes** of Willie McGee; a tragedy of race,
sex, and secrets in the Jim Crow South. Harper 2010
404p il $26.99   **364.66**
1. Trials 2. Veterans 3. Capital punishment 4. Alleged
criminals 5. Mississippi -- Race relations
ISBN 978-0-06-128415-1; 0-06-128415-7

LC 2009-51769

"McGee was mourned in poems, novels and memoirs.
But while he clearly did not get a fair trial, was he inno-
cent? Was Willette Hawkins really the guilty party? 'The
Eyes of Willie McGee' leaves us wondering, and wondering
how many other ghosts remain in Jim Crow's closet." Los
Angeles Times

Prejean, Helen

★ The **death** of innocents; an eyewitness account of wrongful executions. Random House 2005
310p $25.95   **364.66**
1. Capital punishment
ISBN 0-679-44056-9

LC 2004-54154

The author "reexamines the cases of two men she fervently believes were executed for crimes they did not commit. . . . In addition to providing a searing indictment of
capital punishment, Prejean also exposes the fundamental
inadequacies of the American court system. Expect demand
for this extremely thought-provoking book." Booklist
Includes bibliographical references

364.67   Corporal punishment

Spierenburg, Pieter

Violence and punishment; civilizing the body
through time. Pieter Spierenburg. Polity 2013 vi,
223 p.p (hbk.) $69.95   **364.67**
1. Human body 2. Punishment 3. Violence -- History
4. Punishment -- History
ISBN 0745653480; 0745653499; 9780745653488;
9780745653495

LC 2012277159

This book is a "study of historical violence, social control, honor codes, and the transformation of punishment. It

. . . ranges from homicide trends in Amsterdam to modern
notions of the human body, punishment, and even the formation of religions in prehistoric societies. . . . Readers learn
that punishments became infused with religious and political ritual in the early modern period as part of the civilizing
process. This, in turn, reflected aristocratic notions of the
body." (Choice)
Includes bibliographical references (p. [201]-220)
and index

365   Penal and related institutions

Abbott, Jack Henry, 1944-2002

In the belly of the beast; letters from prison. with
an introduction by Norman Mailer. Random House
1981 166p hardcover o.p. pa $12   **365**
1. Prisoners 2. Prisons -- United States
ISBN 0-679-73237-3 pa

LC 80-6038

Abbott's "letters belong with the best prison literature,
not because of their accounts of atrocity, but for their disturbing picture of daily life behind bars." Time

Applebaum, Anne

★ **Gulag**; a history. Doubleday 2003 677p il
maps $35   **365**
1. Convict labor 2. Concentration camps 3. Soviet
Union -- Politics and government
ISBN 0-7679-0056-1

LC 2002-41344

This "describes how, largely under Stalin's watch, a
regulated, centralized system of prison labor—unprecedented in scope—gradually arose out of the chaos of the Russian Revolution. . . . Applebaum details camp life, including strategies for survival; the experiences of women and
children in the camps; sexual relationships and marriages
between prisoners; and rebellions, strikes and escapes. . . .
Applebaum's lucid prose and painstaking consideration of
the competing theories about aspects of camp life and policy
are always compelling." Publ Wkly
Includes bibliographical references

Bernstein, Nell

Burning down the house; the end of juvenile
prison. Nell Bernstein. New Press, The 2014 384 p.
(hardback) $26.95   **365**
1. Juvenile courts 2. Juvenile delinquency 3.
Administration of justice -- United States 4. Juvenile
justice, Administration of -- United States
ISBN 1595589562; 9781595589569

LC 2013043709

In this book journalist Nell Bernstein "turns her attention
to the U.S. juvenile justice system in which more than 66,000
youths are confined. . . . Bernstein introduces adolescents
in and out of detention centers, capturing their struggles to
overcome traumatic histories. . . . Visiting 'therapeutic' prisons in Minnesota, California, and New York, she concludes
that . . . these institutions remain embedded in a larger culture that seems impervious to reform." (Publishers Weekly)

"The combination of muckraking research and absolutism make the book passionate and convincing as advocacy." Kirkus

Includes bibliographical references

Ferro, Jeffrey

Prisons; Rev. ed; Facts On File, Inc. 2011 312p (Library in a book) $45 **365**

1. Prisons -- United States

ISBN 978-0-8160-8236-0; 978-1-4381-3398-0 ebook

LC 2010-49855

First published 2006

This book "examines the state of U.S. prisons and related issues. It focuses on the development of prisons in the United States and how the competing goals of punishment and rehabilitation have shaped the evolution of criminal correction. An overview presents statistics on U.S. prisons and explores the issues behind those statistics, including racial disparity among prisoners and the causes of recidivism. The financial costs of running prisons and the mixed record of private prisons are examined, and laws and legislation relating to issues of incarceration are reviewed." Publisher's note

Includes bibliographical references

Figes, Orlando, 1959-

Just send me word; a true story of love and survival in the Gulag. Orlando Figes. Metropolitan Books/Henry Holt and Company 2012 333 p. **365**

1. Love stories 2. Political prisoners -- Russia 3. Russia -- History -- 1917-1991, Soviet Union 4. Imprisonment -- Soviet Union 5. Fiancées -- Soviet Union 6. Fiancées -- Soviet Union -- Correspondence 7. Labor camps -- Russia (Federation) -- Pechora (Komi) 8. Political prisoners -- Russia (Federation) -- Pechora (Komi) 9. Political prisoners -- Russia (Federation) -- Pechora (Komi) -- Correspondence

ISBN 0805095225; 9780805095227

LC 2011048355

In this book, "[d]rawing on more than 1,200 letters between Lev and Svetlana 'Sveta' Mishchenko, and interviews with the couple, veteran historian Figes . . . tells their remarkable tale of love and devotion during the worst years of the USSR. Having fallen in love as physics students at Moscow University, they were separated for 13 years: first while Lev seized in WWII, and then after he was sentenced to a Siberian labor camp for the 'crime' of serving as a translator for a German officer while a POW. Lev's letters illustrate the extreme hardships of the Stalinist camps. . . . Her letters express her extraordinary devotion and determination to visit Lev, which she managed to do four times, despite the long trek, subterfuges, necessary bribes, and dangers involved in the illegal journeys." (Publishers Weekly)

Includes bibliographical references and index

Kizny, Tomasz

Gulag; life and death inside the Soviet concentration camps. Firefly Books 2004 495p il maps $69.95 **365**

1. Convict labor 2. Concentration camps 3. Soviet Union -- Politics and government

ISBN 1-55297-964-4

LC 2005-357207

This book "contains 550 black-and-white photographs of life in the Soviet Gulag. . . . The photos gathered here range from official archival snapshots, showing both inmates and their captors, to scenes of enormous construction projects and snowbound ruins. Kizny has added his own photographs of the abandoned camps or work projects and included a brief history of the camps and personal accounts of survivors. These rare and historically significant photographs can only hint at the appalling horrors committed within the camps, and the importance of the book cannot be overstated." Booklist

Liao Yiwu

For a song and one hundred songs; a poet's journey through a Chinese prison. Liao Yiwu; translated from the Chinese by Wen Huang. Houghton Mifflin Harcourt 2013 432 p. (hardcover) $26 **365**

1. Political prisoners -- China 2. Tiananmen Square Incident, Beijing (China), 1989 -- Poetry 3. Prisoners -- China -- Biography

ISBN 0547892632; 9780547892634

LC 2012019558

In this book, "exiled Chinese poet Liao [Yiwu] . . . recounts . . . his politicization and imprisonment in the wake of the 1989 government crackdown on the democracy movement centered in Beijing's Tiananmen Square." His poem, "Massacre," about the protest and a subsequent film project resulted in his 1990 arrest. The "bulk of the memoir concerns Liao's four-year imprisonment at a series of facilities in the harrowing Chongqing prison system." (Publishers Weekly)

Oshinsky, David M.

Worse than slavery; Parchman Farm and the ordeal of Jim Crow justice. Free Press 1996 306p il hardcover o.p. pa $14 **365**

1. Prisons -- United States 2. Mississippi State Penitentiary 3. United States -- Race relations

ISBN 0-684-83095-7 pa

LC 95-52880

"Oshinsky's beautifully constructed narrative brings to vivid life one of the most shameful chapters in American history." New Yorker

Includes bibliographical references

Solzhenitsyn, Aleksandr

★ The **Gulag** Archipelago, 1918-1956 v1; an experiment in literary investigation. [by] Aleksandr I. Solzhenitsyn; translated from the Russian by Thomas P. Whitney; foreword by Anne Applebaum. Harper Perennial Modern Classics 2007 xx, 660p pa $21.95 **365**

1. Political prisoners 2. Soviet Union -- Politics and government

ISBN 978-0-06-125371-3; 0-06-125371-5

First published 1974

The first volume of the author's three-volume "'literary investigation' of the network of Soviet prison camps as they existed between 1918 and 1956. . . . A mixture of autobiography, history, and analysis, the relentlessly grim picture of life inside the camps forms the basis for an attack not only on Stalinism and Leninism but also on the whole process of substituting Western rational and secular ideas for Russia's traditional mysticism." Benét's Reader's Ency. 4th edition

★ The **Gulag** Archipelago, 1918-1956 v2; an experiment in literary investigation. [by] Aleksandr I. Solzhenitsyn; translated from the Russian by Thomas P. Whitney; foreword by Anne Applebaum. Harper Perennial Modern Classics 2007 712p il map pa $21.95   **365**
1. Political prisoners 2. Soviet Union -- Politics and government
ISBN 978-0-06-125372-0; 0-06-125372-3
First published 1975
This second volume of a two-volume series describes "the story of Solzhenitsyn's entrance into the Soviet prison camps, where he would remain for nearly a decade." Publisher's note

★ The **Gulag** Archipelago, 1918-1956 v3; an experiment in literary investigation. [by] Aleksandr I. Solzhenitsyn; translated from the Russian by Harry Willetts; foreword by Anne Applebaum. Harper Perennial Modern Classics 2007 558p il map pa $21.95   **365**
1. Political prisoners 2. Soviet Union -- Politics and government
ISBN 978-0-06-125373-7; 0-06-125373-1
First published 1978
The final volume of a three-volume series, this book contains the author's "account of resistance within the Soviet labor camps and his own release after eight years." Publisher's note

Thompson, Heather Ann
Blood in the water; the Attica prison uprising of 1971 and its legacy. Heather Ann Thompson. Pantheon 2016 724 p. illustrations (hardback) $35 **365**
1. Attica Prison 2. Prisoners -- Civil rights 3. Law enforcement -- History 4. Prison riots -- New York (State)
ISBN 0375423222; 9780375423222
              LC 2016000477
National Book Award Finalist: Nonfiction (2016)
This book by Heather Ann Thompson discusses the 1971 uprising by inmates at Attica Prison in New York "to protest years of mistreatment. Holding guards and civilian employees hostage, the prisoners negotiated with officials for improved conditions. . . . On September 13, the state abruptly sent hundreds of heavily armed troopers and correction officers to retake the prison by force. Their gunfire killed thirty-nine men . . . [and] wounded more than one hundred others." (Publisher's note)
"Thompson's superb and thorough study serves as a powerful tale of the search for justice in the face of the abuses of institutional power." Pub Wkly
Includes bibliographical references (pages 579-684) and index.

365.6   Inmates

Bozella, Dewey, 1959-
Stand Tall; Fighting for My Life, Inside and Outside the Ring. by Dewey Bozella. HarperCollins 2016 256 p. $27.99   **365.6**
1. Actual innocence
ISBN 0062208152; 9780062208156
In this memoir "Dewey Bozella recounts his life and the twenty-six years he spent behind bars for a murder he did not commit. . . . Bozella was wrongfully accused of murdering Emma Crapser, a ninety-two-year-old resident of Poughkeepsie, New York. Sentenced to twenty years to life in prison, Bozella fiercely maintained his innocence throughout his ordeal at Sing Sing, and even refused the prosecutor's offer of instant freedom in exchange for admission of guilt." (Publisher's note)
"His writing is concise, never self-congratulatory or self-pitying, and always graceful." Pub Wkly

365.66   Services to prisoners

Brottman, Mikita
The **Maximum** Security Book Club; Reading Literature in a Men's Prison. by Mikita Brottman. HarperCollins 2016 272 p. $26.99   **365.66**
1. Books and reading 2. Prisoners -- Education
ISBN 0062384333; 9780062384331
              LC 2016013355
This book is an "account of the two years literary scholar Mikita Brottman spent reading literature with criminals in a maximum-security men's prison outside Baltimore, and what she learned from them. . . . The book club members struggle with their assigned reading through solitary confinement; on lockdown; in between factory shifts; in the hospital; and in the middle of the chaos of blasting televisions, incessant chatter, and the constant banging of metal doors." (Publisher's note)
"Will not appeal to hard-core law-and-order types, but others will find this a brave and empathetic story of how literature brings light into shadows." Kirkus

366   Secret associations and societies

Ridley, Jasper Godwin
The **Freemasons**; a history of the world's most powerful secret society. [by] Jasper Ridley. Arcade Pub. 2001 357p $25.95; pa $14.95   **366**
1. Freemasons
ISBN 1-55970-601-5; 1-55970-654-6 pa
              LC 2001-45745
The author "traces the origins of freemasonry back to the craft guilds in medieval Europe, and then he chronicles their growth and evolution through the modern era. . . . This work of popular history sheds light on a frequently obscure subject." Booklist
Includes bibliographical references

368 Insurance

Boyd, Roddy

Fatal risk; a cautionary tale of AIG's corporate suicide. Wiley 2011 349p **368**

1. Insurance 2. Financial crises 3. Insurance executives 4. American International Group, Inc.

ISBN 978-0-470-88980-0

LC 2011-01512

"A vivid portrait of the giant insurer at the center of the 2008 financial crisis." Wall Street J

368.4 Government-sponsored insurance

Altman, Nancy J.

The **battle** for Social Security; from FDR's vision to Bush's gamble. Wiley 2005 362p $24.95 **368.4**

1. Social security

ISBN 978-0-471-77172-2; 0-471-77172-4

LC 2005-20700

The author "traces the history of Social Security from its introduction in 1935, and provides a thoughtful, well-researched case against the . . . [Bush] administration's efforts to reduce Social Security protection." Booklist

Includes bibliographical references

Frank, Joshua

The **people's** pension; the struggle to defend social security since Reagan. Eric Laursen, Joshua Frank; [edited by] 674-A 23rd Street. AK Press 2012 818 p. ill. (alk. paper) $13.99 **368.4**

1. Privitization 2. Social security 3. United States -- Politics and government -- 2001-

ISBN 9781849351010

LC 2012933068

This book looks at the issue of Social Security in terms of the U.S. 2012 presidential election. In "the aftermath of the debt reduction deal between Barack Obama and congressional Republicans, the 2012 election promises to be a kind of referendum on the size and role of government—including economic support programs like Social Security. . . . Eric Laursen suggests that the only solution for Social Security is taking it out of the government's hands altogether." (Barnes and Noble)

Includes bibliographical references (p. [727]-783) and index.

Social security handbook; overview of social security programs, 2014. by Social Security Administration. Rowman & Littlefield Publishers, Inc. 2014 703 p. $69 **368.4**

1. Social security

ISBN 1598887068; 9781598887068

This book "provides information about Social Security programs and services, and identifies rights and obligations under the Social Security laws. The handbook also contains information about related programs administered by agencies other than the Social Security Administration." (Publisher's note)

Solman, Paul

Get what's yours; the secrets to maxing out your social security. Laurence J. Kotlikoff, Philip Moeller, Paul Solman. Simon & Schuster 2015 288 p. (hardback) $19.99 **368.4**

1. Social security 2. Personal finance 3. Retirement income 4. Social security -- United States 5. Retirement income -- United States

ISBN 1476772290; 9781476772295

LC 2014034384

This book by Laurence J. Kotlikoff, Philip Moeller, and Paul Solman explains "Social Security benefits in an easy to understand and user-friendly style. . . . It explains what to do if you're a retired parent of dependent children, disabled, or an eligible beneficiary who continues to work, and how to plan wisely before retirement. It addresses the tax consequences of your choices, as well as the financial implications for other investments." (Publisher's note)

"This book works as a thorough overview and as a reference for those with specific questions about Social Security. The authors present the information from the unwieldy system clearly but without dumbing it down." LJ

Includes bibliographical references and index

370 Education

Uncle Tom or new Negro; African Americans reflect on Booker T. Washington and Up from slavery one hundred years later. edited by Rebecca Carroll. Broadway Books/Harlem Moon 2006 320p pa $15.95 **370**

1. Slaves 2. Authors 3. Educators 4. African American educators 5. Memoirists 6. Nonfiction writers 7. Tuskegee Institute 8. Civil rights activists 9. African Americans -- Biography

ISBN 0-7679-1955-6; 978-0-7679-1955-5

LC 2005-50161

"This collection of 20 commentaries by contemporary writers offers new perspectives on Booker T. Washington's autobiography and his place in the struggle for racial equality. Among the commentators are Debra Dickerson, Julianne Malveaux, Bill Ethanson, Ronald Walkers, Earl Ofari Hutchinson, and John McWhorter. The book also includes the complete text of Up from Slavery." Booklist

Includes bibliographical references

370.1 Philosophy and theory, education for specific objectives, educational psychology

Dewey, John, 1859-1952

Democracy and education; an introduction to the philosophy of education. Free Press 1997 378p pa $17.95 **370.1**

1. Education -- Philosophy

ISBN 0-684-83631-9; 978-0-684-83631-7

First published 1916 by Macmillan

"The author's aim here is to detect and state the ideas implied in a democratic society and to apply those ideas to the problems of education." Boston Transcr

370.15   Educational psychology

Levine, Melvin D.

A **mind** at a time; {by} Mel Levine. Simon &
Schuster 2002 352p $26; pa $14   **370.15**
1. Child development 2. Learning disabilities 3.
Educational psychology
ISBN 0-7432-0222-8; 0-7432-0223-6 pa
         LC 2001-57670

The author discusses "eight areas of learning (the memory system, the language system, the spatial ordering system,
the motor system, etc.). He provides chapters describing how
each type of learning works and advises parents and teachers
on how to help kids struggling in these areas. . . . This is a
must-read for parents and educators who want to understand
and improve the school lives of children." Publ Wkly
Includes bibliographical references

370.71   Education

McKeown, Rosalyn

Into the classroom; a practical guide for starting student teaching. Rosalyn McKeown. University of Tennessee Press 2011 xv, 165 p.p (pbk.)
$14.95   **370.71**
1. Teaching 2. Student teaching
ISBN 1572338164; 9781572338166
         LC 2011011282

This book offers suggestions to those "just starting out
in a secondary school classroom. . . . After exploring the
pitfalls of inexperience and providing . . . guidance on maintaining order in the classroom, [Rosalyn] McKeown focuses
on teaching skills. She advises readers on writing objectives
and lesson plans, creating interesting ways to start and end
class, introducing variety into the classroom, lecturing, asking meaningful questions, and using visual aids." (Amazon.
com)
Includes bibliographical references and index.

370.9   History, geographic treatment, biography

Falk, Beverly

Teaching matters; stories from inside city
schools. Beverly Falk and Megan Blumenreich with
Adesina Abani ... [et al.] New Press 2012 xii, 196
p.p ill. (paperback) $19.95   **370.9**
1. Teaching 2. Urban schools 3. Education -- Case
studies 4. Teachers -- United States -- Case studies
ISBN 1595584900; 9781595584908
         LC 2012004564

This book, by Beverly Falk and Megan Blumenreich,
discusses inner city public schools. "As public schools become increasingly embattled . . . , the burden of these restrictions has drastically changed the way children are expected
to learn. . . . Leading education experts Beverly Falk and
Megan Blumenreich provide an enlightening account of
what our students really need--and how teachers are step-

ping up to provide what state standards and political posturing cannot." (Publisher's note)
Includes bibliographical references (p. 189-196)

Hirsch, E. D.

The **schools** we need and why we don't have
them; {by} E.D. Hirsch, Jr. Doubleday 1996 317p
hardcover o.p. pa $14.95   **370.9**
1. Education -- United States
ISBN 0-385-49524-2 pa
         LC 96-2192

This "book presents a sophisticated, scholarly and often
compelling argument and it deserves serious consideration,
whatever one's political predilections." N Y Times Book Rev
Includes bibliographical references

Postman, Neil

The **end** of education; redefining the value
of school. Knopf 1995 209p hardcover o.p. pa
$13.95   **370.9**
1. Multiculturalism 2. Technology and civilization 3.
Education -- United States
ISBN 0-679-75031-2 pa
         LC 94-46605

"Beautifully written, breathtakingly high-minded, this is
Postman's best book on American education." Booklist
Includes bibliographical references

Ripley, Amanda

The **smartest** kids in the world; and how they
got that way. Amanda Ripley. Simon & Schuster
2013 320 p. $28   **370.9**
1. Foreign students 2. Education -- United States
3. Education -- Poland 4. Education -- Finland 5.
Comparative education 6. Education -- Korea (South)
ISBN 1451654421; 9781451654424
         LC 2013002021

This book looks at the educational disparities between
the U.S. and other world nations. Journalist Amanda Ripley
"recounts the experiences of three American teens studying
abroad for a year in the education superpowers. Fifteen-
year-old Kim raises $10,000 so she can go to high school
in Finland; Eric, 18, trades a leafy suburb in Minnesota for
a 'city stacked on top of a city' in South Korea; and Tom,
17, leaves Gettysburg, Pa., for Poland." (Publishers Weekly)
Includes bibliographical references and index

370.922   Educators--biography

McCluskey, Audrey Thomas

A **forgotten** sisterhood; pioneering black women
educators and activists in the Jim Crow South. Audrey Thomas McCluskey. Rowman & Littlefield
2014 192 p. (cloth : alk. paper) $42   **370.922**
1. African American educators 2. Southern States
-- Race relations 3. African Americans -- Education
-- History 4. Southern States -- Social conditions
5. Southern States -- Race relations -- History 6.
African Americans -- Education -- Southern States 7.
Civil rights movements -- Southern States -- History

8. African American women civil rights workers -- Biography 9. African Americans -- Southern States -- Social conditions 10. African American educators -- Southern States -- Biography 11. African Americans -- Segregation -- Southern States -- History 12. African Americans -- Civil rights -- Southern States -- History 13. African American women educators -- Southern States -- Biography

ISBN 9781442211384

LC 2014025293

This book by Audrey Thomas McCluskey reveals how "black activist women Lucy Craft Laney, Mary McLeod Bethune, Charlotte Hawkins Brown, and Nannie Helen Burroughs founded schools aimed at liberating African-American youth from disadvantaged futures in the segregated and decidedly unequal South. . . . These individuals fought discrimination as members of a larger movement . . . [to uplift] future generations through . . . education, social service, and cultural transformation." (Publisher's note)

"McCluskey's well-researched account articulates the importance of this particular movement in education, appropriately and skillfully, to memorialize the four pioneering women at the forefront." Pub Wkly

Includes bibliographical references and index.

371 Schools and their activities; special education

Bedor, Deborah

Getting in by standing out; The New Rules for Admission to America's Best Colleges. Deborah Bedor. Advantage Media Group 2015 194 p. $14.97 **371**

1. College applications 2. Colleges and universities -- Entrance requirements

ISBN 1599325594; 9781599325590

LC 2015936963

In this book on college admissions, author Deborah Bedor "coaxes and inspires students to use their high school years for a personal quest, intellectual passion, or social cause that's in line with their authentic gifts, strengths, and ambitions. All things being equal: grades, scores, and recommendations, it is now your leadership and creative quest towards YOU that reveals the character and intellect that the gatekeepers to Admissions seek." (Publisher's note)

371.01 Specific kinds of schools

Rhee, Michelle A., 1969-

Radical; fighting to put students first. Michelle Rhee. Harper 2013 304 p. (hardcover) $27.99 **371.01**

1. Education -- United States 2. Education -- Aims and objectives 3. Public schools -- United States 4. Educational change -- United States 5. School improvement programs -- United States

ISBN 0062203983; 9780062203984

LC 2012038474

This book, by education reformer Michelle Rhee, "draws on her own life story and delivers her plan for better

American schools. . . . Informing her critique are her . . . experiences in education. . . . Rhee draws on dozens of compelling examples from schools she's worked in and studied, from students who've left behind unspeakable home lives and thrived in the classroom to teachers whose groundbreaking methods have produced unprecedented leaps in student achievement." (Publisher's note)

371.1 Schools and their activities

Kozol, Jonathan

Letters to a young teacher. Crown Publishers 2007 288p hardcover o.p. pa $14 **371.1**

1. Teaching

ISBN 978-0-307-39371-5; 0-307-39371-2; 978-0-307-39372-2 pa; 0-307-39372-0 pa

LC 2007-2689

"The book will delight and encourage first-year (or for that matter, 40th-year) teachers who need Kozol's reminders of the ways that their beautiful profession can bring joy and beauty, mystery and mischievous delight into the hearts of little people in their years of greatest curiosity." Publ Wkly

Includes bibliographical references

Parini, Jay

The **art** of teaching. Oxford University Press 2005 160p $17.95 **371.1**

1. Teaching 2. Vocational guidance

ISBN 0-19-516969-7

LC 2004-5443

The author offers "musings about teaching's demands and what it takes to not lose one's other, creative self while meeting those demands in this memoir-cum-advice book for novice instructors. . . . This warm guide should inform, entertain, and inspire young teachers as they seek to 'waken a student to his or her potential.'" Publ Wkly

371.102 Teaching

Espinoza, Roberta

Pivotal moments; how educators can put all students on the path to college. Roberta Espinoza. Harvard Education Press 2011 200 p. (pbk.) $26.95 **371.102**

1. Higher education

ISBN 1612501192; 9781612501192; 9781612501208

LC 2011937500

In this book, "sociologist Roberta Espinoza introduces the idea of pivotal moments[:] interventions that point the way toward college, particularly for students from working-class or ethnic minority backgrounds. These pivotal encounters and the relationships that spring from them can help students accumulate procedural knowledge about attending college (cultural capital) and interpersonal support (social capital)." (Amazon.com)

Includes bibliographical references and index.

371.2   School administration; administration of student academic activities

Aronica, Lou

Creative schools; the grassroots revolution that's transforming education. Ken Robinson and Lou Aronica. Viking 2015 292 p. illustrations $27.95   **371.2**

1. Creative ability 2. Creative thinking 3. Educational change 4. Education -- United States 5. Educational change -- United States 6. School improvement programs -- United States 7. Creative ability -- Study and teaching -- United States 8. Creative thinking -- Study and teaching -- United States

ISBN 0670016713; 9780670016716

LC 2015001098

This book, by Ken Robinson and Lou Aronica, is a "reappraisal of how to educate our children and young people. . . . [Robinson] argues for an end to our outmoded industrial educational system and proposes a highly personalized, organic approach that draws on today's unprecedented technological and professional resources to engage all students, develop their love of learning, and enable them to face the real challenges of the twenty-first century." (Publisher's note)

"For readers who are ardent about changing education for the better, believing that they can be part of the forces that will revolutionize the future." LJ

Includes bibliographical references and index

Russakoff, Dale

The prize; who's in charge of America's schools? Dale Russakoff. Houghton Mifflin Harcourt 2015 246 p. (hardback) $27   **371.2**

1. Educational change 2. Education -- Government policy 3. Public schools -- United States 4. Education and state -- United States -- History 5. Education and state -- New Jersey 6. Public schools -- New Jersey -- Newark 7. Educational change -- New Jersey -- Newark 8. Education -- Political aspects -- New Jersey -- Newark

ISBN 9780547840055

LC 2015017454

In this book, by Dale Russakoff, "Mark Zuckerberg pledged $100 million to transform Newark's public schools. . . . Then Newark mayor Cory Booker teamed with Governor Chris Christie to turn around one of the most troubled urban school districts in the nation, favoring the creation of charter schools. It would mean massive reform of the way teachers were paid, rewarded, or let go, with accountability tied to student test scores. . . . But along the way, the plan ran into massive resistance." (Booklist)

"An absorbing entry into the burgeoning genre about necessary education reforms." Kirkus

Includes bibliographical references and index

371.26   Examinations and tests; academic prognosis and placement

More Than a Score; The New Uprising Against High-stakes Testing. edited by Jess Hagopian.

Haymarket Books 2014 302 p. illustrations $18   **371.26**

1. Educational change 2. Educational tests and measurements

ISBN 1608463923; 9781608463923

This book, edited by Jesse Hagopian, is a " collection of essays, poems, speeches, and interviews--accounts of personal courage and trenchant insights--from frontline fighters who are defying the corporate education reformers, often at great personal and professional risk, and fueling a national movement to reclaim and transform public education." (Publisher's note)

"An array of outraged, insightful, and inspiring selections, this necessary collection should be required reading for educators, parents, and students affected by unremitting corporate education strategies." Booklist

Reese, William J.

Testing wars in the public schools; a forgotten history. William J. Reese. Harvard University Press 2013 298 p. $45   **371.26**

1. Public schools -- United States 2. Educational tests and measurements 3. Public schools -- United States -- History -- 19th century 4. Educational tests and measurements -- United States -- History -- 19th century

ISBN 0674073045; 9780674073043

LC 2012033665

Author William J. Reese provides an "examination of the roots of the testing culture in American education and the ramifications for administrators, teachers, and students. Reese organizes the book into six chapters, including those that concentrate upon the origins of large-scale testing, the reform-minded reasons for using such instruments, the procedures by which testing was implemented, the effects of testing, how the content was selected, and how the culture of testing evolved." (Choice)

Includes bibliographical references and index

371.3   Methods of instruction and study

Jackson, Rebecca

The learning habit; a groundbreaking approach to homework and parenting that helps our children succeed in school and life. Stephanie Donaldson-Pressman, Rebecca Jackson, Robert Pressman. Perigee Trade 2014 320 p. illustrations (paperback) $17   **371.3**

1. Homework 2. Family life 3. Psychology of learning 4. Families 5. Parenting 6. Study skills

ISBN 0399167110; 9780399167119

LC 2014011124

Written by Stephanie Donaldson-Pressman, Rebecca Jackson, and Robert Pressman, this book "presents new solutions based on the largest study of family routines ever conducted. 'The Learning Habit' offers a blueprint for navigating the maze of homework, media use, and . . . everyday stress . . . turning those 'stress times' into opportunities to develop . . . skills including concentration and focus, time management, decision-making, goal-setting, and self-reliance." (Publisher's note)

"The book lists eight essential skill sets that parents should help children cultivate, from time management to fostering self-reliance. An especially useful chapter focuses on ways to help children concentrate." Pub Wkly

Includes bibliographical references and index

Montessori, Maria

★ The **Montessori** method; introduction by J. McV. Hunt. Schocken Bks. 1964 xxxix, 376p il hardcover o.p. pa $14 **371.3**

1. Montessori method of education

ISBN 0-8052-0922-0 pa

Originally published in Italy; first published 1912 in the United States

This is an introduction to the author's teaching methods. The Montessori system emphasizes the development of individuality in the child and the careful training of the senses. Education is controlled by interpersonal relations between the children rather than between teacher and child

371.33 Teaching aids, equipment, materials

Vander Ark, Tom, 1959-

Getting smart; how digital learning is changing the world. Tom Vander Ark; foreword by Bob Wise. 1st ed. Jossey-Bass 2011 xxi, 213 p.p $26.95 **371.33**

1. Internet in education 2. Computer-assisted instruction 3. Education -- Experimental methods 4. Blended learning -- United States 5. Internet in education -- United States 6. Computer-assisted instruction -- United States

ISBN 1118007239; 9781118007235

LC 2011024028

This book, by Tom Vander Ark, "examines the various facets of educational innovation in the United States and abroad. Vander Ark . . . makes a . . . case for a new model of education that blends online and on-site learning. [He] explains that through the use of technology it is now possible to provide 24/7 access to learning and increase student engagement. . . . By customizing learning . . . each hour of learning can become more effective for all students at all levels." (Publisher's note)

Includes bibliographical references and index

371.4 Student guidance and counseling

Morgan, Genevieve

Undecided; navigating life and learning after high school. Genevieve Morgan. Zest Books 2014 256 p. $14.99 **371.4**

1. College choice 2. Vocational guidance 3. Life skills -- Handbooks, manuals, etc.

ISBN 1936976323; 9781936976324

LC 2013951198

"This comprehensive handbook outlines the different options available to teens after high school and provides suggestions on how to follow each path. . . . It covers everything from SAT preparation and personal statements to trade school pros and cons and advice on how to prepare for life in the military. Full of checklists, anecdotes, brainstorming activities, and journal exercises, 'Undecided' leaves no stone unturned and no option unconsidered." (Publisher's note)

"A helpful guide full of good, sensible advice to teens feeling overwhelmed by the prospect of major life transitions." Kirkus

Includes bibliographical references and index

371.5 School discipline and related activities

Bully; an action plan for teachers and parents to combat the bullying crisis. edited by Lee Hirsch and Cynthia Lowen; with Dina Santorelli. Perseus Books Group 2012 viii, 295 p.p ill. $15.99 **371.5**

1. Bullies 2. Bullying 3. Bullying -- Prevention 4. Cyberbullying -- Prevention 5. Bullying in schools -- Prevention

ISBN 1602861846; 1602861854; 9781602861848; 9781602861855

LC 2012289039

"This companion book to the documentary film Bully was edited by filmmaker [Lee]Hirsch and writer/producer [Cynthia] Lowen, with contributing chapters by a number of celebrities, authors, experts, government officials, and educators. Part homage to the film, part resource, the book interweaves the stories of children who have been bullied with practical information and advice for parents and other readers." (Publishers Weekly)

Includes bibliographical references (p. 281-289) and index

371.7 Student welfare

Fisher, Robin Gaby

Choosing hope; moving forward from life's darkest hours. Kaitlin Roig-DeBellis with Robin Gaby Fisher. G. P. Putnam's Sons, an imprint of Penguin Group (USA) 2015 272 p. $26.95 **371.7**

1. Hope 2. School shootings

ISBN 0399174451; 9780399174452

LC 2015015834

This book, by Kaitlin Roig-DeBellis with Robin Gaby Fisher, is the memoir of "the first-grade teacher at Sandy Hook Elementary School who saved her entire class of fifteen six- and seven-year-olds from the tragic events that took place on December 14, 2012." In it the author describes the events of the tragedy along with the emotional struggles which followed it. (Publisher's note)

"Though it may strike some readers as Pollyannaish, the author's sunny optimism about the teaching profession is sincere. Her account of the shooting, her struggle to keep despair at bay in both herself and her students, and her ultimate triumph as a survivor seeking to make a difference help balance the book and redeem it from excessive sentimentality. A flawed but still courageous and inspiring book from a genuine hero." Kirkus

371.82   Specific groups of students; schools for specific groups of students

Cahill, Sean

✓ **LGBT** youth in America's schools; Jason Cianciotto and Sean Cahill. The University of Michigan Press 2012 236 p. (pbk. : alk. paper) $30   **371.82**
1. Bullies 2. Gay youth 3. Discrimination 4. Schools -- Administration 5. Gay students -- United States 6. Sexual minorities -- Education 7. Lesbian students -- United States 8. Bisexual students -- United States 9. Homosexuality and education -- United States 10. Transgender youth -- Education -- United States
ISBN 0472031406; 9780472028320; 9780472031405; 9780472118229
LC 2011045478
In this book, "[Jason] Cianciotto and [Sean] Cahill use statistics and real-life anecdotes to show the pervasiveness of gender- and sexual orientation-based harassment in American schools, and argue for institutional reform and policy changes. . . . [R]esearch shows that . . . more young people are coming out . . . while still technically a minor, and thus subject to the rules of their educational institutions, and increasingly the abuse of their peers, teachers, and school administrators." (Publishers Weekly)
Includes bibliographical references and index.

Mortenson, Greg

✓ **Three** cups of tea; one man's mission to fight terrorism and build nations--one school at a time. [by] Greg Mortenson and David Oliver Relin. Viking 2006 338p il map $25.95; pa $16   **371.82**
1. Humanitarian intervention 2. Schools -- Pakistan 3. Schools -- Afghanistan
ISBN 0-670-03482-7; 978-0-670-03482-6; 0-14-303825-7 pa; 978-0-14-303825-2 pa
LC 2005-43466
"Laced with drama, danger, romance, and good deeds, Mortenson's story serves as a reminder of the power of a good idea and the strength inherent in one person's passionate determination to persevere against enormous obstacles." Christ Sci Monit

Perez, William

✓ **We** are Americans; undocumented students pursuing the American dream. foreword by Daniel Solorzano. Stylus 2009 xxxiv, 161p $70; pa $22.50   **371.82**
1. Unauthorized immigrants 2. Discrimination in education 3. Illegal aliens 4. United States -- Immigration and emigration
ISBN 978-1-57922-375-5; 978-1-57922-376-2 pa
LC 2009-26206
The author "plumbs the stories of students living with the constant threat of deportation for an answer to the question, 'What does it mean to be an American?' Raised in this country by parents who gained access illegally, the 16 high school, college and postgraduate students profiled here (standing in for 65,000 nationwide) have each embraced our language, culture and collective dream, but are denied pathways to success. . . . No matter what one's position is on legalizing immigrants, this collection of inspiring, heart-

breaking stories puts a number of unforgettable faces to the issue, making it impossible to defend any one side in easy terms or generalities." Publ Wkly
Includes bibliographical references

371.9   Special education

Chura, David

I don't wish nobody to have a life like mine; tales of kids in adult lockup. Beacon Press 2010 xxiii, 216p $24.95; pa $14   **371.9**
1. Juvenile delinquency 2. Prisoners -- Education
ISBN 978-0-8070-0064-9; 978-0-8070-0123-3 pa
LC 2009027664
Shares the experiences of teenagers incarcerated in an adult prison in New York, as well as those of the men and women hired to teach and watch over them.
"Chura offers a compelling personal look at the failings of the juvenile justice system." Booklist

Flink, David

✓ **Thinking** Differently; An Inspiring Guide for Parents of Children With Learning Disabilities. David Flink. HarperCollins 2014 320 p. illustrations $15.99   **371.9**
1. Learning disabilities 2. Students with disabilities
ISBN 0062225936; 9780062225931
This book by David Flink "enlarges our understanding of the learning process and offers powerful, innovative strategies for parenting, teaching, and supporting the 20 percent of students with learning disabilities. . . . Focusing on how to arm students who think and learn differently with essential skills, including meta-cognition and self-advocacy, Flink offers real, hard advice, providing the tools to address specific problems they face." (Publisher's note)
Includes bibliographical references and index

Kozol, Jonathan

✓ **Savage** inequalities; children in America's schools. HarperPerennial 1992 261p pa $14.95   **371.9**
1. Public schools 2. Segregation in education 3. Children with social disabilities
ISBN 0-06-097499-0; 978-0-06-097499-2
First published 1991 by Crown
"Jonathan Kozol has written an impassioned book, laced with anger and indignation, about how our public education system scorns so many of our children. 'Savage Inequalities' is also an important book, and warrants widespread attention" N Y Times Book Rev
Includes bibliographical references

Salzman, Mark

✓ **True** notebooks. Alfred A. Knopf 2003 330p hardcover o.p. pa $13.95   **371.9**
1. Creative writing 2. Juvenile delinquency
ISBN 0-375-41308-1; 0-375-72761-2 pa
LC 2002-43435
"While teaching writing to 17-year-olds detained in Los Angeles Central Juvenile Hall, Salzman found him-

self surprised by the boys' talent. The teens' heartwarming, funny voices are included in his irresistible, provocative memoir." Booklist

Siegel, Lawrence M.

The **complete** IEP guide; how to advocate for your special ed child. 7th ed.; Nolo 2011 380p pa $34.99 **371.9**

1. Special education 2. Children with disabilities 3. Individualized instruction 4. Individuals with Disabilities Education Act

ISBN 978-1-4133-1313-0 pa; 1-4133-1313-2 pa; 978-1-4133-1336-9 ebook; 1-4133-1336-1 ebook

LC 2010-38386

First published 1999. Frequently revised

This legal guide offer strategies and advice for parents of children who need an individualized education program. Includes information on special education laws and eligibility rules, how to draw up a blueprint of a child's educational needs, and what to look for in a special education program.

371.91   Students with physical disabilities

Hauser, Peter C.

★ **How** deaf children learn; what parents and teachers need to know. Marc Marschark Peter C. Hauser. Oxford University Press 2012 156 p. $26.50 **371.91**

1. Teaching 2. Deaf children 3. Elementary education 4. Deaf -- Education 5. Deaf -- Means of communication

ISBN 0195389751; 9780195389753

LC 2011012553

This book is "about teaching deaf children. Written primarily for parents and teachers of deaf or hard-of-hearing children, this work covers general information about their education, gives insights into their cognitive development, and provides steps to their school success. The authors also discuss issues such as the value of cochlear implants and the debate over signing vs. speaking." (Library Journal)

Includes bibliographical references.

372   Specific levels of education

Dewey, John

★ The **school** and society, and The child and the curriculum; introduction by Philip W. Jackson. University of Chicago Press 1990 xli, 209p hardcover o.p. pa $11 **372**

1. Elementary education

ISBN 0-226-14396-1 pa

LC 90-43528

A combined edition of two essays first published separately in 1899 and 1902 respectively

Both of these works stress the functional relationship between classroom learning activities and real life experiences and analyze the social and psychological nature of the learning process. They present and defend the underlying tenets of Dewey's philosophy of education

372.1   Organization and activities in primary education

Tough, Paul

Helping Children Succeed; What Works and Why. by Paul Tough. Houghton Mifflin Harcourt 2016 144 p. $18.99 **372.1**

1. Parenting 2. Child rearing 3. Child development

ISBN 0544935284; 9780544935280

In this book, author Paul Tough "takes on . . . pressing questions: What does growing up in poverty do to children's mental and physical development? How does adversity at home affect their success in the classroom, from preschool to high school? And what practical steps can the adults who are responsible for them—from parents and teachers to policy makers and philanthropists—take to improve their chances for a positive future?" (Publisher's note)

"Tough's research demonstrates that all children have the capacity for self-control, grit, and success if given the right tools to work with from birth. Informative and effective methods to help children overcome issues and thrive at home and in school." Kirkus

372.133   Instructional materials--primary education

Lambert, Megan Dowd

Reading picture books with children; how to shake up storytime and get kids talking about what they see. Megan Dowd Lambert in association with the Eric Carle Museum of Picture Book Art. Charlesbridge 2015 176 p. color illustrations (reinforced for library use) $21.95; (ebook) $64.99 **372.133**

1. Storytelling 2. Language arts 3. Picture books for children 4. School children -- Books and reading 5. Picture books for children -- Educational aspects

ISBN 9781580896627; 9781607346951

LC 2014010501

This book, by Megan Dowd Lambert, is a "a practical guide for reshaping storytime and getting kids to think with their eyes. Traditional storytime often offers a passive experience for kids, but the Whole Book approach asks the youngest of readers to ponder all aspects of a picture book and to use their critical thinking skills." (Publisher's note)

"The author's storytime anecdotes are funny, touching, and ultimately illuminating, highlighting how this approach can open new avenues to explore with children." SLJ

372.21   Preschool education

Christakis, Erika

The **Importance** of Being Little; What Preschoolers Really Need from Grownups. by Erika Christakis. Penguin Group USA 2016 400 p. $28 **372.21**

1. Children 2. Parenting 3. Preschool education

ISBN 0525429077; 9780525429074

In this book, author Erika Christakis "explains what it's like to be a young child in America today. . . . She offers real-life solutions to real-life issues, with nuance and direction that takes us far beyond the usual prescriptions for fewer tests, more play. She looks at children's use of language, their artistic expressions, the way their imaginations grow, and how they build deep emotional bonds to stretch the boundaries of their small worlds." (Publisher's note)

"A deep, provocative analysis of the current modes of teaching preschool e rs and what should be changed to create a more effective learning environment for everyone." Kirkus

Includes bibliographical references (pages [305]-364) and index.

Tough, Paul

★ **How** children succeed; grit, curiosity, and the hidden power of character. Paul Tough. Houghton Mifflin Harcourt 2012 231 p. $27.00   **372.21**
    1. Rich 2. Equality 3. Social classes 4. Poor -- United States 5. Children -- United States 6. Early childhood education -- United States 7. Cognitive styles in children -- United States
    ISBN 0547564651; 9780547564654
                    LC 2012019000

In this book Paul Tough "argues that non-cognitive skills (persistence, self-control, curiosity, conscientiousness, grit and self-confidence) are the most critical to success in school and life. . . . When policymakers favor the belief that disadvantaged kids have insufficient cognitive training, Tough finds that a new generation of researchers are questioning the cognitive hypothesis." (Kirkus Reviews)

"Well-written and bursting with ideas..." Kirkus

Includes bibliographical references and index

372.4   Reading

Fertig, Beth

Why cant U teach me 2 read? three students and a mayor put our schools to the test. Farrar, Straus and Giroux 2009 354p $27   **372.4**
    1. Reading disability 2. Students with disabilities 3. Reading -- Remedial teaching 4. New York (N.Y.) -- Board of Education
    ISBN 978-0-374-29905-7; 0-374-29905-6
                    LC 2009-11520

This is "an overall excellent, thoroughly grounding survey of the state of literacy and education." Publ Wkly

Includes bibliographical references

Flesch, Rudolf Franz

★ **Why** Johnny can't read--and what you can do about it. Harper & Row 1955 222p hardcover o.p. pa $13   **372.4**
    1. Reading 2. Phonetics -- Study and teaching
    ISBN 0-06-091340-1 pa

Companion volume to Why Johnny still can't read (1981)

The author advocates the alphabetic-phonetic system of teaching children to read. He includes step-by-step directions and phonetic drills for use by parents

Grover, Sharon

Listening to learn; audiobooks supporting literacy. by Sharon Grover and Lizette D. Hannegan. American Library Association 2011 xi, 188 p.p (alk. paper) $45   **372.4**
    1. Literacy 2. Audiobooks 3. Educational technology 4. Reading -- United States 5. Children -- Books and reading 6. Libraries -- Special collections -- Audiobooks 7. Literacy -- Study and teaching -- United States 8. School librarian participation in curriculum planning
    ISBN 0838911072; 9780838911075
                    LC 2011041814

Authors Sharon Grover and Lizette D. Hannegan "make the case that audiobooks not only present excellent opportunities to engage the attention of young people but also advance literacy. 'Listening to Learn' connects audiobooks with K-12 curricula and demonstrates how the format can support national learning standards and literacy skills." (Publisher's note)

"This informative resource establishes the literacy benefits of audiobooks as an alternate reading delivery method... Discussions of audiobook formats and recommended sources for building an audiobook collection are also included. The authors provide a collaborative resource that would benefit a classroom, library, or home setting." (Library Media Connection)

Includes bibliographical references (p. 175-178) and index

372.5   The arts

Art and social justice education; culture as commons. edited by Therese Quinn, John Ploof, and Lisa Hochtritt. Routledge 2012 xxiii, 201 p.p ill. (some col.)   **372.5**
    1. Culture 2. Educators 3. Education -- Curricula 4. Arts -- Study and teaching 5. Art in education -- Social aspects 6. Social justice -- Study and teaching 7. Teaching -- Social aspects -- United States 8. Education -- Social aspects -- United States
    ISBN 0415879078; 9780203852477; 9780415879064; 9780415879071
                    LC 2011027006

Editor Therese Quinn "offers inspiration and tools for educators to craft critical, meaningful, and transformative arts education curriculum and arts integration projects. The images, descriptive texts, essays, and resources are grounded within a clear social justice framework and linked to ideas about culture . . . Proposing that art can contribute in a wide range of ways to the work of envisioning and making a more just world, this imaginative . . . sourcebook of contemporary artists' works and education resources advances the field of arts education." (Amazon)

Includes bibliographical references and index

372.6   Language arts (Communication skills)

Maguire, James

American bee; the National Spelling Bee and the culture of word nerds: the lives of five top spellers as they compete for glory and fame. Rodale 2006 371p $24.95   **372.6**

1. Spelling bees 2. English language -- Spelling
ISBN 978-1-59486-214-4; 1-59486-214-1

LC 2005-37443

"From the nail-biting denouement of the 2004 Bee, Maguire . . . moves on to brief sketches of some past winners and then takes an informative and wryly humorous look at the English language itself and the evolution of the American spelling bee from Puritan pastime to major media event." Libr J

Includes bibliographical references

373   Secondary education

Klebold, Sue

A mother's reckoning; living in the aftermath of tragedy. Sue Klebold. Crown 2016 272 p. illustrations (hardcover) $28; (ebook) $65   **373**

1. Columbine High School (Littleton, Colo.) 2. Columbine High School Massacre, Littleton, Colo., 1999 3. School shootings -- Colorado -- Littleton 4. Mothers -- Colorado -- Littleton -- Biography
ISBN 9781101902752; 9781101902769

LC 2015018513

This memoir by Sue Klebold, mother of mass murderer Dylan Klebold of the Columbine High School massacre, chronicles "her journey as a mother trying to come to terms with the incomprehensible. In the hope that the insights . . . she has gained may help other families recognize when a child is in distress, she tells her story in full, drawing upon her personal journals, the videos and writings that Dylan left behind, and on . . . interviews with mental health experts." (Publisher's note)

"Klebold's painful memoir unfolds with more sorrow than drama; readers will be left with the sense that even the 'best' mother cannot know what her child may be feeling or thinking." Booklist

Includes bibliographical references (pages 285-292) and index.

373.1   Organization and activities in secondary education

Keizer, Garret

Getting Schooled; The Reeducation of an American Teacher. Garret Keizer. Henry Holt & Co 2014 320 p. $27   **373.1**

1. Teachers 2. Teaching 3. High schools 4. Rural schools 5. Public schools -- Vermont -- Case studies 6. High school teaching -- Vermont -- Case studies 7. High school teachers -- Professional relationships -- Vermont

-- Case studies
ISBN 0805096434; 9780805096439

LC 2013042594

In this book, "teacher and writer Garret Keizer takes us to school--literally--in this arresting account of his return to the same rural Vermont high school where he taught fourteen years ago. Much has changed since then--a former student is his principal, standardized testing is the reigning god, and smoking in the boys' room has been supplanted by texting in the boys' room." (Publisher's note)

"[A]t once a sympathetic portrait of a school, a searing indictment of a culture that uses working-class children as cannon fodder, and, unexpectedly, a page-turner." Pub Wkly

373.1262   Standardized tests—Secondary education

The official guide to the HiSET exam; Educational Testing Service. McGraw-Hill 2016 768 p. illustrations (paperback) $23   **373.1262**

1. Examinations -- Study guides 2. High school equivalency examinations
ISBN 1259640795; 9781259640797

This resource in the Official Guide to the Hiset Exam series from Educational Testing Service "shows you exactly what the real exam is like. You'll learn how the test is structured, which topics are tested, and how to approach specific HiSET questions, so there will be no surprises on test day. You'll also get HiSET-style exercises, review material, scoring information, and proven test-taking strategies." (Publisher's note)

373.22   Private and public secondary schools

Brick, Michael

Saving the school; the true story of a principal, a teacher, a coach, a bunch of kids, and a year in the crosshairs of education reform. Michael Brick. Penguin Press 2012 288 p. (hardback) $25.95 **373.22**

1. High schools 2. Schools -- Administration 3. School superintendents and principals 4. John H. Reagan High School (Austin, Tex.) 5. School improvement programs -- Texas -- Austin
ISBN 159420344X; 9781594203442

LC 2011050569

This book presents an "account of a troubled Austin, Texas, school that endured a year of tough medicine while facing shutdown. . . . When Reagan was given one more chance to bring up test scores or face closure as part of the national get-tough approach to school reform headed by the new president, . . . [Michael] Brick immersed himself in the lives of the teachers and students. . . . He focuses especially on . . . the school's principal, Anabel Garza." (Kirkus Reviews)

374   Adult education

John, Lauren Z.

Running book discussion groups; a how-to-do-it manual. [by] Lauren Zina John. Neal-Schuman Publishers 2006 250p (How-to-do-it manual for librarians) pa $55   **374**

1. Books and reading 2. Discussion groups

ISBN 1-55570-542-1; 978-1-55570-542-8

LC 2006-704

This is a "step-by-step guide to the tasks and responsibilities librarians are likely to encounter as book-group leaders conducting booktalks both on-site and online. . . . This is essential reading for anyone who may be considering taking on the role of a book-discussion-group leader and a refresher for the more experienced among us." Booklist

Includes bibliographical references

Rose, Mike

Back to school; why everyone deserves a second chance at education. Mike Rose. New Press, The 2012 224 p. (hardcover) $21.95   **374**

1. Adult education 2. College students 3. Higher education

ISBN 9781595587862

LC 2012021135

This book by Mike Rose "look[s] at the schools that serve a growing population of . . . [non-traditional students] exploring what higher education . . . can offer our rapidly changing society." (Publisher's note) "Rose explores the need for a reassessment of the post–K-12 educational system, noting that growing sectors of the labor market require a four- or even two-year degree." (Kirkus Reviews)

Includes bibliographical references

378   Higher education (Tertiary education)

Book of Majors; the only book that describes majors and lists the colleges that offer them. College Board   **378**

1. Colleges and universities -- Curricula 2. Colleges and universities -- United States

Annual. First published 1977 with title: The college handbook index of majors. Variant titles: The College Board book of majors; The College Board index of majors and graduate degrees; Index of majors and graduate degrees

Provides information on over nine hundred college majors, including related fields, prior high school subjects, possible courses of study, and career options and trends for graduates.

Dreifus, Claudia

Higher education? how colleges are wasting our money and failing our kids--and what we can do about it. [by] Andrew Hacker and Claudia Dreifus. Times Books 2010 271p il $26   **378**

1. College costs 2. Higher education 3. College teachers -- United States 4. Colleges and universities

-- Faculty

ISBN 978-0-8050-8734-5; 0-8050-8734-6

LC 2010-07219

Hacker and Dreifus "draw up a powerful, if rambling, indictment of academic careerism. The authors are not shy about making biting judgments along the way. . . . [They conclude] with capsule summaries of, as they put it, 'Schools We Like'—that is, schools that offer superior undergraduate educations at relatively low cost." Wall Street J

Includes bibliographical references

Fiske, Edward B.

Fiske guide to colleges. Sourcebooks   **378**

1. College choice 2. Colleges and universities -- United States

Annual. First published 1982 with title: The New York Times selective guide to colleges

This guide to over 300 of the best colleges and universities nationwide includes information on admissions, costs, financial aid, housing, social life, and academic strengths and weaknesses.

Selingo, Jeffrey J.

College (un)bound; the future of higher education and what it means for students. Jeffrey J. Selingo. Houghton Mifflin Harcourt 2013 xviii, 238 p.p (hardcover) $26   **378**

1. Higher education 2. Colleges and universities -- Finance 3. College students -- United States 4. Educational planning -- United States 5. Universities and colleges -- United States

ISBN 0544027078; 9780544027077

LC 2013001941

This book offers an analysis of "middle-tier American colleges" and highlights "forward-thinking educational models. [Jeffrey J.] Selingo . . . describes a climate in which colleges compete for rankings by improving amenities, falling into an escalating cycle of tuition increases and larger financial aid packages that leave students with crushing debt, and a sense of students as consumers that leads to grade inflation and teaching compromises." (Publishers Weekly)

Includes bibliographical references and index.

Williams, Juan

I'll find a way or make one; a tribute to historically Black colleges and universities. by Juan Williams and Dwayne Ashley. Amistad/HarperCollins 2004 xxiv, 453p il $35   **378**

1. African American universities and colleges 2. African Americans -- Education

ISBN 0-06-009453-2

LC 2004-46450

The authors "explore America's 107 historically black colleges and universities, in existence for 172 years, showing how the schools were created and how black and white abolitionists united to educate newly freed slaves." Libr J

Includes bibliographical references

378.1 Organization and activities in higher education

Albom, Mitch, 1958-

Tuesdays with Morrie; an old man, a young man, and life's greatest lesson. Mitch Albom. Doubleday 1997 192 p. pa $13.99; $20.00 **378.1**
1. Amyotrophic lateral sclerosis 2. Sociologists 3. College teachers 4. Brandeis University -- Faculty -- Biography 5. Death -- Psychological aspects -- Case studies 6. Teacher-student relationships -- United States -- Case studies 7. Amyotrophic lateral sclerosis -- Patients -- United States -- Biography
ISBN 076790592X pa; 0385484518

LC 96052535

This book discusses the author's relationship with his former teacher and mentor, "sociologist Morrie Schwartz. Here [Mitch] Albom recounts how . . . as the old man was dying, he renewed his warm relationship with his revered mentor. This is the . . . record of the teacher's battle with muscle-wasting amyotrophic lateral sclerosis, or Lou Gehrig's disease. The dying man, largely because of his life-affirming attitude toward his death-dealing illness, became a sort of thanatopic guru, and was the subject of three Ted Koppel interviews on Nightline. That was how the author first learned of Morrie's condition. Albom . . . calls his weekly visits to his teacher his last class, and the present book a term paper. The subject: The Meaning of Life . . . Albom does not present a full transcript of the regular Tuesday talks. Rather, he expands a little on the professor's aphorisms." (Kirkus)

"As a student at Brandeis University in the late 1970s, Albom was especially drawn to his sociology professor, Morris Schwartz. On graduation he vowed to keep in touch with him, which he failed to do until 1994, when he saw a segment about Schwartz on the TV program Nightline, and learned that he had just been diagnosed with Lou Gehrig's disease. By then a sports columnist for the Detroit Free Press . . . Albom was idled by the newspaper strike in the Motor City and so had the opportunity to visit Schwartz in Boston every week until the older man died. Their dialogue is the subject of this moving book." Publ Wkly

Bain, Ken

What the best college students do; Ken Bain. The Belknap Press of Harvard University Press 2012 289 p. (alk. paper) $24.95 **378.1**
1. College students 2. Academic achievement 3. College students -- United States 4. Academic achievement -- United States
ISBN 0674066642; 9780674066649

LC 2012015548

In this book, author Ken Bain "identifies the key attitudes that distinguished the best college students from their peers. These individuals started out with the belief that intelligence and ability are expandable, not fixed. This led them to make connections across disciplines, to develop a 'metacognitive' understanding of their own ways of thinking, and to find ways to negotiate ill-structured problems rather than simply looking for right answers." (Publisher's note)

"A soundly encouraging guide for college students to think deeply and for as long as it takes." Kirkus
Includes bibliographical references and index

Beyond the asterisk; understanding Native students in higher education. edited by Heather Shotton, Shelly Lowe, and Stephanie J. Waterman. Stylus 2013 xvi, 189 p.p (cloth : alk. paper) $85 **378.1**
1. Foreign students 2. Students -- United States 3. Native Americans -- Education
ISBN 157922623X; 9781579226237; 9781579226244

LC 2012040238

Editor Heather J. Shotton's book discusses Native American students in higher education. "The purpose of this book is to move beyond the asterisk in an effort to better understand Native students, challenge the status quo, and provide an informed base for leaders in student and academic affairs, and administrators concerned with the success of students on their campuses." (Publisher's note)
Includes bibliographical references and index

Crossman, Anne

Getting the best out of college; insider advice for success from a professor, a dean, and a recent grad. Peter Feaver, Sue Wasiolek, Anne Crossman. Rev. and updated, 2nd ed. Ten Speed Press 2012 xiv, 289 p.p (pbk.) $14.99 **378.1**
1. Counseling 2. College students 3. Colleges and universities -- United States 4. College student orientation -- United States
ISBN 160774144X; 9781607741442

LC 2011051246

This book, by authors Peter Feaver, Sue Wasiolek, and Anne Crossman, "reveals insider advice that makes the hefty price tag worth it: how to impress professors, live with a roommate, pick the best courses (and do well in them), design a meaningful transcript, earn remarkable internships, prepare for a successful career after graduation, and much more." (Publisher's note)

Fiske, Edward B.

Fiske Guide to Getting Into The Right College; Edward B. Fiske & Bruce G. Hammond. 6th edition Sourcebooks 2016 385 p. pbk $16.99 **378.1**
1. College choice 2. College applications 3. Colleges and universities -- United States
ISBN 9781492633303; 1492633305

This book by Edward Fiske and Bruce Hammond is designed to "help you generate a list of schools you love and walk you step-by-step through the process of applying to them. [It] will show you how to: Discover which schools are right for you based on academic programs, size, location, institutional culture, and more." (Publisher's note)

Jager-Hyman, Joie

B + grades, A+ college application; how to present your strongest self, write a stand-out admissions essay, and get into the perfect school for you. by Joie Jager-Hyman, EdD. Random House Inc 2013 ix, 246 p.p (paperback) $14.99 **378.1**
1. Student aid 2. College applications 3. Exposition

(Rhetoric) 4. College applications -- United States 5. Universities and colleges -- United States -- Admission
ISBN 1607743418; 9781607743415

LC 2013004970

In this book, college admissions consultant Joie Jager-Hyman "guides students (and their parents) through the college-admissions process, offering a wealth of insider advice. . . . Jager-Hyman covers the usual steps: developing a list of target, reach, and safety schools; writing essays; prepping for the college interview; taking the SATs; and demystifying financial aid." (Publishers Weekly)

The **Latino** student's guide to college success; Leonard A. Valverde, editor. Greenwood 2012 xiv, 270 p.p (alk. paper) $58   **378.1**
1. Hispanic Americans -- Education (Higher) -- Handbooks, manuals, etc. 2. Universities and colleges -- United States -- Directories 3. Hispanic Americans -- Education (Higher) -- Handbooks, manuals, etc
ISBN 031339797X; 0313397988; 9780313397974; 9780313397981

LC 2012010827

This book, edited by Leonard A. Valverde, provides "advice directed specifically to Latinos contemplating, preparing for, or already in the university or community college setting. This volume contains the 8 Steps to College Success, numerous vignettes of notable Latinos in many fields who give their personal story of how they succeeded in college and their advice for today's students, and a directory of top Latino universities and community colleges." (Publisher's note)

Pekar, Harvey
Students for a Democratic Society; a graphic history. written by Harvey Pekar; art by Gary Dumm; edited by Paul Buhle. Hill & Wang 2008 214p il pa $16; $22   **378.1**
1. Graphic novels 2. College students -- Political activity -- Graphic novels 3. Students for a Democratic Society -- Graphic novels -- History
ISBN 978-0-8090-8939-0 pa; 978-0-8090-9539-1

LC 2007-40641

Students for a Democratic Society formed as an organization in 1960, but had its roots as a New Left group in the League for Industrial Democracy, founded in 1905 with members such as Jack London and Upton Sinclair. The members in 1960 included Al Haber and Tom Hayden, and one of their most famous documents is the Port Huron Statement of 1962. By the late 1960s, with opposition to the Vietnam War in full swing, a radical subgroup called the Weathermen became more violent. Graphic novelist Pekar is joined by members of the SDS in telling the story of the organization, which dissolved soon after its 1969 convention. The book includes some harsh language and violence.

"The book acts like a sophisticated handbook on an often misunderstood organization. It's good comics and excellent history." Publ Wkly

Rosenfeld, Seth, 1956-
Subversives; the FBI's war on student radicals, and Reagan's rise to power. Seth Rosenfeld. Farrar,

Straus and Giroux 2012 752 p. ill., map (alk. paper) $40.00   **378.1**
1. United States. Federal Bureau of Investigation 2. California -- Politics and government -- 1951- 3. Student movements -- California -- Berkeley -- History 4. University of California, Berkeley -- Students -- History 5. Subversive activities -- California -- Berkeley -- History 6. College students -- Political activity -- California -- Berkeley -- History
ISBN 0374257000; 9780374257002

LC 2011041204

This book "traces the FBI's secret involvement with three iconic figures at Berkeley during the 1960s: the ambitious neophyte politician Ronald Reagan, the fierce but fragile radical Mario Savio, and the liberal university president Clark Kerr. Through these converging narratives, the award-winning investigative reporter Seth Rosenfeld tells . . . of FBI surveillance, illegal break-ins, infiltration, planted news stories, poison-pen letters, and secret detention lists." (Publisher's note)
Includes bibliographical references

Shachtman, Tom
Airlift to America; how Barack Obama, Sr., John F. Kennedy, Tom Mboya, and 800 East African students changed their world and ours. St. Martin's Press 2009 273p il $24.99   **378.1**
1. College students 2. African-American Students Federation 3. East Africa -- Foreign relations -- United States 4. United States -- Foreign relations -- East Africa
ISBN 978-0-312-57075-0

LC 2009-13186

"In the late 1950s, before Kenya's independence from Britain, Kenyan leader Tom Mboya and American philanthropist William Scheinman joined to develop a cadre of educated young people to staff the government and schools. Between 1959 and 1963, nearly 800 African students were flown to the U.S. to be educated and to return to become the 'founding brothers and sisters' of their East African nations. Among them were Wangari Maathai, who went on to become an environmentalist and 2004 Nobel Peace Prize winner, and Barack Obama Sr., father of the future president of the U.S. Shachtman provides historical perspective of cold war politics in African nations, countervailing loyalties to European colonial powers, and the appeal of U.S. ideals of independence." Booklist
Includes bibliographical references

Steinberg, Jacques
The **gatekeepers**; inside the admissions process of a premier college. Viking 2002 xxiii, 292p hardcover o.p. pa $15   **378.1**
1. College applications 2. Wesleyan University (Middletown, Conn.)
ISBN 0-670-03135-6; 0-14-200308-5 pa

LC 2002-16884

"This insightful and readable book should be purchased by all academic and large public libraries." Libr J
Includes bibliographical references

Ventrone, Jillian

From the Marine Corps to college; transitioning from the service to higher education. by Jillian Ventrone. Rowan & Littlefield 2014 224 p. (cloth : alk. paper) $35 **378.1**

1. Veterans -- Education 2. United States. Marine Corps 3. Marines -- Education -- United States 4. Veterans -- Education -- United States

ISBN 9781442237209

LC 2014013314

This book, by Jillian Ventrone, was designed "to help Marines navigate the world of higher education and their available state and federal benefits. . . . [It] will better prepare veterans for tackling their new mission: college. . . . [It] can be read as a book from cover-to-cover, or as a reference manual section-by-section. The easy to follow format will assist Marines in furthering their educational goals." (Publisher's note)

"Despite its limitations, this title will appeal to marines and do well in libraries serving this population; otherwise, it is a supplemental purchase." LJ

Includes bibliographical references and index

378.161 Admissions--Higher education

Bruni, Frank

Where You Go Is Not Who You'll Be; An Antidote to the College Admissions Mania. by Frank Bruni. Grand Central Pub 2016 262 p. $14.99 **378.161**

1. College choice 2. College applications

ISBN 1455532681; 9781455532681

LC 2014049043

In this book, author Frank Bruni "shows that the Ivy League has no monopoly on corner offices, governors' mansions, or the most prestigious academic and scientific grants. Through statistics, surveys, and the stories of hugely successful people who didn't attend the most exclusive schools, he demonstrates that many kinds of colleges-large public universities, tiny hideaways in the hinterlands-serve as ideal springboards." (Publisher's note)

"Written in a lively style but carrying a wallop, this is a book that family and educators cannot afford to overlook as they try to navigate the treacherous waters of college admissions." Kirkus

Chatterjee, Pria

The **dirty** little secrets of getting into a top college; Pria Chatterjee. Regan Arts 2015 180 p. illustrations $22.95 **378.161**

1. College choice 2. College applications

ISBN 1941393020; 9781941393024

LC 2014955519

In this book, author Pria Chatterjee "simplifies the complicated process of college admissions, providing parents and students with the tools needed to secure a spot at one of America's most competitive colleges. . . . Through a series of real-world case studies and with a store of deep insider knowledge, Chatterjee will help you navigate the thicket of college admissions." (Publisher's note)

378.3 Student aid and related topics

2015 getting financial aid; by The College Board. Henry Holt & Co 2014 1013 p. $23.99 **378.3**

1. College costs 2. Student loan funds

ISBN 1457303183; 9781457303180

LC 2007227619

This book "is for parents and students challenged by the cost of college. The all-important FAFSA form is explained with step-by-step instructions, and the College Board's CSS/Financial Aid PROFILE® form is explained by the people who administer it. The guide includes information and advice from experts on how to apply for aid, plus easy-to-compare college profiles giving the 'financial aid picture' for more than 3,000 four-year and two-year colleges and technical schools." (Publisher's note)

Collinge, Alan

The **student** loan scam; the most oppressive debt in U.S. history, and how we can fight back. Beacon Press 2008 167p $22.95 **378.3**

1. Student loan funds

ISBN 978-0-8070-4229-8; 0-8070-4229-3

LC 2008-12230

"Comprehensive and stirring, this extraordinary book is whistle-blowing at its finest." Publ Wkly

Includes bibliographical references

Peterson's how to get money for college 2015; Peterson's. Petersons 2014 944 p. $29.95 **378.3**

1. Student aid

ISBN 0768938686; 9780768938685

This book "is a great resource for anyone looking to supplement his or her federal financial aid package with aid from colleges and universities. This comprehensive directory points you to complete and accurate information on need-based and non-need gift aid, loans, work-study, athletic awards, and more. The unique and easy-to-use Colleges-at-a-Glance comparison chart lists the full costs that can be expected, aid packages, and more." (Publisher's note)

378.73 Colleges--United States

Delbanco, Andrew

College; what it was, is, and should be. Andrew Delbanco. Princeton University Press 2012 xiv, 229 p.p (hardcover) $24.95 **378.73**

1. Higher education 2. Colleges and universities

ISBN 0691130736; 9780691130736

LC 2011039399

This book presents an "assessment of how American higher education has lost its way. [Andrew Delbanco] starts with the American ideal, dating back to the Puritans, of college as a place that trained the whole person. . . . In modern America, that focus has shifted: Now it's less about the eternal verities than chasing after dollars, more about filling seats than heads and more about science than the humanities." (Kirkus Reviews)

Includes bibliographical references and index

Mettler, Suzanne

Degrees of inequality; how the politics of higher education sabotaged the American dream. Suzanne Mettler. Basic Books, a member of the Perseus Books Group 2014 272 p. illustrations (hardback) $27.99   **378.73**

1. College costs 2. American dream 3. Higher education 4. Education -- United States 5. Educational change -- United States

ISBN 0465044964; 9780465044962

LC 2013043678

In this book, political scientist Suzanne Mettler "explains why the . . . American Dream is increasingly out of reach for so many. . . . She illuminates how political partisanship has overshadowed America's commitment to equal access to higher education. As politicians capitulate to corporate interests, owners of for-profit colleges benefit, but for far too many students, higher education leaves them with little besides crippling student loan debt." (Publisher's note)

"Though the book orbits the central theme of the for-profits and their outsized political influence, [Mettler] frames this with a history of higher education and its attendant laws, as well as an excellent introduction to political science that explains—in approachable language—the myriad impacts of law and the ways in which the intentions of legislators are often deformed." Pub Wkly

Includes bibliographical references and index

Peterson's four-year colleges 2015; by Peterson's. Petersons 2014 1697 p. illustrations $32.95   **378.73**

1. College choice 2. Colleges and universities

ISBN 0768938635; 9780768938630

LC 2002258012

This book "includes information on every accredited four-year undergraduate institution in the U.S. and Canada (and many international schools). . . . It also includes detailed two-page descriptions written by admissions personnel for over 300 colleges and universities. College-bound students and their parents can access details including campus setting, enrollment, academic programs, entrance difficulty, expenses, student-faculty ratio, application deadline, and contact information." (Publisher's note)

Peterson's two-year colleges 2015; by Peterson's. Petersons 2014 513 p. illustrations $29.95   **378.73**

1. College choice 2. Junior colleges

ISBN 0768938694; 9780768938692

LC 2002258012

This book "includes information on more than 1,900 accredited two-year undergraduate institutions in the United States and Canada, as well as some international schools. It also includes detailed two-page descriptions written by admissions personnel. College-bound students and their parents can research two-year colleges, including community colleges, for information on campus setting, enrollment, majors, expenses, student-faculty ratio, application deadline, and contact information." (Publisher's note)

Profiles of American colleges 2015; by Barron's College Division Staff. Barrons Educational Series Inc 2014 1664 p. $28.99   **378.73**

1. College choice 2. Colleges and universities

ISBN 143800429X; 9781438004297

This guidebook "gives college-bound students online information and guidance to help them match their academic plans and aptitudes with the admission requirements and academic programs of every accredited four-year college in the country. The brand-new 31st edition . . . describes more than 1,650 colleges, with up-to-date facts and figures." (Publisher's note)

379   Public policy issues in education

Greenawalt, Kent

Does God belong in public schools? Princeton University Press 2005 261p $29.95   **379**

1. Church and state 2. Religion in the public schools

ISBN 0691121117

LC 2004-45779

The author "considers issues ranging from the teaching of evolution to parents' rights that their children not be exposed to offensive curriculum. He grounds his analyses in a review of the history and purposes of schooling. . . . His legal and philosophical lines of scholarship come together to produce a nonpartisan consideration of the crucial issues facing US courts and the country." Choice

Includes bibliographical references

Kozol, Jonathan

★ The shame of the nation; the restoration of apartheid schooling in America. Crown Publishers 2005 404p $25; pa $14.95   **379**

1. Segregation in education

ISBN 1-4000-5244-0; 1-4000-5245-9 pa

LC 2005-8626

"Readers interested in public education will appreciate—and be challenged by—this compelling book." Booklist

Includes bibliographical references

Ravitch, Diane, 1938-

The death and life of the great American school system; how testing and choice are undermining education. Basic Books 2010 283p $26.95   **379**

1. School choice 2. Educational tests and measurements 3. Public schools -- United States 4. Educational accountability -- United States 5. Educational tests and measurements -- United States

ISBN 978-0-465-01491-0; 0-465-01491-7

LC 2009-50406

Ravitch critiques "ideas for restructuring schools, including privatization, standardized testing, punitive accountability, and the . . . multiplication of charter schools." (Publisher's note) Index.

The author "provides an important and highly readable examination of the educational system, how it fails to prepare students for life after graduation, and how we can put it back on track. . . . Anyone interested in education should definitely read this accessible, riveting book." Libr J

Includes bibliographical references

379.26 Educational equalization

Green, Kristen
Something Must Be Done About Prince Edward County; A Family, a Virginia Town, a Civil Rights Battle. HarperCollins 2015 336 p. 8 plates; illustrations $25.99 **379.26**
1. Blacks -- Segregation 2. Segregation in education
ISBN 0062268678; 9780062268679
LC 2015295454

This book by Kristen Green "reveals a little-known chapter of American history: the period after the Brown v. Board of Education decision when one Virginia school system refused to integrate. In the wake of the Supreme Court's unanimous decision in the case of Brown v. Board of Education, Virginia's Prince Edward County refused to obey the law. Rather than desegregate, the county closed its public schools." (Publisher's note)

"Green's work brims with real-life detail from the journalist's eye and ear and joins the likes of Diane McWhorter's Carry Me Home in further developing the dimensions of the South's desegregation struggle—particularly from the perspective of white communities—for general readers and scholars of the late 20th-century civil rights movement." LJ

Wilder, Craig Steven
★ Ebony and Ivy; Race, Slavery, and the Troubled History of America's Universities. by Craig Wilder. Bloomsbury 2013 448 p. $30 **379.26**
1. Higher education 2. Slavery -- United States -- History 3. Race discrimination -- United States 4. Slavery -- United States 5. United States -- Race relations 6. Racism in education -- United States 7. African Americans -- Education (Higher) History 8. Discrimination in higher education -- United States 9. Universities and colleges -- United States -- History 10. Minorities -- Education (Higher) -- United States -- History
ISBN 1596916818; 9781596916814
LC 2013011971

In this book, author Craig Steven Wilder examines the relationship among "race, slavery, and the American academy. Wilder shows, our leading universities, dependent on human bondage, became breeding grounds for the racist ideas that sustained them . . . revealing a history of oppression behind the institutions usually considered the cradle of liberal politics." (Publisher's note)

Includes bibliographical references and index

381 Commerce (Trade)

Bond's Top 100 Franchises, 2015; edited by Robert E. Bond. Source Book Publications 2015 392 p. $24.95 **381**
1. Franchises (Retail trade)
ISBN 1887137939; 9781887137935
This book, edited by Robert E. Bond, "assesses a wide variety of variables to give readers the leading franchises out of more than 3,500 under consideration. The final selection is based on a number of factors, including historical perfor-

mance, competitive advantage, franchisee satisfaction, and financial stability." (Publisher's note)

Cassidy, John
How markets fail; the logic of economic calamities. Farrar, Straus and Giroux 2009 390p il **381**
1. Monetary policy 2. Stock exchanges 3. Financial crises 4. Banks and banking
ISBN 0374173206; 9780374173203
LC 2009029529

"Cassidy describes the rising influence of what he calls utopian economics—thinking that is blind to how real people act and that denies the many ways an unregulated free market can produce disastrous unintended consequences." (Publisher's note) Index.

"The author focuses primarily on the rise and fall of free market ideology and the mostly unrealistic ideal of a self-correcting marketplace. An excellent comprehensive history of the economic thought that led to this kind of utopian economics provides a refresher course in Adam Smith, Friedrich August von Hayek, Kenneth Arrow and Hyman Minsky." Publ Wkly

Includes bibliographical references

Dolin, Eric Jay
Fur, fortune, and empire; the epic history of the fur trade in America. W.W. Norton & Co. 2010 442p il map $29.95 **381**
1. Fur trade 2. Europe -- Colonies -- America 3. Fur trade -- North America -- History 4. Fur trade -- Western States -- History 5. Frontier and pioneer life -- North America
ISBN 978-0-393-06710-1
LC 2010016212

This is an "overview of the American fur trade from Colonial times until the beginnings of the conservation movement of the late 19th century. . . . From the Iroquoian 'Beaver Wars' of the mid-1600s to the brutal Russian domination of Alaskan native hunters, Dolin successfully shows how America's natural history is a vital part of our collective national history." Libr J

Includes bibliographical references

Eltis, David
Atlas of the transatlantic slave trade; [by] David Eltis and David Richardson; foreword by David Brion Davis; afterword by David W. Blight. Yale University Press 2010 xxvi, 307p il map (The Lewis Walpole series in eighteenth-century culture and history) $50 **381**
1. Atlases 2. Reference books 3. Slave trade -- Maps
ISBN 978-0-300-12460-6

"For nearly 20 years, the Trans-Atlantic Slave Trade Database project has been diligently tabulating all the slave ship crossings of the Atlantic Ocean, from 1500 to 1900. . . . With 189 informative and handsome maps, Eltis and Richardson relay and interpret the information contained in this rich database, mixing in beautiful historical illustrations and key passages from relevant texts. An accessible narrative, meanwhile, expands on the information in the maps. . . . This marvelous book will change how people think of the slave trade." Foreign Affairs

Mitchell, Stacy

Big-box swindle; the true cost of mega-retailers and the fight for America's independent businesses. Beacon Press 2006 318p $24.95; pa $15   **381**
   1. Chain stores 2. Retail trade 3. Small business
ISBN 978-0-8070-3500-9; 0-8070-3500-9; 978-0-8070-3501-6 pa; 0-8070-3501-7 pa
                LC 2006-13818

Mitchell's "call to action reveals the hidden costs of those 'low prices' promoted by the big-box bullies and gives hope to local entrepreneurs and concerned citizens alike." Booklist
   Includes bibliographical references

Sennett, Frank

Groupon's biggest deal ever; the inside story of how one insane gamble, tons of unbelievable hype, and millions of wild deals made billions for one ballsy joker. Frank Sennett. St. Martin's Press 2012 310 p. (hbk.) $25.99   **381**
   1. Groupon (Firm) 2. Internet industry 3. Internet marketing 4. Coupons (Retail trade) 5. Internet advertising
ISBN 125000084X; 1250014948; 9781250000842; 9781250014948
                LC 2012009440

This book looks at daily deal website Groupon. The firm's "CEO Andrew Mason takes center stage in this story about the company's founding, development, and explosive assent." Author Frank Sennett starts "from November 2006, when Mason first pitched the idea for Policy Tree (Groupon's precursor) to Eric Lefkofsky, the man who became Groupon's chairman, to early November 2011, when Groupon finally went public on the NASDAQ stock exchange." (Publishers Weekly)

Spector, Robert

The **mom** & pop store; how the unsung heroes of the American economy are surviving and thriving. Walker Pub. Co. 2009 293p $26   **381**
   1. Small business 2. Business enterprises
ISBN 978-0-8027-1605-7
                LC 2009-19198

"Lively lessons about business ethics and practices that Fortune 500 companies, the author suggests, would be wise to follow." Kirkus
   Includes bibliographical references

Stanton, Maureen

Killer stuff and tons of money; seeking history and hidden gems in flea-market America. Penguin Press 2011 326p $26.95   **381**
   1. Antiques 2. Flea markets
ISBN 978-1-59420-293-3; 1-59420-293-1
                LC 2010-53099

Before Stanton "reconnected with her pseudonymous old college friend, 'Curt Avery,' who had become a professional antiques dealer, she was 'the self-anointed Queen of the Flea-Market Dollar Table.' Like many Americans, she was on the lookout for an appealing bargain and just as happy with an inexpensive reproduction as the real thing. When

she and Avery met again in 2000, she agreed to fly across the country to attend an auction where some old bottles that he coveted were on offer. He asked her to be his proxy bidder while he hid at the back and signaled his bids. This was her introduction to a fascinating subculture, which she calls 'the flea realm.' Over the years, she attended many fairs and flea markets with Avery as what she calls a 'participant observer,' getting up before dawn to help him set up displays, grabbing food on the run and camping out next to his truck at night. . . . A treasure-trove of a book, especially for would-be antiquers." Kirkus
   Includes bibliographical references

Whitaker, Jan

Service and style; how the American department store fashioned the middle class. St. Martin's Press 2006 342p il $35   **381**
   1. Middle class 2. Department stores
ISBN 978-0-312-32635-7; 0-312-32635-1
                LC 2006-40542

"At their peak, department stores were the nation's largest booksellers and many major chains also sold groceries. But it was clothes that made the stores a prime destination for women of all social classes, and Whitaker discusses at significant length the subtle movements through which major chains from one end of the country to the other cultivated their reputations for being up-to-date with the latest Paris fashions, then tapped into additional markets for young adult and children's wear. More than 100 photographs and illustrations are integrated into the text, aptly demonstrating the lengths to which stores went in order to present themselves as elegant yet modern and convenient." Publ Wkly
   Includes bibliographical references

Ziegler, Mel

Wild company; the untold story of Banana Republic. Mel and Patricia Ziegler. Simon & Schuster 2012 208 p.   **381**
   1. Clothing industry 2. Banana Republic Travel and Safari Company 3. Clothing trade -- United States 4. Fashion merchandising -- United States
ISBN 1451683480; 9781451683486; 9781451683509; 9781451683516
                LC 2012030040

This book, by Mel and Patricia Ziegler, describes how the authors "turned a wild idea into a company that would become the international retail colossus Banana Republic. Re-imagining military surplus as safari and expedition wear, the former journalist and artist created a world that captured the zeitgeist for a generation and spoke to the creativity, adventure, and independence in everyone." (Publisher's note)

382   International commerce (Foreign trade)

Dolin, Eric Jay

When America first met China; an exotic history of tea, drugs, and money in the Age of Sail. Eric Jay Dolin. Liveright Pub. Corp. 2012 394 p.   **382**
   1. China -- History 2. United States -- History 3. China -- Commerce -- United States 4. China -- Foreign economic relations 5. United States -- Foreign

economic relations 6. China -- Commerce -- United States -- History -- 18th century 7. China -- Commerce -- United States -- History -- 19th century 8. United States -- Commerce -- China -- History -- 18th century 9. United States -- Commerce -- China -- History -- 19th century
ISBN 0871404338; 9780871404336

LC 2012016598

In this book, Eric Jay Dolin profiles the early history of United States-China trade. The author "traces . . . [America's] fraught relationship with China back to its roots: . . . a brash, rising naval power . . . [and] a battered ancient empire. . . . [T]he furious trade in furs, opium, and beche-de-mer . . . might have catalyzed America's emerging economy, but it also sparked an ecological and human rights catastrophe . . . that . . . can still be felt today." (Publisher's note)

Includes bibliographical references and index

Goldstein, Natalie

Globalization and free trade; Natalie Goldstein; foreword by Joanna G. Moss. 2nd ed. Facts On File 2012 428 p. (ebook) $54.00; (hardcover) $45.00; (paperback) $18.95; (hardcover) $45.00 **382**
1. Free trade 2. Globalization 3. International economic relations 4. Free trade -- Case studies 5. Globalization -- Economic aspects -- Case studies 6. International economic integration -- Case studies
ISBN 9781438109008; 9780816068081; 9780816077397; 0816083657; 9780816083657

LC 2011004940

This encyclopedia, by Natalie Goldstein, examines international economic issues and "provides an overview of the history of globalization and how it has evolved into its present state." It gives "opinions by proponents and detractors of the issue, and case studies of the United States, East Asia, China, Cochabamba, and Iceland are presented to provide real-world context." (Publisher's note)

Includes bibliographical references and index.

Nabhan, Gary Paul, 1952-

Cumin, camels, and caravans; a spice odyssey. Gary Paul Nabhan. University of California Press 2014 332 p. illustrations some color (California studies in food and culture) (cloth : alk. paper) $29.95 **382**
1. Spices -- History 2. International trade 3. Spice trade 4. Spice trade -- History
ISBN 0520267206; 9780520267206; 9780520956957

LC 2013032714

IACP Cookbook Award Finalist: Culinary History (2015)

In this book author "Gary Paul Nabhan takes the reader on a vivid and far-ranging journey across time and space in this fascinating look at the relationship between the spice trade and culinary imperialism. Drawing on his own family's history as spice traders, as well as travel narratives, historical accounts, and his expertise as an ethnobotanist, Nabhan describes the critical roles that Semitic peoples and desert floras had in setting the stage for globalized spice trade." (Publisher's note)

Includes bibliographical references and index

Rose, Sarah

For all the tea in China; how England stole the world's favorite drink and changed history. Viking 2010 261p $25.95 **382**
1. Tea 2. Horticulturists 3. China -- Description and travel
ISBN 0-670-02152-0; 978-0-670-02152-9

LC 2009-41482

First published 2009 in the United Kingdom

In this book, author Sarah Rose "reconstructs what she posits as the 'greatest theft of trade secrets in the history of mankind.' Tea was grown in China. Great Britain wanted tea. . . . So the East India Company sent hunter [Robert] Fortune, undercover . . . to penetrate the depths of China and surreptitiously gather--steal, in other words--seeds and young plants and send them to India, where they would flourish in soil that was part of the British Empire." (Booklist)

"With her probing inquiry and engaging prose, Sarah Rose paints a fresh and vivid account of life in rural 19th-century China and Fortune's fateful journey into it." Washington Post

Includes bibliographical references

Snyder, Rachel Louise

Fugitive denim; a moving story of people and pants in the borderless world of global trade. W.W. Norton & Company 2008 352p $26.95; pa $16.95 **382**
1. Jeans (Clothing) 2. Clothing industry 3. International trade
ISBN 978-0-393-06180-2; 0-393-06180-9; 978-0-393-33542-2 pa; 0-393-33542-9 pa

LC 2007-24335

"Snyder's investigation is an essential read for those curious about fashion or the globe-spanning business that produces their clothes." Publ Wkly

Includes bibliographical references

383 Communications and transportation

National five digit zip code and post office directory. U.S. Postal Service 2v maps pa $45 **383**
1. Zip code
ISBN 978-1-59804-282-5; 1-59804-282-3

Annual. Continuation of National zip code and post office directory

"Besides ZIP codes and post offices, this directory includes information on the organization of the Postal Service, addressing, parcel weights and sizes, delivery statistics, and other matters." Recomm Ref Books in Paperback. 2d edition

383.49   Postal communication—History, geographic treatment, biography

Gallagher, Winifred

✓ **How** the Post Office Created America; A History. Winifred Gallagher. Penguin Group USA 2016 336 p. (hardcover) $28   **383.49**

1. Postal service -- United States -- History
ISBN 9781594205002; 1594205000

This book, by Winifred Gallagher, "examines the surprising role of the postal service in our nation's political, social, economic, and physical development. . . . This was no conventional mail network but the central nervous system of the new body politic, designed to bind . . . the United States by delivering news about public affairs to every citizen—a radical idea that appalled Europe's great powers." (Publisher's note)

"Gallagher compellingly argues that mail delivery played a vital role in creating American unity via interpersonal communication and points a way forward to a postal service that can remain relevant even in the Internet age." Booklist

384   Communications

Elberse, Anita

✓ **Blockbusters**; hit-making, risk-taking, and the big business of entertainment. Anita Elberse. Henry Holt & Co. 2013 320 p. illustrations (ebook) $40; (hardcover) $30   **384**

1. Celebrities 2. Music trade 3. Motion picture industry 4. Mass media -- Economic aspects
ISBN 9781429945325; 0805094334; 9780805094336
LC 2013014320

This book by Anita Elberse presents "the story of the entertainment blockbuster model and why it isn't going anywhere." It was the author's intent to "identify the strategies entertainment companies employ to maximize profits in a uniquely competitive and unpredictable market. Her . . . conclusion is that there is no surer bet than focusing the lion's share of resources on 'blockbusters,' products intended to make the biggest initial splash with the largest possible audience." (Kirkus Reviews)

"This thought-provoking book will appeal to students of all ages, those in the classroom and well beyond." Booklist
Includes bibliographical references and index

Gertner, Jon

✓ The **idea** factory; Bell Labs and the great age of American innovation. Jon Gertner. Penguin Press 2012 422 p. ill. $29.95   **384**

1. Bell Telephone Laboratories 2. Telecommunication -- History 3. Technological innovations -- History 4. Inventors -- United States -- History -- 20th century 5. Bell Telephone Laboratories -- History -- 20th century 6. Creative ability -- United States -- History -- 20th century 7. Telecommunication -- United States -- History -- 20th century 8. Technological innovations -- United States -- History -- 20th century
ISBN 1594203288; 9781594203282
LC 2011040207

This book "traces the history of Bell Labs through more than five decades of brilliant thinking and innovation. From the transistor to lasers to satellites and cellular technology, Bell Labs and its scientists invented machines and techniques that . . . ultimately presaged all of modern communications. . . . Bell Labs became a haven for creative and technical minds due to a unique culture of encouraged interdisciplinary research." (Kirkus Reviews)

"The book is a celebration of basic exploratory research. . . . [T]he writing and the longitudinal biographical portraits are engaging." LJ

Includes bibliographical references (p. [409]-412) and index

Gordon, Robert

Respect yourself; Stax Records and the soul explosion. Robert Gordon. Bloomsbury 2013 480 p. (alk. paper) $30   **384**

1. Soul music 2. Record producers 3. Stax Records -- History 4. Memphis (Tenn.) -- History
ISBN 1596915773; 9781596915770
LC 2013014533

This book by Robert Gordon on the history of Stax Records "situat[es] the story of Stax within the cultural history of the 1960s in the South. . . . Gordon . . . narrates the stories of the many musicians who called Stax home, from . . . Otis Redding to Isaac Hayes, Sam and Dave, and the Staples Singers, as well as the creative marketing and promotional strategies. . . . By the early 1970s, bad business decisions and mangled personal relationships shuttered the doors of Stax." (Publishers Weekly)

"Although treading much of the same ground as Rob Bowman's Soulsville, U.S.A., Gordon's title brings the story up to the present and is both less dense and more objective. For anyone interested in independent record labels and their music in mid-20th-century America." LJ

Includes bibliographical references and index

Knopper, Steve

✓ **Appetite** for self-destruction; the spectacular crash of the record industry in the digital age. Free Press 2009 301p $26   **384**

1. Music industry
ISBN 978-1-4165-5215-4; 1-4165-5215-4
LC 2008-38739

Knopper "provides a wide-angled, morally complicated view of the current state of the music business. He doesn't let those rippers and burners among us—that is, those who download digital songs without paying for them, and you know who you are—entirely off the hook. But he suggests that with even a little foresight, record companies could have adapted to the Internet's brutish and quizzical new realities and thrived." N Y Times Book Rev

Includes bibliographical references

Lapsley, Phil

✓ **Exploding** the Phone; The Untold Story of the Teenagers and Outlaws Who Hacked Ma Bell. by Phil Lapsley; forward by Steve Wozniak. Grove Press 2013 xvi, 431 p.p (hardcover) $26   **384**

1. AT&T (Firm) 2. Telecommunication -- History
ISBN 080212061X; 9780802120618

In this book, Phil Lapsley "uses more than 100 interviews and 400 Freedom of Information Act requests to present the virtually unknown battle between phone companies and overcurious young tech whizzes determined to explore Ma Bell's networks." He "pieces together a . . . re-creation of 1967, a highly significant period in telecommunications history." (Library Journal)

Wu, Tim, ca. 1973-
The **master** switch; the rise and fall of information empires. Alfred A. Knopf 2010 366p il $27.95   **384**
1. Telecommunication 2. Information technology 3. Mass media -- History 4. Telecommunication -- History 5. Information technology -- History
ISBN 978-0-307-26993-5; 0-307-26993-0
LC 2010-04137
"Policy quibbles aside, there's a sharp insight and a surprising fact on nearly every page of Wu's masterful survey. Above all, Wu shows that each new communications technology spawns the same old quest for power." Boston Globe
Includes bibliographical references

384.1   Telegraphy

Gordon, John Steele
A **thread** across the ocean; the heroic story of the transatlantic cable. Walker & Co. 2002 240p il $26   **384.1**
1. Telegraph 2. Submarine cables
ISBN 0-8027-1364-5
LC 2002-66385
The author "has written a lively, engaging account of the extraordinary efforts that brought about this remarkable scientific, technological, and business feat." Libr J
Includes bibliographical references

384.3   Computer communication

Blum, Andrew
Tubes; a journey to the center of the Internet. Andrew Blum. Ecco 2012 294 p.   **384.3**
1. Internet 2. Computer networks 3. Information networks 4. Information technology 5. Information highway 6. Internet -- History 7. Telecommunication systems 8. Internet -- Social aspects
ISBN 0061994936; 9780061994937
LC 2012009519
In this book, "journalist Andrew Blum goes inside the Internet's physical infrastructure. . . . From the room in Los Angeles where the Internet first flickered to life . . . [to] a ten-thousand-mile undersea cable just two thumbs wide [that] connects Europe and Africa, to the wilds of the Pacific Northwest, where Google, Microsoft, and Facebook have built monumental data centers--Blum chronicles the . . . Internet's development, explains how it all works, and takes . . . [a] look inside its hidden monuments." (Publisher's note)
Includes bibliographical references and index.

Dwyer, Jim
More awesome than money; four boys and their heroic quest to save your privacy from Facebook. Jim Dwyer. Viking 2014 384 p. (hardback) $27.95   **384.3**
1. Business failures 2. Social networking 3. New business enterprises 4. Diaspora (Project) 5. Business failures -- United States 6. Internet industry -- United States 7. Privacy, Right of -- United States 8. Online social networks -- United States 9. New business enterprises -- United States
ISBN 0670025607; 9780670025602
LC 2014004511
"Four NYU undergrads wanted to build a social network that would allow users to control their personal data, instead of surrendering it to big businesses like Facebook. They called it Diaspora. In days, they raised $200,000, and reporters, venture capitalists, and the digital community's most legendary figures were soon monitoring their progress. . . . author Jim Dwyer tells a . . . story of four ambitious and naïve young men who tried to rebottle the genie of personal privacy." (Publisher's note)
"A thoroughly compelling account recommended for those interested in general technology books and business narratives. This book is a welcome addition to the literature on start-ups, particularly for its focus on notions of privacy in the digital era and how entrepreneurs are working to address these critical needs." LJ
Includes bibliographical references and index

384.54   Radiobroadcasting

Heil, Alan L.
Voice of America; a history. Columbia University Press 2003 538p $75; pa $26.50   **384.54**
1. Radio broadcasting 2. Voice of America
ISBN 0-231-12674-3; 0-231-12675-1 pa
LC 2002-41019
This is a "history of America's largest publicly funded overseas broadcasting network. . . . From the crises in eastern Europe to the student uprising in Tiananmen Square, Mr Heil provides countless examples of people clinging to their shortwave radios to listen to VOA and other international broadcasters, in spite of intense jamming, to know what was really going on in their own countries. . . . Readers fascinated by the technical intricacies of radio and the arcana of Washington's broadcasting policies will no doubt be riveted." Economist
Includes bibliographical references

385   Railroad transportation

Ambrose, Stephen E.
Nothing like it in the world; the men who built the transcontinental railroad, 1863-1869. Simon & Schuster 2000 471p $28; pa $16   **385**
1. West (U.S.) -- History 2. Central Pacific Railroad 3. Railroads -- United States 4. Union Pacific Railroad

Company

ISBN 0-684-84609-8; 0-7432-0317-8 pa

LC 00-41005

This is an account of the construction of the transcontinental railroad by the Central Pacific and Union Pacific companies

"Ambrose's scholarship seems impeccable. . . . He writes a brisk, colloquial, straightforward prose that not only is easy to read but also bears the reader on shoulders of wonder and excitement." N Y Times Book Rev

Includes bibliographical references

Bain, David Haward

Empire express; building the first transcontinental railroad. Viking 1999 797p il maps hardcover o.p. pa $30   **385**

1. West (U.S.) -- History 2. Central Pacific Railroad 3. Railroads -- United States 4. Union Pacific Railroad Company

ISBN 0-670-80889-X; 0-14-008499-1 pa

LC 99-33375

"Bain knits together excellent storytelling and exhaustive research in a rich contextual tale of vision, ambition, and, ultimately, political and personal corruption." Libr J

Includes bibliographical references

Drabelle, Dennis

The **great** American railroad war; how Ambrose Bierce and Frank Norris took on the notorious Central Pacific Railroad. Dennis Drabelle. St. Martin's Press 2012 306 p. $26.99   **385**

1. Whistle blowing 2. Central Pacific Railroad Company -- History 3. Norris, Frank, 1870-1902 -- Criticism and interpretation 4. Bierce, Ambrose, 1842-1914? -- Criticism and interpretation 5. Railroads -- California -- History -- 19th century 6. Political corruption -- Press coverage -- California

ISBN 0312667590; 9780312667597; 9781250015051

LC 2012010247

Author Dennis Drabelle "examines the role of literature in battling the Central Pacific Railroad monopoly. He recounts the financing of the transcontinental railroad with U.S. government bonds and how the railroad's owners such as Leland Stanford and Collis Huntington enriched themselves in various quasi-legal ways. Though the railroad worked to make itself untouchable by buying influence, Drabelle chronicles how writers Ambrose Bierce and Frank Norris challenged that position." (Library Journal)

Includes bibliographical references

Hayes, Derek

Historical atlas of the North American railroad. University of California Press 2010 224p il map $39.95   **385**

1. Reference books 2. Historical atlases 3. Railroads -- Canada -- Maps 4. Railroads -- North America -- Maps 5. Railroads -- United States -- Maps 6. North America -- Historical geography 7. Railroads -- North America -- History

ISBN 978-0-520-26616-2

LC 2009-943592

"With 400-plus color maps ranging from 1821 to President Obama's report 'A Vision for High Speed Rail,' this historical atlas reveals the richly variegated visual culture of railroad mapping in the US and Canada. Always utilitarian, railroad maps are differentiated into four types: those required to survey the land for construction and attracting investments, timetable maps for passengers, maps in advertising, and engineering maps. . . . The wealth of visual information, comprehensive coverage, and optimistic stance for the future of railroads on the North American continent make this an important purchase for all reference collections." Choice

Includes bibliographical references

McCommons, James

Waiting on a train; the embattled future of passenger rail service. foreword by James Howard Kunstler. Chelsea Green Pub. Company 2009 285p map pa $17.95   **385**

1. Transportation 2. Railroads -- United States

ISBN 978-1-60358-064-9; 1-60358-064-6

LC 2009-30142

"McCommons spent almost all of 2008 riding Amtrak trains back and forth across the country, telling folks he met along the way that he was doing research for a book on the future of passenger rail. . . . [The resulting work] is part travel log, chronicling both the horrors and the pleasures of riding Amtrak, and part solid political and business reporting on the rail industry that hardly any other journalist is doing." Washington Monthly

White, Richard

Railroaded; the transcontinentals and the making of modern America. Norton 2011 xxxix, 660p il map $35   **385**

1. American national characteristics 2. Railroads -- United States 3. Land settlement -- United States 4. National characteristics, American 5. Railroads -- United States -- History -- 19th century

ISBN 978-0-393-06126-0; 0-393-06126-4

LC 2010-54054

In this book, author Richard White "takes on the task of explaining the achievements and failings of the few transcontinental railroads that spanned North America in the latter half of the 19th century. He concentrates on their financial, political, and social impact. . . . He describes the corruption that made the railroad's founders wealthy but hamstrung the companies . . . , the antipathy between management and workers . . . [and] the antimonopoly movements against railroad practices." (Library Journal)

"Focusing on the entrepreneurs who between the 1860s and 1890s built and operated the transcontinental railroads, White judges them and their companies as failures and malignant influences on the settlement of the West." Booklist

Includes bibliographical references

Wolmar, Christian

Blood, iron, & gold; how the railroads transformed the world. PublicAffairs 2009 376p il map $28.95 **385**
1. Railroads -- History
ISBN 978-1-58648-834-5
LC 2009-38340
First published 2009 in the United Kingdom
This is "a fascinating study not just of a transportation system, but of the Promethean spirit of the modern age." Publ Wkly
Includes bibliographical references

Zoellner, Tom

Train; riding the rails that created the modern world : from the Trans-Siberian to the Southwest Chief. Tom Zoellner. Viking Adult 2014 384 p. (hardback) $27.95 **385**
1. Railroads 2. Railroad engineering 3. Railroad travel -- History
ISBN 0670025283; 9780670025282
LC 2013036816
In this book, Tom Zoellner "examines both the mechanics of the rails and their engines and how they helped societies evolve. Not only do trains transport people and goods in an efficient manner, but they also reduce pollution and dependency upon oil. Zoellner also considers America's culture of ambivalence to mass transit, using the perpetually stalled line between Los Angeles and San Francisco as a case study in bureaucracy and public indifference." (Publisher's note)
"An absorbing and lively reflection on an enduring marvel of modern industrial technology." Booklist
Includes bibliographical references and index

386 Inland waterway and ferry transportation

Bernstein, Peter L.

Wedding of the waters; the Erie Canal and the making of a great nation. W.W. Norton 2005 448p il map $24.95; pa $15.95 **386**
1. Erie Canal (N.Y.)
ISBN 0-393-05233-8; 0-393-32795-7 pa
LC 2004-22792
The author discusses the building of the Erie Canal and how, in his opinion, it changed the course of American history.
This "is an important window into a vital and too often neglected period in the American past." Foreign Affairs
Includes bibliographical references

Karabell, Zachary

Parting the desert; the creation of the Suez Canal. Knopf 2003 310p il map $27.50 **386**
1. Diplomats 2. Suez Canal (Egypt)
ISBN 0-375-40883-5
LC 2002-34209
Karabell "has written a thorough and entertaining work. . . . The author is quite comfortable discussing any issue, period, or personality in the canal's history, and many of the references in his 150-title bibliography are from primary sources. This is simply an excellent book." Libr J

Kelly, Jack

Heaven's ditch; God, Gold, and Murder on the Erie Canal. by Jack Kelly. St. Martin's Press 2016 304 p. illustrations, map (hardback) $27.99 **386**
1. Erie Canal (N.Y.) 2. New York (State) -- History 3. United States -- History -- 1783-1865 4. Erie Canal (N.Y.) -- History 5. New York (State) -- History -- 1775-1865
ISBN 9781137280091
LC 2016003174
In this book by Jack Kelly, "the technological marvel of its age, the Erie Canal grew out of a sudden fit of inspiration. Proponents didn't just dream; they built a 360-mile waterway entirely by hand and largely through wilderness. . . . The Erie Canal made New York the financial capital of America. . . . Kelly illuminates the spiritual and political upheavals along this 'psychic highway' from its opening in 1825 through 1844." (Publisher's note)
"An intriguing account of often overlooked events that significantly impacted the lives and times of individuals living during one of the most tumultuous times in American history." LJ
Includes bibliographical references (pages 265-281) and index.

387.7 Air transportation

Fallows, James

China airborne; James Fallows. Pantheon Books 2012 xiii, 268 p.p **387.7**
1. China -- History -- 1976- 2. Aerospace industry -- China 3. China -- Economic conditions 4. Commercial aeronautics -- China 5. Aeronautics -- China 6. Aerospace industries -- China 7. Aeronautics, Commercial -- China 8. China -- Economic conditions -- 2000-
ISBN 0375422110; 9780375422119
LC 2011046805
This book by James Fallows "analyzes the problems and promises of China's economic development through an examination of the efforts to create a world-class aerospace industry. With its unprecedented manufacturing prowess, China has become a world economic power. But how real and sustainable is the development? The test, writes the author, is how well China succeeds in its current effort to build an aerospace industry." (Kirkus Reviews)
Includes bibliographical references (p. [237]-251) and index

Holmes, Richard, 1945-

★ Falling upwards; how we took to the air. Richard Holmes. Pantheon Books 2013 416 p. $35 **387.7**
1. Flight 2. Balloons 3. Ballooning -- History 4. Balloonists -- History
ISBN 0307379663; 9780307379665
LC 2013011128

This book by Richard Holmes looks at ballooning. He "mentions Daedalus and Icarus, some balloons in literature, films and popular culture, and then lifts off into another of his . . . histories. He notes that the French were the first to use balloons for military purposes (reconnaissance), then tells us about some of the most notable balloon pioneers, including André-Jacques Garnerin, who also pioneered parachutes." (Kirkus Reviews)

Includes bibliographical references and index

McGee, William J.

Attention all passengers; the airlines' dangerous descent and how to reclaim our skies. William J. McGee. HarperCollins 2012 xii, 354 p.p $26.99 **387.7**
1. Airlines 2. Air travel 3. Aeronautics -- Safety measures 4. Airlines -- United States
ISBN 0062088378; 9780062088376
LC 2012026940

Author William J. McGee "derives most of the book from his interviews with, among others, flight attendants, congressmen, [and] an FAA whistleblower. . . . McGee explains how the shortcomings of airlines can and do cost consumers more than a comfortable flight; they result in unsafe conditions. . . . The author exposes the common practice of outsourcing repairs, which can result in crashes because the companies doing the repairs are not as competent or as tightly regulated." (Kirkus Reviews)

Mondor, Colleen Catherine

The map of my dead pilots; Colleen Mondor. Lyons Press 2012 256p **387.7**
1. Alaska 2. Air pilots 3. Aircraft accidents
ISBN 9780762773619
LC 2011033005

This book explores the author's experiences "as operations manager for a commercial airline servicing Alaska's remote villages and hamlets. . . . [Colleen] Mondor has had a bird's-eye view of the rigors of flying cargo that often as not included carcasses as well as crates, sleds as well as the dogs that hauled them, and passengers who had no other means of traversing a state whose isolation was both allure and aggravation. The men who flew these missions are—and, all too sadly, were—a lethal combination of danger junkies and hotshots, dreamers and schemers, dedicated professionals and determined daredevils who reveled in the challenges that Alaska's climate and terrain threw their way." (Booklist)

388 Transportation

McPhee, John A.

Uncommon carriers; [by] John McPhee. Farrar, Straus & Giroux 2006 248p $24 **388**
1. Freight 2. Transportation
ISBN 0-374-28039-8; 978-0-374-28039-0
LC 2006-7953

"McPhee's eye for idiosyncratic detail keeps the stories . . . lively and frequently moves them in interesting directions." Publ Wkly

388.1 Roads

Conover, Ted

The routes of man; how roads are changing the world, and the way we live today. Alfred A. Knopf 2010 333p il map $26.95 **388.1**
1. Roads
ISBN 978-1-4000-4244-9; 1-4000-4244-5
LC 2009-24007

"A readable, fact-filled, well-written exploration of how roads work, for good and ill, and what their future likely holds." Kirkus

Includes bibliographical references

388.3 Vehicular transportation

Sperling, Daniel

Two billion cars; driving toward sustainability. [by] Daniel Sperling [and] Deborah Gordon. Oxford University Press 2009 304p il $24.95 **388.3**
1. Automobile industry 2. Alternative fuel vehicles 3. Automobiles -- Fuel consumption
ISBN 978-0-19-537664-7; 0-19-537664-1
LC 2008-21647

"With statistical data, charts, graphs, and erudite analysis, Sperling and Gordon present the most thorough study of the automobile industry general readers could hope to find." Booklist

Includes bibliographical references and index

390 Customs, etiquette, folklore

Jenkins, Jessica Kerwin

All the time in the world; a book of hours. Jessica Kerwin Jenkins. Nan A. Talese 2013 320 p. (hardback) $28.95 **390**
1. Culture 2. Hobbies 3. Manners and customs -- History 4. Manners and customs -- Miscellanea
ISBN 0385535414; 9780385535410
LC 2013000795

In this book, author Jessica Kerwin Jenkins "uses the template of the medieval book of hours, which provided readings and meditations for certain times of the day and seasons, to create an unusual look at 'how we pass the time.'" (Booklist) "Subjects covered include the daylong ceremony of laying a royal Elizabethan tablecloth; the radicalization of sartorial chic in 1890s Paris; [and] Nostradamus's belief in the aphrodisiac power of jam". (Publisher's note)

Includes bibliographical references

391 Customs

Bowles, Hamish

Vogue and the Metropolitan Museum of Art Costume Institute; parties, exhibitions, people. Hamish

Bowles; [edited by] Chloe Malle. Abrams 2014 272 p. illustrations (chiefly color) $50 **391**

1. Fashion

ISBN 9781419714245

LC 2014934398

This book, by Hamish Bowles and edited by Chloe Malle, profiles "the Metropolitan Museum of Art's annual Costume Institute exhibition. . . . Covering the Costume Institute's history and highlighting exhibitions of the 21st century curated by Harold Koda and Andrew Bolton, this book offers insider access of the first order." (Publisher's note)

Crowe, Lauren Goldstein

The **towering** world of Jimmy Choo; a glamorous story of power, profits and the pursuit of the perfect shoe. [by] Lauren Goldstein Crowe and Sagra Maceira de Rosen. Bloomsbury USA 2009 228p il $26; pa $15 **391**

1. Shoes 2. Fashion design 3. Jimmy Choo (Firm) 4. Clothing industry executives

ISBN 978-1-59691-391-2; 1-59691-391-6; 978-1-60819-040-9 pa; 1-60819-040-4 pa

LC 2008-44378

"A fascinating, well-written chronology that draws a chillingly accurate behind-the-scenes portrait of a contemporary fashion brand." Booklist

Includes bibliographical references

DeJean, Joan E.

The **essence** of style; how the French invented high fashion, fine food, chic cafes, style, sophistication, and glamour. Free Press 2005 303p il $25; pa $15 **391**

1. Kings 2. Fashion -- History 3. France -- Social life and customs

ISBN 0-7432-6413-4; 0-7432-6414-2 pa

LC 2005-40019

"An unusual and delightfully educational perspective on snob appeal." Booklist

Includes bibliographical references

391.009 History, geographic treatment, biography

Dirix, Emmanuelle

Dressing the Decades; Twentieth-Century Vintage Style. Emmanuelle Dirix. Yale University Press 2016 224 p. illustrations (some color) $30 **391.009**

1. Fashion designers 2. Fashion -- History

ISBN 0300215525; 9780300215526

Author Emmanuelle Dirix "examines in depth the origins of the most important luxury garments. Each . . . chapter features a detailed overview of a particular decade, including the historical events, politics, technology, and advertising that inspired its most celebrated designs. The book provides a new perspective on such iconic items and significant trends as the cocktail dress, the Chanel suit, the tunic dress, boho chic, Futuristic chic, and others." (Publisher's note)

"Her well-informed narrative is often laced with socioeconomic observations, including discussion of Holly-

wood's impact on designers and vice versa, the class divisions of haute couture vs. ready-to-wear, and how various social and political movements transformed how we dress and consume fashion. The accompanying photos and illustrations ... are stunning and often drool-worthy." LJ

Includes bibliographical references (pages 218) and index.

Stevenson, N. J.

Fashion; a visual history from regency & romance to retro & revolution : a complete illustrated chronology of fashion from the 1800s to the present day. NJ Stevenson. 1st US ed. St. Martin's Griffin 2012 288 p. ill. (chiefly col.) $29.99 **391.009**

1. Hats 2. Painting 3. Women's clothing 4. Clothing and dress 5. Fashion -- History 6. Fashion design -- History 7. Clothing and dress -- History 8. Fashion -- History -- 19th century 9. Fashion -- History -- 20th century 10. Fashion -- History -- 21st century

ISBN 031262445X; 9780312624453

LC 2011278257

Author N. J. Stevenson describes "when distinctive styles that began as extravagances of the very rich permeated through well-dressed society until a cut of cloth or choice of accessory defined fashion. . . . Each spread focuses on a definitive item--be it bowler hat or little black dress, stiletto or caftan--or identifies key shifts in fashion that reflect excess, liberation, austerity, nostalgia, and technology, displaying it in contemporary images ranging from paintings and illustrated fashion plates to cartoons and photographs." (Publisher's note)

Includes bibliographical references and index

391.6 Personal appearance

Eldridge, Lisa

Face paint; the story of makeup. Lisa Eldridge. Abrams Image 2015 240 p. colour illustrations $29.95 **391.6**

1. Fashion 2. Cosmetics

ISBN 1419717960; 9781419717963

LC 2014959338

This book by Lisa Eldridge "explores the practical and idiosyncratic reasons behind makeup's use, the actual materials employed over generations, and the glamorous icons that people emulate, it is also a social history of women and the ways in which we can understand their lives through the prism and impact of makeup." (Publisher's note)

Peiss, Kathy Lee

Hope in a jar; the making of America's beauty culture. {by} Kathy Peiss. Metropolitan Bks. 1998 334p il hardcover o.p. pa $15.95 **391.6**

1. Cosmetics 2. Personal appearance

ISBN 0-8050-5551-7 pa

LC 97-42706

This is a "social history of the origin and development of the U.S. cosmetics industry. . . . An engrossing, highly readable book that should be welcomed by scholars and general readers alike." Libr J

Includes bibliographical references

392   Customs of life cycle and domestic life

Gollaher, David

Circumcision; a history of the world's most controversial surgery. [by] David L. Gollaher. Basic Bks. 2000 253p hardcover o.p. pa $18   **392**

1. Circumcision

ISBN 0-465-02653-2 pa

LC 99-40015

This history of circumcision discusses Jewish, Muslim, and tribal rituals, medical procedures and complications, reasons for the procedure, and its social significance in various cultures and eras

Jellison, Katherine

It's our day; America's love affair with the white wedding, 1945-2005. University Press of Kansas 2008 297p il (CultureAmerica) $29.95   **392**

1. Marriage customs and rites 2. United States -- Social life and customs

ISBN 978-0-7006-1559-9

LC 2007-35444

The author "takes an in-depth look at the history and popularity of the American 'white wedding' and in doing so provides a unique exploration of late 20th- and early 21st-century American culture. She starts right after World War II and progresses through celebrity, royal, and movie weddings to the 'reality weddings' of today and how the ritual of a white wedding has been adapted in many same-sex marriages. . . . An enlightening and fascinating read, her book is sure to be of interest in most libraries." Libr J

Includes bibliographical references

Mead, Rebecca

One perfect day; the selling of the American wedding. Penguin Press 2007 245p $25.95; pa $15   **392**

1. Weddings

ISBN 978-1-59420-088-5; 978-0-14-311384-3 pa

LC 2006-52461

"Part investigative journalism, part social commentary, Mead's wry, insightful work offers an illuminating glimpse at the ugly underbelly of our Bridezilla culture." Publ Wkly

392.5   Wedding and marriage customs

Style your perfect wedding. DK Publishing 2015 253 p. color illustrations (hardcover) $40 **392.5**

1. Weddings 2. Wedding decorations 3. Weddings -- Planning

ISBN 1465429824; 9781465429827

LC 2015301664

This book presents wedding planning and decoration advice, "from unique wedding ideas to creative wedding themes, from fun bridal shower ideas to handmade wedding crafts, from a beautiful bouquet to the best dresses for your bridal party. . . . It's filled with over 50 . . . projects, including: save-the-date cards, centerpieces, linens, ring cushions, and confetti. This book also has . . . ideas for getting your bridal party involved in designing and planning your wedding." (Publisher's note)

393   Death customs

Jokinen, Tom

Curtains; adventures of an undertaker-in-training. Da Capo Press 2010 279p pa $15.95   **393**

1. Undertakers and undertaking 2. Funeral rites and ceremonies

ISBN 978-0-306-81891-2; 0-306-81891-4

LC 2010-920629

"The narrative pinballs between the many roles Jokinen takes on within the industry—hearse driver, embalming assistant, theatrically solemn host who gestures at coat racks and restrooms. All the while, Jokinen dutifully remains the voice of the curious reader, channeling skepticism, the weirds and awe into laugh-out-loud observations grounded in just enough research to provide context without weighing down the plot." PopMatters

Kammen, Michael G.

Digging up the dead; a history of notable American reburials. [by] Michael Kammen. University of Chicago Press 2010 260p il $25   **393**

1. Burial 2. Exhumation 3. Funeral rites and ceremonies

ISBN 978-0-226-42329-6; 0-226-42329-8

LC 2009-23515

"Kammen has a good sense of the details that make historical stories memorable. His occasional flashes of humor add a winsome, professionally geeky element to the telling." Dallas Morning News

Includes bibliographical references

Pringle, Heather Anne

The mummy congress; science, obsession, and the everlasting dead. {by} Heather Pringle. Hyperion 2001 368p il hardcover o.p. pa $13.95   **393**

1. Mummies 2. Forensic anthropology

ISBN 0-7868-6551-2; 0-7868-8463-0 pa

LC 00-54487

"Besides outstanding members of the scientific association that gathers as the Mummy Congress, Pringle limns the many varieties of mummies, from the world's oldest, preserved by the high-altitude climate of the Andes, to modern Communist dictators, self-mummifying Buddhists, and the subjects of extreme cosmetic surgery. More astounding than all the fright flicks about shambling, gauze-wrapped menaces wound together." Booklist

Includes bibliographical references

394   General customs

Visser, Margaret

The gift of thanks; the roots and rituals of gratitude. Houghton Mifflin Harcourt 2009 458p $27   **394**

1. Gratitude

ISBN 978-0-15-101331-9

LC 2009-14018

First published 2008 in Canada

"A book to be thankful for—sympathetic to human foible, deeply learned and a pleasure to read." Kirkus

Includes bibliographical references

394.1   Eating, drinking; using drugs

Anthony, Jason C.

Hoosh; roast penguin, scurvy day, and other stories of Antarctic cuisine. Jason C. Anthony. University of Nebraska Press 2012 286 p. (pbk. : alk. paper) $26.95   **394.1**

1. Food 2. Scientific expeditions 3. Antarctica -- Exploration 4. Food habits -- Antarctica 5. Outdoor cooking -- Antarctica 6. Antarctica -- History -- Anecdotes 7. Antarctica -- Social life and customs
ISBN 0803226667; 9780803226661

LC 2012011994

This book is "[Jason C.] Anthony's debut . . . [and] traces hardships during Antarctic expeditions and the sometimes disconcerting fare borne of isolation. From blubber to penguin meat, and on infamous occasions, sled dogs and horses, supplemented by canned foods as well as pemmican (a concentrated mixture of fat and protein, the 'perfect endurance food used by Native Americans for millennia'), polar cuisine has always had a storied history." (Kirkus)

Includes bibliographical references.

Cheever, Susan

Drinking in America; Our Secret History. Susan Cheever. Grand Central Publishing 2015 272 p. (hardcover) $28   **394.1**

1. United States -- Civilization 2. Drinking of alcoholic beverages -- United States
ISBN 9781455513871; 1455513873

LC 2015025648

First edition

This book, by Susan Cheever, presents an overview and analysis of the U.S. "national love affair with liquor, taking a long, thoughtful look at the way alcohol has changed . . . [the] nation's history. This is the often-overlooked story of how alcohol has shaped American events and the American character from the seventeenth to the twentieth century." (Publisher's note)

"As implicated as she is in the history of drinking in America, Cheever does not condemn it. Instead, she offers a colorful portrait of a society that, like her own family, has been inde l ibly shaped by its drinking habits. An intelligently argued study of our country's 'passionate connection to drinking.'" Kirkus

Collingham, E. M. (Elizabeth M.)

Curry; a tale of cooks and conquerors. Oxford University Press 2006 315p il maps $28   **394.1**

1. Eating customs 2. India -- Civilization
ISBN 978-0-19-517241-6; 0-19-517241-8

LC 2005-16641

The author "with incredibly engrossing detail, unravels the tantalizing mystery of 'curry' in its innumerable forms, which have ravished the taste buds in far-flung kitchens and dining rooms." MultiCult Rev

Includes bibliographical references

Cowen, Tyler

An **economist** gets lunch; new rules for everyday foodies. Tyler Cowen. Dutton 2012 x, 293 p.p   **394.1**

1. Restaurants 2. Food industry and trade 3. Eating habits -- Economic aspects 4. Food habits -- Economic aspects 5. Food preferences -- Economic aspects
ISBN 0525952667; 9780525952664

LC 2011035174

In this book, economist Tyler Cowen "steers his audience through the contemporary world of eating and drinking. Like many staunch foodies, he respects the local. . . . Cowen finds that, despite what logic may suggest, the most expensive food is not necessarily the best. And he reveals that the same principle holds true in urban America as well as in the Third World. He expands this insight with a survey of barbecue restaurants in the U.S." (Booklist)

Includes bibliographical references and index

Fernandez-Armesto, Felipe

Near a thousand tables; a history of food. Free Press 2002 258p $25; pa $14   **394.1**

1. Food -- History
ISBN 0-7432-2644-5; 0-7432-2740-9 pa

LC 2002-23318

This is a "well-written, thought-provoking overview of food history." Libr J

Includes bibliographical references

The **food** of a younger land; a portrait of American food: before the national highway system, before chain restaurants . . . edited and illustrated by Mark Kurlansky. Riverhead Books 2009 397p il $27.95   **394.1**

1. Cooking 2. Eating customs
ISBN 978-1-59448-865-8

LC 2009-8100

"In the late 1930s the WPA farmed out a writing project with the ambition of other New Deal programs: an encyclopedia of American food and food traditions from coast-to-coast similar to the federal travel guides. After Pearl Harbor, the war effort halted the project for good; the book was never published, and the files were archived in the Library of Congress. . . . [The editor] brought the unassembled materials to light and created this version of the guide that never was. . . . This extraordinary collection—at once history, anthropology, cookbook, almanac and family album—provides a vivid and revitalizing sense of the rural and regional characteristics and distinctions that we've lost and can find again here." Publ Wkly

Mayle, Peter

French lessons; adventures with knife, fork, and corkscrew. Knopf 2001 227p il $24; pa $12.95   **394.1**

1. Eating customs 2. France -- Social life and customs
ISBN 0-375-40590-9; 0-375-70561-9 pa

Mayle "relives some of his most precious moments reveling in the cuisine of his adopted homeland. . . . {He tells} savory, sensual, positively transporting stories about his encounters with Gallic gustatory delights and about his growing appreciation of the central place food occupies in French life." Booklist

McWilliams, James E.

Just food; where locavores get it wrong and how we can truly eat responsibly. Little, Brown and Company 2009 258p $25.99   **394.1**

1. Food industry 2. Natural foods 3. Eating customs
ISBN 978-0-316-03374-9

LC 2009-15514

The author "argues for moderation and compromise in today's raging food fights. Until recently, the author was a locavore—one who eats locally produced food. Though he still believes that it is a dietary commitment with many virtues, he argues that it's also a feeble, ineffective way to feed the world's hungry billions. . . . McWilliams presents some appealing alternatives to the views of both the agrarian romantics on the left and the agribusiness capitalists on the right. . . . Rich in research, provocative in conception and nettlesome to both the right and the left." Kirkus

Includes bibliographical references

Pollan, Michael, 1955-

★ The **omnivore's** dilemma; a natural history of four meals. Penguin Press 2006 450p pa $16; $26.95   **394.1**

1. Eating customs 2. Agriculture -- United States 3. Food supply -- United States 4. Food consumption -- United States
ISBN 0-14-303858-3 pa; 1-59420-082-3

LC 2005-56557

"Pollan has divided The Omnivore's Dilemma into three parts, one for each of the food chains that sustain us: industrialized food, alternative or 'organic' food, and food people obtain by dint of their own hunting, gathering, or gardening. Pollan follows each food chain . . . from the ground up to the table, emphasizing our dynamic co-evolutionary relationship with the species we depend on. He concludes each section by sitting down to a meal—at McDonald's, at home with his family sharing a dinner from Whole Foods, and in a revolutionary 'beyond organic' farm in Virginia. For each meal he traces the provenance of everything consumed, [aiming to] and explain how our taste for particular foods reflects our environmental and biological inheritance." (Publisher's note)

The author "defines the Omnivore's Dilemma as the confusing maze of choices facing Americans trying to eat healthfully in a society that he calls 'notably unhealthy.' He seeks answers to this dilemma by taking readers through the industrial, organic, and hunter-gatherer stages of the food chain. . . . This folksy narrative provides a wealth of information about agriculture, the natural world, and human desires." Libr J

Includes bibliographical references

Schlosser, Eric

★ **Fast** food nation; the dark side of the all-American meal. Houghton Mifflin 2001 356p il $25   **394.1**

1. Restaurants 2. Food industry 3. Convenience foods
ISBN 0-395-97789-4

LC 00-53886

"Schlosser documents the effects of fast food on America's economy, its youth culture, and allied industries. . . . Starting with a young woman who makes minimum wage working at a Colorado fast-food restaurant, Schlosser relates the oft-told story of Ray Kroc's founding of McDonald's. The author also tells about the development of the franchise method of business ownership and the health and nutrition implications of fast-food consumption." Booklist

Includes bibliographical references

Standage, Tom

An **edible** history of humanity. Walker & Company 2009 269p il map $26   **394.1**

1. Food 2. Agriculture 3. Eating customs
ISBN 0-8027-1588-5; 978-0-8027-1588-3

LC 2009-5610

"This meaty little volume [is] cogent, informative and insightful." Kirkus

Includes bibliographical references

A **history** of the world in 6 glasses. Walker & Co. 2005 311p il $25   **394.1**

1. Beverages 2. World history 3. Tea -- History 4. Coffee -- History 5. Beverages -- History 6. Drinking of alcoholic beverages -- History
ISBN 0-8027-1447-1

LC 2004-61209

Mr. Standage's "book divides world history into beer, wine, spirits, coffee, tea and Coca-Cola ages. . . . He begins with humanity's shift from hunting and gathering to agriculture. This transition led to the cultivation of grain, which led to storage and fermentation and, eventually, beer." (N Y Times (Late N Y Ed)) Index.

Standage "has the ability to connect the smallest detail to the big picture and a knack for summarizing vast concepts in a few sentences." Publ Wkly

Includes bibliographical references

394.12   Eating and drinking

Goulding, Matt

Rice, noodle, fish; Deep Travels Through Japan's Food Culture. Matt Goulding; edited by Nathan Thornburgh. HarperWave 2015 352 p. color illustrations (Hardcover) $35; (ebook) $32.99   **394.12**

1. Japanese cooking 2. Food tourism -- Japan 3. Food habits -- Japan
ISBN 9780062394033; 9780062394040

LC 2015005013

This book by Matt Goulding, edited by Nathan Thornburgh, "explores Japan's most intriguing culinary disciplines in seven key regions, from the kaiseki tradition of Kyoto and the sushi masters of Tokyo to the street food of Osaka and the ramen culture of Fukuoka. You . . . will find a brilliant narrative that interweaves immersive food journalism with intimate portraits of the cities and the people who shape Japan's food culture." (Publisher's note)

"Goulding's gift for phrasing and razor-sharp prose elevate what could have been yet another rote travelogue into something much better." Pub Wkly

394.26 Holidays

Baker, James W.

Thanksgiving; the biography of an American holiday. foreword by Peter J. Gomes. University of New Hampshire Press 2009 273p il (Revisiting New England) pa $26.95 **394.26**

1. Thanksgiving Day

ISBN 978-1-58465-801-6

LC 2009-12348

The author shows "how Thanksgiving is seen through each generation's reality, having morphed from a holiday for pilgrim hats and turkeys to a cause for Native American protests to a holy day to several ancient holidays combined and a full-scale orgy of food and football. . . . [This is] an enjoyable, fascinating read both for students and for anyone looking for a good story." Libr J

Includes bibliographical references

Forbes, Bruce David

Christmas; a candid history. University of California Press 2007 179p il $19.95; pa $12.95 **394.26**

1. Christmas

ISBN 978-0-520-25104-5; 978-0-520-25802-0 pa

LC 2007-00366

The author "presents a brief social history of Christmas from pre-Christian winter celebrations to the commercialization of the holiday in American popular culture. The growth of the holiday to include Christmas cards, music and movies are included in this easy to read overview." Univ Press Books for Public and Second Sch Libr, 2008

Includes bibliographical references

Hillstrom, Laurie

The **Thanksgiving** book; [by] Laurie C. Hillstrom. Omnigraphics 2008 328p il $65 **394.26**

1. Thanksgiving Day

ISBN 978-0-7808-0403-6

LC 2007-25708

"This book is definitely a wonderful tribute to the holiday of Thanksgiving." Am Ref Books Annu, 2008

Includes bibliographical references

Holiday symbols and customs; 4th ed.; Omnigraphics 2009 1321p $94 **394.26**

1. Holidays 2. Festivals

ISBN 978-0-7808-0990-1

LC 2008-28403

First published 1998 with title: Holiday symbols

"Describes the origins of 323 holidays around the world. Explains where, when, and how each event is celebrated, with detailed information on the symbols and customs associated with the holiday. Includes contact information and web sites for related organizations." Publisher's note

Includes bibliographical references

Holidays, festivals, and celebrations of the world dictionary; detailing more than 3,000 observances from all 50 states and more than 100 nations: a compendious reference guide to popular, ethnic, religious, national, and ancient holidays. . . edited by Cherie D. Abbey. 4th ed.; Omnigraphics 2010 1323p $144 **394.26**

1. Reference books 2. Holidays -- Dictionaries 3. Festivals -- Dictionaries

ISBN 978-0-7808-0994-9

LC 2009-41138

First edition published 1994 compiled by Sue Ellen Thompson and Barbara W. Carlson

"A comprehensive dictionary that describes more than 3,000 holidays and festivals celebrated around the world. Features both secular and religious events from many different cultures, countries, and ethnic groups. Includes contact information for events; multiple appendices with background information on world holidays; extensive bibliography; multiple indexes." Publisher's note

Rajtar, Steve

United States holidays and observances; by date, jurisdiction, and subject, fully indexed. McFarland & Co. 2003 165p $45 **394.26**

1. Holidays 2. Festivals

ISBN 0-7864-1446-4

LC 2002-154293

This "concentrates on observances and holidays established by statute in the U.S. and American Samoa, District of Columbia, Guam, the Northern Mariana Islands, Puerto Rico, and the U.S. Virgin Islands. In addition, UN-designated holidays are included. . . . The text is arranged by month, and chapters for each month are divided into 'Observances with Variable Dates' and 'Observances with Fixed Dates.' Each entry identifies the observance as federal or specific to a state and offers a description that ranges in length from three or four lines to a quarter page. . . . [This] would be a good addition to ready-reference desks in public libraries and information centers in schools." Booklist

394.264 Halloween

Morton, Lisa

Trick or Treat; A History of Halloween. Lisa Morton. University of Chicago Press 2012 229 p. (hardcover) $29 **394.264**

1. Halloween

ISBN 1780230478; 9781780230474

This book, by Lisa Morton, offers a history of Halloween. "The popularity of Halloween has spread around the globe to places as diverse as Russia, China, and Japan, but its association with death and the supernatural and its inevitable commercialization has made it one of our most misunderstood holidays. How did it become what it is today? . . . Lisa Morton provides a thorough history of this spooky day." (Publisher's note)

395   Etiquette (Manners)

Baldrige, Letitia

Letitia Baldrige's new manners for new times; a complete guide to etiquette. illustrations by Denise Cavalieri Fike. Scribner 2003 xxvi, 709p il $35 **395**
1. Etiquette
ISBN 0-7432-1062-X

LC 2003-65666

First published 1990 with title: Letitia Baldrige's complete guide to the new manners for the 90's

"Combining correctness, consideration, and common sense in equal measure, Baldrige advises readers on proper ways to approach intricate situations. She addresses same-sex unions, pregnant brides, blended and extended families, and sexual harassment with aplomb." Libr J

Blyth, Catherine

The **art** of conversation; a guided tour of a neglected pleasure. Gotham Books 2009 289p $22.50   **395**
1. Conversation
ISBN 978-1-592-40419-3; 1-592-40419-7

LC 2008-24276

"Adopting a chatty, conversational manner to write about conversation, Blyth mixes personal anecdotes into a salmagundi of selected quotes from anthropology, history, literature, philosophy and pop culture to analyze and give advice on the dynamics of good conversation, not to mention the perfect riposte for every situation. She examines everything from small talk to pillow talk, from riotous raconteurs to crashing bores, from flattery to false smiles. . . . Witty, eloquent and insightful, Blyth's book is a delightful encouragement to rediscover conversation as the best communication technology." Publ Wkly

Dresser, Norine

Multicultural manners; essential rules of etiquette for the 21st century. Rev ed; John Wiley & Sons 2005 285p map pa $16.95   **395**
1. Etiquette 2. Manners and customs
ISBN 978-0-471-68428-2; 0-471-68428-7

LC 2004-27079

First published 1996

"From body language and table manners to classroom behavior and gift giving, this guide to etiquette provides fascinating information about relations in our multicultural society." Booklist

Includes bibliographical references

Forni, Pier Massimo

The **civility** solution; what to do when people are rude. [by] P.M. Forni. St. Martin's Press 2008 xxi, 166p $19.95   **395**
1. Courtesy 2. Etiquette
ISBN 978-0-312-36849-4; 0-312-36849-6

LC 2008-9448

"In Part 1 . . . [the author] describes some of the causes of rudeness (e.g., anger, fear, inflated self-worth) and the negative consequences of rude behavior in daily life. . . . In Part 2, Forni provides over 70 examples of situations in which rudeness arises and solutions for dealing with them.

Readers who have been criticized in public or annoyed by a loud cell phone conversation get realistic help." Libr J

Includes bibliographical references

Martin, Judith

Miss Manners' guide to excruciatingly correct behavior; illustrated by Gloria Kamen. freshly updated; Norton 2005 858p il $35   **395**
1. Etiquette
ISBN 0-393-05874-3

LC 2005-00264

First published 1982 by Atheneum Pubs.

"Miss Manners is always as entertaining as she is civilized." Booklist

Morrison, Terri

★ **Kiss,** bow, or shake hands; the bestselling guide to doing business in more than 60 countries. [by] Terri Morrison and Wayne A. Conaway. 2nd ed.; Adams Media 2006 593p il pa $24.95   **395**
1. Negotiation 2. Business etiquette 3. Business communication
ISBN 1-59337-368-6

LC 2006-13587

First published 1994

"The definitive reference for doing business around the world." Libr J

Oliver, Vicky

301 smart answers to tough business etiquette questions. Skyhorse Pub. 2010 370p pa $12.95 **395**
1. Business etiquette
ISBN 978-1-61608-141-6; 1-61608-141-4

LC 2010021474

This guide to business etiquette covers "making a good first impression (and how to fix a bad one!); how to behave in elevators, airplanes, and supply closets; surviving cabs, commutes, and coffee shops; why time is not necessarily money everywhere on the planet; pre-approved conversational topics from A to Z; dining rules and regulations for the twenty-first century; what to do when you are suddenly unemployed; [and] electronic communication." Publisher's note

Includes bibliographical references

Outcalt, Todd

Your beautiful wedding on any budget. Sourcebooks 2009 227p pa $12.99   **395**
1. Weddings
ISBN 978-1-4022-1788-3

LC 2008-46864

"A terrific resource for couples trying to start their marriage on a financially sound footing. The Methodist pastor offers suggestions for building a wedding fund and creative cost-cutting measures based on his debt-free wedding seminars and blog." Libr J

Post, Peggy

Emily Post's etiquette; manners for a new world. by Peggy Post, Anna Post, Lizzie Post, and Daniel Post Senning; illustrations by Janice Richter. 18th

ed. William Morrow 2011 xi, 723 p.p illustrations $39.99 **395**
1. Etiquette
ISBN 0061740233; 9780061740237

LC 2010042228

This book on etiquette, by Peggy Post, Anna Post, Lizzie Post, and Daniel Post Senning, "tackle[s] the latest issues and demands of the twenty-first century—from texting and tweeting to iPhones, Facebook, and all forms of social media. The perfect guide for Millennials living on their own for the first time who wish to establish themselves properly in the workplace, . . . [it] remains the essential handbook to proper social behavior." (Publisher's note)

Includes bibliographical references and index

Emily Post's The etiquette advantage in business; personal skills for professional success. Peggy Post and Peter Post. Third edition HarperResource 2005 xvi, 366 p.p illustrations $30 **395**
1. Job hunting 2. Business etiquette 3. Success in business
ISBN 0060760028; 006227046X; 9780062270467

LC 2005283037

This book, by Peggy Post and Peter Post, "provide[s] you with the all-important tools for building solid, productive relationships with your business associates. . . . In this completely revised and updated edition, which includes three new chapters on ethics, table manners, and electronic communication, the Posts show you how to handle both everyday and unusual situations that are essential to professional and personal success." (Publisher's note)

Vivaldo, Denise
Do it for le$$! weddings; how-to create your dream wedding without breaking the bank. Sellers Pub., Inc. 2008 272p il pa $19.95 **395**
1. Weddings
ISBN 978-1-4162-0519-7

LC 2008-923779

The author "focuses on receptions—venues, logistics, and menus (including numerous recipes). Detailed information and instructive illustrations make this a solid choice for those catering their own affairs." Libr J

Includes bibliographical references

Weiss, Mindy
The **wedding** book; the big book for your big day. by Mindy Weiss with Lisbeth Levine. Workman Pub. Company, Inc. 2007 485p il $35; pa $19.95 **395**
1. Weddings
ISBN 978-0-7611-5094-7; 978-0-7611-3960-7 pa

LC 2008-15510

This book offers wedding planning advice on topics such as announcing the wedding, setting up a budget, planning the ceremony, wedding parties, and designing the dress and tuxedo.

This "comprehensive, well-organized guide offers good details on contracts and setting priorities." Libr J

395.2 Etiquette for stages in life cycle

Post, Lizzie
Emily Post's wedding etiquette; Anna Post and Lizzie Post; with illustrations by Happy Menocal. Sixth edition William Morrow, an imprint of HarperCollins Publishers 2014 xx, 380 p.p illustrations (hardcover) $29.99 **395.2**
1. Weddings 2. Etiquette 3. Wedding etiquette
ISBN 0062326104; 9780062326102

LC 2013498453

This book, by Anna Post and Lizzie Post, "is the classic indispensable, comprehensive guide to creating the wedding of your dream[s], now in its sixth edition. Today's weddings are more complicated than ever, with new traditions replacing old, and new relationships to consider as family life grows more complex. [It] has everything a bride will ever need to know to have the perfect wedding." (Publisher's note)

395.5 Etiquette by situations

Alexander, Liz
Access to Asia; your multicultural guide to building trust, inspiring respect, and creating long-lasting business relationships. Sharon Schweitzer, Liz Alexander. John Wiley & Sons, Inc. 2015 374 p. illustrations (cloth) $30 **395.5**
1. Corporate culture 2. Business etiquette 3. Business communication 4. Cross-cultural studies 5. Management -- Asia 6. Corporate culture -- Asia 7. Business etiquette -- Asia 8. Intercultural communication 9. Management -- Cross-cultural studies
ISBN 9781118919019

LC 2014039933

This book, by Sharon Schweitzer and Liz Alexander, "presents a deeply insightful framework for today's global business leaders and managers, whether traveling from Toronto to Taipei, Baltimore to Bangalore, or San Francisco to Shanghai. . . . Readers will find in-the-trenches advice and stories from 80 regional experts in 10 countries, including China, Hong Kong, India, Japan, and Korea." (Publisher's note)

"Beautifully constructed and expertly written in straightforward language; will make it far easier for anyone to navigate the cultural differences of doing business in Asia." Kirkus

Includes bibliographical references and index

398 Folklore

Bane, Theresa
Encyclopedia of vampire mythology. McFarland & Company, Inc., Publishers 2010 199p $75 **398**
1. Reference books 2. Vampires -- Encyclopedias
ISBN 978-0-7864-4452-6

LC 2010-15576

The "introduction presents a survey of the vampire myth's historical roots and continued evolution. Subsequent entries, organized alphabetically by vampire name, include phonetic pronunciations and define the many tangible and intangible vampiric forms that hail from every continent around the globe. . . . A thorough resource for dark mythologists and vampire enthusiasts." Libr J

Includes bibliographical references

Encyclopedia of American folklife; Simon J. Bronner, editor. M.E. Sharpe 2006 4v il set $399 **398**
1. Reference books 2. Folklore -- United States -- Encyclopedias 3. United States -- Social life and customs -- Encyclopedias
ISBN 0-7656-8052-1; 978-0-7656-8052-5

LC 2005-32119

This encyclopedia "provides a survey of the cultural patterns and experiences of diverse communities throughout the United States and the territories of Guam, Samoa, and Puerto Rico as well as other countries and ethnic groups that have influenced American social practices. . . . The encyclopedia covers crafts, foods, architecture, remedies, customs, holidays, narratives, speech, and stereotypes, with an emphasis on contemporary practices." Libr J

Includes bibliographical references

Guiley, Rosemary Ellen
The **encyclopedia** of vampires & werewolves; foreword by Jeanne Keyes Youngson. 2nd ed; Facts On File 2011 430p il $85; pa $24.95 **398**
1. Reference books 2. Monsters -- Encyclopedias 3. Vampires -- Encyclopedias 4. Werewolves -- Encyclopedias
ISBN 978-0-8160-8179-0; 0-8160-8179-4; 978-0-8160-8180-6 pa; 0-8160-8180-8 pa; 978-1-4381-3632-5 ebook; 1-4381-3632-3 ebook

LC 2010034839

First published 2004 with title: The encyclopedia of vampires, werewolves, and other monsters

"Entries describe supposed true historical accounts, how vampires and werewolves come into existence, beliefs about vampires and werewolves, and real-life creatures and cases that may have inspired their legends. . . . Fictional vampires from a range of media are discussed, along with the people who helped create them." Publisher's note

Includes bibliographical references

Hurston, Zora Neale
Folklore, memoirs, and other writings. Library of Am. 1995 1001p il $35 **398**
ISBN 0-940450-84-4

LC 94-21384

Companion volume to Novels and stories (1995)

"This is the first time the unexpurgated version of Hurston's 1942 autobiography, Dust Tracks on the Road, is being published; sections deemed too provocative (dealing with politics, race, and sex) have been restored. Mules and Men (1935) is a collection of African American folklore she gleaned on travels in the South, while Tell My Horse (1938) tenders her personal findings on African-based religion in Jamaica and Haiti. Additionally, 22 magazine and book articles with anthropological themes . . . that have never been gathered into book form are corralled here." Booklist

Melton, J. Gordon
The **vampire** book; the encyclopedia of the undead. Completely revamped, fully rev. and expanded, 3rd ed.; Visible Ink Press 2010 909p il pa $29.95 **398**
1. Reference books 2. Vampires -- Encyclopedias
ISBN 978-1-57859-281-4

LC 2010-24263

First published 1994

"This vampire lore tome covers legends from around the world, both classical and current, presenting an overview of the historical, literary, mythological, biographical, and popular aspects of vampires. . . . This book is an excellent and comprehensive addition to any collection serving readers interested in learning more about the vampire in time, place, and society. Aficionados of vampires in popular culture will enjoy it." Libr J

Includes bibliographical references

Prahlad, Anand
The **Greenwood** encyclopedia of African American folklore; edited by Anand Prahlad. Greenwood Press 2005 xl, 1557p 3v il set $299.95 **398**
1. Reference books 2. African Americans -- Folklore -- Encyclopedias 3. African Americans -- Social life and customs -- Encyclopedias
ISBN 0-313-33035-2

LC 2005-19214

For a fuller review, see: Booklist, Feb. 1, 2006

"The three volume set gives special attention to music, art, folktales, spiritual beliefs, foodways, proverbs, and other topics central to African American folklore, and discusses the Caribbean and African roots of traditional African American culture." Libr Media Connect

Includes bibliographical references

World folklore for storytellers; tales of wonder, wisdom, fools, and heroes. Josepha Sherman, editor. Sharpe Reference 2010 368p il $95 **398**
1. Folklore 2. Storytelling
ISBN 978-0-7656-8174-4

LC 2009-10525

This is "a wonderfully wide-ranging collection of nearly 200 ethnically diverse folktales. Particularly vital is that the stories are organized thematically rather than geographically, allowing for broader symbolic and anthropological comparisons. Each narrative runs several pages, includes a brief explanatory introduction, and consistently concludes with at least two bibliographic references. Pockets of multipage color plates offer images from native folktale anthologies and other relevant artistic renderings." Libr J

Includes bibliographical references

398.2   Folk literature

Ackroyd, Peter
The **death** of King Arthur; Thomas Malory's Le morte d'Arthur. Sir Thomas Malory; a retelling by Peter Ackroyd. Viking 2011 316p $26.95 **398.2**
1. Authors 2. Kings 3. Britons -- Fiction. 4. Great

Britain -- Kings and rulers -- Fiction. 5. Knights and knighthood -- Great Britain -- Fiction.
ISBN 978-0-670-02307-3; 0-670-02307-8

LC 2011-21800

First published 2010 in the United Kingdom

"Ackroyd takes the daunting Middle English verse and retells the ancient legends in modern English prose. He also omits most of Malory's medieval tales as perhaps too creaky for modern minds, or maybe simply to make his retelling a niftier little book. All the essential stories are here, among them: Arthur lifting the great sword Excalibur from the stone to become king; the adulterous quarter-century-long love affair of Queen Guinevere and Arthur's most powerful and trusted knight, Lancelot du Lake; the love of Tristram and Isolte; Sir Galahad and the search for the Holy Grail; the awesome power of the wizard Merlin, the exquisite evil of Morgan le Fay, Arthur's half-sister, and finally the doom of Camelot and the death of Arthur at the hand of Sir Mordred, his own son born from an incestuous union of Arthur and Morgan le Fay. . . . Ackroyd tells these stories in such simple, vivid language that they seem as new as they must have when first heard around the peat fires of cold and gloomy England perhaps 1,000 years ago. And they're still a lot of fun." Dallas Morning News

Armstrong, Karen

✓ ★ A **short** history of myth. Canongate 2005 159p hardcover o.p. pa $14 **398.2**
1. Mythology
ISBN 1-84195-716-X; 1-84195-800-X pa

This is an "overview of the ever-evolving partnership betweeh myth and man from Paleolithic times to the present. Succinct and cleanly written, it is hugely readable and, in its journey across the epochs of human experience, often moving. . . . Armstrong's exposition is streamlined and uncluttered without being simplistic." N Y Times Book Rev

Includes bibliographical references

Asma, Stephen T.

On monsters; an unnatural history of our worst fears. Oxford University Press 2009 351p il $27.95 **398.2**
1. Monsters
ISBN 978-0-19-533616-0

LC 2009-7219

The author "is insightful and entertaining in his discussion of monsters of the deep, supernatural doppelgangers, zombies, and vampires, and intense in his discussion of Freud and the science of monstrous feelings. . . . Asma's far-reaching book of monsterology is original, captivating, and profoundly elucidating." Booklist

Includes bibliographical references

Brunvand, Jan Harold

The **vanishing** hitchhiker; American urban legends and their meaning. Norton 1981 208p hardcover o.p. pa $13.95 **398.2**
1. Legends -- United States 2. Folklore -- United States
ISBN 0-393-95169-3 pa

LC 81-4744

A collection of modern urban folktales with an ironic or supernatural twist. The author reports on how such tales are disseminated and discusses their inherent messages for contemporary society

Includes bibliographical references

Bulfinch, Thomas

✓ ★ **Bulfinch's** mythology; foreword by Alberto Manguel. Modern Library pbk. ed.; Modern Library 2004 862p pa $17.95 **398.2**
1. Chivalry 2. Emperors 3. Mythology 4. Mabinogion 5. Folklore -- Europe
ISBN 0-375-75147-5

LC 2005-271850

First combined edition published 1913 by Crowell. Originally published in three separate volumes 1855, 1858 and 1862 respectively

"The classic work on mythology, Bulfinch's gives brief summations of Greek, Roman, Norse, Arthurian, and other miscellaneous myths and includes notes on the 'Iliad,' the 'Odyssey,' and the 'Aeneid.'" N Y Public Libr Book of How & Where to Look It Up

Includes bibliographical references

Encyclopedia of Jewish folklore and traditions; Raphael Patai, founding editor; Haya Bar-Itzhak, editor. M.E. Sharpe 2012 44 p. (hardcover : alk. paper) $299 **398.2**
1. Jewish folk literature 2. Judaism -- Encyclopedias 3. Folklore -- Encyclopedias 4. Jews -- Folklore -- Encyclopedias 5. Jews -- Social life and customs -- Encyclopedias
ISBN 0765620251; 9780765620255

LC 2012042203

"This encyclopedia covers the long and multifarious history of Jewish folklore and customs from the Bible to bagels. . . . The eclectic content covers holidays (Purim), material artifacts (illuminated manuscripts), and mythical beliefs (Dybbuk) and offers country studies (Afghanistan, Iran) and biographies of notable Jewish ethnographers." (Library Journal)

Includes bibliographical references and index

✓ **Favorite** folktales from around the world; edited by Jane Yolen. Pantheon Bks. 1986 498p hardcover o.p. pa $18 **398.2**
1. Folklore 2. Fairy tales
ISBN 0-394-75188-4 pa

LC 86-42644

"Selections include tales from the American Indians, the brothers Grimm, Italo Calvino's Italian folk-tales, as well as stories from Iceland, Afghanistan, Scotland, and many other countries. Yolen provides each section with a relevant introduction, often including historical and literary factors, thus alerting readers as to what to look for." SLJ

Haase, Donald

The **Greenwood** encyclopedia of folktales and fairy tales; edited by Donald Haase. Greenwood Press 2008 3v il set $299.95 **398.2**
1. Reference books 2. Folklore -- Encyclopedias 3. Fairy tales -- Encyclopedias
ISBN 978-0-313-33441-2

LC 2007-31698

"Meticulously documented and firmly grounded in scholarly research, most articles feature straightforward language and sufficient background material to be accessible to lay readers and novice researchers." Booklist

Includes bibliographical references

Lavers, Chris

The **natural** history of unicorns. William Morrow 2009 258p il $26.99   **398.2**

1. Unicorns

ISBN 978-0-06-087414-8; 0-06-087414-7

First published 2008 in the United Kingdom

This "is an erudite, scholarly book which uses the unicorn to illuminate millennia of social and geographical change. Unicorns appear in many guises in many cultures. . . . Lavers's achievement is to show how each of these is a chimera based on startlingly accurate reports of real animals, carried over trade routes. . . . Lavers's book offers revelations not only about mythical creatures, but about the extent and effects of globalisation in ancient times. It's eminently readable, too." New Sci

Includes bibliographical references p. 245-248)

Malory, Thomas

Le morte Darthur, or, The hoole book of Kyng Arthur and of his noble knyghtes of the Rounde Table; authoritative text, sources and backgrounds, criticism. [by] Sir Thomas Malory; edited by Stephen H.A. Shepherd. Norton 2004 lii, 954p (A Norton critical edition) pa $16.95   **398.2**

1. Kings

ISBN 0-393-97464-2

LC 2002-26534

Originally published 1485

"The work is a skillful selection and blending of materials taken from the mass of Arthurian legends. The central story consists of two main elements: the reign of King Arthur ending in catastrophe and the dissolution of the Round Table; and the quest of the Holy Grail." Oxford Companion to Engl Lit

Includes bibliographical references

Orenstein, Catherine

Little Red Riding Hood uncloaked; sex, morality, and the evolution of a fairy tale. Basic Bks. 2002 289p il hardcover o.p. pa $14.95   **398.2**

1. Little Red Riding Hood

ISBN 0-465-04126-4 pa; 0-465-04125-6

LC 2002-4240

"Once upon a time, Red Riding Hood was a good little girl. When she foolishly strayed from the path in the forest and spoke to strangers, she fell prey to the wicked wolf, but fortunately, the heroic woodcutter rescued her just in time. . . . With wit and insight, Orenstein makes us look again at the old childhood story, how it has changed and what that says about us. From Perrault and the Brothers Grimm to Bruno Bettelheim and Andrea Dworkin, the lively informal narrative surveys the stories and the scholarship in terms of folklore, psychology, feminism, and pornography." Booklist

Includes bibliographical references

The **Original** Folk and Fairy Tales of the Brothers Grimm; the complete first edition. [Jacob Grimm, Wilhelm Grimm; translated by] Jack Zipes; [illustrated by Andrea Dezsö] Princeton University Press 2014 xliii, 519 p.p illustrations (hardback : acid-free paper) $35   **398.2**

1. Fairy tales 2. Folklore -- Germany 3. Tales -- Germany 4. Fairy tales -- Germany

ISBN 9780691160597

LC 2014004127

"For the very first time, 'The Original Folk and Fairy Tales of the Brothers Grimm' makes available in English all 156 stories from the 1812 and 1815 editions. These narrative gems, newly translated and brought together in one. . . book, are accompanied by . . . new illustrations from . . . artist Andrea Dezsö." (Publisher's note)

Includes bibliographical references and index

Sir Gawain and the Green Knight; a new verse translation. [translated by] Simon Armitage. W. W. Norton & Company 2007 198p $25.95; pa $14.95   **398.2**

1. Arthurian romances 2. Poetry -- By individual authors

ISBN 978-0-393-06048-5; 0-393-06048-9; 978-0-393-33415-9 pa; 0-393-33415-5 pa

LC 2007-28520

Armitage "clearly feels a special kinship with the Gawain poet. He captures his dialect and his landscape and takes great pains to render the tale's alliterative texture and drive. . . . His vernacular translation isn't literal—sometimes he alliterates different letters, sometimes he foreshortens the number of alliterations in a line, sometimes he changes lines altogether and so forth—but his imitation is rich and various and recreates the gnarled verbal texture of the Middle English original, which is presented in a parallel text." N Y Times Book Rev

Wroe, Ann

Orpheus; the song of life. Ann Wroe. Overlook 2012 262 p. $26.95   **398.2**

1. Greek mythology 2. Cross-cultural studies 3. Literature -- History and criticism 4. Orpheus (Greek mythology)

ISBN 9780224091367; 0224091360; 1590207785; 9781590207789

LC 2011508687

This book by Ann Wroe "traces the obscure origins and tangled relationships of the Orpheus myth from ancient times through today." (Library Journal). After tracing "his adventures with Jason and the Argonauts, his eternal love of Eurydice and interminable mourning for her and descent into Hades . . . the author recounts the influence of Orpheus on a veritable pantheon of writers and musicians, including Ovid, Virgil, Milton, Shelley, Keats, Cocteau and a host of others." (Kirkus Reviews)

398.209 History, geographic treatment, biography

Schönwerth, Franz Xaver von, 1809-1886

The **turnip** princess; and other newly created fairy tales. Franz Xaver von Schonwerth; edited by Erika Eichenseer; illustrated by Engelbert Suss; translated by Maria Tatar. Penguin Group USA 2015 288 p. illustrations (paperback) $17 **398.209**
> 1. Fairy tales 2. Princesses -- Fiction
> ISBN 0143107429; 9780143107422
>> LC 2015302549

This book edited by Erika Eichenseer; illustrated by Engelbert Suss; translated by Maria Tatar, presents author Franz Xavier von Schonwerth's fairy tales in English. "Violent, dark, and full of action, and upending the relationship between damsels in distress and their dragon-slaying heroes, these more than seventy stories bring us closer than ever to the unadorned oral tradition in which fairy tales are rooted, revolutionizing our understanding of a hallowed genre." (Publisher's note)

"These eminently enjoyable tales offer a rich new take on the material of the Grimms and Andersen." LJ

Zipes, Jack

The **irresistible** fairy tale; the cultural and social history of a genre. Jack Zipes. Princeton University Press 2012 xvii, 235 p.p (hardcover : alk. paper) $29.95 **398.209**
> 1. Fairy tales 2. Fairy tales -- Social aspects 3. Fairy tales -- History and criticism
> ISBN 0691153388; 9780691153384
>> LC 2011040188

This book, by Jack Zipes, presents "a provocative new theory about why fairy tales were created and retold--and why they became such an indelible and infinitely adaptable part of cultures around the world. . . . Zipes presents a nuanced argument about how fairy tales originated in ancient oral cultures, how they evolved through the rise of literary culture and print, and how, in our own time, they continue to change through their adaptation in an ever-growing variety of media." (Publisher's note)

Includes bibliographical references and index.

398.23   Tales and lore of places and times

Adams, Mark, 1967-

Meet Me in Atlantis; My Obsessive Quest to Find the Sunken City. Mark Adams. Penguin Group USA 2015 336 p. illustrations $27.95 **398.23**
> 1. Exploration 2. Atlantis (Legendary place)
> ISBN 0525953701; 9780525953708
>> LC 2014025735

Author Mark Adams examines why "mateur explorers are still actively searching for [Atlantis] this sunken city all around the world, based entirely on the clues Plato left behind. He visits scientists who use cutting-edge technology to find legendary civilizations once thought to be fictional. He examines the numerical and musical codes hidden in Plato's

writings, and . . . traces their roots back to Pythagoras, the sixth-century BC mathematician." (Publisher's note)

"Adams's excellent examination frames much of Atlantis research on an intimate level. In its own right, this work serves as an important contribution to the search for Atlantis. Readers of history, adventure, travel, scientific inquiry, or the history of science will find this book provocative and entertaining." LJ

398.8   Rhymes and rhyming games

The **Oxford** dictionary of nursery rhymes; edited by Iona and Peter Opie. 2nd ed; Oxford Univ. Press 1997 xxix, 559p il $55 **398.8**
> 1. Reference books 2. Nursery rhymes -- Dictionaries
> ISBN 0-19-860088-7
>> LC 98-140995

First published 1951

"The novice as well as the professional will find it an enjoyable read, as well as a learning experience." Am Ref Books Annu, 1999

398.9   Proverbs

Manser, Martin H.

The **Facts** on File dictionary of proverbs; associate editors, Rosalind Fergusson, David Pickering. 2nd ed.; Facts On File 2006 499p (Facts on File library of language and literature) $55; pa $19.95 **398.9**
> 1. Proverbs
> ISBN 0-8160-6673-6; 978-0-8160-6673-5; 0-8160-6674-4 pa; 978-0-8160-6674-2 pa
>> LC 2006-24535

Original edition published 1983 compiled by Rosalind Fergusson

This dictionary "includes more than 1,700 English-language proverbs . . . that are widely recognized today. Arranged alphabetically, entries provide the meaning of each proverb, the date it was first recorded, variant forms of the proverb, other proverbs that are similar and opposite to it in meaning, and examples of the proverb's use." Publisher's note

Includes bibliographical references

400 LANGUAGE

400 Language

Crystal, David

★ The **Cambridge** encyclopedia of language; 3rd ed; Cambridge University Press 2010 516p il map $99; pa $45 **400**
> 1. Reference books 2. Language and languages -- Encyclopedias
> ISBN 978-0-521-51698-3; 978-0-521-73650-3 pa
>> LC 2010-502889

First published 1987

"A valuable and concise . . . handbook for linguistic beginners, linguistic researchers looking for a quick overview and, most of all, the general reader interested in language." Linguist List

Includes bibliographical references

Everett, Daniel L.

Language; the cultural tool. Daniel L. Everett. Pantheon Books 2012 351 p. ill. $27.95   **400**
    1. Intellect 2. Communication 3. Sociolinguistics 4. Language and culture
    ISBN 0307378535; 9780307378538

LC 2011034829

This book looks at whether language is "a genetically programmed instinct or something we pick up from the culture around us . . . . Challenging Noam Chomsky, Steven Pinker, and other partisans of 'nativism,' which holds that certain kinds of knowledge are hard-wired into us . . . , linguist [Daniel L. Everett . . . argues that language is a practical tool for communicating and social bonding . . . that children learn through general intelligence." (Publishers Weekly)

"Everett unfolds a compelling analysis of how language informs all the activities we recognize as distinctively human. A linguistic study certain to attract many general readers." Booklist

Includes bibliographical references (p. [334]-337) and index

Kenneally, Christine

The first word; the search for the origins of language. Viking 2007 357p $26.95   **400**
    1. Evolution 2. Language and languages
    ISBN 978-0-670-03490-1; 0-670-03490-8

LC 2007-3182

The author "explains difficult ideas concisely and clearly, and she maintains a firm grip on the steering wheel, moving the overall argument along in a straight line. Above all, she is scrupulously fair-minded." N Y Times (Late N Y Ed)

Includes bibliographical references

Pinker, Steven

The language instinct; how the mind creates language. Harper Perennial 2007 526p il pa $15.95   **400**
    1. Language and languages
    ISBN 978-0-06-133646-1; 0-06-133646-7
    First published 1994 by Morrow

The author "argues that an 'innate grammatical machinery of the brain' exists, which allows children to 'reinvent' language on their own. Basing his ideas on Noam Chomsky's Universal Grammar theory, Pinker describes language as a 'discrete combinatorial system' that might easily have evolved via natural selection. Pinker steps on a few toes . . . but his work, while controversial, is well argued, challenging, often humorous, and always fascinating." Libr J

Includes bibliographical references

401   Philosophy and theory

Crystal, David

★ How language works; how babies babble, words change meaning, and languages live or die. Overlook Press 2006 500p $32.50   **401**
    1. Linguistics 2. Language and languages
    ISBN 1-58567-848-1

Crystal "offers an impeccably organized guide to language and communication that brings clarity to a scholarly subject, and is sure to become a standard reference." Publ Wkly

Includes bibliographical references

Pinker, Steven

The stuff of thought; language as a window into human nature. Viking 2007 499p il $29.95   **401**
    1. Thought and thinking 2. Language and languages
    ISBN 978-0-670-06327-7; 0-670-06327-4

LC 2007-26601

The author's "vivid prose and down-to-earth attitude will once again attract an enthusiastic audience outside academia." Publ Wkly

Includes bibliographical references

Words and rules; the ingredients of language. Perennial 2000 349p il pa $15   **401**
    1. Grammar 2. Language and languages
    ISBN 978-0-06-095840-4; 0-06-095840-5
    First published 1999 by Basic Books

This book "with its crisp prose and neat analogies, makes required reading for anyone interested in cognition and language." Publ Wkly

Includes bibliographical references

Yang, Charles

★ The infinite gift; how children learn and unlearn the languages of the world. Scribner 2006 275p il $25   **401**
    1. Language and languages
    ISBN 978-0-7432-3756-7; 0-7432-3756-0

The author explains the "process by which children acquire language. He discusses everything from the sounds they hear in the womb to how they distinguish between different languages at three months to their mastery of their language by age five. Throughout this learning process, posits Yang, a child has tested the grammar and sounds that exist in many other languages (and would presumably have no trouble acquiring them) but ultimately settles on the relevant one, and soon after, can no longer distinguish between or articulate nonrelevant sounds. . . . Anyone with the slightest interest in the English language should read his book." Libr J

410   Linguistics

Crystal, David

★ A dictionary of language; 2nd ed; University of Chicago Press 2001 390p il pa $17.50   **410**
    1. Reference books 2. Language and languages --

Dictionaries
ISBN 0-226-12203-4

LC 00-69076

First published 1992 with title: An encyclopedic dictionary of language and languages; present edition first published in the United Kingdom with title: The Penguin dictionary of language

This dictionary "offers explanations of the most frequently used linguistic terms, particularly those that can occur in texts read by beginners and by interested laypersons. . . . There are also entries concerned with graphology, shorthand writing, and similar peripheral, but interesting, topics. The impression that this dictionary has been written mainly for the general public is enhanced by the humorous jocose caricatures interspersed throughout the text, but the information is still solid. The author has succeeded in creating a handy dictionary that will serve students and laypeople equally well, for both browsing and study." Am Ref Book Annu, 2002

Deutscher, Guy

Through the language glass; why the world looks different in other languages. Metropolitan Books / Henry Holt and Co. 2010 304p il $28; ebook $14.99 **410**

1. Linguistics 2. Language and languages
ISBN 978-0-8050-8195-4; 978-1-4299-7011-2 ebook

LC 2010-1042

Deutscher "combines erudition, wry humor, and serious interpretation in this elegant and charmingly accessible study of the relation among language, culture, and thought and of how we have engaged in and reflected upon language over the years." Libr J

Includes bibliographical references

411 Writing systems of standard forms of languages

Houston, Keith

Shady characters; the secret life of punctuation, symbols, & other typographical marks. Keith Houston. W W Norton & Co Inc 2013 352 p. $25.95 **411**

1. Typography 2. Punctuation 3. Writing -- History 4. Punctuation -- History 5. Signs and symbols -- History 6. Type and type-founding -- History
ISBN 0393064425; 9780393064421

LC 2013017324

This book is a "bestiary of lesser-known punctuation marks. . . . Nearly every punctuation symbol in this book gained its start from the annotation marks of monks, scribes, or scholars. (The chapter on daggers and asterisks, of course, uses those symbols to mark the asides.) Some game-changers, like the sudden confines of the typing press or the yet-more-restrictive typewriter, extend their influence across numerous chapters." (Publishers Weekly)

Includes bibliographical references and index

418 Standard usage (Prescriptive linguistics)

Deheane, Stanislas

Reading in the brain; the science and evolution of a cultural invention. Viking 2009 388p il $27.95 **418**

1. Reading
ISBN 978-0-670-02110-9; 0-670-02110-5

LC 2009-09389

"Dense with ideas and experiments, but richly rewarding for readers willing to put in the effort." Kirkus

Includes bibliographical references

Grossman, Edith

Why translation matters. Yale University Press 2010 135p (Why X matters) **418**

1. Translating and interpreting 2. Literature -- Translations
ISBN 0-300-12656-5; 978-0-300-12656-3

LC 2009-26510

Grossman "argues for the cultural importance of translation and a more encompassing and nuanced appreciation of the translator's role." (Publisher's note) Index.

"In the end, Grossman warmly (after all) and gratefully rehearses the twofold answer to the question of her title: translation matters because it is an expression and an extension of our humanity, the secret metaphor of all literary communication; and because the creation of any literary translation is (or at least must be) an original writing, not a pathetic shadow or tracing of the inaccessible 'original' but the creation, indeed, of a second — and as we have seen, a third and a ninth — but always a new work, in another language." N Y Times Book Rev

Includes bibliographical references

419 Sign languages

Costello, Elaine

Random House Webster's American Sign Language dictionary: unabridged. Random House Reference 2008 xxxii, 1200p $55 **419**

1. Reference books 2. Sign language -- Dictionaries
ISBN 978-0-375-42616-2; 0-375-42616-7

First published 1994 with title: Random House American Sign Language dictionary

This dictionary includes "over 5,600 signs for the novice and experienced user alike. It includes complete descriptions of each sign, plus full-torso illustrations. There is also a subject index for easy reference as well as alternate signs for the same meaning." Publisher's note

Gallaudet University

★ The Gallaudet dictionary of American Sign Language; Clayton Valli, editor in chief; illustrated by Peggy Swartzel Lott, Daniel Renner, and Rob Hills. Gallaudet University Press 2005 xli, 558p il $49.95 **419**

1. Reference books 2. Sign language -- Dictionaries
ISBN 1-56368-282-6; 978-1-56368-282-7

LC 2005-51129

"This is a very valuable language resource for parents, students, and teachers learning ASL as a first language and as a second language." Choice

Includes bibliographical references

Grayson, Gabriel

Talking with your hands, listening with your eyes; a complete photographic guide to American Sign Language. Square One Pubs. 2002 373p il pa $26.95   **419**

1. Sign language
ISBN 0-7570-0007-X

LC 2002-1125

"An outstanding, user-friendly resource for those interested in learning ASL." SLJ

Sternberg, Martin L. A.

American Sign Language; a comprehensive dictionary. illustrated by Herbert Rogoff. Unabridged; HarperCollins Pubs. 1998 xxi, 983p il $60; pa $24   **419**

1. Reference books 2. Sign language -- Dictionaries
ISBN 0-06-271608-5; 0-06-273634-5 pa

LC 98-26649

First published 1981

Arranged alphabetically, this dictionary features 7,000 sign entries, with cross-references and more than 12,000 illustrations

Includes bibliographical references

Tennant, Richard A.

The American Sign Language handshape dictionary; {by} Richard A. Tennant, Marianne Gluszak Brown; illustrated by Valerie Nelson-Metlay. Gallaudet Univ. Press 1998 407p il $39.95   **419**

1. Sign language
ISBN 1-56368-043-2

LC 97-48389

This work organizes "signs by handshape rather than alphabetically by English word order. In so doing, it acts best as a recognition tool for the ASL learner, leading the user quickly to specific signs without having first to refer to an English-equivalent word." Libr J

420   Specific languages

Bragg, Melvyn

The **adventure** of English; the biography of a language. Arcade Pub. 2004 322p il $27.95   **420**

1. English language -- History
ISBN 1-55970-710-0

LC 2003-19583

First published 2003 in the United Kingdom

The author offers a "biography of the English language, highlighting key individuals, places, and literature that advanced it, as well as the political and social trends that influenced it. . . . Bragg discusses its evolution in the English colonies, devoting four chapters to the United States and one each to India, the West Indies, and Australia. . . . Well researched yet more accessible to a wide audience than scholarly treatments by linguists or historians." Libr J

Bryson, Bill

Made in America; an informal history of the English language in the United States. Avon Books 1996 417p pa $14.95   **420**

1. Americanisms 2. English language -- History
ISBN 978-0-380-71381-3; 0-380-71381-0

First published 1994 by Morrow

"For Bryson's wonderfully sane and reasoned discussion of the issues surrounding 'politically correct' language alone, this book is a worthwhile read." Libr J

Includes bibliographical references

Crystal, David

★ The **Cambridge** encyclopedia of the English language; 2nd ed; Cambridge Univ. Press 2003 499p il hardcover o.p. pa $35   **420**

1. English language
ISBN 0-521-82348-X; 0-521-53033-4 pa

LC 2003-272259

First published 1995

This "volume is divided into six broad topics that cover the English language's history, vocabulary, grammar, writing and speech systems, usage, and acquisition. Within these major topics, the book is divided into logical subtopics and finally into the basic unit of the text—the two-page spread. . . . The clear and spirited text is stunning, enhanced with over 500 illustrations, making this a particularly rich reference work and a browser's dream." Libr J {review of 1995 edition}

★ **English** as a global language; David Crystal. 2nd edition Cambridge University Press 2012 212 p. illustrations pbk $16.99   **420**

1. English language -- Social aspects
ISBN 1107611806; 9781107611801

LC 2013498883

First published 1997

Crystal's "account of the rise of English as a global language explores the history, current status and potential of English as the international language of communication. {Includes} sections on the future of English as a world language, English on the Internet, and the possibility of an English 'family' of languages." (Publisher's note)

Hitchings, Henry

The **language** wars; a history of proper English. Farrar, Straus and Giroux 2011 408p $28   **420**

1. English language -- Usage 2. English language -- History
ISBN 978-0-374-18329-5; 0-374-18329-5

LC 2011-10701

"As the author points out, there is probably not a person alive who does not have some bee in his bonnet about the way other people speak and write. Maybe it is the errant apostrophe, the splitting of the poor old infinitive, or the use of 'like' as a comma. Or perhaps it is the exclamation mark, once known as the 'shriek mark'. Mr Hitchings's book is a corrective to some of these linguistic prejudices. It is bracing to learn, for example, that the prohibition on splitting the infinitive is fairly recent. Pre-Victorians did not object. Chaucer was a splitter, and even Shakespeare had a go. Same story with the apostrophe: in the 18th-century authors were sprinkling apostrophes over everything. . . . Mr Hitchings reviews such matters with cool erudition. He is resolutely relaxed about usage, understanding that correctitude and intelligibility are not the same." Economist

Includes bibliographical references

McCrum, Robert

★ The **story** of English; [by] Robert McCrum, Willam Cran [and] Robert MacNeil. 3rd rev ed; Penguin Bks. 2003 xxi, 468p pa $16   **420**
   1. English language -- History
   ISBN 0-14-200231-3
                     LC 2002-29818
   First published 1986 by Viking
   A "companion to the PBS television series of the same name. . . . The text covers the history of our language from its roots in Latin through its transplanting to other shores and its infusions from other cultures and languages. . . . Good for browsing, this book is a must for word and history buffs." SLJ [review of 1986 edition]
   Includes bibliographical references

Metcalf, Allan A.

✓ **Predicting** new words; the secrets of their success. {by} Allan Metcalf. Houghton Mifflin 2002 206p il $22   **420**
   1. New words 2. English language -- Terms and phrases
   ISBN 0-618-13006-3
                     LC 2002-68593
   This book traces the origins of an "array of words and phrases: Marlboro Man, Frankenfood, blurb, skycap, quark, scofflaw. It also introduces us to a fascinating array of would-be words, coinages that never quite caught on. . . . The book is jam-packed with treats for word lovers." Booklist

421 Writing system, phonology, phonetics of standard English

★ **Acronyms**, initialisms, & abbreviations dictionary; 40th ed; Gale Res. 2008 4v set $1,190 **421**
   1. Reference books 2. Acronyms -- Dictionaries
   ISBN 978-1-4144-1902-2; 1-4144-1902-3
   First published 1960 in one volume with title: Acronyms dictionary. Frequently revised
   A guide to acronyms, initialisms, abbreviations, contractions, alphabetic symbols, and similar condensed apellations

Crystal, David

✓ **Spell** It Out; The Curious, Enthralling and Extraordinary Story of English Spelling. David Crystal. St. Martin's Press 2013 336 p. $22.99   **421**
   1. English language -- Spelling 2. English language -- Orthography and spelling 3. English language -- Orthography and spelling -- History
   ISBN 1250003474; 9781250003478
                     LC 2013010521
   In this book author David Crystal "takes readers on a history of English spelling, starting with the Roman missionar-

ies' sixth century introduction of the Roman alphabet and ending with where the language might be going. He looks individually at each letter in the alphabet and its origins. He considers the question of vowels and how people developed a way to tell whether or not it was long or short. He looks at influences from other cultures." (Publisher's note)

Rosen, Michael, 1946-

Alphabetical; how every letter tells a story. Michael Rosen. Counterpoint Press 2015 448 p. illustrations (hardback) $25   **421**
   1. Alphabet 2. Language and languages 3. Writing 4. Alphabet -- History 5. Alphabet in literature
   ISBN 1619024837; 9781619024830
                     LC 2014035051
   This book by Michael Rosen looks at the alphabet. "Each letter receives a brief description of its written evolution and the pronunciation of its name and its sounds, followed by a relevant topic beginning with that letter, such as 'D is for Disappeared Letters' and 'O is for OK.' . . .The diverse topics he covers also include printing fonts, diacritics ('U is for Umlauts'), and the ways that the alphabet can be manipulated to encrypt secrets." (Publishers Weekly)
   "Rosen also is mellow about "correctness" in usage and punctuation ("Our personal histories and feelings are wrapped up in what the letters and their means of transmission mean to each of us") and shows little sorrow for the disappearance of handwriting in schools; in fact, he thinks our current emphasis on it doesn't make much sense. A delightfully informative book about letters, their meanings, and the words and meanings we derive from them." Kirkus
   Includes bibliographical references and index

Truss, Lynne

✓ **Eats,** shoots & leaves; the zero tolerance approach to punctuation. Gotham Books 2004 xxvii, 209p $19.95; pa $12   **421**
   1. Punctuation
   ISBN 1-59240-087-6; 1-59240-203-8 pa
                     LC 2004-40646
   First published 2003 in the United Kingdom
   The author "dissects common errors that grammar mavens have long deplored (often, as she readily points out, in isolation) and makes . . . arguments for increased attention to punctuation correctness. . . . Truss serves up delightful, unabashedly strict and sometimes snobby little book, with cheery Britishisms ('Lawks-a-mussy!') dotting pages that express a more international righteous indignation." Publ Wkly
   Includes bibliographical references

422 Etymology of standard English

✓**Adonis** to Zorro; Oxford dictionary of reference and allusion. edited by Andrew Delahunty and Sheila Dignen. 3rd ed.; Oxford University Press 2010 406p $34.95   **422**
   1. Allusions 2. Reference books
   ISBN 978-0-19-956745-4; 0-19-956745-X
                     LC 2010-549367

First published 2001 with title: The Oxford dictionary of allusions

"This guide to allusions and common references is a moderately priced volume well worth adding to a public, school, community college, or college shelf. Neat and user-friendly, the 1,900 entries, their provenance, definitions, models, and starred cross-references identify a range of familiar terms, from 'Terminator' to 'hobbit,' and from 'My Lai' to the 'sword of Damocles' and 'thirty pieces of silver.' The text makes clever use of fonts, dingbats, and point count to identify authors, sources, and dates." Choice

Crystal, David

The **story** of English in 100 words; David Crystal. St. Martin's Press 2012 260 p. **422**
1. Vocabulary 2. English language -- History 3. English language -- Etymology 4. English language -- Foreign words and phrases 5. English language -- Foreign elements
ISBN 9781250003461; 9781466805088
LC 2012003038

This book presents "information about how English grows, changes, adopts and plays. . . . The author . . . teach[es] 100 lessons about English by picking out 100 words from our history, telling us their origin story and showing us how they've changed and spawned. Roughly chronological-beginning in the fifth century, ending in the 21st-[David] Crystal's text begins with what may be the first written word in our language, raihan, the word for roe-deer, and ends with something awfully recent, twittersphere. In between are not just the stories of individual words but the stories of how words become words. Why do we sometimes spell yogurt with an -h? Has there always been a difference between disinterested and uninterested? Why do only poets use certain words like swain?"(Kirkus)

Forsyth, Mark

The **etymologicon**; a circular stroll through the hidden connections of the English language. Mark Forsyth. Berkley Books 2012 XVIII, 252 p.p $16 **422**
1. English language -- Etymology
ISBN 0425260798; 9780425260791; 9781848313071
LC 2011535421

This book by Mark Forsyth presents a "guide to the strange underpinnings of the English language. It explains: how you get from 'gruntled' to 'disgruntled'; why you are absolutely right to believe that your meager salary barely covers 'money for salt'; how the biggest chain of coffee shops in the world (hint: Seattle) connects to whaling in Nantucket; and what precisely the Rolling Stones have to do with gardening." (Publisher's note)

★ **From** bonbon to cha-cha; Oxford dictionary of foreign words and phrases. edited by Andrew Delahunty. 2nd ed; Oxford University Press 2008 411p $24.95; pa $18.99 **422**
1. Reference books 2. English language -- Foreign words and phrases -- Dictionaries
ISBN 978-0-19-954369-4; 0-19-954369-0; 978-0-19-954368-7 pa; 0-19-954368-2 pa
LC 2008-482026

First published 1997 with title: The Oxford dictionary of foreign words and phrases. Paperback has title: Oxford dictionary of foreign words and phrases

This reference "offers coverage of more than 6,000 foreign words and phrases that are in regular use in English today." Publisher's note

Hendrickson, Robert

★ The **Facts** on File encyclopedia of word and phrase origins; 4th ed., [Updated and expanded ed.]; Facts On File 2008 948p (Facts on File library of language and literature) $95; pa $27.95 **422**
1. Reference books 2. English language -- Terms and phrases 3. English language -- Etymology -- Dictionaries
ISBN 978-0-8160-6966-8; 978-0-8160-6967-5 pa
LC 2007-48223

First published 1987

"Because the entries have both scholarly value and the capacity to entertain, the book is ideal for both linguists and lay readers." Libr J

Hitchings, Henry

The **secret** life of words; how English became English. Farrar, Straus and Giroux 2008 440p $27 **422**
1. English language -- Etymology
ISBN 978-0-374-25410-0; 0-374-25410-9
LC 2008-26055

"Hitchings here provides a colorful, thematic history of the English language. Treating borrowings and coinages as psychological windows to history, the author takes the reader on a tour of the lexicon from Anglo-Saxon to the present day and shows how new words answer linguistic needs. . . . Hitchings treats the reader to some 3,000 word histories. . . . With 90-plus pages of notes, sources, and useful indexes, this is a fine choice for libraries and a 'smorgasbord' for language aficionados." Choice

Includes bibliographical references

Manser, Martin H.

The **Facts** on File dictionary of allusions; David H. Pickering, associate editor. Facts on File 2008 532p (Facts on File library of language and literature) $75; pa $18.95 **422**
1. Allusions 2. Reference books 3. Literature -- Dictionaries
ISBN 978-0-8160-7105-0; 0-8160-7105-5; 978-0-8160-7907-0 pa; 0-8160-7907-2 pa
LC 2007-51375

"In approximately 4,000 entries, this . . . resource explores well-known events, places, people, and phenomena whose names have acquired linguistic significance, conveying a particular message beyond a mere reference to the objects referred to. Entries are drawn from a . . . range of sources, including Shakespeare and the Bible; Greek, Roman, and Norse mythology; texts from literature through the ages; historical events; popular culture; and film and television. Individual entries contain pronunciation guides, defini-

tions, examples, information on derived forms, and more."
Publisher's note
Includes bibliographical references

★ The **Facts** on File dictionary of foreign words and phrases; [by] Martin H. Manser; associate editors: Alice Grandison and David H. Pickering. 2nd ed., [New ed.]; Facts on File 2008 469p (Facts on File library of language and literature) $55; pa $19.95 **422**
  1. Reference books 2. English language -- Foreign words and phrases -- Dictionaries
  ISBN 978-0-8160-7035-0; 978-0-8160-7036-7 pa
LC 2007-29711
First published 2002
This dictionary includes more than 4,500 entries for terms that have entered the English lexicon from foreign languages in the fields of language and literature, religion, law, politics, economics, music, entertainment and cuisine. Examples or quotations are provided to illustrate usage.
"This is a captivating title to browse." SLJ
Includes bibliographical references

More word histories and mysteries; from aardvark to zombie. from the editors of the American Heritage dictionaries. Houghton Mifflin 2006 288p il pa $12.95 **422**
  1. Reference books 2. English language -- Etymology
  ISBN 978-0-618-71681-4; 0-618-71681-5
LC 2006020835
This "emphasizes the huge number of source languages from which English draws its vast vocabulary—from Sanskrit to French and beyond. The introductory pages give the reader a brief overview of the methods and aims of etymology and a potted history of the origins of English. . . . The editors then present an alphabetical listing of words and their etymology. Each of the 300-plus entries is about half a page to a page long and briefly outlines the origins of the word, its use, and the evolution of its meaning. . . . The book's informative yet informal writing style would appeal to the amateur enthusiast, and accessibility is further enhanced by a useful glossary of linguistic terms." Libr J

Quinion, Michael
  ★ **Ballyhoo,** buckeroo, and spuds; ingenious tales of words and their origins. Smithsonian Books 2004 288p $19.95 **422**
  1. English language -- Etymology 2. English language -- Terms and phrases
  ISBN 1-588-34219-0
LC 2004-52235
A look at common English "words and phrases most readers will probably have wondered about. We're all familiar with the phrase 'happy as a clam.' but why a clam? We know what a 10-gallon hat is, but how did it get its name? And what the heck is a ballyhoo, anyway? The book is simply organized—alphabetically, of course—and endlessly illuminating. Quinion's research and documentation are impeccable, and when he needs to make a leap of imagination, he does so gracefully. For word lovers, this book is indispensable." Booklist
Includes bibliographical references

Rosten, Leo
  The **new** joys of Yiddish; revisions and commentary by Lawrence Bush; illustrations by R. O. Blechman. Rev ed; Crown 2001 xxxii, 458p il $35; pa $18 **422**
  1. Yiddish language 2. English language -- Foreign words and phrases
  ISBN 0-609-60785-5; 0-609-80692-0 pa
LC 2001-28366
First published 1968 with title: The joys of Yiddish
This "work explores the nuances and complexities of language, clarifying the interrelationship between Yiddish and English (Yinglish, according to Rosten). The lengthy alphabetical listing not only presents multiple spellings, pronunciation guides, definitions, and cross references but also illustrates usage with background information, anecdotes, and jokes, as well as breezy erudition in the form of tidbits of cultural history, Talmudic and biblical references, tips on pronunciation, and thoughtful commentary. . . . The revision incorporates additional material on modern Yiddish literature and culture and updates on changes in American Jewish life and faith. Also included as an appendix is an English-Yiddish dictionary." Libr J
Includes bibliographical references

Stevens, Christopher
  Written in Stone; A Journey Through the Stone Age and the Origins of Modern Language. Christopher Stevens. W W Norton & Co Inc 2015 272 p. $27.95 **422**
  1. Stone Age 2. Language and languages
  ISBN 160598907X; 9781605989075
In this book author Christopher Stevens "combines detective work, mythology, ancient history, archaeology, the roots of society, technology and warfare, and the sheer fascination of words to explore that original mother tongue, sketching the connections woven throughout the immense vocabulary of English--with some surprising results." (Publisher's note)
"The history of English is fascinating and this is a delightful distraction from a more serious linguistic approach to the topic." LJ

Word histories and mysteries; from abracadabra to Zeus. from the editors of the American Heritage dictionaries. Houghton Mifflin Co. 2004 xvi, 348p il pa $12.95 **422**
  1. Reference books 2. English language -- Etymology
  ISBN 978-0-618-45450-1; 0-618-45450-0
LC 2004014798
"The 400 alphabetically arranged entries here illustrate the diversity from which the English language draws its vocabulary, particularly from the prehistoric base that linguists call Proto-Indo-European. As a result, the editors aim to demonstrate links between the ancient base and modern English. . . . An overall quality resource." Libr J

423   Dictionaries of standard English

Adelson-Goldstein, Jayme

The **Oxford** picture dictionary; [by] Jayme Adelson-Goldstein and Norma Shapiro. 2nd ed.; Oxford University Press 2008 285p il pa $16.95 **423**
1. Reference books 2. Picture dictionaries 3. English language -- Dictionaries
ISBN 978-0-19-436976-3; 0-19-436976-5

                   LC 2007-41017

First published 1998

This picture dictionary features "4,000 words and phrases illustrated with . . . artwork." Publisher's note

The **American** Heritage dictionary of the English language; 5th ed.; Houghton Mifflin Harcourt 2011 xxvii, 2084p il map **423**
1. Reference books 2. Encyclopedias and dictionaries 3. English language -- Usage -- Dictionaries 4. English language -- Dictionaries
ISBN 9780547041018

                   LC 2011004777

First published 1969

This book, "the fifth edition of "The American Heritage Dictionary of the English Language" (AHD)" includes 10,000 new words, with "color photos in the margin to illustrate the definitions. Countries all have a small map with their location and major cities. . . . [U]sage notes . . . . have been updated . . . AHD also includes example sentences, and many of these have been lengthened with the addition of quotations from writers . . . Synonyms for words have been added . . . The purchase of this print edition contains a passkey for a free app version, and there is a free online version at www.ahdictionary.com." (Booklist)

★ **Concise** Oxford American thesaurus. Oxford University Press 2006 996p $19.95 **423**
1. Reference books 2. English language -- Synonyms and antonyms
ISBN 0-19-530485-3; 978-0-19-530485-5

                   LC 2005-35868

First published 1997 in the United Kingdom with title: The concise Oxford thesaurus; Original American edition published 1999 with title: The Oxford American thesaurus of current English

This "thesaurus contains over 15,000 entries with more than 350,000 synonyms and is . . . arranged with the typical synonyms listed first. . . . This simple arrangement makes this thesaurus particularly user-friendly." Libr J

Davidson, Mark

★ **Right,** wrong, and risky; a dictionary of today's American English usage. Norton 2006 570p $29.95 **423**
1. Americanisms 2. Reference books 3. English language -- Usage 4. English language -- Dictionaries
ISBN 0-393-06119-1

                   LC 2005-17628

The author "offers a dictionary that 'views the real world of today's American English, identifying usage questions that are debatable, citing conflicting answers, and offering risk-free solutions for each conflict.' . . . Browsers will enjoy

the colorful, interesting backstories on the origins of terms such as ground zero, on the sudden warming to the phrase girl talk, and on the widely misunderstood use of the word Neanderthal." Booklist

Includes bibliographical references

★ **Dictionary** of confusable words; {edited by} Adrian Room. Fitzroy Dearborn Pubs. 2000 251p $35 **423**
1. English language -- Usage 2. English language -- Synonyms
ISBN 1-57958-271-0

A "guide to potentially confusing words. . . . The brief entries give definitions of each of the terms. Each word is then used in at least one sample sentence, clarifying the differences between like terms. The definitions and examples are in simple language and are easy to understand." Libr J

Espy, Willard R.

Words to rhyme with; a rhyming dictionary. 3rd ed.; Facts On File 2006 683p (Facts on File library of language and literature) $75; pa $19.95 **423**
1. English language -- Rhyme
ISBN 0-8160-6303-6; 978-0-8160-6303-1; 0-8160-6304-4 pa; 978-0-8160-6304-8 pa

                   LC 2005-51122

First published 1986

"Including a primer of prosody, a list of more than 80,000 words that rhyme, a glossary defining 9,000 of the more eccentric rhyming words, and a variety of exemplary verses, one of which does not rhyme at all." Title page

Garner, Bryan A.

★ **Garner's** modern American usage; 3rd ed; Oxford University Press 2009 lx, 942p $45 **423**
1. Reference books 2. Americanisms -- Dictionaries 3. English language -- Usage -- Dictionaries
ISBN 978-0-19-538275-4

                   LC 2009-9539

First published 1998 with title: A dictionary of modern American usage

"One would be tempted to say that this is clearly one of the best works on the topic, but doing so would be using one of Garner's weasel words (intensives such as clearly that 'actually have the effect of weakening a statement'). Suffice it to say that it is highly recommended for most libraries." Booklist

Includes bibliographical references (p. 925-938)

Historical thesaurus of the Oxford English dictionary; with additional material from A Thesaurus of Old English. [edited by] Christian Kay [et al.] Oxford University Press 2009 3952p 2v set $395 **423**
1. Reference books 2. English language -- Synonyms and antonyms
ISBN 978-0-19-920899-9

                   LC 2009-935029

"The knowledge compiled in this 40-year project is stunning, and promises to revolutionize the study of the language by making wholly new kinds of questions possible." Choice

Includes bibliographical references

Houghton Mifflin Co.

★ The **American** Heritage guide to contemporary usage and style. Houghton Mifflin 2005 512p $19.95 **423**

1. English language -- Usage

ISBN 978-0-618-60499-9; 0-618-60499-5

LC 2005-16513

"Drawing on the authoritative knowledge of its lexicographers and the considered collective judgment of a panel of noted writers, the book offers guidance on the simple (the pronunciations of bouquet); the perplexingly redundant (free gift); the often imprecisely used (impeach); the no longer distinct (healthful/healthy); the needless but persistent (irregardless); the easily confused (stationary/stationery); the unfortunately conflated (lay/lie); and many more pitfalls. Articles embodying the precision and lucidity of dictionary definitions explain the history of a word's or expression's usage issue, how and why the issue exists, and the preferred usage." Booklist

Little, Brown & Co. Inc.

★ **Bartlett's** Roget's thesaurus. Little, Brown 1996 xxxii, 1415p $21.95; pa $16.95 **423**

1. Americanisms 2. Reference books 3. English language -- Synonyms and antonyms

ISBN 0-316-10138-9; 0-316-73587-6 pa

LC 96-18343

This thesaurus "reflects the current state of American English, including terminology from the worlds of composers and television, with such sub-categories as 'Living Things,' 'The Arts,' 'Feelings.' But what really makes the book a joy to use is the tremendously useful lists—everything from phobias to styles and periods of furniture." Am Libr

Merriam-Webster Inc.

★ **Merriam-**Webster's collegiate dictionary; Eleventh ed; Merriam-Webster 2003 1623p il $23.95 **423**

1. Reference books 2. English language -- Dictionaries

ISBN 0-87779-808-7

LC 2003-3674

First published 1898

This edition includes over 165,000 entries, 10,000 new words and meanings, 38,000 etymologies, a handbook of style, an essay on the English language, a special section on signs and symbols, and a free one-year subscription to the Collegiate Web site.

★ **Merriam-**Webster's collegiate thesaurus; 2nd ed.; Merriam-Webster 2010 16a, 1162p $21.95 **423**

1. Reference books 2. English language -- Synonyms and antonyms

ISBN 978-0-8777-9269-7; 0-8777-9269-0

LC 2009-42161

First published 1976 with title: Webster's collegiate thesaurus

"Employs a conventional dictionary arrangement, and gives synonyms, related terms, idiomatic equivalents, antonyms, and contrasted words as applicable. Cross-references in small capitals." Guide to Ref Books. 11th edition

★ **Merriam-**Webster's visual dictionary. Merriam-Webster, Inc. 2012 1112 p. (hbk.) $39.95 **423**

1. English language -- Dictionaries

ISBN 0877791511; 9780877791515

This visual dictionary, edited by Jean-Claude Corbeil, has "more than 8,000 highly detailed, full-color illustrations, organized by subject in specialized fields from all aspects of life, . . . [and] nearly 25,000 . . . technical and everyday terms with clear, concise definitions. . . . Themes include a wide variety of fields: astronomy, the earth, human beings, the animal kingdom, plants and gardening, . . . food, arts and architecture, . . . sports and games" and more. (Publisher's note)

Mugglestone, Lynda

Lost for words; the hidden history of the Oxford English Dictionary. Yale University Press 2005 xxi, 273p il $30 **423**

1. Oxford English dictionary

ISBN 0-300-10699-8

LC 2004-29344

"Serious word lovers will appreciate . . . [this book's] fascinating revelations." Booklist

Includes bibliographical references

★ **New** Oxford American dictionary; 3rd ed.; Oxford University Press 2010 xxvi, 2018p il map $60 **423**

1. Reference books 2. Americanisms -- Dictionaries 3. English language -- Dictionaries

ISBN 978-0-19-539288-3

LC 2010-20033

First published 1980 with title: The Oxford American dictionary. Editors vary

"This dictionary arranges definitions by most current usage and provides additional guidance in usage notes. Although U.S. English is the focus here, regionalisms from other English-speaking areas are also included. More than 1000 illustrations (e.g., photos, drawings, diagrams) clarify definitions. . . . A labor of love and an unparalleled gift to writers and readers worldwide, the New Oxford American Dictionary should be on the reference shelves of every library." Libr J

★ **Oxford** American writer's thesaurus; compiled by Christine A. Lindberg. 2nd ed.; Oxford University Press 2008 xxvi, 1052p $40 **423**

1. Reference books 2. English language -- Synonyms and antonyms

ISBN 978-0-19-534284-0; 0-19-534284-4

LC 2008-31259

First published 2004

"This expansive reference . . . is a functional treasure." Libr J

★ **Oxford** dictionary of English idioms; 3rd ed., Oxford pbk ed.; Oxford University Press 2010 408p (Oxford paperback reference) pa $16.95 **423**

1. Reference books 2. English language -- Idioms

ISBN 978-0-19-954378-6

LC 2010-935315

First published 1999 with title: The Oxford dictionary of idioms

This book "contains entries for over 6,000 idioms. . . . These include a range of idioms such as 'the elephant in the corner,' 'go figure,' 'step up to the plate,' 'a walk in the park,' and 'win ugly.'" Publisher's note

The **Oxford** English dictionary; 2nd ed; Oxford Univ. Press 1989 20v apply to publisher for price **423**
1. Reference books 2. English language -- Dictionaries
ISBN 0-19-861186-2

LC 88-5330

First published 1888 with title: New English dictionary on historical principles

"This is an etymological or word-source dictionary. In addition to definitions, this work gives the history of 290,500 words, both current and archaic, in the English language. Slang entries are very limited. Word histories include early forms, variant forms and roots, and first or exemplary usages in English from ancient to modern times. Short explanatory notes are provided for more common words." N Y Public Libr Book of How & Where to Look It Up

Princeton Language Institute

★ **Roget's** 21st century thesaurus in dictionary form; the essential reference for home, school, or office. edited by the Princeton Language Institute; Barbara Ann Kipfer, head lexicographer. 3rd ed; Bantam Dell 2005 962p $15; pa $5.99 **423**
1. Reference books 2. English language -- Synonyms and antonyms
ISBN 0-385-33895-3; 0-440-24269-X pa
First published 1992

This thesaurus, cross referencing each word with the same concept, provides 500,000 synonyms and antonyms in a dictionary format and includes recently coined and common slang terms and commonly used foreign terms.

★ **Random** House Webster's unabridged dictionary; 2nd ed.; Random House 2005 xxvi, 2230p il map $59.95 **423**
1. Reference books 2. English language -- Dictionaries
ISBN 0-375-42599-3

First published 1966 with title: The Random House dictionary of the English language

This dictionary contains over 315,000 entries. A newwords section and an essay on the growth of English are included. 2,400 spot maps and illustrations complement the text

★ **Roget's** international thesaurus; 6th ed; HarperResource 2001 xxv, 1248p $20.95; pa $16.95 **423**
1. Reference books 2. English language -- Synonyms and antonyms
ISBN 0-06-273693-0; 0-06-093544-8 pa

LC 2002-276277

First copyright edition published 1911 with title: The standard thesaurus of English words and phrases classified and arranged so as to facilitate the expression of ideas and assist in literary composition

This edition includes 330,000 words and phrases organized into 1,075 categories and a pinpoint reference system

that directs the user from a comprehensive index to the numbered category of the right word. Cross-references throughout lead to other categories. Also included are supplemental word lists that supply the names of things which have no synonyms (measurements, wines, state mottoes) as well as quotations that amplify the meanings of selected words

★ **Shorter** Oxford English dictionary on historical principles; [editor-in-chief, Lesley Brown] 6th ed.; Oxford University Press 2007 2v il map set $175 **423**
1. Reference books 2. English language -- Dictionaries
ISBN 978-0-19-923324-3; 0-19-923324-1

LC 2007-37226

First published 1933

This dictionary "has more than half a million definitions drawn from the Oxford English Corpus database of more than 1.5 billion words. . . . It includes 'all words in current English from 1700 to the present day, plus the vocabulary of Shakespeare, the Authorized Version of the Bible and other major works from before 1700.'" Booklist

Includes bibliographical references

Simpson, John

The **word** detective; Searching for the Meaning of It All at the Oxford English Dictionary. John Simpson. Basic Books 2016 384 p. (ebook) $18.99; (hardback) $27.99 **423**
1. Lexicographers 2. English language 3. Oxford English dictionary 4. English language -- Lexicography 5. Lexicographers -- Great Britain -- Biography
ISBN 9780465096527; 9780465060696

LC 2016025594

In this book, by John Simpson, "an intensely personal memoir and a joyful celebration of English, he weaves a story of how words come into being (and sometimes disappear), how culture shapes the language we use, and how technology has transformed not only the way we speak and write but also how words are made." (Publisher's note)

"Simpson's vibrant and inspiring memoir gives us a glimpse into life as detective in the realm of words." Pub Wkly

Upton, Clive

★ **Oxford** rhyming dictionary; {by} Clive Upton, Eben Upton. Oxford University Press 2004 659p $37.95 **423**
1. English language -- Rhyme
ISBN 0-19-280115-5

LC 2004-53133

In this dictionary "an index of words leads to numbered sections of phonic groupings of end, double, and triple syllable rhymes, with proximate groupings of near rhymes. But the index (95,000 words) . . . provides many word variations." Choice

Winchester, Simon

The **professor** and the madman; a tale of murder, insanity, and the making of the Oxford English dictionary. HarperCollins Pubs. 1998 242p il $22; pa $13 **423**

1. Surgeons 2. Mentally ill 3. Editors 4. Murderers 5. Lexicographers 6. Oxford English dictionary 7. New English dictionary on historical principles 8. English language -- Lexicography -- History -- 19th century 9. United States -- History -- Civil War, 1861-1865 -- Veterans -- Biography
ISBN 0-06-017596-6; 0-06-099486-X pa

LC 98-10204

Winchester examines the relationship between James Murray, editor of the Oxford English Dictionary, and "William C. Minor (1834-1920), . . . a Civil War surgeon whose war experience caused his personality to change. He became paranoid and was eventually diagnosed as schizophrenic. After three years in an asylum, he went to Europe in 1871. . . . {In London} he killed George Merritt. An English court found him not guilty on the ground of insanity, and Minor was sent to Broadmoor. Coming across a leaflet for volunteers to help compile a history of the English language, Minor offered his services. . . . After 17 years of correspondence, the editor of the Oxford English Dictionary came to meet Minor, who had submitted 10,000 definitions to the project." (Libr J)

The author relates the "story of the Oxford English Dictionary's first editor and the expatriate American murderer who contributed more than 10,000 quotations as examples. Best of all, among the entertaining tangents one learns a great deal about the making of that grandest of all reference works." Libr J

Includes bibliographical references

423.13 Idioms--Dictionaries

Ammer, Christine.
The **American** Heritage dictionary of idioms. Christine Ammer. Houghton Miffliln 2013 506 p (pa) $15.95 **423.13**
ISBN 0547676581; 9780547676586

LC 9780547676586

"This book surveys 10,000 American English expressions. Idioms predominate, but common figures of speech (e.g., blind as a bat), interjections, proverbs, colloquialisms (out in left field), emphatic redundancies whose word order cannot be reversed (far and wide), and slang phrases are also included. Entries and their variants are listed alphabetically in boldface. Where a phrase has more than one meaning, definitions are numbered and ordered by frequency of use. Keywords to phrases are listed alphabetically among the entries and note all the entries that contain that keyword. Entries are labeled to indicate the degree of formality or offensiveness: colloquial, slang, and vulgar slang." (Booklist)

"This book makes for fun browsing and could be very helpful to foreign speakers." Choice

Includes bibliographical references

425 Grammar of standard English

Huddleston, Rodney D.
★ The **Cambridge** grammar of the English language; {by} Rodney Huddleston, Geoffrey K. Pullum in collaboration with Laurie Bauer {et al.} Cambridge Univ. Press 2002 1842p il $160 **425**

1. English language -- Grammar
ISBN 0-521-43146-8

LC 2001-25630

This "comprehensive and detailed look at the principles of the English language . . . {is} an authoritative addition to the fields of both English grammar and linguistics." Libr J

Includes bibliographical references

427 Historical and geographic variations, modern nongeographic variations of English

Axelrod, Alan
Whiskey tango foxtrot; the real language of the modern American military. Alan Axelrod. Skyhorse Publishing 2013 240 p. (pbk. : alk. paper) $12.95 **427**

1. English language -- Slang 2. United States -- Armed forces 3. Sailors -- United States -- Language -- Dictionaries 4. Soldiers -- United States -- Language -- Dictionaries 5. Military art and science -- United States -- Dictionaries 6. English language -- United States -- Slang -- Dictionaries
ISBN 1620876477; 9781620876473

LC 2013011431

In this book, Alan Axelrod "tours modern military slang via six topical chapters, including 'Cake Eaters and Chicken Guts.' As the author acknowledges, the sources for some of his entries are from 'official' authorities such as the Department of Defense Dictionary of Military Terms . . . , but Axelrod's main focus is 'unofficial' terms, such as soldiers' rework of the 'What the . . . ' curse as expressed in this book's title." (Library Journal)

Ayto, John
The **Oxford** dictionary of slang. Oxford University Press 2003 (Oxford paperback reference) pa $16.95 **427**
ISBN 0-19-860763-6

LC 427

A reissue of the title first published 1998

"The 10,000 slang terms defined here originated mainly in the United States, Britain, Australia, or New Zealand and include both old and new coinages. The dictionary's arrangement is topical in thesaurus fashion." Libr J

Bailey, Richard W.
Speaking American; a history of English in the United States. Richard W. Bailey. Oxford University Press 2012 xvi, 207 p.p (alk. paper) $27.95 **427**

1. Americanisms 2. English language -- History 3. English language -- Lexicography -- United States 4. English language -- United States -- Usage 5. English language -- United States -- Grammar 6. English

language -- United States -- History 7. English language -- Variation -- United States

ISBN 019517934X; 9780195179347

LC 2011011042

In this book, Richard W. Bailey "identifies eight major centers of influence on American English and describes how each has helped shape the tongue of today. . . . In his introduction, he" refutes "the idea that language can somehow be perfected and standardized and celebrates the ability of English to change, adapt, adopt, steal and transform. Then he offers a series of . . . chapters, each focusing on a certain region whose influence on the language has been profound." (Kirkus Reviews)

Includes bibliographical references and index.

Crystal, David

By hook or by crook; a journey in search of English. Overlook Press 2008 314p il map $27.95 **427**

1. English language -- Dialects

ISBN 978-1-59020-061-2; 1-59020-061-6

First published 2007 in the United Kingdom

Combines personal reflections, historical allusions, and traveler's observations about the author's encounters with language and its users throughout the English-speaking world.

"In a conversational style that includes plenty of quirky facts, Crystal captures the exploratory, seductive, teasing, quirky, tantalizing nature of language study, and in doing so illuminates the fascinating world of words in which we live." Publ Wkly

Includes bibliographical references

The **stories** of English. Overlook Press 2004 584p il map $35 **427**

1. English language -- History

ISBN 1-585-67601-2

LC 2004-54727

The author "traces the diverse and unpredictable influences that have shaped English into an unruly family of dialects, creoles, and patois. . . . Crystal acknowledges the emergence during the fourteenth and fifteenth centuries of a prestigious standard version of English. Yet he shows in instance after instance that the tempests of linguistic change have often overwhelmed the custodians of the King's English, compelling them to accommodate forces they could not control. And though he never loses his focus on language, Crystal allows some of its more colorful users—including Chaucer, Shakespeare, Samuel Johnson, and Thomas Jefferson—to bring their personalities and voices into the chronicle." Booklist

Includes bibliographical references

Holder, R. W.

★ How not to say what you mean; a dictionary of euphemisms. 4th ed.; Oxford University Press 2007 410p pa $18.95 **427**

1. Reference books 2. Euphemism -- Dictionaries

ISBN 978-0-19-920839-5; 0-19-920839-5

LC 2007-37558

First published 1987 by Bath University Press with title: A dictionary of American and British euphemisms

"Here are almost five thousand euphemistic expressions listed in alphabetical order, ranging from well-known favorites such as 'push up the daisies,' 'fly-by-night,' 'red light district,' 'take to the cleaners,' 'get lucky,' and 'five-fingered discount,' to less amusing expressions from the bureaucratic and military world such as 'restructuring,' 'collateral damage,' and 'extrajudicial killing.' For each word or expression, Holder includes examples from . . . authors, along with . . . explanations of the words' origins and meaning." Publisher's note

Includes bibliographical references

McMahon, Sean

★ **Brewer's** dictionary of Irish phrase & fable; [by] Sean McMahon and Jo O'Donoghue. Brewer's 2009 867p $34.95 **427**

1. Allusions 2. Reference books 3. Folklore -- Ireland 4. Irish literature -- Dictionaries

ISBN 978-0-550-10565-3

First published 2004 by Weidenfeld & Nicholson

"Entries explore the island's history, literature, language, folklore and mythology . . . [with a] mix of people, places, historical events, facts and phrases. . . . 6,000 entries focus on the phrase and fable of Ireland, from ancient myth to modern politics." Publisher's note

MacNeil, Robert

Do you speak American? [by] Robert MacNeil and William Cran. 1st Harvest ed.; Harcourt 2005 228p map pa $13 **427**

1. Americanisms 2. English language -- Dialects

ISBN 978-0-15-603288-9; 0-15-603288-0

LC 2005-23093

Sequel to The story of English (1986)

First published 2005 by Nan A. Talese/Doubleday

"Whether talking to crab fishermen in Maryland or country-and-western singers in Tennessee, the authors discover that regional dialects are thriving despite the uniformity of our national tastes in clothing, fast-food chains, and movies. . . . The authors show how mobility, immigration, and racial and ethnic mixing are rapidly and profoundly changing the language. . . . This is colorful, witty, and insightful commentary on American speech patterns." Booklist

Includes bibliographical references

★ The **new** Partridge dictionary of slang and unconventional English; Tom Dalzell (senior editor) and Terry Victor (editor) Routledge 2006 2v set $220 **427**

1. Reference books 2. English language -- Slang -- Dictionaries

ISBN 0-415-21258-8; 978-0-415-21258-8

First published 1937

This slang dictionary places "emphasis on post-World War II slang and unconventional English." (Publisher's note)

"Entries list the term, identify its part of speech, explain its meaning, identify the country of origin, and cite sources or provide quotations showing how the term is used. . . . This dictionary informs, but it also entertains." Booklist

Includes bibliographical references

Nunberg, Geoffrey

The **ascent** of the A-word; assholism, the first sixty years. Geoffrey Nunberg. PublicAffairs 2012 251 p. (hardcover) $25.99 **427**

1. Popular culture 2. English language -- Slang 3. English language -- History 4. Words, Obscene 5. English language -- Obscene words

ISBN 1610391756; 9781610391757; 9781610391764

LC 2012017027

Author Geoffrey "Nunberg's study of the word 'asshole' . . . breaks down the important place the word 'asshole' occupies in our language and culture. Nunberg begins by charting the rise of 'asshole' from its origins as WWII barracks slang, to its popularization in post-war literature . . . to its eventual adoption as part of Standard English in the 1970s." (Publishers Weekly)

Spears, Richard A.

★ **McGraw**-Hill's dictionary of American slang and colloquial expressions; 4th ed.; McGraw-Hill 2006 xxix, 546p pa $19.95 **427**

1. Americanisms 2. Reference books 3. English language -- Slang -- Dictionaries

ISBN 0-07-146107-8; 978-0-07-146107-8

LC 2005-52220

First published 1989 with title: NTC's dictionary of American slang and colloquial expressions

This book offers "definitions of more than 12,000 slang and informal expressions from various sources, ranging from golden oldies such as . . . golden oldie, to recent coinages like shizzle (gangsta), jonx (Wall Street), and ping (the Internet). Each entry is followed by examples illustrating how an expression is used in everyday conversation and, where necessary, International Phonetic Alphabet pronunciations are given, as well as cautionary notes for crude, inflammatory, or taboo expressions." Publisher's note

Includes bibliographical references

428 Standard English usage (Prescriptive linguistics)

Adolescent literacy in the academic disciplines; general principles and practical strategies. edited by Tamara L. Jetton, Cynthia Shanahan. The Guilford Press 2012 xiv, 274 p.p ill. (paper) $30 **428**

1. Reading 2. Literacy 3. Teaching 4. Secondary education 5. Language arts (Secondary) 6. Language arts -- Correlation with content subjects

ISBN 1462502806; 9781462502806; 9781462502837

LC 2011035689

This book, edited by Tamara L. Jetton and Cynthia Shanahan, "addresses the particular challenges of literacy learning in each of the major academic disciplines. Chapters focus on how to help students successfully engage with texts and ideas in English/literature, science, math, history, and arts classrooms, The book shows that . . . students also need to learn processing strategies that are quite specific to each subject and its typical tasks or problems." (Publisher's note)

Includes bibliographical references and index

Dunn, Patricia A.

Grammar rants. Heinemann/Boynton/Cook Publishers 2011 xvi, 134 p **428**

1. Grammar 2. Textbooks 3. English language -- Grammar

ISBN 0867096055; 9780867096057

LC 2011005689

This book presents an analysis of debates and complaints concerning the moral and social implications of grammar. "Each chapter includes actual rants along with . . . editorial commentary, instructional activities and classroom lessons" intended to facilitate student discussion on the social aspects of grammar and the assumptions people make when they encounter incorrect usage. According to the publisher, these "lessons will promote savvy writing by empowering students and teachers to see for themselves how best to raise the quality of their written and spoken language without resorting to ranting." (Publisher's note)

Includes bibliographical references and index.

Florey, Kitty Burns

Sister Bernadette's barking dog; the quirky history and lost art of diagramming sentences. Melville House 2006 154p $19.95 **428**

1. English language -- Grammar

ISBN 978-1-933633-10-7; 1-933633-10-7

LC 2006-24703

The author "writes with verve about the nuns who taught her to render the English language as a mess of slanted lines, explains how diagrams work, and traces the bizarre history of the men who invented this odd pedagogical tool. And unlike so many of today's microhistorians, who seek to demonstrate how zippers, azaleas, or hopscotch explain the world, Florey is refreshingly content to recount her tale without any suggestion that the diagramming of sentences somehow illuminates the American character. It's a great read." Slate

Fowler, H. W. (Henry Watson), 1858-1933

★ A **dictionary** of modern English usage; H.W. Fowler; with an introduction and notes by David Crystal. Oxford University Press 2010 784 p. **428**

1. English language -- Usage 2. English language -- Idioms 3. English language -- Etymology

ISBN 019958589X; 9780199585892

LC 2011389197

First published 1926

"Much loved for his firm opinions, passion, and dry humor, Fowler has stood the test of time and is still considered by many to be the best arbiter of good practice. Now Oxford is bringing back the original long-out-of-print first edition of this beloved work, enhanced with a new introduction by one of today's leading experts on the language, David Crystal. Drawing on a wealth of entertaining examples, Crystal offers an insightful reassessment Fowler's reputation and his place in the history of linguistic thought. Most important, Crystal examines nearly 300 of Fowler's entries in detail, offering a modern perspective on them, and showing how English has changed since the 1920s." (Publisher's note)

Hult, Christine A.

The **Handy** English grammar answer book; Christine A. Hult. Visible Ink Press 2015 419 p. illustrations (paperback) $21.95   **428**

1. English language -- Usage 2. English language -- Grammar 3. English language -- Grammar -- Handbooks, manuals, etc

ISBN 9781578595204; 1578595207

LC 2015015787

Author Christine A. Hult presnts this "guide to writing with clarity for all occasions. It offers fundamental principles, grammar rules, and punctuation advice, as well as insights on writing for different occasions and audiences. From a brief history of the English language to the deconstruction—and explanation—of the different parts of a sentence, and from showing how to punctuate correctly to how to organize a well-argued essay, this easy-to-use reference answers nearly 500 questions." (Publisher's note)

"This grammar guide distills a lot of technical grammar rules into a digestible format directed toward a wide audience and those new to the English language." Booklist

Includes bibliographical references and index.

Norris, Mary

Between you & me; confessions of a Comma Queen. Mary Norris. W W Norton & Co Inc 2015 240 p. (hardcover) $24.95   **428**

1. English language -- Grammar 2. English language -- Errors of usage 3. Comma 4. English language -- Punctuation 5. English language -- Errors in usage

ISBN 0393240185; 9780393240184

LC 2014043252

In this book, professional editor Mary Norris "brings her vast experience, good cheer, and finely sharpened pencils to help the rest of us in a boisterous language book as full of life as it is of practical advice. . . . [The book offers] descriptions of some of the most common and vexing problems in spelling, punctuation, and usage . . . and her clear explanations of how to handle them." (Publisher's note)

"In countless laugh-out-loud passages, Norris displays her admirable flexibility in bending rules when necessary. She even makes her serious quest to uncover the reason for the hyphen in the title of the classic novel Moby-Dick downright hilarious. A funny book for any serious reader." Kirkus

Includes bibliographical references and index

O'Conner, Patricia T.

★ **Woe** is I; the grammarphobe's guide to better English in plain English. Riverhead Bks. 2003 240p $19.95; pa $14   **428**

1. English language -- Usage 2. English language -- Grammar

ISBN 1-57322-252-6; 1-59448-006-0 pa

LC 2003-41416

First published 1996

This guide to good English offers advice on punctuation, usage, style and grammar as well as e-mail.

"The author doesn't take herself or the subject matter too seriously, offering a delightful romp through the intricacies of our language. . . . She knows her subject, can convey her message with wit and ease, and does it all in a compact,

easy-to-read format. In short, this is an entertaining and useful grammar reference." Libr J

Includes bibliographical references

Peters, Pam

★ The **Cambridge** guide to English usage. Cambridge University Press 2004 608p il $35   **428**

1. Reference books 2. English language -- Usage

ISBN 0-521-62181-X

LC 2004-301888

"Considering the abundance of peculiarities and challenges in English usage, Cambridge will strengthen even a library well stocked with other guides. It is a serious book for those serious about language." Booklist

Strumpf, Michael

The **grammar** bible; everything you always wanted to know about grammar but didn't know whom to ask. [by] Michael Strumpf and Auriel Douglas. Holt 2004 489p pa $18   **428**

1. English language -- Grammar

ISBN 0-8050-7560-7

LC 2003-57129

The authors move "from the parts of speech to the parts of the sentence and then to spelling, vocabulary, and punctuation, even encompassing thorny issues (e.g., sexist language, split infinitives) and complex grammatical terms (e.g., objective complements, gerund phrases). The authors also include a useful list of collocations and intersperse informative and often amusing 'Hot Line' queries throughout. . . This book is thorough, combining practical information not easily found in trade books, and is lively without trying to be too witty, cute, or humorous." Libr J

Includes bibliographical references

433 Dictionaries of standard German

★ **Random** House Webster's German-English, English-German dictionary; Rev. ed; Random House Reference 2006 547p $12.95   **433**

1. Reference books 2. German language -- Dictionaries

ISBN 0-375-72194-0; 978-0-375-72194-6

First published 1997 with title: Random House German-English English-German dictionary

In addition to more than 60,000 entries this dictionary also includes notes on pronunciation, lists of abbreviations, tables of irregular verbs and lists of geographical names.

439 Other Germanic languages

Comprehensive Yiddish-English Dictionary; Hayem Bokhner, Sholem Beynfeld, shef-redaktorn; Berish Goldshteyn, Yankl Salant, asotsyirte redaktorn = Solon Beinfeld, Harry Bochner, editors-in-chief; Barry Goldstein, Yankl Salant, associate editors. Indiana University Press 2013 xxxix, 704 p.p (hardcover) $45   **439**

1. Encyclopedias and dictionaries 2. Yiddish language -- Dictionaries 3. Yiddish language -- Dictionaries --

English
ISBN 0253009839; 9780253009838

LC 2012491596

This book is a Yiddish-English dictionary. It contains "more than 37,000 words and a treasure horde of idiomatic phrases." It provides "readers with the most contemporary grammatical and semantic nuances. . . . Included is a . . . user's guide, an introduction and road map through the difficulties inherent in working with two distinct alphabets and language systems." (Choice)

440 French and related Romance languages

Nadeau, Jean-Benoit

★ The **story** of French; [by] Jean-Benoît Nadeau [and] Julie Barlow. St. Martin's Press 2006 483p map $25.95 **440**
1. French language
ISBN 9780312341831; 0312341830

LC 2006-49348

This book explores the origins and evolution of the French language.

This is "a well-told, highly accessible history of the French language that leads to a spirited discussion of the prospects for French in an increasingly English-dominated world." N Y Times (Late N Y Ed)
Includes bibliographical references

443 Dictionaries of standard French

Correard, Marie-Helene

★ The **Oxford**-Hachette French dictionary; French-English, English-French. edited by Marie-Hélène Corréard, Valerie Grundy. 4th ed.; Oxford University Press/Hachette Livre 2007 xxxviii, 1945p $55 **443**
1. Reference books 2. French language -- Dictionaries
ISBN 978-0-19-861422-7; 0-19-861422-5

LC 2007-14213

First published 1994

This work provides coverage of French and English vocabulary in general as well as scientific and technical areas with over 350,000 words and phrases and over 530,000 translations. Supplementary material includes information on French society and culture, including famous places, people and much practical information for those planning to reside in France.

460 Spanish, Portuguese, Galician

Barlow, Julie

The **story** of Spanish; Jean-Benoit Nadeau and Julie Barlow. St. Martin's Press 2013 496 p. (hardcover) $27.99 **460**
1. Linguistics 2. Spanish language -- History
ISBN 0312656025; 9780312656027

LC 2013002633

This book, by Jean-Benoit Nadeau and Julie Barlow, asks "just how did a dialect spoken by a handful of shepherds in Northern Spain become the world's second most spoken language, the official language of twenty-one countries on two continents, and the unofficial second language of the United States? . . . [The authors] look at the roots and spread of modern Spanish." (Publisher's note)
Includes bibliographical references and index.

463 Dictionaries of standard Spanish

Houghton Mifflin Co.

The **Concise** American Heritage Spanish dictionary; 2nd ed; Houghton Mifflin 2001 xxiv, 616p $14 **463**
1. Reference books 2. Spanish language -- Dictionaries
ISBN 0-618-11769-5

LC 00-66461

"This bilingual dictionary includes more than 70,000 words and phrases. The emphasis on American English and Latin American Spanish as well as the informative guides and tables will assist students of either language." Booklist

470 Latin and related Italic languages

Ostler, Nicholas

Ad infinitum; a biography of Latin. Walker & Company 2007 382p il map $27.95 **470**
1. Latin language
ISBN 978-0-8027-1515-9; 0-8027-1515-X

"In four parts, Ostler covers the origins and development of Latin in the Roman world, Latin's "taking over the church," its medieval continuation and fracturing into vernaculars, and a nuanced rebirth in the Renaissance and its legacy in the contemporary world. Incredibly well documented, with examples from antiquity to the modern era." Libr J

473 Dictionaries of classical Latin

★ **Oxford** Latin dictionary; edited by P. G. W. Glare. Oxford Univ. Press 1982 xxiii, 2126p **473**
1. Reference books 2. Latin language -- Dictionaries 3. Latin language -- Dictionaries -- English
ISBN 0198642245

LC 8208162

This dictionary looks at the meaning and development of more than 40,000 classical Latin words and phrases

"Authorized in 1931 and begun two years later, {this dictionary} appeared in eight fascicles published between 1968 and 1982. These have been combined in a single volume." Wilson Libr Bull

Stone, Jon R.

★ **Latin** for the illiterati; a modern phrase book for an ancient language. 2nd ed.; Routledge 2009 xxii, 338p pa $24.95 **473**

1. Reference books 2. Latin language -- Dictionaries
ISBN 978-0-415-77767-4; 0-415-77767-4
First published 1996

"Organized alphabetically within the categories of verba (common words and expressions), dicta (common phrases and familiar sayings), and abbreviations, this . . . [is a] compendium of more than 7,000 Latin words, expressions, phrases, and sayings taken from the world of art, music, law, philosophy, theology, medicine and the theatre, as well as . . . [remarks and] advice from ancient writers such as Virgil, Ovid, Cicero, and more." Publisher's note

Includes bibliographical references

487 Preclassical and postclassical Greek

Fox, Margalit

★ The **Riddle** of the Labyrinth. HarperCollins 2013 384 p. $27.99 **487**

1. Ciphers 2. Greece -- Antiquities
ISBN 0062228838; 9780062228833

This book looks at the deciphering of Linear B, a "script first found on clay tablets excavated on the island of Crete and later at Pylos on the Greek mainland and dating to the Mycenaean period, circa 1400 BCE." It was deciphered by Michael Ventris. This book focuses on the "work of American classical scholar Alice Kober (1906-50) whose syllabic grids made Ventris's breakthrough possible." (Library Journal)

492.4 Hebrew

Zilkha, Avraham

★ **Modern** English-Hebrew dictionary. Yale Univ. Press 2002 457p (Yale language series) $55; pa $30 **492.4**

1. Reference books 2. Hebrew language -- Dictionaries
ISBN 0-300-09004-8; 0-300-09005-6 pa
LC 2001-26830

This dictionary includes 30,000 entries, with listings for translating words with multiple meanings, newly coined and slang words, common idioms, vocalization of Hebrew words, acronyms, and gender identification and plural forms of irregular nouns

493 Non-Semitic Afro-Asiatic languages

Robinson, Andrew, 1957-

Cracking the Egyptian code; the revolutionary life of Jean-François Champollion. Andrew Robinson. Oxford University Press 2012 272 p. (telework) $29.95 **493**

1. Hieroglyphics 2. Rosetta stone 3. Egyptologists -- France -- Biography 4. Egyptian language -- Writing,

Hieroglyphic
ISBN 0199914990; 9780199914999
LC 2011046769

This book, by Andrew Robinson, "is the first biography in English of [Jean-François] Champollion, widely regarded as the founder of Egyptology.... Robinson ... reconstructs how Champollion cracked the code of the hieroglyphic script, describing how Champollion . . . sailed the Nile for a year, studied the tombs in the Valley of the Kings . . . and carefully compared the three scripts on the Rosetta Stone to penetrate the mystery of the hieroglyphic text." (Publisher's note)

Includes bibliographical references and index.

495.1 Chinese

Cheng & Tsui English-Chinese lexicon of business terms with pinyin; compiled by Andrew C. Chang = [Jianqiao Ying Han shang yong ci hui pin ying ci dian / Zhang Jiezhou bian] Cheng & Tsui Co. 2001 442p (C & T Asian dictionary series) $36.95 **495.1**

1. Reference books 2. Business -- Dictionaries 3. Chinese language -- Dictionaries
ISBN 978-0-88727-394-0; 0-88727-394-7
LC 2001-94244

"A book to hand to your patrons who need to know the Chinese expressions for terms such as Chief Executive Officer, market penetration, and stockholder. More than 9,000 English-language words and phrases are listed with their Chinese simplified characters, with pinyin transliteration equivalents." Booklist

495.7 Korean

Berlitz Korean compact dictionary. Berlitz Publishing 2006 672p pa $12.95 **495.7**

1. Reference books 2. Korean language -- Dictionaries
ISBN 978-981-246-949-6; 981-246-949-4

This book has "45,000 entries that aim to capture the core words of the language. This dictionary features bold, blue headwords [for navigation]." Publisher's note

499 Non-Austronesian languages of Oceania, Austronesian languages, miscellaneous languages

Okrent, Arika

In the land of invented languages; Esperanto rock stars, Klingon poets, Loglan lovers, and the mad dreamers who tried to build a perfect language. Spiegel & Grau 2009 342p il $26 **499**

1. Artificial languages
ISBN 978-0-385-52788-0; 0-385-52788-8
LC 2008-38732

The author "explores some of the themes and shortcomings of 900 years worth of artificial languages. . . . [Her] prose is a model of clarity and grace; through it, she conveys fascinating insights into why natural language, with its corruptions, ambiguities and arbitrary conventions, trips so fluently off our tongues." Publ Wkly

Includes bibliographical references

Pukui, Mary Kawena

Hawaiian dictionary; Hawaiian-English, English-Hawaiian. [by] Mary Kawena Pukui, Samuel H. Elbert. rev & enl ed; University of Hawaii Press 1986 xxvi, 572p $32.95   **499**

1. Reference books 2. Hawaiian language -- Dictionaries
ISBN 0-8248-0703-0

LC 85-24583

Originally published in two separate parts in 1957 and 1964. First combined edition published 1971

"The Hawaiian-English part now comprises 29,000 entries. It is the most comprehensive and up-to-date dictionary for the language." Guide to Ref Books. 11th edition

Includes bibliographical references

500   SCIENCE

500   Natural sciences and mathematics

Aczel, Amir D.

The **artist** and the mathematician; the story of Nicolas Bourbaki, the genius mathematician who never existed. Thunder's Mouth Press 2006 239p il $23.95   **500**

1. Mathematicians
ISBN 978-1-56025-931-2; 1-56025-931-0

"In 1934, a small group of mostly French mathematicians met to reinvent a new math based on a pedagogy of rigorous proofs, clarity, and logical thinking. The group invented a fictitious persona, 'Nicolas Bourbaki,' as a pseudonym under which to author their collective work. Presenting the fascinating story behind the publication of over 40 tomes . . . , Aczel describes the group's cultural context, eccentricities, informal rules, and practices of engagement and offers biographical sketches of such influential members as Andr Weil and Alexandre Grothendieck. Writing in an accessible, conversational style that excludes mathematical proofs, Aczel paints a clear picture of the Bourbaki movement and how it has influenced the way mathematics should be discussed and learned." Libr J

Bais, Sander

In praise of science; curiosity, understanding, and progress. MIT Press 2010 192p il $24.95 **500**

1. Science
ISBN 978-0-262-01435-9; 0-262-01435-1

LC 2009-35675

"Over the course of four short chapters, Sander Bais illustrates in entertaining and often poetic ways not only how all of the sciences are connected to each other, but how they comprise a vital (if not the most vital) endeavor humans has ever undertaken. . . . Among others, the stories in In Praise of Science include the origin of Santa Claus, the history of quantum theory, the invention of the lightning rod, and religious attacks that distorted the theory of evolution and

facts surrounding HIV and AIDS. The polemical nature of Bais' arguments might spark debate for some readers, but he never comes across as ranting. He employs many (at times lengthy) quotes from a variety of sources, and near the end of the book there's a tendency to let the quotes make the case for him. But for the vast majority of the book, Bais seems like the quirky professor everyone loves and/or wishes they had, one who inspires lifelong interests." PopMatters

Includes bibliographical references

Bloom, Howard

The **God** problem; how a godless cosmos creates. by Howard Bloom. Prometheus Books 2012 708 p. (hardcover) $28.00   **500**

1. Cosmology 2. Religion and science 3. Cosmology -- Miscellanea 4. Science -- Social aspects
ISBN 161614551X; 9781616145514

LC 2012013460

This book, by Howard Bloom, asks "how does an inanimate universe generate stunning new forms and unbelievable new powers without a creator? . . . [The book explains] . . . Howard Bloom's provocative new theory of the . . . universe--the Bloom toroidal model, also known as the big bagel theory--which explains two of the biggest mysteries in physics: dark energy and why, if antimatter and matter are created in equal amounts, there is so little antimatter in this universe." (Publisher's note)

Includes bibliographical references and index

Bronowski, Jacob

Science and human values; revised edition with a new dialogue, The abacus and the rose. Harper & Row 1965 119p il hardcover o.p. pa $12   **500**

1. Science
ISBN 0-06-097281-5 pa

First published 1958 by Messner

Contains the following three essays, which were first given as lectures at the Massachusetts Institute of Technology in 1953: The creative mind; The habit of truth; The sense of human dignity. The abacus and the rose was originally broadcast by the BBC Third Programme in 1962

The dialogue "discusses the theme that 'science is as integral a part of the culture of our age as the arts are.'" Sci Am

Brooks, Michael

13 things that don't make sense; the most baffling scientific mysteries of our time. [by] Michael Brooks. Doubleday 2008 240p $23.95   **500**

1. Science
ISBN 0-385-52068-9; 978-0-385-52068-3

LC 2008-12443

This book is based on a 2005 article on scientific anomalies that Brooks wrote for the New Scientist. "13 Things opens at the twenty-third Solvay physics conference, where the scientists present are ready to throw up their hands over an anomaly: is it possible that the universe, rather than slowly drifting apart as the physics of the big bang had once predicted, is actually expanding at an ever-faster speed? . . . [Brooks also examines the questions]: Is a 1977 signal from outer space a transmission from an alien civilization? Might giant viruses explain how life began? Why are some NASA satellites speeding up as they get farther from the sun—and what does that mean for the laws of physics?" (Publisher's note) Index.

This "book examines such mysteries as dark matter and dark energy, the prospect of life on Mars, sex and death, free will and the placebo effect, among other head-scratchers. . . . This elegantly written, meticulously researched and thought-provoking book provides window into how science actually works, and is sure to spur intense debate." New Sci

Includes bibliographical references

Bryson, Bill, 1951-

★ A **short** history of nearly everything. Broadway Bks. 2003 544p $27.50; pa $15.95 **500**
1. Science 2. Science -- Popular works
ISBN 0-7679-0817-1; 0-7679-0818-X pa

LC 2003-46006

"Neither oversimplified nor overstuffed, this exceptionally skillful tour of the physical world covers the basic principles and still has room for profiles of some of the more engaging scientists." N Y Times Book Rev

Includes bibliographical references

Dawkins, Richard

A **devil's** chaplain; reflections on hope, lies, science, and love. Houghton Mifflin 2003 263p il $24; pa $14 **500**
1. Evolution 2. Religion and science 3. Science -- Philosophy
ISBN 0-618-33540-4; 0-618-48539-2 pa

LC 2003-50859

This is "a collection of essays that span 25 years of writing on evolution, education and science versus nonsense. . . . Dawkins is creative, articulate and, above all, emotional." N Y Times Book Rev

Includes bibliographical references

Dyson, Freeman J., 1923-

Dreams of earth and sky; by Freeman Dyson. New York Review Books 2015 300 p. (alk. paper) $27.95 **500**
1. Science 2. Discoveries in science 3. Serendipity in science
ISBN 1590178548; 9781590178546

LC 2014038482

Author "Freeman Dyson's new collection of pieces from 'The New York Review of Books' investigates and celebrates what he calls openness to unconventional ideas in science. His subjects range from the seventeenth-century scientific revolution, to the scientific inquiries of the Romantic generation, to important recent works by Daniel Kahneman and Malcolm Gladwell." (Publisher's note)

"Readers who enjoyed the first volume of reviews will be pleased with this follow-up, and new readers will be delighted by the fascinating insider's view of the scientific community and its intersection with the political establishment." Kirkus

Feynman, Richard Phillips

★ The **meaning** of it all; thoughts of a citizen scientist. Basic Books 2005 133p pa $13.95 **500**
1. Science 2. Religion
ISBN 0-465-02394-0

First published 1998 by Addison-Wesley

"Originally delivered as a three-part lecture series at the University of Washington in 1963, this collection touches on such far-ranging topics as the existence or nonexistence of God; the Constitution; and UFOs. . . . These memorable lectures confirm that Feynman's gift of insight extended from the subatomic world to the cosmic, and to the very human as well." Publ Wkly

The **pleasure** of finding things out; the best short works of Richard P. Feynman. by Richard P. Feynman; edited by Jeffrey Robbins; foreword by Freeman Dyson. Perseus Bks. 1999 270p hardcover o.p. pa $15.95 **500**
1. Science
ISBN 0-7382-0349-1 pa

LC 99-64775

These lectures and interviews are "expositions about [Feynman's] life, about technical topics in computing and physics, and about science's general place in society." Booklist

Gardner, Martin, 1914-2010

★ **Did** Adam and Eve have navels? discourses on reflexology, numerology, urine therapy and other dubious subjects. Norton 2000 333p il hardcover o.p. pa $15.95 **500**
1. Science
ISBN 0-393-32238-6 pa

LC 00-34870

This is a collection of the author's pieces culled from the Skeptical Inquirer. Gardner "gives succinct and amusing critiques of a number of the fallacies that abound in alternative medicine (including the very peculiar urine-therapy treatment) and many other 'dubious subjects.'" Libr J

Includes bibliographical references

Goldacre, Ben

Bad science; quacks, hacks, and big pharma flacks. Faber and Faber 2010 288p il pa $15 **500**
1. Errors 2. Medical misconceptions
ISBN 978-0-86547-918-0

LC 2010-14401

First published 2008 in the United Kingdom

The author "has written a very funny and biting book critiquing what he calls 'Bad Science.' Under this heading he includes homeopathy, cosmetics manufacturers whose claims about their products defy plausibility, proponents of miracle vitamins, and drug companies and physicians who design faulty studies and manipulate the results. . . . While it is a very entertaining book, it also provides important insight into the horrifying outcomes that can result when willful anti-intellectualism is allowed equal footing with scientific methodology." Boston Globe

Includes bibliographical references

Gould, Stephen Jay

The **flamingo's** smile; reflections in natural history. Norton 1985 476p il hardcover o.p. pa $15.95 **500**

1. Natural history

ISBN 0-393-30375-6 pa

LC 85-4916

In this collection "the theme is history, both natural and human. . . . The essays are marked by Gould's usual careful scholarship and erudition and clear and nontechnical language." Sci Books Films

Includes bibliographical references

Gribbin, John R.

Almost everyone's guide to science; the universe, life and everything. [by] John Gribbin with Mary Gribbin. Yale Univ. Press 1999 232p $30; pa $11.95 **500**

1. Science

ISBN 0-300-08101-4; 0-300-08460-9 pa

LC 99-26755

First published 1998 in the United Kingdom

In this "general guide to science for the layperson . . . Gribbin combines biographies and history, on the one hand, with the major theories in science, on the other. . . . The text is clear, is based on solid research, and clearly reflects a lifetime love for science." Sci Books Films

Includes bibliographical references

The **handy** science answer book; compiled by the Carnegie Library of Pittsburgh; [edited by] Naomi E. Balaban and James E. Bobick. 4th ed.; Visible Ink Press 2011 679p il pa $21.95 **500**

1. Science 2. Technology

ISBN 978-1-57859-321-7

LC 2011-429

First published 1994

"The text is divided into various subject areas including physics and chemistry, space, earth, climate and weather, minerals and other materials, energy, technology, and environment, gathering answers to reference questions. . . . A comprehensive index . . . makes the material accessible and easy to find. Pages are full of fascinating tidbits, complemented by illustrations, photos, charts, graphs, and maps." Voice Youth Advocates

Includes bibliographical references

Henderson, Mark

100 most important science ideas; key concepts in genetics, physics and mathematics. [by] Mark Henderson, Joanne Baker, Tony Crilly. Firefly Books 2009 431p il $19.95 **500**

1. Physics 2. Genetics 3. Mathematics

ISBN 978-1-55407-527-0

This book aims to encourage the reader to explore "the 100 most important, groundbreaking ideas that have emerged from the scientific disciplines of genetics, physics, and mathematics. Divided into three sections, each written by one of the authors . . . this work presents complex scientific topics in a simple, understandable way. . . . Text boxes, entertaining quotations, frequent diagrams, and everyday examples hold the reader's attention and make this work engaging to anyone interested in the world of science." Libr J

History of modern science and mathematics; Brian S. Baigrie, editor. Scribner 2002 4v il set $605 **500**

1. Science -- History 2. Mathematics -- History

ISBN 0-684-80636-3

LC 2002-4042

This "set attempts to synthesize the history of scientific developments in anthropology, astronomy, biology, chemistry, mathematics, physics, psychology, and the earth sciences. . . . This work ranges from the 17th century to the present without trying to include the most recent developments." Libr J

Includes bibliographical references

Kipfer, Barbara Ann

How it happens; the extraordinary processes of everyday things. Random House Reference 2005 322p il pa $16.95 **500**

1. Science

ISBN 0-375-72082-0

LC 2005-40453

This "trivia miscellany describes hundreds of processes, from popcorn popping to radio signal transmission to tango dancing." Publisher's note

Munroe, Randall, 1984-

Thing Explainer; Complicated Stuff in Simple Words. by Randall Munroe. Houghton Mifflin Harcourt 2015 64 p. illustrations $24.95 **500**

1. Technological innovations 2. Science -- Juvenile literature 3. Outer space -- Juvenile literature

ISBN 0544668251; 9780544668256

In this book, author Randall Munroe "uses line drawings and only the thousand (or, rather, 'ten hundred') most common words to provide simple explanations for some of the most interesting stuff there is. . . . Funny, interesting, and always understandable, this book is for anyone—age 5 to 105—who has ever wondered how things work, and why." (Publisher's note)

What if? serious scientific answers to absurd hypothetical questions. Randall Munroe. Houghton Mifflin Harcourt 2014 320 p. (hardback) $24 **500**

1. Wit and humor 2. Science -- Miscellanea

ISBN 0544272994; 9780544272996

LC 2014016311

This book, by Randall Munroe, offers "hilarious and informative answers to important questions you probably never thought to ask. . . . In pursuit of answers, Munroe runs computer simulations, pores over stacks of declassified military research memos, solves differential equations, and consults with nuclear reactor operators." (Publisher's note)

"Those who enjoyed the irreverent style of Allie Brosh's best-selling memoir, Hyperbole and a Half, will enjoy Munroe's serious and silly musings on everything from science to romance. One question submitted to his blog: 'If all digital data were stored on punch cards, how big would Google's data warehouse be?' was even answered by the search-engine behemoth. The response, 'No comment.'" LJ

Orzel, Chad

Eureka! discovering your inner scientist. Chad Orzel. Basic Books, a member of the Perseus Books Group 2014 368 p. illustrations (hardcover : alk. paper) $17.99 **500**

1. Discoveries in science 2. Science -- Popular works
ISBN 0465074960; 9780465044917; 9780465074969
LC 2014034615

In this book, author Chad Orzel "shows that science isn't something alien and inscrutable beyond the capabilities of ordinary people, it's central to the human experience. Every human can think like a scientist, and regularly does so in the course of everyday activities. The disconnect between this reality and most people's perception is mostly due to the common misconception that science is a body of (boring, abstract, often mathematical) facts." (Publisher's note)

"Recommended for undergraduate students, science educators, and readers with an amateur interest in science or science history." LJ

★ **Oxford** dictionary of scientific quotations; edited by W.F. Bynum and Roy Porter; assistant editors, Sharon Messenger, Caroline Overy. Oxford University Press 2005 712p $60; pa $18.95 **500**

1. Science 2. Quotations
ISBN 0-19-858409-1; 0-19-861443-8 pa
LC 2005-277260

"This hefty volume is a great reference but it is also a great read—open it up to any page and expand the mind with a sampling of scientific ideas and philosophy." Choice

Park, Robert L.

Voodoo science; the road from foolishness to fraud. Oxford Univ. Press 2000 230p hardcover o.p. pa $17.95 **500**

1. Fraud 2. Science
ISBN 0-19-513515-6; 978-0-19-514710-0 pa; 0-19-514710-3 pa
LC 99-40911

The author "aims to expose various beliefs and schemes put forth in the popular press and other places as scientifically real and factual. . . . {He} turns a critical eye on cold fusion, magnet therapy, homeopathy, perpetual motion, and other recent examples of fringe science. . . . Park's book should be required reading for all science writers, journalists, and politicians." Libr J

Randall, Lisa

Knocking on heaven's door; how physics and scientific thinking illuminate the universe and the modern world. Ecco 2011 xxi, 442p il $29.99; ebook $14.99 **500**

1. Physics 2. Science
ISBN 978-0-06-172372-8; 978-0-06-209689-0 ebook
LC 2011010521

"To explain how science works, Randall analyzes the way two researchers at Bell Labs turned the annoying static coming through their radio telescope into a cosmic breakthrough. For in this piquant episode—and others that Randall examines—science advances by testing theoretical ingenuity against technologically acquired data. . . . Randall

offers an insider's perspective into this cutting-edge science. Yet she illuminates that science with lucid language, laced with references to popular culture, political controversy, and even comic-strip art. The general reader's indispensable passport to the frontiers of science." Booklist

Includes bibliographical references

Rees, Martin J., 1942-

From here to infinity; a vision for the future of science. Martin Rees. W.W. Norton 2012 144 p (hardcover) $23.95 **500**

1. Overpopulation 2. Nuclear warfare 3. Science and civilization 4. Science -- Philosophy
ISBN 0393063070; 9780393063073
LC 2012003421

This book on science by Martin Rees offers "four of the distinguished Reith lectures, delivered annually over BBC radio by renowned thinkers. . . . He reviews our planet's looming problems, from climate change to overpopulation to nuclear war, emphasizing that there are no solutions outside of science. . . . He also warns about the 'tendency for long-term strategies, however important, to be trumped by more immediate issues that can be resolved within an electoral cycle.'" (Kirkus Reviews)

Sagan, Carl

Billions and billions; thoughts on life and death at the brink of the millennium. Random House 1997 241p hardcover o.p. pa $14.95 **500**

1. Science
ISBN 0-345-37918-7 pa
LC 96-52730

This collection of essays covers such topics as: "the invention of chess, life on Mars, global warming, abortion, international affairs, the nature of government, and the meaning of morality. Writing with clarity and an understanding of human nature, Sagan offers hope for humanity's future." Libr J

Includes bibliographical references

★ **Broca's** brain; reflections on the romance of science. Random House 1979 347p hardcover o.p. pa $7.99 **500**

1. God 2. Science 3. Religion 4. Astronomy 5. Machinery 6. Philosophy 7. Physicians 8. Physicists 9. Psychologists 10. Writers on science 11. Nobel laureates for physics
ISBN 0-345-33689-5 pa
LC 78-21810

The author "is a lucid, logical writer with a gift for explaining science to the layman and infecting the reader with his own boundless enthusiasm and curiosity." Natl Rev
Includes bibliographical references

Scientific American's ask the experts; answers to the most puzzling and mindblowing science questions. by the editors of Scientific American. HarperCollins Pubs. 2003 267p il pa $14.95 **500**

1. Science
ISBN 0-06-052336-0
LC 2004-555579

This "is a book that answers questions big, little, and in between. . . . The book uses the familiar question-and-answer format, with a table of contents allowing the reader to flip to a specific question. The questions are answered by a variety of experts. . . . This is one of those books you put on your reference shelf, and pull out whenever the subject turns to matters of scientific interest. Great for trivia buffs, too." Booklist

This **explains** everything; deep, beautiful, and elegant theories of how the world works. edited by John Brockman. 1st ed. Harper Perennial 2013 xx, 411 p.p (paperback) $15.99   **500**
   1. Physics 2. American essays 3. Pattern perception 4. Explanation 5. Science -- Miscellanea
   ISBN 0062230174; 9780062230171

            LC 2012032107

This book is a "collection of brief essays [that] started with a question posed to the readers of Edge.org, founded by [editor John] Brockman . . . : What is your favorite deep, elegant, or beautiful explanation? The result is 150 brief essays that present . . . explanations of the world around us. The authors include Richard Dawkins, Eric Kandel, Alan Alda, and Brian Eno." (Library Journal)

Wiggins, Arthur W.

 ★ The **five** biggest unsolved problems in science; [by] Arthur W. Wiggins [and] Charles M. Wynn; with cartoon commentary by Sidney Harris. J. Wiley & Sons 2003 234p il pa $14.95   **500**
   1. Science
   ISBN 0-471-26808-9

            LC 2003-284262

"The problems discussed in this volume are the dueling concepts of mass and masslessness (physics), the passage from chemicals to living matter (chemistry), the complete structure of the proteome (biology), long-range weather forecasting (geology), and the expansion of the universe (astronomy)." Sci Books Films

   Includes bibliographical references

Wilkinson, Karen

The **Art** of tinkering; meet 150+ makers working at the intersection of art, science & technology. Karen Wilkinson, Mike Petrich. Weldon Owen Inc. 2013 223 p. illustrations (chiefly color) $32.50 **500**
   1. Tinkers -- United States
   ISBN 1616286091; 9781616286095

            LC 2013948536

This book, by Karen Wilkinson and Mike Petrich, "is a collection of exhibits, artwork, and projects that celebrate a whole new way to learn, in which people create their own knowledge through making and doing, working with readily available materials, getting their hands dirty, collaborating with others, problem-solving in the most fun sense of the word, and, yes, oftentimes failing and bouncing back from getting stuck." (Publisher's note)

500.2   Physical sciences

Ball, Philip

Patterns in nature; why the natural world looks the way it does. Philip Ball. University of Chicago Press 2016 288 p. illustrations (chiefly color) (cloth : alk. paper) $35   **500.2**
   1. Nature 2. Ecology 3. Fractals 4. Physical sciences 5. Environmental science 6. Patterns (Mathematics) 7. Geometry in nature 8. Pattern formation (Biology) 9. Pattern formation (Physical sciences)
   ISBN 9780226332420

            LC 2015034568

In this book, by Philip Ball, "Though at first glance the natural world may appear overwhelming in its diversity and complexity, there are regularities running through it, from the hexagons of a honeycomb to the spirals of a seashell and the branching veins of a leaf. Revealing the order at the foundation of the seemingly chaotic natural world, [this book] explores not only the math and science but also the beauty and artistry of nature's awe-inspiring designs." (Publisher's note)

"This is formidable eye candy for the I-love-science crowd, sure to spark a sense of impressed wonder at the beauty of our universe and our ability to photograph it." Pub Wkly

   Includes bibliographical references (page 283) and index.

Ball, Philip, 1962-

 ✓ **Nature's** patterns; a tapestry in three parts. Oxford University Press 2009 308p il $29.95   **500.2**
   1. Shape 2. Chaos (Science) 3. Patterns (Mathematics)
   ISBN 978-0-19-923796-8; 0-19-923796-4

            LC 2009-280579

"From the curl of a ram's horn to patterns of spider webs and the development of an embryo, Mr Ball examines the possible causes of the shapes and forms we observe. His book contains a lot of fascinating detail about the different physical, chemical and evolutionary processes at work." Economist

   Includes bibliographical references

500.5   Space sciences

Launius, Roger D.

Smithsonian atlas of space exploration; [by] Roger D. Launius & Andrew K. Johnston. Collins 2009 230p il map $34.99   **500.5**
   1. Outer space -- Exploration -- Pictorial works
   ISBN 978-0-06-156526-7

            LC 2009-649

This book "relates the story of space exploration in text, photographs, illustrations, and maps from the earliest times to the present. Written at a level geared to the general reader, this topically arranged work is divided into seven parts. . . . Each part contains a number of two or four-page subsections covering topics ranging from the earliest observatories of the ancient world to the possibilities for space flight in the future. . . . Distinguished by outstanding color illustrations and photographs, the very reasonably priced atlas should appeal to a broad audience." Booklist

Includes bibliographical references

501 Philosophy and theory

Arbesman, Samuel

★ The **half**-life of facts; why everything we know has an expiration date. Samuel Arbesman. Current 2012 viii, 242 p.p ill. (hardback) $25.95 **501**
    1. Science 2. Probabilities 3. Theory of knowledge 4. Evolution 5. Science -- Philosophy
    ISBN 159184472X; 9781591844723
                LC 2012019142

This book by Samuel Arbesman presents a "treatise on the nature of facts: what they are, how and why they change and how they sometimes don't (despite being wrong). . . . [Arbesman argues that] what we know 'changes in understandable and systematic ways.' . . . He introduces 'scientometrics,' the science of science. With scientometrics, we can measure the exponential growth of facts, how long it will take, exponentially, for knowledge in any field to be disproved." (Kirkus Reviews)

Includes bibliographical references (pages 215-234) and index

Costa, Rebecca D.

The **watchman's** rattle; thinking our way out of extinction. with a foreword by E.O. Wilson. Vanguard Press 2010 347p $26.95 **501**
    1. Civilization 2. Problem solving 3. Complexity (Philosophy)
    ISBN 978-1-59315-605-3; 1-59315-605-7
                LC 2010-927900

Explains why the human brain has such difficulty dealing with complex global problems and provides a method for surmounting these limitations in order to end the blights of worldwide recession, global warming, fast-spreading viruses, famine, and poverty.

This book "will give concerned readers new hope in human capability." Libr J

Includes bibliographical references

Dawkins, Richard, 1941-

The **magic** of reality; how we know what's really true. illustrated by Dave McKean. 1st Free Press hardcover ed; Free Press 2011 271p il map **501**
    1. Nature 2. Reality 3. Science -- Philosophy
    ISBN 1439192812; 1451628927 ebook;
    9781439192818; 9781451628920 ebook
                LC 2011025607

"In this outstanding 'graphic science book,' evolutionary biologist Dawkins . . . teams up with illustrator Dave McKean . . . to examine questions in everyday science, such as: why seasons occur; what things are made of; and whether there's life on other planets. They explain the answers from mythological and cultural points of view before diving into the chemistry, biology, and physics—all in language that

advanced middle school, or most high school, students can absorb." Publ Wkly

Unweaving the rainbow; science, delusion, and the appetite for wonder. Houghton Mifflin 1998 336p $26; pa $14 **501**
    1. Science -- Philosophy
    ISBN 0-395-88382-2; 0-618-05673-4 pa
                LC 98-40879

Dawkins is a "witty popularizer, whether he is offering a crash course in DNA fingerprinting, explaining the origins of 'mad cow disease' in weird proteins that spread like self-replicating viruses or discussing male birdsong as an auditory aphrodisiac for female birds." Publ Wkly

Includes bibliographical references

Deutsch, David

The **beginning** of infinity; explanations that transform the world. Viking Adult 2011 487p il $30 **501**
    1. Infinite 2. Science -- Philosophy
    ISBN 978-0-670-02275-5; 0-670-02275-6
                LC 2011004120

The book discusses the interaction between humans and the universe they inhabit, challenging concepts such as "the Earth is a maternally inclined spacefaring vessel . . . [and] the utter insignificance of human beings in the cosmic scheme of things. . . . Our cosmic importance derives from our capacity to acquire knowledge, and use it to transform our lives and surroundings. . . . In the short term, this means that we should seek to understand and control the Earth's entire ecosystem. . . . In the medium term we should colonize the Moon, followed by the other planets in our solar system. In the longer term we should aim for the stars - and even beyond: Deutsch argues in some detail that extremely empty intergalactic space is easily capable of sustaining a high population of technologically advanced space-dwellers." (TLS)

"Anyone who loves to grapple with profound ideas should love reading this very ambitious and challenging look at the history and (possibly unlimited) future of human understanding." Sci Books Films

Includes bibliographical references

Firestein, Stuart

Ignorance; how it drives science. Stuart Firestein, Oxford University Press 2012 viii, 195 p.p **501**
    1. Ignorance 2. Discoveries in science 3. Science -- Methodology 4. Science -- Philosophy
    ISBN 0199828075; 9780199828074
                LC 2011051395

This book argues that "[t]he fundamental attribute of successful scientists . . . is a form of ignorance characterised by knowing what you don't know, and being able to ask the right questions. . . . To demonstrate the crucial role of this type of informed ignorance, [Stuart] Firestein highlights two well-known examples. The first, Heisenberg's uncertainty principle, asserts that we cannot know the position and momentum of a particle simultaneously. . . . His second example is Godel's incompleteness theorems. . . . Firestein also includes more modern examples of productive ignorance." (New Scientist)

Includes bibliographical references and index

Henry, John

A **short** history of scientific thought; John Henry. Palgrave Macmillan 2012 xvii, 306 p.p ill. (hbk.) $90 **501**

1. Science -- History 2. Science -- Philosophy 3. Science and civilization 4. Natural history -- History 5. Civilization, Western -- History 6. Science -- Philosophy -- History 7. Science and civilization -- History

ISBN 0230019420; 0230019439; 9780230019423; 9780230019430

LC 2011049038

This book by John Henry offers a "historical survey of the major developments in scientific thought and the impact of science on Western culture, this book takes the reader from ancient times through to the twentieth century. Organized chronologically, the book explores the history of studies of the natural world, and man's role within that world, in a single volume." (Publisher's note)

Includes bibliographical references and index

Mitchell, Melanie

Complexity; a guided tour. Oxford University Press 2009 349p il map $29.95 **501**

1. Complexity (Philosophy) 2. Science -- Philosophy

ISBN 978-0-19-512441-5; 0-19-512441-3

LC 2008023794

The sciences of complexity "seek to explain how large-scale complex, organized, and adaptive behavior can emerge from simple interactions among myriad individuals. . . . Based on her work at the Santa Fe Institute and drawing on its interdisciplinary strategies, Mitchell [attempts to] bring clarity to the workings of complexity across a . . . range of biological, technological, and social phenomena, seeking out the general principles or laws that apply to all of them. She explores as well the relationship between complexity and evolution, artificial intelligence, computation, genetics, information processing, and [other fields]." (Publisher's note) Bibliography. Index.

The author offers a "snapshot of the growing field of complex-systems science. . . . Mitchell explores the historical roots of this area in the work of visionaries such as Henri Poincaré and Edward Lorenz in dynamical-systems theory, and of John von Neumann, Alan Turing and others in computation. . . . The book hits its stride in its latter half, with an insightful survey of recent developments in complex-network theory and scaling in biology." Nature

Includes bibliographical references (p. 326-336)

Nothing; surprising insights everywhere from zero to oblivion. edited by Jeremy Webb. Workman Publishing Company The Experiment 2014 266 p. illustrations $14.95 **501**

1. Science 2. Cosmology 3. Nothing (Philosophy) 4. Science -- Philosophy

ISBN 1615192050; 9781615192052

LC 2014002254

"There's a lot about nothing in this fun assortment of pop science essays culled from the New Scientist. . . . The collection on a whole takes a fun and accessible tone with easily digestable insights and discoveries, like the history and differences between zero as a number and zero as a symbol (which surprisingly people didn't always use it or even have

it to represent nothing) or the critical benefits of doing nothing for certain animals." (Publishers Weekly)

Includes bibliographical references and index

Olson, Randy

★ **Don't** be such a scientist; talking substance in an age of style. Island Press 2009 206p il pa $19.95 **501**

1. Science 2. Communication 3. College teachers 4. Marine biologists 5. Communication in science 6. Motion picture directors 7. Science in motion pictures 8. Science -- Study and teaching

ISBN 1-59726-563-2; 978-1-59726-563-8

LC 2009-7081

Olson discusses his evolution "from science professor to Hollywood filmmaker. In Don't Be Such a Scientist, he . . [discusses] talking substance in an age of style. The key, he argues, is to stay true to the facts while tapping into something more primordial, more irrational, and ultimately more human." (Publisher's note) Filmography of movies by Randy Olson. Index.

The author argues "that 'scientists need artists.' He delves into the principle of 'arouse and fulfill,' suggesting that while scientists are great with the fulfillment part, the power of art can help arouse the interest of the broader audience." Publisher's note

Includes bibliographical references

Poe, Mya

Learning to communicate in science and engineering; case studies from MIT. [by] Mya Poe, Neal Lerner, and Jennifer Craig; foreword by James Paradis. MIT Press 2010 256p il $35 **501**

1. Writing 2. Communication 3. Science -- Study and teaching 4. Engineering -- Study and teaching

ISBN 978-0-262-16247-0

LC 2009-24788

"Case studies and pedagogical strategies to help science and engineering students improve their writing and speaking skills while developing professional identities." Barnes and Noble

Includes bibliographical references

Stannard, Russell

The **end** of discovery. Oxford University Press 2010 228p il $24.95 **501**

1. Physics 2. Theory of knowledge 3. Science -- Philosophy

ISBN 978-0-19-958524-3; 0-19-958524-5

LC 2010-930293

The author "believes that science will eventually come to an end, and that we are living in a 'transient age of human development' in which scientific discoveries can be made. But science won't end because we know everything; it will end because we know everything we can know. . . . [This is] a book worth reading. Lucid and provocative, it is a very polite corrective to both the superstitions of the layman . . . and the triumphalism of the experts." New Statesman

This will change everything; ideas that will shape the future. edited by John Brockman; [introduc-

tion by Daniel C. Dennett] HarperCollins 2010
xxiii, 390p pa $14.99   **501**
1. Science 2. Forecasting
ISBN 978-0-06-189967-6

"With contributions from Ian McEwan, Steven Pinker,
Lee Smolin, Craig Venter, Richard Dawkins and 130 oth-
ers of their ilk, the book is like an intellectual lucky dip."
New Sci

502   Miscellany

Lamothe, Matt

  The **where,** the why, and the how; 75 artists
illustrate wondrous mysteries of science. Matt Lamothe; Julia Rothman; Jenny Volvovski. Chronicle
Books 2012 160 p. ill. (chiefly col.) (hardcover)
$24.95   **502**
  1. Physics 2. Life sciences 3. Earth sciences
ISBN 1452108226; 9781452108223

                     LC 2012289775
  In this book by Matt Lamothe, Julia Rothman, and Jenny
Volvovski, "some of the biggest (and smallest) mysteries of
the natural world are explained in essays by real working
scientists, which are then illustrated by artists given free rein
to be as literal or as imaginative as they like. The result is a
celebration of the wonder that inspires every new discovery." (Publisher's note)

Woodford, Chris

  Atoms Under the Floorboards; The Surprising
Science Hidden in Your Home. Chris Woodford. Excelsior Editions/ State University of New York Press
2015 336 p. illustrations $27   **502**
  1. Houses 2. Science -- Popular works
ISBN 1472912225; 9781472912220

  This book, by Chris Woodford, "presents the fascinating and surprising scientific explanations behind a variety
of common (and often entertainingly mundane) household
phenomena, from gurgling drains and squeaky floorboards
to rubbery custard and shiny shoes. . . . Each chapter focuses
on the objects and processes familiar in everyday life and
slowly unpicks the science behind them." (Publisher's note)

  "The author's writing is clear and precise; he explains
complex matters simply, using scientific terminology without getting bogged down by it, although the book's habit of
expressing weights and measures in both imperial and metric—"160,000 kg/353,000 lb"—can get a little distracting,
especially when it happens several times in a single paragraph. Visual distractions aside, though, this is a lively and
educational book." Booklist

502.8   Auxiliary techniques and procedures; apparatus, equipment, materials

Instruments of science; an historical encyclopedia.
  editors, Robert Bud, Deborah Jean Warner; associate editor, Stephen Johnston; managing editor,
  Betsy Bahr Peterson; picture editor, Simon Chap-

lin. Garland 1998 xxv, 709p il (Garland encyclopedias in the history of science) $175   **502.8**
  1. Reference books 2. Scientific apparatus and
instruments -- Encyclopedias
ISBN 0-8153-1561-9

                     LC 97-15296
  This "encyclopedia presents 325 historically significant
scientific instruments from antiquity to the present. Instruments used for testing and monitoring in addition to those
used for research are studied, including laboratory organisms such as E coli. Each of the signed entries explains how
the instrument works and how it is used, as well as tracing
its invention, development, and distribution. . . . Beautiful
illustrations accompany many of the entries." Am Libr
  Includes bibliographical references

503   Dictionaries, encyclopedias, concordances

The **Encyclopedia** of science and technology; James
  S. Trefil, general editor; contributing editors, Harold Morowitz, Paul Ceruzzi. Routledge 2001
  554p il maps $50   **503**
  1. Reference books 2. Science -- Encyclopedias 3.
Technology -- Encyclopedias
ISBN 0-415-93724-8

                     LC 2001-19983
  This reference includes "1000 entries, arranged alphabetically and color-coded to indicate whether the topic is
related to life science, physical science, or technology. Accessible to the general reader, the articles range widely. . . .
The excellent cross references direct the reader to related articles that cover either more fundamental or more advanced
information. . . . A true pleasure to browse and read; highly
recommended." Libr J
  Includes bibliographical references and index

Encyclopedia of science, technology, and ethics; edited by Carl Mitcham. Macmillan Reference USA
  2005 4v il map set $450   **503**
  1. Reference books 2. Technology -- Encyclopedias 3.
Science -- Ethical aspects -- Encyclopedias
ISBN 0-02-865831-0

                     LC 2005-6968
  This "multivolume work on ethics provides a superb in-
troduction to the issues presented." Booklist
  Includes bibliographical references

McGraw-Hill dictionary of scientific and technical
  terms; 6th ed; McGraw-Hill 2003 2380p il
  $150   **503**
  1. Reference books 2. Science -- Dictionaries 3.
Technology -- Dictionaries
ISBN 0-07-042313-X

                     LC 2002-26436
  First published 1974
  "This continues to be the most comprehensive science
and technology dictionary for the student, researcher, and
layperson." Booklist

McGraw-Hill Publishing Company

McGraw-Hill concise encyclopedia of science & technology; 6th ed.; McGraw-Hill 2009 2v il map set $295 **503**

1. Reference books 2. Science -- Encyclopedias 3. Technology -- Encyclopedias
ISBN 978-0-07-161366-8

LC 2008-50987

First published 1984

This encyclopedia features over 7100 articles on branches of technology and science ranging from acoustics to zoology.

Includes bibliographical references

★ **Van** Nostrand's scientific encyclopedia; 10th ed.; Wiley 2008 3v il map set $450 **503**

1. Reference books 2. Science -- Encyclopedias
ISBN 978-0-471-74338-5

LC 2007-46658

First published 1938

This encyclopedia contains articles contains over 10,000 entries on topics such as biology, chemistry, earth science, mathematics and engineering, anatomy and physiology, physics, botany, and space science.

Includes bibliographical references

506 Organizations and management

Seeing further; the story of science, discovery, and the genius of the Royal Society. edited & introduced by Bill Bryson; contributing editor, Jon Turney. William Morrow 2010 506p il $35; ebook $21.99 **506**

1. Science 2. Royal Society (Great Britain)
ISBN 978-0-06-199976-5; 978-0-06-203622-3 ebook

Bryson "presents a remarkable collection of essays celebrating the 350th anniversary of the founding of the Royal Society of London and its many contributions to science. Society members have included such illustrious names as Darwin, Newton, Leibniz, and Francis Bacon, to name a few. The volume's 23 contributors are both uniformly excellent and remarkable for their diversity." Publ Wkly

Includes bibliographical references (p. 486-489)

507.8 Use of apparatus and equipment in study and teaching

Experiment central; understanding scientific principles through projects. John T. Tanacredi & John Loret, general editors. U.X.L 2000 6v il set $347 **507.8**

1. Science -- Experiments
ISBN 1-4144-0522-7

LC 99-54142

Demonstrates scientific concepts by means of experiments, including step-by-step instructions, lists of materials, troubleshooter's guide, and interpretation and explanation of the results.

Johnson, George

The **ten** most beautiful experiments. Alfred A. Knopf 2008 192p il $22.95 **507.8**

1. Science -- Experiments
ISBN 978-1-4000-4101-5; 1-4000-4101-5

LC 2007-27839

"Writing up Luigi Galvani's study of frog's legs, James Joule's of heat, Albert Michelson's of light's speed, and Robert Millikan's of the electron's charge, Johnson exerts classic appeal to science readers: presenting the lone genius making a great discovery. Good to go in any library." Booklist

Includes bibliographical references

508 Natural history

Alvarez, Walter

A **Most** Improbable Journey; A Big History of Our Planet and Ourselves. Walter Alvarez. W W Norton & Co Inc 2016 288 p. $26.95 **508**

1. Geology 2. Cosmology 3. Evolution 4. Earth sciences
ISBN 039329269X; 9780393292695

This book by geologist Walter Alvarez "expands our view of human history by revealing the cosmic, geologic, and evolutionary forces that have shaped us. . . . Almost fourteen billion years of cosmic history, over four billion years of Earth history, a couple million years of human history . . .--it's staggering to consider. Yet behind everything in our world, . . . lies a similarly grand procession of highly improbable events." (Publisher's note)

Carroll, Sean B.

Remarkable creatures; epic adventures in the search for the origins of species. Houghton Mifflin Harcourt 2009 331p il map $26; pa $14.95 **508**

1. Evolution 2. Naturalists
ISBN 978-0-15-101485-9; 0-15-101485-X; 978-0-547-24778-6 pa; 0-547-24778-8 pa

LC 2008-25438

"A stirring introduction to the wonder of evolutionary biology." Kirkus

Includes bibliographical references

Darwin, Charles

★ The **voyage** of the Beagle; journal of researches into the natural history and geology of the countries visited during the voyage of H.M.S. Beagle round the world. introduction by Steve Jones. Modern Lib. 2001 468p il pa $12.95 **508**

1. Natural history 2. Beagle Expedition (1831-1836) 3. South America -- Description and travel
ISBN 0-375-75680-9

LC 00-46294

This journal records the author's five year voyage around the world as a naturalist aboard H.M.S. Beagle. The trip was influential in the formulation of Darwin's theories of evolution. During the journey he collected data on wildlife, geological formations, weather, and local customs.

De Villiers, Marq

Sahara: a natural history; {by} Marq de Villiers and Sheila Hirtle. Walker & Co. 2002 326p il maps $28; pa $13 **508**

1. Sahara Desert 2. Natural history -- Africa

ISBN 0-8027-1372-6; 0-8027-7678-7 pa

LC 2002-71391

"Insightful and intelligent, this fascinating book will appeal to anyone with a curiosity about the world's largest desert and the people who inhabit it." Booklist

Includes bibliographical references

Flannery, Tim F.

The **eternal** frontier; an ecological history of North America and its peoples. {by} Tim Flannery. Atlantic Monthly Press 2001 404p il maps $27.50; pa $16 **508**

1. Natural history -- North America

ISBN 0-87113-789-5; 0-8021-3888-8 pa

LC 2001-18841

"This book weaves ecological, cultural, and social history together in a marvelous way." Sci Books Films

Fothergill, Alastair

Planet Earth; as you've never seen it before. [by] Alastair Fothergill [et al.]; foreword by David Attenborough. University of California Press 2007 309p il map $39.95 **508**

1. Habitat (Ecology) 2. Earth

ISBN 978-0-520-25054-3; 0-520-25054-0

LC 2006-50073

In this collection of over 400 photographs of natural landscapes and wildlife, the author "takes readers on a kaleidoscopic tour of the flora, fauna and natural history of the Earth's poles, forests, plains, deserts, mountains and oceans." Publ Wkly

Gould, Stephen Jay

★ The **richness** of life; the essential Stephen Jay Gould. edited by Paul McGarr and Steven Rose; with an introduction by Steven Rose and a foreword by Oliver Sacks. Norton 2007 654p il $35 **508**

1. Evolution 2. Natural history

ISBN 978-0-393-06498-8; 0-393-06498-0

LC 2006-29208

Frist published 2006 in the United Kingdom

"For collections that have room for only one volume of his writing, this is the essential one." SLJ

Includes bibliographical references

Leach, Amy

Things that are; Amy Leach; illustrations by Nate Christopherson. Milkweed Editions 2012 xiii, 185 p.p (acid-free paper) $18.00 **508**

1. Essays 2. Natural history 3. Natural history literature

ISBN 1571313346; 9781571313348

LC 2011040887

This book of essays by Amy Leach, winner of a Whiting Writers' Award and a Rona Jaffe Foundation Writers' Award, "explores fantastical and curious subjects pertaining to natural phenomena." It is "divided into two sections -- 'Things of Earth' and 'Things of Heaven' -- containing essays with names such as 'Goats, and Bygone Goats,' 'When Trees Dream of Being Trees' and 'Sail On, My Little Honeybee.' Each of the essays range from three to seven pages, and they are accompanied by . . . pen-and-ink drawings by [Nate] Christopherson." (Kirkus Reviews)

Leopold, Aldo, 1886-1948

A **Sand** County almanac & other writings on ecology & conservation; a sand county almanac & other writings on ecology and conservation. Aldo Leopold; [edited by] Curt Meine. Literary Classics of the United States, Inc. 2013 832 p. illustrations, maps (Library of America) **508**

1. Nature conservation 2. Environmental protection

ISBN 9781598532067

LC 2012948207

A reissue of the title first published 1949

By Aldo Leopold and edited by Curt Meine, "the collection opens with Leopold's classic A Sand County Almanac," which "is joined here by over fifty uncollected articles, essays, speeches, and other writings that chart the evolution of Leopold's ideas over the course of three decades. . . . The volume also presents a freshly prepared version of Leopold's extraordinary field journals." (Publisher's note)

"The volume also includes a chronology of Leopold's life; extensive notes; an index to plants/animals, with a mixture of common and scientific nomenclature; and a general index." Choice

Includes bibliographical references and indexes

Leslie, Clare Walker

The **Curious** Nature Guide; Explore the Natural Wonders All Around You. by Clare Walker Leslie. Storey Publishing 2015 144 p. illustrations (chiefly color) (pbk. : alk. paper) $14.95 **508**

1. Natural history 2. Nature -- Juvenile literature 3. Ecology

ISBN 9781612125091

LC 2015010780

This book, by Clare Walker Leslie, "will inspire you to use all of your senses to notice the colors, sounds, smells, and textures of the trees, plants, animals, birds, insects, clouds, and other features that can be seen right outside your home, no matter where you live. Sketch or write about one exceptional nature image each day; learn to identify cloud types and the weather they bring; or create a record of what you see each day as you walk your dog." (Publisher's note)

"A remarkable book for solitary reading or sharing with children." LJ

Includes bibliographical references and index

Matthiessen, Peter

End of the earth; voyaging to Antarctica. National Geographic Soc. 2003 242p il maps $26 **508**

1. Animals -- Antarctica 2. Antarctica -- Exploration

ISBN 0-7922-5059-1

LC 2003-51254

This account of the author's voyage describes the wildlife he encountered in the region

"Vivid and empathic accounts of the high drama and petty rivalries of Antarctic exploration alternate with Matthiessen's own adventures as he shares his indelible impressions of this cold, white wonderland in the hope that they will inspire readers to appreciate the beauty and bounty of the earth's 'shimmering web of biodiversity' enough to defend and preserve it." Booklist

Includes bibliographical references

Muir, John

Nature writings; the story of my boyhood and youth, my first summer in the Sierra, the mountains of California, Stickeen, selected essays. Library of Am. 1997 888p il $35   **508**
  1. Authors 2. Naturalists 3. Writers on nature
  ISBN 1-88301-124-8
                    LC 96-9664

Muir "is at his best . . . when he is looking intently at something, walking around it, sniffing the air, looking again. As a writer he is a kind of visionary sensualist, a seer who reveals what lies in plain sight." Commentary

Natural history; the ultimate visual guide to everything on Earth. [senior project editor, Kathryn Hennessy] DK 2010 648p il map $50   **508**
  1. Natural history 2. Reference books
  ISBN 978-0-7566-6752-8; 0-7566-6752-6
                LC 2010-283659
"This is an international encyclopedia of life-forms—e.g., fossils, fungi, plants, animals, mammals—that includes vital facts and two to three sentences about each as well as more than 5000 color illustrations in all. Each grouping is introduced by an essay that puts it in biological and evolutionary perspective." Libr J

Nicholls, Steve

Paradise found; nature in America at the time of discovery. University of Chicago Press 2009 524p $30   **508**
  1. Human influence on nature 2. America -- Exploration 3. Natural history -- North America
  ISBN 978-0-226-58340-2; 0-226-58340-6
                LC 2008-36076
The author "turns to the writings of forgotten early naturalists to gain understanding both of the natural abundance of the New World when the first Europeans arrived and of how so much of this living bounty was destroyed so quickly. . . . Not only does Nicholls present arresting material, he also offers fresh interpretations and connections in this grandly spanning and affecting look to the past for guidance in facing a future of further diminishment." Booklist

Includes bibliographical references and index

Rothman, Julia

Nature anatomy; the curious parts & pieces of the natural world. by Julia Rothman, with John Niekrasz. Storey Publishing 2015 224 p. color illustrations, color map (paper w/ flaps : alk. paper) $16.95   **508**
  1. Earth sciences 2. Earth sciences -- Study and teaching (Middle school) -- Pictorial works
  ISBN 1612122310; 9781612122311
                LC 2014033664

This book, by Julia Rothman with John Niekrasz, "celebrates the diverse curiosities and beauty of the natural world. . . . With whimsically hip illustrations, every page is an extraordinary look at all kinds of subjects, from mineral formation and the inside of a volcano to what makes sunsets, monarch butterfly migration, the ecosystem of a rotting log, the parts of a bird, the anatomy of a jellyfish, and much, much more." (Publisher's note)

"With its wide range of topics, from landforms to leaf identification, bird beaks, and water bugs, Nature Anatomy is designed as the ultimate book for browsers with an insatiable curiosity about the great outdoors. Rothman has clearly found a structure and design in which she excels; this title is an informative charmer from start to finish. More, please." Booklist

Safina, Carl

The **view** from Lazy Point; a natural year in an unnatural world. with drawings by Trudy Nicholson; maps by Jon Luoma. Henry Holt and Co. 2011 401p il map $32; ebook $16.99   **508**
  1. Human ecology 2. Marine ecology 3. Coastal ecology 4. Environmental degradation
  ISBN 978-0-8050-9040-6; 0-8050-9040-1; 978-1-4299-5035-0 ebook; 1-4299-5035-8 ebook
                LC 2009-40108
A conservationist explores various global regions to investigate examples of environmental degradation and renewal while identifying a link between environmental dangers and human rights issues.

"A superb work of environmental reportage and reflection." Kirkus

Includes bibliographical references

Sampson, Scott D.

How to raise a wild child; the art and science of falling in love with nature. Scott D. Sampson. Houghton Mifflin Harcourt 2015 352 p. (hardback) $25   **508**
  1. Parenting 2. Child rearing 3. Outdoor education 4. Nature study 5. Child development 6. Natural history -- Study and teaching
  ISBN 0544279328; 9780544279322
                LC 2014048565
This book, by Scott D. Sampson, offers "an easy-to-use guide for parents, teachers, and others looking to foster a strong connection between children and nature, complete with engaging activities, troubleshooting advice, and much more. . . . Distilling the latest research in multiple disciplines, Sampson reveals how adults can help kids fall in love with nature--enlisting technology as an ally, taking advantage of urban nature, and instilling a sense of place along the way." (Publisher's note)

"This timely, significant work carries a far-reaching message for families and the planet." Pub Wkly

Shetterly, Susan Hand

Settled in the wild; notes from the edge of town. Algonquin Books of Chapel Hill 2010 240p $21.95   **508**

1. Wildlife 2. Natural history -- Maine

ISBN 1565126181; 9781565126183

LC 2009-30802

Shetterly "notes the interplay of humanity and wilderness through fishing, forestry, conservation, preservation, hunting, trapping, development and wildlife rehabilitation, but also in quiet, personal appreciation. Shetterly is a less verbose Thoreau, allowing nature's wisdom to seep through her simple yet thorough observations." Kirkus

Steinberg, Ted

★ **Gotham** unbound; an ecological history of greater New York, from Henry Hudson to Hurricane Sandy. Ted Steinberg. Simon & Schuster 2014 544 p. illustrations, maps (hardcover : alk. paper) $32   **508**

1. Natural history -- New York (State) -- New York

ISBN 1476741247; 9781476741246; 9781476741284; 9781476741307

LC 2013036197

This book, by Ted Steinberg, "is a powerful account of the relentless development that New Yorkers wrought as they plunged headfirst into the floodplain and transformed untold amounts of salt marsh and shellfish beds into a land jam-packed with people, asphalt and steel, and the reeds and gulls that thrive among them." (Publisher's note)

A "fascinating and cautionary unnatural history, a staggering epic of human will, might, and folly that affirms a crucial truth, 'the control of nature is an illusion.'" Booklist

Includes bibliographical references and index

Stroud, Patricia Tyson

A **glorious** enterprise; the Academy of Natural Sciences of Philadelphia and the making of American science. Robert McCracken Peck and Patricia Tyson Stroud; photographs by Rosamond Purcell. University of Pennsylvania Press 2012 xvii, 437 p.p (alk. paper) $75   **508**

1. Natural history 2. Science -- History 3. Academy of Natural Sciences of Philadelphia -- History 4. Natural history -- Research -- Pennsylvania -- Philadelphia

ISBN 0812243803; 9780812243802

LC 2011034991

This book by Robert McCracken Peck and Patricia Tyson Stroud focuses on the history of the Academy of Natural Sciences of Philadelphia, which "stands today as the oldest natural history museum in the Western hemisphere.... What began as a small gathering of devoted amateurs has grown into a vibrant international center for scientific education and research." (Publisher's note)

Includes bibliographical references and index.

509   **History, geographic treatment, biography**

Al-Khalili, Jim

The **house** of wisdom; how Arabic science saved ancient knowledge and gave us the Renaissance. Penguin Press 2011 xxix, 302p il map $29.95 **509**

1. Medieval civilization 2. Science -- Philosophy 3. Science -- Arab countries 4. Arab countries -- Intellectual life

ISBN 1-59420-279-6; 978-1-59420-279-7

LC 2010-53136

This is a history of early "Islamic astronomy, mathematics, medicine and philosophy." (N Y Times Book Rev) Glossary. Chronology. Index.

"There is a commonly held view that during the Middle Ages, Arabic scientists focused mainly on translating into Arabic the scientific knowledge of ancient civilizations while contributing little to scientific advancement. Physicist al-Khalili .... challenges this theory by documenting the remarkable contributions of Arabic astronomers, mathematicians, physicians, physicists, chemists, and philosophers, who were scholars at a scientific academy in Baghdad known as the House of Wisdom. .... Al-Khalili brings to life a vibrant intellectual period of Islamic history when there was not only tolerance for other religions and cultures but a synergy between science and Islam. Anyone interested in the early history of science or the development of the scientific method before Galileo will find this an engaging study." Libr J

Includes bibliographical references

Bauer, Susan Wise

The **story** of Western science; From the writings of Aristotle to the big bang theory. Susan Wise Bauer. W.W. Norton & Co. Inc. 2015 336 p. illustrations (hardcover) $26.95   **509**

1. Science -- History 2. Astronomy -- History

ISBN 0393243265; 9780393243260

LC 2015000136

This book by Susan Wise Bauer "shows us the joy and importance of reading groundbreaking science writing for ourselves and guides us back to the masterpieces that have changed the way we think about our world, our cosmos, and ourselves. Each chapter recommends one or more classic books and provides entertaining accounts of crucial contributions to science, vivid sketches of the scientist-writers, and clear explanations of the mechanics underlying each concept." (Publisher's note)

"What is especially enriching in the text is the focus on the science writing of these inquiring pioneers, and each chapter contains names of websites and e-book versions and recommendations for books written by individual scientists. A remarkable resource for a wide audience." Choice

Includes bibliographical references and index

Concise history of science & invention; an illustrated time line. edited by Jolyon Goddard. National Geographic 2010 352 p. ill., maps (some col.) $40.00   **509**

1. Reference books 2. Science -- History 3. Inventions -- History 4. Science -- History -- Chronology 5.

Inventions -- History -- Chronology
ISBN 1426205449; 9781426205446

LC 2009018460

Includes glossary and bibliographical references

Crease, Robert P.

The **great** equations; breakthroughs in science from Pythagoras to Heisenberg. W.W. Norton & Co. 2009 315p il $25.95 **509**

1. Equations 2. Science -- History 3. Science -- Philosophy

ISBN 978-0-393-06204-5; 0-393-06204-X

LC 2008-42494

The author "explores 10 rather beautiful equations. He begins with the beguiling simplicity of the equation that bears Pythagoras' name . . . and moves on to Newton's second law of motion and law of universal gravitation, the second law of thermodynamics, Maxwell's celebrated equations, discoveries by Einstein and Schrödinger and, finally, Heisenberg's famous uncertainty principle. . . . Any reader who aspires to be scientifically literate will find this a good starting place." Publ Wkly

Includes bibliographical references

Dolnick, Edward

The **clockwork** universe; Isaac Newton, the Royal Society, and the birth of the modern world. HarperCollins 2011 378p il $27.99; ebook $23.99 **509**

1. Science 2. Physicists 3. Mathematicians 4. Writers on science 5. Royal Society of London 6. Royal Society (Great Britain) 7. Scientists -- Great Britain -- History

ISBN 9780061719516; 9780062042262

LC 2010-24321

The subject is "how the scientific attempt to describe the underlying order of the cosmos played out in the life of Isaac Newton." (N Y Times Book Rev) Bibliography. Index.

"Colorful, entertainingly written and nicely paced—a fine introductory text on Newton and the scientific revolution." Kirkus

Includes bibliographical references

Encyclopedia of the scientific revolution; from Copernicus to Newton. editor Wilbur Applebaum. Garland 2000 xxxv, 758p il (Garland reference library of the humanities) $160 **509**

1. Reference books 2. Science -- History -- Encyclopedias

ISBN 0-8153-1503-1

LC 00-25149

A "collection of articles on the progress of scientific discovery in the 16th and 17th centuries. . . . The 437 entries vary in length from just half a page to five pages, and each has a short bibliography directing the reader to recent articles and monographs as well as primary sources." Libr J

Includes bibliographical references

Fara, Patricia

★ **Science**; a four thousand year history. Oxford University Press 2009 408p il map pa $18.95; $34.95 **509**

1. Science and civilization 2. Science -- History

ISBN 019922689X; 0199580278 pa; 9780199226894; 9780199580279 pa; 978-0-19-922689-4; 978-0-19-958027-9 pa; 0-19-958027-8 pa; 0-19-922689-X

LC 2008-50975

This "book explores how science has become so powerful by describing the financial interests and imperial ambitions behind its success. . . . [Fara challenges] notions of European superiority by emphasising the importance of scientific projects based around the world. . . . [This] volume challenges scientific supremacy itself, arguing that science is successful not because it is always indubitably right, but because people have said that it is right. Science dominates modern life, but perhaps the globe will be better off by limiting science's powers and undoing some of its effects." (Publisher's note) Index.

"This survey of 4,000 years of scientific discovery from Babylon to the present confirms that historians of science often have quite different perspectives from those of the actual practitioners. . . . Readers learn about the contributions of famous scientists as though they were almost puppets responding to religious, social, and practical influences in both their choices of research topics and their methods of investigation—in contrast to their possessing an inherent desire to better understand the behavior of nature. In this highly readable book that tells a magnificent story, Fara . . . weaves together the bits and pieces in a unique way." Choice

Includes bibliographical references

Freely, John

The **flame** of Miletus; the birth of science in ancient Greece (and how it changed the world) John Freely. I.B. Tauris 2012 238 p. (hbk.) $29.95 **509**

1. Ancient philosophy 2. Greece -- Civilization 3. Science, Ancient 4. Science -- Greece -- History 5. Greece -- Intellectual life -- To 146 B.C

ISBN 1780760515; 9781780760513

LC 2012472537

This book looks at Ancient Greece and "the great scientific thinkers of that distant age. [John Freely] narrates . . . the story of how the ancient flame lit by Thales and others survived the centuries after the fall of Hellas and Rome, resurfaced in the Islamic world, and was transmitted to western Europe. There it rekindled the spirit of scientific inquiry that led to the germination of modern science." (Choice)

Includes bibliographical references (p. 226-235) and index

Green, Bill

Boltzmann's tomb; travels in search of science. Bellevue Literary Press 2011 208p il **509**

1. Scientists 2. Voyages and travels 3. Discoveries in science 4. College deans 5. College teachers 6. Religious scholars

ISBN 1-934137-35-9; 978-1-934137-35-2

This book discusses Green's visits to "the workplaces and graves of . . . famous scientists whose lives and research were affected in some way by unpredicted events." (Sci Books Films) Index.

"This book is very readable and should be especially appealing to young people contemplating a life in science." Sci Books Films

Gribbin, John R.

The **scientists**; a history of science told through the lives of its greatest inventors. [by] John Gribbin. Random House 2003 xxii, 646p il hardcover o.p. pa $16.95   **509**
1. Scientists 2. Science -- History
ISBN 1-4000-6013-3; 0-8129-6788-7 pa
LC 2003-46607
First published 2002 in the United Kingdom with title: Science: a history, 1543-2001

"Replete with scientific clarity, Gribbin's work is the epitome of what a general-interest history of science should be." Booklist

Includes bibliographical references

Hofstadter, Dan

The **Earth** moves; Galileo and the Roman Inquisition. W.W. Norton 2009 240p il   **509**
1. Popes 2. Astronomy 3. Astronomers 4. Inquisition 5. Writers on science 6. Inquisition -- Italy 7. Science, Renaissance 8. Catholic Church -- Italy -- History 9. Astronomy -- Religious aspects -- Christianity 10. Catholic Church -- Doctrines -- History -- 17th century
ISBN 0-393-06650-9; 978-0-393-06650-0
LC 2009-4325
This book examines the Inquisition in relation to Galileo's arrest, trial, conviction, and the legal processes involved. Bibliography. Index.

This book "allows a clear understanding of one of the major events in the history of science." Sci Books Films

Includes bibliographical references

Holmes, Richard, 1945-

★ The **age** of wonder; how the romantic generation discovered the beauty and terror of science. Pantheon Books 2009 xxi, 552p il $40; pa $17.95 **509**
1. Science -- Great Britain -- History
ISBN 978-0-375-42222-5; 978-1-4000-3187-0 pa
LC 2008-49587
"In this big two-hearted river of a book, the twin energies of scientific curiosity and poetic invention pulsate on every page." N Y Times Book Rev

Includes bibliographical references

Lightman, Alan P.

★ The **discoveries**; great breakthroughs in 20th century science. [by] Alan Lightman. Pantheon Books 2005 553p il $32.50; pa $16.95   **509**
1. Science -- History
ISBN 0-375-42168-8; 0-375-71345-X pa
LC 2005-40854
This book "chronicles 25 landmark findings in astronomy, physics, chemistry, and biology in the 20th century. Beginning with Max Planck's quantum theory and ending with Paul Berg's recombinant DNA, these breakthroughs are academically and playfully explored via the nature of the un-

known, the circumstances and influences of discovery, and, most originally, the actual words of the scientists." Libr J
Includes bibliographical references

McCray, W. Patrick

The **visioneers**; how a group of elite scientists pursued space colonies, nanotechnologies, and a limitless future. W. Patrick McCray. Princeton University Press 2012 351 p. (hardback : acid-free paper) $29.95   **509**
1. Nanotechnology 2. Space colonies 3. Visionaries 4. Science -- History
ISBN 0691139830; 9780691139838
LC 2012017061
This book looks at visioneers, a term coined by author W. Patrick McCray "to describe an individual with an an inquiring mind that is not merely scientific or technical but posed imaginatively toward the future. . . . The two primary visioneers examined by McCray are Gerard O'Neil, a prominent Princeton physicist who saw space colonization as an answer to Earth's growing population, and Eric Drexler, who was fascinated by the new field of nanotechnology." (Library Journal)

Includes bibliographical references and index

Mlodinow, Leonard

The **upright** thinkers; the human journey from living in trees to understanding the cosmos. Leonard Mlodinow. Pantheon Books 2015 352 p. illustrations (hard cover : alk. paper) $27.95   **509**
1. Evolution 2. Science -- History
ISBN 0307908232; 9780307908230; 9780307908247
LC 2014040067
This book, by Leonard Mlodinow, offers a "tour through the exciting history of human progress and the key events in the development of science. . . . He presents a . . . new look at the unique characteristics of our species and our society that helped propel us from stone tools to written language and through the birth of chemistry, biology, and modern physics to today's technological world." (Publisher's note)

"Attending to the real people involved in the story he tells, and gifted with a knack for inserting a personal anecdote, a biographical tidbit, or a laugh line just when one is needed, Mlodinow never bores or exhausts. His structuring of the book is also exemplary. It's in three sections, the first ranging from H. habilis to Aristotle and the formalization of reason, the second from Renaissance cosmology to Darwin, and the third from Planck's and Einstein's invention of the quantum onward. Amateur science mavens couldn't ask for a better brief, introductory text." Booklist

Notable black American scientists; Kristine M. Krapp, editor. Gale Res. 1999 xxvi, 349p il $125   **509**
1. Reference books 2. Scientists -- Dictionaries 3. African Americans -- Biography -- Dictionaries
ISBN 0-7876-2789-5
LC 98-36338
The "contributors to this compilation of 254 bibliographic profiles emphasize the achievements of black scientists and physicians, men and women, from Colonial times to the present, in the territory that is now the US. . . . Each

entry begins with basic information about each subject—name, year of birth and death (if deceased), and specialty. A biographical essay follows." Choice

Includes bibliographical references

★ The **Oxford** companion to the history of modern science; editor in chief, J.L. Heilbron; editors, James Bartholomew {et al.} Oxford Univ. Press 2003 xxviii, 941p il $110 **509**
1. Science -- History
ISBN 0-19-511229-6

LC 2002-153783

This reference on the history of science from the Renaissance through the 20th century includes some 600 articles covering "a broad spectrum of topics in all scientific disciplines (e.g., biotechnology, geology) as well as disciplines that influenced science, such as religion and politics. Also included are the biographies of 100 leading figures (e.g., Isaac Newton, Marie Curie) and coverage of scientific instruments (e.g., microscopes, Geiger counters). Organized alphabetically, the well-written articles include plenty of cross references. Over 100 black-and-white illustrations appear within their appropriate articles, but the eight pages of color illustrations in the middle of the volume are not associated with any article." Libr J

Includes bibliographical references

Reader's guide to the history of science; edited by Arne Hessenbruch. Fitzroy Dearborn Pubs. 2000 xxix, 934p $135 **509**
1. Reference books 2. Science -- History -- Encyclopedias
ISBN 1-884964-29-X

LC 2001-270888

"This volume contains about 600 entries on various aspects of the history of science, including individuals (e.g., Galileo), disciplines (e.g., astronomy), and broad topics (e.g., religion)." Libr J

Includes bibliographical references

Reynolds, Moira Davison
American women scientists; 23 inspiring biographies, 1900-2000. McFarland & Co. 1999 149p il hardcover o.p. pa $24.95 **509**
1. Women scientists
ISBN 0-7864-0649-6; 0-7864-2161-4 pa

LC 99-14603

"Four-to-six page profiles of 23 of the century's premier women scientists, representing a wide variety of disciplines. The entries are arranged chronologically beginning with Cornelia Clapp (1849-1934) and ending with Mary Good (1931-). . . . Each entry includes a black-and-white portrait." SLJ

Includes bibliographical references

Snyder, Laura J.
The **philosophical** breakfast club; four remarkable friends who transformed science and changed the world. Broadway Books 2011 439p il map $27; ebook $27 **509**
1. Clergy 2. Economists 3. Scientists 4. Astronomers 5. Philosophers 6. Photographers 7. Mathematicians

8. Writers on science 9. Science -- Philosophy 10. Great Britain -- Intellectual life 11. Scientists -- Great Britain -- History
ISBN 978-0-7679-3048-2; 978-0-7679-3048-2 ebook

LC 2010-25790

This book "gives a unique view of the background and times in which these men lived, and a peek at the implications that their work and philosophy had on today's modern science." Sci Books Films

Includes bibliographical references

Teresi, Dick
Lost discoveries; the ancient roots of modern science, from the Babylonians to the Maya. Simon & Schuster 2002 453p il $27; pa $15 **509**
1. Ancient civilization 2. Science -- History
ISBN 0-684-83718-8; 0-7432-4379-X pa

LC 2002-75457

"Teresi offers a great deal of fascinating material largely ignored by many histories of science." Publ Wkly

Includes bibliographical references

Weinberg, Steven, 1933-
To explain the world; the discovery of modern science. Steven Weinberg. Harper 2015 432 p. illustrations (hardback) $28.99 **509**
1. Ancient history 2. Science -- History 3. Medieval civilization 4. Science -- Greece -- History 5. Science, Ancient 6. Science, Medieval 7. Science -- Methodology -- History
ISBN 0062346652; 9780062346650

LC 2014030253

This book, by Steven Weinberg, is a "commentary on the history of science from the Greeks to modern times. . . . He shows that the scientists of ancient and medieval times . . . did not understand what there is to understand, or how to understand it. Yet over the centuries, through the struggle to solve such mysteries as the curious backward movement of the planets and the rise and fall of the tides, the modern discipline of science eventually emerged." (Publisher's note)

"The author provides an almost 100-page appendix of 'technical notes,' mathematical explanations of many of the theories and ideas discussed in the book. Overall, the book is interesting because it shows a scientist's perspective on the history of science; however, it does not measure up to the strict requirements of historiography expected by professional historians. Summing Up: Optional. General readers." Choice

Includes bibliographical references

Wootton, David
The **Invention** of Science; A New History of the Scientific Revolution. by David Wootton. HarperCollins 2015 784 p. 16 plates; illustrations; maps $35 **509**
1. Science -- History
ISBN 006175952X; 9780061759529

This book, by David Wootton, is an "examination of the . . . the Scientific Revolution, and how it came to change the way we understand ourselves and our world. . . . From gunpowder technology, the discovery of the new world, movable type printing, perspective painting, and the telescope to the practice of conducting experiments, the laws of nature, and the concept of the fact, Wotton shows how these discoveries codified into a social construct and a system of knowledge." (Publisher's note)

"Although academics, who will catch the foreshadowing, will have no trouble following Wootton's argument, casual readers are likely to quit before they reach the payoff." LJ

509.252   Women scientists--Collective biography

Ignotofsky, Rachel

Women in science; 50 Fearless Pioneers Who Changed the World. written and illustrated by Rachel Ignotofsky. Ten Speed Press 2016 127 p. color illustrations (hardcover : alk. paper) $16.99   **509.252**
1. Women scientists 2. Women scientists -- Biography -- Juvenile literature
ISBN 1607749769; 9781607749769
LC 2015050246

This book, by Rachel Ignotofsky, "highlights the contributions of fifty notable women to the fields of science, technology, engineering, and mathematics (STEM) from the ancient to the modern world. . . . The trailblazing women profiled include well-known figures like primatologist Jane Goodall, as well as lesser-known pioneers such as Katherine Johnson, the African-American physicist and mathematician who calculated the trajectory of the 1969 Apollo 11 mission to the moon." (Publisher's note)

Includes bibliographical references and index

510   Mathematics

Adam, John A.

★ A **mathematical** nature walk. Princeton University Press 2009 248p il $27.95   **510**
1. Mathematics 2. Mathematical analysis
ISBN 978-0-691-12895-5; 0-691-12895-2
LC 2008-44828

"The general reader will find here a remarkably lucid explanation of how mathematicians create a formulaic model that mimics the key features of some natural phenomenon. . . . Ordinary math becomes adventure." Booklist

Includes bibliographical references

Barrow, John D.

100 essential things you didn't know you didn't know; math explains your world. by John D. Barrow. W W Norton & Co Inc 2009 284 p. il $16.95   **510**
1. Mathematics
ISBN 0393338673; 9780393070071; 9780393338676
LC 200855910

First published 2008 in the United Kingdom

In this book, author John D. Barrow "takes the most baffling of everyday phenomena and—with simple math, lucid explanations, and illustrations—explains why they work the way they do. His witty, crystal-clear answers shed light on the dark and shadowy corners of the physical world we all think we understand so well." (Publisher's note)

"Barrow (Mathletics), a Cambridge University professor of mathematical sciences and the director of the Millennium

Mathematics Project, delves into the many ways mathematics informs art, and more broadly, our daily lives. Barrow is well versed in mathematics and is fascinated by the topics, but he does not consistently provide accessible explanations. That said, even when he misses, Barrow successfully conveys the idea that mathematics provides a key to understanding both ordinary and extraordinary phenomena." Pub Wkly.

Includes bibliographical references

Benjamin, Arthur

The **Magic** of Math; Solving for X and Figuring Out Why. Basic Books 2015 336 p. illustrations $26.99   **510**
1. Mathematics 2. Sequences (Mathematics)
ISBN 0465054722; 9780465054725
LC 2015936185

This book on mathematics by Arthur Benjamin "empowers you to see the beauty, simplicity, and truly magical properties behind those formulas and equations that once left your head spinning. You'll learn the key ideas of classic areas of mathematics like arithmetic, algebra, geometry, trigonometry, and calculus, but you'll also have fun fooling around with Fibonacci numbers, investigating infinity, and marveling over mathematical magic tricks." (Publisher's note)

"Forget magic. Benjamin delivers a primer generously filled with insights and intuitions that make math approachable, interesting, and, yes, beautiful." Kirkus

Boyer, Carl B.

A **history** of mathematics; [by] Carl B. Boyer and Uta Merzbach. 3rd ed.; Wiley 2010 xx, 668p il (pbk.) $39.95   **510**
1. Mathematics 2. Mathematics -- History
ISBN 9780470525487
LC 2010-3424

First published 1969

This book explores the "history of humankind's relationship with numbers, shapes, and patterns. This revised edition features up-to-date coverage of topics such as Fermat's Last Theorem and the Poincaré Conjecture, in addition to recent advances in areas such as finite group theory and computer-aided proofs." (Publisher's note)

"This good general history of mathematics is understandable to the student as well as authoritative for the mathematician." Malinowsky. Best Sci & Technol Ref Books for Young People

Includes bibliographical references

Darling, David J.

The **universal** book of mathematics; from Abracadabra to Zeno's paradoxes. [by] David Darling. Wiley 2004 383p il $40   **510**
1. Reference books 2. Mathematics -- Encyclopedias
ISBN 0-471-27047-4
LC 2003-24670

"The book's entries include numerous mathematical terms, brief biographies of mathematicians from ancient times to the present, and famous mathematical problems (both solved and unsolved), as well as problems and puzzles of a more recreational nature. It is a spirit of whimsy, the fanciful, and the outrageous that makes this book much more than a dry encyclopedia of mathematical terms, however. Darling's writing style and choice of entries make this an easy book to pick up and page through." Choice

Includes bibliographical references

Dunham, William

The **mathematical** universe; an alphabetical journey through the great proofs, problems, and personalities. Wiley 1994 314p il hardcover o.p. pa $19.95 **510**

1. Mathematics 2. Mathematicians
ISBN 0-471-17661-3 pa

LC 93-46702

In this history of mathematics, "Dunham sheds light not only on the personalities—eccentric, vain, brilliant—of major mathematicians, but also on contemporary social issues, such as multiculturalism and gender equity. Readers who want to understand the cultural significance of mathematics would do well to begin with this book." Booklist

Includes bibliographical references

Ellenberg, Jordan, 1971-

★ **How** not to be wrong; the power of mathematical thinking. Jordan Ellenberg. The Penguin Press 2014 480 p. illustrations (hardback) $27.95 **510**

1. Life skills 2. Mathematics 3. Mathematical analysis
ISBN 1594205221; 9781594205224

LC 2014005394

"The math we learn in school can seem like a dull set of rules, laid down by the ancients and not to be questioned. In 'How Not to Be Wrong,' Jordan Ellenberg shows us how terribly limiting this view is: Math isn't confined to abstract incidents that never occur in real life, but rather touches everything we do--the whole world is shot through with it. . . . Ellenberg chases mathematical threads through a vast range of time and space, from the everyday to the cosmic." (Publisher's note)

"Ellenberg finds the common-sense math at work in the everyday world, and his vivid examples and clear descriptions show how 'math is woven into the way we reason.'" Pub Wkly

Includes bibliographical references and index

Huber, Michael R.

Mythematics; solving the twelve labors of Hercules. Princeton University Press 2009 183p il $24.95 **510**

1. Problem solving 2. Hercules (Legendary character)
ISBN 978-0-691-13575-5

LC 2009-8535

The author takes the ancient Greeks' "early interest in puzzles and the descriptions of Hercules' various labors and reinterpreted each of those labors in terms of several 'tasks,' after which he gives a 'solution' to the mathematical problem(s) implicit in each of the tasks. . . . Given that we tend to think of early Greek mathematics in terms of geometry or, possibly, number theory, the breadth of mathematics required for the various tasks may be surprising." Sci Books Films

Includes bibliographical references

Kanigel, Robert

The **man** who knew infinity; a life of the genius Ramanujan. Washington Sq. Press 1992 438p map il pa $15 **510**

1. Mathematicians
ISBN 0-671-75061-5; 978-0-671-75061-9

LC 91-37763

First published 1991 by Charles Scribner's Sons

"Kanigel deserves high praise for a work of arduous research and rare insight." Booklist

Includes bibliographical references

Mahajan, Sanjoy

Street-fighting mathematics; the art of educated guessing and opportunistic problem solving. MIT Press 2010 134p il pa $25 **510**

1. Problem solving 2. Approximate computation
ISBN 0-262-51429-X; 978-0-262-51429-3

LC 2009-28867

The author argues that the key to solving complex arithmetic questions "lies in having informal tools on hand that let us attack the problem. Though the result may not be perfectly precise, he believes, intuitive mathematical reasoning is often sufficient for our needs. . . . [The book] is not organized around traditional math topics, such as differential equations, but ways of thinking: reasoning by analogy, visualizing geometric problems, and more. Readers can then answer all manner of questions: Guessing the number of babies in the United States, calculating the bond angles in methane, or determining the drag that air exerts on a 747." Dr. Dobb's

Includes bibliographical references

The **New** York Times book of mathematics; edited by Gina Kolata; forward by Paul Hoffman. Sterling 2013 xvi, 480 p.p (hardcover) $24.95 **510**

1. Mathematics
ISBN 1402793227; 9781402793226

LC 2012045019

This book about mathematics is "divided into thematic sections and is only occasionally chronological. Among topics covered are the National Security Agency's (NSA's) threats to mathematicians writing papers with code-breaking applications; the celebrated story of Andrew Wiles's proof of Fermat's Last Theorem; Grigori Perelman's confirmation of the Poincaré conjecture and his subsequent, Bobby Fischer-like, disappearance." (Library Journal)

Parker, Matt

★ **Things** to make and do in the fourth dimension; a mathematician's journey through narcissistic numbers, optimal dating algorithms, at least two kinds of infinity, and more. Matt Parker. Farrar, Straus & Giroux 2014 464 p. illustrations (hardcover) $28 **510**

1. Mathematics
ISBN 0374275653; 9780374275655

LC 2014950271

In this book, "mathematician and comedian Matt Parker . . . sets out to convince his readers to revisit the very math that put them off the subject as fourteen-year-olds. Starting with the foundations of math familiar from school (numbers, geometry, and algebra), he reveals how it is possible to climb all the way up to the topology and to four-dimensional shapes, and from there to infinity--and slightly beyond." (Publisher's note)

"Parker makes it sound easy, even when it is not, and some of the material can be pretty heavy going. However, most important, he reveals the social aspects of the field, describing his interactions with other mathematicians as they bounce problems around, challenging one another's imaginations." LJ

Pasles, Paul C.

Benjamin Franklin's numbers; an unsung mathematical odyssey. Princeton University Press 2008 254p il $26.95   **510**
1. Authors 2. Diplomats 3. Inventors 4. Statesmen 5. Scientists 6. Mathematics 7. Writers on science 8. Members of Congress
ISBN 978-0-691-12956-3; 0-691-12956-8
LC 2006-102508
The author "documents the famous scientist-statesman's lively interest in numerical enigmas, most particularly those known as Magic Squares. . . . An unexpected but welcome perspective on the genial genius of Philadelphia." Booklist
Includes bibliographical references

Pickover, Clifford A.

The math book; from Pythagoras to the 57th dimension, 250 milestones in the history of mathematics. Clifford A. Pickover. Sterling 2009 527 p. il pbk $19.95; $29.95   **510**
1. Mathematics -- History
ISBN 1402788290; 9781402788291; 9781402757969
LC 200843214
In this book, "beginning millions of years ago with ancient 'ant odometers' and moving through time to our modern-day quest for new dimensions, prolific polymath Clifford Pickover covers 250 milestones in mathematical history. Among the numerous concepts readers will encounter as they dip into this inviting anthology: cicada-generated prime numbers, magic squares, and the butterfly effect." (Publisher's note)

"Pickover's love of mathematics shines through the text and images, and it is likely that the reader will catch at least some of his enthusiasm." Choice
Includes bibliographical references

Posamentier, Alfred S.

Magnificent mistakes in mathematics; by Alfred S. Posamentier and Ingmar Lehmann. Prometheus Books 2013 300 p. (hardback) $24   **510**
1. Errors 2. Mathematics 3. Errors, Scientific 4. Discoveries in science
ISBN 1616147474; 9781616147471
LC 2013012126
Authors Alfred S. Posamentier and Ingmar Lehmann "demonstrate how some mistakes had profound consequences for our understanding of mathematics' key concepts. The authors show that when we "prove" that every triangle is isosceles, we are violating a concept not even known to Euclid [and how] even using correct procedures

can sometimes lead to absurd - but enlightening - results." (Publisher's note)
Includes bibliographical references and index

Rudman, Peter Strom

The Babylonian theorem; the mathematical journey to Pythagoras and Euclid. [by] Peter S. Rudman. Prometheus Books 2010 248p il $26   **510**
1. Philosophers 2. Mathematicians 3. Writers on science 4. Mathematics -- History
ISBN 978-1-59102-773-7; 1-59102-773-X
LC 2009-39196
Sequel to How mathematics happened (2007)
"Topics covered include Pythagorean triplets, . . . similar triangles, square-root calculations, and calculations of the volume of a pyramid. . . . This is a well-researched volume on what forms of mathematics existed when similar ideas developed again and again in different cultures. The book's numerous mathematical equations would delight any math student." Sci Books Films
Includes bibliographical references

Seife, Charles

★ Proofiness; the dark arts of mathematical deception. Viking 2010 295p il map $25.95   **510**
1. Mathematics
ISBN 978-0-670-02216-8
LC 2010-12127
The author "examines the many ways that people fudge with numbers, sometimes just to sell more moisturizer but also to ruin our economy, rig our elections, convict the innocent and undercount the needy. . . . [This book] reveals the truly corrosive effects on a society awash in numerical mendacity. This is more than a math book; it's an eye-opening civics lesson." N Y Times Book Rev
Includes bibliographical references

Sherlock Holmes in Babylon; and other tales of mathematical history. edited by Marlow Anderson, Victor Katz, Robin Wilson. Mathematical Association of America 2004 387p il maps (Spectrum series) $51.95   **510**
1. Mathematics -- History
ISBN 0-88385-546-1
LC 2003-113541
This "is a compilation of journal articles written by various mathematical historians and published by the Mathematical Association of America over the past 100 years. The stories deal with many important and fundamental topics from ancient up through 18th-century mathematics. The papers are all self-contained, so the reader with some degree of mathematical maturity can jump around in the book." Sci Books Films
Includes bibliographical references

Singh, Simon

The Simpsons and their mathematical secrets; Simon Singh. Bloomsbury USA 2013 272 p. (hardback) $26   **510**
1. Mathematics 2. Television programs 3. Simpsons

(Television program)
ISBN 1620402777; 9781620402771

LC 2013020884

Author Simon Singh discusses the television series "The Simpsons," examining how "embedded in many plots are subtle references to mathematics, ranging from well-known equations to cutting-edge theorems and conjectures. That they exist, Simon Singh reveals, underscores the brilliance of the shows' writers, many of whom have advanced degrees in mathematics in addition to their unparalleled sense of humor." (Publisher's note)

"Perhaps Simpsons nerds have known this all along, but for the rest of us who think of the TV show as primarily a sharp piece of comic writing, it may come as a surprise to learn that it is riddled with sophisticated mathematics. . ." Kirkus

Includes bibliographical references and index

Stewart, Ian

Professor Stewart's casebook of mathematical mysteries; Ian Stewart. Basic Books, a member of the Perseus Books Group 2014 307 p. black and white illustrations (paperback) $16.99 **510**
1. Mathematics -- Miscellanea
ISBN 0465054978; 9780465054978

LC 2014940655

In this book, by Ian Stewart, "guided by stalwart detective Hemlock Soames and his sidekick, Dr. John Watsup, readers will delve into almost two hundred mathematical problems, puzzles, and facts. Tackling subjects from mathematical dates (such as Pi Day), what we don't know about primes, and why the Earth is round, this clever, mind-expanding book demonstrates the power and fun inherent in mathematics." (Publisher's note)

"Add a few jokes, a few serious applications, and plenty of references for further online exploration, and the result is another fine book from Stewart. Summing Up: Highly recommended. All levels/libraries." Choice

Casebook of mathematical mysteries

Visions of Infinity; The Great Mathematical Problems. Perseus Books Group 2013 352 p. $26.99 **510**
1. Mathematics
ISBN 0465022405; 9780465022403

This looks at mathematical problems. Mathematician Ian Stewart argues that "mathematics is as creative as physics." He discusses Goldbach's Conjecture "that every even number can be written as the sum of two prime numbers," Squaring the Circle, or "constructing a square with an area identical to a given circle," pi, and Newton's laws of motion. (Kirkus)

Strogatz, Steven

★ The **joy** of X; a guided tour of math, from one to infinity. Steven Strogatz. Houghton Mifflin Harcourt 2012 336 p. (hardback) $27.00 **510**
1. Mathematics
ISBN 0547517653; 9780547517650

LC 2012017320

In this book on mathematics, author Steven Strogatz "begins with arithmetic, by way of Sesame Street, then ex-

plores algebra, geometry, and, finally, the wonders of calculus. . . . From addition and subtraction, with a glimpse into negative numbers and 'the black art of borrowing,' it's a quick step into the hardcore detective work of algebra's search for the unknown x, with algorithms like the quadratic equation." (Publishers Weekly)

Szpiro, George G.

Numbers rule; the vexing mathematics of democracy from Plato to the present. Princeton University Press 2010 226p **510**
1. Mathematics 2. Voting 3. Democracy -- History
ISBN 978-0-691-13994-4

LC 2009-28615

Szpiro "traces the quest of philosophers, statesmen and mathematicians throughout history to create a more perfect democracy and adapt to the ever-changing demands of each new generation by analyzing the mathematical anomalies in voting results." (Publisher's note) Index.

The author "presents a refreshingly different presentation of the mathematics of voting and apportionment. Topics are organized chronologically, and historical contexts are presented in an engaging way. Unlike mathematics textbooks, the book reads like a collection of stories describing the origin of many mathematical ideas. The mathematical content is not trivial, and it is well written, very clear, and should be accessible to readers with an understanding of arithmetic and a willingness to play with numbers." Choice

Includes bibliographical references

Poincare's prize; the hundred-year quest to solve one of math's greatest puzzles. Dutton 2007 309p $24.95 **510**
1. Mathematics 2. Mathematicians
ISBN 978-0-525-95024-0; 0-525-95024-9

LC 2007-12792

The author "recounts the story of how a geometrical puzzle worthy of the most voracious sphinx finally yielded to an eccentric Russian genius who has since refused the honors and million-dollar prize proffered by an astonished world. The mathematical puzzle, readers learn, originated with the French polymath Henri Poincaré, whose revolutionary topology generated a tantalizing conjecture about how multidimensional bodies might all be transformed into spheres. . . . Never has mathematics provided more fascinating human drama!" Booklist

Includes bibliographical references

Tammet, Daniel

★ **Thinking** in numbers; on life, love, meaning, and math. Daniel Tammet. Little, Brown and Co. 2013 288 p. $26 **510**
1. Numbers 2. Statistics 3. Mathematics
ISBN 0316187372; 9780316187374

LC 2013935728

This is a book of essays by Daniel Tammet. "His topics include the concept of zero, the calendar, prime numbers, chess, time and statistics. . . . Several of his pieces have an autobiographical component. His essay on infinity shows him as a young boy discovering the infinity of fractions between two points on his walk home from school, and readers learn of his amazing memory in his account of reciting aloud the decimals of pi to 22,514 places at the University of Oxford's Pi Day." (Kirkus Reviews)

Tanton, James S.

★ **Encyclopedia** of mathematics; [by] James Tanton. Facts on File 2005 568p il (Facts on File science library) $75   **510**

1. Reference books 2. Mathematics -- Encyclopedias
ISBN 0-8160-5124-0

LC 2004-16785

This encyclopedia "offers more than 800 entries from abacus and compound interest to Bertrand Russell and vector along with essays on the history and evolution of equations and algebra, calculus, functions, geometry, probability and statistics, and trigonometry." SLJ

Includes bibliographical references

Tymony, Cy

Sneaky math; a graphic primer with projects : ace the basics of algebra, geometry, trigonometry, and calculus with everyday things. by Cy Tymony. Andrews McMeel Pub 2014 179 p. illustrations $12.99   **510**

1. Mathematics
ISBN 1449445209; 9781449445201

In this book, author Cy Tymony "shows us how math is all around us through intriguing and easy projects, including 20 pass-along tools to complement math education programs. The book is divided into seven sections: 1. Fundamentals of Numbers and Arithmetic 2. Algebra Primer 3. Geometry Primer 4. Trigonometry Primer 5. Calculus Primer 6. Sneaky Math Challenges, Tricks, and Formulas [and] 7. Resources." (Publisher's note)

"Math lessons in school have a reputation for being rote and forgettable, but the content has a way of sneaking into everyday life, and by capitalizing on these real-world applications, Tymony helps conquer much of the fear and dread associated with traditional math lessons." Booklist

510.1   Philosophy and theory

Cheng, Eugenia

How to bake pi; an edible exploration of the mathematics of mathematics. Eugenia Cheng. Basic Books 2015 304 p. illustrations (hardcover) $27.50   **510.1**

1. Cooking 2. Mathematics -- Popular works
ISBN 0465051715; 9780465051694; 9780465051717

LC 2014957937

This book, by Eugenia Cheng, "provides an accessible introduction to the logic and beauty of mathematics, powered, unexpectedly, by insights from the kitchen: we learn, for example, how the béchamel in a lasagna can be a lot like the number 5, and why making a good custard proves that math is easy but life is hard." (Publisher's note)

"Despite her zeal for mathematical logic, Cheng recognizes that such logic begins in faith—irrational faith—and ultimately requires poetry and art to complement its findings. A singular humanization of the mathematical project." Booklist

510.92   Mathematicians

Lee Shetterly, Margot

Hidden Figures; The Story of the African-american Women Who Helped Win the Space Race. Margot Lee Shetterly. HarperCollins 2016 384 p. $27.99   **510.92**

1. Women mathematicians 2. African American women 3. United States. National Aeronautics and Space Administration
ISBN 006236359X; 9780062363596

This book, by Margot Lee Shetterly, tells the "true story of the black female mathematicians at NASA whose calculations helped fuel some of America's greatest achievements in space. [It] follows the interwoven accounts of Dorothy Vaughan, Mary Jackson, Katherine Johnson and Christine Darden, four African American women who participated in some of NASA's greatest successes." (Publisher's note)

"Shetterly's highly recommended work offers up a crucial history that had previously and unforgivably been lost. We'd do well to put this book into the hands of young women who have long since been told that there's no room for them at the scientific table." LJ

Includes bibliographical references (pages 273-328) and index.

511   General principles of mathematics

Alexander, Amir

Infinitesimal; how a dangerous mathematical theory shaped the modern world. Amir Alexander. Scientific American/Farrar, Straus and Giroux 2014 368 p. illustrations (hardback) $27   **511**

1. Calculus 2. Geometry 3. Mathematics
ISBN 0374176817; 9780374176815

LC 2013033923

Amir Alexander "look[s] at the history of a . . . mathematical concept. According to classic geometry, a line is made of a string of points, or 'indivisibles,' which cannot be broken down into anything smaller. . . . Churchmen and respected thinkers like Descartes railed against infinitesimals, while Galileo, Newton, and others insisted the concept defined the real world. . . . [B]eginning with the German Jesuit mathematician Christopher Clavius, Alexander explores this war of ideas." (Publishers Weekly)

"The author navigates even the most abstract mathematical concepts as deftly as he does the layered social history, and the result is a book about math that is actually fun to read. A fast-paced history of the singular idea that shaped a multitude of modern achievements." Kirkus

Includes bibliographical references and index

Michael, T. S.

How to guard an art gallery and other discrete mathematical adventures. Johns Hopkins University Press 2009 257p il $60; pa $25   **511**

1. Algorithms 2. Computer science 3. Mathematical analysis
ISBN 978-0-8018-9298-1; 0-8018-9298-8; 978-0-8018-9299-8 pa; 0-8018-9299-6 pa

LC 2009-00435

"The time-honored story problem, central to mathematics and an expression of its fascination or frustration (depending on the student's success), is the protagonist of this delightful work on discrete mathematics. Written for . . . [readers with a knowledge of] algebra and geometry, the text contains 7 chapters, each one devoted to a different story problem and its variations. Pick's formula, art gallery problems, quadratic residues of primes and squares, and stamps and coins and Sylvester's formula are some of the problems presented, with each chapter consisting of a group of problems of increasing difficulty." Sci Tech Book News

Includes bibliographical references

511.3 Mathematical logic (Symbolic logic)

Fortnow, Lance

The **golden** ticket; P, NP, and the search for the impossible. Lance Fortnow. Princeton University Press 2013 188 p. (hardback) $26.95   **511.3**
1. Computer algorithms 2. NP-complete problems
ISBN 0691156492; 9780691156491

LC 2012039523

This book by Lance Fortnow "tackles one of the biggest open problems in mathematics. P vs. NP can be succinctly phrased as the issue of whether some of the hardest and most important questions in mathematics have easily computable solutions. The questions themselves can range from how best to match up organ donors and recipients to how one can use the smallest number of different colors when creating a map." (Library Journal)

Includes bibliographical references and index

Stillwell, John

Roads to infinity; the mathematics of truth and proof. A K Peters 2010 203p il $39   **511.3**
1. Infinite 2. Set theory 3. Symbolic logic 4. Logic, Symbolic and mathematical
ISBN 978-1-56881-466-7; 1-56881-466-6

LC 2010-14077

"This book offers an introduction to modern ideas about infinity and their implications for mathematics. It unifies ideas from set theory and mathematical logic, and traces their effects on mainstream mathematical topics of today, such as number theory and combinatorics." Publisher's note

Includes bibliographical references

512 Algebra

Havil, Julian

The **irrationals**; a story of the numbers you can't count on. Julian Havil. Princeton University Press 2012 298 p. (alk. paper) $29.95   **512**
1. Mathematicians 2. Irrational numbers 3. Mathematics -- History
ISBN 0691143420; 9780691143422

LC 2012931844

This book "tells the story of irrational numbers and the mathematicians who have tackled their challenges, from antiquity to the twenty-first century. Along the way, [author Julian Havil] explains why irrational numbers are surpris-

ingly difficult to define -- and why so many questions still surround them." (Publisher's note)

Livio, Mario

The **equation** that couldn't be solved; how mathematical genius discovered the language of symmetry. Simon & Schuster 2005 353p il $26.95   **512**
1. Symmetry 2. Mathematicians
ISBN 0-7432-5820-7

LC 2005-44123

"Even the mathematically fainthearted can learn a great deal about symmetry from this book." Sci Books Films

Includes bibliographical references

Singh, Simon

Fermat's enigma; the epic quest to solve the world's greatest mathematical problem. foreword by John Lynch. Anchor Books 1998 315p il pa $13.95   **512**
1. Number theory 2. Mathematicians 3. College teachers
ISBN 0-385-49362-2

First published 1997 in the United Kingdom with title: Fermat's last theorem

"This vivid account is fascinating reading for anyone interested in mathematics, its history, and the passionate quest for solutions to unsolved riddles." SLJ

Includes bibliographical references

512.7 Number theory

Conway, John Horton

The **book** of numbers; [by] John Horton Conway, Richard K. Guy. Copernicus 1996 310p il $35   **512.7**
1. Number theory
ISBN 0-387-97993-X

LC 95-32588

"The authors take such joy in the order and patterns of numbers that you can't help being fascinated by what is actually a fairly difficult subject." Libr J

Includes bibliographical references

Derbyshire, John

Prime obsession; Bernhard Riemann and the greatest unsolved problem in mathematics. Plume 2004 422p il pa $16   **512.7**
1. Number theory 2. Mathematicians
ISBN 978-0-452-28525-5; 0-452-28525-9

First published 2003 by Joseph Henry Press

The author "first takes readers through . . . mathematical fundamentals in order to give them a good understanding of Riemann's discovery and its consequences. Interspersed with the hardcore math, other chapters profile Riemann the man and trace the history of mathematics in relation to his still-unproven hypothesis. Derbyshire shows how after 150 years, the world's greatest minds still haven't found a solution." Libr J

512.9   Foundations of algebra

Mackenzie, Dana

The **universe** in zero words; the story of mathematics as told through equations. Dana Mackenzie. Princeton University Press 2012 224 p. ill. (some col.) (hardcover) $27.95   **512.9**
1. Equations 2. Mathematics -- History
ISBN 0691152829; 9780691152820

LC 2011936364

This book "tells the history of twenty-four . . . equations that have shaped mathematics, science, and society -- from the elementary . . . to the sophisticated . . . and from the famous . . . to the arcane. . . . [Dana] Mackenzie . . . explains what each equation means, who discovered it (and how), and how it has affected our lives." (Publisher's note)

Includes bibliographical references (p. 219-221) and index.

513   Arithmetic

Bellos, Alex

Here's looking at Euclid; a surprising excursion through the astonishing world of math. Free Press hardcover ed.; Free Press 2010 319p il $25; ebook $11.99   **513**
1. Number concept
ISBN 978-1-4165-8825-2; 978-1-4165-9634-9 ebook
LC 2009-36815

The author "offers a lively romp through many different fields of mathematics as he incorporates ancient discoveries and modern developments alike. Topics include geometry, number theory, the development of sudoku, numerous aspects of pi and its calculation, statistics, probability and its application to gambling, and many other historical tidbits." Libr J

Includes bibliographical references

513.5   Numeration systems

Aczel, Amir D., 1950-2015

Finding zero; a mathematician's odyssey to uncover the origins of numbers. Amir D. Aczel. Palgrave Macmillan 2015 256 p. (hardback) $26 **513.5**
1. Numerals 2. Zero (The number)
ISBN 1137279842; 9781137279842

LC 2014024462

This book, by Amir D. Aczel, tells the "story of how and where we got . . . numerals. The history begins with the early Babylonian cuneiform numbers, followed by the later Greek and Roman letter numerals. Then Aczel asks the key question: where do the numbers we use today, the so-called Hindu-Arabic numerals, come from? It is this search that leads him to explore uncharted territory, to go on a grand quest into India, Thailand, Laos, Vietnam, and ultimately into the wilds of Cambodia." (Publisher's note)

"The story brims with local color, as well as insights into the history of mathematics and philosophy." Pub Wkly

Includes bibliographical references

Thaller, Bernd

Numbers; their tales, types, and treasures. by Alfred S. Posamentier & Bernd Thaller. Prometheus Books 2015 400 p. illustrations (pbk.) $19 **513.5**
1. Numbers 2. Mathematics 3. Counting 4. Number concept 5. Arithmetic -- Foundations
ISBN 1633880303; 9781633880306

LC 2015011662

This book by Alfred S. Posamentier and Bernd Thaller is designed to "teach you everything you ever wondered about numbers--and more. [It answers] how and why did human beings first start using numbers at the dawn of history? Would numbers exist if we Homo sapiens weren't around to discover them? What's so special about weird numbers like pi and the Fibonacci sequence?" (Publisher's note)

"Overall the book is extremely well written and entertaining. Its rich, satisfying variety encompasses Piaget, multicultural references, Bertrand Russell, number patterns, and historical surprises. Summing Up: Highly recommended. All readers." Choice

Includes bibliographical references and index

515   Analysis

Ash, Avner

Elliptic tales; curves, counting, and number theory. Avner Ash, Robert Gross. Princeton University Press 2012 253 p. (hardcover) $29.95 **515**
1. Number theory 2. Cubic equations 3. Elliptic curves 4. Curves, Elliptic 5. Elliptic functions
ISBN 0691151199; 9780691151199

LC 2011044712

This book explains a major unsolved problem "in contemporary mathematics—the Birch and Swinnerton-Dyer Conjecture. . . . The key to the conjecture lies in elliptic curves, which are cubic equations in two variables. These equations may appear simple, yet they arise from some very deep—and often very mystifying—mathematical ideas. Using only basic algebra and calculus while presenting numerous eye-opening examples, Ash and Gross make these ideas accessible to general readers." (Barnes and Noble)

Includes bibliographical references and index.

Ouellette, Jennifer

The **calculus** diaries; how math can help you lose weight, win in Vegas, and survive a zombie apocalypse. [illustrations by Jason Torchinsky] Penguin Books 2010 318p il pa $15 **515**
1. Calculus
ISBN 978-0-14-311737-7; 0-14-311737-8
LC 2010-25843

The author "shows how she learned to apply calculus to everything from gas mileage to dieting, from the rides at Disneyland to shooting craps in Vegas." Publisher's note

Includes bibliographical references

516 Geometry

Apostol, Tom M., 1923-2016

New Horizons in Geometry; Tom M. Apostol and Mamikon A. Mnatsakanian. Cambridge University Press 2012 520 p. $75   516
1. Calculus 2. Geometry
ISBN 088385354X; 9780883853542

In this book, Tom Apostol and Mamikon A. Mnatsakanian introduce "Mamikon's sweeping-tangent theorem," which "relies on a continuous transformation of a unit tangent to a curve, and then explore its consequences. The authors use this powerful method, which does not fit into the canon of either Euclidean geometry or calculus, to unfold much of classical geometry and to . . . solve problems usually requiring calculus." (Choice)

Lehmann, Ingmar

The **secrets** of triangles; a mathematical journey. by Alfred S. Posamentier and Ingmar Lehmann. Prometheus Books 2012 387 p. ill. (hardcover) $26   516
1. Geometry 2. Triangle 3. Trigonometry
ISBN 1616145870; 9781616145873
                LC 2012013635

This book offers "mathematical insights, intriguing relationships, and surprising results focused on the triangle." Topics include "noteworthy points, special lines, and concentric circles as related to triangles. Ultimately the book is a . . . compendium of results that" may surprise the reader with their simultaneous simplicity and complexity. (Choice)

Includes bibliographical references (p. 367-368) and index.

O'Rourke, Joseph

How to fold it; the mathematics of linkages, origami, and polyhedra. Cambridge University Press 2011 177p il $80; pa $27.99   516
1. Origami 2. Mathematics
ISBN 978-0-521-76735-4; 0-521-76735-0; 978-0-521-14547-3 pa; 0-521-14547-3 pa
                LC 2011001236

The author explains "folding problems starting from high school algebra and geometry and introducing more advanced concepts in tangible contexts as they arise. He shows how variations on these basic problems lead directly to the frontiers of current mathematical research and offers ten . . . unsolved problems for the enterprising reader." Publisher's note

516.2 Euclidean geometry

Berlinski, David

★ The **king** of infinite space; Euclid and his Elements. David Berlinski. Basic Books 2013 172 p. illustrations (hardcover : alk. paper) $24   516.2
1. Geometry 2. Mathematics, Greek 3. Geometry -- History
ISBN 046501481X; 9780465014811
                LC 2012042492

This book by David Berlinski looks at the ancient mathematician Euclid "and the world of axioms and theorems he created--a geometric world that became the basis for much of modern math, from analytic geometry to the idea of curved space-time. To Berlinski, Euclid's fourth-century B.C., 13-volume 'Elements' is a manifestation of his 'intense demand for an idealized world.'" (Publishers Weekly)

Kaplan, Ellen

Hidden harmonies; the lives and times of the Pythagorean theorem. [by] Robert Kaplan and Ellen Kaplan. Bloomsbury Press 2011 290p il $25 516.2
1. Pythagorean theorem 2. Mathematics -- History
ISBN 978-1-59691-522-0; 1-59691-522-6
                LC 2010-19959

The authors discuss "the famous theorem that relates the sides of a right triangle. Going through many of the apparently hundreds of proofs of it, the Kaplans sinuously weave personalities into the history of proving Pythagoras correct. . . . Showing the theorem's endless versatility, the Kaplans and their logic- and symbol-permeated text will engage those who delight in doing the math." Booklist

Includes bibliographical references

Livio, Mario

The **golden** ratio; the story of phi, the world's most astonishing number. Broadway Bks. 2002 294p hardcover o.p. pa $14.95   516.2
1. Geometry
ISBN 0-7679-0815-5; 0-7679-0816-3 pa
                LC 2002-23084

The author examines the history and myths of phi, the "golden ratio" of 1.6180339887 that has been related to phenomena as diverse as the arrangements of petals on roses and the breeding patterns of rabbits.

"Overall, an enjoyable work, amply supported by index, extensive references, and ten appendixes presenting mathematical elaborations of text material." Choice

Includes bibliographical references

519.2 Probabilities

Devlin, Keith J.

The **unfinished** game; Pascal, Fermat, and the seventeenth-century letter that made the world modern. [by] Keith Devlin. Basic Books 2008 191p il (Basic ideas) $24.95   519.2
1. Theologians 2. Probabilities 3. Mathematicians 4. Writers on religion
ISBN 978-0-465-00910-7; 0-465-00910-7
                LC 2008-12222

"This informative book is a lively, quick read for anyone who wonders about the science of predicting what's next and how deeply it affects our lives." Publ Wkly

Includes bibliographical references

Mazur, Joseph

Fluke; the math and myth of coincidences. Joseph Mazur. Basic Books 2016 288 p. illustrations (hardcover) $26.99 **519.2**

1. Chance 2. Mathematics -- Popular works 3. Coincidence 4. Simultaneity (Physics) 5. Coincidence theory (Mathematics)
ISBN 9780465060955

LC 2015043288

In this book, "mathematician Joseph Mazur takes a second look at the seemingly improbable, sharing with us an entertaining guide to the most surprising moments in our lives. He takes us on a tour of the mathematical concepts of probability, such as the law of large numbers and the birthday paradox, and combines these concepts with lively anecdotes of flukes from around the world." (Publisher's note)

"An ideal book . . . for the lay reader who is curious about the nature of coincidence." Booklist

Includes bibliographical references and index

Mlodinow, Leonard

The **Drunkard's** walk; how randomness rules our lives. Pantheon Books 2008 252p il $24.95 **519.2**

1. Chance 2. Probabilities
ISBN 978-0-375-42404-5; 0-375-42404-0

LC 2007-42507

"Mlodinow will help readers sort out Mark Twain's 'damn lies' from meaningful statistics and the choices we face every day." Publ Wkly

Includes bibliographical references

Santos, Aaron

How many licks? or, How to estimate damn near anything. Running Press 2009 175p il pa $14.95 **519.2**

1. Probabilities
ISBN 978-0-7624-3560-9; 0-7624-3560-7

"No matter how you feel about math, Santos' puzzle-solving prowess shows you just how much you can do when you put on your thinking cap." Am Profile

519.3 Game theory

Highfield, Roger

★ **Supercooperators**; altruism, evolution, and why we need each other to succeed. [by] Martin A. Nowak, with Roger Highfield. Free Press 2011 330p $27 **519.3**

1. Evolution 2. Game theory 3. Cooperative societies 4. Evolution (Biology) -- Mathematical models
ISBN 978-1-4391-0018-9; 1-4391-0018-7

LC 2010-35517

"Nowak aims to tackle the mysteries of nature with paper, pencil and computer. By looking at phenomena as diverse as H.I.V. infection and English irregular verbs, he has formally defined five distinct mechanisms that have helped give rise to cooperative behavior, from the first molecules that joined to self-replicate, to the first cells that formed multicellular organisms, all the way to human societies, which exhibit a degree of cooperation unmatched in all creation. In Nowak's view, figuring out how cooperation comes about and breaks down, as well as actively pursuing the 'snuggle for existence,' is the key to our survival as a species." N Y Times Book Rev

Includes bibliographical references

519.5 Statistical mathematics

Everitt, Brian

★ The **Cambridge** dictionary of statistics; [by] B.S. Everitt, A. Skrondal. 4th ed.; Cambridge University Press 2010 468p il $59 **519.5**

1. Reference books 2. Statistics -- Dictionaries
ISBN 978-0-521-76699-9

LC 2010-502891

First published 1998

"This field-specific dictionary explains nearly 4000 terms, concepts, and models relevant to fields employing theoretical, applied, scientific, and survey-related probability methods." Libr J

Reinhart, Alex, 1991-

Statistics done wrong; the woefully complete guide. by Alex Reinhart. No Starch Press 2015 176 p. illustrations (pbk.) $24.95 **519.5**

1. Errors 2. Statistics 3. Statistics -- Methodology 4. Missing observations (Statistics)
ISBN 1593276206; 9781593276201

LC 2015002128

This book, by Alex Reinhart, "is a pithy, essential guide to statistical blunders in modern science that will show you how to keep your research blunder-free. You'll examine embarrassing errors and omissions in recent research, learn about the misconceptions and scientific politics that allow these mistakes to happen, and begin your quest to reform the way you and your peers do statistics." (Publisher's note)

"Overall, this concise guide aims at helping the scientific community better understand the strengths and weaknesses of the research process. A comprehensive bibliography is included, as are numerous references for the statistical misconceptions that are addressed. Choice

Silver, Nate

The **signal** and the noise; why so many predictions fail--but some don't. Nate Silver. Penguin Press 2012 534 p. $27.95 **519.5**

1. Statistics 2. Forecasting 3. Theory of knowledge 4. Knowledge, Theory of 5. Forecasting -- History 6. Forecasting -- Methodology 7. Bayesian statistical decision theory
ISBN 159420411X; 9781594204111

LC 2012027308

This book, by political forecaster Nate Silver, "examines the world of prediction, investigating how we can distinguish a true signal from a universe of noisy data. Most predictions fail, . . . because most of us have a poor understanding of probability and uncertainty. . . . Silver visits the most successful forecasters in a range of areas. . . . He explains and evaluates how these forecasters think and what bonds they share." (Publisher's note)

Includes bibliographical references (p. 459-514)

and index

Smith, Gary

✓ **Standard** deviations; flawed assumptions, tortured data, and other ways to lie with statistics. Gary Smith. Overlook Duckworth 2014 304 p. illustrations (hardback) $28.95 **519.5**

1. Economics 2. Statistics 3. Standard deviations
ISBN 146830920X; 9781468309201

LC 2014017052

In this book, economics professor Gary Smith "walks us through the various tricks and traps that people use to back up their own . . . . theories. Sometimes, the unscrupulous deliberately try to mislead us. Other times, the well-intentioned are blissfully unaware of the mischief they are committing. Today, data is so plentiful that researchers spend precious little time distinguishing between good, meaningful indicators and total rubbish." (Publisher's note)

"We believe these stories if they seem reasonable and love them if they're provocative—see Freakonomics, whose authors have admitted some mistakes."We are too easily seduced by explanations for the inexplicable," writes the author in this amusing, informative account of how many arguments are backed by meaningless statistics." Kirkus

Includes bibliographical references and index

Wheelan, Charles

✓ **Naked** statistics; stripping the dread from the data. Charles Wheelan. W W Norton & Co Inc 2013 304 p. (hardcover) $26.95 **519.5**

1. Statistics
ISBN 0393071952; 9780393071955

LC 2012034411

Wheelan "has provided an intuitive presentation of statistical concepts without getting bogged down by extensive data lists or computation. The author begins by generally introducing each idea with an idealized situation to illustrate that statistical setting and its impact on effective interpretation, and then moves on to current real-world settings to legitimize his discussion. He also clearly discusses subtleties that can be encountered, showing how data users must be careful to avoid oversimplifying the implications of a given result. The presentation is nonthreatening, yet readers will find it a suitably thoughtful consideration of statistical ideas." Choice

Includes bibliographical references and index

520 Astronomy and allied sciences

Astronomy photographer of the year; prize-winning images by top astrophotographers. Firefly Books 2015 287 p. (bound) $39.95 **520**

1. Astronomy 2. Space photography 3. Astronomical photography 4. Astronomy -- Pictorial works 5. Astronomical photography -- Competitions
ISBN 1770854738; 9781770854734

LC 2015458652

This book is a "collection of images from the Astronomy Photographer of the Year competition. Organized by the Royal Observatory, the photographs capture an astounding range of astronomical phenomena both within our solar system and far into deep space. The book features four sections: Earth and Space, Our Solar System, Deep Space, and Overall Winners." (Publisher's note)

"Recommended strongly for anyone with an interest in astronomy or photography, this work would also make for a terrific coffee-table book." Library Journal

Bartusiak, Marcia

✓ The **day** we found the universe. Pantheon Books 2009 337p il $27.95 **520**

1. Astronomy -- History
ISBN 978-0-375-42429-8; 0-375-42429-6

LC 2008-34377

"This is a superb book that interweaves the fascinating story of a major scientific quest with a cast of characters, situations, painstaking observations, and imaginative thinking that reminds us all of the human side of scientific endeavors and the ways in which the universe itself continuously surprises us." Sci Books Films

Includes bibliographical references

Consolmagno, Guy

Turn left at Orion; hundreds of night sky objects to see in a home telescope-- and how to find them. Guy Consolmagno, Dan M. Davis; illustrated by the authors; cover and title page, Mary Lynn Skirvin; additional illustrations by Karen Kotash Sepp, Todd Johnson, and Anne Drogin. 4th edition Cambridge University Press 2011 255 p. illustrations (pbk, spiral) $34.99 **520**

1. Astronomy 2. Constellations
ISBN 9780521153973; 0521153972

LC 2011027048

Originally published 1989

This is a "guidebook to the night sky, providing all the information you need to observe a whole host of celestial objects. . . . Large-format eyepiece views, positioned side-by-side, show objects exactly as they are seen through a telescope, and with improved directions, updated tables of astronomical information and an expanded night-by-night Moon section, it has never been easier to explore the night sky on your own." (Publisher's note)

Includes bibliographical references and index

Couper, Heather

✓ The **history** of astronomy; [by] Heather Couper & Nigel Henbest; foreword by Arthur C. Clarke. Firefly Books 2007 285p il $59.95; pa $29.95 **520**

1. Astronomy -- History
ISBN 978-1-55407-325-2; 1-55407-325-1; 978-1-55407-537-9 pa; 1-55407-537-8 pa

LC 2008-272095

This "history is pieced together through astronomer interviews and visits to historically important astronomy sites around the world. . . . This is a copiously illustrated, straightforwardly written volume that will appeal to readers with and without an astronomy background. In addition to covering astronomy through the ages, the authors do an admirable job explaining current astronomical discoveries and personalities." Choice

Dickinson, Terence

NightWatch: a practical guide to viewing the universe; foreword by Timothy Ferris; illustrations by Adolf Schaller, Victor Costanzo, Roberta Cooke, Glenn LeDrew; principal photography by Terence Dickinson. 4th ed.; Firefly Books 2006 192p il $35   **520**

1. Astronomy
ISBN 978-1-55407-147-0; 1-55407-147-X

LC 2006-491527

Ferris, Timothy

Seeing in the dark; how backyard stargazers are probing deep space and guarding earth from interplanetary peril. Simon & Schuster 2002 379p il hardcover o.p. pa $14   **520**

1. Astronomy 2. Astronomers
ISBN 0-684-86579-3; 0-684-86580-7 pa

LC 2002-20693

"This book should turn many novices on to astronomy and captivate those already fascinated by the heavens." Publ Wkly

Miller, Arthur I.

Empire of the stars; obsession, friendship, and betrayal in the quest for black holes. Houghton Mifflin 2005 364p il $26   **520**

1. Astronomers 2. Mathematicians 3. Black holes (Astronomy) 4. Astrophysicists 5. Writers on science 6. Nobel laureates for physics
ISBN 0-618-34151-X

LC 2004-60909

This history of the discovery of black holes focuses on the bitter rivalry between Indian astrophysicist Subrahmanyan Chandrasekhar and Cambridge astrophysicist Sir Arthur Eddington.

"Astronomy buffs and readers fascinated by the history of science will find this a compelling read." Publ Wkly

Includes bibliographical references

Plait, Philip C.

Death from the skies! these are the ways the world will end . . . [by] Philip Plait. Viking 2008 326p il $25.95   **520**

1. End of the world
ISBN 978-0-670-01997-7; 0-670-01997-6

LC 2008-22943

"The book is extremely informative: Plait explains not only what can destroy the planet but also how it would happen. It's a crash course in astronomy as well as a cautionary tale about the (possibly brief) future of our world." Booklist

Raymo, Chet

An **intimate** look at the night sky. Walker & Co. 2001 242p il $25; pa $16   **520**

1. Astronomy
ISBN 0-8027-1369-6; 0-8027-7670-1 pa

"A delightful, inspiring introduction to astronomy." Booklist

Includes bibliographical references

Ridpath, Ian

★ **Stars** and planets; the most complete guide to the stars, planets, galaxies, and the solar system. illustrated by Wil Tirion. Fully rev. and expanded ed.; Princeton University Press 2007 400p il (Princeton field guides) pa $19.95   **520**

1. Stars 2. Planets 3. Astronomy
ISBN 978-0-691-13556-4; 0-691-13556-8

First published 1998 by DK Pub.

This book features "charts covering all 88 constellations in the Northern and Southern hemispheres; data and notes on all bright stars and other objects of interest; . . . Moon maps and descriptions of the main lunar features; [and] tips on choosing and using binoculars and telescopes." Publisher's note

Sagan, Carl

Cosmos. Random House 2002 365p $35   **520**

1. Astronomy
ISBN 0-375-50832-5

LC 2002-69744

A reissue of the title first published 1980

Based on the author's television series of the same name, this volume covers "the 10- to 20-billion-year history of the universe, from the big bang and subsequent evolution of molecular material through the evolution of human culture." Libr J {review of 1980 edition}

Includes bibliographical references

Pale blue dot; a vision of the human future in space. Ballantine Books 1997 360p pa $14.95 **520**

1. Outer space -- Exploration
ISBN 978-0-345-37659-6; 0-345-37659-5

First published 1994 by Random House

"In a tour of our solar system, galaxy and beyond . . . Sagan meshes a history of astronomical discovery, a cogent brief for space exploration and an overview of life. . . . His exploration of our place in the universe is illustrated with photographs, relief maps and paintings, including high-resolution images made by Voyager 1 and 2, as well as photos taken by the Galileo spacecraft, the Hubble Space Telescope and satellites orbiting Earth." Publ Wkly

Includes bibliographical references

Scagell, Robin

Complete Guide to Stargazing; Robin Scagell. Firefly Books Ltd 2015 320 p. illustrations (some color) (paperback) $39.95   **520**

1. Astronomy -- Encyclopedias 2. Astronomy -- Popular works
ISBN 1770854746; 9781770854741

This book, by Robin Scagell, "is a comprehensive introduction to [the] increasingly popular leisure pursuit [of stargazing.] . . . It explains how and why the sky changes during the night and through the seasons. It gives practical advice on what equipment to choose and describes what you can expect to see. There are also plenty of tips for observing just with the naked eye." (Publisher's note)

"Featuring clear and thorough explanations, this is a worthwhile resource for the beginning stargazer."

Schaaf, Fred

The **50** best sights in astronomy and how to see them; observing eclipses, bright comets, meteor showers, and other celestial wonders. John Wiley 2007 280p il pa $19.95 **520**

1. Astronomy

ISBN 978-0-471-69657-5; 0-471-69657-9

LC 2006-36221

The author "begins with some basic information and terminology (altazimuth system, for example, or right ascension) and then plunges right in with the most easily accessible astronomical sight, the starry sky above our heads. For each sight, he not only explains what it is and the best conditions under which to observe it, he also tells us about its historical, mythological, or scientific importance and explores how these far-off wonders can have a very real effect on our humble home world. This could so easily have been a dry-as-dust tome, but Schaaf's enthusiasm overflows every page." Booklist

Includes bibliographical references

Schilling, Govert

Deep Space; Beyond the Solar System to the End of the Universe and the Beginning of Time. Govert Schilling. Black Dog & Leventhal Pub 2014 224 p. color illustrations $29.95 **520**

1. Astronomy 2. Outer space

ISBN 1579129781; 9781579129781

In this book author Govert Schilling "explores the mysteries of space that lie beyond our solar system on this mind-bending trip to nebulae, galaxies, black holes, and the edge of the observable universe. The book concludes at the edge of the cosmological horizon with a look at dark matter, dark energy, and theories of extraterrestrial life and the Multiverse." (Publisher's note)

"A well-conceived, absorbing survey of the wonders of the cosmos that truly reinforces the author's point that "space is big. Unimaginably big." Recommended for space enthusiasts and astronomy aficionados." LJ

Schneider, Howard

Backyard guide to the night sky; Howard Schneider; foreword by Sandy Wood. National Geographic 2009 21 cm. color illustrations $21.95 **520**

1. Astronomy

ISBN 9781426202810; 1426202814

"Ten chapters cover everything a beginning stargazer will need to know, from understanding the phases of the moon to picking Mars out of a planetary lineup to identifying the kinds of stars twinkling in the constellations. Throughout the book, star charts and tables present key facts in an easy-to-understand format, sidebars and fact boxes present illuminating anecdotes and fun facts." (Publisher's note)

Includes bibliographical references (pages 276-277) and index

Sobel, Dava

A **more** perfect heaven; how Copernicus revolutionized the cosmos. Walker Pub. 2011 273p il map $25 **520**

1. Astronomy 2. Astronomers 3. Solar system

ISBN 978-0-8027-1793-1

LC 2011024772

"Dava Sobel excels in telling the story of Nicholas Copernicus and his almost-shelved masterpiece, On the Revolutions. Along the way, she brings the social and political milieu of the times into sharp relief providing context for the sheer audacity of his insights into planetary motion and his reticence in pursuing their dissemination." Sci Books Films

Includes bibliographical references

Trefil, James

Space atlas; mapping the universe and beyond. James Trefil; foreword by Buzz Aldrin. National Geographic 2012 335 p. col. ill. (hardback) $50 **520**

1. Galaxies 2. Astronomy 3. Solar system 4. Stars -- Atlases 5. Galaxies -- Atlases 6. Solar system -- Atlases 7. Astronomy -- Charts, diagrams, etc

ISBN 1426209711; 9781426209710; 9781426210914

LC 2012020000

Author James Trefil presents a "guide to the planets, stars and outer reaches of the universe." The book "explains the nature of planets, stars, galaxies and exotic objects such as black holes alongside photos and art . . . In addition to the latest imagery coming from space telescopes and diagrams explaining key astronomical concepts, this atlas also includes more than 90 pages of detailed maps." (Publisher's note)

Includes bibliographical references

Trotta, Roberto

The **edge** of the sky; all you need to know about the all-there-is : (using only the ten hundred most-used words in our tongue) Roberto Trotta. Basic Books, a member of the Perseus Books Group 2014 112 p. illustrations (hardcover) $16.99 **520**

1. Astronomy -- Popular works 2. Cosmology -- Popular works

ISBN 0465044719; 9780465044719; 9780465044900

LC 2014020067

This book, by Roberto Trotta, "tells the story of the most important discoveries and mysteries in modern cosmology. . . . The book's lexicon is limited to the thousand most common words in the English language. . . . Through the eyes of a fictional scientist . . . hunting for dark matter . . . , [the author] explores the most important ideas about our universe . . . in language simple enough for anyone to understand." (Publisher's note)

"The book barely qualifies as a book at all, just squeaking past booklet status. An entertaining exercise, in the end, for those student-people who like to ponder the All-There-Is while testing the always-inadequate limits of language." Kirkus

521 Celestial mechanics

Goodstein, David L.

Feynman's lost lecture; the motion of planets around the sun. {by} David L. Goodstein and Judith R. Goodstein. Norton 1996 191p il $35; pa $19.95 **521**

1. Authors 2. Universe 3. Physicists 4. Astrophysics 5. Solar system 6. Writers on science 7. Nobel laureates for physics

ISBN 0-393-03918-8; 0-393-31995-4 pa

LC 95-38719

This "book consists of four chapters. The first and largest is a brief history of the establishment of the Copernican cosmology, which Feynman gave as a lecture to the freshman class at Caltech. Feynman then revisits the work of Isaac Newton and the watershed proof of the Scientific Revolution that separated the ancient world from the modern. There is also a chapter with some wonderful reminiscences of Feynman." Libr J

Includes bibliographical references

522 Techniques, procedures, apparatus, equipment, materials

Dickinson, Terence

The backyard astronomer's guide; [by] Terence Dickinson & Alan Dyer. 3rd ed; Firefly Books 2008 368p il $49.95 **522**

1. Astronomy

ISBN 978-1-55407-344-3; 1-55407-344-8

First published 1991 by Camden House

The authors provide guidance "on the right types of telescopes and other equipment; photographing the stars through a telescope; and star charts, software and other references. They cover daytime and twilight observing, planetary and deep-sky observing, and . . . more." Publisher's note

Includes bibliographical references

Kerrod, Robin

Hubble; the mirror on the universe. [by] Robin Kerrod & Carole Stott. 3rd ed. updated, rev. and expanded.; Firefly Books 2011 224p il pa $29.95 **522**

1. Hubble Space Telescope 2. Outer space -- Exploration

ISBN 978-1-55407-972-8; 1-55407-972-1

LC 2011292195

First published 2003

"Kerrod provides an excellent overview of Hubble's accomplishments (along with a history of the evolution of the telescope), thoughtfully organizing the spellbinding images from space, and clearly and avidly explaining exactly which phenomena they depict." Booklist

Sobel, Dava

★ The glass universe; Dava Sobel. Viking 2016 336 p. **522**

1. Harvard College Observatory 2. Astronomy -- History -- 19th century 3. Astronomy -- History -- 20th century 4. Women in astronomy -- Massachusetts -- History 5. Women mathematicians -- Massachusetts

-- History

ISBN 9780670016952

LC 2016029496

"In the mid-nineteenth century, the Harvard College Observatory began employing women as calculators, or 'human computers,' to interpret the observations their male counterparts made via telescope each night... As photography transformed the practice of astronomy, the ladies turned from computation to studying the stars captured nightly on glass photographic plates. The 'glass universe' of half a million plates that Harvard amassed over the ensuing decades—through the generous support of Mrs. Anna Palmer Draper, the widow of a pioneer in stellar photography—enabled the women to make extraordinary discoveries that attracted worldwide acclaim." Publisher's note

"With grace, clarity, and a flair for characterization, Sobel places these early women astronomers in the wider historical context of their field for the very first time." Pub Wkly

Includes bibliographical references and index

523 Specific celestial bodies and phenomena

The planets; Heather Couper, Robert Dinwiddie, John Farndon, Nigel Henbest, David W. Hughes, Giles Sparrow, Carole Stott, Colin Stuart. Dorling Kindersley 2014 256 p. color illustrations **523**

1. Solar system 2. Astronomy

ISBN 1465424644; 9781465424648

LC 2014451572

This book, by Heather Couper, Robert Dinwiddie, John Farndon, Nigel Henbest, David W. Hughes, Giles Sparrow, Carole Stott, and Colin Stuart, offers "an awe-inspiring journey through the Solar System, from Earth to Mars and beyond. Viewed layer by layer, planets and other objects in the Solar System are taken out of the night sky and presented on a white background, revealing every detail of their surface and internal anatomy in astonishing detail." (Publisher's note)

"This handy volume packed with the latest scientific observational analysis is a must-have for fans of planetary science." LJ

523.1 The universe, galaxies, quasars

Aczel, Amir D.

God's equation; Einstein, relativity, and the expanding universe. Delta Trade Paperbacks 2000 236p il pa $12 **523.1**

1. Cosmology 2. Physicists 3. Relativity (Physics) 4. Nobel laureates for physics

ISBN 978-0-385-33485-3; 0-385-33485-0

First published 1999 by Four Walls Eight Windows

"Though Aczel's analysis of Einstein's work requires familiarity with advanced mathematics, that analysis makes up only a minor portion of his book, and most readers will appreciate the author's inclusion of the great physicist's letters to astronomer Erwin Freundlich." Publ Wkly

Includes bibliographical references

Bell, Jim, 1965-

The **space** book; from the beginning to the end of time, 250 milestones in the history of space & astronomy. Jim Bell. Sterling 2013 528 p. color illustrations; maps (hardcover) $29.95   **523.1**
1. Universe 2. Cosmology 3. Physics -- History 4. Cosmology -- History
ISBN 9781402780714; 1402780710

LC 2013372035

This book by Jim Bell "presents 250 of the most groundbreaking astronomical events, from the formation of galaxies to the recent discovery of water ice on Mars. . . . Open the book to any page to discover some new wonder or mystery about the Universe around us." (Publisher's note)

"This is a fine coffee-table book, suitable for either deep study or a few moments' perusal. Recommended for readers with a casual interest in the history of astronomy and the universe, or for sparking such an interest in others." LJ

Includes bibliographical references (p. 518-525) and index

Benson, Michael

Cosmigraphics; picturing space through time. Michael Benson. Harry N. Abrams 2014 320 p. illustrations, maps $50   **523.1**
1. Maps 2. Astronomy 3. Cosmology
ISBN 1419713876; 9781419713873

LC 2014930552

Los Angeles Times Book Prize Finalist: Science and Technology (2014)

This book by Michael Benson tells the "story of the discovery and description of the universe in a new way. Selecting artful and profound illustrations and maps, many hidden away in the world's great science libraries and virtually unknown today, he chronicles more than 1,000 years of humanity's ever-expanding understanding of the size and shape of space itself." (Publisher's note)

"Perfect for astronomy lovers and of great interest to those who enjoy the histories of art, book making, cartography, philosophy, or theology."

Clark, Stuart

The **Unknown** Universe; A New Exploration of Time, Space, and Modern Cosmology. by Stuart Clark. W W Norton & Co Inc 2016 288 p. illustrations $27.95   **523.1**
1. Universe 2. Cosmology 3. Big bang theory
ISBN 1681771535; 9781681771533

This book, by Stuart Clark, is a "guide to the universe and how our latest deep-space discoveries are forcing us to revisit what we know—and what we don't. On March 21, 2013, the European Space Agency released a map of the afterglow of the Big Bang. Taking in 440 sextillion kilometres of space and 13.8 billion years of time, it is physically impossible to make a better map: we will never see the early universe in more detail." (Publisher's note)

"Since satisfying results have yet to turn up, Clark's book ends on a cliffhanger, but readers will be entirely pleased with the experience." Kirkus

Includes bibliographical references (pages 292-293) and index.

Dauber, Philip M.

The **three** big bangs; comet crashes, exploding stars, and the creation of the universe. [by] Philip M. Dauber, Richard A. Muller. Perseus Books 1997 207p il pa $15   **523.1**
1. Cosmology 2. Supernovas 3. Catastrophes (Geology)
ISBN 978-0-201-15495-5; 0-201-15495-1
First published 1996 by Addison-Wesley

The authors discuss the origins of the universe and of life on Earth.

"Dauber and Muller have not only chosen three 'hot topics' in . . . astronomy but also have masterfully woven the underlying scientific strands together. They paint a colorful picture of the theories and techniques of modern astronomy." Choice

Includes bibliographical references

Frank, Adam

About time; cosmology and culture at the twilight of the Big Bang. Free Press 2011 xxi, 406p il $26   **523.1**
1. Cosmology 2. Space and time 3. Big bang theory 4. Life -- Origin
ISBN 978-1-4391-6959-9; 1-4391-6959-4; 978-1-4391-6961-2 ebook

LC 2011011345

"Frank offers a unique and fascinating look at complex concepts with an accessible style that is both matter-of-fact and thoroughly entertaining." Publ Wkly

Includes bibliographical references

Galfard, Christophe

The **Universe** in Your Hand; A Journey Through Space, Time, and Beyond. by Christophe Galfard. St. Martin's Press 2016 400 p. $27.99   **523.1**
1. Cosmology
ISBN 1250069521; 9781250069528

LC 2016005257

In this book, author Christophe Galfard "employs . . . direct language to show us, not explain to us, the theories that underpin everything we know about our universe. To understand what happens to a dying star, we are asked to picture ourselves floating in space in front of it. To get acquainted with the quantum world, we are shrunk to the size of an atom and then taken on a journey." (Publisher's note)

"Readers looking to expand their knowledge of physics and cosmology will find everything they need here." Pub Wkly

Geach, James

Galaxy; Mapping the Cosmos. by James Geach. University of Chicago Press 2014 256 p. color illustrations $35   **523.1**
1. Galaxies 2. Astronomy
ISBN 1780233639; 9781780233635

In this book, "astronomer James Geach tells the rich stories of both the evolution of galaxies and our ability to observe them, offering a fascinating history of how we've come to realize humanity's tiny place in the vast universe. Taking us on a compelling tour of the state-of-the-art science involved in mapping the infinite, Geach offers a first-hand account of both the science itself and how it is done, describing what we currently know as well as that which we still do not." (Publisher's note)

"Advanced researchers may be frustrated by the purposeful lack of higher-level mathematics, but the casual reader will appreciate how well Geach presents a clear narrative of the science. Choice

Gott, J. Richard

Welcome to the universe; an astrophysical tour. Neil deGrasse Tyson, Michael A. Strauss, and J. Richard Gott. Princeton University Press 2016 472 p. ill. (mostly col.) hbk $39.95   **523.1**
1. Stars 2. Cosmology 3. Relativity (Physics) 4. Stars -- Popular works 5. Cosmology -- Popular works 6. Relativity (Physics) -- Popular works
ISBN 9780691157245; 0691157243

LC 2016013487

"Describing the latest discoveries in astrophysics, the informative and entertaining narrative propels you from our home solar system to the outermost frontiers of space. How do stars live and die? Why did Pluto lose its planetary status? What are the prospects for intelligent life elsewhere in the universe? How did the universe begin? Why is it expanding and why is its expansion accelerating? Is our universe alone or part of an infinite multiverse?" (Publisher's note)

"An accessible and comprehensive overview of our universe by three eminent astrophysicists, based on an introductory course they have taught at Princeton University." Kirkus
Includes bibliographical references and index

Greene, Brian R.

The **fabric** of the cosmos; space, time, and the texture of reality. Knopf 2004 569p il $28.95; pa $15.95   **523.1**
1. Cosmology
ISBN 0-375-41288-3; 0-375-72720-5 pa

LC 2003-58918

"Frogs in bowls, falling eggs, loaves of bread, pennies on balloons, ping pong balls in molasses, and babushka dolls are just some of the analogies used to explain complex concepts cleverly. After reading this book, you will never look at a starry night sky the same way again." Libr J
Includes bibliographical references

Gribbin, John

13.8; the quest to find the true age of the universe and the theory of everything. John Gribbin. Yale University Press 2016 256 p. 16 plates; illustrations $30   **523.1**
1. Cosmology 2. Quantum theory 3. Space and time 4. Relativity (Physics) 5. Cosmochronology
ISBN 0300218273; 9780300218275

LC 2015513118

In this book, author John Gribbin "presents his own version of the Holy Grail of physics, the search that has been going on for decades to find a unified "Theory of Everything" that combines these ideas into one mathematical package... . With his inimitable mixture of science, history, and biography, Gribbin shows how ... these two great theories are very compatible.... The answer lies, intriguingly, with the age of the universe: 13.8 billion years." (Publisher's note)

"In order to bring lay readers up to speed, Gribbin first reprises the crucial developments, beginning in the 19th century, that have led scientists to their current understanding. An exciting chronicle of a monumental scientific accomplishment by a scientist who participated in the measur i ng of the age of the universe." Kirkus
Includes bibliographical references and index

Halpern, Paul

Edge of the universe; a voyage to the cosmic horizon and beyond. by Paul Halpern. John Wiley & Sons 2012 236 p. (cloth) $27.95   **523.1**
1. Universe 2. Big bang theory 3. Dark energy (Astronomy) 4. Cosmology -- Popular works
ISBN 0470636246; 9780470636244

LC 2012002028

This book offers a "look at the mysteries that lurk at the edge of the known universe and beyond." Author Paul Halpern "explains what we know about the Big Bang, the accelerating universe, dark energy, dark flow, and dark matter to examine some of the theories about the content of the universe and why its edge is getting farther away from us faster." (Publisher's note)
Includes bibliographical references and index

Hawking, Stephen, 1942-

Black holes and baby universes and other essays; [by] Stephen Hawking. Bantam Bks. 1993 182p hardcover o.p. pa $18   **523.1**
1. Cosmology 2. Science -- Philosophy
ISBN 0-553-37411-7 pa

LC 93-8269

A collection of essays and speeches ranging from autobiographical sketches to theoretical discussions of black holes, relativity and quantum mechanics.

The author "sprinkles his explanations with a wry sense of humor and a keen awareness that the sciences today delve not only into the far reaches of the cosmos, but into the inner philosophical world as well." N Y Times Book Rev

A **brief** history of time; {by} Stephen Hawking. Updated and expanded tenth anniversary ed; Bantam Bks. 1998 212p il $27.95; pa $16.95   **523.1**
1. Cosmology
ISBN 0-553-10953-7; 0-553-38016-8 pa

LC 98-21874

First published 1988
The author describes concepts about space and time, black holes, the origin and nature of the universe, the uncertainty principle, and the unification of physics. This edition includes a new introduction and a new chapter about wormholes and time travel

★ A **briefer** history of time; [by] Stephen Hawking and Leonard Mlodinow. Bantam Dell 2005 162p il $25   **523.1**
1. Cosmology
ISBN 0-553-80436-7

LC 2005-42949

First published 1988 with title: A brief history of time
The authors describe concepts about space and time, black holes, the origin and nature of the universe, the un-

certainty principle, and the unification of physics. It also discusses string theory, dark matter, and dark energy.

"Hawking and Mlodinow provide one of the most lucid discussions of this complex topic ever written for a general audience. Readers will come away with an excellent understanding of the apparent contradictions and conundrums at the forefront of contemporary physics." Publ Wkly

Includes bibliographical references

Hirshfeld, Alan, ca. 1956-

Starlight Detectives; How Astronomers, Inventors, and Eccentrics Discovered the Modern Universe. by Alan Hirshfeld. Bellevue Literary Press 2014 400 p. illustrations, portraits $19.95 **523.1**
  1. Astronomy 2. Astronomers
  ISBN 1934137782; 9781934137789
This book, by Alan Hirshfeld, focuses on the history of astronomy. "From William Bond, who turned his home into a functional observatory, to John and Henry Draper, a father and son team who were trailblazers of astrophotography and spectroscopy, to geniuses of invention such as Léon Foucault, and George Hale, who founded the Mount Wilson Observatory, Hirshfeld reveals the incredible stories-- and the ambitious dreamers-- behind the birth of modern astronomy." (Publisher's note)

"Although the story fizzles toward the end, this is a well-written and enjoyable title for astronomers—professional and amateur alike—as well as science history fans." LJ

Kaku, Michio

Parallel worlds; a journey through creation, higher dimensions, and the future of the cosmos. Doubleday 2005 428p il hardcover o.p. pa $15.95 **523.1**
  1. Cosmology 2. String theory 3. Big bang theory
  ISBN 0-385-50986-3; 1-4000-3372-1 pa
  LC 2004-56039
"This is a riveting popular treatment of the string revolution in physics written by a pioneering theorist in the field. Kaku expounds comprehensibly on why astrophysicists love strings and branes and the way they resolve various vexatious cosmological paradoxes." Booklist

Krauss, Lawrence M.

A universe from nothing; Lawrence M. Krauss; with a foreword by Christopher Hitchens and an afterword by Richard Dawkins. Free Press 2012 224p (hardback) $24.99 **523.1**
  1. Universe 2. Cosmology 3. Physics -- Philosophy
  ISBN 145162445X; 9781451624458
  LC 2011032519
In this book, "theoretical physicist Lawrence Krauss . . . reveals that modern science 'is' addressing the question of why there is something rather than nothing. . . . Krauss takes us back to the beginning of the beginning, presenting the most recent evidence for how our universe evolved--and the implications for how it's going to end. . . . It looks at the most basic underpinnings of existence" and provides an "entry into the debate about the existence of God and everything that exists." (Publisher's note)

Mitton, Simon

Heart of darkness; unraveling the mysteries of the invisible universe. Jeremiah P. Ostriker, Simon Mitton. Princeton University Press 2013 299 p. (Science essentials) (alk. paper) $27.95 **523.1**
  1. Cosmology 2. Dark matter (Astronomy) 3. Cosmology -- Popular works 4. Dark energy (Astronomy) -- Popular works 5. Dark matter (Astronomy) -- Popular works
  ISBN 0691134308; 9780691134307
  LC 2012950892
This book by Jeremiah P. Ostriker and Mitton explores the history of cosmology. "From humankind's early attempts to comprehend Earth's place in the solar system, to astronomers' exploration of the Milky Way galaxy . . . to the detection of the primordial fluctuations of energy from which all subsequent structure developed, this book explains the physics and the history of how the current model of our universe arose and has passed every test hurled at it by the skeptics." (Publisher's note)

Includes bibliographical references (p. 291-293) and index

Randall, Lisa

Dark Matter and the Dinosaurs; The Astounding Interconnectedness of the Universe. by Lisa Randall. HarperCollins 2015 256 p. illustrations, charts $29.99 **523.1**
  1. Asteroids 2. Dinosaurs 3. Outer space
  ISBN 0062328476; 9780062328472
This book, particle physicist Lisa Randall "uses her research into dark matter to illuminate the startling connections between the furthest reaches of space and life here on Earth. Sixty-six million years ago, an object the size of a city descended from space to crash into Earth, creating a devastating cataclysm that killed off the dinosaurs, along with three-quarters of the other species on the planet. What was its origin?" (Publisher's note)

"Writing in a deceptively chatty narrative style, Randall provides a fascinating window into the ex c itement of discovery and the rigor required to test and elaborate new hypotheses. A top-notch science book from a leading researcher." Kirkus

Rees, Martin J.

Just six numbers; the deep forces that shape the universe. {by} Martin Rees. Basic Bks. 2000 173p il hardcover o.p. pa $14.95 **523.1**
  1. Cosmology 2. Big bang theory
  ISBN 0-465-03673-2 pa
  LC 00-268248
First published 1999 in the United Kingdom
"A brief, readable, and profoundly instructive account of where cosmological knowledge stands at this moment." New Yorker

Includes bibliographical references

Scharf, Caleb

The Copernicus complex; our cosmic significance in a universe of planets and probabilities. Ca-

leb Scharf. Scientific American/Farrar, Straus & Giroux 2014 288 p. illustrations (hardback) $26 **523.1**
1. Universe 2. Astronomy 3. Life -- Origin 4. Life 5. Cosmology 6. Space and time
ISBN 0374129215; 9780374129217; 9780374709464
LC 2014008035

In this book, author "Caleb Scharf takes us on a scientific adventure, from tiny microbes within the Earth to distant exoplanets, probability theory, and beyond, arguing that there is . . . a third way of viewing our place in the cosmos. Bringing us to the cutting edge of scientific discovery, Scharf shows how the answers to fundamental questions of existence will come from embracing the peculiarity of our circumstance without denying the Copernican vision." (Publisher's note)

"Scharf covers a lot of ground, and his entertaining, accessible approach offers valuable insight not just into science, but also into the way our assumptions can make a difficult task, like finding life in the universe, even harder." Pub Wkly

Includes bibliographical references and index

Singh, Simon

Big bang: the origins of the universe. Fourth Estate 2005 532p il $27.95   **523.1**
1. Cosmology 2. Big bang theory
ISBN 0-00716-220-0

The author "presents a brief history of the origins of the universe. . . . He begins with a historical overview of how scientific thought changed from mythology to cosmology, then moves to the debate between the steady state model of an eternal universe and the Big Bang theory, which saw the universe as beginning at a unique moment that was followed by rapid extension. . . . This readable book provides an accessible overview of this complex scientific theory." Libr J

Smoot, George

Wrinkles in time; witness to the birth of the universe. [by] George Smoot and Keay Davidson; with a new preface. Harper Perennial 2007 331p il pa $14.95   **523.1**
1. Cosmology
ISBN 978-0-06-134444-2; 0-06-134444-3
LC 2008-530705

First published 1993 by William Morrow

"Smoot and Davidson present a historical review of cosmology that takes the reader from the work of Galileo to the recent . . . work on 'COBE' (the Cosmic Background Explorer satellite). An excellent nontechnical study of research into what makes the universe the way it is, the book provides a detailed discussion of the search for and the eventual discovery of what are called the 'wrinkles in time' from the viewpoint of the authors' own experiences in the field." Choice [review of 1993 edition]

Includes bibliographical references

Startalk; everything you ever need to know about space travel, sci-fi, the human race, the universe, and beyond. with Neil deGrasse Tyson. National Geographic 2016 304 p. color illustrations hbk $30   **523.1**
1. Cosmology 2. Human beings 3. Earth sciences 4.
Outer space -- Exploration
ISBN 1426217277; 9781426217272
LC 2016019357

This is a companion volume to Neil deGrasse Tyson's podcast and TV show of the same name. "Featuring vivid photography, thought-provoking sidebars, enlightening facts, and fun quotes from science and entertainment luminaries like Bill Nye and Dan Aykroyd, StarTalk reimagines science's most challenging topics--from how the brain works to the physics of comic book superheroes--in a relatable, humorous way that will delight fans and new readers alike." (Publisher's note)

Tegmark, Max

Our mathematical universe; my quest for the ultimate nature of reality. Max Tegmark. Alfred A. Knopf 2014 432 p. illustrations (hardback) $30   **523.1**
1. Physics 2. Cosmology 3. Mathematics 4. Plurality of worlds
ISBN 0307599809; 9780307599803; 9780307744258
LC 2013016020

In this book, author Max Tegmark "leads us . . . through the physics, astronomy and mathematics that are the foundation of his work, most particularly his hypothesis that our physical reality is a mathematical structure and his theory of the ultimate multiverse. He . . . shares with us some of the often surprising triumphs and disappointments that have shaped his life as a scientist." (Publisher's note)

"Lively and lucid, the narrative invites general readers into debates over computer models for brain function, over scientific explanations of consciousness, and over prospects for finding advanced life in other galaxies." Booklist

Tyson, Neil deGrasse

Origins: fourteen billion years of cosmic evolution; {by} Neil deGrasse Tyson, Donald Goldsmith. W.W. Norton 2004 345p il $27.95   **523.1**
1. Cosmology 2. Evolution 3. Life -- Origin
ISBN 0-393-05992-8
LC 2004-12201

"Amateur astronomers—in fact, any reader who enjoys popular science—will find fascinating information presented in clear but never patronizing language." Libr J

Includes bibliographical references

The **universe**; leading scientists explore the origin, mysteries, and future of the cosmos. edited by John Brockman. HarperCollins 2014 379 p. (paperback) $15.99   **523.1**
1. Universe 2. Astrophysics
ISBN 0062296086; 9780062296085

This book, edited by John Brockman, part of the "Best of Edge" series, "brings together the world's best-known physicists and science writers--including Brian Greene, Walter Isaacson, Nobel Prize-winner Frank Wilczek, Benoit Mandelbrot, and Martin Rees--to explain the universe in all wondrous splendor." (Publisher's note)

Universe; general editor, Martin Rees. DK Pub. 2012 528 p. color illustrations $50 **523.1**
1. Astronomy 2. Cosmology -- Popular works
ISBN 0756698413; 9780756698416

LC 2011277855

This book, by Martin Rees, "takes you on the ultimate guided tour of the cosmos. Full of . . . images reflecting recent advances in space imagery, you'll go on a journey from our solar system all the way to the farthest limits of space. . . . [The book includes] information on the nature of the universe, the study of cosmology, Earth's motion, modern telescopes, astrophotography, and even a comprehensive star atlas." (Publisher's note)

Weintraub, David A.

How old is the universe? Princeton University Press 2011 370p il $29.95 **523.1**
1. Universe 2. Cosmology 3. Solar system 4. Earth -- Age
ISBN 978-0-691-14731-4

LC 2010-9117

"This is no-nonsense science writing that will be enjoyed for years: David Weintraub is an expert guide, laying out the evidence in just the right amount of detail." New Sci

523.2 Planetary systems

Baker, David

The **50** most extreme places in our solar system; [by] David Baker and Todd Ratcliff. Belknap Press 2010 290p il $27.95 **523.2**
1. Solar system 2. Extreme environments
ISBN 0-674-04998-5; 978-0-674-04998-7

LC 2010-06126

"Descriptions of physical phenomena are given around themes such as 'Surface and Interior' and 'Extreme Climates.'" (Sci Books Films) Glossary. Bibliography. Index.

The authors "discuss phenomena like the potential for diamond rain on Uranus and Neptune and the hardiness of extremophile life forms. As planetary scientists, they write clearly about the most extreme physical aspects of solar system bodies such as planets, moons, and comets, but deftly mix in more familiar comparisons from planet Earth as well." Choice

Includes bibliographical references

Chown, Marcus

Solar system; a visual exploration of the planets, moons, and other heavenly bodies that orbit our sun. written by Marcus Chown. Black Dog & Leventhal Publishers 2011 224 p. color illustrations hbk $29.95 **523.2**
1. Astronomy 2. Solar system
ISBN 9781579128852; 1579128858

"Every planet and moon is introduced with a big, beautiful, full-page image and a databox that shows the orbit and position of the planet or moon in relation to surrounding bodies, as well as the diameter, mass, volume, surface temperature, atmospheric makeup, and orbital period of the

planet; a scale comparison graphic; and a planet cross-section for the eight planets." (Publisher's note)

Daniels, Patricia

The **new** solar system; ice worlds, moons, and planets redefined. foreword by Robert Burnham. National Geographic Society 2009 223p il map $35 **523.2**
1. Solar system
ISBN 978-1-4262-0462-3; 1-4262-046-20

LC 2009-10117

This is "a sumptuously illustrated book describing the history, composition, and exploration of the solar system. Aimed at a general audience, the text is highly readable and contains numerous side notes providing fascinating anecdotes and facts about the planets, the sun, and astronomers." Choice

Includes bibliographical references

Lang, Kenneth R.

The **Cambridge** guide to the solar system; Kenneth R. Lang. 2nd edition Cambridge University Press 2011 500 p. ill. (some col.) $69.99 **523.2**
1. Solar system
ISBN 0521198577; 9780521198578

LC 2011411432

This book, by Kenneth R. Lang, presents a "comprehensive, up-to-date description of the planets, their moons, and recent exoplanet discoveries. . . . Examples include water on the Moon, volcanism on Mercury's previously unseen half, vast buried glaciers on Mars, geysers on Saturn's moon Enceladus, lakes of hydrocarbons on Titan, encounter with asteroid ltokawa, and sample return from comet Wild 2. The book is further enhanced by hundreds of striking new images of the planets and moons." (Publisher's note)

North, Chris

How to Read the Solar System; A Guide to the Stars and Planets. Chris North and Paul Abel; foreword by Brian May. Pegasus Books 2015 320 p. illustrations hc $26.95 **523.2**
1. Astronomy 2. Solar system
ISBN 9781605986715; 1605986712

Authors Paul Abel and Chris North "look at all the major players, including our more familiar cosmic neighbors--the Sun, the planets and their moons--as well as the occasional visitors to our planet--asteroids, meteors and comets--in addition to distant stars and what might lie beyond our Solar System." (Publisher's note)

'The authors comprehensively cover all the basics, making this book a great primer for readers who are just getting started in their reading on the subject. . . . [T]his chatty, non-technical discussion is perfect for the armchair or budding astronomer who wants a bit of background and history spread widely across the field." Pub Wkly

523.4   Planets, asteroids, trans-Neptunian objects of solar system

Brown, Mike

How I killed Pluto and why it had it coming; Mike Brown. Spiegel & Grau 2010 xiii, 267p 1 ill. (pbk.) $15.00; (alk. paper) o.p.; (alk. paper) o.p.; (ebook) $12.99   **523.4**

1. Planets 2. Astronomers 3. Solar system 4. Pluto (Dwarf planet) 5. Discoveries in science 6. Pluto (Planet) 7. College teachers 8. Eris (Dwarf planet) 9. Discoveries in science -- Anecdotes

ISBN 9780385531108; 0385531087; 9780385531085; 9780385531092

LC 2010015074

This book relates the story of astronomer Mike Brown's research that led to the demotion of Pluto as a planet. "The solar system most of us grew up with included nine planets, with Mercury closest to the sun and Pluto at the outer edge. Then, in 2005, astronomer Mike Brown made the discovery of a lifetime: a tenth planet, Eris, slightly bigger than Pluto. But instead of adding one more planet to our solar system, Brown's find ignited a firestorm of controversy that culminated in the demotion of Pluto from real planet to the newly coined category of 'dwarf' planet. Suddenly Brown was receiving hate mail from schoolchildren and being bombarded by TV reporters—all because of the discovery he had spent years searching for and a lifetime dreaming about." (Publisher's note)

"Deftly pulling readers along on his journey of discovery and destruction, Brown sets the record straight and strongly defends his science with a conversational, rational, and calm voice that may change the public's opinion of scientists as poor communicators." Publ Wkly

Kessler, Andrew

Martian summer; robot arms, cowboy spacemen, and my 90 days with the Phoenix Mars Mission. Pegasus 2011 340p il $27.95   **523.4**

1. Space flight to Mars 2. Phoenix Mars Mission (U.S.) 3. Mars (Planet) -- Exploration

ISBN 978-1-60598-176-5; 1-60598-176-1

The author chronicles the three months he spent in Mission Control for NASA's Phoenix Mars Mission, a project that lead to the discovery of liquid water on Mars, as well as a giant frozen ocean trapped beneath the planet's north pole

"The author provides some fascinating glimpses of the real work of a space mission: planning activities for the lander, dealing with peremptory orders from NASA and JPL, interpreting the sometimes ambiguous data and occasionally letting one's hair down for a party." Kirkus

Levenson, Thomas

The **hunt** for Vulcan; ...and how Albert Einstein destroyed a planet, discovered relativity, and deciphered the universe. Thomas Levenson. Random House Inc 2015 256 p. illustrations $26   **523.4**

1. Relativity (Physics) 2. Vulcan (Hypothetical planet) 3. Relativity

ISBN 0812998987; 9780812998986

LC 2015018989

This book, by Thomas Levenson, tells the "all-but-forgotten story of Isaac Newton, Albert Einstein, and the search for a planet that never existed. For more than fifty years, the world's top scientists searched for the 'missing' planet Vulcan, whose existence was mandated by Isaac Newton's theories of gravity. Countless hours were spent on the hunt . . . and some of the era's most skilled astronomers even claimed to have found it. There was just one problem: It was never there." (Publisher's note)

"Though brief, Levenson's narrative is a well-structured, fast-paced example of exemplary science writing. A scintillating popular account of the interplay between mathematical physics and astronomical observations." Kirkus

Includes bibliographical references

Weintraub, David A.

Is Pluto a planet? a historical journey through the solar system. Princeton University Press 2007 254p il $27.95   **523.4**

1. Planets 2. Pluto (Dwarf planet) 3. Solar system

ISBN 0-691-12348-9; 978-0-691-12348-6

LC 2006-929630

Weintraub "provides a very interesting and thought-provoking history concerning the whole idea of planets, and I recommend the book highly to anyone interested in the solar system." Sci Books Films

Includes bibliographical references

523.43   Mars

Hubbard, Scott

Exploring Mars; chronicles from a decade of discovery. Scott Hubbard; foreword by Bill Nye. University of Arizona Press 2011 xix, 194 p.p (hardcover) $45   **523.43**

1. Space flight to Mars 2. Mars (Planet) -- Exploration 3. United States. National Aeronautics and Space Administration 4. Space flight to Mars -- History

ISBN 0816521115; 0816528969; 9780816521111; 9780816528967

LC 2011036184

This book presents author Scott Hubbard's "perspective on the logistical issues -- technical, scientific, and political -- that . . . [he] faced as NASA's 'Mars Czar' during a reorganization of its Mars Exploration Program. Covering the period between . . . 1999 and the launch of the Mars Odyssey spacecraft in April 2001, Hubbard details the . . . process of simultaneous planning and approval seeking for multiple missions as far as a decade in advance." (Library Journal)

Morton, Oliver

Mapping Mars; science, imagination, and the birth of a world. Picador 2002 357p il maps $30; pa $16   **523.43**

1. Mars (Planet)

ISBN 0-312-24551-3; 0-312-42261-X pa

The author "traces scientists' efforts to map and understand the surface of Mars. . . . Morton writes eloquently and displays a breadth of knowledge not often found in science writing." Publ Wkly

Includes bibliographical references (p. 333-345)

523.5 Meteors, solar wind, zodiacal light

Bevan, A. W. R.

Meteorites: a journey through space and time; [by] Alex Bevan and John de Laeter. Smithsonian Institution Press 2002 215p il maps $35.95 **523.5**
1. Meteorites
ISBN 1-58834-021-X
LC 2001-49551
"Informative and visually appealing, this title meets any library's need for a basic source on meteorites." Booklist
Includes bibliographical references

Cokinos, Christopher

The **fallen** sky; an intimate history of shooting stars. Jeremy P. Tarcher/Penguin 2009 518p $27.95 **523.5**
1. Meteorites
ISBN 978-1-58542-720-8; 1-58542-720-9
LC 2009-17493
"In 1894, fifteen years before his storied expedition to the North Pole, Robert Peary crossed a treacherous expanse of ice in Greenland in search of another prize: a massive meteorite laden with rare metals from outer space. In this hefty, industrious book, Cokinos retraces Peary's steps, and those of other meteor 'obsessives,' in an idiosyncratic hunt of his own." New Yorker
Includes bibliographical references

523.6 Comets

Sagan, Carl

Comet; [by] Carl Sagan and Ann Druyan. Random House 1985 398p il hardcover o.p. pa $23 **523.6**
1. Comets 2. Halley's comet
ISBN 0-345-41222-2
LC 85-8308
"The authors explore the myth and science of comets in a lavishly illustrated, slightly oversize volume that is both fascinating and authoritative." Booklist
Includes bibliographical references

523.7 Sun

Golub, Leon

Nearest star; the surprising science of our sun. {by} Leon Golub & Jay M. Pasachoff. Harvard Univ. Press 2001 267p il $29.95; pa $16.95 **523.7**
1. Sun
ISBN 0-674-00467-1; 0-674-01006-X pa
LC 00-63213
Golub and Pasachoff set out to review what is currently known about the sun. Bibliography. Index.
This is "a brilliant, richly illustrated survey." Booklist
Includes bibliographical references

523.8 Stars

Bartusiak, Marcia

Black hole; how an idea abandoned by Newtonians, hated by Einstein, and gambled on by Hawking became loved. Marcia Bartusiak. Yale University Press 2015 256 p. (clothbound : alk. paper) $27.50 **523.8**
1. Discoveries in science 2. Black holes (Astronomy) 3. Science -- Social aspects
ISBN 030021085X; 9780300210859
LC 2014038950
This book, by Marcia Bartusiak, "tells the story of the fierce black hole debates and the contributions of Einstein and Hawking and other leading thinkers who completely altered our view of the universe. . . . This book celebrates the hundredth anniversary of general relativity, uncovers how the black hole really got its name, and recounts the scientists' frustrating, exhilarating, and at times humorous battles over the acceptance of one of history's most dazzling ideas." (Publisher's note)
"Superior science writing that eschews the usual fulsome biographies of eccentric geniuses, droll anecdotes and breathless prognostication to deliver a persistently fascinating portrait of an odd but routine feature of the cosmos." Kirkus
Includes bibliographical references and index

Kaler, James B.

Extreme stars; at the edge of creation. Cambridge Univ. Press 2001 236p il maps $40 **523.8**
1. Stars
ISBN 0-521-40262-X
LC 00-58522
"Each chapter covers extreme stars of a different kind, including the faintest, the coolest, the brightest, the largest, the smallest, the youngest, the oldest, and the strangest. . . . {Kaler} piques the curiosity of the novice, while encouraging knowledgeable readers to think about stars from a different perspective. There is a wealth of information, much of it not available elsewhere at this semipopular level." Choice

Ridpath, Ian

The **monthly** sky guide; Ian Ridpath; illustrated by Wil Tirion. 9th ed. Cambridge University Press 2012 71 p. col. ill. (paperback) $17.99 **523.8**
1. Astronomy 2. Stars -- Atlases 3. Stars -- Identification 4. Stars -- Observers' manuals
ISBN 1107683157; 9781107683150
LC 2012033599
This book, the ninth edition of Ian Ridpath and Wil Tirion's guide to the night sky, "is updated with planet positions and forthcoming eclipses to the end of the year 2017. It contains twelve chapters describing the main sights visible in each month of the year, providing" information for anyone "wanting to identify prominent stars, constellations, star clusters, nebulae and galaxies; to watch out for meteor showers . . . or to follow the movements of the four brightest planets." (Publisher's note)
Includes bibliographical references and index.

Scharf, Caleb

Gravity's engines; how bubble-blowing black holes rule galaxies, stars, and life in the cosmos. Caleb Scharf. Scientific American/ Farrar, Straus and Giroux 2012 ix, 252 p.p (hardback) $26   **523.8**
1. Gravity 2. Cosmology 3. Black holes (Astronomy)
ISBN 0374114129; 9780374114121

LC 2011047089

Author Caleb Scharf presents a "journey through the endlessly colorful place we call our galaxy and reminds us that the Milky Way sits in a special place in the cosmic zoo--a 'sweet spot' of properties. Is it coincidental that we find ourselves here at this place and time? Could there be a deeper connection between the nature of black holes and their role in the universe and the phenomenon of life?" (Publisher's note)

Includes bibliographical references and index.

The **Stars**; The Definitive Visual Guide to the Cosmos. DK Publishing. Dk Pub 2016 256 p. illustrations (chiefly color) $30   **523.8**
1. Cosmology
ISBN 1465453407; 9781465453402

"Packed with 3-D artworks of each constellation and incredible new imagery from the Hubble Space Telescope, ground-based observatories worldwide, and more, this . . . guide features the most fascinating objects known to astronomy, from glittering star-birth nebulae to supermassive black holes." (Publisher's note)

Tirion, Wil

The **Cambridge** star atlas; Wil Tirion. 4th edition Cambridge University Press 2011 86 p. col ill, col maps $39.99   **523.8**
1. Stars 2. Stars -- Atlases
ISBN 9780521173636; 0521173639

LC 2012589778

This star atlas, by Wil Tirion "is ideal for both beginning astronomers and more experienced observers worldwide. The clear, full-color maps show stars, clusters and galaxies visible with binoculars or a small telescope. The atlas also features constellation boundaries and the Milky Way, and lists objects that are interesting to observe." (Publisher's note)

Tyson, Neil deGrasse

Death by black hole; and other cosmic quandaries. Norton 2007 384p $24.95; pa $15.95   **523.8**
1. Cosmology 2. Space biology 3. Religion and science 4. Black holes (Astronomy) 5. Solar system
ISBN 978-0-393-06224-3; 0-393-06224-4; 978-0-393-33016-8 pa; 0-393-33016-8 pa

LC 2006-22058

"A wonderfully informed viewpoint on the slowly expanding boundaries of human knowledge." Boston Globe

Includes bibliographical references

White, Vivian

The **Total** Skywatcher's Manual; 275+ Skills and Tricks for Exploring Stars, Planets & Beyond. by

Astronomical Society of the Pacific. Simon & Schuster 2015 272 p. color illustrations $29   **523.8**
1. Astronomy
ISBN 161628871X; 9781616288716

This astronomy book "will help you choose the best telescope, identify constellations and objects in the night sky, search for extraterrestrial phenomena, plan star parties, capture beautiful space imagery and much more. . . . With fully illustrated star charts, gorgeous astrophotography and step-by-step project instruction, this family friendly book is the only guide you'll ever need to navigate the nightsky." (Publisher's note)

"Enhanced by gorgeous photos and colorful diagrams, this excellent volume will encourage users to 'engage with and appreciate the extraordinary laboratory unfolding' above them." LJ

523.9   Satellites and rings; eclipses, transits, occultations

Wulf, Andrea

Chasing Venus; the race to measure the heavens. Andrea Wulf. Alfred A. Knopf 2012 xxvi, 304 p.p (hardback) $26.95   **523.9**
1. Astronomy 2. Scientists 3. Venus (Planet) 4. Venus (Planet) -- Transit 5. Astronomy -- History -- 18th century 6. Geodetic astronomy -- History -- 18th century
ISBN 0307700178; 0307958612; 9780307700179; 9780307958617

LC 2011049136

This book "is concerned with Venus's 1761 and 1769 transits, when the international science community dispatched a remarkable set of expeditions to remote parts of the world to observe and measure the planet's passages across the sun. Their primary objective was to use newly acquired observational data to improve knowledge of the distance between Earth and the Sun and the solar system's dimensions. Many of the traveling scientists underwent great travails, and several died." (Library Journal)

526   Mathematical geography

Alder, Ken

The **measure** of all things; the seven-year odyssey and hidden error that transformed the world. Free Press 2002 422p $27; pa $15   **526**
1. Geography 2. Astronomers 3. Metric system
ISBN 0-7432-1675-X; 0-7432-1676-8 pa

LC 2002-70267

"In 1792, two astronomers set out from Paris in opposite directions to measure the meridian and thereby define the length of the meter. Alder's marvelous account of their quest is a dramatic tale of revolution, science, and human error." Libr J

Includes bibliographical references

Danson, Edwin

Weighing the world; the quest to measure the Earth. Oxford University Press 2005 289p il $29.95 **526**

1. Surveying 2. Earth 3. Science -- History
ISBN 978-0-19-518169-2; 0-19-518169-7

LC 2004-66284

The author "enlivens data about geodetic surveying, transforming them into greatly interesting dramas of science." Booklist

Includes bibliographical references

Felt, Hali

Soundings; the remarkable woman who mapped the ocean floor. Hali Felt. Henry Holt and Co. 2012 340 p. (hardback) $30.00 **526**

1. Women cartographers 2. Oceanography -- History 3. Submarine topography 4. Cartographers -- United States -- Biography 5. Geomorphologists -- United States -- Biography 6. Women cartographers -- United States -- Biography
ISBN 0805092153; 9780805092158

LC 2011044178

This book presents a "biography of a groundbreaking geologist who discovered 'a rift valley running down the center of the Atlantic,' essentially transforming 20th-century geophysics despite . . . gender bias and scientific rivalries. . . . From the 1950s through the '70s, Marie Tharp (1920-2006) mapped the entire ocean floor, an accomplishment honored by the Library of Congress in 1997, when she was named 'one of the four greatest cartographers' of the 20th century." (Kirkus Reviews)

Ferreiro, Larrie D.

Measure of the Earth; the enlightenment expedition that reshaped our world. Basic Books 2011 353p il map $28 **526**

1. Geodesy 2. Scientific expeditions 3. Geodesy -- Europe -- History 4. Scientific expeditions -- Europe -- History -- 18th century
ISBN 978-0-465-01723-2; 0-465-01723-1; 978-0-465-02345-5 ebook; 0-465-02345-2 ebook

LC 2011007173

This book "reads like a script from an Indiana Jones adventure film. . . . [It is] very well written and will interest any reader as it gives insight into the 18th Century and introduces some fascinating and unforgettable characters." Sci Books Films

Includes bibliographical references

Nicastro, Nicholas

Circumference; Eratosthenes and the ancient quest to measure the globe. St. Martin's Press 2008 223p il map $23.95 **526**

1. Astronomers 2. Measurement 3. Weights and measures 4. Geographers 5. Writers on science
ISBN 978-0-312-37247-7; 0-312-37247-7

LC 2008-25773

"Nicastro delivers the deeply human story of a multitalented genius whose tenure as the head of Alexandria's famed library occasioned remarkable achievements in literature,

history, linguistics, and philosophy despite the political turmoil that periodically rocked the Ptolemaic world." Booklist

Includes bibliographical references

Raymo, Chet

Walking zero; discovering cosmic space and time along the Prime Meridian. Walker & Co. 2006 194p il maps $22.95 **526**

1. Longitude 2. Great Britain -- Description and travel
ISBN 0-8027-1494-3; 978-0-8027-1494-7

LC 2006-282372

This is the author's "expression of his personal exploration of space, time, and scientific history, inspired partly by his walking the footpaths of southeast England in close proximity to the 0 degrees longitude line. . . . . This work is a thought-provoking, highly enlightening discussion of some of the most fascinating concepts in physics, astronomy, and geology, among other subjects." Sci Books Films

Includes bibliographical references

Reinhartz, Dennis

The **Art** of the Map; An Illustrated History of Map Elements and Embellishments. by Dennis Reinhartz. Sterling Pub Co Inc 2012 240 p. ill. (hardcover) $40 **526**

1. Maps 2. Map drawing
ISBN 1402765924; 9781402765926

This book, by Dennis Reinhartz, offers an "illustrated history of the golden age of cartography, from the sixteenth through the nineteenth centuries, explor[ing] not only the embellishments on maps but also what they reveal about the world in which they were created. Here there be monsters . . . ships actual and archetypical; newly discovered flora such as corn and tobacco; fauna ranging from buffalo to unicorns; [and] godlike beings and fantasy-like depictions of native peoples." (Publisher's note)

Sobel, Dava

★ **Longitude**; the true story of a lone genius who solved the greatest scientific problem of his time. with a new foreword by Neil Armstrong. Hardcover anniversary ed., [10th anniversary ed., 2005 anniversary ed.]; Walker & Co. 2005 184p il $19 **526**

1. Longitude 2. Mechanical engineers 3. Clock and watch makers
ISBN 0-8027-1462-5; 978-0-8027-1462-6
First published 1995

"In 1714, Britain's Parliament offered the modern equivalent of $12 to anybody who could develop a means of determining longitude at sea. While the likes of Isaac Newton and Edmund Halley sought to calculate longitude by celestial measurement, John Harrison, an uneducated clockmaker, solved the problem with his invention of the chronometer. Science writer Sobel tells this story in a way that enables readers 'to see the globe anew.'" Libr J

Includes bibliographical references

Winchester, Simon

The **map** that changed the world; William Smith and the birth of modern geology. illustrations by

Soun Vannithone. HarperCollins Pubs. 2001 329p
il map $26; pa $13.95 **526**
1. Geologists 2. Stratigraphic geology 3. Civil
engineers 4. Writers on science
ISBN 0-06-019361-1; 0-06-093180-9 pa
LC 2001-16603

"In the early years of the nineteenth century, William
Smith created the first geological map of Great Britain, a
time-consuming, solitary project that helped establish geology as one of the 'fundamental fields of study.' . . . Winchester
tells Smith's story, including the dramatic ups and downs of
his personal life. . . . This is just the kind of creative nonfiction that elevates a seemingly arcane topic into popular
fare." Booklist

529   Chronology

Falk, Dan
In search of time; the science of a curious dimension. Thomas Dunne Books, St. Martin's Press 2008
329p il $25.95; pa $15.99 **529**
1. Time 2. Science and civilization
ISBN 978-0-312-37478-5; 0-312-37478-X; 978-0-
312-60351-9 pa; 0-312-60351-7 pa
LC 2008-24875

"The book's scope is audaciously broad. Relying on
reportage and humour to offset writing that is occasionally
prolix, Falk deftly weaves together elements of religion, anthropology, philosophy, and physics into an engaging narrative." Quill Quire
Includes bibliographical references

Galison, Peter Louis
Einstein's clocks and Poincare's maps; empires
of time. by Peter Galison. Norton 2003 389p il
$23.95 **529**
1. Time 2. Physicists 3. Mathematicians 4. Relativity
(Physics) 5. Nobel laureates for physics
ISBN 0-393-02001-0
LC 2002-155114

"Gallison shows how Einstein's work was influenced by
French cartographer Henri Poincaré and by the physicist's
own experience working in a Bern patent office, where the
numerous patent requests for devices designed to coordinate
distant clocks may have prompted further inquiry into the
problem of simultaneity, which lies at the heart of relativity.
Few books have ever made Einstein's theories more accessible—or more engrossing—for general readers." Booklist
Includes bibliographical references

Sims, Michael
Apollo's fire; a day on Earth in nature and imagi-
nation. Viking 2007 xxiv, 296p $24.95 **529**
1. Days 2. Time 3. Astronomy
ISBN 978-0-670-06328-4; 0-670-06328-2
LC 2007-6024

The author "takes a single day and guides readers
through the history of what we know, and what we've imagined, about sunrises, clouds and other natural phenomena.
. . . His delightful tour of day and night skies will inspire

many readers to look up with a marveling new perspective."
Publ Wkly
Includes bibliographical references

530   Physics

Ananthaswamy, Anil
The edge of physics; a journey to Earth's extremes to unlock the secrets of the universe. Houghton Mifflin Harcourt 2010 322p il $25 **530**
1. Physics 2. Cosmology
ISBN 978-0-618-88468-1; 0-618-88468-8
LC 2009-20225

"A meticulous, accessible update of the latest ideas and
instruments that contribute to the clarification of an increasingly puzzling universe." Kirkus
Includes bibliographical references

Balibar, Sebastien
The atom and the apple; twelve tales from con-
temporary physics. translated by Nathanael Stein.
Princeton University Press 2008 190p il $24.95 **530**
1. Physics
ISBN 978-0-691-13108-5
LC 2008-18027

This "is a delightful ramble through many areas of science as well as through the experiences, opinions, passions
and frustrations of a leading research physicist. . . . It is a
very refreshing read that will do much to bring an understanding of scientific culture to the reader." Times Higher Ed
Includes bibliographical references

Buchanan, Mark
Nexus: small worlds and the groundbreaking sci-
ence of networks. Norton 2002 235p $25.95; pa
$14.95 **530**
1. System analysis 2. Patterns (Mathematics)
ISBN 0-393-04153-0; 0-393-32442-7 pa
LC 2002-518

The author "introduces readers to the dynamics of networks and shows how these networks affect behaviors in
both the natural and the social world. . . . [Buchanan] finds
the same patterns taking shape in food chains, in the neuronal networks of insects, in the architecture of the Internet
and in the cultural backgrounds of elite CEOs. . . . Buchanan's ability as an affable, easygoing storyteller makes up for
myriad digressions, and the narrative is, at times, spellbinding." Publ Wkly
Includes bibliographical references

The Cambridge companion to Newton; edited by I.
Bernard Cohen and George E. Smith. Cambridge
Univ. Press 2002 500p il $65; pa $23 **530**
1. Physicists 2. Mathematicians 3. Writers on science
ISBN 0-521-65177-8; 0-521-65696-6 pa
LC 2001-37836

This is "the best available brief overview of Newton's
contributions to mechanics, cosmology, optics, mathematics, alchemy, and theology. The contributors have produced
16 well-written and admirably focused chapters. Some will
be challenging for nonspecialist readers, but even those that

discuss mechanics in detail are so well organized and clearly written that they amply repay close attention." Choice

Includes bibliographical references

Close, F. E.

Nothing; a very short introduction. [by] Frank Close. Oxford University Press 2009 157p (Very short introductions) pa $11.95 **530**

1. Physics -- Philosophy

ISBN 978-0-19-922586-6; 0-19-922586-9

LC 2009-281157

First published 2007 in the United Kingdom with title: The void

This history of "nothing" covers the "history of the vacuum: how the efforts to make a better vacuum led to the discovery of the electron; the ideas of Newton, Mach, and Einstein on the nature of space and time; the mysterious aether and how Einstein did away with it; and the . . . [idea] that the vacuum is filled with the Higgs field." Publisher's note

Includes bibliographical references

Darling, David J.

Gravity's arc; the story of gravity, from Aristotle to Einstein and beyond. [by] David Darling. J. Wiley 2006 278p $24.95 **530**

1. Gravity

ISBN 0-471-71989-7; 978-0-471-71989-2

LC 2005-30772

This is a "historical review of the human understanding of gravity from the ancient Greeks to the 21st century. Included are examinations of Greek philosophers and their debates, medieval and Arabic developments, Galileo, Tycho, Kepler, Newton, Eotvos, [and] Einstein. . . . The writing style is clear and reader friendly. . . . Read this book to learn about gravity and experience a model scientific exposition for the scientist and general reader alike." Sci Books Films

Includes bibliographical references

Einstein, Albert

★ The **evolution** of physics; the growth of ideas from early concepts to relativity and quanta. by Albert Einstein and Leopold Infeld. Simon & Schuster 1938 320p il hardcover o.p. pa $13 **530**

1. Quantum theory 2. Relativity (Physics) 3. Physics -- History

ISBN 0-671-20156-5 pa

An "exposition for the layman of the growth of ideas in physical science." Publ Wkly

The **ultimate** quotable Einstein; collected and edited by Alice Calaprice; with a foreword by Freeman Dyson. Princeton University Press 2011 xxviii, 578p il $24.95; ebook $24.95 **530**

1. Quotations

ISBN 978-0-691-13817-6; 0-691-13817-6; 978-1-4008-3596-6 ebook

LC 2010002855

This collection of Einstein's quotes includes "sections titled 'On and to Children' and 'On Race and Prejudice,' and a brief selection of Einstein's wry verses. The comments are few on the matters of physics and mathematics, concentrat-

ing more on personal, social, political, philosophical, and educational subjects." Choice

Includes bibliographical references

Feynman, Richard Phillips

★ **Six** easy pieces; essentials of physics explained by its most brilliant teacher. [by] Richard P. Feynman; originally prepared for publication by Robert B. Leighton and Matthew Sands; introduction by Paul Davies. Basic Books 2005 xxix, 144p il pa $13.95 **530**

1. Atoms 2. Physics 3. Gravitation 4. Quantum theory 5. Energy conservation

ISBN 978-0-465-02392-9

First published 1995 by Helix Bks.

This book reprints six chapters from Feynman's Lectures on Physics. "In these six chapters, Feynman introduces the general reader to the following: atoms, basic physics, the relationship of physics to other topics, energy, gravitation, and quantum force." Publisher's note

Goldberg, Dave

A **user's** guide to the universe; surviving the perils of black holes, time paradoxes, and quantum uncertainty. [by] Dave Goldberg and Jeff Blomquist. Wiley 2010 296p il $24.95 **530**

1. Physics

ISBN 978-0-470-49651-0; 0-470-49651-7

Surveys the major discoveries of modern physics, from relativity to the Large Hadron Collider. The authors discuss subjects such as special relativity, quantum mechanics, randomness, time travel, and the expanding universe. Illustrated with cartoons

"With a large measure of humor and a minimum of math (one equation), physics professor Goldberg and engineer Blomquist delve into the fascinating physics topics that rarely make it into introductory classes. . . . This nearly-painless guide is . . . involved and scientific, aimed at science hobbyists rather than science-phobes." Publ Wkly

Includes bibliographical references

Hrabovsky, George

The **theoretical** minimum; what you need to know to start doing physics. Leonard Susskind, George Hrabovsky. Basic Books 2013 256 p. illustrations (hardcover) $26.99 **530**

1. Physics

ISBN 046502811X; 9780465028115; 9780465031740

LC 2012953679

This book by "physicist Leonard Susskind and hacker-scientist George Hrabovsky offer[s] a first course in physics and associated math for the ardent amateur. Challenging, lucid, and concise, . . . [it] provides a tool kit for amateur scientists to learn physics at their own pace." (Publisher's note)

"Excellent as an introduction to theoretical physics for the educated layperson, the book will also be useful to students and physicists for its elegant summary of the complete structure of classical mechanics. Summing Up: Highly recommended." Choice

Kragh, Helge

Quantum generations; a history of physics in the twentieth century. Princeton Univ. Press 1999 494p $65; pa $22.95 **530**

1. Physics -- History

ISBN 0-691-01206-7; 0-691-09552-3 pa

LC 99-17903

The author "details the explosive course physics has taken from the introduction of X rays in the mid-1890's to superstring theory in the present day. . . . {He} explains not only how the groundbreaking ideas of physics progressed but also how they are actively applied." Publisher's note

Includes bibliographical references and index

Krauss, Lawrence Maxwell

★ Fear of physics; a guide for the perplexed. [by] Lawrence M. Krauss. Rev ed; Basic Books 2007 257p il pa $29.95 **530**

1. Physics

ISBN 978-0-465-00218-4; 0-465-00218-8

LC 2007-04700

First published 1993

This overview describes what physics is and the work of physicists.

"The writing style genuinely keeps the reader interested. . . . This book is a great resource if you want insight into what physics really is and what physicists do." Sci Books Films

Includes bibliographical references

Levi, Mark

Why cats land on their feet; and 76 other physical paradoxes and puzzles. Mark Levi. Princeton University Press 2012 x, 190 p.p ill. (pbk. : alk. paper) $19.95 **530**

1. Puzzles 2. Science -- Miscellanea

ISBN 0691148546; 9780691148540

LC 2011045728

This book by Mark Levi presents "a compendium of paradoxes and puzzles that readers can solve using their own physical intuition. . . . Levi introduces each physical problem, sometimes gives a hint or two, and then fully explains the solution. Here readers can test their critical-thinking skills against a whole assortment of puzzles and paradoxes. . . . This . . . . collection also features an appendix that explains all physical concepts used in the book." (Publisher's note)

Includes bibliographical references and index

Ohanian, Hans C.

Einstein's mistakes; the human failings of genius. W.W. Norton & Company 2008 394p il $24.95 **530**

1. Physics 2. Physicists 3. Nobel laureates for physics

ISBN 978-0-393-06293-9; 0-393-06293-7

LC 2008-13155

This "clearly written, fascinating, and exciting book is a gem." Sci Books Films

Includes bibliographical references

Pickover, Clifford A.

The physics book; from Olbers' paradox to Schrodinger's cat: from the big bang to quantum resurrection, 250 milestones in the history of physics. Clifford A. Pickover. Sterling Pub Co Inc 2011 527 p. (alk. paper) $29.95 **530**

1. Physics -- History 2. Physics -- Dictionaries

ISBN 1402778619; 9781402778612

LC 2010051365

This book, by Clifford A. Pickover, is "a richly illustrated chronology of physics, containing 250 short, entertaining, and thought-provoking entries. In addition to exploring such engaging topics as dark energy, parallel universes, the Doppler effect, the God particle, and Maxwell's demon, the book's timeline extends back billions of years to the hypothetical Big Bang and forward trillions of years to a time of 'quantum resurrection.'" (Publisher's note)

"This attractive reference by biophysicist, biochemist, and science writer Pickover is composed of lucid one-page explanations of physics concepts, alternating with full-page color illustrations." LJ

Includes bibliographical references and index

Randall, Lisa

Warped passages; unravelling the mysteries of the Universe's hidden dimensions. Ecco 2005 499p il $27.95 **530**

1. Particles (Nuclear physics) 2. Physics -- Philosophy

ISBN 0-713-99699-4; 9780060531089

LC 2004-56376

The author "brings much of the excitement of her field to life as she describes her quest to understand the structure of the universe." Publ Wkly

Includes bibliographical references

Rovelli, Carlo

Seven Brief Lessons on Physics; Carlo Rovelli; translated by Simon Carnell and Erica Segre. Penguin Group USA 2016 96 p. illustrations $18 **530**

1. Gravity 2. Physics 3. Quantum theory 4. Relativity (Physics) 5. Black holes (Astronomy)

ISBN 0399184414; 9780399184413

LC 2016001513

This book, by Carlo Rovelli, is an "introduction to modern physics, offering . . . explanations of Einstein's general relativity, quantum mechanics, elementary particles, gravity, black holes, the complex architecture of the universe, and the role humans play in this weird and wonderful world. He takes us to the frontiers of our knowledge: to the most minute reaches of the fabric of space, back to the origins of the cosmos, and into the workings of our minds." (Publisher's note)

"An intriguing meditation on the nature of the universe and our attempts to understand it that should appeal to both scientists and general readers." Kirkus

Simonyi, Károly, 1916-2011

A cultural history of physics; Károly Simonyi; translated by David Kramer. CRC Press 2012 622 p. (alk. paper) $59.00 **530**

1. Physics 2. Science -- History 3. Science and the humanities 4. Physics -- History

ISBN 1568813295; 9781568813295

LC 2010009407

In this book, "Hungarian scientist and educator Károly Simonyi" describes "the experimental methods and theoretical interpretations that created scientific knowledge, from ancient times to the present day, within the cultural environment in which it was formed." He "explores the interplay of science and the humanities to convey the wonder and excitement of scientific development throughout the ages." (Barnes and Noble)

Includes bibliographical references and index.

530.01   Philosophy and theory

Cole, K. C.

The **hole** in the universe; how scientists peered over the edge of emptiness and found everything. Harcourt 2001 274p il hardcover o.p. pa $14 **530.01**
1. Physics
ISBN 0-15-601317-7 pa

LC 00-44947

Cole discusses the history of nothing, "combining the history of zero (a mathematical nothing) with that of the vacuum (a physical nothing). . . . Until Einstein showed that light needed no tangible medium through which to travel, theorists filled the vacuum with 'ether'—the 'enfant terrible' of substances, as Einstein put it. It was subsequently banished." Atl Mon

Includes bibliographical references

530.092   Physicists

Kaiser, David

How the hippies saved physics; science, counter-culture, and the quantum revival. David Kaiser. 1st ed. W.W. Norton 2011 xxvi, 372 p.p ill. (hardcover) $26.95 **530.092**
1. Quantum theory 2. Counter culture 3. Physicists -- Biography 4. Counterculture -- United States 5. Fundamental Fysiks Group (Berkeley, Calif.)
ISBN 0393076369; 9780393076363

LC 2010053415

This book by David Kaiser looks at "a coterie of physicists who, during the 1970s, embraced New Age fads and sometimes went on to make dramatic discoveries. . . . They explored complex, hitherto ignored areas such as Bell's theorem and quantum entanglement while annoying the establishment by exploring their links to the paranormal. The end result was a transformation in cutting-edge physics and major discoveries in quantum information science, now a thriving industry." (Kirkus Reviews)

"This entertaining, worthwhile read is as much about the nature of society at the dawn of the New Age as it is about quantum physics." Choice

Includes bibliographical references

Schulmann, Robert

An **Einstein** encyclopedia; Alice Calaprice, Daniel Kennefick, and Robert Schulmann. Princeton University Press 2015 376 p. ills., maps, portraits, charts (hardcover : alk. paper) $39.95 **530.092**
1. Physicists 2. Physicists -- Biography -- Encyclopedias 3. Relativity (Physics) -- History -- Encyclopedias 4. Physics -- History -- 20th century -- Encyclopedias
ISBN 0691141746; 9780691141749

LC 2015008233

This book, by Daniel Kennefick, Robert Schulmann, and Alice Calaprice, is a "guide to Albert Einstein's life and work for students, researchers, and browsers alike. [It] contains entries on Einstein's birth and death, family and romantic relationships, honors and awards, educational institutions where he studied and worked, citizenships and immigration to America, hobbies and travels, plus the people he befriended and the history of his archives and the Einstein Papers Project." (Publisher's note)

"This is an extremely well-organized and user-friendly reference title, thoroughly researched and accessible to the general public, students, and scholars alike. Highly recommended for public and academic libraries." Booklist

Includes bibliographical references and index

530.1   Theories and mathematical physics

Baggott, Jim

The **quantum** story; [by] Jim Baggott. Oxford University Press 2011 469p il $29.95 **530.1**
1. Quantum theory 2. Quantum theory -- History
ISBN 978-0-19-956684-6; 0-19-956684-4

In this history of quantum theory, Baggott examines "how, over the space of three decades, Einstein, Bohr, Heisenberg, and others formulated and refined the theory. . . . To take us from the story's beginning to the present day, Baggott organizes his narrative around forty turning-point moments of discovery." (Publisher's note)

"Quantum theory—challenging, disconcerting and heavy on math—is not going to be pinned down and dissected for lay readers without a lot of kicking and screaming. Baggott succeeds, however, imbuing the narrative with important context, his own communicable enthusiasm and the instances of dense theoretical exposition mediated by historical and biographical storytelling. His survey runs roughly chronologically, starting with Max Planck's contention that energy is composed of a definite number of equal finite packages, through Einstein, Bohr, Heisenberg, Dirac, Feynman, Hawking et al. the author then looks at the Standard Model and the more amorphous superstring theory." Kirkus

Includes bibliographical references and index

Bodanis, David

E; a biography of the world's most famous equation. Walker & Company 2005 337p il $25 **530.1**
1. Physicists 2. Space and time 3. Force and energy 4. Nobel laureates for physics
ISBN 0-8027-1463-3

First published 2000

The author relates the story of "Einstein's formulation of the equation in 1905 and its association ever after with relativity and nuclear energy. Parallel with the science, Bodanis populates his tale with dramatic lives." Booklist [review of 2000 edition]

Bolles, Edmund Blair

Einstein defiant; genius versus genius in the quantum revolution. Joseph Henry Press 2004 348p il $27.95   **530.1**

1. Physicists 2. Quantum theory 3. Nobel laureates for physics

ISBN 0-309-08998-0

LC 2003-23735

"This carefully researched book achieves a nice balance between science and history. The author provides enough scientific information to illuminate the unfolding drama for nonscientists and constructs a marvelously choreographed tale of how just about every physicist of note in the last century contributed to the debate." Sci Books Films

Includes bibliographical references

Carroll, Sean M.

★ **From** eternity to here; the quest for the ultimate theory of time. [by] Sean Carroll. Dutton 2009 438p il $25   **530.1**

1. Space and time

ISBN 978-0-525-95133-9; 0-525-95133-4

LC 2009-23828

"Understanding time requires an acquaintance with entropy, relativity, cosmology, thermodynamics and statistical mechanics, which Carroll enthusiastically delivers at great length. Not for the scientifically disinclined, but determined readers will come away with a rewarding grasp of a complex subject." Kirkus

Includes bibliographical references

Close, F. E.

The **infinity** puzzle; quantum field theory and the hunt for an orderly universe. [by] Frank Close. Basic Books 2011 435p il $28.99   **530.1**

1. Infinite 2. Quantum theory

ISBN 978-0-465-02144-4; 978-0-465-02803-0 ebook

LC 2011022966

Close "offers a compelling history and sociology of modern particle theory. We discover the motivations and achievements of a rich cast of brilliant individuals, and get enough of the science to grasp what they were trying to do. Where Close really shines is in exposing the fraught process of recognition in science, focusing on key players such as Pakistani theoretical physicist Abdus Salam and the man after whom the famous boson is named, British physicist Peter Higgs." Nature

Includes bibliographical references

Einstein, Albert

The **meaning** of relativity; 5th ed; Princeton University Press 2005 xxiv, 166p il pa $16.95 **530.1**

1. Relativity (Physics)

ISBN 0-691-12027-7

LC 2004-111082

First published 1922. Translated by Edwin Plimpton Adams, Ernst G. Straus and Bruria Kaufman

"Though few can understand it, most readers in physics and librarians in charge of science collections know this book as one of the landmarks of modern knowledge. . . . The book is not intended for general reading. Instead it is addressed to . . . those whose training enables them to under-

stand the mathematical expressions of relativity." N Y Public Libr. New Tech Books

★ A **stubbornly** persistent illusion; the essential scientific works of Albert Einstein. [edited, with commentary, by Stephen Hawking] Running Press 2007 468p il $29.95   **530.1**

1. Relativity (Physics) 2. Physics -- Philosophy

ISBN 978-0-7624-3003-1; 0-7624-3003-6

LC 2007-935658

The editor presents with introductions writings by Albert Einstein on relativity, the history of physics and philosophy.

"Hawking adds a brief but effective introduction to each section, making this gem of a collection really shine." Publ Wkly

Includes bibliographical references

Ford, Kenneth W.

101 quantum questions; what you need to know about the world you can't see. [by] Kenneth W. Ford. Harvard University Press 2011 291p il   **530.1**

1. Quantum theory

ISBN 9780674050990

LC 2010-34791

"Ford explains the essential concepts of quantum reality, our small-fast world, full of uncertainty and probability, where all matter can exist in more than one state simultaneously. Ford brings interesting and entertaining anecdotal and historical material into his answers, organizing and shaping his book around 15 subjects. By using humor and straight talk to answer questions that often bedevil the nonscientist who attempts to grasp this knotty subject, Ford has created an entertaining read and an excellent companion piece to more detailed popular treatments of modern physics." Publ Wkly

Includes bibliographical references

Gilder, Louisa

The **age** of entanglement; when quantum physics was reborn. Alfred A. Knopf 2008 443p il $27.50   **530.1**

1. Quantum theory

ISBN 978-1-4000-4417-7; 1-4000-4417-0

LC 2008-11796

This is "the story of quantum mechanics and its lively cast of supporters. . . . Gilder's history is rife with curious characters and dramatizes how difficult it was for even these brilliant scientists to grasp the paradigm-changing concepts of quantum science." Publ Wkly

Includes bibliographical references

Greene, B. (Brian), 1963-

★ The **hidden** reality; parallel universes and the deep laws of the cosmos. [by] Brian Greene. Alfred A. Knopf 2011 370p il $29.95   **530.1**

1. Cosmology 2. Quantum theory 3. Relativity (Physics) 4. Physics -- Philosophy 5. General relativity (Physics)

ISBN 0-307-26563-3; 978-0-307-26563-0

LC 2010-42710

The Hidden Reality aims to show how major developments in different branches of fundamental theoretical physics—relativistic, quantum, cosmological, unified, computational—have all led us to consider one or another variety of parallel universe. Index.

The author "explores the possibility that there is not one big uncharted universe, but many. Those universes take the form of Swiss cheese, suds in a bubble bath, passageways right out of 'Star Trek,' and realms right next to us. The danger of writing a mind-blower like 'The Hidden Reality' is that, if the author isn't careful, it can become mind-numbing to read. A caution here upfront: There are points where Greene walks perilously close to that precipice. Black holes, parallel universes, the idea that we and our world may have doppelgängers in different dimensions are heady concepts. For some, such conjecture is religious heresy; for others, it aims to answer the ultimate questions as to how and why we are here, with science, not faith, forming a necessary and—so far—inadequate, bridge to explore the mystery. What Greene . . . does exceedingly well is to lay out the prevailing theories, advanced by the brightest human minds, as to how the whole of everything may be ordered." Christ Sci Monit

Includes bibliographical references

Gribbin, John R.

In search of Schrodinger's cat; quantum physics and reality. Bantam Bks. 1984 302p il pa $15.95   **530.1**
1. Reality 2. Quantum theory
ISBN 0-553-34253-3

         LC 84-2975

This history of quantum mechanics discusses the work of Huygens, Einstein, Schrödinger, Bohr, Planck and Everett

This book "contains many vignettes from the history of science and many insights into the researchers and the work that has led to our current understanding of the quantum theory. Excellent analogies and graphic illustrations are used to present difficult ideas." Sci Books Films

Includes bibliographical references

Schrodinger's kittens and the search for reality; solving the quantum mysteries. {by} John Gribbin. Little, Brown 1995 261p il hardcover o.p. pa $14.95   **530.1**
1. Light 2. Reality 3. Physicists 4. Quantum theory 5. Nobel laureates for physics
ISBN 0-316-32819-7 pa

         LC 95-75652

In this sequel to In search of Schrödinger's cat, Gribbin attempts to "explain recent experimental and theoretical findings about the . . . nature of the submicroscopic world of the atom. The 'Copenhagen interpretation' of quantum mechanics offered by Niels Bohr and his colleagues has prevailed for almost 70 years, but there {are} now . . . competing interpretations. Gribbin reviews this . . . {field and} indicates his personal preference for one of the new theoretical models." Libr J

Includes bibliographical references

Hawking, Stephen, 1942-

★ The **grand** design; [by] Stephen Hawking and Leonard Mlodinow. Bantam Books 2010 198p il $28; ebook $28   **530.1**
1. Universe 2. Cosmology 3. String theory 4. Quantum

theory 5. Life -- Origin 6. Science -- Philosophy
ISBN 978-0-553-80537-6; 0-553-80537-1; 978-0-553-90707-0 ebook; 0-553-90707-7 ebook

"The three central questions of philosophy and science: Why is there something rather than nothing? Why do we exist? Why this particular set of laws and not some other? . . . Along with Caltech physicist Mlodinow . . . Hawking deftly mixes cutting-edge physics to answer those key questions. . . . This is an amazingly concise, clear, and intriguing overview of where we stand when it comes to divining the secrets of the universe." Publ Wkly

Includes bibliographical references

The **nature** of space and time; [by] Stephen Hawking and Roger Penrose. [New ed.]; Princeton University Press 2010 145p il (Isaac Newton Institute series of lectures) pa $14.95; ebook $14.95   **530.1**
1. Astrophysics 2. Quantum theory 3. Space and time
ISBN 978-0-691-14570-9 pa; 978-1-4008-3474-7 ebook

First published 1996

This volume "takes the form of a debate between Hawking and Penrose at Cambridge in 1994. At the center of the discussion is a pair of powerful theories: the quantum theory of fields and the general theory of relativity. The issue is how—if at all—one can merge the two into a quantum theory of gravity. . . . A substantial background in theoretical physics is needed for full comprehension." Libr J

Includes bibliographical references

★ The **universe** in a nutshell; [by] Stephen Hawking. Bantam Bks. 2001 216p il $35   **530.1**
1. Quantum theory
ISBN 0-553-80202-X

         LC 2001-35757

Hawking "explains the basic laws of physics that govern the universe, beginning with a brief history of the concept of relativity, and then he is off and running to explore time, space, the future, and the possibility of time travel, among other fundamental rules of the universe's road. Admirers of Hawking's previous book will continue to appreciate his ability not only to air fresh, provocative ideas but also to say what he means clearly and without watering down his material or condescending to his audience—he even injects humor into his narrative. The profuse, beautifully rendered illustrations contribute greatly to the reader's understanding of his points." Booklist

Kakalios, James

The **amazing** story of quantum mechanics; a math-free exploration of the science that made our world. Gotham Books 2010 318p il $26   **530.1**
1. Quantum theory
ISBN 978-1-59240-479-7; 1-59240-479-0

         LC 2010-29568

"Though the book does not quite live up to the subtitle's promise of a 'math-free' text, readers need no more than basic algebra to accompany comic-book heroes into well-illustrated explanations of quantum packets of light energy, of the wave functions of particles, and even of the angular spin inherent in both energy and matter. These basic principles illuminate the solid-state physics of semiconductors, the atomic magnetism of MRIs, and the nanotechnology of high-capacity storage batteries. And all of this conceptual heavy lifting comes with entertaining episodes from DC Comics and H. G. Wells' fiction. Physics has never been more fun!" Booklist

Includes bibliographical references

Kaku, Michio

Hyperspace; a scientific odyssey through parallel universes, time warps, and the tenth dimension. illustrations by Robert O'Keefe. Oxford Univ. Press 1994 359p il $35   530.1

1. Space and time 2. Relativity (Physics)
ISBN 0-19-508514-0

LC 93-7910

This is an "overview of the major scientists, discoveries, and ideas involved in an ongoing quest for synthesizing quantum mechanics and relativity physics into a superstring theory of our entire universe." Libr J

Includes bibliographical references

Kumar, Manjit

★ **Quantum**; Einstein, Bohr and the great debate about the nature of reality. W.W. Norton 2010 448p il $27.95   530.1

1. Quantum theory
ISBN 978-0-393-07829-9; 0-393-07829-9

LC 2009-51249

"A staggering account of the scientific revolution that still challenges our notions of reality. . . . Kumar evokes the passion and excitement of the period and writes with sparkling clarity and wit. Expertly delineates complex scientific issues in nontechnical language, using telling detail to weave together personal, political and scientific elements." Kirkus

Includes bibliographical references

Lloyd, Seth

★ **Programming** the universe; a quantum computer scientist takes on the cosmos. Knopf 2006 221p il $25.95   530.1

1. Quantum theory 2. Microcomputers
ISBN 1-4000-4092-2; 978-1-4000-4092-6

LC 2005-50408

"Exploring big questions in accessible, comprehensive fashion, Lloyd's work is of vital importance to the general-science audience." Booklist

Includes bibliographical references

Nadis, Steve

The **shape** of inner space; string theory and the geometry of the universe's hidden dimensions. Shing-tung Yau and Steve Nadis; illustrations by Xianfeng (David) Gu and Xiaotian (Tim) Yin. Basic Books 2010 xix, 377 p.p $30   530.1

1. Geometry 2. String theory 3. Fourth dimension 4. Hyperspace 5. String models
ISBN 978-0-465-02023-2; 0-465-02023-2;
9780465020232; 0465020232

LC 2010009956

"It is a testimony to [Yau's] careful prose (and no doubt to the skills of co-author Steve Nadis) that this book so compellingly captures the essence of what pushes string theorists forward in the face of formidable obstacles. It gives us a rare glimpse into a world as alien as the moons of Jupiter, and just as fascinating. . . . Yau and Nadis have produced a strangely mesmerizing account of geometry's role in the universe." New Scientist

Includes bibliographical references (p. 331-343) and index

Rigden, John S.

★ **Einstein** 1905; the standard of greatness. Harvard University Press 2005 173p il $21.95; pa $14.95   530.1

1. Physicists 2. Quantum theory 3. Nobel laureates for physics
ISBN 0-674-01544-4; 0-674-02104-5 pa

LC 2004-54049

"The book is a delight to read, with a lot of interesting, useful information." Choice

Includes bibliographical references

Smolin, Lee

The **trouble** with physics; the rise of string theory, the fall of a science, and what comes next. Houghton Mifflin Co. 2006 392p il $26   530.1

1. String theory 2. Science -- Methodology
ISBN 978-0-618-55105-7; 0-618-55105-0

LC 2006-07235

"This is a well-written, critical profile of the theoretical physics community, free of equations, from the perspective of a member." Libr J

Includes bibliographical references

Susskind, Leonard

The **black** hole war; my battle with Stephen Hawking to make the world safe for quantum mechanics. Little, Brown 2008 470p il $27.99; pa $15.99   530.1

1. Physicists 2. Quantum theory 3. Space and time 4. Relativity (Physics) 5. Black holes (Astronomy) 6. People with disabilities 7. College teachers 8. Writers on science
ISBN 978-0-316-01640-7; 0-316-01640-3; 978-0-316-01641-4 pa; 0-316-01641-1 pa

LC 2007-48355

The author "delves into the related and disturbingly dangerous subject of black holes. Here, he describes disagreements that he and his Dutch friend, Gerard d'Hooft, had with the famous British mathematician/physicist Stephen Hawking on his predictions regarding the interaction of objects with black holes. This book provides an anecdotal, highly readable discussion of the background to black holes and the consequences of their existence." Choice

Includes glossary

Toomey, David M.

The **new** time travelers; a journey to the frontiers of physics. [by] David Toomey. W. W. Norton 2007 391p il $28 **530.1**

1. Space and time

ISBN 978-0-393-06013-3; 0-393-06013-6

LC 2007-11307

This book on the physics of time travel "illustrates dimension-bending concepts with space-time diagrams, M. C. Escher drawings, and the plot of H.G. Wells' Time Machine. Toomey gets a grip on bending the fourth dimension by historically chronicling physicists who have theorized about time travel . . . . If you dream of getting outside your personal light cone, Toomey shows how it might be imagined." Booklist

Includes bibliographical references

Wertheim, Margaret

Physics on the fringe; Smoke rings, circlons, and alternative theories of everything. Margaret Wertheim. Walker & Company 2011 336 p. il **530.1**

1. Physics

ISBN 0802715133; 9780802715135

This book "describes work done by amateur . . . [scientists], people rejected by the academic establishment and rejecting orthodox academic beliefs. . . . Margaret Wertheim's . . . leading character is Jim Carter. . . . Carter's . . . belief in a theory of the universe [is] based on endless hierarchies of circlons. Circlons are mechanical objects of circular shape. . . . He verified the behavior of circlons by doing experiments with smoke rings at his home." (New York Review of Books)

The author "offers a look into the hearts and minds of the 'outsider' physicists: solitary figures who, usually with little or no formal training, strive to explain our world. Wertheim builds the book around the affable Jim Carter, explorer, self-taught physicist, trailer park owner, and proponent of circlon synchronicity, with atoms shaped like tiny circles of coiled spring. . . . This sympathetic portrayal of one outsider's work offers an entry point into a fascinating corner of pseudoscience." Publ Wkly

Includes bibliographical references

Wolfson, Richard

Simply Einstein; relativity demystified. Norton 2003 261p il $24.95 **530.1**

1. Relativity (Physics)

ISBN 0-393-05154-4

LC 2002-2984

"Wolfson's economical and vivid tutorial should open doors for lay readers encountering Einstein's principles for the first time. His popular style, with a minimum of math, should make this a must-have book for Einstein buffs as well." Publ Wkly

Includes bibliographical references

530.11 Relativity theory

Ferreira, Pedro G.

The **perfect** theory; a century of geniuses and the battle over general relativity. Pedro G. Ferreira. Houghton Mifflin Harcourt 2014 304 p. (hardback) $28 **530.11**

1. Relativity (Physics) 2. Physicists -- Biography 3. Physics -- History 4. Science and civilization -- History

ISBN 0547554893; 9780547554891

LC 2013021741

In this book on Albert Einstein's theory of relativity, author Pedro G. Ferreira "shares the story of general relativity's revival and application to previously unobservable objects like quasars and black holes. Ferreira's book is also about the people who find joy and excitement in discovering the secrets of the universe. . . . International collaboration made confirmation of [Einstein's] theory possible, while overturning some initial conclusions." (Publishers Weekly)

"Ferreira does not downplay relativity's complexity and avoids the easy route of oversimplifying it into a cosmic magic show. The result is one of the best popular accounts of how Einstein and his followers have been trying to explain the universe for decades." Kirkus

Includes bibliographical references and index

Gleick, James, 1954-

Time travel; A History. James Gleick. Pantheon Books 2016 352 p. illustrations (ebook) $65.00; (hard cover : alk. paper) $26.95 **530.11**

1. Time travel 2. Space and time 3. Time travel -- Popular works 4. Space and time -- Popular works

ISBN 9780307908803; 9780307908797

LC 2016002323

This book, by James Gleick, "is a mind-bending exploration of time travel: its subversive origins, its evolution in literature and science, and its influence on our understanding of time itself. The story begins at the turn of the previous century, with the young H. G. Wells writing and rewriting the fantastic tale that became his first book and an international sensation: The Time Machine." (Publisher's note)

"Ultimately, readers discern behind the modern mania for the phenomenon a human craving for immortality that—particularly in a secular age—fosters this mania. Both piquant and profound." Booklist

Includes bibliographical references (pages [317]-322) and index.

Gribbin, John

Einstein's Masterwork; 1915 and the General Theory of Relativity. John Gribbin. Icon Books Ltd 2015 240 p. illustrations (ebook) $50.00; (hardcover) $27.95 **530.11**

1. Relativity (Physics)

ISBN 1681772124; 1848318529; 9781848318526; 9781681772653; 9781681772127

This book by John Gribbin reveals "the origins of Einstein's General Theory. . . . In 1915, Albert Einstein presented his masterwork to the Prussian Academy of Sciences—a theory of gravity, matter, space and time: the General Theory of Relativity. . . . It describes the evolution of the universe, black holes, the behavior of orbiting neutron stars, and why clocks run slower on the surface of the earth than in space. It even suggests the possibility of time travel." (Publisher's note)

"Walter Isaacson goes deeper into his life and Dennis Overbye into his work, but readers will find this shorter biography entirely satisfactory." Kirkus

Includes bibliographical references (pages 208-212) and index.

Muller, Richard A., 1944-

Now; The Physics of Time. Richard A. Muller. W W Norton & Co Inc 2016 368 p. illustrations (hardcover) $27.95; (ebook) $50   **530.11**
1. Entropy 2. Space and time 3. Physics -- Philosophy
ISBN 9780393285239; 0393285235; 9780393285246
LC 2016012496

This book by Richard A. Muller "points out that the standard Big Bang theory explains the ongoing expansion of the universe as the continuous creation of new space. [Muller] argues that time is also expanding and that the leading edge of the new time is what we experience as "now." This thought-provoking vision has remarkable implications for some of our biggest questions, not only in physics but also in philosophy—including the ongoing debate about the reality of free will." (Publisher's note)

"Not for the faint of heart or mathematically averse, but Muller is a masterful guide within this survey of cosmology." Kirkus

Musser, George

Spooky action at a distance; the phenomenon that reimagines space and time--and what it means for black holes, the big bang, and theories of everything. George Musser. Scientific American/Farrar, Straus & Giroux 2015 304 p. illustrations (hardcover) $26   **530.11**
1. Space and time 2. Relativity (Physics) 3. Space and time -- Philosophy
ISBN 0374298513; 9780374298517
LC 2015010155

This book, by George Musser, "sets out to answer . . . [questions about space and time,] offering a provocative exploration of nonlocality and a celebration of the scientists who are trying to explain it. Musser guides us on an epic journey into the lives of experimental physicists observing particles acting in tandem, astronomers finding galaxies that look statistically identical, and cosmologists hoping to unravel the paradoxes surrounding the big bang." (Publisher's note)

"Clarity and humor illuminate Musser's writing, and he adroitly captures the excitement and frustration involved in investigating the mysteries of our universe." Pub Wkly

Includes bibliographical references and index

530.12   Quantum mechanics (Quantum theory)

Cox, Brian

The quantum universe; (and why anything that can happen, does) [by] Brian Cox [and] Jeff Forshaw. Da Capo Press 2012 256p   **530.12**
1. Physics 2. Quantum theory 3. Science --

Methodology
ISBN 9780306819643; 9780306820601; 0306819643
LC 2011942393

In this book, "Brian Cox and Jeff Forshaw approach the world of quantum mechanics . . . and make fundamental scientific principles accessible . . . to everyone. The subatomic realm has a reputation for weirdness, spawning any number of profound misunderstandings." This book "asks what observations of the natural world made it necessary, how it was constructed, and why we are confident that, for all its apparent strangeness, it is a good theory." (Publisher's note)

Crease, Robert P.

The quantum moment; how Planck, Bohr, Einstein, and Heisenberg taught us to love uncertainty. Robert P. Crease, Alfred Scharff Goldhaber. W W Norton & Co Inc 2014 352 p. illustrations (hardcover) $29.95   **530.12**
1. Quantum theory 2. Physics -- Popular works 3. Quantum theory -- Popular works
ISBN 0393067920; 9780393067927
LC 2014011427

This book, by Robert P. Crease and Alfred Scharff Goldhaber, offers "the fascinating story of how quantum mechanics went mainstream. . . . The authors--one a philosopher, the other a physicist--draw on their training and six years of co-teaching to dramatize the quantum's rocky path from scientific theory to public understanding. Together, they and their students explored missteps and mistranslations, jokes and gibberish, of public discussion about the quantum." (Publisher's note)

"Though the authors acknowledge that many of those appropriating the jargon of quantum physics have no clue as to its scientific meaning, readers will learn to appreciate the imaginative process that transforms quantum formulas into new metaphors for understanding the human condition. An exhilarating romp for the intellectually adventurous!" Booklist

Includes bibliographical references and index

Parker, Barry R.

Quantum legacy; the discovery that changed our universe. {by} Barry Parker. Prometheus Bks. 2002 282p il $29   **530.12**
1. Quantum theory
ISBN 1-57392-993-X
LC 2002-67966

The author describes the theory of quantum mechanics, its practical applications, and the work of such scientists as Max Planck, Albert Einstein, Niels Bohr, Werner Heisenberg, Erwin Schrodinger, and Richard Feynman

Includes bibliographical references

530.13   Statistical mechanics

Halpern, Paul

Einstein's dice and Schrödinger's cat; how two great minds battled quantum randomness to create a unified theory of physics. Paul Halpern, PhD. Ba-

sic Books 2015 288 p. illustrations (hardcover) $27.99 **530.13**
1. Quantum theory 2. Quantum chaos 3. Physics -- Philosophy 4. Unified field theories 5. Quantum theory -- Philosophy
ISBN 0465075711; 9780465075713

LC 2014041325

In this book, author "Paul Halpern tells the little-known story of how [Albert] Einstein and [Erwin] Schrödinger searched, first as collaborators and then as competitors, for a theory that transcended quantum weirdness. This story of their quest--which ultimately failed--provides readers with new insights into the history of physics and the lives and work of two scientists whose obsessions drove its progress." (Publisher's note)

"Einstein's life feels familiar and true; Schrödinger emerges as someone scarred by envy and not a little opportunistic—e.g., when he composed a 'statement of support for the Anschluss.' Halpern ably explores the clashing personalities and worldviews that had physics in churning ferment during the early part of the 20th century." Kirkus

Includes bibliographical references and index

530.4   States of matter

Frankel, Felice

On the surface of things; images of the extraordinary in science. [by] Felice Frankel and George M. Whitesides. Harvard University Press 2007 160p il pa $26.50 **530.4**
1. Optical images 2. Surfaces (Physics)
ISBN 978-0-674-02688-9

First published 1997 by Chronicle Bks.

Text and photographs explore the way light interacts with various surfaces.

"Materials science bears an unfortunate reputation for dullness, dealing as it does with the stuff of everyday life. A ramble through the pages of this poetic volume, however, exposes the field's underlying luster." Sci Am [review of 1997 ed.]

Includes bibliographical references

530.8   Measurement

Barrow, John D.

The constants of nature; from Alpha to Omega--the numbers that encode the deepest secrets of the universe. Pantheon Books 2002 352p il $26; pa $15 **530.8**
1. Measurement
ISBN 0-375-42221-8; 1-4000-3225-3 pa

LC 2002-75975

"Barrow traces scientists' evolving understanding of natural constants, like the speed of light, in this erudite and enthralling work of popular science." Publ Wkly

Includes bibliographical references

Robinson, Andrew

The story of measurement. Thames & Hudson 2007 224p il map $34.95 **530.8**
1. Measurement
ISBN 978-0-500-51367-5; 0-500-51367-8

LC 2007-921450

"Robinson has the knack to explain any number of complex concepts lucidly and with simplicity, without being condescending. . . . He has produced a highly readable book." Times Lit Suppl

Includes bibliographical references

535   Light and related radiation

Ball, Philip

Invisible; the dangerous allure of the unseen. Philip Ball. The University of Chicago Press 2014 336 p. illustrations (cloth : alk. paper) $27.50 **535**
1. Invisibility
ISBN 022623889X; 1847922899; 9781847922892; 9780226238890

LC 2014035709

In this book, Philip Ball explores "the history of the idea of the invisible. He examines both the why and the how of invisibility, pondering the concept's allure and the opportunity it gives individuals to seize 'power, wealth, or sex,' as well as the intriguing ways that myth, magic, and science intersect in its study. In the Middle Ages, magic books were 'scarcely complete without a spell of invisibility,' but scientists began to test such spells experimentally by the 18th Century." (Publishers Weekly)

"The book is extremely readable, and extensive chapter notes and the bibliography will be useful for those wishing to pursue topics further." Choice

Park, David

The fire within the eye; a historical essay on the nature and meaning of light. Princeton Univ. Press 1997 377p il hardcover o.p. pa $19.95 **535**
1. Light 2. Optics
ISBN 0-691-05051-1 pa

LC 96-45573

A history of the concept and science of light from classical times to the present. Cultural, philosophical, intellectual and theological perspectives are explored and works by Aristotle, Grosseteste, Plotinus and Bohr are among those discussed

"Whether it is Fermat and Huygens on optics or Faraday and Maxwell on electromagnetism, the writing is lively and informed. . . . The very readable style and helpful glossary, along with an excellent bibliography and references, make this work suitable for . . . general readers." Choice

Pendergrast, Mark

Mirror mirror; a history of the human love affair with reflection. Basic Books 2003 404p il $27.50; pa $17 **535**
1. Mirrors
ISBN 0-465-05470-6; 0-465-05471-4 pa

LC 2003-2544

"Those with a historical and scientific bent may profitably read this book for insight into the manufacture of mirrors—along with descendents the telescope and microscope—down through the ages. . . . Whether for pleasure or profit, this well-written, entertaining book, packed with historical information, should be read!" Choice

Includes bibliographical references

535.6 Color

Eckstut, Arielle

The **Secret** Language of Color; Science, Nature, History, Culture, Beauty and Joy of Red, Orange, Yellow, Green, Blue, and Violet. Joann Eckstut and Arielle Eckstut. Black Dog & Leventhal Pub 2013 240 p. color illustrations $29.95 **535.6**
1. Color 2. Vision 3. Physics
ISBN 1579129498; 9781579129491

LC 2014397031

This book, by Joann Eckstut and Arielle Eckstut, is "organized into chapters that begin with . . . [an] explanation of the physics and chemistry of color. . . . In these chapters we learn about how and why we see color, the nature of rainbows, animals with color vision far superior and far inferior to our own, how our language influences the colors we see, and much more." (Publisher's note)

"The book's dynamic design and short entries make it easy to skim, but it's likely that those intending just a casual perusal will find themselves engrossed by this terrifically entertaining and informative volume." Pub Wkly

Includes bibliographical references (p. [234]-235) and index.

536 Heat

Shachtman, Tom

Absolute zero and the conquest of cold. Houghton Mifflin 1999 261p hardcover o.p. pa $14 **536**
1. Thermodynamics 2. Low temperatures -- Research
ISBN 0-395-93888-0; 0-618-08239-5 pa

LC 99-33305

The author "analyzes the social impact of the chill factor, explains the science of cold and tells the curious tales behind inventions like the thermometer, the fridge and the thermos flask." N Y Times Book Rev

Includes bibliographical references

537 Electricity and electronics

Bodanis, David

Electric universe; the shocking true story of electricity. Crown Publishers 2004 308p hardcover o.p. pa $31 **537**
1. Electricity 2. Force and energy
ISBN 1-4000-4550-9; 0-307-33598-4 pa

LC 2004-11275

"As a storyteller, author David Bodanis is wonderful. . . . This book is directed at a general audience, but it should

be required reading for all scientific professionals." Sci Books Films

Includes bibliographical references

539.2 Radiation (Radiant energy)

Blatner, David

Spectrums; our mindboggling universe from infinitesimal to infinity. David Blatner. Walker & Co. 2012 183 p. (hardback) $25 **539.2**
1. Size 2. Science 3. Measurement 4. Spectrum analysis
ISBN 0802717705; 9780802717702

LC 2012010727

This book, by David Blatner, asks "how can we understand the world of the atom or the size of our galaxy? How do we grasp a billionth of a second or a billion years? . . . Blatner re-introduces us to six fundamental spectrums in the world around us: numbers, size, light, sound, heat, and time. Offering fascinating glimpses of hidden realities, full of comparisons, facts, and anecdotes." (Publisher's note)

Jorgensen, Timothy J.

Strange glow; the story of radiation. Timothy J. Jorgensen. Princeton University Press 2016 512 p. illustrations (alk. paper) $35 **539.2**
1. Radiation 2. Radiobiology
ISBN 9780691165035

LC 2015959168

In this book, author Timothy J. Jorgensen "explores how our knowledge of and experiences with radiation in the last century can lead us to smarter personal decisions about radiation exposures today. Jorgensen introduces key figures in the story of radiation—from Wilhelm Roentgen, the discoverer of x-rays, and pioneering radioactivity researchers Marie and Pierre Curie, to Thomas Edison and the victims of the recent Fukushima Daiichi nuclear power plant accident." (Publisher's note)

"Jorgensen's easy-to-follow and enthusiastic style will appeal to readers who are interested in the study of radiation yet have plenty of time on their hands to get to the information they seek." LJ

Includes bibliographical references (pages 411-464) and index.

539.7 Atomic and nuclear physics

Aczel, Amir D.

Present at the creation; the story of CERN and the Large Hadron Collider. [by] Amir Aczel. Harmony Books 2010 271p il $25.99; ebook $12.99 **539.7**
1. Large Hadron Collider (France and Switzerland) 2. CERN
ISBN 978-0-307-59167-8; 978-0-307-59168-5 ebook

LC 2010-14835

Aczel "has produced an excellent review of past, current, and possible future theories of particle physics and how they relate to the field of cosmology. He uses the Large Hadron Collider (LHC), the most energetic particle accelerator ever built, as a focal point for a discussion of these theories." Choice

Includes bibliographical references

Carroll, Sean

The **particle** at the end of the Universe; how the hunt for the Higgs boson leads us to the edge of a new world. Sean Carroll. Penguin Group USA 2012 352 p. $27.95   **539.7**

1. Higgs bosons 2. Dark matter (Astronomy)
ISBN 0525953590; 9780525953593

In this book "Sean Carroll takes readers behind the scenes of the Large Hadron Collider at CERN to meet the scientists and explain . . . the Higgs boson [particle], the key to understanding why mass exists. . . . The fact is, while we have now essentially solved the mass puzzle, there are things we didn't predict and possibilities we haven't yet dreamed. A doorway is opening into the mind boggling, somewhat frightening world of dark matter." (Publisher's note)

Includes bibliographical references and index.

Feynman, Richard Phillips

QED; the strange theory of light and matter. [by] Richard Feynman. Princeton Univ. Press 1985 158p (Alix G. Mautner memorial lectures) $55; pa $15.95   **539.7**

1. Light 2. Electrons 3. Quantum theory
ISBN 0-691-08388-6; 0-691-02417-0 pa
LC 85-42685

The author attempts to describe the interaction between light and electrons

"Feynman describes with accuracy, insight, self-deprecating humor, and clarity the centerpiece of modern elementary particle theory—quantum electrodynamics. . . . 'QED' will challenge the mind." Christ Sci Monit

Goldberg, Dave

The **Universe** in the Rearview Mirror; How Hidden Symmetries Shape Reality. Dave Goldberg. Dutton 2013 336 p. illustrations $27.95   **539.7**

1. Physics 2. Universe 3. Reality 4. Symmetry 5. Cosmology
ISBN 0525953663; 9780525953661
LC 2013016178

Author Dave Goldberg examines "space, time and everything in between showing that our elegant universe--from the Higgs boson to antimatter to the most massive group of galaxies--is shaped by hidden symmetries that have driven all our recent discoveries about the universe and all the ones to come." (Publisher's note)

An "informative, math-free, and completely entertaining look at the concept of symmetry in physics." Pub Wkly

Includes bibliographical references and index

Greene, Brian R.

★ The **elegant** universe; superstrings, hidden dimensions, and the quest for the ultimate theory.

[by] Brian Greene. Vintage Books 2000 448p il pa $15.95   **539.7**

1. Cosmology 2. String theory
ISBN 0-375-70811-1; 978-0-375-70811-4
LC 99-42018

First published 1999 by Norton

The author "makes the terribly complex theory of strings accessible to all. He possesses a remarkable gift for using the everyday to illustrate what may be going on in dimensions beyond our feeble human perception." Publ Wkly

Includes bibliographical references

Lederman, Leon

Beyond the god particle; Leon M. Lederman, Christopher T. Hill. Prometheus Books 2013 340 p. ill hc $24.95   **539.7**

1. Matter 2. Particles (Nuclear physics) 3. Higgs bosons
ISBN 9781616148010
LC 2013022346

The coauthors "discuss the 2012 discovery of the Higgs boson particle . . . and what's next for subatomic particle physics research. This is essentially a sequel to The God Particle, in which the titular term for Higgs boson was coined. Both descriptive and prescriptive, this new book presents enjoyable overviews of discoveries of the physical world, from molecules to atoms and subatomic particles, including a clear description of the need for huge machines to provide energy to accelerate tiny particles. . . . The authors aim to offer "coulds and shoulds," and do, including a directive thoroughly to study strong interactions in particle physics." Booklist

Includes bibliographical references and index

Lincoln, Don

The **large** hadron collider; the extraordinary story of the Higgs boson and other stuff that will blow your mind. by Don Lincoln. Johns Hopkins University Press 2014 240 p. illustrations (hardcover : alk. paper) $29.95   **539.7**

1. Higgs bosons 2. Scientific apparatus and instruments 3. Large Hadron Collider (France and Switzerland)
ISBN 1421413515; 9781421413518
LC 2013040921

In this book, author "Don Lincoln shares an insider's account of the [Large Hadron Collider's] operational history. Lincoln devotes an entire chapter to the Higgs boson and Higgs field, using several extended analogies to help explain the importance of these concepts to particle physics. In the final chapter, he describes what the discovery of the Higgs boson tells us about our current understanding of basic physics." (Publisher's note)

"Readers will be fascinated by the project's sheer mechanical challenges and the failure that caused it to be shut down and rebuilt before being operated at its design power. This engaging story will be appreciated by readers interested in the frontiers of science. Summing Up: Highly recommended. All levels/libraries." Choice

Includes bibliographical references and index

Malley, Marjorie Caroline

Radioactivity; a history of a mysterious science. [by] Marjorie C. Malley. Oxford University Press 2011 xxi, 267p il map $21.95   **539.7**

1. Radioactivity

ISBN 978-0-19-976641-3

LC 2010038979

"Malley presents a timely tale about the discovery of radioactivity, the development of our knowledge of the physical universe, and the way radioactivity has changed our world. . . . [She] manages to make the periodic table and the giants involved in its creation interesting. . . . Malley does a wonderful job of demonstrating how scientific discovery functions, as opposed to the usual approach in which facts and figures are given as tidbits along a chronology." Libr J

Includes bibliographical references

Nelson, Craig

The **age** of radiance; the epic rise and dramatic fall of the atomic era. Craig Nelson. Scribner 2014 416 p. illustrations (hardcover) $29.99   **539.7**

1. Radiation 2. Radioactivity 3. Nuclear energy 4. Nuclear physics 5. Nuclear weapons

ISBN 145166043X; 9781451660432; 9781451660449

LC 2013042192

This book, by Craig Nelson, is a "history of the Atomic Age. . . . From the discovery of X-rays in the 1890s, through the birth of nuclear power in an abandoned Chicago football stadium, to the bomb builders of Los Alamos, . . . Nelson illuminates a pageant of fascinating historical figures: Marie and Pierre Curie, Albert Einstein, Niels Bohr, Franklin Roosevelt, J. Robert Oppenheimer, Harry Truman, Curtis LeMay, John F. Kennedy, Robert McNamara, Ronald Reagan, and Mikhail Gorbachev." (Publisher's note)

"An engaging history that raises provocative questions about the future of nuclear science." Kirkus

Includes bibliographical references and index

Seife, Charles

Sun in a bottle; the strange history of fusion and the science of wishful thinking. Viking 2008 294p il map $25.95   **539.7**

1. Nuclear fusion

ISBN 978-0-670-02033-1; 0-670-02033-8

LC 2008-13135

"Ever since the first hydrogen bomb tests in the 1950s, scientists have hoped to reproduce the sun's magic in a controlled fashion, unlocking an unlimited source of energy. But the dream has been elusive. With great explanatory skill, Seife . . . explains how fusion works and why it is so hard to get power out of it. Seife reviews the parade of hubristic and sometimes comic or outright dishonest claims that fusion scientists have made over the decades." Sci News

Includes bibliographical references

Stewart, Ian

Why beauty is truth; a history of symmetry. Basic Books 2007 290p il $26.95   **539.7**

1. Symmetry

ISBN 978-0-465-08236-0; 0-465-08236-X

LC 2006-38274

"Beginning with the early struggles of the Babylonians to solve quadratics, Stewart guides his readers through the often-tangled history of symmetry, illuminating for non-specialists how a concept easily recognized in geometry acquired new meanings in algebra. . . . An exciting foray for any armchair physicist!" Booklist

Includes bibliographical references

539.72   Particle physics; ionizing radiation

Randall, Lisa

Higgs discovery; the power of empty space. Lisa Randall. Ecco Solo/HarperCollins 2013 99 p. illustrations pbk $9.99   **539.72**

1. Physics 2. Higgs bosons

ISBN 0062300474; 9780062300478

LC 2015300802

"On July 4, 2012, physicists at the Large Hadron Collider in Geneva madehistory when they discovered an entirely new type of subatomic particle that many scientists believe is the Higgs boson. For forty years, physicists searched for this capstone to the Standard Model of particle physics--the theory that describes both the most elementary components that are known in matter and the forces through which they interact. This particle points to the Higgs field, which provides the key to understanding why elementary particles have mass. . . . Lisa Randall explains the science behind this monumental discovery, its exhilarating implications, and the power of empty space." (Publisher's note)

540   Chemistry and allied sciences

Cobb, Cathy

Creations of fire; chemistry's lively history from alchemy to the atomic age. [by] Cathy Cobb and Harold Goldwhite. Perseus Pub. 2001 475p il pa $20.95   **540**

1. Chemistry -- History

ISBN 0-7382-0594-X; 978-0-7382-0594-6

LC 2001-99001

First published 1995 by Plenum Press

This history "begins with chemistry in the Stone Age and ends with current areas of interest such as superheavy elements and the polymerase chain reaction. Along the way, the coverage includes alchemy, cold fusion, and . . . topics like the contributions of Lise Meitner and Marie Lavoisier. . . . This book's light and often humorous style makes it especially appealing to the general reader." Libr J

Includes bibliographical references

The **joy** of chemistry; the amazing science of familiar things. [by] Cathy Cobb & Monty L. Fetterolf. Prometheus Books 2005 393p il hardcover o.p. pa $19   **540**

1. Chemistry

ISBN 1-591-02231-2; 1-591-02771-3 pa

LC 2004-20144

The authors cover "the material of a general chemistry course along with organic, inorganic and analytical chemistry and biochemistry; there's even a chapter on forensic chemistry. . . . They explain everything from flatulence (the chemical composition of intestinal gas) to pizza cheese (why mozzarella rather than, say, parmesan?)." Publ Wkly

Includes bibliographical references

Coffey, Patrick

Cathedrals of science; the personalities and rivalries that made modern chemistry. Oxford University Press 2008 379p il $29.95   **540**
1. Chemists 2. College teachers 3. Chemistry -- History 4. Science -- Ethical aspects 5. Nobel laureates for chemistry
ISBN 978-0-19-532134-0; 0-19-532134-0
LC 2007-48304

The author writes about the careers of such chemists as Gilbert Lewis, Irving Langmuir, Fritz Haber, Glenn Seaborg, Harold Urey, Linus Pauling, and Dorothy Wrinch.

This is "is an engaging, well-written, balanced account of 13 chemists who built modern chemistry." Choice

Includes bibliographical references

CRC Handbook of Chemistry and Physics; W. M. Haynes, editor-in-chief. 95th edition CRC Press 2014 various pagings $169.95   **540**
1. Reference books 2. Physics -- Tables 3. Chemistry -- Tables
ISBN 1482208679; 9781482208672
First published 1913. Periodically revised

A "reference book containing much-used information on mathematics, chemistry, and physics, including tables, physical constants of chemical elements and compounds, definitions, formulae, etc." AAAS Sci Book List for Young Adults

Includes bibliographical references

A dictionary of chemistry; edited by Richard Rennie and Jonathan Law. 7th edition Oxford University Press 2016 577 p. illustrations pbk $19.95 **540**
1. Chemistry -- Dictionaries
ISBN 0198722826; 9780198722823

'Fully revised and updated, the seventh edition of this popular dictionary is the ideal reference resource for students of chemistry, either at school or at university. With over 5000 entries--over 175 new to this edition--it covers all aspects of chemistry, from physical chemistry to biochemistry. The seventh edition boasts broader coverage in areas such as nuclear magnetic resonance, polymer chemistry, nanotechnology and graphene, and absolute configuration." (Publisher's note)

Greenberg, Arthur

From alchemy to chemistry in picture and story. Wiley-Interscience 2007 xxiii, 637p il $69.95 **540**
1. Chemistry -- History
ISBN 978-0-471-75154-0; 0-471-75154-5
LC 2006-33564

According to the author, this "is a combination of his two previous books, A Chemical History Tour and The Art of Chemistry, with some additions and revisions. . . . One could open the book at almost any page to learn something

about the remarkable history of the chemical sciences." Sci Books Films

Includes bibliographical references

★ **Lange's** handbook of chemistry; James G. Speight. 17th edition McGraw-Hill 2016 $199 **540**
1. Chemistry 2. Chemistry -- Tables
ISBN 9781259586095; 125958609X
First published 1934. Periodically revised

"Lange's Handbook of Chemistry, 17th Edition, is divided into six sections--general information and conversion tables, spectroscopy, inorganic chemistry, organic chemistry, petroleum and petroleum products, biomass and biofuels, and environmental science. Existing tables have been thoroughly overhauled and new tables have been added that cover the properties of coal, minerals, natural gas, oil shale, and petroleum." (Publisher's note)

541   Chemistry

Atkins, Peter William, 1940-

Reactions; the private life of atoms. by Peter Atkins. Oxford University Press 2011 191 p.   **541**
1. Chemical reactions
ISBN 9780199695126; 0199695121
LC 2011275047

The author "provides detailed descriptions of the reactions that occur in everyday life, using language that, while elevated, will be accessible for the armchair scientist. Each chapter focuses on a particular type of reaction, including: precipitation, neutralization, combustion, reduction, oxidation separately and in combination, catalysis, and more." Publ Wkly

Gray, Theodore

Molecules; The Elements and the Architecture of Everything. Theodore Gray; photography by Nick Mann. Black Dog & Leventhal Pub 2014 240 p. color illustrations $29.95   **541**
1. Molecules 2. Chemical elements
ISBN 1579129714; 9781579129712

This book by Theodore Grey "begins with an explanation of how atoms bond to form molecules and compounds, as well as the difference between organic and inorganic chemistry. He then goes on to explore the vast array of materials molecules can create." (Publisher's note)

"Readers who wish to learn more about chemistry would be better served with another work that isn't so strongly focused on photography. Those already familiar with the topic are sure to enjoy the images." LJ

546   Inorganic chemistry

Aldersey-Williams, Hugh, 1959-

Periodic tales; a cultural history of the elements, from arsenic to zinc. Ecco 2011 428p il $29.99 **546**
1. Periodic law 2. Chemical elements
ISBN 978-0-06-182472-2; 0-06-182472-0

"Because Aldersey-Williams's ultimate subject is human civilization rather than simply the elements, he gives himself room to expound on just about everything, treating the components of the table as though they were 'sorted by an anthropologist.' So his book is organized (loosely) into five sections: power (elements hoarded as riches or used to exert control); fire (elements that can best be understood by what happens when they are burned); craft (elements used to create and the cultural meaning we ascribe to them); beauty (elements used to 'colour our world'); and earth (elements that have marked the place where they were discovered in a notable way). It's an ambitious project. . . . [The book] is swollen with names, places, and long-forgotten (or simply unknown to most of us) figures, with zigzagging detours into almost every subject imaginable. It is almost more of a question of what the book does not touch upon than what it does." Boston Globe

Includes bibliographical references

Bernstein, Jeremy

Plutonium; a history of the world's most dangerous element. National Academies Press 2007 194p il map $27.95   **546**

1. Plutonium

ISBN 978-0-309-10296-4; 0-309-10296-0

LC 2006-38466

"Bernstein's book should play a useful role by helping to demystify plutonium and by encouraging interested members of the public and Congress to start constructing a more rational policy to deal with the dangers posed by this manmade element." Am Sci

Includes bibliographical references

Challoner, Jack

The **Elements**; The New Guide to the Building Blocks of Our Universe. Sterling Pub Co Inc. 2012 160 p. illustrations (chiefly color) $19.95   **546**

1. Atoms 2. Chemical elements

ISBN 023300436X; 1780971257; 9780233004365; 9781780971254

This book by Jack Challoner presents "both a concise, visual introduction to basic concepts about the atom and a short history of the elements and development of the periodic table, as well as a profile for each element organized by the appropriate color-coded periodic table grouping. Challoner has created an . . . up-to-date collection of profiles on the elements and how they affect our daily lives." (Library Journal)

"Those wishing to add to their collection of guides to the elements may want to examine John Emsley's Nature's Building Blocks: An A-Z Guide to the Elements or Theodore Gray's more recent The Elements: A Visual Exploration of Every Known Atom in the Universe for similar information and presentation. Strongly recommended for all science readers and instructors looking for supplements to their classroom texts." LJ

Gray, Theodore

★ The **elements**; a visual exploration of every known atom in the universe. photographs by Theodore Gray and Nick Mann. Black Dog & Leventhal Publishers 2009 240p il $29.95   **546**

1. Periodic law 2. Chemical elements 3. Chemical elements -- Pictorial works

ISBN 1579128149; 9781579128142

LC 2009-34931

This is a collection of "photographic representations of the 118 elements in the periodic table. . . . [The book also contains] facts, figures, and stories of the elements as well as data on the properties of each, including atomic weight, density, melting and boiling point, valence, electronegativity, and the year and location in which it was discovered." (Publisher's note) Index.

This is a collection of "photographic representations of the 118 elements in the periodic table. . . . Organized in order of appearance on the periodic table, each element is represented by a spread that includes a . . . full-page, full-color photograph that most closely represents it in its purest form. . . . [Also included are] facts, figures, and stories of the elements as well as data on the properties of each, including atomic weight, density, melting and boiling point, valence, electronegativity, and the year and location in which it was discovered." Publisher's note

Includes bibliographical references

Kean, Sam

★ The **disappearing** spoon; and other true tales of madness, love, and the history of the world from the periodic table of the elements. Little, Brown and Co. 2010 391p $24.99   **546**

1. Chemical elements

ISBN 978-0-316-05164-4; 0-316-05164-0

LC 2009-40754

"Kean's traipse among the elements leads him through a warren of subjects, as he examines how these basic building blocks have factored prominently in astronomy, biology, literature, history, politics, and even cryptozoology. With the anecdotal flourishes of Oliver Sacks and the populist accessibility of Malcolm Gladwell, but without the latter's occasional facileness, he makes even the most abstract concepts graspable for armchair scientists. His keen sense of humor is a particular pleasure." Entertainment Wkly

Includes bibliographical references

Rigden, John S.

Hydrogen; the essential element. Harvard Univ. Press 2002 280p il $28; pa $15.95   **546**

1. Hydrogen 2. Science -- History

ISBN 0-674-00738-7; 0-674-01252-6 pa

LC 2001-51708

The author chronicles "how one enduring conundrum—that of explaining the element hydrogen—has challenged two centuries of brilliant scientists. . . . In the process, he clarifies for general readers the nature of the scientific enterprise, in which elegant theories must meet the test of empirical verification." Booklist

Includes bibliographical references

Zoellner, Tom

Uranium; war, energy, and the rock that shaped the world. Viking 2009 337p $26.95; pa $16 **546**
1. Uranium
ISBN 978-0-670-02064-5; 0-670-02064-8; 978-0-14-311672-1 pa; 0-14-311672-X pa
LC 2008-29023

This is an overview of the radioactive mineral.

"Zoellner vividly conveys both the potential benefits and the harm that uranium holds for human civilization. . . . Policymakers and citizens alike need to read 'Uranium.'" Washington Post Book World

Includes bibliographical references

547 Organic chemistry

Gorman, Hugh S.

The story of N; a social history of the nitrogen cycle and the challenge of sustainability. by Hugh S. Gorman. Rutgers University Press 2012 xiii, 241 p.p (Studies in modern science, technology, and the environment) (hardcover : alk. paper) $49.95 **547**
1. Nitrogen 2. Climate change 3. Sustainability 4. Nitrogen cycle 5. Sustainable development 6. Nitrogen -- Environmental aspects 7. Nature -- Effect of human beings on
ISBN 0813554381; 9780813554389; 9780813554396
LC 2012009901

In this book, author Hugh S. "Gorman analyzes the notion of sustainability from a fresh perspective--the integration of human activities with the biogeochemical cycling of nitrogen--and provides a supportive alternative to studying sustainability through the lens of climate change and the cycling of carbon." (Publisher's note)

Includes bibliographical references (p. 209-233) and index

548 Crystallography

Holden, Alan

Crystals and crystal growing; {by} Alan Holden and Phylis Morrison; introduction by Philip Morrison. MIT Press 1982 318p il pa $19.95 **548**
1. Crystals
ISBN 0-262-58050-0
LC 81-23639

First published 1960 by Anchor Bks.

"An excellent introduction to crystallography (and, incidentally, to much basic physics) written in plain language." Libr J

549 Mineralogy

Bonewitz, Ronald

Rocks and minerals; Ronald Louis Bonewitz. 1st American ed. DK Publishing 2012 352 p. col. ill. (DK Smithsonian nature guide) $14.95 **549**
1. Rocks 2. Minerals
ISBN 0756690420; 9780756690427
LC 2012470083

"[P]acked full of stunning images that reveal intricate details and unique characteristics of each rock and mineral. . . . Us[es] close-up photographs of every specimen and profiles containing examples from all over the world [and] brings revealing key facets and details perfect for quick identification." (Publisher's note)

Chaline, Eric

Fifty minerals that changed the course of history; Eric Chaline. Firefly Books 2012 223 p. ill. (chiefly col.), ports. $29.95 **549**
1. Minerals 2. Mines and mineral resources
ISBN 1554079845; 9781554079841

This book by Eric Chaline is a "guide to the minerals that have had the greatest impact on human civilization. These are the materials used from the Stone Age to the First and Second Industrial Revolutions to the Nuclear Age and include metals, ores, alloys, salts, rocks, sodium, mercury, steel and uranium. The book also includes minerals used as currency, as jewelry and as lay and religious ornamentation when combined with gem minerals like diamonds, amber, coral, and jade." (Publisher's note)

Includes bibliographical references and index.

Chesterman, Charles W.

★ The Audubon Society field guide to North American rocks and minerals; scientific consultant, Kurt E. Lowe. Knopf 1979 850p il $19.95 **549**
1. Rocks 2. Minerals
ISBN 0-394-50269-8
LC 78-54893

"Pocket guide providing color photos and descriptions of some 232 mineral species and forty types of rocks. Includes guide to mineral environments, glossary, bibliography, and indexes by name and locality." Ref Sources for Small & Medium-sized Libr. 5th edition

Harlow, George E.

Gems & Crystals; From One of the World's Great Collections. by George E. Harlow and Anna S. Sofianides. Sterling Pub Co Inc 2015 232 p. illustrations (chiefly color) (hardcover) $27.95 **549**
1. Gems 2. Crystals
ISBN 9781454917113; 1454917113

This book, by George E. Harlow and Anna S. Sofianides, "showcases the . . . [American Museum of Natural History's] renowned collection and unlocks the science behind the dazzling properties of each gemstone species. Nearly 150 key varieties of gems and minerals are profiled, with information on their history, lore, and sources, as well as the relationships among the bewildering variety of crystals, minerals, rocks, and gemstones." (Publisher's note)

"Recommended both for its reference value and as a coffee-table book, this title will appeal to geologists and lovers of the lapidary arts." LJ

Includes bibliographical references (pages 201-205) and index.

Johnsen, Ole

Minerals of the world. Princeton Univ. Press 2002 439p il (Princeton field guides) pa $24.95 **549**
1. Crystals 2. Minerals

ISBN 0-691-09537-X

LC 2001-97695

Originally published in hardcover with title: Photographic guide to minerals of the world

The author "provides descriptive information for the identification of more than 500 minerals. . . . This book follows the standard mineralogy textbook approach in which the mineral sections are arranged according to mineral composition and structure. . . . The book's suitability as a field guide is completed by the addition of hundreds of excellent color photographs and drawings. . . . The content material is solid, and superb illustrations on high-quality paper make for an attractive volume." Choice

Klein, Cornelis

Manual of mineral science; [by] Cornelis Klein, Barbara Dutrow. 23rd ed; Wiley 2007 xxi, 675p il $150.95 **549**
1. Minerals

ISBN 978-0-471-72157-4; 0-471-72157-3

LC 2007-273750

First published 1848 under the authorship of James D. Dana. Periodically revised. Variant title: Manual of mineralogy

This is a standard introductory reference book for the use of students and collectors. It covers physical, chemical, determinative, and descriptive mineralogy, discusses mineral occurrence, association, and use, and includes both a subject and mineral index

Includes bibliographical references

Pough, Frederick H.

★ A **field** guide to rocks and minerals; photographs by Jeff Scovil. 5th ed; Houghton Mifflin 1996 396p il hardcover o.p. pa $20 **549**
1. Rocks 2. Minerals

ISBN 0-395-72778-2; 0-395-91096-X pa

LC 94-49005

First published 1953

This illustrated guide utilizes traditional identification methods and includes discussions of crystallography, mineralogy and home laboratory techniques.

Includes bibliographical references

550   Earth sciences

Childs, Craig

Apocalyptic planet; field guide to the everending Earth. Craig Childs. Pantheon Books 2012 xvii, 343 p.p $27.95 **550**
1. Earth 2. End of the world 3. Earth -- History --

Popular works

ISBN 0307379094; 9780307379092

LC 2012006012

In this book "[Craig] Childs makes clear that ours is not a stable planet, that it is prone to sudden, violent natural disasters and extremes of climate. Alternate futures, many not so pretty, are constantly waiting in the wings. Childs refutes the idea of an apocalyptic end to the earth and finds clues to its more inevitable end in some of the most physically challenging places on the globe." (Publisher's note)

Includes bibliographical references (p. 331-343)

★ **Earth**; the definitive visual guide. editors-in-chief, James F. Luhr and Jeffrey E. Post. Revised and updated ed. DK Publishing 2013 528 p. ill. (chiefly col.) (hbk.) $50 **550**
1. Earth

ISBN 1465414371; 9781465414373

LC 2013444093

First published 2003

This book, edited by James F. Luhr, presents "insight into the forces and processes that formed our environment and which continue to influence its evolution. With thousands of . . . photographs and unique visual catalogues of the features and phenomena that take place on Earth -- such as rocks, minerals, and mountains to tropical rain forests and the different types of clouds -- [it] contains the most up-to-date ideas on how our world works." (Publisher's note)

"Specially commissioned new 3-D digital artwork provides a striking, informative guide to the features of our planet, explains the scientific processes that govern our world, and looks at the complex relationship between humans and the natural environment." Publisher's note

Hazen, Robert M.

★ The **story** of Earth; the first 4.5 billion years, from stardust to living planet. Robert M. Hazen. Viking 2012 306 p. **550**
1. Evolution 2. Earth -- Age 3. Earth sciences 4. Earth -- Internal structure 5. Earth

ISBN 0670023558; 9780670023554

LC 2011043713

This book on the history of Earth, by Robert M. Hazen, argues that "'Earth's living and nonliving spheres' have co-evolved over the past four billion years. . . . Describing the 'discoveries of organisms in places long considered inhospitable [to life] - in superheated volcanic vents, acidic pools, Arctic ice and stratospheric dust,' he argues for the dating of the origin of life more than a billion years earlier than estimates based on Nobel Prize winner Harold Urey's groundbreaking experiments." (Kirkus Reviews)

Rudwick, Martin J. S.

Earth's deep history; how it was discovered and why it matters. Martin J. S. Rudwick. University of Chicago Press 2014 392 p. (cloth : alkaline paper) $30 **550**
1. Religion and science 2. Earth sciences -- History 3. Natural history -- History

ISBN 022620393X; 9780226203935

LC 2014010242

This book, by Martin J. S. Rudwick, "begins in the seventeenth century with Archbishop James Ussher, who famously dated the creation of the cosmos to 4004 BC. His narrative then turns to the crucial period of the late eighteenth and early nineteenth centuries, when inquisitive intellectuals, who came to call themselves 'geologists,' began to interpret rocks and fossils, mountains and volcanoes, as natural archives of Earth's history." (Publisher's note)

"Rudwick's descriptions of the personalities and ideas in the development of "deep history" are fascinating, well written, and novel. His effective dismissal of 'young Earth creationism' in the appendix is classic. Summing Up: Essential. All levels/libraries." Choice

Includes bibliographical references and index

Shubin, Neil H., 1960-

The **universe** within; discovering the common history of rocks, planets, and people. Neil Shubin. Pantheon Books 2012 240 p. $25.95 **550**
1. Geology 2. Universe 3. Human body 4. Petrology 5. Earth -- Origin
ISBN 0307378438; 9780307378439

LC 2012007541

This book by Neil Shubin addresses "how . . . the events that formed our solar system billions of years ago [are] embedded inside each of us. . . . Starting . . . with fossils, [Shubin] turns his gaze skyward, showing us how the entirety of the universe's fourteen-billion-year history can be seen in our bodies. As he moves from our very molecular composition . . . to the workings of our eyes, Shubin makes clear how the evolution of the cosmos has profoundly marked our own bodies." (Publisher's note)

Includes bibliographical references and index.

Williams, David B.

Stories in stone; travels through urban geology. Walker 2009 260p il **550**
1. Urban geology
ISBN 978-0-8027-1622-4

LC 2009-5609

The author "describes the mineralogy and history of some of the world's most common building materials. . . . Each chapter showcases a different stone. By describing how the stones formed and how they are used, this book reveals that natural and cultural history may lie no farther than the building next door." Sci News

Includes bibliographical references

551 Geology, hydrology, meteorology

Flannery, Tim, 1956-

Here on Earth; a natural history of the planet. [by] Tim Flannery. Atlantic Monthly Press 2011 316p il **551**
1. Evolution 2. Earth sciences 3. Earth 4. Earth -- Origin 5. Evolution -- History 6. Earth sciences -- History
ISBN 080211976X; 9780802119766

The author "expands on the proposition that humans inherently exhaust their resources, triggering all manner of ecological and societal trauma. To evaluate the idea, he rang-

es over the entirety of human existence, remarking within each subtopic he raises--for example, the Aborigines' relation to Australian ecosystems--the ramifications of human use of available natural resources." Booklist

Includes bibliographical references

Lambert, David

The **field** guide to geology; [by] David Lambert and the Diagram Group. New ed.; Checkmark Books 2006 304p il map $39.95; pa $16.95 **551**
1. Geology
ISBN 0-8160-6509-8; 978-0-8160-6509-7; 0-8160-6510-1 pa; 978-0-8160-6510-3 pa

LC 2006-48533

First published 1988

This is an "overview of the processes that forged the planet and the technologies that have revolutionized the way that scientists investigate Earth's systems." Publisher's note

Includes bibliographical references

Whitehouse, David

Into the Heart of Our World; A Journey to the Center of the Earth: a Remarkable Voyage of Scientific Discovery. by David Whitehouse (Author) W W Norton & Co Inc 2016 288 p. illustrations (some color) $27.95 **551**
1. Geology 2. Planets 3. Earthquakes 4. Plate tectonics 5. Earth -- Internal structure
ISBN 1605989592; 9781605989594

In this book, by David Whitehouse, "The journey to the centre of the earth is a voyage like no other we can imagine. . . . Our planet appears tranquil from outer space. And yet the arcs of volcanoes, the earthquake zones and the auroral glow rippling above our heads are a testimony to something remarkable happenings within the earth's core. For thousands of years, these phenomena were explained in legend and myth. Only in recent times has the brave new science of seismology emerged." (Publisher's note)

"Whitehouse takes readers on a richly rewarding journey through space and time in this scientific travelogue." Kirkus

551.2 Volcanoes, earthquakes, thermal waters and gases

Calderazzo, John

Rising fire: volcanoes and our inner lives. Lyons Press 2004 268p $22.95 **551.2**
1. Volcanoes
ISBN 1-59228-389-6

"Calderazzo climbs volcanoes, presents dramatic accounts of major eruptions, portrays people who live within a volcano's reach, and muses on the impact volcanoes have had on humankind's sense of the sacred." Booklist

Feldman, Jay

★ **When** the Mississippi ran backwards; empire, intrigue, murder, and the new Madrid earthquakes. Free Press 2005 307p il maps $27 **551.2**
1. Mississippi River valley 2. Earthquakes -- United

States
ISBN 0-7432-4278-5

LC 2004-57537

"Through four historical figures, Feldman recreates the frontier world of 1811-12, when the New Madrid earthquakes devastated the lower Ohio and mid-Mississippi valleys. . . . Synthesizing lives and times, Feldman composes a fluent, coherent narrative that culminates in the War of 1812." Booklist

Includes bibliographical references

Gates, Alexander E.

★ **Encyclopedia** of earthquakes and volcanoes; [by] Alexander E. Gates, PH.D and David Ritchie. 3rd ed.; Facts on File 2007 346p il map (Facts on File science library) pa $21.95; $75 **551.2**
1. Reference books 2. Volcanoes -- Encyclopedias 3. Earthquakes -- Encyclopedias
ISBN 9780816071203; 0-8160-6302-8

LC 2005-46619

First published 1994

"The book's entries cover information on key environmental issues, economic dilemmas, ethical concerns, advances in research and technology, organizations, and individuals who have left their mark on the fields of volcanology and seismology." Publisher's note

Includes bibliographical references

Oppenheimer, Clive

Eruptions that shook the world. Cambridge University Press 2011 392p il map $30 **551.2**
1. Volcanoes
ISBN 978-0-521-64112-8

LC 2011004246

The author "pieces together our volcanic past by connecting major historic and prehistoric eruptions to the course of human civilization. . . . A fascinating work that will engage not just volcano experts but also those with an interest in history, climatology, archaeology, and geochronology." Libr J

Includes bibliographical references

Scarth, Alwyn

Vesuvius: a biography. Princeton University Press 2009 342p il map $29.95 **551.2**
1. Volcanoes 2. Vesuvius (Italy)
ISBN 978-0-691-14390-3; 0-691-14390-0

LC 2009-925151

"Vesuvius has been central to Western civilization's unfolding understanding of volcanoes. While the detailed descriptions of historic eruptions here are valuable, if repetitious, the real strength of the book lies in the quotations from primary sources. These range from Pliny the Younger's description of the C.E. 79 eruption that destroyed Pompeii and Herculaneum, to medieval and Counter-Reformation reactions invoking the supernatural (after a brief naturalistic approach in the Renaissance), to the beginnings of a modern scientific understanding of volcanoes in the late 18th century with the work of Sir William Hamilton, the British envoy in Naples. The chronology concludes with current concerns

about the safety of the increasing population around Vesuvius." Libr J

Includes bibliographical references

Winchester, Simon

Krakatoa: the day the world exploded, August 27, 1883. HarperCollins Pubs. 2003 416p il maps $25.95; pa $13.95 **551.2**
1. Volcanoes
ISBN 0-06-621285-5; 0-06-083859-0 pa

"As a rich blend of science and history, this book is highly recommended for most public and academic libraries." Libr J

Includes bibliographical references

551.21 Volcanoes

Thompson, Dick

Volcano cowboys; the rocky evolution of a dangerous science. St. Martin's Press 2000 326p il map $26.95; pa $14.95 **551.21**
1. Volcanoes 2. Mount Saint Helens (Wash.)
ISBN 0-312-20881-2; 0-312-28668-6 pa

LC 00-26158

This describes the work of U.S. Geological Survey scientists in predicting volcanic eruptions, focusing on the eruptions of Mount St. Helens in 1980 and Mount Pinatubo in 1991

"An informative book about science's communication with the lay public." Booklist

Includes bibliographical references

551.22 Earthquakes

Dvorak, John

Earthquake Storms; The Fascinating History and Volatile Future of the San Andreas Fault. by John Dvorak. W W Norton & Co Inc 2014 352 p. illustrations $27.95 **551.22**
1. Faults (Geology) 2. California -- History 3. Earthquakes -- California
ISBN 1605984957; 9781605984957

LC 2014395154

Author John Dvorak "treats Californians and other tectonics enthusiasts to an enjoyable history of the Golden State's earthquakes alongside a bracing look at potential future ones. Dates, locations, magnitudes, and damage figures are all embedded in these stories of quakes and in the stories of those who studied them, like Andrew Lawson, the University of California geology professor who named the San Andreas Fault in 1895, and Charles Richter, developer of the eponymous magnitude scale." (Publishers Weekly)

"Although almost entirely focused on California, this is a fine popular primer on the subject, lucidly written and no more technical than necessary." Kirkus

551.3 Surface and exogenous processes and their agents

Fredston, Jill A.

Snowstruck; in the grip of avalanches. [by] Jill Fredston. Harcourt 2005 342p il $24; pa $14 **551.3**

1. Avalanches 2. Survival skills

ISBN 978-0-15-101249-7; 0-15-101249-0; 978-0-15-603254-4 pa; 0-15-603254-6 pa

LC 2005-20454

"As avalanche experts, . . . [the author and her husband] are often called upon to forecast, trigger, and teach about avalanches as well as rescue survivors—or, sadly, more often to recover remains. Fredston's decades of experience distilled into this instructive and personal narrative will leave readers with a newfound appreciation for the force, the fury, and the cold sorrow of avalanches." Libr J

Gosnell, Mariana

Ice; the nature, the history, and the uses of an astonishing substance. Knopf 2005 560p il $30 **551.3**

1. Ice

ISBN 0-679-42608-6

LC 2005-45126

The author "opens with a description of the sound and sight of a small lake freezing, expanding from there to discuss the seasonal advance and retreat of ice, as on the Great Lakes or Lake Baikal. Taking the next natural step, the persistence of ice through the summer, brings Gosnell to the 1800s origin of glaciology in Louis Agassiz's study of Mont Blanc's Mer de Glace, and subsequently into the contemporary specialty of ice cores in ice-age research. En route through the science, which Gosnell condenses from the technical literature, the author imparts eclectic information through excerpts from poems, adventure and disaster stories, and discussions of ice sports and diversions." Booklist

Pollack, H. N.

A world without ice; [by] Henry Pollack. Avery 2009 287p il map $26; pa $16 **551.3**

1. Ice 2. Glaciers 3. Greenhouse effect

ISBN 978-1-58333-357-0; 978-1-58333-407-2 pa

LC 2009-30326

"Seldom has a scientist written so well and so clearly for the lay reader. Pollack's explanations of how researchers can tell that the climate is warming faster than normal are free of the usual scientific jargon and understandable. All readers concerned about global warming and students writing papers on the topic will want this excellent and important volume." Libr J

Includes bibliographical references

551.41 Geomorphology

Streever, Bill

Heat; adventures in the world's fiery places. Bill Streever. Little, Brown, and Co. 2013 368 p. (hardback) $26.99 **551.41**

1. Fire 2. Heat 3. Arid regions -- Description and travel

ISBN 0316105333; 9780316105330

LC 2012020861

In this book, Bill Streever "explores any place hot or anything that creates heat, like Death Valley, forest fires, coal, oil, nuclear bombs, cooking, and volcanoes. . . . In this . . . companion to 'Cold,' Streever is able to mix the pop science, personal experiences, and historic asides into a . . . commentary on a subject that few people think about." (Publishers Weekly)

551.46 Oceanography and submarine geology

Ballard, Robert D.

The eternal darkness; a personal history of deep-sea exploration. {by} Robert D. Ballard with Will Hively. Princeton Univ. Press 2000 388p il maps $55; pa $18.95 **551.46**

1. Underwater exploration

ISBN 0-691-02740-4; 0-691-09554-X pa

LC 99-43072

Ballard "blends his personal experiences exploring hydrothermal vents and shipwrecks with stories of earlier deep-sea pioneers, focusing especially on the technology. . . . Ballard's volume is easy to read and will be an excellent addition to collections at all levels on oceanography, history of science, and exploration." Libr J

Includes bibliographical references (p. 315-374) and index

Carson, Rachel, 1907-1964

The sea around us. Oxford Univ. Press 2003 274p il maps $45 **551.46**

1. Ocean 2. Oceanography

ISBN 0-19-514701-4

LC 2002-29299

This is a reissue of the title first published 1951

This is a new edition of a "work originally published in 1951 and revised in 1961." (Sci Books Films)

Casey, Susan

The wave; in pursuit of the rogues, freaks and giants of the ocean. Doubleday 2010 326p il map $27.95 **551.46**

1. Surfing 2. Ocean waves

ISBN 978-0-7679-2884-7; 0-7679-2884-9

LC 2010-10193

Casey "estimates that freak waves might have a hand in sinking about two dozen large ships every year. She embarked on a five-year odyssey to meet the people who know these monsters best—from salvagers working a graveyard of ships off the South African coast to a convention of wave scientists, from researchers and mariners who have battled these beasts to surfers who roam the world in search of the ultimate thrill. Reading the 'The Wave' is almost like riding one, paddling in the expositional surf of vivid imagery and colorful description, thrown at you in ever-escalating surges." Cleveland Plain Dealer

Includes bibliographical references

Day, Trevor

Oceans; illustrations by Richard Garratt. rev ed; Facts on File 2008 318p il map (Ecosystem) $70   **551.46**

1. Ocean 2. Oceanography

ISBN 0-8160-5932-2; 978-0-8160-5932-4

LC 2006-100769

First published 1999

This volume describes the oceans of the world with regard to their geography, geology, history, chemistry, biology, ecology, exploration, relationship to the atmosphere, economic resources, and management.

Includes glossary and bibliographical references

Earle, Sylvia A.

The **world** is blue; how our fate and the ocean's are one. National Geographic 2009 303p il map $26   **551.46**

1. Oceanography 2. Marine biology 3. Marine ecology 4. Marine pollution 5. Human influence on nature

ISBN 978-1-4262-0541-5; 1-4262-0541-4

LC 2009-23972

The author "illustrates, in ways both humorous and discomforting, how our cavalier attitude toward the ocean and its inhabitants is causing our slow but certain destruction. Even more importantly, Earle offers solutions and discusses ongoing actions that have been taken to reverse this frightening cycle of obliteration. Even those who do not consider themselves environmentalists will find themselves easily caught up in Earle's heroic fight to save our 'blue world.'" Choice

Includes bibliographical references (p. 286-303)

Hohn, Donovan

★ **Moby**-Duck; The True Story of 28,800 Bath Toys Lost at Sea. Donovan Hohn. Viking 2011 402p. map (pbk) $16   **551.46**

1. Journalism 2. Oceanography

ISBN 0-670-02219-5; 978-0-670-02219-9; 9780143120506

LC 2010-33608

"When the writer Donovan Hohn heard of the mysterious loss of thousands of bath toys at sea, he figured he would interview a few oceanographers, talk to a few beachcombers, and read up on Arctic science and geography... Hohn's accidental odyssey pulls him into the secretive arena of shipping conglomerates, the daring work of Arctic researchers, the lunatic risks of maverick sailors, and the shadowy world of Chinese toy factories." (Publisher's note)

A "thoroughly engaging environmental/travel title that crosses partisan divides with its solid research and apolitical nature." Booklist

Nichols, C. Reid

Encyclopedia of marine science; [by] C. Reid Nichols and Robert G. Williams. Facts on File 2009 626p il map (Facts on File science library) $85   **551.46**

1. Reference books 2. Marine sciences -- Encyclopedias

ISBN 978-0-8160-5022-2; 0-8160-5022-8

LC 2007-45166

"The expert contributors have packed these pages with top-notch information that will be invaluable to students and reference librarians." SLJ

Includes bibliographical references

Prager, Ellen J.

Chasing science at sea; racing hurricanes, stalking sharks, and living undersea with ocean experts. [by] Ellen Prager. University of Chicago Press 2008 162p il $22.50; pa $13   **551.46**

1. Oceanography

ISBN 978-0-226-67870-2; 0-226-67870-9; 978-0-226-67874-0 pa; 0-226-67874-1 pa

LC 2007-49486

This book "assembles anecdotes from colleagues such as marine biologists, geologists and engineers. Their tales range from divers chasing parrotfish poo with plastic bags to oceanographers seeing an actual step in the surface of the sea at the edge of the Gulf Stream. In bringing these briny tales together, Prager explores some of their common themes to convey why many of us study the ocean—and why it matters." Times Higher Ed

Includes bibliographical references

Roberts, Callum

The **ocean** of life; the fate of man and the sea. Callum Roberts. Viking 2012 405 p. paperback $17; hardcover o.p.   **551.46**

1. Ocean 2. Ocean mining 3. Human ecology 4. Climate change 5. Marine ecology 6. Ocean -- History 7. Ocean and civilization

ISBN 9780143123484; 9780670023547; 067002354X

LC 2012000252

This book by Callum Roberts addresses how the ocean "has been used as a dumping ground while being indiscriminately overharvested." It also looks at "noise pollution, invasive species, plastic pollution, and the effects of climate change on reefs and sea levels as well as ocean acidification. . . . Roberts . . . provides . . . arguments against some of the technological 'fixes' some scientists have proposed." (Choice: Current Reviews for Academic Libraries)

Includes bibliographical references and index.

Stow, Dorrik A. V.

★ **Oceans**: an illustrated reference; [by] Dorrik Stow. University of Chicago Press 2006 256p il map $55   **551.46**

1. Ocean 2. Oceanography 3. Marine biology

ISBN 0-226-77664-6

LC 2004-55333

This "reference work presents a thorough overview of the physical, geological, chemical, and biological properties of the world's oceans. . . . [The author's] up-to-date and well-organized volume would make a valuable introduction to a huge field of knowledge." Libr J

Includes bibliographical references

Ulanski, Stan L.

The **Gulf** Stream; tiny plankton, giant bluefin, and the amazing story of the powerful river in the At-

lantic. [by] Stan Ulanski. University of North Carolina Press 2008 212p il map $28; pa $22 **551.46**
1. Gulf Stream
ISBN 978-0-8078-3217-2; 0-8078-3217-0; 978-0-8078-8709-7 pa; 0-8078-8709-9 pa

LC 2008-4746

This "book provides the layperson a synopsis of the physical origin, general biology, and rich exploration history of the Gulf Stream. Ulanski . . . offers a concise, engaging blend of science and history for anyone interested in learning about the general flow dynamics, the intricate food webs, and the human use and exploitation of this vital western-boundary current of the North Atlantic Ocean." Choice

Includes bibliographical references

Winchester, Simon

Atlantic; great sea battles, heroic discoveries, titanic storms, and a vast ocean of a million stories. Harper 2010 495p il map $27.99 **551.46**
1. Atlantic Ocean
ISBN 978-0-06-170258-7; 0-06-170258-7

LC 2010-15229

"Writing the history of the Atlantic Ocean — from tectonic labor pains to its lead role in modern European and American history — might be one of the more difficult tasks Simon Winchester has set for himself. . . . Luckily, the author comes armed with a knowledge almost as vast and deep as his subject, as well as a clever yet functional organizational scheme that divides his oceanic biography Atlantic into the seven ages of a man's life as proposed by Shakespeare. A formidable writer and storyteller, Winchester still gets distracted by the occasional unworthy anecdote or superfluous specificity, but for all the densely packed information in this work, the one thing it never becomes, quite appropriately, is dry." Entertainment Wkly

551.464 Tides

Aldersey-Williams, Hugh, 1959-

The tide; The Science and Stories Behind the Greatest Force on Earth. Hugh Aldersey-Williams. W W Norton & Co Inc 2016 368 p. illustrations (ebook) $50; (hardcover) $27.95 **551.464**
1. Tides
ISBN 9780393243109; 9780393241631

LC 2016018456

This book, by Hugh Aldersey-Williams, is an "exploration into the science and history behind the most mysterious, primal, and powerful force on earth: the tide. . . . He visits the Bay of Fundy in Nova Scotia, where the tides are the strongest in the world; arctic Norway, home of the raging tidal whirlpool known as the maelstrom; and Venice, to investigate efforts to defend the city against flooding caused by the famed acqua alta." (Publisher's note)

"An engaging exploration of the profound historical relationship between science and culture, written in a lively style with clear scientific explanations." Kirkus

Includes bibliographical references and index

551.48 Hydrology

Montgomery, David R.

★ The rocks don't lie; a geologist investigates Noah's flood. David R. Montgomery. W.W. Norton 2012 320 p. (hardcover) $26.95 **551.48**
1. Geology 2. Noah's ark 3. Creationism 4. Paleohydrology 5. Paleolimnology
ISBN 0393082393; 9780393082395

LC 2012015146

In this book, geologist David R. Montgomery "offers a . . . critique of creationist worldviews (including Noah's flood) . . . , reflecting on both ancient and modern debates . . . He admits that geologists have often stifled dissent and stubbornly rejected the idea that massive floods could have ever occurred, discounting such ideas as myths though there have, in fact, been many throughout human history." (Library Journal)

Includes bibliographical references and index

Pielou, E. C.

Fresh water. University of Chicago Press 1998 275p il maps $24; pa $14 **551.48**
1. Water
ISBN 0-226-66815-0; 0-226-66816-9 pa

LC 97-51562

This "is a wonderful natural history of one of life's necessities, a refreshing break from grand theory and special pleading of many a science book. . . . Sometimes Pielou gets political. . . . But the mind-boggling details always hold the attention best." New Scientist

Includes bibliographical references (p. {247}-267) and index

551.5 Meteorology

Buckley, Bruce

★ Weather: a visual guide; [by] Bruce Buckley, Edward J. Hopkins [and] Richard Whitaker. Firefly Books 2004 303p il maps $29.95; pa $27.95 **551.5**
1. Weather 2. Meteorology
ISBN 1-55297-957-1; 978-1-55297-957-0; 1-55407-430-4 pa; 978-1-55407-430-3 pa

LC 2004-303909

This is "a comprehensive academic resource with information and glorious color photographs on virtually every aspect of weather." SLJ

Logan, William Bryant

Air; the restless shaper of the world. William Bryant Logan. W.W. Norton & Co. 2012 416 p. (hardcover) $26.95 **551.5**
1. Air 2. Atmosphere 3. Air pollution 4. Environmental protection 5. Air -- Social aspects
ISBN 039306798X; 9780393067989

LC 2012013823

This environmental book by William Bryant Logan discusses air. "Air sustains the living. Every creature breathes to live, exchanging and changing the atmosphere. . . . Ignorance of the air is costly. The artist Eva Hesse died of inhaling her fiberglass medium. Thousands were sickened after 9/11 by supposedly 'safe' air." The author describes the scope of the atmospheric ecosystem and the importance of its preservation. (Publisher's note)

"For everyone who has wondered just how a 747 manages to get off the ground, luxuriated in the intoxicating aroma of a bed of roses, or marveled at a tropical sunset, Logan's meticulously researched and engagingly presented treatise is a breath of, well, fresh air." Booklist

Includes bibliographical references and index

McGuire, Bill

★ **Waking** the giant; how a changing climate triggers earthquakes, tsunamis, and volcanoes. Bill McGuire. Oxford University Press 2012 xiv, 303 p.p (acid-free paper) $29.95   **551.5**
1. Climate change 2. Natural disasters 3. Tsunamis 4. Earthquakes 5. Volcanic eruptions 6. Climatic changes -- Environmental aspects
ISBN 0199592268; 9780199592265

LC 2011278933

This book by Bill McGuire describes how "an astonishing transformation over the last 20,000 years has seen . . . not only a huge temperature hike but also the Earth's crust bouncing and bending in response to the melting of the great ice sheets and the filling of the ocean basins. . . . McGuire argues that now that human activities are driving climate change as rapidly as anything seen in post-glacial times, the sleeping giant beneath our feet is stirring once again." (Publisher's note)

Includes bibliographical references (p. 271-282) and index

Williams, Jack

★ The **AMS** weather book; the ultimate guide to America's weather. University of Chicago Press 2009 316p il map $35   **551.5**
1. Climate 2. Weather 3. Meteorology
ISBN 0-226-89898-9; 978-0-226-89898-8

LC 2008-35916

This book "provides a clearly written, profusely illustrated narrative guide to weather that affects the US. . . . Topics in this 12-chapter volume range from how rainbows are formed and what makes the wind blow, to climate change and how weather satellites work. In addition, Williams highlights profiles of meteorologists and other scientists influential in weather prediction and research, including many women and minorities. This work, with its attractive, easy-to-understand graphics, offers a useful, engaging basic introduction to a wide variety of weather-related topics." Choice

Includes glossary

551.55   Atmospheric disturbances and formations

Emanuel, Kerry A.

★ **Divine** wind; the history and science of hurricanes. [by] Kerry Emanuel. Oxford Univ. Press 2005 285p il $45   **551.55**
1. Hurricanes
ISBN 0-19-514941-6

LC 2004-.3078

This is a study of hurricanes.

"A gripping popular treatment of peril, that will have great resonance in light of recent disasters." Booklist

Includes bibliographical references

Miles, Kathryn

Superstorm; nine days inside Hurricane Sandy. Kathryn Miles. Dutton, Penguin Group USA 2014 368 p. color illustrations, color map (hardback) $27.95   **551.55**
1. Disaster relief 2. Hurricane Sandy, 2012 3. Weather broadcasting -- United States 4. Hurricanes -- United States -- History -- 21st century
ISBN 0525954406; 9780525954408

LC 2014031087

This book, by Kathryn Miles, profiles the events of Hurricane Sandy in 2012 and offers "the first complete moment-by-moment account of the largest Atlantic storm system ever recorded. . . . Sandy was not just enormous, it was also unprecedented. . . . journalist Kathryn Miles takes readers inside the maelstrom, detailing the stories of dedicated professionals at the National Hurricane Center and National Weather Service." (Publisher's note)

"Miles spends a lot of time talking not just about the storm's severity and significance (there hadn't been anything quite like it before) but also about the people who saw the early warning signs but didn't understand what they meant (one weather-forecasting center was warned the storm was coming, but the forecasted storm seemed so impossible that they dismissed the warnings as a computer anomaly). A fascinating and often moving account of a widely talked about disaster." Booklist

Includes bibliographical references and index

Sandlin, Lee

★ **Storm** kings; the untold history of America's first tornado chasers. Lee Sandlin. Pantheon Books 2013 xxv, 266 p., [16] p. of platesp ill., maps (hardcover) $26.95   **551.55**
1. Tornadoes 2. Storm chasers
ISBN 0307378527; 9780307378521

LC 2012027314

This book, by Lee Sandlin, "explores America's fascination with and unique relationship to tornadoes. . . . Drawing on memoirs, letters, eyewitness testimonies, and archives, Sandlin brings to life the forgotten characters and scientists who changed a nation--including James Espy, America's first meteorologist, and Colonel John Park Finley, who helped place a network of weather 'spotters' across the country." (Publisher's note)

Sobel, Adam

Storm surge; Hurricane Sandy, our changing climate, and extreme weather of the past and future. by Adam Sobel. HarperCollins 2014 336 p. 8 plates; color ills., maps $27.99 **551.55**

1. Weather 2. Hurricanes 3. Climate change 4. Hurricane Sandy, 2012

ISBN 0062304763; 9780062304766

In this book, atmospheric scientist Adam Sobel, "takes us through the devastating and unprecedented events of Hurricane Sandy, using it to explain our planet's changing climate, and what we need to do to protect ourselves and our cities for the future. Was Hurricane Sandy a freak event-- or a harbinger of things to come? Was climate change responsible?" (Publisher's note)

"In 28 absorbing and instructive chapters, Sobel recounts the full history of the hurricane, including its warning signs and an explanation of the weather anomalies that forced Sandy to make a sudden left turn into the New Jersey coastline. He also explores the debate about how much climate change played a role in Sandy's devastating impact and examines how we can better respond to other extreme weather events. Must reading for earth-science and weather buffs and anyone living along the vulnerable passageways of potential future hurricanes." Booklist

551.56   Atmospheric electricity and optics

Bogard, Paul

The end of night; searching for natural darkness in an age of artificial light. Paul Bogard. Little, Brown and Co. 2013 336 p. $27 **551.56**

1. Sky 2. Light 3. Night 4. Light pollution 5. Lighting -- Social aspects 6. Night -- Psychological aspects 7. Lighting -- Physiological aspects

ISBN 0316182907; 9780316182904

LC 2012027287

Author Paul Bogard presents a "blend of environmental and cultural history . . . about light pollution. As he travels the world looking for dark spaces that best reveal the night skies, Bogard considers our affinity for artificial light, the false sense of security it provides, and its implications. He studies the skies of Las Vegas and Paris, Walden Pond and Mantua, Italy. He walks with lighting designers, naturalists, and astronomers while pondering the best way to embrace the night." (Booklist)

"In this artful blend of environmental and cultural history, Bogard manages to make a book about light pollution pure reading pleasure." Booklist

Includes bibliographical references

551.57   Hydrometeorology

Barnett, Cynthia

★ Rain; a natural and cultural history. Cynthia Barnett. Crown Publishers 2014 368 p. (hardcover) $25 **551.57**

1. Rain 2. Weather 3. Droughts 4. Rain and rainfall

5. Physical geography 6. Rainfall anomalies

ISBN 0804137099; 9780804137096; 9780804137119

LC 2014034180

This book by Cynthia Barnett "begins four billion years ago with the torrents that filled the oceans, and builds to the storms of climate change. It weaves together science--the true shape of a raindrop, the mysteries of frog and fish rains--with the human story of our ambition to control rain, from ancient rain dances to the 2,203 miles of levees that attempt to straitjacket the Mississippi River." (Publisher's note)

Barnett "explores every facet of the substance. A seamless blending of personal narrative with scientific and cultural explanations makes the book both informative and entertaining." LJ

Includes bibliographical references and index

Hamblyn, Richard

The invention of clouds; how an amateur meteorologist forged the language of the skies. Picador 2002 292p il pa $15 **551.57**

1. Clouds 2. Chemists 3. Meteorology 4. Meteorologists

ISBN 0-312-42001-3; 978-0-312-42001-7

LC 2002-25152

First published 2001 by Farrar, Straus and Giroux

"A remarkable, remarkably pleasing story." Booklist

Includes bibliographical references

551.6   Climatology and weather

DeBuys, William Eno

A great aridness; climate change and the future of the American southwest. [by] William deBuys. Oxford University Press 2011 369p il map **551.6**

1. Droughts 2. Water supply 3. Southwestern States 4. Climate -- Environmental aspects

ISBN 978-0-19-977892-8

LC 2011033298

The author discusses "the untenable water situation in the Southwest. . . . While he focuses on the environmental science of heat and aridity, he also acknowledges the uncertain nature of climate variability itself. . . . With wide-eyed wonder and the clearest of prose, deBuys explains why we should care about these places, the people he portrays, and the conundrums over land and water he illuminates." Booklist

Includes bibliographical references

Dow, Kirstin, 1963-

The atlas of climate change; mapping the world's greatest challenge. Kirstin Dow and Thomas E. Downing. 3rd edition University of California Press 2011 128 p. col. ill., col. maps pbk $24.95 **551.6**

1. Atlases 2. Climate 3. Reference books

ISBN 9780520268234

LC 2011922284

First published 2006

"This atlas examines the causes of climate change and considers its possible impact on subsistence, water resources, ecosystems, biodiversity, health, coastal megacities, and cultural treasures. It reviews historical contributions to greenhouse gas levels, progress in meeting international commitments, and local efforts to meet the challenge of climate change." Publisher's note

Includes bibliographical references

Dumanoski, Dianne

★ The **end** of the long summer; why we must remake our civilization to survive on a volatile Earth. Crown Publishers 2009 311p $25   **551.6**

1. Climate -- Environmental aspects

ISBN 978-0-307-39607-5; 0-307-39607-X

LC 2009-281272

An environmental journalist discusses the possible ecological consequences beyond global warming resulting from modern human activity and describes the possibility of massive instability and climate swings, including a possible return to ice ages of the past.

"A passionate, precise account of climate change and a persuasive strategy for dealing with 'Nature's return to center stage as a critical player in human history.'" Kirkus

Includes bibliographical references

Fagan, Brian M.

The **long** summer: how climate changed civilization. Basic Books 2003 284p il hardcover o.p. pa $16   **551.6**

1. Climate 2. Civilization -- History

ISBN 0-465-02281-2; 0-465-02282-0 pa

LC 2003-13917

"This book is highly recommended for general audiences considering the implications and the challenges posed by human-induced global climate change." Sci Books Films

Includes bibliographical references

Fleming, James Rodger

Fixing the sky; the checkered history of weather and climate control. [by] James Rodger Fleming. Columbia University Press 2010 325p il (Columbia studies in international and global history) $27.95   **551.6**

1. Global warming 2. Weather control 3. Human influence on nature 4. Climatic changes

ISBN 978-0-231-14412-4

LC 2010-15482

This book "should be read by all who want a better understanding of global climate change and the debate over geoengineering our environment." Sci Books Films

Includes bibliographical references

Fry, Juliane L.

The **encyclopedia** of weather and climate change; a complete visual guide. [authors, Juliane L. Fry ... [et al.] University of California Press 2010 512 p. col. ill., col. maps   **551.6**

1. Reference books 2. Weather -- Encyclopedias 3. Climatology -- Encyclopedias 4. Meteorology -- Encyclopedias 5. Climatic changes -- Encyclopedias

ISBN 0520261011; 9780520261013

LC 2009943908

"Major sections fall under the following headings: Engine, Action, Extremes, Watching, Climate, and Change. Chapters within the sections begin with a broad overview

of a particular topic, then move on to greater detail. The regional climate guide, focusing on 43 specific locations around the world, is particularly noteworthy. ... The profuse illustrations carry the information; this title could be just the thing for visual learners." Libr J

Includes index

Goodell, Jeff

How to cool the planet; geoengineering and the audacious quest to fix Earth's climate. Houghton Mifflin Harcourt 2010 262p $26   **551.6**

1. Greenhouse effect 2. Climate -- Environmental aspects

ISBN 978-0-618-99061-0; 0-618-99061-5

LC 2009-46565

"There is no trace of climate alarmism or political advocacy here. Goodell takes a detailed look at the range of hard choices humanity faces and explores how complicated moral and ethical considerations will dictate our response. Goodell is also a skilled writer. He splices complicated ideas into pithy turns of phrase." Business Week

Includes bibliographical references

Linden, Eugene

The **winds** of change; climate, weather, and the destruction of civilizations. Simon & Schuster 2006 302p il map $26   **551.6**

1. Climate 2. Weather 3. Social change

ISBN 0-684-86352-9; 978-0-684-86352-8

LC 2005-54434

"Relatively restrained in tone, and consequently more persuasive by its sobriety, Linden's presentation of scientists' theories on historical climate change will provoke readers concerned about the implications of global warming for modern civilization." Booklist

Ludlum, David M.

The **Audubon** Society field guide to North American weather. Knopf 1991 656p il maps $19.95   **551.6**

1. Weather forecasting

ISBN 0-679-40851-7

LC 91-52707

"The opening essays provide in-depth information on topics such as clouds, snowstorms, floods, etc. About half of the book is comprised of labelled, high-quality photographs. The third section gives description, environment, season, range, and significance of each type of weather. Clear diagrams, simple definitions, and a readable text make this an excellent selection." SLJ

Lynas, Mark

★ **Six** degrees; our future on a hotter planet. National Geographic 2008 335p $26   **551.6**

1. Environmental influence on humans 2. Greenhouse effect 3. Climate -- Environmental aspects

ISBN 978-1-4262-0213-1

LC 2007-30864

First published 2007 in the United Kingdom

"In 2001, the Intergovernmental Panel on Climate Change released a landmark report projecting average global surface temperatures to rise between 1.4 degrees and 5.8

degrees Celsius (roughly 2 to 10 degrees Fahrenheit) by the end of this century. Based on this forecast, author Mark Lynas outlines what to expect from a warming world, degree by degree." Publisher's note

Includes bibliographical references

Marshall, George

✓ **Don't** Even Think About It; Why Our Brains Are Wired to Ignore Climate Change. George Marshall. St. Martin's Press 2014 272 p. $27; (ebook) $39.00   **551.6**

  1. Climate change -- Public opinion

ISBN 1620401339; 9781620401330; 9781620401347

This book by George Marshall examines why "people have difficulty accepting climate change, even when presented with mountains of evidence. He draws heavily upon interviews with scientists and policy makers, as well as with individuals who have faced the ravages of severe flood or drought. . . . Marshall concludes by pointing out that multiple interpretations of climate change contain the central reason we can ignore it." (Publishers Weekly)

"His work is a much-needed kick in the pants for policymakers, grassroots environmentalists, and the public to induce us to develop effective motivational tools to help us take action to face the reality of climate change before it's too late." Booklist

Includes bibliographical references (pages 243-246) and index.

Pearce, Fred

✓ **With** speed and violence; why scientists fear tipping points in climate change. Beacon Press 2007 xxvi, 278p $24.95; pa $15   **551.6**

  1. Greenhouse effect 2. Climate -- Environmental aspects

ISBN 978-0-8070-8576-9; 0-8070-8576-6; 978-0-8070-8577-6 pa; 0-8070-8577-4 pa

LC 2006-19901

"Important reading for policymakers, climate-change skeptics and anyone planning a future beyond the next decade." Kirkus

Includes bibliographical references

Redniss, Lauren

✓ **Thunder** & Lightning; Weather Past, Present, Future. Lauren Redniss. Random House Inc 2015 272 p. color illustrations $35   **551.6**

  1. Weather 2. Meteorology

ISBN 0812993179; 9780812993172

This book, by Lauren Redniss, focuses on weather. It "roams from the driest desert on earth to a frigid island in the Arctic, from the Biblical flood to the defeat of the Spanish Armada. Redniss visits the headquarters of the National Weather Service, recounts top-secret rainmaking operations during the Vietnam War, and examines the economic impact of disasters like Hurricane Katrina." (Publisher's note)

"This book is not simply a collection of oddments and odd fellows, but rather a genuine demonstration of weather as a phenomena and how it is fantastical on both the symbolic and systematized levels." Kirkus

Includes bibliographical references

Weart, Spencer R.

✓ ★ The **discovery** of global warming; Spencer R. Weart. Rev. and expanded ed. Harvard University Press 2008 x, 230 p.p il pbk $21   **551.6**

ISBN 9780674031890

LC 2008013675

The author "reports the history of global warming theory, including the internal conflicts plaguing the research community and the role government has had in promoting climate studies. . . . Without resorting to fear-mongering, Weart gives an informed history and offers his readers solutions to consider." Publ Wkly

551.63   Weather forecasting and forecasts, reporting and reports

Cullen, Heidi

✓ The **weather** of the future; heat waves, extreme storms, and other scenes from a climate-changed planet. HarperCollins 2010 329p il map $25.99; pa $15.99   **551.63**

  1. Forecasting 2. Climate -- Environmental aspects

ISBN 978-0-06-172688-0; 0-06-172688-5; 978-0-06-172694-1 pa; 0-06-172694-X pa

"A lively and troubling but not entirely doomsday scenario of our warmer future, which will hopefully persuade readers to pay greater attention." Kirkus

Includes bibliographical references

Monmonier, Mark S.

✓ **Air** apparent; how meteorologists learned to map, predict, and dramatize weather. {by} Mark Monmonier. University of Chicago Press 1999 309p il $27.50; pa $17   **551.63**

  1. Meteorology 2. Weather forecasting

ISBN 0-226-53422-7; 0-226-53423-5 pa

LC 98-25797

The author presents a "history of more than 200 years of weather maps, an account that embraces technological advances from the telegraph and mercury barometer to the satellite and Doppler radar." Booklist

Includes index

551.69   Geographic treatment of climate

Tape, Ken D.

✓ The **changing** arctic landscape; Ken D. Tape. University of Alaska Press 2010 viii, 56p ill. (some col.), col. maps (cloth : alk. paper) $35.00   **551.69**

  1. Alaska 2. Arctic regions 3. Climate change 4. Alaska -- Climate 5. Alaska -- Environmental conditions -- Pictorial works 6. Climatic changes -- Environmental aspects -- Alaska -- Pictorial works

ISBN 9781602230804; 1602230803

LC 2009035478

It was the author's intent to demonstrate "how the work of several generations of earth scientists can be integrated into a picture of arctic Alaska landscapes that are responding to both natural and human influences. Decades-old photos from pioneering studies of the geology, vegetation, glaciers, and landforms of Brooks Range and North Slope were used to select specific environments for change detection. . . . The author concludes that the changes are consisted with a warming climate, but the argument for warming is not as solid as the argument for the changes themselves." (Environment)

Includes bibliographical references and index.

551.7 Historical geology

Alvarez, Walter

T. rex and the Crater of Doom. Princeton Univ. Press 1997 185p il $35   **551.7**
1. Dinosaurs 2. Catastrophes (Geology)
ISBN 0-691-01630-5

LC 96-49208

This book "gets the facts across in a lighthearted, almost playful manner. But it's also solid science, a clear and efficient exposition." N Y Times Book Rev

Includes bibliographical references

Bjornerud, Marcia

Reading the rocks; the autobiography of the earth. Basic Books 2005 237p $26   **551.7**
1. Geology
ISBN 0-8133-4249-X

LC 2004-22738

"This wonderful book should be examined by anyone with a curiosity about the natural history of our planet and how one science in particular has done such an impressive job of deciphering key mysteries of its origin and evolution." Sci Books Films

Includes bibliographical references

Fortey, Richard A.

★ **Earth**; an intimate history. by Richard Fortey. Knopf 2004 429p il hardcover o.p. pa $19   **551.7**
1. Stratigraphic geology
ISBN 0-375-40626-3; 0-375-70620-8 pa

LC 2004-46470

The author "relates his walks in places that visually reveal the deep earth (Vesuvius, Hawaii, the Grand Canyon) as well as sites, which, if not so spectacular, contain puzzling elements that provoked great interpretive controversies. . . . The Alps, the Scottish Highlands, Newfoundland, the Deccan Traps of India—these are among Fortey's destinations as he explains the theory of plate tectonics, showing how the theory came to be, as well as the continents and oceans whose skein of connections it explains. This is a marvelously inviting presentation." Booklist

Includes bibliographical references

Hancock, Graham

Underworld: the mysterious origins of civilization; photographs by Santha Faiia. Crown 2002 769p il maps $27.50; pa $16.95   **551.7**
1. Prehistoric peoples 2. Ancient civilization 3. Stratigraphic geology
ISBN 1-4000-4612-2; 1-4000-4951-2 pa

The author presents theories on how "civilization rose about 17,000 years ago (rather than about 6,000) and vanished beneath a rising sea level, leaving its traces in flood myths in Sumerian and Vedic texts, in early maps of the Age of Discovery, and more plausibly, in submerged ruins. Hancock throws up a fantastic amount of data on these points in this work, ranging from his personal textual interpretations to his dives at coastal sites in Malta, India, Japan, and the Bahamas." Booklist

Includes bibliographical references

Macdougall, J. D.

Frozen earth; the once and future story of ice ages. [by] Doug Macdougall. University of California Press 2004 256p il $24.95; pa $15.95   **551.7**
1. Ice Age
ISBN 0-520-23922-9; 0-520-24824-4 pa

LC 2004-8502

The author "presents the scientific history behind ice ages, emphasizing the roles of four great scientists in the field: Louis Agassiz, James Croll, Milutin Milankovitch, and Harlan Bretz. . . . Macdougall's account promotes a welcome reasoning attitude toward ice-age research and its relevance to global warming." Booklist

Includes bibliographical references

Nature's clocks; how scientists measure the age of almost everything. University of California Press 2008 271p il $40; pa $17.95   **551.7**
1. Geochronometry 2. Geological time 3. Radiocarbon dating 4. Radioisotopes in geology
ISBN 978-0-520-24975-2; 978-0-520-26161-7 pa

LC 2007-46955

"Rich in historical titbits, this book is a delightful study of how scientists figured out analytical techniques that revealed the history of the Earth." New Sci

Includes bibliographical references

A short history of planet earth; mountains, mammals, fire, and ice. Wiley 1996 266p il maps (Wiley popular science) hardcover o.p. pa $16.95   **551.7**
1. Stratigraphic geology 2. Life -- Origin
ISBN 0-471-19703-3 pa

LC 95-46399

In "this survey of four-and-a-half billion years of Earth's past . . . MacDougall traces the rise of continents and the origins of life in each era. He discusses tectonic plates, the major extinctions and their probable causes, climate and the Ice Ages, and he speculates on the future of our planet. To compress Earth's history into a single, lucidly written volume is a major achievement." Publ Wkly

Includes bibliographical references

Richet, Pascal

A natural history of time; translated by John Venerella. University of Chicago Press 2007 471p il $29   **551.7**
1. Geological time 2. Earth -- Age
ISBN 978-0-226-71287-1; 0-226-71287-7

LC 2006-33992

Original French edition, 1999

"How old is the Earth? Mr. Richet sets out to explore humanity's attempts to answer this most perplexing of questions, which acted as a spur and a baffle to human ingenuity for 2,500 years. . . . The book is translated from the French—capably, considering how much scientific terminology it contains, but not gracefully—and . . . can be rough going. Still, 'A Natural History of Time' more that repays the effort it requires. Not only does it shed light on key advances in the history of science, from the ancient Greeks to the X-ray, it reminds us of the real heroism and nobility of the scientific enterprise." N Y Sun

552 Petrology

Coenraads, Robert Raymond
Rocks and fossils; a visual guide. [by] Robert R. Coenraads. Firefly Books 2005 304p il $29.95 **552**
1. Rocks 2. Fossils 3. Minerals
ISBN 1-55407-068-6
In this "introduction to geology and paleontology . . . [the author presents the] facts of how fossils are formed, how rocks are formed, and how plate tectonics work. . . . A science work perfectly suited for general use." Booklist

Pellant, Chris
Rocks and Minerals; A Photographic Field Guide. St. Martin's Press 2015 192 p. color illustrations $18 **552**
1. Rocks 2. Minerals
ISBN 1472909933; 9781472909930
In this photographic to rocks and minerals, "a general introduction is followed by a detailed exploration of the three groups of rocks: igneous, metamorphic and sedimentary, including their formation and occurrence, main characteristics and economic uses. . . . The second part of the book begins with an introduction to minerals, including gemstones, explaining their classification, occurrence, formation and characteristics, identification and economic uses." (Publisher's note)
"Students, nature photographers, and budding geologists will find this book both easy to use and highly informative." LJ

553.4 Metals and semimetals

Williams, Susan
Spies in the congo; America's Atomic Mission in World War II. Susan Williams. PublicAffairs 2016 432 p. illustrations, map (hardcover) $28.99 **553.4**
1. Espionage 2. World War, 1939-1945 -- North Africa
ISBN 9781610396547; 9781610396554
LC 2016936154
This book, by Susan Williams, is the "true story of the unsung heroism of a handful of good men—and one woman—in colonial Africa who risked their lives in the fight against fascism and helped deny Hitler his atomic bomb." (Publisher's note)

"While there are numerous books on the Manhattan Project, this is the first to focus on operations related to the origins of the uranium used." LJ
Includes bibliographical references (pages 313-327), filmography (page 329) and index.

553.6 Other economic materials

Kurlansky, Mark
★ Salt: a world history. Penguin Books 2003 484p il map pa $16 **553.6**
1. Salt
ISBN 0-14-200161-9
LC 2004-270006
First published 2002 by Walker & Co.
"Throughout his engaging, well-researched history, Kurlansky sprinkles witty asides and amusing anecdotes. A piquant blend of the historic, political, commercial, scientific and culinary, the book is sure to entertain as well as educate." Publ Wkly
Includes bibliographical references

Welland, Michael
Sand; the never-ending story. University of California Press 2009 343p il map $24.95 **553.6**
1. Sand
ISBN 978-0-520-25437-4
LC 2008-9084
The author "discusses the science, geology, and cultural significance of sand as a critical ingredient in so many aspects of our lives. Learn about arenophiles, sand forensics, extraterrestrial sand, Udden-Wentworth scale, Bagnold formula, and how sand shapes our environment. . . . Anyone who has walked on a beach, run up a sand dune, or built a sand castle will be fascinated by this excellent book." Libr J
Includes bibliographical references

553.7 Water

Fagan, Brian
Elixir; a history of water and humankind. Brian Fagan. 1st U.S. ed. Bloomsbury Press 2011 384 p. ill., maps $28 **553.7**
1. Water supply 2. Human ecology 3. Drinking water 4. Water 5. Water -- History 6. Water and civilization -- History 7. Water -- Social aspects -- History
ISBN 9781608190034; 160819003X
LC 2010032082
Author Brian Fagan presents "anecdotes and historical episodes showing how pre-industrial people . . . properly appreciated water, from the San hunters of the Kalahari, who see the whole world as a sometimes grudging source of the substance, to John Wesley Powell's efforts to create political divisions in the American West not based on surveyors' straight lines but on natural watersheds." (Kirkus Reviews)
"Supplying intriguing historical background, Fagan well informs those pondering freshwater's role in contemporary environmental problems." Booklist
Includes bibliographical references and index.

Kandel, Robert S.

★ **Water** from heaven; the story of water from the big bang to the rise of civilization, and beyond. [by] Robert Kandel. Columbia Univ. Press 2003 311p il maps $29.95; pa $24   **553.7**

1. Water

ISBN 0-231-12244-6; 0-231-12245-4 pa

LC 2002-31229

Original French edition, 1998

"While dense with facts and figures, Kandel's aquatic history is riveting, an exhaustive and complex examination of our most precious chemical compound." Publ Wkly

Includes bibliographical references

Solomon, Steven

Water; the epic struggle for wealth, power, and civilization. Harper 2010 596p il map   **553.7**

1. Water 2. World history 3. Water and civilization 4. Water-supply -- Government policy

ISBN 0060548304; 9780060548308

LC 2009-27500

This is "a narrative account of how water has shaped human society from the ancient past to the present." (Publisher's note) Bibliography. Index.

"Solomon's unprecedented inquiry into the history, science, and politics of water use provides fascinating and ample testimony to the need to place a higher value on water and its preservation." Booklist

Includes bibliographical references

553.8 Gems

Gem; The Definitive Visual Guide. DK, with foreword by Aja Raden. DK Publishing 2016 440 p. color illustrations (ebook) $65; (hardcover) $50   **553.8**

1. Gems 2. Precious metals 3. Precious stones

ISBN 1465453563; 9781465462121; 9781465453563

This book from publisher DK, with foreword by Aja Raden, offers a "guide to precious and semiprecious stones, organic gems, and precious metals. . . . From diamonds to sapphires to obsidian, this compendium profiles all the key gemstones and other precious materials and . . . [shows] the jewels in their different cuts, colors, and uses. . . . The stories, myths, and legends that surround the most celebrated gems and . . . [jewels] from around the world are [also] revealed." (Publisher's note)

Hart, Matthew

Diamond: a journey to the heart of an obsession. Walker & Co. 2001 276p il maps $26   **553.8**

1. Diamonds

ISBN 0-8027-1368-8

LC 2001-26348

Hart's "account of the glittering business of mining and marketing diamonds is also a story of avarice, theft, aesthetics, monopoly, and war. A thoroughly entrancing book." Booklist

Includes bibliographical references

Oldershaw, Cally

★ **Firefly** guide to gems. Firefly Bks. 2004 224p il map $14.95   **553.8**

1. Gems 2. Precious stones

ISBN 1-55297-814-1

This book "opens with extensive introductory material including history, various properties, and lore. Then, each gem is presented with text and charts of specific chemical properties. While most gems are discussed on a single page, some that are well known have longer articles." SLJ

Zoellner, Tom

The **heartless** stone; a journey through the world of diamonds, deceit, and desire. St. Martins Press 2006 293p map hardcover o.p. pa $16   **553.8**

1. Diamonds

ISBN 0-312-33969-0; 978-0-312-33969-2; 0-312-33970-4 pa; 978-0-312-33970-8 pa

LC 2005-33037

The author "probes how 'blood diamonds' are used to fund vicious civil wars in Africa; how De Beers, seeing new markets to exploit, linked diamonds to the ancient yuino ceremony in Japan and played on caste obsession in India; and how India is pushing Belgium and Israel out of the gem trade. . . . This is a superior piece of reportage." Publ Wkly

Includes bibliographical references

560 Paleontology

Eldredge, Niles

Extinction and Evolution; What Fossils Reveal About the History of Life. by Niles Eldredge; introduction by Carl Zimmer. Firefly Books Ltd 2014 256 p. colour illustrations $45   **560**

1. Evolution 2. Extinction (Biology)

ISBN 1770853596; 9781770853591

This book "recounts the work and discoveries of Niles Eldredge, one of the world's most renowned paleontologists, whose research overturned Charles Darwin's theory of evolution as a slow and inevitable process. . . . [It] chronicles how Eldredge made his discoveries and traces the history of life through the lenses of paleontology, geology, ecology, anthropology, biology, genetics, zoology, mammalogy, herpetology, entomology and botany." (Publisher's note)

"Though the text and photo captions are plagued by an assortment of typographical errors, the fossils and theories could not be presented in a more attractive, readable format. This handsome book should appeal to anyone with even the slightest curiosity about how life evolved on this planet. Highly recommended for all science collections." LJ

Fortey, Richard A.

★ **Fossils**; the key to the past. [by] Richard Fortey. 3rd ed; Smithsonian Institution Press 2002 232p il maps $55; pa $27.50   **560**

1. Fossils

ISBN 1-58834-023-6; 1-58834-048-1 pa

LC 2001-49439

First published 1982 by Van Nostrand Reinhold

In this volume, fossils "from earliest Precambrian forms onward are discussed, emphasizing evolutionary trends and extinctions, and relationships with habitat environments and geologic processes, such as volcanism and meteorite impacts, are evaluated. . . . Aspects of preservation, discovery, collection, and identification are discussed." Choice {review of 1991 edition}

Includes bibliographical references

Trilobite! eyewitness to evolution. by Richard Fortey. Knopf 2000 284p il $26; pa $14   **560**
1. Fossils 2. Evolution
ISBN 0-375-40625-5; 0-375-70621-6 pa
LC 00-34908

The author's "unabashed trilobite-centric view of the evolution of life on Earth is full of personal anecdotes and asides, but it's also full of excellent science." Libr J

Includes bibliographical references

Poinar, George O.
The **quest** for life in amber; {by} George and Roberta Poinar. Addison-Wesley 1994 219p il hardcover o.p. pa $18   **560**
1. Amber 2. Fossils
ISBN 0-201-48928-7
LC 94-3043

This is an account of the authors' search for and work with amber, a fossilized resin. The Poinars also include details of their scientific analyses of the insects trapped within this host material

This is "one of those books that educates the general reader about a scientific topic without requiring very much scientific background. Although educational, it is also highly entertaining and should be read for pleasure as much as for knowledge." Choice

Includes bibliographical references

Prothero, Donald R., 1954-
The **story** of life in 25 fossils; tales of intrepid fossil hunters and the wonders of evolution. Donald R. Prothero. Columbia University Press 2015 432 p. illustrations (cloth : alk. paper) $35   **560**
1. Fossils 2. Paleontology 3. Life -- Origin 4. Evolution (Biology)
ISBN 0231171900; 9780231171908
LC 2015003667

This book, by Donald R. Prothero, "describes twenty-five famous, beautifully preserved fossils in a gripping scientific history of life on Earth. Recounting the adventures behind the discovery of these objects and fully interpreting their significance within the larger fossil record, Prothero creates a riveting history of life on our planet." (Publisher's note)

"Of particular appeal to those who enjoy the writings of Stephen Jay Gould but ideal for anyone interested in the origins of life on earth." Library Journal

Includes bibliographical references and index

Rea, Tom
Bone wars; the excavation and celebrity of Andrew Carnegie's dinosaur. University of Pittsburgh Press 2001 276p il hc o.p.; pa $16   **560**
1. Fossils 2. Dinosaurs 3. Philanthropists 4. Metal industry executives
ISBN 0-8229-4173-2; 9780822958468
LC 2001-3336

This describes the history of the excavation of the dinosaur fossil Diplodocus carnegii in 1899 which was financed by Andrew Carnegie

"Rea pieces together countless bits of information to construct an overall picture of this period of scientific discovery." Booklist

Includes bibliographical references and index

Taylor, Paul D.
A **history** of life in 100 fossils; Paul D. Taylor & Aaron O'Dea. Smithsonian Books, in association w/the Natural History Museum, London 2014 224 p. color illustrations $34.95   **560**
1. Fossils 2. Natural history 3. Paleontology 4. Life -- Origin 5. Plants, Fossil 6. Animals, Fossil 7. Fossil hominids 8. Evolution (Biology) 9. Evolutionary paleobiology 10. Fossils -- Pictorial works
ISBN 1588344827; 9781588344823
LC 2014940275

"A History of Life in 100 Fossils showcases 100 key fossils that together illustrate the evolution of life on earth. Iconic specimens have been selected from the renowned collections of the two premier natural history museums in the world, the Smithsonian Institution, Washington, and the Natural History Museum, London. The fossils have been chosen not only for their importance in the history of life, but also because of the visual story they tell. This stunning book is perfect for all readers because its clear explanations and beautiful photographs illuminate the significance of these amazing pieces, including 500 million-year-old Burgess Shale fossils that provide a window into early animal life in the sea, insects encapsulated by amber, the first fossil bird Archaeopteryx, and the remains of our own ancestors." Publisher's note.

"From single-celled foraminifera to gigantic steppe mammoths, this volume presents a sweeping panorama of ancient life and is recommended for nonspecialists interested in paleontology or evolutionary biology.

Includes bibliographical references (page 223) and index

Thompson, Ida
★ The **Audubon** Society field guide to North American fossils; with photographs by Townsend P. Dickinson; visual key by Carol Nehring. Knopf 1982 846p il maps flexible bdg $19.95   **560**
1. Fossils
ISBN 0-394-52412-8
LC 81-84772

"This softbound field guide to fossils is divided into a section of color photographs followed by a section of detailed descriptions. It covers 420 fossils of marine and freshwater invertebrates, insects, plants, and vertebrates that are likely to be found by the amateur." Malinowsky. Best Sci & Technol Ref Books for Young People

Travels with the fossil hunters; edited by Peter Whybrow. Cambridge Univ. Press 2000 211p il $40 **560**

1. Fossils 2. Scientists

ISBN 0-521-66301-6

LC 99-30134

A collection of essays by paleontologists from London's Natural History Museum describing their work in such places as China, India, the Sahara, Latvia, and Antarctica

"The essayists give enough details of their quests to explain their presence in these places and keep science buffs entertained. . . . Heightening the impact of the stories is an abundance of beautiful, colorful photos of the places, the people, and the fossils." SLJ

567.9   Reptiles

Barrett, Paul

Dinosaurs; How They Lived and Evolved. Darren Naish, Paul Barrett. Smithsonian Books 2016 224 p. color ill., color maps (hardcover) $29.95 **567.9**

1. Dinosaurs

ISBN 9781588345820

LC 2016937682

This book by Darren Naish and Paul Barrett traces "the evolution, anatomy, biology, ecology, behavior, and lifestyle of a variety of dinosaurs. [The authors] . . . also remind us that dinosaurs are far from extinct: they present evidence supporting the evolution of dinosaurs to birds that exist today as approximately ten thousand different species. Throughout their narrative Naish and Barrett reveal state-of-the-art new findings shaping our understanding of dinosaurs." (Publisher's note)

"For those who enjoy science but haven't thought about dinosaurs in a while, this volume brings these creatures to mind in a whole new way." LJ

Includes bibliographical references (page 219) and index.

★ **Dinosaurs**; edited by John J. Meier. H.W. Wilson Co. 2011 221p il (Reference shelf) pa $55 **567.9**

1. Dinosaurs

ISBN 978-0-8242-1107-3

LC 2011007540

A collection of articles discussing dinosaurs "from their origins and evolution to their much-debated extinction. . . . Coverage includes . . . background information distilled from the fossil record as well as more speculative and theoretical material." Publisher's note

Includes bibliographical references

Horner, John R.

How to build a dinosaur; extinction doesn't have to be forever. [by] Jack Horner and James Gorman. Dutton 2009 246p il $25.95 **567.9**

1. Dinosaurs 2. Evolution

ISBN 978-0-525-95104-9; 0-525-95104-0

LC 2008-48042

"Dinosaurs could walk the earth again within five years, says paleontologist Jack Horner. It won't happen the way it did in Jurassic Park, the novel and movie inspired in part by Horner's work. No active DNA from history's big lizards is likely ever to be found, he says. But birds carry dinosaur DNA. As embryos, they sprout the beginnings of teeth, claws, and a lizard tail before certain genes cancel and redirect that growth. Horner's dream these days is to bring out a chicken's inner dinosaur by turning off those controlling secondary genes. . . . The great value of How to Build a Dinosaur is that it illuminates how the work of paleontologists has changed in the past few decades." Week

Includes bibliographical references

Larson, Peter L.

Rex appeal; the amazing story of Sue, the dinosaur that changed science, the law, and my life. {by} Peter Larson, Kristin Donnan. Invisible Cities Press 2002 404p il $26.95 **567.9**

1. Fossils 2. Dinosaurs

ISBN 1-931229-07-4

LC 2002-24207

Larson's "team discovered the largest and most complete Tyrannosaurus rex skeleton that the world had seen. Almost immediately, however, the team . . . became embroiled in a dispute with the U.S. government about who owns the fossil, during which the skeleton was seized by the National Guard. . . . The book recounts the heated legal battles but focuses primarily on Larson's adventures in South Dakota, where his group eventually found six more T. rex fossils." Publ Wkly

Includes bibliographical references

Paul, Gregory S.

The **Princeton** field guide to dinosaurs. Princeton University Press 2010 320p il map (Princeton field guides) $35 **567.9**

1. Dinosaurs

ISBN 978-0-691-13720-9; 0-691-13720-X

LC 2010-14916

"Though not a field guide to stuff in your backpack, this exciting addition to dinosaur reference is essential for high school through university libraries and is highly recommended for all students of dinosaurs." Libr J

Includes bibliographical references

Pim, Keiron

Dinosaurs the grand tour; everything worth knowing about dinosaurs from Aardonyx to Zuniceratops. Keiron Pim with field notes by Jack Horner; illustrated by Fabio Pastori. The Experiment 2014 352 p. illustrations (some color) (hardcover) $24.95 **567.9**

1. Fossils 2. Dinosaurs

ISBN 9781615192120; 1615192123

LC 2014018581

This book on dinosaurs, by Keiron Pim and Jack Horner provides "a chronological survey of the group by genus/species from their first appearances in the fossil record in the Triassic through the Jurassic and their final extinction at the end of the Cretaceous. They include information on the initial and later discoveries of parts or whole skeletons and information on many famous dinosaur collectors." (Choice: Current Reviews for Academic Libraries)

"This book provides detailed analyses of more than 300 different dinosaurs, grouped by the period (Triassic, Jurassic, or Cretaceous) in which they lived. Information is provided for each dinosaur on name pronunciation, the creature's diet and weight, where bones have been found, and when it lived. . . . This is a good, inexpensive choice for those who want the most up-to-date, comprehensive information on dinosaurs, and it is suitable for school and public libraries." Booklist

Includes bibliographical references and index

Sampson, Scott D.

Dinosaur odyssey; fossil threads in the web of life. University of California Press 2009 332p il map $29.95   567.9

1. Fossils 2. Dinosaurs

ISBN 978-0-520-24163-3; 0-520-24163-0

LC 2009-6150

"This book draws scientifically accurate pictures in a style that is accessible to researchers and general readers alike." Libr J

Includes bibliographical references

567.91   Specific dinosaurs and other archosaurs

Hone, David

The **Tyrannosaur** Chronicles; The Biology of the Tyrant Dinosaurs. by David Hone. St. Martin's Press 2016 304 p. illustrations (some color) $27   567.91

1. Dinosaurs

ISBN 1472911253; 9781472911254

This book, by David Hone, "tracks the rise of these dinosaurs, and presents the latest research into their biology, showing off more than just their impressive statistics--tyrannosaurs had feathers, and fought and even ate one another. Indeed, David Hone tells the evolutionary story of the group through their anatomy, ecology, and behavior, exploring how they came to be the dominant terrestrial predators of the Mesozoic--and more recently, one of the great icons of biology." (Publisher's note)

"Hone provides a solid meal to feed the popular fascination with these tyrant lizards, easily digestible but made from ingredients that, at least in paleontological terms, are quite fresh." Pub Wkly

Includes bibliographical references (pages 281-289) and index.

569   Fossil mammals

Lister, Adrian

★ **Mammoths**; giants of the ice age. [by] Adrian Lister and Paul Bahn; foreword by Jean M. Auel. Rev ed; University of California Press 2007 192p il $29.95   569

1. Mammoths

ISBN 978-0-520-25319-3; 0-520-25319-1

LC 2007-26369

First published 1994 by Macmillan

This book integrates "research to piece together the story of mammoths, mastodons, and their relatives, icons of the Ice Age." Publisher's note

Includes glossary and bibliographical references

569.9   Humans and related genera

Johanson, Donald C.

Lucy's legacy; the quest for human origins. [by] Donald Johanson and Kate Wong. Harmony Books 2009 309p il map $25   569.9

1. Human origins

ISBN 978-0-307-39639-6; 0-307-39639-8

LC 2008-39907

"In 1974 paleontologist Donald C. Johanson found a female skeleton 3.2 million years old that exhibited both ape and human characteristics. Johanson and Kate Wong . . . recount the stunning discovery of Lucy, and then they venture far beyond that to bring readers up-to-date on what has been unearthed since and the implications of these new finds for what it means to be human. . . . Conversational, knowledgeable, flowing logically from one topic to the next, the book is packed with information of the kind that will be especially intriguing to general readers." Sci Am

Includes bibliographical references

Pyne, Lydia

Seven skeletons; the evolution of the world's most famous human fossils. Lydia Pyne. Viking 2016 288 p. illustrations, map (hardcover) $28   569.9

1. Human origins 2. Fossil hominids 3. Human evolution

ISBN 9780525429852

LC 2016008398

This book, by Lydia Pyne, "explores how seven . . . famous fossils of our ancestors have the social cachet they enjoy today. Drawing from archives, museums, and interviews, Pyne builds a cultural history for each celebrity fossil—from its discovery to its afterlife in museum exhibits to its legacy in popular culture." (Publisher's note)

"Pyne's tales complement and flesh out the well-known narratives already associated with these fossils; her work impressively blends the humanities and science to greatly enrich both." Pub Wkly

Includes bibliographical references and index

Sarmiento, Esteban

★ The **last** human; a guide to twenty-two species of extinct humans. created by G.J. Sawyer and Viktor Deak; text by Esteban Sarmiento, G.J. Sawyer, Richard Milner; with contributions by Donald C. Johanson, Meave Leakey, and Ian Tattersall. Yale University Press 2006 256p il map $45   569.9

1. Evolution 2. Human beings 3. Fossil hominids

ISBN 978-0-300-10047-1; 0-300-10047-7

"This is fascinating stuff, not least because it drives home just how much of our knowledge about the past is based on inference." New Sci

Includes bibliographical references

Walter, Chip

Last ape standing; the seven-million year story of how and why we survived. Chip Walter. Walker & Co. 2013 240 p. $17; $26 **569.9**

1. Evolution 2. Human origins 3. Fossil hominids 4. Human evolution 5. Primates -- Evolution
ISBN 9781620405215; 080271756X; 9780802717566
LC 2012037484

In this book, Chip Walter considers human evolution. He "argues that neotony, 'the retention of juvenile features in the adult animal,' is most responsible for differences between humans and other hominids. . . . In the end, Walter posits that the next evolutionary step might be Cyber sapiens: immortal superhuman hybrids of humans and machines." (Publishers Weekly)

"An exceptionally well-written overview of man's evolutionary history as well as an accessible guide to the underappreciated field of paleoanthropology." Booklist

Includes bibliographical references and index

570 Biology

Carroll, Sean B.

The **Serengeti** Rules; The Quest to Discover How Life Works and Why It Matters. by Sean B. Carroll. Princeton University Press 2016 280 p. illustrations, map $24.95 **570**

1. Ecology 2. Science 3. Developmental biology
ISBN 0691167427; 9780691167428
LC 2015038116

In this book, "biologist and author Sean Carroll tells the stories of the pioneering scientists who sought the answers to . . . simple yet profoundly important questions, and shows how their discoveries matter for our health and the health of the planet we depend upon. One of the most important revelations about the natural world is that everything is regulated." (Publisher's note)

"Carroll superbly animates biological principles while providing important insights." Pub Wkly

Includes bibliographical references and index.

Dawkins, Richard, 1941-

Brief Candle in the Dark; My Life in Science. by Richard Dawkins. HarperCollins 2015 416 p. 24 plates; color illustrations $27.99 **570**

1. Scientists 2. Intellectual life 3. Religion and science
ISBN 0062288431; 9780062288431

In this book, author Richard Dawkins "offers a candid look at the events and ideas that encouraged him to shift his attention to the intersection of culture, religion, and science. He also invites the reader to look more closely at the brilliant succession of ten influential books that grew naturally out of his busy life, highlighting the ideas that connect them and excavating their origins." (Publisher's note)

"Though the narrative could have used some pruning, the author provides an entertaining portrait of his life and times, including the quaint cus t oms still in practice at Oxford. An impressive overview of Dawkins' life's work, written with the freshness of youthful vigor." Kirkus

A dictionary of biology; editor, Robert S. Hine. 7th edition Oxford University Press 2015 662 p. illustrations pbk $19.95 **570**

1. Biology -- Dictionaries
ISBN 9780198714378; 0198714378

"With more than 5,500 clear and concise entries, it provides comprehensive coverage of biology, biophysics, and biochemistry. Over 250 new entries include terms such as Broca's area, comparative genomic hybridization, mirror neuron, and Pandoravirus. Appendices include classifications of the animal and plant kingdoms, the geological time scale, major mass extinctions of species, model organisms and their genomes, Nobel prizewinners, and a new appendix on evolution." (Publisher's note)

Wilson, Edward O., 1929-

★ Letters to a Young Scientist; by Edward O. Wilson. Liveright 2013 256 p. $21.95 **570**

1. Science -- Vocational guidance 2. Observation (Scientific method) 3. Science 4. Biologists -- United States -- Correspondence 5. Naturalists -- United States -- Correspondence
ISBN 0871403773; 9780871403773
LC 2012051412

In this book, author Edward O. Wilson "draws on the experiences of a long career to offer encouraging advice to those considering a life in science. . . . After a prologue in which the author assures would-be scientists of their importance in our technoscientific world, he groups 20 letters into five sections. . . . In Part II, 'The Creative Process,' Wilson discusses the nature of science, the scientific method, how scientists think creatively and what it takes to succeed." (Kirkus Reviews)

570.1 Philosophy and theory

Bulletproof feathers; how science uses nature's secrets to design cutting-edge technology. edited by Robert Allen. University of Chicago Press 2010 192p il $35 **570.1**

1. Robots 2. Bionics
ISBN 978-0-226-01470-8
LC 2009037097

This book "is a fascinating introduction to the field of biomimetics, or bionics. Biomimetics refers to efforts to understand the design and complexity of natural, biological systems and the application of this knowledge to achieve useful new technologies. . . . This book, beautifully illustrated with many real-world examples and explanatory diagrams, will be a joy to read for any fan of science and technology." Choice

Includes bibliographical references

Leroi, Armand Marie

★ The **lagoon**; how Aristotle invented science. Armand Marie Leroi; with translations from the Greek by Simon MacPherson and original illustra-

tions by David Koutsogiannopoulos. Viking 2014 512 p. illustrations, map (hbk) $29.95   **570.1**
1. Biology -- History
ISBN 0670026743; 9780670026746

LC 2014021366

In this book, by Armand Marie Leroi, the author "recovers Aristotle's science. He revisits Aristotle's writings and the places where he worked. He goes to the eastern Aegean island of Lesbos to see the creatures that Aristotle saw, where he saw them. . . . He shows how Aristotle's science is deeply intertwined with his philosophical system and reveals that he was not only the first biologist, but also one of the greatest." (Publisher's note)

"Leroi credits Aristotle with the most basic tenet of empirical science--to understand the world, look first and then try to explain what you see--but resists crediting him with textually unsupported prescience, which highlights beautifully the fact that ideas can be self-consistent, elegant, yet entirely wrong." Pub Wkly

Includes bibliographical references and index

Lovelock, James

The **ages** of Gaia; a biography of our living earth. Norton 1988 xx, 252p il hardcover o.p. pa $13.95   **570.1**
1. Biosphere 2. Life (Biology) 3. Gaia hypothesis 4. Biology -- Philosophy
ISBN 0-393-31239-9 pa

LC 87-36567

"Gaia is the Greek goddess of the earth. For James Lovelock she is the embodiment of a hypothesis: the earth is not merely the abode of life but is a single living organism. He proposes that all living species are components of that organism, as cells are components of the human body," N Y Times Book Rev

Includes bibliographical references

Margulis, Lynn

What is life? foreword by Niles Eldredge. University of California Press 2000 288p il pa $24.95   **570.1**
1. Life (Biology) 2. Life -- Origin 3. Biological diversity 4. Biology -- Philosophy
ISBN 0-520-22021-8

LC 00-25833

First published 1995 by Simon & Schuster

"Continuing Margulis's contention that organelles within cells, such as mitochondria, were originally free-living organisms that fused with others to form complex cells and bodies, the authors extend this concept to the Earth as a superorganism. Although following traditional evolutionary pathways, the authors argue that life has played a role in its own evolution." Choice

Includes bibliographical references

Thomas, Lewis

The **lives** of a cell; notes of a biology watcher. Viking 1974 153p hardcover o.p. pa $13   **570.1**
1. Biology -- Philosophy
ISBN 0-14-004743-3 pa

In this collection of twenty-nine short essays "the author does not confine his scientist's eye to a microscope. He

takes a much wider view of the world, looking at insect behavior and the possibility of intelligent life in outer space or bird songs and the evolution of language. He also offers a modest proposal for saving ourselves from nuclear self-destruction." Time

Includes bibliographical references

Yoon, Carol Kaesuk

Naming nature; the clash between instinct and science. W.W. Norton 2009 344p il $27.95   **570.1**
1. Names 2. Biology -- Classification
ISBN 978-0-393-06197-0; 0-393-06197-3

LC 2009-14332

This is "a wondrous history of taxonomy—the science of ordering and naming living things—and how it has disconnected us from the natural world. . . . Yoon is an outstanding science writer who takes a seemingly dull topic and rivets unsuspecting readers to the page. Superb." Kirkus

Includes bibliographical references

570.9   History, geographic treatment, biography

Gerald, Michael C.

The **Biology** Book; From the Origin of Life to Epigenetics, 250 Milestones in the History of Biology. by Michael C. Gerald, with Gloria E. Gerald. Sterling Pub Co Inc 2015 528 p. color illustrations $29.95   **570.9**
1. Biology
ISBN 1454910682; 9781454910688

This book on biology, by Michael C. Gerald, "introduce[s] readers to every major subdiscipline, including cell theory, genetics, evolution, physiology, thermodynamics, molecular biology, and ecology. With information on such varied topics as paleontology, pheromones, nature vs. nurture, DNA fingerprinting, bioenergetics, and so much more, this lively collection will engage everyone who studies and appreciates the life sciences." (Publisher's note)

"Well suited to reference collections in secondary schools; also an optimal pick for general readers with an interest in biology or the history of science." LJ

571   Internal biological processes and structures

Roach, Mary, 1959-

★ **Packing** for Mars; the curious science of life in the void. W.W. Norton 2010 334p il   **571**
1. Space biology
ISBN 0-393-06847-1; 978-0-393-06847-4

LC 2010-17113

This book examines space travel and life without gravity. (Publisher's note)

The author "explores the organic aspects of the space program, such as the dangerous bane of space motion sickness and the challenges of space hygiene. . . . She devotes one chapter to space food and another to zero-gravity elimination, which is a serious matter, even with a term like 'fecal popcorning.' An impish and adventurous writer with a gleefully inquisitive mind and a standup comic's timing, Roach celebrates human ingenuity (the odder the better), and calls for us to marshal our resources, unchain our imaginations, and start packing for Mars." Booklist

Includes bibliographical references

Toomey, David

Weird Life; The Search for Life That Is Very, Very Different from Our Own. David Toomey. 1st ed. W W Norton & Co Inc 2013 288 p. ill pbk $15.95; (hardcover) $25.95 **571**

1. Life 2. Ecology 3. Organisms 4. Life (Biology) 5. Adaptation (Biology) 6. Extreme environments 7. Life on other planets 8. Curiosities and wonders
ISBN 9780393348262; 0393071588; 9780393071580
LC 2012042391

This book looks at living organisms. The "author begins by describing 'extremophiles,' which thrive in wildly harsh conditions: chemical hot springs, inside sea ice, . . . or at the ocean's bottom. Having dealt with creatures that, however weird, exist, he proceeds to even stranger life that may exist on Earth, the planets, elsewhere throughout the universe, and in the minds of writers and philosophers. Along the way, he addresses surprisingly difficult questions, such as how to define life." (Kirkus)

"Toomey manages to make this panoply of life forms at once strange and familiar, and in doing so will entrance his readers." LJ

Includes bibliographical references and index.

571.7   Biological control and secretions

Foster, Russell G.

Rhythms of life; the biological clocks that control the daily lives of every living thing. Yale University Press 2004 276p il $30; pa $18 **571.7**

1. Biological rhythms
ISBN 0-300-10574-6; 978-0-300-10574-2; 0-300-10969-5 pa; 978-0-300-10969-6 pa
LC 2004-105609

The authors "survey the biological clocks that dictate circadian rhythms, the daily cycles that affect creatures from cockroaches to humans. . . . Biology buffs will marvel at the fascinating material." Publ Wkly

Includes bibliographical references

571.8   Reproduction, development, growth

Carroll, Sean B.

Endless forms most beautiful; the new science of evo devo and the making of the animal kingdom. with illustrations by Jamie W. Carroll, Josh P. Klaiss, Leanne M. Olds. W.W. Norton & Co. 2005 350p il $25.95 **571.8**

1. Evolution
ISBN 0-393-06016-0
LC 2004-29388

The author's "highly detailed and well-illustrated technical discussions are enriched by his appreciation for the philosophical, aesthetic, and ethical implications of the biologi-

cal wonders he decodes, adding up to a vital and enjoyable introduction to a field with profound implications." Booklist

Includes bibliographical references

Haycock, David Boyd

Mortal coil; a short history of living longer. Yale University Press 2008 308p il **571.8**

1. Aging 2. Longevity 3. Death 4. Medicine -- Philosophy 5. Immortality (Philosophy)
ISBN 0-300-11778-7; 9780300117783
LC 2007-35341

This book "explores the medical, scientific, and philosophical theories behind the quest for the prolongation of human life. [According to Haycock], it was a conundrum that intrigued Sir Francis Bacon and underpinned the scientific revolution; ideas of ultimate perfectibility, indefinite progress, and worldly rather than heavenly immortality fed directly into the spirit of the Enlightenment and even further into the nineteenth and twentieth centuries. In today's world of genetic research, cryonics, and nanotechnology, we still seek the same elusive philosopher's stone." (Publisher's note) Index.

This book is "fully successful in managing to drum up excitement for the future of human development while steering clear of propaganda." PopMatters

Includes bibliographical references

572   Biochemistry

Finkel, Elizabeth

The **Genome** Generation; by Elizabeth Finkel. Melbourne University Publishing 2012 256 p. $32.95 **572**

1. Genomes 2. Evolution 3. Medical technology
ISBN 0522856470; 9780522856477

This book, by Elizabeth Finkel, covers revolutionary genetic developments in areas as diverse as medicine, agriculture, and evolution. From Botswana to Boston and from Australia to Mexico, the contributors to this work reveal what it means to be part of the genome generation. [It answers questions] such as What have we learned about evolution? How has it changed the way we practice medicine, grow crops, and breed livestock? and Is the genomic revolution an overhyped flop?" (Publisher's note)

McFadden, Johnjoe

Life on the Edge; The Coming of Age of Quantum Biology. Jim Al-Khalili and Johnjoe Macfadden. Random House Inc 2015 368 p. illustrations, map $28 **572**

1. Life -- Origin 2. Quantum theory
ISBN 0307986810; 9780307986818
LC 2015018948

In this book on quantum biology by Jim Al-Khalili and Johnjoe McFadden, "by explaining the fundamentals of quantum mechanics, and exploring recent theories and findings, they aim to convince the reader that quantum effects are more than simply the deep substrate on which biology exists--without recourse to a single equation." (New Scientist)

"Of interest to readers curious about the inner workings of life; suitable for public and undergraduate academic libraries." LJ

Morton, Oliver

★ **Eating** the sun; how plants power the planet. HarperCollins 2008 457p il $28.95 **572**
1. Photosynthesis
ISBN 978-0-00-716364-9; 0-00-716364-9
LC 2008-23433

First published 2007 in the United Kingdom

This book "is a work of flowing prose that makes vivid why our leafy nub of cosmic dust, swirling around an average star, is an extraordinarily beautiful and rare place to reside in the universe." Christ Sci Monit

Includes bibliographical references

Wilcox, Christie

Venomous; How Earth's Deadliest Creatures Mastered Biochemistry. Christie Wilcox. Scientific American/Farrar, Straus and Giroux 2016 256 p. illustrations (hardcover) $26 **572**
1. Biochemistry 2. Poisonous animals 3. Venom
ISBN 9780374283377; 9780374712211
LC 2016001951

In this book, "biologist Christie Wilcox investigates and illuminates the animals of our nightmares. . . . She reveals just how venoms function and what they do to the human body. With Wilcox as our guide, we encounter a jellyfish with tentacles covered in stinging cells that can kill humans in minutes; a two-inch caterpillar with toxic bristles that trigger hemorrhaging; and a stunning blue-ringed octopus capable of inducing total paralysis." (Publisher's note)

"Whether she's discussing snakes and pufferfish or Komodo dragons and spiders—not to mention octopuses, snails, platypuses, and bees—Wilcox relates technical biochemical and physiological information in a manner that is accessible and enjoyable. " Pub Wkly

Includes bibliographical references and index

572.8 Biochemical genetics

Arney, Kat

Herding Hemingway's Cats; Understanding How Our Genes Work. Kat Arney. St. Martin's Press 2016 288 p. (hardcover) $27 **572.8**
1. Genetics
ISBN 1472910044; 9781472910042

This book, by Kat Arney, is "a survey of recent research and thinking on genes. What are genes, asks science writer Arney, and what do they do? . . . Genetic knowledge has the power to save us, she writes at the beginning of the book. Of course, it's not nearly that simple, but by the end of the book, Arney has arrived at a simplified definition of a gene." (Kirkus Reviews)

"A robust, bouncy, pellucid introduction to DNA and genetics." Kirkus

Includes bibliographical references (pages [263]-279) and index.

Carroll, Sean B.

★ **The making** of the fittest; DNA and the ultimate forensic record of evolution. with illustrations by Jamie W. Carroll and Leanne M. Olds. W.W. Norton & Co. 2006 301p il map $25.95 **572.8**
1. DNA 2. Evolution
ISBN 978-0-393-06163-5; 0-393-06163-9
LC 2006-17197

The author presents "discoveries gathered from DNA evidence that confirm Charles Darwin's theory of evolution 'beyond any reasonable doubt.' . . . Readers will gain insight into the evolutionary process and expand their knowledge of how the 'fittest' species were made, from fish that live in subfreezing water to birds that communicate via ultraviolet colors." Libr J

Includes bibliographical references

Cobb, Matthew

Life's Greatest Secret; The Race to Crack the Genetic Code. Matthew Cobb. Basic Books 2015 464 p. 16 plates; illustrations $29.99 **572.8**
1. DNA 2. Genetic code 3. Life -- Origin
ISBN 0465062679; 9780465062676

Author Matthew Cobb presents "the story of the discovery and cracking of the genetic code, the thing that ultimately enables a spiraling molecule to give rise to the life that exists all around us. Cobb gives the full and rich account of the cooperation and competition between the eccentric characters--mathematicians, physicists, information theorists, and biologists--who contributed to this revolutionary new science." (Publisher's note)

"Like Cobb's other titles, this scholarly work reflects extensive research and draws upon primary documents. Upper-level students and researchers in biology or the history of science are best equipped to appreciate this detailed book. Other readers should consider Michel Morange's A History of Molecular Biology." LJ

Francis, Richard C.

Epigenetics; the ultimate mystery of inheritance. W.W. Norton 2011 234p il $25.95 **572.8**
1. Genetics 2. Adaptation (Biology)
ISBN 978-0-393-07005-7; 0-393-07005-0
LC 2011-00696

The author "sets out to dethrone the notion that genes are the 'directors' of the 'plays' that are our lives, orchestrating our development and determining our risk for disease and sundry physical and behavioral traits. Yes, genes are important, writes the author, but they are subject to regulation by forces that can turn them on or off, sometimes for a lifetime, sometimes across generations. These forces can come via the cell housing of the genes, other parts of the body or the environment, in each instance initiating the actions of chemicals that bind (or unbind) one or more parts of a gene, preventing (or activating) its transcription. This is an 'epigenetic' process—epigenetics is the science that studies the ways in which DNA can undergo long-term regulatory changes that do not involve mutations of the genes themselves. To illustrate, Francis provides a dizzying array of examples." Kirkus

Includes bibliographical references

Kean, Sam

The **violinist's** thumb; and other lost tales of love, war, and genius, as written by our genetic code. Sam Kean. Little, Brown and Co. 2012 ix, 401 p.p (hardback) $25.99   **572.8**

1. DNA 2. Genetics 3. Human genome 4. Behavior genetics 5. Human genetics -- Miscellanea

ISBN 0316182311; 9780316182317

LC 2012007029

In this book, author Sam Kean "attempts to take the mystery out of DNA by explaining its structure, its historical impact, and how the science of genetics continues to influence our lives. A good portion of the book examines how modern genetic breakthroughs have helped to explain our evolutionary and historical past. . . . The latter part of the book concentrates on what the future may hold as computer technology and our base of genetic knowledge expands." (Library Journal)

Includes bibliographical references and index.

Segrè, Gino

Ordinary geniuses; Max Delbruck, George Gamow, and the origins of genomics and big bang cosmology. Gino Segrè. Viking 2011 xxi, 330 p.p $27.95   **572.8**

1. Physicists -- United States -- Biography 2. Molecular biologists -- United States -- Biography

ISBN 9780670022762; 0670022764

LC 2011009309

The author "explores the extraordinary lives and scientific accomplishments of two far-from-ordinary men, Max Delbrück and George Gamow. . . . An exuberant dual biography that integrates developments in quantum physics, cosmology and genetics since the 1920s with the lives of these two scientists." Kirkus

Includes bibliographical references (p. 309-318) and index

Sulston, John

The **common** thread; a story of science, politics, ethics, and the human genome. [by] John Sulston, Georgina Ferry. Joseph Henry Press 2002 310p il $24.95   **572.8**

1. Human Genome Project

ISBN 0-309-08409-1

LC 2002-14007

The author gives an "account of the excitement, hard work, vision, and daring needed to move from worm biology to recommending sequencing of the human genome, while senior and influential colleagues argued vigorously against it. He speaks forcefully of the necessity of keeping the sequence public and freely available. . . . {This title is} recommended for almost any library, particularly those with readers willing to go beyond sound bites and media hype." Libr J

Includes bibliographical references

Wagner, Andreas

Arrival of the fittest; the hidden mechanism of evolution. Andreas Wagner. Current 2014 304 p. illustrations $27.95   **572.8**

1. Evolution 2. Natural selection 3. Evolutionary genetics

ISBN 1591846463; 9781591846468

LC 2014009774

In this book "evolutionary biologist Andreas Wagner draws on over fifteen years of research to present the missing piece in [Charles] Darwin's theory. Using experimental and computational technologies that were heretofore unimagined, he has found that adaptations are not just driven by chance, but by a set of laws that allow nature to discover new molecules and mechanisms in a fraction of the time that random variation would take." (Publisher's note)

"A book of startling congruencies, insightful flashes and an artful enthusiasm that delivers knowledge from the inorganic page to our organic brains." Kirkus

Includes bibliographical references and index

Watson, James D., 1928-

★ The **annotated** and illustrated double helix; James D. Watson; edited by Alexander Gann & Jan Witkowski. Simon & Schuster 2012 345 p. (hardcover) $30   **572.8**

1. DNA 2. Genetic Code 3. Molecular Biology

ISBN 1476715491; 9781476715490; 9781476715506; 9781476715513

LC 2012037483

This book, by James D. Watson, Alexander Gann and Jan Witkowski, was "published to mark the 50th anniversary of the Nobel Prize for Watson and Crick's discovery of the structure of DNA, an annotated and illustrated edition of . . , his 1968 memoir, 'The Double Helix,' the brash young scientist James Watson chronicled the drama of the race to identify the structure of DNA, a discovery that would usher in the era of modern molecular biology." (Publisher's note)

"Numerous appendices include a chapter about his Nobel Prize experiences, the first letters about the double helix, a previously unpublished chapter, and reviews of the original edition. Watson strikes a balance between science for the layman and science for the scientist, resulting in a memoir that will hold the interest of a broad, scientifically-minded audience." Pub Wkly

Includes bibliographical references and index

573.7   Musculoskeletal system

Winchester, Simon

Skulls; An Exploration of Alan Dudley's Curious Collection. Black Dog & Leventhal Pub 2012 240 p. $29.95   **573.7**

1. Skull

ISBN 1579129129; 9781579129125

This book by Simon Winchester focuses on the "story of skulls, both human and animal, from every perspective imaginable: historical, biographical, cultural, and iconographic. . . . At the center of 'Skulls' is a . . . never-before-seen-in-any-capacity visual array of the skulls of more than 300 animals. . . . The skulls are from the collection of Alan Dudley, a British collector and owner of what is probably the largest and most complete private collection of skulls in the world." (Publisher's note)

573.8 Nervous and sensory systems

Hughes, Howard C.

Sensory exotica; a world beyond human experience. MIT Press 1999 345p $40; pa $18.95 **573.8**
1. Senses and sensation 2. Comparative physiology
ISBN 0-262-08279-9; 0-262-58204-X pa

LC 98-51875

This is a compendium of stories and information regarding the vast array of sensory systems that are utilized by different species, ranging from insects to aquatic mammals to humans. . . . Hughes does an excellent job of presenting the facts and the science behind the vast array of sensory systems." Sci Books Films

Includes bibliographical references and index

Iacoboni, Marco

Mirroring people; the new science of how we connect with others. Farrar, Straus and Giroux 2008 308p il $25 **573.8**
1. Nervous system
ISBN 978-0-374-21017-5; 0-374-21017-9

LC 2007-47322

The author introduces "readers to the world of mirror neurons and what they imply about human empathy, which, the author says, underlies morality. . . . Iacoboni's expansive style and clear descriptions make for a solid introduction to cutting-edge neurobiology." Publ Wkly

Includes bibliographical references

575.5 Roots and leaves

Vogel, Steven, 1940-2015

The life of a leaf; Steven Vogel. The University of Chicago Press 2012 xi, 303 p.p (hardcover : alkaline paper) $35 **575.5**
1. Leaves 2. Leaves -- Growth 3. Leaves -- Physiology
ISBN 0226859398; 9780226859392

LC 2011037295

In this book, Steven Vogel "demonstrates how a scientist can unite micro and macro perspectives in looking at the natural world. Using the leaf of a plant as his model system of life, he explores aspects of structure, function, and physiology while embedding specific questions in a broader evolutionary context. Thus, as we learn how a leaf . . . uses various strategies to maintain appropriate water balance, we also learn why these strategies are important." (Publishers Weekly)

Includes bibliographical references (pages 287-293) and index

576 General and external biological phenomena

Dawkins, Richard

★ The selfish gene; 30th anniversary ed; Oxford University Press 2006 xxiii, 360p il pa $15.95 **576**
1. Genetics 2. Evolution
ISBN 978-0-19-929115-1; 0-19-929115-2 pa

LC 2007-271478

First published 1976

The author examines evolution and contends that genes that benefit individual members of a species will be passed on to future generations, rather than those which may benefit the entire group

Includes bibliographical references

576.5 Genetics

Endersby, Jim

A guinea pig's history of biology. Harvard University Press 2007 499p il $27.95; pa $18.95 **576.5**
1. Genetics 2. Heredity 3. Biology -- History
ISBN 978-0-674-02713-8; 0-674-02713-2; 978-0-674-03227-9 pa; 0-674-03227-6 pa

LC 2007-20824

"This book would be of interest to anyone fascinated or intrigued by genetics or biological research, as well as any professional or lay student of history and science." Sci Books Films

Includes bibliographical references

Henig, Robin Marantz

★ The monk in the garden: how Gregor Mendel and his pea plants solved the mystery of inheritance. Houghton Mifflin 2000 292p il $24; pa $14 **576.5**
1. Geneticists
ISBN 0-395-97765-7; 0-618-12741-0 pa

LC 00-24341

The author explores "Mendel's personality and experiments. The latter lasted but a few years in the 1850s and 1860s, ending when Mendel became the abbot of his monastery in what is now Brno in the Czech Republic. Henig crisply conveys how the laws of inheritance that Mendel derived from his statistical analysis remained unnoticed until several botanists who discovered them independently in 1900 also learned that Mendel found them first. This biography itself rediscovers a scientist often mentioned but insufficiently known." Booklist

Knight, Jeffrey A.

★ Genetics & inherited conditions; editor, Jeffrey A. Knight. Salem Press 2010 3v il (Salem health) set $395 **576.5**
1. Reference books 2. Genetics -- Encyclopedias 3. Medical genetics -- Encyclopedias
ISBN 978-1-587-65650-7; 1-587-65650-7

LC 2010-5289

First published 1999 with title: Encyclopedia of genetics

"The subjects covered include all aspects of genetics, such as diseases, biology, genetic engineering, social issues, and more. . . . Articles covering diseases and syndromes include such information as definition, risk factors, etiology and genetics, symptoms, screening and diagnosis, treatment and therapy, and prevention and outcomes. For other types of articles, essays are preceded by a brief summary of the significance of the topic and definitions of key terms." Booklist

Includes bibliographical references

Monosson, Emily

Unnatural selection; how we are changing life, gene by gene. Emily Monosson. Island Press 2014 232 p. (cloth : alk. paper) $30   **576.5**

1. Pollution 2. Natural selection 3. Pesticides and wildlife

ISBN 1610914988; 1610914996; 9781610914987; 9781610914994

                 LC 2014939900

This book by Emily Monosson presents "evidence of how human activities drive evolution for the unintended benefit of certain organisms . . . . In part 1, she uses case studies to investigate the anthropogenic selective pressures that cause unnatural selection in pest and disease organisms. . . . . In part 2, she investigates the impacts of pollutants on natural selection of organisms in the wild." (Choice: Current Reviews for Academic Libraries)

"The author stresses how some organisms have the genetic diversity to evolve successfully, and others lack the genes to adapt. She asserts that early life evolved in a toxic, chaotic environment that left behind highly adaptive traits. In effect, many organisms can survive the changes. However, Monosson also cautions that unnatural evolution can lead to a future world in which new biodiversity is not conducive to human survival." Choice

576.8   Evolution

Ayala, Francisco Jose, 1934-

Darwin's gift to science and religion. Joseph Henry Press 2007 237p il map $24.95   **576.8**

1. Evolution 2. Creationism 3. Naturalists 4. Natural selection 5. Travel writers 6. Writers on science 7. Evolution (Biology) 8. Intelligent design (Teleology)

ISBN 0-309-10231-6; 978-0-309-10231-5

                 LC 2007-05821

"With the publication in 1859 of On the Origin of Species by Means of Natural Selection, Charles Darwin established evolution. . . . [Francisco Ayala offers] explanations of the science [and] reviews the history that led us to ratify Darwin's theories." (Publisher's note)

"This elegant book provides the single best introduction to Darwin and the development of evolutionary biology now available." Publ Wkly

Includes bibliographical references

Barnosky, Anthony D.

Dodging extinction; power, food, money and the future of life on Earth. Anthony D. Barnosky. University of California Press 2014 256 p. (cloth : alk. paper) $29.95   **576.8**

1. Human ecology 2. Mass extinctions 3. Human influence on nature 4. Extinction (Biology) 5. Conservation of natural resources

ISBN 0520274377; 9780520274372

                 LC 2013048773

In this book, by Anthony D. Barnosky, "weaves together evidence from the deep past and the present to alert us to the looming Sixth Mass Extinction and to offer a practical, hopeful plan for avoiding it. . . . He presents compelling evidence that unless we rethink how we generate the power we

use to run our global ecosystem, where we get our food, and how we make our money, we will trigger what would be the sixth great extinction on Earth, with dire consequences." (Publisher's note)

"The author is an optimist who suggests a way through the present crisis: implement reasonable and responsible resource management and sustainable agricultural and energy practices along with habitat restoration and conservation biology. It can be done. This is a must read for college students and a well-informed citizenry. Summing Up: Essential. All levels/libraries." Choice.

Includes bibliographical references and index

Billings, Lee

Five billion years of solitude; the search for life among the stars. by Lee Billings. Current 2013 304 p. $27.95   **576.8**

1. Universe 2. Life -- Origin 3. Extrasolar planets 4. Life on other planets

ISBN 1617230065; 9781617230066

                 LC 2013017672

This book presents an "overview of the still-evolving field of 'exoplanetary' research (discovery and characterization of planets orbiting other stars). Early dreams that we would locate and visit intelligent, technologically sophisticated beings elsewhere in space have been tempered as declining governmental funding has restricted our planet hunting." (Library Journal)

"A great outline of the subject, bringing what's often treated as science fiction down to Earth, where it can be understood." Kirkus

Includes bibliographical references and index

Browne, Janet

★ **Darwin's** Origin of species; a biography. Atlantic Monthly Press 2007 174p (Books that changed the world) hardcover o.p. pa $14   **576.8**

1. Naturalists 2. Travel writers 3. Writers on science

ISBN 0-87113-953-7; 978-0-87113-953-5; 0-8021-4346-6 pa; 978-0-8021-4346-4 pa

                 LC 2007-275116

"This excellent introduction is highly recommended for all readers who want to better understand the heated debates that this book still causes today." Publ Wkly

Includes bibliographical references

Byrne, Eugene

Darwin; a graphic biography. by Eugene Byrne; illustrated by Simon Gurr. Smithsonian Books 2013 96 p. ill. (paperback) $9.95   **576.8**

1. Evolution 2. Graphic novels 3. Natural selection -- Comic books, strips, etc 4. Evolution (Biology) -- Comic books, strips, etc

ISBN 1588343529; 9781588343529

                 LC 2012951786

This work of graphic nonfiction by Eugene Byrne and Simon Gurr presents a "summary of [Charles] Darwin's life and achievement. . . . Darwin was an indifferent student . . .until he received an invitation to take a voyage that 'would change the course of history.' . . .The animals he encountered seemed so different . . . that he theorized that if it weren't a matter of different conditions that resulted in such 'transmutation,' they might well have had a different creator." (Kirkus Reviews)

Includes bibliographical references.

Catling, David C.

Astrobiology; a very short introduction. David C. Catling. Oxford University Press 2013 142 p. illustrations (Very short introductions) (pbk.) $11.95 **576.8**

1. Space biology 2. Life on other planets 3. Exobiology
ISBN 0199586454; 9780199586455

LC 2013940856

In this book "David C. Catling introduces [astrobiology] through our understanding of the factors that allowed life to arise and persist on our own planet, and for the signs we are looking for in the search for extraterrestrial life. Astrobiologists seek to understand the origin and evolution of life on Earth in order to illuminate and guide the search for life on other planets." (Publisher's note)

A "very good treatment of astrobiology. In eight chapters and just about 130 pages, it covers the full gamut of the discipline, which really only came about in the 1990s. Importantly, in spite of the necessary requirement of brevity, Catling . . . does not neglect key historical elements in his topical discussions." Choice

Includes bibliographical references and index

Coyne, Jerry A.

★ Why evolution is true. Viking 2009 xx, 282p il map $27.95 **576.8**

1. Evolution
ISBN 978-0-670-02053-9

LC 2008-33973

Presents the threads of modern work in genetics, paleontology, geology, molecular biology, and anatomy that demonstrate the stamp of the evolutionary processes first proposed by Darwin.

"Readers looking to understand the case for evolution and searching for a response to many of the most common creationist claims should find everything they need in this powerful book, which is clearer and more comprehensive than the many others on the subject." Publ Wkly

Includes bibliographical references

Darwin, Charles

The Beagle letters; edited by Frederick Burkhardt; with an introduction by Janet Browne. Cambridge University Press 2008 xxx, 470p il map $32 **576.8**

1. Evolution 2. Beagle Expedition (1831-1836)
ISBN 978-0-521-89838-6; 0-521-89838-2

LC 2009-417801

"The complete correspondence both to and from Charles Darwin during his five years circumnavigating the globe on the HMS Beagle, beginning in 1831, documents his growth as a naturalist and offers a picture of life in the England he left behind. . . . It is fascinating to watch Darwin attempt to come to grips with the huge amount of data he collected and make sense of the patterns he observed. We get an intimate look at an adventurous young Darwin, so unlike his more

familiar, sedentary older self who would write On the Origin of Species." Publ Wkly

Includes bibliographical references

The Darwin reader; edited by Mark Ridley. 2nd ed; Norton 1996 315p il pa $21.30 **576.8**

1. Evolution 2. Natural selection
ISBN 0-393-96967-3

LC 95-50297

First published in the United Kingdom with title: The essential Darwin; first Norton edition published 1987

This collection presents excerpts from Darwin's most important works including Origin of the species, The descent of man and Coral reef. Illustrations are taken from the original editions

Includes bibliographical references

On the origin of species; David Quammen, general editor. Illustrated ed.; Sterling Pub. 2008 544p il $35 **576.8**

1. Heredity 2. Evolution 3. Human origins 4. Natural selection
ISBN 978-1-4027-5639-9

LC 2008-6902

Illustrated edition of the book first published 1859 with title: The origin of species by means of natural selection

"As a milestone not only in the history of science but also in cultural history, On the Origin of Species belongs in every library, high school and above. . . . [Quammen] offers a gloriously illustrated and richly annotated volume, which testifies to the book's enduring legacy. Throughout the text, relevant sidebars from other of Darwin's writings, including his Autobiography, field notes from the HMS Beagle, and his myriad letters, are presented for their insight. Illustrations include historical images, such as sketches, woodcuts, and portraits of people and places, but also included are contemporary photographs of the flora and fauna that Darwin described." Libr J

Includes bibliographical references

★ The origin of species by means of natural selection, or, The preservation of favored races in the struggle for life. Modern Library 1993 689p $21.95 **576.8**

1. Heredity 2. Evolution 3. Human origins 4. Natural selection
ISBN 0-679-60070-1

LC 93-3598

First published 1859. Variant title: The origin of species by means of natural selection

The classic exposition of the "theory of evolution by natural selection. Darwin argues that every species develops or evolves from a previous one and that all life is a continuing pattern. His objects of study were the variations from generation to generation in domestic plants and animals. . . . While subsequent investigation has superseded some of Darwin's arguments, Origin of Species remains one of the most influential books ever published." Reader's Ency. 4th edition

Davies, P. C. W.

The **eerie** silence; renewing our search for alien intelligence. [by] Paul Davies. Houghton Mifflin Harcourt 2010 241p il $27   **576.8**
    1. Life on other planets 2. Extraterrestrial beings 3. Unidentified flying objects
ISBN 978-0-547-13324-9; 0-547-13324-3
                       LC 2010-3088

"After 50 years of scanning the skies for signs of extraterrestrial intelligence, astronomers have only silence to report — an eerie silence, Davies argues. Part history of the search, part road map for its future and (large) part mind-stretching exercise, the book provides Davies' perspective on profound questions that have implications far beyond alien hunting." Sci News
    Includes bibliographical references

Dawkins, Richard

★ The **ancestor's** tale; a pilgrimage to the dawn of evolution. with additional research by Yan Wong. Houghton Mifflin 2004 673p il $28; pa $16.95   **576.8**
    1. Evolution
ISBN 0-618-00583-8; 0-618-61916-X pa
                       LC 2004-59864

The author "sets out on a pilgrimage tracing the history of the human species back to the very origins of life, marking along the way 39 rendezvous points where the human genealogical path crosses that of other terrestrial species. . . . Lively and daring, a book certain to draw even casual readers deep into the adventure—and controversy—of science." Booklist
    Includes bibliographical references

The **greatest** show on Earth; the evidence for evolution. Free Press 2009 470p il map $30 **576.8**
    1. Evolution
ISBN 978-1-4165-9478-9; 1-4165-9478-7
                       LC 2009-25330

"A pleasure in the face of so much scientific ignorance—biology rendered accessible and relevant to the utmost degree." Kirkus
    Includes bibliographical references

Eiseley, Loren C.

★ The **immense** journey; [by] Loren Eisley. Random House 1957 210p hardcover o.p. pa $10   **576.8**
    1. Evolution 2. Human origins
ISBN 0-394-70157-7 pa

Dr Eiseley's "style is beautiful, compelling in impact and poetic in its imagery. His subject is one of the epics of natural science—the 'immense journey' of life as known on this planet." Christ Sci Monit

★ **Evolution**; the first four billion years. edited by Michael Ruse [and] Joseph Travis; with a foreword by Edward O. Wilson. Belknap Press of Harvard University Press 2009 979p il map $39.95   **576.8**
    1. Evolution
ISBN 9780674031753
                       LC 2008-30270

"If ever there were an education in a book, there's one in this massive volume." Booklist
    Includes bibliographical references

Evolution, the whole story; edited by Steve Parker. Firefly Books Ltd 2015 576 p. col. ill., map, chart, table $39.95   **576.8**
    1. Evolution 2. Evolution (Biology) 3. Evolution (Biology) -- Popular works
ISBN 1770854819; 9781770854819
                       LC 2015452843

This book, edited by Steve Parker, "provides an in-depth and up-to-the- minute account of evolution. . . . Ten esteemed experts thoroughly survey how each of Earth's major groups of living things diversified and evolved through time and using visual features that make the story comprehensible. . . . Along with profiles of the most important scientists that have influenced evolutionary theory, the book reveals how these advances have added to and often changed the story." (Publisher's note)

"The coverage here is exhaustive, but the writing is easy to follow, and the short-entry format makes for a very readable book. This is an important work and is highly recommended for all types of libraries, where it will serve both general readers and students." Booklist

Fortey, Richard A.

★ **Life**; a natural history of the first four billion years of life on earth. [by] Richard Fortey. Knopf 1998 346p il $32.59; pa $15   **576.8**
    1. Evolution 2. Life -- Origin
ISBN 0-375-40119-9; 0-375-70261-X pa
                       LC 97-49466

First published 1997 in the United Kingdom with subtitle: an unauthorized biography

This work is "written for readers with no science. It will help them understand the specialized and often technical books on evolution that make headlines but leave most people wondering why." N Y Times Book Rev
    Includes bibliographical references

Gould, Stephen Jay, 1941-2002

★ **Hen's** teeth and horse's toes. Norton 1983 413p il hardcover o.p. pa $15.95   **576.8**
    1. Evolution
ISBN 0-393-31103-1 pa
                       LC 82-22259

The theme of this collection is "biological evolution. {The author} has grouped the 30 essays into seven categories: Sensible Oddities, Personalities, Adaptation and Development, Teilhard and Piltdown, Science and Politics, Extinction and a Zebra Trilogy." America
    Includes bibliographical references

The **structure** of evolutionary theory. Belknap Press 2002 xxii, 1433p il $39.95   **576.8**
    1. Evolution 2. Evolution (Biology) 3. Punctuated

equilibrium (Evolution)
ISBN 0-674-00613-5

LC 2001-43556

This is a summation of the author's "life work, building on Darwinism to provide a . . . synthesis of how {in Gould's view} evolution has shaped the living world. . . . Gould says of his book that it 'cycles through the three central themes of Darwinian logic at three scales—by brief mention of a framework in (the introduction), by full exegesis of Darwin's presentation in Chapter 2, and by lengthy analysis of the major differences and effects in historical (part 1) and modern critiques (part 2) of these three themes in the rest of the volume.'" (N Y Rev Books) Index.

This is a "history and analysis of classical and twentieth-century evolutionary theory." Booklist

Includes bibliographical references

Johnson, Paul, 1928-
Darwin; portrait of a genius. Paul Johnson. Viking 2012 176 p. $25.95 **576.8**
1. Biography 2. Evolution 3. Social Darwinism 4. Naturalists -- England -- Biography
ISBN 0670025712; 9780670025718

LC 2012003433

In this book, Paul Johnson presents a biography of Charles Darwin. He "summarizes the key events of Darwin's formative days, then devotes the meat of the book to his development of the theory and the publication of 'The Origin of Species.' . . . Johnson also points to what he considers two central flaws in Darwin's work: a too-literal acceptance of Malthus' theories and insufficient understanding of anthropology." He also discusses social Darwinism. (Kirkus Reviews)

Jones, Steve
Darwin's ghost; the origin of species updated. Random House 2000 xxix, 377p il hardcover o.p. pa $15.95 **576.8**
1. Evolution 2. Natural selection
ISBN 0-345-42277-5 pa

LC 99-53246

First published 1999 in the United Kingdom with title: Almost like a whale

Jones "has updated Charles Darwin's On the origin of species (1859) so that the fact of organic evolution is both understandable and relevant to today's general reader. . . . Very informative and cogently argued, this book is an important addition to the natural history literature." Libr J

Includes bibliographical references

Kaufman, Marc
First contact; scientific breakthroughs in the hunt for life beyond Earth. Simon & Schuster 2011 213p il $26; ebook $12.99 **576.8**
1. Life on other planets
ISBN 978-1-4391-0900-7; 978-1-4391-3030-8 ebook
LC 2010-44630

Kaufman "takes us from beneath the surface of our planet, where scientists hunt for and study 'extremophile' microbes that alter our views of what is necessary for life to exist, to observatories and labs searching deep space for extraterrestrial signals or exoplanets, planets outside the solar system. Not only does the book suggest the breadth of the effort, it reveals how each aspect reveals ideas and science never before suspected. . . . [The author] does what excellent science reporters do—he translates at times difficult concepts into language those of us who barely passed 'Bonehead Chemistry' can understand." Seattle Post-Intelligencer

Includes bibliographical references

Keller, Michael
Charles Darwin's On the Origin of Species; a graphic adaptation. [by] Michael Keller; art by Nicolle Rager Fuller. Rodale 2009 192p il $19.99; pa $14.99 **576.8**
1. Naturalists 2. Graphic novels 3. Travel writers 4. Writers on science 5. Heredity -- Graphic novels 6. Evolution -- Graphic novels 7. Human origins -- Graphic novels 8. Natural selection -- Graphic novels
ISBN 978-1-60529-697-5; 1-60529-697-X; 978-1-60529-948-8 pa; 1-60529-948-0 pa

LC 2009-11387

"The graphic novel follows Origin's original chapters, combining snippets of Darwin's text with quotes from letters, illustrative examples from his time and from the present, and occasional invented dialog. Fuller's images of people seem clumsy, but her full-color plants, animals, charts, maps, and scientific accoutrements are attractive and effective. . . . [This] version well conveys both the science and the wonder of Origin." Libr J

Kirschvink, Joseph
A new history of life; the radical new discoveries about the origins and evolution of life on earth. Peter Ward & Joe Kirschvink. Bloomsbury Press 2015 416 p. illustrations (alk. paper) $30 **576.8**
1. Life sciences 2. Life -- Origin 3. Evolution
ISBN 160819907X; 9781608199075

LC 2014029828

Authors Peter Ward and Joe Kirschvink "show that many of our long-held beliefs about the history of life are wrong. First, the development of life was not a stately, gradual process. Second, life consists of carbon, but three other molecules have determined how it evolved: oxygen, carbon dioxide, and hydrogen sulfide. Third, ever since Darwin we have thought of evolution in terms of species. Yet it is the evolution of ecosystems-from deep-ocean vents to rainforests-that has formed the living world." (Publisher's note)

Includes bibliographical references and index

Kolbert, Elizabeth
★ The **sixth** extinction; an unnatural history. Elizabeth Kolbert. First edition. Henry Holt and Co 2014 336 p. illustrations, map (hardback) $28 **576.8**
1. Extinction (Biology) 2. Environmental degradation 3. Human influence on nature 4. Mass extinctions 5. Environmental disasters
ISBN 0805092994; 9780805092998

LC 2013028683

Pulitzer Prize: General Nonfiction (2015)
Carnegie Medal Shortlist: Nonfiction (2015)
Los Angeles Times Book Prize: Science and Technology (2014)

"In 'The Sixth Extinction,' [author] Elizabeth Kolbert draws on the work of scores of researchers in half a dozen disciplines, accompanying many of them into the field: geologists who study deep ocean cores, botanists who follow the tree line as it climbs up the Andes, marine biologists who dive off the Great Barrier Reef. She introduces us to a dozen species, some already gone, others facing extinction." (Publisher's note)

"Kolbert . . . weaves a relatable element into the at-times heavily scientific discussion, bringing the sites of past and present extinctions vividly to life with fascinating information that will linger with readers long after they close the book. A highly significant eye-opener rich in facts and enjoyment." Kirkus

Includes bibliographical references and index

Larson, Edward J.

Evolution: the remarkable history of a scientific theory. Modern Library 2004 337p il (Modern Library chronicles) $21.95; pa $14.95   **576.8**

1. Evolution

ISBN 0-679-64288-9; 0-8129-6849-2 pa

LC 2003-64888

This is an "overview of evolutionary thought from ancient speculations to the emergence of a neo-Darwinian synthesis. It focuses on those essential facts, events, and ideas that have contributed to the successes of scientific evolutionism. . . . Larson is to be commended for stressing the value of both scientific inquiry and the evolutionary framework. This outstanding book is highly recommended for all academic and public libraries." Libr J

Includes bibliographical references

Margulis, Lynn

Symbiotic planet; a new look at evolution. Basic Bks. 1998 147p il (Science masters series) hardcover o.p. pa $14   **576.8**

1. Evolution 2. Symbiosis 3. Gaia hypothesis

ISBN 0-465-07272-0 pa

LC 98-38921

"From the origin of life to the classification and phylogeny of living organisms, from a discussion of Gaia—the belief that Earth operates like a living being—to a discussion of the underlying reasons for sex, iconoclastic biologist Margulis . . . takes on many of the big questions in biology. . . . In a book that is part autobiography and part biological primer, Margulis . . . advances the idea that a large part of organic evolution can be explained by symbiosis." Publ Wkly

Includes bibliographical references

Mayr, Ernst

What evolution is. Basic Bks. 2001 318p il maps hardcover o.p. pa $16   **576.8**

1. Evolution

ISBN 0-465-04426-3 pa

LC 2001-36562

"A wise and illuminating examination, by an illustrious evolutionary biologist, that sorts out the complexities of evolution." N Y Times Book Rev

Includes bibliographical references

McCalman, Iain, 1947-

Darwin's armada; four voyages and the battle for the theory of evolution. W.W. Norton & Co. 2009 422p il map   **576.8**

1. Botanists 2. Evolution 3. Biologists 4. Naturalists 5. Essayists 6. Travel writers 7. Writers on science

ISBN 0-393-06814-5; 978-0-393-06814-6

LC 2009-16055

"This geographically expansive account of the rise of evolutionary theory traces the lives and travels of four titans of nineteenth-century biology: Darwin, the botanist Joseph Hooker, the physiologist Thomas Huxley, and Alfred Russel Wallace, a fearless globetrotter whose dangerous and often unpleasant journeys in the Amazon and the Malay Archipelago were the source of biological epiphanies and tens of thousands of specimens. Though these stories have been told before, McCalman's central conceit—that the four naturalists, who all travelled at length in the Southern Hemisphere, share a 'special bond of the salt'—supplies a fresh, antipodean perspective." New Yorker

Includes bibliographical references

Mesler, Bill

A Brief History of Creation; Science and the Search for the Origin of Life. by Bill Mesler and H. James Cleaves II. W W Norton & Co Inc 2015 336 p. illustrations $27.95   **576.8**

1. Biology 2. Creation 3. Theology 4. Evolution

ISBN 0393083551; 9780393083552

LC 2015024251

This book, by Bill Mesler and H. James Cleaves II, is the "epic story of the scientists through the ages who have sought answers to life's biggest mystery: How did it begin? . . . [They] examine historical discoveries in the context of philosophical debates, political change, and our evolving understanding of the complexity of biology. The story they tell is rooted in metaphysical arguments, in a changing understanding of the age of the Earth, and even in the politics of the Cold War." (Publisher's note)

"This lively, accessible book is recommended for science enthusiasts interested in origin of life issues and the history of science." LJ

Newitz, Annalee

Scatter, adapt, and remember; how humans will survive a mass extinction. Annalee Newitz. Doubleday 2013 320 p. illustrations, maps (hardcover : alk. paper) $26.95   **576.8**

1. Human beings 2. Survival skills 3. Extinction (Biology) 4. Survival

ISBN 0385535910; 9780385535915

LC 2012042409

LA Times Book Prize Finalist: Science & Technology (2013)

In this book, author Annalee Newitz "explains that although global disaster is all but inevitable, our chances of long-term species survival are better than ever. [She] focuses on humanity's long history of dodging the bullet, as well as on new threats that we may face in years to come. Most important, it explores how scientific breakthroughs today will help us avoid disasters tomorrow." (Publisher's note)

"Humans may be experts at destroying the planet, but we are no slouches at preserving it, either, and Newitz's shrewd speculations are heartening." Kirkus

Includes bibliographical references and index

Novacek, Michael J.

Terra; our 100-million-year-old ecosystem--and the threats that now put it at risk. [by] Michael Novacek. Farrar, Straus and Giroux 2007 xxiv, 451p il map $27 576.8

1. Ecology 2. Evolution 3. Environmental degradation 4. Human influence on nature

ISBN 978-0-374-27325-5; 0-374-27325-1

LC 2007-9126

The author takes a "look at what humans have done over time and in more recent years. Combining paleontology, evolutionary biology, and environmental science, he shows how these three perspectives can bring us to a better understanding of the 'mass extinction event' that threatens this planet if changes aren't implemented now." Libr J

Includes bibliographical references

Nye, Bill, 1955-

Undeniable; evolution and the science of creation. Bill Nye with Corey Powell. St Martin's Press 2014 320 p. illustrations (hardcover : alk. paper) $25.99 576.8

1. Evolution 2. Creationism 3. Natural history 4. Religion and science 5. Creationism -- Popular works 6. Evolution (Biology) -- Popular works 7. Natural history -- Philosophy -- Popular works

ISBN 1250007135; 9781250007131

LC 2014027163

"Revealing the mechanics of evolutionary theory, the scientist, engineer and inventor presents a compelling argument for the scientific unviability of creationism and insists that creationism's place in the science classroom is harmful not only to our children, but to the future of the greater world as well." Publisher's Note

"The straightforward, accessible language and clear explanations make this ideal reading to understand life's origins, especially for those new to the evidence of evolution. While firm about the fact of evolution, the tone is friendlier to religious viewpoints and more upbeat than that in Richard Dawkins's The Greatest Show on Earth." LJ

Includes bibliographical references and index

Rutherford, Adam

Creation; how science is reinventing life itself. Adam Rutherford. Current 2013 288 p. (hardback) $27.95 576.8

1. Life -- Origin 2. Genetic engineering 3. Biogenesis -- Popular Works

ISBN 1617230057; 9781617230059

LC 2013013441

Author Adam Rutherford's book brings "genomics and synthetic biology to life in this accessible overview of the past and future of the fields. In the first half," Rutherford "describes what we know about cellular biology, while the second portion explores where and how we might apply our growing knowledge base in the future. He argues that the theory of evolution does not aim to explain the origin of life,

but he also insists that in order to know where we're going, we have to know where we're from, and one of the best ways to do that is to trace evolution at the cellular level." (Publisher's note)

Includes bibliographical references and index

Sasselov, Dimitar

The life of super-Earths; Dimitar Sasselov. Basic Books 2012 xvi, 202 p.p ill. 576.8

1. Exobiology 2. Extrasolar planets 3. Life on other planets 4. Life -- Origin 5. Synthetic biology

ISBN 9780465021932; 9780465023400

LC 2011036888

This book discusses the research supporting the claim for extra-terrestrial life beyond Earth. Author Dimitar "Sasselov (Astronomy/Harvard Univ.) reviews the hard evidence in favor . . . before proceeding to explain discoveries and simulations that suggest we are not alone. No telescope has directly observed an extra-solar planet, but the author delivers a[n] . . . explanation of how instruments and, since 2009, a satellite are detecting subtle changes in a star's light or movement that reveal not only the presence of planets (600 so far) but their size, orbits and a hint of their composition. Sasselov maintains that the minority of 'super-earths' possess conditions favorable to life: proper temperature, protective atmosphere, volcanism and tectonic movements." (Kirkus)

Includes bibliographical references and index

Stott, Rebecca

★ Darwin's ghosts; the secret history of evolution. Rebecca Stott. Spiegel & Grau 2012 xviii, 396 p.p 576.8

1. Evolution 2. Naturalists 3. Biology -- History 4. Scientists -- Biography 5. Naturalists -- Biography 6. Evolution (Biology) -- History

ISBN 1400069378; 9781400069378

LC 2011041951

This book "draws for readers stories of the people who came before [Charles] Darwin and who presented ideas that were precursors to the theory of evolution. . . . Many of the thinkers and ideas presented in this book . . . Darwin was not aware of until after the publication of 'On the Origin of Species.' After receiving a critical letter, he compiled a list of his scientific predecessors to be included in the foreword of later editions . . . including Aristotle, Al-Jahiz, Leonardo da Vinci, and Denis Diderot." (Library Journal)

Includes bibliographical references (p. [357]-376) and index

Switek, Brian

Written in stone; evolution, the fossil record and our place in nature. Brian Switek. 1st ed. Bellevue Literary Press 2010 320p il pa $17.95 576.8

1. Fossils 2. Evolution 3. Fossil hominids 4. Human evolution

ISBN 1-934137-29-4 pa; 978-1-934137-29-1 pa

This is a "history of evolutionary discovery." (Publisher's note) Index.

The author "presents a popular account of fossil discoveries, historical debates related to evolution, and how the unearthing of these missing links is filling in the gaps in evolutionary history. . . . Armchair scientists and general readers interested in evolution will enjoy this informative book." Libr J

Ward, Peter Douglas

Life as we do not know it; the NASA search for (and synthesis of) alien life. Peter D. Ward. Viking 2005 xxvii, 292p ill. hardcover o.p. (pbk.) $15.00; o.p. **576.8**

1. Science 2. Solar system 3. Life (Biology) 4. Life on other planets 5. Life -- Origin
ISBN 9780143038498; 0670034584
LC 2005056299

This book "sets a research agenda aimed at unraveling science's most profound questions: What is life, and where does it exist? To that query, he adds this philosophical discussion: What is humanity's role in life's unfolding on Earth and in the rest of the Solar System? . . . [Author Peter] Ward begins with a generally agreed-upon set of criteria—life metabolizes, has complexity and organization, reproduces, develops, evolves, and is autonomous—but then proposes the controversial hypothesis that this definition should include viruses. . . . Ward leaves no solar-system world unvisited. He quickly dismisses Mercury but spends a number of pages discussing the possibility of life floating high in the sulfuric-acid-laced clouds of Venus. . . . Mars gets the most attention outside of Earth." (National Space Society)

The author "believes researchers might be taking the wrong approach by looking only for earthly DNA-based life forms. Truly alien life, he argues, might have completely different origins. . . . The science is neatly laid out, and readers willing to follow his daring, scientifically based speculations will find their imaginations spurred." Publ Wkly

Includes bibliographical references (p. [257]-278) and index

Wilson, David Sloan

★ Evolution for everyone; how Darwin's theory can change the way we think about our lives. Delacorte Press 2007 390p $24 **576.8**

1. Evolution
ISBN 978-0-385-34021-2; 0-385-34021-4
LC 2006-23685

"Rather than catalog its successes, denounce its detractors or in any way present evolutionary theory as the province of expert tacticians like himself, Wilson invites readers inside and shows them how Darwinism is done, and at lesson's end urges us to go ahead, feel free to try it at home. The result is a sprightly, absorbing and charmingly earnest book that manages a minor miracle, the near-complete emulsifying of science and the 'real world,' ingredients too often kept stubbornly, senselessly apart." N Y Times Book Rev

Includes bibliographical references

Young, Christian C.

★ Evolution and creationism; a documentary and reference guide. [by] Christian C. Young and Mark A. Largent. Greenwood Press 2007 298p il $85 **576.8**

1. Evolution 2. Creationism
ISBN 978-0-313-33953-0; 0-313-33953-8
LC 2007-10682

"This reference work provides over 40 of the most important documents to help readers understand the [evolution versus creationism] debate in the eyes of the people of the time. Each document is from a major participant in the debates from the predecessors of Darwin to the judges of the influential court cases of the present day." Publisher's note

Includes bibliographical references

577 Ecology

Burdick, Alan

★ Out of Eden; an odyssey of ecological invasion. Farrar, Straus & Giroux 2005 324p il $25; pa $14 **577**

1. Ecology 2. Biological invasions
ISBN 0-374-21973-7; 0-374-53043-2 pa
LC 2005-922517

"A sober report, Burdick's work still sounds an alarm for readers concerned with the way humans alter nature." Booklist

Carroll, Sean

The Big Picture; On the Origins of Life, Meaning, and the Universe Itself. by Sean Carroll. Penguin Group USA 2016 496 p. illustrations $28 **577**

1. Universe 2. Quantum theory
ISBN 0525954821; 9780525954828
LC 2015050590

In this book, by Sean Carroll, "readers learn the difference between how the world works at the quantum level, the cosmic level, and the human level--and then how each connects to the other. Carroll's presentation of the principles that have guided the scientific revolution from Darwin and Einstein to the origins of life, consciousness, and the universe is dazzlingly unique." (Publisher's note)

"Carroll is the perfect guide on this wondrous journey of discovery. A brilliantly lucid exposition of profound philosophical and scientific issues in a language accessible to lay readers." Kirkus

Includes bibliographical references and index.

Christopher, Thomas

Garden revolution; How Our Landscapes Can Be a Source of Environmental Change. Larry Weaner and Thomas Christopher. Timber Press 2016 328 p. color illustrations $39.95 **577**

1. Gardening 2. Landscape ecology
ISBN 9781604696165
LC 2015036650

This book, by Larry Weaner and Thomas Christopher, "shows how an ecological approach to planting can lead to beautiful gardens that buck much of conventional gardening's counter-productive, time-consuming practices. Instead of picking the wrong plant and then constantly tilling, weeding, irrigating, and fertilizing, Weaner advocates for choosing plants that are adapted to the soil and climate of a specific site and letting them naturally evolve over time." (Publisher's note)

"With accompanying stunning color photographs, the authors invite readers into a world of new landscape possibilities with an eye toward natural beauty and sustainability." Pub Wkly

Includes bibliographical references and index

Roston, Eric

The **carbon** age; how life's core element has become civilization's greatest threat. Distributed to the trade by Macmillan 2008 309p il $25.99 **577**

1. Carbon 2. Atmosphere

ISBN 978-0-8027-1557-9; 0-8027-1557-5

LC 2008-2754

"The first half traces carbon's history from the beginning of the universe, the Big Bang, and the nucleosynthesis (the formation of the elements) through the life cycle of stars, and then covers the development of life and dynamics of the 'natural' carbon cycle of Earth. The second section spans the last 150 years and delves into the impact of humans on the climate in creating what Roston calls the 'industrial carbon cycle.' Without using a great deal of scientific jargon, Roston leads us patiently and clearly through this complex issue." Libr J

Includes bibliographical references

Wills, Christopher

Green Equilibrium; The Vital Balance of Humans and Nature. Christopher Wills. Oxford University Press 2013 320 p. $34.95 **577**

1. Ecology 2. Evolution 3. Ecosystem health 4. Biotic communities 5. Ecosystem management 6. Nature -- Effect of human beings on 7. Human beings -- Effect of environment on

ISBN 0199645701; 9780199645701

LC 2012277418

In this book, Christopher Wills "recounts visits to diverse wildlife reserves around the world, illustrated with his photographs, while discussing many aspects of evolution. The author describes a green equilibrium as balance among organisms that maintains a local ecosystem. No paradise, it includes predation, disease, and starvation." Humans' effects, both positive and negative, on ecosystems are considered. (Library Journal)

Includes bibliographical references (p. 247-267) and index

577.2 Specific factors affecting ecology

Global weirdness; severe storms, deadly heat waves, relentless drought, rising seas, and the weather of the future. produced by Climate Central. Pantheon Books 2012 214 p. ill. $22.95 **577.2**

1. Meteorology 2. Climate change 3. Global warming 4. Climatic changes 5. Weather forecasting 6. Global environmental change 7. Climatic changes -- Forecasting 8. Climatic changes -- Mathemathical models 9. Greenhouse gases -- Environmental aspects

ISBN 0307907309; 9780307907301

LC 2011047699

This book, "[p]roduced by Climate Central, . . . summarizes . . . everything we know about the science of climate change; explains what is likely to happen to the climate in the future; and lays out in practical terms what we can and

cannot do to avoid further shifts. Sixty . . . entries tackle such questions as: Is climate ever 'normal'? . . . [and w] hat risks does climate change pose for human health?" (Publisher's note)

Includes bibliographical references (p. 201-214).

Montaigne, Fen

Fraser's penguins; a journey to the future in Antarctica. Henry Holt and Co. 2010 288p il map $26 **577.2**

1. Penguins 2. Human influence on nature 3. Ecologists 4. Climate -- Environmental aspects 5. Antarctica -- Description and travel

ISBN 978-0-8050-7942-5; 0-8050-7942-4

LC 2010-07151

The author "spent five months tracking penguins through the breeding season on the northwestern Antarctica peninsula with the scientist Bill Fraser, and his book is a bittersweet account of the stark beauty of the continent and the climate change that threatens its delicate ecosystem. . . . Montaigne poetically portrays the daunting Antarctic landscape and gives readers an intimate perspective on its rugged, audacious, and charming penguin and human inhabitants." Publ Wkly

Includes bibliographical references

577.3 Ecology of specific environments

Haskell, David George

The **forest** unseen; a year's watch in nature. David George Haskell. Viking 2012 268 p **577.3**

1. Seasons 2. Nature study 3. Philosophy of nature 4. Natural history -- Tennessee 5. Forests and forestry -- Tennessee 6. Seasons -- Tennessee 7. Nature observation -- Tennessee 8. Old growth forests -- Tennessee 9. Old growth forest ecology -- Tennessee

ISBN 9780670023370

LC 2011037552

In this book, "biologist David Haskell uses a one-square-meter patch of old-growth Tennessee forest as a window onto the entire natural world. Visiting it almost daily for one year to trace nature's path through the seasons, he brings the forest and its inhabitants to . . . life. Each of this book's short chapters begins with a simple observation: a salamander scuttling across the leaf litter; the first blossom of spring wildflowers. From these, Haskell spins a . . . web of biology and ecology, explaining the science that binds together the tiniest microbes and the largest mammals and describing the ecosystems that have cycled for thousands- sometimes millions-of years." (Publisher's note)

Includes bibliographical references and index

Preston, Richard

The **wild** trees; a story of passion and daring. Random House 2007 294p il map $25.95; pa $16 **577.3**

1. Redwood 2. Botanists 3. College teachers

ISBN 978-1-4000-6489-2; 1-4000-6489-9; 978-0-8129-7559-8 pa; 0-8129-7559-6 pa

LC 2006-48646

The author tells the story of Steve Sillett, Marie Antoine and other naturalists and researchers who climb and explore giant redwoods in northern California

"There is something so elementally boyish in searching out the biggest and tallest, poring over maps and measurements, dubbing these trees with names lifted from J.R.R. Tolkein's Middle Earth. . . . Preston knows how to fold the science into the seams of his narrative, and his dry humor crops up, pleasurably, at the edges of his observations." Cleveland Plain Dealer

577.34   Rain forest ecology

Lowman, Margaret

Life in the treetops; adventures of a woman in field biology. [by] Margaret D. Lowman. Yale Univ. Press 1999 219p il maps hardcover o.p. pa $13.95   **577.34**

1. Botanists 2. Women scientists
ISBN 0-300-07818-8; 978-0-300-07818-3; 0-300-08464-1 pa; 978-0-300-08464-1 pa

LC 98-48691

Lowman "gives a funny, unassuming and deeply idiosyncratic chronicle of her trials and triumphs as a field biologist of tree canopies and other ecosystems in Australia, New England, Belize, Panama and elsewhere." N Y Times Book Rev

Includes bibliographical references
Followed by It's a jungle up there! (2006)

Royte, Elizabeth

The Tapir's morning bath; mysteries of the tropical rain forest and the scientists who are trying to solve them. Houghton Mifflin 2001 328p maps $25; pa $14   **577.34**

1. Rain forest ecology 2. Panama -- Description
ISBN 0-395-97997-8; 0-618-25758-6 pa

LC 2001-24989

Royte discusses time spent with scientists studying the ecology of Barro Colorado, an island in the Panama Canal.

This is "a superb introduction to tropical ecology and theoretical biology, as well as original and thoroughly engaging travel writing." Publ Wkly

Includes bibliographical references

577.5   Ecology of miscellaneous environments

Barilla, James

★ My Backyard Jungle; The Adventures of an Urban Wildlife Lover Who Turned His Yard into Habitat and Learned to Live With It. James Barilla. Yale University Press 2013 376 p. $28   **577.5**

1. Wildlife conservation 2. Human-animal relationship 3. Habitat (Ecology) 4. Urban ecology (Biology) 5. Animals and civilization
ISBN 0300184018; 9780300184013

LC 2012040298

In this book, James Barilla "takes readers on his personal journey to explore human and animal relationships in shared

habitats around the world. To begin with, he had his own property in Columbia, SC, certified by the National Wildlife Federation as a wildlife habitat. . . . Going between his backyard and distant locations, his chapters cover topics from idealized children's toys . . . to the illegal wildlife trade." (Library Journal)

Includes bibliographical references (pages 349-353) and index

577.6   Aquatic ecology

Douglas, Marjory Stoneman

The Everglades; river of grass. illustrated by Robert Fink; [update by Michael Grunwald] 60th anniversary ed; Pineapple Press 2007 447p $19.95   **577.6**

1. Everglades (Fla.)
ISBN 978-1-56164-394-3

LC 2007-28384

First published 1947 by Rinehart

A natural history of South Florida focusing on the unique ecosystem of the Everglades. Discusses environmental changes, scientific research, and political responses to conservation efforts.

Includes bibliographical references

577.7   Marine ecology

Carson, Rachel

The edge of the sea; with illustrations by Bob Hines. Houghton Mifflin 1955 276p il hardcover o.p. pa $14   **577.7**

1. Seashore 2. Marine biology
ISBN 0-395-92496-0 pa

"The seashores of the world may be divided into three basic types: the rugged shores of rock, the sand beaches, and the coral reefs and all their associated features. Each has its typical community of plants and animals. The Atlantic coast of the United States [provides] clear examples of each of these types. I have chosen it as the setting for my pictures of shore life." Preface

Ellis, Richard

★ The empty ocean; plundering the world's marine life. written and illustrated by Richard Ellis. Island Press 2003 367p il hardcover o.p. pa $25; pa $37.50   **577.7**

1. Marine ecology 2. Endangered species
ISBN 1-55963-974-1; 1-55963-637-8 pa; 9781559636377

"Rather than writing the 'Silent Spring' of the oceans, [Ellis] has produced a book that is likely to provide the inspiration and source materials for such a badly needed work . . . It is also a splendid example of history illuminating ecology, with well-chosen facts that enable us to picture a largely invisible catastrophe." N Y Times Book Rev

Includes bibliographical references

578 Natural history of organisms and related subjects

Weidensaul, Scott

★ Return to wild America; a yearlong journey in search of the continent's natural soul. North Point Press 2005 xx, 394p il map $26; pa $15   **578**
1. Artists 2. Illustrators 3. Ornithologists 4. Writers on nature 5. Natural history -- North America
ISBN 0-8654-7688-8; 0-8654-7731-0 pa

LC 2005-47720

Fifty years after the publishing of Roger Tory Peterson's and James Fisher's Wild America, the author retraces Peterson and Fisher's steps "from Newfoundland's craggy coastline, down the East Coast, into Mexico and up the West Coast to Alaska. . . . This engrossing state-of-nature memoir, making a vibrant case for preserving America's wild past for future Americans, promises to become a classic in its own right." Publ Wkly

Includes bibliographical references

578.4 Adaptation

Barrington, Rupert

Life; extraordinary animals, extreme behaviour. [by] Martha Holmes and Mike Gunton; [with] Rupert Barrington ... [et al.] University of California Press 2010 311p il map   **578.4**
1. Animal behavior 2. Adaptation (Biology)
ISBN 0-520-26537-8; 978-0-520-26537-0

LC 2009-31158

First published 2009 in the United Kingdom

"In 2009, to commemorate the 200th anniversary of Charles Darwin's birth, the BBC premiered the ten-episode television documentary Life to great acclaim. . . . Written by the documentary's producers, this impressive companion volume showcases species of fish, amphibians, reptiles, insects, birds, mammals, and plants that have developed unique or unusual strategies for solving 'the eternal problems of life': finding food, escaping predators, attracting mates, and raising young. . . . Even the most casual reader will be awed by the beauty, complexity, and ingenuity of nature as celebrated here."

"In 2009, to commemorate the 200th anniversary of Charles Darwin's birth, the BBC premiered the ten-episode television documentary Life to great acclaim. . . . Written by the documentary's producers, this impressive companion volume showcases species of fish, amphibians, reptiles, insects, birds, mammals, and plants that have developed unique or unusual strategies for solving 'the eternal problems of life': finding food, escaping predators, attracting mates, and raising young. . . . Even the most casual reader will be awed by the beauty, complexity, and ingenuity of nature as celebrated here." Libr J

Forbes, Peter

Dazzled and deceived; mimicry and camouflage. Yale University Press 2009 283p il map $27.50   **578.4**
1. Camouflage (Biology)
ISBN 978-0-300-12539-9; 0-300-12539-9

LC 2009-23577

"Forbes has produced a colorful look at camouflage in nature and battle, with a focus on the two world wars. . . . [The book] straddles the worlds of evolutionary biology, art, and military strategy with a world-class cast of characters, among them Charles Darwin, Pablo Picasso, Vladimir Nabokov, Theodore Roosevelt, and Winston Churchill. A pivotal character is Abbott Henderson Thayer, the eccentric New England painter who studied the animals near his summer home in Dublin, N.H., and is one of the few artists to have a scientific law (Thayer's Law of Concealing Coloration) named after him." Boston Globe

Includes bibliographical references

578.6 Miscellaneous nontaxonomic kinds of organisms

Hamilton, Garry

Super species; the creatures that will dominate the planet. Firefly Books 2010 271p il $35   **578.6**
1. Nonindigenous pests 2. Biological invasions
ISBN 978-1-55407-630-7; 1-55407-630-7

LC 2011286604

"Well researched and written, with an abundance of excellent photos, this work provides an outstanding, balanced look at this group of species." Choice

Includes bibliographical references

578.68 Rare and endangered species

Ackerman, Diane, 1948-

The rarest of the rare; vanishing animals, timeless worlds. Random House 1995 xxi, 184p hardcover o.p. pa $12   **578.68**
1. Rare animals 2. Endangered species
ISBN 0-679-77623-0 pa

LC 95-8499

"Every species that is endangered or becomes extinct deserves so poetic a chronicler as Ackerman." Libr J

578.7 Organisms characteristic of specific kinds of environments

Burt, William

Marshes; the disappearing Edens. Yale University Press 2007 179p il $35   **578.7**
1. Marshes
ISBN 978-0-300-12229-9; 0-300-12229-2

LC 2006-26961

This book combines photographs of marsh life with information about wetland habitat in North America.

"This well-structured, readable book will be valuable for students, teachers, researchers, and sundry readers interested in a unique kind of wetland. Reading this book is an excellent way to understand marshes as wild places." Choice

Includes bibliographical references

Carson, Rachel

Under the sea wind; introduction by Linda Lear; illustrations by Howard Frech. Penguin Books 2007 xx, 184p il (Penguin classics) pa $15   **578.7**

1. Marine biology

ISBN 978-0-14-310496-4

LC 2006-50707

First published 1941 by Simon & Schuster

A series of narratives describe the birds and sea creatures that inhabit the Eastern coasts of North America.

Includes bibliographical references

Cramer, Deborah

Smithsonian ocean; our water, our world. Smithsonian Books 2008 295p il map $39.95 **578.7**

1. Marine biology 2. Marine ecology

ISBN 978-0-06-134383-4; 0-06-134383-8

LC 2008-15633

"With its hundreds of beautiful photographs, the volume is visually enchanting. It is also a vividly, accurately, and clearly written survey of the state of our understanding . . . of the history and current condition of the ocean." Sci Books Films

Includes bibliographical references

Crist, Darlene Trew

World ocean census; a global survey of marine life. [by] Darlene Trew Crist, Gail Scowcroft, James M. Harding, Jr. Firefly Books 2009 256p il map $40   **578.7**

1. Marine animals 2. Marine biology 3. Science -- Methodology 4. Census of Marine Life (Project)

ISBN 978-1-55407-434-1; 1-55407-434-7

The authors "have produced a highly readable text with stunning photos that should fully engage the public imagination." Publ Wkly

Includes bibliographical references

DeStefano, Stephen

Coyote at the kitchen door; living with wildlife in suburbia. Harvard University Press 2010 196p il $24.95   **578.7**

1. Coyotes 2. Urbanization 3. Suburban life 4. Wildlife conservation

ISBN 978-0-674-03556-0; 0-674-03556-9

The author "examines the expanding field of 'urban ecology' in this pithy volume. Urban ecologists study changes in human-animal interactions caused by factors like sprawl, traffic, and noise pollution, in an attempt to understand why some species (the mountain lion, say) are badly disrupted by human developments, while others, such as the coyote, appear to be thriving—turning up in more and more Eastern back yards. DeStefano cites some alarming facts . . . but, having experienced the benefits of a suburban childhood, he

refuses to reduce his thinking to a view in which wilderness preservation is the only solution." New Yorker

Includes bibliographical references

Kirby, Richard R.

Ocean drifters; a secret world beneath the waves. Firefly Books 2011 192p il $29.95   **578.7**

1. Marine plankton

ISBN 978-1-55407-982-7; 1-55407-982-9

LC 2011284690

"Kirby (Marine Inst. Research Fellow, Plymouth Univ., UK), who has published widely in scientific journals, combines in this book his area of expertise-plankton-with magnificent color photography of each species. He details the importance of the ocean's plankton layer to the health of the globe and its effects on sea and human life in the photos' descriptions...Recommended for readers interested in the smaller denizens of the natural world, the ocean, or microphotography." (Library Journal)

Koslow, J. Anthony

★ The **silent** deep; the discovery, ecology, and conservation of the deep sea. [by] Tony Koslow. University of Chicago Press 2007 270p il map $35   **578.7**

1. Marine ecology 2. Marine resources 3. Conservation of natural resources

ISBN 978-0-226-45125-1; 0-226-45125-9

LC 2006-22282

"This important book should be read by everyone who cares about Earth's future." Choice

Includes bibliographical references

Rice, Stanley A.

Encyclopedia of biodiversity; author, Stanley A Rice. Facts On File 2012 598 p. $95   **578.7**

1. Biology -- Encyclopedias 2. Evolution -- Encyclopedias 3. Biodiversity -- Encyclopedias

ISBN 0816077266; 9780816077267

LC 2010050557

This biology and evolutionary science encyclopedia, by Stanley A. Rice, provides "information about groups of organisms (from bacteria to mammals) and about ecological concepts and processes (such as biogeography and ecological succession). . . . Tables at the end of each entry . . . allow . . . readers to see how environmental conditions and biodiversity have changed through evolutionary time." (Publisher's note)

"The text is suitable for high school students but advanced enough for adult readers, too. Although there are many encyclopedias on ecology, resources, and science, this one presents important biodiversity topics in one volume, providing a handy overview for term papers and class presentations." LJ

Includes bibliographical references and index

Sardet, Christian

Plankton; wonders of the drifting world. Christian Sardet; edited by Rafael D. Rosengarten and Theodore Rosengarten; translated from the French by Christian Sardet and Dana Sardet; prologue by Mark Ohman. University of Chicago Press 2015 224 p.

illustrations (chiefly color) (cloth : alkaline paper)
$45   **578.7**

1. Marine biology 2. Marine ecology 3. Plankton
-- Pictorial works

ISBN 022618871X; 9780226188713

LC 2014034445

This book by Christian Sardet "transports readers into the currents, where jeweled chains hang next to phosphorescent chandeliers, spidery claws jut out from sinuous bodies, and gelatinous barrels protect microscopic hearts. The creatures' vibrant colors pop against the black pages, allowing readers to examine every eye and follow every tentacle. Jellyfish, tadpoles, and bacteria all find a place in the book, representing the broad scope of organisms dependent on drifting currents." (Publisher's note)

"A fascinating book that will cause readers to think deeply about plankton and its importance to human and animal life. A biology or general science background is not necessary to read this book; the reader needs only a desire to learn more about these intriguing organisms." LJ

Includes bibliographical references and index

Wolfe, David W.

Tales from the underground; a natural history of subterranean life. Perseus Bks. 2001 221p il hardcover o.p. pa $18   **578.7**

1. Soil microbiology

ISBN 0-7382-0679-2 pa

The author discusses the ecology of life in the soil and the earth's rocky crust, including Darwin's experiments with earthworms, Lewis and Clark's first encounter with prairie dogs, the use of genetic tools, and the possible role of primitive underground microbes in evolution.

Wolfe "explains in a straightforward, readable style that there is probably as much biodiversity and even as much biomass below ground as above." New Sci

Includes bibliographical references

579   Natural history of microorganisms, fungi, algae

Ben-Barak, Idan

The **invisible** kingdom; from the tips of our fingers to the tops of our trash, inside the curious world of microbes. Basic Books 2009 204p $24   **579**

1. Microbiology

ISBN 978-0-465-01887-1; 0-465-01887-4

LC 2009-19655

The author "gives an enthusiastic tour of single-celled life. . . . He touches on myriad microbes in a range of environments, from the abyss of the sea to the inside of humans, explaining how they defend themselves, eat, move, and reproduce." Booklist

Includes bibliographical references

Dunn, Rob

The **wild** life of our bodies; predators, parasites, and partners that shape our evolution. Harper 2011 290p $26.99   **579**

1. Evolution 2. Parasites 3. Human ecology 4.

Microorganisms

ISBN 978-0-06-180648-3; 0-06-180648-X

LC 2010-43564

The author "shares the view of modern human life as a paradise lost, but the loss he laments is not merely of a vague sense of being one with nature. What we have sacrificed, he argues, is a physical connection with the species that shaped our bodies from our physique to the immune system. As humans became urban and industrial, we also separated ourselves from other species. Pets aside, we have laboured to rid our houses and cities of creatures — not just visible predators and pests but also the microbes on our countertops and hands. Some of these steps were sensible acts of self-preservation, but others were driven by an ideology of humans as separate from nature. Dunn . . . catalogues the dangers of that ideology." New Scientist

Includes bibliographical references

Montgomery, David R.

The **hidden** half of nature; the microbial roots of life and health. David R. Montgomery and Anne Bikle. W W Norton & Co. 2016 320 p. (hardcover) $26.95   **579**

1. Health 2. Farm produce 3. Soil microbiology 4. Conservation of natural resources

ISBN 9780393244403

LC 2015027979

In this book, authors David R. Montgomery and Anne Bikle study "how microbes are transforming the way we see nature and ourselves—and could revolutionize agriculture and medicine. . . . They are abruptly plunged further into investigating microbes when Biklé is diagnosed with cancer. . . . The authors also discover startling insights into the similarities between plant roots and the human gut." (Publisher's note)

"Recommended for general readers wishing to learn more about gardening, sustainability, and nutrition, as well as students and scholars of geology, microbiology, botany, the history of science, public health, agriculture, and nutrition." LJ

Includes bibliographical references and index

Sankaran, Neeraja

★ **Microbes** and people: an A-Z of microorganisms in our lives. Oryx Press 2000 297p il $62.95   **579**

1. Reference books 2. Microbiology -- Dictionaries

ISBN 1-57356-217-3

LC 00-10117

"Because it provides very readable coverage of topics so much in the news lately, this dictionary will be much used in high school, undergraduate, and public libraries." Booklist

Includes bibliographical references

Yong, Ed

★ **I** Contain Multitudes; The Microbes Within Us and a Grander View of Life. Ed Yong. HarperCollins 2016 256 p. color illustrations (hardcover) $27.99   **579**

1. Microbiology 2. Microorganisms

ISBN 9780062368591; 0062368591

This book, by Ed Yong, offers an "informative and vastly entertaining examination of the most significant revolution in biology since Darwin—a 'microbe's-eye view' of the world that reveals a marvelous, radically reconceived picture of life on earth. . . . Many people think of microbes as germs to be eradicated, but those that live with us—the microbiome—build our bodies, protect our health, shape our identities, and grant us incredible abilities." (Publisher's note)

"The author excels at objectively navigating the large body of research related to the microbiome without overselling its curative potential or sacrificing any of the deliciously icky details, and he delivers some of the finest science writing out there in language that will appeal to a wide audience." Kirkus

Includes bibliographical references (pages 299-338) and index

579.3 Prokaryotes (Bacteria)

Tetro, Jason

The **Germ** Files; The Surprising Ways Microbes Can Improve Your Health and Life (And How to Protect Yourself from the Bad Ones) by Jason Tetro. Random House Inc 2016 288 p. illustrations $19   **579.3**

1. Bacteria 2. Microbiology 3. Microorganisms 4. Germ theory of disease
ISBN 0385685777; 9780385685771

This book, by Jason Tetro, "is a one-stop source of the most up-to-date, life-changing information on our relationship with microbes, presented in concise and highly readable items grouped by theme. Areas covered include health, hygiene, sex, childcare, nutrition and dieting." (Publisher's note)

"Written in an engaging, fluid style that is nonacademic, this book also imparts a plethora of in-depth information." LJ

Zimmer, Carl

Microcosm; E. coli and the new science of life. Pantheon Books 2008 243p il $25.95   **579.3**

1. Bacteria
ISBN 978-0-375-42430-4; 0-375-42430-X

LC 2007-37155

The author "renders an absorbing picture of what E. coli says about the history and future of life." Booklist

Includes bibliographical references

579.5 Fungi

Hudler, George W.

Magical mushrooms, mischievous molds. Princeton Univ. Press 1998 248p il hardcover o.p. pa $18.95   **579.5**

1. Fungi
ISBN 0-691-07016-4 pa

LC 98-10163

The author shows how fungi "have dramatically influenced the course of human history. With chapters on yeasts used to make bread and to brew alcoholic beverages, on the medicinal uses of fungi from penicillin to possible treatments for AIDS, on edible mushrooms like the common button mushroom and the more exotic truffle, and on hallucinogenic mushrooms, Hudler takes readers on an enthralling and informative tour of this much maligned kingdom." Publ Wkly

Includes bibliographical references

579.6 Mushrooms

McKnight, Kent H.

A **field** guide to mushrooms, North America; [by] Kent H. McKnight and Vera B. McKnight; illustrations by Vera B. McKnight. Houghton Mifflin 1987 429p il hardcover o.p. pa $21   **579.6**

1. Mushrooms
ISBN 0-395-91090-0 pa

LC 86-27799

"More than 500 species [of mushrooms] are described and depicted. . . . Edibility of each species is noted and signified by marginal pictograms both in the text and on the color-plates. . . . Appended: a genial chapter of recipes by Anne Dow, glossary, selected references, and index." Booklist

Smith, Alexander Hanchett

The **mushroom** hunter's field guide; {by} Alexander H. Smith and Nancy Smith Weber. all color & enlarged; University of Mich. Press 1980 316p il $24.95   **579.6**

1. Mushrooms
ISBN 0-472-85610-3

LC 80-10514

First published 1958

This is a "field guide for both novices and experts alike. The introductory chapter explains basic terminology and what to look for when identifying fungi. More than 280 mushrooms are described, including identifying marks, edibility, habitat, native range, and type of spore. A color photograph . . . of each mushroom is most valuable for accurate information." Booklist

Includes bibliographical references

580 Natural history of plants and animals

Goodall, Jane, 1934-

Seeds of Hope; Wisdom and Wonder from the World of Plants. Jane Goodall with Gail Hudson. 1st ed. Grand Central Pub. 2013 384 p. (hardcover) $26.99   **580**

1. Plants 2. Philosophy of nature 3. Hope 4. Trees 5. Human-plant relationships
ISBN 1455513229; 9781455513222

LC 2012045482

This book, by Jane Goodall with Gail Hudson, "examines the critical role that trees and plants play in our world. . . . She introduces us to botanists around the world, as well as places where hope for plants can be found, such as The Millennium Seed Bank, where one billion seeds are preserved.

She shows us the secret world of plants with all their mysteries and potential for healing our bodies as well as Planet Earth." (Publisher's note)

Kassinger, Ruth

✓ ★ A **Garden** of Marvels; How We Discovered That Flowers Have Sex, Leaves Eat Air, and Other Secrets of Plants. Ruth Kassinger. HarperCollins Publishers 2014 416 p. illustrations $25.99 **580**
1. Botany 2. Gardens 3. Botanists 4. Gardening 5. Botany -- Humor 6. Botanists -- United States -- Anecdotes 7. Women gardeners -- United States -- Anecdotes
ISBN 0062048996; 9780062048998
LC 2014002824

In this book, author Ruth Kassinger "sets out to understand the basics of botany in order to become a better gardener. She retraces the progress of the first botanists who banished myths and misunderstandings and discovered that flowers have sex, leaves eat air, roots choose their food, and hormones make morning glories climb fence posts. She also visits modern gardens, farms, and labs to discover the science behind extraordinary plants." (Publisher's note)

"[A]n informal, entertaining account of how early researchers discovered how plants work and what scientists are still learning about plants today." Kirkus

Includes bibliographical references and index

Mabey, Richard

The **cabaret** of plants; forty thousand years of plant life and the human imagination. by Richard Mabey. W W Norton & Co Inc 2016 400 p. color illustrations (hardcover) $29.95 **580**
1. Botany -- History
ISBN 9780393239973
LC 2015033568

This book, by Richard Mabey, "explores dozens of plant species that for millennia have challenged our imaginations, awoken our wonder, and upturned our ideas about history, science, beauty, and belief. Going back to the beginnings of human history, Mabey shows how flowers, trees, and plants have been central to human experience not just as sources of food and medicine but as objects of worship, actors in creation myths, and symbols of war and peace, life and death." (Publisher's note)

"What Mabey does best is invite readers to think about plants in a radical new way, even posing the question as to whether a plant's sensory abilities—electrostatic charges, chemical communication through pheromones and bio- acoustic sound waves—actually constitute intelligence. An unusual and vastly entertaining journey into the world of mysterious plant life as experienced by a gifted nature writer." Kirkus

Includes bibliographical references and index

★ **Magill's** encyclopedia of science; plant life. editor, Bryan D. Ness. Salem Press 2002 4v il map set $457 **580**
1. Reference books 2. Botany -- Encyclopedias
ISBN 1-58765-084-3
LC 2002-13319

This encyclopedia provides "information for any study related to plants, archaea, bacteria, algae, or fungi, from molecular-level processes to planet-wide economic or environmental issues. The 379 signed articles, about half of which are published with revisions and updated bibliographies from several of the publisher's earlier reference books, are arranged into a single alphabet." SLJ

Includes bibliographical references

Marder, Michael

The **philosopher's** plant; an intellectual herbarium. Michael Marder; with drawings by Mathilde Roussel. Columbia University Press 2014 288 p. illustrations (pbk. : alk. paper) $24.95 **580**
1. Botany 2. Philosophy 3. Botany -- History 4. Botany -- Philosophy 5. Plants -- Adaptation 6. Human-plant relationships
ISBN 0231169035; 9780231169028; 9780231169035
LC 2014010349

This book, by Michael Marder and illustrated by Mathilde Roussel, explores how "philosophers have used germination, growth, blossoming, fruition, reproduction, and decay as illustrations of abstract concepts. . . . Choosing twelve botanical specimens that correspond to twelve significant philosophers, . . . [the author] recasts the development of philosophy through the evolution of human and plant relations." (Publisher's note)

Includes bibliographical references and index

581.4   Adaptation

Dunn Chace, Teri

Seeing seeds; discover the unexpected beauty in seedheads, pods, and fruit. Robert Llewellyn and Teri Dunn Chace. Timber Press 2015 284 p. color illustrations $29.95 **581.4**
1. Fruit 2. Seeds 3. Seeds -- Pictorial works
ISBN 1604694920; 9781604694925
LC 2015006910

This book by Teri Dunn Chace and Robert Llewellyn reveals "there is much more to a seed than the plant it will someday become: seeds, seedheads, pods, and fruits have their own astounding beauty that rivals, and sometimes even surpasses, the beauty of flowers. In these stunning pages you'll gain an understanding of how seeds are formed and dispersed, why they look the way they do, and how they fit into the environment." (Publisher's note)

Includes bibliographical references and index

Hanson, Thor

The **triumph** of seeds; how grains, nuts, kernels, pulses, and pips, conquered the plant kingdom and shaped human history. Thor Hanson. Basic Books, a member of the Perseus Books Group 2015 304 p. illustrations (hardcover : alk. paper) $26.99 **581.4**
1. Seeds
ISBN 0465055990; 9780465048724; 9780465055999
LC 2014047078

In this book, author Thor Hanson explains that "[w]e live in a world of seeds. From our morning toast to the cotton in our clothes, they are quite literally the stuff and staff of life, supporting diets, economies, and civilizations around the globe. . . . Spanning the globe, . . . from gardens and flower patches to the spice routes of Kerala, this is a book of knowledge, adventure, and wonder." (Publisher's note)

"Hanson argues that evolutionary intelligence finds the right balance—evolution acts like a gardener, saving the most successful experiments. From cotton to orchids, the future of seeds looks promising. Summing Up: Recommended. All readers." Choice

Includes bibliographical references and index

581.6 Miscellaneous nontaxonomic kinds of plants

Angier, Bradford

Field guide to edible wild plants; revisions by David K. Foster; illustrations by Arthur J. Anderson; additional illustrations by Jacqueline Mahannah, Michelle L. Meneghini, and Kristen E. Workman. 2nd ed.; Stackpole Books 2008 282p il pa $21.95 **581.6**
1. Edible plants
ISBN 978-0-81173-447-9; 0-81173-447-1

LC 2007-40125

First published 1974

"Plants are arranged alphabetically by one of their common names. Each entry includes genus, family affiliation, other common names, a lengthy plant description (including many interesting facts about the plant), notes on distribution, and a statement concerning edibility and preparation of the plant parts." Libr J

Foster, Steven

★ **Peterson** field guide to medicinal plants and herbs of eastern and central North America; Steven Foster and James A. Duke; photographs by Steven Foster. Houghton Mifflin Harcourt 2014 456 p. col. ill. (Peterson field guides) $21 **581.6**
1. Medical botany 2. Plants -- Identification
ISBN 0547943989; 9780547943985

In this book, authors "Steven Foster and James A. Duke have used recent advances in the study of medicinal plants and their combined experience of over 100 years to completely update the 'Peterson Field Guide to Medicinal Plants.' The clear and concise text identifies the key traits, habitats, uses, and warnings for more than 530 of the most significant medicinal plants in the eastern and central United States and Canada including both native and alien species." (Publisher's note)

"A hefty handbook to haul over marsh and meadow, but invaluable to searchers and researchers alike." LJ

Includes bibliographical references (p. 422-425) and indexes

Gibbons, Euell

Stalking the wild asparagus; with illustrations by Margaret F. Schroeder; including a remembrance of the author by John McPhee. 25th anniversary

ed; Hood, A.C. 1987 303p il hardcover o.p. pa $17.50 **581.6**
1. Cooking 2. Edible plants
ISBN 0-911469-036 pa

LC 87-16933

A reprint of the title first published 1962 by McKay

In this series of brief anecdotal essays the naturalist discourses on the identification and preparation of roots, flowers and plants, old Indian legends, and wilderness survival.

Stewart, Amy

★ The **drunken** botanist; the plants that create the world's great drinks. Amy Stewart. Algonquin Books of Chapel Hill 2013 400 p. $19.95 **581.6**
1. Edible plants 2. Alcoholic beverages 3. Cocktails 4. Plants, Edible 5. Plants, Useful
ISBN 1616200464; 9781616200466

LC 2012041725

This book by Amy Stewart "explores the botanical beginnings of our favorite drinks. . . . Each plant description includes history, propagation, and usage details. Stewart includes sidebars with recipes, field guides, planting instructions, a description of the role of bugs in getting from seed to plant to table, and in-depth historical details. She includes archaeological finds such as the presence of barley beer on clay pot fragments dated to 3400 B.C.E." (Library Journal)

Sumner, Judith

The **natural** history of medicinal plants; foreword by Mark Plotkin. Timber Press 2000 235p il hardcover o.p. pa $24.95 **581.6**
1. Medical botany
ISBN 0-88192-483-0; 978-0-88192-957-7 pa; 0-88192-957-3 pa

LC 99-76555

Sumner presents an "accessible introduction to the world of medicinal plants. . . . Some of her most interesting revelations are about the relationships that animals have with plants." Booklist

Includes bibliographical references

Turner, Nancy J.

★ The **North** American guide to common poisonous plants and mushrooms; [by] Nancy J. Turner and Patrick von Aderkas. Timber Press 2009 375p il $29.95 **581.6**
1. Mushrooms 2. Poisonous plants
ISBN 0-88192-929-8; 978-0-88192-929-4

LC 2008-35095

First published 1991 with title: Common poisonous plants and mushrooms of North America

"The book is split into four main categories: mushrooms, wild plants, ornamental and crop plants, and houseplants. Each plant entry includes a . . . photograph to aid the task of identification, a description of the plant, notes on where they commonly occur, and a description of their toxic properties." Publisher's note

Includes bibliographical references

Van Wyk, Ben-Erik

★ **Food** plants of the world; an illustrated guide. Timber Press 2005 480p il $39.95 **581.6**

1. Edible plants

ISBN 0-88192-743-0; 978-0-88192-743-6

LC 2005-44048

This is an "illustrated guide to more than 350 commercially important plants that are sources of cereals, nuts, fruits, vegetables, drinks, herbs, and spices." Choice

Includes bibliographical references

582.1 Herbaceous and woody plants, plants noted for their flowers

Symonds, George W. D.

The **shrub** identification book; the visual method for the practical identification of shrubs, including woody vines and ground covers. photos by A. W. Merwin. William Morrow & Company 1963 379p il pa $22 **582.1**

1. Shrubs

ISBN 978-0-688-05040-5; 0-688-05040-9

First published 1963 by Barrow

"Part I gives pictorial keys for thorns, leaves, flowers, fruit, twigs and bark of broad-leaved upright shrubs. Part II contains 200 master pages arranged under four categories, with data on habitat, blooming period, etc., accompanying the photographs." Wilson Libr Bull

Includes bibliographical references

582.13 Plants noted for their flowers

Heywood, V. H.

Flowering plant families of the world; [by] V.H. Heywood . . . [et al.] Updated & rev.; Firefly Books 2007 424p il map $59.95 **582.13**

1. Flowers

ISBN 978-1-55407-206-4; 1-55407-206-9

LC 2007-272849

First published 1978 in the United Kingdom with title: Flowering plants of the world

"At the core of the book are . . . entries on 504 flowering plant families. Each entry describes distribution, anatomy, habitat, classification and commercial uses." Publisher's note

Includes bibliographical references

Spellenberg, Richard

National Audubon Society field guide to North American wildflowers, western region; 2nd ed rev; Knopf 2001 862p il map $19.95 **582.13**

1. Wild flowers

ISBN 0-375-40233-0

LC 2001-269242

First published 1979

"More than 940 . . . full-color images show the wildflowers of western North America close-up and in their natural habitats. . . . Images are grouped by flower color and shape

and keyed to . . . descriptions that reflect current taxonomy." Publisher's note

Thieret, John W.

National Audubon Society field guide to North American wildflowers: eastern region; revising author, John W. Thieret; original authors, William A. Niering and Nancy C. Olmstead. Knopf 2001 879p il map (National Audubon Society field guide series) $19.95 **582.13**

1. Wild flowers

ISBN 0-375-40232-2

LC 2001-269241

First published 1979 under the authorship of William A. Niering and Nancy C. Olmstead

"Covers the area east of the Rockies and east of the Big Bend area of Texas to the Atlantic. Color photographs together with family and species descriptions make this a most useful field guide." Sci News {review of 1979 edition}

Wells, Diana

100 flowers and how they got their names; illustrated by Ippy Patterson. Algonquin Bks. 1997 257p il $17.95 **582.13**

1. Flowers 2. Popular plant names

ISBN 1-56512-138-4

LC 96-22296

The author "describes the mythology and history behind 100 favorite garden plants, emphasizing the exploits of botanists and plant explorers who brought them out of their native habitats." Libr J

Includes bibliographical references

582.16 Trees

Hugo, Nancy Ross

★ **Seeing** trees; Nancy Ross Hugo; photography by Robert J. Llewellyn. 1st ed; Timber Press 2011 242p. col. ill. **582.16**

1. Trees

ISBN 9781604692198

LC 2010052455

National Outdoor Book Awards: Nature and the Environment (2011)

This book, "[f]ocusing on widely grown trees, . . . describes the rewards of careful and regular tree viewing, outlines strategies for improving your observations, and describes some of the most visually interesting tree structures, including leaves, flowers, buds, leaf scars, twigs, and bark. . . . [P]rofiles of ten familiar species -- including such beloved trees as white oak, southern magnolia, white pine, and tulip poplar -- show you how to recognize and understand many of their most compelling (but usually overlooked) physical features." (Publisher's note)

Includes bibliographical references and index.

Johnson, Hugh

The **world** of trees; consultant editor, John Grimshaw; preface by Thomas Pakenham. University of California Press 2010 400p il map $34.95 **582.16**

1. Trees

ISBN 978-0-520-24756-7

First published 1973 with title: The international book of trees

"The first section of the book provides general information on how trees grow, the life cycle of trees, their classification, and morphological characteristics. Next comes a compendium of more than 600 taxa of trees, divided into conifers and broadleaves. Beautiful color photographs, including portraits and landscape scenes, grace every page. The last section includes a guide to choosing trees for the landscape and a chart comparing the ornamental traits of trees throughout the seasons." Am Gardener

Kingsbury, Noël

The **glory** of the tree; an illustrated history. by Noel Kingsbury; photography by Andrea Jones. Firefly Books Ltd 2014 288 p. colour illustrations $39.95 **582.16**

1. Trees

ISBN 1770852654; 9781770852655

This book, written by Noel Kingsbury, with photography by Andrea Jones, "describes 90 species of tree that collectively span the millennia of evolution and cross the globe. Organized into six categories -- Antiquity, Ecology, Sacred, Utility, Food and Ornament -- the trees are presented in short chapters that touch on botany, history, culture and more." (Publisher's note)

"Notable for splendid color photographs and authoritative commentary, The Glory of the Tree is highly recommended for public libraries and the collections of garden and landscape enthusiasts." Booklist

Little, Elbert Luther

★ The **Audubon** Society field guide to North American trees; [by] Elbert L. Little; photographs by Sonja Bullaty and Angelo Lomeo [et. al.]; visual key by Susan Rayfield and Olivia Buehl. Knopf 1980 2v il v1 $19.95; v2 $19.95 **582.16**

1. Trees -- North America

ISBN 0-394-50760-6 v1; 0-394-50761-4 v2

LC 79-3474

These "guides are unusual in that they contain many color photographs of parts of a living tree. The identification keys are easy to use, being based on an arrangement by leaf shapes, flowers, fruit, and fall leaves, and giving drawings of winter silhouettes. The eastern guide covers 364 species, the western guide describes 314 species; they divide the country at central Texas and the Rockies." Libr J

Nadkarni, Nalini

Between earth and sky; our intimate connections to trees. [by] Nalini M. Nadkarni. University of California Press 2008 322p il $45; pa $17.95 **582.16**

1. Trees

ISBN 978-0-520-24856-4; 978-0-520-26165-5 pa

LC 2008-2162

"This book presents a multifaceted, multidisciplined approach to the appreciation of trees that combines science, art, literature, poetry, and spirituality, including a discussion of the practical use of trees throughout history. . . . Beginning with a very enlightening chapter defining just what a tree is and describing the attributes of trees, the book thoroughly explores the human affinities to trees, explaining that trees fulfill human needs at every level of our existence. The chapters cover physical needs, security, health, recreation, time and history, symbols and language, and finally spirituality and mindfulness." Choice

Includes bibliographical references

Sibley, David

The **Sibley** guide to trees; written and illustrated by David Allen Sibley. Alfred A. Knopf 2009 xxxviii, 426p il map $39.95 **582.16**

1. Trees -- North America

ISBN 978-0-375-41519-7

LC 2009-927625

This "is an outstanding book that should be available in all public libraries, schools, colleges, universities, and homes. The text is comprehensive and the illustrations are pertinent, accurate, and clear." Sci Books Films

Wohlleben, Peter

The **Hidden** Life of Trees; What They Feel, How They Communicate—Discoveries from a Secret World. by Peter Wohlleben. Greystone Books 2016 288 p. illustrations (ebook) $24.99; $24.95 **582.16**

1. Trees 2. Forests and forestry

ISBN 9781771642491; 1771642483; 9781771642484

In this book, author Peter Wohlleben "draws on groundbreaking scientific discoveries to describe how trees are like human families: tree parents live together with their children, communicate with them, support them as they grow, share nutrients with those who are sick or struggling, and even warn each other of impending dangers. Wohlleben also shares his deep love of woods and forests, explaining the amazing processes of life, death, and regeneration he has observed in his woodland." (Publisher's note)

"In this spirited exploration, he guarantees that readers will never look at these life forms in quite the same way again." LJ

Includes bibliographical references (pages 252-260) and index.

583 Dicotyledons

Anderson, Edward F.

★ The **cactus** family; with a foreword by Wilhelm Barthlott; and a chapter on cactus cultivation by Roger Brown. Timber Press 2001 776p il maps $99.95 **583**

1. Cactus

ISBN 0-88192-498-9; 978-0-88192-498-5

LC 00-60700

This reference work on cactaceae covers 125 genera and 1810 species

"While more than 1,000 photographs overall illustrate the extraordinary diversity and beautiful flowers of cacti, the main section—an alphabetically arranged reference—will arguably rank as the definitive work readers will use to examine and identify cactus genera, species, and subspecies." Booklist

Includes bibliographical references

Pappalardo, Joe

Sunflowers; the secret history; the unauthorized biography of the world's most beloved weed. Overlook Press 2008 256p il $22.95 **583**

1. Sunflowers

ISBN 978-1-58567-991-1; 1-58567-991-7

A "look at a flower so ubiquitous that its critical role in cultural development since the dawn of time often goes overlooked. A glib, upbeat writer and fiercely determined researcher, Pappalardo intrepidly investigates everything from the sunflower's genetic history and recent bioengineering discoveries to its influence on global economies from the U.S. to Uganda." Booklist

590 Animals

Jones, Richard

House Guests, House Pests; A Natural History of Animals in the Home. by Richard Jones. St. Martin's Press 2015 288 p. illustrations $28 **590**

1. Household pests

ISBN 1472906233; 9781472906236

In this book, author Richard Jones notes that from "bats in the belfry to beetles in the cellar, moths in the wardrobe and mosquitoes in the bedroom, humans cannot escape the attentions of the animal kingdom. . . . [He] poses questions such as where these animals came from, can we live with them, can we get rid of them, and should we?" (Publisher's note)

"Although not the intended audience, curious U.S. readers can still enjoy this gentle perspective on creatures that share our sacred space." LJ

Stewart, Tracey

Do unto animals; a friendly guide to how animals live, and how we can make their lives better. Tracey Stewart; illustrated by Lisel Ashlock. Artisan 2015 200 p. color illustrations (alk. paper) $19.95 **590**

1. Animal welfare 2. Human-animal relationship 3. Pets 4. Livestock 5. Animal communication 6. Animals -- Habitations 7. Human-animal relationships

ISBN 9781579656232; 1579656234

LC 2015010995

In this book, "through hundreds of charming illustrations, a few homemade projects, and her humorous, knowledgeable voice, [Tracey] Stewart provides insight into the secret lives of animals and the kindest ways to live with and alongside them. [Its] part practical guide, part memoir of her life with animals, and part testament to the power of giving back." (Publisher's note)

"Rich in informed insights on animal behavior, augmented by creative craft projects, and alluring with clever watercolor illustrations, Stewart's passionate and practical guide to living with domestic pets, backyard critters, and

farm animals artfully combines sensible advice with grassroots advocacy." Booklist

Includes bibliographical references and index

590.73 Collections and exhibits of living mammals

Baratay, Eric

★ Zoo: a history of zoological gardens in the West; [by] Eric Baratay, Elisabeth Hardouin-Fugier. Reaktion Bks. 2002 400p il $40 **590.73**

1. Zoos

ISBN 1-86189-111-3

In this history of zoos the authors "take a social history focus, examining how people view wild animals and how that has changed over time. . . . One can read the text or spend hours simply enjoying the images. Libraries that have other titles on zoos will still want to purchase this." Libr J

Includes bibliographical references

French, Thomas

Zoo story; life in the garden of captives. Hyperion 2010 288p $24.99 **590.73**

1. Zoos 2. Lowry Park Zoo

ISBN 978-1-4013-2346-2

The author "chronicles the rise of Lowry Park from one of the worst zoos in the country to one of the best. . . . This behind-the-scenes look will both entertain and enlighten animal lovers. It is a story that needs to be told, and French does it superbly." Libr J

Includes bibliographical references

Robinson, Phillip T.

★ Life at the zoo: behind the scenes with the animal doctors. Columbia University Press 2004 293p il $27.95; pa $17.95 **590.73**

1. Zoos

ISBN 0-231-13248-4; 0-231-13249-2 pa

LC 2004-43893

"It would be difficult to cover even one aspect, such as animal health, that might affect the overall management of a zoo, but Dr. Philip Robinson manages to provide an excellent coverage of just about everything that might be involved in the operation of a zoo." Sci Books Films

Includes bibliographical references

590.75 Museum activities and services

Milgrom, Melissa

Still life; adventures in taxidermy. Houghton Mifflin Harcourt 2010 285p $25 **590.75**

1. Taxidermy

ISBN 978-0-618-40547-3

LC 2009-13511

"An animated initiation to the realm of taxidermy—its cultural significance, its hybrid status between art, craft and science, and the obsessive, idiosyncratic personalities who practice it. . . . Brimming with respect and immersive vitality." Kirkus

591 Specific topics in natural history of animals

Wildlife of the world; contributors Jamie Ambrose [and nine others] DK Publishing 2015 480 p. illustrations, color maps $50 **591**
1. Animals 2. Animals -- Pictorial works
ISBN 1465438041; 9781465438041

LC 2015458474

This book, by DK Publishing, foreword by Don E. Wilson and produced in association with the Smithsonian Institution,"takes you on a journey through some of the most scenic and rich animal habitats--from the Amazon rain forests to the Himalayas, the Sahara to the South Pole--meeting the most important animals in each ecosystem along the way.... An additional eighty-page illustrated reference section on the animal kingdom explains the animal groups and profiles additional species." (Publisher's note)

591.3 Genetics, evolution, age characteristics

Nielsen, Claus
Animal evolution; interrelationships of the living phyla. Claus Nielsen. Oxford University Press 2012 x, 402 p.p (hbk) $69.99 **591.3**
1. Evolution 2. Developmental biology 3. Unicellular organisms 4. Phylogeny 5. Evolution (Biology)
ISBN 0199606021; 019960603X; 9780199606023; 9780199606030

LC 2011941928

In this book, Claus Nielsen "examines the unity of the animal kingdom by tracing the evolution of all the 31 living phyla from their unicellar ancestor. The second edition incorporates new morphological data and new topic areas from the past decade, including histological/ultrastructural and embriological data, numerical cladistic analyses, DNA sequencing and developmental biology." (Booknews)
Includes bibliographical references and index.

591.47 Protective and locomotor adaptations, color

Emlen, Douglas J.
Animal weapons; the evolution of battle. by Douglas J. Emlen; illustrated by David J. Tuss. Henry Holt & Co. 2014 288 p. 16 plates; color illustrations (hardcover) $30 **591.47**
1. Weapons 2. Animal defenses 3. Military art and science 4. Animal weapons 5. Defensive (Military science)
ISBN 0805094504; 9780805094503

LC 2014004772

This book, by Douglas J. Emlen, is the "story behind the stunning, extreme weapons we see in the animal world--teeth and horns and claws--and what they can tell us about the way humans develop and use arms and other weapons. .... He looks at everything from our armor and camouflage to the evolution of the rifle and the structures human populations have built across different regions and eras to protect their homes and communities." (Publisher's note)

"Emlen's excellent writing will draw in readers intrigued by astonishingly powerful weapons, both in the wild and in the military, and how they have evolved owing to selective pressures. Though Philip Street's Animal Weapons describes a greater variety of animal defenses, Emlen's book is a more compelling read because it focuses on the parallels between animal and humans in this regard." LJ
Includes bibliographical references and index

Wilkinson, Matt
Restless creatures; the story of life in ten movements. Matt Wilkinson. Basic Books 2015 320 p. illustrations (hardcover) $28.99 **591.47**
1. Anatomy 2. Evolution 3. Human locomotion 4. Animal locomotion 5. Extremities (Anatomy) -- Evolution
ISBN 9780465065721; 9780465098699

LC 2015037173

In this book, author Matt Wilkinson "makes the bold new argument that the true story of evolution is the story of locomotion, from the first stirrings of bacteria to the amazing feats of Olympic athletes. By retracing the four-billion-year history of locomotion, evolutionary biologist Matt Wilkinson shows how the physical challenges of moving from place to place—when coupled with the implacable logic of natural selection—offer a uniquely powerful means of illuminating the living world." (Publisher's note)

"Through all of this lucidly detailed narrative, readers see how evolution endowed life with powers of movement, and how those powers opened dramatic new possibilities for evolutionary metamorphoses." Booklist
Includes bibliographical references and index

591.5 Behavior

American Museum of Natural History
Animal life; Charlotte Uhlenbroek, [editor in chief] DK Pub. 2008 512p il map $50 **591.5**
1. Animal behavior 2. Animals -- Pictorial works
ISBN 978-0-7566-3986-0; 0-7566-3986-7

LC 2008-300010

This book "provides an excellent overview of the animal world written at a level accessible to students and the general public. Introductory sections cover basics of animal life such as evolution, animal history, classification, and anatomy. Animal behavior receives the most extensive treatment, encompassing living space, hunting and feeding, defense mechanisms, sex and reproduction, birth and development, society, communication, and intelligence." Booklist

Balcombe, Jonathan
The **exultant** ark; a pictorial tour of animal pleasure. University of California Press 2011 214p il $34.95 **591.5**
1. Pleasure 2. Animal behavior
ISBN 978-0-520-26024-5; 0-520-26024-4

LC 2010-43747

"As animal behaviourist Jonathan Balcombe sees it, too often the animal kingdom is portrayed solely as a realm of dire and perpetual struggle for survival. He argues that observations of playfulness or expressions of pleasure by nonhuman creatures of all stripes, feathers and fins are depicted as nothing more than evolutionary adaptation. The Exultant Ark, his pictorial exploration of pleasure among creatures from primate to porpoise, challenges this idea. It intersperses glorious images of animals preening, grooming and gallivanting with snippets of studies suggesting such behaviours belie an overly utilitarian interpretation." New Sci

Includes bibliographical references

Second nature; the inner lives of animals. foreword by J.M. Coetzee. Palgrave Macmillan 2010 242p il $27.00; $27.00 **591.5**
1. Animal behavior 2. Animal intelligence 3. Animal psychology 4. Social behavior in animals
ISBN 0230613624; 9780230613621

LC 2009-30770

The author of Pleasurable Kingdom (2006) argues that animals are "sentient beings capable of feelings and pain and emotions." (Publisher's note) Index.

The author "draws on the latest research, observational studies and personal anecdotes to reveal the full gamut of animal experience—from emotions, to problem solving, to moral judgment. Balcombe challenges the widely held idea that nature is red in tooth and claw, highlighting animal traits we have disregarded until now: their nuanced understanding of social dynamics, their consideration for others, and their strong tendency to avoid violent conflict." Publisher's note

Includes bibliographical references

Bekoff, Marc

Wild justice; the moral lives of animals. [by] Marc Bekoff and Jessica Pierce. University of Chicago Press 2009 188p il $26; pa $17 **591.5**
1. Animal behavior 2. Animal intelligence 3. Animal psychology 4. Motivation in animals 5. Social behavior in animals
ISBN 0-226-04161-1; 0-226-04163-8 pa; 978-0-226-04161-2; 978-0-226-04163-6 pa

LC 2008-40173

Bekoff and Pierce argue "that animals exhibit a broad repertoire of moral behaviors, including fairness, empathy, trust, and reciprocity. Underlying these behaviors is a complex and nuanced range of emotions, backed by a high degree of intelligence and surprising behavioral flexibility. . . . [The authors draw] conclusion that there is no moral gap between humans and other species: morality is an evolved trait that we unquestionably share with other social mammals." (Publisher's note) Index.

The authors "discuss recent scientific studies documenting that great apes, monkeys, wolves, coyotes, hyenas, dolphins, whales, elephants, rats, and mice are capable of a wide range of moral behavior. They strongly urge the scientific and philosophical communities to recognize that these animals can act as moral agents within the context of their own social groups. This provocative and well-argued view of animal morality may surprise some readers as it challenges outdated assumptions about animals." Libr J

Includes bibliographical references

Benyus, Janine M., 1958-

The **secret** language of animals; A Guide to Remarkable Behavior. by Janine M. Benyus; illustra-

tions by Juan Carlos Barberis. Black Dog & Leventhal Pub 2014 480 p. illustrations $22.95 **591.5**
1. Animal behavior 2. Wildlife watching 3. Zoo animals -- Behavior
ISBN 1579129684; 9781579129682

LC 98028743

In this book, "biologist Janine Benyus takes us inside the animal kingdom and shows us the whys and the hows behind the distinctive behavior of creatures great and small in their natural environments. Divided geographically into five sections—Africa, Asia, North America, the oceans, and the poles—the book examines and describes the behavior, body language, and patterns of communication of 20 different animals." (Publisher's note)

"The narrative is extremely accessible, and readers of all ages will enjoy learning something new about their favorite zoo animals. Recommended for most public libraries, where this would do well in the circulating collection." Booklist

Includes bibliographical references (p. 444-455) and index

Berger, Joel

The **better** to eat you with; fear in the animal world. University of Chicago Press 2008 305p il map $29 **591.5**
1. Fear 2. Animal behavior
ISBN 978-0-226-04363-0; 0-226-04363-0

LC 2008-00418

This is "an engaging book about how an understanding of predator-prey dynamics can inform conservation biology." Times Higher Ed

Includes bibliographical references (p. 287-292)

Boysen, Sarah Till

The **smartest** animals on the planet; with a contribution from Deborah Custance. Firefly Books 2009 192p il map $35 **591.5**
1. Animal behavior 2. Animal intelligence
ISBN 978-1-5540-7456-3; 1-5540-7456-8

"Succinctly written and sumptuously illustrated with photographs and diagrams, this appealing book is sure to fascinate the general reader and inspire the science student considering a career in animal behavior or cognition." Libr J

Braitman, Laurel

Animal madness; how anxious dogs, compulsive parrots, and elephants in recovery help us understand ourselves. Laurel Braitman. Simon & Schuster 2014 384 p. (hardback) $28 **591.5**
1. Mental illness 2. Animal behavior 3. Comparative psychology 4. Animal psychology
ISBN 1451627009; 9781451627008

LC 2014000791

This book by Laurel Braitman "draws evidence from across the world to show how humans and other animals are astonishingly similar when it comes to their feelings and the ways in which they lose their minds. . . . Nonhuman animals can lose their minds. And when they do, it often looks a lot like human mental illness." (Publisher's note)

"Braitman's gradual accretion of reasons to believe in animal emotional states that we can relate to, including the loopy ones, gives pause and sparks curiosity." Kirkus

★ **Encyclopedia** of animal behavior; edited by Marc Bekoff; foreword by Jane Goodall. Greenwood Press 2004 3v il set $349.95   **591.5**
1. Animal behavior
ISBN 0-313-32745-9

LC 2004-56073

This encyclopedia describes "what makes animals tick using techniques that range from molecular approaches to analysis of species. The 300 entries, some stretching to 7000 words, discuss topics as diverse as concept learning in pigeons and stress in dolphins." Libr J

Includes bibliographical references

Fagan, Brian
The **intimate** bond; how animals shaped human history. Brian Fagan. Bloomsbury Press 2014 304 p. illustrations, maps (alk. paper) $28   **591.5**
1. Working animals -- History 2. Human-animal relationships -- History
ISBN 1620405725; 9781620405727

LC 2014027152

Animals, and our ever-changing relationship with them, have left an indelible mark on human history. From the dawn of our existence, animals and humans have been constantly redefining their relationship with one another, and entire civilizations have risen and fallen upon this curious bond we share with our fellow fauna. Brian Fagan unfolds this fascinating story from the first wolf who wandered into our prehistoric ancestors' camp and found companionship, to empires built on the backs of horses, donkeys, and camels, to the industrial age when some animals became commodities, often brutally exploited, and others became pets, nurtured and pampered, sometimes to absurd extremes." McMillan Palgrave

"History, anthropology, and cultural studies enthusiasts will enjoy this excellent, intelligent book, as will animal lovers of all stripes." LJ

Includes bibliographical references and index

Foster, Charles
Being a Beast; Adventures Across the Species Divide. Charles Foster. Henry Holt & Co. 2016 256 p. (hardcover) $28   **591.5**
1. Animal behavior 2. Human-animal relationships -- History
ISBN 1627796339; 9781627796330

In this book author Charles Foster "explores what it's really like to be an animal--by living like them. He lived alongside badgers for weeks, sleeping in a sett in a Welsh hillside and eating earthworms. He caught fish in his teeth while swimming like an otter; rooted through London garbage cans as an urban fox; was hunted by bloodhounds as a red deer. And he followed the swifts on their migration route over the Strait of Gibraltar, discovering himself to be strangely connected to the birds." (Publisher's note)

"This approach, along with his willingness to address and avoid the temptation for anthropomorphism, makes his book interesting and informative." Pub Wkly

Includes bibliographical references (pages [219]-226) and index.

Grandin, Temple
★ **Animals** in translation; using the mysteries of autism to decode animal behavior. [by] Temple Grandin and Catherine Johnson. Scribner 2010 356p $28; ebook $18.99   **591.5**
1. Autism 2. Animal behavior
ISBN 978-1-4391-8710-4; 978-1-4391-3084-1 ebook
First published 2005

"This fascinating book will teach readers to see as animals see, to be a little more visual and a little less verbal, and, as a unique analysis of animal behavior, it belongs in all libraries." Booklist

Includes bibliographical references

Griffin, Donald Redfield
Animal minds; beyond cognition to consciousness. {by} Donald R. Griffin. {Rev and expanded}; University of Chicago Press 2001 355p $27.50 **591.5**
1. Animal behavior
ISBN 0-226-30865-0

LC 00-10006

First published 1992

"Griffin's book will enlighten, delight and even ruffle some feathers." Publ Wkly

Includes bibliographical references

Masson, J. Moussaieff
When elephants weep; the emotional lives of animals. {by} Jeffrey Moussaieff Masson and Susan McCarthy. Delacorte Press 1995 xxiii, 291p il hardcover o.p. pa $15.95   **591.5**
1. Animal behavior 2. Animal intelligence
ISBN 0-385-31428-0 pa

LC 94-23819

The authors gather "the evidence to date for the existence of emotions and, hence, something approaching human consciousness in animals. . . . Masson and McCarthy do a commendable job of synthesizing the material they tackle . . . making it efficiently readable." Booklist

Includes bibliographical references

McCarthy, Susan
★ **Becoming** a tiger; how baby animals learn to live in the wild. HarperCollins 2004 418p hardcover o.p. pa $13.95   **591.5**
1. Animal intelligence
ISBN 0-06-620924-2; 0-06-093484-0 pa

LC 2003-67553

"McCarthy writes clearly and her penchant for humor . . . makes the book an easy read, both for students of learning and those who can't get enough of television's Animal Planet." Publ Wkly

Includes bibliographical references

Morell, Virginia
Animal wise; the thoughts and emotions of our fellow creatures. Virginia Morell. Random House Inc 2013 304 p. $26   **591.5**
1. Animal behavior 2. Thought and thinking 3.

Cognition in animals 4. Human-animal communication
ISBN 0307461440; 9780307461445

LC 2012031503

This book, by Virginia Morell, "explores the frontiers of research on animal cognition and emotion. . . . [The book] takes us . . . into the inner world of animals, from ants to elephants to wolves, and from sharp-shooting archerfish to pods of dolphins that rumble like rival street gangs. . . . She probes the moral and ethical dilemmas of recognizing that even 'lesser animals' have cognitive abilities such as memory, feelings, personality, and self-awareness." (Publisher's note)

Smoller, Jordan

The **other** side of normal; how biology is providing the clues to unlock the secrets of normal and abnormal behavior. Jordan Smoller. HarperCollins 2012 390 p. **591.5**

1. Psychology 2. Human behavior 3. Mental illness 4. Behavior genetics 5. Abnormal psychology 6. Psychobiology 7. Norm (Philosophy) 8. Biological psychiatry
ISBN 0061492191; 9780061492198; 9780061492204

LC 2011040827

In this book, "[t]he author uses the 2010 announcement by the American Psychiatric Association of provisional plans to revise the Diagnostic and Statistical Manual of Mental Disorders as an opportunity to revisit the hot-button issue of what constitutes mental disease. In his opinion, one of the shortcomings of the DSM is its creation of 'categories from constellations of symptoms' without understanding how they connect to the 'functional organization of the mind and brain.'" (Kirkus)
Includes bibliographical references

Waal, F. B. M. de (Frans B. M.), 1948-

★ **Are** We Smart Enough to Know How Smart Animals Are? Frans de Waal. W W Norton & Co Inc 2016 352 p. illustrations $27.95 **591.5**

1. Psychology 2. Animal intelligence
ISBN 0393246183; 9780393246186

LC 2015049994

This book by Frans de Waal "based on research involving crows, dolphins, parrots, sheep, wasps, bats, whales, and of course chimpanzees and bonobos, . . . explores both the scope and the depth of animal intelligence. He offers a firsthand account of how science has stood traditional behaviorism on its head by revealing how smart animals really are, and how we've underestimated their abilities for too long." (Publisher's note)

"This insightful and fascinating work by a scientist who has been at the forefront of new thinking about primates and what it means to be human is highly recommended. De Waal fans and general readers interested in the field of animal cognition will be delighted." Library Journal

Weiner, Jonathan

Time, love, memory; a great biologist and his quest for the origins of behavior. Knopf 1999 300p il $27.50; pa $14 **591.5**

1. Behavior genetics 2. Biophysicists 3. Neuroscientists

4. College teachers
ISBN 0-679-44435-1; 0-679-76390-2 pa

LC 98-43128

An exploration of the work of "one of the unsung pioneers of molecular biology: brash, eccentric physicist-turned-biologist Seymour Benzer. By studying tiny genetic mutations in the fruit fly, Benzer seeks to shed light on the question of whether genes determine behavior. Weiner . . . presents an elegant scientific detective story." Publ Wkly
Includes bibliographical references

591.56   Behavior relating to life cycle

Bagemihl, Bruce

Biological exuberance; animal homosexuality and natural diversity. illustrated by John Megahan. St. Martin's Press 1999 751p il map $40; pa $21.95 **591.56**

1. Homosexuality 2. Animal behavior
ISBN 0-312-19239-8; 0-312-25377-X pa

LC 98-28528

The author "challenges the belief that homosexuality is an aberration in nature by revealing the documented homosexual or transgendered behavior of 450 animal species. Contesting the idea that scarcity and functionality are the primary agents of biological change, biologist Bagemihl persuasively argues that abundance and extravagance are just as crucial to the mosaic of life." Publ Wkly
Includes bibliographical references

Safina, Carl

Beyond words; what animals think and feel. Carl Safina. Henry Holt & Co. 2015 480 p. 16 plates; illustrations (hardcover) $32 **591.56**

1. Animal behavior 2. Animal intelligence 3. Animal psychology 4. Whales -- Psychology 5. Wolves -- Psychology 6. Elephants -- Psychology 7. Psychology, Comparative
ISBN 0805098887; 9780805098884

LC 2014045385

This book, by Carl Safina, "offers an intimate view of animal behavior to challenge the fixed boundary between humans and nonhuman animals. . . . [It] brings forth . . . insight into the unique personalities of animals through extraordinary stories of animal joy, grief, jealousy, anger, and love. The similarity between human and nonhuman consciousness, self-awareness, and empathy calls us to re-evaluate how we interact with animals." (Publisher's note)

"With forays into neurology and diverse animal-behavior studies, Safina reveals that ours is just one of many powerful minds at work on Earth and that we share many profound traits with our fellow animals. By turns mesmerizing, thrilling, and tragic, Safina's enlightening inquiry into animal intelligence calls for a new, compassionate perspective before we unwittingly drive our precious animal kin into extinction." Booklist
Includes bibliographical references and index

Wilcove, David S.

No way home; the decline of the world's great animal migrations. with illustrations by Louise Zemaitis. Island Press/Shearwater Books 2008 253p il map $24.95 **591.56**

1. Environmental degradation 2. Animals -- Migration
ISBN 978-1-55963-985-9; 1-55963-985-7

LC 2007-26205

"Absorbing and thought provoking, [this work] deserves to be widely read and used to promote conservation action." Science

Includes bibliographical references

Zuk, M.

Sexual selections; what we can and can't learn about sex from animals. {by} Marlene Zuk. University of Calif. Press 2002 239p il $40; pa $16.95 **591.56**

1. Sexual behavior in animals
ISBN 0-520-21974-0; 0-520-24075-8 pa

LC 2001-5771

"Fascinating and persuasive. Zuk is not an idealogue, just an unusually clear-eyed scholar." N Y Times Book Rev

Includes bibliographical references and index

591.562 Sexual behavior

Bondar, Carin

Wild Sex; The Science Behind Mating in the Animal Kingdom. by Carin Bondar Ph. D. W.W. Norton & Co Inc. 2016 400 p. $27.95 **591.562**

1. Sexual behavior in animals
ISBN 1681771667; 9781681771663

This book, by Carin Bondar Ph. D., is a "guide to the reproductive habits of creatures great and small. . . . She looks at the evolution of sexual organs (and how they've shaped social hierarchies), tactics of seduction, and the mechanics of sex. She investigates a wide range of topics, from whether animals experience pleasure from sex to what happens when females hold the reproductive power." (Publisher's note)

"A fascinating peek into the intimate behavior of our animal cousins that provides new insight into the benefits of being human." Kirkus

Includes bibliographic references (pages 295-366) and glossary.

591.59 Communication

Friend, Tim

Animal talk; breaking the codes of animal language. Free Press 2004 274p il $25; pa $15 **591.59**

1. Animal communication
ISBN 0-7432-0157-4; 0-7432-0158-2 pa

LC 2003-63107

"The author describes the methods of, and reasons behind, animal communication and demonstrates that human and animal communication are not so widely disparate as once believed. Friend also gives background details on the basics of communication theory, genetics, evolution, and the progression of scientific thought regarding animal communication. . . . His humorous and engaging prose style makes this a captivating read." Libr J

Includes bibliographical references

591.6 Miscellaneous nontaxonomic kinds of animals

Quammen, David

★ **Monster** of God; the man-eating predator in the jungles of history and the mind. Norton 2003 513p maps $26.95; pa $15.95 **591.6**

1. Dangerous animals 2. Predatory animals 3. Endangered species
ISBN 0-393-05140-4; 0-393-32609-8 pa

LC 2003-7812

"Rich with personal stories that clarify humanity's true place in the universe, this book will leave the reader eager for more. . . . This has all the makings of a science book of the year. Highly recommended." Libr J

Includes bibliographical references

591.68 Rare and endangered animals

DeBuys, William

The **last** unicorn; a search for one of Earth's rarest creatures. William DeBuys. Little, Brown & Co. 2015 368 p. $18 **591.68**

1. Saola 2. Laos -- Description and travel 3. Nakai-Nam Theun National Biodiversity Conservation Area (Laos) 4. Saola -- Laos -- Nakai-Nam Theun National Biodiversity Conservation Area 5. Endangered species -- Laos -- Nakai-Nam Theun National Biodiversity Conservation Area 6. Wildlife conservation -- Laos -- Nakai-Nam Theun National Biodiversity Conservation Area
ISBN 0316232874; 9780316232869; 9780316232876

LC 2014020923

In this book, William DeBuys "recounts his journey to the Nakai-Nam Theun region of Laos in search of the saola, an endangered antelopelike creature that has rarely been seen by man. . . . The creature recalls the mythical unicorn as it has largely evaded discovery, leaving scientists to piece together information based on bone samples, hunter accounts, and photographic evidence." (Library Journal)

"Recommended for readers of popular science, travel, and autobiography." LJ

Girling, Richard

The **Hunt** for the Golden Mole; All Creatures Great & Small and Why They Matter. Richard Girling. Counterpoint Press 2014 312 p. illustrations $26 **591.68**

1. Hunting 2. Rare animals 3. Moles (Animals) 4. Golden moles -- Somalia 5. Extinct animals -- Somalia 6. Biodiversity -- South Africa 7. Nature conservation -- South Africa 8. Hunting -- Moral and ethical aspects
ISBN 1619024500; 9781619024502

LC 2014022506

This book, "taking as its narrative engine the hunt for an animal that is legendarily rare, Richard Girling writes [a] . . . history of humankind's interest in hunting and collecting--what prompts us to do this? What good might come of our need to catalog all the living things of the natural world?" (Publisher's note)

"Though Girling presents a sobering assessment of the state of the world's fauna, he does so with the dramatic flair of a novelist and eye for detail of a travel journalist. The result is a page-turning, thought-provoking treatise on a desperate environmental crisis." Booklist

Includes bibliographical references and index

O'Connor, M. R.

Resurrection Science; Conservation, De-extinction and the Precarious Future of Wild Things. M.R. O'Connor. St. Martin's Press 2015 266 p. $25.99 **591.68**
1. Climate change 2. Extinction (Biology)
ISBN 113727929X; 9781137279293

LC 2015004485

This book, by M.R. O'Connor, "explores the extreme measures scientists are taking to try and save them, from captive breeding and genetic management to de-extinction. In stories of sixteenth-century galleon excavations, panther-tracking in Florida swamps, ancient African rainforests, Neanderthal tool-making, and cryogenic DNA banks, O'Connor investigates the philosophical questions of an age in which we 'play god' with earth's biodiversity." (Publisher's note)

"A book as thought-provoking as it is fascinating." Booklist

Includes bibliographical references and index.

Shapiro, Beth

How to Clone a Mammoth; The Science of De-extinction. Beth Shapiro. Princeton University Press 2015 256 p. illustrations (some color) $24.95 **591.68**
1. Genetic engineering 2. Extinction (Biology)
ISBN 0691157057; 9780691157054

LC 2014049574

This book, by Beth Shapiro, "walks readers through the astonishing and controversial process of de-extinction. From deciding which species should be restored, to sequencing their genomes, to anticipating how revived populations might be overseen in the wild, . . . [the author] vividly explores the extraordinary cutting-edge science that is being used--today--to resurrect the past." (Publisher's note)

"The beauty of this work is in its honesty: Shapiro, who is invested in this science as a practitioner, does not attempt to woo the masses. She takes the ethical concerns head on, not as an advocate but as an honest broker. This book is appropriate for undergraduate biology as well as graduate courses and seminars in environmental ethics, human dimensions, and conservation genetics or for a reading seminar. Summing Up: Highly recommended. Upper-division undergraduates and graduate students; general readers." Choice

591.7 Animal ecology, animals characteristic of specific environments

Heinrich, Bernd

Life everlasting; the animal way of death. Bernd Heinrich. Houghton Mifflin Harcourt 2012 xiv, 236 p.p **591.7**
1. Death 2. Zoology 3. Animal behavior 4. Animal communication 5. Life cycles (Biology) 6.

Animal ecology 7. Animal life cycles 8. Animals -- Psychological aspects
ISBN 0547752660; 9780547752662

LC 2012010583

This book "explores the taboos and relevance of scavengers, the 'life-giving links that keep nature's systems humming along smoothly.' After a friend asked if he could be buried on the author's woodland property in Maine, he reexamined his curiosity with the natural world . . . [Bernd] Heinrich presents five major sections outlining how bodies and plants are recycled and broken down: small to large . . . north to south . . . plant undertakers . . . watery deaths . . . and changes (metamorphosis and death rituals). Above all, temperature affects how and what breaks down carrion as the flies and insects of summer are replaced by various birds in the winter. The author also tracks how trees decompose, a process that often begins before they die." (Kirkus Reviews)

Summer world; a season of bounty. Ecco 2009 253p il $26.95 **591.7**
1. Summer 2. Animals
ISBN 978-0-06-074217-1; 0-06-074217-8

A discussion of animal survival in the hot season explores the ways in which animals make the most of the summer's short span by efficiently compacting most of their procreative and survival activities.

"Heinrich presents natural science at its engaging best." Kirkus

Includes bibliographical references

Hoyt, Erich

Creatures of the deep; in search of the sea's monsters and the world they live in. Erich Hoyt. Firefly Books 2014 288 p. color illustrations $39.95 **591.7**
1. Ocean bottom 2. Marine biology 3. Abysses 4. Abyssal zone 5. Faune marine 6. Marine animals
ISBN 1770852816; 9781770852815

LC 2014901153

In this book author "Erich Hoyt gives readers a glimpse of the amazing variety of creatures found in the deepest parts of the ocean. Weaving together details from the latest scientific research about sharks, giant squid, dragonfish, huge tube worms, clams and tiny microbes of the deep-sea vents, Hoyt embarks on a magical journey roaming across the abyssal plains and descending into deep-sea trenches more than 20,000 feet down." (Publisher's note)

"From the surface-dwelling manta ray to the marine spider of the hadal zone (appropriately named for Hades), Hoyt describes life cycles and family trees of marine flora and fauna, as well as the scientific community's efforts to understand them. Startling facts abound, and Hoyt's enthusiasm for his subject shows on every page." Pub Wkly

Includes bibliographical references and index

Naskrecki, Piotr

The smaller majority; the hidden world of the animals that dominate the tropics. Belknap Press of Harvard University Press 2005 278p il $35 **591.7**
1. Invertebrates 2. Tropics 3. Animals -- Pictorial works
ISBN 0-674-01915-6; 978-0-674-01915-7

LC 2005-46060

"Naskrecki's exuberant, expert knowledge of this microscopic world has been distilled down to the most arresting details. Crisp, enjoyable prose, clearly explains complex biological processes." Publ Wkly

Includes bibliographical references

591.9   Animals by specific continents, countries, localities

Bambaradeniya, Channa N. B.

The **illustrated** atlas of wildlife; [by] Channa Bambaradeniya [et al.] University of California Press 2009 288p il map $39.95   **591.9**

1. Atlases 2. Biogeography 3. Reference books

ISBN 978-0-520-25785-6; 0-520-25785-5

LC 2008-40625

"This gorgeous book, featuring detailed, customized maps and more than 800 photographs . . . and original artworks, presents a spectacular visual survey of wild animals across the globe and describes in detail their habitats, physical characteristics, diet, and behavior. . . . [It also includes] conservation and preservation data, information about human impact upon the world's complex ecosystems, and chronicles of the evolution and adaptation of animals over the ages." Education Digest

Includes glossary and bibliographical references

592   Specific taxonomic groups of animals

Attenborough, David

Life in the undergrowth. Princeton University Press 2006 288p il $29.95   **592**

1. Invertebrates

ISBN 0-691-12703-4

LC 2005-934727

"This wonderful exploration of invertebrates exceeds the requirements for a great nature book through the strength of its photographs and the quality of its prose." Publ Wkly

Stewart, Amy

The **earth** moved; on the remarkable achievements of earthworms. Algonquin Bks. 2004 223p $23.95; pa $12.95   **592**

1. Worms 2. Earthworms

ISBN 1-56512-337-9; 1-56512-468-5 pa

LC 2003-52379

Stewart discusses earthworms. "This peaceful, delicate creature, Stewart writes, has posed a large task for scientists, who have taken more than 100 years to piece together a portrait of the earthworm's dark life. But the subterrestrials still have more to teach us, even as creatures like the giant Oregon earthworm are being pushed to the brink of extinction." (Christ Sci Monit)

The author explores "the impact worms have on humans and on our planet. . . . {She} educates on the vital roles these creatures play in growing crops, how they can neutralize the effects of nuclear waste on soil, and their ability to regenerate new body parts. . . . A book that's as enlightening as it is entertaining." SLJ

Includes bibliographical references

594   Mollusks and molluscoids

Harasewych, M. G.

The **book** of shells; a life-size guide to identifying and classifying six hundred seashells. [by] M.G. Harasewych & Fabio Moretzsohn. University of Chicago Press 2010 655p il map $55   **594**

1. Shells 2. Mollusks 3. Reference books

ISBN 978-0-226-31577-5; 0-226-31577-0

LC 2009-34321

This book "provides an excellent introduction to the major classes of sea-living mollusks worldwide. Students and the lay enthusiast will find the 600 entries accessible and engaging. . . . A table lists the family, shell-size range, distribution, abundance, depth, habitat, feeding habit, and the presence or absence of an operculum. A color range map, genus and species and common name, a paragraph-long description of the species, a listing of related species, a color life-size illustration, and, for small shells, a larger, more detailed image complete the information." Booklist

Includes bibliographical references

Montgomery, Sy

The **soul** of an octopus; a joyful exploration into the wonder of consciousness. Sy Montgomery. Atria Books 2015 272 p. color illustrations (hardback) $26   **594**

1. Octopuses 2. Animal intelligence 3. Octopuses -- Behavior

ISBN 1451697716; 9781451697711

LC 2014038751

National Book Award Finalist: Nonfiction (2015)

In this book, author "Sy Montgomery explores the emotional and physical world of the octopus--a surprisingly complex, intelligent, and spirited creature--and the remarkable connections it makes with humans. Montgomery chronicles this growing appreciation of the octopus, but also tells a love story." (Publisher's note)

"Along with an abundance of fascinating octopus lore, Montgomery illuminates her own quest to understand the creatures better and paints vivid portraits of the people who are similarly drawn to them. Her affection for her subjects, both human and cephalopod, shines through." LJ

Includes bibliographical references and index

Scales, Helen

Spirals in Time; The Secret Life and Curious Afterlife of Seashells. by Helen Scales. St. Martin's Press 2015 304 p. 8 plates; color illustrations $27   **594**

1. Shells

ISBN 1472911369; 9781472911360

In this book, marine biologist Helen Scales "shows how seashells have been sculpted by the fundamental rules of mathematics and evolution; how they gave us color, gems, food, and new medicines. After surviving multiple mass extinctions millions of years ago, molluscs and their shells still face an onslaught of anthropogenic challenges. . . . But rather than dwelling on all that is lost, Scales emphasizes that seashells offer an accessible way to reconnect people with nature." (Publisher's note)

"Aiming to inspire a sympathetic public, Scales tells the story of mollusks and reveals their importance in human economy and culture. Never dull or overly technical, this book is a welcome introduction to mollusks and seashells." Booklist

Williams, Wendy

Kraken; the curious, exciting, and slightly disturbing science of squid. Abrams Image 2011 223p il $21.95   **594**

1. Squids

ISBN 978-0-8109-8465-3

LC 2010032489

This book "traces sightings of the giant squid throughout the centuries. . . . Discussion of the anatomy, physiology, reproduction, evolution, and taxonomy of Architeuthis is provided, along with accounts of the author's visits to various scientific laboratories and descriptions of research studies being conducted on the animal. . . . This serves as a good introduction to the subject for general readers and an inspiration to young people interested in marine biology." Libr J

Includes filmography and bibliographical references

595   Arthropods

Fortey, Richard

Horseshoe crabs and velvet worms; the story of the animals and plants that time has left behind. by Richard Fortey. Alfred A. Knopf 2012 320 p. ill. (some col.) $28.95   **595**

1. Botany 2. Zoology 3. Paleontology 4. Worms 5. Plant conservation 6. Arthropoda -- Conservation 7. Invertebrates -- Conservation 8. Limulus polyphemus -- Conservation

ISBN 9780307263612

LC 2011039941

This book by Richard Fortey introduces "the reader to organisms that seemingly have undergone little change since their ancient origins. . . . Evolution has never stopped, and Fortey discusses changes that occur at the molecular level in response to predation pressure and other changing environmental conditions. He starts his journey by witnessing the spectacular spawning of horseshoe crabs, the closest living relatives of his specialty, the trilobites." (Choice: Current Reviews for Academic Libraries)

"Informative, engrossing and delightful." Kirkus

595.4   Chelicerates

Beccaloni, Jan

Arachnids. University of California Press 2009 320p il $39.95   **595.4**

1. Mites 2. Ticks 3. Spiders

ISBN 978-0-520-26140-2; 0-520-26140-2

LC 2009-18657

"This book is overflowing with scientific data and crystal-clear images of strange insects that are certain to make your skin crawl. Free of myths and misconceptions, this book delivers the real facts on the diverse arachnid family which includes a wide variety of scorpions, ticks, mites, and

over 38,000 species of spiders. They vary from bizarre to beautiful and a few are even deadly but all are interesting and sure to spark your imagination." Shutterbug

Includes bibliographical references

595.7   Insects

Brock, James P.

★ Kaufman field guide to butterflies of North America; [by] Jim P. Brock and Kenn Kaufman; with the collaboration of Rick and Nora Bowers and Lynn Hassler. Houghton Mifflin 2006 391p il map pa $19.95   **595.7**

1. Butterflies

ISBN 0-618-76826-2; 978-0-618-76826-4

LC 2006-287515

First published 2003 with title: Butterflies of North America

"Each species is listed by common name and scientific name and receives a several-sentence description, including flight time and larval food plants. All except very local or accidental species also are shown on range maps. The illustrations are opposite the written description, with most species pictured in multiple images. . . . The illustrations are created by digital enhancement of photographs. . . . An essential purchase for all libraries." Booklist [review of 2003 edition]

Capinera, John L.

Field guide to grasshoppers, crickets, and katydids of the United States; [by] John L. Capinera, Ralph D. Scott, and Thomas J. Walker. Cornell University Press 2004 249p il maps hardcover o.p. pa $29.95   **595.7**

1. Crickets 2. Grasshoppers

ISBN 0-8014-4260-5; 0-8014-8948-2 pa

LC 2004-10727

"The highlight is certainly the 50 pages of Scott's color illustrations. . . . For those who want to know what's plaguing them when locusts descend, this is the book." Publ Wkly

Includes bibliographical references

Carde, Ring T.

Encyclopedia of insects; editors, Vincent H. Resh, Ring T. Cardé. 2nd ed; Elsevier/Academic Press 2009 xxxiii, 1132p il map $120   **595.7**

1. Reference books 2. Insects -- Encyclopedias

ISBN 978-0-12-374144-8

First published 2003

This book covers "all aspects of insect anatomy, physiology, evolution, behavior, reproduction, ecology, and disease, as well as issues of exploitation, conservation, and management." Publisher's note

Includes bibliographical references

Eisner, Thomas

For love of insects. Belknap Press of Harvard University Press 2003 448p il $35; pa $19.95 **595.7**

1. Insects

ISBN 0-674-01181-3; 0-674-01827-3 pa

LC 2003-44399

"Ranging from a caterpillar who feeds on flowers while disguising as one by affixing petals to his back, to a beetle who can resist a pull 200 times his own weight, the book is full of little known information about how insects feed, fight, and reproduce." Univ Press Books for Public and Second Sch Libr, 2006

Includes bibliographical references

★ **Secret** weapons; defenses of insects, spiders, scorpions, and other many-legged creatures. [by] Thomas Eisner, Maria Eisner, Melody V.S. Siegler. Belknap Press of Harvard University Press 2005 372p il $29.95; pa $18.95 **595.7**

1. Insects 2. Spiders 3. Animal defenses 4. Arachnida
ISBN 0-674-01882-6; 0-674-02403-6 pa

LC 2005-41042

"This volume presents 69 case studies of organisms from 4 orders of spiders, 2 of centipedes, 5 of millipedes, and 10 of insects. Most of the studies address defensive chemistry and identify the chemical(s) involved, how each is acquired, stored, and deployed." (Sci Books Films) Index.

"This very readable and well-illustrated book will appeal to all those interested in disciplines like biology, entomology, and ecology." Choice

Includes bibliographical references

Ellis, Hattie

Sweetness & light; the mysterious history of the honeybee. Harmony Books 2004 243p il hardcover o.p. pa $13.95 **595.7**

1. Bees 2. Beekeeping
ISBN 1-4000-5405-2; 1-4000-5406-0 pa

LC 2004-4116

"What a delightful volume on the honeybee this is: Not only is the reader treated to a wealth of information on the biology, ecology, and economic importance of that insect, but the interrelationship of the honeybee and humanity throughout history is very nicely presented." Sci Books Films

Includes bibliographical references

Evans, Arthur V.

An **inordinate** fondness for beetles; [by] Arthur V. Evans, Charles L. Bellamy; photography by Lisa Charles Watson; illustrations by Patricia Wynne. University of California Press 2000 208p il pa $31.95 **595.7**

1. Beetles
ISBN 0-520-22323-3; 978-0-520-22323-3

LC 99-46118

First published 1996 by Henry Holt and Company

"The incredible full-color photographs bring readers up close without a magnifying lens at hand, and the seemingly infinite variations within the species due to size, structure, and color are easily seen. . . . While the text is scientific, it is very readable." SLJ

Includes bibliographical references

Himmelman, John

Cricket radio; tuning in the night-singing insects. Belknap Press of Harvard University Press 2011 254p il $22.95 **595.7**

1. Crickets 2. Katydids
ISBN 978-0-674-04690-0

LC 2010-35203

The author explores "what moves crickets and katydids to sing, how they produce their distinctive sounds, how they hear the songs of others, and how they vary cadence, volume, and pitch to attract potential mates, warn off competitors, and evade predators." Publisher's note

Includes bibliographical references

Holldobler, Bert

The **leafcutter** ants; civilization by instinct. [by] Bert Hölldobler and Edward O. Wilson. Norton 2010 160p il pa $19.95 **595.7**

1. Ants
ISBN 978-0-393-33868-3

LC 2010-16202

The authors "introduce the general reader to earth's most evolved animal society. With the colony's queen as its reproductive organ; the various ages and types of workers as the brain, heart, and other organs; and the communication among the ants similar to the communication of nerves and ganglia, a leafcutter ant colony can be truly considered as a superorganism." Booklist

Includes bibliographical references

The **superorganism**; the beauty, elegance, and strangeness of insect societies. [by] Bert Hölldobler and Edward O. Wilson; line drawings by Margaret C. Nelson. W.W. Norton & Company 2009 xxi, 522p il $55 **595.7**

1. Insects
ISBN 978-0-393-06704-0; 0-393-06704-1

LC 2008-38547

"This study covers mathematical analysis as well as field data, but in a straightforward manner that guides readers from one remarkable fact or concept to the next, inspiring wonder at the origin of our own societies." Publ Wkly

Includes bibliographical references

Keller, Laurent

The **lives** of ants; by Laurent Keller and Élisabeth Gordon; translated by James Grieve. Oxford University Press 2009 252p il $27.95; pa $15.95 **595.7**

1. Ants
ISBN 978-0-19-954186-7; 0-19-954186-8; 978-0-19-954187-4 pa; 0-19-954187-6 pa

LC 2008-943416

The authors "provide a lucid . . . overview of any evolution, ecology, biology, behavior, and genetics that easily communicates complex research in these areas to a wide audience." Sci Books Films

Includes bibliographical references

Milne, Lorus Johnson

The **Audubon** Society field guide to North American insects and spiders; [by] Lorus and Margery Milne; visual key by Susan Rayfield. Knopf 1980 989p il $19.95 **595.7**

1. Insects 2. Spiders
ISBN 0-394-50763-0

LC 80-7620

The authors "have based their field guide on 702 excellent color photographs (75 of which are of spiders and other arachnids). In addition to some general information, the text (two thirds of the book) is made up of brief comments on each kind of arthropod pictured." Choice

Includes glossary

Moffett, Mark W.

Adventures among ants; a global safari with a cast of trillions. University of California Press 2010 280p il $29.95 **595.7**

1. Ants 2. Ants -- Ecology 3. Ants -- Behavior
ISBN 978-0-520-26199-0; 0-520-26199-2

LC 2009-40610

"This superb book by a first-class writer with an unsurpassed feel for ants begins at the ground level as we come face to face with the creatures, move into their minds, and begin to understand what makes them tick. Moffett organizes his text around six ant lifestyles, each represented by an insect that dominates its habitat: Indian Marauder ants, African army ants, African Weaver ants, Amazon slavemaking ants, Neotropical leaf cutter ants, and the Argentine ant, a global invader. . . . This marvelous volume illustrated with the author's closeup photographs will delight biologists, naturalists, and general readers with a natural history bent." Libr J

Includes bibliographical references

The monarch butterfly; biology & conservation. edited by Karen S. Oberhauser & Michelle J. Solensky. Cornell University Press 2004 248p il maps (A Comstock book) $39.95 **595.7**

1. Monarch butterflies 2. Wildlife conservation
ISBN 0-8014-4188-9

LC 2004-884

"Covered is every facet of monarch breeding, migration, and overwintering, as well as population modeling and management. . . . The text is clearly written, and the mathematical formulas included in certain chapters are not essential to understanding the main ideas. The most up-to-date and comprehensive publication on monarch butterfly biology, this will be an important reference tool." Libr J

Includes bibliographical references

Pyle, Robert Michael

★ The **Audubon** Society field guide to North American butterflies; visual key by Carol Nehring and Jane Opper. Knopf 1981 916p il $19.95 **595.7**

1. Butterflies
ISBN 0-394-51914-0

LC 80-84240

This guide "introduces more than 600 species of North American butterfly, including those native to the Hawaiian Islands. A section of brilliant color plates (more than 1,000 of them) featuring butterflies in their natural habitats, follows a general introduction and notes on text organization and use." Booklist

Raffles, Hugh

Insectopedia. Pantheon Books 2010 465p il **595.7**

1. Insects 2. Human-animal relationships
ISBN 0375423869; 9780375423864

LC 2009-24302

"For as long as humans have existed, insects have existed, too. Wherever we've traveled, they've traveled, too. Yet we hardly know them. . . . Organizing his book alphabetically with one entry for each letter, weaving together brief vignettes, meditations, and extended essays, Raffles embarks on an . . . exploration of history and science, anthropology and travel, economics, philosophy, and popular culture to show us how insects have triggered our obsessions, stirred our passions, and beguiled our imaginations." (Publisher's note) Index

"In addition to the fine writing, Raffles includes many intriguing drawings and illustrations, as well as a fascinating Notes section. Because of his manner of organization, there is little reason to read the book in order; you can simply open it anywhere and discover a new way to reflect on not only insects but people." Seattle Times

Includes bibliographical references

Schmidt, Justin O.

The **sting** of the wild; Justin O. Schmidt. Johns Hopkins University Press 2016 280 p. color illustrations (hardcover : alk. paper) $24.95 **595.7**

1. Insect pests 2. Poisonous animals 3. Poisonous arthropoda
ISBN 1421419289; 1421419297; 9781421419282; 9781421419299

LC 2015026989

In this book, author Justin O. Schmidt "takes us on a journey inside the lives of stinging insects, seeing the world through their eyes as well as his own. He explains how and why they attack and reveals the powerful punch they can deliver with a small venom gland and a 'sting,' the name for the apparatus that delivers the venom. We learn which insects are the worst to encounter and why some are barely worth considering." (Publisher's note)

"Schmidt's tales will prove infectiously engaging even to entomophobes." Pub Wkly

Includes bibliographical references and index

Stokes, Donald W.

The **butterfly** book; an easy guide to butterfly gardening, identification, and behavior. {by} Donald and Lillian Stokes and Ernest Williams. Little, Brown 1991 95p il maps pa $12.95 **595.7**

1. Butterflies
ISBN 0-316-81780-5

LC 91-15323

This book discusses plants which will attract butterflies, explains butterfly life cycles and behavior, and provides information for identification of over 140 species

Van Dokkum, Pieter, 1972-

Dragonflies; Magnificent Creatures of Water, Air, and Land. Pieter van Dokkum. Yale University

Press 2015 176 p. color illustrations (alk. paper)
$35 **595.7**
1. Dragonflies 2. Dragonflies -- United States 3.
Dragonflies -- United States -- Pictorial works
ISBN 030019708X; 9780300197082

LC 2014025844

This book, by Pieter van Dokkum, "begins . . . when an
alien-looking larva crawls out of the water and transforms
into a fully formed dragonfly. In the following chapters we
witness dew-covered dragonflies sparkling in the morning
sun, then a pair of mating dragonflies moving through the
air. . . . In the final chapter, one generation dies as the next
prepares to leave the water and begin its own winged journey." (Publisher's note)

"A lovely volume to pair with Forrest L. Mitchell and
James L. Lasswell's A Dazzle of Dragonflies, van Dokkum's
vivid compilation of photographs is a treat for nature lovers. The accompanying text is poetically written and a fascinating introduction to the distinct characteristics of these
creatures."LJ

Includes bibliographical references and index

Waldbauer, Gilbert

★ **What** good are bugs? insects in the web of
life. Harvard University Press 2003 384p il hardcover o.p. pa $17.50 **595.7**
1. Insects
ISBN 0-674-01027-2; 0-674-01632-7 pa

LC 2002-27335

This "is an excellent work about the beneficial insects,
that vast majority of insect species of which we are generally
unaware. . . . The author is an excellent writer and provides
many interesting examples." Choice

Includes bibliographical references

Zuk, Marlene

Sex on six legs; lessons on life, love, and language from the insect world. [by] Marlene Zuk.
Houghton Mifflin Harcourt 2011 262p $25 **595.7**
1. Insects 2. Sexual behavior in animals
ISBN 978-0-15-101373-9

LC 2010025829

"Despite the title, . . . the book gives clear accounts of
a wide range of research beyond sex: insect personalities,
wasp facial recognition, fruit flies artificially bred for intelligence, slave-making ants, hitchhiking blister beetles and
much more." Sci News

Includes bibliographical references

595.77 Flies (Diptera) and fleas

Spielman, A.

Mosquito; a natural history of man's most persistent and deadly foe. {by} Andrew Spielman and
Michael D'Antonio. Hyperion 2001 247p il maps
hardcover o.p. pa $12 **595.77**
1. Mosquitoes
ISBN 0-7868-8667-6 pa

LC 2001-16815

The authors tell us about the mosquito's "life cycle, its
natural enemies and predators, and, of course, its monumental impact on human history. . . . This is truly an unexpected
delight, an informative, entertaining, and sometimes skin-
crawly book that should appeal to anyone with a taste for
popular science." Booklist

595.78 Moths and butterflies

Leach, William

Butterfly people; an American encounter with
the beauty of the world. William R. Leach. Pantheon
Books 2012 416 p. $32.50 **595.78**
1. Butterflies 2. Entomologists -- United States 3.
Butterflies -- United States -- History -- 19th century 4.
Entomologists -- United States -- History -- 19th century
5. Industrial revolution -- United States -- History --
19th century
ISBN 0375422935; 9780375422935

LC 2012000389

This book, by William R. Leach, "is [a] . . . chronicle
of nineteenth-century America's infatuation with butterflies,
and the story of the naturalists who unveiled the mysteries of
their existence. . . . Leach focuses on the correspondence and
scientific writings of half a dozen pioneering lepidopterists
who traveled across the country and throughout the world,
collecting and studying unknown and exotic species." (Publisher's note)

Includes bibliographical references and index

Orenstein, Ronald

Butterflies. Firefly Books Ltd 2015 288 p. color
illustrations $45 **595.78**
1. Butterflies
ISBN 1770855807; 9781770855809

This book on butterflies, by Ronald Orenstein, "reveals
a rare and close up look at the odd beauty and behavior of
some of the strangest of these tiny creatures. Despite their
large numbers, the world of these particularly weird insects
exists largely hidden from our view. Included in the book are
some of the most interesting species from North and South
America, Europe, the Caribbean, Australia, New Zealand
and beyond." (Publisher's note)

"Though one might quibble with the infrequent identification of plant life in the photographs, or perhaps wish for
exact-size measurements of pictured species to be included
in the captions, this gorgeous book reveals a wonder on
nearly every page and will enthrall natural history enthusiasts both amateur and expert alike." LJ

595.79 Hymenoptera

Holldobler, Bert

The **ants**; [by] Bert Hölldobler and Edward O.
Wilson. Belknap Press 1990 732p il $95 **595.79**
1. Ants
ISBN 0-674-04075-9

LC 89-30653

"Science is rarely good literature. 'The Ants' is an exalting exception." N Y Times Book Rev

Includes bibliographical references

✓ **Journey** to the ants; a story of scientific exploration. {by} Bert Hölldobler and Edward O. Wilson. Belknap Press 1994 228p il $27.50; pa $16.95 **595.79**

1. Ants

ISBN 0-674-48525-4; 0-674-48526-2 pa

LC 94-13386

"A skillful blend of natural lore, autobiography, and history." Libr J

595.799   Apoidea

The **bee** book; Fergus Chadwick, Steve Alton, Emma Sarah Tennant, Bill Fitzmaurice, Judy Earl. DK Publishing 2016 221 p. illustrations (some color) $25 **595.799**

1. Beekeeping 2. Bees 3. Honeybee 4. Bumblebees 5. Bee culture

ISBN 1465443835; 9781465443830

LC 2015458993

This book "shows you step-by-step how to create a bee-friendly garden, get started in beekeeping, and harness the power of honey for well-being. Fully illustrated with full-color photographs throughout, this . . . guide covers everything you need to know to start your own backyard hive, from setup to harvest. Practical beekeeping techniques are explained with clear step-by-step sequences, photos, and diagrams." (Publisher's note)

"This is a charming, information-rich book that should lead readers to appreciate bees and welcome them into their gardens and wild places and even encourage some to keep honeybees." Booklist

Frey, Kate

The **bee**-friendly garden; Kate Frey and Gretchen LeBuhn. Ten Speed Press 2016 224 p. color illustrations (trade pbk.) $19.99 **595.799**

1. Bees 2. Gardening 3. Honey plants 4. Gardening to attract wildlife

ISBN 9781607747635

LC 2015025815

In this book, "garden designer Kate Frey and bee expert Gretchen LeBuhn provide everything you need to know to create a dazzling garden that helps both the threatened honeybee and our own native bees. No matter how small or large your space, and regardless of whether you live in the city, suburbs, or country, just a few simple changes to your garden can fight the effects of colony collapse disorder and the worldwide decline in bee population that threatens our global food chain." (Publisher's note)

"Frey and LeBuhn's accessible and inspiring advice, if correctly followed by growers around the world, could profoundly help restore diminishing bee populations to thriving good health, which is essential to our crops and our well-being." Booklist

Includes bibliographical references (page 184) and index.

Seeley, Thomas D.

Honeybee democracy. Princeton University Press 2010 273p $29.95 **595.799**

1. Bees 2. Democracy 3. Honeybee -- Behavior

ISBN 978-0-691-14721-5

LC 2010-10265

Seeley's "enthusiasm and admiration for honeybees is infectious. His accumulated research seems truly masterly, doing for bees what E. O. Wilson did for ants." N Y Times Book Rev

Includes bibliographical references

596   Chordates

Dinerstein, Eric

The **kingdom** of rarities; Eric Dinerstein. Island Press 2013 312 p. (cloth : alk. paper) $29.95 **596**

1. Ecology 2. Rare animals 3. Rare vertebrates

ISBN 1610911954; 1610911962; 9781610911955; 9781610911962

LC 2012025535

In this book, Eric Dinerstein "demonstrates that while rarity is a phenomenon of nature, few scientists have sought to study the more 'uncommon' species in a given ecosystem, and therefore may be missing key issues to better understand the natural world. He has cumulated over 40 years of his studies and experiences to highlight how rare species have developed intricate and complex webs, and how their existence has profound impacts on the ecosystem(s) in which they live." (Choice)

Includes bibliographical references and index

597   Cold-blooded vertebrates

Balcombe, Jonathan

What a Fish Knows; The Inner Lives of Our Underwater Cousins. by Jonathan Balcombe. Farrar, Straus & Giroux 2016 304 p. color illustrations $27 **597**

1. Fishes 2. Animal behavior

ISBN 0374288216; 9780374288211

LC 2015048629

This book on fish, by Jonathan Balcombe, "draws on the latest science to present a fresh look at these remarkable creatures in all their breathtaking diversity and beauty. Fishes conduct elaborate courtship rituals and develop lifelong bonds with shoalmates. They also plan, hunt cooperatively, use tools, curry favor, deceive one another, and punish wrongdoers." (Publisher's note)

"This is a lively and surprising work that makes a strong argument for sport and food fishing reform." LJ

Includes bibliographical references and index.

Behnke, Robert J.

★ **Trout** and salmon of North America; illustrated by Joseph R. Tomelleri; foreword by Thomas McGuane; introduction by Donald S. Proebstel; edited by George Scott. Free Press 2002 359p il maps $40 **597**

1. Trout 2. Salmon

ISBN 0-7432-2220-2

LC 2002-69256

"Along with full and clearly written scientific explanations, statistics and analysis, the author provides anecdotal and historical details that make this not just a field guide, but a fascinating read for those interested in the natural world." Publ Wkly

Includes bibliographical references

Compagno, Leonard J. V.

Sharks of the world; [by] Leonard Compagno, Marc Dando, Sarah Fowler. Princeton University Press 2005 368p il map (Princeton field guides) hardcover o.p. pa $29.95 **597**

1. Sharks

ISBN 0-691-12071-4; 0-691-12072-2 pa

LC 2004-111901

First published in the United Kingdom with title: Field guide to the sharks of the world

The authors cover "over 450 species, including many as-yet-unnamed species and some that are only known from a single specimen. Each is illustrated with both a line drawing and a beautifully rendered color painting; in most cases a ventral view of the head and illustrations of the teeth are included. . . . Packed with information, this is an invaluable guide for anyone interested in this fascinating group." Choice

Includes bibliographical references

Eilperin, Juliet

Demon fish; travels through the hidden world of sharks. Pantheon Books 2011 xxi, 295p il $26.95 **597**

1. Sharks

ISBN 978-0-375-42512-7

LC 2010-30264

Eilperin "describes her travels throughout Asia, South Africa, and the United States in search of shark information and folklore. . . . The author provides a well-written overview of current and past attitudes toward sharks and discusses shark species, physiology, genetics, reproduction, evolution, navigation, and attacks on swimmers." Libr J

Includes bibliographical references

Gilbert, Carter Rowell

★ **National** Audubon Society field guide to fishes, North America; [by] Carter R. Gilbert, James D. Williams. rev ed, 2nd ed, fully rev; Alfred A. Knopf 2002 607p il maps pa $19.95 **597**

1. Fishes -- North America

ISBN 0-375-41224-7

LC 2002-20773

First published 1983 with title: The Audubon Society field guide to North American fishes, whales, and dolphins

This guide covers over 600 freshwater and saltwater species in detail, with notes on 771 more species.

Page, Lawrence M.

★ **Peterson** field guide to freshwater fishes of North America north of Mexico; [by] Lawrence M. Page, Brooks M. Burr; illustrations by Eugene C. Beckham III . . . [et al.]; maps by Griffin E. Sheehy. 2nd ed.; Houghton Mifflin Harcourt 2011 663p il map pa $21 **597**

1. Fishes -- North America

ISBN 978-0-547-24206-4; 0-547-24206-9

LC 2010-49219

First published 1991 with title: A field guide to freshwater fishes: North America north of Mexico

This guide to identifying different species of freshwater fish in North America includes "maps and information showing where to locate each species of fish—whether that species can be found in miles-long stretches of river or small pools that cover only dozens of square feet." Publisher's note

Includes glossary and bibliographical references

Pepperell, Julian G.

Fishes of the open ocean; a natural history & illustrated guide. illustrated by Guy Harvey. University of Chicago Press 2010 266p il map $35 **597**

1. Fishes

ISBN 978-0-226-65539-0; 0-226-65539-3

LC 2009032290

This book "details the biology and brief ecology of various open-ocean fishes. The first half of the book details the importance of pelagic fish in the oceans, the food web of oceanic life, and the relationship between form (fish shape) and function, along with a historical perspective of interactions between fish and humans. The second half of the book illustrates the distribution range, migratory patterns and behavior, reproductive patterns, and trophic information of various fishes. . . . the book is not exhaustive in detail, it provides a very useful overall description of various fishes and their life in the oceans." Choice

Includes bibliographical references

Rigney, Matt

In pursuit of giants; one man's global search for the last of the great fish. Matt Rigney. Viking 2012 336 p. ill., map $26.95 **597**

1. Fishes 2. Overfishing 3. Corporations -- Environmental aspects 4. Fishing -- History 5. Fisheries -- History 6. Wildlife conservation 7. Marine fishes -- Ecology 8. Rare fishes -- Conservation 9. Fish populations -- Research 10. Marine fishes -- Conservation 11. Endangered species -- Research

ISBN 0670023353; 9780670023356

LC 2012003442

Author Matt Rigney "debuts with this personal investigation into the decline of big-game fish like marlin, swordfish and bluefin tuna. His travels took him to the Mediterranean, Japan, Cabo San Lucas, Mexico, Georges Bank off Nova Scotia, the Great Barrier Reef, and New Zealand. . . . Everywhere he traveled he discovered a similar story: Corporations entered an area, manipulated or ignored government regulations, and, using long lines and huge nets, laid waste to massive populations of sea creatures." (Kirkus Reviews)

Includes bibliographical references and index

Schultz, Ken

Ken Schultz's field guide to saltwater fish. Wiley 2004 274p il pa $17.95 **597**

1. Fishes

ISBN 0-471-44995-4

LC 2003-15773

"Arranged alphabetically by species, each entry covers the identification, size/age, distribution, habitat, life history/behavior, and feeding habits of each fish." Publisher's note

Schweid, Richard

Consider the eel. University of North Carolina Press 2002 181p il map pbk $27.95 **597**

1. Eels

ISBN 9781469615134; 0-8078-2693-6

LC 2001-48067

The author "tries to fill in the gaps in the eel's astonishing natural history and tie that to sketches of fishery traditions, folklore, literary excerpts and reportage. . . . Anyone with a curiosity about the sea will find Schweid's taste of the eel strangely appealing." Publ Wkly

Includes bibliographical references

Smith, C. Lavett

National Audubon Society field guide to tropical marine fishes of the Caribbean, the Gulf of Mexico, Florida, the Bahamas, and Bermuda. Knopf 1997 720p il maps $19.95 **597**

1. Tropical fish

ISBN 0-679-44601-X

LC 97-7690

This illustrated guide to tropical fishes describes nearly 1,200 species and includes color photographs, classification and identification information.

597.176   Freshwater fishes

Voigt, Emily

The dragon behind the glass; a true story of power, obsession, and the world. Emily Voigd. Scribner 2016 336 p. illustrations, maps (alk. paper) $26 **597.176**

1. Fishes 2. Black market 3. Endangered species 4. Scleropages formosus

ISBN 9781451678949; 9781451678956; 9781451678963

LC 2015040075

This book, by Emily Voigd, is a "journey into the bizarre world of the Asian arowana or 'dragon fish'—the world's most expensive aquarium fish. . . . Treasured as a status symbol believed to bring good luck, the Asian arowana is bred on high-security farms in Southeast Asia. . . . In the United States, however, it's protected by the Endangered Species Act and illegal to bring into the country—though it remains the object of a thriving black market." (Publisher's note)

"A fresh, lively look at an obsessive desire to own a piece of the wild." Kirkus

Includes bibliographical references and index

597.3   Selachii, Holocephali, fleshy-finned fishes

Ebert, David A.

A pocket guide to sharks of the world; David A. Ebert, Sarah Fowler, Marc Dando. Princeton University Press 2015 256 p. illustrations, map (Princeton pocket guides) (paper) $19.95 **597.3**

1. Sharks

ISBN 0691165998; 9780691165998

LC 2014951471

This book, by David A. Ebert, Sarah Fowler, and Marc Dando, "is the first field guide to identify, illustrate, and describe the world's 501 shark species. Its compact format makes it handy for many situations, including recognizing living species, fishery catches, or parts sold at markets. The book also contains useful sections on identifying shark teeth and the shark fins most commonly encountered in the fin trade." (Publisher's note)

"This well-organized, well-written guide is ideal for scholars, professionals, and enthusiasts. Leonard Compagno et al's Sharks, while slightly older, is an engaging introduction for beginners." LJ

Weinberg, Samantha

A fish caught in time; the search for the coelacanth. HarperCollins Pubs. 2000 xx, 220p il map hardcover o.p. pa $13 **597.3**

1. Coelacanth

ISBN 0-06-093285-6 pa

LC 99-44800

First published 1999 in the United Kingdom

"In 1938, a fish believed to be extinct for 70 million years was caught off the South African coast, triggering the 'greatest scientific find of the century.' The search for the coelacanth . . . is a fascinating story, and Weinberg . . . tells it well." Libr J

Includes bibliographical references

597.8   Amphibians

Moore, Robin

In search of lost frogs; The Campaign to Discover the World's Rarest Amphibians. Robin Moore. Firefly Books Ltd 2014 256 p. illustrations, color portraits $35 **597.8**

1. Frogs 2. Rare animals

ISBN 1770854649; 9781770854642

In this book, author Robin Moore "seeks to raise the profile of frogs in the consciousness of a public largely unaware that in recent years 'amphibians have been at the forefront of the largest mass extinction.' Moore spearheaded an international effort to search for species feared to be extinct. Following Moore on his global odyssey and riding the rollercoaster of his hopes, disappointments and triumphs brings the reader closer to his beloved frogs." (Publishers Weekly)

"This is a superb resource for general readers and for specialists with advanced training in herpetology. It not only makes fascinating reading but also provides numerous, excellent color photos of rare frogs and salamanders. Summing Up: Highly recommended. All readership levels and libraries." Choice

597.9   Reptiles

Attenborough, David

Life in cold blood. Princeton University Press 2008 288p il $29.95   **597.9**

1. Reptiles 2. Amphibians

ISBN 978-0-691-13718-6; 0-691-13718-8

LC 2007-938089

"The writing is crisp and lively, the examples are up to date, and the photography is beautiful. . . . This is a very interesting book, which provides many examples of organisms some of us often overlook." Am Biology Teacher

Conant, Roger

A field guide to reptiles & amphibians; eastern and central North America. [by] Roger Conant and Joseph T. Collins; illustrated by Isabelle Hunt Conant and Tom R. Johnson. 3rd ed, expanded; Houghton Mifflin 1998 616p il map (Peterson field guide series) pbk $21   **597.9**

1. Reptiles 2. Amphibians

ISBN 9780395904527

LC 98-13622

First published 1958 with title: A field guide to reptiles and amphibians of the United States and Canada east of the 100th meridian

This guide describes 595 species and subspecies, featuring color photos, black and white drawings, and color distribution maps of reptiles and amphibians of the region. Also includes information on transporting live reptiles and amphibians

Includes glossary and bibliographical references

Ernst, Carl H.

Venomous reptiles of the United States, Canada, and northern Mexico; Carl H. Ernst and Evelyn M. Ernst. Johns Hopkins University Press 2011 424 p. ill. (some col.), maps (v. 2 : alk. paper) $75   **597.9**

1. Reptiles 2. Poisonous animals 3. Animals -- North America 4. Heloderma -- North America 5. Poisonous snakes -- North America

ISBN 0801898757; 0801898765; 9780801898754; 9780801898761

LC 2010036966

This book presents a reference guide to the venomous reptiles of North America. "The first volume contains species accounts of the venomous lizards and elapid and viperid snakes found north of Mexico's twenty-fifth parallel. Volume 2 of this definitive work covers the twenty-one species of the genus Crotalus found in the United States, Canada, and . . . northern Mexico." (Publisher's note)

"A current, vital addition to herpetology collections." LJ

Includes bibliographical references and index

Firefly Encyclopedia of Reptiles and Amphibians; edited by Chris Mattison. Firefly Books Ltd 2015 272 p. color illustrations, maps (hardcover) $49.95   **597.9**

1. Reptiles 2. Amphibians

ISBN 1770855939; 9781770855939

This encyclopedia, edited by Chris Mattison, "covers every family [of reptile and amphibian], ranging from large, predatory constrictors and crocodilians to miniature tree frogs and salamanders. This third edition adds 32 extra pages to incorporate numerous important updates based on the latest scientific findings and interpretations." (Publisher's note)

"Some 320 color photographs complement topical essays, evenly split into 'amphibian' and 'reptile' parts, which together weave what Mattison calls the 'threads' of taxonomy and other key themes regarding these complex creatures." LJ

Includes bibliographical references (pages 259-261) and index

Stebbins, Robert C.

A field guide to Western reptiles and amphibians; text and illustrations by Robert C. Stebbins. 3rd ed newly rev; Houghton Mifflin 2003 533p il map (Peterson field guide series) pa $22   **597.9**

1. Reptiles 2. Amphibians

ISBN 0-395-98272-3

LC 2002-27561

First published 1966

This "covers all the species of reptiles and amphibians found in western North America. More than 650 full-color paintings and photographs show key details for making accurate identifications. . . . Color range maps give species' distributions. . . . [Includes] information on conservation efforts and survival status." Publisher's note

Includes bibliographical references

Tyning, Thomas F.

A guide to amphibians and reptiles; edited by Donald W. Stokes and Lillian Q. Stokes; illustrations by Andrew Finch Magee; range maps by Thomas F. Tyning and Timothy J. Flanagan. Little, Brown 1990 400p il hardcover o.p. pa $14.95   **597.9**

1. Reptiles 2. Amphibians

ISBN 0-316-81713-9 pa

LC 89-28444

This guide covers common frogs, salamanders, alligators, snakes, turtles, and lizards

Includes bibliographical references

597.92   Turtles

Safina, Carl

Voyage of the turtle; in pursuit of the Earth's last dinosaur. Holt 2006 383p il map $27.50; pa $17   **597.92**

1. Turtles

ISBN 978-0-8050-7891-6; 0-8050-7891-6; 978-0-8050-8318-7 pa; 0-8050-8318-9 pa

LC 2005-55023

"This is a well-written natural history/conservation narrative. General readers will enjoy the book and hopefully will become excited to learn more about critical environmental issues." Sci Books Films

Includes bibliographical references

Spotila, James R.

Sea turtles; a complete guide to their biology, behavior, and conservation. Johns Hopkins University Press 2004 227p il $24.95 **597.92**

1. Sea turtles

ISBN 0-8018-8007-6

LC 2004-8935

"The author is eloquent in his appeal for the conservation of sea turtles. The best single book on the subject." Booklist

Includes bibliographical references

597.96 Snakes

Campbell, Jonathan

The **venomous** reptiles of the Western Hemisphere; by Jonathan A. Campbell and William W. Lamar, with contributions by Edmund D. Brodie III [et al.] Comstock Pub. Associates 2004 2v il maps (Comstock books in herpetology) set $149.95 **597.96**

1. Reptiles 2. Poisonous animals

ISBN 0-8014-4141-2

LC 2003-7834

The authors "describe two species of lizards (the Gila monster and the beaded lizard) and 190 species of dangerously venomous snakes of North, Central and South America. Provided are . . . accounts of each species—from the smallest to the largest—complete with descriptions, habitats, and geographic distribution." Libr J

Includes bibliographical references

Ernst, Carl H.

Snakes of the United States and Canada; [by] Carl H. Ernst, Evelyn M. Ernst. Smithsonian Books 2003 668p il map $70 **597.96**

1. Snakes

ISBN 1-58834-019-8

LC 2002-26924

"This current and comprehensive volume contains all the information currently available on the 131 species of snakes living in North America." Libr J

Includes bibliographical references

Mattison, Christopher

The **new** encyclopedia of snakes. Princeton University Press 2007 272p il map $35 **597.96**

1. Reference books 2. Snakes -- Encyclopedias

ISBN 0-691-13295-X; 978-0-691-13295-2

LC 2007-922951

First published 1995 by Facts on File with title: The encyclopedia of snakes

This encyclopedia "covers all aspects of snake biology and habitat. This is not a field guide aimed at snake identification. . . . But the work contains a wealth of information about our scaled friends, including patterns of distribution and matters relating to evolution and morphology, feeding, reproduction, and defensive strategies. . . . This captivating

work will appeal to students and snake lovers everywhere." Libr J

Includes bibliographical references

★ **Snakes** of the world; [by] Chris Mattison. Facts on File 2003 190p il map $35 **597.96**

1. Snakes

ISBN 0-8160-5213-1

LC 2002-34737

A reissue of the title first published 1986

Snake morphology, reproduction, diet, self-defense, ecology and behavior are discussed

"Mattison provides an enjoyable introduction to snake biology and snake diversity for the interested general reader. . . . Many of the numerous color photographs are spectacular." Choice [review of 1986 edition]

Includes bibliographical references

O'Shea, Mark

Venomous snakes of the world. Princeton University Press 2005 160p il map $29.95 **597.96**

1. Snakes 2. Poisonous animals

ISBN 0-691-12436-1

LC 2005-920576

"Fascinating photographs and descriptions will make this title a favorite." Univ Press Books for Public and Second Sch Libr, 2006

Includes bibliographical references

Perez, Larry

Snake in the grass; an Everglades invasion. Larry Perez. Pineapple Press 2012 xvii, 220 p.p col. ill., col. maps (paperback) $16.95 **597.96**

1. Pythons 2. Everglades (Fla.) 3. Biological invasions 4. Snakes -- Florida -- Everglades National Park

ISBN 1561645133; 9781561645138

LC 2011043280

This book, by Larry Perez, explores the ecological disruption of the Florida Everglades due to the introduction of Burmese pythons. "Over the past decade, thousands of pythons have made themselves at home across the landscape. And . . . methods of control remain elusive. Many questions remain in the wake of this troubling discovery. . . . The story unfolding in the Florida Everglades provides new opportunities to revisit our understanding of wilderness and man's place within it." (Publisher's note)

Includes bibliographical references and index

Rubio, Manny

Rattlesnake; portrait of a predator. Smithsonian Institution Press 1998 xxvii, 239p il $49.95 **597.96**

1. Rattlesnakes

ISBN 1-56098-808-8

LC 98-22935

This book contains "more than 120 color photographs of various North American rattlesnakes. . . . The text discusses many aspects of rattlesnake evolution, anatomy and physiology, and ecology, including several chapters on interactions between snakes and people." Sci Books Films

Includes bibliographical references

598   Birds

Ackerman, Jennifer

★ The **Genius** of Birds; by Jennifer Ackerman. Penguin Group USA 2016 352 p. illustrations $28   **598**

1. Birds 2. Animal intelligence 3. Birds -- Behavior 4. Birds -- Psychology

ISBN 1594205213; 9781594205217

In this book, author Jennifer Ackerman "explores the newly discovered brilliance of birds and how it came about. As she travels around the world to the most cutting-edge frontiers of research . . . Ackerman not only tells the story of the recently uncovered genius of birds but also delves deeply into the latest findings about the bird brain itself that are revolutionizing our view of what it means to be intelligent." (Publisher's note)

"Ackerman (Ah-Choo! The Uncommon Life of Your Common Cold; Sex Sleep Eat Drink Dream: A Day in the Life of Your Body) documents the amazing and almost unbelievable abilities of birds to migrate great distances, remember where thousands of food items are stored, and adapt to nonnative areas. Also described are the virtuoso skills of birdsong (some creatures are capable of hundreds of vocalizations) and the artistry of nest builders, such as bowerbirds, which favor artificial blue objects. . . . Highly recommended for all interested in natural history, behavior, and ecotravel." LJ

Alderfer, Jonathan

★ **National** Geographic birding essentials; all the tools, techniques, and tips you need to begin and become a better birder. [by] Jonathan Alderfer and Jon L. Dunn. National Geographic 2007 224p il pa $15.95   **598**

1. Bird watching

ISBN 978-1-4262-0135-6; 1-4262-0135-4

LC 2007-30960

This "book offers data on how to begin and how to improve your bird-watching skills. Chapters deal with the pleasures of birding, getting started, where and when birds are found, how common or rare they are at different seasons, parts of a bird, how to identify them, and variations in birds. . . . With a helpful glossary, this is an essential volume for all bird-watchers." Booklist

Includes bibliographical references

Arctic wings; birds of the Arctic National Wildlife Refuge. edited by Stephen Brown; foreword by Jimmy Carter; introduction by David Allen Sibley. Mountaineers Books 2006 192p il map $39.95; pa $27.95   **598**

1. Birds

ISBN 0-89886-975-7; 978-0-89886-975-0; 0-89886-976-5 pa; 978-0-8988-6976-7 pa

LC 2006-865

"The unique aspect of this book is the vivid photographs of bird behavior and the birds in their habitats, showing the importance of the habitats to the birds' continued existence. A great addition is a CD with 60 bird calls recorded on the refuge." Sci Books Films

Includes bibliographical references

★ The **atlas** of bird migration; tracing the great journeys of the world's birds. general editor Jonathan Elphick; foreword by Thomas E. Lovejoy. Firefly Books 2007 176p il map hardcover o.p. pa $24.95   **598**

1. Birds -- Migration

ISBN 978-1-55407-248-4; 1-55407-248-4; 978-1-55407-971-1 pa; 1-55407-971-3 pa

First published 1995 by Random House

"The first section is a primer on bird migration and habitat usage patterns, consisting of short, illustrated essays on topics like the evolution of migration, the mechanics of flight, birds' navigational methods and how human development affects migration patterns. Succeeding sections examine different families of migrating birds according to geographical distribution, and each has carefully designed maps that show birds' seasonal ranges and migratory routes. The use of color to describe, clarify, distinguish and compare migration patterns is exceptional, and clear explanations of complicated topics (e.g., how birds fly) make it an excellent text for middle and high school students as well as adults." Publ Wkly

Attenborough, David

The **life** of birds. Princeton Univ. Press 1998 320p il $29.95   **598**

1. Birds

ISBN 0-691-01633-X

LC 98-30705

"Well illustrated with color photographs, Attenborough's latest goes a long way to converting all readers into bird lovers." Booklist

Includes bibliographical references

Birkhead, Tim

Bird sense; what it's like to be a bird. by Tim Birkhead. Walker & Company 2012 265 p. $25   **598**

1. Nightingales 2. Birds -- Behavior 3. Senses and sensation in animals 4. Birds -- Physiology 5. Birds -- Psychology

ISBN 0802779662; 9780802779663

LC 2011043684

This book attempts to answer the question "what would an avian existence be like?" Zoologist Tim Birkhead examines "a bird's basic senses. . . . Birkhead describes, for example, ducks that keep half of their brain awake during sleep so they can still spot predators. Then there are the great grey owls that pinpoint their rodent prey using asymmetric ears." (New Scientist)

Includes bibliographical references and index.

The **Most** Perfect Thing; Inside (and Outside) a Bird's Egg. by Tim Birkhead. St. Martin's Press 2016 304 p. illustrations (some color) $27   **598**

1. Eggs

ISBN 1632863693; 9781632863690

This book, by Tim Birkhead, "is about how eggs in general are made, fertilized, developed, and hatched. The eggs of most birds spend just 24 hours in the oviduct; however, that journey takes 48 hours in cuckoos, which surreptitiously lay their eggs in the nests of other birds. From the earliest times, the study of birds' ovaries and ova (eggs) played a vital role in the quest to unravel the mysteries of fertilization and embryo development in humans." (Publisher's note)

"Birkhead manages to contain what could have become an unwieldy topic, and readers with little familiarity in guillemot eggs specifically will still find the material fascinating." Pub Wkly

Includes bibliographical references (pages [221]-265) and index.

★ **Ten** thousand birds; ornithology since Darwin. Tim Birkhead, Jo Wimpenny, Bob Montgomerie. Princeton University Press 2014 544 p. ill (some color), color maps **598**
1. Birds 2. Evolution 3. Ornithologists 4. Evolution (Biology) 5. Ornithology -- History -- 19th century 6. Ornithology -- History -- 20th century 7. Ornithology -- History -- 21st century
ISBN 9780691151977; 0691151970

LC 2013939390

This book, by Tim Birkhead, "provides a . . . history of modern ornithology, tracing how the study of birds has been shaped by a succession of visionary and often-controversial personalities, and by the unique social and scientific contexts in which these . . . individuals worked. . . . It describes how in the early 1900s pioneering individuals such as Erwin Stresemann, Ernst Mayr, and Julian Huxley recognized the importance of studying live birds in the field." (Publisher's note)

An "engaging, readable history of ornithology, replete with dozens of color and black-and-white illustrations and vivid, frequently humorous descriptions of the people who advanced ornithology because of, and often in spite of, their personalities. The charming and witty work fills the needs of academic scientists and researchers as well as serious birders." Choice

Includes bibliographical references (pages 467-496) and index

Bull, John L.
★ The **National** Audubon Society field guide to North American birds, Eastern region; [by] John Bull and John Farrand, Jr.; revised by John Farrand, Jr.; visual key by Amanda Wilson and Lori Hogan. rev ed; Knopf 1994 797p il maps pa $19.95 **598**
1. Birds -- North America
ISBN 0-679-42852-6

LC 94-7768

Companion volume to National Audubon Society field guide to North American birds, Western region, by Miklos D. F. Udvardy

First published 1977

This pictorial guide to 508 eastern species arranges birds by color and shape to simplify identification. It also includes information on bird-watching and conservation status

Includes bibliographical references

Clark, William S.
★ A **field** guide to hawks of North America; {by} William S. Clark and Brian K. Wheeler; illustra-

tions by Brian K. Wheeler. 2nd ed; Houghton Mifflin 2001 316p il maps $30; pa $22 **598**
1. Hawks
ISBN 0-395-67068-3; 0-395-67067-5 pa

LC 2001-2477

First published 1987

"Accounts are presented for all 39 of North America's diurnal raptors, including eagles, falcons, and vultures. Each species account reviews details of plumages and molts, useful identification features, patterns of flight, and general behavior. . . . The guide also provides size data (weight, length, and wingspread) for all species, as well as the etymology of common and scientific names. Basically, the reference is essential for any student of raptors and useful for serious birders in general." Am Ref Books Annu, 2002

Includes bibliographical references

Dunne, Pete
Pete Dunne's essential field guide companion. Houghton Mifflin Co. 2006 710p $29.95 **598**
1. Birds -- North America
ISBN 0-618-23648-1; 978-0-618-23648-0

LC 2005-21110

Dunne presents "information on status, distribution, habitat, cohabitants, movement and migration, behavior, flight, and vocalizations for all species of North American birds." (Sci Books Films)

This "title should appeal . . . to the serious birder striving to become more accomplished. No serious bird collection should be without it." Libr J

Dunne, Pete, 1951-
Pete Dunne on bird watching; the how-to, where-to, and when-to of birding. Houghton Mifflin 2003 334p il pa $12 **598**
1. Bird watching
ISBN 0-395-90686-5

LC 2002-27558

This "book is a superlative introduction to bird watching." Libr J

Includes bibliographical references

Elphick, Jonathan
The **World** of Birds; by Jonathan Elphick. Firefly Books Ltd 2014 608 p. illustrations (chiefly colour) $75 **598**
1. Birds
ISBN 1770853049; 9781770853041

LC 2014451570

This book, by Jonathan Elphick, "is a comprehensive and authoritative guide to every aspect of bird life and a concise survey of the world's orders and families. . . . Elphick begins by defining the distinguishing features of birds before going on to describe their evolution since the age of the dinosaurs. With the aid of fact boxes and clear photographs, he then explores in greater detail each of the significant elements of bird life." (Publisher's note)

"This work has less family information than Perrins's titles but is attractive and easy to use; highly recommended for those interested in natural history, birding, and biology." LJ

Floyd, Ted

Smithsonian field guide to the birds of North America; [by] Ted Floyd; edited by Paul Hess and George Scott; designed by Charles Nix; maps by Paul Lehman; photographs by Brian E. Small . . . [et al.] HarperCollins Publishers 2008 512p il map pa $24.95 **598**

1. Birds -- North America

ISBN 978-0-06-112040-4; 0-06-112040-5

LC 2008-1395

"Ideal for beginners, but also has formidable resources for experienced birders. . . . Perfect for field use. Birders of any experience level will be happy with this volume on their bookshelf." Publ Wkly

Includes bibliographical references

Gehrman, Elizabeth

Rare birds; the extraordinary tale of the Bermuda petrel and the man who brought it back from extinction. Elizabeth Gehrman. Beacon Press 2012 256 p. **598**

1. Rare birds 2. Bermuda petrel

ISBN 0807010766; 9780807010761

LC 2012014237

This book by Elizabeth Gehrman is the "story of David Wingate . . . who brought . . . the cahow, or Bermuda petrel . . . back from presumed extinction. . . . In 1951, two scientists invited fifteen-year-old Wingate along on a bare-bones expedition to find the bird. The team . . . locat[ed] seven nesting pairs, and Wingate knew his life had changed forever. He would spend the next fifty years battling natural and man-made disasters, bureaucracy, and personal tragedy." (Publisher's note)

Includes bibliographical references and index

Hanson, Thor

Feathers; the evolution of a natural miracle. Basic Books 2011 336p il **598**

1. Birds 2. Feathers

ISBN 0-465-02013-5; 978-0-465-02013-3

LC 2011003272

Hanson "presents the natural history of feathers, applying the findings of paleontologists, ornithologists, biologists, engineers and art historians to answer questions about the origin of feathers, their evolution and their uses throughout the ages." (Publisher's note) Index.

"Divided into sections that cover such categories as evolution, insulation, flight and adornment, 'Feathers' stretches from the ancient mists of the late Jurassic to the laboratories of today's Smithsonian Museum, where 'snarge'—science slang for what's produced when a bird meets a plane—is analyzed for data. In between, you learn that a falcon thrown out of an airplane can dive at a speed of 242 miles per hour, that the word pen is itself derived from the Latin word for feather and that the most valuable cargo on the Titanic wasn't gold or jewels but more than 40 cases of plumes intended for women's hats, a fashion craze that nearly caused the extinction of several species and led to the formation of the Audubon Society, as well as America's first National Wildlife Refuge, Florida's Pelican Island. Mr. Hanson may be a scientist but he writes like a man who believes in the value of story. . . . [He] offers more than a fanciful, associa-

tive style. He is a very good explainer of serious biology." Wall Street J

Includes bibliographical references

Hayward, Neil

Lost among the birds; Accidentally Finding Myself in One Very Big Year. Neil Hayward. Bloomsbury USA 2016 416 p. (hardback) $28 **598**

1. Bird watching 2. Bird watchers -- Anecdotes 3. Bird watching -- Anecdotes 4. Birds -- Counting -- Anecdotes

ISBN 9781632865793

LC 2015045570

In this book, by Neil Hayward, "birding was a lifelong passion. It was only among the birds that Neil found a calm that had eluded him in the confusing world of humans. But this time he also found competition. His growing list of species reluctantly catapulted him into a Big Year--a race to find the most birds in one year." (Publisher's note)

"Readers will be intrigued and inspired." Booklist

Karlson, Kevin T.

Birding by Impression; A Different Approach to Knowing and Identifying Birds. by Kevin Karlson, Dale Rosselet. Houghton Mifflin Harcourt 2015 304 p. color illustrations $30 **598**

1. Bird watching 2. Birds -- Identification

ISBN 0547195788; 9780547195780

This book, by Kevin Karlson and Dale Rosselet, offers a "highly visual guide to identifying birds in the field based on the important, unchanging features of size, shape, structure, and behavior. . . . Using this approach, birders can quickly assess all birds and distinguish new and uncommon species from familiar ones. They can then examine more detailed field marks to fine-tune the identification." (Publisher's note)

"This is not a guide for use in the field but a work to study when readers want to have a broader understanding of the differences among similar species. Roger Tory Peterson would be pleased that the institute that bears his name sponsored this work. This reference belongs in all libraries with natural-history collections." Booklist

Kaufman, Kenn

Kaufman field guide to birds of North America; with the collaboration of Rick and Nora Bowers and Lynn Hassler Kaufman. Houghton Mifflin 2005 392p il map pa $18.95 **598**

1. Birds -- North America

ISBN 0-618-57423-9; 978-0-618-57423-0

First published 2000 with title: Birds of North America

For this identification guide "Kaufman selected over 2000 digitally edited photographs, enhanced to improve contrast, color, and the like. The excellent result will appeal to beginning birders perhaps intimidated by illustrations. . . . Kaufman's text is simple and uncluttered, a plus for novices." Libr J

Kiser, Joy M.

America's other Audubon; Joy M. Kiser. Princeton Architectural Press 2012 191 p. (hardcover : alk. paper) $45.00   **598**

1. Birds 2. Nature study 3. Animal painting and illustration 4. Birds in art 5. Birds -- North America -- Pictorial works 6. Ornithological illustration -- North America 7. Ornithologists -- United States -- Biography
ISBN 1616890592; 9781616890599

LC 2011039605

This book is a reprinted collection of "almost unknown late 19th-century color paintings of birds' nests and eggs by an obscure Ohio family. Begun by Genevieve Jones, who died young, it was eventually completed by her brother Howard, mother Virginia, and friend Eliza Schulze. . . . The accompanying detailed notes and paintings of the eggs are more in the nature of a scientific contribution at a time when there were no guides to such." (Library Journal)

Kroodsma, Donald E.

The singing life of birds; the art and science of listening to birdsong. drawings by Nancy Haver. Houghton Mifflin 2005 482p il $28   **598**

1. Birdsongs
ISBN 0-618-40568-2

LC 2004-65130

"Kroodsma is a warm, encouraging guide to the world of birdsong, and his enthusiasm is contagious." Publ Wkly

Includes bibliographical references

Leahy, Christopher W.

The birdwatcher's companion to North American birdlife; illustrations by Gordon Morrison. Princeton University Press 2004 1039p il hardcover o.p. pa $19.95   **598**

1. Birds -- North America
ISBN 0-691-09297-4; 0-691-11388-2 pa

LC 2003-66383

First published 1982 by Hill & Wang

"This alphabetical compendium of ornithology offers entries ranging from single-line definitions of avian terminology ('Erne') to 12-page essay-style articles ('Systemics') that concentrate primarily on the US and Canada. Entries include a substantial number of biographies and black-and-white drawings. . . . Comprehensive entries on conservation, evolution of birdlife, optical equipment, and human threats to birdlife provide welcome up-to-date information. . . . Leahy's style is by turns serious and scholarly or personal and whimsical, appropriate to a comprehensive reference for both novice and expert birders. There is no recent comparable work." Choice

Includes bibliographical references

Lederer, Roger J.

Beaks, bones, and bird songs; How the Struggle for Survival Has Shaped Birds and Their Behavior. Roger J. Lederer. Timber Press 2016 282 p. illustrations, maps (hardcover) $24.95   **598**

1. Birds -- Behavior 2. Birds -- Evolution
ISBN 9781604696486

LC 2015045261

This book, by Roger J. Lederer, "guides the reader through the myriad, and often almost miraculous, things that birds do every day to merely stay alive. . . . Lederer shares how and why birds use their sensory abilities to see ultraviolet, find food without seeing it, fly thousands of miles without stopping, change their songs in noisy cities, navigate by smell, and much more." (Publisher's note)

"This is an exceptional overview of the life, adaptations, and impressive skill sets of wild birds." LJ

Includes bibliographical references (pages 245-261) and index.

Marzluff, John M.

Welcome to subirdia; sharing our neighborhoods with wrens, robins, woodpeckers, and other wildlife. John M. Marzluff; illustrations by Jack DeLap. Yale University Press 2014 320 p. illustrations (cloth : alk. paper) $30   **598**

1. Birds 2. Bird watching 3. Habitat (Ecology) 4. Urban animals 5. Birds -- Habitat 6. Bird watchers -- Anecdotes 7. Bird watching -- Washington (State) -- Seattle 8. Birds -- Washington (State) -- Seattle -- Identification
ISBN 0300197071; 9780300197075

LC 2014012257

In this book, author John M. Marzluff "reveals how our own actions affect the birds and animals that live in our cities and towns, and he provides ten specific strategies everyone can use to make human environments friendlier for our natural neighbors." (Publisher's note)

"Readers visit ten cities around the world and marvel at the simplicity of the author's ten rules for saving the situation. And readers are left with an optimistic list of deeply rewarding projects accessible to anyone. This is therapy for people who worry. Beautifully illustrated in black-and-white by Jack Delap, with accuracy and touches of humor. For scientists, bird lovers, philosophers—and everyone else. Summing Up: Highly recommended. All levels/libraries." Choice

Includes bibliographical references and index

Masear, Terry

Fastest Things on Wings; Rescuing Hummingbirds in Hollywood. Terry Masear. Houghton Mifflin Harcourt 2015 320 p. 8 plates; color illustrations $25   **598**

1. Hummingbirds 2. Birds -- Anatomy 3. Motion picture industry
ISBN 0544416031; 9780544416031

LC 2014

In this book, author Terry Masear presents her "account of the trials and triumphs a hummingbird rehabber encounters while caring for her tiny, fragile patients. During the four months that Terry worked with Gabriel, [an Anna's hummingbird] she took in 160 hummingbirds, from a miniature nestling rescued by a bulldog and a fledgling trapped inside a skydiving wind tunnel at Universal CityWalk, to Pepper, a female Anna's injured on a film set." (Publisher's note)

"Not just for birders, this captivating book brims with warmth, humor, and drama that will have wide appeal." Kirkus

Montgomery, Sy

Birdology; lessons learned from a pack of hens, a peck of pigeons, cantankerous crows, fierce falcons, hip hop parrots, baby hummingbirds, and one murderously big cassowary. Free Press 2010 260p il $25 **598**

1. Birds
ISBN 978-1-4165-6984-8; 1-4165-6984-7
LC 2009-31303

"Montgomery assists a hummingbird rehabilitator in the delicate raising of two tiny orphans, and meets the 'most dangerous bird on earth,' the enormous, razor-clawed cassowary in Australia, one bird whose dinosaur ancestry is blazingly apparent. She also writes from unexpected perspectives about falcons, crows, pigeons, chickens, and parrots. . . . Inspired equally by all that we share with birds—similarities in intelligence, emotion, language, and music—and all that is mysterious (birds 'remain fundamentally wild'), Montgomery expresses profound appreciation for the living web of life in a book that both bird lovers and readers new to bird lore will find evocative, enlightening, and uplifting." Booklist

Includes bibliographical references

National Audubon Society

Bird; the definitive visual guide. Audubon; [senior editor, Peter Frances; contributors, BirdLife International, David Burnie] DK Pub. 2007 512p il map $50 **598**

1. Birds
ISBN 978-0-7566-3153-6; 0-7566-3153-X
LC 2007-282186

"From flyleaf to fore edge, the visuals are astounding. . . . An enclosed CD with bird calls and songs adds yet another dimension to a glorious work." Libr J

National Geographic complete birds of North America; edited by Jonathan Alderfer with Jon L. Dunn; maps by Paul Lehman; contributing authors, Jessie H. Barry ... [and 24 others] National Geographic 2014 743 p. color illustrations, color map $40 **598**

1. Birds -- North America
ISBN 1426213735; 9781426213731
LC 2014451569

This book, edited by Jonathan Alderfer, "is an astonishing resource that covers every bird species found in North America as well as all the seasonal visitors. Entries are organized by family group, the taxonomic organization newly updated to match current American Ornithologists' Union guidelines. Within a family, each separate bird entry has dozens of tips and illustrations on species' gender, age group, behavior, habitat, nesting and feeding habits, and migration routes." (Publisher's note)

"The introductory material is brief, as are the bibliography and website list (which omits the National Audubon Society). The binding is supple; that of the first edition is too tight. Summing Up: Highly recommended. All academic and public libraries." Choice

Includes bibliographical references and index

Nigge, Klaus

Whooping crane; images from the wild. introduction by Krista Schlyer. Texas A&M University Press 2010 217p il map $45 **598**

1. Cranes (Birds)
ISBN 978-1-60344-209-1; 1-60344-209-X
LC 2009048496

"On the flock's wintering grounds at Aransas National Wildlife Refuge in Texas, photographer Klaus Nigge has captured the daily activity of a single family over several weeks in two separate years, documenting their life in the salt marshes of the central Texas coast and, in one year, the happy arrival from the north of twin adolescents. . . . Then, with the backing of National Geographic magazine, he received unprecedented permission from the Canadian government to photograph the cranes' summer nesting sites in remote areas of Wood Buffalo National Park. . . . [This collection of his photos is divided into] three galleries, each containing portfolios of images of these magnificent birds in their natural habitat." Publisher's note

Includes bibliographical references

Peterson, Roger Tory

Peterson field guide to birds of Eastern and Central North America; [by] Roger Tory Peterson, with contributions from Michael DiGiorgio [et al.] 6th ed; Houghton Mifflin Harcourt 2010 445p il map (Peterson field guide series) $19.95 **598**

1. Birds -- North America
ISBN 978-0-547-15246-2; 0-547-15246-9
LC 2009-37681

First published 1934 with title: A field guide to the birds
This guide to birds found east of the Rocky Mountains contains colored illustrations painted by the author, with a description of each species on the facing page. Views of young birds and seasonal variations in plumage are included.

Peterson field guide to birds of Western North America; with contributions from Michael DiGiorgio [et al.] 4th ed; Houghton Mifflin Harcourt 2010 493p il map (Peterson field guide series) pa $19.95 **598**

1. Birds -- North America
ISBN 978-0-547-15270-7; 0-547-15270-1
LC 2009-39158

First published 1941 with title: A field guide to western birds
This guide illustrates over 600 species of birds on 176 color plates. In addition, over 588 range maps are included.

Peterson, Roger Tory, 1908-1996

★ **Peterson** field guide to birds of North America; with contributions from Michael DiGiorgio . . . [et al.] Houghton Mifflin Co. 2008 527p il map (Peterson field guide series) $26 **598**

1. Birds -- North America
ISBN 0-618-96614-5; 978-0-618-96614-1
LC 2007-39803

First published 1934 with title: A field guide to the birds. Previously published in two separate parts as A field guide to western birds (1990) and A field guide to the birds of eastern and central North America (2002)

This guide to birds found in North America contains colored illustrations painted by the author, with a description of each species on the facing page. Views of young birds and seasonal variations in plumage are included. The book also includes a URL to video podcasts.

"This field guide is of high quality and should be in millions of birders' and other nature lovers' backpacks." Sci Books Films

★ The **Princeton** encyclopedia of birds; edited by Christopher Perrins. Princeton University Press 2009 656p il map pa $35   **598**
1. Reference books 2. Birds -- Encyclopedias
ISBN 978-0-691-14070-4; 0-691-14070-7

First published 1985 by Facts on File with title: The encyclopedia of birds. Previous edition published 2003 by Firefly Bks. with title: Firefly encyclopedia of birds

The editor "combines the work of 150 contributors and more than 1000 great color photographs, maps, and other illustrations to produce a stunning book that informs both amateurs and experts. Coverage includes form and function, distribution, diet, breeding biology, and conservation and environment." Libr J

Includes bibliographical references

Sibley, David
  ★ The **Sibley** field guide to birds of Eastern North America; written and illustrated by David Allen Sibley. Knopf 2003 431p il pa $19.95   **598**
1. Birds -- North America
ISBN 0-679-45120-X

LC 2002-114931

"All the qualities to be expected in a field guide are here. . . . Image reproduction is crisp, colors are distinct, shading shows well, and despite the very small size, range map colors are clear. . . . Sibley has accomplished the difficult task of condensing . . . [The Sibley guide to birds] to practical field size." Libr J

★ The **Sibley** field guide to birds of Western North America; written and illustrated by David Allen Sibley. Knopf 2003 473p il pa $19.95   **598**
1. Birds -- North America
ISBN 0-679-45121-8

LC 2002-114930

"All the qualities to be expected in a field guide are here. . . . Image reproduction is crisp, colors are distinct, shading shows well, and despite the very small size, range map colors are clear. . . . Sibley has accomplished the difficult task of condensing . . . [The Sibley guide to birds] to practical field size." Libr J

★ The **Sibley** guide to bird life & behavior; illustrated by David Allen Sibley; edited by Chris Elphick, John B. Dunning, Jr., David Allen Sibley. Knopf 2001 588p il maps hardcover o.p. pa $39.95   **598**
1. Birds -- North America
ISBN 0-679-45123-4; 1-4000-4386-7 pa

LC 2001-33903

This companion volume to The Sibley guide to birds provides "information about birds' lives and behavior. . . . Part 1 ('The World of Birds') discusses basic avian biology, including form, distribution, population, and conservation, in about 100 pages. Part 2 ('Bird Families of North America'), to which over 40 ornithologists contributed, uses a standard format to describe taxonomy, foraging, breeding, range, nests, eggs, longevity, conservation, and more." Libr J

★ The **Sibley** guide to birds; written and illustrated by David Sibley. Knopf 2000 544p il maps pa $35   **598**
1. Birds -- North America
ISBN 0-679-45122-6

LC 00-41239

"The treatments of each of the 810 species have detailed paintings to show the natural variations in plumage (e.g., juveniles, male/female adults, seasonal and geographic changes). In all, there are more than 6,600 full-color illustrations. . . . The text for each species has a short summary of identification key points, description of vocalizations, and an up-to-date range map." Choice

★ **Sibley's** birding basics; written and illustrated by David Allen Sibley. Knopf 2002 154p il pa $15.95   **598**
1. Birds 2. Bird watching
ISBN 0-375-70966-5

LC 2002-20768

Sibley "explores general aspects of birding such as getting started, misidentification, voice, understanding feathers, age variation, ethics and conservation, taxonomy, and finding birds. If being a field naturalist is a craft, then this book is essential in helping to develop and understand the required skills." Libr J

Stokes, Donald
  The **new** stokes field guide to birds; western region. Donald Stokes, Lillian Stokes. Little, Brown and Co. 2013 574 p. $19.99   **598**
1. Birds -- North America 2. Birds -- Handbooks, manuals, etc.
ISBN 0316213926; 9780316213929

LC 2012945368

This guide offers information about North American birds in two volumes, one devoted to the eastern region and one to the western region. "Much of the data is directly taken from the earlier 1996 editions," but there are "many new photos and inclusions. . . . The tiny range maps include not only the year-round, summer, and winter ranges, but migration routes as well." (Library Journal)

Stokes, Donald W.
  The **bird** feeder book; an easy guide to attracting, identifying, and understanding your feeder birds. {by} Donald and Lillian Stokes; illustrations of feeders by Gordon Morrison; range maps by Leslie Cow-

perthwaite. Little, Brown 1987 90p il maps pa
$12.95 **598**
   1. Bird watching
   ISBN 0-316-81733-3

                           LC 87-3016

   "This guide for beginners features 72 dramatic color photographs of the most common backyard birds. The text offers chapters on attracting and identifying birds (which types of feeders to use, etc.), dealing with squirrels and other yard pests, and planting shrubbery layouts that offer food and nest sites. A nicely illustrated, logically organized handbook." Booklist
   Includes bibliographical references

Strycker, Noah

   The **thing** with feathers; the surprising lives of birds and what they reveal about being human. Noah Strycker. Riverhead Books, a member of Penguin Group (USA) 2014 304 p. illustrations (hardback) $27.95 **598**
   1. Birds -- Behavior 2. Human-animal relationship 3. Bird watching -- Anecdotes
   ISBN 1594486352; 9781594486357

                       LC 2013030320

   Written by Noah Strycker, "'The Thing with Feathers' explores the astonishing homing abilities of pigeons, the good deeds of fairy-wrens, the influential flocking abilities of starlings, the deft artistry of bowerbirds, the extraordinary memories of nutcrackers, the lifelong loves of albatross, and other mysteries--revealing why birds do what they do, and offering a glimpse into our own nature." (Publisher's note)
   "Strycker . . . here combines the latest in ornithological science with snippets of history and his own vast experience in the field to hatch a thoroughly entertaining examination of bird behavior." Booklist
   Includes bibliographical references and index

Swash, Andy

   The **world's** rarest birds; Erik Hirschfeld, Andy Swash & Robert Still; with contributions by Nick Langley ... [et al.]; and illustrations by Tomasz Cofta. Princeton University Press 2013 360 p. ill. (chiefly col.), col. maps (WILDGuides) $45 **598**
   1. Birds 2. Extinct animals 3. Endangered species 4. Extinct birds 5. Birds -- Conservation 6. Rare birds -- Identification 7. Rare birds -- Geographical distribution
   ISBN 0691155968; 9780691155968

                       LC 2012945960

   This book, by Erik Hirschfeld, Andy Swash & Robert Still, "depicts the most endangered birds in the world and provides the latest information on the threats each species faces and the measures being taken to save them. Today, 571 bird species are classified as critically endangered or endangered, and a further four now exist only in captivity. . . . [It] has introductory chapters that explain the threats to birds, the ways threat categories are applied, and the distinction between threat and rarity." (Publisher's note)
   "The scope, depth and organization is exemplary. The links to regularly updated information through the QR codes means the book's value will continue." LJ

Tudge, Colin

   The **bird**; a natural history of who birds are, where they came from, and how they live. Crown Publishers 2009 462p il $30 **598**
   1. Birds
   ISBN 978-0-307-34204-1
   First published 2008 in the United Kingdom with title: Consider the birds
   "The author writes with clarity and cheerful wit about the physics and mechanics of flight, evolution and the archaeological record [of birds] . . . [Tudge] covers the avian landscape like a tarp, from amusing anecdotes about bird behavior, to a critique of behavioralism, to the abuse of Darwin's theories, to the complex structure of avian taxonomy. . . Entertaining, charming and knowledgeable." Kirkus
   Includes bibliographical references

Udvardy, Miklos D. F.

   ★ **National** Audubon Society field guide to North American birds, Western region; revised by John Farrand, Jr.; visual key by Amanda Wilson and Lori Hogan. rev ed; Knopf 1994 822p il maps pa $19.95 **598**
   1. Birds -- North America
   ISBN 0-679-42851-8

                       LC 94-7415

   Companion volume to National Aududon Society field guide to North American birds, Eastern region by John L. Bull
   First published 1977
   In this guide, "virtually every bird found in North America is brought to life in a full-color photograph and with textual information on the bird's voice, nesting habits, habitat, range, and interesting behaviors. Accompanying range maps; overhead flight silhouettes; sections on birdwatching, accidental species, and endangered birds" are also included. (Publisher's note)
   Includes bibliographical references

Unwin, Mike

   The **atlas** of birds; diversity, behavior, and conservation. Princeton University Press 2011 144p il map pa $22.95 **598**
   1. Birds 2. Atlases 3. Reference books
   ISBN 978-0-691-14949-3

                       LC 2011920367

   This "is neither a textbook nor an encyclopedia but rather a compendium of interesting factoids and bird trivia, with each two-page layout addressing one aspect of bird biology. This is a book for general readers who enjoy studying birds." Choice
   Includes bibliographical references

Weidensaul, Scott

   Living on the wind; across the hemisphere with migratory birds. North Point Press 1999 420p il hardcover o.p. pa $15 **598**
   1. Birds -- Migration
   ISBN 0-86547-591-1 pa

                       LC 99-11693

"The book will be of interest to biologists and amateur naturalists; birders will particularly appreciate the discussion of key 'fallout' areas." Libr J

Includes bibliographical references

Of a feather; a brief history of American birding. Harcourt, Inc. 2007 358p il $25; pa $15   **598**
1. Bird watching 2. Bird watching -- United States
ISBN 0-15-101247-4; 0-15-603355-0 pa; 978-0-15-101247-3; 978-0-15-603355-8 pa
LC 2007-07364

This narrative history of birding in America "begins in colonial America, where new arrivals from Europe 'made awed note of the continent's teeming skies and waterways.'" (N Y Times Book Rev)

The author's "vivid descriptions of his own experiences should send many a reader out of doors to look for the small, contained miracle that is a bird." Publ Wkly

Includes bibliographical references

Williamson, Sheri L.
A **field** guide to hummingbirds of North America; {by} Sheri L. Williamson. Houghton Mifflin 2001 263p il maps $30; pa $22   **598**
1. Hummingbirds
ISBN 0-618-02495-6; 0-618-02496-4 pa
LC 2001-24473

"The habits, habitats, migratory patterns, physical traits, diet, mating practices, where to find them in short, all the information that a good wildlife guide offers are the stuff of Williamson's book. Clear, engaging prose and 180 full color photographs make this a natural for birdwatchers everywhere." Publ Wkly

Zickefoose, Julie
Baby Birds; An Artist Looks into the Nest. Julie Zickefoose. Houghton Mifflin Harcourt 2016 352 p. color illustrations $28   **598**
1. Birds 2. Nest building
ISBN 0544206703; 9780544206700

In this book, by Julie Zickefoose, "more than 400 watercolor paintings show the breathtakingly swift development of seventeen different species of wild birds. Sixteen of those species nest on Julie's wildlife sanctuary, so she knows the birds intimately, and writes about them with authority. Julie shares a lifetime of insight about bird breeding biology, growth, and cognition." (Publisher's note)

"This is not a field guide; rather, it is for learning about baby birds and savoring watercolor paintings of them in more contemplative settings. It will appeal to lovers of nature art and bird-watching enthusiasts." Library Journal

Includes bibliographical references (pages 326-327) and index

The **bluebird** effect; uncommon bonds with common birds. Julie Zickefoose. Houghton Mifflin Harcourt Co. 2012 355 p.   **598**
1. Naturalists 2. Bird watching 3. Birds -- Behavior 4. Wildlife rehabilitation 5. Human-animal relationship 6. Birds -- United States
ISBN 9780547003092
LC 2011036692

This book by bird rehabilitator Julie Zickefoose presents an "account of her rescues of cardinals, robins and more than 20 other bird species. . . . The birds are a disparate lot: the starlings with their imitations of car alarms and barking dogs; the potentially home-wrecking chickadees; the lean and sinewy ospreys; the barn sparrows that haunt the eaves of large home-improvement stores." (Kirkus Reviews)

Includes bibliographical references and index

598.47 Penguins

Jones, Mark
Penguins; the ultimate guide. Tui De Roy, Mark Jones, Julie Cornthwaite. Princeton University Press 2014 240 p. color illustrations, col. maps (cloth) $35   **598.47**
1. Penguins
ISBN 0691162999; 9780691162997
LC 2013956959

This book by Tui de Roy, Mark Jones, and Julie Cornthwaite "provides a unique look at [penguins] and the cutting-edge science that is helping us to better understand them. Featuring more than 400 breathtaking photos, this is the ultimate guide to all 18 species of penguins, including those with retiring personalities or nocturnal habits that tend to be overlooked and rarely photographed." (Publisher's note)

"Most highly recommended for all interested, whether the lay public or scientists, in natural history and Antarctic and sub-Antarctic places." LJ

598.7 Miscellaneous orders of land birds

Davies, Nick, 1953-
Cuckoo; Cheating by Nature. by Nick Davies. St. Martin's Press 2015 320 p. 8 plates; illustrations $27   **598.7**
1. Cuckoos 2. Birds -- Nests
ISBN 1620409526; 9781620409527

In this book, scientist Nick Davies asks "how does the cuckoo get away with laying its eggs in the nests of other birds and tricking them into raising young cuckoos rather than their own offspring? . . . Davies and his colleagues studied adult cuckoo behavior, cuckoo egg markings, and cuckoo chick begging calls to discover exactly how cuckoos trick their hosts." (Publisher's note)

"He describes experiments involving recorded bird calls, radio transmitters, and egg substitutions, and he reports findings that suggest how predators and prey continue to adapt. Readers may gain some respect, if not affection, for a hard-to-understand bird." Booklist

Gallagher, Tim
★ **Imperial** Dreams; Tracking the Imperial Woodpecker Through the Wild Sierra Madre. Tim Gallagher. Pocket Books 2013 304 p. $26   **598.7**
1. Woodpeckers 2. Sierra Madre Mountains 3. Imperial woodpecker 4. Natural history -- Mexico 5. Sierra Madre Occidental Region (Mexico) -- Description

and travel
ISBN 1439191522; 9781439191521

LC 2013005233

In this book by explorer and naturalist Tim Gallagher, he journeys "deep into Mexico's . . . Sierra Madre Occidental, home to rich wildlife, as well as to Mexican drug cartels, in a perilous quest to locate the most elusive bird in the world--the imperial woodpecker. Gallagher's . . . quest takes a harrowing turn as he encounters armed drug traffickers, burning houses, and fleeing villagers. His mission becomes a life-and-death drama that . . . as he chases truth in the most dangerous of habitats." (Publisher's note)

Includes bibliographical references and index

Gorman, Gerard

Woodpeckers of the World; A Photographic Guide. by Gerard Gorman. Firefly Books Ltd 2014 528 p. illustrations, maps $49.95 **598.7**
1. Woodpeckers
ISBN 177085309X; 9781770853096

This book, by Gerard Gorman, "is the first definitive guide to all 239 species of woodpecker. Beautiful color photographs of male, female and juvenile woodpeckers taken in their natural habitat reveal the birds' coloring, markings, and sexual dimorphism. . . . Identification notes are followed by brief entries on food, voice, drumming, habitat, status, distribution, geographic variation and confusion species." (Publisher's note)

"Highly recommended for birders, naturalists, and biologists." LJ

Orenstein, Ronald

Hummingbirds; by Ronald I. Orenstein; photographs by Michael Fogden and Patricia Fogden. Firefly Books Ltd 2014 256 p. color illustrations $35 **598.7**
1. Hummingbirds
ISBN 1770854002; 9781770854000

LC 2014497430

This book, by Ronald I. Orenstein, "covers all aspects of hummingbird natural history, their relationship with the plants on which they feed, the miracle of their flight, their elaborate social life and nesting behavior, and their renowned feats of migration." (Publisher's note)

"Of optional interest to naturalists, nature buffs, and birders." LJ

Shunk, Stephen A.

Peterson Reference Guide to Woodpeckers of North America; Stephen Shunk. Houghton Mifflin Harcourt 2016 320 p. ill. (some color), color maps (hardcover) $35 **598.7**
1. Woodpeckers 2. Natural history
ISBN 9780618739950; 0618739955

This book, by Stephen Shunk, offers "a complete guide to the natural history, ecology, and conservation of North America's 23 woodpecker species. . . . It explores their unique anatomy and their fascinating and often comical behaviors; it covers each species' North American conservation status; and it showcases over 250 stunning photographs of woodpeckers in their natural habitats, plus easy-to-read figures and range maps." (Publisher's note)

"A colorful guide to the 'carpenters' within the world of birds." LJ

Includes bibliographical references (pages 264-293) and index.

598.8 Perching birds (Passeriformes)

Young, Jon

What the robin knows; how birds reveal the secrets of the natural world. Jon Young; with science and audio editing by Dan Gardoqui. Houghton Mifflin Harcourt 2012 xxviii, 241 p.p **598.8**
1. Birdsongs 2. Bird watching 3. Philosophy of nature 4. Nature observation 5. Songbirds -- Behavior 6. Natural history -- New Jersey
ISBN 0547451253; 9780547451251

LC 2012002403

In this book naturalist Jon Young teaches "three basic premises: the robin, junco, and other songbirds know everything important about their environment, be it backyard or forest; by tuning in to their vocalizations and behavior, we can acquire much of this wisdom for our own pleasure and benefit; and the birds' companion calls and warning alarms are just as important as their songs. Birds are the sentries—and our key to understanding the world beyond our front door. Unwitting humans create a zone of disturbance that scatters the wildlife. Respectful humans who heed the birds acquire an awareness that radically changes the dynamic. We are welcome in their habitat." (Publisher's note)

Includes bibliographical references and index.

598.9 Falconiformes, Caprimulgiformes, owls

MacDonald, Helen

★ **H** is for Hawk; Helen Macdonald. Grove Press 2015 320 p. (hardcover) $26 **598.9**
1. Grief 2. Hawks 3. Falconry
ISBN 9780802123411; 0802123414

LC 2014472504

Carnegie Medal Shortlist: Nonfiction (2016)

National Book Critics Circle Award Finalist: Autobiography (2015)

In this memoir, "following the sudden death of her father, [Helen] Macdonald . . . tried staving off deep depression with a unique form of personal therapy: the purchase and training of an English goshawk, which she named Mabel. Although a trained falconer, the author chose a raptor both unfamiliar and unpredictable, a creature of mad confidence that became a means of working against madness." (Kirkus Reviews)

"Macdonald, a trained falconer, rediscovers a favorite book of her childhood, T.H. White's The Goshawk (1951), in which White, author of The Once and Future King, recounts his mostly failed but illuminating attempts at training a goshawk. . . . The book moves from White's frustration at training his bird to Macdonald's sure, deliberate efforts to get Mabel to fly to her." Pub Wkly

Includes bibliographical references

Mikkola, Heimo

Owls of the world; a photographic guide. Heimo Mikkola. Firefly Books 2012 512 p. $49.95 **598.9**
1. Owls 2. Hiboux 3. Owls -- Identification 4. Owls -- Pictorial works 5. Owls -- Geographical distribution 6. Hiboux -- Ouvrages illustrés
ISBN 1770851364; 9781770851368

LC 2012288505

This book is "a complete guide to identifying the world's owls. Photographers spend hours waiting to capture them and birders seek them out with determination, but owls have been tough to identify--until now. . . .Owls are shown as adults from a perspective that clearly shows markings which assist in identification. Photographs of similar-looking species are included where identification is particularly difficult." (Publisher's note)

Includes bibliographical references (p. 504) and index

Taylor, Marianne

Owls; [text by Marianne Taylor; photos by Markus Varesvuo ... et al.] Cornell University Press 2012 224 p. col. ill. (hardcover) $35 **598.9**
1. Owls
ISBN 0801451817; 9780801451812

LC 2012023191

This book, by Marianne Taylor, presents an introduction to various species of owls. "From tiny Elf and Pygmy Owls through the familiar Tawny and Barn Owls to the giant Eagle and Fish Owls, these fierce hunters of dawn, dusk and night have long held a fascination for people around the world. This . . . book, covering all owl species found in the northern hemisphere, looks closely at how owls live their lives, and how best to recognize them." (Publisher's note)

Includes bibliographical references (p. 220) and index.

599 Mammals

Elbroch, Mark

Mammal tracks & sign; a guide to North American species. Stackpole Bks. 2003 779p il maps $44.95 **599**
1. Mammals 2. Animal tracks
ISBN 0-8117-2626-6

LC 2002-10549

The author "brings an ideal combination of practical experience and careful research to this work. . . . A definitive treatment, Elbroch's book will set the standard for years to come and is essential to anyone interested in tracking this continent's mammals." Libr J

Includes bibliographical references

★ The **Peterson** field guide to animal tracks; [by] Mark Elbroch and Olaus J. Murie. 3rd ed.; Houghton Mifflin Company 2005 (The Peterson field guide series) hardcover o.p. pa $19.95 **599**
1. Animal tracks
ISBN 978-0-618-51742-8; 978-0-618-51743-5 pa

LC 2005-13108

First published 1954

"Murie's handbook is recognized as the classic work on the subject. . . . The illustrated guide describes the tracks, droppings, and marks left on bones and leaves by an army of wild animals-bats, bears, rabbits, reptiles, moles, weasels, and others. A fascinating collection of miscellaneous information about the habits of these creatures is part of the descriptive text." Wynar. Ref Books in Paperback. 2d edition

Nowak, Ronald M.

Walker's mammals of the world; 6th ed; Johns Hopkins Univ. Press 1999 2v il set $135 **599**
1. Mammals 2. Reference books
ISBN 0-8018-5789-9

LC 98-23686

First published 1964

"A goal of the work . . . [is] to provide a quality photograph of a living representative of every genus of mammal. . . . Each genus entry contains information on the number of species known, key literature references, physical description, comparison of characteristics of representative species, description of habitat, general behavior, breeding and care of young, and information on the species' endangered status." Am Ref Books Annu, 2000

Includes bibliographical references

Owens, Mark

Secrets of the savanna; twenty-three years in the African wilderness unraveling the mysteries of elephants and people. [by] Mark and Delia Owens. Houghton Mifflin 2006 230p il map $26; pa $14.95 **599**
1. Elephants 2. Wildlife conservation
ISBN 978-0-395-89310-4; 0-395-89310-0; 978-0-618-87250-3 pa; 0-618-87250-7 pa

LC 2005-23842

Sequel to The eye of the elephant

"This book, full of adventure and a few hair-raising moments, deserves a wide readership." Libr J

Includes bibliographical references

★ The **Princeton** encyclopedia of mammals; edited by David W. Macdonald. Princeton University Press 2009 936p il map pa $45 **599**
1. Reference books 2. Mammals -- Encyclopedias
ISBN 978-0-691-14069-8; 0-691-14069-3

This encyclopedia features a "general introduction to mammals followed by . . . accounts of species and groups that . . . describe form, distribution, behavior, status, conservation, and more." Publisher's note

Includes bibliographical references

Whitaker, John O.

★ **National** Audubon Society field guide to North American mammals; rev ed; Knopf 1996 937p il maps pa $19.95 **599**
1. Mammals
ISBN 0-679-44631-1

LC 95-81456

First published 1980

This field guide describes 390 species of mammals of North America and includes keys for identification, range maps, information on tracks and anatomy, and 375 color photos

599.2   Marsupials and monotremes

Flannery, Tim F.

Chasing kangaroos; a continent, a scientist, and a search for the world's most extraordinary creature. Grove Press 2007 258p il map hardcover o.p. pa $14   **599.2**

1. Kangaroos 2. Australia -- Description and travel
ISBN 978-0-8021-1852-3; 0-8021-1852-6; 978-0-8021-4371-6 pa; 0-8021-4371-7 pa

LC 2006-52628

First published 2004 in Australia with title: Country
"In a time where pride in one's country is a rarity, Flannery has written a love letter to his. . . . Just as much as Chasing Kangaroos is about the evolution of a creature, it's also Flannery's acknowledgement of Australia's inherent uniqueness, a uniqueness he begs is not casually lost in the growing conformity of the global landscape." Paste

599.5   Cetaceans and sea cows

Bortolotti, Dan

Wild blue; a natural history of the world's largest animal. Thomas Dunne Books 2008 315p il map $24.95   **599.5**

1. Whales
ISBN 978-0-312-38387-9; 0-312-38387-8

LC 2008-24933

The author "provides the most comprehensive title yet on blue whales for the general reader. Encapsulating everything from statistical analysis of geographic populations to the reports of whalers from centuries past, Wild Blue is an effective twenty-first-century fusion of marine biology and international politics." Booklist
Includes bibliographical references

Folkens, Pieter A.

National Audubon Society guide to marine mammals of the world; illustrated by Pieter A. Folkens; written by Randall R. Reeves [et al.] Knopf 2002 527p il maps $26.95   **599.5**

1. Marine mammals
ISBN 0-375-41141-0

LC 2001-38103

"Just about everything one could hope for in a guide can be found in this info-packed yet extremely user-friendly tome. . . . A liberal dose of superb, high-quality action color photographs shows the creatures in their natural surroundings." SLJ
Includes bibliographical references

Herzing, Denise L.

Dolphin diaries; my 25 years with spotted dolphins in the Bahamas. St. Martin's Press 2011 xxi, 314p $26.99; ebook $12.99   **599.5**

1. Dolphins
ISBN 978-0-312-60896-5; 978-1-4299-8744-8 ebook

LC 2011005995

"Tales of diving with wild dolphins, recalcitrant equipment, living on boats, and hurricanes really bring both the excitement and the drudgery of field research to life." Booklist
Includes bibliographical references

Hoare, Philip

The **whale**; in search of the giants of the sea. Ecco 2010 453p il map $27.99   **599.5**

1. Whales 2. Whaling
ISBN 978-0-06-197621-6; 0-06-197621-0

First published 2009 in the United Kingdom with title: Leviathan; or, The whale
A "chronicle of the tragic interaction between humans and whales. Using Herman Melville's life and 'Moby-Dick' as touchstones, Hoare traces the whaling industry from its origins in 18th century New England to the present." Los Angeles Times
Includes bibliographical references

Kelsey, Elin

Watching giants; the secret lives of whales. with photographs by Doc White; additional photographs by Francois Gohier. University of California Press 2009 201p il $24.95   **599.5**

1. Whales
ISBN 978-0-520-24976-9; 0-520-24976-3

LC 2008-7782

"An appealing, agitating foray into the world of whales that ignites both protective instincts and a hungry curiosity to know more." Kirkus
Includes bibliographical references

Rothenberg, David

Thousand mile song; whale music in a sea of sound. Basic Books 2008 287p il $27.50   **599.5**

1. Whales
ISBN 978-0-465-07128-9; 0-465-07128-7

LC 2007-48161

"Biologists know that whale songs, which may carry for hundreds of miles, change over time and are passed on from one generation to the next, but they don't fully understand what these complex sounds are for. . . . [The author] proposes that music played by humans can help us find answers. He tested this theory by playing his clarinet into an underwater speaker and recording the whales' responses on an underwater hydrophone. His intriguing book includes sonograms and a CD demonstrating that the orcas, belugas and humpbacks he played for seemed to interact with his music. . . . His paean to the beautiful music these great mammals make should lend further support to attempts to save the whales at a time when they are increasingly threatened." Publ Wkly
Includes bibliographical references

599.53   Dolphins and porpoises

Casey, Susan

Voices in the Ocean; A Journey into the Wild and Haunting World of Dolphins. Susan Casey. Random House Inc 2015 320 p. 16 plates; illustrations $27.95 **599.53**

1. Dolphins 2. Human-animal relationship
ISBN 0385537301; 9780385537308

LC 2015011763

This book by Susan Casey offers a "look into the mysterious world of dolphins and their conflicted history with man. For two years Casey traveled the world, and now she has written a thrilling book about the other intelligent life on the planet. Since the dawn of recorded history, humans have felt a kinship with the sleek and beautiful dolphin, an animal whose playfulness, sociability, and intelligence seems like an aquatic mirror of mankind." (Publisher's note)

"This book does not provide scientific background as does Justin Gregg's Are Dolphins Really that Smart? but will interest general and YA readers, as well as nature lovers, who will lose their eagerness to visit dolphin shows and may be motivated toward further reading on the subject." LJ

Hargrove, John

Beneath the surface; killer whales, SeaWorld, and the truth beyond Blackfish. John Hargrove with Howard Chua-Eoan. Palgrave Macmillan 2015 272 p. 8 plates; color illustrations (alk. paper) $26 **599.53**

1. Whales 2. Animal rights 3. Marine aquariums 4. Sea World 5. Killer whale 6. Aquatic animal welfare 7. Captive marine mammals 8. Killer whale -- Habitat
ISBN 1137280107; 9781137280107

LC 2014039895

This book by authors John Hargrove and Howard Chua-Eoan "paints a compelling portrait of these highly intelligent and social creatures, including [Hargrove's] favorite whales Takara and her mother Kasatka, two of the most dominant orcas in SeaWorld. And he includes vibrant descriptions of the lives of orcas in the wild, contrasting their freedom in the ocean with their lives in SeaWorld." (Publisher's note)

"Hargrove, with coauthor Chua-Eoan, blends natural history and corporate indictment into an emotional story about a man changing sides in the argument over human domination of the animal world. Recommended for animals-rights collections in public libraries." Booklist

Kirby, David

Death at SeaWorld; Shamu and the dark side of killer whales in captivity. David Kirby. St. Martin's Press 2012 469 p. (hardcover) $26.99 **599.53**

1. Amusement parks 2. Captive marine mammals 3. Marine mammals -- Behavior 4. Sea World 5. Killer whale 6. Animal attacks 7. Marine biologists 8. Aquatic animal welfare 9. Humane Society of the United States
ISBN 1250002028; 9781250002020; 9781250008312

LC 2012009433

In this book, investigative journalist David Kirby examines the marine mammal theme park SeaWorld. "SeaWorld trainer Dawn Brancheau's death in 2010 after being attacked by a killer whale made headlines, but the story goes deeper.

Marine biologist and animal advocate Naomi Rose had already spent two decades challenging SeaWorld's captivity of killer whales as dangerous to both whales and humans." (Library Journal)

Montgomery, Sy

Journey of the pink dolphins; an Amazon quest. Simon & Schuster 2000 317p il maps hardcover o.p. pa $16 **599.53**

1. Dolphins 2. Amazon River valley
ISBN 0-7432-0026-8 pa

LC 99-45840

The author "recounts her Amazonian adventures in search of the botos, the famously elusive freshwater pink dolphins, a quest that yields not only invaluable scientific observations but profound insights into the significance of myth." Booklist

Includes bibliographical references

Neiwert, David

Of orcas and men; what killer whales can teach us. David Neiwert. The Overlook Press 2015 320 p. illustrations $27.95 **599.53**

1. Killer whales 2. Human-animal relationship 3. Killer whale 4. Human-animal relationships
ISBN 1468308653; 9781468308655

LC 2015010796

This book, by David Neiwert, is a "history of orcas, and an exploration of their relationship with human beings. . . . Beginning with their role in myth and contemporary popular culture, Neiwert shows how killer whales came to capture our imaginations, and brings to life the often catastrophic environmental consequences of that appeal." (Publisher's note)

"This narrative is perhaps a bit long but accessible and persuasive. The author authoritatively presents his facts and will likely inspire readers to share what they've learned from his call to action to ensure the orcas' survival. His tone isn't alarmist or strident, but his message is urgent. A wide-ranging, interesting book that should be required reading for school-aged environmentalists." Kirkus

Includes bibliographical references and index

599.638   Giraffe and okapi

Peterson, Dale

★ **Giraffe** reflections; text by Dale Peterson; photographs by Karl Ammann. University of California Press 2013 221 p. (cloth : alk. paper) $39.95 **599.638**

1. Animals -- Pictorial works 2. Giraffe
ISBN 0520266854; 9780520266858

LC 2012038611

Author Dale Peterson's book features a book on endangered giraffes. The book presents "a natural and cultural history of the world's tallest and second-biggest land animals, describing in detail their biology and behavior. He offers a new perspective on the giraffes' place in our world, and argues for the stronger protection of these imposing yet endangered creatures and their elusive forest relatives, the okapis." (Publisher's note)

Includes bibliographical references and index

599.64 Bovids

Rinella, Steven

  American buffalo; in search of a lost icon. Spiegel & Grau 2008 277p il map $24.95   **599.64**

  1. Bison

  ISBN 978-0-385-52168-0; 0-385-52168-5

LC 2008-13624

  "In 2005, [Rinella] won an Alaska state lottery permit making him one of 24 hunters allowed to kill one wild buffalo each to thin out the Copper River herd in the Wrangell-Saint Elias National Park. The book's core is Rinella's entertaining and often harrowing account of that hunting trip into Alaska's frozen south-central wilderness, where he bagged his first buffalo. But entwined throughout that story line is an engaging back story — a stampede of facts and factoids, legends and lore, hard-core science and staggering history of North America's largest land animal. Everything you ever wanted to know about the buffalo — or didn't — going back to Pleistocene days." USA Today

  Includes bibliographical references

599.67 Elephants

Ammann, Karl

  Elephant reflections; photographs by Karl Ammann; text by Dale Peterson. University of California Press 2009 272p il $39.95   **599.67**

  1. Elephants

  ISBN 978-0-520-25377-3; 0-520-25377-9

LC 2008-42391

  "Ammann's photographs capture an astonishing range of elephant behavior, but Peterson's text—with its scope, synthesis of history and observation, précis of the ivory trade and conservation—is what distinguishes this book. He spins the history of elephant research into mini-mysteries of how scientists struggled to understand elephants' secretive behaviors. . . . The photographs and text complement each other beautifully in their respective odes to the 'improbable' physicality of the elephant's body." Publ Wkly

  Includes bibliographical references

Anthony, Lawrence, 1950-2012

  The **elephant** whisperer; my life with the herd in the African wild. [by] Lawrence Anthony with Graham Spence. Thomas Dunne Books/St. Martin's Press 2009 368p il $24.99   **599.67**

  1. Elephants 2. Wildlife refuges

  ISBN 978-0-312-56578-7

LC 2009-23815

  This is the author's "robust portrait of Thula Thula, the game land he owns, in cooperation with a number of Zulu tribes, in Zululand—5,000 acres of raw landscape that is thought to have been part of the exclusive hunting grounds of the Zulu king. No longer, since Anthony now runs it as a conservationist lodge, but it continues to produce colorful tales of wild discovery. Most prominent are the many fascinating stories that surround his adoption of the elephants, an unruly bunch he endeavors to make at home on the reserve. With a combination of intuition and experience, the author intelligently discusses many aspects of elephant behavior." Kirkus

599.7 Carnivores

Nicholls, Henry

  The **way** of the panda; the curious history of China's political animal. Pegasus Books 2011 319p il map $25   **599.7**

  1. Giant panda 2. Wildlife conservation 3. China -- Foreign relations

  ISBN 978-1-60598-188-8; 1-60598-188-5

  First published 2010 in the United Kingdom

  "When the Chinese government brings Giant Pandas to the negotiating table, the stakes change. Whole populations and their leaders clamor for access to these animals, as if they were toddlers reaching for toys. Washington, London and Moscow have all succumbed to this awesome (a chorus of 'Awwwwwww!' accompanies every panda appearance) force. That is only one reason that Henry Nicholls refers to the Giant Panda as a political animal in his charmingly written 'The Way of the Panda.' At times everything concerning the creatures seems to have a political angle: not only their value as state gifts (with heavy strings attached) but also their precise scientific classification; their mating habits and offspring; and the efforts to ensure their preservation. The author compares the history of the panda in the modern world to that of China itself, complete with a 'great leap forward' in the 1960s, when the captive breeding of pandas first became possible." Wall Street J

  Includes bibliographical references

599.75 Cat family

Adamson, Joy

  Born free; a lioness of two worlds. Pantheon Bks. 1987 220p il hardcover o.p. pa $14.95 **599.75**

  1. Lions 2. Kenya -- Description and travel

  ISBN 0-375-71438-3 pa

LC 86-42972

  A reissue of the title first published 1960

  This is the "story of a lioness who bridged the gulf between two worlds, that of the jungle and of man. The author and her husband, a Kenya game warden, reared a cub to kill and fend for herself when she was returned to the jungle. At the same time they were able to preserve the bond of confidence and affection established with her as a pet." Cincinnati Public Libr

Hunter, Luke

  Wild cats of the world; by Luke Hunter. St. Martin's Press 2015 240 p. ill. (chiefly color), maps $40   **599.75**

  1. Cats 2. Wild cats

  ISBN 1472912195; 9781472912190

  This book, by Luke Hunter, "explores the spectacular Cat Family in unprecedented depth. Drawing on thousands of scientific papers and direct observations in the field, each species is profiled at length, covering all aspects of felid behaviour and ecology. The book is profusely illustrated with colour plates, black-and-white sketches showing important aspects of cat life, and accurate images of every species' skull." (Publisher's note)

"The authoritative and accessible text is accompanied by charming drawings and documentary photographs, including some showing the capturing and killing of prey. Location maps, size data, and conservation status introduce each species' information." Booklist

Includes bibliographical references (page 235) and index.

Sunquist, Fiona

The **wild** cat book; Fiona Sunquist and Mel Sunquist; with photos by Terry Whittaker and others. University of Chicago Press 2014 v, 268 p.p color illustrations (cloth) $35   **599.75**
1. Wild cats 2. Photography of animals 3. Felidae
ISBN 0226780260; 9780226780269

LC 2013048755

In this book, authors and "cat experts Fiona and Mel Sunquist introduce us to the full panoply of the purring, roaring feline tribe. Illustrated throughout with Terry Whittaker's . . . color photographs as well as unique photos from biologists in the field--some the highest quality images ever captured of exceptionally rare species--'The Wild Cat Book' . . . also serves as a valuable and accessible reference on cat behavior and conservation." (Publisher's note)

"An extensive bibliography for each species provides sources of additional information for interested readers. The clearly written text and attractive layout of photographs make this book a valuable resource for both academic and public libraries." Choice

Includes bibliographical references (pages 245-259) and index

Vaillant, John

The **tiger**; a true story of vengeance and survival. Alfred A. Knopf 2010 329p il map $26.95; pa $15   **599.75**
1. Tigers 2. Tiger hunting 3. Tigers -- Behavior 4. Human-animal relationships 5. Siberia (Russia) -- Description and travel 6. Russian Far East (Russia) -- Description and travel
ISBN 978-0-307-26893-8; 0-307-26893-4; 978-0-307-38904-6 pa; 0-307-38904-9 pa; 978-0-307-59379-5 ebook; 0-307-59379-7 ebook

LC 2010-04068

"What makes 'The Tiger' a grand addition to the animal-pursuit subgenre is the sensitive way in which Vaillant . . . evokes his cat. Few writers have taken such pains to understand their monsters, and few depict them in such arresting prose." N Y Times Book Rev

Includes bibliographical references

599.756   Tiger

Matthiessen, Peter

Tigers in the snow; introduction and photographs by Maurice Hornocker. Farrar, Straus & Giroux 1999 169p il hardcover o.p. pa $15   **599.756**
1. Tigers 2. Endangered species
ISBN 0-86547-596-2 pa

LC 99-44866

"Mixing information about the lives of all the races of wild tigers with firsthand tales of his visits to Russia, the author brings an immediacy to his narrative that stirs the reader to awe of these great cats. . . . [An] evocative look at one of our rarest animals." Booklist

Includes bibliographical references

Sooyong Park

Great Soul of Siberia; Passion, Obsession, and One Man's Quest for the World's Most Elusive Tiger. Sooyong Park. Greystone Books 2015 340 p. 16 plates; ills.; maps; ports. $27.95   **599.756**
1. Tigers 2. Wildlife conservation
ISBN 1771641134; 9781771641135

Author "Sooyong Park tracks three generations of Siberian tigers living in remote southeastern Russia. Reminiscent of the way Timothy Treadwell . . . immersed himself in the lives of bears, Park sets up underground bunkers to observe the tigers, living thrillingly close to these beautiful but dangerous apex predators. At the same time, he draws from twenty years of experience and research to focus on the Siberian tigers' losing battle against poaching and diminishing habitat." (Publisher's note)

"Living in solitary confinement during the brutal winter months, waiting patiently for Bloody Mary to appear, Park felt he had gained access to 'the intimate depths of nature,' and he shares this intimacy with readers. A heartfelt memoir that reflects the author's respect and love for a wild and pitiless world." Kirkus

599.77   Dog family

Busch, Robert

The **wolf** almanac; a celebration of wolves and their world. by Robert H. Busch. New & rev ed; Lyons Press 2007 274p il map pa $19.95   **599.77**
1. Wolves
ISBN 978-1-59921-069-8; 1-59921-069-X
First published 1995

This offers information about "the evolution and history of wolves; their biology and physiology; their behavior and sociology; and their influence in ancient cultures and mythology. . . . The author also discusses the conservation politics of all wolf species." Publisher's note

Includes bibliographical references

Flores, Dan

Coyote America; Dan Flores. Basic Books 2016 288 p. illustrations (hardcover) $27.5   **599.77**
1. Coyotes 2. Animals -- North America 3. Coyote

-- North America -- History
ISBN 9780465052998; 0465052991

LC 2015043370

This book, by Dan Flores, "is both an environmental and a deep natural history of the coyote. It traces both the five-million-year-long biological story of an animal that has become the 'wolf' in our backyards, as well as its cultural evolution from a preeminent spot in Native American religions to the hapless foil of the Road Runner." (Publisher's note)

"Flores's mix of edification and entertainment is a welcome antidote to a creature so often viewed with fear." Pub Wkly

Includes bibliographical references (pages 249-256) and index.

Lopez, Barry Holstun

★ Of wolves and men; with photographs by John Bauguess; including a new afterword by the author and expanded bibliography. 1st Scribner Classics ed.; Scribner Classics 2004 323p il $45 **599.77**
1. Wolves
ISBN 0-7432-4936-4

LC 2004-45429

First published 1978

The author "infuses his natural history of the long relationship between wolves and humankind with both myth and science, then revisits the controversial subject of wolf reintroduction." Booklist
Includes bibliographical references

McAllister, Ian

The last wild wolves; ghosts of the rain forest. with contributions by Chris Darimont; introduction by Paul C. Paquet. University of California Press 2007 191p il map $39.95 **599.77**
1. Wolves
ISBN 978-0-520-25473-2; 0-520-25473-2

LC 2007-10887

"The text is particularly well written and engaging. . . . However, it is the dozens of unique photos sprinkled liberally throughout the book that provide the greatest appeal." Sci Books Films

Smith, Douglas W.

★ Decade of the wolf; returning the wild to Yellowstone. [by] Douglas W. Smith & Gary Ferguson. Lyons Press 2005 212p il maps $23.95; pa $16.95 **599.77**
1. Wolves 2. Endangered species 3. Yellowstone National Park
ISBN 1-59228-700-X; 1-59228-886-3 pa

LC 2005-40767

"Well illustrated with black-and-white and color photographs, this intimate history of the return of the top predator to Yellowstone will find an eager audience." Booklist
Includes bibliographical references

Thomas, Elizabeth Marshall, 1931-

The **hidden** life of dogs; Elizabeth Marshall Thomas. Mariner Books 2010 xxiii, 168 p.p illustrations (pbk.) $13.95 **599.77**
1. Dogs -- Behavior 2. Dogs -- Psychology
ISBN 0547416857; 9780547416854

LC 2010483554

"In this . . . account, based on thirty years of living with and observing dogs, we meet Misha, a friend's husky, whom [author Elizabeth Marshall] Thomas followed on his daily rounds of more than 130 square miles, and who ultimately provided the simple and surprising answer to the question What do dogs want most? Not food, not sex, but other dogs." (Publisher's note)

"Although Thomas draws on her knowledge of philosophy and the theory of animal consciousness, this book never bogs down in theory and remains very readable. A title worth considering for libraries where there is client interest." LJ
Includes bibliographical references (p. [167]-168)

599.78   Bears

Croke, Vicki

★ The **lady** and the panda; the true adventures of the first American explorer to bring back China's most exotic animal. [by] Vicki Constantine Croke. Random House 2005 372p il $25.95; pa $14.95 **599.78**
1. Explorers 2. Giant panda
ISBN 0-375-50783-3; 0-375-75970-0 pa

LC 2004-51356

"This well-written, exhaustively researched and documented book should be on every library's shelves." Libr J
Includes bibliographical references

Ellis, Richard

On thin ice; the changing world of the polar bear. Alfred A. Knopf 2009 400p il $28.95 **599.78**
1. Polar bear 2. Greenhouse effect
ISBN 978-0-307-27059-7; 0-307-27059-9

LC 2009-20017

This profile of the habitat and life cycle of the polar bear covers the species' venerated position in Inuit culture, its reproductive habits, and the environmental factors that are compromising its ability to survive.

"The real strength of the book is its focus on the polar bear as the poster child of global warming, of how tied the bears are to the arctic ice and what will happen if the ice melts, and of the national and international wrangling over the politics of climate change and the listing of the bear as an endangered species. The polar bear could not ask for a better champion than Ellis in this highly recommended work." Booklist
Includes bibliographical references

599.79 Marine carnivores

Williams, Terrie M.

The **odyssey** of KP2; an orphan seal, a marine biologist, and the fight to save a species from extinction. Terrie M. Williams. Penguin Press 2012 xvi, 283 p.p ill. (hardcover) $27.95   **599.79**
1. Animal rescue 2. Seals (Animals) 3. Wildlife rehabilitation 4. Endangered species -- Hawaii 5. Wildlife conservation -- Hawaii 6. Wildlife rehabilitation -- Hawaii 7. Hawaiian monk seal -- Conservation
ISBN 1594203393; 9781594203398
LC 2011050415

AAAS/Subaru SB&F Prize for Excellence in Science Books: Young Adult Science Book (2013)

This book "chronicles . . . . an orphaned Hawaiian monk seal's . . . rescue and first years of life. . . . [Terrie M.] Williams and her team of researchers began an intense study of the young male, and they collected important data on KP2's growth rates, feeding habits and sociability, with the 'survival of [the] entire species' resting on his shoulders." (Kirkus Reviews)

599.8 Primates

Among African apes; stories and photos from the field. edited by Martha M. Robbins and Christophe Boesch. University of California Press 2011 182p il map pa $29.95; ebook $29.95   **599.8**
1. Apes
ISBN 978-0-520-26710-7 pa; 978-0-520-94883-9 ebook
LC 2010033131

This book on apes contains some violent content. "The authors want to raise awareness about the plight of African apes. To do so, they draw upon research careers that go back at least 30 years. Included in the text are day-to-day accounts of what it takes to organize and find a research site in Africa, what it's like to track a gorilla, what it's like to experience a chimp or bonobo community, and what happens to these communities as a result of their encounters with various human communities. . . . Rarely does a book so perfectly illustrate the scientific process. The interaction between researcher and subject comes alive in these pages." Sci Books Films

Includes bibliographical references

Bearzi, Maddalena

Beautiful minds; the parallel lives of great apes and dolphins. [by] Maddalena Bearzi & Craig B. Stanford. Harvard University Press 2008 351p $24.95; pa $14.95   **599.8**
1. Apes 2. Dolphins 3. Comparative psychology
ISBN 978-0-674-02781-7; 0-674-02781-7; 978-0-674-04627-6 pa; 0-674-04627-7 pa
LC 2007-46199

"Endowed through evolution with large brains, the great apes (chimpanzees, bonobos gorillas and orangutans) and the cetaceans (dolphins and whales) are second only to humans in intelligence. In this delightful and intriguing

book, . . . [the authors] discuss the similarities between these groups." Publ Wkly
Includes bibliographical references

Goodall, Jane

★ **In** the shadow of man; photographs by Hugo van Lawick; [with a new preface; foreword by Richard Wrangham] Mariner Books 2009 xxx, 302p il map pa $15.95   **599.8**
1. Chimpanzees
ISBN 978-0-547-33416-5
LC 2009044848

First published 1971

The author describes the chimpanzee group she studied during ten years of field observation in the Gombe Stream Chimpanzee Reserve in Tanzania.

Includes bibliographical references

Through a window; my thirty years with the chimpanzees of Gombe. [with a new preface and a new afterword] Houghton Mifflin Harcourt 2010 xx, 337p il map pa $15.95   **599.8**
1. Chimpanzees
ISBN 978-0-547-33695-4; 0-547-33695-0
LC 2009045230

First published 1990

This continuation of In the shadow of man "tells two stories: first of how the chimps of Gombe in Tanzania have grown, changed and died, and second, how Goodall and her dedicated group of Tanzanian observers have survived the rigours of the past thirty years. It is beautifully written, and evokes both sympathy and understanding of these animals." Times Lit Suppl

Includes bibliographical references

Morris, Desmond

Planet ape; [by] Desmond Morris with Steve Parker. Firefly Books 2009 288p il $49.95   **599.8**
1. Apes
ISBN 978-1-55407-566-9

Detail of the great apes, including: where they live, how they live and the challenges they face. Illustrations compare apes with human beings, including their anatomy, social life, physical and mental development, diet and communication.

"Published in a large format (approximately 10 by 11 inches) with hundreds of full-color glossy photographs and illustrations, this beautiful volume is a cross between a coffee-table book and a thorough compendium of ape behavior, anatomy, taxonomy, and lore. . . . The book reads well, is packed full of exciting information, and is just plain fun to browse for hours." Sci Books Films

Redmond, Ian

The **primate** family tree; the amazing diversity of our closest relatives. foreword by Jane Goodall. Firefly Books 2008 176p il map $35; pbk $24.95   **599.8**
1. Primates
ISBN 978-1-55407-378-8; 1-55407-378-2; 9781554079643

The Primate Family Tree "is beautifully designed, and the contents are well organized and will be interesting to all.

... This is a very attractive, interesting, and informative publication." Sci Books Films

Includes bibliographical references

Sapolsky, Robert M.

A **primate's** memoir. Scribner 2001 304p pa $14; $25   **599.8**
1. Baboons 2. Baboons -- Behavior -- Africa, East -- Anecdotes
ISBN 0-7432-0241-4 pa; 0-7432-0247-3

LC 00-63522

This is an account of the author's experiences observing baboons in Kenya

"One closes Sapolsky's book a lot more knowledgeable about plenty of baboon-related matters. But mostly one has already begun to miss the company of this sometimes cranky but always impassioned, learned and winningly irreverent man." N Y Times Book Rev

★ **World** atlas of great apes and their conservation; edited by Julian Caldecott and Lera Miles; foreword by Kofi A. Annan. University of California Press, in association with UNEP-WCMC 2005 456p il map $45   **599.8**
1. Apes 2. Atlases 3. Biogeography 4. Reference books 5. Wildlife conservation
ISBN 0-520-24633-0; 978-0-520-24633-1

LC 2006-272653

"Each great ape specie is given a separate chapter that contains information on behavior and ecology, communication and tool use, threats and conservation, and exceptionally detailed distribution maps. What sets this book apart is the section that details each country in which apes are found and exactly what conservation efforts are underway." Univ Press Books for Public and Second Sch Libr, 2006

Includes bibliographical references

599.88   Great apes and gibbons

Fossey, Dian

★ **Gorillas** in the mist. Houghton Mifflin 1983 326p il hardcover o.p. pa $14   **599.88**
1. Gorillas
ISBN 0-618-08360-X pa

LC 82-23332

This book "recounts some of the events of the thirteen years that I have spent with the mountain gorillas in their natural habitat and includes data from the fifteen years of continuing field study. . . . The region inhabited by the gorillas is some twenty-five miles long and varies in width from six to twelve miles. Two thirds of the conservation area lies in Zaire (formerly known as the Democratic Republic of the Congo) in the Parc National des Virungas; about 30,000 acres of conservation area lie in Rwanda and are known as the Parc National des Volcans. The small remaining northeastern portion of the mountain gorillas' habitat lies in Uganda and is known as the Kigezi Gorilla Sanctuary." (Preface) Bibliography. Index.

This book "recounts some of the events of the thirteen years that I have spent with the mountain gorillas in their

natural habitat and includes data from the fifteen years of continuing field study." Preface

Includes bibliographical references

Stanford, Craig B.

Planet without apes; Craig B. Stanford. Belknap Press of Harvard University Press 2012 262 p. ill. (hardcover) $25.95   **599.88**
1. Apes 2. Endangered species 3. Extinct animals
ISBN 0674067045; 9780674067042

LC 2012023985

This book, by Craig B. Stanford, "warns that extinction of the great apes--chimpanzees, bonobos, gorillas, and orangutans--threatens to become a reality within just a few human generations. We are on the verge of losing the last links to our evolutionary past, and to all the biological knowledge about ourselves that would die along with them. The crisis we face is tantamount to standing aside while our last extended family members vanish from the planet." (Publisher's note)

"Stanford has brilliantly distilled scientific research, African and Asian economic issues, and ethical concerns surrounding the exploitation of these intelligent, highly social creatures into a powerful plea for primate protection." LJ

Includes bibliographical references and index

Waal, Frans de

Bonobo; the forgotten ape. photographs, Frans Lanting. University of Calif. Press 1997 210p il maps $50; pa $29.95   **599.88**
1. Apes
ISBN 0-520-20535-9; 0-520-21651-2 pa

LC 96-41095

The subject of this monograph is the bonobo, a species of ape. "In six chapters, de Waal describes the history of the discovery of bonobos as a separate species; he compares them with common chimps; he describes their natural habitat and their . . . use of sex as social currency, particularly in moderating aggression; he examines bonobo social structure in relation to that of common chimps and humans; and he finishes with an exploration of bonobos' highly developed sense of empathy." New Sci

Includes bibliographical references

599.885   Chimpanzees

Halloran, Andrew R.

The **song** of the ape; Andrew R. Halloran. 1st ed. St. Martin's Press 2012 x, 276p.p   **599.885**
1. Chimpanzees 2. Animal sounds 3. Animal communication 4. Zoo keepers 5. Primatologists
ISBN 9780312563110; 9781429933278

LC 2011041344

The premise for this book began when, "working as a zookeeper at a drive-through animal park in south Florida, [author and primatologist Andrew R.] Halloran witnessed the escape of a group of chimpanzees who capitalized on an unsecured boat to flee from their island habitat and an upstart group of rival chimps. To react so quickly and uniformly, the group, Halloran surmises, must have been communicating in a complex manner that allowed them to plan and orchestrate such an escape. To examine this idea further, Halloran . . . embarks on a . . . study of five of the chimps involved, delving into their histories, their calls, and the meaning of their calls. The result is an . . . account of communication development among these intelligent animals . . . showing how they communicate with each other on their own terms and how numerous factors cause dialects to emerge." (Publishers Weekly)

Includes bibliographical references and index

599.9 Humans

Fabian, Ann

The **skull** collectors; Ann Fabian. The University of Chicago Press 2010 xi, 270 p.p ill.   **599.9**
1. Anthropometry 2. Race relations 3. Craniology -- History

ISBN 978-0-226-23348-2; 0-226-23348-0

LC 2009047712

This book tells the "story of [naturalist Samuel] Morton, his contemporaries, and their search for a scientific foundation for racial difference. From cranial measurements and museum shelves to heads on stakes, bloody battlefields, and the 'rascally pleasure' of grave robbing, [author Ann] Fabian paints a . . . picture of scientific inquiry in service of an agenda of racial superiority, and of a society coming to grips with both the deadly implications of manifest destiny and the mass slaughter of the Civil War. . . . Fabian also . . . traces the continuing implications of this history, from lingering traces of scientific racism to debates over the return of the remains of Native Americans that are held by museums to this day." (Publisher's note)

Includes bibliographical references and index

Olson, Steve

Mapping human history; discovering the past through our genes. Houghton Mifflin 2002 292p il $25; pa $14   **599.9**
1. Human beings 2. Physical anthropology

ISBN 0-618-09157-2; 0-618-35210-4 pa

LC 2001-51880

The author "traces the history of human civilization in five regions of the world—Africa, the Middle East, Asia, Australia, and Europe and the Americas, plus a final chapter on Hawaii—to explain how physical differences originated and to provide evidence of our essential sameness." Publ Wkly

Includes bibliographical references and index

599.93 Genetics, sex and age characteristics, evolution

Johanson, Donald C.

★ **From** Lucy to language; [by] Donald Johanson & Blake Edgar; principal photography, David

L. Brill. Rev., updated, and expanded; Simon and Schuster 2006 288p il map $65   **599.93**
1. Human origins 2. Fossil hominids

ISBN 0-7432-8064-4; 978-0-7432-8064-8

LC 2007-270098

First published 1996

This is a "photographic showcase of the essential physical evidence of human origins. . . . Permitting a face-to-face encounter with human ancestors, this work furnishes essential information, [and] an incomparable visual experience." Booklist

Includes bibliographical references

Lucy: the beginnings of humankind; [by] Donald C. Johanson and Maitland A. Edey. Simon & Schuster 1981 409p il hardcover o.p. pa $16   **599.93**
1. Human origins 2. Fossil mammals

ISBN 0-671-72499-1 pa

LC 80-21759

In November 1974 at a place called Hadar in Ethiopia Donald Johanson "discovered the partial skeleton of an extremely primitive female, erect-walking primate or hominid. . . . The skeleton received the name 'Lucy.' Much later, Lucy received the scientific name, Australopithecus afarensis, and it was determined she was some 3.5 million years old. . . . This book is Johanson's own story of the events leading up to and subsequent to Lucy's discovery." Best Sellers

Includes bibliographical references

Jolly, Alison

Lucy's legacy; sex and intelligence in human evolution. Harvard Univ. Press 1999 518p il hardcover o.p. pa $18.95   **599.93**
1. Evolution 2. Intellect

ISBN 0-674-00069-2; 0-674-00540-6 pa

LC 99-32252

"Lucy is the name given to the fossil skeleton of an Australopithecine, a human ancestor, discovered in Ethiopia. The name may be a misnomer, since there's no way yet of telling whether Lucy was female. No matter. Primatologist Jolly's interest is not so much in Lucy as in the crucial role that females in general have played in human evolution. . . . In clear and clever prose, Jolly shows us how we got so smart, what sex had to do with it, and how our brains have become the central force in evolution." Booklist

Includes bibliographical references

Leakey, Richard E.

The **origin** of humankind; [by] Richard Leakey. Basic Bks. 1994 171p il maps (Science masters series) hardcover o.p. pa $14.95   **599.93**
1. Human origins

ISBN 0-465-05313-0 pa

LC 94-3617

This "is a worthwhile addition to many kinds of libraries—public, general, science, biological, and psychological." Sci Books Films

Includes bibliographical references

Origins reconsidered; in search of what makes us human. [by] Richard Leakey and Roger Lewin.

Doubleday 1992 375p il hardcover o.p. pa $16.95   **599.93**
1. Human origins
ISBN 0-385-46792-3 pa

LC 92-6661

"Leakey and Lewin discuss how conceptions of human anatomical and behavioral development have been radically altered within the last 12 years by new discoveries and research in other fields. They review the developments and assert Leakey's own hypotheses based on these discoveries. ... . This is an engrossing book written for the layperson, fully explaining anthropological terms and theories when necessary. It's a solid introduction to current theory concerning human development." SLJ

Marks, Jonathan
★ **What** it means to be 98[percent] chimpanzee; apes, people, and their genes. University of Calif. Press 2002 312p $27.50   **599.93**
1. Genetics 2. Evolution 3. Human beings
ISBN 0-520-22615-1

LC 2001-7085

"With plenty of entertaining sarcasm as well as scientific argument and moral indignation, Marks blasts the pretensions of grandiose geneticists pretty thoroughly out of the water. This may be the science book to read this year." Booklist

Includes bibliographical references

Ridley, Matt
Genome; the autobiography of a species in 23 chapters. HarperCollins Pubs. 2000 344p hardcover o.p. pa $14.95   **599.93**
1. Genomes 2. Genetics
ISBN 0-06-019497-9; 978-0-06-089408-5 pa; 0-06-089408-3 pa

LC 99-40933

Ridley presents a "summation of our ever increasing understanding of the roles that genes play in disease, behavior, sexual differences, and even intelligence. More important, though, he addresses not only the ethical quandaries faced by contemporary scientists but the reductionist danger in equating inheritability with inevitability." New Yorker

Includes bibliographical references

Swisher, Carl C.
Java Man; how two geologists changed our understanding of human evolution. [by] Carl C. Swisher III, Garniss H. Curtis, Roger Lewin. University of Chicago Press 2001 256p il pa $16   **599.93**
1. Human origins 2. Fossil hominids
ISBN 978-0-226-78734-3; 0-226-78734-6

LC 2001-37337

First published 2000 by Scribner

The authors "offer a lively writeup of the technicalities of geochronology, bio-sketches of the discoverers of the erectus fossils, travelogues of their travel in Java, and their side of a spat with paleoanthropology celebrity Don Johansen. An engrossing contribution to the general-interest literature about human origins." Booklist

Includes bibliographical references

Sykes, Bryan
Adam's curse; a future without men. Norton 2004 318p il $25.95; pa $15.95   **599.93**
1. Genetics 2. Chromosomes 3. Sex (Biology)
ISBN 0-393-05896-4; 0-393-32680-2 pa

LC 2004-3628

First published 2003 in the United Kingdom
"This book incorporates many genres—scientific protocol, biography, harlequin romance, and historical fiction—all expertly executed by Sykes." Sci Books Films

DNA USA; a genetic portrait of America. Bryan Sykes. Liveright Pub. Corp. 2012 369 p.   **599.93**
1. Genetics 2. Genealogy 3. Chromosomes 4. DNA fingerprinting 5. United States -- Population 6. Human genetics -- Popular works 7. Human population genetics -- United States -- Popular works
ISBN 0871404125; 9780871404121

LC 2011053182

In this book, "America's gorgeous mosaic emerges from its DNA in this . ... treatise on genetics and genealogy. Oxford geneticist [Bryan] Sykes . . . traveled across the United States collecting DNA samples, recording family histories. . . . The resulting 'chromosomal portraits,' painted by analyzing markers that correlate with African, European, or Asian-Native American populations, reveal DNA tell-tales of unsuspected centuries-old migrations and mixings: Mexican-American Catholics descended from Spanish Jews; white Southerners with substantial African-American ancestry; possible journeys from Europe to North America 10,000 years ago, Sykes gives .... explanations of new genetic techniques and their startling success at tracing familial ties across continents and millennia." (Publishers Weekly)

Includes bibliographical references and index

Tattersall, Ian
The **fossil** trail; how we know what we think we know about human evolution. 2nd ed.; Oxford University Press 2009 xxiii, 327p il map pa $24.95   **599.93**
1. Fossils 2. Evolution 3. Human origins
ISBN 978-0-19-536766-9

LC 2008-13654

First published 1995
"The task of organising such complex material into a narrative account would have defeated most writers, but Tattersall has mastered it with remarkable skill." New Sci [review of 1995 edition]

Includes bibliographical references

Masters of the planet; Ian Tattersall. Palgrave Macmillan 2012 272p.   **599.93**
1. Biology 2. Evolution 3. Human origins
ISBN 9780230108752

LC 2011034415

'This book examines the evolution of humans. "When homo sapiens made their entrance 100,000 years ago they were confronted by a wide range of other early humans - homo erectus, who walked better and used fire; homo habilis who used tools; and of course the Neanderthals, who were brawny and strong. .... [Author Ian Tattersall] explores how the physical traits and cognitive ability of homo sapiens distanced them from the rest of nature. Even more importantly, 'Masters of the Planet' looks at how our early ancestors acquired these superior abilities; it shows that their strange and unprecedented mental facility is not, as most of us were taught, simply a basic competence that was refined over unimaginable eons by natural selection. Instead, it is an emergent capacity that was acquired quite recently and changed the world definitively." (Publisher's note)

Includes bibliographical references and index.

Taylor, Timothy

The **artificial** ape; how technology changed the course of human evolution. Palgrave Macmillan 2010 256p il $27   **599.93**
1. Evolution 2. Human origins
ISBN 9780230617636

LC 2010-7924

The author "proposes that it was our early adoption of tools, objects, and, now, technology that changed us [from apes], demonstrating how: baby slings made out of animal fur freed up our arms up to use tools; clothes kept us warm, reducing our need for body hair; [and] shelter protected us from the elements and led our bodies to become slighter and physically weaker. . . . Taylor shows how humans made choices that assumed greater control over their own evolution." Publisher's note

Includes bibliographical references

Wade, Nicholas

Before the dawn; recovering the lost history of our ancestors. Penguin Press 2006 312p il map $24.95   **599.93**
1. Evolution 2. Social change
ISBN 1-59420-079-3; 978-1-59420-079-3

LC 2005-55293

"This is highly recommended for readers interested in how DNA analysis is rewriting the history of mankind." Publ Wkly

Includes bibliographical references

Walker, Alan

The **wisdom** of the bones; in search of human origins. [by] Alan Walker and Pat Shipman. Knopf 1996 338p il maps hardcover o.p. pa $14 **599.93**
1. Evolution 2. Human origins 3. Fossil hominids
ISBN 0-679-74783-4 pa

LC 95-37525

"In 1984 Walker, along with colleague Richard Leakey and their 'hominidgang' of experienced Kenyan excavators, discovered a near-intact fossil of Homo erectus. The find was a veritable trove of theory-busting information, which the authors take up after recounting the scientists who preceded Walker in investigating the species. . . . A fluidly presented portrait of the people and process of paleoanthropology." Booklist

Includes bibliographical references

Wilson, Edward O., 1929-

★ The **social** conquest of earth; Edward O. Wilson. W. W. Norton & Co 2012 viii, 330 p.p **599.93**
1. Evolution 2. Human origins 3. Human behavior 4. Natural selection 5. Human evolution -- Philosophy 6.

Social evolution -- Philosophy 7. Evolution (Biology) -- Philosophy
ISBN 0871404133; 9780871404138

LC 2011052680

This book by Edward O. Wilson provides an "explanation of why humans rule the Earth. After a respectful nod to the old favorites (big brains, tools, language, fire), the author maintains that these merely provide the background to our overpowering 'eusociality'; we are the world's most intensely social creatures, living in complex societies of mutually dependent individuals. . . . Group selection--as opposed to kin selection . . . --is the author's big idea." (Kirkus Reviews)

Includes bibliographical references and index.

600   TECHNOLOGY

600   Technology (Applied sciences)

Doorley, Rachelle

Tinkerlab; a hands-on guide for little inventors. Rachelle Doorley. Roost Books 2014 xv, 219 p.p color illustrations (pbk. : alk. paper) $21.95 **600**
1. Inventions 2. Creative activities 3. Playrooms 4. Creative activities and seat work
ISBN 161180065X; 9781611800654

LC 2013027910

This book, by Rachelle Doorley, offers "55 playful experiments that encourage tinkering, curiosity, and creative thinking. . . . [It offers] hands-on activities that explore art, science, and more . . . for children two and up. . . . In addition to offering a host of activities that parents and teachers can put to use right away, this book also includes a buffet of recipes . . . and a detailed list of materials to include in the art pantry." (Publisher's note)

"Young children will relish the projects provided here. From paper houses to marble runs to marker explosions, Doorley's designs have more of an engineering essence than those found in the standard arts and crafts book, and they will also take more preparation, but early educators, in particular, will delight in the volume's possibilities. For all budding inventors." LJ

Includes bibliographical references (page 216)

Harman, Jay

The **shark's** paintbrush; biomimicry and how nature is inspiring innovation. Jay Harman. White Cloud Press 2013 326 p. ill $26.95 **600**
1. Biomimicry 2. Sustainable development
ISBN 1935952846; 9781935952848

LC 2012015185

This book, by Jay Harman, describes how, "in a world of depleted natural resources, entrepreneurs and scientists are turning to nature to inspire future products that are more energy- and cost-efficient. Biomimicry, the science of employing nature to advance sustainable technology, is arguably one of the hottest new business concepts." Harman "shows business leaders and aspiring entrepreneurs how we can reconcile creating more powerful, lucrative technologies with maximizing sustainability." (Publisher's note)

"A useful update on recent developments in biomimicry and an intriguing case for innovative green technology that goes beyond sustainability." Kirkus

Macaulay, David

The **Way** Things Work Now; From Levers to Lasers, Windmills to Wi-fi, a Visual Guide to the World of Machines. [by] David Macaulay with Neil Ardley. Houghton Mifflin Harcourt 2016 400 p. illustrations hbk $35   **600**

1. Machinery 2. Inventions 3. Technology
ISBN 9780544824386; 0544824385

Originally published 1988 and 1998 as The Way Things Work and The New Way Things Work

"Famously packed with information on the inner workings of everything from windmills to Wi-Fi, this extraordinary and humorous book both guides readers through the fundamental principles of machines, and shows how the developments of the past are building the world of tomorrow. This sweepingly revised edition embraces all of the latest developments, from touchscreens to 3D printer." (Publisher's note)

"Macaulay's brilliantly designed, engagingly informal diagrams and cutaways bring within the grasp of even casual viewers a greater understanding of the technological wonders of both past and present." Kirkus

607   Education, research, related topics

Tirella, Joseph

Tomorrow-land; the 1964-65 World's Fair and the transformation of America. Joseph Tirella. Lyons Press, an imprint of Globe Pequot Press 2014 197 p. illustrations $26.95   **607**

1. Exhibitions 2. United States -- Politics and government -- 20th century 3. Social change -- United States -- History -- 20th century 4. United States -- Social conditions -- 20th century 5. United States -- Social life and customs -- 20th century 6. Political culture -- United States -- History -- 20th century 7. Technological innovations -- United States -- History -- 20th century
ISBN 0762780355; 9780762779840; 9780762780358
LC 2013015055

This book, by Joseph Tirella, tells the "story of New York's second World's Fair in the context of its tumultuous times. Robert Moses, the city's . . . master builder . . . who had a hand in the construction of the first World's Fair in 1939, maneuvered his way to power for the entire 1964-1965 version. His ultimate goal was to turn the fair's grounds in Flushing Meadow Park in Queens into a rival for the jewel in Manhattan's crown, Central Park." Kirkus Reviews

"A model of accessible narrative, showing the author's immersion in archival research, this book will be appreciated most by those who love reading about Sixties or New York City history or, of course, world's fairs." LJ

Includes bibliographical references and index

609   History, geographic treatment, biography

Popular mechanics magazine.

The **wonderful** future that never was; flying cars, mail delivery by parachute, and other predictions from the past. Gregory Benford and the editors of Popular mechanics. Hearst Communications 2010 207p il $24.95   **609**

1. Forecasting 2. Technological innovations 3. Inventions -- History
ISBN 978-1-58816-822-1
LC 2010-3998

"Profusely illustrated (there's something on nearly every page), the book is endlessly fascinating, a collage of snapshots of the present the way people saw it when it was still the distant future." Booklist

609.2   Biography

Kendall, Joshua

★ **America's** obsessives; the compulsive energy that built a nation. Joshua Kendall. GCP 2013 304 p. (hardcover) $27   **609.2**

1. Success 2. Compulsive behavior 3. United States -- Biography 4. Scholars -- United States -- Biography 5. Inventors -- United States -- Biography 6. Successful people -- United States -- Biography 7. Motivation (Psychology) -- United States -- Case studies 8. Compulsive behavior -- Social aspects -- United States -- Case studies
ISBN 1455502383; 9781455502387; 9781611138320
LC 2012051196

Author Joshua Kendall "profiles a 'ticker-tape parade of American icons' in an effort to understand how their 'obsessions and compulsions. . . fueled their stratospheric success.' Across a range of disciplines, from sexuality to sports, these seven legendary figures revolutionized their fields, and they all likely had obsessive-compulsive personality disorder (OCPD)." Subjects include Thomas Jefferson, Henry Heinz, Melvil Dewey, Alfred Kinsey, Charles Lindbergh, and Ted Williams. (Publishers Weekly)

Includes bibliographical references and index

Vare, Ethlie Ann

Patently female; from AZT to TV dinners: stories of women inventors and their breakthrough ideas. [by] Ethlie Ann Vare, Greg Ptacek. Wiley 2002 220p il $27.95   **609.2**

1. Women inventors
ISBN 0-471-02334-5
LC 2001-26950

Sequel to: Mothers of invention (1988)

The authors "detail how women's ideas like the cotton gin, automatic sewing machine and even the Brooklyn Bridge have often been attributed to men and how history books and museums like the Smithsonian and the National Inventors Hall of Fame have ignored women's achievements." Publ Wkly

Includes bibliographical references

610 Medicine and health

Adler, Robert E.

Medical firsts; from Hippocrates to the human genome. Wiley 2004 232p il $24.95   **610**
1. Medicine -- History
ISBN 0-471-40175-7

LC 2003-14212

"Adler ably combines good storytelling, clear and cogent scientific explanations [and] a respect for science over superstition." Publ Wkly
Includes bibliographical references

Anderson, Julie

The **art** of medicine; over 2,000 years of images and imagination. [by] Julie Anderson, Emm Barnes, and Emma Shackleton; foreword by Antony Gormley. Ilex Press 2011 256 p. $50.00   **610**
1. Medicine in art 2. Medicine -- History 3. Medical illustration 4. Medical illustration -- History 5. Medicine -- History -- Pictorial works
ISBN 0226749363; 9780226749365

LC 2011019933

This book on visual representations of medicine "offers a . . . gallery of rarely seen paintings, artifacts, drawings, prints, and extracts from manuscripts and manuals to provide . . . visual insight into our knowledge of the human body and mind, and how both have been treated with medicine. Julie Anderson, Emm Barnes, and Emma Shackleton take readers on a . . . journey through the history of medical practice, exploring contemporary biomedical images, popular art, and caricature." (Publisher's note)
Includes bibliographical references and index

Bortolotti, Dan

Hope in hell; inside the world of Doctors Without Borders. Firefly Bks. 2004 303p il $29.95; pa $19.95   **610**
1. Médecins Sans Frontières (Organization)
ISBN 1-55297-865-6; 1-55407-142-9 pa

LC 2005-357206

"Much of what Bortolotti reports is noticeably absent from the daily headlines, so this eye-opening account is all the more chilling, and MSF's efforts achingly more compelling." Booklist
Includes bibliographical references

The **Cambridge** illustrated history of medicine; edited by Roy Porter. Cambridge Univ. Press 1996 400p il maps hardcover o.p. pa $35   **610**
1. Medicine -- History
ISBN 0-521-44211-7; 0-521-00252-4 pa

LC 95-38000

This is a history of medicine from antiquity to the present. In ten "chapters, Roy Porter and his collaborators examine the changing form of medicine and . . . {the} technical successes that it has achieved." Sci Am
Includes bibliographical references

Current medical diagnosis and treatment; edited by Maxine A. Papadakis and Stephen J. McPhee; as-

sociate editor Michael W. Rabow. McGraw-Hill illustrations   **610**
1. Medicine
Annual. First published 1974 as a successor to Current diagnosis & treatment. Editors vary
"Provides concise information on the diagnosis and treatment of diseases and disorders for medical practitioners. Uses common medical terminology, but is generally understandable to the layperson." N Y Public Libr Book of How & Where to Look It Up

★ **Dorland's** illustrated medical dictionary; 32nd ed; Elsevier/Saunders 2011 xxvii, 2147p il $51.95   **610**
1. Reference books 2. Medicine -- Dictionaries
ISBN 978-1-4160-6257-8

LC 2011-9789

First published 1900. Periodically revised
This standard reference includes terms used in medicine, surgery, dentistry, pharmacy, chemistry, nursing, veterinary science, biology, and medical biology. Pronunciation, derivation, and definitions are given.
"This is considered one of the most comprehensive medical dictionaries in print." N Y Public Libr Book of How & Where to Look It Up
Includes bibliographical references

Groopman, Jerome E.

★ **How** doctors think; [by] Jerome Groopman. Houghton Mifflin Co. 2007 307p il $26   **610**
1. Medicine 2. Diagnosis 3. Physicians
ISBN 978-0-618-61003-7; 0-618-61003-0

LC 2006-35718

This book is comprised of a series of "essays that explore the rational and irrational factors that influence medical decision-making. By turns inspired and dismaying, it explains how even the best doctor can draw the wrong conclusion, and why that same doctor might also come up with a brilliant diagnosis that has eluded his peers. Uncertainty hovers over the practice of medicine, which Dr. Groopman, a clear writer and a humane thinker, presents as an art as well as a science, despite the spectacular advances in medical technology." N Y Times (Late N Y Ed)
Includes bibliographical references

Your medical mind; how to decide what is right for you. [by] Jerome Groopman and Pamela Hartzband. Penguin Press 2011 308p $27.95   **610**
1. Medicine 2. Decision making 3. Physician-patient relationship
ISBN 978-1-59420-311-4

LC 2011019808

The authors "present readers with a fascinating look into medical decision making. Through detailed portraits of socially and ethnically diverse real-life individuals who must make medical choices, the authors show how patients' family history, culture, profession, and attitudes toward medicine and technology can shape their decisions about treatment. . . . This engaging, insightful, and illuminating book should be read by general audiences as well as medical and healthcare professionals, who are often baffled by the choices their patients make." Libr J

Includes bibliographical references

Magill's medical guide; medical editors: Bryan C. Auday, Ph.D., Gordon College, Michael A. Buratovich, Ph.D., Spring Arbor University, Geraldine F. Marrocco, Ed.D., APRN, CNS, ANP-BC, Yale University School of Nursing, Paul Moglia, Ph.D., South Nassau Communities Hospital. 6th ed.; Salem Press 2014 2537 p. 6v il (Salem health) $425   **610**
1. Reference books 2. Medicine -- Encyclopedias
ISBN 1619252147; 9781619252141

LC 2010-31862

First published 1995

Covers diseases, disorders, treatments, procedures, specialties, anatomy, biology, and issues in an A-Z format, with sidebars addressing recent developments in medicine and concise information boxes for all diseases and disorders.

Includes bibliographical references and index.

Mukherjee, Siddhartha

The **laws** of medicine; field notes from an uncertain science. Siddhartha Mukherjee. Simon & Schuster 2015 96 p. (hardcover) $16.99   **610**
1. Medicine 2. Science -- Philosophy
ISBN 9781476784847; 1476784841

This book, by Siddhartha Mukherjee, discusses "philosophy on the little-known principles that govern medicine--and how understanding these principles can empower us all. . . . Is medicine a 'science'? Sciences must have laws—statements of truth based on repeated experiments that describe some universal attribute of nature. But does medicine have laws like other sciences?" (Publisher's note)

"This mininarrative, packed with complex ideas translated into easily accessible language and an engaging style, leaves the readers time to ponder the author's ideas at greater length, and the result is a fascinating and illuminating trek through a beautiful mind. A splendid exploration of how medicine might be transformed." Kirkus

Orbinski, James

An **imperfect** offering; humanitarian action in the twenty-first century. Walker & Co. 2008 431p il $27   **610**
1. War relief 2. Medical assistance 3. Médecins Sans Frontières (Organization)
ISBN 978-0-8027-1709-2; 0-8027-1709-8

"Orbinski was president of Doctors Without Borders when it received the Nobel Peace Prize in 1999, and this book echoes and expands on his acceptance speech. He argues that humanitarian action must be free of political influence, must not become a tool of war and must not be silent in the face of human-rights violations. . . . An important, consciousness-raising work." Kirkus

Includes bibliographical references

Parker, Steve

Kill or cure; an illustrated history of medicine. Steve Parker. Dorling Kindersley 2013 400 p. illustrations; portraits (hbk.) $30   **610**
1. Popular medicine 2. Medicine -- History 3. Medicine, Popular 4. Medicine -- History -- Popular works
ISBN 1465408428; 9781465408426

LC 2013474432

This illustrated reference book, by Steve Parker, relates "compelling stories behind mankind's never-ending quest to cure every disease. . . . Beginning with early healers, chance discoveries, technological advancement, and 'wonder' drugs, . . . [the volume] highlights information about human anatomy, surgical instruments, and medical breakthroughs while telling the dramatic tale of medical progress." (Publisher's note)

Includes bibliographical references (page 392) and index

Pogrebin, Letty Cottin

How to be a friend to a friend who's sick; Letty Cottin Pogrebin. PublicAffairs 2013 304 p. (hardcover) $24.99   **610**
1. Sick 2. Caregivers 3. Helping behavior 4. Diseases -- Psychological aspects 5. Care of the sick -- Psychological aspects
ISBN 1610392833; 9781610392839

LC 2012049749

"Throughout her recent bout with breast cancer, Letty Cottin Pogrebin became fascinated by her friends' and family's diverse reactions to her and her illness: how awkwardly some of them behaved; how some misspoke or misinterpreted her needs; and how wonderful it was when people read her right. She began talking to her fellow patients and dozens of other veterans of serious illness, seeking to discover what sick people wished their friends knew." (Publisher's note)

"A useful refresher course on navigating the complicated territory of compassionate companionship." Kirkus

Includes bibliographical references and index

Pollack, Robert

The **missing** moment; how the unconscious shapes modern science. Houghton Mifflin 1999 240p $25   **610**
1. Psychology 2. Medicine -- Philosophy
ISBN 0-395-70985-7

LC 99-26241

"The collective myth of science and of biomedicine, in Pollack's diagnosis, involves misplaced beliefs in the omnipotence of rational thought, absolute control over nature and triumph over death. With eloquence and wit, he contends that biomedicine's heroic goals of beating infectious microbes into total submission, of eradicating cancer and of dramatically extended life expectancy should give way to emphasis on disease prevention and methods to slow the aging process." Publ Wkly

Includes bibliographical references

Porter, Roy

The **greatest** benefit to mankind; a medical history of humanity. Norton 1998 831p il $35; pa $18.95 **610**

1. Medicine -- History 2. Social medicine -- History
ISBN 0-393-04634-6; 0-393-31980-6 pa
LC 98-10219

First published 1997 in the United Kingdom

Porter's "study traces Western medical thought and practices from their origins in classical Greece to today's biomedical developments. Although scholarly, the text is elegantly written, accessible to the general reader, and filled with fascinating details." Libr J

Includes bibliographical references

Szczeklik, Andrzej

★ **Kore**; on sickness, the sick, and the search for the soul of medicine. Andrzej Szczeklik; translated by Antonia Lloyd-Jones; with an introduction by Adam Zagajewski. Counterpoint 2012 320 p. (hardback : alk. paper) $26 **610**

1. Sick 2. Soul 3. Medicine 4. Humanities 5. History of Medicine 6. Philosophy, Medical 7. Physician-Patient Relations
ISBN 161902019X; 9781619020191; 9781619021389
LC 2012042867

In this book, translated by Antonia Lloyd-Jones, author Andrzej Szczeklik "insists that only with a curiosity thoroughly at home in both [science and the humanities] . . . can one expect to discover what we should mean about sickness and about the soul. . . . Anecdotes drawn from a personal immersion in art, music, and literature are woven with reports on experimental medicine and daily clinical experience." (Publisher's note)

Includes bibliographical references and index

Teresi, Dick

The **undead**; organ harvesting, the ice-water test, beating heart cadavers : how medicine is blurring the line between life and death. Dick Teresi. Pantheon Books 2012 256 p. **610**

1. Death 2. Brain death 3. Medical ethics 4. Physicians -- Attitudes 5. Transplantation of organs, tissues, etc. -- Ethical aspects 6. Attitude to Death 7. Death -- Autobiography 8. Persistent Vegetative State 9. Tissue and Organ Harvesting
ISBN 9780375423710
LC 2011032025

"In this . . . look at how doctors determine the moment of death, skeptical science writer . . . [Dick] Teresi . . . relishes ripping into the 1968 Harvard team that formulated new criteria for determining death: 'loss of personhood,' or brain death. Doctors, Teresi says, can now 'declare a person dead in less time than it takes to get a decent eye exam' by testing reflexes: 'a flashlight in the eyes, ice water in the ears, and then an attempt to gasp for air' when the respirator is disconnected. Teresi interviews scientists who question the finality of brain death when the heart is still beating, and even the concept that personhood is located solely in the brain. . . . Teresi charges that the brain-death revolution is

driven by the $20 billion-a-year organ transplant business." (Publishers Weekly)

Includes bibliographical references and index

610.28 Auxiliary techniques and procedures; apparatus, equipment, materials

Gawande, Atul

★ The **checklist** manifesto; how to get things right. Metropolitan Books 2010 209p $24.50 **610.28**

1. Lists 2. Medical care -- Quality control
ISBN 9780805091748
LC 2009-46888

"We live in a world of great and increasing complexity, where even the most expert professionals struggle to master the tasks they face. Longer training, ever more advanced technologies—neither seems to prevent grievous errors. But in [this book], . . . Gawande finds a remedy in the . . . simplest of techniques: the checklist. First introduced decades ago by the U.S. Air Force, checklists have enabled pilots to fly aircraft of mind-boggling sophistication. Now innovative checklists are being adopted in hospitals around the world. . . . Gawande takes us from Austria, where an emergency checklist saved a drowning victim who had spent half an hour underwater, to Michigan, where a cleanliness checklist in intensive care units virtually eliminated a type of deadly hospital infection. He explains how checklists actually work to prompt striking and immediate improvements." (Publisher's note) Index.

"Few medical writers working today can transmit the gore-drenched terror of an operation that suddenly goes wrong—a terror that has a special resonance when it is Dr. Gawande himself who makes the initial horrifying mistake. And few can make it as clear as he can what exactly is at stake in the effort to minimize calamities." N Y Times (Late N Y Ed)

Includes bibliographical references

Topol, Eric

The **creative** destruction of medicine; Eric Topol. Basic Books 2012 xi, 303p.p **610.28**

1. Medical technology 2. Access to health care 3. Technological innovations 4. Internet 5. Health Communication 6. Biomedical Technology 7. Diffusion of Innovation 8. Medical Informatics Applications 9. Delivery of Health Care -- trends
ISBN 9780465025503; 9780465029341
LC 2011041162

This book offers information about "how academic healthcare organizations . . . can collaborate with for-profit companies to accelerate technological progress in medicine. . . . The author says that no single innovation will have a more profound effect than the conversion of biological data. . . . Dr. [Eric] Topol focuses much of his attention on the development of 'theranostics,' or the integrated use of treatments and diagnostics . . . to better guide therapy." (Wall Street Journal)

Includes bibliographical references and index.

Wachter, Robert

The **digital** doctor; hope, hype, and harm at the dawn of medicine's computer age. by Robert Wachter. McGraw-Hill 2015 330 p. illustrations (hardback : alk. paper) $30   **610.28**
1. Medical technology 2. Physician-patient relationship 3. Clinical Medicine 4. Clinical Competence 5. Medical Informatics 6. Physician-Patient Relations
ISBN 0071849467; 9780071849463

LC 2015001206

This book, by Robert Wachter, "examines healthcare at the dawn of its computer age. It tackles the hard questions, from how technology is changing care at the bedside to whether government intervention has been useful or destructive. And it does so with clarity, insight, humor, and compassion. Ultimately, it is a hopeful story." (Publisher's note)

"Wachter writes about the complexity of health-care IT systems, patient access and contributions to their office notes, IBM's Watson (the Jeopardy-champion supercomputer), and intelligent, biosensing underwear. Maybe the best take on modern medicine's 'man versus machine' debate is provided by Warner Slack, a physician and informatics expert: 'Any doctor who could be replaced by a computer should be.'"

610.3 Medicine--dictionaries

Magill's medical guide; medical editors: Bryan C. Auday, Ph.D., Gordon College, Michael A. Buratovich, Ph.D., Spring Arbor University, Geraldine F. Marrocco, Ed.D., APRN, CNS, ANP-BC, Yale University School of Nursing, Paul Moglia, Ph.D., South Nassau Communities Hospital. Seventh edition Salem Press 2014 5 volumes ill **610.3**
1. Medicine -- Encyclopedias
ISBN 9781619252141; 1619252147

This medical reference book "covers diseases, disorders, treatments, procedures, specialties, anatomy, biology, and issues in an A-Z format, with sidebars addressing recent developments in medicine and concise information boxes for all diseases and disorders." (Publisher's note)

"Covers diseases, disorders, treatments, procedures, specialties, anatomy, biology, and issues in an A-Z format, with sidebars addressing recent developments in medicine and concise information boxes for all diseases and disorders." Publisher's note

Includes bibliographical references and index.

Mosby's medical dictionary; editor, Marie T. O'Toole. 10th edition Elsevier 2016 1942 p. ill. (chiefly col.) hbk $43.95   **610.3**
1. Medicine 2. Medicine -- Dictionaries
ISBN 9780323414258; 0323414257

"Over 56,000 entries offer detailed definitions, as well as the latest information on pathophysiology, treatment and interventions, and nursing care.More than 2,450 color photographs and line drawings demonstrate and explain complex conditions and abstract concepts.Strict, common-sense alphabetical organization makes it easy to find key terms and definitions." (Publisher's note)

Taber's cyclopedic medical dictionary; editor, Donald Venes ... [et. al.] 22nd ed F.A. Davis 2013 2846 p. col. ill. (indexed) $42.95   **610.3**
1. Medical care 2. Medicine -- Dictionaries
ISBN 080362977X; 9780803629783; 9780803629790; 9780803629776

LC 2012034064

First published 1940. Periodically revised

"In hand, online, or on your mobile device--anywhere and everywhere, 'Taber's 22' is the all-in-one, go-to source in the classroom, clinical, and beyond. Under the editorial direction of Donald Venes, MD, MSJ, a team of expert consulting editors and consultants, representing nearly every health care profession, ensures that the content reflects the most current healthcare information." (Publisher's note)

This work gives "definitions of medical terms and words. Pronunciation is given for all but very common terms and the etymology of most words is included. Appendixes include such information as emergency treatment, dietetic charts, Latin and Greek nomenclature, and normal reference laboratory values." Guide to Ref Books

Includes bibliographical references and index

610.69 Medical personnel and relationships

Berger, Zackary

Talking to your doctor; a patient's guide to communication in the exam room and beyond. Zackary Berger. "Rowman & Littlefield Publishers, Inc. 2013 208 p. illustrations (cloth : alk. paper) $34 **610.69**
1. Communication 2. Patient participation 3. Physician-patient relationship 4. Physician and patient 5. Communication in medicine
ISBN 1442220503; 9781442220508

LC 2013014172

This book, by Zackary Berger, "helps readers navigate the new, more promising waters of doctor-patient collaboration, starting at the simplest and most human interaction --the conversation between two people in a room-- and ending with the benefits that can be obtained by cultivating an effective partnership. While patients need to take control of the visit and set their agenda, the latest research shows that doctors and patients need to connect on a more emotional level as well." (Publisher's note)

"Every visit to the doctor's office is an opportunity for a new beginning and an important dialogue about remaining healthy or feeling better. Patients should feel comfortable about expressing their concerns, and physicians need to listen carefully. Berger's book lays a strong foundation for constructing solid relationships between patients and their physicians." Booklist

Includes bibliographical references and index

Michelson, Leslie D.

The **patient's** playbook; how to save your life and the lives of those you love. by Leslie D. Michelson. Alfred A. Knopf 2015 336 p. (hardback) $24.95   **610.69**
1. Medical care 2. Decision making 3. Patient advocacy 4. Patient education 5. Self-care, Health 6. Medicine -- Decision making 7. Medical errors --

Prevention
ISBN 038535228X; 9780385352284

LC 2015014325

This book, by Leslie D. Michelson, seeks to "show you how to choose the right doctor, coordinate the best care, and get to the No-Mistake Zone in medical decision making. . . . [The book] is an essential guide to the most effective techniques for getting the best from a broken system: sourcing excellent physicians, selecting the right treatment protocols, researching with precision, and structuring the ideal support team." (Publisher's note)

"In a fluid, informative, and educated manner, Michelson delivers an impassioned call to arms for patients and caregivers to be their best advocate, ready to organize, question, and ask for second opinions." LJ

Ofri, Danielle

What doctors feel; how emotions affect the practice of medicine. Danielle Ofri. Beacon Press 2013 232 p. (alk. paper) $24.95 **610.69**
1. Physicians 2. Physician-patient relationship
ISBN 0807073326; 9780807073322

LC 2012049349

Here, Dr. Danielle Ofri offers a "take on the inner life of medical professionals, describing not only her own bumpy path from med student to M.D., but also the difficulty of maintaining empathy for patients over the years. 'Emotional layers' in medicine are more subtle and pervasive than anyone wants to believe, and they often become the 'dominant players in medical decision-making,' she argues." (Publishers Weekly)

Includes bibliographical references

Reilly, Brendan

One doctor; close calls, cold cases, and the mysteries of medicine. Brendan Reilly. Atria Books 2013 352 p. $28 **610.69**
1. Physician-patient relationship
ISBN 1476726299; 9781476726298; 9781476726366

LC 2013006739

In this book, phyisican Brendan Reilly "relates his most challenging cases, beginning in the present--when he sees 19 ER patients on an average day--before backtracking to his early career at Dartmouth in 1985. That year, Reilly struggled to identify the cause of an eccentric and lovable patient's delirium. By the time he figured it out, the patient--Fred--had died." (Publishers Weekly)

Reilly's "book is about more than the joy of saving lives and the sadness of losing them—it's an intimate exploration of modern medicine and the human condition." Pub Wkly

Includes bibliographical references and index

610.730   Organizations and management

Makary, Marty

Unaccountable; what hospitals won't tell you and how transparency can revolutionize health care. by Marty Makary. Bloomsbury Press 2012 246 p. ill. (hardback) $26 **610.730**
1. Medical records 2. Health care reform -- United States 3. Medical errors 4. Patient education 5.

Medical personnel and patient 6. Medical care -- Quality control 7. Health facilities -- Public relations
ISBN 1608198367; 9781608198368

LC 2012007740

In this book, surgeon Marty Makary "suggests that providing patients with more access to their own medical information, as well as to the volume and safety records of facilities and doctors, would improve the overall quality of health care and save money. . . . He takes on what he believes is the health-care profession's inept self-regulation, poor communication caused by fear of speaking up, obfuscation of available statistics, and nonprofit hospital CEO compensation." (Library Journal)

Includes bibliographical references and index

610.9   Medicine--history

Mattern, Susan P.

Prince of medicine; Galen in the Roman world. Susan P. Mattern. Oxford University Press 2013 368 p. $29.95 **610.9**
1. Medicine -- History 2. Roman World 3. History, Ancient 4. History of Medicine 5. Physicians -- Biography
ISBN 019976767X; 9780199767670

LC 2012035656

Susan P. Mattern presents a "biography of Galen of Pergamum (circa 130-212 C.E.), a Greek who practiced medicine and philosophy in the Roman-dominated Mediterranean, first rising to fame at home in Asia Minor before becoming preeminent in Rome during the reign of Marcus Aurelius." (Library Journal)

Includes bibliographical references and index

610.92   Biography

Sweet, Victoria

God's hotel; a doctor, a hospital, and a pilgrimage to the heart of medicine. Victoria Sweet. Riverhead Books 2012 384 p. ill. (hardback) $27.95 **610.92**
1. Medicine 2. Hospitals 3. Physicians 4. MEDICAL -- Essays 5. Laguna Honda Hospital (San Francisco, Calif.) -- History 6. Hospital care -- California -- San Francisco -- Anecdotes
ISBN 1594488436; 9781594488436

LC 2011049340

This book offers a "portrait of a . . . physician on a quest to understand the heart, as well as the art, of medicine. Laguna Honda Hospital, the last remaining almshouse in the United States--a therapeutic community that houses and cares for the chronically ill or impoverished--offers . . . [author and physician Victoria] Sweet . . . a[n] . . . education in ministering to the body, heart, and soul." (Library Journal)

Includes bibliographical references

611   Human anatomy, cytology, histology

Balaban, Naomi E.

The **handy** anatomy answer book; [by] Naomi E. Balaban and James E. Bobick. Visible Ink Press 2008 362p il pa $21.95   **611**

1. Physiology 2. Human anatomy
ISBN 978-1-57859-190-9

"This book can provide an excellent way to read and self-test for health and human biology classes. Adults wanting to know more about the subjects covered will also find a wealth of useful and accessible information." Voice Youth Advocates

Gray's anatomy; the anatomical basis of clinical practice. editor-in-chief, Susan Standring. 41st edition Elsevier 2015 1562 p. ill. (some col.) hbk $228.99   **611**

1. Anatomy
ISBN 9780702052309; 0702052302

LC 2015027527

A comprehensive standard reference work with illustrations, descriptions and definitions.

Includes bibliographical references and index

Roach, Mary

★ **Stiff**; the curious lives of human cadavers. Norton 2003 303p il $23.95; pa $13.95   **611**

1. Dead 2. Dissection 3. Human experimentation in medicine
ISBN 0-393-05093-9; 0-393-32482-6 pa

LC 2002-152908

"For those who are interested in the fields of medicine or forensics and are aware of some of the procedures, this book makes excellent reading." SLJ

Includes bibliographical references

Shubin, Neil

Your inner fish; a journey into the 3.5-billion-year history of the human body. Pantheon Books 2008 229p il map $24   **611**

1. Evolution 2. Human anatomy
ISBN 978-0-375-42447-2; 0-375-42447-4

LC 2007-24699

This is a "look at how the human body evolved into its present state. . . . Shubin excels at explaining the science, making each discovery an adventure, whether it's a Pennsylvania roadcut or a stony outcrop beset by polar bears and howling Arctic winds." Publ Wkly

Includes bibliographical references

612   Human physiology

Ashcroft, Frances

The **spark** of life; electricity in the human body. Frances Ashcroft; illustrations by Ronan Mahon. Norton 2012 339 p. ill.   **612**

1. Biology 2. Physiology 3. Electrophysiology 4. Human physiology 5. Electrophysiology -- Popular works
ISBN 0393078035; 9780393078039

LC 2012021264

This book, by Frances Ashcroft, presents an "exploration of the surprising role that electricity plays in our bodies. What happens during a heart attack? Can someone really die of fright? What is death, anyway? How does electroshock treatment affect the brain? What is consciousness? The answers to these questions lie in the electrical signals constantly traveling through our bodies, driving our thoughts, our movements, and even the beating of our hearts." (Publisher's note)

Includes bibliographical references and index

Francis, Gavin

Adventures in human being; a grand tour from the cranium to the calcaneum. Gavin Francis. Basic Books, a member of the Perseus Books Group 2015 272 p. (hardback) $26.99   **612**

1. Human body 2. Physiology 3. Human anatomy 4. Human physiology
ISBN 0465079687; 9780465079681

LC 2015015371

"Drawing on his experiences as a surgeon, ER specialist, and family physician, Francis blends stories from the clinic with episodes from medical history, philosophy, and literature to describe the body in sickness and in health, in life and in death. When assessing a young woman with paralysis of the face, Francis reflects on the age-old difficulty artists have had in capturing human expression. A veteran of the war in Iraq suffers a shoulder injury that Homer first described three millennia ago in the Iliad. And when a gardener pricks her finger on a dirty rose thorn, her case of bacterial blood poisoning brings to mind the comatose sleeping beauties in the fairy tales we learn as children." Publisher's Note.

"His skill as a writer and an observer of human nature become obvious when he is able to make a chapter entitled "Large Bowel & Rectum" thoroughly engaging. Francis writes with humility and makes the point that being a good medical practitioner is not "about dramatically saving lives, but quietly, methodically, trying to postpone death." Pub Wkly.

Includes bibliographical references and index

The **Human** body; an illustrated guide to its structure, function, and disorders. editor-in-chief, Charles Clayman. Dorling Kindersley 1995 240p il $30   **612**

1. Physiology 2. Human anatomy
ISBN 1-56458-992-7

LC 94-37165

"This absolutely stunning book succeeds immeasurably as a guide to the human body." Sci Books Films

Lieberman, Daniel, 1964-

The **story** of the human body; evolution, health, and disease. Daniel Lieberman. Pantheon Books 2013 464 p. illustrations $27.95   **612**

1. Evolution 2. Human body 3. Adaptation (Biology)
ISBN 0307379418; 9780307379412

LC 2013011811

This book, by Daniel E. Lieberman, presents the "story of human evolution consisting of five biological transformations (walking upright, eating a variety of different foods, accumulating physical traits aligned to hunting and gathering, gaining bigger brains with larger bodies, and developing unique capacities for cooperation and language) and two cultural ones (farming and reliance on machines)." (Booklist)

"Lieberman's discussion of type 2 diabetes, heart disease, and breast cancer are as clear as any yet published, and he offers a well-articulated case for why an evolutionary perspective can greatly enrich the practice of medicine." Pub Wkly

Includes bibliographical references and index

612.044   Exercise and sports

Fitzgerald, Matt

How bad do you want it? mastering the psychology of mind over muscle. Matt Fitzgerald; foreword by Samuele Marcora, PhD. VeloPress 2015 xiii, 282 p.p (pbk. : alk. paper) $18.95   **612.044**

1. Physical fitness 2. Sports -- Psychological aspects 3. Endurance sports 4. Endurance sports -- Physiological aspects 5. Endurance sports -- Psychological aspects

ISBN 1937715418; 9781937715410

LC 2015048381

This book, by Matt Fitzgerald, "examines more than a dozen pivotal races to discover the surprising ways elite athletes strengthen their mental toughness. . . . Their own words reinforce what the research has found: strong mental fitness lets us approach our true physical limits. . . . Each chapter explores the how and why of an elite athlete's transformative moment, revealing powerful new psychobiological principles you can practice to flex your own mental fitness." (Publisher's note)

Includes bibliographical references (pages 267-271) and index

612.1   Specific functions, systems, organs

Amidon, Stephen

The sublime engine; a biography of the human heart. [by] Stephen Amidon and Thomas Amidon. Rodale 2011 242p $24.99   **612.1**

1. Heart

ISBN 978-1-60529-584-8

LC 2010-30227

This book "presents a multifaceted picture of the heart's influences on mythology, science, and popular culture through the ages. In six lyrically written chapters, they trace humanity's perennial fascination with the heart through the eyes of history's greatest artists and medical explorers, beginning with the Greeks and fancifully ending with a peek into the future of cardiological innovation." Booklist

Includes bibliographical references

612.3   Digestive system

Collen, Alanna

10% human; how your body's microbes hold the key to health and happiness. Alanna Collen. Harper 2015 336 p. color illustrations (hardback) $26.99   **612.3**

1. Health 2. Biology 3. Viruses 4. Microbial metabolism 5. Intestines -- Microbiology 6. Microorganisms -- Therapeutic use

ISBN 0062345982; 9780062345981; 9780062345998

LC 2015004721

In this book, author "Alanna Collen draws on the latest scientific research to show how our personal colony of microbes influences our weight, our immune system, our mental health, and even our choice of partner. She argues that so many of our modern diseases--obesity, autism, [and] mental illness . . . have their root in our failure to cherish our most fundamental and enduring relationship: that with our personal colony of microbes." (Publisher's note)

"Collen never claims that she has uncovered the answers to modern health woes, but she points out the markers that may one day lead to such answers. Everything you wanted to know about microbes but were afraid to ask." Kirkus

Price, Catherine

Vitamania; our obsessive quest for nutritional perfection. Catherine Price. The Penguin Press 2015 336 p. (hardback) $27.95   **612.3**

1. Vitamins 2. Nutrition 3. Dietary supplements 4. Food -- United States 5. Vitamins -- History 6. Food -- United States -- Psychological aspects 7. Nutrition -- United States -- Psychological aspects 8. Dietary supplements -- Social aspects -- United States 9. Vitamins in human nutrition -- Social aspects -- United States

ISBN 1594205043; 9781594205040

LC 2014036657

In this book, author Catherine Price "offers a lucid and lively journey through our cherished yet misguided beliefs about vitamins, and reveals a straightforward, blessedly anxiety-free path to enjoyable eating and good health. . . . Her travels to vitamin manufacturers and food laboratories and military testing kitchens--along with her deep dive into the history of nutritional science--provide a witty and dynamic narrative." (Publisher's note)

"Price's sharp wit, skillful and vivid translation of science into story, and valiant inquisitiveness (she insists on tasting synthetic vitamins and gets buzzed on the military's caffeinated meat sticks) make for an electrifying dissection of our vitamin habit in contrast to our irrevocable need for naturally nutrient-rich food." Booklist

Includes bibliographical references and index

Roach, Mary, 1959-

★ Gulp; adventures on the alimentary canal. Mary Roach. W W Norton 2013 336 p.   **612.3**

1. Alimentary canal -- Popular works 2. Digestive organs -- Popular works 3. Gastrointestinal system -- Popular works

ISBN 9780393081572

LC 2012050391

In this book, science writer Mary Roach explores "the alimentary canal. Roach asks the questions that some readers may have always wondered: Does saliva have curative properties? Do pets taste food differently than their owners do? Could Jonah have survived three days in a whale's stomach? . . . As she investigates these questions, Roach encounters many an eccentric scientist who has worked tirelessly to unlock the mysteries of saliva, gastrointestinal gases, and mastication." (Library Journal)

"Roach's approach is grounded in science, but the virtuosic author rarely resists a pun, and it's clear she revels in giving readers a thrill... Adventurous kids and doctors alike will appreciate this fascinating and sometimes ghastly tour of the gastrointestinal system." Pub Wkly

Includes bibliographical references

612.6   Reproduction, development, maturation

Angier, Natalie

Woman; an intimate geography. Houghton Mifflin 1999 398p $25   **612.6**
1. Physiology 2. Gender role 3. Sex role 4. Women -- Psychology
ISBN 0-395-69130-3

LC 98-47634

"Angier proves a knowledgeable, witty guide on our illustrative journey through hordes of cultures and species." Ms

Includes bibliographical references

Eliot, Lise

Pink brain, blue brain; how small differences grow into trouplesome gaps--and what we can do about it. Houghton Mifflin Harcourt 2009 420p il $25   **612.6**
1. Child development 2. Sex differences (Psychology)
ISBN 978-0-618-39311-4

LC 2009-14746

"This is an important book and highly recommended for parents, teachers, and anyone who works with children." Libr J

Includes bibliographical references

Jensen, Frances E.

The **teenage** brain; a neuroscientist's survival guide to raising adolescents and young adults. Frances E. Jensen; with Amy Ellis Nutt. Harper 2014 384 p. illustrations (hardback) $27.99   **612.6**
1. Parenting 2. Neurosciences 3. Adolescent psychology 4. Brain -- Growth 5. Parent and teenager 6. Developmental neurobiology 7. Developmental psychobiology
ISBN 0062067842; 9780062067845; 9780062067852; 9780062067869

LC 2014009600

In this book, by Frances E. Jensen, with Amy Ellis Nutt, "drawing on her research knowledge and clinical experience, [a] neurologist and mother of two boys" . . . offers a revolutionary look at the science of the adolescent brain, providing . . . insights that translate into practical advice for both parents and teenagers." (Publisher's note)

"Recommended for readers who enjoyed Laurence Steinberg's Age of Opportunity, this title applies new science to the frustrating dilemma of how to live with teenage kids." LJ

Katz, Rebecca

The **longevity** kitchen; satisfying, big-flavor recipes featuring the top 16 age-busting power foods [120 recipes for vitality and optimal health] Rebecca Katz with Mat Edelson; photography by Leo Gong. Ten Speed Press 2013 256 p. color illustrations (hardback) $29.99   **612.6**
1. Health 2. Cookbooks 3. Longevity 4. Natural foods 5. Physical fitness 6. Natural foods -- Recipes 7. Longevity -- Nutritional aspects 8. Older people -- Health and hygiene
ISBN 1607742942; 9781607742944

LC 2012035097

This cookbook presents a "collection of 125 delicious whole-foods recipes showcasing 16 antioxidant-rich power foods, developed by wellness authority Rebecca Katz to combat and prevent chronic diseases such as diabetes, heart disease, high blood pressure, inflammation, arthritis, and other conditions that plague American adults, enabling readers to live longer, healthier lives." (Publisher's note)

"The authors' introductions to each recipe can be tiresomely silly, so readers should skip straight to the ingredient list and start cooking up something healthy and delicious." Pub Wkly

Includes bibliographical references and index

Kim, Susan

Flow; the cultural story of menstruation. [by] Elissa Stein and Susan Kim. St. Martin's Griffin 2009 270p $27.99   **612.6**
1. Menstruation
ISBN 978-0-312-37996-4

LC 2009-17046

"There is probably no better book for moms who want their daughters to respect themselves in every aspect, and for female preteens and teens who would never say a word about their moms reading a book about menses but surely would like several sneak peeks into its pages." Booklist

Includes bibliographical references

Lachs, Mark

Treat me, not my age; a doctor's guide to getting the best care as you or a loved one gets older. Viking 2010 386p il $27.95   **612.6**
1. Aging 2. Elderly -- Health and hygiene
ISBN 978-0-670-02210-6

LC 2010-17487

The author "discusses for seniors and their caregivers the aging process, ageism in society, choosing and communicating with a physician, financial issues, medications, complementary and alternative medicine, and end-of-life planning. Writing in a witty, conversational style, Lachs provides a great deal of useful information." Libr J

Includes bibliographical references

Martin, Robert

How we do it; the evolution and future of human reproduction. Robert Martin. Basic Books 2013 xii, 304 p.p (hardcover) $27.99 **612.6**

1. Evolution 2. Reproduction 3. Human fertility 4. Human evolution 5. Human reproduction 6. Evolution (Biology)

ISBN 0465030157; 0465037844; 9780465030156; 9780465037841

LC 2012278031

In this book, "primatologist Robert Martin draws on forty years of research to locate the roots of everything from our sex cells to the way we care for newborns. He examines the procreative history of humans as well as that of our primate kin to reveal what's really natural when it comes to making and raising babies, and distinguish which behaviors we ought to continue--and which we should not." (Publisher's note)

"The author explains potentially complicated topics in a marvelously clear manner; although the focus is clearly evolutionary, he does not shy from considering practical implications." Choice

Includes bibliographical references and index

Nilsson, Lennart

A child is born; [photography], Lennart Nilsson; text, Lars Hamberger; translated from the Swedish by Linda Schenck. 4th ed, completely rev and updated; Delacorte Press 2003 239p il $35; pa $21 **612.6**

1. Pregnancy 2. Childbirth 3. Embryology

ISBN 0-385-33754-X; 0-385-33755-8 pa

LC 2003-43854

Original Swedish edition, 1965; first United States edition, 1966

An illustrated look at male and female reproductive anatomy and physiology, the processes of ovulation and fertilization, fetal development, and labor and delivery.

Roach, Mary, 1959-

Bonk; the curious coupling of science and sex. Norton 2008 319 p. il **612.6**

1. Sex (Biology)

ISBN 0393064646; 9780393064643

LC 2007-51990

This is an overview of the research on sexual physiology.

"Tucked between the jokes and anecdotes, you will find lessons on impotence, orgasm, unusual and unusually brave scientists, and the sexual behaviour of other species, including a hilarious description of porcupine sex." New Sci

Includes bibliographical references (p. 307-319)

Stipp, David

The youth pill; scientists at the brink of an anti-aging revolution. Current 2010 308p $26.95 **612.6**

1. Longevity 2. Drug industry

ISBN 978-1-61723-000-4; 1-61723-000-6

LC 2010-7114

The author possesses "a singular style, crafting complex explanations of scientific discoveries (and failures) into eminently enjoyable reading. Whether or not the notion of liv-

ing energetically to the age of 150 appeals, Stipp makes the research compelling." Booklist

Includes bibliographical references

Weil, Andrew

Healthy aging; a lifelong guide to your physical and spiritual well-being. Alfred A. Knopf 2005 293p $27.95 **612.6**

1. Aging

ISBN 0-375-40755-3

LC 2005-45183

The author "explores common Western beliefs and attitudes about aging and urges readers to develop healthier perspectives. The 60-year-old author assesses the growing and lucrative field of anti-aging medicine, takes the position that aging is not reversible, and offers many ways for readers to prevent conditions and illnesses that limit mortality and ensure well-being into the later years. . . . The real value is Weil's courageous stand, one likely to meet resistance in a culture devoted to external indicators of eternal youth." Publ Wkly

Includes bibliographical references

Williams, Florence

Breasts; a natural and unnatural history. Florence Williams. W.W. Norton & Co. 2012 338 p. ill. (hardcover) $25.95 **612.6**

1. Breast 2. Breast cancer 3. Human ecology 4. Cancer -- Environmental aspects 5. Breast -- History 6. Breast -- Psychological aspects

ISBN 0393063186; 9780393063189

LC 2011053153

This book is a "comprehensive 'environmental history' of the only human body part without its own medical specialty, [in which] . . . [Florence] Williams . . . the reader along a journey extending from the evolution of human breasts from sweat glands, through cosmetic breast enhancements, the science and politics of breastfeeding, and possible links between pollutants and breast cancer in both women and men." (Publishers Weekly)

Includes bibliographical references

612.67 Aging

Sagan, Dorion

Cracking the aging code; Josh Mitteldorf and Dorion Sagan. Flatiron Books 2016 336 p. (hardback) $27.99 **612.67**

1. Aging 2. Aging -- Physiological aspects

ISBN 9781250061706

LC 2016001602

In this book, "theoretical biologist Josh Mitteldorf and award-winning writer and ecological philosopher Dorion Sagan reveal that evolution and aging are even more complex and breathtaking than we originally thought. Using meticulous multidisciplinary science, as well as reviewing the history of our understanding about evolution, this book makes the case that aging is not something that 'just happens,' nor is it the result of wear and tear or a genetic inevitability." (Publisher's note)

"A thoughtful examination of the role of aging and death in supporting life." Kirkus

Includes bibliographical references (pages 309-318) and index.

612.8 Nervous system

Aftel, Mandy

Fragrant; the secret life of scent. Mandy Aftel. Riverhead Books 2014 288 p. illustrations (hardback) $27.95 **612.8**

1. Perfumes 2. Cosmetics 3. Odors 4. Smell 5. Jasmine 6. Cinnamon 7. Ambergris 8. Frankincense 9. Mints (Plants)

ISBN 1594631417; 9781594631412

LC 2014018554

In this book by Mandy Aftel "through five major players in the epic of aroma, she explores the profound connection between our sense of smell and the appetites that move us. Cinnamon, queen of the Spice Route, touches our hunger for the unknown. Mint, homegrown the world over, speaks to our affinity for the familia. Frankincense, an ancient incense ingredient, taps into our longing for transcendence. And exquisite jasmine exemplifies our yearning for beauty." (Publisher's note)

"Targeted toward those new to the perfume world, this book is strongly recommended for casual readers interested in the basics of scent and perfumery." LJ

Alter, David

Staying sharp; 9 keys for a youthful brain through modern science and ancient wisdom. Henry Emmons, MD And David Alter, PhD. Touchstone, a imprint of Simon & Schuster, Inc. 2015 288 p. (hardcover) $25 **612.8**

1. Brain 2. Intellect 3. Brain -- Care and hygiene

ISBN 1476758948; 9781476758947; 9781501116810

LC 2015000723

Authors Henry Emmons and David Alter "demonstrate how to blend the best of modern science and Eastern holistic medicine together to form a powerful drug-free program to maintain a youthful mind and a happy life. [They] have taken their expertise and translated the fundamentals of brain science into an easily accessible collection of the nine key lessons proven to preserve and strengthen mental acuity." (Publisher's note)

"The authors, who have worked together for over 25 years, dub their approach an intersection of Eastern tradition and Western science. Some readers may be skeptical, but for those open to new ways of thinking and acting, this book will provide a valuable start." Pub Wkly

Biever, John A.

The **wandering** mind; understanding disassociation, from daydreams to disorders. John A. Biever and Maryann Karinch. Rowman & Littlefield Publishers 2012 xv, 167 p.p (hardcover) $35; (ebook) $34.99 **612.8**

1. Mental illness 2. Dissociation (Psychology) 3.

Consciousness 4. Mental health

ISBN 1442216158; 1442216174; 9781442216150; 9781442216174 pdf

LC 2012013303

In this book by John A. Biever and Maryann Karinch, Biever "describes daydreaming, fantasy-prone personalities, and charismatic leaders. He differentiates dissociate identity disorder (DID) from dissociative fugue, dissociative amnesia, depersonalization disorders, and false memories, using examples from the literature as well as his own case studies." (Choice)

Includes bibliographical references (p. 155-156) and index.

Buonomano, Dean

Brain bugs; how the brain's flaws shape our lives. W. W. Norton & Co. 2011 310p $25.95 **612.8**

1. Brain 2. Memory

ISBN 978-0-393-07602-8

LC 2011014934

The author explains "that as the human brain has evolved over the past 100,000 years, it has added layer upon layer of networked neural connections to cope with a rapidly changing world. But, he writes, the brain's most detrimental malfunctions are often traceable to its most ancient structures—those that compose the limbic system. . . . Drawing on real-world examples and current research in neuroscience, Buonomano guides the reader through the unexpected ways in which our lives are influenced by the messiness of our busiest, most intricate, and often most error-prone organ." The Scientist

Includes bibliographical references

Burnett, Dean

Idiot brain; What Your Head Is Really Up To. Dean Burnett. W W Norton & Co Inc 2016 336 p. (hardcover) $26.95 **612.8**

1. Brain 2. Memory 3. Consciousness 4. Neurosciences 5. Brain -- Popular works 6. Memory -- Popular works 7. Consciousness -- Popular works 8. Neurosciences -- Popular works

ISBN 9780393253788

LC 2016009451

In this book, "neuroscientist Dean Burnett celebrates blind spots, blackouts, insomnia, and all the other downright laughable things our minds do to us, while also exposing the many mistakes we've made in our quest to understand how our brains actually work." (Publisher's note)

"Burnett manages to both entertain and inform in engaging ways that would benefit the performance of the most humorless pedant." Kirkus

Includes bibliographical references and index

Carr, Nicholas G., 1959-

The **shallows**; what the Internet is doing to our brains. W.W. Norton 2010 276p $26.95 **612.8**

1. Internet 2. Neuropsychology 3. Neurophysiology 4. Internet -- Psychological aspects

ISBN 978-0-393-07222-8; 0-393-07222-3

LC 2010-07639

"Drawing from neuroscience, history and social-science research, Carr reviews evidence that learning how to solve a problem, how to play a piece of music or how to speak a language physically changes the brain. It's a mistake, he argues, to think of the brain as a hard drive that stores information; it's far more than that and changes dynamically as it processes information, altering itself as it confronts challenges — for better or worse. Reading a book, he notes, is vastly different from reading hyperlinked Internet text. Reading a book is solitary, requiring deep thought, analysis of the text and sustaining a narrative thread for the duration. By contrast, Internet reading invites shallow skimming for relevant passages, incessant clicking to hyperlinked articles and reliance on Google's search algorithms to determine relevance. . . . Carr argues that the result is an emerging nation of shallow and impatient readers." Seattle Times

Includes bibliographical references

Churchland, Patricia S.

Braintrust; what neuroscience tells us about morality. [by] Patricia S. Churchland. Princeton University Press 2011 273 p. (hardcover) $24.95   **612.8**
1. Ethics 2. Philosophy 3. Neuropsychology 4. Neurobiology 5. Neurosciences
ISBN 069113703X; 9780691137032
LC 2010043584
In this book, "[Patricia S.] Churchland argues that morality originates in the biology of the brain. She describes the 'neurobiological platform of bonding' that, modified by evolutionary pressures and cultural values, has led to human styles of moral behavior. . . . Moral values, Churchland argues, are rooted in a behavior common to all mammals -- the caring for offspring." (Publisher's note)

Includes bibliographical references and index

DeSalle, Rob

The **brain**; big bangs, behaviors, and beliefs. Rob DeSalle and Ian Tattersall; illustrated by Patricia J. Wynne. Yale University Press 2012 xiv, 354 p.p ill. (clothbound : alk. paper) $29.95   **612.8**
1. Brain 2. Evolution 3. Nervous system 4. Cognition 5. Neurophysiology 6. Brain -- Evolution
ISBN 0300175221; 9780300175226
LC 2011044329
This book by Rob DeSalle and Ian Tattersall presents a "step-by-step account of the evolution of the brain and nervous system." The authors "explain how the cognitive gulf that separates us from all other living creatures could have occurred. They discuss the development and uniqueness of human consciousness, how human and nonhuman brains work, the roles of different nerve cells, the importance of memory and language in brain functions, and much more." (Publisher's note)

Includes bibliographical references (p. 327-336) and index

Doidge, Norman

The **brain** that changes itself; stories of personal triumph from the frontiers of brain science. Viking 2007 427p $24.95   **612.8**
1. Brain 2. Neuroplasticity
ISBN 978-0-670-03830-5; 0-670-03830-X
LC 2006-49224

"A woman who perpetually feels like she's falling, a man addicted to hard-core pornography, an amputee with excruciating pain in his phantom elbow: all cured thanks to neuroplasticity, the brain's ability to rewire itself. Doidge provides a history of the research in this growing field, highlighting scientists at the edge of groundbreaking discoveries and telling fascinating stories of people who have benefited. An engaging read for anyone interested in the science behind how our surprisingly moldable brains are changed by our experiences." Psychology Today

The **brain's** way of healing; remarkable discoveries and recoveries from the frontiers of neuroplasticity. Norman Doidge, M.D. Viking 2015 432 p. (hardback) $29.95   **612.8**
1. Neuroplasticity 2. Brain -- Physiology 3. Brain 4. Healing
ISBN 067002550X; 9780670025503
LC 2014038471
This book by Norman Doidge shows "how the amazing process of neuroplastic healing really works. It describes natural, non-invasive avenues into the brain provided by the forms of energy around us--light, sound, vibration, movement--which pass through our senses and our bodies to awaken the brain's own healing capacities without producing unpleasant side effects. Doidge explores cases where patients alleviated years of chronic pain or recovered from debilitating strokes or accidents." (Publisher's note)

"A fascinating study on brain science that shows the way to major therapeutic discoveries." LJ

Includes bibliographical references and index

Eliot, Lise

What's going on in there? how the brain and mind develop in the first five years of life. Bantam Bks. 1999 533p hardcover o.p. pa $18   **612.8**
1. Brain 2. Developmental psychology
ISBN 0-553-37825-2 pa
LC 99-35423
"This book is both theoretical and practical, combining scientific reportage with 'how-to' advice for new parents. . . . With clear, mostly simple language, {Eliot} guides readers through a fascinating array of new research—on infant balance, the development of language and memory, and the relationship between the birthing process and the brain." Libr J

Gazzaniga, Michael S.

Human; the science behind what makes us unique. Ecco 2008 447p $27.50   **612.8**
1. Brain 2. Human beings 3. Consciousness
ISBN 978-0-06-089288-3; 0-06-089288-9
LC 2008-297703
"A savvy, witty guide to neuroscience today." Kirkus

Includes bibliographical references

Kaku, Michio

The **future** of the mind; the scientific quest to understand, enhance, and empower the mind. Dr. Michio Kaku, professor of Theoretical Physics, City University of New York. Doubleday 2014 400 p. illustrations $28.95   **612.8**
1. Mind and body 2. Neurosciences 3. Neuropsychology

4. Brain-computer interfaces 5. Cognitive neuroscience 6. Brain -- Mathematical models
ISBN 038553082X; 9780385530828

LC 2013017338

In this book, "theoretical physicist [Michio] Kaku . . . explores fantastical realms of science fiction that may soon become our reality. His futurist framework merges physics with neuroscience to model how our brains construct the future, and is loosely applied to demonstrations that 'show proof-of-principle' in accomplishing what was previously fictional: that minds can be read, memories can be digitally stored, and intelligences can be improved to great extents." (Publishers Weekly)

Kaku "delivers ingenious predictions extrapolated from good research already in progress." Kirkus

Includes bibliographical references

Kounios, John, 1956-

The **Eureka** factor; aha moments, creative insight, and the brain. John Kounios and Mark Jung-Beeman. Random House Inc 2015 288 p. illustrations $28   **612.8**

1. Intuition 2. Cognitive styles 3. Thought and thinking 4. Insight 5. Cognition -- Physiological aspects 6. Higher nervous activity -- Measurement 7. Thought and thinking -- Physiological aspects
ISBN 1400068541; 9781400068548

LC 2014022220

First edition.

In this book, neuroscientists John Kounios and Mark Jung-Beeman "explain how insights arise and what the scientific research says about stimulating more of them. They discuss how various conditions affect the likelihood of your having an insight, when insight is helpful and when deliberate methodical thought is better suited to a task, what the relationship is between insight and intuition, and how the brain's right hemisphere contributes to creative thought." (Publisher's note)

"An excellent title for those interested in neuroscience or creativity, or those who enjoy reading about brain research." LJ

Kurzweil, Ray, 1948-

How to create a mind; the secret of human thought revealed. Ray Kurzweil. Viking 2012 336 p. $27.95   **612.8**

1. Brain 2. Consciousness 3. Artificial intelligence 4. Self-consciousness (Awareness) 5. Brain -- Localization of functions
ISBN 0670025291; 9780670025299

LC 2012027185

In this book, "[Ray] Kurzweil . . . provides insight into how the human brain functions, while speculating on the possibilities and philosophical implications of creating a nonbiological mind. Underlying this analysis is the Pattern Recognition Theory of Mind, a process in the neocortex, the seat of higher brain functions such as perception, memory, and language and, by extension, consciousness." (Publishers Weekly)

Includes bibliographical references and index.

Lilienfeld, Scott O.

Brainwashed; The Seductive Appeal of Mindless Neuroscience. Sally Satel and Scott O. Lilienfeld. Perseus Books Group 2013 256 p. $26.99   **612.8**

1. Mind and body 2. Neurosciences
ISBN 0465018777; 9780465018772

In this book, "a psychiatrist and a clinical psychologist . . . argue against the use of brain scans as the basis for marketing efforts, addiction treatment, lie detection, and decisions in criminal trials. . . . The authors explain how particular mental states cannot be pinned directly onto active brain regions. They assert that a comprehensive understanding of behavior requires consideration of not only brain activity but also psychological, social, and cultural influences." (Library Journal)

Linden, David J.

Touch; the science of hand, heart, and mind. David J. Linden. Viking 2015 261 p. illustrations (hardback) $28.95   **612.8**

1. Touch 2. Emotions -- Physiological aspects 3. Touch -- Physiological aspects 4. Touch -- Psychological aspects
ISBN 0670014877; 9780670014873

LC 2014038475

This book by David J. Linden "combines anecdotes, stories, history, and neuroscience research" to explore touch in humans. "Chapters address how we sense what we actively touch, how we sense things that come in contact with our skin (other people as well as substances), how touch interacts with emotions in intimate forms of touching, and how our touch sensors can cause problems or be fooled." (Library Journal)

"An exciting book for those interested in learning more about the sense of touch and how the brain performs." LJ

Includes bibliographical references and index Includes bibliographical references and index

McAuliffe, Kathleen

This is your brain on parasites; How Tiny Creatures Manipulate Our Behavior and Shape Society. Kathleen McAuliffe. Houghton Mifflin Harcourt 2016 288 p. (hardback) $27   **612.8**

1. Parasites 2. Microbiology 3. Nervous system -- Diseases 4. Parasitology
ISBN 9780544192225

LC 2016002949

This book, by Kathleen McAuliffe, is an "investigation of the myriad ways that parasites control how other creatures—including humans—think, feel, and act. These tiny organisms can only live inside another animal, and as McAuliffe reveals, they have many evolutionary motives for manipulating their host's behavior. Far more often than appreciated, these puppeteers orchestrate the interplay between predator and prey." (Publisher's note)

"McAuliffe presents her collected research—often from small, nearly anecdotal studies—less as fact than in a spirit of exploration." Pub Wkly

Includes bibliographical references and index.

Palca, Joe

Annoying; the science of what bugs us. [by] Joe Palca and Flora Lichtman. Wiley 2011 272p $25.95 **612.8**
1. Physiology 2. Neuropsychology
ISBN 978-0-470-63869-9

LC 2010-54046

Palca and Lichtman "skitter all over the map in pursuit of their subject, and at first their progress seems peculiarly random, like one of those robotic vacuums. But in the end they do indeed cover every part of the terrain: from physics and psychology to aesthetics, genetics and even treatment for the miserably, terminally annoyed." N Y Times (Late N Y Ed)

Includes bibliographical references

Randall, David K.

Dreamland; adventures in the strange science of sleep. David K. Randall. W.W. Norton 2012 304 p. $25.95; (hardcover) $25.95 **612.8**
1. Sleep 2. Dreams 3. Sleepwalking
ISBN 039308020X; 9780393080209

LC 2012014932

This book offers an "examination of the science behind the little-known world of sleep. . . . [David K.] Randall explores the research that is investigating those dark hours that make up nearly a third of our lives. Taking readers from military battlefields to children's bedrooms, [the book] shows that sleep isn't as simple as it seems. Why did the results of one sleep study change the bookmakers' odds for certain Monday Night Football games? Do women sleep differently than men? And if you happen to kill someone while you are sleepwalking, does that count as murder?" (Publisher's note)

Includes bibliographical references

Suskind, Dana

Thirty Million Words; How to Build Your Child's Brain. Dana Suskind. Penguin Group USA 2015 320 p. $28 **612.8**
1. Child rearing 2. Child development 3. Parent-child relationship
ISBN 0525954872; 9780525954873

LC 2015016306

In this book, author "Dana Suskind, explains why the most important--and astoundingly simple--thing you can do for your child's future success in life is to talk to him or her, reveals the recent science behind this truth, and outlines precisely how parents can best put it into practice." (Publisher's note)

"Parents, other caregivers, and early childhood educators will be moved and inspired by this work." LJ

Zimmer, Carl

Soul made flesh; the discovery of the brain--and how it changed the world. Free Press 2004 367p il $26 **612.8**
1. Brain
ISBN 0-7432-3038-8

LC 2003-63144

Zimmer tells "the story of the 'discovery' of the human brain by physician Thomas Willis. Exploring the effects of this breakthrough on 17th-century Oxford, the author traces and investigates the subsequent discoveries and theories in neurology and medicine that flowed from Willis and others (e.g., Harvey, Hobbes, Descartes, Boyle, and Locke) in Oxford and on the continent. . . . Zimmer's elegant writing combines these multiple perspectives to produce a fascinating tour-de-force of a man, a time, and a place that readers will greatly enjoy." Libr J

Includes bibliographical references

612.82 Central nervous system

Carter, Rita

The human brain book; Rita Carter, Susan Aldridge, Martyn Page, Steve Parker; consultants Chris Frith, Utal Frith Melanie Shulman. DK Publishing 2014 264 p color illustrations hc $40 **612.82**
1. Brain 2. Human anatomy 3. Brain -- Physiology
ISBN 9781465416025; 1465416021

LC 2013444872

Written by Rita Carter, this second edition uses "the latest findings from neuroscience with new brain imaging techniques, as well as developments on infant brains, telepathy, and brain modification, this new edition of DK's 'The Human Brain Book' covers brain anatomy, function, and disorders. . . . With its . . . 22-page atlas, illustrated with MRI scans, and an interactive DVD, 'The Human Brain Book' is a . . . resource for . . . human biology, anatomy, and neuroscience." (Publisher's note)

"Using computer-generated three-dimensional images, graphics, and clear explanatory text presented in brief sections, the follow-up to The Human Body Book (2007) examines each aspect of the brain's structure and functions... This is a valuable resource for any high-school, college, and public library collection. Libraries should be aware that it comes with a DVD." Booklist

Eagleman, David

The brain; the story of you. David Eagleman. Pantheon Books 2015 218 p. color illustrations (hardback) $28.95 **612.82**
1. Self 2. Brain 3. Reality 4. Neurosciences
ISBN 1101870532; 9781101870532

LC 2015023281

This book, by David Eagleman, is "a journey into the questions at the mysterious heart of our existence. What is reality? Who are 'you'? How do you make decisions? Why does your brain need other people? How is technology poised to change what it means to be human? In the course of his investigations, Eagleman guides us through the world of extreme sports, criminal justice, facial expressions, genocide, brain surgery, gut feelings, robotics, and the search for immortality." (Publisher's note)

"This is a straightforward, stimulating companion book to the PBS series on the subject." Pub Wkly

Includes bibliographical references (pages 204-213).

Ros, Hana

Neurocomic; Hana Ros; illustrated by Matteo Farinella. Nobrow Press 2014 144 p. illustrations $24.95 **612.82**
1. Brain 2. Psychology 3. Neurosciences
ISBN 1907704701; 9781907704703

This book by Hana Ros, illustrated by Matteo Farinella, is a "journey through the human brain: a place of neuron forests, memory caves, and castles of deception. Along the way, you'll encounter Boschean beasts, giant squid, guitar-playing sea slugs, and the great pioneers of neuroscience. Hana Ros and Matteo Farinella provide an insight into the most complex thing in the universe." (Publisher's note)

"The information relayed is sufficiently genuine for the book to be a neophyte's primer on brain science, and the manner of its presentation is certainly exciting enough to sustain interest." Booklist

613　Personal health and safety

Boston Women's Health Book Collective

★ **Our** bodies, ourselves; [by the] Boston Women's Health Book Collective. 40th anniversary ed.; Touchstone 2011 928p il pa $26; ebook $12.99　　　　　　　　　　　　　　　　　　**613**
1. Women -- Psychology 2. Women -- Health and hygiene
ISBN 978-1-4391-9066-1 pa; 1-4391-9066-6 pa; 978-1-4391-9665-6 ebook; 1-4391-9665-6 ebook
LC 2011022749

First published 1971

This encyclopedia of women's health covers such topics as body image, food, alcohol and drugs, holistic healing, psychotherapy, occupational health, violence, relationships and sexuality, sexual health and controlling fertility, childbearing, aging and politics of women and health.

This is "the bible for women's health; an outstanding resource that belongs in all health collections." Libr J

Brewer, Stephen C.

The **Canyon** Ranch guide to men's health; a doctor's prescription for male wellness. Stephen C. Brewer. SelectBooks, Inc. 2016 256 p. illustrations (hardbound book : alk. paper) $24.95　　　**613**
1. Exercise 2. Nutrition 3. Heart diseases 4. Men -- Health and hygiene 5. Heart -- Diseases 6. Medicine and psychology
ISBN 9781590793626
LC 2015026737

This book, by Stephen C. Brewer, "is a sustainable, real-world approach to men's health. The book is divided into four sections designed to target a specific phase on your journey to well-being. In-depth detail is tailored to target five specific age groups and then subdivided by function. The guide takes a comprehensive look at every aspect of men's health from sexual health to cardiovascular and prostate." (Publisher's note)

"This accessible handbook is equal parts factual and friendly, and it will help men conquer their health fears and make wise choices for healthy, long lives." Pub Wkly

Columbia University/Health Service

The **Go** ask Alice book of answers; a guide to good physical, sexual, and emotional health. [by] Co-

lumbia University's Health Education Program. Holt & Co. 1998 345p pa $15.95　　　　　　**613**
1. Adolescence 2. Sex education 3. Youth -- Health and hygiene
ISBN 0-8050-5570-3
LC 98-3318

"The title within the title refers to a Web site maintained by Columbia University Health Services. Set up to answer questions about relationships, sex, physical and mental health, nutrition, and related matters, the site eventually was opened to the general public as a quick-reference forum. The book's seven chapters round up queries the site has received and responses to them from Columbia-associated health educators." Booklist

Includes bibliographical references

Dietert, Rodney

The **human** superorganism; How the Microbiome Is Revolutionizing the Pursuit of a Healthy Life. Rodney Dietert. Dutton 2016 352 p. (hardcover) $28　　　　　　　　　　　　　　　　　　　**613**
1. Health 2. Microbiology 3. Microbiota
ISBN 9781101983904
LC 2015041110

This book, by Rodney Dietert, "makes a sweeping, paradigm-shifting argument. It demolishes two fundamental beliefs that have blinkered all medical thinking until very recently: 1) Humans are better off as pure organisms free of foreign microbes; and 2) the human genome is the key to future medical advances. The microorganisms that we have sought to eliminate have been there for centuries supporting our ancestors." (Publisher's note)

"Dietert makes a fascinating case for an exciting, emerging field that offers a new way of thinking about the human body and health." Pub Wkly

Includes bibliographical references and index

Grigore, Adina

Skin cleanse; the simple, all-natural program for clear, calm, happy skin. Adina Grigore. HarperWave 2015 237 p. illustrations (hardback) $24.99　　**613**
1. Health 2. Skin -- Care 3. Nutrition 4. Self-care, Health 5. Detoxification (Health) 6. Skin -- Care and hygiene
ISBN 0062332554; 9780062332554
LC 2014044382

This book by Adina Grigore "helps readers diagnose and understand the underlying causes of their individual skin problems and offers all-natural recipes--using inexpensive ingredients that can be found at the grocery store to treat them effectively. From learning about how diet and lifestyle factors affect the quality of your skin to examining what is in the dozens of products we use every day, Grigore helps you take control over what goes on your skin." (Publisher's note)

Guiliano, Mireille

French women don't get facelifts; the secret of aging with style and attitude. Mireille Guiliano. Grand Central Life & Style 2013 272 p. (hardcover) $25　　　　　　　　　　　　　　　　　　　　**613**
1. Women -- France 2. Women -- Health and hygiene 3. Aging -- Psychological aspects 4. Older women

-- France -- Attitudes 5. Older women -- Health and hygiene -- France
ISBN 1455524115; 9781455524112

LC 2013017824

Author Mireille Guiliano's book "presents an insightful guide to the French way of aging with style, grace, and attitude. She encourages midlife women to adopt French-inspired remedies for aging woes, such as antiaging foods, regular exercise, sufficient sunlight, proper skin care, and plenty of water . . . The author provides a list of superfoods paired with easy-to-follow recipes, a straightforward skincare routine, product recommendations, and ways to stay physically active." (Library Journal)

Northrup, Christiane

Goddesses never age; the secret prescription for radiance, vitality, and well-being. Christiane Northrup, M.D. Hay House, Inc. 2015 408 p. illustration (hardback) $25.99   **613**
1. Aging 2. Women -- Health and hygiene 3. Physical fitness
ISBN 1401945163; 9781401945169

LC 2014029338

This book, by Christiane Northrup, "in chapters that blend personal stories and practical exercises with the latest research on health and aging, . . . lays out the principles of ageless living, from rejecting processed foods to releasing stuck emotions, from embracing our sensuality to connecting deeply with our Divine Source." (Publisher's note)

Pollan, Michael

In defense of food; an eater's manifesto. Penguin Press 2008 244p $21.95; pa $16   **613**
1. Nutrition 2. Eating customs
ISBN 978-1-59420-145-5; 1-59420-145-5; 978-0-14-311496-3 pa; 0-14-311496-4 pa

LC 2007037552

"Pollan will succeed in making you think twice about what you are piling up in your grocery cart or on your plate." Christ Sci Monit
Includes bibliographical references

Roizen, Michael F.

This is your do-over; the 7 secrets to losing weight, living longer, and getting a second chance at the life you want. Michael F. Roizen and Ted Spiker. Scribner 2015 358 p. illustrations (hardback) $26   **613**
1. Health 2. Weight loss 3. Vitality 4. Rejuvenation 5. Self-care, Health
ISBN 1501103334; 9781501103339; 9781501103346

LC 2014049798

In this book author Michael Roizen "provides the tools you need to halt bad health and start living at your peak vitality. In this book, he addresses all the areas that contribute to total-body wellness, including nutrition, exercise, sex, stress, sleep, and the brain. Using concrete strategies available to anyone of any age, Dr. Roizen shows you how to reset your health with his seven simple secrets to earning a Do-Over." (Publisher's note)

Smith, Rick

Toxin toxout; getting harmful chemicals out of our bodies and our world. Bruce Lourie, Rick Smith. St. Martin's Press 2014 304 p. (hardcover) $25.99   **613**
1. Pesticides 2. Environmental health 3. Detoxification (Health) 4. Environmentally induced diseases -- Nutritional aspects
ISBN 1250051339; 9781250051332

LC 2013049688

This book presents a "guide to the toxins in our everyday environment and how best to avoid them or get them out of our bodies. . . . The authors . . . focus on providing practical advice on how to avoid toxins (the short answer is to buy organic and natural products) and eliminate those that have accumulated from our bodies. . . . Toward the end of their book, [Bruce] Lourie and [Rick] Smith discuss some of the broader implications of their findings." (CCPA Monitor)

"In a collegial, straightforward style, Lourie and Smith quiz doctors and researchers, converse with wellness activists, visit organic stores and companies and, most interestingly, engage in a variety of experiments to track how the more than 80,000 synthetic chemicals in use today got into our bodies and what it will take to get them out." Booklist

Includes bibliographical references and index

Tanzi, Rudolph E.

Super genes; the hidden key to total well-being. Deepak Chopra, M.D. & Rudolph E. Tanzi, Ph.D. Harmony 2015 336 p. illustrations (hardback) $26   **613**
1. Heredity 2. Health self-care 3. Nature and nurture 4. Genes -- Popular works 5. Self-care, Health -- Popular works
ISBN 9780804140133; 9780804140157

LC 2015028562

This book, by Deepak Chopra and Rudolph E. Tanzi, "present[s] a bold new understanding of our genes and how simple changes in lifestyle can boost genetic activity. . . . You will always have the genes you were born with, but genes are dynamic, responding to everything we think, say, and do. Suddenly they've become our strongest allies for personal transformation." (Publisher's note)

"Chopra's name, along with his trademark blend of concrete suggestions with spiritual principles, will guarantee popularity." Booklist

Weil, Andrew

Eight weeks to optimum health; a proven program for taking full advantage of your body's natural healing power. Knopf 1997 276p $25; pa $13.95   **613**
1. Health self-care 2. Alternative medicine
ISBN 0-679-44715-6; 0-449-00026-5 pa

LC 96-51918

The book's "strength lies in its design, which uses small easy steps to achieve big changes. . . . As a physician, Weil is careful to substantiate every claim, and he debunks some of today's more extreme alternative health theories." Libr J
Includes bibliographical references

613.042   Personal health of specific sex groups

Vonn, Lindsey

Strong Is the New Beautiful; Embrace Your Natural Beauty, Eat Clean, and Harness Your Power. by Lindsey Vonn. HarperCollins 2016 256 p. color illustrations (ebook) $26.99; $27.99   **613.042**
1. Women -- Health and hygiene
ISBN 9780062400604; 0062400584; 9780062400581
In this book, author Lindsey Vonn "lays out the never-before-seen training routines and her overall philosophy that have helped her become the best female skier in the world—tailored for women of all shapes and sizes. Lindsey backs up her fitness program with advice on what to eat and how to work out, and kicks readers into high-gear, helping bolster their self-confidence and build a better body image, with the tips and tricks she's learned as a pro." (Publisher's note)
"Vonn has created an inspiring narrative, along with a seductive means of getting healthy and fit." Pub Wkly

613.2   Dietetics

Abbott, Christmas

The **Badass** Body Diet; The Breakthrough Diet and Workout for a Tight Booty, Sexy Abs, and Lean Legs. Christmas Abbott. HarperCollins 2015 384 p. color illustrations $27.99   **613.2**
1. Diet 2. Exercise
ISBN 0062390953; 9780062390950
In this book, author "Christmas Abbott shows how to attain the body of your dreams with a targeted eating strategy and total-body workout plan that will whip glutes and hips--and every problem area--into top shape. She dispels the myth of the health benefits of a "pear shape" body, teaches readers how to spot-reduce excess fat with targeted meal plans and recipes that zap cellulite, and galvanizes them with a quick and simple workout plan." (Publisher's note)
"Abbott's unadorned focus on fitness should appeal to any woman seeking to improve her body, regardless of body type." Pub Wkly

Bittman, Mark

Food matters; a guide to conscious eating with more than 75 recipes. Simon & Schuster 2009 326p il $24   **613.2**
1. Nutrition 2. Agriculture 3. Weight loss 4. Food industry 5. Eating customs
ISBN 978-1-4165-7564-1; 1-4165-7564-2
LC 2008-39593
The "Minimalist" columnist and author of How to Cook Everything outlines an eating plan that is comprised of environmentally responsible choices, in a guide that shares insight into the risks associated with livestock production.

Brown, Harriet

Body of truth; how science, history, and culture drive our obsession with weight--and what we can do about it. Harriet Brown. Da Capo Lifelong Books 2015 273 p. (hardback) $25.99   **613.2**
1. Body image 2. Body weight 3. Weight loss 4.

Reducing diets -- Evaluation 5. Weight loss -- Social aspects 6. Weight loss -- Psychological aspects
ISBN 0738217697; 9780738217697
LC 2014043431
In this book author Harriet Brown "systematically unpacks what's been offered as 'truth' about weight and health. Starting with the four biggest lies, Brown shows how research has been manipulated; how the medical profession is complicit in keeping us in the dark; how big pharma and big, empty promises equal big, big dollars; how much of what we know (or think we know) about health and weight is wrong. And how all of those affect all of us every day, whether we know it or not." (Publisher's note)
"A solid general overview of the scientific and cultural issues surrounding fatness and weight loss with an excellent starter bibliography." LJ
Includes bibliographical references and index

Buettner, Dan

The **Blue** Zones solution; eating and living like the world's healthiest people. Dan Buettner. National Geographic 2015 320 p. illustrations (hardcover : alk. paper) $26   **613.2**
1. Diet 2. Health 3. Nutrition 4. Functional foods
ISBN 1426211929; 9781426211928
LC 2014044932
Author "Dan Buettner . . . lays out a proven plan to maximize your health based on the practices of the world's healthiest people. Buettner reveals how to transform your health using smart eating and lifestyle habits gleaned from new research on the diets, eating habits, and lifestyle practices of the communities he's identified as 'Blue Zones'--those places with the world's longest-lived, and thus healthiest, people." (Publisher's note)
"Readers seeking a healthier lifestyle will appreciate this warm and encouraging book." LJ
Includes bibliographical references and index

Davis, Brenda

Becoming vegan; the complete reference on plant-based nutrition. Brenda Davis, RD, Vesanto Melina, MS, RD. Book Publishing Company 2014 ix, 611 p.p color illustrations (pbk.) $29.95 **613.2**
1. Veganism 2. Nutrition 3. Veganism -- Health aspects
ISBN 1570672970; 9781570672972
LC 2014018034
Authors "Brenda Davis and Vesanto Melina specifically designed this fully referenced, comprehensive edition to meet the needs of health professionals, academic librarians, and curriculum developers as well as lay readers with a deep interest in nutrition.
The authors explore the health benefits of vegan diets compared to other dietary choices; explain protein and amino acid requirements at various stages of life; describe fats and essential fatty acids and their value in plant-based diets." (Publisher's note)
"The book also carefully considers specific issues surrounding veganism during pregnancy and lactation, infancy, childhood, the teen years, and adulthood and provides practical advice for athletes and for those seeking to maintain a healthy weight. The science behind the recommendations is well documented with extensive chapter refer-

ences. Summing Up: Highly recommended. All nutrition collections." Choice

Includes bibliographical references (pages 449-532) and index

Duyff, Roberta Larson

American Dietetic Association complete food and nutrition guide; Roberta Larson Duyff. 4th ed. rev. and updated John Wiley & Sons Inc 2012 708 p. ill. (paper) $24.95   **613.2**

1. Diabetes 2. Nutrition

ISBN 9780470912072; 0470912073

LC 2012382537

This book, by Roberta Larson Duyff, "covers the basics on nutrition, managing weight, and healthy eating. It also provides easy steps and how-tos for selecting, preparing, and storing foods safely to get the most nutrition and flavor for your dollar, and more. Comprehensive, accessible, and easy-to-use, this valuable reference shows how to make healthy food choices to fit any lifestyle." (Publisher's note)

"The author's goal is 'to answer the whats, hows, and whys about food and nutrition' for wellness. This new edition . . . is divided into six sections covering food choices for wellness; the basics of nutrition; food selection and safety; special needs for various life stages; food choices for some selected health problems; and a selected list of resources." Choice

Includes bibliographical references and index

Esmonde-White, Miranda

Aging backwards; reverse the aging process and look 10 years younger in 30 minutes a day. Miranda Esmonde-White. HarperWave 2014 278 p. illustrations (hardback) $27.99   **613.2**

1. Aging 2. Longevity 3. Physical fitness 4. Rejuvenation 5. Aging -- Prevention

ISBN 0062313339; 9780062313331

LC 2014028452

In this book, author Miranda Esmonde-White "offers an eye-opening guide to anti-aging that provides essential tools to help anyone turn back the clock and look and feel younger no matter what age. . . . Miranda offers a groundbreaking guide on how to maintain and repair our cells, through scientifically designed workouts. Healthy cells prevent joint pain, muscle loss and weak bones—helping to control weight, increase energy, and improve strength and mobility." (Publisher's note)

Friedman, Howard S.

The **longevity** project; surprising discoveries for health and long life from the eight-decade study. [by] Howard S. Friedman and Leslie R. Martin. Hudson Street Press 2010 248p $25.95   **613.2**

1. Longevity

ISBN 978-1-594630-75-0; 1-594630-75-5

LC 2010-22833

"Analyzing the data from the Terman study and following up on the 1500 participants, . . . [the authors] investigate why some people live until old age while others die or become ill prematurely. Unlike most studies, this work looks at key psychological factors, habits, and patterns that affect health and longevity over time. Some of the authors' con-

clusions about achieving longevity are surprising. Factors such as the study participants' sociability, conscientiousness, happiness, and religious involvement were analyzed to show which patterns lead over time to an increased life span. The authors have provided a well-written and easy-to-follow analysis of this interesting study." Libr J

Includes bibliographical references

Hartwig, Melissa

The **whole30**; the 30-day guide to total health and food freedom. Melissa Hartwig and Dallas Hartwig; with Chef Richard Bradford; photography by Alexandra Grablewski. Houghton Mifflin Harcourt 2015 ix, 421 p.p color illustrations (hardcover) $30 **613.2**

1. Diet 2. Nutrition 3. Weight loss 4. Nutrition -- Popular works 5. Food habits -- Popular works 6. Weight loss -- Popular works 7. Diet therapy -- Popular works 8. Self-care, Health -- Popular works

ISBN 0544609719; 9780544609716

LC 2015007139

This book, by Melissa Hartwig and Dallas Hartwig, is a "step-by-step plan to break unhealthy habits, reduce cravings, improve digestion, and strengthen your immune system. . . . [It] features more than 100 chef-developed recipes, like Chimichurri Beef Kabobs and Halibut with Citrus Ginger Glaze, designed to build your confidence in the kitchen and inspire your taste buds. The book also includes real-life success stories, community resources, and an extensive FAQ." (Publisher's note)

"For those interested in trying the Whole30, this book is an invaluable guide that shouldn't be overlooked." Whole thirty

Heller, Marla

The **everyday** DASH diet cookbook; over 150 fresh and delicious recipes to speed weight loss, lower blood pressure, and prevent diabetes. by Marla Heller, MS, RD; with Rick Rodgers. Grand Central Life & Style 2013 214 p. (hardback) $26   **613.2**

1. Cookbooks 2. Hypertension -- Prevention 3. Reducing diets -- Recipes 4. Salt-free diet -- Recipes 5. Diabetes -- Diet therapy -- Recipes

ISBN 1455528064; 9781455528066

LC 2012045485

This cookbook looks at the "research-based DASH (dietary approaches to stop hypertension) diet," which "emphasizes 'real foods' and minimizes processed sugars, salt, cholesterol, and fats. Writing with veteran cookbook author [Rick] Rodgers . . . , leading DASH expert [Marla] Heller . . . offers easy recipes (e.g., crunchy broccoli slaw, rosemary pork chops with balsamic glaze) for readers living a healthy lifestyle." (Library Journal)

Includes bibliographical references and index

Hever, Julieanna

The **Vegiterranean** Diet; The New and Improved Mediterranean Eating Plan--with Deliciously Satisfying Vegan Recipes for Optimal Health. by Ju-

lieanna Hever. Da Capo Lifelong Books 2014 288 p. illustrations $17.99   **613.2**
1. Mediterranean cooking
ISBN 0738217891; 9780738217895

LC 2015304766

This Mediterranean diet cookbook, by Julieanna Hever, offers "comprehensive nutrition info, shopping lists with everyday ingredients, more than 40 delicious, budget-friendly recipes, flexible meal plans (great for families, too!), [and] strategies for overall health." (Publisher's note)

"Readers may recognize Hever from her Veria Living show What Would Julieanna Do? and appearances on programs such as The Dr. Oz Show. The author's strong media presence, combined with early accolades from established vegan chefs and advocates such as Colleen Patrick-Goudreau, increase the likelihood of demand. Readers seeking nutritional guidance will be pleased with the range of coverage." LJ

Jacobson, Howard

Proteinaholic; how our obsession with meat is killing us and what we can do about it. Garth Davis, M.D. HarperOne 2015 384 p. (hardback) $27.99   **613.2**
1. Diet in disease 2. Proteins in human nutrition 3. Meat
ISBN 9780062279309; 9780062279316

LC 2015020233

In this book, by Garth Davis, a "surgeon specializing in weight loss delivers a paradigm-shifting examination of the diet and health industry's focus on protein, explaining why it is detrimental to our health, and can prevent us from losing weight. . . . This . . . book reveals the truth about the dangers of protein and shares a proven approach to weight loss, health, and longevity." (Publisher's note)

"This title is easy to understand and, despite its infomercial-like tone, gives sound information that will motivate readers to improve their health." LJ

Leake, Lisa

100 days of real food; how we did it, what we learned, and 100 easy, wholesome recipes your family will love. by Lisa Leake. HarperCollinsPublishers 2014 360 p. color illustrations $29.99   **613.2**
1. Health 2. Cookbooks 3. Natural foods 4. Cooking -- Natural foods
ISBN 0062252550; 9780062252555

LC 2015303205

In this book, author Lisa Leake "draws from her hugely popular website to offer simple, affordable, family-friendly recipes and practical advice for eliminating processed foods from your family's diet. . . . Illustrated with 125 photographs and filled with step-by-step instructions, this hands-on cookbook and guide includes [a]dvice for navigating the grocery store and making smart purchases, [t]ips for reading ingredient labels, [and] 100 quick and easy recipes." (Publisher's note)

Includes bibliographical references and index

Lee, Janet

The **supplement** handbook; a trusted expert's guide to what works & what's worthless for more

than 100 conditions. Mark Moyad, MD, MPH; with Janet Lee, LAc. Rodale 2014 ix, 502 p.p (paperback) $24.99   **613.2**
1. Dietary supplements
ISBN 1623360358; 9781623360351

LC 2014035702

This handbook on supplements, by Mark Moyad, will "guide you through the proven (or debunked) treatment options for more than 100 common conditions--everything from arthritis, heartburn, and high cholesterol to fibromyalgia, migraines, and psoriasis. Dr. Moyad provides clear guidelines, sifting through conflicting information for a definitive answer you can use today." (Publisher's note)

"This book explains what supplements are, what they can and can't do, and when to use them. It also tells readers how to evaluate the information that is available about supplements.The bulk of the book discusses specific medical conditions, with recommendations for supplements based on evidence from research." Booklist

Ludwig, David

Always hungry? conquer cravings, retrain your fat cells, and lose weight permanently. David Ludwig. Grand Central Life & Style 2016 384 p. illustrations (hardback) $28   **613.2**
1. Hunger 2. Weight loss 3. Self-care, Health 4. Metabolism -- Regulation 5. Reducing diets -- Recipes
ISBN 1455533866; 9781455533862

LC 2015032645

This book, by David Ludwig, "explains why traditional diets don't work, and presents a radical new plan to help you lose weight without hunger, improve your health, and feel great. [It] turns dieting on its head with a three-phase program that ignores calories and targets fat cells directly. The recipes and meal plan include luscious high fat foods (like nuts and nut butters, full fat dairy, avocados, and dark chocolate), savory proteins, and natural carbohydrates." (Publisher's note)

"Ludwig's meal plans and recipes are excellent. This quality book on the basics of losing weight will appeal to all types of readers." Library Journal

Includes bibliographical references and index

Mann, Traci

Secrets from the eating lab; the science of weight loss, the myth of willpower, and why you should never diet again. Traci Mann, PhD. HarperWave 2015 272 p. illustrations (hardback) $26.99   **613.2**
1. Diet 2. Weight loss 3. Eating habits 4. Weight loss -- Social aspects 5. Reducing diets -- Social aspects 6. Weight loss -- Psychological aspects 7. Reducing diets -- Psychological aspects
ISBN 0062329235; 9780062329233

LC 2014049872

In this book, author Traci Mann "challenges assumptions--including those that make up the very foundation of the weight loss industry--about how diets work and why they fail. The result of more than two decades of research, it offers cutting-edge science and exciting new insights into the American obesity epidemic and our relationship with eating and food." (Publisher's note)

"Mann cites study after study to make her case; titles her last chapter, 'Final Words: Diet Schmiet'; and declares that no single eating plan will ever make the pounds melt away forever. 'The fragility of willpower' and 'a culture of ubiquitous temptations' conspire against the best-laid plans. Her bottom-line recommendation: 'reach your leanest livable weight.' Sold." Booklist

Mercola, Joseph M., 1954-

Effortless healing; 9 simple ways to sidestep illness, shed excess weight, and help your body fix itself. Joseph Mercola. Random House Inc 2015 323 p. illustrations (hardback) $26   **613.2**
1. Nutrition 2. Health self-care
ISBN 0553417975; 9780553417975; 9781781805091
LC 2014022046

In this book, "online health pioneer, natural medicine advocate, and . . . author Dr. Joseph Mercola reveals the nine simple secrets to a healthier, thinner you." His advice includes "avoiding certain meat and fish, but enjoying butter. . ., eating sauerkraut (and other fermented foods) to improve your immune system and your mood . . . , [and] walking barefoot outside to decrease system-wide inflammation (and because it just feels great)." (Publisher's note)

Moss, Michael

★ **Salt,** sugar, fat; how the food giants hooked us. Michael Moss. Random House Inc 2013 480 p. (hardcover) $28   **613.2**
1. Obesity 2. Junk food -- Marketing 3. Food industry -- United States 4. Food industry and trade -- United States 5. Nutrition -- Economic aspects -- United States 6. Food habits -- Economic aspects -- United States
ISBN 1400069807; 9780679604778; 9781400069804
LC 2012033034

Pulitzer prize winner Michael Moss offers an exposé of the U.S. food industry. He "explains the two-faced science of salt, sugar, and fat, which impart tantalizing tastes and luscious mouth-feel that light up the same neural circuits that narcotics do . . . while causing epidemic obesity, cardiovascular disease, and diabetes. But he also crafts an . . . insiders' view of the food industry, where these ingredients are the main weapons in a brutally competitive war for stomach-share." (Publishers Weekly)

Nesheim, Malden

Why calories count; from science to politics. Marion Nestle and Malden Nesheim. University of California Press 2012 288 p. (California studies in food and culture) (hardback : alk. paper) $29.95   **613.2**
1. Diet 2. Nutrition 3. Weight loss 4. Eating customs 5. Food -- Caloric content 6. Food Industry
ISBN 9780520262881
LC 2011044785

This book "assists readers in evaluating diet claims, formulating strategies to lose, gain, or maintain weight, and learning how to make healthy food choices. [Marion] Nestle . . . and [Malden] Nesheim . . . focus on the history of the calorie and its relationship to body weight, the science behind metabolism, how to estimate calories in a given portion, and

. . . the role of big business in creating calorie-laden food." (Library Journal)
Includes bibliographical references and index.

Netzer, Corinne T.

The **complete** book of food counts; Corinne T. Netzer. Dell 2012 903 p. (pbk.) $8.99   **613.2**
1. Diet therapy 2. Low-calorie diet 3. Nutrition -- Tables 4. Food -- Composition -- Tables 5. Brand name products -- Composition -- Tables
ISBN 0440245613; 9780440245612
LC 2014415863

Written by Corinne T. Netzer, "this vital reference provides all the essential counts you need to know for generic and brand-name foods--as well as the latest gourmet and health foods and a variety of ethnic cuisines. Whether it's fresh or frozen, fast-food or slow-cooked, 'The Complete Book of Food Counts' is an A to Z guide to the choices in your supermarket aisles, at your local farmer's market, or served in your favorite restaurants!" (Publisher's note)

Wansink, Brian

Slim by design; mindless eating solutions for home, school, grocery stores, restaurants, and more. Brian Wansink. William Morrow 2014 320 p. color illustrations, color map $26.99   **613.2**
1. Diet 2. Architectural design
ISBN 0062136526; 9780062136527
LC 2015304142

In this book "author Brian Wansink introduces groundbreaking solutions for designing our most common spaces--schools, restaurants, grocery stores, and home kitchens, among others--in order to make positive changes in how we approach and manage our diets. Wansink presents compelling research conducted at the Food and Brand Lab at Cornell University by way of cartoons, drawings, charts, graphs, floor plans, and more." (Publisher's note)
"Every plant or office manager, school lunch supervisor, restaurateur, and parent should have this book." LJ

613.25   Weight-losing diet

Cruikshank, Tiffany

Meditate your weight; the 21-day retreat to optimize your metabolism and feel great. Tiffany Cruikshank. Harmony 2016 336 p. (hardback) $22   **613.25**
1. Meditation 2. Metabolism 3. Weight loss 4. Metabolism -- Regulation 5. Weight loss -- Psychological aspects
ISBN 9780804187961
LC 2015033619

This book, by Tiffany Cruikshank, "helps you explore and release what's weighing you down physically, emotionally, and mentally—the mental blocks, thoughts, habits, and behaviors that stand in your way—to make it easier to think more clearly, make better choices, and maximize metabolism. As you lighten up on the inside, you'll lighten up on the outside." (Publisher's note)
Includes bibliographical references (pages 305-311) and index.

613.6 Personal safety and special topics of health

Bailey, Elizabeth

Safe kids, smart parents; what parents need to know to keep their children safe. Rebecca Bailey, Ph.D. with Elizabeth Bailey; introduction by Terry Probyn. Simon & Schuster 2013 224 p. (trade paper : alk. paper) $15   **613.6**

1. Children 2. Safety education 3. Parenting 4. Children -- Protection 5. Critical thinking in children 6. Children -- Crimes against -- Prevention

ISBN 1476700443; 9781476700441

LC 2012047452

This book is a guide to children's safety. It is "divided into two sections, one intended for parents and guardians, the other written especially for children. The message in both is the same: the need for parents and children (whether toddlers or teens) to be aware of their environment and vigilant. The authors emphasize the difficult reality that, these days, children must be taught to be wary of all strangers, even those who appear to be in trouble and are requesting help." (Kirkus Reviews)

Canterbury, Dave

Bushcraft 101; a field guide to the art of wilderness survival. Dave Canterbury. Adams Media 2014 256 p. (pb) $16.99   **613.6**

1. Camping 2. Wilderness survival 3. Camping -- Handbooks, manuals, etc 4. Outdoor life -- Handbooks, manuals, etc 5. Outdoor recreation -- Handbooks, manuals, etc 6. Wilderness survival -- Handbooks, manuals, etc 7. Camping -- Equipment and supplies -- Handbooks, manuals, etc

ISBN 1440579776; 9781440579776

LC 2014012976

This book, by Dave Canterbury, "gets you ready for your next backcountry trip with advice on making the most of your time outdoors. Based on the 5Cs of Survivability--cutting tools, covering, combustion devices, containers, and cordages--this valuable guide offers only the most important survival skills to help you craft resources from your surroundings and truly experience the beauty and thrill of the wilderness." (Publisher's note)

Dorn, Michael

Staying alive; how to act fast and survive deadly encounters. Michael Dorn, Stephen Satterly, Dr. Sonayia Shepherd, Chris Dorn. Barrons Educational Series, Inc. 2014 292 p. illustrations $14.99 **613.6**

1. Survival skills 2. Survival

ISBN 1438004087; 9781438004082

LC 2013031901

In this book, authors Michael Dorn, Stephen Satterly, Dr. Sonayia Shepherd, and Chris Dorn "take the successful strategies that have been used to avert planned school shootings, bombings, and other deadly events and demonstrate how those techniques can be utilized by the average person. . . . With an in-depth look at mass casualty attacks across the centuries, . . . [it] offers everything the average person needs to know in order respond to, and recover from, a crisis." (Publisher's note)

"A chilling and comprehensive crisis-preparedness guide." LJ

Includes bibliographical references and index

Gervasi, Lori Hartman

Fight like a girl-- and win; defense decisions for women. St. Martin's Griffin 2007 285p pa $14.99   **613.6**

1. Safety education 2. Self-defense for women

ISBN 978-0-312-35772-6; 0-312-35772-9

LC 2007-17216

"Although the author has a black belt in karate, she maintains that 90 percent of self-defense is awareness and common sense. She helps readers set up absolute rules and boundaries, sharpen their observation skills, and trust in their intuition. Physical fitness is stressed, and resources are provided for further training." Libr J

Includes bibliographical references

Kostigen, Thomas M.

National Geographic extreme weather survival guide; understand, prepare, survive, recover. by Thomas M. Kostigen. Random House Inc 2014 384 p. illustrations, maps (pbk. : alk. paper) $30 **613.6**

1. Extreme weather 2. Survival skills 3. Weather 4. Severe storms 5. Natural disasters 6. Emergency management -- Handbooks, manuals, etc

ISBN 142621376X; 9781426213762

LC 2014005362

This book, by Thomas M. Kostigen, "tells you how to plan ahead and prepare, respond to emergencies, and survive the worst-case scenarios. From the risks of building on changing coastlines to the safety kit you should have packed up at home, from the telltale signs of a hurricane on the horizon to how to power up when the grid goes down--this will be the one book to carry with you through all kinds of bad weather." (Publisher's note)

"Readers intending to use this as a reference will want to purchase a copy to keep at home. Libraries may wish to purchase for the book's excellent photographs, along with the browsable short sections and checklists. A young readers' version, Extreme Weather: Surviving Tornadoes, Sandstorms, Hailstorms, Blizzards, Hurricanes, and More! is available through National Geographic Kids." LJ

Includes bibliographical references and index

Extreme weather survival guide

Marquis, Sarah

Wild by nature; from Siberia to Australia, three years alone in the wilderness on foot. Sarah Marquis. Thomas Dunne Books/St. Martin's Press 2016 272 p. color illustrations, maps (hardcover) $26.99 **613.6**

1. Hiking 2. Wilderness survival

ISBN 9781250081971

LC 2015039458

This travel memoir, by Sarah Marquis, "takes you on the trail of her ten-thousand-mile solo hike across the remote Gobi desert from Siberia to Thailand, at which point she was transported by boat to complete the hike at her favorite tree in Australia. Against nearly insurmountable odds and relying on hunting and her own wits, Sarah Marquis survived the Mafia, drug dealers, . . . temperatures from subzero to scorching, . . . and a life-threatening abscess." (Publisher's note)

"Her tales of whom she meets and what she sees are as bracing as she is. Straightforward and forthright, this is adventure writing as it was meant to be." Booklist

Moore, Alexis

Cyber self-defense; expert advice to avoid online predators, identity theft, and cyberbullying. Alexis Moore and Laurie J. Edwards. Lyons Press 2014 272 p. illustration (paperback) $16.95   **613.6**
   1. Computer crimes 2. Computer security 3. Internet -- Safety measures 4. Cyberbullying 5. Online identity theft -- Prevention
   ISBN 1493005693; 9781493005697
                 LC 2014027221

This book, by Alexis Moore and Laurie J. Edwards, offers advice for online personal security. It "introduces the ten most common personality profiles of cyberstalkers—such as Attention-Getting, Jealous, Manipulative, Controlling, and Narcissistic—and their threatening online behaviors. . . . Case studies illustrate how that particular cybercriminal operates, and . . . offer[] tips to prevent and/or recover from each type of cybercrime." (Publisher's note)

Includes bibliographical references and index

Rawles, James Wesley

Tools for survival; what you need to survive when you're on your own. James Wesley Rawles. Plume 2014 368 p. (paperback) $18   **613.6**
   1. Self-reliance 2. Survival skills 3. Alternative lifestyles 4. Survival 5. Self-reliant living
   ISBN 0452298121; 9780452298125
                 LC 2014032904

This book, by James Wesley Rawles, provides "essential survival advice from the world's preeminent expert in preparedness. . . . [He] details the tools needed to survive anything from a short-term disruption to a long-term, grid-down scenario." (Publisher's note)

Stilwell, Alexander

The encyclopedia of survival techniques. Lyons Press 2007 192p il map pa $19.95   **613.6**
   1. Survival skills 2. Wilderness survival
   ISBN 978-1-59921-314-9
   First published 2000
This guide covers preparation, basic skills, equipment, various terrains, natural disasters, and first aid.

Wiseman, John

SAS survival handbook; the ultimate guide to surviving anywhere. John "Lofty" Wiseman. 3rd edition William Morrow 2014 672 p. illustrations pbk $21.99   **613.6**
   1. Survival skills 2. Wilderness survival
   ISBN 0062378074; 9780062378071
                 LC 2014956877

"The ultimate guide to surviving anywhere, now updated with more than 100 pages of additional material. Revised to reflect the latest in survival knowledge and technology, and covering new topics such as urban survival and terrorism, the internationally bestselling SAS Survival Handbook

is the definitive resource for all campers, hikers, and outdoor adventurers." (Publisher's note)

Zeisler, Avital

Weapons of fitness; the women's ultimate guide to fitness, self-defense, and empowerment. Avital Zeisler. Avery 2015 240 p. $20   **613.6**
   1. Self-defense for women 2. Women -- Physical fitness 3. Physical fitness
   ISBN 1583335692; 9781583335697
                 LC 2014044613

This book, by Avital Zeisler, offers a "self-defense and fitness book for women by a ballerina-turned-self-defense expert. . . . After ballerina Avital Zeisler was savagely attacked as a young woman, she . . . took action to train with experts in self-defense from around the world. Seeking a method specific to women and using Krav Maga as a base, she created her own self-defense program: the Soteria Method." (Publisher's note)

613.69   Survival

Canterbury, Dave

Advanced bushcraft; an expert field guide to the art of wilderness survival. Dave Canterbury. Adams Media 2015 256 p. illustrations (paperback) $16.99   **613.69**
   1. Wilderness survival 2. Camping -- Handbooks, manuals, etc 3. Outdoor life -- Handbooks, manuals, etc 4. Outdoor recreation -- Handbooks, manuals, etc 5. Wilderness survival -- Handbooks, manuals, etc 6. Camping -- Equipment and supplies -- Handbooks, manuals, etc
   ISBN 1440587965; 9781440587962
                 LC 2015008301

This book, by Dave Canterbury, "goes beyond bushcraft basics to teach you how to survive in the backcountry with little or no equipment. . . . He covers crucial survival skills like tracking to help you get even closer to wildlife, crafting medicines from plants, and navigating without the use of a map or compass. He also offers ways to improvise and save money on bushcraft essentials like fire-starting tools and packs." (Publisher's note)

613.7   Physical fitness

American College of Sports Medicine

★ Complete guide to fitness & health; Barbara Bushman, editor. Human Kinetics 2011 396p il pa $21.95   **613.7**
   1. Health 2. Exercise 3. Physical fitness
   ISBN 978-0-7360-9337-8; 0-7360-9337-0
                 LC 2011-6563

"Contributions from a range of academics (many affiliated with the ACSM) distill the current thinking on nutrition and exercise for all ages and for adults with chronic conditions such as arthritis and diabetes. They discuss how to determine your current levels of fitness, create a graduated fitness plan and coordinate it with proper eating habits, and measure your progress and maintain your optimum level. Chapters include recommendations for those with special health and medical conditions, such as diabetes, high cholesterol, high blood pressure, and arthritis. . . . Anyone who is serious about getting in shape will want this guide." Libr J

Includes bibliographical references

Bonifonte, Philip

T'ai chi for seniors; how to gain flexibility, strength, and inner peace. New Page Bks. 2004 213p il pa $16.99   **613.7**

1. Tai chi

ISBN 1-564-14697-9

LC 2003-60207

The author describes the ancient Chinese exercise that focuses "on easy, gentle movements that increase aerobic capacity, decrease blood pressure and stress, and improve balance and joint function. Along with a short history of various tai chi styles philosophies, the text features breathing techniques, warm-up exercises, movement forms, and meditation exercises with modifications for those with limited mobility." Libr J

Broad, William J.

The science of yoga; William J. Broad. Simon & Schuster 2012 xxxi, 298p ill.   **613.7**

1. Exercise 2. Hatha yoga 3. Yoga -- History

ISBN 9781451641424; 9781451641431; 9781451641448

LC 2011020408

This book, "[f]ive years in the making, . . . draws on more than a century of . . . research to present the first impartial evaluation of a practice thousands of years old. It celebrates what's real and shows what's illusory, describes what's uplifting and beneficial and what's flaky and dangerous--and why. Broad illuminates how yoga can lift moods and inspire creativity. He exposes moves that can cripple and kill. . . . [The book] presents a . . . body of evidence that raises questions about whether humans have latent capabilities for entering states of suspended animation and unremitting sexual bliss. 'The Science of Yoga' takes us on a . . . tour of unknown yoga that goes from old archives in Calcutta to the world capitals of medical research, from storied ashrams to spotless laboratories, from sweaty yoga studios with master teachers to the cozy offices of yoga healers." (Publisher's note)

Budig, Kathryn

Aim true; love your body, eat without fear, nourish your spirit, discover true balance! Kathryn Budig. William Morrow 2016 336 p. (paperback) $24.99   **613.7**

1. Self 2. Yoga 3. Health 4. Exercise 5. Hatha yoga 6. Physical fitness 7. Women -- Health and hygiene

ISBN 0062419714; 9780062419712

LC 2015034599

In this book author Kathryn Budig "extends her empowering message beyond the [yoga] mat. Whether your goal is to love who you are right now, reshape the way you view food, develop a meditation practice, or discover new ways to embrace the great balancing act that is life, this holistic

approach to yoga, diet, and mindfulness has something for you." (Publisher's note)

"In an age that increasingly commercializes the ancient practice of yoga, Budig's wholesome, down-to-earth outlook is welcome, sure to aid readers of all shapes and sizes in establishing healthy food and exercise patterns while practicing self-love and acceptance." Publisher's Weekly

Contreras, Bret

Strong curves; a woman's guide to building a better butt and body. Victory Belt Pub. 2013 320 p. color illustrations $34.95   **613.7**

1. Exercise 2. Women -- Health and hygiene

ISBN 1936608642; 9781936608645

Written by Bret Contreras, "'Strong Curves' offers an extensive fitness and nutrition guide for women seeking to improve their physique, function, strength, and mobility. . . . Each page is packed with information decoding the female anatomy, providing a better understanding as to why most fitness programs fail to help women reach their goals." (Publisher's note)

Cordoza, Glen

Becoming a supple leopard; the ultimate guide to resolving pain, preventing injury, and optimizing athletic performance. by Kelly Starrett, Glen Cordoza. Victory Belt Pub. 2013 400 p. color illustrations $59.95   **613.7**

1. Human locomotion 2. Physical education

ISBN 1936608588; 9781936608584

This book, by Kelly Starrett with Glen Cordoza, "maps out a detailed system comprised of more than two hundred techniques and illuminates common movement errors that cause injury and rob you of speed, power, endurance, and strength. Whether you are a professional athlete, a weekend warrior, or simply someone wanting to live healthy and free from restrictions, . . . [this book] will teach you how to maintain your body and harness your genetic potential." (Publisher's note)

Durant, John

Spartan Fit; 30 Days. Transform Your Mind. Transform Your Body. Commit to Grit. by Joe De Sena and John Durant. Houghton Mifflin Harcourt 2016 256 p. illustrations $24   **613.7**

1. Physical fitness

ISBN 0544439600; 9780544439603

This book, by Joe De Sena and John Durant, presents "a complete 30-day workout and diet plan to help you reach peak performance. . . . De Sena designed the Spartan races to test overall conditioning: strength, flexibility, endurance, and speed. His signature take-no-prisoners approach to achieving physical and mental fitness has taken the endurance world by storm and inspired millions." (Publisher's note)

"This book is ideal for workout enthusiasts who want to push themselves to the limit." Pub Wkly

Includes bibliographical references (page 201) and recipes.

Epstein, David

The **sports** gene; inside the science of extraordinary athletic performance. David Epstein. Current 2013 352 p. $26.95   **613.7**
  1. Athletes 2. Genetics 3. Human genetics 4. Sports -- Physiological aspects
  ISBN 1591845114; 9781591845119
                    LC 2013013443

In this book, David Epstein investigates the connection between genetics and athletic ability. "Drawing on interviews with athletes and scientists, he points out that 'a nation succeeds in a sport not only by having many people who practice prodigiously at sport-specific skills, but also by getting the best all-around athletes into the right sports in the first place.'" (Publishers Weekly)

"[T]his book is essential reading for sports fans interested in the science of sports, and for readers (not scholars) interested in the science of human differences." LJ
Includes bibliographical references and index

Fitness and exercise sourcebook; edited by Amy L. Sutton. 3rd ed; Omnigraphics 2007 663p il (Health reference series) $87   **613.7**
  1. Exercise 2. Physical fitness
  ISBN 978-0-7808-0946-8; 0-7808-0946-7
                    LC 2006-36852
  First published 1996
  Includes bibliographical references

Grossman, Gail Boorstein

Restorative yoga for life; Gail Boorstein Grossman, E-RYT, CYKT. Adams Media Corp 2014 254 p. color illustrations (pb) $19.99   **613.7**
  1. Rest 2. Yoga 3. Hatha yoga 4. Relaxation
  ISBN 1440575207; 9781440575204
                    LC 2014026432

This book, by Gail Boorstein Grossman, "teaches you how to practice restorative yoga--a form of yoga that focuses on physical and mental relaxation through poses aided by props. . . . While restorative yoga is beneficial for your entire body, Gail also shows you how to treat more than twenty ailments, such as headaches, digestive issues, and anxiety, through specific yoga poses and sequences." (Publisher's note)

Hanoch, Doron

The **yoga** lifestyle; Using the Flexitarian Method to Ease Stress, Find Balance, and Create a Healthy Life. Doron Hanoch. Llewellyn Publications 2016 384 p. illustrations $19.99   **613.7**
  1. Health 2. Hatha yoga 3. Vegetarianism 4. Stress management 5. Vegetarians 6. Medicine, Ayurvedic
  ISBN 9780738748665
                    LC 2016002999

This book, by Doron Hanoch, "expands on the concept of the flexitarian diet to help you build an entire flexitarian lifestyle. Integrating yoga, Ayurveda, breathing practices, meditation, nutrition, and recipes—the flexitarian method takes a holistic approach to cultivating health and joy. Presenting techniques that can be utilized immediately, this book helps you become flexible in mind and body so that

you can adapt to the needs and changes of today's world." (Publisher's note)

"It is clear from this thoughtful guide that Hanoch has the determination and know-how to introduce readers from all walks of life to a happier and healthier mode of living." Pub Wkly
Includes bibliographical references

Hesson, James L.

Weight training for life; 9th ed.; Wadsworth/Cengage Learning 2010 178p il $59.95   **613.7**
  1. Weight lifting
  ISBN 978-0-495-55909-2; 0-495-55909-1
                    LC 2010291364
  First published 1985 by Morton

"The text contains hundreds of full-color photos demonstrating exercises and proper techniques. It also contains forms for writing goals, planning a personal weight-training program, and recording circumference, strength, and muscle endurance measurements." Publisher's note
Includes bibliographical references

Hines, Emmett W.

Fitness swimming; [by] Emmett Hines. 2nd ed.; Human Kinetics 2008 224p il pa $18.95   **613.7**
  1. Swimming 2. Physical fitness
  ISBN 978-0-7360-7457-5; 0-7360-7457-0
                    LC 2008-13353
  First published 1999

The author "has created 60 . . . workouts and 16 sample programs, each arranged into suggested training zones to correspond to your fitness level and performance goals. . . . The text covers stretching, warm-up and cool-down methods, heart rate zone targets, expanded instruction for stroke efficacy, progressive drills, conditioning tips, and fitness assessments." Publisher's note
Includes bibliographical references

Isacowitz, Rael

Pilates; Rael Isacowitz. 2nd ed Human Kinetics 2014 373 p. illustrations $22.95   **613.7**
  1. Pilates method
  ISBN 1450434169; 9781450434164
                    LC 2013019507

This book, by Rael Isacowitz, is a "comprehensive guide on Pilates. . . . In this second edition, [a] world-renowned Pilates expert . . . shows you the same repertoire that he has used to train multiple Olympians as well as an elite group of professional instructors who work with celebrities and athletes around the world." (Publisher's note)
Includes bibliographical references and index

Krasno, Jeff

Wanderlust; A Modern Yogi's Guide to Discovering Your Best Self. Jeff Krasno, Sarah Herrington, and Nicole Lindstrom. St. Martin's Press 2015 304 p. illustrations (chiefly color) $24.99   **613.7**
  1. Yoga 2. Self-perception
  ISBN 1623363500; 9781623363505
                    LC 2015023375

This book by Jeff Krasno, Sarah Herrington, and Nicole Lindstrom "a road map for the millions of people engaged in cultivating their best selves. For the 20 million people who grab their yoga mats in the United States every week, this book gives a completely unique way to understand 'yoga'--not just as something to do in practice, but as a broader principle for living." (Publisher's note)

"A reader can, in effect, experience the festival's essence through the book, which includes yoga routines, meditation guidance, blank pages for guided journaling and drawing, and recipes for conscious eating. The richly illustrated volume is a souvenir, a sampler of yoga lifestyle activities, and, perhaps, a vicarious trip for those who have yet to go in search of their own 'true north.'" Pub Wkly

Kunitz, Daniel

Lift; Fitness Culture, from Naked Greeks and Acrobats to Jazzercise and Ninja Warriors. Daniel Kunitz. Harper Wave 2016 336 p. (hardback) $26.99   **613.7**

1. Exercise 2. Physical fitness 3. Sports -- History 4. Exercise -- Social aspects 5. Physical fitness -- Social aspects 6. Physical education and training -- Social aspects
ISBN 9780062336187

LC 2016004087

This book by Daniel Kunitz explores "the ways in which human exercise and physical ideals have changed over time—and what we can learn from our past. . . . Humans have been conditioning our bodies . . . for a variety of reasons: to imitate gods, to be great warriors, to build nations, . . . to achieve physical perfection. . . . Behind each of these goals is a story and method of exercise that . . . sheds light on aspects of . . . multi-faceted fitness culture of today." (Publisher's note)

"Kunitz includes his own challenges with fitness along the way, making this a book not just for those interested in the roots of fitness, but for anyone who struggles to live healthily." Pub Wkly

Includes bibliographical references ([291] - 304) and index.

Lacerda, Daniel

2,100 Asanas; the complete yoga poses. Daniel Lacerda, Founder of Mr. Yoga, Inc. Black Dog & Leventhal 2015 736 p. color illustrations (hardback) $35   **613.7**

1. Hatha yoga 2. Yoga 3. Exercise
ISBN 9781631910104

LC 2015026283

This book, by Daniel Lacerda, "is a . . . meticulously crafted catalog of yoga poses and modifications. . . . Each photograph features an expert yogi performing the pose to perfection. . . . The book is organized into eight major types of poses-standing, seated, core, quadruped, backbends, inversions, prone, and supine-and further broken down by families of poses that progress from easiest to more challenging." (Publisher's note)

"For readers with an interest in yoga, from beginners to advanced experts." Library Journal

Twenty-one hundered Asanas

Two thousand and one hundred Asanas

Liebman, Hollis Lance

Encyclopedia of Exercise Anatomy; by Hollis Liebman. Firefly Books Ltd 2014 392 p. color illustrations $49.95   **613.7**

1. Exercise
ISBN 1770854436; 9781770854437

LC 2015301045

This book on exercise, by Hollis Liebman, "enables the reader to tailor a personalized and professional program that will meet specific needs. A runner can dip into yoga to improve his breathing; a muscle builder can shape her legs with cycling workouts; a gymnast can combine yoga with core stability and strength exercises, and a woman over 50 can design a program that fits into her busy life." (Publisher's note)

"This useful title, which will also work well as a circulating item, presents that something extra for fitness enthusiasts who want to become serious about their conditioning." LJ

McClusky, Mark

Faster, higher, stronger; how sports science is creating a new generation of superathletes, and what we can learn from them. Mark McClusky. Hudson Street Press 2014 288 p. (alk. paper) $25.95 **613.7**

1. Sports science 2. Sports medicine 3. Athletes -- Training 4. Sports sciences 5. Athletes -- Training of
ISBN 1594631530; 9781594631535

LC 2014021223

This book, by Mark McClusky, explores how "today, it's impossible to separate the achievements of athletes from the scientists who support them. . . . [This volume] brings readers behind the scenes with a new generation of athletes, coaches, and scientists whose accomplishments are changing our understanding of human physical achievement and completely redefining the limits of the human body." (Publisher's note)

"All of this trickles down to amateur athletics as well, and McClusky does a good job of relating cutting-edge science to people wanting to run their 5K a little faster or shave a few strokes off their golf handicap." Booklist

Includes bibliographical references and index

Pagano, Joan

Strength training exercises for women; exercises for women. Joan Pagano. DK Publishing 2014 336 p. color illustrations $22.95   **613.7**

1. Weight lifting 2. Women -- Health and hygiene 3. Muscle strength 4. Exercise for women 5. Weight training for women 6. Physical fitness for women
ISBN 1465415807; 9781465415806

LC 2014397527

Written by Joan Pagano, "Packed with more than 200 visual step-by-step exercises designed to burn calories, strengthen the core, and tone the body, 'Strength Training for Women' is a must-have for core-conscious women who want to target key areas of their body and maintain all-round strength and fitness." (Publisher's note)

Strength training for women; tone up, burn calories, stay strong. Dorling Kindersley 2005 160p il pa $15   **613.7**

1. Weight lifting 2. Physical fitness 3. Women --

Health and hygiene
ISBN 0-7566-0595-4; 978-0-7566-0595-7

LC 2005-295208

The author "begins with a three-part fitness test and questionnaire to assess whether the reader should consult a doctor before beginning her program. For true beginners, she provides an anatomy chart that depicts the major muscle groups and the exercises that are best suited to them. She dispels fitness myths like 'lifting weights will bulk you up' and 'you can spot reduce,' and talks about the risk factors, exercise guidelines and restrictions of osteoporosis. . . . This book may be one of the best substitutes for pricey gym memberships and personal trainers." Publ Wkly

Reynolds, Gretchen

The **first** 20 minutes; surprising science reveals how we can exercise better, train smarter, live longer. Gretchen Reynolds. Hudson Street Press 2012 xvii, 266 p.p **613.7**

1. Health 2. Exercise 3. Physical fitness 4. Exercise -- Popular Works 5. Exercise -- Physiological aspects 6. Physical Fitness -- Popular Works 7. Exercise -- physiology -- Popular Works 8. Physical education and training -- Physiological aspects
ISBN 1594630933; 9781594630934

LC 2012000321

This book by Gretchen Reynolds offers "findings about the mental and physical benefits of exercise, personal stories from scientists and laypeople alike, as well as researched-based prescriptions for readers, . . . show[ing] what kind of exercise—and how much—is necessary to stay healthy, get fit, and attain a smaller jeans size. Inspired by Reynolds's . . . 'Phys Ed' column for 'The New York Times,' this book explains how exercise affects the body in distinct ways and provides the tools readers need to achieve their fitness goals, whether that's a faster 5K or staying trim." (Publisher's note)

Schuler, Lou

Strong; Nine Workout Programs for Women to Burn Fat, Boost Metabolism, and Build Strength for Life. by Lou Schuler and Alwyn Cosgrove. Avery, an imprint of Penguin Random House 2015 304 p. illustrations (hardback) $27.95 **613.7**

1. Exercise 2. Weight lifting 3. Women -- Health and hygiene 4. Exercise for women 5. Weight training for women
ISBN 9781583335758

LC 2015015248

In this book, fitness author Lou Schuler and strength coach Alwyn Cosgrove "present a comprehensive strength and conditioning plan to help women burn fat and build muscle by getting them off the machines and revolutionizing how they work out." (Publisher's note)

"This book is thoughtful, precise, and well-geared to providing women of all ages and fitness backgrounds with the knowledge and tools necessary for building strength." Pub Wkly

Starrett, Kelly

Ready to run; unlocking your potential to run naturally. Simon & Schuster 2014 288 p. $29.95 **613.7**

1. Running 2. Athletes -- Wounds and injuries
ISBN 1628600098; 9781628600094

"The harsh effects of too much sitting and too much time wearing the wrong shoes has left us shackled to lower back problems, chronic knee injuries, and debilitating foot pain. In this book [by Kelly Starrett and T. J. Murphy], you will learn the 12 standards that will prepare your body for a lifetime of top-performance running." (Publisher's note)

Taubes, Gary

Why we get fat and what to do about it. Alfred A. Knopf 2011 257p $24.95 **613.7**

1. Obesity 2. Weight loss 3. Low-carbohydrate diet
ISBN 978-0-307-27270-6; 0-307-27270-2

LC 2010-34248

The author "assures readers that overweight and obesity are not character flaws but a disorder of fat accumulation; most of the book deals with this issue in detail. This brave, paradigm-shifting man uses logic and the primary literature to unhinge the nutritional mantra of the last 80 years that an imbalance of 'calories in versus calories out' leads to weight change." Choice

Includes bibliographical references

613.794 Sleep

Huffington, Arianna Stassinopoulos, 1950-

The **sleep** revolution; transforming your life, one night at a time. Arianna Huffington. Harmony 2016 400 p. (hardback) $26 **613.794**

1. Sleep 2. Sleep deprivation 3. Sleep -- Health aspects
ISBN 9781101904008

LC 2015039918

This book, by Arianna Huffington, is an "exploration of sleep from all angles, from the history of sleep, to the role of dreams in our lives, to the consequences of sleep deprivation, and the new golden age of sleep science that is revealing the vital role sleep plays in our every waking moment and every aspect of our health–from weight gain, diabetes, and heart disease to cancer and Alzheimer's." (Publisher's note)

"So compelling and informative is Huffington's book that everyone should read it and sleep!" Booklist

Includes bibliographical references (pages [315]-375) and index.

613.9 Birth control, reproductive technology, sex hygiene, sexual techniques

Comfort, Alex, 1920-2000

The **joy** of sex; The Ultimate Revised Edition. Alex Comfort, Susan Quilliam. Rev. ed. Crown Publishers 2008 288 p. ill. (some col.) (hc) $29.95 **613.9**

1. Sex 2. Sex education 3. Sex -- Psychological aspects
ISBN 9780307452030; 0307452034

LC 2008017531

"An international bestseller since it was first published in 1972, Dr. Alex Comfort's classic work dared to celebrate the joy of human physical intimacy with such authority and candor that a whole generation felt empowered to enjoy sex. . . . Substantial revisions from sex expert and relationship psychologist Susan Quilliam include new information on [k] ey scientific discoveries in the fields of psychology, physiology, and sexology." (Publisher's note)

Includes bibliographical references and index

Nagoski, Emily

Come as you are; the surprising new science of women's sexual wellbeing. Emily Nagoski, Ph.D. Simon & Schuster 2015 400 p. (hardcover) $16 **613.9**
1. Sex education 2. Sexual hygiene 3. Women -- Sexual behavior 4. Women -- Health and hygiene 5. Sexual health 6. Sex instruction for women
ISBN 1476762090; 9781476762098; 9781476762104
LC 2014017773

This book, by Dr. Emily Nagoski, is an "exploration of why and how women's sexuality works. . . . Cutting-edge research across multiple disciplines tells us that the most important factor for women in creating and sustaining a fulfilling sex life, is not what you do in bed or how you do it, but how you feel about it. Which means that stress, mood, trust, and body image are not peripheral factors in a woman's sexual wellbeing; they are central to it." (Publisher's note)

"An essential purchase for consumer health and women's health collections. This book will empower women to fully understand why their sexual desire is so different from men's." LJ

Includes bibliographical references

Vernacchio, Al

For goodness sex; changing the way we talk to teens about sexuality, values, and health. Al Vernacchio, with Brooke Lea Foster. HarperWave 2014 272 p. (hardback) $25.99 **613.9**
1. Sex education 2. Teenagers -- Sexual behavior 3. Sexual ethics 4. Parent and teenager 5. Sex instruction for teenagers
ISBN 0062269518; 9780062269515
LC 2014019134

This book by Al Vernacchio offers a "progressive, effective, and responsible approach to sex education for parents and teens that challenges traditional teaching models and instead embraces 21st century realities by promoting healthy sexuality, values, and body image in young people." The book contains "examples from the classroom, exercises and quizzes, and a wealth of sample discussions and crucial information." (Publisher's note)

Weschler, Toni

Taking charge of your fertility; the definitive guide to natural birth control, pregnancy achievement, and reproductive health. Toni Weschler, MPH. 20th anniversary edition William Morrow/HarperCollins 2015 536 p. illustrations pbk $25.99 **613.9**
1. Birth control 2. Human fertility
ISBN 9780062326034; 0062326031
Includes bibliographical references and index

This book, by Toni Weschler, is "a thoroughly revised and expanded edition of the leading book on fertility and women's reproductive health. Since [it was first published] two decades ago, Toni Weschler has taught a whole new generation of women how to become pregnant, avoid pregnancy naturally and gain better control of their gynecological and sexual health by taking just a couple minutes a day using the proven Fertility Awareness Method." (Publisher's note)

613.907 Education

Roffman, Deborah

Talk to me first; everything you need to know to become your kids' "go-to" person about sex. by Deborah Roffman. 1st ed. Da Capo Lifelong 2012 xii, 281 p.p (pbk. : alk. paper) $14.99 **613.907**
1. Parenting 2. Conversation 3. Sex education 4. Parent and child 5. Parent and teenager 6. Sexual ethics for teenagers 7. Sex instruction for children 8. Sex instruction for teenagers
ISBN 0738215082; 9780738215082; 9780738215877
LC 2012006068

This book presents a "guide for parents contemplating how to talk to their children about [sex]. . . . [Deborah] Roffman discusses a laundry list of commonly used statements about sex and doesn't shy away from more sensitive material such as abstinence, gay and transgendered kids, sexually transmitted infections and rape. Throughout, she emphasizes the importance of positive, direct interaction with children." (Kirkus Reviews)

Includes bibliographical references (p. 245-251) and index.

614 Forensic medicine; incidence of injuries, wounds, disease; public preventive medicine

Bass, William M.

Death's acre; inside the legendary forensic lab the Body Farm where the dead do tell tales. [by] Bill Bass and Jon Jefferson; foreword by Patricia Cornwell. Putnam 2003 304p il $24.95; pa $15 **614**
1. Forensic anthropology
ISBN 0-399-15134-6; 0-425-19832-4 pa
LC 2003-46908

"The author explains the process of decomposition and how bones give clues to identify: approximate age, sex, height, and race, all of which are needed to bring the forensic scientist one step closer to putting a name to a corpse. He describes some of the cases he has been involved with and laughs at himself when he shares stories of mistakes and assumptions. Young adults will gain insight into the forensic process and appreciate Bass's dedication to the truth and his work." SLJ

Blum, Deborah

The **poisoner's** handbook; murder and the birth of forensic medicine in Jazz Age New York. Penguin Press 2010 319p pa $16; $25.95 **614**
1. Toxicology 2. Forensic sciences 3. Poisons and

poisoning 4. Poisoning 5. Forensic toxicology 6. Forensic sciences -- History 7. Crime -- New York (N.Y.) -- History -- 20th century

ISBN 0-14-311882-X pa; 1-59420-243-5; 978-0-14-311882-4 pa; 978-1-59420-243-8

LC 2009-26461

This "history of the development of forensics in New York City . . . spans the years from 1915 to 1936." (N Y Times Book Rev) Index.

"Blum effectively balances the fast-moving detective story with a clear view of the scientific advances that her protagonists brought to the field. Caviar for true-crime fans and science buffs alike." Kirkus

Includes bibliographical references

Maples, William R.

Dead men do tell tales; [by] William R. Maples and Michael Browning. Doubleday 1994 292p il hardcover o.p. pa $15.95 **614**

1. Forensic anthropology

ISBN 0-385-47968-9 pa

LC 94-12290

Maples, a forensic anthropologist, "describes the remains (or, when burnt, cremains) presented to him, describes what he looks for, and guides us through his thinking and the search for additional clues and information. His most difficult, fascinating, and perplexing case dealt with a 1985 apparent double murder and burning, while among historic bodies, Maples dealt with those of Francisco Pizarro, Zachary Taylor, Czar Nicholas II, and Joseph Merrick, 'the Elephant Man.'" Booklist

Mitchell, T. J.

Working stiff; two years, 262 bodies, and the making of a medical examiner. Judy Melinek, MD and T.J. Mitchell. First Scribner hardcover ed Scribner 2014 272 p. (hardback) $25 **614**

1. Forensic sciences 2. Medical jurisprudence 3. Forensic pathologists -- New York (State) -- New York -- Biography 4. Medical examiners (Law) -- New York (State) -- New York -- Biography

ISBN 1476727252; 9781476727257; 9781476727264

LC 2014017610

This book, by Judy Melinek and T. J. Mitchell, offers a "memoir of a young forensic pathologist's 'rookie season' as a NYC medical examiner, and the cases--hair-raising and heartbreaking and impossibly complex--that shaped her as both a physician and a mother. . . . [It] offers a firsthand account of daily life in one of America's most arduous professions, and the unexpected challenges of shuttling between the domains of the living and the dead." (Publisher's note)

"Though some sections call for a strong stomach, armchair detectives and would-be forensic pathologists will find Melinek's well-written account to be inspiring and engaging." Pub Wkly

614.4 Incidence of and public measures to prevent disease

Allen, Arthur

Vaccine; the controversial story of medicine's greatest lifesaver. Norton 2007 523p il $27.95 **614.4**

1. Vaccination

ISBN 0-393-05911-1; 978-0-393-05911-3

LC 2006-19480

The author "records the miracles, controversies, and tragedies that have accompanied the development of vaccines since Edward Jenner first combated smallpox in the 18th century. . . . This compelling narrative of the vaccine's undoubted triumphs and troubling challenges is highly recommended to serious readers interested in medicine and public health." Libr J

Includes bibliographical references

Conis, Elena

Vaccine nation; America's changing relationship with immunization. Elena Conis. University of Chicago Press 2015 344 p. (cloth : alkaline paper) $27.50 **614.4**

1. Vaccination 2. Immunization 3. Vaccination -- United States -- History -- 20th century

ISBN 0226923762; 9780226923765

LC 2014009846

This book by Elena Conis "opens in the 1960s, when government scientists--triumphant following successes combating polio and smallpox--considered how the country might deploy new vaccines against what they called the 'milder' diseases, including measles, mumps, and rubella. In the years that followed, Conis reveals, vaccines fundamentally changed how medical professionals, policy administrators, and ordinary Americans came to perceive the diseases they were designed to prevent." (Publisher's note)

"This fascinating book is for those interested in the history of medicine and in the relationship between medicine and American culture. Scholars, public health officials, and some general readers will find Conis's thesis—that changing social attitudes about the role of government in health, the place of individual freedoms, and an individual's duty to a larger society shaped how citizens thought about vaccines—to be cogent and carefully argued." LJ

Includes bibliographical references and index

Encyclopedia of plague and pestilence; from ancient times to the present. George Childs Kohn, editor. 3rd ed; Facts On File 2008 529p il map (Facts on File library of world history) $85 **614.4**

1. Reference books 2. Epidemics -- Encyclopedias

ISBN 978-0-8160-6935-4; 0-8160-6935-2

LC 2006-41296

First published 1995

This encyclopedia provides "descriptions of more than 700 epidemics, listed alphabetically by location of the outbreak. Each . . . entry includes when and where a particular epidemic began, how and why it happened, whom it affected, how it spread and ran its course, and its outcome and significance." Publisher's note

Includes bibliographical references

Garrett, Laurie

The **coming** plague; newly emerging diseases in a world out of balance. Penguin 1995 750p maps pa $20   **614.4**

1. Viruses 2. Epidemics 3. Ebola virus 4. AIDS (Disease) 5. Communicable diseases

ISBN 0-14-025091-3; 978-0-14-025091-6

First published 1994 by Farrar, Straus & Giroux

"The author demonstrates that the emerging global village means not only superior communication and trade among nations but also the deadly swap of microbes. Analyzing the spread of both familiar diseases like cholera and new viruses like Ebola, this is 'a meticulously researched, genuinely disturbing' account." N Y Times Book Rev

Includes bibliographical references

McNeill, William H. (William Hardy), 1917-2016

Plagues and peoples; William H. McNeill. Anchor Press 1998 340 p. map $17   **614.4**

1. Epidemics -- History 2. Civilization -- History

ISBN 9780385121224; 0385121229

LC 89027689

This book, by William Hardy McNeill, offers an interpretation "of world history as seen through the extraordinary impact . . . of disease on cultures. From the conquest of Mexico by smallpox as much as by the Spanish, to the bubonic plague in China, to the typhoid epidemic in Europe, the history of disease is the history of humankind. With the identification of AIDS in the early 1980s, another chapter has been added to this chronicle of events." (Publisher's note)

Offit, Paul A.

★ **Deadly** choices; how the anti-vaccine movement threatens us all. Basic Books 2010 270p il $27.50   **614.4**

1. Vaccination 2. Vaccination of children 3. Vaccination of children -- Complications

ISBN 0-465-02149-2; 978-0-465-02149-9

LC 2010-22446

Offit examines the history of the anti-vaccine movement, opening with the "introduction of smallpox vaccination in 19th-century England and continuing to present-day anti-vaccine activism in the United States." (Sci Books Films) Bibliography. Index.

This "is a thorough dismantling of antivaccine notions and a sober warning about the resurgence of deadly childhood infections stemming from declining vaccination rates. Worried parents, especially, will find this a lucid, compelling riposte to antivaccine fear-mongering." Publ Wkly

Includes bibliographical references

Oldstone, Michael B. A.

Viruses, plagues, and history; past, present, and future. by Michael B.A. Oldstone. Rev and updated ed; Oxford University Press 2010 383p il map $17.95   **614.4**

1. Viruses 2. Epidemics 3. Communicable diseases

ISBN 978-0-19-532731-1; 0-19-532731-4

LC 2009-03550

First published 1998

Oldstone "focuses his tale on a few of the most famous viruses humanity has battled, beginning with some we have effectively defeated, such as smallpox, polio, and measles. . . . [He] then describes the fascinating viruses that have captured headlines in more recent years: Ebola and other hemorrhagic fevers, which literally turn their victims' organs to a bloody pulp; the Hantavirus outbreaks in the southwestern United States and elsewhere; mad cow disease, a frightening illness made worse by government mishandling and secrecy; and, of course, AIDS." Publisher's note

Includes bibliographical references (p. 343-369) and index. (BLCM)

Quammen, David, 1948-

★ **Spillover;** animal infections and the next human pandemic. David Quammen. W.W. Norton & Co. 2012 587 p. (hardcover) $28.95   **614.4**

1. Epidemics 2. Animals -- Diseases 3. Animals as carriers of disease

ISBN 0393066800; 9780393066807

LC 2012029300

This book by David Quammen "sums up . . . what we know about some of the world's scariest scourges: Ebola, AIDS, pandemic influenza--and what we can do to thwart the 'NBO,' the Next Big One. The author discusses zoonoses, infectious diseases that originate in animals and spread to humans. . . . They persist because they are endemic in a reservoir population through a process of mutual adaptation." (Kirkus Reviews)

Includes bibliographical references and index

Sears, Robert W.

The **vaccine** book; making the right decision for your child. Robert W. Sears. 2nd ed. Little, Brown & Co. 2011 335 p. (Sears parenting library) pbk $16   **614.4**

1. Vaccination 2. Children -- Health and hygiene 3. Vaccination of children 4. Immunization of children

ISBN 9780316180528; 0316180521

LC 2011293797

In this book, author Robert W. Sears "devotes each chapter in the book to a disease/vaccine pair and offers a comprehensive discussion of what the disease is, how common or rare it is, how serious or harmless it is, the ingredients of the vaccine, and any possible side effects from the vaccine." (Publisher's note)

"The first 12 chapters discuss each vaccination in the childhood series, providing explanation of the relative disease, how the vaccine is made and points to assess a child's at-risk level when considering if the vaccine is necessary. Sears does offer guidance for those who are indecisive, offering his opinion based on clinical experience and 13 years of research taken from product inserts, pediatric reference books, articles and databases. Additional chapters illuminate more controversial aspects of the debate, such as how vaccine safety is researched and what the findings are, side effects and how to minimize them, common myths and questions." Pub Wkly

Includes bibliographical references and index

614.5   Incidence of and public measures to prevent specific diseases and kinds of diseases

Allen, Arthur

★ The **fantastic** laboratory of Dr. Weigl; how two brave scientists battled typhus and sabotaged the Nazis. Arthur Allen. W.W. Norton & Co. Inc 2014 400 p. illustrations, maps (hardcover) $26.95 **614.5**
1. Typhus 2. Zoologists 3. World War, 1939-1945 -- Poland 4. Anti-Nazi movement -- Poland 5. Scientists -- Poland -- Biography 6. Typhus fever -- Poland -- History 7. World War, 1939-1945 -- Underground movements -- Poland
ISBN 039308101X; 9780393081015

LC 2014003246

This book by Arthur Allen describes how "In the 1920s, [zoologist Rudolf] Weigl had created the first typhus vaccine . . . . giving him cover during the Nazi's violent occupation of Lviv. His lab soon flourished as a hotbed of resistance. Weigl hired otherwise doomed mathematicians, writers, doctors, and other thinkers, protecting them from atrocity. Among the scientists saved by Weigl, who was a Christian, was a gifted Jewish immunologist named Ludwik Fleck." (Publisher's note)

"Allen is unflinching in his retelling of this monstrous era, but he manages to avoid writing a depressing narrative. Instead, Weigl, Fleck and their vaccines illuminate the inherent social complexities of science and truth and reinforce the overriding good of man." Kirkus

Includes bibliographical references and index

Barry, John M.

The **great** influenza; the epic story of the deadliest plague in history. Viking 2004 546p il $29.95; pa $16 **614.5**
1. Influenza
ISBN 0-670-89473-7; 0-14-303649-1 pa

LC 2003-57646

In this account of the 1918 influenza pandemic, the author "explores how the deadly confluence of biology (a swiftly mutating flu virus that can pass between animals and humans) and politics (President Wilson's all-out war effort in WWI) created conditions in which the virus thrived, killing more than 50 million worldwide and perhaps as many as 100 million in just a year." Publ Wkly
Includes bibliographical references

Cantor, Norman F.

In the wake of the plague; the Black death and the world it made. 1st Perennial ed.; Perennial/HarperCollins 2002 245p il map pa $13.95 **614.5**
1. Plague
ISBN 0-06-001434-2

LC 2001-51819

First published 2001 by Free Press

"By animating history and demonstrating our times' connections to even as remote an event as the Black Death, Cantor's erudite excursion proves most engrossing." Booklist
Includes bibliographical references

Foege, William H., 1936-

House on fire; the fight to eradicate smallpox. University of California Press/Milbank Memorial Fund 2011 218p il map (California/Milbank books on health and the public) $29.95 **614.5**
1. Smallpox
ISBN 978-0-520-26836-4

LC 2010-41703

"Foege's emphasis on the personal does enliven the myriad statistics he presents. But he seems a reluctant memoirist, uncomfortable with the spotlight, and as a consequence, the story gets bogged down, at times, by Foege's need to mention (and compliment) every colleague with whom he ever collaborated. Still, though Foege is anything but self-congratulatory, it is impossible to read 'House on Fire' without admiring him and feeling grateful for the gift he gave to mankind." Boston Globe
Includes bibliographical references

Halperin, Daniel

Tinderbox; How the West Sparked the AIDS Epidemic and How the World Can Finally Overcome It. Craig Timberg and Daniel Halperin. Penguin Press HC 2012 421 p. ill. (hardback) $29.95 **614.5**
1. Imperialism 2. AIDS (Disease) 3. Communicable diseases -- History 4. Epidemiology -- Africa -- History 5. Pakistan -- History 6. Colonialism -- Africa 7. Western World -- Africa 8. India -- History -- Partition, 1947 9. HIV Infections -- etiology -- Africa 10. India -- Foreign relations -- Pakistan 11. Pakistan -- Foreign relations -- India 12. HIV Infections -- epidemiology -- Africa 13. Acquired Immunodeficiency Syndrome -- etiology -- Africa 14. Acquired Immunodeficiency Syndrome -- epidemiology -- Africa
ISBN 159420327X; 9781594203275

LC 2011040206

It was the authors' intent to "trace the history, growth and spread of HIV and present what will in the minds of many be a controversial approach to addressing the disease. . . . The key factor in the spread of the disease was the expansion of European colonialism in Africa. . . . [Craig] Timberg and [Daniel] Halperin examine how to confront it." (Kirkus Reviews)
Includes bibliographical references and index.

Holt, Nathalia

Cured; how the Berlin patients defeated HIV and forever changed medical science. Nathalia Holt. Dutton, published by the Penguin Group 2014 336 p. $27.95 **614.5**
1. Gene therapy 2. HIV infections 3. Gene therapy -- Germany -- Berlin -- History 4. HIV infections -- Treatment -- Germany -- Berlin
ISBN 0525953922; 9780525953920

LC 2013037181

In this book, HIV researcher Nathalia Holt "offers increasing hope for a cure by spotlighting the two male 'Berlin Patients' . . . who chemically bombarded and expunged the HIV virus from their bodies. The author tracks the enduring histories of these men--German-born Christian Hahn and Timothy Brown, an American. . . . Holt also profiles

HIV specialists Heiko Jessen, Bruce Walker and David Ho."
(Kirkus Reviews)

"[I]n this accessible and fascinating account, Holt . . .
juggles genetic mysteries, research perils, the agonies of
these two reserved and sensitive men diagnosed with what
was considered a death sentence, and the dogged doctors
who successfully treated them during the later stages of
AIDS epidemic." Pub Wkly

Includes bibliographical references

Johnson, Steven

The **ghost** map; the story of London's most terrifying epidemic--and how it changed science, cities,
and the modern world. Riverhead 2006 299p il map
$26.95   **614.5**
1. Cholera 2. Physicians 3. Writers on medicine
ISBN 1-59448-925-4; 978-1-59448-925-9

LC 2006-23114

"From Snow's discovery of patient zero to Johnson's
compelling argument for and celebration of cities, this
makes for an illuminating and satisfying read." Publ Wkly

Includes bibliographical references

Kelly, John

The **great** mortality; an intimate history of the
Black Death, the most devastating plague of all time.
HarperCollins Publishers 2005 364p hardcover o.p.
pa $14.95   **614.5**
1. Plague
ISBN 0-06-000692-7; 0-06-000693-5 pa

LC 2004-54213

"Western Europe is the primary focus of Kelly's compact history, which is 'intimate' in that it highlights many
particular persons' passages through the crucible years,
1348-49. . . . Kelly proceeds chronologically, beginning with
the plague's prehistory in north central Asia and its spread
through China before empire-building Mongols brought it
west. . . . This sweeping, viscerally exciting book contributes to a literature of perpetual fascination: the chronicles of
pestilence." Booklist

Includes bibliographical references

Kolata, Gina

★ **Flu**; the story of the great influenza pandemic
of 1918 and the search for the virus that caused it.
Simon & Schuster 2001 330p il pa $15   **614.5**
1. Influenza 2. Epidemiology 3. Influenza -- History
-- 20th century
ISBN 0-7432-0398-4; 978-0-7432-0398-2

LC 00-64861

First published 1999 by Farrar, Straus & Giroux

"Clearly explaining both the science and the social toll
of the pandemic, Kolata writes an admirable history and
soberly spells out how the U.S. government is prepared—
or unprepared—for a similar public health threat today."
Publ Wkly

Includes bibliographical references

Murphy, Monica, 1970-

Rabid; a cultural history of the world's most diabolical virus. Bill Wasik and Monica Murphy. Viking 2012 240 p. $25.95   **614.5**
1. Rabies 2. Diseases in literature 3. Communicable
diseases -- History 4. Rabies -- Treatment -- History 5.
Rabies -- Epidemiology -- History
ISBN 0670023736; 9780670023738

LC 2011043903

This book "chart[s] four thousand years in the history,
science, and cultural mythology of rabies. . . . A disease that
spreads avidly from animals to humans, rabies has served
throughout history as a symbol of savage madness, of inhu-
man possession. And today, its history can help shed light on
the wave of emerging diseases, from AIDS to SARS to avian
flu, that we now know to originate in animal populations."
(Publisher's note)

Pisani, Elizabeth

The **wisdom** of whores; bureaucrats, brothels,
and the business of AIDS. W. W. Norton & Co. 2008
372p $25.95   **614.5**
1. Sexual behavior 2. AIDS (Disease) -- Prevention
ISBN 978-0-393-06662-3; 0-393-06662-2

LC 2007-51396

The author discusses various aspects of international
AIDS prevention.

This is "an eye-opening look at who gets AIDS how,
when and where. . . . Delivers a strong, well-told and believable message." Kirkus

Includes bibliographical references

Preston, Richard

The **hot** zone. Random House 1994 300p hardcover o.p. pa $14   **614.5**
1. Ebola virus 2. Animal experimentation
ISBN 0-385-49522-6 pa

LC 94-13415

This book by Richard Preston "tells the true story of how
a deadly virus from the central African rain forest suddenly
appears in a Washington, D.C., animal test lab. In a matter of
days, 90% of the primates exposed to the virus are dead, and
secret government forces are mobilized to stop the spread
of this exotic 'hot' virus." (SB&F: Your Guide to Science
Resources For All Ages)

"Ebola, a lethal virus that slumbers in an unknown host
somewhere in the rain forest, sneaked into the United States
in 1989 in a shipment of primates that ended up in a monkey house in Reston, Virginia. This virus jumps between
species easily, and takes only weeks to kill its victim, with
gory hemorrhaging from various orifices. Preston tells the
suspenseful tale of its detection, and gives vivid life to the
members of the SWAT team that, for eighteen bio-hazardous
days, combatted the strain now known as Ebola Reston."
New Yorker

Quammen, David, 1948-

Ebola; the natural and human history of a deadly virus. David Quammen. W W Norton & Co Inc
2014 128 p. map (paperback) $13.95   **614.5**
1. Ebola virus 2. Public health 3. Disease Reservoirs
-- Popular Works 4. Disease Outbreaks -- history

-- Popular Works 5. Ebola virus -- pathogenicity -- Popular Works 6. Hemorrhagic Fever, Ebola -- history -- Popular Works
ISBN 0393351556; 9780393351552
LC 2014038144
In this book author David Quammen examines how "Ebola has emerged sporadically, each time to devastating effect. It can kill up to 90 percent of its victims. In between these outbreaks, it is untraceable, hiding deep in the jungle. The search is on to find Ebola's elusive host animal. And until we find it, Ebola will continue to strike." (Publisher's note)

"This book will appeal to a wide range of readers. Those who have not previously read Spillover but want to learn more about Ebola will find much to interest them here. Summing Up: Recommended. All levels/libraries." Choice
Includes bibliographical references

Shah, Sonia
The **fever**; how malaria has ruled humankind for 500,000 years. Sarah Crichton Books/Farrar, Straus, and Giroux 2010 307p $26 **614.5**
1. Malaria 2. Malaria -- History
ISBN 0-374-23001-3; 978-0-374-23001-2
LC 2010-2374
This is a chronicle of the illness and its influence on human lives. (Publisher's note) Index.

"This fascinating, mordant pop-sci account tells us why malaria is one of the world's greatest scourges, killing a million people every year and debilitating another 300 million, and why we have remained complacent about it. . . . [This] is an absorbing account of human ingenuity and progress, and of their heartbreaking limitations." Publ Wkly
Includes bibliographical references

Spurlock, Morgan
Don't eat this book; fast food and the supersizing of America. G. P. Putnam's Sons 2005 308p hardcover o.p. pa $14 **614.5**
1. Restaurants 2. Food industry 3. Convenience foods
ISBN 0-399-15260-1; 0-425-21023-5 pa
LC 2005-43196
The author "describes America's obesity epidemic, its relation to the fast food industry, the industry's cozy relations to U.S. government agencies and how the problem is spreading worldwide. . . . His book is a powerful tool in his rip-roaring campaign to turn around America's love-hate relationship with fast food." Publ Wkly
Includes bibliographical references

Tayman, John
The **Colony**; John Tayman. Scribner 2006 421p il maps $27.50 **614.5**
1. Leprosy 2. Hawaii -- History
ISBN 0-7432-3300-X
LC 2005-47767
This is a "history of the leper colony at the Hawaiian island Molokai. . . . Tayman's crisp, flowing writing and inclusion of personal stories and details make this an utterly engrossing look at a heartbreaking chapter in Hawaiian history." Booklist

615 Pharmacology and therapeutics

Griffith, H. Winter
Complete Guide to Prescription & Nonprescription Drugs; H. Winter Griffith, revised and updated by Stephen W. Moore. Tarcherperigree **615**
1. Drugs 2. Pharmacology
Annual
This is a "guide to all major prescription and nonprescription drugs, featuring revised, up to date FDA information and an A-Z list of illnesses for easy reference. [It] includes coverage of dosage and length of time before drug takes effect; side effects, special precautions; interactions with other food and drugs; standards for use by different age groups, and more." (Publisher's note)

O'Neil, Maryadele J.
★ The **Merck** index; an encyclopedia of chemicals, drugs, and biologicals. Maryadele J. O'Neil, editor; Patricia E. Heckelman, senior associate editor; Cherie B. Koch, associate editor; Kristin J. Roman, assistant editor; Catherine M. Kenny, editorial assistant; Maryann R. D'Arecca, administrative assistant. 14th ed.; Merck 2006 various paging il $125 **615**
1. Reference books 2. Drugs -- Dictionaries 3. Materia medica -- Dictionaries
ISBN 0-911910-00-X; 978-0-911910-00-1
First published 1889. Periodically revised
"Technical descriptions of the preparation, properties, uses, commercial names, and toxicity of drugs and medicines." N Y Public Libr Book of How & Where to Look It Up

PDR for nonprescription drugs. Physicians Desk Reference Inc 2014 360 p. $59.95 **615**
1. Pharmacology 2. Nonprescription drugs
ISBN 1563638274; 9781563638275
This book, by the editorial staff of the Physicians' Desk Reference, "offers . . . [a] guide to hundreds of the most commonly used OTC medications, including analgesics, cough and cold preparations, fever reducers, allergy medications, and more. Organized for easy use, . . . [the volume] offers comprehensive drug information such as usage, dosage, warnings and precautions, side effects, ingredients, and more." (Publisher's note)

Physicians' desk reference. Physicians Desk Reference Inc **615**
1. Pharmacology
Annual. First published 1947. Title varies
"Latest available information intended for physicians on over 2,000 products. Covers dosage, contraindications, precautions, side effects, and undesirable interactions. The information is furnished by the manufacturers of the various products. Product identification in color." N Y Public Libr Book of How & Where to Look It Up

615.107 Research

Goldacre, Ben

Bad Pharma; How Drug Companies Mislead Doctors and Harm Patients. Ben Goldacre. Faber & Faber 2013 448 p. $28   **615.107**

1. Drug industry 2. Drugs -- Testing 3. Drugs --Testing 4. Drugs --Quality control 5. Clinical trials --Moral and ethical aspects 6. Drugs --Testing --Moral and ethical aspects 7. Pharmaceutical industry --Moral and ethical aspects

ISBN 0865478007; 9780865478008

LC 2012038902

In this book, physician Ben Goldacre "reveals how pharmaceutical companies mislead doctors and hurt patients. They 'sponsor' trials, which tend to yield favorable results, while negative results often remain unreported. He also reports that drug companies spend twice as much on marketing and advertising as on researching and developing new drugs." (Booklist)

Includes bibliographical references and index.

615.3 Organic drugs

Orr, Stephen

The **new** American herbal; Stephen Orr. Clarkson Potter 2014 384 p. color illustrations $27.50 **615.3**

1. Herbs 2. Herb gardening 3. Herbals 4. Herbs -- Handbooks, manuals, etc 5. Herbs -- Utilization -- Handbooks, manuals, etc

ISBN 0449819930; 9780449819937

LC 2013043040

"With more than 900 entries, each accompanied by brand new photography and helpful growing advice, 'The New American Herbal' takes the study of herbs to [a] . . . new level. [author Stephen] Orr covers the entire spectrum of herbaceous plants, from culinary to ornamental to aromatic and medicinal, presenting them in an easy to use A to Z format packed with recipes, DIY projects, and . . . examples of garden design highlighting herbal plantings."

Pursell, J. J.

The **herbal** apothecary; 100 medicinal herbs and how to use them. JJ Pursell; with photos by Shawn Linehan. Timber Press 2016 292 p. color illustrations (hardcover) $34.95   **615.3**

1. Medical botany 2. Herbs -- Therapeutic use -- Handbooks, manuals, etc 3. Materia medica, Vegetable -- Handbooks, manuals, etc

ISBN 9781604695670; 9781604696622

LC 2015009786

This book, by J. J. Pursell, with photos by Shawn Linehan, "provides an accessible and comprehensive introduction to medicinal plants, explaining how they work and how to use them safely. Incorporating traditional wisdom and scientific information, . . . [it also] includes advice on growing and foraging for healing plants and recommendations for plant-based formulations to fight common ailments." (Publisher's note)

"It is not a quick read, but will quickly become indispensable for understanding a neglected field that is ripe with great benefits." Pub Wkly

Includes bibliographical references and index

One hundred medicinal herbs and how to use them

615.5 Therapeutics

Bland, Jeffrey S.

The **disease** delusion; conquering the causes of chronic illness for a healthier, longer, and happier life. HarperCollins 2014 409 p. illustrations $26.99   **615.5**

1. Chronic diseases 2. Diseases -- Causes

ISBN 0062290738; 9780062290731

"In 'The Disease Delusion,' Dr. [Jeffrey] Bland explains what Functional Medicine is and what it can do for you. While advances in modern science have nearly doubled our lifespans in only four generations, our quality of life has not reached its full potential. Outlining the reasons why we suffer chronic diseases from asthma and diabetes to obesity, arthritis and cancer to a host of other ailments, Dr. Bland offers achievable, science-based solutions." (Publisher's note)

Borins, Mel

A **doctor's** guide to alternative medicine; what works, what doesn't, and why. Mel Borins, MD.; foreword by Dr. Bernie Siegel. Lyons Press 2014 336 p. (paperback) $19.95   **615.5**

1. Alternative medicine

ISBN 1493005952; 9781493005956

LC 2014015122

In this book, doctor Mel Borins uses "the latest scientific research and double-blind studies to educate patients and physicians alike on which alternative treatments work, which don't, and why. . . . Written in clear, accessible language for the layperson while providing citations to full studies for the medical professional, the book covers traditional healing and herbal remedies, physical therapies, psychological therapies, and natural health products." (Publisher's note)

Fondin, Michelle S.

The **wheel** of healing with ayurveda; an easy guide to a healthy lifestyle. Michelle S. Fondin. New World Library 2015 288 p. illustrations (paperback) $15.95   **615.5**

1. Ayurveda 2. Lifestyles 3. Medicine, Ayurvedic -- Popular works

ISBN 1608683524; 9781608683529

LC 2015001783

This book, by Michelle S. Fondin, presents a guide to "Ayurveda, the 'science of life,' is a complete wellness system that includes all that we associate with medical care-prevention of disease, observation, diagnosis, and treatment--as well as self-care practices that are generally absent from Western medicine. This truly holistic approach considers not just diet, exercise, and genetics but also relationships, life purpose, finances, environment, and past experiences." (Publisher's note)

"A strong beginning text for those seeking wellness beyond the bounds of traditional medicine." LJ

Includes bibliographical references and index

The **Gale** encyclopedia of alternative medicine; Laurie J. Fundukian, editor. 4th ed Gale / Cengage Learning 2014 2848 p. 4v (set : hbk. : alk. paper) $714   **615.5**
1. Reference books 2. Alternative medicine -- Encyclopedias 3. Internal Medicine -- Encyclopedias 4. Complementary Therapies -- Encyclopedias -- English
ISBN 1573027308; 9781573027304
                  LC 2013045439

"The four volumes contain more than 800 entries, approximately 400 color images, and many informative illustrations and charts pertaining to herbs and flowers, therapies and procedures, nutrition, and diseases and conditions. More than 50 new entries were added" for the fourth edition. (Publisher's note)

Includes bibliographical references and index

Low Dog, Tieraona

Healthy at home; get well and stay well without prescriptions. Tieraona Low Dog, M.D. National Geographic 2014 335 p. (hardback) $26   **615.5**
1. Naturopathy 2. Diet therapy 3. Health self-care
ISBN 1426212585; 9781426212581
                  LC 2013034581

This book, by Tieraona Low Dog, "helps you take charge of health care guided by a physician expert in natural healing, herbal medicine, and home remedies. . . . [The author] guides us in identifying, responding to, and caring for all the most common ailments, so that when it's time to take care at home, you have a doctor's advice on how." (Publisher's note)

"Accessible and reliable, this title will appeal to readers interested in alternative medicine and those who enjoyed the author's other books (Life Is Your Best Medicine: A Woman's Guide to Health, Healing, and Wholeness at Every Age; National Geographic Guide to Medicinal Herbs: The World's Most Effective Healing Plants). Recommended." LJ

Murray, Michael T.

The **encyclopedia** of natural medicine; Michael T. Murray, Joseph E. Pizzorno. 3rd ed Atria Books 2012 x, 1219 p.p ill. (trade paper : alk. paper) $29.99   **615.5**
1. Naturopathy 2. Alternative medicine 3. Naturopathy -- Encyclopedias
ISBN 1451663005; 9781451663006; 9781451663013; 9781451687347
                  LC 2012023268
First published 1991

In this book, authors "Michael Murray and Joseph Pizzorno focus on promoting health and treating disease with nontoxic, natural therapies. This . . . book . . . shows you how to improve your health through a positive mental attitude, a healthy lifestyle, a health-promoting diet, and supplements, along with plenty of practical tips. Murray and Pizzorno present an evidence-based approach to wellness, based on firm scientific findings." (Publisher's note)

Includes bibliographical references and index

Speid, Lorna

Clinical trials; what patients and healthy volunteers need to know. Oxford University Press 2010 186p il pa $19.95   **615.5**
1. Drugs -- Testing
ISBN 978-0-19-973416-0
                  LC 2010-9154

"If informed consent is the gold standard for clinical-trial participants, this book raises the bar to become the platinum standard. A must-have for anyone—healthy or sick—who is considering volunteering." Booklist

Includes bibliographical references

615.7   Pharmacokinetics

Backes, Michael

Cannabis Pharmacy; the practical guide to medical marijuana. Michael Backes. Black Dog & Leventhal Pub 2014 272 p. illustrations, map $22.95 **615.7**
1. Marijuana 2. Alternative medicine
ISBN 157912951X; 9781579129514

This book, by Michael Backes, offers "evidence-based information on using cannabis for ailments and conditions, plus a comprehensive guide to the most popular varieties. . . . [It] begins with the history of medical marijuana and an explanation of how cannabis works with the body's own endocannabinoid system. . . . [It then] goes on to explore in detail 27 of the most popular cannabis varieties . . . and the medical conditions for which patients have reported effectiveness." (Publisher's note)

"Suitable as an at-home reader for patients (and their families) considering medicinal marijuana as a treatment option." LJ

Blaser, Martin J.

★ **Missing** microbes; how the overuse of antibiotics is fueling our modern plagues. Dr. Martin Blaser. Henry Holt & Co. 2014 288 p. illustrations (hardback) $28   **615.7**
1. Bacteria 2. Antibiotics 3. Drug resistance in microorganisms
ISBN 0805098100; 9780805098105; 9780805098112
                  LC 2013042578
Los Angeles Times Book Prize Finalist: Science and Technology (2014)

"In 'Missing Microbes,' Dr. Martin Blaser invites us into the wilds of the human microbiome where for hundreds of thousands of years bacterial and human cells have existed in a peaceful symbiosis that is responsible for the health and equilibrium of our body. . . . Taking us into both the lab and deep into the fields where these troubling effects can be witnessed firsthand, Blaser . . . provides cutting edge evidence for the adverse effects of antibiotics." (Publisher's note)

A "masterful work of preventive health and superb science writing." Booklist

Includes bibliographical references (pages 221-256) and index

Kramer, Peter D.

★ **Ordinarily** well; the case for antidepressants. Peter D. Kramer. Farrar, Straus & Giroux 2016 336 p. (hardback) $27   **615.7**

1. Drug therapy 2. Antidepressants 3. Depression (Psychology) 4. Psychotropic drugs 5. Antidepressants -- History 6. Antidepressants -- Effectiveness

ISBN 9780374280673

LC 2015036472

In this book, Peter D. Kramer "examines the growing controversy about the popular medication [of antidepressants]. A practicing doctor who trained as a psychotherapist and worked with pioneers in psychopharmacology, Kramer combines moving accounts of his patients' dilemmas with an eye-opening history of drug research to cast antidepressants in a new light." (Publisher's note)

"Kramer (Listening to Prozac), a psychiatrist and professor at Brown Medical School, makes an energetic and personal case for the role of antidepressants in easing crippling depression. Starting with the history of psychotherapy, when "infinite patience was the norm" in treatment for depression, Kramer delves into the breakthrough use of imipramine for treatment in the mid-1950s that helped "redefine the disorder" and "invigorate" psychopharmacology. . . . Kramer shows that the tools may be imperfect, but people battling severe depression are "lucky to have them." PW

Kuhn, Cynthia

Buzzed; the straight facts about the most used and abused drugs from alcohol to ecstasy. Cynthia Kuhn, Ph.D., Scott Swartzwelder, Ph.D., Wilkie Wilson, Ph.D., Duke University and Duke University School of Medicine; with Leigh Heather Wilson and Jeremy Foster. 4th edition W.W. Norton & Company 2014 385 p. pbk $19.95   **615.7**

1. Drugs 2. Drug abuse

ISBN 0393344517; 9780393344516

LC 2014011441

This book, by Cynthia Kuhn, Scott Swartzwelder, Wilkie Wilson, with Leigh Heather Wilson and Jeremy Foster, is "the fourth edition of the essential, accessible source for understanding how drugs work and their effects on body and behavior. . . . It includes new information about biological and behavioral changes in addiction, the prescription-drug abuse epidemic, distinctive drug effects on the adolescent brain, and trends from synthetic cannabinoids to e-cigarettes." (Publisher's note)

"[S]urveys the most used and abused drugs from caffeine to heroin to methamphetamine. In both quick-reference summaries and in-depth analysis, it reports on how these drugs enter the body, how they manipulate the brain, their short-term and long-term effects, the different highs they produce, and the circumstances in which they can be deadly." Publisher's note

Includes bibliographical references and index

Shroder, Tom

Acid test; LSD, Ecstasy, and the power to heal. Tom Shroder. Blue Rider Press, a member of Penguin Group (USA) 2014 448 p. (hardback) $27.95 **615.7**

1. LSD (Drug) 2. Hallucinogens 3. Ecstasy (Drug) 4. Mental illness 5. Post-traumatic stress disorder

6. Mental illness -- Treatment 7. LSD (Drug) -- Therapeutic use 8. Ecstasy (Drug) -- Therapeutic use 9. Hallucinogenic drugs -- Therapeutic use 10. Mentally ill -- United States -- Biography 11. Post-traumatic stress disorder -- Treatment 12. Post-traumatic stress disorder -- Patients -- United States -- Biography

ISBN 0399162798; 9780399162794

LC 2014016115

This book, by Tom Shroder, focuses on "LSD and MDMA (better known as Ecstasy) [and how they] have proven . . . effective in treating anxiety disorders such as PTSD yet . . . remain illegal. . . . [It] covers the first heady years of experimentation in the fifties and sixties, through the backlash of the seventies and eighties, when the drug subculture exploded and uncontrolled use of street psychedelics led to a PR nightmare that created the drug stereotypes of the present day." (Publisher's note)

"Shroder both informs readers about the drugs' shadowy pasts and provides insight into the future of mental health." Pub Wkly

615.8   Specific therapies and kinds of therapies

Quest, Penelope

Reiki for life; the complete guide to reiki practice for levels 1, 2 & 3. Jeremy P. Tarcher/Penguin 2010 310p il pa $16.95   **615.8**

1. Reiki (Healing system)

ISBN 978-1-58542-790-1

LC 2009-51213

This book covers "basic routines, details about the power and potential of each level, special techniques for enhancing Reiki practice, and . . . direction on the use of Reiki toward spiritual growth. Penelope Quest also compares the origins and development of Reiki in the West and the East, revealing methods specific to the original Japanese Reiki tradition." Publisher's note

Includes bibliographical references

616   Diseases

Bacci, Ingrid

Effortless pain relief; a guide to self-healing from chronic pain. Free Press 2005 255p $24 **616**

1. Chronic pain

ISBN 0-7432-6075-9

LC 2005-295415

This book presents an "explanation of how stress creates chronic pain, along with . . . self-help techniques for reducing and even eliminating pain." Publisher's note

Biddle, Wayne

A **field** guide to germs; 2nd Anchor Books ed; Anchor Bks. (NY) 2002 209p il pa $13.95 **616**

1. Microbiology 2. Germ theory of disease

ISBN 1-400-03051-X

LC 2002-511927

First published 1995 by Holt & Co.

"Relaying essential information about the 100 most prevalent, powerful, or literarily famous microbiological malefactors in dictionary-encyclopedia style, Biddle injects social and political history into the exposition to provide fuller understanding of germs, their roles in society, their histories, and their current statuses. . . . Eminently entertaining, the book yet has the serious purpose of showing how concerns other than science and the relief of human suffering have affected the course of medical history." Booklist {review of 1995 edition}

Includes bibliographical references

Collins, Francis S.

The **language** of life; DNA and the revolution in personalized medicine. Harper 2010 332p il $26.99 **616**

1. Medical genetics 2. Genetic screening

ISBN 978-0-06-173317-8; 0-06-173317-2

LC 2009-25832

"This readable book . . . can help anyone understand more about how genetics and our DNA contribute to our health." Libr J

Includes bibliographical references

Gawande, Atul

Better; a surgeon's notes on performance. Metropolitan 2007 273p $24 **616**

1. Medicine 2. Medical ethics

ISBN 978-0-8050-8211-1; 0-8050-8211-5

LC 2006-46962

"Mostly, and repeatedly, the question Gawande pose at the heart of each of his essays is deceptively straightforward and can-do: How do we get it right, or barring that, just an ioat better? . . . Gawande is unassuming in every way, and yet his prose is infused with steadfast determination and hope." Boston Globe

Groopman, Jerome E.

The **anatomy** of hope; how people prevail in the face of illness. [by] Jerome Groopman. Random House 2004 248p hardcover o.p. pa $14.95 **616**

1. Hope 2. Physician-patient relationship

ISBN 0-375-50638-1; 0-375-75775-9 pa

LC 2003-46692

The author "discovered that hope could actually cause physiological change, blocking pain and improving respiratory, circulatory, and motor function. He shares personal experiences from his own life and his patients' case histories that illustrate the power and importance of hope. . . . An excellent narrative for public libraries." Libr J

Includes bibliographical references

Kaplan, Gary

Total recovery; Solving the mystery of chronic pain and depression. Dr. Gary Kaplan, DO, with Donna Beech. Rodale 2014 250 p. (hardcover) $26.99 **616**

1. Chronic pain 2. Depression (Psychology) 3. Chronic pain -- Complications

ISBN 162336275X; 9781623362751

LC 2013046868

"In 'Total Recovery,' Dr. Gary Kaplan argues that we've been thinking about disease all wrong. Drawing on dramatic patient stories and cutting-edge research, the book reveals

that chronic physical and emotional pain are two sides of the same coin. New discoveries show that disease is not the result of a single event but an accumulation of traumas. Every injury, every infection, every toxin, and every emotional blow generates the same reaction: inflammation." (Publisher's note)

Includes bibliographical references and index

Kenneally, Christine

The **invisible** history of the human race; how DNA and history shape our identities and our futures. Christine Kenneally. Viking 2014 368 p. (hardback) $27.95 **616**

1. DNA 2. Genetics 3. Human beings 4. Pedigree 5. DNA -- history 6. Genetics -- history 7. Human Migration -- history

ISBN 0670025550; 9780670025558

LC 2014021679

In this book, "Christine Kenneally draws on cutting-edge research to reveal how both historical artifacts and DNA tell us where we come from and where we may be going. While some books explore our genetic inheritance and popular television shows celebrate ancestry, this is the first book to explore how everything from DNA to emotions to names and the stories that form our lives are all part of our human legacy." (Publisher's note)

"Those interested in learning basic human genetics or seeking a more accurate story of eugenics might prefer Ricki Lewis's Human Genetics: The Basics or Paul A. Lombardo's A Century of Eugenics in America. For appreciating genealogy and family history in a new light, Kenneally's work shines." LJ

Includes bibliographical references and index

Lewis, Moshe

Understanding pain; an introduction for patients and caregivers. Naheed Ali and Moshe Lewis. Rowman & Littlefield 2015 376 p. (cloth : alk. paper) $38 **616**

1. Physiology 2. Psychology 3. Pain -- Treatment 4. Pain -- Popular Works

ISBN 1442233605; 9781442233607

LC 2014042262

In this book authors Naheed Ali and Moshe Lewis "walks readers through the various types of pain, the causes and symptoms, as well as the methods of treatment currently available. From prescription medication to acupuncture and massage therapy, various approaches may work for some but not for others. Here, the authors provide a comprehensive introduction to the subject, covering self-care as well as caring for others in pain, and addressing alternative as well as traditional methods of pain management." (Publisher's note)

"Medical doctors Lewis and Ali (author of books about diabetes, obesity, Alzheimer's, and arthritis) deliver a hefty overview of the history, causes, symptoms, and treatment of pain... Fortunately, they provide a glossary at the end, along with such helpful resources as names and addresses of nationally recognized clinics. As for their advice, much of it seems quite basic: exercise, reduce stress, eat a well-balanced diet... Still, the millions of Americans who suffer from acute pain (less than six months) or chronic pain (more than six months) and the doctors, friends, and family who look out for them will find much good information here." Booklist

Includes bibliographical references and index

Moalem, Sharon

Survival of the sickest; a medical maverick discovers why we need disease. [by] Sharon Moalem, with Jonathan Prince. William Morrow 2007 267p $25.95   **616**

1. Diseases 2. Genetics 3. Evolution 4. Natural selection

ISBN 978-0-06-088965-4; 0-06-088965-9

LC 2006-50128

The author "uses numerous examples to show how analyzing history might help explain why a certain genetic trait that seems useless—even harmful—to us now made perfect sense in our ancestors' environment. He also introduces such recent research topics as host manipulation, noncoding DNA, and epigenetics. The particularly coherent writing style makes complex ideas accessible to people without a science background. With the book's emphasis on evolution's goals of survival and reproduction, readers will gain insights into why evolution may have selected for certain traits and why having that insight may better our lives." Libr J

Murphree, Rodger H.

Treating and beating fibromyalgia and chronic fatigue syndrome; a step-by-step program proven to help you feel good again. by Rodger H. Murphree. Cardinal Pub Group 2014 544 p. $21.95   **616**

1. Fibromyalgia 2. Chronic fatigue syndrome

ISBN 0972893873; 9780972893879

In this book on fibromyalgia and chronic fatigue syndrome, Dr. Rodger H. Murphree "explains in easy to understand terms how and why using scientifically researched and clinically proven natural vitamins, minerals, amino acids, and other over the counter supplements, corrects the problems associated with these illnesses." (Publisher's note)

Parks, Tim

Teach us to sit still; a skeptic's search for health and healing. Rodale Books 2011 322p il   **616**

1. Chronic pain 2. Mind and body

ISBN 1609611586; 9781609611583

LC 2011-08512

First published 2010 in the United Kingdom

"In a hallmark of conversion narratives, the original mania reproduces itself as a mirror image: in the old days, hyperbolically anxious; in the new, hyperbolically anxious to enumerate the old anxiety. To his credit, Parks doesn't pretend otherwise. Moreover, his personal account, never preachy, engages some serious matters about contemporary life, notably what it's like to be a patient, as nearly all of us, sooner or later, are or will be." N Y Times Book Rev

Twelve breaths a minute; end-of-life essays. edited by Lee Gutkind; foreword by Karen Wolk Feinstein; introduction by Francine Prose. Southern

Methodist University Press 2011 267p (Medical humanities) $23.95   **616**

1. Death 2. Caregivers 3. Terminal care 4. Terminally ill

ISBN 978-0-87074-571-3; 0-87074-571-9

LC 2010-45874

"A collection of creative nonfiction essays about end-of-life issues. How depressing, a friend said. I thought the same thing until I read one and then another and then another. Sad, yes. But depressing? No. 'Twelve Breaths a Minute,' a book commissioned by the Jewish Healthcare Foundation as part of its ongoing end-of-life initiative, is uplifting. The 23 essays, chosen from among more than 400 submissions, also are beautifully written. The writers are the sons, daughters and parents who have had to deal with the deaths of family, as well as members of the medical profession who have had to balance the oath to save lives with the desires of a patient to die without extraordinary medical measures. Sometimes they are both." Pittsburgh Post-Gazette

616.02   Special topics of diseases

Anthes, Emily

Frankenstein's cat; cuddling up to biotech's brave new beasts. Emily Anthes. 1st ed. Scientific American / Farrar, Straus and Giroux 2013 256 p. (hardcover) $26   **616.02**

1. Biotechnology 2. Transgenic animals

ISBN 0374158592; 9780374158590

LC 2012029045

This book, by Emily Anthes, "takes us from petri dish to pet store as she explores how biotechnology is shaping the future of our furry and feathered friends. . . . [Visiting] a 'frozen zoo' where scientists are storing DNA from the planet's most exotic creatures, she discovers how we can use cloning to protect endangered species, craft prosthetics to save injured animals, and employ genetic engineering to supply farms with disease-resistant livestock." (Publisher's note)

"[A] quick, often surprising review of current advances, giving accessible treatment to a weighty subject and employing clear descriptions of complex science." Booklist

Includes bibliographical references and index.

Brody, Jane E.

Jane Brody's guide to the great beyond; a practical primer to help you and your loved ones prepare medically, legally, and emotionally for the end of life. [by] Jane Brody. Random House 2009 xxiv, 287p il $26   **616.02**

1. Death 2. Terminal care 3. Terminally ill

ISBN 978-1-4000-6654-4

LC 2008-16583

"With bulleted lists itemizing what needs to be done and how to do it, short portraits and anecdotes throughout, Brody covers the importance of preparation; the necessity of an advance directive and why a living will is not enough; funeral plans; living with a bad prognosis and dealing with uncertainty; caregiving; hospice; communicating with doctors; assisted dying; organ donation and autopsy; and legacies. An instructive, inspiring and reassuring work full of compassion and humor (along with several cartoons from various New

Yorker illustrators), this volume belongs on every family's bookshelf." Publ Wkly

Brown, Theresa

The **shift**; one nurse, twelve hours, four patients' lives. Theresa Brown. Algonquin Books of Chapel Hill 2015 204 p. $24.95 **616.02**

1. Nurses 2. Patients 3. Medical care 4. Cancer -- Nursing 5. Interpersonal relations 6. Intensive Care Units -- Pennsylvania -- Popular Works

ISBN 161620320X; 9781616203207

LC 2015010992

In this book, author "Theresa Brown invites us to experience not just a day in the life of a nurse but all the life that happens in just one day on a hospital's cancer ward. . . . In Brown's skilled hands . . . we are given an unprecedented view into the individual struggles as well as the larger truths about medicine in this country, and by shift's end, we have witnessed something profound about hope and healing and humanity." (Publisher's note)

"At its best, Brown's memoir increases empathy for nurses, who work hard and often must care for difficult patients and cope with a caste system that gives them less respect than MDs. This account also raises important ethical questions, such as just how fully informative healthcare workers should be when the prognosis isn't good." Booklist

Butler, Katy

Knocking on Heaven's Door; the path to a better way of death. Katy Butler. Simon & Schuster 2013 336 p. illustrations $25 **616.02**

1. Death 2. Right to die 3. Terminal care -- Decision making 4. Euthanasia -- Moral and ethical aspects 5. Adult children of aging parents -- Family relationships

ISBN 1451641974; 9781451641974

LC 2013017659

In this book, "when doctors refused to disable the pacemaker that caused her eighty-four-year-old father's heart to outlive his brain, Katy Butler . . . embarked on a quest to understand why modern medicine was depriving him of a humane, timely death. After his lingering death, Katy's mother, nearly broken by years of nonstop caregiving, defied her doctors, refused open-heart surgery, and insisted on facing death the old-fashioned way: bravely, lucidly, and head on." (Publisher's note)

"With candidness and reverence, Butler examines one of the most challenging questions a child may face: how to let a parent die with dignity and integrity when the body has stopped functioning." Kirkus

Includes bibliographical references

Casarett, David

Shocked; adventures in bringing back the recently dead. David Casarett. Current 2014 304 p. $27.95 **616.02**

1. Cardiac resuscitation 2. Science -- Popular works 3. Resuscitation -- Popular Works

ISBN 1591846714; 9781591846710

LC 2014004313

This book, by David Casarett, explores how "not too long ago, there was no coming back from death. But now, with revolutionary medical advances, death has become just

another serious complication. . . . [The author] chronicles his exploration of the cutting edge of resuscitation and reveals just how far science has come." (Publisher's note)

"This book may work for readers of Mary Roach's Stiff, in which the author's interest is more theoretical." LJ

Includes bibliographical references and index

First aid manual; the step-by-step guide for everyone. American College of Emergency Physicians; medical editor-in-chief, Gina M. Piazza, DO, FACEP. DK Publishing 2014 288 p. color illustrations $14.95 **616.02**

1. First aid 2. Medicine -- Handbooks, manuals, etc. 3. First aid in illness and injury -- Handbooks, manuals, etc

ISBN 9781465419507

LC 2014430333

This book, edited by Gina M. Piazza, "looks at more than 100 different conditions, from splinters and sprained ankles to strokes and unconsciousness, and shows exactly what to do with step-by-step photographic sequences. Every condition is clearly explained, outlining causes, symptoms and signs, and action plans." (Publisher's note)

American College of Emergency Physicians first aid manual

Gibney, Mike

Something to chew on; challenging controversies in food and health. Mike Gibney. University College Dublin Press 2012 xiv, 177 p.p (paperback) $38.95 **616.02**

1. Food 2. Nutrition 3. Food supply 4. Public health 5. Genetic engineering

ISBN 1906359679; 9781906359676

LC 2012405919

This book, by Mike Gibney, discusses the scientific perspective on many of "the worldwide controversies dominating the popular press in relation to the modern food chain. It deals with the topics of organic food, GM foods, obesity, growing old, the integrity of food research, global warming, global malnutrition, consumer perception of food-borne risk, our gut bacteria, and how nutrition during pregnancy primes us for health in later life." (Publisher's note)

Volandes, Angelo E., 1971-

The **conversation**; a revolutionary plan for end-of-life care. Angelo Volandes. Bloomsbury 2015 256 p. illustrations (hardback) $26 **616.02**

1. Terminal care 2. Palliative treatment 3. Elderly -- Medical care

ISBN 1620408546; 9781620408544

LC 2014028386

This book, by Angelo Volandes, "through the stories of seven patients and seven very different end-of-life experiences, . . . demonstrates that what people with a serious illness, who are approaching the end of their lives, need most is not new technologies but one simple thing: The Conversation." (Publisher's note)

"Written with passion and clarity, this book moves beyond others on the topic by including empirical evidence of how to make such conversations about end-of-life care most effective." LJ

Includes bibliographical references and index

616.042 Genetic diseases (Hereditary diseases)

Mukherjee, Siddhartha

★ The **gene**; an intimate history. Siddhartha Mukherjee. Scribner 2016 592 p. illustrations (some color) (hardcover) $30 **616.042**
1. Genetics 2. Heredity 3. Genes 4. Genetics -- history

ISBN 9781476733500; 9781476733524

LC 2015039962

In this book, author Siddhartha Mukherjee "has a written a biography of the gene. . . . Weaving science, social history, and personal narrative to tell us the story of one of the most important conceptual breakthroughs of modern times, Mukherjee animates the quest to understand human heredity and its surprising influence on our lives, personalities, identities, fates, and choices." (Publisher's note)

"Sobering, humbling, and extraordinarily rich reading from a wise and gifted writer who sees how far we have come—but how much farther we have to go to understand our human nature and destiny." Kirkus

Includes bibliographical references and index

616.07 Pathology

Biss, Eula

★ **On** immunity; an inoculation. Eula Biss. Graywolf Press 2014 216 p. (alk. paper) $24 **616.07**
1. Immunity 2. Immunization

ISBN 1555976891; 9781555976897

LC 2014935701

In this book, author Eula Biss "addresses a chronic condition of fear--fear of the government, the medical establishment, and what is in your child's air, food, mattress, medicine, and vaccines. She finds that you cannot immunize your child, or yourself, from the world. . . . Biss investigates the metaphors and myths surrounding our conception of immunity and its implications for the individual and the social body." (Publisher's note)

Includes bibliographical references

Franscell, Ron

Morgue; a life in death. Dr. Vincent Di Maio and Ron Franscell; foreword by Dr. Jan Garavaglia. St. Martin's Press 2016 288 p. illustrations (hardback) $26.99 **616.07**
1. Physicians -- Biography 2. Pathologists -- New York (State) -- Brooklyn -- Biography

ISBN 1250067146; 9781250067142

LC 2016001125

In this book, Dr. Vincent Di Maio "guides us into the inner sanctum, through the cases that have made him famous, from the exhumation of assassin Lee Harvey Oswald and the racially charged shooting of Florida teen Trayvon Martin, to the unmasking of a serial baby-killer and the mysterious death of troubled genius Vincent van Gogh." (Publisher's note)

"Di Maio and Franscell deliver a well-paced, thoughtful, and absorbing work that will fascinate crime buffs and scholars alike." Pub Wkly

Nuland, Sherwin B.

How we die; reflections on life's final chapter. Knopf 1994 278p hardcover o.p. pa $14 **616.07**
1. Death

ISBN 0-679-74244-1 pa

LC 93-24590

"Nuland is one of those rare physicians who know a great deal about a great deal, not only medicine but also its history and, beyond that, literature and the humanities." Commentary

Pagana, Timothy J.

Mosby's diagnostic and laboratory test reference; Kathleen Deska Pagana, Timothy J. Pagana, and Theresa N. Pagana. 13th edition Mosby Inc. 2016 1040 p. pbk $57.95 **616.07**
1. Medicine 2. Diagnosis 3. Laboratories

ISBN 0323399576; 9780323399579

First published 1992. Frequently revised

This medical handbook, by Kathleen Deska Pagana, Timothy J. Pagana, and Theresa N. Pagana, provides "concise test entries are arranged alphabetically and reflect the latest in research and diagnostic testing. Each test entry includes vital information such as type of test, alternate or abbreviated test names, test explanation, normal and abnormal findings, possible critical values, contraindications, potential complications, interfering factors, and patient care." (Publisher's note)

Sanders, Lisa

Every patient tells a story; medical mysteries and the art of diagnosis. Broadway 2009 xxvii, 276p $25 **616.07**
1. Diagnosis

ISBN 0-7679-2246-8; 978-0-7679-2246-3

LC 2008-41478

The author "discusses how doctors deal with diagnostic dilemmas. . . . Sanders not only collects difficult cases, she reflects on what each means for both patient and struggling physician. . . . Readers who enjoy dramatic stories of doctors fighting disease will get their fill, and they will also encounter thoughtful essays on how doctors think and go about their work, and how they might do it better." Publ Wkly

Includes bibliographical references

Zuk, M.

Riddled with life; friendly worms, ladybug sex, and the parasites that make us who we are. Harcourt 2007 328p il $25 **616.07**
1. Diseases 2. Parasites 3. Pathology 4. Human ecology 5. Adaptation (Biology)

ISBN 978-0-15-101225-1; 0-15-101225-3

LC 2006-28642

"Zuk has an amazing gift for turning experiments and facts into stories. . . . She is urging the public to take a new look at disease, though it's one that's well supported by the research. There are moments where she's speculating ahead of the science a bit, but those moments are clearly marked. Riddled with Life will change the way you look at public and private health." PopMatters

Includes bibliographical references

616.1 Specific diseases

Forrester, James

The **Heart** Healers; The Misfits, Mavericks, and Rebels Who Created the Greatest Medical Breakthrough of Our Lives. James S. Forrester. St. Martin's Press 2015 400 p. 16 plates; illustrations $27.99   **616.1**
1. Heart diseases 2. Medicine -- Research
ISBN 1250058392; 9781250058393
LC 2015017977

In this book author "James Forrester tells the story of the mavericks and rebels who defied the accumulated medical wisdom of the day to begin conquering heart disease. Forrester tells the story of these rebels and the risks they took with their own lives and the lives of others to heal the most elemental of human organs - the heart. The result is a compelling chronicle of a disease and its cure, a disease that is still with us, but one that is slowly being worn away." (Publisher's note)

"Forrester brings history to life and explains complex procedures for lay readers in this excellent book for readers interested in medical history and those who want to understand modern medical procedures." LJ

Khan, Joel

The **whole** heart solution; halt heart disease now with the best alternative and traditional medicine. Joel Kahn, MD, Preventive Cardiologist and Clinical Professor of Medicine at Wayne State University School of Medicine. The Reader's Digest Association, Inc. 2013 308 p. (alk. paper) $24.99   **616.1**
1. Heart diseases 2. Holistic medicine 3. Heart -- Diseases -- Alternative treatment
ISBN 1621451437; 9781621451433; 9781621451518
LC 2013040399

In this book, holistic doctor Joel Kahn "reveals more than 75 simple, low-cost things you can do right away—from drinking your veggies to opening your windows to walking barefoot—to make yourself heart attack proof." (Publisher's note)
Includes bibliographical references (pages 293-302) and index.

616.12 Diseases of heart

Fuhrman, Joel

The **end** of heart disease; the eat to live plan to prevent and reverse heart disease. Joel Fuhrman, MD. HarperOne 2016 448 p. illustrations (hardback) $28.99   **616.12**
1. Heart diseases -- Prevention 2. Heart -- Diseases -- Prevention -- Popular works 3. Heart -- Diseases -- Diet therapy -- Popular works 4. Heart -- Diseases -- Nutritional aspects -- Popular works
ISBN 9780062249357
LC 2015033616

This book, by Joel Fuhrman, MD, "presents a scientifically proven, practical program to prevent and reverse heart disease—coinciding with the author's new medical study.

. . . [It] shows us how we can significantly lower cholesterol and blood pressure, reduce weight, heal obstructive coronary artery disease, and even eradicate advanced heart disease—all without the need for dangerous procedures like angioplasty or bypass surgery." (Publisher's note)

"It's obvious Furhman's zeal is genuine as he passionately tries to convince the general public to make smarter choices." Booklist

Includes bibliographical references (pages [383]-422) and index.

616.2 Diseases of respiratory system

Ackerman, Jennifer

Ah-choo! the uncommon life of your common cold. Twelve 2010 245p $22.99   **616.2**
1. Cold (Disease)
ISBN 978-0-446-54115-2; 978-0-446-57401-3 ebook
LC 2010-4794

The author "parses the variety and durability of the cold, its wellknown miseries, paradoxes (a highly active immune system may actually make you sicker with a cold), and myriad mysteries (why do poorer people get more colds? what roles do stress and sleep play? is our clean obsession making us more susceptible to sickness?) with the thoroughness of a scientist, the doggedness of a journalist, and the verve of a thriller writer. . . . There's a nifty collection of comforting recipes as well, including a nonalcoholic hot toddy (and a delicious sounding boozy one, too), banana pudding, and yes, chicken soup." Publ Wkly

Includes bibliographical references

616.3 Diseases of digestive system

Ali, Naheed

Understanding celiac disease; an introduction for patients and caregivers. Naheed Ali. Rowman & Littlefield Pub Inc 2014 332 p. (cloth : alk. paper) $38   **616.3**
1. Celiac disease 2. Celiac Disease
ISBN 1442226552; 9781442226555
LC 2014016086

"Celiac disease is being diagnosed more and more frequently, as people recognize their digestive issues may be linked to their gluten intake and sensitivity to various foods that include gluten. Here, Ali, in typical fashion, reviews the biology of celiac disease, its various symptoms, causes, and outcomes, and includes information about treatment, prevention, and living well with celiac." Publisher's note.

"Those who want a more technical description of celiac disease will find this book useful; readers looking for a basic overview and understanding of the condition and how to live with it may want to consider David L. Burns's 100 Questions & Answers About Celiac Disease and Sprue or Celiac Disease by Sylvia Llewelyn Bower, et al." LJ

Includes bibliographical references and index

Lacy, Brian E.

Making sense of IBS; a physician answers your questions about irritable bowel syndrome. Brian E.

Lacy, Ph.D., M.D. The Johns Hopkins University Press 2013 xii, 380 p.p illustrations (pbk. : alk. paper) $21.95 **616.3**

1. Irritable bowel syndrome 2. Irritable colon

ISBN 1421411156; 9781421411156

LC 2013006074

This book, by Brian E. Lacy, discusses irritable bowel syndrome. "Today more than ever before, physicians are able to diagnose this complex disorder, understand and explain its origins, and develop a treatment plan that effectively meets the individual needs of a patient. . . . [The author] explains normal digestion, the causes of IBS, how IBS is diagnosed, and what to expect with treatment." (Publisher's note)

Includes bibliographical references and index

Making sense of irritable bowel syndrome

Steinhart, A. Hillary

Crohn's & colitis diet guide; Includes 175 Recipes. by Dr. Hillary Steinhart and Julie Cepo. Robert Rose 2014 336 p. illustrations $24.95 **616.3**

1. Diet 2. Chronic diseases 3. Digestive system

ISBN 077880478X; 9780778804789

Second edition

This book on Crohn's disease and ulcerative colitis, by Dr. Hillary Steinhart and Julie Cepo, "provides all the necessary guidelines regarding the specific foods that might cause problems, as well as delicious and nutritious recipes that can be enjoyed without compromising this difficult condition." (Publisher's note)

"The guide is written in easy-to-understand language, provides answers to commonly asked questions and many useful illustrations, although there are no photos of the recipes. Steinhart and Cepo are both knowledgeable, and clearly interested in helping those with IBD lead healthier lives. They have produced an invaluable guide that is highly recommended for those with IBD and those who care for them." Pub Wkly

616.4 Diseases of endocrine, hematopoietic, lymphatic, glandular systems; diseases of male breast

American Diabetes Association

American Diabetes Association complete guide to diabetes; 5th ed.; American Diabetes Association 2011 499p il pa $22.95 **616.4**

1. Diabetes

ISBN 978-1-58040-330-6

LC 2010-41272

First published 1996

This book describes types of insulin and the best ways to use them, insulin pumps and injection-free insulin techniques in research, new oral diabetes medications and therapies, the use of carbohydrate counting techniques as a meal planning tool as well as information on diabetes in the workplace, school, and day care.

Includes bibliographical references

Ask the experts; expert answers about your diabetes from the pages of Diabetes forecast. American Diabetes Association. American Diabetes Association 2014 159 p. (pbk.) $12.95 **616.4**

1. Diabetes -- Miscellanea

ISBN 1580405398; 9781580405393

LC 2013046542

This book, by the editors of the American Diabetes Association, provides advice for managing diabetes, "written by physicians, nurse practitioners, physician assistants, dietitians, diabetes educators, and other experts in the diabetes research and clinical communities. . . . Unlike most self-care titles for people with diabetes, the unique format . . . creates an open forum for people to ask the specific and individualized questions that normally don't get answered." (Publisher's note)

Flippin, Royce

The **diabetes** reset; the revolutionary plan to reverse, control, and avoid Type 2 diabetes. George King, M.D. with Royce Flippin. Workman Publishing Company, Inc. 2014 326 p. illustrations (alk. paper) $25.95 **616.4**

1. Diet 2. Diabetes 3. Exercise 4. Weight loss 5. Self-care, Health 6. Non-insulin-dependent diabetes -- Alternative treatment

ISBN 076117592X; 9780761175926

LC 2014034312

This book, by Dr. George King, presents "a plan that will let readers avoid, control, and even reverse type 2 diabetes. The program begins with losing weight—and shows why losing only 5% of body weight makes a life-changing difference. It explains how a good's night sleep can significantly lower blood glucose levels. . . . It disentangles the carbohydrate confusion, reveals how to decrease the body's inflammatory response, and explains the importance of moderate exercise." (Publisher's note)

"While the promise of a "reset" may set off some red flags for skeptics, readers searching for a hopeful look at life with Type 2 diabetes or a step-by-step guide to making lifestyle changes will be attracted to this book." LJ

Includes bibliographical references and index

Mayo Clinic, the essential diabetes book; how to prevent, control & live well with diabetes. medical editor, M. Regina Castro, M.D. 2nd ed Time Home Entertainment, Inc. 2014 vii, 223 p.p color illustrations (pbk.) $19.95 **616.4**

1. Diabetes

ISBN 0848743393; 9780848743390

LC 2014933598

This book, edited by M. Regina Castro, presents a guidebook to diabetes, including discussion of how to manage "the pre-diabetes stage . . . types of diabetes; symptoms and risk factors; treatments and strategies for managing your blood sugar; avoiding serious complications; advances in insulin delivery [and more.]" (Publisher's note)

"This title covers: the pre-diabetes stage - taking charge to prevent diabetes; types of diabetes; symptoms and risk factors; treatments and strategies for managing your blood sugar; avoiding serious complications; advances in insulin delivery and new medications; and recipes." Publisher's note

Rubin, Richard R.

The **Johns** Hopkins guide to diabetes; for patients and families. Christopher D. Saudek, M.D., Richard R. Rubin, Ph.D., CDE, Thomas W. Donner, M.D. Johns Hopkins University Press 2014 xi, 488 p.p illustrations (pbk. : alk. paper) $22.95 **616.4**

1. Diabetes 2. Therapeutics 3. Diabetes -- Treatment -- Handbooks, manuals, etc

ISBN 1421411792; 1421411806; 9781421411798; 9781421411804

LC 2013015256

Written by Christopher D. Saudek, Richard R. Rubin, and Thomas W. Donner, "'The Johns Hopkins Guide to Diabetes' is a comprehensive and easy-to-read guide to this complex condition, answering questions such as: What are the differences between Type 1 and Type 2 diabetes? How are the different forms of this disease treated? Can gestational diabetes become a permanent condition? Can diabetes ever be managed successfully with diet and exercise alone?" (Publisher's note)

Wright, Hillary

The **prediabetes** diet plan; how to reverse prediabetes and prevent diabetes through healthy eating and exercise. Hillary Wright, MEd, RD. Ten Speed Press 2013 ix, 245 p.p (trade paperback) $15.99 **616.4**

1. Preventive medicine 2. Diabetes -- Diet therapy 3. Physical fitness 4. Diabetes -- Prevention 5. Prediabetic state -- Patients -- Diet therapy

ISBN 1607744627; 9781607744627

LC 2013018751

This book by Hillary Wright tells how, "While diabetes cannot be cured, prediabetes can be reversed, so it is critical to take action at an early stage. In straightforward, jargon-free language, 'The Prediabetes Diet Plan' explains insulin resistance (the underlying cause of prediabetes and type 2 diabetes) and offers a comprehensive strategy of diet and lifestyle change, which has been proven more effective than medication." (Publisher's note)

"This excellent introduction for readers recently diagnosed with (or at risk for) prediabetes will also interest readers with other forms of insulin resistance." LJ

Includes bibliographical references and index

616.5   Diseases of integument

Yosipovitch, Gil

Living with itch; a patient's guide. Gil Yosipovitch, M.D., and Shawn G. Kwatra, M.D. Johns Hopkins University Press 2013 160 p. color illustrations (A Johns Hopkins Press health book) (pbk. : alk. paper) $16.95 **616.5**

1. Skin -- Diseases 2. Itching -- Popular works 3. Dermatology -- Popular works 4. Skin -- Diseases -- Popular works

ISBN 1421412330; 9781421412337

LC 2013016433

In this book, authors Gil Yosipovitch and Shawn G. Kwatra "explain the cascade of physiological events that causes us to experience itch. They describe the many skin diseases, from atopic dermatitis (eczema) to psoriasis, and conditions like chronic kidney disease, lymphoma, HIV, and neuropathies that cause itch. . . . Patient and parent narratives illustrate how people cope with itch and how, with medical and social support, itch can be managed." (Publisher's note)

"Although there is no simple cure, the book offers hope as well as treatment options, useful charts, and links to on-line resources. Those seeking support, information, and relief will benefit from this forthright guide." LJ

Includes bibliographical references (page 135) and index

616.6   Diseases of urogenital system

Kang, Mandip S.

The **doctor's** kidney diets; a nutritional guide to managing and slowing the progression of chronic kidney disease. Mandip S. Kang, MD, FASN. Square One Publishers 2015 208 p. (pbk.) $17.95 **616.6**

1. Kidneys -- Diseases 2. Self-care, Health 3. Kidneys -- Diseases -- Diet therapy 4. Kidneys -- Diseases -- Nutritional aspects

ISBN 9780757003738

LC 2015018370

This book, by Dr. Mandip S. Kang, "is divided into two parts. Part One provides a clear overview of kidney function, kidney disease, and the role that nutrition plays in the treatment of kidney problems. The doctor then reviews the special dietary considerations of individuals with CKD, including the need to limit certain nutrients, fluids, and other dietary components." (Publisher's note)

"This well-written manual is essential for anyone diagnosed with kidney disease, or their caregivers, and is a needed addition for all consumer health collections." LJ

Includes bibliographical references and index

616.7   Diseases of musculoskeletal system

Pizzorno, Lara

Your bones; how you can prevent osteoporosis & have strong bones for life-naturally. Lara Pizzorno, MA, LMT; with Jonathan V. Wright, MD. Praktikos Books 2013 xiii, 496 p.p illustrations (some color) (pbk.) $12 **616.7**

1. Osteoporosis 2. Preventive medicine 3. Osteoporosis -- Prevention -- Popular works 4. Osteoporosis -- Diet therapy -- Popular works 5. Osteoporosis -- Exercise therapy -- Popular works 6. Osteoporosis -- Nutritional aspects -- Popular works

ISBN 160766013X; 9781607660132

LC 2012047340

Written by Lara Pizzorno, "'Your Bones' contains everything you need to know for healthy bones in one book, providing scientifically based advice which highlights natural prevention and treatment strategies. This updated and expanded edition includes many new studies on the dangers of the bisphosphonate drugs and an in depth discussion of two new drugs with potential adverse effects." (Publisher's note)

"Consumer health collections looking for another book about the natural ways to prevent osteoporosis would do well to choose this title. Those looking for recipes or photos of recommended exercises need to look elsewhere." LJ

Includes bibliographical references and index

Thomas, Donald E.

The **lupus** encyclopedia; a comprehensive guide for patients and families. Donald E. Thomas, Jr., M.D., FACP, FACR. Johns Hopkins University Press 2013 912 p. illustrations (A Johns Hopkins Press health book) (pbk. : alk. paper) $34.95   **616.7**
1. Systemic lupus erythematosus 2. Systemic lupus erythematosus -- Encyclopedias
ISBN 1421409836; 1421409844; 9781421409832; 9781421409849
LC 2012042648

This book on the topic of lupus, by doctor Donald E. Thomas, "is an authoritative compendium that provides detailed explanations of every body system potentially affected by the disease, along with practical advice about coping. People with lupus, their loved ones, caregivers, and medical professionals-- all will find here an invaluable resource." (Publisher's note)

"This book supplies a caring, comprehensive guide to understanding and coping with lupus." LJ

Includes bibliographical references and index

616.8   Diseases of nervous system and mental disorders

Bowling, Allen C.

Optimal health with multiple sclerosis; a guide to integrating lifestyle, alternative, and conventional medicine. Allen C. Bowling, MD, PhD, Physician Associate, Colorado Neurological Institute, Englewood, Colorado and Clinical Professor of Neurology, University of Colorado, Aurora, Colorado. Demos Medical Publishing, LLC 2014 402 p. (alk. paper) $24.95   **616.8**
1. Multiple sclerosis 2. Alternative medicine 3. Multiple sclerosis -- Treatment 4. Multiple sclerosis -- Alternative treatment
ISBN 1936303701; 9781936303700
LC 2014027383

This book, by doctor Allen C. Bowling, provides "evidence-based information on the relevance, safety, and effectiveness of various alternative and lifestyle medicine approaches to MS treatment and the best ways to safely integrate them with conventional medicine. . . . [It] provides the accurate and unbiased information people with MS, their friends and family, health care professionals, and educators need to make responsible decisions and achieve the very best outcome." (Publisher's note)

Includes bibliographical references and index

Cahalan, Susannah

Brain on fire; my month of madness. by Susannah Cahalan. Free Press 2012 264 p. illustrations $25   **616.8**
1. Encephalitis 2. Brain -- Diseases 3. Autoimmune diseases 4. Diagnostic errors -- United States -- Case

studies 5. Encephalitis -- Patients -- United States -- Biography 6. Autoimmune diseases -- Patients -- United States -- Biography 7. Frontal lobes -- Diseases -- Patients -- United States -- Biography 8. Limbic system -- Diseases -- Patients -- United States -- Biography
ISBN 145162137X; 9781451621372
LC 2012012670

This book chronicles how "when she was twenty-four years old, [Susannah] Cahalan had a seizure that was accompanied by delusions, paranoia, hallucinations, and violent mood swings. Over the course of a month, she was hospitalized with an autoimmune disease that caused her body to attack her brain. She remembers almost nothing of this month. . . . She began researching what happened to her and recreating, in words, her month of madness." (Voice of Youth Advocates)

"Cahalan expertly weaves together her own story and relevant scientific and medical information about autoimmune diseases, which are about two-thirds environmental and one-third genetic in origin. So, she writes, an external trigger, such as a sneeze or a toxic apartment, probably combined with a genetic predisposition toward developing aggressive antibodies to create her problem. A compelling health story." Booklist

Includes bibliographical references

Estep, Preston

The **mindspan** diet; reduce Alzheimer's risk, minimize memory loss, and keep your brain young. Preston Estep, III. Ballantine Books 2016 304 p. illustrations (hardcover : alk. paper) $27   **616.8**
1. Diet therapy 2. Alzheimer's disease 3. Alzheimer's disease -- Diet therapy
ISBN 9781101886120
LC 2016003594

This book, by Preston Estep, III, presents a "plan for curbing memory loss and improving cognitive longevity that will forever change how you think about diet and aging. . . . Complete with food recommendations, shopping lists, advice on reading nutrition labels, and more than seventy delicious recipes, [it] shows that you can enjoy the richest flavors life has to offer and remain lean, healthy, and cognitively intact for a very long life." (Publisher's note)

"Presenting a sensible regimen that people can follow easily, this recommended diet book with useful information about aging is for most consumer health collections." LJ

Includes bibliographical references and index

Gillies, Andrea

Keeper; one house, three generations, and a journey into Alzheimer's. Broadway Books 2010 323p $25; ebook $25   **616.8**
1. Caregivers 2. Journalists 3. Alzheimer's disease 4. Memoirists
ISBN 978-0-307-71911-9; 978-0-307-71913-3 ebook
LC 2010-6659

First published 2009 in the United Kingdom

In this "chronicle of her troubled two years taking care of her mother-inlaw in the throes of dementia, . . . Gillies reveals the 'dehumanizing' toll of the disease on the whole family. Gillies, her husband, and three children moved to a rambling Victorian house in the wilds of a Scottish peninsula and took in Chris's parents, Edinburgh residents who had been showing signs of needing increasing care: irascible Morris had 'bad legs,' while his strong-willed wife, Nancy, at 79, was spiraling deeper into Alzheimer's. As Nancy's memory deteriorated the entire family unit began to collapse under the strain of constant caretaking. . . . [This] memoir is an invaluable resource on the stages of Alzheimer's, history, drugs, brain function, care-giving options, even literary works." Publ Wkly

Includes bibliographical references

Ingram, Jay
The **End** of Memory; A Natural History of Aging and Alzheimer's. by Jay Ingram. St. Martin's Press 2015 304 p. $26.99   **616.8**
  1. Alzheimer's disease
  ISBN 125007648X; 9781250076489
                       LC 2015019167

In this book on Alzheimer's, "science author Jay Ingram writes a biography of this disease that attacks the brains of patients. He charts the history of the disease from before it was noted by Alois Alzheimer through to the twenty-first century, explains the fascinating science of plaques and tangles, recounts the efforts to understand and combat the disease, and introduces us to the passionate researchers who are working to find a cure." (Publisher's note)

Highly readable and informative, this work is strongly recommended for readers interested in medicine, scientific research or pathology." Library Journal

Kosik, Kenneth S.
Outsmarting alzheimer's; what you can do to reduce your risk. Kenneth S. Kosik, MD, with Alisa Bowman. The Reader's Digest Association, Inc. 2015 320 p. illustrations (hardback) $24.99   **616.8**
  1. Dementia 2. Nervous system 3. Health self-care 4. Alzheimer's disease 5. Self-care, Health 6. Alzheimer's disease -- Prevention
  ISBN 9781621452447
                       LC 2015025509

This book, by Kenneth S. Kosik, "is an easy-to-follow, research-based guide to the simple, low-cost choices that give the reader the power to reduce the risk of developing Alzheimer's disease and dementia. . . . [This book] gives you 80 simple lifestyle prescriptions in the six key areas with the most scientific evidence for protecting your brain health: Social Smarts, Meal Smarts, Aerobics Smarts, Resilience to Stress Smarts, Train Your Brain Smarts, and Sleep." (Publisher's note)

"Kosik offers a very reasonable and feasible program, aimed at both avoiding Alzheimer's disease and achieving overall enhanced physical and mental well-being." Pub Wkly

Includes bibliographical references and index

Kuhn, Daniel
Alzheimer's early stages; first steps for families, friends and caregivers. 2nd ed; Hunter House 2003 306p hardcover o.p. pa $15.95   **616.8**
  1. Alzheimer's disease
  ISBN 0-89793-398-2; 0-89793-397-4 pa
                     LC 2002-151932

First published 1999
This book covers "the importance of getting a diagnosis, risk factors (including the role of depression), early symptoms, treatment and prevention, and information on physical health, safety concerns, caring for the caregiver, and financial and end-of-life planning—all illustrated with brief, first-person narratives. Of special interest are chapters on relationships, including telling others about the diagnosis, and the . . . section on current available treatments. . . . Intelligently written with numerous references to professional and consumer literature, this book is an excellent choice for Alzheimer's and consumer health collections." Libr J

Includes bibliographical references

Lang, Anthony E.
 ★ **Parkinson's** disease; a complete guide for patients and families. [by] William J. Weiner, Lisa M. Shulman, Anthony E. Lang. 2nd ed.; Johns Hopkins University Press 2007 278p il $55; pa $17.95 **616.8**
  1. Parkinson's disease
  ISBN 0-8018-8545-0; 978-0-8018-8545-7; 0-8018-8546-9 pa; 978-0-8018-8546-4 pa
                     LC 2006-18814
  First published 2001
This book contains "information for managing this complex condition, including details on the use of medications, diet, exercise, complementary therapies, and surgery." Publisher's note

Mace, Nancy L.
 ★ The **36**-Hour Day; A Family Guide to Caring for People Who Have Alzheimer Disease, Related Dementias and Memory Loss. [by] Nancy L. Mace, Peter V. Rabins. 5th ed Johns Hopkins University Press 2011 353 p. hc $45   **616.8**
  1. Alzheimer's disease
  ISBN 1421402793; 9781421402796

This book, by Nancy L. Mace and Peter V. Rabins, is "the definitive guide for people caring for someone with dementia. Now in a new and updated edition, this best-selling book features thoroughly revised chapters on the causes of dementia, managing the early stages of dementia, the prevention of dementia, and finding appropriate living arrangements for the person who has dementia when home care is no longer an option." (Publisher's note)

Palfreman, Jon
Brain storms; the race to unlock the mysteries of Parkinson's disease. Jon Palfreman. Scientific American/Farrar, Straus & Giroux 2015 272 p. illustrations (hardback) $26   **616.8**
  1. Parkinson's disease 2. Parkinson Disease -- Personal Narratives
  ISBN 0374116172; 9780374116170
                     LC 2015003861

This book, by Jon Palfreman, named a Publisher's Weekly Top 10 Science Book form Fall 2015, "chronicles how scientists have worked to crack the mystery of [Parkinson's Disease,] what was once called the shaking palsy, from the earliest clinical descriptions of tremors, gait freezing, and micrographia to the cutting edge of neuroscience, and charts the victories and setbacks of a massive international effort to best the disease." (Publisher's note)

"In this illuminating book, Palfreman reminds patients that exercise and a positive attitude help, and he urges them to participate in clinical trials and take to task drug companies reluctant to initiate huge trials for what they dismiss as a non-life-threatening disease." Kirkus

Ramachandran, V. S.

The **tell**-tale brain; a neuroscientist's quest for what makes us human. W. W. Norton 2011 xxvi, 357p il $26.95   **616.8**
1. Brain 2. Nervous system
ISBN 978-0-393-07782-7
        LC 2010-44913
"Ramachandran produces an exhilarating and at times funny text that invites discussion and experimentation." Kirkus
Includes bibliographical references

Ropper, Allan H.

Reaching down the rabbit hole; a renowned neurologist explains the mystery and drama of brain disease. Dr. Allan H. Ropper and Brian David Burrell. St. Martin's Press 2014 272 p. (hardback) $25.99   **616.8**
1. Neurosciences 2. Nervous system 3. Brain -- Diseases 4. Neurology -- Anecdotes 5. Brain -- Diseases -- Anecdotes 6. Neurologists -- Massachusetts -- Boston -- Biography
ISBN 1250034981; 9781250034984
        LC 2014017011
In this book, authors Dr. Allan H. Ropper and Brian David Burrell "take the reader behind the scenes at Harvard Medical School's neurology unit to show how a seasoned diagnostician faces down bizarre, life-altering afflictions." (Publisher's note)

Sacks, Oliver W.

An **anthropologist** on Mars; seven paradoxical tales. [by] Oliver Sacks. Knopf 1995 327p il hardcover o.p. pa $14   **616.8**
1. Nervous system -- Diseases
ISBN 0-679-75697-3 pa
        LC 94-26733
In this "collection of previously published essays, the noted neurologist describes his meetings with seven people whose 'abnormalities' in brain function generate new perspectives on the workings of that organ, the nature of experience and concepts of personality and consciousness. . . Writing with eloquent particularity and compassionate respect, Sacks enlarges our view of the nature of human experience." Publ Wkly
Includes bibliographical references

★ The **man** who mistook his wife for a hat and other clinical tales; [by] Oliver Sacks. Simon & Schuster 1998 243p il pa $14   **616.8**
1. Nervous system -- Diseases
ISBN 0-684-85394-9
        LC 98-4723
First published 1985 by Summit Bks.

"Sacks introduces the reader to real people who suffer from a variety of neurological syndromes which includes symptoms such as amnesia, uncontrolled movements, and musical hallucinations. Sacks recounts their stories in a riveting, compassionate, and thoughtful manner." Libr J
Includes bibliographical references

Uncle Tungsten; memories of a chemical boyhood. [by] Oliver Sacks. Knopf 2001 337p il hardcover o.p. pa $14   **616.8**
1. Physicians 2. Neurologists 3. Writers on science 4. Writers on medicine
ISBN 0-375-40448-1; 0-375-70404-3 pa
        LC 2001-33738
"Sacks' first scientific love was chemistry, and he presents an avid history of the field within a memoir that pays tribute to his uncle, who welcomed Sacks into his lab, thus encouraging his passion for chemistry and learning." Booklist

Small, Gary

2 weeks to a younger brain; Gary Small, Gigi Vorgan. Humanix Books 2015 308 p. illustrations (hardback : alk. paper) $24.95   **616.8**
1. Brain 2. Self-improvement
ISBN 1630060305; 9781630060305; 9781630060312
        LC 2014958068
This book, by Gary Small and Gigi Vorgan, "translates the latest brain science into practical strategies and exercises that yield quick and long-lasting benefits. It will not only improve your memory, but will also strengthen your physical health by reducing your risk for diabetes, heart disease, and stroke. The latest research confirms that there is a lot we can do to boost our memory and keep our brains young." (Publisher's note)
Includes bibliographical references (pages 245-282) and index

What if it's not Alzheimer's? a caregiver's guide to dementia. edited by Gary Radin and Lisa Radin; foreword by Murray Grossman, MD EdD. Prometheus Books 2014 340 p. illustrations (paperback) $19   **616.8**
1. Dementia 2. Caregivers -- Handbooks, manuals, etc. 3. Caregivers -- Handbooks, manuals, etc 4. Dementia -- Nursing -- Handbooks, manuals, etc 5. Dementia -- Patients -- Care -- Handbooks, manuals, etc
ISBN 161614968X; 9781616149680
        LC 2014015843
This book, edited by Gary Radin and Lisa Radin, is a "comprehensive guide dealing with frontotemporal degeneration (FTD), one of the largest groups of non-Alzheimer's dementias. . . . The first part defines and explores FTD as an illness distinct from Alzheimer's disease. . . . In the following section on caregiver resources, the contributors identify professional and government assistance programs along with private resources and legal options." (Publisher's note)
"While there is some overlap among the individual chapters, this guide presents a wealth of medical information, written in terms the interested layperson can understand, as well as practical advice. One of the few books to discuss

FTD specifically, this is an invaluable resource for patients, family, and friends, as well as health-care providers." LJ

Includes bibliographical references and index

616.85 Miscellaneous diseases of nervous system and mental disorders

Adam, David

The **man** who couldn't stop; OCD and the true story of a life lost in thought. David Adam. Farrar, Straus and Giroux 2015 336 p. (hardcover) $26 **616.85**

1. Obsessive-compulsive disorder
ISBN 0374223955; 9780374223953; 9780374710514
LC 2014017387

This book, by David Adam, is an "intimate look at the power of intrusive thoughts, how our brains can turn against us, and living with obsessive compulsive disorder. . . . Adam explores the weird thoughts that exist within every mind, and how they drive millions of us toward obsession and compulsion." (Publisher's note)

"For all the impressive marshaling of information, it is Adam's own story of his struggles with the condition, which his infant daughter forced him to confront instead of uneasily accepting, that is the most captivating aspect of this impressive work." Booklist

Includes bibliographical references

Bass, Ellen

The **courage** to heal; a guide for women survivors of child sexual abuse. by Ellen Bass and Laura Davis. 20th anniversary edition; 4th revised edition; Collins Living 2008 xxxiv, 606p pa $22.95 **616.85**

1. Child sexual abuse 2. Adult child sexual abuse victims 3. Women -- Psychology
ISBN 978-0-06-128433-5; 0-06-128433-5
LC 2008-11616
First published 1988

"This book offers help and encouragement to women who were sexually abused in childhood. Through moving firstperson narratives, it illustrates how to come to terms with the past and work constructively towards the future. Along the way it describes the effects of sexual abuse, maps the stages survivors pass through, and offers practical guidance on dealing with self-defeating behaviors and building self-esteem. . . . Compassionate and supportive." Libr J

Includes bibliographical references

Boyes, Alice

The **anxiety** toolkit; strategies for fine-tuning your mind and moving past your stuck points. Alice Boyes. Perigee 2015 240 p. (paperback) $16 **616.85**

1. Anxiety 2. Psychology 3. Anxiety -- Popular works 4. Anxiety -- Treatment -- Popular works
ISBN 0399169253; 9780399169250
LC 2014040065

In this book, author "Alice Boyes translates powerful, evidence-based tools used in therapy clinics into tips and tricks you can employ in everyday life. Whether you have an anxiety disorder, or are just anxiety-prone by nature, you'll

discover how anxiety works, strategies to help you cope with common anxiety 'stuck' points and a confidence that - anxious or not - you have all the tools you need to succeed in life and work." (Publisher's note)

Boyes's tone is friendly but never saccharine, and endlessly practical. Her tips and exercises, drawn from cognitive behavioral therapies that she herself has administered, should make a valuable reference for anxiety sufferers, and an ideal companion to readers undergoing psychotherapy themselves." Pub Wkly

Bulik, Cynthia M.

Midlife eating disorders; your journey to recovery. Cynthia M. Bulik, Ph. D. Walker & Company 2013 352 p. $17 **616.85**

1. Eating disorders 2. Middle aged persons 3. Middle-aged persons 4. Middle age -- Psychological aspects
ISBN 080271269X; 9780802712691
LC 2012037481

In this book, clinical psychologist and director of the University of North Carolina Eating Disorders Program Cynthia M. Bulik "reviews the causes, features, and age-appropriate treatments of midlife eating disorders from anorexia nervosa to binge eating, bulimia nervosa, and purging. She explores some of the challenges facing adults with eating problems, including parenting, intimacy, pregnancy, and breastfeeding." (Booklist)

"[Bulik] discusses treatment options, finding compassionate care, and the importance of support from health professionals as well as family and friends. The book has extensive notes as well as a resource list of American and British organizations." LJ

Includes bibliographical references and index

Dittrich, Luke

★ **Patient** H.M. a story of memory, madness and family secrets. Luke Dittrich. Random House 2016 320 p. illustrations (hardback) $28 **616.85**

1. Memory 2. Memory Disorders 3. Memory, Long-Term 4. Epilepsy -- surgery 5. Amnesia, Anterograde
ISBN 9780812992731
LC 2015048638

This book, by Luke Dittrich, describes how "in 1953, a twenty-seven-year-old factory worker named Henry Molaison . . . received a radical new version of the then-common lobotomy. . . . The operation failed to eliminate Henry's seizures, but it did have an unintended effect: Henry was left profoundly amnesic, unable to create long-term memories. Over the next sixty years, Patient H.M., as Henry was known, became the most studied individual in the history of neuroscience." (Publisher's note)

"Though long, there's not a wasted word in the book, which should make readers glad we live in the age of Prozac and not the scalpel. A mesmerizing, maddening story and a model of journalistic investigation." Kirkus

Donvan, John

★ **In** a different key; the story of autism. John Donvan and Caren Zucker. Crown Publishers 2016 688 p. (hardback) $30 **616.85**

1. Autism 2. Mental health 3. People with disabilities 4. Autism spectrum disorders 5. Autism spectrum

disorders -- History

ISBN 0307985679; 9780307985675; 9780307985705

LC 2015024706

This book on autism by authors John Donovan and Caren Zucker "tells the extraordinary story of this often misunderstood condition, and of the civil rights battles waged by the families of those who have it. Unfolding over decades, it is a beautifully rendered history of ordinary people determined to secure a place in the world for those with autism—by liberating children from dank institutions; campaigning for their right to go to school, challenging expert opinion on what it means to have autism." (Publisher's note)

"This book will not educate researchers with new information on autism. It will, however, introduce a human aspect to the chronology. Parents of autistic children will recognize themselves in many of these stories but also learn more about the truth behind them. Autistic individuals will take away lessons to forgive the past and to recognize the vast spectrum of difference—not just among those on the autism spectrum but among all people, who are always learning and growing." LJ

Frost, Randy O.

Stuff. Houghton Mifflin Harcourt 2010 290p
$27   **616.85**

1. Compulsive hoarding 2. Collectors and collecting 3. Obsessive-compulsive disorder

ISBN 978-0-15-101423-1; 0-15-101423-X

LC 2009-28273

"Writing with authority and compassion, the authors tell the stories of diverse men and women who acquire and accumulate possessions to the point where their apartments or homes are dangerously cluttered with mounds of newspapers, clothing and other objects. . . . An absorbing, gripping, important report." Kirkus

Includes bibliographical references

Gambaro, Jill, 1959-

The **truth** about carpal tunnel syndrome; finding answers, getting well. Jill Gambaro. Rowman & Littlefield Pub Inc 2014 151 p. (cloth : alk. paper)
$34   **616.85**

1. Stress (Physiology) 2. Occupational health and safety 3. Carpal tunnel syndrome 4. Overuse injuries -- Miscellanea 5. Carpal tunnel syndrome -- Treatment

ISBN 1442225793; 9781442225794

LC 2013051337

Written by Jill Gambaro, "'The Truth About Carpal Tunnel Syndrome' is a . . . patient account of this controversial injury. Using layman's terms, the book describes why it's so difficult to treat, how the author learned to manage hers, and how the medical and legal systems work in conflict to those suffering such injuries. Offering hope to sufferers and their loved ones, this book captures the reality of carpal tunnel syndrome." (Publisher's note)

Includes bibliographical references and index

Grandin, Temple, 1947-

★ The **autistic** brain; thinking across the spectrum. Temple Grandin and Richard Panek. Hough-

ton Mifflin Harcourt 2013 256 p. (hardcover)
$28   **616.85**

1. Autism 2. Neurosciences 3. Autism -- Research 4. Psychology, Pathological 5. Autism spectrum disorders 6. Autistic people -- Mental health

ISBN 0547636458; 9780547636450

LC 2013000662

This book, by Temple Grandin and Richard Panek, presents an "account of the latest science of autism. . . . Autism studies have moved from the realm of psychology to neurology and genetics, and there is far more hope today than ever before thanks to groundbreaking new research into causes and treatments. Now Temple Grandin reports from the forefront of autism science, bringing her singular perspective to a thrilling journey into the heart of the autism revolution." (Publisher's note)

Grinker, Roy Richard, 1961-

Unstrange minds; remapping the world of autism. Basic Books 2006 340p hardcover o.p.   **616.85**

1. Autism

ISBN 0465027636; 0465027644; 9780465027637; 9780465027644

LC 2006-23003

Part 1 of this work examines "the history of the classification of psychiatric disorders. . . . The second part of the book explores the cultural issues related to autism in . . . India, South Korea, and South Africa and how the place of the autistic child is changing in those countries." (Sci Books Films) Index.

"The first part of the book is an expanded essay on the history of the classification of psychiatric disorders and how these definitions continue to evolve. . . . The second part of the book explores the cultural issues related to autism in societies as diverse as those of India, South Korea, and South Africa and how the place of the autistic child is changing in those countries. Grinker's experiences as a father of an autistic child are woven throughout the volume. . . . The text is scholarly, but easily read, and is useful not only for providing an understanding of autism, but also for understanding the issues associated with changing diagnoses of psychiatric disorders." Sci Books Films

Includes bibliographical references

Hallowell, Edward M.

Driven to Distraction; Recognizing & Coping With Attention Deficit Disorder From Childhood to Adulthood. by Edward M. Hallowell and John Ratey. Rev. and updated ed. Anchor Books 2011 382 p.
$15.95   **616.85**

1. Attention deficit disorder

ISBN 0307743152; 9780307743152

LC 2011292194

The authors of this book, Edward M. Hallowell and John Ratey, "explore the varied forms ADHD takes, from hyperactivity to daydreaming. They dispel common myths, offer helpful coping tools, and give a thorough accounting of all treatment options as well as tips for dealing with a diagnosed child, partner, or family member. But most importantly, they focus on the positives that can come with this 'disorder'—

including high energy, intuitiveness, creativity, and enthusiasm." (Publisher's note)

Includes bibliographical references and index

Hornbacher, Marya

Wasted: a memoir of anorexia and bulimia. HarperCollins Pubs. 1998 268p hardcover o.p. pa $13.95   **616.85**

1. Bulimia 2. Anorexia nervosa

ISBN 0-06-018739-5; 978-0-06-085879-7 pa; 0-06-085879-6 pa

LC 97-21375

This "is a gritty, unflinching look at eating disorders. . . . Hornbacher is at her best when she zeroes in on the specifics of eating disorders and their origins." N Y Times Book Rev

Includes bibliographical references

Kluger, Jeffrey

The **Narcissist** Next Door; Understanding the Monster in Your Family, in Your Office, in Your Bed-in Your World. Jeffrey Kluger. Riverhead Books 2014 288 p. $27.95   **616.85**

1. Narcissism

ISBN 1594486360; 9781594486364

LC 2014006297

This book, by Jeffrey Kluger, is an "exploration of narcissism, how to recognize it, and how to handle it. . . . Kluger frames the surprising new research on narcissism and explains the complex, exasperating personality disorder. He reveals how narcissism and narcissists affect our lives at work and at home, on the road, and in the halls of government; what to do when we encounter narcissism; and how to neutralize its effects before it's too late." (Publisher's note)

"In addition to being informative and engaging, Kluger's account provides some effective tools for dealing with potential narcissists." Pub Wkly

Kramer, Peter D.

Listening to Prozac; a psychiatrist explores mood-altering drugs and the new meaning of the self. Viking 1993 409p hardcover o.p. pa $15   **616.85**

1. Psychiatry 2. Psychotherapy 3. Psychotropic drugs 4. Personality disorders

ISBN 0-14-026671-2 pa

LC 92-50733

"Kramer's thesis is that Prozac, in addition to its antidepressant effects, can also act upon aspects of the personality that were previously conceptualized as enduring individual traits (i.e., sensitivity to rejection, social inhibition, and reactivity to stressors). Medication with Prozac appears to have beneficial effects on self-esteem, the ability to experience pleasure, and mental acuity. Kramer is favorable to Prozac, although he documents its side effects, unknown long-term affects, and controversial publicity." Choice

Lask, Bryan

Can I tell you about eating disorders? a guide for friends, family and professionals. Bryan Lask and Lucy Watson; illustrated by Fiona Field. Jessica

Kingsley Publishers 2015 56 p. illustrations (alk. paper) $14.95   **616.85**

1. Eating disorders 2. Eating disorders -- Juvenile literature

ISBN 1849054215; 9781849054218

LC 2014025450

In this book, by Bryan Lask and Lucy Watson, "[m]eet Alice - a teenage girl with anorexia nervosa. Alice invites readers to learn about anorexia nervosa and how it makes her see herself differently from how other people see her. She also introduces readers to Beth who has bulimia nervosa, Sam who has selective eating problems, Francesca who has functional dysphagia and Freddie who has food avoidance emotional disorder." (Publisher's note)

Eating disorders; a parents' guide. Rachel Bryant-Waugh and Bryan Lask. Routledge 2013 xv, 180 p.p illustrations (pbk.) $26.95   **616.85**

1. Eating disorders in children 2. Eating disorders in adolescence 3. Eating disorders in children -- Popular works 4. Eating disorders in adolescence -- Popular works

ISBN 0415501563; 9780203375228; 9780415501569; 9780415814775

LC 2012034666

This book, by Rachel Bryant-Waugh and Bryan Lask, "is dedicated to clarifying the subject of eating disorders. Combining an accessible and straightforward introduction to the subject with practical advice, this book represents the first step towards recognising, understanding and dealing with the problem." (Publisher's note)

Lintala, Janet

The **un**-prescription for Autism; a natural approach for a calmer, happier, and more focused child. Janet Lintala with Martha W. Murphy; foreword by Elizabeth Mumper; illustrations by Jill Seale. AMACOM, American Management Association 2016 304 p. (paperback) $18.95   **616.85**

1. Autism 2. Autistic children 3. Asperger's syndrome 4. Autism spectrum disorders 5. Asperger's syndrome -- Patients -- Care 6. Asperger's syndrome -- Patients -- Biography

ISBN 9780814436639

LC 2015038238

In this book, "Dr. Janet Lintala, founder of the Autism Health center and an autism mom herself, shares the natural protocols used in her practice to dramatically improve the function and well-being of children on the spectrum. Drawing on the latest research developments, as well as personal and clinical experience, she targets the underlying issues . . . associated with the behavior, bowel, and sleep problems so common to autism." (Publisher's note)

"In prose that is easy to understand and sometimes humorous, Lintala relates going through the protocols with her own son as well as patients." LJ

Includes bibliographical references and index

Unprescription for Autism

Lock, James

Help your teenager beat an eating disorder; James Lock, Daniel Le Grange. Guilford Pubn 2015 310 p. $18.95   **616.85**
1. Parenting 2. Eating disorders 3. Eating disorders in adolescence
ISBN 146251748X; 9781462517480
LC 200416664

In this book, authors James Lock and Daniel Le Grange "explain what you need to know about eating disorders, which treatments work, and why it is absolutely essential to play an active role in your teen's recovery--even though parents have often been told to take a back seat. Learn how to monitor your teen's eating and exercise, manage mealtimes, end weight-related power struggles, and partner successfully with health care providers." (Publisher's note)

Matlen, Terry

The **queen** of distraction; how women with ADHD can conquer chaos, find focus, and get more done. Terry Matlen, MSW; foreword by Sari Solden, MS LMFT. New Harbinger Publications, Inc. 2014 200 p. (paperback) $16.95   **616.85**
1. Women -- Mental health 2. Attention deficit disorder 3. Women -- Life skills guides 4. Mothers -- Life skills guides 5. Women -- Mental health -- Popular works 6. Attention-deficit disorder in adults -- Popular works 7. Attention-deficit disordered adults -- Life skills guides
ISBN 1626250898; 9781626250895
LC 2014015747

This book "presents practical skills to help women with ADHD achieve focus and balance in all areas of life. . . . Psychotherapist Terry Matlen delves into the feminine side of ADHD—the elements of this condition that are particular to women, such as: relationships, skin sensitivities, meal-planning, parenting, and dealing with out-of-control hormones. In addition, the book offers helpful tips and strategies to get your symptoms under control." (Publisher's note)

"Whether or not one actually suffers from ADHD, this work is helpful for regaining focus and control over the events of everyday." LJ
Includes bibliographical references

McBride, Karyl

Will I ever be good enough? healing the daughters of narcissistic mothers. Free Press 2008 243p il $24   **616.85**
1. Narcissism 2. Self-acceptance 3. Mother-daughter relationship
ISBN 978-1-4165-5132-4; 1-4165-5132-8
LC 2008-14676

In this book aimed at women whose mothers have narcissistic personality disorder, "McBride presents specific steps toward recovery that daughters of any age can use as they grieve for the love and support they didn't receive, set healthy boundaries with their mothers and access an 'internal mother' as a source of self-comforting. The author provides parenting tips as well as advice on maintaining healthy love relationships and friendships—all of which tend to be weak points of the daughters of narcissistic mothers." Publ Wkly
Includes bibliographical references

Morris, David J.

The **evil** hours; a biography of post-traumatic stress disorder. David J. Morris. Houghton Mifflin Harcourt 2015 336 p. (hardback) $27   **616.85**
1. War 2. Post-traumatic stress disorder 3. Post-traumatic stress disorder -- United States 4. Post-traumatic stress disorder -- Patients -- United States -- Biography
ISBN 0544086619; 9780544570320; 9780544086616
LC 2014034487

This book, by David J. Morris, offers "a moving, eye-opening exploration of PTSD. . . . Through interviews with individuals living with PTSD, forays into the scientific, literary, and cultural history of the illness, and memoir, Morris crafts a . . . work that will speak not only to those with the condition and to their loved ones, but also to all of us struggling to make sense of an anxious and uncertain time." (Publisher's note)

"Though its incidence among combat veterans has brought post-traumatic stress disorder to the fore, the National Institute of Mental Health estimates that one in every 30 American adults suffers from the condition. Seasoned war correspondent Morris, also a former marine infantry officer with PTSD, here draws on personal experience, interviews, and scientific studies to present the big picture." LJ

Nathan, Debbie

Sybil exposed; the extraordinary story behind the famous multiple personality case. Free Press 2011 xxi, 297p il $26; ebook $12.99   **616.85**
1. Artists 2. Painters 3. Mentally ill 4. Multiple personality
ISBN 978-1-4391-6827-1; 978-1-4391-6829-5 ebook
LC 2011009164

The author "claims that the subject of the 1973 international bestseller, Sybil by Flora Schreiber, and the blockbuster film that followed, was a deliberate fabrication that not only fooled a mass popular audience but shaped the practice of psychiatry, opening the door to mass hysteria and misdiagnosis. . . . A nuanced, not-entirely-unsympathetic account of the women who perpetrated a sensational literary fraud." Kirkus
Includes bibliographical references

Raine, Adrian

The **anatomy** of violence; the biological roots of crime. Adrian Raine. 1st ed. Pantheon Books 2013 xv, 478 p.p ill. (some col.) (hardcover) $35 **616.85**
1. Genetics 2. Violence 3. Mind and body 4. LAW -- General 5. Violence -- Physiological aspects 6. Violence -- Psychological aspects
ISBN 0307378845; 9780307378842
LC 2012036952

This book, by Adrian Raine, researches "the biological roots of violence. . . . Raine documents from genetic research that the seeds of sin are sown early in life, giving rise to abnormal physiological functioning that cultivates crime. Drawing on classical case studies of well-known killers in history . . . Raine illustrates how impairments to brain areas controlling our ability to experience fear, make good decisions, and feel guilt predispose us to violence." (Publisher's note)

Includes bibliographical references (pages 375-453) and index.

Robison, John Elder

Switched on; a memoir of brain change and emotional awakening. John Elder Robison. Spiegel & Grau 2015 320 p. (hardback) $28   **616.85**
1. Asperger's syndrome 2. Autism -- Treatment 3. Asperger's syndrome -- Patients -- Treatment 4. Asperger's syndrome -- Patients -- United States -- Biography
ISBN 9780812996890; 9780812996906
LC 2015014112

In this memoir, author John Elder Robison "wrote . . . 'Look Me in the Eye,' a memoir about growing up with Asperger's syndrome. Amid the blaze of publicity that followed, he received a unique invitation: Would John like to take part in a study led by one of the world's foremost neuroscientists, who would use an experimental new brain therapy known as TMS, or transcranial magnetic stimulation, in an effort to understand and then address the issues at the heart of autism?" (Publisher's note)

"Fascinating for its insights into Asperger's and research, this engrossing record will make readers reexamine their preconceptions about this syndrome and the future of brain manipulation." Booklist

Includes bibliographical references

Rodriguez, Ana Maria

Autism spectrum disorders; the complete guide to understanding autism, Asperger's syndrome, pervasive developmental disorder, and other ASDs. Chantal Sicile-Kira. Berkeley Pub. Group 2004 xxi, 360 p.p (USA Today health reports: diseases and disorders) $17   **616.85**
1. Autism 2. Autistic children 3. Asperger's syndrome 4. Autism -- Popular works 5. Autism in children -- Popular works 6. Asperger's syndrome -- Popular works 7. Developmental disabilities -- Popular works
ISBN 0399166637; 0399530479; 9780399166631
LC 2004052935

This book on autism spectrum disorders, by Chantal Sicile-Kira, "explains all aspects of the condition, and is written for parents, educators, caregivers, and others looking for accurate information and expert insight. Newly updated to reflect the latest research, treatment methods, and DSM-V criteria." (Publisher's note)

"Sicile-Kira draws on 20 years' experience as both a professional and a parent in this single-volume guide to Autistic Spectrum Disorders (ASD), first published in Britain in 2003. She covers many topics (e.g., education, diagnosis, treatments, family life, resources, and life for adults with autism) but does not usually provide enough detail to be truly informative, even in an introductory manner... Sicile-Kira does, however, provide a few strong chapters, such as education especially when discussing getting through an Individualized Education Plan (IEP) meeting and services for adults with ASD. For a better single volume on ASD, see Mitzi

Waltz's Autistic Spectrum Disorders. An optional purchase for public libraries." LJ

Includes bibliographical references (p. [337]-350) and index

Ronson, Jon

The psychopath test; Jon Ronson. Riverhead Books 2011 275 p.   **616.85**
1. Research 2. Abnormal psychology 3. Mentally ill -- Institutional care 4. Psychopaths
ISBN 978-1-59448-801-6; 1-59448-801-0
LC 201103133

This book provides an "exploration of psychiatry's attempts to understand and treat psychopathy, [in which] British journalist Ronson . . . reveals that psychopaths are more common than we'd like to think. Visiting Broadmoor Psychiatric Hospital, where some of Britain's worst criminal offenders are sent, Ronson discovers the difficulties of diagnosing the complex disorder when he meets one inmate who says he feigned psychopathy to get a lighter sentence, and instead has spent 12 years in Broadmoor. The psychiatric community's criteria for diagnosing psychopathy . . . is a checklist developed by the Canadian prison psychologist Robert Hare. Using Hare's rubric, which includes 'glibness,' 'grandiose sense of self-worth,' and 'lack of remorse,' Ronson sets off to interview possible psychopaths, many of them in positions of power, from a former Haitian militia leader to a power-hungry CEO." (Publishers Weekly)

Includes bibliographical references (p. [273]-275).

Sacks, Oliver, 1933-2015

The mind's eye. Alfred A. Knopf 2010 263p il $26.95   **616.85**
1. Perception 2. Nervous system 3. Vision disorders 4. Communicative disorders 5. Neurology 6. Face perception 7. Cognition disorders
ISBN 978-0-307-27208-9; 0-307-27208-7
LC 2010-12791

Sacks "offers case histories of six individuals adjusting to major changes in their vision. A renowned pianist has lost the ability to read music scores and must cope with the fear of an ever-shrinking life as her vision worsens. A prolific writer develops 'word blindness' and is unable to read even what he himself writes, forcing him to develop memory books in his mind, adaptations that he later incorporates into his fiction writing. Sacks recalls his own struggle to cope with a tumor in his eye that left him unable to perceive depth. He includes diary entries and drawings of his harrowing experience. . . . [A] riveting exploration of how we use our vision to perceive and understand the world and our place in it and how our brains teach us to 'see' those things we need to lead a complete, fulfilled life." Booklist

Includes bibliographical references

Schreiber, Flora Rheta

Sybil. Warner Books 1995 460p il pa $7.99   **616.85**
1. Multiple personality
ISBN 978-0-446-35940-5; 0-446-35940-8
First published 1973 by Regnery Pub.

This is the "true story of Sybil I. Dorsett, a battered child possessed by 16 different personalities. . . . The author skillfully evokes Sybil's patient work during 11 years of psychoanalysis and her eventual success in integrating these selves into a unified personality." Libr J

Senator, Susan

Autism Adulthood; Strategies and Insights for a Fulfilling Life. Susan Senator. Skyhorse Publishing 2016 320 p. $26.99   **616.85**
  1. Autistic people 2. People with disabilities
  ISBN 151070423X; 9781510704237

This book by Susan Senator "features thirty interviews with autistic adults, their parents, caregivers, researchers, and professionals. Each vignette reveals firsthand a family's challenge, their circumstances, their thought processes, and their unique solutions, and plans of action. Sharing the wisdom that emerges from parents' and self-advocates' experiences, Senator adds her own observations and conclusions based on her long-term experience with autism." (Publisher's note)

"Straightforward and to the point, Senator's book addresses many parents' worst fears and inspires them to step up and create a situation and a community that can support their child in their absence. This is a must-read for any parent with a child on the autism spectrum as well as caregivers, siblings, and extended family. Suitable for any library with parenting and autism collections." Library Journal

Smith, Daniel

Monkey mind; a memoir of anxiety. Daniel B. Smith. 1st Simon & Schuster hardcover Simon & Schuster 2012 viii, 212 p.p (hardcover) $25 **616.85**
  1. Anxiety 2. Journalists 3. Interpersonal relations 4. Anxiety disorders 5. Mentally ill -- United States -- Biography
  ISBN 1439177309; 9781439177303; 9781439177327
                 LC 2011025971

In this memoir, "afflicted journalist and editor [Daniel] Smith uses humor . . . as he explains the excess of thought and emotion also known as 'Monkey Mind' in Buddhism." After college "graduation, he embarks on his first romance and lands a fact-checking job at the Atlantic. . . . Reading the harsh comments posted online about his article and tracking his thoughts and behavior for triggers helps him reroute his psychological circuitry and win his ex back." (Publishers Weekly)

Smith, R. Garth

ASD, the complete autism spectrum disorder health & diet guide; The complete Autism Spectrum Disorder health & diet guide. by R. Smith, Susan Hannah, Elke Sengmueller. Firefly Books Ltd 2014 408 p. illustrations $24.95   **616.85**
  1. Autism 2. Autistic children 3. Children -- Health and hygiene
  ISBN 0778804739; 9780778804734

This book on autism spectrum disorder (ASD), by R. Smith, Susan Hannah, and Elke Sengmueller, "will be a valuable resource for parents, caregivers and health professionals as well, with its combination of years of practical experience and a range of skills and knowledge. . . . 175 recipes and gluten-free/cassein-free meal plans help to build a nutritious, varied and tasty diet that may improve gastro-

intestinal and ASD symptoms for some children." (Publisher's note)

"With sections for all parts of the day, there are plenty of recipes to work through for even the pickiest/limited eater. This should be required reading for anyone wanting to best address healthy options for Autistic people." Pub Wkly

Solomon, Andrew

The **noonday** demon; an atlas of depression. Scribner 2001 569p $28; pa $16   **616.85**
  1. Depression (Psychology)
  ISBN 0-684-85466-X; 0-684-85467-8 pa
               LC 2001-18884

"The author draws on his own life story and other sources for a deeply moving and provocative exploration of depression." Booklist
Includes bibliographical references

Stossel, Scott

My age of anxiety; fear, hope, dread, and the search for peace of mind. Scott Stossel. Alfred A. Knopf 2014 416 p. (hardcover) $27.95   **616.85**
  1. Anxiety 2. Anxiety -- Chemotherapy 3. Anxiety disorders -- Epidemiology 4. Tranquilizing drugs -- Social aspects
  ISBN 0307269876; 9780307269874; 9780307390608
               LC 2013006336

This book, by Scott Stossel, presents an "account of the author's struggles with anxiety, and of the history of efforts by scientists, philosophers, and writers to understand the condition. . . . He ranges from the earliest medical reports of Galen and Hippocrates, through later observations by Robert Burton and Soren Kierkegaard, to the investigations by great nineteenth-century scientists, such as Charles Darwin, William James, and Sigmund Freud." (Publisher's note)

"[T]he author's beautiful prose and careful research combine to make this book informative, thoughtful and fun to read. Powerful, eye-opening and funny." Kirkus
Includes bibliographical references

Styron, William

Darkness visible; a memoir of madness. Random House 1990 84p hardcover o.p. pa $11 **616.85**
  1. Depression (Psychology)
  ISBN 0-679-73639-5 pa
               LC 90-53141

This is an account of the author's experience of suicidal depression and his recovery

"The book's virtues—considerable—are twofold. First, it is a pitiless and chastened record of a nearly fatal human trial far commoner than assumed—and then a literary discourse on the ways and means of our cultural discontents." Publ Wkly

Van der Kolk, Bessel A., 1943-

The **body** keeps the score; brain, mind, and body in the healing of trauma. Bessel A. van der Kolk. Viking 2014 464 p. illustrations $27.95   **616.85**
  1. Stress (Psychology) 2. Post-traumatic stress disorder 3. Stress Disorders, Post-Traumatic -- therapy 4. Stress

Disorders, Post-Traumatic -- physiopathology
ISBN 0670785938; 9780670785933

LC 2014021365

In this book, author Bessel A. van der Kolk "transforms our understanding of traumatic stress, revealing how it literally rearranges the brain's wiring specifically areas dedicated to pleasure, engagement, control, and trust. He shows how these areas can be reactivated through innovative treatments including neurofeedback, mindfulness techniques, play, yoga, and other therapies." (Publisher's note)

"This valuable work for psychologists, therapists, and public health professionals walks the line between academic medical text and popular nonfiction. More important, it offers hope for the millions of sufferers and their families seeking meaningful treatment and relief from the ongoing pain of trauma." LJ

Includes bibliographical references and index

Wansink, Brian

Mindless eating; why we eat more than we think. Bantam Books 2006 276p il hardcover o.p. pa $14   **616.85**
1. Eating habits
ISBN 978-0-553-80434-8; 0-553-80434-0; 978-0-553-38448-2 pa; 0-553-38448-1 pa

LC 2006-47532

The author "explores some of the psychological aspects of overeating to explain why we in fact consume more than we believe we do.... Wansink's dual approach emphasizing food knowledge and self-knowledge offers a sensible route to permanent weight loss." Booklist

Includes bibliographical references

616.86   Substance abuse (Drug abuse)

Beattie, Melody

Beyond codependency; and getting better all the time. Hazelden Foundation 1989 252p pa $15.95   **616.86**
1. Drug abuse 2. Applied psychology
ISBN 0-89486-583-8

The author discusses "the process of recovering from the self-defeating behaviors adopted as survival tactics by adult children of families rendered dysfunctional by parental alcoholism or similar traumas." Publ Wkly

Includes bibliographical references

★ **Codependent** no more; how to stop controlling others and start caring for yourself. 2nd ed.; Hazelden 1992 250p pa $15.95   **616.86**
1. Drug abuse 2. Codependency 3. Health self-care
ISBN 0-89486-402-5

LC 2004-351623

First published 1987

This guide offers advice on how to overcome codependency, aimed at the spouses and other caretakers of people who abuse drugs or alcohol.

Includes bibliographical references

Goldfarb, Toni L.

American Lung Association 7 steps to a smoke-free life; [by] Edwin B. Fisher, Jr. with Toni L. Goldfarb. Wiley 1998 226p pa $14.95   **616.86**
1. Tobacco habit 2. Smoking cessation programs
ISBN 0-471-24700-6

LC 97-38826

"Based on the American Lung Association's smoking cessation program, this book coaches smokers through discovering their own personal motivations and obstacles to quitting, planning effective strategies to meet and conquer the temptation to pick up a cigarette, and tailoring a cessation program to individual lifestyles." Libr J

616.89   Mental disorders

Adamec, Christine

When your adult child breaks your heart; coping with mental illness, substance abuse, and the problems that tear families apart. Joel L. Young, MD., Christine Adamec. Lyons Press, an imprint of Globe Pequot Press 2013 251 p. (pbk.) $19.95   **616.89**
1. Mental illness 2. Substance abuse 3. Self-care, Health 4. Parent and adult child 5. Parents of mentally ill children -- Psychology
ISBN 0762792973; 9780762792979

LC 2013023047

"Behind nearly every adult who is accused of a crime, ... addicted to drugs or alcohol, or ... severely mentally ill ... there is ... one extremely stressed-out parent." This book by Joel L. Young, with Christine Adamec, "presents families with quotations and scenarios from real suffering parents ..., practical advice, and tested strategies for coping. It also discusses the fact that parents of adult children may themselves need therapy and medications." (Publisher's note)

"The book offers practical advice, stories, and resources—and, perhaps most importantly, comfort for any parent facing one of the biggest parenting challenges." Pub Wkly

Includes bibliographical references and index

Bollas, Christopher

When the Sun Bursts; The Enigma of Schizophrenia. by Christopher Bollas. Yale University Press 2015 240 p. 1 illustration $28   **616.89**
1. Schizophrenia
ISBN 0300214731; 9780300214734

This book on schizophrenia, by Christopher Bollas, "asserts that schizophrenics can be helped by much more humane treatments, and that they have a chance to survive and even reverse the process if they have someone to talk to them regularly and for a sustained period, soon after their first breakdown. ... [Bollas] offers his interpretation of how schizophrenia develops, typically in the teens, as an adaptation in the difficult transition to adulthood." (Publisher's note)

"A vastly informative, coherent, and valuable assessment; useful and accessible for both mental health professionals and laypeople—even those who don't share the author's unique perspectives and treatment alternatives." Kirkus

Burns, Tom

★ **Our** Necessary Shadow; The Nature and Meaning of Psychiatry. Tom Burns. W.W. Norton & Co Inc. 2014 384 p. $27.95   **616.89**

1. Psychiatry 2. Medicine -- History
ISBN 1605985708; 9781605985701

Introduction: What is psychiatry and what is it for? -- What to expect if you are referred to a psychiatrist -- Part one. How modern psychiatry developed. The origins of institutional psychiatry -- The discovery of the unconscious -- The rise and fall of psychoanalysis -- The first medical model (between the wars) -- The impact of war -- Out of the asylum - the origins of community care -- Part two. The questions psychiatry asks about us and the questions we ask of it. Is mental illness real? Psychiatry's legitimacy -- Is psychiatry trustworthy? Psychiatry's sins and abuses -- Is bad behavior any of our business? Psychiatry and the law -- A diagnosis for everything and the medicalization of everyday life -- New treatments but old dilemmas -- The rise of neuroscience and the future of psychiatry -- Epilogue

"This is the first attempt in a generation to explain the whole subject of psychiatry. . . . Tom Burns reviews the historical development of psychiatry, throughout alert to where psychiatry helps, and where it is imperfect. What is clear is that mental illnesses are intimately tied to what makes us human in the first place and the drive to relieve the suffering they cause is even more human." (Publisher's note)

"There are fine chapters on neuroscience and pharmaceuticals . . ., and Burns covers antipsychiatry movements, the insanity defense, and the impact of war." LJ

Includes bibliographical references (p. 306-309) and index

Earley, Pete

Resilience; two sisters and a story of mental illness. Jessie Close with Pete Earley. Grand Central Publishing 2015 320 p. 16 plates; illustrations (hardback) $27   **616.89**

1. Mentally ill -- Family relationships 2. Sisters 3. Psychoses 4. Manic-depressive illness
ISBN 1455548820; 9781455530229; 9781455548804; 9781455548828

LC 2014024743

This book, by Jessie Close with Pete Earley, is the memoir of actress Glenn Close's sister after "Jessie first started to exhibit symptoms of severe bipolar disorder. . . . Glenn was always by her side throughout. . . . It wasn't until [Jessie's son] Calen entered McLean's psychiatric hospital that Jessie herself was diagnosed. Fifteen years and twelve years of sobriety later, Jessie is a stable and productive member of society." (Publisher's note)

"Close's story alternates with brief corroborative vignettes written by her sister in a belabored and grim memoir that will nonetheless reach its intended audience thanks to the author's famous sister and their shared nonprofit group geared toward mental health, Bring Change 2 Mind." Pub Wkly

Frances, Allen

★ **Saving** Normal; An Insider's Revolt Against Out-of-control Psychiatric Diagnosis, Dsm-5, Big Pharma, and the Medicalization of Ordinary Life. Allen Frances. HarperCollins 2013 xx, 314 p.p (hardcover) $27.99   **616.89**

1. Psychiatry 2. Mental health 3. Mental illness
ISBN 0062229257; 9780062229250

This book, by Allen Frances, "warns that mislabeling everyday problems as mental illness has shocking implications for individuals and society. . . . We also shift responsibility for our mental well-being away from our own naturally resilient and self-healing brains . . . into the hands of 'Big Pharma,' who are reaping multi-billion-dollar profits." (Publisher's note)

Greenberger, Dennis

Mind over mood; change how you feel by changing the way you think. Dennis Greenberger and Christine A. Padesky. Guilford Press 2016 341 p. (pbk. : alk. paper) $26.95   **616.89**

1. Human behavior 2. Cognitive therapy 3. Mood (Psychology) 4. Affective disorders -- Treatment 5. Cognitive therapy -- Popular works
ISBN 1462520421; 9781462520428

LC 2015025241

Authors Dennis Greenberger and Christine A. Padesky present this book with "steps you can take to overcome emotional distress--and feel happier, calmer, and more confident. The second edition contains numerous new features: expanded content on anxiety; chapters on setting personal goals and maintaining progress; happiness rating scales; gratitude journals; innovative exercises focused on mindfulness, acceptance, and forgiveness." (Publisher's note)

"Recommended for dedicated readers willing to spend an hour a day working on new skills." LJ

Includes bibliographical references and index

Kalb, Claudia

Andy Warhol was a hoarder; inside the minds of history's great personalities. Claudia Kalb. National Geographic Books 2016 320 p. illustrations (hardback) $24   **616.89**

1. Celebrities 2. Mental health 3. Fame -- Psychological aspects 4. Celebrities -- Psychology -- Biography
ISBN 1426214669; 9781426214660

LC 2015024370

In this book, author "Claudia Kalb gives readers a glimpse into the lives of high-profile historic figures through the lens of modern psychology, weaving groundbreaking research into biographical narratives that are deeply embedded in our culture. From Marilyn Monroe's borderline personality disorder to Charles Darwin's anxiety, Kalb provides . . . insight into a broad range of maladies, using historical records and interviews with leading mental health experts." (Publisher's note)

"In all, Kalb's well-written exercise in applying modern psychiatric theory to historical figures, from Marilyn Monroe to Albert Einstein to Charles Darwin, certainly makes for some very entertaining armchair speculation." Booklist

Includes bibliographical references

Lieberman, Jeffrey A.

Shrinks; the untold story of psychiatry. Jeffrey Lieberman, MD, Ogi Ogas. Little, Brown & Co. 2015 352 p. illustrations (hardcover) $28 **616.89**
1. Psychiatry 2. Psychoanalysis
ISBN 0316278866; 9780316278980; 9780316278867
LC 2014956581

This book by Jeffrey A. Lieberman "offers a broad historical perspective of how the mental health profession acquired its notoriously pseudoscientific reputation through chapters mining the processes of diagnosis and treatment, including a generous section highlighting the trailblazing career of Sigmund Freud. . . . Lieberman also discusses psychiatry's historic role regarding issues of sexual orientation, the treatment of PTSD and the riddles involved in diagnosing schizophrenia." (Kirkus Reviews)

"A lively defense of psychiatry that extols brain science and pharmaceutical treatment. A contrasting approach is found in Philip Thomas's Psychiatry in Context; critical of routine overuse of pharmaceuticals, Thomas makes a case for understanding the unique experience of each patient, even in schizophrenia." LJ

Marchant, Jo

Cure; a journey into the science of mind over body. by Jo Marchant. Crown Publishers 2016 320 p. (hardback) $26 **616.89**
1. Mental healing 2. Alternative medicine 3. Mind and body therapies
ISBN 9780385348157; 9780385348171
LC 2015024707

This book, by Jo Marchant, presents a "look at the new science behind the mind's surprising ability to heal the body. . . . We learn how meditation protects against depression and dementia, how social connections increase life expectancy and how patients who feel cared for recover from surgery faster. We meet Iraq war veterans who are using a virtual arctic world to treat their burns and children whose ADHD is kept under control with half the normal dose of medication." (Publisher's note)

"A balanced, informative review of a controversial subject." Kirkus

Includes bibliographical references (pages 257-286) and index.

Porter, Roy

Madness; a brief history. Oxford Univ. Press 2002 241p il hardcover o.p. pa $12.95 **616.89**
1. Psychiatry 2. Mental illness
ISBN 0-19-280267-4 pa
LC 2001-52329

This is a study on the many ways madness has been perceived and misperceived from antiquity to modern times. The author "also discusses topical issues, including the relationship between lunacy and creativity, the drive to institutionalize, which peaked in the mid-20th century; the rise and demise of psychoanalysis; and the development of the antipsychiatry movement. This book combines the appeal of history as narrative with the intellectual stimulation derived from cogent analysis." Libr J

Includes bibliographical references

Scull, Andrew

Madness in civilization; a cultural history of insanity, from the Bible to freud, from the madhouse to modern medicine. Andrew Scull. Princeton University Press 2015 432 p. 32 plates : illustrations (cloth) $39.50 **616.89**
1. Social conditions 2. Mental illness -- History
ISBN 0691166153; 9780691166155
LC 2014956046

This book, by Andrew Scull, explores the cultural history of insanity. "From the Bible to Sigmund Freud, from exorcism to mesmerism, from Bedlam to Victorian asylums, from the theory of humors to modern pharmacology, the book explores the manifestations and meanings of madness, its challenges and consequences, and our varied responses to it." (Publisher's note)

"Scull is sharp on every point, but some of his best moments come when he explains the introduction of psychoanalysis into pop culture in the postwar period, thanks in good part to Hollywood, and when he takes a sidelong look at both the drug-dependent psychiatry of today and its discontents, such as Scientology. To be read as both corrective and supplement to Foucault, Szasz, and Rieff. Often brilliant and always luminous and rewarding." Kirkus

Sederer, Lloyd I.

The **family** guide to mental health care; Lloyd I Sederer, MD; foreword by Glenn Close. W.W. Norton & Co Inc. 2013 xxii, 312 p.p (hardcover) $25.95 **616.89**
1. Mental health services 2. Families of terminally ill 3. Mental illness -- United States 4. Mental health services -- United States 5. Families of the mentally ill -- Counseling of
ISBN 0393707946; 9780393707946
LC 2013007244

This book, by Lloyd I. Sederer, offers advice for families navigating the U.S. mental health care system. "More than fifty million people a year are diagnosed with some form of mental illness. . . . Family members and friends are often the first to realize when someone has a problem. . . . From understanding depression, bipolar illness and anxiety to eating and traumatic disorders, schizophrenia, and much more, readers will learn what to do and how to help." (Publisher's note)

Includes bibliographical references and index.

Shorter, Edward

A **history** of psychiatry; from the era of the asylum to the age of Prozac. Wiley 1997 436p il hardcover o.p. pa $30 **616.89**
1. Psychiatry
ISBN 0-471-24531-3 pa
LC 96-15292

This "social history of 200 years of psychiatry in the U.S., Great Britain, France, and Germany is informative and at times lively. . . . Dealing ably with the major trends, Shorter does not fail to also illuminate such engaging and horrifying byways as the 'fever cure' and ice pick lobotomy." Booklist

Includes bibliographical references

Slater, Lauren

Prozac diary. Penguin Bks. 1999 203p pa
$15   **616.89**
    1. Mental illness 2. Psychotropic drugs
    ISBN 0-14-026394-2; 978-0-14-026394-7
                                        LC 97-35727
    First published 1998 by Random House
    The author "was among the first patients to be given Pro-
zac, and she has now been on it, almost without interruption,
for ten years. She credits the drug with enabling her, after an
incapacitating adolescence, not only to taste and see but to
complete a doctorate; marry; and, as director of a clinic, be
useful. But she also ponders what it means to one's sense of
self to be more or less permanently under the influence of a
personality (and libido) altering drug." New Yorker

Torrey, E. Fuller (Edwin Fuller), 1937-

Surviving schizophrenia; a manual for families, consumers, and providers. E. Fuller Torrey.
3rd ed; HarperCollins 2013 488 p. illustrations
$16.99   **616.89**
    1. Mentally ill 2. Schizophrenia
    ISBN 0062268856; 9780062268853
    Written by E. Fuller Torrey, "Since its first publication
in 1983, 'Surviving Schizophrenia' has become the standard
reference book on the disease and has helped thousands of
patients, their families, and mental health professionals. In
clear language, this . . . book describes the nature, causes,
symptoms, treatment, and course of schizophrenia and also
explores living with it from both the patient's and the family's point of view." (Publisher's note)

Washington, Harriet A.

Infectious madness; the surprising science of
how we catch mental illness. Harriet A. Washington.
Little, Brown & Co./Hachette Book Group 2015 304
p. illustrations $28   **616.89**
    1. Psychology 2. Mental illness
    ISBN 0316277800; 9780316277808
                                        LC 2015935999
    Author Harriet Washington "presents the new germ the-
ory, which posits not only that many instances of Alzheimer's, OCD, and schizophrenia are caused by viruses, prions,
and bacteria, but also that with antibiotics, vaccinations,
and other strategies, these cases can be easily prevented or
treated." (Publisher's note)
    "Recommended for fans of science journalism and
readers interested in the next 'hot topic' in biological
psychiatry." LJ

Whitaker, Robert

Anatomy of an epidemic; magic bullets, psychiatric drugs, and the astonishing rise of mental illness in America. Crown Publishers 2010 404p il
$26   **616.89**
    1. Psychiatry 2. Mental illness 3. Psychotropic drugs
    ISBN 978-0-307-45241-2; 0-307-45241-7
                                        LC 2009-49467
    This is the "first book to investigate the long-term out-
comes of patients treated with psychiatric drugs, and Whitaker finds that, overall, the drugs may be doing more harm

than good. Adhering to studies published in prominent
medical journals, he argues that, over time, patients with
schizophrenia do better off medication than on it. Children
who take stimulants for ADHD, he writes, are more likely
to suffer from mania and bipolar disorder than those who
go unmedicated. Intended to challenge the conventional wisdom about psychiatric drugs, 'Anatomy' is sure to provoke
a hot-tempered response, especially from those inside the
psychiatric community." Salon
    Includes bibliographical references

616.9   Other diseases

Finlay, B. Brett

Let Them Eat Dirt; Saving Your Child from an
Oversanitized World. B. Brett Finlay; Marie-Claire
Arrieta. Workman Pub Co 2016 304 p. (ebook)
$26.95; (hardcover) $26.95   **616.9**
    1. Microbiota 2. Microorganisms 3. Children -- Health
and hygiene
    ISBN 9781616206710; 9781616206499; 1616206497
                                        LC 2016018794
    In this book, microbiologists Brett Finlay and Marie-
Claire Arrieta "explain how the trillions of microbes that
live in and on our bodies influence childhood development;
why an imbalance of those microbes can lead to obesity,
diabetes, and asthma, among other chronic conditions; and
what parents can do--from conception on--to positively affect their own behaviors and those of their children." (Publisher's note)
    "Solid, easily assimilated evidence showing how mi-
crobes are an integral part of a child's healthy life." Kirkus
    Includes bibliographical references (pages 263-274)
and index.

Horowitz, Richard I.

Why can't I get better? solving the mystery
of lyme and chronic disease. Richard Horowitz,
M.D. St. Martin's Press 2013 544 p. (hardback)
$29.99   **616.9**
    1. Diagnosis 2. Lyme disease 3. Chronic diseases 4.
Symptoms
    ISBN 1250019400; 9781250019400
                                        LC 2013013336
    This book, by doctor Richard Horowitz, is "about di-
agnosing, treating and healing Lyme, and peeling away the
layers that lead to chronic disease. . . . [He] covers in detail
Lyme's leading symptoms and co-infections, including immune dysfunction, sleep disorders, chronic pain and neuro-
degenerative disorders–providing a . . . health care model . .
. for physicians and health care providers to effectively treat
Lyme and other chronic illnesses." (Publisher's note)
    "Less self-help and more educational, this work is rec-
ommended for health sciences professionals and medically
literate audiences, not necessarily for introductory or casual
readers." LJ
    Includes bibliographical references) and index

Masterson, Karen M.

The malaria project; the U.S. government's secret mission to find a miracle cure. Karen Masterson.

New American Library 2014 406 p. 16 plates; ills. $26.95 **616.9**
1. Malaria 2. Human experimentation in medicine 3. Malaria -- history -- United States 4. Malaria -- drug therapy -- United States 5. Antimalarials -- history
ISBN 0451467329; 9780451467324

LC 2014018351

This book, by Karen M. Masterson, "is the story of America's secret mission to combat malaria during World War II—a campaign modeled after a German project which tested experimental drugs on men gone mad from syphilis. . . . The project tasked dozens of the country's top research scientists and university labs to find a treatment to remedy half a million U.S. troops incapacitated by malaria." (Publisher's note)

Includes bibliographical references and index

McKenna, Maryn
Superbug; the fatal menace of MRSA. Free Press 2010 271p $26 **616.9**
1. Methicillin-Resistant Staphylococcus aureus
ISBN 978-1-4165-5727-2; 1-4165-5727-X

LC 2009-37793

"McKenna suggests that vaccines might be the answer, but it seems a distant hope — and too late for the patients whose heartbreaking stories she tells. A meticulously researched, frightening report on a deadly pathogen." Kirkus

Includes bibliographical references

Preston, Richard
The **demon** in the freezer; a true story. Random House 2002 240p hardcover o.p. pa $7.99 **616.9**
1. Smallpox 2. Biological warfare
ISBN 0-375-50856-2; 0-345-46663-2 pa

The author explains "the chemical properties of the smallpox virus; how a single infected person . . . can set off an epidemic; and what this horrendous disease can be like. . . . We learn how the disease was eliminated by an international vaccination campaign in the 1970's; why there are reasons to believe that the Soviet Union grew staggering quantities of the virus, allegedly in part to arm intercontinental missiles; and how the virus might now be used by others as a 'strategic weapon.'" N Y Times Book Rev

Weintraub, Pamela
Cure Unknown; inside the Lyme epidemic. Pamela Weintraub. Revised ed. St. Martin's Press 2013 456 p. ill $17.99 **616.9**
1. Lyme disease
ISBN 1250044561; 9781250044563

This book, by Pamela Weintraub, is an "investigation into Lyme disease--the science, history, medical politics, and patient experience. . . . In this nuanced picture of the intense controversy and crippling uncertainty surrounding Lyme disease, Pamela Weintraub sheds light on one of the angriest medical disputes raging today." (Publisher's note)

"When Pamela Weintraub, a science journalist, learned that her oldest son tested positive for Lyme disease, she thought she had found an answer to the symptoms that had been plaguing her family for years. . . . Almost everything about Lyme disease turned out to be deeply controversial, from the microbe causing the infection, to the length and

type of treatment and the kind of practitioner needed." Publisher's note

Includes bibliographical references and index

616.95 Sexually transmitted diseases, zoonoses

Sexually transmitted disease; an encyclopedia of diseases, prevention, treatment, and issues. Jill Grimes, MD, editor; Kristyn Fagerberg, MD and Lori Smith, MD, coeditors. Greenwood 2013 2 volumes (xxxiii, 784 p.)p illustrations $189 **616.95**
1. Reference books 2. Sexually transmitted diseases -- Encyclopedias
ISBN 1440801347; 9781440801341

LC 2013016319

This encyclopedia, edited by Jill Grimes, MD, "contains over 230 entries that span the history and wide range of topics regarding [sexually transmitted diseases], from the birth of condoms over 3,000 years ago through discovery of the infectious agents and the invention of effective vaccines to the legal and societal implications of STDs." (Publisher's note)

"Many entries include boxed case studies, black-and-white photographs, or diagrams to supplement the text. Volume 1 features a time line, from 400 BCE to 2012, offering historical context." Booklist

Includes bibliographical references and index

616.97 Diseases of immune system

Blum, Susan
Your immune system recovery plan; a doctor's 4-step program to feel better now. by Susan S. Blum, MD, MPH; with Michele Bender. Simon & Schuster 2013 384 p. illustrations (hardcover) $27.99 **616.97**
1. Immune system 2. Health self-care 3. Autoimmune diseases -- Treatment 4. Self-care, Health
ISBN 1451694970; 1451694997; 9781451694970; 9781451694994

LC 2012031929

In this book, by Susan S. Blum, with Michele Bender, the author "shares her . . . four-step program to treat, reverse, and prevent autoimmune conditions and repair your immune system. . . . The program she used to treat her own serious autoimmune condition and help countless patients reverse their symptoms, heal their immune systems, and prevent future illness" is outlined in full detail. (Publisher's note)

"By cycling back to the nonnegotiable role of food (for example, Blum expresses frustration with people who think low-calorie packaged snacks are healthy and states that most people are guilty of "food amnesia") and examining the effects of infections on specific conditions, Blum encourages readers to play detective, find the root causes of their problem, and take control of recovery." Pub Wkly

Includes bibliographical references and index

Myers, Amy

The **autoimmune** solution; prevent and reverse the full spectrum of symptoms and diseases. Amy Myers, MD. HarperOne 2015 416 p. illustrations (hardback) $27.99　　　　　　　　**616.97**

1. Popular medicine 2. Autoimmune diseases 3. Autoimmune diseases -- Popular works

ISBN 0062347470; 9780062347473; 9780062347480

LC 2014017620

In this book, by Amy Myers, "a renowned leader in functional medicine . . . offers her medically proven approach to prevent a wide range of inflammatory-related symptoms and diseases, including allergies, obesity, asthma, cardiovascular disease, fibromyalgia, lupus, IBS, chronic headaches, and Hashimoto's thyroiditis." (Publisher's note)

"Americans who suffer from psoriasis, type 1 diabetes, and other autoimmune diseases and want to treat them without conventional medicine will find many alternative ideas in this guide from medical doctor Myers." Booklist

Sicherer, Scott H.

Food allergies; a complete guide for eating when your life depends on it. Scott H. Sicherer; foreword by Maria Laura Acebal; introduction by Hugh A. Sampson. Johns Hopkins University Press 2013 279 p. ill. (hdbk. : alk. paper) $45　　　　　　**616.97**

1. Food allergy 2. Food allergy -- Diet therapy

ISBN 1421408449; 1421408457; 1421408988; 9781421408446; 9781421408453; 9781421408989

LC 2012025274

In this book, Scott H. Sicherer "addresses the full spectrum of food allergies, from mild to life threatening, from single foods to food families, clearing up misconceptions along the way. He explains how exposure to foods can bring about an allergic response, describes the symptoms of food allergy, and illuminates how food allergies develop. He also recommends tests for diagnosing both food allergies and chronic health problems caused by food allergies." (Publisher's note)

"This book is practical and informative without being overwhelming." LJ

Includes bibliographical references and index

Velasquez-Manoff, Moises

An **Epidemic** of Absence; A New Way of Understanding Allergies and Autoimmune Diseases. by Moises Velasquez-Manoff. Simon & Schuster 2012 vii, 385 p.p ill.　　　　　　　　**616.97**

1. Health 2. Immune system 3. Parasitic diseases

ISBN 1439199388; 9781439199381

LC 2012289041

Author Moises Velasquez-Manoff looks at "worm theory"--deliberate infection with parasitic worms--in development to treat autoimmune disease. It explains why farmers' children so rarely get hay fever, why allergy is less prevalent in former Eastern Bloc countries, and how one cancer-causing bacterium may be good for us. It probes the link between autism and a dysfunctional immune system. It investigates the newly apparent fetal origins of allergic disease--that a mother's inflammatory response imprints on her unborn child, tipping the scales toward allergy." (Publisher's note)

Includes bibliographical references (p. 313-356) and index.

616.99　Tumors and miscellaneous communicable diseases

Aaronson, Naomi

Pilates for breast cancer survivors; a guide to recovery, healing, and wellness. Naomi Aaronson, Ann Marie Turo. Demos Medical Publishing, LLC 2014 176 p. illustrations $21.95　　　　　　**616.99**

1. Breast cancer 2. Pilates method 3. Cancer patients 4. Relaxation Therapy -- Popular Works 5. Breathing Exercises -- Popular Works 6. Exercise Movement Techniques -- Popular Works 7. Breast Neoplasms -- rehabilitation -- Popular Works

ISBN 1936303574; 9781936303571

LC 2014020932

This book, by Naomi Aaronson and Ann Marie Turo, presents a guide to Pilates exercises for breast cancer survivors. "No matter where you are in treatment, what side effects you may be experiencing, or your general fitness level, Pilates is a safe and effective way to help you regain flexibility, power, and endurance while relieving treatment side effects such as lymphedema, fatigue, depression, peripheral neuropathy, osteoporosis, and upper extremity impairment." (Publisher's note)

"Strengthening the body and spurring recovery through pilates seems like a win-win. For patient health and fitness collections." LJ

Includes bibliographical references and index

Ahuja, Nita

Johns Hopkins patients' guide to colon and rectal cancer; Nita Ahuja, Brenda S. Nettles. Jones & Bartlett Learning 2013 166 p. illustrations (alk. paper) $27.95　　　　　　　　**616.99**

1. Colon cancer 2. Rectum cancer 3. Rectum -- Cancer -- Popular works 4. Colon (Anatomy) -- Cancer -- Popular works

ISBN 0763774286; 9780763774288

LC 2012023015

This book, by Nita Ahuja and Brenda S. Nettles, "is a concise patient guide on treating and coping with colorectal cancer. . . . The Johns Hopkins Patients' Guides are designed to alleviate your anxiety, empower you with information, and enable you to fully understand your treatment options. . . . The information is there to help lighten your burden and to assist you in becoming an active participant in your care." (Publisher's note)

Ali, Naheed

Understanding lung cancer; an introduction for patients and caregivers. Naheed Ali. Rowman & Littlefield Publishers, Inc. 2014 363 p. (cloth : alk. paper) $38　　　　　　　　**616.99**

1. Caregivers 2. Lung cancer 3. Cancer patients 4. Caregivers -- Popular works 5. Lung -- Cancer --

Popular works
ISBN 1442223235; 9781442223233

LC 2013036194

In this book, Dr. Naheed Ali "helps readers to understand what lung cancer is, how it develops, its different forms, and how both patients and caregivers can approach healing and treatment. Offering a clear background on the disease and its development, this work will help lung cancer sufferers and their friends and family better cope with and understand the diagnosis." (Publisher's note)

Includes bibliographical references and index

Fullbright, Colleen Dolan

How to help your friend with cancer; by Colleen Dolan Fullbright. American Cancer Society/Health Promotion 2014 112 p. illustrations (paperback) $12.95 **616.99**
1. Cancer patients 2. Helping behavior 3. Cancer -- Psychological aspects
ISBN 1604432241; 9781604432244

LC 2014030700

This book, by Colleen Dolan Fullbright, "provides insight into a friend's cancer experience in each part of the journey, answering questions such as 'What do caregivers cite as their number one need?' and 'What does a cancer patient fear most when active treatment is over?' It contains suggestions for expressing concern and helping in practical ways throughout a friend's cancer experience, from diagnosis, through treatment, and after active treatment." (Publisher's note)

Includes bibliographical references and index

Gazella, Karolyn A.

The **definitive** guide to thriving after cancer; a five-step integrative plan to reduce the risk of recurrence and build lifelong health. Lise N. Alschuler, ND, FABNO and Karolyn A. Gazella. Ten Speed Press 2013 224 p. (trade pbk.) $15.99 **616.99**
1. Health 2. Diet therapy 3. Cancer patients 4. Cancer -- Prevention 5. Cancer -- Diet therapy
ISBN 160774564X; 9781607745648

LC 2013014557

In this book, authors Lise N. Alschuler and Karolyn A. Gazella "teach you not just how to survive, but also how to thrive after cancer by integrating the best of conventional, natural, and alternative cancer prevention therapies to support and enhance your body's five critical pathways. With simple, empowering daily actions that you can start today, it is the only program that provides the comprehensive approach needed for optimal health and recurrence prevention." (Publisher's note)

"For cancer survivors and caregivers who need a well-organized, comprehensible manual for healthy living after cancer and who don't already have the previous titles by these authors." LJ

Gubar, Susan, 1944-

Memoir of a debulked woman; enduring ovarian cancer. Susan Gubar. W.W. Norton & Co. 2012 288 p. **616.99**
1. Ovaries -- Cancer -- Patients 2. Ovaries -- Cancer -- Treatment 3. Women -- United States -- Biography

4. Cancer -- Psychological aspects 5. Ovaries -- Cancer -- Patients -- United States -- Biography
ISBN 9780393073256

LC 2011053073

This book presents an "account of the author's ovarian cancer treatment and a staunch protest against the state of contemporary approaches to the disease. In telling her personal story, feminist scholar Gubar . . . remains the academic, looking for understanding not just in the medical literature but also in Frida Kahlo's art . . . and other women's writings." (Kirkus Reviews)

Includes bibliographical references

Hutton, Andrea

Bald Is Better With Earrings; A Survivor's Guide to Getting Through Breast Cancer. Andrea Hutton. HarperCollins 2015 224 p. $17.99 **616.99**
1. Cancer patients 2. Breast cancer -- Treatment
ISBN 0062375652; 9780062375650

This book is author Andrea Hutton's "answer for women diagnosed with breast cancer: a straightforward handbook, leavened with humor and inspiration, to shepherd them though the experience. Warm and down-to-earth, Hutton explains what to expect and walks you through this intense and emotional process: tests, surgery, chemo, losing your hair and shaving your head, being bald, radiation treatments." (Publisher's note)

"Readers will be equally overwhelmed and overjoyed by Hutton's prescriptions. This book could be a lifesaver for breast cancer club members." LJ

Jacobs, Hollye

The **Silver** Lining; A Supportive and Insightful Guide to Breast Cancer. text by Hollye Jacobs, RN, MS, MSW; photography by Elizabeth Messina. Pocket Books 2014 288 p. ill. (some col.) $35 **616.99**
1. Breast cancer 2. Cancer patients 3. Cancer -- Patients -- Attitudes
ISBN 147676350X; 9781476763507

LC 2013019103

Author Hollye Jacobs "offers an unabashedly candid account of her experience with breast cancer. Each chapter . . . focuses on a particular point in the breast cancer journey and discusses how to handle challenges . . . including: diagnosis; relaying the news; . . . surgery; chemotherapy; the isolating nature of the disease; radiation; nutritional and other therapies to ease treatment; discovering the new normal; and redefining your life post-treatment." (Publishers Weekly)

"With her humorous and approachable style, Jacobs has written an essential title for patients facing a cancer diagnosis." LJ

Kalanithi, Paul, 1977-2015

When breath becomes air; Paul Kalanithi. Random House 2016 256 p. 1 illustration (hardback) $25 **616.99**
1. Surgeons 2. Lung cancer 3. Husband and wife 4. Neurosurgeons -- Biography 5. Lungs -- Cancer -- Patients -- United States -- Biography
ISBN 081298840X; 9780812988406

LC 2015023815

In this memoir, author Paul Kalanithi tells how "at the age of thirty-six, on the verge of completing a decade's worth of training as a neurosurgeon, [he] was diagnosed with stage IV lung cancer. [It] chronicles Kalanithi's transformation from a naïve medical student . . . into a neurosurgeon at Stanford working in the brain, the most critical place for human identity, and finally into a patient and new father confronting his own mortality." (Publisher's note)

"This eloquent, heartfelt meditation on the choices that make life worth living, even as death looms, will prompt readers to contemplate their own values and mortality." Booklist

Leaf, Clifton

The **truth** in small doses; why we're losing the war on cancer-and how to win it. Clifton Leaf. 1st S&S hardcover ed Simon & Schuster 2013 512 p. illustrations (hbk. : alk. paper) $27   616.99

1. Cancer 2. Medicine -- Research 3. Drug Discovery -- History

ISBN 1476739986; 9781476739984; 9781476739991; 9781476740003

LC 2013005817

This book, by Clifton Leaf, offers a "history of the war on cancer. . . . [The author] began to investigate why we had made such limited progress fighting this terrifying disease. The result is a gripping narrative that reveals why the public's immense investment in research has been badly misspent." (Publisher's note)

"Leaf believes that the system must be revamped now, arguing that free exchange of information and a major upgrade in preventative medicine are the keys to improvement. An important evaluative study meriting serious public discussion." Kirkus

Includes bibliographical references and index

Leifer, John

After you hear it's cancer; a guide to navigating the difficult journey ahead. John Leifer; with Lori Lindstrom Leifer. Rowman & Littlefield 2015 320 p. (cloth : alk. paper) $36   616.99

1. Cancer patients 2. Cancer -- Popular works 3. Cancer -- Patients -- Popular works 4. Cancer -- Treatment -- Popular works

ISBN 1442246251; 9781442246256

LC 2015000013

This book, by John Leifer, "guides cancer patients along their journey where no one knows the duration or the destination. Divided into the three parts of being a cancer patient—the diagnosis, initial treatment, and on to survivorship—the book will help the newly diagnosed cancer patient navigate a complex health care system, make astute decisions at difficult junctures, and manage the emotional turbulence that can rock his or her world." (Publisher's note)

"Recommended for medically literate cancer patients who want to make well-informed decisions about their treatments." LJ

Includes bibliographical references and index

Mukherjee, Siddhartha

★ The **emperor** of all maladies. Scribner 2010 571p il $30; ebook $14.99   616.99

1. Cancer

ISBN 978-1-4391-0795-9; 1-4391-0795-5; 978-1-4391-8171-3 ebook; 1-4391-8171-3 ebook

LC 2010-24114

The author explores how cancer has been perceived throughout history.

"Mukherjee's formidable intelligence and compassion produce a stunning account of the effort to disrobe the 'emperor of maladies.'" Publ Wkly

Includes bibliographical references

Port, Elisa

★ The **new** generation breast cancer book; how to navigate your diagnosis and treatment options--and remain optimistic--in an age of information overload. Elisa Port, MD, FACS, Chief of Breast Surgery at Mount Sinai Medical Center and Co-director of the Dubin Breast Center. Ballantine Books 2015 320 p. (paperback) $20   616.99

1. Breast cancer -- Diagnosis 2. Breast cancer -- Treatment 3. Breast -- Cancer 4. Women -- Health and hygiene 5. Breast -- Cancer -- Treatment

ISBN 1101883154; 9781101883150

LC 2015022841

This book, by Elisa Port, offers a "definitive guide to managing breast cancer in the information age—a comprehensive resource for diagnosis, treatment, and peace of mind. The breast cancer cure rate is at an all-time high, and so is the information, to say nothing of the misinformation, available to patients and their families. . . . Dr. Elisa Port describes every possible test and every type of doctor visit, providing a comprehensive, empathetic guide." (Publisher's note)

"Over the years there have been many excellent texts for patients from physicians in the field. Port's title is as up-to-date as one can get, with lots to offer people facing a cancer diagnosis or hoping to support someone with the disease." LJ

Prijatel, Patricia

Surviving triple negative breast cancer; hope, treatment, and recovery. Patricia Prijatel. Oxford University Press 2013 256 p. (hardback : alk. paper) $7.95   616.99

1. Breast cancer 2. Cancer patients 3. Breast cancer -- Treatment 4. Breast -- Cancer -- Treatment -- Popular works 5. Breast -- Cancer -- Patients -- United States -- Biography

ISBN 1616518898; 9780195387629

LC 2012012425

This book, by health journalist Patricia Prijatel, "delivers . . . information on . . . [triple-negative breast cancer]; the role of genetics, family history, and race; how to navigate treatment options; understanding a pathology report; and a plethora of strategies to reduce the risk of recurrence. . . . Woven throughout the book are stories of women who have faced TNBC, . . . who went through a variety of medical treatments and then got on with life." (Publisher's note)

Includes bibliographical references and index.

Ross, Theodora

A **cancer** in the family; take control of your genetic inheritance. Theodora Ross. Avery 2016 304 p. illustration (hardback) $25   **616.99**

1. Cancer 2. Genetics 3. Families -- History 4. Cancer -- Genetic aspects 5. Oncologists -- United States -- Biography

ISBN 1101982837; 9781101982839

LC 2015026294

This book, by Theodora Ross, "shows readers how to spot the patterns of inherited cancer, how to get tested for cancer-causing genes, and what to do if you have one. With a foreword by Siddartha Mukherjee, prize winning author of 'The Emperor of All Maladies,' this will be the first authoritative, go-to for people facing inherited cancer, this book empowers readers to face their genetic heritage without fear." (Publisher's note)

"Recommended for readers seeking appropriate information on hereditary cancers, including their causes, and risk management as well as those beyond the target audience who are interested in sound writing on medical topics." Library Journal

Roth, Andrew J.

Managing prostate cancer; a guide for living better. Andrew J. Roth. Oxford University Press 2016 368 p. (paperback) $21.95   **616.99**

1. Prostate gland -- Cancer 2. Men -- Health and hygiene 3. Physician and patient 4. Prostate -- Cancer -- United States 5. Men -- Health and hygiene -- United States 6. Prostate -- Cancer -- Psychological aspects

ISBN 019933692X; 9780199336920

LC 2015016699

This book, by Andrew J. Roth, "provides the emotional skills and strategies necessary to help patients deal with the challenges a prostate cancer diagnosis brings to everyday life. These tools, which Dr. Roth terms 'Emotional Judo,' effectively teach patients to identify what their fears are rooted in, how to distinguish the rational and irrational aspects of their thoughts and behaviors, make healthier choices to promote a more positive approach." (Publisher's note)

"Roth offers a first-rate overview of how best to respond to a diagnosis of prostate cancer." Booklist

Includes bibliographical references and index

Schwalbe, Will

★ The **end** of your life book club; Will Schwalbe. 1st ed. Alfred A. Knopf 2012 viii, 336 p.p (hardcover) $25.00; (paperback) $15.00; (ebook) $25.00   **616.99**

1. Terminally ill 2. Books and reading 3. Mother-son relationship 4. Families of terminally ill 5. Cancer -- Patients -- United States -- Biography 6. Cancer -- Patients -- Family relationships -- United States

ISBN 0307594033; 9780307594037; 9780307739780; 9780307961112

LC 2012018989

In this book by Will Schwalbe, after his mother is "diagnosed with a form of advanced pancreatic cancer" the pair "start a 'book club' that brings them together as her life comes to a close. . . . Their list jumps from classic to popular, from poetry to mysteries, from fantastic to spiritual. The

issues they discuss include questions of faith and courage as well as everyday topics such as expressing gratitude and learning to listen." (Publisher's note)

Scott, Walter J.

Lung cancer; a guide to diagnosis and treatment. Walter J. Scott. 2nd ed. Addicus Books 2012 vii, 110 p.p ill. (pbk.) $19.95   **616.99**

1. Lung cancer

ISBN 1886039097; 9781886039094

LC 2011042503

"The completely revised second edition has been updated to include a discussion of the movement towards customized chemotherapy; treatment options for early-stage lung cancer including minimally invasive surgery; and the most promising treatments, among them multimodality therapy--a combination of surgery, chemotherapy, and radiation." Publisher's note

Includes bibliographical references and index

Sikka, Madhulika

A **breast** cancer alphabet; Madhulika Sikka. Crown Publishers 2014 224 p. $19   **616.99**

1. Breast cancer 2. Cancer patients 3. Breast -- Cancer -- Miscellanea

ISBN 0385348517; 9780385348515

LC 2013003652

In this book, Madhulika Sikka "has gathered together her reflections and discoveries of being in 'Cancerland' in an A-to-Z guidebook to the entire process of cancer diagnosis, treatment and life afterward. The author examines the process of coping with the waves of feelings one will experience (anxiety, guilt, indignity and others), the need for pampering and the odds of a diagnosis--one in eight women in the United States will get breast cancer." (Kirkus Reviews)

"Whether discussing turbans and other headwear, omnipresent anxiety, or the relief that pillows can provide from post-surgery pain, Sikka's voice is calm and earnest, poetic and descriptive, and occasionally even uplifting." Pub Wkly

Includes bibliographical references

Silver, Marc

Breast cancer husband; how to help your wife (and yourself) through diagnosis, treatment, and beyond. foreword by Frederick P. Smith. Rodale 2004 319p pa $14.95   **616.99**

1. Caregivers 2. Breast cancer

ISBN 1-579-54833-4

LC 2004-7914

"Silver's prose is funny, tender, and filled with rock-solid advice." Libr J

Smith, Claire Bidwell, 1978-

The **rules** of inheritance; a memoir. Claire Bidwell Smith. Hudson Street Press 2012 298 p.   **616.99**

1. Bereavement 2. Autobiographies 3. Self-realization 4. Women -- United States -- Biography 5. Bereavement -- Psychological aspects 6. Daughters -- United States -- Biography 7. Psychotherapists -- United States -- Biography 8. Women psychotherapists -- United States -- Biography 9. Children of cancer patients -- United

States -- Biography
ISBN 1594630887; 9781594630880

LC 2011025136

This memoir by Claire Bidwell Smith describes "a young woman who loses her family but finds herself in the process. . . . Smith is just fourteen years old when both of her charismatic parents are diagnosed with cancer. With an impatience typical of youth, Claire throws herself at anything she thinks might help her cope with the weight of this harsh reality: boys, alcohol, traveling, and the anonymity of cities like New York and Los Angeles. By the time she is twenty-five years old they are both gone and Claire is very much alone in the world." (Publisher's note)

Stark, Lizzie

Pandora's DNA; tracing the breast cancer genes through history, science, and one family tree. Lizzie Stark. Chicago Review Press 2014 336 p. (hardback) $26.95   **616.99**
1. Mastectomy 2. Breast cancer 3. Cancer -- Genetic aspects 4. BRCA genes 5. Breast -- Cancer -- Genetic aspects 6. Mastectomy -- Patients -- United States -- Biography
ISBN 1613748604; 9781613748602

LC 2014018310

In this book, Lizzie Stark "uses her family's experience to frame a larger story about the so-called breast cancer genes, exploring the morass of legal quandaries, scientific developments, medical breakthroughs, and ethical concerns that surround the BRCA mutations, from the troubling history of prophylactic surgery . . . to the landmark lawsuit against Myriad Genetics, which held patents on the BRCA genes every human carries." (Publisher's note)

"The book is a must-read for women questioning whether to be tested for the BRCA mutations and for women considering their options after testing positive. A gutsy, deeply revealing account that more than fulfills the promise of the subtitle." Kirkus

Includes bibliographical references and index

Walsh, Patrick C.

Dr. Patrick Walsh's guide to surviving prostate cancer; Patrick C. Walsh and Janet Farrar Worthington. Grand Central Life & Style 2012 590 p. illustrations $19   **616.99**
1. Prostate gland -- Cancer 2. Prostate -- Cancer
ISBN 1455504181; 9781455504183

LC 2011942040

This book, by Patrick C. Walsh and Janet Farrar Worthington, "offers a message of hope to every man facing . . . [prostate cancer.] Prostate cancer is a different disease in every man, which means that the right treatment varies for each man. Readers will discover their risk factors, simple changes that can reduce the risk of developing the disease, treatment options, and more." (Publisher's note)

Wapner, Jessica

The **Philadelphia** chromosome; a mutant gene and the quest to cure cancer at the genetic level. Jessica Wapner; foreword by Robert A. Weinberg, PhD.

The Experiment, LLC 2013 320 p. ill. (some col.) (pbk.) $25.95   **616.99**
1. Chromosomes 2. Gene therapy 3. Philadelphia Chromosome -- United States
ISBN 1615190678; 9781615190676; 9781615191659

LC 2012047686

This book by Jessica Wapner "describes the path from the first description of a chromosomal abnormality in cancer cells to the successful deployment of a gene-targeted medicine against what had previously been a lethal leukemia. Along the way, she pays homage to various scientific underdogs. . . . In the last chapter, Wapner surveys the current landscape of cancer research, noting hurdles to continued progress such as difficulties in sequencing tumors." (Science)

"Wapner weaves together the basic and applied science with the stories of the dedicated researchers, the broader supporting superstructure of modern medicine and the process of bringing pharmaceuticals to market. An absorbing, complex medical detective story." Kirkus

Includes bibliographical references and index

Will my cancer come back? staying healthy after treatment. edited by Julia H. Rowland, PhD, Julie K. Silver, MD. American Cancer Society 2015 240 p. (paperback) $19.95   **616.99**
1. Cancer patients 2. Cancer -- Diet therapy 3. Cancer -- Treatment 4. Cancer -- Exercise therapy 5. Cancer -- Psychological aspects
ISBN 160443211X; 9781604432114

LC 2014030908

"Although no one can predict whether cancer will recur in any one individual, certain behaviors reduce the risk of cancer recurrence for cancer survivors as a group." Edited by Julia H. Rowland and Julie K. Silver, "This book looks at the scientific evidence behind these behaviors; the chapters included cover diet and nutrition, physical activity, social support, psychological interventions, coping strategies, and everything in between."

617 Surgery, regional medicine, dentistry, ophthalmology, otology, audiology

Current surgical diagnosis & treatment; edited by Gerard M. Doherty, Lawrence W. Way. 12th ed; Lange Medical Books/McGraw-Hill 2006 1453p il pa $66.95   **617**
1. Surgery
ISBN 978-0-07-142315-1; 0-07-142315-X

LC 2006-278501

First published 1977. Periodically revised

This book "covers over 1,000 diseases and disorders managed by surgeons . . . {and} emphasizes quick recall of major diagnostic features and succinct descriptions of disease processes, followed by procedures for definitive diagnosis and treatment, epidemiology, pathophysiology, and pathology." Publisher's note

Includes bibliographical references

Doherty, Gerard M.

Current Diagnosis and Treatment Surgery; Gerard M. Doherty. 14th edition McGraw-Hill 2015 1395 p. illustrations pbk $93 **617**

1. Surgery 2. Medicine 3. Diagnosis

ISBN 9780071792110; 0071792112

First published 1977. Periodically revised

This book, by Gerard M. Doherty, provides "evidence-based, point-of-care information on 1000 diseases and disorders most often treated by surgeons. . . . [It includes] coverage of general surgery and all subspecialties you need to be versed in, including otolaryngology, plastic and reconstructive surgery, gynecology, orthopedics, urology, and pediatrics." (Publisher's note)

Gawande, Atul

Complications: a young surgeon's notes on an imperfect science. Metropolitan Bks. 2002 269p $24 **617**

1. Surgery

ISBN 0-8050-6319-6

LC 2001-55884

The author describes the work of a trainee surgeon. The pieces "range from edgy accounts of medical traumas to sobering analyses of doctors' anxieties and burnout. . . . These exquisitely crafted essays, in which medical subjects segue into explorations of much larger themes, place Gawande among the best in the field." Publ Wkly

Includes bibliographical references

617.1   Injuries and wounds

Fainaru, Steve

League of Denial; The NFL, Concussions and the Battle for Truth. Mark Fainaru-Wada and Steve Fainaru. Random House Inc 2013 416 p. illustrations (chiefly color) $27 **617.1**

1. Brain -- Concussion 2. National Football League 3. Sports medicine -- United States 4. Football injuries -- United States

ISBN 0770437540; 9780770437541

LC 2012276088

"Both ESPN investigative reporters, the authors reveal how the NFL, over a period of nearly two decades, sought to cover up and deny mounting evidence of the connection between football and brain damage. This narrative moves between the NFL trenches, America's research labs and the boardrooms where the NFL went to war against science; it examines how the league used its power and resources to attack independent scientists and elevate its own flawed research." Publisher's note

"The narrative is fast-paced and almost cinematic in the way it describes the culture of the gridiron, and in the picture it provides of the NFL research labs where scientists drew their conclusions, and the NFL boardrooms where football executives decided to go to war." Pub Wkly

Yaeger, Don

Any given Monday; sports injuries and how to prevent them for athletes, parents, and coaches :

based on my life in sports medicine. James R. Andrews with Don Yaeger. Scribner 2013 288 p. (hardcover : alk. paper) $25 **617.1**

1. Sports medicine 2. Athletes -- Wounds and injuries 3. Sports injuries

ISBN 1451667086; 9781451667080; 9781451667097; 9781451667103

LC 2012028374

This book, by James R. Andrews and Don Yaeger, presents a "sport-by-sport guide to injury prevention and treatment, written specifically for the parents, grandparents, and coaches of young athletes. From identifying eating disorders to preventing career-ending ACL tears and concussions, 'Any Given Monday' . . . reveals how young athletes can maximize their talent and maintain a lifetime of health both on the field and off." (Publisher's note)

"While it is unlikely that many will read this cover to cover, it makes a great pass-around for parents and grandparents and demands to be read by youth coaches, trainers, and sports administrators, who, hopefully, will heed Andrews' call for change." Booklist

Sports injuries and how to prevent them for athletes, parents, and coaches

617.4   Surgery by systems and regions

Esty, Mary Lee

Conquering Concussion; by Mary Lee Esty, C. M. Shifflett. Round Earth Publishing 2014 310 p. 8 plates; color illustrations $24.95 **617.4**

1. Brain -- Concussion 2. Brain -- Wounds and injuries

ISBN 0965342506; 9780965342506

This book on concussion, by Mary Lee Esty and C. M. Shifflett, "presents history, new research, treatments, and 20 years of clinical case histories. These are real stories about real people struggling with post-concussion symptoms: terrible fatigue, headache and body pain, emotional swings, mental fog, insomnia, weight gain and balance problems. . . . It features neurotherapy, but presents additional therapies that can aid recovery." (Publisher's note)

"Clear figures, photos and illustrations; a glossary; and a list of supplemental resources make the book even more user-friendly.An eye-opener for anyone concerned about concussion—which the authors persuasively argue should include everyone." Kirkus

Kean, Sam

The **tale** of the dueling neurosurgeons; the history of the human brain as revealed by true stories of trauma, madness, and recovery. Sam Kean. Little, Brown & Co. 2014 407 p. illustrations (hardcover) $27 **617.4**

1. Physicians 2. Neurosciences 3. Brain -- Diseases 4. Brain Diseases -- Popular Works 5. Brain -- Physiology -- Popular Works 6. Physicians -- History -- Popular Works 7. Neurosciences -- History -- Popular Works 8. Neurologic Manifestations -- Popular Works

ISBN 9780316286480 (international); 0316182346; 9780316182348

LC 2014004910

In this book, author "Sam Kean travels through time with stories of neurological curiosities: phantom limbs, Siamese twin brains, viruses that eat patients' memories, blind people who see through their tongues. . . . Kean explores the brain's secret passageways and recounts the forgotten tales of the ordinary people whose struggles, resilience, and deep humanity made neuroscience possible." (Publisher's note)

"Entertaining and quotable, Kean's writing is sharp, and each individual story brings the history of neuroscience to life. Compulsively readable, wicked scientific fun." Kirkus

Includes bibliographical references and index

Krug, Louise

Louise; amended. Louise Krug. Black Balloon Pub. 2012 192 p. (trade paper : alk. paper) $14   **617.4**

1. Brain -- Wounds and injuries
ISBN 1936787016; 9781936787012

LC 2011938591

This memoir by Louise Krug describes "A beautiful young woman from Kansas [who] is about to embark on the life of her dreams--California! Glossy journalism! French boyfriend!--only to suffer a brain bleed that collapses the right side of her body, leaving her with double vision, facial paralysis, and a dragging foot. . . . The memoir presents not only Louise's perspective, but also the reaction of her loved ones. . . in fictional interludes." (Publisher's note)

Snyder, Rich, d. 1993

What you must know about dialysis; the secrets to surviving and thriving on dialysis. Rich Snyder. Square One Publishers 2013 197 p. (pbk.) $17.95   **617.4**

1. Chronic disease 2. Kidneys -- Diseases 3. Hemodialysis -- Patients 4. Hemodialysis -- Popular works
ISBN 0757003494; 9780757003493

LC 2012028692

In this book, "osteopathic physician and nephrologist [Rich] Snyder . . . arms patients with . . . information to aid in coping with chronic kidney conditions that require dialysis or a kidney transplant. . . . Focusing primarily on controlling fluid intake and blood pressure, Snyder discusses a dietary regimen, diet supplements, and caring for emotional and spiritual as well as physical well-being." (Publishers Weekly)

Includes bibliographical references and index

Stoler, Diane Roberts

Coping with concussion and mild traumatic brain injury; a guide to living with the challenges associated with post concussion syndrome and brain trauma. Diane Roberts Stoler, Ed.D., and Barbara Albers Hill. Avery 2013 400 p. illustrations (alk. paper) $18   **617.4**

1. Brain -- Concussion 2. Brain -- Wounds and injuries 3. Brain damage 4. Brain damage -- Psychological aspects
ISBN 1583334769; 9781583334768

LC 2013016860

This book, by Diane Roberts Stoler and Barbara Albers Hill, is a "guide for improving memory, focus, and quality of

life in the aftermath of a concussion. Often presenting itself after a head trauma, concussion-- or mild traumatic brain injury (mTBI)-- can cause chronic migraines, depression, memory, and sleep problems that can last for years, referred to as post concussion syndrome (PCS)." (Publisher's note)

"Filled with practical advice on understanding and living with concussion and TBI, this well-written and well-organized volume is an excellent resource for patients who have suffered from this condition and for their family members." LJ

Includes bibliographical references and index

617.5   Regional medicine

Deyo, Richard A.

Watch your back! how the back pain industry is costing us more and giving us less, and what you can do to inform and empower yourself in seeking treatment. Richard A. Deyo MD. ILR Press, an imprint of Cornell University Press 2014 232 p. (Culture and politics of health care work) (cloth : alk. paper) $21.95   **617.5**

1. Backache 2. Backache -- Treatment 3. Back -- Diseases -- Treatment
ISBN 0801453240; 9780801453243

LC 2014006972

In this book, Dr. Richard A. Deyo "proposes an approach to managing back pain . . . that empowers the individual and leads more directly to effective care. . . . [It] exposes [the] flaws in the current approach to back pain, along with the profit motives and conflicts of interest behind many of them. The book dramatizes the problems with stories of prominent individuals who encountered high-tech pitfalls, then found low-tech solutions suited to their lifestyles and the nature of their back pain." (Publisher's note)

"Concise, clearly written, and evidence based, Deyo's work would be invaluable to those facing the onset of back pain and the dizzying range of treatment choices, as well as to practitioners and policy makers." LJ

Includes bibliographical references and index

Laskas, Jeanne Marie, 1958-

Concussion; Jeanne Marie Laskas. Random House Inc 2015 288 p. 8 plates; illustrations (acid-free paper) $16   **617.5**

1. Brain -- Concussion 2. National Football League 3. Sports injuries 4. Head -- Wounds and injuries
ISBN 0812987578; 9780812987577

LC 2015020171

Author Jeanne Marie Laskas presents the "story of Dr. Bennet Omalu, the pathologist who made one of the most significant medical discoveries of the twenty-first century, a discovery that challenges the existence of America's favorite sport and puts Omalu in the crosshairs of . . . the [National Football League]. Omalu discovered in [Mike] Webster's brain . . . proof that Iron Mike's mental deterioration was . . . a disease caused by blows to the head that could affect everyone playing [football]." (Publisher's note)

"Effectively sobering. Suffice it to say that Pop Warner parents will want to armor their kids from head to toe upon reading it." Kirkus

617.6   Dentistry

Artemis, Nadine, 1971-

Holistic dental care; the complete guide to healthy teeth and gums. Nadine Artemis; foreword by Victor Zeines. North Atlantic Books 2013 xvii, 130 p.p color illustrations (pbk.) $16.95   **617.6**
   1. Health self-care 2. Dentistry -- Popular works
   ISBN 1583947205; 9781583947203; 9781583947210
                  LC 2013014011

This book, by Nadine Artemis, is "a comprehensive guide to natural, do-it-yourself oral care, [which] . . . introduces simple, at-home dental procedures that anyone can do. Highlighted with fifty-three full-color photos and illustrations, this book offers dental self-care strategies and practices that get to the core of the problems in our mouths--preventing issues from taking root and gently restoring dental health." (Publisher's note)

Includes bibliographical references   (p. 115-121) and index

Best-Boss, Angie

Your child's teeth; a complete guide for parents. Evelina Weidman Sterling, Angie Best-Boss. Johns Hopkins University Press 2013 296 p. illustrations (hardcover : alk. paper) $40   **617.6**
   1. Children -- Dental care 2. Pedodontics
   ISBN 1421410621; 142141063X; 9781421410623; 9781421410630
                  LC 2012047776

In this book, authors Evelina Weidman Sterling and Angie Best-Boss "team up with pediatric dentists and oral health experts to answer parents' many questions about children's teeth. Topics include: how thumb sucking and pacifiers affect teeth, how to brush your young children's teeth, . . . how to help special needs children get proper dental care, how medical problems affect teeth, how fluoride rinses and dental sealants work, how a root canal is done." (Publisher's note)

"Untypical, too, but much appreciated are Day's admissions of difficult times and how to overcome them. A super (and superquirky) memoir." Booklist

Wynbrandt, James

The **excruciating** history of dentistry; toothsome tales & oral oddities from Babylon to braces. St. Martin's Press 1998 248p il hardcover o.p. pa $14.95   **617.6**
   1. Dentistry -- History
   ISBN 0-312-26319-8 pa
                  LC 98-9794

The author "discusses the development of dentistry as a profession, the use of different anesthetics, and the evolution of dentures and dental prosthetics, among other topics. Much of the book is devoted to anecdotes illustrating discontinued dental practices." Libr J

Includes bibliographical references

617.7   Ophthalmology

Sacks, Oliver W.

The **island** of the colorblind; and, Cycad island. {by} Oliver Sacks. Knopf 1997 298p il maps hardcover o.p. pa $13   **617.7**
   1. Color blindness 2. Parkinson's disease 3. Islands of the Pacific
   ISBN 0-375-70073-0 pa
                  LC 96-34252

First published 1996 in the United Kingdom

"As a travel writer, Sacks ranks with Paul Theroux and Bruce Chatwin. As an investigator of the mind's mysteries, he is in a class by himself." Publ Wkly

Includes bibliographical references

617.8   Otology and audiology

Bouton, Katherine

   ★ **Shouting** won't help; why I - and 50 million other Americans - can't hear you. Katherine Bouton. Sarah Crichton Books/Farrar, Straus, and Giroux 2013 288 p. (hardcover : alk. paper) $26   **617.8**
   1. Deaf 2. Hearing impaired 3. Deafness 4. Deaf women -- New York (State) -- New York -- Biography
   ISBN 0374263043; 9780374263041
                  LC 2012029096

This book, by Katherine Bouton, describes the author's personal experiences struggling with hearing loss. "For twenty-two years, Katherine Bouton had a secret that grew harder to keep every day. . . . She had gone profoundly deaf in her left ear; her right was getting worse. . . . Using her experience as a guide, Bouton examines the problem [of hearing loss] personally, psychologically, and physiologically." (Publisher's note)

Includes bibliographical references and index

618.1   Gynecology and obstetrics

Anstett, Patricia

Breast cancer surgery and reconstruction; What's Right for You. Patricia Anstett; with photography by Kathleen Galligan. Rowman & Littlefield 2016 224 p. illustrations (cloth : alk. paper) $35   **618.1**
   1. Breast cancer 2. Plastic surgery 3. Breast -- Surgery
   ISBN 9781442242623
                  LC 2016003294

This book, by Patricia Anstet, "offers a glimpse into the big picture of the various stages and types of breast reconstruction using stories and photos of real women. It offers a true picture of what breast reconstruction entails, and offers hope to those facing it." (Publisher's note)

"This important, well-reported guide should empower women with breast cancer to figure out their own best treatment." Booklist

Includes bibliographical references and index

Eig, Jonathan

★ The **birth** of the pill; how four crusaders reinvented sex and launched a revolution. Jonathan Eig. W W Norton & Co Inc 2014 416 p. (hardcover) $27.95 **618.1**

1. Oral contraceptives
ISBN 0393073726; 9780393073720

LC 2014019355

This book on this history of birth control, by Jonathan Eig, "revolves around four principal characters: . . . feminist Margaret Sanger, who was a champion of birth control, . . . Katharine McCormick, who owed her fortune to her wealthy husband, . . . scientist Gregory Pincus, who was dismissed by Harvard in the 1930s as a result of his experimentation with in vitro fertilization, . . . and the telegenic John Rock, a Catholic doctor from Boston." (Publisher's note)

Includes bibliographical references and index

Greer, Germaine

The **change**; women, aging and the menopause. Ballantine 1993 422p pa $23 **618.1**

1. Aging 2. Menopause 3. Self-realization 4. Women -- Psychology
ISBN 0-449-90853-4; 978-0-449-90853-2

First published 1991 in the United Kingdom

This is a discussion of menopause in Western society. Greer looks at medical, psychological and social aspects of the cessation of menstruation and the aging process. She views the climateric as an important turning-point in a woman's life.

"In a wise, witty and inspiring book, Greer rebukes doctors, psychiatrists—and women themselves—who blame the aging female for her menopausal distress. . . . Greer dispels all manner of myths and misconceptions about menopause." Publ Wkly

Includes bibliographical references

Love, Susan M.

Dr. Susan Love's Breast Book; Susan M. Love, M.D.; with Elizabeth Love and Karen Lindsey; illustrations by Marcia Williams. 6th edition Da Capo Lifelong Books 2015 704 p. illustrations pbk $24 **618.1**

1. Breast 2. Breast cancer
ISBN 9780738218212; 0738218219

LC 2015458675

This book covers breast development, plastic surgery, common problems, and breast cancer diagnosis, treatment, and screening.

"New to this edition is the use of 'liquid biopsy,' blood tests that trace metastases, and ways of lessening the side effects of chemotherapy and radiation." LJ

Includes bibliographical references and index

Potter, Daniel A.

What to do when you can't get pregnant; the complete guide to all the options for couples facing fertility issues. by Daniel A. Potter, MD, and Jennifer S. Hanin, MA; foreword by Pamela Madsen. Da Capo Press, a member of the Perseus Books Group 2013 xxii, 329 p.p illustrations (paperback) $18.99 **618.1**

1. Infertility 2. Reproductive technology 3. Infertility -- Treatment -- Popular works 4. Human reproductive technology -- Popular works
ISBN 0738216917; 9780738216911

LC 2013372225

This book, by doctor Daniel A. Potter and journalist Jennifer S. Hanin, is a "guide to all the options for couples facing fertility issues, now revised and updated. . . . Drawing on the latest science, Potter and Hanin offer sound advice for choosing the right doctor, asking the right questions, and living a healthy, fertile lifestyle." (Publisher's note)

"This solid, up-to-date resource supplants Debra Fulghum Bruce and Samuel Thatcher's Making a Baby: Everything You Need To Know To Get Pregnant. Recommended for most consumer health collections." LJ

Sheehy, Gail

The **silent** passage: menopause; Rev and updated with four brand-new chapters; Pocket Bks. 1998 xxvi, 293p pa $7.50 **618.1**

1. Menopause
ISBN 0-671-56777-2

LC 98-65873

First published 1992

The author examines the medical, psychological, and social aspects of menopause and includes interviews with women in various stages of menopause and with experts. Discussions of herbal remedies, exercise and diet, menopause in the workplace, estrogen and brainpower, and new frontiers in treatment are included

Silverstone, Alicia, 1976-

The **kind** mama; a simple guide to supercharged fertility, a radiant pregnancy, a sweeter birth, and a healthier, more beautiful beginning. Alicia Silverstone. Rodale 2014 354 p. color illustrations (paperback) $23.99 **618.1**

1. Pregnancy 2. Women -- Health and hygiene 3. Infants -- Nutrition 4. Pregnancy -- Nutritional aspects 5. Childbirth -- Psychological aspects 6. Infertility, Female -- Diet therapy
ISBN 1623360404; 9781623360405

LC 2013049183

"In 'The Kind Mama,' Alicia Silverstone has created a comprehensive and practical guide empowering women to take charge of their fertility, pregnancy, and first 6 months with baby. Drawing on her own experience, as well as that of obstetricians, midwives, nutritionists, holistic health counselors, and others, Silverstone offers advice on getting one's 'baby house' in order through nutrient-rocking foods that heal and nourish." (Publisher's note)

"In addition to her birth story, Silverstone discusses morning sickness, circumcision (not recommended) and the family bed (create a safe sleep sanctuary for the whole family). In "For Gentlemen Only" sections, she doles out useful tips for dads on how to be supportive partners. Health-conscious moms-to-be will enjoy and learn from this heart-centered guide." Pub Wkly

Streicher, Lauren F., 1956-

The **essential** guide to hysterectomy; advice from a gynecologist on your choices before, during, and after surgery. Lauren F. Streicher, M.D. M. Evans 2013 xiv, 466 p.p illustrations (pbk. : alk. paper) $22.95 **618.1**

1. Hysterectomy 2. Women -- Health and hygiene 3. Patient education 4. Hysterectomy -- Popular works
ISBN 1590772113; 9781590772119

LC 2012043565

In this book, author "Lauren Streicher . . . reveals the following: What your doctor isn't telling you; robotic hysterectomy and why it is becoming so popular; new nonsurgical ways to control heavy bleeding; the latest on hormone therapy, including bioidentical hormones; how to decrease your risk of uterine or ovarian cancer without removing your uterus or ovaries; new methods for treating fibroids; and a comprehensive guide to websites and resources." (Publisher's note)

618.178 Infertility

Boggs, Belle

The **art** of waiting; On Fertility, Medicine, and Motherhood. Belle Boggs. Graywolf Press 2016 224 p. (alk. paper) $16 **618.178**

1. Motherhood 2. Infertility
ISBN 9781555977498

LC 2016931135

In this book, author Belle Boggs "recounts her realization that she might never be able to conceive. She searches the apparently fertile world around her--the emergence of thirteen-year cicadas, the birth of eaglets near her rural home, and an unusual gorilla pregnancy at a local zoo--for signs that she is not alone. Boggs also explores other aspects of fertility and infertility." (Publisher's note)

"Readers struggling with infertility may find reassurance and comfort in Boggs's experiences; their loved ones will gain insight into the painful experience of infertility. All readers will appreciate the engaging prose and thought-provoking information." LJ

618.2 Obstetrics

Epstein, Randi Hutter

Get me out; a history of childbirth from the Garden of Eden to the sperm bank. W.W. Norton 2010 302p il $24.95 **618.2**

1. Childbirth
ISBN 978-0-393-06458-2

LC 2009-34751

The author "provides a sharp, sassy history of childbirth. The book is as much a study in sociology as historical snapshot of human birthing practices and gynecological advances, with particular emphasis on developments in the late 19th- and 20th-century United States. . . . The author's engaging sarcasm . . . lends this chronicle a welcome punch and vitality often absent from medical histories." Kirkus

Includes bibliographical references

Mayo Clinic guide to a healthy pregnancy; [by the pregnancy experts at Mayo Clinic; medical editors, Roger Harms, Myra Wick] Good Books 2011 509 p. ill. (chiefly ill.) (pbk.) $19.95 **618.2**

1. Pregnancy 2. Childbirth 3. Prenatal care
ISBN 1561487171; 9781561487172

LC 2011920078

This book, by Roger Harms and Myra Wick, presents a centralized reference to pregnancy, prenatal care and childbirth. "Features include week-by-week updates on baby's growth and month-by-month changes for mom, a 40-week pregnancy calendar, a symptoms guide, and a review of important pregnancy decisions. In this illustrated book you'll also receive advice on how to get pregnant, meal planning, exercise, medication use and parenthood." (Publisher's note)

Guide to a healthy pregnancy

The **mommy** docs' ultimate guide to pregnancy and birth; [by] Yvonne Bohn, Allison Hill, Alane Park with Melissa Jo Peltier. Da Capo Lifelong 2011 526p il pa $15.95 **618.2**

1. Pregnancy 2. Childbirth 3. Infants -- Care
ISBN 978-0-7382-1460-3

"Chapters are arranged from preparing for pregnancy to first, second, and third trimesters; birth; and early days at home. Additional chapters handle complications of early pregnancy, high-risk pregnancies, and 'frequently asked questions . . . and frequently repeated myths.' They offer reassurance for a healthy pregnancy even for those with health conditions such as hypertension or diabetes. Throughout, the authors deliver practical tips and emotional support for coping with both complicated and uncomplicated pregnancies as well as the things that can go wrong, such as miscarriages or infertility. . . . A great resource for anyone seeking information on pregnancy, childbirth, and the first weeks after birth." Libr J

Includes bibliographical references

Murkoff, Heidi

★ **What** to expect when you're expecting; by Heidi Murkoff and Sharon Mazel; foreword by Charles J. Lockwood, MD. 5th edition Workman Pub. Co. 2016 644 p. illustrations hardcover $29.95 **618.2**

1. Pregnancy 2. Childbirth
ISBN 0761189246; 9780761189244

LC 2015044527

"The revised fifth edition of 'America's pregnancy bible' has completely updated medical information, including the latest on prenatal screening, a brand-new section on postpartum birth control, and effects of current lifestyle trends, such as juice bars, raw diets, e-cigarettes, and omega-3 fatty acids, on pregnant women." LJ

Pregnancy day by day; an illustrated daily countdown to motherhood, from conception to childbirth and beyond. consultant editor, Paula Amato; editor-in-chief, Maggie Blott. DK Publishing 2009 496 p. col. ill. $40 **618.2**

1. Childbirth 2. Women -- Health and hygiene 3. Pregnancy -- Popular works 4. Pregnancy -- Pictorial

works
ISBN 0756650410; 1465415904; 9780756650414;
9781465415905

LC 2010280671

Edited by Maggie Blott, "For expectant parents who want to know everything about their developing baby at every stage, 'Pregnancy Day by Day' provides a daily countdown to the date of delivery. Covering each day of pregnancy in detail, as well as labor, birth, and life with a new baby, 'Pregnancy Day by Day' is [a] . . . guide that is written by a team of experts." (Publisher's note)

Includes bibliographical references (p. 480-481) and index

The **pregnancy** encyclopedia; all your questions answered. consultant editor, Paula Amato, M.D.; editor-in-chief, Dr. Chandrima Biswas, consultant obstetrician. DK Publishing 2016 351 p. color illustrations (hbk) $40   **618.2**
1. Infants 2. Pregnancy 3. Childbirth 4. Pregnancy -- Popular works 5. Childbirth -- Popular works 6. Obstetrics -- Popular works 7. Newborn infants -- Popular works
ISBN 1465443789; 9781465443786

LC 2016304347

This book "is an engaging and accessible question-and-answer guide to some of the most commonly asked questions about pregnancy, packed with full-color photographs and illustrations. . . . Top experts in the field offer encyclopedic coverage of the topics relating to pregnancy and birth, from fertility and family planning to nutrition and exercise to lifestyle changes, planning for the future, and more." (Publisher's note)

"This book will be a very useful resource. It has a detailed index and a glossary to help readers find what they need. This is an excellent addition to public and consumer-health library collections." Booklist

Romm, Aviva Jill

The **natural** pregnancy book; your complete guide to a safe, organic pregnancy and childbirth with herbs, nutrition, and other holistic choices. Aviva Jill Romm; foreword by Ina May Gaskin. Ten Speed Press 2014 xvi, 288 p.p (paperback) $17.99 **618.2**
1. Pregnancy 2. Holistic medicine 3. Pregnancy -- Popular works 4. Holistic medicine -- Popular works 5. Alternative medicine -- Popular works
ISBN 1607744481; 9781607744481; 9781607744498

LC 2014008356

Written by Aviva Jill Romm, this is "A revised and updated edition of the classic handbook for women seeking a safe, organic, eco-friendly, and natural pregnancy, featuring an integrative-based approach with new medical, herbal, and nutritional information. . . . Dr. Romm takes a holistic approach, emphasizing natural remedies wherever possible and providing up-to-date advice on herbs that promote wellness during pregnancy." (Publisher's note)

Includes bibliographical references and index

Sears, William

The **healthy** pregnancy book; month by month, everything you need to know from America's baby experts. Williams Sears, MD, and Martha Sears, RN, with Linda Holt, MD, and BJ Snell, PhD, CNW. Little, Brown & Co. 2013 xviii, 446 p.p illustrations $17   **618.2**
1. Pregnancy 2. Women -- Health and hygiene 3. Childbirth
ISBN 0316187437; 9780316187435

LC 2013946521

In this book, author William Sears and Martha Sears "address emotional and physical changes that take place during pregnancy, baby's brain development, healthy pregnancy habits, pregnancy superfoods, optimal weight gain, fitness, managing stress, sleep, choosing the right healthcare provider, birthing choices, the transition into parenthood, engaging personal stories, and more." (Publisher's note)

Includes bibliographical references (pages 425-427) and index

Simkin, Penny

The **Birth** Partner; A Complete Guide to Childbirth for Dads, Doulas & All Other Labor Companions. HougHton Mifflin Harcourt 2013 396 p. illustrations $18.95   **618.2**
1. Pregnancy 2. Childbirth 3. Pregnancy -- Popular works
ISBN 155832819X; 9781558328198

LC 891763

"Since the original publication of 'The Birth Partner,' new mothers' mates, friends, and relatives and doulas (professional birth assistants) have relied on Penny Simkin's guidance in caring for the new mother from the last few weeks of pregnancy through the early postpartum period. Fully revised in its fourth edition, 'The Birth Partner' remains the definitive guide for preparing to help a woman through childbirth and the essential manual to have at hand during the event." (Publisher's note)

Vincent, Peggy

Baby catcher; chronicles of a modern midwife. Scribner 2002 336p $26; pa $13   **618.2**
1. Midwives
ISBN 0-7432-1933-3; 0-7432-1934-1 pa

LC 2001-54988

This is an account of a midwife specializing in home births who "over the course of 40 years, brought some 2,000 babies into the world. . . . A solid writer, Vincent doesn't preach the virtues of unmedicated birthing; she just lays consistent stories of women doing it—Christian Science moms, Muslim moms, spiritualist moms, lesbian moms, teen moms and just plain ordinary moms." Publ Wkly

★ **Your** pregnancy week by week; Glade B. Curtis, M.D., M.P.H., OB/GYN and Judith Schuler, M.S. 8th edition DaCapo Lifelong 2016 463 p. illustrations pbk $15.99   **618.2**
1. Fetus 2. Pregnancy
ISBN 9780738218939; 0738218936

LC 2016303069

First published 1989 by Fisher Books

This book, by Glade B. Curtis and Judith Schuler, "provides everything expectant parents need for a healthy, happy pregnancy, including descriptions of the fetus's development each week, up-to-date information about medical tests and procedures, safe weekly exercises to help expectant moms stay in shape, and helpful hints for the father-to-be." (Publisher's note)

618.3 Diseases, disorders, management of pregnancy, childbirth, puerperium

Ilse, Sherokee

The **prenatal** bombshell; help and hope when continuing or ending a precious pregnancy after an abnormal diagnosis. Stephanie Azri and Sherokee Ilse. Rowman & Littlefield 2015 254 p. (cloth : alk. paper) $37 **618.3**

1. Pregnancy 2. Prenatal care 3. Bereavement -- Personal Narratives 4. Decision Making -- Personal Narratives 5. Abortion, Induced -- Personal Narratives 6. Patient Education as Topic -- Personal Narratives 7. Prenatal Diagnosis -- psychology -- Personal Narratives
ISBN 1442239425; 9781442239425

LC 2014040890

Authors Stephanie Azri and Sherokee Ilse present this "companion guide through the journey from diagnosis and beyond once you've decided to either continue or end your precious pregnancy. Issues such as managing the pregnancy, delivery, termination, creating memories, future babies, and the long term impact of such a traumatic experience are all covered in detail. The lived experiences of other women who have gone through this journey are also included to provide hope, support, and guidance through difficult times." (Publisher's note)

"The book's underlying message for parents is to look clearly at what is happening and to accept, not try to deny, the difficult emotions that it will bring. This book is an excellent vehicle for coming to grips with a very difficult situation." Pub Wkly

Includes bibliographical references and index

618.4 Childbirth

Gaskin, Ina May

Ina May's guide to childbirth. Bantam Books 2003 348p il pa $14.95 **618.4**

1. Natural childbirth
ISBN 0-553-38115-6

LC 2002-29901

Gaskin "explains that the female body is well designed for normal birth and provides techniques for dealing with the discomforts of labor. A whole chapter devoted to women's birthing experiences supports her stance. More than a childbirth guide, this comprehensive book provides insight into the sociological and historical aspects of the natural childbirth movement." Libr J

Includes bibliographical references

Leboyer, Frédérick, 1918-

Birth without violence; Frédérick Leboyer; new translation by Yvonne Fitzgerald and the author. 3rd

ed Healing Arts Press 2009 xiii, 130 p.p ill. (pbk.) $14.95 **618.4**

1. Childbirth 2. Natural childbirth
ISBN 1594772975; 9781594772979

LC 2009001028

Original French edition, 1974; first English translation published 1975 by Knopf

This book, by Frédérick Leboyer, translated by Yvonne Fitzgerald, advocates that "babies are born complete human beings with the ability to experience a full range of emotions. First published in 1974, it revolutionized the way we perceive the process of birth. . . . Examining alternatives to technocentric approaches to childbirth, this new edition . . . shows us how we can ease the transition from womb to world without trauma or fear." (Publisher's note)

A new edition of the book that "revolutionized the way we perceive the process of birth, urging us to consider birth from the infant's point of view." It shows how to "ease the transition from womb to world without trauma or fear." (Publisher's note)

618.92 Pediatrics

Barkley, Russell A.

Taking Charge of ADHD; The Complete, Authoritative Guide for Parents. Russell A. Barkley, PHD. 3rd ed The Guilford Press 2013 363 p. pbk $19.95; hc $55 **618.92**

1. Child psychology 2. Adolescent psychology 3. Attention deficit disorder 4. Child rearing 5. Attention-deficit hyperactivity disorder
ISBN 1462508510; 1462507891; 9781462507894; 9781462508518
First published 1995

Presents "science-based information . . . about attention-deficit/hyperactivity disorder (ADHD) and its treatment. It also presents a proven eight-step behavior management plan specifically designed for 6- to 18-year-olds with ADHD. Updated throughout with current research and resources, the third edition includes the latest facts about medications and about what causes (and doesn't cause) ADHD." Publisher's note

Includes bibliographical references and index

Barnett, Kristine

The **spark**; raising a genius. Kristine Barnett. Random House 2013 272 p. illustrations $25 **618.92**

1. Autism 2. Genius 3. Parents of autistic children 4. Autism in children -- Case studies 5. Autistic children -- Rehabilitation 6. Mothers of autistic children -- Case studies
ISBN 0812993373; 9780679645245; 9780812993370

LC 2012032774

This book, by Kristine Barnett is a "memoir that attempts to answer the question, how do we determine the differences between gifted and disabled? . . . Her son Jake received a diagnosis [of autism] at the age of 2, which set off a series of standard educational responses. . . . Barnett took an approach that instead focused on what she would refer to as his 'spark.' . . . Her success with Jake is unimpeachable: He is a 'prodigy in math and science.'" (Kirkus Reviews)

"Barnett even runs a day-care center, takes in foster kids, and starts a sports program for autistic kids. Jake is unusual, but so is his superhuman mom." Booklist

Bashe, Patricia Romanowski, 1949-

Asperger Syndrome; The Oasis Guide: Advice, Inspiration, Insight, and Hope, from Early Intervention to Adulthood. Patricia Romanowski Bashe. 3rd ed Random House Inc 2014 592 p. illustrations $17   **618.92**

1. Autism 2. Asperger's syndrome
ISBN 0385344651; 9780385344654
First published 2001

This book, by Patricia Romanowski Bashe, offers a "comprehensive, authoritative guide to Asperger syndrome. This fully revised, updated, and expanded edition captures the latest in research, strategies, and parenting wisdom, and delivers it all in the empathetic, practical, and hope-filled style 'The OASIS Guide' is famous for." (Publisher's note)

"This edition includes new developments made in AS research over the past four years, new thinking on diagnosis and evaluation, the latest approaches to medication and social skills development, and tips on navigating the maze of interventions, therapies, and special education." Publisher's note

Includes bibliographical references

The **big** book of symptoms; A-Z guide to your child's health. American Academy of Pediatrics; [edited by] Steven P. Shelov, MD, MS, FAAP, Shelly Vaziri Flais, MD, FAAP. American Academy of Pediatrics 2014 260 p. illustrations $16.95   **618.92**

1. Diagnosis 2. Children -- Health and hygiene
ISBN 1581108400; 9781581108408

LC 2013945504

Edited by Steven P. Shelov and Shelly V. Flais, "This book is designed to help you distinguish minor everyday concerns with more serious conditions, and to suggest a reasonable course of action. Organized into 2 sections, an A to Z directory of the 100 or so most common childhood symptoms and an illustrated first aid manual, 'Symptoms' will help parents determine the best way to help their sick child." (Publisher's note)

"In July 2011, the American Academy of Pediatrics (AAP) published My Child Is Sick: Expert Advice for Managing Common Illnesses and Injuries by Barton D. Schmitt, whose bulleted and numbered triage system was more helpful. While any AAP title is worthy of consideration for libraries, those owning Schmitt's can pass on this." LJ

Camarata, Stephen M.

Late-talking children; a symptom or a stage? Stephen M. Camarata. The MIT Press 2014 256 p. (hardcover : alk. paper) $19.95   **618.92**

1. Child development 2. Children -- Language 3. Language disorders in children 4. Language disorders in children -- Diagnosis 5. Developmentally disabled children -- Education
ISBN 0262027798; 9780262027793

LC 2014003809

In this book, author Stephen Camarata "describes in accessible language what science knows about the characteristics and causes of late talking. He explains that late talking is only one of a constellation of autism symptoms. Although all autistic children are late talkers, not all late-talking children are autistic." (Publisher's note)

"Camarata, while wanting to support parents, sometimes has an alarmist tone, even when referring to colleagues. The text, therefore, is more appropriate for academic audiences and scientific readers than the distressed parent. Undergraduate libraries and colleges with speech therapy programs will want to consider." LJ

Includes bibliographical references and index

Chansky, Tamar E.

Freeing your child from anxiety; practical strategies to overcome fears, worries, and phobias and be prepared for for life--from toddlers to teens. Tamar Chansky, Ph.D.; illustrations by Phillip Stern. Harmony Books 2014 viii, 468 p.p illustrations (paperback) $16.99   **618.92**

1. Anxiety 2. Child psychology 3. Anxiety in children
ISBN 0804139806; 9780804139809

LC 2013050665

This book, by Tamar Chansky, "contains easy, fun, and effective tools for teaching children to outsmart their worries and take charge of their fears. This revised and updated edition also teaches how to prepare children to withstand the pressure in our competitive test-driven culture." (Publisher's note)

Includes bibliographical references (pages 449-450) and index

Chicoine, Brian

The **guide** to good health for teens & adults with Down syndrome; [by] Brian Chicoine & Dennis McGuire. Woodbine House 2010 391p il pa $29.95   **618.92**

1. Down syndrome
ISBN 978-1-890627-89-8

LC 2010-18783

"This excellent book provides a wealth of information for DS caregivers. . . . The authors describe diagnosis, treatment, and prevention of common health conditions impacting DS people and cover mental and emotional issues that can affect physical health. Sexuality and birth control are discussed, as is abuse prevention. The book also includes information on residential options as well as coverage of end of life issues." Libr J

Includes bibliographical references

Cohen, Scott W.

Eat, sleep, poop; a common sense guide to your baby's first year--essential information from an award-winning pediatrician and new dad. Scribner 2010 291p il pa $16   **618.92**

1. Infants -- Care
ISBN 978-1-4391-1706-4; 1-4391-1706-3

LC 2009-37966

"Cohen is great at identifying parental concerns, and he responds with reassuring answers, providing just enough information to assuage worries. Of the multitude of baby guides out there, this is, hands down, one of the best in years." Libr J

Includes bibliographical references

Dawson, Geraldine

A **parent's** guide to high-functioning autism spectrum disorder; how to meet the challenges and help your child thrive. Sally Ozonoff, Geraldine Dawson, James C. McPartland. The Guilford Press 2015 308 p. (paperback) $18.95   **618.92**
1. Autism 2. Autistic children 3. Asperger's syndrome 4. Parents of autistic children 5. Asperger's syndrome -- Popular works 6. Autism spectrum disorders -- Popular works
ISBN 1462517471; 9781462517473; 9781462517954
    LC 2014026326

In this book on high-functioning autism spectrum disorder (ASD), authors Sally Ozonoff, Geraldine Dawson, and James C. McPartland "show how you can work with your child's unique impairments--and harness his or her capabilities. Vivid stories and real-world examples illustrate ways to help kids with ASD relate more comfortably to peers, learn the rules of appropriate behavior, and succeed in school. You'll learn how ASD is diagnosed and what treatments and educational supports really work." (Publisher's note)

Includes bibliographical references and index

Estreich, George

The **Shape** of the Eye; A Memoir. George Estreich. Penguin Group USA Jeremy P. Tarcher/Penguin 2013 336 p. $16.95   **618.92**
1. Heredity 2. Down syndrome 3. Children with disabilities 4. Authors, American -- Biography 5. Stay at home fathers -- Biography 6. Down syndrome -- Patients -- Biography 7. Children with disabilities -- Biography 8. Down syndrome -- Patients -- Family relationships 9. Parents of children with disabilities -- Biography
ISBN 0399163344; 9780399163340
    LC 2013009657

"In this . . . memoir, George Estreich, a poet and stay-at-home dad, tells his daughter's story, reflecting on her inheritance--from the literal legacy of her genes, to the family history that precedes her, to the Victorian physician John Langdon Down's diagnostic error of 'Mongolian idiocy.' Against this backdrop, Laura takes her place in the Estreich family as a unique child, quirky and real, loved for everything ordinary and extraordinary about her." (Publisher's note)

"An elegantly written, luminous, and profoundly human portrait of pain and sorrow, hope and cautious optimism." Booklist

Includes bibliographical references (pages [299]-314)

Foss, Ben

The **dyslexia** empowerment plan; a blueprint for renewing your child's confidence and love of learning. by Ben Foss. Ballantine Books 2013 336 p. (hardback) $27   **618.92**
1. Parents 2. Dyslexia 3. Child psychology 4. Dyslexic children -- Rehabilitation 5. Parents of children with disabilities
ISBN 0345541235; 9780345541239
    LC 2013023931

In this book, author Ben Foss "describes dyslexia as a characteristic and a disability that should be accommodated in the same way as blindness or mobility issues. Foss reframes the use of film, audiobooks, and material read aloud as ear-reading, in contrast to the eye-reading that is the educational standard. He hopes that parents can learn to explain their child's needs in a way that will win them essential support, and that they can help their child build self-esteem." (Publishers Weekly)

Includes bibliographical references and index

French, Thomas

Juniper; The Girl Who Was Born Too Soon. Kelley French, Thomas French. Little, Brown & Co. 2016 336 p. illustrations $26   **618.92**
1. Parents 2. Premature infants
ISBN 0316324426; 9780316324427
    LC 2016933403

In this memoir, by Kelley French and Thomas French, "a micro preemie fights for survival. . . . Juniper French was born four months early, at 23 weeks gestation. She weighed 1 pound, 4 ounces, and her twiggy body was the length of a Barbie doll. . . . Premature babies like Juniper, born at the edge of viability, trigger the question: Which is the greater act of love--to save her, or to let her go?" (Publisher's note)

"A fierce and fact-filled love story with few holds barred." Kirkus

Gnaulati, Enrico

Back to normal; why ordinary childhood behavior Is mistaken for ADHD, bipolar disorder, and Autism Spectrum Disorder. Enrico Gnaulati. Beacon Press 2013 256 p. (alk. paper) $26.95   **618.92**
1. Mental health 2. Child psychology 3. Adolescent psychology
ISBN 0807073342; 9780807073346; 9780807073353
    LC 2013009182

This book, by clinical psychologist Enrico Gnaulati, is a "definitive account of why our kids are being dramatically overdiagnosed-- and how parents and professionals can distinguish between true psychiatric disorders and normal childhood reactions to stressful life situations. . . . Gnaulati tells detailed stories of wrongly diagnosed kids, . . . with information about the developmental, temperamental, and environmentally driven symptoms that . . . can mimic a psychiatric disorder." (Publisher's note)

"Gnaulati makes a strong case that an incorrect diagnosis of behavioral problems can be stigmatizing and that prescription drugs frequently have overlooked, negative side effects. A valuable guide for parents and educators that includes tips on choosing a therapist and parenting strategies." Kirkus

Includes bibliographical references and index

Harris, Sandra L.

Essential first steps for parents of children with autism; helping the littlest learners. by Lara Delmolino & Sandra L. Harris. 1st edition Woodbine

House 2014 154 p. illustrations (Topics in autism)
$21.95   **618.92**

1. Autism 2. Parents of autistic children 3. Autistic children

ISBN 1606131893; 9781606131893

LC 2013038047

The authors "offer a detailed, authoritative guide that discusses everything from early indicators of autism to likely behaviors (including those rooted in sensory issues), how-to's for increasing communication and social skills, and family support. Case studies and reviews of promising research and interventions make this the go-to guide for parents of autistic children." LJ

Includes bibliographical references and index

Siblings of Children With Autism; A Guide for Families. [by] Sandra L. Harris and Beth A. Glasberg. Woodbine House 2012 163 p. illustrations
$21.95   **618.92**

1. Autism 2. Siblings 3. Autistic children 4. Autistic children -- Family relationships

ISBN 1606130749; 9781606130742

LC 20031239

This book, by Sandra L. Harris and Beth A. Glasberg, "takes a fresh look at what it's like to grow up as the brother or sister of a child with autism--the basics of sibling relationships at all ages and how autism can affect these dynamics. Parents get important advice about balancing responsibilities for each child, encouraging their kids to share feelings, explaining autism to other children, and initiating play and interaction between siblings." (Publisher's note)

Hayden, Torey L.

Twilight children; three voices no one heard until a therapist listened. [by] Torey Hayden. William Morrow 2005 331p $24.95   **618.92**

1. Child abuse 2. Psychotherapy

ISBN 0-06-056088-6

LC 2004-47376

"The author documents the particulars of her approach to treating a volatile, manipulative nine-year-old abuse victim; a mute but sociable and atypically charismatic four-year-old; and, in a change of pace, an 82-year-old stroke victim. The dysfunctional family dynamics impacting each patient are explored, as are impediments to the therapist's interfacing with relatives." SLJ

Jackson, Luke

Freaks, geeks and asperger syndrome; a user guide to adolescence. foreword by Tony Attwood. Kingsley, J. 2002 217p il pa $17.95   **618.92**

1. Autism 2. Asperger's syndrome 3. Adolescent psychology 4. Autistic youth 5. Asperger's syndrome -- Patients 6. Asperger's syndrome -- Patients -- Family relationships

ISBN 1-8431-0098-3

LC 2002-70930

"In this terrific book that is sure to inspire other adolescents with the same condition, 13-year-old Jackson offers a teenager's perspective on what it's like to live with

Asperger's. He also writes about his younger brother, who has a more severe condition on the ASD spectrum." Libr J

Includes bibliographical references

Sex, drugs and Asperger's syndrome (ASD) a user guide to adulthood. Luke Jackson; foreword by Tony Attwood. Jessica Kingsley Publishers 2016 208 p. (alk. paper) $25   **618.92**

1. Adulthood 2. Autistic people -- Life skills guides 3. Autistic youth -- Life skills guides 4. Asperger's syndrome -- Patients -- Family relationships

ISBN 9781849056458

LC 2015027315

This book, by Luke Jackson, is an "unabridged and sparkling sequel to his . . . user guide to adolescence 'Freaks, Geeks and Asperger Syndrome.' . . . With devastating clarity, Luke focuses on the pitfalls involved in navigating the transition to adulthood, and the challenges of adult life. He covers everything from bullying and drugs to socialising, sex, negotiating relationships, and finding and keeping your first job." (Publisher's note)

"Jackson's personal and brutally honest take on being an adult with ASD is eye-opening and refreshing. A valuable read for teens and adults with ASD as well as parents, siblings, employers, teachers, caregivers, friends, and partners of those on the spectrum." LJ

Jassey, Jonathan

The **newborn** sleep book; a simple, proven method for training your new baby to sleep through the night. Dr. Lewis Jassey and Dr. Jonathan Jassey. Perigee Trade 2014 224 p. (paperback) $15 **618.92**

1. Sleep 2. Infants -- Health and hygiene 3. Infants -- Sleep

ISBN 0399167986; 9780399167980

LC 2014011339

This book by Lewis Jassey and Jonathan Jassey provides advice on getting newborn babies to sleep through the night by strictly regulating feeding times despite an infant's hunger. "The Jassey Way uses a feeding schedule that allows newborns (and their parents) a full night's sleep at a younger age than other sleep training techniques." (Publisher's note)

"Parent testimonials and numerous checklists are appended to this manageable plan." Pub Wkly

Includes bibliographical references

Lazebnik, Claire

Overcoming Autism; Finding the Answers, Strategies and Hope That Can Transform a Child's Life. by Lynn Kern Koegel and Claire LaZebnik. Penguin Group USA 2014 398 p. $17   **618.92**

1. Child rearing 2. Autistic children 3. Parents of autistic children 4. Autism in children

ISBN 0143126547; 9780143126546

LC 2013046676

This book, by Lynn Kern Koegel and Claire LaZebnik, is "a fully revised and updated edition of the definitive guide to reducing symptoms of autism spectrum disorder. . . . This revised edition has also been expanded to clarify the importance of community support to affected families and the effect of societal acceptance on a child's life." (Publisher's note)

"The book has the feel of a reference work with a structure that uses questions to open each section. More accessible and straightforward than most books detailing treatments, including Bryna Siegel's Helping Children with Autism Le'tn, this book is strongly recommended." LJ

Leach, Penelope

Your Baby and Child From Birth to Age Five; Penelope Leach; photographs by Camilla Jessel. Alfred A. Knopf 2010 559 p. color illustrations $23.95 **618.92**
1. Parenting 2. Child development
ISBN 0375712038; 9780375712036
LC 2010022848

This book, by Penelope Leach, "encompasses the latest research and thinking on child development and learning, and reflects the realities of today's changing lifestyles and new approaches to parenting. . . . Dr. Leach describes--in easy-to-follow stages, from birth through starting school-- what is happening to your child, what he or she is doing, experiencing and feeling." (Publisher's note)

"In addition to physical growth and progress, Leach addresses the psychosocial needs of children. She also includes parent concerns and responses similar to those found in Workman's 'What To Expect' series. Public and academic libraries would do well to stock the new version of this primer on children and their development for circulation as well as for the reference shelf." LJ

Linden, Dana Wechsler

Preemies; the essential guide for parents of premature babies. Dana Wechsler Linden, Emma Trenti Paroli, and Mia Wechsler Doron. 2nd ed Gallery Books 2010 xxii, 633 p.p ill. $26.99 **618.92**
1. Infants -- Care 2. Premature infants 3. Infants -- Health and hygiene 4. Premature infants -- Care 5. Pregnancy -- Complications 6. Birth weight, Low -- Complications
ISBN 1416572325; 9781416572329
LC 2011289347

"'Preemies, Second Edition' is the only parents' reference resource of its kind--delivering up-to-the-minute information on medical care in a warm, caring, and engaging voice. Authors Dana Wechsler Linden and Emma Trenti Paroli are parents who have 'been there.' Together with neonatologist Mia Wechsler Doron, they answer the dozens of questions that parents will have at every stage." (Publisher's note)

This guide "covers risk factors, the first day, the first week, surgery, taking the baby home and many other topics. Each section contains personal observations from parents of preemies, insightful comments from 'the doctor's perspective' and information on procedures, equipment, common problems and other issues." Publ Wkly

Porto, Anthony

The **pediatrician's** guide to feeding babies and toddlers; practical answers to your questions on nutrition, starting solids, allergies, picky eating, and more. Anthony Porto, M.D. and Dina DiMaggio, M.D. Ten

Speed Press 2016 256 p. illustrations (paperback) $18.99 **618.92**
1. Child rearing 2. Bottle feeding 3. Breast feeding 4. Infants -- Nutrition 5. Food habits 6. Children -- Nutrition 7. HEALTH & FITNESS -- Children
ISBN 9781607749011; 9781607749028
LC 2015031409

This book, by Anthony Porto, M.D. and Dina DiMaggio, M.D, is a "comprehensive manual that takes the guesswork out of feeding [babies and toddlers]. . . . With recipes, parenting stories, and recommendations based on the latest pediatric guidelines, this book will allow you to approach mealtime with confidence so you can spend more time enjoying your new family." (Publisher's note)

"Parents will find the chapters useful to read through as their children reach each stage, and well enough organized to use as a reference when particular concerns come up." Pub Wkly

Includes bibliographical references and index

Prizant, Barry M.

Uniquely human; a different way of seeing autism. Barry Prizant, Ph.D.; with Tom Fields-Meyer. Simon & Schuster 2015 272 p. (hardcover) $26 **618.92**
1. Autism 2. Psychotherapy 3. Autism in children
ISBN 9781476776231; 9781476776248
LC 2014035241

This book, by Barry Prizant with Tom Fields-Meyer, challenges "autism therapy [that] typically focuses on ridding individuals of 'autistic' symptoms. . . . Now Dr. Barry M. Prizant offers a new . . . paradigm: the most successful approaches to autism don't aim at fixing a person by eliminating symptoms, but rather seeking to understand the individual's experience and what underlies the behavior." (Publisher's note)

"This positive volume should reassure parents and caregivers of kids with autism and any other disability that their kids are not broken, but, indeed, special." Booklist

Includes bibliographical references and index.

Rapp, Emily

The **still** point of the turning world; Emily Rapp. The Penguin Press 2013 272 p. (hardcover) $25.95 **618.92**
1. Tay-Sachs disease 2. Parents of children with disabilities
ISBN 1594205124; 9781594205125
LC 2012039516

This book, by Emily Rapp, is a memoir of a mother struggling to parent her terminally ill child. "Ronan was diagnosed at nine months old with Tay-Sachs disease, a rare and always-fatal degenerative disorder. . . . Rapp and her husband were forced to re-evaluate everything they thought they knew about parenting. They would have to learn to live with their child in the moment; to find happiness in the midst of sorrow; to parent without a future." (Publisher's note)

Saul, Richard

ADHD does not exist; the truth about attention deficit and hyperactivity disorder. Richard Saul. HarperWave 2013 336 p. (hardback) $25.99 **618.92**
1. Psychology 2. Hyperactivity 3. Mental health 4. Attention deficit disorder 5. Attention-deficit hyperactivity disorder
ISBN 006226673X; 9780062266736

LC 2013030794

In this book, "behavioral neurologist Dr. Richard Saul draws on five decades of experience treating thousands of patients labeled with Attention Deficit and Hyperactivity Disorder--one of the fastest growing and widely diagnosed conditions today--to argue that ADHD is actually a cluster of symptoms stemming from over 20 other conditions and disorders." (Publisher's note)

Includes bibliographical references and index

Schwarz, Alan

ADHD nation; children, doctors, big pharma, and the making of an American epidemic. Alan Schwarz. Scribner 2016 338 p. (hardback) $28 **618.92**
1. Ritalin 2. Hyperactive children -- United States 3. Attention-deficit hyperactivity disorder -- United States 4. Diagnostic errors -- United States
ISBN 1501105914; 9781501105913

LC 2016018493

This book about ADHD in America by Alan Schwarz examines "this cultural and medical phenomenon: The father of ADHD, Dr. Keith Conners, spends fifty years advocating drugs like Ritalin before realizing his role in . . . 'a national disaster of dangerous proportions'; a troubled young girl and a studious teenage boy get entangled in the growing ADHD machine and take medications that backfire horribly; and big Pharma egregiously over-promotes the disorder and earns billions." (Publisher's note)

"In this powerful, necessary book, Schwarz exposes the dirty secrets of the growing ADHD epidemic." Kirkus

Includes bibliographical references and index

Sears, William

The **allergy** book; solving your family's nasal allergies, asthma, food sensitivities, and related health and behavioral problems. by Robert Sears, MD, FAAP, William Sears, MD FRCP. Little, Brown & Co. 2015 352 p. $16 **618.92**
1. Allergy 2. Food allergy
ISBN 0316324809; 9780316324809

LC 2014954181

This book, by doctors Robert and William Sears, is "a comprehensive guide to treating and preventing nasal allergies, asthma, food allergies and intolerances, and more. Allergies are one of the most common ailments, causing children to miss school and parents to miss work. Left untreated or unresolved, stuffy noses, itchy skin, and irritated bellies can lead to chronic asthma, eczema, inflammatory bowel disease, and neurological disorders." (Publisher's note)

"The authors warn readers about hidden sources of allergens (eggs can turn up in canned soups and in salad dressings), and discuss healthy eating, favoring fruits and vegetables over gluten-filled foods. Even allergy-free people will benefit from checking out the Searses' easy-to-read, clearly laid-out guidebook." Booklist

Shetreat-Klein, Maya

The **Dirt** Cure; Growing Healthy Kids With Food Straight from Soil. Maya Shetreat-Klein. Pocket Books 2016 384 p. $26 **618.92**
1. Food industry 2. Children -- Nutrition
ISBN 1476796971; 9781476796970

Author Maya Shetreat-Klein examines the "contents of children's food, how it's seriously harming their bodies and brains, and what we can do about it. [She] explains how food is constantly changing kids' bodies, brains, and even genes--for better or for worse. She also shares success stories from her practice and tips as a working mother of three on stocking healing foods (from veggies to chocolate!), reading labels, and getting even picky eaters into the new menu." (Publisher's note)

"The text is full of scientific information presented in a fun and informative way, giving concrete evidence that good food can transform one's life." Pub Wkly

Includes bibliographical references (pages 333-358) and index.

Sicherer, Scott H.

Understanding and managing your child's food allergies. Johns Hopkins University Press 2006 312p il $45; pa $18.95 **618.92**
1. Parenting 2. Food allergy
ISBN 0-8018-8491-8; 978-0-8018-8491-7; 0-8018-8492-6 pa; 978-0-8018-8492-4 pa

LC 2006-5261

This "book provides parents with practical advice for managing a child's environment at home, at school, or out in the world at large. In Part 2, 'Diagnosing a Food Allergy,' the practice of taking a detailed medical history is espoused and case studies serve to bring the issue home. An action plan for anaphylaxis, a life-threatening type of allergic reaction, as well as a chapter on food allergy resources are included." Libr J

Includes bibliographical references

Sleep; what every parent needs to know. American Academy of Pediatrics; [edited by] Rachel Moon, MD, FAAP. American Academy of Pediatrics 2013 250 p. ill. $16.95 **618.92**
1. Sleep 2. Parenting 3. Sleep therapy
ISBN 1581107811; 9781581107814

LC 2012953639

This book, edited by Rachel Moon, "incorporates the expertise of more than 20 pediatricians and covers numerous issues regarding how to create and maintain healthy sleep habits in children. . . . The book is divided into two sections: Ages, Stages and Phases and Childhood Sleep Challenges. Part one guides readers from the first year of life through adolescence, with chapters along the way about toddlers, preschoolers, and school-age kids." (Publisher's note)

Suskind, Ron

Life, animated; a story of sidekicks, heroes, and autism. by Ron Suskind. Kingswell 2014 358 p. illustrations, some color (hardback) $26.99 **618.92**
1. Autism 2. Communication 3. Animated films 4. Parents of autistic children 5. Autistic children
ISBN 1423180364; 9781423180364
LC 2014006760

"This is the real-life story of Owen Suskind, the son of the Pulitzer Prize-winning journalist Ron Suskind and his wife, Cornelia. An autistic boy who couldn't speak for years, Owen memorized dozens of Disney movies, turned them into a language to express love and loss, kinship, brotherhood.The family was forced to become animated characters, communicating with him in Disney dialogue and song; until they all emerge, together, revealing how, in darkness, we all literally need stories to survive." (Publisher's note)

"The Disney effect may be distinctive to this experience, but the family dynamic should resonate with a much wider readership." Kirkus

Thurow, Roger

The **first** 1,000 days; a crucial time for mothers and children-and the world. Roger Thurow. PublicAffairs 2016 304 p. (hardback) $26.99 **618.92**
1. Pregnancy 2. Infants -- Nutrition 3. Children -- Health and hygiene 4. Infants -- Nutrition -- Case studies 5. Infants -- Health and hygiene -- Case studies
ISBN 9781610395854
LC 2015050285

This book, by Roger Thurow, focuses on women who "were participating in an unprecedented international initiative designed to transform their lives, the lives of their children, and ultimately the world. The 1,000 Days movement, a response to recent, devastating food crises and new research on the economic and social costs of childhood hunger and stunting, is focused on providing proper nutrition during the first 1,000 days of children's lives, beginning with their mother's pregnancy." (Publisher's note)

"You may find yourself cheering and crying with the families you meet. 1,000 Days is a valuable addition to larger public and academic libraries, and for any library where mothers and healthcare providers can share the information." Booklist

Includes bibliographical references and index.

Trainor, Kathleen

Calming your anxious child; words to say and things to do. Kathleen Trainor. Johns Hopkins University Press 2016 264 p. (hardcover : alk. paper) $45 **618.92**
1. Anxiety -- Treatment 2. Parent-child relationship 3. Parent and child -- Popular works 4. Anxiety in children -- Popular works 5. Anxiety disorders -- Treatment -- Popular works
ISBN 1421420090; 1421420104; 9781421420097; 9781421420103
LC 2015034014

In this book, "Dr. Kathleen Trainor builds on cognitive behavioral therapy to provide practical steps for guiding parents through the process of helping their children manage their anxieties. . . . Dr. Trainor's method involves identify-

ing the anxieties and the behaviors, rating them, agreeing on what behaviors to work on changing, identifying strategies for changing behaviors, noting and charting progress, offering incentives, and reinforcing progress." (Publisher's note)

"Anxiety can be a tough condition to beat, but parents with the organizational skills to stick to the Trainor approach will in all likelihood achieve improvement. A solid offering." LJ

Includes bibliographical references and index

Turbo, Richard

★ **Caring** for your baby and young child; birth to age 5. Steven P. Shelov, editor-in-chief; Tanya Remer Altmann, medical editor; Robert E. Hannemann, associate medical editor; Richard Turbo, writer. 6th edition Bantam 2014 917 p. illustrations (paperback) $23 **618.92**
1. Child care 2. Infants -- Care 3. Child development
ISBN 0553393820; 9780553393828
LC 2014013096

This book, edited by Steven P. Shelov, Tanya Remer Altmann, Robert E. Hannemann, with writings by Richard Turbo, is an infant and early child care handbook "covering everything from preparing for childbirth to toilet training to nurturing your child's self-esteem. Whether it's resolving common childhood health problems or detailed instructions for coping with emergency medical situations, this new and revised edition . . . has everything you need." (Publisher's note)

Wedge, Marilyn

A **Disease** Called Childhood; Why ADHD Became an American Epidemic. by Marilyn Wedge. Penguin Group USA 2015 272 p. $26.95 **618.92**
1. Attention deficit disorder
ISBN 1583335633; 9781583335635
LC 2014045248

This book, by Marilyn Wedge, presents a "look at the rise of ADHD in America, arguing for a better paradigm for diagnosing and treating our children. . . . Wedge examines how myriad factors have come together, resulting in a generation addictied to stimulant drugs, and a medical system that encourages diagnosis instead of seeking other solutions." (Publisher's note)

"While Wedge offers options not every medical professional or concerned parent will swallow willingly, her affable a pproach and compassionate universal concern for the wellness of children are evident throughout. In an important read for open-minded parents, Wedge offers fresh perspectives and practical approaches to the continuing ADHD conundrum." Kirkus

618.97 Geriatrics

Serani, Deborah

Depression in later life; Deborah Serani. Rowman & Littlefield Pub Inc 2016 286 p. illustrations (cloth : alk. paper) $35 **618.97**
1. Elderly -- Psychology 2. Depression (Psychology)

3. Depression in old age -- Popular works
ISBN 144225582X; 9781442255821

LC 2015045280

This book, by Deborah Serani, "introduces readers to depression among the aging and elderly. It looks at both sufferers who've been diagnosed in their younger years as well as those with a new diagnosis, and reviews the symptoms, the diagnostic process, treatment options including alternative and holistic approaches, and long term care for those experiencing mild, moderate, or severe depression." (Publisher's note)

"Though the author uses a lot of technical jargon, overall this is a valuable resource that can help improve the quality of life for a highly at-risk group." Booklist

Includes bibliographical references and index

620 Engineering and allied operations

Molotch, Harvey Luskin

Where stuff comes from; how toasters, toilets, cars, computers, and many other things come to be as they are. [by] Harvey Molotch. Routledge 2003 324p il $35; pa $29.95 **620**
1. Engineering
ISBN 0-415-94400-7; 0-415-95042-2 pa

LC 2003-1191

The author examines "the complicated, dynamic relationships between inventor, society, corporation, regulator, shopkeeper, community, family and customer. . . . Myriad links, he argues, ultimately produce and constantly change what we want, buy, keep and throw away; thus, neither consumers nor producers are to be blamed for our numerous possessions. . . . Molotch's description of systemic person-product complexes could work to end blame-the-consumer guilt-mongering in the popular discourse." Publ Wkly

Includes bibliographical references

Petroski, Henry

The **essential** engineer; why science alone will not solve our global problems. Alfred A. Knopf 2010 274p il $26.95 **620**
1. Engineering 2. Technological innovations 3. Technology and civilization
ISBN 978-0-307-27245-4; 0-307-27245-1

LC 2009-21216

"Petroski presents a book-length argument for the place of engineering in humanity's future, especially when it comes to ensuring that future in the face of climate change, natural disasters, dwindling oil supplies and other global problems. . . . Scientists get the credit for everything from the moon landing to the construction of the Large Hadron Collider, he complains, when in reality those and myriad other projects large and small couldn't have been achieved

without the creative, intelligent and rigorous input of engineers." Washington Post Book World

Includes bibliographical references

Success through failure; the paradox of design. Princeton University Press 2006 235p il hardcover o.p. pa $21.95 **620**
1. Design 2. Engineering
ISBN 978-0-691-12225-0; 0-691-12225-3; 978-0-691-13642-4 pa; 0-691-13642-4 pa

LC 2005-34126

An "engaging and readable book. . . . Petroski uses countless interesting case histories to show how failure motivates technological advancement." IEEE Spectrum

Includes bibliographical references

Petroski, Henry, 1942-

★ **To** forgive design; understanding failure. Henry Petroski. Belknap Press of Harvard University Press 2012 xii, 410 p.p ill. **620**
1. Design 2. Engineering 3. Structural failures 4. System failures (Engineering)
ISBN 0674065840; 9780674065840

LC 2011044194

This book, by Henry Petroski, "looks not only at how people contribute to the failure of engineering designs but also at how analyzing those failures can improve subsequent models. He considers many different types of failures, from several infamous bridge collapses to carefully designed intentional failures, which are engineered specifically to prevent greater failures." (Library Journal)

"Even the layman will find Petroski's study to be accessible, informative, and interesting." Pub Wkly

Includes bibliographical references and index.

620.009 History, geographic treatment, biography

Brain, Marshall

The **engineering** book; From the Catapult to the Curiosity Rover: 250 Milestones in the History of Engineering. Marshall Brain. Sterling Pub Co Inc 2015 528 p. illustrations (some color) (hardcover) $29.95 **620.009**
1. Engineering 2. Encyclopedias and dictionaries
ISBN 1454908092; 9781454908098

This book, by Marshall Brain, the "creator of the 'How Stuff Works' series and a professor at the Engineering Entrepreneurs Program at NCSU provides a detailed look at 250 milestones in the discipline [of engineering]. He covers the various areas, including chemical, aerospace, and computer engineering, from ancient history to the present." (Publisher's note)

"Despite some problems, this book is a solid introduction to its topic and can serve to generate interest in the applied sciences and engineering. For report use, however, it lacks the depth that high-school students and older readers would expect, thus it's recommended for middle schoolers only." LJ

620.1 Engineering mechanics and materials

Freinkel, Susan

    Plastic; a toxic love story. Houghton Mifflin Harcourt 2011 324p $27   **620.1**

    1. Plastics

    ISBN 978-0-547-15240-0

                    LC 2010-43019

    "At first a godsend, [plastic] reduced dependence on shrinking natural resources, such as the shell of the hawksbill turtle (combs) or elephants' ivory (billiard balls and piano keys.) Ultimately it democratized materialism, making everything available to everybody, cheaply. Now, the partner we've found in plastic 'can rightly inspire both our deepest admiration and our strongest disgust.' To describe its history, wonders and dangers, journalist Freinkel reviews eight products: the comb, the chair, the Frisbee, the IV bag, the disposable lighter, the grocery bag, the soda bottle and the credit card. You will not look casually at any of them again." Cleveland Plain Dealer

    Includes bibliographical references

Miodownik, Mark

    Stuff matters; exploring the marvelous materials that shape our manmade world. Mark Miodownik. Houghton Mifflin Harcourt 2014 272 p. illustrations (hardback) $26   **620.1**

    1. Materials 2. Physical sciences 3. Materials science -- Popular works

    ISBN 0544236041; 9780544236042

                    LC 2013047575

    In this book, author Mark Miodownik "entertainingly examines the materials he encounters in a typical morning, from the steel in his razor and the graphite in his pencil to the foam in his sneakers and the concrete in a nearby skyscraper. He offers a compendium of the most astounding histories and marvelous scientific breakthroughs in the material world." (Publisher's note)

    "At a time when science is maligned, first-rate storyteller Miodownik entertains and educates with pop-culture references, scholarly asides, and nods to everyone from the Six Million Dollar Man to the Luminère brothers. A delight for the curious reader." Booklist

Waldman, Jonathan

    Rust; the longest war. Jonathan Waldman. Simon & Schuster 2015 304 p. 8 unnumbered pages of plates (hardcover) $26.95   **620.1**

    1. Engineering 2. Structural steel 3. Corrosion and anticorrosives 4. Corrosion and anti-corrosives -- History 5. Corrosion and anti-corrosives -- Anecdotes

    ISBN 1451691599; 9781451691597; 9781451691603

                    LC 2014043291

    In this book on rust and corrosion author "Jonathan Waldman travels from Key West, Florida, to Prudhoe Bay, Alaska, to meet the colorful and often reclusive people who are fighting our mightiest and unlikeliest enemy. The result is a fresh and often funny account of an overlooked engineering endeavor that is as compelling as it is grand, illuminating a hidden phenomenon that shapes the modern world." (Publisher's note)

    "A brilliantly written and fascinating close-up look at one of nature's most neglected threats to man-made structures and machines." Booklist

621 Applied physics

Alley, Richard B., 1957-

    Earth; the operators' manual. W.W. Norton 2011 479p il $27.95   **621**

    1. Energy development 2. Renewable energy resources 3. Greenhouse effect

    ISBN 978-0-393-08109-1

                    LC 2010-54016

    The author "presents a primer on combatting global warming. The book begins with a history of how fuel—from trees, whale oil, and petroleum—has been instrumental to civilization and how we tend to exhaust our sources. He goes on to explain how scientists study climate change and why the evidence is convincing, and ends with a call to action and an overview of possible solutions. . . . This optimistic book ought to convince even the most obstinate climate-change denier." Publ Wkly

    Includes bibliographical references

Marks' standard handbook for mechanical engineers; [edited by] Eugene A. Avallone, Theodore Baumeister, Ali Sadegh. 11th ed; McGraw-Hill 2006 1800p il $199.95   **621**

    1. Mechanical engineering -- Handbooks, manuals, etc.

    ISBN 978-0-07-142867-5; 0-07-142867-4

    First published 1916 under the editorship of Lionel S. Marks with title: Mechanical engineers' handbook. Periodically revised. Editors vary

    This volume presents concisely the basic scientific and technical data of mechanical engineering, covering theory, basic mechanism, standard practice, often-needed mathematical formulae and technical data

    Includes bibliographical references

621.3 Electrical, magnetic, optical, communications, computer engineering; electronics, lighting

American electricians' handbook; Terrell Croft, Frederic P. Hartwell, Wilford I. Summers [editors] 16th ed McGraw-Hill 2013 1712 p. ill. $90   **621.3**

    1. Electrical engineering -- Handbooks, manuals, etc. 2. Electric engineering -- Handbooks, manuals, etc

    ISBN 0071798803; 9780071798808

    This handbook, edited by Terrell Croft, Frederic P. Hartwell, and Wilford I. Summers, is "the definitive industry reference for information on designing, installing, operating, and maintaining electrical systems and equipment. The Sixteenth Edition is revised to comply with the 2011 National Electrical Code and the 2012 National Electrical Safety Code, and covers current energy-efficient technologies, such as photovoltaics and induction lighting." (Publisher's note)

"The Sixteenth Edition is revised to complywith the 2011 National Electrical Code and the 2012 National Electrical Safety Code, and covers current energy-efficient technologies, such as photovoltaics and induction lighting. Detailed photos, diagrams, charts, tables, and calculations are included throughout." Publisher's note

National electrical code handbook 2014; [edited by] Mark W. Earley, P.E., Christopher D. Coache, Mark Cloutier, Gil Moniz. National Fire Protection Association 2013 1259 p. $165.50 **621.3**
1. Electrical engineering -- Handbooks, manuals, etc.
ISBN 1455905445; 9781455905447
LC 2013941415
First published 1978. Periodically revised

This book, edited by Mark W. Earley, Christopher D. Coache, Mark Cloutier, and Gil Moniz, is a professional handbook on the electrical safety codes published by the National Fire Protection Association. It "explains the reasoning behind NFPA 70®: NEC concepts, provides real-world examples, and gives you the background behind Code revisions, so you can work with authority." (Publisher's note)

This "is a nationally accepted guide to the safe installation of electrical conductors and equipment, and is, in fact, the basis for all electrical codes used in the United States." Ref Sources for Small & Medium-sized Libr. 5th edition

Shulman, Seth
★ The **telephone** gambit; chasing Alexander Graham Bell's secret. W. W. Norton & Co. 2008 256p il $24.95 **621.3**
1. Inventors 2. Telephone 3. Teachers of the deaf 4. Telecommunications executives
ISBN 978-0-393-06206-9; 0-393-06206-6
LC 2007-30904
The author argues that Alexander Graham Bell is not the true inventor of the telephone.

This book "does a neat job of painting, in rapid brush strokes, a portrait of the thrilling era of innovation in which Bell lived and also of the interesting circumstances of his life. . . . [He] also manages to lace his work with just enough technology to tell his story without losing the interest of any low-tech readers." Christ Sci Monit
Includes bibliographical references

Standard Handbook for Electrical Engineers; H. Wayne Beaty, Donald G. Fink. 16th ed McGraw-Hill 2012 2144 p. ill $150 **621.3**
1. Green technology 2. Electrical engineering -- Handbooks, manuals, etc.
ISBN 0071762329; 9780071762328
First published 1908. Periodically revised
16th ed
"Completely revised throughout to address the latest codes and standards, the 16th Edition of this renowned reference offers new coverage of green technologies such as smart grids, smart meters, renewable energy, and cogeneration plants. Modern computer applications and methods for securing computer network infrastructures that control power grids are also discussed." (Publisher's note)

621.31 Generation, modification, storage, transmission of electric power

Fletcher, Seth
Bottled lightning; superbatteries, electric cars, and the new lithium economy. Hill and Wang 2011 260p $26 **621.31**
1. Lithium 2. Electronics 3. Electric batteries
ISBN 978-0-8090-3053-8; 0-8090-3053-5
LC 2010-47695
"Provides an entertaining, surprisingly eventful history of human efforts to harness energy in the form of battery power . . . . A fine, readable work of popular science." Kirkus
Includes bibliographical references

621.319 Transmission

The **complete** guide to wiring; current with 2014-2017 electrical codes. 6th ed Cool Springs Press 2014 335 p. color illustrations (paperback) $24.99 **621.319**
1. Electric wiring 2. Houses -- Maintenance and repair 3. Electric wiring, Interior -- Amateurs' manuals 4. Dwellings -- Electric equipment -- Amateurs' manuals 5. Dwellings -- Maintenance and repair -- Amateurs' manuals
ISBN 159186612X; 9781591866121
LC 2014000449
First published 1998 by Cowles Creative Pub.
"The modern home can include dozens of electronic components unknown just a few years ago, and this book provides essential information on wiring for those devices. It includes information on security systems, home theaters and surround-sound systems, computer networks, and a host of kitchen amenities like espresso machines to grind-and-brew coffee machines." (Publisher's note)
Includes "an overview of electricity and wiring safety; wire, cable, and conduits; boxes and panels; switches; and receptacles. . . [and] foolproof circuit maps for 30 common wiring set-ups and step-by-step walkthroughs of every essential home wiring and electrical repair project." Publisher's note
Includes bibliographical references and index

Richter, H. P.
Wiring simplified; Based on the 2014 National Electrical Code. Park Publishing, Inc. 2014 256 p. $14.95 **621.319**
1. Electric wiring 2. Houses -- Maintenance and repair
ISBN 097929455X; 9780979294556
Written by H. P. Richter, W. C. Schwan, and F. P. Hartwell, "This 44th edition--part of a series continuously published for more than 80 years and based on the 2014 National Electrical Code--is a handy instruction manual that has been used by generations of readers who learn the 'why' as well as the 'how-to' of wiring practices. Encouraging readers to tackle jobs small and large, the guide covers everything from repairing a table lamp to wiring a whole house." (Publisher's note)

621.32 Lighting

Brox, Jane

Brilliant; the evolution of artificial light. Houghton Mifflin Harcourt 2010 360p $25   **621.32**

1. Lighting

ISBN 978-0-547-05527-5; 0-547-05527-7

         LC 2009-35441

The author "examines our relationship with light, our attempts to harness it to brighten places we cannot see, and its impact on American psychology and culture. . . . This well-written, well-researched, and thought-provoking book has much to offer. The general reader with an interest in the (social) history of technology will find it . . . a source of inspiration for considering technology's impact on our lives." Libr J

Includes bibliographical references

621.381 Electronics

Horowitz, Paul

The **art** of electronics; Paul Horowitz, Harvard University, Winfield Hill, Rowland Institute. Cambridge University Press 2015 1223 p. illustrations (hardback) $120   **621.381**

1. Electronic circuits 2. Electronics -- Handbooks, manuals, etc. 3. Electrical engineering -- Handbooks, manuals, etc. 4. Electronics 5. Electronic circuit design

ISBN 9780521809269

         LC 2015002303

This book, by Paul Horowitz and Winfield Hill, "is the thoroughly revised and updated third edition of the . . . authoritative book on electronic circuit design. In addition to new or enhanced coverage of many topics, the third edition includes 90 oscilloscope screenshots illustrating the behavior of working circuits, [and] dozens of graphs giving highly useful measured data of the sort that is often buried or omitted in datasheets but which you need when designing circuits." (Publisher's note)

Includes bibliographical references and index

Platt, Charles

Make; more electronics: journey deep into the world of logic chips, amplifiers, sensors, and randomicity. Charles Platt. Oreilly & Associates Inc 2014 357 p. $34.99   **621.381**

1. Electronics 2. Electrical engineering

ISBN 1449344046; 9781449344047

This book, by Charles Platt, "picks up where 'Make: Electronics' left off: you'll work with components like comparators, light sensors, higher-level logic chips, multiplexers, shift registers, encoders, decoders, and magnetic sensors. . . . With step-by-step instructions, and hundreds of color photographs and illustrations, this book will help you use -- and understand -- intermediate to advanced electronics concepts and techniques." (Publisher's note)

Schultz, Mitchel E.

Grob's basic electronics; 11th ed.; McGraw-Hill 2011 xxvi, 1206p il $155.31   **621.381**

1. Electricity 2. Electronics

ISBN 978-0-07-351085-9; 0-07-351085-8

         LC 2010-8273

First published 1959 under the authorship of Bernard Grob. Periodically revised

An introductory text on the fundamentals of electricity and electronics for technicians in radio, television, and industrial electronics.

Includes glossary

621.384 Specific topics in general radio

The ARRL handbook for radio communications. American Radio Relay League various pagings il   **621.384**

1. Radio -- Handbooks, manuals, etc.

ISBN

Annual. Began publication 1926. Editions 1 through 61 published with title: The Radio amateur's handbook. Editions 62 through 79 published with title: The ARRL handbook for radio amateurs

"Chapters cover fundamentals and changing technology in the field and include many tables, circuit diagrams, photographs, and occasional references." Guide to Ref Books. 11th edition

Silver, H. Ward

Ham radio for dummies; by H. Ward Silver. John Wiley & Sons Inc 2013 xvi, 358 p.p illustrations $24.99   **621.384**

1. Amateur radio stations 2. Radio -- Handbooks, manuals, etc. 3. Radio -- Amateurs' manuals

ISBN 1118592115; 9781118592113

         LC 2013938107

This book, by H. Ward Silver, offers "first step[s] for learning about ham radio. . . . This hands-on beginner guide reflects the operational and technical changes to amateur radio over the past decade and provides you with updated licensing requirements and information, changes in digital communication (such as the Internet, social media, and GPS), and how to use e-mail via radio." (Publisher's note)

Includes bibliographical references and index

621.388 Television

Abramson, Albert

The **History** of Television 1880 to 1941. McFarland & Company, Inc. 2009 354 p. $49.95 **621.388**

1. Inventions -- History 2. Television -- History 3. Television

ISBN 0786440864; 9780786440863

         LC 8643091

"A sole inventor of television does not exist. Instead, it came about through a remarkable interaction of several hundred scientists. Interviews with the scientists whose imagination and enterprise combined to make television a reality, extensive archival research worldwide, and rare photos make this book [by Albert Abramson] the one definitive history and the only authoritative account." (Publisher's note)

The **history** of television, 1942 to 2000; foreword by Christopher H. Sterling. McFarland & Co. 2003 309p il hardcover o.p. pa $75   **621.388**
1. Television -- History
ISBN 0-7864-1220-8; 978-0-7864-3243-1 pa; 0-7864-3243-8 pa

LC 2002-326

"No reference work available in print right now matches the attention to detail that is obvious here. A significant work on how the machinery of television has evolved, this . . . should stand as the authority for years to come." Libr J
Includes bibliographical references

621.389   Security, sound recording, related systems

Zen and the art of recording; Mixerman. Hal Leonard Books 2014 291 p. $24.99   **621.389**
1. Sound recordings 2. Popular music -- Writing and publishing 3. Popular music -- Production and direction 4. Sound recording industry -- Vocational guidance 5. Sound recordings -- Production and direction -- Vocational guidance
ISBN 1480387436; 9781480387430

LC 2014035146

In this book, author Mixerman "distills the inescapable technical realities of recording down to understandable and practical terms. Whether musician or self-taught recordist, whether at home or in a full-blown studio complex, you'll discover a definitive blueprint for recording within the current realities of the business, without ever losing focus on the core consideration--the music itself." (Publisher's note)

621.43   Internal-combustion engines

★ **Small** engines and outdoor power equipment; a care & repair guide for lawn mowers, snowblowers & small gas-powered implements. edited by Peter Hunn. Cool Springs Press 2014 144 p. color illustrations (pbk) $19.99   **621.43**
1. Household equipment and supplies -- Maintenance and repair 2. Small gasoline engines -- Maintenance and repair 3. Gardening -- Equipment and supplies -- Maintenance and repair
ISBN 1591865875; 9781591865872

LC 2013028515

"Small engine repair and maintenance is well covered here, starting with an introduction to common engine types, with interior systems and components clearly illustrated. Tools needed and safety considerations are carefully detailed, followed by a lengthy troubleshooting chart. A section on annual maintenance is accompanied by large photos and step-by-step instructions; it's followed by basic repairs, which focus on common issues. The book finishes with more difficult repairs that involve interior systems, such as rebuilding or replacing parts." LJ

621.48   Nuclear engineering

Smith, Gar
  Nuclear roulette; the truth about the most dangerous energy source on earth. Gar Smith; foreword by Jerry Mander and Ernest Callenbach. Chelsea Green Pub. 2012 xxx, 279 p.p (hardcover) $29.95 **621.48**
1. Nuclear energy 2. Nuclear power plants 3. Nuclear power plants -- Accidents 4. Nuclear power plants -- Risk assessment 5. Nuclear power plants -- Natural disaster effects
ISBN 1603584773; 9781603584340; 9781603584357; 9781603584777

LC 2012027407

Author Gar Smith argues that "nuclear power is not clean, cheap, or safe. . . . While some critiques are familiar-nuclear power is too costly, too dangerous, and too unstable-others are surprising: Nuclear Roulette exposes historic links to nuclear weapons, impacts on Indigenous lands and lives, and the ways in which the Nuclear Regulatory Commission too often takes its lead from industry, rewriting rules to keep failing plants in compliance." (Publisher's note)
Includes bibliographical references (p. [233]-267) and index

621.56   Low-temperature technology

Jackson, Tom
  Chilled; How Refrigeration Changed the World and Might Do So Again. Tom Jackson. St. Martin's Press 2015 272 p. (hardcover) $27   **621.56**
1. Refrigeration 2. Technology -- History
ISBN 9781472911438; 1472911431

This book on refrigeration by Tom Jackson examines "how experts through the ages have attempted to understand the elemental laws that govern our universe and then to allow for the possibility of manipulating temperature. Aristotle, Fahrenheit, Joule, and many lesser-known scientists make appearances, as do the early icebox and refrigeration prospectors who created a global market for preserving food through controlled chilling as opposed to salting, pickling, or canning." (Booklist)
"Jackson's spirited explanations of centuries-old scientific experiments relating to the transmutation of gases into water, finding absolute zero, and identifying chemical elements—to name a few—will be most appreciated by readers with a strong interest in the physical sciences." Booklist
Includes bibliographical references (page [268]) and index.

621.9   Tools

Horne, Richard
  3d printing for dummies; Kalani K. Hausman and Richard Horne. John Wiley & Sons Inc 2014 368 p. illustrations (pbk.) $29.99   **621.9**
1. Three-dimensional printing 2. Industrial arts --

Handbooks, manuals, etc.
ISBN 1118660757; 9781118660751
LC 2013952422

This handbook, by Kalani K. Hausman and Richard Horne, "examines each type of 3D printing technology available today and gives artists, entrepreneurs, engineers, and hobbyists insight into the amazing things 3D printing has to offer. You'll discover methods for the creation of 3D printable objects using software, 3D scanners, and even photographs with the help of this timely 'For Dummies guide.'" (Publisher's note)

Rigsby, Mike

A **beginner's** guide to 3D printing; 14 simple toy designs to get you started. Mike Rigsby. Chicago Review Press 2014 291 p. illustrations (paperback) $17.95   **621.9**
 1. Computer-aided design 2. Three-dimensional printing 3. Computer-aided design software 4. SketchUp 5. CAD--CAM systems 6. Rapid prototyping
ISBN 1569761973; 9781569761977
LC 2014026069

In this book on 3D printing, "engineer Mike Rigsby leads readers step-by-step through fourteen simple toy projects, each illustrated with screen caps of Autodesk 123D Design, the most common free 3D software available. The projects are later described using Sketchup, another free popular software package." (Publisher's note)

Beginner's guide to three-D printing

622   Mining and related operations

Carter, Bill

Boom, Bust, Boom; A Story About Copper, the Metal That Runs the World. Bill Carter. Simon & Schuster 2012 288 p. $26   **622**
 1. Copper 2. Copper mines and mining
ISBN 1439136440; 9781439136447

This book by Bill Carter is "a sweeping account of civilization's complete dependence on copper and what it means for people, nature, and our global economy. Copper is a miraculous and contradictory metal, essential to nearly every human enterprise. . . . Yet . . . copper mining causes irrevocable damage to the Earth . . . and the mines themselves have significant effects on the economies and wellbeing of the communities where they are located." (Publisher's note)

Includes bibliographical references and index.

Prud'homme, Alex

Hydrofracking; Alex Prud'homme. Oxford University Press 2013 184 p. (What everyone needs to know) (pbk. : alk. paper) $16.95   **622**
 1. Hydraulic fracturing 2. Environmental protection 3. Hydraulic fracturing -- Popular works 4. Shale gas reservoirs -- Popular works 5. Gas wells -- Hydraulic fracturing -- Popular works 6. Oil wells -- Hydraulic fracturing -- Popular works
ISBN 0199311250; 9780199311255; 9780199311262
LC 2013028962

"A timely addition to Oxford's What Everyone Needs to Know series, 'Hydrofracking' tackles this contentious topic, exploring both sides of the debate and providing a clear guide to the science underlying the technique. In . . . question-and-answer format, Alex Prud'homme . . . [covers] key points, from the economic and political benefits of fracking to the health dangers and negative effects on the environment." (Publisher's note)

"Most useful are the point/counterpoint discussions on the pros and cons of fracking." Choice

Includes bibliographical references and index

623.4   Ordnance

Gun digest 2015; edited by Jerry Lee. F & W Media Inc 2014 560 p. illustrations $34.99   **623.4**
 1. Guns 2. Firearms industry
ISBN 1440239126; 9781440239120
LC 44032588

This guidebook, edited by Jerry Lee, "has been regarded by the shooting industry, hunters, competitive shooters, collectors, and hobbyists everywhere as the shooter's No. 1 resource. . . . With in-depth articles about today's most fascinating guns, both old and new, testfire stories on the industry's hot-off-the-line guns, insights on fine collectibles and custom creations, and up to date reports on new optics, guns, ammo, and reloading equipment, this book has something for everyone." (Publisher's note)

Hodge, Nathan

A **nuclear** family vacation; travels in the world of atomic weaponry. [by] Nathan Hodge and Sharon Weinberger. Bloomsbury 2008 324p $24.99 **623.4**
 1. Arms control 2. Nuclear weapons 3. Nuclear engineering
ISBN 978-1-59691-378-3; 1-59691-378-9
LC 2008-2013

This "is a book that is both entertaining and informative. Hodge and Weinberger are shrewd and observant nuclear tour guides who are knowledgeable about their subject without being didactic." Am Sci

Includes bibliographical references

Sheinkin, Steve

Bomb; the race to build and steal the world's most dangerous weapon. Steve Sheinkin. Roaring Brook Press 2012 266 p. ill. (hc) $19.99   **623.4**
 1. Nuclear warfare 2. Nuclear weapons 3. World War, 1914-1918 -- Chemical warfare 4. Atomic bomb -- History 5. Operation Freshman, 1942 6. Atomic bomb -- Germany -- History 7. World War, 1939-1945 -- Secret service -- Soviet Union 8. World War, 1939-1945 -- Secret service -- Great Britain
ISBN 1596434872; 9781596434875
LC 2011044096

Robert F. Sibert Informational Book Medal (2013)
YALSA Award for Excellence in Nonfiction for Young Adults (2013)
John Newbery Honor Book (2013)

Author Steve Sheinkin's "story unfolds in three parts, covering American attempts to build the [atomic] bomb, how the Soviets tried to steal American designs and how the Americans tried to keep the Germans from building a bomb. It was the eve of World War II, and the fate of the world was at stake . . . all along the way spies in the United States were feeding sensitive information to the KGB." (Kirkus Reviews)

Includes bibliographical references (p. [243]-259) and index

Weapons & warfare; editor, John Powell. 2nd ed.; Salem Press 2010 3v il map set $395 623.4
1. Reference books 2. Military weapons 3. Military art and science
ISBN 978-1-58765-594-4

LC 2009-50491

First published 2001

"Volume 1, Ancient & Medieval, . . . covers warfare from prehistoric times to approximately 1500; Volume 2, Modern, covers 1500 to the present. The organization is chronological by geographic region, and both volumes open with essays discussing weapons and forces used in that era of history, how and why those tools of warfare have evolved or been discontinued, and the military achievement of the forces, weapons, uniforms and armor, military organizations, and doctrine strategy and tactics. In the third volume, Culture and Concepts, essays cover social aspects of war, technological achievements used in warfare, and morality of behavior during war. . . . This useful overview of warfare's evolution will be appreciated by students as well as general readers." Libr J

623.7 Communications, vehicles, sanitation, related topics

Cockburn, Andrew
Kill Chain; Drones and the Rise of the High-tech Assassins. by Andrew Cockburn. Henry Holt & Co. 2015 320 p. illustrations $28 623.7
1. Drone aircraft 2. Military art and science 3. National security -- United States
ISBN 0805099263; 9780805099263

LC 2014029340

This book, by Andrew Cockburn, is a "narrative on the history of drone warfare. . . . Taking the reader inside the well-guarded world of national security, the book reveals the powerful interests - military, CIA and corporate - that have led the drive to kill individuals by remote control. Most importantly of all, the book describes what has really happened when the theories underpinning the strategy -- and the multi-billion dollar contracts they spawn -- have been put to the test." (Publisher's note)

"Despite some problems, this is an informative and easy-to-read book for those interested in this hot topic. Perhaps a drone will drop it off at your front door." LJ

623.74 Vehicles

Whittle, Richard
Predator; The Secret Origins of the Drone Revolution. Richard Whittle. Henry Holt & Co. 2014 352 p. illustrations $30 623.74
1. Drone aircraft 2. Aerospace engineering 3. Military

art and science 4. Drone aircraft -- United States -- History 5. Aerospace industries -- California, Southern -- History 6. Drone aircraft -- United States -- Design and construction
ISBN 0805099646; 9780805099645

LC 2014014070

This book, by Richard Whittle, is the "untold story of the birth of the Predator drone, a wonder weapon that transformed the American military, reshaped modern warfare, and sparked a revolution in aviation. . . . The remarkable cast of characters responsible for developing the Predator includes a former Israeli inventor, . . . two billionaire brothers, . . . a pair of fighter pilots, . . . a cunning Pentagon operator, . . . and a secretive Air Force organization known as Big Safari." (Publisher' snote)

"Military and aviation aficionados will learn from and enjoy this in-depth work that employs a readable, journalistic style." LJ

Includes bibliographical references and index

623.8 Nautical engineering and seamanship

Naranjo, Ralph
The Art of Seamanship; Evolving Skills, Exploring Oceans, and Handling Wind, Waves, and Weather. McGraw-Hill 2014 544 p. illustrations $50 623.8
1. Sailing 2. Navigation
ISBN 0071493425; 9780071493420

LC 2015300840

In this book, "Around-the-world sailor Ralph Naranjo . . . delivers a . . . reference for anything that comes up while on the water, sharing all the knowledge today-s sailors need to -hand, reef, and steer'--an enduring reference to the collective skills of the bluewater sailor. Naranjo's vast knowledge is supported by real-life examples of sailing mishaps, sample itineraries, vibrant photos, as well as first-hand accounts and sidebars from top sailors and marine experts." (Publisher's note)

Ujifusa, Steven
A man and his ship; America's greatest naval architect and his quest to build the S.S. United States. Steven Ujifusa. Simon & Schuster 2012 x, 437 p., [32] p. of platesp ill. (hc : alk. paper) $29.99 623.8
1. Ocean liners 2. United States -- Military history 3. World War, 1939-1945 -- Naval operations 4. United States (Steamship) 5. Gibbs & Cox -- History -- 20th century 6. Naval architects -- United States -- Biography 7. Ocean liners -- United States -- History -- 20th century
ISBN 9781451645071; 9781451645088

LC 2011049883

Author Steven Ujifusa tells the story of William Francis Gibbs, who, in 1915, "completed plans for the world's largest and fastest superliner . . . Setting up his own company in 1922, Gibbs made his name building modest liners for American companies . . . As World War II loomed, Gibbs became the leading designer for the U.S. Navy and Merchant Marine. It took the Cold War and energetic lobbying to achieve Gibbs' dream . . . Launched in 1952 to national acclaim, the SS United States was a technological triumph;

rival liners never matched her speed, reliability or safety." (Kirkus)

Includes bibliographical references and index

623.88 Seamanship

Bigon, Mario

The **Morrow** guide to knots; for sailing, fishing, camping, climbing. Mario Bigon and Guido Regazzoni; translated from the Italian by Maria Piotrowska. W. Morrow 1982 255 p. color illustrations $16.99 **623.88**

1. Knots and splices 2. Life skills -- Handbooks, manuals, etc.

ISBN 0688012256; 0688012264; 9780688012267

LC 82006308

"Included . . . are a section on decorative knots, a cross-reference list of the many applications of knots, and a detailed glossary." Written by Mario Bigon and Guido Regazzoni and edited by Kennie Lyman, "'The Morrow Guide to Knots' is a . . . reference tool for all sportsmen and campers, homeowners, and youngsters as well." (Publisher's note)

Bibliography: p. 252

Chapman piloting & seamanship; edited by Elbert S. Maloney, Peter A. Janssen, and Jonathan Eaton. Sterling Pub Co Inc 2013 919 p. color illustrations $60 **623.88**

1. Boats and boating 2. Navigation -- Handbooks, manuals, etc.

ISBN 1588169618; 9781588169617

LC 2013018755

This book, edited by Elbert S. Maloney, Peter A. Janssen, and Jonathan Eaton, is the 67th edition of "a single comprehensive reference that combines the best traditions of seamanship with cutting-edge practices, gear, and technology. . . . [It includes] how-to maintenance information for . . . engines; a complete integration of the tools and techniques of electronic navigation . . . with . . . unsurpassed treatment of traditional chart-and-compass piloting skills." (Publisher's note)

Pawson, Des

The **handbook** of knots; Expanded ed.; DK 2004 176p il pa $17 **623.88**

1. Rope 2. Knots and splices

ISBN 0-7566-0374-9; 978-0-7566-0374-8

LC 2004-274491

First published 1998

"This is a step-by-step guide to tying and using more than 100 knots. . . . There's a chapter on rope construction, rope materials, and properties of ropes and their main uses. It's very informative and put together concisely." BAYA Book Rev [review of 1998 edition]

Rousmaniere, John

The **Annapolis** Book of Seamanship; John Rousmaniere; illustrated by Mark Smith. 4th edition

Simon & Schuster 2014 403 p. illustrations hbk $49.99 **623.88**

1. Sailing 2. Navigation

ISBN 9781451650198; 1451650191

LC 2014412287

"Completely revised and updated to address changes in technology and safety standards, this new edition is the definitive guide to the art and science of sailing." (Publisher's note)

623.89 Navigation

Cutler, Thomas J.

Dutton's nautical navigation; [by] Thomas J. Cutler; with the U.S. Naval Institute Navigation Board. 15th ed; Naval Inst. Press 2004 447p il map $55 **623.89**

1. Navigation

ISBN 1-557502-48-X

LC 2003-11183

First published 1926 under the authorship of Benjamin Dutton with title: Navigation and nautical astronomy. Variant title: Dutton's navigation & piloting

This guide for the coastal and seagoing mariner focuses on piloting, celestial navigation, radio navigation and dead reckoning

624.2 Bridges

Blockley, D. I.

Bridges; the science and art of the world's most inspiring structures. Oxford University Press 2010 312p il $29.95 **624.2**

1. Bridges

ISBN 978-0-19-954359-5

"In this fascinating exploration for lay readers, Blockley lucidly explains both the basic forces at work on every bridge—tension, compression, and shear—and the structural elements combating those forces: beams, arches, trusses, and suspension cables. . . . Bold, insightful statements help make this a remarkable work." Publ Wkly

Includes bibliographical references

625.1 Railroads

Train; the definitive visual history. DK Publishing. DK Publishing 2014 320 p. illustrations (some color) $40 **625.1**

1. Railroads 2. Engineering 3. Railroads -- History 4. Locomotives -- History 5. Railroads -- History -- Pictorial works 6. Locomotives -- History -- Pictorial works

ISBN 1465422293; 9781465422293

LC 2012287667

This book from DK Publishing is a "celebration of all things train and track, with stories of key innovators, designers, and iconic rail journeys. Iconic trains, such as the Orient Express and Mallard are showcased in 'virtual tours' that reveal the anatomy of these legendary engines. This guide provides a truly international view of trains through time, from English steam to Japanese electric." (Publisher's note)

DK Smithsonian

625.2   Railroad rolling stock

Jensen, Joel

Steam: an enduring legacy; the railroad photographs of Joel Jensen. introduction by Scott Lothes; essay by John Gruber; afterword by Jeff Brouws. W. W. Norton & Company 2011 160p il $50   **625.2**

1. Steam engines 2. Railroads -- Pictorial works

ISBN 978-0-393-08248-7; 0-393-08248-2

"Jensen has been photographing trains and rail stations west of the Mississippi River for some 25 years, and this long-overdue collection of his work features black-and-white shots that capture the bygone majesty and sense of history inspired by these steam-powered machines, preserved and operated in the latter-day era by dedicated rail-fans. Besides the 150 photos, there are essays by John Gruber and Scott Lothes—both of the Center for Railroad Photography and Art—examining the economics and cultural importance of trains in America." BookPage

627   Hydraulic engineering

Hiltzik, Michael A.

Colossus; Hoover Dam and the making of the American century. Free Press 2010 496p il map $30   **627**

1. Hoover Dam (Ariz. and Nev.) 2. Civil engineers

ISBN 978-1-4165-3216-3; 1-4165-3216-1

LC 2009-33833

In this account of the Hoover Dam story, Hiltzik "explains the technological and physical difficulties posed by the dam project, but he also fixes the endeavor in its time and captures the personalities of the people involved. . . . The author is at his best in a masterly portrayal of Frank Crowe, the central figure in the dam's construction. A born engineer who demanded much from his workmen, Crowe had to solve a myriad of problems on the fly as he confronted the unexpected difficulties of an unprecedented project in an unprecedented location. . . . One of the nice things about nonfiction such as 'Colossus' is that the stories don't need to be believable; they just need to be true." Wall Street J

Includes bibliographical references and index

Matson, Tim, 1943-

Earth ponds; the country pond maker's guide to building, maintenance, and restoration. Tim Matson. 3rd ed Countryman Press 2012 150 p. ill. $21.95   **627**

1. Ponds 2. Water supply engineering

ISBN 9781581571479; 158157147X

This book, by Tim Matson, is "the bible of pond-making in a fully redesigned 30th-anniversary edition. . . .For thirty years now . . . [this book] has guided an entire generation of pond makers on everything from site planning to soil sampling to drainage and wildlife management. It's a complete overview of the country pond. Illustrations guide the pond builder through every step of the process; chapters carefully describe the issues and decisions in a wonderfully personal way." (Publisher's note)

Includes bibliographical references

628.4   Waste technology, public toilets, street cleaning

Humes, Edward

Garbology; our dirty love affair with trash. Edward Humes. Avery 2012 277 p.   **628.4**

1. Pollution 2. Consumption (Economics) 3. United States -- Social life and customs 4. Refuse and refuse disposal -- United States 5. Salvage (Waste, etc.) -- China 6. Environmental engineering -- United States

ISBN 1583334343; 9781583334348

LC 2012001701

In this book, "Edward Humes . . . [makes the case] that the United States—the world's largest generator of trash—will soon confront a new crisis of garbage. . . . Humes spotlights a turning point in the history of American garbage: the postwar rise of consumer culture, birthed by a new generation of advertisers who saw their mission in life as persuading Americans to throw away perfectly good things in order to buy bigger, better replacements. . . . Humes argues that an economy whose health depends on how much disposable stuff people buy is driving us toward a precipice. Making and trashing all those things will generate economic activity and jobs, to be sure, but the waste-driven model of mass consumption also eats up tremendous amounts of increasingly scarce resources." (Bookforum)

Includes bibliographical references and index

628.5   Pollution control technology and industrial sanitation engineering

Sengo, Zenaida

Air plants; the curious world of Tillandsias. Zenaida Sengo; photographs by Caitlin Atkinson. Timber Press, Inc. 2014 224 p. color illustrations $19.95   **628.5**

1. House plants 2. Ornamental plants 3. Epiphytes 4. Tillandsia

ISBN 1604694890; 9781604694895

LC 2014009480

This book, by Zenaida Sengo, illustrated by Caitlin Atkinson, "shows how simple and rewarding it is to grow, craft, and design with these modern beauties. Decorating with air plants is made easy with . . . photographs that showcase ideas for using them mounted on walls, suspended from the ceiling, as living bows and jewelry, as screens, and in unique containers, like leather pouches, dishes, and baskets." (Publisher's note)

"The coverage of air-plant display, design, and decor is dazzling as Sengo offers guidance in using these "virtually weightless" plants in ceiling suspensions and wall displays and even as wearable, living art. This comprehensive guide is an invaluable resource that delights the eye with the dizzying variety and beauty of air plants and the possibilities for inventive installments." Booklist

Curious world of Tillandsias

628.9 Other branches of sanitary and municipal engineering

National Fire Protection Association

Fire protection handbook; Arthur E. Cote, editor-in-chief; Casey C. Grant, John R. Hall, Jr., Robert E. Solomon, asoociate editors; Pamela A. Powell, managing editor. 20th ed; National Fire Protection Assn. 2008 2v il $233.75 **628.9**

1. Fire prevention

ISBN 978-0-87765-758-3; 0-87765-758-0

LC 2007-928644

First published 1896. Periodically revised. Title varies

"A handbook of approved practice in the fields of fire prevention and fire protection. Will be useful to owners and superintendents of buildings, and to architects and engineers interested in designing safe buildings and planning for their protection against fire." Carnegie Libr of Pittsburgh

Walliser, Jessica

Attracting beneficial bugs to your garden; a natural approach to pest control. Jessica Walliser. Timber Press 2014 240 p. col. ill. $24.95 **628.9**

1. Gardening 2. Beneficial insects 3. Garden pests -- Biological control

ISBN 1604693886; 9781604693881

LC 2013015303

Written by Jessica Walliser, "'Attracting Beneficial Bugs to Your Garden' is a book about bugs and plants, and how to create a garden that benefits from both. In addition to information on companion planting and commercial options for purchasing bugs, there are 19 detailed bug profiles and 39 plant profiles." (Publisher's note)

"While the subject matter and close-up photographs of insects eating insects may make some readers squirm, dedicated gardeners will discover enough solid information and genuine motivation to finally put down their bug spray." Booklist

Includes bibliographical references and index

629.1 Aerospace engineering

Branson, Richard

Reach for the skies; ballooning, birdmen, and blasting into space. Current 2011 343p il $26.95 **629.1**

1. Aeronautics -- History

ISBN 978-1-61723-003-5

LC 2010-52340

"The Virgin Atlantic Airlines founder and billionaire adventurer celebrates the exploits of airborne daredevils—his own prominently among them—in this lively history of aviation pioneers. Branson ranges from the Montgolfier brothers' 1783 invention of the hot-air balloon to today's nascent space tourism industry . . . highlighting men and women who risked their money and lives to advance aerial technology or just put on a good show. It's a colorful assemblage of engineers, test pilots, barnstormers, and fighter aces. . . . Branson's enthusiasm for avant-garde flight and his firsthand understanding of its rigors make this a rousing—sometimes even elevating—read." Publ Wkly

Includes bibliographical references

Hickam, Homer H.

★ **Rocket** boys; a memoir. [by] Homer H. Hickam, Jr. Delacorte Press 1998 368p $25.95; pa $14 **629.1**

1. Authors 2. Novelists 3. Aerospace engineers 4. Memoirists 5. West Virginia 6. Authors, American 7. Writers on science

ISBN 0-385-33320-X; 0-385-33321-8 pa

LC 98-19304

"Even if Hickam stretched the strict truth to metamorphose his memories into Stand By Me-like material for Hollywood . . . the embellishing only converts what is a good story into an absorbing, rapidly readable one that is unsentimental but artful about adolescence, high school, and family life." Booklist

629.13 Aeronautics

Alexander, David E.

Why don't jumbo jets flap their wings? flying animals, flying machines, and how they are different. Rutgers University Press 2009 278p il $26.95 **629.13**

1. Aeronautics 2. Animal flight

ISBN 978-0-8135-4479-3; 0-8135-4479-3

LC 2008-35425

Alexander discusses the mechanics and physics of how animals and aircraft fly.

"Anyone interested in the flight of birds or insects or the flight of various types of aircraft will find this volume fascinating. . . . [This book] is very well written and approaches complex topics in a manner that readers at any level of expertise will find understandable and interesting." Sci Books Films

Includes glossary and bibliographical references

Butler, Susan

East to the dawn; the life of Amelia Earhart. Da Capo Press 1999 489p il map pa $15.95 **629.13**

1. Air pilots 2. Missing persons 3. Women air pilots 4. Memoirists

ISBN 978-0-306-81837-0

First published 1997 by Addison-Wesley

In this biography of the pilot and women's rights advocate "Butler shows a mastery of aviation history, and considerable sophistication about the technology of flight and navigation . . . The mountain of new material it marshals guarantees 'East to the Dawn' a permanent place on the shelf of Amelia Earhart references." N Y Times Book Rev

Includes bibliographical references

Goldstone, Lawrence

★ **Birdmen**; The Wright Brothers, Glenn Curtiss, and the Battle to Control the Skies. Lawrence Goldstone. Random House Inc 2014 448 p. illustrations $28   **629.13**
1. Aeronautics -- History
ISBN 034553803X; 9780345538031
         LC 2014001424

This book, by Lawrence Goldstone, tells the "story of the . . . feud between . . . great air pioneers, the Wright brothers and Glenn Curtiss. . . . On one side, a pair of tenacious siblings who together had solved the centuries-old riddle of powered, heavier-than-air flight. On the other, an audacious motorcycle racer whose innovative aircraft became synonymous in the public mind with death-defying stunts. For more than a decade, they battled each other in court, at air shows, and in the newspapers." (Publisher's note)

"A superbly crafted retelling of a story familiar to aviation buffs, here greatly strengthened by fresh perspectives, rigorous analyses, comprehensible science, and a driving narrative." LJ

Includes bibliographical references (pages 401-404) and index

Grant, R. G.

Flight: 100 years of aviation. DK Pub. 2002 440p il hardcover o.p. pa $24.95   **629.13**
1. Aeronautics -- History
ISBN 0-7894-8910-4; 0-7566-1902-5 pa
         LC 2002-73935

"The impressive illustrations include over 300 gorgeous, full-color profiles of the world's major military and civilian aircraft and space vehicles." Libr J

Gubert, Betty Kaplan

Distinguished African Americans in aviation and space science; {by} Betty Kaplan Gubert, Miriam Sawyer, and Caroline M. Fannin. Oryx Press 2002 319p il (Distinguished African Americans series) $64.95   **629.13**
1. Astronauts 2. African American pilots
ISBN 1-57356-246-7
         LC 2001-34821

This profiles 80 men and 20 women in aviation and space science covering 80 years of the 20th century

"Libraries should not hesitate to add this title to their collections." Booklist

Includes bibliographical references

Haynsworth, Leslie

Amelia Earhart's daughters; the wild and glorious story of American women aviators from World War II to the dawn of the space age. {by} Leslie Haynsworth and David Toomey. Morrow 1998 322p il hardcover o.p. pa $14   **629.13**
1. Air pilots 2. Women air pilots 3. Women astronauts 4. Cosmetics industry executives
ISBN 0-380-72984-9 pa
         LC 98-8727

This "study of American women aviators concentrates almost exclusively on the WASPs of World War II and the would-be female astronauts of the early 1960s." Booklist

Includes bibliographical references

Lindbergh, Charles

The **spirit** of St. Louis; [by] Charles A. Lindbergh. Scribner 1998 562p il hardcover o.p. pa $20   **629.13**
1. Spirit of St. Louis (Airplane) 2. Aeronautics -- Flights
ISBN 0-684-85277-2; 0-7432-3705-6 pa
         LC 98-33556

First published 1953

This is an account of the first solo transatlantic flight from New York to Paris, as well as a detailed description of the preparation for the flight which in turn mirrors aviation of the 1920's.

Mortimer, Gavin

Chasing Icarus; the seventeen days in 1910 that forever changed American aviation. Walker & Co 2009 305p il $26   **629.13**
1. Aeronautics -- History
ISBN 978-0-8027-1711-5

The author "argues that three aeronautic events in 1910 vouchsafed the primacy of U.S. aviation and the triumph of heavier-than-air flight. Interweaving the events—Walter Wellman's failed attempt to cross the Atlantic in his dirigible, America; the International Balloon Cup Race, which embarked from St. Louis; and the country's first international aircraft contest, held above the Belmont Park racetrack in New York—Mortimer effectively places the reader at the vital center of all three. . . . A singular contribution to early aviation history." Libr J

Includes bibliographical references

Smithsonian atlas of world aviation; charting the history of flight from the first balloons to today's most advanced aircraft. [compiled by] Dana Bell. HarperCollins 2008 230p il map $39.95 **629.13**
1. Reference books 2. Historical atlases 3. Aeronautics -- History
ISBN 978-0-06-125144-3; 0-06-125144-5
         LC 2007-47574

"Bell's writing . . . adds immeasurably to the value of this atlas: it is articulate, clear, informative, and, above all, accurate." SLJ

Includes bibliographical references

Trzebinski, Errol

The **lives** of Beryl Markham; Out of Africa's hidden free spirit and Denys Finch Hatton's last great love. Norton 1993 396p il maps hardcover o.p. pa $12   **629.13**
1. Air pilots 2. Memoirists 3. Horse trainers
ISBN 0-393-31252-6 pa
         LC 93-9919

The author offers "confirmation of the rumor that Beryl's third husband actually wrote her best-selling memoir, West with the Night." Booklist

Includes bibliographical references

629.130 Biography of flight

Jackson, Joe

Atlantic fever; Lindbergh, his competitors, and the race to cross the Atlantic. Joe Jackson. Farrar, Straus and Giroux 2012 x, 525 p.p   **629.130**

1. Aeronautics -- History 2. Air pilots -- Biography 3. Aeronautics -- Competitions 4. Transatlantic flights -- History -- 20th century 5. Aeronautics -- Competitions -- History -- 20th century

ISBN 0374106754; 9780374106751

LC 2011046068

In this book, Joe Jackson "places Lindbergh's historic flight of May 20-21, 1927, in the dramatic framework of the 'Great Atlantic Air Race,' which began eight years earlier when Franco-American hotelier Ramond Orteig sponsored a $25,000 prize to the first aviator to cross the Atlantic. . . . Jackson traces the futile attempts to win the Orteig Prize until the spring of 1927, when a bevy of pilots stepped forth to compete for the honor no matter the cost. Jackson's compelling portraits of these contenders . . . place Lindbergh's successful bid in perspective. The reader is reminded that 'Lindy' was the last contestant to arrive in New York but the first to depart, owing to the simplicity of his effort compared with the technical, funding, and personnel complexities of his rivals' preparations." (Libr J)

Includes bibliographical references and index

629.132 Mechanics of flight; flying and related topics

Vanhoenacker, Mark

Skyfaring; a journey with a pilot. Mark Vanhoenacker. Alfred A. Knopf 2015 368 p. (hardback) $25.95   **629.132**

1. Airplanes -- Piloting 2. Aeronautics -- Popular works 3. Airplanes -- Piloting -- Popular works

ISBN 038535181X; 9780385351812

LC 2014041159

In this book, Mark Vanhoenacker explores his experiences as a pilot. He "recalls how he came to become a long-haul pilot, abandoning postgraduate work at Cambridge University. . . .The author describes in detail his classroom instruction together with various exams for his Boeing 747-type rating before entering the cockpit as a licensed pilot." Vanhoenacker draws on "autobiography, avionics, history, geography, physics, and poetry" to explain his experiences of flight. (Library Journal)

"The author loves travel and encountering new cities and situations, and his job makes this possible for him. This is a delightful and entertaining work, a genuine pleasure to read, and likely to be enjoyed by all. Highly recommended. Summing Up: Highly recommended. All levels." Choice

629.133 Aircraft types

Botting, Douglas

Dr. Eckener's dream machine; the great Zeppelin and the dawn of air travel. Holt & Co. 2001 331p il maps $27.50; pa $16   **629.133**

1. Airships 2. Aeronautics -- Flights 3. Graf Zeppelin (Airship) 4. Aircraft industry executives

ISBN 0-8050-6458-3; 0-8050-6459-1 pa

LC 2001-24770

Botting discusses the history of the Zeppelin, a rigid airship designed by a Prussian army officer, Ferdinand Count von Zeppelin, and the career of Hugo Eckener, who promoted and flew the dirigible

"A truly exciting book, filled with colorful characters and plenty of derring-do and laced with just the right amount of sadness and tragedy." Booklist

Includes bibliographical references

Chiles, James R.

The **god** machine; from boomerangs to black hawks, the story of the helicopter. Bantam Dell 2007 354p il hardcover o.p. pa $16   **629.133**

1. Helicopters

ISBN 978-0-553-80447-8; 978-0-553-38352-2 pa

LC 2007-28575

This "is an engaging blend of pop science and pop culture." Publ Wkly

Includes bibliographical references

629.2 Motor land vehicles, cycles

Lessing, Hans-Erhard

Bicycle design; an illustrated history. Tony Hadland and Hans-Erhard Lessing; with contributions from Nick Clayton and Gary W. Sanderson. The MIT Press 2014 xiii, 564 p.p illustrations (hardcover : alk. paper) $34.95   **629.2**

1. Bicycles -- History 2. Bicycles -- Parts -- History 3. Bicycles -- Design and construction -- History

ISBN 0262026759; 9780262026758

LC 2013023698

This book, by Tony Hadland and Hans-Erhard Lessing, with contributions from Nick Clayton and Gary W. Sanderson, gives a "comprehensive account of the bicycle's technical and historical evolution, from the earliest velocipedes . . . to modern racing bikes, mountain bikes, and recumbents. It traces the bicycle's development in terms of materials, ergonomics, and vehicle physics, as carried out by inventors, entrepreneurs, and manufacturers." (Publisher's note)

Includes bibliographical references (pages 29-548) and index

629.22 Types of vehicles

Harley-Davidson; the complete history, by Darwin Holmstrom. Motorbooks 2016 240 p. illustrations (chiefly color) (hc w/jacket) $50 **629.22**
1. Motorcycles 2. Harley-Davidson motorcycle
ISBN 0760350000; 9780760350003
LC 2016937974

This book on the history of Harley-Davidson by Darwin Holmstrom "celebrates these iconic motorcycles. . . . Pages in the book reveal historic images as well as modern photos from the top motorcycle photographers working today. Additionally, there are chapters from some of the most celebrated motorcycle writers of all time--Peter Egan, Kevin Cameron, Ed Youngblood, Allan Girdler, Steve Anderson, and many more." (Publisher's note)

629.222 Gasoline-powered, oil-powered, man-powered vehicles

The **Beaulieu** encyclopedia of the automobile; editor in chief, Nick Georgano; foreword by Lord Montagu of Beaulieu. Fitzroy Dearborn Pubs. 2000 2v il set $325 **629.222**
1. Reference books 2. Automobiles -- Encyclopedias
ISBN 1-57958-293-1
LC 2001-316285

"The most comprehensive automobile encyclopedia available today." Am Libr

Car; the definitive visual history of the automobile. [senior project editor, Kathryn Hennessy; US editor, Beth Landis Hester] DK Pub. 2011 360 p. ill. (chiefly col.) (hbk.) $40 **629.222**
1. Automobiles -- History 2. Automobiles -- Pictorial works 3. Automobiles -- History -- Chronology
ISBN 0756671671; 9780756671679
LC 2011282325

This book, edited by Kathryn Hennessy and Beth Landis, "tracing the history of the automobile, from the first prototypes to the super cars of today, . . . covers the technological developments and manufacture of cars, the cultural backdrop against which the various models arose, and the enduring impact the car has had on society as an object of curiosity, symbol of luxury, and item of necessity." (Publisher's note)

Gross, Ken
Dream cars; innovative design, visionary ideas. Sarah Schleunung, Ken Gross. Random House Inc 2014 134 p. color illustrations (hardback) $40 **629.222**
1. Antique and classic cars 2. Automobiles -- Design and construction 3. Product design -- Exhibitions 4. High Museum of Art -- Catalogs 5. Automobiles -- Drawings -- Exhibitions 6. Antique and classic cars -- Exhibitions 7. Experimental automobiles -- Exhibitions
ISBN 0847842630; 9780847842636
LC 2014000794

This book, by Sarah Schleunung and Ken Gross, "presents some of the world's most breathtaking concept cars built between 1934 and 2001, a series of visionary designs that influenced the automotive industry and challenged notions of what is possible both aesthetically and technologically." (Publisher's note)
Includes bibliographical references and index

Ingrassia, Paul
Engines of change; a history of the American dream in fifteen cars. Paul Ingrassia. 1st Simon & Schuster hc ed. Simon & Schuster 2012 xx, 395 p., [32] p. of platesp ill. (some col.) (hardcover) $30.00; (paperbook) $18.00 **629.222**
1. Popular culture -- United States 2. Automobiles -- United States -- History 3. Automobiles -- Social aspects -- United States -- History
ISBN 1451640633; 9781451640632; 9781451640649; 9781451640656
LC 2012002303

This book, by Paul Ingrassia, offers a cultural history of automobiles in the United States. "From the assembly lines of Henry Ford to the open roads of Route 66, from the lore of Jack Kerouac to the sex appeal of the Hot Rod, America's history is a vehicular history. . . . Ingrassia offers a[n] . . . epic in fifteen automobiles, . . . as well as the personalities and tales behind them." (Publisher's note)
Includes bibliographical references (p. 373-375) and index.

Parissien, Steven
The **life** of the automobile; a history of the motor car. Steven Parissien. Thomas Dunne Books 2014 448 p. (hardback) $27.99 **629.222**
1. Automobiles -- History
ISBN 1250040639; 9781250040633
LC 2013045750

This book, by Steven Parissien, "is the first comprehensive world history of the car. . . . The author examines the advances of the interwar era, the Golden Age of the 1950s, and the iconic years of the 1960s to the decades of doubt and uncertainty following the oil crisis of 1973, the global mergers of the 1990s, the bailouts of the early twenty-first century, and the emergence of the electric car." (Publisher's note)
"This elegant and authoritative work demonstrates the historical links among people, machines, and cultures on a global scale." LJ
Includes bibliographical references and index

Swift, Earl
Auto Biography; A Classic Car, an Outlaw Motorhead, and 57 Years of the American Dream. by Earl Swift. HarperCollins 2014 368 p. illustrations (some color) $26.99 **629.222**
1. American dream 2. Criminals 3. Automobiles
ISBN 0062282662; 9780062282668

This book, by Earl Swift, "follows an outlaw auto dealer as he struggles to save a rusted '57 Chevy--a car that has already passed through twelve pairs of hands before his--while financial ruin, government bureaucrats and the FBI close in on him. . . . [H]assled by a growing assortment of challengers, the Chevy's thirteenth owner--an orphan, grade-school dropout and rounder, a felon arrested seventy-odd times, and a man who's been written off as a ruin himself--embarks on a mission to save the car." (Publisher's note)

"A big, weird, heartfelt book about a badass who could give a damn whether you root for him or not." Kirkus

Includes bibliographical references

629.225 Work vehicles

Tractor; the definitive visual history. Jemima Dunne (ed.) DK Publishing 2015 256 p. illustrations (chiefly color) $30 **629.225**
1. Agricultural machinery 2. Tractors -- Pictorial works 3. Tractors -- History
ISBN 1465435999; 9781465435996

LC 2015288087

This book, edited by Jemima Dunne and the Dorling Kindersley company, "showcases the complete history of farm machinery--from steam and vintage tractors to the latest combine harvesters. . . . Packed with images and tractor data on more than 200 iconic machines, . . . [the book] explores the entire range of tractors and farming machines from around the world." (Publisher's note)

"There is also a chapter on 'How Tractors Work: Tractor Technology,' a glossary, and an index. While the photographs are the obvious draw, the narrative is surprisingly informative and well-researched. Suitable for public libraries, this book will do well in the circulating collection." Booklist

629.227 Cycles

Hallett, Richard

Bike deconstructed; a grand tour of the modern bicycle. Richard Hallett. Princeton Architectural Press 2014 192 p. color illustrations (alk. paper) $29.95 **629.227**
1. Bicycles 2. Bicycles -- Parts 3. Bicycles -- Design and construction -- History
ISBN 1616892285; 9781616892289

LC 2013029264

In this book, author Richard Hallett "dismantles the modern bicycle to uncover the origin, design, and evolution of every integral part. Through stunning photography, accessible writing, and clear diagrams, Hallett examines every aspect of the bike in detail-- from the anatomy of the drive chain to the geometry of the main frame, and from spoke weaving patterns to the effect of fork rake on steering and stability." (Publisher's note)

"The author includes historical background for many topics, as well as the advantages and disadvantages of different materials used in terms of weight, strength, and flexibility. A fascinating work of interest to a wide audience. Summing Up: Recommended. All cycling enthusiasts, undergraduate students, and general readers. General Readers; Lower-division Undergraduates; Upper-division Undergraduates; Two-year Technical Program Students." Choice

Zinn, Lennard

Zinn & the art of road bike maintenance; the world's best-selling bicycle repair and maintenance

guide. Lennard Zinn; illustrated by Todd Telander and Mike Reisel. 5th edition VeloPress 2016 28 cm illustrations pbk $26.95 **629.227**
1. Bicycles -- Maintenance and repair
ISBN 9781937715373; 193771537X

LC 2015039577

"From basic repairs like how to fix a flat tire to advanced overhauls of drivetrains and brakes, Zinn's clearly illustrated guide makes every bicycle repair and maintenance job easy for everyone. Zinn's friendly step-by-step guide explains the tools you'll need and how to know you've done the job right. The two-color interior is easy to read—even in a dimly-lit garage or workshop. Hundreds of hand-drawn illustrations and exploded parts diagrams show just the right level of detail to lead you through every bicycle repair task." (Publisher's note)

Includes bibliographical references (page 447) and indexes

629.28 Tests, driving, maintenance, repair

Downs, Todd

Essential road bike maintenance handbook; Todd Downs with Brian Fiske. Rodale 2014 ix, 166 p.p illustrations (pbk.) $14.99 **629.28**
1. Bicycles -- Maintenance and repair 2. Bicycles -- Maintenance and repair -- Handbooks, manuals, etc
ISBN 1623361664; 9781623361662

LC 2012474514

This book, by Todd Downs with Brian Fiske, "distills the core fundamentals and serves as a guide to repairing and maintaining one's bike, focusing specifically on instructions with step-by-step photos, troubleshooting tips, links to videos, and helpful sidebar material. The book is clearly organized . . . so that readers can find quickly and efficiently the information they need." (Publisher's note)

Bicycling essential road bike maintenance handbook

Henderson, Bob

The **Haynes** bicycle book; the Haynes repair manual for maintaining and repairing your bike. by Bob Henderson. 3rd edition Haynes North America 2013 224 p. ill. (chiefly col.) pbk $29.95 **629.28**
1. Cycling 2. Bicycles -- Maintenance and repair
ISBN 9781620920404; 1620920409

LC 2013930927

This bicycle manual, by Bob Henderson, presents information on "how to set up your bike, routine maintenance, troubleshooting, and easy-to-follow repair procedures for road, mountain, hybrid, cruiser and BMX bikes." (Publisher's note)

McCormick, Danielle

Essential car care for women; Jamie Little and Danielle McCormick. Seal Press 2013 192 p. color illustrations (pbk.) $16 **629.28**
1. Automobiles -- Maintenance and repair 2. Automobiles -- Maintenance and repair -- Amateurs'

manuals
ISBN 1580054366; 9781580054362

LC 2011045604

In this guidebook, authors Jamie Little and Danielle Mc-Cormick "offer the indispensable, hard-won advice women need to buy, sell, and care for their cars with confidence. . . . [They] explain what an alternator, regulator, distributor, and timing belt are; how to change a tire, recharge a flat battery, check the oil, and assess tire pressure; what to do when a car breaks down or when an accident occurs; how to buy a car without being taken advantage of; and more." (Publisher's note)

"This is a good update for Julie Sussman & Stephanie Glakas-Tenet's Dare To Repair Your Car. As it lacks an overwhelming amount of mechanical instruction, this book proves useful and approachable. It will appeal to high school to adult audiences, male or female, though guys may be leery of the pink cover. Very strongly recommended." LJ

Ramsey, Dan
   Teach yourself visually car care & maintenance; by Dan Ramsey and Judy Ramsey. Visual / Wiley 2009 210p il (Visual read less, learn more) pa $24.95   **629.28**
   1. Automobiles -- Maintenance and repair
   ISBN 978-0-470-37727-7

LC 2009-920042

This book covers "how to change oil and other fluids; rotate tires; replace fuel pumps, air filters, and batteries; and . . . more." Publisher's note
   Includes glossary

Vanderbilt, Tom
   Traffic; why we drive the way we do (and what it says about us) Alfred A. Knopf 2008 402p $24.95   **629.28**
   1. City traffic 2. Automobile drivers
   ISBN 978-0-307-26478-7

LC 2008-11507

"This may be the most insightful and comprehensive study ever done of driving behavior and how it reveals truths about the types of people we are." Booklist
   Includes bibliographical references

629.295   Vehicles for extraterrestrial surfaces

Manning, Rob
   Mars Rover Curiosity; an inside account from curiosity's chief engineer. Rob Manning, William L. Simon. Smithsonian Books 2014 240 p. illustrations $29.95   **629.295**
   1. Space vehicles 2. Mars (Planet) -- Exploration 3. United States. National Aeronautics and Space Administration
   ISBN 1588344738; 9781588344731

LC 2014941274

This book on the Mars rover Curiosity by Rob Manning and William L. Simon "tells of bringing the groundbreaking spacecraft to life. Manning and his team at NASA's Jet Propulsion Laboratory, tasked with designing a lander many times larger and more complex than any before, faced

technical setbacks, fights over inadequate resources, and the challenges of leading an army of brilliant, passionate, and often frustrated experts." (Publisher's note)

"It will be an enjoyable read for anyone interested in Mars, the exploration of Mars, or how NASA designs its missions. Summing Up: Highly recommended. Lower- and upper-division undergraduates; general readers." Choice

629.4   Astronautics

Clegg, Brian
   Final Frontier; The Pioneering Science and Technology of Exploring the Universe. Brian Clegg. St. Martin's Press 2014 304 p. $26.99   **629.4**
   1. Science 2. Technology 3. Outer space -- Exploration 4. Astronautics -- Popular works 5. Interplanetary voyages -- Popular works 6. Outer space -- Exploration -- Popular works
   ISBN 1250039436; 9781250039439

LC 2014010056

In this book, by Brian Clegg, "we discover the massive challenges that face explorers, both human and robotic, to uncover the current and future technologies that could take us out into the galaxy and take a voyage of discovery where no one has gone before-- but one day someone will." (Publisher's note)

"This fine work belongs in all college libraries. Summing Up: Highly recommended." Choice
   Includes bibliographical references and index

Dean, Margaret Lazarus
   Leaving orbit; notes from the last days of american spaceflight. Margaret Lazarus Dean. Graywolf Press 2015 240 p. (alk. paper) $16   **629.4**
   1. Astronautics -- United States 2. United States. National Aeronautics and Space Administration
   ISBN 155597709X; 9781555977092

LC 2014960047

This book, by Margaret Lazarus Dean, winner of the Graywolf Press Nonfiction Prize, presents an "elegy to the waning days of human spaceflight as we have known it. In the 1960s, humans took their first steps away from Earth, and for a time our possibilities in space seemed endless. But in a time of austerity and in the wake of high-profile disasters . . . that dream has ended." (Publisher's note)

"Dean deftly captures the thrill and discovery of American space exploration, as well as the disappointment and outrage she believes everyone should feel at its ending." Pub Wkly

Holt, Nathalia
   Rise of the Rocket Girls; The Women Who Propelled Us, from Missiles to the Moon to Mars. by Nathalia Holt (Author) Little, Brown & Co. 2016 352 p. illustrations (some color) $27   **629.4**
   1. Satellites 2. Jet propulsion 3. Women mathematicians 4. Rockets (Aeronautics) 5. Women -- United States -- Biography
   ISBN 0316338923; 9780316338929

LC TL862.J48

"In the 1940s and 50s, when the newly minted Jet Propulsion Laboratory needed quick-thinking mathematicians to calculate velocities and plot trajectories, they didn't turn to male graduates. Rather, they recruited an elite group of young women who, with only pencil, paper, and mathematical prowess, transformed rocket design, helped bring about the first American satellites, and made the exploration of the solar system possible." (Publisher's note)

"This is an excellent contribution to American history, valuable not only for what it reveals about the space program and gender equality but even more as great reading. Book clubs will be lining up." Booklist

Milestones of space; eleven iconic objects from the Smithsonian National Air and Space Museum. Michael J. Neufeld, [editor] Smithsonian National Air & Space Museum in assoc. w/Zenith Press 2014 176 p. illustrations (mostly color) (hardback) $30   **629.4**
1. Astronautics 2. United States. National Aeronautics and Space Administration 3. National Air and Space Museum -- Catalogs 4. Astronautics -- United States -- Equipment and supplies -- Pictorial works
ISBN 0760344442; 9780760344446
LC 2013045152
This book, edited by Michael J. Neufeld, "select curators of the Smithsonian National Air and Space Museum present a . . . photographic celebration of some of the most groundbreaking artifacts that played key parts in giving humanity its first steps into the cosmos. Focusing on the most iconic objects and technology . . . , this book extensively profiles eleven of the NASM's most important breakthroughs in space technology." (Publisher's note)
Includes bibliographical references (page 172) and index

Teitel, Amy Shira
Breaking the Chains of Gravity; The Story of Spaceflight Before Nasa. Amy Shira Teitel. St. Martins Press 2016 304 p. 8 plates; illustrations $27   **629.4**
1. Space flight 2. United States. National Aeronautics and Space Administration
ISBN 1472911172; 9781472911179
LC 2015046643
"NASA's history is a familiar story, culminating with the agency successfully landing men on the moon in 1969, but its prehistory is an important and rarely told tale. America's space agency drew together some of the best minds the non-Soviet world had to offer." Written by Amy Shira Teitel, "'Breaking the Chains of Gravity' looks at the evolving roots of America's space program." (Publisher's note)

"Aircraft and rocketry geeks will find the most to love in this jet-powered history, but it's a great primer for anyone interested in the origins of space travel." LJ

Tyson, Neil deGrasse, 1958-
Space chronicles; facing the ultimate frontier. Neil deGrasse Tyson; edited by Avis Lang. W.W. Norton 2012 364 p. ill. $26.95   **629.4**
1. Space flight -- Forecasting 2. Astronautics -- United States 3. Astronautics and state -- United States 4. United States. National Aeronautics and Space

Administration 5. Astronautics 6. Space flight 7. Outer space -- Exploration
ISBN 0393082105; 9780393082104
LC 2011032481
In this book, Neil DeGrasse Tyson "delivers . . . [an] argument for space exploration even in the face of a disastrous economy. In this collection of articles and talks, the author investigates what space travel means to us as a species and, more specifically, what NASA means to America. . . . 'When science does advance, when discovery does unfold . . . ,' he writes, 'they happen as an auxiliary benefit and not as a primary goal of NASA's geopolitical mission statement.'" (Kirkus Reviews)

"Tyson is an articulate popularizer of astrophysics. . . . His writing style, while necessarily a bit technical, is as engaging as his screen presence." LJ

629.43   Unmanned space flight

Zimmerman, Robert
The **universe** in a mirror; the saga of the Hubble Telescope and the visionaries who built it. Princeton University Press 2008 287p il $29.95   **629.43**
1. Hubble Space Telescope
ISBN 978-0-691-13297-6; 0-691-13297-6
LC 2007-943159
"Must reading for armchair astrophysicists." Booklist
Includes bibliographical references

629.44   Auxiliary spacecraft

Aldrin, Buzz, 1930-
Mission to mars; my vision for space exploration. by Buzz Aldrin and Leonard David. National Geographic 2013 272 p. $26   **629.44**
1. Outer space -- Exploration 2. Mars (Planet) -- Exploration
ISBN 1426210175; 9781426210174
LC 2012953599
In this book, by Buzz Aldrin and Leonard David, Aldrin "speaks out as a vital advocate for the continuing quest to push the boundaries of the universe as we know it. As a pioneering astronaut who first set foot on the moon during mankind's first landing of Apollo 11--and as an aerospace engineer who designed an orbital rendezvous technique critical to future planetary landings--Aldrin has a vision, and in this book he plots out the path he proposes, taking humans to Mars by 2035." (Publisher's note)

"Aldrin makes a daring proposal for further space exploration in this exciting glimpse of the new new frontier." Pub Wkly

White, Rowland
Into the Black; the extraordinary untold story of the first flight of the space shuttle Columbia and the men who flew her. Rowland White. Simon & Schus-

ter 2016 464 p. ill. (some color), maps (hardcover) $29.99   **629.44**

1. Columbia (Spacecraft) 2. Outer space -- Exploration
ISBN 9781501123634; 9781501123627; 1501123629

LC 2016006784

This book, by Rowland White, "using interviews, NASA oral histories, and recently declassified material, . . . pieces together the dramatic untold story of the Columbia mission and the brave people who dedicated themselves to help the United States succeed in the age of space exploration. On April 12, 1981, NASA's Space Shuttle Columbia blasted off from Cape Canaveral." (Publisher's note)

"Bolstering technological insights with personal information from his interviews with astronauts and engineers, White produces a space history aerospace enthusiasts will very much enjoy." Booklist

Includes bibliographical references (pages 403-412) and index.

629.45   Manned space flight

Ackmann, Martha

The **Mercury** 13: the untold story of thirteen American women and the dream of space flight. Random House 2003 239p il hardcover o.p. pa $13.95   **629.45**

1. Women astronauts 2. Project Mercury
ISBN 0-375-50744-2; 0-375-75893-3 pa

LC 2002-37118

"Mercury 13 is both an outstanding work of research and an exceptionally readable and well-told story. Readers will gain new perspectives on space, medicine, women, and American culture, and will appreciate the magnitude of what was lost when the women were grounded." SLJ

Includes bibliographical references

Koppel, Lily

The **Astronaut** Wives Club; A True Story. Lily Koppel. Grand Central Pub. 2013 384 p. (hardcover) $28   **629.45**

1. United States -- History 2. Astronauts' spouses -- Biography 3. Astronautics -- United States -- History 4. Astronauts' spouses -- Texas -- Houston -- Biography 5. Women -- Texas -- Houston -- Social life and customs -- 20th century
ISBN 1455503258; 9781455503254

LC 2012045976

This book, by Lily Koppel, profiles the lives of U.S. astronauts' wives during the 1960s and onward. "As America's Mercury Seven astronauts were launched on death-defying missions, television cameras focused on the brave smiles of their young wives. Overnight, these women were transformed from military spouses into American royalty. . . . They formed the Astronaut Wives Club, meeting regularly to provide support and friendship." (Publisher's note)

Kranz, Eugene F.

Failure is not an option; mission control from Mercury to Apollo 13 and beyond. {by} Gene Kranz. Simon & Schuster 2000 415p il $26   **629.45**

1. Space flight 2. Astronautics -- United States 3. United States -- National Aeronautics and Space Administration
ISBN 0-7432-0079-9

LC 00-27720

"A welcome contribution to the history of space flight. More than any previous book, it gives the view of that history as lived by the brotherhood of Mission Control. The writing, like Kranz himself, is brisk, unadorned and informative, but warmed from time to time by characteristic expressions of irony and humor." N Y Times Book Rev

Mailer, Norman, 1923-2007

Of a fire on the moon; Norman Mailer. Random House Trade Paperbacks 2004 463 p. (acid-free paper) $16   **629.45**

1. Apollo project 2. Space flight to the moon 3. Project Apollo (U.S.) 4. Astronauts -- United States 5. United States -- Civilization -- 1945-
ISBN 0553390619; 9780553390612

LC 2014415502

This book, by Norman Mailer, is a "chronicle of the Apollo 11 mission . . . , America's reach for greatness in the midst of the Cold War. . . . [This volume] compiles the reportage [Norman] Mailer published between 1969 and 1970 in 'Life' magazine: gripping firsthand dispatches from inside NASA's clandestine operations in Houston and Cape Kennedy; technical insights into the magnitude of their awe-inspiring feat; and prescient meditations that place the event in human context." (Publisher's note)

Nelson, Craig

Rocket men; the triumph and tragedy of the first Americans on the moon. Viking 2009 404p il $27.95   **629.45**

1. Apollo project 2. Space flight to the moon 3. Astronautics -- United States
ISBN 978-0-670-02103-1

LC 2008-51175

"A thorough recounting—as full in human terms as in scientific and technical detail—of NASA's first manned Moon landing. . . . The definitive account of a watershed in American history." Kirkus

Includes bibliographical references

Piantadosi, Claude A.

Mankind beyond Earth; the history, science, and future of human space exploration. Claude A. Piantadosi. Columbia University Press 2012 336 p. (cloth : alk. paper) $35   **629.45**

1. Interplanetary voyages 2. Outer space -- Exploration 3. Outer space -- Exploration -- Popular works 4. Manned space flight -- History -- Popular works 5. Astronautics -- United States -- Forecasting -- Popular works
ISBN 0231162421; 9780231162425; 9780231531030

LC 2012017631

In this book, Claude A. Piantadosi "offers a brief history of human space exploration; a discussion of various strategies for extending human excursions to asteroids, the Moon (again), Mars, the outer planets of the Sun, and even targets beyond the solar system; and a rigorous examination of the very special and expensive conditions needed for human survival on such trips." (Library Journal)

Includes bibliographical references and index

Pyle, Rod

Destination moon; the Apollo missions in the astronauts' own words. HarperCollins Publishers 2005 192p il $24.95; pa $14.95 **629.45**

1. Space flight to the moon 2. Project Apollo
ISBN 0-06-087349-3; 0-06-087350-7 pa

LC 2005-51350

This "survey of the Apollo moon program includes a brief summary of each flight and attempted flight of the great effort, from the fatal fire on Pad 34 in 1967 to the landing of a scientist on the moon in Apollo 17 in 1972. . . . Space collections of all sizes should welcome Pyle's book, and smaller ones will find it invaluable." Booklist

Wolfe, Tom

★ The **right** stuff. Picador 2008 352p pa $16 **629.45**

1. Astronauts 2. Astronautics -- United States
ISBN 0-312-42756-5; 978-0-312-42756-6

First published 1979 by Farrar, Straus & Giroux

This volume chronicles "the handful of adrenaline-junkie military test pilots who became the Mercury astronauts. Their story is juxtaposed against that of Chuck Yeager, the ace of aces pilot who broke the sound barrier but couldn't apply to the space program because he lacked a college degree. . . . A terrific read from beginning to end." Libr J

629.455   Planetary flights

Wohlforth, Charles

Beyond Earth; Our Path to a New Home in the Planets. Charles Wohlforth and Amanda R. Hendrix, Ph.D. Pantheon Books 2016 320 p. (hard cover : alk. paper) $27.95 **629.455**

1. Astronautics 2. Space colonies 3. Titan (Satellite) 4. Interplanetary voyages 5. Manned space flight 6. Space flight -- Physiological effect 7. Space flight -- Psychological aspects
ISBN 9780804197977

LC 2016009498

This book by Charles Wohlforth and Amanda R. Hendrix offers an "account of the developments . . . that have transformed the dream of space colonization into something that may well be achievable. . . . [It] is grounded not only in the human capacity for invention . . . but also in the bureaucratic, political, and scientific realities. . . . The authors . . . [claim] that . . . Titan . . . offers the most realistic . . . prospect of life without support from Earth." (Publisher's note)

"On the whole, the fictional chapters are entertaining, chilling, and put the science in a more human context. The two halves work together to create a striking, reality-based

possible future that's seen through the lens of current knowledge." Pub Wkly

629.47   Astronautical engineering

Guthrie, Julian

How to make a spaceship; A Band of Renegades, an Epic Race, and the Birth of Private Spaceflight. by Julian Guthrie. Penguin Group USA 2016 448 p. illustrations (ebook) $65; $28 **629.47**

1. Space flight
ISBN 9780698405851; 1594206724; 9781594206726

This book, by Julian Guthrie, is about "the historic race that reawakened the promise of manned spaceflight. Alone in a Spartan black cockpit, test pilot Mike Melvill rocketed toward space. He had eighty seconds to exceed the speed of sound. . . . The spectacle defied reason, the result of a competition dreamed up by entrepreneur Peter Diamandis, whose vision for a new race to space required small teams to do what only the world's largest governments had done before." (Publisher's note)

"Guthrie well captures the high-risk, buccaneering spirit of privately financed spaceflight." Booklist

629.8   Automatic control engineering

Bascomb, Neal

The **new** cool; a visionary teacher, his FIRST robotics team, and the ultimate battle of smarts. Crown Publishers 2010 337p il $25; ebook $12.99 **629.8**

1. Robots 2. FIRST (Organization)
ISBN 978-0-307-58889-0; 978-0-307-58891-3 ebook

LC 2010-21646

The author "charts the marathon play-by-play teamwork of a group of fourth-year Southern California students from Dos Pueblos High School Engineering Academy as they competed in a robot-building contest. Since 2002, physics teacher and mentor Amir Abo-Shaeer has administered an experimental science curriculum culminating in a team entry in 'FIRST' (For Inspiration and Recognition of Science and Technology), a worldwide robotics competition created by Dean Kamen. . . . Aside from a mind-numbing plethora of physics terminology, Bascomb skillfully translates the exhilarating challenge to the page via intricately descriptive, expertly paced sketches of the group and their combined handiwork. A nail-biting thrill ride for techies and armchair engineers." Kirkus

Includes bibliographical references

Davis, Joshua

Spare parts; four undocumented teenagers, one ugly robot, and the battle for the American dream. Joshua Davis. Farrar Straus & Giroux 2014 240 p. illustrations (hardcover) $25 **629.8**

1. Robots -- Competitions 2. Mexicans -- United States 3. Mexican Americans -- Economic conditions 4. Robotics -- Competitions -- United States 5. Phoenix (Ariz.) -- Social life and customs 6. Mexican American boys -- Education -- United States 7. Remote

submersibles -- Competitions -- United States
ISBN 0374183376; 9780374183370; 9780374534981
LC 2014018569

This book, by Joshua Davis, profiles how "In 2004, four Latino teenagers arrived at the Marine Advanced Technology Education Robotics Competition. . . . They were born in Mexico but raised in Phoenix, Arizona. . . . No one had ever suggested . . . that they might amount to much--but two inspiring science teachers had convinced these impoverished, undocumented kids from the desert who had never even seen the ocean that they should try to build an underwater robot." (Publisher's note)

"Davis pulls no punches as he describes the grim sociopolitical atmosphere that allows the oppression of talented people for no morally acceptable reason. The four young inventors and their struggles helped spur the DREAMers movement, and their story will also be told in a forthcoming Hollywood movie. This is important reading." Booklist

Dufty, David F.

How to build an android; the true story of Philip K. Dick's robotic resurrection. David F. Dufty. 1st US ed. H. Holt 2012 272 p. ill. (hbk.) $26.00 **629.8**
1. Robots 2. Artificial intelligence 3. Roboticists -- Biography 4. Androids -- Popular works 5. Robotics -- Popular works 6. Artificial intelligence -- Popular works
ISBN 0805095519; 9780805095517
LC 2011043674

This book by David F. Dufty tells "the story of the roboticists who created a fully functioning android replica of renowned writer Philip K. Dick." (Kirkus Reviews) "Dufty focuses on two main developers . . . David Hanson . . . who created Phil's head only to later lose it on an airplane, and Andrew Olney, a computer programmer who was obsessed with science fiction books as a youngster. Dufty examines how their differing outlooks influenced the project." (Publishers Weekly)

Long, John

Darwin's devices; what evolving robots can teach us about the history of life and the future of technology. John Long. Basic Books 2012 273 p. **629.8**
1. Biology -- Simulation methods 2. Evolution -- Study and teaching 3. Robots -- Design and construction 4. Technological innovations -- Forecasting 5. Evolutionary robotics 6. Technological forecasting 7. Evolution -- Simulation methods
ISBN 0465021417; 9780465021413; 9780465029280
LC 2011051804

The author "traces his path from a doctoral student studying the evolution of fish vertebrae to his present position as director of Vassar's Interdisciplinary Robotics Laboratory. . . . [John] Long explains how a blunder in an early version of his doctoral thesis led to his later work with robots. . . . Long's first self-propelled robot had a fairly simple design--an embedded minicomputer, one light sensor and a backbone built to mimic varying structural aspects of a marlin vertebrae. . . . More complex robots allowed him to model predator/prey relationships and target acquisition more realistically, and he was able to consider broader issues such as

the relationship between goal-directed behavior and animal intelligence." (Kirkus)
Includes bibliographical references and index

Mindell, David A.

Our Robots, Ourselves; Robotics and the Myths of Autonomy. David A. Mindell. Penguin Group USA 2015 272 p. illustrations $27.95 **629.8**
1. Robots 2. Technological innovations
ISBN 0525426973; 9780525426974

Author "David Mindell offers a . . . behind-the-scenes look at the cutting edge of robotics today, debunking commonly held myths and exploring the rapidly changing relationships between humans and machines. Drawing on firsthand experience, extensive interviews, and the latest research from MIT and elsewhere, Mindell takes us to extreme environments--high atmosphere, deep ocean, and outer space--to reveal where the most advanced robotics already exist." (Publisher's note)

"An expansively researched and enjoyably accessible treatment of robotic automation, recommended for readers of popular science and those with an interest in artificial intelligence and automation." LJ

630 Agriculture and related technologies

Berry, Wendell

Bringing it to the table; on farming and food. introduction by Michael Pollan. Counterpoint 2009 234p pa $14.95 **630**
1. Family farms 2. Sustainable agriculture 3. Agriculture -- United States
ISBN 978-1-58243-543-5
LC 2009-24437

"The essays [included] address such concerns as: How does organic measure up against locally grown? What are the differences between small and large farms, and how does that affect what you put on your dinner table? What can you do to support sustainable agriculture?" Publisher's note
Includes bibliographical references

Hanson, David

Breaking through concrete; building an urban farm revival. David Hanson and Edwin Marty; photographs by Michael Hanson; foreword by Mark Winne. University of California Press 2012 xv, 181 p.p (cloth : alk. paper) $29.95 **630**
1. Gardening 2. Teenage mothers 3. Homeless persons 4. Community gardens 5. Urban agriculture 6. Community gardens -- United States 7. Urban agriculture -- United States
ISBN 0520270541; 9780520270541
LC 2011024485

For this book, "[b]rothers David (a freelance journalist) and Michael (a freelance photographer) Hanson, together with Marty, founder of the nonprofit Jones Valley Farm in downtown Birmingham, AL, traveled cross-country to 12 urban gardens, starting in Seattle and ending in Illinois. Featured projects include a Santa Cruz garden tended by the homeless, a New Orleans congregational garden run by Vietnamese immigrants, and a Detroit teaching farm for teenage mothers." (Library Journal)

Includes bibliographical references.

Levatino, Audrey

Woman-powered farm; manual for a self-sufficient lifestyle from homestead to field. Audrey Levatino. The Countryman Press 2015 343 p. color illustrations (pbk.) $24.95　　　**630**
1. Women farmers 2. Farm management
ISBN 1581572417; 9781581572414
LC 2015006642

In this book, by Audrey Levatino with photography by Michael Levatino, the author "shares her experiences of running a farm and offers invaluable advice on how to get started, whether you have hundreds of acres or a simple lot for an urban community garden. [The book is] filled with personal anecdotes and stories from other women farmers, from old hands to brand new ones, from agricultural icons like Temple Grandin, to her own sister." (Publisher's note)

"A comprehensive volume on farming for women beginning to contemplate the industry, whether as a hobby or for a living. Personal anecdotes and a friendly tone don't overshadow the wealth of information in this book." LJ

Includes bibliographical references and index

631.5　Cultivation and harvesting

Dirr, Michael A.

The Reference Manual of Woody Plant Propagation; by Michael A. Dirr and Charles W. Heuser, Jr. Varsity Press 2009 410 p. illustrations $49.95 **631.5**
1. Horticulture 2. Plant propagation
ISBN 1604690046; 9781604690040
LC 2009497202

"Over 1,100 species and their propagation requirements by seeds, cuttings, grafting and budding, and tissue culture are discussed in exhaustive detail. Essentially a recipe book for making more trees and shrubs, this reference is a high-level how-to." (Publisher's note)

Lowe, Judy

Pruning; an illustrated guide : foolproof methods for shaping and trimming trees, shrubs, vines, and more. Judy Lowe. Cool Springs Press 2014 144 p. color illustrations; map (softcover) $19.99　　**631.5**
1. Pruning 2. Gardening
ISBN 159186562X; 9781591865629
LC 2013026162

"In 'Pruning: An Illustrated Guide,' award-winning gardening writer Judy Lowe imparts over two decades of expertise, focusing on the most common backyard pruning needs for the most commonly grown landscape plants. From trees and shrubs to hydrangeas, azaleas, roses, and other perennials, Lowe takes an in-depth approach to all the pruning essentials." (Publisher's note)

Includes bibliographical references and index

631.6　Clearing, drainage, revegetation

Fukuoka, Masanobu

Sowing seeds in the desert; natural farming, global restoration, and ultimate food security. Masanobu Fukuoka; edited by Larry Korn. Chelsea Green Pub. 2012 168 p. (hardback) $22.50　　　**631.6**
1. Sustainable agriculture 2. Agricultural innovations 3. Agriculture -- Environmental aspects 4. Revegetation 5. Desert reclamation 6. Desertification -- Control
ISBN 9781603584180; 1603584188; 9781603584197
LC 2012007330

This book "calls on modern-day farmers to reconsider their methods and heed the needs of the land. . . . [Masanobu Fukuoka] illuminates regional disparities in environmental and agricultural thought and practice. . . . In clarifying popular misconceptions about organic and natural farming, he advises that we must not focus on cash crops. . . . Only by the co-existence of myriad micro-organisms and vegetation will we be able to preserve and maintain our land." (Publishers Weekly)

Includes bibliographical references.

631.8　Fertilizers, soil conditioners, growth regulators

Pleasant, Barbara

★ The complete compost gardening guide; banner batches, grow heaps, comforter compost, and other amazing techniques for saving time and money, and producing the most flavorful, nutritious vegetables ever. [by] Barbara Pleasant & Deborah L. Martin. Storey Pub. 2008 319p il map $29.95; pa $19.95　　　**631.8**
1. Compost 2. Gardening
ISBN 978-1-58017-703-0; 978-1-58017-702-3 pa
LC 2007-49729

The authors "provide both a reference guide and an introduction to composting. The first section . . . includes a number of interesting facts, definitions, and even recipes (e.g., for Miracle Leaf Mold). The second section, on compost gardening techniques, examines easy methods of composting with piles, bins, and cans as well as more elaborate approaches involving pits and trenches. It also discusses the use of earthworms in composting. Finally, the third section treats in detail the kinds of plants that will do well in a composter's garden. . . . Essential reading for any gardener interested in composting, this should find its way into many public libraries with active gardening communities and academic and special libraries with an interest in horticulture and gardening." Libr J

632　Plant injuries, diseases, pests

Dickinson, Richard

Weeds of North America; Richard Dickinson and France Royer. University of Chicago Press 2014

797 p. illustrations (chiefly color) (pbk. : alk. paper)
$35   **632**

1. Weeds 2. Weeds -- North America -- Identification 3. Weeds -- North America -- Handbooks, manuals, etc

ISBN 022607644X; 9780226076447

LC 2013038953

This book, by Richard Dickinson and France Royer, "is the first to cover North American weeds at every stage of growth. The book is organized by plant family, and more than five hundred species are featured. Each receives a two-page spread with images and text identification keys. Species are arranged within family alphabetically by scientific name, and entries include vital information on seed viability and germination requirements." (Publisher's note)

"This comprehensive identification guide will aid in weed ecology and control." LJ

Includes bibliographical references and index

Mabey, Richard

Weeds; in defense of nature's most unloved plants. HarperCollins 2011 324p il $25.99; ebook $12.99   **632**

1. Weeds

ISBN 978-0-06-206545-2; 978-0-06-206547-6 ebook

LC 2011010483

First published 2010 in the United Kingdom

"This lively, erudite work invites readers to take a new look at the lowly and unloved weed. Mabey explains how weeds have cunningly evolved to survive natural disasters, human devastation, climate change, and almost every attempt to eradicate them. He weaves together a complex, fascinating tale of history and botany that travels from the first farm fields of Mesopotamia to the bomb craters of the London Blitz and the lowly industrial outfields of our modern cities." Publ Wkly

Includes bibliographical references

Stewart, Amy

Wicked bugs; the louse that conquered Napoleon's army & other diabolical insects. etchings and drawings by Briony Morrow-Cribbs. Algonquin Books of Chapel Hill 2011 271p il $18.95   **632**

1. Mites 2. Ticks 3. Spiders 4. Insect pests

ISBN 978-1-56512-960-3

LC 2011-3629

"Ranging from verdant South American jungles to Manhattan's cold concrete canyons, Stewart amusingly but analytically profiles the baddest bugs around in quick but attention-grabbing snapshots of little creatures that pack a lot of punch. Bed bugs and bookworms, rat fleas and filth flies all come under Stewart's curious gaze as she exposes their evil habits and lethal charms. No alarmist setting out to stoke preexisting phobias, Stewart shares her natural fascination with the insect world to help readers recognize both the threats and the wonders that could be lurking in corner crevices or come wafting in on the next gentle breeze." Booklist

Includes bibliographical references

633.1   Cereals

Yafa, Stephen

Grain of truth; the real case for and against wheat and gluten. Stephen Yafa. Avery 2015 304 p. illustrations (hardcover) $25.95   **633.1**

1. Wheat 2. Gluten-free diet 3. Gluten 4. Wheat-free diet

ISBN 1594632499; 9781594632495

LC 2015005944

In this book, author Stephen Yafa "sets the record straight, breaking down the botany of the wheat plant we've hijacked for our own use, the science of nutrition and digestion, the effects of mass production on our health, and questions about gluten and fiber-- all to point us towards a better, richer diet." (Publisher's note)

"Well researched and accessible, this title is recommended for libraries where people look for Michael Pollan's titles (Cooked; Food Rules; The Omnivore's Dilemma). Worth considering for any collection with copies of William Davis's Wheat Belly or David Perlmutter's Grain Brain." LJ

Includes bibliographical references and index

633.5   Fiber crops

Fine, Doug

Hemp bound; dispatches from the front lines of the next agricultural revolution. Doug Fine. Chelsea Green Publishing Company 2014 192 p. (pbk.) $14.95   **633.5**

1. Hemp 2. Agriculture -- United States 3. Hemp industry

ISBN 1603585435; 9781603585439; 9781603585446

LC 2013048926

"In 'Hemp Bound: Dispatches from the Front Lines of the Next Agricultural Revolution,' . . . author Doug Fine embarks on a . . . journey to meet the men and women who are testing, researching, and pioneering hemp's applications for the twenty-first century. . . . Fine learns how . . . possible it is for this misunderstood plant to help us end dependence on fossil fuels, heal farm soils damaged [by] growing monocultures, and bring . . . taxable revenue into the economy." (Publisher's note)

"A short, sweet, logical and funny argument for the potential of one of the world's most dynamic cash crops." Kirkus

Includes bibliographical references and index

633.79   Marijuana

Cervantes, Jorge

The **Cannabis** Encyclopedia; The Definitive Guide to Cultivation & Consumption of Medical Marijuana. Jorge Cervantes. Van Patten Publishing 2015 596 p. color illustrations, map $50   **633.79**

1. Marijuana 2. Herbs -- Therapeutic use

ISBN 1878823345; 1878823396; 9781878823342; 9781878823397

Author Jorge Cervantes presents this "guide to medical marijuana cultivation and consumption. It explains all the essential techniques to grow indoors, outdoors and in greenhouses. All gardening practices are well-researched and illustrated with easy step-by-step examples and instructions. More than 2,000 . . . color images illustrate this 596-page book." (Publisher's note)

"Essential where patrons grow, or are interested in growing, their own cannabis." LJ

634   Orchards, fruits, forestry

Bowling, Barbara L.

Homegrown berries; successfully grow your own strawberries, raspberries, blueberries, blackberries, and more. Barbara L. Bowling. Timber Press, Inc. 2014 224 p. color illustrations $19.95   **634**
1. Berries 2. Gardening 3. Ornamental berries
ISBN 1604693177; 9781604693171
LC 2014009483
This book, by Barbara L. Bowling, is a guidebook to growing berries in home gardens. This volume "covers the entire process, from planting to picking that first nutritious, luscious fruit. You'll learn the best varieties for your region, how to fit them into your landscape, and how to maintain them for peak harvest year after year." (Publisher's note)

"From 'Berry Basics' to the listings of recommended cultivars by region, suggested reading, and resources, this comprehensive guide will inspire and instruct everyone interested in homegrown berries." Booklist

Successfully grow your own strawberries, raspberries, blueberries, blackberries, and more

Deardorff, David

What's wrong with my fruit garden? 100% organic solutions for berries, trees, nuts, vines, and tropicals. David Deardorff and Kathryn Wadsworth. Timber Press 2014 312 p. color illustrations $24.95   **634**
1. Gardening 2. Fruit culture 3. Fruit-culture 4. Organic gardening 5. Fruit -- Diseases and pests -- Control 6. Fruit trees -- Wounds and injuries -- Diagnosis
ISBN 1604693584; 9781604693584; 9781604694888
LC 2013009257
Written by David Deardorff and Kathryn Wadsworth, "'What's Wrong With My Fruit Garden?' offers a path toward a healthy garden packed with fresh fruit. In addition to learning how to diagnose a plant problem through clear visual keys, you will also learn the most effective organic solutions for every problem. Detailed plant portraits include information on growth; seasonality; temperature, light, and soil requirements; and planting techniques." (Publisher's note)

"Deardorff and Wadsworth arm the gardener with needed strategies that lessen the risk of failure and encourage robust growth." Pub Wkly

Includes bibliographical references and index

Jacobsen, Rowan

Apples of uncommon character; heirlooms, modern classics, and little-known wonders. Rowan Jacobsen; photographs by Clare Barboza. Bloomsbury

USA 2014 320 p. color illustrations (alk. paper) $35   **634**
1. Fruit 2. Apples 3. Apples -- Varieties
ISBN 1620402270; 9781620402276
LC 2013044004
In this book on apples, author Rowan Jacobsen "shows us the fruit in all its glory. Jacobsen collected specimens both common and rare from all over North America, selecting 120 to feature, including the best varieties for eating, baking, and hard-cider making. Each is accompanied by a photograph, history, lore, and a list of characteristics. The book also includes 20 recipes." (Publisher's note)

"Full-color photographs help with identification. Twenty-plus recipes show off the fruit to best advantage, and there is a formula for the perfect apple pie." Booklist

Ralph, Ann

Grow a little fruit tree; simple pruning techniques for small-space, easy-harvest fruit trees. by Ann Ralph. Storey Publishing 2015 168 p. color illustrations (pbk. : alk. paper) $16.95   **634**
1. Pruning 2. Fruit trees -- Pruning
ISBN 1612120547; 9781603428897; 9781612120546
LC 2014025665
With this book, by Ann Ralph, "grow your own apples, plums, cherries, and peaches in even the smallest backyard! . . . Ralph reveals a simple yet revolutionary secret that keeps an ordinary fruit tree much smaller than normal. These great little trees take up less space, require less care, offer easy harvest, and make a fruitful addition to any home landscape." (Publisher's note)

"Every gardener who has previously felt too intimidated to cultivate his or her own mini orchard will find enough well-seasoned advice and inspiration here to begin planting a fruit tree or two during the next growing season."

Simple pruning techniques for small-space, easy-harvest fruit trees

634.8   Grapes

Cox, Jeff

From vines to wines; the complete guide to growing grapes and making your own wine. by Jeff Cox. Storey Publishing 2015 264 p. illustrations (pbk. : alk. paper) $18.95   **634.8**
1. Vineyards 2. Wine and wine making 3. Viticulture 4. Viticulture -- United States
ISBN 1612124380; 9781612124384
LC 2014033708
In this book, by Jeff Cox, "every aspect of growing flawless grapes and making extraordinary wine is covered in this classic guide. Fully illustrated instructions clearly show you how to choose and prepare a vineyard site; build effective trellising systems; select, plant, prune, and harvest the right grapes for your climate; press, ferment, age, and bottle wine; and judge wine for clarity, color, aroma, and taste." (Publisher's note)

"A must-have for anyone interested in making their own wine." LJ

634.9   Forestry

Brown, Daniel

Under a flaming sky; the great Hinckley firestorm of 1894. [by] Daniel James Brown. Lyons Press 2006 256p il map $22.95   **634.9**
1. Forest fires 2. Minnesota
ISBN 1-59228-863-4; 978-1-59228-863-2

"On September 1, 1894, a firestorm consumed timber-boomtown Hinckley, Minnesota, and three nearby hamlets. Brown, grandson of an 11-year-old survivor, makes riveting, affecting, white-knuckle reading of that horrifying, internationally reported day's lethal passage." Booklist

Includes bibliographical references

Connors, Philip

Fire season; field notes from a wilderness lookout. Ecco 2011 246 p. (trade) $24.99   **634.9**
1. Authors 2. Solitude 3. New Mexico 4. Forest fires 5. Essayists 6. Fire lookouts 7. Newspaper editors 8. Writers on nature 9. Fire lookout stations 10. Gila National Forest (N.M.)
ISBN 0061859362; 9780061859366

The content of this book is based on author "Philip Connors['time] . . . spent . . . in a seven-by-seven foot fire-lookout tower, ten thousand feet above the ground in one of the remotest territories of New Mexico. One of the least developed parts of the country, the first region designated as an official wilderness area in the world, the section he tends is also one of the most fire-prone, suffering more than thirty thousand lightning strikes each year. . . . Connors' time up on the peak is filled with drama—there are fires large and small; spectacular midnight lightning storms and silent mornings awakening above the clouds; surprise encounters with long-distance hikers, smokejumpers, bobcats, black bears, and an abandoned, dying fawn." (Blackstone Audio)

"For almost a decade, former Wall Street Journal reporter Connors has spent half a year keeping vigil over 20,000 square miles of desert, forest, and mountain chains from atop a tower 10,000 feet above sea level. One of a handful of seasoned, seasonal fire-watchers in New Mexico's Gila National Forest, Connors introduces us to his wilderness in this ruminative, lyrical, occasionally suspenseful account." Publ Wkly

Henry, Jeff

The year Yellowstone burned; a twenty-five-year perspective. Jeff Henry; foreword by Bob Barbee. Taylor Trade Publishing 2015 296 p. color illustrations; maps (pbk. : alk. paper) $24.95   **634.9**
1. Forest fires 2. Yellowstone National Park 3. Fire ecology -- Yellowstone National Park 4. Forest fires -- Yellowstone National Park 5. Forest fires -- Environmental aspects -- Yellowstone National Park
ISBN 1589799038; 9781589799035

LC 2014046126

This book, by Jeff Henry, discusses "the Yellowstone fires of 1988 [which] consumed nearly 800,000 acres. . . . In the years following, spectacular wildflowers rose from the ashes and trees rapidly reclaimed the landscape. In this twenty-five-year look back at the fires, . . . Jeff Henry recalls not only the summer of 1988, when he witnessed and

photographed nearly every aspect of the fires, but also the years since as nature healed the charred landscape." (Publisher's note)

"The author's stunning photographs and the firsthand observations and opinions are the highlights of this book and make it a must-have." LJ

MacLean, Norman

Young men & fire. University of Chicago Press 1992 301p pl maps $19.95   **634.9**
1. Forest fires 2. Fire fighters 3. Large print books 4. United States -- Forest Service
ISBN 0226500616; 9780226500614

LC 92-11890

"On Aug. 5, 1949, 16 Forest Service smoke jumpers landed at a fire in remote Mann Gulch, Mont. Within an hour, 13 were dead or irrevocably burned, caught in a 'blowup'--a rare explosion of wind and flame. . . . [A]n engrossing account of human fallibility and natural violence." Pub Wkly

Mytting, Lars, 1968-

Norwegian wood; chopping, stacking, and drying wood the Scandinavian way. Lars Mytting. Abrams Image 2015 192 p. color illustrations $24.95 **634.9**
1. Wood 2. Drilling and boring (Metal, wood, etc.)
ISBN 1419717987; 9781419717987

LC 2014959349

Author Lars Mytting presents this book "about chopping, stacking, and burning wood that has sold more than 200,000 copies in Norway and Sweden and has been a fixture on the bestseller lists there for more than a year. Norwegian Wood provides useful advice on the rustic hows and whys of taking care of your heating needs, but it's also a thoughtful attempt to understand man's age-old predilection for stacking wood and passion for open fires." (Publisher's note)

635   Garden crops (Horticulture)

Allaby, Michael

The gardener's guide to weather and climate; How to Understand the Weather and Make It Work for You. Michael Allaby. Timber Press, Inc. 2015 336 p. color illustrations, maps $29.95   **635**
1. Climate 2. Weather 3. Gardening 4. Crops and climate
ISBN 1604695544; 9781604695540

LC 2014040762

This book by Michael Allaby offers "practical advice on adapting your garden to create optimum conditions for plants. You'll learn how weather works, how to predict different conditions, and how to make the best of meteorological highs and lows. And you'll discover fascinating insights into climate change, cloud formation, jet streams, and much more." (Publisher's note)

"Color illustrations enhance the value of this book for the reference shelf; it's probably best read in winter by those seeking the really big picture for their gardens." Pub Wkly

Balick, Michael J.

Rodale's 21st-century herbal; a practical guide for healthy living using nature's most powerful plants.

Michael J. Balick; foreword by Andrew Weil. Rodale 2013 498 p. color illustrations (hardcover) \$35 **635**
1. Herbs -- Therapeutic use 2. Encyclopedias and dictionaries 3. Herbs 4. Herbals 5. Herb gardening 6. Organic gardening
ISBN 1609618041; 9781609618049

LC 2013022312

Written by Michael J. Balick, "'Rodale's 21st-Century Herbal' first explores the historical relationship between people and herbal plants and how it has evolved over time. In the second part, readers will delve into an A-to-Z encyclopedia of 180 of the most useful herbs from around the globe. . . . The final section highlights how herbs create a 'fuller' life and features herbal cooking techniques, ways to use herbs for beauty and the bath, ideas for daily herbal use." (Publisher's note)

Bartholomew, Mel, 1931-2016

All new square foot gardening; the revolutionary way to grow more in less space. Mel Bartholomew. 2nd ed. Cool Springs Press 2013 272 p. col. ill. (softcover) \$24.99 **635**
1. Vegetable gardening 2. Vertical gardening 3. Square foot gardening 4. Gardening for children
ISBN 1591865484; 9781591865483

LC 2012042837

In this book, author and gardener Mel Bartholomew "furthers his discussion on one of the most popular gardening trends today: vertical gardening. He also explains how you can make gardening fun for kids by teaching them the square foot method. Finally, an expanded section on pest control helps you protect your precious produce." (Publisher's note)

Square foot gardening high-value veggies; homegrown produce ranked by value. Mel Bartholomew. Cool Springs Press 2016 128 p. color illustrations (pb) \$17.99 **635**
1. Home economics 2. Vegetable gardening 3. Rate of return 4. Square foot gardening 5. Vegetable gardening -- Economic aspects
ISBN 1591866685; 9781591866688

LC 2015040351

This book, by Mel Bartholomew, helps you "Calculate the return on investment for your vegetable garden and get the most bang for your gardening bucks! [The book] is an easy-to-use reference book helping gardeners choose edibles that make the most financial and spatial sense. Explore the thought processes and math behind growing vegetables and herbs in order to craft the best plan for your produce." (Publisher's note)

Bellamy, Andrea

Small-space vegetable gardens; growing great edibles in containers, raised beds, and small plots. Andrea Bellamy. Timber Press, Inc. 2014 224 p. color illustrations \$19.95 **635**
1. Small farms 2. Vegetable gardening
ISBN 1604695471; 9781604695472

LC 2014009485

This book, by Andrea Bellamy, offers advice on growing vegetable gardens in limited spaces. The author "explains

the basics of growing a bounty of edibles in a minimal amount of space . . . [and] shares all the knowledge she's gained from years of gardening small: how to find and assess a space, and how to plan and build a garden." (Publisher's note)

"Recommended for readers interested in gardening on a smaller scale or growing food where lack of physical space is challenging." LJ

Includes bibliographical references and index

Growing great edibles in containers, raised beds, and small plots

Biodynamic gardening; DK Publishing. Dk Publishing 2015 253 p. color illustrations \$22.95 **635**
1. Gardening 2. Organic farming
ISBN 1465429867; 9781465429865

DK Publishing offers this "resource for learning more about the biodynamic method of organic gardening. This clear, practical guide gives you tried-and-true advice on biodynamic gardening and tips on this ultra-green, organic gardening method. Full-color photographs and easy-to-understand charts and graphs are helpful tools in organizing information in a way anyone can understand and use in biodynamic gardening." (Publisher's note)

"For people with an interest in environmentally aware gardening and a willingness to experiment with nontraditional methods." LJ

Bradley, Fern Marshall

Saving vegetable seeds; by Fern Marshall Bradley. Storey Publishing 2014 91 p. illustrations (pbk. : alk. paper) \$8.95 **635**
1. Seeds 2. Vegetable gardening 3. Vegetables -- Seeds 4. Vegetables -- Seeds -- Harvesting
ISBN 1612123635; 9781612123639; 9781612123646

LC 2014011272

"This illustrated, step-by-step guide shows you how to save seeds from 20 of the most popular vegetable garden plants, including beans, carrots, peas, peppers, and tomatoes. You'll learn how each plant is pollinated (key to determining how the seed should be saved), how to select the seeds to collect, and how to process and store collected seeds." (Publisher's note)

"Five stages—plant maintenance for producing topquality seeds, harvesting, cleaning and drying, packaging and storing, and testing for viability—are thoroughly explored for each crop, including lettuce, radishes, cucumbers, and more. Wonderfully user-friendly, this will be in demand." Booklist

Campbell, Stu

How to mulch; save water, feed the soil, and suppress weeds. Stu Campbell and Jennifer Kujawski. Storey Publishing 2015 96 p. (Storey basics) (pbk. : alk. paper) \$8.95 **635**
1. Soils 2. Gardening 3. Mulching
ISBN 1612124445; 9781612124445; 9781612124452

LC 2014029013

This book, by Stu Campbell and Jennifer Kujawski, part of the "Storey basics" series, "shows you exactly how to mulch for any situation, covering sheet mulching, feeding mulches, and living mulches for use in the yard, garden, and home landscape. It even includes a quick-reference chart of mulch types and a section on mulching for success with specific vegetables." (Publisher's note)

"Campbell's sound, experienced advice, supported by excellent illustrations, makes this handbook an indispensable one for both veteran and novice gardeners." Booklist

Coleman, Eliot

Winter harvest handbook; year-round vegetable production using deep-organic techniques and unheated greenhouses. Chelsea Green Pub. Co. 2009 247p il map pa $29.95   **635**
1. Greenhouses 2. Organic farming 3. Vegetable gardening
ISBN 978-1-60358-081-6
LC 2008-53184

"Coleman's opus is as much a call to action for town planners to embrace local farms as it is a bible for small farmers. This book is for people who know what they're doing." N Y Times Book Rev

Includes bibliographical references

Coombes, Allen J.

The **A** to Z of plant names; a quick reference guide to 4000 garden plants. Allen J. Coombes. 1st ed. Timber Press 2012 312 p. $19.95   **635**
1. Popular plant names 2. Botany -- Nomenclature 3. Botany -- Great Britain -- Dictionaries 4. Botany -- North America -- Dictionaries 5. Plants -- Great Britain -- Nomenclature -- Dictionaries 6. Plants -- North America -- Nomenclature -- Dictionaries
ISBN 1604691964; 9781604691962
LC 2011029271

This guide to plant names "features the botanic names of the plants that gardeners really grow. Additional information includes suggested pronunciation, the common name, the derivation of the scientific name, the number of species currently accepted, the type of plant and the distribution." (Publisher's note)

Includes bibliographical references (p. 311-312).

Coronado, Shawna

Grow a living wall; create vertical gardens with purpose : pollinators - herbs & veggies - aromatherapy - many more. Shawna Coronado. Cool Springs Press 2015 160 p. color illustrations (sc) $24.99   **635**
1. Vertical gardening
ISBN 1591866243; 9781591866244
LC 2014035466

This book, by Shawna Coronado, "is the first wall-gardening book to focus exclusively on the needs of home gardeners. . . . In addition to the comprehensive, step-by-step information that explains the basics of vertical gardening, each of the 20 featured gardens has its own chapter filled with useful tips, stunning photography, and fascinating background stories that point out how much difference a small garden can make." (Publisher's note)

"A green thumbs up! All levels of garden hobbyists and landscapers will enjoy this upbeat book." LJ

Create vertical gardens with purpose

Culp, David L.

The **layered** garden design lessons for year-round beauty from Brandywine Cottage; design lessons for year-round beauty from Brandywine Cottage. David L. Culp; with Adam Levine; photographs by Rob Cardillo. Timber Press 2012 312 p. illustrations $34.95   **635**
1. Gardens 2. Gardening 3. Garden design 4. Gardens -- Pennsylvania -- Design 5. Gardening -- Pennsylvania -- Anecdotes
ISBN 1604692367; 9781604692365
LC 2012007640

This gardening guidebook, by David L. Culp, "starts with a basic lesson in layering -- how to choose the correct plants by understanding how they grow and change throughout the seasons, how to design a layered garden, and how to maintain it. To illustrate how layering works, Culp takes you on a personal tour through each part of his celebrated garden: the woodland garden, the perennial border, the kitchen garden, the shrubbery, and the walled garden." (Publisher's note)

"In the tradition of classics like Beverly Nichols's Merry Hall, this is a marvelous account of how one gardener created his garden and a sense of place. It's an essential title in the 'how I did it' genre of garden writing." LJ

Includes bibliographical references and index

Damrosch, Barbara

The **garden** primer; illustrations by Linda Heppes Funk, Ray Maher, and Carol Bolt. 2nd ed.; Workman Pub. 2008 820p il map $28.95; pa $18.95 **635**
1. Gardening
ISBN 978-0-7611-4856-2; 978-0-7611-2275-3 pa
LC 2007-51425

First published 1988

This is a "book for the new gardener that clearly explains the basics of garden planning, plant care, and equipment. Detailed chapters on the different categories of plants—annuals, perennials, vegetables, fruits, lawns, shrubs, roses, vines, trees, wildflowers, and even house plants—give general advice on how to use and care for these varieties. A valuable book for public libraries." Libr J

Includes bibliographical references

Deardorff, David

What's wrong with my vegetable garden? 100% organic solutions for all your vegetables, from artichokes to zucchini. David Deardorff and Kathryn Wadsworth. Timber Press 2012 p. cm. color illustrations (pbk.) $24.95   **635**
1. Organic gardening 2. Vegetable gardening 3. Vegetables -- Diseases and pests -- Control
ISBN 9781604691849; 9781604692839; 1604691840
LC 2011018443

This book on gardening, by David Deardorff and Kathryn Wadsworth, "teaches you how to keep your vegetables healthy so they're less susceptible to attack, and when problems do occur, it shows you how to recognize the problem and find the right organic solution. Among the book's highlights are . . . detailed portraits of the most commonly grown vegetables, . . . illustrated problem-solving guides, . . . [and]

discussions of the most effective organic solutions." (Publisher's note)

"With this attractive book, organic gardeners will find it easy to grow vegetables and diagnose and organically treat common problems. Recommended." LJ

Includes bibliographical references and index

Deardorff, David C.

What's wrong with my plant (and how do I fix it?) a visual guide to easy diagnosis and organic remedies. [by] David Deardorff and Kathryn Wadsworth. Timber Press 2009 451p il pa $24.95   **635**

1. Plant diseases 2. Ornamental plants 3. Natural pesticides

ISBN 978-0-88192-961-4; 0-88192-961-1
     LC 2009-19447

"The book allows readers to select a suitable starting point that describes a plant's symptom—for example, wilting leaves or holes in the stems—and answer simple questions that eventually lead to a solution to the problem. . . . The book is divided into three parts. The first features clear keys that help identify the cause. . . . Once the problem is identified, the reader just goes to the suggested page in the second section, which contains a hierarchy of remedies. The third section, also referenced by individual page numbers in the previous two, contains excellent pictures of symptoms to help confirm the diagnosis of the problem and offer remedies. . . . [This book] is an important reference that will help gardeners successfully diagnose their own plant problems and make educated decisions about how to solve them." Am Gardener

Includes bibliographical references

Deppe, Carol

The **Tao** of vegetable gardening; cultivating tomatoes, greens, peas, beans, squash, joy, and serenity. Carol Deppe. Chelsea Green Publishing 2015 288 p. 16 plates; color illustrations (pbk.) $24.95   **635**

1. Vegetable gardening

ISBN 1603584870; 9781603584876; 9781603584883
     LC 2014036464

This book, by Carol Deppe, "explores the practical methods as well as the deeper essence of gardening. . . . [It] focuses on some of the most popular home garden vegetables—tomatoes, green beans, peas, and leafy greens—and through them illustrates the key principles and practices that gardeners need to know to successfully plant and grow just about any food crop." (Publisher's note)

"The advice for raising tomatoes and greens will benefit the gardener, but the magic of the book is the way it teaches the gardener how to grow with the garden." Pub Wkly

The **gardener's** year. Dorling Kindersley 2015 317 p. color illustrations $24.95   **635**

1. Gardening 2. Horticulture 3. Gardens

ISBN 1465424571; 9781465424570
     LC 2015430167

This book from publisher DK features "gardening tips for a wide variety of garden projects, covering flowers and plants, fruits, vegetables and herbs, and trees and shrubs. Its vibrant galleries of what and when to plant, photo sequences of key techniques, and season-by-season approach make it accessible for even the most inexperienced of gardeners." (Publisher's note)

"This is a great book for daydreaming over. Experienced gardeners may take away a few new ideas." Library Journal

Gardiner, Mary M.

Good garden bugs; everything you need to know about beneficial predatory insects. Mary M. Gardiner, Ph.D. Quarry Books 2015 176 p. color illustrations $24.99   **635**

1. Agricultural pests 2. Beneficial insects 3. Predatory insects 4. Garden pests -- Biological control

ISBN 1592539092; 9781592539093
     LC 2014049089

This book, by Mary M. Gardiner, "is an easy-to-follow reference to beneficial insects that provide pest control, allowing your garden to grow full and bountiful. Aphids, caterpillars, grubs, and slugs are not only creepy-crawlies: They can wreak havoc on your garden and plants. But fear not! You don't need dangerous chemicals to enjoy a lively, healthy garden. The secret? More lady beetles, fewer aphids! Wildlife in your garden--especially insects--can be natural pesticide alternatives." (Publisher's note)

Includes bibliographical references and index

Everything you need to know about beneficial predatory insects

Grow All You Can Eat in Three Square Feet; by DK Publishing. DK Pub 2015 256 p. color illustrations $22.95   **635**

1. Gardening

ISBN 1465429808; 9781465429803

This book, for "small-space gardeners," is "packed with information on window boxes, potted plants, patio gardening, raised beds, small square-foot gardening, container gardening, and everything else related to growing your own small garden." (Publisher's note)

"While the title may be overly optimistic, this book is useful for beginning and experienced gardeners alike because of the multiple projects and sample gardens that are provided. However, Andrea Bellamy's Small-Space Vegetable Gardens offers expanded contextual material and provides specific growing instructions for additional edible plants." LJ

Harrison, Lorraine

Heirloom Plants; A Complete Compendium of Heritage Vegetables, Fruits, Herbs & Flowers. by Lorraine Harrison and Thomas Etty. Chicago Review Press 2016 224 p. illustrations (some color) $29.99   **635**

1. Gardening

ISBN 1613735758; 9781613735756

This book, by Lorraine Harrison and Thomas Etty, "includes information on almost 500 exciting cultivars to be grown and harvested, along with detailed profiles and cultivation tips for each plant. In addition to edibles, the book also has chapters on antique herbs and flowers, from Cup and Saucer vines to Sweet William carnations to Empress of India nasturtiums." (Publisher's note)

"This encyclopedic delineation of 'directories' of vegetable, fruit, herbs, and flowers offers practical help to the gardener who's interested in preserving heirloom cultivars and turning a green-thumb hobby into an all-out mission." Pub Wkly

Includes bibliographic references (pages 218-219) and index.

Hatch, Peter J.

A **rich** spot of earth; Thomas Jefferson's revolutionary garden at Monticello. Peter J. Hatch; foreword by Alice Waters. Yale University Press 2012 263 p. (clothbound : alk. paper) $35.00 **635**
1. Gardens 2. Presidents -- United States 3. Vegetable gardening -- United States 4. Monticello (Va.) 5. Vegetable gardening -- Virginia
ISBN 9780300171143
LC 2011038043

This book presents an account of U.S. President Thomas Jefferson's garden at his estate, Monticello. "Beginning with an extensive examination of Jefferson's structural plans and implementation strategies for Monticello's complex system of vegetable gardens, [Peter J.] Hatch then chronicles his own lengthy effort at the helm of a vast restoration project that owes much of its success to the meticulous records Jefferson left behind. Along with providing plant profiles of the myriad vegetables cultivated there over the centuries, he also offers . . . insights into the arduous physical tasks involved in eighteenth-century gardening as well as Jefferson's prudent establishment of seed-saving techniques that continue to affect the marketplace." (Booklist)

Includes bibliographical references and index.

Homegrown harvest; a season-by-season guide to a sustainable kitchen garden. Rita Pelczar, editor in chief. Rev. American ed.; American Horticultural Society 2011 304p il $32.50 **635**
1. Vegetable gardening
ISBN 978-1-84533-560-1

"The American Horticultural Society shows temperate-climate gardeners how to make their ways through the gardening year. The book is arranged by season, from early spring to late winter, with how-to advice on growing vegetables and fruits, subdivided into tasks for the different vegetable families and fruit trees, bushes, and vines in each subseason, individualized for mild-winter, medium-temperature, and cold-winter regions. . . . The book's sumptuous tone, instructive photographs, and detailed directions should give beginning gardeners the enthusiasm and confidence to get started and organizationally challenged old-timers a sigh of relief that they won't have to figure out what to do next." Publ Wkly

Houbein, Lolo

One Magic Square Vegetable Gardening; The Easy, Organic Way to Grow Your Own Food on a Three-Foot Square. Lolo Houbein. The Experiment 2016 352 p. color illustrations (pbk.) $18.95 **635**
1. Organic gardening 2. Vegetable gardening 3. Kitchen gardens
ISBN 1615193251; 9781615193257
LC 2015041550

This book on organic vegetable gardening, by Lolo Houbein, "will help first-time gardeners get started—and help

veteran gardeners get results—on a small, easy-to-maintain plot. No actual magic is required!" (Publisher's note)

"Australian gardener Houbein has a personal and intimate understanding of food security, having survived famine during the Nazi occupation in Holland." Pub Wkly

Includes bibliographical references and index
Vegetable gardening

Hutchinson, Carolyn

Time-saving gardener; tips and essential tasks, season by season. Firefly Books 2008 144p il pa $19.95 **635**
1. Gardening
ISBN 978-1-55407-372-6; 1-55407-372-3

First published 1999 in the United Kingdom with title: The once-a-week gardener

"For gardeners too busy to plan, this eminently practical book takes care of the distracting work of planning, organizing and prioritizing." Publ Wkly

Jabbour, Niki

Groundbreaking food gardens; 73 plans that will change the way you grow your garden. by Niki Jabbour. Storey Pub. 2014 272 p. col. ill. (pbk. : alk. paper) $19.95 **635**
1. Fruit 2. Vegetables 3. Edible plants 4. Vegetable gardening 5. Food crops 6. Edible landscaping
ISBN 161212061X; 9781603428446; 9781612120614
LC 2013030517

In this book, author Niki Jabbour "has collected 73 plans for novel and inspiring food gardens from her favorite superstar gardeners, including Amy Stewart, Amanda Thomsen, Barbara Pleasant, Dave DeWitt, and Jessi Bloom. You'll find a garden that provides salad greens 52 weeks a year, another that supplies your favorite cocktail ingredients, one that you plant on a balcony, one that encourages pollinators, one that grows 24 kinds of chile peppers, and dozens more." (Publisher's note)

"Every plan is accompanied by full-color illustrations, growing tips, and tweakable lists of crop possibilities. The abundance of creative advice here will help perk up the gardens of both novice and professional growers." Booklist

Seventy-three plans that will change the way you grow your garden

Joffe, Daron

Citizen farmers; the biodynamic way to grow healthy food, build thriving communities, and give back to the Earth. by Daron "Farmer D" Joffe; with Susan Puckett; photography by Rinne Allen. Stewart, Tabori & Chang, an imprint of Abrams 2014 224 p. color illustrations $24.95 **635**
1. Gardening 2. Organic gardening 3. Sustainable agriculture 4. Sustainable living 5. Biodynamic agriculture
ISBN 1617691011; 9781617691010
LC 2013945633

IACP Cookbook Award Winner: Food Matters (2015)

In this book, Daron "Farmer D" Joffe "teaches us to not only create sustainable gardens but also to develop a more holistic, community-minded approach to how our food is grown and how we live our lives in balance with nature.

. . . [T]he book is . . . packed with advice on establishing a biodynamic garden, composting, soil composition and replenishment, controlling pests and disease, cooperative gardening practices, and even creating delicious meals." (Publisher's note)

Includes bibliographical references (pages 218-219) and index

Joy, LaManda
Start a community food garden; the essential handbook. LaManda Joy. Timber Press, Inc. 2014 224 p. illustrations $24.95   **635**
1. Community gardens 2. Food crops 3. Vegetables
ISBN 160469484X; 9781604694840
LC 2014020842

This book, by LaManda Joy, offers a guide to community gardening and "covers every step of the process: fundraising, community organizing, site sourcing, garden design and planning, finding and managing volunteers, and managing the garden through all four seasons. A section dedicated to the basics of growing was designed to be used by community garden leaders as an educational tool for teaching new members how to successfully garden." (Publisher's note)

"A valuable reference for building a strong foundation for anyone new to organizing or community gardening." LJ

Karsten, Joel
Straw bale gardens complete; Joel Karsten. Cool Springs Press 2015 176 p. color illustrations (sc) $24.99   **635**
1. Gardens 2. Garden design
ISBN 1591869072; 9781591869078
LC 2014955422

This book by Joel Kartsen "contains all of the original information that has set the gardening world on fire. But it also goes much deeper, with nearly 50 pages of all-new advice and photos on subjects such as growing in a tight urban setting, making your straw bale garden completely organic, and using new fertilizers and conditioning products. There is even information on using straw bale techniques to grow veggies in other organic media for anyone who has a hard time finding straw." (Publisher's note)

LeHoullier, Craig
Epic tomatoes; How to Select and Grow the Best Varieties of All Time. by Craig LeHoullier. Storey Publishing 2015 255 p. color illustrations (hbk. : alk. paper) $29.95   **635**
1. Tomatoes
ISBN 161212464X; 9781612122083; 9781612124643
LC 2014029010

In this book, author Craig LeHoullier "offers everything a tomato enthusiast needs to know about growing more than 200 varieties of tomatoes—from sowing seeds and planting to cultivating and collecting seeds at the end of the season. He also offers a comprehensive guide to the various pests and diseases of tomatoes and explains how best to avoid them." (Publisher's note)

"The many charming illustrations and color photos include images of vintage seed packets and ads, and the appen-

dix offers lists of resources and sources, all immensely useful for growers of America's most popular home crop." Booklist

Includes bibliographical references and index

Markham, Brett L.
Mini farming; self sufficiency on a 1/4 acre. rev. and expanded; Skyhorse Pub. 2010 227p il pa $16.95   **635**
1. Farms 2. Agriculture 3. Self-reliance
ISBN 978-1-60239-984-6
LC 2009041561

"An excellent guide for gardeners wanting to eliminate most of their grocery bills. Markham's approach combines his own experience with the best practices from several raised-bed methods. Advice includes how to select vegetables that are calorie-dense and budget friendly, how to raise poultry, how to build both a plucker and a thresher, and how to preserve food." Libr J

Includes bibliographical references

McCrate, Colin
High-yield vegetable gardening; grow more of what you want in the space you have. by Colin McCrate and Brad Halm. Workman Pub Co. 2015 319 p. illustrations $18.95   **635**
1. Vegetable gardening
ISBN 1612123961; 9781612123967

In this book, authors Colin McCrate and Brad Halm "show how you can make your food garden much more productive, no matter how big or small it is. You'll learn their secrets for preparing the soil, selecting and rotating your crops, and mapping out a specific customized plan to make the most of your space and your growing season." (Publisher's note)

"With worksheets, charts, and tables galore, the volume also includes an extensive collection of links for people who prefer to do their record keeping, an essential tool of the high-yield garden arsenal, on a computer. Appendixes and a list of suppliers round out this rich, thoughtful resource." LJ

Includes bibliographical references (pages 307-308) and index

Mikolajski, Andrew
Pruning plant by plant; Andrew Mikolajski. DK Publishing 2012 480 p. color illustrations $14.95   **635**
1. Pruning 2. Gardening 3. Horticulture
ISBN 0756692725; 9780756692728
LC 2011277776

"With clear text and illustrations that explain the reasons for pruning and exactly where and how to cut, 'Pruning Plant by Plant' is a handy visual guide that covers all the most popular plants. Whether its fruit trees, soft fruits, or vines, 'Pruning Plant by Plant' includes advice on pruning 170 of the most widely-grown shrubs and climbers, with easy-to-follow instructions for gardeners of all levels." (Publisher's note)

Obama, Michelle, 1964-

American grown; the story of the White House kitchen garden and gardens across America. Michelle Obama. Crown Publishers 2012 271 p. $30.00 **635**

1. United States. White House Office 2. Vegetable gardening -- United States 3. Gardening -- United States 4. Food habits -- United States 5. Kitchen gardens -- Washington (D.C.) 6. White House Gardens (Washington, D.C.)

ISBN 0307956024; 9780307956026; 9780307956033

LC 2012015935

In this book U.S. "First Lady [Michelle] Obama presents the . . . tale of the White House Kitchen Garden." In 2009, "the first food-producing garden since Eleanor Roosevelt's WWII-era 'victory garden'" was planted. Here, Obama details the evolution of the current 1,100 square foot patch, and expands her story to touch on community gardens, farmers' markets, the importance of the availability of fresh foods, and her 'Let's Move!' initiative to fight childhood obesity." (Publishers Weekly)

Includes bibliographical references and index.

Pleasant, Barbara

Starter vegetable gardens. Storey Pub. 2010 179p il pa $19.95 **635**

1. Vegetable gardening

ISBN 978-1-60342-529-2

LC 2009-49114

"From simple bag gardens to bountiful food cornucopias, each garden plan is . . . laid out with precise lists of materials and plants based on detailed landscape plans suitable for small city gardens as well as larger suburban backyards. Along with year-by-year overviews that allow gardeners to anticipate growth and adapt to changes, Pleasant provides essential cultivation and maintenance techniques." Booklist

Rodale's ultimate encyclopedia of organic gardening; the indispensible green resource for every gardener. edited by Fern Marshall Bradley, Barbara W. Ellis, and Ellen Phillips. Newly rev. and updated; Rodale 2009 707p il map pa $24.99 **635**

1. Reference books 2. Organic gardening -- Encyclopedias

ISBN 978-1-59486-917-4; 1-59486-917-0

LC 2008-35329

First published 1959 with title: Rodale's encyclopedia of organic gardening; this is a revision of the 1992 edition published with title: Rodale's all-new encyclopedia of organic gardening

This volume presents alphabetically arranged entries about topics relating to organic gardening.

"The book marches through its business, Acer to Zucchini. The chart of common organic fertilizers is nifty, especially for those of us who can ferret out that blood meal we've lost in the pantry. Scarification, permaculture, crop rotation and cover crops are clarified. Diagrams are used judiciously." N Y Times Book Rev

Includes bibliographical references

Russell, Stephen

The **essential** guide to cultivating mushrooms; by Stephen Russell. Storey Publishing 2014 232 p. color illustrations (pbk. : alk. paper) $24.95 **635**

1. Mushrooms 2. Edible plants 3. Edible mushrooms

ISBN 1612121462; 9781612121468; 9781612124636

LC 2014015198

This book, by Stephen Russell, "shows you how to cultivate mushrooms in your own home, producing shiitakes, oysters, lion's manes, maitakes, and portabellas for your kitchen or for a small business. Beginners will learn the best way to use a mushroom kit, as well as how to maintain the sterile procedures and controlled environment that cultivation requires." (Publisher's note)

"Thorough and clearly written with helpful photos on nearly every page, this guide is a must for anyone who wants to move beyond premade growing kits. With Russell's emphasis on building basic skills, advice for avoiding common mistakes, and sections on troubleshooting, the book will be a valuable resource for those interested in growing a variety of gourmet mushrooms." LJ

Smith, Edward C.

★ The **vegetable** gardener's bible; discover Ed's high-yield W-O-R-D system for all North American gardening regions. 2nd ed., [Fully updated 10th anniversary ed.]; Storey Pub. 2009 351p il map $34.95; pa $24.95 **635**

1. Organic gardening 2. Vegetable gardening

ISBN 978-1-60342-476-9; 978-1-60342-475-2 pa

LC 2009-23862

First published 2000

The author "explains everything novice and experienced gardeners need to know to grow vegetables and herbs using his system of wide, deep, raised beds. He gives detailed instructions on siting, preparing, and planning a vegetable garden, then goes on to cover choosing plant varieties, starting seed, and growing plants. Smith discusses compost creation, companion planting, crop rotation, succession planting, and ecologically friendly methods of dealing with plant diseases and pests." Libr J

Includes bibliographical references

The **vegetable** gardener's container bible. Storey Pub. 2011 263p il map $29.95; pa $19.95 **635**

1. Container gardening 2. Vegetable gardening

ISBN 978-1-60342-976-4; 978-1-60342-975-7 pa

LC 2010-51167

First published 2006 with title: Incredible vegetables from self-watering containers

The author discusses "how to choose the right plants, select containers and tools, care for plants throughout the growing season, control pests without chemicals, and . . . more." Publisher's note

Smith, Jeremy N.

Growing a garden city; how farmers, first graders, counselors, troubled teens, foodies, a homeless shelter chef, single mothers, and more are transforming themselves and their neighborhoods through the intersection of local. [by] Jeremy N. Smith; foreword by Bill McKibben; photographs by Chad Harder and Sepp Jannotta. Skyhorse Pub. 2010 225p il $24.95 **635**

1. Community gardens
ISBN 978-1-61608-108-9

LC 2010-12369

"Bright, vibrant, and buoyantly accessible, this effervescent celebration of the local food movement thrums with regional, national, and international implications." Booklist

Speichert, C. Greg

Encyclopedia of water garden plants; [by] Greg Speichert & Sue Speichert; foreword by Ann Lovejoy. Timber Press 2004 386p il $49.95 **635**

1. Freshwater plants 2. Landscape gardening
ISBN 0-88192-625-6

LC 2003-16619

"The authors devote separate chapters to hardy waterlilies, tropicals, lotus, marginal plants, irises, waterlily-like plants (such as water snowflakes), floaters, and submerged plants. . . . This is the most comprehensive guide to all types of water plants and would make an excellent addition to gardening collections." Libr J

Springer, Lauren

Passionate gardening; good advice for challenging climates. essays and photography by Lauren Springer & Rob Proctor. Fulcrum 2000 336p il $34.95 **635**

1. Gardening
ISBN 1-55591-348-2

LC 99-49511

The "authors dispense practical advice to gardeners facing difficult growing conditions, such as poor soil, dry shade, etc. . . . {They also} discuss what plants to select—whether working with bulbs or ornamental grasses—and how to use them in conjunction with other plants." Libr J

Includes bibliographical references

Swift, Vivian

Gardens of awe and folly; a traveler's journal of the meaning of life and gardening. Vivian Swift. St. Martins Press 2016 176 p. color illustrations (alk. paper) $28 **635**

1. Gardens 2. Voyages and travels
ISBN 9781632860279; 1632860279

LC 2015019652

This book, by Vivian Swift, offers "a charming stroll through some public gardens. Swift . . . plainly loves the experience of gardens: the plentitude and solitude they offer, the colors and the scents, the tea rooms that provide the opportunity to relax and reflect. She . . . proves an engaging guide to gardens in locales ranging from Key West and post-Katrina New Orleans to Paris . . . and Marrakech." (Kirkus Reviews)

"A breezy, whimsical book that does its best to approximate the renewal one might feel upon visiting a garden." Kirkus

Tucker, Arthur O.

The **encyclopedia** of herbs; a comprehensive reference to herbs of flavor and fragrance. [by] Arthur O. Tucker and Thomas DeBaggio; edited by Francesco DeBaggio. [2nd ed.]; Timber Press 2009 604p il $39.95 **635**

1. Reference books 2. Herbs -- Encyclopedias
ISBN 978-0-88192-994-2

LC 2009-16700

First published 2000 by Interweave Press with title: The big book of herbs

The authors "describe more than 500 herbs that are most common in home gardens, catalogs, restaurants, and markets used for flavor or fragrance, from the acorus (sweet flag) used in the Oil of Holy Ointment to Zingiber mioga (mioga ginger) used for soups and stir fry." Libr J

Includes bibliographical references

What's wrong with my vegetable garden? 100% organic solutions for all your vegetables, from artichokes to zucchini. David Deardorff and Kathryn Wadsworth. Timber Press 2012 249 p. (pbk.) $24.95 **635**

1. Organic gardening 2. Vegetable gardening 3. Vegetables -- Diseases and pests -- Control
ISBN 1604691840; 9781604691849; 9781604692839

LC 2011018443

Includes bibliographical references and index

Wulf, Andrea

The **brother** gardeners; botany, empire, and the birth of an obsession. Alfred A. Knopf 2008 354p il map $35 **635**

1. Gardening 2. Horticulture
ISBN 978-0-307-27023-8; 0-307-27023-8

LC 2008-55080

First published 2008 in the United Kingdom

"A garden will never look quite the same after you've read this book. . . . Wulf's book will be of interest to anyone with a garden, even if it's on a windowsill." Libr J

Includes bibliographical references

Wyman, Donald

Wyman's gardening encyclopedia; new expanded 2nd ed; Macmillan 1986 xxvi, 1221p il $65 **635**

1. Reference books 2. Gardening -- Encyclopedias 3. Ornamental plants -- Encyclopedias
ISBN 0-02-632070-3

LC 86-12509

First published 1961

Contains information on major horticultural practices, including use of pesticides and herbicides, and on ornamental and agricultural plant species. Includes scientific names according to Hortus third, with cross-references for common names

635.09 Gardening--history

Kristal, Marc

At home in the garden; Carolyne Roehm; photographs by Carolyne Roehm; written with Marc Kristal. Potter Style/Publishers 2015 304 p. color illustrations $85   **635.09**
1. Gardens 2. Connecticut 3. Gardens -- Connecticut 4. Gardens -- Connecticut -- Pictorial works
ISBN 1101903570; 9781101903575

LC 2015009054

In this book, author "Carolyne Roehm celebrates her gardens as outdoor living rooms, revealing how she chooses the plants, flowers, and layouts; how she entertains guests with gorgeous table settings and breathtaking arrangements; and how she savors the hours among the blooms." (Publisher's note)

McDowell, Marta

All the presidents' gardens; Madison's cabbages to Kennedy's roses: how the White House grounds have grown with America. Marta McDowell. Timber Press, Inc. 2016 328 p. illustrations (chiefly color), $29.95   **635.09**
1. Gardens 2. White House (Washington, D.C.) 3. Gardens -- Washington (D.C.) -- History 4. Horticulture -- Washington (D.C.) -- History 5. White House Gardens (Washington, D.C.) -- History
ISBN 1604695897; 9781604695892

LC 2015029811

This book, by Marta McDowell, "tells the untold history of the White House Grounds, starting with the seed-collecting, plant-obsessed George Washington and ending with Michelle Obama's kitchen garden. Filled with fascinating details about Lincoln's goats, Ike's putting green, Jackie's iconic roses, Amy Carter's tree house, and information on the plants whose favor has come and gone over the years." (Publisher's note)

"Photographs, line drawings, paintings, maps, and other documents add to the interesting stories. Short biographies of the 14 head gardeners, a lengthy chart of the plants in the gardens, and two bibliographies add to this delightful and elucidating work." Booklist

Includes bibliographical references and index

635.65 Garden legumes

Malone, Hilary

The Power of Pulses; Saving the World With Peas, Beans, Chickpeas, Favas & Lentils. by Dan Jason, Hilary Malone, and Alison Malone Eathorne. Douglas & McIntyre 2016 240 p. $24.95   **635.65**
1. Vegetable gardening 2. Cooking -- Vegetables
ISBN 1771621028; 9781771621021

LC 2016026118

This book, by Dan Jason, Hilary Malone, and Alison Malone Eathorne, "provides tips on how North American home gardeners can grow and save their own delicious, vividly hued heirloom beans, peas, chickpeas, lentils and favas. As well as being incredibly versatile in the kitchen, pulses

are also rich in fiber, high in vitamin B, gluten-free and remarkably low on the glycemic index—contributing to good health." (Publisher's note)

"This is a perfect book for gardeners, vegetarians, and others looking to expand beyond their tried-and-true pulses." Booklist

635.9 Flowers and ornamental plants

American Horticultural Society encyclopedia of plants & flowers; editor-in-chief, Christopher Brickell. Rev ed DK Publishing 2011 744 p. col. ill., maps $60   **635.9**
1. Horticulture 2. Ornamental plants 3. Plants -- Encyclopedias
ISBN 0756668573; 9780756668570

LC 2011290703

First published 1989 in the United Kingdom with title: The Royal Horticultural Society gardeners' encyclopedia of plants and flowers

"Packed with 8,000 plants for every climate . . . from trees, shrubs, perennials, annuals, biennials, bulbs, water plants, and cacti, the 'AHS Encyclopedia of Plants & Flowers' is a . . . reference for . . . gardeners. This fully revised and updated edition features a brighter, clearer design and improved navigation--cataloging plants by color, season, and size--that makes the book more intuitive for the reader." (Publisher's note)

Armitage, Allan M.

Armitage's garden perennials; 2nd ed., fully rev. and updated; Timber Press 2011 347p il $49.95   **635.9**
1. Reference books 2. Perennials -- Encyclopedias
ISBN 978-1-60469-038-5

LC 2011293867

First published 2000

This is an "illustrated compilation of 136 genera of garden-worthy perennials. Alphabetical entries feature illuminating descriptions of plant habits and forms, along with essential cultural advice. Armitage recommends countless varieties that can be depended on to perform well or are particularly lovely specimens. Appropriate U.S.D.A. zones and regions where the plants will thrive are noted, too. With its accessible writing style, abundant color photographs, and final section listing plants suggested for specific conditions or purposes, Armitage's latest work should be considered an essential addition to gardening collections." Booklist

Armitage's native plants for North American gardens. Timber Press 2006 451p il $49.95   **635.9**
1. Ornamental plants
ISBN 0-88192-760-0; 978-0-88192-760-3

LC 2005-22495

This book provides "information on more than 630 native species and cultivars of perennials, biennials, and annuals that are readily available to mainstream gardeners... . With more than 400 color photos, this is an essential reference book for nursery people and horticulturalists, home gardeners, and all libraries." Libr J

Includes bibliographical references

Armitage's vines and climbers. Timber Press 2010 212p il $29.95 **635.9**
1. Climbing plants 2. Ornamental plants
ISBN 978-1-60469-039-2

LC 2009-32437

This book is "written with authority, in simple language, with humor. Anyone trying to build a gardening library should think about adding this one." Philadelphia Inquirer

Includes bibliographical references

Bainbridge, David A.
Gardening with less water; low-tech, low-cost techniques for using up to 90% less water in your garden. by David A. Bainbridge. Storey Publishing 2015 128 p. color illustrations (pbk. : alk. paper) $14.95 **635.9**
1. Xeriscaping
ISBN 9781612125824; 9781612125831

LC 2015036487

This book "offers simple, inexpensive, low-tech techniques for watering your garden much more efficiently -- using up to 90% less water for the same results. With illustrated step-by-step instructions, David Bainbridge shows you how to install buried clay pots and pipes, wicking systems, and other porous containers that deliver water directly to a plant's roots with no or minimal evaporation." (Publisher's note)

"Beyond soaker hoses, the title offers a varied range of scalable options for growers of all types committed to the exploration and use of optimal water-sparing techniques." LJ

Baldwin, Debra Lee
Succulents simplified; growing, designing, and crafting with 100 easy-care varieties. Debra Lee Baldwin. Timber Press 2013 272 p. color illustrations $24.95 **635.9**
1. Succulent plants 2. Succulent plants -- Varieties
ISBN 1604693932; 9781604693935

LC 2012038829

This book, by Debra Lee Baldwin, "is a complete primer on choosing, growing and designing with succulents. Along with gorgeous photos packed with design ideas, Debra offers her top 100 plant picks and explains how to grow and care for succulents no matter where you live. Step-by-step projects, including a cake-stand centerpiece, special-occasion bouquets, a vertical garden, and a succulent topiary sphere, will inspire you to express your individual style." (Publisher's note)

"This fresh and entertaining volume certainly deserves a green thumbs up." LJ

Includes bibliographical references and index

Bender, Richard W.
Bountiful bonsai; create instant indoor container gardens with edible fruits, herbs and flowers.

Richard Bender. Tuttle Pub. 2015 128 p. (pbk.) $14.95 **635.9**
1. Bonsai 2. Indoor gardening
ISBN 480531270X; 9784805312704

LC 2013040431

This book, by Richard Bender, "presents a radical new approach that applies bonsai techniques to everyday container gardening, instantly turning houseplants and herbs into beautiful and unusual bonsai sculptures!" (Publisher's note)

Christopher, Thomas
Essential perennials; the complete reference to 2700 perennials for the home garden. Ruth Rogers Clausen and Thomas Christopher; photographs by Alan L. Detrick and Linda Detrick. Timber Press, Inc. 2015 452 p. color illustrations $39.95 **635.9**
1. Perennials 2. Flower gardening 3. Perennials -- Handbooks, manuals, etc
ISBN 1604693169; 9781604693164

LC 2014020896

"Perennials are the mainstay of any garden. But how do you choose from the thousands available, and care for the ones you already have? Essential Perennials helps you decide exactly which plants will bring you the beauty you want and will thrive in the conditions you can provide. Trusted garden experts Ruth Rogers Clausen and Thomas Christopher focus on what every gardener needs to know. For each plant you'll find information on flower color; season of bloom; foliage characteristics; height and width; light requirements; and hardiness and heat sensitivity. You'll also learn cultural tips, the most outstanding cultivars for each species, and whether a plant has any special requirements or potential problems." Publisher's Note.

"This update to Clausen's lauded Perennials in American Gardens (1989) is enthusiastically recommended for both academic and public libraries and is an essential purchase for libraries where there is an interest in gardening." Booklist

Colletti, Maria
Terrariums; gardens under glass: designing, creating, and planting modern indoor gardens. by Maria Colletti. Cool Springs Press 2015 176 p. illustrations, color (sc) $24.99 **635.9**
1. Terrariums 2. Indoor gardening 3. Glass gardens
ISBN 9781591866336

LC 2015012059

In this book, author Maria Colletti "makes designing your very own interior gardens easy with step-by-step photos of over twenty of her own designs. Get all of the information you need on the 'it' plants of today--tillandsias (air plants), orchids, mosses, cacti, and succulents, along with 'traditional' terrarium ferns." (Publisher's note)

"Colletti includes plant ideas and design schemes for ecosystems such as the tropical terrarium (lots of air plants), the woodland (ferns and mosses), or the desert (succulents, cacti), all illustrated with abundant color photos. In all cases the basic premise is the same: a thriving ecosystem that sits on the dining table, rendering the joy of watching nature in progress in a small world you created." Pub Wkly

Gardens under glass

Cullina, William

Native trees, shrubs & vines; a guide to using, growing, and propagating North American woody plants. William Cullina. HougHton Mifflin Harcourt 2002 xi, 354 p.p color illustrations $40 **635.9**
1. Native plants 2. Cultivated plants 3. Ornamental plants 4. Ornamental woody plants -- Canada 5. Native plants for cultivation -- Canada 6. Ornamental woody plants -- United States 7. Native plants for cultivation -- United States

ISBN 0618098585; 9780618098583

LC 2002022586

This book, by William Cullina, "is a comprehensive reference to almost one thousand native woody plants. A . . . guide for naturalists, restorationists, nursery owners, landscape architects, and designers as well as gardeners, it points out that ecological gardening offers specific benefits to the individual as well as the environment." (Publisher's note)

"Cullina's writing is a pleasure to read beautifully descriptive, informative, and personal. His useful, authoritative work is highly recommended for North American libraries." LJ

Includes bibliographical references (p. 338-339) and index

Native trees, shrubs, and vines

Understanding perennials; a new look at an old favorite. Houghton Mifflin Harcourt 2009 247p il $40 **635.9**
1. Perennials

ISBN 978-0-618-88346-2; 0-618-88346-0

LC 2008-36760

This book provides "a chance to learn what soil is composed of, why it's acid or alkaline and why you should care. Cullina will straighten out your understanding of roots, bulbs, rhizomes, stolons, corms and tubers; he clarifies osmosis, photosynthesis, secretory structures, nitrogen fixes and plant hormones. . . . [He] is an engaging, clear and congenial writer." N Y Times Book Rev

Includes bibliographical references

Darke, Rick

The **American** woodland garden; capturing the spirit of the deciduous forest. text and photography by Rick Darke. Timber Press 2002 377p il $49.95 **635.9**
1. Gardening 2. Forest plants

ISBN 0-88192-545-4

LC 2002-20474

This "is both a pictorial and narrative account of a wooded locale in Pennsylvania that the author spent years studying, as well as a design and planting guide. . . . He explains the different elements of a woodland garden and thoroughly describes the plants (features, zones, and growth ranges) that will perform well. The author's photographs illustrate both the overall effect and the beauty of individual plants." Libr J

Includes bibliographical references

Dash, Mike

Tulipomania; the story of the world's most coveted flower and the extraordinary passions it aroused. Crown 2000 273p hardcover o.p. pa $13.95 **635.9**
1. Tulips 2. Netherlands -- History

ISBN 0-609-80765-X pa

LC 99-39186

"The centerpiece of this story is a stunning two months, December 1636 and January 1637, when fortunes were made and lost in the Netherlands—in tulip bulb futures trading. Stripped to its basics, this would be a dry case study in an economics textbook. But Dash adds depth to the tale by including relevant bits of botany, sociology and history, as well as glimpses of the personalities involved in the creation of the tulip market." Publ Wkly

Includes bibliographical references

Deardorff, David

What's wrong with my houseplant? save your indoor plants with 100% organic solutions. David Deardoff, Kathryn Wadsworth. Timber Press 2016 292 p. color illustrations (hardcover) $34.95 **635.9**
1. House plants 2. Indoor gardening 3. Organic gardening

ISBN 9781604695908; 9781604696332

LC 2015013389

This book, by David Deardoff and Kathryn Wadsworth, "shows you how to keep indoor plants healthy by first teaching you how to identify the problem. This hardworking guide includes plant profiles for 148 plants organized by type, visual keys to the most of common problems, and the related organic solutions that will lead to a healthy plant. This easy-to-navigate book is for anyone who loves and has struggled with their indoor plants—it will turn even the brownest thumbs green!" (Publisher's note)

"Clearly and expertly written, the finder is easy to follow whether readers are looking to add plants inside their homes or salvaged the ones they already have." Pub Wkly

Includes bibliographical references and index

Dirr, Michael

Dirr's encyclopedia of trees and shrubs; Michael A. Dirr. Timber Press 2011 951 p. col. ill. $79.95 **635.9**
1. Trees 2. Shrubs 3. Ornamental plants 4. Ornamental trees -- Encyclopedias 5. Ornamental shrubs -- Encyclopedias

ISBN 0881929018; 9780881929010

LC 2011007951

This reference book, by Michael A. Dirr, focuses on trees and shrubs. "From majestic evergreens to delicate vines and flowering shrubs, Dirr features thousands of plants and all the essential details for identification, planting, and care, plus full-color photographs showing a tree's habit in winter, distinctive bark patterns, fall color, and more." (Publisher's note)

"With beautiful, artistic photographs and succinct text, this volume is nearly as attractive as one of the gorgeous blossoming shrubs discussed within. . . . The chatty descriptions incorporate information often limited to tables—disease resistance, size, shape, and zone hardiness as well as some history and taxonomy. These descriptions are accompanied by high-quality photographs." Booklist

Includes bibliographical references and index

Dirr's Hardy trees and shrubs; an illustrated encyclopedia. by Michael A. Dirr. Timber Press 1997 493p il $69.95   **635.9**

1. Trees 2. Shrubs 3. Landscape gardening

ISBN 0-88192-404-0

LC 96-54032

"Depicting both character and traits (fruit, flower, bark, or autumn color), the volume covers over 500 species and some additional varieties and cultivars. Each entry enumerates scientific name, common name, detailed plant description, environmental conditions, place in the landscape, i.e., woodlawn tree or lawn tree, and hardiness zones." Libr J

Dirr's trees and shrubs for warm climates; an illustrated encyclopedia. by Michael A. Dirr. Timber Press 2002 446p il map $69.95   **635.9**

1. Trees 2. Shrubs 3. Ornamental plants 4. Landscape gardening

ISBN 0-88192-525-X

LC 2001-35810

"This volume, in conjunction with Dirr's Hardy Trees and Shrubs, completes [the author's] coverage of the woody ornamentals cultivated in North America. In a witty and informative style, Dirr presents botanic, cultural, and landscaping details on over 400 species. Entries are accompanied by magnificent color photos." Libr J

Manual of woody landscape plants; their identification, ornamental characteristics, culture, propagation and uses. Michael A. Dirr; illustrations by Bonnie Dirr ... [et al.] 6th ed; Stipes Pub. 2009 1325 p. illustrations, map   **635.9**

1. Ornamental plants 2. Landscape gardening

ISBN 9781588748706; 1588748685; 9781588748683

LC 2009905492

This book, by Michael A. Dirr, is the sixth edition of the guide to woody landscape gardening. "It features expanded descriptions of former entries, over 2,000 new species and cultivars, trademark names and patent numbers, as well as all species, subspecies and variety names verified using the GRIN taxonomic data base (germplasm resources information network) and other sources." (Publisher's note)

DiSabato-Aust, Tracy

The **well-tended** perennial garden; planting & pruning techniques. Expanded ed; Timber Press 2006 383p il map $34.95   **635.9**

1. Perennials

ISBN 978-0-88192-803-7; 0-88192-803-8

LC 2006-10388

First published 1998

In addition to details on pruning and maintenance this work contains an A-Z encyclopedia of perennials

Includes bibliographical references

Duffield, Mary Rose

Plants for dry climates; how to select, grow, and enjoy. {by} Mary Rose Duffield and Warren D. Jones. rev ed; Perseus Pub. 2001 216p il pa $27.50   **635.9**

1. Gardening 2. Desert plants

ISBN 1-55561-251-2

LC 2001-280011

First published 1981

The authors "explore strategies for gardening in dry or arid climates. . . . They cover climate conditions and pre-design concerns such as possible planting restrictions by neighborhood covenants, the use of professional landscaping services, costs, and maintenance. A detailed plant guide identifies more than 300 species best suited to arid gardens, explaining conditions in which they thrive or are compromised." Libr J

Includes bibliographical references

Ellis, Barbara W.

Covering ground; unexpected ideas for landscaping with colorful, low-maintenance ground covers. Storey Pub. 2007 224p il map $29.95; pa $19.95   **635.9**

1. Grasses 2. Climbing plants 3. Ornamental plants

ISBN 1-58017-664-X; 978-1-58017-664-4; 1-58017-665-8 pa; 978-1-58017-664-4 pa

LC 2007-335

"Divided into three main sections, the book addresses why one should consider using ground covers, types of plants for different areas, and planting, growing, and propagating. . . . Suitable for all gardening collections, this easy and fun read is essential for the home gardener looking for low-maintenance or problem-area ground covers." Libr J

Taylor's guide to annuals; how to select and grow more than 400 annuals, biennials, and tender perennials. Houghton Mifflin 1999 441p il (Taylor's guides to gardening) pa $23   **635.9**

1. Annuals (Plants) 2. Flower gardening

ISBN 0-395-94352-3

LC 99-33188

First published 1986

This guide features information on over five hundred popular plants and cultivars for landscaping and gardening

Taylor's guide to perennials; more than 600 flowering and foliage plants, including ferns and ornamental grasses. Houghton Mifflin 2001 490p il map (Taylor's guide to gardening) pa $23   **635.9**

1. Perennials 2. Flower gardening

ISBN 0-395-98363-0

LC 00-33436

First published 1986

Text and numerous illustrations cover popular perennials, their cultivars, ornamental grasses, and ferns

Fisher, Kathleen

Taylor's guide to shrubs; how to select and grow more than 500 ornamental and useful shrubs for privacy, ground covers, and specimen plantings. Houghton Mifflin 2001 441p il map (Taylor's guides to gardening) pa $23 **635.9**

1. Shrubs
ISBN 0-618-00437-8

LC 00-36941

First published 1987

This guide covers information on popular shrubs and their cultivars and includes growing instructions

Flora: a gardener's encyclopedia; over 20,000 plants. chief consultant, Sean Hogan. Timber Press 2003 2v il map set $99.95 **635.9**

1. Flowers 2. Reference books 3. Ornamental plants -- Encyclopedias
ISBN 0-88192-538-1

LC 2003-59663

"Although gardening books abound, none matches this work's range of detail." Libr J

Gardiner, Jim

The **Timber** Press encyclopedia of flowering shrubs; Jim Gardiner. Timber Press 2011 p. cm. **635.9**

1. Shrubs 2. Gardening 3. Garden design 4. Flowering shrubs -- Encyclopedias 5. Flowering shrubs -- Pictorial works
ISBN 9780881928235

LC 2011020264

This book, by Jim Gardiner, is a reference work for gardening with flowering shrubs. "Rich attributes . . . make flowering shrubs the most rewarding of garden plants, but this vast group with its scores of tempting plants . . . requires careful navigation. Leading expert on woody plants Jim Gardiner has distilled several decades of knowledge and experience into . . . [a] pictorial reference of hardy shrubs that excel in temperate-zone gardens." (Publisher's note)

Includes bibliographical references and index

Greenlee, John

The **American** meadow garden; creating a natural alternative to the traditional lawn. photography by Saxon Holt. Timber Press 2009 278p il $34.95 **635.9**

1. Grasses 2. Landscape gardening
ISBN 978-0-88192-871-6; 0-88192-871-2

LC 2009-19438

"Meadow gardening is an exciting, fresh approach to horticulture. By taking advantage of native plant life and soil conditions, gardeners can create an ecologically friendly yard that requires less water and mowing. Greenlee . . . focuses on the conditions of regional types of American grasslands, emphasizing throughout that gardeners must first understand local ecology (using professional help where necessary) to be successful. With Holt's photographs, this is a large and colorful showcase of Greenlee's extensive knowledge and great passion for gardening." Libr J

Includes bibliographical references

Hansen, Eric

Orchid fever; a horticultural tale of love, lust, and lunacy. Pantheon Bks. 2000 288p hardcover o.p. pa $13 **635.9**

1. Orchids
ISBN 0-679-77183-2 pa

LC 99-44582

"Most of Hansen's sketches are fundamentally vehicles for illustrating his serious and provocative argument against CITES (the Convention on International Trade in Endangered Species of Wild Fauna and Flora). According to the author, CITES thwarts orchid conservation and perversely legitimizes plant smuggling by botanical institutions." Libr J

Heffernan, Cecelia

Flowers A to Z; buying, growing, cutting, arranging. photography T.K. Hill. Abrams 2001 160p $49.50; pa $17.95 **635.9**

1. Flowers 2. Flower gardening 3. Flower arrangement
ISBN 0-8109-3348-9; 0-8109-2122-7 pa

LC 00-64282

"Recommendations for the best tools and containers are followed by in-depth profiles of 55 of the most popular garden and hothouse flowers, in which Heffernan shares such trade secrets as the flower's vase life and its cost at different seasons. . . .Straightforward directions are supported by close-up photographs." Booklist

Heibel, Tara

Rooted in design; Sprout Home's guide to creative indoor planting. Tara Heibel and Tassy de Give; photography by Ramsay de Give and Maria Lawson. Ten Speed Press 2015 224 p. illustrations (chiefly color) (hardcover) $25 **635.9**

1. House plants 2. Indoor gardening
ISBN 1607746972; 9781607746973; 9781607746980

LC 2014036284

This book, by Tara Heibel and Tassy de Give, is a "guide to creatively integrating indoor plants with home decor. . . . [They] offer expert advice for choosing plant varieties and pairing them with unique design ideas. Sharing practical tips honed through hundreds of plant design classes, Heibel and DeGive tell readers everything they need to know to care for their one-of-a-kind green creations." (Publisher's note)

"While the authors concentrate more on design than the practicalities of indoor gardening, they do address many common issues, such as watering and lighting. Buried in the last few pages is a plant directory that answers questions of what plants work best in low light and with varying levels of water and soil." Pub Wkly

Sprout Home's guide to creative indoor planting
Guide to creative indoor planting

Helm, Bennett

The **water** gardener's bible; Ben Helm, Kelly Billing. Rodale 2008 192 p. color illustrations; maps (pbk.) $21.95 **635.9**

1. Water gardens
ISBN 1594866589; 9781594866586

LC 2007045129

In this book, authors Ben Helm and Kelly Billing explain how "installing a beautiful water garden has become a feasible undertaking for the average homeowner. . . . The pages are crammed with specifics about pond biology and chemistry, beneficial bacteria, fish health, nuisance algae, and electrical and child safety—all that is necessary to duplicate the sights, sounds, and sanctuary of a babbling brook, splashing fountain, or cascading waterfall right in the backyard." (Publisher's note)

Includes bibliographical references and index
Water gardener's bible

Hewitt, Terry
The **complete** book of cacti & succulents. Dorling Kindersley 1993 176p il hardcover o.p. pa $20   **635.9**
1. Cactus 2. Succulent plants
ISBN 1-56458-337-6; 0-7894-1657-3 pa
LC 93-22107

An illustrated look at the history and cultivation of more than 300 plants. Ideas for containers and display are included.

The **Hillier** gardener's guide to trees & shrubs; editor, John Kelly; consultant editor, John Hillier. Reader's Digest Assn. 1997 640p il maps $50   **635.9**
1. Trees 2. Shrubs
ISBN 0-89577-973-0
LC 97-4282

First published 1995 in the United Kingdom
"Alphabetically arranged plant directory covering more than 4000 plants with over 400 genres represented. . . . {It discusses} basic biology, theory and practice, selection and purchase, care and maintenance, pest and diseases, plant propagation, plant names, and plant selection." Libr J

Hodgson, Larry
Perennials for every purpose; choose the plants you need for your conditions, your garden, and your taste. Rodale 2000 502p il $29.95; pa $19.95 **635.9**
1. Perennials
ISBN 0-87596-823-6; 0-87596-893-7 pa
LC 99-6968

"Preliminary chapters cover the basics such as getting started, creating a design, and keeping plants healthy. The highlight, however, is the 14 chapters that profile perennials that can be used in unique situations (e.g., dry, wet, sunny, shade, easy-care). Each plant profile includes a photograph, a sidebar listing plant characteristics, and informative paragraphs detailing good companion plants, problems and solutions, and the top performers and recommended varieties for each plant." Libr J

Includes bibliographical references

Kelaidis, Gwen Moore
Hardy succulents; tough plants for every climate. photography by Saxon Holt. Storey Pub. 2008 159p il map $29.95; pa $19.95   **635.9**
1. Succulent plants
ISBN 978-1-58017-701-6; 978-1-58017-700-9 pa
LC 2007-39890

The author "offers practical tips on siting, planting, soil requirements, and care of succulents for every hardiness zone in a clear and confident voice. Advice on pairing succulents with perennials, using them as focal points in the garden, and protecting them from the cold of winter is dispensed in lively prose. . . . This delightful book will be practical and inspiring for both novice and experienced gardeners." Libr J

Keville, Kathi
The **aromatherapy** garden; growing fragrant plants for happiness and well-being. Kathi Keville. Timber Press 2016 276 p. color illustrations $24.95   **635.9**
1. Gardening 2. Aromatherapy 3. Fragrant gardens 4. Aromatic plants -- Therapeutic use
ISBN 9781604695496
LC 2015029697

This book, by Kathi Keville, "explains how fragrant plants can be as therapeutic as they are intoxicating, and how easy it is to add this captivating element to gardens large and small. . . . Revealed here are the scents, secrets, and science behind plant aromatherapy, and how to optimize its full benefits. Detailed plant profiles will help you create a beautiful source of restorative aromas, oils, sachets, teas, and more." (Publisher's note)
"With such rich descriptions, readers will long for the actual aroma." Pub Wkly

Kukielski, Peter E.
Roses without chemicals; 150 disease-free varieties that will change the way you grow roses. Peter E. Kukielski. Timber Press, Inc. 2015 256 p. color illustrations $19.95   **635.9**
1. Roses 2. Gardening 3. Roses -- Varieties -- North America 4. Roses -- Disease and pest resistance -- North America
ISBN 1604693541; 9781604693546
LC 2014020741

In this book on rose gardening, author Peter E. Kukielski "highlights 150 . . . . tough, new varieties, rating them for disease resistance, flowering, and fragrance. He also tells which perform best in each region and teaches simple cultivation techniques that will result in gorgeous, easy-care gardens filled with healthy roses." (Publisher's note)
"This valuable guide for gardeners wanting to try roses that are less disease-prone is recommended for public libraries and horticultural collections." LJ

One hundred fifty disease free varieties that will change the way you grow roses

Martin, Tovah
The **indestructible** houseplant; 200 beautiful plants that everyone can grow. Tovah Martin; photography by Kindra Clineff. Timber Press 2015 288 p. color illustrations (alk. paper) $22.95   **635.9**
1. Plants 2. Interior design 3. House plants
ISBN 1604695013; 9781604695014
LC 2014042918

In this book author Tovah Martin "shows that anyone can grow healthy houseplants. It all boils down to a simple set of skills and--here's the crucial part--picking the right plants. These tough but beautiful plants can thrive in less-than-ideal conditions, and they're easy to find. You'll also learn how to pot, repot, water, and fertilize; pick up some great ideas for fun, funky containers; and benefit from Tovah's tips on how to display your plants." (Publisher's note)

"The green-thumb-challenged will give Martin a standing ovation for this much-needed book created for "windowsill-gardener wannabees" desiring plants to "survive tough love" and "transform" lives. New England-based Martin appreciates interest in an indoor gardening approach requiring minimal time investment." Booklist

Includes bibliographical references and index

The **new** terrarium; creating beautiful displays for plants and nature. [by] Tovah Martin and Kindra Clineff. Clarkson Potter/Publishers 2009 176p il $25   **635.9**
    1. Terrariums
    ISBN 978-0-307-40731-3; 0-307-40731-4
                                          LC 2008-27713
"With beguiling photographs by Kindra Clineff, this attractive volume contains everything you need to know about growing plants under glass." N Y Times Book Rev

The **unexpected** houseplant; 220 extraordinary choices for every room in your home. Tovah Martin; photography by Kindra Clineff. 1st ed. Timber Press 2012 328 p. col. ill. (paperback) $22.95; (ebook) $22.95   **635.9**
    1. House plants 2. Indoor gardening 3. Container gardening
    ISBN 160469243X; 9781604692433; 1604694262; 9781604694260
                                          LC 2011045164
It was author Tovah Martin's intent to demonstrate "how correctly chosen plants placed in creative containers can enhance indoor living space. Martin shows how imagination and use of fundamental ground rules for growing and proper placement should result in an indoor horticultural paradise year round. Martin covers over 220 plants, ranging from exotic to conventional. . . .Growth requirements, propagation advice, problems, and attributes of plants are outlined." (Library Journal)

Includes bibliographical references and index.

McGowan, Alice
    Bulbs in the basement, geraniums on the windowsill; how to grow and overwinter 165 tender plants. [by] Alice McGowan, Brian McGowan. Storey Pub. 2008 208p il pa $17.95   **635.9**
    1. Perennials 2. Greenhouses 3. Ornamental plants
    ISBN 978-1-60342-042-6; 1-60342-042-8
                                          LC 2008-22440
"After offering readers a brief history of gardening with 165 plants, the McGowans give advice on choosing a container, on container combinations, and on the best type of soil to use. They stress the importance of the correct temperature and give instructions on setting up a site. There's a color photograph of each plant, along with information on its shape, color, and foliage, what the genus comprises, and

design ideas. There also are instructions on how to use the guide, as well as suggested reading." Booklist

Includes bibliographical references

McIndoe, Andy
    The **creative** shrub garden; eye-catching combinations for year-round interest. Andy McIndoe. Timber Press 2014 248 p. color illustrations $29.95   **635.9**
    1. Shrubs 2. Gardening 3. Ornamental shrubs
    ISBN 9781604694345
                                          LC 2013040985
This book, by Andy McIndoe, "shows you how to make the most of the many benefits of shrubs—including their hardiness, year-long beauty, size, and low-maintenance nature—by making them the main element in a garden design. McIndoe teaches you the basics first, with tips on choosing shrubs based on a garden's size, determining soil and climate needs, and pruning and maintenance." (Publisher's note)

"A plant directory; alphabetical guide for planting and maintaining various shrubs, including container planting; suggested readings; and an index round out this comprehensive text sure to please gardeners who love perennials." Booklist

Includes bibliographical references and index

Michener, David
    Taylor's guide to ground covers; more than 400 flowering and foliage ground covers for every garden situation. {by} David Michener and Nan Sinton. completely rev and updated; Houghton Mifflin 2001 375p il maps (Taylor's guides to gardening) pa $23   **635.9**
    1. Grasses 2. Climbing plants 3. Ornamental plants
    ISBN 0-618-03010-7
                                          LC 2001-39566
First published 1987 with title: Taylor's guide to ground covers, vines & grasses

"In this guide luscious photographs of 400 ground covers are paired with information about gardening zones and sun tolerance. . . . The splendor of the photography aside, the no-nonsense approaches are recommended." Am Ref Books Annu, 2003

The **New** Southern Living Garden Book; The Ultimate Guide to Gardening. by The Editors of Southern Living Magazine. Oxmoor House 2015 768 p. $34.95   **635.9**
    1. Gardening
    ISBN 0848742982; 9780848742980
This book is a "definitive source on gardening from the brand Southern gardeners have turned to for nearly 50 years. Completely redesigned and updated for the first time in 10 years, the new edition features over 1,700 beautiful color photographs and over 7,000 featured plants. Enhanced features include a monthly garden checklist, a Q&A section to tackle everyday problems, and garden design solutions." (Publisher's note)

O'Sullivan, Penelope

The **homeowner's** complete tree & shrub handbook; the essential guide to choosing, planting and maintaining perfect landscape plants. photography by Karen Bussolini. Storey Pub. 2007 408p il map $39.95; pa $29.95 **635.9**

1. Trees 2. Shrubs 3. Ornamental plants

ISBN 978-1-58017-571-5; 978-1-58017-570-8 pa

LC 2007-10718

This guide to planting trees and shrubs discusses planning the landscape and buying, planting and caring for trees and shrubs. Includes descriptions of 348 trees and shrubs.

"The real jewel of this volume is the extensive AZ directory of nearly 350 trees and shrubs, many offering more than one season of interest. There is even a handy pronounciation guide for every plant name." Libr J

Includes webliography and bibliographical references

Ondra, Nancy J.

Grasses; versatile partners for uncommon garden design. Nancy J. Ondra; photography by Saxon Holt. Storey Books 2002 143 p. illustrations, map $19.95 **635.9**

1. Grasses 2. Gardening 3. Ornamental plants 4. Ornamental grasses

ISBN 158017423X; 9781580174237

LC 2001049845

This book, by Nancy J. Ondra, with photographs by Saxon Holt, "is a complete introduction to using ornamental grasses in combination with perennials, annuals, shrubs, and other garden plants. [The volume includes] full-color photos [that] illuminate complete plans for 24 gardens featuring grasses." (Publisher's note)

"Supported by Saxon Holt's captivating color photographs, Ondra elevates grasses from garden understudies to starring roles." Booklist

Taylor's guide to roses; how to select, grow, and enjoy more than 380 roses. Houghton Mifflin 2001 474p il maps (Taylor's guides to gardening) pa $23 **635.9**

1. Roses

ISBN 0-618-06888-0

LC 00-68248

First published 1986

Text and numerous full color illustrations describe classes of roses including floribundas, grandifloras, miniatures, and climbers. Suggestions are provided for carefree border and ground cover roses. Entries are given for each plant, noting its uses and limitations

Pavord, Anna

Bulb. Mitchell Beazley 2009 544p il map $39.99 **635.9**

1. Bulbs

ISBN 978-1-84533-532-8

This book features "advice on the purchase and care of bulbs. The approximately 600 entries include detailed descriptions of the blooms, some comparisons with related cultivars, plant size, hardiness, native areas, and bloom season. . . . The entries are accompanied by photographs of individual

blossoms. These are interspersed with lush two-page-spread images of gardens, masses of blooms, and single spectacular blooms. Pavord's writing style is delightfully conversational while providing important technical information for the gardener." Booklist

Includes bibliographical references

Penick, Pam

The **water**-saving garden; how to grow a gorgeous garden with a lot less water. by Pam Penick. Ten Speed Press 2016 240 p. color illustrations (trade pbk.) $19.99 **635.9**

1. Gardening 2. Xeriscaping 3. Water conservation 4. Drought-tolerant plants

ISBN 9781607747932

LC 2015025964

This book, by Pam Penick, offers "a guide to growing beautiful gardens in drought-prone areas utilizing minimal water for maximum results. . . . [It] provides gardeners and homeowners with a diverse array of techniques and plentiful inspiration for creating outdoor spaces that are so beautiful and inviting, it's hard to believe they are water-thrifty. Including a directory of 100 plants appropriate for a variety of drought-prone regions of the country." (Publisher's note)

"With the growing popularity of permaculture and sustainable cultivation techniques, Penick's how-to offers gardeners at all levels of experience much timely advice on working with one of the Earth's most precious natural resources." Booklist

The **plant** finder; the right plants for every garden. senior consultants, Tony Rodd and Geoff Bryant. Firefly Books 2007 992p il map $49.95 **635.9**

1. Gardening 2. Ornamental plants 3. Landscape gardening

ISBN 978-1-55407-265-1; 1-55407-265-4

LC 2007-298960

This book "gives basic descriptions and growing conditions for more than 5,000 plants, with a focus on the temperate zones. . . . Beginning gardeners as well as plant fanatics may find this comprehensive volume an indispensable midwinter reference for yearly garden planning, as well as a useful outdoor planting companion come spring." Publ Wkly

Pleasant, Barbara

The **complete** houseplant survival manual; essential know-how for keeping (not killing) more than 160 indoor plants. photography by Rosemary Kautzky. Storey Pub. 2005 365p il pa $24.95 **635.9**

1. House plants

ISBN 1-58017-569-4

LC 2005-14205

"Following an enlightening introduction that discusses the history, uses, and benefits that houseplants bestow, the manual is divided into three main sections. The first two are plant directories offering in-depth plant profiles of first flowering, then foliage, houseplants. The third is an extensive compilation of houseplant-care topics, from acclimatization to watering. With vivid color photographs, precise illustrations, appendixes listing helpful resources, definitions, and a cross-reference chart of botanical and common names, this is a must-have manual for anyone who shares home or office space with potted plants." Booklist

Silver, Johanna

The **bold** dry garden; Lessons from the Ruth Bancroft Garden. Johanna Silver; photographs by Marion Brenner. Timber Press 2016 236 p. color illustrations (hardcover) $34.95   **635.9**
    1. Gardens 2. Xeriscaping 3. Landscape gardening 4. Landscape gardening -- Water conservation 5. Ruth Bancroft Garden (Walnut Creek, Calif.)
    ISBN 9781604696707
                        LC 2016001680

This book, by Johanna Silver, with photographs by Marion Brenner, helps you "celebrate and recreate the beauty of The Ruth Bancroft Garden! Ruth Bancroft is a dry gardening pioneer. Her lifelong love of plants led to the creation of one of the most acclaimed public gardens, The Ruth Bancroft Garden in Walnut Creek, California. . . . [This book] offers unparalleled access to the garden and the extraordinary woman responsible for it." (Publisher's note)

"Replete with brilliant color photography, this hopeful book will win over anyone who doubts that a desolate landscape can support thriving life." Pub Wkly

Includes bibliographical references and index

Wiley, Keith

Designing and planting a woodland garden; plants and combinations that thrive in the shade. Keith Wiley. Timber Press, Inc. 2014 280 p. color illustrations $34.95   **635.9**
    1. Gardening 2. Woodland gardening 3. Shade-tolerant plants 4. Woodland garden plants
    ISBN 1604693851; 9781604693850
                        LC 2014011045

In this book, author and gardener Keith Wiley "offers comprehensive information on hundreds of woodland plants and details how to use them in a well-designed garden. Information on planting a woodland garden includes design tips and instruction on how to create shade in a garden. Plant profiles for woodland trees, shrubs, perennials, bulbs, ferns, and grasses include complete growing information, along with the botanical and common name and zone requirements." (Publisher's note)

"The helpful garden designs and diagrams (such as how to plant a tree), along with hundreds of color photographs, facilitate choosing perennials, shrubs, trees, bulbs, tubers, and ferns. Gardeners, who are dreamers, writes Wiley, can dream that, once established, this magical garden will in fact grow itself." PW

636   Animal husbandry

Belozerskaya, Marina

The **Medici** giraffe; and other tales of exotic animals and power. Little, Brown and Co. 2006 414p il $24.99   **636**
    1. Exotic animals
    ISBN 0-316-52565-0; 978-0-316-52565-7
                        LC 2006-09659

"This is a sumptuous read—smart, funny and utterly compelling." Publ Wkly

Includes bibliographical references

Francis, Richard C.

Domesticated; evolution in a man-made world. Richard C. Francis. W W Norton & Co Inc 2015 400 p. illustrations (hardcover) **$27.95**   **636**
    1. Evolution 2. Human-animal relationship 3. Animals and civilization 4. Domestic animals -- History
    ISBN 0393064603; 9780393064605
                        LC 2014046934

In this book, author Richard C. Francis "investigates the nature of domestication, focusing mostly on the biological rather than anthropological factors responsible for a wide array of human/animal partnerships. He ranges widely across species, including house pets, livestock, and pack animals, discussing the types of genetic changes that commonly occur during the process of domestication and the developmental implications such changes have." (Publishers Weekly)

"The cited literature is extensive and an excellent source for those wishing to pursue specific topics further. This treatise will be valuable to a wide readership, from animal lovers to a large array of professionals. Summing Up: Highly recommended. All readers." Choice

Includes bibliographical references and index

Galaxy, Jackson

Catification; designing a happy and stylish home for your cat (and you!) Jackson Galaxy, Kate Benjamin. Tarcher 2014 304 p. color illustrations (paperback) $21.95   **636**
    1. Cats 2. Interior design 3. Cats -- Housing 4. Interior decoration 5. Cats -- Equipment and supplies
    ISBN 0399166017; 9780399166013
                        LC 2014019022

This book, by Jackson Galaxy and Kate Benjamin, "shows cat owners everywhere how to make their homes both cat-friendly and chic. . . . [It] includes more than twenty fun DIY projects, from kitty beds and litter boxes to catios (cat patios) that will be sure to make readers-- and their cats- - purr in approval." (Publisher's note)

"If you have cats, you need this book." LJ

Grandin, Temple

★ **Animals** make us human; creating the best life for animals. [by] Temple Grandin and Catherine Johnson. Houghton Mifflin Harcourt 2009 342p $26   **636**
    1. Animal behavior
    ISBN 978-0-15-101489-7; 0-15-101489-2
                        LC 2008-34892

"Packed with fascinating insights, unexpected observations and a wealth of how-to tips, Grandin's peppy work ably challenges assumptions about what makes animals happy." Publ Wkly

Halligan, Karen

Doc Halligan's What every pet owner should know; prescriptions for happy, healthy cats and dogs.

illustrations by Liz Wells. HarperCollins Publishers 2007 324p il $24.95; pa $15.95   **636**

1. Cats 2. Dogs 3. Pets -- Health and hygiene
ISBN 978-0-06-089859-5; 0-06-089859-3; 978-0-06-089860-1 pa; 0-06-089860-7 pa

LC 2007-60869

"Emphasizing canine (and feline) wellness, . . . [the author] gives clear advice about preventing illness and injuries through sensible nutrition, regular grooming, dental care, and partnering with your veterinarian." Libr J

Katz, Jon

Dog days; dispatches from Bedlam Farm. Villard Books 2007 273p il $23.95   **636**

1. Domestic animals 2. Farm life -- New York (State)
ISBN 978-1-4000-6404-5; 1-4000-6404-X

LC 2006-52804

This is a "collection of stories from upstate New York's Bedlam Farm. . . . Bedlam Farm, a cross between a working and a hobby farm, is the home of the animals that are . . . [the author's] inspiration. . . . A must-read for all animal lovers." Booklist

636.08   Specific topics in animal husbandry

Pierce, Jessica

Run, Spot, run; the ethics of keeping pets. Jessica Pierce. University of Chicago Press 2016 256 p. (cloth : alk. paper) $26   **636.08**

1. Animal welfare 2. Pets -- Ethical aspects 3. Human-animal relationships 4. Pets -- Moral and ethical aspects 5. Animal welfare -- Moral and ethical aspects 6. Human-animal relationships -- Moral and ethical aspects
ISBN 9780226209890

LC 2015038627

In this book, Jessica Pierce, "a lover of pets herself (including, over the years, dogs, cats, fish, rats, hermit crabs, and more), . . . understands the joys that pets bring us. But she also refuses to deny the ambiguous ethics at the heart of the relationship, and through a mix of personal stories, philosophical reflections, and scientifically informed analyses of animal behavior and natural history, she puts pet-keeping to the test. Is it ethical to keep pets at all?" (Publisher's note)

"A thoughtful book that should spark debate, with the author stressing that bringing a companion animal into one's life is an ethical commitment that should not to be taken lightly." Kirkus

Includes bibliographical references and index

636.088   Animals for specific purposes

Link, Tim

Talking with dogs and cats; joining the conversation to improve behavior and bond with your animals. Tim Link. New World Library 2015 240 p. (pbk. : alk. paper) $14.95   **636.088**

1. Cats 2. Dogs 3. Animal communication 4. Pets -- Behavior 5. Pets -- Psychology 6. Human-animal communication
ISBN 1608683222; 9781608683222

LC 2015004274

In this book, author and "animal communicator Tim Link's approach respects the personality and feelings of animals, and his simple, accessible methods can facilitate the understanding and communication that all animal lovers crave. If you've ever wondered what your animal was trying to tell you with a bark, meow, or tweet, this is the book for you." (Publisher's note)

"For readers who enjoyed Amelia Kinkade's Straight from the Horse's Mouth, Link's easygoing attitude and sincerity will be a welcome addition to those interested in alternative forms of animal communication." LJ

Includes bibliographical references

636.089   Veterinary medicine

Black's veterinary dictionary; edited by Edward Boden and Anthony Andrews. 22nd ed A. & C. Black 2015 790 p. il $52   **636.089**

1. Veterinary medicine 2. Veterinary medicine -- Dictionaries
ISBN 0713663626; 140817572X; 9781408175729

First published 1928 by Macmillan with title: Black's veterinary cyclopedia

This book, edited by Edward Boden and Anthony Andrews, "is an essential reference tool for all with a professional or leisure interest in the care of animals. . . . For the 22nd edition much new and updated information has been included, reflecting the numerous developments that have taken place in animal care and husbandry, and welfare. There is greatly expanded coverage of topics relating to popular breeds of dog and cat, and the inheritable conditions that might affect their health." (Publisher's note)

"There is greatly expanded coverage of topics relating to popular breeds of dog and cat, and the inheritable conditions that might affect their health.

Advances in medicine, surgery and diagnostic techniques; descriptions of newly identified diseases such as Schmallenberg virus; the resurgence of old scourges such as TB in cattle, and ongoing enzootic infections such as bird flu are included in this new edition." Publisher's note

Boston, Sarah

Lucky Dog; How Being a Veterinarian Saved My Life. Sarah Boston. Pgw 2014 288 p. 8 plates; illustrations $14.95   **636.089**

1. Veterinarians 2. Cancer patients 3. Veterinary medicine 4. Human-animal relationship
ISBN 1770893512; 9781770893511

LC 2013918885

This book, by Sarah Boston, "is not your typical cancer memoir. She takes us on a hysterical and thought-provoking journey through the human healthcare system from the perspective of an animal doctor. Weaving funny and poignant stories of dogs she's treated along the way, this is an insightful memoir about what the human medical world can learn from the way we treat our canine counterparts." (Publisher's note)

"Readers will count themselves fortunate, too, as they accompany Boston on her unexpected journey and spend time with some wonderful dogs along the way." Pub Wkly

Bowers, Kathryn

Zoobiquity; What Animals Can Teach Us About Health and the Science of Healing. Barbara Natterson-Horowitz and Kathryn Bowers. Alfred A. Knopf 2012 308 p.   **636.089**

1. Medicine 2. Pathology 3. Veterinary medicine 4. Comparative psychology 5. Pathology, Veterinary 6. Disease Models, Animal 7. Physiology, Comparative 8. Psychology, Comparative

ISBN 0307593487; 9780307593481

LC 2012005051

"In this . . . book, cardiologist and psychiatrist [Barbara] Natterson-Horowitz, along with science journalist [Kathryn] Bowers, explore some of humanity's most pressing health problems (cancer, obesity) through the eyes of the animal kingdom. The authors argue in favor of the 'One Health' worldview, which brings doctors and veterinarians into close collaboration to discuss causation and treatment of diseases." (Publishers Weekly)

"Clearly, we have much to learn from animals and from this profoundly illuminating new fusion of veterinary, human, and evolutionary medicine." Booklist

Includes bibliographical references and index

Goldstein, Martin

The **nature** of animal healing; the path to your pet's health, happiness, and longevity. Knopf 1999 357p hardcover o.p. pa $16   **636.089**

1. Pets 2. Veterinary medicine

ISBN 0-345-43919-8 pa

LC 98-38193

"Goldstein outlines an approach to healing that revolves around strengthening the immune system through diet and such holistic healing techniques as acupuncture and homeopathy, so that an animal can heal itself. . . . This is a life-affirming book that should interest any pet owner." Publ Wkly

Herriot, James

Every living thing. St. Martin's Press 1992 342p $22.95   **636.089**

1. Authors 2. Veterinarians 3. Large print books 4. Memoirists

ISBN 0-312-08188-X

LC 92-18526

Sequel to The Lord God made them all, entered in main catalog

"Herriot regales us with additional tales of his veterinary practice in Yorkshire. He picks up his story after World War II, when medicines and treatment have improved, his children are growing up and the family moves to a new house. . . . There are no surprises here, just the expected mix of gentle humor and compassion for animals and people alike. Herriot's many fans will not be disappointed." Publ Wkly

James Herriot's animal stories; with an introduction by Jim Wright; illustrations by Lesley Holmes. St. Martin's Press 1997 142p il   **636.089**

1. Domestic animals 2. Large print books 3. Veterinary

medicine

LC 97-13863

This is a compilation of ten previously published stories from the author's autobiographical accounts of the practice of veterinary medicine in 1930's Yorkshire England

Kahn, Cynthia M.

The **Merck** veterinary manual; [edited by Cynthia M. Kahn and Scott Line] 10th ed. Merck 2010 2945 p. $60   **636.089**

1. Veterinary medicine

ISBN 091191093X; 9780911910933

LC 2010923995

This book, edited by Cynthia M. Kahn and Scott Line, "is the most comprehensive, reliable reference for veterinary professionals. . . . [It has] been updated to reflect the latest advances in veterinary medicine. . . . The section on behavior has been thoroughly revised, and includes the most current information on diagnosing and treating behavioral disorders in dogs, cats, and other domestic animals." (Publisher's note)

Schoen, Allen M.

Kindred spirits; how the remarkable bond between humans and animals can change the way we live. Broadway Bks. 2001 280p hardcover o.p. pa $14   **636.089**

1. Pets 2. Veterinary medicine

ISBN 0-7679-0431-1 pa

LC 00-57891

This book "covers the benefits of the human-animal bond; seven ways to foster a spiritual bond with your animal; wellness approaches, such as diet therapy and preventing and treating cancer the natural way; finding veterinary support; and how to let go when there is nothing further that can be done." Libr J

Includes bibliographical references

636.1   Horses

Hill, Cherry

How to think like a horse; the essential handbook for understanding why horses do what they do. Cherry Hill. Storey Publishing 2006 ix, 181 p.p ill. (chiefly col.) $19.95   **636.1**

1. Horses -- Behavior 2. Human-animal relationship 3. Horsemanship 4. Human-animal communication

ISBN 1580178359; 1580178367; 9781580178358

LC 2005027792

In this book, by Cherry Hill, "horse trainer and instructor Cherry Hill believes that every human/horse relationship benefits from a greater human understanding of what motivates horses, how they experience the world, what makes them happy, and what worries them. Journey through the equine mind with Hill as she explores what makes a horse tick." (Publisher's note)

Includes bibliographical references (p. 178) and index

Katz, Jon

Saving Simon; how a rescue donkey taught me the meaning of compassion. Jon Katz. Ballantine Books 2014 209 p. illustrations (hardcover : alk. paper) $25   **636.1**
1. Donkeys 2. Compassion 3. Animal rescue 4. Donkeys -- New York (State) -- West Hebron -- Anecdotes 5. Animal rescue -- New York (State) -- West Hebron -- Anecdotes
ISBN 0345531191; 9780345531193
LC 2014027915
"In the spring of 2011, [author] Jon Katz received a phone call that would challenge every idea he ever had about mercy and compassion. An animal control officer had found a neglected donkey on a farm in upstate New York, and she hoped that Jon and his wife, Maria, would be willing to adopt him. . . . Jon came to understand compassion and mercy in a new light." (Publisher's note)

"More introspective than previous stories, perhaps reflecting his desire for a slower pace in life, this book handles the emotional highs and lows of living with animals with empathy and thoughtfulness, forcing readers to re-examine their own meanings of compassion and mercy. A heartwarming tale of rescue and redemption." Kirkus

Richards, Susan

Chosen by a horse; a memoir. Soho Press 2006 248p $20   **636.1**
1. Horses
ISBN 1-56947-419-2
LC 2005-52337
"Richards adopts an emaciated mare and her foal, overriding the small voice telling her that she already has three horses to care for and a herniated disk. Her experience with her new charges proves profoundly instructive in terms of how love can foster growth of the human spirit and help in overcoming pain and loss. The abused mare, Lay Me Down, proves to be one of those rare creatures that remain gentle despite years of mistreatment, responding profoundly to the kind treatment that is part of everyday life for Richards' animals. Fascinated by the affection this animal accords a stranger, Richards notes the mare's courage and slowly begins to emulate it in her own life, opening up to a love affair and its aftermath." Booklist

Storey's horse-lover's encyclopedia; an English and Western A-to-Z guide. edited by Deborah Burns. Storey Bks. 2001 471p il $37.50; pa $24.95   **636.1**
1. Horses
ISBN 1-58017-336-5; 1-58017-317-9 pa
LC 00-46329
"The alphabetically arranged entries vary in length from a few sentences to a few pages, with the most thorough coverage going to extensive topics like breeding, foot care, and feeding. Most entries consist of one or two paragraphs and provide a good definition of the term at hand." Libr J

Williams, Wendy

The **horse**; the epic history of our noble companion. Wendy Williams. Scientific American/Farrar, Straus & Giroux 2015 320 p. illustrations (some color) (hardcover) $26   **636.1**
1. Horses 2. Human-animal relationships -- History 3. Horses -- History 4. Horses -- Evolution
ISBN 0374224404; 9780374224400
LC 2015003860
In this book, author Wendy Williams "chronicles the 56-million-year journey of horses as she visits with experts around the world, exploring what our biological affinities and differences can tell us about the bond between horses and humans, and what our longtime companion might think and feel. . . . Williams charts the course that leads to our modern Equus-from the protohorse to the Dutch Warmbloods, Thoroughbreds, and cow ponies of the twenty-first century." (Publisher's note)

"Williams's book educates, entertains, and enthralls; it's part scientific discovery, part social commentary, and part history lesson, while always focusing on the relationship between horses and humans. This accessible profile of equines through the ages pays homage to an animal that had a crucial role in the modernization of the world." Pub Wkly
Includes bibliographical references and index

636.2   Cattle and related animals

Lewis, Celia

The **illustrated** guide to cows; how to choose them. [Celia Lewis]; with a foreword by the Prince of Wales. St Martins Pr 2014 160 p. color illustrations $25   **636.2**
1. Beef cattle 2. Dairy cattle
ISBN 1408181355; 9781408181355
LC 2011278365
Written by Celia Lewis, "'The Illustrated Guide to Cows' covers the 58 most familiar breeds of cattle in Europe and North America. Breed profiles are written in engaging text that covers the history of each breed, its main characteristics and how to look after them, and each one has been beautifully illustrated by the author." (Publisher's note)

"Lewis concludes with instructions on milking, dairy production, tanning, and more. This guide, with its abundance of friendly illustrations, is an informative and fun homage to an animal of great importance." Pub Wkly
Chickens

636.4   Swine

Estabrook, Barry

Pig tales; an omnivore's quest for sustainable meat. Barry Estabrook. W. W. Norton & Company 2015 320 p. illustration (hardcover) $26.95 **636.4**
1. Pigs 2. Meat industry
ISBN 039324024X; 9780393240245
LC 2014048321
This book, by Barry Estabrook, offers an "investigation of the commercial pork industry and an inspiring alternative to the way pigs are raised and consumed in America. . . . [The author] shows how these creatures are all too often subjected to lives of suffering in confinement and squalor, sustained on a drug-laced diet just long enough to reach

slaughter weight, then killed on mechanized disassembly lines. But it doesn't have to be this way." (Publisher's note)

"An enjoyable and erudite read, the book will appeal to a broad audience. It includes detailed notes; photos and illustrations would have been welcome." Choice

Montgomery, Sy

The **good** good pig; the extraordinary life of Christopher Hogwood. Ballantine Books 2006 228p il $21.95; pa $13.95   **636.4**

1. Pigs

ISBN 0-345-48137-2; 978-0-345-48137-5; 0-345-49609-4 pa; 978-0-345-49609-6 pa

LC 2005-57094

This is a "description of the 14-year life of a 750-pound pet pig who was named after the conductor [Christopher Hogwood]. Anyone who has ever loved a pet can enjoy reading about the relationship between Montgomery and her Christopher." Sci Books Films

636.5   Chickens and other kinds of domestic birds

Johnson, Samantha

How to build chicken coops; everything you need to know. Samantha Johnson and Daniel Johnson. Voyageur Press 2015 176 p. color illustrations (sc) $19.99   **636.5**

1. Chickens 2. Animal housing 3. Chickens -- Housing

ISBN 0760347336; 9780760347331

LC 2014039439

This book, by Samantha Johnson and Daniel Johnson, provides instruction on raising chickens and building chicken coops, but "is not just a collection of plans, but a compendium of the background and insider information for chicken owners. How much space will you need? What is dust bathing? How many nest boxes and windows will your coop need? How much will it cost? What steps do you need to take to keep your chickens safe from predators?" (Publisher's note)

"This book is ideal for high school students or adults who need an introduction on raising chickens and coop building." LJ

Lawler, Andrew

Why did the chicken cross the world? the epic saga of the bird that powers civilization. Andrew Lawler. Atria Books 2014 336 p. (hardback) $26   **636.5**

1. Chickens 2. Civilization -- History 3. Animals and civilization 4. Human-animal relationship 5. Chickens -- History 6. Animals and civilization -- History 7. Human-animal relationships -- History

ISBN 1476729891; 9781476729893

LC 2014031979

In this book, author Andrew Lawler "delivers a sweeping history of the animal that has been most crucial to the spread of civilization across the globe—the chicken. . . . Beginning with the recent discovery in Montana that the chicken's unlikely ancestor is T. rex, . . . [it] track[s] the chicken from its

original domestication in the jungles of Southeast Asia some 10,000 years ago to postwar America, where it became the most engineered of animals." (Publisher's note)

"Recommended for readers of popular nonfiction as well as those with a specific interest in accessible scientific and anthropological studies." LJ

Includes bibliographical references and index

Rude, Emelyn

Tastes Like Chicken; A History of America's Favorite Bird. by Emelyn Rude. W W Norton & Co Inc 2016 272 p. illustrations (ebook) $50; $27.95 **636.5**

1. Poultry 2. Chickens 3. Eating customs 4. Cooking (Chicken)

ISBN 9781681771984; 1681771632; 9781681771632

A fowl introduction -- The early bird -- A healing broth -- The general chicken merchants -- Of chicken and champagne -- The poor man's chicken -- America's egg basket -- Calories and constituents -- The kosher chicken wars -- Celia Steele's modest endeavor -- They saw in hens a way -- A chicken for every grill -- A nugget worth more than gold -- The tale of the colonel and the general -- The modern chicken -- the end and the beginning.

In this book, author Emelyn Rude "details the ascendancy of chicken from its humble origins to its centrality on grocery store shelves and in restaurants and kitchens. Along the way, she reveals startling key points in its history, such as the moment it was first stuffed and roasted by the Romans, how the ancients' obsession with cockfighting helped the animal reach Western Europe, and how slavery contributed to the ubiquity of fried chicken today." (Publisher's note)

"Readers of food histories such as Mark Kurlansky's Cod will appreciate this engaging, well-researched, and thorough history of America's changing food preferences." LJ

Includes bibliographical references (pages 201-263) and index.

636.7   Dogs

American Kennel Club

★ The **complete** dog book; American Kennel Club. 20th ed.; Ballantine Books 2006 xxi, 858p il $35   **636.7**

1. Dogs

ISBN 0-345-47626-3; 978-0-345-47626-5

LC 2005-48263

First published 1935. Periodically revised

"The official guide to 124 AKC registered breeds and their history, appearance, selection, training, care and feeding, and first aid. Some color plates." N Y Public Libr. Ref Books for Child Collect. 2d edition

The **American** Kennel Club's meet the breeds; dog breeds from A to Z. an official publication of the American Kennel Club. The American Kennel Club and I-5 Press 2013 215 p. color illustrations (pbk.) $15.95   **636.7**

1. Dog shows 2. Dogs -- Breeding 3. Dogs 4. Dog breeds

ISBN 1621870871; 9781621870876

LC 2014412543

"The fourth edition of the best-selling new owner's breed guide, 'The American Kennel Club's Meet the Breeds' now presents profiles and photographs of 199 breeds, representing every AKC-recognized breed. Nearly 400 color photographs on 216 pages, the new edition includes the four new breeds entering the AKC in 2014: the American Hairless Terrier, the Grand Basset Griffon Vendéen, the Norrbottenspets, and the Portuguese Podengo." (Publisher's note)

Anderson, Teoti

The **ultimate** guide to dog training; puppy training to advance techniques plus 50 problem behaviors solved. by Teoti Anderson. I-5 Press 2014 239 p. color illustrations (alk. paper) $19.95   **636.7**
    1. Dogs -- Behavior 2. Dogs -- Training
    ISBN 1621870901; 9781621870906
                  LC 2014015365

This dog training guide "encompasses every topic from the puppy's first lessons and house-training to advance training methods and retraining rescue dogs, rebellious teens, and seniors. . . . Dog trainer and behavior expert Teoti Anderson offers straightforward advice and easy-to-follow instructions for each topic, all based on her success-oriented positive-training methods." (Publisher's note)

Bendersky, Jorge

DIY dog grooming, from puppy cuts to best in show; everything you need to know, step by step. Jorge Bendersky. Quarry Books 2013 160 p. illustrations (chiefly color) $24.99   **636.7**
    1. Dogs -- Care 2. Dogs -- Grooming
    ISBN 1592538886; 9781592538881
                  LC 2013038975

This book, by Jorge Bendersky, "will show you how to take the best care of your dog, regardless of breed, temperament, or age. Practical step-by-step photos will take you through everything you need to know to bathe and trim your dog, plus care for her nails, ears, teeth, and more. Learn how to train her to relax and enjoy grooming." (Publisher's note)

Do it yourself dog grooming, from puppy cuts to best in show

Dog grooming, from puppy cuts to best in show

Blackwell, Lewis

The **life** and love of dogs; Lewis Blackwell. Abrams 2014 216 p. color illustrations $50   **636.7**
    1. Dogs -- Pictorial works 2. Human-animal relationship
    ISBN 1419713930; 9781419713934
                  LC 2014930772

This book, by Lewis Blackwell, "offers hundreds of incredible images by acclaimed photographers from around the world. A textual exploration of our unique relationship with dogs-- including a surprising analysis of the qualities that make a dog attractive in our eyes, a detailed look at how the breeds we see today are a product of our own needs and desires, and more." (Publisher's note)

"Readers who have enjoyed Blackwell's other books will delight in this beautiful, contemplative analysis of dogs as a species and as human companions." LJ

Bradshaw, John

★ **Dog** sense; how the new science of dog behavior can make you a better friend to your pet. John Bradshaw. Basic Books 2011 xxiv, 324 p.p il $25.99   **636.7**
    1. Dogs -- Behavior 2. Dogs -- Psychology 3. Human-animal relationship 4. Animal intelligence 5. Human-animal relationships
    ISBN 0465019447; 9780465019441
                  LC 2010054337

The author discusses "how humans can live in harmony with their canine friends, explaining why positive reinforcement is a more effective way to control behavior and how to weigh a dog's unique personality against the stereotypes of its breed." (Publisher's note) Bibliography. Index.

"Pet owners and those interested in the animal mind will learn from this balanced, well-referenced guide to the science of canine behavior." LJ

Includes bibliographical references and index

Burch, Mary R.

Citizen canine; ten essential skills every well-mannered dog should know. Kennel Club Books 2010 256p il pa $14.95   **636.7**
    1. Dogs -- Training
    ISBN 978-1-593786-44-1
                  LC 2009-28847

"Often a component of therapy dog assessment, the Canine Good Citizen (CGC) test has become a popular way to document a dog's manners. . . . [The author] outlines the ten test items and demonstrates how to teach your dog these skills. . . . This well-indexed guide is essential reading for dog owners, whether the goal is obedience training, therapy dog work, or simply polite pets." Libr J

Coile, D. Caroline

Encyclopedia of dog breeds. Barron's Educational Series 2005 352p il $29.95   **636.7**
    1. Reference books 2. Dogs -- Encyclopedias
    ISBN 0-7641-5700-0
                  LC 2004-52977

First published 1998

"More than 150 breed descriptions are grouped along American Kennel Club divisions: the sporting group, the hound group, the working group, and so on. . . . Breed descriptions are organized into subsections entitled 'History,' 'Temperament,' 'Upkeep,' 'Health,' and 'Form and Function.'" Booklist

Coppinger, Raymond

Dogs; a new understanding of canine origin, behavior, and evolution. [by] Raymond Coppinger and Lorna Coppinger. University of Chicago Press 2002 352p il pa $18   **636.7**
    1. Dogs
    ISBN 0-226-11563-1
                  LC 2002-20404

First published 2001 by Scribner

"This important book belongs in all libraries." Booklist
Includes bibliographical references

Coren, Stanley

Why we love the dogs we do; how to find the dog that matches your personality. Free Press 1998 308p il hardcover o.p. pa $13   **636.7**

1. Dogs

ISBN 0-684-85502-X pa

LC 97-50333

"Coren offers insight into dog-and-owner personality conflicts and shows prospective owners how to choose the dog that is right for them. His book shows why some breeds of dogs turn out to be disasters for certain people, provides personality tests for readers to determine their own distinctive personality types, and includes amusing 'famous pet' anecdotes. Humanitarian, witty, and full of common sense, this is a perfect primer for novice dog owners." Booklist

Includes bibliographical references

★ Decoding Your Dog; The Ultimate Experts Explain Common Dog Behaviors and Reveal How to Prevent or Change Unwanted Ones. by American College of Veterinary Behaviorists; edited by Debra Horwitz, John Ciribassi, and Steve Dale. Houghton Mifflin Harcourt 2014 384 p. illustrations $27   **636.7**

1. Dogs -- Behavior 2. Dogs -- Training

ISBN 0547738919; 9780547738918

LC 2014395601

This book, edited by Debra Horwitz, John Ciribassi, and Steve Dale, is a "dog behavior guide. . . . Experts analyze problem behaviors, decipher the latest studies, and correct common misconceptions and outmoded theories. The book includes: effective, veterinary-approved positive training methods [and] expert advice on socialization, housetraining, diet, and exercise." (Publisher's note)

"A fascinating and detailed exploration of the reasons behind common dog behaviors and of how to interpret dogs' communication signals in order to train them to be happy, healthy, obedient companions." LJ

Eldredge, Debra

Dog owner's home veterinary handbook; [by] Debra M. Eldredge . . . [et al.] 4th ed; Wiley Pub. 2007 xxviii, 628p il $34.99   **636.7**

1. Dogs -- Diseases

ISBN 978-0-4700-6785-7; 0-4700-6785-3

LC 2007-16275

First published 1980

"The authors discuss all of the major organ systems with descriptions of normal functions and infectious and parasitic diseases. Writing in easy-to-understand terms, they identify emergency situations and explain first-aid care. . . . It contains information on Lyme disease and other recently recognized problems." Libr J [review of 1992 edition]

Fogle, Bruce

Dog owner's manual. DK Pub. 2003 288p il pa $25   **636.7**

1. Dogs

ISBN 0-7894-9321-7

LC 2002-41146

"Fogle's succinct writing style packs a tremendous amount of information into each sentence. Heavily illustrated with beautiful photographs." Booklist

Franklin, Jon

★ The wolf in the parlor; the eternal connection between humans and dogs. Henry Holt 2009 283p $25   **636.7**

1. Dogs

ISBN 978-0-8050-9077-2; 0-8050-9077-0

LC 2009-2227

Building on evolutionary science, archaeology, behavioral science, and the firsthand experience of watching his own dog evolve from puppy to family member, Franklin posits that man and dog are more than just inseparable; they are part and parcel of the same creature.

"Among a plethora of books on breeding, disciplining, loving and lamenting the loss of man's best friend, this thoughtful discourse is a best of breed." Publ Wkly

The good dog; true stories of love, loss, and loyalty. [edited by] David DiBenedetto & the editors of Garden & Gun. HarperWave 2014 336 p. illustrations $25.99   **636.7**

1. Dogs 2. Pets 3. Human-animal relationship 4. Dogs -- Anecdotes 5. Human-animal relationships -- Anecdotes

ISBN 0062242350; 9780062242358

LC 2014015874

This book presents a "collection of true stories celebrating the unique relationship between humans and their canine companions, penned by some of today's top writers, including Jon Meacham, Roy Blount, Jr, Dominique Browning, and P.J. O'Rourke." (Publisher's note)

"Other contributors include Ace Atkins, Rick Bragg, Roy Blount Jr., Jon Meacham and Julia Reed. Bird lovers may blanch at feather-in-the-mouth hunting tales, but this selection of vignettes is varied, entertaining and frequently heartwarming." Kirkus

Herriot, James

James Herriot's dog stories. St. Martin's Press 1986 xxxiii, 426p il $23.95; pa $7.99   **636.7**

1. Dogs

ISBN 0-312-43968-7; 0-312-92558-1 pa

LC 86-6637

Herriot "has gathered 50 recollections of canines, some of them sentimental, a few tragic and at least one—the story of a terrier male who abruptly becomes attractive to other males—as odd as anything in the Decameron. Herriot recalls that in his student days domestic animals were customarily listed in descending order of importance: horse, ox, sheep, pig, dog. In the latest work, he has brought his favorites to the front and given them a new leash on life." Time

James Herriot's favorite dog stories; illustrations by Lesley Holmes. St. Martin's Press 1996 169p il $17.95   **636.7**

1. Dogs 2. Large print books

ISBN 0-312-14841-0

LC 96-18796

This is a collection of 10 previously published dog "stories written in Herriot's heartwarming style. Each tale is accompanied by new attractive watercolor illustrations. A dog-lover's delight." SLJ

Horowitz, Alexandra

Inside of a dog; what dogs see, smell, and know. Scribner 2009 353p $27 **636.7**
1. Dogs -- Psychology
ISBN 1-4165-8340-8; 978-1-4165-8340-0
LC 2008-45842

This book examines "the sensations and thought processes of dogs." (N Y Times Book Rev)
Includes bibliographical references

Kaplan, Laurie

Help Your Dog Fight Cancer; Empowerment for Dog Owners, Turn Despair into Confidence, Become Your Best Friend's Best Advocate. Laurie Kaplan; edited by Alice Villalobos. Jangen Press 2016 258 p. ill. (some col.) (paperback) $29.99 **636.7**
1. Cancer 2. Dogs -- Care 3. Veterinary medicine
ISBN 0975479431; 9780975479438
LC 2004107152

This book, by Laurie Kaplan, edited by Alice Villalobos, discusses "Canine cancer causes and prevention . . . , the most common types of cancer in dogs, diagnostic tests and treatment options . . . , [and] communicating clearly with your veterinarian and making informed decisions . . . about testing and treatment." (Publisher's note)

"A unique contribution to the field of animal care, this work is highly recommended for most public libraries." LJ

Katz, Jon

★ **Katz** on dogs; a commonsense guide to training and living with dogs. Villard 2005 xxviii, 240p il $24.95 **636.7**
1. Dogs -- Training
ISBN 1-4000-6403-1
LC 2005-46209

Katz's "commonsense approach and skill as a storyteller make this an appealing, informative book." Libr J
Includes bibliographical references

The **new** work of dogs; tending to life, love, and family. Villard Bks. 2003 xxiii, 225p $19.95; pa $13.95 **636.7**
1. Dogs
ISBN 0-375-50814-7; 0-375-76055-5 pa
LC 2002-44915

The author "explores the bond between dogs and their owners. Focusing on 12 people-dog relationships in Montclair, N.J., and drawing on current research into attachment theory, interviews with animal workers and psychiatrists, as well as conversations with dog owners, Katz offers nuanced portraits of what happens when humans depend on dogs to satisfy their emotional needs. . . . In this well-written and thoughtful account, Katz makes a convincing case that dog owners must be more self-aware and responsible when they use their pets as human substitutes." Publ Wkly

Kavin, Kim

The **Dog** Merchants; Inside the Big Business of Breeders, Pet Stores, and Rescuers. by Kim Kavin. W W Norton & Co Inc 2016 336 p. $27.95 **636.7**
1. Dogs -- Breeding
ISBN 1681771403; 9781681771403

This book, by Kim Kavin, "is the first book to explain the complex and often surprisingly similar business practices that extend from the American Kennel Club to local shelters, from Westminster champions to dog auctions. . . . Kavin reveals how dog merchants create markets for dogs, often in defiance of the usual rules of supply and demand. She takes an investigative approach and meets breeders and rescuers at all levels." (Publisher's note)

"A scathing indictment of an industry run amok; belongs on every pet lover's bookshelf." Kirkus
Includes bibliographic references (pages 273-296) and index.

Kerasote, Ted

Merle's door; lessons from a freethinking dog. Harcourt, Inc. 2007 398p $25 **636.7**
1. Dogs
ISBN 978-0-15-101270-1
LC 2006-38041

"In telling Merle's story, Kerasote also explores the science behind canine behavior and evolution, weaving in research on the human-canine bond and musing on the way dogs see the world. Merle is a true character, yet Merle is also Everydog. An absolute treasure of a book." Booklist
Includes bibliographical references

Pukka's Promise; The Quest for Longer-lived Dogs. Ted Kerasote. Houghton Mifflin Harcourt 2013 464 p. $28 **636.7**
1. Dogs 2. Animals -- Longevity 3. Dog owners -- Anecdotes
ISBN 0547236263; 9780547236261
LC 2012289472

This book, by Ted Kerasote, discusses dogs as pets and their health and longevity, "questioning our conventional wisdom and emerging with vital new information that will surprise even the most knowledgeable dog lovers. . . . Interviewing breeders, veterinarians, and leaders of the animal-welfare movement, Kerasote pulls together the latest research to help us rethink the everyday choices we make for our companions." (Publisher's note)

McConnell, Patricia

For the love of a dog; understanding emotion in you and your best friend. Ballantine Books 2006 332p il hardcover o.p. pa $15.95 **636.7**
1. Dogs
ISBN 0-345-47714-6; 978-0-345-47714-9; 0-345-47715-4 pa; 978-0-345-47715-6 pa
LC 2006-45200

"This is not a book on how to train dogs, but McConnell's examination of cases from her veterinary practice, backed up by her scientific study of animal behavior, will help readers better understand their closest companions." Booklist

Monks of New Skete

The **art** of raising a puppy; the Monks of New Skete; [photographs by the Monks of New Skete] Little, Brown & Co. 2011 x, 341 p.p illustrations (hbk.) $26   **636.7**

1. Dogs -- Care 2. Animal rescue 3. Puppies 4. Puppies -- Training
ISBN 0316083275; 9780316083270

LC 2011002744

"This new edition of 'The Art Of Raising a Puppy' features new photographs throughout, along with updated chapters on play, crating, adopting dogs from shelters and rescue organizations, raising dogs in an urban environment, and the latest developments in canine health and canine behavioral theory." (Publisher's note)

Includes bibliographical references (p. [329]-331) and index

How to be your dog's best friend; the classic training manual for dog owners. {by} the Monks of New Skete. completely rev and updated, 2nd ed; Little, Brown 2002 336p il $25.95   **636.7**

1. Dogs -- Training
ISBN 0-316-61000-3

LC 2002-102894

First published 1978

This guide to dog training focuses on important aspects of the canine-human relationship, including discipline and choosing a breed that fits the owner's personality and lifestyle

This book's "unique value lies in the monks' insights and thoughts about the human-canine bond. . . . Without devolving into New Age psychobabble, the monks make philosophical and spiritual observations that no dog lover could resist." Publ Wkly

Includes bibliographical references

The **new** complete dog book; by the American Kennel Club. I-5 Press 2014 912 p. color illustrations (alk. paper) $49.95   **636.7**

1. Dogs 2. Photography of animals 3. Dog breeds 4. Dogs -- Standards -- United States
ISBN 162187091X; 9781621870913

LC 2014015369

"'The Complete Dog Book' first appeared 85 years ago and now for the first time has been reformatted and published in full color. A celebration of every breed of dog recognized by the American Kennel Club--over 200 breeds--this volume offers readers [an] . . . official standard for every AKC-recognized breed." (Publisher's note)

Orlean, Susan

★ **Rin** Tin Tin. Simon & Schuster 2011 324p il $26.99; ebook $12.99   **636.7**

1. Working dogs 2. Rin-Tin-Tin (Dog)
ISBN 978-1-4391-9013-5; 978-1-4391-9015-9 ebook

LC 2011024476

This book discusses the "story of Lee Duncan (1893-1960), a young American soldier and dog-lover who found the German shepherd puppy that became Rin Tin Tin (Rinty) in France, got the dog home and spent the rest of his life training and promoting Rinty, breeding other German shep-

herds. . . . [The author] also provides the biography of Duncan, as well as Bert Leonard, writer and producer, and she includes interviews with Duncan's daughter, the current keeper of the latest Rinty and scores of others. The author tells the story of silent films (where Rinty began his career), the transition to talkies and to color, the rise of television, the popularity of dog ownership in America (especially of German shepherds and collies--because of Lassie) and the evolving tastes of American youth." (Kirkus)

"A terrific dog's tale that will make readers sit up and beg for more." Kirkus

Includes bibliographical references

Pierson, Melissa Holbrook

The **secret** history of kindness; learning from how dogs learn. Melissa Holbrook Pierson. W W Norton & Co Inc 2015 320 p. (hardcover) $26.95   **636.7**

1. Kindness 2. Dogs -- Training 3. Positive psychology 4. Dogs -- Psychology 5. Dog trainers -- Psychology 6. Dogs -- Training -- Philosophy
ISBN 0393066193; 9780393066197

LC 2014045932

This book, by Melissa Holbrook Pierson, is an "intimate, surprising look at man's best friend and what the leading philosophies of dog training teach us about ourselves. . . . Pierson draws surprising connections in her exploration of how kindness works to motivate all animals, including the human one." (Publisher's note)

"A well-researched and thorough examination of current methods of dog training based on psychology; useful to those who want a deeper, beyond-the-basics understanding of the techniques." LJ

Includes bibliographical references

Rosenfelt, David

Dogtripping: 25 rescues, 11 volunteers, and 3 RVs on our canine cross-country adventure. David Rosenfelt. St. Martin's Press 2013 288 p. color illustrations (hardcover) $25.99   **636.7**

1. Dogs 2. Moving 3. Human-animal relationship 4. Dog adoption 5. Dogs -- Biography 6. Human-animal relationships 7. Authors, American -- 21st century -- Biography
ISBN 1250014697; 9781250014696

LC 2013009168

This book, by David Rosenfelt, is an "account of a cross-country move from California to Maine, and the beginnings of a dog rescue foundation. When . . . Rosenfelt and his family moved from Southern California to Maine, he thought he had prepared for everything. . . . But traveling with twenty-five dogs turned out to be a bigger ordeal than he anticipated, despite the RVs, the extra kibble, volunteers, and camping equipment." (Publisher's note)

"Spirited and absolutely absorbing reading for fans of canine capers." Booklist

Rutherford, Clarice

How to raise a puppy you can live with; [by] Clarice Rutherford, David H. Neil. 4th ed., rev. &

updated; Alpine Blue Ribbon Books 2005 153p il
pa $11.95 **636.7**
1. Dogs -- Training
ISBN 1-57779-076-6

LC 2005-41038
First published 1981
This book features "practical advice on puppy selection,
development, training, and problem-solving." Libr J
Includes bibliographical references

Stavrinides, Liz
Miracle dogs; rescue stories. Liz Stavrinides.
St. Martin's Press 2014 272 p. illustrations (hard-
cover) $21.99 **636.7**
1. Pets 2. Rescue dogs 3. Dogs -- Care 4. Dogs
-- Anecdotes 5. Dog owners -- Anecdotes 6. Dogs
-- Pictorial works 7. Dog adoption -- Anecdotes 8.
Animal rescue -- Anecdotes
ISBN 1250045770; 9781250045775

LC 2014021151
This book by Liz Stavrinides "celebrates and honors the
rescuers and the dogs whose lives they've saved. It features
wonderful stories and photographs of dog rescuers, dog
trainers, and rescue organizations such as The Gentle Barn
and Tamar Geller's Operation Heroes and Hounds, along
with celebrity pet owners " (Publisher's note)
"Essential for dog lovers and those who are active in rescue as well as animal photography fans." LJ

Stilwell, Victoria
Train your dog positively; understand your dog
and solve common behavior problems including
separation anxiety, excessive barking, aggression,
housetraining, leash pulling, and more! Victoria Stilwell. Ten Speed Press 2013 248 p. illustrations
$14.99 **636.7**
1. Dogs -- Behavior 2. Dogs -- Training
ISBN 1607744147; 9781607744146

LC 2012045637
In this book, author "Victoria Stilwell provides a comprehensive toolbox designed to help dog owners overcome
the most persistent, annoying and dangerous behavior problems in their dogs. Far from being merely another dog training manual, however, it also serves as [a] . . . roadmap for
understanding where our dogs come from, how they experience the world and what we need to teach them most effectively." (Publisher's note)
Includes bibliographical references and index

Thomas, Elizabeth Marshall
The **social** lives of dogs; the grace of canine
company. illustrated by Jared Taylor Williams. Simon & Schuster 2000 253p hardcover o.p. pa
$13.95 **636.7**
1. Dogs
ISBN 0-7434-2236-8 pa

LC 99-87357
Thomas discusses how dogs interact with various members of the household, including other dogs and pets of
other species

The author "draws upon her extensive knowledge of the
behavior and treatment of feral dogs in East Africa to explain
the domestication of the dog. Appendixes containing advice
on controlling dogs' behavior and on keeping parrots as pets
conclude this entertaining and informative book." Libr J

Toutonghi, Pauls
Dog Gone; a lost pet's extraordinary journey and
the family who brought him home. Pauls Toutongh-
hi. Alfred A. Knopf, a division of Penguin Random
House LLC 2016 272 p. illustrations, map (hardcover) $25 **636.7**
1. Dogs 2. Rescue work
ISBN 9781101947012; 1101947012; 1101971010

LC 2015034739
This book, by Pauls Toutonghi, tells a "true story of a
lost dog's journey and a family's furious search to find him
before it is too late. . . . Saturday, October 10, 1998. Fielding Marshall is hiking on the Appalachian Trail. His beloved
dog—a six-year-old golden retriever mix named Gonker—
bolts into the woods. Just like that, he has vanished. And
Gonker has Addison's disease. If he's not found in twenty-
three days, he will die." (Publisher's note)
"This book offers a poignant reminder of the important
role dogs often fill as they help their human companions traverse difficult life passages." LJ

Warren, Cat
What the dog knows; the science and wonder of
working dogs. Cat Warren. Simon & Schuster 2013
352 p. $26.99 **636.7**
1. Working dogs 2. Search dogs -- Anecdotes
ISBN 1451667310; 9781451667318

LC 2013012006
This book, by Cat Warren, focuses on working dogs.
She "interviews cognitive psychologists, historians, medical
examiners, epidemiologists, and forensic anthropologists, as
well as the breeders, trainers, and handlers who work with
and rely on these . . . animals daily. Along the way, she discovers story after story that proves the . . . capabilities—as
well as the . . . limits—of working dogs and their human
partners." (Publisher's note)
"Warren writes with verve and provides rare insight into
our working partnership with canines." Kirkus

Zheutlin, Peter
Rescue road; one man, thirty thousand dogs, and
a million miles on the last hope highway. Peter Zheutlin. Sourcebooks, Inc. 2015 236 p. illustrations
(paperback) $14.99 **636.7**
1. Dogs 2. Animal rescue 3. Dog rescue 4. Animal
welfare
ISBN 9781492614074

LC 2015012970
This book, by Peter Zheutlin, presents "the extraordinary story of one man who has driven more than 1 million
miles to rescue thousands of dogs from hunger, abuse and
neglect and give them a second chance at life and love . . .
from Houston's impoverished Fifth Ward--where thousands
of strays roam the streets--and high-kill animal shelters in
Louisiana, to joyous scenes of adopters embracing their new
pups in the Northeast." (Publisher's note)

"An unabashedly sentimental and affecting portrait of a modern-day animal-loving hero."

636.755 Terriers

Dickey, Bronwen

Pit bull; the battle over an American icon. by Bronwen Dickey. Alfred A. Knopf 2016 352 p. illustrations (hardcover) $26.95 **636.755**
1. Dogs -- Breeding 2. Pit bull terriers
ISBN 9780307961761; 0307961761

LC 2015033292

This book, by Bronwen Dickey, offers an "illuminating story of how a popular breed of dog became the most demonized and supposedly the most dangerous of dogs—and what role humans have played in the transformation. . . . Dickey offers us a clear-eyed portrait of this extraordinary breed, and an insightful view of Americans' relationship with their dogs." (Publisher's note)

"This exceptional, thoroughly researched, and expertly written work is a must for all libraries." LJ

Includes bibliographical references

636.8 Cats

Bradshaw, John, 1950-

★ **Cat** sense; how the new feline science can make you a better friend to your pet. John Bradshaw. Basic Books 2013 336 p. (hardcover) $27.99 **636.8**
1. Cats 2. Pets 3. Animal intelligence 4. Cat owners 5. Cats -- Behavior 6. Cats -- Psychology 7. Human-animal relationships
ISBN 0465031013; 9780465031016

LC 2013020749

In this book, author John Bradshaw takes readers "further into the mind of the domestic cat . . . using cutting-edge scientific research to dispel the myths and explain the true nature of our feline friends. Tracing the cat's evolution from lone predator to domesticated companion, Bradshaw shows that although cats and humans have been living together for at least eight thousand years, cats remain independent, predatory, and wary of contact with their own kind." (Publisher's note)

"Bradshaw teases out a better understanding of what our cats want (and need) from their owners. . . . This fascinating book will be a bible for cat owners." Booklist

Includes bibliographical references and index

The **trainable** cat; a practical guide to making life happier for you and your cat. John Bradshaw and Sarah Ellis. Basic Books 2016 352 p. illustrations (hardcover) $27.99 **636.8**
1. Cats 2. Cats -- Behavior 3. Cats -- Training
ISBN 0465050905; 9780465050901; 9780465096497

LC 2016019146

This book, by John Bradshaw and Sarah Ellis, "show[s] that not only can cats be trained, but they absolutely must be in order to strengthen the bond between pet and owner, reduce their anxiety, and maximize their happiness. . . . Once

we understand our beloved pet's journey from wild predator to domesticated animal, we can train them to overcome their natural inhibitions, fears, and anxieties." (Publisher's note)

"Cat lovers will appreciate the sensible advice and in-depth explanations of feline behavior." Pub Wkly

Includes bibliographical references and index

The **cat** encyclopedia. DK Publishing 2014 320 p. color illustrations, col. maps $40 **636.8**
1. Cats -- Encyclopedias 2. Animals -- Encyclopedias
ISBN 1465419594; 9781465419590

"Offering everything you need to know about cats in one easy-reference volume, 'The Cat Encyclopedia' features stunning photographs of cat breeds from around the world combined with expert advice on kitten and cat care, and a celebration of cats in art and culture. 'The Cat Encyclopedia' is packed with information on the characteristics, origins, and behaviors of each type of cat, and includes beautifully photographed profiles of the world's cat breeds." (Publisher's note)

The **complete** cat breed book; consultant editor, Kim Dennis-Bryan. DK Publishing 2013 256 p. color illustrations $22 **636.8**
1. Cats 2. Pets 3. Cat breeds
ISBN 1465408517; 9781465408518

LC 2012554447

"Combining cat breeds, behavior, and training tips in one easy volume, 'The Complete Cat Breed Book' is an essential reference to the basics of choosing and looking after a cat. Packed with practical advice on cat maintenance, from handling and grooming to nutrition, exercise, and health, current and prospective cat owners will discover the best cat breed for their lifestyle." (Publisher's note)

Includes index

DK the complete cat breed book

Cooper, Gwen

Homer's odyssey; a fearless feline tale, or how I learned about love and life with a blind wonder cat. Delacorte Press 2009 287p il $20 **636.8**
1. Cats
ISBN 978-0-385-34385-5; 0-385-34385-X

LC 2009-17602

A pet rescue volunteer and literacy outreach coordinator describes her relationship with a three-pound blind cat whose daredevil character and affectionate personality saw the author through six moves, a burglary, and the healing of her broken heart.

"This tender and affecting book reveals Homer's lessons about love and acceptance—and how he transformed Cooper into the woman she had always wanted to be." Pub Wkly

Cox, Tom

Close encounters of the furred kind; New Adventures with My Sad Cat & Other Feline Friends. Tom Cox. Thomas Dunne Books, St. Martin's Press 2016 256 p. illustrations (hardcover) $24.99 **636.8**
1. Cats 2. Cats -- England -- Norfolk -- Anecdotes
ISBN 9781250077325

LC 2016003326

This book by Tom Cox "is the follow-up to The Good, The Bad, and the Furry, . . . it tells the story of Tom Cox's life with his charismatic cats--The Bear, Shipley, Ralph, and recent recruit Roscoe. . . . Readers who became attached to The Bear's magical, owlish persona during his previous adventures will become more so here as he proves, once again, that he's a cat with endless secrets and significantly more than nine lives." (Publisher's note)

"Cox is endlessly funny, speaking for his cats and poking good-natured fun at every human he encounters, including himself." Booklist

Hart, Benjamin L.

Your ideal cat; insights into breed and gender differences in cat behavior. Benjamin L. Hart, DVM, PhD, and Lynette A. Hart, PhD. Purdue University Press 2013 x, 147 p.p illustrations (pbk. : alk. paper) $15 **636.8**
1. Cats 2. Animal behavior 3. Cat breeds 4. Cats -- Behavior
ISBN 1557536481; 9781557536488
LC 2012034713

Written by Benjamin L. Hart and Lynette A. Hart, this "book takes the process of selecting a cat to the next level by offering data-based behavioral profiles of a wide range of cat breeds. Developed over a lifetime of research and through extensive interviews with eighty veterinary experts, the profiles are presented in easy-to-use graphical form." (Publisher's note)

Includes bibliographical references (pages 135-140) and index

Herriot, James

James Herriot's cat stories; with illustrations by Lesley Holmes. St. Martin's Press 1994 161p $17.95 **636.8**
1. Cats
ISBN 0-312-11342-0
LC 94-20131

A "collection of favorite cat tales from Herriot's veterinary practice. Retired after over 50 years in practice, Herriot continues to entertain young and old alike with his storytelling ability. His current collection includes 'Alfred, the Sweet-Shop Cat,' 'Boris and Mrs. Bond's Cat Establishment,' 'Moses Found Among the Rushes,' and others." Libr J

Myron, Vicki

Dewey; a small-town library cat who touched the world. Grand Central Publisher 2008 277p il $19.99 **636.8**
1. Cats
ISBN 978-0-446-40741-0; 0-446-40741-0
LC 2008-4498

The story of Dewey Readmore Books, the beloved library cat of Spencer, Iowa.

"Myron's beguiling, poignant, and tender tale of survival, loyalty, and love is an unforgettable study in the mysterious and wondrous ways animals, and libraries, enrich humanity." Booklist

Nagelschneider, Mieshelle

The **cat** whisperer; why cats do what they do-- and how to get them to do what you want. Mieshelle Nagelschneider. Bantam Books 2011 310 p. illustrations $25 **636.8**
1. Cats 2. Cats -- Behavior 3. Cats -- Psychology
ISBN 0553807854; 9780553807851; 9780553907230
LC 2010038747

In this book, cat behaviorist Mieshelle Nagelschneider provides "practical and effective strategies for solving every feline behavior problem imaginable-- from litter box issues to scratching, spraying, biting, and beyond. . . . Central to her approach is a keen understanding of the unique way cats see the world-- their need for safety and security, their acute territoriality, and their insatiable desire to catch and kill prey." (Publisher's note)

"Using the author's methods, readers learn how to successfully introduce (or reintroduce) cats, curb feline aggression, retrain cats who eliminate outside their litter boxes, reduce excessive meowing, stop destructive behaviors (like scratching furniture), and curb compulsive behaviors. Full of "think like a cat" advice, Nagelschneider's work will make for happier human-feline households." Booklist

Includes bibliographical references (p. [293]-297) and index

636.9 Other mammals

Westoll, Andrew

The **chimps** of Fauna Sanctuary; a true story of resilience and recovery. Houghton Mifflin Harcourt 2011 268p il $25 **636.9**
1. Chimpanzees 2. Wildlife refuges 3. Animal rescue 4. Fauna Foundation 5. Chimpanzees -- Behavior 6. Animal experimentation -- Moral and ethical aspects
ISBN 978-0-547-32780-8; 0-547-32780-3
LC 2010049783

"This is both an inspiring and a disturbing book. It is inspiring because of the devotion of caregivers to welfare of the chimps; it is disturbing because of the callous treatment to which chimps in research are subjected." Sci Books Films

Includes bibliographical references

637 Processing dairy and related products

Caldwell, Gianaclis

Mastering artisan cheesemaking; the ultimate guide for home-scale and market producers. Gianaclis Caldwell; foreword by Ricki Carroll. Chelsea Green Publishing 2012 vi, 345 p.p color illustrations $40 **637**
1. Cooking 2. Cheesemaking
ISBN 1603583327; 9781603583329
LC 2012023148

This cheese-making book, by Gianaclis Caldwell, "thoroughly explains the art and science that allow milk to be transformed into epicurean masterpieces. Caldwell offers a deep look at the history, science, culture, and art of making artisan cheese on a small scale, and includes detailed information on equipment and setting up a home-scale operation." (Publisher's note)

"Recipes are offered and explained in very easy terms. A complete package." Booklist

Includes bibliographical references (pages 327-328) and index

English, Ashley

Home dairy with Ashley English; all you need to know to make cheese, yogurt, butter & more. Lark Crafts 2011 135p il (Homemade living) $19.95 **637**

1. Dairy products

ISBN 978-1-60059-627-8

LC 2010020669

"English is no slouch at demystifying the intricacies of home dairy; from the simplicities of churning out your own delectable butter to pressing your very first gouda, the author covers it all in clean, unpretentious, step-by-step instruction. Excellent for those looking to take a slight step off the grid." Kirkus

Includes bibliographical references

Lucero, Claudia

One-hour cheese; ricotta, mozzarella, chèvre, paneer--even burrata, fresh and simple cheeses you can make in an hour or less! by Claudia Lucero, founder of Urban Cheesecraft and Creator of DIY Cheese Kit. Workman Pub. Company, Inc. 2014 260 p. color illustrations (alk. paper) $14.95 **637**

1. Cheesemaking

ISBN 0761177485; 9780761177487

LC 2014001166

In this cookbook Claudia Lucero "shows step by step—with every step photographed—exactly how to make sixteen fresh cheeses at home, using easily available ingredients and tools, in an hour or less. The approach is basic and based on thousands of years of cheesemaking wisdom: Heat milk, add coagulant, drain, salt, and press. Simple variations produce delicious results across three categories—Creamy and Spreadable, Firm and Chewy, and Melty and Gooey." (Publisher's note)

"A fantastic introduction for novices who want simple, delicious, DIY cheese." LJ

Includes bibliographical references and index

638 Insect culture

Black, Scott Hoffman,

Gardening for butterflies; How You Can Attract and Protect Beautiful, Beneficial Insects. the Xerces Society (Scott Hoffman Black, Brianna Borders, Candace Fallon, Eric Lee-Mader, Matthew Shepherd); foreword by Robert Michael Pyle. Timber Press 2016 287 p. color illustrations $24.95 **638**

1. Gardening 2. Butterflies 3. Butterfly gardening

ISBN 9781604695984

LC 2015029810

This book, "by the experts at the Xerces Society, introduces you to a variety of colorful garden guests who need our help, and shows you how to design a habitat where they

will thrive. This optimistic call to arms is packed with everything you need to create a beautiful, beneficial, butterfly-filled garden." (Publisher's note)

"This book will help even those without green thumbs support the much-needed effort to assist and protect pollinators." Booklist

Includes bibliographical references (pages 269-274) index.

Goulson, Dave

A **Buzz** in the Meadow; The Natural History of a French Farm. Dave Goulson. Picador 2015 288 p. $25 **638**

1. Farms 2. France 3. Insects

ISBN 1250065887; 9781250065889

In this book, author Dave "Goulson returns to tell the tale of how he bought a derelict farm in the heart of rural France. Over the course of a decade, on thirty-three acres of meadow, he created a place for his beloved bumblebees to thrive. But other creatures live there too, myriad insects of every kind, many of which Goulson had studied before in his career as a biologist." (Publisher's note)

"Unexpectedly, Goulson also moves beyond his home to reflect on the work of biologists of the past and present, particularly when considering the critical state of the world's pollinators, for whom he issues a gentle call to arms. The book is, therefore, less a meditative reflection of wildlife in the country and more an artful blend of E. O. Wilson and Barry Lopez, with a continental flair. Backyard naturalists, regardless of their locale, will delight in the amiable company of this witty and thoughtful guide." Booklist

Hubbell, Sue

A **book** of bees; and how to keep them. drawings by Sam Potthoff. Houghton Mifflin 1998 193p il pa $13 **638**

1. Bees

ISBN 0-395-88324-5

LC 98-10191

First published 1988 by Random House

"Following the seasons of the beekeeper's year the author imparts practical hints along with literary, mythological, entomological, and anecdotal commentary." Booklist

Jacobsen, Rowan

Fruitless fall; the collapse of the honey bee and the coming agricultural crisis. Bloomsbury USA 2008 279p il $25 **638**

1. Bees

ISBN 978-1-59691-537-4; 1-59691-537-4

LC 2008-26126

The author "celebrates the marvels of the honeybee, reveals the many ways we've endangered this essential pollinator, and calls for action to prevent a 'fruitless fall'." Booklist

Includes bibliographical references

Nordhaus, Hannah

The **beekeeper's** lament; how one man and half a billion honey bees help feed America. Harper Perennial 2011 269p il pa $14.99 **638**

   1. Bees 2. Beekeeping 3. Beekeepers

   ISBN 978-0-06-187325-6; 0-06-187325-X

"Nordhaus centers her account on John Miller, a migratory beekeeper who hauls truckloads of bees from crop to crop to help farmers who don't have natural pollinators. Honey bees are crucial to American agriculture, pollinating crops of 90 different fruits and vegetables. We would lose our almond crops almost entirely without bees, for example. Nordhaus meticulously details this process, demonstrating how modern apiculture affects everyone from keeper to bee to farmer to consumer. . . . [She] provides an almost overwhelming amount of information in a relatively short amount of space, but it's a fascinating read from cover to cover, and Miller makes a genuinely likable American hero." Stamford Advocate

638.1   Beekeeping

Flottum, Kim

The **backyard** beekeeper; an absolute beginner's guide to keeping bees in your yard and garden. Kim Flottum. Quarry Books 2010 208 p. color illustrations $24.99 **638.1**

   1. Beehives 2. Beekeeping 3. Honeybee 4. Bee culture

   ISBN 159253919X; 9781592539192

                        LC 2010287519

Written by Kim Flottum, 'The Backyard Beekeeper,' now revised and expanded, makes the time-honored and complex tradition of beekeeping an enjoyable and accessible backyard pastime that will appeal to gardeners, crafters, and cooks everywhere. This expanded edition gives . . . even more information on 'greening' your beekeeping with sustainable practices, pesticide-resistant bees, and urban and suburban beekeeping." (Publisher's note)

"Flottum (editor, Bee Culture magazine) brings beekeeping into the backyard with this handbook on keeping hives and harvesting their products. New material on natural beekeeping and "extreme urban beekeeping" will satisfy most readers." LJ

Sammataro, Diana

The **beekeeper's** handbook; Diana Sammataro and Alphonse Avitabile; foreword by Dewey M. Caron. Comstock Pub. Associates 2011 x, 308 p.p illustrations (pbk. : alk. paper) $29.95 **638.1**

   1. Beekeeping 2. Bee culture -- Handbooks, manuals, etc

   ISBN 0801476941; 9780801449819; 9780801476945

                        LC 2010050047

This book, by Diana Sammataro and Alphonse Avitabile, is a "guide to the hobby and profession of beekeeping. Featuring clear descriptions and authoritative content, this handbook provides step-by-step directions accompanied by more than 100 illustrations for setting up an apiary, handling bees, and working throughout the season to maintain a healthy colony of bees and a generous supply of honey. This book

explains the various colony care options and techniques." (Publisher's note)

   Includes bibliographical references and index

639   Hunting, fishing, conservation, related technologies

Blanchard, Zechariah

Saltwater Fish and Reef Tanks; From Beginner to Expert. by Zechariah James Blanchard. Createspace Independent Publishing Platform 2014 154 p. $9.97 **639**

   1. Marine aquariums

   ISBN 1499203160; 9781499203165

This book, by Zechariah James Blanchard, "is the premier source of information for new and experienced saltwater aquarium owners. . . . Whether you're looking to setup a saltwater reef or a fish only tank, this book was written as an explanation and road-map to success in caring for your aquarium equipment, fish, corals, and invertebrates." (Publisher's note)

Greenlaw, Linda

The **lobster** chronicles; life on a very small island. Hyperion 2002 238p $22.95; pa $13.95 **639**

   1. Lobster fisheries 2. Isle au Haut (Maine)

   ISBN 0-7868-6677-2; 0-7868-8591-2 pa

In this companion to The hungry ocean, the author gives "up swordfishing to return to her parents' home on Isle Au Haut off the coast of Maine and fish for lobster. . . . She intersperses her narrative with plenty of eccentrics who live on her tiny island. . . . Self-speculation and uncertainties . . . nicely balance her delightfully cocky essays of island life." Publ Wkly

639.2   Commercial fishing, whaling, sealing

Dolin, Eric Jay

Leviathan; the history of whaling in America. W.W. Norton & Company 2007 479p il $27.95 **639.2**

   1. Whaling -- History

   ISBN 978-0-393-06057-7; 0-393-06057-8

                        LC 2007-06113

The author "chronicles the long history of whaling in North America, from the voyages of Capt. John Smith, who, like many after him, 'found this Whale-fishing a costly conclusion,' to the last voyage of the Wanderer, a whaler that set sail from the once-teeming port of New Bedford, Mass., in 1924 and promptly wrecked in the shallows before a crowd of curious onlookers. . . . Anyone whose knowledge of whaling begins and ends with 'MobyDick' will get a solid education from Mr. Dolin, who fills in the historical record and sets the stage for the glory years when men like Melville set out from Nantucket, New Bedford, Sag Harbor and dozens of other ports on voyages lasting as long as four years." N Y Times (Late N Y Ed)

   Includes bibliographical references

Greenlaw, Linda

The **hungry** ocean; a swordboat captain's journey. Hyperion 1999 265p map $22.95; pa $14   **639.2**

1. Fishing

ISBN 0-7868-6451-6; 0-7868-8541-6 pa

LC 98-51985

The author "details a 30-day swordfishing trip from Gloucester to the Grand Banks. Greenlaw describes her boat, equipment, and various electronic gear, including the 'temperature bird' that is lowered to measure the temperature at the fishing depth, as well as her technique for finding just the right area to fish. . . . An exciting and detailed look inside the commercial fishing industry." Libr J

Kurlansky, Mark

★ The **last** fish tale; the fate of the Atlantic and survival in Gloucester, America's oldest fishing port and most original town. Riverhead Books 2009 xxix, 269p il map pa $16   **639.2**

1. Commercial fishing 2. Gloucester (Mass.)

ISBN 978-1-59448-374-5

First published 2008 by Ballantine Books

The author "provides a delightful, intimate history and contemporary portrait of the quintessential northeastern coastal fishing town: Gloucester, Mass., on Cape Anne. Illustrated with his own beautifully executed drawings, Kurlansky's book vividly depicts the contemporary tension between the traditional fishing trade and modern commerce, which in Gloucester means beach-going tourists." Publ Wkly

Includes bibliographical references

639.3   Culture of cold-blooded vertebrates

Halverson, Anders

An **entirely** synthetic fish; how rainbow trout beguiled America and overran the world. Anders Halverson. Yale University Press 2010 xxi, 257 p.p   **639.3**

1. Rainbow trout 2. Fisheries -- United States 3. Introduced fishes -- United States 4. Rainbow trout industry -- United States -- History

ISBN 0300140878; 9780300140873

LC 2009036200

Halverson provides an "account of the rainbow trout and why it has become the most commonly stocked and controversial freshwater fish in the United States. Discovered in the remote waters of northern California, rainbow trout have been artificially propagated and distributed for more than 130 years by government officials eager to present Americans with an opportunity to get back to nature by going fishing. . . . Dubbed 'an entirely synthetic fish' by fisheries managers, the rainbow trout has been introduced into every state and province in the United States and Canada and to every continent except Antarctica, often with devastating effects on the native fauna, [according to the author]." (Publisher's note) Bibliography. Index.

this is not one of those whiny, hand-wringing catalogs of environmental gloom and doom. With prose as engaging as it is thoughtful, Halverson has crafted an absorbing cautionary tale of ecological trial and error, documenting our tardy

but increasing understanding of biological interdependence and its immeasurable value. Washington Post

Includes bibliographical references (p. 211-244) and index

Mattison, Chris

What reptile? a buyer's guide for reptiles and amphibians. by Chris Mattison. Barron's Educational Series, Inc. 2013 208 p. color illustrations (pbk.) $16.99   **639.3**

1. Pets 2. Reptiles 3. Amphibians 4. Captive reptiles 5. Captive amphibians 6. Captive reptiles -- Breeding 7. Captive amphibians -- Breeding

ISBN 1438001622; 9781438001623

LC 2012932104

This book on reptiles, by Chris Mattison, "provides prospective owners with vital advice for choosing and caring for more than 150 species of reptiles and amphibians. Each entry details Animal temperament and habits, Special equipment and housing, Daily care needs and breeding habits, Animal pricing and care costs, [and] Potential drawbacks that new owners should know." (Publisher's note)

639.34   Fish culture in aquariums

Bailey, Mary

The **Ultimate** Encyclopedia of Aquarium Fish & Fish Care; A definitive guide to identifying and keeping freshwater and marine fishes. by Mary Bailey and Gina Sandford. Natl Book Network 2015 256 p. color illustrations $13.99   **639.34**

1. Fishes 2. Aquariums

ISBN 1780193416; 9781780193410

This book, by Mary Bailey and Gina Sandford, is a "comprehensive manual on planning, building, stocking and maintaining all types of aquaria, fully illustrated with 700 photographs and diagrams." (Publisher's note)

Mills, Dick

Aquarium fish. DK 2004 72p il (101 essential tips) pa $5   **639.34**

1. Fishes 2. Aquariums

ISBN 0-7566-0611-X; 978-0-7566-0611-4

LC 2004-303366

Reprint of paperback printed by DK Pub. in 1996

This book offers advice on choosing fish for aquariums, aquarium equipment, decoration, feeding, and health care, and describes various species of tropical, coldwater, freshwater, and marine fishes.

"Accurate, clear, and concise writing is enhanced with wonderful color photographs on each page." Voice Youth Advocates [review of 1996 edition]

639.9 Conservation of biological resources

Jacobsen, Rowan

The **living** shore; rediscovering a lost world. illustrated by Mary Elder Jacobsen. Bloomsbury 2009 167p il map $20   **639.9**
1. Oysters 2. Commercial fishing 3. Puget Sound region (Wash.)
ISBN 978-1-59691-684-5; 1-59691-684-2

LC 2009-8903

A marine scientist, together with Rowan and a conservancy group interested in habitat restoration, suggests a possible blueprint for cleaning up our oceans by observing an isolated pocket of oysters living on the western side of Vancouver Island.

"Lovely science writing, and a smart look into where the work of ecological restoration is headed." Kirkus

Includes bibliographical references

Varty, Boyd

Cathedral of the wild; an African journey home. Boyd Varty. Random House Inc 2014 304 p. illustrations (acid-free paper) $27   **639.9**
1. Game reserves 2. Africa -- Social conditions 3. Londolozi Game Reserve (South Africa) -- History 4. Wildlife conservation -- South Africa -- Londolozi Game Reserve -- History
ISBN 1400069858; 9781400069859

LC 2013022706

Author Boyd Varty presents a "memoir of his life in [Londolozi Game Reserve in South Africa]. At Londolozi, Varty gained the confidence that emerges from living in Africa. It was there that young Boyd and his equally adventurous sister learned to track animals, raised leopard and lion cubs, followed their larger-than-life uncle on his many adventures filming wildlife, and became one with the land. An intense spiritual quest takes him across the globe and back again." (Publisher's note)

An "intense, insightful memoir that brings together several wise observations about the relationship between nature and humanity." Pub Wkly

Includes bibliographical references and index

639.97 Specific kinds of animals

Bradley, Carol

Last chain on Billie; how one extraordinary elephant escaped the big top. Carol Bradley. St. Martin's Press 2014 336 p. (hardcover) $25.99 **639.97**
1. Circus 2. Elephants 3. Animal rescue 4. Animal welfare 5. Animal rescue -- United States 6. Animal welfare -- United States 7. Elephants -- United States -- Anecdotes 8. Circus animals -- United States -- Anecdotes 9. Captive elephants -- United States -- Anecdotes
ISBN 1250025699; 9781250025692

LC 2014008568

This book, by Carol Bradley, "charts the history of elephants in America, the . . . story of the Elephant Sanctuary and the . . . tale of a resilient elephant who defied the system. . . . Left in the wild, Billie the elephant would have spent her

days surrounded by family. . . . Instead, traders captured her as a baby and shipped her to America, where she learned . . . the full repertoire of elephant tricks. . . . But behind the scenes she lived a life of misery." (Publisher's note)

"Graphic details of animal abuse may offend some readers, but the overall story is worth enduring those passages. A moving and informative account of the plight of trained elephants in the U.S. and the efforts of those who have created an asylum for them." Kirkus

Mills, J. A.

Blood of the tiger; a story of conspiracy, greed, and the battle to save a magnificent species. J.A. Mills. Beacon Press 2015 272 p. illustrations (hardback) $27.95 **639.97**
1. Tiger trade -- China
ISBN 0807074969; 9780807074961

LC 2014015760

This book, by J.A. Mills, "takes readers on a wild ride to save one of the world's rarest animals from a band of Chinese billionaires. . . . There may be only three thousand wild tigers left in the entire world. More shocking is the fact that twice that many-- some six thousand-- have been bred on farms, not for traditional medicine but to supply a luxury-goods industry that secretly sells tiger-bone wine, tiger-skin décor, and exotic cuisine enjoyed by China's elite." (Publisher's note)

"The author provides a list of resources for readers inspired to take action, in addition to a substantial set of notes. A telling inside view of 20 years in international tiger conservation work, including the successes, failures and the work that is still required." Kirkus

Includes bibliographical references and index

Raffin, Michele

The **birds** of Pandemonium; life among the exotic and the endangered. by Michele Raffin. Algonquin Books of Chapel Hill 2014 240 p. 16 plates; color illustrations $24.95 **639.97**
1. Birds -- Protection 2. Wildlife conservation 3. Pandemonium Aviaries 4. Birds -- Conservation -- California
ISBN 1616201363; 9781616201364

LC 2014023612

In this book, author "Michele Raffin steps outside into the bewitching bird music that heralds another day at Pandemonium Aviaries. . . . Pandemonium, the home and bird sanctuary that Raffin shares with some of the world's most remarkable birds, is a conservation organization dedicated to saving and breeding birds at the edge of extinction, with the goal of eventually releasing them into the wild. . . . Their amazing stories make up the heart of this book." (Publisher's note)

"Animal lovers will likely forgive the author her stylistic lapses and read appreciatively of her many strong works." LJ

640 Home and family management

Alink, Merissa

Little house living; the make-your-own guide to a frugal, simple, and self-sufficient life. Merissa

Alink. Gallery Books 2015 320 p. color illustrations $26.99   **640**

1. Home economics 2. Household budgets 3. Housekeeping

ISBN 1501104268; 9781501104268; 9781501104282

LC 2015024538

Author Merissa A. Alink presents this "homemaking book, inspired by Laura Ingalls Wilder's 'Little House on the Prairie,' featuring creative, fun ways to live . . . life simply and frugally. With over 130 practical, simple DIY recipes, . . . full-color photographs, and [Alink's] trademark charm in personal stories and tips, 'Little House Living' is the epitome of heartland warmth and prairie inspiration." (Publisher's note)

"With chapters on Body and Beauty, Household, Children and Pets, and Make-Ahead Mixes, plus additional stories, Alink brings a bit of Wilder's life into the present." LJ

Bried, Erin

How to sew a button; and other nifty things your grandmother knew. Ballantine Books 2009 xxii, 278p il pa $15   **640**

1. Handicraft 2. Life skills 3. Home economics

ISBN 978-0-345-51875-0; 0-345-51875-6

LC 2009036046

"These anecdotes and tutorials gleaned from subject experts and grandmothers who were children during the Great Depression cover a broad swath of homemaking skills. Instead of systematic how-tos, Bried presents these lessons as a means to improve the quality of the reader's life. Excellent information, but definitely written to a female audience." Libr J

Mendelson, Cheryl

Home comforts; the art and science of keeping house. illustrations by Harry Bates. Scribner 1999 884p il hardcover o.p. pa $21   **640**

1. Home economics

ISBN 0-684-81465-X; 0-7432-7286-2 pa

LC 99-37555

Mendelson includes "sections on food, clothing, cleanliness, daily life, and safety, with information on negligence, domestic employment laws, insurance, and even the impact of clothing label laws on our laundry. Preferred methods are explained in detail, and some alternatives are offered for those who need to compromise. This is a valuable tool." Libr J

Includes bibliographical references

Stewart, Martha, 1941-

Martha Stewart's Homekeeping Handbook; the essential guide to caring for eveything in your home. Martha Stewart. Clarkson Potter 2006 744 p. illustrations $45   **640**

1. Home economics

ISBN 0517577003; 9780517577004

LC 2006050267

This book, by Martha Stewart, offers the author's "expertise in home maintenance and care. . . . With charts, sidebars, illustrated techniques, and personal anecdotes from . . . decades of experience caring for . . . homes–this is far more than just a compendium of ways to keep your house clean.

It covers everything from properly executing a living room floor plan to setting a formal table . . . , to polishing your silver and caring for family heirlooms." (Publisher's note)

Tracy, Brian

Eat that frog! 21 great ways to stop procrastinating and get more done in less time. by Brian Tracy. Berrett-Koehler Publishers 2006 128 p. $15.95 **640**

1. Time management 2. Procrastination

ISBN 1576754227; 9781576754221

LC 0013189

Second Edition

This book, by Brian Tracy, "provides the 21 most effective methods for conquering procrastination and accomplishing more. This new edition is revised and updated throughout, and includes brand new information on how to keep technology from dominating our time." (Publisher's note)

Includes index

Walsh, Peter

How to organize just about everything; more than 500 step-by-step instructions for everything from organizing your closets to planning a wedding to creating a flawless filing system. Free Press 2005 501p $25   **640**

1. Home economics

ISBN 0-7432-5494-5

LC 2004-56277

"Inside the 16 sections are 501 activities, both the usual and out-of-the-ordinary tasks, from getting organized and planning a remodeling project to joining the Peace Corps or becoming an astronaut. Each features the step-by-step procedures, tips, a warning (if necessary), and 'who knew?'— additional advice designed to make the activity a success. . . . A great humane reference anytime, anywhere, for any occasion." Booklist

640.73   Evaluation and purchasing guides

Levine, Judith

Not buying it; my year without shopping. Simon & Schuster 2006 274p $25   **640.73**

1. Shopping 2. Consumer education

ISBN 0-7432-6935-7

LC 2005-55517

The author discusses her experiences when she decided not to buy any nonessential items for a year.

"This honest and humorous tale of a nonspending year is well worth putting aside a few hours to read." Christ Sci Monit

641   Food and drink

101 classic cookbooks; 501 classic recipes. Marvin J. Taylor, Clark Wolf, The Fales Library, New York University. Rizzoli 2012 688 p. $50   **641**

1. Cookbooks 2. American cooking

ISBN 0847837939; 9780847837939

LC 2012940384

This "collection, edited by [Marvin J.] Taylor . . . and food consultant [Clark] Wolf, offers signature recipes from 20th-century classics such as Fannie Farmer's 'The Boston Cooking-School Cook Book,' James Beard's 'American Cookery,' and Mark Bittman's 'How To Cook Everything.' Books are organized chronologically in entries that explain each title's historical significance and include bibliographic information, images of the first edition, and a list of notable recipes." (Library Journal)

The **backyard** homestead; edited by Carleen Madigan. Storey Pub. 2009 367p il pa $18.95 **641**
1. Vegetable gardening 2. Food -- Preservation
ISBN 978-1-60342-138-6
LC 2009-01338

"Madigan presents the information in clear chapters, starting with vegetables, herbs, and fruit and nut trees; moving on through growing grains and grinding them into flour; and then tackling keeping chickens, cows, pigs, and more. The last chapter, 'Food from the Wild,' delves into beekeeping, foraging for berries and mushrooms, and making your own maple syrup. None of the information is particularly in-depth—if you decide to pursue something, you'll likely want to get another book on that one subject. But as an inspiration and an introduction to the various possibilities, it's perfect." Epicurious

Includes bibliographical references

Bourdain, Anthony, 1956-
Appetites; a cookbook. Anthony Bourdain, Laurie Woolever. HarperCollins 2016 304 p. (hardcover) $37.50 **641**
1. Cooking 2. Cookbooks
ISBN 0062409956; 9780062409959

This cookbook, by Anthony Bourdain and Laurie Woolever, "boils down forty-plus years of professional cooking and globe-trotting to a tight repertoire of personal favorites—dishes that everyone should (at least in Mr. Bourdain's opinion) know how to cook. . . . After years of traveling more than 200 days a year, he now enjoys entertaining at home." (Publisher's note)

"In what might be his most accessible book yet, Bourdain reveals his 'Ina Garten–like need to feed the people around me' with a terrific collection of recipes for family and friends." Pub Wkly

A **cook's** tour; global adventures in extreme cuisines. Ecco 2002 274p il pa $14.99 **641**
1. Food 2. Cooking
ISBN 0-06-001278-1
LC 2002-23507

First published 2001 by Bloomsbury Press

This is an "account of the author's global search for the 'perfect mix of food and context' that takes the reader to the culinary corners of the earth: from Vietnam (a live cobra heart) and Japan (poisonous blowfish) to England (roasted bone marrow) and Scotland (deep-fried Mars bar)." N Y Times Book Rev

Cowin, Dana
Food & Wine Annual Cookbook 2015; An Entire Year of Recipes. Dana Cowin. Oxmoor House 2015 408 p. (hardcover) $34.95 **641**
1. Cookbooks 2. Seasonal cooking
ISBN 0848746708; 9780848746704

This cookbook, by Dana Cowin, presents "more than 650 recipes and perfected each one in the 'Food & Wine' Test Kitchen. Home cooks will find tasty ideas for every occasion-from simple weeknight dinners and Sunday brunch to fabulous holiday meals and cocktail parties contributed by some of the biggest names in food, including Jacques Pépin, Alice Waters, David Chang, Dorie Greenspan, Marcus Samuelsson, and Giada De Laurentiis." (Publisher's note)

Davidson, Alan, 1924-2003
The **Oxford** companion to food; Alan Davidson; edited by Tom Jaine; illustrations by Soun Vannithone. 3rd ed Oxford University Press 2014 xxx, 921p illustrations $65 **641**
1. Food 2. Reference books
ISBN 9780199677337
LC 2013957569

First published 1999

"There is new coverage of attitudes to food consumption, production and perception, such as food and genetics, food and sociology, and obesity. New entries include terms such as convenience foods, drugs and food, Ethiopia, leftovers, medicine and food, pasta, and many more. There are also new entries on important personalities who are of special significance within the world of food." Publisher's note

Includes bibliographical references and index

Fisher, M. F. K. (Mary Frances Kennedy), 1908-1992
The **art** of eating; M.F.K. Fisher; with an introduction by Clifton Fadiman; an appreciation by James A. Beard; and a retrospective essay by Joan Reardon. Wiley Pub. 2004 xxxiv, 749 p.p $24.95 **641**
1. Cooking 2. Eating habits 3. Gastronomy
ISBN 0764542613; 9780764542619
LC 2003026124

IACP Culinary Classics Book Award (2012)
James Beard Cookbook Hall of Fame (1990)

This book, by Mary Frances Kennedy Fisher, is a "50th anniversary paperback reprint . . . [of the author's collected best writings on food and cooking. M. F. K.] Fisher (1908-1992) was one of this country's earliest food writers. . . . The 784-page collection brings together five works originally published under separate titles. . . . There are also recipes scattered throughout." (Publisher's note)

A **stew** or a story; an assortment of short works by M.F.K. Fisher. gathered and introduced by Joan Reardon. Shoemaker & Hoard 2006 364p $28; pa $15.95 **641**
1. Food 2. Cooking
ISBN 978-1-59376-115-8; 1-59376-115-5; 978-1-59376-165-3 pa; 1-59376-165-1 pa
LC 2006-08708

"Fisher's food writing was ahead of its time; a frequent contributor to Gourmet, Bon App tit, and other publications, Fisher had lived in both France and the California wine country and offered cooking tips that predate the American culinary 'revolution' of the 1960s. As these enjoyable pieces show, she was also a witty writer who offered astute observations along with the occasional recipe. The topics chosen for this collection include coffee making, borscht, olives, picnics, holidays, and places." Libr J

Includes bibliographical references

Fraioli, James O.

The **Canon** Cocktail Book; Recipes from the Award-Winning Bar. by Jamie Boudreau and James O. Fraioli. Houghton Mifflin Harcourt 2016 352 p. (ebook) $28; $28   **641**

1. Bars 2. Cocktails

ISBN 9780544631595; 054463103X; 9780544631038

This book, by Jamie Boudreau and James O. Fraioli, focuses on "Seattle bar Canon. . . . offers 100 cocktail recipes ranging from riffs on the classics, like the Cobbler's Dream and Corpse Reviver, to their lineup of original house drinks, such as the Truffled Old Fashioned and the Banksy Sour. In addition to tips, recipes, and formulas for top-notch cocktails, syrups, and infusions, Boudreau breaks down the fundamentals and challenges of opening and running a bar." (Publisher's note)

"This terrific resource is sure to send armchair bartenders scurrying to their shakers." Pub Wkly

Jordan, Christy

Sweetness; Southern recipes to celebrate the warmth, the love, and the blessings of a full life. Christy Jordan. Workman Pub Co 2016 304 p. (paperback) $16.95   **641**

1. Desserts 2. Southern cooking

ISBN 0761189424; 9780761189428

This Southern cookbook, by Christy Jordan, "shares 197 recipes for sweet things to eat and drink—recipes that are deeply delicious, rich with tradition, often reaching through generations, and designed with today's hectic schedules in mind. Because life is just better when you add a little sweetness." (Publisher's note)

"Filled with family stories and cheerful advice, this cookbook is a reasonably priced volume of easy-to-make sweets." LJ

Kamp, David

The **United** States of Arugula; how we became a gourmet nation. Broadway Books 2006 392p il $26   **641**

1. Dining 2. Gastronomy 3. Cookery, American

ISBN 0-7679-1579-8

LC 2006-42599

In this book, David Kamp "details the development of fine dining in the U.S. and proves healthy, even exotic food movements are having an effect on our diet. . . . Historically, the rich always had high-end restaurants; the rest contented themselves with recipes in the ladies' sections of newspapers and magazines. But thanks to 'the Big Three'--James Beard, Julia Child and Craig Claiborne-America had an eating revolution." (Publishers Weekly)

The author "details the development of fine dining in the U.S. and proves healthy, even exotic food movements are having an effect on our diet. . . . This cultural history makes for an engrossing read, documenting the dramas and rivalries of the food industry." Publ Wkly

Includes bibliographical references

Kingsolver, Barbara, 1955-

★ **Animal,** vegetable, miracle; a year of food life. [by] Barbara Kingsolver, with Steven L. Hopp and Camille Kingsolver; original drawings by Richard A. Houser. HarperCollins Publishers 2007 370p il $26.95; pa $15.99   **641**

1. Farm life 2. Eating customs 3. Appalachian region 4. Agriculture and energy

ISBN 978-0-06-085255-9; 0-06-085255-0; 978-0-06-085256-6 pa; 0-06-085256-9 pa

LC 2006-53516

"This is a serious book about important problems. Its concerns are real and urgent. It is clear, thoughtful, often amusing, passionate and appealing. It may give you a serious case of supermarket guilt, thinking of the energy footprint left by each out-of-season tomato, but you'll also find unexpected knowledge and gain the ability to make informed choices about what—and how—you're willing to eat." Washington Post Book World

Includes bibliographical references

Krissoff, Liana

Canning for a New Generation; Bold, Fresh Flavors for the Modern Pantry. by Liana Krissoff; photographs by Rinne Allen. Harry N Abrams Inc 2016 400 p. $27.50   **641**

1. Canning and preserving

ISBN 1617691852; 9781617691850

This book on canning, by Liana Krissoff, "is filled with fresh and new ways to preserve nature's bounty throughout the year. Organized by season and illustrated with beautiful photographs, it offers detailed instructions and recipes for making more than 150 canned, pickled, dried, and frozen foods, as well as 50 inventive recipes for dishes using these foods. Basic information on canning techniques and lively sidebars round out this refreshing take on a classic cooking tradition." (Publisher's note)

Lappé, Anna, 1973-

Diet for a hot planet; the climate crisis at the end of your fork and what you can do about it. with a forward by Bill McKibben. Bloomsbury 2010 xxi, 313p il   **641**

1. Food supply 2. Food industry 3. Eating customs 4. Greenhouse effect

ISBN 1-59691-659-1; 978-1-59691-659-3

LC 2010-17363

The author "argues that food is 'the integrating lens' for the innumerable responses to climate change. At three meals or more per day, Lappe writes, we are faced with either supporting or resisting industrial food production. So-called conventional food production and distribution—ecologically and economically fragile—contributes to nearly one-third of total human-caused global warming and paradoxically creates hunger out of plenty. Organic, local, plant-based foods, on the other hand, have the potential to not only mitigate but ultimately repair this damage. Lappe bolsters her support for a local, organic diet with a substantial bibliography of peer-reviewed science, studies, policies and interviews." Kirkus

Includes bibliographical references

Manfield, Christine

Dessert Divas; by Christine Mansfield. Trafalgar Square Books 2015 240 p. $69.95   **641**

1. Desserts

ISBN 1921383534; 9781921383533

IACP Cookbook Award Finalist: Photography (2015)

In this book, "chef Christine Manfield believes that desserts should appeal to all the senses. They should be utterly seductive, ethereal, and delicious, with aesthetics that capture your imagination. . . . In a sumptuously illustrated tribute to the desserts created at her Sydney restaurant Universal, Christine unveils the mystery, elegance, whimsy, and fantasy behind . . . iconic desserts." (Publisher's note)

O'Neill, Laura

Van Leeuwen Artisan Ice Cream; by Laura O'Neill, Benjamin Van Leeuwen, Peter Van Leeuwen, Olga Massov. HarperCollins 2015 256 p. illustrations (chiefly color) (hardcover) $29.99   **641**

1. Cookbooks 2. Ice cream, ices, etc.

ISBN 9780062329585; 0062329588

This ice cream cookbook, by Laura O'Neill, Benjamin Van Leeuwen, Peter Van Leeuwen, and Olga Massov, "includes . . . recipes for every palate and season, from beloved favorites like Vanilla to adventurous treats inspired by a host of international culinary influences, such as Masala Chai with Black Peppercorns and Apple Crumble with Calvados and Crème Fraîche." (Publisher's note)

"This engagingly written cookbook is a recommended purchase for all libraries." LJ

Oliver, Jamie, 1975-

Jamie's dinners; with photographs by David Loftus and Chris Terry and illustrations by Marion Deuchars. Hyperion 2004   **641**

1. Cooking

ISBN 1-4013-0194-0

"The Naked Chef grows up: Oliver, the ebullient British lad who enchanted the Friends generation of Food Network viewers, turns his focus from throwing impromptu dinner parties to cooking family meals and school lunches. As always, the emphasis is on tasty food that anyone can prepare-and the book's best sections are devoted to simple fare such as sandwiches and pasta, where Oliver brings new life to staples like grilled cheese, with his Double-Decker Cheddar Cheese Sandwich with Pickled Onions and Potato Chips. The chef romps through shopping, kitchen tools, basic ingredients and core dishes, tying together his 120 recipes with the family-friendly theme of value for money." PW

Srulovich, Itamar

Honey & Co the Baking Book; Sarit Packer and Itamar Srulovich. Hodder & Stoughton 2015 304 p. $39.95   **641**

1. Food 2. Cooking

ISBN 1444735004; 9781444735000

This cookbook by Sarit Packer and Itamar Srulovich features recipes for "sticky buns full of cherries and pistachios in the morning; a loaf of rich dough rolled with chocolate, hazelnuts and cinnamon that has been proving since dawn and comes out of the oven fresh for elevenses. Lunch is a crisp, crumbly shell of pastry filled with spiced lamb or burnt aubergine, and at teatime there are cheesecakes and fruit cakes, small cakes and massive cookies." (Publisher's note)

Young, Catherine

The Beetlebung Farm cookbook; a year of cooking on Martha's Vineyard. by Chris Fischer, with Catherine Young. Little, Brown & Co. 2015 320 p. color illustrations; color map $35   **641**

1. American cooking 2. Martha's Vineyard (Mass.)

ISBN 0316404071; 9780316404075

LC 2014957428

This book, by Chris Fischer, presents a "year of fresh, simple, seasonal cooking. . . . Beetlebung Farm, his grandparents' five-acre parcel in the town of Chilmark, [Martha's Vineyard] is both Fischer's inspiration and the source for the fine raw materials he showcases. These recipes express the unique understanding of ingredients that comes from a life spent hauling in lobster pots, cultivating vegetables, tracking game in the woods, and butchering his own meat." (Publisher's note)

"This superb collection is a must-have for every cook interested in simple yet flavorful food that's guaranteed to please." Pub Wkly

641.01   Philosophy and theory

Wilson, Bee

First bite; how we learn to eat. Bee Wilson; with illustrations by Annabel Lee. Basic Books, a member of the Perseus Books Group 2015 352 p. illustrations (hardcover) $27.99   **641.01**

1. Gastronomy 2. Eating customs 3. Food preferences

ISBN 9780465064984

LC 2015027683

In this book, "food writer Bee Wilson draws on the latest research from food psychologists, neuroscientists, and nutritionists to reveal that our food habits are shaped by a whole host of factors: family and culture, memory and gender, hunger and love. . . . The way we learn to eat holds the key to why food has gone so disastrously wrong for so many people. But Wilson also shows that both adults and children have immense potential for learning new, healthy eating habits." (Publisher's note)

"This work will appeal to food scientists, parents wishing to know the roots of their children's meal choices, and curious readers in general." LJ

Includes bibliographical references and index

641.2   Beverages (Drinks)

Acitelli, Tom

The **audacity** of hops; the history of America's craft beer revolution. Tom Acitelli. Chicago Review Press 2013 416 p. (pbk.) $19.95   **641.2**

1. Beer 2. Brewing 3. Microbreweries 4. Beer --
United States
ISBN 1613743882; 9781613743881

LC 2013002264

This book by Tom Acitelli is a "look at craft beer from the 1960s onward, from its birth out of the home brewing movement to ultimately revitalize an industry—and the drinking habits of millions. The author traces craft brewing's passage from an unorthodox business decision to a potentially logical investment. His book provides the histories of dozens of breweries, from familiar names to more obscure, long-shuttered institutions, and takes in numerous industry-wide controversies." (Library Journal)

Includes bibliographical references and index

Alworth, Jeff

The **beer** bible; the essential beer lover's guide. Jeff Alworth. Workman Publishing 2015 656 p. illustrations (alk. paper) $19.95   **641.2**

1. Beer
ISBN 0761168117; 9780761168119

LC 2015024777

This book, by Jeff Alworth, "is the ultimate reader- and drinker-friendly guide to all the world's beers. . . . Divided into four major families—ales, lagers, wheat beers, and tart and wild ales—there's everything a beer drinker wants to know. . . . Each style is a chapter unto itself, delving into origins, ingredients, description and characteristics, substyles, and tasting notes, and ending with a recommended list of the beers to know in each category." (Publisher's note)

"Beer enthusiasts will welcome this guide that feels like one is spending time with a well-versed drinking pal." LJ

Includes bibliographical references and index

Beaumont, Stephen

The **world** atlas of beer; The Essential Guide to the Beers of the World. Sterling Epicure 2012 256 p. (hardcover) $30   **641.2**

1. Beer 2. Brewing
ISBN 1402789610; 9781402789618

This book presents the "global history of beer. . . . Color photographs accompany the text, which offers information on buying and drinking beer, as well as a geographic survey of beers around the world. Other topics covered include the various types of beer, brewing methods and technologies, trends, brands, and more." (Booklist)

Broom, Dave

The **World** Atlas of Whisky; More Than 200 Distilleries Explored and 750 Expressions Tasted. by Dave Broom. Octopus Pub Group 2014 336 p. $39.99   **641.2**

1. Whiskey
ISBN 1845339428; 9781845339425

IACP Cookbook Award Finalist: Food and Beverage/Reference/Technical (2015)

In this whisky guidebook, author Dave Broom "explores over 200 distilleries and examines over 400 expressions. Detailed descriptions of the Scottish distilleries can be found here, while Ireland, Japan, the USA, Canada and the rest of the world are given exhaustive coverage. There are tasting notes on single malts from Aberfeldy to Tormore, Yoichi (and coverage of the best of the blends)." (Publisher's note)

"A perfect complement to Dominic Roskrow's expansive The World's Best Whiskies, which includes distiller interviews." LJ

Kolpan, Steven

Exploring wine; The Culinary Institute of America's Complete Guide to Wines of the World. Steven Kolpan, Brian H. Smith, Michael A. Weiss. 3rd ed Wiley 2010 792 p. col. ill., col. maps (cloth) $70   **641.2**

1. Wine and wine making
ISBN 0471770639; 9780471770633

LC 2009014016

This book, by Steven Kolpan, Brian H. Smith, and Michael A. Weiss, "thoroughly demystifies wine, from the basics of wine production to the nuances of wine lists, wine marketing, and wine service. Completely revised and updated, this new edition of the critically acclaimed guide features more comprehensive coverage of the wine regions of the world, grape varietals, winemaking, purchasing, tasting, service, and pairing." (Publisher's note)

"This new edition of the critically acclaimed guide features more comprehensive coverage of the wine regions of the world, grape varietals, winemaking, purchasing, tasting, service, and pairing." Publisher's note

Includes bibliographical references and index

Winewise; your complete guide to understanding, selecting, and enjoying wine. Steven Kolpan, Brian H. Smith, and Michael A. Weiss, The Culinary Institute of America. Revised edition Houghton Mifflin Harcourt 2014 376 p. illustrations, maps $35 **641.2**

1. Wine and wine making
ISBN 0544334620; 9780544334625

LC 2014016316

This book, by Steven Kolpan, Brian Smith, and Michael Weiss, offers an "essential consumer guide to wine [that] features all the most current information for today's wine landscape. The authors, longtime wine educators at The Culinary Institute of America, have added all the latest and most relevant information to their award-winning book, including new picks for the best regional producers, off-the-beaten-path finds, and bargain bottles." (Publisher's note)

"Brevity is the soul of keeping a reader's attention, and a lot of ground is covered here by breaking out the material into hundreds of short entries grouped across 17 chapters. . . . Back-of-book gems include best practices for at-home wine tastings, a list of value wines, and full permission to enjoy wine from a box." Pub Wkly

Old, Marnie

Wine; a tasting course. Marnie Old. DK Publishing 2013 256 p. color ills, color maps (hardcover) $25 **641.2**

1. Wine and wine making 2. Wine tasting
ISBN 1465405887; 9781465405883

LC 2013454888

IACP Cookbook Award Finalist: Food and Beverage/Reference/Technical (2015)

This book, by Marnie Old, "[offers] a visual tour of wine styles, explaining the big-picture concepts, and encouraging readers to recognize the connections between wines. . . . [Old] challenges all the stuffy orthodoxies about wine, and teaches that best way to learn is through tasting." (Publisher's note)

Peynaud, Emile

The **taste** of wine; the art and science of wine appreciation. {by} Emile Peynaud; with the assistance of Jacques Blouin; translated from the French by Michael Schuster; with a foreword by Michael Broadbent. 2nd ed; Wiley 1996 xxi, 346p il $95 **641.2**

1. Wine and wine making
ISBN 0-471-11376-X

LC 96-24181

Original French edition 1980; first English translation published 1987 in the United Kingdom

"Long considered the definitive tome on winetasting." Libr J

Includes bibliographical references

Proulx, Annie, 1935-

Cider; making, using & enjoying sweet & hard cider. Annie Proulx & Lew Nichols. 3rd ed; Storey Pub. 2003 iv, 219 p.p illustrations $14.95 **641.2**

1. Cider 2. Brewing 3. Apples
ISBN 1580175201; 9781580175203

LC 2003272271

In this brewing cookbook, Annie Proulx and Lew Nichols "take you step-by-step through the cidermaking process, covering everything from the various types of apple presses to how to filter, fine, rack, and store your cider. They also provide recipes for making six types of cider---still, sparkling, champagne, barrel, French, and flavored---and advise you on which apples to use to achieve particular flavor qualities." (Publisher's note)

Risen, Clay

American Whiskey, Bourbon & Rye; A Guide to the Nation's Favorite Spirit. by Clay Risen. Sterling Pub Co Inc 2013 304 p. color illustrations $24.95 **641.2**

1. Whiskey 2. Alcoholic beverages
ISBN 1402798407; 9781402798405

This book, by Clay Risen, is a "guide devoted solely to US-made whiskey, rye, and bourbon. Arranged alphabetically by distillery and/or brand, it offers histories, ratings, and tasting notes for over 200 whiskeys. Each main account includes the name and address of the maker, including website URL and contact information, along with its various products." (Publisher's note)

"Risen . . . deftly combines history and assessment in this informative volume that covers more than 200 of the titular spirits." LJ

Includes bibliographical references (pages 281-284) and index

Tardi, Alan

Champagne, uncorked; the house of Krug and the timeless allure of the world's most celebrated drink. Alan Tardi. PublicAffairs 2016 296 p. illustrations (chiefly color) (hardcover) $26.99 **641.2**

1. Alcohol 2. Wine and wine making 3. Champagne (Wine)
ISBN 161039688X; 9781610396882; 9781610396899

LC 2016007400

In this book author "Alan Tardi journeys into the heartland of the world's most beloved wine. Anchored by the year he spent inside the prestigious and secretive Krug winery in Reims, the story follows the creation of the superlative Krug Grande Cuvée. Tardi also investigates the evocative history, quirky origins, and cultural significance of Champagne." (Publisher's note)

"Tardi deftly melds the process of creating champagne with the story of the winery from its earliest days. The result is fascinating, all the more so for the rich side stories captured in endnotes." LJ

Includes bibliographical references (page 263).

Wallace, Benjamin

The **billionaire's** vinegar; the mystery of the world's most expensive bottle of wine. Crown Publishers 2008 319p $24.95; pa $14.95 **641.2**

1. Wine and wine making
ISBN 978-0-307-33877-8; 0-307-33877-0; 978-0-307-33878-5 pa; 0-307-33878-9 pa

LC 2007-31645

"This is a gripping story, expertly handled by Benjamin Wallace who writes with wit and verve, drawing the reader into a subculture strewn with eccentrics and monomaniacs. . . . Full of detail that will delight wine lovers. It will also appeal to anyone who merely savours a great tale, well told." Economist

Includes bibliographical references

Zraly, Kevin

Windows on the World Complete Wine Course; Kevin Zraly. 30th anniv ed Sterling Epicure 2014 368 p. il $27.95 **641.2**

1. Wine and wine making
ISBN 1454913649; 9781454913641

Annual. First published 1985

IACP Cookbook Award Finalist: Wine, Beer and Spirits (2015)

Zraly's "definitive . . . bestselling guide to wine receives a complete update. As always, [Kevin] Zraly deftly takes the mystery out of wine, recommending hundreds of new wines . . . and providing the latest information on vintage wines. But this thoroughly redesigned edition also presents a beautiful tribute to the renowned restaurant, Windows on the World, where Zraly's course began." (Publisher's note)

"Zraly deftly takes the mystery out of choosing wine, explains the basics, and suggests hundreds of new wines to try. . . . [T]his thoroughly redesigned edition also presents a beautiful tribute to Windows on the World, the renowned restaurant where Zraly's course began. User-friendly smartphone tags and audio guides are featured throughout." Publisher's note

Windows on the World complete wine course; 2010 ed.; Sterling 2009 338p il map $27.95 **641.2**
1. Wine and wine making
ISBN 978-1-4027-6767-8
Annual. First published 1985

Looks at how and where wine is made and how this affects its quality and pricing, including information on how the professionals taste and rate wine and a country-by-country tour of the latest vintages.

"The casual browser will find fascinating trivia and facts about wine in numerous sidebars, but may not be able to resist becoming involved in the main text, making this difficult to put down. Highly recommended for all wine connoisseurs." Libr J

641.22 Wine

★ The **Oxford** companion to wine; edited by Jancis Robinson; assistant editor, Julia Harding; advisory editor, viticulture: Richard E. Smart; advisory editors, oenology: Valérie Lavigne & Denis Dubourdieu. Oxford University Press 2015 xlvii, 859 p.p color illustrations, maps (hardcover) $65 **641.22**
1. Wine and wine making
ISBN 9780198705383; 0198705387
LC 2015941385

This book, edited by Jancis Robinson with Julia Harding, part of the publisher's "Oxford Companions" series, is the fourth edition of the work, which "presents almost 4,000 entries on every wine-related topic imaginable, from regions and grape varieties to the owners, connoisseurs, growers, and tasters in wine through the ages; from viticulture and oenology to the history of wine, from its origins to the present day." (Publisher's note)

"This hefty volume is certain not just to answer both broad and obscure questions on viniculture, but also to pique the interest of the reader who dips into its pages." LJ

Includes bibliographical references

641.23 Brewed and malted beverages

Huckelbridge, Dane

The **United** States of beer; a freewheeling history of the all-American drink. Dane Huckelbridge. HarperCollins 2016 289 p. illustrations (hbk.) $25.99 **641.23**
1. Beer 2. Brewing 3. United States -- Civilization
ISBN 0062389750; 9780062389756
LC 2016302473

This book, by Dane Huckelbridge, offers a "cultural history [that] charts the . . . complex story of our favorite alcoholic drink, showing how America has been under the influence of beer at almost every stage. From the earliest Native American corn brew (called chicha) to the waves of immigrants who brought with them their unique brewing traditions, to the seemingly infinite varieties of craft-brewed suds found on tap today, beer has claimed an outsized place in our culture." (Publisher's note)

"The author's breezy style is a perfect match for his subject." LJ

Includes bibliographical references (pages [271]-277) and index.

641.3 Food

Adarme, Adrianna

The **year** of cozy; 125 Recipes, Crafts, and Other Homemade Adventures. Adrianna Adarme. Rodale Books 2015 259 p. color illustrations (trade hardcover) $24.99 **641.3**
1. Cooking 2. Handicraft 3. Comfort food 4. Do-it-yourself work
ISBN 1623365104; 9781623365103
LC 2015034972

This book, by Adrianna Adarme, presents "recipes and projects. . . . Organized by the months of the year and by categories as 'Live,' 'Do,' and 'Make,' [it] offers ideas for activities, recipes, and DIY projects that make the little moments in life just as exciting as the big. Adarme gives us special (but totally doable) things we can do for others and ourselves. From quick recipes to easy crafts, she focuses on simple, inexpensive undertakings that have a big reward: happiness." (Publisher's note)

Barber, Dan

★ The **third** plate; field notes on the future of food. by Dan Barber. The Penguin Press 2014 496 p. illustrations (hardback) $29.95 **641.3**
1. Agriculture 2. Natural foods 3. Eating customs 4. Seasonal cooking
ISBN 1594204071; 9781594204074
LC 2013039966

James Beard Foundation Award Winner: Writing and Literature (2015)

This book, by Dan Barber, advocates for "an integrated system of vegetable, grain, and livestock production that is fully supported--in fact, dictated--by what we choose to cook for dinner. The third plate is where good farming and good food intersect. While the third plate is a novelty in America, Barber demonstrates that this way of eating is rooted in worldwide tradition." (Publisher's note)

"In this bold and impassioned analysis, Barber insists that chefs have the power to transform American cuisine to achieve a sustainable and nutritious future." Kirkus

Includes bibliographical references and index

Best food writing 2014; edited by Holly Hughes. Da Capo Lifelong Books 2014 373 p. (paperback) $15.99 **641.3**
1. Food writing
ISBN 0738217913; 9780738217918

This book on food writing, edited by Holly Hughes, "offers the tastiest prose of the year, from a range of voices:

food writing stars, James Beard Award winners, writer-chefs, bestselling authors, and up-and-coming bloggers alike. With new sections devoted to 'A Table for Everyone' and 'Back to Basics,' you'll find a topic and a flavor for every appetite." (Publisher's note)

"Recommended for all libraries, this collection has something for connoisseurs, short story fans, and anyone hungry for a good read." LJ

Bittman, Mark

The **food** matters cookbook; 500 revolutionary recipes for better living. Simon & Schuster 2010 645p $35; ebook $16.99   **641.3**
   1. Food 2. Health 3. Cooking 4. Nutrition
   ISBN 978-1-4391-2023-1; 978-1-4391-4123-6 ebook
                                              LC 2010-28623
The author "provides a rational approach to eating that not only improves health but also helps the environment. Extolling the benefits of a plant-heavy diet, Bittman offers more than 500 healthful recipes that feature unprocessed fruits, vegetables, legumes, nuts, and whole grains and reduce all types of meat to backup players. In addition, he shares five basic principles for sane eating that are easy to implement and understand as well as an unusually helpful pantry section and handy charts for substituting produce and seafood by season. . . . Practical and balanced, this collection will shape the way we cook at home for years to come." Publ Wkly

Blount, Roy

Save room for pie; food songs and chewy ruminations. Roy Blount, Jr. Sarah Crichton Books/ Farrar, Straus & Giroux 2016 304 p. (hardcover) $26   **641.3**
   1. Food 2. Wit and humor 3. Food -- Anecdotes 4. Food in literature
   ISBN 9780374175207
                                              LC 2015036049
In this book, the author and comedian Roy Blount Jr. "applies his much-praised wit and charm to a rich and fundamental topic: food. As a lifelong eater, Blount always got along easy with food. . . . But food doesn't exist in a vacuum; there's the global climate and the global economy to consider, not to mention Blount's chronic sinusitis, which constricts his sense of smell, and consequently his taste buds." (Publisher's note)

"Eminently quotable, informative, and entertaining, Blount makes for a genial host, regaling the reader with story after story." Pub Wkly

Includes bibliographical references

Britton, Sarah

My new roots; Sarah Britton. Clarkson Potter/Publishers 2015 256 p. color illustrations $29.99   **641.3**
   1. Plants 2. Cooking 3. Cooking (Natural foods)
   ISBN 0804185387; 9780804185387
                                              LC 2014018135
This book by Sarah Britton "is the ultimate guide to revitalizing one's health and palate, one delicious recipe at a time: no fad diets or gimmicks here. Whether readers are newcomers to natural foods or are already devotees,

they will discover how easy it is to eat healthfully and happily when whole foods and plants are at the center of every plate." (Publisher's note)

Chaplin, Amy

★ **At** home in the whole food kitchen; celebrating the art of eating well. Amy Chaplin. Roost Books, an imprint of Shambhala Publications, Inc. 2014 386 p. color illustrations hbk $35   **641.3**
   1. Cookbooks 2. Cooking -- Natural foods 3. Natural foods
   ISBN 1611800854; 9781611800852
                                              LC 2013043411
   IACP Cookbook Award Finalist: Julia Child First Book (2015)
   IACP Cookbook Award: Health & Special Diet (2015)
   James Beard Foundation Award: Vegetable Focused and Vegetarian (2015)
This natural foods cookbook, by Amy Chaplin, offers a "vegetarian cookbook with all the tools you need to be at home in your kitchen, cooking in the most nourishing and delicious ways--from the foundations of stocking a pantry and understanding your ingredients, to preparing elaborate seasonal feasts." (Publisher's note)

"After introducing whole food pantry essentials ranging from ancient grains to superfoods, [Chaplin] presents mostly vegan and gluten-free recipes. . . . [She] also offers lifestyle advice, weighing in on the benefits of cleansing and eating organic." LJ

Includes bibliographical references and index

Crosby, Guy

The **science** of good cooking; master 50 simple concepts to enjoy a lifetime of success in the kitchen. the editors at America's Test Kitchen and Guy Crosby; illustrations by Michael Newhouse and John Burgoyne. America's Test Kitchen 2012 486 p. $40   **641.3**
   1. Food 2. Cooking 3. Cookbooks
   ISBN 1933615982; 9781933615981
                                              LC 2012012807
This book by the editors of America's Test Kitchen and Guy Crosby, part of the Cook's Illustrated Cookbooks series, "brings science to the stove. . . . In addition to explaining how food science works (and why you should care), 'The Science of Good Cooking' shows you the science. This book brings you into the test kitchen with 50 . . . experiments engineered to illustrate (and illuminate) the science at work." (Publisher's note)

Darlington, Tenaya

Dibruno Bros. House of Cheese; by Tenaya Darlington; photographs by Jason Verney. 1st ed. Running Press 2013 256 p. (hardcover) $25.00   **641.3**
   1. Cheese
   ISBN 0762446048; 9780762446049
                                              LC 2012942524
In this book, Tenaya Darlington "draws on the offerings at long-established Philadelphia cheese monger Di Bruno Bros. and the expertise of its staff to highlight a range of cheeses according to such personalities as 'mountain men,' 'vixens,' 'quiet types,' and 'pierced punks.' . . . The descrip-

tion of each cheese briefly captures its history and its flavor, complemented with suggestions for beverage pairings and accompaniments." (Library Journal)

David, Laurie

The **family** cooks; 100+ recipes to get your family craving food that's simple, tasty, and incredibly good for you. Laurie David; foreword by Katie Couric. Rodale Books 2014 277 p. color illustrations (hardback) $27.99   **641.3**

    1. Nutrition 2. Cooking -- Natural foods 3. Families -- Nutrition 4. Cooking (Natural foods)

    ISBN 1623362504; 9781623362508

                  LC 2014003505

IACP Cookbook Award Finalist: Children, Youth and Family (2015)

In this cookbook, author Laurie David "inspires parents and kids to take control of what they eat by making it themselves. With her longtime collaborator, Kirstin Uhrenholdt, David offers more than 100 recipes that are simple, fast, 'low in the bad stuff and high in the good stuff,' and designed to bring kids into the cooking process. The authors also demystify cooking terms and break down basic prep techniques, creating stress-free meals that foster health, togetherness, and happy palates." (Publisher's note)

"Written primarily for busy families with children, David's attractive guide to reclaiming the family dinner will also appeal to young couples and professionals trying to shop smarter and eat less-processed meals at home." LJ

Family cooks, one hundred plus recipes to get your family craving food that's simple, tasty, and incredibly good for you

100+ recipes to get your family craving food that's simple, tasty, and incredibly good for you

Del Mar Sacasa, María

The **quinoa** [keen-wah] cookbook; Maria del Mar Sacasa. HarperWave 2015 193 p. color illustrations (hardback) $23.99   **641.3**

    1. Quinoa 2. Cooking 3. Cooking (Quinoa)

    ISBN 0062411217; 9780062411211

                  LC 2015009849

In this book by Maria del Mar Sacasa readers "will find more than seventy-five recipes that utilize quinoa in unexpected, creative, and delicious ways. From Nutty Quinoa Granola to Breakfast Coconut Quinoa; Roasted Peppers with Lamb-Quinoa Stuffing to Matzo Ball–Style Quinoa Soup; Charred Romaine Greek Salad with Quinoa-Crusted Feta to Quinoa, Sweet Potato, and Walnut Veggie Burgers; Quinoa, Cashew, and Orange Blossom Brittle." (Publisher's note)

Quinoa cookbook

Foer, Jonathan Safran

Eating animals. Little, Brown and Company 2009 341p $25.99; pa $14.99   **641.3**

    1. Vegetarianism

    ISBN 978-0-316-06990-8; 978-0-316-06988-5 pa

                  LC 2009-34434

The novelist presents a critique of the food industry and explores arguments in favor of humane agriculture and vegetarianism.

"A blend of solid—and discomforting—reportage with fierce advocacy that will make committed carnivores squeal." Kirkus

Includes bibliographical references

Forte, Sara

The **sprouted** kitchen; a tastier take on whole foods. Sara Forte; photography by Hugh Forte. Ten Speed Press 2012 241 p. color illustrations (hbk.) $25   **641.3**

    1. Cookbooks 2. Cooking -- Natural foods 3. Cooking (Cereals) 4. Cooking (Natural foods) 5. Sugar-free diet -- Recipes

    ISBN 1607741148; 1607741156; 9781607741145; 9781607741152

                  LC 2012008143

This cookbook by Sara Forte "features 100 of her most mouthwatering recipes. Illustrated by her photographer husband, Hugh Forte, [it] celebrates the simple beauty of seasonal foods with original recipes--plus a few favorites from her popular Sprouted Kitchen food blog. The collection features tasty snacks on the go like Granola Protein Bars, gluten-free brunch options like Cornmeal Cakes with Cherry Compote, dinner party dishes like Seared Scallops on Black Quinoa." (Publisher's note)

Tastier take on whole foods

The **sprouted** kitchen bowl and spoon; simple and inspired whole foods recipes to savor and share. Sara Forte; photography by Hugh Forte. Ten Speed Press 2015 256 p. color illustrations $25   **641.3**

    1. Salads 2. Cooking -- Natural foods 3. Cooking (Natural foods)

    ISBN 1607746557; 9781607746553

                  LC 2014036843

In this cookbook "author Sara Forte turns her attention to bowl food, which combines vegetables, whole grains, and lean proteins in one vessel to make a simple, complete, and nutritious meal. . . . Sara offers delicious, produce-forward recipes for every meal, such as Golden Quinoa and Butternut Breakfast Bowl; Spring Noodles with Artichokes, Pecorino, and Charred Lemons; Turkey Meatballs in Tomato Sauce; and Cocoa Nib Pavlovas with Mixed Berries." (Publisher's note)

"Vegetarians and flexitarians will find plenty to love here, as will vegans, though they'll have fewer choices. Readers interested in healthy bowl foods may also like Ruth Tal and Jennifer Houston's Fresh: New Vegetarian and Vegan Recipes from Fresh Restaurants." LJ

Ganeshram, Ramin

Future Chefs; recipes by tomorrow's cooks across the nation and the world. Ramin Ganeshram; photography by Jean Paul Vellotti. Rodale 2014 xi, 276 p.p color illustrations (paperback) $24.99 **641.3**

    1. Cooking 2. Teenagers -- United States 3. Cooking -- United States 4. Teenage cooks -- United States

    ISBN 1623362067; 9781623362065

                  LC 2014025322

IACP Cookbook Award Winner: Children, Youth and Family (2015)

This cookbook, by Ramin Ganeshram, is a "curated collection of 150 recipes drawn from the experience and kitchens of young cooks all over America. . . . Whether they've taken to it because of necessity, inspiration, or sheer passion, these are kids, teens, and tweens who are very serious about food." (Publisher's note)

Future chefs

Hamilton, Gabrielle

★ **Prune**; Gabrielle Hamilton. Random House Inc 2014 576 p. illustrations (chiefly color) (hardback) $45   **641.3**
1. French cooking 2. American cooking 3. Prune (Restaurant)
ISBN 0812994094; 9780812994094
LC 2014003617

This cookbook, by Gabrielle Hamilton, is "filled with signature recipes from her celebrated New York City restaurant Prune. . . . A self-trained cook turned James Beard Award–winning chef, . . . Hamilton opened Prune on New York's Lower East Side fifteen years ago. . . . A deeply personal and gracious restaurant, in both menu and philosophy, Prune uses the elements of home cooking and elevates them in unexpected ways." (Publisher's note)

" Recipes range from a complex cold pork with tuna sauce to a simple butter-and-sugar sandwich. . . . Despite the book's address to fellow restaurateurs, skilled home chefs can find a number of ways to profit from a fair number of Hamilton's creations." Booklist

Hamshaw, Gena

Choosing raw; making raw foods part of the way you eat. Gena Hamshaw. Da Capo Lifelong, a member of the Perseus Books Group 2014 276 p. color illustrations (paperback) $19.99   **641.3**
1. Veganism 2. Cooking -- Natural foods 3. Cooking (Natural foods)
ISBN 0738216879; 9780738216874
LC 2014017394

This book, by Gena Hamshaw, "addresses the questions and concerns for any newcomer to veganism; makes a plant-based diet with many raw options feel easy instead of intimidating; provides a starter kit of delicious recipes; and offers a mainstream, scientifically sound perspective on healthy living." (Publisher's note)

"Among vegan cookbooks, this volume will appeal most to those who are interested in better understanding a vegan diet and curious about raw foods. Cooks looking for vegan recipes without the raw focus have lots of other great recent titles to choose from, such as The Oh She Glows Cookbook by and Isa Does It by Isa Chandra Moskowitz." LJ

Includes bibliographical references and index

Hemphill, Ian

The **spice** & herb bible; Ian Hemphill with recipes by Kate Hemphill. 2nd ed; Robert Rose 2014 800 p. color illustrations (bound) $49.95   **641.3**
1. Herbs 2. Spices 3. Cooking -- Herbs 4. Cookbooks
ISBN 0778804968; 9780778804963
LC 2014472224

James Beard Foundation Award Nominee: Reference and Scholarship (2015)

This cookbook, by Ian Hemphill, with recipes by Kate Hemphill, "is a fascinating and authoritative guide. Hemphill describes a wide range of global herbs and spices used in modern kitchens either alone or in wonderful blends. He completely demystifies the art of combining herbs and spices and home cooks can meet and enjoy a world of flavors previously found only at internationally inspired restaurants." (Publisher's note)

"This truly beautiful and quite comprehensive volume will appeal to lovers of food, amateur and professional chefs, and everyone in between. While other works may address similar information, the author gives a personal touch to this one, which creates an uncommon warmth." LJ

The spice and herb bible

Hoffmann, James

The **world** atlas of coffee; from beans to brewing--coffees explored, explained, and enjoyed. by James Hoffmann. Firefly Books Ltd 2014 256 p. color illustrations; maps $35   **641.3**
1. Coffee 2. Coffeehouses 3. Coffee industry
ISBN 1770854703; 9781770854703

This book on coffee, by James Hoffmann, "presents the bean in full-color photographs and concise, informative text. It shows the origins of coffee -- where it is grown, the people who grow it; and the cultures in which coffee is a way of life -- and the world of consumption -- processing, grades, the consumer and the modern culture of coffee." (Publisher's note)

"An unusual offering that will be of value in collections serving agriculture, business, and nutrition students." LJ

Jurafsky, Dan

The **language** of food; a linguist reads the menu. Dan Jurafsky. W.W. Norton & Co. Inc. 2014 272 p. illustrations, maps (hardcover) $26.95   **641.3**
1. Linguistics 2. Eating customs 3. English language -- Terms and phrases 4. Food -- History 5. Food habits -- History 6. Food -- Terms and phrases 7. English language -- Etymology 8. Dinners and dining -- Terms and phrases
ISBN 0393240835; 9780393240832
LC 2014020202

James Beard Foundation Award Nominee: Writing and Literature (2015)

In this book, author "Dan Jurafsky peels away the mysteries from the foods we think we know. Thirteen chapters evoke the joy and discovery of reading a menu dotted with the sharp-eyed annotations of a linguist. From ancient recipes preserved in Sumerian song lyrics to colonial shipping routes that first connected East and West, Jurafsky paints a vibrant portrait of how our foods developed." (Publisher's note)

"A highly informative and entertaining compendium of food and word facts sure to appeal to foodies and etymologists alike." Kirkus

Includes bibliographical references and index

Katzinger, Jennifer

Gluten-free & vegan pie; more than 50 sweet and savory pies to make at home. Jennifer Katzinger; photographs by Charity Burggraaf. Sasquatch Books

2013 xvii, 140 p.p color illustrations (alk. paper) $23.95 **641.3**

1. Pies 2. Veganism 3. Cookbooks 4. Gluten-free diet 5. Vegetarian cooking 6. Gluten-free diet -- Recipes

ISBN 1570618682; 9781570618680

LC 2012050141

This book, by Jennifer Katzinger with photographs by Charity Burggraaf, offers "more than 55 gluten-free and vegan pie recipes. . . . Baking your favorite pies without dairy, eggs, gluten, or animal products calls for a different approach to both fillings and dough. Here you'll find techniques and tips for mixing and working with dough that doesn't contain butter or lard, and for luscious fillings that contain neither cream nor egg." (Publisher's note)

"Katzinger presents a breadth of pastry doughs, press-in crusts, and sweet and savory fillings that can be used to make pies, turnovers, cobblers, crisps, galettes, tarts, and more." LJ

Gluten-free and vegan pie

★ **Larousse** gastronomique; the world's greatest culinary encyclopedia. with the assistance of the Gastronomic Committee, president Joël Robuchon. Clarkson Potter Publishers 2009 1206p il map $90 **641.3**

1. French cooking 2. Reference books 3. Food -- Encyclopedias 4. Cooking -- Encyclopedias

ISBN 978-0-307-46491-0

Original French edition published 1938 under the authorship of Prosper Montagné; first United States edition 1961

"The alphabetical entries range in length from a few sentences to several pages. They cover types of food (Apples, Locusts); cooking techniques (Braising, Grilling); famous chefs (Auguste Escoffier, Alice Waters); culinary jobs (Maître d'hôtel, Sommelier); countries (China, Greece); and tools of the trade (Knife, Saucepan). . . . This is an essential resource for most library reference collections as well as a wonderful book to browse." Booklist

Le, Stephen

One hundred million years of food; what our ancestors ate and why it matters today. Stephen Le. Picador 2015 320 p. (hardcover) $26 **641.3**

1. Nutrition 2. Food -- History 3. Natural foods 4. Prehistoric peoples -- Food

ISBN 9781250050410

LC 2015029501

This book, by Stephen Le, offers a "tour through the evolution of the human diet, and how we can improve our health by understanding our complicated history with food. . . . Travelling around the world to places as far-flung as Vietnam, Kenya, India, and the US, Stephen Le introduces us to people who are growing, cooking, and eating food using both traditional and modern methods, striving for a sustainable, healthy diet." (Publisher's note)

"An intriguing viewpoint on how dietary practices have changed over time, but further research is needed to support some of Le's healthy living recommendations." Library Journal

McLagan, Jennifer

Odd bits; how to cook the rest of the animal. photography by Leigh Beisch. Ten Speed Press 2011 248p il $35 **641.3**

1. Cooking -- Meat

ISBN 978-1-58008-334-8

LC 2011-11575

A "unique, informative, and readable cookbook. The ingredients used for the 100 recipes include lungs, necks, spleens, tongues, cheeks, testicles, and feet, as well as a few more common cuts (ribs, brisket, and shanks). In her introduction, McLagan traces the history of eating meat and why in earlier times the odd bits were considered the prime parts. In the last 75 to 100 years, most of these parts have been discarded or used for cat and dog food in the United States. McLagan encourages readers with a detailed and clear discussion of how to choose, prepare, and cook them. She draws the line at eyeballs and notes that lungs are not sold in the United States." Libr J

Medrich, Alice

★ **Flavor** flours; Alice Medrich with Maya Klein. Artisan Books 2014 368 p. Illustrations $35 **641.3**

1. Flour 2. Baking 3. Cookbooks

ISBN 1579655130; 9781579655136

LC 2014004631

IACP Cookbook Award Finalist: Baking: Savory or Sweet (2015)

James Beard Foundation Award Winner: Baking and Dessert (2015)

In this cookbook, author "Alice Medrich applies her baking precision and . . . palate to flavor flours--wheat-flour alternatives including rice flour, oat flour, corn flour, sorghum flour, teff, and more. The resulting (gluten-free!) recipes show that baking with alternate flours adds an extra dimension of flavor." (Publisher's note)

Mitchell, Andie

Eating in the middle; Andie Mitchell. Clarkson Potter 2016 240 p. color illustrations $27.99 **641.3**

1. Diet 2. Eating habits 3. Food 4. Health 5. Nutrition

ISBN 9780770433277; 0770433278

LC 2015034879

In this cookbook, author Andie Mitchell "gives readers the dishes that helped her reach her goals and maintain her new size. In 80 recipes, she shows how she eats: mostly healthy meals that are packed with flavor, like Lemon Roasted Chicken with Moroccan Couscous and Butternut Squash Salad with Kale and Pomegranate, and then the 'sometimes' foods, the indulgences such as Peanut Butter Mousse Pie with Marshmallow Whipped Cream." (Publisher's note)

"Mitchell's middle ground philosophy is woven into the chatty, bloggish storytelling, and abundant recipe notes describe her journey away from emotional eating and toward a practical, balanced approach to food, but this cookbook is not a diet book." Pub Wkly

O'Connell, John

The **Book** of Spice; From Anise to Zedoary. by John O'Connell. W.W. Norton & Co Inc. 2016 248 p. illustrations $26.95 **641.3**

1. Spices 2. Spices -- History

ISBN 1681771527; 9781681771526

This book, by John O'Connell, "reveals the amazing history of spices both familiar and esoteric. . . . O'Connell's erudite chapters combine history with insights into art, religion, medicine, science, and is richly seasoned with anecdotes and recipes." (Publisher's note)

"Libraries should have a variety of spice books, and this one not only supplies a piquant perspective but makes readers want to get in the kitchen and start cooking." LJ

Includes bibliographical references (pages 254-272).

Olmsted, Larry

Real food/fake food; Why You Don't Know What You're Eating and What You Can Do about It. Larry Olmsted. Algonquin Books of Chapel Hill 2016 336 p. illustrations $27.95 **641.3**

1. Fraud 2. Nutrition 3. Food additives 4. Artificial foods 5. Consumer education 6. Fraud -- Popular works 7. Nutrition. -- Popular works 8. Food additives -- Popular works 9. Food -- Quality -- Popular works 10. Artificial foods -- Popular works 11. Food substitutes -- Popular works 12. Consumer education -- Popular works

ISBN 9781616204211

LC 2016018797

This book by Larry Olmsted discusses "why real food matters and empowers consumers to make smarter choices. Olmsted brings readers into the unregulated food industry, revealing the shocking deception . . . from high-end foods . . . to everyday staples. . . . It's a massive bait . . . in which counterfeiting is rampant and in which the consumer . . . pays the price. . . . He travels to the sources of the real stuff to help us recognize what to look for, eat, and savor." (Publisher's note)

"A provocative yet grounded look at the U.S. food industry. Though the prospect of finding quality food products may prove increasingly challenging for most consumers, Olmsted provides encouraging tips to help navigate the many obstacles." Kirkus

Includes bibliographical references (pages 293-315).

Ornelas, Kriemhild Conee

The **Cambridge** world history of food; editors, Kenneth F. Kiple, Kriemhild Coneè Ornelas. Cambridge Univ. Press 2000 2v set $190 **641.3**

1. Diseases 2. Nutrition 3. Edible plants 4. Food -- History

ISBN 0-521-40216-6

LC 00-57181

"The two volumes are arranged in eight parts covering the diet of early man, staple foods, dietary liquids, nutrients and food-related disorders, food and drink around the world, nutrition and health, current food-related issues and concluding with a dictionary of plant foods. . . . The Cambridge World History of Food is a thorough study of a topic that

is eternally popular. It should become a standard source in reference collections." Booklist

Includes bibliographical references

The **Oxford** encyclopedia of food and drink in America; Andrew F. Smith, editor in chief. Oxford University Press 2004 2v il set $250 **641.3**

1. Beverages 2. Reference books 3. Food 4. Cookery, American 5. Food -- Encyclopedias

ISBN 0-19-515437-1; 978-0-19-515437-5

LC 2003-24873

In some 800 articles, this work "covers the significant events, inventions, and social movements in American history that have affected the way Americans view, prepare, and consume food and drink. In an A-Z format, this two-volume set details the regions, people, ingredients, foods, drinks, publications, advertising, companies, historical periods, and political and economic aspects pertinent to American cuisine."

"Whether readers make a living studying culinary traditions or just enjoy eating, they'll find this book a marvel. . . . For food lovers of all stripes, this work inspires, enlightens and entertains." Publ Wkly

Pierson, Stephanie

The **brisket** book; a love story with recipes. photographs by Roger Sherman. Andrews McMeel Publishing 2011 208p il $29.99 **641.3**

1. Cooking -- Meat

ISBN 978-1-4494-0697-4

LC 2011-921500

"The book is both humorous and serious: from a section called Found in Translation—how to order brisket in sixteen languages—to The Last Brisket, a joke by David Minkoff. Pierson shares cooking tips, chef interviews, information on beef cuts, different cooking techniques and more than 30 brisket recipes. It took Stephanie a year to select and test the recipes that are included in the book. They come from notable chefs, cookbook authors, cowboys, pit masters and home cooks." KosherEye

Reese, Jennifer

Make the bread, buy the butter; what you should and shouldn't cook from scratch--over 120 recipes for the best homemade foods. Jennifer Reese. 1st Free Press hardcover ed; Free Press 2011 295 p. il $24 **641.3**

1. Cookbooks 2. Natural foods 3. Agricultural processing 4. Processed foods -- Costs 5. Natural foods -- Processing

ISBN 1451605870; 9781451605877; 9781451605891 ebook

LC 2011009088

This book, by Jennifer Reese, "gives 120 recipes with . . . practical yet . . . fun 'Make or buy' recommendations. Reese . . . relates her food and animal husbandry adventures. . . . Her tales include living with a backyard full of . . . chickens, . . . ducks, and . . . baby goats. . . . Here's . . . what is involved in a truly homemade life--with the good news that you shouldn't try to make everything yourself--and how to get the most out of your time in the kitchen." (Publisher's note)

Rodale, Maria

Scratch; Home Cooking for Everyone Made Simple, Fun, and Totally Delicious. by Maria Rodale. St. Martin's Press 2016 384 p. color illustrations $35; (ebook) $27.99   **641.3**

1. Cooking

ISBN 1623366437; 9781623366438; 9781623366445

This cookbook, by Maria Rodale, "is full of comfort food recipes that aren't focused on any one healthy trend, but are instead innately healthy. . . . Besides sharing her family's favorite recipes, Maria's book also gives you a peek into her life as a Rodale, with personal family portraits and stories." (Publisher's note)

"This down-to-earth, totally accessible cookbook will take any cook from breakfast to dessert." Pub Wkly

Rosenblum, Mort

Chocolate: a bittersweet saga of dark and light. North Point Press 2005 290p il $24; pa $14 **641.3**

1. Chocolate

ISBN 0-86547-635-7; 0-86547-730-2 pa

LC 2004-54734

The author "unveils chocolate's history and its various incarnations, including in his fresh and insightful discussions the origins of mole; the differences between, say, Hershey's kisses and Valrhona's products; the invention of Nutella; and the small boutique chocolate artisans found nearly everywhere. . . . A compelling and tasty read." Booklist

Sacks, Stefanie

What the fork are you eating? an action plan for your pantry and plate. Stefanie Sacks, MS, CNS, CDN. Jeremy P. Tarcher/Penguin, a member of Penguin Group, (USA) 2014 400 p. (paperback) $16.95   **641.3**

1. Nutrition 2. Natural foods 3. Food additives 4. Grocery shopping

ISBN 039916796X; 9780399167966

LC 2014027015

In this book, by Stefanie Sacks, "we learn exactly what the most offensive ingredients in our food are and how we can remove (or at least minimize) them in our diets. Sacks gives us an aisle-by-aisle rundown of how to shop for healthier items and create simple, nutritious, and delicious meals, including fifty original recipes." (Publisher's note)

"While Sacks writes in a similar style to Marion Nestle and Michael Pollan, her book is more accessible and practical for people seeking the motivation and tools to follow a healthier lifestyle, emphasizing that even very small changes in diet can make a big difference in health. Although some readers may object to the mildly offensive language she deploys as part of her no-nonsense shtick, this is a valuable guide to evaluating, choosing, and preparing food for wellness." LJ

Includes bibliographical references and index

Schatzker, Mark

The Dorito effect; the surprising new truth about food and flavor. Mark Schatzker. Simon & Schuster 2015 272 p. (hardcover) $27   **641.3**

1. Nutrition 2. Food industry -- United States 3. Junk food 4. Food portions 5. Reducing diets

ISBN 1476724210; 9781476724218; 9781476724232

LC 2014044543

This book by Mark Schatzker "examines the state of the American food industry and its role in the rising obesity epidemic. He contends that foods such as tomatoes are losing flavor owing to modern agricultural practices; meanwhile, 'things' such as chips and fast food have become highly flavored to taste more appealing. . . .Schatzker makes his case for curing this problem by seeking out several foods that were specifically cultivated for their taste." (Library Journal)

"This is a provocative new take on American eating." Booklist

Tea; history, terroirs, varieties. edited by Kevin Gascoyne, Francois Marchand, Jasmin Desharnais, and Hugo Americi. Firefly Books 2014 271 p. color ills., color maps (pbk.) $24.95   **641.3**

1. Tea 2. Tearooms 3. Tea industry 4. Thé 5. Cooking (Tea) 6. Tea -- History 7. Cuisine (Thé) 8. Thé -- Histoire

ISBN 1770853197; 9781770853195

LC 2014415257

This book on tea, edited by Kevin Gascoyne, Francois Marchand, Jasmin Desharnais, and Hugo Americi, is "concise and authoritative with dozens of photographs and images of the teas themselves, revealing the surprising variety of color and opacity of each variety. The book is an escorted tour of the world's tea-growing countries -- China, Japan, Taiwan, India, Sri Lanka, Nepal, Vietnam and East Africa." (Publisher's note)

"While there is no shortage of tea-related tomes, this definitive guide will appeal to die-hard tea enthusiasts interested in learning about the modern, global industry as well as the history and enjoyment of this ubiquitous beverage." LJ

Includes bibliographical references (page 269) and index

The **tea** book. Dk Pub 2015 224 p. $22   **641.3**

ISBN 1465436065; 9781465436061

This book "is your world tour of the art of tea. Visit tea plantations from India to Kenya and explore maps of the world's most important growing regions. Learn to recognize tea-leaf varietals and spot the best types from each region. Recreate a Japanese tea ceremony with a guide to storied traditions and practical implements. Discover the health benefits of green tea. Craft the perfect Chai tea." (Publisher's note)

White, Dana Angelo

First bites; superfoods for babies and toddlers. Dana Angelo White, MS, RD, ATC. Published by the Penguin Group 2015 192 p. (paperback) $14.95   **641.3**

1. Toddlers 2. Infants -- Nutrition 3. Infants -- Health and hygiene 4. Baby foods 5. Toddlers -- Nutrition

ISBN 0399172467; 9780399172465

LC 2014040028

Author Dana Angelo White presents this book " introducing 50 superfoods into baby and toddler diets, with tips and recipes to show parents how to raise healthy eaters for life. Recipes are designed to help to foster healthy eating habits and create a diet filled with 50 fresh, minimally processed superfoods that are just as delicious as they are healthy." (Publisher's note)

"Most parents eventually conclude that little ones can eat whatever healthy dish you are enjoying (just smash up or blend), but White's focus on the known 50 superfoods will get everyone off to a great start. Bon Appetit!" LJ

World cheese book; edited by Juliet Harbutt. DK Publishing 2015 352 p. il map (pbk.) $25 **641.3**
1. Cheese 2. Cooking -- Cheese 3. Cooking (Cheese)
ISBN 1465436057; 9781465436054

LC 2015413323

This book, edited by Juliet Harbutt, is a "comprehensive guide to cheese and covers more world cheeses, with more photography, than any other book on the subject. Discover the flavor profile, shape, and texture of just about every imaginable cheese in this exhaustive, at-a-glance reference." (Publisher's note)

"A must for cheese connoisseurs, this title will delight with its extensive detail and full-color, up-close pictures. The tasting and enjoyment notes for each entry will guide the new cheese enthusiast." LJ

Includes bibliographical references

Wrangham, Richard W.
Catching fire; how cooking made us human. [by] Richard Wrangham. Basic Books 2009 309p $26.95 **641.3**
1. Fire 2. Cooking 3. Eating customs 4. Prehistoric peoples
ISBN 978-0-465-01362-3

LC 2009-1742

This "is a plainspoken and thoroughly gripping scientific essay that presents nothing less than a new theory of human evolution. . . . [This book] contains serious science yet is related in direct, no-nonsense prose. It is toothsome, skillfully prepared brain food." N Y Times (Late N Y Ed)

Includes bibliographical references

Ying, Chris
The **wurst** of Lucky peach; a treasury of encased meat. Chris Ying and the editors of Lucky peach. Clarkson Potter/Publishers 2016 240 p. illustrations (chiefly color) (hardcover) $26 **641.3**
1. Sausages
ISBN 9780804187770

LC 2015038559

In this book, Chris Ying and the editors of Lucky Peach present "a cookbook as a scrapbook, stuffed with curious local specialties, like cevapi, a caseless sausage that's traveled all the way from the Balkans to underneath the M tracks in Ridgewood, Queens; a look into the great sausage trails of the world, from Bavaria to Texas Hill Country and beyond; and the ins and outs of making your own sausages, including fresh chorizo." (Publisher's note)

"Refreshingly enthusiastic about their subject material (and damning when the situation calls for it), the team has done a great favor for the world's carnivores." Pub Wkly

641.302   Health foods

Hill, McKel
Nutrition Stripped; 100 Whole-Food Recipes Made Deliciously Simple. by McKel Hill. HarperCollins 2016 304 p. color illustrations (ebook) $22.99; $23.99 **641.302**
1. Cooking
ISBN 9780062419934; 0062419927; 9780062419927

This book, by McKel Hill, "based on the popular Nutrition Stripped blog, featur[es] more than 100 exciting and good-for-you recipes and color photography throughout. . . . Drawing inspiration from nature, the turning of the seasons, the world of plants, nutrient dense foods and hidden gems in the world of superfoods, Hill celebrates simplicity, and shares her vast professional knowledge and expertise." (Publisher's note)

"Best known for the anti-inflammatory turmeric milk recipe on her healthy living site, Nutrition Stripped, Hill offers elixirs and more in her first cookbook. But this is more than a cookbook; it's a healthy living guide." Booklist

Lillien, Lisa
Hungry girl clean & hungry; all-natural recipes for clean eating in the real world. Lisa Lillien. St. Martin's Griffin 2016 348 p. illustrations (trade pbk.) $19.99 **641.302**
1. Cookbooks 2. Cooking -- Natural foods 3. Cooking (Natural foods) 4. Women -- Health and hygiene
ISBN 9780312676773

LC 2015048585

This cookbook, by Lisa Lillien, "gives mainstream America delicious, satisfying, and clean recipes, using healthy ingredients found in supermarkets everywhere. The best part? The recipes are so easy, anyone can make 'em! Featuring 90 vegetarian recipes, 108 gluten-free recipes, 56 recipes in 30 minutes or less, [and] 43 recipes with 5 ingredients or less." (Publisher's note)

"Most readers will simply rejoice at the fact that pumpkin spice waffles, barbecue meatloaf , and fudgy flourless chocolate cake are now legit diet foods." Pub Wkly

Seo, Danny
Naturally, delicious; 100 Recipes for Healthy Eats That Make You Happy. Danny Seo. Pam Krauss Books 2016 240 p. color illustrations (hardcover) $30 **641.302**
1. Cookbooks 2. Cooking -- Natural foods
ISBN 9781101905302

LC 2015038829

This cookbook by Danny Seo "will show home cooks that preparing healthy, delicious food on a daily basis doesn't have to feel like an expensive, time-consuming chore. By following Danny's emphasis on clever kitchen hacks, kitchen efficiency strategies, and eye-catching presentations, readers will be able to create simple, delicious meals with minimal effort and time, making eating healthfully and well a sustainable practice anyone can introduce to their everyday routine." (Publisher's note)

"Overall, this is an interesting approach to good-for-you food without sacrificing flavor and appeal." Pub Wkly

Ward, Tess

The **naked** cookbook; Tess Ward; photography by Columbus Leth. Ten Speed Press 2016 128 p. (hardcover) $24.99   **641.302**

1. Cookbooks 2. Cooking -- Natural foods 3. Health 4. Cooking (Natural foods)

ISBN 1607749947; 9781607749943

LC 2015039084

This cookbook, by Tess Ward, with photography by Columbus Leth, offers "a transformative approach to healthy eating that strips back one's diet to simple, clean, and pure foods that cleanse, restore, and nourish the body, featuring 60 recipes and a chapter on detoxing. . . . This is not a deprivation diet but an achievable lifestyle where food is enjoyed and celebrated in its purest form." (Publisher's note)

641.35   Vegetable juices

Dinki, Nikki

Meat on the side; Delicious Vegetable-Focused Recipes for Every Day. Nikki Dinki; photographs by Ellen Silverman. St. Martin's Griffin 2016 288 p. color illustrations (hardback) $27.99   **641.35**

1. Cooking -- Vegetables 2. Cooking (Vegetables)

ISBN 9781250067166

LC 2015043188

This cookbook, by Nikki Dinki, presents "100 recipes to put meat in the passenger seat. You won't miss the beef in these Eggplant Meatballs; you'll marvel that pasta can be made from a parsnip using just a peeler; and you'll never want traditional nachos again after trying Nikki's Cabbage Nachos." (Publisher's note)

"For those who like flexible recipes that can be both meaty and meatless, this cookbook provides excellent choices." LJ

641.36   Meat

Venezia, Ray

The **everyday** meat guide; a neighborhood butcher's advice book. Ray Venezia with Chris Peterson. Chronicle Books Llc 2016 184 p. illustrations $19.95   **641.36**

1. Meat 2. Cooking -- Meat

ISBN 9781452142883

LC 2015008240

This book "condenses [Ray] Venezia's expert advice from 25 years behind the butcher block, giving every weeknight shopper and grill enthusiast the need-to-know information on meat grades, best values, and common cuts for poultry, pork, lamb, veal, and beef. [It] includes easy-to-follow illustrations and instructions for the questions butchers are most often asked, plus a handy photo gallery for quick identification at the market." (Publisher's note)

"Venezia clearly and succinctly leads consumers through the butcher shop, from poultry—including ducks, geese, turkey, and, of course, chicken—right up to beef." LJ

641.4   Food preservation and storage

Barrow, Cathy

Mrs. Wheelbarrow's practical pantry; recipes and techniques for year-round preserving. Cathy Barrow; photographs by Christopher Hirsheimer and Melissa Hamilton. W.W. Norton & Co. Inc. 2014 432 p. color illustrations (hardcover) $35   **641.4**

1. Cooking 2. Canning and preserving

ISBN 0393240738; 9780393240733

LC 2014017291

IACP Cookbook Award Winner: Single Subject (2015)

In this book, author "Cathy Barrow presents a beautiful collection of essential preserving techniques for turning the fleeting abundance of the farmers' market into a well-stocked pantry full of canned fruits and vegetables, jams, stocks, soups, and more. Beyond the core techniques of water-bath canning, advanced techniques for pressure canning, salt-curing meats and fish, smoking, and even air-curing pancetta are broken down." (Publisher's note)

"Barrow offers a well-rounded look at home preserving and this book will appeal to those looking to expand their pantry." LJ

Includes bibliographical references and index

Complete book of home preserving; 400 delicious and creative recipes for today. edited by Judi Kingry and Lauren Devine. R. Rose 2006 448 p. 32 plates; color illustrations $22.95   **641.4**

1. Fruit -- Preservation 2. Canning and preserving 3. Vegetables -- Preservation 4. Cooking (Fruit) 5. Cooking (Vegetables)

ISBN 0778801314; 077880139X; 9780778801313; 9780778801399

LC 2007701974

This cookbook, edited by Judi Kingry and Lauren Devine, sponsored by the Ball Home Canning Products company, "includes comprehensive directions on safe canning and preserving methods plus lists of required equipment and utensils. [The book includes both] specific instructions for first-timers and handy tips for the experienced." (Publisher's note)

Home preserving

Costenbader, Carol W.

The **big** book of preserving the harvest; {foreword by Joanne Lamb Hayes} rev ed; Storey Bks. 2002 347p il pa $18.95   **641.4**

1. Canning and preserving

ISBN 1-58017-458-2

LC 2002-21172

First published 1997

In addition to recipes this book provides instructions for food preservation techniques, including canning, drying, freezing, the preparation of jams and jellies, pickles, relishes and chutneys, vinegars and seasonings, and cold storage. Includes a section on gift giving, directions on building a food dehydrator, a table of equivalents, and a conversion chart to metric measures

Includes bibliographical references

Field, Rick

The **Art** of preserving; authors, Lisa Atwood, Rebecca Courchesne, Rick Field; photographer, France Ruffenach. Weldon Owen 2010 239 p. col. ill. (pbk) $19.95   **641.4**

1. Food -- Preservation 2. Canning and preserving
ISBN 9781740899789; 9781616283834; 1616283831

This book, by Lisa Atwood, Rick Field, and Rebecca Courchesne, "[p]acked with . . . recipes for preserves, from Apricot Jam to Pickled Fennel with Orange Zest to Preserved Lemons, . . . provides a wealth of ideas for making the most of the harvest. Additional recipes showcase the many ways that preserved foods can be used in finished dishes, from savory starters to flavorful main courses to sweet desserts." (Publisher's note)

Foolproof preserving; a guide to small batch jams, jellies, pickles, condiments, and more. by the editors at America's Test Kitchen. America's Test Kitchen 2016 310 p. color illustrations (paperback) $26.95   **641.4**

1. Condiments 2. Canning and preserving 3. Jam
ISBN 9781940352510

LC 2015045561

This book, by the editors and staff of America's Test Kitchen, presents instructions on "the art of preserving produce by canning and preserving. . . . This detailed guide to home preserving is perfect for novice canners and experts alike and offers more than 100 foolproof recipes across a wide range of categories, from sweet jams and jellies to savory jams, vegetables, condiments, pickles, whole fruits, and more." (Publisher's note)

"An exceptional resource for novice canners, though preserving veterans will find plenty here to love as well." LJ

The **Good** Housekeeping step-by-step cookbook; edited by Susan Westmoreland with the assistance of Susan Deborah Goldsmith and Elizabeth Brainerd Burge. Hearst Books 2008 576p il $29.95 **641.4**

1. Cooking
ISBN 978-1-58816-760-6; 1-58816-760-7
First published 1997

This offers over 1,000 basic recipes illustrated by 1,800 color photographs divided into sections such as appetizers, soups, eggs and cheese, shellfish, poultry, meat, vegetables, pasta, grains and beans, breads, and desserts.

Macdonald, Emma

Artisan Preserving; Over 100 Recipes for Jams, Chutneys and Relishes, Pickles, Sauces and Cordials, and Cured Meats and Fish. by Emma Macdonald. Osprey Pub Co 2014 224 p. color illustrations $29.95   **641.4**

1. Canning and preserving
ISBN 1848991959; 9781848991958

This book, by Emma Macdonald, "is a one-stop resource for all of your preserving needs. . . . Learn the lost arts of curing, drying, pickling, bottling/canning, crystalizing and jellying; make all kinds of jams, jellies, pickles, chutneys, relishes, cordials, fruit liqueurs, sauces, ketchups, confits

and salamis, fruit curds, cheeses and butters, and dried fruits and veggies." (Publisher's note)

"This chic, thoughtful overview of many types of food preservation has the potential to become a staple for novice and veteran cooks alike." LJ

Mackenzie, Jennifer

The **complete** book of pickling; 250 recipes from pickles & relishes to chutneys & salsas. Robert Rose 2009 335p il pa $24.95   **641.4**

1. Canning and preserving
ISBN 978-0-77880216-7; 0-7788-0216-7

This is a "terrific collection of 250 pickles, sauces, chutneys and relishes. . . . Even readers without an appreciation for the tang of a good pickle will appreciate MacKenzie's 50 chutneys, including variations such as Sangria Citrus, classic cranberry and peach, pineapple ginger and spiced tomato; six chili sauces; 18 salsas; and homemade ketchup." Publ Wkly

West, Kevin

Saving the season; the essential guide to home canning, pickling, and preserving. by Kevin West. Alfred A. Knopf 2013 544 p. (hardback) $35 **641.4**

1. Fruit -- Preservation 2. Canning and preserving
ISBN 0307599485; 9780307599483

LC 2012037844

In this book, Kevin West "explores the various preserves available through the four seasons. Each base recipe includes variations to please any palate; the recipe for Black Mission Fig Jam offers directions to flavor it with Syrah, Madeira, or Smoky Black Tea. . . . Appendixes of peak seasons by region and tables of fruit varieties provide extensive information for cooks in any region. More than just recipes, the book also contains stories of the author's travels." (Library Journal)

Includes bibliographical references and index

641.42   Canning

The **all** new ball book of canning and preserving; Over 350 of the Best Canned, Jammed, Pickled, and Preserved Recipes. Jarden Home Brands. Oxmoor House 2016 368 p. illustrations $22.95   **641.42**

1. Fruit -- Preservation 2. Canning and preserving 3. Vegetables -- Preservation
ISBN 0848746783; 9780848746780

LC 2015958285

This book on canning and preserving "covers water bath and pressure canning, pickling, fermenting, freezing, dehydrating, and smoking. Straightforward instructions and step-by-step photos ensure success for beginners, while practiced home canners will find more advanced methods and inspiring ingredient twists." (Publisher's note)

"These 200-plus recipes prove that jellies and chutneys, salsas and syrups contain enough seasoning magic to flavor any meal. The book also shows how thoroughly the experts at Ball approach the subject." Booklist

641.5 Cooking

The **150** best American recipes; edited by Fran Mc-Cullough and Molly Stevens; foreword by Rick Bayless; photography by Ben Fink; [selected by the editors of The best American recipes] Houghton Mifflin 2006 352p il $30 **641.5**
1. Cooking
ISBN 978-0-618-71865-8; 0-618-71865-6
LC 2006-5604

The editors "have selected the 'best of the best' recipes from . . . [The Best American Recipes series], choosing from more than 1000 contenders. The recipes come from a variety of sources, from cookbooks to web sites to cooking schools, and the result is a mouthwatering array: Charred Tomatillo Guacamole; Tuscan Pork Roast with Herbed Salt; Mussels with Smoky Bacon, Lime, and Cilantro; and Mocha Fudge Pudding." Libr J

Ahern, Shauna James

Gluten-free girl every day; Shauna James Ahern, with Daniel Ahern; photography by Penny De Los Santos. John Wiley & Sons, Inc. 2013 319 p. col. ill. (cloth) $29.99 **641.5**
1. Cookbooks 2. Gluten-free diet 3. Gluten-free diet -- Recipes
ISBN 111811521X; 9781118115213
LC 2012030520

James Beard Award (2014)

This cookbook, by Shauna James Ahern, was the winner of a James Beard Foundation cookbook award. "Vegetables in season are the key to these healthy, relatively simple recipes, along with whole grains, beans, and a few key spices and homemade sauces. . . . [The book] also includes practical tips on how to stock a gluten-free pantry, as well as helpful insights into how to bake gluten-free." (Publisher's note)

Alford, Jeffrey

Beyond the Great Wall; recipes and travels in the other China. [by] Jeffrey Alford and Naomi Duguid; studio photography by Richard Jung; location photographs by Jeffrey Alford and Naomi Duguid. Artisan 2008 376p il map $40 **641.5**
1. Chinese cooking 2. Tibet (China) -- Description and travel
ISBN 978-1-57965-301-9
LC 2007-28556

The authors "explore the food and peoples of the outlaying regions of present-day China, historically home to those not ethnically Chinese. Part travel guide and part cookbook, this collection looks at the cultural survival and preservation of food in smaller societies including that of the Tibetan, Mongol, Tuvan and Kirghiz peoples, among others. . . . A handsome and engaging collection suitable for travelers and cooks alike, this book will delight anyone with an interest in this part of the world." Publ Wkly

Includes bibliographical references

The **America's** Test Kitchen healthy family cookbook; a new, healthier way to cook everything from America's most trusted test kitchen. the editors at America's test kitchen; photography, Daniel J. Van Ackere, Carl Tremblay. America's Test Kitchen 2010 viii, 520 p.p ill. (chiefly col.) (looseleaf) $34.95 **641.5**
1. Cookbooks 2. American cooking 3. Cooking, American 4. Families -- Health and hygiene
ISBN 1933615567; 9781933615561
LC 2011278441

This cookbook, produced by the editors at America's Test Kitchen, "[p]resents advice on cooking techniques, equipment, food preparation, and selection of ingredients, along with more than 750 recipes for healthy dishes, including appetizers, soups, meats, fish, vegetables, sauces, breads, and desserts." (Publisher's note)

"[A] well-tested collection of more than 750 recipes that employ vetted techniques and abundant flavor to create dishes that are as healthy as they can be, given what they are, without sacrificing a pleasurable eating experience." Pub Wkly

The **America's** Test Kitchen new family cookbook; all-new edition of the best-selling classic with 1,100 new recipes. the editors at America's Test Kitchen. America's Test Kitchen 2014 928 p. col. ill. $40 **641.5**
1. Cookbooks 2. American cooking
ISBN 1936493853; 9781936493852
LC 2014009517

"The 'America's Test Kitchen New Family Cookbook' contains more than 1,100 new recipes accompanied by new photography and a brand-new package. The result is a comprehensive but approachable tome that every cook will want in the kitchen, for many years to come. . . . This new edition is hardcover (rather than ringbound) and features a fresh design with four-color food photography throughout." (Publisher's note)

American food writing; an anthology with classic recipes. edited by Molly O'Neill. Library of America 2007 753p il $40 **641.5**
1. Cooking
ISBN 978-1-59853-005-6; 1-59853-005-4

This "collection of essays, anecdotes, and recipes spans three centuries of American food writing, from Meriwether Lewis's account of killing 'two bucks and two buffaloe' during his famous trek across the continent, to Michael Pollan's up-to-the-minute account of the politics of organic food. . . . With so many wonderful ingredients, this rich, delectable treat is a must-have for American foodies." Publ Wkly

Includes bibliographical references

American Institute for Cancer Research

The **new** American plate cookbook; recipes for a healthy weight and a healthy life. American Institute for Cancer Research. University of California Press 2005 306p il $24.95 **641.5**
1. Cooking
ISBN 0-520-24234-3
LC 2004-17993

The recipes in this book are "built around vegetables and whole grains, with an emphasis on brown rice, wheat pasta, and other healthful foods, rather than protein. . . . Recipes are appealing and easy to make and cover every course of a meal. Well-known dishes are reworked, e.g., New England Clam Chowder, to help with the transition to healthier eating." Libr J

Anderson, Jean

The **food** of Portugal; color photography by the author. Morrow 1986 304p il map hardcover o.p. pa $19.95 **641.5**

1. Portuguese cooking

ISBN 0-688-13415-7 pa

LC 86-2510

The author "first covers Portugal's geography and touches on distinctive regional cooking styles. The following glossary delineates Portuguese food, drink, and dining terminology. . . . Part 2, . . . is a guide to the country's best food." Booklist

Includes bibliographical references

Anderson, Pam

How to cook without a book; recipes and techniques every cook should know by heart. Broadway Bks. 2000 290p $25 **641.5**

1. Cooking

ISBN 0-7679-0279-3

LC 99-43776

"Former executive editor of Cook's magazine and author of The Perfect Recipe, Anderson wants to teach Americans a new way to cook without relying on recipes. It's somewhat surprising, then, to discover that this book is full of recipes. However, readers may cotton to Anderson's method: each chapter consists of a simple technique, basic recipe, variations, key points and a little mnemonic device used to recall the technique. The techniques are, for the most part, terrific time-savers." Pub Wkly

Perfect recipes for having people over; photographs by Rita Maas. Houghton Mifflin 2005 304p il $35 **641.5**

1. Cooking 2. Entertaining

ISBN 0-618-32972-2

LC 2005-46370

Anderson "offers 200 recipes from entrées to desserts. Most are easy to make; some require guest participation, such as shish kebabs, with a variety of ingredients for all tastes. The book begins with main courses since they will dictate the accompaniments. Each recipe has a question section–e.g., 'Any Shortcuts?' 'What Should I Serve with It?' 'How Far Ahead Can I Make It?' There are many familiar dishes like macaroni and cheese and deviled eggs, but readers will also encounter innovative recipes." Libr J

Andrews, Colman

Country cooking of Ireland; photographs by Christopher Hirsheimer; foreword by Darina Allen. Chronicle 2009 383p il map $50 **641.5**

1. Irish cooking

ISBN 978-0-8118-6670-5

The author "provides new perspectives on the often maligned Irish cuisine. The breathtakingly beautiful photographs are alone enough to convince, but Andrews, calling Irish cuisine one of the most exciting food stories in the

world today, lets the dishes make his case. Robust soups such as butternut and apple and roast pork belly start the mouth juices flowing. Andrews offers a culinary feast with everything from nested eggs and steak-and-kidney pie to Arlington chicken liver pâté and battered sausages. . . . Andrews has done the near impossible in elevating a cuisine thought to be humble and drab into tantalizing fare that will have worldwide appeal." Publ Wkly

Includes bibliographical references

Antine, Stacey, 1968-

Appetite for life; the thumbs up, no yucks guide to getting your kid to be a great eater-including over 100 kid-approved recipes. Stacey Antine. HarperCollins 2012 272 p. ill. $26.99 **641.5**

1. Cooking 2. Cookbooks 3. Children -- Nutrition

ISBN 0062103709; 9780062103703

LC 2012002471

This book, by Stacey Antine, founder of HealthBarn USA, offers advice for encouraging healthy, nutritious eating in children and families along with multiple cooking recipes. The book "encourages giving children a voice: with her 'no yucks allowed' method, kids use a thumbs-up/thumbs-down rating system for each new food they try, but they always have to try at least one bite." (Publisher's note)

"Frustrated parents will find plenty of encouraging and practical ideas as well as more than 100 recipes for breakfast, lunch, dinner, and snack time." Pub Wkly

Includes bibliographical references and index

Atlas, Nava

Plant power; transform your kitchen, plate, and life with fresh and flavorful vegan recipes. by Nava Atlas; photographs by Hannah Kaminsky. HarperOne 2014 384 p. color illustrations (hardback) $29.99 **641.5**

1. Cooking 2. Veganism 3. Nutrition 4. Vegan cooking 5. Cooking (Vegetables) 6. Kitchens -- Management 7. Veganism -- Health aspects 8. Veganism -- Moral and ethical aspects

ISBN 9780062273291; 9780062273314; 0062273299

LC 2013043023

This cookbook by Nava Atlas "focuses on the basics, from setting up a plant-powered pantry and fridge to choosing the best fresh foods for each season and streamlining daily meal preparation. Each of the . . . recipes is easy to make and customizable, with tips on variations from turning up the heat and mixing up ingredients, to kid-friendly, gluten-free, and seasonal options." (Publisher's note)

"Atlas succeeds more as a recipe writer than a diet guru. Her new book may not compel readers to overhaul their lifestyles, but it will provide them with new, delicious, and practical vegan recipes." LJ

Banfield, Kelsey

The **family** calendar cookbook; Kelsey Banfield. Running Press 2015 336 p. color illustrations (paperback) $23 **641.5**

1. Cooking 2. Cookbooks

ISBN 0762451076; 9780762451074

LC 2014956344

This cookbook, by Kelsey Banfield, "is organized by your family's timetable, featuring no-fuss recipes for every occasion (no matter how big or small). Whether you're serving snacks for your daughter's slumber party, or throwing a Winter Chili Night for friends, or providing allergy-sensitive treats to take to your son's classroom--author Kelsey Banfield has crafted the most reliable, most delicious recipe for everything that crops up." (Publisher's note)

"Recommended for families that need a perfect recipe in a pinch." LJ

Bastianich, Lidia

Lidia cooks from the heart of Italy; by Lidia Matticchio Bastianich and Tanya Bastianich Manuali, with David Nussbaum; full-page photographs by Christopher Hirsheimer; other photographs by Lidia Matticchio Bastianich. Alfred A. Knopf 2009 411p il $35   **641.5**

1. Italian cooking

ISBN 978-0-307-26751-1; 0-307-26751-2

         LC 2009-22021

"Bastianich and daughter Tanya take readers on a culinary tour of Italy's 12 regions. Grouped by those areas, the recipes are simple enough for novice cooks. Included are appetizers, soups, salads and side dishes, condiments, pastas and risottos/rice, vegetarian main courses (aside from pasta), fish and seafood, meat and poultry, and desserts. In addition, there are stories about the history of the dishes." Libr J

★ **Lidia's** family table; Lidia Matticchio Bastianich, with David Nussbaum; photographs by Christopher Hirsheimer. Random House Inc 2004 419 p. col. ill. $35   **641.5**

1. Cookbooks 2. Italian cooking

ISBN 1400040353; 9781400040353

         LC 2004022411

In this cookbook, author and television chef "Lidia Bastianich, ... gives us her most generous, instructive, and creative cookbook. The emphasis here is on cooking for the family, and her book is filled with unusually delicious basic recipes for everyday eating Italian-style, as well as imaginative ideas for variations and improvisations." (Publisher's note)

"Step-by-step photographs illustrate kitchen techniques, and charming photos of the author's grandchildren and other family scenes add to the appeal of this engaging, immensely practical book." LJ

Batali, Mario

Italian grill; [by] Mario Batali with Judith Sutton; photography by Beatriz da Costa; art direction by Lisa Eaton and Douglas Riccardi. Ecco 2008 246p il $29.95   **641.5**

1. Italian cooking 2. Barbecue cooking

ISBN 978-0-06-145097-6; 0-06-145097-9

A collection of eighty recipes for grilled Italian food is divided into categories for antipasti, pizza, meat, fish, and vegetables, and includes information on grilling basics, different heat-source options, and differences in grilling equipment.

"This is an essential collection for any serious backyard cook." Publ Wkly

Bayless, Rick

Fiesta at Rick's; fabulous food for great times with friends. [by] Rick Bayless with Deann Groen Bayless; photographs by Paul Elledge. W. W. Norton 2010 348p il $35   **641.5**

1. Menus 2. Entertaining 3. Mexican cooking

ISBN 978-0-393-05899-4

         LC 2010-13128

"The book loosely packages recipes around fiestas, from a luxury guacamole and cocktail party for 12 to classic mole for 24, complete with game-plan checklists. . . . The hardest thing about using this book isn't finding the ingredients (today, practically every small town has a great Mexican grocery), it's keeping yourself from eating everything before the guests arrive." N Y Times Book Rev

Beard, James

The **armchair** James Beard; edited by John Ferrone; foreword by Barbara Kafka. Lyons Press 1999 346p $24.95   **641.5**

1. Cooking

ISBN 1-55821-737-1

         LC 98-29728

This collection assembles "essays on everything from main courses to condiments; dining in restaurants, hospitals, and al fresco; libations and desserts; and broader philosophical concerns on gastronomy. Each chapter has captured Beard's feeling for food, his wicked sense of humor, his consummate excellence as a writer, and even his love of controversy. . . . The 150 recipes cover the globe and honor the palate." Libr J

The **fireside** cook book; a complete guide to fine cooking for beginner and expert. [by] James A. Beard; illustrated by Alice Provensen and Martin Provensen; foreword by Mark Bittman. Simon & Schuster 2008 336p il $30   **641.5**

1. Cooking

ISBN 978-1-4165-8967-9; 1-4165-8967-8

         LC 2008-25094

First published 1949

This volume "includes more than 12,000 recipes and variations, with chapters on every course of a meal, as well as 'Outdoor Cookery,' 'Frozen Foods and PickUp Meals,' and more. This 60th-anniversary edition includes the original watercolor illustrations and a brief new foreword by cookbook author Mark Bittman. While some of the information and language is dated, of course, it's amazing how ahead of his time Beard often was. . . . The amount of information the book provides is equally impressive, and Beard's straightforward, opinionated prose remains a delight to read." Libr J

★ **James** Beard's American cookery. Little, Brown 1972 877p hardcover o.p. pa $24.95 **641.5**

1. Cooking

ISBN 0-316-08566-9 pa

"Comprehensive in scope the cookbook gives eighteenth-and nineteenth-century recipes as well as modern directions for preparation of a full range of U.S. cookery. . . . The format is attractive and the historical data add to the value of an authoritative guide." Booklist

Includes bibliographical references

Behr, Edward

The **Food** and Wine of France; Eating and Drinking from Champagne to Provence. by Edward Behr. Penguin Group USA 2016 320 p. $28 **641.5**
1. Eating customs 2. French cooking
ISBN 1594204527; 9781594204524

In this book, "food writer Edward Behr investigates French cuisine and what it means, in encounters from Champagne to Provence. He tells the stories of French artisans and chefs who continue to work at the highest level. Many people in and out of France have noted for a long time the slow retreat of French cuisine, concerned that it is losing its important place in the country's culture and in the world culture of food." (Publisher's note)

"What resonates is that whether a cuisine is defined by its ingredients, techniques, or even the logistical structure of its menu, it is perhaps the story and the telling that remain most important." LJ

Besh, John

Cooking from the heart; my favorite lessons learned along the way. John Besh. Andrews McMeel Pub., LLC 2013 320 p. $40 **641.5**
1. Cooking 2. Cookbooks
ISBN 1449430562; 9781449430566
LC 2013936654

In this book "James Beard Award-winning chef John Besh shares the lessons he learned from his mentors through 140 accessible recipes and cooking lessons. . . . From Germany's Black Forest to the mountains of Provence, each chapter highlights . . . memories and . . . recipes--the framework for his love of food." (Publisher's note)

The **best** recipe; by the editors of Cook's illustrated; illustrations by John Burgoyne; photography by Carl Tremblay. Boston Common Press 1999 575 p. illustrations $29.95 **641.5**
1. Cooking 2. Cookbooks
ISBN 0936184388; 9780936184388
LC 2002512594

"'The Best Recipe' is a collection of the editors' picks from the pages of 'Cook's Illustrated.' The recipes have been edited, organized, and annotated with in-depth descriptions of how we developed the 'best' recipe. And they appear alongside dozens of equipment ratings and taste tests of supermarket foods, as well as more than 200 illustrations demonstrating the most efficient food preparation methods." (Publisher's note)

Better homes and gardens

Better homes and gardens new cook book; 15th ed.; J. Wiley 2010 660p il $29.95 **641.5**
1. Cooking
ISBN 978-0-470-55686-3
LC 2010-25417

First published 1930 with title: My Better Homes and Gardens cook book. Periodically revised

"A standard cookbook . . . with staple recipes and types of cooking." N Y Public Libr. Book of How & Where to Look It Up

★ **Better** Homes and Gardens New Cook Book; Better Homes and Gardens. 16th edition HougHton Mifflin Harcourt 2014 658 p. color illustrations (loose leaf) $29.99 **641.5**
1. Cooking 2. Cookbooks 3. Canning and preserving
ISBN 0544307070; 9780544307070
LC 2014012314

This Better Homes and Gardens cookbook is "the fully updated and revised [16th] edition. . . . [It] includes more than 1,200 recipes, 1,000 color photos, and more tips and how-to information than ever. . . . Along with the best recipes for favorite foods, this indispensable volume offers information on new cooking trends and fresh ideas, a new fruit and vegetable guide with ID photos, and expanded coverage of canning." (Publisher's note)

★ **Betty** Crocker cookbook; 1500 recipes for the way you cook today. Betty Crocker. 11th edition Betty Crocker 2011 684 p. ill (some col) (looseleaf) $29.99 **641.5**
1. Cooking 2. Cookbooks
ISBN 0470906022; 9780470906026
LC 2011009744

This 11th edition of the Betty Crocker cookbook "includes hundreds of new recipes, three new chapters, and icons that showcase how we cook today--faster, healthier, and with many more flavors. New features celebrate the book's expertise and heritage with repertoire-building recipe lessons and fresh twists on American classics." (Publisher's note)

Betty Crocker's cooking basics; learning to cook with confidence. Macmillan 1998 280p il $19.95 **641.5**
1. Cooking
ISBN 0-02-862451-3
LC 98-20522

In addition to recipes, this illustrated volume contains tips on food selection, grocery shopping, thawing, and nutrition. Cooking equipment is discussed

Bittman, Mark

★ **How** to cook everything; 2,000 simple recipes for great food. illustrations by Alan Witschonke. 2nd ed.; J. Wiley 2008 1044p il $35 **641.5**
1. Cooking
ISBN 978-0-76-457865-6; 0-76-457865-0
LC 2008-18984

First published 1998 by Macmilllan

The author presents "more than 1000 basic recipes and simple and inventive variations. The enormous breadth of recipes along with Bittman's engaging, straightforward prose will appeal to cooks looking for reliable help with kitchen fundamentals." Publ Wkly

Includes bibliographical references

How to Cook Everything Fast; A Better Way to Cook Great Food. Mark Bittman; illustrations by Olivia de Salve Villedieu. Houghton Mifflin Harcourt 2014 1056 p. illustrations $35   **641.5**

1. Cooking 2. Cookbooks 3. Quick and easy cooking
ISBN 0470936304; 9780470936306

LC 2014427729

In this book, author Mark Bittman "provides a game plan for becoming a better, more intuitive cook while you wake up your weekly meal routine with 2,000 main dishes and accompaniments that are simple to make, globally inspired, and bursting with flavor. . . . Time management-- the essential principle of fast cooking-- is woven into revolutionary recipes that do the thinking for you." (Publisher's note)

"Bittman's latest is fantastic for busy, novice, and noncooks. It's also a practical tool for anyone who aspires but struggles to cook more often." LJ

★ **How** to cook everything vegetarian; simple meatless recipes for great food. illustrations by Alan Witschonke. Wiley 2007 996p il $35   **641.5**

1. Vegetarian cooking
ISBN 978-0-7645-2483-7; 0-7645-2483-6

LC 2006-36937

This vegetarian cookbook "presents more than 2000 recipes and variations. Most of the recipes are quick and easy; prep times are given for each one, and icons indicate those that are especially fast, can be made ahead, and/or are vegan. . . . An essential purchase for all cookery collections." Libr J

Mark Bittman's Kitchen express; 404 inspired seasonal dishes you can make in 20 minutes or less. Simon & Schuster 2009 233p $26   **641.5**

1. Quick and easy cooking
ISBN 978-1-4165-7566-5

LC 2008-54823

"Bittman here offers a sampling of 404 inspiring recipes. . . . The no-sweat recipes are divided into four sections: summer, fall, winter and spring, capitalizing on the freshest ingredients of each season while whittling down the prep time of ordinarily elaborate dishes like coq au vin and ricotta cheesecake to 10 minutes or less. The book includes a drill-down of how best to stock your kitchen, and given the impromptu nature of the book, the substitution grid proves indispensable." Publ Wkly

Mark Bittman's kitchen matrix; more than 700 simple recipes & techniques to mix & match for endless possibilities. Mark Bittman. Pam Krauss Books 2015 304 p. illustrations (hardback) $35   **641.5**

1. Cooking 2. Cookbooks
ISBN 0804188017; 9780804188012

LC 2015020733

This book, by Mark Bittman, "anthologizes his popular Matrix series in a boldly graphic new cookbook that emphasizes creativity, improvisation, and simplicity as the keys to varied cooking. . . . Accompanied by striking photographs and brief, straightforward instructions, these thematic matrices show how simple changes in preparation and ingredient swaps in a master recipe can yield dishes that are each completely different from the original, and equally delicious." (Publisher's note)

"This unconventional cookbook can help proficient cooks develop ideas for creating their own recipe variations." LJ

The **VB6** cookbook; 320 all-new recipes that help you eat healthy vegan meals all day and delicious flexitarian dinners at night. Mark Bittman; photographs by Quentin Bacon. Clarkson Potter 2014 272 p. color illustrations $29.95   **641.5**

1. Veganism 2. Cookbooks 3. Vegetarian cooking 4. Vegan cooking 5. Reducing diets -- Recipes
ISBN 0385344821; 9780385344821

LC 2013050637

"When [author Mark] Bittman committed to a vegan before 6:00 pm diet, he quickly realized that everything about it became easier if he cooked his own meals at home. In The VB6 Cookbook he makes this proposition more convenient than you could imagine. Drawing on a varied and enticing pantry of vegan staples strategically punctuated with 'treat' foods . . . , he has created a versatile repertoire of recipes that makes following his plan simple, satisfying, and sustainable." (Publisher's note)

"Rather than overload readers with prescriptive rules, unfamiliar ingredients, and complicated preparations, Bittman gives them a memorable charge (eat more plants, less meat and processed foods) and tools to help them follow it." LJ

Bracken, Peg

The **I** hate to cook book; with a new foreword by Jo Bracken; drawings by Hilary Knight. 50th anniversary ed.; Grand Central Pub. 2010 207p $22.99; ebook $10.99   **641.5**

1. Cooking 2. Quick and easy cooking
ISBN 978-0-446-54592-1; 978-0-446-56894-4 ebook

LC 2009-1249

First published 1960 by Harcourt, Brace

"This book's strident title belies both its usefulness and its popularity. Peg Bracken faced the burden of being a full-time writer, a full-time mother and a full-time housewife. To buy herself a bit more time for other pursuits, she and her friends collected a host of easy, stress-free recipes. What's truly wonderful is Bracken's droll delivery and the more than 200 recipes that run the gamut from appetizers to desserts." Washington Post

Brennan, Kathy

Keepers; two home cooks share their tried-and-true weeknight recipes and the secrets to happiness in the kitchen. Kathy Brennan and Caroline Campion; photographs by Christopher Testani. Rodale Books 2013 256 p. color illustrations (hardcover) $26.99   **641.5**

1. Menus 2. Cookbooks 3. American cooking 4. Quick and easy cooking 5. Cooking, American 6. Low budget cooking 7. Cooking -- Philosophy 8. Kitchens -- Management
ISBN 1609613546; 9781609613549

LC 2013005481

IACP Cookbook Award (2014)

In this cookbook, chefs Kathy Brennan and Caroline Campion "offer 120 appealing, satisfying recipes ideal for weeknight meals. There's an array of master recipes for classic dishes with options for substitutions, updated old favorites, one-pot meals, 'international' dishes, super-fast ones, and others that reheat well or can be cooked in individual portions." (Publisher's note)

Briscione, James

The **great** cook; essential techniques and inspired flavors to make every dish better. James Briscione. Oxmoor House 2015 367 p. color illustrations (hardcover) $29.95 **641.5**
1. Cookbooks 2. Cooking -- Study and teaching
ISBN 0848739914; 9780848739911

LC 2015930569

This cookbook, by James Briscione, "will show you how to confidently turn out a pie with a flaky, tender crust, make homemade pasta, and master a wow-the-crowd Coq Au Vin. Chef and culinary instructor James Briscione guides readers through 36 in-depth, recipe-oriented lessons: Roast chicken. Seafood. Layer Cakes. Each lesson is detailed with instructive photos of every step, and variation recipes will help build on newly acquired skills." (Publisher's note)

"Filled with attractive food photography and doable gourmet recipes, this cookbook will entice calorie-conscious readers who enjoyed such titles as Dana Cowin's Mastering My Mistakes in the Kitchen." LJ

Brown, Alton, 1962-

Everydaycook; Alton Brown. Random House Inc. 2016 256 p. color illustrations (ebook) $65; (hardcover) $35 **641.5**
1. Cookbooks
ISBN 1101885718; 9781101885727; 9781101885710

This book by cooking show host Alton Brown discusses how he got into cooking and why he wrote the book. "I was sitting around trying to organize my recipes, and I realized that I should put them into a personal collection. One thing led to another, and here's EveryDayCook. There's still plenty of science and hopefully some humor in here . . . , but unlike in my other books, a lot of attention went into the photos . . . . As for the recipes, . . . they're pretty darned tasty." (Publisher's note)

Brown, Leanne

★ **Good** and cheap; eat well on $4/day. Leanne Brown. Workman Publishing 2015 208 p. color illustrations (alk. paper) $16.95 **641.5**
1. Cooking 2. Household budgets 3. Low budget cooking
ISBN 0761184996; 9780761184997

LC 2015011072

IACP Cookbook Award: Judge's Choice (2015)
IACP Cookbook Award Finalist: Food Matters (2015)

This book, by Leanne Brown, is a "cookbook filled with delicious, healthful recipes created for everyone on a tight budget. . . . While studying food policy as a master's candidate at NYU, Leanne Brown asked a simple yet critical question: How well can a person eat on the $4 a day given by SNAP, the U.S. government's Supplemental Nutrition Assistance Program informally known as food stamps? The answer is surprisingly well." (Publisher's note)

"Brown estimates the cost per serving for all dishes, including potato leek pizzas, dark and spicy chili, and peanut chicken and broccoli with coconut rice." LJ

Includes bibliographical references and index

Bryant, George

The **paleo** kitchen; finding primal joy in modern cooking. George Bryant and Juli Bauer. Victory Belt Publishing Inc 2014 327 p. color illustrations $34.95 **641.5**
1. Cookbooks 2. Paleo cooking
ISBN 1628600101; 9781628600100

This cookbook, by George Bryant and Juli Bauer, "bring[s] a myriad of bold and delectable gluten & grain-free Paleo recipes straight from their kitchens to yours in their new cookbook. . . . [It] boasts over 100 brand new recipes consisting of appetizers, entrées, side dishes, and decadent desserts that are sure to invigorate and please the fearless caveman palate." (Publisher's note)

Includes bibliographical references (page 314) and index

Buford, Bill

Heat; an amateur's adventures as kitchen slave, line cook, pasta-maker, and apprentice to a Dante-quoting butcher in Tuscany. Knopf 2006 318p $25.95 **641.5**
1. Cooks 2. Italian cooking 3. Television personalities 4. Restaurateurs 5. Cookbook writers
ISBN 1-4000-4120-1; 978-1-4000-4120-6

LC 2005-57868

"Mr Buford also has a biographer's gift of bringing characters to life. . . . [He] fills his book with people as pungent and spicy as the food." Economist

Chang, David

Momofuku; [by] David Chang and Peter Meehan; photographs by Gabriele Stabile. Clarkson Potter 2009 303p il $40 **641.5**
1. Asian cooking
ISBN 978-0-307-45195-8

"Chang's Virginia upbringing, upscale restaurant experience and love of certain Korean and Japanese flavors result in the kind of dishes that will jam your eyeballs into the back of your head, like brussels sprouts with bacon and kimchi puree. This fawningly produced book . . . is fueled by Chang's hard-core attitude and punctuated with a 'Hell's Kitchen' season's worth of unprintable words. The dude's intense, and he wants you to know it. The food is intense, too, especially as the recipes increase in difficulty as the chapters move up the Momofuku restaurant scale, from Noodle Bar to Ssam Bar to Ko." N Y Times Book Rev

Chang, Joanne

Baking with less sugar; recipes for desserts using natural sweeteners and little-to-no white sugar. by Joanne Chang; photographs by Joseph De Leo.

Chronicle Books LLC 2015 224 p. color illustrations $25　　**641.5**
1. Baking
ISBN 145213300X; 9781452133003

LC 2014023855

In this cookbook on baking with less sugar, author Joanne Chang "warmly shares her secrets for playing up delicious ingredients and using natural sweeteners, such as honey, maple syrup, and fruit juice. In addition to entirely new go-to recipes, she's also revisited classics from 'Flour' and her lines-out-the-door bakeries to use minimal refined sugar." (Publisher's note)

Child, Julia

From Julia Child's kitchen; photographs and drawings by Paul Child; additional technical photographs by Albie Walton. Knopf 1975 687, xxvip il $13.99　　**641.5**
1. French cooking
ISBN 0-517-20712-5

The author "has taken many of the recipes she demonstrated in her 72 'French Chef' TV shows; grouped them by subject {soups, appetizers, egg dishes, fish, poultry, meat, vegetables, salads, bread} added variations and additional recipes; and introduced each section and most recipes with commentaries." Libr J
Includes bibliographical references

★ **Mastering** the art of French cooking; by Julia Child, Louisette Bertholle, Simone Beck. updated ed; Knopf 1983 2v il v1 $40; v1 pa $30; v2 $60; v2 pa $30　　**641.5**
1. French cooking
ISBN 0-375-41340-5 v1; 0-394-72178-0 v1 pa; 0-394-40152-2 v2; 0-394-72177-2 v2 pa

LC 83-48113

Volume 1 first published 1961 with Beck's name first; volume 2 by Julia Child and Simone Beck
Volume one includes, in addition to usual categories, a chapter dealing with entrees and luncheon dishes, including quiches, pâtés, and crepes, and other cold buffet items. Volume two emphasizes French bread and pastries, with chapters also devoted to soups, meats, chickens, vegetables, and desserts. Appendices discuss stuffings and kitchen equipment.

★ **The** **way** to cook; photographs by Brian Leatart and Jim Scherer; food designer, Rosemary Manell. Knopf 1989 511p il $65; pa $39.95 **641.5**
1. Cooking
ISBN 0-394-53264-3; 0-679-74765-6 pa

LC 88-45838

The author aims at "blending classic techniques with free-style American cooking and with added emphasis on lightness, freshness, and simpler preparations. . . . She structures the chapters (from Soups to Cakes & Cookies) around master recipes, . . . grouping the recipes according to method; these are followed . . . {by} variations that are . . . made once the basics are understood." (Publisher's note) Index.
"With her sensible-as-always approach to food, Child has produced a comprehensive cooking bible, filled with stunning photographs and practical illustrations, that will

aid the novice {and} inspire the gourmet. . . . A masterwork from a master chef." Libr J

Chitnis, Christine

Little bites; 100 healthy, kid-friendly snacks. Christine Chitnis and Sarah Waldman; photographs by Christine Chitnis. Roost Books 2015 x, 277 p.p color illustrations (paperback) $24.95　　**641.5**
1. Cookbooks 2. Snack foods 3. Children -- Nutrition
ISBN 161180177X; 9781611801774

LC 2014022055

This cookbook, by Christine Chitnis and Sarah Waldman, "offers 100 wholesome, seasonal, vegetarian snacks perfect for active families. When you're on the go with little ones, snacks are essential. Whether it's an energetic pick-me-up after school or a nutritional boost at the playground, the 100 wholesome snacks in this book will help everyone get through the day." (Publisher's note)
Includes bibliographical references and index

Clark, Melissa

Cook this now; 120 easy and delectable dishes you can't wait to make. Hyperion 2011 396p il $29.99　　**641.5**
1. Cooking
ISBN 978-1-4013-2398-1

LC 2011010420

"Clark presents readers with 120 recipes organized by season and month. With a candid opening essay on weekly trips to her local NYC farmers' market in the dead of winter—think frosty fingers, and ice-topped milk—Clark sets the course for this down-to-earth, realistic guide to cooking throughout the year, finding and highlighting seasonal gems in mains, side dishes, and desserts. . . . Even with a multitude of cooking-by-season titles in the marketplace, the author's inspiring use of fresh ingredients and flexible attitude toward cooking make this a solid addition to any kitchen cookbook shelf." Publ Wkly

In the kitchen with a good appetite. Hyperion 2010 444p il $27.50　　**641.5**
1. Cooking
ISBN 978-1-4013-2376-9

LC 2010-5760

"A Good Appetite," Melissa Clark's weekly feature in the New York Times Dining Section, is about dishes that are easy to cook and that speak to everyone, either stirring a memory or creating one. Now, Clark takes the same freewheeling yet well-informed approach that has won her countless fans and applies it to one hundred and fifty delicious, simply sophisticated recipes." (Publisher's note)
Includes bibliographical references

Coe, Andrew

A **square** meal; A Culinary History of the Great Depression. Jane Ziegelman and Andrew Coe. Harper 2016 336 p. illustrations (hardback) $26.99 **641.5**
1. American cooking -- History 2. Great Depression, 1929-1939 3. United States -- History -- 20th century 4. Depressions -- 1929 -- United States 5. Cooking, American -- History -- 20th century 6. United States -- Social conditions -- 1933-1945 7. Diet -- United States

-- History -- 20th century 8. Crises -- United States -- History -- 20th century 9. Food supply -- United States -- History -- 20th century 10. Social change -- United States -- History -- 20th century 11. Home economics -- United States -- History -- 20th century 12. United States -- Environmental conditions -- History -- 20th century

ISBN 9780062216410; 9780062216427

LC 2016016051

This book by Jane Ziegelman and Andrew Coe offers "an in-depth exploration of the greatest food crisis the nation has ever faced--the Great Depression--and how it transformed America's culinary culture. . . . [It] examines the impact of economic contraction and environmental disaster on how Americans ate then--and the lessons and insights those experiences may hold for us today. [It] features 25 black-and-white photographs." (Publisher's note)

"Coe and Ziegelman have written an engaging social history illustrated throughout with historically authentic recipes. Even if the period cuisine doesn't make the reader's mouth water, the vivid recreation of American eating at a historical crossroads is engrossing." Pub Wkly

Includes bibliographical references and index

Colwin, Laurie

Home cooking; a writer in the kitchen. Laurie Colwin; illustrated by Anna Shapiro. Vintage Books 2010 x, 193 p.p ill. $15.95 **641.5**
1. Cooking 2. Cookbooks
ISBN 0307474410; 9780307474414

LC 2010455796

James Beard Cookbook Hall of Fame (2012)

This autobiographical cookbook, "is [author] Laurie Colwin's manifesto on the joys of sharing food and entertaining. From the humble hotplate of her one-room apartment to the crowded kitchens of bustling parties, Colwin regales us with tales of meals gone both magnificently well and disastrously wrong." (Publisher's note)

The **complete** vegetarian cookbook; a fresh guide to eating well with 700 foolproof recipes. by the editors at America's test kitchen. America's Test Kitchen 2015 463 p. illustrations (chiefly color) $29.95 **641.5**
1. Vegetarian cooking
ISBN 1936493969; 9781936493968

LC 2014042807

This book presents "a collection of. . .vegetarian recipes covering hearty vegetable mains, rice and grains, beans and soy as well as soups, appetizers, snacks, and salads. More than 300 recipes are fast (start to finish in 45 minutes or less), 500 are gluten-free, and 250 are vegan and are all highlighted with icons on the pages." (Publisher's note)

Cook's illustrated (Periodical)

The **best** International recipe; a home cook's guide to the best recipes in the world. by the editors of Cook's Illustrated. America's Test Kitchen 2007 579p il $35 **641.5**
1. Cooking
ISBN 978-1-933615-17-2; 1-933615-17-6

This volume contains more than 300 recipes from around the world. Each has been tested to ensure success. Includes explanations of ingredients and what to look for, and in some cases, what you can substitute without compromising flavor. Specialty equipment is also discussed. Core techniques are highlighted throughout the book.

The **new** best recipe; by the editors of Cook's illustrated; photography, Carl Tremblay, Daniel J. Van Ackere; illustrations, John Burgoyne. 2nd ed.; America's Test Kitchen 2004 1028p il $35 **641.5**
1. Cooking
ISBN 978-0-936184-74-6; 0-936184-74-4

First published 1999 by Boston Common Press

A compendium of more than 1,000 recipes. "Twenty-two chapters cover appetizers to desserts. Even the simplest tasks, such as blanching vegetables or peeling an egg, are explained and illustrated in detail. More involved techniques include brining poultry and roasting a turkey. . . . Well organized and extremely clear." Publ Wkly

Cowin, Dana

Mastering My Mistakes in the Kitchen; 55 Great Chefs Teach Me How to Cook. Dana Cowin. HarperCollins 2014 272 p. color illustrations $34.99 **641.5**
1. Cooks 2. Cooking
ISBN 0062305905; 9780062305909

In this book, author Dana Cowin "spills the secret of her culinary ineptitude, while learning--finally--to cook, side-by-side with some of the greatest chefs working today, from David Chang to Alice Waters to Thomas Keller." (Publisher's note)

"More accessible than Adam Roberts's Secrets of the Best Chefs, this cookbook is foremost a collection of reliable recipes and straightforward advice. Like Ina Garten's Barefoot Contessa Foolproof, it relies on simple equipment, techniques, and ingredients." LJ

Craig, Caroline

The **little** book of lunch; 100 recipes & ideas to reclaim the lunch hour. Caroline Craig, Sophie Missing; photography by David Loftus. Regan Arts 2015 207 p. color illustrations $24.95 **641.5**
1. Luncheons
ISBN 1941393225; 9781941393222

LC 2014955542

This book about lunch, by Caroline Craig and Sophie Missing, is a "beautiful, internationally acclaimed guide to turning your midday meal into a masterpiece—featuring 100 easy, inexpensive, delicious recipes designed to be made ahead of time with just a few ingredients." (Publisher's note)

Crandall, Russell

Paleo takeout; restaurant favorites without the junk. Russ Crandall. Simon & Schuster 2015 320 p. color illustrations (paperback) $34.95 **641.5**
1. Cookbooks 2. Paleo cooking
ISBN 162860087X; 9781628600872

This paleo cookbook, by Russ Crandall, offers "over 200 weeknight-friendly dishes that taste so good, you'll finally throw out that emergency stack of takeout menus hiding in your kitchen drawer. . . . [The author] re-creates everyone's favorite takeout meals using wholesome ingredients and some seriously inventive techniques." (Publisher's note)

Crumpacker, Bunny

How to slice an onion; cooking basics and beyond--hundreds of tips, techniques, recipes, food facts, and folklore. Thomas Dunne Books 2009 303p il $25.99   **641.5**
1. Cooking
ISBN 978-0-312-53718-0
LC 2009-16741
"Beginning with the properly sliced onion, Crumpacker explains the hows of cooking as well as the whys: readers will learn why roasting a chicken upside-down is preferable (it keeps the white meat moist), how you can salvage overcooked scrambled eggs (a little butter or sour cream), and the best way to crush tomatoes for homemade marinara sauce (by hand). These and other tips won't bowl over veteran cooks, but Crumpacker's simple advice will rapidly build cookery confidence in those used to dining on canned or premade products. . . . Though bolstered with recipes, Crumpacker's crisp prose makes this volume a winner—the next best thing to having a chef at your side as you prepare to tackle a new dish." Publ Wkly
Includes bibliographical references

Cunningham, Marion

The **Fannie** Farmer cookbook; illustrated by Lauren Jarrett. 13th ed; Knopf 1996 874p il $30   **641.5**
1. Cooking
ISBN 0-679-45081-5
LC 97-162330
First published 1896 under the authorship of Fannie Merritt Farmer. Periodically revised
This standard cookbook focuses on the selection, preparation, and serving of a wide variety of foods

David, Elizabeth

A **book** of Mediterranean food; decorated by John Minton. 2nd rev. ed.; New York Review Books 2002 203p il (New York Review Books classics) pa $14.95   **641.5**
1. Mediterranean cooking
ISBN 978-1-59017-003-8; 1-59017-003-2
LC 2002-749
First published 1950 in the United Kingdom
This is a "mixture of recipes, culinary lore, and frank talk. In bleak postwar Great Britain, when basics were rationed and fresh food a fantasy, David set about to cheer herself—and her audience—up with dishes from the south of France, Italy, Spain, Portugal, Greece, and the Middle East." Publisher's note

French provincial cooking. Grub Street 2008 519p il $34.95   **641.5**
1. French cooking
ISBN 978-1-904943-71-6; 1-904943-71-3
LC 2008-411778
First published 1960 in the United Kingdom
This book "should be approached and read as a series of short stories, as well as written and evocative as the best lit-

erature. The voice is highly personal and opinionated, sometimes sharp but always true and always entertaining. This book is a long essay on French cuisine, offering background stories and sketches of recipes very different from the prescriptive type of recipes that most modern readers might be used to today." Living France

Italian food; rev ed; Penguin Books 1999 xxxiii, 376p pa $16   **641.5**
1. Italian cooking
ISBN 978-0-14-118155-4; 0-14-118155-9
LC 99-200031
First published 1958 in the United Kingdom
"David studies and analyzes cooking the way a scholar analyzes literature, and, as a result, her titles are far more than just cookbooks. Along with the recipes, of which there are many, she explains at length the histories of the dishes and offers splendid advice on serving wine with the meals." Libr J
Includes bibliographical references

Summer cooking; illustrated by Adrian Daintrey. New York Review Books 2002 234p il (New York Review Books classics) pa $12.95   **641.5**
1. British cooking
ISBN 978-1-59017-004-5; 1-59017-004-0
LC 2002-744
First published 1955 in the United Kingdom
"Don't let the unsophisticated subject fool you into expecting only cheese sandwiches and potato salads. For all its simplicity, 'Summer Cooking' is a wonderfully subversive volume — every bit as unexpected and enchanting to read today as it must have been 50 years ago, when England was just stirring from its wartime fast and garlic was an ingredient still capable of provoking controversy. . . . David earned her place in gastronomic history by being one of the first writers to suggest that thoughtful food and cooking itself could be a means of escape. Now, 15 years after her death, that voice remains a singular note in the chorus of her contemporaries and acolytes, neither frankly amiable like Julia Child, nor seductively literate like M.F.K. Fisher, nor playfully mod like Nigella Lawson. No matter how trivial the point, David speaks her mind." Salon.com

Davies, Katie Quinn

What Katie Ate; Recipes and Other Bits and Pieces. photography by Katie Quinn Davies. Penguin Group USA 2012 304 p. col. ill. $40   **641.5**
1. Cookbooks 2. Cooking
ISBN 0670026182; 9780670026180
LC 2012289524
James Beard Foundation Award: Photography (2013)
In this book, food photographer Katie Quinn Davies "shares her favorite simple dishes with a . . . collection of recipes and . . . images. . . . Showcasing her extraordinary eye, this debut cookbook is a unique combination of food diary and how-to, with tips and tricks, photographs, recipes, and stories. . . . Featured dishes range from Wild Mushrooms on Toast with Parmesan and Herbs to Roasted Pork Tenderloin with Apple, Prune & Pine Nut Stuffing and Cider Cream Gravy." (Publisher's note)

"Davies built her fan base with a blog that chronicles her meals and work, and her debut book gives readers a tangible record—part recipe collection, part scrapbook, laden with sumptuous color and extravagant, full-page layouts." Pub Wkly

De Laurentiis, Giada, 1970-

Happy cooking; Giada De Laurentiis. Pam Krauss Books 2015 320 p. color illustrations $35 **641.5**

1. Family 2. Cooking

ISBN 0804187924; 9780804187923; 9780804187930

LC 2015022028

Author Giada de Laurentis presents "nearly 200 new recipes and helpful advice on everything from hosting a potluck or open house to what to pack along for lunch every day. Drawing on the time-saving tips and healthy eating strategies that keep her functioning at the highest possible level in her roles as working mom, restaurateur, and tv personality, she has assembled a year-round roadmap to vibrant good health and delicious eating." (Publisher's note)

Devlin, Naomi

River Cottage Gluten Free; by Naomi Devlin. St. Martin's Press 2016 272 p. $25 **641.5**

1. Gluten-free diet

ISBN 1408858479; 9781408858479

LC 2016026345

In this cookbook, "nutritionist Naomi Devlin gives clear advice for gluten-free eating, including detailed guidance on alternative flours, methods of fermentation, and baking ideas. 120 tasty recipes [are included] for breakfasts, breads, pastries, soups, salads, snacks, main dishes, and desserts." (Publisher's note)

Dickerman, Sara

The **food** lover's cleanse; 140 delicious, nourishing recipes that will tempt you back into healthful eating. by Sara Dickerman. HarperCollins 2015 341 p. color illustrations $35 **641.5**

1. Diet 2. Cooking

ISBN 0062390236; 9780062390233

In this book, by Sara Dickerman, "you'll find four different two-week cleanse plans, one for each season, and 140 fabulous recipes that use fresh, flavorful, unprocessed ingredients. High in fruits, vegetables, and whole grains . . . the program emphasizes eating mindfully, controlling portion size, and curbing grazing impulses. Empty calories are replaced with filling protein- or fiber-rich snacks." (Publisher's note)

"Dickerman's approachable guide to whole foods-centric, occasionally meatless healthy eating can help readers curb their postholiday guilt and adopt sustainable life changes. For vegetarians and vegans, Mark Bittman's The VB6 Cookbook is a better choice." Library Journal

DiSpirito, Rocco

Now eat this! 150 of America's favorite comfort foods, all under 350 calories. Ballantine Books 2010 xxiii, 246p il pa $22; ebook $22 **641.5**

1. Cooking 2. Low-calorie diet

ISBN 978-0-345-52090-6 pa; 0-345-52090-4 pa;

978-0-307-76753-0 ebook; 0-307-76753-1 ebook

LC 2009-52470

"Lower-calorie brownies, gravy, spaghetti and meatballs, and beef stroganoff will delight readers who have been avoiding favorite foods." Libr J

Dojny, Brooke

The **New** England cookbook; 350 recipes from town and country, land and sea, hearth and home. illustrations by John MacDonald. Harvard Common Press 1999 652p il $29.95; pa $21.95 **641.5**

1. Cooking

ISBN 1-55832-138-1; 1-55832-139-X pa

LC 99-14393

This volume includes traditional dishes as well as "dozens of ethnic specialties from the various immigrant groups who have helped populate New England: Oregano-Scented Greek Lamb Shanks, Portuguese Tuna Escabeche, and Garlicky Mussels, Italian-style, to name a few." Libr J

Includes bibliographical references and index

Donofrio, Jeanine

The **Love** and Lemons Cookbook; An Apple-to-zucchini Celebration of Impromptu Cooking. by Jeanine Donofrio. Penguin Group USA 2016 320 p. color illustrations $35 **641.5**

1. Cooking -- Vegetables 2. Quick and easy cooking

ISBN 1583335862; 9781583335864

LC 2016006543

This cookbook, by Jeanine Donofrio, "features more than one hundred simple recipes that help you turn your farmers market finds into delicious meals. . . . Organized by ingredient, [it] teaches readers how to make beautiful food with what's on hand. . . . The book also features resources to show readers how to stock their pantry, gluten-free and vegan options for many of the recipes, as well as ideas on mixing and matching ingredients, so that readers always have something new to try." (Publisher's note)

"Celebrating spontaneity in cooking with plant-based inspiration, this imaginative recipe collection will please cooks who take their cue from ingredients as much as from recipes." Pub Wkly

Duclos, Andrea

The **plantiful** table; easy, from-the-earth recipes for the whole family. Andrea Duclos. Experiment, LLC 2015 311 p. color illustrations (cloth) $24.95 **641.5**

1. Vegetarian cooking

ISBN 1615192476; 9781615192472

LC 2015003784

This cookbook, by Andrea Duclos, presents "Over 125 full-flavored, plant-based dishes sure to please even the pickiest kids and the hungriest adults. . . . Throughout, Drea gives kid-friendly tips so that one meal can feed everyone. Plus, she takes the guesswork out of reviving leftovers. So, from Drea's family to yours—large or small, all-vegan or not—here are hearty meals straight from the earth, perfect for your happy home, every day!" (Publisher's note)

Duguid, Naomi

Taste of Persia; A Cook's Travels Through Armenia, Azerbaijan, Georgia, Iran, and Kurdistan. by Naomi Duguid. Artisan, a division of Workman Publishing Company, Inc. 2016 400 p. color ill., color maps (ebook) $35; (hardback, with dust jacket) $35 **641.5**
1. Middle Eastern cooking 2. Cooking, Iranian 3. Cooking, Kurdish 4. Cooking, Armenian 5. Cooking, Azerbaijani 6. Cooking, Georgian (South Caucasian)
ISBN 9781579657277; 9781579655488

LC 2016012875

This book, by Naomi Duguid, focuses on "the Persian culinary region. . . . Nearly 125 recipes, framed with stories and photographs of people and places, introduce us to a culinary paradise where ancient legends and ruins rub shoulders with new beginnings—where a wealth of history and culinary traditions makes it a compelling place to read about for cooks and travelers and for anyone hankering to experience the food of a wider world." (Publisher's note)

"This gorgeous and compelling title will transport home cooks and armchair travelers to another time and place." LJ

Includes bibliographical references (pages 375-379) and index.

Dunlop, Fuchsia

Land of fish and rice; Recipes from the Culinary Heart of China. Fuchsia Dunlop. W W Norton & Co Inc 2016 368 p. (hardcover) $35 **641.5**
1. Cookbooks 2. Chinese cooking 3. Cooking, Chinese
ISBN 9780393254389

LC 2016013124

This cookbook by Fuchsia Dunlop "draws on years of study and exploration to present the recipes, techniques, and ingredients of the Jiangnan kitchen. You will be inspired to try classic dishes such as Beggar's Chicken and sumptuous Dongpo Pork, as well as fresh, simple recipes such as Clear-Steamed Sea Bass and Fresh Soybeans with Pickled Greens." (Publisher's note)

"The Jiangnan is an exquisite 'crucible of Chinese gastronomy,' and Dunlop's scholarly homage to the region will captivate the culinary imagination." Pub Wkly

Includes bibliographical references and index

Durand, Faith

The Kitchn cookbook; Sara Kate Gillingham-Ryan and Faith Durand; photographs by Leela Cyd. Clarkson Potter/Publishers 2014 304 p. color illustrations $32.50 **641.5**
1. Cooking 2. Kitchens
ISBN 0770434436; 9780770434434; 9780770434441

LC 2014029477

James Beard Foundation Award Winner: General Cooking (2015)

In this book by Sara Kate Gillinghma and Faith Durand "comes 150 recipes and a cooking school with 50 essential lessons, as well as a guide to organizing your kitchen--plus storage tips, tool reviews, inspiration from real kitchens, maintenance suggestions, 200 photographs, and much more." (Publisher's note)

Kitchen cookbook

Dusoulier, Clotilde

The French market cookbook; vegetarian recipes from my Parisian kitchen. by Clotilde Dusoulier. Clarkson Potter Publishers 2013 224 p. (pbk.) $22.50 **641.5**
1. French cooking 2. Vegetarian cooking 3. Cooking, French
ISBN 0307984826; 9780307984821

LC 2012554926

In this book author Clotilde Dusoulier "takes [readers] through the seasons in 82 recipes--and explores the love story between French cuisine and vegetables. [Recipes include] carrots are lightly spiced with star anise and vanilla in a soup made with almond milk; tomatoes are jazzed up by mustard in a gorgeous tart; winter squash stars in golden Corsican turnovers; and luscious peaches bake in a cardamom-scented custard." (Publisher's note)

"Organized by season and peppered with tips on how to select and store vegetables, this cookbook will excite readers looking for substantial vegetarian meals they can feel good about eating." LJ

The Eat Like a Man Guide to Feeding a Crowd; how to cook for family, friends, and spontaneous parties. by Ryan D'Agostino; foreword by Bryan Voltaggio; introduction by David Granger and Mario Batali. Chronicle Books 2015 224 p. illustrations (chiefly color) (alk. paper) $30 **641.5**
1. Entertaining 2. Quantity cooking
ISBN 1452131848; 9781452131849

LC 2014031085

This cookbook, by Ryan D'Agostino, "is the ultimate resource for guys who want to host big crowds and need the scaled-up recipes, logistical advice, and mojo to pull it off whether they're cooking breakfast for a houseful of weekend guests, producing an epic spread for the playoffs, or planning the backyard BBQ that trumps all. With tantalizing photos and about 100 recipes for lazy breakfasts, afternoon noshing, dinner spreads, and late-night binges." (Publisher's note)

"Well, men may not need this follow-up volume, timed for Father's Day, but they just might want it. Maintaining a formula similar to the original, 80 recipes from a distinguished line-up of chefs are offered, interspersed with brief essays from Esquire authors." Pub Wkly

The essential New York times grilling cookbook; more than 100 years of sizzling food writing and recipes. edited by Peter Kaminsky; foreword by Mark Bittman; other contributors include Craig Claiborne, Pierre Franey, Florence Fabricant, Steven Raichlen, Molly O'Neill, Julia Moskin, and many more. Sterling Epicure 2014 400 p. illustrations (some color) $24.95 **641.5**
1. Cookbooks 2. Barbecue cooking 3. Barbecuing
ISBN 1402793243; 9781402793240

LC 2013026602

Edited by Peter Kaminsky, this book shows how "Over the past 100 years, the 'New York Times' has published thousands of articles on barbecuing and grilling, along with mouthwatering recipes--and this unique collection gathers the very best. These essential pieces are worth savoring not only for their time-tested advice and instruction, but also for the quality of the storytelling: even non-cooks will find them a delight to read." (Publisher's note)

"A fascinating look at how various innovators, personalities, and cultural trends have shaped the evolution of grilling and barbecue." LJ

Includes bibliographical references and index

Estrine, Darryl

Harvest to heat; cooking with America's best chefs, farmers, and artisans. [by] Darryl Estrine and Kelly Kochendorfer; foreword by Alice Waters. Taunton Press 2010 295p il $40   641.5
1. Cooking
ISBN 978-1-60085-254-1
LC 2010-11943

"The authors match farmers and artisans with chefs and restaurants across the country to present 100 original recipes from, e.g., Eric Ripert (Le Bernardin, New York), Paul Kahan (Blackbird, Chicago), and Vitaly Paley (Paley's Place, Portland, OR), for the home cook, for starters and salads, main courses, sides, and desserts. . . . Each recipe is accompanied by a description of the farmer or artisan who provided the main ingredients. Sustainable food is in, and this book will encourage home cooks to follow the tenets of the movement." Libr J

Fairchild, Barbara

The **Bon** appetit cookbook. Wiley 2006 xxiv, 792p il $34.95   641.5
1. Cooking
ISBN 0-7645-9686-1; 978-0-7645-9686-5
LC 2005-5181

"Mirroring the magazine on which it is based, this collection of 1,200 recipes is accessible, applicable to most home cooks' lives and a pleasure to cook from." Publ Wkly

The **Bon** appetit fast easy fresh cookbook. J. Wiley 2008 xxix, 770p il $34.95   641.5
1. Cooking
ISBN 978-0-470-22630-8
LC 2007-44562

This cookbook "presents hundreds of quick and simple recipes from the magazine's popular 'Fast Easy Fresh' feature. An introductory 'Shopping Guide' covers buying and storing produce, meat, and fish, and dozens of sidebars and boxes provide more information on ingredients and techniques. . . . Sure to appeal to any busy cook as well as the magazine's numerous fans, this is highly recommended." Libr J

Falk, Daina

The **hungry** fan's game day cookbook; 165 recipes for eating, drinking & watching sports. Daina Falk. Oxmoor House 2016 256 p. color illustrations (paperback) $22.95   641.5
1. Cooking 2. Cookbooks 3. Sports spectators
ISBN 0848745833; 9780848745837
LC 2016943633

This cookbook, by Daina Falk, "celebrates game day cooking at its best, from pulled pork sandwiches at the tail-

gate to sky-high stadium chili at home. . . . [In this collection,] Daina presents more than 100 crowd-pleasing recipes to jazz up your tailgate and score points with any home game-watching guest." (Publisher's note)

"Regardless of culinary preferences or skill level, every hungry sports fan can find something appealing in this go-to guide for game days all year long." Pub Wkly

Fearnley-Whittingstall, Hugh

River Cottage every day; photography by Simon Wheeler. Ten Speed Press 2011 415p il $32.50   641.5
1. British cooking 2. Cooking -- Natural foods
ISBN 978-1-60774-098-8
LC 2010-46949

First published 2009 in the United Kingdom

"An advocate of a back-to-basics approach to cooking and sustainable agriculture, . . . [the author] delivers thoughtful insight and colorful narratives that celebrate the joy of good family food, which will inspire and compel readers into the kitchen, book in hand. Simple ingredients become brilliant when combined in fresh and easy recipes like Baked Breakfast Cheesecake, Curried Fish Pie, breads, boxed lunches, and frittatas." Libr J

River Cottage Veg; 200 Inspired Vegetable Recipes. Hugh Fearnley-Whittingstall. Random House Inc. 2013 416 p. (hardcover) $35   641.5
1. Cookbooks 2. Vegetarian cooking
ISBN 1607744724; 9781607744726

This book, by Hugh Fearnley-Whittingstall, offers "a comprehensive collection of 200+ recipes that embrace vegetarian cuisine as the centerpiece of a meal. . . . In this . . . illustrated cookbook, you'll find handy weeknight one-pot meals, pure and simple raw dishes, and hearty salads as well as a chapter of meze and tapas dishes to mix and match." (Publisher's note)

Fernald, Anya

Home cooked; 100 essential recipes for a new way to cook. Anya Fernald with Jessica Battilana. Ten Speed Press 2016 304 p. color illustrations (hardback) $35   641.5
1. Cooking 2. Family life
ISBN 9781607748403; 9781607748410
LC 2015033515

Authors Anya Fernald and Jessica Battilana present this "recipe collection and how-to guide for preparing base ingredients that can be used to make simple, weeknight meals, while also teaching skills like building and cooking over a fire, and preserving meat and produce, written by a sustainable food expert and founder of Belcampo Meat Co." (Publisher's note)

"Fernald's approach advances the importance of celebration, traditional ways of food and farm, and viable food production techniques." Pub Wkly

Includes bibliographical references and index

Fertel, Rien

The **one** true barbecue; fire, smoke, and the pitmasters who cook the whole hog. by Rien Fertel; photographs by Denny Culbert. Touchstone 2016

288 p. ill.(chiefly color), map (hardcover : alk. paper) $25   **641.5**
1. Barbecue cooking 2. Southern cooking 3. Cooks -- Southern States -- Biography 4. Barbecuing -- Southern States -- History 5. Southern States -- Social life and customs
ISBN 9781476793979

LC 2015033791

In this book, author Rien Fertel "chronicles the uniquely southern art of whole hog barbecue—America's original barbecue—through the professional pitmasters who make a living firing, smoking, flipping, and cooking 200-plus pound pigs." (Publisher's note)

"Fertel is well-aware that the ground he covers isn't entirely new, but food fans and lovers of Americana alike will go wh o le hog for this loving paean to a distinct tradition." Kirkus

Includes bibliographical references and index

Fertig, Judith
The **back** in the swing cookbook; recipes for eating and living well every day after breast cancer. Barbara C. Unell and Judith Fertig; foreword by Rachel S. Beller; photography by Sara Remington. Andrews McMeel Pub., LLC 2012 261 p. col. ill. $29.99   **641.5**
1. Cookbooks 2. Breast cancer 3. Breast -- Cancer -- Prevention 4. Breast -- Cancer -- Diet therapy -- Recipes
ISBN 1449418325; 9781449418328

LC 2011944354

IACP Cookbook Award (2013)

This cookbook, by Barbara C. Unell and Judith Fertig, "is . . . full of 150 feel-good recipes that are easy to prepare, with fresh ingredients specifically designed to help breast cancer survivors get back in the swing of joyful, healthy living. . . . In addition to . . . food and drinks, . . . [it] include[s] . . . friendly nuggets on topics ranging from genetics, lifestyle choices, and the environment to the influence of all three on living a full and happy life." (Publisher's note)

Flay, Bobby, 1964-
Brunch @ Bobby's; 140 Recipes for the Best Part of the Weekend. Bobby Flay with Stephanie Banyas and Sally Jackson; photographs by Ben Fink. Clarkson Potter/Publishers 2015 256 p. color illustrations $29.99   **641.5**
1. Brunches 2. Brunch @ Bobby's (Television program)
ISBN 0385345895; 9780385345897

LC 2014012752

This cookbook, by celebrity chef Bobby Flay, "includes 140 recipes starting with the lip-smacking cocktails, both spiked and virgin, . . . along with hot and iced coffees and teas. He then works his way through eggs; pancakes, waffles, and French toast (including flavored syrups and spreads); pastries (a first) and breads; salads and sandwiches; and side dishes. . . . This is how Bobby does brunch." (Publisher's note)

"These bold, flavorful moves from Flay's breakfast playbook will leave readers salivating." Pub Wkly

Bruch at Bobby's

Flinn, Kathleen
The **kitchen** counter cooking school; how a few simple lessons transformed nine culinary novices into fearless home cooks. Viking Adult 2011 285p il $26.95   **641.5**
1. Cooking -- Study and teaching
ISBN 978-0-670-02300-4

LC 2011016222

"A successful, ambitious graduate of Paris' Le Cordon Bleu culinary academy, Flinn scrutinized average American supermarket shoppers and concluded that far too many rely on prepackaged, processed foods. Pressing them about their food choices, she learned that these timid souls simply believed that they lacked the time and certainly the ability to regularly prepare meals for their families from fresh, seasonal ingredients. Flinn eventually recruited nine motivated volunteers who spent time with her to learn how to plan meals confidently, shop effectively, cook thoughtfully, and serve attractively. She taught them such basic techniques as braising as well as simple but important recipes such as roasted chicken. . . . Flinn winningly offers inspiration to anyone who cares about cooking but lacks basic tools and skills." Booklist

Includes bibliographical references

Fong, Henry
Nom nom paleo; food for humans. Michelle Tam + Henry Fong. Andrews McMeel Publishing 2013 277 p. color illustrations (hbk.) $35   **641.5**
1. Paleo cooking 2. Cooking (Natural foods) 3. Gluten-free diet -- Recipes 4. High-protein diet -- Recipes 5. Prehistoric peoples -- Nutrition
ISBN 1449450334; 9781449450335

LC 2013942801

James Beard Foundation Award Nominee: Focus on Health (2015)

This cookbook, by Michelle Tam and Henry Fong, presents "more than 100 fool-proof Paleo and gluten-free recipes, and over 900 step-by-step photographs and cartoons. . . . Building blocks such as Paleo Sriracha, Magic Mushroom Powder, and Paleo Mayonnaise lay the flavor foundation for many of the dishes in the rest of the book." (Publisher's note)

Includes bibliographical references (page 268) and index

Nomnom paleo

Foose, Martha Hall
★ **Screen** doors and sweet tea; recipes and tales from a Southern cook. Clarkson Potter/Publishers 2008 248p il $32.50   **641.5**
1. Southern cooking
ISBN 978-0-307-35140-1; 0-307-35140-8

LC 2007031646

"Born and raised in Mississippi, Foose cooks Southern food with a contemporary flair: Sweet Potato Soup is enhanced with coconut milk and curry powder; Blackberry Limeade gets a lift from a secret ingredient–cardamom; and her much-ballyhooed Sweet Tea Pie combines two great Southern staples–sweet tea and pie, of course–to make one phenomenal signature dessert. The more than 150 original recipes are not only full of flavor, but also rich with local color and characters." (Publisher's note)

Foung, Jessica Goldman

Sodium girls limitless low-salt cookbook; Jessica Goldman; photography by Matt Armendariz. Wiley 2012 256 p. (pbk.) $24.99   **641.5**

1. Cookbooks 2. Food -- Sodium content 3. Salt-free diet -- Recipes

ISBN 1118123778; 9781118123775

LC 2011040042

This is a cookbook by blogger Jessica Goldman Foung, who documents her experiences with living a low-sodium lifestyle on her blog Sodium Girl. Here, "she shares . . . recipes (some new, some from her blog, and some from celebrity chefs) and useful advice, such as how to cut salt from your favorite recipes, including buffalo wings and Bloody Marys. Also provided is information on handling diet-challenging situations and environments (e.g., restaurant outings, trips abroad, college dining halls)." (Library Journal)

Friedman, Andrew

Knives at dawn; the American quest for culinary glory at the legendary Bocuse d'Or competition. Free Press 2009 304p $26   **641.5**

1. Cooking -- Competitions

ISBN 978-1-4391-5307-9

LC 2009-35271

"A vibrant portrait of the world's most significant cooking competition, the Bocuse d'Or, in Lyon, France. . . . [The author] dynamically illustrates the colorful personalities, ego-battering conflicts, career-defining aspirations, politicking, precision planning, naked missteps and the final judges' decisions regarding the 2009 U.S. team's shot for the culinary gold medal. . . . The book is infused with the muscular, meticulous gusto of a sportswriter covering the Olympics. Edge-of-your-seat food writing of the highest caliber." Kirkus

Includes bibliographical references

Fuentes, Laura

The best homemade kids' lunches on the planet; make lunches your kids will love with over 200 deliciously nutritious lunchbox ideas. Laura Fuentes. Fair Winds Press 2014 240 p. color illustrations $24.99   **641.5**

1. Cookbooks 2. School children -- Food 3. Lunchbox cooking

ISBN 1592336086; 9781592336081

LC 2013049151

This cookbook dedicated to school child lunches, written by Laura Fuentes, "[f]ull of recipes to suit every age and stage, . . . shows you how simple and easy it is to prepare food that'll be the envy of the lunch table. . . . There are even entire lunchbox meals that are gluten-, soy-, and/or nut-free." (Publisher's note)

The best homemade kids' snacks on the planet; more than 200 healthy homemade snacks you and your kids will love. Laura Fuentes. Quarto Pub Group USA 2015 240 p. illustrations $24.99 **641.5**

1. Snack foods 2. Eating habits

ISBN 1592336612; 9781592336616

LC 2014047820

In this book by Laura Fuentes readers will "find more than 200+ great ideas for solving the snack conundrum. Recipes and ideas you can whip up in minutes, without fuss in the kitchen, or fuss from your kid! So whether you're packing snacks for your purse, the school bag, the sports bag, or the can't-make-it-until-dinner whining hour, you'll find quick and healthy ideas everyone in your family will love." (Publisher's note)

"Stocked with good ideas, these recipes will give families (not just the kids!) nutritional snacking options." LJ

Gand, Gale

Gale Gand's brunch! Clarkson Potter/Publishers 2009 208p il $27.50   **641.5**

1. Cooking

ISBN 978-0-307-40698-9

LC 2008-36988

Gand "starts with an enticing assortment of drinks (e.g., white hot chocolate and a three-alarm Bloody Mary), then a chapter on brunch's eggy foundations—omelets, stratas, frittatas, quiches and crêpes, each with appetizing variations—that will please any brunch crowd. In subsequent chapters, Gand hits the sweet and savory high points, from pancakes and doughnuts to onion tarts and cheddar grits. . . . Accessible instructions, basic preparation tips and make-ahead hints ensure that both beginners and those who think cooking brunch is too bothersome will find this volume to be inspiring." Publ Wkly

Garten, Ina

Barefoot Contessa at home; everyday recipes you'll make over and over again. photographs by Quentin Bacon. Clarkson Potter 2006 p. cm. **641.5**

1. Menus. 2. Cookery.

ISBN 1400054346

LC 2006014257

Barefoot Contessa family style; easy ideas and recipes that make everyone feel like family. photographs by Maura McEvoy; food styling by Rori Trovato. Potter 2002 240p il $35   **641.5**

1. Cooking

ISBN 0-609-61066-X

LC 2002-74979

This is "simple, elegant home cooking with good ingredients and a minimum of fuss. It takes a certain amount of chutzpah to include ordinary chicken noodle soup and mashed potatoes and gravy in a cookbook, but Garten pulls it off with heart and style." Publ Wkly

Barefoot Contessa, how easy is that? Ina Garten. 1st ed.; Clarkson Potter 2010 p. cm. $35   **641.5**

1. Cooking 2. Barefoot Contessa (East Hampton, N.Y.: Store)

ISBN 978-0-307-23876-4

LC 2010-2025

Barefoot in Paris; easy French food you really can make at home\Ina Garden; photographs by Quentin Bacon; Food Stuyleing by Rori Trovato; Prop

Styling by Miguel Flores-Vianna. Clarkson Potter\ Publishers 2004 p. cm **641.5**

ISBN 1-400-04935-0 (hardcover)

LC 2004-3280

Cooking for Jeffrey; A Barefoot Contessa Cookbook. Ina Garten. Clarkson Potter/Publishers 2016 256 p. color illustrations (hardcover) $35 **641.5**

1. Cookbooks 2. Quick and easy cooking

ISBN 9780307464897

LC 2016025974

This cookbook by Ina Garten, "is filled with the recipes . . . [her husband] and their friends request most often. . . . Traditional dishes that she's updated, such as Brisket with Onions and Leeks, and Tsimmes, . . . and new favorites, like Skillet-Roasted Lemon Chicken and Roasted Salmon Tacos, . . . salads, including Maple-Roasted Carrot Salad and Kale Salad. . . . Ina has included a chapter devoted to bread and cheese, with recipes and tips." (Publisher's note)

"True to form, this culinary love letter is as warm and comforting as Garten's dishes." Pub Wkly

Make it ahead; Ina Garten; photographs by Quentin Bacon; garden photographs by John M. Hall. Clarkson Potter 2014 272 p. color illustrations (hardback) $35 **641.5**

1. Cooking 2. Cookbooks 3. Make-ahead cooking 4. Barefoot Contessa (Store)

ISBN 0307464881; 9780307464880; 9780770434496

LC 2014004486

This cookbook, by Ina Garten, focuses on make-ahead practices in cooking. "Each recipe includes clear instructions for what you can do ahead of time, and how far in advance, so you can cook with confidence and eliminate last-minute surprises. . . . With beautiful photographs and hundreds of invaluable make-ahead tips, this is your new go-to guide for preparing meals that are stress-free yet filled with those fabulously satisfying flavors." (Publisher's note)

"Throughout, her tips and tricks, from a sidebar to one page, will simply help transform the cooking and the entertaining; she'll recommend storing pasta sauce in plastic freezer bags as well as spotlight the 10 make-ahead tips for parties. A quieter, simpler, more accessible version of Martha Stewart in the kitchen. Make-ahead meals appended." Booklist

Gentry, Ann

The **Real** Food Daily cookbook; really fresh, really good, really vegetarian. [by] Ann Gentry with Anthony Head. Ten Speed Press 2005 232p $24.95 **641.5**

1. Vegetarian cooking

ISBN 1-58008-618-7

LC 2005-16245

The author presents "what she has learned about seasonal, organic, macrobiotic and vegan cooking. Gentry doesn't break new ground—sandwiches made with tempeh instead of meat, and nut cheeses like cashew cheddar will be familiar to most vegans—but she provides clear and comprehensive directions on how to make them more interesting and flavorful. . . . Gentry explains the basics without preaching

or condescending to readers, and discusses nutritional benefits without unnecessary jargon." Publ Wkly

Gerson, Fany

My sweet Mexico; recipes for authentic breads, pastries, candies, beverages, and frozen treats. Ten Speed Press 2010 215p il $30 **641.5**

1. Desserts 2. Mexican cooking

ISBN 978-1-58008-994-4

LC 2010-14469

The author "has dutifully catalogued the confections of her native Mexico. . . . American readers who have only encountered the occasional tres leches cake in a Mexican restaurant will be stunned by the breadth and depth of recipes here, ranging from coffee-flavored corn cookies to guava caramel pecan rolls and hibiscus ice pops, all culled from Gerson's family, friends, and generous strangers. . . . Gerson's vivid descriptions, exacting instruction, and obvious passion for her subject matter make this volume a substantial read about the most tempting indulgences." Publ Wkly

Includes bibliographical references

Goin, Suzanne

★ **Sunday** suppers at Lucques; [by] Suzanne Goin with Teri Gelber; photographs by Shimon and Tammar. Knopf 2005 398p il $35 **641.5**

1. French cooking

ISBN 1-4000-4215-1

LC 2004-58604

The author "writes with passion and humor, and while her recipes are sophisticated and sometimes complicated, they are written with the home cook in mind." Libr J

Goldberg, Dan

Cuba! Recipes and Stories from the Cuban Kitchen. written by Dan Goldberg, Andrea Kuhn, and Jody Eddy. Ten Speed Press 2016 256 p. color illustrations (hardcover : alk. paper) $30 **641.5**

1. Cookbooks 2. Cuban cooking 3. Caribbean cooking 4. Cooking, Cuban

ISBN 9781607749868; 9781607749875

LC 2016011291

This cookbook written by Dan Goldberg, Andrea Kuhn, and Jody Eddy "explores the magic of this country through recipes and stories. . . . Goldberg and Kuhn . . . with renowned food writer Jody Eddy, bring the best of Cuban food to home kitchens with more than 75 meticulously tested recipes. From Cuban-Style Fried Chicken . . . to Squid-ink Empanadas. . . . This cookbook offers a unique opportunity to bring a little slice of Cuba into your home and onto your plate." (Publisher's note)

"Photographer Goldberg, art director Kuhn, and food writer Eddy made three visits to Havana and its environs over a five-year period, feasting on the local cuisine and meeting the proud cooks and farmers of the area. They now report back on their sightseeing, with scores of photos and 75 recipes in tow." Pub Wkly

Includes bibliographical references and index

Goldstein, Joyce

The **new** Mediterranean Jewish table; Old World recipes for the modern home. Joyce Goldstein. Uni-

versity of California Press 2016 468 p. (cloth : alk. paper) $39.95 **641.5**
1. Jewish cooking 2. Mediterranean cooking 3. Cooking, Mediterranean
ISBN 9780520284999

LC 2015043306

This book, by Joyce Goldstein, is a "guide to Jewish home cooking. . . . It is . . . filled with . . . seasonal recipes . . . that embrace fresh fruits and vegetables; grains and legumes; small portions of meat, poultry, and fish; and a healthy mix of herbs and spices. It is also the story of how Jewish cooks successfully brought the local ingredients, techniques, and traditions of their new homelands into their kitchens." (Publisher's note)

"Thorough research and excellent recipes make Goldstein's latest an instant classic, worthy of shelf space alongside complementary works by Claudia Roden and Joan Nathan." LJ

Includes bibliographical references and index

Good housekeeping (Periodical)
★ The **Good** Housekeeping cookbook; 1,275 recipes from America's favorite test kitchen. edited by Susan Westmoreland. 125th anniversary ed.; Hearst Books 2010 752p il $35 **641.5**
1. Cooking
ISBN 978-1-58816-813-9

LC 2010-18437

Provides over 1,200 traditional and contemporary American recipes and offers information on cooking techniques, tools, ingredients, food handling, nutrition, canning, freezing, and holiday celebrations.

"Quick recipes and simple dessert preparations, like Fire-Roasted Nectarines and Coffee Granita, will please anyone pressed for time, but the encyclopedic inclusion of recipes for everything from Egg Salad, Lobster Bisque, and Chocolate Souffle to Pad Thai, Salmon with Mustard-Dill Sauce, and Muffuletta is its true benefit, making it a cookbook readers will grow with." Publ Wkly

Goodall, Tiffany
The **ultimate** student cookbook; from chicken to chili. photography by Claire Peters. Firefly Books 2010 160p il pa $14.95 **641.5**
1. Cooking 2. Quick and easy cooking
ISBN 978-1-55407-602-4

The author "outlines basic kitchen equipment, pantry ingredients, and food hygiene. Writing for the student with no cooking experience, she offers step-by-step photos that will make cooking a breeze. Goodall discusses basics like how to cook noodles, rice, and potatoes and presents dishes like wraps, salads, soups, chili, pizza, kebabs, and cakes. Two alcoholic drinks are included. Highly recommended for the numerous photographs and the variety of recipes." Libr J

The **gourmet** cookbook; more than 1000 recipes. edited by Ruth Reichl. Houghton Mifflin 2004 1040p $40 **641.5**
1. Cooking
ISBN 0-618-37408-6

LC 2004-47873

Recipes culled from issues of Gourmet magazine include "concoctions like Coq au Vin, Beef Wellington, Coulibiac, Chop Suey, Bananas Foster, and Black Forest Cake. . . . Every chapter begins with an overview of its subject; each recipe has an introduction; and many dishes feature helpful 'cook's notes,' which give tips for food preparation, technique and storage." Publ Wkly

Gourmet today; more than 1000 all-new recipes for the contemporary kitchen. edited by Ruth Reichl. Houghton Mifflin Harcourt 2009 1008p il $40 **641.5**
1. Cooking
ISBN 978-0-618-61018-1

LC 2009-19781

The editor "offers a diverse range of recipes that reflect the ever-changing American palate and the many cultures that have influenced it. Alongside Stilton cheese puff are recipes for babaghanouj, bangers and mash, Armenian lamb pizza, arepas with black beans and feta, and Vietnamese fried spring rolls. Informative sidebars provide details on a huge array of topics, from what salt to use when to preserving fish. . . . Comprehensive, appetizing and thoroughly tested, this mammoth collection is the book no kitchen should be without." Publ Wkly

Greenspan, Dorie
Around my French table; more than 300 recipes from my home to yours. photographs by Alan Richardson. Houghton Mifflin Harcourt 2010 530p il $40 **641.5**
1. French cooking
ISBN 978-0-618-87553-5; 0-618-87553-0

LC 2010-14232

"A part-time Paris resident for more than a decade, Greenspan focuses on what French people really eat at home: easy-to-prepare yet flavorful dishes that are suitable for just about any time of day. From Bacon and Eggs and Asparagus Salad to Chicken in a Pot to Veal Chops with Rosemary Butter, her offerings are hardy, mostly uncomplicated, and superbly appetizing. She also provides sidebars on a wide range of topics, including whether or not to wash raw chicken, several ways of cooking beets, mussels, and more." Publ Wkly

Griffin, Brooke
Skinny suppers; 125 lightened up, healthier meals for your family. Brooke Griffin. William Morrow, an Imprint of HarperCollins Publishers 2016 320 p. color illustrations (hardcover) $29.99 **641.5**
1. Low-calorie diet 2. Quick and easy cooking 3. Low-calorie diet -- Recipes
ISBN 9780062419156

LC 2015034595

This cookbook, by Brooke Griffin, offers "125 suppers and sides (including 25 fan favorites) like Philly Cheesesteak Stuffed Peppers, Supreme Pizza Pasta Casserole, Un-Sloppy Janes, and Loaded Nacho Soup. These are recipes you can feel good about—they're satisfying, lower in fat and calories, and, most important, delicious! Plus, most are under 350 calories per serving and take less than 30 minutes from prep to table." (Publisher's note)

"Having this cookbook on hand will be like having your own personal cheerleader in the kitchen." Booklist

The **grilling** book; the definitive guide from Bon Appetit. edited by Adam Rapoport; photography by Peden + Munk. Andrews McMeel Pub., LLC 2013 432 p. color illustrations $45　　**641.5**
1. Cookbooks 2. Barbecue cooking
ISBN 1449427529; 9781449427528
LC 2012952341

This cookbook, edited by Adam Rapoport, focuses on grilling. "Offering more than 350 foolproof recipes, dozens of luscious full-color photographs, crystal clear illustrations, and plenty of plainspoken, here's-how-to-do-it guidelines, [it] welcomes you to everything that is sensational (and sensationally simple) about grilling." (Publisher's note)

Gur, Janna

The **book** of New Israeli food; a culinary journey. photography, Eilon Paz; contributing writers Rami Hann . . . [et al.] Schocken Books 2008 303p il $35　　**641.5**
1. Israeli cooking
ISBN 978-0-8052-1224-2; 0-8052-1224-8
First published 2007 in Israel

"Beautiful and comprehensive, this book will become an immediate favorite with anyone with even a passing interest in Israeli cuisine." Publ Wkly

Hair, Jaden

The **steamy** kitchen cookbook; 101 Asian recipes simple enough for tonight's dinner. photography by Jaden Hair. Tuttle Pub. 2009 160p il $27.95 **641.5**
1. Asian cooking
ISBN 978-0-8048-4028-6
LC 2009-17461

The author, a food blogger, "shares recipes drawn from her mother's kitchen, other food bloggers, and her own delightful archives. Her focus is mostly simple Asian dishes (from China, Vietnam, Japan, and Thailand), with several more complicated ones thrown into the mix. . . . For home cooks of all levels of experience seeking to expand their repertoire of Asian recipes, Hair has written an extremely accessible cookbook that blends great recipes with mouthwatering photographs she took." Libr J

Hamilton, Alissa

Got milked? the great dairy deception and why you'll thrive without milk. Alissa Hamilton. HarperCollins 2015 336 p. $26.99　　**641.5**
1. Milk 2. Dairy products
ISBN 0062362054; 9780062362056

In this book, author Alissa Hamilton "proves why we don't need dairy in our daily diets, how our dependence on it is actually making many people sick, and what we can do to change it. Hamilton turns a critical eye on the Dairy Food Group and the promotional programs it supports to dispel misconceptions about milk and its crucial role in our health. Interweaving cutting-edge science in a lively narrative, Got Milked opens our eyes to the many ways in which dairy can actually be harmful to our bodies." (Publisher's note)

"Recommended reading for anyone who is skeptical about health claims of food items." LJ

Hasselbrink, Kimberley

Vibrant food; celebrating the ingredients, recipes, and colors of each season. written and illustrated by Kimberley Hasselbrink. Ten Speed Press 2014 224 p. colored illustrations (hardback) $25　**641.5**
1. Seasonal cooking 2. Color of food 3. Food -- Pictorial works
ISBN 1607745410; 9781607745419
LC 2013040310

IACP Cookbook Award Finalist: Health & Special Diet (2015)

In this book, author Kimberley Hasselbrink "invites you to look at ingredients differently and let their colors inspire you: the shocking fluorescent pink of a chard stem, the deep reds and purples of baby kale leaves, the bright shades of green that emerge in the spring, and even the calm yellows and whites of so many winter vegetables. Thinking about produce in terms of color can reinvigorate your relationship with food." (Publisher's note)

"This enjoyable title would be a nice addition to the shelves of voracious seasonal cookbook readers, but it does not do enough to distinguish itself for most cooks, other than readers of the author's blog, to seek it out specifically." LJ

Hazan, Marcella, 1924-2013

Ingredienti; Marcella's Guide to the Market. by Marcella Hazan and Victor Hazan. Simon & Schuster 2016 256 p. illustrations $20　　**641.5**
1. Cookbooks 2. Italian cooking 3. Grocery shopping
ISBN 145162736X; 9781451627367

This book by Marcella Hazan and Victor Hazan presents a guide "on how to shop for the best ingredients and prepare the most delicious meals. . . . Her husband and . . . collaborator . . . translated and transcribed these vignettes on how to buy and what to do with the fresh produce used in Italian cooking. . . . Her clear, practical guidance in acquiring the components of good cooking is helpful wherever you choose to shop—in supermarkets, farmers' markets, . . . or online." (Publisher's note)

"This little volume offers a treasury of lifetime observations to serious, inquisitive cooks." Booklist
Includes bibliographical references.

Marcella says . . . Italian cooking wisdom from the legendary teacher's master classes, with more than 120 of her irresistible new recipes. HarperCollins Publishers 2004 390p il $29.95　　**641.5**
1. Italian cooking
ISBN 0-06-620967-6
LC 2004-42892

The author shares lessons in Italian cooking, discussing techniques, ingredients and planning and preparing Italian dishes

Henry, Diana

A **Change** of Appetite; where healthy meets delicious. Diana Henry. Octopus Pub Group 2014 336 p. color illustrations $34.99　　**641.5**
1. Cookbooks 2. Asian cooking 3. Middle Eastern

cooking
ISBN 1845338928; 9781845338923

LC 2014412876

James Beard Foundation Award Nominee: Focus on Health (2015)

"What happened when one of today's best-loved food writers had a change of appetite? Here are the dishes that Diana Henry created when she started to crave a different kind of diet--less meat and heavy food, more vegetable-, fish-, and grain-based dishes--often inspired by the food of the Middle East and Far East, but also drawing on cuisines from Georgia to Scandinavia." (Publisher's note)

"Broken down by season, the book offers a nice mix of food from around the world that will not take a toll on the digestive system." Pub Wkly

Includes bibliographical references (page 328-329) and index

Roast figs, sugar snow; food to warm the soul. photographs by Jason Lowe. Mitchell Beazley 2009 191p il pa $19.99 **641.5**
1. Cooking
ISBN 978-1-84533-524-3
First published 2005 in the United Kingdom

This "is an appealing collection of winter dishes from the Northern Hemisphere (including northern Italy, France, Russia, Switzerland, and Vermont), certain to make cooks yearn for a long winter." Libr J

Simple; by Diana Henry. Octopus Pub Group 2016 320 p. $32.99 **641.5**
1. Cookbooks 2. Quick and easy cooking
ISBN 1784722049; 9781784722043

This cookbook by Diana Henry features "ingenious ideas such as no-hassle starters and sauces that will lift any dish. From Turkish Pasta with Caramelized Onions, Yoghurt and Dill and Paprika-baked Pork Chops with Beetroot, . . . to Parmesan-roasted Cauliflower with Garlic and Thyme, [Henry] takes the kind of ingredients we are most likely to find in our cupboard and fridge . . . and provides recipes that will become your friends for life." (Publisher's note)

"Those looking to enliven their daily toast, eggs, pastas, and salads will find particularly fabulous choices here, along with other delicious mains and desserts." LJ

Hesser, Amanda

The **essential** New York Times cook book; classic recipes for a new century. W.W. Norton 2010 932p il $40 **641.5**
1. Cooking
ISBN 978-0-393-06103-1; 0-393-06103-5

LC 2010-33311

The author "spent six years combing the Times's vast recipe archive, cooking her way through more than 1000 recipes to assemble this indispensible tome culled from 150 years of the paper's food columns. This daunting compendium features both noteworthy classics (Osso Buco) and modern recipes (Smoked Mashed Potatoes) that have been tested and, in some cases, updated for the contemporary cook. Chapters begin with a time line and are arranged by type of food (e.g., soups, vegetables, cakes) then chronologi-

cally within the chapter, making for a fascinating historic overview of the interests of American cooks." Libr J

Includes bibliographical references

Hirsheimer, Christopher

Canal house cooks every day; Melissa Hamilton, Christopher Hirsheimer. Andrews McMeel Pub., LLC 2012 359 p. col. ill. $45 **641.5**
1. Cooking 2. Cookbooks
ISBN 1449421474; 9781449421472

LC 2012936742

James Beard Foundation Award: General Cooking (2013)

This book, by Melissa Hamilton and Christopher Hirsheimer, was the 2013 James Beard Foundation Award winner for General Cooking. "The delicious, easy-to-prepare recipes celebrate the everyday practice of simple cooking and the enjoyment of eating. . . . In addition to the recipes, this wonderful cookbook includes menus for all the great holidays throughout the year, plus twelve intimate essays . . . that introduce each month and capture the feeling and vibe of that special time of the year." (Publisher's note)

Hyman, Gwen

Urban Italian; simple recipes and true stories from a life in food. [by] Andrew Carmellini, and Gwen Hyman; photographs by Quentin Bacon. Bloomsbury 2008 311p il $35 **641.5**
1. Italian cooking
ISBN 978-1-59691-470-4

The author "presents spectacular recipes while opening a window onto his life with food, from his Italian-American boyhood and cooking school to revelations while traveling in Italy and being a top New York chef. . . . The recipes, which come from all over Italy and mix regional Italian and American influences, are arranged classically, from antipasti to dolci." Publ Wkly

The **illustrated** kitchen bible; editor-in-chief, Victoria Blashford-Snell. DK Pub 2008 544 p. color illustrations $24.95 **641.5**
1. Cooking 2. International cooking
ISBN 0756639743; 1465451552; 9780756639747; 9781465451552

LC 2009275493

This book, by Victoria Blashford-Snell, is "a comprehensive kitchen resource of over 1,000 delicious, achievable, and international recipes, with sumptuous photography, precise text, and innovative ideas, now with a refreshed new look." (Publisher's note)

"The sheer number of options and clear instructions will ensure success no matter the cook's skill level, and the curated recipes make this a book that cooks of all tastes and skill levels can grow with." Pub Wkly

Kitchen bible

Iyer, Raghavan

660 curries; the gateway to the world of Indian cooking. by Raghavan Iyer. Workman Pub. 2008 809p il $32.50; pa $22.95 **641.5**
1. Indian cooking 2. Cooking -- Curry
ISBN 978-0-7611-4855-5; 0-7611-4855-8; 978-0-

7611-3787-0 pa; 0-7611-3787-4 pa

LC 2008-1288

"A wide-ranging guide to the curries of the Indian subcontinent, including Pakistan, Nepal, and Sri Lanka. Iyer explains that Indian curries are not based on a can of curry powder and that the term 'curry' refers to any dish simmered in or covered with a fragrant, spicy (though not necessarily hot) sauce or gravy. The hundreds of recipes include appetizer curries such as Skewered Chicken with Creamy Fenugreek Sauce, main-course curries like Yogurt-Marinated Lamb with Ginger and Garlic, and 'contemporary curries' such as Wild Salmon with Chiles, Scallions, and Tomato; there are also recipes for 'curry cohorts'—rice, bread, and other accompaniments." Libr J

Jaffrey, Madhur

At home with Madhur Jaffrey; simple, delectable dishes from India, Pakistan, Bangladesh, and Sri Lanka. Alfred A. Knopf 2010 301p il $35; ebook $35   **641.5**

1. Asian cooking

ISBN 978-0-307-26824-2; 978-0-307-59440-2 ebook

LC 2010-19678

This is a "cookbook of easily prepared, thoughtful, and unusual dishes from India, Pakistan, Bangladesh, and Sri Lanka. Anyone looking to explore Indian cooking for the first time will find this volume uniquely helpful." Booklist

Madhur Jaffrey's world vegetarian. Potter 1999 760p $40; pa $24.95   **641.5**

1. Vegetarian cooking

ISBN 0-517-59632-6; 0-609-80923-7 pa

LC 98-30318

A compendium of vegetarian "recipes from all over the world. Grouped mostly into broad categories by main ingredient (beans, grain, vegetables, etc.), they are as likely to come from a Palestinian restaurant in Toronto, the nuns at the Ormylia Monastery in Macedonia, or a home cook in Mexico as from Jaffrey's own Indian background or her experience as a cooking teacher." Libr J

Madhur Jaffrey's ultimate curry bible; India, Singapore, Malaysia, Indonesia, Thailand, South Africa, Kenya, Great Britain, Trinidad, Guyana, Japan, USA. Ebury 2003 352p il $51.65   **641.5**

1. Cooking -- Curry

ISBN 978-0-09-187415-5; 0-09-187415-7

With over 150 recipes, "Madhur starts with the best curry recipes in India today, moves on to Asian curries, and even includes European curry ideas such as French curry sauces. Some recipes have never before appeared in print, such as fish seasoned with tamarind and coconut and lamb braised with oranges. Also included are Madhur's tips for the best accompanying foods — she gives us ideas for rice, bread, chutneys, relishes and sweets — the perfect complement for any curry." Publisher's note

Jamison, Cheryl Alters

The **big** book of outdoor cooking and entertaining; spirited recipes and expert tips for barbecuing, charcoal and gas grilling, rotisserie roasting, smok-

ing, deep-frying, and making merry. [by] Cheryl and Bill Jamison. Morrow 2006 548p $24.95   **641.5**

1. Entertaining 2. Barbecue cooking

ISBN 0-06-073784-0; 978-0-06-073784-9

LC 2006-41918

This book features "more than 850 recipes and information on every aspect of backyard cooking. There are dozens of 'Party-Time Tips' and other helpful hints, menu suggestions, and sidebars and boxes on techniques, ingredients, and more. . . . New grilling books appear as the season approaches every year, but this one is an essential purchase." Libr J

Jenkins, Nancy Harmon

The **new** Mediterranean diet cookbook; a delicious alternative for lifelong health. with a foreword by Marion Nestle. Bantam Books 2009 496p $26.95   **641.5**

1. Low-fat diet 2. Mediterranean cooking

ISBN 978-0-553-38509-0; 0-553-38509-7

LC 2008-40982

First published 1994 with title: The Mediterranean diet cookbook

Jenkins' "knowledge of these cuisines is both personal and informed. . . . An essential purchase." Libr J

Includes bibliographical references

Jinich, Pati

Mexican today; new and rediscovered recipes for contemporary kitchens. Pati Jinich; photography by Ellen Silverman. Houghton Mifflin Harcourt 2016 320 p. color illustrations (paper over board) $30   **641.5**

1. Mexican cooking 2. Mexican American cooking 3. Cooking, Mexican

ISBN 0544557247; 9780544557246

LC 2015042717

In this Mexican cookbook, chef Pati Jinich "shares easy, generous dishes, both traditional ones and her own new spins. Some are regional recipes she has recovered from the past and updated, like Miners' Enchiladas with fresh vegetables and cheese or Drunken Rice with Chicken and Chorizo, a specialty of the Yucatán." (Publisher's note)

"Many of her recipes can be made in advance or in less than 30 minutes and rely on easy-to-find ingredients. A highlight of this cookbook is its playful variations such as baked huevos rancheros casserole." LJ

Jones, Anna

A **modern** way to eat; 200+ Satisfying Vegetarian Recipes. by Anna Jones. Ten Speed Press 2014 352 p. color illustrations (hardback) $35   **641.5**

1. Cookbooks 2. Vegetarian cooking

ISBN 1607748037; 9781607748038

LC 2014035561

This book, by Anna Jones, offers a "modern vegetarian cookbook packed with quick, healthy, and fresh recipes that explore the full breadth of vegetarian ingredients--grains, nuts, seeds, and seasonal vegetables--from Jamie Oliver's London-based food stylist and writer Anna Jones." (Publisher's note)

"Attuned to the latest dietary trends, this excellent vegetarian cookbook blends the cozy, clever charm of Sophie

Dahl's Very Fond of Food with the varied textures and flavors from Yotam Ottolenghi's Plenty and the quick, bonus meal ideas (e.g., one soup: 1,000 variations, ten ways with avocado on toast) of Mark Bittman's "How To Cook Everything" series."LJ

Jones, Judith

The **pleasures** of cooking for one. Alfred A. Knopf 2009 273p il $27.95 **641.5**
1. Cooking
ISBN 978-0-307-27072-6
LC 2009-12307

Counsels readers on how to enjoy a solitary culinary life by preparing meals in accordance with one's own preferences, outlining a range of basic through sophisticated recipes that work in weekly menus and make use of leftovers.

This is a "civilized, unfussy guide to cooking—and cooking well—for solitary diners. . . . [The author] doesn't skip desserts, entertaining or self-indulgence, and best of all, her whole book benefits from the diverse and cumulative gleanings of work with many of the great cooks and cookbook writers (including Julia Child, of course) of the latter half of the 20th century." Publ Wkly

Includes bibliographical references

Joulwan, Melissa

Well fed; Paleo recipes for people who love to eat. by Melissa Joulwan; foreword by Melissa and Dallas Hartwig; photos by David Humphreys; design by Kathleen Shannon. Greenleaf Book Group Llc 2012 160 p. ill. (chiefly col.) $29.95 **641.5**
1. Cookbooks 2. Paleo cooking 3. Reducing diets 4. High-protein diet -- Recipes 5. Prehistoric peoples -- Nutrition
ISBN 061557226X; 9780615572260

This paleo-diet cookbook, by Melissa Joulwan, "explains how to get in the habit of a Weekly Cookup so that you have ready-to-go food for snacks and meals every day. It will also show you how to make Hot Plates, a mix-and-match approach to combining basic ingredients with spices and seasonings. . . . The recipes are as simple as possible, without compromising taste." (Publisher's note)

Kamozawa, Aki

Ideas in food; great recipes and why they work. [by] Aki Kamozawa and H. Alexander Talbot. Clarkson Potter 2010 320p il $25 **641.5**
1. Cooking 2. Chemistry
ISBN 978-0-307-71740-5; 978-0-307-71974-4 ebook
LC 2010-17633

"The authors break down the science behind correctly and deliciously preparing everything from bread, pasta, and eggs (including soft scrambled eggs; hardboiled eggs, and brown butter hollandaise sauce) to homemade butter and yogurt. Most recipes fall into the 'Ideas for Everyone' category, which composes about the first three-quarters of the book; the final section is 'Ideas for Professionals,' which explores trendy molecular gastronomy topics like liquid nitrogen-used to make popcorn gelato-and carbon dioxide, a necessary tool for making coffee onion rings. Straightforward prose and anecdotes with personality keep this from being a dry food science tome. And accessible recipes for

such dishes as a simple roast chicken, green beans almondine, and root beer-braised short ribs mean it never gets too lofty." Publ Wkly

Includes bibliographical references

Katz, Rebecca

The **cancer**-fighting kitchen; nourishing big-flavor recipes for cancer treatment and recovery. [by] Rebecca Katz with Mat Edelson. Celestial Arts 2009 222p il $32.50 **641.5**
1. Cooking for the sick 2. Cancer -- Diet therapy
ISBN 978-1-58761-344-9
LC 2009-14359

"Katz's experience with cancer patients and their long, often frustrating recovery lends authority to her wise, common-sense approach, suitable for cooks of all skill levels." Publ Wkly

Includes bibliographical references

Katzen, Mollie

Get cooking; 150 simple recipes to get you started in the kitchen. [by] Mollie Katzen, with photographs by the author. HarperStudio 2009 xx, 268p il pa $24.99 **641.5**
1. Cooking
ISBN 978-0-06-173243-0
LC 2009-32815

This book "offers an invaluable list of equipment and advice (you can never have too many cutting boards), plus an illustrated vegetable-chopping guide. The 150 recipes for such common dishes as chicken noodle soup, potato salad, and spaghetti and meatballs are a good starting place for beginners. The recipes note variations, complementary dishes, and vegan dishes. Highly recommended for new cooks." Libr J

The **heart** of the plate; vegetarian recipes for a new generation. Mollie Katzen; photographs and illustrations by Mollie Katzen. Houghton Mifflin Harcourt 2013 464 p. $34.99 **641.5**
1. Cookbooks 2. Vegetarian cooking 3. International cooking 4. Cooking (Natural foods)
ISBN 0547571593; 9780547571591
LC 2013010180

This cookbook by Mollie Katzen promotes vegetables, focusing "on their natural flavors rather than rich accompaniments such as butter, cream, and cheese." The recipes "combine everyday vegetables in appetizing ways." Chapters on soups, salads, grains, burgers, pasta, and desserts are included. (Publishers Weekly)

The **Moosewood** Cookbook; 40th Anniversary Edition. by Mollie Katzen. Random House Inc 2014 231 p. illustrations $19.99 **641.5**
1. Cooking 2. Vegetarian cooking
ISBN 1607747391; 9781607747390
LC 2014015685

This cookbook, by Mollie Katzen, originally published in 1974, "has inspired generations to cook simple, healthy, and seasonal food. . . . Katzen hand-wrote, illustrated, and locally published a spiral-bound notebook of recipes for vegetarian dishes inspired by those she and fellow cooks served at their small restaurant co-op in Ithaca, N.Y. . . . [It] continues to be a seminal, timely, and wholly personal work." (Publisher's note)

Keller, Thomas

★ Ad Hoc at home. Artisan Books 2009 359p il $50 **641.5**

1. Cooking

ISBN 978-1-57965-377-4

LC 2009-13258

For this cookbook, the author focuses on "family-style meals for the home cook in this accessible and dazzlingly beautiful book based on the fare served at his Ad Hoc restaurant, in Napa, Calif. . . . [He provides] a thorough primer on the foundations of cooking, offering clear and easy-to-follow instructions on techniques such as butchering and trussing chickens and tying a pork loin. . . . Dishes such as braised beef short ribs, buttermilk fried chicken, and fig-stuffed roast pork loin highlight a vast array of offerings that range from crab cakes to shortbread cookies." Publ Wkly

Kennedy, Diana

From my Mexican kitchen; techniques and ingredients. photographs by Michael Calderwood; and styled by the author. Clarkson Potter 2003 320p il $40 **641.5**

1. Mexican cooking

ISBN 0-609-60700-6

LC 2002-70405

The author "explains how to produce authentic enchiladas, tacos, tamales, sopes, panuchos, and other Mexican classics. Kennedy also provides a guide to wild greens, items rarely seen outside provincial markets. Her advice on freezing excess quantities of cuitlacoche (corn fungus) will reward fans of that uncommon mushroom. This is an indispensable addition to any library cookbook collection." Booklist

Kiros, Tessa

Food from many Greek kitchens. Andrews McMeel Pub. 2011 333p il $35 **641.5**

1. Greek cooking

ISBN 978-1-4494-0652-3

LC 2010943021

First published 2010 in Australia

"For each recipe, [the author] gives the title in English and Greek and offers an introduction to the dish and thorough instruction. From Baklava to Keftedes Fried Meatballs to Pita Bread, the accessible dishes are accompanied by beautiful photography. Greek cookbooks written for the beginner are rare, so this book is a gem. It provides a good foundation and is sure to be a gateway to more advanced Greek cooking." Lirb J

Ko, Genevieve

Home cooking with Jean-Georges; [by] Jean-Georges Vongerichten with Genevieve Ko. Clarkson Potter/Publishers 2011 256p il $40 **641.5**

1. Cooking

ISBN 978-0-307-71795-5; 0-307-71795-X

LC 2010-53808

"After working 18-hour days six days a week, Vongerichten buys a weekend country home and rediscovers the joys of unfussy cooking. He shares recipes for the meals he and his family enjoy in this pleasingly accessible volume. Chicken liver and pancetta crostini, swiss chard braised in shiitake butter, shortbread are among the recipes that cover salads, fish and seafood, meat, desserts, and brunch. All focus on flavor yet rely on a minimal number of ingredients that don't take a lot of time and effort to prepare. . . . Dotted with culinary reminiscences both personal and professional, this book shows Vongerichten at his simple best and offers his many fans the opportunity to cook and enjoy his favorite meals without being chained to the kitchen for hours." Publ Wkly

Koenig, Leah

Modern Jewish cooking; recipes & customs for today's kitchen. Leah Koenig; photographs by Sang An. Chronicle Books 2014 352 p. color illustrations (hardcover) $35 **641.5**

1. Cookbooks 2. Jewish cooking

ISBN 1452127484; 9781452127484

LC 2014012075

This cookbook, by Leah Koenig, with photographs by Sang An, "shares 175 recipes showcasing handmade, seasonal, vegetable-forward dishes. Classics of Jewish culinary culture--such as latkes, matzoh balls, challah, and hamantaschen--are updated with smart techniques and vibrant spices." (Publisher's note)

"The beautiful photography, pleasing layout on heavy paper, and excellent recipes make this a fine gift book as well as a suitable purchase for cookbook collections, especially in communities with large Jewish populations." LJ

Krieger, Ellie

You have it made! delicious, healthy do-ahead meals. Ellie Krieger; photography by Quentin Bacon. Houghton Mifflin Harcourt 2016 352 p. chiefly color illustrations (paper over board) $30 **641.5**

1. Quick and easy cooking 2. Make-ahead cooking

ISBN 9780544579309

LC 2015028798

This cookbook, by Ellie Krieger, is "devoted to . . . make-ahead meals. . . . Her recipes . . . can all be prepared ahead of time, making putting food on the table that much easier. Each recipe includes instructions for refrigerating and/or freezing as well as storing and reheating directions. With exciting dishes like the Pumpkin Spice Overnight Oats in Jars and the Herbed Salmon Salad, you'll be able to have meals ready days in advance." (Publisher's note)

"Healthy cooking often requires many steps and a reliance on daily visits to farmers' markets, but Krieger's new collection makes truly nourishing food more accessible to the average household." Pub Wkly

Lagasse, Emeril

From Emeril's kitchens; favorite recipes from Emeril's restaurants. William Morrow/HarperCollins 2003 342p il $27.50 **641.5**

1. Cooking

ISBN 978-0-06-018535-0; 0-06-01853-5

LC 2002-27568

"Spreading his philosophy and history in the introduction, [Emeril] entreats the user not to be put off by the complexity of many of the recipes, but to use the components and mix and match the dishes. The first chapter, 'Basics,' contains the building blocks of many of the dishes, ranging from the customary stocks to Hard Boiled Eggs and Roast Duck. Subsequent chapters are structured in the usual manner ranging from appetizers and first courses through desserts. Each dish is attributed to its restaurant or chef and results in a range of styles and inspirations." Publ Wkly

Lagasse, Emeril, 1959-

Essential Emeril; favorite recipes and hard-won wisdom from a life in the kitchen. by Emeril Lagasse. Oxmoor House 2015 304 p. color illustrations $29.95 **641.5**
1. Cooking
ISBN 0848744780; 9780848744786

LC 2015944368

In this cookbook, chef Emeril Lagasse "presents his favorite recipes, best-kept cooking secrets, and behind-the-scenes stories from his life in the kitchen. Discover more than 130 iconic dishes . . . each tested and perfected for today's home cook. . . . Anecdotes reveal the inspiration behind each recipe, with cameos from A-list names including Mario Batali, Roy Choi, and Nobu Matsuhira, alongside memories of family, friends, and early influences such as Julia Child and Charlie Trotter." (Publisher's note)

"More advanced than some of his other titles, Lagasse's latest showcases his skill. Emeril fans will savor these delicious and iconic dishes." LJ

Lang, Adam Perry

Serious barbecue; smoke, char, baste, and brush your way to great outdoor cooking. [by] Adam Perry Lang, with J.J. Goode and Amy Vogler. Hyperion Books 2009 390p il $35 **641.5**
1. Barbecue cooking
ISBN 978-1-4013-2306-6

LC 2009-1765

The author's "definition of barbecue includes grilling as well as 'low and slow cooking,' and he presents a wide variety of tasty recipes here, along with a detailed introduction to barbecue basics and many useful sidebars on techniques and other tips. Highly recommended for all collections." Libr J

Lawson, Nigella, 1960-

How to Eat; The Pleasures and Principles of Good Food. Nigella Lawson. John Wiley 2002 474 p. $35 **641.5**
1. Cooking 2. Cookery
ISBN 0471257508; 9780471257509

This cookbook, by celebrity chef Nigella Lawson, is an "all-purposed cookbook, brimming with easygoing mealtime strategies and 350 mouthwatering recipes, from a truly

sublime Tarragon French Roast Chicken to a totally decadent Chocolate Raspberry Pudding Cake." (Publisher's note)

Nigella express; good food, fast. photographs by Lis Parsons. Hyperion 2007 390p il $35 **641.5**
1. Cooking
ISBN 978-1-4013-2243-4; 1-4013-2243-3

"Recipes in this book run the gamut from retro crepe suzettes to modern favorites like quesadillas and smoothies; and from orange French toast for breakfast to cocktail nibbles for a party. In the interest of speed Lawson uses prepared ingredients, but they're the ones many of us use already, like mayonnaise from a jar or frozen puff pastry. And if her tastes are sometimes nostalgically British (Eton mess, roly poly pudding) she also has a whole chapter on quick Tex-Mex food." WeightWatchers.com

Simply Nigella; feel good food. Nigella Lawson; photographs by Keiko Oikawa. Flatiron Books 2015 416 p. color illustrations (hardcover) $35 **641.5**
1. Cooking 2. Well-being 3. Comfort food
ISBN 1250073758; 9781250073754

LC 2015036267

This cookbook by Nigella Lawson "taps into the rhythms of our cooking lives with recipes that are uncomplicated and relaxed yet always satisfying. From quick and calm workday dinners (Miso Salmon; Cauliflower & Cashew Nut Curry) to stress-free ideas when feeding a crowd (Chicken Traybake with Bitter Orange & Fennel) to the instant joy of bowlfood for cozy nights on the sofa (Thai Noodles with Cinnamon and Shrimp), here is food guaranteed to make everyone feel good." (Publisher's note)

"Home cooks who love planning relaxed meals by whim will be well served by Lawson's latest, which offers a winning selection of recipes for all occasions." Library Journal

Le, Stephanie

Easy Gourmet; Awesome Recipes Anyone Can Cook. by Stephanie Le. St. Martin's Press 2014 240 p. color illustrations $21.99 **641.5**
1. Cooking 2. Cookbooks 3. Quick and easy cooking
ISBN 1624140629; 9781624140624

This cookbook, by Stephanie Le, "is full of updated modern twists on your favorite classics like Chicken and Waffles, Maple-Glazed Duck, Miso Cod and Quinoa, and Sriracha Hot Wings. Her must-have recipes cover every meal and everything in between, all paired with stunning photography and clean, modern design." (Publisher's note)

"Simple recipes, attractive photographs, an easy-to-read layout, and a functional lie-flat binding make this a great choice for young and aspiring cooks, small families, and anyone looking for easy meal ideas." LJ

Lee, Cecilia Hae-Jin

Quick and easy Korean cooking; more than 70 everyday recipes. photographs by Julie Toy and Cecilia Hae-Jin Lee. Chronicle Books 2009 168p il pa $22.95 **641.5**
1. Korean cooking
ISBN 978-0-8118-6146-5

LC 2008-33629

"Quality, accessible, authentic Korean cookbooks are hard to come by. Ably filling that gap is [this book]. .... It's filled with more than 70 recipes, most of which only call for about six ingredients. If you're skeptical that such simple recipes can produce the flavor bombs that are Korean dishes, know that three recipes were tested, and all worked perfectly as written. Each one was lively with the flavors of garlic, chiles, soy sauce, and sesame." Village Voice

Lee, Jennifer Tyler

The **52** new foods challenge; a family cooking adventure for each week of the year. by Jennifer Tyler Lee. Penguin Group USA 2014 316 p. $20 **641.5**

1. Cooking 2. Parenting

ISBN 1583335560; 9781583335567

IACP Cookbook Award Finalist: Children, Youth and Family (2015)

In this book, author Jennifer Tyler Lee "gives parents practical tips to dramatically change the way their families eat. Her helpful advice . . . . will show parents how to start eating healthy every week of the year. Each week offers a healthy new food to try, from artichokes to zucchini, and includes easy recipes and fun activities to work on as a family-- from learning to cook together to enjoying the farmers' market to even experimenting with growing your own food." (Publisher's note)

"A fun way to engage children in creating meals and trying new things." LJ

Lee, Matthew

★ The **Lee** Bros. southern cookbook; stories and recipes for southerners and would-be southerners. [by] Matt Lee and Ted Lee; color photography by Gentl & Hyers. W.W. Norton 2006 589p il $35 **641.5**

1. Southern cooking

ISBN 978-0-393-05781-2; 0-393-05781-X

LC 2006-22745

This "cookbook begins with a collection of drink recipes, from sweet tea to potent planters' punch. To accompany these beverages, the Lee brothers array a long series of snack and party foods. A section on preserves and pickles documents some rarely seen regional treats, such as Jerusalem artichoke relish. Meats, seafood, sweets, and breads round out the book. Every recipe has a story attached, and the large format makes for easy reading." Booklist

Leidich, Shari Koolik

Two Moms in the Raw; simple, clean, irresistible recipes for your family's health. Shari Koolik Leidich; photography by Iain Bagwell. Rux Martin/ Houghton Mifflin Harcourt 2015 288 p. color illustrations (hardback) $22 **641.5**

1. Cookbooks 2. Quick and easy cooking 3. Cooking -- Natural foods 4. Raw foods 5. Cooking (Natural foods) 6. Raw food diet -- Recipes 7. Two Moms in the Raw (Firm)

ISBN 0544253256; 9780544253254

LC 2014036934

This raw, cooked and gluten-free cookbook, by Shari Koolik Leidich, offers "130-plus dishes, like Brunchy Poached Eggs on Spinach with Roasted Red Pepper Sauce,

or Plum and Tatsoi Salad. . . . Indulgent snacks like Creamy Olive and Artichoke Dip and Butternut-Lemongrass Soup satisfy cravings, and chicken and fish . . . come bolstered with plenty of raw produce and grains. Desserts ditch processed sugar in favor of natural sweeteners and power nutrients." (Publisher's note)

"Home cooks may be daunted by her inclusive list of basic "exotics"—including gomaiso, ashwagandha, coconut aminos, and psyllium husks—but her kid-friendly 'coconutty' chicken breasts and raw key lime pie bring a fun nutritional boost to the family table." Pub Wkly

Includes bibliographical references (page 276) and index

Leite, David

The **new** Portuguese table; exciting flavors from Europe's western coast. photographs by Nuno Correia. Clarkson Potter 2009 256p il $32.50 **641.5**

1. Portuguese cooking

ISBN 978-0-307-39441-5; 0-307-39441-7

LC 2008-51283

The author "begins by outlining Portugal's diverse regional cuisines and then describes traditional ingredients. From there it is a straightforward listing of appetizers, soups, fish, meat, poultry, vegetable/egg/rice dishes, breads, sweets, liqueurs, and condiments, with approximately 150 recipes overall. . . . Full of delicious-sounding recipes, this title is sure to appeal to adventurous cooks wanting to try a new ethnic cuisine and will also be popular with Portuguese American communities." Libr J

Levine, Sarabeth

Sarabeth's good morning cookbook; Breakfast, Brunch, and Baking. by Sarabeth Levine. Random House Inc 2015 282 p. color illustrations $40 **641.5**

1. Baking 2. Brunches 3. Breakfasts

ISBN 0847846385; 9780847846382

In this cookbook, author Sarabeth Levine "shares her most beloved breakfast and brunch recipes. . . . A comprehensive guide to morning meals, this . . . . book covers the dishes everyone desires. Sarabeth's signature pancakes and muffins are quick enough for weekdays, while her quiches and coffee cakes are guaranteed to impress weekend guests. In addition to her sophisticated twists on the standards, Sarabeth surprises with such innovative breakfast treats as morning cookies." (Publisher's note)

Lewis, Edna

★ The **taste** of country cooking; [with a foreword by Alice Waters] 30th anniversary ed.; Knopf 2006 xxi, 268p il $22.95 **641.5**

1. Southern cooking

ISBN 0-307-26560-9; 978-0-307-26560-9

First published 1976

"Recipes are categorized by the four seasons and are ones . . . [the author] grew up with in a small Virginia farming community (personal reminiscences about her family life appear throughout the text)." Booklist

Liddon, Angela

The **oh** she glows cookbook; over 100 vegan recipes to glow from the inside out. Angela Liddon.

Avery, a member of Penguin Group (USA) 2016 352 p. color illustrations (print : alk. paper) $27 **641.5**
1. Veganism 2. Cookbooks 3. Vegetarian cooking 4. Vegan cooking
ISBN 9781583335741; 1583335749
LC 2016009038

This cookbook, by Angela Liddon, presents collected recipes taken from the author's "blog, ohsheglows.com, to spread the word about her journey to health and the powerful transformation that food can make. . . . [This book] is packed with more than 100 delicious recipes such as go-to breakfasts, protein-packed snacks, hearty entrées, and decadent desserts." (Publisher's note)

"Liddon's authentic voice and candidly shared successes will motivate nonvegans to try healthy recipes." LJ

Includes bibliographical references and index

Lim, Allen

The **feed** zone cookbook; fast and flavorful food for athletes. Biju Thomas & Allen Lim. Velo Press 2011 xi, 315 p.p col. ill. (hardcover : alk. paper) $24.95 **641.5**
1. Cookbooks 2. Athletes -- Nutrition 3. Snack foods
ISBN 1934030767; 9781934030769
LC 2011028918

In this athlete-centered cookbook, by Biju Thomas and Allen Lim, "provides 150 delicious recipes that even the busiest athletes can prepare in less time than it takes to warm up for a workout. . . . [The book] strikes the perfect balance between science and practice so that athletes will change the way they think about food, replacing highly processed food substitutes with real, nourishing foods that will satisfy every athlete's cravings." (Publisher's note)

Feed zone portables; a cookbook of on-the-go food for athletes. Biju Thomas & Allen Lim. VeloPress 2013 xv, 271 p.p color illustrations (hardback) $24.95 **641.5**
1. Cookbooks 2. Athletes -- Nutrition 3. Snack foods
ISBN 1937715000; 9781937715007
LC 2013003073

In this cookbook, author "[Allen] Lim joined professional chef Biju Thomas to make eating delicious and practical. . . . Their groundbreaking 'Feed Zone Cookbook' brought the favorite recipes of the pros to everyday athletes. In [this,] their new cookbook . . . , Chef Biju and Dr. Lim offer 75 all-new portable food recipes for cyclists, runners, triathletes, mountain bikers, climbers, hikers, and backpackers." (Publisher's note)

Link, Donald

Real Cajun; rustic home cooking from Donald Link's Louisiana. [by] Donald Link with Paula Disbrowe; photographs by Chris Granger. Clarkson Potter Publishers 2009 255p il $35 **641.5**
1. Cooking -- Louisiana
ISBN 978-0-307-39581-8; 0-307-39581-2
LC 2008-36989

"Link shares the fare he ate growing up on the bayou, as well as what he cooks for family, friends and funerals. Some recipes are aspirationally insane—fried chicken and andouille gumbo, or 'game day' choucroute with sausage,

tasso and duck confit—while others I simply aspire to make, like a fried oyster and bacon sandwich (bacon recipe included), and Link's outstanding boudin, which he also uses as a heart-stopping beignet filling. The tone is easygoing, the explanations clear." N Y Times Book Rev

Lukins, Sheila

The **Silver** Palate cookbook; Julee Rosso & Sheila Lukins with Michael McLaughlin; photographs by Patrick Tregenza and Susan Goldman; illustrations by Sheila Lukins. Workman Pub Co 2007 xi, 452 p.p col. ill. (pbk) $22.95 **641.5**
1. Cookbooks 2. American cooking 3. Cooking
ISBN 9780761145981; 9780761145974; 0761145974
LC 2007276244

James Beard Cookbook Hall of Fame (1992)

IACP Culinary Classics Book Award (2014)

This cookbook, by Julee Rosso & Sheila Lukins, is a 25th anniversary edition that "brings a new passion for food and entertaining into American homes. Its 350 . . . dishes make every occasion special, and its recipes, featuring vibrant, pure ingredients, are a pleasure to cook. Brimming with kitchen wisdom, cooking tips, information about domestic and imported ingredients, menus, quotes, and lore, this . . . book feels as fresh and exciting as the day it was first published." (Publisher's note)

Lundy, Ronni

Victuals; An Appalachian Journey, with Recipes. Ronni Lundy; photographs by Johnny Autry. Clarkson Potter/Publishers 2016 320 p. illustrations (some color) (hardback) $32.50; (ebook) $65 **641.5**
1. American cooking 2. Appalachian Region 3. Cooking, American 4. Cooking -- Appalachian Region, Southern 5. Appalachian Region, Southern -- Social life and customs
ISBN 9780804186742; 9780804186759
LC 2016013454

This book, by Ronni Lundy, "explores the diverse and complex food scene of the Mountain South through recipes, stories, traditions, and innovations. Each chapter explores a specific defining food or tradition of the region--such as salt, beans, corn (and corn liquor). The essays introduce readers to their rich histories and the farmers, curers, hunters, and chefs who define the region's contemporary landscape." (Publisher's note)

"Fans of locally sourced foods and Southern cooking will find a lot to like here, as Lundy does a terrific job of showcasing Appalachia's breadth and depth." Pub Wkly

Madison, Deborah

The **new** vegetarian cooking for everyone; Deborah Madison. Ten Speed Press 2014 665 p. $40 **641.5**
1. Cookbooks 2. Vegetarian cooking
ISBN 1607745534; 9781607745532
LC 2013046540

Originally published: New York: Broadway Books, 1997

This cookbook, by Deborah Madison, "originally published in 1997, . . . has endured as one of the world's most popular vegetarian cookbooks, winning both a James Beard Foundation award and the IACP Julia Child Cookbook of the Year Award. Now, . . . [this edition] picks up where that culinary legacy left off, . . . including a new introduction, more than 200 new recipes, and comprehensive, updated information on vegetarian and vegan ingredients." (Publisher's note)

★ **Vegetarian** cooking for everyone; 10th anniversary ed; Broadway Books 2007 742p il $40   **641.5**
1. Vegetarian cooking
ISBN 978-0-7679-2747-5; 0-7679-2747-8
LC 2007-10075
First published 1997
Following information on ingredients and techniques, the recipes focus "mainly on vegetables and grains, aiming at flavor and variety, both often arrived at via assorted ethnic approaches." Publ Wkly

Vegetarian suppers from Deborah Madison's kitchen; Deborah Madison. Broadway Books 2005 228 p. ill. (pbk) $19.99   **641.5**
1. Cookbooks 2. Vegetarian cooking 3. Suppers
ISBN 076792472X; 9780767916271; 9780767924726
LC 2004045899
This vegetarian cookbook, by Deborah Madison, "solves the perennial question of what to cook for dinner in her first collection of suppertime solutions, with more than 100 inspiring recipes to enjoy every night of the week. . . . For vegetarians and health-conscious nonvegetarians, the quest for recipes that don't call for meat often can seem daunting." (Publisher's note)
"[O]ffers everything from quickie suppers to subtle, sophisticated dinner-party dishes while encouraging local, seasonal eating and unfussy kitchen artisanship. . . . Madison's recipes do call for good kitchen gear (Dutch ovens, double-boilers, numerous gratin pans and casseroles) and some hard-to-find ingredients (fromage blanc, blanched nettles, Thai basil), but they're flexible enough to allow for substitutions." Pub Wkly

Makan, Chetna
The **Cardamom** Trail; Chetna Bakes With Flavours of the East. by Chetna Makan. Octopus Pub Group 2016 240 p. color illustrations $29.99 **641.5**
1. Spices 2. Indian cooking
ISBN 1784721298; 9781784721299
In this cookbook, by Chetna Makan, "Indian influences will transform your baking from the familiar to the exotic, from the ordinary to the extraordinary. Discover rare but precious traditional bakes from India, as well as new spice-infused recipes. Delve into the history of Indian herbs and spices and learn how to match foods and flavors." (Publisher's note)
"Infuse the vibrant flavors of India into your baked goods with this beautiful volume of recipes redolent with herbs, spices, and surprising ingredients." Booklist

The **make-ahead** cook; 8 smart strategies for dinner tonight. by the editors at America's Test Kitchen. America's Test Kitchen 2014 328 p. illustrations (chiefly color) $26.95   **641.5**
1. Dinners 2. Cookbooks 3. Dinners and dining 4.

Make-ahead cooking
ISBN 1936493845; 9781936493845
LC 2014014386
This cookbook, by the editors at America's Test Kitchen, "reinvents make-ahead cooking so that you can cook when you want and still eat well every night of the week. While most make-ahead cookbooks focus only on stocking your freezer, this book takes a new approach, with 8 strategies that show you how a little advance work and planning can reap huge benefits." (Publisher's note)
"Indispensable for busy families and anyone who has limited time to cook during the week." LJ

Mallmann, Francis
Seven fires; grilling the Argentine way. [by] Francis Mallmann, with Peter Kaminsky. Artisan 2009 278p il $35   **641.5**
1. Outdoor cooking 2. Barbecue cooking 3. Argentine cooking
ISBN 978-1-57965-354-5
LC 2008-37367
"Mallmann cooks with the elegant purity achieved only after attaining a mastery of complicated food. . . . He also reconnects us to the primal simplicity and visceral pleasure of cooking over a fire—though his recipes can be made over charcoal or in a grill pan, too." N Y Times Book Rev

Marks, Gil
The **world** of Jewish cooking; more than 500 traditional recipes from Alsace to Yemen. Simon & Schuster 1996 406p il hardcover o.p. pa $17 **641.5**
1. Jewish cooking
ISBN 0-684-83559-2 pa
LC 96-2848
This cookbook is "loosely arranged by food category, with chapters on appetizers, soups, and main dishes, as well as side items, breads, and desserts. . . . You'll find recipes from India, Africa, even China, here, alongside many dishes that originated in one of the two major Jewish cultural communities, Ashkenazic and Sephardic." Booklist

Massaad, Barbara Abdeni
Man'oushé; inside the Lebanese street corner bakery. Barbara Abdeni Massaad; photography by Barbara Abdeni Massaad and Raymond Yazbeck. Interlink Books, An imprint of Interlink Publishing Group, Inc. 2014 200 p. color illustrations $30 **641.5**
1. Cookbooks 2. Lebanese cooking
ISBN 1566569281; 9781566569286
LC 2013032109
This cookbook, by Barbara Abdeni Massaad, "is dedicated entirely to the art of creating the perfect man'oushé. With over 70 simple recipes, it offers you a way to enjoy these typical [Lebanese] pies traditionally baked in street corner bakeries in the comfort of your own home." (Publisher's note)
"A reasonably adept home baker will find Massaad's recipes easy to follow. . . . The book's full-color photographs bring into focus not just the foods but also the lively characters who constitute a remarkably diverse nation." Booklist

McDonnell, Imen

The **Farmette** cookbook; recipes and adventures from my life on an Irish farm. Imen McDonnell. Roost Books 2016 361 p. color illustrations (hardcover : alk. paper) $35   **641.5**

1. Ireland 2. Country life 3. Irish cooking 4. Cooking, Irish 5. Country life -- Ireland
ISBN 9781611802047

LC 2015026646

This cookbook "documents Imen McDonnell's extraordinary Irish country cooking journey, which began the moment she fell in love with an Irish farmer and moved across the Atlantic to County Limerick. This book's collection of 150 recipes and colorful stories chronicles nearly a decade-long adventure of learning to feed a family (and several hungry farmers) while adjusting to her new home (and nursing a bit of homesickness)." (Publisher's note)

"An outstanding debut, with just the right amount of sentimentality." LJ

Miglore, Kristen

Food52 genius recipes; 100 recipes that will change the way you cook. Kristen Miglore; photography by James Ransom. Ten Speed Press 2015 272 p. color illustrations (hardback) $35   **641.5**

1. Cooking
ISBN 1607747979; 9781607747970

LC 2014034413

This cookbook presents what author "Kristen Miglore calls genius recipes. Passed down from the cookbook authors, chefs, and bloggers who made them legendary, these foolproof recipes rethink cooking tropes, solve problems, get us talking, and make cooking more fun. Every week, Kristen features one such recipe and explains just what's so brilliant about it in the James Beard Award-nominated Genius Recipes column on Food52. Here, in this book, she compiles 100 of the most essential ones." (Publisher's note)

"Miglore's addition to Food52's growing list of cookbooks is a treat for readers who enjoy casual gourmet food." LJ

Genius recipes

Miller, Laura

Raw, vegan, not gross; all vegan and mostly raw recipes for people who love to eat. Laura Miller. Flatiron Books 2016 215 p. color illustrations (hardback) $25.99   **641.5**

1. Veganism 2. Cookbooks 3. Vegetarian cooking 4. Raw foods 5. Vegan cooking
ISBN 1250066905; 9781250066909

LC 2016014385

This cookbook, by Laura Miller, "offers more than a hundred entirely vegan and mostly raw recipes for all people who want to eat deliciously. . . . [It seeks to] engage your taste buds with strengthening breakfasts . . . , easy weeknight dinners . . . , crowd-pleasing party food . . . , irresistible drinks & desserts . . . , and many more nutritious, satisfying dishes that are as beautiful and fun to make as they are healthful." (Publisher's note)

Moore, Russell

This is Camino; Russell Moore and Alison Hopelain with Chris Colin and Maria Zizka; photographs by Yoko Takahashi. Ten Speed Press 2015 272 p. color illustrations (hardcover) $35   **641.5**

1. California 2. Restaurants 3. American cooking 4. Camino (Restaurant) 5. Cooking, American -- California style 6. Cooking -- California -- San Francisco
ISBN 1607747286; 9781607747284

LC 2015013757

This cookbook, by Russell Moore and Alison Hopelain, is "about the unique, fire-based cooking approach and ingredient-focused philosophy of Camino restaurant in Oakland, CA, with approximately 100 recipes." (Publisher's note)

"A compelling look at an innovative restaurant. Aspiring chefs and advanced cooks may also enjoy Suzanne Goin's The A.O.C. Cookbook and Nancy Silverton's The Mozza Cookbook (also from California restaurants)." LJ

Moosewood Restaurant cooks at home; fast and easy recipes for any day. the Moosewood Collective. Simon & Schuster 1994 416 p. ill. $25   **641.5**

1. Cookbooks 2. Vegetarian cooking 3. Cooking -- Natural foods 4. Moosewood Restaurant 5. Cooking (Natural foods)
ISBN 0671679929; 0671879545; 9780671679927

LC 93039126

James Beard Award (1995)

Written by the Moosewood Collective, this book features "over 150 carefully honed and tested recipes calling for the best ingredients, accompanied by time-saving tips and planning suggestions, add up to a delicious whole-foods cuisine that is versatile and healthful and can be prepared with a minimum of effort." (Publisher's note)

Moosewood restaurant favorites; the 250 most-requested, naturally delicious recipes from one of America's best-loved restaurants. The Moosewood Collective. St. Martin's Press 2013 416 p. ill. (chiefly col.) (hardback) $29.99   **641.5**

1. Veganism 2. Vegetarian cooking 3. Cooking -- Vegetables 4. Cooking -- Natural foods 5. Moosewood Restaurant
ISBN 1250006252; 9781250006257

LC 2013013841

This book focuses on "Moosewood Restaurant, founded in 1973. . . . [It] contains 250 of their most requested recipes completely updated and revised to reflect the way they're cooked now--increasingly vegan and gluten-free, benefitting from fresh herbs, new varieties of vegetables, and the wholesome goodness of newly-rediscovered grains." (Publisher's note)

"This collection of some of Moosewood's cooks' and customers' most admired recipes has something for just about everyone." Booklist

Morgan, Jeff

The **covenant** kitchen; food and wine for the new Jewish table. Jeff Morgan and Jodie Morgan.

Schocken Books, OU Press 2015 262 p. color illustrations (hardback) $35   **641.5**
1. Kosher food 2. Jewish cooking 3. Food and wine pairing
ISBN 0805243259; 9780805243253

LC 2014025769

Authors Jeff Morgan and Jodie Morgan present "the ultimate kosher cookbook for food lovers, with more than one hundred mouthwatering recipes complete with suggested wine pairings, from the veteran cookbook authors and owners of the acclaimed Covenant Winery in California. [It] includes informative sidebars on how to select the right wine for any occasion, on the requirements for kosher food preparation, and on how to prepare the basics." (Publisher's note)

"This hip, fresh cookbook is just the thing for foodies desiring to keep kosher while elevating their repertoire of dishes for the benefit of themselves or their dinner guests—and there's plenty to interest cooks who lack a kosher kitchen as well." LJ

Morris, Julie
Superfood Kitchen; Cooking with Nature's Most Amazing Foods. Sterling Pub Co Inc 2012 256 p.   **641.5**
1. Cookbooks 2. Nutrition 3. Cooking -- Natural foods
ISBN 145490352X; 9781454903529

This cookbook, by Julie Morris, presents "dishes . . . entirely composed of plant-based, nutrient-dense, and whole foods that energize, nourish, and taste delicious. Each recipe . . . combines natural ingredients that deliver . . . antioxidants, essential fatty acids (like omega-3), minerals, vitamins, and more. The . . . superfood meals--from Goldenberry Pancakes to Quinoa Spaghetti with Cashew Cream Sauce and Chard--will make you feel as good as they taste." (Publisher's note)

Moskowitz, Isa Chandra
Vegan pie in the sky; 75 out-of-this-world recipes for pies, tarts, cobblers & more. [by] Isa Chandra Moskowitz & Terry Hope Romero. Da Capo Lifelong 2011 223p il pa $17   **641.5**
1. Pies 2. Vegetarian cooking
ISBN 978-0-7382-1274-6

The authors focus on "dessert in this collection of 75 egg, dairy and animal-free pies, cheesecakes, cobblers and tarts. . . . The duo deserves plaudits for their user-friendly approach as well as their ability to keep scarcer ingredients to a minimum. Bakers who fear they won't be able to recreate these will be happy to discover that once they've mastered a crust or two they'll be able to whip together a Strawberry Field Hand Pie, Chocolate Mousse Tart, or even a Coconut Cream with confidence." Publ Wkly

Moulton, Sara
Sara Moulton's Home Cooking 101; How to Make Everything Taste Better. by Sara Moulton. Oxmoor House 2016 368 p. color illustrations $35   **641.5**
1. American cooking
ISBN 0848744411; 9780848744410

LC 2015956841

This cookbook, by Sara Moulton, "is packed with essential techniques, expert tips, and practical advice to sharpen

your sense of taste and cultivate confidence in the kitchen. . . . Sara guide[s] readers through the fundamentals, then offers 150 hit recipes to illustrate, step-by-step, the time-tested methods that make each so delicious. You'll learn to navigate your stove, season like a pro, and add umami to a dish while discovering new ideas for weeknight dinners." (Publisher's note)

"Busy home cooks will find much to savor in this approachable, elegant collection of recipes." Pub Wkly
Includes indexes.

Nathan, Joan
Jewish cooking in America; expanded ed; Knopf 1998 518p il $35   **641.5**
1. Jewish cooking
ISBN 0-375-40276-4

LC 98-27952

First published 1994

This companion volume to the PBS television series contains nearly 300 recipes. It "is also a history of the Jewish people through their food. Nathan introduces both people and food in a preface that discusses dietary laws, Jewish holidays, Jewish immigration to the U.S., and the impact of Jews—and their food—on American culture. With every recipe comes an original story or a reprint of an article or a personal vignette that intrigues and/or edifies." Booklist
Includes bibliographical references

Quiches, kugels, and couscous; my search for Jewish cooking in France. Alfred A. Knopf 2010 387p il $39.95; ebook $40   **641.5**
1. French cooking 2. Jewish cooking 3. Jews -- France
ISBN 978-0-307-26759-7; 978-0-307-59450-1 ebook
LC 2010-20280

"Nathan's multi-layered, narrative approach makes this treasury of tempting flavors an entertaining and compelling read." Publ Wkly
Includes bibliographical references

Nathan, Zoe
Breakfast at Huckleberry; recipes, stories, and secrets from our kitchen. by Zoe Nathan; with Laurel Almerinda and Josh Loeb; photographs by Matt Armendariz. Chronicle Books 2014 288 p. illustrations (chiefly color) $35   **641.5**
1. Baking 2. Cookbooks 3. Breakfasts 4. Huckleberry (Restaurant)
ISBN 1452123527; 9781452123523

LC 2013037996

This cookbook, by Zoe Nathan, with Laurel Almerinda and Josh Loeb, "collects more than 115 recipes and more than 150 color photographs, including how-to sequences for mastering basics such as flaky dough and lining a cake pan. [The Los Angeles-based restaurant] Huckleberry's recipes span from sweet (rustic cakes, muffins, and scones) to savory (hot cereals, biscuits, and quiche)." (Publisher's note)

"Filled with entertaining behind-the-scenes stories and technical tips relayed in plain English, this cookbook will thrill meticulous bakers and Huckleberry's devotees." LJ

Natkin, Michael

Herbivoracious; a flavor revolution with 150 vibrant and original vegetarian recipes. Michael Natkin. Harvard Common Press 2012 367 p.   **641.5**

1. Cookbooks 2. Nutrition 3. Vegetarian cooking
ISBN 1558327452; 9781558327450

LC 2011030819

This vegetarian cookbook "offers up 150 . . . recipes. . . . A third of the book is taken up with hearty main courses, ranging from a robust Caribbean Lentil-Stuffed Flatbread across the Atlantic to a comforting Sicilian Spaghetti with Pan-Roasted Cauliflower and around the Cape of Good Hope to a delectable Sichuan Dry-Fried Green Beans and Tofu. An abundance of soups, salads, sauces and condiments, sides, appetizers and small plates, desserts, and breakfasts round out the recipes. [Michael] Natkin . . . provides lots of advice on how to craft vegetarian meals that amply deliver protein and other nutrients, and the . . . . menus he presents deliver balanced and complementary flavors. . . . The many dozens of vegan and gluten-free recipes are clearly noted." (Publisher's note)

Neely, Pat

Down home with the Neelys; a Southern family cookbook. [by] Patrick Neely and Gina Neely; with Paula Disbrowe. Alfred A. Knopf 2009 278p il $27.95   **641.5**

1. Barbecue cooking 2. Southern cooking
ISBN 978-0-307-26994-2; 0-307-26994-9

LC 2008-54393

This cookbook written by "husband-and-wife television personalities with their own Tennessee chain of barbecue joints . . . [is] full of 120 recipes that pull back the curtain on their award-winning seasonings, sauce, and fixings. Emphasizing their personal story and family recipes, this cookbook is brimming with down-home personality . . . and dishes that are 'simple, stylish, and not too fussy.'" Publ Wkly

New American Heart Association cookbook

The new American Heart Association cookbook; 8th ed.; Clarkson Potter 2010 xxi, 696p il $35 **641.5**

1. Cooking 2. Low-cholesterol diet 3. Heart diseases
-- Diet therapy
ISBN 978-0-307-40757-3

LC 2009-44692

First published 1973 with title: American Heart Association cookbook

"Each recipe comes with a breakdown of calories, protein content, carbohydrates, cholesterol, fats (broken down by saturated, polyunsaturated and monounsaturated) and sodium content, along with a table of dietary exchange. . . . This book remains a basic in many heart-conscious kitchens." Publ Wkly

The **New** York Times Jewish cookbook; more than 825 traditional and contemporary recipes from around the world. edited by Linda Amster; introduction by Mimi Sheraton. St. Martin's Press 2003 xxvi, 614p $35   **641.5**

1. Jewish cooking
ISBN 978-0-312-29093-1; 0-312-29093-4

LC 2002-68358

"Included here are hundreds of recipes from Jewish communities all over the world, reflecting Mimi Sheraton's introductory comment that Jewish food is 'the world's oldest fusion cuisine.' Recipes range from Persian Chicken Soup with Chickpea Dumplings to Alain Ducasse's Rib-Eye Steaks with Peppered Cranberry Marmalade to Fresh Corn and Red Pepper Blini. All the classics are here, too, and there's a separate chapter on 'Trimmings,' including an array of condiments and garnishes. . . . This is an essential purchase." Libr J

The **New** York Times Passover cookbook; more than 200 holiday recipes from top chefs and writers. edited by Linda Amster. Morrow 1999 xxii, 328p il $25   **641.5**

1. Passover 2. Jewish cooking
ISBN 0-688-15590-1

LC 98-41282

This book's recipes "range from the traditional to the innovative and are drawn from European, Mediterranean and Middle Eastern traditions. . . . Amster has produced what may be the definitive word in Passover cookbooks, from recipes to the feelings evoked by sitting at a beautifully set, bountifully laden table." Publ Wkly

Includes bibliographical references

O'Neill, Molly

One big table; a portrait of American cooking 600 recipes from the nation's best home cooks, farmers, fishermen, pit-masters, and chefs. Simon & Schuster 2010 864p il $50; ebook $37.99   **641.5**

1. Cooking
ISBN 978-0-7432-3270-8; 978-1-4516-0977-6 ebook

LC 2010-28841

"This collection celebrates the nation's culinary diversity, both ethnically and agriculturally, and offers a uniquely intimate look at what home cooking in America is truly like today. O'Neill crossed the country, interviewing home cooks and spending time in the kitchens of recent immigrants. The results are enticing recipes that intertwine family stories, personal histories, and food. From stuffed Danish pancakes in Utah to tamales in Santa Fe and Vietnamese shrimp pancakes in Mississippi, this eclectic collection showcases the best this country has to offer." Publ Wkly

Oliver, Jamie, 1975-

Cook with Jamie; my guide to making you a better cook. photography: David Loftus and Chris Terry. Hyperion 2007 447p il $37.50   **641.5**

1. Cooking
ISBN 978-1-4013-2233-5; 1-4013-2233-6

"Aiming to educate readers on cooking basics, Oliver offers more than 175 recipes, which emphasize flavor and freshness over labor-intensive preparation. With a conversational style that favors general guidelines over strict instructions—recipes often call for a 'knob of butter,' a 'handful of shelled peas' or 'a big handful of freshly grated Parmesan'— Oliver's friendly and enthusiastic approach handily deflates new-cook anxiety. Loaded with photos that cover common skills like cleaning and preparing fresh lobster, discerning degrees of doneness in meat and crafting homemade pasta, Oliver's patient explanations leave little room for confusion.

His dishes, many of which are updated versions of classics, are impressive and accessible." Publ Wkly

Jamie Oliver's comfort food; The Ultimate Weekend Cookbook. by Jamie Oliver. HarperCollinsPublishers 2014 406 p. color illustrations, portraits $34.99 **641.5**
1. Cooking 2. Cookbooks
ISBN 0062305611; 9780062305619
LC 2015460582

This book, by celebrity chef Jamie Oliver, "brings together 100 ultimate comfort food recipes from around the world. . . . Recipes include everything from mighty moussaka, delicate gyoza with crispy wings, steaming ramen and katsu curry to super eggs Benedict, scrumptious sticky toffee pudding and tutti frutti pear tarte tatin." (Publisher's note)

Ortega, Simone
1080 recipes; [by] Simone and Ines Ortega; illustrations, Javier Mariscal. Phaidon 2007 975p il $39.95 **641.5**
1. Spanish cooking
ISBN 978-0-7148-4836-5; 0-7148-4836-0
First published 1977 in Spain

"Something like the Joy of Cooking for the Spanish home cook, . . . [this book] includes recipes for both traditional regional fare and dishes inspired by a variety of other cuisines. . . . An essential purchase." Libr J

Oseland, James
Saveur; The New Classics Cookbook: More Than 1,000 of the World's Best Recipes for Today's Kitchen. James Oseland. Simon & Schuster 2014 624 p. illustrations (some color) $40 **641.5**
1. Cooking 2. Cookbooks
ISBN 1616287357; 9781616287351
IACP Cookbook Award Finalist: General (2015)
James Beard Foundation Award Nominee: General Cooking (2015)

This cookbook, by James Oseland, presents several selections from the culinary magazine "Saveur." It "features more than 1,000 well-curated global recipes in an essential collection for home cooks everywhere. This . . . selection celebrates the brand's authority, heritage, and depth of worldwide culinary knowledge." (Publisher's note)

"Highly recommended for most collections and home cooks who'd like a contemporary, all-purpose kitchen reference." LJ

Ottolenghi, Yotam
★ **Jerusalem**; a cookbook. Yotam Ottolenghi, Sami Tamimi. Ten Speed Press 2012 318 p. (hardcover) $35.00 **641.5**
1. Cookbooks 2. Jewish cooking 3. Israeli cooking 4. Cooking, Middle Eastern 5. Jerusalem -- Description and travel
ISBN 1607743949; 9781607743958; 9781607743941
LC 2012017560
James Beard Foundation Award: International (2013).

This is a cookbook of recipes from Jerusalem. "London chefs and business partners [Yotam] Ottolenghi and [Sami] Tamimi both grew up in Jerusalem (the former in the Jewish

west, the latter in the Arab east). Drawing on their childhood experiences for inspiration, they've updated traditional recipes (e.g., Falafel, Tabbouleh, Lamb Shawarma) to suit the lifestyles and preferences of modern home cooks." (Library Journal)

Nopi; the cookbook. Yotam Ottolenghi, Ramael Scully; with Tara Wigley. Ten Speed Press 2015 352 p. color illustrations (hardback) $40 **641.5**
1. Cookbooks 2. Mediterranean cooking 3. Middle Eastern cooking 4. Nopi (Restaurant) 5. Cooking, Mediterranean 6. Cooking, Middle Eastern
ISBN 9781607746232; 9781607746249
LC 2015017809

This book, by Yotam Ottolenghi, Ramael Scully, with Tara Wigley, offers "a cookbook from acclaimed London restaurant Nopi, by . . . author Yotam Ottolenghi and Nopi head chef Ramael Scully. Pandan leaves meet pomegranate seeds, star anise meets sumac, and miso meets molasses in this collection of 120 new recipes from Yotam Ottolenghi's restaurant." (Publisher's note)

"Although Ottolenghi's latest will challenge readers in ways its predecessors did not, it reliably delivers unique recipes with flavor combinations unmatched in their inventiveness." LJ

Ottolenghi; the cookbook. Yotam Ottolenghi and Sami Tamimi. Ebury 2008 288 p. col. ill. (hardcover) $35 **641.5**
1. Cookbooks 2. Mediterranean cooking 3. Cooking 4. Ottolenghi (Restaurant)
ISBN 9781607744184; 160774418X
LC 2014397522

This cookbook, by Yotam Ottolenghi and Sami Tamimi, "features 140 recipes culled from the popular Ottolenghi restaurants and inspired by the diverse culinary traditions of the Mediterranean. . . . The recipes reflect the authors' upbringings in Jerusalem yet also incorporate culinary traditions from California, Italy, and North Africa, among others." (Publisher's note)

"This vibrant and bold collection lives up to the authors promise that 'cooking can be enjoyable, simple, and fulfilling, yet look and taste amazing.'" Pub WKly

Page, Karen
The **flavor** bible; the essential guide to culinary creativity, based on the wisdom of America's most imaginative chefs. [by] Karen Page and Andrew Dornenburg; photographs by Barry Salzman. Little, Brown and Company 2008 380p il $35 **641.5**
1. Cooking
ISBN 978-0-316-11840-8; 0-316-11840-0
LC 2007-33064

"The authors first discuss the four basic tastes and the roles played by weather, the season of the year, and other environmental factors in cooking. The rest of the book is an extensive alphabetic guide to different culinary ingredients. . . . Rather than just another collection of recipes, this is a unique resource that both beginning cooks and serious chefs will find wonderfully inspiring and immensely useful." Libr J

Paltrow, Gwyneth, 1972-

It's all easy; delicious weekday hacks for the super-busy home cook. Gwyneth Paltrow with Thea Baumann; photographs by Ditte Isager. Life & Style 2016 288 p. illustrations (chiefly color) (hardcover) $35 **641.5**

1. Cookbooks 2. Quick and easy cooking
ISBN 9781455584215

LC 2015044440

In this cookbook, by Gwyneth Paltrow with Thea Baumann and photographs by Ditte Isager, the author shares "more than 125 of her favorite recipes that can be made in the time it would take to order takeout (which often contains high quantities of fat, sugar, and processed ingredients). All the dishes are surprisingly tasty, with little or no sugar, fat, or gluten." (Publisher's note)

"Paltrow's recipes offer refreshing ways for home cooks to regain balance in their lives and on their plates in face of today's on-the-go lifestyle."

Pascal, Cybele

The **whole** foods allergy cookbook; two hundred gourmet & homestyle recipes for the food allergic family. Vital Health Pub. 2006 213p pa $18.95 **641.5**

1. Cooking 2. Diet therapy 3. Food allergy
ISBN 1-890612-45-6; 978-1-890612-45-0

LC 2005-931263

"Each and every dish offered is free of dairy, eggs, wheat, soy, peanuts, tree nuts, fish, and shellfish. . . . [The book includes] recipes for breakfast pancakes, breads, and cereals; lunch soups, salads, spreads, and sandwiches; dinner entrées and side dishes; dessert puddings, cupcakes, cookies, cakes, and pies; and even after-school snacks ranging from trail mix to pizza and pretzels. Included is a resource guide to organizations that can supply information and support, as well as a shopping guide for hard-to-find items." Publisher's note

Includes bibliographical references

Patalsky, Kathy

Healthy happy vegan kitchen; Kathy Patalsky. Houghton Mifflin Harcourt 2015 352 p. color illustrations (trade paper) $25 **641.5**

1. Health 2. Veganism 3. Cookbooks 4. Vegan cooking 5. Cooking (Natural foods)
ISBN 0544379802; 9780544379800

LC 2014014408

This cookbook by Kathy Patalsky presents "vegan recipes from the author behind the blog HealthyHappy-Life.com. Along with the inventive recipes, the book also includes guides to help 'veganize' your kitchen, cooking techniques for vegan staples, and wellness tips, making it the perfect book for both long-time vegans and newcomers alike." (Publisher's note)

"Headnotes and information on the author's own vegan journey offer encouragement and background for anyone interested in embracing the meatless life or simply incorporating meatless meals into their diet." Pub Wkly

Peltre, Beatrice

My French family table; Recipes for a Life Filled with Food, Love, and Joie de Vivre. Béatrice Peltre. Roost Books, an imprint of Shambhala Publications, Inc. 2016 392 p. color illustrations (hardcover : alk. paper) $35 **641.5**

1. French cooking 2. Cooking, French
ISBN 9781611801361

LC 2015026649

This cookbook, by Beatrice Peltre, "offers a beautiful assortment of over 120 recipes for naturally gluten-free dishes that feature whole grains, colorful produce, and distinctive spices. Every meal is an inspired work of love." (Publisher's note)

"Peltre's latest shows how cooking for gluten-free eaters doesn't have to be stressful. Highly recommended for foodies, flexitarians, and confident home cooks who are new to gluten-free cooking." LJ

Pepin, Jacques

The **apprentice**; my life in the kitchen. Houghton Mifflin 2003 318p il $26 **641.5**

1. Cooks 2. Cooking 3. Television personalities 4. Cookbook writers
ISBN 0-618-19737-0

LC 2002-192158

"Pépin relates how his interest in food and culinary techniques developed into passions for cooking and teaching. He does this deftly, neatly capturing personalities and events with clear, concise writing." Libr J

Essential Pepin; more than 700 all-time favorites from my life in food. Houghton Mifflin Harcourt 2011 685p il $40 **641.5**

1. French cooking
ISBN 978-0-547-23279-9

LC 2011-16057

Pepin "offers more than 700 of his best French and French-accented dishes from decades of cooking and teaching. They're simple without being dumbed down; approachable yet still adventurous. Whether he's explaining how to make Escoffier quenelles with mushroom sauce; black sea bass gravlax; chicken livers sautéed with vinegar; duck cassoulet; artichoke hearts with tarragon and mushrooms; or tarte tatin, he makes it seem doable and shares tidbits of wisdom to boost confidence and kitchen knowledge. His head notes are brief but informative, warm but not cloying. Pepin's own line drawings accompany the recipes, and they are, appropriately, at once homey and sophisticated. A DVD teaching a variety of cooking techniques accompanies the book, promising to make even the more challenging recipes less intimidating. For serious cooks and beginners alike, this is an instant classic." Publ Wkly

Jacques Pepin celebrates; by Jacques Pépin with Claudine Pépin; photographs by Christopher Hirsheimer; illustrations by Jacques Pépin. Knopf 2001 458p il $40 **641.5**

1. Cooking 2. Entertaining
ISBN 0-375-41209-3

LC 2001-29929

"In this companion to a new PBS series, Pépin builds on a broad definition of celebrations—encompassing holidays, special occasions, and simply nice weather—to present a collection of typically solid French recipes and numerous useful tips and techniques. . . . More valuable than the recipes . . . are the many notes on chopping, garnishing, carving and so forth." Publ Wkly

Perelman, Deb

★ The **smitten** kitchen cookbook; Deb Perelman. Alfred A. Knopf 2012 p. cm.   **641.5**
1. Cooking 2. Kitchens 3. Cookbooks
ISBN 9780307595652

LC 2012007711

This book is a cookbook by "Deb Perelman of Smitten Kitchen--home cook, photographer, and celebrated food blogger." The book is "all about approachable, uncompromised home cooking. Here you'll find better uses for your favorite vegetables: asparagus blanketing a pizza; ratatouille dressing up a sandwich; cauliflower masquerading as pesto. . . . Deb tells you her favorite summer cocktail; how to lose your fear of cooking for a crowd; and the essential items you need for your own kitchen." (Publisher's note)

Peternell, Cal

A **Recipe** for Cooking; by Cal Peternell. HarperCollins 2016 352 p. $29.99; (ebook) $27.99 **641.5**
1. Cooking
ISBN 0062427865; 9780062427861; 9780062427878
LC 2016046678

This cookbook, by Cal Peternell, "gives you everything you need to cook for big get-togethers, holiday feasts, family occasions, and for a special dinner for two. He organizes the recipes by season to help cooks plan their meals from first bite to last—how a meal should start, what should be the main attraction, what should be served alongside, and how to choose the perfect finish." (Publisher's note)

"Cookbooks for relaxed entertaining are making a comeback." LJ

★ **Twelve** Recipes; Cal Peternell. 1st ed HarperCollins 2014 304 p. ill. (chiefly col.) hbk $26.99   **641.5**
1. Cooking 2. Cookbooks
ISBN 0062270303; 9780062270306

LC 2015303204

IACP Cookbook Award: General (2015)

"Based on the life-altering course of instruction [author Cal Peternell] prepared and honed through many phone calls with his son, 'Twelve Recipes' is [an] . . . introduction to the kitchen. Peternell focuses on the core foods and dishes that comprise a successful home cook's arsenal, each building skill upon skill--from toast, eggs, and beans, to vinaigrettes, pasta with tomato, and rice, to vegetables, soup, meats, and cake."

"Marked by Peternell's zeal for good, simple food, this title takes a very different approach from cooking handbooks that emphasize science or technical precision." LJ

Peterson, James

Cooking. Ten Speed Press 2007 534p il $40   **641.5**
1. Cooking
ISBN 978-1-580-08789-6; 1-580-08789-2

LC 2007-21065

This book "opens with a fairly brief description of ten basic cooking techniques and then moves on to Recipes To Learn By, organized by course or main ingredient. Many of the recipes are traditional French standbys, from Celeriac Rémoulade to Beef à la Mode, although there are dishes inspired by Thai, Mexican, and other cuisines as well. . . . Essentially an intensive course for home cooks in the classic techniques that underlie good cooking, this is recommended for all cookery collections." Libr J

Glorious French food; a fresh approach to the classics. Wiley 2002 xxv, 742p il map $45 **641.5**
1. French cooking
ISBN 0-471-44276-3

LC 2001-46972

The author presents "50 classic recipes as the starting point for his wide-ranging exploration of French food and techniques; each recipe serves both to demonstrate a variety of techniques and as the inspiration for a diverse collection of other recipes related to it in one way or another. . . . Each chapter includes boxes and charts on improvising with different ingredients and flavors. The suggested variations for individual recipes, often mini-essays in themselves, open up dozens of other possibilities. Peterson is both passionate and knowledgeable about his subject, and his . . . book is an essential purchase." Libr J

Includes bibliographical references

Kitchen simple; essential recipes for everyday cooking. Ten Speed Press 2011 244p il $30 **641.5**
1. Cooking
ISBN 978-1-58008-318-8

LC 2011-04435

"With a solid background in culinary instruction, Peterson easily articulates the basics of cooking and baking the selected recipes for even the most adventurous cook. This diverse assortment of 200 recipes strikes a perfect balance between fundamental and more advanced dishes, making it a useful source for cooks at every level of expertise. The straightforward language and full-color photographs, taken by Peterson himself, combine to create an accessible, well-organized guide to cooking for any occasion." Shelf Awareness

Phillips, Carolyn

All under heaven; Recipes from the 35 Cuisines of China. written and illustrated by Carolyn Phillips; introduction by Ken Hom. Ten Speed Press 2016 524 p. illustrations, map (hardcover : alk. paper) $40   **641.5**
1. Cookbooks 2. Chinese cooking 3. Cooking, Chinese
ISBN 9781607749820

LC 2015029244

This cookbook by Carolyn Phillips is "a comprehensive, contemporary portrait of China's culinary landscape and the geography and history that has shaped it. . . . With hundreds of recipes--from simple Fried Green Onion Noodles to Lotus-Wrapped Spicy Rice Crumb Pork--written with clear, step-by-step instructions, [it] serves as both a handbook for the novice and a source of inspiration for the veteran chef." (Publisher's note)

"Those who enjoy the thoroughly researched cookbooks of experts such as Claudia Roden (The New Book of Middle Eastern Food) will appreciate Phillips's comprehensive treatment, which includes historical information, an extensive ingredient glossary, suggested menus, and useful advice." LJ

Includes bibliographical references and index

Pierson, Joy

Vegan holiday cooking from Candle Cafe; celebratory menus and recipes from New York's premier plant-based restaurants. Joy Pierson, Angel Ramos, and Jorge Pineda. Ten Speed Press 2014 176 p. color illustrations (hardback) $22.99 **641.5**
1. Veganism 2. Cookbooks 3. Holiday cooking 4. Candle Cafe 5. Vegan cooking 6. Candle 79 (Restaurant)
ISBN 1607746476; 9781607746478; 9781607746485
LC 2014005259

"This collection of vegan holiday recipes—the first of its kind from award-winning chefs—elevates plant-based fare to a new level. With fresh, inventive menus for Thanksgiving, Christmas, New Year's Eve, Lunar New Year, Super Bowl Sunday, Valentine's Day, Passover, Easter, Cinco de Mayo, and Independence Day, this cookbook blends favorite traditions with a modern sensibility. Tantalizing dishes include Sweet Potato Latkes with Almond Crème Fraîche for Passover; Porcini-Crusted Seitan with Glazed Cipollini Onions and Mushroom Gravy for Thanksgiving; and Red, White, and Blue Margaritas for the Fourth of July.

Now home cooks can entertain in the spirit of New York's premier vegan restaurants, Candle Cafe, Candle 79, and Candle Cafe West. With forewords by Alicia Silverstone and Laura and Woody Harrelson, plus sumptuous photography throughout, this festive cookbook invites vegans and omnivores alike to gather around the holiday table and enjoy." Publisher's Note

"You'll be proud to serve and eat these vegan foods, and party hosts won't be tempted to hide them at the end of their holiday buffet." LJ

Pollan, Michael, 1955-

★ **Cooked**; a natural history of transformation. Michael Pollan. Penguin Press 2013 480 p. (hardback) $27.95 **641.5**
1. Cooking 2. Food industry -- United States 3. Cooks
ISBN 1594204217; 9781594204210
LC 2012039705

In this book, author Michael Pollan shows that "taking back control of cooking may be the single most important step anyone can take to help make the American food system healthier and more sustainable. Reclaiming cooking as an act of enjoyment and self-reliance, learning to perform the magic of these everyday transformations, opens the door to a more nourishing life." (Publisher's note)

"The author mixes journalistic encounters with tales of skilled, often relentlessly obsessive cooks who demonstrated the art of transforming the products of nature into tasty food and then tried, with spotty success, to teach him to do the same. Four sections describe this transformation with the four classical elements: fire, water, air and earth." Kirkus
Includes bibliographical references

The **professional** chef; the Culinary Institute of America. 8th ed; Wiley 2006 1215p il map $70 **641.5**
1. Cooking 2. Restaurants
ISBN 978-0-7645-5734-7; 0-7645-5734-3
LC 2004-27110

First published 1962
"The nation's most prestigious training school for food careerists concentrates the essence of its course work within a comprehensive volume that competent students must master. Every aspect of the restaurant business is addressed, from nutrition and portion sizing to fiscal and human resource management. Sections on equipment, from major appliances to handheld tools, show the bond between chef and technology. Chapters on world cooking identify the most typical cooking processes and give examples of commonly appearing ingredients in each style. Recipes record classic preparations that form the foundation for myriad elaborations and personalization to move cooking from mere technique to high art. Although beyond the need of most home cooks, this massive tome is a necessary reference-collection purchase for any library whose community includes foodservice-training programs." Booklist

Psilakis, Michael

How to roast a lamb; new Greek classic cooking. [by] Michael Psilakis with Brigit Binns & Ellen Shapiro; foreword by Barbara Kafka; photography, Christopher Hirsheimer & Melissa Hamilton. Little, Brown and Company 2009 288p il $35 **641.5**
1. Greek cooking 2. Mediterranean cooking
ISBN 978-0-316-04121-8
LC 2008-54932

This "cookbook is an emotional autobiography in narrative and recipe form. It's also an introduction to the marvels of Hellenic cuisine. Psilakis, beginning with childhood favorites, moves from simple home cooking to complex restaurant fare. The bulk of the dishes—precise and lavishly illustrated—are easy enough to replicate (although some of his Anthos creations require dozens of ingredients and could take all day to make)." Time Out N Y

Puck, Wolfgang

Live, love, eat! the best of Wolfgang Puck. Gramercy Books 2006 243p il $14.99 **641.5**
1. Cooking
ISBN 978-0-517-22868-5; 0-517-22868-8
LC 2006-41232

First published 2002 by Random House
This volume contains more than 125 recipes for appetizers, a variety of seasonal soups and salads, and, along with pasta and risotto recipes, the California-style pizzas that first made Puck and his original Spago Hollywood a favorite of international celebrities. Puck also serves up all manner of

main courses, including seafood recipes, poultry dishes, and meat recipes. To round out the collection, he offers a variety of vegetable and other side-dish recipes, plus desserts. A section covering basics, sauces, and techniques provides guidance for beginning and experienced cooks alike. Illustrated throughout with more than 150 color images of finished dishes and closeup how-to shots demonstrating key techniques and tips.

Pépin, Jacques, 1935-

Heart & soul in the kitchen; Jacques Pepin; photography by Tom Hopkins Studio. Houghton Mifflin Harcourt 2015 ix, 435 p.p illustrations $35 **641.5**
1. Cooking
ISBN 0544301986; 9780544301986
LC 2015490299

This book, by author Jacques Pépin "is an intimate look at the celebrity chef and the food he cooks at home with family and friends—200 recipes in all. There are the simple dinners Jacques prepares for his wife, like the world's best burgers (the secret is ground brisket). There are elegant dinners for small gatherings. . . . And there are the dishes for backyard parties, including grilled chicken tenderloin in an Argentinean chimichurri sauce." (Publisher's note)

"Readers can expect effortless, entertaining-worthy fare...along with humorous and informative anecdotes from Pépin's storied career...Highly recommended for fans of the chef and most public libraries." LJ

Quessenberry, Sara

The **good** neighbor cookbook; 125 easy and delicious recipes to surprise and satisfy the new moms, new neighbors, recuperating friends, community-meeting members, book club cohorts, and block party pals in your life! [by] Sara Quessenberry and Suzanne Schlosberg. Andrews McMeel 2011 195p il pa $16.99 **641.5**
1. Cooking
ISBN 978-0-7407-9355-4

Provides 125 recipes for appetizers, soups, salads, entrées, and snacks suitable for a variety of gatherings, including block parties, potluck dinners, book clubs, and recuperating friends.

"This distinctive approach that highlights the communality of cooking is highly recommended." Libr J

Raichlen, Steven

★ The **barbecue!** bible; photography by Ben Fink. 10th anniversary edition; Workman Pub. 2008 556p il **641.5**
1. Barbecue cooking
ISBN 978-0-7611-4944-6; 978-0-7611-4943-9
First published 1998

Raij, Alex

The **Basque** book; a love letter in recipes from the kitchen of Txikito. Alex Raij with Eder Montero and Rebecca Flint Marx; photography by Penny De Los Santos. Ten Speed Press 2016 304 p. color illustrations (hardcover : alk. paper) $29.99 **641.5**
1. Basque cooking 2. Basque Provinces (France and

Spain) 3. Cooking, Basque
ISBN 9781607747611; 9781607747628
LC 2015041924

This Basque cookbook, by Alex Raij with Eder Montero and Rebecca Flint Marx, with photography by Penny De Los Santos, "share[s] more than one hundred recipes from [the authors' New York City restaurant] Txikito—all inspired by the home cooking traditions of the Basque Country—that will change the way you cook." (Publisher's note)

"Part cookbook, part travelog, this richly descriptive title is a pleasure to read and recalls evocative, landscape photography-rich works such as Giorgio Locatelli's Made in Sicily." LJ

Includes bibliographical references and index

Ramineni, Shubhra

Entice with spice; easy Indian recipes for busy people. photography by Masano Kawana; styling by Christina Ong and Magdalene Ong. Tuttle Pub. 2010 160p il map $27.95 **641.5**
1. Indic cooking
ISBN 978-0-8048-4029-3
LC 2009-49092

This is a "cookbook full of traditional Indian recipes adapted for busy American kitchens. Beginning with thorough explanations, from terminology to spice mixtures, she provides time-saving suggestions and tips for preparing ingredients. . . . This may be the Indian cookbook that American foodies have been waiting for." Publ Wkly

Ramsay, Gordon, 1966-

Gordon Ramsay's fast food; more than 100 delicious, super-fast, and easy recipes. by Gordon Ramsay. Sterling 2012 208 p. col. ill. $24.95 **641.5**
1. Cookbooks
ISBN 1402797877; 9781402797873

In this cookbook, celebrity chef Gordon Ramsay "serves up a feast of doable ideas: more than 100 recipes and 15 great menus for putting food on the table each and every day. Many of the dishes take only 15 minutes to prepare and cook; none takes longer than half an hour--and you can put together an entire meal in only 30-45 minutes. Ramsay also offers time-saving shortcuts, plus info on how to stock your pantry." (Publisher's note)

Recipes from an Italian summer; [translation by Mary Consoni; photographs by Joel Meyerowitz, Andy Sewell; illustrations by Jeffrey Fisher] Phaidon Press Limited 2010 431p il $39.95 **641.5**
1. Italian cooking
ISBN 978-0-714857732

This collection, "from the editors behind The Silver Spoon cookbook, is comprised of a glorious 400+ pages of recipes for picnics, barbecues, light suppers and summer entertaining (with the chapters thus organized, along with chapters on salads, desserts and ice cream/beverages). It's a compilation of dishes from popular Italian vacation regions. . . . The dishes are simple yet glorious in that Italian way (meaning without good ingredients first press olive oil, farmers market greens, real Parmigiano-Reggiano, there's little point in making many of the recipes)." L A Wkly

Reichl, Ruth, 1948-

My kitchen year; 136 recipes that saved my life. Ruth Reichl. Random House Inc. 2015 336 p. color illustrations (hardcover) $30   **641.5**
1. Seasonal cooking
ISBN 9781400069989; 140006998X

LC 2014029197

This book, by Ruth Reichl, describes the author's experiences re-learning to appreciate cooking after she lost her job as a food magazine editor. It "follows the change of seasons--and Reichl's emotions--as she slowly heals through the simple pleasures of cooking. While working 24/7, Reichl would 'throw quick meals together' for her family and friends. Now she has the time to rediscover what cooking meant to her." (Publisher's note)

"Reichl has written some classics in food literature, including Tender at the Bone (1998); therefore, much attention will be accorded her latest book." Booklist

Rice, Valentina

Recipes from many kitchens; celebrated local food artisans share their signature dishes. by Valentina Rice. Page Street Publishing Co. 2016 192 p. color illustrations (pbk) $21.99   **641.5**
1. Cooking 2. Cookbooks
ISBN 1624142028; 9781624142024

LC 2015948086

This cookbook by Valentina Rice offers a multi-cultural artisinal "collection of over 80 recipes will see you through every occasion, from a decadent French Breakfast to an exotic Indian Feast. Learn to make the fluffiest of scones from a master baker or the creamiest of croquetas from Spanish aristocracy. Valentina introduces you to this talented community of makers in this extraordinary collection of flavorful menus." (Publisher's note)

"As founder of Many Kitchens (manykitchens.com), an online marketplace for artisanal foods, Rice has access to a distinct community of food entrepreneurs. When asked to contribute recipes to this cookbook, she came back with an eclectic mix of tastes and techniques." LJ

Ridge, Brent

The **Beekman** 1802 heirloom dessert cookbook; 100 delicious heritage recipes from the farm and garden. by Brent Ridge, Josh Kilmer-Purcell, and Sandy Gluck. Rodale Books 2013 272 p. (hardback) $32.50   **641.5**
1. Farm produce 2. American cooking 3. Farm life -- United States 4. Desserts 5. Cooking, American 6. Farm life -- New York (State) -- Upstate New York 7. Farm produce -- New York (State) -- Upstate New York
ISBN 1609615735; 9781609615734

LC 2013010502

This book, by Josh Kilmer-Purcell, Brent Ridge, and Sandy Gluck, "will show off the delicious and decadent recipes that the Beekman Boys have collected from across the generations of their family, from Brent's grandmother's Fourth of July Fruitcake to Josh's mother's Hot Chocolate Dumplings. Each recipe will be accompanied by a personal memory from the authors or a story about how that recipe came to be." (Publisher's note)

Robertson, Robin

Robin Robertson's vegan without borders; easy everyday meals from around the world. Robin Robertson. Andrews McMeel Pub., LLC 2014 304 p. illustrations $40   **641.5**
1. Cooking 2. Veganism
ISBN 1449447082; 9781449447083

LC 2014930776

Author Robin Robertson presents a cookbook of her "favorite dishes from the great cuisines of the world and shows how cooking vegan makes borders disappear. Whether the recipe hails from Ecuador or Ethiopia, these plant-based dishes invite you to travel the culinary world and sample 150 of Robin's all-time favorites." (Publisher's note)

"Robertson's existing fans will be joined by many new ones on this tasty whirlwind tour of the globe." LJ

Vegan planet; more than 425 irresistible recipes with fantastic flavors from home and around the world. Robin Robertson. The Harvard Common Press 2014 xii, 532 p.p (pbk.) $19.95   **641.5**
1. Veganism 2. Vegan cooking 3. International cooking
ISBN 1558328319; 9781558328310

LC 2013022919

This vegan cookbook, by Robin Robertson, "is back in a thoroughly revised edition. . . . [U]pdates cover such things as: the newly expanded range of whole grains that are available; super greens, such as kale and chard, that are rising in popularity; new facts concerning which cooking oils are healthiest and most earth-friendly; and new saucing and flavoring ideas from the global pantry." (Publisher's note)

Includes bibliographical references and index

Roden, Claudia

Arabesque: a taste of Morocco, Turkey, and Lebanon. Knopf 2006 341p il $35   **641.5**
1. Turkish cooking 2. Lebanese cooking 3. Moroccan cooking
ISBN 0-307-26498-X; 978-0-307-26498-5

LC 2006-45258

First published 2005 in the United Kingdom

The author "has chosen more than 150 recipes from Morocco, Turkey, and Lebanon, some newly discovered, some variations on more familiar dishes, and a selection of favorite classic dishes. Each section opens with a fascinating insider's guide, providing both cultural and culinary history as well as information on specific ingredients and techniques. . . . An essential purchase." Libr J

The **book** of Jewish food; an odyssey from Samarkand to New York. Claudia Roden. Knopf 1996 668 p. il $45   **641.5**
1. Cookbooks 2. Jewish cooking 3. Jewish civilization
ISBN 0394532589; 9780394532585

LC 96028758

James Beard Award (1997)

This cookbook, written by Claudia Roden, "traces the development of both Ashkenazic and Sephardic Jewish communities and their cuisine over the centuries. The 800 . . . recipes, many never before documented, represent trea-

sures garnered by Roden through nearly 15 years of traveling around the world." (Publisher's note)

Includes bibliographical references and index

The **food** of Spain. Ecco Press 2011 $39.99 **641.5**
1. Spanish cooking
ISBN 978-0-06-196962-1

Rombauer, Irma von Starkloff

★ **Joy** of cooking; [by] Irma S. Rombauer, Marion Rombauer Becker, Ethan Becker; illustrated by
John Norton. 75th anniversary ed.; Scribner 2006
1132p il $30   **641.5**
1. Cooking
ISBN 978-0-7432-4626-2; 0-7432-4626-8
                                        LC 2006-51231
First published 1931

This is the "backbone for any library's cookery reference
collection, its nearly 4,000 recipes defining essential American home cooking." Booklist

Rose, Evelyn

100 Best Jewish Recipes; Evelyn Rose with Judi
Rose. Interlink Pub Group Inc 2015 208 p. color
illustrations $30   **641.5**
1. Cookbooks 2. Jewish cooking
ISBN 156656073X; 9781566560733

"100 Best Jewish Recipes is comprised of the highlights
from Evelyn Rose's culinary life, which spanned several decades and earned her the recognition as one of the world's
foremost Jewish food writers. Packed with mouthwatering
ideas for both family meals and those special occasions
when you want to impress without spending hours in the
kitchen, this book contains 100 fail-safe recipes for which
the author is justly celebrated." (Publisher's note)

"Condensing the world's vast tradition of Jewish cookery to just 100 dishes presents a formidable challenge. The
late Evelyn Rose spent a lifetime scouring Europe, Africa,
and Asia and documenting the foods consumed in those continents' Jewish communities. Duck breast glazed with ginger, honey, and soy recalls the seasonings of Chinese food.
Sephardi-style pizza evokes Armenian or Turkish lahmacun,
and further topping it with kosher salami transforms it almost into American pepperoni pizza. . . . Because Jewish
holidays have so many food traditions supplementing religious ones, Rose gives advice on dishes to celebrate the
eight major festivals that Jews observe. An excellent addition to most library collections." Booklist

Rosenthal, Mitchell

Cooking my way back home; recipes from San
Francisco's Town Hall, Anchor & Hope, and Salt
House. Mitchell Rosenthal with Jon Pult, foreword
by wolfgang Puck; photography by Paige Green.
Ten Speed Press 2011 vii, 263 p.p col. ill. (hbk.)
$35   **641.5**
1. Cookbooks 2. American cooking 3. Southern
cooking 4. Salt House (Restaurant) 5. Anchor & Hope
(Restaurant) 6. Cooking, American -- Southern style
7. Cooking, American -- California style 8. Town Hall

(Restaurant : San Francisco, Calif.)
ISBN 158008592X; 9781580085922
                                        LC 2011011631

This cookbook, by Mitchell Rosenthal with Jon Pult,
"blends Southern-inspired comfort food with urban sophistication and innovation, for exciting results. Reflecting on
the classics (Shrimp Étouffée), updating regional specialties
(Poutine), elevating family favorites (Chopped Liver), and
reveling in no-holds-barred, all-out indulgences (Butterscotch Chocolate Pot de Crème) are what's on order in this
collection of 100 . . . recipes." (Publisher's note)

Includes bibliographical references

Roux, Michel

The **French** kitchen; recipes from the master of
French cooking. by Michel Roux Jr. Simon & Schuster 2016 352 p. $40   **641.5**
1. French cooking
ISBN 1681880601; 9781681880600
                                        LC 2015057875

In this cookbook, by Michel Roux Jr., "you'll find 200
classics recipes . . . to master French cooking. No topic is
breezed over: and with chapters for soup, terrines and pâtés,
eggs and cheese, fish and shellfish, chicken, duck and game
birds, meat, vegetables and salads, desserts, bread and crois-
sants, and stocks and sauces." (Publisher's note)

"Today, chefs of all statures are adored, revered for
their kitchen talent, devotion to the "cause," and painstaking meticulousness in this art and craft of food. Yet not all
can translate those competencies into a collection of recipes
for the home cook to follow. Roux, of London's Michelin-
starred La Gavroche, can..." Booklsit

Ruggiero, Tina

The **truly** healthy family cookbook; mega-nutritious meals that are inspired, delicious and fad free.
by Tina Ruggiero. Page Street Publishing 2013 224
p. (pbk.) $22.99   **641.5**
1. Cookbooks 2. Nutrition
ISBN 1624140084; 1624140092; 9781624140082;
9781624140099
                                        LC 2013933895

This book, by Tina Ruggiero, contains "recipes based
on modern nutrition science. It takes a flexitarian approach
that includes the best parts of the current health movements.
Ruggiero offers up her best 120 mega-nutritious recipes . .
. that focus on . . . tasty, fresh, real food ingredients, simple
preparation and proven nutrition." (Publisher's note)

Ruhlman, Michael

Ratio; the simple codes behind the craft of everyday cooking. Scribner 2009 xxv, 224p il $27 **641.5**
1. Cooking
ISBN 978-1-416-56611-3; 1-416-56611-2
                                        LC 2008-32679

"While Ruhlman was attending the Culinary Institute
of America for a book project, a chef showed him a copy
of the golden rules, which boiled down the elements of
(French) cooking into ratios. . . . [In this volume] Ruhlman
guides readers through the ratios for a variety of doughs,
batters, stocks, sauces, custards and sausages, explaining
their chemical and culinary basis in clear, earnest prose and

providing tasteful recipes that lay out the technique for each formula." N Y Times Book Rev

Ruhlman's twenty; the ideas and techniques that will make you a better cook. Michael Ruhlman; photographs by Donna Turner Ruhlman. Chronicle Books 2011 367 p. col. ill. (alk. paper) $40 **641.5**
1. Cooking 2. Cookbooks
ISBN 9780811876438
LC 2011036735
IACP Award (2012)
James Beard Award (2012)

This cookbook "distills [author Michael] Ruhlman's decades of cooking, writing, and working with the world's greatest chefs into twenty essential ideas from ingredients to processes to attitude that are guaranteed to make every cook more accomplished. Whether cooking a multi-course meal, the juiciest roast chicken, or just some really good scrambled eggs, Ruhlman reveals how a cook s success boils down to the same twenty concepts." (Publisher's note)

"Thorough, clearly explained, and stunningly beautiful, this collection will appeal to cooks of all levels." Pub Wkly
Includes bibliographical references and index

Saltsman, Amelia

The **Santa** Monica Farmers' Market Cookbook; seasonal foods, simple recipes, and stories from the market and farm. Amelia Saltsman; foreword by Deborah Madison. Blenheim 2007 216 p. col. ill. $22.95 **641.5**
1. Markets 2. Cookbooks 3. Farm produce 4. Santa Monica (Calif.) 5. Cooking 6. Santa Monica Farmers' Market (Santa Monica, Calif.)
ISBN 0979042909; 9780979042904
LC 2007901323

This cookbook, by Amelia Saltsman, is "a celebration of the [Santa Monica Farmers' Market]. . . . What s the difference between white and green zucchini? What are amaranth, sapote, and ramps? With Amelia as your guide, you'll learn the answers to these questions and more. You'll also find advice on how to select and store produce, stories about farmers and their crops, chef and farmer cooking tips, and more than 100 of Amelia's simple, tempting recipes." (Publisher's note)

Includes bibliographical references (p. 205-206) and index

Samuelsson, Marcus, 1970-

Marcus off duty; the recipes I cook at home. Marcus Samuelsson with Roy Finamore; photography by Paul Brissman. Houghton Mifflin Harcourt 2014 352 p. illustrations (chiefly color) (paper over board) $35 **641.5**
1. Cooking 2. Cookbooks
ISBN 0470940581; 9780470940587
LC 2014018169
James Beard Foundation Award Nominee: General Cooking (2015)

This book, by chef Marcus Samuelsson, "serves up the dishes he makes at his Harlem home for his wife and friends. The recipes blend a rainbow of the flavors he experienced in his travels-- Ethiopian, Swedish, Mexican, Caribbean, Ital-

ian, and Southern soul. His eclectic, casual food includes dill-spiced salmon; coconut-lime curried chicken; mac, cheese, and greens; chocolate pie spiced with Indian garam masala; and for kids, peanut noodles with slaw." (Publisher's note)

"Highly recommended for adventurous and well-traveled home cooks, as well as fans of Susan Feniger's Street Food." LJ

Red Rooster Cookbook; The Story of Food and Hustle in Harlem. Marcus Samuelsson; photographs by Bobby Fisher; text with April Reynolds; recipes and text with Roy Finamore; illustrations by Rebekah Maysles and Leon Johnson. Houghton Mifflin Harcourt 2016 384 p. color illustrations (paper over board) $37.50 **641.5**
1. Restaurants 2. American cooking 3. Harlem (New York, N.Y.) 4. International cooking 5. Red Rooster (Restaurant) 6. Food -- New York (State) -- New York 7. Cooking -- New York (State) -- New York
ISBN 9780544639775
LC 2016037226

This cookbook, by Marcus Samuelsson, presents "Southern comfort food and multicultural recipes. . . . When . . . Samuelsson opened Red Rooster on Malcolm X Boulevard in Harlem, he envisioned more than a restaurant. It would be the heart of his neighborhood and a meet-and-greet for both the downtown and the uptown sets, serving Southern black and cross-cultural food." (Publisher's note)

"Fisher's food and street photography colorfully captures the character of Samuelsson's dishes as well as the characters that inhabit his neighborhood." Pub Wkly

The **soul** of a new cuisine; a discovery of the foods and flavors of Africa. foreword by Desmond Tutu. Wiley 2006 xxii, 344p il map $40 **641.5**
1. African cooking
ISBN 0-7645-6911-2

For this African cookbook, the author "traveled to Africa and even took cooking lessons in Ethiopia, the country of his birth. Samuelsson emphasizes that this is not the definitive cookbook of an area with over 800 languages and dialects, but an overview of what he saw and ate in his travels. . . . This is a unique cookbook about a little-known cuisine, including travel essays and enhanced by beautiful color photographs that depict the food and the people of Africa. A necessary acquisition for international cookery collections." Libr J
Includes bibliographical references

Sanfilippo, Diane

Practical paleo; a customized approach to health and a whole-foods lifestyle. Diane Sanfillipo, with photography by Bill Staley. Victory Belt Pub. 2012 416 p. col. ill. $39.95 **641.5**
1. Cookbooks 2. Paleo cooking
ISBN 1936608758; 9781936608751

This Paleo cookbook, by Diane Sanfilippo, illustrated by Bill Staley, "explains why avoiding both processed foods and foods marketed as 'healthy'--like grains, legumes, and pasteurized dairy--will improve how you look and feel and lead to lasting weight loss. . . . [This book] is jam-packed with over 120 easy recipes, all with special notes about common food allergens including nightshades and FODMAPs. Meal plans are also included." (Publisher's note)

Sauvage, Jeanne

Gluten-free wish list; sweet & savory treats you've missed the most. Jeanne Sauvage; photographs by Eva Kolenko. Chronicle Books Llc 2015 256 p. color illustrations (hardcover) $29.95 **641.5**
1. Cookbooks 2. Gluten-free diet 3. Baking 4. Gluten-free diet -- Recipes
ISBN 9781452138336

LC 2015000533

This gluten-free cookbook, by Jeanne Sauvage, with photographs by Eva Kolenko, includes "recipes for pizza crust, bagels, and all of the other wheat-laden staples folks miss most after eliminating gluten from their diets. Here author Jeanne Sauvage proves that gluten-free should never be anything less than delicious." (Publisher's note)

"For those looking to expand their specialty cooking section or who are thinking of going gluten-free themselves, this book would seem to be the ticket. For all cookbook collections." LJ

Includes bibliographical references and index

Schroeder, Keith

Cooking light mad delicious; The Science of Making Healthy Food Taste Amazing. by Keith Schroeder. Oxmoor House 2014 384 p. color illustrations $35 **641.5**
1. Cooking
ISBN 0848704282; 9780848704285

LC 2014944834

James Beard Foundation Award Winner: Focus on Health (2015)

This cookbook, by Keith Schroeder, "takes the kitchen science genre to the next level. . . . Schroeder teaches home cooks about the nature of ingredients, how to maximize texture and flavor with clever cooking techniques, . . . smooth moves in the kitchen for better work flow, and how all the sciences-geography, meteorology, chemistry, physics, botany, biology, even human sociology and anthropology-can help home cooks master the science of light cooking." (Publisher's note)

Shaw, Diana

The **essential** vegetarian cookbook; your guide to the best foods on earth. Diana Shaw; illustrated by Kathy Warriner. Clarkson Potter/Publishers 1997 611 p. illustrations hardcover o.p. $24.95 **641.5**
1. Vegetarian cooking
ISBN 051788268X; 9780517882689

LC 9622290

Author Diana Shaw "presents the one book that full-time and part-time vegetarians need on their shelves--a book that contains more than 600 contemporary low-fat recipes and invaluable nutritional and culinary information about the vegetarian way of life." (Publisher's note)

"There are plenty of innovative vegetable dishes, such as Spicy Spinach Nuggets with Cooling Chive Sauce, and ethnic favorites, for example, Spring Rolls with Peanut Sauce. From soups (Barley Soup with Zucchini) to "one-dish din-

ners" (Potato-Fennel Stew with Mixed Beans and Tofu) and tasty pasta sauces (Three-Mushroom Sauce), Shaw offers much to prod the appetites and imaginations of dedicated cooks." Publisher's Weekly

Shepherd, Sue

The **2**-step low-FODMAP eating plan; How To Build a Custom Diet that Relieves the Symptoms of IBS, Lactose Intolerance, and Gluten Sensitivity. Sue Shepherd. Experiment 2016 288 p. (pbk.) $19.95 **641.5**
1. Diet therapy 2. Digestive system 3. Irritable colon -- Diet therapy -- Recipes 4. Malabsorption syndromes -- Diet therapy -- Recipes
ISBN 9781615193158

LC 2015042268

In this book, Dr. Sue Shepherd "presents a reliable approach to identify what foods you can enjoy, and eliminate only those that cause symptoms [of your digestive disorder]. . . . With menu plans for adults, kids, vegetarians and vegans, anyone can do it. Dr. Shepherd also delivers a guide to shopping and how to approach food labels, travel information and tips for eating out, and over 80 crave-worthy recipes." (Publisher's note)

"This superlative guide, as deeply informative and accessible as it is hunger-inducing and eye-catching, will benefit not only those with IBS, celiac, and lactose intolerance, but health-cognizant gourmands as well." Pub Wkly

Shulman, Martha Rose

The **simple** art of vegetarian cooking; templates and lessons for making delicious meatless meals every day. Martha Rose Shulman. Rodale Books 2014 270 p. color illustrations (hardback) $32.50 **641.5**
1. Cookbooks 2. Vegetarian cooking 3. Quick and easy cooking
ISBN 162336129X; 9781623361297

LC 2013049184

"In 'The Simple Art of Vegetarian Cooking,' . . . Martha Rose Shulman offers a . . . method for creating delicious plant-based meals every day. . . . It teaches the reader how to cook basic dishes via templates--master recipes with simple guidelines for creating an essential dish, such as a frittata or an omelet, a stir-fry, a rice bowl, a pasta dish, a soup--and then how to swap in and out key ingredients as desired based on seasonality and freshness." (Publisher's note)

The **very** best of recipes for health; 250 recipes and more from the popular feature on NYTimes.com. Martha Rose Shulman. Rodale 2010 xvi, 352 p.p col. ill. (hardcover) $37.50 **641.5**
1. Cookbooks 2. Cooking -- Natural foods 3. Health 4. Nutrition
ISBN 9781605295732; 1605295736

LC 2010021608

This cookbook, by Martha Rose Shulman, "shows how to fill your refrigerator, freezer, and cabinets with healthy staples such as beans, grains, extra virgin olive oil, tuna, eggs, yogurt, and tomato sauce, so that you are prepared to cook delicious dishes like Asparagus and Herb Frittata, Quinoa Salad with Lime Ginger Dressing and Shrimp, or

Pizza Marinara with Tuna and Capers in minutes." (Publisher's note)

Shulman, Martha Rose

Mediterranean harvest; vegetarian recipes from the world's healthiest cuisine. Martha Rose Shulman. Rodale 2007 p. cm.   **641.5**
1. Vegetarian cookery. 2. Cookery, Mediterranean.
ISBN 9781594862342 (hardcover); 1594862346 (hardcover)

LC 2007031561
Includes bibliographical references and index..

The **silver** spoon. Phaidon Press 2005 1263p il $39.95   **641.5**
1. Italian cooking
ISBN 978-0-7148-4531-9; 0-7148-4531-0
Original Italian edition, 1950

"The book contains recipes for everything from basic sauces and marinades to salads, game, fish and baked goods, with each section color-coded for easy browsing. Recipes emphasize fresh ingredients and are to-the-point, typically summed up in a paragraph sans photo illustrations. Those who know their way around a kitchen will appreciate the brevity. . . . Almost all of the ingredients called for can be found in a typical supermarket. . . . Globe-trotting gourmands will appreciate the menu and 'signature dish' contributions by famous Italian chefs that round out the book. The most exhaustive Italian cookbook in recent memory, this volume offers something for every cook, regardless of their skill level, and deserves to be a fixture in American kitchens." Publ Wkly

Silverton, Nancy

Mozza at home; More than 150 Crowd-Pleasing Recipes for Relaxed, Family-Style Entertaining. by Nancy Silverton with Carolynn Carreño; photographs by Christopher Hirsheimer. Alfred A. Knopf 2016 432 p. (hardcover) $35   **641.5**
1. Entertaining 2. Italian cooking 3. Pizzeria Mozza 4. Cooking, Italian
ISBN 9780385354325

LC 2015029125
In this cookbook, author Nancy Silverton "shares her renewed passion and provides nineteen menus packed with easy-to-follow recipes that can be prepared in advance (with no fancy restaurant equipment needed!) and are perfect for entertaining. Organized by meal, each menu provides a main dish along with a complementary selection of appetizers and side dishes." (Publisher's note)

"The exceptional foods of Nancy Silverton's wildly popular Los Angeles restaurants now come to delight home kitchens. Silverton's recipes reflect her attention to detail, her sophistication, and her creative imagination." Booklist

Simmons, Marie

Whole world vegetarian; Marie Simmons; photography by Teri Lynn Fisher and Jenny Park. Houghton Mifflin Harcourt 2016 320 p. color illustrations (paperback) $23   **641.5**
1. Vegetarian cooking
ISBN 9780544018457

LC 2015044198
This cookbook, by Marie Simmons, presents "big-flavored vegetarian dishes from around the globe. . . . Simmons follows her culinary wanderlust, bringing together a collection of bold, imaginative dishes and seamlessly adapting them to contemporary tables." (Publisher's note)

"Simmons employs a wide range of ingredients, but few will prove difficult to source readily. Experienced cooks may handily transform some of the egg and cheese dishes here into vegan counterparts." Booklist

Simonds, Nina

★ Spices of life; simple and delicious recipes for great health. Nina Simonds; photographs by Tina Rupp. 1st ed.; Random House Inc 2005 383 p. col. ill. $24.95   **641.5**
1. Cookbooks 2. Cooking -- Herbs 3. Quick and easy cooking 4. Spices 5. Cooking (Herbs)
ISBN 0375411607; 9780375411601

LC 2004021089
James Beard Award (2006)
IACP Cookbook Award (2006)
In this cookbook, author and chef "Nina Simonds offers us more than 175 . . . recipes, along with practical tips for a sensible lifestyle, that demonstrate that health-giving foods not only provide pleasure but can make a huge difference in our lives. With her emphasis on the tonic properties of a wide variety of foods, herbs, and spices, this book also brings us up to date on the latest scientific research" (Publisher's note)

Simonds' book is "full of straightforward but practical recipes, and peppered with loads of health information." Pub Wkly
Includes bibliographical references (p. 362-364) and index

Slonecker, Andrea

Beer bites; tasty recipes and perfect pairings for brew lovers. Christian DeBenedetti and Andrea Slonecker; photographs by John Lee. Chronicle Books Llc 2015 168 p. color illustrations $24.95   **641.5**
1. Beer 2. Cooking 3. Food and beer pairing
ISBN 145213524X; 9781452135243

LC 2014032763
This cookbook, by Christian DeBenedetti and Andrea Slonecker, "n serves up 65 globe-roaming and simple recipes from appetizers to snacks and main courses that go beyond typical pub grub with recommendations of beer styles and widely available must-try brews for each dish. Beer Bites is ideal for the growing cadre of craft beer lovers eager to explore the basics and nuances of beer and food pairings." (Publisher's note)

This superb collection features of recipes that are sure to be hits at any gathering. Highly recommended for all cooking collections." Library Journal

Sobel, Adam

Street vegan; recipes and dispatches from the Cinnamon Snail food truck. Adam Sobel; photographs by Kate Lewis. Clarkson Potter/Publishers 2015 272 p. $25   **641.5**

1. Veganism 2. Vegan cooking 3. Street food -- New York (State) -- New York

ISBN 0385346190; 9780385346191; 9780385346207

LC 2014047446

This cookbook, by Adam Sobel, presents "[m]eatless meals revamped by the Cinnamon Snail, the vegan food truck with a cult following. . . . Adam brings his food straight to your kitchen, along with stories of the challenges of working on a food truck while still finding ways to infuse food with imagination, love, and a pinch of perspective." (Publisher's note)

Spieler, Marlena

Paris; authentic recipes celebrating the foods of the world. recipes and text Marlena Spieler; photographs Jean-Blaise Hall; general editor Chuck Williams. Oxmoor House 2004 191p il map (Williams-Sonoma foods of the world) $24.95   **641.5**

1. French cooking

ISBN 978-0-8487-2854-8

Illustrated with full-color photographs. "Dozens of stories reveal the secrets of making long-cherished foods and profile people, places, and influences that have shaped the Parisian food scene. More than 45 recipes allow you to sample traditional dishes, such as Boeuf en Daube, Steak withe Shallot Sauce, or Raspberry Charlotte, as well as such innovations as Duck Breasts with Port and Figs or Strawberry Soup." Publisher's note

Spungen, Susan

Recipes; a collection for the modern cook. Susan Spungen; foreword by Martha Stewart; photographs by Maria Robledo. William Morrow 2005 272 p. col. ill. $34.95   **641.5**

1. Cooking 2. Cookbooks

ISBN 0060731249; 9780060731243

LC 2005045710

IACP Cookbook Award Winner (2006)

In this cookbook, by Susan Spungen, the "founding food editor and editorial director for food at 'Martha Stewart Living Omnimedia' for twelve years presents her own easy, unfettered ideas for cooking simple food rich with freshness and flavors to share with family and friends." This cookbook is organized primarily by technique. (Publisher's note)

Stabiner, Karen

Generation chef; Risking It All for a New American Dream. Karen Stabiner. Avery, an imprint of Penguin Random House, LLC 2016 320 p. $26   **641.5**

1. Cooks 2. Restaurants 3. Entrepreneurs

ISBN 9781583335802

LC 2016026428

This book by Karen Stabiner tells "the story of Jonah Miller, who at age twenty-four attempts to fulfill a lifelong dream by opening the Basque restaurant Huertas in New York City. . . . Miller, a rising star who has been named to the 30-Under-30 list of both Forbes and Zagat, quits his job as a sous chef, creates a business plan, lines up investors, leases a space, hires a staff, and gets ready to put his reputation and his future on the line." (Publisher's note)

"Stabiner takes the reader beyond the shiny surface of food celebrity and Instagrammed plates to expose the beating hearts of those who get up every day to create something inspiring for strangers to consume." Pub Wkly

Stewart, Martha

Martha Stewart's cooking school; lessons and recipes for the home cook. by Martha Stewart with Sarah Carey; photographs by Marcus Nilsson; portraits by Ditte Isager. Clarkson Potter 2008 504p il $45   **641.5**

1. Cooking 2. Entertaining

ISBN 978-0-307-39644-0; 0-307-39644-4

LC 2008-531117

This "cookbook is the result of what Stewart refers to as her 'mission to teach the methods of home cooking.' Chapters are organized by technique, from 'How To Make White Stock' to 'How To Make Pâte à Choux.' Master recipes are followed by others that build on them, and there are hundreds of color photographs, including many step by steps for essential techniques. The illustrated 'Basics' section that opens the book covers equipment, knife skills, herbs and spices, 'the onion family,' and citrus fruits. Charts, buying guides, and sidebars are featured throughout, along with dozens of tips on ingredients, special techniques, and more." Libr J

Streiff, Fritz

The art of simple food; notes, lessons, and recipes from a delicious revolution. [by] Alice Waters, with Patricia Curtan, Kelsie Kerr & Fritz Streiff; illustrations by Patricia Curtan. Clarkson Potter 2007 405p il $35   **641.5**

1. Quick and easy cooking

ISBN 978-0-307-33679-8; 0-307-33679-4

LC 2007-300393

"After a useful discussion of ingredients and equipment come chapters on techniques, such as making broth and soup. Each of these includes three or four recipes that rely on the technique described. . . . The final third of the book divides many more recipes traditionally into salads, pasta and so forth. Waters taps an almost endless supply of ideas for appealing and fresh yet low-stress dishes." Publ Wkly

Sunset the great outdoors cookbook; Adventures in Cooking Under the Open Sky. by The Editors of Sunset Magazine. Time Home Entertainment Inc. 2014 254 p. color illustrations $24.95   **641.5**

1. Outdoor cooking

ISBN 0376028076; 9780376028075

LC 2013939860

IACP Cookbook Award Winner: Compilations (2015)

This cookbook "draws on the long tradition of cooking and living in the great outdoors. Discover the tradition and evolution of outdoor cooking in the West with stories, quotes, and historical photos. . . . With 200+ fresh recipes and 150+ full-color photos, this book has everything readers need to experience the ultimate outdoor cooking adventure - from menu planning and packing tips, to easy step-by-step cooking techniques." (Publisher's note)

Swanson, Heidi

Super natural every day; well-loved recipes from my natural foods kitchen. Heidi Swanson. Ten Speed Press 2011 p. cm. pa $23 **641.5**

1. Cooking -- Natural foods

ISBN 978-1-58008-277-8

LC 2010-43749

'A collection of 100 vegetarian recipes for nutritious, weekday-friendly dishes from the blogger behind 101 Cookbooks'--

Swift, Sally

The **Splendid** table's how to eat supper; recipes, stories, and opinions from public radio's award-winning food show. [by] Lynne Rossetto Kasper and Sally Swift. Clarkson Potter/Publishers 2008 338p il $35 **641.5**

1. Dining 2. Cooking

ISBN 978-0-307-34671-1

LC 2007-24749

"This superb book should grace the shelves of even the most infrequent of cooks." Publ Wkly

Tanis, David

Heart of the artichoke and other kitchen journeys. Artisan 2010 344p il $35 **641.5**

1. Menus 2. Cooking 3. Entertaining

ISBN 978-1-57965-407-8

LC 2010-4538

The author "begins with 14 'Kitchen Rituals' (ordinary pleasures perfect for one or two people) such as Jalapeño Pancakes and raw artichokes for lunch. Menus are arranged by season and feature, e.g., Fork-Mashed Potatoes and Spring Lamb with Rosemary. There are also menus for a long table (for a large crowd) such as A Perfect Suckling Pig. Simple recipes, eloquent writing, and Tanis's great reputation make this an essential purchase." Libr J

A **platter** of figs and other recipes; foreword by Alice Waters; photographs by Christopher Hirsheimer. Artisan 2008 294p il $35 **641.5**

1. Menus 2. Cooking 3. Entertaining

ISBN 978-1-57965-346-0; 1-57965-346-4

LC 2007-49384

This volums is "both a meditation on the powerful rites of cooking and serving a meal and a gentle but serious education in doing both. . . . With 24 menus distributed over the course of a year, Tanis emphasizes seasonality with ingredients (blueberry-blackberry crumble in summer; celery root mashed potatoes in winter) and with the types of dishes provided for each menu (as with a divine, warming lobster risotto as part of a menu for a cold spring day). Anecdotes from his peripatetic life of enjoying good food around the world, from Venice to Morocco to New Mexico, add another intimate dimension and help the book appear written just for the reader by a kind, patient friend." Publ Wkly

Includes bibliographical references

Tarlow, Andrew

Dinner at the Long Table; Andrew Tarlow and Anna Dunn. Ten Speed Press 2016 336 p. color illustrations (ebook) $65.00; (hardcover) $40 **641.5**

1. Dinners 2. Cookbooks 3. Cooking

ISBN 9781607748472; 9781607748465

LC 2016012177

This cookbook by Andrew Tarlow and Anna Dunn "brings Tarlow's keen eye for combining design and taste to a collection of seventeen seasonal menus ranging from small gatherings to blow-out celebrations. The menus . . . include recipes like a leisurely ragu, followed by fruit and biscotti; paella with tomato toasts, and a Catalan custard; fried calamari sandwiches and panzanella; or a lamb tajine with spiced couscous, pickled carrots, and apricots in honey." (Publisher's note)

"With nine outer-borough eateries and shops in his portfolio, Tarlow, more than anyone, has been responsible for defining Brooklyn's artisinal food scene." Pub Wkly

Tausend, Marilyn

Cocina de la familia; more than 200 authentic recipes from Mexican-American home kitchens. {by} Marilyn Tausend with Miguel Ravago. Simon & Schuster 1997 415p hardcover o.p. pa $20 **641.5**

1. Mexican American cooking

ISBN 0-684-85259-4 pa

LC 97-26979

This cookbook includes recipes for "Green Enchiladas with Spinach and Tofu, Chicken with Spicy Prune Sauce made with Coca-Cola, and Mexican Beef Chow Mein, {as well as} more traditional Mexican fare like Guacamole and Braised Chicken with Rice and Vegetables." Publ Wkly

Includes bibliographical references

Terry, Bryant

Vegan Soul kitchen; fresh, healthy, and creative African American cuisine. Da Capo Press 2009 223p il pa $18.95 **641.5**

1. Southern cooking 2. African American cooking

ISBN 978-0-7382-1228-9; 0-7382-1228-8

LC 2008-46945

Includes bibliographical references

Theroux, Jessica

Cooking with Italian grandmothers; recipes and stories from Tuscany to Sicily. introduction by Alice Waters. Welcome Books 2010 296p $25.99 **641.5**

1. Italian cooking

ISBN 978-1-59962-089-3

LC 2010-21657

"American chef Jessica Theroux spent a year traveling throughout Italy, cooking and talking with Italian grandmothers, learning their secrets and listening to their stories. The result is a charming and authentic collection of recipes, techniques, anecdotes, and photographs that celebrate the rustic and sustainable culinary traditions of Italy's most experienced home cooks." (Publisher's note)

Thomas, Anna

Love soup; 160 all-new vegetarian recipes from the author of The Vegetarian Epicure. illustrations by Annika Huett. W. W. Norton & Company 2009 528p il $35; pa $22.95 **641.5**

1. Soups 2. Vegetarian cooking

ISBN 978-0-393-06479-7; 978-0-393-33257-5 pa

LC 2009-19632

The author presents 160 "enticing recipes that may just charm even a die-hard carnivore. Soups are organized by season and range from hearty selections like rustic leek and potato, and minestrone for a crowd, to lighter summer options including tomato and fennel soup with blood orange and sweet corn. . . . Recipes for breads, dips and spreads, salads and a collection of desserts, as well as sample menus at the start of each chapter, make it easy to plan a full meal." Publ Wkly

Vegan, vegetarian, omnivore; dinner for everyone at the table. Anna Thomas; photography by Victoria Pearson. W W Norton & Co Inc 2016 496 p. color illustrations (hardcover) $35 **641.5**

1. Cookbooks 2. Vegetarian cooking 3. Cooking

ISBN 9780393083019

LC 2015043951

This cookbook, by Anna Thomas with photography by Victoria Pearson, "shows us how to cook for today's table, with over 150 recipes for all tastes, and menus for every occasion. For a casual evening with friends, Farro with Lentils and Lavender served with Ratatouille from the Charcoal Grill makes a beautiful vegan supper—and also pairs wonderfully with garlic-and-herb rubbed lamb chops for the omnivores." (Publisher's note)

"Armed with nearly 200 of Thomas's versatile recipes, hosts can feel confident cooking one menu for all their guests." LJ

Thompson, David

Thai food; with photography by Earl Carter. Ten Speed Press 2002 673p $40 **641.5**

1. Thai cooking

ISBN 978-1-580-08462-8; 1-580-08462-1

LC 2002-18117

"The first section of the book provides detailed cultural and social history and a guide to the regions and regional cuisines of Thailand. Then a detailed glossary of ingredients and a guide to techniques introduce the hundreds of recipes. These are grouped into chapters on relishes, soups, curries, salads, and sides, followed by one of menus with recipes. . . . [This] culinary history/cookbook is unique and will be an important purchase for any Asian cookery collection." Libr J

Includes bibliographical references

Thug Kitchen; eat like you give a f*ck. by Thug Kitchen. Rodale 2014 212 p. color illustrations (hardback) $24.99 **641.5**

1. Vegetarian cooking 2. Cooking -- Vegetables 3. Cooking (Vegetables)

ISBN 1623363586; 9781623363581

LC 2014036430

In this cookbook "Thug Kitchen wants to show everyone how to take charge of their plates and cook up some real f*cking food. . . . [T]hey're throwing down more than 100 recipes for their best-loved meals, snacks, and sides for beginning cooks to home chefs. . . . Plus they're going to arm you with all the info and techniques you need to shop on a budget and go and kick a bunch of ass on your own." (Publisher's note)

Tourles, Stephanie L.

Raw energy; 124 raw food recipes for energy bars, smoothies, and other snacks to supercharge your body. [by] Stephanie Tourles. Storey Pub. 2009 271p il pa $16.95 **641.5**

1. Snack foods 2. Vegetarian cooking 3. Cooking -- Natural foods

ISBN 978-1-60342-467-7

LC 2009-28675

"This delightful addition is easily accessible even to readers looking to make small changes in their diets. . . . [The author] shares a list of ingredients with pictures of each item. A list of kitchen equipment is also provided to accompany these recipes for shakes, bars, and soups, some of which require the use of a juicer or dehydrator. For libraries that don't have any books on the topic, this is an excellent introduction." Libr J

Includes bibliographical references

Trang, Corinne

Essentials of Asian cuisine; fundamentals and favorite recipes. black-and-white photographs by Corinne Trang; color photographs by Christopher Hirscheimer. Simon & Schuster 2003 592p il hardcover o.p. pa $34.99 **641.5**

1. Asian cooking

ISBN 0-7432-0312-7; 1-4391-9108-5 pa

LC 2002-30490

"Authoritative and thoroughly researched, this will be invaluable as both a reference and a cookbook." Libr J

Includes bibliographical references

Tsai, Ming

Blue Ginger; East-meets-West cooking with Ming Tsai. by Ming Tsai and Arthur Boehm. Potter 1999 275p $32.50 **641.5**

1. Cooking 2. Asian cooking

ISBN 0-609-60530-5

LC 99-36393

"Chapters divide the 125-plus recipes into soups, dim sum, rice and noodles, poultry, meat, seafood, elaborate side dishes and desserts, with mail-order sources. . . . Instructions are clearly written and often include tips for wine and food pairings and advice on ingredient substitutions and techniques." Publ Wkly

Turner, Kristy

But I could never go;-vegan!- 125 recipes that prove you can live without cheese, it's not all rabbit food, and your friends will still come over for dinner. by Kristy Turner, photographs by Chris Miller. The Experiment 2014 xi, 308 p.p color illustrations (pbk.) $23.95 **641.5**

1. Veganism 2. Cookbooks 3. Vegetarian cooking 4.

Vegan cooking
ISBN 1615192107; 9781615192106; 9781615192113
LC 2014020051

This vegan cookbook, by Kristy Turner, with photographs by Chris Miller, "deliciously refutes every excuse you've ever heard with 125 bursting-with-flavor vegan recipes for every meal of the day--including dessert! . . . You'll find you can get enough protein, fit in at a potluck, learn to love cauliflower, and enjoy pizza, nachos, brownies, and more--without any animal products at all." (Publisher's note)

"Vegan foodies and foodies considering becoming vegan will be eager to break out their farro, sriracha, and liquid smoke, and have fun in the kitchen." LJ

Vetri, Marc

Il viaggio di Vetri; a culinary journey. [by] Marc Vetri with David Joachim; wine notes by Jeff Benjamin; photography by Douglas Takeshi Wolfe. Ten Speed Press 2008 289p il $40   **641.5**
1. Italian cooking
ISBN 978-1-58008-888-6; 1-58008-888-0
LC 2008-21667

"More than a cookbook, this . . . is a guide through the particular Italian cuisine and culture on which . . . [the author] has based his career. . . . Amateur chefs may have only dreamed of having a culinary journey like Vetri's, but with this book he has given them a reliable key to turning dream into reality." Publ Wkly

Vinton, Sherri Brooks

Eat it up! 150 Recipes to Use Every Bit and Enjoy Every Bite of the Food You Buy. Sherri Brooks Vinton. Da Capo Lifelong Books, a member of the Perseus Books Group 2016 256 p. (pbk.) $18.99 **641.5**
1. Cooking 2. Food conservation 3. Food waste -- Prevention
ISBN 9780738218182
LC 2015045183

In this cookbook, author Sherri Brooks Vinton "helps you make the most out of the food you bring home. These 150 delicious recipes mine the treasure in your kitchen—the fronds from your carrots, leaves from your cauliflower, bones from Sunday's roast, even the last lick of jam in the jar are put to good, tasty use." (Publisher's note)

"A sterling resource for the ecologically minded cook." Booklist

Includes bibliographical references and index

Voltaggio, Bryan

Home; recipes to share with family and friends. Bryan Voltaggio. Little, Brown & Co. 2015 272 p. color illustrations (hardcover) $35   **641.5**
1. Entertaining 2. American cooking
ISBN 0316323888; 9780316323888
LC 2014944089

This cookbook is author "Bryan Voltaggio's tribute to the American comfort food he enjoyed growing up, elevated with sophisticated and irresistible new recipes. Voltaggio brings an authentic love for seasonal, farm-to-table cooking and a playful and distinctive approach to classic dishes in his first solo cookbook. Many of the recipes celebrate his Middle-Atlantic roots in inventive ways." (Publisher's note)

"This is a celebrity chef cookbook that readers will want to use, not relegate to the coffee table." LJ

Waters, Alice

In the green kitchen; techniques to learn by heart. photographs by Hirsheimer & Hamilton. Clarkson Potter/Publishers 2010 151p il $28   **641.5**
1. Slow food movement 2. Vegetarian cooking 3. Cooking -- Natural foods
ISBN 978-0-307-33680-4; 0-307-33680-8
LC 2010-278664

The author "showcases basic cooking techniques every cook can and should master along with recipes using each method in this slim and attractive book. Derived from a Slow Food Nation event she helped organize, where notable chefs and foodies provided demonstrations on foundational procedures, Waters highlights a set of techniques that are universal to all cuisines. She covers the most basic of the basics, from stocking the pantry and washing lettuce to boiling pasta and wilting greens. . . . Ideal for the cooking novice, this gem of a book captures the expertise of world-class chefs in an accessible, straightforward manner." Publ Wkly

Weight Watchers 50th anniversary cookbook; 280 delicious recipes for every meal. St. Martin's Griffin 2013 335 p. $29.99   **641.5**
1. Cookbooks 2. Weight loss
ISBN 1250036402; 9781250036407

This cookbook of updated recipes "supplements the new Weight Watchers 360 program. Emphasizing retro comfort foods like chicken cordon bleu, cheddar corn pudding, and Boston cream pie, the book aims to dispel notions that diet food can't be crave-worthy. Each recipe includes nutritional analysis and a 'PointsPlus' value based on the amount of protein, carbohydrates, fat, and fiber per serving. Using the secondary index, readers can easily choose recipes by points value." (Library Journal)

Weil, Andrew

The **healthy** kitchen; recipes for a better body, life, and spirit. {by} Andrew Weil and Rosie Daley; photographs by Sang An, Amy Haskell, and Eric Studer. Knopf 2002 xxxvii, 325p il $24.95; pa $16.95   **641.5**
1. Cooking 2. Natural foods
ISBN 0-375-41306-5; 0-375-71031-0 pa
LC 2001-50391

This is "a stimulating invitation to healthy, pleasurable eating." Publ Wkly

Weinstein, Bruce

Cooking know-how; be a better cook with hundreds of easy techniques, step-by-step photos, and ideas for over 500 great meals. [by] Bruce Weinstein & Mark Scarbrough; photography by Lucy Schaeffer. John Wiley 2009 406p il $34.95   **641.5**
1. Cooking
ISBN 978-0-470-18080-8
LC 2008-44375

"The recipes are structured without being fussy and the majority are relatively easy. This is a welcome rarity, imparting a useful, innovative framework as well as the confidence to depart from it." Publ Wkly

The **Great** Big Pressure Cooker Book; 500 easy recipes for every day and every machine. Bruce Weinstein and Mark Scarborough; photographs by Tina Rupp. Clarkson Potter/Publishers 2015 512 p. 16 plates; color illustrations $25   **641.5**
1. Cookbooks 2. Quick and easy cooking 3. Pressure cooking
ISBN 0804185328; 9780804185325
LC 2014022862
This cookbook by Bruce Weinstein and Mark Scarbrough " has recipes for every device, stovetop and electric, no matter the manufacturer. Whether you're seeking an adventurous array of spices, found in dishes such as Cherry Chipotle Pulled Chicken or Smashed Sweet Potatoes with Pineapple and Ginger, or pure comfort food, like French Toast Bread Pudding or Classic Pot Roast and Potatoes, you'll find the perfect recipe." (Publisher's note)

Vegetarian dinner parties; 150 meatless meals good enough to serve to company. Bruce Weinstein & Mark Scarbrough; photographs by Eric Medsker. Rodale 2014 304 p. color illustrations (hardcover) $32.50   **641.5**
1. Vegetarian cooking
ISBN 1609615018; 9781609615017
LC 2014018558
James Beard Foundation Award Nominee: Vegetable Focused and Vegetarian (2015)
IACP Cookbook Award: People's Choice (2015)
IACP Cookbook Award Finalist: Health & Special Diet (2015)
In this cookbook, food writers Bruce Weinstein & Mark Scarbrough "take the reader by the hand and teach them not only how to make extraordinarily delicious and modern vegetarian and vegan dishes that everyone will love, . . . they show readers how to actually build dinner parties starting with flavors, seasonality and availability, and even time and skill." (Publisher's note)
"The authors consider the different foods at a dinner party to be distinct courses rather than parts of the same meal: each course must stand on its own. Vegan dishes, which make up nearly half of the collection, are clearly identified, and many recipes suggest an accompanying beer or wine that pairs well." Pub Wkly

Weir, Joanne
Sunset kitchen gypsy; Joanne Weir. Time Home Entertainment 2015 288 p. illustrations $35 **641.5**
1. Food 2. Cooking 3. Creation (Literary, artistic, etc.)
ISBN 0848746031; 9780848746032
LC 2014954434
Author Joanne Weir "shares the spark that led to her love of cooking, how she learned to taste and develop a palate, the meal that would forever change her life, her years working with Alice Waters at Chez Panisse during the beginning of the farm-to-table movement, and her continued travels teaching cooking classes the world over. Throughout, she offers the cherished dishes and lessons that have shaped her culinary journey." (Publisher's note)

"A compelling read with worldly recipes and evocative writing. If you like this title, try following it with Alex Guarnaschelli's Old-School Comfort Food or Hubert Keller's Souvenirs." Library Journal

Wells, Patricia
Patricia Wells' trattoria; simple and robust fare inspired by the small family restaurants of Italy. William Morrow 2003 338p il pa $18.95 **641.5**
1. Italian cooking
ISBN 978-0-06-093652-5
First published 1993
This "collection of informal, robust recipes, gathered from Italy's small family-run restaurants, should appeal to anyone who appreciates the unmasked flavors of high-quality fresh ingredients, simply but lovingly prepared. Wells's often lengthy headnotes are full of personal reminiscences but also paint a colorful picture of the country's relaxed, generous lifestyle. Wine suggestions follow each recipe, and there are sensible cooking tips throughout." Libr J

The **Provence** cookbook; 175 recipes and a select guide to the markets, shops, & restaurants of France's sunny south. HarperCollins 2004 338p il $29.95 **641.5**
1. French cooking
ISBN 978-0-06-050782-4; 0-06-050782-9
LC 2003-56977
Wells offers "her own recipes, along with some from her butcher, fishmonger, other merchants, neighborhood restaurants, and other sources slightly farther afield. Most of the dishes are simple, allowing the flavors of Provence's wonderfully fresh produce and other ingredients to come through. . . . Wine suggestions are included throughout—sometimes for Wells's own label, since her vineyard is now productive—and she provides addresses and other relevant details about her favorite restaurants and purveyors." Libr J

Wex, Michael
Rhapsody in schmaltz; Yiddish food and why we can't stop eating it. Michael Wex. St. Martin's Press 2016 320 p. (hardback) $26.99 **641.5**
1. Jewish cooking 2. Jews -- Social life and customs 3. Jews -- Food 4. Ashkenazim -- Social life and customs
ISBN 9781250071514
LC 2015044974
This book, by Michael Wex, "traces the pathways of Jewish food from the Bible and Talmud, to Eastern Europe, to its popular landing pads in North America today. With an eye for detail and a healthy dose of humor, Michael Wex also examines how these impact modern culture, from temple to television." (Publisher's note)
"Informative, merrily entertaining culinary and cultural history." Kirksu

Wilson, Jose
Beard on food; the best recipes and kitchen wisdom from the Dean of American cooking. James Beard; assisted by José Wilson; illustrations by Karl

Stuecklen. Bloomsbury 2007 xii, 335 p.p illustrations $26.50 **641.5**
1. Cookbooks 2. American cooking 3. Cooking
ISBN 1596914467; 9781596914469
LC 2009368426

In this book, by James Beard, assisted by José Wilson with illustrations by Karl Stuecklen, "one of America's . . . culinary thinkers and teachers collects his best essays, ranging from the perfect hamburger to the pleasures of oxtails, from salad dressing to Sauce Diable. The result is not just a compendium of fabulous recipes and delicious bites of writing. It's a philosophy of food--unfussy, wide-ranging, erudite, and propelled by Beard's exuberance and sense of fun." (Publisher's note)

Wolfert, Paula
The **slow** Mediterranean kitchen; recipes for the passionate cook. Wiley 2003 350p il $34.95 **641.5**
1. Mediterranean cooking
ISBN 0-471-26288-9
LC 2002-153265

The author offers "dishes from all the countries of the region: brodetto Pasquale (Italian Easter Lamb Soup), Expatriate Roast Chicken with Lemon and Olives from Morocco, and Catalonian Fall-Apart Lamb Shanks. Although many recipes call for braising, stewing, and other techniques of long cooking, others are not limited to those techniques, for Wolfert's definition of slow cooking also encompasses marinating and similar techniques." Libr J

Workman, Katie
Dinner solved! 100 ingenious recipes that make the whole family happy, including you. by Katie Workman. Workman Publishing 2015 384 p. (alk. paper) $17.95 **641.5**
1. Cooking
ISBN 0761181873; 9780761181873
LC 2015011304

In this cookbook, author Katie Workman "her attention to the biggest problem that every family cook faces: how to make everyone at the table happy without turning into a short-order cook. . . . Katie shows you how Asian Spareribs can start mild and sweet for less adventurous eaters—and then, in no time, become a zesty second version for spice lovers. She shakes up the usual chicken for dinner with Chicken Tikka Masala-ish—and feeds vegetarians, too." (Publisher's note)
"Families can use this practical, mix-and-match recipe collection to lessen the stress of meal planning." LJ

The **mom** 100 cookbook; 100 recipes every mom needs in her back pocket. Katie Workman; photographs by Todd Coleman. Workman Pub Co 2012 xxix, 366 p.p col. ill. (alk. paper) $16.95 **641.5**
1. Cooking 2. Cookbooks 3. Parenting
ISBN 0761166033; 9780761166030
LC 2012001330

This cookbook, by Katie Workman, "offers recipes, tips, techniques, attitude, and wisdom for staying happy in the kitchen while proudly keeping it homemade--because homemade not only tastes best, but is also better (and most economical) for you. . . . [It presents] 20 dilemmas every mom

faces, with 5 solutions for each: including terrific recipes for the vegetable-averse, the salad-rejector, for the fish-o-phobe, or the overnight vegetarian convert." (Publisher's note)

Worrall-Thompson, Antony
The **essential** diabetes cookbook; good healthy eating from around the world. [by] Anthony Worrall Thompson, with Louise Blair. Kyle: Kyle Cathie 2010 287p il $35 **641.5**
1. Cooking 2. Diabetes -- Diet therapy
ISBN 978-1-906868-15-4
LC 2010-932221

200 recipes for diabetics that take their inspiration from cuisines around the world, including nutritional information for each recipe.
"From fish (Grilled Sea Bass with Spiced Cabbage) to crepes (Asian Surf and Turf Crêpes) to pork (Tofu, Pork, and Shellfish Hot Pot), these dishes bring life back into diabetic cooking. . . . Adventurous cooks will cheer for this diabetes cookbook." Libr J

Zakarian, Geoffrey, 1959-
My perfect pantry; Geoffrey Zakarian; with Amy Stevenson and Margaret Zakarian; photographs by Sara Remington. Clarkson Potter 2014 304 p. color illustrations $30 **641.5**
1. Cookbooks 2. American cooking 3. Cooking
ISBN 0385345666; 9780385345668
LC 2013050636

This cookbook, by Geoffrey Zakarian, with Amy Stevenson and Margaret Zakarian, and featuring photographs by Sara Remington, focuses on household cooking from stock pantry items. "Forget exotic condiments and specialty foods. With a working base of 50 readily available ingredients, from oats and honey to almonds and canned chickpeas, you will always have the makings of a delicious home-cooked meal." (Publisher's note)
Zakarian's "list of 50 pantry necessities includes beans, oils, pastas, sauces, and nuts. For each of these staples he proffers a trio of recipes. Color photographs enhance the text and encourage readers to pursue Zakarian's culinary vision." Booklist

641.502 Auxiliary techniques and procedures

Warner, Justin
The **Laws** of Cooking; And How to Break Them. by Justin Warner. St. Martin's Press 2015 336 p. color illustrations $35 **641.502**
1. Cooking
ISBN 1250065135; 9781250065131
LC 2015034388

This cookbook, by Justin Warner, "encourages improvisation and play. . . . By introducing eleven laws based on familiar foods, . . . [Warner] will teach you why certain flavors combine brilliantly, and then show how these combinations work in 110 more complex and inventive recipes " (Publisher's note)
"Warner's focus is on the food, and encouraging readers to stretch their palates and skills to create something truly

unique. This is a refreshingly new take from an author to watch." Pub Wkly

641.509   History, geographic treatment, biography

Cherniavsky, Mark

The **cookbook** library; four centuries of the cooks, writers, and recipes that made the modern cookbook. Anne Willan; with Mark Cherniavsky and Kyri Claflin. University of California Press 2012 xii, 328 p.p (cloth : alk. paper) $50   **641.509**
1. Cooking -- History
ISBN 0520244001; 9780520244009

LC 2011024489
Includes bibliographical references (p. 296-306) and indexes

Prud'homme, Alex

The **French** chef in America; Julia Child's Second Act. Alex Prud'homme. Alfred A. Knopf 2016 336 p. (hardcover : alk. paper) $27.95   **641.509**
1. Cooks -- Biography 2. Cooks -- United States -- Biography
ISBN 9780385351751; 9780804168793

LC 2015043441
This book, by Alex Prud'homme, "shows us [Julia] Child in the aftermath of the publication of Mastering the Art of French Cooking, suddenly finding herself America's first lady of French food and under considerable pressure to embrace her new mantle. We see her dealing with difficult colleagues and the challenges of fame." (Publisher's note)

"Kelsey provides as much information as possible about all of the participants in these journeys and manages to keep it interesting." Pub Wkly

Includes bibliographical references and index

641.53   Light meals

Olivier, Michele

Little Bento; 32 Irresistible Bento Box Lunches for Kids. Michele Olivier. Sonoma Press 2016 178 p. color illustrations $16.99   **641.53**
1. Cookbooks 2. Japanese cooking 3. Quick and easy cooking
ISBN 1943451281; 9781943451289
This cookbook by Michele Olivier "shows parents how to turn their picky children into healthy, adventurous eaters through creative, easy-to-assemble bento box lunches. . . . [It] contains over 100 recipes and 32 photos of fully-composed, seasonally-organized bento box lunches, which include . . . comprehensive bento box ingredient lists, . . . pros and cons of various bento box options, . . . and bento meal planning tips and a weekly meal planning worksheet." (Publisher's note)

641.555   Timesaving cooking

Dinner Made Simple; 35 Everyday Ingredients, 350 Easy Recipes. Oxmoor House 2016 352 p. color illustrations (pbk.) $24.95   **641.555**
1. Dining 2. Cooking
ISBN 0848746899; 9780848746896

LC 2015958963
This cookbook, from "Real Simple Magazine," is "filled with 350 easy, quick dishes-many ready in 30 minutes or less-to help you get out of your recipe rut. With 10 ideas for every ingredient, you'll never look at a box of spaghetti, a bunch of carrots, or a ball of pizza dough the same way again." (Publisher's note)

"With plenty of ideas for meals that can be prepared in less than 30 minutes, this cookbook will satisfy busy home cooks and eaters who enjoy browsing by photo." LJ

641.563   Cooking for health, appearance, personal reasons

Flanagan, Shalane

Run fast, eat slow; nourishing recipes for athletes. by Shalane Flanagan and Elyse Kopecky. St. Martin's Press 2016 242 p. color illustrations $24.99; (ebook) $19.99   **641.563**
1. Cooking 2. Nutrition
ISBN 162336681X; 9781623366810; 9781623366827
This cookbook, by Shalane Flanagan and Elyse Kopecky, "proves food can be indulgent and nourishing at the same time. Finally here's a cookbook for runners that shows fat is essential for flavor and performance and that counting calories, obsessing over protein, and restrictive dieting does more harm than good." (Publisher's note)

Includes bibliographical references (pages 220-222) and index.

Hay, Donna

Life in Balance; Donna Hay. HarperCollins 2016 240 p. color illustrations $34.99   **641.563**
1. Diet 2. Cookbooks
ISBN 1460750322; 9781460750322
This cookbook by Donna Hay "is about embracing food and all its benefits. Each chapter, from breakfast to baking, has simple recipes enriched with nature's superfoods. . . . From new ideas for power dinners to tempting grills, from super-charged breakfasts to low-carb options. . . . The only kind of diet that works, after all, is the balanced diet - the one you can sustain long term. And when your life is in balance, you feel great and it shows - from the inside out." (Publisher's note)

"Recommended for readers who dislike the idea of dieting but want to explore popular health foods." LJ

Perlmutter, David

The **grain** brain cookbook; more than 150 life-changing gluten-free recipes to transform your health.

David Perlmutter. Little, Brown & Co. 2014 352 p. color illustrations (hardcover) $30 **641.563**
   1. Cookbooks 2. Gluten-free diet
   ISBN 0316334251; 9780316334259
                      LC 2014940575
This gluten free cookbook, by David Perlmutter, builds off the author's previous work arguing "the devastating effects of wheat, sugar, and carbs on the brain. . . . [This book] presents more than 150 delectable recipes to keep your brain vibrant and your body fit, all while dramatically reducing your risk for--and treating--Alzheimer's, depression, ADHD, and epilepsy, as well as relieving everyday conditions like headaches, insomnia, and forgetfulness." (Publisher's note)
"Recommended only for libraries where Perlmutter's books are in high demand." LJ

Roll, Rich, 1972-
The **plantpower** way; whole food plant-based recipes and guidance for the whole family. Penguin Group USA 2015 319 p. color illustrations $39.95 **641.563**
   ISBN 1583335870; 9781583335871
In this book authors Rich Roll and Julie Piatt "shares the joy and vibrant health they and their whole family have experienced living a plant-based lifestyle. Bursting with inspiration, practical guidance, and beautiful four-color photography, The Plantpower Way has more than 120 delicious, easy-to-prepare whole food recipes, including hearty breakfasts, lunches, and dinners, plus healthful and delicious smoothies and juices, and decadent desserts." (Publisher's note)

Walker, Danielle
Danielle Walker's against all grain; meals made simple : gluten-free, dairy-free, and paleo recipes to make anytime. by Danielle Walker. Simon & Schuster 2014 319 p. color illustrations $34.95 **641.563**
   1. Gluten-free diet
   ISBN 162860042X; 9781628600421
This cookbook, by Danielle Walker, presents "recipes that make cooking for the grain-free family both easy and enjoyable. . . . Walker takes the guesswork out of meal planning with eight weeks' worth of dinner ideas, complete with full shopping lists and recipes for using up leftovers. Whether we're moms, students, or business owners, at the end of the day we all want fresh, home-cooked meals that are easy to prepare." (Publisher's note)

Weil, Andrew, 1942-
Fast Food, Good Food; More Than 150 Quick and Easy Ways to Put Healthy, Delicious Food on the Table. Andrew Weil. Little, Brown & Co. 2015 304 p. color illustrations $30 **641.563**
   1. Health 2. Cooking
   ISBN 0316329428; 9780316329422
                      LC 2015931944
The recipes in author Andrew Weil's cookbook "showcase fresh, high-quality ingredients and hearty flavors, like Buffalo Mozzarella Bruschetta, Five-Spice Winter Squash Soup, Greek Style Kale Salad, Pappardelle with Arugula Walnut Pesto, Pan-Seared Halibut with Green Harissa, Coconut Lemon Bars, and Pomegranate Margaritas. With

guidance on following an anti-inflammatory diet and mouth-wateringly gorgeous photographs, FAST FOOD, GOOD FOOD will inspire the inner nutritionist and chef in every reader." (Publisher's note)
"Weil's accessible recipes will attract flexitarians, especially those with a penchant for seafood, vegetables, whole grains, and olive oil." LJ

641.564 Seasonal cooking

Tomlinson, Steve
Agricola cookbook; Josh Thomsen, Kate Winslow, Steve Tomlinson. Burgess Lea Press 2015 240 p. color illustrations $30 **641.564**
   1. Cooking 2. Restaurants 3. Farm produce
   ISBN 1941868002; 9781941868003
                      LC 2014954376
Authors Josh Thomsen, Kate Winslow, and Steven Tomlinson present "official cookbook of Agricola, the celebrated farm-to-table restaurant in Princeton, NJ. It's a farm-supported restaurant with its heart in the right place--and now, a cookbook with 100 inspired recipes, including Sweet Corn Soup with Bacon and Smoked Paprika Oil, Flatiron Steak with Green Garlic Gremolata and a kale salad." (Publisher's note)

641.568 Cooking for special occasions

Rosenstrach, Jenny
How to celebrate everything; Recipes & Rituals for Birthdays, Holidays, Family Dinners & Every Day in Between. Jenny Rosenstrach. Ballantine Books 2016 336 p. color illustrations (hardback) $30 **641.568**
   1. Dinners 2. Cookbooks 3. Entertaining 4. Holiday cooking 5. Families 6. Dinners and dining
   ISBN 9780804176309
                      LC 2016001416
This cookbook by Jenny Rosenstrach is "a warm and inviting guide to turning birthdays, holidays, and everyday occasions into cherished traditions, with more than 100 time-tested recipes. . . . [It includes] complete menus for Thanksgiving, Christmas, and New Year's Eve and, of course, dozens of Rosenstrach's signature family dinners: Grilled Soy-Glazed Pork Chops, Harissa Roasted Chicken, [and] Crispy Chickpeas with Yogurt Sauce." (Publisher's note)
"This book is a delicious and delightful ode to the ways family and food intertwine, reinforcing each other." Booklist

641.578 Outdoor cooking

Master of the grill; foolproof recipes, top-rated gadgets, gear, & ingredients plus clever test kitchen tips & fascinating food science. by the editors at America's Test Kitchen. America's Test Kitchen

2016 464 p. illustrations (chiefly color) (paperback) $29.95   **641.578**
1. Outdoor cooking 2. Barbecue cooking 3. Barbecuing
ISBN 9781940352541

LC 2015040405

This cookbook, edited by America's Test Kitchen, "features a wide variety of kitchen-tested recipes. . . . Everyone should know how to make—the juiciest burgers, barbecue chicken that's moist not tough, tender grill-smoked pork ribs, the greatest steak. . . . Learn how to make Cowboy Steaks, Alabama BBQ Chicken, and Kansas City Sticky Ribs. . . . Covers the pros and cons of gas and charcoal grills and which might be right for you, as well as the tools you'll use with them." (Publisher's note)

"The recipes are presented thoughtfully and often accompanied by step-by-step photos guiding readers through processes such as trimming asparagus and arranging coals. This is a fabulous addition to the ATK canon." Pub Wkly

641.59   Cooking characteristic of specific geographic environments, ethnic cooking

Acheson, Hugh
A **New** Turn in the South; Southern Flavors Reinvented for Your Kitchen. Hugh Acheson. Clarkson Potter 2011 299 p. color illustrations $35   **641.59**
1. Cookbooks 2. American cooking 3. Southern cooking
ISBN 0307719553; 9780307719553

LC 2010052632

James Beard Award (2012)
In this cookbook, by Hugh Acheson, "you'll find libations, seasonal vegetables that take a prominent role, salads and soups, his prized sides, and fish and meats--all of which turn Southern food on its head every step of the way. Hugh's recipes include: Oysters on the Half Shell with Cane Vinegar and Chopped Mint Sauce; . . . Chanterelles on Toast with Mushrooms; . . . Braised and Crisped Pork Belly with Citrus Salad; . . . and Lemon Chess Pies with Blackberry Compote." (Publisher's note)

Acquista, Angelo
The **Mediterranean** Family Table; 125 Simple, Everyday Recipes Made With the Most Delicious and Healthiest Food on Earth. by Acquista Angelo, M.D. and Laurie Anne Vandermolen. HarperCollins 2015 336 p. color illustrations $29.99   **641.59**
1. Diet 2. Mediterranean cooking
ISBN 006240718X; 9780062407184
In this book, Dr. Acquista Angelo "combines his medical experience and Sicilian roots to outline the guiding principles of the Mediterranean diet and takes it one step further with a collection of easy, wholesome, and delicious recipes the entire family will love." (Publisher's note)

"For those interested in changing their life through diet, Acquista is an infectiously positive coach, and his recipes make a fine playbook." Pub Wkly

Alford, Jeffrey
★ **Hot,** sour, salty, sweet; a culinary journey through Southeast Asia. Jeffrey Alford and Naomi Duguid; studio photographs by Richard Jung; location photographs by Jeffrey Alford and Naomi Duguid. Artisan 2000 346 p. col. ill. $45   **641.59**
1. Cookbooks 2. Southeast Asian cooking 3. Cookery, Southeast Asian
ISBN 1579651143; 9781579651145

LC 00022092

In this cookbook, written by Jeffrey Alford and Naomi Duguid, "more than 175 recipes for spicy salsas, welcoming soups, grilled meat salads, and exotic desserts are accompanied by evocative stories about places and people. The recipes and stories are . . . illustrated throughout with more than 150 full-color food and travel photographs." (Publisher's note)

"Part travel essay and part culinary exploration, this is a perfect choice for both adventurous cooks and armchair travelers." LJ
Includes bibliographical references (p. 325-327) and index

Algar, Ayla Esen
Classical Turkish cooking; traditional Turkish food for the American kitchen. {by} Ayla Algar. HarperCollins Pubs. 1991 306p $35; pa $17 **641.59**
1. Turkish cooking
ISBN 0-06-016317-8; 0-06-093163-9 pa

LC 91-55096

"A cuisine that melds the fragrances and flavors of the Far East, Central Asia, Iran, Anatolia, and the Mediterranean is enriched by Algar as she goes well beyond the standard recipes (160 of them) to explain Turkey's historical, cultural, and culinary traditions—and, along the way, to include a glimpse of her personal family heritage." Booklist
Includes bibliographical references

Alger, Kajsa
Susan Feniger's street food; Susan Feniger, Kajsa Alger, and Liz Lachman. Random House Inc. 2012 224 p. $27.50   **641.59**
1. Salads 2. Cooking 3. Asian cooking 4. Street food 5. International cooking
ISBN 0307952584; 9780307952585

LC 2011041175

Author Susan Feniger "shares 83 of her favorite recipes with home cooks, giving them a taste of these . . . dishes. On her globe-trotting adventures, with cooking and eating as the only shared language, Susan has forged friendships with rice farmers in Vietnam, women baking flatbread in Turkey, and nomadic cheesemakers in Mongolia. . . . [Recipes are featured, such as] Saigon Chicken Salad, . . . Thai Drunken Shrimp with Rice Noodles, or sweet-savory Korean Glazed Short Ribs with Sesame and Asian Pear." (Publisher's note)

Balla, Nicolaus
★ **Bar** Tartine; techniques & recipes. Nicolaus Balla and Cortney Burns; photographs by Chad

Robertson. Chronicle Books 2014 256 p. hbk $40 **641.59**

1. Cookbooks 2. Restaurants 3. Bar Tartine (San Francisco, Calif.) 4. Cooking, American -- California style

ISBN 1452126461; 9781452126463

LC 2014011157

James Beard Foundation Award: Cooking from a Professional Point of View (2015)

IACP Cookbook Award: Chefs and Restaurants (2015)

"Chefs Balla and Burns, at their much-praised Bar Tartine, in San Francisco, have transformed the craft of drying all sorts of herbs, flowers, vegetables, fruits, and meats into an art form. They share their methods for creating dehydrated delicacies, be it via oven-drying, sun-drying, or a food dehydrator, and offer a selection of recipes that utilize those ingredients." (Publishers Weekly)

"Many of these techniques are doable for home cooks, though it's hard to imagine amateurs making their own bottarga (which involves drying cured sacs of fish roe for five to seven weeks)." LJ

Barr, Luke

Provence, 1970; M.F.K. Fisher, Julia Child, James Beard, and the Reinvention of American Taste. Luke Barr. Clarkson Potter 2013 320 p. (alkaline paper) $26 **641.59**

1. Cooks 2. French cooking 3. Provence (France) -- Biography 4. Cooking, American -- Philosophy 5. Cooking, American -- History -- 20th century 6. Provence (France) -- Social life and customs -- 20th century

ISBN 0307718344; 9780307718341

LC 2013007782

This book discusses winter 1970, when "culinary icons M.F.K. Fisher, Julia Child, James Beard, Simone Beck, and Richard Olney all found themselves in Provence, France. This period was a turning point both for these figures and for the culture of food. . . . [Luke] Barr, Fisher's great-nephew, pieces together the events of that winter from diaries and letters, chronicling the dinner parties that took place and the food that was eaten." (Library Journal)

Includes bibliographical references and index

Barrenechea, Teresa

The **Basque** table; passionate home cooking from one of Europe's great regional cuisines. {by} Teresa Barrenechea, with Mary Goodbody. Harvard Common Press 1998 232p il hardcover o.p. pa $16.95 **641.59**

1. Basque cooking

ISBN 1-55832-140-3; 978-1-55832-327-8 pa; 1-55832-327-9 pa

LC 98-29295

The author's "Basque dishes are characterized by fresh, lively flavors; garlic, hot chilis, and roasted sweet peppers, fish of all types, and beef and lamb are favorite ingredients. While home-style dishes are her emphasis here, there are some entries from nueva cocina as well. A chapter on pinchos, the Basque version of tapas, is a highlight, and there are sidebars on Basque ingredients and traditions throughout." Libr J

Bastianich, Lidia

Lidia's commonsense Italian cooking; 150 delicious and simple recipes everyone can master. by Lidia Matticchio Bastianich and Tanya Bastianich Manuali; photographs by Marcus Nilsson. Alfred A. Knopf 2013 304 p. color illustrations hbk $35 **641.59**

1. Cookbooks 2. Italian cooking

ISBN 0385349440; 9780385349444

LC 2013005067

In this cookbook, it was the authors' intent to "creat[e] a new sort of Italian cooking for American kitchens that crosses time-honored boundaries and looks to fashion a more relaxed . . . cuisine." Recipes include "potatoes baked in beer, eggplant and rice parmigiana, and veggie 'meatballs.' Traditionally unadorned pasta carbonara gets some sliced artichokes in its cream-and-egg sauce. Desserts include an apple cake, cookies, and several variations of rice pudding." (Booklist)

Includes bibliographical references and index

Lidia's Italian-American kitchen; by Lidia Matticchio Bastianich; photographs by Christopher Hirsheimer. Knopf 2001 xxvi, 432p il $35 **641.59**

1. Italian cooking

ISBN 0-375-41150-X

LC 2001-45009

"Bastianich has a warm, engaging style, and she's a teacher as well as a chef: throughout, she provides thoughtful head-notes and sidebars along with useful boxes on cooking with wine, 'resting' soup, and other such practicalities." Libr J

Baxter, John, 1939-

The **perfect** meal; in search of the lost tastes of France. John Baxter. Harper Perennial 2013 382 p. ill. (pbk.) $14.99 **641.59**

1. French cooking 2. France -- Description and travel 3. Cooking (Game)

ISBN 0062088068; 9780062088062

LC 2012019240

IACP Cookbook Award (2014)

This book, by John Baxter is "part grand tour of France, part history of French cuisine, taking readers on a journey to discover and savor some of the world's great cultural achievements before they disappear completely. Some of the most revered and complex elements of French cuisine are in danger of disappearing as old ways of agriculture, butchering, and cooking fade and are forgotten." (Publisher's note)

"Baxter skillfully blends what could be considered merely entertaining food trivia into a satisfying full-course meal." Pub Wkly

Bayless, Rick

Rick Bayless's Mexican kitchen; capturing the vibrant flavors of a world-class cuisine. [by] Rick Bayless with Deann Groen Bayless and JeanMarie Brownson; photographs by Maria Robledo; illus-

trations by John Sandford. Scribner 1996 448p il
$35   **641.59**
   1. Mexican cooking
ISBN 0-684-80006-3
                          LC 96-218444
This cookbook "includes more than 200 tantalizing recipes and is packed with information on Mexican ingredients
and cooking techniques, regional cuisine, and history. . . .
A serious guide to an often underestimated cuisine, this is
important as both a reference and a cookbook." Libr J
   Includes bibliographical references

Besh, John
   My family table; a passionate plea for home
cooking. John Besh. Andrews McMeel Pub., LLC
2011 264 p. col. ill. $35   **641.59**
   1. Family 2. Kitchens 3. American cooking 4.
Cooking, American
ISBN 1449407870; 9781449407872
                       LC 2011923008
IACP Cookbook Award (2012)
In this book, "[r]enowned chef and James Beard award-
winner John Besh invites us into his home and shows us
how we can put good, fresh, healthy food on the table for
our families every day. . . . From organizing your kitchen
and stocking your pantry to demystifying fish cookery, [he]
shares his favorite recipes he cooks with his family every
day." (Publisher's note)
   "Recipes like Risotto of Almost Anything and Whole
Roasted Sole with Brown Butter reinforce Besh's Jamie
Oliver-like argument that practical home cooking does not
require reliance on processed products. Includes some excellent holiday recipes." LJ

   My New Orleans; the cookbook : 200 of my fa-
vorite recipes & stories from my hometown. by John
Besh. Andrews McMeel Universal 2009 374 p. ill.
(chiefly col.) $45   **641.59**
   1. Cookbooks 2. Cooking -- Louisiana 3. New Orleans
(La.) -- Social life and customs 4. Cooking, Cajun
5. Cooking, Creole 6. Cooking -- Louisiana -- New
Orleans 7. Cooking, American -- Louisiana style
ISBN 0740784137; 9780740784132
                       LC 2009920846
IACP Cookbook Award (2010)
In this cookbook, by John Besh, "archival, four-color, location photography along with ingredient information make
the Big Easy easy to tackle in home kitchens. Cooks will
salivate over the 200 recipes that honor and celebrate everything New Orleans. . . . From Mardi Gras, to the shrimp season, to the urban garden, to gumbo weather, boucherie (the
season of the pig), and everything tasty in between, Besh
gives a sampling of New Orleans." (Publisher's note)

Bishara, Rawia
   Olives, lemons & za'atar; the best middle eastern
home cooking. Rawia Bishara. Kyle Books 2014
224 p. (hardcover) $29.95   **641.59**
   1. Cookbooks 2. Middle Eastern cooking
ISBN 1906868840; 9781906868840
                       LC 2013952643

This cookbook by Rawia Bishara is "Organized by
Breakfasts, Mezze, Salads, Soups and Stews, Main Courses
(including vegetarian, fish, chicken, lamb and beef), Sides,
Pickles and Sauces, and Desserts. . . . A dish like Egyptian
Rice with Lamb and Pine Nuts shows this cookbook goes
beyond Nazareth, and is more of a bible of Middle Eastern
food." (Publisher's note)
   "Themes of food, family, and personal growth flow
throughout this gorgeous cookbook, which balances both
simple and challenging recipes." LJ

Brock, Sean
   ★ **Heritage**; Sean Brock with contributions by
Marion Sullivan and Jeff Allen; photographs by Peter
Frank Edwards. Artisan 2014 336 p. illustrations
(chiefly color) hbk $40   **641.59**
   1. Cookbooks 2. American cooking 3. Southern
cooking
ISBN 1579654630; 9781579654634
                       LC 2014005022
IACP Cookbook Award Winner: Julia Child First Book
(2015)
James Beard Foundation Award Winner: American
Cooking (2015)
   IACP Cookbook Award Finalist: American (2015)
   IACP Cookbook Award Finalist: Chefs and Restaurants
(2015)
   This cookbook, by Sean Brock, "offers all of his inspired
recipes. With a drive to preserve the heritage foods of the
South, Brock cooks dishes that are ingredient-driven and
reinterpret the flavors of his youth in Appalachia and his adopted hometown of Charleston. The recipes include all the
comfort food (think food to eat at home) and high-end restaurant food (fancier dishes when there's more time to cook)
for which he has become so well-known." (Publisher's note)
   "The recipes (e.g., butter-bean chowchow; pork belly
with herbed farro, pickled elderberries, chanterelles, and sumac; buttermilk pie with cornmeal crust) range from simple
to sophisticated, and some call for unusual preparations. .
. . Within chapters, Brock profiles producers who supply
his restaurants, explains various ingredient categories, and
touches on topics from industrial agriculture to the origins
of bourbon to 19th-century books on food and drink." LJ

Caggiano, Biba
   Biba's Italy; favorite recipes from the splendid
cities. Biba Caggiano. Artisan 2006 xv, 320 p.p ill.
$29.95   **641.59**
   1. Italian cooking 2. Italy -- Description and travel 3.
Cooking, Italian
ISBN 1579653170; 9781579653170
                       LC 2006045951
This cookbook, by Biba Caggiano, presents "the very
best food from our very favorite cities--the glorious dining
destinations Rome, Florence, Bologna, Milan, and Venice.
. . . The 100 delicious, simple recipes range from time-
honored home-cooking traditions to restaurant classics and
even startling innovations by Italy's star chefs, and are accompanied by invaluable cooking tips and rich, evocative
atmosphere. And each chapter offers travel tips galore."
(Publisher's note)

Carrillo Arronte, Margarita

★ Mexico; The Cookbook. Margarita Carrillo Arronte. Phaidon Inc Ltd 2014 704 p. color illustrations hbk $49.95 **641.59**
1. Cookbooks 2. Mexican cooking
ISBN 0714867527; 9780714867526

This book Margarita Carrillo Arronte by "features an unprecedented 700 recipes from across the entire country, showcasing the rich diversity and flavors of Mexican cuisine. [It includes] notes on recipe origins, ingredients, and techniques, along with contributions from top chefs such as Enrique Olvera and Hugo Ortega." (Publisher's note)

"Full-color photos of food, landscapes, and people round out this hefty and appealing collection. For those interested in learning how to make authentic Mexican cuisine, Arronte has provided the definitive guide." Pub Wkly

Includes bibliographical references and index

Child, Julia

Julia and Jacques cooking at home; by Julia Child and Jacques Pepin, with David Nussbaum. Knopf 1999 430p il $40 **641.59**
1. French cooking
ISBN 0-375-40431-7
LC 98-32418

A companion volume to the PBS series. "For each show, the two chefs started out with ideas and ingredients but no set recipes, so they improvised as they went along, cooking a lot of their favorite traditional dishes and coming up with new ones as well. . . . Dozens of boxes throughout the text provide information on a wide variety of topics." Libr J

Cook, Steven

★ Zahav; a world of Israeli cooking. Michael Solomonov and Steven Cook; produced by Dorothy Kalins; photography by Mike Persico. Houghton Mifflin Harcourt 2016 368 p. color illustrations (hardcover) $35 **641.59**
1. Cookbooks 2. Israeli cooking 3. Cooking, Israeli
ISBN 9780544373280
LC 2015004346

This Israeli cookbook, by Michael Solomonov and Steven Cook, "showcases the melting-pot cooking of Israel, especially the influences of the Middle East, North Africa, the Mediterranean, and Eastern Europe [sold at the Philadelphia-based restaurant Zahav]. Solomonov's food includes little dishes called mezze, such as the restaurant's insanely popular fried cauliflower; a hummus so ethereal that it put Zahav on the culinary map; and a pink lentil soup with lamb meatballs." (Publisher's note)

"Readers with an adventurous palate and an open mind will be richly rewarded by this terrific debut." Pub Wkly

Cramby, Jonas

Tex-Mex from Scratch; Jonas Cramby. Sterling Pub Co Inc. 2015 144 p. color illustrations $24.95 **641.59**
1. Mexican cooking 2. Barbecue cooking
ISBN 145491629X; 9781454916291

In this book by Jonas Cramby "along with 70 mouthwatering recipes--from antojitos like shrimp taquitos to sweet Helado de Cajeta (caramel ice cream) to top it all off—this collection takes you through all the basics. Learn how to prepare your own tortillas, assemble the best taco, knock together the perfect guacamole, and make your own barbecue smoker." (Publisher's note)

"Texas BBQ is a treat for armchair cooks and can broaden regional collections. Cramby, whose daughters are named Dixie Margarita and Lone Star, has an infectious passion for Tex-Mex food and a talent for food photography. Of his available and forthcoming titles, Tex-Mex from Scratch offers the best value." LJ

Currence, John

Pickles, pigs & whiskey; recipes from my three favorite food groups and then some. John Currence. Andrews McMeel Pub., LLC 2013 259 p. col. ill. $40 **641.59**
1. Cookbooks 2. American cooking 3. Southern cooking
ISBN 1449428800; 9781449428808
LC 2013940033

This cookbook, by John Currence, presents "130 recipes organized by 10 different techniques, . . . [including] Pickled Sweet Potatoes, Whole Grain Guinness Mustard, Deep South 'Ramen' with a Fried Poached Egg, Rabbit Cacciatore, Smoked Endive, Fire-Roasted Cauliflower, and Kitchen Sink Cookie Ice Cream Sandwiches. Each recipe has a song pairing with it." (Publisher's note)

"Recipes for mint julep redux, deep South "ramen" with fried poached eggs, hill country cioppino, and bourbon-pecan pie with tonka bean ice cream, showcase some of the most exciting trends in Southern food and drink." LJ

Deuki Hong

Koreatown; a cookbook. Deuki Hong and Matt Rodbard; photographs by Sam Horine. Clarkson Potter/Publishers 2015 272 p. color illustrations (hardcover) $30 **641.59**
1. Korean cooking 2. Korean Americans 3. Cooking, Korean
ISBN 9780804186131; 0804186138
LC 2015009587

This cookbook, by Deuki Hong and Matt Rodbard, is based on the authors' "love affair with the grit and charm of Korean cooking in America. Koreatowns around the country are synonymous with mealtime feasts and late-night chef hangouts, and Deuki Hong and Matt Rodbard show us why with stories, interviews, and over 100 delicious, super-approachable recipes." (Publisher's note)

"Hong, with coauthor Robard, celebrates Korean cooking in America, and his recipes cover a wide spectrum of meat, seafood, and vegetable offerings." Booklist

Disbrowe, Paula

Down south; soulful recipes and slow-simmered recollections. Donald Link with Paula Disbrowe. Clarkson Potter 2014 256 p. color illustrations (hardback) $35 **641.59**
1. Southern States 2. American cooking 3. Cooking, Cajun 4. Cooking, American -- Southern style
ISBN 0770433189; 9780770433185
LC 2013020280

IACP Cookbook Award Winner: American (2015)

In this cookbook author Donald Link, with Paula Disbrowe, "combines his talents to unearth true down home Southern cooking so everyone can pull up a seat at the table and sample some of the region's finest flavors. Along the way, he introduces all sorts of characters and places, including pitmaster Nick Pihakis of Jim 'N Nick's BBQ, Louisiana goat farmer Bill Ryal, beloved Southern writer Julia Reed, a true Tupelo honey apiary in Florida, and a Texas lamb ranch with a llama named Fritz." (Publisher's note)

Soulful recipes and slow-simmered recollections

Dixon, Kirsten

The **Tutka** Bay Lodge cookbook; coastal cuisine from the wilds of Alaska. by Kirsten Dixon and Mandy Dixon; photography by Tyrone Potgieter. Alaska Northwest Books 2014 224 p. color illustrations (hardcover) $29.99 **641.59**
1. Alaska 2. American cooking 3. Cooking -- Alaska 4. Tutka Bay Lodge (Alaska) 5. Cooking, American -- Pacific Northwest style
ISBN 1941821154; 9781941821152
LC 2014017785
IACP Cookbook Award Winner: E-Cookbook (2015)

This cookbook, by Kirsten Dixon and Mandy Dixon, offers "personal stories, evocative photographs, and recipes that are purposefully simple and designed for the home cook. . . . This recipe collection represents the cuisine at Tutka Bay Lodge, the Dixons' seaside lodge nestled within the curve of a quiet cove at the entrance to Tutka Bay, a deep seven-mile fjord in Kachemak Bay, Alaska." (Publisher's note)

Duguid, Naomi

★ **Burma**; rivers of flavor. Naomi Duguid. Artisan 2012 372 p. col. ill. $35 **641.59**
1. Myanmar 2. Cookbooks 3. Asian cooking 4. Food -- Burma 5. Cooking (Spices) 6. Cooking, Burmese 7. Burma -- Social life and customs
ISBN 1579654134; 9781579654139
LC 2011052121
IACP Cookbook Award (2013)

"Located at the crossroads between China, India, and the nations of Southeast Asia, Burma has long been a land that absorbed outside influences into its everyday life. . . . Interspersed throughout the 125 recipes are intriguing tales from the author's many trips to this fascinating but little-known land." (Publisher's note)

"A colorful immersion into the daily market and table of the Burmese people, this volume is an invitation to celebrate the Burmese people and their transformation." Pub Wkly

Includes bibliographical references and index

Dunlop, Fuchsia

Every grain of rice; simple Chinese home cooking. Fuchsia Dunlop; photography by Chris Terry. W W Norton & Co Inc 2013 351 p. illustrations (hardcover) $35 **641.59**
1. Cookbooks 2. Chinese cooking
ISBN 0393089045; 9780393089042
LC 2012004741
James Beard Award (2014)

In this book, author "Fuchsia Dunlop trained as a chef in China's leading Sichuan cooking school and possesses the rare ability to write recipes for authentic Chinese food that you can make at home. Following her two seminal volumes on Sichuan and Hunan cooking, . . . [this cookbook] is inspired by the vibrant everyday cooking of southern China, in which vegetables play the starring role, with small portions of meat and fish." (Publisher's note)

Dupree, Nathalie

Mastering the art of Southern cooking; Nathalie Dupree & Cynthia Graubart; photographs by Rick McKee; with a foreword by Pat Conroy. Gibbs Smith 2012 720 p. col. ill. $45 **641.59**
1. Cookbooks 2. American cooking 3. Southern cooking
ISBN 1423602757; 9781423602750
LC 2012017365
James Beard Foundation Award: American Cooking (2013)

"Through more than 600 recipes and hundreds of step-by-step photographs, Dupree and Graubart make it easy to learn the techniques for creating the South's fabulous cuisine. . . . Traditional Southern recipes and ingredients are also given modern twists to make them relevant for today's healthy lifestyle." (Publisher's note)

Includes bibliographical references and index

Eddy, Jody

North; the new Nordic cuisine of Iceland. Gunnar Karl Gíslason and Jody Eddy; foreword by René Redzepi. Ten Speed Press 2014 352 p. color illustrations (hardback) $40 **641.59**
1. Cooking 2. Iceland 3. Restaurants 4. Cooking, Icelandic
ISBN 1607744988; 9781607744986
LC 2014003525
IACP Cookbook Award: Judge's Choice (2015)
IACP Cookbook Award Finalist: International (2015)

This book, by Gunnar Karl Gíslason and Jody Eddy, offers a "look into the food and culture of Iceland. . . . Perhaps no Icelandic restaurant is as well-loved and critically lauded as . . . Gíslason's Restaurant Dill, which opened in Reykjavík's historic Nordic House in 2009. 'North' is Gíslason's wonderfully personal debut: equal parts recipe book and culinary odyssey, it offers an unparalleled look into a star chef's creative process." (Publisher's note)

"Many of the recipes reflect the natural resources of Iceland, for example, the sea-salt employed is Icelandic and the fact that so many recipes involve pickled items is a direct product of the necessity of storing food items in a harsh climate. . . . There are many recipes, though, for which the chef does not need to have access to Iceland." Pub Wkly

Foose, Martha Hall

A **southerly** course; recipes & stories from close to home. Martha Hall Foose. Clarkson Potter 2011 256 p. col. ill. $32.50 **641.59**
1. Cookbooks 2. American cooking 3. Southern cooking
ISBN 0307464288; 9780307464286
LC 2010022969

This cookbook, by Martha Hall Foose, "delves deep into Mississippi Delta flavors and foodways. . . . In her signature style, she pairs each recipe with an anecdote or words of advice. . . . Martha's beloved Southern cuisine is a fresh take on homey favorites fiercely protected by the locals, including Skillet Fried Corn, Sweet Pickle Braised Pork Shoulder, and Blackberry Jelly Roll." (Publisher's note)

"Offering meditations on subjects like congealed salads and family china, Foose has all the savvy of a local tour guide, leading the way through her native state with poetry and wit." Pub Wkly

Friedman, Andrew, 1967-

Classico e moderno; Michael White and Andrew Friedman. Ballantine Books 2013 448 p. (hardcover : alk. paper) $50   **641.59**

1. Italian cooking 2. Cooking, Italian
ISBN 0345530527; 9780345530523

LC 2013009625

In this book by Michael White and Andrew Friedman, "White brings his passion for authentic Italian cuisine to the home kitchen, with recipes--nearly 250--that cover both the traditional and contemporary dishes of the region. White shares such iconic dishes as Meatballs Braised in Tomato Sauce; Pasta and Bean Soup; Cavatelli with Lamb Ragù and Bell Peppers; and Roasted Pork Leg with Rosemary and Black Pepper." (Publisher's note)

Includes bibliographical references and index

Galimberti, Gabriele

In her kitchen; stories and recipes from grandmas around the World. Gabriele Galimberti. Clarkson Potter/Publishers 2014 248 p. color illustrations, maps $30   **641.59**

1. Cooking 2. Grandmothers 3. International cooking 4. Galimberti, Gabriele -- Travel
ISBN 0804185557; 9780804185554

LC 2013050635

James Beard Foundation Award Winner: Photography (2015)

In this book, author Gabriele Galimberti presents "beautiful portraits of grandmothers from all over the world with their signature recipes. . . . These vibrant and intimate profiles and photographs pay homage to grandmothers and their cooking everywhere. From a Swedish housewife and her homemade lox and vegetables to a Zambian villager and her Roasted Spiced Chicken, this collection features a global palate." (Publisher's note)

"While drawing on some academic sources, this book is written in lively narrative prose that is more appropriate for general readers than scholars." LJ

Grimes, Dixie

The **B.T.C.** old-fashioned grocery cookbook; recipes and stories from a Southern revival. Alexe van Beuren; with recipes by Dixie Grimes. Clarkson Potter 2014 240 p. color illustrations hbk $29.99   **641.59**

1. Cookbooks 2. Southern cooking 3. B.T.C. Old-Fashioned Grocery 4. Water Valley, Miss. -- Social life

and customs
ISBN 0385345003; 9780385345002

LC 2013019690

"'The B.T.C. Old-Fashioned Grocery Cookbook' shares 120 of the store's best recipes, giving home cooks everywhere a taste of the food that brought a community together." (Publisher's note)

"Water Valley, Miss., is a small, rural village saved from obscurity by being just 25 minutes from the campus town of Oxford, and by being fortunate enough to be the home of chef Grimes and self-made business woman van Beuren. . . . Van Beuren's unadorned prose keeps the character studies pure, with a refreshingly minimal amount of folksiness, while Grimes's 120 recipes alternate between classic and surprising." Pub Wkly

Includes bibliographical references and index

Hazan, Marcella, 1924-2013

★ **Essentials** of classic Italian cooking; illustrated by Karin Kretschmann. Knopf 1992 688p il $30   **641.59**

1. Italian cooking
ISBN 0-394-58404-X

LC 92-52954

Revised and updated edition of the author's The classic Italian cookbook (1973) and More classic Italian cooking (1978)

This volume combines revised and updated versions of the author's The Classic Italian Cook Book (BRD 1973) and More Classic Italian Cooking (BRD 1979). Index.

This "could readily assume the mantle of the definitive resource for Italian cuisine." Booklist

Marcella cucina; photography by Alison Harris, design by Joel Avirom. HarperCollins Pubs. 1997 471p il $35   **641.59**

1. Italian cooking
ISBN 0-06-017103-0

LC 97-1253

This book includes both the author's "old favorites and recent creations, along with her versions of regional dishes from chefs and home cooks throughout Italy. . . . She offers an intimate, at times nostalgic glimpse at her life with cooking." Libr J

Helou, Anissa

Mediterranean street food; stories, soups, snacks, sandwiches, barbecues, sweets, and more, from Europe, North Africa, and the Middle East. Anissa Helou. William Morrow 2006 277 p. ill. $19.99   **641.59**

1. Cookbooks 2. Mediterranean cooking 3. Cookery, Mediterranean
ISBN 0060891513; 9780060891510

LC 2001051451

In this cookbook by Anissa Helou, readers will "join her on a fascinating adventure around the Mediterranean, where eating on the street is a way of life. . . . With . . . black-and-white photographs from Anissa's travels and more than eighty-five fast, flexible, flavorful recipes, . . . [this book] offers home cooks the chance to experience the tastes of distant lands without leaving the kitchen." (Publisher's note)

Includes bibliographical references and index

Hiroko Shimbo

Hiroko's American kitchen; cooking with Japanese flavors. Hiroko Shimbo; photography by Frances Janisch. Andrews McMeel Pub., LLC 2012 215 p. col. ill. $24.99   **641.59**

1. Cookbooks 2. Japanese cooking
ISBN 1449409784; 9781449409784

LC 2012936725

IACP Cookbook Award (2013)

This cookbook, by Hiroko Shimbo, presents "125 . . . recipes that highlight the best of Japanese cuisine. . . . The recipes are organized in chapters, each using one of two stocks or four sauces. By preparing and storing these easily made items, with a minimum of time and fuss you can enjoy a wide variety of delicious dishes every day. These are recipes . . . are prepared and served in dishes that are familiar to American tastes and dining habits." (Publisher's note)

Hoyer, Daniel

Mayan cuisine; recipes from the Yucatan region. Daniel Hoyer; photographs by Marty Snortum. Gibbs Smith 2008 224 p. ill. (chiefly col.) $34.95 **641.59**

1. Cookbooks 2. Mayan cooking 3. Maya cooking 4. Cooking -- Mexico -- Yucatán (State)
ISBN 1423601319; 9781423601319

LC 2007033541

In this cookbook, author "Daniel Hoyer brings us the authentic recipes of the . . . [Maya of the Yucatan Region,] along with his personal experiences that make the historical and cultural background of this people accessible and enjoyable." Recipes include "Sweet Corn and Cilantro Cream Soups, Yucatan BBQ Shrimp, Smoked Pork Loin, Jicama-Orange Salad, and Chicken in Red Chile and Pumpkinseed Sauce." (Publisher's note)

"Hoyer is encouraging and enthusiastic, offering salient tips for key techniques like working with tamale wrappers and charring tomatoes, as well as sources for hard-to-locate ingredients." Pub Wkly

Humm, Daniel

I love New York; ingredients and recipes : a moment in New York cuisine. Daniel Humm and Will Guidara. Ten Speed Press 2013 512 p. col. ill. $50   **641.59**

1. Local foods 2. American cooking 3. New York (State) 4. Cooking, American 5. Cooking -- New York (State) -- New York
ISBN 1607744406; 9781607744405

LC 2012026491

IACP Cookbook Award (2014)

Chef Daniel Humm and restaurant manager Will Guidara present a "cookbook showcasing the foods, ingredients, and culinary history of New York. . . . [They take] an in-depth look at the region's centuries-old farming traditions along with nearly 150 recipes that highlight its outstanding ingredients. . . . Included among these dishes designed explicitly for the home cook are reinterpretations of New York classics." (Publisher's note)

Iyer, Raghavan

Indian cooking unfolded; a master class in Indian cooking, with 100 easy recipes using 10 ingredients or less. by Raghavan Iyer; photography by TK. Workman Publishing 2013 340 p. color illustrations (alk. paper) $19.95   **641.59**

1. Cookbooks 2. Indian cooking 3. Cooking, Indic
ISBN 0761165215; 9780761165217

LC 2013004247

This cookbook, by Raghavan Iyer, focuses on Indian cooking. "The book's 100 authentic recipes use only ingredients readily available at the local supermarket. Taking into account time restraints, each dish can be quickly assembled and will give home cooks the confidence to create knockout Tandoori Chicken, Coconut Squash with Chiles, Turmeric Hash Browns, Saffron-Pistachio Ice Cream Bars, and Mango Bread Pudding with Chai Spices." (Publisher's note)

Includes bibliographical references and index

Jaffrey, Madhur

An **invitation** to Indian cooking; Madhur Jaffrey; with a new preface by the author. Ecco Press/ Alfred A. Knopf 1999 285, 15 p.p ill hardcover o.p.; paperback $16.95   **641.59**

1. Cookbooks 2. Indian cooking 3. Cooking, Indic
ISBN 0880016647; 9780375712111; 0375712119

LC 98030321

First published 1973

IACP Culinary Classics Book Award (2014)

James Beard Cookbook Hall of Fame (2006)

This cookbook, by Madhur Jaffrey, "originally published in 1973, introduced the richly fascinating cuisine of India to America--and changed the face of American cooking. Now, as Indian food enjoys an upsurge of popularity in the United States, a whole new generation of readers and cooks will find all they need to know about Indian cooking in Madhur Jaffrey's . . . book." (Publisher's note)

Jamison, Bill

The **border** cookbook; authentic home cooking of the American Southwest and Northern Mexico. {by} Cheryl Alters Jamison and Bill Jamison. Harvard Common Press 1995 500 p. ill. pbk $21.95; hardcover o.p.   **641.59**

1. Cookbooks 2. American cooking 3. Cooking 4. Mexican cooking 5. Cooking -- Southwestern style
ISBN 9781558321038; 9781558321021; 1558321039

LC 95010799

James Beard Award (1996)

In this "James Beard Book Award-winning cookbook, authors Cheryl Alters Jamison and Bill Jamison combine the best of Mexican and Southwest cooking, bringing together this large region's Native American, Spanish, Mexican, and Anglo culinary roots into one big, exuberant book. . . . In over 300 recipes they explore the common elements and regional differences of border cooking." (Publisher's note)

Joachim, David

Cooking light global kitchen; the world's most delicious food made easy. David Joachim. Oxmoor

House 2014 319 p. color illustrations (hardcover) $29.95 **641.59**
1. Cooking 2. Cookbooks
ISBN 9780848739980; 0848739981
LC 2013956992

This cookbook, by David Joachim and the editors of 'Cooking Light Magazine,' "brings a world of flavor, texture, and enticing aromas to your everyday meals. In this book, the sometimes intimidating topic of preparing your favorite ethnic-inspired dishes is made easy, approachable, and, most importantly, doable for home cooks of any skill level, by using ethnic ingredients easy-to-find in your local grocery store!" (Publisher's note)

Rustic Italian food; Marc Vetri with David Joachim; beverage notes by Jeff Benjamin; photography by Kelly Campbell; foreword by Mario Batali. Ten Speed Press 2011 291 p. col. ill. $35 **641.59**
1. Sauces 2. Cookbooks 3. Italian cooking 4. Cooking -- Pasta products 5. Cooking, Italian
ISBN 158008589X; 9781580085892
LC 2011015301

In this cookbook, "Philadelphia chef Marc Vetri celebrates the handcrafted cuisine of Italy, advocating a hands-on, back-to-the-basics approach to cooking. . . . [It presents] an education in kitchen fundamentals, with detailed, step-by-step instructions for making terrines, dry-cured salami, and cooked sausage; a thorough guide to bread and pasta making; and a primer on classic Italian preserves and sauces." (Publisher's note)

"Advanced cooks looking to master bread and pasta will value Vetri's patient, masterful explanation of underlying techniques." LJ

Jones, Catherine Cheremeteff
A **year** of Russian feasts; Catherine Cheremeteff Jones; illustrations by Barbara Stott McCoy. Jellyroll Press 2002 192 p. ill. $16.95 **641.59**
1. Russian cooking 2. Religious holidays 3. Russian Orthodox Church 4. Cooking, Russian 5. Food habits -- Russia (Federation) 6. Russia (Federation) -- Social life and customs
ISBN 0971601305; 9780971601307
LC 2001129493

This cookbook, by Catherine Cheremeteff Jones, illustrated by Barbara Stott McCoy, "explains to Western readers the regularly recurring Russian Orthodox feasts, those traditional dishes associated with them, and the holidays' significance in the life of the church and the people. In Orthodoxy, prior to feasting comes fasting, so Jones' first recipes exemplify ascetic vegetarian dishes. Then it's on to the celebrations . . . : beet soups, meat-stuffed dumplings, sweetly spiced and aromatic Easter bread, and many variations on potatoes." (Booklist)

Kennedy, Diana
The **essential** cuisines of Mexico. Potter 2000 526p $35 **641.59**
1. Mexican cooking
ISBN 0-609-60355-8
LC 00-23156

The author has gathered "the recipes from her first cookbook, the groundbreaking Cuisines of Mexico (1972), as well its two successors, The Tortilla Book (1975) and Mexican Regional Cooking (1978) . . . in this new collection. She's revised the recipes and simplified some, and there are also 30 or so new recipes. Kennedy's books became classics long ago; this compilation of her early works is an essential purchase." Libr J
Includes bibliographical references

Khanna, Vikas
Return to the rivers; recipes and memories of the Himalyan River Valleys. Vikas Khanna, Andrew Blackmore-Dobbyn. Lake Isle Press 2013 444 p. color illustrations, map (hardback : alk. paper) $35 **641.59**
1. Himalaya Mountains
ISBN 1891105531; 9781891105531
LC 2013951725
IACP Cookbook Award Finalist: Culinary Travel (2015)

This book, by Vikas Khanna and Andrew Blackmore-Dobbyn, "is an incredible collection of recipes, photos, and memories as a means to preserve and share the sacred foodways, values, and simple gifts of friendship that the Himalayan people bestowed Khanna. Exploring the regions the great Himalayas directly touch upon–Bhutan, Nepal, Tibet, Northern India, Myanmar, Western China, Pakistan–Khanna was met with immeasurable kindness and hospitality." (Publisher's note)

Kijac, Maria Baez
The **South** American table; the flavor and soul of authentic home cooking from Patagonia to Rio de Janeiro, with 450 recipes. Maria Baez Kijac; foreword by Charlie Trotter. Houghton Mifflin Harcourt 2003 478 p. ill., 1 map (alk. paper) $29.95 **641.59**
1. Cookbooks 2. Latin American cooking 3. Cookery, Latin American 4. Cookery -- South America 5. South America -- Social life and customs
ISBN 9781558322486; 1558322485
LC 2003011100

This South American-themed cookbook, by Maria Baez Kijac, "reflects a true mix of history and cultures, melding the bounty of the New World (tomatoes, potatoes, corn, beans, hot peppers) and the cooking traditions of its indigenous peoples with the influences and culinary heritage of the Conquistadors, African slaves, and immigrants from Italy, Germany, China, and elsewhere." (Publisher's note)

Author Kijac "offers a thorough volume that is part reference book and part cookbook. Long chapters about the geography of South America and its pre-Columbian civilizations, as well as a history of cooking in South America precede the hundreds of recipes. A glossary of South American ingredients as well as a dictionary of ingredients are included as well. The recipes are wonderful, if overwhelming in number." Pub Wkly

Kochilas, Diane

The **glorious** foods of Greece. Morrow 2000
496p map $40   **641.59**
1. Greek cooking
ISBN 0-688-15457-3

LC 00-28158

This cookbook includes over 400 recipes from various
"regions, starting with the Peloponnesus and the Ionian Islands, moving on to Macedonia, the islands of the Aegean,
and Crete, and finishing up in the city of Athens. . . . Kochilas also provides extensive historical background, cultural as
well as culinary, along with detailed descriptions and explanations of ingredients." Libr J

Includes bibliographical references and index

Koehler, Jeff

Spain; Recipes and Traditions from the Verdant
Hills of the Basque Country to the Coastal Waters of
Andalucía. by Jeff Koehler; location photographs by
Jeff Koehler, plated food photographs by Kevin Mi-
yazaki. Chronicle Books 2013 352 p. color illustra-
tions (hardback) $40   **641.59**
1. Spanish cooking 2. Cooking, Spanish
ISBN 0811875016; 9780811875011

LC 2013026594

This book of Spanish recipes, by food writer Jeff
Koehler, is "organized by food type rather than local. . . . A
tasty section on tapas covers classics like dates wrapped in
bacon, as well as more intense options, such as Galician octopus with paprika on potatoes. . . . In addition to the food itself, Koehler explores a variety of the country's food-related
traditions." (Publishers Weekly)

Kostow, Christopher, 1976-

★ A **new** Napa cuisine; Christopher Kostow;
photography by Peden + Munk. Ten Speed Press
2014 304 p. illustrations (hardback) $50   **641.59**
1. American cooking 2. Napa Valley (Calif.) 3.
Cooking, American -- California style 4. Napa Valley
(Calif.) -- Description and travel
ISBN 1607745941; 9781607745945

LC 2014010462

IACP Cookbook Award: Cookbook of the Year (2015)
IACP Cookbook Award: Global Design (2015)
James Beard Foundation Award Nominee: Photography
(2015)

This cookbook on Napa, California, by Christopher
Kostow, "celebrates the local artisans, products, growers,
and wilds that have played a role in the creation of a nascent style of cooking specific to this small American valley. Through tales of designing china with local ceramicists
or discovering wild edibles along the creek while walking
his dog; planting seeds both literal and figurative--Kostow's
story is a personal and engaging one." (Publisher's note)

"This sort of food lies beyond even the most ambitious
amateur, but culinary students will appreciate the challenge
of seeing where their art and craft are headed, and the restaurant's patrons will love documentation of a once-in-a-
lifetime dinner." Booklist

Lebovitz, David

★ **My** Paris kitchen; recipes and stories. David
Lebovitz. Ten Speed Press 2014 345 p. ill. (chiefly
col.) (hardback) $35   **641.59**
1. French cooking 2. Paris (France) -- Civilization 3.
Paris (France) -- Description and travel 4. Food habits
-- France 5. Paris (France) -- Social life and customs
ISBN 1607742675; 9781607742678

LC 2013032561

IACP Cookbook Award Finalist: International (2015);
James Beard Foundation Award Nominee: International
(2015)
IACP Cookbook Award Finalist: Literary Food Writing
(2015)

"In 'My Paris Kitchen,' [author] David [Lebovitz] re-
masters the classics, introduces lesser-known fare, and presents 100 sweet and savory recipes that reflect the way modern Parisians eat today. You'll find Soupe à l'oignon, Cassoulet, Coq au vin, and Croque-monsieur, as well as Smoky
barbecue-style pork, Lamb shank tagine, Dukkah-roasted
cauliflower, Salt cod fritters with tartar sauce, and Wheat
berry salad with radicchio, root vegetables, and pomegranate." (Publisher's note)

"French food personalized and demystified for the home
cook in the best way." Pub Wkly

Includes bibliographical references and index

Lee, Matt

The **Lee** Bros. Charleston kitchen; Matt Lee and
Ted Lee. Clarkson Potter 2012 240 p. col. ill., col.
maps $35   **641.59**
1. Cookbooks 2. American cooking 3. Southern
cooking 4. Cooking, American -- Southern style 5.
Cooking -- South Carolina -- Charleston
ISBN 0307889734; 9780307889737

LC 2012013331

IACP Cookbook Award (2014)

This cookbook, by Matt Lee and Ted Lee, features recipes for Southern U.S. cuisine. "The 100 offerings represent
a mix of the classic and the newfangled. There's peach
leather, a Charleston chew dating back to the 19th century,
which requires two days of sun-drying. And then there's a
totally nontraditional tomato and watermelon gazpacho with
shrimp." Chapters "cover drinks, snacks, soups, vegetables,
fish, meat, and desserts." (Publishers Weekly)

"The brothers also provide two excellent addendums: a
comprehensive bibliography of Charleston cookbooks dating back to 1756 and directions for a walking or driving tour
featuring eateries from which many of their recipes were
derived." Pub Wkly

Includes bibliographical references (p. 232-[235])
and index

Lewis, Edna, 1916-2006

The **gift** of Southern cooking; recipes and revelations from two great Southern cooks. by Edna
Lewis and Scott Peacock. Knopf 2003 352p il
$29.95   **641.59**
1. Southern cooking 2. Cookery, American -- Southern
style
ISBN 0-375-40035-4

LC 2002-73153

This is a collection of recipes by Edna Lewis, author of The Taste of Country, and Scott Peacock, the chef at Watershed in Decatur, Alabama. "Together they share their secrets for such Southern basics as pan-fried chicken, . . . creamy grits, . . . and genuine Southern biscuits. . . . {According to the authors}, the way everything is put together—with the condiments and relishes and preserves and wealth of vegetables all spread out on the table—is what makes the meal uniquely Southern. . . . {The book includes} twenty-two seasonal menus, from A Spring Country Breakfast for a Late Sunday Morning and A Summer Dinner of Big Flavors to An Alabama Thanksgiving and A Hearty Dinner for a Cold Winter Night." (Publisher's note) Index.

"If you care—and I mean really care—about coleslaw, pan-fried chicken, trout, . . . greens simmered in pork stock and Southern-style ketchups, relishes and vinegars, this is a book you shouldn't be without." N Y Times Book Rev

Lo, Eileen Yin-Fei

Mastering the art of Chinese cooking; Eileen Yin-Fei Lo; photographs by Susie Cushner; brush calligraphy by San Yan Wong. Chronicle Books 2009 384 p. col. ill. $50   **641.59**
  1. Cookbooks 2. Chinese cooking
ISBN 0811859339; 9780811859332
                       LC 2010027670
IACP Cookbook Award (2010)

This cookbook, by Eileen Yin-Fei Lo, offers "a series of lessons [to] build skill, knowledge, and confidence as Lo guides the home cook step by step through the techniques, ingredients, and equipment that define Chinese cuisine. With more than 100 classic recipes and technique illustrations throughout, . . . [It] makes . . . this ancient cuisine utterly accessible." (Publisher's note)

"[V]isually stunning—with brush calligraphy, decorative borders, and full-page color photographs—as well as a comprehensive and educational guide that fulfills the promise of how to master Chinese cooking." Pub Wkly

Miller, Adrian

Soul food; the surprising story of an American cuisine, one plate at a time. by Adrian Miller. University of North Carolina Press 2013 344 p. (cloth : alk. paper) $30   **641.59**
  1. American cooking 2. African American cooking 3. African American cooking -- History 4. Cooking, American -- Southern style
ISBN 146960762X; 9781469607627
                       LC 2013002823

In this book author Adrian Miller "delves into the influences, ingredients, and innovations that make up the soul food tradition. Focusing each chapter on the culinary and social history of one dish--such as fried chicken, chitlins, yams, greens, and 'red drinks'--Miller uncovers how it got on the soul food plate and what it means for African American culture and identity." (Publisher's note)

"An engaging, tradition-rich look at an often overlooked American cuisine--certainly to be of interest to foodies from all walks of life." Kirkus

Includes bibliographical references and index

Nguyen, Andrea

Asian dumplings; mastering gyoza, spring rolls, samosas, and more. Andrea Quynhgiao Nguyen; photography by Penny De Los Santos. Ten Speed Press 2009 234 p. col. ill. (hardcover) $30 **641.59**
  1. Dumplings 2. Asian cooking 3. Cooking, Asian
ISBN 1580089755; 9781580089753
                       LC 2010286323

This cookbook, by Andrea Quynhgiao Nguyen, focuses on preparing Asian style dumplings. "Plump pot stickers, spicy samosas, and tender bāo (stuffed buns) are enjoyed by the million every day in dim sum restaurants, streetside stands, and private homes worldwide. Wrapped, rolled, or filled; steamed, fried, or baked--Asian dumplings are also surprisingly easy to prepare, as [the author] . . . demonstrates." (Publisher's note)

Includes bibliographical references (p. 227-228) and index

Nguyen, Luke

The **food** of Vietnam; Luke Nguyen. Hardie Grant Books 2013 367 p. $50   **641.59**
  1. Cookbooks 2. Vietnamese cooking 3. Vietnam -- Description and travel
ISBN 1742706207; 9781742706207

A journey to discover food & heritage -- Saigon & south -- From coast to countryside -- Salt water people -- Princes & paupers -- The dragon & the turtle -- Mountain people -- Basic recipes -- Glossary -- Index

This cookbook and travel memoir, by Luke Nguyen, "follows his trip from northern Vietnam down to the south, through marketplaces and kitchens of strangers and family alike to find the best recipes Vietnam has to offer. Luke records his experiences with the people he meets and the places he visits along the way, breathing life into the classic recipes of Vietnam, from pho to banh mi and everything in between." (Publisher's note)

Oliver, Jamie, 1975-

Jamie's Italy; Jamie Oliver; photographs by David Loftus and Chris Terry. Hyperion 2006 319 p. il $34.95   **641.59**
  1. Cookbooks 2. Italian cooking
ISBN 1401301959; 9781401301958
                       LC 2006445348

This cookbook by Jamie Oliver focuses on Italian cuisine. "Italy and its wonderful flavors have always had a major influence on Jamie Oliver's food and cooking. . . . [Here] he travels this famously gastronomic country paying homage to the classic dishes of each region and searching for new ideas to bring home. The result is a . . . collection of Italian recipes, old and new." (Publisher's note)

Olney, Richard

Lulu's Provencal table; the food and wine from Domaine Tempier Vineyard. by Richard Olney; foreword by Alice Waters; photographs by Gail Skoff. Grub Street 2013 364 p. il (hc) $29.95   **641.59**
  1. Cookbooks 2. Vineyards 3. French cooking 4. Domaine Tempier 5. Domaine Tempier Vineyard 6. Cookery, French -- Provencal style
ISBN 9781909166189; 1909166189

First published 1994

This book, by Richard Olney, describes how the author "moved to Provence[, France] in 1961 and had the good fortune to befriend Lulu and Lucien Peyraud, the owners of the noted Domaine Tempier vineyard in Provence, not far from Marseilles. . . . [The book provides] Olney's descriptions of the regional food served as the vineyard meals at the domaine. Then he lovingly transcribes Lulu's recipes." (Publisher's note)

Simple French food; Richard Olney; new foreword by Mark Bittman; foreword by James Beard; introduction by Patricia Wells; drawings by Richard Olney. Houghton Mifflin Harcourt 2014 455 p. ill. (hbk.) $24.99   **641.59**
1. Cookbooks 2. French cooking 3. Cooking, French 4. Cooking, French -- Provencal style
ISBN 0544242203; 9780544242203
LC 2014012324
IACP Culinary Classics Book Award (2013)

"This new edition of [Richard Olney's] classic cookbook includes a fresh cover, new interior design, and a foreword by Mark Bittman. . . . Olney's 175 recipes are so straightforward that cooks will be inspired to go right into the kitchen: herb omelets, fish with zucchini, lamb shanks with garlic, and many more. He also shares techniques (several featuring his own illustrations), such as fermenting vinegar, in line with the back-to-basics trend in cooking." (Publisher's note)

Palmer, Charlie

Charlie Palmer's American fare; everyday recipes from my kitchens to yours. Charlie Palmer. Grand Central Life & Style 2015 272 p. color illustrations (hardback) $40   **641.59**
1. Entertaining 2. American cooking 3. Cooking, American
ISBN 1455530999; 9781455530991
LC 2014048819

Author Charlie Palmer presets the "book about favorite American recipes he loves to share with family and friends. Included will be over 100 recipes that any cook can make with ease-from Charlie's Famous Corn Chowder with Shrimp to Cheese Strata to Prosciutto-Wrapped Zucchini to Baked Lemon Chicken; plus snacks like Crispy Chickpeas and desserts like Double-Trouble Chocolate Chip Cookies, Lemon Shortbread and Fig Crostata." (Publisher's note)

"While Palmer covers the basics, he also offers appealing quick and easy lunches, including croque monsieur with mornay sauce, and baked ratatouille. His standout chapter explores family favorites, which include chicken liver pâté, baked littleneck clams, lentil–butternut squash soup, and oatmeal cookies. Fans will delight in this exceptional, accessible cookbook." Pub Wkly

American fare

Pelaez, Ana Sofia

The **Cuban** table; a celebration of food, flavors, and history. Ana Sofia Pelaez; photographs by Ellen Silverman. St. Martin's Press 2014 336 p. illustrations (hardback) $35   **641.59**
1. Cookbooks 2. Cuban cooking 3. Cooking, Cuban
ISBN 1250036089; 9781250036087
LC 2014026974
James Beard Foundation Award Nominee: International (2015)

This cookbook, by Ana Sofia Pelaez, with photographs by Ellen Silverman, "is a comprehensive, contemporary overview of Cuban food, recipes and culture as recounted by serious home cooks and professional chefs, restaurateurs and food writers. . . . Here you'll find documented recipes for everything from iconic Cuban sandwiches to rich stews with Spanish accents and African ingredients, accompanied by details about historical context and insight into cultural nuances." (Publisher's note)

"Let's hope Pelaez and Silverman undertake more collaborations. Their thorough and respectful treatment of their subject results in a compelling cookbook that conveys a strong sense of place." LJ

Includes bibliographical references and index

Phan, Charles

★ The **slanted** door; modern Vietnamese food. Charles Phan with Janny Hu; photography by Ed Anderson. Ten Speed Press 2014 288 p. ill. (chiefly col.) (hardcover) $40   **641.59**
1. Vietnamese cooking
ISBN 1607740540; 9781607740544
LC 2014015943
IACP Cookbook Award: Photography (2015)
IACP Cookbook Award Finalist: Chefs and Restaurants (2015)

"Charles Phan opened The Slanted Door in San Francisco in 1995, inspired by the food of his native Vietnam. . . . The Slanted Door is a love letter to the restaurant, its people, and its food. Featuring stories in addition to its most iconic recipes,The Slanted Door both celebrates a culinary institution and allows home cooks to recreate its excellence." (Publisher's note)

"Phan's cuisine illustrates the synthesis that is Vietnam's culinary heritage: Chinese ingredients and traditions blended with French techniques. The Slanted Door's bar also mixes extensive lists of innovative cocktails, and these, along with Phan's cooking, are here documented." Booklist

Vietnamese home cooking; Charles Phan with Jessica Battilana; photography by Eric Wolfinger. Ten Speed Press 2012 xxix, 222 p.p col. ill. $35 **641.59**
1. Cookbooks 2. Vietnamese cooking 3. Cooking, Vietnamese
ISBN 1607740532; 9781607740537; 9781607743859
LC 2012014119
IACP Cookbook Award (2013)

In this cookbook, chef Charles Phan "introduces traditional Vietnamese cooking to home cooks by focusing on fundamental techniques and ingredients. . . . With solid instruction and encouraging guidance, perfectly crispy imperial rolls, tender steamed dumplings, delicately flavored whole fish, and meaty lemongrass beef stew are all deliciously close at hand." (Publisher's note)

Phillips, Michael

The **Chelsea** Market cookbook; 100 recipes from New York's premier indoor food market. by Michael Phillips with Rick Rodgers. Stewart, Tabori & Chang 2013 223 p. color illustrations $29.95 **641.59**
    1. Cookbooks 2. American cooking 3. Cooking, American 4. International cooking 5. Chelsea Market (New York, N.Y.)
    ISBN 1617690376; 9781617690372

LC 2013009924

IACP Cookbook Award (2014)

This book, by Michael Phillips and Rick Rodgers, "collects the most interesting and famous recipes from the [Chelsea New York City] market's eclectic vendors and celebrity food personalities. Archival images, gorgeous food photography, and cooking and entertaining tips and anecdotes accompany the 100 recipes, ranging from Buddakan's Hoisin Glazed Pork Belly, to Sarabeth's Velvety Cream of Tomato Soup, to Ruthy's Rugelach." (Publisher's note)

Plum, Camilla

The **Scandinavian** Kitchen; Camilla Plum; photography by Anne-Li Engstrom. Natl Book Network 2011 272 p. col. ill. hardcover o.p. $35 **641.59**
    1. Cookbooks 2. Scandinavian cooking 3. Cooking, Scandinavian
    ISBN 1906868476; 9781906868475

This cookbook, by Camilla Plum, "shares Scandinavian tastes, broken down by group of ingredient, easy to recreate in your own kitchen. Scandinavian cooking achieves a delicate balance between extravagance and the humble, producing a wealth of seasonal daily food, and more luxurious festive food." (Publisher's note)

"Plum, a leading Danish food writer, broadcaster, and cookbook author, extols the virtues of Scandinavian cuisine in this beautiful and fascinating collection. More of a guide to Scandinavian agriculture and its bounty than a full-fledged cookbook, this work showcases the diverse ingredients that make up the Scandinavian diet, including the wide array of both fresh and preserved fish, meat, and vegetables. Recipes are numerous but feel almost secondary." Pub Wkly

Randall, Alice

Soul food love; 100 years of cooking and eating in one Black family, with recipes. Alice Randall and Caroline Randall Williams; photographs by Penny De Los Santos. Clarkson Potter/Publishers 2015 224 p. illustrations (chiefly color) **641.59**
    1. Cookbooks 2. African American cooking
    ISBN 9780804137935

LC 2014014423

NAACP Image Award: Outstanding Literary Work - Instructional (2016)

In this cookbook, by Alice Randall and Caroline Randall Williams, with photographs by Penny De Los Santos, "a mother-daughter duo reclaims and redefines soul food by mining the traditions of four generations of black women and creating 80 healthy recipes to help everyone live longer and stronger." (Publisher's note)

"The Wind Done Gone author Randall and daughter, poet Randall Williams, write about the history of black

cooking in America and offer recipes that are both traditional and nutritious." LJ

Ray, Rachael, 1968-

Everyone is Italian on Sunday; Rachael Ray. Atria Paperback 2015 408 p. color illustrations (hardcover : alk. paper) $39.99 **641.59**
    1. Cookbooks 2. Italian cooking 3. Cooking, Italian
    ISBN 9781476766072

LC 2014043645

This Italian cookbook, by Rachael Ray, brings "together signature recipes for the traditional Italian staples that [the author] grew up with and still cooks for her family and friends today. From arancini to saffron gnocchetti sardi, from small bites to hearty meals, from her sister's favorite Italian desserts to her husband's Italian ingredient-inspired cocktails, here is a treasury of delicious dishes to prepare with love and devour with gusto." (Publisher's note)

"For those who are looking for a new angle , this cookbook satisfies in spades." Pub Wkly

Richardson, Alan

The **breath** of a wok; unlocking the spirit of Chinese wok cooking through recipes and lore. Grace Young and Alan Richardson; with text and recipes by Grace Young. Simon & Schuster 2004 240 p. ill. (some col.) $37.50 **641.59**
    1. Cookbooks 2. Wok cooking 3. Cooking, Chinese 4. Food habits -- China
    ISBN 0743238273; 9780743238274

LC 2003070403

IACP Cookbook Award (2005)

This cookbook, written by Grace Young and Alan Richardson, "brings the techniques and flavors of old-world wok cooking into today's kitchen, enabling anyone to stir-fry with wok hay. . . . The 125 recipes are a testament to the versatility of the wok, with stir-fried, smoked, pan-fried, braised, boiled, poached, steamed, and deep-fried dishes." (Publisher's note)

Includes bibliographical references and index

Roden, Claudia

The **new** book of Middle Eastern food; rev ed; Knopf 2000 513p il $35 **641.59**
    1. Middle Eastern cooking 2. Cookery, Middle Eastern
    ISBN 0-375-40506-2

LC 00-708864

Originally published 1968 in the United Kingdom; first United States edition published 1972 with title: A book of Middle Eastern food

This volume "includes 800 recipes and variations, as well as historical background, an introduction to essential ingredients and regional dietary practices, folktales, and a vast amount of other information." Libr J

Includes bibliographical references

Rodriguez, Jessamyn Waldman

The **Hot** Bread Kitchen cookbook; artisanal baking from around the world. Jessamyn Waldman Rodriguez and the Bakers of Hot Bread Kitchen with

Julia Turshen. Clarkson Potter/Publishers 2015 301 p. (hardcover) $35   **641.59**
1. Bread 2. Cookbooks 3. International cooking
ISBN 9780804186179

LC 2014048697

This cookbook, by Jessamyn Waldman Rodriguez and the Bakers of Hot Bread Kitchen with Julia Turshen, "Hot Bread Kitchen is a bakery that employs and empowers immigrant women, providing them with the skills to succeed in the culinary industry. The tasty corollary of this . . . is a line of authentic breads you won't find anywhere else . . . [but] these ethnic gems can now be made at home." (Publisher's note)

'Hot Bread Kitchen's first cookbook foray is essential reading for serious foodies, bakers and anyone inspired by the bakery's philanthropic mission." LJ

Includes bibliographical references and index

Ronnen, Tal
Crossroads; extraordinary recipes from the restaurant that is reinventing vegan cuisine. Tal Ronnen with Scot Jones and Serafina Magnussen with JoAnn Cianciulli. Artisan 2015 304 p. color illustrations $35   **641.59**
1. Veganism 2. Cookbooks 3. Vegetarian cooking 4. Vegan cooking 5. Cooking, Mediterranean
ISBN 1579656366; 9781579656362

LC 2015010988

In this cookbook, chef Tal Ronnen with Scot Jones and Serafina Magnussen with JoAnn Cianciulli, "teaches readers to make his recipes and proves that the flavors we crave are easily replicated in dishes made without animal products. With accessible, unfussy recipes, [the book] . . . takes plant-based eating firmly out of the realm of hippie health food and into a cuisine that fits perfectly with today's modern palate." (Publisher's note)

"Vegan cooking taken to a new level of refinement. Epicures and professionals should take note." LJ

Rouxel, Sebastien
★ **Bouchon** Bakery; Thomas Keller, with Sebastien Rouxel and Matt McDonald; along with Susie Heller, Michael Ruhlman, and Amy Vogler; photographs by Deborah Jones. Artisan 2012 399 p. col. ill. $50   **641.59**
1. Baking 2. Pastry 3. Cookbooks 4. Bouchon Bakery
ISBN 1579654355; 9781579654351

LC 2012000695

IACP Cookbook Award (2013)

This cookbook, by Thomas Keller, was the winner of the 2013 IACP Cookbook Award for Food Photography & Styling. "[I]n this . . . amalgam of American and French baked goods, you'll find recipes for the beloved TKOs and Oh Ohs (Keller's takes on Oreos and Hostess's Ho Hos) and all the French classics he fell in love with as a young chef apprenticing in Paris: the baguettes, the macarons, the millefeuilles, the tartes aux fruits." (Publisher's note)

"[T]his lovely volume is a must-have for cooks who want to take baking to the next level." Pub Wkly

Includes index

Santibañez, Roberto
Truly Mexican; Essential Recipes and Techniques for Authentic Mexican Cooking. [by] Roberto Santibanez, with J.J. Goode and Shelley Wiseman. John Wiley & Sons, Inc. 2011 264 p. col. ill. $35   **641.59**
1. Cookbooks 2. Mexican cooking 3. Sauces
ISBN 0470499559; 9780470499559

LC 2010013151

This cookbook, by Roberto Santibanez, is "[a]n introduction to Mexican cooking. [It] covers the main ingredients as well as how they're best prepared--from toasting tortillas to roasting tomatoes--and offers a few simple kitchen commandments that make great results a given. Recipes cover main dishes, sides, salsas, guacamoles, moles, adobos, and more." (Publisher's note)

"[T]he author's expertise is conveyed in a straightforward and inspiring tone that will instill confidence in cooks eager to prepare Mexican meals at home, regardless of previous experience or skill level." Pub Wkly

★ The **Silver** Spoon; 2nd English edition Phaidon Press 2011 1504 p. ill. (chiefly col.), map hbk $49.95   **641.59**
1. Italian cooking
ISBN 0714862568; 9780714862569

LC 2011293278

This classic Italian cookbook "features over 2,000 revised recipes and is illustrated with 400 brand new, full-color photographs. A comprehensive and lively book, its uniquely stylish and user-friendly format makes it accessible and a pleasure to read. The new updated edition features new introductory material covering such topics as how to compose a traditional Italian meal, typical food traditions of the different regions, and how to set an Italian table." (Publisher's note)

"Globe-trotting gourmands will appreciate the menu and 'signature dish' contributions by famous Italian chefs that round out the book. The most exhaustive Italian cookbook in recent memory, this volume offers something for every cook, regardless of their skill level, and deserves to be a fixture in American kitchens." Pub Wkly

Speck, Maria
Ancient grains for modern meals; Mediterranean whole grain recipes for barley, farro, kamut, polenta, wheat berries & more. Maria Speck; photogaphy by Sara Remington. Ten Speed Press 2011 ix, 210 p.p col. ill. (hardback) $29.99   **641.59**
1. Cookbooks 2. Cooking -- Grains 3. Alternative grains 4. Grain 5. Cooking (Cereals) 6. Cooking, Mediterranean
ISBN 1580083544; 9781580083546

LC 2010045867

IACP Cookbook Award (2012)

This cookbook, by Maria Speck, presents recipes for alternative, traditional grains including "farro, barley, polenta, and wheat berries." It contains "rustic but elegant dishes--Creamy Farro with Honey-Roasted Grapes, Barley Salad with Figs and Tarragon-Lemon Dressing, Lamb Stew with

Wheat Berries in Red Wine Sauce, and Purple Rice Pudding with Rose Water Dates." (Publisher's note)

Includes bibliographical references and index

Sterling, David

★ **Yucatán**; recipes from a culinary expedition. by David Sterling. University of Texas Press 2014 576 p. ill. (chiefly col.), col. map (hardbound : alk. paper) $60   **641.59**

1. Maya cooking 2. Yucatan (Mexico) 3. Cooking -- Yucatan Peninsula 4. Mayas -- Social life and customs 5. Yucatán Peninsula -- Description and travel 6. Yucatán Peninsula -- Social life and customs

ISBN 0292735812; 9780292735811

LC 2013021911

James Beard Foundation Award Winner: International (2015)

James Beard Foundation Award Winner: Cookbook of the Year (2015)

This book, by David Sterling, "takes you on a gastronomic tour of the [Yucatan] peninsula in this unique cookbook. . . . Throughout the journey, Sterling serves up over 275 authentic, thoroughly tested recipes. . . . He also discusses pantry staples and basic cooking techniques and offers substitutions for local ingredients that may be hard to find elsewhere." (Publisher's note)

"Some recipes are multiday affairs, but they're clearly written and intended for home cooks. An introductory index provides an invaluable reference to unique Mesoamerican ingredients." LJ

Includes bibliographical references and index

Swanson, Heidi

Near & far; recipes inspired by home and travels. Heidi Swanson. Ten Speed Press 2015 336 p. color illustrations (hardcover : alk. paper) $29.99   **641.59**

1. International cooking

ISBN 1607745496; 9781607745495

LC 2014047586

In this cookbook author Heidi Swanson "describes the fragrance of flatbreads hot off a Marrakech griddle, soba noodles and feather-light tempura in Tokyo, and the taste of wild-picked greens from the Puglian coast. Recipes such as Fennel Stew, Carrot & Sake Salad, Watermelon Radish Soup, Brown Butter Tortelli, and Saffron Tagine use healthy, whole foods ingredients and approachable techniques." (Publisher's note)

"Highly recommended for anyone who loves unassuming and easy gourmet cooking. Fans of David Tanis (One Good Dish) and Alice Waters (The Art of Simple Food) will love this." LJ

Includes bibliographical references and index

Near and far

Terry, Bryant

Afro-vegan; farm-fresh African, Caribbean & Southern flavors remixed. Bryant Terry; photography by Paige Green. Ten Speed Press 2014 215 p. ill. (chiefly col.), col. map (hardback) $27.50   **641.59**

1. Veganism 2. Caribbean cooking 3. African American cooking 4. Vegan cooking 5. Cooking, African 6. Cooking, Caribbean 7. Cooking, American

-- Southern style

ISBN 1607745313; 9781607745310

LC 2013048560

"With more than 100 modern and delicious dishes that draw on [author Bryant] Terry's personal memories as well as the history of food that has traveled from the African continent, Afro-Vegan takes you on an international food journey. Accompanying the recipes are Terry's insights about building community around food, along with suggested music tracks from around the world and book recommendations." (Publisher's note)

Includes bibliographical references and index

Thielen, Amy

The **New** Midwestern table; 200 heartland recipes. Amy Thielen. Clarkson Potter/Publishers 2013 399 p. color illustrations (hardback) $35   **641.59**

1. Cookbooks 2. Midwestern cooking

ISBN 0307954870; 9780307954879

LC 2012047058

James Beard Award (2014)

This cookbook, by Amy Thielen, "reveals all that she's come to love--and learn--about the foods of her native Midwest, through updated classic recipes and numerous encounters with spirited home cooks. . . . [The book also contains] 150 color photographs capturing these fresh-from-the-land dishes and the striking beauty of the terrain." (Publisher's note)

Van Aken, Norman

New World kitchen; Latin American and Caribbean cuisine. Norman Van Aken, with Janet Van Aken; photographs by Tim Turner. Ecco 2003 xiv, 322 p.p ill. (some col.) $34.95   **641.59**

1. Cookbooks 2. Caribbean cooking 3. Latin American cooking 4. Cooking, Caribbean 5. Cooking, Latin American

ISBN 0060185058; 9780060185053

LC 2002027158

This cookbook, by Norman Van Aken with Janet Van Aken, "explores the rich influence of Latin American cuisine on the American palate. From the African-influenced Creole cuisines of Cuba, Puerto Rico, and Jamaica to South American flavors from Brazil, Peru, and Argentina to the distinct tastes of Mexico, Van Aken works his particular magic on this luscious cornucopia and emerges with a wealth of brilliant recipes." (Publisher's note)

"Combined with Van Aken's many thoughtful sidebars and notations, the sophistication of these recipes make this a treat for serious home cooks." Pub Wkly

Includes bibliographical references and index

Von Bremzen, Anya

Mastering the art of Soviet cooking; a memoir of love and longing. by Anya von Bremzen. Crown Publishers 2013 352 p. $26   **641.59**

1. Russian cooking 2. Russia -- History -- 1917-1991, Soviet Union 3. Food habits -- Soviet Union 4. Moscow (Russia) -- Biography 5. Russian Americans -- Biography 6. Soviet Union -- Social life and customs 7. Women cooks -- Soviet Union -- Biography 8. Food writers -- United States -- Biography 9.

Cooking, Russian -- History -- 20th century 10. Russia
(Federation) -- Social conditions -- 1991-
ISBN 0307886816; 9780307886811

LC 2013007787

This book by Anya von Bramzen presents "a memoir
of life in Soviet Russia. The book is subdivided by decade,
and von Bremzen . . . weaves her own memories together
with stories from her grandmother and mother, beginning in
1910. The common denominator--and recurring touchstone-
-is food. . . . Von Bremzen concludes with nine recipes."
(Library Journal)

"With anecdotes, history and recipes, the author delivers
a lively, precisely detailed cultural chronicle." Kirkus

Includes bibliographical references

Wadi, Sameh

The **new** mediterranean cookbook; incredible
dishes inspired by cooking traditions spanning three
continents. Sameh Wadi. Page Street Pub. Co. 2015
224 p. color illustrations (pbk.) $28   **641.59**
1. Mediterranean cooking
ISBN 1624140955; 1624141048; 9781624140952;
9781624141041

LC 2014950215

In this Mediterranean cookbook, chef Sameh Wadi "offers a collection of recipes that represent an exceptional look
into his rich heritage, the culinary foundation that has propelled him to the top of the American restaurant scene. . .
. He takes influences from everything from Mediterranean
street food to top gourmet offerings and gives you the best of
the Mediterranean, one recipe at a time." (Publisher's note)

Wells, Patricia

Patricia Wells at home in Provence; recipes inspired by her farmhouse in France. Patricia Wells;
photographs by Robert Freson. Fireside 1999 355 p.
col il (paperback) $24   **641.59**
1. Cookbooks 2. French cooking 3. Provence (France)
-- Description 4. French cooking -- Provencal style
ISBN 9780684815695; 9780684863283; 0684863286

LC 00266924

James Beard Award (1997)

In this French cookbook, Patricia Wells, "the award-
winning journalist and author invites readers to share the
passion, the joy, and, best of all, the cooking of her adopted
home. Provence is uniquely blessed with natural beauty as
well as some of the world's most appealing foods and liveli-
est wines. . . . Here are 175 recipes from Patricia's farmhouse kitchen." (Publisher's note)

Willan, Anne

The **country** cooking of France; by Anne Willan;
photographs by France Ruffenach. Chronicle Books
2007 390 p. ill. (chiefly col.), col. map $50 **641.59**
1. Cookbooks 2. French cooking 3. Cooking, French
ISBN 0811846466; 9780811846462

LC 2007004773

James Beard Award (2008)

This cookbook, by Anne Willan, "combines years of
hands-on experience with extensive research to create a
brand new classic. More than 250 recipes range from the
time-honored La Truffade, with its crispy potatoes and

melted cheese, to the Languedoc specialty Cassoulet de Toulouse, a bean casserole of duck confit, sausage, and lamb."
(Publisher's note)

Wolfert, Paula

Couscous and other good food from Morocco;
Introd. by Gael Green. Color photos. by Bill Bayer.
Drawings by Sidonie Coryn. Harper & Row 1973
xv, 351 p.p illus. (part col.) $19.99   **641.59**
1. Cookbooks 2. Moroccan cooking 3. Cooking,
Moroccan
ISBN 0060147210; 0060913967; 9780060913960

LC 72009165

IACP Culinary Classics Book Award (2013)
James Beard Cookbook Hall of Fame (2008)

"Since it was first published in 1973, 'Couscous and
Other Good Food from Morocco' has established itself as
the classic work on one of the world's great cuisines, and in
2008 it was inducted into the James Beard Cookbook Hall
of Fame. From the magnificent bisteeyas . . . to endless varieties of couscous, [author] Paula Wolfert reveals not only
the riches of the Moroccan kitchen but also the variety and
flavor of the country itself." (Publisher's note)

Bibliography: p. 342

The **food** of Morocco; Paula Wolfert; photographs by Quentin Bacon; drawings by Mark Mar-
thaler. Ecco 2011 518 p. ill. (chiefly col.), col. maps
$45   **641.59**
1. Cookbooks 2. Moroccan cooking
ISBN 0061957550; 9780061957550

LC 2011278431

James Beard Award (2012)

This cookbook, by Paula Wolfert, "provides food lovers
with the definitive guide to the food of Morocco. Lavishly
photographed and packed with tantalizing recipes to please
the modern palate, . . . [the book] provides helpful preparation techniques for chefs, home cooks, and any serious
student of the culinary arts and culture." (Publisher's note)

Deftly balancing authenticity with ease of preparation, .
. . Wolfert is an eager and encouraging host, walking readers through the various regions and their signature dishes as
well as the handful of ingredients that make the cuisine so
distinctive." Pub Wkly

Includes bibliographical references and index

Mediterranean clay pot cooking; traditional and
modern recipes to savor and share. Paula Wolfert.
John Wiley & Sons 2009 xviii, 334 p.p ill. (chiefly
col.) (cloth) $34.95   **641.59**
1. Cookbooks 2. Clay pot cooking 3. Mediterranean
cooking
ISBN 076457633X; 9780764576331

LC 2008055912

In this cookbook, author Paula Wolfert, "shares her inimitable passion for detail and insatiable curiosity about cultural traditions and innovations. . . . Here, the self-confessed
clay pot 'junkie'--having collected in her travels ceramic
pots of all sorts . . . shares recipes as vibrant as the Mediterranean itself along with the delightful stories behind the
earthy pots, irresistible dishes, and outstanding cooks she
has met along the way." (Publisher's note)

"Wolfert is a true cook's author, and . . . this book is not for the casual home cook. But for those willing to tackle them, Wolfert's clay pot dishes do indeed merit the hype." Pub Wkly

Includes bibliographical references and index

Wong, Lee Anne

Dumplings All Day Wong; A Cookbook of Asian Delights from a Top Chef. by Lee Anne Wong. St. Martin's Press 2014 256 p. color illustrations $22.99 **641.59**

1. Cookbooks 2. Dumplings 3. Asian cooking
ISBN 1624140599; 9781624140594

LC 2013922991

This book, by celebrity chef Lee Anne Wong, "will have you creating one-of-a-kind dumplings that wow your family and friends. Folds such as Potstickers, Gyozas, Shumai, Har Gow, Wontons and more, along with countless fillings and different cooking methods such as steaming, pan-frying, baking or deep-frying, allow you to create awe-inspiring dumplings in innumerable ways." (Publisher's note)

"This excellent dumpling cookbook highlights a wealth of flavors and techniques and advocates a from-scratch approach. The simpler dumplings in Bee Yin Low's Easy Chinese Recipes would make a great starting point for novices." LJ

641.594 Cooking--Europe

Bastianich, Lidia

Lidia's favorite recipes; 100 foolproof Italian dishes, from basic sauces to irresistible entrées. by Lidia Matticchio Bastianich and Tanya Bastianich Manuali; photographs by Marcus Nilsson. Alfred A. Knopf 2012 240 p. color illustrations $24.95 **641.594**

1. Cookbooks 2. Italian cooking
ISBN 0307595668; 9780307595669

LC 2012023455

This book by Lidia Matticchio Bastianich and Tanya Bastianich Manuali presents "the recipes for dishes that [have been] raved and written about over and over--the best, the most comforting, and the most delicious dishes in [Lidia's] repertoire. With new information about the affordability, seasonality, and nutritional value of the ingredients, this book shows there is no question why these dishes are the easiest and most enjoyable to bring to the family table." (Publisher's note)

"More compact than Bastianich's other titles, this practical collection is perfect for families as well as readers who enjoyed Viana La Place and Evan Kleiman's Cucina Rustica." LJ

Lidia's mastering the art of Italian cuisine; everything you need to know to be a great Italian cook. by Lidia Mattichio Bastianich, with Tanya Bastianich

Manuali. Alfred A. Knopf 2015 480 p. (hardcover) $37.50 **641.594**

1. Italian cooking 2. Cooking, Italian
ISBN 0385349467; 9780385349468

LC 2015001871

Author Lidia Mattichho Bastianich presents this "guide to Italian cooking, coauthored with her daughter, Tanya [Bastianich Manuali]--covering everything from ingredients to techniques to tools, plus more than 400 delectable recipes. Lidia introduces us to the full range of standard ingredients--meats and fish, vegetables and fruits, grains, spices and condiments--and how to buy, store, clean, and cook with them." (Publisher's note)

"The book completes its course with a charming chapter on Italian culture and language, as well as an extensive glossary of food terms. With this passionate treatise on Italian food and culture, readers dreaming of la dolce vita may find armchair travels enough to satisfy their hunger." Pub Wkly

Mastering the art of italian cuisine

Bottura, Massimo

Never Trust a Skinny Italian Chef; Massimo Bottura. Phaidon Inc Ltd 2014 296 p. color illustrations $59.95 **641.594**

1. Cooking 2. Italian cooking
ISBN 0714867144; 9780714867144

James Beard Foundation Award Nominee: Cooking from a Professional Point of View (2015)

This cookbook by Massimo Bottura is "a tribute to [his] twenty-five year career and the evolution of Osteria Francescana, his three Michelin star restaurant based in Modena, Italy. Divided into four chapters, each one dealing with a different period, the book features 50 recipes and stories explaining Bottura's inspirations (including the music and art that motivates him), ingredients, and techniques." (Publisher's note)

"Quirky dishes such as a deconstructed mortadella sandwich made with mortadella foam; bread, butter, and anchovies; and a compression of pasta and beans make this a fun collection to peruse, but one unlikely to inspire home cooks. Professionals, however, will relish the opportunity for guided experimentation with Italian classics." Pub Wkly

Clark, Melissa

Franny's; simple seasonal Italian. by Andrew Feinberg, Francine Stephens, Melissa Clark. Artisan 2013 ix, 366 p.p ill. (some col.) (hardcover) $35.00 **641.594**

1. Cooking 2. Cookbooks 3. Cooking, Italian 4. Cooking -- New York (State) -- Brooklyn
ISBN 1579654649; 9781579654641

LC 2012028954

In this book, Andrew Feinberg and Francine Stephens, owners of the Brooklyn, New York restaurant Franny's, offer recipes "for everything from soups, salads, and fritti to fish, vegetables, and cocktails." For more complicated recipes, "the authors provide straightforward step-by-step instructions accompanied by photos that demonstrate the proper technique." (Publishers Weekly)

Includes index.

Hercules, Olias

Mamushka; A Cookbook. Olia Hercules. Weldon Owen 2015 240 p. color illustrations $35 **641.594**

1. Cooking 2. Ukraine 3. Eastern Europe
ISBN 1616289619; 9781616289614

This cookbook by Olia Hercules is a "celebration of the food, flavors, and heritage of Eastern Europe--from the Black Sea to Baku, Kiev to Kazakhsta--[and] features over 100 recipes for fresh, delicious, and unexpected dishes from this dynamic yet underappreciated region. [It] showcases the cuisine from Ukraine and beyond, weaving together vibrant food with descriptive narratives and stunning lifestyle photography." (Publisher's note)

Hercules's unexpected Ukranian, Azerbaijani, Russian, and Armenian comfort foods can help home cooks transition to colder months." LJ

Hoffman, Susanna

The olive and the caper; adventures in Greek cooking. by Susanna Hofman; in collaboration with Victoria Wise. Workman Pub. Co. 2004 xvii, 589 p.p ill. (some col.) $19.95 **641.594**

1. Greek cooking 2. Greece -- Social life and customs 3. Cooking, Greek 4. Food habits -- Greece
ISBN 0761134689; 1563058480; 9781563058486
LC 2004040862

This book, by Susanna Hofman, combines "recipes and adventure. . . . Including 325 recipes developed in collaboration with Victoria Wise, . . . [it] celebrates all things Greek: Chicken Neo-Avgolemeno. Fall-off-the-bone Lamb Shanks. . . . Siren-like sweets, from world-renowned Baklava to uniquely Greek preserves. . . . In addition, it . . . has dozens of lively essays throughout the book--about the origins of Greek food, about village life, history, language, [and] customs." (Publisher's note)

"With its fascinating trove of information, this work will please armchair cooks and traveling foodies. For those willing to surrender to its searingly bright palate of flavors, it's a boon to the kitchen, too. Photos, illus. (July)Forecast: With the Olympics in Athens next month, interest should be strong." Pub Wkly

Includes bibliographical references and index

How to eataly; a guide to buying, cooking, and eating Italian food. Written by Eataly, Foreword by Mario Batali, Lidia Bastianich, Joseph Bastianich and Oscar Farinetti. Rizzoli International Publications 2014 304 p. illustrations (chiefly color) $35 **641.594**

1. Cookbooks 2. Italian cooking
ISBN 0847843351; 9780847843350
LC 2014941649

This cookbook, by Eataly, with a foreword by Mario Batali, Lidia Bastianich, Joseph Bastianich and Oscar Farinetti, offers "the secrets to Italian cooking, straight from the source—the wildly popular food emporium that is founded in Italy. . . . Learn how to assemble an antipasto platter, how to eat breakfast like an Italian, and how to use pantry flavor boosters like capers and anchovies." (Publisher's note)

Italian Comfort Food; by The Editors of Saveur. Simon & Schuster 2015 224 p. color illustrations $35 **641.594**

1. Italian cooking
ISBN 1616289643; 9781616289645

This cookbook, by The Editors of Saveur, "features 100 recipes from the magazine's archives and editors. . . . With classic and brand new recipes, this cookbook presents the flavors, ingredients and techniques you need for Italian comfort food. This masterful selection illuminates SAVEUR's authority, heritage, and culinary wealth." (Publisher's note)

Kochilas, Diane

Ikaria; lessons on food, life, and longevity from the Greek island where people forget to die. Diane Kochilas; photographs by Vassillis Stenos. Rodale 2014 306 p. color illustrations (hardback) $35 **641.594**

1. Longevity 2. Greek cooking 3. Greece -- Description and travel 4. Cooking, Greek 5. Ikaria (Greece : Municipality) 6. Food -- Greece -- Ikaria (Municipality) 7. Cooking -- Greece -- Ikaria (Municipality)
ISBN 1623362954; 9781623362959
LC 2014032164

IACP Cookbook Award Winner: International (2015)

This book, by Diane Kochilas, is "[p]art cookbook, part travelogue, filled with gorgeous photography, stunning recipes, and interviews with locals. . . . We'll learn about the life-giving benefits of delicious salads both raw and cooked, the gorgeous breads and savory pies that are a part of every meal, the bean dishes that are passed down through generations, and the seafood that is at the root of the Ikarian culinary culture." (Publisher's note)

Includes bibliographical references and index

Loomis, Susan Herrmann

In a French kitchen; tales and traditions of everyday home cooking in France. Susan Herrmann Loomis. Gotham Books 2015 320 p. $26.95 **641.594**

1. French cooking 2. Cooking, French 3. Food habits -- France
ISBN 1592408869; 9781592408863
LC 2014035856

In this book, expat Susan Herrmann Loomis "demystifies . . . the seemingly effortless je ne sais quoi behind a simple French meal. One by one, readers are invited to meet the busy people of Louviers and surrounding villages and towns of Loomis's adopted home, from runway-chic Edith, who has zero passion for cooking--but a love of food that inspires her to whip up an array of mouthwatering dishes--to Nathalie, who becomes misty-eyed as she talks about her mother's Breton cooking." (Publisher's note)

"Loomis also shares scores of recipes from her own repertoire and those of her friends, including a 12-month meal plan based on fresh, seasonal ingredients. A tempting and helpful guide to delectable food." Kirkus

Minchilli, Elizabeth

Eating Rome; living the good life in the Eternal City. Elizabeth Minchilli. St. Martin's Griffin 2015 256 p. illustrations (trade pbk.) $24.99 **641.594**

1. Rome (Italy) 2. Italian cooking 3. Cooking, Italian

4. Restaurants -- Italy -- Rome 5. Grocery shopping -- Italy -- Rome 6. Dinners and dining -- Italy -- Rome
ISBN 1250047684; 9781250047687

LC 2014044288

This book, by Elizabeth Minchilli, "is a personal . . . look at some of the city[of Rome]'s monuments to food culture. Join her as she takes you on a stroll through her favorite open air markets; stop by the best gelato shops; order plates full of carbonara and finish the day with a brilliant red Negroni." (Publisher's note)

"Minchilli is biased toward family-run specialty shops in certain neighborhoods, and she reflects on the changing culinary scene with the rise of the Roman brunch and the closing of many traditional spots." Pub Wkly

Moulle, Jean Pierre

French roots; two cooks, two countries, and the beautiful food along the way. Jean-Pierre Moullé and Denise Lurton Moullé. Ten Speed Press 2014 272 p. color illustrations (hardcover) $35 **641.594**
1. Cooks 2. California 3. French cooking 4. Cooking, French 5. Cooks -- United States -- Biography
ISBN 160774547X; 9781607745471

LC 2014023823

IACP Cookbook Award Finalist: Julia Child First Book (2015)

This book, by Jean-Pierre Moullé and Denise Lurton Moullé, "is the story of their lives told through the food they cook-- beginning with the dishes of old-world France, the couple's birthplace, and focusing on the simple, pared-down preparations of French food common in the postwar period. The story then travels to the San Francisco Bay Area in the 1970s, where Jean-Pierre was appointed executive chef at Chez Panisse when California cuisine was just emerging." (Publisher's note)

"Readers who have an active imaginary life in France will relish poring over this cookbook's extensive narrative. Fans of Chez Panisse will enjoy pairing it with titles from other chef alums, such as David Tanis and David Lebovitz." LJ

Nolen, Jeremy

German cooking now; 100 recipes for family-style meals. by Jeremy and Jessica Nolen with Drew Lazor; photographs by Jason Varney. Chronicle Books LLC 2014 248 p. color illustrations (hardcover) $40 **641.594**
1. Cookbooks 2. German cooking 3. Cooking, German
ISBN 9781452128061; 1452128065

LC 2014000717

This cookbook, by Jeremy and Jessica Nolen with Drew Lazor, with photography by Jason Varney, "celebrates fresh vegetables, grains, herbs, and spices as obsessively as it does pork, pretzels, and beer. Chefs Jeremy and Jessica Nolen share recipes from their family table, inspired by their travels in Germany." (Publisher's note)

"Despite its traditional leanings, this German cookbook is refined and chic, with very clear instructions." LJ

Includes bibliographical references (page 228) index

Thorisson, Mimi

A **kitchen** in France; a year of cooking in my farmhouse. Mimi Thorisson; photographs by Oddur Thorisson. Clarkson Potter/Publishers 2014 304 p. illustrations (print edition : alkaline paper) $40 **641.594**
1. Cookbooks 2. French cooking 3. Country life -- France 4. Cooking, French 5. Cooking -- France -- Médoc 6. Seasons -- France -- Médoc 7. Médoc (France) -- Biography 8. Farmhouses -- France -- Médoc 9. Seasonal cooking -- France -- Médoc 10. Médoc (France) -- Description and travel 11. Médoc (France) -- Social life and customs
ISBN 080418559X; 9780804185592

LC 2013049107

IACP Cookbook Award Finalist: Photography (2015)

This cookbook, by Mimi Thorisson, "chronicles the family's seasonal meals and life in an old farmhouse, all photographed by her husband, Oddur. Mimi's convivial recipes--such as Roast Chicken with Herbs and Crème Fraîche, Cèpe and Parsley Tartlets, Winter Vegetable Cocotte, Apple Tart with Orange Flower Water, and Salted Butter Crème Caramel--will bring the warmth of rural France into your home." (Publisher's note)

"And while the appeal of this collection rests firmly on its recipes, the incredible photographs capture life in the French countryside. Sidebars on everything from dried grapevines and wine to garlic and visits the butcher add little details that transport the reader to this bucolic, idyllic world where Thorisson is the perfect host."

Waters, Alice, 1944-

My pantry; Alice Waters; illustrations by Fanny Singer. Pam Krauss Books 2015 144 p. illustrations $24.99 **641.594**
1. Cooking 2. Grocery shopping 3. Spices 4. Cooking, French
ISBN 080418528X; 9780804185288; 9780804185295

LC 2014042977

Author Alice Waters, with Fanny Singer, "invites readers to step not into the kitchen at Chez Panisse, but into her own, sharing how she shops, stores, and prepares the pantry staples and preserves that form the core of her daily meals. Ranging from essentials like homemade chicken stock, red wine vinegar, and tomato sauce to the unique artisanal provisions that embody Alice's unadorned yet delightful cooking style, she shows how she injects even simple meals with nuanced flavor." (Publisher's note)

"The truly ambitious may make their own simple, unaged cheeses. Not everyone has access to the sorts of ingredients available in Waters' Mediterranean climate, but creative cooks can adapt local produce in season to Waters' techniques." Booklist

Weiss, Jeffrey

Charcuteria; the soul of Spain. Jeffrey Weiss. Surrey Books 2013 460 p. (hardcover) $39.95 **641.594**
1. Cooking -- Meat 2. Spanish cooking 3. Cooking (Meat)
ISBN 1572841524; 9781572841529

LC 2013018755

This cookbook, by Jeffrey Weiss, "is the first book to introduce authentic Spanish butchering and meat-curing techniques to America. Included are more than 100 traditional Spanish recipes, straightforward illustrations providing easy-to-follow steps for amateur and professional butchers, and gorgeous full-color photography of savory dishes, Iberian countrysides, and centuries-old Spanish cityscapes." (Publisher's note)

Wells, Patricia

The **French** kitchen cookbook; recipes and lessons from Paris and Provence. Patricia Wells; photographs by Jeff Kauck. HarperCollinsPublishers 2013 312 p. color illustrations $35   **641.594**
1. French cooking 2. Cooking, French 3. Cooking -- France -- Paris 4. Cooking -- France -- Provence
ISBN 0062088912; 9780062088918

LC 2013013311

In this cookbook, chef Patricia Wells "invites home cooks into her life in France, making the fresh and delicious recipes from her popular classes. . . . Here are some of her best recipes for appetizers, desserts, and everything in between, dishes inspired by the vibrant Provençal countryside and the bustle of Parisian life." (Publisher's note)

641.595   Cooking--Asia

Chattman, Lauren

Maangchi's real Korean cooking; authentic dishes for the home cook. Maangchi with Lauren Chattman; photographs by Maangchi. Houghton Mifflin Harcourt 2015 320 p. color illustrations (hardcover) $30   **641.595**
1. Cooking 2. Korean cooking
ISBN 054412989X; 9780544129894; 9780544465756

LC 2015004571

In this book on Korean cooking, author Maangchi " shows how to cook all the country's best dishes, from few-ingredient dishes (Spicy Napa Cabbage) to those made familiar by Korean restaurants (L.A. Galbi, Bulgogi, Korean Fried Chicken) to homey one-pots like Bibimbap." (Publisher's note)

"Like Robert Danhi's Easy Thai Cooking and Bee Yin Low's Easy Chinese Recipes, this encouraging and instructional cookbook demystifies Asian home cooking. First-timers to Korean restaurants and grocery stores will be grateful for Maangchi's introductory chapters." LJ

Erway, Cathy

The **food** of Taiwan; recipes from the beautiful island. Cathy Erway; photography by Pete Lee. Houghton Mifflin Harcourt 2015 256 p. color illustrations (paper over board) $30   **641.595**
1. Cookbooks 2. Taiwanese cooking 3. Food -- Taiwan 4. Taiwan -- Description and travel 5. Cooking, Chinese -- Taiwanese style
ISBN 0544303016; 9780544303010

LC 2014016524

This book, by Cathy Erway, photography by Pete Lee, "offers an insider's look at Taiwanese cooking--from home-

style dishes to authentic street food. . . . Recipes range from the familiar, such as Pork Belly Buns, Three Cup Chicken, and Beef Noodle Soup, to the exotic, like the Stuffed Bitter Melon, Oyster Noodle Soup, and Dried Radish Omelet." (Publisher's note)

"A fabulous addition to any collection." LJ

Ghayour, Sabrina

Persiana; recipes from the Middle East & beyond. by Sabrina Ghayour. Interlink Books, an imprint of Interlink Publishing Group, Inc. 2015 240 p. $35   **641.595**
1. Cookbooks 2. Middle Eastern cooking 3. International cooking 4. Cooking, Middle Eastern
ISBN 1566569958; 9781566569958

LC 2014021227

This book, by Sabrina Ghayour, is "a celebration of the food and flavors from the regions near the Southern and Eastern shores of the Mediterranean Sea, with over 100 recipes for modern and accessible Middle Eastern dishes, including Lamb & Sour Cherry Meatballs; . . . Blood Orange & Radicchio Salad; . . . and Spiced Carrot, Pistachio & Coconut Cake with Rosewater Cream." (Publisher's note)

"Though the decidedly 70's font and presentation wears a little thin, this is an outstanding collection that will surely win readers over and inspire many a meal." Pub Wkly

Greeley, Alexandra

Nong's Thai kitchen; 84 classic and contemporary recipes that are healthy and delicious. Nongkran Daks and Alexandra Greeley. Tuttle Publishing 2015 160 p. color illustrations (pbk.) $14.95   **641.595**
1. Cookbooks 2. Thai cooking 3. Cooking, Thai
ISBN 0804843317; 9780804843317

LC 2014030057

In this cookbook, author Nongkran Daks "shares her secrets for creating Thai cuisine's most beloved dishes at home--using ingredients that can be found in most grocery stores. Daks teams up with veteran food writer Alexandra Greeley to show readers how to prepare classic Thai recipes." (Publisher's note)

"Chef in suburban Washington, D.C., Daks offers recipes for all manner of Thai dishes to re-create at home. Ever-popular satay can be grilled indoors or out, and the spicy peanut-coconut sauce that makes satay almost universally appreciated turns out to be easy to reproduce from ingredients available in most well-stocked supermarkets." Booklist

Ha, Robin

Cook Korean! a comic book with recipes. Robin Ha. Ten Speed Press 2016 176 p. color illustrations (paperback) $19.99   **641.595**
1. Cookbooks 2. Korean cooking 3. Cooking, Korean -- Comic books, strips, etc
ISBN 9781607748878

LC 2015047866

This cookbook and graphic novel by Robin Ha "is the ideal introduction to cooking Korean cuisine at home. Ha's colorful and humorous one- to three-page comics fully illustrate the steps and ingredients needed to bring more than sixty traditional (and some not-so-traditional) dishes to life. . . . You'll learn how to create everything from easy kimchi (mak kimchi) and soy garlic beef over rice (bulgogi dupbap) to seaweed rice rolls (gimbap) and beyond." (Publisher's note)

"Like Maangchi's Real Korean Cooking, this highly recommended collection is a solid introduction for readers who feel daunted by Korean cooking and ingredients." LJ

Includes bibliographical references and index

Jaffrey, Madhur

★ **Vegetarian** India; a journey through the best of Indian home cooking. Madhur Jaffrey. Alfred A. Knopf 2015 448 p. illustrations (hardcover : alk. paper) $35 **641.595**
  1. Vegetarianism 2. Indian cooking 3. Cooking, Indic 4. Vegetarian cooking
  ISBN 1101874864; 9781101874868
LC 2014048953

Author Madhur Jaffrey "shares the delectable, healthful, vegetable- and grain-based foods enjoyed around the Indian subcontinent. Jaffrey travels from north to south, and from the Arabian Sea to the Bay of Bengal, collecting recipes for the very tastiest dishes along the way. She visits the homes and businesses of shopkeepers, writers, designers, farmers, doctors, weavers, and more, gathering their stories and uncovering the secrets of their most delicious family specialties." (Publisher's note)

"Jaffrey's fresh compilation features extraordinary variety and achieves approachability without oversimplification. Highly recommended for vegetarians and Indian food enthusiasts." LJ

Joo, Judy

Korean food made simple; Judy Joo; With Vivian Jao; Photography by Jean Cazals. Houghton Mifflin Harcourt 2016 288 p. (hardback) $30 **641.595**
  1. Cookbooks 2. Korean cooking 3. Cooking, Korean
  ISBN 9780544663305
LC 2015049784

This cookbook, by Judy Joo, with Vivian Jao, and photography by Jean Cazals, "brings Korean food to the masses, proving that it's fun and easy to prepare at home. . . . The book has over 100 recipes including well-loved dishes like kimchi, sweet potato noodles (japchae), beef and vegetable rice bowl (bibimbap), and Korean fried chicken, along with creative, less-traditional recipes." (Publisher's note)

"Cooks looking to make a first foray into Korean cooking or those wishing to enhance their knowledge will delight in Joo's uncommon approach and her tasty creations." Pub Wkly

Kian Lam Kho

Phoenix claws and jade trees; essential techniques of authentic Chinese cooking. Kian Lam Kho; photographs by Jody Horton. Clarkson Potter 2015 368 p. color illustrations $35 **641.595**
  1. Chinese cooking 2. China -- Social life and customs
  ISBN 0385344686; 9780385344685
LC 2014046694

This cookbook by Kian Lam Kho "offers a unique introduction to Chinese home cooking, demystifying it by focusing on its basic cooking methods. In outlining the differences among various techniques--such as pan-frying, oil

steeping, and yin-yang frying--and instructing which one is best for particular ingredients and end results, culinary expert Kian Lam Kho provides a practical, intuitive window into this unique cuisine." (Publisher's note)

"Kho rounds out his excellent book with recipes and lessons on smoking as well as cold and sweet dishes. This extraordinary collection is a must-have for anyone interested in Chinese cuisine." Pub Wkly

Includes bibliographical references and index

Maffei, Yvonne

My halal kitchen; Global Recipes, Cooking Tips, and Lifestyle Inspiration. by Yvonne M. Maffei. Surrey, an Agate imprint 2016 224 p. color illustrations (hardback) $29.95 **641.595**
  1. Middle Eastern cooking 2. Islamic cooking 3. Cooking, Middle Eastern 4. Food -- Religious aspects -- Islam
  ISBN 1572841745; 9781572841741
LC 2016001808

This book, by Yvonne M. Maffei, "celebrates halal cooking and shows readers how easy it can be to prepare halal meals. Her cookbook collects more than 100 recipes from a variety of culinary traditions, proving that halal meals can be full of diverse flavors. Home cooks will learn to make classic American favorites and comfort foods, as well as international dishes that previously may have seemed out of reach: Coq without the Vin, Shrimp Pad Thai, Chicken Tamales, and many more." (Publisher's note)

"An approachable introduction to halal home cooking for Muslim and non-Muslim families alike." LJ

Includes bibliographical references and index

Meehan, Peter

Lucky Peach 101 easy Asian recipes; Peter Meehan and the editors of Lucky Peach; Photographs by Gabriele Stabile. Clarkson Potter/Publishers 2015 272 p. color illustrations $35 **641.595**
  1. Asian cooking 2. Southeast Asian cooking
  ISBN 0804187797; 9780804187794
LC 2015015729

Author Peter Meehan "present[s] a compendium of recipes that hit the sweet spot between craveworthy and stupid simple and are destined to become favorites. Your friends and lovers will marvel as you show off your culinary worldliness, whipping up meals with fish-sauce-splattered panache and all the soy-soaked, ginger-scalliony goodness you could ever want--all for dinner tonight." (Publisher's note)

"Readers will also appreciate the surprising lack of prep for many dishes; few require chopping and dicing multitudes of vegetables or sourcing ingredients that are difficult to find in the U.S. This is an outstanding, practical guide sure to inspire even the most discouraged home cook." Pub Wkly

Sodha, Meera

Made in India; recipes from an Indian family kitchen. Meera Sodha. St. Martin's Press 2015 319 p. color illustrations $35 **641.595**
  1. Indian cooking 2. India -- Social life and customs
  ISBN 1250071011; 9781250071019

In this cookbook author Meera Sodha presents "over 130 delicious recipes collected from three generations of her family. On the menu is everything from hot chapatis to street food (chili paneer; beet and feta samosas), fragrant curries (spinach and salmon, or perfect cinnamon lamb curry) to colorful side dishes (pomegranate and mint raita; kachumbar salad), and mouthwatering desserts (mango, lime, and passion fruit jello; pistachio and saffron kulfi)." (Publisher's note)

"Sodha offers helpful sections explaining how each Indian ingredient tastes and the best ways to use it, and how to fix a dish that's too spicy or salty. The power of this book lies in its simplicity—both in terms of ingredients and technique." Publisher's Weekly

Srulovich, Itamar

Honey & Co. the cookbook. Itamar Srulovich, Sarit Packer. Little, Brown & Co. 2015 304 p. color illustrations $35   **641.595**
1. Cooking 2. Restaurants 3. Middle Eastern cooking
ISBN 0316284300; 9780316284301

LC 2014953286

In this cookbook by Itamar Srulovich and Sarit Packer, "recipes include spreads and dips, exquisitely balanced salads, one-pan dishes, simple fragrant soups, rich Persian entrees, the tagines of North Africa, the Sofritos of Jerusalem, and the herb-infused stews of Iran. HONEY & CO. brings the flavors of the Middle East to life in a wholly accessible way, certain to entice and satisfy in equal measure." (Publisher's note)

"This restaurant cookbook is representative of the hottest trends and has enough variety to be suitable for everyday use." LJ

West, Da-Hae

K-food; Korean home cooking and street food. Da-Hae West, Gareth West. Octopus Pub Group 2016 240 p. color illustrations (hardcover) $24.99   **641.595**
1. Cookbooks 2. Korean cooking
ISBN 9781784721596; 178472159X

This cookbook, by Da-Hae West and Gareth West, offers instruction on Korean cuisine "from a run-down on the basics of Korean cooking, including now readily available sauces, pastes and other ingredients, through chapters on kimchi and the etiquette of the famous Korean BBQ, to recipes for everything from the irresistible Bulgogi Burger and spicy, sticky spare ribs to Panjeon (seafood pancakes) and corn on the cob with kimchi butter." (Publisher's note)

"Korean cookbooks are very popular right now—this one will satisfy adventurous cooks looking for contemporary recipes." LJ

Ying, Chris

The Mission Chinese Food Cookbook; Danny Bowien and Chris Ying. HarperCollins 2015 336 p. color illustrations (hardcover) $34.99   **641.595**
1. Cookbooks 2. Restaurants 3. Chinese cooking
ISBN 9780062243416; 0062243411

This cookbook, by Danny Bowien and Chris Ying, "tracks the fascinating, meteoric rise of the [Mission Chinese Food] restaurant and its chef. Each chapter in the story—from the restaurant's early days, to an ill-fated trip to China, to the opening of the first Mission Chinese in New York—unfolds as a conversation between Danny and his collaborators, and is accompanied by detailed recipes for the addictive dishes that have earned the restaurant global praise." (Publisher's note)

"To hear Bowien in his own words is a treat, and his debut cookbook is not to be missed. Like Gabrielle Hamilton's Prune, this will thrill foodies and aspiring chefs." LJ

641.597   Cooking—North America

Acheson, Hugh

The broad fork; recipes for the wide world of vegetables and fruits. Hugh Acheson; photographs by Rinne Allen. Clarkson Potter/Publishers 2015 336 p. color illustrations $35   **641.597**
1. Farm produce 2. American cooking 3. Seasonal cooking 4. Southern cooking
ISBN 038534502X; 9780385345026

LC 2014023531

This book, by Hugh Acheson, is "a seasonal cookbook of 200 recipes designed to make the most of your farmers' market bounty, your CSA box, or your grocery produce aisle. . . . Beautifully written, this book brings fresh produce to the center of your plate. It's what both your doctor and your grocery bill have been telling you to do, and Hugh gives us the knowledge and the inspiration to wrap ourselves around produce in new ways." (Publisher's note)

Ahern, Shauna James

Gluten-Free Girl American classics reinvented; Shauna James Ahern and Daniel Ahern; photography by Lauren Volo. Houghton Mifflin Harcourt 2015 320 p. color illustrations (paper over board) $29.99   **641.597**
1. Cookbooks 2. American cooking 3. Gluten-free diet 4. Cooking, American 5. Gluten-free diet -- Recipes
ISBN 0544219880; 9780544219885

LC 2015007133

This cookbook, by Shauna James Ahern and Daniel Ahern, with photography by Lauren Volo, offers "a collection of comfort-food classics that are all . . . gluten-free. Cinnamon Rolls with Cream Cheese Frosting, Chicken-Fried Steak, New England Clam Chowder--the country's most beloved dishes, reinvented. Of course, it wouldn't be true comfort food without dessert, and Shauna aptly provides plenty of delicious recipes for sweets lovers." (Publisher's note)

"Those who feel limited on a gluten-free diet will rejoice in this extensive and appetizing collection of family favorites that can once again be on the menu." Pub Wkly

The America's test kitchen do-it-yourself cookbook; 100+ foolproof kitchen projects for the adventurous home cook. by the editors at America's test kitchen; photography by Anthony Tieuli. America's Test Kitchen 2012 viii, 360 p.p $26.95   **641.597**
1. Cookbooks 2. American cooking 3. Cooking, American
ISBN 193649308X; 9781936493081

LC 2012022144

In this book, the editors of the television cooking show America's Test Kitchen "walk home cooks step-by-step through more than 100 of their favorite D.I.Y. kitchen projects. . . . This book delivers a wide variety of projects, from jams and pickles like Grandma used to make to artisanal cheeses and cured meats that you usually have to pay top dollar for at a specialty shop." (Publisher's note)

Batali, Mario, 1960-
America--farm to table; simple, delicious recipes celebrating local farmers. Mario Batali and Jim Webster; food photography by Quentin Bacon; farm photography by Christine Birch Ferrelli and Lara Cerri. Grand Central Life & Style 2014 302 p. color illustrations (hardback) $35 **641.597**
1. Farms 2. Local foods 3. Farm produce 4. American cooking 5. Cooking, American 6. Local foods -- United States 7. Farms, small -- United States
ISBN 1455584681; 9781455584680; 9781455584697
LC 2014011984
In this book "author and . . . chef Mario Batali pays homage to the American farmer-from Maine to Los Angeles-in stories, photos, and recipes. . . . Batali asked his chef friends from Nashville, Tennessee, to San Francisco, to tell him who their favorite farmers were, and those farmers graciously shared their personal stories along with their top-of-the-line produce and products." (Publisher's note)
"No particular ingredient is sacred; all ingredients are celebrated in the unique farmer-chef-home-cook collaboration." Booklist

Mario Batali Big American cookbook; 250 favorite recipes from across the USA. Mario Batali with Jim Webster; photographs by Quentin Bacon. Grand Central Life & Style 2016 512 p. color illustrations (hardcover) $40 **641.597**
1. American cooking 2. Cooking, American 3. Local foods -- United States
ISBN 1455584711; 9781455584710; 9781455569663
LC 2016022712
This cookbook, by celebrity chef Mario Batali, presents "over 250 simple recipes celebrating the treasures of the state fairs and the dishes of the local rotary clubs and ethnic groups. Batali has interpreted these regional gems with the same excitement and passion that he has approached traditional Italian food." (Publisher's note)
"Boosting recipes with color photographs, Batali makes every dish look like great fun, and it's impossible not to share his enthusiasm." Booklist

Bayless, Rick, 1953-
Authentic Mexican; regional cooking from the heart of Mexico. Rick Bayless with Deann Groen Bayless; illustrations by John Sandford. William Morrow 1987 384 p. color illustrations; map $35 **641.597**
1. Mexican cooking
ISBN 0061373265; 0688043941; 9780061373268
LC 86012706
This Mexican cookbook, by Rick Bayless, "offers the full range of dishes, from poultry, meat, fish, rice, beans,

and vegetables to eggs, snacks made of corn masa, tacos, turnovers, enchiladas and their relatives, tamales, and moles, ending with desserts, sweets, and beverages. . . . Menu suggestions and timing and advance-preparation tips make these dishes perfectly convenient for today's working families. And traditional and contemporary variations accompany each recipe." (Publisher's note)
Bibliography: p. [357]-361

Mexican everyday; Rick Bayless, with Deann Groen Bayless; color photographs by Christopher Hirsheimer. 1st ed.; Norton 2005 336 p. col. ill. (hbk.) $29.95 **641.597**
1. Mexican cooking 2. Cooking, Mexican
ISBN 039306154X; 9780393061543
LC 2005023129
This Mexican cookbook, by Rick Bayless, "is a collection of 90 full-flavored recipes—like Green Chile Chicken Tacos, Shrimp Ceviche Salad, Chipotle Steak with Black Beans—that meet three criteria for 'everyday' food: 1) most need less than 30 minutes' involvement; 2) they have the fresh, clean taste of simple, authentic preparations; and 3) they are nutritionally balanced, full-featured meals—no elaborate side dishes required." (Publisher's note)
"Befitting the Mexican origins of these dishes, Bayless uses a wide variety of chiles, especially the deeply flavorful poblano. With virtually every recipe in the book, Bayless adds "riffs" that offer imaginative variations on the main recipe's techniques." Booklist

Mexico: one plate at a time; {by} Rick Bayless, with Jeanmarie Brownson and Deann Groen Bayless; color photographs by Bentl & Hayers; Mexican location photographs by James Baigrie. Scribner 2000 x, 374 p.p color illustrations $35 **641.597**
1. Mexican cooking
ISBN 068484186X; 9780684841861
LC 00058327
In this book, author Rick Bayless "takes us . . . through Mexican markets, street stalls and home kitchens to bring us the great dishes of Mexico, one 'plate' at a time. . . . To complete the journey into the Mexican mindset, Rick, with help from his testers, ends each 'plate' with a question-and-answer section. . . . Rick draws from his years of living in Mexico, pulling us into the Mexican kitchen, to teach us how to create authentic Mexican dishes in our American kitchens." (Publisher's note)
"There are helpful questions and answers at the end of each section, based on questions generated by recipe testers, an addition that may be unique to the cookbook genre. There is much here for both neophytes and experienced cooks. Highly recommended for all public libraries." LJ
Includes bibliographical references and index
Mexico one plate at a time

More Mexican everyday; simple, seasonal, celebratory. Rick Bayless, with Deann Groen Bayless and David Tamarkin; photographs by Hirsheimer and Hamilton. W.W. Norton & Co. Inc. 2015 384 p. color illustrations (hardcover) $35 **641.597**
1. Mexican cooking 2. Seasonal cooking 3. Cooking,

Mexican
ISBN 0393081141; 9780393081145

LC 2015005985

This Mexican cookbook, by Rick Bayless, "teaches home cooks how to build tasty meals with a few ingredients in a short amount of time. . . . He explains fully the classic techniques that create so many much-beloved Mexican meals, from tacos and enchiladas to pozole and mole. Home cooks under his guidance will be led confidently to making these their go-to recipes night after night." (Publisher's note)

"Recipes conclude with quick summaries of ingredients to ease shopping. An effective starting point for the would-be home Mexican cook." Booklist

Bryson, Francine

Blue ribbon baking from a redneck kitchen; Francine Bryson; foreword by Jeff Foxworthy; photographs by Ben Fink. Clarkson Potter/Publishers 2014 240 p. color illustrations $22   **641.597**
1. Desserts 2. Cookbooks 3. American cooking 4. Baking 5. Cooking, American -- Southern style
ISBN 0804185786; 9780804185783

LC 2014018086

In this cookbook, by Francine Bryson, the author explains, "here are the recipes and tricks I was taught by my Great-Granny, Granny, Nana, and Mama—the women who schooled me on the ways a Southern woman keeps a kitchen—and that I learned from twenty-plus years of competing on the baking circuit." (Author's note)

"Bryson is an eager and enthusiastic teacher, more concerned with instructing readers on how to get things right (they will do well to heed her many tips sprinkled throughout the book) than waving ribbons in their faces. She's not above including a classic like soda pop cake, peach cobbler, or store-bought cake mix to achieve her results. It adds up to a warm and welcoming collection that's sure to get plenty of use. Home bakers might as well pick up two copies, as the first one's likely to get dog-eared and butter-stained in a short amount of time." Pub Wkly

Christensen, Kate

How to cook a moose; my life in the northeast corner: a culinary memoir. Kate Christensen. Island-port Press 2015 298 p. (hardcover with dust jacket) $24.95   **641.597**
1. Cooking 2. New England 3. Food writing 4. Portland (Me.)
ISBN 1939017734; 9781939017734

LC 2014959692

This memoir, by Kate Christensen, is an "account of the unexpected fulfillment she found in New England, living, loving, cooking, and eating. . . . Christensen celebrates the land, food, and people of Maine. The state became her home after she and her partner, Brendan, decided to leave a beloved New Hampshire farmhouse. . . . They settled in the quietly cosmopolitan city of Portland, where they discovered restaurants that . . . rivaled those in larger cities like New York." (Kirkus Reviews)

"Christensen is eating well, in love, and radiating the 'quiet internal daily joy of living in a culture based on authenticity and integrity.' A warmly engaging culinary memoir." Kirkus

Cook's Country eats local; 150 regional recipes you should be making no matter where you live. by the editors at America's Test Kitchen. America's Test Kitchen 2015 320 p. (alk. paper) $26.95   **641.597**
1. American cooking 2. Cooking, American
ISBN 1936493993; 9781936493999

LC 2015005574

This cookbook provides "150 Regional Recipes. . . . From Maine's hearty Joe Booker Stew to pineapple-packed Hawaiian Fried Rice, this collection of recipes brings bold local flavors and tried-and-true cooking techniques home—no matter where that may be. Home cooks will discover little-known specialties and revamped classics in each of the four chapters: New England and the Mid-Atlantic, Appalachia and the South, The Midwest and Great Plains, Texas and the West." (Publisher's note)

"For families and home cooks seeking foolproof classic fare for potlucks, picnics, tailgates, and other occasions." LJ

Includes bibliographical references and index

Erickson, Renee

A boat, a whale, and a walrus; a year of menus. by Renee Erickson with Jess Thomson. Sasquatch Books 2014 320 p. illustrations (some color) (alk. paper) $40   **641.597**
1. American cooking 2. Seasonal cooking 3. Cooking, American -- Pacific Northwest style
ISBN 1570619263; 9781570619267

LC 2014021808

IACP Cookbook Award Finalist: Photography (2015)

This cookbook, by chef Renee Erickson, is "for anyone who loves the fresh seasonal food of the Pacific Northwest. Defined by the bounty of the Puget Sound region, as well as by French cuisine, [it] is filled with seasonal, personal menus like Renee's Fourth of July Crab Feast, Wild Foods Dinner, and a fall pickling party." (Publisher's note)

"If a trip to Seattle isn't possible, this book provides the next best way to enjoy Erickson's beautiful seafood." LJ

Includes bibliographical references and index

Flinn, Kathleen

Burnt toast makes you sing good; recipes of love, loss, and adventure from an American Midwest family. Kathleen Flinn. Viking 2014 288 p. illustrations $27.95   **641.597**
1. Family 2. American cooking 3. Cooks -- Untied States -- Biography 4. Cooking, American -- Midwestern style
ISBN 067001544X; 9780670015443

LC 2014004497

IACP Cookbook Award Finalist: Literary Food Writing (2015)

This memoir by Kathleen Flinn "offers a flavorful tale spanning three generations as Flinn returns to the mix of food and memoir readers loved in her New York Times best-seller 'The Sharper Your Knife, the Less You Cry.' From a Route 66 trek to San Francisco to their Michigan farm to the shores of Florida, humor and adventure defines her family even in the worst of times." (Publisher's note)

"As a young adult, Flinn aspired to attend her culinary idol Julia Child's alma mater, Le Cordon Bleu. More than a decade later, following along the well-worn path of a family love affair with food, she lived out her dream. A warm, quietly poignant treat." Kirkus

Includes bibliographical references and index

Food in the Civil War era; the North. edited by Helen Zoe Veit. Michigan State University Press 2014 205 p. illustrations (American food in history) (cloth : alkaline paper) $29.95 **641.597**

1. American cooking 2. Eating customs -- United States -- History 3. United States -- History -- 1861-1865, Civil War 4. Cooking, American -- History -- 19th century 5. Food -- United States -- History -- 19th century 6. Cookbooks -- United States -- History -- 19th century 7. Cooking, American -- History -- 19th century -- Sources 8. Food habits -- United States -- History -- 19th century 9. Food -- Social aspects -- United States -- History -- 19th century 10. United States -- History -- Civil War, 1861-1865 -- Social aspects

ISBN 1611861225; 9781611861228

LC 2013025306

IACP Cookbook Award Finalist: Culinary History (2015)

This book, edited by Helen Zoe Veit, "presents a variety of Civil War-era recipes from the South, accompanied by eye-opening essays describing this tumultuous period in the way people lived and ate. . . . Together, these recipes and essays provide a unique portrait of Southern life via the flavors, textures, and techniques that grew out of a time of crisis." (Publisher's note)

"The only criticism of this volume is that it does not sufficiently address the culinary diversity of the North, show popular cookbooks written by nonwhite authors, or discuss what the rural and urban poor consumed. Summing Up: Recommended. All food history collections." Choice

Gartland, Ashley

Heartlandia; heritage recipes from the Country Cat. by Adam and Jackie Sappington with Ashley Gartland. Houghton Mifflin Harcourt 2015 304 p. (hardcover) $30 **641.597**

1. Restaurants 2. Portland (Or.) 3. American cooking 4. Cooking, American 5. Country Cat Dinner House & Bar (Portland, Ore.)

ISBN 9780544363779; 0544363779

LC 2014036933

This cookbook "is based on husband-and-wife team Adam and Jackie Sappington's acclaimed Portland restaurant, The Country Cat Dinner House & Bar. . . . Some of the . . . dishes include Autumn Squash Soup with Apple Cider and Brown Butter, Red Wine-Braised Beef with Wild Mushroom Steak Sauce, and Crispy Fried Oysters with Smoky Bacon and Green Apple Ragout. . . . The sweets are just as enticing. . . . Additional chapters include one for drinks and another for pickles and preserves." (Publisher's note)

"A beautiful restaurant cookbook to have on hand in colder months, when you'll crave comforting meals." LJ

Humm, Daniel

The **NoMad** cookbook; Daniel Humm, Will Guidara, and Leo Robitschek. Ten Speed Press 2015 552 p. color illustrations, map (hardcover) $100 **641.597**

1. Cooking 2. Cocktails 3. NoMad Hotel (New York, N.Y.)

ISBN 9781607748229

LC 2015007694

This book, by Daniel Humm, Will Guidara, and Leo Robitschek, is a "uniquely packaged cookbook. . . . What appears to be a traditional cookbook is in fact two books in one: upon opening, readers discover that the back half contains false pages in which a smaller cocktail recipe book is hidden. The result is a wonderfully unexpected collection of both sweet and savory food recipes and cocktail recipes." (Publisher's note)

"Superb in both substance and scope, this collection offers a feast for the senses that will be savored at length." Pub Wkly

O'Brady, Tara

Seven spoons; my favorite recipes for any and every day. Tara O'Brady. Ten Speed Press 2015 296 p. color illustrations (hardback) $27.50 **641.597**

1. Cooking 2. Canadians 3. Cooking, Canadian

ISBN 1607746379; 9781607746379

LC 2014036366

In this cookbook, Tara O'Brady "shares stories and recipes from her Canadian home. . . . Recipes like Roasted Carrots with Dukkah and Harissa Mayonnaise, Braised Beef Short Ribs with Gremolata, and Plum Macaroon Cake are wholesome, hearty, and showcase the myriad culinary influences at work in O'Brady's kitchen. . . . Impeccable food photography and a lavish package round out this beautiful, personal collection." (Publisher's note)

"Recommended for fans of O'Brady's blog (sevenspoons.net) and readers who'd like a globally influenced home cooking collection." LJ

Includes bibliographical references and index

Presilla, Maricel E.

★ **Gran** cocina latina; the food of Latin America. Maricel E. Presilla; photography by Gentl & Hyers/Edge; illustrations by Julio Figueroa. Norton & Company 2012 vii, 901 p., [32] p. of platesp ill. (some col.) (hardcover) $45 **641.597**

1. Cookbooks 2. Latin American cooking 3. Cooking, Mexican 4. Cooking, Caribbean

ISBN 0393050696; 9780393050691

LC 2012017701

James Beard Foundation Award: Cookbook of the Year (2013)

Author Maricel E. Presilla, "who runs a restaurant in Hoboken, N.J., and holds a doctorate in medieval Spanish history, offers this bible of Latin American food." It "covers dishes from Mexico, Argentina, and the Hispanic Caribbean. . . . Presilla includes more than 500 recipes for everything from tropical roots to empanadas and meat dishes of every kind." (Publishers Weekly)

Rodgers, Rick

The **essential** James Beard cookbook; 400 recipes that shaped the tradition of American cooking.

James Beard with Rick Rodgers. St. Martin's Press 2012 380 p. illustrations (hardback) $35   **641.597**
1. Cookbooks 2. American cooking
ISBN 0312642180; 9780312642181

LC 2012028372

This cookbook is a "compilation of some of [chef James] Beard's best recipes" and "spans the breadth of his culinary achievement. In true American fashion, he draws from French, Italian, Indian, African, and other cuisines and adapts them to American kitchens and techniques, often simplifying otherwise complex dishes, such as cassoulet, without compromising flavor. Betty Fussell contributes a perceptive essay on Beard's complicated life and his teaching talents." (Booklist)

"Home cooking has evolved considerably since Beard's cookbooks were first published, so it's wonderful to see his recipes reprinted in this functional collection." LJ

Rollins, Kent

A **taste** of cowboy; ranch recipes and tales from the trail. Kent Rollins with Shannon Rollins; photographs by Shannon Keller Rollins. Houghton Mifflin Harcourt 2015 248 p. color illustrations (hardback) $30   **641.597**
1. Cowhands 2. American cooking 3. Ranch life -- West (U.S.) 4. Cooking, American -- Western style 5. Cowboys -- West (U.S.) -- Social life and customs
ISBN 0544275004; 9780544275003

LC 2014036936

In this cookbook, author Kent Rollins takes readers "into his frontier world with simple food anyone can do. Kent offers labor-saving breakfasts like Egg Bowls with Smoked Cream Sauce. For lunch or dinner, there's 20-minute Green Pepper Frito Pie, hands-off, four-ingredient Sweet Heat Chopped Barbecue Sandwiches, or mild and smoky Roasted Bean-Stuffed Poblano Peppers." (Publisher's note)

"Though Rollins offers sage advice on choosing and caring for cast-iron cookware, readers won't need to worry about building a fire, since these recipes have been adjusted to allow followers to recreate cowboy fare in the comfort of their own kitchens. However, Rollins remains true to his methods by incorporating a wide variety of boxed, canned, and prepared ingredients such as creamed soups and processed cheese. Rollins's campfire stories and DIY cures for ailments such as arthritis (honey in your coffee) and spider bites (tape a penny on it) give warmth and personality to a book that even city slickers will enjoy spending time with." PW

Sewall, Jeremy

The **New** England kitchen; fresh takes on seasonal recipes. Jeremy Sewall, Erin Byers Murray, Baron Seaver. Rizzoli International Publications 2014 255 p. color illustrations (hardcover) $39.95   **641.597**
1. New England 2. American cooking
ISBN 0789327473; 9780789327475

LC 2014942046

James Beard Foundation Award Nominee: American Cooking (2015)

In this New England cookbook, chef Jeremy Sewall "adapts the region's fresh, simple flavors into refined dishes for the home cook. More than one hundred delectable reci-
pes highlight the area's celebrated farms and fisheries to incorporate distinct flavors throughout the year. . . . The book also includes profiles of a New England farmer, fishermen, and an artisanal beer brewer to capture the new revolutionary spirit." (Publisher's note)

Tellez, Lesley

Eat Mexico; recipes from Mexico City's streets, markets and fondas. Lesley Tellez. Kyle Books 2015 192 p. color illustrations (hardcover : alk. paper) $24.95   **641.597**
1. Mexican cooking 2. Mexico City (Mexico)
ISBN 1909487279; 9781909487277

LC 2014960085

This book by Lesley Tellez is "a culinary love letter to one of the biggest cities in the world--a chaotic, vibrant place where residents eat from sidewalk grills and stands, and markets and casual restaurants serve up fresh, hot food daily. Tellez takes you through [Mexico City's] most classic dishes, offering recipes from her favorite haunts on the streets, in city markets, and in small, homestyle fondas." (Publisher's note)

Thompson-Anderson, Terry, 1946-

Texas on the Table; people, places, and recipes celebrating the flavors of the Lone Star State. by Terry Thompson-Anderson; photos by Sandy Wilson. University of Texas Press 2014 452 p. illustrations (chiefly color) (cl. : alk. paper) $45   **641.597**
1. Texas 2. American cooking 3. Southern cooking 4. Cooking -- Texas 5. Terroir -- Texas 6. Cooking, American -- Southwestern style
ISBN 0292744099; 9780292744097

LC 2013048386

James Beard Foundation Award Nominee: American Cooking (2015)

This cookbook, by Terry Thompson-Anderson, "presents 150 new and classic recipes, along with stories of the people—farmers, ranchers, shrimpers, cheesemakers, winemakers, and chefs—who inspired so many of them and who are changing the taste of Texas food. The recipes span the full range from finger foods and first courses to soups and breads, salads, seafood, chicken, meat (including wild game), sides and vegetarian dishes, and sweets." (Publisher's note)

Werner, Eric

Hartwood; bright, wild flavors from the edge of the Yucatan. Eric Werner and Mya Henry. Artisan 2015 301 p. illustrations (chiefly color) (alk. paper) $40   **641.597**
1. Mexican cooking 2. Yucatan (Mexico) 3. Maya cooking 4. Cooking, Mexican 5. Hartwood (Restaurant : Tulum, Mexico)
ISBN 157965620X; 9781579656201

LC 2015013061

This cookbooks is also the "the story of [authors] Eric Werner and Mya Henry, an intrepid young couple who gave up their restaurant jobs in New York City to start anew in the one-road town of Tulum, Mexico. Here they built Hartwood, one of the most exciting and inspiring restaurants in the world. Werner's passion for dazzling flavors and natural ingredients is expertly translated into recipes anyone can cook at home." (Publisher's note)

"Vibrant flavors dominate this warm and welcoming collection, bringing the local tastes of the Yucatán region into the home kitchen." Pub Wkly

Includes bibliographical references and index

641.598 Cooking--South America

Acurio, Gastón

Peru; the cookbook. Gastón Acurio. Phaidon Inc Ltd 2015 400 p. color illustrations (hardcover) $49.95 **641.598**

1. Peru 2. Cooking

ISBN 0714869201; 9780714869209

This Peruvian cookbook, by Gastón Acurio, offers "500 traditional home cooking recipes from the country's most acclaimed and popular chef. . . . [The author] guides cooks through the full range of Peru's vibrant cuisine from popular classics like quinoa and ceviche, and lomo saltado to lesser known dishes like amaranth and aji amarillo." (Publisher's note)

"In chef and restaurant owner Acurio's first foray into English-language cookbooks, the cuisine of Peru shines. The color-coded sections book break down the usual Western groupings of dishes (appetizers, first course, etc.) with a more Peruvian sensibility in mind." Pub Wkly

Castanho, Thiago

Brazilian Food; Thiago Castanho, Luciana Bianchi. Firefly Books Ltd 2014 256 p. illustrations; portraits (col) $39.95 **641.598**

1. Cookbooks 2. Brazilian cooking

ISBN 177085472X; 9781770854727

This cookbook, by Thiago Castanho and Luciana Bianchi, "explores the best of Brazilian food and its traditions. Along with three award-winning guest chefs, . . . [the authors] selected more than 100 recipes that adventurous cooks will want to try at home, even if they have never been to Brazil." (Publisher's note)

"With beautiful, splashy photos of the recipes, markets, food producers and even street artists at work, this book is elevated above a simple collection of recipes. It's an ode to the author's foodscape, and his passion for it is infectious. Readers who have never heard of manteiga de garrafa or tried pickled peppers will be excited about Castanho's recipes and may be inspired to visit Brazil." Pub Wkly

Kaminsky, Peter

Mallmann on fire; Francis Mallmann with Peter Kaminsky and Donna Gelb. Artisan 2014 320 p. color illustrations $40 **641.598**

1. Cookbooks 2. Outdoor cooking 3. Frying 4. Broiling 5. Barbecuing 6. Cooking, Argentine 7. Cooking -- Patagonia (Argentina and Chile)

ISBN 9781579655372; 1579655378

LC 2014004632

This cookbook, by Francis Mallmann with Peter Kaminsky and Donna Gelb, "takes us grilling in magical places . . ., each locale inspiring new discoveries as revealed in 100 recipes for meals both intimate and outsized. We encounter

legs of lamb and chicken hung from strings, coal-roasted delicata squash, roasted herbs, a parrillada of many fish, and all sorts of griddled and charred meats, vegetables, and fruits, plus rustic desserts cooked on the chapa and baked in wood-fired ovens." (Publisher's note)

"Though the author targets serious outdoor cooks, his title is suitable for amateurs and armchair travelers. Not all of the recipes require a fire, and those that do can usually be adapted to the stovetop." LJ

Includes index

641.6 Cooking specific materials

Aidells, Bruce

The **complete** meat cookbook; a juicy and authorative guide to selecting, seasoning, and cooking today's beef, pork, lamb, and veal. {by} Bruce Aidelle and Denis Kelly; photographs by Beatriz Da Costa; illustrations by Mary De Palma. Houghton Mifflin 1998 604p il $35 **641.6**

1. Cooking -- Meat

ISBN 0-618-13512-X

LC 98-28216

"More than 230 recipes, many with several variations, are presented along with charts and illustrations to help the reader understand different types of meat." Libr J

Anthony, Michael, 1968-

V Is for Vegetables; Inspired Recipes & Techniques for Home Cooks: From Artichokes to Zucchini. Michael Anthony. Little, Brown & Co. 2015 384 p. color illustrations $40 **641.6**

1. Diet 2. Cooking -- Vegetables

ISBN 0316373354; 9780316373357

LC 2015931409

In this cookbook author Michael Anthony "celebrates the act of cooking vegetables he loves. Anthony shows how unlocking the secrets of vegetables can be as simple as roasting a beet, de-knobbing a Jerusalem artichoke, peeling a gnarly celery root, slicing a bright radish, washing a handful of just-picked greens." (Publisher's note)

"With its distinctive recipes, this title can augment and supplement collections that already include classics such as James Peterson's Vegetables, Revised and Deborah Madison's Vegetable Literacy." Library Journal

Bevill, Amanda

World spice at home; New Flavors for 75 Favorite Dishes. Amanda Bevill and Julie Kramis Hearne. Sasquatch Books 2014 240 p. color illustrations (alk. paper) $24.95 **641.6**

1. Spices 2. Cooking 3. Cookbooks 4. Cooking (Spices)

ISBN 1570619077; 9781570619076

LC 2014011114

This cookbook, by Amanda Bevill and Julie Kramis Hearne, "brings the world's exotic spices to your home kitchen to breath new life into favorite, familiar, and traditional dishes with wonderful new flavors. Transform a grilled ribeye steak using an Arabic baharat spice blend;

add drama to your carrot cake using Kashmiri garam masala. Spices add gratifying dimension to foods, and while the spice blends come from around the world, these recipes are friendly and familiar." (Publisher's note)

"Bevill and Kramis Hearnes's spice blends, which contain 7–14 spices (compared to 40-plus in some ethnic cookbooks), taste superior to many premade and shelf-weary equivalents. Their approachable recipes offer home cooks a gentle introduction to new flavorings." LJ

Includes bibliographical references and index

Byres, Tim
Smoke; new firewood cooking: how to build flavor with fire, on the grill and in the kitchen. Tim Byres. Rizzoli International Publications 2013 255 p. ill. (chiefly col.) $40 **641.6**
1. Cookbooks 2. Barbecue cooking
ISBN 0847839796; 9780847839797
LC 2012950104
James Beard Award (2014)

This cookbook, by Tim Byres, was the winner of the 2014 James Beard Award in the General Cooking Category. "Byres . . . gives innovative ideas for easy ways to use smoke in your everyday kitchen arsenal of flavors--such as smoking safely on the stovetop with woodchips, putting together relishes and salsas made with smoked peppers and other vegetables, grilling with wood planks, and using smoke-cured meats to add layers of flavor to a dish." (Publisher's note)

Cameron, Angus
The **L.L.** Bean game and fish cookbook; by Angus Cameron and Judith Jones; illustrations by Bill Elliott. Random House 1983 475p il $25.95 **641.6**
1. Cooking -- Fish 2. Cooking -- Game
ISBN 0-394-51191-3
LC 82-15089
"With handsome wildlife and botanical drawings by Bill Elliott, the book was written by two experts and is complete and comprehensive." Christ Sci Monit

Carreño, Carolynn
Meat; everything there is to know : recipes and stories from America's gretest Butcher. Pat LaFrieda and Carolynn Carreño. Atria Books 2014 256 p. color illustrations (hardback) $39.99 **641.6**
1. Meat industry 2. Cooking -- Meat
ISBN 1476725993; 9781476725994; 9781476726007; 9781476726014
LC 2014000898
IACP Cookbook Award Finalist; Single Subject (2015)

"In 'Meat,' [author] Pat [LaFrieda] introduces you to cuts beyond chops and tenderloins--including inexpensive and unusual cuts--so you can venture outside your everyday selections. With detailed, step-by-step photos, he provides instruction in the best butchering skills for the home cook, such as needling, frenching, rolling, and tying." (Publisher's note)

"LaFreida's emphasis is in educating readers on the various animals, diagramming cuts, and showing how to best utilize them. Tips like how to break down a chicken or cut pockets in veal or pork chops for stuffing make this a valuable reference that will give readers a greater appreciation

for not only their favorite cuts of meat, but their butcher as well." Pub Wkly
Includes bibliographical references and index

Cole, Tyson
Uchi: the cookbook; by Tyson Cole and Jessica Dupuy; foreword by Lance Armstrong. Umaso Publishing 2011 268p $39.95 **641.6**
1. Sushi 2. Japanese cooking 3. Cooking -- Seafood 4. Uchi (Austin, Tex.: Restaurant)
ISBN 978-0-292-77129-1; 0-292-77129-0

"Every now and then a cookbook comes along that is such a great read and has such dazzling photography that I can't put it down. Uchi, the Cookbook is one of those." Texas Monthly

Cook's illustrated (Periodical)
The **best** chicken recipes; by the editors of Cook's illustrated; photography, Keller + Keller, Carl Tremblay, and Daniel J. Van Ackere; illustrations, John Burgoyne. America's Test Kitchen 2008 422p il $35 **641.6**
1. Cooking -- Poultry
ISBN 978-1-933615-23-3; 1-933615-23-0

This volume "offers more than 300 recipes for chicken, along with a primer called 'Chicken 101,' information on techniques (including step-by-step illustrations), and ratings of equipment and ingredients." Libr J

The **cook's** illustrated meat book; the game-changing guide that teaches you how to cook meat and poultry with 425 bulletproof recipes. the editors of America's Test Kitchen. America's Test Kitchen 2014 504 p. illustrations (some color) $40 **641.6**
1. Cookbooks 2. Cooking -- Meat
ISBN 1936493861; 9781936493869
LC 2014016170

This cookbook "begins with a 27-page master class in meat cookery, which covers shopping, . . . storing, . . . and seasoning meat. . . . 425 bulletproof and rigorously tested recipes for beef, pork, lamb, veal, and poultry provide plenty of options for everyday meals and special occasion dinners and you'll learn new (and better) ways to cook favorites such as Pan-Seared Thick-Cut Steak, Juicy Pub-Style Burgers, Weeknight Roast Chicken, Barbecued Pulled Pork, and more." (Publisher's note)

"That said, carnivores with an obsession for perfection will likely have found their new bible in this comprehensive collection." Pub Wkly

Culinary Institute of America
Vegetables; recipes and techniques from the world's premier culinary college. the Culinary Institute of America; photography by Ben Fink. Lebhar-Friedman Books 2007 293p il $40 **641.6**
1. Cooking -- Vegetables
ISBN 978-0-86730-918-8; 0-8673-0918-0
LC 2007-298057

Includes "over 150 recipes for soups, appetizers, salads, entrees, side dishes, and a chapter devoted to sauces and relishes made from vegetables or perfect to serve with vegetables. Accompanied by 75 full-color photos." Publisher's note

Fraioli, James O.
Culinary birds; the ultimate poultry cookbook. Chef John Ash, James O. Fraioli. Running Press 2013 319 p. color illustrations (hardcover) $30 **641.6**
1. Cookbooks 2. Cooking -- Poultry
ISBN 0762444843; 9780762444847

LC 2013938633
James Beard Award (2014)
This cookbook, by John Ash and James O. Fraioli, "offers more than 170 savory ways to enjoy poultry. . . . Because it is important to know where your bird comes from, [the book also] . . . provides a brief history of poultry, the rise of factory farms, and the progression of the sustainability movement." (Publisher's note)
Includes index

Grescoe, Taras
Bottomfeeder; how to eat ethically in a world of vanishing seafood. Bloomsbury USA 2008 327p $24.99; pa $16 **641.6**
1. Seafood 2. Marine resources 3. Conservation of natural resources 4. Cooking -- Seafood
ISBN 978-1-59691-225-0; 1-59691-225-1; 978-1-59691-625-8 pa; 1-59691-625-7 pa

LC 2007-49843
The author, a food and travel writer, presents an account of his experiences eating fish and seafood around the world and looks at the ecological ramifications of our diet. He argues that we need to redesign our relationship with seafood.
This is "a comprehensive, lively and illuminating guide." Nation
Includes bibliographical references

Grigson, Jane
Charcuterie and French pork cookery; Jane Grigson. Grub Street 2001 347 p. ill. $34.95 **641.6**
1. French cooking 2. Cooking -- Pork 3. Cookery (Pork) 4. Cooking, French
ISBN 1902304888; 9781902304885

LC 2008426563
IACP Culinary Classics Book Award (2013)
This book, by Jane Grigson, "first published in 1969 but unavailable for many years, . . . is a guidebook and a recipe book. She describes every type of charcuterie available for purchase and how to make them yourself. She describes how to braise, roast, pot-roast and stew all the cuts of pork, how to make terrines, how to cure your own ham and make your own sausages." (Publisher's note)

Guggiana, Marissa
Primal cuts; cooking with America's best butchers. Marissa Guggiana; foreword by Dario Cecchini; introduction by Andrew Zimmern. Welcome Books 2012 287 p. col. ill. (hardcover) $40 **641.6**
1. Cookbooks 2. Cooking -- Meat 3. Carving (Meat, etc.) 4. Cooking (Meat) 5. Meatcutting -- United States
ISBN 1599621150; 9781599621159

LC 2012018389

This cookbook describes how "Marissa Guggiana, food activist, writer, and fourth generation meat purveyor traveled the country to discover 50 of our most gifted butchers and share their favorite dishes, personal stories, and cooking techniques. From the Michelin star chef to the small farmer who raises free-range animals--butchers are the guide for this unique visual cookbook, packed with tons of their most prized recipes and good old-fashioned know-how." (Publisher's note)

Guittard, Amy
Guittard Chocolate cookbook; irresistible family recipes and stories from San Francisco's bean-to-bar chocolate company. Amy Guittard; photographs by Antonis Achilleos. Chronicle Books Llc 2015 177 p. color illustrations $25 **641.6**
1. Cooking 2. Chocolate 3. Cooking, Chocolate
ISBN 1452135339; 9781452135335

LC 2014033173
Author "Amy Guittard presents tried-and-true favorite recipes from five generations of Guittards [San Francisco's oldest continuously family-owned chocolate company], ranging from start-your-day-right Chocolate Cherry Scones to fudgey Mocha Cookies and deep, dark Chocolate Caramel Pecan Bundt Cake. Leave it to the people who really know chocolate to make a collection of recipes that are sure to make every chocolate lover long for one bite more." (Publisher's note)

Higgins, Katie
Chocolate-covered Katie; over 80 delicious recipes that are secretly good for you. Katie Higgins. Life & Style 2015 207 p. color illustrations (trade pbk.) $20 **641.6**
1. Desserts 2. Cooking -- Chocolate 3. Chocolate desserts
ISBN 1455599700; 9781455599707

LC 2014017846
In this cookbook, Katie Higgins "shares over 80 never-before-seen recipes, such as Chocolate Obsession Cake, Peanut Butter Pudding Pops, and Ultimate Unbaked Brownies, that use only real ingredients, without any unnecessary fats, sugars, or empty calories. These desserts prove once and for all that health and happiness can go hand-in-hand-you can have your dessert and eat it, too!" (Publisher's note)

Jacoby, Kate
Vedge; 100 plates, large and small, that place vegetables in the spotlight. Rich Landau and Kate Jacoby. The Experiment 2013 256 p. (cloth) $24.95 **641.6**
1. Veganism 2. Cooking -- Fruit 3. Vegetarian cooking 4. Cooking -- Vegetables 5. Vegan cooking
ISBN 1615190856; 9781615190850

LC 2013012098
In this cookbook, chefs Rich Landau and Kate Jacoby "share their passion for ingenious vegetable cooking. The more than 100 recipes here--such as Fingerling Potatoes with Creamy Worcestershire Sauce, Pho with Roasted Butternut Squash, Seared French Beans with Caper Bagna Cauda, and Eggplant Braciole--explode with flavor but are surprisingly straightforward to prepare." (Publisher's note)

Kafka, Barbara

★ **Vegetable** love; a book for cooks. [by] Barbara Kafka with Christopher Styler; photographs by Christina Cornish. Artisan 2005 708p il $35 **641.6**

1. Vegetables 2. Cooking -- Vegetables

ISBN 1-57965-168-2

LC 2005-47818

The author "has triumphed with an outstanding, indispensable cookbook that not only summons the reader to get into the kitchen and cook but also constitutes a valuable and comprehensive reference tool." Booklist

Includes bibliographical references

La Place, Viana

Verdura; vegetables, Italian style. Viana La Place. Grub Street 2010 320 p. il (pbk) $24.95 **641.6**

1. Cookbooks 2. Cooking -- Vegetables 3. Italian cooking

ISBN 1906502781; 9781906502782

LC 2010537034

Originally published: New York: Morrow, 1991. London: Macmillan, 1994

This cookbook, by Viana La Place, offers "300 irresistible recipes [that] represent the best of the Italian approach to vegetable preparation, an earthy yet spirited technique that celebrates fresh ingredients simply treated. . . . Contending that eating well-prepared vegetables helps us to appreciate life's natural cycles, [the volume] . . . presents recipes for antipastos, salads, soups, sandwiches, pasta, risottos, pizzas, and much more." (Publisher's note)

Includes bibliographical references (p. 307) and index

Lobel, Stanley

The **meat** bible; all you need to know about meat and poultry from America's master butchers. by Stanley Lobel ... [et al.]; with Mary Goodbody and David Whiteman; photographs by Lucy Schaeffer. Chronicle Books 2009 319p il $40 **641.6**

1. Cooking -- Meat 2. Cooking -- Poultry

ISBN 978-0-8118-5826-7; 0-8118-5826-X

LC 2008-33441

"Recipes number 135, well photographed and indexed." Publ Wkly

Madison, Deborah

Vegetable literacy; exploring the affinities and history of the vegetable families, with 300 recipes. Deborah Madison. 1st ed. Ten Speed Press 2013 416 p. col. ill. (hardcover) $40.00 **641.6**

1. Cooking (Vegetables) 2. Food crops -- Identification

ISBN 9781607741916; 1607741911

LC 2012030968

Includes bibliographical references (page 395) and index.

Mast, Rick

Mast Brothers Chocolate; a family cookbook. Rick Mast & Michael Mast; foreword by Thomas Keller; photography by Tuukka Koski. Little Brown & Co 2013 276 p. illustrations, some color (hbk.) $40 **641.6**

1. Desserts 2. Cookbooks 3. Cooking -- Chocolate 4.

Chocolate 5. Cooking (Chocolate) 6. Mast Brothers Chocolate

ISBN 0316234842; 9780316234849

LC 2013938865

IACP Cookbook Award (2014)

In this cookbook, authors Rick Mast and Michael Mast "share their unique story and recipes for classic American desserts like chocolate cookies and cakes, brownies, bars, milkshakes, and even home-made whoopie pie. There are mouthwatering savory dishes as well, like Pan-seared Scallops with Cocoa Nibs and Cocoa Coq au Vin." (Publisher's note)

Moonen, Rick

Fish without a doubt; the cook's essential companion. [by] Rick Moonen and Roy Finamore; photographs by Ben Fink. Houghton Mifflin Co. 2008 496p il $35 **641.6**

1. Cooking -- Fish 2. Cooking -- Seafood

ISBN 978-0-618-53119-6; 0-618-53119-X

LC 2007-52084

In this cookbook that covers the preparing of sustainable fish, the authors "show how to clean, bone, and portion both finfish and shellfish. Recipes are organized by cooking method—broiling, poaching, roasting, grilling, steaming, [and] frying. . . . Succeeding chapters cover such fish basics as chowders, fish cakes, and salads. . . . Both the book's organization and its comprehensive coverage make this a necessary addition to any cookbook collections." Booklist

Music, Debra

Theo Chocolate; recipes & sweet secrets from Seattle's favorite chocolate maker. Debra Music and Joe Whinney with Leora Bloom. Sasquatch Books 2015 256 p. (alk. paper) $24.95 **641.6**

1. Chocolate 2. Cookbooks 3. Theo Chocolate 4. Chocolate candy 5. Chocolate desserts

ISBN 1570619972; 9781570619977

LC 2015011364

This book, by Debra Music and Joe Whinney with Leora Bloom, presents "sweet and savory chocolate recipes, along with the fascinating story of how North America's first organic and Fair Trade chocolate factory came to be (and why they are so passionate about how their chocolate is made)." (Publisher's note)

"Though light on technical instruction, this book contains a compelling range of sweet and savory recipes." Library Journal

Includes bibliographical references and index

Ottolenghi, Yotam

★ **Plenty**; vibrant vegetable recipes from London's Ottolenghi. by Yotam Ottolenghi. Chronicle Books 2011 287p il $35 **641.6**

1. Cooking -- Vegetables 2. Ottolenghi (Restaurant)

ISBN 978-1-4521-0124-8

LC 2011036741

Includes bibliographical references

★ **Plenty** more; vibrant vegetable cooking from London's Ottolenghi. Yotam Ottolenghi. Ten Speed

Press 2014 352 p. color illustrations (hardcover) $35 **641.6**

1. Cookbooks 2. Vegetarian cooking 3. Cooking (Vegetables) 4. Ottolenghi (Restaurant)

ISBN 1607746212; 9781607746218

LC 2014017924

IACP Cookbook Award Finalist: Chefs and Restaurants (2015)

James Beard Foundation Award Nominee: Vegetable Focused and Vegetarian (2015)

In this vegetarian cookbook, author Yotam Ottolenghi "continues to explore the diverse realm of vegetarian food with a wholly original approach. Organized by cooking method, more than 150 dazzling recipes emphasize spices, seasonality, and bold flavors." It also includes "120 vegetarian dishes organized by cooking method." (Publisher's note)

While the recipes "require time and finesse . . . they are often revelatory, introducing textures and flavor combinations that readers won't find elsewhere." LJ

Peterson, James

Meat; a kitchen education. Ten Speed Press 2010 326p il $35 **641.6**

1. Cooking -- Meat

ISBN 978-1-58008-992-0; 1-58008-992-5

LC 2010-21759

"Though his introduction addresses vegans, admonishing all to 'follow your conscience' about the consumption of animals, the rest of [Peterson's] text advocates only the use of the best lamb, rabbit, beef, and chicken available. Thoroughly review the first two chapters; in them Peterson sets forth the proper ways to sauté, grill, braise, and poach (among other methods), illustrates such fundamental preparation methods as julienning a leek and sectioning a turnip, and identifies the flavors associated with different international cuisines. Next, the fun: 175 recipes and, more important, instructions and sidebars to ensure that expensive roasts and whole birds emerge with great taste." Booklist

Pollinger, Ben

School of fish; Ben Pollinger. Simon & Schuster 2014 439 p. colored illustrations (hardback) $35 **641.6**

1. Cooking -- Seafood 2. Cooking (Seafood)

ISBN 145166513X; 9781451665130; 9781451665147

LC 2014000760

IACP Cookbook Award Finalist: General (2015)

In this cookbook, chef Ben Pollinger "distills years of experience working in some of the world's best restaurants in this no-nonsense book that demystifies the art of cooking seafood. With more than 100 recipes organized by technique from the easiest to the most advanced, Pollinger takes you through the ins and outs of baking, roasting, braising, broiling, steaming, poaching, grilling, frying, sautéing, and of course seasoning." (Publisher's note)

Raichlen, Steven

Project smoke; by Steven Raichlen. Workman Publishing 2016 336 p. (alk. paper) $22.95 **641.6**

1. Cooking 2. Barbecue cooking 3. Smoked foods 4.

Smoking (Cooking) 5. Cooking (Smoked foods)

ISBN 9780761181866

LC 2015044528

This cookbook, by Steven Raichlen, "a step-by-step guide to cold-smoking, hot-smoking, and smoke-roasting, and a collection of 100 innovative recipes for smoking every kind of food, from starters to desserts. . . . Illustrated throughout with full-color photographs, it's a book that inspires hunger at every glance, and satisfies with every recipe tried." (Publisher's note)

"An excellent how-to for those fired up about smoke." Booklist

Rule, Cheryl Sternman

Yogurt culture; a global look at how to make, bake, sip, and chill the world's creamiest, healthiest food. Cheryl Sternman Rule; photography by Ellen Silverman. Houghton Mifflin Harcourt 2015 352 p. color illustrations (paper over board) $22 **641.6**

1. Cookbooks 2. Dairy products 3. Cooking (Yogurt)

ISBN 0544252322; 9780544252325

LC 2014039690

This cookbook, by Cheryl Sternman Rule, with photography by Ellen Silverman, "presents 115 flavorful recipes, taking yogurt farther than the breakfast table, lunchbox, or gym bag. . . . In chapters like Flavor, Slurp, Dine, and Lick, [the author] pairs yogurt not just with fruit but with meat, not just with sugar but with salt, not just with herbs but with fragrant spices whose provenance spans the globe." (Publisher's note)

"This excellent cookbook belongs in most collections, along with Arto de Hartounian's The Yogurt Cookbook." LJ

Seaver, Barton

For cod and country. Sterling Epicure 2011 294p il $30 **641.6**

1. Cooking -- Seafood

ISBN 978-1-4027-7775-2

A "a user's manual for any seafood lover who wants to eat sustainably—and very well. Seaver's book vibrates with personality, practical advice, photographs (both evocative and how-to), and stovetop wisdom: never be shy about adding butter, but go easy on the black pepper. With the help of step-by-step photographs, he demonstrates seafood-savvy techniques, everything from how to fillet a bass to how to open an oyster without severing one of your arteries. He also provides a list of substitutions for overexploited species: Use Pacific cod in place of Atlantic cod; sablefish instead of Chilean sea bass; squid instead of octopus." Atlantic

Slater, Nigel

Ripe; a cook in the orchard. Nigel Slater; photography by Jonathan Lovekin. Ten Speed Press 2012 591 p. col. ill. (hardback) $40 **641.6**

1. Cookbooks 2. Gardening 3. Cooking -- Fruit

ISBN 1607743329; 9781607743323

LC 2011043551

James Beard Foundation Award: Single Subject (2013)

This cookbook, by food writer Nigel Slater, "focuses on sweet and savory applications for fruits grown in his London garden. Organized alphabetically, the fruit-focused chapters offer historical and varietal information, gardening tips, and suggested flavor pairings, followed by simple recipes like Baked Peaches with Maple Syrup and Vanilla, Slow-Cooked Quinces with Cassis, and Roast Leg of Pork with Spiced Rhubarb." (Library Journal)

Speck, Maria

Simply ancient grains; fresh and flavorful whole grain recipes for living well. by Maria Speck. Ten Speed Press 2015 272 p. color illustrations (hard-cover) $27.50   **641.6**
1. Cookbooks 2. Cooking -- Grains 3. Grain 4. Cooking (Cereals) 5. Heirloom varieties (Plants)
ISBN 1607745887; 9781607745884

LC 2014036879

This cookbook, by Maria Speck and photography by Erin Kunkel, presents recipes for cooking Ancient grains. "From black rice to red quinoa to golden Kamut berries, ancient grains are showing up on restaurant menus and store shelves in abundance. . . . [The author] makes cooking with these fascinating and nourishing staples easy and accessible with sumptuous recipes for breakfast, lunch, dinner, and dessert." (Publisher's note)

"Speck simplifies cooking with grains without sacrificing flavor. Her recipes—including minted barley and fennel stew with marinated feta, New England cider mussels with fresh cranberries and bulgur, and walnut spelt biscotti with olive oil—are deliciously nourishing and not to be missed." LJ

Includes bibliographical references and index

Stein, Rick

Rick Stein's complete seafood; a step-by-step reference with over 150 recipes and 550 photographs. Rick Stein [photography by James Murphy] Ten Speed Press 2004 264 p. col. ill. $27.99   **641.6**
1. Cookbooks 2. Cooking -- Fish 3. Cooking -- Seafood 4. Cooking (Fish) 5. Cooking (Seafood) 6. Cookery, International
ISBN 1580085687; 1580089143; 9781580089142

LC 2006298920

James Bead Award (2005)

This cookbook, by Rich Stein, "offers an almost limitless repertoire [of seafood recipes], with detailed instructions and extensive charts. Hundreds of photographs and illustrations show how to scale and gut fish for the grill, bake whole fish in a salt or pastry casing, hot-smoke fish, prepare live crabs, and clean and stuff squid, along with other essential techniques." (Publisher's note)

Vegetables from an Italian garden; season-by-season recipes. Phaidon 2011 431p il $39.95   **641.6**
1. Vegetable gardening 2. Cooking -- Vegetables
ISBN 978-0-7148-6117-3; 0-7148-6117-0

This book, assembled by the editors at Phaidon Press, "is divided into four chapters, following the four seasons. Each chapter has its own colored ribbon, which makes it easy to go to the season you want to cook from. . . . Each season starts with an explanation of the vegetables available that season. There is a short history of the vegetable, then an explanation of how to select and buy them, along with stunning photos by Andy Sewell. Following this is a description of how and when to plant these vegetables in your own

garden. The scrumptious recipes are taken from all parts of Italy. Well written and clear, they let you jump in and start cooking." Super Chef

Vinton, Sherri Brooks

Put 'em up! a comprehensive home preserving guide for the creative cook, from drying and freezing to canning and pickling. Storey Pub. 2010 303p il pa $19.95   **641.6**
1. Cooking -- Fruit 2. Cooking -- Vegetables 3. Fruit -- Preservation 4. Vegetables -- Preservation
ISBN 978-1-60342-546-9

LC 2010009609

"Vinton provides an excellent introduction to multiple food preservation methods. Organized first by technique, then by fruit or vegetable, this volume contains many easy-to-follow options for prepared and preserved foods." Libr J

Includes bibliographical references

Wells, Patricia

Vegetable harvest; vegetables at the center of the plate. William Morrow 2007 324p il $34.95 **641.6**
1. Cooking -- Vegetables
ISBN 978-0-06-075244-6; 0-06-075244-0

LC 2006-43723

"After surveying the bounty of her backyard garden, Wells became inspired to build meals around vegetables rather than starting with meat, fish or poultry. She tripled the number she served at each meal and tried different cooking methods, looking for the best-tasting, most wholesome ways of cooking each type. She includes nutritional information and an equipment list for each recipe, and selectively offers wine suggestions, translations of French food idioms, and nuggets of folklore connected to the dish or main ingredient. . . . This collection is highly recommended for cooks and gardeners alike." Publ Wkly

641.65   Vegetables--cooking

Bloomfield, April

A **Girl** and Her Greens; Hearty Meals from the Garden. HarperCollins 2015 272 p. color illustrations $34.99   **641.65**
ISBN 006222588X; 9780062225887

LC 2015490298

This cookbook by April Blomfield "reflects the lighter side of the renowned chef whose name is nearly synonymous with nose-to-tail eating. In recipes such as Pot-Roasted Romanesco Broccoli, Onions with Sage Pesto, and Carrots with Spices, Yogurt, and Orange Blossom Water, April Bloomfield demonstrates the basic principle of her method: that unforgettable food comes out of simple, honest ingredients, an attention to detail, and a love for the sensual pleasures of cooking and eating." (Publisher's note)

"Bloomfield's latest is an excellent companion to its popular predecessor, offering a second helping of narrative-rich recipes and Sun Young Park's charming illustrations." LJ

Eatingwell Vegetables. Houghton Mifflin Harcourt 2016 516 p. color illustrations $35   **641.65**
1. Cooking 2. Vegetables
ISBN 0544715284; 9780544715288

This book, from the editors of "EatingWell" magazine, "guides both vegetable lovers and novices through the world of produce, including must-know basics, shopping notes, growing advice, and cooking tips on 100 common and less common vegetables, from arugula to yucca." (Publisher's note)

"Food trends such as the cauliflower pizza crust and raw kale salads also get their due. Throughout, bonus tips for growing cucumbers and "stale-ing" bread offer added value. This is a useful addition to a veg-centric cook's collection." Pub Wkly

Lang, Rebecca

The **Southern** vegetable book; A Root-to-Stalk Guide to the South's Favorite Produce. Rebecca Lang. Oxmoor House 2016 256 p. color illustrations (hardcover) $27.95   **641.65**
1. Southern cooking 2. Cooking -- Vegetables
ISBN 0848746880; 9780848746889

This cookbook, by Rebecca Lang, "brings you to the table to celebrate the versatility of vegetables with Southern flair. . . . The classic vegetables that we all know and love are represented, but lesser-known but equally-celebrated ones, such as Jerusalem artichokes and ramps, also make an appearance. The recipes in the book pay homage to classic Southern dishes while offering modern interpretations for the home cook, whether you call the South home or not." (Publisher's note)

" Many recent cookbooks feature creative vegetable preparations... this one has a distinct Southern twist." LJ

Mangini, Cara

The **Vegetable** Butcher; How to Select, Prep, Slice, Dice, and Masterfully Cook Vegetables from Artichokes to Zucchini. Cara Mangini. Workman Pub Co 2016 352 p. color illustrations (hardcover) $29.95   **641.65**
1. Cookbooks 2. Cooking -- Vegetables
ISBN 9780761180524; 0761180524
LC 2016004215

In this cookbook, by Cara Mangini, "the skills of butchery meet the world of fresh produce. . . . In step-by-step photographs, [a] 'vegetable butcher' . . . shows how to break down a butternut squash, cut a cauliflower into steaks, peel a tomato properly, chiffonade kale, turn carrots into coins and parsnips into matchsticks, and find the meaty heart of an artichoke. Additionally, more than 150 original, simple recipes put vegetables front and center." (Publisher's note)

"Blending practical aspects found in such manuals as Jacque Pepin's New Complete Techniques with the varied recipes familiar to titles such as Michael Anthony's V Is for Vegetables, Mangini's debut will augment most vegetable cooking collections." LJ

Wilkinson, Matt

Mr. Wilkinson's vegetables; a cookbook to celebrate the garden. Matt Wilkinson. Black Dog & Leventhal Pub. 2013 287 p. $27.95   **641.65**
1. Cooking -- Vegetables
ISBN 157912934X; 9781579129347

In this cookbook, "Melbourne, Australia-based chef [Matt] Wilkinson takes a 'veg-first approach' to cooking, building dishes around fresh, seasonal produce. In 25 chapters named for vegetables, he shares inspiring and beautifully photographed recipes that range from rustic (braised eggplant, tomato and meatballs) to playful ('Shepherd's Pie' croquettes) to unconventional (frozen vanilla syrup-coated fennel)." (Library Journal)

641.658   Mushrooms--cooking

Selengut, Becky

Shroom; mind-bendingly good recipes for cultivated and wild mushrooms. Becky Selengut. Andrews McMeel Pub., LLC 2014 205 p. color illustrations $35   **641.658**
1. Cooking -- Mushrooms
ISBN 1449448267; 9781449448264
LC 2014931303

This cookbook by Becky Selengut focuses on mushrooms. "She answers common questions about buying, cleaning . . ., storing, and eating mushrooms. . . . Each chapter includes five recipes that are presented in order from easy to advanced, with suggested wine pairings." Recipes include "banh mi sandwiches with red curry roasted portobellos and pickled vegetables [and] silken scrambled eggs with shaved Alba white truffles." (Library Journal)

"A delight to read and cook from, this is one of the most welcoming and unintimidating mushroom books to hit shelves in ages." LJ

641.66   Meat--cooking

Burgers; 125 Mouthwatering Recipes and Tips. edited by Jane Francisco. Hearst Books 2016 127 p. color illustrations (hardcover) $16.95 **641.66**
1. Cooking 2. Cookbooks 3. Hamburgers 4. Cooking (Meat)
ISBN 9781618372017; 1618372017
LC 2016427269

In this hamburger cookbook, edited by Jane Francisco and the Good Housekeeping publishing company, "you'll discover something exciting and delicious—including Texas Chicken Burgers, Rosemary-Cabernet Sliders, Greek Lamb Burgers, Salmon Burgers with Cajun Rémoulade Sauce, and Portobello Pesto Burgers." (Publisher's note)

"A reasonably priced cookbook for burger lovers working with a modest budget." LJ

641.665   Poultry--cooking

Flores, Eva Kosmas

Adventures in chicken; 150 Amazing Recipes from the Creator of AdventuresInCooking.com. Eva Kosmas Flores. Houghton Mifflin Harcourt 2016 288 p. color illustrations (paper over board) $30   **641.665**
1. Cookbooks 2. Cooking (Chicken)
ISBN 9780544558205

LC 2015038041

This cookbook by Eva Kosmas Flores is aimed at "home cooks who want to push their cooking to the next level with the best versions of classics like Chicken Marsala with Balsamic Caramelized Onions and Pork Belly or innovative temptations such as Korean Barbecue Drumsticks with Ginger-Pear Sauce. There are sections on chicken cooking techniques, how to make perfect stock, and more." (Publisher's note)

"An aptly titled book that takes everyday chicken to the ends of the earth." Booklist

Henry, Diana

A **Bird** in the Hand; Chicken Recipes for Every Day and Every Mood. by Diana Henry. Mitchell Beazley 2015 224 p. color illustrations $19.02 **641.665**
1. Cooking (Chicken)
ISBN 1845338960; 9781845338961

This chicken cookbook, by Diana Henry, presents a "collection of recipes for every day and every mood. . . . From quick Vietnamese lemon grass and chilli chicken thighs and a smoky chicken salad with roast peppers and almonds, through to a complete feast with pomegranate, barley and feta stuffed roast chicken with Georgian aubergines, there is no eating or entertaining occasion that isn't covered in this book." (Publisher's note)

"Whether herbaceous, aromatic, sweet, or spicy, these new chicken dishes promise to reinvigorate even the tiredest taste buds." LJ

641.675   Eggs--cooking

Ruhlman, Michael

★ **Egg**; a culinary exploration of the world's most versatile ingredient. Michael Ruhlman; photography by Donna Turner Ruhlman. Little Brown & Co 2014 xix, 235 p.p col. ill. $40   **641.675**
1. Cooking -- Eggs
ISBN 0316254061; 9780316254069

LC 2013948058

James Beard Foundation Award Nominee: Single Subject (2015)

In this cookbook Michael Ruhlman "explains why the egg is the key to the craft of cooking. . . . He starts with perfect poached and scrambled eggs and builds up to brioche and Italian meringue. Along the way readers learn to make their own mayonnaise, pasta, custards, quiches, cakes, and other preparations that rely fundamentally on the hidden powers of the egg." (Publisher's note)

"Ruhlman's regard for this simple ingredient is evident as he describes the multiple functions it serves and then offers up recipes for a wide array of appetizing dishes." Pub Wkly

641.691   Game--cooking

Canterbury, Dave

The **Bushcraft** field guide to trapping, gathering, and cooking in the wild; Dave Canterbury, New York Times bestselling author of Bushcraft. Adams Media 2016 264 p. (pbk.) $16.99   **641.691**
1. Camping 2. Wilderness survival 3. Cooking (Game) -- Technique 4. Cooking (Wild foods) -- Technique 5. Camping -- Handbooks, manuals, etc 6. Hunting -- Handbooks, manuals, etc 7. Wilderness survival -- Handbooks, manuals, etc
ISBN 1440598525; 9781440598524

LC 2016024921

This book, by Dave Canterbury, " provides you with all you need to know about packing, trapping, and preparing food for your treks and wilderness travels. Whether you're headed out for a day hike or a weeklong expedition, you'll find everything you need to survive--and eat well--out in the wild." (Publisher's note)

641.692   Fish--cooking

Seaver, Barton

Two if by sea; Delicious Sustainable Seafood. Barton Seaver. Sterling Pub Co Inc 2016 304 p. color illustrations (hardcover) $30   **641.692**
1. Cooking -- Seafood
ISBN 1454917873; 9781454917878

This seafood cookbook, by Barton Seaver, "offers more than 150 new mouthwatering recipes, including entrees, salads, appetizers, soups, pastas, stews, sides, and sauces. . . . Each of Seaver's fresh-tasting, casual (and always delicious) recipes features seafood that hasn't been overfished or caught in an environmentally destructive way." (Publisher's note)

"From a quick weeknight meal of canned shrimp and pasta to a show-stopping stew for guests, the ideas here will fit any bill. Essential for seafood lovers." LJ

Thompson, Jennifer Trainer

Fresh Fish; A Fearless Guide to Grilling, Shucking, Searing, Poaching & Roasting Seafood. by Jennifer Trainer Thompson. Workman Pub Co 2016 352 p. illustrations (chiefly color)   **641.692**
1. Cooking -- Fish 2. Cooking -- Seafood
ISBN 1612128084; 9781612128085

LC 2015041612

This book on seafood, by Jennifer Trainer Thompson, "offers simple step-by-step instructions for all of the essential cooking methods, including baking, pan-frying, braising, broiling, steaming, poaching, roasting, marinating, and grilling—along with 175 mouthwatering recipes that bring out the best in everything from fish fillets and whole fish to shrimp, mussels, lobster, clams, calamari, and more." (Publisher's note)

"A capable, reasonably priced all-purpose seafood cookbook that focuses primarily on recipes."

641.694 Mollusks--cooking

Jacobsen, Rowan

The **Essential** Oyster; A Salty Appreciation of Taste and Temptation. by Rowan Jacobsen. St. Martin's Press 2016 304 p. color illustrations $35 **641.694**
1. Oysters
ISBN 1632862565; 9781632862563

This book, by Rowan Jacobsen, "is the definitive book for oyster-lovers everywhere, featuring stunning portraits, tasting notes, and backstories of all the top oysters, as well as recipes from America's top oyster chefs and a guide to the best oyster bars." (Publisher's note)

"A handful of recipes from top chefs round out the book, chased down with a dirty oyster-brine martini." Pub Wkly

641.7 Specific cooking processes and techniques

Blonder, Greg

Meathead; the science of great barbecue and grilling. text and photos by Meathead Goldwyn; with Greg Blonder, Ph.D. A Rux Martin Book, Houghton Mifflin Harcourt 2016 400 p. illustrations (chiefly color) (hardback) $35 **641.7**
1. Cookbooks 2. Barbecue cooking 3. Barbecuing
ISBN 9780544018464

LC 2015049143

This cookbook, by Meathead Goldwyn with Greg Blonder, offers a "definitive guide to the concepts, methods, equipment, and accessories of barbecue and grilling. The founder and editor of the world's most popular BBQ and grilling website, AmazingRibs.com, Meathead applies the latest research to backyard cooking more than 100 thoroughly tested recipes." (Publisher's note)

"This highly recommended food-science focused guide to grilling and barbecue will satisfy amateurs and professionals alike." LJ

Science of great barbecue and grilling

Carroll, Joe

Feeding the fire; recipes and strategies for better barbecue and grilling. Joe Carroll with Nick Fauchald. Artisan Books 2015 264 p. illustrations $29.95 **641.7**
1. Cookbooks 2. Barbecue cooking 3. Barbecuing
ISBN 1579655572; 9781579655570

LC 2014035876

This grilling cookbook, by Joe Carroll with Nick Fauchald, "teaches the hows and whys of live-fire cooking: how to create low and slow fires, how to properly grill chicken (leave it on the bone), why American whiskey blends so nicely with barbecued meats (both are flavored with charred

wood), and how to make the best sides to serve with meat (keep it simple)." (Publisher's note)

"With dishes like smoked and grilled hot dogs, charred corn with compound cream cheese, and butcher's steaks with garlic butter, this cookbook is a master class in minimal and well-prepared barbecue." LJ

Child, Julia

Baking with Julia; based on the PBS series hosted by Julia Child. written by Dorie Greenspan; photographs by Gentl & Hyers. Morrow 1996 480p il $40 **641.7**
1. Baking
ISBN 0-688-14657-0

LC 96-23061

"The 200 recipes are organized as a course in baking, with an early, energetic section on the basic batters and doughs for cakes and pastries. The book moves on to recipes of varying degrees of complexity. . . . But the book's success is due to more than organization: the text never misses a chance to explain, expand and entertain." N Y Times Book Rev

Includes bibliographical references

Cook it in cast iron; kitchen-tested recipes for the one pan that does it all. by the editors at America's Test Kitchen. America's Test Kitchen 2016 304 p. color illustrations (alk. paper) $26.95 **641.7**
1. Skillet cooking
ISBN 9781940352480

LC 2015037708

This cookbook, by the editor's of America's Test Kitchen, "will show you everything you need to know about cast-iron cookware and the many (and often surprising) dishes you can cook and bake in this multitasker of a pan, from the classic dishes everyone knows and loves like steak, perfect fried eggs, and cornbread, to innovative and inspiring recipes like skillet apple pie, pizza, and cinnamon swirl bread." (Publisher's note)

"The editors of Cook's Country undertake a comprehensive exploration of the classic cast iron skillet, as well as the panoply of meals it can provide." Pub Wkly

Includes bibliographical references and index

Cook's illustrated (Periodical)

Best skillet recipes; a best recipe classic. by the editors of Cook's illustrated; photography, Keller + Keller, Carl Tremblay, and Daniel J. Van Ackere; illustrations, John Burgoyne. America's Test Kitchen 2009 335p il $35 **641.7**
1. Cooking
ISBN 978-1-933615-41-7; 1-933615-41-9

This cookbook celebrates the "versatility of that ordinary workhorse, the 12-inch skillet. An indispensable tool for eggs, pan-seared meats and sautéed vegetables, the skillet can also be used for stovetop-to-oven dishes such as All-American Mini Meatloaves; layered dishes such as tamale pie and Tuscan bean casserole; and even desserts such as hot fudge pudding cake. . . . Whether or not you properly appreciate your skillet, this book will at least teach you to wield it gracefully." Publ Wkly

Cunningham, Marion, 1922-2012

The **Fannie** Farmer baking book; illustrated by Lauren Jarrett. Alfred A. Knopf 1984 624p il hardcover o.p. pa $12.99 **641.7**

1. Baking

ISBN 0-517-14829-3

LC 84-47862

This baking book is a "guide to the making of . . . pies, cakes, breads and cookies. . . . {Recipes range from} French bread and cornbread, rugelach and scones, Election Cake from the 18th century and Schrafft's Butterscotch Cookies." (Newsweek) Index.

"Separate chapters cover pies and tarts, cookies, cakes, yeast breads, quick breads, and crackers in encyclopedic detail with brisk but reassuring professionalism. Many of the 800 recipes are standard favorites." Libr J

Davis, Timothy Charles

The **hot** chicken cookbook; the fiery history and red-hot recipes of Nashville's beloved bird. Timothy Charles Davis. Spring House Press 2015 128 p. ill. (chiefly color), portrait (pbk. : alk. paper) $19.95 **641.7**

1. Cooking (Chicken) 2. Nashville (Tenn.)

ISBN 9781940611198

LC 2015951464

In this book, by Timothy Charles Davis, "Nashville-style Hot Chicken is the Music City's claim to culinary fame. . . . Davis, a chef, writer, and Nashville resident, traces the dish's origins back to the late 1930's at Prince's Hot Chicken Shack, a story of love gone wrong, and follows the trail to its white-hot buzz of today." (Publisher's note)

"Reading Davis's cookbook, it's easy to understand why hot chicken has a cult following. A fascinating exploration of food culture and highly recommended." LJ

Fine cooking roasting; favorite recipes & essential tips for chicken, beef, veggies & more. editors and contributors of Fine cooking. The Taunton Press, Inc. 2014 153 p. colored illustrations $14.95 **641.7**

1. Cooking 2. Roasting (Cooking)

ISBN 1627108076; 9781627108072

LC 2014024594

IACP Cookbook Award Finalist: Compilations (2015)

This roasting cookbook, by the editors of Fine Cooking magazine "serves up the best recipes and techniques so home cooks can successfully produce bold-flavored, juicy meat and vegetable dishes time and again.'. . . You will easily learn the age-old art of: Slow roasting, Quick searing, Braising, [and] Simmering." (Publisher's note)

Roasting

Kaminsky, Peter

Charred & scruffed; Bold New Techniques for Explosive Flavor On and Off the Grill. Adam Perry Lang with Peter Kaminsky. Artisan 2012 xiv, 266 p.p col. ill. **641.7**

1. Barbecue cooking 2. Barbecuing

ISBN 9781579654658

LC 2011031786

In this book, chef Adam Perry Land "employs his extensive culinary background to refine and concentrate the flavors and textures of barbecue and reimagine its possibilities. Adam's new techniques, from roughing up meat and vegetables ('scruffing') to cooking directly on hot coals ('clinching') to constantly turning and moving the meat while cooking ('hot potato'), produce crust formation and layers of flavor." (Publisher's note)

Includes index

Mackay, Jordan

Franklin barbecue; a meat-smoking manifesto. Aaron Franklin and Jordan Mackay; photography by Wyatt McSpadden. Ten Speed Press 2015 224 p. illustrations (chiefly color) (hardcover) $29.99 **641.7**

1. Barbecue cooking 2. Barbecuing

ISBN 1607747200; 9781607747208

LC 2014036177

This cookbook, by Aaron Franklin and Jordan Mackay, "is a definitive resource for the backyard pitmaster, with chapters dedicated to building or customizing your own smoker; finding and curing the right wood; creating and tending perfect fires; sourcing top-quality meat; and of course, cooking mind-blowing, ridiculously delicious barbecue, better than you ever thought possible." (Publisher's note)

Franklin "spends most of the book exploring the general mechanics and intangibles behind creating a delicious brisket."

Ruhlman, Michael

Ruhlman's how to braise; foolproof techniques and recipes for the home cook. Michael Ruhlman. Little, Brown & Co. 2015 147 p. color illustrations (hardcover) $25 **641.7**

1. Braising (Cooking)

ISBN 0316254134; 9780316254137

LC 2014941487

This cookbook, by Michael Ruhlman, focuses on braising. "Among the recipes featured . . . are Moroccan Lamb Tagine, Classic Yankee Pot Roast, Mexican Pork and Posole Stew with Dried Chilis, Braised Fennel, and a Corned Beef and Cabbage Braise." (Publisher's note)

"... Ruhlman (How to Roast) notes, 'There is pleasure to be had in the aroma of floured meat sizzling in hot fat.' Anyone who shares that sentiment will want to dive into this handy guide, and anyone without a Dutch oven would be well advised to purchase one along with the book." Pub Wkly

Stevens, Molly

★ **All** about braising; the art of uncomplicated cooking. Molly Stevens; color photographs by Gentl & HyersEdge; black-and-white illustrations by Yevgeniy Solovyev; wine notes and selections by Tim Gaiser. 1st ed; W W Norton & Co Inc 2004 481 p. ill. (some col.) $35 **641.7**

1. Cookbooks 2. Braising (Cooking)

ISBN 0393052303; 9780393052305

LC 2004017907

IACP Award (2005)

James Beard Foundation Award (2005)

This book, by Molly Stevens, offers a cookbook dedicated to braising. "Written to instruct a cook at any level . . . , [it includes] 125 . . . recipes for meat, poultry, seafood, and vegetables, ranging from quick-braised weeknight dishes to slow-cooked weekend braises." It also includes "a thorough explanation of the principles of good braising with helpful advice on the best cuts of meat, the right choice of fish and vegetables, and the right pots." (Publisher's note)

"[T]he book contains interesting tasting notes and cultural information, and Stevens's lengthy instructions will be particularly valuable to beginners." Pub Wkly

Includes bibliographical references and index

All about roasting; a new approach to a classic art. photographs by Quentin Bacon; wine pairings by Tim Gaiser. W. W. Norton 2011 573p il $35 **641.7**
1. Roasting (Cooking)
ISBN 978-0-393-06526-8
LC 2011022692

The author "begins with a 45-page introduction to the art and science of roasting that should be required reading for anyone in possession of a chunk of meat and an oven. Topics covered include the differences in employing high versus low heat, the reasons to rest meat before carving, the joys of convection ovens, and why fat is always a critical component. Next come 150 recipes divided into chapters on beef, pork, poultry, fish, and vegetables. . . . [This] is a compelling collection that drives home the difference between a chef merely showing off some recipes and a teacher exploring her craft." Publ Wkly

Includes bibliographical references

641.76   Barbecuing, broiling, grilling

Carruthers, John
Eat street; the ManBQue guide to making street food at home. John Carruthers, John Scholl, Jesse Valenciana. Running Press 2016 328 p. color illustrations (paperback) $23   **641.76**
1. Cooking -- Meat 2. Barbecue cooking 3. Barbecuing 4. International cooking 5. Street food -- United States
ISBN 9780762458691; 0762458690
LC 2015959425

This book, by John Carruthers, Jesse Valenciana, and John Scholl, "presents 200 recipes for . . . street food. Starting with the setups, [readers] discover how to get the most out of everything from flat-top griddles to outdoor brick ovens to earthenware pots. Then dig into the greatest hand-held grub from around the world: Philly Cheese Steaks, Pork Belly Gyoza Dumplings, Arepas, and more." (Publisher's note)

"Recommend this humorous, unconventional cookbook to readers who like meaty and fried comfort foods with a healthy dose of sarcasm." LJ

641.8   Cooking specific kinds of dishes and preparing beverages

Alexander, William
52 loaves; one man's relentless pursuit of truth, meaning, and a perfect crust. Algonquin Books of Chapel Hill 2010 339p il $23.95   **641.8**
1. Bread
ISBN 978-1-56512-583-4
LC 2009-49656

Charts the author's attempts to bake the perfect loaf of bread, including growing, harvesting, and milling his own wheat.

"Bakers will delight in his often humorous mission as he relates leaving out salt, growing his own wheat, discovering parchment paper, and splashing water into the oven in an effort to create steam. . . . This humorous memoir is recommended for anyone who has ever tried to bake a loaf." Libr J

Includes bibliographical references

Alford, Jeffrey
Flatbreads and flavors; a baker's atlas. Jeffrey Alford and Naomi Duguid. Morrow 1995 xvi, 441 p.p ill. (some col.) $21.99   **641.8**
1. Bread 2. Cookbooks 3. International cooking
ISBN 0061673269; 0688114113; 9780061673269
LC 94030892

James Beard Award (1996)

In this cookbook, "Jeffrey Alford and Naomi Duguid have found an internationally shared and nourishing element of culture and cuisine: flatbreads, humankind's simplest, oldest, and most remarkably varied form of bread. . . . In addition, they provide 150 recipes for traditional accompaniments to the flatbreads, from chutneys and curries, salsas and stews." (Publisher's note)

Includes bibliographical references (p. 421-425) and index

The **America's** test kitchen family baking book; [by] the editors at America's Test Kitchen; photography, Daniel J. Van Ackere, Carl Tremblay, Keller + Keller. America's Test Kitchen 2008 544p il $34.95   **641.8**
1. Baking 2. America's test kitchen (Television program)
ISBN 978-1-933615-22-6; 1-933615-22-2

"Expert bakers and novices scared of baking's requisite exactitude can all learn something from this hefty, all-purpose home baking volume." Publ Wkly

Anderson, Pam
Perfect one-dish dinners; all you need for easy get-togethers. photographs by Judd Pilossof. Houghton Mifflin Harcourt 2010 266p il $32   **641.8**
1. Entertaining 2. One-dish cooking
ISBN 978-0-547-19595-7
LC 2010-21447

This is an "accessible, engaging collection of meals based around a singular dish. Grouped into four sections—summer salads and grilled platters; casseroles; the roasting pan; and stews—Anderson smartly mixes classics like Osso

Bucco, Paella, and Lasagna with riffs on standards like Coq Au Vin (here with white wine and spring vegetables) and a Spanish beef stew (with bell peppers, chickpeas, saffron, paprika, and orange). . . . Whether readers are new to cooking or simply looking for new ideas for meals, Anderson's winning collection is sure to encourage and inspire." Publ Wkly

Andres, Jose

Tapas; a taste of Spain in America. [by] José Andrés with Richard Wolffe. Clarkson Potter 2005 256p il $35　　**641.8**
1. Appetizers 2. Spanish cooking
ISBN 1-4000-5359-5

LC 2004-27466

The author presents some of the small-plate dishes "he serves at his tapas restaurants, including traditional favorites recreated with American ingredients. . . . Recipes are organized by ingredient, from olives and olive oil to citrus to fish, shellfish, and meat, and they are mouth-watering: Oven-Roasted Potatoes and Oyster Mushrooms, for example, or Lobster with Pimentón and Olive Oil." Libr J

Includes bibliographical references

Baking illustrated; a best recipe classic. by the editors of Cook's illustrated; illustrations, John Burgoyne; photography, Carl Tremblay, Keller + Keller, Daniel Van Ackere. America's Test Kitchen 2004 515p il $35　　**641.8**
1. Baking
ISBN 0-936184-75-2

"Test kitchen cooks analyzed brand-name baking ingredients and equipment and . . . make 'best buy' recommendations. . . . The test summaries preceding each recipe include both successes and failures; the resulting recipes (more than 350) cover everything from the simplest quick breads to more complex yeast breads and cookies and pastries. . . . This is the best instructional book on baking this reviewer has seen." Libr J

Bauer, Jeni Britton

Jeni's splendid ice creams at home. Artisan 2011 217p il $23.95　　**641.8**
1. Ice cream, ices, etc.
ISBN 978-1-57965-436-8; 1-57965-436-3

LC 2010-39453

"This inspiring collection of seasonal ice cream recipes from Ohio-based ice cream whiz Bauer stands apart for its creative, unconventional flavors like Sweet Basil & Honeyed Pine Nut and Sweet Potato with Torched Marshmallows." Libr J

Beard, James

Beard on bread; drawings by Karl Stuecklen. Knopf 1973 230p il hardcover o.p. pa $15 **641.8**
1. Bread
ISBN 0-679-75504-7 pa

"An inclusive guide to the preparation of a variety of breads with recipes for coffee cakes, rolls, flat breads, fried cakes. . . . The recipes included are those Beard considers the best from around the world which can be made in a U.S. kitchen." Booklist

Beranbaum, Rose Levy

The **cake** bible; edited by Maria D. Guarnaschelli; photographs by Vincent Lee; foreword by Maida Heatter. Morrow 1988 555p il　　**641.8**
1. Cake
ISBN 0-688-04402-6; 978-0-688-04402-2

LC 8801369

This collection of cake recipes includes "discussions on ingredients and equipment and concludes with a . . . section on the chemistry of cake baking and on making . . . professional wedding cakes." (Libr J) Bibliography. Index.

Includes bibliographical references

The **best** one-dish suppers; a best recipe classic. by the editors of Cook's Illustrated; photography, Keller + Keller, Carl Tremblay, and Daniel J. Van Ackere; illustrations, John Burgoyne. America's Test Kitchen 2011 342p il $35　　**641.8**
1. One-dish cooking 2. Quick and easy cooking
ISBN 978-1-933615-81-3

"This volume presents recipes (180 of them, further clarified by 169 illustrations) for supremely simple meals (including many versions of tempting classics) prepared in one cooking vessel. There are dinners that can be made in just a sheet pan, a single pot, a dutch oven, or a slow cooker, plus stews and chilis, casseroles, and stir-frys. . . . This book could easily become a go-to resource for busy home cooks." Publ Wkly

Blakeslee, Robert L.

Your time to bake; a first cookbook for the novice baker. by Robert L. Blakeslee. Square One Publishers 2012 384 p. (hardback) $29.95　　**641.8**
1. Baking 2. Desserts 3. Cookbooks 4. Cake decorating
ISBN 9780757003554

LC 2011014622

In this cookbook, "[Robert L.] Blakeslee includes 'step by step photo instructions, with a finished shot of each recipe.' . . . He provides recipes for every simple sweet treat imaginable. . . . Explaining that baking is 'more about chemistry,' Blakeslee . . . discusses 'important baking variables and how to control them,' with helpful tips: measuring ingredients exactly and making sure ingredients such as eggs and butter are the correct temperature. Also . . . [included] are sections on essential items needed for baking--such as different flours, sugars, spices and cheeses--important equipment, and baking terms from A to Z. . . . [T]here are more than 150 recipes . . . and a final chapter on decorating cookies, tarts, and cupcakes and making fondant." (Publishers Weekly)

Boyle, Tish

The **cake** book; the definitive guide to making great cakes with nearly 200 recipes. Tish Boyle; photography by John Uher. Houghton Mifflin Harcourt 2006 376 p. ill. (some col.) $39.95　　**641.8**
1. Cake 2. Cookbooks 3. Cake decorating
ISBN 0471469335; 9780471469339

LC 2005021384

This cake cookbook, written by Tish Boyle, "includes recipes ranging from pound cakes and coffee cakes to meringue, mousse, and ice cream cakes to fillings, frostings, and more. Throughout, color and black-and-white photographs and drawings show you important techniques and spectacular end results. A difficulty rating with each recipe helps you decide which to make, depending on how much time--or ambition--you have." (Publisher's note)

"Well written, easy to read, and beautifully photographed." LJ

Colicchio, Tom

'wichcraft; craft a sandwich into a meal--and a meal into a sandwich. [by] Tom Colicchio with Sisha Ortúzar; text by Rhona Silverbush; photographs by Bill Bettencourt. Clarkson Potter/Publishers 2009 208p il $27.50   641.8

1. Sandwiches

ISBN 978-0-609-61051-0

LC 2008-27803

The authors offer "an entire cookbook featuring the sandwiches served at . . . [their] New York restaurant, 'wichcraft. . . . This book's table of contents alone will have grab-and-go eaters and sophisticated gastronomes alike salivating." Booklist

The **Complete** book of pasta and noodles; by the editors of Cook's illustrated; preface by Christopher Kimball; illustrations by Judy Love; photographs by Daniel J. van Ackere. Potter 2000 483p il hardcover o.p. pa $19.95   641.8

1. Cooking -- Pasta products

ISBN 0-609-80930-X pa

LC 99-40076

This work brings "together information and recipes covering pasta's worldwide range from North America's beloved macaroni and cheese through Italy's sophisticated sauces, across China's exotic rice noodles, and up to Japan's modest Zen noodles in broth. . . . Content and organization combine to make this a superior cooking reference book for libraries." Booklist

Corriher, Shirley

BakeWise; the hows and whys of successful baking with over 200 magnificent recipes. [by] Shirley O. Corriher. Scribner 2008 532p $40   641.8

1. Baking

ISBN 978-1-4165-6078-4; 1-4165-6078-5

LC 2008-32681

This "collection of more than 200 recipes offers amateur and expert bakers alike clear, numbered steps and a plethora of information on ingredients, equipment and method. Invaluable troubleshooting sections solve pesky problems on everything from pale and crumbly cookies to fallen soufflés. . . . Astute references to a variety of chefs, cookbook authors and restaurants add a knowing punch to this solid collection that's sure to please bakers of all skill levels." Publ Wkly

Crocker, Betty

★ Betty Crocker cookie book; rev ed; Wiley 2003 xxix, 322p il $22.95   641.8

1. Cookies

ISBN 0-7645-3940-X

LC 2003-270127

First published 1963 by Golden Press with title: Cooky book

This book features "over 240 cookie favorites, from heirloom showstoppers to contemporary treats . . . [including] everything from chocolate chip cookies to brownies, oatmeal cookies to date bars and more." Publisher's note

Daley, Regan

In the sweet kitchen; the definitive baker's companion. Artisan 2001 692p il hardcover o.p. pa $24.95   641.8

1. Baking

ISBN 1-57965-208-5; 1-57965-427-4 pa

LC 2001-41289

"While other books include some details on baking ingredients and tools as part of their introduction to the craft, . . . [this] is the definitive guide to all the equipment, techniques, and ingredients a baker uses." Libr J

Includes bibliographical references

DeMasco, Karen

The craft of baking; cakes, cookies, & other sweets with ideas for inventing your own. [by] Karen DeMasco & Mindy Fox; photographs by Ellen Silverman. Clarkson Potter Publishers 2009 256p il $35   641.8

1. Cake 2. Candy 3. Baking 4. Cookies 5. Desserts

ISBN 978-0-307-40810-5; 0-307-40810-8

"In the first sections, [DeMarco] covers ingredients and techniques accessible even to novice bakers. Then come her 'new modern-day treats,' created with 'traditional recipes and familiar home baking techniques,' e.g., Lemon Olive Cake (an interesting variation on the traditional lemon cake using butter and extra virgin olive oil). Sources are listed for hard-to-find items. Owing to DeMasco's well-respected culinary pedigree, home bakers will want this." Libr J

Desaulniers, Marcel

Death by chocolate cakes; an astonishing array of chocolate enchantment. recipes with Brett Bailey and Kelly Bailey; photography by Duane Winfield. Morrow 2000 216p il $35   641.8

1. Cake 2. Cooking -- Chocolate

ISBN 0-688-16297-5

LC 00-56247

This "cookbook features indulgent showstoppers, from Happy All the Time Cakes to Excessively Expressive Espresso Ecstasy, each one shown in a full-page color photograph. Although many of the recipes are complicated, instructions are detailed and clear; there are no headnotes per se to introduce these creations, but 'The Chef's Touch' section at the end of each recipe provides tips and some background." Libr J

Includes bibliographical references

Fine cooking appetizers; 200 recipes for small bites with big flavor. from the editors and contributors of Fine cooking. Taunton Press 2010 252 p. col. ill. $19.95   **641.8**
1. Cookbooks 2. Appetizers
ISBN 1600853307; 9781600853302
LC 2010028598

"In [this collection] the editors of Fine Cooking have gathered a tempting--and satisfying--range of recipes on favorite topics. . . . As always, clear instructions, full-color photos, plus tips and techniques help you get delicious results." This cookbook features 200 recipes for appetizers. (Publisher's note)

The **Gourmet** cookie book; the single best recipe from each year 1941-2009. Houghton Mifflin Harcourt 2010 161p il $18   **641.8**
1. Cookies
ISBN 978-0-547-32816-4
LC 2010-18882

This cookbook "features one recipe for every year Gourmet magazine was in business. . . . The recipes are grouped by decade, from the ration-era pluck of the 1940s (honey refrigerator cookies and Scotch oat crunchies), when the magazine was published out of a penthouse in the Plaza Hotel, to the twisted classics of the oughts (cranberry turtle bars and glittering lemon sandwich cookies). The wistful headnotes offer historical insight into our past tastes and aspirations." N Y Times Book Rev

Haedrich, Ken
★ **Pie**: 300 tried-and-true recipes for delicious homemade pie. The Harvard Common Press 2004 639p il $37.95; pa $24.95   **641.8**
1. Baking
ISBN 1-558-32253-1; 1-558-32254-X pa
LC 2004-3635

Haedrich's "zeal and solid expertise make this book a worthy addition to the baker's bookshelf." Publ Wkly

Heatter, Maida
Maida Heatter's book of great desserts; drawings by Toni Evins. Andrew McMeel 1999 xxxii, 528p il $26.95   **641.8**
1. Desserts
ISBN 0-8362-7861-5
LC 98-45993

First published 1974 by Knopf

This cookbook features nearly 300 dessert recipes for both light and rich desserts including Queen Mother's Cake, Mushroom Meringues, and East 62nd Street Lemon Cake

Maida Heatter's brand-new book of great cookies; illustrations by the author. Random House 1995 244p il hardcover o.p. pa $19   **641.8**
1. Cookies
ISBN 0-8129-9175-3 pa
LC 95-5250

First published 1977 with title: Book of great cookies
"The instructions here are true to a long line of Heatter recipes: foolproof. Ms. Heatter's instructions are famously

meticulous. They are also lengthy and chatty, full of learned asides." N Y Times Book Rev

Maida Heatter's cookies; by Maida Heatter; illustrations by Melanie Marder Parks. Cader Books Andrews McMeel 1997 xii, 308 p.p illustrations $19.99   **641.8**
1. Baking 2. Cookies
ISBN 0836237331; 1449401155; 9781449401153
LC 97031043

This book is a "classic cookie collection from Maida Heatter, James Beard Lifetime Hall of Fame member. . . . [It] offers 225 classic cookie recipes for drop cookies, bar cookies, icebox cookies, rolled cookies, hand-formed cookies, dessert crackers, ice creams, sauces, and more, accompanied by two-color, line-drawn illustrated pages." (Publisher's note)
Cookies

Hellmich, Mittie, 1960-
Ultimate bar book; the comprehensive guide to over 1,000 cocktails. by Mittie Hellmich; illustrations by Arthur Mount. Chronicle Books 2006 474 p. ill. (jacket) $19.95   **641.8**
1. Cocktails 2. Bartending
ISBN 0811843513; 9780811843515
LC 2005030720

This alcoholic mixed-drinks guidebook, by Mittie Hellmich, features "essential-to-know topics such as barware, tools, and mixing tips. . . . Illustrations show precisely what type of glass should be used for each drink. With dozens of recipes for garnishes, rims, infusions, and syrups; punches, gelatin shooters, hot drinks, and non-alcoholic beverages." (Publisher's note)
Includes bibliographical references and indexes

Hensperger, Beth
The **best** quick breads; 150 recipes for muffins, scones, shortcakes, gingerbreads, cornbreads, coffeecakes, and more. Beth Hensperger. Harvard Common Press 2000 256p pa $22.95   **641.8**
1. Bread
ISBN 1-55832-171-3
LC 00-36962

First published 1994 by Chronicle Books with title: The art of quick breads

This book includes about 150 recipes. "In addition to quick loaves, both sweet and savory, there are waffles, dumplings, biscuits, popovers, and a variety of other easy baked goods, along with some tasty accompaniments, such as the Fruit Salsa for her Hopi Blue Corn Hotcakes." Libr J

Hirigoyen, Gerald
Pintxos; small plates in the Basque tradition. [by] Gerald Hirigoyen with Lisa Weiss; photography by Maren Caruso. Ten Speed Press 2009 201p il $24.95   **641.8**
1. Cooking 2. Basque cooking
ISBN 978-1-58008-922-7; 1-58008-922-4
LC 2008-43518

Lebovitz, David

The **perfect** scoop; ice creams, sorbets, granitas, and sweet accompaniments. David Lebovitz; photography by Lara Hata. Ten Speed Press 2007 256 p. il (pbk) $18.99; (hbk) $24.99   **641.8**
 1. Desserts 2. Cookbooks 3. Ice cream, ices, etc.
 ISBN 9781580082198; 9781580088084; 158008219X
                             LC 2006037610

This cookbook, by David Lebovitz, offers a "guide to the pleasures of homemade ice creams, sorbets, granitas, and more. With an emphasis on intense and sophisticated flavors and a bountiful helping of the author's expert techniques, this collection of frozen treats ranges from classic . . . to comforting . . . , contemporary . . . to cutting edge." (Publisher's note)

"The author's 25 years of experience as a frozen-dessert maker are put to excellent use in this wittily written, detailed volume. Step-by-step photos and advice on selecting an ice cream machine will reassure ice cream amateurs." Pub Wkly

Matheson, Christie

Flour; spectacular recipes from Boston's Flour Bakery + Cafe. by Joanne Chang, with Christie Matheson; photographs by Keller + Keller. Chronicle Books 2010 319 p. col. ill. (hbk.) $35   **641.8**
 1. Flour 2. Baking 3. Cookbooks 4. Baked products 5. Flour Bakery + Cafe 6. Baking -- Massachusetts -- Boston 7. Cooking -- Massachusetts -- Boston
 ISBN 081186944X; 9780811869447
                             LC 2011377998

This baking cookbook, by Joanne Chang with Christie Matheson, features Boston, Massachusetts-based "Flour Bakery-owner Joanne Chang's repertoire of baked goods. . . . Almost 150 Flour recipes such as Milky Way Tart and Dried Fruit Focaccia are included, plus Joanne's essential baking tips." (Publisher's note)

Medrich, Alice

Chewy gooey crispy crunchy melt-in-your-mouth cookies. Artisan Books 2010 384p il $25.95 **641.8**
 1. Cookies
 ISBN 978-1-57965-397-2
                             LC 2010-19491

"Medrich presents a compendium of exciting and enticing cookie recipes that reflects every aspect of our widening culinary landscape. . . . The recipes are organized by texture, hence the title, but there's also a section grouping cookies into categories like those containing whole grains, those that keep at least two weeks, ridiculously quick and easy cookies, and cookies to make with kids. This book has redesigned and reframed the often-overlooked cookie and is a boon to the modern, conscious baker." Publ Wkly

Mix shake stir; cocktails for the home bar: recipes from Danny Meyer's acclaimed New York City restaurants. foreward by Danny Meyer. Little, Brown 2009 223p il $29.99   **641.8**
 1. Cocktails
 ISBN 978-0-316-04512-4; 0-316-04512-8
                           LC 2008-934947

Restauranteur Meyers "delivers a terrific collection of 140 tempting recipes for cocktails created by bartenders in his award-winning dining establishments. Included are old favorites like the Ritz as well as new classics like the Winter Mojito, and the book's clear instructions and luscious photographs will inspire even nondrinkers to pick up a cocktail shaker. As a bonus, basic tips on mixing drinks, recipes for simple syrups and garnishes, and a concise collection of recipes for bar snacks are offered." Libr J

Mushet, Cindy

The **art** and soul of baking; [by] Sur La Table with Cindy Mushet; foreword by Alice Medrich; photography by Maren Caruso. Andrews McMeel Pub. 2008 454p il $40   **641.8**
 1. Baking
 ISBN 978-0-7407-7334-1; 0-7407-7334-8
                             LC 2008-8232

This guide to baking "covers both sweet and savory baking. . . . Two lengthy introductory chapters cover techniques, equipment, and ingredients, and dozens of sidebars on 'Tips for Success' and 'What the Pros Know' offer further helpful insider advice. . . . Mushet's style is engaging and never intimidating. Essential." Libr J

Ojakangas, Beatrice

The **Best** Casserole cookbook ever; by Beatrice Ojakangas; photographs by Susie Cushner. Chronicle Books 2008 640 p. col. ill. (alk. paper) $24.95 **641.8**
 1. Baking 2. Cookbooks 3. Casserole cooking
 ISBN 0811856240; 9780811856249
                             LC 2007042019

This cookbook, by Beatrice Ojakangas, with photography by Susie Cushner, is dedicated to baking casseroles. "From a breakfast of Eggs Florentine to a dinner of Pork Chops with Apple Stuffing, soon even the most casserole-wary cook will be dishing about these delights. Yummy treats like Parmesan and Sun-Dried Tomato Quiche and Strawberry Rhubarb Crisp are just right for parties. Even appetizers are reinvented in casserole form!" (Publisher's note)

Parsons, Brad Thomas

Bitters; a spirited history of a classic cure-all, with cocktails, recipes, and formulas. Brad Thomas Parsons; photographs by Ed Anderson. Ten Speed Press 2011 231 p. col. ill. $24.99   **641.8**
 1. Cocktails 2. Alcohol -- History 3. Alcoholic beverages 4. Bitters
 ISBN 1580083595; 9781580083591
                             LC 2011017774
 IACP Award (2012)
 James Beard Award (2012)
 A brief history of bitters -- A bitters boom -- Making your own bitters -- Setting up your bar -- Bitters hall of fame -- Old-guard cocktails -- New-look cocktails -- Bitters in the kitchen

This book, by Brad Thomas Parsons with photography by Ed Anderson, "traces the history of the world's most storied elixir, [bitters,] from its earliest 'snake oil' days to its near evaporation after Prohibition to its ascension as a beloved (and at times obsessed-over) ingredient on the contemporary bar scene." (Publisher's note)

Includes bibliographical references and index

Pasta, atlante dei prodotti tipici/English
  Encyclopedia of pasta; translated by Maureen B. Fant; with a foreword by Carol Field. University of California Press 2009 xxi, 374p il map (California studies in food and culture) $29.95   **641.8**
  1. Italian cooking 2. Reference books 3. Cooking -- Pasta products 4. Pasta products -- Encyclopedias
  ISBN 978-0-520-25522-7
                                                          LC 2009-10522
  This book provides "a complete history of pasta in Italy, showcasing more than 300 types of pasta—from bucatini and gnocchetti to tortellini and ziti. . . . Each entry is nicely displayed in a box and includes an overview of each pasta type: the primary ingredients, preparation techniques, the different names for each kind of pasta, how it is served, the region where it is found, and the author's remarks. . . . This wonderful resource is destined to become the definitive book on pasta. It succeeds both as a scholarly achievement and as an entertaining and authentic overview of Italian history and geography." Libr J
  Includes bibliographical references

Patent, Greg
  Baking in America; traditional and contemporary favorites from the past 200 years. Houghton Mifflin 2002 552p il $35   **641.8**
  1. Baking
  ISBN 0-618-04831-6
  "Patent's cookbook will be irresistible to anyone interested in the rich traditions and history of American baking." Libr J

Peterson, James
  Baking. Ten Speed Press 2009 378p il $40 **641.8**
  1. Baking
  ISBN 978-1-58008-991-3
  "This workhorse of a guidebook . . . is a worthy baking school between covers. . . . The work features over 300 recipes, mostly classics based in the French tradition. The five chapters—Cakes; Pies, Tarts and Pastries; Cookies; Breads, Quick Breads, and Bread-based Desserts; and Custards, Soufflés, Fruit Curds and Mousses—include a comprehensive overview, sidebars on techniques and recipes designed to teach techniques that can be used in more than the recipe listed." Publ Wkly

Pillsbury Co.
  Pillsbury best cookies cookbook; favorite recipes from America's most-trusted kitchens. [by] the Pillsbury Company. Wiley Pub 2003 255p il $22.95   **641.8**
  1. Cookies
  ISBN 0-7645-8854-0; 978-0-7645-8854-9
  First published 1997 by Potter
  This "cookbook includes more than 175 recipes for cookies, brownies, and other bars, from old favorites like Chocolate Chips to new ones like Cherry Poppy Seed Twinks. . . . There are also lots of tips and hints, suggestions to 'Make It Special,' and variations, as well as 'real-time' prep times and nutrition analyses for each recipe." Libr J [review of 1997 edition]

Robertson, Chad
  Tartine; by Elisabeth M. Prueitt and Chad Robertson; foreword by Alice Waters; photographs by France Ruffenach. Chronicle Books 2006 223 p. ill. (chiefly col.) $35   **641.8**
  1. Pastry 2. Desserts 3. Cookbooks 4. Tartine (Bakery)
  ISBN 0811851508; 9780811851503
                                                          LC 2006004651
  In this cookbook, "pastry chef Elisabeth Prueitt and . . . baker Chad Robertson share not only their fabulous recipes, but also the secrets and expertise that transform a delicious homemade treat into a great one." Recipes featured include "moist Brioche Bread Pudding; luscious Banana Cream Pie; [and] the sweet-tart perfection of Apple Crisp. . . . Practical advice comes in the form of handy Kitchen Notes. These "hows" and "whys" convey the authors' know-how." (Publisher's note)

  Tartine bread; photographs by Eric Wolfinger. Chronicle Books 2010 304p il $40   **641.8**
  1. Bread
  ISBN 978-0-8118-7041-2
  "This 'baker's guidebook' is divided into four parts: Basic Country Bread; Semolina and Whole-Wheat Breads; Baguettes and Enriched Breads; and Day-Old Bread. Robertson's basic recipe is explained in depth with numbered steps, and consists of making a natural leaven and baking in a cast-iron cooker. The author's passionate tone and tales of baking apprenticeships, along with top-notch step-by-step photos, elevate the title from mere manual to enjoyable read." Publ Wkly

Sax, Richard
  ★ **Classic** home desserts; a treasury of heirloom and contemporary recipes from around the world. Richard Sax; photography by Alan Richardson. Houghton Mifflin Harcourt 2010 648 p. col il $35   **641.8**
  1. Desserts 2. Cookbooks 3. International cooking
  ISBN 0618057080; 9780618057085
                                                          LC 2010025552
  IACP Cookbook Award (1995)
  James Bead Award (1995)
  This dessert cookbook, by Richard Sax with photography by Alan Richardson, winner of the James Beard Award and the Julia Child Award, offers "350 of the best and most beloved home desserts. Everything the cook longs for is here: cobblers and crisps, cakes and cookies, puddings and soufflés, pies and pastries, ice creams and sauces." (Publisher's note)
  Includes bibliographical references and index

Schreiber, Cory
  Rustic fruit desserts; crumbles, buckles, cobblers, pandowdies, and more. [by] Cory Schreiber and Julie Richardson; photography by Sara Remington. Ten Speed Press 2009 164p il $22   **641.8**
  1. Desserts 2. Cooking -- Fruit
  ISBN 978-1-58008-976-0; 1-58008-976-3
                                                          LC 2008-49349

"A seasonal mini-bible that goes beyond basics." N Y Times Book Rev

Tosi, Christina

Momofuku Milk Bar; Christina Tosi. 1st ed.; Clarkson Potter 2011 p. cm. $35 **641.8**
1. Baking 2. Desserts 3. Momofuku Milk Bar
ISBN 978-0-307-72049-8

LC 2011007720

"Momofuku Milk Bar finally shares the recipes for these now-legendary riffs on childhood flavors and down-home classics—all essentially derived from ten mother recipes—along with the compelling narrative of the unlikely beginnings of this quirky bakery's success. It all started one day when Momofuku founder David Chang asked Christina to make a dessert for dinner that night. Just like that, the pastry program at Momofuku began, and Christina's playful desserts helped the restaurants earn praise from theNew York Times and the Michelin Guide and led to the opening of Milk Bar, which now draws fans from around the country and the world." (Publisher's note)

Walter, Carole

Great cookies; secrets to sensational sweets. Carole Walter; photographs by Duane Winfield. 1st ed; Clarkson Potter 2003 418 p. col. ill. $35 **641.8**
1. Cookbooks 2. Cookies
ISBN 0609609696; 9780609609699

LC 2003007633

IACP Cookbook Award Winner (2004)

This cookbook, by Carole Walter with photography by Duane Winfield, is "packed with more than 200 . . . recipes and more than 150 . . . photographs [of cookies,] . . . from traditional favorites like Snickerdoodles, Oatmeal Raisin, and Favorite Lemon Squares to future stars of the cookie jar like the trail mix-inspired Teton Trailers and chewy, chocolaty Midnight Macaroons." (Publisher's note)

Includes bibliographical references (p. 404) and index

Wells, Patricia

Salad as a meal; healthy main-dish salads for every season. Patricia Wells; photography by Jeff Kauck. William Morrow 2011 360 p. illustrations $34.99 **641.8**
1. Salads
ISBN 006123883X; 9780061238833

LC 2010027043

This book, by Patricia Wells is a "definitive guide to creating delicious and hearty salads for any occasion—including more than 150 recipes and gorgeous color photographs. . . . You can experience a whole world in a salad—with tender greens, savory meat, seafood, and vegetable accompaniments, and versatile dressings—and salad-friendly sides such as homemade bread and home-cured olives." (Publisher's note)

"Given Wells's high profile and the book's useful focus, this can't miss wherever cookbooks are popular." LJ

Zabar, Tracey

One sweet cookie; celebrated chefs share favorite recipes. photography by Ellen Silverman. Rizzoli 2011 191p il $30 **641.8**
1. Cookies
ISBN 978-0-8478-3666-6

LC 2011927545

"When cookie-obsessed baker Zabar couldn't convince friends to participate in a cookie swap, she orchestrated a virtual exchange, the result of which is this outstanding collection of recipes from more than 50 well-known New York City chefs. . . . [It features] contributions from Dorie Greenspan, Michael Laiskonis, Maury Rubin, Laurent Tourondel, and others." Libr J

Includes bibliographical references

641.81   Side dishes, sauces, garnishes

Baker, Lucy

Fat witch bake sale; 67 recipes from the beloved Fat Witch Bakery for your next bake sale or party. Patricia Helding with Lucy Baker. Rodale Books 2014 184 p. color illustrations (hardback) $22.99 **641.81**
1. Baking 2. Baked products 3. Fat Witch Bakery
ISBN 1623362261; 9781623362263

LC 2014038513

This cookbook, by Patricia Helding, presents a "collection of yummy brownies, blondies, barks, bars, and more . . . along with tips and tricks for packaging and selling them at your next bake sale. Here are mouthwatering recipes for Pecan Caramel Brownies; Red Velvet Brownies; Five Layer Chocolate Bars; Jelly Blondies; Cinnamon Bars; Pumpkin Oatmeal Bars; Coconut Macadamia Cookies; uniquely grownup flavors like Fruitcake Brownies and Rum Raisin Spice Bars; and even gluten-free treats." (Publisher's note)

Beranbaum, Rose Levy

★ The **baking** Bible; Rose Levy Beranbaum. Houghton Mifflin Harcourt 2014 576 p. color illustrations (hardback) $40 **641.81**
1. Baking 2. Cookbooks
ISBN 1118338618; 9781118338612

LC 2014016319

IACP Cookbook Award: Baking: Savory or Sweet (2015)

"With all-new recipes for the best cakes, pies, tarts, cookies, candies, pastries, breads, and more, this magnum opus draws from [author] Rose [Levy Beranbaum's] passion and expertise in every category of baking. As is to be expected from the woman who's been called 'the most meticulous cook who ever lived,' each sumptuous recipe is truly foolproof--with detail-oriented instructions that eliminate guesswork, 'plan-aheads,' ingenious tips, and highlights for success." (Publisher's note)

"Berenbaum successfully bridges the gap between popular home baking collections and professional texts." LJ

Black, Sarah

One dough, ten breads; making great bread by hand. Sarah Black; photography by Lauren Volo.

Houghton Mifflin Harcourt Publishing Co. 2016 224 p. color illustrations (hardcover) $25   **641.81**
1. Bread 2. Baking
ISBN 9780470260951

LC 2015004574

This bread cookbook, by Sarah Black with photography by Lauren Volo, offers an "introduction to making bread by hand, from one easy dough to ten classic loaves to infinite possibilities. . . . instructor Sarah Black starts with the simplest 'plain white' dough, then makes small changes to ingredients, proportions, and shapes to take the reader through ten 'foundation' breads." (Publisher's note)

"Black, who believes "getting your hands in the dough is the best way to learn about bread," provides easy-to-follow directions for 10 types of bread, each created from one dough and with less than 30 minutes of active time." Pub Wkly

Day, Cheryl
Back in the Day Bakery, made with love; more than 100 recipes and make-it-yourself projects to create and share. Cheryl Day and Griffith Day. Artisan Books 2015 312 p. color illustrations $24.95 **641.81**
1. Baking 2. Cookbooks 3. Cake 4. Pies 5. Back in the Day Bakery (Savannah, Ga.)
ISBN 1579655564; 9781579655563

LC 2014035874

This baking cookbook, by Cheryl Day and Griffith Day, "features more than 100 . . . recipes, including some of the[ir] bakery's most requested treats, such as Star Brownies and the Cakette Party Cake, as well as savories like Chive Parmigiano-Reggiano Popovers and Rosemary Focaccia. Cheryl and Griff share their baking techniques and also show readers how to put together whimsical decorations, like a marshmallow chandelier and a best-in-show banner." (Publisher's note)

"Though the Days are wordy at times, the narrative is instructive and warming. The inclusion of crafts like a marshmallow chandelier and a "keepsake cake topper" seems jarring rather than jovial, the only off note. This is a terrific sequel, and fans of Southern baking (not to mention baking in general) will want to add it to their collection." Pub Wkly
Includes bibliographical references and index

Daykin, Rosie
Butter baked goods; nostalgic recipes from a little neighborhood bakery. Rosie Daykin; photography by Janis Nicolay. Alfred A. Knopf 2015 272 p. color illustrations (hardcover) $29.95   **641.81**
1. Baking 2. Cooking 3. Cake 4. Pastry 5. Baked products
ISBN 1101875089; 9781101875087

LC 2014039534

This cookbook by Rosie Daykin "has simple instructions written in an accessible and easy-to-follow style, plus tips on how to stock your pantry and your toolbox with everything that you'll need to get started. Rosie's baking is not about trickery . . . but about great-tasting, homemade treats that celebrate life's milestones: birthdays, Thanksgiving, Christmas, Easter, baby showers, bridal showers, or just that gloomy afternoon when you need a little pick-me-up." (Publisher's note)

"Daykin's enchanting collection of traditional goodies made from scratch (with plenty of butter, sugar, and heavy cream) can help home bakers improve their skills and expand their repertoire."

Food52 baking; 60 sensational treats you can pull off in a snap. by the editors of Food52; photography by James Ransom. Ten Speed Press 2015 172 p. color illustrations (hardback) $22.99   **641.81**
1. Baking 2. Desserts
ISBN 1607748010; 9781607748014

LC 2015027663

This cookbook "curated by the editors of Food52, [shows how] you can have homemade treats far superior to the store-bought variety, even when it feels like you're too busy to turn on the oven. From Brown Butter Cupcake Brownies to 'Cuppa Cuppa Sticka' Peach and Blueberry Cobbler, these sixty reliable, easy-to-execute recipes won't have you hunting down special equipment and hard-to-find ingredients." (Publisher's note)

"A troubleshooting guide collects tips scattered through the book, explaining how to stale fresh bread in a hurry, how to pit cherries without a cherry pitter, and how to package cookies for the mail. This title may just become that one baking book kept out on the counter for use time and time again." Pub Wkly
Baking

Forkish, Ken
Flour water salt yeast; the fundamentals of artisan bread and pizza. Ken Forkish; photographs by alan Weiner. Ten Speed Press 2012 265 p. col. ill. (hardback) $35   **641.81**
1. Bread 2. Pizza 3. Baking 4. Cookbooks
ISBN 160774273X; 9781607742739; 9781607742746

LC 2012012080

IACP Cookbook Award (2013)
James Beard Foundation Award: Baking and Dessert (2013)

This book, by Ken Forkish, is "[d]ivided into four sections ('The Principles of Artisan Bread,' 'Basic Bread Recipes,' 'Levain Bread Recipes,' and 'Pizza Recipes'), with recipes broken down by breads made with store-bought yeast, breads made with long-fermented simple doughs, and doughs made with pre-ferments. . . . [The] book presents recipes accessible to novices, while providing a different approach for making dough to experienced bakers." (Publishers Weekly)

Fromartz, Samuel
★ **In** search of the perfect loaf; a home baker's odyssey. Samuel Fromartz. Viking 2014 256 p. illustrations (hardback) $26.95   **641.81**
1. Bread
ISBN 0670025615; 9780670025619

LC 2014004522

In this memoir, journalist Samuel Fromartz "was offered the assignment of a lifetime: to travel to France to work in a boulangerie. So began his quest to hone not just his homemade baguette . . . but his knowledge of bread, from seed to table. For the next four years, Fromartz traveled across the United States and Europe, perfecting his sourdough in California, his whole grain rye in Berlin, and his country wheat in the South of France." (Publisher's note)

"Richly detailed history and lively anecdotes make this book a consummate celebration of the deceptively simple loaf of bread." Kirkus

Includes bibliographical references and index

Goldman, Duff

Duff Bakes; Duff Goldman. HarperCollins 2014 304 p. color illustrations $27.50 **641.81**

1. Cake 2. Baking 3. Pastry 4. Cookies

ISBN 0062349805; 9780062349804

This book, by celebrity baker Duff Goldman, is a "full-color baking book filled with more than 100 recipes for irresistible must-bake favorites, from cakes to cookies to brownies to muffins to breads. . . . [It] includes chapters on different types of pastry dough, a variety of cookies, brownies, muffins, bread, biscuits, pies, cakes and cake decorating, gluten-free and vegan desserts, and much more." (Publisher's note)

"Rounded out with plenty of salient tips on everything from selecting the right blowtorch (hit the hardware store) to getting cheesecake out of a cake pan (briefly warm the bottom over the stove top), Goldman and Gonzalez's thoughtful instructions are sure to inspire and embolden readers." Pub Wkly

Kulaga, Agatha

Ovenly; sweet and salty recipes from New York's most creatvie bakery. Agatha Kulaga & Erin Patinkin; photography by Winona Barton-Ballentine. Harlequin Nonfiction 2014 240 p. color illustrations (alk. paper) $29.95 **641.81**

1. Bread 2. Baking 3. Baked products 4. Ovenly (Bakery)

ISBN 0373892950; 9780373892952

LC 2014005173

This cookbook by Erin Patinkin and Agatha Kulaga is based on "Ovenly . . . an award-winning bakery headquartered in Greenpoint, Brooklyn. Since 2010, their innovative baked goods have found their way into cafés, restaurants and stores nationwide." (Publisher's note)

"Complemented by an attractive design and step-by-step photographs of important techniques, this is a satisfying everyday baking collection—perfect for readers who like substantial baked goods with a salty streak." LJ

Peacock, Julie

The **soup** club cookbook; feed your friends, feed your family, feed yourself. Courtney Allison, Tina Carr, Caroline Laskow, and Julie Peacock. Clarkson Potter Publishers 2014 240 p. illustrations (mostly color) (paperback) $25 **641.81**

1. Soups 2. One-dish cooking 3. One-dish meals

ISBN 0770434622; 9780770434625; 9780770434632

LC 2014009496

In this book, authors Courtney Allison, Tina Carr, Caroline Laskow, and Julie Peacock "share not only their formula for starting a soup club--which gives you at least three meals every month when you don't have to worry about dinner--but also 150 fantastic recipes for soups and sides and stor-

ing tips for stretching those meals across the week." (Publisher's note)

Peterson, James

★ **Sauces;** classical and contemporary sauce making. James Peterson. 3rd ed.; J. Wiley 2008 612 p. ill. (chiefly col.) $49.95 **641.81**

1. Sauces 2. Cookbooks

ISBN 0470194960; 9780470194966

LC 2007046546

James Bead Award (1992)

This cookbook, the third edition by James Peterson, is the "former winner of the prestigious James Beard Cookbook-of-the-Year award and the ultimate reference for saucemaking. . . . With more 325 recipes in all, [it] includes all-new chapters on Asian sauces and pasta sauces, plus new recipes that cater to lighter, contemporary tastes. Includes a 32-page color insert with more than 100 color photos of sauce-making techniques." (Publisher's note)

"In the third edition, the sections have been organized so the entries are easier to use as a reference. Peterson has also added 60 recipes that showcase the sauces with a variety of foods." LJ

Includes bibliographical references and index

Robertson, Chad

Tartine Book No. 3; modern, ancient, classic, whole. Chad Robertson. Chronicle Books 2013 336 p. color illustrations $40 **641.81**

1. Baking 2. Cookbooks 3. Alternative grains 4. Pastry 5. Cooking (Bread) 6. Tartine (Bakery)

ISBN 1452114307; 9781452114309

LC 2012276745

This book, by Chad Robertson, the third cookbook published "from Tartine Bakery & Cafe. . . . is a revolutionary, and altogether timely, exploration of baking with whole grains. The narrative of Chad Robertson's search for ancient flavors in heirloom grains is interwoven with 85 recipes for whole-grain versions of Tartine favorites." (Publisher's note)

"Acclaimed baker and Tartine Bakery cofounder Robertson's third cookbook is as visually impressive as its predecessors. . . . Its recipes, however, are far more challenging, providing spare instructions and assuming considerable technical knowledge. Robertson breaks up chapters of intriguing and innovative breads, crispbreads, and pastries (e.g., sprouted quinoa kamut bread, lemon-poppy-kefir pound cake) with accounts of baking-related travels in Denmark, Sweden, Germany, Austria, France, and Mexico." LJ

Trattner, Douglas

Michael Symon's 5 in 5 for every season; 150 quick dinners, sides, and holiday dishes. Michael Symon, with Douglas Trattner; photographs by Jennifer May. Clarkson Potter 2015 255 p. color illustrations $19.99 **641.81**

1. Cooking 2. Seasons 3. Holiday cooking 4. Dinners and dining 5. Side dishes (Cooking) 6. Quick and easy cooking

ISBN 0804186561; 9780804186568

LC 2015006128

This cookbook by Michael Symon "delivers 165 quick, easy, fresh recipes organized by season with an entire section devoted to making the holidays simpler than ever. Each chapter features inspired main courses as well as recipes for sides and 5 fun ways to celebrate the season, including no-bake summer fruit desserts and spiked drinks to warm up with in winter." (Publisher's note)

5 in 5 for every season

Michael Symon's five in five for every season

Volger, Lukas

Bowl; vegetarian recipes for ramen, pho, bibim-bap, dumplings, and other one-dish meals. Lukas Volger; photography by Michael Harlan Turkell. Houghton Mifflin Harcourt 2016 256 p. color illustrations (paperback) $25   **641.81**
1. Soups 2. Asian cooking 3. Vegetarian cooking 4. Stews 5. Cooking, Asian 6. One-dish meals
ISBN 0544325281; 9780544325289

LC 2015037777

This cookbook tells how author Lukas Volger's "ramen explorations led him from a simple bowl of miso ramen to a glorious summer ramen with corn broth, tomatoes, and basil. From there, he went on to the Vietnamese noodle soup pho, with combinations like caramelized spring onions, peas, and baby bok choy. Volger also includes many tips, techniques, and indispensable base recipes perfected over years of cooking, including broths, handmade noodles, sauces, and garnishes." (Publisher's note)

"A go-to cookbook for Asian-inspired vegetarian soups, noodle bowls, and dumplings." Library Journal

Volland, Susan

Mastering Sauces; The Home Cook's Guide to New Techniques for Fresh Flavors. by Susan Volland. W W Norton & Co Inc 2015 464 p. 16 plates; color illustrations $39.95   **641.81**
1. Sauces
ISBN 0393241858; 9780393241853

LC 2015017677

This cookbook, by Susan Volland, "presents sauce-making in a whole new way. . . . In addition to over 150 recipes that reflect today's tastes for seasonal produce, international ingredients, and alternative dietary choices, there are dozens of tips and tables suggesting ways to adapt and customize sauces." (Publisher's note)

"This is an excellent culinary reference with a thoroughness that recalls titles such as Shirley Corriher's Cookwise and Karen Page and Andrew Dornenburg's The Flavor Bible. Highly recommended, along with Martha Holmberg's Modern Sauces." LJ

Weber, Kathleen

Della Fattoria bread; Kathleen Weber; with Amy Albert and Amy Vogler; photographs by Ed Anderson. Workman Publishing Company, Inc. 2014 336 p. illustrations $29.95   **641.81**
1. Bread 2. Della Fattoria (Bakery)
ISBN 1579655319; 9781579655310

LC 2014004630

James Beard Foundation Award Nominee: Baking and Dessert (2015)

This book, by Kathleen Weber, "is filled with . . . bread-baking secrets . . . and features recipes for all levels of

bakers. Beginners can learn to bake yeasted breads using pans. Advanced bakers can jump right into making free-form loaves of naturally leavened breads in all shapes and flavors. Other chapters include recipes for enriched breads like brioche and challah; pre-fermented breads, including baguettes; and crackers, breadsticks, naan, and more." (Publisher's note)

"Highly recommended for serious home bakers, especially those looking to move on from easier titles such as Jeff Hertzberg and Zoe Francois's Artisan Bread in Five Minutes a Day." LJ

Includes an index

641.813   Soups

Thomas, Heather

Broth; Nature's cure-all for health and nutrition, with delicious recipes for broths, soups, stews and risottos. by Vicki Edgson and Heather Thomas. Motorbooks Intl 2016 176 p. color illustrations $30   **641.813**
1. Soups 2. Stews
ISBN 1910254487; 9781910254486

This cookbook, by Vicki Edgson and Heather Thomas, "explains why bone broth is so healthy and nutritious and how you can harness its essential goodness in your everyday diet. The delicious recipes can be used by people who are detoxing or following the Paleo Diet as well as the 5:2 Diet (especially on fasting days). All the broths, soups and stews featured are easy to prepare and do not require any specialist skills, making them accessible and user-friendly." (Publisher's note)

641.815   Bread and bread-like foods

Dodge, Abigail Johnson

The everyday baker; recipes & techniques for foolproof baking breads, pastries, cakes, pies, cookies, and more. Abigail Johnson Dodge. Taunton Press, Inc. 2015 624 p. color illustrations $40   **641.815**
1. Bread 2. Baking 3. Desserts
ISBN 9781621138105

LC 2015032688

This cookbook, by Abigail Johnson Dodge, is a "resource for anyone who likes, loves, or lives to bake. This definitive collection serves as a delicious roadmap through a baker's sweet and savory kitchen and includes over 176 foolproof, innovative recipes all featuring must-know tips and techniques, comprehensive instructions, 80 stunning photographs of the finished dishes, and almost 1,000 step-by-step photographs designed to revolutionize the home baking experience." (Publisher's note)

"Filled with step-by-step photographs of essential techniques and precise recipes that include both weight and volume measurements, her book will help home bakers of all skill levels feel more confident when making easy and advanced treats." LJ

Kaminsky, Peter

Bien Cuit; Zachary Golper, Peter Kaminsky. Regan Arts 2015 324 p. illustrations (chiefly color) $50 **641.815**

1. Bread 2. Baking

ISBN 9781941393413; 1941393411

LC 2015938343

This cookbook, by Zachary Golper and Peter Kaminsky "introduces a new approach to a proudly old-fashioned way of baking bread. In the oven of his Brooklyn bakery, Chef Zachary Golper creates loaves that are served in New York's top restaurants and sought by bread enthusiasts around the country. His secret: long, low-temperature fermentation, which allows the dough to develop deep, complex flavors." (Publisher's note)

"This essential addition for serious bread enthusiasts, especially those who work exclusively by hand, will also interest novice and intermediate bakers, but they should be prepared to read recipes several times, use metric measurements and specialty flours, and budget considerable time." Library Journal

Lawson, Nigella, 1960-

How to be a domestic goddess; baking and the art of comfort cooking. Nigella Lawson; photography by Petrina Tinslay. Hyperion 2001 viii, 374 p.p color illustrations $35 **641.815**

1. Baking

ISBN 0786867973; 9780786867974

LC 2001024170

This cookbook, by celebrity chef Nigella Lawson, "is not about being a goddess, but about feeling like one. . . . Filled with over 220 gorgeously illustrated recipes, this book understands our anxieties, feeds our fantasies, and puts cakes, pies, pastries, preserves, puddings, breads, and cookies back in our own kitchens." (Publisher's note)

"Timed to launch with her television series Nigella Bites on the E! channel and Style networks this fall, this book will bask in the warm, fuzzy and competent glow of Lawson's renown. She'll be a hit in the U.S.; her book will get ample promo and fly off the shelves." Pub Wkly

Includes bibliographical references (p. 364-365) and index

Moore, Christine

Little Flower baking; Christine Moore with Cecilia Leung; photographs by Staci Valentine. Prospect Park Books 2016 288 p. color illustrations (alk. paper) $35 **641.815**

1. Baking 2. Cookbooks 3. American cooking 4. Cooking, American 5. Little Flower (Restaurant)

ISBN 9781938849602

LC 2015042873

This cookbook, by Christine Moore with Cecilia Leung, with photographs by Staci Valentine, offers "one of California's most acclaimed bakers is sharing her very best recipes, all adapted and carefully tested for the home cook. Extensively photographed . . . , it inspires home cooks to make her rustically beautiful, always delicious cookies, cakes, pastries, savory baked goods, breads, rolls, bars, puddings, and so much more." (Publisher's note)

"Recipes are written clearly enough, even for kitchen novices, and she includes a helpful prologue of baking and ingredient tips. This one's a must-read for serious bakers." Booklist

641.82   Main dishes

Bastianich, Joseph

Healthy pasta; the sexy, skinny, and smart way to eat your favorite food. Joseph Bastianich and Tanya Bastianich Manuali. Alfred A. Knopf 2015 185 p. color illustrations (hardcover) $26.95 **641.82**

1. Cookbooks 2. Cooking -- Pasta products 3. Cooking (Pasta) 4. Cooking, Italian

ISBN 0385352247; 9780385352246

LC 2014025460

This cookbook by Joseph Bastianich and Tanya Bastianich Manuali presents "100 recipes, each under 500 calories per serving, that are as good for you as they are delectable. This wonderfully informative, easy-to-use cookbook provides simple ways to make pasta an integral part of a healthy and well-balanced lifestyle, even if you're gluten-free." (Publisher's note)

"Though their sexiness is debatable, these recipes are tasty, practical, and in line with current dietary trends. Recommended for pasta lovers in search of healthier everyday recipes." LJ

Carluccio, Antonio

Pasta; The Essential New Collection from the Master of Italian Cookery. Antonio Carluccio. Chronicle Books Llc 2015 224 p. color illustrations $29.95 **641.82**

1. Italian cooking 2. Cooking -- Pasta products

ISBN 1849496641; 9781849496643

This cookbook by Antonio Carluccio "combines his inimitable knowledge with his expert taste buds to provide over 100 original and irresistible pasta recipes in this definitive book. The book begins with an instructional masterclass, teaching the reader everything they will need to know about pasta--how to cook it and how to marry it with the perfect sauce--with accompanying step-by-step photography." (Publisher's note)

"This is a superb addition to shelves already groaning with Italian cookbooks. Pasta lovers will want to give this one some serious consideration." Pub Wkly

Forkish, Ken

The **elements** of pizza; Ken Forkish; photography by Alan Weiner. Ten Speed Press 2016 256 p. color illustrations (hardcover : alk. paper) $30 **641.82**

1. Pizza

ISBN 9781607748380

LC 2015032247

In this cookbook, Ken Forkish "breaks down each step of the pizza-making process, from choosing a dough to shaping your pie to selecting cheeses and toppings that will work for your home kitchen setup. Forkish offers more than a dozen different dough recipes. . . . His clear, expert instructions will have you shaping pies and loading a pizza peel with the confidence of a professional pizzaiolo. And his innovative, seasonal topping ideas will surprise and delight any pizza lover." (Publisher's note)

"Committed bakers will find plenty here to keep ovens hot and families' plates filled with honest versions of one of the nation's most beloved foods." Booklist

Includes bibliographical references and index

Green, Aliza

Making artisan pasta; how to make a world of handmade noodles, stuffed pasta, dumplings, and more. [Aliza Green; with photography by Steve Legato] Quarry Books 2012 176 p. col. ill. (pbk.) $24.99　　　　　　　　　　　　　　**641.82**

　　1. Cookbooks 2. Cooking -- Pasta products 3. Noodles
ISBN 1592537324; 9781592537327

　　　　　　　　　　　　　　　　　LC 2011031326

This cookbook offers "chef Aliza Green's pasta expertise and encyclopedic knowledge of all things culinary, plus hundreds of . . . photos by acclaimed food photographer Steve Legato, [so that readers can] learn how to use the best ingredients and simple, classic techniques to make fresh, homemade pasta in . . . [their] own kitchen." (Publisher's note)

"The book contains many useful extras such as nutrition information, resources, and a glossary, but those who want to serve a homemade sauce along with their pasta fresca may need to consult another resource." LJ

Includes bibliographical references (p. 168-169) and index

Joachim, David

Mastering pasta. Ten Speed Press 2015 272 p. color illustrations hardcover $29.99　　　　**641.82**

　　1. Cookbooks 2. Italian cooking
ISBN 1607746077; 9781607746072

　　　　　　　　　　　　　　　　　LC 2014020868

"Vetri's personal stories of travel and culinary discovery in Italy appear alongside his easy-to-follow, detailed explanations of how to make and enjoy fresh handmade pasta. Whether you're a home cook or a professional, you'll learn how to make more than thirty different types of pasta dough, from versatile egg yolk dough, to extruded semolina dough, to a variety of flavored pastas—and form them into shapes both familiar and unique. In dishes ranging from classic to innovative, Vetri shares his coveted recipes for stuffed pastas, baked pastas, and pasta sauces. He also shows you how to make light-as-air gnocchi and the perfect dish of risotto." Publisher's Note.

"This lavish pasta cookbook has lots of science-based information and an overview of 15 types of wheat flours. Perfect for dedicated pasta lovers looking to hone their skills." LJ

Louis, Jenn

Pasta by hand; a collection of Italy's small pasta shapes and dumplings. Jenn Louis; photographs by Ed Anderson. Chronicle Books LLC 2015 208 p. illustrations (hardback) $25　　　　　　　　**641.82**

　　1. Cookbooks 2. Cooking -- Pasta products 3. Dumplings 4. Pasta products
ISBN 1452121885; 9781452121888

　　　　　　　　　　　　　　　　　LC 2014032602

This cookbook, by Jenn Louis, with photographs by Ed Anderson, "includes more than 65 recipes for hand-shaped traditional pastas and dumplings, along with deeply satisfying sauces to mix and match. Louis shares her recipes and expertise in hand-forming beloved shapes such as gnocchi, orecchiette, gnudi, and spatzli as well as dozens of other regional pasta specialties." (Publisher's note)

"The luxurious sauce recipes in the last chapter are worth the price of admission alone and feature traditional ragús of lamb, rabbit, porcini, tomato, beef, and wild boar. This single-focus cookbook is written with both authority and a passion for 'some of the most soulful Italian food we can eat.'" Pub Wkly

Marchetti, Domenica

The **glorious** pasta of Italy; by Domenica Marchetti. Chronicle Books 2011 280 p. col. ill. (alk. paper) $30　　　　　　　　　　　　　　**641.82**

　　1. Cookbooks 2. Italian cooking 3. Cooking -- Pasta products
ISBN 0811872599; 9780811872591

　　　　　　　　　　　　　　　　　LC 2011030010

This pasta-centered Italian cookbook, by Domenica Marchetti, "draws from her Italian heritage to share 100 classic and modern recipes. Step-by-step instructions for making fresh pasta offer plenty of variations on the classic egg pasta, while a glossary of pasta shapes, a source list for unusual ingredients, and a handy guide for stocking the pantry with pasta essentials encourage the home cook to look beyond simple spaghetti." (Publisher's note)

Includes index

One pot; 120-plus easy recipes for your stockpot, skillet, slow cooker, and more. from the kitchens of Martha Stewart Living. Clarkson Potter/Publishers 2014 256 p. color illustrations $26　　　　　　　　　　　　　　**641.82**

　　1. Cooking 2. Quick and easy cooking 3. Stews 4. One-dish meals 5. Electric cooking, Slow
ISBN 0307954412; 9780307954411

　　　　　　　　　　　　　　　　　LC 2013050638

In this book "editors of 'Martha Stewart Living' present a brand-new collection of 120 recipes--organized by vessel--to help you do just that, all while adding savory new dishes to your weekly rotation. With chapters devoted to your essential cooking vessels--stockpot, skillet, slow cooker, and more--this book is [designed] to streamline your meals." (Publisher's note)

"Useful for weeknight home cooking, this survey of one-pot preparations features consistent, classic recipes and vibrant photographs. Readers interested in the slow-cooking chapters will also enjoy Andrew Schloss's Cooking Slow." LJ

Parachini, Chris

Roberta's; Carlo Mirarchi, Brandon Hoy, Chris Parachini and Katherine Wheelock, art direction by Ryan Rice. Clarkson Potter 2013 287 p. color illustrations $35　　　　　　　　　　　　　　**641.82**

　　1. Pizza 2. Cookbooks 3. Restaurants 4. Roberta's

(Restaurant)
ISBN 0770433715; 9780770433710

LC 2013004300

The authors of this cookbook, Carlo Mirarchi, Brandon Hoy, Chris Parachini and Katherine Wheelock, "share recipes, photographs, and stories meant to capture the experience of [the Brooklyn-based pizza restaurant] Roberta's for those who haven't been, and to immortalize it for those who've been there since the beginning." (Publisher's note)

Segan, Francine

Pasta modern; new & inspired recipes from Italy. Francine Segan. Stewart, Tabori & Chang 2013 208 p. $35 **641.82**
1. Italian cooking 2. Cooking -- Pasta products
ISBN 1617690627; 9781617690624

LC 2013935989

In this book, author Francine Segan "challenges the notion that pasta must be traditional or old-world. . . .Segan details . . . unusual pasta dishes from Italy's food bloggers, home cooks, artisan pasta makers, and vanguard chefs. . . . Tips and anecdotes culled from Segan's Italian travels enhance the easy-to-follow directions, and a glossary of more than 50 . . . dried pastas showcases shapes to revive any pasta lover's repertoire." (Publisher's note)

"Meticulously researched, thoughtfully curated, and artfully designed, this unique collection will inspire readers to try new preparations and flavors." LJ

Tanis, David

One good dish; by David Tanis. Artisan 2013 256 p. $25.95 **641.82**
1. Cookbooks 2. One-dish meals
ISBN 1579654673; 9781579654672

LC 2013006289

Author David Tanis "turns his focus to an eclectic array of simple, casual meals that satisfy and are appropriate to be eaten at any time of day. Tanis's whimsy runs from bread, snacks, and condiments to vegetables, griddled foods, desserts, and more. Waffle-iron grilled cheese, gorgonzola and walnut crostini; and ham and gruyere bread pudding are highlights among the rustic offering of bread entries." (Publishers Weekly)

641.83 Salads

Romero, Terry Hope

Salad samurai; 100 cutting-edge, ultra-hearty, easy-to-make salads you don't have to be vegan to love. Terry Hope Romero. Da Capo Lifelong 2014 180 p. col. ill. (pbk.) $19.99 **641.83**
1. Salads 2. Veganism 3. Cookbooks 4. Vegan cooking
ISBN 0738214876; 9780738214870

LC 2014002618

This vegan cookbook, by Terry Hope Romero, offers a "guide to real salad bushido: a hearty base, a zesty dressing, and loads of seriously tasty toppings. . . . Based on whole food ingredients and seasonal produce, these versatile meatless, dairy-free dishes are organized by season for a full year of memorable meals." (Publisher's note)

641.84 Sandwiches and related dishes

García, Lorena

Lorena Garcia's new taco classics; Lorena Garcia. Celebra 2015 368 p. color illustrations $29.95 **641.84**
1. Mexican cooking 2. Latin American cooking 3. Tacos
ISBN 0451476913; 9780451476913

LC 2015008294

In this cookbook, "breaking down each new-style taco into its elements, [author Lorena Garcia] shows you how to create each delicious layer--from the shell to the fillings to the toppings, including slaws, salads, and sauces. These flavor-packed recipes are made for pairing and sharing, depending on your craving or occasion." (Publisher's note)

"Traditionalists will appreciate the inclusion of tamales with green tomatillo and pulled chicken and tostadas al pastor, as well as tips on making the best chile de arbol sauce. This book is approachable enough for the novice, and packed with must-try dishes for everyday dining as well as special occasions. Readers might want to buy two copies, since the first one's going to be stained and tattered in no time." Pub Wkly

New taco classics

Kord, Tyler

A **super** upsetting cookbook about sandwiches; Tyler Kord; photography by Noah Fecks; artwork by William Wegman. Clarkson Potter/Publishers 2016 191 p. (hardcover) $22.99 **641.84**
1. Cookbooks 2. Sandwiches
ISBN 0804186413; 9780804186414

LC 2015028505

This book, by Tyler Kord, with photography by Noah Fecks and artwork by William Wegman, presents "careless ruminations on sandwich philosophy, love, self-loathing, pay phones, getting drunk in the shower, Tom Cruise, food ethics, and what it's like having the names of two different women tattooed on your body. Most of these ruminations also happen to be truly excellent recipes." (Publisher's note)

Stupak, Alex

Tacos; recipes and provocations. Alex Stupak and Jordana Rothman; photographs by Evan Sung. Clarkson Potter 2015 240 p. color illustrations (hardback) $32.50 **641.84**
1. Cooking -- Meat 2. Mexican cooking 3. Tacos 4. Tortillas
ISBN 0553447297; 9780553447293

LC 2015006214

"Superstar chef Alex Stupak's love of real Mexican food changed his life; it caused him to quit the world of fine-dining pastry and open the smash-hit Empellón Taqueria in New York City. Now he'll change the way you make--and think about--tacos forever.

TACOS is a deep dive into the art and craft of one of Mexico's greatest culinary exports. We start by making fresh tortillas from corn and flour, and variations that look to innovative grains and flavor infusions. Next we master salsas, from simple chopped condiments to complex moles that simmer for hours and have flavor for days. Finally we explore fillings, both traditional and modern--from a pine-apple-topped pork al pastor to pastrami with mustard seeds.

But TACOS is more than a collection of beautiful things to cook. Wrapped up within it is an argument: Through these recipes, essays, and sumptuous photographs by Evan Sung, the 3-Michelin-star veteran makes the case that Mexican food should be as esteemed as the highest French cooking." Publisher's Note

641.86   Desserts

Adams, Jocelyn Delk

Grandbaby cakes; modern recipes, vintage charm, soulful memories. Jocelyn Delk Adams. Surrey Books, An Agate Imprint 2015 224 p. $22.95   641.86
   1. Cake 2. Baking
   ISBN 1572841737; 9781572841734
                                                      LC 2015013216
NAACP Image Award Nominee: Outstanding Literary Work - Instructional (2016)

This cookbook is author Jocelyn Delk Adams's "love note to her family, thanking those who came before and passing on this touching tradition with 50 brilliant cakes. Adams creates sophisticated flavor combinations based on [her grandmother] Big Mama's gorgeous centerpiece cakes, giving each recipe something familiar mixed with something new." (Publisher's note)

"Adams's cake recipes are familiar yet unlike any you'll find in similar cookbooks. An instant classic, this title belongs in most baking collections." LJ

Ansel, Dominique

Dominique Ansel; the secret recipes. foreword by Daniel Boulud. Simon & Schuster 2014 272 p. color illustrations (hardback) $35   641.86
   1. Pastry 2. Cookbooks
   ISBN 1476764190; 9781476764191
                                                      LC 2014024377
This cookbook, by Dominique Ansel, "shares the secret to transforming the most humble ingredients into the most extraordinary, tempting, and satisfying pastries imaginable. . . . [The book] reveals the stories and recipes behind his most sought-after creations and teaches lovers of dessert everywhere how to make magic in their own kitchens." (Publisher's note)

"Ansel's essays will delight his fans, as well as foodies who enjoy learning about the creative processes of famous chefs. Those new to French pastry will prefer collections with more recipes and instruction." LJ

Beddall, Catherine

The magic of gingerbread; 16 Beautiful Projects to Make and Eat. written and photographed by Catherine Beddall. Peter Pauper Press, Inc. 2016 176 p. illustrations (chiefly color) (hardcover : alk. paper) $22.99   641.86
   1. Gingerbread
   ISBN 1441319808; 9781441319807
                                                      LC 2016003632

In this book, pastry artist Catherine Beddall "shares her secrets for creating classic gingerbread houses and a bounty of other gingerbread whimsies, including a gingerbread space rocket, robot, and chess set!" (Publisher's note)
   Includes bibliographical references

Bilderback, Leslie

No-churn ice cream; over 100 simply delicious no-machine frozen treats. Leslie Bilderback. St. Martin's Griffin 2015 168 p. color illustrations (trade pbk.) $22.99   641.86
   1. Cookbooks 2. Ice cream, ices, etc. 3. Ice cream, ices, etc
   ISBN 1250054389; 9781250054388
                                                      LC 2015007286
This dessert cookbook, by Leslie Bilderback, gives instruction for ice-cream making. "What if you could make your own ice cream at home without all of the fuss, for a fraction of the cost of buying it, and without any special equipment? . . . [This book] is a mouthwatering collection of shortcuts and classic culinary techniques that help you achieve delicious, artisanal results." (Publisher's note)

"Supplemented by Bilderback's professional pastry knowledge, this easy yet informative ice cream cookbook will appeal to a wide audience. Highly recommended for college students, apartment dwellers, and anyone lacking kitchen equipment or space." LJ

Bittman, Mark, 1950-

★ How to Bake Everything; Simple Recipes for the Best Baking. Mark Bittman. Houghton Mifflin Harcourt 2016 704 p. illustrations (hardcover) $35; (ebook) $35   641.86
   1. Baking 2. Cookbooks
   ISBN 9780470526880; 9780544798861; 0470526882
                                                      LC 2016449439
This cookbook by Mark Bittman offers "the simplest way to bake everything, from American favorites (Crunchy Toffee Cookies, Baked Alaska) to of-the-moment updates (Gingerbread Whoopie Pies). It explores global baking, too: Nordic ruis, New Orleans beignets, Afghan snowshoe naan. The recipes satisfy every flavor craving thanks to more than 2,000 recipes and variations." (Publisher's note)

"This compendium is the next best thing to having the master himself in the kitchen, and should be a staple for all public library collections." Booklist

Boyle, Tish

Flavorful; 150 irresistible desserts in all-time favorite flavors. Tish Boyle; photography by Andrew Meade. Houghton Mifflin Harcourt 2015 384 p. color illustrations (hardcover) $35   641.86
   1. Baking 2. Desserts 3. Cookbooks
   ISBN 1118523555; 9781118523551
                                                      LC 2015004678
This baked goods and desserts cookbook, by Tish Boyle with photography by Andrew Meade, describes how "pastry chefs . . . [use] vanilla, berry and cherry, apple, citrus, cheese, nuts, caramel, coffee, and chocolate. . . . Author Tish Boyle has translated this list of go-to ingredients into a stunning collection of more than 150 recipes for baked goods

and other desserts, with a chapter dedicated to each singular flavor." (Publisher's note)

"Reliable and technically informative, Boyle's latest functions like nine single-subject titles in one. Highly recommended for readers who enjoy classic dessert collections such as Sherry Yard's The Secrets of Baking and Flo Braker's The Simple Art of Perfect Baking." LJ

Includes bibliographical references

Byrn, Anne

American cake; From Colonial Gingerbread to Classic Layer, the Stories and Recipes Behind More Than 125 of Our Best-Loved Cakes. Anne Byrn. Rodale 2016 352 p. illustrations (chiefly color) (trade hardcover : acid-free paper) $29.99   **641.86**
1. Cookbooks 2. Cake decorating 3. Cake -- United States -- History 4. Cake
ISBN 9781623365431

LC 2016029092

This cookbook by Anne Byrn takes "a journey through America's past to present with more than 125 authentic recipes for our best-loved and beautiful cakes and frostings. Tracing cakes chronologically from the dark, moist gingerbread of New England to the elegant pound cake, the hardscrabble Appalachian stack cake, . . . Hawaiian Chantilly, and the modern California cakes. . . . Byrn shares . . . stories, and a behind-the-scenes look into what cakes we were baking back in time." (Publisher's note)

"These well researched and written pages go far beyond the average baking guide." Pub Wkly

Includes bibliographical references (pages 325-329) and index.

Greenspan, Dorie

★ **Baking** chez moi; recipes from my paris home to your home anywhere. Dorie Greenspan; photographs by Alan Richardson. Houghton Mifflin Harcourt 2014 496 p. ill. (chiefly col.) (hardback) $40   **641.86**
1. Baking 2. Desserts 3. French cooking
ISBN 0547724241; 9780547724249

LC 2014016312

IACP Cookbook Award Finalist: Baking: Savory or Sweet (2015)

IACP Cookbook Award Finalist: International (2015)

James Beard Foundation Award Nominee: Baking and Dessert (2015)

In this cookbook, author Dorie Greenspan "explores the fascinating world of French desserts, bringing together a charmingly uncomplicated mix of contemporary recipes, including original creations based on traditional and regional specialties, and drawing on seasonal ingredients, market visits, and her travels throughout the country." (Publisher's note)

"Combining everyday desserts with doable versions of extremely popular treats (think macarons, éclairs, and crack-

le-top cream puffs), Greenspan's new collection is an instant classic." LJ

★ **Dorie's** cookies; Dorie Greenspan. Houghton Mifflin Harcourt 2016 528 p. color illustrations (ebook) $35; (paper over board) $35   **641.86**
1. Cookies
ISBN 9780547614854; 9780547614847

LC 2015042719

This cookbook, by Dorie Greenspan, presents "cookies for every taste and occasion. . . . There are company treats like Portofignos, with chocolate dough and port-soaked figs, and lunch-box Blueberry Buttermilk Pie Bars. They Might Be Breakfast Cookies are packed with goodies—raisins, dried apples, dried cranberries, and oats' while Almond Crackle Cookies have just three ingredients. [And] there are dozens of choices for the Christmas cookie swaps." (Publisher's note)

"Accomplished bakers will be challenged and inspired by the breadth of recipes and the many suggestions Greenspan offers throughout the book to modify recipes. This is a cookbook to read, bake, and eat your way through." Pub Wkly

Greenstein, Elaine

A **Jewish** baker's pastry secrets; George Greenstein with Elaine Greenstein, Juia Greenstein, and Isaac Bleicher. Ten Speed Press 2015 202 p. (hardback) $29.99   **641.86**
1. Pastry 2. Jewish cooking 3. Cooking, European
ISBN 1607746735; 9781607746737

LC 2015025814

In this cookbook, author George Greenstein "crafts master dough recipes for Jewish holiday baking and European classics. . . . Greenstein's expert guidance for making doughs like bundt, babka, strudel, gugelhopf, stollen, pressburger, puff pastry, and Danish create a jumping-off point for more than 200 variations of classic pastries. . . . The book also offers an in-depth guide to ingredients and equipment, . . . as well as basic recipes for fillings, icings, and glazes." (Publisher's note)

Includes bibliographical references (pages 197) and index

Harris, Miriam

Magpie; Sweets and Savories from Philadelphia's Favorite Pie Boutique. by Holly Ricciardi, with Miriam Harris. Running Press 2015 256 p. color illustrations (hardcover) $27.50   **641.86**
1. Pies 2. Cookbooks
ISBN 9780762454532; 0762454539

LC 2015937006

This cookbook, by Holly Ricciardi, with Miriam Harris, "serves up Magpie [Artisan Pie Boutique's] . . . seasonal menu for home bakers everywhere: the fruity, creamy, and nutty pies; hand pies, pot pies, and quiches; and even pie shakes and pie 'fries,' all fine-tuned to exacting standards and with lots of step-by-step instruction for that all-important crust." (Publisher's note)

"Versatile enough to be used year-round, this pie cookbook will complement most baking collections." LJ

Holiday cookies; prize-winning family recipes from the Chicago Tribune for cookies, bars, brownies and more. Chicago Tribune Surrey Books 2014 222 p. color illustrations (hard cover) $24.95   **641.86**
1. Baking 2. Cookies 3. Holiday cooking
ISBN 1572841648; 9781572841642
LC 2014026785

IACP Cookbook Award Finalist: Compilations (2015)

This book by the staff of the "Chicago Tribune" "is a comprehensive collection of the best holiday cookies as curated from nearly three decades worth of reader submissions. These delicious recipes represent an eclectic mix of traditional and modern recipes from diverse cultural background and skill levels, such as Tropical Nuevo Latino Cookies, Dorie's Dark and Stormies, and Grandma Grump's Peanut Butter Drizzles." (Publisher's note)

"A timely cookie collection that's big on variety and nostalgia." LJ

Jaronsky, Shelly

The **cookies** & cups cookbook; let's all agree to eat dessert first: 100 recipes to make your life sweet, plus 25 recipes for the weirdos who like to eat dinner. by Shelly Jaronsky. Gallery Books 2016 320 p. (trade pbk.) $23.99   **641.86**
1. Cookies 2. Desserts
ISBN 9781501102516
LC 2015027541

This cookbook, by Shelly Jaronsky, "features . . . sweet treats 100% guaranteed to make you want to eat dessert first. . . . With recipes ranging from the deliciously decadent (her S'mores Fudge Bars will make you seriously reconsider everything you thought you knew about baked goods) to the deceptively simple (her Favorite Chocolate Chip Cookie will become an instant staple in your baking repertoire), [it] truly has something for everyone." (Publisher's note)

"Jaronsky, the creator of the website Cookies & Cups, presents over 125 selections with sweets in the front. Her casual tone and concise recipes with numbered steps are inviting for those new to the kitchen." Pub Wkly

Kave, Allison

First prize pies; Shoo-fly, candy apple & other deliciously inventive pies for every week of the year (and more) Allison Kave. Stewart, Tabori & Chang 2014 224 p. color illustrations $29.95   **641.86**
1. Pies 2. Cookbooks
ISBN 161769102X; 9781617691027
LC 2013945638

In this cookbook, author "Allison Kave made pies as a hobby, until one day her boyfriend convinced her to enter a Brooklyn pie-making contest. . . . [Now] people can't get enough of her Bourbon Ginger Pecan pie, her whimsical Root Beer Float Pie, her addictive Chocolate Peanut Butter Pretzel Pie. . . . Organized by month, the book includes pies for every sweet tooth, from inventive pies like Chocolate Lavender Teatime to old-school comfort pies like Candy Apple." (Publisher's note)

Includes bibliographical references and index

Lane, Christina

Dessert for Two; Small Batch Cookies, Brownies, Pies, and Cakes. Christina Lane. W W Norton & Co Inc 2015 240 p. color illustrations $24.95 **641.86**
1. Desserts 2. Cookbooks 3. Cooking for two
ISBN 1581572840; 9781581572841

This cookbook, by Christina Lane, offers "well-loved desserts and scales them down to make only two servings. . . . Cakes are baked in small pans and ramekins. Pies are baked in small pie pans or muffin cups. Cookie recipes are scaled down to make 1 dozen or fewer. . . . Now you can have your own personal-sized cake and eat it, too." (Publisher's note)

McDermott, Kate

Art of the pie; A Practical Guide to Homemade Crusts, Fillings, and Life. Kate McDermott, photographed by Andrew Scrivani. Countryman Press, a division of W W Norton & Co. 2016 352 p. color illustrations (hardcover) $35   **641.86**
1. Pies 2. Baking 3. Cookbooks
ISBN 9781581573275
LC 2016017593

This cookbook, by Kate McDermott, photographed by Andrew Scrivani, gives "detailed instructions for making, rolling, and baking crusts. A pie needs filling, too, and [McDermott] does not neglect a single detail when describing her ingredients, methods, and tricks for making the filling and finishing off the pie. Recipes include: Blackberry Pie for Julia Child,The Best Peach Pie in the World, and Old-Fashioned Rhubarb Pie."(Publisher's note)

"It's really all about the standards... McDermott excels, giving readers an informative guide they'll be referring to for years to come." Pub Wkly

Milk Bar Life; Sweet and Savory Recipes to Make Right Now. Christina Tosi. Random House Inc Clarkson Potter 2015 256 p. $35   **641.86**
1. Cooking 2. Desserts 3. Momofuku Milk Bar
ISBN 0770435106; 9780770435103
LC 2014041740

Moore, Kathy

Delicious dump cakes; 50 Super Simple Desserts to Make in 15 Minutes or Less. Roxanne Wyss and Kathy Moore; photographs by Staci Valentine. St. Martin's Griffin 2016 128 p. color illustrations (trade pbk.) $19.99   **641.86**
1. Cake 2. Baking 3. Cobblers (Cooking)
ISBN 9781250082633
LC 2015049003

In this cookbook, by Roxanne Wyss and Kathy Moore, "you'll find a wide array of cakes and desserts that require minimal utensils to prepare. For nearly all of the recipes, simply open readily available cans or a package of cake mix and layer in the pan. Never again will you have to struggle with complex steps or deal with lots of dirty dishes." (Publisher's note)

"Whatever readers' level of experience or inexperience in the kitchen, this cookbook will have them serving up delicious desserts in a flash." LJ

Naturally sweet; Bake All Your Favorites with 30% to 50% Less Sugar. by the editors at America's Test Kitchen. America's Test Kitchen 2016 336 p. color illustrations $26.95; (ebook) $25.99 **641.86**
1. Baking 2. Desserts 3. Sugar-free diet
ISBN 9781940352589; 9781940352596
LC 2016009055

This cookbook by the editors of America's Test Kitchen, tackles the "challenge of creating foolproof, great-tasting baked goods that contain less sugar and rely only on natural alternatives to white sugar. . . . Changing the sugar in a recipe can have disastrous results: Baked goods turn out dry . . . [and] inedible. . . . [This book] address these issues . . . with 120 foolproof, great-tasting recipes . . . that reduce the overall sugar content by at least 30%." (Publisher's note)

"Cooks with a powerful sweet tooth should scoop up this well-researched recipe book for healthier takes on classic sweet treats." Booklist

Payard, Francois

Payard cookies; François Payard with Anne E. McBride; photography by Rogério Voltan. Houghton Mifflin Harcourt 2015 272 p. color illustrations (hardcover) $30 **641.86**
1. Cookies 2. French cooking 3. Cooking, French
ISBN 0544512987; 9780544512986
LC 2014044010

Author "François Payard shares his favorite cookie recipes—the bestsellers at his popular New York City patisseries and cafés, the recipes he learned from his father, and the ones he makes at home. They range from the simplest sablés (butter cookies) to the most picture-perfect macarons, with everything in between." (Publisher's note)

"Experienced bakers will have no trouble with Payard's pleasing and precise cookie recipes." LJ

Ptak, Claire

The **Violet** Bakery cookbook; Claire Ptak. Ten Speed Press 2015 272 p. color illustrations (hardcover) $29.99 **641.86**
1. Baking 2. Desserts 3. Violet Bakery (London, England)
ISBN 1607746719; 9781607746713
LC 2014036768

This book, by Claire Ptak, is a "design-forward cookbook for sweet and savory baked goods from London's popular Violet Bakery that focuses on quality ingredients, seasonality, and taste (as opposed to science) as the keys to creating satisfying, delightful homemade pastries, tarts, sweets, and more. . . . Over 100 recipes include nourishing breakfasts, midday snacks, desserts to share, fruit preserves, and stylish celebration cakes." (Publisher's note)

"Highly recommended for fans of baking books such as Elisabeth Prueitt and Chad Robertson's Tartine and Zoe Nathan's Huckleberry. Aspiring pastry chefs will find inspiration in Ptak's impressive career highlights." LJ

Richardson, Julie

Vintage cakes; timeless cupcakes, flips, rolls, layer, angel, snack, chiffon, and icebox cakes for to-day's sweet tooth. Julie Richardson; photography by Erin Kunke. Ten Speed Press 2012 166 p. col. ill. (hbk,) $24 **641.86**
1. Cake 2. Cookbooks
ISBN 1607741024; 9781607741022
LC 2011041262

This cookbook by Julie Richardson focuses on cakes. She "consulted classic cookbooks, submissions from family and friends, and vintage recipes dating back to the 1920s. . . . Richardson includes familiar (e.g., Wacky, Texas Sheet, Red Velvet, Caramel, and Watergate cakes) and lesser-known classics and a few originals, all updated to suit modern palates." (Library Journal)

Includes bibliographical references (p. 157) and index

Robicelli, Allison

Robicelli's; A Love Story, With Cupcakes: With 50 Decidedly Grown-up Recipes. by Allison Robicelli and Matt Robicelli. Penguin Group USA 2013 320 p. $35 **641.86**
1. Baking 2. Family 3. Cupcakes
ISBN 0670785873; 9780670785872

Authors Allison Robicelli and Matt Robicelli present a "guide to gourmet cupcakes, featuring grown-up flavors (figs! whiskey! fried chicken!) and the delicious story of a family saved by a love of sweets. Nixing cutesy, pastel-colored dollops of fluff for real ingredients and rich French buttercreams, the husband and wife team have reinvented the cupcake craze for a more sophisticated palate." (Publisher's note)

"Photos are lick-the-page enticing and proof that home bakers are going to enjoy the best bleeping cupcakes their side of the Brooklyn Bridge." Pub Wkly

Seneviratne, Samantha

Sugar and spice; Samantha Seneviratne; photography by Erin Kunkel. Ten Speed Press 2015 240 p. (hardcover) $27.50 **641.86**
1. Pastry 2. Cookies 3. Cooking (Spices)
ISBN 1607747464; 9781607747468
LC 2015005473

In this book, author Samantha Senevirante presents a "collection of more than eighty unique, unexpected, and uniformly delicious recipes for spice-centric sweets. [It is] filled with fascinating histories, origin stories, and innovative uses for the world's most enticing spices--including vanilla, cinnamon, peppercorns, and cardamom." (Publisher's note)

"Marked by a sense of the exotic, Seneviratne's recipes will lure many home cooks, including fans of Alice Medrich's Pure Dessert and Claudia Fleming's The Last Course." LJ

Shulman, Martha Rose

★ The **art** of French pastry; Jacquy Pfeiffer; with Martha Rose Shulman; photographs by Paul Strabbing. Alfred A. Knopf 2013 432 p. (hardback) $85 **641.86**
1. Baking 2. Pastry 3. French cooking
ISBN 0307959368; 9780307959355
LC 2013017643

In this cookbook, pastry chef Jacquy Pfeiffer provides "an intimate knowledge of the fundamentals of pastry. . . .

By teaching you how to make everything from pâte à choux to pastry cream, Pfeiffer builds on the basics until you have an understanding of the science behind the ingredients used, how they interact with one another, and what your hands have to do to transform them into pastry." (Publisher's note)

"Anyone studying to be a professional baker will profit from Pfeiffer's guidance, and the amateur cook can vastly improve family desserts." Booklist

Tosi, Christina

Milk Bar Life; Sweet and Savory Recipes to Make Right Now. Christina Tosi. "Random House Inc Clarkson Potter" 2015 256 p. color illustrations $35 **641.86**
1. Cooking 2. Eating habits 3. Desserts 4. Momofuku Milk Bar
ISBN 0770435106; 9780770435103
LC 2014041740

In this cookbook author Christina Tosi "bakes one-bowl treats, grills with skills, and embraces simple, nostalgic--and often savory--recipes made from supermarket ingredients. For anyone addicted to crack pie®, compost cookies®, and cake truffles, here are their savory counterparts--such as Kimcheezits with Blue Cheese Dip, Burnt Honey–Butter Kale with Sesame Seeds, and Choose Your Own Adventure Chorizo Burgers." (Publisher's note)

Wright, Caroline

Mix + Match Cakes; Mix & Match Your Way to 100 Amazing Combinations. by Caroline Wright (Author) Workman Pub Co 2016 192 p. $17.95 **641.86**
1. Cake 2. Baking 3. Desserts
ISBN 0761182039; 9780761182030
LC 2013036826

This book, by Caroline Wright, "is a full-color visual cookbook—photos in the front, recipes in the back—and the first step in every baker's cake adventure. It includes valuable baking tips, vegan and gluten-free variations, plus how to tweak the recipes to make sheet cakes, Bundt cakes, and cupcakes, too." (Publisher's note)

"Baking purists may turn up their spatulas, but this is a kid-friendly title that's downright fun for adults, too."

641.865 Pastries

Berry, Mary

Baking with Mary Berry; cakes, cookies, pies, and pastries from the British queen of baking. Mary Berry. DK Publishing 2015 192 p. color illustrations (paperback) $19.95 **641.865**
1. Baking 2. Cookbooks
ISBN 1465453237; 9781465453235

This baking cookbook, by Mary Berry, "draws on Mary's more than 60 years in the kitchen, with tips and step-by-step instructions for bakers just starting out and full-color photographs of finished dishes throughout. The recipes follow Mary's prescription for dishes that are no fuss, practical, and foolproof—from breakfast goods to cookies, cakes, pastries, and pies, to special occasion desserts such as cheesecake and soufflés, to British favorites that will inspire." (Publisher's note)

"The recipes themselves are clear and concise and the offerings wide ranging, everything from the usual, brownies and lemon meringue pie, to the unusual, almond and apricot tartlets to the exotic, figgy-seeded bites. A solid guide, not just for fans of the show—but it's those fans (and their numbers are growing in the U.S.) who will be clamoring for copies." Booklist

Farrow, Joanna

Gingerbread Houses, Animals and Decorations; Explore the Delicious Versatility of Gingerbread in 24 Delightful Projects. Joanna Farrow. Natl Book Network 2012 64 p. color illustrations (hardcover) $9.99 **641.865**
1. Cookbooks 2. Gingerbread
ISBN 9780754825081; 0754825086

This cookbook, by Joanna Farrow, presents multiple holiday recipes using gingerbread. "Gingerbread is deliciously tasty, fun and very versatile; there are light dark gingerbreads, chocolate varieties and even gingerbread laden with fruits, nuts and candies. . . . Make delectable cottages, castles, a Christmas tree, a Noah's ark, a rocking horse, festive decorations and classic cookies, all shown step by step in 150 fabulous photographs." (Publisher's note)

"Farrow (Dress Your Gingerbread) goes beyond gingerbread houses to make edible centerpieces (wreathes, cookie-trimmed Christmas trees), gifts (autumnal plaques, boxes), ornaments, and jewelry. This versatile book also contains a template for a marvelous gingerbread steam train." LJ

Johnstone, Christi Farr

Smart cookie; transform store-bought cookies into amazing treats. Christi Farr Johnstone; [edited by] Jordana Tusman. Running Press 2014 192 p. color illustrations $16 **641.865**
1. Cookies
ISBN 0762452528; 9780762452521
LC 2013958111

This book, by Christi Farr Johnstone, "includes 50 simple and fun cookie creations made entirely from easy-to-find store-bought ingredients-- no baking required! Projects include rainbows, monster pops, balloons, robots, ladybugs, and much more, with lots of ideas for tips, techniques, packaging, and displays. From birthdays to graduations and baby showers to Christmas, there is a cookie in this book for any and all occasions." (Publisher's note)

"Johnstone's charming decorated cookies require minimal time and equipment and no baking. This is her debut title and a great resource for kid-friendly decorating projects and last-minute party favors." LJ

Lebo, Kate

Pie school; lessons in fruit, flour and butter. by Kate Lebo. Sasquatch Books 2014 227 p. color illustrations (paperback) $24.95 **641.865**
1. Pies 2. Cookbooks 3. Baking
ISBN 1570619107; 9781570619106
LC 2014021810

This book, by Kate Lebo, with photography by Rina Jordan, offers "recipes for fifty perfect pies. Included are apple (of course), five ways with rhubarb, lemon chiffon, several blueberry pie variations, galettes, and more. . . . In addition to recipes, Lebo invites readers to ruminate on the social history, the meaning, and the place of pie in the pantheon of favorite foods." (Publisher's note)

"An informed and rather romantic take on the art of the handmade pie." LJ

Includes bibliographical references and index

Weinstein, Bruce

A **la** mode; 120 recipes in 60 pairings : pies, tarts, cakes, crisps, and more topped with ice cream, gelato, frozen custard, and more. Bruce Weinstein and Mark Scarbrough. St. Martin's Griffin 2016 224 p. color illustrations (trade pbk.) $24.99 **641.865**
1. Cake 2. Pies 3. Desserts 4. Ice cream, ices, etc
ISBN 1250072131; 9781250072139

LC 2016000033

This book, by Mark Scarbrough and Bruce Weinstein, "offers not just solid dessert recipes, from raspberry oat bars to bear claws, from chocolate pecan pie to a white chocolate pavlova, but also gives you the unforgettable pairings that make these desserts smash hits: apple cranberry pie with Camembert ice cream, chocolate sheet cake with salt caramel frozen custard, and espresso cream jelly roll with mascarpone ice cream." (Publisher's note)

"This isn't your average ice cream cookbook. Rather than providing just a few suggested accompaniments, Weinstein and Scarbrough (The Great Big Pressure Cooker Book) pair each of the 60 ice cream recipes with a complementary dessert. They also forego a master ice cream base in favor of multiple ice cream types and techniques. . . . As with Jeni Britton Bauer's Jeni's Splendid Ice Cream Desserts, this cookbook is a playful collection of unusual ice cream pairings." LJ

641.87 Preparing beverages

Arnold, Dave

★ **Liquid** intelligence; the art and science of the perfect cocktail. Dave Arnold; photography by Travis Huggett. 1st ed W W Norton & Co Inc 2014 416 p. color illustrations (hardcover) $35 **641.87**
1. Cocktails 2. Bartending 3. Measuring instruments
ISBN 0393089037; 9780393089035

LC 2014022332

IACP Cookbook Award: Jane Grigson Award (2015)
James Beard Foundation Award: Beverage (2015)

This book, by Dave Arnold, "is the beginning of a new method of making drinks, a problem-solving approach grounded in attentive observation and creative techniques. Readers will learn how to extract the sweet flavor of peppers without the spice, why bottling certain drinks beforehand beats shaking them at the bar, and why quinine powder and succinic acid lead to the perfect gin and tonic." (Publisher's note)

"Professional bartenders will drink up this remarkable manual, and amateurs will find Arnold's step-by-step guide to gathering requisite hardware both achievable and fun." Booklist

Includes bibliographical references and index

Conigliaro, Tony, 1971-

The **cocktail** lab; unraveling the mysteries of flavor and aroma in drink, with recipes. Tony Conigliaro. Ten Speed Press 2013 224 p. color illustrations (hardback) $29.99 **641.87**
1. Bartending 2. Alcoholic beverages 3. Cocktails
ISBN 1607745674; 9781607745679

LC 2013004969

James Beard Award (2014)

In this book, bartender Tony Conigliaro presents a "collection of 60 revolutionary cocktails, all grounded in the classics but utilizing technologies and techniques from the molecular gastronomy movement. . . . Tony presents his best and boldest creations: drinks like the Vintage Manhattan, Dirty Martini by the Sea, and Cosmo Popcorn." (Publisher's note)

Includes bibliographical references (pages 217-218) and index

Del Mar Sacasa, María

Summer cocktails; margaritas, mint juleps, punches, party snacks, and more. Maria del Mar Sacasa. Quirk Books 2015 160 p. color illustrations (hardcover) $22.95 **641.87**
1. Cocktails 2. Cookbooks
ISBN 1594747857; 9781594747854

LC 2014944415

This book, by Maria del Mar Sacasa, "features more than 100 seasonal recipes for punches and pitchers, frosty drinks, classics and throwbacks, and more. Craft your beverages from the bottom up with underpinnings straight from your summer garden, including Strawberry-Rosemary Shrub, Rhubarb Syrup, or Tomatillo and Coriander Tequila. Plus, round out the perfect party with savory snacks to match your cool drinks." (Publisher's note)

"With clear instructions and bright color photographs it's easy to make a Pulparindo or a Pimm's your new summer staple, while handy guides to tools and prep techniques round out this essential primer." LJ

Fauchald, Nick

★ **Death** & Co; modern classic cocktails. David Kaplan, Nick Fauchald, Alex Day; photographs by William Hereford; illustrations by Tim Tomkinson. Ten Speed Press 2014 320 p. ill. (some col.) (hardcover) $40 **641.87**
1. Bars 2. Cocktails 3. Bartending 4. Death & Co.
(Bar : New York, N.Y.)
ISBN 1607745259; 9781607745259

LC 2014004245

IACP Cookbook Award Finalist: Global Design (2015)
James Beard Foundation Award Nominee: Beverage (2015)

This book, by David Kaplan, Nick Fauchald, and Alex Day, is a "guide to the contemporary craft cocktail movement. . . . [M]ore than just a collection of recipes, [it] is also a complete cocktail education, with information on the theory and philosophy of drink making, a complete guide to buying and using spirits, and step-by-step instructions for mastering key bartending techniques." (Publisher's note)

"There's a clear, unpretentious spirits primer for those who have been bluffing their way through in-vogue varieties of rum, tequila, and whiskey; other sections tackle bitters, ice, glassware, and additional details without dictating. More than half the book is devoted to 450-plus recipes for classics, variations, and riffs." LJ

Includes bibliographical references and index

Helwig, Jenna

Smoothie-licious; power-packed smoothies and juices the whole family will love. Jenna Helwig. Houghton Mifflin Harcourt Publishing Co. 2015 159 p. color illustrations $14.99   **641.87**
   1. Health 2. Beverages 3. Natural foods 4. Smoothies (Beverages)
   ISBN 0544370082; 9780544370081
                                         LC 2015431117
Author "Jenna Helwig shows how to make 75 smoothies and whole-fruit juices that are both healthy and delicious. Kids will love the bright colors and playful names like Peanut Berry Blast and Mexican Frozen Hot Chocolate; parents will love that they feature nutrient-dense seeds, dark greens and fresh fruit, and use no refined sugars." (Publisher's note)

McDonnell, Duggan

Drinking the devil's acre; a love letter to San Francisco and her cocktails. Duggan McDonnell; photographs by Luke Abiol. Chronicle Books 2015 256 p. $24.95   **641.87**
   1. Cocktails 2. San Francisco (Calif.) 3. Bars (Drinking establishments) -- California -- San Francisco -- History
   ISBN 1452135258; 9781452135250
                                         LC 2014044040
This book by Duggan McDonnelp is a "mix of barman's memoir and literary journalism, with layers of spirited history and liquid wisdom. A tender tale of love for delicious drink, and for one's city, a book for anyone with a passion for history, cocktails, San Francisco, and the wanderlust of travel." (Publisher's note)

"Not just another cocktail recipe book but a great read peppered with drinks to be made. Highly recommended where books on cocktails are popular." LJ

Includes bibliographical references and index

Morgenthaler, Jeffrey

Bar Book; Elements of Cocktail Technique. Jeffrey Morgenthaler with Martha Holmberg; photographs by Alanna Hale. Chronicle Books Llc 2014 288 p. color illustrations (hc) $30   **641.87**
   1. Cocktails 2. Bartending 3. Alcoholic beverages
   ISBN 9781452113845; 145211384X
   IACP Cookbook Award Finalist: Wine, Beer and Spirits (2015)
"Written by renowned bartender and cocktail blogger Jeffrey Morgenthaler, 'The Bar Book' is the only technique-driven cocktail handbook out there. . . . More than 60 recipes illustrate the concepts explored in the text, ranging from juicing, garnishing, carbonating, stirring, and shaking to choosing the correct ice for proper chilling and dilution of a drink." (Publisher's note)

"Straightforward directions are matched with beautifully clear photographs that make homemade grenadine, limoncello, and ginger beer look enticingly simple. The author also demystifies shaking, muddling, and presentation." LJ

Muldoon, Sean

The **Dead** Rabbit drinks manual; secret recipes and barroom tales from two Belfast boys who conquered the cocktail world. Jack McGarry, Sean Muldoon, Ben Schaffer; photography by Brent Herrig. Houghton Mifflin Harcourt 2015 288 p. color illustrations (hardcover) $27   **641.87**
   1. Bars 2. Cocktails 3. Dead Rabbit Grocery and Grog (New York, N.Y.)
   ISBN 9780544373204
                                         LC 2014043215
This book is a "cocktail collection from . . . Dead Rabbit Grocery & Grog in Lower Manhattan. . . . [A]long with its inventive recipes, [it] also details founder Sean Muldoon and bar manager Jack McGarry's inspiring rags-to-riches story that began in Ireland and has brought them to the top of the cocktail world. . . . Dead Rabbit's award-winning drinks . . . range from fizzes to cobblers to toddies, each with its own historical inspiration." (Publisher's note)

"Like the best Irish bartender, this book is warm, welcoming, full of great stories, and dedicated to excellent drinks." LJ

Reiner, Julie

The **craft** cocktail party; amazing drinks for every occasion. Julie Reiner with Kaitlyn Goalen; photographs by Daniel Krieger. Grand Central Life & Style 2015 240 p. color illustrations (hardcover) $26   **641.87**
   1. Cocktails
   ISBN 1455581593; 9781455581597; 9781455581603
                                         LC 2014049853
This book of cocktails, by Julie Reiner, "provides inspiration for the rest of us, not only the cocktail geeks. . . . Recipes are organized around seasonality and occasion, with different events and themes appropriate to the specific time of the year. Each section will include a mixture of holiday-inspired drinks, classic cocktails, and innovative new drinks, all along with fun cocktail lore." (Publisher's note)

Simonson, Robert

A **proper** drink; The Untold Story of How a Band of Bartenders Saved the Civilized Drinking World. Robert Simonson. Ten Speed Press 2016 352 p. (hardcover : alk. paper) $27   **641.87**
   1. Bars 2. Bartenders 3. Cocktails -- History 4. Bartenders -- Biography 5. Bars (Drinking establishments)
   ISBN 9781607747543
                                         LC 2016014120
This book by Robert Simonson tells the "story of the contemporary craft cocktail revival. . . . Simonson interviewed more than 200 key players from around the world . . . --bars, bartenders, patrons, and visionaries--who in the last 25 years have changed the course of modern drinkmaking. The book also features a curated list of about 40 cocktails--25 modern classics, plus an additional 15 to 20 rediscovered classics and classic contenders--to emerge from the movement." (Publisher's note)

"No matter which side of the bar readers are on, they're sure to work up a powerful thirst." Pub Wkly

Includes bibliographical references and index

Sultan, Tim

Sunny's nights; lost and found at a bar on the edge of the world. Tim Sultan. Random House 2016 288 p. illustrations, map $27   **641.87**

1. Bars 2. Bartending -- New York (State) -- New York 3. Red Hook (N.Y.) -- Social life and customs 4. Brooklyn (New York, N.Y.) -- Social life and customs 5. Bartenders -- New York (State) -- New York -- Biography

ISBN 1400067278; 9781400067275

LC 2015019985

This memoir, by Tim Sultan, is a "portrait of the dream experience we're all searching for every time we walk into a bar, and an enchanting memoir of an unlikely and abiding friendship. The first time he saw Sunny's Bar, in 1995, Tim Sultan was lost, thirsty for a drink, and intrigued by the single bar sign among the forlorn warehouses lining the Brooklyn waterfront. Soon enough, Sultan has quit his office job to bartend full-time for Sunny Balzano, the bar's owner." (Publisher's note)

"An indelible portrait of an unusual man and a nearly forgotten part of NYC."

Tanguay, Paul

The **Tippling** bros. a lime and a shaker. Tad Carducci and Paul Tanguay, the Tippling bros., with Alia Akkam; foreword by Doug Frost; photography by Lauren Volo. Houghton Mifflin Harcourt 2015 256 p. color illustrations $18.99   **641.87**

1. Cocktails 2. Cookbooks

ISBN 054430232X; 9780544302327

LC 2014023051

This mixed drink cookbook, by Tad Carducci and Paul Tanguay, with Alia Akkam, illustrated by Lauren Volo, offers "Mexican cocktail culture and vibrant mezcal- and tequila-based recipes from renowned drinks experts The Tippling Bros. . . . Their 72 exciting recipes go past the classic margarita and include traditional, craft, and spicy drinks." (Publisher's note)

"A title that is sure to have readers looking for opportunities to try the recipes contained within. Highly recommended for any collection in which books on cocktails are prevalent." LJ

The Tippling brothers

Lime and a shaker

641.874   Alcoholic beverages

Jones, Carey

The **Brooklyn** bartender; a modern guide to cocktails and spirits. Carey Jones; photographs by Lucy Schaeffer. Black Dog & Leventhal Publishers 2016 304 p. (hardcover : alk. paper) $24.99 **641.874**

1. Cocktails 2. Brooklyn (New York, N.Y.) 3. Liqueurs

ISBN 9780316390255

LC 2015050472

This book, by Carey Jones, "gathers 300 of the most innovative and exciting cocktail recipes from . . . Brooklyn. . . . Organized by spirit, the recipes allow readers to replicate bartenders' signature drinks, from the ornate juleps and cobblers of Maison Premiere to the party-friendly 'Frozemonade' at Extra Fancy to the namesake gin cocktail of Clover Club." (Publisher's note)

"Even the staunchest teetotaler will work up quite a thirst while perusing what is easily one of the best cocktail books this year." Pub Wkly

Parsons, Brad Thomas

Amaro; The Spirited World of Bittersweet, Herbal Liqueurs, with Cocktails, Recipes, and Formulas. Brad Thomas Parsons; photography by Ed Anderson. Ten Speed Press 2016 280 p. color illustrations (hardcover : alk. paper) $26   **641.874**

1. Cocktails 2. Cookbooks 3. Wine and wine making 4. Bitters 5. Sweetness (Taste) 6. Bitterness (Taste)

ISBN 9781607747482

LC 2016012981

In this book by Brad Thomas Parsons with photographs by Ed Anderson, "the European tradition of making bittersweet liqueurs--called amari in Italian--has been around for centuries. But it is only recently that these herbaceous digestifs have moved . . . and become a key ingredient on cocktail lists in the country's best bars and restaurants. . . . [The book includes] more than 100 recipes for amaro-centric cocktails, DIY amaro, and even amaro-spiked desserts." (Publisher's note)

"Bitter flavors may not be for everyone, but Parsons succeeds at opening up exciting possibilities to try at home or seek out at bars." LJ

Includes bibliographical references and index

642   Meals and table service

Battista, Maggie

Food gift love; more than 100 recipes to make, wrap, and share. Maggie Battista, founder of Eat Boutique; photography Heidi Murphy. Houghton Mifflin Harcourt 2015 255 p. (paper over board) $25 **642**

1. Gifts 2. Cookbooks 3. Snack foods 4. Gift baskets

ISBN 9780544387676

LC 2015004480

This book, by Maggie Battista, presents a "food-gift guide for crafty cooks and food-DIY fans. . . . [It] features 100 memorable, edible gifts for any occasion with simple, delicious recipes, detailed wrapping instructions, and stunning photography. . . . [It includes diverse projects from] simple homemade infused salts and sugars to instant-gratification gifts like fresh ricotta and flavored butters." (Publisher's note)

"An exquisite book for browsing and inspiration. Best for readers with plenty of time to cook and wrap their edible, special-occasion treasures." LJ

Colwin, Laurie

More home cooking; a writer returns to the kitchen. Laurie Colwin. HarperPerennial 2000 224 p. $12.99　　　　**642**

1. Cookbooks 2. Food 3. Cookery 4. Cooking 5. Entertaining

ISBN 0060955317; 9780060955311

James Beard Cookbook Hall of Fame (2012)

This book, "like its predecessor, 'Home Cooking,' is an expression of [author] Laurie Colwin's lifelong passion for cuisine. In this . . . mix of recipes, advice, and anecdotes, she writes about often overlooked food items such as beets, pears, black beans, and chutney. . . . Colwin also discusses the many pleasures and problems of cooking at home in essays such as 'Desserts That Quiver,' 'Turkey Angst,' and 'Catering on One Dollar a Head.'" (Publisher's note)

Hanel, Marnie

The picnic; recipes and inspiration from basket to blanket. Marnie Hanel, Andrea Slonecker, and Jen Stevenson. Artisan 2014 192 p. color illustrations $19.95　　　　**642**

1. Picnics

ISBN 1579656080; 9781579656089

LC 2014036496

This book, by Marnie Hanel, Andrea Slonecker, and Jen Stevenson, "shares everything you need to plan an effortless outdoor get-together: no-fail recipes, helpful checklists, and expert advice. With variations on everyone's favorite deviled eggs, 99 uses for a Mason jar, . . . rules for scoring lawn games, and refreshing drinks to mix up in crowd-friendly batches, let 'The Picnic' take the stress out of your next party and leave only the fun." (Publisher's note)

"A fresh look at outdoor entertaining that's just in time for spring and summer. Highly recommended." LJ

Includes an index

Rosenstrach, Jenny

Dinner; the playbook : a 30-day plan for mastering the art of the family meal. Jenny Rosenstrach. Ballantine Books Trade Paperbacks 2014 240 p. illustrations (chiefly color) (pbk.) $20　　　　**642**

1. Dinners 2. Eating customs 3. Cooking 4. Families 5. Dinners and dining

ISBN 0345549805; 9780345549808

LC 2013033023

In this book author Jenny Rosenstrach "shares her story, offering weekly meal plans, tons of organizing tips, and eighty-plus super-simple, kid-vetted recipes. She and her husband, Andy, would cook thirty new dishes in a single month--and her kids would try them all. Was it nuts for two working parents to take on this challenge? Yes. But did it transform family dinner from stressful grind to happy ritual? Completely." (Publisher's note)

"Families and novice cooks who accept Rosenstrach's challenge will definitely find a few "keepers" here to add to their repertoire." LJ

642.4　　Meals for social and public occasions

Reed, Julia

Julia Reed's south; Spirited Entertaining and High-Style Fun All Year Long. Julia Reed, Paul Costello; [edited by] SandyG. Rizzoli International Publications, Inc. 2016 224 p. color illustrations (hardcover) $50　　　　**642.4**

1. Entertaining

ISBN 9780847848287

LC 2015958266

In this book, author Julia Reed "offers up a feast of options for holiday cocktails, spring lunches, formal dinners, and even a hunt breakfast. Eleven seasonal events feature delicious, easy-to-prepare recipes, ranging from fried chicken to Charlotte Russe and signature cocktails or wine-pairings—she introduces her talented friends (rum makers, potters, fabric designers, bakers) along the way." (Publisher's note)

643　　Housing and household equipment

101 Saturday morning projects; organize, decorate, rejuvenate. The Reader's Digest Association. Reader's Digest Association 2010 144 p. col. ill. $14.95　　　　**643**

1. Self-instruction 2. Storage in the home 3. Houses -- Remodeling 4. Do-it-yourself work 5. Storage in the home -- Amateurs' manuals 6. Dwellings -- Remodeling -- Amateurs' manuals 7. Dwellings -- Maintenance and repair -- Amateurs' manuals

ISBN 1606520180; 9781606520185

LC 2009038049

This book "is a storehouse of practical ideas and projects for keeping things running smoothly around your home or apartment. From storage ideas to plumbing fixes, these sensible projects provide easy-to-follow answers to keeping your home and yard in tip-top shape-with no project taking more than four hours." (Publisher's note)

Black & Decker Corp.

The complete guide to finishing basements; step-by-step projects for adding living space without adding on. Creative Pub. International 2009 255p il pa $24.99　　　　**643**

1. Basements 2. Houses -- Remodeling

ISBN 978-1-58923-454-3; 1-58923-454-5

LC 2008-45813

"Thorough and filled from beginning to end with handy reference information, this tome more than adequately demostrates how to evaluate, upgrade, and remodel the . . . . basement." Booklist

The complete photo guide to home improvement; [created by the editors of Creative Publishing International, Inc., in cooperation with Black & Decker] Creative Pub. International 2009 560p il $35　　　　**643**

1. Houses -- Remodeling 2. Houses -- Maintenance

and repair
ISBN 978-1-58923-452-9; 1-58923-452-9
LC 2008-45755
First published 2001
This home improvement guide covers such topics as flooring, ceilings and walls, windows and doors, and remodeling different rooms including kitchens, bathrooms, and basements.

This "guide is basic, easy to follow, and completely illustrated. The organization is sensible and information easy to find." Libr J

The **complete** photo guide to home repair. Creative Pub. International 2008 559p il $35   643
1. Houses -- Maintenance and repair
ISBN 978-1-58923-417-8; 1-58923-417-0
LC 2008-16520
First published 1999
"Features more than 200 . . . home repair projects, including common wiring, plumbing, interior and exterior repairs." Publisher's note

The **book** of home how-to; complete photo guide to home repair & improvement. Black+Decker. Cool Springs Press 2014 600 p. (hardback) $35   643
1. Dwellings -- Maintenance and repair -- Amateurs' manuals
ISBN 1591865980; 9781591865988
LC 2013047686

Bray, Ilona M.
Nolo's essential guide to buying your first home; [by] Ilona Bray, Alayna Schroeder & Marcia Stewart. 3rd ed.; Nolo 2010 426p il pa $24.99   643
1. Houses -- Buying and selling
ISBN 978-1-4133-1322-2 pa; 1-4133-1322-1 pa; 978-1-4133-1348-2 ebook; 1-4133-1348-5 ebook
LC 2010-31334
First published 2007. Frequently revised
Provides information on selecting the right house, the right mortgage, the right agent, the right inspections and more. CD-ROM contains a "Homebuyer's Toolkit" with forms and other resources.
Includes bibliographical references

Bryson, Bill
At home; a short history of private life. Doubleday 2010 497p il $28.95   643
1. Rooms 2. Houses
ISBN 978-0-7679-1938-8; 0-7679-1938-6
LC 2010-04008
The author takes readers on a tour of his house, a rural English parsonage, showing how each room has figured in the evolution of private life.

"It takes a very particular kind of thoughtfulness, as well as a bold temperament, to stuff all this research into a mattress that's supportive enough to loll about on while pondering the real subject of this book—the development of the modern world. . . . Bryson is fascinated by everything, and his curiosity is infectious." N Y Times Book Rev
Includes bibliographical references

Complete do-it-yourself manual; by Editors Of Family Handyman. Simon & Schuster 2014 528 p. color illustrations $35   643
1. Self-instruction 2. House construction
ISBN 1621452018; 9781621452010
This book is a "manual for home improvements. . . . Written in a style of text that addresses readers in a very accessible, conversational tone for easy, user-friendly assistance with every do-it-yourself task. All instructions and materials have been updated to address current codes (electrical, plumbing and building), and revised to indicate the very latest in materials, tools, and technology." (Publisher's note)

"A worthy competitor to this old standby is Black and Decker's The Complete Photo Guide to Home Repair , but the Complete Do-It-Yourself Manual is still more comprehensive and detailed. Recommended for all libraries." LJ

The **complete** guide to finishing basements; projects and practical solutions for converting basements into livable space. by Editors of Cool Springs Press. Cool Springs Press 2013 239 p. color illustrations (softcover) $24.99   643
1. Basements 2. Houses -- Remodeling 3. Basements -- Remodeling -- Amateurs' manuals
ISBN 1591865883; 9781591865889
LC 2013009481
This book "covers every aspect of designing and planning a basement conversion/remodeling project. . . . It deals comprehensively with adapting home mechanical systems to basement conditions. The many featured projects include finishing a bathroom stub-out, installing an all-new basement bathroom, insulating, repairing foundation walls, installing sump pumps, dehumidification strategies, as well as many other projects designed for livability." (Publisher's note)

Black & Decker complete guide to finishing basements

Corbett, Michael
Before you buy! the homebuyer's handbook for today's market. Plume 2011 xxiii, 277p il pa $15   643
1. Real estate investment 2. Houses -- Buying and selling
ISBN 978-0-452-29680-0
LC 2010050910
A real estate developer offers advice on buying a home during the economic crisis, covering common mistakes made by buyers and offering advice on how to handle foreclosure, mortgages, inspections, and other issues.

Crook, David
The **Wall** Street Journal complete home owner's guidebook; make the most of your biggest asset in any market. Three Rivers Press 2008 260p il pa $14.95   643
1. Real estate investment 2. Houses -- Buying and selling
ISBN 978-0-307-40592-0; 0-307-40592-3
LC 2008-25355
This is a "look at the pros and cons of owning a home—rather than renting one from a bank via a mortgage—along with its ultimate costs. . . . For those aspiring to own a home

and those trying to manage the affordability of their biggest asset, this is a must read." Publ Wkly

Includes bibliographical references

Do it yourself kitchens; stunning spaces on a shoe-string budget. Wiley 2011 192p   **643**
    1. Kitchens
    ISBN 9781118031629

"Ranked by budget, from $1000 up to $10,000, sample kitchen makeovers showcased here illustrate a range of possibilities. With spending breakdowns, stunning before-and-after shots, and lots of tips that make big differences, this book has wide appeal. For each makeover there are detailed instructions for selected projects, such as installing fixtures, resurfacing, and tiling. This is not in-depth how-to, but ideas and inspiration. Each sample kitchen is brimming with creativity and innovation."

Family Handyman

Refresh your home; simple projects and tips to save money, update, and renovate. editors of the Family handyman. Reader's Digest 2011 287p il pa $16.95   **643**
    1. Houses -- Remodeling
    ISBN 978-1-60652-201-1
                                   LC 2010029903
First published 2010 with title: Family handyman home improvement 2010

"The coverage of a wealth of home fixes with a dose of humor makes this DIY guide a delight. . . . There are tips and insights on every page. New gadgets, considerations for appliance purchases, and fun little projects populate this book. The section on power tool safety is important, and 'dos and don'ts' suggestions are peppered throughout. Even common goofs are shared with chuckles. A charming and friendly collection of tips and projects." Libr J

German, Roger

Remodeling a basement; Rev. ed.; Taunton Press 2010 170p il (Taunton's build like a pro) pa $19.95   **643**
    1. Basements 2. Houses -- Remodeling
    ISBN 978-1-60085-292-3
                                   LC 2009-33545
First published 2004

"Beginning with solving moisture problems, then renovating space, this book walks the reader through a logical process for repair and remodeling, with easy-to-follow instruction and illustrations. Design ideas and the latest building code data are also included." Libr J

Home Depot, Inc.

Home improvement 1-2-3; 3rd ed., Newly expanded and rev.; Home Depot Books 2008 607p il $34.95   **643**
    1. Interior design 2. Houses -- Remodeling 3. Houses -- Maintenance and repair
    ISBN 978-0-696-23850-5
                                   LC 2008-924090
First published 1995

This book offers illustrated instructions for home remodeling, decorating, and repair.

Jackson, Albert

Popular mechanics complete home how-to; [by] Albert Jackson and David Day. Hearst Books 2004 514p il $24.95   **643**
    1. Houses -- Maintenance and repair
    ISBN 1-58816-302-4
                                   LC 2003-56853
"Interior and exterior repairs are included, from simple tasks like replacing an electrical switch to difficult ones like constructing a wall or building a pond, as well as common upgrades. Everything is explained in detail, with a wealth of clear photos and illustrations. A section on skills and tools shows the use of woodworking, building, decorating, plumbing, and electrical equipment, and a reference section describes hardware/materials and defines commonly used terminology. A great general guide to home repairs of all types, this book will see heavy use in most collections." Libr J

Litchfield, Michael W.

Renovation; [by] Michael Litchfield; Chip Harley, technical editor. The Taunton Press, Inc. 2012 615 p. color illustrations $50   **643**
    1. Houses -- Remodeling
    ISBN 1600854923; 9781600854927
                                   LC 2005110
This book, in its fourth edition, "contains the collective wisdom of hundreds of contractors, architects and tradespeople who shared their first-hand experience with [author] Mike Litchfield as he interviewed and photographed them on job sites across North America. . . . [It] contain[s] extensively revised chapters on planning; doors, windows and skylights; electrical wiring; and energy conservation." (Publisher's note)

New fix-it-yourself manual; by Reader's Digest. The Reader's Digest Association, Inc. 1996 448 p. color illustrations $35   **643**
    1. Self-instruction 2. Furniture -- Repairing 3. Electric household appliances -- Maintenance and repair 4. Do-it-yourself work 5. Furniture -- Repairing -- Amateurs' manuals 6. Household appliances -- Maintenance and repair -- Amateurs' manuals 7. Household appliances, Electric -- Maintenance and repair -- Amateurs' manuals
    ISBN 0895778718; 9780895778710
                                   LC 96015189
This book is a "reference guide for every homeowner, guaranteed to help you maintain and improve your home while saving time and money. Covering everything from replacing faulty faucets and showerheads to curing the quirks of an air conditioner, this book provides step-by-step illustrated instructions, plus a comprehensive chapter on tools. Includes more than 3,000 instructional photographs, illustrations, charts, and diagrams." (Publisher's note)

Reader's digest new fix-it-yourself manual

O'Connor, Kevin

The best homes from This old house; Kevin O'Connor; photographs by Michael Casey. Stewart, Tabori & Chang 2011 225 p. color illustrations $35   **643**
    1. House construction 2. Domestic architecture 3.

Architecture, Domestic -- United States 4. Dwellings -- Remodeling -- United States 5. Dwellings -- United States -- Maintenance and repair
ISBN 1584799358; 9781584799351

LC 2011018212

Author Kevin O'Connor "chronicle[s] 10 of the finest transformations rendered by the craftsmen and artists from the past decade of filming the show ['This Old House']. Never before have completed projects from This Old House been displayed in such detail. From interiors to exteriors, with insights from every step of the process, the works presented in this book will give devotees of 'This Old House' something they've never had before—the rarely shown finished spaces." (Publisher's note)

Reader's Digest Association, Inc.

Complete do-it-yourself manual; with the editors of Family handyman. rev and updated; Reader's Digest 2005 528p il $35   **643**
1. Houses -- Maintenance and repair
ISBN 0-7621-0579-8

LC 2004-50945

First published 1973 with title: Reader's Digest complete do-it-yourself manual

This manual for homeowners covers topics such as power tools, plumbing, landscaping, and storage projects with photos, diagrams and illustrations

"Intriguing sidebars on wood refinishers (the fastest drying versus the safest), the financial benefits of renting specialty tools for a large drywall project and other subjects round out this must-have guide." Publ Wkly

Solakian, Susan E.

The **homeowner's** guide to managing a renovation; tough-as-nails tactics for getting the most from your money. Sterling 2008 288p il pa $19.95 **643**
1. Houses -- Remodeling
ISBN 978-1-4027-2754-2

LC 2008-03797

"While dollar figures used will quickly be outdated, the principles presented are constant. This is really an underrepresented topic in how-to collections, and Solakian's book is an especially good offering." Libr J

Soles, Clyde

The **fire** smart home handbook; preparing for and surviving the threat of wildfire. Clyde Soles; foreword by Molly Mowery. Lyons Press 2014 288 p. illustrations (some color) (pbk.) $19.95   **643**
1. Wildfires 2. Houses -- Safety measures 3. Wildfires -- United States -- Prevention and control 4. Dwellings -- Fires and fire prevention -- United States
ISBN 0762796901; 9780762796908

LC 2013050242

Written by Clyde Soles, "this highly detailed and practical guide will help you live safely in the wildfire zone and save you time and money along the way, providing various methods of risk mitigation along with the financial level of each action. . . . This book will help you create a survivable space that will not only enhance the scenery but may increase the value of your home." (Publisher's note)

"While not everyone has to worry about wildfire, some of this advice applies to fire preparedness in most any home." Pub Wkly

Sussman, Julie

Dare to repair; a do-it-herself guide to fixing (almost) anything in the home. {by} Julie Sussman and Stephanie Glakas-Tenet; illustrations by Yeorgos Lampathakis. HarperCollins Pubs. 2002 253p il pa $14.95   **643**
1. Houses -- Maintenance and repair
ISBN 0-06-095984-3

LC 2002-27625

The authors "show women how to perform a number of the most common repairs, including unclogging drains and toilets, replacing electrical switches and outlets, leveling appliances, lighting pilot lights, unsticking windows, and installing a door peephole. . . . This is a wonderful book that should be purchased by every public library." Libr J

Ultimate guide: home repair and improvement; 3rd ed.; Creative Homeowner 2011 607p il $29.95   **643**
1. Houses -- Remodeling 2. Houses -- Maintenance and repair
ISBN 978-1-58011-528-5

First published 2000 with title: Home book

This guide "completely covers the repairs most home owners need. . . . This strong manual is highly recommended." Libr J

Wilson, Bee

Consider the fork; a history of how we cook and eat. Bee Wilson; with illustrations by Annabel Lee. Basic Books 2012 xxiii, 327 p.p (hardback) $26.99   **643**
1. Food writing 2. Eating habits 3. Eating customs 4. Cooking -- History 5. Kitchen utensils -- History 6. Dinners and dining -- History
ISBN 9780465021765; 9780465033324

LC 2012016283

Author Bee Wilson presents an "evolution of cooking around the world, revealing the hidden history of everyday objects we often take for granted. Knives . . . predate the discovery of fire, whereas the fork endured centuries of ridicule before gaining widespread acceptance . . . Blending history, science, and anthropology, Wilson reveals how our culinary tools and tricks came to be, and how their influence has shaped modern food culture." (Publisher's note)

Includes bibliographical references and index.

Wing, Charlie

How Your House Works; A Visual Guide to Understanding and Maintaining Your Home. by Charlie Wing. RSMeans 2012 192 p. color illustrations $24.95   **643**
1. Houses -- Maintenance and repair
ISBN 1118099400; 9781118099407

LC 2011046745

This book, by Charlie Wing, "uncovers the mysteries behind just about every major appliance and building element in your house. Clear, full-color drawings show you exactly how these things should be put together and how they function, including what to check if they don't work. Covering topics such as electrical systems, heating and air conditioning, plumbing, major household appliances, foundation, framing, doors, and windows, this updated Second Edition has considerable additional information." (Publisher's note)

"This book is more a 'how' than a 'how-to' and fills its role quite nicely. Highly recommended for all collections." LJ

643.12   Selecting, buying, selling homes

Scott, Drew
   Dream home; the Property Brothers' ultimate guide to finding & fixing your perfect house. Jonathan Scott, Drew Scott; photography by David Tsay. Houghton Mifflin Harcourt Publishing Company 2016 304 p. color illustrations (paper over board) $30   **643.12**
   1. Houses -- Remodeling 2. Houses -- Buying and selling 3. House buying 4. Dwellings -- Inspection 5. Dwellings -- Remodeling
   ISBN 0544715675; 9780544715677

                 LC 2015037674

Authors Jonathan Scott and Drew Scott present this "comprehensive source, covering the ins and outs of buying, selling, and renovating a house, with hundreds of full-color photos throughout. The brothers cover numerous topics including the hidden costs of moving, savvy negotiating tactics, and determining your home must-haves. Other handy features include a calendar of key dates for finding the best deals on home products and a cheat sheet of worth-it fix-its." (Publisher's note)

"Dream Home is full of ideas and is a good source for anyone looking to buy, sell, or renovate a property. " Booklist

643.7   Renovation, improvement, remodeling

Susanka, Sarah
   Not so big remodeling; tailoring your home for the way you really live. by Sarah Susanka and Marc Vassallo. Taunton Press 2012 329 p. illustrations (chiefly color) $24.95   **643.7**
   1. Houses -- Remodeling
   ISBN 1600858244; 9781600858246

                 LC 2008046632

In this book, authors Sarah Susanka and Marc Vassallo "demonstrate how carefully chosen tweaks and simple additions can make a home seem much larger and more inviting. . . . [They] show readers how to think like an architect, so they can accurately assess their home's shortcomings, apply 'Not So Big' principles to their remodeling plan, and phase in their project incrementally over time." (Publisher's note)

645   Household furnishings

Montano, Mark
   The **big**-ass book of home decor; photographs by Auxy Espinoza. Stewart, Tabori & Chang 2010 271p il pa $22.50   **645**
   1. Interior design
   ISBN 978-1-58479-825-5

                 LC 2009-36376

The author "presents over 100 projects for decorating, creating, and repurposing furniture and decorative accessories. He offers clearly written instructions illustrated with color photographs of the steps. The wealth of inspiring projects that require only basic skills—e.g., decoupage, spray paint, glue gun—will make this a popular choice for both experienced and inexperienced crafters." Libr J

Petersik, Sherry
   Lovable livable home; how to add beauty, get organized, and make your house work for you. Sherry and John Petersik of Young House Love. Artisan 2015 336 p. color illustrations (alk. paper) $27.50   **645**
   1. Houses 2. Interior design 3. Interior decoration 4. Dwellings -- Remodeling
   ISBN 1579656226; 9781579656225

                 LC 2015010991

In this book authors Sherry Petersik and John Peterski " set out to prove that just because you have kids or pets doesn't mean you're sentenced to floors overrun with toys or furniture covered in plastic. Through never-before-seen makeovers in the Petersiks' own house, doable DIY projects, and a gallery of other inspiring spaces, Lovable Livable Home shows how beautiful homes can be functional too." (Publisher's note)

"The clever ideas developed by these amateurs that adapt to the needs of busy families will motivate others to tackle their own spaces." LJ

Includes bibliographical references and index

646   Sewing, clothing, management of personal and family life

Moebes, Deborah
   Stitch Savvy; 25 Skill-Building Projects to Take Your Sewing Technique to the Next Level: Home Decor, Patchwork & Quilting, Bags, Sewing for Children, Clothing. F & W Media Inc 2012 224 p. (hardcover) $27.99   **646**
   1. Sewing -- Technique
   ISBN 1440229473; 9781440229473

This book by Deborah Moebes "focuses on sewists who are ready to move past basic beginner projects. The title is organized into five 'tracks' (home decor, patchwork and quilting, bags, sewing for children, and clothing), each with five progressively more difficult projects. The author's goal is to further refine basic sewing skills and bring beginners to the next level. . . . [E]ach project includes a sidebar that serves as a guide to possible 'next steps'." (Library Journal)

Stanley, Suzannah Hamlin

DIY wardrobe makeovers; alter, refresh & refashion your clothes: step-by-step sewing tutorials. Suzannah Hamlin Stanley. C&T Publishing, Inc. 2015 160 p. color illustrations (soft cover) $26.95 **646**

1. Sewing 2. Fashion 3. Clothing and dress 4. Clothing and dress -- Remaking
ISBN 1617450421; 9781617450426

LC 2014036813

In this book, author Suzannah Hamlin Stanley shows readers how to "unlock your closet's potential with simple wardrobe fixes and refashions to express your style. These basic alterations and step-by-step restyling tutorials will help you fit and reassemble garments into newfound faves. No sloppy shortcuts here--learn how to alter sweaters, pants, and everything in your wardrobe for a more flattering fit. Take it in, take it up, or let it out—all on your home sewing machine." (Publisher's note)

"The title is slightly misleading, as the majority of the tutorials are more about mending, repairing, and customizing rather than transforming existing pieces into something completely different. However, the instructions are excellent, and sewists who want to customize ready-to-wear garments to create a more flattering fit will appreciate this guide." LJ

646.2   Sewing and related operations

Bednar, Nancy

The **encyclopedia** of sewing machine techniques; [by] Nancy Bednar, JoAnn Pugh-Gannon. Sterling Pub. 2007 336p il pa $24.95 **646.2**

1. Sewing
ISBN 1-4027-4293-2; 978-1-4027-4293-4
First published 1999

Among the techniques covered in this illustrated step-by-step guide are beading, fringing, pintucks, and puffing.

Bull, Jane

Get set, sew; the beginner's sewing machine book. Jane Bull. Dk Pub 2015 125 p. color illustrations (hardcover) $20 **646.2**

1. Sewing 2. Handicraft
ISBN 1465435875; 9781465435873

LC 2015472670

This handicraft book, by Jane Bull, "is a clear, fresh, enjoyable introduction to sewing on a machine. Jane's friendly, jargon-free instructions and step-by-step photos will walk you through everything you need to know to learn how to use a sewing machine. Master sewing machine basics one at a time, then put newly learned skills to work with 20 simple sewing projects to make--including creative and original bags, accessories, cushions, and toys." (Publisher's note)

Cheetham, Kathleen

Singer perfect plus; sew a mix-and-match wardrobe in plus and petite-plus sizes. Quayside Pub. Group 2009 144p il $25 **646.2**

1. Sewing 2. Tailoring 3. Women's clothing
ISBN 978-1-58923-394-2; 1-58923-394-8

LC 2008-30415

"Cheetham's projects for casual and workplace fashions are accessible for beginning sewers. The mix-and-match tips are reminiscent of fashion magazine features, providing hints for assembling creative outfits. It's refreshing to see the clothes modeled on an actual plus-sized woman (the author herself)." Libr J

Colgrove, Debbie

Teach yourself visually sewing. Wiley 2006 283p il (Visual read less, learn more) pa $24.99 **646.2**

1. Sewing
ISBN 0-471-74991-5; 978-0-471-74991-2

LC 2005-939196

This visual guide explains the "basics of hand sewing and sewing with a machine. . . . [It includes] information about tools and fabrics." Publisher's note

Creative Publishing International, Inc.

★ The **complete** photo guide to sewing; 1200 full-color how-to photos. [created by the editors of Creative Publishing International] Rev. + expanded ed.; Creative Pub. International 2009 352p il pa $24.99 **646.2**

1. Sewing
ISBN 978-1-58923-434-5; 1-58923-434-0

LC 2008-31264

First published 1999

"Sections include choosing the right tools and notions, using conventional machines and sergers, fashion sewing, tailoring, and home décor projects. Included are step-by-step instructions for basic projects like pillows, tablecloths, and window treatments." Publisher's note

The **complete** photo guide to window treatments; [edited by Linda Neubauer] 2nd ed; Creative Publisher International 2011 320p il pa $24.99 **646.2**

1. Draperies
ISBN 978-1-58923-607-3

LC 2010046925

First published 2007

"Fabric recommendations and materials lists introduce each style of window treatment, with clear, step-by-step instructions. Organization is consistent and well thought out, making this an easy manual to follow." Libr J

Includes bibliographical references

First time sewing; the absolute beginner's guide. by the editors of Creative Publishing international. Creative Publishing international, a member of Quayside Publishing Group 2014 127 p. (pbk.) $19.99; (ebook) $19.99 **646.2**

1. Sewing 2. Machine sewing
ISBN 1589238044; 9781589238046; 9781627880091

LC 2015430813

This book, by the editors of Creative Publishing international, is a "guide that . . . teaches you how to sew using hand stiches as well as sewing machines. Filled with detailed descriptions of materials and tools, the easy step-by-step instructions for all the basic sewing techniques will have you creating projects like aprons, pillows, and even pants and shorts in no time." (Publisher's note)

Sewing
Sewing

Gardiner, Wendy

The **sewing** machine accessory bible; get the most out of your machine from using basic feet to mastering specialty feet. [by] Wendy Gardiner & Lorna Knight. Griffin: St. Martin's 2011 128p il pa $22.99   **646.2**

1. Sewing machines
ISBN 978-0-312-67658-2

This book focuses "on sewing machine accessories—feet, needles, and other attachments. . . . [The authors] briefly cover the basics of sewing machines, but they focus on the specialized feet that come with the machine. A photo of a sewing machine foot is included at the top left corner of each spread, allowing for quick and easy identification. There's also information about how to use each foot—what it's for and how to sew with it. Beginners will find this book especially handy." Libr J

Handmade interiors; DK Publishing. DK Publishing 2015 304 p. color illustrations $40   **646.2**

1. Furniture 2. Interior design
ISBN 1465427082; 9781465427083

This book by DK Publishing "shows you how to create your own soft furnishings, such as cushions and curtains, and transform every room in the house. Clear step-by-step pictures show how to create your version of the inspiration pieces shown, while advice on fabrics and suggested variations are provided to help you tailor each project to your own unique space and budget." (Publisher's note)

"This book will soon become a well-worn reference." LJ

Ishida, Sanae

Sewing happiness; A Year of Simple Projects for Living Well. Sanae Ishida. Sasquatch Books 2016 225 p. illustrations $22.95   **646.2**

1. Sewing 2. Autobiography 3. Machine sewing
ISBN 9781570619953

LC 2015040697

In this book, "twenty simple sewing projects are tied together with a thread of memoir that tells the story of how sewing brought Sanae Ishida profound happiness. Each seasonal project, specially designed to promote health, creativity, relationships and more, provides gentle inspiration to live your best life." (Publisher's note)

"The instructions are thorough, the tips and advice are generous, and the overall presentation is thoughtful." LJ

Includes bibliographical references

James, Chris

The **complete** serger handbook. Sterling 1997 159p il hardcover o.p. pa $17.95   **646.2**

1. Sewing 2. Sewing machines
ISBN 0-8069-9807-5 pa

LC 96-39316

This "is a concise guide to the serger and serger techniques. Major sections of the book include identifying the parts of a serger (with photos of each part), serger accessories, types of threads, threading and testing the threading, learning to regulate tension, and techniques." Libr J

Lee, Linda

Sewing edges and corners. Taunton Press 2000 134p il pa $19.95   **646.2**

1. Sewing
ISBN 1-56158-418-5

LC 00-29919

The author offers about 40 corner and edge techniques for garments and home decorating projects

"Readers appreciate the clarity of Lee's instructions, since each step is numbered, photographs and other illustrations ease difficult tasks, and sidebars ensure the comfortableness of the sewing." Booklist

Lindsay, Virginia

Sewing to sell; the beginner's guide to starting a craft business : bonus, 16 starter projects : how to sell locally & online. Virginia Lindsay. C&T Publishing 2014 152 p. color illustrations (soft cover) $25.95   **646.2**

1. Sewing 2. Arts and crafts movement 3. Selling -- Handbooks, manuals, etc 4. Small business -- Management -- Handbooks, manuals, etc 5. Handicraft industries -- Management -- Handbooks, manuals, etc 6. Home-based businesses -- Management -- Handbooks, manuals, etc
ISBN 1607059037; 9781607059035

LC 2014013070

Author Virginia Lindsay presents "a book that's half-helpful suggestions for those who want to start a home-based sewing business and half a selection of 16 sewing patterns that can be used to make projects to sell. The first section contains valuable information on everything from identifying potential customers to taking good photos for online sales and setting prices for craft shows." (Publishers Weekly)

"Most appropriate for crafters who need a very basic guide to selling their handmade goods. Those looking to take their business to the next level will benefit from Kari Chapin's Grow Your Handmade Business and The Handmade Marketplace, which provide a more comprehensive view of operating a craft-based enterprise." LJ

Includes bibliographical references

New complete guide to sewing; step-by-step techniques for making clothes and home accessories. Reader's Digest. Reader's Digest Association 2011 384 p. ill. (some col.) $35   **646.2**

1. Sewing 2. Tailoring 3. Dressmaking 4. Household linens
ISBN 1606522086; 9781606522080

LC 2010029616

This book is the "ultimate stitch-and-seam reference book for both beginners and seasoned sewers. . . . In this updated edition, sewers will find 20 new modern projects from Simplicity patterns; Instructions for making smart trousers, traditional curtains, a light summer dress, kids' clothes, a beach towel, patchwork bag, and more." (Publisher's note)

The **new** sewing essentials; Updated and rev. ed.; Creative Publishing International 2008 144p il pa $16.99   **646.2**
1. Sewing
ISBN 978-1-58923-432-1; 1-58923-432-4
First published 1984 by Random House with title: Sewing essentials
This guide to sewing clothes and other items includes information on equipment, patterns, fabrics, and techniques.

Paganelli, Jennifer
Happy home; twenty-one sewing and craft projects to pretty up your home. by Jennifer Paganelli; with Dolin O'Shea; photographs by Tim Geaney. Chronicle Books 2012 175 p. illustrations $27.50   **646.2**
1. Sewing 2. Interior design 3. Machine sewing 4. House furnishings
ISBN 0811874451; 9780811874458
LC 2011018891
In this book, author Jennifer Paganelli "shows readers how to whip up twenty-one beautiful accessories to transform their space into a sunny, happy home. Each project showcases Jennifer's . . . style—from luxe drapery to cheery tablecloths and napkins. Featuring simple step-by-step instructions, a comprehensive glossary of techniques, pattern sheets tucked into a handy front pocket, and lush color photos, this book makes it exceptionally easy to pretty up every room in the house." (Publisher's note)

Reader's Digest Association, Inc.
New complete guide to sewing; step-by-step techniques for making clothes and home accessories. from the editors at Reader's digest. Reader's Digest Assn. 2002 384p il $35   **646.2**
1. Sewing
ISBN 0-7621-0420-1
LC 2002-69944
First published 1976 with title: Complete guide to sewing
This illustrated guide begins with an overview of basic equipment and techniques. A discussion of patterns and fabrics is included. The bulk of the book provides step-by-step instructions for making clothes and home furnishings.

Shore, Debbie
Half yard gifts; easy sewing projects using left-over pieces of fabric. Debbie Shore. Search Press 2015 96 p. color illustrations (paperback) $19.95   **646.2**
1. Gifts 2. Sewing
ISBN 9781782211501; 1782211500
This book "is the latest title from sewing guru Debbie Shore, and the next book in her best-selling half yard series. . . . It contains 22 projects to sew and give away, each

made using less than half a yard of fabric. The book contains gifts for all your family and friends: the projects range from pincushions, bags and paperweights to aprons for budding chefs, kneeling pads for gardeners and tool belts for DIY-enthusiasts." (Publisher's note)
"Gift sewing is popular, and there's a wide range of projects here. Sewists looking for cute, feminine gift designs will enjoy." LJ

Smith, Alison
The **sewing** book; An Encyclopedic Resource of Step-by-Step Techniques. Alison Smith. DK Pub. 2009 400 p. illustrations (some color) (ebook) $65; $40   **646.2**
1. Sewing
ISBN 9780756657185; 0756642809; 9780756642808
This book, by Alison Smith, "is the only sewing book you'll ever need. Every tool and every technique you require for making your own home furnishings or clothing is closely and sharply photographed, carefully annotated, and clearly explained." (Publisher's note0

Staples, Heidi
Sew organized for the busy girl; tips to make the most of your time & space : 23+ quick and clever sewing projects you'll love. by Heidi Staples. C&T Publishing, Inc. 2015 112 p. illustrations (some color) (softcover) $22.95   **646.2**
1. Sewing 2. Time management 3. House furnishings
ISBN 1607059797; 9781607059790
LC 2014031103
This book, by Heidi Staples, describes how to "fit sewing into your busy lifestyle with practical tips that will help you put hours back on the clock! . . . Revive your creative life and make the most of your time with easy-to-implement advice. Stitch up 23 projects, ranging from handcrafted quilts to home decor, children's gifts, and attractive storage cases." (Publisher's note)
"Staples's suggestions range from useful (gathering items related to an ongoing project into a project bag) to a little silly (using a weekly "family meeting" to declare your need for some sewing time), but the chronically disorganized—and those seeking a better system—will appreciate her low-stress, creative approach." LJ

Yaker, Rebecca
Little one-yard wonders; by Rebecca Yaker and Patricia Hoskins. Storey Publishing 2014 360 p. color illustrations (One-yard wonders series) (paper w/concealed wire-o and patterns : alk. paper) $29.95   **646.2**
1. Handicraft 2. Children's clothing 3. Machine sewing 4. Children's paraphernalia
ISBN 1612121241; 9781612121246
LC 2013045043
Written by Rebecca Yaker and Patricia Hoskins, "[t]his newest addition to the best-selling One-Yard Wonders series features 101 . . . projects for babies and kids, each using just one yard of fabric and many requiring just a few hours to complete. Step-by-step illustrated instructions, . . . close-up photographs, and pattern pieces included in a bound-in en-

velope make it easy and fun to create all kinds of adorable items." (Publisher's note)

"This title is a treasure trove of handmade kid's stuff, and sewists of all skill levels will find ideas and inspiration in this lighthearted collection." LJ

One-yard wonders; look how much you can make with just one yard of fabric! Rebecca Yaker and Patricia Hoskins; photography by John Gruen; photo styling by Raina Kattelson. Storey Pub. 2009 303 p. ill. (some col.) $24.95   **646.2**
  1. Sewing 2. Interior design 3. Clothing and dress 4. Machine sewing 5. House furnishings
  ISBN 1603424490; 9781603424493
                                    LC 2009023721
This book, by Rebecca Yaker and Patricia Hoskins, "presents a delightful array of simple, stylish projects that can be made with just a single yard of fabric - from apparel to accessories, from plush toys to pet beds, from baby items to bags, and from home decor to 'Happy Birthday' banners. Projects have a hip, contemporary flair, and most can be completed in a few hours." (Publisher's note)

"This is a fundamental crafts book appropriate for most crafts collections." Booklist
  1-yard wonders

646.21   Construction of home furnishings

Ellis, Cassandra
  Home sewn; projects and inspiration for every room. Cassandra Ellis. Random House Inc. 2016 160 p. color illustrations (hardcover) $24.99 **646.21**
  1. Sewing 2. Handicraft
  ISBN 9781101906958; 1101906952
                                    LC 2015030531
This craft book, by Cassandra Ellis, "features distinctive sewing projects dedicated to living, resting, eating, and sharing. Use quality materials—from rustic linen to leather—to create simple ottomans, pendant light shades, a voile bed skirt, and more. With dreamy lifestyle photography and ideas for every room." (Publisher's note)

646.4   Clothing and accessories construction

Abousteit, Nora
  BurdaStyle sewing vintage modern; mastering iconic looks from the 1920s to 1980s. Nora Abousteit with Jamie Lau and David Leon Morgan. 1st ed. Potter Craft 2012 216 p. illustrations (chiefly color) (hardcover) $29.99; (ebook) $85.00   **646.4**
  1. Sewing 2. Dressmaking -- Patterns
  ISBN 0307586758; 9780307586759; 9780770434397
                                    LC 2012010976
This book is a collection of sewing patterns. "Five adaptable master patterns for tops, dresses, and pants are transformed into nineteen unique projects for both women and men that draw inspiration from key fashion moments. These influential looks—from the Roaring Twenties to the Awe-

some Eighties—are all modernized and reinterpreted for today's sewing enthusiasts." (Publisher's note)

Armstrong, Helen Joseph
  Patternmaking for fashion design; technical illustrator, Vincent James Maruzzi; fashion illustrator, Kathryn Hagen. 4th ed; Pearson Prentice Hall 2006 xxi, 805p il $104.40   **646.4**
  1. Dressmaking -- Patterns
  ISBN 978-0-13-194893-9; 0-13-194893-8
                                    LC 2005-283500
First published 1987 by Harper & Row
"Covers the three steps in the development of design patterns—dart manipulation, added fullness, and contouring—with a central theme that all designs are based on one, or more of these three major patternmaking and design principles." Publisher's note
Includes bibliographical references

Betzina, Sandra
  Power sewing step-by-step. Taunton Press 2000 231p il $34.95; pa $24.95   **646.4**
  1. Sewing 2. Dressmaking
  ISBN 1-56158-363-4; 1-56158-572-6 pa
                                    LC 00-23431
"Vests, pants, shirts, dresses, and jackets for women are the focus of this book, with Betzina guiding the reader step by step through her thinking process in planning, constructing, fitting, customizing, and finishing each type of garments. More than 500 color photos illustrate many tricks of the trade, shortcuts, and tips. This will be a core title in any sewing collection." Libr J

BurdaStyle modern sewing; edited by Michelle Bredeson. Interweave 2014 127 p. $29.99 **646.4**
  1. Sewing 2. Dressmaking -- Patterns 3. Skirts 4. Blouses 5. Tailoring (Women's)
  ISBN 1620339129; 9781620339121
                                    LC 2014005783
This book, edited by Michelle Bredeson, "includes 21 projects from the archives of BurdaStyle magazine. All of the must-have basics of a woman's wardrobe are covered in this collection: jackets, pants, blouses, skirts, and dresses. The designs include versatile separates as well as combinations that further expand the possibilities for the modern woman's wardrobe." (Publisher's note)

"The BurdaStyle name is popular among sewists, and this collection of workplace-friendly garments from the magazine's archives will appeal to young professionals who want to put a distinct stamp on their wardrobe." LJ
Wardrobe essentials

Butler, Amy
  Amy Butler's style stitches; 12 Easy Ways to 26 Wonderful Bags. by Amy Butler. Chronicle Books 2010 182 p. illustrations $29.95   **646.4**
  1. Sewing 2. Handbags 3. Fancy work
  ISBN 0811866696; 9780811866699
                                    LC 2009025698
This book on handbag sewing, by Amy Butler, "offers 12 basic patterns with enough variations to achieve 26 unique looks. Ranging from chic clutches and delicate wristlets to

pretty hobo bags and handy coin purses, with instructions for altering dimensions, straps, and embellishments to get the desired look, each project incorporates Butler's fresh, modern style and attention to detail." (Publisher's note)

Doh, Jenny

Signature styles; 20 stitchers craft their look. Lark Crafts 2011 144p il pa $19.95   **646.4**
1. Sewing 2. Dressmaking 3. Fashion accessories 4. Dress accessories
ISBN 978-1-60059-791-6; 1-60059-791-2
LC 2010040531

Reveals how 20 women authors, bloggers, entrepreneurs and more developed their own distinctive looks. Each crafter shares her studio, style, a key technique, and an exclusive project.

This is "a surprisingly varied collection, ranging from costumey retroquirk to urban couture to modern country." Libr J

Hirsch, Gretchen

Gertie's ultimate dress book; a modern guide to sewing fabulous vintage styles. Gretchen Hirsch. STC Craft 2016 236 p. color illustrations (hardcover) $35   **646.4**
1. Sewing 2. Dressmaking
ISBN 9781617690754
LC 2015948555

This book, by Gretchen Hirsch, with photography by Karen Pearson, "is packed with all the information and patterns you could ever need to create a wardrobe filled with stunning vintage frocks. The book begins with all the essential techniques for dressmaking and includes instructions and patterns for 23 dresses for a variety of occasions." (Publisher's note)

"Though these garments are less suitable for everyday wear than the ones featured in her previous book, Gertie Sews Vintage Casual, the retro-style dresses will appeal to sewists interested in customizing their own 1950s style frock." LJ

Includes bibliographical references (page 230) and index.

A **modern** guide to sportswear styles of the 1940s and 1950s; Gretchen Hirsch. STC Craft/A Melanie Falick Book 2014 223 p. ills; folded patterns $35   **646.4**
1. Sewing 2. Fashion 3. Women's clothing
ISBN 1617690740; 9781617690747
LC 2014930803

Author "Gretchen 'Gertie' Hirsch celebrates the classic casual styles that icons like Katharine Hepburn, Audrey Hepburn, and Rosie the Riveter made famous--think wide-legged trousers, fitted capri pants, beach rompers, shorts, knit tops, jeans, and day dresses. In Part I, Hirsch introduces key techniques for sportswear construction--from working with knit fabrics to the intricacies of pant-making--and in Part II, she showcases a 30-plus-piece vintage-inspired casual wardrobe." (Publisher's note)

"The audience for Hirsch's second book will likely be wider than that for her first, since casualwear is more accessible than retro-cocktail dresses. Though a few pieces veer toward the costumey, women will find that the garments in this collection fall well within contemporary workplace and casual styles but with a clever, retro flair." LJ

Ito, Michiyo

Simply sewn; clothes for every season. Michiyo Ito. Interweave 2015 128 p. illustrations (some color) $24.99   **646.4**
1. Sewing 2. Women's clothing 3. Dressmaking -- Patterns
ISBN 1620337290; 9781620337295
LC 2014037464

This book on sewing, by Michiyo Ito, presents "easy-to-wear and easy-to-make clothing and accessories for all seasons. . . . The 31 versatile, contemporary clothing designs in this book include dresses, shirts, pants, and jackets that are comfortable and appropriate for all figures. Uncomplicated accessories--including scarfs, wraps and bags--add even more options to the collection." (Publisher's note)

Kim, Sue

Boutique bags; classic style for modern living - 19 projects 76 bags. Sue Kim. C&T Publishing, Inc. 2015 160 p. illustrations, color (soft cover) $24.95   **646.4**
1. Handbags 2. Handicraft
ISBN 1607059851; 9781607059851
LC 2014038488

This handicraft book, by Sue Kim, offers "19 fashionable projects [for making handbags], from a metal-framed clutch to a ruffled carryall, you'll have a match for every outfit. Learn to sew darts, ruffles, and other design elements for a professional finish. Make multiples of your favorites and see for yourself how a simple change in fabric offers a whole new look." (Publisher's note)

"Sewists who enjoy bags designed by Lexie Barnes, Amy Butler, or Sara Lawson will enjoy Kim's stylish designs." LJ

Mallalieu, Nicole

The **better** bag maker; an illustrated handbook of handbag design--techniques, tips, and tricks. Nicole Claire Mallalieu. Stash Books, an imprint of C&T Publishing 2014 192 p. color illustrations (soft cover) $26.95   **646.4**
1. Sewing 2. Handbags
ISBN 1607058057; 9781607058052
LC 2013034373

In this book, by Nicole Claire Mallalieu, "accomplished bag maker, Nicole Mallalieu, reveals her high-end techniques, shortcuts, and secrets for professional design and finishes. The 10 featured projects teach a range of expert skills from adjusting the proportion of the pattern to constructing pockets, straps, flaps, and bases." (Publisher's note)

"While these plans are useful, the technique tutorials are the highlight here—they contain information that can be applied to many bag patterns, not just the ones in this collection. Sewists of every ability level will appreciate having a wealth of bag-making information in a single volume." LJ

Includes bibliographical references (page 191)

Mitnick, Sarai

The **Colette** sewing handbook; inspired styles and classic techniques for the new seamstress. Sarai Mitnick. Krause Publications 2011 176 p. color illustrations $29.99   **646.4**

1. Sewing 2. Dressmaking 3. Dressmaking -- Patterns
ISBN 1440215456; 9781440215452

LC 2011275711

This book, by Sarai Mitnick, presents "simple fundamentals [that] can help you perfect any sewing project. . . . [It] includes five beautiful patterns for modern classic pieces, including a scalloped-hem skirt, flutter-sleeve blouse, sweetheart neck sheath dress, asymmetrical flounce dress, and a lined dress with gathered sleeves. Each project will help you put the fundamentals into practice as you sew." (Publisher's note)

"Though the book is intended for beginners, it is appropriate for sewers of all levels who appreciate a well-tailored garment." LJ

Smith, Alison

Dressmaking; The Complete Step-by-Step Guide to Making your Own Clothes. Alison Smith. DK Publishing 2015 224 p. color illustrations (paperback) $15.95   **646.4**

1. Sewing 2. Dressmaking 3. Clothing and dress 4. Tailoring (Women's)
ISBN 1465429816; 9781465429810

LC 2015300522

This book, by Alison Smith, "covers everything one needs to know to make, alter, and customize clothes. Sewers will discover what supplies to buy and how to use them, the best fabrics to choose based on drape and weave, how to understand patterns and alter them, and the essential general techniques to master—plus patterns and detailed step-by-step instructions are provided for a skirt, dress, shirt, tee, jacket, and pair of pants—including suggested variations!" (Publisher's note)

Veblen, Sarah

The **complete** photo guide to perfect fitting; Sarah Veblen. Creative Pub. International 2012 224 p. color illustrations (pbk.) $24.99   **646.4**

1. Dressmaking 2. Patternmaking 3. Dressmaking -- Pattern design -- Pictorial works 4. Clothing and dress measurements -- Pictorial works 5. Clothing and dress -- Alteration -- Pictorial works
ISBN 1589236084; 9781589236080

LC 2011023810

This book, by Sarah Veblen, "is the ultimate reference for fitting test garments and transferring accurate adjustments to patterns! . . . Rather than making commonly accepted changes to a commercial pattern, the method presented in this guide focuses on the way a test garment fits the body. The fabric is manipulated to improve the fit, and then those specific changes are made to the pattern." (Publisher's note)

White, Betz

Sewing green; projects and ideas for stitching with organic, repurposed, and recycled fabrics: plus tips and resources for earth-friendly stitching. Stewart, Tabori & Chang 2009 143p il pa $24.95 **646.4**

1. Recycling 2. Clothing and dress
ISBN 978-1-58479-758-6; 1-58479-758-4

LC 2008023649

"White's collection of green sewing projects features garments and accessories made from thrift-store clothing, scrap fabric, and recycled goods. The looks are contemporary—you won't find any 1970s-era hippie patchwork dresses—and the designer profiles and tips are inspirational. Nicely cutting edge." Libr J

646.7   Management of personal and family life

Atik, Chiara

Modern Dating; A Field Guide. Chiara Atik; foreword by Brian Schechter & Aaron Schildkrout. Harlequin Books 2013 224 p. illustrations $19.95   **646.7**

1. Online dating 2. Dating (Social customs) 3. Interpersonal relations
ISBN 0373892772; 9780373892778

LC 2013478066

This book, by Chiara Atik, is a "guide for navigating the modern dating world. . . . Rather than listing a set of 'rules,' [it] offers advice on modern challenges, like how to send a relatively unembarrassing sext, how to create a failproof first date idea, and how to make sure you're getting into a relationship for the right reasons." (Publisher's note)

"Atik's smart, youthful appraisal of today's social landscape makes her seem like an expert that's just one step ahead of you. Informed by research and delivered with style, this is big-sister advice at its best." Pub Wkly

Becker-Phelps, Leslie

Love; The Psychology of Attraction. by DK (Author) DK Pub 2016 224 p. color illustrations, charts $19.95   **646.7**

1. Courtship 2. Dating (Social customs) 3. Interpersonal relations 4. Love -- Psychological aspects
ISBN 1465429891; 9781465429896

This book "explores the nature of intimate relationships. . . . The book is divided into five chapters, beginning with 'You' and ending with 'Together,' with all the complexities of seeking and dating in between. Specific topics include determining whether a second date is appropriate and deciding whether and when to become physically intimate with a new partner. Interactive exercises guide couples onto the road to harmony." (Publishers Weekly)

"This is one of the most straightforward guides to dating available." LJ

Berg, Rona

Beauty: the new basics; illustrations by Anja Kroencke; photography by Deborah Jaffe. Workman 2001 404p il pa $19.95   **646.7**

1. Personal appearance
ISBN 0-7611-0186-1

LC 00-43631

The author discusses "hair and skin care, bath and body, aging, skin cancer, makeup, home spa treatments, aromatherapy, and cosmetic surgery. She includes a directory of day and destination spas and recommended salons. Amusing time lines give thumbnail histories of style and popular products. Essential for small collections in particular." Libr J

Blake, Jenny

Life after college; the complete guide to getting what you want. Jenny Blake. Running Press 2011 293 p. (pbk.) $17   **646.7**
1. Personal finance 2. College graduates 3. Life skills -- Handbooks, manuals, etc. 4. Professional developmen -- Handbooks, manuals, etc. 5. College graduates -- Employment 6. Young men -- Life skills guides 7. Young women -- Life skills guides 8. Young adults -- Life skills guides 9. College graduates -- Life skills guides
ISBN 0762441275; 9780762441273
LC 2010940614
The book is "full of . . . advice to encourage young adults who are on the precipice of a new life, a life that can be tenuous and daunting. It covers money, relationships (both romantic and familial), friends, health, fun and relaxation, life planning, and personal and professional growth." (Library Journal)

Brandon, Ruth

Ugly beauty; Helena Rubinstein, L'Oreal, and the blemished history of looking good. Harper 2011 290p il $26.99; ebook $21.99   **646.7**
1. Chemists 2. Personal appearance 3. L'Oreal SA 4. Cosmeticians 5. Art collectors 6. Cosmetics industry executives
ISBN 978-0-06-174040-4; 0-06-174040-3; 978-0-06-204156-2 ebook; 0-06-204156-8 ebook
LC 2010-24435
"A clearheaded discussion of current beauty standards, vanity, and the gender politics of the modern cosmetic industry rounds out this lively history of the founding of the beauty business as we know it." Publ Wkly
Includes bibliographical references

Cullinane, Jan

The new retirement; the ultimate guide to the rest of your life. [by] Jan Cullinane and Cathy Fitzgerald. Rev. and updated ed.; Rodale 2007 484p pa $19.95   **646.7**
1. Retirement
ISBN 978-1-59486-479-7; 1-59486-479-9
LC 2007-15947
First published 2004
This guide provides "information about particular locales, financial planning and tax considerations, lifelong learning opportunities, leisure and volunteer activities, and working after retirement." Publisher's note
Includes bibliographical references

DuPriest, Laura

Natural beauty; pamper yourself with salon secrets at home. Prima Pub. 2002 230p il pa $10.95   **646.7**
1. Cosmetics 2. Personal appearance 3. Skin -- Care
ISBN 0-7615-2099-6
LC 2002-72554
The author's "obvious knowledge about everything from waxing to massaging to not being taken in at the cosmetics counter, as well as her inventive concoctions . . . make this a solid beauty resource." Publ Wkly

Essence total makeover; body, beauty, spirit. [by the editors of Essence]; Patricia Mignon Hinds, editor; introduction by Susan L. Taylor. Crown 2000 216p il hardcover o.p. pa $18   **646.7**
1. Personal appearance 2. African American women -- Health and hygiene
ISBN 0-609-80527-4 pa
LC 99-14442
"Hinds provides practical tips on caring for skin, hair, body, and spirit. Glossy and attractive, this comprehensive volume is aimed at African American women." Libr J
Includes bibliographical references

Hinden, Stan

How to retire happy; the 12 most important decisions you must make before you retire. [foreword by John C. Bogle] 3rd ed., fully rev. and updated; McGraw-Hill 2010 233p pa $18.95; ebook $18.95   **646.7**
1. Retirement
ISBN 978-0-07-170247-8 pa; 978-0-07-171298-9 ebook
First published 2001
This retirement planning guide covers such topics as Social Security, pension plans, investments after retirement, health insurance, preparing for serious illness, and where to live after retirement.
Includes bibliographical references

Kashuk, Sonia

Real beauty; concept by Sonia Kashuk; written with Amie Valentine. Potter 2003 137p il + 1 DVD ROM $27.50   **646.7**
1. Personal appearance 2. Women -- Health and hygiene
ISBN 1-4000-4774-2
LC 2003-535298
The author "showcases women of all ages and ethnic types, covering nutrition and fitness in addition to the usual hair and skin care. The accompanying DVD shows the suggested makeup techniques being performed." Libr J

Kirsch, Melissa

The girl's guide to absolutely everything. Workman Pub. 2006 477p il $26.95; pa $15.95 **646.7**
1. Young women 2. Conduct of life
ISBN 978-0-7611-4213-3; 0-7611-4213-4; 978-0-7611-3579-1 pa; 0-7611-3579-0 pa
LC 2006-41840

The author provides "advice for women in their twenties and thirties on everything from body image and friendship to first jobs and money. . . . Her well-designed book is pleasurable to read and encourages healthy, responsible behavior." Libr J

Includes bibliographical references

Lofas, Jeannette

Stepparenting; Rev. and updated.; Citadel Press 2004 241p pa $12.95   **646.7**
1. Parenting 2. Stepparents 3. Stepchildren
ISBN 0-8065-2652-1; 978-0-8065-2652-2
LC 2004-556219
First published 1985 by Zebra Books
"Acknowledging the difficulty of a stepparent's role, this standout title guides readers through carefully forming a stepfamily, with straightforward coverage of the usual issues (e.g., etiquette, praising positive behavior)." Libr J

Massey, Lorraine

Curly girl; more than just hair--it's an attitude: a celebration of curls: how to cut them, care for them, love them & set them free. Workman 2001 148p il pa $9.95   **646.7**
1. Hair
ISBN 0-7611-2300-8
LC 2001-26842
This book features "tips on shampoo . . . conditioners . . . drying, combing . . . styling, getting the right cut, and how to Heal Thy Hair after years of strong detergents and damaging blow-dryers. There are before-and-after photographs . . . self-help tests, confessions from curly girls {and} advice." Publisher's note

Romanowski, Perry

Can you get hooked on lip balm? top cosmetic scientists answer your questions about the lotions, potions, and other beauty products you use every day. [by] Perry Romanowski and the creators of TheBeautyBrains.Com. Harlequin 2011 194p pa $16.95   **646.7**
1. Cosmetics
ISBN 978-0-373-89234-1
LC 2010-44199
"Women who subscribe to such magazines as InStyle and Self will devour this question-and-answer guide to cosmetics, shampoos, and nail polishes." Booklist
Includes bibliographical references

Soukup, Ruth

Unstuffed; Ruth Soukup. Zondervan 2016 219 p. (softcover) $16.99   **646.7**
1. Simplicity 2. Conduct of life 3. Simplicity -- Religious aspects -- Christianity
ISBN 0310337690; 9780310337690
LC 2015031891
In this book, author Ruth Soukup, "through personal stories, Biblical truth, and practical action plans, . . . will inspire and empower each of us to finally declutter not just our home, but our mind and soul as well. 'Unstuffed' is real, honest, and gets right down to the question we are all facing-

-how can we take back our lives from the stuff that is weighing us down?" (Publisher's note)

"Commonsense suggestions, personal anecdotes, and Soukup's Christian perspective give the book a friendly, nonthreatening feel. Hopefully delving into the why as well as the how may allow some of us to break the 'stuff' cycle." Booklist

Thomas, Mathilde

The **French** beauty solution; time-tested secrets to look and feel beautiful inside and out. by Mathilde Thomas. Gotham Books 2015 263 p. illustrations (hardback) $26.95   **646.7**
1. Skin -- Care 2. Health self-care 3. Personal grooming 4. Personal appearance 5. Women -- Health and hygiene 6. Beauty, Personal 7. Self-care, Health 8. Skin -- Care and hygiene
ISBN 1592409512; 9781592409518
LC 2015003934
In this book, author Mathilde Thomas "shares the simple, natural, time-tested beauty secrets she learned growing up in France that any woman can use to look younger, healthier, and more radiant without harsh products or drastic procedures. . . . [It] covers everything from how to use natural ingredients such as oil and honey to wash your face; what foods to eat for healthier hair, skin, and nails; and the amazing properties of grapes and grapeseed oil." (Publisher's note)

647   Management of public households (Institutional housekeeping)

Ripert, Eric

On the line; [by] Eric Ripert, Christine Muhlke. Artisan 2008 239p il $35   **647**
1. Restaurants 2. Le Bernardin (New York, N.Y.: Restaurant)
ISBN 978-1-57965-369-9; 1-57965-369-3
LC 2008-05930
"A behind-the-scenes look at the famed New York restaurant Le Bernardin. . . . Chef Ripert and New York Times writer Muhlke recount the restaurant's history, from its founding in 1986 by Gilbert and Maguy Le Coze, through Ripert's joining the team in 1991, to the present day. This thorough guide to how the restaurant operates teaches about various kitchen stations, tools of the trade, key personnel and their duties, how new dishes are born and what it's like to spend a night 'on the line.' . . . [Some recipes are included.] A huge treat for industry insiders, fans of Le Bernardin and foodies everywhere." Publ Wkly

647.9   Specific kinds of public households and institutions

Brown, Pete, 1968-

Shakespeare's Pub; A Barstool History of London As Seen Through the Windows of Its Oldest Pub -

the George Inn. Pete Brown. St. Martin's Press 2013 368 p. (hardcover) $26.99   **647.9**
1. Bars 2. George Inn (Enfield, London, England) -- History 3. Great Britain -- History
ISBN 1250033888; 9781250033888

LC 2013010139

This book, by Pete Brown, offers a history of London through focusing on the "George Inn near London Bridge; a cosy, wood-paneled, galleried coaching house a few minutes' walk from the Thames. . . . Chaucer and his fellow pilgrims almost certainly drank in the George on their way out of London to Canterbury. It's fair to say that Shakespeare popped in from the nearby Globe for a pint, and we know that Dickens certainly did." (Publisher's note)

Schultz, Howard

Onward; how Starbucks fought for its life without losing its soul. [by] Howard Schultz with Joanne Gordon. Rodale 2011 350p il $25.99   **647.9**
1. Leadership 2. Coffee industry 3. Starbucks Coffee International (Firm)
ISBN 978-1-60529-288-5

LC 2011003239

"Throughout this book, readers get a very intimate look at the conviction that drives leaders, the resiliency of employees, the passion that customers feel about a brand, and the global community that one brand can inspire. Whether or not you are a coffee lover or have a fondness for the Starbucks experience, Onward details tremendous leadership lessons from which everyone can learn." T + D

647.95   Eating and drinking places

Cate, Martin

Smuggler's Cove; Exotic Cocktails, Rum, and the Cult of Tiki. by Martin Cate and Rebecca Cate. Random House Inc 2016 352 p. $30   **647.95**
1. Cocktails
ISBN 1607747324; 9781607747321

LC 2016012487

In this book, authors Martin Cate and Rebecca Cate "take you on a colorful journey into the lore and legend of tiki: its birth as an escapist fantasy for Depression-era Americans; how exotic cocktails were invented, stolen, and re-invented; Hollywood starlets and scandals; and tiki's modern-day revival." (Publisher's note)

"Even the most serious single-malt sipper will be charmed by this richly illustrated ode to escapism." LJ

Includes bibliographical references (pages 340-341) and index.

Wizenberg, Molly

Delancey; a man, a woman, a restaurant, a marriage. Molly Wizenberg. Simon & Schuster 2014 256 p. illustrations (hardback) $25.00; (trade paperback) $15.99   **647.95**
1. Marriage 2. Restaurants 3. Married people 4. Delancey (Pizzaria : Seattle, Wash.) 5. Food writers -- United States -- Biography 6. Pizzerias -- Washington (State) -- Seattle 7. Restaurateurs -- United States --

Biography
ISBN 9781451655094; 9781451655117; 9781451655124

LC 2013034429

In this memoir, author Molly Wizenberg "recounts how opening a restaurant sparked the first crisis of her young marriage. . . . [W]hen Brandon decided to open a pizza restaurant, Molly was supportive. . . . The restaurant, Delancey . . . became a success, and Molly tried to convince herself that she was happy in their new life until--in the heat and pressure of the restaurant kitchen--she realized that she hadn't been honest with herself or Brandon." (Publisher's note)

"Wizenberg candidly describes her fears and doubts, as well as her struggles with trying to be a supportive wife." LJ

648   Housekeeping

Friedman, Virginia M.

Field guide to stains; how to identify and remove virtually every stain known to man. by Virginia M. Friedman, Melissa Wagner, and Nancy Armstrong. Quirk Bks. 2003 280p il pa $14.95   **648**
1. Cleaning
ISBN 1-931686-07-6

LC 2002-104065

This guide to identifying and removing over 100 stains features sections on sauces, fruits and vegetables, office products, and yard and garage stains. It also includes information on when and where certain stains are most likely to occur

Kerr, Jolie

My boyfriend barfed in my handbag ... and other things you can't ask Martha; Jolie Kerr. Penguin Group 2014 256 p. $15   **648**
1. House cleaning
ISBN 0142196932; 9780142196939

LC 2013022730

In this book, author Jolie Kerr "offers a . . . guide to cleaning up life's little emergencies. Life is filled with spills, odors, and those oh-so embarrassing stains you just can't tell your parents about. And let's be honest: no one is going to ask Martha Stewart what to do when your boyfriend barfs in your handbag. . . . Jolie takes on questions ranging from the basic-- how do I use a mop? -- to the esoteric-- what should I do when bottles of homebrewed ginger beer explode in my kitchen?" (Publisher's note)

Kondo, Marie

The **life**-changing magic of tidying up; the Japanese art of decluttering and organizing. Marie Kondo; translated from Japanese by Cathy Hirano. Ten Speed Press 2014 213 p. (hardcover) $16.99   **648**
1. Home economics 2. House cleaning 3. Housekeeping
ISBN 1607747308; 9781607747307

LC 2014017930

This book is a "guide to decluttering your home from Japanese cleaning consultant Marie Kondo. . . . Most methods advocate a room-by-room or little-by-little approach, which doom you to pick away at your piles of stuff forever.

The KonMari Method, with its revolutionary category-by-category system, leads to lasting results." (Publisher's note)

Leeds, Regina

Rightsize . . . right now! the eight-week plan to organize, declutter, and make any move stress-free. Regina Leeds. Da Capo Lifelong, a member of the Perseus Books Group 2015 xii, 244 p.p (paperback) $15.99 **648**

    1. Moving 2. Orderliness 3. Moving, Household
    ISBN 0738218014; 9780738218014

                              LC 2014039459

In this book on household moving, professional organizer Regina Leeds "outlines her 8-week plan to clear clutter, organize, pack, and relocate without stress, with: Helpful guidance on making a moving plan, from hiring movers down to forwarding mail; Strategies to tackle each room in the house in a smart, efficient way; Rightsizing projects to weed out unneeded possessions; [and] Expert advice on organizing your belongings for the move and the new home." (Publisher's note)

    "Although focusing on traditional moves, there are also suggestions for college students and downsizing retirees. Leeds' logical, practical advice will be welcomed by anyone eyeing a new residence." Booklist

    Right size . . . right now!

Mendelson, Cheryl

Laundry; the home comforts book of caring for clothes and linens. Cheryl Mendelson; illustrated by Harry Bates. Scribner 2005 xvi, 400 p.p $24.99 **648**

    1. Laundry 2. Home economics
    ISBN 0743271459; 0743271467; 9780743271455;
    9780743271462

                              LC 2005051602

    This book, edited by Cheryl Mendelson and illustrated by Harry Bates, is a "comprehensive, entertaining, and inspiring book on the art of laundering. Culled from the bestselling 'Home Comforts,' with revised and updated information and a new introduction, . . . [it] is an indispensable guide to caring for all the cloth in one's home." (Publisher's note)

    Includes bibliographical references (p. [371]-380) and index

Platt, Stacey

What's a disorganized person to do? Artisan 2010 277p il pa $16.95 **648**

    1. House cleaning 2. Storage in the home
    ISBN 978-1-57965-372-9

                              LC 2009-13493

    The author "offers quick tips (e.g., storing sterling silver with chalk to prevent tarnish), instructions (e.g., folding silk scarves correctly), and one-hour projects (e.g., taking back the junk drawer) that anyone can immediately put into practice. Guidelines for organizing office space are designed for those who like to file and those who prefer to pile, and detailed steps for vacation packing and cross-country moving are also included. The employment of one idea alone is worth the price of the book." Libr J

    Includes bibliographical references

648.5   Housecleaning

Ewer, Cynthia Townley

Cut the Clutter; by Cynthia Ewer. DK Publishing 2016 240 p. color illustrations $16.95   **648.5**

    1. House cleaning
    ISBN 1465453059; 9781465453051

                              LC 2016387148

This book, by Cynthia Ewer, is "a guide to conquering clutter and cleaning your home. . . . Step-by-step instructions, household routines, and quick tips make these daunting tasks easier to tackle, and will leave you with more time and energy for the good things in life." (Publisher's note)

    The book delves into the nitty-gritty of list-making, menu planning, and the cycles of cleaning. It's best used as a reference guide for specific chores... rather than as a method to follow strictly. This practical guide will be a solid resource for young adults and new parents." Pub Wkly

649   Child rearing; home care of people with disabilities and illnesses

Agnew, Connie L.

Twins! pregnancy, birth, and the first year of life. [by] Connie L. Agnew, Alan H. Klein, and Jill Alison Ganon; illustrations by Victor Robert. 2nd ed.; Collins 2005 360p il pa $18.95   **649**

    1. Twins
    ISBN 0-06-074219-4; 978-0-06-074219-5

                              LC 2005-45585

First published 1997

An overview of the physical, medical, emotional, and psychological issues involved in having twins. Fetal and embryonic development, nutrition, and exercise are among the topics covered. Includes interviews with parents of twins.

    Includes bibliographical references

American Academy of Pediatrics

Caring for your school-age child; ages 5 to 12. editor-in-chief, Edward L. Schor. rev trade pa. ed; Bantam Bks. 1999 xxviii, 624p il pa $19.95   **649**

    1. Child care 2. Child rearing
    ISBN 0-553-37992-5

                              LC 99-12639

First published 1995

This book "offers comprehensive information about the growth, development, and behavior of children from five to 12 years of age. . . . Bicycle safety, latchkey children, dealing with violence and crime, guns in the home, prejudice, gender identity and sexual orientation, and physical and sexual abuse appear along with the usual information about immunization, diet, school problems, illness, and first aid. The text also offers sound, practical advice about how parents in traditional and nontraditional families can handle a wide variety of situations, stating clearly when they should seek professional help. . . . This book belongs in all parenting and consumer health collections." Libr J {review of 1995 edition}

Ames, Louise Bates

Your eight-year-old; lively and outgoing. by Louise Bates Ames and Carol Chase Haber; illustrated with photographs by Betty David. Delacorte Press 1989 147p il hardcover o.p. pa $12.95 **649**
1. Child rearing
ISBN 0-440-50681-6 pa

LC 88-31150

A discussion of the basic personality and typical physical and mental development of the eight-year-old
Includes bibliographical references

Your five-year-old; sunny and serene. by Louise Bates Ames and Frances L. Ilg, Gesell Institute of Child Development; illustrated with photographs by Betty David. Delacorte Press 1979 123p il hardcover o.p. pa $12.95 **649**
1. Child rearing
ISBN 0-440-50673-5 pa

LC 78-11622

Beginning with a description of the general characteristics of the five-year-old, the authors go on to discuss how the child relates to parents and others
Includes bibliographical references

Your four-year-old; wild and wonderful. by Louise Bates Ames and Frances L. Ilg, Gesell Institute of Child Development. Delacorte Press 1976 152p il hardcover o.p. pa $12.95 **649**
1. Child rearing
ISBN 0-440-50675-1 pa

A discussion of the basic personality and typical physical and mental development of the four-year-old
Includes bibliographical references

Your one-year-old; the fun-loving, fussy 12-to-24-month-old. by Louise Bates Ames, Frances L. Ilg, and Carol Chase Haber (Gesell Institute of Child Development); illustrated with photographs by Betty David. Delacorte Press 1982 178p il hardcover o.p. pa $12.95 **649**
1. Child rearing
ISBN 0-440-50672-7 pa

LC 81-17275

A discussion of the basic personality and typical physical and mental development of the one-year-old
Includes bibliographical references

Your seven-year-old; life in a minor key. by Louise Bates Ames and Carol Chase Haber; illustrated with photographs by Betty David. Delacorte Press 1985 165p il hardcover o.p. pa $12.95 **649**
1. Child rearing
ISBN 0-440-50650-6 pa

LC 84-15627

A discussion of the basic personality and typical physical and mental development of the seven-year-old
Includes bibliographical references

Your six-year-old; defiant but loving. by Louise Bates Ames and Frances L. Ilg, Gesell Institute of Child Development. Delacorte Press 1976 132p il hardcover o.p. pa $12.95 **649**
1. Child rearing
ISBN 0-440-50674-3 pa

A discussion of the basic personality and typical physical and mental development of the six-year-old
Includes bibliographical references

Your two-year-old; terrible or tender. by Louise Bates Ames, and Frances L. Ilg, Gesell Institute of Child Development. Delacorte Press 1976 149p il hardcover o.p. pa $12.94 **649**
1. Child rearing
ISBN 0-440-50638-7 pa

A discussion of the basic personality and typical physical and mental development of the two-year-old
Includes bibliographical references

Bowers, Mark

8 keys to raising the quirky child; how to help a kid who doesn't (quite) fit in. Mark Bowers; foreword by Babette Rothschild. W W Norton & Co Inc. 2015 320 p. (pbk.) $19.95 **649**
1. Parenting 2. Child rearing 3. Autistic children 4. Exceptional children 5. Parents of autistic children 6. Parents of exceptional children
ISBN 0393709205; 9780393709209

LC 2015004622

This book, by Mark Bowers, "defines quirky markers and offers strategies for parents to understand their children's brains and behaviors; to know what is developmentally appropriate, and what isn't; to understand how to reach their kids; and to help facilitate their social functioning in the world." (Publisher's note)
"Frustrated parents who believe their child is well-described by the 'quirky' profile will find Bowen's attitude supportive, his psychological explanations of their child's motivations satisfying, and his specific strategies for helping these kids accept breadth of experience and build social competency usable and encouraging." Pub Wkly.
Includes bibliographical references and index
Eight keys to raising the quirky child

Brazelton, T. Berry

Touchpoints birth to 3; your child's emotional and behavioral development. revised with Joshua Sparrow. 2nd ed.; Da Capo Lifelong Books 2006 xxvi, 500p il pa $17.95 **649**
1. Child rearing 2. Child psychology 3. Child development
ISBN 978-0-7382-1049-0; 0-7382-1049-8

LC 2008-274711

First published 1992 by Addison-Wesley with title: Touchpoints

The author "defines 'touchpoints' as the periods of development and regression which every child experiences while growing up. He describes the first six years of life and the touchpoints of that period. . . . Worried new parents will be put at ease after reading this book. Brazelton is knowledgeable, warm, and kind, and his book is a pleasure to read." Libr J

Includes bibliographical references

Brooks, Robert B.

Raising resilient children; fostering strength, hope, and optimism in your child. {by} Robert Brooks, Sam Goldstein. Contemporary Bks. 2001 317p hardcover o.p. pa $14.95 **649**
1. Child rearing 2. Parent-child relationship
ISBN 0-8092-9765-5 pa

LC 00-60316
The authors "synthesize research on children's coping skills; define and describe resilience (the capacity to cope and feel competent); and offer specific strategies for nurturing resilience in children." Booklist

Includes bibliographical references

Brott, Armin A.

The **expectant** father; facts, tips, and advice for dads-to-be. [by] Armin A. Brott and Jennifer Ash. 3rd ed.; Abbeville Press 2010 373p il $18.95; pa $12.95 **649**
1. Fathers 2. Pregnancy
ISBN 978-0-7892-1079-1; 978-0-7892-1077-7 pa

LC 2010-15973
First published 1995
This book "gives dads-to-be a month-by-month breakdown of what to expect as they prepare to welcome a baby into their family. For each month, Brott and Ash give a rundown of what mothers, babies, and fathers are experiencing physically and emotionally, from moodiness and food cravings (which fathers aren't exempt from) to balancing fatherhood with work. . . . Brott and Ash's measured, experienced tone offers assurance and guidance for those new to the stresses and worries of impending fatherhood, making this a must-have for anyone expecting." Publ Wkly

Includes bibliographical references

Brown, Christia Spears

Parenting beyond pink and blue; how to raise your kids free of gender stereotypes. Christia Spears Brown, PhD. Ten Speed Press 2014 240 p. illustrations (pbk) $14.99 **649**
1. Parenting 2. Gender role 3. Sex differences (Psychology) 4. Stereotype (Social psychology)
ISBN 160774502X; 9781607745020

LC 2014001259
This book, by developmental psychologist Christia Spears Brown, is "a guide that helps parents focus on their children's unique strengths and inclinations rather than on gendered stereotypes to more effectively bring out the best in their individual children, for parents of infants to middle schoolers. . . . [It] addresses all the issues that contemporary parents should consider--from gender-segregated birthday parties and schools to sports, sexualization, and emotional intelligence." (Publisher's note)

Brown "argues that children are 'free to flourish' when gender is deemphasized and covers both the neuroscience and cultural influences of sex in language that is accessible and at times even humorous." LJ

Includes bibliographical references and index

Bullard, Sara

Teaching tolerance; raising open-minded empathetic children. Doubleday 1996 235p hardcover o.p. pa $19 **649**
1. Children 2. Parenting 3. Prejudices 4. Toleration
ISBN 0-385-47265-X pa

LC 95-36045
Bullard "states the principles of tolerance adults need to impart to children and provides guidelines for modeling the behavior we want to encourage." Libr J

Cohen, Lawrence J.

Playful parenting; a bold new way to use play in raising your children. Ballantine Bks. 2001 307p $23.95; pa $14 **649**
1. Play 2. Games 3. Parenting
ISBN 0-345-43897-3; 0-345-44286-5 pa

LC 00-66809
"According to Cohen, children of all ages have an ongoing need for connectedness, security and attachment; playful interaction with parents is an important way to develop such bonds. Through play, parents can help their kids develop greater confidence, express bottled up or difficult feelings, recover from daily emotional upheavals, negotiate agreements, express love and—not least—have fun." Publ Wkly

Dawson, Peg

Smart but scattered; the revolutionary 'executive skills' approach to helping kids reach their potential. [by] Peg Dawson [and] iRichard Guare. Guilford Press 2009 vi, 314 p.p illustrations $53 **649**
1. Parenting 2. Life skills 3. Parent and child 4. Child development 5. Executive ability in children 6. Children -- Life skills guides
ISBN 1593859872; 9781593854454; 9781593859879

LC 2008026078
This parenting book, by Peg Dawson and Richard Guare, "shows that many kids who have the brain and heart to succeed lack or lag behind in crucial 'executive skills'--the fundamental habits of mind required for getting organized, staying focused, and controlling impulses and emotions. Learn easy-to-follow steps to identify your child's strengths and weaknesses, use activities and techniques proven to boost specific skills, and problem-solve daily routines." (Publisher's note)

"As the first books on the subject to speak directly, comprehensively, and universally to parents, both titles are recommended for parenting collections in public and school libraries; Dawson and Guare's work should be considered essential." LJ

Includes bibliographical references (p. 303-309) and index

Deak, JoAnn

Girls will be girls; a parent's guide to cultivating confident, competent and connected daughters.

by JoAnn Deak with Teresa Barker. Hyperion 2002
287p $23.95; pa $14.95   **649**
   1. Girls 2. Teenagers 3. Child rearing
   ISBN 0-7868-6768-X; 0-7868-8657-9 pa
                       LC 2001-39247
"Deak discusses the differences between fathers and
daughters and mothers and daughters and also some of the
more common problems faced by teens, such as body image
and peer pressure." Publ Wkly

Edgerton, Clyde

Papadaddy's book for new fathers; advice to
dads of all ages. Clyde Edgerton; drawings by Daniel
Wallace. Little, Brown and Co. 2013 192 p. $25 **649**
   1. Fatherhood 2. Child rearing 3. Father-child
relationship
   ISBN 0316056928; 9780316056922
                       LC 2012033851
Author Clyde Edgerton "is a 68-year-old father with
four children between the ages of 6 and 30. Here, he offers
the fruits of the many ruminations and experiences that informed them, coming at his subject with a wisdom that is
still being surprised, daily. Enjoy the good stuff, he writes,
and make sure your children are the best of the good stuff."
(Kirkus Reviews)

Egan, Amy

Is it a big problem or a little problem? when to
worry, when not to worry, and what to do. [by] Amy
Egan . . . [et al.] St. Martin's Press 2007 335p il pa
$15.95   **649**
   1. Child psychology 2. Child development
   ISBN 978-0-312-35412-1
                       LC 2007-17218
The authors "divide the book into three sections, 'The
Basics,' 'Understanding Development,' and 'Where Children Struggle.' Within these, they illustrate specific concerns
(e.g., 'She can hear, why doesn't she understand?'), explore
the range of normal, and examine signals that indicate a need
for professional intervention. . . . Never using an alarmist
tone, the authors strike a perfect balance between advocating
for early intervention and appreciating the ups and downs of
typical childhood behavior." Libr J
   Includes bibliographical references

Elman, Natalie Madorsky

The **unwritten** rules of friendship; simple strategies to help your child make friends. by Natalie Madorsky Elman and Eileen Kennedy-Moore. Little,
Brown 2003 340p il pa $14.95   **649**
   1. Friendship 2. Child rearing 3. Socialization
   ISBN 0-316-91730-3
                       LC 2002-40611
The authors "formulate nine prototypes of children with
friendship problems. These range from passive (e.g., 'sensitive soul') to more aggressive (e.g., 'intimidating' children, 'short-fused' children, and born leaders) personalities.
Chapters provide checklists for evaluation, social rules such
children need to know, learning activities, and case studies.
. . . Colorfully written and practical, Unwritten Rules offers
many tips for anxious parents." Libr J
   Includes bibliographical references

Ezzo, Gary

On becoming baby wise; giving your infant the
gift of nighttime sleep. by Gary Ezzo and Robert
Buckman. Hawksflight & Assoc Inc 2012 279 p.
illustrations $13.95   **649**
   1. Infants -- Care 2. Parent-child relationship
   ISBN 1932740139; 9781932740134
This book, by Gary Ezzo and Robert Buckman, is a
"newborn parenting manual for naturally synchronizing
your baby's feeding time, waketime and nighttime sleep
cycles, so the whole family can sleep through the night. The
authors demonstrate how order and stability are mutual allies of every newborn's metabolism and how parents can
take advantage of these biological propensities. In particular,
they note how an infant's body responds to the influences of
parental routine or the lack thereof." (Publisher's note)

Fonseca, Christine

Raising the shy child; a parent's guide to social
anxiety : advice for helping kids make friends, speak
up, and stop worrying. Christine Fonseca. Prufrock
Press, Inc. 2015 xvi, 223 p.p illustrations (pbk.)
$16.95   **649**
   1. Shyness 2. Parenting 3. Child rearing 4. Social
phobia 5. Bashfulness in children 6. Social phobia in
children
   ISBN 1618213989; 9781618213983
                       LC 2014048544
This book, by Christine Fonseca, "takes a fresh look at
social anxiety disorder, coupling the latest in research trends
with evidence-based strategies and real-world stories to untangle the complexities of this disorder. . . . [It] uses a combination of real-world examples and stories from adults and
children with social anxiety disorder to show parents and
educators how to help children find a path through their fear
and into social competence." (Publisher's note)
   "Parents who have seen educators minimize their child's
struggles as normal shyness, felt herded into one-size-fits-all
solutions, or struggled to comprehend apparently nonsensi-
cal behavior from bright children will find this comprehensive resource grounding and practical." Pub Wkly
   Includes bibliographical references (pages 213 -222)

Foster, Joanne

Beyond intelligence; secrets of raising happily
productive kids. Dona Matthews, Joanne Foster.
House of Anansi Press Inc. 2014 280 p. (pbk. : alk.
paper) $15.95   **649**
   1. Intellect 2. Parenting
   ISBN 1770894772; 9781770894778; 9781770894785
                       LC 2014935195
In this book, authors Dona Matthews and Joanne Foster "show that intelligence is not fixed rather, it can be increased. Through myriad anecdotes from personal experience and case studies, they reveal how parents can identify
a child's abilities, foster creativity, and bolster effort and
persistence. They also address how to prevent or alleviate
emotional and social problems, and how to embrace failures
as learning opportunities." (Publisher's note)
   "Parents who have read other child rearing books may
recognize but still appreciate the information and advice

provided here: listen to, understand, and nurture children in order to foster their growth." LJ

Furedi, Frank

Paranoid parenting; why ignoring the experts may be best for your child. Chicago Review Press 2002 233p pa $14.95   **649**
1. Parenting 2. Child rearing 3. Parent-child relationship
ISBN 1-55652-464-1

LC 2002-4121

"This book is provocative, well argued, and clearly written, though the rhetoric can be stinging." Libr J
Includes bibliographical references and index

Gold, Tammy

Secrets of the nanny whisperer; a practical guide for finding and achieving the gold standard of care for your child. by Tammy Gold. Perigee 2015 288 p. (paperback) $16   **649**
1. Child care services 2. Nannies -- Recruiting 3. Child care services -- United States 4. Nannies -- Employment -- United States 5. Nannies -- Selection and appointment -- United States
ISBN 0399169881; 9780399169885

LC 2014040010

This book by Tammy Gold focuses on the hiring and managing of child care workers. "In Part 1, the author explains the value of the nanny-family match and outlines how to best pursue the nanny relationship for long-term success. Part 2 equips readers with a Family Needs Assessment and the author's eponymous 'Gold Standard' hiring process, including screenings, in-home trials, and background checks. Part 3 focuses on managing the nanny relationship and resolving conflicts." (Library Journal)

"While many families view their nanny as a part of the family, Gold reminds readers that this is ultimately an employment relationship. She dispenses exceptional advice that will help families avoid common pitfalls and is especially strong when illustrating scenarios from the nanny's point of view. From her needs assessment to interview questions to problem-solving language, Gold's examples and crisp narrative gives readers one-stop shopping for nanny know-how. A required purchase. Well done." LJ

Huggins, Kathleen

The **nursing** mother's companion; Kathleen Huggins; foreword by Ruth A. Lawrence. Harvard Common Press 2010 x, 358 p.p illustrations (pbk. : alk. paper) $16.95   **649**
1. Breast feeding 2. Breastfeeding -- Popular works
ISBN 1558327207; 9781558327191; 9781558327207
LC 2010005981

This book "has been among the best-selling books on breastfeeding for 25 years, and is respected and recommended by professionals and well loved by new parents for its encouraging and accessible style. Kathleen Huggins equips breastfeeding mothers with all the information they need to overcome potential difficulties and nurse their babies successfully from the first week through the toddler years, or somewhere in between." (Publisher's note)

Includes bibliographical references (p. 341-347) and indexes

Hurley, Katie

The **happy** kid handbook; how to raise joyful children in a stressful world. Katie Hurley. Tarcher 2015 320 p. (paperback) $16.95   **649**
1. Happiness 2. Parenting 3. Child rearing 4. Happiness in children
ISBN 9780399171819

LC 2015022156

This book, by Katie Hurley, "shows parents how happiness is the key to raising confident, capable children. . . . Happiness is about parenting the individual, because not every child is the same. . . . By exploring the differences among introverts, extroverts, and everything in between, this definitive guide to parenting offers parents the specific strategies they need to meet their child exactly where he or she needs to be met from a social-emotional perspective." (Publisher's note)

"Her book is highly recommended for people who seek a parenting orientation rather than a method but still want a substantial toolbox of specific activities to use in understanding and connecting with their children." Pub Wkly
Includes bibliographical references and index

Ilg, Frances Lillian

Your three-year-old; friend or enemy. by Louise Bates Ames, and Frances L. Ilg, Gesell Institute of Child Development. Delacorte Press 1976 168p il hardcover o.p. pa $12.95   **649**
1. Child rearing
ISBN 0-440-50649-2 pa

A discussion of the basic personality and typical physical and mental development of the three-year-old
Includes bibliographical references

Karp, Harvey

The **happiest** baby guide to great sleep; simple solutions for kids from birth to 5 years. by Harvey Karp. William Morrow 2012 367 p. illustrations; charts $15.99   **649**
1. Sleep 2. Parenting
ISBN 0062113313; 0062113321; 9780062113313; 9780062113320

In this book on regulating young children's sleep patterns, "[Harvey] Karp lays a number of myths to rest in his latest book, including the idea that babies, who have shorter sleep cycles than adults, can't learn better sleep habits before three months of age. In fact, he gets right to work giving parents tips and tools to help their newborns develop good sleeping patterns, and then moves on to older babies and toddlers." (Publishers Weekly)

"While the advice is sound, the book is embarrassingly long while the author belabors the obvious, and the pace is insufferable. Despite the critique, patrons may likely request." LJ

The **happiest** baby on the block; the new way to calm crying and help your baby sleep longer. Bantam Bks. 2002 267p il $21.95; pa $13.95   **649**
1. Child rearing 2. Parent-child relationship 3. Infants

-- Care

ISBN 0-553-80255-0; 0-553-38146-6 pa

LC 2001-56734

To calm a crying baby the author "recommends a series of five steps designed to imitate the uterus. These steps include swaddling, side/stomach position, shhh sounds, swinging and sucking. The book includes detailed advice on the proper way to swaddle a child, the difference between a gentle rocking versus shaking and more." Publ Wkly

Kazdin, Alan E.

The **Everyday** Parenting Toolkit; The Kazdin Method for Easy, Step-by-step, Lasting Change for You and Your Child. Alan E. Kazdin. Houghton Mifflin Harcourt 2013 208 p. $25 **649**

1. Child rearing 2. Parent-child relationship 3. Parenting

ISBN 0547985541; 9780547985541

LC 2012537349

Here, Alan E. Kazdin "offers practical strategies to help parents manage everyday behavioral problems. His science-based method may surprise some readers, particularly those who favor a more authoritarian approach. The core of the book focuses on the 'ABC's': antecedents, behavior, and consequences. According to Kazdin, parents can effect desired behavior in their children by offering choices and speaking in pleasant tones." (Publishers Weekly)

Includes bibliographical references (p. [178]-181) and index

Kennedy, Janet Krone

The **good** sleeper; the essential guide to sleep for your baby--and you. Janet Krone Kennedy, PhD. Holt Paperbacks 2015 304 p. (paperback) $16 **649**

1. Sleep 2. Infants -- Care 3. Naps (Sleep) 4. Infants -- Sleep 5. Parent and infant

ISBN 0805099433; 9780805099430

LC 2014019607

This book, by Janet Krone Kennedy, offers a "straightforward method for training infants to become great sleepers for life. . . . For something so important, there's too much conflicting information about how best to get your baby to sleep through the night and nap successfully during the day. This book is a straightforward, no-nonsense answer to one of the biggest challenges new parents face when they welcome a brand new baby home." (Publisher's note)

"Proposing 'authoritative parenting' (rather than attachment parenting), Kennedy is making an argument about more than infant rest... This approach is sure to draw strong reactions from the mommy-blogosphere, whether it's ire from moms who like to sleep in the same bed as baby, or praise from exhausted parents who will no doubt be eager to try Kennedy's program." Pub Wkly

Kennedy-Moore, Eileen, 1964-

Smart parenting for smart kids; nurturing your child's true potential. Eileen Kennedy-Moore, Mark S. Lowenthal. John Wiley & Sons inc. 2011 xii, 306 p.p (pbk.) $16.95 **649**

1. Child rearing 2. Academic achievement 3. Parent-child relationship 4. Gifted children 5. Parents of

gifted children

ISBN 0470640057; 9780470640050

LC 2010043005

Author Eileen Kennedy-Moore discusses child-rearing and offers "a perceptive guide to help smart children succeed academically and socially." The author offers suggestions for parents on how they can "help lead their children to new intellectual and emotional growth. Near the end of each chapter are suggestions for how parents can model healthy behaviors for their kids. . . . This . . . look at raising smart children will help parents teach their kids that there's more to life than academic achievement." (Kirkus Reviews)

Includes bibliographical references and index.

La Leche League International

The **Womanly** art of breastfeeding; 7th rev ed; Plume 2004 463p il pa $18 **649**

1. Breast feeding

ISBN 978-0-452-28580-4; 0-452-28580-1

LC 2004-557599

First published 1956. Periodically revised

This guide explains the benefits of breastfeeding and offers advice on avoiding problems, breastfeeding and working mothers, family life, and weaning.

Includes bibliographical references

Lahey, Jessica

The **gift** of failure; how the best parents learn to let go so their children can succeed. Jessica Lahey. Harper 2015 304 p. (hardback) $26.99 **649**

1. Parenting 2. Failure (Psychology) 3. Parental overprotection 4. Self-reliance in children 5. Parenting -- United States 6. Child rearing -- United States 7. Early childhood education -- United States

ISBN 0062299239; 9780062299239

LC 2014039146

This book, by Jessica Lahey, "focuses on the critical school years when parents must learn to allow their children to experience the disappointment and frustration that occur from life's inevitable problems so that they can grow up to be successful, resilient, and self-reliant adults. . . . Even though . . . parents see themselves as being highly responsive to their children's well being, they aren't giving them the chance to experience failure." (Publisher's note)

"Lahey's conversational tone, combined with research and narratives from both children and parents, delivers in-depth insight into the value of mistakes. With chapters on specific age groups (middle schoolers and high schoolers) and hot-button issues, such as household chores, homework, and friendships, any parent who needs assistance reining in the supermom tendencies will find sound advice here." LJ

Leach, Penelope

The **essential** first year. DK Publishing 2010 288p il pa $17.95 **649**

1. Child rearing 2. Infants -- Care

ISBN 978-0-7566-5799-4

"Leach empowers parents without overwhelming or guilting them, ultimately making the world a better place for families and children everywhere. Warning: this will make you want to have babies." Libr J

Includes bibliographical references

Your baby & child; from birth to age five. photographs by Jenny Matthews. 3rd ed completely rev; Knopf 1997 559p il $35; pa $20   **649**
1. Child care 2. Child development 3. Infants -- Care
ISBN 0-375-40007-9; 0-375-70000-5 pa
LC 97-29325
First published 1977 in the United Kingdom with title: Baby and child; first United States edition 1978

The author explores the psychosocial needs of children along with their physical growth and progress. Parental concerns are addressed

"Public and academic libraries would do well to stock . . . this primer on children and their development for circulation as well as for the reference shelf." Libr J

Lev, Arlene Istar
The **complete** lesbian & gay parenting guide; Berkeley trade pbk. ed.; Berkley Books 2004 379p pa $17   **649**
1. Parenting 2. Gay parents
ISBN 0-425-19197-4; 978-0-425-19197-2
LC 2004-57080
"This book addresses the concerns of transgendered parents, as well as those of lesbian and gay parents. . . . [The author] knows how to tackle relevant issues, e.g., dealing with the homophobia that children of GLBT parents will inevitably encounter. Humorous and replete with valuable narratives." Libr J

Includes bibliographical references

Lippincott, Jenifer Marshall
7 things your teenager won't tell you; and how to talk about them anyway. [by] Jenifer Marshall Lippincott and Robin M. Deutsch. Ballantine Books 2005 223p pa $14.95   **649**
1. Parenting 2. Teenagers 3. Adolescent psychology 4. Parent-child relationship
ISBN 0-8129-6959-6
LC 2005-297256
"The first section of the book reviews psychological and physiological research on brain development in adolescents. The authors then identify seven important facts to keep in mind, among them: truth is a malleable concept for teens, they suffer from distorted self-images, and they are attracted to risks. . . . Parents of teens will recognize the us-and-them dialogues and will find encouragement and guidance." Booklist

Includes bibliographical references

Margulis, Jennifer
The **business** of baby; what doctors don't tell you, what corporations try to sell you, and how to put your pregnancy, childbirth, and baby before their bottom line. Jennifer Margulis. Scribner 2013 368 p. (hardcover) $27   **649**
1. Pregnancy -- Economic aspects 2. Parenthood --

Economic aspects
ISBN 1451636083; 1451636091; 9781451636086; 9781451636093
LC 2012031245
This book, by Jennifer Margulis, "exposes how our current cultural practices during pregnancy, childbirth, and the first year of a baby's life are not based on the best evidence or the most modern science, . . . [but are] being undermined by corporate interests. . . . [Combining] research and in-depth interviews . . . , Margulis's . . . critique . . . arms parents with the information they need to make informed decisions about their own health and the health of their infants." (Publisher's note)

Includes bibliographical references and index.

Mayes, Linda C.
The **Yale** Child Study Center guide to understanding your child; healthy development from birth to adolescence. {by} Linda C. Mayes and Donald J. Cohen with John E. Schowalter and Richard H. Granger; J. L. Bell, editorial consultant; W. Rodney Torbert, illustrator. Little, Brown 2002 548p $40; pa $21.95   **649**
1. Child rearing 2. Child development 3. Parent-child relationship
ISBN 0-316-95432-2; 0-316-79432-5 pa
LC 00-39116
"The book offers three perspectives: the scientific, with basic information about meeting a growing child's needs; the emotional, with attention to understanding a child's feelings; and the parental, with emphasis on the feelings and expectations the parent brings to the relationship. . . . The objective is to help parents balance the three perspectives. . . . This approach lends the guide a broad and deep perspective on parenting even as it covers typical issues such as imaginary friends and sibling rivalry." Booklist

Medina, John, 1956-
Brain rules for baby; how to raise a smart and happy child from zero to five. John Medina. 2nd ed; updated Pear Press 2014 323 p. ill pbk $15.95 **649**
1. Child psychology 2. Parent-child relationship 3. Parenting 4. Child rearing 5. Child development
ISBN 0983263388; 9780983263388
Medina "presents the best of the refereed literature to examine how infants process information at the molecular, cellular, and behavioral levels. . . . Covering such topics as pregnancy, relationships, and 'moral' babies, the book will educate even the most learned parents. Medina's humorous, conversational style makes this an absolute pleasure to read." LJ

Miller, Lisa
The **Spiritual** Child; The New Science on Parenting for Health and Lifelong Thriving. by Lisa Miller. St. Martin's Press 2015 400 p. $27.99 **649**
1. Parenting 2. Spiritual life 3. Child development
ISBN 125003292X; 9781250032928
LC 2015005940
In this book, author Lisa Miller "presents the next big idea in psychology: the science and the power of spirituality. . . . Combining cutting-edge research with broad an-

ecdotal evidence from her work as a clinical psychologist to illustrate just how invaluable spirituality is to a child's mental and physical health, Miller translates these findings into practical advice for parents, giving them concrete ways to develop and encourage their children's .... well-being." (Publisher's note)

"If the plights of Marin and Kurt had been introduced earlier, Miller could have established more emotional connection with her readers, who would then be more engaged with the science she presents. New science or a leap of faith? Either way, nurturing spirituality in your children may save them a world of pain." Kirkus

Murkoff, Heidi

★ **What** to Expect the First Year; by Heidi Murkoff with Sharon Mazel. 3rd edition Workman Pub. Co. 2014 704 p. illustrations pbk $16.95 **649**
1. Child rearing 2. Infants -- Care
ISBN 0761181504; 9780761181507

LC 8740647

This book, by Heidi Murkoff, "is the world's best-selling, best-loved guide to the instructions that babies don't come with, but should. And now, it's . . . completely updated. Keeping the trademark month-by-month format that allows parents to take the potentially overwhelming first year one step at a time, . . . [it's] packed with even more practical tips, realistic advice, and relatable, accessible information than before." (Publisher's note)

Murkoff, Heidi Eisenberg

What to expect the first year; [by] Heidi Murkoff, Arlene Eisenberg & Sandee Hathaway. 2nd ed, rev and updated; Workman 2003 704p $25.95; pa $15.95 **649**
1. Child rearing 2. Infants -- Care
ISBN 0-7611-3184-1; 0-7611-2958-8 pa

LC 2003-57578

First published 1996 with Eisenberg's name appearing first

This guide to "taking care of a newborn through the milestone of his or her first birthday . . . [covers] issues such as newborn screening, home births and the resulting at-home newborn care, vitamins and vaccines, milk allergies, causes of colic, sleep problems, SIDS, returning to work, dealing with siblings, weaning, sippy cups, . . . [and] the expanded role of the father." Publisher's note

★ **What** to expect the second year; from 12 to 24 months. [by] Heidi Murkoff and Sharon Mazel; foreword by Mark D. Widome. Workman Pub Co 2011 512p il $24; pa $15.95 **649**
1. Toddlers 2. Child rearing
ISBN 978-0-7611-6364-0; 978-0-7611-5277-4 pa

This is a "look at the toddler from 12 to 24 months. In 15 chapters the authors cover feeding, sleeping, learning, playing, health and safety, injuries and developmental disorders, discipline, and other issues with a meaty center section on behavior. . . . Murkoff offers sound advice and reassurance that will help parent and toddler stay grounded during this whirlwind period of growth and change." Publ Wkly

Neifert, Marianne R.

Great expectations; the essential guide to breastfeeding. [by] Marianne Neifert. Sterling 2009 312p il pa $14.95 **649**
1. Breast feeding
ISBN 978-1-4027-5817-1

LC 2009-5248

"The author combines detailed, readable medical explanations with practical tips for success and addresses potential challenges honestly rather than glossing over them with bland reassurances. Each chapter seems designed to stand alone, making it easy for time-pressed mothers to find the information they need without reading the entire book." Libr J

Palmer, Sara

Just one of the kids; raising a resilient family when one of your children has a physical disability. Kay Harris Kriegsman, Ph.D., and Sara Palmer, Ph.D. Johns Hopkins University Press 2013 240 p. (hardcover : alk. paper) $49 **649**
1. Children with physical disabilities 2. Parents of children with disabilities 3. Children with disabilities -- Family relationships
ISBN 1421409305; 1421409313; 9781421409306; 9781421409313

LC 2012035771

This book, by psychologists Kay Harris Kriegsman and Sara Palmer, presents a guide for parents of children with physical disabilities. "The authors show families how to be pragmatic and inclusive when solving problems and setting expectations. The real family stories and personal experiences of the authors, one of whom has such a disability, create an intimate and nonjudgmental tone with a degree of optimism." (Library Journal)

"A valuable resource for families looking for encouragement as they try to create an inclusive environment for their child with a physical disability." LJ

Includes bibliographical references and index

Phelan, Thomas W.

★ **1-2-3** magic; effective discipline for children 2-12. Thomas W. Phelan, PhD. Sourcebooks 2016 288 p. illustrations (hardcover : alk. paper) $24.99 **649**
1. Parenting 2. Child rearing 3. Children -- Conduct of life 4. Discipline of children
ISBN 9781492629887; 9781492631828; 149262988X

LC 2015021612

This book, by Thomas W. Phelan, Ph.D. "compiles two decades of research and experience into an easy-to-use program designed for parents striving to connect more deeply with their children and help them develop into healthy, capable teenagers and adults. [Readers will] find tools to use in virtually every situation, as well as real-life stories from parents who have successfully navigated common parenting challenges such as reluctance to do chores, talking back, and refusing to go to bed." (Publisher's note)

Phelan's 1-2-3 is the gold standard of child discipline for good reason. All libraries should update to the new edition and purchase in sufficient quantities." Library Journal

Includes bibliographical references and index

Pitman, Teresa

Sweet sleep; nighttime and naptime strategies for the breastfeeding family. Diane Wiessinger and [three others] Ballantine Books 2014 512 p. illustrations (paperback : acid-free paper) $20   **649**

> 1. Parenting 2. Breast feeding 3. Sleeping customs 4. Sleep 5. Breastfeeding 6. Breastfeeding -- Safety measures
>
> ISBN 0345518470; 9780345518477
>
> LC 2014019411

Written by Diane Wiessinger, Diana West, Linda J. Smith, and Teresa Pitman, "'Sweet Sleep' includes extensive information on creating a safe sleep space, helping children learn to sleep on their own and defusing criticism of your family's choices. . . . This book is nothing but supportive of whatever your choices are about nursing and sleeping." (BookPage)

"The core of the book offers detailed, practical advice on bed sharing and breast-feeding, with basic guidelines for safe bed sharing outlined in seven steps." Pub Wkly

Includes bibliographical references and index

The **womanly** art of breastfeeding; by Diane Wiessinger, Diana West, and Teresa Pitman. Ballantine Books 2010 xxiv, 550 p.p illustrations (pbk.) $20   **649**

> 1. Breast feeding
>
> ISBN 0345518446; 9780345518446
>
> LC 2010014031

This guide to breastfeeding, by Diane Wiessinger, Diana West, and Teresa Pitman, "has been retooled, refocused, and updated for today's mothers and lifestyles. Working mothers, stay-at-home moms, single moms, and mothers of multiples will all benefit from the book's range of nursing advice, stories, and information—from preparing for breastfeeding during pregnancy to feeding cues, from nursing positions to expressing and storing breast milk." (Publisher's note)

Includes bibliographical references (p. [499]-535) and index

Richey, Mary Anne

The **impulsive,** disorganized child; solutions for parenting kids with executive functioning difficulties. James W. Forgan, Ph.D., & Mary Anne Richey. Prufrock Press Inc. 2015 xiv, 258 p.p illustrations (pbk.) $17.95   **649**

> 1. Self-control 2. Child rearing 3. Children with mental disabilities 4. Child psychology 5. Self-control in children 6. Executive functions (Neuropsychology) 7. Children with mental disabilities -- Care
>
> ISBN 1618214012; 9781618214010
>
> LC 2015001880

This book, by James W. Forgan and Mary Anne Richey, "helps parents pinpoint weak executive functions in their children, then learn how to help their kids overcome these deficits with practical, easy solutions. Children who can't select, plan, initiate, or sustain action toward their goals are children who simply struggle to succeed in school and other aspects of life." (Publisher's note)

"The advice presented has practical context and gives specifics for action. Using the "SMART" model (goals should be: specific, measurable, attainable, realistic, and timely), kids can join their parents in improving impulse control and organization." LJ

Includes bibliographical references

Sears, William

The **baby** book; everything you need to know about your baby from birth to age two. William Sears, MD, Martha Sears, RN, Robert Sears, MD, and James Sears, MD. 3rd ed Little, Brown & Co. 2013 xiv, 770 p.p ill., charts (pbk.) $21.99   **649**

> 1. Infants -- Care 2. Infants -- Development 3. Newborn infants -- Care
>
> ISBN 0316198269; 9780316198264
>
> LC 2012953605

Written by William Sears, Martha Sears, Robert Sears, and James Sears, this book "presents a practical, contemporary approach to parenting that reflects the way we live today. Focusing on the essential needs of babies--eating, sleeping, development, health, and comfort--it addresses the questions of greatest concern to parents. The Searses acknowledge that there is no one way to parent a baby." (Publisher's note)

"The authors teach new parents how to bond with their babies through seven fundamental behaviors, including breastfeeding, 'babywearing' and setting proper boundaries. . . . From tips for a healthy birth, getting your baby to sleep and feeding him the 'right fats,' to information about early health concerns, the major steps in infant development and troublesome but typical toddler behavior, the authors of this comprehensive volume . . . are assured and reassuring experts." Publ Wkly

Includes bibliographical references and index

Parenting the fussy baby and high-need child; everything you need to know--from birth to age five. {by} William Sears and Martha Sears. Little, Brown 1996 237p il hardcover o.p. pa $12.95   **649**

> 1. Parenting 2. Child psychology
>
> ISBN 0-316-77916-4 pa
>
> LC 95-48381

To cope with a high-need child the authors "recommend the approach they label attachment parenting; it includes such techniques as on-demand feeding and weaning; night-time parenting; sharing sleep; soothing through motion, sound, visual distraction, and physical contact; and learning via close study how to anticipate the baby's needs." Booklist

Includes bibliographical references

Siegel, Daniel J.

No-drama discipline; the whole-brain way to calm the chaos and nurture your child's developing mind. Daniel J. Siegel, M.D., Tina Payne Bryson, Ph.D. Bantam Books 2014 288 p. illustrations (hardback) $26   **649**

> 1. Parenting 2. Child rearing 3. Child development
>
> ISBN 0345548043; 9780345548047
>
> LC 2014008270

Written by Daniel J. Siegel and Tina Payne Bryson, "'No-Drama Discipline' provides an effective, compassionate road map for dealing with tantrums, tensions, and tears--without causing a scene." It includes "strategies that help parents identify their own discipline philosophy--and master the best methods to communicate the lessons they are trying to impart." (Publisher's note)

"With lucid, engaging prose accompanied by cartoon illustrations, Siegel and Bryson help parents teach and communicate more effectively." Pub Wkly

The **whole**-brain child; 12 revolutionary strategies to nurture your child's developing mind. Daniel J. Siegel, Tina Payne Bryson. Delacorte Press 2011 xiii, 176 p.p illustrations $24   **649**
1. Parenting 2. Child rearing 3. Child development
ISBN 0553807919; 9780553807912; 9780553907254
LC 2010052988

In this book, authors Daniel J. Siegel and Tina Payne Bryson "demystify the meltdowns and aggravation, explaining the new science of how a child's brain is wired and how it matures. . . . By applying these discoveries to everyday parenting, you can turn any outburst, argument, or fear into a chance to integrate your child's brain and foster vital growth." (Publisher's note)

"Siegel and Bryson reveal that an integrated brain with parts that cooperate in a coordinated and balanced manner creates a better understanding of self, stronger relationships, and success in school, among other benefits. With illustrations, charts, and even a handy 'Refrigerator Sheet,' the authors have made every effort to make brain science parent-friendly." Pub Wkly

Small, Meredith F.
Our babies, ourselves; how biology and culture shape the way we parent. Anchor Bks. (NY) 1998 xxii, 292p il hardcover o.p. pa $14.95   **649**
1. Parent-child relationship 2. Infants -- Care 3. Infants -- Development
ISBN 0-385-48362-7 pa
LC 97-44348

The author "explores ethnopediatrics, an interdisciplinary science that combines anthropology, pediatrics, and child development research in order to examine how child-rearing styles across cultures affect the health and survival of infants. Small describes the different parenting styles of several cultures, including . . . the nomadic Ache tribe of Paraguay, the agrarian !Kung San society of the Kalahari Desert in Africa, and the American industrialized society." Libr J
Includes bibliographical references

Spock, Benjamin, 1903-1998
Dr. Spock's baby and child care; by Benjamin Spock. Gallery Books 2012 xx, 1130 p.p illustrations $19.99   **649**
1. Child care 2. Child rearing 3. Infants -- Care
ISBN 1439189285; 9781439189283
LC 2012382318

Author Benjamin Spock offers "advice on age-old topics such as caring for a new baby, as well as accidents, illness, and injuries, [and] this revised edition also covers: medical opinion on immunizations . . . obesity and nutrition . . . [and] cultural diversity, and non-traditional family structures." (Publisher's note)

Doctor Spock's baby and child care

Dr. Spock on parenting; sensible advice from America's most trusted child care expert. Simon & Schuster 1988 318p hardcover o.p. pa $16.95 **649**
1. Parenting
ISBN 0-7434-2683-5 pa
LC 88-15792

"The author presents a personal critique on parenting, often bordering on the autobiographical. . . . He discusses in depth and with great conviction contemporary and traditional parent concerns, such as divorce, discipline, sex education, and the father's role." Libr J

Dr. Spock's the first two years; the emotional and physical needs of children from birth to age two. edited by Martin T. Stein. Pocket Bks. 2001 153p pa $13.95   **649**
1. Child care 2. Child rearing 3. Child development
ISBN 0-7434-1122-6

In these articles culled from Redbook and Parenting Spock's advice to parents is that they should "trust themselves" and "expands on this idea in his reply to the question, 'What has eroded so many parents' self-assurance in asking for reasonably good behavior?'" Libr J

Dr. Spock's the school years; the emotional and social development of children. edited by Martin T. Stein. Pocket Bks. 2001 283p pa $15.95 **649**
1. Child care 2. Child rearing 3. Child development
ISBN 0-7434-1123-4

This volume collects Spock's essays published in Redbook and Parenting. They address "our contemporary culture's tendency to overschedule children." Libr J

Wiseman, Rosalind, 1969-
Masterminds and wingmen; helping our boys cope with schoolyard power, locker-room tests, girl-friends, and the new rules of Boy World. Rosalind Wiseman. Harmony Books 2013 384 p. illustrations $25   **649**
1. Masculinity 2. Boys -- Psychology 3. Adolescent psychology 4. Parent and teenager 5. Teenage boys -- Psychology
ISBN 0307986659; 9780307986658
LC 2013372427

This book offers information "for every parent--or anyone who cares about boys--to know. Collaborating with a large team of middle- and high-school-age editors, Rosalind Wiseman has created an unprecedented guide to the life your boy is actually experiencing--his on-the-ground reality. Not only does Wiseman challenge you to examine your assumptions, she offers innovative coping strategies aimed at helping your boy develop a positive, authentic, and strong sense of self." (Publisher's note)

"Wiseman's sound and steady assistance provides a calm response to every twist and turn on the multifaceted road of parenthood. . . . A wealth of sensible information for parents of boys." Kirkus
Includes bibliographical references (pages 365-366) and index

Wright, Julie

The **happy** sleeper; the science-backed guide to helping your baby get a good night's sleep-newborn to school age. Heather Turgeon, Julie Wright; illustrations by Jack Sheehy. Jeremy P. Tarcher/Penguin 2014 368 p. illustrations (paperback) $16.95   **649**

1. Sleep 2. Child rearing 3. Infants -- Sleep 4. Children -- Sleep

ISBN 0399166025; 9780399166020

                 LC 2014035240

This book, by Heather Turgeon and Julie Wright, presents a guide for infant sleeping habits. The authors "show parents how to be sensitive and nurturing, but also clear and structured so that babies and young children develop the self-soothing skills they need to fall asleep independently . . ., sleep through the night . . . , take healthy naps . . . , [and] grow into natural, optimal sleep patterns for day and night." (Publisher's note)

"Different approaches are given for kids up to age six, making this a manual that will grow with the child. Turgeon and Wright's compassionate but firm system reminds parents that even the smallest infants are already learners, and to be more cognizant of what they want to teach." Pub Wkly

Includes bibliographical references and index

649.1   Child rearing

Faber, Adele

★ **How** to Talk So Kids Will Listen and Listen So Kids Will Talk; Adele Faber, Elaine Mazlish; ill. by Kimberly Ann Coe. 30th anniversary edition Scribner Classics 2012 345 p. illustrations hbk $26   **649.1**

1. Parenting 2. Communication 3. Parent-child relationship

ISBN 1451663870; 9781451663877

First published 1980 by Rawson, Wade Publishers

This book on parenting, by Adele Faber and Elaine Mazlish, "includes fresh insights and suggestions as well as the author's time-tested methods to solve common problems and build foundations for lasting relationships." (Publisher's note)

The authors "keep true to the style of the original, while also updating their text with new scenarios and including feedback and letters they have received from readers over the years. Praised for its down-to-earth and respectful approach to communication, this book helps parents acknowledge their child's feelings, engage their cooperation, and encourage autonomy." LJ

Includes bibliographical references and index

Glickman, Elaine Rose

Your kid's a brat and it's all your fault; nip the attitude in the bud--from toddler to tween. Elaine Rose Glickman. Tarcher 2016 320 p. (paperback) $16   **649.1**

1. Parenting 2. Parent-child relationship 3. Emotionally disturbed children 4. Parent and child 5. Pampered child syndrome 6. Problem children -- Behavior

modification

ISBN 9780399173127

                 LC 2015045423

In this book, author "Elaine Rose Glickman tells parents that—when it comes to their bratty kids—the buck stops with them! . . . Divided into three sections—'Your Budding Brat' for toddlers and preschoolers, 'Your Bratty Child' for grade-schoolers, and 'Your Bratty Tween'—this book is packed with wisdom and tips culled from the trenches of child-rearing." (Publisher's note)

"Most parents will find this humorous guide refreshing and truly helpful." Booklist

Ingall, Marjorie

Mamaleh knows best; What Jewish Mothers Do to Raise Successful, Creative, Empathetic, Independent Children. Marjorie Ingall. Harmony Books 2016 245 p. (hardback) $25; (ebook) $65   **649.1**

1. Parenting 2. Parent-child relationship 3. Child rearing -- Religious aspects -- Judaism

ISBN 080414141X; 9780804141413; 9780804141420

                 LC 2016010796

This book by Marjorie Ingall "shares Jewish secrets for raising self-sufficient, ethical, and accomplished children. [Ingall] offers abundant examples showing how Jewish mothers have nurtured their children's independence, fostered discipline, . . . stressed education, and maintained a sense of humor. These . . . strategies have proven successful in a wide variety of settings. . . . . But you don't have to be Jewish to cultivate the same qualities in your own children." (Publisher's note)

"Ingall's engaging guide will help parents, Jewish or not, navigate the jagged terrain of child-rearing with a hearty dose of confidence and laughter." Pub Wkly

Includes bibliographical references (pages 232-235) and index.

Raeburn, Paul

The **game** theorist's guide to parenting; how the science of strategic thinking can help you deal with the toughest negotiators you know--your kids. Paul Raeburn and Kevin Zollman. Scientific American/Farrar, Straus & Giroux 2016 240 p. (hardcover) $25   **649.1**

1. Parenting 2. Game theory 3. Negotiation 4. Game theory -- Social aspects

ISBN 9780374160012

                 LC 2015036381

In this book, authors Paul Raeburn and Kevin Zollman "pair up to highlight tactics from the worlds of economics and business that can help parents. . . . [They] show that some of the same strategies successfully applied to big business deals and politics—such as the Prisoner's Dilemma and the Ultimatum Game—can be used to solve such titanic, age-old parenting problems as dividing up toys, keeping the peace on long car rides, and sticking to homework routines." (Publisher's note)

"Tantalizing perspectives on cultivating sharing, honesty, and cooperation via game theory." Kirkus

Includes bibliographical references and index

Swanson, Wendy Sue

Mama doc medicine; finding calm and confidence in parenting, child health, and work-life balance. Wendy Sue Swanson, MD, MBE, FAAP. American Academy of Pediatrics 2014 389 p. illustrations $16.95 **649.1**

1. Parenting 2. Mother-child relationship 3. Parent-child relationship

ISBN 1581108370; 9781581108378

LC 2013943971

Pediatrician Wendy Sue Swanson "helps decipher today's conflicting medical opinions, offers helpful online resources, and shares what she's learned over many years from her patients, friends and family in this . . . guide to parenting." (Publisher's note)

"Arranged in four sections ("Prevention," "Social-Emotional Support," "Immunizations," and "Work-Life Balance/ Mothering"), [Swanson's] guide is practical as well as personal."

Includes bibliographical references and index.

Willingham, Emily

The **informed** parent; a science-based resource for your child's first four years. Tara Haelle and Emily Willingham, Ph.D. Perigee Books 2016 336 p. (paperback) $20 **649.1**

1. Parenting 2. Child rearing 3. Child development 4. Pregnancy 5. Parenthood 6. Infants -- Care 7. Families -- Health and hygiene

ISBN 9780399171062

LC 2015046759

This book, by Tara Haelle and Emily Willingham, Ph.D, offers the "latest scientific research on home birth, breastfeeding, sleep training, vaccines, and other key topics—to help parents make their own best-informed decisions. . . . The ultimate resource for today's science-minded generation, [this book] was written for readers who prefer facts to "friendly advice," and who prefer to make up their own minds, based on the latest findings as well as their own personal preferences." (Publisher's note)

"For anyone headed into parenthood, this is a must-read, as it answers so many questions new parents are bound to ask. Easy-to-read, up-to-date information on the latest research into pregnancy, childbirth, and early childhood." Kirkus

649.122 Infants--home care

Cross, Claire

The **baby** book; pregnancy, birth, baby & childcare from 0 to 3. writers Shaoni Bhattacharya, Claire Cross, Carol Dyce, Kate Ling, Susannah Marriott, Karen Sullivan, and Jo Wiltshire. DK Publishing 2016 320 p. color illustrations (paperback) $24.95 **649.122**

1. Parenting 2. Pregnancy 3. Child rearing

ISBN 1465444785; 9781465444783

LC 2015458963

This book, by Shaoni Bhattacharya, Claire Cross, Carol Dyce, Kate Ling, Susannah Marriott, Karen Sullivan, and Jo Wiltshire, "is a guide to caring for your child—from

pregnancy through age three. . . . [The book] . . . provides everything you need to know as a parent—from pregnancy superfoods and labor tips to first check-ups and breastfeeding secrets—while presenting this part of life as something you should celebrate, not fear." (Publisher's note)

"While books on this subject are abundant, readers will be naturally drawn to the warm style and sheer beauty of the DK titles. Libraries can't go wrong with this acquisition." LJ

DeSouza, Luiza

Eat, Play, Sleep; The Essential Guide to Your Baby's First Three Months. Luiza DeSouza. Pocket Books 2015 304 p. illustrations $25 **649.122**

1. Infants 2. Parenting 3. Child rearing

ISBN 1451650922; 9781451650921

This parenting book, by Luiza DeSouza, offers a "practical and reassuring guide to the first three months with your new baby. . . . [The author suggests to new mothers:] Take your time, trust your maternal instincts, and choose a course that fits your needs--and your baby's personality." (Publisher's note)

"Moms without a nurse or a more experienced relative on hand should find these suggestions very helpful, particularly because such specifics can get lost in books by more academic or medically oriented experts. Though never effusive, her voice does convey steadiness with just a bit of toughness, lending credibility to her statement that coolly confident mothers make for calm, happy babies. She doesn't hide her disdain for certain modern parenting ideas, singling out the attachment theory behind cosleeping as particularly misguided. Families who want a traditional nurse's approach to care, but can't afford help at home, may find this manual a good alternative." Pub Wkly

Watch my baby grow; DK Publishing. DK Publishing 2014 220 p. color illustrations $25 **649.122**

1. Infants 2. Child development

ISBN 1465429778; 9781465429773

LC 2015303153

This book "shows you everything that happens in the first year of life in step-by-step pictures with detailed explanations. Every milestone of baby development, from gurgles to coos to first words, is documented and explained." (Publisher's note)

"This is a truly beautiful book that any new parent would love to own. Its single-subject photographic approach gives depth to understanding infant development. The text has a calm and encouraging tone that celebrates the loveliness of babies and families. A must-have for all public library collections, this is unequivocally recommended." LJ

649.3 Feeding children

Altmann, Tanya Remer

What to feed your baby; a pediatrician's guide to the eleven essential foods to guarantee veggie-loving, no-fuss, healthy-eating kids. Tanya Altmann. HarperOne 2016 336 p. (paperback) $17.99 **649.3**

1. Eating customs 2. Infants -- Nutrition 3. Food habits

ISBN 9780062404947

LC 2015033614

In this book, pediatrician Tanya Altmann "provides the latest nutritional recommendations and best practices for feeding babies and young children. The simple, fool-proof program focuses on serving eleven foundation foods: eggs, prunes, avocado, fish, yogurt/cheese/milk, nuts, chicken/beans, fruit, green veggies, whole grains, and water." (Publisher's note)

"This clear, thorough guide will take the angst and confusion out of feeding time for parents and youngsters alike." Pub Wkly

Includes bibliographical references (pages 311-314) and index.

649.33   Breast feeding

Shortall, Jessica

Work. Pump. Repeat. The New Mom's Survival Guide to Breastfeeding and Going Back to Work. Jessica Shortall. Harry N Abrams Inc 2015 208 p. $19.95   **649.33**

  1. Breast feeding 2. Working mothers
  ISBN 9781419718700; 1419718703

                                          LC 2015934789

Author Jessica Shortall presents this "book to give women what they need to know beyond the noise of the "Mommy Wars" and judgment on breastfeeding choices. Jessica Shortall shares the nitty-gritty basics of surviving the working world as a breastfeeding mom, offering a road map for negotiating the pumping schedule with colleagues, navigating business travel, and problem-solving when forced to pump in less-than-desirable locales." (Publisher's note)

649.58   Children--Reading and related activities

Newman, Nancy

  Raising passionate readers; 5 easy steps to success in school and life. Nancy Newman. Tribeca View Press 2014 222 p. $16.95   **649.58**

  1. Literacy 2. Children -- Books and reading
  ISBN 0615847544; 9780615847542

                                          LC 2013951969

In this book, by Nancy Newman, "bridging the gap between scientists and busy parents by combining the latest scientific research with what she has learned as a teacher and mother, . . . [the author] offers a simple, practical, and joyful approach that boosts children's literacy skills and instills an enduring love of reading." (Publisher's note)

"While the subject literature has not changed much over the years, it is still widely accepted that reading is the greatest indicator of future academic success. Recommended for collections needing an update on the topic." LJ

649.7   Moral and character training of children

Borba, Michele

  Unselfie; why empathetic kids succeed in our all-about-me world. Michele Borba. Touchstone 2016 288 p. (hardback) $25   **649.7**

  1. Empathy 2. Child rearing 3. Interpersonal relations
  ISBN 9781501110030

                                          LC 2015049137

This book, by Michele Borba, "offers a 9-step program to help parents cultivate empathy in children, from birth to young adulthood—and explains why developing a healthy sense of empathy is a key predictor of which kids will thrive and succeed in the future. . . . Borba offers a framework for parenting that yields the results we all want: successful, happy kids who also are kind, moral, courageous, and resilient." (Publisher's note)

"Her thought- provoking and practical book may very well tip over the parenting priority applecart—and rightly so." Pub Wkly

Includes bibliographical references and index.

Prosek, Jen

  Raising Can-Do Kids; Giving Children the Tools to Thrive in a Fast-Changing World. Richard Rende, Jen Prosek. Penguin Group USA 2015 272 p. $24.95   **649.7**

  1. Parenting 2. Child development
  ISBN 0399168966; 9780399168963

This book by Richard Rende and Jen Prosek attempts to "make a link between the essential qualities that make great entrepreneurs tick and what we know about how children learn and grow, offering parents proven ways to raise kids who embrace the uncertain, challenging adventure that is growing up in today's (and tomorrow's) changing world. Each chapter is devoted to a quality—including curiosity, inventiveness, optimism, opportunity-seeking, compassion, and service." (Publisher's note)

"The authors' suggestions and insights cover a wide spectrum of child-raising situations and should, when properly applied, deliver lasting results." Kirkus

649.8   Home care of people with disabilities and illnesses

American Cancer Society complete guide to family caregiving; the essential guide to cancer caregiving at home. by Julia A. Bucher, Peter S. Houts, Terri Ades. American Cancer Society/Health Promotions 2011 354 p. illustrations (pbk. : alk. paper) $24.95   **649.8**

  1. Cancer patients 2. Caregivers -- Handbooks, manuals, etc. 3. Caregivers 4. Cancer -- Palliative treatment 5. Cancer -- Patients -- Home care
  ISBN 094423500X; 9780944235003

                                          LC 2010015968

This book, by Julia A. Bucher, Peter S. Houts, and Terri Ades, "offers manageable solutions to the many conditions and situations caregivers may face. From physical and emotional conditions, to dealing with health care providers and insurance carriers this resource helps teach caregivers to take care of their own needs as well as those of the person with cancer." (Publisher's note)

Includes bibliographical references and index

Carter, Rosalynn

Helping yourself help others; a book for caregivers. {by} Rosalynn Carter with Susan K. Golant. Times Bks. 1994 278p hardcover o.p. pa $14 **649.8**
1. Caregivers 2. Home care services
ISBN 0-8129-2591-2 pa

LC 94-11924

The authors "describe the stages the caregiver progresses through, from first facing the illness or declining health of a loved one to the 'long-term, hard-work phase of caregiving.' Questions regarding in-home professional care and nursing homes are addressed, and the authors provide information on strategies, support groups, program recommendations, helpful organizations, and books." Booklist

McFarlane, Rodger

The **complete** bedside companion; no-nonsense advice on caring for the seriously ill. {by} Rodger McFarlane, Philip Bashe. Simon & Schuster 1998 544p hardcover o.p. pa $25.95 **649.8**
1. Caregivers 2. Home nursing 3. Terminal care
ISBN 0-684-84319-6 pa

LC 97-43746

"This primer provides information on general illness and specific diseases, questions to ask the physician, basic nursing skills, making hospital visits, dealing with insurance companies, sources of additional information, and support groups. The authors . . . supplement this material with case studies and personal experiences." Libr J

Includes bibliographical references

650.1 Personal success in business

Bolles, Richard

★ **What** color is your parachute? 2017; a practical manual for job-hunters and career-changers. by Richard N. Bolles. Ten Speed Press 2016 355 p. hbk $29.99 **650.1**
1. Job hunting 2. Cover letters 3. Resumes (Employment)
ISBN 9780399578212; 0399578218
First published 1972; revised annually

"This revised and updated edition combines classic elements like the famed Flower Exercise with updated tips on social media and search tactics. Bolles demystifies the entire job-search process, from resumes to interviewing to networking, expertly guiding job-hunters toward their dream job." (Publisher's note)

Chideya, Farai

The **episodic** career; how to thrive at work in the age of disruption. Farai Chideya. Atria Books 2016 288 p. (hardback) $26 **650.1**
1. Job hunting 2. Vocational guidance 3. Job hunting -- United States -- History -- 21st century 4. Vocational

guidance -- United States -- History -- 21st century
ISBN 1476751501; 9781476751504

LC 2015029936

This book, by Farai Chideya, "explores the landscape of employment in America. Profiling the rich, the poor, and people from every strata in between, Chideya seeks to understand the many kinds of work we do--for example, not just job fields, but whether we seek to build institutions or seek social change while earning money. In addition, Chideya provides a self-diagnostic tool to help you find your work/life 'sweet spot.'" (Publisher's note)

"A fun, useful, and informative book for any stage of the career path. Recommended for public libraries and career collections." LJ

Includes bibliographical references and index.

Evans, Dave

Designing your life; how to think like a designer and build a well-lived, joyful life. William Burnett and David J. Evans. Alfred A. Knopf 2016 304 p. (hardcover) $26.95 **650.1**
1. Design 2. Quality of life 3. Vocational guidance 4. Decision making 5. Self-realization 6. Design -- Social aspects
ISBN 1101875321; 9781101875322

LC 2016008862

In this book authors "Bill Burnett and Dave Evans show . . . how design thinking can help . . . create a life that is both meaningful and fulfilling. The same design thinking responsible for amazing technology, products, and spaces can be used to design and build your career and your life, a life of fulfillment and joy, constantly creative and productive, one that always holds the possibility of surprise." (Publisher's note)

"With useful fact-finding exercises, an empathetic tone, and sensible advice, this book will easily earn a place among career-finding classics." Pub Wkly

Goulston, Mark

Just listen; discover the secret to getting through to absolutely anyone. foreword by Keith Ferrazzi. American Management Association 2009 234p il $24.95 **650.1**
1. Business communication 2. Interpersonal relations
ISBN 978-0-8144-1403-3

LC 2009-14386

This is "a primer on dealing with hard-to-reach people in virtually every scenario—defiant executives, angry employees, families in turmoil, warring couples—through use of well-honed psychological techniques. . . . Chapter summaries feature action steps preparing readers to encounter similar scenarios, yielding a guide that is as entertaining as it is useful." Publ Wkly

Harris, Carla A.

Strategize to win; the new way to start out, step up, or start over in your career. Carla A. Harris. Hudson Street Press 2014 256 p. (hardback) $25.95 **650.1**
1. Career changes 2. Vocational guidance 3. Career

development 4. Success in business
ISBN 1594633053; 9781594633058

LC 2014031571

This book, by Carla A. Harris, "offers a new way to conceptualize career strategies and gives us proven tools for successful change. . . . [The author] gives readers the tools they need to get started; get 'unstuck' from bad situations; redirect momentum; and position themselves to manage their careers no matter the environment." (Publisher's note)

"Advice to those in the 'Starting Over' phase covers knowing when it's time to jump ship and recognizing what factors motivate one, whether it's increased compensation, improved chances for advancement, or escaping current unfair treatment. She also provides an informative chapter on repositioning oneself, which many will find especially insightful. Most professionals should be able to find something of value, whether they're just starting out, ready to move on, or somewhere in between." Pub Wkly

Hill, Napoleon
Think and grow rich; the landmark bestseller--now revised and updated for the 21st century. rev. and expanded by Arthur R. Pell. 1st Jeremy P. Tarcher/Penguin ed.; Jeremy P. Tarcher/Penguin 2005 302p pa $10   **650.1**
1. Success 2. Entrepreneurship
ISBN 1-585-42433-1

LC 2005-44133
First published 1937 by The Ralston Society
A motivational guide to achieving wealth and success, drawing upon stories of successful millionaires as examples.

Jacobs, Bert
Life is good; the book. Bert Jacobs and John Jacobs. National Geographic 2015 271 p. color illustrations (hardback) $25   **650.1**
1. Optimism 2. Happiness 3. Life Is Good (Firm) 4. Clothing trade -- United States 5. Businesspeople -- United States -- Conduct of life
ISBN 9781426215636

LC 2015020909
This book, by Bert Jacobs and John Jacobs, "celebrates the power of optimism: the driving force behind their beloved, socially conscious clothing and lifestyle brand. Following the chronology of their personal and professional journeys, Bert and John share their unique ride—from their scrappy upbringing outside Boston to the unlikely runaway success of their business. The brothers illuminate ten key superpowers accessible to us all [including:] openness, courage, [and] simplicity." (Publisher's note)

"An outstanding book for all ages. One cannot browse through it without smiling and feeling that, despite everything, life is good." LJ

Includes bibliographical references (pages 269-270).

Kerpen, Dave
The **art** of people; 11 Simple People Skills That Will Get You Everything You Want. Dave Kerpen. Crwon Business 2016 276 p. $27   **650.1**
1. Communication 2. Industrial psychology 3. Interpersonal relations 4. Psychology, Industrial 5.

Interpersonal communication
ISBN 0553419404; 9780553419405

LC 2015016366

In this book, author Dave Kerpen argues "the key to getting ahead is being the person others like, respect, and trust. Because no matter who you are or what profession you're in, success is contingent less on what you can do for yourself, but on what other people are willing to do for you. Here, through 53 bite-sized, easy-to-execute, and often counterintuitive tips, you'll learn to master the 11 People Skills that will get you more of what you want at work, at home, and in life." (Publisher's note)

Kotter, John P., 1947-
Buy-in; saving your good idea from being shot down. [by] John P. Kotter and Lorne A. Whitehead. Harvard Business Review Press 2010 192p   **650.1**
1. Creative ability 2. Public relations
ISBN 978-1-4221-5729-9

LC 2010016497
"This book explains how to protect a good idea and win support for it. The authors welcome naysayers, nitpickers, and handwringers into the room during the discussion, because they show you in this book how to respond to the unfair attacks to find success. Readers learn about the four attack strategies—death by delay, confusion, fear mongering, and character assassination—and how to show respect for all and use simple, clear, and common-sense responses. . . . This book helps you gain the upper hand by giving you practical responses to more than 24 generic attacks that people often use to shoot down good ideas." T + D

Kramer, Andrea S.
Breaking through bias; communication techniques for women to succeed at work. Andrea S. Kramer and Alton B. Harris. Bibliomotion, Inc. 2016 256 p. (hardcover : alk. paper) $27.95   **650.1**
1. Vocational guidance 2. Business communication 3. Women in the workplace 4. Sex discrimination 5. Women -- Communication 6. Vocational guidance for women 7. Stereotypes (Social psychology) 8. Communication in management -- Sex differences 9. Communication in organizations -- Sex differences
ISBN 9781629561042

LC 2015040059
This book, by Andrea S. Kramer and Alton B. Harris, "explains that it is the stereotypes about women, men, work, leadership, and family that hold women back, and it presents an integrated set of communication techniques that women can use to avoid the discriminatory consequences of these stereotypes." (Publisher's note)

"In addition to providing intelligent guidance, it reminds us all that we have a long way to go when it comes to achieving gender equality in the workplace." Booklist

Includes bibliographical references and index

Kreamer, Anne
Risk/reward; why intelligent leaps and daring choices are the best career moves you can make. by Anne Kreamer. Random House Inc. 2015 224 p. (hardback) $26   **650.1**
1. Career changes 2. Success in business 3. Risk-

taking (Psychology) 4. Risk management 5. Career development

ISBN 1400067987; 9781400067985

LC 2014046074

In this book, author Anne Kreamer "makes the compelling case that embracing risk is essential to managing a twenty-first-century career. Risk-taking isn't just for entrepreneurs, nor does it require working on a figurative tight-rope. Rather, Kreamer says, conscious, consistent, and modest risk-taking can help us become more able to recognize opportunity when it appears, and more likely to seize the chance to make the right change at the right moment." (Publisher's note)

"Well-written with intriguing findings, this quick and relevant read is recommended for public libraries and career collections." LJ

Includes bibliographical references

Licht, Aliza

Leave Your Mark; Land Your Dream Job. Kill it in Your Career. Rock Social Media. Aliza Licht. Grand Central Publishing 2015 259 p. (hardback) $26 **650.1**

1. Success 2. Vocational guidance 3. Social media 4. Career development

ISBN 1455584142; 9781455584147

LC 2014049281

In this book, author Aliza Licht, "shares advice, inspiration, and a healthy dose of real talk. . . . She delivers personal and professional guidance for people just starting their careers and for people who are well on their way. With a particular emphasis on communicating and building your personal brand." (Publisher's note)

McCormack, Mark H.

What they don't teach you at Harvard Business School. Bantam Bks. 1984 256p hardcover o.p. pa $16.95 **650.1**

1. Success 2. Management

ISBN 0-553-34583-4 pa

LC 84-45172

McCormack's firm, the International Management Group, merchandises professional sports figures and markets the international television rights to sporting events. In this book, McCormack offers advice on business management.

Mohr, Tara

Playing big; find your voice, your mission, your message. by Tara Sophia Mohr. Gotham Books 2014 304 p. (hardcover) $27 **650.1**

1. Success 2. Women -- Psychology 3. Self-help techniques 4. Success in business 5. Self-actualization (Psychology)

ISBN 1594206074; 9781594206078

LC 2014021945

This book by Tara Mohr "provides real, practical tools to help women quiet self-doubt, identify their callings, 'unhook' from praise and criticism, unlearn counterproductive good girl habits, and begin taking bold action. The book offers tools to help every woman play bigger--whether she's an executive, community volunteer, artist, or stay-at-home mom." (Publisher's note)

"Recommended for women who have good ideas but are unsure of themselves or how to implement their innovative concepts. A useful book for public libraries and those with strong feminist or career collections." LJ

Includes bibliographical references

Newport, Cal

Deep work; rules for focused success in a distracted world. Cal Newport. Grand Central Publishing 2016 304 p. (hardback) $28 **650.1**

1. Attention 2. Distraction (Psychology) 3. Success 4. Cognition 5. Distraction 6. Mental work

ISBN 9781455586691

LC 2015032646

This book, by Cal Newport, "instead of arguing distraction is bad, . . . celebrates the power of its opposite. Dividing this book into two parts, he first makes the case that in almost any profession, cultivating a deep work ethic will produce massive benefits. He then presents a rigorous training regimen, presented as a series of four 'rules,' for transforming your mind and habits to support this skill." (Publisher's note)

"It's tempting to blow off the message as the complaints of an admitted non-technophile, but Newport's disarming self-awareness... and emphasis on a meaningful work practice that's 'rich with productivity and meaning' makes for an excellent lesson in focusing on quality rather than quantity at work." Pub Wkly

Includes bibliographical references and index

Power, Katherine

The career code; Must-Know Rules for a Strategic, Stylish, and Self-Made Career. Hillary Kerr, Katherine Power. Abrams Image 2016 168 p. illustrations $19.95 **650.1**

1. Success in business

ISBN 9781419718021

LC 2015949324

In this book, authors Hillary Kerr and Katherine Power "bring you the Everygirl's guide for creating your own professional success, on every level, flawlessly. . . . Chapters include advice on résumé building, dressing for the job you want, and how to effectively communicate at work—even with the most difficult colleagues—all done with the Who What Wear girls' practical and polished signature style." (Publisher's note)

"This savvy, smart guide will benefit professionals at all career stages." LJ

RoAne, Susan

How to work a room; the ultimate guide to making lasting connections, in person and online. Susan RoAne. William Morrow 2014 xxviii, 370 p.p illustrations (pbk.) $15.99 **650.1**

1. Public relations 2. Business etiquette 3. Business entertaining 4. Interpersonal relations

ISBN 0062295349; 9780062295347

LC 2007935900

This book, by Susan RoAne, "is the fully revised and updated edition of the ground-breaking self-help book on improving communicating and socializing skills in business and life. [It] lays down the fundamentals for savvy socializing, whether at a party, a conference, or even communicating online." (Publisher's note)

Includes bibliographical references (p. [349]-354) and index

Samit, Jay

Disrupt you! master personal transformation, seize opportunity, and thrive in the era of endless innovation. Jay Samit. Flatiron Books 2015 304 p. (hardback) $27.99 **650.1**

1. Decision making 2. Success in business 3. Creative ability in business 4. Technological innovations -- Economic aspects

ISBN 1250059372; 9781250059376

LC 2015017121

In this book, author Jay Samit "describes the unique method he has used to invent new markets and expand established businesses. . . . Incorporating stories from his own experience and anecdotes from other innovators and disruptive businesses-including Richard Branson, Steve Jobs, Elon Musk, YouTube, Circ du Soleil, Odor Eaters, Iams, Silly Putty, and many more-Samit shows how personal transformation can reap entrepreneurial and professional rewards." (Publisher's note)

"Throughout, Samit incorporates elements of his own success story as well as those of prominent figures such as actor Jim Carrey, Benihana founder Hiroaki Aoki, and Zappos CEO Tony Hsieh. Samit closes with a motivational 'Self-Disruptor's Manifesto.' For readers seeking to get more out of their lives and careers, Samit is a wise teacher with valuable lessons to impart." Pub Wkly

Shell, G. Richard

Springboard; launching your personal search for success. G. Richard Shell. Portfolio/Penguin 2013 320 p. $26.95 **650.1**

1. Success 2. Vocational guidance 3. Satisfaction 4. Job satisfaction 5. Self-realization

ISBN 1591845475; 9781591845478

LC 2013017451

Author G. Richard Shell "offers a guide to a more fruitful life. . . . The reader learns about developing his or her own definition of success. . . . Citing research on happiness and wealth, as well as anecdotes and spiritual wisdom, Shell concludes that meaningful work--i.e., work that uses your talents, 'ignites you emotionally,' and is financially rewarding, in addition to building health and strong relationships--is the true measure of success." (Publishers Weekly)

Includes bibliographical references and index

Smith, Larry R., 1943-

No fears, no excuses; what you need to do to have a great career. Larry Smith. Houghton Mifflin Harcourt 2016 272 p. (hardback) $26 **650.1**

1. Self-realization 2. Vocational guidance 3. Career development

ISBN 9780544663336

LC 2015037676

This book, by Larry Smith, offers "a provocative new approach to discovering your true calling in life and achieving not just a good career, but a great one. . . . In his straightforward, no-nonsense approach, Smith itemizes and dis-

misses all the usual excuses, fears, and worries that people hide behind when trying to find their true direction." (Publisher's note)

"This compelling book offers a highly readable blueprint for career success. Readers willing to invest the time and effort required to finding their true direction and achieving their goals will appreciate." LJ

Sull, Donald

Simple Rules; How to Thrive in a Complex World. by Donald Sull, Kathleen Eisenhardt. Houghton Mifflin Harcourt 2015 256 p. $27 **650.1**

1. Conduct of life

ISBN 0544409906; 9780544409903

LC 2014044513

This book, by by Donald Sull and Kathleen Eisenhardt, is "a hands-on tool to achieve some of our most pressing personal and professional objectives, from overcoming insomnia to becoming a better manager or a smarter investor. Simple rules can help solve some of our most urgent social challenges. . . . Drawing on more than a decade of rigorous research, the authors provide a clear framework for developing effective rules and making them better over time." (Publisher's note)

"Feeling info-ed out? Sull, a senior lecturer at the MIT Sloan School of Management and a global expert on market strategy and execution, and Eisenhardt, professor of strategy and organization at Stanford University, offer a framework for the creation of a few simple rules to manage it all." LJ

Vaden, Rory

Procrastinate on purpose; 5 permissions to multiply your time. Rory Vaden. Perigee Trade 2014 236 p. illustrations (hardback) $24.95 **650.1**

1. Time management 2. Labor productivity

ISBN 0399170626; 9780399170621

LC 2014040004

This book, by Rory Vaden, offers a "high-energy approach and can-do spirit to the most nagging problem in our professional lives: stalled productivity. Millions are overworked, organizationally challenged, or have a motivation issue that's holding them back. Vaden presents a simple yet powerful paradigm that will set readers free to do their best work--on time and without stress and anxiety." (Publisher's note)

Includes bibliographical references and index

Verveer, Melanne

Fast forward; how women can achieve power and purpose. Melanne Verveer and Kim K. Azzarelli; foreword by Hillary Rodham Clinton. Houghton Mifflin Harcourt 2015 256 p. 8 plates; color illustrations (hardback) $24 **650.1**

1. Success 2. Businesswomen 3. Work-life balance 4. Women executives 5. Success in business 6. Women in the professions 7. Women in economic development

ISBN 0544527194; 9780544527195; 9780544664357

LC 2015019683

This book by Melanne Veveer and Kim K. Azzarelli, "through interviews with a network of more than seventy trailblazing women, . . . shows women how to accelerate their growing economic power and combine it with purpose to find both success and meaning in their lives. Through clear, practical advice and personal stories of women around the world -- including Hillary Clinton, Geena Davis, Christine Lagarde, and Diane von Furstenberg -- Fast Forward shows every woman how to know her power." (Publisher's note)

Wasmund, Shaa

Do less, get more; how to work smart and live life your way. Shaa Wasmund. Portfolio Penguin 2015 218 p. $27.95 **650.1**

1. Success 2. Time management 3. Success in business
ISBN 1591847168; 9781591847168

LC 2015295904

This book, by Sháá Wasmund, argues that "when you stop trying to do so much, you get so much more done. . . . [The author] reveals that when we embrace a 'less is more' attitude, we can appreciate all the good things we already have and find the courage to prune the nonessentials. And then we can find the space in which to pursue exciting new opportunities." (Publisher's note)

"Wasmund ultimately brings her reader to a place where they believe, along with her, that the 'things that will create your best life are perfectly attainable if you are willing to stop doing what's not important and start prioritizing what is.' Sage and sane advice." Booklist

Includes bibliographical references (pages 216-217)

Do get

Webb, Caroline

How to have a good day; harnessing the power of behavioral science to transform our working lives. Caroline Webb. Crown Business 2016 368 p. (hardback) $26 **650.1**

1. Neuropsychology 2. Job satisfaction 3. Industrial psychology 4. Psychology, Industrial 5. Performance -- Psychological aspects 6. Job satisfaction -- Psychological aspects
ISBN 9781447276517; 9780553419634

LC 2015026815

In this book, "economist and former McKinsey partner Caroline Webb shows readers how to use recent findings from behavioral economics, psychology, and neuroscience to transform our approach to everyday working life. Advances in these behavioral sciences are giving us ever better understanding of how our brains work, why we make the choices we do, and what it takes for us to be at our best." (Publisher's note)

Includes bibliographical references and index.

Williams, Joan, 1952-

What works for women at work; four patterns working women need to know. Joan C. Williams, Rachel Dempsey; [foreword by] Anne-Marie Slaughter. NYU Press 2014 384 p. (hardback) $24.95 **650.1**

1. Gender role 2. Work environment 3. Women -- Employment 4. Women -- Psychology 5. Sex role in the work environment
ISBN 1479835455; 9781479835454

LC 2013029819

This book, by Joan C. Williams and Rachel Dempsey, "is a comprehensive and insightful guide for mastering office

politics as a woman. . . . Distilling over 35 years of research, Williams and Dempsey offer four crisp patterns that affect working women: Prove-It-Again!, the Tightrope, the Maternal Wall, and the Tug of War. Each represents different challenges and requires different strategies—which is why women need to be savvier than men to survive and thrive in high-powered careers." (Publisher's note)

"[F]illed with street-smart advice and plain old savvy about the way life works in corporate America." Booklist

Includes bibliographical references and index

650.14   Success in obtaining jobs and promotions

Berger, Lauren

All work, no pay; finding an internship, building your resume, making connections, and gaining job experience. Lauren Berger. Ten Speed Press 2012 xii, 194 p.p $12.99 **650.14**

1. Job hunting 2. Internship programs 3. Employees -- Training 4. Vocational guidance
ISBN 1607741687; 9781607741688

LC 2011034540

This book is a "guide [that] reveals insider secrets to scoring the perfect internship, building invaluable connections, boosting transferable skills, and ultimately moving toward your dream career." Topics include "internship opportunities," writing "effective resumes and cover letters," and "network[ing] like a pro." (Publisher's note)

Includes bibliographical references and index.

Citrin, James M.

The career playbook; essential advice for today's aspiring young professional. by James M. Citrin. Random House Inc 2015 241 p. illustrations $14 **650.14**

1. Job hunting 2. Success in business 3. Vocational guidance
ISBN 0553446967; 9780553446968

LC 2015288094

This book, by James M. Citrin, "offers recent graduates and aspiring young professionals actionable advice for excelling. From his practical tips on generating valuable introductions, nailing interviews, and negotiating compensation to strategic advice on the arc of a career, the importance of relationships, how to cultivate a mentor, and knowing when to change jobs or industries, Citrin provides an invaluable guide to the most urgent questions." (Publisher's note)

Kay, Andrea

This is how to get your next job; an inside look at what employers really want. Andrea Kay; foreword by Richard Nelson Bolles. American Management Association 2013 245 p. (pbk.) $16 **650.14**

1. Job hunting 2. Vocational guidance 3. Career development 4. Employment interviewing
ISBN 0814432212; 9780814432211

LC 2012051814

In this book, Andrea Kay "offers practical advice for the job seeker based on her expertise as a career consultant. The first chapter, 'You Are What You Seem,' lists 17 characteristics employers look for, such as consistent, stable behavior; clear, critical thinking; and initiative. Her approach highlights multiple ways to reassess strengths and weaknesses and offers readers the opportunity to glean the employer's perspective." (Library Journal)

Mackay, Harvey

Use your head to get your foot in the door; job search secrets no one else will tell you. Portfolio 2010 329p il $25.95; pa $16   650.14

1. Job hunting

ISBN 978-1-59184-321-4; 1-59184-321-9; 978-1-59184-343-6 pa; 1-59184-343-X pa

LC 2009039791

"This collection of job search tips by Mackay . . . [comes] complete with humorous examples and 'Quickie' one-page stories that illustrate his main points. Don't let the cover or any worry about his sense of humor dissuade you: this is a very useful book. The short chapters with descriptive titles make it easy to navigate, and Mackay offers tips—from changing your attitude to getting hired—both for those currently employed but wishing to position themselves better in their current companies and for those who are out of work." Libr J

Includes bibliographical references

Raskin, Donna

The **dirty** little secrets of getting your dream job; Don Raskin. Regan Arts 2016 192 p. illustrations (paperback) $22.95   650.14

1. Job hunting 2. Vocational guidance

ISBN 1942872763; 9781942872764

LC 2015951639

This book, by Don Raskin, "offers all the necessary tools for navigating the tough job market and securing your dream job. Don Raskin owns and operates . . . an advertising and marketing agency in New York City. During his twenty-five years at the agency he has interviewed hundreds of new college graduates for positions within his agency and has placed a strong emphasis on entry-level recruitment for positions in creative, account management, traffic, and production." (Publisher's note)

Selingo, Jeffrey J.

There Is Life After College; What Parents and Students Should Know About Navigating School to Prepare for the Jobs of Tomorrow. by Jeffrey J. Selingo. HarperCollins 2016 288 p. $25.99   650.14

1. College graduates -- Vocational guidance

ISBN 006238886X; 9780062388865

LC 2015046199

This book, by Jeffrey J. Selingo, "offers students, parents, and even recent graduates the practical advice and insight they need to jumpstart their careers. . . . Selingo answers key questions—Why is the transition to post-college life so difficult for many recent graduates? How can graduates market themselves to employers that are reluctant to provide on-the-job training? . . . —and offers a practical step-by-step plan every young professional can follow." (Publisher's note)

"Levelheaded advice for students and parents on the best path to take from high school to employment." Kirkus

Includes bibliographical references and index.

Yate, Martin

Knock 'em dead cover letters; Martin Yate. Adams Media Corp 2012 320 p.   650.14

1. Job hunting 2. Cover letters 3. Resumes (Employment)

ISBN 9781440536809

LC 2012025589

In this book, author Martin Yate "shows you how to dramatically increase your chances of landing an interview with a dynamic cover letter. Using his 25+ years of experience, he has built a practical, easy-to-follow approach to creating every type of letter you will use in a job search. Inside this book, you'll find all-new examples of cover letters and learn how to use his proven methods." (Publisher's note)

Knock 'em dead resumes; Resumes that knock 'em dead. Martin Yate, CPC. Adams Media Corp 2014 320 p. (pb) $14.99   650.14

1. Resumes (Employment) 2. Résumés (Employment)

ISBN 1440579075; 9781440579073

LC 2014019106

In this book on resume writing, author Martin Yate "shows you how to beat the competition. Using his 25+ years of experience, he has built a practical, easy-to-follow approach to writing killer resumes. This new edition of the perennially bestselling guide includes cutting-edge advice on the latest and most effective resume-writing tactics and has completely new sample resumes." (Publisher's note)

652.1   Penmanship

Trubek, Anne

The **History** and Uncertain Future of Handwriting; by Anne Trubek. St. Martin's Press 2016 192 p. illustrations (some color) $26   652.1

1. Handwriting

ISBN 1620402157; 9781620402153

In this book, author Anne Trubek "uncovers the long and significant impact handwriting has had on culture and humanity--from the first recorded handwriting on the clay tablets of the Sumerians some four thousand years ago and the invention of the alphabet as we know it, to the rising value of handwritten manuscripts today. Each innovation over the millennia has threatened existing standards and entrenched interests." (Publisher's note)

"An absorbing and concise book that will engage readers who are curious about communications." LJ

Includes bibliographical references (pages 157-166) and index.

657   Accounting

Shim, Jae K.

Accounting handbook; by Joel G. Siegel, Jae K. Shim, Nick Dauber, and Anique A. Qureshi. 6th edition. Barrons Educational Series Inc 2015 1062 p. $39.99 **657**

1. Accounting 2. Accounting -- Handbooks, manuals, etc

ISBN 0764166573; 9780764166570

LC 2014009657

This reference book, by Joel G. Siegel, Jae K. Shim, Nick Dauber, and Anique A. Qureshi, is an accounting handbook. "An opening overview of financial accounting describes financial statements and presents details on financial reporting requirements and compliance, and U.S. GAAP (Generally Accepted Accounting Principles) and IFRS (International Financial Reporting Standards). Chapters that follow cover cost management, as well as taxation forms and their preparation." (Publisher's note)

Includes bibliographical references and index

658 General management

Collins, James C.

Good to great; why some companies make the leap, and others don't. {by} Jim Collins. Harper-Business 2001 300p il $27.50 **658**

1. Leadership 2. Management

ISBN 0-06-662099-6

LC 2001-24818

"Starting with every company that ever appeared in the Fortune 500, Collins identifies 11 great ones and looks for similarities among them, and what he finds will both surprise and fascinate anyone involved in management." Booklist

Includes bibliographical references

Drucker, Peter F.

The **Drucker** lectures; essential lessons on management, society, and economy. edited and with an introduction by Rick Wartzman. McGraw-Hill 2010 266p $29.95; ebook $29.95 **658**

1. Management

ISBN 978-0-07-170045-0; 0-07-170045-5; 978-0-07-175950-2 ebook; 0-07-175950-6 ebook

LC 2010484567

This book presents thirty-three of Peter F. Drucker's speeches and talks delivered at professional gatherings and in the classroom.

"From his concern with continuous and full employment in the 1950s to globalization, nonprofit management, and the future of the corporation in the early 2000s, these lectures reflect a Drucker that many scholars and practitioners knew, but they also reveal new insights into the currency . . . of his thinking." Choice

Includes bibliographical references

Horstman, Mark

The **effective** manager; Mark Horstman. John Wiley & Sons Inc. 2016 208 p. (hardback) $28 **658**

1. Management 2. Executive ability 3. Personnel management 4. Teams in the workplace 5. Supervision of employees 6. Teams in the workplace -- Management

ISBN 1119244609; 9781119244608

LC 2016018227

This book, by Mark Horstman, "is a hands-on practical guide to great management at every level. . . . First, you'll identify what 'effective management' actually looks like: can you get the job done at a high level? Do you attract and retain top talent without burning them out? Then you'll dig into the four critical behaviors that make a manager great, and learn how to adjust your own behavior to be the leader your team needs." (Publisher's note)

Michelli, Joseph A.

Driven to delight; delivering world-class customer experience the Mercedes-Benz way. Joseph Michelli. McGraw-Hill 2016 304 p. illustrations (alk. paper) $27 **658**

1. Customer services 2. Automobile industry 3. DaimlerChrysler 4. Mercedes automobiles 5. Automobile industry and trade -- Germany -- Management 6. Automobile industry and trade -- Customer services -- Germany

ISBN 007180630X; 9780071806305

LC 2015029398

In this book, author Joseph Michelli "shares the greatest customer-driven insights behind one of the most iconic brand names in the world: Mercedes-Benz USA. . . . It reveals the action plan Mercedes-Benz USA used to catapult the company to first place rankings in national customer satisfaction studies while at the same time growing sales and profits." (Publisher's note)

Thompson, Mark

Now, build a great business! 7 ways to maximize your profits in any market. [by] Mark Thompson and Brian Tracy; foreword by Frances Hesselbein. American Management Association 2011 xxii, 228p $24.95 **658**

1. Marketing 2. Leadership

ISBN 978-0-8144-1697-6; 0-8144-1697-7

LC 2010030612

The authors "offer easy, tried-and-true ways to think about and plan organizational growth, especially in tough economic times. In seven steps (with a chapter devoted to each), the authors identify sustainable strategies for attracting customers and recruiting better leaders. They share seven simple questions that leaders ask themselves and provide helpful checklist exercises on a variety of key topics including creating a great business plan, designing an effective marketing plan, and creating a good customer experience." Publ Wkly

Wall Street journal

The **Wall** Street Journal essential guide to management; lasting lessons from the best leadership minds of our time. Harper Business 2010 xxvii, 207p pa $16.99 **658**

1. Management

ISBN 978-0-06-184033-3

LC 2010-2879

The author "lays out in helpful order and understandable prose what he considers the best practices for a good manager to follow; especially instructive are his discussions of 'six different styles that leaders use to motivate others.'. . . . For serious consideration for any library business collection." Booklist

Includes bibliographical references

Wooldridge, Adrian

Masters of management; how the business gurus and their ideas have changed the world--for better and for worse. HarperBusiness 2011 446p $29.99 **658**

1. Management

ISBN 978-0-06-177113-2; 9780061771132

LC 2011015690

First published 1996 by Times Bks. with title: The witch doctors

"The core of the book is a solid examination of the effects of entrepreneurship, globalization, and the free-agency economy on corporate governance. Wooldridge offers a balanced look at how business schools have spawned a guru industry that offers a gamut of theories on learning, innovation, and strategy. Peter Drucker, Tom Peters, and the 'Journo-Gurus' (Thomas Friedman, Malcolm Gladwell, and Chris Anderson) receive focused attention as the main influences in contemporary theory. . . . This is one of the best overviews of management theory in the 20th century. It is written in a clear and accessible style that will appeal to both MBA students and the general reader." Libr J

658.02   Management of enterprises of specific sizes and scope

Sarillo, Nick, 1963-

A slice of the pie; how to build a big little business. Nick Sarillo. Portfolio 2012 272 p. $26.95 **658.02**

1. Small business 2. Entrepreneurship 3. Business planning 4. Success in business 5. Industrial management 6. Employees -- Training of 7. New business enterprises

ISBN 1591844584; 9781591844587

LC 2012019321

In this book, Nick Sarillo, "founder and CEO of Nick's Pizza & Pub, offers a personal account of being a small business owner, sharing his perspectives, challenges he's faced and overcome, and the way he's transformed his company into a thriving success. More than a mere autobiography, it's also the story of his company and the people he works with. Sarillo expounds on the paths that he has chosen and why, what those choices have produced, and where the results have led." (Publishers Weekly)

Strauss, Steven D.

The small business bible; everything you need to know to succeed in your small business. Steven D. Strauss. Wiley 2012 xiii, 578 p.p (pbk.) $22.95 **658.02**

1. Small business 2. New business enterprises 3. New business enterprises -- United States 4. Small business -- United States -- Finance 5. Small business -- United States -- Management

ISBN 1118135946; 9781118135945

LC 2011042848

This book, by Steven D. Strauss, is a "comprehensive guide to small business success. . . . It shows you what really works (and what doesn't!) and includes scores of tips, insider information, stories, and proven secrets of success. . . . This Third Edition includes entirely new chapters devoted to social media, mobility and apps, and new trends in online discounting and group buying that are vital to small business owners everywhere." (Publisher's note)

658.1   Organization and financial management

Barringer, Bruce

Launching a Business; The First 100 Days. Bruce Barringer. Business Expert Pr 2013 254 p. illustrations (Entrepreneurship and small business management collection) $43.95 **658.1**

1. Management 2. Entrepreneurship 3. New business enterprises

ISBN 1606493973; 9781606493977

This book by Bruce R. Barringer "focuses on the tasks that a new business owner must complete in the first 100 days of launching a business. . . . Examples include securing the proper business licenses and permits, setting up a bookkeeping system, negotiating a lease, buying insurance, entering into contracts with vendors, recruiting and hiring employees, making the first sale, and so on." (Publisher's note)

"[Offers] tactical advice on things important during early launch of a business that an experienced founder should know but a novice likely will not." Choice

Duffy, Scott

Launch! the critical ninety days from idea to market. Scott Duffy. Portfolio Hardcover 2013 240 p. (hardback) $26.95 **658.1**

1. New products 2. Entrepreneurship 3. New business enterprises

ISBN 1591846064; 9781591846062

LC 2013039077

In this book, entrepreneur Scott Duffy "has developed a practical approach for turning your big idea into a thriving venture by focusing on the crucial period of 90 days immediately before, during, and after starting your business. Based on his own experiences, . . . Duffy . . . emphasizes the personal side of entrepreneurship, including balancing finances, relationships, and your health." (Publisher's note)

"A breezy handbook for entrepreneurs on how to launch a new business, product or service. . . . Solid advice for novice risk-takers." Kirkus

Includes bibliographical references and index

Guillebeau, Chris, 1979-

The $100 startup; how to fire your boss and create a new future. by Chris Guillebeau. Crown Business 2012 xviii, 285 p.p illustrations (hbk.) $23 **658.1**

1. Entrepreneurship 2. Vocational guidance 3. New business enterprises -- Management

ISBN 0307951529; 9780307951526

LC 2012003093

This book, by Chris Guillebeau, seeks to show "how to lead of life of adventure, meaning and purpose--and earn a good living. . . . . [The author presents] the most valuable lessons from those who've learned how to turn what they do into a gateway to self-fulfillment. It's all about finding the intersection between your 'expertise'-- even if you don't consider it such--and what other people will pay for." (Publisher's note)

One hundred dollar startup

Johnson, Victoria M.

Grant writing 101; everything you need to start raising funds today. McGraw-Hill 2011 269p pa $20; ebook $20 **658.1**

1. Fund raising 2. Grants-in-aid

ISBN 978-0-07-175018-9 pa; 978-0-07-175018-9 ebook

LC 2010039599

This guide to grant writing offers "ten tactics for writing a compelling proposal; tips for finding the best grantor for your needs; important components of various types of grants; [and] next steps for when you're approved." Publisher's note

Karlgaard, Rich

Team Genius; The New Science of High-Performing Organizations. Rich Karlgaard and Michael S. Malone. HarperCollins 2015 304 p. $27.99 **658.1**

1. Management 2. Teams in the workplace

ISBN 006230254X; 9780062302540

This book by Rich Karlgaard and Michael S. Malone "shows managers and executives that the planning, design, and management of great teams no longer have to be a black art. It explores solutions to essential questions that could spell the difference between success and obsolescence. Do you know how to reorganize your subpar teams to turn them into top performers? Can you identify which of the top-performing teams in your company are reaching the end of their life span?" (Publisher's note)

"Gems of insight and wisdom are offered here, such as the need for balance between creative and analytical skills to maintain a team's forward momentum, but not all readers will persevere to find and employ them. For fans of business history and theory." LJ

Kawasaki, Guy

The **art** of the start 2.0; the time-tested, battle-hardened guide for anyone starting anything. by Guy Kawasaki. Penguin Group USA 2015 326 p. illustrations $29.95 **658.1**

1. Success in business

ISBN 1591847842; 9781591847847

This book, by Guy Kawasaki, is a "guide to launching and making your new product, service, or idea a success. . . . Guy understands the seismic changes in business over the last decade: . . . Many of the basics of getting established have become easier, cheaper, and more democratic. Business plans are no longer necessary. Social media has replaced PR and advertising as the key method of promotion." (Publisher's note)

"An excellent guide packed with valuable information for students, would-be entrepreneurs, and practicing entrepreneurs." LJ

Kidder, David S.

The **Startup** playbook; secrets of the fastest-growing startups from their founding entrepreneurs / David S. Kidder. David S. Kidder. Chronicle Books 2013 292 p. $29.99 **658.1**

1. Entrepreneurs 2. Entrepreneurship 3. New business enterprises 4. New business enterprises -- Management

ISBN 1452105049; 9781452105048

LC 2012019684

This book by David S. Kidder "shares the hard-hitting experiences of some of the world's most influential entrepreneurs and CEOs, revealing their most closely held advice. Face-to-face interviews with 40 founders give readers key insights into what it took to build PayPal, LinkedIn, AOL, TED, Flickr, and many others into household names. Special sections include topics ranging from how to select the right idea to pursue to finding funding and overcoming inevitable obstacles." (Publisher's note)

Wasserman, Noam

The **founder's** dilemmas; anticipating and avoiding the pitfalls that can sink a startup. Noam Wasserman. Princeton University Press 2012 p. cm. **658.1**

1. Management 2. Entrepreneurship 3. New business enterprises 4. New business enterprises -- Management

ISBN 9780691149134

LC 2011037954

This book, by Noam Wasserman, is part of the Kauffman Foundation Series on Innovation and Entrepreneurship. "Often downplayed in the . . . starting up a new business venture is . . . [the question] should they go it alone, or bring in co-founders, hires, and investors to help build the business? . . . Bad decisions at the inception of a promising venture lay the foundations for its eventual ruin. . . . Wasserman reveals the common pitfalls founders face and how to avoid them." (Publisher's note)

Includes bibliographical references and index

658.11 Initiation of business enterprises

Buelow, Beth L.

The **Introvert** Entrepreneur; Amplify Your Strengths and Create Success on Your Own Terms. by Beth Buelow. Penguin Group USA 2015 272 p. $15.95; (ebook) $16.99 **658.11**

1. Entrepreneurship 2. Success in business

ISBN 0399174834; 9780399174834; 9781101992647

In this book, author Beth Buelow "shows readers how to harness their natural gifts (including curiosity, independence, and a love of research) and counteract their challenges (such as an aversion to networking and self-promotion). She addresses a wide range of topics . . . informed by interviews with introverts who have created successful businesses without compromising their core personality." (Publisher's note)

"This is a thoughtful, kind, and helpful guide for all those who are looking to strike out on their own, but concerned that their need for alone time may get in the way." Pub Wkly

Includes bibliographical references (pages 245-248)

and index.

658.15   Financial management

Goldfayn, Alex

The **revenue** growth habit; the simple art of growing your business by 15% in 15 minutes per day. Alex Goldfayn. Wiley 2015 256 p. illustrations (hardback) $25   **658.15**

1. Management 2. Strategic planning 3. Revenue management
ISBN 1119084067; 9781119084068

LC 2015013431

In this book, author Alex Goldfayn "shows how to grow your organization by 15% or more in 15 minutes or less per day without spending a penny of your money. . . . [He] shows how to request and collect testimonials and how to communicate these testimonials to grow your business. You will discover how to write powerful case studies, ask for (and get!) referrals, grow your lists, and send a revenue-growing newsletter." (Publisher's note)

McKeever, Mike

How to write a business plan; Mike P. McKeever. 13th edition Nolo 2016 pbk $34.99   **658.15**

1. Small business 2. Business planning 3. New business enterprises
ISBN 9781413323191; 1413323197

LC 2016026296

"This bestselling, newly updated book contains clear, step-by-step instructions to make realistic financial projections, develop effective marketing strategies and refine your overall business goals. . . . Updated 13th Edition includes the latest laws and banking regulations that could affect businesses and their investors, plus an expanded collection of resources for putting together the best plan." (Publisher's note)

658.3   Personnel management (Human resource management)

Elton, Chester

All in; how the best managers create a culture of belief and drive big results. Adrian Gostick and Chester Elton. Free Press 2012 viii, 243 p.p (hbk.) $25   **658.3**

1. Leadership 2. Executive ability 3. Personnel management 4. Corporate culture 5. Employee motivation 6. Organizational behavior
ISBN 1451659822; 9781451659825

LC 2011045590

Author Adrian Gostick answers today's leadership questions, such as why are managers "able to get their employees to commit wholeheartedly to their culture and give that extra push that leads to outstanding results? . . . [The author presents] a simple seven-step road map for creating a culture of belief: define a burning platform; create a customer focus; develop agility; share everything; partner with your talent;

root for each other; and establish clear accountability." (Publisher's note)

Includes bibliographical references and index.

Hallowell, Edward M.

Shine; using brain science to get the best from your people. Harvard Business Review Press 2011 197p il $26.95   **658.3**

1. Management 2. Job satisfaction 3. Interpersonal relations 4. Motivation (Psychology)
ISBN 978-1-59139-923-0; 1-59139-923-8

LC 2010024950

"Edward Hallowell draws on brain science, performance research, and his own experience helping people maximize their potential to present a . . . process for getting the best from your people." Publisher's note

Includes bibliographical references

Kelly, Matthew

The **dream** manager. Hyperion 2007 158p $19.95   **658.3**

1. Employee morale 2. Personnel management 3. Motivation (Psychology)
ISBN 978-1-4013-0370-9; 1-4013-0370-6

LC 2007-13597

This "business fable extols the virtues of helping those working for and with you to achieve their dreams. In this way . . . managers can boost morale and control turnover. . . . This one's sure to appeal to business readers." Libr J

Tracy, Brian

Full engagement! inspire, motivate, and bring out the best in your people. American Management Association 2011 226p $22   **658.3**

1. Employee morale 2. Personnel management 3. Motivation (Psychology)
ISBN 978-0-8144-1689-1; 0-8144-1689-6

LC 2010048293

The author "shows managers how they can supercharge their employees' efforts." Publisher's note

658.4   Executive management

Bock, Laszlo

Work rules! insights from inside Google that will transform how you live and lead. Laszlo Bock. Twelve 2015 416 p. illustrations (hardback) $30   **658.4**

1. Leadership 2. Management 3. Google (Firm) 4. Corporate culture 5. Google (Firm) -- Management
ISBN 1455554790; 9781455554799

LC 2014020843

This book by Laszlo Bock explains "how Google hires and manages its employees. . . . The company aims to 'keep people in an environment of freedom, creativity, and play.' However, there are rules underlying this culture, and values underlying these rules, to each of which Bock devotes one of the book's 14 chapters. Its bedrock is trust in the fundamental goodness of people." (Library Journal)

"Bock makes a persuasive case for ceding power to individual employees and teams. For visionary managers." LJ

Includes bibliographical references and index

Bolman, Lee G.

How great leaders think; the art of reframing. Lee G. Bolman, Terrence E. Deal. Jossey-Bass 2014 228 p. (hardback) $30   **658.4**

1. Leadership 2. Thought and thinking 3. Organizational change

ISBN 1118140982; 9781118140987

LC 2014013595

This book "uses compelling, contemporary examples to show how more complex thinking is the key to better leadership.[Authors Lee] Bolman and [Terrence] Deal's influential four-frame model of leadership and organizations . . . offers leaders an accessible guide for understanding four major aspects of organizational life: structure, people, politics, and culture." (Publisher's note)

Chan, Ronald W.

Behind the Berkshire Hathaway curtain; lessons from Warren Buffett's top business leaders. John Wiley & Sons 2010 178p il $24.95; ebook $16.99   **658.4**

1. Success 2. Business 3. Management 4. Executive ability 5. Financiers 6. Berkshire Hathaway Inc.

ISBN 978-0-470-56062-4; 0-470-56062-2; 978-0-470-64297-9 ebook

LC 2010281776

"Chan shares some of the business philosophies, strategies, and mindsets learned from exclusive interviews with leaders of Buffett's Berkshire Hathaway, including David Sokol of MidAmerican Energy, Cathy Baron Tamraz of Business Wire, Brad Kinstler of See's Candies, and Maria Gottschalk of Pampered Chef. The detailed stories of these executives' early career decisions bring to life practical lessons for personal and professional success." T + D

Chapman, Bob

Everybody matters; the extraodinary power of caring for your people like family. by Bob Chapman and Raj Sisodia. Penguin Group USA 2015 260 p. charts $27.95   **658.4**

1. Employees 2. Job satisfaction 3. Work environment

ISBN 1591847796; 9781591847793

LC 2015303330

In this book, authors Bob Chapman and Raj Sisodia "show how any organization can reject the traumatic consequences of rolling layoffs, dehumanizing rules, and hypercompetitive cultures. Once you stop treating people like functions or costs, disengaged workers begin to share their gifts and talents toward a shared future. Uninspired workers stop feeling that their jobs have no meaning. Frustrated workers stop taking their bad days out on their spouses and kids." (Publisher's note)

"Chapman is convincing in his appeal for a more human approach to management in all kinds of organizations. This inspirational read is recommended for all types of business collections." LJ

Includes bibliographical references (pages 249-253) and index.

Conant, Douglas R.

Touchpoints; creating powerful leadership connections in the smallest of moments. [by] Douglas R. Conant, Mette Norgaard. Jossey-Bass 2011 xxxi, 173p (Warren Bennis signature series) $26.95; ebook $12.99   **658.4**

1. Leadership

ISBN 978-1-1180-0435-7; 978-1-1180-7554-8 ebook

LC 2011008907

"In an engaging personal style, Doug Conant, the CEO of Campbell Soup Company, discusses a leadership philosophy that he and leadership development expert Mette Norgaard refer to as 'TouchPoints'—those daily encounters with staff, co-workers, or colleagues that leaders can use to 'touch' others in meaningful ways, such as influencing, inspiring, or providing clarity. The book highlights ways to develop that ability and ways to practice leadership in the moment." T + D

Covey, Sean

The **4** disciplines of execution; achieving your wildly important goals. Chris McChesney, Sean Covey, Jim Huling. 1st Free Press hardcover ed. Free Press 2012 xxvi, 326 p.p ill. (hbk.) $28   **658.4**

1. Leadership 2. Responsibility 3. Executive ability 4. Organization 5. Goal -- Psychology 6. Goal setting in personnel management

ISBN 145162705X; 9781451627053

LC 2012001672

Authors Chris McChesney and Sean Covey provide "a simple repeatable, and proven formula for executing on your most important strategic priorities in the midst of the whirlwind. . . . Leaders can produce breakthrough results, even when executing the strategy requires a significant change in behavior from their teams [through] focusing on the wildly important, acting on lead measures, keeping a compelling scoreboard, [and] creating a cadence of accountability." (Publisher's note)

Includes bibliographical references and index

Davidds, Yasmin

★ **Your** own terms; a woman's guide to taking charge of any negotiation. Yasmin Davidds, PsyD with Ann Bidou. American Management Association 2015 256 p. illustrations (pbk. : alk. paper) $16.95   **658.4**

1. Negotiation 2. Businesswomen 3. Negotiation in business

ISBN 9780814436028

LC 2015009457

This book, by Yasmin Davidds, with Ann Bidou, "helps women strike a balance, merging our natural strengths (collaboration, relationship building, listening) with a firm grasp of established tactics. Guidelines, stories, and exercises illuminate the psychology of negotiation and reveal how women can: control how they are perceived; eliminate self-sabotaging beliefs and behaviors; discover their personal negotiation style; . . . and set the bar high and negotiate to get there." (Publisher's note)

"This is that rare guide that matches big-picture strategy with specific advice, worksheets, and scripts. It's indispensable for women looking to effectively negotiate a salary, ca-

reer move, or new opportunity with confidence and ease."
Pub Wkly

Includes bibliographical references and index

Ferrazzi, Keith

Never eat alone and other secrets to success; one relationship at a time. Keith Ferrazzi with Tahl Raz. 1st ed.; Random House Inc 2014 379 p. $27 **658.4**

1. Interpersonal relations

ISBN 0385346654; 9780385346658

LC 2004061757

In this book, author Keith Ferrazzi "lays out the specific steps—and inner mindset—he uses to reach out to connect with the thousands of colleagues, friends, and associates on his Rolodex. . . . Ferrazzi's form of connecting to the world around him is based on generosity, helping friends connect with other friends. Ferrazzi distinguishes genuine relationship-building from the crude, desperate glad-handling usually associated with 'networking.'" (Publisher's note)

"In addition to variations on the theme of hard work, Ferrazzi offers counterintuitive perspectives that ring true: 'vulnerability... is one of the most underappreciated assets in business today'; 'too many people confuse secrecy with importance.' No one will confuse this book with its competitors" Pub Wkly

Gallo, Carmine

Talk like TED; the 9 public speaking secrets of the world's top minds. Carmine Gallo. St. Martin's Press 2014 288 p. illustrations (hardcover : alk. paper) $24.99 **658.4**

1. Public speaking 2. Business presentations

ISBN 1250041120; 9781250041128

LC 2013031049

In this book about public speaking, author Carmine Gallo "identifies the common elements that make TED Talks so successful. He offers nine secrets, including mastering the art of storytelling, being passionate about the subject matter, speaking conversationally, using humor, . . . and keeping presentations to 18 minutes. Gallo divides the lessons into three parts, focusing on the emotional, novel, and memorable." (Booklist)

"The author . . . includes successful outlines and guides to using both audio-visual aides and effective body language. Dramatic composition and vigorous presentation make this a powerful tool to improve mastery of speaking skills." Kirkus

Includes bibliographical references and index

Goleman, Daniel

Primal Leadership; Unleashing the Power of Emotional Intelligence. Daniel Goleman, Richard Boyatzis, Annie McKee. 2nd edition Harvard Business Review Press 2013 336 p. $22 **658.4**

1. Emotions 2. Management

ISBN 1422168034; 9781422168035

LC 2013018294

This book, by Daniel Goleman, Richard Boyatzis, and Annie McKee, "established 'emotional intelligence' in the business lexicon-- and made it a necessary skill for leaders. . . . This refreshed edition, with a new preface by the authors, vividly illustrates the power . . . . of leadership that is self-aware, empathic, motivating, and collaborative in a world

that is ever more economically volatile and technologically complex." (Publisher's note)

Johnson, Whitney

Disrupt yourself; putting the power of disruptive innovation to work. by Whitney Johnson. Bibliomotion 2015 208 p. illustrations (hardback) $24.95 **658.4**

1. Strategic planning 2. Success in business 3. Organizational change 4. Career changes 5. Disruptive technologies

ISBN 1629560529; 9781629560526

LC 2015019271

"As president and cofounder of Rose Park Advisors' Disruptive Innovation Fund with Clayton Christensen, Whitney Johnson used the theory of disruptive innovation to invest in publicly traded stocks and private early-stage companies. In [this book], she helps you understand how the frameworks of disruptive innovation can apply to your particular path." (Publisher's note)

"Johnson astutely highlights the value of constraints, the dangers of entitlement, and the necessity of changing plans when circumstances call for it. Her chapter on learning from failure contains particularly wise advice that everyone should embrace. In Johnson's closing chapter, she emphasizes the value of a "discovery-driven career" and the possibilities it offers. Savvy and often counterintuitive, this superb book offers the tools, mind-set guidance, and rationale for avoiding complacency and embracing a new career path." Pub Wkly

Klubeck, Martin

Why organizations struggle so hard to improve so little; overcoming organizational immaturity. Martin Klubeck, Michael Langthorne, and Donald Padgett. Praeger Pub 2010 xvi, 222 p.p ill. (hardcover : alk. paper) $34.95; (ebook) $49.00 **658.4**

1. Organizational change 2. Organizational behavior

ISBN 0313380228; 0313380236; 9780313380228; 9780313380235

LC 2009046410

This book by Martin Klubeck, Michael Langthorne, and Donald Padgett "explains the difficulties and dangers of organizational immaturity, then provides proven, effective tools and ideas for achieving change within the limitations of an immature organization. With this guide, leaders and other stakeholders will be able to determine the maturity level of an organization, get beyond prevailing myths about how change gets derailed, and identify potential areas for improvement." (Publisher's note)

Includes bibliographical references and index.

Kouzes, James M.

The **truth** about leadership; the no-fads, heart-of-the-matter facts you need to know. [by] James M. Kouzes, Barry Z. Posner. Jossey-Bass 2010 xxv, 197p $24.95; ebook $16.99 **658.4**

1. Leadership 2. Executive ability

ISBN 978-0-470-63354-0; 978-0-470-87243-7 ebook

LC 2010018715

"It's hard to think of a better introduction for a new manager—or back-to-basics review for a veteran." Conference Board Rev

Includes bibliographical references

Kowitz, Braden

Sprint; How to Solve Big Problems and Test New Ideas in Just Five Days. by Jake Knapp (Author), John Zeratsky (Author), Braden Kowitz (Author) Simon & Schuster 2016 288 p. illustrations $28 **658.4**

1. Success 2. Management 3. Decision making 4. Problem solving

ISBN 150112174X; 9781501121746

This book, by Jake Knapp and John Zeratsky, presents "a unique five-day process for solving tough problems, proven at more than a hundred companies. Entrepreneurs and leaders face big questions every day: What's the most important place to focus your effort, and how do you start? What will your idea look like in real life? . . . Now there's a surefire way to answer these important questions: the sprint." (Publisher's note)

"This workbook is a solid guide to getting unstuck and generating your next great idea." Pub Wkly

Meyer, Jennifer

Decision quality; Value Creation from Better Business Decisions. Carl Spetzler, Hannah Winter, Jennifer Meyer. John Wiley & Sons, Inc. 2016 237 p. (hardback) $30 **658.4**

1. Decision making

ISBN 9781119144670; 1119144671

LC 2015043777

This book, by Carl Spetzler, Hannah Winter, and Jennifer Meyer, "empowers you to make the best possible choice and get more of what you truly want from every decision. . . . [They] show you how to frame a problem or opportunity, create a set of attractive alternatives, identify relevant uncertain information, clarify the values that are important in the decision, apply tools of analysis, and develop buy-in among stakeholders.' (Publisher's note)

Peshawaria, Rajeev

Too many bosses, too few leaders; the art of being a true leader. Free Press 2011 xxii, 222p $26; ebook $12.99 **658.4**

1. Leadership

ISBN 978-1-4391-9774-5; 978-1-4391-9776-9 ebook

"Peshawaria's book ought to become required reading for all business people—from students to executives." Publ Wkly

Includes bibliographical references

Peters, Thomas J.

The **little** big things; 163 ways to pursue excellence. [by] Tom Peters. HarperStudio 2010 xxix, 538p $24.99; ebook $11.99 **658.4**

1. Management

ISBN 978-0-06-189408-4; 978-0-06-196350-6 ebook

LC 2009051160

The author "combines observations he has gleaned from his travels, current news items, conversations, and followers of his blog in a compact guide that aims to help readers realize effective projects, customer contentment, employee engagement, and business profitability. No doubt, Peters is on target as he advises readers to appreciate the angry customer, work on their last impressions, make sure that the restroom is clean, and 160 other ways to guarantee success. Each suggestion contains a rationale, example, and method of implementation, all in two pages apiece." Libr J

Pimsleur, Julia

Million Dollar Women; The Essential Guide for Female Entrepreneurs Who Want to Go Big. Julia Pimsleur. Simon & Schuster 2015 256 p. illustrations (hbk) $28 **658.4**

1. Success 2. Businesswomen 3. Entrepreneurship 4. Fund raising 5. New business enterprises 6. Women-owned business enterprises

ISBN 0349406316; 1476790299; 9781476790299

LC 2015011025

In this book author Julia Pimsleur "introduces you to seven women who, instead of 'leaning in,' simply left corporate America and 'marched in' to the world of entrepreneurship. They have raised capital, developed powerful networks, and generated multimillion-dollar companies from scratch." (Publisher's note)

"A useful book on angel investing and funding opportunities, primarily aimed at women entrepreneurs. Recommended for public libraries with strong business collections." LJ

Includes bibliographical references

Pinson, Linda

Anatomy of a business plan; the step-by-step guide to building your business and securing your company's future. Linda Pinson. 8th edition Out of Your Mind...and Into the Marketplace 2008 372 p. $22.95 **658.4**

1. Business planning 2. New business enterprises 3. New business enterprises -- Planning

ISBN 0944205550; 9780944205556

This book, by Linda Pinson, "provides any entrepreneur the tools to create a well-constructed business plan. All steps are included—from initial considerations to envisioning the organizational structure to creating a growth-powering marketing plan and building for the future with airtight financial documents. The book offers proven, step-by step advice for developing and packaging the components of the plan and keeping them up to date." (Publisher's note)

Port, Michael

Steal the show; from speeches to job interviews to deal-closing pitches, how to guarantee a standing ovation for all the performances in your life. Michael Port. Houghton Mifflin Harcourt 2015 272 p. (hardback) $27 **658.4**

1. Communication 2. Job interviews 3. Business communication 4. Business presentations 5. Employment interviewing 6. Interpersonal

communication
ISBN 9780544555181

LC 2015017313

In this book on presentations, author Michael Port "draws on his experience as an actor and as a highly successful corporate speaker and trainer to teach readers how to make the most of every presentation and interaction. He demonstrates how the methods of successful actors can help you connect with, inspire, and persuade any audience." (Publisher's note)

"Required reading for anyone preparing for a job interview, serving in a leadership position, or speaking to the public." LJ

Sandberg, Sheryl, 1969-
Lean in; women, work, and the will to lead. Sheryl Sandberg. Alfred A. Knopf 2013 240 p. (hardcover) $24.95   **658.4**
1. Leadership 2. Women in the workplace 3. Women executives 4. Leadership in women
ISBN 0385349947; 9780385349949

LC 2012043371

This book, by Sheryl Sandberg, "examines why women's progress in achieving leadership roles has stalled, explains the root causes, and offers compelling, commonsense solutions that can empower women to achieve their full potential. . . . Sandberg digs . . . into these issues, combining personal anecdotes, hard data, and compelling research to cut through the layers of ambiguity and bias surrounding the lives and choices of working women." (Publisher's note)

Tarr-Whelan, Linda
Women lead the way; your guide to stepping up to leadership and changing the world. Berrett-Koehler Publishers 2009 213p $24.95   **658.4**
1. Leadership 2. Women executives
ISBN 978-1-60509-135-8; 1-60509-135-9

LC 2009-21826

"Conversational and eye-opening, with many narrative illustrations and concrete advice, Tarr-Whelan's text could prove an important volume for working women looking to advance and enrich their careers." Publ Wkly

Includes bibliographical references

Taylor, William
Practically radical; not-so-crazy ways to transform your company, shake up your industry, and challenge yourself. [by] William C. Taylor. William Morrow 2011 xxi, 293p $27.99; pa $14.99   **658.4**
1. Leadership 2. Business enterprises
ISBN 978-0-06-173461-8; 0-06-173461-6; 978-0-06-203522-6 pa; 0-06-203522-3 pa

LC 2010028021

The author "takes us on an inside look at 25 companies that have grown ever more adaptive to not merely survive but thrive in today's challenging environment. . . . An engaging and briskly written read, this will captivate and benefit business people interested in change and innovation." Publ Wkly

Includes bibliographical references

Walsh, Bill
The **score** takes care of itself; my philosophy of leadership. [by] Bill Walsh with Steve Jamison and Craig Walsh. Portfolio 2009 251p $25.95   **658.4**
1. Leadership 2. Management 3. Football -- Coaching
ISBN 978-1-59184-266-8

LC 2009-10651

"This posthumous leadership guide by the acclaimed head coach of the San Francisco 49ers is a fascinating compendium of Walsh's philosophy, as compiled by his son and Jamison. . . . Walsh reveals a simple and strict philosophy that prizes people above all and focuses on core values, principles and ideals. . . . Enlightening, informative and engaging, this powerful book is a must-read for executives and managers at every level." Publ Wkly

Wheeler, Michael
The **art** of negotiation; how to improvise agreement in a chaotic world. by Michael Wheeler. Simon & Schuster 2013 320 p. (hardcover : alk. paper) $26   **658.4**
1. Negotiation 2. Business planning 3. Negotiation in business
ISBN 1451690428; 9781451690422; 9781451690439

LC 2013005793

This book, by Michael Wheeler, "hows how master negotiators thrive in the face of chaos and uncertainty. Wheeler illuminates the improvisational nature of negotiation, drawing on his own research and his work with Program on Negotiation colleagues. He explains how the best practices of diplomats such as George J. Mitchell, dealmaker Bruce Wasserstein, and Hollywood producer Jerry Weintraub apply to everyday transactions." (Publisher's note)

658.452   Management--Oral communication

Duarte, Nancy
Resonate; present visual stories that transform audiences. Nancy Duarte, author of slide:ology. Wiley 2010 xxi, 248 p.p color illustrations $29.95 **658.452**
1. Communication 2. Public speaking 3. Business presentations
ISBN 0470632011; 9780470632017

LC 2010284662

This public speaking handbook, by Nancy Duarte, "helps you make a strong connection with your audience and lead them to purposeful action. The author's approach is simple: building a presentation today is a bit like writing a documentary. Using this approach, you'll convey your content with passion, persuasion, and impact." (Publisher's note)

Includes bibliographical references (p. 234-236) and index

McGowan, Bill
Pitch Perfect; How to Say It Right the First Time, Every Time. by Bill McGowan. HarperCollins 2014 288 p. illustrations $27.99   **658.452**
1. Communication
ISBN 0062273221; 9780062273222

In this book, Bill McGowan "teaches you how to get your message across and get what you want with pitch perfect communication. . . . Saying the right thing the right way can make the difference between sealing the deal or losing the account, getting a promotion, or getting a pink slip. It's essential to be pitch perfect--to get the right message across to the right person at the right time." (Publisher's note)

"In this engaging, enlightening, and full-of-practical-advice text, McGowan calls out poor public speaking doctrine and replaces it with examples of better ways to persuade and communicate." LJ

658.5 Management of production

Kolko, Jon

Well-designed; how to use empathy to create products people love. Jon Kolko. Harvard Business Review Press 2014 224 p. (hardback) $28 **658.5**
1. Design 2. Empathy 3. New products 4. Product design 5. Consumer behavior 6. Marketing research
ISBN 9781625274793; 1625274793

LC 2014032507

This book, by Jon Kolko, presents advice for product design, "demonstrating how . . . [to] conceive and build successful, emotionally resonant products again and again. . . . You need to deeply understand customer needs and feelings, and this understanding must be reflected in the product. . . . We see how leading companies use a design process of storytelling and iteration that evokes positive emotions, changes behavior, and creates deep engagement." (Publisher's note)

"Passion and energy are left out of the writer's equation, and the pale, gray typeface and bland charts lack the pizzazz the subject calls for. Because of these deficiencies, the book is recommended with reservations for graduate design and marketing students, faculty, and practitioners. Summing Up: Recommended. With reservations. Graduate students, faculty, and practitioners." Choice

658.8 Management of marketing

Burcher, Nick

Paid, owned, earned; maximizing marketing returns in a socially connected world. Nick Burcher. Kogan Page 2012 xiv, 279 p.p **658.8**
1. Marketing 2. Mass media 3. Social media 4. Digital media 5. Internet marketing 6. Online social networks 7. Marketing -- Management
ISBN 074946562X; 9780749465629; 9780749465636
LC 2011038487

This book by Nick Burcher "defines the constituents of each area of paid, owned and earned media and shows how they are linked together. The complexity of media that now sees multiple channels accessed through multiple devices has created major challenges for today's marketing and advertising professionals. [Burcher] proposes a blueprint for how to think and navigate across this space." (Publisher's note)

Includes bibliographical references and index

Cook, Sarah

Customer care excellence; how to create an effective customer focus. 6th ed.; Kogan Page 2011 278p il pa $39.95; ebook $39.95 **658.8**
1. Quality control 2. Customer services 3. Customer relations
ISBN 978-0-7494-5705-1 pa; 0-7494-5705-8 pa; 978-0-7494-6257-4 ebook

LC 2010023892

First published 1992 with title: Customer care

"This book explains how to develop and sustain a customer-service focus within a company. Emphasizing both strategic and practical aspects of customer service, the author explains how gaining customer commitment and motivating employees to deliver excellent service can ensure successful results and satisfied customers." Publisher's note

Includes bibliographical references

Handley, Ann

Content rules; how to create killer blogs, podcasts, videos, ebooks, webinars (and more) that engage customers and ignite your business. [by] Ann Handley & C.C. Chapman. Wiley 2011 xxii, 282p il (New rules of social media series) $24.95; ebook $9.99 **658.8**
1. Internet marketing 2. Digital media 3. Web sites -- Design
ISBN 978-0-470-64828-5; 0-470-64828-7; 978-0-470-94872-9 ebook

LC 2011280622

A one-stop source on the art and science of developing marketing content that people care about. This coverage is interwoven with case studies of companies successfully spreading their ideas online—and using them to establish credibility and build a loyal customer base.

Includes bibliographical references

Jantsch, John

The **referral** engine; teaching your business how to market itself. Portfolio 2010 243p $25.95 **658.8**
1. Marketing 2. Advertising
ISBN 978-1-59184-311-5

LC 2009-49521

"This practical, smart, and original guide is essential reading for any company looking to grow without a fat marketing budget." EContent

Lindström, Martin

Small Data; The Tiny Clues That Uncover Huge Trends. Martin Lindstrom. St. Martin's Press 2016 256 p. illustrations (hardback) $25.99 **658.8**
1. Consumers 2. Marketing 3. Brand name products 4. Consumer behavior 5. Branding (Marketing)
ISBN 9781250080684

LC 2015030202

In this book, author Martin Lindstrom "harnesses the power of 'small data' in his quest to discover the next big thing. Hired by the world's leading brands to find out what makes their customers tick, Martin Lindstrom spends 300 nights a year in strangers' homes, carefully observing every detail in order to uncover their hidden desires, and, ultimately, the clues to a multi-million dollar product." (Publisher's note)

"Lindstrom's uncanny ability to detect and decipher seemingly unrelated clues will inspire reporters and detectives as well as companies looking for ways to develop new products and ideas." Krikus

Includes bibliographical references (pages 235-239) and index.

Miles, Jason

YouTube marketing power; how to use video to find more prospects, launch your products, and reach a massive audience. by Jason Miles. McGraw-Hill 2014 xvii, 231 p.p illustrations (pbk.) $20 **658.8**
1. Advertising 2. Internet marketing 3. YouTube (Electronic resource) 4. Internet videos 5. Internet advertising 6. Video tape advertising
ISBN 0071830545; 9780071830546

LC 2013030881

In this book, author Jason Miles "shows you how to get up and running on YouTube and offers best practices for using it to drive traffic to websites to increase sales. . . . This fast-paced but highly detailed guide reveals why companies frequently fail at YouTube marketing and how you can succeed by avoiding the same mistakes." (Publisher's note)

Schaefer, Mark W.

Return on influence; the revolutionary power of Klout, social scoring, and influence marketing. Mark Schaefer. McGraw-Hill 2012 xviii, 215 p.p (alk. paper) $25 **658.8**
1. Social influence 2. Internet marketing 3. Online social networks 4. Social media -- Marketing
ISBN 0071791094; 9780071791090

LC 2011052315

This book, by Mark Schaefer, "is the first book to explore how brands are identifying and leveraging the world's most powerful bloggers, tweeters, and YouTube celebrities to build product awareness, brand buzz, and new sales. . . . [In it] marketing consultant and college educator Mark W. Schaefer shows you how to use the latest breakthroughs in social networking and influence marketing to achieve your goals." (Publisher's note)

Includes bibliographical references and index.

Siegel, David

Pull; the power of the Semantic Web to transform your business. Portfolio 2009 270p il $27.95 **658.8**
1. Internet marketing 2. Electronic commerce 3. Information technology
ISBN 978-1-59184-277-4

LC 2009-35779

"This thought-provoking read is sure to spark ideas about what it will take to succeed in tomorrow's marketplace." Publ Wkly

Includes bibliographical references

Underhill, Paco

★ **Why** we buy; the science of shopping. Updated and rev.; Simon & Schuster Pbks. 2009 306p pa $16; ebook $12.99 **658.8**
1. Shopping 2. Consumers 3. Marketing
ISBN 978-1-4165-9524-3 pa; 1-4165-9524-4 pa; 978-1-4165-6174-3 ebook; 1-4165-6174-9 ebook

LC 2010-483248

First published 1999

"Each chapter delves into a particular aspect of a store environment and its interface with customers: the importance of signage and why less is more, how men shop, . . . and clues about waiting time. Throughout, insights are peppered with one or several examples." Booklist [review of 1999 edition]

Watkins, Alexandra

Hello, my name is awesome; how to create brand names that stick. Alexandra Watkins. Berrett-Koehler Publishers 2014 112 p. (paperback) $16.95 **658.8**
1. Marketing 2. Brand name products 3. Branding (Marketing)
ISBN 1626561869; 9781626561861

LC 2014018994

In this book, the author Alexandra Watkins, a "naming consultant . . . , explains how anyone--even noncreative types--can create memorable and buzz-worthy brand names. . . . She also provides up-to-date advice, . . . and you'll see dozens of examples--the good, the bad, and the 'so bad she gave them an award.'" (Publisher's note)

"Useful for readers who are naming anything more important than a household pet." LJ

659.1 Advertising

Turow, Joseph

The **daily** you; how the new advertising industry is defining your identity and your world. Joseph Turow. Yale University Press 2011 xi, 234 p.p (hardback) $28.00 **659.1**
1. Advertising 2. Internet marketing 3. Consumer profiling 4. Marketing -- Technological innovations 5. Customer services -- Technological innovations
ISBN 0300165013; 9780300165012

LC 2011028202

This book presents "a warning about the impact of the 'Web 3.0' revolution . . . on individual freedom and privacy. . . . It is via this avalanche of personal data, available through networks like Facebook . . . [Joseph] Turow warns, 'the new advertising industry is defining your identity and your world.' . . . The root of the problem, Turow explains, is the disappearance of boundaries between advertising and content that shaped 20th-century media." (New Scientist)

Includes bibliographical references and index.

659.2   Public relations

Gramm, Jeff

Dear chairman; boardroom battles and the rise of shareholder activism. Jeff Gramm. Harper Business 2016 320 p. (hardcover) $29.99   **659.2**
1. Stockholders 2. Corporate governance 3. Stockholders -- United States -- History 4. Corporate governance -- United States -- History 5. Corporations -- Investor relations -- United States -- History
ISBN 9780062369833

LC 2015038177

This book, by Jeff Gramm, is a "history of one of [American] capitalism's longest running tensions—the conflicts of interest among public company directors, managers, and shareholders—told through entertaining case studies and original letters from some of our most legendary and controversial investors and activists." (Publisher's note)

"Entertaining as well as intriguing, Gramm's work is a great read for both students of business and interested general readers." LJ

Includes bibliographical references and index

660.6   Biotechnology

Kurpinski, Kyle

How to defeat your own clone; and other tips for surviving the biotech revolution. [by] Kyle Kurpinski and Terry D. Johnson. Bantam Books Trade Paperbacks 2010 180p il pa $14   **660.6**
1. Cloning 2. Biotechnology
ISBN 978-0-553-38578-6; 0-553-38578-X

LC 2009-45899

"Kurpinski and Johnson have written a science book that is irreverent, timely, accessible, and, best of all, compulsively readable." Publ Wkly

663   Beverage technology

Bryson, Lew

Tasting whiskey; An Insider's Guide to the Unique Pleasures of the World's Finest Spirits. by Lew Bryson. Storey Publishing 2014 256 p. (pbk. : alk. paper) $18.95   **663**
1. Whiskey
ISBN 1612123015; 9781612123011

LC 2014023260

IACP Cookbook Award Finalist: Wine, Beer and Spirits (2015)

This book, by Lew Bryson, is a "comprehensive guide to everything there is to know about the world's whiskeys, including Scotch and bourbon as well as Tennessee, Irish, Japanese, and Canadian whiskeys. You'll learn about the types of whiskey and the distilling traditions of the regions where they are made, how to serve and taste whiskeys to best appreciate and savor them, how to collect and age whiskey for great results, and much more." (Publisher's note)

Kirk, Mimi

The **ultimate** book of modern juicing; more than 200 fresh recipes to cleanse, cure, and keep you healthy. by Mimi Kirk. W W Norton & Co Inc 2015 312 p. $24.95   **663**
1. Fruit 2. Vegetables
ISBN 1581572603; 9781581572605

This book on juicing, by Mimi Kirk, "is the only book on the topic you'll ever need. Kirk has been juicing vegetables and fruits for more than 40 years, yet she doesn't look a day over 50. (And yes, those two things are connected.) She recently became more interested in how to use juicing to feel and look even better. Her discoveries—genuinely up-to-the-minute—are shared here, along with vibrant photographs of her creations." (Publisher's note)

Mitenbuler, Reid

Bourbon empire; the past and future of America's whiskey. Reid Mitenbuler. Viking Adult 2015 320 p. illustrations (hardback) $27.95   **663**
1. Whiskey 2. Alcoholic beverages -- United States 3. Bourbon whiskey -- United States
ISBN 0670016837; 9780670016839

LC 2015001100

This book, by Reid Mitenbuler, "unraveling the many myths and misconceptions surrounding [Bourbon,] America's most iconic spirit, . . . traces a history that spans frontier rebellion, Gilded Age corruption, and the magic of Madison Avenue. Whiskey has profoundly influenced America's political, economic, and cultural destiny, just as those same factors have inspired the evolution and unique flavor of the whiskey itself." (Publisher's note)

"An illuminating, well-paced narrative that will interest students and imbibers of the wee drap, American-style." Kirkus

Includes bibliographical references and index

Rogers, Adam

★ **Proof**; the science of booze. Adam Rogers. Houghton Mifflin Harcourt 2014 272 p. (hardcover) $26   **663**
1. Alcohol -- History 2. Alcohol -- Research 3. Liquors 4. Distillation 5. Alcoholic beverages
ISBN 0547897960; 9780547897967

LC 2013045770

IACP Cookbook Award Winner: Wine, Beer and Spirits (2015)

In this book, author "Adam Rogers puts our alcoholic history under the microscope, from our ancestors' accidental discovery of fermented drinks to the cutting-edge laboratory research that proves why--or even if--people actually like the stuff. From fermentation to distillation to aging, 'Proof' offers a unique glimpse inside the barrels, stills, tanks, and casks that produce iconic drinks." (Publisher's note)

"The science here can be intimidating to process, but when enjoyed in leisurely sips, Rogers's cheeky and accessible writing style goes down smoothly, capturing the essence of this enigmatic, ancient social lubricant." Pub Wkly

Includes bibliographical references and index

Wood, Stephen M.

Apples to cider; how to make sweet and hard cider at home. April White with Stephen M. Wood of Farnum Hill Ciders. Quarry Books 2015 152 p. color illustrations (alk. paper) $24.99   **663**

1. Apples 2. Brewing 3. Cider
ISBN 1592539181; 9781592539185

LC 2015000551

In this book, brewers April White and Stephen M. Wood "share decades of experience and a simple philosophy: Cider is all about the apples. Whether you are a home brewer, a home winemaker, or simply a cider lover, you can join the growing community of cidermakers that are reviving this thousand-year-old craft." (Publisher's note)

"The authors detail how to set up tasting sessions to compare different ciders. They also offer instructions for making French cidre and ice cider, the apple version of ice wine. Savvy adepts can even turn cider into elegant apple champagne." Booklist

Includes bibliographical references and index

How to make sweet and hard cider at home

664   Food technology

Adamchak, Raoul W.

Tomorrow's table; organic farming, genetics, and the future of food. [by] Pamela C. Ronald [and] Raoul W. Adamchak. Oxford University Press 2008 208p il map $29.95   **664**

1. Organic farming 2. Genetic engineering 3. Genetically modified foods 4. Food -- Biotechnology
ISBN 9780195301755

LC 2007-7071

"The format is easy to follow and effective at highlighting . . . [the authors'] seemingly adverse positions on the subject. By the book's conclusion, their argument is elegantly presented in a logical fashion." Choice

Includes bibliographical references (p. 179-197)

Danforth, Adam

★ **Butchering** poultry, rabbit, lamb, goat, and pork; the comprehensive photographic guide to humane slaughtering and butchering. by Adam Danforth. Storey Publishing 2014 456 p. color illustrations (pbk. : alk. paper) $24.95   **664**

1. Meat 2. Animal welfare 3. Slaughtering and slaughterhouses 4. Meat animals 5. Meat cutting 6. Meat -- Preservation 7. Game and game-birds, Dressing of
ISBN 1612121829; 9781603429313; 9781612121826; 9781612121888

LC 2013030702

IACP Cookbook Award: Beverage/Reference/Technical (2015)

James Beard Foundation Award: Reference and Scholarship (2015)

In this book, author Adam Danforth "shows you exactly how to humanely slaughter and butcher chickens and other poultry, rabbits, sheep, pigs, and goats. From creating the right pre-slaughter conditions to killing, skinning, keeping cold, breaking the meat down, and creating cuts of meat you'll recognize from the market, Danforth walks you through every step, leaving nothing to chance." (Publisher's note)

Includes bibliographical references and index

Ivanko, John D.

Homemade for Sale; How to Set Up and Market a Food Business from Your Home Kitchen. by Lisa Kivirist, John D. Ivanko. New Society Publishers 2015 240 p. illustrations (paperback) $22.95   **664**

1. Entrepreneurship 2. Home-based business
ISBN 9780865717862; 0865717869

LC 2014481269

This book, by Lisa Kivirist and John D. Ivanko, offers an "authoritative guide to conceiving and launching your own home-based food start-up. Packed with profiles of successful cottage food entrepreneurs, this comprehensive and accessible resource covers everything you need to get cooking for your customers, creating items that by their very nature are specialized and unique." (Publisher's note)

"An excellent, eminently practical resource to make a successful home-based food business a reality. Recommended for public libraries." LJ

Katz, Sandor Ellix

The **art** of fermentation; an in-depth exploration of essential concepts and processes from around the world. Sandor Ellix Katz; foreword by Michael Pollan. Chelsea Green Pub. 2012 498 p. ill. (some col.) (hardback) $39.95   **664**

1. Fermentation 2. Canning and preserving 3. Fermented foods
ISBN 160358286X; 9781603582865; 9781603583640

LC 2011052014

James Beard Foundation Award: Reference and Scholarship (2013)

This book, by Sandor Ellix Katz, was the winner of the 2013 James Beard Foundation Book Award for Reference and Scholarship. "Readers will find detailed information on fermenting vegetables; sugars into alcohol; . . . sour tonic beverages; milk; grains and starchy tubers; beers (and other grain-based alcoholic beverages); beans; seeds; nuts; fish; meat; and eggs, as well as growing mold cultures, using fermentation in agriculture, art, and energy production, and considerations for commercial enterprises." (Publisher's note)

"Katz takes fermentation down to the molecular level while keeping it conversational and accessible to the generalist." LJ

Includes bibliographical refererences and index

López-Alt, J. Kenji

The **food** lab; better home cooking through science. J. Kenji López-Alt; photographs by the author. W W Norton & Co Inc. 2015 938 p. color illustrations (hardcover) $49.95   **664**

1. Food 2. Cooking 3. Science 4. Food -- Analysis 5. Cooking -- Research 6. Food -- Experiments 7. Cooking -- Technique
ISBN 0393081087; 9780393081084

LC 2015016358

In this book author J. Kenji Lopez "focuses on the science behind beloved American dishes, delving into the interactions between heat, energy, and molecules that create great food. Kenji shows that often, conventional methods don't work that well, and home cooks can achieve far better results using new--but simple--techniques." (Publisher's note)

"This indispensable kitchen manual, which suggests visualizing heat capacity as a coop full of Red Bull-energized chickens, makes food science accessible." LJ

McLagan, Jennifer

★ **Bitter**; a taste of the world's most dangerous flavor, with recipes. Jennifer McLagan; photography by Aya Brackett. Ten Speed Press 2014 272 p. color illustrations (hardback) $29.99 **664**
1. Taste 2. Cooking 3. Bitterness (Taste)
ISBN 160774516X; 9781607745167

LC 2014023824

James Beard Foundation Award: Single Subject (2015)
IACP Cookbook Award Finalist: Single Subject (2015)

In this book, author Jennifer McLagan "laments the disappearance of bitter tastes from mainstream diets and sets to reintroduce them to readers. In 100 recipes that incorporate chicories (frisee), beverages (coffee), brassicas (rutabaga), and other foods (almonds, cardoons), the author sheds light on how bitter tastes and smells affect the brain and palate." (Library Journal)

Includes bibliographical references and index

Mueller, Tom

Extra virginity; Tom Mueller. 1st ed. W. W. Norton 2011 238 p. **664**
1. Fraud 2. Olive oil 3. Food adulteration and inspection 4. Olive -- History 5. Olive -- Folklore 6. Olive oil -- History 7. Olive oil industry -- Moral and ethical aspects
ISBN 9780393070217

LC 2011041459

In this book, author "Tom Mueller . . . [an] expert on olive oil and olive oil fraud . . . [tells] a story of globalization, deception, and crime in the food industry from ancient times to the present, and a[n] . . . indictment of today's lax protections against fake and even toxic food products in the United States. . . . [The book] is also an . . . account of the artisanal producers, chemical analysts, chefs, and food activists who are defending the extraordinary oils that truly deserve the name 'extra-virgin.'" (Publisher's note)

Robinson, Jancis

Wine grapes; a complete guide to 1,380 vine varieties, including their origins and flavors. by Jancis Robinson, Julia Harding, and Jose Vouillamoz. Ecco/HarperCollins 2012 1242 p. (hardback) $175 **664**
1. Grapes 2. Wine and wine making 3. Viticulture 4. Grapes -- Varieties
ISBN 0062206362; 9780062206367

LC 2012019224

James Beard Foundation Award: Beverage (2013)

This book by Jancis Robinson, Julia Harding, and Jose Vouillamoz provides information "about the . . . fruit that care, love, skill, and time transform into [wine]. [It] is the first complete compendium in more than a century to all

grape varieties relevant to the wine lover. 'Wine Grapes' charts the relationships of the grapes . . . ., discusses . . . where and how they are grown, and, most importantly, what the wines made from them will ultimately taste like." (Publisher's note)

Shetterly, Caitlin

Modified; GMOs and the Threat to Our Food, Our Land, Our Future. Caitlin Shetterly. G.P. Putnam's Sons 2016 352 p. (ebook) $65; (print) $28 **664**
1. Genetically modified foods
ISBN 9780698160224; 9780399170676

LC 2016011424

This book, by Caitlin Shetterly, "look[s] at the issue that started the biggest food fight of our time--GMOs. From a journalist and mother who learned that genetically modified corn was the culprit behind what was making her and her child sick, a must-read book for anyone trying to parse the incendiary discussion about genetically modified foods." (Publisher's note)

"Shetterly's accessible, well-researched, and damning work brings clarity to an often fuzzy debate." Pub Wkly

Winter, Ruth

A **consumer's** dictionary of food additives; 7th ed.; Three Rivers Press 2009 595p pa $17.95; ebook $17.95 **664**
1. Reference books 2. Food additives -- Dictionaries
ISBN 978-0-307-40892-1 pa; 978-0-307-45259-7 ebook

LC 2008-40601

First published 1972. Periodically revised

This guide provides "facts about the safety and side effects of more than 12,000 ingredients—such as preservatives, food-tainting pesticides, and animal drugs—that end up in food as a result of processing and curing." Publisher's note

Includes bibliographical references

666 Ceramic and allied technologies

Macfarlane, Alan

Glass: a world history; {by} Alan Macfarlane and Gerry Martin. University of Chicago Press 2002 255p il $27.50 **666**
1. Glass
ISBN 0-226-50028-4

LC 2002-20493

The authors "make the case for the centrality of glass in the artistic renaissance and scientific revolution that took place in Western Europe from the 14th to 17th centuries. They discuss the origins of glass making and trace its development and usage across centuries and multiple cultures (Europe, the Middle East, China, India, and Japan). Their discussion combines cultural, artistic, and aesthetic viewpoints of glass within these cultures with history and developments in science. The result is a thoroughly readable, carefully argued work, filled with delightful surprises. . . . An excellent example of microhistory . . . this is required for history of science collections and recommended for large public and academic collections." Libr J

Includes bibliographical references

667 Cleaning, color, coating, related technologies

Garfield, Simon

Mauve; how one man invented a color that changed the world. Norton 2001 222p il hardcover o.p. pa $13.95 **667**

1. Chemists 2. Dyes and dyeing 3. Mauve 4. Dye industry -- Great Britain 5. Chemists -- England -- Biography
ISBN 0-393-32313-7 pa

LC 00-69533

This volume discusses how a British student, William Henry Perkin, while trying to synthesize quinine from coal tar, developed mauve, "the first mass-produced artificial dye. . . . By the turn of the 20th century, because of Perkin's novel idea, dye makers had 2,000 synthesized colors at their disposal." (N Y Times Book Rev) Index.

"The text is understandable by the average layman and is enjoyable reading for the scientist and non-scientist alike." Sci Books Films

Includes bibliographical references

Greenfield, Amy Butler

A **perfect** red; empire, espionage, and the quest for the color of desire. Amy Butler Greenfield. 1st ed; HarperCollins 2005 338p il $26.95 **667**

1. Dyes and dyeing
ISBN 0-06-052275-5

LC 2004-42376

The author "combines the investigative prowess of a detective with the intellectual reasoning of an academician to create an eminently entertaining and educational read." Booklist

Includes bibliographical references

668 Technology of other organic products

Turin, Luca

The **secret** of scent; adventures in perfume and the science of smell. Ecco 2006 207p il $23.95; pa $13.95 **668**

1. Perfumes
ISBN 0-06-113383-3; 978-0-06-113383-1; 0-06-113384-1 pa; 978-0-06-113384-8 pa

LC 2006-46273

The author "investigates the reason things smell they way they do." N Y Times Book Rev

Includes bibliographical references

Winter, Ruth

A **consumer's** dictionary of cosmetic ingredients; Complete Information About the Harmful and Desirable Ingredients Found in Cosmetics and Cos-

meceuticals. Ruth Winter. Three Rivers Press 2009 567 p. $18 **668**

1. Chemicals 2. Cosmetics 3. Cosmetics -- Dictionaries
ISBN 0307451119; 9780307451118

LC 2010292417

This book, by Ruth Winter, presents "[e]verything you need to know about the safety and efficacy of cosmetics and cosmeceuticals. . . . This updated and expanded edition gives you the facts you need to protect yourself and your family from possible irritants, confusing chemical names, and the exaggerated claims of gimmicky additives. With 800 new ingredients found in toiletries, cosmetics, and cosmeceuticals . . . this alphabetically organized guide evaluates them all." (Publisher's note)

Includes bibliographical references (p. [565]-567)

674 Lumber processing, wood products, cork

The **Encyclopedia** of wood; a tree-by-tree guide to the world's most versatile resource. general editor, Aidan Walker. Facts on File 2005 192p il map $35 **674**

1. Reference books 2. Wood -- Encyclopedias
ISBN 0-8160-6181-5

LC 2004-60849

First published 1989

"A nice addition to libraries with strong interior design or DIY collections." Libr J

Includes bibliographical references

Petroski, Henry

The **pencil**; a history of design and circumstance. Knopf 1990 434p il hardcover o.p. pa $20 **674**

1. Pencils
ISBN 0-394-57422-2; 0-679-73415-5 pa

LC 89-45362

The author discusses the manufacture, design, history, and sociological significance of the pencil.

"An incredibly rich and complex history of this entirely unremarkable instrument of communication." SLJ

Includes bibliographical references

676 Pulp and paper technology

Basbanes, Nicholas A., 1943-

★ **On** paper; the everything of its two-thousand-year history. Nicholas A. Basbanes. Alfred A. Knopf 2013 448 p. $35 **676**

1. Paper 2. Paper industry 3. Paper -- History 4. Papermaking -- History 5. Paper industry -- History
ISBN 0307266427; 9780307266422

LC 2012050267

Andrew Carnegie Medal for Excellence in Nonfiction Shortlist (2014)

This book, by Nicholas A. Basbanes, presents "a consideration of all things paper: its invention that revolutionized human civilization; its thousand-fold uses (and misuses), proliferation, and sweeping influence on society; its makers, shapers, collectors, and pulpers. Basbanes writes about the ways in which paper has been used to record history, make laws, conduct business, and establish identities." (Publisher's note)

Includes bibliographical references

Grummer, Arnold E.

Trash-to-treasure papermaking. Storey Publishing 2011 207p il pa $16.95 **676**

1. Paper 2. Papermaking

ISBN 978-1-60342-547-6

LC 2010-43056

"Grummer begins with basic papermaking, then progresses to more advanced skills. Ample tips on everything from proper technique to troubleshooting problems with finished paper are included. A gallery of clever projects with directions rounds out this friendly, accessible guide to papermaking." Libr J

Includes bibliographical references

Hiebert, Helen, 1965-

The **papermaker's** companion; the ultimate guide to making and using handmade paper. Helen Hiebert. Storey Books 2000 219 p. $18.95 **676**

1. Papermaking 2. Paper, Handmade

ISBN 1580172008; 9781580172004

LC 99087351

This book by Helen Hiebert "covers absolutely everything you need to know about papermaking, from the basics to advanced techniques such as shaped sheets, embossing, laminating, and watermarking. . . . [The book] also includes thorough step-by-step instructions for processing pulp, building papermaking equipment, and making paper-based projects." (Publisher's note)

Includes bibliographical references and index.

Kurlansky, Mark, 1948-

Paper; Paging Through History. Mark Kurlansky. W.W. Norton & Company 2016 416 p. illustrations (hardcover) $27.95 **676**

1. Papermaking 2. Paper -- History 3. Papermaking -- History 4. Paper industry -- History

ISBN 9780393239614; 0393239616

LC 2016007084

This book, by Mark Kurlansky, offers "a definitive history of paper and the astonishing ways it has shaped today's world. Paper is one of the simplest and most essential pieces of human technology. For the past two millennia, the ability to produce it in ever more efficient ways has supported the proliferation of literacy, media, religion, education, commerce, and art; it has formed the foundation of civilizations, promoting revolutions and restoring stability." (Publisher's note)

"Kurlansky profiles key individuals, from inventors to master printers, writers, artists, and revolutionaries, while incisively parsing technological breakthroughs and social conundrums." Booklist

Includes bibliographical references (pages [347]-354) and index.

Monro, Alexander

The **paper** trail; an unexpected history of a revolutionary invention. Alexander Monro. Alfred A.

Knopf 2016 384 p. illustrations, maps (hardback) $30 **676**

1. Paper 2. Papermaking 3. Paper industry 4. Paper -- History 5. Papermaking -- History

ISBN 9780307271662

LC 2015036988

This book, by Alexander Monro, is a "detailed history that tells the fascinating story of how paper—the simple Chinese invention of two thousand years ago—wrapped itself around our world, humankind's most momentous ideas imprinted on its surface. . . . [It] explores how the new substance was used to solidify social and political systems that influenced China even into our own time." (Publisher's note)

"The result is an engaging, lively, informative examination of a ubiquitous resource and its multimillennia influence on the world." Pub Wkly

Includes bibliographical references and index

677 Textiles

Ekarius, Carol

The **field** guide to fleece; 100 sheep breeds and how to use their fibers. by Deborah Robson and Carol Ekarius. Storey Publishing LLC 2013 231 p. color illustrations (pbk. : alk. paper) $14.95 **677**

1. Wool

ISBN 1612121780; 9781612121789

LC 2013003107

This book, by Deborah Robson and Carol Ekarius, offers a "portable reference . . . [for crafters to] quickly and easily look up any of 100 sheep breeds, the characteristics of their fleece, and the kinds of projects for which their fleece is best suited. Each breed profile includes a photo of the animal and information about its origin and conservation status, as well as the weight, staple length, fiber diameter, and natural colors of its fleece." (Publisher's note)

"This pocket-size guide is perfect for spinners and other fiber enthusiasts who want quick information on the characteristics of a wide variety of fleeces and would be a worthwhile book to have on hand at a fiber festival."

Includes bibliographical references (page 232) and index

Parkes, Clara

The **knitter's** book of yarn; the ultimate guide to choosing, using, and enjoying yarn. by Clara Parkes. 1st ed.; Potter Craft 2007 255 p. ill. (chiefly col.); **677**

1. Yarn 2. Knitting

ISBN 9780307352163; 0307352161

LC 2007009363

Includes bibliographical references (p. 242) and index.

Schoeser, Mary

World textiles: a concise history. Thames & Hudson 2003 224p il (World of art) pa $14.95 **677**

1. Fabrics 2. Textile industry

ISBN 0-500-20369-5

LC 2002-110919

"Arranged roughly into chronological periods, the book . . . details technique, materials, and designs and puts them in historical and cultural context. This is truly a fantastic history of textile arts. . . . The text itself is a delight to read and more comprehensive than in other comparable works." Libr J

Includes bibliographical references

681.1   Instruments for measuring time, counting and calculating machines and instruments

Marchant, Jo

Decoding the heavens; a 2,000-year-old computer--and the century-long search to discover its secrets. Da Capo Press 2009 328p il $25   **681.1**
  1. Clocks and watches 2. Greece -- Antiquities
  ISBN 978-0-306-81742-7; 0-306-81742-X
                          LC 2008-939733
First published 2008 in the United Kingdom
The author "relates the century-long struggle of competing amateurs and scientists to understand the secrets of a 2000-year-old clock-like mechanism found in 1901 by Greek divers off the coast of Antikythera, a small island near Tunisia. . . . This globe-trotting, era-spanning mystery should absorb armchair scientists of all kinds." Publ Wkly

Includes bibliographical references

682   Small forge work (Blacksmithing)

Parkinson, Peter

The **artist** blacksmith; design and techniques. Crowood Press 2002 160p il $40   **682**
  1. Blacksmithing
  ISBN 1-86126-428-3
"Parkinson explains the tools, materials, and equipment needed by blacksmiths as well as the most commonly used techniques. Numerous illustrations of beautiful creations (such as gates, sculptures, household items, and furniture) appear throughout this fascinating title." Libr J

683.4   Small firearms

Baum, Dan

Gun guys; a road trip. Dan Baum. 1st ed. Knopf 2013 352 p. (hardcover) $26.95   **683.4**
  1. Firearms industry 2. United States -- Social conditions 3. Firearms ownership -- United States 4. Firearms owners -- United States 5. Firearms -- Social aspects -- United States
  ISBN 0307595412; 9780307595416
                     LC 2012028767
This book, by Dan Baum, discusses gun culture in the United States. "Many Americans love guns--which horrifies and fascinates many other Americans, and much of the rest of the world. . . . [The author] grabs his licensed concealed handgun and hits the road to meet some of the 40 percent of Americans who own guns." Baum interviews gun owners and enthusiasts along with victims of gun crime. (Publisher's note)

Includes bibliographical references (pages [321]-323)

and index

Firearms; an illustrated history. Dorling Kindersley, Limited. Dk Pub 2014 320 p. color illustrations $40   **683.4**
  1. Guns 2. Firearms industry
  ISBN 1465416056; 9781465416056
This book is a "definitive visual guide to the history of firearms and guns. . . . [It] charts the evolution and history of the gun, from the pistol, flintlock musket and rifle to the shotgun, machine gun and revolver. This book features over 300 firearms and guns spanning centuries of development, with the world's most iconic gun brands such as Colt, Smith and Wesson, Maxim and the Kalashnikov AK-47 covered with amazing photographic features." (Publisher's note)

"This is one of the best visual overviews available of the historical development of firearms, with brilliant photography and an emphasis on artistic as well as technological achievements. The material will be appreciated by readers interested in the history of technology as well as basic firearms enthusiasts." LJ

684   Furnishings and home workshops

Abram, Norm

Measure twice, cut once; lessons from a master carpenter. Little, Brown 1996 196p il $18.95 **684**
  1. Woodwork 2. Carpentry
  ISBN 0-316-00494-4
                      LC 96-7584
In this book about woodwork and carpentry the author "deals mainly with hand tools. Abram covers items such as levels, chalk lines, and plumb-bobs, detailing his experiences with them and his preferences. . . . Even experienced woodworkers will pick up a tip or two from this book." Libr J

Hoadley, R. Bruce

Understanding wood; a craftsman's guide to wood technology. 2nd ed; Taunton Press 2000 280p il $39.95   **684**
  1. Wood 2. Woodwork
  ISBN 1-56158-358-8
                   LC 00-44322
First published 1980
This guide "covers the nature of wood and its properties, the basics of wood technology, and the woodworker's raw materials." Publisher's note

Includes bibliographical references and index

Kelsey, John

Woodworking; Techniques & Projects for the First Time Woodworker. John Kelsey. Fox Chapel Publishing 2013 111 p. ill. (chiefly col.) $14.99 **684**
  1. Woodwork 2. Woodwork -- Handbooks, manuals, etc 3. Carpentry -- Handbooks, manuals, etc
  ISBN 156523801X; 9781565238015
                  LC 2013017981
This book, by John Kelsey, is a guidebook for woodworking. "Each of the woodworking projects in this book can be completed in just a few hours. Designed to teach

basic woodworking skills, they require only ordinary lumber and simple hand and power tools that you may already own. Each new project builds on what you learned before, allowing you to become more self-confident as your skills increase." (Publisher's note)

"Aimed at nine-year-olds through adults, this beautifully arranged title starts logically with wood selection and tool overviews and contains simple skill-building tasks that will develop DIYers' confidence and help them to learn technique. The quality of instruction is high, with large color photos showing each step." LJ

Warner, Pat

The **router** book. Taunton Press 2001 185p pa $19.95 **684**

1. Woodwork 2. Power tools

ISBN 1-56158-423-1

LC 2001-27149

"Warner shows readers how to get the most from their router, covering tools, accessories, and its use. Fixed-base, plunge routers, and laminate trimmers are introduced with excellent evaluations of specific models of each type." Libr J

684.1 Furniture

Blair, Barb

Furniture Makeovers; Simple Techniques for Transforming Furniture With Paint, Stains, Paper, Stencils, and More. by Barb Blair; forward by Holly Becker; photography by J. Aaron Greene. Chronicle Books 2013 192 p. (hardcover) $24.95 **684.1**

1. Furniture finishing

ISBN 1452104158; 9781452104157

This book looks at refinishing furniture. Author Barb Blair describes, with illustrations, 24 refinishing techniques, "ranging from . . . stripping and sanding" to "adding wallpaper. Little tips abound: use an overhead projector to display an image for tracing onto a piece of furniture; e-mail artwork to an office supply store to print instead of buying a pack of expensive transparencies for use at home." (Publishers Weekly)

Furniture makes the room; Barb Blair, founder of Knack Studios; Photographs by Paige French. Chronicle Books 2016 190 p. color illustrations $27.95 **684.1**

1. Interior design 2. Furniture finishing 3. Furniture painting 4. Interior decoration -- Themes, motives

ISBN 1452139997; 9781452139999

LC 2015015943

This book, by Barb Blair, "goes beyond the nuts and bolts of furniture refinishing to show how to style rooms with each customized piece. For instance, she transforms a well-worn coffee table with a painted ombré design, and then reveals how to incorporate it into a bright and sunny den, a cozy reading nook, and a cheerful bedroom. With instructions for 15 before-and-after furniture projects—dressers, tables, beds, armoire, and more—in Blair's signature bold style." (Publisher's note)

Bruno, Isabelle

Reinventing Ikea; Isabelle Bruno, Christine Baillet. Abrams Image 2016 216 p. color illustrations (paperback) $24.95 **684.1**

1. Ikea (Company) 2. Interior design 3. Furniture making 4. Furniture finishing

ISBN 1419722670; 9781419722677

LC 2016932043

This book features "70 customization projects conceived from popular Ikea products. Authors Isabelle Bruno and Christine Baillet share the best DIY projects for every room in your home—from the bedroom to the kitchen, the living room to the office. Organized by four levels of difficulty . . . , the projects are perfect for anyone interested in quick crafts—like a cake stand—or more involved—like constructing a kitchen island or a Mondrian-inspired desk." (Publisher's note)

Cone, Steve

Singer upholstery basics plus; complete step-by-step photo guide. Creative Pub. International 2007 155p il pa $19.95 **684.1**

1. Upholstery

ISBN 978-1-58923-329-4; 1-58923-329-8

LC 2007-7252

First published 1997 with title: Upholstery basics

"If there ever was an upholstery bible, this is it." Libr J

Dobson, Cherry

The **complete** guide to upholstery; stuffed with step-by-step techniques for professional results. St. Martin's Griffin 2009 143p il pa $24.95 **684.1**

1. Upholstery 2. Furniture -- Repairing

ISBN 978-0-312-38327-5; 0-312-38327-4

"Want to recycle your old furniture with reupholstery? This lovely manual . . . contains fine step-by-step photos and tips on technique. Master upholsterer Dobson easily walks the confident beginner through the basics." Libr J

Hingley, Brian D.

Furniture repair & restoration. Creative Homeowner 2010 175p il pa $14.95 **684.1**

1. Furniture finishing 2. Furniture -- Repairing

ISBN 978-1-58011-478-3

First published 1998 with title: Furniture repair & refinishing

"With special sections on evaluation and repair of structural issues, this volume features an array of valuable information on furniture repair and refinishing. . . . Geared toward beginners in wood restoration, the book highlights the author's professional experience, which shows through in the advice and thorough directions." Libr J

Jones, Stephanie

Upstyle your furniture; Kathleen Ballos. Barrons Educational Series, Inc. 2015 160 p. color illustrations $21.99 **684.1**

1. Furniture finishing

ISBN 1438005563; 9781438005560

LC 2014932020

In this book, Stephanie Jones "compiles her techniques for furniture transformation. . . . She begins with the basics: how to select those pieces that are worth the work of transformation, and then how to decide on the style, color, and process that will make each one look its best. Using examples from her own studio to colorfully illustrate the text, Jones shows the reader the best techniques for preparing, making repairs, finishing, and embellishing each project." (Publishers Weekly)

"Overall, this is a great example of styles that will appeal to a wide range of tastes and abilities. Don't let this be the only furniture project book on the shelf, though—pair it with another that has better step-by-step illustrations, such as Christophe Pourny's The Furniture Bible." LJ

Paolini, Gregory

Arts & crafts furniture projects; Gregory Paolini. The Taunton Press 2015 170 p. color illustrations $24.95   **684.1**

1. Furniture making 2. Arts and crafts movement
ISBN 1600857817; 9781600857812
LC 2014046454

This book, by professional woodworker Gregory Paolini, "showcases nine iconic furniture projects that vary in difficulty. Timeless and always in style, Arts & Crafts is a perennial favorite and a style that works nicely with almost any home decor." (Publisher's note)

"Highly recommended for strong intermediate to more expert woodworkers who are well equipped to take on these beautiful projects, as there are no basic instructions for tool use or general techniques, though special tips appear throughout." LJ

Arts and crafts furniture projects

Pourny, Christophe

★ The **furniture** bible; everything you need to know to identify, restore and care for furniture. Christophe Pourny with Jen Renzi; foreword by Martha Stewart. Artisan 2014 304 p. color illustrations hbk $35   **684.1**

1. Furniture finishing 2. Furniture -- Repairing
ISBN 1579655351; 9781579655358
LC 2014004628

This book, by Christophe Pourny with Jen Renzi, "teaches readers everything they need to know about the provenance and history of furniture, as well as how to restore, update, and care for their furniture--from antiques to mid-century pieces, family heirlooms or funky flea-market finds. The heart of the book is an overview of . . . [the author's] favorite techniques." (Publisher's note)

"Pourny explains how to assess damage, make repairs, and complete a final finish. A strong section on furniture care and cleaning argues that using the right methods will prolong the life of furniture. This guide will find a wide audience among those who simply want to learn about and appreciate good furniture, as well as those who are more hands-on." Pub Wkly

Includes bibliographical references and index

White, Ana

The **handbuilt** home; 34 simple, stylish, and budget-friendly woodworking projects for every room. Ana White. Potter Craft 2012 192 p. color illustrations (alk. paper) $22.99   **684.1**

1. Woodwork 2. Furniture making 3. Woodwork -- Amateurs' manuals 4. Furniture making -- Amateurs' manuals
ISBN 0307587320; 9780307587329; 9780307587336
LC 2012936933

This book, by Ana White, offers advice on how to create "beds, organizers, Adirondack chairs, a play table, and more! It's easy to build inexpensive, quality furnishings with this . . . collection of woodworking projects from Ana White, the popular blogger who has inspired millions of homemakers with her stylish furniture plans and DIY spirit." (Publisher's note)

"Generally a nice collection, but beginners will need tool instruction. Pair this with Fox Chapel's "Missing Shop Manual" series (Table Saw: The Tool Information You Need at Your Fingertips & others). Recommended for public libraries with popular woodworking collections." LJ

686 Printing and related activities

Lee, Marshall

Bookmaking: editing, design, production; technical consultant Joseph Gannon. 3rd ed; Norton 2004 494p il $49.95   **686**

1. Books 2. Book industry
ISBN 0-393-73018-2
LC 2003-59672

First published 1965 by Bowker

This book describes "the business and art of transmitting an author's manuscript to readers by means of a book. The process includes editing, physical and visual design, costing, production planning, scheduling, procurement, and distribution. . . . This timeless classic should be acquired while it is still available." Choice

Includes bibliographical references

Rivers, Charlotte

Little book of book making; timeless techniques and fresh ideas for beautiful handmade books. Charlotte Rivers. Potter Craft 2014 192 p. color illustrations (hardback) $22.99   **686**

1. Book design 2. Bookbinding 3. Artists' books 4. Book designers
ISBN 0770435149; 9780770435141
LC 2013044724

This book, by Charlotte Rivers, is a "guide to 30 top bookmakers working today, plus 21 tutorials for essential techniques to make your own books. . . . Packed with wonderfully eclectic examples, this book explores the intriguing creative possibilities of bookmaking as a modern art form, including a wide range of bindings, materials, and embellishments. Featured techniques include everything from Coptic to concertina binding, as well as experimental page treatments." (Publisher's note)

686.2   Printing

Garfield, Simon

Just my type; a book about fonts. Gotham Books 2011 356p il $27.50   **686.2**
1. Printing 2. Fonts 3. Type and type-founding -- History
ISBN 978-1-59240-652-4

LC 2011379019

First published 2010 in the United Kingdom

"Conveying the richness and the personality of typefaces with love and passion, this is an accessible and entertaining introduction to the world of lettering." Blueprint

Includes biblliographical references

Lupton, Ellen

Thinking with type; a critical guide for designers, writers, editors, & students. Ellen Lupton. Princeton Architectural Press 2010 224 p. color illustrations (alk. paper) $24.95   **686.2**
1. Typography 2. Type and type-founding 3. Graphic design (Typography)
ISBN 1568989695; 9781568989693

LC 2010005389

This book, by Ellen Lupton, "is the definitive guide to using typography in visual communication, from the printed page to the computer screen. This revised edition includes . . . the latest information on style sheets for print and the web, the use of ornaments and captions, lining and non-lining numerals, the use of small caps and enlarged capitals, as well as information on captions, font licensing, mixing typefaces, and hand lettering." (Publisher's note)

Includes bibliographical references and index

Spiekermann, Erik

★ **Stop** Stealing Sheep and Find out How Type Works; Erik Spiekerman. 2nd ed; Pearson P T R 2013 213 p. il (some col) $39.99   **686.2**
1. Typography 2. Graphic design 3. Type and type-founding
ISBN 0321934288; 9780321934284

LC 2014378096

"In this third edition, acclaimed type designer Erik Spiekermann brings his type classic fully up to date on mobile and web typography. . . . If you use type--and these days, almost everyone does--Spiekermann's engaging, common-sense style will help you understand how to look at type, work with type, choose the best typeface for your message, and express yourself more effectively through design." (Publisher's note)

"This updated edition uses an easygoing style to get readers from a variety of backgrounds up to speed on good use of type and general typography. The examples, images, and guidance not only are helpful to illustrate concepts, but also are up-to-date with current web and mobile trends and technologies." Choice

Includes bibliographical references and indexes

686.209   Printing--History

Kluger, Richard

★ **Indelible** ink; The Trials of John Peter Zenger and the Birth of America's Free Press. Richard Kluger. W W Norton & Co Inc 2016 368 p. illustrations (hardcover) $27.95   **686.209**
1. Freedom of the press 2. Civil rights -- United States -- History 3. Printers -- United States -- Biography 4. Trials (Seditious libel) -- New York (State) 5. Printing -- New York (State) -- History -- 18th century 6. Freedom of the press -- United States -- History -- 18th century
ISBN 9780393245462

LC 2016011040

This book by Richard Kluger presents the "untold story of the battle to legalize free expression in America. . . . When in 1733 a small newspaper . . . printed scathing articles assailing the new British governor, William Cosby, as corrupt and abusive, colonial New York was scandalized. The paper's publisher, an impoverished printer named John Peter Zenger . . . , became the endeavor's courageous fall guy." (Publisher's note)

"Event by compelling event, readers follow Zenger through the drama that eventually landed him in jail on libel charges--before a liberty-loving jury freed him with a 1735 verdict signaling a clear American commitment to the unfettered reporting that can check abuse of power." Booklist

Includes bibliographical references and index

686.3   Bookbinding

Cambras, Josep

Bookbinding; techniques and projects. [translation from the Spanish, Michael Brunelle and Beatriz Cortabarria] Barron's 2007 143p il (Decorative techniques) pa $26.99   **686.3**
1. Bookbinding
ISBN 978-0-7641-6084-4; 0-7641-6084-2

LC 2007-924989

"Beginning with a historical overview, continuing to an explanation of tools and materials, Cambras showcases his expertise in chapters devoted to half a dozen techniques and the same quantity of paper-painting methods." Booklist

Diehn, Gwen

Real life journals: designing & using handmade books. Lark Books 2010 180p il (Live & learn) $24.95   **686.3**
1. Diaries 2. Bookbinding
ISBN 978-1-60059-492-2

LC 2009-32647

"Chapters on tools, covers, paper choices, and bindings are detailed and fully illustrated, but Diehn . . . goes well beyond that, making a point to include information on creating a purposeful design, enriching textual content, and binding the words to the visual elements to reflect a bookmaker's interests and personality. . . [This is] a lovely, helpful volume that will inspire and attract journalers and scrapbookers alike." Booklist

Ekrem, Erica

Bound; making 30 artful handmade books. Erica Ekrem. Lark Crafts 2015 144 p. color illustrations (paperback) $19.95   **686.3**

1. Book design 2. Bookbinding 3. Book design -- Handbooks, manuals, etc 4. Bookbinding -- Handbooks, manuals, etc

ISBN 1454708670; 9781454708674

LC 2013049059

Bookbinder Erica Ekrem "has devised creative fun for book artists of all levels. Choose from three categories: Vintage, Nature, and Leather. Make books from mason jars and seashells, a classic leather-bound photo album, and other works of art." (Publisher's note)

"This fresh look at an old art will be in demand and is highly recommended." LJ

Golden, Alisa

Making handmade books; 100+ bindings, structures & forms. Lark Crafts 2010 256p il pa $19.95   **686.3**

1. Books 2. Bookbinding

ISBN 978-1-60059-587-5

LC 2010-1546

"This volume updates and combines Golden's previous Creating Handmade Books and Unique Handmade Books to provide an introduction to the fascinating world of artists' books. The specimens highlighted are far from your traditional book—they are works of art that will challenge readers' ideas of what books can be. Though there are plenty of inspiring photographs, there is also ample direction to guide readers interested in creating their own books. Golden also intersperses tidbits of bookmaking history and lore throughout, making this guide not only pleasurable and inspiring to look at but fun to read. " Libr J

Includes bibliographical references

LaPlantz, Shereen, 1947-2003

Cover to cover; creative techniques for making beautiful books, journals & albums. Shereen LaPlantz. Sterling Pub Co Inc 2015 144 p. illustrations (some color) $19.95   **686.3**

1. Bookbinding

ISBN 1454708484; 9781454708483

This book, by Liz Shareen, "[f]irst published in 1995, . . . quickly became renowned in the bookmaking community as the definitive guide to the art. This . . . revised 20th anniversary edition . . . features updated photography and a fresh interior design. . . . After introducing all the bookbinding basics, it shows readers, step by step, how to create, fold, assemble, and stitch a wide range of books and journals . . . using a variety of materials." (Publisher's note)

688.7   Recreational equipment

Gathercole, Peter

Fly tying for beginners; how to tie 50 failsafe flies. Peter Gathercole. Barron's 2006 256 p. color illustrations $24.99   **688.7**

1. Fly casting 2. Fly tying 3. Fly fishing 4. Flies,

Artificial

ISBN 0764158457; 9780764158452

LC 2005921781

This book, by Peter Gathercole, "shows beginners how to craft 50 professional-looking flies for trout and salmon fishing. Each fly-tying project consists of step-by-step instructions accompanied by close-up photos of the work in progress and a large photo of the finished fly. Beginners will learn how to make dry flies, wet flies, bugs, nymphs, hairwings, and streamers. They'll also get advice on which flies are best for catching which variety of fish." (Publishers note)

The **fly-tying bible**; 100 deadly trout and salmon flies in step-by-step photographs. Peter Gathercole. Barron's 2003 256 p. color illustrations $24.95   **688.7**

1. Artificial flies 2. Fly tying 3. Trout fishing 4. Salmon fishing 5. Flies, Artificial

ISBN 0764155504; 9780764155505

LC 2002109917

In this book, by Peter Gathercole, "fly-tying is a highly prized fisherman's craft, but it's also an art form, wonderfully captured in this volume's hundreds of color photos. Each of 100 fly patterns is presented in a two-page spread: an enlarged photo and textual description on the left-hand page, complemented with a set of step-by-step, clearly captioned photos on the facing page." (Publisher's note)

688.722   Dolls, puppets, marionettes

Capella, Massimiliano

Barbie; The Icon. Massimiliano Capella. Natl Book Network 2016 208 p. color illustrations $65   **688.722**

1. Barbie dolls 2. Popular culture

ISBN 1943876118; 9781943876112

This book, by Massimiliano Capella, "celebrates the impact Barbie has had in culture for three generations in everything from style, to fashion, to careers, that makes her the voice of the contemporary woman, the voice of pop culture, and the image of a genuine living legend." (Publisher's note)

"This is a charming book for all ages, and older readers will especially enjoy revisiting their childhoods." Publisher's Weekly

690   Construction of buildings

The **Art** of natural building; design, construction, resources. editors: Joseph F. Kennedy, Michael Smith, Catherine Wanek; illustrated by Joseph F. Kennedy. New Soc. Pubs. 2002 291p il pa $26.95   **690**

1. Building 2. Building materials 3. House construction

ISBN 0-86571-433-9

"The authors, who are practitioners in the natural building movement, introduce a variety of nontraditional construction options, including underground building and building with alternative materials such as adobe, recycled agricultural materials, rammed earth, and straw bale. They also address energy efficiency, design, and the desire to create a healthy environment. The final chapters include case studies." Libr J

Includes bibliographical references

Black & Decker Corp.

The **complete** guide to patios & walkways; money-saving do-it-yourself projects for improving outdoor living space. Creative Pub. International 2010 255p il pa $24.99 **690**
1. Patios
ISBN 978-1-58923-481-9

This is a guide to plan, build, repair, and maintain patios and walkways. It "stands out for its detailed photos and step-by-step, logically arranged instructions. . . . There is an original section on drainage options with projects." Libr J

Bollinger, Don

Hardwood floors; laying, sanding and finishing. Taunton Press 1990 137p il pa $19.95 **690**
1. Floors
ISBN 0-942391-62-4

LC 90-11065

The author "addresses the three types of flooring: strip, plank, and parquet—covering such topics as estimating costs; selecting wood types and grades; preparing the underlayment; planning the layout; sanding; and applying various finishes." Libr J

Includes bibliographical references

The **complete** outdoor builder; from arbors to walkways : 150 DIY projects. Creative Pub. International 2009 528 p. (pbk.) $19.99 **690**
1. Masonry 2. Garden structures 3. Masonry -- Amateurs' manuals 4. Woodwork -- Amateurs' manuals 5. Building, Wooden -- Amateurs' manuals 6. Do-it-yourself work -- Amateurs' manuals 7. Outbuildings -- Design and construction -- Amateurs' manuals 8. Garden structures -- Design and construction -- Amateurs' manuals
ISBN 1589234839; 9781589234833

LC 2009028983

This book, edited by Mark Johnson, Tracy Stanley, and Jennifer Gehlhar, provides advice on adding "patios and walkways to the yard. . . . From low-cost, curb-appeal walkways to expansive, estate-quality decorative concrete patios ,. . . this book presents each project with step-by-step instructions and full-color photographs as well as . . . tips, tricks, and inspiration. Each project uses the most current materials, tools, common practices, codes, and construction techniques." (Publisher's note)

Includes bibliographical references and index.

Cory, Steve

Ultimate guide: porches; building techniques for adding a new porch to your home. Creative Homeowner 2011 191p il pa $16.95 **690**
1. Porches
ISBN 978-1-58011-491-2

LC 2009941175

In this manual, the author "shares numerous, clear illustrations and detailed construction information and tech-

niques. His confident, expert instruction . . . is apparent in the projects presented here. . . . A solid addition to any home improvement collection." Libr J

Diedricksen, Derek

Microshelters; 59 creative cabins, tiny houses, tree houses, and other small structures. Derek Diedricksen. Storey Publishing 2015 255 p. illustrations (chiefly color) (pbk. : alk. paper) $18.95 **690**
1. Houses 2. Log cabins and houses 3. Outbuildings
ISBN 1612123538; 9781612123530

LC 2015009864

Author Derek Diedricksen presents this "collection of creative and inspiring ideas for tiny houses, cabins, forts, studios, and other microshelters. Created by a wide array of builders and designers around the United States and beyond, these 59 unique and innovative structures show you the limits of what is possible. Each is displayed in full-color photographs accompanied by commentary by the author." (Publisher's note)

"A handy source for tiny-house enthusiasts. Pair this with Ryan Mitchell's Tiny House Living or Jay Shafer's The Tumbleweed DIY Book of Backyard Sheds & Tiny Houses." Library Journal

Johnston, Amy

What your contractor can't tell you; the essential guide to building and renovating. Amy Johnston. Shube Pub. 2008 208 p. $24.95 **690**
1. House construction 2. Houses -- Remodeling
ISBN 0979983800; 9780979983801

This book by Amy Johnston "is a comprehensive guide to getting the best results while building or renovating a home. . . . Chapters give detailed coverage of critical topics: design; selecting and supervising the architect and contractor; cost estimates; budget; plan specifications; contracts; dealing with town officials; and keeping track of everything along the way. For each stage of the project, there is detailed information on common pitfalls and how to avoid them." (Publisher's note)

Includes bibliographical references and index.

Kidder, Tracy

House. Houghton Mifflin 1985 341p il hardcover o.p. pa $14 **690**
1. House construction
ISBN 0-618-00191-3 pa

LC 85-7630

"The saga of a couple who supervised the building of their house in Massachusetts, this report interweaves the personal lives of those involved in the project with New England history, the sociology of building, popular lore and practical tips for would-be homebuilders." Publ Wkly

Includes bibliographical references

Levy, Matthys

Why buildings fall down; how structures fail. {by} Matthys Levy and Mario Salvadori; illustrations

by Kevin Woest. Norton 1992 334p il hardcover
o.p. pa $14.95 **690**
1. Building failures 2. Structural failures
ISBN 0-3933-1152-X pa

LC 91-34954

"Two structural engineers examine puzzling structural
failures and collapses and the destruction of ancient and
modern buildings, bridges, dams, and other constructions.
Plenty of illustrations accent the lively text." Booklist

Stiles, David
Backyard Building; Treehouses, Sheds, Arbors,
Gates and Other Garden Projects. Jeanie Stiles and
David Stiles. W.W. Norton & Co. Inc 2014 256 p.
col. ill. $19.95 **690**
1. Building 2. Garden structures 3. Life skills --
Handbooks, manuals, etc.
ISBN 1581572387; 9781581572384

This book by Jeanie Stiles and David Stiles, part of the
Countryman Know How series, covers "backyard accessories, the fundamentals of tools and materials, and useful
tips based on real-life questions from the couple's popular
website." It features "hand-drawn illustrations to guide the
reader through the building process in a user-friendly way."
(Publisher's note)

695 Roof covering

Black & Decker Corp.
The **complete** guide to roofing, siding & trim;
created by: the editors of Creative Publishing International, Inc., in cooperation with Black & Decker.
Updated 2nd ed.; Creative Pub. International 2008
271p il pa $24.99 **695**
1. Roofs 2. Siding (Building materials)
ISBN 978-1-58923-418-5

LC 2008-26823
First published 2004 with title: The complete guide to
roofing & siding

This guide to installing and maintaining roofing and siding includes a "section on trim work as well as a section on
ecofriendly roofs. . . . The photo gallery is quite attractive
and fresh, reflecting current and popular house styles. The
evaluation of materials—relating to home style, maintenance, duration, and drawbacks—is particularly nice. Text
is matter-of-fact and clear, with no topic overdone. A useful
and usable guidebook, this is recommended for all public
libraries." Libr J

The **complete** guide to roofing & siding; Choose,
Install & Maintain Roofing & Siding Materials.
by Editors of Creative Publishing. Creative Pub.
International 2012 255 p. illustrations (chiefly
color) (soft cover) $24.99 **695**
1. Houses -- Remodeling 2. Siding (Building materials)
3. Roofs -- Maintenance and repair 4. Roofing --
Handbooks, manuals, etc 5. Roofing -- Installation --
Handbooks, manuals, etc 6. Siding (Building materials)
-- Handbooks, manuals, etc 7. Roofs -- Maintenance

and repair -- Handbooks, manuals, etc
ISBN 158923717X; 9781589237179

LC 2011052377
This book "covers all traditional materials, from wood
lap siding, brick, concrete block, stucco, stone veneer, and
wooden shakes to vinyl, raised-ridge metal roofing, and
fiber/cement lap siding. Less traditional roof-covering materials, such as EPDM rubber, architectural shingles, and
fully bonded selvage edge and metal shingles are also featured with clear how-to photos and instructions." (Publisher's note)
Complete guide to roofing and siding
Black & Decker?

696 Utilities

Black & Decker Corp.
The **complete** guide to plumbing; modern materials and current codes all new guide to working with
gas pipe. Expanded 4th ed.; Creative Pub. International 2008 334p il pa $24.99 **696**
1. Plumbing
ISBN 978-1-58923-378-2; 1-58923-378-6

LC 2008-8636
First published 1998

This guide to plumbing covers fixtures, installations, repairs, materials, tools, and skills.

"The sequential directions for many common household
repairs are the real asset here. Excellent photos with simple
instruction for each project are also valuable. Includes a
DVD with demonstrations of many of the jobs described in
the book." Libr J

The **complete** guide to plumbing; faucets & fixtures -
PEX - tubs & toilets - water heaters? troubleshoot-
ing & repair - much more. by Editors of Creative
Publishing. Creative Pub. International 2012
335 p. color illustrations (soft cover) $24.99 **696**
1. Plumbing 2. Houses -- Remodeling 3. Plumbing
-- Amateurs' manuals 4. Dwellings -- Remodeling --
Amateurs' manuals
ISBN 1589237005; 9781589237001

LC 2011052378
This book "has the answer to any home plumbing problem you're likely to find. . . . The basics of home plumbing systems are explained with clarity, and all of the most
popular plumbing projects are shown with beautiful step-by-
step photos. New information in this edition includes how to
winterize a house and how to install a state-of-the-art, on-
demand water heater." (Publisher's note)

Henkenius, Merle
Plumbing: complete projects for the home; New
expanded ed.; Creative Homeowner 2006 287p il
pa $19.95 **696**
1. Plumbing
ISBN 1-58011-311-7; 978-1-58011-311-3

LC 2006-924699
First published 2002 with title: Plumbing: basic, intermediate & advanced projects

The author "shows homeowners how to tackle expensive plumbing repairs (e.g., replacing a washer in a leaky faucet). . . . The skill level of each project is rated, and photos walk users step by step through the instructions. . . . Strongly recommended for all collections." Libr J

697 Heating, ventilating, air-conditioning engineering

Ewing, Rex A.

Got sun? go solar; harness nature's free energy to heat and power your grid-tied home. [by] Rex A. Ewing and Doug Pratt. Expanded 2nd ed.; PixyJack Press 2009 191p il map pa $20 **697**
1. Wind power 2. Solar energy 3. Photovoltaic power generation
ISBN 978-0-9773724-6-1
LC 2009-19053
First published 2005
"This is an excellent primer on home application of solar energy. Written in a chatty and amusing style, the book is more informational than mechanical." Libr J
Includes bibliographical references

697.1 Heating with open fires (Radiative heating)

Thurkettle, Vincent

The Wood Fire Handbook; The Complete Guide to a Perfect Fire. by Vincent Thurkettle. Octopus Pub Group 2015 224 p. illustrations $16.99 **697.1**
1. Fire
ISBN 1845336704; 9781845336707
This wood fire handbook, by Vincent Thurkettle, "shows you that the soothing effect of dancing flames and glowing embers is a simple pleasure to have in our lives. Understanding everything that underpins the perfect wood fire makes it even more enjoyable." (Publisher's note)
"In times when utility costs can prove prohibitive, this book will enable anyone to explore the possibilities and benefits of maintaining a good fire in the hearth." Pub Wkly

698 Detail finishing

Jenkins, Alison

300 tips for painting & decorating; tips, techniques & trade secrets. Alison Jenkins. Firefly Books Ltd 2014 176 p. ill. (chiefly col.) $19.95 **698**
1. Painting 2. Interior design
ISBN 1770854525; 9781770854529
This book, by Alison Jenkins, offers "a professional decorator shares hundreds of her personal tips, techniques and trade secrets that will guide homeowners in attractive decorating and regular maintenance tasks, from repainting a ceiling to finding and fixing energy-sucking drafts. These are the how-to's, the wisdom and the time-saving shortcuts that do-it-yourself homeowners will appreciate for years to come." (Publisher's note)

"All of the tips are illustrated, if not with photographs and drawings, then with graphic design. What counts most are the author's know-how sections. . . . Great advice made accessible." Booklist

Santos, Brian

Painting and wallpapering secrets from Brian Santos, the Wall Wizard. Wiley 2011 240p il pa $21.99 **698**
1. Paperhanging 2. House painting
ISBN 978-0-470-59360-8; 0-470-59360-1
LC 2010-28548
"This guide contains useful information for wall treatments. The practical and reassuring advice includes important directions on what not to do. This is nitty-gritty do-it-yourself, with outstanding prep instruction, tool selection, well-thought-out tips and tricks, and technique photos. While inspirational wall-treatment photo books abound, . . . this is the guide you'll need to achieve those looks." Libr J

700 ARTS

700 The arts

★ Arts and humanities through the eras. Gale 2004 5v il set $450 **700**
1. Arts -- History 2. Civilization -- History
ISBN 0-7876-5695-X
LC 2004-10243
"Each volume consists of nine chapters covering the major branches of the humanities: architecture and design, dance, fashion, literature, music, philosophy, religion, theater, and visual arts. . . . This outstanding series offers a wealth of information; the chapters on architecture, dance, and theater alone are worth the price of each volume." Libr J
Includes bibliographical references

Cumming, Robert

Art; a visual history. by Robert Cumming. DK Publishing 2015 416 p. color illustrations $30 **700**
1. Art -- History 2. Art -- Handbooks, manuals, etc
ISBN 1465436618; 9781465436610
LC 2015473824
This book, by Robert Cumming, "is the complete visual guide to Western art, now updated and repackaged in a themed slipcase. How to tell Impressionism from Expressionism, a Degas from a Monet, early Medieval art from early Christian? [This book] explains it all—painting, sculpture, great artists, styles, and schools." (Publisher's note)
"With its solid, accessible information and hundreds of excellent, full-color reproductions, this is ideal for high school or college students as well as any art lover or museumgoer." LJ

Galitz, Kathryn Calley

The **Metropolitan** Museum of Art; masterpiece paintings. Kathryn Calley Galitz. Skira Rizzoli Publications, Inc. 2016 544 p. (hardcover) $75   **700**
1. Art museums 2. Art -- Exhibitions
ISBN 0847846598; 9780847846597

LC 2016938042

This book, by Kathryn Calley Galitz, "offers an exquisite tour, unique in its lavish illustration, scholarship, extent, and graceful packaging. As the first large survey published in 30 years, and the first large general survey of the Met's paintings collection it is the first to celebrate the greatest and most iconic paintings of one of the largest, most important, and most beloved museums in the world." (Publisher's note)

Impelluso, Lucia

Gods and heroes in art; edited by Stefano Zuffi; translated by Thomas Michael Hartmann. Getty Mus. 2003 383p il pa $19.95   **700**
1. Reference books 2. Art and mythology -- Dictionaries
3. Classical mythology -- Dictionaries
ISBN 0-89236-702-4

LC 2002-13422

The characters of ancient Greek and Roman mythology "are each described in entries summarizing their distinctive stories, their special attributes, and the ways in which artists have depicted them. Each entry is . . . illustrated with reproductions of works of art in which the god or hero is pictured. . . . The book concludes with . . . indexes, including a list of iconographic symbols associated with the subjects, and a bibliography." Publisher's note

Includes bibliographical references

The **muses** go to school; inspiring stories about the importance of arts in education. edited by Herbert Kohl and Tom Oppenheim. New Press 2012 xxvii, 200 p.p   **700**
1. Celebrities 2. Arts -- Study and teaching 3. Education -- Aims and objectives
ISBN 1595585397; 9781595585394

LC 2011042803

In this book, edited by Herbert Kohl and Tom Oppenheim, "autobiographical pieces with well-known artists and performers are paired with . . . essays by . . . educators to produce a . . . case for positioning the arts at the center of primary and secondary school curriculums. Spanning a range of genres from acting and music to literary and visual arts, these . . . voices make surprising connections between the arts and the development of intellect, imagination, spirit, emotional intelligence, self-esteem, and self-discipline of young people." (Publisher's note)

Updike, John, 1932-2009

Always looking; essays on art. by John Updike; edited by Christopher Carduff. Alfred A. Knopf 2012 xiii, 204 p.p ill. $45   **700**
1. Art criticism 2. Art -- Psychology
ISBN 0307957306; 9780307957306

LC 2012005986

This book presents "the previously uncollected art writings of the prolific and award-winning novelist and critic [John] Updike, who died in 2009. . . . The essays explore works by artists including [Claude] Monet . . . [Edgar] Degas . . . [and Rene] Magritte; the major movements of Impressionism, Surrealism, Pop art, and Minimalism; and the habits and tastes of the collectors who shape our understanding of fine art's place in American culture." (Publishers Weekly)

700.1   Philosophy and theory of the arts

Larson, Kay

Where the heart beats; John Cage, Zen Buddhism, and the inner life of artists. Kay Larson. Penguin Press 2012 474 p. (hardcover) $29.95   **700.1**
1. Zen Buddhism 2. Postmodernism 3. Zen Buddhism -- Influence
ISBN 1594203407; 9781594203404

LC 2011044714

This book, by Kay Larsen, "part biography, part cultural history," presents "reflections on [John] Cage's encounters with and absorption of Zen Buddhism. . . . Weaving threads of the teachings of Zen Buddhist writer D.T. Suzuki and Alan Watts, along with Cage's own reflections and writings on art, music, dance, and life. [Kay] Larson . . . covers Cage's growing understanding of the nature of noise and silence and the roles that each plays in music." (Publishers Weekly)

Includes bibliographical references and index

700.19   Arts--psychological aspects

James, Jamie

The **glamour** of strangeness; artists and the last age of the exotic. Jamie James. Farrar, Straus & Giroux 2016 368 p. (hardback) $27   **700.19**
1. Artists 2. Identity (Psychology) 3. Alienation (Social psychology) 4. Artists -- Biography 5. Artists -- Psychology
ISBN 9780374163358

LC 2015041555

This book, by Jamie James, focuses on six "artists . . . ., Walter Spies, the . . . German painter who remade his life in Bali; Raden Saleh, the Javanese painter who found fame in Europe; Isabelle Eberhardt, a Russian-Swiss writer who roamed the Sahara; . . . the American experimental filmmaker Maya Deren, who went to Haiti. . . . From France, Paul Gauguin left for Tahiti; and Victor Segalen, a naval doctor, poet, and novelist, immersed himself in . . . imperial Peking." (Publisher's note)

"Abundant primary sources inform James' sharply drawn, sympathetic portraits." Kirkus

Includes bibliographical references and index

700.92   Biography

Byatt, A. S. (Antonia Susan), 1936-

Peacock & vine; On William Morris and Mariano Fortuny. A.S. Byatt. Alfred A. Knopf 2016 192 p. color illustrations (hardback) $26.95   **700.92**
ISBN 9781101947470

LC 2016008946

This book, by A.S. Byatt, "opens a window into the lives, designs, and passions of Mariano Fortuny and William Morris. . . . Born a generation apart in the mid-1800s, Fortuny and Morris were seeming opposites: Fortuny a Spanish aristocrat thrilled by the sun-baked cultures of Crete and Knossos; Morris a member of the British bourgeoisie, enthralled by Nordic myths. Through their revolutionary inventions and textiles, both men inspired a new variety of art." (Publisher's note)

"Although brief, this is an inspiring homage that forges illuminating connections between two dynamos." Kirkus

Includes bibliographical references.

Davis, Deborah

The **trip**; Andy Warhol's plastic fantastic cross-country adventure. Deborah Davis. Atria Books 2015 324 p. illustrations (hardback) $26   **700.92**
1. Automobile travel -- United States -- History -- 20th century

ISBN 1476703515; 9781476703510

LC 2015016732

This book by Deborah Davis "captures [Andy] Warhol's interactions with Dennis Hopper, Peter Fonda, Marcel Duchamp, Elizabeth Taylor, Elvis Presley, and Frank Sinatra. Along the way he also met rednecks, beach bums, underground filmmakers, artists, poets, socialites, and newly minted hippies, and they each left an indelible mark on his psyche." (Publisher's note)

"Davis's prose mirrors the zeitgeist Warhol brought to his art: bright, breezy, and easy to understand. She may not convince readers that the L.A. trip was Warhol's artistic turning point, but she immerses them in his gossipy, kitschy, crowded, materialistic, and off-kilter world. For Warhol aficionados, this book may add a few twists to familiar territory. For readers less familiar with the pop artist, it provides an entertaining and accessible introduction to his work and a beginner's guide to the social scene of the pop art world." Pub Wkly

Kaplan, Carla

Miss Anne in Harlem; The White Women of the Black Renaissance. by Carla Kaplan. Harper 2013 512 p. $28.99   **700.92**
1. Whites 2. Harlem Renaissance 3. Women -- United States

ISBN 0060882387; 9780060882389

In this book, author Carla Kaplan "focuses on white women, collectively called 'Miss Anne,' who became Harlem Renaissance insiders. [She] focuses on six of the unconventional, free-thinking women, some from Manhattan high society, many Jewish, who crossed race lines and defied social conventions to become a part of the culture and heartbeat of Harlem." (Publisher's note)

Ross, Clifford

The **world** of Edward Gorey; by Clifford Ross and Karen Wilkin. Abrams 1996 190p il hardcover o.p. pa $19.95   **700.92**
1. Artists 2. Authors 3. Novelists 4. Illustrators 5. Set designers 6. Children's authors

ISBN 0-8109-9083-0 pa

LC 95-47900

This book includes an "interview with Mr. Ross, {in which} Edward Gorey speaks of his likes and dislikes and aspects of his career. . . . Ms. Wilkin discusses Gorey's work as illustrator, author, stage designer, and miscellaneous creator." Atl Mon

Includes bibliographical references

Rynecki, Elizabeth

Chasing portraits; a great-granddaughter's quest for her lost art legacy. Elizabeth Rynecki. NAL, New American Library 2016 385 p. illustrations (some color) (hardback) $28   **700.92**
1. Jewish artists -- Poland -- Biography 2. Jews in art 3. Art, Polish -- 20th century

ISBN 1101987669; 9781101987667

LC 2016012588

This memoir by Elizabeth Rynecki focuses on her "quest to find the art of her Polish-Jewish great-grandfather, lost during World War II. . . . Before Moshe was deported to the ghetto, he entrusted his work to friends who would keep it safe. After he was killed in the Majdanek concentration camp, the art was dispersed all over the world. With the help of historians, curators, and admirers of Moshe's work, Elizabeth began the incredible . . . task of rebuilding his collection." (Publisher's note)

"A wonderful story beautifully told. Rynecki's yearslong search, successes, frustrations, and failures are a study in perseverance." Kirkus

Includes bibliographical references.

Smee, Sebastian

The **art** of rivalry; Four Friendships, Betrayals, and Breakthroughs in Modern Art. Sebastian Smee. Random House 2016 416 p. illustrations (some color) (hardback) $28   **700.92**
1. Artists -- Psychology 2. Creation (Literary, artistic, etc.)

ISBN 9780812994803

LC 2015050361

In this book, "art critic Sebastian Smee tells the fascinating story of four pairs of artists—Manet and Degas, Picasso and Matisse, Pollock and de Kooning, Freud and Bacon—whose fraught, competitive friendships spurred them to new creative heights." (Publisher's note)

"This ambitious and impressive work is an utterly absorbing read about four important relationships in modern art." Pub Wkly

Includes bibliographical references

701   Philosophy and theory of fine and decorative arts

Snyder, Laura J.

Eye of the beholder; Johannes Vermeer, Antoni van Leeuwenhoek, and the reinvention of seeing. Laura J. Snyder. W W Norton & Co Inc 2015 448 p. color illustrations; map (hardcover) $27.95   **701**
1. Art and science 2. Art and science -- Netherlands

-- Delft -- History -- 17th century
ISBN 0393077462; 9780393077469

LC 2014038143

"In 'Eye of the Beholder,' Laura J. Snyder transports us to the streets, inns, and guildhalls of seventeenth-century Holland, where artists and scientists gathered, and to their studios and laboratories, where they mixed paints and prepared canvases, ground and polished lenses, . . . and invented the modern notion of seeing. With charm and narrative flair Snyder brings Vermeer and Van Leeuwenhoek--and the men and women around them--vividly to life." (Publisher's note)

"Though it is only speculation that these great thinkers knew each other personally, Snyder expertly brings to life their shared social milieu of artists and scientists, all seeking new ways to investigate nature. These intertwined biographies weave a story of two men whose insistence on "daring to see" revolutionized our understanding of perception itself." Booklist

Includes bibliographical references and index

701.85   Color

Atwood, Rebecca

Living with pattern; color, texture, and print at home. Rebecca Atwood. Clarkson Potter Publishers 2016 288 p. (ebook) $65; (hardback) $32.50 **701.85**
1. Interior design 2. Color in interior decoration 3. Texture in interior decoration 4. Repetitive patterns (Decorative arts) in interior decoration
ISBN 9780553459456; 0553459449; 9780553459449

LC 2016008549

This book, by Rebecca Atwood, presents "ideas for how to use pattern to decorate your home. . . . She covers pattern usage you probably already have, such as on your duvet cover or in the living room rug, and she also reveals the unexpected places you might not have thought to add it: bathroom tiles, an arrangement of book spines in a reading nook, or windowpane gridding in your entryway." (Publisher's note)

Includes bibliographical reference (pages 279-281) and index

702   Miscellany of fine and decorative arts

Congdon, Lisa

Art, Inc. the essential guide for building your career as an artist. Lisa Congdon; Edited by Meg Mateo Ilasco. Chronicle Books 2014 184 p. illustrations $16.95   **702**
1. Artists 2. Art -- Economic aspects 3. Art -- Vocational guidance
ISBN 145212826X; 9781452128269

LC 2014035328

In this book "Lisa Congdon reveals the many ways you can earn a living by making art--through illustration, licensing, fine art sales, print sales, teaching, and beyond. Including industry advice from such successful art-world pros as Nikki McClure, Mark Hearld, Paula Scher, and more." (Publisher's note)

"A useful resource for young adults, emerging artists, and creative people of all ages who seek a career change." LJ

702.8   Auxiliary techniques and procedures; apparatus, equipment, materials

Amore, Anthony M.

The art of the con; the most notorious fakes, frauds, and forgeries in the art world. Anthony M. Amore. Palgrave Macmillan Trade 2015 272 p. 8 plates; color illustrations (hardback) $26   **702.8**
1. Art thefts 2. Art -- Forgeries
ISBN 1137279877; 9781137279873

LC 2014046676

This book, by Anthony M. Amore, "tells the stories of some of history's most notorious yet untold cons. They involve stolen art hidden for decades; elaborate ruses that involve the Nazis and allegedly plundered art; . . . the use of online and television auction sites to scam buyers out of millions; and other confidence scams incredible not only for their boldness but more so because they actually worked." (Publisher's note)

"Of significant interest to art world aficionados, brokers, collectors, dealers, lawyers, professionals, and general readers, this ambitious, well-presented and well-documented survey belongs in public as well as academic and special libraries." LJ

703   Dictionaries, encyclopedias, concordances of fine and decorative arts

Frazier, Nancy

The Penguin concise dictionary of art history. Penguin Ref. 1999 774p hardcover o.p. pa $20 **703**
1. Reference books 2. Art -- Dictionaries
ISBN 0-14-051420-1 pa

LC 98-56089

"An easy-to-read, scholarly yet not lofty, fascinating, and very well-organized book." Libr J

Includes bibliographical references (p. {731}-736) and index

704   Special topics in fine and decorative arts

The female gaze; women artists making their world. edited by Robert Cozzolino with contributions by Glenn Adamson, Linda Lee Alter, Diane Burko, Anna C. Chave, Robert Cozzolino, Anna Havemann, Joanna Gardner-Huggett, Melanie Anne Herzog, Janine Mileaf, Mey-Yen Moriuchi, Jodi Throckmorton, Michele Wallace. Pennsylvania Academy of the Fine Arts 2012 335 p. (alk. paper) $60   **704**
1. Women artists 2. Art -- Exhibitions 3. Women artists -- Exhibitions 4. Art, Modern -- 20th century -- Exhibitions 5. Art, Modern -- 21st century -- Exhibitions 6. Art -- Pennsylvania -- Philadelphia -- Exhibitions 7.

Pennsylvania Academy of the Fine Arts -- Exhibitions
ISBN 1555953891; 9781555953898

LC 2012036714

This "catalog was created in conjunction with an exhibition of the same title at the Pennsylvania Academy of the Fine Arts, where [art collector Linda Lee] Alter eventually donated her collection" of women-made art. The book features "essays by an internationally diverse group of scholars and curators who focus on Alter's collection." (Library Journal)

Includes bibliographical references (pages 323-330)

Holladay, Wilhelmina Cole

A **museum** of their own; National Museum of Women in the Arts. text contributions by Philip Kopper. Abbeville Press 2008 240p il $50   **704**
1. Women artists 2. National Museum of Women in the Arts (U.S.)
ISBN 978-0-7892-1003-6; 0-7892-1003-7

LC 2008-21646

"The National Museum of Women in the Arts . . . opened in 1987. It changed the status of women artists and the life of its founder, who now tells the museum's fascinating success story in an entertainingly anecdotal, inspiring, and beautifully illustrated [book]. . . . This invaluable work of art history is enlivened by Holladay's encounters with artists . . . and gorgeous reproductions, many of works that will be new to even the most art-expert readers." Booklist

In **harmony**; the Norma Jean Calderwood collection of Islamic art. edited by Mary McWilliams; with essays by Jessica Chloros and Katherine Eremin, Walter B. Denny, Penley Knipe, Oya Pancaroğlu, David J. Roxburgh, Sunil Sharma, Anthony B. Sigel, Marianna Shreve Simpson. Harvard Art Museum 2013 303 p. (Yale University Press) $75   **704**
1. Art collections 2. Islamic art -- Exhibitions 3. Art, Iranian -- Exhibitions 4. Arthur M. Sackler Museum -- Exhibitions 5. Art -- Private collections -- Massachusetts -- Cambridge -- Exhibitions
ISBN 9781891771620; 9780300176414; 0300176414

LC 2012030304

Editor Mary McWilliams' book features the Norma Jean Calderwood collection of Islamic art. The book features nine essays that "explore issues of conservation as well as the cultural and historical significance of various objects in this largely unpublished collection. Topics include the influence of calligraphic line and physical gesture on Safavid drawings; figurative imagery on Iranian ceramics; and what cobalt pigment reveals about an object's origins." (Publisher's note)

Includes bibliographical references (pages 274-290) and index

704.03   Ethnic and national groups

The **James** T. Bialac Native American Art Collection; Selected Works. Mark Andrew White, General Editor. University of Oklahoma Press 2012

xi, 223 p.p ill. (hardcover) $49.95; (paperback) $29.95   **704.03**
1. Art collections 2. Native American art 3. Indian art -- Catalogs 4. Fred Jones Jr. Museum of Art -- Catalogs 5. Art -- Private collections -- Oklahoma -- Norman -- Catalogs
ISBN 0806143045; 9780806142999; 9780806143040

LC 2012003005

This book, published by the Fred Jones Museum of Art, presents a catalogue of the James T. Bialac Native American Art Collection of "easel paintings and three-dimensional works. . . . The collection comprises nearly four thousand items, including drawings, sculptures, prints, kachinas, jewelry, ceramics, rattles, baskets, and textiles. . . . The Bialac Collection represents indigenous cultures across North America." (Publisher's note)

Includes bibliographical references (pages 205-209) and index

Patton, Sharon F.

African-American art. Oxford Univ. Press 1998 319p il maps (Oxford history of art) hardcover o.p. pa $18.95   **704.03**
1. African American art
ISBN 0-19-284213-7 pa

LC 98-190459

"Comprehensively and with sharp, scholarly accuracy, Patton has closed gaps between the chronological and thematic directions of Black American art and complexities of Euro-American art history." Choice

Russell, Karen Kramer

Shapeshifting; transformations in native american art. Karen Kramer Russell. Yale University Press 2012 248 p. $65   **704.03**
1. Indian art 2. Native American art 3. Native Americans -- North America
ISBN 0300177321; 9780300177329

LC 2011928735

Author Karen Kramer Russell "aims to dispel the notion that Native American art is 'predictable.' . . . This confluence of past and present is enacted in many of the pieces featured in this . . . volume, such as Brian Jungen's Cetology . . . [and] Dwayne Wilcox's After Two or Three Hundred Years You Will Not Notice. . . . Russell and her colleagues . . . achieve their goal of asserting the . . . relevancy of Native American art." (Publishers Weekly)

The **visual** blues; Natalie A. Mault, R. A. Lawson, John Lowe; [edited by] Natalie A. Mault. University of Washington Press 2014 88 p. color illustrations (alk. paper) $40   **704.03**
1. Art and music 2. Harlem Renaissance 3. Jazz music -- History and criticism
ISBN 061587830X; 9780615878300

LC 2013949519

This book, edited by Natalie A. Mault, "explores the enormous impact that blues and jazz music emanating from the Deep South and moving north had on artists associated with the Harlem Renaissance. . . . The art scene in Harlem from 1919 to approximately 1940 encouraged a melding of art, music, literature, and poetry, providing a creative haven and outlet for transcending hardships and shattering racial stereotypes." (Publisher's note)

"Highly recommended for anyone interested in art and African American cultural history." LJ

704.9 Iconography

Bussagli, Marco

Angels. Abrams 2007 780p il $19.95   **704.9**
1. Angels 2. Art and religion
ISBN 978-0-8109-9436-2; 0-8109-9436-4
           LC 2007-010749

"Art historian Marco Bussagli has organized the book by significant Biblical events. . . . Each work of art is accompanied by the Biblical passage it illustrates, along with a commentary exploring its form and meaning." Publisher's note

Includes bibliographical references

Levine, Lee I.

Visual Judaism in late antiquity; historical contexts of Jewish art. Lee I. Levine. Yale University Press 2012 x, 582 p.p (cloth : alk. paper) $75 **704.9**
1. Antiquities 2. Jewish art and symbolism 3. Middle East -- Civilization -- To 622
ISBN 0300100892; 9780300100891
           LC 2012003770

Here, Lee I. Levine "focuses on the art of the Jewish people inside and outside the synagogue, from c. 1200 BCE to seventh century CE, using 'the immediate social, cultural, and religious contexts as the main points of reference in interpreting Jewish art of Late Antiquity.' . . . Levine argues: 'the picture that emerges from the archaeological remains of Late Antiquity is far more diverse, heterogeneous, and locally oriented than that derived from literary sources.'" (Library Journal)

Includes bibliographical references (pages 483-557) and index

★ The **Renaissance** portrait; from Donatello to Bellini. edited by Keith Christiansen and Stefan Weppelmann; essays by Patricia Rubin ... [et al.] Metropolitan Museum of Art -- Distributed by Yale University Press 2011 xii, 420 p.p (hc: Yale University Press) $65   **704.9**
1. Renaissance portrait painting -- Italy 2. Art, Italian -- Exhibitions 3. Portraits, Renaissance -- Italy -- Exhibitions
ISBN 0300175914; 1588394255; 1588394263; 9780300175912; 9781588394255; 9781588394262
           LC 2011027471

This book, edited by Keith Christiansen and Stefan Weppelmann, "provides new research and insight into the early history of portraiture in Italy, examining in detail how its major art centers--Florence, the princely courts, and Venice--saw the rapid development of portraiture as closely linked to Renaissance society and politics, ideas of the individual, and concepts of beauty." (Publisher's note)

Includes bibliographical references and index.

707.5 Art--collecting

Obrist, Hans-Ulrich, 1968-

Ways of curating; Hans Ulrich Obrist with Asad Reza. Faber & Faber, Inc. 2014 176 p. (hardback) $23   **707.5**
1. Art museum curators 2. Art museums 3. Museums -- Curatorship
ISBN 0865478198; 9780865478190
           LC 2014016970

This book "is a compendium of the insights [Hans Ulrich] Obrist has gained from his years of extraordinary work in the art world. It skips between centuries and continents, flitting from meetings with the artists who have inspired him . . . to biographies of influential figures such as Diaghilev and Walter Hopps. It describes some of the greatest exhibitions in history, as well as some of the greatest exhibitions never realized." (Publisher's note)

"An essential title for museum professionals, curators, and students aspiring to these professions." LJ

708 Galleries, museums, private collections of fine and decorative arts

The **art** of music; edited by Patrick Coleman. Yale University Press 2015 318 p. (hardback) $65   **708**
1. Artists 2. Art and music 3. Creative ability
ISBN 0300215479; 9780300215472
           LC 2015017781

This book, edited by Patrick Coleman, is an "illustrated and . . . interdisciplinary look at the mutual influence between music and the visual arts across cultures and eras. The book sheds new light on more familiar artists at the intersection of the visual and the musical, such as Wassily Kandinsky and Arnold Schoenberg, and presents new scholarship on less well-known examples in the arts of Asia, Africa, the Americas, and Europe." (Publisher's note)

Includes bibliographical references and index

Meier, Richard

Building the Getty. University of California Press 1999 204p il pa $25.95   **708**
1. Getty Center (Los Angeles, Calif.)
ISBN 0-520-21730-6; 978-0-520-21730-0
           LC 99-20219

First published 1997 by Knopf

"Charting his involvement in the Getty's construction, Meier recounts in an intriguingly candid, eminently personal style the formidable bureaucratic process entailed upon undertaking to realize this grandiose endeavor. Beginning with the competition itself, Meier's detailed reminiscences offer fascinating insights into the design process and the extraordinarily intricate procedures and systems, as well as endless setbacks, associated with executing a modern-day megalithic structure." Booklist

National Gallery of Art (U.S.)

★ **National** Gallery of Art; [foreword by Earl A. Powell III] 2nd ed.; Thames and Hudson 2006 332p il (World of art) pa $18.95 **708**

1. National Gallery of Art (U.S.)

ISBN 0-500-20390-3; 978-0-500-20390-3

LC 2005-904459

First published 2004 by National Gallery of Art; Based on John Walker's National Gallery of Art, published 1984

"The collection of the National Gallery of Art in Washington includes works by the greatest masters of Western art from the twelfth century to the present. . . . [In this] look at the National Gallery's masterpieces . . . the works are illustrated in full color, and the curators have written the texts." Publisher's note

708.1   Geographic treatment

Walsh, John

The **J.** Paul Getty Museum and its collections; a museum for the new century. {by} John Walsh, Deborah Gribbon. Getty Mus. 1997 288p hardcover o.p. pa $40 **708.1**

1. Philanthropists 2. Art collectors 3. J. Paul Getty Museum 4. Energy industry executives

ISBN 0-89236-476-9 pa

LC 97-12170

This volume is a history of the J. Paul Getty Museum and a guide to its collections

This is "a lavish visual compendium of J. Paul Getty's amazing art collection; in addition, the text reveals important background details surrounding Getty's life and his passion for art. Walsh and Gribbon communicate just how the magnate's fortunes were put to the test as planned acquisitions of artwork flourished." Booklist

709   History, geographic treatment, biography

The **Art** Book; Phaidon Press. Phaidon Press 2012 592 p. (hardcover) $59.95 **709**

1. Art 2. Artists

ISBN 0714864676; 9780714864679

This book by Phaidon Press is an "A - Z guide to artists from medieval times to the present day . . . including paintings, photographs, sculptures, video, installations and performance art. Each artist is represented on a full page with a definitive work and explanatory . . . information." The book features "examples of all periods, schools, visions and techniques." (Publisher's note)

Atlas of world art; edited by John Onians. Oxford University Press 2004 352p il maps $150 **709**

1. Art -- History -- Maps

ISBN 0-19-521583-4

LC 2003-55029

This atlas offers a "framework for coverage of art activity around the world from prehistoric times to 2000. . . . Each of the book's seven parts (each covers a period in art history) includes a brief illustrated introduction followed

by a standardized sequence of sections on World, American, European, African, Asian and Pacific Art." Choice

Includes bibliographical references

Bailey, Gauvin Alexander

Art in time; a world history of styles and movements. Gauvin Alexander Bailey [and twenty four others] Phaidon Press 2014 367 p. illustrations (chiefly color) $69.95 **709**

1. Art 2. Art -- History 3. Art movements

ISBN 0714867373; 9780714867373

LC 2014466680

This book, by Gauvin Alexander Bailey and others, "is the first book to embed art movements within the larger context of politics and history. Global in scope and featuring an innovative present-to-past arrangement, the book's accessible text looks back on the most significant art styles and movements, from the present day to antiquity." (Publisher's note)

"Regardless, this is an ambitious attempt to rethink the survey in light of contemporary art's global turn and a valuable addition to any library." LJ

Barnitz, Jacqueline

Twentieth-century art of Latin America. University of Tex. Press 2001 400p il $70; pa $34.95 **709**

1. Latin American art 2. Art -- 20th century 3. Art, Latin American 4. Art, Modern -- 20th century -- Latin America

ISBN 0-292-70857-2; 0-292-70858-0 pa

LC 99-50871

A survey of 20th century Latin American art which includes coverage of regional movements, and discussion of historical, political, and cultural influences

"Latin American art, the fruit of violent collisions among diverse indigenous, European, and African cultures, is revealed as provocative and vibrant in Barnitz's well-illustrated and groundbreaking overview of its dazzling twentieth-century flowering." Booklist

Includes bibliographical references

Beckett, Wendy

Sister Wendy's American collection; {by} Sister Wendy Beckett. HarperCollins Pubs. 2000 288p il $40 **709**

1. Art appreciation 2. Art -- History

ISBN 0-06-019556-8

LC 00-40953

The author provides a "discussion of works in six of America's renowned art museums. . . . {She} includes a variety of media-- paintings, sculpture, decorative arts, armor, and other art objects-- and the individual works originate from a dizzying array of time periods and several countries." Libr J

Bramly, Serge

Leonardo; the artist and the man. translated by Sian Reynolds. Penguin Bks. 1994 493p il pa $25 **709**

1. Artists 2. Painters 3. Scientists 4. Artists, Italian 5. Writers on science

ISBN 0-14-023175-7; 978-0-14-023175-5

Original French edition, 1988

In this account Bramly "sheds light on the more personal aspects of Leonardo. . . . As he follows da Vinci's often frustrating career and ever-widening sphere of inquiries, inventions, and discoveries, he also patches together overlooked clues about his private life, causing us to marvel anew at Leonardo's fertile and versatile mind while acquiring a sharper image of Leonardo the man. A richly detailed, expansive, and thoroughly enjoyable portrait." Booklist

Includes bibliographical references

Craven, Wayne

American art; history and culture. McGraw-Hill 2003 687p il pa $69   **709**
1. American art
ISBN 978-0-07-282329-5; 0-07-282329-1
LC 2002-035777
First published 1994

The author "establishes seven main stylistic periods—colonial, Federal, romantic, the American Renaissance, early modern, postwar modern, and postmodern—and then goes into great detail within each section, profiling individual artists and discussing the effects of various social, political, and technological changes on aesthetics and the role of art in daily life. . . . Coverage of American photography and twentieth-century art are particularly dynamic, but his examples and emphases prove to be insightful and creative throughout." Booklist

Includes bibliographical references

Cuba: art and history, from 1868 to today; [edited by Nathalie Bondil; translation, Timothy Bernard et al.] Montreal Museum of Fine Arts 2008 424p il map $85   **709**
1. Cuban art
ISBN 3-7913-4019-0; 978-3-7913-4019-7
LC 2008-396997

"This momentous, dazzling volume interweaves history, biography, and artistic expression to explicate Cuba's distinctive vibrancy and glorious creativity." Booklist

Includes bibliographical references

Dippie, Brian W.

The **Frederic** Remington Art Museum collection. Abrams 2000 264p il $49.50   **709**
1. Artists 2. Painters 3. Sculptors 4. West (U.S.) in art 5. Drafters
ISBN 0-8109-6711-1
LC 00-49339

This biography examines the artist's life and work and follows his evolution from illustrator to artist

"Photographs and comparative images enhance the author's discussions of Remington himself and of the individual paintings, drawings, and sculptures." Libr J

Includes bibliographical references

Encyclopedia of artists; [consulting editor, William Vaughan; contributors, Christopher Ackroyd, et al.] Oxford Univ. Press 2000 6v il set $195 **709**
1. Reference books 2. Art -- Dictionaries 3. Artists

-- Dictionaries
ISBN 0-19-521572-9
LC 00-27167

"This set is beautifully written and illustrated. It will not only provide reliable information for researchers but will also entertain the interested browser." Am Ref Books Annu, 2001

Encyclopedia of Latin American & Caribbean art; edited by Jane Turner. Oxford University Press 2006 803p il (Grove library of world art) $250   **709**
1. Reference books 2. Caribbean art -- Encyclopedias 3. Latin American art -- Encyclopedias
ISBN 978-0-19-531075-7; 0-19-531075-6
First published 1999 by Grove's Dictionaries

"This work covers the art of every country in Central and South America and the Caribbean, from the colonial period to the present. The entries, expanded and updated from the publisher's mammoth Dictionary of Art, cover countries, artists, and artistic styles, with cross-referencing where appropriate." Libr J [review of 1999 edition]

Includes bibliographical references

Farrington, Lisa E.

Creating their own image; the history of African-American women artists. Oxford University Press 2005 354p il $55   **709**
1. Women artists 2. African American women 3. African American artists
ISBN 0-19-516721-X
LC 2003-66171

"A richly detailed yet fluent work of trailblazing research, fresh interpretations, and cogent argument, Farrington's treatise discusses vital aesthetic as well as social and cultural issues and creates a vibrant context for such seminal artists as Augusta Savage, Faith Ringgold, Barbara Chase-Riboud, Kara Walker, and many more." Booklist

FitzGerald, Michael C.

★ **Picasso** and American art; [by] Michael FitzGerald; with a chronology by Julia May Boddewyn. Whitney Museum of American Art; in association with Yale University Press 2006 400p il $65   **709**
1. Artists 2. Painters 3. American art
ISBN 9780300114522; 0-300-11452-4
LC 2006-1402

A "study of Picasso's influence on some of the most significant American artists of the 20th century. Fitzgerald moves chronologically, from the earliest Americans who engaged cubism in the teens (Max Weber, Mardsen Hartley, Man Ray, Stuart Davis), through the modernist investigations of Arshile Gorky, Willem De Kooning and Jackson Pollack, and winds up with Roy Lichtenstien's pop-art and Jasper Johns' postmodern responses to Picasso. Fitzgerald takes great pains to triangulate exhibition specifics with the work and words of each artist to document the precise nature and extent of the influence in each case. . . . There is a generous supply of images presented with the text, and they are as successful as Fitzgerald's prose in illuminating the complexities of Picasso's influence on these artists." Publ Wkly

Includes bibliographical references

Gardner, Helen

★ **Gardner's** art through the ages; a global history. [revised by] Fred S. Kleiner. Enhanced 13th ed.; Wadsworth, Cengage Learning 2010 1088p il map $165.99   **709**

1. Art -- History

ISBN 978-0-495-79986-3; 0-495-79986-6

        LC 2009-932089

First published 1926 by Harcourt Brace & Co.

This book surveys world art from prehistoric times to the present day. Painting, sculpture, architecture and some decorative arts are considered. Although the focus is on European art, there are also chapters on ancient Near Eastern, Asian, pre-Columbian, American Indian, African and Oceanic art.

Includes bibliographical references

Gombrich, E. H.

★ The **story** of art; 16th ed rev and expanded; Phaidon Press 1995 688p il $49.95; pa $29.95 **709**

1. Art -- History

ISBN 0-7148-3355-X; 0-7148-3247-2 pa

        LC 96-140698

First published 1950

This survey of art examines artistic achievements in historical context to consider how prevailing social, political, and economic factors may have influenced the succession and popularity of certain artistic styles.

Includes bibliographical references

Gompertz, Will

What Are You Looking at? the Surprising, Shocking & Sometimes Strange Story of 150 Years of Modern Art. Will Gompertz. Dutton 2012 432 p. (hardcover) $28.95   **709**

1. Art -- 20th century 2. Art -- 21st century

ISBN 0525952675; 9780525952671

        LC 2012027995

It was author Will "Gompertz's aim . . . to demystify modern art, to provide a basic history of each of its 'isms,' and show how these movements are interconnected." He "begins with [Marcel] Duchamp's omnipresent influence on the history of modern art and then chronicles movements that led up to and followed Duchamp's Fountain (1917), from pre-Impressionist artists Manet and Courbet to contemporary artists Banksy and Ai Weiwei." (Publishers Weekly)

The Grove encyclopedia of American art; editor in chief, Joan Marter. Oxford University Press 2011 5 v. ill. (some col.), map   **709**

1. American art -- Encyclopedias

ISBN 9780195335798; 0199739269; 9780199739264; 0195335791

        LC 2010030274

This reference book "contains entries . . . that comprise a . . . survey . . . art history. It covers American painting, architecture, sculpture, and photography from the Pre-Columbian sources to the colonial period to the twenty-first century devoting coverage to many previously underrepresented areas of inquiry, including African American artists, Asian American artists, and Native American art, both historical and contemporary. Artists, major movements, institutions, critics, and the architecture found in major cities of the United States are covered, as are new media and methodologies, including digital art, performance art, and installation art. In addition to American artists such as John Singer Sargent, Robert Rauschenberg, Maya Lin, and Kiki Smith, attention is also paid to individuals who have had a significant impact on American art and art history through their activity in the United States, including Marcel Duchamp, Erwin Panofsky, Renzo Piano, and Max Beckmann." (Publisher's note)

Includes bibliographical references and index.

Harvey, Eleanor Jones

The **Civil** War and American art; Eleanor Jones Harvey. Smithsonian American Art Museum 2012 xvii, 316 p.p ill. (hardcover) $65   **709**

1. American art 2. Art collections 3. United States -- History -- 1861-1865, Civil War -- Pictorial works 4. Art, American -- 19th century -- Themes, motives -- Exhibitions 5. Art and society -- United States -- History -- 19th century -- Exhibitions

ISBN 0300187335; 9780300187335; 9780937311981

        LC 2012029342

This book, by Eleanor Jones Harvey and released by the Smithsonian American Art Museum, "looks at the range of artwork created before, during, and following the [U.S. Civil War], in the years between 1852 and 1877. [The] author . . . surveys paintings made by some of America's finest artists, including Frederic Church, Sanford Gifford, Winslow Homer, and Eastman Johnson, and photographs taken by George Barnard, Alexander Gardner, and Timothy H. O'Sullivan." (Publisher's note)

Includes bibliographical references (pages 274-293) and index.

Haskell, Barbara

The **American** century; art and culture. Norton 2000 2v il boxed set $120   **709**

1. American art 2. Arts -- United States

ISBN 978-0-393-04859-9; 0-393-04859-4

A reissue of the title first published 1999

Based on exhibitions at the Whitney Museum, these illustrated volumes cover 20th century American painting, sculpture, printmaking, and photography through political, historical, social, economic, and culture contexts

Hassrick, Peter H.

Art of the American West; the Haub family collection at Tacoma Art Museum. Laura F. Fry, Peter H. Hassrick, Scott Manning Stevens. Tacoma Art Museum 2014 312 p. color illustrations (hardback) $65   **709**

1. American art 2. West (U.S.) in art 3. Native American art 4. Tacoma Art Museum -- Catalogs 5. West (U.S.) -- In art -- Catalogs 6. Art, American -- West (U.S.) -- Catalogs 7. Art -- Private collections -- Washington (State) -- Tacoma -- Catalogs

ISBN 0300207603; 9780300207606

        LC 2014020864

This book "was prepared to celebrate the opening of the Taub Family Collection of the Art of the American West at the Tacoma Art Museum. The 320 color reproductions in the volume, representing the work of 140 artists who sought to chronicle life in the American West, provide a visual chronicle of the peoples, topography, flora, and fauna of lands that would play a vital role in the evolution of the nation." (Choice: Current Reviews for Academic Libraries)

"As expected in a work of this nature, essays on the collection, and themes in western art appropriate to the collection, as well as concise but informative artist biographies, complement the work. This extensive and vibrant collection is unique in the Pacific Northwest. Summing Up: Recommended. All readership levels." Choice

Includes bibliographical references

Hauptman, Jodi

Degas; A Strange New Beauty. Jody Hauptman; with essays by Carol Armstrong [and 11 others] The Museum of Modern Art 2016 239 p. illustrations (chiefly color) $50   709
1. Engraving 2. Monotype (Engraving) -- 19th century -- Exhibitions
ISBN 1633450058; 9781633450059
                                                                LC 2015960601
This book, by Jody Hauptman, focuses on Edgar Degas. "Degas was introduced to the monotype process, a technique in which the artist draws in ink on a metal plate that is then run through a press, typically resulting in a single print. Degas embraced the medium with enormous enthusiasm, inventing a new repertoire of mark-making that included wiping, scraping, scratching, fingerprinting and rendering via removal." (Publisher's note)

"Each chapter, authored by a Degas specialist, includes helpful endnotes. A catalog of the exhibition and over 176 images are also included." LJ

Includes bibliographical references (pages 236-238)

Hearn, Maxwell K.

Splendors of Imperial China; treasures from the National Palace Museum, Taipei. Metropolitan Mus. of Art 1996 144p il hardcover o.p. pa $29.95 709
1. Chinese art 2. National Palace Museum (Taipei, Taiwan)
ISBN 0-87099-766-1 pa
                                                                LC 95-46590
Hearn "selected more than 100 works to present here, drawn from an extensive traveling exhibition featuring Neolithic and Bronze Age works, as well as Sung, Ming, and other dynasty masterpieces. This beautifully produced book contains fine quality reproductions that illuminate a splendid collection of rare artwork.... The text describes in accessible terms important background information, including cultural climate, historical events, and artistic elements." Booklist

Herrera, Hayden

Frida: a biography of Frida Kahlo. Harper & Row 1983 507p il hardcover o.p. pa $24.95   709
1. Artists 2. Painters 3. Artists, Mexican
ISBN 0-06-008589-4 pa
                                                                LC 80-8688

This biography of the Mexican painter and wife of Diego Rivera "is a mesmerizing story of radical art, romantic politics, bizarre loves and physical suffering. . . . Herrera resolves Kahlo the public figure and Kahlo the artist in a perceptive portrait of a woman who rose above a circumscribed content with a grand style." Time

Includes bibliographical references

Hoving, Thomas

Art for dummies; foreword by Andrew Wyeth. IDG Books Worldwide, Inc 1999 382p il (--For dummies) $24.99   **709**
1. Art appreciation 2. Art -- History
ISBN 978-0-7645-5104-8; 0-7645-5104-3
                                                                LC 99-65838
"In this delightful book, Hoving . . . leads readers gently through thousands of years of art history. . . . His breathless enthusiasm is avuncular, scholarly, and quite infectious—an attitude that happily precludes condescension. . . . A terrific book for students, travelers, tyros, and old hands alike." Libr J

Includes bibliographical references

Hughes, Robert

American visions; the epic history of art in America. Knopf 1997 635p il $65; pa $39.95 **709**
1. American art
ISBN 0-679-42627-2; 0-375-70365-9 pa
                                                                LC 96-45111
"Hughes has orchestrated a spectacular integration of facts, observations, and insights in this ambitious, lively, and gloriously illustrated volume." Booklist

Includes bibliographical references

Janson, H. W.

★ **Janson's** history of art; the western tradition. Penelope J.E. Davies ... [et. al] 8th ed.; Prentice Hall 2011 xxxi, 1152p il map $170.40   **709**
1. Art -- History
ISBN 978-0-205-68517-2; 0-205-68517-X
                                                                LC 2009-22617
First published 1962 by Abrams with title: History of art

A history of art from prehistoric cave paintings to video art. While the focus is primarily on Western art, brief discussions of Oriental, Near Eastern, Islamic, African and Latin American arts are included.

Includes bibliographical references

Johnson, Paul

★ **Art**: a new history. HarperCollins Pubs. 2003 777p il $39.95   **709**
1. Art -- History
ISBN 0-06-053075-8
"While {Johnson's} narrative is for the most part a conventional journey through the canon, his headlong pace, quirky views and pungent prose make it anything but dull." Publ Wkly

Kettenmann, Andrea

Frida Kahlo : 1907-1954; Pain and Passion. by Andrea Kettenmann. Taschen America Llc 2015 96 p. $14.99   **709**

ISBN 383650085X; 9783836500852

This book, by Andrea Kettenmann, focuses on "Mexican artist Frida Kahlo. . . . Two events in her life were of crucial importance. When she was eighteen, a bus accident put her in hospital for a year with a smashed spinal column and fractured pelvis. It was in her sick bed that she first started to paint. Then, aged twenty-one, she married the world-famous Mexican mural artist Diego Rivera." (Publisher's note)

Khalili, Nasser D.

Islamic art and culture; a visual history. Overlook Press 2006 186p il $60   **709**

1. Islamic art 2. Islamic civilization

ISBN 1-58567-839-2; 978-1-58567-839-6

This "visual history of Islamic art introduces readers to the diverse peoples, cultures, and styles making up Islam today. Spanning 12 centuries and covering everything from miniature painting to architecture, it shows, e.g., various Qur'ans, coins, armor, and scientific instruments. . . . This is an excellent introduction to the subject that combines aptly chosen and beautifully reproduced photographs with a concise and informative text." Libr J

Includes bibliographical references

King, Ross

Art: over 2,500 works from cave to contemporary; foreword by Ross King. DK Pub. 2008 612p il $50   **709**

1. Reference books 2. Art appreciation 3. Art -- History

ISBN 978-0-7566-3972-3; 0-7566-3972-7

LC 2008-301471

Within each time period, provides examples of significant works in painting, sculpture, drawing and other media. Highlights themes that were important at various times such as nudes, landscape, still life, and love. Includes brief biographies of some artists and a "closer look" in depth for the most significant works.

"Easy to read and use, . . . both newcomers to art and art connoisseurs will enjoy this picturesque work." Libr J

Includes glossary

Klein, Stefan

Leonardo's legacy; how Da Vinci reimagined the world. translated by Shelley Frisch. Da Capo Press 2010 291p il $26   **709**

1. Artists 2. Painters 3. Inventors 4. Scientists 5. Artists, Italian 6. Writers on science

ISBN 978-0-306-81825-7; 0-306-81825-6

LC 2010-00130

Original German edition, 2008

The author "makes a compelling case that DaVinci's ability to trigger an empathetic physical response in the viewer lay in his scientific acumen: the asymmetry of the Mona Lisa's smile, for instance, deliberately reflects the asymmetry of the human brain. While Leonardo is remembered primarily as an artist, his accomplishments as a scientist were at least as important. . . . Including a detailed

chronology of the artist's life, this makes an illuminating new look at Leonardo's unique genius." Publ Wkly

Includes bibliographical references

Langdon, Helen

Caravaggio; a life. Westview Press 2000 436p il map pa $22   **709**

1. Artists 2. Painters 3. Artists, Italian

ISBN 0-8133-3794-1; 978-0-8133-3794-4

First published 1998 in the United Kingdom

In this study of the Renaissance painter, "Langdon's masterly achievement is to integrate Caravaggio's art and life in a convincing and vividly delineated recreation of his world." Libr J

Includes bibliographical references

Little, Stephen

. . . isms: understanding art. Universe 2004 159p il pa $16.95   **709**

1. Art -- History

ISBN 0-7893-1209-3

LC 2004-94996

The author "identifies four types of isms: trends specific to the visual arts (perspectivism), broad cultural trends (romanticism), artist-defined movements (cubism), and retrospectively named movements (mannerism). He then moves forward chronologically, deftly defining more than 50 isms, naming key artists, and showcasing splendid examples." Booklist

Lottman, Herbert R.

Man Ray's Montparnasse. Abrams 2001 261p il $29.95   **709**

1. Artists 2. Painters 3. Photographers 4. Paris (France) -- Intellectual life

ISBN 0-8109-4333-6

LC 2001-633

Lottman presents a "snapshot of Man Ray between the two world wars, emphasizing the 1920s, with the developing Montparnasse section of Paris as the backdrop. Here are the cutting-edge dadaists and surrealists flanking Man Ray and his unerring camera eye, along with poets and artists, collectors, lovers, and other assorted characters. . . . Lottman's vivid exploration of 20th-century art events will serve the art historian and student of Paris very well in documenting an essential epoch and place." Libr J

Includes bibliographical references and index

Marin, Cheech

Chicano visions; American painters on the verge. essays by Max Benavidez, Constance Cortez, Tere Tomo. Little, Brown 2002 160p il $35; pa $19.95   **709**

1. American painting 2. Mexican Americans

ISBN 0-8212-2805-6; 0-8212-2806-4 pa

LC 2002-104645

"Marin's extraordinary collection forms the foundation for this exciting and invaluable showcase . . . {which includes works by} John Valadez, Gronk, Diane Gamboa, Patssi Valdez, Adan Hernandez, and Carlos Almaraz." Booklist

Includes bibliographical references

Martin, Barnaby

Hanging man; the arrest of Ai Weiwei. Barnaby Martin. Faber and Faber, Inc. 2013 256 p. (hardback) $27   **709**

1. Political activists 2. China -- Social conditions -- 2000- 3. China -- Politics and government -- 2002- 4. Dissenters, Artistic -- China -- Social conditions -- 21st century

ISBN 0374167753; 9780374167752

LC 2013015010

This book focuses on the arrest of Chinese artist and activist Ai Weiwei. Journalist Barnaby Martin interviewed "the artist about his experience, to inform the larger world of his treatment, to learn why he was arrested and ultimately released, and, finally, to shed light on the current state of the Chinese government itself. . . . Martin covers . . . the political trajectory of China through the 20th century, contemporary art movements in the post-Mao era, and Ai Weiwei's own life." (Library Journal)

"A book that offers great clarity on an important subject without succumbing to oversimplification." Kirkus

McPhee, John A.

The **ransom** of Russian art; {by} John McPhee. Farrar, Straus & Giroux 1994 181p il $20; pa $12   **709**

1. Economists 2. Russian art 3. Art collectors 4. College teachers

ISBN 0-374-24682-3; 0-374-52450-5 pa

LC 94-14723

"McPhee's engaging narrative sheds light on this suppressed creative milieu." Publ Wkly

Muller, Melissa, 1967-

Lost lives, lost art; Jewish collectors, Nazi art theft, and the quest for justice. [by] Melissa Muller [and] Monika Tatzkow; with contributions from Thomas Blubacher and Gunnar Schnabel; foreword by Ronald S. Lauder. Vendome Press 2010 248p il $40   **709**

1. Art thefts 2. Jews -- Europe 3. Art -- Collectors and collecting 4. World War, 1939-1945 -- Destruction and pillage

ISBN 9780865652637

LC 2010-15337

The authors "cover 15 Jewish/possibly Jewish families with vast art collections looted by the Nazis. Jewish collectors either had to sell their treasures for a pittance or had them seized. The Bloch-Bauer family's story is famous, but the unknown histories of other prominent families are compellingly told here, and there is a final historical-legal commentary by expert Gunnar Schnabel on Nazi-looted art and the German laws that perpetuated these crimes. . . . Richly illustrated with excellent art reproductions and family photographs." Libr J

Nuland, Sherwin B.

Leonardo da Vinci. Viking 2000 170p il (Penguin lives series) pa $13   **709**

1. Artists 2. Painters 3. Scientists 4. Artists, Italian

5. Writers on science

ISBN 0-670-89391-9; 978-0-14-303510-7 pa; 0-14-303510-X pa

LC 00-32061

"Nuland . . . elegantly sketches Leonardo's life of constant employment by noblemen eager to enjoy the prestige he reflected on them and of even more constant curiosity, which drove him to become the greatest anatomist before Vasari. . . . A scintillating addition." Booklist

Paquet, Marcel

Magritte; by Marcel Paquet. Taschen America Llc 2015 96 p. $14.99   **709**

1. Magritte, Rene, 1898-1967 2. Art

ISBN 3836503573; 9783836503570

This book, by Marcel Paquet, focuses on "the influence of René Magritte. . . . His surrealistic painting turns the usual order of things ironically on its head, thus restoring mystery to a world that has lost its magic." (Publisher's note)

Contains biographical information

Penrose, Roland

Picasso: his life and work; 3rd ed; University of Calif. Press 1981 517p il hardcover o.p. pa $21.95   **709**

1. Artists 2. Painters

ISBN 0-520-04207-7 pa

LC 80-54015

First published 1958 by Harper

The author "has produced a painstaking, comprehensive biography . . . and, what is more, a popular biography, assuming neither knowledge of nor sympathy with twentieth-century art on the part of the reader." Times Lit Suppl {review of 1958 edition}

Includes bibliographical references

Petropoulos, Jonathan

The **Faustian** bargain; the art world in Nazi Germany. Oxford Univ. Press 2000 395p il $42.50 **709**

1. Art thefts 2. National socialism 3. World War, 1939-1945 -- Destruction and pillage

ISBN 0-19-512964-4

LC 99-33372

"Spotlighting five groups--art museum directors, art dealers, art journalists, art historians, and artists--Petropoulos . . . details how each of these groups either directly or indirectly facilitated the theft of countless works of art and legitimized the Nazi regime." Libr J

Includes bibliographical references

Robinson, Roxana

Georgia O'Keeffe: a life. University Press of New England 1999 639p il pa $22.95   **709**

1. Artists 2. Painters

ISBN 0-87451-906-3

LC 98-30944

A reissue of the title first published 1989 by Harper & Row

"This biography, the first to draw on sources unavailable during O'Keeffe's lifetime—and the first to be granted her family's cooperation—offers a persuasive feminist analysis of the life and work of an iconic figure in American art. .

. . [The author's] detailed, sensitive critique of O'Keeffe's work . . . alternates with an absorbing, intimate narrative of O'Keeffe's personal life." Publ Wkly

Includes bibliographical references

Schama, Simon

The **power** of art. Ecco 2006 448p il $50 **709**
1. Art -- History
ISBN 0-06-117610-9; 978-0-06-117610-4
LC 2007-270937

The author "presents eight remarkable artists who created their masterworks against a backdrop of personal and professional distress. From politically charged commentaries (David, Picasso, Turner and Rembrandt) to intensely personal visions of the world (van Gogh and Rothko) and the reinvention of the divine (Bernini and Caravaggio), Schama takes these masters' hallowed works off the museum wall and drags them through the mud and muck that went into their creation." Publ Wkly

Includes bibliographical references

Scott, John F.

Latin American art; ancient to modern. University Press of Fla. 1999 xxiv, 240p il $49.95; pa $29.95 **709**
1. Latin American art
ISBN 0-8130-1645-2; 0-8130-1826-9 pa
LC 98-46535

A study "of Latin American art from pre-Columbian times to the present, encompassing media ranging from sculpture, pottery, and painting to architecture. Scott . . . addresses the major styles and artists that define each period." Libr J

Includes bibliographical references

Tomkins, Calvin

Duchamp; a biography. Holt & Co. 1996 550p il map hardcover o.p. pa $20 **709**
1. Artists 2. Painters 3. Artists, French
ISBN 0-8050-5789-7
LC 96-3080

"Tomkins organizes the facts of Duchamp's life and work into a sober, coherent whole, and for this alone his book makes valuable reading for anyone seeking to understand how art's cutting edge was honed." New Repub

Includes bibliographical references

Tregear, Mary

Chinese art; rev ed; Thames & Hudson 1997 216p il maps (World of art) pa $14.95 **709**
1. Chinese art
ISBN 0-500-20299-0
First published 1980 by Oxford Univ. Press

An introduction to major decorative, ceremonial, figurative and narrative aspects of Chinese art. Coverage ranges from works of Neolithic groups and the bronzes of the Shang dynasty to Buddhist sculpture, ceramics, garden design and architecture. Emphasis is also placed on the interaction of poetry, painting and calligraphy.

Includes bibliographical references

Visona, Monica Blackmun

A **history** of art in Africa; [by] Monica Blackmun Visona, Robin Poynor, Herbert M. Cole; with contributions by Suzanne Preston Blier (introduction), Rowland Abiodun (preface) and Michael D. Harris (chapter 16) 2nd ed; Pearson/Prentice Hall 2007 560p il pa $111 **709**
1. African art
ISBN 978-0-13-612872-4; 0-13-612872-6
LC 2007-15831
First published 2000

"Treating the subject from an art historical rather than an anthropological perspective, this groundbreaking book is organized geographically to cover the entire continent. Each of the five regional sections focuses on selected major art traditions. . . . Accompanying the text are over 700 photos and scores of maps, plans, drawings, etc." Libr J [review of 2000 edition]

Includes bibliographical references (p. 544-551)

709.01 Periods of development, and arts of nonliterate peoples

Berlo, Janet Catherine

Native North American art; by Janet Catherine Berlo and Ruth B. Phillips. Oxford Univ. Press 1999 291p il map (Oxford history of art) hardcover o.p. pa $24.95 **709.01**
1. Native American art
ISBN 0-19-284218-8 pa
LC 99-177938

This survey covers the "artistic output of most Native American tribes across the northern hemisphere over a period of more than eight centuries. . . . In an introduction that stresses the commonality of themes—cosmology, vision quests, love of ornament, reverence of materials—[the authors] emphasize the importance of today's Native art as a natural extension. Five regional chapters then incorporate history, outstanding crafts and arts, some prominent figures, and social, religious, and cultural aspects." Libr J

709.02 6th-15th centuries, 500-1499

Adams, Laurie

Italian Renaissance art. Westview Press 2001 420p il map $75; pa $65 **709.02**
1. Italian art 2. Art -- 15th and 16th centuries
ISBN 978-0-8133-3690-9; 0-8133-3690-2; 978-0-8133-3691-6 pa; 0-8133-3691-0 pa
LC 2001-269582

"Adams has produced a near-perfect introduction to the people, places, and events of the Italian Renaissance. . . . The text follows Italian art as it transforms from a highly religious activity into a very human one, and culminates with a focus on the multitalented genius of da Vinci, Raphael, and Michelangelo. . . . The side boxes are helpful and provide further information about the religious figures, ideas, and historical events that directly influenced the era, such as Dante and the black death. . . . This, along with numerous superb photographs, adds incalculable value to the understanding of the Italian Renaissance." Booklist

Includes bibliographical references

709.03 Modern period, 1500-

Craske, Matthew

Art in Europe, 1700-1830; a history of the visual arts in an era of unprecedented urban economic growth. Oxford Univ. Press 1997 320p il (Oxford history of art) hardcover o.p. pa $21.50 **709.03**

1. Art -- 19th century 2. World history -- 18th century

ISBN 0-19-284206-4 pa

LC 96-37917

This study analyzes "the fundamental historical causes of change that took place from the early 1700s to 1839. . . . Craske . . . provides a series of four stimulating chapters devoted respectively to the function of the artist, art worlds, the appreciation of the visual arts, and evolving ideas of history and civilization. The text is enhanced by 129 high-quality illustrations." Choice

709.04 20th century, 1900-1999

Arnason, H. Harvard

★ History of modern art; painting, sculpture, architecture, photography. [by] H.H. Arnason, Elizabeth C. Mansfield. 6th ed.; Pearson Prentice Hall 2009 830p il $130.67; pa $122.67 **709.04**

1. Modern art

ISBN 0-205-67367-8; 978-0-205-67367-4; 0-13-606206-7 pa; 978-0-13-606206-6 pa

LC 2009-15436

First published 1969

This covers artists and movements in art from the 19th century to the present, discussing such schools as cubism, surrealism, and abstract impressionism. Video, installation and performance art, sculpture, architecture, and photography are also surveyed.

"An ideal primer on modern art." Libr J

Includes glossary and bibliographical references

★ Art deco 1910-1939; edited by Charlotte Benton, Tim Benton, and Ghislaine Wood. Bulfinch Press 2003 464p il $65 **709.04**

1. Art deco

ISBN 0-8212-2834-X

LC 2002-113762

This exhibition catalog includes 40 essays about the Art Deco movement and its sources and expression throughout the world in such fields as architecture, ceramics, fashion, jewelry, graphic design, metalwork, glasswork, and film

Includes bibliographical references

Barnes, Julian, 1946-

Keeping an eye open; essays on art. Julian Barnes. Alfred A. Knopf 2015 288 p. color illustrations (hardback) $30 **709.04**

1. Art -- History 2. Art -- 20th century 3. Art, Modern

-- 19th century 4. Art, Modern -- 20th century

ISBN 9781101873373; 9781101874783; 9781101874790

LC 2015014317

In this collection of essays, author Julian Barnes notes that "Flaubert believed that it was impossible to explain one art form in terms of another, and that great paintings required no words of explanation. Braque thought the ideal state would be reached when we said nothing at all in front of a painting. . . . The seventeen essays gathered here help trace the arc from Romanticism to Realism and into Modernism." (Publisher's note)

"Barnes knows that one of the immeasurable pleasures of art is its capacity to approach us from unexpected angles and excite our senses of wonder. The same may be said of his scholarly and astute yet accessible and exciting essays." Kirkus

Includes bibliographical references.

Brandon, Ruth

Surreal lives; the surrealists, 1917-1945. Grove Press 1999 527p il hardcover o.p. pa $16 **709.04**

1. Surrealism

ISBN 0-8021-3727-X pa

LC 99-25492

This study of surrealism "gives an account of the school's major practitioners, from Apollinaire to Dali; their flamboyant eccentricities and unconventional sexual entanglements prove a lively and absorbing complement to their work." New Yorker

Includes bibliographical references

Dempsey, Amy

Art in the modern era; a guide to styles, schools & movements 1860 to the present. Abrams 2002 304p il $55 **709.04**

1. Reference books 2. Modern art -- Encyclopedias 3. Art -- 20th century -- Encyclopedias

ISBN 0-8109-4172-4

LC 2001-46261

This guide to art from 1860 to the present describes 300 schools and movements and includes a fold-out timeline

"All major and minor movements are mentioned in this very comprehensive guide, which could easily become a standard for modern art survey courses, making it a sensible purchase for most libraries." Libr J

Includes bibliographical references

Dickerman, Leah

★ Dada; Zurich, Berlin, Hannover, Cologne, New York, Paris. with essays by Brigid Doherty [et al.] National Gallery of Art in association with Distributed Art Publishers 2005 519p il $65 **709.04**

1. Dadaism

ISBN 1-933045-20-5

LC 2005-17984

"Seven scholars and curators contribute essays that examine each of the various Dada centers in turn. . . . Each essay examines key locations (e.g., the Cabaret Voltaire), individuals, publications (including Merz magazine), and inventions (such as ready-mades and photomontage.) . . . Its comprehensive scholarship and color illustrations of many rarely seen works make this book essential for all art collections." Choice

Includes bibliographical references

Homburg, Cornelia

Neo-impressionism and the dream of realities; painting, poetry, music. Cornelia Homburg, Paul Smith, Laura D. Corey. Yale University Press 2015 191 p. illustrations; portraits (cloth : alk. paper) $60   **709.04**
1. Impressionism (Art) 2. Symbolism in literature
ISBN 0300190832; 9780300190830

LC 2014937873

This book, by Cornelia Homburg, Paul Smith, and Laura D. Corey, "explores the creative exchange between Neo-Impressionist painters and Symbolist writers and composers in the late 1880s and early 1890s. Symbolism, with its emphasis on subjectivity, dream worlds, and spirituality, has often been considered at odds with Neo-Impressionism's approach to portraying color and light. This book repositions the relationship between these movements." (Publisher's note)

"All in all, this is a superb and much-needed assessment. Profusely and well illustrated. Summing Up: Recommended. Upper-division undergraduate, graduate, and research collections." Choice

Livingstone, Marco

Pop art; a continuing history. 2nd ed. Thames & Hudson 2000 272p il $29.95   **709.04**
1. Pop art
ISBN 978-0-500-28240-3; 0-500-28240-4

LC 00-100788

First published 1991 in the United Kingdom

With 300 color plates this volume chronicles the work of 130 artists of the Pop Art movement, including Jasper Johns, Robert Rauschenberg, Andy Warhol, and Roy Lichtenstein.

"Recommended as the best single historical survey on Pop Art." Libr J

Salle, David, 1952-

How to see; Looking, Talking, and Thinking about Art. David Salle. W W Norton & Co Inc 2016 256 p. (ebook) $50; (hardcover) $29.95   **709.04**
1. Art appreciation 2. Art, Modern -- 20th century 3. Art, Modern -- 21st century
ISBN 9780393248142; 9780393248135

LC 2016025215

This book, by David Salle, is a "master class in contemporary art. . . . Engaging with a wide range of Salle's friends and contemporaries—from painters to conceptual artists such as Jeff Koons, John Baldessari, Roy Lichtenstein, and Alex Katz, among others—[this book] explores not only the multilayered personalities of the artists themselves but also the distinctive character of their oeuvres." (Publisher's note)

"Sharp insights and an affable tone make this collection equivalent to a hearty discussion with a mentor—recommended for anyone interested in visual arts." Pub Wkly

709.05   21st century, 2000-2099

Perry, Grayson, 1960-

Playing to the gallery; helping contemporary art in its struggle to be understood. Grayson Perry. Penguin Books 2015 128 p. color illustrations $25   **709.05**
1. Art criticism 2. Art -- 21st century 3. Art appreciation 4. Art, Modern -- 20th century -- Public opinion 5. Art, Modern -- 21st century -- Public opinion
ISBN 0143127357; 9780143127352

LC 2014032486

This book by Grayson Perry and "Based on his hugely popular Reith Lectures and full of words and pictures, [is a] . . . personal journey through the art world answers the basic questions that might occur to us in an art gallery but seem too embarrassing to ask. Questions such as: What is 'good' or 'bad' art--and does it even matter?" (Publisher's note)

"Well read but not pretentious, skeptical but not cynical, this book will have anyone interested in (or puzzled by) contemporary art laughing as they ponder major issues that define how we think about and experience art." LJ

Thornton, Sarah

Seven days in the art world. W.W. Norton 2008 274p il $24.95   **709.05**
1. Art -- Marketing 2. Art -- Exhibitions
ISBN 978-0-393-06722-4; 0-393-06722-X

LC 2008-35056

"The book is cleverly divided into seven day-in-the-life chapters, each focusing on a different facet of the contemporary art world: an auction (at Christie's New York), an art school 'crit' (at the California Institute of the Arts in Valencia), an art fair (Art Basel), an artist's studio (that of the Japanese star Takashi Murakami), a prize (Britain's prestigious Turner Prize), a magazine (Artforum) and a biennale (Venice). Thornton is a smart and savvy guide with a keen understanding of the subtle power dynamics that animate each of these interconnected milieus." N Y Times Book Rev

Includes bibliographical references

709.1   Areas, regions, places in general

O'Kane, Bernard

★ Treasures of Islam; artistic glories of the Muslim world. Duncan Baird; Distributed in the USA by Sterling Pub. 2007 224p il map $35 **709.1**
1. Islamic art 2. Islamic civilization
ISBN 978-1-84483-483-9; 1-84483-483-2

The author "combines an overview of Islamic art and architecture with a cursory history of Islam's empires and dynasties. Beginning with a brief discussion of the earliest mosque from the seventh century, and showing how Islamic architects created a distinctive artistic tradition, O'Kane . . . follows architectural and artistic ideas to the 19th century. . . . The wealth of glorious full-color illustrations make this beautifully designed book an excellent introduction to the art of Islam." Publ Wkly

Includes bibliographical references

709.2   Biography

Henri Matisse; the cut-outs. edited by Karl Buchberg, Nicholas Cullinan, Jodi Hauptman, and Nicholas Serota. The Museum Of Modern Art 2014 298 p. illustrations (chiefly color) $60   **709.2**

1. Artists 2. Paper crafts
ISBN 0870709151; 0870709488; 9780870709159; 9780870709487

LC 2014934445

This book, edited by Karl Buchberg, Jodi Hauptman, and Nicholas Cullinan, "presents approximately 150 works in a groundbreaking reassessment of the . . . . [Henri Matisse's] colorful and innovative final years. From the late 1940s on, Henri Matisse (1869-1954) worked almost exclusively with paper and scissors, cutting painted sheets into various shapes and sizes and arranging them into lively compositions, striking for their chromatic harmonies and economy of means." (Publisher's note)

"The beautifully produced catalog of this exhibition includes essays that explore Matisse's innovative process, brought to life by photographs of the artist with his assistants at work in his studio as well as a generous and representative selection of high-quality color reproductions of significant milestones from a decade of cut-out projects. Essential for art studio, history, and conservation collections. Summing Up: Essential. All readership levels." Choice

Includes bibliographical references and index
Cut-outs

Hirst, Michael

Michelangelo; v1 Michael Hirst. Yale University Press 2011 x, 438 p.p v1 ill. (some col.) $40.00   **709.2**

1. Poets 2. Italian art 3. Mural painting and decoration 4. Artists 5. Painters 6. Sculptors 7. Architects 8. Biography, Individual
ISBN 0300118619; 9780300118612

LC 2011042294

In this book, author Michael Hirst presents a biography of Michelangelo, following "the artist from his apprenticeship in Ghirlandaio's workshop to his final move to Rome in 1534, when, at the age of 59, he left behind his native Florence, never to return. During these years he created such outstanding works as the marble 'Pietà,' the giant marble 'David,' commissioned for the cathedral in Florence, the Sistine Ceiling frescoes, and the new sacristy and library for the Medici family at San Lorenzo." (Publisher's note)

Includes bibliographical references (p. [378]-415) and index

Rothkopf, Scott

Jeff Koons; a retrospective. Scott Rothkopf. Whitney Museum of American Art Distrib. by Yale University Press 2014 303 p. illustrations (mostly color) (hb) $65   **709.2**

1. Artists
ISBN 0300195877; 9780300195873

LC 2014003418

Author "Scott Rothkopf carefully examines the evolution of [Jeff] Koons' work and his development over the past thirty-five years, offering a fresh scholarly perspective on the artist's multi-faceted career. In addition, short essays by a wide range of interdisciplinary contributors--from academics to novelists--probe provocative topics such as celebrity and media, markets and money, and technology and fabrication." (Publisher's note)

"Rothkopf couples such analyses with personal anecdotes recalling his initial and repeated engagements with Koons and his work before characterizing the artist as not just a "child of our time but an active agent of it." Beautifully designed, this volume is a crucial acquisition for art libraries. Summing Up: Highly recommended. Lower-division undergraduates and above." Choice

Includes bibliographical references (pages 253-271) and index

709.3   Specific continents, countries, localities

Boardman, John

Greek art; 4th ed, rev and expanded; Thames & Hudson 1996 304p il map (World of art) pa $16.95   **709.3**

1. Greek art
ISBN 0-500-20292-3

LC 96-60184

First published 1964 by Praeger Pubs.

Partial contents: The beginnings and geometric Greece; Greece and the arts of the East and Egypt; Archaic Greek art; Classical sculpture and architecture; Hellenistic art; Selected bibliography

"This is a classic in the field made even more readable and useful than before. Highly recommended for all collections." Libr J

Robins, Gay

The **art** of ancient Egypt; Rev ed; Harvard University Press 2008 271p il map pa $27.95   **709.3**

1. Egyptian art 2. Egypt -- Antiquities
ISBN 978-0-674-03065-7; 0-674-03065-6

LC 2008-4264

First published 1997

"The first chapter orients the reader in the cultural, technical, and iconographic contexts needed to explore the evolution of the Egyptian artistic tradition in subsequent chapters. Beginning with the predynastic origins (5000 BCE) and concluding in the Ptolemaic Period (304-30 BCE), Robins traces the development of sculpture, painting, funerary and religious art, and architecture with over 300 illustrations, many in color." Libr J [review of 1997 edition]

Includes bibliographical references (p. 256-266)

709.5

Brougher, Kerry

Ai weiwei; according to what? Kerry Brougher, Mami Kataoka, Charles Merewether; edited by Kerry Brougher, Mami Kataoka, Charles Merewether. Del

Monico Books 2012 176 p. ill. (some col.) (hardcover) $39.95 **709.5**

1. Artists, Chinese 2. Installations (Art) -- Exhibitions
ISBN 3791352407; 9783791352404

LC 2012949559

This book features dissident Chinese artist Ai Weiwei's work, ranging from furniture, videos, and photographs to sculpture and ceramics, [and] is published in conjunction with an exhibition . . . . Curator Mami Kataoka (Mori) summarizes the artist's life . . . and influences on his work. Two short chapters follow: Charles Merewether . . . elaborates on Ai's social concerns; Kerry Brougher . . . presents an interview with the artist." (Choice)

Includes bibliographical references (p. 142-144)

Brysac, Shareen Blair

The **China** collectors; America's century-long hunt for Asian art treasures. Karl E. Meyer and Shareen Blair Brysac. Palgrave Macmillan Trade 2015 432 p. illustrations (some color) (hardback) $30 **709.5**

1. Chinese art 2. Art -- Collectors and collecting 3. Art, Chinese -- Appreciation -- United States 4. Art -- Collectors and collecting -- United States -- History -- 19th century 5. Art -- Collectors and collecting -- United States -- History -- 20th century
ISBN 1137279761; 9781137279767

LC 2014031029

This book, by Karl E. Meyer and Shareen Blair Brysac, "is the first full account of a century-long treasure hunt in China from the Opium Wars and the Boxer Rebellion to Mao Zedong's 1949 ascent. The principal gatherers are mostly little known and defy invention. They included 'foreign devils' who braved desert sandstorms, bandits and local warlords in acquiring significant works." (Publisher's note)

"While the lack of a comprehensive bibliography may reduce the usefulness of the book for scholarly purposes, this title will appeal to readers with an interest in the history of Chinese art curation and the founding of American museum collections." LJ

Includes bibliographical references

711 Area planning (Civic art)

McGregor, James H.

Rome from the ground up; [by] James H.S. McGregor. Belknap Press of Harvard University Press 2005 344p il map $29.95; pa $18.95 **711**

1. Rome -- History 2. City planning -- Rome
ISBN 0-674-01911-3; 0-674-02263-7 pa

LC 2005-48213

The author "chronologically traces the successive periods of intense architecture and planning that helped Rome achieve strategic greatness, from the Etruscan management of the Tiber Island ford 3,000 years ago, to the city's unparalleled artistic stamp by Bramante and Michelangelo during the Renaissance, to Mussolini's monumental Fascist vision, to the precarious repairs heralding the Jubilee Year of 2000. . . . Here is a walking tour in stately, inviting prose that ren-

ders wonderfully manageable a massive history lesson for the intellectually curious and adept." Publ Wkly

Includes bibliographical references

712 Landscape architecture (Landscape design)

Buchanan, Rita

Taylor's master guide to landscaping. Houghton Mifflin 2000 384p il $40 **712**

1. Landscape gardening
ISBN 0-618-05590-8

LC 99-54110

Companion volume to Taylor's master guide to gardening

"Buchanan offers a comprehensive treatment of landscape design, emphasizing designing with plants and including extensive information about choosing and caring for plants, trees, shrubs, vines, and ground covers. . . . A landmark work destined to become a classic." Libr J

Cox, Madison

The **Gardener's** Garden; edited by Phaidon Editors. Phaidon Inc Ltd 2014 480 p. color illustrations $79.95 **712**

1. Gardens 2. Gardening
ISBN 0714867470; 9780714867472

This book is "both a collection of gardens from around the world and a resource for those seeking inspiration on garden design and planting. . . . [It features] over 250 permanent gardens by leading garden designers, horticulturalists and landscape architects, from the 14th century to the present day, and covering all key types and styles of garden." (Publisher's note)

"The density of visuals displayed with relatively little text leaves the reader a lot to digest, making it difficult at times to pinpoint the intended takeaway. Readers who can explore slowly will be transported around the world into lovely, curious, and distinctly human landscapes." Pub Wkly

Graham, Wade

American Eden; from Monticello to Central Park to our backyards: what our gardens tell us about who we are. Harper 2011 459p il $35; ebook $27.99 **712**

1. Gardens 2. Landscape architecture
ISBN 978-0-06-158342-1; 978-0-06-207886-5 ebook

LC 2010-24940

"Graham unveils the aesthetic, political, psychological, and ethical dimensions of the American garden. . . . Graham is able to gently mock the fashions of history while astutely observing that we are still as vulnerable to gardening fads today. After more than 250 years, the American gardening tradition has bequeathed to us treasured public parks, suburban sprawl, Kentucky bluegrass lawns in the desert, and kitchen gardens at the White House. Graham's history is a fascinating and illuminating tour of this American landscape." Publ Wkly

Includes bibliographical references

Hayward, Gordon

Stone in the garden; inspiring designs and practical projects. Norton 2001 224p il $39.95   **712**

1. Landscape gardening

ISBN 0-393-04779-2

LC 00-69945

"The book's first half focuses on the philosophical and design considerations of stone forms as varied as walls, paths, terraces, and even benches. The second half is more practical, covering topics such as estimating the amount of stone needed for a wall, the methods of cutting and laying stone, and building pools and fountains." Libr J

Includes bibliographical references

Majerus, Marianne

Garden Design; a book of ideas. Heidi Howcroft, Marianne Majerus. Firefly Books Ltd 2015 320 p. color illustrations (hardcover) $49.95   **712**

1. Gardens 2. Garden design

ISBN 1770855246; 9781770855243

This book, by Heidi Howcroft and Marianne Majerus, offers "takes the reader through the entire process [of garden design]: assessing the garden situation, developing a design, installing the components, and finally, dressing the space. The . . . color photographs show an enormous variety of gardens and their elements in detail, varying from large and small, to urban and rural, covering a wide range of styles, including contemporary, modern, city, Mediterranean and natural." (Publisher's note)

"Paging through the exquisite photographs in this coffee-table book is like being given a sneak peek into some of the world's most gorgeous private outdoor spaces. It includes sections on types of paving, enclosures, garden furniture, and art. This book will inspire readers to envision what is possible even in the smallest, most improbable space." Pub Wkly

Nagel, Vanessa Gardner

Understanding garden design; the complete handbook for aspiring designers. Timber Press 2010 235p il $34.95   **712**

1. Garden design

ISBN 978-0-88192-943-0

LC 2009-53692

"Thorough and thoroughly accessible, Nagel's reasoned yet personable approach to an often intimidating subject will benefit both homeowners and design professionals." Booklist

Includes bibliographical references

Rybczynski, Witold

A clearing in the distance: Frederick Law Olmsted and America in the nineteenth century. Scribner 1999 480p il $28; pa $15.95   **712**

1. Travel writers 2. Urban planners 3. Landscape architects

ISBN 0-684-82463-9; 0-684-86575-0 pa

LC 99-18094

"Rybczynski, celebrated for his sparkling prose as well as for his deep knowledge of architectural history, adeptly chronicles the life of the man who 'was a landscape architect before that profession was founded.'" Booklist

Includes bibliographical references

Wulf, Andrea

Founding gardeners; the revolutionary generation, nature, and the shaping of the American nation. Knopf 2011 349p il map $30; ebook $14.99 **712**

1. Gardens 2. Gardening 3. American national characteristics 4. Statesmen -- United States

ISBN 978-0-307-26990-4; 0-307-26990-6; 978-0-307-59554-6 ebook

LC 2010-52920

The book discusses how the "leaders of the American Revolution and the early republic were engaged plantation owners keenly interested in scientific agriculture. Andrea Wulf argues that this interest, shared by other Founding Fathers, was no mere sideline activity, but rather something central to their identities as leaders and political thinkers." The author examines "the political role of horticulture/agriculture in the Constitutional Convention and the landmark battle over the Hamilton Bank Bill in 1791 that brought party political differences into the open." (Journal of American History)

The author demonstrates "that the garden, the natural world and the shape of a new nation were, for the men who launched the United States, parts of a whole. The image of the farmer-statesman is an ideal of republican government dating back to Romans. It's no accident that the men who led the Revolution and wrote the Constitution owned plantations and farms. . . . [Wulf is a] writer of considerable grace and breadth of vision, and 'Founding Gardeners' is an excellent portrait of the early years of the federal republic. It will delight the general reader, not just the garden buff. But for the garden enthusiast, this is a book of special interest, reminding us that a garden has a purpose, a character, a soul—that it's an expression of our relationship not just to the soil, but to a vision of the world." Cleveland Plain Dealer

712.6   Private parks and grounds

Greayer, Rochelle

Cultivating garden style; inspired ideas and practical advice to unleash your garden personality. Rochelle Greayer. Timber Press, Inc. 2014 320 p. color illustrations $35   **712.6**

1. Gardens 2. Garden design 3. Gardening 4. Gardens -- Styles

ISBN 1604694777; 9781604694772

LC 2014009479

In this book author "Rochelle Greayer shares ways to create outdoor areas that are charming, comfortable, appealing, and reflect individuality. It features twenty-three unique garden styles accompanied by advice on how to recreate the look. Simple step-by-step projects, like how to make a macramé plant hanger, help the reader personalize the space." (Publisher's note)

"The extravagant use of color photos on each page brings visual clarity to otherwise improbable schemes. Whether depicting "retro rockery," topiary, trellising, Danish or Zen features, the book offers needed guidance for designing outdoor space in a way that helps gardeners bring unique personality to their living, growing outdoor decor." Pub Wkly

Pember, Mat

The **Little** Veggie Patch Co. DIY Garden Projects; by Mat Pember and Dillon Seitchik-Reardon. Random House Inc. 2016 272 p. color illustrations $34.95 **712.6**

1. Gardening 2. Recycling 3. Handicraft

ISBN 1743790996; 9781743790991

This book, by Mat Pember and Dillon Seitchik-Reardon, "includes over 38 . . . projects for those young and old wanting to transform their outdoor living space. It is broken into 6 categories from Kids, Recycled/Upcyled, X-Factor, Vertical Gardening, Gardening basics and Kitchen, and includes a variety of projects for experienced handy folk to quirky ideas that will involve the youngest members of the family." (Publisher's note)

"Charming and hip projects emphasize recycled materials and small space gardens that will be attractive in urban settings. Highly recommended, especially where variety is desired." LJ

715 Woody plants in landscape architecture

Hobson, Jake

The **art** of creative pruning; inventive ideas for training and shaping trees and shrubs. Jake Hobson. Timber Press 2011 200 p. color illustrations $34.95 **715**

1. Pruning 2. Topiary work

ISBN 160469114X; 9781604691146

LC 2011007954

In this book, by Jake Hobson, "[n]othing brings a touch of artistry to the garden like ornamental pruning. . . . Drawing on both eastern and western styles, . . . Hobson moves beyond the traditional lollipops and animals and teaches a wholly new approach to ornamental pruning that appeals to modern sensibilities. . . . All the practical considerations are here as well, including pruning to improve a view, remedial pruning to fix problems, and pruning fruit trees to increase yield." (Publisher's note)

"Libraries already well stocked with titles such as Christopher Brickell and David Joyce's The American Horticultural Society Pruning & Training or Lewis Hill and Penelope O'Sullivan's The Pruning Answer Book will find Hobson's gorgeously illustrated, more philosophical book a good counterpart to those more nuts-and-bolts guides. Written with passion, verve, and a dash of dry wit, this title will inspire any gardener who wants to understand the how and why of creative pruning before picking up the shears and hacking off branches." LJ

Includes bibliographical references and index

How to train and shape trees and shrubs

720 Architecture

Cornille, Didier

Skyscrapers; who built that? : an introduction to skyscrapers and their architects. Didier Cornille.

Princeton Architectural Press 2014 84 p. illustrations (alk. paper) $16.95 **720**

1. Skyscrapers -- Juvenile literature 2. Architecture -- Juvenile literature

ISBN 1616892706; 9781616892708

LC 2014004388

This juvenile book, by Didier Cornille, "is a colorful tour of the world's tallest buildings and the larger-than-life personalities who built them. Beginning with a brief biographical sketch of each architect, illustrator Didier Cornille imaginatively depicts the construction of eight of the world's most impressive skyscrapers." (Publisher's note)

"Though the information is a little slight, the spare illustrations easily make up for it—all of Cornille's drawings unmistakably reveal architectural components not visible in photographs, such as interior structures or foundations, and although they're very minimalistic, it's impossible not to see the structures' grandeur in each illustration. Though this resembles a picture book, the sometimes elevated language makes this better suited to middle- or even high-school students who already have an interest in architecture or graphic design." Booklist

Davies, Colin

Thinking about architecture; an introduction to architectural theory. Colin Davies. Chronicle Books Llc. 2011 160 p. ill. (paperback) $29.95; (ebook) $29.95 **720**

1. Architecture -- Philosophy

ISBN 185669755X; 9781856697552; 9781780670911

It was author Colin Davies' intent "to provide designers, teachers, students, and interested laypersons with a set of ideas that will enrich their conversation, their writing, and above all their thinking about architecture." The book introduces "basic concepts such as representation, form, and space." (Publisher's note)

Palladio, Andrea

The **four** books on architecture; translated by Robert Tavernor and Richard Schofield. MIT Press 1997 xxxv, 436p il $69.95; pa $24.95 **720**

1. Architecture

ISBN 0-262-16162-1; 0-262-66133-0 pa

LC 96-36406

"Drawing on the monuments of ancient Rome as well as the author's own villas and public works, this philosophical treatise and practical guide served as the pattern book for countless Palladian buildings by other architects around the world. Elegantly translated (in the first new English translation since 1738) and illustrated with the lyrical, rarely seen woodcuts of Palladio's original." N Y Times Book Rev

Includes bibliographical references

Rybczynski, Witold

Mysteries of the mall; and other essays. Witold Rybczynski. Farrar, Straus & Giroux 2015 336 p. (hardcover) $27 **720**

1. Architecture -- United States 2. City planning -- United States 3. Cities and towns -- United States 4. Architecture and society -- United States 5. Cities and

towns -- United States -- History
ISBN 0374269939; 9780374269937

LC 2014046633

This collection of essays on urban planning and architecture, by Witold Rybczynski, "ranges over subjects as varied as shopping malls, Central Park, the Paris opera house, and America's shrinking cities. Along the way, he examines our post-9/11 obsession with security, the revival of the big-city library, the rise of college towns, and our fascination with vacation homes, and he visits Disney's planned community of Celebration." (Publisher's note)

"A superb book for those interested in architectural history, written in an e asygoing style by a man with encyclopedic knowledge and an obvious great love for building." Kirkus

Watkin, David, 1941-

A **history** of Western architecture; David Watkin. 6th edition Laurence King Pub 2015 736 p. ill. (some col.) pbk $45   **720**
1. Architecture -- History
ISBN 9781780675978; 1780675976
First edition 1986
Includes bibliographical references and index.

"David Watkin traces the history of western architecture from the earliest times in Mesopotamia and Egypt to the eclectic styles of the twenty-first century. The author emphasizes the ongoing vitality of the Classical language of architecture, underlining the continuity between, say, the work of Ictinus in fifth-century BC Athens and that of McKim, Mead and White in twentieth-century New York." (Publisher's note)

720.9   History, geographic treatment, biography

Architecture; the whole story. general editor, Denna Jones; foreword by Richard Rogers & Philip Gumuchdjian. Prestel Pub. 2014 576 p. color illustrations $34.95   **720.9**
1. Architecture 2. Architecture -- Themes, motives
ISBN 3791349155; 9783791349152

LC 2014937907

"This latest addition to the Whole Story series offers an encyclopedic and lavishly illustrated survey of architecture throughout human history. Sweeping in reach and exhaustive in detail, [it] is an indispensible reference for anyone interested in the evolution of our built environment. Ranging chronologically from the Neolithic period to the sustainability movement of today, it looks at hundreds of examples of structures, their designers, and their contextual significance." (Publisher's note)

"Over 1,000 images illustrate buildings, details, and an occasional cross-section or floor plan. Considering the book's worldwide focus, however, a map would have been a welcome addition. Similar comprehensive reference works, such as the two-volume Oxford Companion to Architecture, edited by Patrick Goode (CH, Mar'10, 47–3549), are more systematic but lack the vitality of Jones's work. Summing Up: Highly recommended. Lower-division undergraduates through graduate students; general readers." Choice

Includes bibliographical references and index

Boucher, Bruce

Andrea Palladio; the architect in his time. principal photography by Paolo Marton. 2nd ed; Abbeville Press 2007 324p il pa $39.95   **720.9**
1. Architects
ISBN 978-0-7892-0940-5; 0-7892-0940-3
First published 1994

"In this careful, comprehensive, stunningly illustrated survey, Boucher . . . capably illuminates Palladio's stylistic evolution. . . . Among the 300 plates are more than 100 newly commissioned photographs of building interiors and exteriors, which superbly capture Palladio's distincitve blend of simplicity and grandeur." Publ Wkly

Includes bibliographical references (p. 301-312)

Glancey, Jonathan

The **story** of architecture. Dorling Kindersley 2000 240p il hardcover o.p. pa $25   **720.9**
1. Architecture -- History
ISBN 0-7894-5965-5; 0-7894-9334-9 pa

LC 00-30434

"Devoting nearly half the text to the modern period, Glancey condenses history's panorama into a series of colorful vignettes, each described as having some contemporary relevance. Driven by a contagious enthusiasm, the narrative is enlivened by chatty, sometimes offbeat commentary." Libr J

Hollis, Edward

The **secret** lives of buildings; from the ruins of the Parthenon to the Vegas Strip in thirteen stories. Metropolitan Books 2009 338p il $28   **720.9**
1. Buildings 2. Architecture
ISBN 978-0-8050-8785-7; 0-8050-8785-0

LC 2009-18715

This book is "built around thirteen chapters, each telling the story of a building that changed dramatically over time, either in physical terms (the Parthenon, Gloucester Cathedral) or conceptual ones (the Venetian hotel and casino in Las Vegas, which seeks to capture the image of the Most Serene Republic if not, exactly, the spirit). Hollis's stories are engrossing—his history of the Hulme housing estates in Manchester, and their role as incubator for British post-punk rock, was completely new to me—and his writing is engaging." Bookforum

Includes bibliographical references (p. 315-322)

Jarzombek, Mark

A **global** history of architecture; Francis D.K. Ching, Mark Jarzombek, Vikramaditya Prakash. Wiley 2011 848 p. illustrations, maps hbk $115 **720.9**
1. Architecture -- History
ISBN 0470402571; 9780470402573

LC 2010040984

"It differs from other architectural survey books in that its chapters are organized not by period or country but according to 18 chronological time-cuts, each encompassing a period of 200 to 400 years and crossing over multiple styles and geographical locations. Even as it features most of the major monuments included in other architectural surveys, this volume has countless more, especially from the non-Western world. The text provides a thorough and detailed analysis of the patronage, historical context, and architecture of each building." Choice

Includes bibliographical references and index

Rybczynski, Witold

The **perfect** house: a journey with the Renaissance architect Andrea Palladio. Scribner 2002 266p il $25; pa $15   **720.9**

1. Architects 2. Architecture -- 15th and 16th centuries

ISBN 0-7432-0586-3; 0-7432-0587-1 pa

LC 2002-66838

The author offers a historical and architectural analysis of ten villas attributed to 16th century Italian architect Andrea Palladio

"With its intriguing biographical detail, precise descriptions of design elements, and engaging insights into daily life in the 16th century, Rybczynski's book is a small but lasting gift to the reader." Libr J

Includes bibliographical references

The Seventy wonders of the modern world; 1500 years of extraordinary feats of engineering and construction. edited by Neil Parkyn. Thames & Hudson 2002 304p il $40   **720.9**

1. Architecture 2. Curiosities and wonders

ISBN 0-500-51047-4

LC 2002-100549

Published in the United Kingdom with title: The seventy architectural wonders of our world

"Most of the featured 'wonders' date from the second half of the 20th century. The selections are divided into seven categories: churches, palaces, public buildings, towers and skyscrapers, bridges and railways, canals and dams, and statues. Each entry includes basic information on history, structural and engineering details, innovations, aesthetics, and a sidebar 'fact-file.'" Libr J

Includes bibliographical references

Storrer, William Allin

The **Frank** Lloyd Wright companion; Rev ed; University of Chicago Press 2006 492p il $99 **720.9**

1. Architects 2. Nonfiction writers

ISBN 0-226-77621-2

LC 2006-44502

First published 1993

This "volume covers more than 450 buildings designed by master architect Wright between 1886 and 1959. Storrer documents each structure with plans, drawings, photographs, and commentary. Each presentation is both complete and concise, following each stage of Wright's aesthetic development, each leap of his imagination, and each instance of technical innovation." Booklist

Wolfe, Tom

From Bauhaus to our house. Bantam Books 1999 111p il pa $15   **720.9**

1. Bauhaus -- Influence 2. Architecture -- 20th century 3. Architecture -- United States

ISBN 978-0-553-38063-7; 0-553-38063-X

First published 1981 by Farrar, Straus & Giroux

A humorous history of American architecture in the 20th century.

720.973 Architecture--United States

Howard, Hugh

Architecture's odd couple; Frank Lloyd Wright and Philip Johnson. Hugh Howard. Bloomsbury Press 2016 352 p. illustrations (some color) (hardback) $28   **720.973**

1. Architecture 2. Architecture -- United States -- History -- 20th century

ISBN 1620403757; 9781620403754

LC 2015042135

This book, by Hugh Howard, "traces the historical threads connecting [architects Frank Lloyd Wright and Philip Johnson] and offers readers a distinct perspective on the era they so enlivened with their designs. Featuring many of the structures that defined modern space--from Fallingwater to the Guggenheim, from the Glass House to the Seagram Building--this book presents an arresting portrait of modern architecture's odd couple and how they shaped the American landscape by shaping each other." (Publisher's note)

"Written with wit and flair and supported by solid research, this thoughtful and well-built book will delight architecture buffs." Booklist

Includes bibliographical references (pages 285-320) and index.

721 Architectural materials

Rybczynski, Witold

The **look** of architecture. Oxford Univ. Press 2001 130p il hardcover o.p. pa $9.95   **721**

1. Design 2. Architecture

ISBN 0-19-513443-5; 0-19-515633-1 pa

LC 00-53077

"The author's deeply informed enthusiasm is infectious, and his removal of architectural writing from an airily theoretical discourse to the realm of practical experience is empowering for the lay reader." Publ Wkly

Includes bibliographical references

Smith, Nathan

Color concrete garden projects; make your own planters, furniture, and fire pits using creative techniques and vibrant finishes. Nathan Smith and Michael Snyder; photographs by Charles Coleman. Timber Press 2015 208 p. color illustrations $19.95 **721**

1. Concrete construction 2. Garden ornaments and furniture 3. Concrete construction -- Formwork 4. Garden ornaments and furniture -- Design and construction

ISBN 1604695390; 9781604695397

LC 2014048495

In this book, by Nathan Smith and Michael Snyder, "[d]iscover the countless ways you can craft with color and concrete! . . . This hands-on guide will take your outdoor space from gray to great. . . . Twenty creative step-by-step projects for furniture, planters, and art include an elegant tabletop planter, a modern birdhouse, and a charming chair for kids." (Publisher's note)

"This book has taken concrete projects to a new high; there's nothing else quite as focused on the subject. For a general concrete container book, see Malin Nilsson and Camilla Arvidsson's Concrete Garden Projects. A true standout—superior instructions and innovative design and use of pigment. A must for any DIY collection." LJ

724 Architecture from 1400

Curtis, William J. R.

Modern architecture since 1900; 3rd ed [rev, expanded, and redesigned]; Phaidon 1996 736p il $59.95; pa $39.95   **724**

1. Architecture -- 20th century
ISBN 978-0-7148-3524-2; 0-7148-3524-2; 978-0-7148-3356-9 pa; 0-7148-3356-8 pa

LC 97-112837
First published 1982
"The volume's well-detailed text is buttressed with 650 color and black-and-white illustrations. This should be a standard volume in all architecture collections." Lib J
Includes bibliographical references

Gropius, Walter

The **new** architecture and the Bauhaus; translated from the German by P. Morton Shand; with an introduction by Frank Pick. MIT Press 1965 112p il pa $14.95   **724**

1. Bauhaus 2. Architecture -- 20th century
ISBN 0-262-57006-8

LC 65-10279
Original German edition, 1925; this is a reissue of the translation first published 1935 in the United Kingdom
The founder of the Dessau Bauhaus describes the work of that institution, and his own architectural theories

Huxtable, Ada Louise

On architecture; collected reflections on a century of change. Walker 2008 478p il $35   **724**

1. Architecture -- 20th century
ISBN 978-0-8027-1707-8; 0-8027-1707-7
The author "presents her penetrating and tough-minded criticism spanning half a century. . . . Centering largely on modernism, its masters and its discontents, the volume opens with an overview of the past four decades, including startlingly powerful pieces on the late '60s urban decay and the '90s reinvention of architecture." Publ Wkly

726 Buildings for religious and related purposes

King, Ross

Brunelleschi's dome; how a Renaissance genius reinvented architecture. Penguin Books 2001 194p il pa $14   **726**

1. Artists 2. Sculptors 3. Architects 4. Church buildings 5. Santa Maria del Fiore (Cathedral: Florence, Italy)
ISBN 0-14-200015-9

LC 2001-280068
First published 2000 by Walker & Co.

"King illuminates the mysterious sources of inspiration and the secretive methods of architectural genius Filippo Brunelleschi in a fascinating chronicle of the building of his masterwork, the dome of Santa Maria del Fiore in Florence. A remarkable saga of how one incandescent mind performed the one matchless feat that would forever transform architecture from a mechanical craft into a creative art." Booklist
Includes bibliographical references

727 Buildings for educational and research purposes

Holway, Tatiana

The **flower** of empire; the Amazon's largest water lily, the quest to make it bloom, and the world it helped create. Tatiana Holway. Oxford University Press 2013 328 p. $29.95   **727**

1. Botany -- History 2. Victorian architecture 3. Victoria amazonica 4. Botanical gardens -- England -- History -- 19th century
ISBN 0195373898; 9780195373899

LC 2012034518
The "central narrative of [Tatiana] Holway's book pivots around an 1837 British discovery in Guiana of an immense water lily, and the mission to make one bloom in England. Along with the story of a quest for germination is the author's . . . description of the botany-obsessed Victorian England where the building of glass greenhouses influenced the design of the Crystal Palace in Hyde Park for the Great Exposition of 1851." (Library Journal)

728 Residential and related buildings

Eck, Jeremiah

The **distinctive** home; a vision of timeless design. Taunton Press 2003 234p il $40   **728**

1. Building 2. Domestic architecture -- Designs and plans
ISBN 1-561-58528-9

LC 2002-151820
"Eck firmly believes it is possible to build creative houses without a large budget. He discusses a home's site placement, examines the flow of activity within a modern home, and encourages the reader to think of rooms beyond their traditional uses. Eck's book encourages creativity and provides a series of color photographs for developing sound ideas." Libr J

★ The **elements** of style; an encyclopedia of domestic architectural detail. general editor, Stephen Calloway; consultant editor, Elizabeth Cromley. Firefly Books 2005 592 p. ill. (some col.) $85   **728**

1. Domestic architecture 2. Architecture -- Great Britain 3. Architecture -- United States 4. Interior architecture 5. Architecture -- Details 6. Architecture, Domestic -- Great Britain 7. Architecture, Domestic -- United States
ISBN 1554070791; 9781770850866

LC 2006276161

This book, edited by Stephen Calloway, Alan Powers, and Elizabeth Cromley, presents a "visual survey, period by period, feature by feature, of the key styles in American and British domestic architecture from the Tudor period to present day. . . . The book is designed for owners of period houses, restorers, architects, interior designers and all those interested in our architectural heritage." (Publisher's note)

Includes bibliographical references (p. 581-583) and index

The Greenwood encyclopedia of homes through American history; Thomas W. Paradis, general editor. Greenwood Press 2008 4v il set $399.95   **728**
1. Reference books 2. Decorative arts -- Encyclopedias 3. Domestic architecture -- Encyclopedias
ISBN 978-0-313-33496-2; 0-313-33496-X

LC 2008-2946

"The set covers ten historical eras beginning with the Colonial era and ending with the period 1986 to present. Each era is introduced by a time line and short historical essay. Other essays synthesize research under topics such as building materials, house plans, interior design, and landscaping. . . .The value of the set lies behind the pretty facade of the American home, in the contributors' exploration of the interaction of physical house and family life." Choice

Includes bibliographical references

Jordan, Wendy Adler
Universal design for the home; great looking, great living design for all ages, abilities, and circumstances. Quarry Books 2008 207p il pa $24.99 **728**
1. Domestic architecture -- Designs and plans
ISBN 978-1-59253-381-7; 1-59253-381-7

LC 2007-32663

This book "shows how a home that is accommodating to all can also have a stylish decor. . . . Color photographs and some before-and-after floor plans show how accessibility standards have been incorporated. A list of resources is provided." Libr J

McAlester, Virginia Savage
A **field** guide to American houses; the definitive guide to identifying and understanding America's domestic architecture. Virginia Savage McAlester; with drawings by Suzanne Patton Matty and photographs by Steve Clicque. Random House Inc 2013 848 p. ill. $50   **728**
1. Architecture -- United States 2. Domestic architecture -- Guidebooks 3. United States -- Guidebooks 4. Architecture, Domestic -- United States -- Guidebooks
ISBN 140004359X; 9781400043590

LC 2013018432

This book "covers more than 50 styles of American residential architecture, from early settlement homes of the seventeenth century to the modern 'Millennium Mansions' of the present day. Expanded and completely revised from the 1984 edition, this edition includes American house design from the last three decades and adds more than 600 new photographs and illustrations." (Booklist)

Includes bibliographical references and index

Mitchell, Ryan
Tiny house living; ideas for building and living well in less than 400 square feet. F & W Media Inc 2014 175 p. color illustrations $26.99   **728**
1. Simplicity 2. Small houses
ISBN 1440333165; 9781440333163

LC 2015490704

"This book explores the philosophies behind the tiny house lifestyle, helps you determine whether it's a good fit for you, and guides you through the transition to a smaller space. For inspiration, you'll meet tiny house pioneers and hear how they built their dwellings (and their lives) in unconventional, creative and purposeful ways. They'll invite you in, show you around their cozy abodes, and share lessons they learned along the way." (Publisher's note)

Petroski, Henry, 1942-
The **house** with sixteen handmade doors; a tale of architectural choice and craftsmanship. Henry Petroski; with photographs by Catherine Petroski. W.W. Norton & Co. Inc. 2014 384 p. illustrations, maps (hardcover) $27.95   **728**
1. Maine 2. Domestic architecture 3. Architecture, Domestic -- Maine 4. Arrowsic (Me.) -- Buildings, structures, etc
ISBN 0393242048; 9780393242041

LC 2014006423

"When Henry Petroski and his wife Catherine bought a . . . six-decades-old island retreat in coastal Maine, Petroski couldn't help but admire its unusual construction. An . . . expert on engineering, history, and design, he began wondering about the place's origins and evolution. . . . Sleuthing around dimly lit closets, knotty-pine wall panels, and even a secret passage . . . Petroski zooms in on the details but also steps back to examine the structure in the context of its time and place." (Publisher's note)

"Though this fascinating history of a house includes painstaking attention to woodcrafting techniques that may excite professional and amateur architects and carpenters a bit more than general readers, the book is replete with Petroski's usual fascinating details and elegant prose." Booklist

Includes bibliographical references and index

Pierce, Deborah
The **accessible** home; designing for all ages and abilities. Deborah Pierce. The Taunton Press 2012 234 p. illustrations (ebook) $23.99; (pbk.) $32.95   **728**
1. Houses -- Maintenance and repair 2. Architecture and people with disabilities 3. Universal design 4. Dwellings -- Barrier-free design
ISBN 9781621136910; 1600854915; 9781600854910

LC 2012029176

This book, by Deborah Pierce, "goes beyond ramps and grab-bars to help aging boomers, or those faced with disabilities, accomplish home accessibility on a deeper level. With a focus on closing the gap between home and homeowner, architect Deborah Pierce leads readers through the steps of universal design—from hiring the right architect to creating a pleasing space with the final details." (Publisher's note)

Susanka, Sarah

Creating the not so big house; insights and ideas for the new American home. photographs by Grey Crawford. Taunton Press 2000 258p il $34.95; pa $24.95   **728**

1. Interior design 2. Domestic architecture
ISBN 1-56158-377-4; 1-56158-605-6 pa

LC 00-44323

Susanka provides photographs and plans of houses that are designed to look bigger than their actual size

"Architect Susanka has big ideas about small design. . . . {This book promotes} well-designed, efficient, interesting modest-size homes. . . . {She} includes 25 delightful examples of houses designed by architects from around the country." Booklist

The **not** so big house; a blueprint for the way we really live. {by} Sarah Susanka, with Kira Obolensky. Expanded edition Taunton Press 1998 199p il col il pbk $24.95   **728**

1. Domestic architecture
ISBN 1600851509; 9781600851506

LC 2009018546

Originally published 1998

"Architect Susanka believes that the large homes being built today place too much emphasis on square footage rather than on current lifestyles. Here she shows how homes can be designed to feature 'adaptable spaces open to one another, designed for everyday use.' She describes how to examine occupants' lifestyles, how to incorporate the kitchen as the focal point of the home, how to give the illusion of space, and how, with storage, lighting, and furniture arrangement, a smaller home can be comfortably livable." (Library Journal)

Includes bibliographical references and index

Not so big solutions for your home. Taunton Press 2002 155p il pa $22.95   **728**

1. Interior design 2. Domestic architecture -- Designs and plans
ISBN 1-56158-613-7

LC 2002-7101

The author presents a compilation of 31 essays from her "Drawing Board" column in Fine Homebuilding magazine "that offer a number of solutions to household design problems both big and small. . . . Susanka offers an eclectic mix: tips on site selection, mud room design, planning to fit specific furniture, creating a family room that works, personalizing with tile, and planning window seats, pantries, TV placement, and floor plan changes." Libr J

Van Doren, Adam, 1962-

The **house** tells the story; homes of the American presidents. by Adam Van Doren; foreword by David McCullough. David R. Godine 2015 196 p. color ill., color maps (alk. paper) $40   **728**

1. Houses 2. Presidents -- United States -- Homes 3. Dwellings in art 4. Presidents -- Dwellings -- United States -- Pictorial works
ISBN 1567925421; 9781567925425

LC 2015000579

In this book, "historian David McCullough and noted artist Adam Van Doren unite for an excursion to the celebrat-

ed homes of fifteen American presidents, past and present. The text is personal and unaffected; Van Doren visited these homes to ensure that he recorded every detail accurately, often becoming acquainted with the former presidents themselves, always trying to portray them in the human environment they created for themselves." (Publisher's note)

"Warm, accessible, and harmonious, this book marries history with art for a uniquely American vision." Pub Wkly

Versaci, Russell

Creating a new old house; yesterday's character for today's home. Russell Versaci; photographs by Erik Kvalsvik. The Taunton Press, Inc. 2003 218 p. color illustrations $24.95   **728**

1. Domestic architecture 2. Architecture -- United States 3. Architecture, Domestic -- United States
ISBN 1561586153; 1561587923; 9781561587926

LC 2003004993

In this book, author Russell Versaci "explores how architects, builders, and craftsmen are reinterpreting the traditional American house. Through photographs and engaging text, brief discussions of history and craftsmanship, and occasional sidelong glances at the workings of real old houses, Versaci employs his 'Pillars of Traditional Design' to explain how traditional houses go together and what gives them their unique design appeal." (Publisher's note)

Wilhide, Elizabeth

Scandinavian Home; A Comprehensive Guide to Mid Century Modern Scandinavian Designers. Elizabeth Wilhide. Chronicle Books Llc 2016 192 p. (hardcover) $29.95   **728**

1. Interior design 2. Modernism in architecture 3. Scandinavian architecture
ISBN 1849497494; 9781849497497

This book, by Elizabeth Wilhide, profiles "Scandinavian Modern . . . , the most influential and enduring design movement of the 20th century, dominating the international scene in the 1950s and continuing to shape the way we live today. Architects and designers from Denmark, Sweden, Norway, and Finland, were responsible for a range of contemporary homes, furniture, textiles, ceramics, glassware, and other products that defined an entire approach to modern post-war living." (Publisher's note)

"This solid entry point into the Scandinavian school of design has the elegance of a coffee-table book combined with the information of a reference guide." Pub Wkly

Wolfson, Elissa

Audubon birdhouse book; building, placing, and maintaining great homes for great birds. by Margaret A. Barker and Elissa Wolfson. Voyageur Press 2013 160 p. ills. (col.), col. maps (softcover) $24.99 **728**

1. Woodwork 2. Birdhouses 3. Bird attracting -- United States 4. Birdhouses -- Design and construction
ISBN 0760342202; 9780760342206

LC 2013018947

This book, by Margaret A. Barker and Elissa Wolfson, "produced in association with the National Audubon Society, . . . explains how to build and place functional . . . bird homes that are safe and appropriate for more than 20 classic North American species, from wrens to raptors. Each of the easy-to-build boxes and shelves within is accompanied by cut lists, specially created line diagrams, and step-by-step photography." (Publisher's note)

Includes bibliographical references and index

728.37   Houses

Susanka, Sarah

Inside the not so big house; discovering the details that bring a home to life. Sarah Susanka and Marc Vassallo; photographs by Ken Gutmaker. Taunton Press 2005 210 p. color illustrations $21.95; (ebook) $17.99   **728.37**

1. Architecture 2. Interior design 3. Small houses 4. Interior architecture 5. Architecture -- Details 6. Room layout (Dwellings)

ISBN 1561586811; 1561589845; 9781561589845; 9781600857300

LC 2005008228

In this book, authors Sarah Susanka and Marc Vassallo "focus their lens on the tangible and sometimes intangible details that bring an otherwise ordinary home to life. Incorporating such details as dropped ceilings, built-in shelves, pocket doors, window seats, and well-placed alcoves infuses a home with the character of its owners. .... From Rhode Island to San Diego, the 23 homes featured here illustrate exceptional attention to detail." (Publisher's note)

728.8   Large and elaborate private dwellings

Wiencek, Henry

National Geographic guide to America's great houses; more than 150 outstanding mansions open to the public. by Henry Wiencek and Donna M. Lucey. National Geographic Soc. 1999 320p il pa $25   **728.8**

1. Domestic architecture 2. American architecture 3. Architecture -- United States

ISBN 0-7922-7424-5

LC 98-53013

Arranged by state, this guide includes information on past owners, furnishings, renovations, room descriptions, and excursion plans for other nearby houses of note. The text is accompanied by 170 full-color photos

736   Other plastic arts

Brown, Nancy Marie

Ivory Vikings; The King, the Walrus, the Artist and the Empire That Created the World's Most Famous Chessmen. Nancy Marie Brown. Palgrave Macmillan Trade 2015 288 p. illustrations, maps (hardback) $26.99   **736**

1. Chess 2. Antiquities 3. Viking civilization 4. Lewis chessmen 5. Lewis with Harris Island (Scotland) -- Antiquities 6. Viking antiquities -- Scotland -- Lewis with Harris Island 7. Ivories, Romanesque -- Scotland

-- Lewis with Harris Island

ISBN 1137279370; 9781137279378

LC 2015002532

This book, by Nancy Marie Brown, explores the history of the Vikings through focusing on the Lewis Chessmen artifacts. The narrative connects "medieval Icelandic sagas with modern archaeology, art history, forensics, and the history of board games. In the process, ... [the author] presents a vivid history of the 400 years when the Vikings ruled the North Atlantic, and the sea-road connected countries and islands we think of as far apart and culturally distinct." (Publisher's note)

"This book is a delight for chess players, of course, but also for gamers of all sorts as well as anyone interested in the intricacies of the provenance of art and in endlessly fascinating minutiae—the strength and uses of walrus skin, how to carve walrus ivory, and so much more." Booklist

Includes bibliographical references

Hayakawa, Hiroshi

Kirigami menagerie; 38 paper animals to copy, cut & fold. Sterling Pub. 2009 128p il pa $17.95   **736**

1. Paper crafts 2. Animals in art

ISBN 978-1-60059-318-5

LC 2008-50622

The author shows how to cut and fold paper shapes to make 38 different types of animals, including sheep, pandas, and dragons.

Van Sicklen, Margaret

The joy of origami. Workman 2005 152p il pa $16.95   **736**

1. Origami

ISBN 0-7611-3988-5; 978-0-7611-3988-1

LC 2005-43687

"The 57 [origami] models [included] range in difficulty from a simple Elephant in Pajamas to a more challenging Tyrannosaurus Rex." Publisher's note

737.4   Coins

Krause, Chester L.

Standard catalog of world coins; 1901-2000. by Chester L. Krause and Clifford Mishler. Krause Publs. il   **737.4**

1. Coins

ISBN

First published 1972. Periodically revised

This illustrated volume currently covers coins from throughout the world minted 1901-2000. Prices are provided for each coin in up to four grades of preservation. Includes commemorative issues.

Yeoman, R. S.

A guide book of United States coins; The official red book. R.S. Yeoman; editor, Kenneth Bressett; research editor, Q. David Bowers; valuations editor,

Jeff Garrett. Whitman Pub. 429p il (Official red book series)   **737.4**

1. Coins 2. Reference books

Annual. First published 1946 by Whitman

This guide "known as the 'Red Book' is an outstanding reference on U.S. coins designed for use in identifying and grading coins. All issues from 1616 to the present are covered. The guide provides historical data, statistics, values, and detailed photographs for each coin. Additional sections deal with specialties such as Civil War and Hard Times tokens, misstruck coins, and uncirculated and proof sets." Nichols. Guide to Ref Books for Sch Media Cent. 4th edition

Handbook of United States coins; the official Blue Book. by R. S. Yeoman; edited by Kenneth Bressett. Whitman Publishing 2008 various pagings il   **737.4**

1. Coins

ISBN

Annual. First published 1942

This companion volume to A Guide book of United States coins gives the wholesale values of U.S. coins from colonial times to the present

738   Ceramic arts

Kovel, Ralph M.

Kovels' dictionary of marks: pottery and porcelain; by Ralph M. and Terry H. Kovel. 2nd ed; Crown 1995 278p il $17   **738**

1. Pottery -- Marks 2. Porcelain -- Marks

ISBN 0-517-70137-5

LC 95-3361

First published 1953 with title: Dictionary of marks—pottery and porcelain

This is a guide to identification of American, English, and European pottery and porcelain including an "index of 5,000 marks, listed by prominent features and with a complete cross-reference {showing} at a glance (a) geographical location of mark, (b) factory or family name of manufacturer, (c) type of ware, (d) method of producing the mark on the object, (e) color of the mark, and (f) date when the mark was used. The authors have included a foreword, bibliography, index of manufacturers and a . . . guide to the often misunderstood marks of Delft, Sevres, and England 1842-1883." Publisher's note

Kovels' new dictionary of marks; {by} Ralph and Terry Kovel. Crown 1986 290p il $19   **738**

1. Pottery -- Marks 2. Porcelain -- Marks

ISBN 0-517-55914-5

LC 85-15146

Covering pottery and porcelain from 1850 to the present this volume is regarded as a complimentary volume to the one covering 1650 to 1850

Scott, Marilyn

The **potter's** bible; an illustrated guide for beginners. by Marylin Scott. A&C Black 2007 illustrations   **738**

1. Pottery

ISBN 9780785821434

This book, by Marylin Scott, is "essential illustrated reference for both beginner and advanced potters. . . . Learn about essential tools and equipment, different types and constituencies of clay, methods of production and much more. Includes dozens of ideas for creating textured surface effects and decorations." (Publisher's note)

738.1   Techniques, procedures, apparatus, equipment, materials

Burnett, Jason Bige

Graphic clay; ceramic printing and image transfer techniques. Jason Bige Burnett. Lark Crafts 2014 160 p. color illustrations $27.95   **738.1**

1. Ceramics 2. Art pottery 3. Transfer printing 4. Pottery craft 5. Transfer-printing 6. Glazing (Ceramics)

ISBN 1454707755; 9781454707752

LC 2014016141

This book, by Jason Bige Burnett, "offers a wealth of techniques for transferring images onto clay vessels. . . . [It] addresses such topics as staining sculptural work, glazing, brush application, screenprinting patterns on pottery, and slip, drawing, bisque, decal, stencils, and more. Question-and-answer sessions with top artists show how they developed their signature method and personal style." (Publisher's note)

"Intermediate and experienced artists with some existing ceramics skills can find much inspiration here." LJ

Muller, Kristin

The **potter's** studio handbook; a start-to-finish guide to hand-built and wheel-thrown ceramics. Quarry Books 2007 192p il (Back yard series) pa $24.99   **738.1**

1. Pottery

ISBN 978-1-59253-373-2; 1-59253-373-6

LC 2007-16693

The author "guides beginners through advanced students in equipping a ceramic studio, handling the design, preparing the clay, constructing slab projects, throwing on a wheel, glazing, and firing. The 16 clay projects featured here include teapots, vases, and dinner plates. Readers can draw inspiration from the creative painting and underglazing examples, as well as the unusual firing techniques for color and texture." Libr J

Nelson, Glenn C.

Ceramics: a potter's handbook; [by] Glenn C. Nelson, Richard Burkett. 6th ed; Wadsworth/Thomson Learning 2002 439p il pa $90.95   **738.1**

1. Pottery 2. Ceramics

ISBN 0-03-028937-8

LC 2001-96329

First published 1960. Periodically revised

This manual for beginner to advanced potters presents forming and decorating techniques, body and glaze recipes, and sources for raw materials and equipment.

Includes bibliographical references

Pavelka, Lisa

The **complete** book of polymer clay; step-by-step instructions, original projects, inspirational gallery. Taunton Press 2010 221p il pa $24.95 **738.1**
1. Clay 2. Modeling
ISBN 978-1-60085-128-5

LC 2009-42430

This book presents projects with complete instructions showing readers how to make pendants, curio boxes, a necklace and a bracelet.

Includes bibliographical references

Taylor, Brian

Glaze; the ultimate ceramic artist's guide to glaze and color. Kate Doody, Brian Taylor. Barrons Educational Series, Inc. 2014 320 p. color illustrations $34.99 **738.1**
1. Glazes 2. Ceramics
ISBN 0764166425; 9780764166426

LC 2014942859

In this book by Brian Taylor and Kate Doody "potters will find a wealth of guidance on the glazing process as several of today's leading ceramicists share the recipes and techniques behind their most stunning works of art--each selected specifically for its unique glaze." (Publisher's note)

"Pottery was never so alluring. Appended are a glossary, a bibliography, an Orton cone chart, a directory of ceramic materials, and teachers and artists." Booklist

738.209 History and geographic treatment of porcelain

De Waal, Edmund

The **white** road; journey into an obsession. Edmund de Waal. Farrar, Straus & Giroux 2015 416 p. illustrations (hardback) $27 **738.209**
1. Ceramics 2. Porcelain -- History
ISBN 0374289263; 9780374289263; 9780374709099

LC 2015022207

This book, by Edmund de Waal, "gives us an intimate narrative history of his lifelong obsession with porcelain, or 'white gold.' A potter who has been working with porcelain for more than forty years, de Waal describes how he set out on five journeys to places where porcelain was dreamed about, refined, collected and coveted-and that would help him understand the clay's mysterious allure." (Publisher's note)

"De Waal's passionately and elegantly elucidated story of porcelain, laced with memoir and travelogue, serves as a portal into the madness and transcendence of our covetous obsession with beauty." Booklist

Includes bibliographical references

739.2 Work in precious metals

Faber, Toby

Fabergé's eggs; the extraordinary story of the masterpieces that outlived an empire. Random House 2008 302p il $30 **739.2**
1. Artists 2. Emperors 3. Empresses 4. Artisans 5. Jewelers 6. Metalworkers
ISBN 978-1-4000-6550-9; 1-4000-6550-X

LC 2007-49635

"Faber moves beyond mere description and illustration as he traces the fascinating history and sociology of these turn-of-the-century status symbols." Booklist

Includes bibliographical references

Von Habsburg, Geza

Faberge revealed; at the Virginia Museum of Fine Arts. Géza von Habsburg; with contributions by Carol Aiken ... [et al.] Virginia Museum of Fine Arts Skira Rizzoli 2011 xiii, 421 p.p illustrations (some color) (trade) $75 **739.2**
1. Art objects 2. Jewelry -- Russia -- Catalogs 3. Art objects, Russian -- Catalogs 4. Fabergé (Firm) -- Catalogs 5. Virginia Museum of Fine Arts -- Catalogs 6. Jewelry -- Virginia -- Richmond -- Catalogs 7. Art objects -- Virginia -- Richmond -- Catalogs
ISBN 0847837386; 0917046900; 0917046919; 9780847837380; 9780917046902; 9780917046919

LC 2011016388

This book, by Geza Von Habsburg, "present[s] new findings on Fabergé, his workshops, and the creation of these extraordinary objects. . . . Also included is a section on forgeries that bravely confronts this vexing question. Every object has been splendidly re-photographed for this book - and the detailed photography alone should provide inestimable value for future Fabergé scholarship." (Publisher's note)

Includes bibliographical references and index

739.27 Jewelry

Codina, Carles

The **complete** book of jewelry making. Lark Bks. 2000 160p il hardcover o.p. pa $19.95 **739.27**
1. Jewelry
ISBN 1-57990-188-3; 1-57990-304-5 pa

LC 00-42809

This book covers "the basics, from the ABCs of metallurgy to such complicated techniques as enameling and lacquering. . . . Most of the examples are contemporary, taken from European designers, and all blessed with great color photographs." Booklist

DeCoster, Marcia

★ **Marcia** DeCoster's beaded opulence; elegant jewelry projects with right angle weave. Lark Books 2009 128p il (Beadweaving master class) $24.95 **739.27**
1. Jewelry 2. Beadwork
ISBN 978-1-60059-292-8

LC 2008-50857

This book features jewelry projects using beading stitches with right-angle weave designs.

Haab, Sherri

The **art** of metal clay; techniques for creating jewelry and decorative objects. Rev. and expanded ed.; Watson-Guptill Publications 2010 160p il pa $24.99   **739.27**

1. Jewelry 2. Metalwork 3. Precious metal clay
ISBN 978-0-82309-932-0

LC 2009-43781

First published 2003

"An essential project book for anyone interested in learning to work with metal clay. . . . [The projects included involve] bronze and copper metal clays, etching, and enameling. An included DVD has additional projects." Libr J

McGrath, Jinks

The **complete** jewelry making course; Principles, Practice and Techniques: A Beginner's Course for Aspiring Jewelry Makers. Jinks McGrath. Barron's 2007 144 p. color illustrations (pbk.) $21.99 **739.27**

1. Jewelry making
ISBN 0764136607; 9780764136603

LC 2006936734

This book, by Jinks McGrath, "teaches the craft of jewelry making to students looking to create professional quality items. The author covers every step of the process, from creating original design concepts to fashioning professionally finished pieces of jewelry. She lists all required tools and equipment, explains their uses, advises on safe working practices, and then guides her readers through every stage of the jewelry making process in a series of carefully structured tutorials." (Publisher's note)

Includes bibliographical references (p. 144) and index

Miller, Judith

Miller's costume jewelry. Miller's 2010 256p il $34.99   **739.27**

1. Jewelry
ISBN 978-1-84533-563-2

"The highly informative and entertaining introduction highlights the rise and continued use of costume jewelry from ancient times to the present and features many of the influences that make vintage costume jewelry so popular. The book's remainder is divided into four sections focusing on major designers, classic designers, galleries (special collections), and designers to watch. . . . This delightful book will captivate costume jewelry enthusiasts." Libr J

Raden, Aja

Stoned; Jewelry, Obsession, and How Desire Shapes the World. HarperCollins 2015 368 p. 8 plates; color illustrations $27.99   **739.27**

ISBN 0062334697; 9780062334695

"What makes a stone a jewel? What makes a jewel priceless? And why do we covet beautiful things? In this brilliant account of how eight jewels shaped the course of history, jeweler and scientist Aja Raden tells an original and often startling story about our unshakeable addiction to beauty and the darker side of human desire." (Publisher's note)

"History enthusiasts will be entertained by Raden's knowledge of famous names as well as her narrative approach to the topic. Occasional injections of humor will keep readers interested." Library Journal

Young, Anastasia

The **workbench** guide to jewelry techniques. Interweave Press LLC 2009 320p il $34.95 **739.27**

1. Jewelry
ISBN 978-1-59668-169-9

LC 2009-41385

This is a "reference guide for all jewelers, amateur or professional. Includes extensive photographic illustrations of virtually all techniques needed to create quality jewelry. Also has an excellent chapter on design, and additional sections on photographing, exhibiting, marketing, and selling work." Libr J

Includes bibliographical references

740   Graphic arts

Eskilson, Stephen J.

Graphic design; a new history. [by] Stephen J. Eskilson. Yale University Press 2011 464 p. il (cloth : alk. paper) $65.00 **740**

1. Graphic arts -- History 2. Commerical art -- History 3. Commercial art -- History
ISBN 0300172605; 9780300172607

LC 2011025963

This book on "the history of graphic design explores its evolution from the 19th century to the present day. Author Stephen J. Eskilson demonstrates how a new era began for design arts under the influence of Victorian reformers, tracing the emergence of modernist design styles in the early 20th century, and examining the wartime politicization of regional styles." (Publisher's note)

The author focuses "on the evolution of graphic design since the 19th century as well as on what recent developments in the field of information technology mean for today's designers. . . . The result is an effective description of the political effects of design (e.g., strategies used by illustrators of war posters) and countercultural influences (e.g., drugs and graffiti) supported beautifully by 400-plus large color reproductions." Libr J

Includes bibliographical references and index

741   Drawing and drawings

Salisbury, Martin

Children's Picturebooks; The Art of Visual Storytelling. by Martin Salisbury. Chronicle Books Llc 2012   **741**

1. Illustration of books 2. Picture books for children
ISBN 185669738X; 9781856697385

Author Martin Salisbury's "book covers the key stages of conceiving a narrative, creating a visual language, and developing storyboards and design of a picturebook. There are interviews with leading children's picturebook illustrators, as well as case studies of their work. The picturebooks and artists featured hail from Australia, Belgium, Cuba, France,

Germany, Hungary, Ireland, Italy, Japan, Norway, Poland, Portugal, Russia, Singapore, South Korea, Spain, Taiwan, the UK, and the USA." (Publisher's note)

Satrapi, Marjane

Embroideries. Pantheon Books 2005 134p il $16.95 **741**

1. Graphic novels 2. Iran -- Graphic novels 3. Women -- Iran -- Graphic novels

ISBN 0-375-42305-2

LC 2004-58660

"Discussions of sex are frank and explicit and laced with high humor. . . . Satrapi's simple black-and-white cartooning style is tremendously effective, expertly portraying emotional nuances with just a few lines." Libr J

741.092 Biography

Bair, Deirdre

Saul Steinberg; a biography. Deirdre Bair. Nan A.Talese/Doubleday 2012 732 p. illustrations (some color) (alk. paper) $40 **741.092**

1. Artists -- United States -- Biography

ISBN 038552448X; 9780385524483

LC 2011050601

This book by Deirdre Bair is a "biography of Saul Steinberg, one of The New Yorker's most iconic artists. . . . Born in Romania, Steinberg was educated in Milan and was already famous for his satirical drawings when World War II forced him to immigrate to the United States. . . . His wife was the artist Hedda Sterne, . . . but his truly great love was the United States, where he traveled extensively by bus, train, and car, drawing, observing, and writing." (Publisher's note)

Includes bibliographical references and index

Lester, Toby

Da Vinci's ghost; genius, obsession, and how Leonardo created the world in his own image. Toby Lester. 1st ed.; Free Press 2012 275 p. **741.092**

1. Art criticism 2. Art -- History 3. Figure drawing

ISBN 1439189234; 9781439189238; 9781439189252 (ebook)

LC 2011027966

This book tells "the story of Vitruvian Man: Leonardo da Vinci's famous drawing of a man in a circle and a square. Deployed today to celebrate subjects as various as the nature of genius, the beauty of the human form, and the universality of the human spirit . . . it has become the world's most famous cultural icon, yet almost nobody knows anything about it. . . . Toby Lester weaves together a century-spanning saga of people and ideas. Assembled here is an eclectic cast of . . . characters . . . and, of course, in the starring role, Leonardo himself—whose ghost Lester resurrects in the . . . unfamiliar context of his own times." (Publisher's note)

Includes bibliographical references.

Genius, obsession, and how Leonardo created the world in his own image

741.2 Techniques, procedures, apparatus, equipment, materials

Birch, Helen (Artist)

Freehand; sketching tips and tricks drawn from art. by Helen Birch. Chronicle Books 2013 224 p. color illustrations (pbk.) $18.95 **741.2**

1. Composition (Art) 2. Drawing -- Technique 3. Creation (Literary, artistic, etc.)

ISBN 1452119775; 9781452119779

LC 2013036430

This book, written and illustrated by Helen Birch, "breaks down basic drawing techniques . . . and reveals their practical application in dazzling examples by today's coolest artists. Over 200 innovative works of art demonstrate all the fundamentals--line, tone, composition, texture, and more--and are presented alongside friendly text explaining the simple techniques used to achieve each stylish effect." (Publisher's note)

"Employing the formula of examples + explanations = inspiration, journalist and artist Birch presents the work of dozens of practicing contemporary artists, highlighting prominent techniques so that the reader can emulate and build upon them. Illustrations can be found on nearly every page, including many close-up views that break down for the reader what is happening in the more elaborate drawings." LJ

Includes bibliographical references and index

De Reyna, Rudy

How to draw what you see; by Rudy De Reyna. Watson-Guptill 2005 175 p. illustrations (ebook) $59.97; $19.99 **741.2**

1. Drawing -- Technique

ISBN 9780307786357; 0823023753; 9780823023752

This book, by Rudy De Reyna, "shows artists how to recognize the basic shape of an object—cube, cylinder, cone, or sphere—and use that shape to draw the object, no matter how much detail it contains." (Publisher's note)

"This compact 35th anniversary edition touches on still life, landscapes, and figure drawing in pencil, charcoal, watercolor wash, acrylic, and ink. De Reyna's dedication and enthusiasm are evident on every page." LJ

Edwards, Betty

Drawing on the Right Side of the Brain; A Course in Enhancing Creativity & Artistic Confidence. Betty Edwards. 4th ed. Tarcher/Penguin 2012 xxxiii, 284 p.p ill. (hbk.) $32.95; (pbk.) $19.95; (deluxe) $29.95; (hbk.) $32.95; (pbk.) $19.95; (deluxe) $29.95 **741.2**

1. Laterality 2. Drawing -- Technique 3. Visual perception 4. Cerebral dominance

ISBN 1585429198; 1585429201; 158542921X; 9781585429196; 9781585429202; 9781585429219

LC 2012001232

"This new edition of the hugely popular and influential drawing manual first published over 30 years ago incorporates new findings from neuroscience, like the discovery of brain plasticity, together with the tried-and-true exercises included in past editions." LJ

Includes bibliographical references (p. 270-274) and index

Kaupelis, Robert

Experimental drawing; 30th anniversary ed.; Watson-Guptill 2010 192p il pa $22.99   **741.2**
1. Drawing -- Technique
ISBN 978-0-8230-1622-8; 0-8230-1622-6
LC 2009-931354
First published 1980
"This classic work is a perfect next step for artists who have mastered the basics." Libr J
Includes bibliographical references

Micklewright, Keith

Drawing: mastering the language of visual expression. Harry N. Abrams 2005 168p il (Abrams studio) pa $29.95   **741.2**
1. Drawing -- Technique
ISBN 0-8109-9238-8
LC 2005-5862
"Using examples of master artists such as Ingres and Michelangelo as well as more contemporary work of Cezanne, Hockney, and others, different aspects of drawing are examined. Each chapter ends with 'Ideas to Explore,' in which the reader is given suggestions for practice. . . . This book is valuable for those learning the theory behind the elements of drawing and for those looking for practical instruction." Voice Youth Advocates
Includes bibliographical references

Price, Maggie

Painting with pastels; easy techniques to master the medium. North Light Books 2007 128p il pa $24.99   **741.2**
1. Pastel drawing
ISBN 978-1-58180-819-3; 1-58180-819-4
LC 2006-029048
"This book shows the reader . . . [how] to paint with pastels, from materials and techniques to painting from photographs. . . . Hand-in photos show how to hold and apply the pastel, and the twenty-two step-by-step demonstrations cover . . . preparing your surface, underpainting, figure drawing and more." Publisher's note

Willenbrink, Mark

Drawing for the absolute beginner; a clear & easy guide to successful drawing. Mark and Mary Willenbrink. North Light Books 2006 128 p. chiefly illustrations (pbk. : alk. paper) $19.99; (ebook) $19.99   **741.2**
1. Drawing 2. Drawing -- Technique
ISBN 1581807899; 9781581807899; 9781600616013
LC 2006008900
This book, by Mark and Mary Willenbrink, "makes drawing in a realistic style easier than you may think and more fun than you ever imagined! . . . [It] cover[s] it all—from choosing materials and the correct way to hold your pencil, to expert advice on the tricky stuff, like getting proportions and perspective right, drawing reflections, and designing strong compositions." (Publisher's note)

741.235   Pastel

Creevy, Bill

The **pastel** book; materials and techniques for today's artist. by Bill Creevy. Watson-Guptill 1991 175p illustrations $32.50   **741.235**
1. Pastel drawing
ISBN 0-8230-3902-1; 9780823039050
This book, by Bill Creevy, is "for anyone working with pastels. . . . Defining the pastel medium broadly—color in stick form to be used for drawing and painting simultaneously—the author creates works of sensuous textures and colors, ranging from subtle to intense. He uses traditional soft and hard pastels, as well as oil pastels and oil sticks, showing the effects produced by each in step-by-step demonstrations." (Publisher's note)

Eagle, Ellen

Pastel painting atelier; essential lessons in techniques, practices, and materials. Ellen Eagle; foreword by Maxine Hong Kingston. Watson-Guptill Publications 2013 192 p. illustrations $35; (ebook) $65   **741.235**
1. Pastel drawing 2. Pastel drawing -- Technique
ISBN 082300841X; 9780823008414; 9780823008421
LC 2012018761
This book, by Ellen Eagle, "explores pastel's rich but relatively unexamined past, reveals her own personal influences and approaches, and guides you toward the discovery and mastery of your own vision." (Publisher's note)

McKinley, Richard

Pastel pointers; top secrets for beautiful pastel paintings. Richard McKinley. North Light Books 2010 127 p. illustrations (chiefly color) (pbk. : alk. paper) $26.99; (ebook) $33.74   **741.235**
1. Pastel drawing 2. Pastel drawing -- Technique
ISBN 144030839X; 9781440308390; 9781440313912
LC 2010028709
This book on pastel painting, by Richard McKinley, "covers everything from the fundamentals to get you going (how to lay out your palette, create an underpainting, evoke luminous effects) to inspirations that will keep you growing (plein air painting, working in a series, keeping a painting journal). Whether you're a beginner or an experienced painter anxious to explore the expressive possibilities of pastel, this is your guide to making the most of the medium." (Publisher's note)
Includes bibliographical references and index

741.5   Cartoons, graphic novels, caricatures, comics

101 top tips from professional manga artists; Sonia Leong, Hayden Scott Baron. Barrons Educational Series, Inc. 2013 176 p. $22.99   **741.5**
1. Japanese art 2. Drawing -- Technique 3. Manga -- Study and teaching
ISBN 1438002068; 9781438002064
LC 2012948428

This book, by Sonia Leong and Hayden Scott Baron, focuses on the Japanese drawing known as manga. "With additional insights from a select group of fellow professionals, this illustration-packed book covers all aspects of manga art, presenting advice and instruction on . . . everything an illustrator needs to know in order to create successful manga art for a variety of media." (Publisher's note)

"Freelance comic artist and illustrator Leong and several contributing artists provide over 100 tips grouped and organized around basic topics, highlighting key aspects of manga such as character design, backgrounds, props, software and media, and even practices of successful professionals." LJ

Abel, Jessica

Drawing words & writing pictures; making comics: from manga, graphic novels, and beyond. [by] Jessica Abel & Matt Madden. First Second Books 2008 xxi, 282 p.p il $34.99　　741.5
1. Drawing -- Technique 2. Cartooning -- Technique 3. Comic books, strips, etc. 4. Graphic novels -- Authorship 5. Comic books, strips, etc. -- Authorship
ISBN 1596431318; 9781596431317

LC 2007044125

Authors Jessica Abel and Matt Madden present "a course on comic creation -- for college classes or for independent study -- that centers on storytelling and concludes with making a finished comic. With chapters on lettering, story structure, and panel layout, the fifteen lessons offered -- each complete with homework, extra credit activities and supplementary reading suggestions -- provide a solid introduction for people interested in making their own comics." (Publisher's note)

This "book offers step-by-step entry into a complicated series of skills in a nonscary and approachable way." Libr J

Includes bibliographical references (p. 261-265) and index

Mastering comics; drawing words & writing pictures continued. by Jessica Abel and Matt Madden. 1st ed. First Second 2012 xvii, 318 p.p chiefly ill. (some col.) (hardcover) $34.99　　741.5
1. Drawing 2. Cartoonists 3. Cartooning -- Technique 4. Comic books, strips, etc. -- Technique
ISBN 1596436174; 9781596436176

LC 2011037023

Jessica Abel's book "Mastering Comics," written with her husband Matt Madden, is a "course of study for the budding cartoonist. Covering advanced topics such as story composition, coloring, and file formatting, [the book] is a vital companion to the introductory content of the first volume" entitled "Drawing Words & Writing Pictures." (Publisher's note)

Andelman, Bob

Will Eisner: A Spirited Life; 1st M Press ed. M Presss 2005 375p illustrations $14.95　　741.5
1. Graphic novels 2. Arts -- Biography 3. Artists -- Biography 4. Authors -- Biography 5. Literature -- Biography 6. Cartoonists -- Biography 7. Cartoonists -- United States -- Biography
ISBN 1-59582-011-6

LC 2005026326

"Michael Chabon contributes a heartfelt introduction to Andelman's first-ever biography of Will Eisner (1917-2005) . . . Eisner revolutionized the field . . . from his 1940s stories featuring masked crime fighter the Spirit to his later, pioneering graphic novels but also as businessman and entrepreneur, teacher, mentor, and the inspiration of countless young artists [like Art Spiegelman]. . . . Besides verifying Eisner's impact on nearly every artist who drew comics in his wake, Andelman shows that Eisner's influence extends to such film directors as Spielberg and Tarantino." Booklist

B., David

Epileptic. Pantheon Books 2005 361p il $25; pa $18.95　　741.5
1. Graphic novels 2. Autobiographical graphic novels 3. Epilepsy -- Graphic novels
ISBN 0-375-42318-4; 0-375-71468-5 pa; 9780375423185

LC 2004-53419

Original French edition, 2002

The author's "artwork is magnificent—gorgeously bold, impressionistic representations of the world not as it is but as he's taught himself to perceive it. . . . B.'s illustrations constantly underscore his writing's wrenching psychological depth; readers can literally see how the chaos of his childhood shaped his vision and mind." Publ Wkly

Barry, Lynda

What it is. Drawn & Quarterly 2008 209p il $24.95　　741.5
1. Authorship -- Graphic novels 2. Creative writing -- Graphic novels
ISBN 978-1-897299-35-7; 1-897299-35-4

LC c2007-9047319

Independent cartoonist Lynda Barry presents an unconventional book that encourages its readers to write by using her colorful art and asking questions such as "How are monsters different? And how are they the same?" "Can/Do images exist without thinking?" "What is the difference between lying and pretending?" Each question appears with illustrated writing prompts and Barry's own ruminations on the topics. It's a workbook of sorts, but it also exists as a book to be read for itself.

"Every so often a book comes along that surpasses expectations, taking readers on an inspirational voyage that they don't want to leave. This is one such book." SLJ

Beatty, Scott

★ The **DC** Comics encyclopedia; the definitive guide to the characters of the DC universe. text by Scott Beatty . . . [et al.]; updated text by Dan Wallace. Updated and expanded; DK Pub. 2008 399p il $40　　741.5
1. Reference books 2. DC Comics Group 3. Comic books, strips, etc. -- Encyclopedias
ISBN 978-0-7566-4119-1; 0-7566-4119-5

LC 2008-300609

First published 2004

The authors "meticulously profile 1000 DC heroes and villains created since DC's 1935 founding. The entries are organized alphabetically, by character name, while introductory insets consistently detail first appearance, hero/villain status, physical statistics, and special powers. A genuinely essential DC character reference." Libr J

Bechdel, Alison, 1960-

Are you my mother? a comic drama. Alison Bechdel. Houghton Mifflin Harcourt 2012 286 p. **741.5**
1. Cartoonists -- Biography 2. Autobiographical graphic novels 3. Mother-daughter relationship -- Graphic novels 4. Cartoonists -- United States -- Comic books, strips, etc
ISBN 0618982507; 9780618982509
LC 2012010582
In this book, "[Alison] Bechdel not only searches for keys to [her relationship with her mother] but perhaps even for surrogate mothers, through therapy, girlfriends and the writing of Virginia Woolf, Adrienne Rich, Alice Miller and others. Yet the primary inspiration in this literary memoir is psychoanalyst Donald Winnicott, whose life and work Bechdel explores along with her own." (Kirkus Reviews)

★ **Fun** home; a family tragicomic. Houghton Mifflin 2006 232p il $19.95 **741.5**
1. Artists 2. Authors 3. Novelists 4. Cartoonists 5. Graphic novels 6. Autobiographical graphic novels 7. Essayists 8. Comic book writers 9. Biography, Individual
ISBN 0-618-47794-2; 978-0-618-47794-4
LC 2005-30304
Time Magazine Book of the Year for 2006
This is a memoir in graphic novel format about the author's "childhood, her father's death and their shared homosexuality. . . . The death was deemed an accident—a truck hit [Mr. Bechdel] as he crossed a road with an armful of garden brush—but Ms. Bechdel suspects suicide." (N Y Times (Late N Y Ed))
This "is one of the very best graphic novels ever." Booklist

Backderf, Derf

My friend Dahmer; written & illustrated by Derf Backderf. Abrams ComicArts 2012 221 p. **741.5**
1. Comic books, strips, etc. 2. Friendship -- Graphic novels 3. High school -- Graphic novels 4. Autobiographical graphic novels
ISBN 9781419702167
LC 2011285306
Alex Award (2013)
This book is an "exploration of notorious serial killer Jeffrey Dahmer by his high-school classmate. . . . In this graphic novel, [Derf] Backderf interweaves his memories of Dahmer with additional information gleaned from news reports, public interviews, and the memories of other classmates and community members. The book traces Dahmer's progression from experimenting with roadkill to . . . his first human victim just post-high school." (Bulletin of the Center for Children's Books)

Brunetti, Ivan

★ An **anthology** of graphic fiction, cartoons & true stories, vol. 2; edited by Ivan Brunetti. Yale University Press 2008 400p il $28 **741.5**
1. American wit and humor 2. Comic books, strips, etc.
ISBN 978-0-300-12671-6; 0-300-12671-9
"Brunetti's second collection of his favorite cartoonists' work is even better than the first—more far-ranging, more personal and eccentric. Clearly a tour of one person's singular tastes, it's arranged in a stream-of-consciousness 'oh, and you have to see this one' sort of way: work by 80-odd cartoonists, mostly from the past few decades, but also incorporating some early-1900s comic strips, a 1940s-vintage Fletcher Hanks story and several circa 1950 Harvey Kurtzman pieces as well as a smattering of previously unpublished gems." Publ Wkly

★ An **Anthology** of graphic fiction, cartoons, and true stories; edited by Ivan Brunetti. Yale University Press 2006 400p il $28 **741.5**
1. American wit and humor 2. Comic books, strips, etc.
ISBN 978-0-300-11170-5; 0-300-11170-3
LC 2006-14095
Brunetti presents "an overview of the art-comics movement, complete with a handful of the classic newspaper strips that informed today's creators. He finds room for such established veterans as R. Crumb, Lynda Barry, Gilbert and Jaime Hernandez, Daniel Clowes, Gary Panter, and Chester Brown as well as many less-familiar creators. . . . Brunetti admits that his selection criteria are highly personal, but as a cartoonist himself, whose work combines a socially transgressive spirit and impressive formal capability, his idiosyncratic approach is based in professional expertise. If his choices are sometimes arguable, his iconoclasm makes the book livelier and less predictable than such anthologies are wont to be." Booklist

Cartooning; philosophy and practice. Yale University Press 2011 77p il pa $13 **741.5**
1. Cartooning -- Technique
ISBN 978-0-300-17099-3; 0-300-17099-8
LC 2010-940419
"The first half of the book is devoted to the basic terminology and materials of the medium, while the second half is devoted to an intensive and full 15-week comics course. The course should make the non-draftsperson comfortable with drawing and progressively able to translate the panels of the story from head to page. It also breaks down the drawing process so that anyone can draw a couple characters without having to fret about making realistic, Marvel-style, detailed renderings or obsessive crosshatch shading. Cartooning is set to become the next de-facto book for breaking into the comics medium." Molossus
Includes bibliographical references

Chast, Roz

★ **Can't** We Talk About Something More Pleasant? A Memoir. Roz Chast. St. Martin's Press 2014 240 p. color illustrations hc $28 **741.5**
1. Aging parents
ISBN 9781608198061; 1608198065
Kirkus Prize: Nonfiction (2014)

National Book Critics Circle Award: Autobiography (2014)

In this memoir, author Roz Chast "brings her signature wit to the topic of aging parents. Spanning the last several years of their lives and told through four-color cartoons, family photos, and documents, and a narrative as rife with laughs as it is with tears, Chast's memoir is both comfort and comic relief for anyone experiencing the life-altering loss of elderly parents." (Publisher's note)

Chast "brings her parents and herself to life in the form of her characteristic scratchy-lined, emotionally expressive characters, making the story both more personal and universal." Pub Wkly

★ The **complete** cartoons of the New Yorker; edited by Robert Mankoff; foreword by David Remnick. Black Dog & Leventhal 2004 655p il $60 **741.5**
1. Cartoons and caricatures 2. New Yorker (Periodical) 3. New Yorker Magazine, Inc.
ISBN 1-579-12322-8

LC 2004-46371

"Issued as part of the New Yorker's eightieth anniversary celebration, this . . . volume collects, in two formats, the cartoons that have appeared in the pages of that magazine over the course of its distinguished publishing history. . . . The book itself gathers 2,500 of the most representative cartoons for display, but two accompanying CDs contain all the cartoons (68,647, to be exact) ever published in the magazine. Arrangement is by chapter, with each covering a decade of the New Yorker's existence. . . . A testament—a tribute—to the great magazine but also an absolutely special way to spend quality time." Booklist

Crumb, R.

The **book** of Genesis; illustrated by R. Crumb. W.W. Norton 2009 un il map $24.95 **741.5**
1. Graphic novels
ISBN 978-0-393-06102-4; 0-393-06102-7

LC 2009-14303

An illustrated adaptation of the entire book of Genesis, providing the biblical accounts of the Creation, Adam and Eve, Cain and Abel, Noah and the ark, the Tower of Babel, and other people and events.

"This is the Bible that distressed 19th-century English philanthropist and man of letters Thomas Bowdler: not stories for sweet-faced kiddies, but sex and blood. . . . We could not expect less from the patriarch of underground comix—themselves notorious for sex and violence and deals gone sour. Indeed, Crumb's muscular, detailed black-and-white seems ideally suited to Old Testament scuffles and seaminess." Libr J

De Haven, Tom

Our hero; Superman on Earth. Yale University Press 2010 224p il $24 **741.5**
1. Superman (Fictitious character)
ISBN 978-0-300-11817-9; 0-300-11817-1

LC 2009-18206

De Haven "offers an extended meditation on the role the flying Krypton orphan has played in comic books, cartoons, movies, and TV. Our Hero: Superman on Earth is part history — a summary of the ways Superman creators Jerry Siegel and Joe Shuster were ripped off will break your heart — and

part philosophy. De Haven contends that since his creation in 1938, Superman has seen many reinventions, but he always represents a uniquely American desire: to have 'the freedom to act in ways that are satisfying to him. It makes him feel good, dammit.' This book will make you feel the same." Entertainment Wkly

Includes bibliographical references

Delisle, Guy

★ **Pyongyang**: a journey in North Korea; translated by Helge Dascher. Drawn & Quarterly 2005 176p il map hardcover o.p. pa $14.95 **741.5**
1. Graphic novels 2. Korea (North) -- Graphic novels
ISBN 1-896597-89-0; 1-897299-21-4 pa

"Pyongyang will appeal to multiple audiences: current events buffs, Persepolis fans and those who just love a good yarn." Publ Wkly

Diffee, Matthew

Hand drawn jokes for smart attractive people; by Matthew Diffee. Simon & Schuster 2015 241 p. black and white illustrations $22 **741.5**
1. Jokes 2. Wit and humor 3. Cartoons and caricatures
ISBN 1476748748; 9781476748740

LC 2015452520

This book, by cartoonist Matthew Diffee, presents his "funniest drawings and writings from the past decade as well as all-new cartoons and sketches organized into categories that will appeal to smart attractive people in all walks of life, based on profession and circumstance: smart attractive Medical Professionals, sharp and good-looking Old People; beautiful geniuses in Prison; brainy handsome Lumberjacks; and more." (Publisher's note)

Eisner, Will

★ **Comics** and sequential art; principles and practices from the legendary cartoonist. W.W. Norton 2008 175p il (The Will Eisner library) pa $22.95 **741.5**
1. Drawing -- Technique 2. Graphic novels -- Authorship 3. Comic books, strips, etc. -- Authorship
ISBN 978-0-393-33126-4; 0-393-33126-1

LC 2008-20042

First published 1985 by Poorhouse Press

This book offers the author's ideas, theories, and advice about graphic storytelling and the uses to which the comic book art form can be applied.

Glidden, Sarah

How to understand Israel in 60 days or less; writer & artist, Sarah Glidden; letterer Clem Robins. Vertigo/DC Comics 2010 206p il map $24.99; $19.99 **741.5**
1. Graphic novels 2. Israel-Arab conflicts -- Graphic novels 3. Israel -- Description and travel -- Graphic novels
ISBN 978-1-4012-2233-8; 9781401222345

This book "is Sarah [Glidden]'s memoir not only of her Israeli governmentsponsored trip through Tel Aviv, Jerusalem, the Golan Heights, Masada and other famous locations, but of the emotional journey she never expected to take while she was there. Her experience clashes with her preconceived notions again and again, particularly when she tries to take a non-chaperoned trip into the West Bank. Sarah is forced to question first her political beliefs and, ultimately, her own sense of identity." (Publisher's note)

"Glidden's soft, watercolor palette and realistic art complement without overshadowing this thoughtful exploration of the role that cultural heritage plays in the search for personal identity." SLJ

Goldstein, Nancy

Jackie Ormes; the first African American woman cartoonist. University of Michigan Press 2008 225p il $35 **741.5**

1. Cartoonists 2. African American women -- Biography
ISBN 978-0-472-11624-9; 0-472-11624-X

LC 2007-35395

This book covers the life and career of Jackie Ormes, who was the first African American woman cartoonist. She wrote and drew comic strips that ran in Black newspapers such as the Pittsburgh Courier and the Chicago Defender. She was part of the Black elite in Chicago and knew other luminaries such as singer Eartha Kitt and musician/composer/conductor Duke Ellington. She was also investigated by the FBI because of her Leftist political ideas and activities. While she did such things as create Torchy paper dolls, based on her beautiful and sexy cartoon character, and cute Patty-Jo dolls, Ormes also used her comic strips to put forth her political views. This book reproduces some of her cartoons and comic strips, in both black and white and in color.

Includes bibliographical references

Guibert, Emmanuel

Alan's war. First Second 2008 304p il pa $24 **741.5**

1. Soldiers 2. Veterans 3. Graphic novels 4. Biographical graphic novels 5. Soldiers -- Graphic novels 6. World War, 1939-1945 -- Graphic novels
ISBN 978-1-59643-096-9; 1-59643-096-6

LC 2007-46190

French cartoonist Guibert met and became friends with Alan Cope and interviewed him at length to create this book. It recreates Cope's memories of being an eighteen-year-old G.I. during World War II. Unlike the war movies that focus on battles, this book focuses on more everyday, mundane memories of the day-to-day life of a soldier. Cope frankly describes a bout with crabs (genital lice), matter-of-factly tells of casual man-to-man sexual encounters among the soldiers, and gives the reader a feel for what happened back then. He also talks about postwar relationships and travels.

This is a "poignant and frank graphic memoir of young soldier who was told to serve his country in WWII and how it changed him forever. . . . Cope and Guibert forge a story that resonates with humanity." Publ Wkly

Hajdu, David

The **ten**-cent plague; the great comic-book scare and how it changed America. Farrar, Straus and Giroux 2008 434p $26 **741.5**

1. Comic books, strips, etc.
ISBN 978-0-374-18767-5; 0-374-18767-3

LC 2007-25024

"Hajdu offers captivating insights into America's early bluestocking-versus-blue-collar culture wars, and the later tensions between wary parents and the first generation of kids with the buying power to mold mass entertainment." Village Voice

Includes bibliographical references

Hart, Christopher

Cartooning for the beginner. Watson-Guptill 2000 144p il pa $19.95 **741.5**

1. Cartooning -- Technique
ISBN 0-8230-0586-0

LC 00-101905

This guide to cartooning techniques "covers the world of cartoon animals, animation, and 'edgy 'toons.'" Libr J

Hayden, Jennifer

The **Story** of My Tits; by Jennifer Hayden. Top Shelf Productions 2015 352 p. illustrations $29.99 **741.5**

1. Breast cancer -- Graphic novels
ISBN 1603090541; 9781603090544
Eisner Nominee: Best Reality-Based Work (2016)

This book is a "graphic memoir and a cancer narrative. . . When Jennifer Hayden was diagnosed with breast cancer at the age of 43, she realized that her tits told a story. Across a lifetime, they'd held so many meanings: hope and fear, pride and embarrassment, life and death. And then they were gone. Now, their story has become a way of understanding her story." (Publisher's note)

"Using famous works of art as metaphors for her own experiences and limiting her drawings to four equally measured panels per page, Hayden's work is matter-of-fact and unsentimental without becoming cold or heartless. The pacing of her storytelling is seamless, as if she were telling the story to the reader across a kitchen table." Booklist

Hirschfeld, Al

Hirschfeld on line. Applause Theatre Bk. Pubs. 1998 343p $59.95 **741.5**

1. Entertainers 2. Cartoons and caricatures
ISBN 1-55783-356-7

Hirschfeld "is the irreplaceable M.V.P. of the New York theatre world, and this compendium of his drawings amounts to a historic work of droll, generous-minded theatre criticism. The artist himself has annotated the drawings, which cover a range of the performing arts . . . and his comments are as swooping and witty as his lines." New Yorker

Holtz, Allan

American newspaper comics; an encyclopedic reference guide. Allan Holtz. The University of Michigan Press 2011 624 p. (cloth : alk. paper) $150 **741.5**

1. Cartooning 2. Cartoons and caricatures 3. Newspapers -- Sections, columns, etc. -- Comics 4. Comic books, strips, etc. -- United States -- History and criticism
ISBN 0472117564; 9780472117567

LC 2010033752

The author Allan Holtz focuses on the history of the newspaper comic strip, discussing "the evolution of newspaper cartoon features and . . . [correcting] misinformation that has circulated for years in other references. . . . [The book includes] start and end dates of features, their format, frequency, creators, and distribution companies. . . . [It also] includes a CD with samples of more than 2,000 cartoon features." (Publisher's note)

Howe, Sean

Marvel Comics; the untold story. by Sean Howe. Harper 2012 485 p. (hardback) $26.99 **741.5**

    1. Superhero comic books, strips, etc. 2. Comic books, strips, etc. -- History 3. United States -- History -- 20th century 4. Marvel Comics Group 5. Comic books, strips, etc. -- United States -- History and criticism

    ISBN 0061992100; 9780061992100

LC 2012015058

Author Sean Howe presents a book on the history of Marvel Comics. Howe "reveals the outsized personalities behind the scenes, including Martin Goodman, the self-made publisher who forayed into comics after a get-rich-quick tip in 1939 . . . and Jack Kirby, the World War II veteran who'd co-created Captain America in 1940 and, twenty years later, developed with Lee the bulk of the company's marquee characters in a three-year frenzy of creativity that would be the grounds for future legal battles and endless debates." (Publisher's note)

Includes bibliographical references and index

Humbug; [editor, Harvey Kurtzman; art, Jack Davis . . . [et al.]] Fantagraphics 2009 2v il set $60 **741.5**

    1. American wit and humor 2. Comic books, strips, etc.

    ISBN 978-1-56097-933-3; 1-56097-933-X

"MAD's early years have been justly lauded for their japing assault on postwar American culture, but this . . . two-volume boxed set reflects the history of comedy in the period after staff stars like Kurtzman jumped ship in 1956. . . . [Humbug's] 11 monthly issues published in 1957 and 1958 are all collected here." Publ Wkly

Jacobson, Sidney

The **9** /11 report; a graphic adaptation. by Sid Jacobson and Ernie Colón; [with a foreword by Thomas H. Kean and Lee H. Hamilton] Hill and Wang 2006 133p il $30; pa $16.95 **741.5**

    1. Graphic novels 2. September 11 terrorist attacks, 2001 -- Graphic novels

    ISBN 0-8090-5738-7; 978-0-8090-5738-2; 0-8090-5739-5 pa; 978-0-8090-5739-9 pa

"The book aims to make . . . [The 9/11 Commission Report] more accessible to all readers and draw in young adults. . . . This graphic adaptation is an important and necessary part of any collection." Libr J

Jones, Gerard

Men of tomorrow; geeks, gangsters and the birth of the comic book. Basic Books 2004 320p il $26; pa $15 **741.5**

    1. Cartoonists 2. Comic books, strips, etc.

    ISBN 0-465-03656-2; 0-465-03657-0 pa

LC 2004-9031

This book tells "the surprising story of the young Jewish misfits, hustlers and nerds who invented the superhero and the comic book industry. . . . Springing unheralded out of working-class Jewish immigrant neighborhoods in the depths of the Depression, these young men transformed an odd mix of geekdom, science fiction, and outsider yearnings into blue-eyed chisel-nosed crime-fighters and adventurers who quickly captured the mainstream imagination. . . . He chronicles how the comics sparked a frightened counterattack that nearly destroyed the industry in the 1950's and how later they surged back at an underground level, to inspire a new generation to transmute those long-ago fantasies into art, literature, blockbuster movies and graphic novels." Publisher's note

Karp, Jesse

Graphic novels in your school library; Jesse Karp; illustrated by Rush Kress. American Library Association 2012 xi, 146 p.p ill. (alk. paper) $50 **741.5**

    1. School libraries 2. Graphic novels -- Bibliography 3. Libraries -- Collection development 4. Graphic novels 5. Graphic novels in education -- United States 6. Libraries -- Special collections -- Graphic novels 7. School libraries -- Collection development -- United States

    ISBN 0838910890; 9780838910894

LC 2011026353

This book, by Jesse Karp, "takes a look at the term graphic novel, how the format has become entwined in our culture, and the ways in which graphic novels can be used in the library and in the classroom. . . . Karp . . . [i]ntroduces the history . . . and the conventions of the form, . . . [p]rovides annotated lists of core titles, [and] . . . [o]ffers lesson plans that use graphic novels . . . from life skills and dating to history." (Publisher's note)

Includes bibliographical references (p. 131-132) and index

Kitchen, Denis

The **art** of Harvey Kurtzman; the mad genius of comics. by Denis Kitchen and Paul Buhle; introduction by Art Spiegelman; designed by Kitchen, Lind & Associates. Abrams Comicarts 2009 241p il $40 **741.5**

    1. Cartoonists 2. Cartoons and caricatures

    ISBN 978-0-8109-7296-4; 0-8109-7296-4

LC 2008-04809

"Retrace the strands that led to a lot of current American satire — including The Simpsons, Saturday Night Live and The Daily Show — and sooner or later you end up at Harvey Kurtzman. A comic mastermind who created Mad Magazine and Playboy's 'Little Annie Fanny,' Kurtzman also happened to discover Robert Crumb and gave Gloria Steinem her first job. . . . [This volume] explores the life and art of the famous satirist, weaving together the story of Kurtzman's career with a collection of the artist's images and illustrations." NPR

Kneece, Mark

The **art** of comic book writing; the definitive guide to outlining, scripting, and pitching your se-

quential art stories. by Mark Kneece. Watson-Guptill Publications 2015 192 p. illustrations (some color) (paperback) $24.99   **741.5**
  1. Comic books, strips, etc. -- Authorship
  ISBN 9780770436971

LC 2015007716

This book, by Mark Kneece, is a "practical guide for beginner and advanced comic book writers that outlines the steps needed to successfully craft a story for sequential art. . . . He provides a practical set of guidelines favored by many comic book publishers and uses a unique trial and error approach to show would-be scribes the potential pitfalls they might encounter when seeking a career in comics writing." (Publisher's note)

"This guide isn't the first to discuss how to write for comics, yet it is by far the most in-depth treatment given to the subject in recent years. Although Kneece's works may not be well known, his legacy may well be this text, which will serve as a relevant resource to any program teaching comics and/or creative writing." LJ

Includes bibliographical references and index

Lee, Stan, 1922-
  Stan Lee's How to draw comics; from the legendary co-creator of Spider-Man, the Incredible Hulk, Fantastic Four, X-Men, and Iron Man. Watson-Guptill Publication 2010 224p il pa $24.99 **741.5**
  1. Graphic novels 2. X-Men (Fictional characters) 3. Fantastic Four (Fictional characters) 4. Drawing -- Technique 5. Comic books, strips, etc. -- Authorship
  ISBN 978-0-8230-0083-8

LC 2010-5781

The author "includes chapters on creating comics with computer programs and online resources and how to get work in the 21st century. The book begins with a brief history of comics, then focuses on action-adventure style, romance, humor, horror, and Japanese manga. This is the one book anyone interested in drawing comics should own." Libr J

Includes bibliographical references

Leopold, David
  The **Hirschfeld** century; portrait of an artist & his age. by David Leopold. Alfred A. Knopf 2015 336 p. illustrations (some color) (hardcover : alk. paper) $40   **741.5**
  1. Cartoonists
  ISBN 110187497X; 9781101874974

LC 2014047134

This book, by David Leopold, showcases how "Al Hirschfeld redefined caricature and exemplified Broadway and Hollywood, enchanting generations with his mastery of line. . . . [This volume] brings together for the first time the artist's extraordinary eighty-two-year career, . . . his influences, his techniques, [and] his evolution from his earliest works to his last drawings." (Publisher's note)

"An intelligent, carefully representative look at Hirschfeld's work that ably shows why the artist deserves to be remembered today." Kirkus

Lepore, Jill
  The **Secret** History of Wonder Woman; by Jill Lepore. Alfred A. Knopf 2014 448 p. 16 plates; color illustrations (hc : alk. paper) $29.95   **741.5**
  1. Feminism in literature 2. Wonder Woman (Fictitious character) 3. Literature and society -- United States
  ISBN 0385354045; 9780385354042

LC 2014011064

This book, by Jill Lepore, is a "work of historical detection revealing that the origin of one of the world's most iconic superheroes hides within it a fascinating family story--and a crucial history of twentieth-century feminism. Wonder Woman, created in 1941, is the most popular female superhero of all time. . . . Lepore has uncovered an astonishing trove of documents, including the never-before-seen private papers of William Moulton Marston, Wonder Woman's creator." (Publisher's note)

"Lepore demonstrates the power of exploring popular culture as history, and her readable style, as well as the subject matter, allows her to introduce this more nuanced understanding of a complex past to a wide audience. Summing Up: Highly recommended. All readers." Choice

Includes bibliographical references and index

Masters of American comics; essay by John Carlin; with contributions by Stanley Crouch . . . [et al.]; edited by John Carlin, Paul Karasik, and Brian Walker. Yale University Press 2005 316p il $45   **741.5**
  1. Cartoonists 2. Comic books, strips, etc.
  ISBN 0-300-11317-X

LC 2005-19449

"Hundreds of color reproductions allow the ingenuity of the artists' work to speak for itself." New Yorker

Includes bibliographical references

McCloud, Scott
  Making comics; storytelling secrets of comics, manga, and graphic novels. HarperCollins 2006 264p il pa $22.95   **741.5**
  1. Graphic novels -- Drawing 2. Comic books, strips, etc. -- Authorship
  ISBN 0-06-078094-0; 978-0-06-078094-4

The author "explores practical matters, including comics devices such as panels, word balloons, and sound effects; facial expressions and body language; the creation of convincing and evocative settings; and the different tools artists can use for the job, from pencils to computers. He also delves into the framing of images in panels, the flow of panels on a page, and the relationships between words and pictures in comics. . . . This is thoughtful, fascinating, stimulating, potentially controversial, and inspiring." Libr J

Includes bibliographical references

Reinventing comics; how imagination and technology are revolutionizing an art form. Paradox Press 2000 237p il pa $22.95   **741.5**
  1. Cartoons and caricatures 2. Comic books, strips, etc.
  ISBN 0-06-095350-0

LC 00-710457

The author maps out "'12 revolutions', which, he believes, need to take place for comics to survive and finally be recognized as a legitimate art form. The topics progress from the oldest of comic-related arguments (seeking respect) to the use of computer technology to renew and expand its audience. These brilliantly presented discussions concern comics as literature, comics as art, creators' rights, industry innovation, and public perception, among other topics." Libr J

★ **Understanding** comics; the invisible art. HarperPerennial 1994 215p il pa $22.95 **741.5**
1. Comic books, strips, etc.
ISBN 0-06-097625-X; 9780060976255
First published 1993 by Kitchen Sink Press

McCloud "conducts a genial, well-researched and funny tour of virtually every historical and perceptual aspect of comics, which he calls 'sequential art,' that is, art that consists of sequences of words and pictures. Beginning in the 11th century with the Bayeux tapestry, he examines pre-Columbian picture languages and the printing press, presenting a quick survey of the historical development of early sequential pictures into the specialized visual language of comics. . . . He dissects the vocabulary of the medium, cheerfully analyzing the psychological power of comics and their central role in our ultra-visual culture." (Publishers Weekly)
Includes bibliographical references

Morrison, Grant
Supergods; what masked vigilantes, miraculous mutants, and a sun god from Smallville can teach us about being human. Spiegel & Grau 2011 444p il **741.5**
1. Superheroes 2. Comic books, strips, etc. 3. Heroes 4. Comic books, strips, etc. -- United States
ISBN 1-4000-6912-2; 978-1-4000-6912-5
LC 2010053712

A graphic novelist presents a history of the superhero in American comic books and movies. Index.

Morrison chronicles the "rise, fall, rise, fall and rise again of comic-book superheroes, from Superman's auspicious beginning as a Depression-era symbol of the power of the individual to Wolverine's rise to prominence in a more morally ambiguous era." Kirkus
Includes bibliographical references

Nadel, Dan
Art in time; unknown comic book adventures 1940-1980. Abrams ComicArts 2010 301p il $40 **741.5**
1. Comic books, strips, etc.
ISBN 978-0-8109-8824-8; 0-8109-8824-0
LC 2009-31672

Nadel "rescues from oblivion an array of fascinatingly offbeat comics in a variety of genres (superhero, thriller, Western). In Art in Time, these meticulously reprinted full-length comic-book stories range from a terrifically sexy noir comic by Harry Lucey, 'The Cutie Killer Caper,' to Matt Fox's 'I Was a Vampire,' whose weirdly wooden art can be downright terrifying. Throughout, Nadel offers plenty of biographical details and brisk art criticism that make these riotous pages even more thrilling to rediscover." Entertainment Wkly
Includes bibliographical references

O'Neil, Dennis
Batman unauthorized; vigilantes, jokers, and heroes in Gotham City. edited by Dennis O'Neil. Benbella Books, Inc. 2008 219p il (Smart pop series) $17.95 **741.5**
1. Graphic novels 2. Batman (Fictional character) 3. Comic books, strips, etc. -- History and criticism
ISBN 978-1-93377130-4; 1-933771-30-5
LC 2007-46504

Former Batman comics editor and comic book writer O'Neil edits this collection of essays about Batman and his world, written by comics writers, magazine editors, and others. Topics include the cost of being Batman, calculated to the last dollar; why Batman is the most American of superheroes; whether Bruce Wayne might be mentally ill; why Batman needs Robin more than Robin needs Batman; why Arkham Asylum is doing more harm than good for Gotham City; why Batman works better when his world remains closer to reality; and more.
Includes bibliographical references

The **DC** comics guide to writing comics; introduction by Stan Lee. Watson-Guptill 2001 128p il $19.95 **741.5**
1. Comic books, strips, etc. -- Authorship
ISBN 0-8230-1027-9
LC 2001-26101

"O'Neil addresses the universals of writing in a way that makes the book useful to all aspiring scripters, regardless of their knowledge of comics." Booklist

Papadatos, Alecos
Democracy; concept, Alecos Papadatos; story, Alecos Papdatos & Abraham Kawa; script, Abraham Kawa; art direction & drawings, Alecos Papdatos; colouring, Annie Di Donna. Bloomsbury 2015 236 p. color illustrations $27 **741.5**
1. Democracy 2. War stories 3. Athens (Greece) -- Fiction
ISBN 1608197190; 9781608197194

This book by Alecos Papadatos, Abraham Kawa, and Annie Di Donna "opens in 490 B.C., with Athens at war. The hero of the story, Leander, is trying to rouse his comrades for the morrow's battle against a far mightier enemy, and begins to recount his own life, having borne direct witness to the evils of the old tyrannical regimes and to the emergence of a new political system. The tale that emerges is one of daring, danger, and big ideas, of the death of the gods and the tortuous birth of democracy." (Publisher's note)

"Papadatos's lively and energetic art illuminates battles, alliances, political machinations, and vivid personalities, and Di Donna's intense coloring is gloriously rich without a touch of gaudiness. For those interested in further background, the extensive back matter features useful commentary on both legendary and historical figures and concepts." Pub Wkly

Satrapi, Marjane, 1969-
★ The **complete** Persepolis. Pantheon Books 2007 341p il pa $24.95 **741.5**
1. Artists 2. Authors 3. Novelists 4. Cartoonists 5.

Graphic novels 6. Autobiographical graphic novels 7. Memoirists 8. Iran -- Graphic novels
ISBN 978-0-375-71483-2

LC 2007-60106

Originally published in two separate volumes 2003-2004

Ignatz Award: Outstanding Graphic Novel (2005)

This "is the story of Satrapi's . . . childhood and coming of age within a large and loving family in Tehran during the Islamic Revolution; of the contradictions between private life and public life in a country plagued by political upheaval; of her high school years in Vienna facing the trials of adolescence far from her family; of her homecoming—both sweet and terrible; and, finally, of her self-imposed exile from her beloved homeland." Publisher's note

Small, David, 1945-

Stitches; a memoir. W.W. Norton 2009 329p il $23.95   **741.5**

1. Artists 2. Authors 3. Illustrators 4. Graphic novels 5. Comic books, strips, etc. 6. Autobiographical graphic novels 7. Art teachers 8. Children's authors 9. Cancer -- Graphic novels 10. Family life -- Graphic novels
ISBN 978-0-393-06857-3; 0-393-06857-9

LC 2009-22526

David Small grew up in a dysfunctional family, with a radiologist father who was distant, an angry mother who expressed her anger in eloquent silences, and an older brother who played drums a lot to express his frustrations. When he was eleven, he had a lump, a growth, on the side of his neck. Nothing was done until he was fourteen. He thought he was going in for a minor surgery to remove the cyst from his neck; instead, there were two surgeries, and when he woke up, he had no voice—a vocal cord was removed. He later learned he had cancer, something his parents refused to discuss. After he finds his mother in bed with another woman and his father confesses that he exposed him to x-rays when he was very young, Small leaves home at age sixteen, with little except his dreams that his art could be his life. In one early scene, Small shows the indignities wrought upon his body by his father, including an enema. In another scene, young Small and his older brother look at their father's medical books and see a woman's breast and a man's penis; towards the end of the book, Small draws his grandmother stripping all her clothes off and dancing wildly after setting her house on fire. Other than these few images, Small's depictions of his horrible childhood and teen years are quiet and low-key.

"Emotionally raw, artistically compelling and psychologically devastating graphic memoir of childhood trauma." Kirkus

Spiegelman, Art, 1948-

★ **Co-Mix**; A Retrospective of Comics, Graphics, and Scraps. by Art Spiegelman. Farrar Straus & Giroux 2013 120 p. $39.95   **741.5**

1. Comic books, strips, etc.
ISBN 1770461140; 9781770461147

Harvey Nominee: Best Biographical, Historical, or Journalistic Presentation (2014)

This book, "a companion piece to a retrospective exhibition . . . collects some of [Art] Spiegelman's best work spanning nearly six decades along with biographical information and critical essays. The editors trace his career from com-

mercial work for Playboy to his underground, experimental work, including the Raw anthology where he first serialized 'Maus'. . . . The book also features many of Spiegelman's controversial 1990's New Yorker covers and autobiographical comics." (Publishers Weekly)

"Maus did much to 'legitimize' comics to the wider world, but this thoughtfully curated, elegantly presented volume is an even more convincing testament to the potential of the medium." Booklist

Spiegelman, Nadja

I'm supposed to protect you from all this; a memoir. Nadja Spiegelman. Penguin Group USA 2016 320 p. (hardcover) $27   **741.5**

ISBN 9781594631924; 1594631921

LC 2016010834

This memoir, by Nadja Spiegelman, is about "mothers and daughters—and mothers as daughters—traced through four generations, from Paris to New York and back again. . . . More than . . . [the author's] famous father, Maus creator Art Spiegelman, and even more than most mothers, hers—French-born New Yorker art director Françoise Mouly—exerted a force over reality that was both dazzling and daunting." (Publisher's note)

"A fascinating, gracefully written glimpse into the complexities of family life, full of secrets, hidden wounds, and survival tips." Kirkus

Steinberg, Saul

Steinberg at the New Yorker; introduction by Ian Frazier. H.N. Abrams 2005 239p il $50   **741.5**

1. Artists 2. Cartoonists 3. Illustrators 4. Cartoons and caricatures 5. New Yorker Magazine, Inc.
ISBN 0-8109-5901-1

LC 2004-19498

The author "surveys six decades of Steinberg's pieces, including all 89 New Yorker covers (in full color), cartoons, wartime sketches from overseas, evocative (but never literal-minded) illustrations for articles, and unpublished items from the artist's portfolio. The material is arranged thematically, examining such recurring motifs as cats, pedestals and rubber-stamped figures and documenting the turn to visual metaphor in Steinberg's later work. . . . Steinberg's cartoons usually made readers think before they laughed, and so will this splendid memorial to a 20th-century artistic landmark." Publ Wkly

Includes bibliographical references

Thomas, Roy

75 years of Marvel Comics; from the golden age to the silver screen. by Roy Thomas, edited by Josh Baker. Taschen America 2014 720 p. illustrations (hardcover) $200   **741.5**

1. Marvel Comics Group 2. Superhero comic books, strips, etc. -- History and criticism
ISBN 3836548453; 9783836548458

LC 2014026069

This book, by Roy Thomas and edited by Josh Baker, "presents a magnum opus of the most influential comic book publisher today, with an inside look not only at its celebrated characters, but also at the 'bullpen' of architects whose names are almost as familiar as the protagonists they brought to life. . . . This book delves into the heart of thousands of costumed characters who continue to fight the good fight in comics, movies, and toy aisles of the world." (Publisher's note)

Torres, Alissa

American widow; illustrated by Sungyoon Choi. Villard Books 2008 209p il $22   **741.5**
1. Educators 2. Graphic novels 3. Autobiographical graphic novels 4. Memoirists 5. Widows -- Graphic novels 6. September 11 terrorist attacks, 2001 -- Graphic novels
ISBN 978-0-345-50069-4

LC 2008-08396

Alissa Torres' husband Luis had just started his new job in the World Trade Center on September 10, 2001. The next day, he died in the terrorist attacks that destroyed the twin towers. Alissa was more than seven months pregnant. In this book, she recounts the personal struggles she suffered as a pregnant "terror widow," first heaped upon with sympathy, then publicly scorned. She describes the tragedies suffered by all the families who lost loved ones on September 11, 2001 and the frustrations they experienced dealing with bureaucrats as they tried to get even the smallest physical trace of their loved ones.

The author's "tragedy of errors inspires anger on her behalf, although the story is calmly and beautifully told. Choi's simple and attractive line art is set off by turquoise wash, yielding to a full-color photo at the end when Alissa embraces her life anew." Libr J

Tran, G. B. (Gia-Bao), 1976-

Vietnamerica; a family's journey. written and illustrated by GB Tran. Villard Books 2010 279 p. chiefly col. ill. $30   **741.5**
1. Artists 2. Illustrators 3. Graphic novels 4. Vietnamese Americans -- Biography 5. Cartoonists 6. Vietnamese refugees -- Graphic novels 7. Vietnamese Americans -- Graphic novels 8. Vietnam War, 1961-1975 -- Graphic novels
ISBN 0345508726; 9780345508720

LC 2011283144

"GB Tran is a young Vietnamese American artist who grew up distant from (and largely indifferent to) his family's history. Born and raised in South Carolina as a son of immigrants, he knew that his parents had fled Vietnam during the fall of Saigon. But even as they struggled to adapt to life in America, they preferred to forget the past--and to focus on their children's future. It was only in his late twenties that GB began to learn their extraordinary story. When his last surviving grandparents die within months of each other, GB visits Vietnam for the first time and begins to learn the tragic history of his family, and of the homeland they left behind." (Publisher's note)

"The comic utilizes a dizzying barrage of effects to depict the characters' confusing experience: different lettering styles, realistic action set against full-page government posters, sound effects swirling from panel to panel, action-packed panoramas breaking apart as South Vietnam collapses." Pub Wkly

Tyler, Carol

Soldier's heart; the campaign to understand my WWII veteran father - a daughter's memoir. by Carol Tyler. Fantagraphics 2015 362 p. color illustrations, color map $39.99   **741.5**
1. Father-daughter relationship 2. World War, 1939-1945 -- Biography -- Graphic novels
ISBN 160699896X; 9781606998960

Originally published as three separate volumes

"The phrase 'soldier's heart' is the predecessor to today's post-traumatic stress disorder (PTSD). This is the underlying theme in Tyler's . . . biography of her father's life in this book, originally released as the trilogy You'll Never Know, between 2009 and 2012. Tyler tells the story of her father, Charles, his upbringing as a plumber's son in Chicago before he enlists in the army during World War II; his war experience; after the war as he raises his family with his beloved wife, Red; and their lives into the present. The time line jumps between the current day, as Tyler deals with her own troubled marriage and raising her daughter, and the past (her own, her father's, and her mother's)." (Library Journal)

Watterson, Bill

The **complete** Calvin and Hobbes. Andrews McMeel Pub. 2005 3v il set $150   **741.5**
1. Comic books, strips, etc.
ISBN 0-7407-4847-5; 978-0-7407-4847-9

LC 2004-62709

This is a collection of the entire run of the comic strip Calvin and Hobbes, which ran from 1985 to 1995.

"This is one of the all-time great comic strips, absolutely essential for every library." Libr J

Wednesday comics. DC Comics 2010 200p il $49.99   **741.5**
1. Superhero graphic novels 2. Comic books, strips, etc.
ISBN 978-1-401227470; 1-401227473

LC 2010-282211

"A must-have book for DC comics fans, fans of any comic art, or even those who used to read comics but haven't done so for years. These classic characters still captivate our imaginations – as they have for decades." Christ Sci Monit

Weiner, Stephen

101 outstanding graphic novels; Stephen Weiner; [edited by] Daniel J. Fingeroth. 3rd edition NBM Pub. 2015 80 p. (hardcover) $15.99   **741.5**
1. Graphic novels
ISBN 1561639443; 9781561639441

LC 2014958652

Previously called 101 Best Graphic Novels

"The popular primer on the best graphic novels, initially called The 101 Best Graphic Novels, is back in its third updated edition. Expert librarian Stephen Weiner--with the crowdsourcing help of professionals in the field, from artists to critics to leading comic store owners--has sifted through the bewildering thousands of graphic novels now available to come up with an outstanding, not-to-be-missed 101." (Publisher's note)

741.58   Cartoon animation

Ghez, Didier

They drew as they pleased; Part 1 the hidden art of Disney's musical years: 1930s. By Didier Ghez; Foreword by John Musker. Chronicle Books 2016 207 p. illustrations (some color (hardcover) $40   **741.58**

1. Cartoonists 2. Walt Disney Productions 3. Walt Disney Productions -- History -- 20th century 4. Animated films -- United States -- History and criticism

ISBN 9781452137438; 9781452137445

LC 2015040121

Vol. 1 of 6-volume series

This book, by Didier Ghez, describes how "as the Walt Disney Studio entered its first decade and embarked on some of the most ambitious animated films of the time, Disney hired a group of 'concept artists' whose sole mission was to explore ideas and inspire their fellow animators. [This volume] . . . showcases four of these early pioneers and features artwork developed by them for the Disney shorts from the 1930s." (Publisher's note)

"This is a gem for film buffs and Disney enthusiasts looking for an absorbing title to fill out their collections." LJ

Includes bibliographical references and index

741.6   Graphic design, illustration, commercial art

Crumb, R.

R. Crumb: the complete record cover collection. W. W. Norton & Co. 2011 un il $27.95   **741.6**

1. Popular music 2. Sound recordings -- Album covers

ISBN 978-0-393-08278-4

This volume is "filled with the artist's designs for such ephemera as 'Unknown Detroit Bluesmen' or Cliff Edwards's 'I'm a Bear in a Ladies' Boudoir.' Starting in the 1970s, Mr. Crumb produced covers for reissues from labels like Yazoo, Blue Goose and Barrelhouse Records, and his love for the music is evident—a stippled Robert Johnson stares out in stark black and white, Bessie Smith sings 'Put a Little Sugar in My Bowl' and Charlie Patton gets his own mini-graphic novel. . . . (The biggest act here is Big Brother and the Holding Company, with Janis Joplin done over to fit Crumb's zaftig ideal.) In this journeyman work, however, the discipline of playing second fiddle to his favorite musicians keeps the artist's self-loathing in check without taming the ribald humor that is also a hallmark of the blues. Few Crumb projects seem like so much fun—to read about, to look at or to listen along to." Wall Street J

Hayes, Clay

Gig posters volume 1; rock show art of the 21st century. Quirk Books 2009 208p il $40   **741.6**

1. Posters 2. Rock music

ISBN 978-1-59474-326-9; 1-59474-326-6

LC 2008-938830

"There is no single style for gig posters — they are punk, grunge, new wave, neo-modern, comic, retro, parodic and satirical. Some are beautiful, others ugly; some derivative, others novel. Most are eye-catching, and some are memo-rable. Those that are wheat-pasted on hoardings or taped to lampposts are usually removed within days, so GigPosters has been a terrific archive of the good, the bad and the ugly. But digital versions just don't compare with the printed posters, which is why . . . [this book, compiled by the] founder of GigPosters, is such a useful resource. The book contains posters by leaders of the art form (including Emek, Eleanor Grosch, Lil Tuffy and Luke Drozd), who offer brief commentaries about their work." N Y Times Book Rev

Heller, Steven, 1950-

Becoming a graphic & digital designer; a guide to careers in design. Steven Heller & Veronique Vienne. 5th edition John Wiley & Sons, Inc. 2015 335 p. color illustrations pbk $44.95   **741.6**

1. Graphic arts 2. Commercial art 3. Computer graphics

ISBN 1118771982; 9781118771983

LC 2015011294

"With an emphasis on portfolio requirements and job opportunities, this guide helps both students and individuals interested in entering the design field prepare for successful careers. Coverage includes design inspiration, design genres, and design education, with discussion of the specific career options available in print, interactive, and motion design. Interviews with leading designers like Michael Bierut, Stefan Sagmeister, and Mirko Ilic give readers an insider's perspective on career trajectory and a glimpse into everyday operations and inspirations at a variety of companies and firms." (Publisher's note)

Includes bibliographical references (pages 330-331) and index.

Neuburger, Emily K.

Show me a story; 40 craft projects and activities to spark children's storytelling. by Emily K. Neuburger. Storey Pub. 2012 144 p. ill. (pbk. : alk. paper) $16.95; (hardcover) $26.95   **741.6**

1. Storytelling 2. Handicraft for children 3. Illustrators -- Interviews 4. Illustrated children's books

ISBN 1612121489; 9781603429887; 9781612121482

LC 2012004610

This book presents "40 creative projects and activities [designed to] encourage [children] to free their storytelling instincts." Activities for "[y]ounger children" include "making story stones and a storytelling jar . . . while older kids will enjoy word grab bags, story walks, and journaling exercises." The book is intended "[f]or everyone ages 5 to 12". (Publisher's note)

Includes bibliographical references and index.

The poster; 1,000 posters from Toulouse-Lautrec to Sagmeister. edited by Cees V. de Jong, Alston W. Purvis, Martijn F. Le Coultre; text by Alston W. Ourvis; intorduction by Cees W. de Jong. Abrams 2010 567p il pa $35   **741.6**

1. Posters

ISBN 978-0-8109-9588-8; 0-8109-9588-3

LC 2010-14458

"In the history of art, the poster occupies a strange no-man's-land, a middle ground at the intersection of design and commerce. However masterful they might be in terms of composition and execution, the fact remains that posters are used to sell something else—a product, an idea, a critical bit of wartime propaganda. Whether it's cookies or patriotism that is on the block, the purpose of a poster seems to rest uneasily alongside the artistic spirit that impels it. The Poster is a book that aims not to apologize for this duality, but to acknowledge it and then move on. In purely artistic terms, posters can be marvelous works of skill and imagination— powerfully designed and skillfully executed. . . . Overall, the collection succeeds admirably." PopMatters

Includes bibliographical references

Rees, Darrell

How to Be an Illustrator; by Darrel Rees. Chronicle Books LLC 2014 167 p. ill (some col) $24.95 **741.6**
1. Illustrators 2. Vocational guidance
ISBN 1780673280; 9781780673288

This book, by Darrel Rees, "offers practical help and guidance to aspiring illustrators. . . . International illustrators are interviewed, discussing how they got their break in the industry, their experiences with clients, their methods of promoting work, and more. In addition, leading art directors describe their approach to commissioning illustration, how they spot new talent, their thoughts on promotional material, and their advice to up-and-coming illustrators." (Publisher's note)

'This guide . . . shares the author's insights on everything except the artistic aspects of the occupation, i.e., business concerns such as education, job hunting, project management, billing, and promoting yourself." LJ

Includes bibliographical references

Rendgen, Sandra

Understanding the world; the atlas of infographics. Sandra Rendgen; ed. Julius Wiedemann. Taschen 2014 456 p. color ills; color maps $69.99 **741.6**
1. Atlases 2. Information visualization 3. Maps -- Design 4. Visual communication 5. Communication -- Graphic methods
ISBN 3836548836; 9783836548830
LC 2015588511

This book by Sandra Rendgen and Julius Wiedemann presents "more than 280 contemporary and vintage visualizations to help us understand our world, including seven fold-out spreads. Spanning the present state, and historical shaping, of society, culture, technology, economics and the environment, this is at once a showcase of . . . data design work, and a . . . digest of where and how we live." (Publisher's note)

Salisbury, Martin

Illustrating children's books; creating pictures for publication. Barron's Educational Series 2004 144p il pa $22.95 **741.6**
1. Illustrators 2. Illustration of books 3. Picture books for children
ISBN 0-76412-717-9

The author "surveys the genre's distinguished history with examples from Caldecott, Greenaway, N. C. Wyeth, Maxfield Parrish, and Howard Pyle. . . . Through sketches and annotations, Salisbury explains how to create fantasy,

fairy tale, realism, and nature drawing. Written for advanced students, the book covers storyboards and layouts, contracts, copyrights, and how to present one's work professionally. Highly recommended for all collections." Libr J

Includes bibliographical references

Schiller, Justin

Maurice Sendak; a celebration of the artist and his work. by Justin Schiller and illustrated by Maurice Sendak. Harry N. Abrams 2013 223 p. (alk. paper) $45 **741.6**
1. Artists -- Biography
ISBN 1419708260; 9781419708268
LC 2013007227

In this book, by Justin Schiller, "the preeminent children's book artist of the twentieth century, Maurice Sendak and his sixty-year career are celebrated in this full-color catalog of more than two hundred images being exhibited at the Society of Illustrators in New York City. [Images are] accompanied by twelve essays by such noted scholars and historians as Leonard S. Marcus, Iona Opie, Steven Heller, and Paul O. Zelinsky." (Publisher's note)

Includes bibliographical references and index

741.945   Italian drawing

Kline, Fred R.

Leonardo's holy child; the discovery of a Leonardo da Vinci masterpiece: a connoisseur's search for lost art in America: a memoir of discovery. by Fred R. Kline. Pegasus Books 2016 360 p. illustrations (some color) (hardcover) $29.95 **741.945**
1. Art -- 15th and 16th centuries 2. Art -- Expertising
ISBN 1605989797; 9781605989792
LC 2016387139

This book, by Fred R. Kline, "is about the discovery of one [art] piece in particular: About ten years ago, . . . a beautiful little drawing caught [the author's] eye. Attributed to Carracci, . . . but Kline's every instinct told him that the attribution was wrong. He . . . bought the drawing outright. And that was the beginning of how Kline discovered Leonardo da Vinci's model drawing for the Infant Jesus and the Infant St. John." (Publisher's note)

"Even the most casual museum goer will find something to appreciate in this fascinating account." booklist

742   Perspective in drawing

Brehm, Matthew

Drawing perspective; How to See It and How to Apply It. Paul Heaston. Barrons Educational Series, Inc. 2015 144 p. color illustrations $19.99 **742**
1. Drawing 2. Perspective
ISBN 9781438006598
LC 2014945484

This book, by Paul Heaston, is "a hands-on guide to perspective that's for anyone who wants to draw or paint—in any genre or medium. It's partly about learning how to draw a set of straight lines that meet at a point, but it's not filled with lots of dull, dry theory (although it does explain how it all works)." (Publisher's note)

"Dynamic layouts and simple structure make this guide fun to read and easy to comprehend." LJ

Includes bibliographical references (page 144) and index.

Norling, Ernest R.

Perspective made easy; Ernest R. Norling. Dover Publications 1999 xii, 203 p.p illustrations $10.95; (ebook) $9.95 **742**

　1. Drawing 2. Perspective 3. Drawing -- Technique
　ISBN 0486404730; 9780486404738; 9780486130002

LC 99010310

This book, by Ernest R. Norling, is "devoted entirely to clarifying the laws of perspective. . . . Beginning with clear, concise, immediately applicable discussions of the horizon, vanishing point, and the crucial relationship of eye level to perspective drawing, you'll learn how to place figures and objects in a drawing, depict interiors, create shade and shadows, and achieve all the other elements necessary for a successful perspective drawing." (Publisher's note)

743.4　Drawing human figures

Bradley, Barbara

Drawing people; how to portray the clothed figure. Barbara Bradley. North Light Books 2003 175 p. illustrations (some color) $26.99; (ebook) $33.74 **743.4**

　1. Drawing 2. Figure drawing 3. Drapery in art 4. Human figure in art 5. Drawing -- Technique
　ISBN 1581803591; 9781581803594; 9781440317798

LC 2003042043

This book, by Barbara Bradley, "provides all the information you need to render clothed human figures with energy, detail and control. Bradley begins by teaching the basics of any drawing, including proportion, perspective and value. Next, you'll learn how to overcome the special challenges posed by clothing, including fabric folds and draping effects. Bradley illustrates how they're constructed and how to draw them in different situations." (Publisher's note)

"Watson's Life Drawing Class is a rich and dynamic volume on the human form, clothed and unclothed, flabby and buff, indoors and out. Using pencil, charcoal, ink, and watercolor, Watson (Artists Sketchbook) utilizes photographs to complement lessons in balance and proportion, lighting, mood, and composition." LJ

Hart, Christopher

Human anatomy made amazingly easy. Watson-Guptill 2000 114p il pa $19.95 **743.4**

　1. Figure drawing 2. Artistic anatomy
　ISBN 0-8230-2497-0

LC 00-43514

In this work for the beginning artist "Hart simplifies the process in an accessible manual that concentrates on line and forgoes the complexity of color." Libr J

Huston, Steve

Figure drawing for artists; making every mark count. by Steve Huston. Quarto Pub Group USA 2016 192 p. $24.99 **743.4**

　1. Drawing
　ISBN 1631590650; 9781631590658

LC 2016021567

In this book, "artist Steve Huston shows beginners and pros alike the two foundational concepts behind the greatest masterpieces in art and how to use them as the basis for their own success. Embark on a drawing journey and discover how these twin pillars of support are behind everything from the Venus De Milo to Michelangelo's Sibyl to George Bellow's Stag at Sharkey's." (Publisher's note)

Loomis, Andrew, 1892-1959

Figure drawing for all it's worth; Andrew Loomis. Titan Books 2011 204 p. illustrations $39.95 **743.4**

　1. Figure drawing 2. Anatomy, Artistic 3. Figure drawing -- Technique
　ISBN 0857680986; 9780857680983

LC 2011381456

This book focuses on illustrator Andrew Loomis. "His hugely influential series of art instruction books have never been bettered, and Figure Drawing is the first in Titan's programme of facsimile editions, returning these classic titles to print for the first time in decades." (Publisher's note)

Ryder, Anthony

The **artist's** complete guide to figure drawing; a contemporary perspective on the classical tradition. Anthony Ryder. Watson-Guptill Publications 2000 160 p. illustrations $24.99; (ebook) $65 **743.4**

　1. Figure drawing 2. Figure drawing -- Technique
　ISBN 0823003035; 9780823003037; 9780770434748

LC 99022843

In this book, by Anthony Ryder, "amateur and experienced artists alike are guided toward [a] new way of seeing and drawing the figure with a three-step drawing method. . . . [It] starts with the block-in, an exercise in seeing and establishing the figure's shape. It then build to the contour, a refined line drawing that represents the figure's silhouette. The last step is tonal work on the inside of the contour, when light and shadow are shaped to create the illusion of form." (Publisher's note)

Figure drawing

Vanderpoel, John H.

The **human** figure; [by] John H. Vanderpoel. Dover Publications 1958 143 p. illustrations $7.95; (ebook) $7.95 **743.4**

　1. Figure drawing
　ISBN 0486204324; 9780486204321; 9780486133782

LC 57014883

This book, by John H. Vanderpoel, presents a "clear, detailed presentation of thousands of fundamental features of the human figure. Every element of the body . . . is carefully and concisely pointed out in the text. Even more helpful are the 430 pencil and charcoal drawings that illustrate each feature so that you are, in effect, shown what to look for by a master teacher." (Publisher's note)

743.42 Portraiture

Parks, Carrie Stuart

Secrets to drawing realistic faces; Carrie Stuart Parks. North Light Books 2002 140 p. illustrations $23.99; (ebook) $23.99   **743.42**
1. Face in art 2. Drawing -- Technique
ISBN 1581802161; 9781581802160; 9781600614958
LC 2002023509

This book, by Carrie Stuart Parks, will help you "render strikingly realistic faces and self-portraits! . . . . Proven, hands-on exercises and before-and-after examples from Parks' students ensure instant success! It's all the guidance and inspiration you need to draw realistic faces with precision, confidence and style!" (Publisher's note)

"Her useful and far-ranging discussion of materials includes an evaluation of pencils' graphite grades, kneaded and electric erasers, blending tools, and papers." Booklist

743.49 Anatomy for artists

Winslow, Valerie L.

Classic human anatomy; the artist's guide to form, function, and movement. Valerie L. Winslow. Watson-Guptill Publications 2009 303 p. illustrations (some color) (hbk.) $40   **743.49**
1. Human anatomy 2. Anatomy, Artistic 3. Figure drawing -- Technique
ISBN 0823024156; 9780823024155
LC 2009280099

This book, by Valerie L. Winslow, "provides simple, insightful approaches to the complex subject of human anatomy, using drawings, diagrams, and reader-friendly text. Three major sections–the skeletal form, the muscular form and action of the muscles, and movement–break the material down into easy-to-understand pieces." (Publisher's note)

"A significant contribution to the literature of art reference." LJ

Includes glossary, bibliographical references (p. 295-296) and index

743.6 Drawing animals

Hand, Diana

Draw Horses in 15 Minutes; Capture the beauty of the equine form. by Diana Hand. Octopus Pub Group 2016 112 p. illustrations $12.99   **743.6**
1. Drawing 2. Animal painting and illustration
ISBN 1781572496; 9781781572498

This book by Diana Hand "shows you how to express your love of horses through drawing. In a series of tutorials, [Hand] describes every stage from finding your model and learning the basic skills of drawing to portraying the movement and spirit of the individual horse. [The book] will inspire you to make your own expressive drawings based on the principles of equine anatomy. Furthermore, you will discover a skill you never thought you had." (Publisher's note)

"Artist Hand provides short horse drawing sessions that can function as confidence builders for wobbly beginners and offer an achievable time investment for anyone." LJ

745 Decorative arts

Akiyama, Lance

Rubber band engineer; build slingshot powered rockets, rubber band rifles, unconventional catapults, and more guerrilla gadgets from household hardware. Lance Akiyama. Quarto Pub Group USA 2016 144 p. color illustrations (paperback) $22.99   **745**
1. Handicraft 2. Rubber bands
ISBN 9781631591044; 1631591045

In this book, by Lance Akiyama, "discover unexpected ways to turn common materials into crafty contraptions that range from surprisingly simple to curiously complex. In vivid color photos, you'll be guided to create slingshot rockets, unique catapults, and even hydraulic-powered machines. Whether you build one or all 19 of these designs, you'll feel like an ingenious engineer when you're through." (Publisher's note)

"Wonderfully illustrated, with clear and straightforward instructions, these projects provide great, mischievous fun that's very much in the vein of William Gurstelle's Defending Your Castle." LJ

American Folk Art Museum

Encyclopedia of American folk art; Gerard C. Wertkin, editor; Lee Kogan, associate editor; in association with the American Folk Art Museum. Routledge 2004 xxxiii, 612p il $125   **745**
1. American folk art
ISBN 0-415-92986-5
LC 2003-18051

This volume "covers more than three centuries of folk artists and provides information about museum collections, institutions that collect and sponsor folk art, and subjects related to the various forms of folk art. Entries tend to be detailed, and in some cases, extensive. . . . The work is heavily and usefully cross-referenced. Most entries end with brief bibliographies. Although not heavily illustrated, the work offers a number of interesting color and black-and-white illustrations keyed to specific entries." Choice

Includes bibliographical references

Frisoni, Christine-Lea

The Big Book of a Miniature House; Create and Decorate a House Room by Room. by Christine-Lea Frisoni. GMC Publications 2015 192 p. $35   **745**
1. Doll furniture 2. Interior design 3. Miniature objects
ISBN 1861089546; 9781861089540

In this book, author Christine-Lea Frisoni "explains how to make a beautiful miniature French country house. . . . Having made the dolls' house, Christine explains how to build up the wall panels to provide deep recesses, fancy panelling and wall niches to add character - ideas that can be translated to any existing dolls' house. Instructions to make a range of French-style furniture, fittings and even flowers are included." (Publisher's note)

745.1 Antiques

Miller, Judith

Miller's antiques handbook & price guide; [edited by] Judith Miller. Octopus Books various pagings il   **745.1**

1. Antiques

Annual. First published 1979. Variant title: Miller's international antiques price guide

This guide includes photographs, prices and brief descriptions of museum-quality antiques sold at auction or by dealers during the past year.

"Although this is a best-of resource, not covering attic knickknacks, it is an alluring look book with inherent educational value." Libr J

745.2 Industrial art and design

Norman, Don

The **design** of everyday things; Don Norman. Basic Books 2013 xviii, 347 p.p illustrations (pbk.) $17.99   **745.2**

1. Human engineering   2. Industrial design -- Psychological aspects

ISBN 0465050654; 9780465050659

LC 2013024417

"The Design of Everyday Things shows that good, usable design is possible. The rules are simple: make things visible, exploit natural relationships that couple function and control, and make intelligent use of constraints." Author "Don Norman hails excellence of design as the most important key to regaining the competitive edge in influencing consumer behavior." (Publisher's note)

"The revised edition updates examples; the original work preceded the Web and mobile devices. It also expands and refines the treatment of psychology, analyzing how affordances are signified to people, how emotion impacts everything people do and experience, and how culture can modulate what is 'natural' in design. Most notably, the revised edition articulates a broader view of design's goals and constraints." Choice

Includes bibliographical references (pages 321-330) and index

745.4 Pure and applied design and decoration

Albrecht, Donald

The **Work** of Charles and Ray Eames; a legacy of invention. essays by Donald Albrecht . . . {et al.} Abrams 1997 205p il hardcover o.p. pa $24.95   **745.4**

1. Design 2. Architects 3. Exhibit designers 4. Interior designers 5. Furniture designers 6. Industrial designers 7. Motion picture producers

ISBN 0-8109-1799-8; 978-0-8109-9232-0 pa; 0-8109-9232-9 pa

LC 97-4086

This overview of the work of two prominent American postwar designers features "pictures of famous furniture,

toys, exhibitions, promotional material, informal snapshots, stills from films, comics, advertisements, exhibitions for the federal government, and much more. The work features six major essays, each with extensive notes, by scholars, designers, academics, and architecture/design writers." Choice

Includes bibliographical references

Miller, Judith, 1951-

Miller's arts & crafts; living with the arts & crafts style. by Judith Miller. Octopus Pub Group 2014 239 p. color illustrations $39.99   **745.4**

1. Arts and crafts movement

ISBN 1845339436; 9781845339432

This book on the arts & crafts movement, by Judith Miller, "covers furniture, ceramics, silver and metalware, glass, textiles, jewellery, books and posters, and includes fascinating profiles of key designers such as William Morris, the Stickleys, Liberty & Co, Tiffany Studios, George Ohr, Rookwood and many more. It comes with a pictorial design directory, price ranges and a wealth of essential information for collectors." (Publisher's note)

"Noteworthy for its breadth and its superb color images, this is an up-to-date resource for any art collection." LJ

745.5 Handicrafts

Chapin, Kari

★ The **handmade** marketplace; how to sell your crafts locally, globally, and online. Kari Chapin. 2nd edition Storey Publishing 2014 247 p. pbk $15.95   **745.5**

1. Handicraft 2. Internet marketing

ISBN 161212335X; 9781612123356

LC 2014004540

Chapin "provides advice on starting from the ground up, covering everything from choosing a catchy name to developing a logo and marketing strategies. There's a strong focus on using social media and blogs to promote one's business--a must in today's connected world--and Chapin gives thoughtful guidance on how to do so without overwhelming followers with your message. Online sales aren't everything, so there's also facts about selling at craft fairs and through brick-and-mortar stores." (Library Journal)

Includes bibliographical references and index

Corwin, Lena

Printing by hand; a modern guide to printing with handmade stamps, stencils, and silk screens. by Lena Corwin; photography by Thayer Allyson Gowdy. Stewart, Tabori & Chang 2008 144 p. (alk. paper) $29.95   **745.5**

1. Handicraft 2. Stencil work 3. Silk screen printing 4. Rubber stamp printing 5. Screen process printing

ISBN 1584796723; 9781584796725

LC 2007044503

In this book, author Lena Corwin "teaches crafters everything they need to know to master stamping, stenciling, and screen printing, from making their own printing devices to trouble-shooting when plans go awry. Her . . . collection of projects ranges from stamped stationery and simple-to-sew pouches, to stenciled tote bags and furniture, to screen-printed bed linens and upholstery fabric." (Publisher's note)

Joyce, Anna

Stamp stencil paint; making extraordinary patterned projects by hand. Anna Joyce. STC Craft 2015 144 p. illustrations (some color) $27.50 **745.5**
1. Stencil work 2. Patternmaking
ISBN 9781617691775; 1617691771

LC 2014959128

In this book, author Anna Joyce "shares her signature hand-printing techniques and infectious enthusiasm for adding patterns to ready-made surfaces such as fabric, ceramics, paper, leather, furniture, walls, and more. Following beautiful step-by-step photography, crafters learn new, easy skills to stamp, stencil, and hand-paint wonderful projects for their homes, wardrobes, families, and friends." (Publisher's note)

"Crucially, sound advice about matching particular types of pigments and paints to specific surfaces is liberally dispensed." LJ

Martha Stewart living

Martha Stewart's encyclopedia of crafts; an A-to-Z guide with detailed instructions and endless inspiration. [by the editors of Martha Stewart living] Potter Craft 2009 416p il $35 **745.5**
1. Handicraft
ISBN 978-0-307-45057-9

LC 2008-33415

"In alphabetical order, from albums to wreaths, with intermediate stops at beading, jewelry making, mosaics, quilling, soap making, and more, Stewart presents easily absorbed directions for 200 projects; in each project profile, sumptuous illustrations are partnered with rich, full, stimulating discussion of materials, techniques, and tips. . . . Of primary importance to all crafts collections." Booklist

Pester, Sophie

Supercraft; easy projects for every weekend. Sophie Pester, Catharina Bruns. DK Publishing 2016 175 p. illustrations (chiefly color) $14.95 **745.5**
1. Handicraft
ISBN 1465449205; 9781465449207

LC 2016287005

"Supercraft is packed with DIY craft and sewing projects that use everyday materials and innovative techniques so you can upcycle your way to creating something new and stylish. Embroider a notebook, print fabric with starfruit, make a hanging garden for your bathroom, and much, much more. Each of the 52 projects in this book include everything you need to know, with step-by-step photographs and detailed instructions, and are simple enough to finish in a weekend." (Publisher's note)

"The aesthetic is fresh and contemporary, with lots of bright colors and modern art-inspired style. Numerous techniques are covered, including paper craft, painting, crochet, embroidery, weaving, origami, and sewing, making this a veritable buffet of ideas." LJ

Pigza, Jessica

Bibliocraft; the modern crafter's guide to finding inspiration at the library. Jessica Pigza. STC Craft/A

Melanie Falick Book 2014 208 p. illustrations (chiefly colour) $27.50 **745.5**
1. Handicraft 2. Library resources
ISBN 1617690961; 9781617690969

LC 2013945655

In this book, author Jessica Pigza "hones her literary hunting-and-gathering skills to help creatives of all types, from DIY hobbyists to fine artists, develop projects based on library resources. In Part I, she explains how to take advantage of the riches libraries have to offer—both in person and online. In Part II, she presents 20+ projects inspired by library resources." (Publisher's note)

"Though bibliophiles and fans of libraries will be drawn in by the theme of the book, crafters who haven't visited a library since childhood will be thrilled with the wealth of talented artists whose projects are featured. (Bibliophiles will also be pleased that no books are harmed in the making of these crafts.)" LJ

Samuell, Kristine

A **year** of gingerbread houses; making & decorating gingerbread houses for all seasons. by Kristine Samuell. Sterling Pub Co Inc 2015 135 p. illustrations (some color) $19.95 **745.5**
1. Gingerbread
ISBN 1454708913; 9781454708919

In this book, by Kristine Samuell, "[n]othing's more enticing for any holiday or special occasion than an awesome, lusciously decorated gingerbread house. With designs for Christmas, Halloween, Valentine's Day, and birthdays, these exquisite projects include a cottage, chalet, and two-story house. Options as customized windows, doors, chimneys, paths, trees, topiaries, and even lighting add to the charm." (Publisher's note)

"One of the best gingerbread books available, Samuell's debut is essential for serious gingerbread architects and decorators." LJ

Van't Hul, Jean

The **artful** parent; simple ways to fill your family's life with art and creativity. Jean Van't Hul. Roost Books 2013 xxi, 320 p.p color illustrations (pbk. : alk. paper) $21.95 **745.5**
1. Handicraft for children 2. Parent-child relationship 3. Child artists 4. Parent and child 5. Creative activities and seat work
ISBN 1590309642; 9781590309643

LC 2012021168

This book, by Jean Van't Hul, offers "more than 60 kids' art activities from the creator of www.ArtfulParent.com. Art making is a wonderfully fun way for young children to tap into their imagination, deepen their creativity, and explore new materials, all while strengthening their fine motor skills and developing self-confidence. . . . [This book gives] all the tools and information you need to encourage your children's creativity through art." (Publisher's note)

"Parents, teachers, and child-care providers will all find useful ideas and inspiration here." LJ

745.54   Papers

Farrell, Patrick

Paper to petal; 75 whimsical paper flower ideas to craft by hand. Rebecca Thuss and Patrick Farrell; Foreward by Martha Stewart. Potter Craft 2013 256 p. color illustrations (print edition) $24.99   **745.54**

1. Paper flowers

ISBN 0385345054; 9780385345057

LC 2012048675

This book on paper flowers, by Rebecca Thuss and Patrick Farrell, "walks you through the easy basics of transforming simple materials into a vibrant display of fanciful handmade blooms suitable for every occasion. . . . Customize every petal, leaf or stem to go dramatic or delicate; mimic nature or fashion your blossoms in any color you can imagine to make something uniquely personal. You'll be amazed how easy it is to produce these gorgeous flower projects." (Publisher's note)

Helfand, Jessica

Scrapbooks: an American history; A Winterhouse edition; Yale University Press 2008 244p il $45   **745.54**

1. Scrapbooks 2. Paper crafts

ISBN 978-0-300-12635-8; 0-300-12635-2

The author "offers both an overview of the history of the creation of scrapbooks and a visual feast for readers via the integration of texts, images, and memorabilia of all types. . . . Helfand has made a brilliant selection of unusual examples by visiting numerous archives, and she weaves a narrative based on examples that she found. . . .The book is sumptuous, a superb marriage in fine design, paper, and print." Choice

Rodabaugh, Katrina

The **paper** playhouse; awesome art projects for kids : using paper, boxes, and books. by Katrina Rodabaugh, photographs by Leslie Sopia Lindell. Quayside Pub Group 2015 144 p. color illustrations $22.99   **745.54**

1. Handicraft 2. Paper crafts

ISBN 1592539807; 9781592539802

In this book, artist Katrina Rodabaugh, with photographs by Leslie Sopia Lindell, "with simple techniques including sculpture, printmaking, bookbinding, collage, and even ideas for public art, families work through step-by-step instructions while using imagination and budding aesthetics." (Publisher's note)

"Craft projects using recycled or upcycled materials are perennially popular, and the kid-friendly angle adds a fun dimension." LJ

745.572   Plastics

Heaser, Sue

The **polymer** clay techniques book; by Sue Heaser. North Light Books 1999 128 p. color illustrations $22.99   **745.572**

1. Modeling

ISBN 1581800088; 9781581800081

With this book, by Sue Heaser, "readers can create polymer clay buttons or boxes or anything in between. Starting with the very basics (such as rolling, baking and gluing), it then moves on to more advanced methods: marbling, texturing, millefiori, bead-making, faux-stone effects and more. Feature spreads show exciting ways to combine techniques." (Publisher's note)

"The Polymer Clay Technique Book, in particular, has detailed step-by-step instructions for many techniques such as marbling, cutting, and making millefiori canes." LJ

Includes bibliographical references (p. 126) and index.

745.59   Making specific objects

Michaels, Chris Franchetti

Teach yourself visually jewelry making & beading. Wiley Publishing 2007 290p il (Visual read less, learn more) pa $24.99   **745.59**

1. Beads 2. Jewelry 3. Beadwork

ISBN 978-0-470-10150-6; 0-470-10150-4

This book explains how "to craft designs that are chic but inexpensive. With hundreds of detailed photos, this book covers tools and supplies, bead stringing and weaving, wire wrapping, and more." Publisher's note

Oppenheimer, Betty

Candlemaker's companion; a complete guide to rolling, pouring, dipping, and decorating your own candles. Completely rev and updated; Storey Bks. 2001 199p il pa $18.95   **745.59**

1. Candles

ISBN 1-58017-366-7

LC 00-53802

First published 1997

This offers a brief history of candles followed by information about wicks, waxes and additives, color and scent, and equipment. Step-by-step instructions on candlemaking techniques and decoration, and a list of suppliers

Includes bibliographical references

745.592   Toys, models, miniatures, related objects

Davis, Todd

Handy dad; 25 awesome projects for dads and kids. by Todd Davis; photographs by Juli Stewart and Todd Davis; illustrations by Nik Schulz. Chronicle Books 2010 167 p. col. ill., plans (pbk.) $24.95   **745.592**

1. Handicraft 2. Toy making 3. Father-child relationship

4. Family recreation 5. Handicraft -- Design
ISBN 081186958X; 9780811869584

LC 2009026020

This book, by extreme sports athlete Todd Davis, "presents 25 awesome projects for dads to build with their kids. Busy dads can choose projects that range from simple to challenging and take anywhere from five minutes to a full weekend. Readers are given all the directions they need to grab materials that can be found around the house or at the local hardware store and get to work." (Publisher's note)

Finnanger, Tone, 1973-
Tilda's toy box; Sewing Patterns for Soft Toys and More from the Magical World of Tilda. by Tone Finnanger. F & W Media Inc. 2015 135 p. color illustrations $24.99 **745.592**
  1. Soft toy making
  ISBN 1446306151; 9781446306154

This book, by Tone Finnanger, "will show you how to make a wide range of beautiful soft toys and gifts for kids, plus amazing accessories for their bedrooms. Discover simple sewing patterns for adorably plump dolls with a range of outfits and accessories, cute jungle creatures like monkeys, and sea-themed creations - pirates, whales and fish--all reproduced at full-size to trace from the page." (Publisher's note)

745.594 Decorative objects

Bluhm, Lisa
Creative soldered jewelry & accessories; Lisa Bluhm. Lark Crafts 2014 128 p. color illustrations $21.95 **745.594**
  1. Jewelry 2. Soldering 3. Handicraft 4. Jewelry making 5. Solder and soldering
  ISBN 1454708166; 9781454708162

LC 2013044513

This book, Lisa Bluhm, presents "more than 20 trendy new projects and the hottest techniques [of soldered jewelry]. Thanks to a robust basics section crafters will easily master the fundamentals of using either a soldering torch or iron, and make such gorgeous items as fashionable earrings, playful tiaras, unique frames, and pretty boudoir bottles." (Publisher's note)

"This is a practical introduction and overview of both hard and soft soldering for hobbyists. Creating fun pieces as part of the learning process is an added bonus." LJ

Creative soldered jewelry and accessories

Brown, Carrie
The **new** Christmas tree; 25 dazzling trees and over 100 handcrafted projects for an inspired holiday. Carrie Brown; photographs by Paige Green. Artisan 2015 296 p. color illustrations (alk. paper) $29.95 **745.594**
  1. Handicraft 2. Christmas trees 3. Christmas tree ornaments
  ISBN 9781579655914

LC 2015010993

This book, by Carrie Brown with photographs by Paige Green, presents "one-of-a-kind trees that celebrate food, nature, fashion, folk art, typography, color, and art history. Each spectacular design is easily replicated, with step-by-step instructions for crafting coordinating ornaments, garlands, and toppers, plus advice on selecting the right tree, choosing lights, and more." (Publisher's note)

"There's no shortage of clever ideas, especially for those who'd like to produce ornaments without much fuss. Brown is at her best in suggesting simple crafts that will make an impressive statement." Pub Wkly

Includes bibliographical references and index

Brown, Stephen
Glitterville's handmade christmas; Stephen Brown. Andrews McMeel Publishing 2012 181 p. color illustrations $24.99 **745.594**
  1. Christmas 2. Handicraft
  ISBN 1449414559; 9781449414559

LC 2011944595

Author Stephen Brown presents "twenty new whimsical, winter-wonderful craft projects that will fill your home with sleighfuls of cheer. Hundreds of beautiful, easy-to-follow, step-by-step full-color photos and how-tos make the crafting fun and the results foolproof. From a Jolly Dolly Holly Wreath or a charming Glittery Village you can nestle into its own Sparkle Forest, to the frostiest Magic Snow and the jolliest pine-cone-bodied Glitter Gnome." (Publisher's note)

Glitterville's handmade Halloween; a glittered guide for whimsical crafting! Stephen Brown. Andrews McMeel Publishing 2012 xxiv, 178 p,p color illustrations (pbk.) $19.99 **745.594**
  1. Halloween 2. Handicraft 3. Halloween decorations
  ISBN 1449414524; 9781449414528

LC 2011944594

This book by Stephen Brown is "full of bright, colorful photos, step-by-step holiday how-tos, and over-the-harvest-moon decorating ideas to make your home sparkle and shine this spooktacular season. [Its designed to] delight readers as they make their way through the playfully photographed pages of the book, which include full, never-before-published instructions for making some of Glitterville's most sought-after items." (Publisher's note)

Handmade Halloween

Cetti, Livia
The **exquisite** book of paper flowers; a guide to making unbelievably realistic paper blooms. Livia Cetti. STC Craft/A Melanie Falick Book 2014 192 p. colour illustrations $24.95 **745.594**
  1. Origami 2. Artificial flowers
  ISBN 1617691003; 9781617691003

LC 2013945659

This book, by Livia Cetti, offers a "comprehensive how-to manual showcasing . . . techniques for creating 27 popular [tissue paper] blooms, including peonies, poppies, roses, and hibiscus. Clear instructions and . . . step-by-step photographs show crafters of all levels how to make individual flowers as well as how to combine blooms to form 20 exquisite garlands, centerpieces, wreaths, corsages, and boutonnieres." (Publisher's note)

Combs, Rebecca Ann

Kumihimo: basics & beyond; 24 braided and beaded jewelry projects on the kumihimo disk. by Rebecca Combs. Kalmbach Books 2013 95 p. $21.99   **745.594**
    1. Jewelry 2. Handicraft
    ISBN 1627000437; 9781627000437

This book, by Rebecca Combs, "presents techniques for creating all-cord braids and beaded braids, then teaches beaders how to transform them into finished jewelry. Short demonstrations of the key techniques needed for each project are presented in easy-to-grasp portions, allowing beaders to learn and practice as they go." (Publisher's note)

Crowther, Janet

Make a statement; Katie Covington and Janet Crowther. Chronicle Books 2014 143 p. color illustrations (alk. paper) $22.95   **745.594**
    1. Jewelry making 2. Fashion 3. Costume jewelry
    ISBN 1452133204; 9781452133201
                                                    LC 2014004103

In this book on "statement jewelry . . . jewelry designers Janet Crowther and Katie Covington share their trade secrets for using basic techniques and easy-to-source materials to make stylish jewelry and accessories, from a gold bib necklace and geometric hoop earrings to a classic charm bracelet and elegant shoe clips." (Publisher's note)

Includes bibliographical references and index

Deeb, Margie

The **beader's** color palette; 20 creative projects, 220 inspired combinations for beaded and gemstone jewelry. Watson-Guptill 2008 192p il pa $24.95   **745.594**
    1. Color 2. Jewelry 3. Beadwork
    ISBN 978-0-8230-0474-4; 0-8230-0474-0
                                                    LC 2007-936519

The author "provides meticulously worked-out color palettes to capture the essence of period artworks or natural objects. Each palette indicates the proportion of dominant and secondary hues so that the finished piece will reflect the colors of the original period artwork or natural object." Libr J

Includes bibliographical references

Geary, Theresa Flores

The **illustrated** bead bible; terms, tips & techniques. photographs by Debra Whalen. Sterling Pub. 2008 406p il $29.95   **745.594**
    1. Beads 2. Beadwork
    ISBN 978-1-4027-2353-7; 1-4027-2353-9
                                                    LC 2007-026120

"This may be the ultimate bead reference book. The majority of the text is made up of an illustrated alphabetical encyclopedia of beads, broadly defined, and beading terms. Additional chapters include tips and techniques, charts illustrating bead characteristics, and stitch diagrams." Libr J

Includes glossary and bibliographical references

Gedeon, Jade

Beautiful bracelets by hand; seventy-five one-of-a-kind baubles, bangles and other wrist adornments you can make at home. Jade Gedeon. Page Street Pub. Co. 2014 224 p. color illustrations (pbk.) $21.99   **745.594**
    1. Bracelets 2. Handicraft
    ISBN 1624140904; 1624140920; 9781624140907; 9781624140921
                                                    LC 2014939128

In this book on bracelets, author Jade Gedeon "offers seventy-five of her favorite designs, and gives readers all the secrets for making talk-of-the-town adornments. With so many different materials and methods to choose from, you'll have multiple artistic, unique and vintage-looking bracelets to add to your collection. . . . Materials include beads, chain, cord, fabric, leather, metal, plastic and wood so you can convey a multitude of looks and feels." (Publisher's note)

"The majority of the bracelets in this book are so simple and easy to make that absolute beginners can duplicate them successfully. Much of the writing reads like corny catalog copy, but there's enough Gedeon to make this a worthwhile purchase, especially where beginners' jewelry-making titles are popular." LJ

Kan, Lisa

Bead metamorphosis; exquisite jewelry from custom components. Lisa Kan. Interweave A division of F+W Media, Inc. 2014 159 p. (pbk.) $25.99   **745.594**
    1. Beadwork 2. Jewelry making
    ISBN 1596688254; 9781596688254
                                                    LC 2014028517

This book, by Lisa Kan, presents "[b]eautiful bead-woven jewelry that is convertible, reversible, or interchangeable. . . . Create beautiful bead-woven earrings, necklaces, bracelets, and brooches-all of which transform by disassembling, reassembling, reversing, or interchanging separate beadwork components." (Publisher's note)

Karon, Karen

Advanced chain maille jewelry workshop; weaving with rings and scales. Karen Karon. Interweave 2014 159 p. $26.99   **745.594**
    1. Metalwork 2. Jewelry making 3. Metal-work 4. Chains (Jewelry)
    ISBN 1620336596; 9781620336595
                                                    LC 2014011104

This book, by Karen Karon, "begins by reviewing basic chain maille weaves. . . . [It] is then divided into 4 sections, each devoted to a particular type of weave: new Persian weaves, Elf-based weaves, Hybrid weaves, and Scale Maille weaves that incorporate sheet metal scales into traditional weaves for a striking effect. Sprinkled throughout the illustrated step-by-step instructions for each weave technique are valuable tips from Karen." (Publisher's note)

"For experienced jewelry makers, since basic chain maille techniques such as opening and closing jump rings properly are not covered. Those looking to go beyond the techniques addressed in most related books will find a wealth of information within these pages." LJ

Katz, Amy

Seed bead chic; 25 elegant projects inspired by fine jewelry. Amy Katz. Lark Jewelry & Beading 2014 128 p. illustrations (Lark jewelry & beading bead inspirations) (paperback) $24.95 **745.594**
1. Jewelry 2. Beadwork 3. Jewelry making 4. Beadwork -- Patterns
ISBN 1454708174; 9781454708179
LC 2013047476

This book by Amy Katz, "featuring a variety of stitches--including the author's newly created right-angle ladder stitch--these stunning pieces cover everything from earrings to brooches. Photographs, diagrams, and helpful tips make the beading process simple and pleasurable!" (Publisher's note)

"Katz's projects are sophisticated in both style and technique. Jewelry makers looking for a challenge will find one here." LJ

Papp, Csilla

Sensational soutache jewelry making; Braided Jewelry Techniques for 15 Statement Pieces. by Csilla Papp. F & W Media Inc 2016 128 p. color illustrations $24.99 **745.594**
1. Jewelry making
ISBN 1440243743; 9781440243745
LC 2016302298

In this book, by Csilla Papp, "you'll learn the basic techniques of soutache embroidery, and then get creative with 15 easy-to-follow projects for bracelets, earrings, brooches, rings and necklaces. . . . Color and stone choice combine with elaborate braids to make these pieces distinctly yours." (Publisher's note)

"Jewelrymakers interested in experimenting with soutache, as well as fans of statement jewelry, will be drawn to Papp's intricate designs." LJ

Sheldon, Kathy

Felt-o-ween; 40 scary-cute projects to celebrate Halloween. Kathy Sheldon. Lark Crafts 2014 132 p. illustrations (chiefly color) (alk. paper) $14.95 **745.594**
1. Halloween 2. Handicraft 3. Felt craft 4. Halloween decorations
ISBN 1454708514; 9781454708513
LC 2013039868

This book by Kathy Sheldon and Amanda Carestio "brings you 40 BOO-tiful decorations and costumes for a festive Halloween. Requiring little or no stitching, these felted projects are 100% beginner-friendly, including pumpkin candy bags, a huggable vampire stuffy, a creepy crawly wreath, and plenty of ears, headbands, and other wearables for revelers young and old." (Publisher's note)

Includes bibliographical references and index

Van't Hul, Jean

The **artful** year; celebrating the seasons & holidays with family arts and crafts. Jean Van't Hul. Roost 2015 351 p. color illustrations (alk. paper) $24.95 **745.594**
1. Family 2. Cooking 3. Arts and crafts movement 4.

Handicraft 5. Seasonal cooking 6. Family recreation 7. Holiday decorations
ISBN 1611801494; 9781611801491
LC 2013048889

Author Jean Van't Hul presents "art activites, crafts, recipes, and more to help make each season special. By doing so, your family will create memories and mementos, you'll develop creative growth in your children and yourself, and you'll have lots of fun! The book includes: Arts and crafts, using the materials, colors, and themes of the season . . . Decorations to make as a family [and] . . . Favorite seasonal recipes that are fun for children to help make." (Publisher's note)

Includes bibliographical references and index

Watanabe, Judi

The **Complete** Photo Guide to Cardmaking; More than 800 Large Color Photos. by Judi Watanabe. Quarto Pub Group USA 2016 256 p. color illustrations $24.99 **745.594**
1. Handicraft 2. Greeting cards
ISBN 1589238826; 9781589238824

This book, by Judi Watanabe, "is the ultimate resource on card making. All paper-crafting techniques that can be employed for card making are thoroughly covered, including a comprehensive description of paper types available, folding options and techniques, coloring and image transfer methods, and adding embellishments. Inside, you'll also find methods for using a computer to design and print cards." (Publisher's note)

"Although this is a cardmaking book, scrapbookers, art journalers, and mixed-media artists will also appreciate the image-based tutorials and the abundance of inspiring photos." LJ

Wiseman, Jillian

Jill Wiseman's beautiful beaded ropes; 24 wearable jewelry projects in multiple stitches. Jill Wiseman. Lark Crafts 2012 119 p. color illustrations (hardback) $27.95 **745.594**
1. Beads 2. Jewelry 3. Jewelry making 4. Beadwork -- Patterns
ISBN 1454703563; 9781454703563
LC 2012002269

Author Jill Wiseman "presents 24 beaded rope designs in this . . . entry in Lark Jewelry & Beading's popular Beadweaving Master Class series. From dainty to heavy, and from simple to outrageously textured, these . . . wearable necklace, lariat, bangle, and bracelet projects (plus a few earrings!) utilize such popular stitch techniques." (Publisher's note)

"Wiseman's designs have a lot of appeal and are easily customizable to suit individual tastes, and the variety of stitches used in the projects will pique beaders' interest." LJ

745.6 Calligraphy, heraldic design, illumination

Doh, Jenny

Creative lettering; techniques & tips from top artists. Jenny Doh. Lark Crafts 2013 144 p. color illustrations $19.95 **745.6**

1. Lettering 2. Lettering -- Technique
ISBN 1454704004; 9781454704003

LC 2012021130

In this book, edited by Jenny Doh, "[s]ixteen accomplished contributors-- including calligraphers, painters, collagists, card makers, fiber artists, and graphic designers-- give their personal perspectives on lettering. They all offer their favorite tools, how they use them, their signature technique with step-by-step instructions and photos, and an alphabet sampler of their own font." (Publisher's note)

"Artists of all skill levels can enjoy this title." LJ

More creative lettering; techniques & tips from top artists. Jenny Doh. Sterling Pub Co Inc 2015 144 p. color illustrations (paperback) $19.95 **745.6**

1. Lettering 2. Decoration and ornament
ISBN 1454708921; 9781454708926

This book, by Jenny Doh, "has gathered a variety of big names and talented up-and-coming artists, who all provide tips on their favorite forms on hand lettering and tools, along with complete alphabets and how-to projects based on their signature styles. With everything from posters and cards to signs, collages, and journals, this . . . collection will inspire readers as they create their own, personalized work." (Publisher's note)

"With lots of practical and creative applications, this book can be appreciated by a wide range of audiences." LJ

Godfrey-Nicholls, Gaye

Mastering calligraphy; the complete guide to hand lettering. by Gaye Godfrey-Nicholls. Chronicle Books 2013 288 p. color illustrations $40 **745.6**

1. Calligraphy
ISBN 1452101124; 9781452101125

This book, by Gaye Godfrey-Nicholls, offers a "comprehensive and up-to-date volume on this traditional craft [of caligraphy] and its contemporary practice. . . . Inside are step-by-step instructions accompanied by examples of current work, plus historical information, artist profiles, troubleshooting tips, and an extensive resource section." (Publisher's note)

"Godfrey-Nicholls, an Australia-based artist, elucidates the art of hand-lettering in this comprehensive work. The majority of the book is devoted to calligraphic hands, or different styles of writing. Each hand includes a brief history, exercises for practicing the basic shapes and strokes, foundational groups of letters arranged by type, and variations on the alphabet. Appropriate supplies are suggested for each hand." LJ

Includes bibliographical references (pages 278-281) and index

Shepherd, Margaret

Learn calligraphy; the complete book of lettering and design. Broadway Bks. 2001 167p il pa $16.95 **745.6**

1. Calligraphy
ISBN 0-7679-0732-9

LC 00-53016

This guide presents historical background, and advice on materials, technique, and workspace organization. Also included are recommended usages for the various alphabets. Step-by-step illustrations are provided

Thorpe, Molly Suber

Modern calligraphy; everything you need to know to get started in script calligraphy. Molly Suber Thorpe; photography by Molly Suber Thorpe. St. Martin's Griffin 2013 vi, 184 p.p illustrations (chiefly color) (softcover) $24.99 **745.6**

1. Calligraphy 2. Writing -- Materials and instruments
ISBN 1250016320; 9781250016324

LC 2013013847

This book, by Molly Suber Thorpe, "breaks the calligraphy process down into simple steps so anyone can learn to create their own stunning wedding invitations, thank you cards, gift tags, and more. Starting with an overview of the supplies—from paper to ink to pens—you will learn how to form letters, words, and then phrases by following Molly's clear step-by-step instructions, and by practicing with the provided templates." (Publisher's note)

745.92 Floral arts

Chezar, Ariella

★ The **flower** workshop; lessons in arranging blooms, branches, fruits, and foraged materials. by Ariella Chezar, with Julie Michaels. Ten Speed Press 2016 256 p. color illustrations (hardcover : alk. paper) $25 **745.92**

1. Flower arrangement
ISBN 9781607747659

LC 2015027664

This book, by floral designer Ariella Chezar, "provides step-by-step instructions for more than forty-five stunning floral projects from simple to spectacular, but also equips you with the skills to customize arrangements at home. . . . Chezar walks you through the nuts and bolts of creating a variety of small flourishes, tonal arrangements, branch arrangements, handheld bouquets, wreathes, garlands, grand gestures, and more—all accompanied by detailed photography." (Publisher's note)

"Infused with overwhelming appreciation for nature and including quotes from others and Chezar's own poetic phrases, the book offers beauty and inspiration to flower arrangers at most levels of skill." Booklist

Includes bibliographical references and index

Cylinder, Carly

The **flower** chef; A Modern Guide to Do-It-Yourself Floral Arrangements. Carly Cylinder; edited by Amara Holstein. Grand Central Life & Style 2016 223 p. color illustrations (hardcover) $28 **745.92**

1. Flower arrangement

ISBN 1455555495; 9781455555499

LC 2015039431

This book, by Carly Cylinder, "is a modern, comprehensive guide to floral design that caters to all readers--from beginners who have never worked with flowers before, . . . to decorators, party planners and photographers looking to liven up their spaces. . . . This book teaches you everything you need to know about flower arranging including tips on how to buy and care for flowers, how to cut and prepare them, and how to use . . . decorative elements." (Publisher's note)

"This book creates a needed foundation for aspiring designers." LJ

Harampolis, Alethea

The **flower** recipe book; Alethea Harampolis and Jill Rizzo of Studio Choo. Artisan 2013 272 p. $24.95 **745.92**

1. Flower arrangement

ISBN 1579655300; 9781579655303

LC 2012046704

This book, by Alethea Harampolis and Jill Rizzo, is a "flower-arranging bible for today's aesthetic. Filled with an array of stunning, easy-to-find flowers, it features 400 high-resolution photos,more than 40 step-by-step slideshows,and tappable pop-tips throughout. The arrangements run the gamut of styles and techniques: some are wild and some are structured; some are time-intensive and some are astonishingly simple." (Publisher's note)

746   Textile arts

Adams, Liza

Needle felting; from basics to bears with step-by-step photos and instructions for creating cute little bears and bunnies from natural wools. Liza Adams. Stackpole Books 2016 128 p. color illustrations (pbk.) $22.95 **746**

1. Handicraft 2. Felt work 3. Textile crafts

ISBN 0811716627; 9780811716628

LC 2015045254

With this book on needle felting, by Liza Adams, "make the cutest little creatures from wool! Needle felting is all the rage, and this book shows you how to create tiny bears, rabbits, dogs, cats, fairies, dolls, cupcakes, and more." (Publisher's note)

Bardwell, Sandra

Sewing Basics; All You Need to Know about Machine and Hand Sewing. Sandra Bardwell. Murdoch 2011 272 p. $17.72 **746**

1. Sewing 2. Handicraft

ISBN 1741967503; 9781741967500

Author Sandra Bardwell presents this book "covering fabrics, sewing machines, hand sewing, fitting, finishing, trouble-shooting and much more. For beginners learning how to hem and for more experienced sewers who need help dealing with difficult fabrics, 'Sewing Basics' is an invalu-

able reference to keep on the bookshelf for many years to come." (Publisher's note)

Fassett, Kaffe

Kaffe Fassett's Bold Blooms; Kaffe Fassett, Liza Prior Lucy. Harry N Abrams Inc 2016 224 p. (hardcover) $35 **746**

1. Quilts 2. Flowers in art

ISBN 1419722360; 9781419722363

This book, by Kaffe Fassett with Liza Prior Lucy, "guide and vibrant pattern collection of 25 new patchwork and needlepoint projects, from renowned color expert and quilt and fabric designer Kaffe Fassett. Drawing inspiration from the natural beauty of flowers, [it] . . . invites crafters to explore the behind-the-scenes process and fascinating design methods used to create Kaffe's bold fabrics and modern color palettes." (Publisher's note)

"Patterson's photographs enhance the artistic aspect, making the book not just a craft guide but a beautiful keepsake of its own. The whole book is just smashing." PubWkly

Glass, Alison

Alison Glass Appliqué; The Essential Guide to Modern Appliqué. Lucky Spool Media 2014 144 p. $28.95 **746**

ISBN 194065503X; 9781940655031

This book by Alison Glass "is for the advanced beginner interested in heirloom and slow sewing. It [offers a] way to learn about incorporating inventive textile treatments and embellishments to achieve one-of-a-kind, modern designs. All of the techniques, from old-school to cutting-edge, are clearly demonstrated with step-by-step instruction, 20 helpful illustrations, and 60 detailed, how-to photographs." (Publisher's note)

Stewart, Martha, 1941-

Martha Stewart's encyclopedia of sewing and fabric crafts; basic techniques for sewing, appliqué, embroidery, quilting, dyeing, and printing, plus 150 inspired projects from A to Z. by Martha Stewart Living Magazine. Potter Craft 2010 400 p. illustrations (chiefly color) $35; (ebook) $65 **746**

1. Sewing 2. Handicraft 3. Textile crafts

ISBN 0307450589; 9780307450586; 9780307965516

LC 2009040548

This book, by the editors of Martha Stewart Living Magazine, "covers everything a home sewer craves: the basics of sewing by hand or machine, along with five other time-honored crafts techniques, and step-by-step instructions for more than 150 projects that reflect not only Martha Stewart's depth of experience and crafting expertise, but also her singular sense of style." (Publisher's note)

Includes index and resources (p.378-387)

White, Christine

Uniquely felt; dozens of techniques from fulling and shaping to nuno and cobweb: includes 46 creative projects. Storey Pub. 2007 311p il pa $24.95 **746**

1. Fabrics 2. Handicraft

ISBN 978-1-58017-673-6; 1-58017-673-9

LC 2007-23531

The author covers "basic feltmaking techniques as well as needle, nuno, cobweb, 3-D, and carved techniques and featuring 46 projects. . . . What makes this a title of lasting value for libraries is the depth of solid information it offers on the craft and its history, on various artists, and on related topics like setting up a feltmaking studio, teaching felt making, and leading community feltmaking projects." Libr J

Includes bibliographical references

746.1　Products and processes

Dixon, Anne

The **handweaver's** pattern directory; over 600 weaves for 4-shaft looms. Interweave Press 2007 254p il $34.95　　**746.1**
　　1. Weaving
　　ISBN 978-1-59668-040-1
　　　　　　　　　　　　　　LC 2007-26351

This "guide to more than 600 different weaving patterns for four-shaft looms divides weaves into basic groups by structure (e.g., basic threadings, block drafts). Each weave is accompanied by warp threading and weaving drafts (the latter, explained in a handy extended flap), a tieup grid, closeup photos of the weave, and color photos of the actual woven fabric. Beginning weavers will appreciate the sections on weaving basics and finishing techniques as well as the glossary of common weaving terms." Libr J

Mitchell, Syne

Inventive weaving on a little loom; discover the full potential of the Rigid-Heddle loom, for beginners and beyond. Syne Mitchell. Storey Publishing 2015 295 p. color illustrations (pbk. : alk. paper) $29.95　　**746.1**
　　1. Looms 2. Weaving 3. Handlooms 4. Hand weaving
　　ISBN 9781603429726; 1603429727
　　　　　　　　　　　　　　LC 2015019702

In this book author Syne Mitchell "covers everything rigid-heddle weavers need to know about the craft, from the basics -- how to select a loom, set it up, and get started -- to a wide variety of fun techniques that yield beautiful results. Begin by exploring a variety of weave structures, including finger-manipulated laces, tapestry, and color play." (Publisher's note)

"Notable for its full coverage of rigid heddle weaving, one of the most accessible pathways into this ancient art, this is an essential addition to weavers' bookshelves." LJ

Includes bibliographical references and index

Murphy, Marilyn

Woven to wear; 17 thoughtful designs with simple shapes. Marilyn Murphy. Interweave Press 2013 143 p. color illustrations (pbk.) $26.95　　**746.1**
　　1. Weaving 2. Clothing and dress 3. Hand weaving
　　ISBN 1596686510; 9781596686519
　　　　　　　　　　　　　　LC 2012048056

This garment-weaver's handbook, by Marilyn Murphy, "offers guidance for weaving scarves, wraps, and more. She also provides advice for designing garments, cutting and sewing fabric, adding edgings and closures, and combining woven fabrics with other techniques. In addition, nine

contributing designers share their working philosophies." (Publisher's note)

"Beginners (or experienced weavers who could use a refresher) will appreciate the thorough introduction to weaving tools and technique." LJ

Patrick, Jane

The **weaver's** idea book; creative cloth on a rigid-heddle loom. Interweave Press 2010 239p il $29.95　　**746.1**
　　1. Weaving
　　ISBN 978-1-59668-175-0
　　　　　　　　　　　　　　LC 2009-39518

"Patrick's collection of patterns and projects explores the possibilities of weaving on a rigid heddle loom. From basic plain weaves to finger-controlled and pick-up techniques, Patrick guides weavers of all skill levels. . . . This is an excellent addition to any weaving collection." Libr J

Includes bibliographical references

746.12　Spinning, twisting, reeling

Boggs, Jacey

Spin art; mastering the craft of spinning textured yarn. Jacey Boggs. Interweave Press 2011 143 p. color illustrations $26.95　　**746.12**
　　1. Yarn 2. Spinning 3. Hand spinning
　　ISBN 1596683627; 9781596683624
　　　　　　　　　　　　　　LC 2011276733

This book, by Jacey Boggs, offers a guide for craft spinning yarn. "The yarn styles explored in this comprehensive spinning guide are as well made as they are inventive. Jacey walks you through each of her techniques, with a refreshing mixture of quirky, fanciful, and unexpected designs that are always skillfully constructed." (Publisher's note)

746.14　Weaving

Anderson, Sarah

The **spinner's** book of yarn designs; techniques for creating 80 yarns. Sarah Anderson; foreword by Judith MacKenzie. Storey Publishing 2012 255 p. color illustrations (ebook) $27.50　　**746.14**
　　1. Yarn 2. Spun yarns 3. Hand spinning
　　ISBN 1603427384; 9781603427388; 9781603429023
　　　　　　　　　　　　　　LC 2012039869

This book, by Sarah Anderson, "shows you how to create 80 distinctive yarn types, from classics like mohair bouclé to novelties like supercoils. . . . Anderson describes the unique architecture of each type of yarn and shares expert techniques for manipulating and combining fibers. Take your crafting to a new level and ensure that you have the best yarn available by spinning it yourself." (Publisher's note)

"Inventive, accessible, and fun, this book is an invitation to spinners of all skill levels to venture into uncharted territory and try out something new. This beautiful reference is an essential addition to any spinner's library." Pub Wkly

Includes bibliographical references (pages 248-249) and index

746.3 Pictures, hangings, tapestries

Brosens, Koenraad

European tapestries in the Art Institute of Chicago; [by] Koenraad Brosens; with contributions by Pascal-Francois Bertrand [et al.]; Christa C. Mayer Thurman, general editor. Yale University Press 2008 407p il $75 **746.3**

1. Tapestry

ISBN 978-0-300-11960-2; 0-300-11960-7

LC 2008-930401

Brosens, "along with a distinguished group of art historians and curators, argues for the historical and artistic importance of tapestry as an art form. Designed to accompany the Art Institute of Chicago's exhibition The Divine Art: Four Centuries of European Tapestries, this is a genuinely unique text. Its pioneering scholarship is both precise in its claims and accessibly written for a wide audience. After introductory essays, the tapestries are arranged by region and then subdivided by chronology. These works range from medieval through baroque art styles. The color illustrations and the essays that analyze each tapestry are exquisite." Libr J

Includes bibliographical references

746.4 Needlework and handwork

Finnanger, Tone, 1973-

Tilda Homemade & Happy. F & W Media Inc 2014 144 p. color illustrations $22.99 **746.4**

1. Sewing 2. Handicraft 3. Interior design

ISBN 1446305902; 9781446305904

This book by designer Tone Finnanger presents a "collection of inspirational home accessories including quilts, cushions and decorative items to make Christmas even more special." These include "gold-winged reindeer and sheep, round-eyed owls, plump pigs with flower applique detail, angels, stars and darling decorative cakes . . . all in Tone's unique range of fabulous fabrics. The projects are photographed in the author's own log cabin" in Norway. (Publisher's note)

Zimmermann, Elizabeth

★ **Knitting** without tears; basic techniques and easy-to-follow directions for garments to fit all sizes. by Elizabeth Zimmermann. Scribner 1971 120 p. ill. pbk $16.95 **746.4**

1. Knitting

ISBN 0684135051; 9780684135052

LC 70140776

This book, by Elizabeth Zimmermann, "puts the fun back into knitting with easy-to-follow instructions and timeless designs. . . . This . . . book is poised to inspire a whole new generation of knitters who have yet to discover the joys and comforts of knitting." (Publisher's note)

Includes bibliography

746.42 Nonloom weaving and related techniques

Hartmann, Kat

Hot knots; fresh macrame ideas for jewelry, home and fashion. Kat Hartmann. Barrons Educational Series, Inc. 2015 128 p. illustrations $21.99 **746.42**

1. Macrame

ISBN 1438005652; 9781438005652

LC 2014956306

This book, by Kat Hartmann, "explores a variety of macramé techniques--from historical, centuries-old designs, to modern fusion knots--and guides readers through 18 cool and contemporary projects for jewelry, housewares, accessories, and more." (Publisher's note)

"Up-to-date titles about macramé are difficult to find, and while Hartmann includes nods to 1970s-era classics such as owls and plant hangers, contemporary crafters will find that macramé is both simple and versatile." LJ

746.43 Knitting, crocheting, tatting

Anderson, Susan B.

Susan B. Anderson's kids' knitting workshop; The Easiest and Most Effective Way to Learn to Knit! Susan B. Anderson. Artisan 2015 200 p. color illustrations $17.95 **746.43**

1. Knitting 2. Handicraft for children 3. Knitting -- Patterns -- Juvenile literature

ISBN 1579655904; 9781579655907

LC 2015013064

Knitter Susan B. Anderson "presents her first book targeted at a young audience. This accessible introduction to knitting in the round includes easy-to-follow illustrated tutorials on techniques from casting on and binding off to joining colors to make stripes, and 17 progressively challenging knitting projects—beginning with simple infinity scarves and hats and building to supersweet toys and decor." (Publisher's note)

Includes bibliographical references and index

Kids' knitting workshop

Bassetti, Amanda

Arm knitting; 30 home and fashion projects for all your no-needle needs. Amanda Bassetti. Barrons Educational Series, Inc. 2015 144 p. color illustrations $17.99 **746.43**

1. Knitting 2. Handicraft

ISBN 1438007302; 9781438007304

LC 2015941220

Author Amanda Bassetti presents this guide to knitting that features "clear, step-by-step instructions and photographs . . . 30 home and fashion projects, including a winter snood, scarves, boot warmers, blankets, a chunky rug, footstool, pet bed, baby blanket, super-fast mug cozy, and more . . . [and] helpful suggestions on techniques and materials." (Publisher's note)

"Hands down (or arms up), one of the best-ever beginner craft books." Booklist

Bernard, Wendy

Up, down, all-around stitch dictionary; a collection of stitch patterns to knit top down, bottom up, back and forth, and in the round. Wendy Bernard; photography by Thayer Allyson Gowdy. Stewart Tabori & Chang 2014 288 p. ill. (some col.) $29.95   **746.43**
    1. Knitting 2. Handicraft 3. Life skills -- Handbooks, manuals, etc.
    ISBN 1617690996; 9781617690990
                                            LC 2013945660
"In the 'Up, Down, All-Around Stitch Dictionary,' designer Wendy Bernard . . . presents instructions for working 150 popular stitch patterns four different ways: top down, bottom up, back and forth, and in the round. This hefty collection, ranging from lace and cables to colorwork and fancy edgings, is loaded with . . . swatches of each pattern, plus charted and text instructions." (Publisher's note)

"As with any solid stitch dictionary, the swatches show multiple repeats of the pattern, and the color photos are clear and large enough to display detail. Charts are present as needed." LJ

Bestor, Leslie Ann

Cast on, bind off; 54 step-by-step methods. by Leslie Ann Bestor. Storey Pub. 2012 215 p. color illustrations (paper w/partially concealed wire-o : alk. paper) $16.95   **746.43**
    1. Knitting 2. Knitting -- Technique
    ISBN 1603427244; 9781603427241
                                            LC 2012002769
This book on knitting by Leslie Ann Bestor "presents more than 50 ways to cast on and bind off, creating edges that are tighter, looser, stretchier, lacier, longer-lasting, prettier. . . . Detailed instructions for each technique are combined with step-by-step photography. . . . At-a-glance charts identify the best cast on or bind off for various types of knitting, as well as cast on/bind off pairs that work well together." (Publisher's note)

Includes bibliographical references (page 209) and indexes

Budd, Ann

The knitter's handy book of patterns; basic designs in multiple sizes and gauges. Interweave Press 2002 112p pa $24.95   **746.43**
    1. Knitting
    ISBN 1-931499-04-7
                                            LC 2001-59208
The patterns in this book "allow the knitter to create garments in any size from toddler to extra-large adult in any weight of yarn, from fingering to bulky. The knitter has only to knit a generous swatch with yarn and needles of her/his choice and plug the resulting gauge information into the charted instructions and schematics provided. Highly recommended for all knitting collections." Libr J

Chachula, Robyn, 1978-

Unexpected afghans; innovative crochet designs with traditional techniques. Robyn Chachula.

Interweave Press 2012 159 p. illustrations (pbk.) $22.99   **746.43**
    1. Crocheting 2. Afghans (Coverlets) 3. Crocheting -- Patterns
    ISBN 159668299X; 9781596682993
                                            LC 2012001563
This book, by Robyn Chachula, "presents 29 innovative interpretations of [crocheted afghan blankets.] . . . Expert designers including Kristin Omdahl, Kathy Merrick, Kimberly McAlindin, and many more, provide an abundance of fresh patterns and projects that are perfect for new and advanced crocheters as they start out beginner-friendly and become more complex, allowing a crocheter to build skills and confidence." (Publisher's note)

"With almost 30 different projects encompassing a variety of styles and techniques, this is an excellent value." LJ
    Includes bibliographical references and index

Crochet at home; 25 clever projects for colorful living. edited by Brett Bara. Interweave Press 2013 143 p. illustrations (chiefly color) (pbk.) $22.95   **746.43**
    1. Crocheting 2. Interior design 3. Household linens 4. House furnishings 5. Crocheting -- Patterns
    ISBN 1596688378; 9781596688377
                                            LC 2012048922
In this book "editor Brett Bara and a team of crochet experts bring 25 . . . home projects to life. Explore a collection of practical, pretty pieces for your kitchen, living room, and bedroom: from a riotously colorful blanket, to a delicate bunting of crocheted snowflakes, to flower-inspired trivets that are anything but dull-and even a full-sized ottoman! Techniques such as felting, lace, and crocheting with wire will appeal to beginner and advanced crocheters alike." (Publisher's note)

Crowfoot, Jane

Ultimate crochet bible; a complete reference with step-by-step techniques. Collins & Brown; Distributed in the U.S. and Canada by Sterling Pub. 2010 304p il (C & B crafts) $29.95   **746.43**
    1. Crocheting
    ISBN 978-1-84340-563-4
This guide begins "with an overview of the craft's origins and its requirements and necessities (for instance, hooks, needles, and knowledge of how to read a chart). Each chapter truly exposes the how-to details, not only in words but also, most important, in oversize illustrations. Included are a well-explained section of basics (for instance, how to differentiate between front and reverse sides and how to work crochet for left-handed crafters) and specific stitch categories: texture and lace, thread, Tunisian entrelac, color, beads and sequins, edgings, and professional finishing techniques." Booklist

Delany, Sarah

How to crochet; learn the basic stitches and techniques. Sara Delaney. Storey Publishing 2014 iv, 124 p.p **746.43**
1. Crocheting 2. Crocheting -- Patterns
ISBN 9781612123929

LC 2014018168

In this book "Sara Delaney shows you her techniques for working a basic chain and creating single and double chain stitches. You'll learn about changing colors, joining, fastening off, reading crochet patterns, and working with different shapes. Working on small projects, such as a simple potholder or scarf, gives you the practice and experience you need." (Publisher's note)

"Beginning crocheters looking for a no-frills guide will find exactly what they're looking for here." LJ

Includes bibliographical references and index

Dosen, Stephanie

Woodland knits; over 20 enchanting patterns: a Tiny Owl Knits Collection. by Stephanie Dosen; photographer, Tiffany Mumford. The Taunton Press, Inc. 2013 128 p. color illustrations $19.95 **746.43**
1. Knitting 2. Dress accessories 3. Knitting -- Patterns
ISBN 1627100245; 9781627100243

LC 2013026929

This book on knitting, by Stephanie Dosen, offers "delicately beautiful patterns that incorporate deer, fox, owl, and other woodland themes (plus pretty flowers and vines) and look like nothing else on the market. Here are 20 cute, contemporary projects to knit—including all the quick-to-make favorites—hats, scarves, wristlets, bags, wraps, and mitts." (Publisher's note)

Durant, Judith

Increase, decrease; by Judith Durant. Storey Publishing 2015 256 p. color illustrations (paper w/ partially concealed wire-o : alk. paper) $16.95 **746.43**
1. Knitting 2. Cross-stitch 3. Stitches (Sewing) 4. Knitting -- Patterns 5. Knitting -- Technique
ISBN 1612123317; 9781612123318

LC 2014042919

Author Judith Durant presents "a comprehensive guide to 99 different methods for increasing and decreasing knitting stitches. Each method is clearly described and includes step-by-step how-to photographs, swatches showing the look of the featured stitch, and a list of best uses. You'll find the best technique for every situation, whether you want to increase from the center, shape sleeves and necklines, work shaped lace, or decrease for the top of a hat." (Publisher's note)

Durham, Teva

Loop-d-loop crochet; more than 25 novel designs for crocheters (and knitters taking up the hook) Teva Durham; photographs by Adrian Buckmaster. Stewart, Tabori & Chang 2007 144 p. color illustrations $29.95 **746.43**
1. Crocheting 2. Crocheting -- Patterns
ISBN 1584795808; 9781584795803

LC 2006025052

In this book on crochet, author Teva Durham "presents more than 25 designs that are as up-to-the-minute, stylewise, as they are thoroughly steeped in crochet stitchwork tradition. Each of the projects, which range from purses, skirts, shawls, and sweaters for the whole family to a hammock and a pair of brocade boots, epitomizes Durham's signature design sensibility." (Publisher's note)

Includes bibliographical references (p. 142) and index

Eckman, Edie

Around the corner crochet borders; 150 colorful, creative crocheted edgings with charts & instructions for turning the corner perfectly every time. Edie Eckman. Storey Publishing 2010 316 p. color illustrations $16.95 **746.43**
1. Crocheting 2. Decoration and ornament 3. Crocheting -- Patterns 4. Borders, Ornamental (Decorative arts)
ISBN 1603425381; 9781603425384

LC 2010001461

This book, by Edie Eckman, offers "a collection of 150 colorful crochet frames, each with detailed instructions for working around a corner. Instructions are offered both as text and as charts for working in-the-round; back-and-forth charts are also included for when that method is more appropriate. Photographs of finished borders, each turning a 90-degree corner, allow readers to see the details up close." (Publisher's note)

Crochet borders

Connect-the-shapes crochet motifs; creative techniques for joining motifs of all shapes. by Edie Eckman. Storey Publishing 2012 272 p. color illustrations (hardcover with concealed wire-o : alk. paper) $19.95 **746.43**
1. Crocheting 2. Needlework -- Patterns 3. Crocheting -- Patterns
ISBN 1603429735; 9781603429733

LC 2012013934

Author Edie Eckman presents "a book that teaches 100 original motif designs and a variety of techniques to join them. The emphasis is squarely on motifs; only a few patterns are included. Each motif, gathered in 'families' of grannies, chains, clusters, flowers, swirls, radials and more, is shown in written directions, charted, and in full-color illustrations." (Publishers Weekly)

"Eckman's eye for color and design make this an excellent addition to any crafter's crochet collection." LJ

The crochet answer book; solutions to every problem you'll ever face, answers to every question you'll ever ask. Edie Eckman. 2nd edition Storey Publishing 2015 408 p. illustrations $14.95 **746.43**
1. Crocheting
ISBN 1612124062; 9781612124063

LC 2014033696

In this book, by Edie Eckman, "you'll find helpful answers to . . . crochet questions, including . . . questions on broomstick lace, linked stitches, crochet cables, and much more. You'll also find illustrations for left-handed crocheters; up-to-the-minute information on new internet resources; and an expanded section on unusual techniques like Tunisian crochet." (Publisher's note)

Eckman "presents a definitively revised guide that reflects the latest trends. In her inimitable question-and-answer style, she features the most recently unearthed techniques (do remember: what's old is new again in this and other needlework books), like Tunisian crochet and Bruges and Clones laces. There are brief illustrations, now, for both left- and right-handed stitchers. And new yarns and new tools (or adaptive ones) are explored with helpful tips and caveats." Booklist

Herzog, Amy

Knit to flatter; by Amy Herzog. Stewart, Tabori & Chang 2013 159 p. color illustrations (alk. paper) $24.95 **746.43**
1. Knitting 2. Human body 3. Knitting -- Patterns 4. Clothing and dress measurements
ISBN 1617690171; 9781617690174

LC 2012022908

In this book, author Amy Herzon "teaches you how to assess your shape--top-heavy, bottom-heavy, or proportiona-- and then knit accordingly. With a great sense of fun and acceptance, Amy Herzog presents silhouettes and styles that work with each body shape, along with four ideal sweater patterns per category." (Publisher's note)

"Featuring a variety of models and a beauty-at-all-sizes attitude, Herzog's positive, inspiring book will help knitters create attractive garments that make them feel gorgeous." LJ

Includes bibliographical references and index

Hiatt, June Hemmons

The **principles** of knitting; methods and techniques of hand knitting. June Hemmons Hiatt; illustrations by Jesse Hiatt. Simon & Schuster 2012 xx, 712 p.p $45 **746.43**
1. Knitting
ISBN 1416535179; 9781416535171

LC 2012418278

This book, by June Hemmons Hiatt and illustrated by Jesse Hiatt, "is the definitive book on knitting techniques, with valuable information for everyone from beginners to experienced knitters. June Hiatt presents not only a thorough, thoughtful approach to the craft, but also a passion for carrying on the art of knitting to future generations." (Publisher's note)

"This new edition of one of the great knitting references will bring Hiatt's clear explanations and comprehensive information to a new generation of knitters." LJ

Includes bibliographical references (pages 665-672) and index

Hubert, Margaret

10 Granny Squares 30 Blankets; Color Schemes, Layouts, and Edge Finishes for 30 Unique Looks. by Margaret Hubert. Quarto Pub Group USA 2015 128 p. illustrations, color (chiefly) $19.99 **746.43**
1. Crocheting
ISBN 1589238931; 9781589238930

In this book, author Margaret Hubert "shows how you can crochet 30 completely different blankets. Each square is used three times with different yarns, color schemes, motif arrangements, and edge finishes. . . . You can crochet blankets that are perfect for babies, boys, girls, college kids, and

grown-ups. Some are crazy, colorful, and fun; others are serene, classic, and sophisticated. Crochet them for bedrooms, family rooms, or dorms." (Publisher's note)

"Hubert is one of the crocheters responsible for rescuing granny squares from the 1970s nostalgia heap, and here she continues her quest to modernize this tried-and-true favorite." Library Journal

The **complete** photo guide to crochet. Creative Pub. International 2010 272p il pa $24.99 **746.43**
1. Crocheting
ISBN 978-1-58923-472-7

LC 2009-31798

"Reference for crocheters; includes instructions and diagrams for 200 stitch patterns, basic information about how to crochet, plus 20 patterns." Publisher's note

The **granny** square book; timeless techniques and fresh ideas for crocheting square by square. Margaret Hubert. Creative Pub. International 2011 176 p. illustrations (chiefly color) (ebook) $24.99; (spiral bound) $24.99 **746.43**
1. Crocheting 2. Crocheting -- Patterns
ISBN 9781610581646; 1589236386; 9781589236387

LC 2011013365

This book, by Margaret Hubert, "shows the evolution of the granny square, how it can be used and interpreted in different ways with different yarns, and how today's crocheter can design her own projects using the granny squares of her choice with the yarn choices of today. Just as Margaret learned from her grandmother and mother and then passed the skill down to her daughter and granddaughter, each generation finds new uses and artistic ways to interpret granny squares." (Publisher's note)

"Crocheters looking to move beyond basic granny squares, as well as new crocheters drawn to these traditional motifs, will enjoy this collection." LJ

Keim, Cecily

Teach yourself visually crochet; [by] Cecily Keim and Kim P. Werker. 2nd ed.; Wiley Publishing, Inc. 2011 333p il (Visual read less, learn more) pa $24.99 **746.43**
1. Crocheting
ISBN 978-0-470-87997-9

LC 2010-941213

First published 2006 with authors' names in reverse order

This guide to crocheting contains techniques, color photos, step-by-step instructions and tips for additional guidance.

Knight, Erika

500 crochet stitches; the ultimate crochet stitch bible. Erika Knight. St. Martin's Press 2015 287 p. illustrations (chiefly color) (paper over board) $24.99 **746.43**
1. Sewing 2. Crocheting 3. Stitches (Sewing) 4. Crocheting -- Technique
ISBN 9781250067302

LC 2015016931

This book, by Erika Knight, "is both a stitch guide and a how-to-crochet primer, all in one volume. You get all the information needed to get started, including how to choose yarn and needles, read patterns, work basic stitches, how to check gauge, increase and decrease, join pieces and finish projects and care for your crochet items." (Publisher's note)

"There are a number of crochet stitch dictionaries on the market, but most are focused on a specific type of stitch (e.g., edgings) or on motifs. This comprehensive work makes an excellent reference for crocheters of all skill levels." LJ

Five hundred crochet stitches

Marchant, Nancy

Knitting brioche; the essential guide to the brioche stitch. Nancy Marchant. North Light Books 2009 256 p. illustrations (alk. paper) $27.99 **746.43**
1. Knitting 2. Needlework 3. Knitting -- Patterns 4. Knitting -- Netherlands
ISBN 1600613012; 9781600613012

LC 2009038643

This book, by Nancy Marchant, is "devoted exclusively to brioche stitch, a knitting technique that creates a double-sided fabric. This complete guide will take you from your first brioche stitches to your first (or hundredth) project, and even to designing with brioche stitch, if you desire." (Publisher's note)

Includes bibliographical references (p. 254-255)

Knitting fresh brioche; creating two-color twists & turns : 75 stitches--12 stunning scarves & wraps. Nancy Marchant. Sixth & Spring Books 2014 240 p. illustrations (some color) (paperback) $24.95 **746.43**
1. Knitting 2. Needlework -- Patterns 3. Knitting -- Patterns
ISBN 1936096773; 9781936096770

LC 2014017015

This book, by Nancy Marchant, presents patterns and advice for needlework stitching with the brioche technique. The author "works brioche in two colors, forming graceful, undulating textures with increases and decreases. She explains everything from how to hold the yarn and cast on (offering multiple options) to creating the basic fabric and reading two-color charts." (Publisher's note)

"Marchant is widely recognized as the expert on brioche stitch, and her continued explorations of such knitting will appeal to experienced knitters looking for the next big trend." LJ

Includes bibliographical references and index

Melville, Sally

Knitting pattern essentials; adapting and drafting knitting patterns for great knitwear. Sally Melville. Potter Craft 2013 224 p. color illustrations (alk. paper) $24.99 **746.43**
1. Knitting 2. Sweaters 3. Knitting -- Patterns 4. Knitwear -- Pattern design
ISBN 0307965570; 9780307965578; 9780307965585

LC 2012015715

This book, by Sally Melville, is a "comprehensive guide to sweater construction. ... [Sally] reveals the secrets to creating or modifying a pattern so the finished project looks and fits exactly how you want it to. Pattern drafting has never been easier to understand as Sally breaks down each skill." (Publisher's note)

Newton, Deborah

Finishing school; a master class for knitters. Deborah Newton. Sixth&Spring Books 2011 164 p. color illustrations (hardback) $29.95 **746.43**
1. Knitting 2. Knitting -- Patterns
ISBN 1936096196; 9781936096190

LC 2011013424

In this book, knitter Deborah Newton "shares her expertise and love of finishing techniques in an on-the-page master class. Deborah patiently takes her student-readers step by step through the ins and outs of blocking, seaming, edging, and embellishing, giving them the confidence and skills to create professional-looking knitwear. In addition to Deborah's expert instructions, the book includes patterns for 12 sweaters, jackets, and scarves, many with variations." (Publisher's note)

Omdahl, Kristin

The **finer** edge; crocheted trims, motifs & borders. Kristin Omdahl. Interweave Press 2013 144 p. ill. (chiefly col.) (pbk.) $22.95 **746.43**
1. Crocheting 2. Handicraft 3. Crocheting -- Patterns
ISBN 1596685549; 9781596685543

LC 2012029110

In this book, author Kristin Omdahl "explores crocheted edge motifs in this colorful pattern dictionary. The edgings are organized by type of construction (top-down, bottom-up, side-to-side, miscellaneous) and each contains written and charted instructions as well as a full-color swatch. Patterns for crocheted garments and accessories round out the collection and show the edgings in use on real-world projects." (Library Journal)

"Several crocheted edging/motif books have been published in the last few years. Omdahl is a big name in the field, and crocheters will appreciate this nicely curated ensemble." LJ

Includes bibliographical references and index

One-skein wonders for babies; 101 knitting projects for infants & toddlers. edited by Judith Durant. Storey Publishing 2015 288 p. (pbk. : alk. paper) $18.95 **746.43**
1. Knitting 2. Infants' clothing 3. Knitting -- Patterns
ISBN 9781612124803

LC 2015010744

This book, edited by Judith Durant, "offers 101 original knitting projects for babies and toddlers--each using just a single skein of yarn! From mittens and hats to tees, sweaters, hoodies, pants, dresses, socks, and bootees, you'll find the perfect wearable for every child and every occasion." (Publisher's note)

"This is a popular series, and the collection of projects will appeal to knitters with little ones in their lives." LJ

Radcliffe, Margaret

Circular knitting workshop; essential techniques to master knitting in the round. by Margaret Radcliffe. Storey Publishing LLC 2012 319 p. color illustrations (pbk.) $24.95 **746.43**
1. Knitting 2. Arts and crafts movement 3. Knitting

-- Patterns
ISBN 1603429999; 9781603429993
LC 2011025033
Author "Margaret Radcliffe covers everything you need to know to master the art of circular knitting, presenting Fair Isle, twined, helix, tubular, and other classic techniques in detailed step-by-step photographic sequences. Thirty-five demonstration projects let you try out each technique on a mini sock, hat, bag, mitten, sweater, or vest before applying it to a larger project." (Publisher's note)

"All knitters, from novice to expert, will find something new and useful in this comprehensive guide. Essential for knitting collections." LJ

The **knitting** answer book; solutions to every problem you'll ever face; answers to every question you'll ever ask. by Margaret Radcliffe. 2nd edition Storey Publishing 2015 439 p. illustrations pbk $14.95   **746.43**
1. Knitting 2. Knitting -- Miscellanea
ISBN 9781612124056; 9781612124049; 1612124046
LC 2014033661
"Margaret Radcliffe's classic Q&A guide is better than ever! This thoroughly revised and updated new edition gives expert answers to scores of new questions that knitters have asked since the first edition was published. You'll find more than a dozen new cast ons and bind offs; new techniques for beading and knitting backwards; tips for making smooth stripes when knitting in the round and for measuring gauge on tricky fabrics, such as ribbing and lace; fresh information on interpreting patterns and adjusting patterns to fit; and much more." (Publisher's note)
Includes bibliographical references (pages 415-428) and index

The **knowledgeable** knitter; understand the inner workings of knitting and make every project a success. by Margaret Radcliffe. Storey Publishing 2014 296 p. ill. (chiefly col.) (hardcover : alk. paper) $34.95   **746.43**
1. Knitting 2. Needlework -- Patterns 3. Knitting -- Patterns
ISBN 1612124143; 9781612120409; 9781612124148
LC 2014016057
This book by Margaret Radcliffe is a "reference for any knitter seeking better results, whether the challenge is reading a pattern chart, substituting yarn, modifying a pattern, fixing a mistake, shaping a collar, or adjusting an armhole." It "covers everything from how to identify a well-written pattern to evaluating schematics, revising a pattern so it fits perfectly, and making adjustments throughout a project." (Publisher's note)
Includes bibliographical references and index

Righetti, Maggie
Crocheting in plain English; 2nd ed.; Thomas Dunne Books 2008 268p il pa $16.95   **746.43**
1. Crocheting
ISBN 978-0-312-35354-4; 0-312-35354-5
LC 2008-43913
First published 1988

This is "one of the most comprehensive and accessible guides to crochet available. This isn't a quick-start guide: Righetti provides an overview of the necessary supplies, a brief history of crochet, and information about gauge before guiding beginners through their first stitch, an ideal approach for readers who wish to understand crochet in-depth." Libr J
Includes bibliographical references

Knitting in plain English. St. Martin's Press 1986 241p il pa $14.95   **746.43**
1. Knitting
ISBN 0-312-45853-3
LC 86-1800
This compendium is divided into four sections: preliminaries to knitting; the work itself; finishing; and patterns. Black-and-white photos accompany the text

Square, Vicki
The **knitter's** companion; Expanded and updated, deluxe ed.; Interweave 2010 138p il $24.95   **746.43**
1. Knitting
ISBN 978-1-59668-314-3
First published 1996
This is "an excellent ready reference for a variety of knitting techniques, including cast-ons, bind-offs, finishing, and other basics. . . . The demonstrations on the DVDs show knitters exactly what they should be doing. Every knitting collection needs a reference; this one is affordable and accessible." Libr J

Starmore, Alice
Alice Starmore's book of Fair Isle knitting; Alice Starmore. Dover Publications 2009 199 p. ill. (some col.) (pbk.) $29.95   **746.43**
1. Knitting 2. Knitting -- Scotland -- Fair Isle -- Patterns
ISBN 0486472183; 9780486472188
LC 2009026197
In this book, author Alice Starmore "explains the traditional Fair Isle techniques of circular knitting and presents detailed tutorials on incorporating classic motifs, exploring color schemes, and creating unique patterns and designs. She shares fourteen of her own original designs, including patterns for cardigans, vests, fishermen's sweaters, hats, gloves, and mittens. More than 250 photographs, drawings, and easy-to-follow charts illustrate sources of inspiration." (Publisher's note)
Includes bibliographical references and index

Stoller, Debbie
★ **Stitch** 'n bitch; the knitter's handbook. illustrations by Adrienne Yan; fashion photography by John Dolan. Workman 2003 248p il hardcover o.p. pa $13.95   **746.43**
1. Knitting
ISBN 0-7611-3258-9; 0-7611-2818-2 pa
LC 2003-53543
"An introduction chronicles the history of knitting from the female perspective, while subsequent chapters cover topics such as yarn type, instruments, stitches, and patterns. Perhaps the most exciting bit is Stoller's 'knit as you learn' technique: with every new stitch, she presents a new pattern,

thereby allowing knitters to build on their knowledge. . . . Essential for all crafts collections and perfect for a display." Libr J

Stitch 'n bitch superstar knitting; go beyond the basics. Debbie Stoller; with photography by Gabrielle Revere. Workman Pub. Co. 2010 xii, 356 p.p color illustrations (pbk. : alk. paper) $17.95 **746.43**
1. Knitting
ISBN 0761135979; 9780761135975
LC 2010051402
This book, by Debbie Stoller, "is the only knitter's handbook to teach the full array of advanced knitting techniques and skills, such as double-knitting, knitting lace, complicated color work, beading, and more. . . . There's also a whole section on DIY—which gives a tutorial on creating your own knitting patterns." (Publisher's note)
"Essential for the well-rounded knitting collection owing to the sections on techniques and designing; a few of the patterns are destined to be popular. The Frilly Filly Scarf (see pattern, above) is simple and sophisticated." LJ

Turner, Sharon
Teach yourself visually knitting; 2nd ed.; Wiley Pub. 2010 339p il (Visual read less, learn more) pa $22.99 **746.43**
1. Knitting
ISBN 978-0-470-52832-7; 0-470-52832-X
LC 2009-941352
First published 2006
This guide to knitting contains techniques, color photos, step-by-step instructions and tips for additional guidance.

Vogue knitting; the ultimate knitting book. by the editors of Vogue Knitting Magazine. Sixth & Spring 2003 280p il $38.95 **746.43**
1. Knitting
ISBN 1-931543-16-X
LC 2002-17571
Reissue of the title first published 1989 by Pantheon Bks.
"Following an introductory chapter on the history of knitting, the editors offer tips on how to understand knitting instructions and advice on the whole range of basic and advanced techniques. A stitch dictionary containing instructions and a photo for over 120 stitches is a real bonus. The book also contains patterns for what are referred to as 'classic sweaters.'" Booklist {review of 1989 edition}

746.432 Knitting

Budd, Ann
Knitter's handy book of top-down sweaters; basic designs in multiple sizes and gauges. Ann Budd. Interweave Press LLC 2012 263 p. illustrations (ebook) $22.95; (hardback) $29.95 **746.432**
1. Knitting 2. Sweaters 3. Knitting -- Patterns
ISBN 9781620330524; 1596684836; 9781596684836
LC 2012001366
This book, by Ann Budd, "offers instructions for knitting five basic sweater types: circular yoke, raglan, modified-

drop shoulder, set-in sleeve, and saddle shoulder. Patterns are offered in multiple sizes and yarn gauges and for a broad age group." (Publisher's note)
"Knitters who want to design their own sweaters but don't want to figure out all the math will appreciate Budd's straightforward approach to sweater design, while knitters who are just looking for patterns will enjoy the variety of ready-to-knit patterns in this collection." LJ
Includes bibliographical references and index

New directions in sock knitting; 18 innovative designs knitted from every which way. Ann Budd. F & W Media Inc 2016 167 p. illustrations (chiefly color) (paperback) $26.99 **746.432**
1. Socks 2. Knitting 3. Needlework -- Patterns
ISBN 9781620339435; 1620339439
LC 2016301981
This book, by Ann Budd, offers "eighteen designs [for sock knitting] . . . that range from traditional sock patterns to more challenging and innovative sock constructions. The socks in this collection use a variety of knitting techniques including double knitting, intarsia in the round, short-row shaping, mirrored color and texture patterns, and multi-directional knitting in both traditional and innovative ways." (Publisher's note)
"Most of the patterns are extremely detailed, but patient knitters will find the process rewarding, and the finished results are gorgeous." LJ

Sock knitting master class; innovative techniques + patterns from top designers. Ann Budd. Interweave 2011 183 p. color illustrations $26.99 **746.432**
1. Socks 2. Knitting 3. Knitting -- Patterns
ISBN 1596683120; 9781596683129
LC 2010049008
This book, by Ann Budd, "showcases methods for designing and knitting creative socks, featuring signature elements and techniques from 16 top designers. You'll learn what makes good sock design, and then dive into knitting 18 spectacular, brand-new patterns featuring the widest variety of techniques." (Publisher's note)
"This is an excellent addition to sock-knitting collections." LJ
Includes bibliographical references (p. 182) and index

Drysdale, Rosemary
Entrelac; the essential guide to interlace knitting. Rosemary Drysdale. Sixth&Spring Books 2010 160 p. color illustrations $24.95 **746.432**
1. Knitting 2. Knitting -- Patterns
ISBN 1936096005; 9781936096008
LC 2010932159
This book on entrelac knitting, by Rosemary Drysdale, "introduces both the history and how-to of this fun style, along with 20 patterns for a variety of garments, home décor items, and baby accessories. Comprehensive instructions and a wide array of swatches provide endless possibilities in lace, colorwork, and much more." (Publisher's note)

Durant, Judith

Cable left, cable right; 94 Knitted Cables. Judith Durant. Storey Publishing 2016 216 p. (pbk. : alk. paper) $16.95   **746.432**

1. Knitting 2. Cable knitting 3. Knitting -- Technique
ISBN 9781612125169

LC 2015044820

This book on kitting, by Judith Durant, "eliminates the mystery with detailed, in-depth instructions for creating 94 different styles of cable, from perfectly plain to fantastically fancy. Close-up photos and clear instructions teach you the techniques you need, including design options like braids, diamonds, and pretzels so you can make your cables truly one-of-a-kind." (Publisher's note)

"Each of the cables includes a full-color, close-up swatch illustrating clearly how the cables are formed as well as charted instructions. Helpful tips for troubleshooting—including a clever approach to remedying loose stitches before and after cables—are supplied throughout." LJ

Gaughan, Norah

Norah Gaughan's Knitted Cable Sourcebook; A Breakthrough Guide to Knitting With Cables and Designing Your Own. by Norah Gaughan; photography by Jared Flood. Harry N Abrams Inc 2016 276 p. color illustrations $29.95; (ebook) $23.32 **746.432**

1. Knitting
ISBN 1419722395; 9781419722394; 9781613122914

LC 2016956329

This book on knitting, by Norah Gaughan, "presents more than 150 new and innovative cable stitch patterns ranging from basic to complex and offers enlightening insight into how cables are engineered, how knitters can design their own, and how knitters can mix and match cables in a knitting pattern." (Publisher's note)

Herzog, Amy

Knit wear love; foolproof instructions for knitting your best-fitting sweaters ever in the styles you love to wear. Amy Herzog. Stewart, Tabori & Chang 2015 192 p. color illustrations $24.95 **746.432**

1. Knitting 2. Clothing and dress
ISBN 1617691399; 9781617691393

LC 2014942999

In this book about knit wear, author Amy Herzog "guides us through picking a base pattern that not only works for our inherent shape, but also suits our size and style—all with the skill of a top-notch teacher and designer and the honesty and humor of a BFF." (Publisher's note)

"This classic-in-the-making will inspire knitters to make sweaters that fit well and suit their personal style." LJ

You can knit that; foolproof instructions for fabulous sweaters. by Amy Herzog. Harry N Abrams Inc 2016 175 p. illustrations (some color) $24.95; (ebook) $18.65 **746.432**

1. Knitting 2. Sweaters
ISBN 1419722476; 9781419722479; 9781613122938

This book, by Amy Herzog, "is a clear, simple reference book and pattern collection that gives knitters the sweater-making confidence they need. Whether you're knitting a sweater for the first time or seeking to expand your skills to knit sweaters in styles you've never tried before, this essential guide starts with basic sweater know-how and moves into instructions for knitting six must-have sweater styles." (Publisher's note)

"Herzog's expertise, combined with her ability to explain clearly the hows and whys of sweater knitting, will build confidence even in the most reluctant knitters." LJ

Includes bibliographical references.

Knight, Erika

750 knitting stitches; the ultimate knit stitch bible. Erika Knight. St. Martin's Griffin 2015 287 p. color illustrations (paper over board) $24.99 **746.432**

1. Stitches (Sewing) 2. Sewing -- Technique 3. Knitting -- Technique
ISBN 9781250067180

LC 2015017155

This book, by Erika Knight, is "both a stitch guide and a how-to knit primer, all in one volume. . . . The comprehensive pattern library includes 750 knitting stitches, from simple to ornate, including knit and purl patterns, basic and complex cables, Fair Isles and intarsia designs, and rib and edging patterns. Each is fully explained with instructions and accompanied by a full-color photo of a sample knitted swatch." (Publisher's note)

"A close-up, full-color swatch is also included for each design, giving the knitter an idea of what multiple pattern repeats look like in a knitted sample. A directory of basic knitting abbreviations and a guide to knitting elementals appear in the introduction." LJ

Knitting masterclass; with over 20 technical workshops and 15 beautiful patterns. by The Knitter; edited by Juliet Bernard. Sterling Pub Co Inc 2013 160 p. color illustrations $24.95 **746.432**

1. Knitting
ISBN 1908449020; 9781908449023

This book on knitting, edited by Juliet Bernard, presents "techniques drawn from the magazine [The Knitter's] popular Masterclass series. The 'seminars'—led by top teachers, lavishly photographed, and featuring exclusive projects—include Creating Perfect Lace, Steeking without Fear, Confident Cables, Provisional Cast On Methods, Flawless Fair Isle, and more." (Publisher's note)

Nico, Brooke

More Lovely Knitted Lace; Contemporary Patterns in Geometric Shapes. Brooke Nico. Sterling Pub Co. Inc. 2016 128 p. illustrations (chiefly color) (paperback) $19.95 **746.432**

1. Knitting 2. Lace and lace making 3. Needlework -- Patterns
ISBN 9781454709183; 1454709189

This book, by Brooke Nico, "presents 16 new projects that offer a fresh and original take on lace knitting. Think sweaters, capelets, tunics and cowls, knit in yarns both thick and thin—contemporary designs that give knitters a wealth of new possibilities. Organized by overall shape—circle, square, triangle, and rectangle—these lovely garments will change the way you look at lace knitting." (Publisher's note)

"Using geometric shapes as the basic foundation of knitted designs is not a new concept, but Nico's latest book offers a fresh take." Booklist

Starmore, Alice
Tudor roses; by Alice Starmore. Dover Pubns 2013 175 p. color illustrations $40 **746.432**
1. Knitting 2. Great Britain -- History -- 1485-1603, Tudors
ISBN 1606600478; 9781606600474
This book, by Alice Starmore, is a "stunning collection of hand-knitted designs inspired by members of the Tudor dynasty. . . . [It] features charts and instructions as well as a fascinating historical background on the royal family. Glorious full-color photography spotlights the completed works." (Publisher's note)

Weil, Anne
Knitting without needles; by Anne Weil. Potter Craft 2015 191 p. color illustrations (ebook) $59.97; (alk. paper) $19.99 **746.432**
1. Knitting 2. Finger weaving 3. Knitting -- Patterns 4. Knitting -- Technique
ISBN 9780804186537; 0804186529; 9780804186520
LC 2014036650
This book on knitting, by Anne Weil, "shows you how to loop yarn with your fingers or your forearms with thirty patterns that are simple to follow and produce stylish results. Best of all, many of them knit up fast—in less than an hour! " (Publisher's note)

Wood, Jennifer
Refined knits; Sophisticated Lace, Cable, and Aran Lace Knitwear. Jennifer Wood. Interweave Books 2016 156 p. illustrations (some color) $25.99 **746.432**
1. Knitting 2. Knitting -- Patterns
ISBN 163250068X; 9781632500687
LC 2016388252
This book on cable and lace knitting patterns, by Jennifer Wood, "concentrates on these two techniques, along with incredibly unique Aran Lace which combines the two, and the results are sure to impress." (Publisher's note)
"The patterns are comprehensive, including written and charted instructions, schematics, and notes on construction as needed." LJ
Includes bibliographical references and index

746.434 Crocheting

★ **A** to Z of crochet; [editor: Sue Gardner] Martingale & Company 2008 160 p. col. ill. (pbk.) $18.99 **746.434**
1. Crocheting 2. Crocheting -- Technique 3. Crocheting -- Handbooks, manuals, etc
ISBN 156477998X; 9781564779984
LC 2010282406
"Here's everything you ever wanted to know about crochet. This indispensable reference will guide you through everything from beginner's basics through stitches and techniques for every shape and texture Imaginable. With step-

by-step instructions and close-up photos, there's no easier way to learn to crochet! Whether you're a new crocheter or you just want to try new techniques, this must-have resource offers all the know-how you'll ever need." Publisher's Note.

Crochet one-skein wonders for babies; 101 projects for infants & toddlers. edited by Judith Durant & Edie Eckman; photography by Geneve Hoffman. Storey Publishing 2016 288 p. color illustrations (pbk. : alk. paper) $18.95 **746.434**
1. Crocheting 2. Infants' clothing 3. Crocheting -- Patterns
ISBN 9781612125763; 161212576X
LC 2015050175
This book, edited Judith Durant and Edith Eckman, is a "collection of 101 projects . . . to crochet . . . clothes, toys, and accessories for the babies and toddlers. Each project uses just one skein of yarn, many take just a few hours to complete, and plenty are suitable for beginners. Hats and caps, bootees and socks, mitts, dresses, tops and bottoms— plus blankets, bibs, soft toys, bottle cozies, diaper bags, and more." (Publisher's note)
"Handy tips on topics such as sizing and safety are scattered throughout, featuring valuable information the crocheter will continue to use in future projects. Covering a lot of ground in one volume, this thorough collection would be a valuable addition to libraries where crochet books are in demand." Booklist

Eckman, Edie
Beyond the square crochet motifs; 144 circles, hexagons, triangles, squares, and other unexpected shapes. Edie Eckman. Storey Publishing 2008 vi, 201 p.p illustrations (some color) (ebook) $18.95; (hardcover with concealed wire-o : alk. paper) $18.95 **746.434**
1. Crocheting 2. Crocheting -- Patterns
ISBN 9781603428149; 1603420398; 9781603420396
LC 2008018090
This book, by Edie Eckman, " opens up the door to crocheting creativity with more than 140 motifs of every shape and size. Embellish your clothing, linens, housewares, and bags with colorful patterns as you put odd yarn leftovers to good use. Step-by-step instructions and color photographs provide the building blocks to limitless possibilities. Open up your imagination and let your crochet follow." (Publisher's note)

Gullberg, Maria
Tapestry crochet and more; A Handbook of Crochet Techniques and Patterns. Maria Gullberg. Trafalgar Square Books 2016 84 p. color illustrations (concealed spiral) $17.95 **746.434**
1. Crocheting
ISBN 9781570767678
LC 2015958246
This book, by Maria Gullberg, "is the perfect introduction to a whole new set of [crocheting] techniques that will broaden your crochet horizons. Experiment with color, shape, and structure, using ribbed, relief, double-layer, and tapestry crochet to create bags, totes, hats, wrist warmers,

lace, and flowers with striking designs you almost won't believe are crocheted." (Publisher's note)

"This concealed ring-bound book focuses on tapestry crochet but also offers several other types of projects, including granny squares and three-dimensional flowers. The look of tapestry crochet is very distinctive and is rarely represented in craft books published in the U.S." Booklist

Todhunter, Tracey

Crochet; Techniques and Projects to Build a Lifelong Passion For Beginners Up. Tracy Todhunter. Barrons Educational Series, Inc. 2016 160 p. $18.99   **746.434**

1. Crocheting 2. Needlework
ISBN 9781438007595
                                        LC 2015951472

This crochet resource book by Tracey Todhunter, published as part of the "Learn It! Love It!" series, features "hundreds of detailed how-to photographs, carefully annotated, . . . guest designers sharing some of their favorite crochet patterns, . . . 'quick start projects' for beginners . . . [and] clinics to help students solve project dilemmas. Find the techniques necessary to learn crochet and love it--in no time at all!" (Publisher's note)

"The tone is straightforward but friendly, and the written and photographed instructions are thorough, making this appropriate for crafters who learn best either visually or by following written instructions." LJ

746.44   Embroidery

A-z of Ribbon Embroidery. Search Press 2016 132 p. color illustrations $19.95   **746.44**

1. Embroidery 2. Ribbon work
ISBN 178221173X; 9781782211730

In this book from Country Bump, readers "will find every stitch and technique fully explained with step by step photographs and clear instructions. Accomplished embroiderers have compiled advice on choosing ribbons, fabrics, needles and frames, as well as a host of other hints and tips. There are forty exquisite designs with full detail provided on the materials and stitches used for every element and a helpful Ribbon Embroidery Index." (Publisher's note)

"Search Press, as always in this British series, excels, giving its readers good instructions and traditional designs, including Victorian bouquet, roses, violets, baby bears, and other animals and flowers. Occasional tips (e.g., test ribbons first for color fastness by washing) ensure that beginners are on the same page as experienced embroiderers. A fresh, instructive approach to a wonderful tradition." Booklist

A-Z of Whitework; compiled by Country Bumpkin. Search Press 2015 128 p. color illustrations $19.95   **746.44**

1. Embroidery 2. Needlework
ISBN 1782211799; 9781782211792

This book is the "ultimate resource for beginning and experienced needlecrafters who want to discover the timeless appeal of whitework in its many forms. Whitework is white on white embroidery where the texture of the stitchery, whether it be delicate or bold, creates the beauty and inter-

est. Over 1,000 step-by-step photos illustrate the creation of this beautiful traditional white-on-white embroidery which has inspired needlecrafters for centuries." (Publisher's note)

"Traditional whitework embroidery—especially Mountmellick and cutwork—is starting to get some attention on embroidery blogs, and these classic techniques will appeal to stitchers with sophisticated tastes." LJ

Christensen, Jo Ippolito

★ The **needlepoint** book; Jo Ippolito Christensen; foreword by Amy Bunger. 3rd edition Simon & Schuster 2014 560 p. ill. (some col.) (hardcover) $60   **746.44**

1. Needlepoint 2. Canvas embroidery
ISBN 147675408X; 9781476754086; 9781476754109
                                        LC 2014023165

This is a "revised and expanded edition" of Jo Ippolito Christensen's book on needlepoint, including "a crash course on how to use new fibers; updated information on materials, as well as how to work with and care for them; dozens of new stitches; and diagrams and stitch guides for select projects included in book. Also featured are thirty-two pages of color photographs with all-new projects . . . and a new ribbon stitch chapter." (Publisher's note)

"Even though the book is a reference, the text is enjoyable to read. Sage advice from Christensen and a variety of other needle artists can be found throughout." LJ

Includes bibliographical references and index

Ganderton, Lucinda

★ Embroidery; Lucinda Ganderton. DK Publishing 2015 160 p. color illustrations (paperback) $15.95   **746.44**

1. Embroidery 2. Needlework
ISBN 1465436030; 9781465436030
                                        LC 2015431417

Author Lucinda Ganderton presents "a comprehensive guide to inspire and inform sewers of all levels. Find advice on which thread, needles, or fabrics work with which techniques, and take a look at an incredible 200 stitches -- with levels of difficulty, step-by-step instructions, and ideas on where and how to use them." (Publisher's note)

"It's straightforward, simple, and easy to access, thanks not only to an appended index but also to an upfront visual table of contents. The quintessentially perfect reference." Booklist

Prain, Leanne

Hoopla; the art of unexpected embroidery. photography by Jeff Christenson. Arsenal Pulp Press 2011 400p il pa $29.95   **746.44**

1. Embroidery
ISBN 978-1-55152-406-1

"In this combination overview of embroidery and exploration of its current trends, Prain takes a traditional approach, beginning with a cursory look at the craft's history and highlighting practicalities, such as tools and equipment, finishing techniques, and stitching resources. But it is between these lines that the author's true innovation and fun starts: specifically, with interviews with 28 working embroiderers and the same number of unusual projects to complete. . . . Projects don't disappoint, with directions as clear as the designs are funky: handkerchiefs emblazoned with microbes, a modern cuckoo clock stitched on Aida cloth, and knuckle-tattoo church gloves." Booklist

Includes bibliographical references

Reader's Digest Association

The **big** book of cross-stitch designs; over 900 simple-to-stitch decorative motifs. Reader's Digest Association 2007 320p il $29.95   **746.44**

1. Cross-stitch 2. Needlework -- Patterns
ISBN 0-7621-0673-5; 978-0-7621-0673-8

LC 2006-044634

"When editors at Reader's Digest identify a subject to publish, they explore its history, plumb the most popular techniques, then apply those learnings pragmatically. Here, cross-stitching takes on a more artistic bent, starting with the book's layout-big type fonts, step-by-step illustrations with full-color photographs of the projects—and ending with more than 900 designs." Booklist

Ringquist, Rebecca

★ **Rebecca** Ringquist's embroidery workshops; a bend-the-rules primer. Rebecca Ringquist. Stewart, Tabori & Chang 2015 160 p. illustrations $29.95   **746.44**

1. Embroidery
ISBN 1617691410; 9781617691416

LC 2014943000

In this book on embroidery, author Rebecca Ringquist "teaches everything from the 'proper' way to form a French knot and transfer a design to a canvas to new ways to stitch three-dimensionally, work with nontraditional threads and fabrics, draw with thread freeform, and mix and match machine- and hand-stitching. Also featured are instructions for 20 innovative projects, including a cloth sampler designed especially for the book, . . . table linens, wall art, and clothing embellishments." (Publisher's note)

"Ringquist is a skilled instructor with a great deal of experience. Crafters who are intimidated by embroidery will find her free-spirited approach refreshing." LJ

Shimoda, Naoko

Artfully embroidered; motifs and patterns for bags and more. Naoko Shimoda. Interweave 2014 120 p. illustrations (chiefly color) (pbk.) $24.99   **746.44**

1. Embroidery 2. Needlework -- Patterns 3. Embroidery -- Patterns
ISBN 9781620337288; 1620337282

LC 2014036871

This book, by Naoko Shimoda, "reinvents vintage embroidery through a modern aesthetic. Traditional Japanese and western motifs are made new with color and embellishment, and 25 embroidered patterns demonstrate the beauty of the traditional designs while keeping the projects fresh and modern-looking for today's sewists." (Publisher's note)

"Shimoda is a master at combining fabric and thread for impressive effects. Sewists interested in exploring the world of embroidery will find a wealth of inspiration here, though beginners may need to consult a reference or an online tutorial to get themselves up to speed on the basics." LJ

Thomas, Mary

Mary Thomas's dictionary of embroidery stitches; by Mary Thomas and Jan Eaton. Trafalgar Square Pub. 1998 208 p. color illustrations $26.95 **746.44**

1. Embroidery 2. Embroidery -- Dictionaries
ISBN 1570761183; 9781570761188

LC 97081406

This book on embroidery, by Mary Thomas, was "[f]irst published in 1934. . . . Updated by Jan Eaton, it pictures and describes over 400 embroidery stitches arranged by usage, ranging from basic outline and border stitches to more complex detached-filling and pulled-fabric stitches." (Publisher's note)

"A comprehensive dictionary offering more than 400 stitches, this edition includes 100 new stitches, all described and pictured in full-color diagrams. Essential for public libraries and embroidery collections." LJ

Dictionary of embroidery stitches

Watson, Sarah

Pen to thread; 750+ hand-drawn embroidery designs to inspire your stitches. Sarah Watson. Interweave 2015 159 p. illustrations (some color) (pbk.) $26.99   **746.44**

1. Embroidery 2. Needlework -- Patterns 3. Embroidery -- Patterns 4. Embroidery -- Instruction and study
ISBN 1620339528; 9781620339527

LC 2016288028

This book, by Sarah Watson, "more than 750 whimsical, imaginative motifs [of embroidery.] . . . From every day objects like birdcages and backpacks to sophisticated poodles, playful mermaids, and punchy pinatas, each pattern is more charming than the next. Sarah has also included embroidery and stitching basics in case you're new to this fun and addictive hobby." (Publisher's note)

"Illustrator and fabric designer Watson brings her whimsical, hand-drawn designs to embroiderers in this collection of small and medium motifs." LJ

Includes bibliographical references and index

746.46   Patchwork and quilting

Arkison, Cheryl

Sunday morning quilts; 16 modern scrap projects: sort, store, and use every last bit of your treasured fabrics. Amanda Jean Nyberg and Cheryl Arkison. StashBooks 2012 143 p. color illustrations (pbk.) $22.95   **746.46**

1. Quilts 2. Quilting 3. Patchwork 4. Quilting -- Patterns 5. Patchwork -- Patterns
ISBN 1607054272; 9781607054276

LC 2011034028

In this book, authors Amanda Jean Nyberg and Cheryl Arkison "share a passion for scraps, and they're here to help you get creative with 16 scrappy quilt projects that include piecing, appliqué, and improvisational work. This book has ideas on how to adapt patterns for your own personal 'Sunday morning' style, plus tips for effectively cutting, storing, and organizing your scraps." (Publisher's note)

Baumgarten, Linda

Four centuries of quilts; the Colonial Williamsburg collection. Linda Baumgarten, Kimberly Smith Ivey. The Colonial Williamsburg Foundation 2014 355 p. illustrations $75 **746.46**

1. Quilts 2. Quilting -- History 3. Quilts -- Catalogs 4. Colonial Williamsburg Foundation -- Catalogs 5. Quilts -- Virginia -- Williamsburg -- Catalogs
ISBN 0300207360; 9780300207361 (Yale); 9780879352646

LC 2013049064

This book, by Linda Baumgarten and Kimberly Smith Ivey, "trace[s] the evolution of quilting styles and trends as they relate to the social, political, and economic issues of their time. The collection includes quilts made by diverse religious and cultural groups over 400 years and across continents, from the Mediterranean, England, France, America, and Polynesia." (Publisher's note)

"The catalog's arc is roughly chronological across categories (ethnic groups, quilting techniques, genres, materials, and pattern names) that reflect collection strengths. Its best feature is the authors' efforts to recover the identities of individual quilt makers." Choice

Includes bibliographical references and index

Beyer, Jinny

The **quilter's** album of patchwork patterns; more than 4050 pieced blocks for quilters. Breckling Press 2009 488p il $49.95 **746.46**

1. Quilting
ISBN 978-1-933308-08-1

LC 2009-21009

The author "pored through newspapers, catalogs, patterns, and magazines of the 1800s and 1900s to prepare illustrations—along with grids, dates, and multiple names—of more than 4,000 quilting blocks, the foundation of this genre of stitching. Yet providing that resource wasn't enough; Beyer enhances her encyclopedic reference by featuring mini catalogs of like-minded design styles, like bow ties, airplanes, the Red Cross, and kaleidoscope blocks. She also details her sources with commentary and explains how she categorized the blocks. Worthy of any quilting (and quilter's) library." Booklist

Includes bibliographical references

Four century of quilts; the Colonial Williamsburg collection. Linda Baumgarten, Kimberly Smith Ivey. The Colonial Williamsburg Foundation 2014 355 p. **746.46**

1. Quilts -- Catalogs 2. Colonial Williamsburg Foundation -- Catalogs 3. Quilts -- Virginia -- Williamsburg -- Catalogs
ISBN 9780300207361; 9780879352646

LC 2013049064

Includes bibliographical references and index

Gering, Jacquie

Quilting modern; techniques and projects for improvisational quilts. Jacquie Gering, Katie Pedersen.

Interweave Press 2012 175 p. color illustrations (pbk.) $26.99 **746.46**

1. Quilts 2. Quilting 3. Patchwork 4. Patchwork -- Patterns 5. Machine quilting -- Patterns
ISBN 1596683872; 9781596683877

LC 2011039245

This book, by Jacquie Gering and Katie Pedersen, "teaches quilters how to use improvisational techniques to make graphic, contemporary quilts and quilted projects. Explore seven core techniques and multiple projects using each technique--all presented with detailed instructions..... New and seasoned quilting artists will love making stunning bed, wall hanging, pillowcase, and table accessory quilts with this must-have resource." (Publisher's note)

Includes bibliographical references and index

Gilleland, Diane

All points patchwork; English paper piecing beyond the hexagon, for quilts & small projects. by Diane Gilleland. Storey Publishing 2015 224 p. color illustrations (pbk. : alk. paper) $19.95 **746.46**

1. Quilting 2. Patchwork 3. Paper work 4. Quilting -- Patterns 5. Patchwork -- Patterns
ISBN 1612124208; 9781612124209

LC 2014048235

This book on patchwork, by Diane Gilleland, focuses on the "traditional technique known as English paper piecing..... [It] takes you far beyond traditional hexagons with step-by-step photos showing you how to connect triangles, octagons, diamonds, jewels, triangles, tumblers, pentagons, and curved shapes. It even provides dozens of ideas for incorporating the pattern designs into clothing, pillows, quilts, and home decor items!" (Publisher's note)

"An essential reference for quilters interested in EPP." LJ

Includes bibliographical references and index

Hartman, Elizabeth

Modern patchwork; 12 quilts to take you beyond the basics. Elizabeth Hartman. StashBooks 2012 143 p. color illustrations (soft cover) $24.95 **746.46**

1. Quilts 2. Quilting 3. Patchwork 4. Patchwork quilts 5. Quilting -- Patterns
ISBN 1607055481; 9781607055488

LC 2011040928

With this book, by Elizabeth Hartman, you can "[e]xpand your patchwork skills with . . . new designs and techniques. . . . These projects are bold, bright, graphic, and designed to give modern quilters new challenges. You can learn new skills like curved seam piecing and create your best modern quilt yet. Make it fresh, make it fun, make it something you will use and cherish for years to come." (Publisher's note)

Pink, Tula

Quilts from the house of Tula Pink; 20 fabric projects to make, use and love. Tula Pink. Krause Publications 2012 144 p. color illustrations (pbk.) $24.99 **746.46**

1. Quilts 2. Quilting 3. Quilting -- Patterns
ISBN 1440218188; 9781440218187

LC 2012471570

In this book, fabric designer Tula Pink "offers 20 patterns with her signature flair for color, design and original style. Between 10 amazing quilts and 10 extra-cool companion projects, you'll be inspired to play with fabric, color and design in a way like never before!" (Publisher's note)

Includes bibliographical references and index

Tula Pink's city sampler; 100 modern quilt blocks. Tula Pink. David & Charles 2013 255 p. ill. (chiefly col.) $27.99   746.46

1. Quilts 2. Quilting
ISBN 1440232148; 9781440232145

In this book, author "Tula Pink gives you an inspiring quilt block collection. . . . Make a beautiful, modern quilt of your own design with the 100 original quilt blocks or try one of the 5 city-themed sampler quilts designed by Tula." (Publisher's note)

Schmidt, Denyse

Denyse Schmidt; modern quilts, traditional inspiration : 20 new designs with historic roots. Denyse Schmidt; photographs by John Gruen. Stewart, Tabori & Chang 2012 160 p. color illustrations; patterns $29.95   746.46

1. Quilting 2. Quilts -- Design 3. Quilting -- Patterns
ISBN 1584799005; 9781584799009

LC 2011021075

Author Denise Schmidt "pays homage to the quilters and quilts that came before her. Each of the 20 traditional quilt designs she has reinterpreted here (among them are Irish Chain, Mariner's Compass, and Orange Peel, to name a few) is introduced with a lively overview of the pattern's history. Instructions are illustrated, templates are provided at full size on a pullout pattern sheet, and a complete techniques section is included at the back of the book." (Publisher's note)

"It's wonderful to see quilting traditions treated with reverence in a modern quilting book, and the variety of designs, combined with the wealth of information on both quilting and the traditions of each design, make this an essential addition to quilting collections." LJ

Denyse Schmidt quilts; 30 colorful quilt and patchwork projects. text by Denyse Schmidt with Bethany Lyttle; photographs by Susie Cushner. Chronicle Books 2005 175 p. color illustrations $24.95   746.46

1. Quilting 2. Patchwork 3. Quilts -- Design 4. Quilting -- Patterns 5. Patchwork -- Patterns
ISBN 0811844420; 9780811844420

LC 2004023094

In this book on quilting, author Denyse Schmidt "reveals the secrets behind her most popular designs. Thirty projects range from the simple to the challenging, from patchwork slippers and aprons to tote bags and pillows to her beloved quilt patterns, offering something for every level of quilter. Schmidt reviews the fundamentals of quilting and provides easy-to-follow instructions, patterns, sewing tips, and an artful approach to design basics." (Publisher's note)

Wood, Sherri Lynn

Improv handbook for modern quilters; a guide to creating, quilting, and living courageously. Sherri

Lynn Wood. Stewart, Tabori & Chang 2015 176 p. color illustrations $27.50   746.46

1. Quilts 2. Cross-stitch
ISBN 1617691380; 9781617691386

LC 2014942998

In this book author "Sherri Lynn Wood presents a flexible approach to quilting that breaks free of old paradigms. Instead of traditional instructions, she presents 10 frameworks (or scores) that create a guiding, but not limiting, structure. To help quilters gain confidence, Wood also offers detailed lessons for stitching techniques key to improvisation." (Publisher's note)

"Improv quilting may not be to everyone's taste—it can be visually jarring at times—but many who love this style are downright passionate about it, and Wood provides a comprehensive overview of improvisational techniques." LJ

746.6   Printing, painting, dyeing

Callahan, Gail

Hand dyeing yarn and fleece; dip-dyeing, hand-painting, tie-dyeing, and other creative techniques. photography by John Polak. Storey Pub. 2010 168p il $18.95   746.6

1. Wool 2. Yarn 3. Dyes and dyeing
ISBN 1-60342-468-7; 978-1-60342-468-4

LC 2009-28676

This guide to dyeing yarn and fleece "includes instructions for designing self-striping and multicolored yarns with dip-dyeing, tie-dyeing, hand-painting, and other [techniques, as well as] . . . advice on color theory and types of dyes, including food colors and other 'grocery store' dyes." Publisher's note

Includes bibliographical references

Corwin, Lena

Lena Corwin's made by hand; a collection of projects to print, sew, weave, dye, knit, and otherwise create. by Lena Corwin. Stewart, Tabori & Chang 2013 176 p. illustrations (chiefly color) $29.95 746.6

1. Weaving 2. Handicraft 3. Sewing 4. Knitting 5. Textile crafts 6. Dyes and dyeing 7. Textile printing
ISBN 1617690597; 9781617690594

LC 2013010186

Author Lean Corwin "re-creates and builds upon her popular workshop series in order to reach crafters in Brooklyn and beyond. For this "best of" collection, she has chosen expert teachers and her favorite projects: Jenny Gordy introduces us to knitted socks and elegantly sewn tops and dresses; Cal Patch teaches how to make a modern embroidery sampler as well as a braided rag rug; and Corwin herself presents her favorite screen-printing." (Publisher's note)

Swearington, Jen

Printing on fabric; techniques with screens, stencils, inks, & dyes. Jen Swearington. 1st ed. Lark Crafts 2013 160 p. (paperback) $21.95   746.6

1. Textile design 2. Textile printing
ISBN 1454703946; 9781454703945

LC 2012006729

This book, by Jen Swearington, offers "an essential and accessible guide to printing by hand on fabric. She starts by explaining how to translate design ideas into prints, from single motifs to repeating patterns. Jen then goes on to cover various methods of transfer: stencils, photo emulsion, dye baths, bleach resists, and more." (Publisher's note)

746.7 Rugs

Denny, Walter B.

How to read Islamic carpets; Walter B. Denny. Metropolitan Museum of Art/Yale University Press 2014 143 p. color illustrations (How to read series) $25   746.7
1. Islamic art 2. Rugs and carpets 3. Islamic rugs -- History 4. Islamic rugs -- Technique 5. Metropolitan Museum of Art (New York, N.Y.) 6. Islamic rugs -- New York (State) -- New York
ISBN 030020809X; 9780300208092 (Yale University Press); 9781588395405 (The Metropolitan Museum of Art)

LC 2014035553

This book, by Walter B. Denny, part of the "How to read" series, "explores the history, design techniques, materials, craftsmanship, and socioeconomic contexts of these . . . [Islamic carpets], promoting a better understanding and appreciation of these frequently misunderstood pieces. Fifty-five examples . . . are illustrated with new photographs and revealing details." (Publisher's note)

"This slim, affordable book is highly recommended to both public and academic libraries of all sizes with collections on art, art history, or textile arts." LJ

Includes bibliographical references

Tiede, Karen

Knitting fabric rugs; 28 colorful designs for crafters of every level. Karen Tiede. Storey Publishing 2015 184 p. color illustrations (pbk. : alk. paper) $18.95   746.7
1. Knitting 2. Rugs and carpets 3. Rugs 4. Knitting -- Patterns
ISBN 1612124488; 9781612124483

LC 2015008211

Author Karen Tiede "gives you directions for making 28 different rugs, with designs that use age-old motifs, including stripes and spirals; traditional quilt patterns, such as tessellations and log cabin designs; and freeform inventions. She shows how to create a wide range of color modulations, as well as different shapes, from rectangles to circles." (Publisher's note)

"Tiede tries to take a "knitting curmudgeon" approach à la Elizabeth Zimmerman, but unlike Zimmerman, Tiede's tone can be off-puttingly grumpy, especially when she complains about her dislike of particular colors or the physical pain that cutting and knitting with recycled fabric causes her. Still, green crafts are popular, and Tiede's techniques are tried and true, so ecoconscious knitters may be drawn in." LJ

746.9 Other textile products

Faerm, Steven

Fashion: design course. Barron's 2010 144p il pa $23.99   746.9
1. Fashion design
ISBN 978-0-7641-4423-3

LC 2009-940543

The author "takes readers through a thorough exploration of the fashion industry, from history to inspiration to the design process to landing a job. There are also 14 practical assignments to help budding designers learn more about the industry. Teens exploring careers in fashion will enjoy the practical advice from industry insiders, and fashion-mad readers of all ages will appreciate the information about how fashion design works." Libr J

Givhan, Robin

The Battle of Versailles; the night American fashion stumbled into the spotlight and made history. Robin Givhan. Flatiron Books 2015 320 p. illustrations (some color) (hardback) $27.99   746.9
1. Fashion shows 2. Social change 3. Château de Versailles (Versailles, France) 4. Fashion merchandising -- Social aspects 5. Fashion shows -- France -- Versailles -- History 6. Fashion merchandising -- United States -- History
ISBN 1250052904; 9781250052902; 9781250053855

LC 2014040369

This book, by Robin Givhan, tells how, "Conceived as a fund-raiser for the restoration of King Louis XIV's palace, in the late fall of 1973, five top American designers faced off against five top French designers in an over-the-top runway extravaganza. . . . By the end of the evening, the Americans had officially taken their place on the world's stage, prompting a major shift in the way race, gender, sexuality, and economics would be treated in fashion for decades to come." (Publisher's note)

"Readers need not be fashion mavens to enjoy this entertaining episode of history, enhanced by Givhan's effortless ability to illustrate the models and designers (particularly Lambert) who changed how we dress." Kirkus

Grumbach, Didier

History of international fashion; Didier Grumbach; photo editor Isabelle d'Hauteville. Interlink Books, an imprint of Interlink Publishing Group, Inc. 2014 462 p. illustrations (chiefly color) $45 746.9
1. Fashion design 2. Fashion designers 3. Fashion -- History 4. Fashion design -- History 5. Fashion -- France -- History -- 20th century 6. Fashion design -- France -- History -- 20th century
ISBN 1566569761; 9781566569767

LC 2014004755

In this book, author "Didier Grumbach walks you down the runways of fashion history and unfolds the secrets of the industry with stories and accounts from those who have played an active part in its development from the 1920s to the present. . . . The heroes are Dior, Saint Laurent, Kenzo, Sonia Rykiel, Prada, Hermès, and others. Their adventures are presented in an innovative chronological--and logical--order." (Publisher's note)

"Much of this is channeled through Grumbach's own extensive experiences, beginning with his family's textile company, where he strove "to create ready-to-wear that had the same quality manufacturing as haute couture." Grumbach concludes with a shrewd look at today's globalized fashion industry. Just like the best designer clothes, this exposé is both dazzling and enduring." Booklist

Includes bibliographical references (pages 436-437) and index

Lowit, Roxanne
Yves Saint Laurent; Roxanne Lowit. Thames & Hudson 2014 208 p. illustrations (some colour) (hardcover) $50 **746.9**
1. Fashion designers
ISBN 0500517606; 9780500517604
LC 2014930896
This biography is author "Roxanne Lowit's personal photographic history of [Yves] Saint Laurent, the man and the fashion, from 1978, the year she first met him, to the last show he gave in 2002. With contributions from YSL's muses and admirers, including Catherine Deneuve, Betty Catroux, Lucie de la Falaise, Pat Cleveland, and Valerie Steele, this book represents the backstage experience at YSL's shows as Lowit experienced them herself." (Publisher's note)

The **Mood** guide to fabric and fashion; the essential guide from the world's most famous fabric store. Harry N Abrams Inc 2015 184 p. illustrations (chiefly color) $27.50 **746.9**
1. Fabrics 2. Fashion
ISBN 1617690880; 9781617690884
LC 2014959131
This book is a "guide for home-sewers, fashion students, aspiring designers, and Project Runway fans who want to learn everything they need to know to choose and use quality fabric. Drawing upon the expertise of the Mood staff, the book teaches readers the fundamentals—from where fabric is produced to the ins and outs of its construction—and features a fabric-by-fabric guide to cottons and other plant fibers, wools, silks, knits, and other specialty fabrics." (Publisher's note)

"A pleasingly presented layperson's introduction to the world of fashion fabrics. The name recognition will be a big draw." LJ

Schuman, Emily
Cupcakes and cashmere at home; Emily Schuman. Abrams Image 2015 175 p. color illustrations $19.95 **746.9**
1. Entertaining 2. Interior design
ISBN 1419715836; 9781419715839
LC 2014942738
In this book, author Emily Schuman "expands on the personal lifestyle advice that her fans loved in her first book and on her popular blog, with a focus on interior design and entertaining at home. The book features never-before-seen content and explores Emily's accessible design philosophy for decorating and creating a fashionable personal space. In addition, the book includes DIY design projects and party planning ideas." (Publisher's note)

746.92   Costume

Linett, Andrea
The **cool** factor; Andrea Linett. Artisan 2016 208 p. color illustrations $24.95 **746.92**
1. Fashion 2. Women's clothing 3. Womens' clothing
ISBN 9781579656485
LC 2015034242
This book, by stylist Andrea Linett, "offers easy-to-implement, actionable tips that will change the way women dress. The tips are modeled by real-life style icons like Kim Gordon of Sonic Youth and Christene Barberich, founder of Refinery29, as Andrea highlights the ingenious ways in which they skillfully pile on layers, or dress up denim for work or a party." (Publisher's note)

"There's at least one tip or rule-busting—potentially game-changing—suggestion for any woman looking to cultivate a coherent wardrobe and unique style by using her eyes, judgment, and Linett's six principles." Pub Wkly

Moses, Susan
The **art** of dressing curves; the best-kept secrets of a fashion stylist. Susan Moses. Harper Design Intl 2016 254 p. illustrations (some color) (hardcover) $35 **746.92**
1. Fashion 2. Women's clothing
ISBN 9780062362032; 0062362038
LC 2014937017
In this book, author Susan Moses, "the go-to celebrity stylist for curvy women both on and off the red carpet presents the first inspirational, confidence-building, prescriptive style guide for plus-size women who want to dress fashionably and look their beautiful best. . . . [The author] gives plus-size women the confidence and know-how to dress beautifully for their particular body shape." (Publisher's note)

Includes bibliographical references (pages 248-251).

747   Interior decoration

Becker, Holly
Decorate; 1,000 professional design ideas for every room in your home. Holly Becker & Joanna Copestick; photographs by Debi Treloar. Chronicle Books 2011 288 p. color illustrations $35 **747**
1. Interior design 2. Decoration and ornament 3. Interior decoration
ISBN 0811877892; 9780811877893
LC 2010048053
In this book by Holly Becker and Joanna Copestick "the world's top designers and leading decor experts including Kelly Wearstler, Amy Butler, Jonathan Adler, and many others come together to share over 1,000 professional tips, ideas, and solutions for every room and every budget." (Publisher's note)

1,000 professional design ideas for every room in your home

One thousand professional design ideas for every room in your home

Blair, Gabrielle Stanley

Design mom; how to live with kids: a room-by-room guide. Gabrielle Stanley Blair. Artisan Books 2015 288 p. color illustrations $29.95   **747**

1. Family life 2. Interior design 3. Families 4. Interior decoration 5. Interior decoration -- Human factors

ISBN 1579655718; 9781579655716

LC 2014038734

In this design book, mom Gabrielle Stanley Blair "offers a room-by-room guide to keeping things sane, organized, creative, and stylish. She provides advice on getting the most out of even the smallest spaces; simple fixes that make it easy for little ones to help out around the house; ingenious storage solutions for the never-ending stream of kid stuff; rainy-day DIY projects; and much, much more." (Publisher's note)

"Blair even finds a way to keep mass-marketed character decor out of a child's bedroom by substituting NASA photos for Buzz Lightyear pinups. This is a happy marriage of interior design book and parenting guide." Pub Wkly

Includes bibliographical references and index

Blakeney, Justina

The **new** Bohemians; cool and collected homes. Justina Blakeney. Stewart, Tabori & Chang 2015 304 p. color illustrations $35   **747**

ISBN 1617691518; 9781617691515

LC 2014942982

In this book, author "Justina Blakeney defines the New Bohemians as creative individuals who are boutique owners and bloggers, entrepreneurs and ex-pats, artists and urban farmers. [It] explores 20 homes located primarily on the East and West coasts. Exclusive interviews with the owners, 12 DIY projects created by Blakeney and inspired by objects found in the homes, and a 'Plant-O-Pedia' offer insight into achieving this aesthetic." (Publisher's note)

"The youthful exuberance shown in these interiors will encourage amateurs to discover their own bohemian style." LJ

Bonney, Grace

Design*Sponge at home; Grace Bonney. Artisan 2011 ix, 390 p.p color illustrations $35   **747**

1. Interior design 2. Decoration and ornament 3. Interior decoration -- Amateurs' manuals

ISBN 1579654312; 9781579654313

LC 2010039458

Author Grace Bonney presents a "guide, which includes: Home tours of 70 real-life interiors featuring artists and designers . . .Fifty DIY projects, with detailed instructions for personalizing your space . . . Step-by-step tutorials on everything from stripping and painting furniture to hanging wallpaper and doing your own upholstery . . .[and] Fifty Before & After makeovers." (Publisher's note)

"A highly recommended compendium of ideas to inspire amateur decorators." LJ

Includes bibliographical references (p. 372-379) index

Borsics, Angelin

Styled; secrets for arranging rooms, from tabletops to bookshelves. Emily Henderson, with Angelin Borsics; photographs by David Tsay. Potter Style 2015 304 p. color illustrations $32.50   **747**

1. Interior design 2. Interior decoration -- Handbooks, manuals, etc

ISBN 0804186278; 9780804186278; 9780804186285

LC 2014045185

This book, by Emily Henderson, is a "guide to thinking like a stylist, with 1,000 design ideas for creating the most beautiful, personal, and livable rooms. . . . From editing out what you don't love to repurposing what you can't live without to arranging the most eye-catching vignettes on any surface, you'll learn how to make your own style magic." (Publisher's note)

Bradbury, Dominic

The **iconic** interior; private spaces of leading artists, architects, and designers. Dominic Bradbury; with photographs by Richard Powers. Abrams Books 2012 351 p. (alk. paper) $65   **747**

1. Interior design 2. Domestic architecture 3. Interior decoration -- History -- 20th century -- Themes, motives 4. Interior decoration -- History -- 21st century -- Themes, motives

ISBN 1617690058; 9781617690051

LC 2012007221

In this book, author Dominic Bradbury "visits homes whose interiors 'sum up a design movement or define a particular style' of 20th-century interior design. Descriptions of the homes, located primarily in the United States and Europe, include text, color photographs . . . , and a brief biography of the resident or designer. The inhabitants, including Alvar Aalto, Billy Baldwin, Donna Karan, Todd Oldham, and Russel Wright, represent the epitome of 20th-century design and style." (Library Journal)

Includes bibliographical references and index

Brown, Amanda

★ **Spruce**; a step-by-step guide to upholstery and design. by Amanda Brown. Storey Publishing 2013 400 p. ill. (chiefly col.) (hardcover : alkaline paper) $35   **747**

1. Upholstery

ISBN 1612121373; 9781612121376

LC 2013012590

This book, by Amanda Brown, "is the only book you'll need to learn the craft and art of upholstery from start to finish. With clear instructions illustrated by more than 900 step-by-step photographs, the five projects included here are designed to teach all of the techniques and skills you need to reupholster any piece of furniture to suit your own taste and style." (Publisher's note)

"[P]erfectly matches complete, precisely written directions with correspondingly crisp, helpful photographs." Booklist

Includes bibliographical references and index

Carlson, Julie

Remodelista; a manual for the considered home. Julie Carlson with the editors of Remodelista. Artisan 2013 400 p. color illustrations $37.50   **747**

1. Interior design 2. Houses -- Remodeling 3. Dwellings -- Remodeling 4. Interior decoration --

Themes, motives

ISBN 157965536X; 9781579655365

LC 2013006278

This interior decorating book, by Julie Carlson with the editors of Remodelista.com, "has a singular and clearly defined aesthetic: classic pieces trump designs that are trendy and transient, and well-edited spaces take precedence over cluttered environments. . . . [This guide] decodes the secrets to achieving this aesthetic, with in-depth tours and lessons from 12 enviable homes." (Publisher's note)

"An excellent source of inspiration for those interested in renovating their house or just revamping a room." LJ

Chapman, Emma

A **beautiful** mess happy handmade home; a room-by-room guide to painting, crafting, and decorating a cheerful, more inspiring space. Elsie Larson and Emma Chapman. Potter Style 2014 240 p. color illustrations (paperback) $21.99 **747**

1. Handicraft 2. Interior design 3. House furnishings 4. Interior decoration -- Amateurs' manuals

ISBN 0770434053; 9780770434052

LC 2014008902

In this book, authors Elsie Larson and Emma Chapman "overhauled each room in their first homes with DIY projects using family photos, vibrant fabrics, flea-market finds, and affordable furniture. Now, you can learn how to paint, craft, and decorate your way to a happy, bright space with distinct personality. In the same upbeat spirit and modern style found on their blog, you'll find fresh, all-new projects." (Publisher's note)

"In the introduction, the authors instruct readers to identify what features stand out in "favorite spaces" of all kinds, to make lists of how rooms might be used unconventionally (playing cards in a dining room), and to do some soul searching ("Make a list of 100 things about YOU.") The idea is to make home an expression of one's personality, a skill that the authors have clearly mastered." Pub Wkly.

Includes bibliographical references (page 237) and index

Crochet, Treena

Bungalow style; creating classic interiors in your arts and crafts home. Taunton Press 2005 186p il $29.95 **747**

1. Interior design 2. Domestic architecture 3. Houses -- Remodeling

ISBN 978-1-56158-623-3; 1-56158-623-4

LC 2004-9748

This book pictures a "variety of interior details and describes how to add or restore elements that suggest a historic flair while keeping the home comfortable and functional. Common problems such as integrating modern conveniences or gaining needed space are also addressed." Publisher's note

DeGeneres, Ellen, 1958-

Home; Ellen DeGeneres. Grand Central Life & Style 2015 304 p. color illustrations (hardcover) $35 **747**

1. Interior design

ISBN 1455533564; 9781455533558; 9781455533565

LC 2015940081

In this book, comedian Ellen DeGeneres "will, for the first time, share her passion for home design and style. . . . DeGeneres offers a personal look at every room in each of her homes. . . . An added bonus is a look at the homes of her friends and collaborators-some of the finest designers in the country. They share their advice on home design, furnishings, as well as a glimpse at their awe-inspiring rooms." (Publisher's note)

"Written with DeGeneres's typical candor and wit, this book will spark interest with her fans." LJ

Domino: your guide to a stylish home; editors of Domino, Jessica Romm Perez, Shani Silver. Simon & Schuster 2016 224 p. (hardcover) $35; (ebook) $23.99 **747**

1. Interior design 2. Interior decoration

ISBN 1501151878; 9781501151873; 9781501151880

LC 2016031819

This book, by the editors of Domino, is a "guide to discovering your personal style and creating a space you love. . . . [It] provides a trusted filter, using the friendly and authoritative voice of domino to teach readers about attainable, stylish design and how to make it uniquely your own." (Publisher's note)

Gates, Erin

Elements of style; designing a home and a life. Erin T. Gates. Simon & Schuster 2014 318 p. color illustrations (hardback) $35 **747**

1. Interior design 2. Interior decoration

ISBN 1476744874; 9781476744872

LC 2014012101

This book, by Erin T. Gates, "is a uniquely personal and practical decorating guide that shows how designing a home can be an outlet of personal expression and an exercise in self-discovery. Drawing on her ten years of experience in the interior design industry, Erin combines honest design advice and . . . photographs and illustrations with personal essays about the lessons she has learned while designing her own home and her own life—the first being: none of our homes or lives is perfect." (Publisher's note)

Giramonti, Lisa Borgnes

Novel interiors; Lisa Borgnes Giramonti. Potter Style 2014 288 p. color illustrations $35 **747**

1. Literature 2. Interior design 3. Decoration and ornament 4. Interior decoration in literature 5. Interior decoration -- Themes, motives

ISBN 0385345992; 9780385345996

LC 2013036923

In this book, author Lisa Borgnes Giramonti "inspires a new approach to decorating: by teaching us through the lens of worlds we may already know and love. With gorgeous photographs by World of Interiors photographer Ivan Terestchenko, aspirational quotes, and tailored reading lists, Novel Interiors reveals the essence and details of interiors mentioned in great literary works." (Publisher's note)

Gura, Judith

The **guide** to period styles for interiors; Judith Gura. Bloomsbury, Fairchild Books, an imprint of

Bloomsbury Publishing Inc. 2016 xvi, 479 p.p (alk. paper) $90 **747**

1. Interior design -- History 2. Interior decoration -- History

ISBN 9781628924718

LC 2015005290

This book, by Judith Gura, "makes it a snap to identify period styles from the 17th century to the present day. . . . Including examples and analysis on 17th-century Louis XIV through 20th-century Late Modern and each style in between, this new edition is also updated with the latest trends of the 21st century, including computer design, sustainable design, and modern office design." (Publisher's note)

"Sidebars offer information on movements, designers, and styles. Enough here has changed that libraries owning the first edition will want to consider this update." Booklist

Includes bibliographical references and index

Lee, Vinny

Kitchenalia; Furnishing and Equipping Your Kitchen With Flea Market Finds and Period Pieces. by Vinny Lee. Motorbooks Intl 2014 224 p. color illustrations $40 **747**

1. Kitchens 2. Flea markets 3. Interior design

ISBN 1909342491; 9781909342491

This book, by Vinny Lee, "is an inspiring guide to putting together a unique and creative kitchen using reclaimed and reinvented surfaces, furniture, objects and equipment. Period pieces, whether farmhouse furniture, salvaged surfaces, vintage textiles or retro cooking utensils and gadgets, are the antithesis of the mass-produced modern alternatives and have a timeless integrity. Sourcing such items from flea markets and antiques fairs is a unique and rewarding way to kit out a kitchen." (Publisher's note)

"The variety of styles makes this book an inspiring choice for those looking for ideas on decorating kitchens." LJ

Lemieux, Christiane

The **Finer** Things; Timeless Furniture, Textiles, and Details. Christiane Lemieux with Rumaan Alam. Potter Style 2014 416 p. color illustrations $60 **747**

1. Interior design 2. House furnishings 3. Interior decoration

ISBN 0770434290; 9780770434298; 9780770434304

LC 2013047267

In this book, by Christiane Lemieux, "quality matters. Just as a home's foundation should be built to stand the test of time, so, too, should the furniture, objects, and elements of our rooms speak to an enduring sense of beauty and comfort. They should outlast trends and our loving day-to-day use. But how does one recognize quality and judge whether something is well made?" (Publisher's note)

Includes bibliographical references and index.

Moss, Charlotte

Charlotte Moss; garden inspirations. Charlotte Moss. Rizzoli 2015 288 p. color illustrations (hardcover) $50 **747**

1. Gardens 2. Interior design

ISBN 0847844773; 9780847844777

LC 2014956849

In this book, "celebrated interior designer and renowned tastemaker Charlotte Moss turns her eye to the garden as a resource for interiors, entertaining, and good living. Charlotte Moss's greatest muse is the garden, and this book shows the myriad ways the garden provides inspiration every day--indoors and outdoors." (Publisher's note)

Needleman, Deborah

The **book** of decorating; a room-by-room guide to creating a home that makes you happy. Deborah Needleman, Sara Ruffin Costello, & Dara Caponigro. Simon & Schuster 2008 271 p. color illustrations (alk. paper) $32 **747**

1. Interior design 2. Interior decoration -- Handbooks, manuals, etc

ISBN 1416575464; 9781416575467

LC 2008015072

This book, by Deborah Needleman, Sara Ruffin Costello, and Dara Caponigro, "cracks the code to creating a beautiful home, bringing together inspiring rooms, how-to advice and insiders' secrets from today's premier tastemakers in an indispensable style manual. The editors take readers room by room, tapping the best ideas from domino magazine and culling insights from their own experiences." (Publisher's note)

"Different styles are shown for each in plenty of color photographs, with suggested furnishings and advice on how to mix styles. Each chapter concludes with a look at how a Domino staff member has decorated a similar room with a description of her approach to design. Recommended for large public libraries." LJ

Includes bibliographical references (p. 252-263)

The **perfectly** imperfect home; Deborah Needleman. Clarkson Potter 2011 255 p. color illustrations $30 **747**

1. Home economics 2. Interior design 3. Interior decoration

ISBN 0307720136; 9780307720139

LC 2011020194

This book, by Deborah Needleman and illustrated by Virginia Johnson, offers home decoration advice. "Ranging from classics such as 'A Really Good Sofa' and 'Pretty Table Settings' to unusual surprises like 'A Bit of Quirk' and 'Cozifications,' the essential elements of style are treated in witty and wonderfully useful little essays. You'll learn what to look for, whether you are at a flea market or a fancy boutique-- or just mining what you already own." (Publisher's note)

"Books such as Grace Bonney's Design*Sponge at Home and Christiane Lemieux's Undecorate explain how to add a personal touch to decor, while Needleman shows how professionals approach interior design." LJ

New decorating book. John Wiley & Sons 2011 312 p. (paperback) $24.99 **747**

1. Interior design

ISBN 0470887141; 9780470887141

This book on interior design "mix[es] styles for personal expression with an awareness of budget. Organized in two parts, the first section is filled with room-by-room decorating guides and home tours to cover broad sweeps of decorating topics. The second section is organized by integral design topic: color, furniture arrangement, flooring, lighting, etc." (Publisher's note)

Petersik, Sherry

Young house love; 251 ways to paint, craft, update, organize, and show your home some love. Sherry and John Petersik. Artisan 2012 336 p. $25.95 **747**

1. Houses -- Maintenance and repair 2. Housekeeping -- Miscellanea 3. Interior decoration -- Miscellanea 4. Dwellings -- Remodeling -- Miscellanea 5. Dwellings -- Maintenance and repair -- Miscellanea

ISBN 1579654789; 9781579654788

LC 2012009849

This book by Sherry Petersik and John Petersik provides "home design ideas for every style, skill level and budget. . . . Sherry and John are home-improvement enthusiasts primed to pass on a slew of projects, tricks, and techniques to do-it-yourselfers. . . . Learn to trick out a thrift-store mirror, spice up plain old roller shades, 'hack' your Ikea table to create three distinct looks, and so much more." (Publisher's note)

Richardson, Sarah

Sarah style; Sarah Richardson. Gallery Books 2014 352 p. illustrations (hardback) $26 **747**

1. Interior design 2. Life skills -- Handbooks, manuals, etc. 3. Interior decoration -- Canada

ISBN 147678437X; 9781476784373; 9781476784380

LC 2014016081

In this book, author Sarah Richardson "walks you through each room in your home, from the master bedroom to the kids' rooms, to the kitchen, the bathroom, and everywhere in between, showing you how to turn a house into a home--Sarah style. Featuring full-page design spreads with . . . attention to detail, 'Sarah Style' is a cache of creative, unique ideas for transforming your living spaces." (Publisher's note)

"Richardson's descriptions of how she approached the design for each area and the abundance of color photographs will inspire readers to tackle their own interiors." LJ

Spencer, Lara

Flea market fabulous; designing gorgeous rooms with vintage treasures. Lara Spencer. Stewart, Tabori & Chang 2014 182 p. color illustrations $25.95 **747**

1. Flea markets 2. Interior design

ISBN 1617690953; 9781617690952

LC 2013945640

In this book, author Lara Spencer "shows readers that all it takes is planning, shopping know-how, and a little imagination to create beautiful and comfortable homes that reflect their personal style. . . . She identifies the design dilemma; comes up with a decorating plan; makes a mood board for inspiration; compiles a shopping list; scours flea markets for furniture and accessories that fit the bill; restores, repurposes, and reinvents the pieces she finds, giving them new life." (Publisher's note)

Van der Meer, Antonia

Coastal living beach house happy; the joy of living by the water. Antonia van der Meer. Oxmoor

House 2015 224 p. color illustrations (hardcover) $40 **747**

1. Houses 2. Beaches

ISBN 9780848744298; 0848744292

LC 2014953432

This book, by Antonia van der Meer, describes how "with a unique attachment to their homes, coastal dwellers and their homes exude a certain warmth and beauty found nowhere else.. . . . [The author] reveals six routes to the happiness found in beach houses, exposing how the walls and windows, doors and floors, décor and architecture combine to create an atmosphere in which we can breathe easier and be our best." (Publisher's note)

"Whether looking to create an interior for a beachfront cottage or just add a coastal touch to a room, one will find an abundance of inspiring ideas in this book." LJ

747.94 Decorating with color

Studholme, Joa

Farrow & Ball How to Decorate; Joa Studholme and Charlotte Crosby. Octopus Pub Group 2016 256 p. color illustrations $39.99 **747.94**

1. Interior design 2. Decoration and ornament

ISBN 1784720879; 9781784720872 •

This book, by Joa Studholme and Charlotte Crosby, "provides a highly practical and inspirational guide to the successful use of paint and paper in any home, large or small, urban or country. The book brings together the expertise of Joa Studholme and Farrow & Ball's creative team to demystify the nitty-gritty of transforming a home - from deciding which colors work best in a north-facing room to creating accents with paint and making the most of a feature wall." (Publisher's note)

"The wealth of information on topics such as room accessories, color combinations, and even ceilings makes this book an invaluable tool for the novice who feels inspired to give a living space a makeover." Pub Wkly

748.2 Blown, cast, decorated, fashioned, molded, pressed glass

Chihuly; edited by Diane Charbonneau. Montreal Museum of Fine Arts; DelMonico Books, an imprint of Prestel 2013 230 p. illustrations (chiefly color) (Del Monico Books/Prestel) $65 **748.2**

1. Glass sculpture 2. Glass art -- 20th century -- Exhibitions 3. Glass art -- 21st century -- Exhibitions

ISBN 2891923685; 3791353241; 9782891923682; 9783791353241

LC 2012277913

In this book on artist Dale Chihuly, the authors "examine Chihuly's personal and artistic development, working environment and collections, and collaborative working methods, in addition to recognizing Chihuly's important achievements and contributions to craft and art history." Particular focus is given to his studio glass artwork. "Also included are Chihuly's energetic acrylic paintings and innovative burned drawings." (Choice)

The book "covers a rich set of vibrant work inspired predominantly by natural forms and makes the most of its large format. The documentation is superb, the scope is expansive, and the text is expertly presented." LJ

Includes bibliographical references

Ward, Gerald W. R.

Chihuly; through the looking glass. Gerald W.R. Ward. MFA Publications Available through D.A.P. / Distributed Art Publishers 2011 149 p. color illustrations, portraits $50   **748.2**

1. Glass sculpture 2. Site-specific installations (Art) -- Exhibitions 3. Glass art -- United States -- History -- 20th century -- Exhibitions 4. Glass art -- United States -- History -- 21st century -- Exhibitions 5. Glass sculpture -- United States -- History -- 20th century -- Exhibitions 6. Glass sculpture -- United States -- History -- 21st century -- Exhibitions

ISBN 0878467645; 0878467653; 9780878467648; 9780878467655

LC 2010941797

In this book, by Gerald W.R. Ward, "Dale Chihuly has been credited with elevating blown glass from delicate decorative object to groundbreaking fine art. . . . [It] focuses on the artist's pieces and installations in relation to the spaces that generate, shape and surround them." (Publisher's note)

Includes bibliographical references

Through the looking glass

748.5   Stained, painted, leaded, mosaic glass

Rich, Chris

Stained glass basics; techniques & projects. by Chris Rich with Martha Mitchell and Rachel Ward. Sterling 1996 144p il $24.95; pa $14.95   **748.5**

1. Glass painting and staining

ISBN 0-8069-4876-0; 0-8069-4877-9 pa

LC 95-54102

"This book presents the fundamental techniques of working with stained glass and is intended for those getting started in the craft. Excellent color photographs and diagrams show materials and tools, as well as the cutting, assembling, and soldering of glass items. The projects . . . include hanging glass panels, boxes, and lamps." Libr J

Stevenson, Christine

Creative stained glass; modern designs & simple techniques. Christine Kellmann Stevenson. Lark Books 2004 128 p. illustrations (chiefly color) $14.95   **748.5**

1. Glass painting and staining 2. Glass craft

ISBN 1579904874; 1600591329; 9781600591327

LC 2003024958

This book, by Christine Kellmann Stevenson, presents "27 stained-glass projects. . . . More than 70 color photos present the techniques, all worked with easy-to-acquire, modern, and efficient tools. Try two methods of cutting, with or without making a pattern. Use overlays, plating, and patinas to color the finish, creatively combine different techniques, and see how to work with brass and copper came." (Publisher's note)

749   Furniture and accessories

Kistler, Vivian Carli

The **complete** photo guide to framing & displaying artwork; 500 full-color how-to photos. Creative Pub. International 2009 192p il pa $24.99   **749**

1. Picture frames and framing

ISBN 978-1-58923-422-2; 1-58923-422-7

LC 2008-46612

In this guide, the author "teaches the do-it-yourselfer to frame like a pro. Hundreds of photos illustrate conservation matting, working with premade elements or frame-building from scratch, glazing, and hanging." Libr J

Logan, M. David

Mat, mount and frame it yourself. Watson-Guptill 2002 160p il pa $24.95   **749**

1. Decoration and ornament 2. Picture frames and framing

ISBN 0-8230-3038-5

LC 2001-93246

This describes how to mat, mount, and frame art on paper or cloth, how to determine measurements and proportions, select colors, and glaze, install, and hang framed art

"Logan does a great job of explaining everything and supplements the text with attractive photos. . . . There is something here for framers of all skill levels." Libr J

Miller, Judith

Furniture; [world styles from classical to contemporary] [foreword by David Linley] DK Publishing 2005 560p il $60   **749**

1. Furniture

ISBN 0-7566-1340-X

LC 2005-296398

The author "presents a lavish four-color and highly educational book, and the result will never lose its library-patron appeal." Booklist

Includes bibliographical references

749.03   Furniture and accessories—Dictionaries, encyclopedias, concordances

Aronson, Joseph

The **encyclopedia** of furniture; by Joseph Aronson. Crown Publishers 1965 484 p. illustrations $35   **749.03**

1. Furniture

ISBN 0517037351; 9780517037355

LC 65024334

This book on furniture, by Joseph Aronson, "cover[s] every period and development to the present, the designers and makers, the woods and other materials, the architecture and decoration." (Publisher's note)

749.32 Chairs

Rybczynski, Witold

Now I sit me down; Witold Rybczynski. Farrar, Straus & Giroux 2016 256 p. illustrations (hardback) $25 **749.32**
1. Posture 2. Chairs -- History 3. Sitting customs -- History
ISBN 9780374223212

LC 2015041604

This book, by Witold Rybczynski, "chronicles the history of the chair from the folding stools of pharaonic Egypt to the ubiquitous stackable monobloc chairs of today. He tells the stories of the inventor of the bentwood chair, Michael Thonet, and of the creators of the first molded-plywood chair, Charles and Ray Eames. He reveals the history of chairs to be a social history--of different ways of sitting, of changing manners and attitudes, and of varying tastes." (Publisher's note)

"Rybczynski is totally engaging in this smoothly flowing, sharp, witty narrative—another winner from a top-notch writer on design." Kirkus

Includes bibliographical references and index.

751 Techniques, procedures, apparatus, equipment, materials, forms

Ganz, Nicholas

★ **Graffiti** world; street art from five continents. edited by Tristan Manco. Updated ed.; Abrams 2009 391p il $35 **751**
1. Graffiti 2. Street art 3. Mural painting and decoration
ISBN 978-0-8109-8049-5

LC 2009-922509

First published 2004

Ganz's survey of graffiti art includes "upward of 2,000 full-color photographs. . . . An ephemeral, often despised, yet irrefutably powerful mode of expression, graffiti has always been political, and although many of the street artists Ganz succinctly profiles have moved away from illegal spray painting, they have not compromised the inherent subversiveness of their work. . . . Ganz's global array captures the power and synergy of this vibrant alternative art world in which artists form crews and collectiveness to ensure that their art is seen." Booklist [review of 2004 edition]

Includes bibliographical references

751.4 Techniques and procedures

Artist's painting techniques; DK. DK Publishing 2016 304 p. color illustrations (hardcover) $30 **751.4**
1. Painting 2. Acrylic painting 3. Watercolor painting 4. Painting -- Technique
ISBN 1465450955; 9781465450951

LC 2016448564

This book from publisher DK offers a "practical guide to learning how to bring out your inner artist with a wide range of painting styles, whether you want to learn how to use acrylics, watercolors, or oil paints. With progression in mind, this master class will teach you the basic principles of painting and then inspire you to move on to new challenges and create masterpieces of your own. It explains which tools, materials, and methods should be used along the way." (Publisher's note)

"This handbook will be a foundational and popular addition to any art instruction shelf." LJ

Crilley, Mark

The **realism** challenge; drawing and painting secrets from a modern master of hyperrealism. Mark Crilley. Watson-Guptill 2015 160 p. color illustrations (paperback) $19.99 **751.4**
1. Drawing 2. Realism in art 3. Photo-realism 4. Drawing -- Technique 5. Painting -- Technique
ISBN 0385346298; 9780385346290

LC 2014024085

In this book, author "Mark Crilley takes you step-by-step through his process for producing stunning, hyperrealistic recreations of everyday items. Based on Crilley's mega-popular 'Realism Challenge' YouTube videos, The Realism Challenge contains thirty lessons demonstrating how to render mirror-like duplicates in the trompe l'oeil tradition of everything from shells, leaves, and candy bars to your very own still life arrangements." (Publisher's note)

"Those with modest artistic skills can greatly improve their ability to draw and paint realistic objects by following the tips and tricks detailed here." LJ

Includes bibliographical references and index

Marine, Carol

Daily painting; paint small and often to become a more creative, productive, and successful artist. Carol Marine. Watson-Guptill 2014 182 p. illustrations (chiefly color) (paperback) $22.99; (ebook) $65 **751.4**
1. Painting 2. Painting -- Technique
ISBN 0770435335; 9780770435332; 9780770435349

LC 2014009131

This book on painting, by Carol Marine, presents "a unique system for jump-starting artistic creativity, encouraging experimentation and growth, and increasing sales for artists of all levels, from novices to professionals. . . . The idea is simple: do art (usually small) often (how often is up to you), and if you'd like, post and sell it online. Soon you'll find that your block dissolves and you're painting work you love—and more of it than you ever thought possible!" (Publisher's note)

751.42 Use of water-soluble mediums

Kersey, Geoff

Painting successful watercolours from photographs; by Geoff Kersey. Search Press 2015 128 p. color illustrations $24.95 **751.42**
ISBN 1844489981; 9781844489985

This book, by Geoff Kersey, is for painters "who work from photographic source material. . . . Reference photographs, colour charts and preparatory sketches are shown alongside all the finished paintings in this book, with full details of the adaptations and creative processes involved. There are plenty of clear tips and advice, and an illustrated glossary of all the painting terms used." (Publisher's note)

"This guide has solid crossover potential among avid travelers, hobbyist watercolor painters, and amateur photographers." LJ

O'Connor, Birgit

Watercolor essentials; hands-on techniques for exploring watercolor in motion. North Light Books 2009 127p il $29.99   **751.42**
1. Watercolor painting -- Technique
ISBN 978-1-60061-094-3
LC 2008-36576

This guide to watercolor painting covers topics such as types of watercolor paint, painting tools and materials, using color, values, and painting techniques.

"This is an exciting, comprehensive package for the beginning watercolor artist. O'Connor . . . keys her lessons to a 70-minute DVD. Her wet and loose technique and the personal touch of the DVD make this a great choice at a good price." Libr J

751.422   Watercolor painting

Robinson, Mario Andres

Lessons in realistic watercolor; A Contemporary Approach to Painting People and Places in the Classical Tradition. Mario Andres Robinson. The Monacelli Press 2016 176 p. $25   **751.422**
1. Realism in art 2. Watercolor painting -- Technique
ISBN 9781580934459
LC 2015038871

This book, by Mario Andres Robinson, "shows us how to create beautiful, timeless, classical watercolor paintings through the use of simple, yet sophisticated, contemporary techniques every watercolorist needs to know. . . . Robinson simplifies the process and teaches artists to layer colors from light to dark and to focus on the highlighted areas first." (Publisher's note)

"Artists of intermediate skill level are best poised to benefit from these lessons." LJ

751.426   Acrylic painting

Kloosterboer, Lorena

Painting in acrylics; the indispensable guide. Lorena Kloosterboer. Firefly Books 2014 320 p. color illustrations $35   **751.426**
1. Acrylic painting 2. Acrylic painting -- Technique
ISBN 1770854088; 9781770854086
LC 2015472146

This book, by Lorena Kloosterboer, "provides comprehensive guidance for painters of all experience. Realist painter Lorena Kloosterboer, known for her exceptional technical skill, starts with the basics and progresses to advanced techniques and professional practice." (Publisher's note)

751.45   Oil painting

Gorst, Brian

The **complete** oil painter; the essential reference source for beginning to professional artists. Brian Gorst. Watson-Guptill 2003 128 p. color illustrations $24.99   **751.45**
1. Oil painting 2. Painting -- Technique
ISBN 082300855X; 9780823008551
LC 2003103063

This book on oil painting, by Brian Gorst, "is an essential, one-stop guide to becoming an expert in every aspect of this medium. Artists will discover everything they need to know about materials (pigments, supports, canvases); tools and equipment (palettes, brushes); paint application (wet-into-wet, alla-prima, glazing, impasto); form and color (light and dark, expression, color mixing); exploring themes (still life, portraiture, figure painting); and much more." (Publisher's note)

Painting the great masters; Parramon Editorial Team. Barrons Educational Series, Inc. 2014 143 p. color illustrations $24.99   **751.45**
1. Painting -- Technique 2. Art -- Study and teaching
ISBN 1438005490; 9781438005492
LC 2014930732

From the Parramon Editorial Team, "the trade secrets of the great masters are uncovered in this exhaustive study of 14 of the world's most famous paintings. Both amateur and experienced artists will find hundreds of instructional images, detailed explanations, and additional hints and tips that will enable them to make successful copies or interpretations of classic works of art." (Publisher's note)

"Beginning and intermediate artists may enjoy a return to this traditional method of learning through imitation." LJ

Scott, Marilyn

The **Oil** Painter's Bible; A Essential Reference for the Practicing Artist. by Marylin Scott. Book Sales 2005 192 p. illustrations $14.99   **751.45**
1. Oil painting
ISBN 0785819428; 9780785819424

This book, by Marylin Scott, "is a must for anyone who has not used oil paints before, and even those who are familiar with the medium may find some surprises among the range of techniques—and hopefully some new inspiration in the gallery of finished pictures. The book is divided into four main sections: Materials, Color, Techniques, and Subjects. Advanced techniques like glazing, impasto, knife painting, and scumbling will give even the most advanced artists inspiration." (Publisher's note)

Willenbrink, Mark

Oil painting for the absolute beginner; a clear & easy guide to successful oil painting. by Mark and Mary Willenbrink. North Light Books 2010 127p il pa $24.99   **751.45**
1. Painting -- Technique
ISBN 978-1-60061-784-3
LC 2010-5056

"Unlike less successful art books for beginners, this one starts simply and takes the rank amateur to a satisfying level of accomplishment. . . . The accompanying DVD offers useful demonstrations of two complete paintings." Libr J

751.7 Specific forms

Felisbret, Eric
Graffiti New York; Eric Felisbret DEAL CIA; contributions by Luke Felisbret SPAR ONE; foreword by James Prigoff. Abrams 2009 339 p. ill. (chiefly col.) **751.7**
1. Street art 2. Artists -- United States 3. Mural painting and decoration 4. Graffiti -- New York (N.Y.) -- History 5. Graffiti -- New York (State) -- New York 6. Street art -- New York (State) -- New York 7. Mural painting and decoration, American -- New York (State) -- New York
ISBN 0810951460; 9780810951464
LC 2009011736
This book explores the history and influence of New York City as a "mecca of graffiti culture. . . . This is the city where it all began, yet few know the back story. 'Graffiti New York' fills that gap, detailing the concepts, aesthetics, ideals, and social structures that have served as a cultural blueprint for graffiti movements across the world. The book features approximately 1,000 images, complemented by texts by the authors and relevant players in the movement, as well as descriptive graphics and sidebars. [The book describes] . . . the birth of simple signature tags to today's vibrant murals, and covering the ups and downs of the movement, the culture's value system, its social framework, the various forms of graffiti, and significant artists and crews." (Publisher's Note)

759 History, geographic treatment, biography

Bailey, Anthony
Velazquez: surrendering at Breda. Holt 2011 264p il $32; ebook $16.99 **759**
1. Artists 2. Painters 3. Artists, Spanish
ISBN 978-0-8050-8835-9; 978-1-4299-7377-9 ebook
LC 2010049809
The author "uses Velázquez's painting of the 1625 surrender of the Dutch town of Breda to Spanish forces as an entry point into a richly detailed portrait of the court of King Philip IV as Spain's Hapsburg empire crumbled around him." Kirkus
Includes bibliographical references

Baillio, Joseph
Claude Monet, 1840-1926; Paris, Galeries nationales, Grand Palais, September 22, 2010-January 24, 2011. [authors of the catalogue, Joseph Baillio . . . [et al.]] Abrams 2010 384p il $65 **759**
1. Artists 2. Painters 3. Impressionism (Art)
ISBN 978-0-8109-9709-7
"In this splendid retrospective catalog for a show at the Galéries Nationales, Grand Palais in Paris through January 2011, Monet's paintings are presented in philosophical, psychological, physical, and personal context in a series of

concise, thoughtful, informative, and well-translated essays by noted art historians. . . . This book is what a retrospective catalog should be—expansive and precise, looking over a beloved artist's life and work with many color reproductions." Libr J
Includes bibliographical references

Brainard, Joe
The Nancy book; essays by Ann Lauterbach [and] Ron Padgett; collaborations with Bill Berkson . . . [et al.] Siglio Press 2008 144p il **759**
1. Cartoonists 2. Poets 3. Artists 4. Authors 5. Set designers 6. Nancy (Fictitious character)
ISBN 097995620X; 9780979956201
From 1963 to 1978 Joe Brainard created some 100 Nancy comic strips. "The Nancy Book includes 78 full page reproductions . . . and features collaborations with poets Bill Berkson, Ted Berrigan, Robert Creeley, Frank Lima, Frank O'Hara, Ron Padgett, and James Schuyler." (Publisher's note)
"The guileless heroine of Ernie Bushmiller's long-running comic strip 'Nancy' is an unlikely icon in contemporary art, recurring in work by postmodern cartoonists like Bill Griffith and Scott McCloud, in an Andy Warhol painting, and in rock posters by Frank Kozik. But no one put her to better use than Joe Brainard, in whose irreverent, effervescent paintings, drawings, and collages (occasionally produced in collaboration with poet friends like Ron Padgett and Frank O'Hara) Nancy appears as an ashtray; a medical illustration; the subject of pieces by de Kooning, Picasso, and Leonardo; and part of Mt. Rushmore. Updating the old 'Tijuana Bibles,' Brainard also gleefully depicts Nancy in flagrante delicto and tripping on hallucinogens. Brash but never bratty, fanciful without descending into preciousness." New Yorker

Brewer, John
The American Leonardo; a tale of obsession, art and money. Oxford University Press 2009 310p il $24.95 **759**
1. Artists 2. Painters 3. Scientists 4. Art collections 5. Art dealers 6. Art collectors 7. Art -- Expertising 8. Writers on science 9. Patrons of the arts 10. Art -- 15th and 16th centuries 11. Art -- Collectors and collecting 12. Painting, Renaissance -- Expertising
ISBN 978-0-19-539690-4; 0-19-539690-1
LC 2009008681
"In 1919, a Midwestern auto salesman named Harry Hahn and his French war bride, Andrée, got in touch with Joseph Duveen, the famous New York art dealer, with an offer to sell what they claimed was an original painting by Leonardo da Vinci. Duveen publicly dismissed the work as a fake, and the Hahns, taking him to court for slander, began a decades-long struggle for authentication that scrutinized not only the art world's élitism but the validity of connoisseurship itself. Brewer skillfully outlines the conditions that made America ripe for such an incident and explores how Old Master art became the currency with which the country's new millionaires established their cultural credibility." New Yorker
Includes bibliographical references and index

Brown, David Alan

Leonardo da Vinci; origins of a genius. Yale Univ. Press 1998 240p il $65 **759**

1. Artists 2. Painters 3. Scientists 4. Writers on science

ISBN 0-300-07246-5

LC 98-15164

The author traces the "early influences and the emergence of da Vinci's intense curiosity about nature and ability to re-create it in drawing and painting. The chapter on 'Ginevra de' Benci' is a splendid example of how art history and contemporary scientific techniques can be combined in the examination and attribution of a painting. The excellent full page reproductions and small detail examples are carefully placed within the text for ease of reference." Libr J

Includes bibliographical references

Kelder, Diane

The **great** book of French impressionism; 2nd Abbeville ed; Abbeville Press 2001 400p il $85 **759**

1. French painting 2. Impressionism (Art)

ISBN 978-0-7892-0688-6; 0-7892-0688-9

LC 2001-266313

First published 1980

This book "traces the development of Impressionism from its roots in landscape and Realist painting through its focus on modern urban life. . . . The works of the major Impressionists and Post Impressionists, Manet, Monet, Renoir, Degas, Toulouse-Lautrec, Seurat, and Cezanne, are featured." Publisher's note

Includes bibliographical references

King, Ross

The **judgment** of Paris; the revolutionary decade that gave the world impressionism. Walker 2006 448p il $28 **759**

1. Artists 2. Painters 3. Sculptors 4. French art 5. Illustrators 6. Impressionism (Art)

ISBN 0-8027-1466-8

LC 2005-31089

"The book serves as an entertaining if broad account of a revolutionary transformation in vision—not least of all through art." Libr J

Includes bibliographical references

★ **Leonardo** and the Last supper; Ross King. Walker & Company 2012 352 p. $28.00 **759**

1. Religious art 2. Art -- History 3. Last Supper in art 4. Italy -- Politics and government -- 1268-1559

ISBN 0802717055; 9780802717054

LC 2012005358

This book presents an account "of the political situation in 15th-century Italy and how it informs our understanding of [Leonardo da Vinci's] 'The Last Supper' . . . interspersed with analysis of history's many interpretations of the painting. . . . The book addresses such topics as the groupings of the apostles and their hand placement; readings of the painting as glorifying faith; and whether the figure next to Jesus depicts the apostle John or Mary Magdalene." (Publishers Weekly)

Michelangelo & the Pope's ceiling. Walker & Co. 2002 371p il hardcover o.p. pa $15 **759**

1. Artists 2. Painters 3. Sculptors 4. Architects 5. Mural painting and decoration 6. Italy -- History -- 0-1559 7. Vatican -- Cappella Sistina

ISBN 0-8027-1395-5; 0-14-200369-7 pa

LC 2002-38074

"This engaging narrative sets the record straight on a few points and is highly recommended for most public library collections." Libr J

Includes bibliographical references

Leal, Brigitte

The **ultimate** Picasso; {by} Brigitte Léal, Christine Piot, Marie-Laure Bernadac; preface by Jean Leymarie. Abrams 2000 535p il hardcover o.p. pa $ **759**

1. Artists 2. Painters

ISBN 0-8109-9114-4 pa

These "essays detail events in Picasso's life and the circumstances surrounding the creation of his art, his influences, and world events. This lavish, handsome book contains more than 1200 reproductions, nearly 800 in full color." SLJ

Includes bibliographical references

National Gallery of Art (U.S.)

Edouard Vuillard; [by] Guy Cogeval with Kimberly Jones [et al.] National Gallery of Art, in association with Yale University Press 2003 501p il $70 **759**

1. Artists 2. Painters

ISBN 0-300-09737-9

LC 2002-151120

"A superb display of the surprising colors, forceful textures, and mysterious atmosphere of Vuillard's paintings, accompanied by commentaries in which aesthetics, art history, and biography are perfectly balanced." Booklist

Includes bibliographical references

Robb, Peter

M: the man who became Caravaggio. Holt & Co. 2000 570p il pa $20 **759**

1. Artists 2. Painters 3. Artists, Italian

ISBN 0-8050-6356-0; 978-0-312-27474-0 pa; 0-312-27474-2 pa

LC 99-43576

First published 1998 in Australia

The author examines the life and work of the Italian painter

Robb's "mettlesome assertions regarding M's ruthlessness, 'hairtriggered touchiness,' resiliency, and homosexuality, as well as his confident theories regarding his crimes and punishments, make for great narrative vitality and drama." Booklist

Includes bibliographical references

Roe, Sue

The **private** lives of the impressionists. Harper-Collins Publishers 2006 356p il map $29.95 **759**

1. Artists, French 2. Impressionism (Art)

ISBN 0-06-054558-5; 978-0-06-054558-1

LC 2006-43621

This is a "group portrait of the revolutionary artists dubbed the impressionists for their atmospheric landscapes and forthright depictions of everyday life. Here, masterfully set against a panoramic rendering of their turbulent times, are Manet, Pissarro, Degas, Monet, Renoir, Cezanne, Sisley, Morisot, and Cassatt, each incisively defined as an individual and in terms of their complex interactions as they devoted themselves to paintings that met only with derision." Booklist

Includes bibliographical references

Sassoon, Donald

Becoming Mona Lisa; the making of a global icon. Harcourt 2001 337p il $30; pa $16 **759**

1. Artists 2. Painters 3. Scientists 4. Writers on science

ISBN 0-15-100828-0; 0-15-602711-9 pa

LC 2001-24956

This is a history of Leonardo's most famous portrait and its meanings and popularization in the centuries since it was painted

"Sassoon's knowledge of the minutiae of history and his respect for the image drive the narrative. . . . {This work is} thoroughly researched and highly readable." Libr J

Includes bibliographical references

Scotti, R. A.

Vanished smile; the mysterious theft of Mona Lisa. Knopf 2009 241p il map $24.95 **759**

1. Artists 2. Painters 3. Art thefts 4. Scientists 5. Writers on science

ISBN 978-0-307-26580-7; 0-307-26580-3

LC 2008-47851

The author reports on the "1911 theft of Mona Lisa. The lovely woman with the enigmatic smile was simply lifted off the wall and spirited away. The scandal was immense, the investigation feverish, the headlines screaming, and Scotti revels in every turn. Her lively, expert coverage encompasses the fascinating, many-chaptered story of Mona Lisa and ironic revelations about the frenzy among America's robber barons for old masters and the corresponding renaissance in art fraud. . . . Scotti's avid, exciting true-life mystery yields intriguing disclosures and reaffirms Mona Lisa's unique powers." Booklist

759.06 Painting -- 1900-1999

Godfrey, Tony

Painting today. Phaidon Press 2009 448p il $75 **759.06**

1. Painting -- 20th century 2. Painting -- 21st century

ISBN 978-0-7148-4631-6

"Weighing in at over ten pounds, the book is overflowing with gorgeous full-page reproductions of paintings sprinkled with Godfrey's smartly organized commentary. . . . The most

exciting part of the book is how the image placement creates a rowdy dialogue between paintings. If this book could talk, it would roar like a raging party in an echoing art museum." KQED

759.13 United States

Biel, Steven

American Gothic; a life of America's most famous painting. W.W. Norton & Co. 2005 215p il $21.95; pa $13.95 **759.13**

1. Artists 2. Painters

ISBN 0-393-05912-X; 0-393-32855-4 pa

LC 2005-4726

"In this ingenious gem of a book, Stephen Biel . . . weaves together a rich cultural history of this unforgettable picture and asks why it has become, for better or for worse, America's most popular painting." Economist

Includes bibliographical references

Carter, Alice A.

The **Red** Rose girls; an uncommon story of art and love. Abrams 2000 216p il hardcover o.p. pa $19.95 **759.13**

1. Artists 2. Painters 3. Illustrators

ISBN 0-8109-9068-7 pa

LC 99-39866

"Three of the first American women artists to achieve fame and fortune in the Victorian era—Jessie Willcox Smith, Elizabeth Shippen Green and Violet Oakley—lived unconventional lives marked by a remarkable degree of collaboration. In this . . . study, Carter explores the trio's internecine artistic and romantic relations." Publ Wkly

Includes bibliographical references

Cikovsky, Nicolai

Winslow Homer; {by} Nicolai Cikovsky, Jr., Franklin Kelly; with contributions by Judith Walsh and Charles Brock. National Gallery of Art 1995 420p il $80 **759.13**

1. Artists 2. Painters

ISBN 0-300-06555-8 Yale Univ. Press

LC 95-19025

In this catalog of the American artist's retrospective exhibition, the contributors "present a contextually rich and vibrant analysis of Homer's life and groundbreaking work." Booklist

Includes bibliographical references

Cohen-Solal, Annie

Mark Rothko; toward the light in the chapel. Annie Cohen-Solal. Yale University Press 2015 296 p. 8 plates; color illustrations (Jewish lives) (hardback) $25 **759.13**

1. Painters 2. Jewish men 3. Painters -- United States -- Biography

ISBN 030018204X; 9780300182040

LC 2014037767

Author Annie Cohen-Solal's biography on Mark Rothko, "based on considerable archival research, tells the unlikely story of how a young immigrant from Dvinsk became a crucial transforming agent of the art world. His integration into American society began with a series of painful experiences, especially as a student at Yale, where he felt marginalized for his origins and ultimately left the school. The decision to become an artist led him to a new phase in his life." (Publisher's note)

"A defining and affecting tribute to a modern master." Booklist

Includes bibliographical references and index

Elderfield, John

De Kooning: a retrospective; [by] John Elderfield; with Lauren Mahoney [et al.]; edited by David Frankel. Museum of Modern Art 2011 504p il $75   **759.13**
1. Artists 2. Painters
ISBN 978-0-87070-797-1

"A superlative exhibition. (Its catalogue is equally fantastic.)." ARTINFO

Includes bibliographical references

Fortune, Brandon Brame

Elaine de kooning; portaits. Brandon Brame Fortune, Ann Eden Gibson, Simona Cupic. DelMonico Books - Prestel 2015 160 p. illustrations, color portraits $49.95   **759.13**
1. Painters -- Biography
ISBN 3791354388; 9783791354385

LC 2014958601

This book, by Brandon Brame Fortune, "explores the portraiture of Elaine de Kooning. . . . John F. Kennedy, Frank O'Hara, Allen Ginsberg, Merce Cunningham, and Fairfield Porter were just some of the figures who sat for portraits by Elaine de Kooning. Famous for her marriage to the Abstract Expressionist Willem de Kooning, Elaine was herself a groundbreaking artist and writer who challenged many conventions during her career." (Publisher's note)

"Fortune reveals how de Kooning "simultaneously transgressed and upheld" gender stereotyping with a sensibility to the "masculine" abstract expressionist painterly style that retained a vital naturalism, which was her key contribution to the movement. Summing Up: Recommended. All readership levels." Choice

Gerdts, William H.

American impressionism; William H. Gerdts. 2nd ed; Abbeville Press 2001 368p il $85 **759.13**
1. American art 2. Impressionism (Art)
ISBN 978-0-7892-0737-1; 0-7892-0737-0

LC 2001-22419

First published 1984

"The best general source available on American Impressionism. . . . [The] book covers the major artists in the movement, including expatriates working in Europe and regional schools throughout the United States during the late 19th and early 20th centuries. . . .The well-chosen illustrations include many full-page color reproductions as well as photographs of many of the artists." Libr J

Includes bibliographical references

Hennessey, Maureen Hart

Norman Rockwell; pictures for the American people. [by] Maureen Hart Hennessey and Ann Knutson. Abrams 1999 199p il $35   **759.13**
1. Artists 3. Painters 3. Illustrators
ISBN 0-8109-6392-2

LC 99-73071

A catalogue of a traveling exhibition of Rockwell's work. "Colorplates reproduce Rockwell's paintings in detail, and the essays set them in fresh contexts, discussing such themes as Rockwell's urban scenes; the reaction by both black and white Southerners to Rockwell's historic civil rights painting The Problem We All Live With; and Rockwell's role in the development of American illustration." Publisher's note

Includes bibliographical references

Kamensky, Jane

A revolution in color; The World of John Singleton Copley. Jane Kamensky. W W Norton & Co Inc 2016 480 p. illustrations (hardcover) $35 **759.13**
1. Artists -- United States -- Biography 2. United States -- History -- 1775-1783, Revolution 3. American loyalists -- Biography 4. Painters -- United States -- Biography 5. United States -- History -- Revolution, 1775-1783 -- Biography 6. United States -- History -- Revolution, 1775-1783 -- Social aspects
ISBN 9780393240016

LC 2016019022

This book by Jane Kamensky offers a biography of Boston-born painter John Singleton Copley, whose "brush captured the faces of his neighbors—ordinary men like Paul Revere, John Hancock, and Samuel Adams—who would become the revolutionary heroes of a new United States. . . . The artist, however, did not share his subjects' politics. Copley's nation was Britain; his capital, London. . . . He painted America's revolution from a far shore, as Britain's American War." (Publisher's note)

"There may never be a better biography of Copley than this sumptuous, exquisitely told story of a man and his time." Kirkus

Includes bibliographical references and index

Livingston, Jane

The paintings of Joan Mitchell; with essays by Linda Nochlin, Yvette Lee. University of Calif. Press 2002 237p il $65; pa $35   **759.13**
1. Artists 2. Painters
ISBN 0-520-23568-1; 0-520-23570-3 pa

LC 2001-58514

This is a "vivid portrait of the artist. . . . Mitchell's compositions {are} gorgeously reproduced here in vibrant color." Booklist

Includes bibliographical references

Mathews, Nancy Mowll

Mary Cassatt; a life. Yale Univ. Press 1998 383p il pa $21   **759.13**
1. Artists 2. Painters 3. Artists -- United States
ISBN 0-300-07754-8

LC 98-8028

First published 1994 by Villard Bks.

This "is an evenly written, well-documented, and sympathetic—but not patronizing—biography that should be acquired by most libraries." Libr J

Includes bibliographical references

Philadelphia Museum of Art

Thomas Eakins; organized by Darrel Sewell with essays by Kathleen A. Foster {et al.}; chronology by Kathleen Brown. Yale Univ. Press 2001 xli, 446p il $75 **759.13**

1. Artists 2. Painters 3. Sculptors 4. Art teachers
ISBN 0-300-09111-7

LC 2001-53142

"This enormous volume accompanies the largest retrospective of {Eakins' work}. . . . {It} includes some 120 photographs as well as examples of his work in watercolor, drawing, and sculpture. . . . Several lengthy and interesting biocritical essays, themselves making up 175 pages of text, separate four sections of color plates. This is clearly the definitive monograph on one of the most significant artists America has produced." Libr J

Includes bibliographical references

Staiti, Paul

Of Arms and Artists; The American Revolution Through Painters' Eyes. Paul Staiti. St. Martin's Press 2016 400 p. (hardcover) $30 **759.13**

1. Artists -- United States 2. United States -- History -- 1775-1783, Revolution
ISBN 9781632864659; 1632864657

LC 2016007703

This book by Paul Staiti reveals that "the lives of the five great American artists of the Revolutionary period--Charles Willson Peale, John Singleton Copley, John Trumbull, Benjamin West, and Gilbert Stuart--were every bit as eventful as those of the Founders with whom they continually interacted. . . . The collective stories of these five artists open a fresh window on the Revolutionary era, making more human the figures we have long honored as our Founders." (Publisher's note)

"Throughout, Staiti provides insightful, in-depth discussions of many key paintings, and the book is lavishly illustrated with illustrations and color plates. A lively, splendid history that captures the times with insight, acumen, and a juggler's finesse." Kirkus

Includes bibliographical references and index.

Vaill, Amanda

Everybody was so young; Gerald and Sara Murphy, a lost generation love story. Broadway Bks. 1999 470p il pa $16.95 **759.13**

1. Artists 2. Painters 3. Patrons of the arts 4. Artists -- United States 5. Spouses of prominent persons
ISBN 0-7679-0370-6; 978-0-7679-0370-7

LC 99-10416

First published 1998 by Houghton Mifflin

"Often considered minor Lost Generation celebrities, the Murphys were in fact much more than legendary party givers. Vaill's compelling biography unveils their role in the European avant-garde movement of the 1920s." Libr J

Includes bibliographical references

Wilton, Andrew

American sublime; landscape painting in the United States, 1820-1880. {by} Andrew Wilton & Tim Barringer. Princeton Univ. Press 2002 284p il $49.95; pa $35 **759.13**

1. American painting 2. Landscape painting
ISBN 0-691-09670-8; 0-691-11556-7 pa

"Wilton, of the Tate Gallery, considers the influence of Edmund Burke's theory of sublimity and the surge in scientific development on American painters, while Barringer . . . discusses the profound effect on the painters' imaginations of a pristine land free of Western religious, literary, and historical associations. . . . Wilton and Barringer's commentary is stimulating and important, and the exceptional plates are bliss unadulterated." Booklist

Includes bibliographical references

759.2   European painting

Asleson, Robyn

Albert Moore. Phaidon Press 2000 240p il hardcover o.p. pa $29.95 **759.2**

1. Artists 2. Painters
ISBN 0-7148-3846-2; 978-0-7148-4392-6 pa; 0-7148-4392-X pa

LC 00-421386

"This book focuses on the artist's interaction with the Victorian art world as well as his formal pictorial concerns. . . . In addition, the author looks at the politics of Victorian art institutions. This is an excellent book filled with gorgeous color reproductions. Recommended for general collections as well as libraries that support art programs." Libr J

Includes bibliographical references

Peppiatt, Michael

Francis Bacon in Your Blood; A Memoir. Michael Peppiatt. St. Martin's Press 2015 416 p. $28 **759.2**

1. Artists
ISBN 1632863448; 9781632863447

This memoir by author Michael Peppiatt "has a different vigor, revealing the artist [Francis Bacon] at his most intimate and indiscreet, and his London and Paris milieus in all their seediness and splendor. Bacon is felt with immediacy, as Peppiatt draws from contemporary diaries and records of their time together, giving us the story of a friendship, and a new perspective on an artist of enduring fascination." (Publisher's note)

"Even if true to life, this unfiltered discourse does not make for the best reading. Similarly, too much of the narrative consists of avid dining and drinking with the artist, which is repetitive and only interesting to a point. Still, Peppiatt's book emerges as a credible document of a life spent under the heady influence of a tremendous talent and personality." Pub Wkly

759.36   Austrian painting

O'Connor, Anne-Marie

The **lady** in gold; the extraordinary tale of Gustav Klimt's masterpiece, Portrait of Adele Bloch-Bauer. by Anne-Marie O'Connor. Knopf 2012 349 p.   **759.36**

1. Jews -- Austria 2. Portrait painting 3. Vienna (Austria) -- History

ISBN 9780307265647

LC 2011033578

This book explores "one of Gustav Klimt's most celebrated paintings. . . . [Anne-Marie] O'Connor traces the multifaceted history of Portrait of Adele Bloch-Bauer (1907). . . . The [book] . . . evokes the intellectually precocious and ambitious Adele's rich cultural and social milieu in Vienna, and how she became entwined with the charismatic, sexually charged, and irreverent Klimt, who may have been Adele's lover before and also during her marriage. During WWII, Adele's portrait was renamed by the Nazis as the Dame in Gold to erase her Jewish identity. O'Connor's final arguments about the tragic yet redemptive symbolism of Adele's portrait . . . while it represents the failure of the dream of Jews like Adele to assimilate, through the painting she achieves "her dream of immortality."" (Publishers Weekly)

Includes bibliographical references and index.

759.4   French painting

Bocquet, José-Louis

Kiki de Montparnasse; Catel & Bocquet; [translated from the Belgian edition by Nora Mahony] SelfMadeHero 2011 416 p. chiefly ill. (pbk.) $24.95   **759.4**

1. Painters 2. Artists' models 3. Women -- France -- History 4. Artists' models -- France -- Biography -- Comic books, strips, etc

ISBN 9781906838256

LC 2011431146

This book offers a graphic biography of artist model and actress Alice Prin, better known as Kiki de Montparnasse. In "bohemian Montparnasse [in Paris, France] of the 1920s, Kiki escaped poverty to become one of the most charismatic figures of the avant-garde years between the wars. Partner to [artist] Man Ray, and one of the first emancipated women of the 20th century, Kiki made her mark with her freedom of style, word, and thought that could be learned from only one school—the school of life." (Amazon.com)

Includes bibliographical references (p. 413-415)

Danchev, Alex

Cézanne; a life. Alex Danchev. Pantheon Books 2012 xx, 488 p.p (hardback) $40   **759.4**

1. French painting 2. Artists -- Biography 3. Painters -- France -- Biography

ISBN 0307377075; 9780307377074

LC 2012007182

Author Alex Danchev presents a biography on Paul Cézanne. "One of the most influential painters of his time and beyond, Cézanne was the exemplary artist-creator of the modern age who changed the way we see the world. .

. . Danchev tells the story of an artist who was originally considered a madman, a barbarian, and a sociopath. . . . [He] shows us how the beliefs Cézanne held and the life he led became the obsession and inspiration of artists, writers, poets, and philosophers from Henri Matisse and Pablo Picasso to Samuel Beckett and Allen Ginsberg." (Publisher's note)

Includes bibliographical references and index.

King, Ross

★ **Mad** enchantment; Claude Monet and the painting of the water lilies. Ross King. Bloomsbury USA 2016 416 p. ill. (some color), maps, table (hardcover) $30   **759.4**

1. French painting 2. Water lilies in art

ISBN 9781632860125

LC 2015049404

This book by Ross King tells the story behind the creation of the painting series the Water Lilies by Claude Monet. "By early 1914, French newspapers were reporting that Monet, by then 73 and one of the world's wealthiest, most celebrated painters, had retired his brushes. He had lost his beloved wife, Alice, and his eldest son, Jean. . . . And yet, despite ill health, self-doubt, and advancing age, Monet began painting again on a more ambitious scale than ever before." (Publisher's note)

"Never before has the full drama and significance of Monet's magnificent Water Lilies been conveyed with such knowledge and perception, empathy and wonder." Booklist

Includes bibliographical references

Shackelford, George T. M.

Gustave Caillebotte; the painter's eye. Mary Morton, George T.M. Shackelford; Essays by Michael Marrinan, Alexandra K. Wettlaufer, Elizabeth Benjamin, Stéphane Guégan, Sarah Kennel. "National Gallery of Art" "Kimbell Art Museum" "in association w/University of Chicago Press" 2015 283 p. ill. (chiefly color), portrait (hardback) $60 **759.4**

ISBN 9780226263557; 9780894683930

LC 2015004438

In this book, by Mary Morton and George Shackelford, "Gustave Caillebotte (1848–94) has come to be recognized as one of the most dynamic and original artists of the impressionist movement in Paris. His paintings are favorites of museum-goers, and recent restoration of his work has revealed more color, texture, and detail than was visible before while heightening interest in all of Caillebotte's artwork." (Publisher's note)

Includes bibliographical references (pages 271-275)

The **World** Is an Apple; The Still Lifes of Paul Cézanne. edited by Benedict Leca. Giles 2014 240 p. color illustrations $54.95   **759.4**

1. Still-life painting

ISBN 1907804285; 9781907804281

This book, edited by Benedict Leca, "offers a reappraisal of Paul Cézanne's achievement in the genre of still life. It examines his paintings within the context of his artistic development and professional self-fashioning, and probes the shifting scientific and critical discourses that shaped both his practice and the reception of his pictures." (Publisher's note)

"Specialists in modern and French art will especially appreciate this finely designed volume that may be considered for special and public libraries alike." LJ

759.5 Italian painting

Hales, Dianne

Mona Lisa; a life discovered. Dianne Hales. Simon & Schuster 2014 336 p. map, genealogical table (hardback) $28 **759.5**

1. Mona Lisa (Painting) 2. Renaissance portrait painting -- Italy 3. Florence (Italy) -- History -- 1421-1737 4. Artists' models -- Italy -- Florence -- Biography
ISBN 1451658966; 9781451658965; 9781451658972
LC 2013042086

This book on the "Mona Lisa" painting by Dianne Hales, "a blend of biography, history, and memoir, truly is a book of discovery--about the world's most recognized face, most revered artist, and most praised and parodied painting. Who was she, this ordinary woman who rose to such extraordinary fame? Why did the most renowned painter of her time choose her as his model?" (Publisher's note)

"This engaging account of a Renaissance woman will appeal to a general audience." LJ

Includes bibliographcial references (pages 293-300) and index

King, Ross

Florence; the paintings & frescoes, 1250-1743. Introductions and Essays by Ross King; Painting Descriptions by Anja Grebe. Black Dog & Leventhal 2015 708 p. chiefly col. ill, maps **759.5**

1. Italian art 2. Art -- History 3. Florence (Italy) -- History 4. Painting -- Italy -- Florence
ISBN 1631910019; 9781631910012
LC 2015026785

Authors Ross King and Anje Gerbe present this "comprehensive book on the paintings and frescoes of Florence . . . with nearly 2,000 beautifully reproduced artworks from the city's great museums and churches. Every painted work that is on display in the Uffizi Gallery, The Pitti Palace, the Accademia, and the Duomo is included in the book, plus many or most of the works from 28 of the city's other magnificent museums and churches." (Publisher's note)

"Written in an easy-to-read style, this surprisingly affordable tome, given its size and lavish illustrations, will interest general readers through art historians." LJ

Includes bibliographical references

759.6 Spanish painting

Cumming, Laura

The **Vanishing** Velazquez; a 19th century bookseller's obsession with a lost masterpiece. by Laura Cumming. Scribner 2016 304 p. illustrations (some color) (hardcover) $28 **759.6**

1. Art -- Attribution 2. Booksellers and bookselling 3. Portrait painting -- History 4. Portrait painting -- Attribution 5. Booksellers and bookselling -- England

-- Reading
ISBN 9781476762159; 9781476762180
LC 2015040220

In this book, by Laura Cumming, "[Diego] Velazquez (1599–1660) was the official painter of the Madrid court. . . . When Prince Charles of England—a man wealthy enough to help turn Spain's fortunes--ventured to the court to propose a marriage with a Spanish princess, he allowed just a few hours to sit for his portrait. [John] Snare believed only Velazquez could have met this challenge. But in making his theory public, Snare was ostracized." (Publisher's note)

"Snare's story is noteworthy, but it is Cumming's spirited and clever narration that makes this enigma utterly engrossing." Pub Wkly

Includes bibliographical references (pages [275]-287) and index.

Descharnes, Robert, 1926-2014

Salvador Dalí, 1904-1989; the paintings. by Robert Descharnes and Gilles Néret. Taschen America Llc 2013 780 p. illustrations (chiefly color) $19.99; (ebook) $27.07 **759.6**

1. Surrealism
ISBN 383654492X; 9783836544924; 9781599283517
LC 2015005265

This book, by Robert Descharnes and Gilles Néret, "explor[es] Dalí's grandiose and grotesque oeuvre. . . . Dalí (1904-1989) was one of the century's greatest exhibitionists and eccentrics—and was rewarded with fierce controversy wherever he went. He was one of the first to apply the insights of Sigmund Freud and psychoanalysis to the art of painting, approaching the subconscious with extraordinary sensitivity and imagination." (Publisher's note)

759.9 Other geographic areas

Fischer, Stefan

Hieronymus Bosch; The Complete Works. by Stefan Fischer. Taschen America Llc 2016 300 p. illustrations $39.99 **759.9**

ISBN 3836538350; 9783836538350

This book, by Stefan Fischer, "presents the complete [Hieronymus] Bosch oeuvre, celebrating the artist's staggering compositional scope and most bizarre and intricate details through full-page reproductions, abundant details, and a fold-out spread drawn from The Last Judgement." (Publisher's note)

Gohr, Siegfried

★ **Magritte**; attempting the impossible. Siegfried Gohr. D.A.P./Distributed Art Publishers 2009 323 p. illustrations (chiefly color) (alk. paper) $85 **759.9**

1. Surrealism 2. Surrealism -- Belgium
ISBN 1933045930; 9781933045931
LC 2009022403

This book, by Siegfried Gohr, focuses on "Belgian painter René Magritte. . . . Magritte's paintings offer a space for the viewer to contemplate the emptiness of signs and to locate that emptiness in a world we recognize--indeed, the artist relies on the props of normalcy in order to upend, invert and collapse them into the terra incognita where life leaves off and art begins." (Publisher's note)

Includes bibliographical references (p. 318-319) and indexes

Attempting the impossible

Liedtke, Walter A.

Vermeer and the Delft school; by Walter Liedtke in collaboration with Michiel C. Plomp and Axel Rüger; with contributions by Reinier Baarsen {et al.} Metropolitan Mus. of Art 2001 626p il $85   **759.9**

1. Artists 2. Painters 3. Dutch painting

ISBN 0-300-08848-5

LC 00-49550

"This is the catalog of an exhibition held at the Metropolitan Museum of Art, New York, N.Y., Mar. 8-May 27, 2001 and at the National Gallery, London, June 20-Sept. 16, 2001. It includes fifteen works by Vermeer and paintings, tapestries and drawings by other Delft artists, including Gerard Houckgeest, Emanuel de Witte, Carel Fabritius, Paulus Potter, Leonaert Bramer, Jan de Bisschop and Pieter de Hooch. . . . Liedtke believes that Vermeer was nurtured and goaded exclusively by Dutch art of his time and by the traditions of his hometown." N Y Rev Books

Includes bibliographical references

Lozano, Luis-Martin

Frida Kahlo. Bulfinch Press 2001 245p il $85   **759.9**

1. Artists 2. Painters

ISBN 0-8212-2766-1

LC 2001-89093

Original Mexican edition, 2000

In this "illustrated survey of Frida Kahlo's work Lozano . . . explores her life and paintings in a series of essays that range from a poetic study by noted Mexican cultural critic Carlos Monsiváis to a short, prosaic piece written in 1943 by her husband, Diego Rivera, to an academic essay by Lozano himself. . . . Lozano uses Kahlo's own stunning images, offering high-quality reproductions of some of Kahlo's most famous works as well as some of her lesser-known pieces. Previously unseen photos of Kahlo at work in her studio are also included. The detail and clarity of the images is incredible." Libr J

Thomson, Belinda

Van Gogh paintings; the masterpieces. Thames & Hudson 2007 190p il $45   **759.9**

1. Artists 2. Painters

ISBN 978-0-500-23838-7; 0-500-23838-3

This book "offers a general survey of Van Gogh's paintings. . . . [and] discusses Van Gogh's paintings in terms of a chronological and biographical progression . . . . Filled with beautifully written descriptive passages of the works and careful analysis of the artist's style. . . . This book is a solid introduction to Van Gogh's paintings." Choice

Includes bibliographical references

760   Printmaking and prints

Hughes, Robert

Goya. Knopf 2003 429p il $40   **760**

1. Artists 2. Etchers 3. Painters 4. Printmakers

ISBN 0-394-58028-1

LC 2002-43281

This is "a remarkably vital, delectably discursive, and deeply affecting study." Booklist

Includes bibliographical references

770   Photography, computer art, cinematography, videography

Arnold, Eve

All about Eve; the photography of Eve Arnold. Eve Arnold. TeNeues 2012 216 p. (hardcover : alk. paper) $85   **770**

1. Portrait photography 2. Women photographers -- United States

ISBN 383279641X; 9783832796419

LC 2011943114

Eve Arnold "may be best known for her black and white images of Marilyn Monroe, but she has chronicled figures as diverse as migrant potato workers and heads of state in addition to screen icons during her assignments, which involved everything from politics, social issues, travel, to current events and a little glamour. Guided by her own words, this volume features Arnold's now iconic photographs as well as many never-before published images." (Publisher's note)

Bajac, Quentin

Photography at MOMA; 1920-1960. Quentin Bajac, Lucy Gallun, Roxana Marcoci. Museum of Modern Art 2016 392 p. $75   **770**

1. Modern art -- Exhibitions 2. Photography -- Exhibitions

ISBN 1633450139; 9781633450134

LC 2016941489

This book on photography at the Museum of Modern Art, by Quentin Bajac, Lucy Gallun, and Roxana Marcoci, "comprises a comprehensive catalogue of the collection post-1960s and brings much-needed new critical perspective to the most prominent artists working with the photographic medium of the late 20th and early 21st centuries." (Publisher's note)

Campany, David

The **open** road; photography and the American road trip. David Campany. Aperture Foundation 2014 336 p. illustrations, color maps (hardcover : alk. paper) $65   **770**

1. Travel writing 2. Automobile travel 3. United States -- Description and travel 4. Photography, Artistic 5. Photographic criticism 6. United States -- Pictorial works 7. United States -- Description and travel -- Pictorial works 8. United States -- Social life and customs -- Pictorial works

ISBN 1597112402; 9781597112406

LC 2014020321

This book, edited by David Campany, "considers the photographic road trip as a genre in and of itself, and presents the story of photographers for whom the American road is muse. The book features David Campany's introduction to the genre and 18 chapters presented chronologically, each exploring one American road trip in depth through a portfolio of images and informative texts." (Publisher's note)

Includes bibliographical references

Cardozo, Christopher

Edward S. Curtis; one hundred masterworks. Christopher Cardozo; with contributions by A. D. Coleman, Louise Erdrich, Eric J. Jolly, and Michael Charles Tobias. DelMonico Books/Prestel 2015 184 p. illustrations (some color) (hardcover) $65 **770**
1. Native Americans -- History 2. Photography in ethnology 3. Photographers -- United States -- Biography
ISBN 9783791354217; 9783791365800
LC 2014049053

In this book, "author Christopher Cardozo has curated a groundbreaking monograph on internationally renowned photographer Edward Curtis. Curtis's magnum opus, The North American Indian, the most extensive photographic portrait of Native Americans, is a crucial contribution to the history of America's Native peoples as well as a testament to his tireless efforts to document and express the spirit of over eighty distinct tribal groups." (Publisher's note)

One hundred masterworks

Cartier-Bresson, Henri, 1908-2004

The **Decisive** Moment; photography by Henri Cartier-Bresson. Steidl 2015 160 p. chiefly illustrations (hbk.) $125 **770**
1. Portrait photography 2. Photography, Artistic -- 20th century
ISBN 9783869307886; 3869307889

This book, by Henri Cartier-Bresson, was "originally published in 1952. . . . This new publication—the first and only reprint since the original 1952 edition—is a meticulous facsimile of the original book that launched the artist to international fame, with an additional booklet on the history of The Decisive Moment by Centre Pompidou curator Clément Chéroux." (Publisher's note)

Foresta, Merry A.

Irving Penn; Beyond Beauty. by Merry Foresta. Yale University Press 2015 240 p. color ill., plates, portraits $45 **770**
1. Photographers
ISBN 0300214901; 9780300214901
LC 2015934207

This book, by Merry Foresta, presents an "overview of the work of legendary American photographer Irving Penn. . . . Drawing from the extensive holdings of the Smithsonian American Art Museum, including a major gift from The Irving Penn Foundation, this . . . catalogue compiles 161 of Penn's iconic images, including a number of unpublished works." (Publisher's note)

Includes bibliographical references (pages 238) and index.

Gatcum, Chris

The **Beginner's** photography guide; [written by Chris Gatcum] DK Publishing 2013 192 p. color photos (ebook) $58.95; $19.95 **770**
1. Photography
ISBN 9781465416346; 1465408452; 9781465408457
LC 2012278016

This book, by Chris Gatcum, is a "manual for any novice photographer who wants to unlock the potential of their new digital camera. . . . It takes you through every technique you need to create stunning images, from exposure to flash to image enhancement. Handy checklists provide a quick rundown of the equipment and camera settings for each technique, and at-a-glance comparison images show how camera settings can produce remarkably different results." (Publisher's note)

"Though perfect for novices, this manual will also be helpful to readers with prior knowledge of analog photography wishing to translate their skills to the digital realm." LJ

Beginner's photography guide :

the ultimate step-by-step manual for getting the most from your digital camera

Getting the most from your digital camera

Gulbrandsen, Don

Edward Sheriff Curtis; visions of the first Americans. [photographs selected and essay by] Don Gulbrandsen. Chartwell Books Compendium 2006 256 p. chiefly ill., col. map, ports. $24.99 **770**
1. Native Americans 2. Native Americans -- Biography 3. Native Americans -- Pictorial works
ISBN 0785821147; 0785826505; 9780785821144; 9780785826507
LC 2008300121

This book on Edward S. Curtis, by Don Gulbrandsen, "is a tribute to the photographer, his work, but above all to the Native Americans he photographed. Chapters on many different Native American tribes make this collection unique." (Publisher's note)

Hallett, Tracy

Digital photography complete course; written by David Taylor, Tracy Hallett, Paul Lowe, Paul Sanders. DK Publishing 2015 360 p. illustrations (chiefly color) $30 **770**
1. Photography 2. Photography -- Digital techniques
ISBN 1465436073; 9781465436078
LC 2015451543

This book "uses a combination of tutorials, step-by-step demonstrations, practical assignments, and Q&As to help you understand and use your camera to the max. Choose your own pace to work through the modules—the program is totally customizable to your schedule. As you work through the lessons, test your new knowledge and troubleshoot common issues." (Publisher's note)

"An affordable, uncomplicated way to learn about digital photography." LJ

Horenstein, Henry

Digital photography; a basic manual. Henry Horenstein with Allison Carroll. Little, Brown &

Co. 2011 240 p. illustrations (some color) (pbk.)
$30 **770**
1. Digital photography 2. Photography -- Digital
techniques
ISBN 0316020745; 9780316020749

LC 2011018758

This book, by Henry Horenstein, is a " guide to capturing digital photographs. . . . All concepts are fully illustrated
with sample work by internationally renowned professionals, representing editorial work, photojournalism, and everything in between. Topics covered include essential information for both film and digital photography, . . . as well as
digital-specific information on image editing, printing methods, and even file storage." (Publisher's note)

Magnum Photos, Inc.
New York September 11; by Magnum photographers; introduction by David Halberstam. Power-
House Bks. 2001 140p il $29.95 **770**
1. Documentary photography 2. World Trade Center
terrorist attack, 2001
ISBN 1-57687-130-4

LC 2001-52330

This collection of photographs documents the attack on
the World Trade Center on September 11, 2001. The book
is organized essentially as a series of picture essays by
individual photographers

Matter, Jordan
Dancers among us; a celebration of joy in the
everyday. Jordan Matter. Workman Publishing 2012
229 p. color illustrations (alk. paper) $17.95 **770**
1. Dance in art 2. Dance -- Pictorial works 3. Dancers
-- Portraits 4. Portrait photography
ISBN 0761171703; 9780761171706

LC 2012033655

This book by Jordan Matter presents photographs of
"dancers leaping, laughing, reclining, and soaring in some
of the most unconventional spots: in offices, crossing a
busy street, high up in a leafy tree limb, and even in the
shower!" The "images [are] around themes like work, play,
love, exploration, and dreaming." Also included are "Matter's personal anecdotes about life, learning, and family".
(Dance Magazine)

Stieglitz, Alfred
★ Alfred Stieglitz: the key set; the Alfred Stieglitz collection of photographs. [text by] Sarah Greenough. Abrams 2002 2v il set $150 **770**
ISBN 0-8109-3533-3

LC 2002-5066

This is a "captioned catalog of 1,642 Stieglitz photographs. . . . It contains 'the finest print of every mounted
photograph in Stieglitz's possession at the time of his death.'
. . . Greenough's essay examines 'what is and is not in the
key set in order to clarify the evolution of Stieglitz's understanding of modernist photography. . . .' The set contains
very useful, dense chronologies of Stieglitz's process and
techniques (1882-1944) and of exhibitions (1888-1944), a
bibliography (1875-2001), and an essay on Stieglitz's concern with reproduction printing and publishing." Choice
Includes bibliographical references

Szarkowski, John
Ansel Adams at 100; Ansel Adams, John Szarkowski. Little, Brown & Co. 2003 191 p. (Paperback) $40 **770**
1. Photographers -- United States 2. Photography,
Artistic -- Exhibitions
ISBN 9780821228654; 082122865X

LC 0069941

This book "commemorates the birth of the famous native
San Franciscan photographer with 114 of [Ansel] Adams's
rich, beloved images spanning his oeuvre, and some delightful photos of the artist. The book and accompanying centennial exhibit at San Francisco's Museum of Modern Art . .
. , curated by John Szarkowski, director of the department
of photography at New York's Museum of Modern Art, re-
evaluate the impact of Adams's work on photography, landscapes and the audience." (Publishers Weekly)

Weston, Edward
Edward weston; 125 Photographs. Edward
Weston; [edited by] Steve Crist. AMMO Books 2012
262 p. $50 **770**
1. Photography
ISBN 1934429309; 9781934429303

LC 2012933925

This book, edited by Steve Crist, "contains 125 of [Ed-
ward] Weston's well-known images and many lesser-known
gems. Additionally, a detailed introduction, along with reproductions of many unseen photographs and ephemera help
round out this ultimate tribute to a legendary photographer."
(Publisher's note)

770.1　　Philosophy and theory

Peterson, Bryan
Learning to see creatively; design, color, and
composition in photography. Bryan Peterson. 3rd
edition Amphoto Books 2015 144 p. color illustrations pbk $25.99 **770.1**
1. Photography 2. Composition (Art)
ISBN 9781607748274; 1607748274

LC 2014049147

"Fully revised with 100 percent new photography, this
best-selling guide takes a radical approach to creativity by
explaining how it is not just an inherent ability but a skill
that can be learned and applied. Using inventive photos from
his own stunning portfolio, author and veteran photographer
Bryan Peterson deconstructs creativity for photographers.
He details the basic techniques that go into not only taking
a particular photo, but also provides insights on how to improve upon it--helping readers avoid the visual pitfalls and
technical dead ends that can lead to dull, uninventive photographs." (Publisher's note)
Includes bibliographical references and index

770.82　　Women photographers

Women of vision; National Geographic Photographers on Assignment. foreword by Ann Curry, in-

troduction by Chris Johns. National Geographic Society 2013 222 p. mostly colored illustrations (hardcover : alk. paper) $30 **770.82**
1. Photojournalism 2. Women photographers 3. Women photographers -- Biography
ISBN 1426212720; 9781426212727

LC 2013012585

"Women photographers have produced many of National Geographic's most powerful photo-narratives of the past decade. These talented photojournalists are celebrated in this captivating photography book, covering places and subjects around the globe and sharing the same passion and commitment to storytelling that has come to define National Geographic magazine, with more than 31 million readers worldwide." (Publisher's note)

770.9 History, geographical treatment, biography

Ang, Tom
  Photography; The Definitive Visual History. Tom Ang. DK Pub. 2014 480 p. color illustrations, portraits $50 **770.9**
1. Photographers 2. Photography -- History 3. Photographers -- Biography 4. Photography -- History -- Pictorial works
ISBN 1465422889; 9781465422880

LC 2014453689

This book, by Tom Ang, "lavishly celebrates the most iconic photographs and photographers of the past 200 years. Tracing the history of photography from its origins in the 1800s to the digital age, . . . [this book] is the only book of its kind to give a comprehensive account of the people, the photographs, and the technologies that have shaped the history of photography." (Publisher's note)

"While too basic for a professional or serious student, this volume will appeal to photo enthusiasts and general readers. Those wanting an extensive single-volume overview should stick with Michael R. Peres's The Focal Encyclopedia of Photography." LJ

Morris, Errol, 1948-
  Believing is seeing; observations on the mysteries of photography. Penguin Press 2011 xxv, 310p il map $40 **770.9**
1. Documentary photography
ISBN 978-1-59420-301-5; 1-59420-301-6

LC 2011013101

The book "takes the reader on a walking tour of photojournalistic hot spots, from 1855 to 2006 to 2003 to 1936 to 2006 to 1863 , in that order . . . Mostly, Morris tries to clear up unsolved mysteries in the crevices of the history of photography—things like whether Walker Evans moved some knickknacks in a sharecropper's house he photographed; which of two photographs by Roger Fenton, from the Crimean War, was taken first; and how much guilt can be inferred from a digital photo of an American soldier grinning over a dead Iraqi at Abu Ghraib." (Nation)

"Morris' assiduous and profound inquiry into the relationship between reality and photography is eye-opening,

mind-expanding, and essential in this age of ubiquitous digital images." Booklist
  Includes bibliographical references

770.92 Biography

Alinder, Mary Street
  Group f.64; Edward Weston, Ansel Adams, Imogen Cunningham, and the community of artists who revolutionized American photography. Mary Street Alinder. Bloomsbury USA 2014 416 p. 16 plates; illustrations (alk. paper) $35 **770.92**
1. Photography 2. Modernism (Aesthetics) 3. Group f.64 -- History 4. Photography -- United States -- History 5. Modernism (Art) -- West (U.S.) -- History 6. Photographers -- United States -- Biography
ISBN 1620405555; 9781620405550

LC 2014011040

"In this . . . group biography about the California photographers known as Group f.64, [Mary Street] Alinder . . . tells a distinctly West Coast story about an ambitious, broad-minded, and unusually diverse movement. Originally founded at a party in Berkeley, Calif., in 1932 by Edward Weston, Ansel Adams, Imogen Cunningham, and Willard Van Dyke, among others, Group f.64 advocated for 'straight' photography over pictorialism's painterly affectations." (Publishers Weekly)

"As she chronicles the photographers' friendships, tempestuous love lives, epic parties, scrambles to survive, passionate manifestos, heated public debates, social and environmental concerns, and hard-won exhibitions, Alinder achieves an f.64 degree of crisp and commanding detail in this landmark group portrait of the visionary photographers who succeeded in 'forever changing our way of seeing.'" Booklist
  Includes bibliographical references and index

Burrows, Larry
  Vietnam; introduction by David Halberstam. Knopf 2002 243p il $50 **770.92**
1. Vietnam War, 1961-1975 -- Pictorial works
ISBN 0-375-41102-X

LC 2002-19100

This "confirms that {Burrows} was an artist as well as a journalist, capable of arousing the great tragic emotions, pity and terror." Booklist
  Includes bibliographical references

Egan, Timothy
  ★ **Short** nights of the Shadow Catcher; the epic life and immortal photographs of Edward Curtis. Timothy Egan. Houghton Mifflin Harcourt 2012 384 p. ill. (hardback) $28.00 **770.92**
1. Photographers 2. Native Americans -- History 3. Native Americans -- Pictorial works 4. Photographers -- United States -- Biography
ISBN 0618969020; 9780618969029

LC 2012022390

This book by "National Book Award winner Timothy Egan" is a biography of photographer Edward Curtis that "recaptures the story of a man both entrapped by his time and ahead of it." In 1900, Curtis "made a decision that changed his life . . . . He largely abandoned his lucrative portrait studio work and began a thirty-year project to record images of Native Americans who, he believed, were doomed to extinction, [which] destroyed his marriage and left him destitute." (Barnes and Noble)

Gross, Michael, 1952-

Focus; Michael Gross. Atria Books 2016 416 p. illustrations (some color) (hardcover) $28   **770.92**
1. Photography 2. Clothing industry 3. Models (Persons) -- Biography 4. Fashion photography -- History 5. Fashion photographers -- Biography 6. Fashion merchandising -- Social aspects 7. Fashion photographers -- Conduct of life
ISBN 9781476763460

LC 2015045564

This book, by Michael Gross, "probes the lives, hang-ups, and artistic triumphs of more than a dozen of fashion photography's greatest visionaries: Richard Avedon, Irving Penn, Melvin Sokolsky, Bert Stern, David Bailey, Bill King, Deborah Turbeville, Helmut Newton, Gilles Bensimon, Bruce Weber, Steven Meisel, Corinne Day, Bob and Terry Richardson, and more." (Publisher's note)

"The subject matter will be historically significant to those who are concerned with the photo artist's role in the golden age of modern fashion photography. " LJ

Huffman, Alan

Here I Am; The Story of Tim Hetherington, War Photographer. Alan Huffman. Grove Press 2013 256 p. (hardcover) $25   **770.92**
1. War photography
ISBN 0802120903; 9780802120908

This book, by Alan Huffman, offers a biography of "Tim Hetherington (1970-2011) . . . , one of the world's most distinguished and dedicated photojournalists, whose career was tragically cut short when he died in a mortar blast while covering the Libyan Civil War. . . . Huffman recounts Hetherington's life from his first interests in photography, through his critical role in reporting the Liberian Civil War, to his tragic death in Libya." (Publisher's note)

Panzer, Mary

Mathew Brady and the image of history; with an essay by Jeana K. Foley. Smithsonian Institution Press 1997 xxiii, 232p il hardcover o.p. pa $19.95   **770.92**
1. Photographers 2. United States -- History -- 1861-1865, Civil War -- Pictorial works
ISBN 1-56098-793-6; 978-1-58834-143-3 pa; 1-58834-143-7 pa

LC 97-9493

In this reassessment of the life and work of the iconic 19th-century photographer, the author "points out that Brady seldom stood behind the camera, preferring the role of studio chief executive officer and entrepreneur to that of a mere 'operator.' . . . Moreover, Brady was an incompetent businessman, often leaving his creditors in the lurch, and ended his career in bankruptcy. This is enough to make us think twice about Brady, but Panzer's most audacious assertion

is that we also need to think twice about the meaning of the pictures attributed to him." N Y Times Book Rev

Includes bibliographical references

Willis, Deborah

Reflections in Black; a history of Black photographers, 1840-1999. Norton 2000 348p il $50; pa $35   **770.92**
1. African Americans in art 2. African American photographers 3. Photography -- History
ISBN 0-393-04880-2; 0-393-32280-7 pa

LC 99-55185

Companion volume to A Smithsonian traveling exhibition
"Willis sketches important figures and traces both developments in photographic techniques and the practice of photography by African Americans. . . . A beautiful and informative album." Booklist

Includes bibliographical references and index

Wilson, Robert

Mathew Brady; Portraits of a Nation. Robert Wilson. St. Martin's Press 2013 320 p. $28 **770.92**
1. United States -- History -- 1861-1865, Civil War -- Photography 2. Photographers -- United States -- Biography
ISBN 1620402033; 9781620402030

LC 2013016928

In this biography of photographer Mathew Brady, author Robert Wilson "examines surviving business registers, articles, advertisements, and documents of Brady's associates and prestigious clients. . . . Wilson shows how Brady's artistic genius . . . his awareness of the commercial value and historical impact of his art; his congenial personality; and his relentless and savvy promotion of himself, his business, and his craft made him the preeminent 19th-century photographer." (Library Journal)

Includes bibliographical references and index

771   Techniques, procedures, apparatus, equipment, materials

Miotke, Jim

BetterPhoto basics; the absolute beginner's guide to taking photos like the pros. Jim Miotke. Amphoto Books 2010 239 p. color illustrations (alk. paper) $21.99; (ebook) $65   **771**
1. Photography 2. Photography -- Amateurs' manuals
ISBN 081740502X; 0817405313; 9780817405021; 9780817405311; 9780817400248

LC 2009045259

In this book, photographer Jim Miotke "shares tips and tricks to improve your photos right away, no matter what camera you're using. Too busy to read a book? No problem—flip to any page for an instant tip to use right away! Learn to compose knockout shots, make the most of indoor and outdoor light, and photograph twenty popular subjects, from sunsets and flowers to a family portrait." (Publisher's note)

Peterson, Bryan

Understanding exposure; how to shoot great photographs with any camera. Bryan Peterson. 4th edition AmPhoto Books 2016 176 p. color illustrations pbk $26.99 **771**

1. Photography 2. Photography -- Exposure
ISBN 1607748509; 9781607748502

LC 2015025905

"This latest edition of [Peterson's] very popular, user-friendly guide suitable for beginners explains exposure--the key to successful photographic images--in plain, easily understood language. Peterson breaks down complex theories into simpler concepts, offering many helpful tips and short-cuts along the way. Following an introductory chapter defining exposure, subsequent sections cover aperture, shutter speed, light, special techniques, including use of filters and multiple exposure, and electronic flash." (Library Journal)

Includes bibliographical references and index

775 Digital photography

Ang, Tom

Digital photographer's handbook; Tom Ang. 5th edition DK 2012 408 p. ill. (chiefly col.) pbk $24.95 **775**

1. Digital cameras 2. Digital photography
ISBN 0756692423; 9780756692421

LC 2012418315

The latest edition of this book has been updated with "new photographic and image-manipulation projects, up-to-the-minute information on the latest technology and equipment, with revised and updated text and new pictures." (Publisher's note0

Includes bibliographical references and index

Digital photography masterclass; Tom Ang. 2nd edition DK 2013 360 p. color illustrations hbk $30 **775**

1. Digital photography 2. Photography -- Processing
ISBN 1465408568; 9781465408563

Ang "teaches how to look at the world with a photographer's eye and offers tutorials, photographic assignments, and step-by-step image-manipulation exercises. Combining technical and artistic aspects of photography, Ang completes the volume with sections on travel, documentary, portrait, nature, sports, and architecture photography." (Library Journal)

Freeman, Michael

The **photographer's** mind; creative thinking for better digital photos. Focal Press 2011 192p il pa $29.95 **775**

1. Digital photography
ISBN 978-0-240-81517-6

The author "shares experience he has gained as a professional photographer to improve the quality of the digital pictures nearly everyone is now creating. The content is streamlined into three chapters, on intent, style, and process, that tackle both the practical and the intangible aspects of photography more thoughtfully than many similar books.

Freeman is as adept at explaining composition as he is at discussing the problem of cliché or the philosophy of the sublime." Libr J

Includes bibliographical references

777 Cinematography and videography

Ascher, Steven

The **filmmaker's** handbook; a comprehensive guide for the digital age. Steven Ascher & Edward Pincus; drawings by Carol Keller and Robert Brun; original photographs by Ted Spagna and Stephen McCarthy completely revised and updated by Steven Ascher With contributions by David Leitner. Plume 2012 xii, 818 p.p (pbk.) $30; (ebook) $65 **777**

1. Cinematography 2. Motion pictures -- Production and direction 3. Digital video -- Handbooks, manuals, etc 4. Cinematography -- Handbooks, manuals, etc 5. Digital cinematography -- Handbooks, manuals, etc 6. Motion pictures -- Production and direction -- Handbooks, manuals, etc
ISBN 0452297281; 9780452297289; 9781101613801

LC 2012036572

This book, by Steven Ascher and Edward Pincus, is an "authoritative guide to producing, directing, shooting, editing, and distributing your video or film. . . . [It] is now updated with the latest advances in HD and new digital formats. For students and teachers, professionals and novices, this indispensable handbook covers all aspects of movie making." (Publisher's note)

Includes bibliographical references (pages 791-793) and index

778 Specific fields and special kinds of photography

National Geographic, the photographs. National Geographic Soc. 1994 336p il $50 **778**

1. Photojournalism 2. Documentary photography
ISBN 0-87044-986-9

LC 94-29971

"A treasury of 350 full-color photographs from the archives of the National Geographic shares a stunning array of work, reflecting the themes of The Land, Underwater, Science, The United States, and The World." (Publisher's note)

778.3 Special kinds of photography

Benson, Michael

Far out; a space-time chronicle. Abrams 2009 328p il **778.3**

1. Space photography
ISBN 0810949482; 9780810949485

LC 2009-929096

This is a "collection of astronomical images from observatories around the world and in space." (Publisher's note) Index.

"Here are stars packed like golden sand, gas combed in delicate blue threads, piled into burgundy thunderheads and carved into sinuous rilles and ribbons, and galaxies clotted with star clusters dancing like spiders on the ceiling. . . . You can sit and look through this book for hours and never be bored, . . . or you can actually read the accompanying learned essays. Mr. Benson's prose is up to its visual surroundings, no mean feat." N Y Times (Late N Y Ed)

Includes bibliographical references

778.5 Cinematography and videography

Harryhausen, Ray

The **art** of Ray Harryhausen; [by] Ray Harryhausen & Tony Dalton; with a foreword by Peter Jackson. Billboard Books 2006 230p il $50 **778.5**
1. Animated films 2. Cinematography
ISBN 0-8230-8400-0
LC 2005-930364

First published 2005 in the United Kingdom

"The text is fun and informative, but the main feast here is the art, and the reproductions of the concept drawings and photos of the models are superb." Libr J

778.53 Animation

Williams, Richard, 1933-

The **animator's** survival kit; A Manual of Methods, Principles and Formulas for Classical, Computer, Games, Stop Motion and Internet Animators. Richard Williams. Faber & Faber 2009 x, 382 p.p illustrations (some color) $35 **778.53**
1. Animation (Cinematography) 2. Drawing -- Technique
ISBN 0571238335; 0571238343; 086547897X; 9780571238330; 9780571238347; 9780865478978
LC 2010294449

This book, by Richard Williams, "provides the underlying principles of animation that every animator--from beginner to expert, classic animator to computer animation whiz --needs. . . . [Williams] illustrates his points with hundreds of drawings, distilling the secrets of the masters into a working system in order to create a book that will become the standard work on all forms of animation for professionals, students, and fans." (Publisher's note)

778.7 Photography under specific conditions

Rotman, Jeffrey L.

The **last** fisherman; witness to the endangered oceans. by Jeffrey L. Rotman and Yair Harel; introduction by Les Kaufman. Abbeville Press Publishers 2014 276 p. color illustrations (hardcover : alk. paper) $49.95 **778.7**
1. Overfishing 2. Underwater photography 3. Marine photography 4. Saltwater fishing -- Pictorial works
ISBN 0789211912; 9780789211910
LC 2014016848

This book, by by Jeffrey L. Rotman and Yair Harel, "with breathtaking images and compelling stories, an underwater photographer chronicles the glory, and devastation, of our changing oceans. . . . His journey mirrors our view of the oceans as places of wonder, to the fragile hunting grounds they are today." (Publisher's note)

"An excellent cautionary tale, this work offers much to celebrate, too. Highly recommended to all interested in nature, the oceans, and fishing." LJ

Includes bibliographical references and index

778.71 Outdoor photography

Manwaring, Jed

Extraordinary everyday photography; awaken your vision to create stunning images wherever you are. Brenda Tharp and Jed Manwaring. Amphoto Books 2012 160 p. illustrations (chiefly color) $25.99 **778.71**
1. Photography 2. Outdoor photography -- Amateurs' manuals 3. Photography -- Technique -- Amateurs' manuals
ISBN 081743593X; 9780817435936; 9780817435943
LC 2011040810

In this book, by Brenda Tharp and Jed Manwaring, "readers learn to use composition, available light, color, and point of view to create stunning photographs in any environment. Photographers are born travelers. They'll go any distance to capture the right light, beautiful landscapes, wildlife, and people. But exotic locales aren't necessary for interesting photographs. Wonderful images are hiding almost everywhere; you just need to know how to find them." (Publisher's note)

Includes bibliographical references and index

778.9 Photography of specific subjects

Cox, Rosamund Kidman

Wildlife Photographer of the Year; 50 Years. by Rosamund Kidman Cox. Firefly Books Ltd 2014 256 p. illustrations, portraits $49.95 **778.9**
1. Wildlife photography
ISBN 1770854622; 9781770854628

This book is a "collection of nature photography [that] features all the winning pictures from the prestigious 50th . . .Wildlife Photographer of the Year competition. . . . The photographs are chosen by an international jury for their artistic merit and originality, from categories that together represent a diversity of natural subjects. The range of styles is also diverse, as is the genre of photography, whether action, macro, underwater, landscape, or environmental reportage." (Publisher's note)

"Spare text offers readers a glimpse into how each image was made, its back story and why it deserves to be in the book. Clear the coffee table—this book has substance, beauty and will draw readers in again and again." Pub Wkly

Shaw, John

John Shaw's nature photography field guide; by John Shaw. rev ed; AMPHOTO 2000 p. cm color illustrations **778.9**
1. Nature photography
ISBN 0-8174-4059-3; 9780817440596
LC 00-42013

This book, by John Shaw, "contains state-of-the-art instruction on how any photographer can aim for . . . impressive results every time a camera is focused on the great outdoors. . . . Using his own exceptional work as examples, the author discusses each type of nature subject and how to approach photographing it." (Publisher's note)

"Shaw's book will be of great value to anyone wishing to make better landscapes and wildlife photographs." LJ

Watkins, Carleton Emmons

Carleton Watkins: the complete mammoth photographs; Weston Naef and Christine Hult-Lewis; with contributions by Michael Hargraves, Jack von Euw, and Jennifer A. Watts. J. Paul Getty Museum 2011 xxv, 572p il map $195 **778.9**
1. Photography 2. California -- Pictorial works
ISBN 978-1-60606-005-6; 1-60606-005-8
LC 2011-05241

"A monumental achievement in the pictorial historiography of 19th-century America, loaded with new images and data, this will be an indispensable resource for students of photography and U.S. history." Libr J

Includes bibliographical references

779 Photographic images

Brandow, Todd

Edward Steichen; lives in photography. [by] Todd Brandow and William A. Ewing. W. W. Norton & Company 2008 355p il $100 **779**
1. Photographers 2. Artistic photography
ISBN 978-0-393-06626-5
LC 2007-20128

"One of the finest photography books published in many years; highly recommended for all libraries." Libr J

Includes bibliographical references (p. 309-316)

Carter, Graydon

Vanity Fair, the portraits; a century of iconic images. by Graydon Carter and the editors of Vanity Fair; foreword by Graydon Carter; essays by Christopher Hitchens, David Friend, and Terence Pepper. Abrams 2008 383p il $65 **779**
1. Celebrities 2. Portrait photography
ISBN 978-0-8109-7298-8; 0-8109-7298-0
LC 2008-05033

"Culled from the pages of Vanity Fair magazine by its editor, Graydon Carter, and his staff, and shot by many of the greatest photographers in the history of the medium, these pictures are engrossing less because of the people they portray than because of the breathtaking ingenuity with which each subject is captured. . . . Whether taken by Baron de Meyer, Edward Steichen or Man Ray, or by latter-day ge-

niuses like [Annie] Leibovitz, Helmut Newton or Herb Ritts, these pictures stand as some of the finest examples of photographic craft ever to appear in the mainstream press." N Y Times Book Rev

Evans, Walker, 1903-1975

American photographs; Walker Evans; with an essay by Lincoln Kirstein. Museum of Modern Art Distributed by New York Graphic Society Books 1988 205 p. chiefly illustrations $40 **779**
1. Photography 2. United States -- Pictorial works 3. Photography, Artistic 4. United States -- Social conditions -- 1918-1932 -- Pictorial works 5. United States -- Social conditions -- 1933-1945 -- Pictorial works
ISBN 0870702378; 0870702386; 087070835X; 9780870708350
LC 88062926

This book, by Walker Evans, "was a carefully prepared letterpress production, published by The Museum of Modern Art in 1938 to accompany an exhibition of photographs by Evans that captured scenes of America in the early 1930s. . . . This version, like the fiftieth-anniversary edition produced by the Museum in 1988, captures the look and feel of the very first edition with the aid of new digital technologies." (Publisher's note)

Friedman, Elias Weiss

The Dogist; Photographic Encounters With 1,000 Dogs. by Elias Weiss Friedman. Workman Pub Co 2015 304 p. color illustrations $24.95 **779**
1. Dogs 2. Animals -- Pictorial works
ISBN 1579656714; 9781579656713
LC 2015036708

This book, by Elias Weiss Friedman, "is a beautiful, funny, and inspiring tribute to the beloved dogs in our lives. Every page presents dog portraits that command our attention. Whether because of the look in a dog's eyes, its innate beauty, or even the clothes its owner has dressed it in, the photos will make you ooh and aah, laugh, and fall in love." (Publisher's note)

"This delightful collection of photographs is likely to catch the eye of readers who follow Friedman's blog, Facebook page, tweets, and/or Instagram account. Animal portraiture enthusiasts may be especially interested in this title as an exemplar of the genre." LJ

Haas, Robert B.

Through the eyes of the Vikings; an aerial vision of Arctic lands. Robert B. Haas. Ragged Bears [distributor] 2010 219p il map $50 **779**
1. Aerial photography 2. Arctic regions -- Pictorial works
ISBN 978-1-4262-0638-2; 1-4262-0638-0
LC 2010549763

Hitchcock, Susan Tyler

National geographic rarely seen; photographs of the extraordinary. [compiled by] Susan Tyler Hitchcock; foreword by Stephen Alvarez. National

Geographic Society 2015 399 p. color illustrations (hardcover : alk. paper) $40 **779**
1. Photography 2. Nature photography 3. Travel photography 4. Landscape photography 5. Documentary photography 6. Geography -- Pictorial works
ISBN 1426215614; 9781426215612
LC 2015014900
This book, by National Geographic, "features striking images of places, events, natural phenomena, and manmade heirlooms seldom seen by human eyes. It's all here: 30,000-year-old cave art sealed from the public; animals that are among the last of their species on Earth; volcanic lightning; giant crystals that have grown to more than 50 tons; the engraving inside Abraham Lincoln's pocket watch." (Publisher's note)

Leibovitz, Annie
Annie Leibovitz at work; [Sharon DeLano, editor] Random House 2008 237p il $40 **779**
1. Portrait photography
ISBN 978-0-375-50510-2; 0-375-50510-5
LC 2008-933724
Leibovitz "discusses her personal approaches, trials, and discoveries as a professional photographer, pairing detailed memories and technical discussions with images of her most iconic celebrity portraits (including the Rolling Stones, Demi Moore, John Lennon, and Queen Elizabeth). The book adheres to a chronological format—from Leibovitz's earliest black-and-white photos of the Rolling Stones and John Lennon to her conceptual color portraits from the 1980s. . . . Also included are personal and family photographs as well as her most recent photo shoots for Vanity Fair, including the Obama and Clinton campaigns." Libr J

A **photographer's** life, 1990-2005. Random House 2006 un il $75 **779**
1. Portrait photography
ISBN 978-0-375-50509-6; 0-375-50509-1
LC 2006-45765
This is a collection of Leibovitz's "work from 1990-2005. . . . [Portraits of] Johnny Cash, Nicole Kidman, Mikhail Baryshnikov, Keith Richards, Michael Jordan, Joan Didion, R2-D2, Patti Smith, Nelson Mandela, Jack Nicholson, William Burroughs, [and] George W. Bush with members of his Cabinet appear alongside pictures of Leibovitz's family and friends, reportage from the siege of Sarajevo in the early Nineties, and landscapes." Publisher's note

Women; {photographs by} Annie Leibovitz; {essay by} Susan Sontag. Random House 1999 239p il $75; pa $49.95 **779**
1. Women -- Portraits
ISBN 0-375-50020-0; 0-375-75646-9 pa
LC 99-24968
"Leibovitz greatly increases our lexicon of womanhood with her brilliant photographs of musicians, doctors, teachers, trapeze artists, gangbangers, nude women, a woman in chador, women soldiers, and girls with their Barbies, all commanding attention and respect." Booklist

Life: World War 2; history's greatest conflict in pictures. edited by Richard B. Stolley. Little, Brown 2001 351p il hardcover o.p. pa $29.95 **779**
1. World War, 1939-1945 -- Pictorial works 2. World history -- 20th century -- Pictorial works
ISBN 0-8212-2771-8; 0-8212-5713-7 pa
LC 2001-93633
This "album of 665 photographs taken from the archives of Life magazine and other collections begins with the years 1919 to 1939, the two decades leading up to World War II. Editor Stolley then proceeds to chronicle the war, year by year through 1945, and ends with what he calls 'the war's aftermath,' 1946 to 2001. . . . For World War II buffs, the book is a natural treasure." Booklist

Lyon, Danny
Memories of myself; essays. Phaidon 2009 207p il $90 **779**
1. Documentary photography
ISBN 978-0-7148-4851-8; 0-7148-4851-4
"What happens when you hang out in brothels, derby pits, and dark alleys for forty years? For starters, you take some damn memorable photos. That's been the path of American photographer Danny Lyon, who, like a Method actor, immersed himself in the subcultures he documented. His iconic work from the '60s (pre–Easy Rider photos of bikers on the road) led to exhibitions in MoMA and the Whitney and two Guggenheim fellowships, and he's credited with pioneering the New Journalism movement in photography. In Memories of Myself . . . he shares 134 mostly unpublished pictures—of Colombian prostitutes in hair curlers, chain-smoking greasers, and Brooklyn teens playing Wiffle Ball—that are so intimate they could have come from the photo albums of the subjects themselves. This is the genius of Lyon's work: He inhabits, rather than invades, the personal space of his subjects." GQ

McCartney, Linda
Life in photographs; texts by Paul McCartney, Linda McCartney, Annie Leibovitz, Mary McCartney, Martin Harrison, Stella McCartney; edited by Alison Castle. Taschen 2011 un $69.99 **779**
1. Portrait photography
ISBN 978-3-8365-2728-6
This volume "offers a portrait of Beatledom from a singularly intimate point of view: that of Paul's wife of nearly three decades, the late Linda McCartney. While the couple's famous friends — Mick Jagger, Steve McQueen, Willem de Kooning — are well represented, the fly-on-the-wall shots of the McCartneys' idyllic intercontinental life . . . are just as enthralling. But the real highlights are the images of Paul with John Lennon, capturing the electric chemistry and childlike joy that informed the Beatles' greatest work." Entertainment Wkly

National Geographic Society (U.S.)
★ **In** focus; National Geographic greatest portraits. National Geographic Society 2004 504p il $30 **779**
1. Portrait photography
ISBN 0-7922-7363-X
LC 2004-44953

"Comprising 280 portraits by 150 of National Geographic's celebrated photographers . . . the book spans over 100 years and covers the entire globe. Organized chronologically as well as thematically and enriched with essays on the development of photographic styles through decades, it is a tasteful celebration of the medium but even more so of human diversity." Libr J

Through the lens; National Geographic greatest photographs. National Geographic Soc. 2003 504p il $30   **779**
1. Documentary photography
ISBN 0-7922-6164-X

LC 2003-52757

This is a "collection of 250 photos, mostly in color and drawn from the National Geographic Society's archive. . . . The society's signature blend of dramatic, rigorously composed natural shots and 'family of nations'-style culture peeps are backed by broad captions and text. . . . The six sections ('Europe'; 'Asia'; 'Africa & the Middle East'; 'The Americas'; 'Oceans and Isles'; 'The Universe') include the first color underwater photographs, as well as collaborative work with NASA, and prominently credit the 84 photographers whose work is featured." Publ Wkly

Schles, Ken
Invisible City; by Ken Schles. Steidl 2015 80 p. chiefly illustrations $40   **779**
1. Photography 2. New York (N.Y.) 3. Bohemianism -- New York (N.Y.)
ISBN 3869306912; 9783869306919
This book, by Ken Schles, is "one of the twentieth century's great depictions of nocturnal bohemian experience. Documenting his life in New York City's East Village during its heyday in the tumultuous 1980s, Schles captured its look and attitude in delirious and dark honesty." (Publisher's note)

The **Scurlock** Studio and Black Washington; picturing the promise. edited by Paul Gardulo . . . [et al.] National Museum of African American History and Culture: In collaboration with the National Museum o 2009 224p il $35   **779**
1. Scurlock Studio (Firm) 2. African Americans -- Pictorial works 3. Washington (D.C.) -- Social life and customs
ISBN 978-1-58834-262-1; 1-58834-262-X

LC 2008-32847

"In 1911 Addison Scurlock opened a photography studio in Washington, D.C., and went on to chronicle the aspirations and ambitions of the black community into the 1990s. . . . Photographs include the famous (Marian Anderson, Duke Ellington, Ralph Bunche, W. E. B. DuBois, and Muhammad Ali) as well as the influential but perhaps less well known (business owners, churchgoers, civic leaders, members of high society). With more than 100 images, this book is a proud celebration of a vibrant community from the early to the late twentieth century." Booklist
Includes bibliographical references

Shaughnessy, Jim
The **call** of trains; railroad photographs of Jim Shaughnessy. text by Jeff Brouws. W.W. Norton 2008 224p il $65   **779**
1. Railroads -- Pictorial works
ISBN 978-0-393-06592-3; 0-393-06592-8

LC 2008-1295

"Shaughnessy began shooting trains in downtown Troy, New York (his hometown), in the middle 1940s. He eventually took lengthy trips, first in New England and Canada, later across the Midwest to the Southwest, to photograph trains. He initially focused on the big engines but quickly extended his purview to include railway workers, railway buildings, and the countrysides through which the trains rolled. A civil engineer rather than a professional photographer, he became as skilled as any pro. . . . Appearing on full pages of this oversize volume, his pictures are engrossing, stunning masterpieces of photodocumentation." Booklist
Includes bibliographical references

Smith, Joel
Edward Steichen: the early years. Princeton Univ. Press 1999 167p il $65   **779**
1. Photographers 2. Artistic photography
ISBN 0-691-04873-8

LC 99-26617

Smith examines the photography of Edward Steichen. Alfred Stieglitz was a patron of Steichen's, and Smith discusses "the interrelationship between Steichen's work and Stieglitz's shifting aesthetic interests, as well as the influence of Paris on Steichen's development." N Y Times Book Rev
Includes bibliographical references

Stepan, Peter
Photos that changed the world; the 20th century. edited by Peter Stepan; with contributions by Claus Biegerd [et al.] Prestel-Verlag 2000 183p il pa $19.95   **779**
1. Photojournalism
ISBN 3-7913-2395-4; 3-7913-3628-2 pa
Stepan provides "105 images that had the lasting visual power to capture a moment that could be the image of an era held in the instant of a shutter's click for distribution to a generation. . . . The photos are well reproduced and gain from the explanations of time, place, and context included in the excellent short essays that accompany each." Libr J

Szarkowski, John
William Eggleston's Guide; essay by John Szarkowski. Museum of Modern Art distributed by the MIT Press 1976 110 p. illustrations, portraits $45   **779**
1. Artistic photography 2. Photography, Artistic
ISBN 087070317X; 0870703781; 9780870703782

LC 77358661

This book of photography by William Eggleston "was the first one-man show of color photographs ever presented at The Museum of Modern Art, New York, and the Museum's first publication of color photography. . . . For this edition, . . . The Museum of Modern Art has made new color separations from the original 35 mm slides, producing a facsimile edition in which the color will be freshly responsive to the photographer's intentions." (Publisher's note)

Thompson, Michael

Michael Thompson: Portraits; edited by Vince Aletti. Damiani 2011 216p il $65   **779**
1. Artistic photography
ISBN 978-8-86208-156-6; 8-86208-156-1

"There aren't very many successful commercial photographers whose work is considered to be fine art and exhibited in galleries. . . . It's a fine line that one walks to gain that respect, especially for a photographer who specializes in fashion and celebrity. . . . Michael Thompson is one such photographer who has blurred the line and broken the boundary. The memorable portraits in this book of celebrity tell a story of our culture as much as about the person being photographed." Full Frontal Fashion

779.092   Photographers

Benton, Maya

Roman vishniac rediscovered; Maya Benton. DelMonico Books - Prestel 2015 384 p. illustrations (some color) $75   **779.092**
1. Photography
ISBN 9783791353951

LC 2015943008

This book, by Maya Benton, "emphasiz[es] Roman Vishniac's prodigious talents as one of the great documentary photographers of the 20th century. . . . In addition to featuring Vishniac's best-known work—the iconic images of Jewish life in Eastern Europe before the Holocaust—this publication also introduces many previously unpublished photographs spanning more than six decades of Vishniac's work." (Publisher's note)

Includes bibliographical references.

McCurry, Steve

The **Iconic** Photographs. by Steve McCurry. Phaidon Inc Ltd 2012 chiefly color illustrations   **779.092**
1. Photography
ISBN 0714865133; 9780714865133

Pictures of the Year International Book Award, Best Photography Book Award, Judges' Special Recognition, 2012

This book, by Steve McCurry, "brings together some of the most beautiful of [his] photographs from around the world, including iconic images from Southeast Asia, Africa and Europe.New edition of a previously limited edition work." (Publisher's note)

Magnum contact sheets; edited by Kristin Lubben.

Thames & Hudson 2011 508 p. illustrations (some color) $75   **779.092**
1. Photography 2. Photojournalism 3. Photography -- History 4. Documentary photography 5. Photographers -- Biography
ISBN 0500543992; 050054431X; 9780500543993; 9780500544310

LC 2011922610

This photography book, by Kristin Lubben, "presents a remarkable selection of contact sheets and ancillary material, revealing for the first time how the most celebrated Magnum photographers capture and edit the very best shots. Addressing key questions of photographic practice, the book illuminates the creative methods, strategies, and editing processes behind some of the world's most iconic images." (Publisher's note)

Includes bibliographical references and index

779.2   Portraits--photographs

Arbus, Diane, 1923-1971

Diane Arbus; An Aperture Monograph. by Diane Arbus. Aperture Monograph Thames & Hudson [distributor] 2012 15 p. illustrations $39.95   **779.2**
1. Photography 2. Portrait photography 3. Photography, Artistic
ISBN 1597111759; 9781597111751

LC 2013456957

This book, by Diane Arbus, first published in 1972, "offered the general public its first encounter with the breadth and power of her achievements. . . . A quarter of a century has done nothing to diminish the riveting impact of these pictures or the controversy they inspire. Arbus' photographs penetrate the psyche with all the force of a personal encounter and, in doing so, transform the way we see the world and the people in it." (Publisher's note)

779.3   Nature—photographic images

Malin, Gray

Beaches; Gray Malin. Harry N Abrams Inc 2016 143 p. color illustrations, color map (hardcover) $40   **779.3**
1. Beaches 2. Aerial photography
ISBN 1419720899; 9781419720895

LC 2016012939

This book, by Gray Malin, documents the work of the author, "the artist of the moment for the Hollywood and fashion elite. His . . . aerial photographs of beaches around the world are shot from doorless helicopters, creating playful and stunning celebrations of light, shape, and perspective, as well as summer bliss." (Publisher's note)

779.9796   Sports—photographic images

Buckland, Gail

Who shot sports; a photographic history, 1843 to the present. Gail Buckland. Alfred A. Knopf 2016 329 p. illustrations (some color) (hardcover : alk. paper) $45   **779.9796**
1. Sports -- History 2. Photography of sports 3. Photography of sports -- History
ISBN 0385352239; 9780385352239

LC 2015038089

This book, by Gail Buckland, "brings together the work of 165 extraordinary photographers, most of their images heralded, most of their names unknown; photographs that capture the essence of athletes' mastery . . . and showing what human will, discipline, drive, and desire look like when suspended in time." (Publisher's note)

"Buckland writes with such authority that her thoughts on photography, as an art form, and her analysis of individual images in and out of the sports context make this a must-read for pop culture enthusiasts and anyone interested in photography." Pub Wkly

Includes bibliographical references and index

779.99 History—photographic images

Frank, Robert, 1924-

The **Americans**; by Robert Frank; introduction by Jack Kerouac. Steidl 2008 180 p. chiefly illustrations $40   **779.99**

1. Documentary photography 2. United States -- Social life and customs -- 1945-1970

ISBN 386521584X; 9783865215840

This book, by Robert Frank, was "published in France in 1958, then in the United States in 1959. . . . In 83 photographs, Frank looked beneath the surface of American life to reveal a people plagued by racism, ill-served by their politicians and rendered numb by a rapidly expanding culture of consumption. Yet he also found novel areas of beauty in simple, overlooked corners of American life." (Publisher's note)

"Preceding an exhibition that will tour U.S. galleries in 2009, this volume will no doubt introduce new generations to Frank's inimitable record of daily life fifty years ago." Pub Wkly

780 Music

The **complete** classical music guide; general editor, John Burrows with Charles Wiffen and contributions from Robert Ainsley ... [et al.] DK Pub. 2012 352 p. ill. (hc) $25   **780**

1. Music 2. Musical instruments 3. Music appreciation

ISBN 0756692563; 9780756692568

LC 2012562384

This "illustrated guide is arranged by period—'early' (ie 1000-1600), baroque, classical, romantic (with additional chapters on romantic opera and national schools) and modern. Each period is introduced by an overview, and the book opens with a general guide to classical music—its elements, instruments and performance." (Classical Music)

Forney, Kristine

★ The **enjoyment** of music; an introduction to perceptive listening. Kristine Forney, Joseph Machlis. W. W. Norton 2011 xxxiii, 595 p.p ill. (chiefly col.), col. maps (hardcover) $116.45   **780**

1. Music appreciation 2. Music -- Social aspects 3. Music -- History and criticism

ISBN 0393935205; 9780393935202

LC 2010026215

This book by Kristine Forney and Joseph Machlis "reflects how today's students learn, listen to, and live with mu-

sic. . . . It emphasizes context to show how music fits in the everyday lives of people throughout history, and connects culture, performance, and technology to the lives of students today. The new edition features . . . cultural and historical context, and in-text features that encourage and develop critical thinking skills." (Publisher's note)

Includes bibliographical references and index

Gilbert, Steven E.

The **music** of Gershwin. Yale Univ. Press 1995 255p music (Composers of the twentieth century) $47   **780**

1. Composers

ISBN 0-300-06233-8

LC 95-12086

This book analyzes major musical works of George Gershwin including Rhapsody in Blue, Concerto in F, An American in Paris, Porgy and Bess, and some of his popular songs and lesser known works

"With this book, Gershwin's music finally gets the attention it deserves. . . . Gilbert's book is not for the casual reader, since it requires an understanding of music theory and notation." Libr J

Includes bibliographical references

The **Harvard** biographical dictionary of music; edited by Don Michael Randel. Belknap Press 1996 1013p il $39.95   **780**

1. Reference books 2. Music -- Bio-bibliography

ISBN 0-674-37299-9

LC 96-16456

"International in scope and covering all eras of music from the ancient to the present, this important new reference source has information concerning 5,500 individuals. Most are associated with classical concert music, although prominent jazz, rock , folk, and popular personalities are also represented: Madonna, Mozart, Zoot Sims, Mick Jagger, and Dolly Parton are included. Musicologists, educators, teachers, and reviewers, no matter how influential, are excluded. Entries consist of brief to long paragraphs that may include a bibliography or a list of compositions. . . . This is an authoritative and significant new reference work which all libraries must purchase." Choice

The **Harvard** concise dictionary of music and musicians; edited by Don Michael Randel. Belknap Press 1999 757p il hardcover o.p. pa $18.95 **780**

1. Reference books 2. Music -- Dictionaries 3. Music -- Bio-bibliography

ISBN 0-674-00084-6; 0-674-00978-9 pa

LC 99-40644

"Entries are arranged alphabetically and encompass terms, musical forms and styles, individual works, and instruments, as well as composers, performers, and theorists." Booklist

★ The **Harvard** dictionary of music; edited by Don Michael Randel. 4th ed; Belknap Press 2003

978p il (Harvard University Press reference library) $39.95 **780**

1. Reference books 2. Music -- Dictionaries

ISBN 0-674-01163-5

LC 2003-58262

First published 1944 under the authorship of Willi Apel

This reference "includes entries on all the styles and forms in Western music; . . . articles on the music of Africa, Asia, Latin America, and the Near East; descriptions of instruments . . . {with} historical background, and articles that reflect today's best, including popular music, jazz, and rock." Publisher's note

Hoffman, Miles

The **NPR** classical music companion; an essential guide for enlightened listening. Houghton Mifflin 2005 306p pa $15 **780**

1. Reference books 2. Music -- Dictionaries

ISBN 978-0-618-61945-0; 0-618-61945-3

LC 2006-273343

First published 1997 with title: The NPR classical music companion: terms and concepts from A to Z

This musical guide includes This musical guide includes "entries that are at least a good-size paragraph in length and liable to include, besides technical information, historical and listener's advisory material." Booklist

Lockwood, Lewis

Beethoven: the music and the life. Norton 2002 604p il music $39.95 **780**

1. Composers

ISBN 0-393-05081-5

LC 2002-75397

The author "concentrates primarily on his subject's music and development as a composer before dedicating separate chapters to biography and the historical, political, and cultural milieus. . . . All of Lockwood's narrative, including the discussion of specific compositions, will be accessible to serious music lovers with only a modest technical background. This results partly from an interesting innovation . . . 100 additional musical examples are available on a companion web site. . . . Lockwood's study offers a new and authoritative interpretation of a prodigiously gifted and complex man and artist." Libr J

Includes bibliographical references

★ The **New** Grove dictionary of music and musicians; edited by Stanley Sadie; executive editor, John Tyrrell. 2nd ed; Oxford University Press 2004 29v set $1, 500 **780**

1. Reference books 2. Music -- Dictionaries

ISBN 978-0-19-517067-2

First published 1980 in twenty volumes to supersede Grove's dictionary of music and musicians; this edition first published 2000

"Grove is not fat, it is limitless. Whether Grove is on the reference shelf or online, teachers, students, researchers, and the common reader will find it an abiding source of satisfaction." Commonweal

Includes bibliographical references

Norton Anthology of Western Music; edited by J. Peter Burkholder and Claude V. Palisca. 7th ed. W W Norton & Co Inc 2014 883 p. pa $48.30 **780**

1. Music appreciation 2. Music -- History and criticism 3. Musical analysis 4. Music collections

ISBN 0393921611; 9780393921618

LC 2009543431

This book, edited by J. Peter Burkholder and Claude V. Palisca, "feature[s] outstanding teaching pieces that reveal the sweep of history through changing genres, styles, conventions, forms, techniques, and materials. The Seventh Edition includes new twentieth- and twenty-first-century works by Adams, Bernstein, Carter, Golijov, Higdon, Revueltas, Saariaho, Strauss, and Villa-Lobos." (Publisher's note)

★ The **Oxford** companion to music; edited by Alison Latham. Oxford Univ. Press 2002 1434p il $65 **780**

1. Reference books 2. Music -- Dictionaries 3. Musicians -- Dictionaries

ISBN 0-19-866212-2

LC 2002-537302

"Among the 8000 entries are articles on composers, theorists, and some performers; instruments, forms, and terms; subjects like electronic music, individual countries, and politics and music; and some pieces (and even some famous arias). Each entry is presented in a dictionary format, with a select index of names appended and sometimes with bibliographic references. . . . The bias is still English, but the book provides cross references to American terms and includes plenty of American composers and musical subjects. A solid reference with a grand pedigree, usefully improved for home and general library use, this is highly recommended for all public libraries." Libr J

Includes bibliographical references

Ross, Alex

Listen to this. Farrar, Straus and Giroux 2010 364p il $27; ebook $12.99 **780**

1. Musical criticism 2. Music -- History and criticism

ISBN 978-0-374-18774-3; 0-374-18774-6; 978-1-4299-7761-6 ebook; 1-4299-7761-2 ebook

LC 2010-10283

"Though the bulk of the book examines classical work both historical and contemporary, Ross veers effortlessly from Mozart to Radiohead, from Kurt Cobain to Brahms, bringing a pop fan's enthusiasm to the composers and treating the rock stars seriously as musicians. . . . The triumph of 'Listen to This' is that Ross dusts off music that's centuries old to reval the passion and brilliance that's too often hidden from a contemporary audience. It's a joy for a pop fan or a classical aficionado." N Y Times Book Rev

Includes bibliographical references

Schonberg, Harold C.

★ The **lives** of the great composers; 3rd ed; Norton 1997 653p il $35 **780**

1. Composers

ISBN 0-393-03857-2

LC 96-13308

First published 1970

This book traces the lives of important musical figures from Monteverdi to Ives and includes information on the serialists, minimalist composers and the new tonalists of the 1990s

"Schonberg writes for the lay reader. His intention is to humanize the composers and the writing, always highly readable, emphasizes biographical information rather than musical analysis." Libr J

Includes bibliographical references

Tolan, Sandy

Children of the stone; the healing power of music in a hard land. Sandy Tolan. Bloomsbury USA 2014 453 pages chiefly col. ill., maps $28   **780**
1. Intifada, 2000- 2. Music -- Study and teaching 3. Violists -- West Bank -- Biography 4. Music -- Social aspects -- West Bank 5. Music -- Instruction and study -- West Bank 6. Refugees, Palestinian Arab -- West Bank -- Education

ISBN 1608198138; 9781608198139

LC 2014032528

Author Sandy Tolan presents this stroy of "Ramzi Hussein Aburedwan, a child from a Palestinian refugee camp, confronts an occupying army, gets an education, masters an instrument, dreams of something much bigger than himself, and then, through his charisma and persistence, inspires scores of others to work with him to make that dream real. The dream: a school to transform the lives of thousands of children--as Ramzi's life was transformed--through music." (Publisher's note)

"This is an engrossing and powerful story, moving skillfully amid the failure of the never-ending battles and 'peace' talks between Israel and Palestine and the determination of one brave young man to change his world." Booklist

Includes bibliographical references and index

Walker-Hill, Helen

From spirituals to symphonies; African-American women composers and their music. Greenwood Press 2002 401p il $94.95   **780**
1. Poets 2. Singers 3. Teachers 4. Composers 5. Violinists 6. African American women

ISBN 0-313-29947-1

LC 2001-40600

This profiles the lives and works of Undine Smith Moore, Julia Perry, Margaret Bonds, Irene Britton Smith, Dorothy Rudd Moore, Valerie Capers, Mary Watkins, and Regina Harris Baiocchi

This is "an accessible, thoughtful, and humanist study. . . . Detailed works lists and an appendix enumerating other black women composers add reference value." Libr J

Includes bibliographical references

780.2   Miscellany; texts; treatises on music scores and recordings

Calamar, Gary

Record store days; from vinyl to digital and back again. [by] Gary Calamar and Phil Gallo. Sterling 2010 238p il $19.95   **780.2**
1. Record stores 2. Music industry

ISBN 978-1-4027-7232-0

"Packed with quotes from musicians, shop owners, and fans, this volume is a treat for readers, with its inside look at the importance of vinyl in people's lives throughout the 20th century. Major vinyl shops such as Tower Records, Rhino Records, and Bleecker Bob's are profiled. Nearly every page is graced with vintage photographs and interesting sidebars filled with facts, from the format history of recorded music over the century to vinyl oddities. The authors stress the importance of record stores as community meeting places and discuss the demise of the record industry, the rise of digital music, and the comeback of vinyl thanks to bands releasing limited-edition vinyl singles." Libr J

Cutler, David

The **savvy** musician; building a career, earning a living & making a difference. Helius Press 2009 350p il pa $19.99   **780.2**
1. Music industry -- Vocational guidance

ISBN 978-0-9823075-0-2

This book "is a guide to the aspiring musician who wants to make their living doing what they love. A . . . blend of music and marketing book, David Cutler encourages musicians to learn how to sell themselves and adapt technology to their approaches, to get themselves out there with a recognizable brand. An honest book about making it in the music industry, 'The Savvy Musician' is a read that can't be missed by music lovers." Midwest Book Rev

Includes bibliographical references

Kot, Greg

★ **Ripped**; how the wired generation revolutionized music. Scribner 2009 262p $25; pa $14 **780.2**
1. Music industry 2. Music -- Internet resources

ISBN 978-1-4165-4727-3; 1-4165-4727-4; 978-1-4165-4731-0 pa; 1-4165-4731-2 pa

LC 2008-40839

The author's "breezy, entertaining, journalistic style and sympathetic tone consistently draw in the reader. Essential for all those interested in the intersection of music and technology." Libr J

780.26   Texts; treatises on music scores and recordings

Day, Timothy

★ A **century** of recorded music; listening to musical history. Yale Univ. Press 2000 306p il $40; pa $19   **780.26**
1. Sound recordings -- History 2. Music -- History and criticism 3. Sound -- Recording and Reproducing

-- History
ISBN 0-300-08442-0; 0-300-09401-9 pa
LC 00-43490

This work provides a "narrative of the evolution of recording from cylinders (1887), shellac discs, and acoustic rerecording through the reproducing piano, electrical amplifications (1925), and magnetic tape to the long-playing record (1948) and compact disc of the 1980s. Day also discusses studio practices and the emergence of influential record producers, the role of radio and recordings in creating a mass audience, the expansion of recorded repertoire, and new ways to experience music. Recommended for all music collections." Choice

Includes bibliographical references

780.3   Music dictionaries

Bourne, Joyce

The **Oxford** Dictionary of Music; Tim Rutherford-Johnson; Michael Kennedy; Joyce Bourne. Oxford Univ Pr 2012 976 p. $49.95   **780.3**
1. Music 2. Music -- Dictionaries
ISBN 0199578109; 9780199578108

This book by Tim Rutherford-Johnson, Michael Kennedy, and Joyce Bourne, "offers broad coverage of a wide range of musical categories spanning many eras, including composers, librettists, singers, orchestras, important ballets and operas, and musical instruments and their history. Over 250 new entries have been added to this [sixth] edition to expand coverage of popular music, ethnomusicology, modern and contemporary composers, music analysis, and recording technology." (Publisher's note)

780.7   Education, research, related topics; performances

Tunstall, Tricia

Changing lives; Tricia Tunstall. Norton 2012 320 p.   **780.7**
1. Conductors (Music) 2. Music -- Study and teaching 3. Music -- Instruction and study -- Venezuela 4. Music -- Instruction and study -- United States 5. Fundación del Estado para el Sistema Nacional de las Orquestas Juveniles e Infantiles de Venezuela -- History
ISBN 9780393078961
LC 2011026504

This book tells the "story of conductor . . . Gustavo Dudamel, and the music education program, El Sistema, . . . the music education program that nurtured his musical talent, first as a young violinist and then as a budding conductor under the mentorship of its founder, José Antonio Abreu. . . . No matter the location, the overarching goal of El Sistema is unwavering: to rescue children from the depredations of poverty through music." (Publisher's note)

780.89   Ethnic and national groups

Murray, Albert

The **blue** devils of Nada; a contemporary American approach to aesthetic statement. Pantheon Bks. 1996 238p $23; pa $12   **780.89**
1. Poets 2. Artists 3. Authors 4. Singers 5. Pianists 6. Composers 7. Novelists 8. Blues music 9. Jazz musicians 10. African American arts 11. Band leaders 12. Trumpet players 13. Short story writers 14. Nobel laureates for literature
ISBN 0-679-44213-8; 0-679-75859-3 pa
LC 95-23331

In these essays Murray "presents Louis Armstrong, Count Basie, Duke Ellington, painter Romare Bearden and Ernest Hemingway as embodying, in their work and their lives, a peculiarly American strain of existential improvisation and epic storytelling. His theme, variously elaborated, is the effort of the engaged artist to document and give shape to the rootlessness and chaos underlying contemporary life in general—and African American life, in particular—in a way that transcends 'agitprop journalism.'" Publ Wkly

780.9   History, geographic treatment, biography

Blanning, T. C. W.

The **triumph** of music; the rise of composers, musicians and their art. [by] Tim Blanning. Belknap Press of Harvard University Press 2008 416p il $29.95   **780.9**
1. Musicians 2. Music -- Social aspects
ISBN 978-0-674-03104-3; 0-674-03104-0
LC 2008-26753

"This is not intended to be a history of music; it is a brilliantly written history of the steady growth of the power of music and its performers." Libr J

Includes bibliographical references (p. 343-352)

Crawford, Richard

America's musical life; a history. Norton 2000 976p il hardcover o.p. pa $23.95   **780.9**
1. American music -- History and criticism
ISBN 0-393-04810-1; 978-0-393-32726-7 pa; 0-393-32726-4 pa
LC 99-47565

This survey of music in America covers "blues, jazz, swing, pop, rock, hip hop . . . with economics and history as cultural backdrops. Well researched and sensitively constructed, this is highly recommended." Libr J

Includes bibliographical references

Mithen, Steven J.

The **singing** neanderthals; the origins of music, language, mind, and body. [by] Steven Mithen. Harvard University Press 2006 374p il map $25.95; pa $16.95   **780.9**
1. Music 2. Evolution
ISBN 0-674-02192-4; 978-0-674-02192-1; 978-0-674-02559-2 pa; 0-674-02559-8 pa
LC 2005-30187

First published 2005 in the United Kingdom

The author argues "that as a species, humans most likely made musical noises that led to language, not the other way around. . . . This book is a rich resource." Choice

Includes bibliographical references

Moody, Rick

On celestial music; and other adventures in listening. Rick Moody. Little, Brown and Company 2012 439 p. **780.9**

1. American essays 2. Music appreciation 3. Popular music -- History and criticism 4. Music -- History and criticism

ISBN 9780316105217

LC 2011030556

This book offers a collection of essays on music. ""On Celestial Music," which was included in "Best American Essays," 2008, begins with a lament for the loss in recent music of the vulnerability expressed by Otis Redding's masterpiece, "Try a Little Tenderness;" moves on to [Rick] Moody's infatuation with the . . . music of the Velvet Underground; and ends with an appreciation of Arvo Part and Purcell. . . . Contemporary groups covered include Magnetic Fields (their love songs), Wilco (the band's and Jeff Tweedy's evolution), Danielson Famile (an evangelical rock band), The Pogues (Shane McGowan's problems with addiction), The Lounge Lizards (John Lurie's brilliance), and Meredith Monk." (Publisher's note)

Includes bibliographical references and index

Music; the definitive visual history. DK Publishing. DK Publishing 2015 480 p. illustrations (some color) $24.95 **780.9**

1. Music -- History and criticism

ISBN 1465442464; 9781465442468

LC 2015667167

This book "guides readers through the progression of music since its prehistoric beginnings. . . . Telling the story of musical developments, era by era, linking musical theory, technology, and human genius into the narrative, [it] profiles the lives of groundbreaking musicians from Mozart to Elvis, takes an in-depth look at the history and function of various instruments, and includes listening suggestions for each music style." (Publisher's note)

Palisca, Claude V.

A history of Western music; J. Peter Burkholder, Donald Jay Grout, Claude V. Palisca. 9th edition W.W. Norton & Co. Inc. 2014 1009 p. illustrations hbk $144.85 **780.9**

1. Music -- History and criticism

ISBN 0393918297; 9780393918298

LC 2013035016

First published 1960

The authors survey the course of Western music from the ancient world to modern atonalism and dodecaphony. They cover vocal and instrumental forms, notation, performance, music-printing, the development of instruments, and biographical information on composers.

Includes bibliographical references and index

Rosen, Charles

The classical style; Haydn, Mozart, Beethoven. expanded ed; Norton 1997 xxx, 533p il $35; pa $19.95 **780.9**

1. Composers 2. Music -- History and criticism

ISBN 0-393-04020-8; 0-393-31712-9 pa

LC 96-27335

First published 1971 by Viking

"This remains simply the most important book on the classical style in music." Choice

Includes bibliographical references

The romantic generation. Harvard Univ. Press 1995 723p il hardcover o.p. pa $18.95 **780.9**

1. Music -- History and criticism

ISBN 0-674-77934-7 pa

LC 94-46239

The author "explains and describes the first half of the 19th century in conjunction with literature, art, and social changes. . . . Rosen also examines the lives of the composers and pursues some detailed analysis of numerous compositions to make his points. The result is a fresh, challenging, and stimulating view of the society in which Chopin, Liszt, Berlioz, and Schumann flourished." Libr J

Terkel, Studs, 1912-2008

And they all sang; adventures of an eclectic disc jockey. New Press 2005 xxii, 301p $25.95; pa $16.95 **780.9**

1. Musicians

ISBN 978-1-59558-003-0; 1-59558-003-4; 978-1-59558-118-1 pa; 1-59558-118-9 pa

LC 2005-43866

In this "collection of 40 interviews, . . . Terkel recalls his venerable radio program, The Wax Museum, which premiered shortly after the end of WWII in 1945, profiling composers, entertainers and impresarios of nearly every type of music. . . . Insightful and daring, Terkel always asks the right questions, whether culturally or musically." Publ Wkly

780.92 Biography

The Norton/Grove dictionary of women composers; edited by Julie Anne Sadie & Rhian Samuel. Norton 1995 xliii, 548p il $45 **780.92**

1. Reference books 2. Women composers -- Dictionaries

ISBN 0-393-03487-9

First published 1994 in the United Kingdom with title: The New Grove dictionary of women composers

"This important volume does not merely recycle material from the 1980 New Grove but collects 900 newly written articles, the longer ones signed." Libr J

Porter, Cecelia Hopkins

Five lives in music; women performers, composers, and impresarios from the baroque to the present. Cecelia Hopkins Porter. University of Illinois Press 2012 xiv, 244 p.p ill. (cloth : alk. paper) $45 **780.92**

1. Women composers -- Biography 2. Women musicians -- Biography 3. Composers -- Biography 4.

Musicians -- Biography
ISBN 0252037014; 9780252037016

LC 2011051102

This book, by Cecelia Hopkins Porter, profiles women musicians through history. It "brings to light the private and performance lives of five remarkable women musicians and composers. . . . Porter probes each musician's social and economic status, her education and musical training, the cultural expectations within the traditions and restrictions of each woman's society, and other factors." (Publisher's note)

Includes bibliographical references (p. [229]-237) and index

781 Principles, forms, ensembles, voices, instruments

Mannes, Elena

The **power** of music; pioneering discoveries in the new science of song. foreword by Dr. Aniruddh Patel. Walker & Company 2011 263p il $26 **781**

1. Music and science 2. Music -- Psychological aspects
ISBN 978-0-8027-1996-6; 0-8027-1996-1

LC 2010-48255

An "investigation of how music affects people and other animals. Detailing a variety of scientific experiments, [the author] shows the effects of sound frequencies and vibrations on body organs and brain waves; her study culminates in documentation supporting music therapy. Mannes's intercontinental explorations range from songbird studies to infants' melodic preferences to the origins of the universe (one topic on which her discussions seem rather far-fetched if fascinating). Interviews with influential musicians such as Bobby McFerrin help lighten an otherwise rather dense text." Libr J

Includes bibliographical references.

781.1 Basic principles of music

Byrne, David, 1952-

★ **How** Music Works; David Byrne. Pgw 2012 **781.1**

ISBN 1936365537; 9781936365531

In this book, David Byrne "explores how profoundly music is shaped by its time and place, and he explains how the advent of recording technology in the twentieth century forever changed our relationship to playing, performing, and listening to music. Acting as historian and anthropologist, raconteur and social scientist, he searches for patterns." (Publisher's note)

Includes bibliographical references.

781.2 Elements of music

Piston, Walter

Counterpoint. Norton 1947 235p music $41.75 **781.2**

1. Counterpoint
ISBN 978-0-393-09728-3; 0-393-09728-5

This work covers the principles and techniques of counterpoint as represented in the works of 18th and 19th century composers

Harmony; 5th ed; Norton 1987 575p $59.95 **781.2**

1. Harmony
ISBN 0-393-95480-3

LC 86-23901

First published 1941

A presentation of the harmonic structures utilized by composers of the 18th and 19th centuries. Includes examples and exercises

781.49 Recording of music

Milner, Greg

Perfecting sound forever; an aural history of recorded music. Faber and Faber 2009 416p il $35 **781.49**

1. Sound recordings 2. Musical perception 3. Music -- Computer programs 4. Sound -- Recording and reproducing 5. Sound -- Recording and reproducing -- History
ISBN 0-571-21165-8; 978-0-571-21165-4

LC 2008-55444

This is a history of recording music from 1915, the year in which "Thomas Edison proclaimed that he could record a live performance and reproduce it perfectly, shocking audiences who found themselves unable to tell whether what they were hearing was an Edison Diamond Disc or a flesh-and-blood musician. Today, [according to the author], the equation is reversed. Whereas Edison proposed that a real performance could be rebuilt with absolute perfection, Pro Tools and digital samplers now allow musicians and engineers to create the illusion of performances that never were. . . . [Milner asks the question]: Should a recording document reality as faithfully as possible, or should it improve upon or somehow transcend the music it records?" (Publisher's note) Index.

"The author begins in the late 19th century, tracing the evolution from Edison's invention of the phonograph to the contemporary use of digital music files. Broad in scope and steeped in detail, the book strikes a mostly well-maintained balance between the history of the technological development of recordings and the more approachable accounts of the people and events surrounding it." Kirkus

781.6 Traditions of music

Horowitz, Joseph

★ **Classical** music in America; a history of its rise and fall. W. W. Norton & Company 2005 606p il $39.95; pa. $19.95 **781.6**

1. Music -- United States
ISBN 0-393-05717-8; 9780393330557

LC 2004-27754

"As a comprehensive, convincing analysis of the contemporary dilemma, and a riveting portrait of the century and a half of events and personalities which brought it about, Mr Horowitz's account would be hard to beat." Economist

Includes bibliographical references

781.62 Folk music

American ballads and folk songs; [compiled by] John A. Lomax and Alan Lomax; with a foreword by George Lyman Kittredge. Dover Publications 1994 xxxix, 625p pa $21.95 **781.62**
1. Ballads 2. Folk music -- United States
ISBN 0-486-28276-7; 978-0-486-28276-3
First published 1934 by MacMillan

Treasury of authentic songs, many recorded on location by noted father-and-son folklorists. Music and lyrics for over 200 ballads about the railroads, mountain songs, chain gang songs, creole songs, songs about cocaine and whisky, reels, minstrel songs, songs of childhood and much more. Includes such time-honored favorites as John Henry, Goin Home, Frankie and Albert, Down in the Valley, Little Brown Jug, Alabama-Bound, Shortenin Bread, Skip to My Lou, Frog Went a-Courtin and a host of others. Notes about the origin of each melody, a bibliography and an index are included.

★ **Our** singing country; folk songs and ballads. collected and compiled by John A. Lomax and Alan Lomax; music editor. Ruth Crawford Seeger; introduction to the Dover edition by Judith Tick; includes bibliography by Harold W. Thompson. Dover 2000 pa $16.95 **781.62**
1. Ballads 2. Folk music -- United States
ISBN 978-0-486-41089-0 pa; 0-486-41089-7 pa
First published 1941 by MacMillan

This includes melodies and words for tunes from all parts of the United States. Songs include spirituals, hollers, game songs, lullabies, courting songs, chain-gang work songs, Cajun airs, breakdowns, and many more. Includes over 200 authentic folk songs and ballads.

Sandburg, Carl

The **American** songbag; [compiled by] Carl Sandburg; introduction by Garrison Keillor. Harcourt Brace Jovanovich 1990 xxix, 495p pa $35 **781.62**
1. Folk music -- United States
ISBN 978-0-15-605650-2 pa; 0-15-605650-X pa
A reissue of the title first published 1927

"Sandburg was not only a poet but also a noted collector and performer of American folk music. This anthology contains words and music to 290 songs that people have sung in the making of Americanca." Publisher's note

Strom, Yale

The **book** of Klezmer; the history, the music, the folklore. A Cappella Bks. 2002 381p il music $28 **781.62**
1. Klezmer music
ISBN 1-55652-445-5

LC 2002-2701

This history of Klezmer music is divided into "four chapters: 'From King David to Duvid the Klezmer,' 'From

the Enlightenment to the Holocaust,' 'Klezmer in the New World, 1880-1960,' and 'From Zev to Zorn: The Masters of the Culture.' The first appendix, 'Klezmer Memories in the Memorial Books,' is one of the most moving sections, featuring a collection of commentaries on klezmer music and musicians from hundreds of memorial books written by Holocaust survivors." Libr J

Includes discography and bibliographical references

Wade, Stephen

The **beautiful** music all around us; field recordings and the American experience. Stephen Wade. University of Illinois Press 2012 xvii, 477 p.p ill., music (Music in American life) (hardcover) $24.95 **781.62**
1. Sound recordings 2. Folk music -- United States 3. Archive of Folk Culture (U.S.) 4. Field recordings -- United States -- History 5. Folk music -- United States -- History and criticism
ISBN 0252036883; 9780252036880

LC 2011044092

This book, by Stephen Wade, is part of the "Music in American Life" series. It describes the "backstories of thirteen performances captured on Library of Congress field recordings between 1934 and 1942 in locations reaching from Southern Appalachia to the Mississippi Delta and the Great Plains. . . . Alongside loving and expert profiles of these performers and their locales and communities, Wade also untangles the histories of these iconic songs and tunes." (Publisher's note)

Includes bibliographical references (p. [423]-445) and index.

Ware, Charles Pickard

Slave songs of the United States; the complete 1867 collection of slave songs. [collected and compiled] by William Francis Allen, Charles Pickard Ware, and Lucy McKim Garrison; piano accompaniments by Irving Schlein; Peter Schlein, editor. Hal Leonard 2007 183p pa $15.95 **781.62**
1. Spirituals (Songs) 2. African American music 3. Folk music -- United States 4. Slavery -- United States -- Songs
ISBN 978-1-42342-262-4 pa; 1-42342-262-7 pa

"One of the first documentary collections of Negro folk songs was compiled in 1867 by William Francis Allen, Charles Pickard Ware and Lucy McKim Garrison. . . . This collection of 136 authentic folk songs of the Negro people revolutionized America's understanding of this music. The book, which contains spirituals, work songs, field hollers, soldier songs of Civil War days, and freedom songs, has become a classic of its kind. . . . In 1965, composer Irving Schlein created . . . piano settings for every song from the original edition. Chords for guitar have also been added to the musical notation." Publisher's note

Young, Rob

Electric Eden; unearthing Britain's visionary music. Faber and Faber 2011 664p il pa $25 **781.62**
1. Folk music -- Great Britain
ISBN 978-0-86547-856-5; 0-86547-856-2

LC 2011-01987

First published 2010 in the United Kingdom

"It is a commonplace that rock and R&B came out of the folk and blues revivals of the early 1960s, and Young shows, through enchanting storytelling and brilliant commentary, that a similar revival in England inspired the Beatles and Pink Floyd, Led Zeppelin and Traffic, Kate Bush and Talk Talk. Folklorists notated old songs and dances. Marxists put folk music forward as the true voice of the people. Composers like Benjamin Britten and Ralph Vaughan Williams devised rich neo-traditional pageantry. Today, the pioneers of the "acid folk" movement see this music as a model for their own." (Publisher's Note)

"Young's narrative slips fluidly forward, backward, and through the cracks of canonical music history. And he doesn't just stick to music; like Greil Marcus with a thirst for ancient paganism and postmodern urban theory, Young weaves a poetic, philosophical tapestry as rich and heady as the songs he champions." AV Club

Includes bibliographical references and discography

781.64   Western popular music

Bradley, Andy

House of hits; the story of Houston's Gold Star/ SugarHill Recording Studios. by Andy Bradley and Roger Wood. University of Texas Press 2010 334p il (Brad and Michele Moore roots music series) $34.95   **781.64**

1. Popular music 2. Music industry 3. SugarHill Recording Studios (Firm)

ISBN 978-0-292-71919-4

LC 2009-44441

"A complete and well-annotated history of Gold Star/ SugarHill, the oldest continuously operating recording studio in the U.S., the book is a trove of interesting stories and first-person narratives from many of the major players who made the records that are now an indelible part of the lexicon of American music." Houston Press

Includes bibliographical references

Broven, John

Record makers and breakers; voices of the independent rock 'n' roll pioneers. University of Illinois Press 2008 584p il $50   **781.64**

1. Popular music 2. Music industry

ISBN 978-0-252-03290-5; 0-252-03290-X

LC 2008-27204

"This volume is an engaging and exceptional history of the independent rock 'n' roll record industry from its raw regional beginnings in the 1940s with R & B and hillbilly music through its peak in the 1950s and decline in the 1960s. John Broven combines narrative history with extensive oral history material from numerous recording pioneers including Joe Bihari of Modern Records; Marshall Chess of Chess Records; Jerry Wexler, Ahmet Ertegun, and Miriam Bienstock of Atlantic Records; Sam Phillips of Sun Records; Art Rupe of Specialty Records; and many more." (Publisher's Note)

"The depth of factual detail is incredible, but it's presented in the style of a rich oral history. . . . It's a chronicle of the entrepreneurial American spirit, liberally punctuated by the creation of some of the most exciting and innovative music of all time." Record Collector

Includes bibliographical references (p. 545-556)

Chang, Jeff

Can't stop, won't stop; a history of the hip-hop generation. introduction by D.J. Kool Herc. St. Martin's Press 2005 546p il hardcover o.p. pa $16   **781.64**

1. Rap music

ISBN 0-312-30143-X; 0-312-42579-1 pa

LC 2004-56656

"A fascinating, far-reaching must for pop-music and pop-culture collections." Booklist

Includes bibliographical references, discography, and filmography

Charnas, Dan

The **big** payback; the history of the business of hip-hop. New American Library 2010 660p il $24.95   **781.64**

1. Hip-hop 2. Rap music 3. Music industry

ISBN 978-0-451-22929-8; 0-451-22929-0

LC 2010-16062

On this four-decade-long journey from the studios where the first rap records were made to the boardrooms where the big deals were inked, "The Big Payback" tallies the list of who lost and who won along the 40-year road to hip-hop's dominance.

This "history of the rap industry is a classic of music-business dirt-digging as well as a kind of pulp epic. . . . Tomorrow's Diddys should sleep with this book under their pillow." Rolling Stone

The **Encyclopedia** of Country Music; the ultimate guide to the music. compiled by the staff of the Country Music Hall of Fame and Museum; edited by Paul Kingsbury, Michael McCall, and John W. Rumble with the assistance of Michael Gray and Jay Orr. 2nd ed. Oxford University Press 2012 xi, 626 p.p $65.00   **781.64**

1. Music industry 2. Country musicians 3. Folk music -- United States 4. Country music -- Encyclopedias

ISBN 0195395638; 9780195395631

LC 2010045104

This country music encyclopedia, edited by Michael McCall, John Rumble, and Paul Kingsbury, is a revised edition of the previous 1998 publication. "This . . . edition includes more than 1,200 A-Z entries covering nine decades of history and artistry. . . . Compiled by . . . experts at the Country Music Hall of Fame and Museum, the encyclopedia has been brought completely up-to-date, with new entries on the artists who have profoundly influenced country music in recent years." (Publisher's note)

Govenar, Alan B.

Texas blues; the rise of a contemporary sound. [by] Alan Govenar. Texas A&M University Press

2008 599p il (John and Robin Diskson series in Texas music) $40 **781.64**

1. Blues music 2. Rhythm and blues music 3. Texas
ISBN 978-1-58544-605-6; 1-58544-605-X

LC 2007-39152

As this "study shows, the importance of Texas Blues is demonstrated by the number of musicians who have practiced or are practicing this art. The coverage is expansive, with introductory essays, interviews conducted by Govenar and others, and a wealth of photographs. Govenar . . . manages to profile an amazing number of guitarists, pianists, singers, and others, both well known and obscure, who show how much pioneering blues musicians like T-Bone Walker and Lightnin' Hopkins influenced their own development. The discussion of the role played by tiny establishments, radio stations, country music, and several key record labels is particularly enlightening." Libr J

Includes discography and bibliographical references

Hermes, Will

Love goes to buildings on fire; five years in New York that changed music forever. Faber and Faber 2011 368p il $30 **781.64**

1. Popular music 2. Music -- New York (N.Y.)
ISBN 978-0-86547-980-7

LC 2011-08445

"New York City might have been dead broke, crime-ridden and garbage-infested in the 1970s, but the music sure was great. Bob Marley opened a club date for Bruce Springsteen, Bronx DJs stole power from streetlights to fiddle with turntables in new ways, Philip Glass drove classical purists nuts with his sweeping, hypnotic compositions, and The Fania All Stars remade salsa. Down at CBGB's, the Talking Heads were double-billed with the Ramones. New York City has been pumping out great music from Gershwin to Gaga, but veteran music writer Will Hermes shows in his episodic and idiosyncratic book, 'Love Goes to Buildings on Fire,' how 1973 through 1977 stood out as a time for innovation. Not only did the grimy time plant the seeds of hip-hop, it also fostered the highly influential scenes in jazz, Latino music, punk, disco, new wave and classical." Huffington Post

Includes bibliographical references

Houghton, Mick

Becoming Elektra; the true story of Jac Holzman's visionary record label. Jawbone 2010 304p il pa $29.95 **781.64**

1. Popular music 2. Music industry 3. Elektra Records (Firm) 4. Recording industry executives
ISBN 978-1-906002-29-9

Includes "full-color reproductions of virtually every title in Elektra's catalog, themselves a revealing portrait of changing tastes and evolving consumer sophistication. Houghton's research is meticulous but he avoids the minutia that clogs many music books." Seattle Post-Intelligencer

The **riot** grrrl collection; edited, with an introduction by Lisa Darms. Feminist Press 2013 362 p. illustrations (chiefly color) $34.95 **781.64**

1. Fanzines 2. Punk culture 3. Women's movement 4. Zines 5. Punk rock music -- Periodicals 6. Riot grrrl

movement -- Periodicals
ISBN 1558618228; 9781558618220

LC 2013014331

"Against the backdrop of the culture wars and before the rise of the Internet or desktop publishing, the zine and music culture of the Riot Grrrl movement empowered young women across the country to speak out against sexism and oppression." This book, edited by Lisa Darms, "reproduces a sampling of the original zines, posters, and printed matter for the first time since their initial distribution in the 1980s and '90s, and includes an original essay by Johanna Fateman." (Publisher's note)

"The writers' desperation, anger, and desire translate vividly into the 21st century and will resonate strongly with today's feminists, misfits, and punks." Pub Wkly

Includes bibliographical references

Roden, Steve

. . . i listen to the wind that obliterates my traces; music in vernacular photographs, 1880-1955. Dust-to-Digital 2011 un $50 **781.64**

1. Folk music 2. Popular music 3. Artistic photography 4. Musical instruments -- Pictorial works
ISBN 978-09817342-4-8

This volume is "compiled from the personal collection of interdisciplinary sound and visual artist Steve Roden. It contains a book of photographs of musicians mostly unknown and others related to the hearing of music. This beautifully hardbound book also contains two CDs containing 51 songs recorded between approximately 1914-1955, taken from 78s and acetates. The music ranges from the well known Bradley Kincaid's 1928 recording of 'Froggie Went A-Courtin' and Ukulele Ike's '(I'm Cryin' 'Cause I Know I'm) Losing You' to virtually unknown sides taken from home recordings. This is all annotated by a lengthy poetic essay by Roden that attempts to create a social and poetic context from the ephemeral, and is underscored by epigraphs from writers from James Agee, Joseph Roth, and William Wordsworth to Pär Lagerqvist and Gerhart Hauptmann." Allmusic.com

Seabrook, John

The **song** machine; inside the hit factory. by John Seabrook. W W Norton & Co Inc 2015 352 p. (hardcover) $26.95 **781.64**

1. Music industry 2. Popular music -- Writing and publishing 3. Music trade 4. Sound recording industry 5. Popular music -- Production and direction
ISBN 9780393241921

LC 2015022305

In this book, author John Seabrook explains that "songs are highly processed products. . . . [Through the] stories of artists like Katy Perry, Britney Spears, and Rihanna, as well as expert songsmiths like Max Martin, Stargate, Ester Dean, and Dr. Luke, [Seabrook] shows what life is like in an industry that has been catastrophically disrupted—spurring innovation, competition, intense greed, and seductive new products." (Publisher's note)

"Seabrook goes deeper into the career developments of Rihanna and Katy Perry, but most of the artists hold insignificant power within the international behemoth that this industry has become and even less control over their own musical progression. A revelatory ear - opener, as the music business remains in a state of significant flux." Kirkus

Includes bibliographical references and index

Smirnoff, Marc

The **Oxford** American book of great music writing; edited by Marc Smirnoff; foreword by Van Dyke Parks. University of Arkansas Press 2008 xxii, 421p il $34.95   781.64

1. Popular music -- History and criticism

ISBN 978-1-557-28887-5; 1-557-28887-9

LC 2008-26298

A collection of fifty-five essays taken from Oxford American magazine's Southern Music Issues from 1996 to 2007.

"With contributions from Nick Tosches, Robert Palmer, Robert Gordon, and Peter Guralnick, some of the top music writers, Smirnoff reminds us what good music writing is. This compilation is full of little gems, including Susan Straight's tender reminiscence of the music of Al Green, Tom Piazza's harrowing account of his encounter with bluegrass legend Jimmy Martin, and John Fergus Ryan's report of his time backstage with Jerry Lee Lewis in 1970. Also included are Jerry Wexler on Dusty Springfield, Roy Blount Jr. on Ray Charles, and John Jeremiah Sullivan on Chris Bell (of Big Star)." Booklist

Includes bibliographical references

Stanley, Bob

Yeah! Yeah! Yeah! the story of pop music from Bill Haley to Beyonce. Bob Stanley. W W Norton & Co Inc 2014 624 p. (hardcover) $29.95   781.64

1. Music appreciation 2. Popular music -- History and criticism

ISBN 9780393242690

LC 2014002223

This book, by Bob Stanley, is a "work of musical history, tracing the story of pop music through individual songs, bands, musical scenes, and styles from Bill Haley and the Comets . . . to Beyoncé's first megahit. . . . It covers the birth of rock, soul, R&B, punk, hip hop, indie, house, techno, and more, and it will remind you why you fell in love with pop music in the first place." (Publisher's note)

"The assemblage of irresistible, bite-size histories of top-of-the-charts stars is joyful, smart, and addictive, just like the best pop songs, and a must for music fans everywhere." Booklist

Includes bibliographical references and index

Wald, Elijah

How the Beatles destroyed rock 'n' roll; an alternative history of American popular music. Oxford University Press 2009 323p il $24.95   781.64

1. Popular music -- History and criticism

ISBN 978-0-19-534154-6

LC 2008-42265

"A bracing, inclusive look at the dramatic transformation in the way music was produced and listened to during the 20th century." Kirkus

Includes bibliographical references (p. 281-289)

Watkins, S. Craig

★ **Hip** hop matters; politics, pop culture, and the struggle for the soul of a movement. Beacon Press 2005 295p $24.95; pa $16   781.64

1. Rap music

ISBN 0-8070-0982-2; 0-8070-0986-5 pa

LC 2004-24187

The author "presents a concise, clear history of the hip-hop movement in the US and uses it as a springboard for discussion of contemporary issues of politics, pop culture, and struggle." Choice

Includes bibliographical references

Westhoff, Ben

Dirty South; Outkast, Lil Wayne, Soulja Boy, and the Southern rappers who reinvented hip-hop. Chicago Review Press 2011 298p il pa $14.95 781.64

1. Rap music

ISBN 978-1-56976-606-4; 1-56976-606-1

LC 2010-53907

An "exploration of the musical and personal terrain of what has come to be known as the Southern sound of rap by such artists as Lil Wayne, Young Jeezy, and Ludacris. Westhoff convincingly details how Southern rap music—'party music, full of hypnotic hooks and sing-along choruses'—took over from dominant East Coast and West Coast rap styles by replacing 'normal rap structures and metaphor-heavy rhymes. . . in favor of chants, grunts and shouts.' In fact, the beauty of Westhoff's descriptions of the genre as a whole and various songs in particular will make old fans as well as newbies want to search out and play classic CDs such as OutKast's 'Aquemini' and 'Kings of Crunk' by Lil Jon. And Westhoff's personal trips to the home bases of each artist he presents show how the personalities of the artists reinforce their music." Publ Wkly

Includes bibliographical references

781.642   Country music

Jennings, Dana Andrew

Sing me back home; love, death, and country music. [by] Dana Jennings. Faber and Faber 2008 257p $24   781.642

1. Country music -- History and criticism

ISBN 978-0-86547-960-9; 0-86547-960-7

LC 2007-47955

This "quirky, endearing combination memoir, family history, music criticism, and love-of-place offering, made up of short, punchy chapters and sharp observations about country's appeal and how country has expressed the inchoate emotions of its largely rural following, essentiallypresents the music as the portrayal of a way of life and a way of being." Booklist

Includes discography and bibliographical references

Kagarise, Leon

Pure country; the Leon Kagarise archives 1961-1971. foreword by Robert Gordon; introduction and

text by Eddie Dean. Process Media 2008 191p il
$35 **781.642**
1. Country music -- Pictorial works
ISBN 978-1-93417-003-8

"Kagarise was an obsessive fan of 'real' country and
bluegrass musics, and he amassed a giant collection of records, live tapes and ephemera, mostly during the 1960s.
This volume collects many of the color slides he shot at a
couple of outdoor venues in Maryland and Pennsylvania,
and the views of this lost scene they provide is unparalleled.
Well-known figures like Johnny Cash, George Jones and
Skeeter Davis mix with more legendary unknowns (at least
to proles), like the Stoneman family, with whom Kagarise
had a special connection, and who he rates far above the
Carter family in terms of sheer talent. The main text . . .
provides a very boss thumbnail history of country music in
the pre-modern era." Arthur

Russell, Tony
Country music originals; the legends & the
lost. Oxford University Press 2007 258p il
$29.95 **781.642**
1. Country music 2. Country musicians
ISBN 978-0-19-532509-6
LC 2007-8471

"Russell has accomplished a spectacular feat in that he
has written a thorough reference book that is as pleasing to
read as the best of narrative nonfiction." Publ Wkly

Includes bibliographical references

Zwonitzer, Mark
Will you miss me when I'm gone? the Carter
Family and their legacy in American music. [by] Mark
Zwonitzer with Charles Hirshberg. Simon & Schus-
ter 2002 417p il hardcover o.p. pa $15 **781.642**
1. Carter family (Musical group)
ISBN 0-684-85763-4; 0-7432-4382-X pa
LC 2002-22395

The author "follows the Carter family's history from the
1891 birth of A.P. Carter, the musical founder, up through
the late 1970s, offering background on the social, economic
and technological developments that spawned American
folk, country and rock music. . . . Zwonitzer writes with flair,
weaving anecdotes into a compelling study that will intrigue
historians and music lovers alike." Publ Wkly

781.643 Blues

Ferris, William
Give my poor heart ease; voices of the Mississippi blues. [interviews by] William Ferris. University
of North Carolina Press 2009 302p il $35 **781.643**
1. Blues music 2. African Americans -- Mississippi
ISBN 0-8078-3325-8; 978-0-8078-3325-4
LC 2009-16647

Ferris "presents transcriptions of stories he captured via
films and recording devices from the 1960s and 1970s of
Mississippi blues practitioners, preachers, and Parchman
Prison inmates. The enclosed CD and DVD bring the package together with stories, blues songs, and gospel record-

ings. B.B. King and Willie Dixon are the most famous artists
included, but the stories of desperately poor sharecroppers
and ex-inmates are just as engrossing. The comprehensive
bibliography is a great resource." Libr J

Includes bibliographical references

Gioia, Ted
Delta blues; the life and times of the Mississippi
Masters who revolutionized American music. artwork by Neil Harpe. W. W. Norton 2008 449p il
$27.95; pa $16.95 **781.643**
1. Blues music
ISBN 978-0-393-06258-8; 0-393-06258-9; 978-0-393-
33750-1 pa; 0-393-33750-2 pa
LC 2008-09412

Gioia describes the "beginnings of the Delta sound with
Charley Patton and former Parchman inmates Son House
and Bukka White. He relates the stories of such obscure
Delta artists as Tommy Johnson and Big Joe Williams before
delivering the bulk of the book, which describes the lives
and influences of Delta blues icons Robert Johnson, Muddy
Waters, Howlin' Wolf, B.B. King, and John Lee Hooker.
Gioia ends with a chapter about the rediscovery of Delta
legends by rabid blues collectors during the 1960s and then
oddly leaps to 1990s performers such as Chris Thomas King
and Junior Kimbrough in the last few pages. . . . Though presenting little new information and not geared for the blues
fanatic, this is an excellent introduction to Delta blues for the
novice and the general reader." Libr J

Includes bibliographical references

King, B. B.
★ **Blues** all around me; the autobiography of
B.B. King. [by] B.B. King with David Ritz. Avon
Bks. 1996 336p il pa $15.99 **781.643**
1. Singers 2. Guitarists 3. Blues music 4. Blues
musicians 5. African American musicians
ISBN 0-380-97318-9; 0-06-206103-8 pa
LC 96-27773

King recounts his humble beginnings and his career as a
prominent blues guitarist.

"This is one of the best recent pop-music bios. King
speaks straight from the soul, it seems, just like he plays the
guitar." Booklist

Lomax, Alan
★ The **land** where the blues began. New Press
2002 539p il pa $21.95 **781.643**
1. Blues music 2. African American music 3. African
Americans -- Mississippi
ISBN 1-56584-739-3; 978-1-56584-739-2
LC 2004-268632

First published 1993 by Pantheon

This is an account of the folklorist and musicologist's
travels in the Mississippi Delta in the 1940s as he recorded
the work of African American blues musicians.

"If it were a novel, Alan Lomax's long-awaited account
of his adventures in the Mississippi Delta would be called
'sprawling' and a 'must read.' . . . It is as delightful and hard
to put down as any fictional epic." Booklist

Includes bibliographical references, discography and
filmography

Nothing but the blues; the music and the musicians. {edited by} Lawrence Cohn. Abbeville Press 1993 432p il hardcover o.p. pa $39.95 **781.643**

1. Blues music

ISBN 0-7892-0607-2 pa

LC 93-2791

The essays in this volume aim to :trace the metamorphosis of the blues from its African roots and the 'hollers,' work songs, and party music of the rural south to the . . . rhythms of urban blues and on to R & B and blues rock. . . . Blues styles associated with specific regions are described. . . . Other topics include the impact of radio and recording technology on the popularity of the blues, the link between gospel and blues, and the blues revival of the 1960s." (Booklist)

This "illustrated compilation of articles by 10 notable writers examines the origins of blues and the music's various styles and artists, including women." Booklist

Includes discography and bibliographical references

781.646   Reggae

Bradley, Lloyd

This is reggae music; the story of Jamaica's music. Grove Press 2001 572p il pa $17   **781.646**

1. Reggae music

ISBN 0-8021-3828-4

LC 2001-33462

First published 2000 in the United Kingdom with title: Brass culture: when reggae was king

Presented "in a witty and engaging manner. . . . For enthusiasts, this book is fabulous." Libr J

Includes bibliographical references

781.648   Electronica

Matos, Michaelangelo

The **underground** is massive; how electronic dance music conquered America. Michaelangelo Matos. HarperCollins 2015 448 p. 16 plates; illustrations $25.99   **781.648**

1. Dance music 2. Electronic music 3. Popular culture -- United States

ISBN 0062271784; 9780062271785

LC 2015563599

This book, by Michaelangelo Matos, offers a "definitive chronicle of one of the hottest trends in popular culture--electronic dance music--from the noted authority covering the scene. . . . Drawing on a vast array of resources, including hundreds of interviews and a library of rare artifacts, from rave fanzines to online mailing-list archives, Matos reveals how EDM blossomed in tandem with the nascent Internet-message boards and chat lines connected partiers from town to town." (Publisher's note)

781.65   Jazz

Cook, Richard

The **Penguin** guide to jazz recordings; [by] Richard Cook and Brian Morton. 9th ed.; Penguin 2008 pa $37.50   **781.65**

1. Jazz music -- Discography 2. Sound recordings -- Reviews

ISBN 978-0-14-102327-4; 0-14-102327-9

Biannual. First published 1992

"Entries include very brief descriptions of the artists and a list of their recordings, with reviews and ratings by the authors. The lengths of the CD entries vary from very short (label, catalog number, issue date, and performers) to extensive, multiparagraph descriptions of the album's history, reception, and individual songs. The authors are clearly devout jazz historians, and the character of the entries is as much admiring as it is strictly factual. Their detailed descriptions of albums, songs, and even artists' tone colors and interpretations within specific songs are testament to their expertise." Booklist

Cooke, Mervyn

The **chronicle** of jazz; Mervyn Cooke. Oxford University Press 2013 272 p. illustrations (hardback : alk. paper) $39.95   **781.65**

1. Jazz ensembles 2. Jazz musicians 3. Jazz music -- History and criticism 4. Jazz -- Chronology 5. Jazz -- History and criticism

ISBN 0199341001; 9780199341009

LC 2013019617

This book, by Mervyn Cooke, "charts the evolution of jazz from its roots in Africa and the southern United States to the myriad urban styles heard around the world today. . . . Featuring hundreds of rare images, from record-cover artwork to pictures of live performances, each chronologically arranged section contains special box features on such topics as the unique tonal qualities of the bass clarinet, jazz clubs in Paris, personality sketches, and seminal gigs and albums." (Publisher's note)

"This handsome and attractive volume by music professor and writer Cooke covers the entire history of the jazz medium in one accessible and colorful resource." Booklist

Includes discography (pages 264-265), bibliographical references (page 266), and indexes

Feather, Leonard

The **biographical** encyclopedia of jazz; [by] Leonard Feather and Ira Gitler, with the assistance of Swing journal, Tokyo. Oxford Univ. Press 1999 xx, 718p hardcover o.p. pa $29.95   **781.65**

1. Jazz musicians

ISBN 0-19-507418-1; 978-0-19-532000-8 pa; 0-19-532000-X pa

LC 98-15485

This book is based in part on Leonard Feather's Encyclopedia of jazz, The new encyclopedia of jazz, The encyclopedia of jazz in the sixties, and on a subsequent work by Mr. Feather and Ira Gitler, The encyclopedia of jazz in the seventies

This reference source "is made up of more than 3,000 biographies, listed in alphabetical order. Musicians, singers, songwriters, and producers are included. Each entry begins with birth and death information, instruments played, and music-education information. This is followed by a listing of groups each individual played with for significant periods of time. Concluding each entry are lists of recordings, broadcast appearances, and record labels. . . . An indispensable reference source for its comprehensiveness and quality of scholarship." Booklist

Includes discographies

Giddins, Gary

Jazz; Gary Giddins & Scott DeVeaux. 2nd edition W W Norton & Co 2015 ML3508 ill., music pbk $159.05 **781.65**
1. Jazz music -- History and criticism
ISBN 0393937062; 9780393937060
LC 2014038121

"Enhanced with diagrams and references to specific recordings, the opening chapters walk the reader through some basic definitions and concepts required for critical listening. The authors write in a nonthreatening blend of academic and conversational language, gently guiding the novice toward deeper understanding while simultaneously offering the scholar opportunity for reflection. In the remainder of the book, the authors discuss jazz by period, providing rich detail and social, economic, and historical context." (Choice Reviews)

Visions of jazz; the first century. Oxford Univ. Press 1998 690p hardcover o.p. pa $18.95 **781.65**
1. Jazz musicians 2. Jazz music -- History and criticism
ISBN 0-19-513241-6 pa
LC 98-12199

"Alongside his virtuoso considerations of Ellington, Monk, Mingus, and the predictable greats, Giddins illuminates the contributions to be found in the likes of Al Jolson's minstrel posing and Stan Kenton's florid kitsch. His writing, like the music he loves, is joyously polyphonic, with history, legend, musicology, biography, and performance all rising out of the mix." New Yorker

Weather bird; jazz at the dawn of its second century. Gary Giddins. Oxford University Press 2004 xxiv, 632p $35 **781.65**
1. Jazz music -- History and criticism
ISBN 0-19-515607-2
LC 2004-654

"This book collects more than 140 essays, articles, and reviews that Giddins wrote from 1990 to November 2003. . . . The breadth and depth of his knowledge is extremely impressive, his ear is astounding, and his masterly style routinely achieves the near impossible in writing engagingly about something that inherently eludes description." Libr J

Gioia, Ted

The history of jazz; 2nd ed.; Oxford University Press 2011 444p il pa $19.95 **781.65**
1. Jazz music -- History and criticism
ISBN 978-0-19-539970-7; 0-19-539970-6
LC 2010-23182

First published 1997

The author "relates the story of African American music from its roots in Africa to the international respect it enjoys today. . . . This well-researched, extensively annotated volume covers the major trends and personalities that have shaped jazz. The excellent bibliography and list of recommended listening make this a valuable purchase for libraries building a jazz collection." Libr J

Includes discography and bibliographical references

Kahn, Ashley

The **house** that Trane built; the story of Impulse Records. Norton 2006 338p il $29.95 **781.65**
1. Jazz music 2. Jazz musicians 3. Saxophonists 4. Impulse Records (Firm)
ISBN 0-393-05879-4
LC 2005-037218

The author "offers a fascinating insider's view of the sessions that produced not only Coltrane's classics but also top-grade albums by both fiery radicals and such timeless stars as Duke Ellington, Coleman Hawkins and Benny Carter." Economist

Lees, Gene

You can't steal a gift; Dizzy, Clark, Milt, and Nat. foreword by Nat Hentoff. Yale Univ. Press 2001 269p il $27.95 **781.65**
1. Singers 2. Pianists 3. Photographers 4. Jazz musicians 5. Bassists 6. Band leaders 7. Flugelhornists 8. Trumpet players 9. United States -- Race relations
ISBN 0-300-08965-1
LC 2001-3444

Lees discusses the lives and careers of four jazz musicians: Dizzy Gillespie, Terry Clark, Milt Hinton, and Nat King Cole. A theme of the book is how these artists were affected by race relations in the United States

The author "has a natural ease with words and a graceful prose style that captures the reader's attention." Booklist

Marsalis, Wynton

Moving to higher ground; how jazz can change your life. [by] Wynton Marsalis with Geoffrey C. Ward. Random House 2008 181p il **781.65**
1. Jazz music -- History and criticism
ISBN 1400060788; 9781400060788
LC 2008-16560

The author "explains in lay readers' terms how jazz works as a diverse musical genre and, more important, how an understanding and appreciation of jazz can enrich one's life. . . . This work is highly recommended." Libr J

Morgenstern, Dan

Living with jazz; a reader. edited by Sheldon Meyer. Pantheon Books 2004 712p $35 **781.65**
1. Jazz music -- History and criticism
ISBN 0-375-42072-X
LC 2004-43432

This is a compilation of "nearly half a century of Morgenstern's profiles, liner notes, record and show reviews and other musings. . . . Morgenstern reminisces about his introduction to jazz in a brief opening memoir, then segues into lengthy sections on his greatest heroes, Louis Armstrong and Duke Ellington. . . . His exuberant characterizations make this monumental volume a stimulating guide to jazz in the second half of the 20th century." Publ Wkly

Myers, Marc

Why jazz happened; Marc Myers. University of California Press 2013 267 p. (hardcover) $34.95   **781.65**
1. Jazz music -- History and criticism 2. Jazz -- History and criticism
ISBN 0520268784; 9780520268784
    LC 2012022218

This book, by Marc Myers, offers a "social history of jazz. It provides a . . . look at the many forces that shaped this most American of art forms and the many influences that gave rise to jazz's post-war styles. . . . This book views jazz's evolution through the prism of technological advances, social transformations, changes in the law, economic trends, and much more." (Publisher's note)

Includes bibliographical references and index

Paulo, Joaquim

Jazz covers; ed. Julius Wiedemann; interviews with Bob Ciano . . . [et al.] by Joaquim Paulo; top-10 favorite records lists by jazz DJs Amir Abdullah . . . [et al.] Taschen 2008 494p il pa $39.99   **781.65**
1. Jazz music 2. Sound recordings -- Album covers
ISBN 978-3-8228-2366-8; 3-8228-2366-X

This volume "manages to sum up the genre with the thoroughness of a scholarly essay. Vivid photographs are accompanied by pithy back-story writeups of the jazz artists and album designers." Time Out Hong Kong

Ratliff, Ben

The jazz ear; conversations over music. Times Books 2008 256p il $25   **781.65**
1. Jazz music -- History and criticism
ISBN 978-0-8050-8146-6; 0-8050-8146-1
    LC 2008-10122

"Originally published as a series in the New York Times, the 15 conversations presented here consist of Ratliff sitting down with such diverse and talented luminaries as Sonny Rollins, Pat Metheny, Paul Motian, and Dianne Reeves. The treasure of these conversations is not just their fluid and intimate manner but their focus on the recordings that had the greatest influence on the artists and their musical paths. . . . An added bonus is the recommended-listening section, in which Ratliff shares his list of his subjects' seminal recordings. Highly recommended." Libr J

Includes bibliographical references

Sandke, Randall

Where the dark and the light folks meet; race and the mythology, politics, and business of jazz. Scarecrow Press 2010 277p (Studies in jazz) $40; ebook $40   **781.65**
1. Jazz music -- History and criticism
ISBN 0-8108-6652-8; 0-8108-6990-X ebook; 978-0-8108-6652-2; 978-0-8108-6990-5 ebook
    LC 2009-37977

The author "tackles a controversial question: Is jazz the product of an insulated African-American environment, shut off from the rest of society by strictures of segregation and discrimination, or is it more properly understood as the juncture of a wide variety of influences under the broader umbrella of American culture?" Publisher's note

Includes bibliographical references

Strayhorn; an illustrated life. edited by A. Alyce Claerbaut and David Schlesinger. Bolden 2015 208 p. illustrations (some color) (hardback) $35   **781.65**
1. Composers -- Biography 2. Jazz musicians -- Biography 3. Composers -- United States -- Biography 4. Jazz musicians -- United States -- Biography 5. Composers -- United States -- Biography -- Pictorial works 6. Jazz musicians -- United States -- Biography -- Pictorial works
ISBN 1932841989; 9781932841985
    LC 2015021651

This book, edited by A. Alyce Claerbaut and David Schlesinger, "is a stunning collection of essays, photographs, and ephemera celebrating Billy Strayhorn, one of the most significant yet under-appreciated contributors to 20th century American music. Released in commemoration of Strayhorn's centennial, this luxurious coffee-table book offers intimate details of the composer's life from musicians, scholars, and Strayhorn's closest relatives." (Publisher's note)

"Readers with even the slightest interest in jazz will be delighted with the endlessly fascinating array of visual treats and star-studded reminiscences that tenderly pay tribute to an often overlooked yet extremely important figure in jazz history." LJ

Includes bibliographical references and index

Ward, Geoffrey C.

Jazz; a history of America's music. based on a documentary film by Ken Burns written by Geoffrey C. Ward; with a preface by Ken Burns. Knopf 2000 489p il $65; pa $29.95   **781.65**
1. Jazz music
ISBN 0-679-44551-X; 0-679-76539-5 pa
    LC 00-22604

The authors "have assembled a comprehensive history with a focus on the musicians and the sociology of jazz. . . . The short articles by Wynton Marsalis, Dan Morgenstern, Gerald Early, Stanley Crouch, and Gary Giddins, which are woven into the text, provide a . . . specific focus on a number of jazz's aspects." Libr J

Includes bibliographical references

781.66   Rock (Rock 'n' roll)

Almond, Steve

Rock and roll will save your life; a book by and for the fanatics among us (with bitchin' soundtrack) Random House 2010 216p $23   **781.66**
1. Rock music -- History and criticism 2. Popular music -- History and criticism
ISBN 978-1-4000-6620-9; 1-4000-6620-4

"As a young writer plagued by self-doubt, Almond reveled in the emotional escape of music; the joy of his fanaticism is conveyed poignantly—and so completely—

that we're infected with his touted salvation too. With well-placed 'interludes' or 'reluctant exegeses,' Almond peppers his pages with biting insights and funny vignettes; dismissing, for instance, Toto's 'Africa' as ', . . the lovechild of Muzak and Imperialism.' Though the language feels a bit highbrow, Almond ultimately crafts a playful and intelligent read." Paste

Browne, David

Fire and rain; the Beatles, Simon & Garfunkel, James Taylor, CSNY, and the lost story of 1970. Da Capo Press 2011 369p il $26 **781.66**

1. Singers 2. Rock music 3. Beatles 4. Songwriters 5. Simon and Garfunkel 6. Rock music -- History and criticism 7. Crosby, Stills and Nash (Musical group) 8. Crosby, Stills, Nash and Young (Musical group)

ISBN 9780306818509; 0-306-81850-7

"Browne skillfully interleaves the stories of these musicians during this tumultuous year, making room for substantial walk-ons by other significant industry figures like Bill Graham, Peter Yarrow, Phil Spector, Rita Coolidge, Carole King and Joni Mitchell. Intimately familiar with the music, fully comprehending the cross-pollination among the artists, thoroughly awake to the dynamics of the decade's last gasp, the author expertly captures a volatile and hugely interesting moment in rock history." Kirkus

Includes bibliographical references

Buckland, Gail

Who shot rock & roll; a photographic history, 1955 to the present. Alfred A. Knopf 2009 319p il $40 **781.66**

1. Rock music -- Pictorial works

ISBN 978-0-307-27016-0; 0-307-27016-5

LC 2009-19122

"Here are nearly 300 iconic photographs by those photographers who understood the power of the image in the formation and sustenance of rock-and-roll culture from 1955 onward. The care with which Buckland selects representative photographers and their most significant images is matched by her interpretive prowess. . . . [She] carefully but deliberately argues that the art of rock photography has been sacrificed to the paparazzi and corporate art departments. In light of this inclusive, heady and visceral collection of the genre's best, it would be hard to argue otherwise." Publ Wkly

Includes bibliographical references

Cohen, Mitchell

All These Things That I've Done; My Insane, Improbable Rock Life. Matt Pinfield; Mitchell Cohen. Simon & Schuster 2016 272 p. illustrations $25 **781.66**

1. Rock music 2. Specialists

ISBN 1476793891; 9781476793894

LC 2016024686

In this book by Matt Pinfield with Mitchell Cohen, "Pinfield offers the ultimate music fan's memoir, a chronicle of the songs and artists that inspired his improbable career alongside some of the all-time greats, from The Beatles to KISS to U2 to The Killers. . . . Pinfield shares his five decades of stories from the front lines of rock and roll, exploring how

. . . he became a sought-after reporter, unlikely celebrity, and the last word in popular music." (Publisher's note)

"His own recurring struggles with addiction flesh out the narrative, grounding his enthusiasm for music in an awareness of the somber side of the rock lifestyle. His encyclopedic knowledge of contemporary sounds makes the memoir as informative as it is personal." Pub Wkly

Cutler, Sam

You can't always get what you want; my life with the Rolling Stones, the Grateful Dead and other wonderful retrobates. ECW Press 2010 326p il pa $17.95 **781.66**

1. Rock music 2. Rolling Stones 3. Grateful Dead (Musical group)

ISBN 978-1-55022-932-5

First published 2008 in Australia

"Effortlessly readable, packed with entertaining, sleazy, behind-the-scenes tales." Portland Mercury

German, Bill

Under their thumb; how a nice boy from Brooklyn got mixed up with the Rolling Stones (and lived to tell about it) Villard Books 2009 354p il $25 **781.66**

1. Rolling Stones

ISBN 978-1-4000-6622-3; 1-4000-6622-0

LC 2008-45533

"The epic tale of an obsessive teenager who launched a Rolling Stones fanzine and spent the next two decades capturing the band's whirlwind metamorphosis from behind the scenes. . . . First-rate, firsthand account of the world's greatest rock 'n' roll band, and a disenchanted chronicle of its increasingly crass commercialization." Kirkus

Gruen, Bob

New York Dolls; the photographs of Bob Gruen. introduction by Lenny Kaye; featuring commentary by David Johansen and Sylvain Sylvain and quotes collected by Legs McNeil; afterword by Morrissey. Abrams Image 2008 158p il $24.95 **781.66**

1. Rock musicians 2. New York Dolls (Musical group)

ISBN 978-0-8109-7271-1; 0-8109-7271-9

LC 2008-13074

"Gruen met singer David Johansen, guitarists Johnny Thunders and Sylvain Sylvain, drummer Jerry Nolan and bassist Arthur 'Killer' Kane at the beginning of 1973, months after the untimely death of original drummer Billy Murcia. The book chronicles the glam-rock band's career over 230 photographs, only 30 of which have previously been seen by the public. The last picture in the book is of their 2004 reunion in London. Lenny Kaye wrote the book's foreword and interviewed the group's surviving members, Johansen and Sylvain Sylvain." Rolling Stone

Lang, Michael

The road to Woodstock; with Holly George-Warren. Ecco 2009 304p il $29.99 **781.66**

1. Woodstock Festival, 1969

ISBN 978-0-06-157655-3; 0-06-157655-7

"The author is a generous raconteur with a good memory for specifics, but what elevates this book above the level of most rock memoirs is the inclusion of voices other than Lang's—including scenesters and key Woodstock players like Jimi Hendrix, Roger Daltrey, Pete Townshend, Jerry Garcia, Abbie Hoffman, John Sebastian, Greil Marcus and Wavy Gravy. . . . Well-written, informative and tons of fun, Lang's book will be appreciated by rockers and musicologists of all ages." Kirkus

Includes bibliographical references

Margotin, Philippe

All the Songs; The Story Behind Every Beatles Release. Jean-Michel Guesdon & Philippe Margotin; preface by Patti Smith; Scott Freiman, consulting editor. Black Dog & Leventhal Pub 2013 672 p. ill, portraits (chiefly color) $50   **781.66**
1. Beatles
ISBN 1579129528; 9781579129521

In this book, by Philippe Margotin and Jean-Michel Guesdon, "every album and every song ever released by the Beatles—from 'Please Please Me' to 'The Long and Winding Road'—is dissected, discussed, and analyzed. . . . Here, we learn that one of John Lennon's favorite guitars was a 1958 Rickenbacker 325 Capri. . . . We also learn that 'Love Me Do,' recorded in Abbey Road Studios in September 1962, took 18 takes to get right, even though it was one of the first songs John and Paul ever wrote together." (Publisher's note)

"Arranged chronologically by album, the book includes for each song basic information (songwriter, track length, number of takes, etc.), a brief discussion of how it was written and recorded, and an overall assessment. . . . [N]umerous anecdotes and quotations from the group keep the book entertaining and accessible even to more casual music fans." LJ

Includes bibliographical references, discography, and indexes

Marshall, Jim

Trust; photographs of Jim Marshall. Omnibus Press 2009 165p il $39.95   **781.66**
1. Rock music -- Pictorial works
ISBN 978-1-84772-110-5; 1-84772-110-9

Jim Marshall "devoted himself to photographing musicians. But more than just taking pictures, Marshall had a knack for capturing moments, snapshots of when the music and the individual collided, which, in turn, revealed something special or private about the artist. His pictures were often windows into the souls of those who were so revered but not always understood. . . . Dr. John sits backstage in full concert regalia, beside him a shrunken human head. Bob Dylan and Johnny Cash casually chat on the set of The Johnny Cash Show. John Coltrane looks contemplative in the backyard of his Queens, NY home. The vast majority of pictures in Trust are split among jazz, blues, and '60s rock and roll. . . . The photographs are paired with short anecdotes about the artists or stories about the images, and in doing this, Marshall lends just enough of his own story to the pictures he presents. But largely, it is Marshall's body of work that does the talking, and, in that, these photographs are revelatory." Under the Radar

McMurray, Jacob

Taking punk to the masses; from nowhere to Nevermind; a visual history from the permanent collection of Experience Music Project. Fantagraphics Books 2011 253p il pa $29.99   **781.66**
1. Punk rock music
ISBN 978-1-60699-433-7

This volume "visually documents the explosion of Grunge, the Seattle Sound, within the context of the underground punk subculture that was developing throughout the U.S. in the late 1970s and 1980s. This musical journey is represented entirely through the collection of Experience Music Project, Seattle's museum of music and popular culture . . . . . Featuring over 100 key artifacts from EMP's collection, Taking Punk to the Masses illustrates the evolution of punk rock from underground subculture to mainstream embrace." Publisher's note

Moore, Thurston

No wave; post-punk, underground, New York, 1976-1980. by Thurston Moore and Byron Coley; introduction by Lydia Lunch. Abrams Image 2008 143p il $24.95   **781.66**
1. Punk rock music 2. Experimental music
ISBN 978-0-8109-9543-7; 0-8109-9543-3

LC 2007-34093

"A treasure trove of rare photographs and oral history of a fleeting moment of New York underground that continues to reverberate 30 years later." Booklist

Richardson, Peter

No simple highway; a cultural history of the Grateful Dead. Peter Richardson. St. Martin's Press 2015 373 p. 16 plates; ills.; portraits (hardback) $26.99   **781.66**
1. Rock music 2. Grateful Dead (Musical group) 3. Rock musicians -- United States -- Biography 4. Rock music -- Social aspects
ISBN 1250010624; 9781250010629

LC 2014036345

This book on the rock band the Grateful Dead, by Peter Richardson, "vividly recounts the Dead's colorful history, adding new insight into everything from the Acid Tests to the band's formation of their own record label to their massive late career success, while probing the riddle of the Dead's vast and durable appeal." (Publisher's note)

Includes bibliographical references (pages 339-353) and index

Robb, John

Punk rock; an oral history. John Robb; edited by Oliver Craske; introduction by Henry Rollins. PM 2012 xv, 562 p.p illustrations $19.95   **781.66**
1. Punk culture 2. Punk rock music 3. Rock musicians -- Anecdotes 4. Punk rock musicians -- Anecdotes 5. Punk rock music -- History and criticism
ISBN 1604860057; 9781604860054

LC 2011939680

Author John Robb presents a history of punk rock music. "John Robb talks to many of those who cultivated the movement, such as John Lydon, Lemmy, Siouxsie Sioux, Mick

Jones, Chrissie Hynde, Malcolm McLaren, Henry Rollins, and Glen Matlock, weaving together their accounts to create a . . . history of UK punk. . . . Over 150 interviews" are presented from groups like The Clash, the Stranglers, and The Sex Pistols on the period's "roots in the late 1960s to its enduring influence on the bands, fashion, and culture of today" are presented. (Publisher's note)

Russell, Ethan A.

Let it bleed; the Rolling Stones, Altamont, and the end of the sixties. Ethan A. Russell, with Gerard Van der Leun. Springboard Press 2009 239p il $35   **781.66**
1. Rolling Stones 2. Altamont Festival
ISBN 978-0-446-53904-3
LC 2008-53229
"In 1969, Russell was one of 16 people and the only photographer to join the Rolling Stones on their tour of America. . . . Russell's 200-plus photos, most in stark and clear black and white, range from the band rehearsing and relaxing in a bucolic setting before the tour to Mick Jagger in front of a mirror applying makeup to a closeup of Keith Richards intensely tuning up. Wide onstage shots illustrate the band's relationship with their adoring public. Including interviews and comments from many of the members of the touring group and a haunting narrative of the desolation at Altamont, Russell, with Van Der Leun . . . presents a definitive and authoritative picture of the Stones." Libr J

Savage, Jon

★ 1966; The Year the Decade Exploded. by Jon Savage. Faber & Faber 2016 620 p. illustrations $29.95   **781.66**
1. Popular culture 2. Nineteen sixties 3. Rock music -- 1961-1970 -- History and criticism.
ISBN 0571277624; 9780571277629
In this book, by Jon Savage, the "pop world accelerated and broke through the sound barrier in 1966. In America, in London, in Amsterdam, in Paris, revolutionary ideas slow-cooking since the late '50s reached boiling point. . . . A unique chemistry of ideas, substances, freedom of expression and dialogue across pop cultural continents created a landscape of immense and eventually shattering creativity." (Publisher's note)

Turman, Katherine

Louder Than Hell; The Definitive Oral History of Metal. By Jon Wiederhorn and Katherine Turman. HarperCollins 2013 736 p. $32.50   **781.66**
1. Rock musicians 2. Heavy metal (Music)
ISBN 006195828X; 9780061958281
Written by Jon Wiederhorn and Katherine Turman, this book is an "oral history of heavy metal," which "includes hundreds of interviews with the giants of the movement, conducted over the past 25 years." It "features more than 250 interviews with some of the biggest bands in metal, including Black Sabbath, Metallica, Megadeth, Anthrax, Slayer, Iron Maiden, Judas Priest, Spinal Tap, Pantera, White Zombie, Slipknot, and Twisted Sister." (Publisher's note)

Victor, Adam

The Elvis encyclopedia. Overlook Duckworth 2008 598p il $65   **781.66**
1. Actors 2. Singers 3. Rock musicians
ISBN 978-1-58567-598-2; 1-58567-598-9
An alphabetical compendium of topics related to Elvis Presley. Includes personal and place names, movie and song titles, events, and general subjects.
"This obsessively detailed and completely entertaining chronicle . . . of every possible aspect of Elvis Preley's life is mesmerizing and deserves a wide audience." Publ Wkly

Waksman, Steve

This ain't the summer of love; conflict and crossover in heavy metal and punk. University of California Press 2009 408p   **781.66**
1. Punk rock music 2. Heavy metal (Music)
ISBN 0520253108; 0520257170; 9780520253100; 9780520257177
LC 2008025957
This survey of heavy metal and punk music "begins on the cusp of the '70s with the colossal arena performances of Grand Funk Railroad, setting up the relationship between performer and (in this case, enormous) audience, which is an ongoing point of reference. From here, Waksman uses subsequent artists to deconstruct the rock concert, moving through the performative stage antics of Alice Cooper and Iggy Pop, to the metal and hardcore bands of the early '80s. . . . The number of fanzines and interviews cited is evidence that this is a comprehensively and enthusiastically researched book. As a critical study it provides an original critique of both the genres involved, and of genre itself; the only flipside is that this ends up playing second fiddle to a damn good story." PopMatters
Includes discography and bibliographical references

Wald, Elijah

Dylan Goes Electric! Newport, Seeger, Dylan, and the Night That Split the Sixties. Elijah Wald. HarperCollins 2015 256 p. 8 plates; illustrations $26.99   **781.66**
1. Music festivals -- Rhode Island -- Newport
ISBN 0062366688; 9780062366689
This book, by Elijah Wald, analyzes "the day [musician Bob] Dylan 'went electric' at the Newport Folk Festival, timed to coincide with the event's fiftieth anniversary. . . . Elijah Wald explores the cultural, political and historical context of this seminal event that embodies the transformative decade that was the sixties." (Publisher's note)
"Some of this material has been covered before, but rarely has it been done so knowingly, lovingly, and felicitously. All the players, too, are here (Joan Baez, Dave Van Ronk, Johnny Cash, et al.), and, though nostalgic, the book makes a major contribution to modern musical history." Booklist

Yarm, Mark

Everybody loves our town; an oral history of Grunge. Crown Archetype 2011 567p il $25; ebook $12.99   **781.66**
1. Rock music -- History and criticism
ISBN 978-0-307-46443-9; 978-0-307-46445-3 ebook
LC 2011009192

A tribute to the Pacific Northwest's grunge genre draws on the observations of individuals at the forefront of the movement from Soundgarden and the Melvins to Nirvana and Pearl Jam, citing such influences as the rise of Seattle's Sub Pop record label and the death of Kurt Cobain.

"Yarm's affectionate, gossipy, detailed look at the highs and lows of the contemporary Seattle music scene is one of the most essential rock books of recent years." Kirkus

782.1   Vocal forms

Abbate, Carolyn
A **history** of opera; Carolyn Abbate and Roger Parker. W.W. Norton 2012 603 p. illustrations (hardcover) $45; (paperback) $21.95   **782.1**
1. Opera -- History 2. Opera
ISBN 9780393057218; 9780393348958
LC 2012031546

This book by Carolyn Abbate and Roger Parker chronicles the history of opera from its "birth . . . in the 17th century up through the most recent technological innovations that bring operatic performances to wider and wider audiences. While the authors cover the breadth of operatic history . . . they focus their attention on the composers whose works are most performed today: Verdi, Mozart, Puccini, Wagner, Rossini, Donizetti, Strauss, Bizet, and Handel." (Publishers Weekly)

Includes bibliographical references and index

Berger, William
Verdi with a vengeance; an energetic guide to the life and complete works of the king of opera. Vintage Bks. 2000 497p il pa $15   **782.1**
1. Composers
ISBN 0-375-70518-X
LC 00-42261

The author "provides a brief overview of the composer's life and times and examines the connections between contemporary politics and Verdi's creative output. . . . A glossary and recommended recordings, films, and soundtracks are included. Informative and eminently readable for the novice and scholar alike." Libr J

Includes bibliographical references

McCarter, Jeremy
Hamilton; the revolution. Lin-Manuel Miranda, Jeremy McCarter. Grand Central Pub. 2016 287 p. illustrations (chiefly color) (hardcover) $45   **782.1**
1. Historical drama
ISBN 9781455539741; 9781455567539; 9781478938323; 9781478939351
LC 2015957946

This book, by Lin-Manuel Miranda and Jeremy McCarter, provides the libretto of the Broadway musical "Hamilton" and accounts of its creation, concept, and success. It "gives readers an unprecedented view of both revolutions, from the only two writers able to provide it. [The playwright] Miranda, along with Jeremy McCarter, a cultural critic and theater artist who was involved in the project from its earliest stages." (Publisher's note)

"A treasure trove of information, they highlight his writing process, musical influences (ranging from show tunes to pop to hip-hop), amusing anecdotes, and so much more." LJ

Mordden, Ethan
Anything goes; a history of American musical theatre. Ethan Mordden. Oxford University Press 2013 360 p. illustrations (alk. paper) $29.95 **782.1**
1. Musicals 2. Theater -- United States -- History 3. Musicals -- United States -- History and criticism
ISBN 0199892830; 9780199892839
LC 2013000208

This book by Ethan Mordden examines "the musical from the 1920s through the 1970s. . . . He also explores the changing structure of musical comedy and operetta, and the evolution of the role of the star. " (Publisher's note)

"Mordden brightly differentiates those forms, citing hundreds and analyzing dozens of examples of them in a sweeping narrative that, with plenty of sass and tang, wit and even a little snark, not to mention scholarly precision, is obviously the best-ever history of the musical and likely to remain so for a very long time." Booklist

Includes bibliographical references, discography and index

The **Richard** Rodgers reader; edited by Geoffrey Block. Oxford Univ. Press 2002 356p il music (Readers on American musicians) $55; pa $38   **782.1**
1. Composers 2. Composers -- United States
ISBN 0-19-513954-2; 0-19-531343-7 pa
LC 2001-37505

"A fine combination of anecdote, music criticism, and biography, this is recommended for all libraries interested in American popular culture and American musical theater." Libr J

Includes bibliographical references

Rose, Michael
The **birth** of an opera; fifteen masterpieces from Poppea to Wozzeck. Michael Rose. W.W. Norton & Company 2013 480 p. (hardcover) $35   **782.1**
1. Opera 2. Composers 3. Librettists 4. Operas -- Analysis, appreciation
ISBN 0393060438; 9780393060430
LC 2012039470

This book by Michael Rose discusses "how operas are written and the personalities . . . and musical circumstances that have shaped their composition. . . . From Monteverdi and Mozart to Puccini and Berg, each chapter focuses on a well-known opera and tells the story that lies behind its creation." Rose describes "Verdi deep in Shakespearian discussion with Boito as they remodel . . . 'Otello;' and Debussy coming almost literally to blows with Maeterlinck over . . . 'Pelléas et Mélisande.'" (Publisher's note)

Includes bibliographical references and index

Sondheim, Stephen, 1930-
Finishing the hat; collected lyrics (1954-1981) with attendant comments, principles, heresies, grudg-

es, whines and anecdotes. Knopf 2010 445p il $39.95 **782.1**

1. Songs 2. Musicals 3. Composers 4. Lyricists 5. Biography, Individual 6. Musical theater -- History 7. Popular music -- Writing and publishing
ISBN 0-679-43907-2; 978-0-679-43907-3

LC 2010-11056

"Along with the lyrics for all of his productions from 1954 to 1981—including West Side Story, Company, Follies, A Little Night Music, and Sweeney Todd—Sondheim discusses his relationship with his mentor, Oscar Hammerstein II, and his collaborations with . . . Leonard Bernstein, Arthur Laurents, Ethel Merman, Richard Rodgers, Angela Lansbury, Hal Prince, and [others]. . . . Sondheim [also seeks to] analyze his work and dissect his own songs as well as those of others." (Publisher's note) Index.

"There's so much more to 'Finishing the Hat' than witty, profound and groundbreaking lyrics. In chapters and annotations every budding lyricist and musical fan will relish, Sondheim covers everything from the history of musical theater and views of major lyricists to stories about the making of his shows and lessons in the craft of lyric writing. . . . The 80-year-old Sondheim, not surprisingly, turns out to be a remarkable writer, even when no rhymes are in sight. He's at turns funny and poignant, ornery and instructive. His honesty often stings, especially in analytical sidebars that detail the varied flaws of such heralded lyric-writing comrades as Noel Coward, Ira Gershwin, Lorenz Hart, Alan Jay Lerner and (heresy!) even Oscar Hammerstein II, his mentor." Cleveland Plain Dealer

Includes bibliographical references

Look, I made a hat; collected lyrics (1981-2011) with attendant comments, amplifications, dogmas, harangues, wafflings, diversions and anecdotes. by Stephen Sondheim. 1st ed; Alfred A. Knopf 2011 480p hardcover $45 **782.1**

1. Musicals 2. Lyricists 3. Popular song lyrics 4. Composers -- United States 5. Songs--Texts. 6. Musicals--Excerpts--Librettos.
ISBN 978-0307593412

LC 2011014604

"Picking up where he left off in Finishing the Hat, Sondheim gives us all the lyrics, along with excluded songs and early drafts, of the Pulitzer Prize winning Sunday in the Park with George, Into the Woods, Assassins and Passion. Here, too, is an in-depth look at the evolution of Wise Guys, which subsequently was transformed into Bounce and eventually became Road Show. Sondheim takes us through his contributions to both television and film, some of which may surprise you, and covers plenty of never-before-seen material from unproduced projects as well." (Publisher's Note)

"With this chronological continuation of Finishing the Hat, musical theater lyricist and composer Sondheim has produced another delightful book that melds lyrics, anecdotes, opinions, and whimsy...As in the previous volume, Sondheim includes descriptions about each show, as well as running commentary. Sondheim's general essays (the "harangues" and "dogmas" of the subtitle) show him at his opinionated and literate best....certainly all libraries owning the first volume will want the second." (Library Journal)

Includes bibliographical references and index.

782.27 Hymns

Christ-Janer, Albert

American hymns old and new; {compiled by} Albert Christ-Janer, Charles W. Hughes, Charles Sprague Smith. Columbia Univ. Press 1980 838p music $130 **782.27**

1. Hymns
ISBN 9780231034586

This is an interdenominational compilation of 625 hymns sung in America since 1615

782.4 Secular forms

Bostridge, Ian

Schubert's winter journey; anatomy of an obsession. Ian Bostridge. Alfred A. Knopf 2015 528 p. illustrations (chiefly color), (hardcover) $29 **782.4**

1. Music -- History and criticism
ISBN 9780307961631

LC 2014020088

This book, by Ian Bostridge, examines the song cycle "Winterrreise" (Winter Journey) by Franz Schubert. An "English tenor . . . who has sung these pieces frequently offers his take on the meaning and enduring power of Winterreise. . . . Bostridge probes the historical context of each piece and explores its connections to other arts." (Publishers Weekly)

Includes bibliographical references and index

Starr, Ringo, 1940-

Photograph; Ringo Starr. Genesis Publications 2015 304 p. ills., facsimiles, portraits $50 **782.4**

1. Beatles 2. Musicians
ISBN 1905662335; 9781905662333

In this collection of photographs, musician Ringo Starr "opens his archives to share memories of his childhood, The Beatles and beyond. are and unseen photographs taken by Ringo, with others reproduced from his family albums, are showcased here for fans of The Beatles and anyone passionate about modern music. Accompanied by Ringo's original manuscript of over 15,000 words, 'Photograph' gives unprecedented insight into the life of one of the world's greatest musicians." (Publisher's note)

782.42 Songs

Cohen, Rich

The **Sun** and the Moon and the Rolling Stones; Rich Cohen. Spiegel & Grau 2016 400 p. illustrations $30 **782.42**

1. Bands (Music) 2. Rock musicians -- England -- Biography 3. Rolling Stones
ISBN 9780804179232

LC 2015035782

This book, by Rich Cohen, is a "narrative history that will give readers a new understanding of the Rolling Stones. . . . The story begins at the beginning: the fateful meeting of Mick Jagger and Keith Richards on a train platform in

1961—and goes on to span decades, with a focus on the golden run—from the albums Beggars Banquet (1968) to Exile on Main Street (1972)—when the Stones were prolific and innovative and at the height of their powers." (Publisher's note)

"A compact and conversant history that makes the story new again, capturing the Rolling Stones in all their Faustian glory." Kirkus

Includes bibliographical references (pages 351-360) and index.

Edwards, Paul

The **concise** guide to hip-hop music; a fresh look at the art of hip-hop, from old-school beats to freestyle rap. Paul Edwards. St. Martin's Griffin 2015 240 p. (trade pbk.) $14.99   **782.42**
   1. Hip-hop -- Encyclopedias 2. Rap music -- History and criticism 3. Rap (Music) -- History and criticism 4. Rap (Music) -- Analysis, appreciation
   ISBN 9781250034816
                              LC 2014034012

This book, by Paul Edwards, "breaks down the difference between old school and new school [hip-hop music from its beginning in 1973 to the present], recaps the biggest influencers of the genre, and sets straight the myths and misconceptions of the artists and their music." (Publisher's note)

Includes bibliographical references

Gioia, Ted

Work songs; [by] Theodore Gioia. Duke University Press 2006 352p $27.95   **782.42**
   1. Folk music 2. Labor -- Songs
   ISBN 0-8223-3726-6; 978-0-8223-3726-3
                              LC 2005026241

Gioia "poignantly tells the story of work songs sung by everyone from prehistoric hunters to today's consumers. His task involved drawing on multilayered and diverse resources that include travel literature, slave narratives, historical accounts and personal journals, myths and legends, biographies, and labor union writings; the focus is on the rhythms, melodies, and lyrics of music that has accompanied such tasks as raising and lowering sails, felling trees, and weaving and sewing garments. . . . This book provides an opportunity to re-experience the history and dignity of our human toils. Highly recommended for public and academic libraries." Libr J

Includes bibliographical references

Gray, Michael

The **Bob** Dylan encyclopedia. Continuum 2006 832p il $40   **782.42**
   1. Singers 2. Folk musicians 3. Songwriters
   ISBN 0-82646-933-7; 978-0-82646-933-5
                            LC 2006-12728

This book "covers many of his songs, albums, and film work, as well as just about every personality associated with the folk singer/rock star. . . . Overall, this is an amazingly well-researched and surprisingly readable work." Libr J

Includes bibliographical references

Lehman, David

A **fine** romance; Jewish songwriters, American songs. Nextbook/Schocken 2009 249p (Jewish encounters) $23   **782.42**
   1. Composers 2. Lyricists 3. Songwriters and songwriting 4. Jews -- United States 5. Popular music -- History and criticism
   ISBN 978-0-8052-4250-8; 0-8052-4250-3
                          LC 2009-05942

"Lehman investigates the lasting impact of 20th-century Jewish popular songwriters in America, ranging from Irving Berlin's and Jerome Kern's early efforts in the 1910s through George Gershwin, Harold Arlen, Richard Rodgers, Lorenz Hart, and Oscar Hammerstein II to Leonard Bernstein and the early 1960s. In fluid prose and expert foreshadowing and summations, the author conveys the personality of each musician or writer and recommends selected versions of his favorite songs." Libr J

Includes bibliographical references

Lynskey, Dorian

33 revolutions per minute; a history of protest songs, from Billie Holiday to Green Day. Ecco 2011 660p il pa $19.99   **782.42**
   1. Political ballads and songs 2. Popular music -- 20th century 3. Popular music -- 21st century 4. Popular music -- Political aspects 5. Popular music -- History and criticism 6. Protest songs -- History and criticism
   ISBN 0061670154; 9780061670152
                          LC 2010-24247

The author presents a history of protest music through an examination of thirty-three songs, from Strange Fruit (1939) to American Idiot (2008). Index.

The author "delves into the protest song movement from 1939 to the present. Dividing the time into discrete sections, he focuses on particular examples but also provides information on related songs. The author traces the historical context, using valuable contemporary sources and quotations from the artists. . . . Lynskey's flowing prose and well-turned phrases bring the times to life. He is especially adept at integrating the songs into the wider social milieu, which extends the appeal to cultural historians as well as music lovers." Libr J

Includes bibliographical references

Margotin, Philippe

Bob Dylan; all the songs : the story behind every track. Philippe Margotin, Jean-Michel Guesdon. Hachette Books 2015 703 p. illustrations (some color) (hardcover) $50   **782.42**
   1. Composition (Music)
   ISBN 9781579129859; 1579129854
                          LC 2015667168

This book, by Philippe Margotin and Jean-Michel Guesdon, is a "comprehensive account of Bob Dylan's work yet published with the full story of every recording session, every album, and every single released during his remarkable and illustrious 53-year career. . . . [The volume] focuses on Dylan's creative process and his organic, unencumbered style of recording." (Publisher's note)

"A Dylan fan could live inside this book for weeks. Hard-core enthusiasts will be enthralled by the details of the many outtakes." Library Journal

Mehr, Bob

Trouble boys; the true story of the Replacements. Bob Mehr. Da Capo Press 2015 520 p. illustrations (hardcover : alk. paper) $27.5 **782.42**
1. Replacements (Musical group) 2. Rock musicians -- United States -- Biography
ISBN 9780306818790; 9780306822032
LC 2015026791

This book, by Bob Mehr, is a biography of the rock band the Replacements. "Written with the participation of the group's key members, including reclusive singer-songwriter Paul Westerberg, bassist Tommy Stinson, and the family of late guitarist Bob Stinson, Trouble Boys is a deeply intimate and nuanced portrait, exposing the primal factors and forces—addiction, abuse, fear—that would shape one of the most brilliant and notoriously self-destructive groups of all time." (Publisher's note)

"Though hefty, Mehr's book is a page-turner from beginning to end and should find its way onto every music fan's bookshelf. It offers a master class on how to pen a rock biography." LJ

Includes bibliographical references and index

★ **National** anthems of the world; edited by Michael Jamieson Bristow. 11th ed.; Weidenfeld & Nicolson 2006 629p $90 **782.42**
1. National songs
ISBN 0-304-36826-1

First published 1943 in the United Kingdom with title: National anthems of the United Nations and France

This volume contains national anthems of about 198 nations, including melody and accompaniment. Words are presented in the native language with transliteration provided where necessary. English translations follow. Brief historical notes on the adoption of each anthem are included

"An essential reference resource for all libraries." Libr J

Polenberg, Richard

Hear my sad story; the true tales that inspired "Stagolee," "John Henry," and other traditional American folk songs. Richard Polenberg. Cornell University Press 2015 304 p. illustrations (cloth : alk. paper) $26 **782.42**
1. Folklore -- United States 2. Folk songs -- United States 3. Folk songs, English -- United States -- History and criticism
ISBN 9781501700026
LC 2015016652

This book, by Richard Polenberg, "describes the historical events that led to the writing of many famous American folk songs that served as touchstones for generations of American musicians, lyricists, and folklorists. Those events, which took place from the early nineteenth to the mid-twentieth centuries, often involved tragic occurrences: murders, sometimes resulting from love affairs gone wrong; [and] desperate acts borne out of poverty and unbearable working conditions." (Publisher's note)

"A well-written primer of American folk culture that should be in any serious popular music collection." LJ
Includes bibliographical references and index

Porter, Cole

Selected lyrics; Robert Kimball, editor. Library of America 2006 178p (American poets project) $20 **782.42**
1. American songs
ISBN 978-1-93108-294-5; 1-93108-294-4
LC 2006-40809

"For those hankering after a happy medium between American poetry and American Idolatry, Kimball's reading edition affords a golden opportunity to brush up on your Porter—just be sure to listen up, too, if you really want to be wowed." N Y Times Book Rev

Ritz, David

After the Dance; My Life with Marvin Gaye. Jan Gaye and David Ritz. HarperCollins 2015 304 p. 16 plates; portraits $25.99 **782.42**
1. Wives 2. Drug abuse
ISBN 0062135511; 9780062135513
NAACP Image Award Nominee: Outstanding Literary Work- Biography/Autobiography (2016)

In this book, author Jan Gaye, with David Ritz, presents a "cautionary tale about the ecstasy and dangers of loving Marvin Gaye, a performer passionately pursued by all--and a searing memoir of drugs, sex, and old school R&B from the wife of legendary soul icon Marvin Gaye." (Publisher's note) "Marvin's drug-crazed behavior became increasingly unhinged and unpredictable, right up until he was tragically shot dead in an argument with his father." (Kirkus Reviews)

"Gaye's explicitly confessional account of her doomed uphill struggle to stay with Marvin is a prime example of how obsessive celebrity worship can so easily (and dangerously) masquerade as enduring love. A fascinating, unsentimental account of a be-careful-what-you-wish-for romance." Kirkus

Smith, Patti, 1946-

Patti Smith Collected Lyrics, 1970-2015; Patti Smith. HarperCollins 2015 336 p. illustrations, facsimiles (hardcover) $29.99 **782.42**
1. Rock music 2. Popular song lyrics
ISBN 006234501X; 9780062345011
LC 2016560739

This book, by Patti Smith, is "a revised and updated version of the iconic artist's collected lyrics. This . . . collection from 'rock and roll's poet laureate' is a testimony to the fierce passion and uncompromising originality of Patti Smith's music and writing. Building on the collection originally published in 1998, this new edition features more than thirty-five new songs, new artwork, and an introduction from Patti Smith herself." (Publisher's note)

"To see Smith's galvanizing lyrics on the page, without musical embellishment, is to encounter the essence of her art—the radiant spectrum of her concerns, the razor-edge of her wit, and the depth of her emotions." Booklist

782.421 Rock (Rock 'n' roll) songs

The **Beatles** anthology. Chronicle Bks. 2000 367p
il $60; pa $35   **782.421**
1. Beatles
ISBN 0-8118-2684-8; 0-8118-3636-3 pa
                                    LC 00-23685
The story of the Beatles as "told through quotes from
John, Paul, George, and Ringo, as well as the group's closest
aides: George Martin, Neil Aspinall, and Derek Taylor. . . .
The density of the text is daunting, but the book's browsabil-
ity makes it as appealing to casual readers as it is indispensable to Beatlemaniacs." Libr J
Includes bibliographical references

Lil Wayne, 1982-
Gone 'til November; A Journal of Rikers Island.
by Lil Wayne. Penguin Group USA 2016 176 p.
$23   **782.421**
1. Prisoners 2. Rap musicians
ISBN 0735212112; 9780735212114
                                    LC 2016034964
This memoir, by rap musician Lil Wayne, is "a deeply
personal and revealing account of his time spent incarcerated on Rikers Island for eight months in 2010." (Publisher's note)

McNally, Dennis
A **long** strange trip; the inside history of the
Grateful Dead. Broadway Bks. 2002 684p il $30;
pa $18.95   **782.421**
1. Grateful Dead (Musical group)
ISBN 0-7679-1185-7; 0-7679-1186-5 pa
                                    LC 2002-25561
A history of the rock music group led by Jerry Garcia
which first became popular in the 1960's
"As the Dead's publicist for more than 20 years, Mc-
Nally packs this . . . full of intimate details otherwise un-
available. . . . The most exhaustively researched book on the
band to date." Publ Wkly
Includes bibliographical references

782.5 Vocal executants

Steinberg, Michael
Choral masterworks; a listener's guide. Michael Steinberg. Oxford University Press 2005 321p
$30   **782.5**
1. Choral music
ISBN 0-19-512644-0
                                    LC 2004-13619
"Well-written, concise introductions that record collectors, concertgoers, and chorus members alike should
enjoy." Booklist

784 Instruments and their music

Piston, Walter
Orchestration. Norton 1955 477p il music
$56.75   **784**
1. Musical instruments 2. Instrumentation and
orchestration
ISBN 978-0-393-09740-5; 0-393-09740-4
This text on writing for the orchestra begins with a discussion of individual instruments and their playing techniques. The last two sections cover analysis and specific
problems of orchestration

784.19 Instruments

Wilkinson, Philip
The **history** of music in fifty instruments; written
by Philip Wilkinson. Firefly Books Ltd 2014 224 p.
illustrations; portraits (hardcover) $29.95   **784.19**
1. Musical instruments 2. Music -- History and criticism
ISBN 1770854282; 9781770854284
                                    LC 2014900697
This book, by Philip Wilkinson, "outlines musical history in [50] well-written nuggets of information. Profiling
one instrument at a time, it describes the history of music
since the 1700s, when orchestras first took the formal shape
familiar to us. The concise text explains the role of each instrument in the orchestra and its importance in the development of music in general." (Publisher's note)
"Wilkinson's history unfolds like a symphonic work
with instrument makers, composers and virtuosic performers picking up these incredible creations and exposing
their beauty and capability. To open it up is to be instantly
hooked." Pub Wkly

784.192 Techniques and procedures for
instruments themselves

Pagliaro, Michael
The **musical** instrument desk reference; a guide
to how band and orchestral instruments work. Michael J. Pagliaro. Scarecrow Press 2012 189 p.
(cloth : alk. paper) $65   **784.192**
1. Musical instruments 2. Wind instruments --
Construction 3. Bowed stringed instruments --
Construction
ISBN 0810882701; 9780810882706; 9780810882713
                                    LC 2012007244
This book "begins with an 'easy-reference quick start'
section on woodwinds, followed by more in-depth chapters
on the flute, clarinet, saxophone, oboe, and the bassoon.
For the brass instruments, there are fingering charts, an expanded in-depth study chapter, and a chapter on functioning.
Nonfretted string instruments . . . are also given a chapter on
producing sound and an expanded in-depth study chapter.
The final chapter consists of an overview of percussion instruments." (Booklist)

784.2 Full orchestra (Symphony orchestra)

Steinberg, Michael

The **symphony**; a listener's guide. Oxford Univ. Press 1995 678p music $42.50; pa $25   **784.2**

1. Symphony 2. Composers 3. Music appreciation

ISBN 0-19-506177-2; 0-19-512665-3 pa

LC 95-5568

"Steinberg describes 36 composers and, movement by movement, 118 symphonies, including all the standard repertory . . . as well as a few by less well known composers such as Gorecki, Harbison, Martinu, and Sessions. The writing varies from formal and factual to chatty, with candid asides and stories relevant to the composer, the composition, or an important performance." Libr J

Includes bibliographical references

785 Ensembles with only one instrument per part

Sachs, Harvey

The **Ninth**; Beethoven and the world in 1824. Random House 2010 225p il   **785**

1. Composers 2. Romanticism in music 3. Music -- Social aspects 4. Music -- Political aspects 5. Music -- History and criticism 6. Music -- Social aspects -- Europe -- History

ISBN 1-4000-6077-X; 1-58836-981-1 ebook; 978-1-4000-6077-1; 978-1-58836-981-9 ebook

LC 2009-19716

This analysis of Beethoven's seminal Ninth Symphony identifies it as a key cultural event that reflected major social upheavals, including the emergence of a dynamic Western world and changes in philosophical perspectives on individuality.

"This discussion of the cornerstone of Romantic music, whose influence extended deep into the twentieth century, is concise, thorough, and written from the heart of a great biographer, musicologist, and lover of fine music." Booklist

Includes bibliographical references

786.2 Keyboard instruments

Isacoff, Stuart

A **natural** history of the piano; the instrument, the music, the musicians--from Mozart to modern jazz, and everything in between. Alfred A. Knopf 2011 361p il   **786.2**

1. Pianos 2. Piano music -- History and criticism

ISBN 9780307266378; 978030770142-8 ebook

LC 2011011557

"Isacoff offers an encyclopedic history of the beloved instrument and profiles such masters as Beethoven, Gershwin, and Oscar Peterson in this big slice of heaven for piano lovers." Booklist

Includes bibliographical references

786.5 Organs

Whitney, Craig R.

All the stops; the glorious pipe organ and its American masters. Public Affairs 2003 xxv, 323p il $30; pa $17.95   **786.5**

1. Organs (Musical instruments)

ISBN 1-586-48173-8; 1-586-48262-9 pa

LC 2002-37025

"Whitney extolls the organ's eclectic heritage at a time when the instrument seems poised for a return to the mainstream, and his glossary of its colorful terminology will help novices tell a windchest from a bombarde." New Yorker

Includes bibliographical references

787.3 Violas

Siblin, Eric

The **cello** suites; J.S. Bach, Pablo Casals, and the search for a Baroque masterpiece. Atlantic Monthly Press 2009 319p $24   **787.3**

1. Composers 2. Music appreciation 3. Cellists

ISBN 978-0-8021-1929-2; 0-8021-1929-8

The author explores the history of Bach's six suites for unaccompanied cello.

"Siblin's curiosity and passion for his subject is evident throughout, and his method of structuring the story according to the arrangement of the music is inspired. . . . Meticulous in his research, as evidenced by copious notes and resources collected over his travels to several European countries, Siblin makes convincing connections and offers possible answers to the questions surrounding the suites. In the process, he sheds considerable light on the lives of Bach and Casals." Quill Quire

Includes bibliographical references

787.8 Plectral lute family

Seeger, Pete

How to play the 5-string banjo; a manual for beginners. 3rd ed; Oak Publications 2002 72p il pa $16.95   **787.8**

1. Banjos

ISBN 9781597731645 pa; 1597731641 pa

First published 1948 by People's Songs

A basic manual for banjo players, with melody line, lyrics, and banjo accompaniment and solos notated in standard form of tablature. Appendix includes material on where to buy a banjo, books on the banjo, books of songs to sing and phonograph records

787.87 Guitars

Chapman, Richard

The **new** complete guitarist; rev American ed;
DK 2003 208p il pa $20   **787.87**
   1. Guitars
   ISBN 0-7894-9701-8
                 LC 2004-271630

First published 1993 with title: The complete guitarist

This work ranges "from fundamentals such as tuning,
scales, chords, picking, and strumming, to advanced techniques of various styles such as rock, blues, and jazz.
[It also] includes discussions on such topics as sound and
amplification, choosing a guitar, studio and home recording,
plus care and maintenance of the instrument. An appealing
book in the style of the 'Eyewitness' series." SLJ [review of
1993 edition]

Includes bibliographical references

Chappell, Jon

Guitar All-in-one for Dummies; by Jon Chappell, Mark Phillips, and Desi Serna. 2nd edition Wiley 2014 628 p. illustrations pa. $34.99   **787.87**
   1. Guitars 2. Guitars -- Study and teaching 3. Guitar
4. Guitar -- methods -- self instruction
   ISBN 9781118872024; 1118872029

This book is a "complete compendium of guitar instruction, written in clear, concise For Dummies style. It covers everything from positioning and basic chords to guitar
theory and playing styles, and even includes maintenance
advice to keep your instrument sounding great. It's an amazing resource for newbies and veterans alike, and offers you
the opportunity to stretch beyond your usual genre." (Publisher's Note)

Murray, Charles Shaar

Crosstown traffic: Jimi Hendrix and the post-war
rock'n'roll revolution. St. Martin's Press 1990 247p
il hardcover o.p. pa $12   **787.87**
   1. Singers 2. Guitarists 3. Rock musicians 4.
Biography, Individual
   ISBN 0-312-06324-5 pa
                 LC 89-77681

First published 1989 in the United Kingdom with title:
Crosstown traffic: Jimi Hendrix and post-war pop

This is a biography of the rock guitarist who died in
1970. Discography. Bibliography. Index.

"This informed, textured account will be irresistible to
devotees of Hendrix and psychedelic rock as well as fans of
blues, funk, jazz and rock 'n' roll." Booklist

Includes discography and bibliographical references

790 Recreational and performing arts

Denmead, Ken

Geek dad; awesomely geeky projects and activities for dads and kids to share. foreword by Chris Anderson. Gotham Books 2010 222p pa $17; ebook
$9.99   **790**
   1. Amusements 2. Father-son relationship
   ISBN 978-1-59240-552-7 pa; 978-1-101-40431-7
ebook
                 LC 2010-8860

This book contains projects for activities such as creating a customized comic strip, building a lamp with CDs and
LEGOs, and launching a video camera with balloons.

Includes bibliographical references

790.1 General kinds of recreational activities

Conner, Bobbi

Unplugged play; no batteries, no plugs, pure fun.
illustrations by Amy Patacchiola. Workman Pub.
2007 xxv, 401p il $27.95; pa $16.95   **790.1**
   1. Play 2. Games
   ISBN 978-0-7611-4114-3; 978-0-7611-4390-1 pa
               LC 2007-23999

"Conner has compiled more than 710 games and activities sorted by age level. Good old-fashioned play and fun are
the motto here with simple props from around the house or
just an imagination. The book is separated into three major
parts: 'Toddler Play,' 'Preschool Play,' and 'Grade School
Play.' Each has a section on solo play, ideas for parent and
child, playing with others, and birthday-party activities.
Each chapter and section is loaded with ideas and suggestions for simple crafts. There is such a wealth of information
in this book." SLJ

791 Public performances

Austen, Jake

Darkest America; black minstrelsy from slavery
to hip-hop. Yuval Taylor and Jake Austen. W. W.
Norton 2012 368 p. (hardcover) $26.95   **791**
   1. Hip-hop culture 2. African Americans -- History
3. Popular culture -- United States 4. Blackface
entertainers -- United States -- History 5. Hip-hop --
United States -- History 6. Minstrel shows -- United
States -- History
   ISBN 0393070980; 9780393070989

               LC 2012007307

This book, by Yuval Taylor and Jake Austen,
"investigate[s] the complex history of black minstrelsy, adopted in the mid-nineteenth century by . . . performers who
played the grinning blackface fool to entertain . . . audiences.
We now consider minstrelsy an embarrassing relic, but once
blacks and whites alike saw it as a black art form. . . . And .
. . black minstrelsy remains deeply relevant to popular black
entertainment, particularly in the work of contemporary artists." (Publisher's note)

"An innovative, marvelous book about comedy, stereotypes and the struggle to steer through the sometimes-fierce
internal debates over African-American identity in a society
still struggling with its racial past." Kirkus

Includes bibliographical references and index

Fine, Marshall

Accidental genius; how John Cassavetes invented the American independent film. Miramax Books 2006 482p il $27.95   791

1. Actors 2. Motion picture directors

ISBN 1-4013-5249-9

The author "argues that mainstream moviegoers ought to care about maverick director Cassavetes (1929-89) as the progenitor of today's American independent film movement." Booklist

Moore, Rachel S.

The **artist's** compass; the complete guide to building a life and a living in the performing arts. Rachel Moore, President and CEO of the Los Angeles Music Center. Touchstone 2016 224 p. (hardback) $24.99   791

1. Success 2. Performing arts 3. Performing arts -- Economic aspects 4. Performing arts -- Vocational guidance

ISBN 9781501105951; 9781501126642

LC 2015037025

In this book, "Los Angeles Music Center CEO Rachel Moore shares how to make life as a performer more successful, secure, and sustainable by approaching a career in the arts like an entrepreneur. A former dancer in the American Ballet Theatre's corps de ballet, Moore knows firsthand what it's like to struggle and succeed as an artist. Now in an off-stage role as CEO, Moore shares the hard-won lessons she's learned about making one's own success." (Publisher's note)

"Moore is qualified to become a mentor to a whole new generation of artists, and they will benefit greatly from her advice." Pub Wkly

Includes bibliographical references and index

791.3   Circuses

Daly, Michael

Topsy; The Startling Story of the Crooked Tailed Elephant, P.T. Barnum, and the American Wizard, Thomas Edison. by Michael Daly. Pgw 2013 viii, 369 p.p $27   791.3

1. Circus 2. Elephants

ISBN 0802119042; 9780802119049

This book, by Michael Daly, examines how "in 1903, on Coney Island, an elephant named Topsy was electrocuted, and over the past century, this bizarre, ghoulish execution has reverberated through popular culture with the whiff of urban legend. But it really happened, and many historical forces conspired to bring Topsy, Thomas Edison, and those 6600 volts of alternating current together that day. Daly weaves together a fascinating popular history, the first book on this astonishing tale." (Publisher's note)

Jensen, Dean

Queen of the air; a true story of love and tragedy at the circus. Dean Jensen. Crown Publishers 2012 336 p. $26   791.3

1. Circus 2. Interpersonal relations 3. Aerialists -- United States -- Biography 4. Woman circus performers

-- United States -- Biography

ISBN 030798656X; 9780307986566

LC 2012018066

This book by Dean Jensen presents the "true story of renowned trapeze artist and circus performer Leitzel, Queen of the Air, the most famous woman in the world at the turn of the 20th century, and her star-crossed love affair with Alfredo Codona, of the famous Flying Codona Brothers." (Publisher's note)

Macy, Beth

Truevine; Two Brothers, a Kidnapping, and a Mother's Quest: A True Story of the Jim Crow South. Beth Macy. Little, Brown & Co. 2016 432 p. $28   791.3

1. Circus 2. Brothers 3. Kidnapping 4. African Americans -- Biography

ISBN 9780316337540

LC 2015959853

This book, by Beth Macy, is the "true story of two African-American brothers who were kidnapped and displayed as circus freaks, and whose mother endured a 28-year struggle to get them back. The year was 1899 and the place a sweltering tobacco farm in the Jim Crow South town of Truevine, Virginia. George and Willie Muse were two little boys born to a sharecropper family. One day a white man offered them a piece of candy, setting off events that would take them around the world." (Publisher's note)

"A rambling, colorful, and thought-provoking medley of human stories intersecting with one another in carnival tents and Virginia backlands, this solid popular history has much to offer regarding issues of race, family, disability, and spectacle." LJ

791.43   Motion pictures

1001 Movies You Must See Before You Die; general editor, Steven Jay Schneider; updated by Ian Haydn Smith. Updated edition Barrons 2015 960 p. illustrations hbk $35   791.43

1. Motion pictures

ISBN 9780764167904; 0764167901

Originally published 2003

"Thorough essays for each movie combine important plot points, vital statistics, commentary, context, and informative trivia for films spanning 1902-2014. The movies are listed by decade and include a color-coded system for quickly locating titles. Schneider researched many top film lists to assist in his effort to include entries that exemplify a well-rounded collection deemed significant for various reasons. He states that the result is not intended to be a 'best of' list but rather a 'provocation' providing fodder for stimulating discussion and debate." (Library Journal)

Allen, Woody, 1935-

Woody Allen on Woody Allen; in conversation with Stig Björkman. Grove Press 1995 288 p. $22; $15.95   791.43

1. Motion picture producers and directors -- United

States -- Interviews

ISBN 080211556X; 0802142036; 9780802142030

LC 94026866

This book by Woody Allen is "a unique self-portrait of this uncompromising filmmaker that offers a revealing account of his life and work. In a series of rare, in-depth interviews, Allen brings us onto the sets and behind the scenes of all his films. Since its original publication, 'Woody Allen on Woody Allen' has been the primary source of Allen's own thoughts on his work, childhood, favorite films, and inspirations." (Publisher's note)

Includes filmography.

Arnold, Jeremy

The **essentials**; 52 must-see movies and why they matter. Jeremy Arnold; foreword by Robert Osborne. Running Press 2016 288 p. illustrations (some color) (paperback) $25; (ebook) $16.99   **791.43**

1. Motion pictures -- Appreciation 2. Motion pictures -- Reviews

ISBN 0762459468; 9780762459469; 9780762459476

LC 2015959543

This book, by Jeremy Arnold, "showcas[es] 52 Essential films from the golden age to the present. . . . These are movies that define what it means to be a classic. Readers can enjoy one film per week, for a year of stellar viewing, or indulge in their own classic movie festival." (Publisher's note)

Includes bibliographical references (pages 272-279) and index

Biskind, Peter

Easy riders, raging bulls; how the sex-drugs-and-rock-'n'-roll generation saved Hollywood. Simon & Schuster 1998 506p il hardcover o.p. pa $15   **791.43**

1. Motion pictures 2. Motion picture producers and directors

ISBN 0-684-85708-1 pa

LC 98-2919

"Biskind does relish the tales of outlandish behaviour. . . . But in kicking over the traces of survivors' more or less reliable memories, he shows that libidinal and pharmaceutical urges were intrinsic to the film-makers' ferocious need to outdo each other as auteurs along the lines of the European greats they studied and worshipped." Sight Sound

Includes filmography and bibliographical references

My Lunches With Orson; Conversations Between Henry Jaglom and Orson Welles. edited by Peter Biskind. Henry Holt and Co. 2013 320 p. $28 **791.43**

1. Motion picture producers and directors -- United States 2. Motion picture producers and directors -- United States -- Anecdotes

ISBN 0805097252; 9780805097252

LC 2013000291

Here, film historian Peter Biskind has edited recordings captured when Orson Welles lunched with his friend, film director Henry Jaglom. In the montage offered, "Welles offers a montage of opinion on his career, his disappointments, and acquaintances from Marlene Dietrich and Laurence Olivier to Winston Churchill." (Library Journal)

Bogle, Donald

Bright boulevards, bold dreams; the story of Black Hollywood. One World Ballantine Books 2005 411p il $26.95; pa $15.95   **791.43**

1. African American actors 2. African Americans in motion pictures

ISBN 0345454189; 0345454197 pa

LC 2004-54781

"Starting with Madame Sul-Te-Wan's work in D.W. Griffith's 1915 The Birth of a Nation and ending with the 1960s deaths of Louise Beavers, Nat 'King' Cole and Dorothy Dandridge, Bogle tells the stories of the stars of Black Hollywood: their outfits, their love affairs and their struggles for better roles. . . . Bogle's lively style . . . and his many anecdotes will entertain and inform film students and black history buffs alike." Publ Wkly

Includes bibliographical references

Cavalier, Stephen

The **world** history of animation; Stephen Cavalier. University of California Press 2011 416 p. ill. (some col.) (cloth : alk. paper) $39.95   **791.43**

1. Animated films 2. Animation (Cinematography) 3. Animated television programs 4. Animators 5. Animated films -- History and criticism

ISBN 0520261127; 9780520261129

LC 2010931052

This book on animation by Stephen Cavalier "tells the genre's 100-year-old story around the globe, featuring key players in Europe, North America, and Asia." It is "organized chronologically and covers pioneers, feature films, television programs, digital films, games, independent films, and the web. . . . The book explains the evolution of animation techniques, from rotoscoping to refinements of cel techniques, direct film, claymation, and more." (Publisher's note)

Includes bibliographical references (p. 404-405) and index.

Conversations at the American Film Institute with the great moviemakers; the next generation. edited and with an introduction by George Stevens, Jr. Alfred A. Knopf 2012 xxiii, 737 p.p (hbk.) $39.95   **791.43**

1. Motion pictures 2. Motion picture industry 3. Motion picture producers and directors 4. Motion pictures -- Production and direction 5. Motion picture producers and directors -- United States -- Interviews

ISBN 0307273474; 9780307273475

LC 2011043741

This book presents conversations with "directors, producers, writers, actors, cameramen, composers, editors": "men and women working in pictures, beginning in 1950, when the studio system was collapsing and people could no longer depend on, or were bound by, the structure of studio life to make movies." Others, "who began to work long after the studio days were over," are featured as well. (Barnes and Noble)

Includes bibliographical references and index.

Corliss, Richard, 1944-2015

Mom in the movies; the iconic screen mothers you love (and a few you love to hate) by Richard Corliss; foreword by Debbie Reynolds and Carrie Fisher; [with editorial assistance from Turner Classic Movies] Simon & Schuster 2014 192 p. illustrations $35 **791.43**

1. Mothers 2. Women in motion pictures 3. Mothers in motion pictures

ISBN 1476738262; 9781476738260

LC 2013044850

"Turner Classic Movies and film historian Richard Corliss present 'Mom in the Movies: The Iconic Screen Mothers You Love (and a Few You Love to Hate),' the . . . . fully illustrated book that shares the many ways Hollywood has celebrated, vilified and otherwise memorialized dear old Mom. . . . Here, you will meet the Criminal Moms . . . and the eccentric Showbiz Moms. . . . You'll also find Great American Moms, as warm and nourishing as apple pie." (Publisher's note)

A "comprehensive retrospective of mothers as portrayed on film from the earliest "Silent Moms" . . . to the most recent figures." LJ

D'Alessandro, Emilio

Stanley Kubrick and me; thirty years at his side. Emilio D'Alessandro with Filippo Ulivieri; translated by Simon Marsh. Arcade Publishing 2016 384 p. illustrations (some color) (hardback) $27.99 **791.43**

1. Motion picture producers and directors -- Biography 2. Motion picture producers and directors -- United States -- Biography

ISBN 9781628726695

LC 2015050645

This book, Emilio D'Alessandro, focuses on filmmaker Stanley Kubrick. "Emilio was the silent guy in the room when the script for The Shining was discussed. He still has the coat Jack Nicholson used in the movie. He was an extra on the set of Eyes Wide Shut, Kubrick's last movie. He knew all the actors and producers Kubrick worked with; he observed firsthand Kubrick's working methods down to the smallest detail." (Publisher's note)

"Hard-core Kubrick devotees won't learn much, but this easygoing and likable memoir humanizes an eccentric titan of cinema." LJ

Dixon, Wheeler W., 1950-

A **Short** History of Film; Wheeler Winston Dixon & Gwendolyn Audrey Foster. 2nd edition Rutgers University Press 2013 449 p. illustrations (some color) pa. $29.95 **791.43**

1. Motion picture industry 2. Motion picture industry -- History 3. Motion pictures -- History

ISBN 9780813560557

LC 2012533144

This book, by Wheeler Winston Dixon and Gwendolyn Audrey Foster, "provides a concise and accurate overview of the history of world cinema, detailing the major movements, directors, studios, and genres from 1896 through 2012. Accompanied by more than 250 rare color and black-and-white stills - including many from recent films - the new edition .

. . [conveys] a sense of cinema's sweep in the twentieth and early twenty-first centuries." (Publisher's note)

"This excellent introduction stands out in a crowded field with its lively, accessible writing, broad coverage, and particular focus on traditionally marginalized figures in film history...The most striking aspect of the book is the coverage of women, African Americans, and Third World filmmakers, which strongly complements its solid coverage of American and European film. Illustrations abound, and even the best-versed cineaste will find new films to track down after reading the breezy, enthusiastic analysis in this book. Highly recommended for all collections, this text would also make an excellent textbook for introductory film-studies courses." (Library Journal)

Film noir; the encyclopedia. edited by Alain Silver . . . [et al.]; co-editor: Carl Macek; designed by Bernard Schleifer. [4th ed.]; Overlook Duckworth 2010 511p il **791.43**

1. Mystery films 2. Motion pictures

ISBN 978-1-590201442

First published 1979

An introductory essay "lays out the history and parameters of noir in a succinct but undogmatic way, offering an intro for the new viewer as well as food for thought for the hardboiled fan. Most of the rest of the book consists of synopses of noir films, providing a brief plot summary followed by a paragraph or two detailing key aspects of each film. Important flicks like Kiss Me Deadly and Double Indemnity get a bit more space and consideration, and the authors, for the most part, avoid subjective reviews and concentrate on chasing down each film's address in the naked city of noir. . . . This new edition of the definitive text on film noir is a perfect companion for a foray into the dreamlike world of some of the most dark and mesmerizing movies ever made." PopMatters

Fischer, Paul

★ A **Kim** Jong-Il production; the extraordinary true story of a kidnapped filmmaker, his star actress, and a young dictator's rise to power. Paul Fischer. Flatiron Books 2015 368 p. illustrations (some color) (hardcover) $27.99 **791.43**

1. Kidnapping 2. Korea (North) 3. Actresses -- Korea (South) -- Biography 4. Motion pictures -- Korea (North) -- History -- 20th century 5. Motion picture producers and directors -- Korea (South) -- Biography

ISBN 1250054265; 9781250054265

LC 2014040366

"Before becoming the world's most notorious dictator, Kim Jong-Il ran North Korea's Ministry for Propaganda and its film studios. Conceiving every movie made, he acted as producer and screenwriter. Despite this control, he was underwhelmed by the available talent and took drastic steps, ordering the kidnapping of Choi Eun-Hee (Madam Choi)--South Korea's most famous actress--and her ex-husband Shin Sang-Ok, the country's most famous filmmaker." (Publisher's note)

"The most compelling facets of this book of astonishments are Fischer's insights into the relationships between Choi, Shin, and their diabolical captor and Fischer's canny perception of how Kim Jong-Il turned his oppressed, corrupt, and starving country into one vast theatrical production of fantasy, deceit, and terror, scripting lives of fear, ignorance, obedience, and deprivation." Booklist

Includes bibliographical references (pages 345- 353)

Gleiberman, Owen

Movie freak; my life watching movies. Owen Gleiberman. Hachette Books 2016 352 p. (hardback) $28   **791.43**
1. Critics 2. Motion pictures -- History and criticism 3. Film critics -- United States -- Biography
ISBN 0316382965; 9780316382960
LC 2015039430

In this memoir, author Owen Gleiberman "paints a bittersweet portrait of his complicated and ultimately doomed friendship with Pauline Kael, the legendary New Yorker film critic who was his mentor and muse. He also offers an unprecedented inside look at what the experience of being a critic is really all about, detailing his stint at The Boston Phoenix and then, starting in 1990, at [Entertainment Weekly]." (Publisher's note)

"A story of societal change, rich in cultural as well as personal history." Kirkus

Goldman, William

Adventures in the screen trade; a personal view of Hollywood and screenwriting. Warner Bks. 1983 418p $17.50   **791.43**
1. Motion picture industry 2. Motion picture authorship. 3. Hollywood (Los Angeles, Calif.)--History.
ISBN 0-446-51273-7
LC 82-17602

"No one knows the writer's Hollywood more intimately than William Goldman. Two-time Academy Award-winning screenwriter and the bestselling author of Marathon Man, Tinsel, Boys and Girls Together, and other novels, Goldman now takes you into Hollywood's inner sanctums...on and behind the scenes for Butch Cassidy and the Sundance Kid, All the President's Men, and other films...into the plush offices of Hollywood producers...into the working lives of acting greats such as Redford, Olivier, Newman, and Hoffman...and into his own professional experiences and creative thought processes in the crafting of screenplays. You get a firsthand look at why and how films get made and what elements make a good screenplay." (Publisher's Note)

Goldman devotes several "chapters to separate categories like Stars, Producers, Executives, the basic elements a screenplay requires, then other chapters to specific reminiscences of movies with which he was associated (e.g., 'Harper,' 'The Great Waldo Pepper,' 'Marathon Man,' 'A Bridge Too Far'), and he ends with a sequence of . . . examples of how a short story (he uses one of his own as illustration) could be adapted first into a screenplay and gradually into a movie." (America) Index.

Which Lie Did I Tell? more adventures in the screen trade. William Goldman. Vintage Books 2001 485 p. $17.95   **791.43**
1. Screenwriters 2. Motion picture industry 3. Motion picture authorship 4. Motion picture industry -- California -- Los Angeles
ISBN 0375703195; 9780375703195

This book by William Goldman, "the Oscar-winning screenwriter of 'Butch Cassidy and the Sundance Kid' and 'The Princess Bride' (he also wrote the novel), and the bestselling author of 'Adventures in the Screen Trade' . . . is as much a screenwriting how-to (and how-not-to) manual as it is a feast of insider information. "Which Lie Did I Tell?" is [designed] for anyone even slightly intrigued by the process of how a movie gets made." (Publisher's Note)

"[Goldman] discusses screenwriting perils, explains how successful movies like Charade and The Sound of Music wreaked havoc by siring copycat films, describes how Andre the Giant always paid for lunch, complains that MTV's impact on quick-cutting has helped make 1990s films awful, reveals that only Clint Eastwood and Sean Connery are tall, investigates how great comedy scenes worked in When Harry Met Sally and There's Something About Mary, debunks auteurs, and divulges why no big star would play Superman in 1978...An engaging expos that is not mean-spirited; recommended for public and academic libraries and film collections." (Library Journal)

Harris, Mark

★ **Five** Came Back; A Story of Hollywood and the Second World War. Mark Harris. Penguin Group USA 2014 480 p. illustrations $29.95   **791.43**
1. Motion picture industry 2. World War, 1939-1945 -- Motion pictures and the war 3. Motion picture producers and directors -- United States 4. Motion pictures -- United States -- History 5. Motion picture industry -- California -- Los Angeles -- History
ISBN 1594204306; 9781594204302
LC 2013039983

Los Angeles Times Book Prize Finalist: History (2014)

This book tells "the untold story of how Hollywood changed World War II, and how World War II changed Hollywood, through the prism of five film directors caught up in the war: John Ford, William Wyler, John Huston, Frank Capra, and George Stevens." (Publisher's note) "Some of the five worked together (Capra and Stevens), but others worked separately on feature-length documentaries, short subjects and films for military use only." (Kirkus Reviews)

"Narrative nonfiction that is as gloriously readable as it is unfailingly informative." Booklist

Includes bibliographical references and index

Pictures at a revolution; five movies and the birth of the new Hollywood. Penguin Press 2008 490p il $27.95   **791.43**
1. Motion pictures
ISBN 978-1-59420-152-3; 1-59420-152-8
LC 2007-32633

The author examines the five films nominated for the Academy Award for Best Picture in 1967: Bonnie and Clyde, The Graduate, Guess Who's Coming To Dinner, In the Heat of the Night, and Dr. Dolittle.

"Harris gives us a juicy, multilayered chronicle of a turning point in American culture. This is page-turning social history; someone reading this book who didn't live through those days would understand why 'the '60s' had to happen." Newsweek

Includes bibliographical references

Kael, Pauline

The **age** of movies; selected writings of Pauline Kael. edited by Sanford Schwartz. Library of America 2011 xxiv, 828p $40 **791.43**

1. Motion pictures -- Reviews

ISBN 978-1-59853-109-1; 1-59853-109-3

LC 2011-23053

"Spanning 1965 to 1990, the volume holds many sparkling radio essays [Kael] delivered over the East Bay airwaves and had reprinted in places like Film Quarterly before heading east, and a wealth of reviews from magazines, especially from her residency at The New Yorker, where she opined from 1967 to 1991. The full range of Kael's smarts, vision, wit, prejudices, and downright cruelty are on full, wicked display." Millions

Karp, Josh

Orson Welles's last movie; the making of The other side of the wind. Josh Karp. St. Martin's Press 2015 352 p. 8 plates; illustrations (hardback) $26.99 **791.43**

1. Motion pictures -- Production and direction 2. Other side of the wind (Motion picture)

ISBN 1250007089; 9781250007087

LC 2015002464

This book, by Josh Karp, presents a history of the "legendary but self-destructive director Orson Welles" and the production of his final film "The Other Side of the Wind." This book "is a fast-paced, behind-the-scenes account of the bizarre, hilarious and remarkable making of what has been called 'the greatest home movie that no one has ever seen.'" (Publisher's note)

"A fascinating story, much more than your typical making-of book." Booklist

Lane, Anthony

Nobody's perfect; writings from the New Yorker. Knopf 2002 xx, 752p $30; pa $16.95 **791.43**

1. Motion pictures -- Reviews

ISBN 0-375-41448-7; 0-375-71434-0 pa

LC 2002-20809

"One of the best aspects of Lane's column, and of this anthology, is that it wanders across cultural and intellectual borders." Libr J

Lanzmann, Claude, 1925-

The **Patagonian** hare; a memoir. Claude Lanzmann; translated from the French by Frank Wynne. Farrar, Straus & Giroux 2012 x, 528 p.p ill. **791.43**

1. Autobiographies 2. Journalists -- Biography 3. Motion picture producers and directors -- Biography 4. Journalists -- France -- Biography 5. Motion picture producers and directors -- France -- Biography

ISBN 0374230048; 9780374230043

LC 2011048058

This book is the memoir of the "journalist and filmmaker Claude Lanzmann. . . . Raised as a secular Jew in a family with deep communist sympathies . . . the author served in the French Resistance and narrowly missed capture by the Nazis. . . . He became editor of Jean-Paul Sartre's journal 'Le Temps Modernes' . . . and had an intense seven-year affair with Sartre's lover, Simone de Beauvoir, who was happy to take him on as her 'sixth man.' Faithfulness wasn't anyone's game then, and Lanzmann seemed to seduce nearly every woman he ever met. He also became deeply immersed in his own Jewish heritage and documentary filmmaking, ultimately resulting in his nine-hour magnum opus Shoah." (Kirkus)

Longworth, Karina

Hollywood frame by frame; the unseen silver screen in contact sheets, 1915-1997. Karina Longworth. Princeton Architectural Press 2014 1 p. (hardback) $30 **791.43**

1. Hollywood (Calif.) 2. Motion picture industry 3. Contact printing -- United States 4. Stills (Motion pictures) -- United States 5. Motion pictures -- United States -- Pictorial works

ISBN 1616892595; 9781616892593

LC 2013051020

This book by Karina Longworth "presents hundreds of never-before-published photos from the sets of some of the greatest films of the twentieth century. Hollywood's biggest stars are caught with their guard down behind the scenes of movie classics from Some Like It Hot and Breakfast at Tiffany's to Taxi Driver and The Silence of the Lambs." (Publisher's note)

"Cinephiles will relish these moments captured from another era." LJ

Lumet, Sidney

Making movies. Knopf 1995 220p hardcover o.p. pa $12 **791.43**

1. Motion pictures -- Production and direction

ISBN 0-679-75660-4 pa

LC 94-34449

"A fascinating look at the artist at work." Libr J

Mann, William J.

Behind the screen; how gays and lesbians shaped Hollywood, 1910-1969. Viking 2001 xxiv, 422p il $29.95; pa $16 **791.43**

1. Motion picture industry 2. Homosexuality in motion pictures

ISBN 0-670-03017-1; 0-14-200114-7 pa

LC 2001-17984

In this study "Mann examines how the movie capital of the world was transformed by a host of writers, directors, designers, actors, and producers often at odds with the official codes, and mores of the times. . . . Mann's book is important reading for anyone interested in the history of American film. Essential for all film and gay studies collections." Libr J

Muir, John Kenneth

The **encyclopedia** of superheroes on film and television; 2nd ed.; McFarland & Co. 2008 696p il $75 **791.43**

1. Reference books 2. Superhero films -- Encyclopedias 3. Superhero television programs -- Encyclopedias

ISBN 978-0-7864-3755-9; 0-7864-3755-3

LC 2008-19724

First published 2004

"Entries start with description and background of the hero. Live-action films are presented with reviewer comments and cast and crew. TV series also present reviewer comments and a description of the series. Episode guides include title, writer and director credits, and air dates as well as episode descriptions and guest casts. . . . A good addition to the pop-culture collection." Booklist

Includes bibliographical references

Osborne, Robert A.

75 years of the Oscar; the official history of the Academy Awards. {by} Robert Osborne. Abbeville Press 2013 416p il $75   **791.43**

1. Academy Awards (Motion pictures)

ISBN 9780789211422

First published 1989 with title: 60 years of the Oscar. Published every five years.

This includes a history of the Academy of Motion Picture Arts and Sciences, overviews of Academy Award nominees and winners, award ceremonies, and a complete listing of nominees and winners in every category

Includes bibliographical references

Rabin, Nathan

My year of flops; the A.V. Club presents one man's journey deep into the heart of cinematic failure. Scribner 2010 264p il pa $15   **791.43**

1. Motion pictures

ISBN 978-1-4391-5312-3; 1-4391-5312-4

LC 2010-18224

"Follow Nathan Rabin on his quest 'to provide a sympathetic reappraisal of some of the most reviled films of all time,' and what do you learn? 'Pennies From Heaven' and 'Freddy Got Fingered' are better than you might think, and 'Ishtar' offers an 'exquisitely jaundiced take' on American foreign policy. Mostly, though, Mr. Rabin sits slack-jawed watching the everlasting dreadfulness of 'Mame,' 'Battlefield Earth' and 'Exit to Eden' ('the mother of all unsexy sex films'). Always glad to snark it up, Mr. Rabin can also be mournful when reflecting on how worthwhile failures like 'Heaven's Gate' diminished Hollywood's ambitions, then and now. The book, which collects columns that first appeared on The Onion's pop-culture Web site, includes more bad movies and interviews with actors caught up in the cinematic wreckage." N Y Times Book Rev

Rough Guides (Firm)

The **Rough** Guide to film; [by] Richard Armstrong . . . [et al.] Distributed by Penguin Putnam 2007 649p il pa $27.99   **791.43**

1. Reference books 2. Motion picture producers and directors -- Biography -- Dictionaries

ISBN 978-1-84353-408-2; 1-84353-408-8

LC 2007-300132

"This volume looks beyond the Hollywood mainstream to provide assistance to anyone who is browsing rental-store shelves or online DVD catalogs in search of something new. More than 800 directors from around the globe are profiled, and more than 2,000 of their most important films are briefly reviewed. . . . If you're in a hurry, you can turn to the various categorized lists of five great directors, five classic films, and five 'lesser-known gems.'" Booklist

Santopietro, Tom

The **sound** of music story; how one young nun, one handsome Austrian captain, and seven singing Von Trapp children inspired the most beloved film of all time. by Tom Santopietro. St. Martin's Press 2015 336 p. illustrations (hardcover) $28.99 **791.43**

1. Sound of music (Motion picture)

ISBN 9781250064462

LC 2014033795

Includes bibliographical references and index.

In this book on the film "The Sound of Music," Tom Santopietro "chronicles the initial faltering financial commitment of 20th Century Fox, and the torturous search for a director, a cinematographer, the actors and actresses, and other staff. . . . Although the Von Trapp family, and Austria, initially distanced themselves from the film because they thought it inaccurately portrayed their family and the times, they later accepted . . . [it] because of what it means to people." (Publishers Weekly)

"A fun-to-read book, perfect for musical-lovers, aspiring moviemakers, and film buffs." Booklist

Schickel, Richard, 1933-

Keepers; the greatest films-and personal favorites-of a moviegoing lifetime. Richard Schickel. Alfred A. Knopf 2015 320 p. (hardcover) $26.95; (ebook) $51   **791.43**

1. Film criticism 2. Motion pictures 3. Motion pictures -- Evaluation

ISBN 9780375424595; 9781101874714

LC 2014034997

This book by film critic Richard Schickel offers a "history of film as he's seen—and lived—it, a tour of his favorites, a master class in what makes a film soar or flop. [His] no-holds-barred, often raucously irreverent opinions can range from panning classics, to spotlighting forgotten treasures, to defending the art of 'popular' genres such as horror, westerns, screwball comedy, and noir. Beyond his picks and pans, Schickel offers a wealth of behind-the-scenes anecdotes." (Publisher's note)

"Schickel, who posits in his introduction that movies are about both nothing and everything, wholly succeeds in making readers care about every film he's seen." Pub Wkly

Spoto, Donald

The **dark** side of genius; the life of Alfred Hitchcock. {with a new introduction by the author} Centennial ed; Da Capo Press 1999 594p il pa $22   **791.43**

1. Motion picture directors

ISBN 0-306-80932-X

LC 99-37941

This is a reissue of the title first published 1983 by Little, Brown

This is a biography of the director of such films as The man who knew too much, The thirty-nine steps, The lady vanishes, Rebecca, Spellbound, Strangers on a train, Rear window, and Psycho

This "is a vivid and perceptive portrait of a man whose character was as strange and shadowed as his films. . . . Hitchcock's final obsession was secretiveness, but he has been well served by a knowledgeable and revealing biography." Time

Includes bibliographical references

Szostak, Phil

The **art** of Star Wars; the force awakens. Phil Szostak. Abrams 2015 256 p. color illustrations $40 **791.43**

1. Art 2. Star Wars films

ISBN 1419717804; 9781419717802

LC 2014959560

Author Phil Szostak's book on the film "Star Wars: The Force Awakens" goes "inside the Lucasfilm art departments for the creation of fantastical worlds, unforgettable characters, and unimaginable creatures. [It covers] from the earliest gathering of artists and production designers at Lucasfilm headquarters in San Francisco to the fever pitch of production at Pinewood Studios to the conclusion of post-production at Industrial Light & Magic." (Publisher's note)

Thomson, David, 1941-

The **big** screen; the story of the movies. David Thomson. 1st ed. Farrar, Straus and Giroux 2012 viii, 595 p.p (alk. paper) $35.00 **791.43**

1. Motion pictures -- Social aspects 2. Motion pictures -- United States -- History 3. Motion pictures -- Social aspects -- United States

ISBN 9780374191894; 0374191891

LC 2012009140

This book by David Thomson is "is a wide-ranging narrative about the movies and their signal role in modern life. Thomson takes us around the globe, through time, and across many media--moving from Eadweard Muybridge to Steve Jobs, from 'Sunrise' to 'I Love Lucy,' from John Wayne to George Clooney, from television commercials to streaming video--to tell the complex, gripping, paradoxical story of the movies." (Publisher's note)

Includes bibliographical references and index.

How to watch a movie; David Thomson. Alfred A. Knopf 2015 256 p. (ebook) $65; (hardcover) $24.95 **791.43**

1. Cinematography 2. Motion pictures -- Appreciation

ISBN 9781101875407; 9781101875391; 9781101910849

LC 2014046757

In this book about cinema, author David Thomson "offers his most inventive exploration of the medium yet: guiding us through each element of the viewing experience, considering the significance of everything from what we see and hear on-screen—actors, shots, cuts, dialogue, music—to the specifics of how, where, and with whom we do the viewing." (Publisher's note)

"An enjoyably deep dive into the interaction between cinema and psyche." Kirkus

The **whole** equation; a history of Hollywood. Knopf 2005 402p il hardcover o.p. pa $15 **791.43**

1. Motion picture industry -- History 2. Motion pictures -- History and criticism

ISBN 0-375-40016-8; 0-375-70154-0 pa

LC 2004-48358

"Peeling back the layers, goring sacred cows, correcting misconceptions, and revealing truth rather than reprinting legends, Thomson offers history, yes, but also a philosophical meditation on how the movie industry has inspired and influenced L.A. and America, and vice versa." Booklist

Includes bibliographical references

Turan, Kenneth

Not to be missed; 54 favorites from a lifetime of film. Kenneth Turan. PublicAffairs 2014 368 p. (hardback) $25.99; (ebook) $11.99 **791.43**

1. Motion pictures -- History and criticism 2. Motion pictures

ISBN 9781586483968; 9781610393676

LC 2014007773

This book presents Kenneth Turan's "fifty-four favorite films. . . . [It] blends cultural criticism, historical anecdote, and inside-Hollywood controversy. Turan's selection of favorites ranges across all genres. From 'All About Eve' to 'Seven Samurai' to 'Sherlock Jr.,' these are all timeless films." (Publisher's note)

"Turan's illuminating reflections do what the best essays on film always do: send us to watch the movie, whether for the first time or the 20th." Pub Wkly

Includes bibliographical references and index

Urwand, Ben

The **collaboration**; Hollywood's pact with Hitler. Ben Urwand. The Belknap Press of Harvard University Press 2013 320 p. (hardcover : alk. paper) $26.95 **791.43**

1. National socialism 2. Germany -- History -- 1933-1945 3. Motion picture industry -- History 4. National socialism and motion pictures 5. Germany -- Civilization -- American influences 6. Motion picture industry -- United States -- History -- 20th century

ISBN 0674724747; 9780674724747

LC 2013013576

This book looks at the "alliance Hollywood made with the Nazis, which allowed both to keep packing movie theaters in Germany up until the outbreak of war. Concomitant with Hollywood's golden era of the 1930s was the rise of the Nazi Party, whose chief officials admired American films. . . . The result of this complicated and slippery relationship . . . was the absolute disappearance from film of Nazis and Jews until the end of the decade." (Kirkus Reviews)

Includes bibliographical references and index

Warren, Bill

Keep watching the skies! American science fiction movies of the fifties. research associate, Bill Thomas; foreword by Howard Waldrop. 21st century ed.; McFarland & Co. 2010 1004p il $99 **791.43**

1. Reference books 2. Science fiction films

ISBN 978-0-7864-4230-0; 0-7864-4230-1

LC 2009-20594

First published in two volumes 1982-1986

Covers "nearly 300 films released between 1950 and 1962. . . . Although prominent films like Forbidden Planet, Them! The Time Machine, and The Fly receive more extensive coverage, all of the essays . . . include production, cast, and distribution credits; a plot synopsis; production details and fun background facts; discussion of the direction, acting, effects, and other prominent elements of the film; and information about public and critical reaction. Attractive photos accompany most of the essays, and posters for the best-known films are reproduced in 35 color plates. . . . Although the audience for 1950s science fiction may be dwindling, this is the kind of reference that not only informs but also creates new fans." Booklist

Includes bibliographical references

Wasson, Sam

Fifth Avenue, 5 AM; Audrey Hepburn, Breakfast at Tiffany's, and the dawn of the modern woman. HarperStudio 2010 xx, 231p il map $19.99 **791.43**
    1. Actors 2. Breakfast at Tiffany's (Motion picture)
    ISBN 978-0-06-177415-7

                     LC 2009-52439

The author "presents an irresistibly gossipy account of the production of Breakfast at Tiffany's (1961), charting the transformation of actress Audrey Hepburn into an icon of emerging sexual liberation—the good/bad girl, the lovable 'kook,' independent and sexually experienced but sufficiently charming to bring home to mother. Rich in incident and set among the glitterati of America's most glamorous era, the book reads like a novel." Kirkus

Wieland, Karin

Dietrich & Riefenstahl; Hollywood, Berlin, and a century in two lives. Karin Wieland; translated by Shelley Frisch. Liveright Publishing Corp. 2015 624 p. illustrations (hardcover) $35   **791.43**
    1. Women entertainers -- Germany -- Biography 2. Motion picture actors and actresses -- Germany -- Biography 3. Women motion picture producers and directors -- Germany -- Biography
    ISBN 9780871403360

                     LC 2015026548

National Book Critics Circle Award Finalist: Biography (2015)

This book, by Karin Wieland, translated by Shelley Frisch, named Best Book of 2015 by the "Boston Globe" and "Washington Post" newspapers, offers a dual biography of the 20th century women actresses Leni Riefenstahl and Marlene Dietrich. "Skillfully juxtaposing these two fascinating lives, Wieland brings to vivid life a time of international upheaval, chronicling radical evolutions of politics, fame, and femininity on a grand stage." (Publisher's note)

"Wieland deftly traces both lives through their many ups and downs. A sweeping, revelatory dual biography." Kirkus

Includes bibliographical references and index
Dietrich and Riefenstahl

791.44   Radio

Ely, Melvin Patrick

The **adventures** of Amos 'n' Andy; a social history of an American phenomenon. University Press of Va. 2001 xxi, 322p il pa $18.50   **791.44**
    1. African Americans on television 2. Amos 'n' Andy (Radio program) 3. Amos 'n' Andy (Television

program)
    ISBN 0-8139-2092-2

                     LC 2001-45538

First published 1991 by Free Press

A "historian examines one of America's greatest cultural enigmas—the amazing popularity, among blacks as well as whites, of 'Amos 'n' Andy' on radio for more than 30 years." N Y Times Book Rev

Includes bibliographical references

Schwartz, A. Brad

★ **Broadcast** hysteria; Orson Welles's War of the worlds and the art of fake news. A. Brad Schwartz. Hill & Wang 2015 352 p. illustrations (hardcover) $35   **791.44**
    1. Radio broadcasting 2. War of the worlds (Radio program) 3. Science fiction radio programs -- Psychological aspects 4. Radio broadcasting -- United States -- History -- 20th century
    ISBN 9780809031610; 0809031612

                     LC 2014040510

In this book author "A. Brad Schwartz boldly retells the story of [Orson] Welles's famed radio play and its impact. Schwartz is the first to examine the hundreds of letters sent to Orson Welles himself in the days after the broadcast, and his findings challenge the conventional wisdom. Schwartz shows that Welles's broadcast became a major scandal, prompting a different kind of mass panic as Americans debated the bewitching power of the radio." (Publisher's note)

"A gripping and informative look at the War of the World broadcast, as well as contemporary issues in the early 20th-century industry of radio. Highly recommended for students of journalism, fans of Welles, and general readers interested in radio or broadcasting." LJ

Includes bibliographical references and index

791.45   Television

Burnett, Carol, 1933-

In such good company; Eleven Years of Laughter, Mayhem, and Fun in the Sandbox. Carol Burnett. Crown Archetype 2016 320 p. illustrations (ebook) $65; (hardback) $28   **791.45**
    1. Women comedians 2. Comedy television programs 3. Carol Burnett Show (Television program : 1967-1978)
    ISBN 9781101904664; 9781101904657

                     LC 2016008433

In this book, comedian Carol Burnett "delves into little-known stories of the guests, sketches and improvisations that made The Carol Burnett Show legendary, as well as some favorite tales too good not to relive again. While writing this book, Carol rewatched all 276 episodes and screen-grabbed her favorite video stills from the archives to illustrate the chemistry of the actors and the improvisational magic that made the show so successful." (Publisher's note)

"Burnett watched every episode afresh to research this book, and that attention to detail shows in her exhaustive accounts of major sketches. However, even nonfans will enjoy the nuggets of intrigue Burnett scatters throughout, in which she shines a light on the sexism she faced during her tenure as a leading lady of the small screen." Pub Wkly

Kelly, Megyn, 1970-

Settle for More; Megyn Kelly. HarperCollins 2016 304 p. hardcover $29.99   **791.45**
  1. Women journalists -- Biography 2. Television personalities -- Biography
  ISBN 9780062494603; 0062494600
                LC 2016041059

This memoir by Megyn Kelly details "her rise as one of the most respected journalists working today. From the values and lessons that have shaped her career, to her time at the center of the chaotic 2016 Republican presidential primary, this book offers an inside look at an uncompromising woman's journey to the top of the news business. . . . Kelly goes behind the scenes of the stories and the storms that have made her one of the most talked about public figures in America." (Publisher's note)

Miller, James Andrew

Those guys have all the fun; inside the world of ESPN. [by] James Andrew Miller and Tom Shales. Little, Brown and Company 2011 763p il $27.99   **791.45**
  1. ESPN, Inc. 2. Television broadcasting of sports
  ISBN 0316043001; 9780316043007

This book "presents the history of sports channel ESPN based on interviews with . . . current and former employees, featuring announcers and analysts as well as sports stars including LeBron James, Peyton Manning, and Jeff Gordon." (Publisher's note) Index.

"Compiled from more than 550 interviews, Those Guys traces ESPN from its birth as an underdog to its current status as a money-printing behemoth. Some of the best sections deal with the early days of cable, when the network invented itself through savvy business decisions and slow-pitch-softball coverage. But it's the big libidos and bigger egos that will get the most attention. The book is packed with entertaining stories of unpleasant people and awful behavior: booze-fueled boorishness, absurdly arrogant execs, and the endlessly fascinating Olbermann. . . . Miller and Shales offer compelling behind-the-scenes tales of many major sports moments, including the Rush Limbaugh–Donovan McNabb flap and ESPN's takeover of Monday Night Football." Entertainment Wkly

Mulgrew, Kate, 1955-

Born With Teeth; A Memoir. Kate Mulgrew. Little Brown & Co 2015 320 p. illustrations $28   **791.45**
  1. Actresses 2. Motherhood
  ISBN 0316334316; 9780316334310
                LC 2015930445

In this memoir, actress Kate Mulgrew details how "at twenty-two, just as her career was taking off, she became pregnant. Having already signed the adoption papers, she was allowed only a fleeting glimpse of her child. As her star continued to rise, her life became increasingly demanding and fulfilling, a whirlwind of passionate love affairs, life-saving friendships, and bone-crunching work. Mulgrew remained haunted by the loss of her daughter, until, two

decades later, she found the courage to face the past." (Publisher's note)

"Mulgrew's enjoyable narrative is compelling as she portrays her decades of acting work, personal triumphs and heartbreaks, and her mesmerizing life." Library Journal

Seitz, Matt Zoller

TV (the book) Two Experts Pick the Greatest American Shows of All Time. Alan Sepinwall & Matt Zoller Seitz. Grand Central Publishing 2016 432 p. (ebook) $60; (paperback) $19.99   **791.45**
  1. Television programs 2. Television series -- United States -- History and criticism
  ISBN 9781455537419; 9781455588190
                LC 2016015540

In this book, authors Alan Sepinwall and Matt Zoller Seitz "have identified and ranked the 100 greatest scripted shows in American TV history. Using a complex, obsessively all- encompassing scoring system, they've created a Pantheon of top TV shows, each accompanied by essays delving into what made these shows great." (Publisher's note)

"The great debate: how do you pick the best show of all time? -- The inner circle -- No-doubt-about-it classics -- Groundbreakers and workhorses -- Outlier classics -- Works in progress -- A certain regard -- Miniseries -- TV-movies -- Live plays made for television." Kirkus

Shales, Tom

Live from New York; an uncensored story of Saturday Night Live. Tom Shales and James Andrew Miller. Little, Brown & Co. 2015 800 p. 24 plates; illustrations $19.99   **791.45**
  1. Comedy television programs 2. Saturday Night Live (TV program) 3. Saturday night live (Television program)
  ISBN 031629506X; 9780316295062
                LC 200272958

Authors James Andrew Miller and Tom Shales present this book on the television show "Saturday Night Live. "Trail-blazing talents recalled three turbulent decades of on-camera antics and off-camera escapades. Now a fourth decade has passed---and bestselling authors James Andrew Miller and Tom Shales have returned to Studio 8H. Over more than 100 pages of new material, they raucously and revealingly take the SNL story up to the present, adding a constellation of iconic new stars, surprises, and controversies." (Publisher's note)

Stelter, Brian

Top of the morning; inside the cutthroat world of morning tv. Brian Stelter. Grand Central Pub. 2013 320 p. (hardcover) $28   **791.45**
  1. Television broadcasting of news 2. Today show (Television program) 3. Good morning America (Television program)
  ISBN 1455512877; 9781455512874; 9781455545360
                LC 2013932327

This book looks at the struggles between the morning news television programs "Today" and "Good Morning America." It "commences with the decision of producer Jim Bell to remove struggling co-host Ann Curry from Today. As that story unfolds, Stelter periodically returns us to the earliest days of Today (1952: with Dave Garroway and chimp J. Fred Muggs) and to the beginnings of GMA in 1975." (Kirkus Reviews)

791.450　History, geographic treatment, biography

Lunden, Joan, 1950-

Had I Known; A Memoir of Survival. Joan Lunden. HarperCollins 2015 304 p. 16 plates; illustrations $26.99　　**791.450**

1. Journalists 2. Breast cancer 3. Cancer patients
ISBN 0062404083; 9780062404084

In this memoir, journalist Joan Lunden "speaks candidly about her battle against breast cancer, her quest to learn about it and teach others, and the transformative effect it's had on her life. As Joan reveals, while her journey was not easy, it profoundly changed her in unexpected ways. Her odyssey helped Joan redefine herself, her values, and most of all, her health." (Publisher's note)

"And Lunden's fans will enjoy learning more about her life. With longtime coauthor and friend Morton, Lunden offers a chatty book with an empowering message for women with breast cancer." Booklist

Martin, Brett

Difficult men; behind the scenes of a creative revolution: from The Sopranos and The Wire to Mad Men and Breaking Bad. by Brett Martin. The Penguin Press 2013 320 p. (hardcover) $27.95 **791.450**

1. Television -- History 2. Characters and characteristics on television 3. Television series -- United States 4. Television program genres -- United States 5. Cable television -- United States -- History 6. Television broadcasting -- Social aspects -- United States
ISBN 1594204195; 9781594204197

LC 2012047001

Here, Brett Martin "names the period spanning 1999 to 2013 'the third golden age of television,'" and considers what made it possible. He looks at the rise of shows with a "serialized narrative, as opposed to the syndication-friendly stand-alone episodes common in broadcast television. A little later, shows like The Wire, The Sopranos, and Mad Men subverted network formulas to present flawed, even nihilistic antiheros wrestling with inner demons." (Publishers Weekly)

Includes bibliographical references.

791.5　Puppetry and toy theaters

Blumenthal, Eileen

★ **Puppetry**; a world history. Abrams 2005 272p il $65　　**791.5**

1. Puppets and puppet plays
ISBN 0-8109-5587-3

LC 2004-29349

This is a "history of the puppet world, from prehistoric times to Tony-winning Broadway hit Avenue Q. . . . This would be a welcome addition to the libraries of perform-

ing arts buffs who want to learn more about a lesser known form." Publ Wkly

Includes bibliographical references

791.8　Animal performances

Hemingway, Ernest

★ **Death** in the afternoon. Scribner 1999 397p il $35　　**791.8**

1. Bullfights
ISBN 0-684-85922-X

LC 99-231717

First published 1932

"A loosely organized book on bullfighting in Spain. . . . Hemingway depicts the bullfight as an emblematic tragedy, a test of courage, with a bloody and not entirely predictable end. Throughout, he digresses to philosophize on life and death in exchanges with a character he calls the Old Lady." HarperCollins Reader's Ency of Am Lit. 2nd edition

Hemingway, Ernest, 1899-1961

The **dangerous** summer; introduction by James A. Michener. Scribner 1985 228p il hardcover o.p. pa $13　　**791.8**

1. Bullfights 2. Spain -- Description
ISBN 0-684-83789-7 pa

LC 84-27578

"In the summer of 1959—between The Old Man and the Sea {BRD 1952} and the completion of A Moveable Feast {BRD 1964}—{Hemingway} contracted with Life magazine to write a series of articles on the personal and professional rivalry of the two greatest bullfighters since the death of Manolete in 1947: Luis Miguel Dominguín and Antonio Ordóñez. The Dangerous Summer narrated 'the gradual destruction of one person by another with all the things that led up to it and made it.'" (Natl Rev)

A look at the "personal and professional rivalry of the two greatest bullfighters since the death of Manolete in 1947: Luis Miguel Dominguín and Antonio Ordóñez. The Dangerous Summer provides an insider's view based on extensive experience, mingles memory and desire, and is essential reading for anyone interested in the subject or the author." Natl Rev

Peter, Josh

Fried twinkies, buckle bunnies & bull riders; a year inside the professional bull riders tour. Rodale 2005 246p il $24.95　　**791.8**

1. Bull riding 2. Professional Bull Riders, Inc.
ISBN 1-59486-119-6

LC 2005-17297

"The argument can be made that the Professional Bull Riders Tour may be the most dangerous, least financially rewarding of all sporting endeavors. Skull fractures, punctured lungs, and destroyed knees are all relatively routine injuries. At least now there is a million-dollar payout for the overall champion each season, but even that is in deferred dollars. Peter, a sportswriter for the New Orleans Times-Picayune, spent the 2004 season with the PBR tour and offers a penetrating portrait of a sport that stands at that awkward stage between minor league and national acceptance. . . . Fried

Twinkies are a genuine but rare concession delicacy, and buckle bunnies are the young ladies who curry the favor of the young macho men who ride the bulls. This is a tough book to walk away from." Booklist

792   Stage presentations

Adler, Stella

Stella Adler: the art of acting; compiled and edited by Howard Kissel. Applause Theatre Bk. Pubs. 2000 271p il $25.95   792
1. Acting
ISBN 1-55783-373-7

In this collection of Adler's papers Kissel "has taken tapes, transcriptions, notebooks, and other sources to reconstruct an acting course in 22 lessons. . . . The lessons are graduated from very basic matters to quite complex issues of textual analysis and decorum. Though mostly monologs, they include enough exercises and student responses to get the flavor of Adler's work. . . . This is required reading for anyone interested in theater practice." Libr J

The **Best** Men's Stage Monologues 2016; edited by Lawrence Harbison. Smith & Kraus 2016 210 p. pbk $14.95   792
1. Acting 2. Monologues
ISBN 9781575259079; 1575259079

Annual. First published 1991 for the 1990 theater season under the editorship of Jocelyn Beard

"Here you will find a rich and varied selection of monologues for men from plays which were produced and/or published in the 2015-2016 theatrical season. Most are for younger performers (teens through 30s) but there are also some excellent pieces for older actors as well. Some are comic, some are dramatic. Some are short, some are long." (Publisher's note)

The **Best** Women's Stage Monologues 2016; by Lawrence Harbison. Smith & Kraus Pub Inc 2016 204 p. $14.95   792
1. Monologues
ISBN 1575259060; 9781575259062

This book, by Lawrence Harbison, presents "a rich and varied selection of monologues for men from plays which were produced and/or published in the 2015-2016 theatrical season. Most are for younger performers (teens through 30s) but there are also some excellent pieces for older actors as well. Some are comic, some are dramatic. Some are short, some are long. All represent the best in contemporary playwriting.(Publisher's note)

Brook, Peter

The **empty** space. Atheneum 1968 141p hardcover o.p. pa $11   792
1. Drama 2. Theater
ISBN 0-684-82957-6 pa
LC 68-12531

The author "distinguishes four types of theater: the Deadly Theatre (conventional), the Holy Theatre (ritualistic), the Rough Theatre (combative), and the Immediate

Theatre (mutative and organic). An impassioned treatise that is also very accessible and direct." Libr J

Browar, Ken

The **art** of movement; Deborah Ory, Ken Browar, NYC Dance Project. Black Dog & Leventhal 2016 304 p. (hardcover) $50   792
1. Dance 2. Dancers
ISBN 0316318582; 9780316318587
LC 2016939031

This book, by Deborah Ory and Ken Browar, is a "celebration of movement and dance in hundreds of breathtaking photographs of more than 70 dancers from American Ballet Theater, New York City Ballet, Alvin Ailey American Dance Theater, Martha Graham Dance Company, Boston Ballet, Royal Danish Ballet, the Royal Ballet, and many more." (Publisher's note)

Chekhov, Michael

To the actor; {rev and expanded ed. by Mala Powers}; Routledge 2002 lii, 222p il $75; pa $19.95   792
1. Acting
ISBN 0-415-25875-8; 0-415-25876-6 pa
First published 1953 by Harper & Row

"Chekhov is among a handful of master acting teachers who have profoundly influenced not only a constellation of famous stars but also shaped an acting style and sensibility. . . . This new edition contains all of Chekhov's brilliant insights, techniques, and exercises, as well as a previously unpublished chapter on the 'Psychological Gesture,' a central precept of his system." Libr J
Includes bibliographical references

Corson, Richard

Stage makeup; [by] Richard Corson, Beverly Gore Norcross, James Glavan. 10th ed.; Ally & Bacon/Pearson 2009 xx, 407p il $141.40   792
1. Theatrical makeup
ISBN 978-0-205-64454-4
LC 2008-53845

First published 1942 by Appleton. Periodically revised
The authors discuss the art and technique of theatrical makeup, covering such topics as facial anatomy, various methods for applying greasepaint and other makeup, and the use of beards, wigs, and prosthetic pieces.

Gillette, J. Michael

Designing With Light: An Introduction to Stage Lighting; an introduction to stage lighting. Michael Gillette, Michael J. McNamara. 6th ed. McGraw-Hill 2013 379 p. ill. (some col.) pa. $143.45   792
1. Stage lighting
ISBN 0073514233; 9780073514239
LC 2012034637

This book, by J. Michael Gillette and Michael J. McNamara, "is a comprehensive survey of the practical and aesthetic aspects of stage lighting design. The authors approach stage lighting design as an art that integrates the vision of director, actor, and playwright, and as a craft that provides practical solutions for the manipulation of stage space. The sixth edition offers a wealth of new information on new trends in lighting design." (Publisher's Note)

The author "divides his standard text for undergraduate lighting design students into the two constituent elements of his craft—technology and design. He clearly and completely presents both technical and aesthetic design aspects." Libr J

Hagen, Uta

Respect for acting; by Uta Hagen with Haskel Frankel. Macmillan 1973 227p $19.95   **792**

1. Acting

ISBN 0-02-547390-5

This "classic treatise on the process and craft of acting has significantly benefited actors for three decades. Juxtaposed with Hagen's aesthetic is a wealth of practical information, creative ideas, and her uniquely useful object exercises." Libr J

Lane, Stewart F.

Black Broadway; African Americans on the great white way. Stewart F. Lane. Square One Publishers 2015 288 p. illustrations (some color) (hardback) $39.95   **792**

1. African American actors 2. African American theater 3. Musicals -- United States 4. Broadway (New York, N.Y.) -- History 5. American drama -- African American authors -- History and criticism 6. African American theater -- New York (State) -- New York -- History -- 20th century 7. African Americans in the performing arts -- New York (State) -- New York -- History -- 20th century

ISBN 9780757003882; 0757003885

LC 2014006513

In this book on the history of Broadway, author "Stewart F. Lane uses words and pictures to capture this tumultuous century and to highlight the rocky road that black actors have travelled to reach recognition on the Great White Way. Like the doors of many professions, those of the theater world were shut to minorities for decades. While the Civil War may have freed the slaves, it was not until the Civil Rights Movement of the 1960s that the playing field began to level." (Publisher's note)

"This volume's superior presentation of visual theatrical elements make it essential for any theater collection." Library Journal

Includes bibliographical references

Mamet, David

True and false; heresy and common sense for the actor. Pantheon Bks. 1997 127p hardcover o.p. pa $11   **792**

1. Acting

ISBN 0-679-77264-2 pa

LC 97-19336

"Mamet exhorts actors to show up early, have their lines down cold, and have a single objective for each scene. He contends that overthinking and too much emotional interpretation is not the actor's role. Essential reading for theater collections." Libr J

Moore, Sonia

★ The **Stanislavski** system; the professional training of an actor. digested from the teachings of Konstantin S. Stanislavski. 2nd rev ed; Penguin Bks. 1984 96p pa $12.95   **792**

1. Acting 2. Actors 3. Theatrical directors

ISBN 0-14-046660-6

LC 84-2855

First published 1960 with title: The Stanislavski method

This is a concise, simplified guide to the teachings of the great master of the Moscow Art Theater

The **Oxford** companion to theatre and performance; edited by Dennis Kennedy. Oxford University Press 2010 689p $45   **792**

1. Reference books 2. Theater -- Encyclopedias 3. Performing arts -- Encyclopedias

ISBN 978-0-19-957419-3

"This is a one-volume updated version of the two-volume Oxford Encyclopedia of Theatre & Performance published in 2003. Kennedy . . . has succeeded in pulling together 2400 entries intended to educate, delight, and encourage the reader to pursue more in-depth information." Libr J

Stanislavsky, Konstantin

★ An **actor's** work; a student's diary. [by] Konstantin Stanislavski; translated and edited by Jean Benedetti. Routledge 2008 693p $35   **792**

1. Acting

ISBN 9780415422239; 0-415-42223-X

LC 2007-45357

A combined translation of Stanislavsky's An actor prepares and Building a character, which describe and illustrate the principles of method acting.

This "translation by Benedetti of Stanislavski's famous works . . . will be greeted with excitement by actors everywhere." Libr J

Includes bibliographical references

Creating a role; [by] Constantin Stanislavski; translated by Elizabeth Reynolds Hapgood; edited by Hermine I. Popper; foreword by Robert Lewis. Routledge 2003 271p pa $19.95   **792**

1. Acting

ISBN 0-87830-981-0

LC 91-228412

"Stanislavski unifies his conceptual canon and applies it to detailed preparatory work for the roles of Othello and Gogol's Inspector General." Libr J

792.02   Miscellany

Douglas, Illeana, 1965-

I blame Dennis Hopper; and other stories from a life lived in and out of the movies. Illeana Douglas. Flatiron Books 2015 304 p. illustrations (hardback) $25.99   **792.02**

1. Motion picture actors and actresses -- United States -- Biography 2. Actresses -- United States -- Anecdotes

3. Actresses -- United States -- Biography
ISBN 9781250052919

LC 2015022208

This book, by Illeana Douglas, is "a memoir about learning to survive in Hollywood. . . . Writing from the perspective of the ultimate show business fan, Douglas packs each page with hilarious anecdotes, bizarre coincidences, and fateful meetings that seem, well, right out of a plot of a movie." (Publisher's note)

"The author's warm portraits and disarming honesty infuse the memoir with an endearing sweetness and charm." Kirkus

Gillette, J. Michael

Theatrical design and production; An Introduction to Scene Design and Construction, Lighting, Sound, Costume, and Makeup. J. Michael Gillette. 7th ed. McGraw-Hill Higher Education 2012 624 p. ill. (some col.) hardcover $192.45 **792.02**
1. Theaters -- Stage setting and scenery 2. Stage management. 3. Theater--Production and direction. .
ISBN 0073382221; 9780073382227

LC 2012020022

This book, by J. Michael Gillette, "is a comprehensive and practical survey that examines the technical and design aspects of play production, including scene design and construction, lighting, sound, costume, and makeup. Design is presented as both an art closely integrated with the director's, actor's, and playwright's visions, and a craft that provides practical solutions for the physical manipulation of stage space." (Publisher's note)

Includes bibliographical references

Lahr, John

Joy ride; show people and their shows. John Lahr. W.W. Norton & Co. Inc. 2015 576 p. illustrations (hardcover) $29.95 **792.02**
1. Theater -- Reviews 2. Dramatists -- Biography 3. Dramatists, American -- Biography 4. Theater -- New York (State) -- New York -- Reviews 5. Theatrical producers and directors -- United States -- Biography
ISBN 9780393246407

LC 2015013987

This book, by John Lahr, presents a collection of the author's biographical profiles and reviews from the 'New Yorker' magazine, focusing on contemporary theater. The book "throws open the stage door and introduces readers to such makers of contemporary drama as Arthur Miller, Tony Kushner, Wallace Shawn, Harold Pinter, David Rabe, David Mamet, Mike Nichols, and August Wilson." (Publisher's note)

"Faithful readers of The New Yorker will enjoy revisiting these articles. Anyone interested in the history of the American theater and contemporary drama will applaud these thoughtful and critical pieces." LJ

792.09 History, geographic treatment, biography

Brockett, Oscar G.

History of the theatre; [by] Oscar G. Brockett, Franklin J. Hildy. 10th ed; Pearson 2008 688p il map $113 **792.09**
1. Theater -- History 2. Drama -- History and criticism
ISBN 978-0-205-51186-0

LC 2009-291794

First published 1968

This work traces the development of the theater from primitive times to the present, with an emphasis on European theater.

Includes bibliographical references

Levy, Reynold

They told me not to take that job; tumult, betrayal, heroics, and the transformation of Lincoln Center. Reynold Levy. PublicAffairs 2015 376 p. 8 plates; color ills., maps (hardback) $28.99 **792.09**
1. Opera 2. Centers for the performing arts -- New York (State) -- New York 3. Lincoln Center for the Performing Arts 4. Performing arts -- New York (State) -- New York -- Management
ISBN 1610393619; 9781610393614

LC 2014049065

In this book, author Reynold "Levy tells the inside story of the demise of the New York City Opera, the Metropolitan Opera's need to use as collateral its iconic Chagall tapestries in the face of mounting operating losses, and the New York Philharmonic's dalliance with Carnegie Hall." (Publisher's note)

Includes bibliographical references and index

Riedel, Michael

Razzle Dazzle; The Battle for Broadway. Michael Riedel. Simon & Schuster 2015 464 p. 16 plates; illustrations $27 **792.09**
1. Theater 2. Musicals
ISBN 1451672160; 9781451672169

Author Michael Riedel presents this "narrative account of the people and the money and the power that re-invented an iconic quarter of New York City, turning its gritty back alleys and sex-shops into the glitzy, dazzling Great White Way--and bringing a crippled New York from the brink of bankruptcy to its glittering glory." (Publisher's note)

"While not functioning as an introduction or a detailed history of the American commercial theater, this book articulates a neglected but historically essential point of view." LJ

792.5 Opera

Osborne, Charles

The **complete** operas of Mozart; a critical guide. Da Capo Press 1986 349p il pa $17.95 **792.5**
1. Composers 2. Opera -- Stories, plots, etc.
ISBN 978-0-306-80190-7; 0-306-80190-6
First published 1978 by Atheneum

In this introduction to Mozart's operas, "each opera is treated as a separate chapter. . . . Each chapter begins with a separate page containing the dramatis personae and their voice range . . . the date, place, and cast for the first performance . . . the name of the librettist, and the Kochel number." Choice

The **complete** operas of Puccini; a critical guide. Da Capo Press 1983 279p il pa $9.95   **792.5**

1. Composers 2. Opera -- Stories, plots, etc.

ISBN 0-306-80200-7; 978-0-306-80200-3

LC 83-10142

First published 1982 by Atheneum

The author "provides general background information on all 13 Puccini operas. . . . Unencumbered by technical language, this enjoyably written book is accessible to all admirers of one of the most popular opera composers of all time." Choice

Includes bibliographical references

The **complete** operas of Richard Wagner. Da Capo Press 1993 288p il pa $16.95   **792.5**

1. Composers 2. Opera -- Stories, plots, etc.

ISBN 0-306-80522-7; 978-0-306-80522-6

LC 92-34417

First published 1990 in the United Kingdom

In this book, "biography—often in Wagner's own words—combined with criticism by Wagner's contemporaries, literary background, Wagner's librettos, plot summaries, descriptions of musical elements illustrated with musical examples, and Osborne's own insights form a clear picture of Wagner, his world, and the operas." Libr J

Includes bibliographical references

Sadie, Stanley

The **Grove** book of operas; edited by Stanley Sadie; revised by Laura Macy. 2nd ed; Oxford University Press 2009 xxiii, 740p il $39.95; pa $27.95; $27.95   **792.5**

1. Reference books 2. Opera -- Encyclopedias

ISBN 978-0-19-530907-2; 0-19-530907-3; 0-19-538711-2 pa; 9780195387117 pa

LC 2006-15323

First published 1996 by Macmillan with title: The new Grove book of operas

"A vital reference on the subject." Libr J

Includes bibliographical references

792.6   Musical plays

Bloom, Ken

Broadway musicals; the 101 greatest shows of all time. [by] Ken Bloom & Frank Vlastnik; new preface by Broadway's leading ladies; foreword by Jerry Orbach. Rev. and updated ed.; Black Dog & Leventhal 2010 344p il $40   **792.6**

1. Musicals

ISBN 978-1-57912-849-4

First published 2004

This is a history of Broadway musicals from the past 100 years. Each entry features commentary, photos and brief features on performers and creators.

Boland, Robert

Musicals! directing school and community theatre. {by} Robert Boland and Paul Argentini. Scarecrow Press 1997 xxv, 202p il pa $35   **792.6**

1. Musicals -- Production and direction

ISBN 0-8108-3323-9

LC 97-11996

This is "a handbook for novice directors of the musical. This illustrated nuts-and-bolts compendium includes 22 chapters divided among three major sections addressing preparation, production, and performance. Through accessible prose and a you-can-do-it tone, the authors provide an overview of preproduction planning, auditioning and casting, blocking, stage composition, rehearsals, and choreography, as well as the more technical layers of set design, costumes, and lights." Libr J

Includes bibliographical references

Hischak, Thomas

The **Oxford** companion to the American musical; theatre, film, and television. [by] Thomas S. Hischak. Oxford University Press 2008 923p il $39.95 **792.6**

1. Reference books 2. Musicals -- Dictionaries

ISBN 9780195335330

LC 2007-52436

This is an "overview of the American musical theater on the stage, silver screen, and small screen. The 2000-plus entries are brief but detailed accounts of plots; production histories; careers of actors, dancers, musicians, lyricists, composers, choreographers, and directors; organizations; and genres (animated musicals, frontier musicals). . . . This thorough work provides enjoyable reading for anyone interested in American theatrical history in general and musicals in particular." SLJ

Includes discography and bibliographical references (p. 899-902)

Maslon, Laurence

★ **Broadway**; the American musical. Laurence Maslon; based on the documentary film by Michael Kantor; foreword by Julie Andrews. 2nd edition Applause Theatre & Cinema Books 2010 497p illustrations, maps pbk $40   **792.6**

1. Musicals -- United States

ISBN 1423491033; 9781423491033

"A companion to the six-part PBS documentary series, Broadway: The American Musical is the first comprehensive history of the musical, from its roots at the turn of the 20th century through the smashing successes of the new millennium. The in-depth text is lavishly illustrated with a treasure trove of photographs, sheet-music covers, posters, scenic renderings, production stills, rehearsal shots and caricatures, many previously unpublished." (Publisher's note)

Stempel, Larry

Showtime; a history of the Broadway musical theater. W. W. Norton & Company 2010 xx, 826p il $39.95 **792.6**

1. Musicals 2. Musicals -- New York (N.Y.)
ISBN 978-0-393-06715-6; 0-393-06715-7

LC 2010-19704

Beginning in the seventeenth-century United States, well before Broadway existed, Stempel presents the multiple theatrical adventures that would lead from various directions to 'West Side Story' (1957) and 'Les Misérables' (1987). He examines not only minstrelsy, vaudeville, and European operetta—the musical's well-known precursors—but also the Astor Place riot of 1849, an event that publicly performed the ever-hardening divisions of class and culture among American audiences. Later, Stempel describes off-Broadway performances . . . beginning with the Works Progress Administration and the Little Theatre movement, progressing to 'Hair' (1968), which eventually transferred to Broadway, and nodding to regional theaters where many shows originated." (Journal of American History)

"Theater buffs will be delighted to find that this scholarly, definitive work is also a hugely entertaining read." Publ Wkly

Includes discography and bibliographical references

Viertel, Jack

The secret life of the American musical; how classic Broadway shows are built. Jack Viertel. Sarah Crichton Books 2016 336 p. (hardcover) $28 **792.6**

1. Musicals 2. Musicals -- United States -- History and criticism 3. Musicals -- United States -- Analysis, appreciation
ISBN 9780374256920; 9780374711252

LC 2015023713

This book, by Jack Viertel, "begins with an overture and concludes with a curtain call. . . . Viertel has spent three decades on Broadway, working on dozens of shows old and new as a conceiver, producer, dramaturg, and general creative force. . . . He shows us patterns in the architecture of classic shows and charts the inevitable evolution that has taken place in musical theater as America itself has evolved socially and politically." (Publisher's note)

"An enlightening trip for lovers of musicals." Kirkus

792.7 Variety shows and theatrical dancing

Apatow, Judd, 1967-

Sick in the head; conversations about life and comedy. by Judd Apatow. Random House Inc. 2015 512 p. 16 plates; illustrations (hardback) $27 **792.7**

1. Actors 2. Comedians 3. Stand-up comedy -- United States 4. Comedians -- United States -- Interviews 5. Television actors and actresses -- United States -- Interviews 6. Motion picture actors and actresses -- United States -- Interviews
ISBN 0812997573; 9780812997576

LC 2015008155

This book "gathers [filmmaker Judd] Apatow's most memorable and revealing conversations into one hilarious, wide-ranging, and incredibly candid collection that spans not only his career but his entire adult life. Here are the comedy legends who inspired and shaped him, from Mel Brooks to Steve Martin. Here are the contemporaries he grew up with in Hollywood, from Spike Jonze to Sarah Silverman. And here, finally, are the brightest stars in comedy today." (Publisher's note)

"An exceptional volume; in a field where shallowness is a hallmark, these artists reveal an unexpected depth. For all libraries." LJ

Downer, Lesley

Women of the pleasure quarters; the secret history of the geisha. Broadway Bks. 2001 288p il hardcover o.p. pa $14.95 **792.7**

1. Geishas 2. Japan -- Social life and customs
ISBN 0-7679-0490-7 pa

LC 00-49409

The author "skillfully intertwines her profiles of Kyoto personalities and tea-house customs with a fluidly written geisha history that's unabashedly aimed at a Western audience. . . . Written in dynamic, highly readable prose, the book is supported by exhaustive research and a lengthy bibliography." Publ Wkly

Includes bibliographical references and index

Faleiro, Sonia

Beautiful thing; inside the secret world of Bombay's dance bars. Sonia Faleiro. Black Cat 2012 216 p. **792.7**

1. Dancers 2. Poverty 3. Bombay (India) 4. Women -- India 5. Human trafficking
ISBN 9780670084050

LC 2010347432

In this book, author Sonia Faleiro "mines the gritty underworld of Bombay's dance bars, where dancers perform for male patrons in . . . the hope of escape from poverty. She spent five years shadowing Leela, a teenage dancer. . . . Leela and . . . Priya, her confidante and fellow dancer, consider themselves a cut above women who sell their services on the streets and in brothels. But when a self-seeking politician . . . shut[s] down Bombay's dance bars, the two are left with few options. Faleiro paints a . . . picture of rape, physical abuse, and sexual slavery, often perpetrated on women like Leela by their own families. But Leela's fearlessness keeps her afloat . . . where the cops are as corrupt as the gangsters and HIV an unspoken but constant threat." (Publishers Weekly)

Hart, Hannah

Buffering; Unshared Tales of a Life Fully Loaded. by Hannah Hart. HarperCollins 2016 240 p. $23.99 **792.7**

1. Essays
ISBN 0062457519; 9780062457516

In this book, author Hannah Hart is "stirring up memories and tales from her past. By combing through the journals that Hannah has kept for much of her life, this collection of narrative essays deliver a fuller picture of her life, her experiences, and the things she's figured out about family, faith, love, sexuality, self-worth, friendship and fame." (Publisher's note)

Josephson, Barney

Cafe Society; the wrong place for the right people. Barney Josephson; with Terry Trilling-Josephson; foreword by Dan Morgenstern. University of Illinois Press 2009 376p il (Music in American life) $32.95　　　　**792.7**

　　1. Café Society (New York, N.Y.: Nightclub) 2. Greenwich Village (New York (N.Y.) -- Social life and customs

　　ISBN 978-0-252-03413-8; 0-252-03413-9

　　　　　　　　　　　　　LC 2008-27205

"An epic ode to personal integrity, creative vision and entrepreneurial tenacity, shedding timely light on the germination of the civil-rights movement." Kirkus

　　Includes bibliographical references

Nesteroff, Kliph

The **Comedians**; Drunks, Thieves, Scoundrels, and the History of American Comedy. by Kliph Nesteroff. Grove Press 2015 432 p. 16 plates; ills; portraits $28　　　　**792.7**

　　1. Comedy 2. Comedians 3. Comedy films 4. Comedy radio programs 5. Comedy television programs

　　ISBN 0802123988; 9780802123985

In this book, "comedy historian Kliph Nesteroff brings to life a century of American comedy with real-life characters, forgotten stars, mainstream heroes and counterculture iconoclasts. Based on over two hundred original interviews and extensive archival research, Nesteroff's groundbreaking work is a narrative exploration of the way comedians have reflected, shaped, and changed American culture over the past one hundred years." (Publisher's note)

"Both pop culture enthusiasts and entertainment scholars will relish this important history of American comedy." LJ

Seibert, Brian

What the eye hears; a history of tap dancing. Brian Seibert. Farrar, Straus & Giroux 2015 624 p. illustrations (hardback) $35　　　　**792.7**

　　1. Jazz music 2. Tap dancing 3. Tap dancing -- History

　　ISBN 0865479534; 9780865479531

　　　　　　　　　　　　　LC 2015005010

National Book Critics Circle Award Finalist: Nonfiction (2015)

Author Brian Seibert "offers an authoritative account of the great American art of tap dancing. Brian Seibert, a dance critic for The New York Times, begins by exploring tap's origins as a hybrid of the jig and clog dancing from the British Isles and dances brought from Africa by slaves. He tracks tap's transfer to the stage through blackface minstrelsy and charts its growth as a cousin to jazz." (Publisher's note)

"Drawing on primary sources of every kind, from written accounts by slave traders in the early 17th century to personal interviews conducted in the 21st, the author breaks down not merely the origins art of tap dancing itself, but the racial and gender constructs that forced the industry--and its performers--to develop in the ways they did, while acknowledging his own white male privilege." Pub Wkly

Includes bibliographical references (pages [541]-574) and index

Trav S. D.

No applause, just throw money; or, The book that made vaudeville famous; a high-class, refined entertainment. Faber and Faber 2005 328p il $25 **792.7**

　　1. Vaudeville

　　ISBN 0-571-21192-5

　　　　　　　　　　　　　LC 20050-9787

This book documents the history and legacy of vaudeville in the United States.

"One of the year's best historical performing arts texts; a wonderful story wonderfully told." Libr J

　　Includes bibliographical references

792.8　Ballet and modern dance

Craine, Debra

The **Oxford** dictionary of dance; [by] Debra Craine, Judith Mackrell. 2nd ed.; Oxford University Press 2010 502p il (Oxford paperback reference) pa $18.95　　　　**792.8**

　　1. Reference books 2. Dance -- Dictionaries

　　ISBN 978-0-19-956344-9; 0-19-956344-6

　　　　　　　　　　　　　LC 2010-930321

Based on The concise Oxford dictionary of ballet by Horst Kroegler. First published 2000

"The work covers all aspects of the diverse dance world from classical ballet to modern, from flamenco to hip-hop, from tap to South Asian dance forms and includes . . . entries on technical terms, steps, styles, works and countries, in addition to many biographies of dancers, choreographers, and companies." Publisher's note

　　Includes bibliographical references

Fuhrer, Margaret

American dance; the complete illustrated history. Margaret Fuhrer. Voyageur Press 2014 288 p. illustrations (chiefly color) (hardback) $45　　**792.8**

　　1. Performance art 2. Dance -- United States 3. Dance -- United States -- History 4. Modern dance -- United States -- History

　　ISBN 0760345996; 9780760345993

　　　　　　　　　　　　　LC 2014022261

This book by Margaret Fuhrer "explores centuries of innovation, individual genius and collaborative exploration. Some of its stories - such as Fred Astaire dancing on the ceiling or Alvin Ailey founding the trailblazing company that bears his name - will be familiar to anyone who loves dance." (Publisher's note)

"A dance sampler that should prompt readers to further explore the multifaceted history of dance and maybe take a class!" Library Journal

Homans, Jennifer

★ **Apollo's** angels. Random House 2010 643p il $35　　　　**792.8**

　　1. Ballet 2. Ballet -- History

　　ISBN 978-1-4000-6060-3; 1-4000-6060-5

　　　　　　　　　　　　　LC 201006945

This book "places ballet . . . in the larger context of the times and societies in which it evolved, flourished and flagged, only be revitalized by an infusion of fresh ideas. That revitalization could come from a ballet master like Jean-Georges Noverre, presented by Homans as an important Enlightenment figure whose ideas on reforming ballet were consonant with those of Diderot on reforming theater. Renewal came from the genius of dancers like Marie Taglioni, the incarnation of romanticism . . . But in a closing section . . . [the author]sounds a despairing note: "ballet is dying," she declares. Not only is the creative well running dry and performances dull, but more crucially, Homans sees today's values as inimical to those of ballet." (Publishers Weekly)

"A book of this breadth is going to have its own biorhythms—chapters that engage the author's mind and heart wholly, where everything clicks and the thinking is virtually kinetic, and chapters that don't come as easily. Ms. Homans is at her best when the ideological agenda at hand aspires to discipline, precision and refinement. Her French section is masterful, as are the chapters on the rise of the ballerina, the Danish style, Imperial Russian classicism, and British ballet." Wall Street J

Includes bibliographical references

Minden, Eliza Gaynor

The **ballet** companion; a dancer's guide to the technique, traditions, and joys of ballet. Eliza Gaynor Minden. Touchstone Books 2005 xv, 331 p.p illustrations (some color) $29.95   **792.8**
1. Ballet 2. Ballet dancers 3. Ballet dancing -- Handbooks, manuals, etc
ISBN 9780743264075; 074326407X
LC 2005044102

This book, by Eliza Gaynor Minden "is a fresh, comprehensive, and thoroughly up-to-date reference book for the dancer. With 150 stunning photographs of ballet stars Maria Riccetto and Benjamin Millepied demonstrating perfect execution of positions and steps, this elegant volume brims with everything today's dance student needs" (Publisher's note)

"[The Author's] explanation of the differences between the six major ballet styles, along with the superb glossaries of terms and dance history timeline, make this book a valuable resource for dance studios and a great primer for dancers in the early stages of training." Publishers Weekly

Includes bibliographical references (p. [316]-317) and index

Reynolds, Nancy

No fixed points; dance in the twentieth century. [by] Nancy Reynolds and Malcolm McCormick. Yale Univ. Press 2003 907p il $50   **792.8**
1. Dance 2. Ballet 3. Modern dance
ISBN 0-300-09366-7
LC 2003-10754

"Although everyone will be using the book for reference, Reynolds and McCormick have produced a work that is completely unlike a standard reference book; you don't just look things up in it—you read it. Here is a coherent, reasoned and entertaining chronicle of dance performance in the West over the hundred years that are unquestionably the fullest and most complicated in the long history of this fragmented and elusive art." N Y Times

Includes bibliographical references

793.2   Parties and entertainments

Sedaris, Amy

I like you; hospitality under the influence. Warner Books 2006 303p il $27.99   **793.2**
1. Cooking 2. Entertaining
ISBN 978-0-446-57884-4; 0-446-57884-3
LC 2006-07521

"Novice party-planners will actually find some helpful hints along the way as Sedaris offers instructions and real recipes. . . . [This book] is an outrageous and deadpan delight, greatly enhanced by her deliriously kitschy illustrations and photos." Publ Wkly

793.3   Social, folk, national dancing

Soffee, Anne Thomas

Snake hips; belly dancing and how I found true love. Chicago Review Press 2002 xxii, 262p $22.95   **793.3**
1. Belly dancing
ISBN 1-55652-458-7
LC 2002-572

This is the author's story of how she cured a broken heart and changed her life for the better through belly-dancing

"Soffee's witty, flowing prose draws readers into this unlikely but captivating story." Booklist

Includes bibliographical references

793.7   Games not characterized by action

The **official** Scrabble players dictionary; 5th edition Merriam-Webster 2014 728 p, pbk $8.50 **793.7**
1. Scrabble (Game) -- Dictionaries
ISBN 0877798222; 9780877798224

This is a dictionary of words which can be used in the game of Scrabble.

Roberts, Cokie

Capital dames; the Civil War and the women of Washington, 1848-1868. Cokie Roberts. Harper/HarperCollins 2015 512 p. illustrations, maps, portraits (hardcover : alk. paper) $27.99   **793.7**
1. Women -- Washington (D.C.) 2. Washington (D.C.) -- History 3. United States -- History -- 1861-1865, Civil War -- Women 4. Women -- Washington (D.C.) -- Biography 5. Women -- United States -- History -- 19th century 6. United States -- History -- 1815-1861 -- Biography 7. Washington (D.C.) -- History -- Civil War, 1861-1865 8. Reconstruction (U.S. history, 1865-1877) -- Biography 9. Politicians' spouses -- Washington (D.C.) -- Biography
ISBN 0062002767; 9780062002761; 9780062002778
LC 2015001049

In this book author "Cokie Roberts marks the sesquicentennial of the Civil War by offering a . . . look at Washington, D.C. and the experiences, influence, and contributions of its women during this momentous period of American history. Roberts chronicles these women's increasing independence, their political empowerment, their indispensable role in keeping the Union unified through the war, and in helping heal it once the fighting was done." (Publisher's note)

"An enlightening account detailing how the Civil War changed the nation's capital while expanding the role of women i n politics, health care, education, and social services." Kirkus

Includes bibliographical references and index

793.74   Mathematical games and recreations

Tahan, Malba

The **man** who counted; a collection of mathematical adventures. illustrated by Patricia Reid Baquero & translated by Leslie Clark and Alastair Reid. Norton 1993 244p il hardcover o.p. pa $15.95 **793.74**
    1. Mathematical recreations
    ISBN 0-393-30934-7 pa
                                                      LC 92-18822
"This small book is a joy. . . . These are beautifully expressive tales that find mathematical puzzles and numerical intrigue in human situations and speak not just of solving the problems but of the needs we all have for friendship, love, and beauty." Booklist

793.8   Magic and related activities

Gardner, Martin, 1914-2010

The **colossal** book of short puzzles and problems; combinatorics, probability, algebra, geometry, topology, chess, logic, cryptarithms, wordplay, physics and other topics of recreational mathematics. edited by Dana Richards. Norton 2006 494p il $35   **793.8**
    1. Scientific recreations 2. Mathematical recreations
    ISBN 0-393-06114-0; 978-0-393-06114-7
                                                      LC 2005-24080
This is a compilation of puzzles from Martin Gardner's "column, 'Mathematical Games,' which appeared for over 25 years in Scientific American. . . . [The topics] include combinatorics, probability, algebra, plane and solid geometry, topology, games, chess, logic, wordplay, and physics, among others. . . . Anyone interested in recreational mathematics should like this book. The puzzles are fascinating and the book is easily browsed. It can also serve as a good reference for (high school and college) teachers seeking interesting problems to complement routine ones in mathematics texts." Sci Books Films

Miles, Bryan

101 magic tricks; discover powerful magic for every occasion. Bryan Miles. Quarry Books 2015 208 p. colour illustrations $19.99   **793.8**
    1. Magic tricks
    ISBN 1631590723; 9781631590726
                                                      LC 2015025881
This book, by Bryan Miles, presents "101 Magic Tricks! Astonish and amaze everyone you know with easy-to-master tricks and illusions. Learn classic sleight of hand techniques that are simple enough for any apprentice to grasp.

Conquer magical ruses that require no special equipment, and are explained with simple step-by-step instructions." (Publisher's note)
    One hundred one magic tricks
    One hundred and one magic tricks

Stone, Alex

Fooling Houdini; magicians, mentalists, math geeks, and the hidden powers of the mind. Alex Stone. Harper 2012 x, 301 p.p ill. (hardback) $26.99   **793.8**
    1. Magicians 2. Perception 3. Magic tricks 4. Autobiographies 5. Magic -- Social aspects 6. Magicians -- United States 7. Magic -- Psychological aspects 8. Magicians -- United States -- Biography
    ISBN 0061766216; 9780061766213
                                                      LC 2011041927
This book by Alex Stone recounts his "quest to join the ranks of master magicians. As he navigates this . . . subculture, Stone pulls back the curtain on a community shrouded in secrecy . . . and organized around a single overriding need: to prove one's worth by deceiving others. . . . In trying to understand how expert magicians manipulate our minds to create their astonishing illusions, Stone uncovers . . . insight into human nature and the nature of perception." (Publisher's note)

794   Indoor games of skill

Botermans, Jack

The **book** of games; strategy, tactics & history. [by] Jack Botermans; [translated from the Spanish by Edgar Loy Fankbonner] Sterling 2008 736p il $29.95   **794**
    1. Board games 2. Indoor games
    ISBN 978-1-4027-4221-7; 1-4027-4221-5
                                                      LC 2007-10173
"Some 65 international games are described and demonstrated in this colorful book. Ranging from dominoes to mancala and shogi to Yut, each entry highlights the game's origins, versions, and playing rules. . . . Color illustrations and diagrams are used liberally to illustrate strategic moves and the variations of game boards and pieces, while photographs show the games being played. . . . Libraries should consider this for their circulating collections." Booklist

Kearney, Kirsten

Block city; how to build incredible worlds in minecraft. Yazur Strovoz. Abrams 2015 256 p. color illustrations (paperback) $22.50   **794**
    1. Design 2. Computer games
    ISBN 1419716182; 9781419716188
                                                      LC 2014945989
This book, by Yazur Strovoz, focuses on "Minecraft--a humble computer game about placing blocks-- . . . that has captured the imagination of more than 36 million players around the world. . . . The most impressive and spectacular achievements in Minecraft design are its cities. . . . The product of thousands of hours of work by devoted Minecraft players, these virtual places are the envy of millions who aspire to master the skills to create them." (Publisher's note)

794.1 Chess

Fischer, Bobby

Bobby Fischer teaches chess; by Bobby Fisher, Stuart Margulies, Donn Mosenfelder. Bantam 1972 334p il pa $7.99   **794.1**
1. Chess
ISBN 0-553-26315-3; 978-0-553-26315-2
First published 1966 by Basic Systems, Inc.

In this book the authors give specific advice and hints aimed at both the beginning and advanced player. Each step-by-step lesson is fully illustrated.

Hallman, J. C.

The **chess** artist. Thomas Dunne Bks. 2003 334p il map $25.95; pa $13.95   **794.1**
1. Chess
ISBN 0-312-27293-6; 0-312-33396-X pa
LC 2003-46872

"Educational, fanciful, entertaining, this is a book that will make every reader see the game of chess in an entirely new—if slightly weird—light." Booklist
Includes bibliographical references

U.S. Chess Federation's official rules of chess; Tim Just, chief editor, National Tournament Director. 6th edition Random House 2014 369 p. pbk $19.99   **794.1**
1. Chess
ISBN 9780375724008; 0375724001
LC 2014009874

"This comprehensive rulebook is the only guide sanctioned and compiled by the U.S. Chess Federation (USCF), the governing body for chess in the United States. It is designed to be a useful reference for all chess players, especially tournament directors and chess club teachers." (Publisher's note)

794.6 Bowling

Manzione, Gianmarc

Pin Action; Small-time Gangsters, High-stakes Gambling, and the Teenage Hustler Who Became a Bowling Champion. by Gianmarc Manzione. W W Norton & Co Inc. 2014 336 p. 16 plates; illustrations $27.95   **794.6**
1. Bowling 2. Organized crime
ISBN 1605986453; 9781605986456
LC 2015410656

This book, by Gianmarc Manzione, explains how "in the 1960s, New York City was the center of . . . a form of high-stakes gambling in which bowlers—often teenagers—faced off for thousands of dollars. . . . You can bet the pressure is on . . . and losses come with dire consequences. But for a few kids, the world of action bowling would turn out to be a ticket off the mean streets and onto the Professional Bowlers Association Tour. For Ernie Schlegel, it would be a chance to shed his hustler ways and become a bonafide champion." (Publisher's note)

"This well-researched account is for those who remember the glory days of bowling. Others will be fascinated by the gritty side of the sport, which few knew existed." LJ

794.7 Ball games

Byrne, Robert

Byrne's new standard book of pool and billiards. Harcourt Brace & Co. 1998 xxv, 406p il hardcover o.p. pa $20   **794.7**
1. Billiards 2. Pool (Game)
ISBN 0-15-100325-4; 0-15-600554-9 pa
LC 98-14656

First published 1978 with title: Byrne's standard book of pool and billiards

The author explains the rules of pool and billiards and offers advice on strategy with diagrams of various shots.
Includes bibliographical references

McCumber, David

Playing off the rail; a pool hustler's journey. Avon Books 1997 384p pa $14.95   **794.7**
1. Pool (Game) 2. Pool players
ISBN 0-380-72923-7
First published 1996 by Random House

A "look at the game of pool, which is a gambling sport not yet sanitized by what McCumber calls the 'Fellowship of Christian Athletes types.' He plays financial backer to a sharp-tongued player named Tony Annigoni, and takes him on the road across North America in search of highstakes games. . . . This is a terrific book." New Yorker

794.8 Electronic games

Bissell, Tom

Extra lives; why video games matter. Pantheon Books 2010 218p   **794.8**
1. Video games
ISBN 0-307-37870-5; 978-0-307-37870-5
LC 2009-39602

This is a volume of essays about video games. Portions of the work originally appeared in The New Yorker, Tin House, and Kill Screen. Mr Bissell explains: "I wrote this book as a writer who plays a lot of games, and in these pages you will find one man's opinions and thoughts on what playing games feels like, why he plays them, and the questions they make him think about. In the portions of the book where I address game design and game designers, it is . . . to a formally explanatory rather than technically informative end." (Author's note) Index.

The "first truly indispensable work of literary nonfiction about society's most lucrative entertainment medium. Bissell's commentary is marvelously astute and his enthusiasm for games makes even his words on the printed page feel positively backlit. Any breathless adoration for the medium he doles out, however, takes on additional weight because of his willingness to admit when a game falls on its face." Paste

Parkin, Simon

An **illustrated** history of 151 video games; a detailed guide to the most important games. by Simon Parkin. Natl Book Network 2014 255 p. color illustrations $29.99   **794.8**

1. Video games

ISBN 0754823903; 9780754823902

This book, by Simon Parkin, "charts the evolution of videogames through 151 most influential titles, with 500 photographs and screenshots." (Publisher's note)

795.4   Card games

Gibson, Walter Brown

Hoyle's modern encyclopedia of card games; rules of all the basic games and popular variations. {by} Walter B. Gibson. Dolphin Bks. (NY) 1974 398p il pa $12.95   **795.4**

1. Card games

ISBN 0-385-07680-0

This guide to the rules and techniques of various card games includes special sections on pinochle, poker and solitaire

Ho, Oliver

The **Ultimate** Book of Family Card Games; by Oliver Ho. Sterling 2010 118 p. color illustrations (hc-plc with jacket : alk. paper) $9.95   **795.4**

1. Card games 2. Card games -- Juvenile literature

ISBN 1402750412; 9781402750410

LC 2010026522

This book, by Oliver Ho, presents family card games. "Everyone loves to play cards, and this ultimate collection has all the fun favorites, including rummy, spades, war, old maid, go fish, snip snap snorem, and hearts. There are over 50 games in all, organized by type and difficulty, and complete with instructions, rules, strategies, color illustrations, and a brief note on each one's origins." (Publisher's note)

Hoyle, Edmond

Hoyle's rules of games; descriptions of indoor games of skill and chance, with advice on skillful play: based on the foundations laid down by Edmond Hoyle, 1672-1769. edited by Albert H. Morehead and Geoffrey Mott-Smith. 3rd rev. & updated ed.; Plume 2001 362p il pa $14   **795.4**

1. Card games

ISBN 0-452-28313-2

LC 2002-278550

This guide "includes rules, strategies, and playing odds for more than 250 games." Publisher's note

Includes bibliographical references

McManus, James

Cowboys full; the story of poker. Farrar, Straus, and Giroux 2009 516p il $30   **795.4**

1. Poker

ISBN 978-0-374-29924-8; 0-374-29924-2

LC 2009-29533

The story of poker, from its roots in China, the Middle East, and Europe to its ascent as a global—but especially an American—phenomenon, braiding history with poker's relevance to our military, diplomatic, business, and personal affairs.

"The epic story of how poker has grown from disreputable roots to become America's—and the world's—game. . . . A satisfying, useful overview." Kirkus

Includes bibliographical references (p. 471-474)

Positively Fifth Street; murderers, cheetahs, and Binion's World Series of Poker. Farrar, Straus & Giroux 2003 422p il $26   **795.4**

1. Poker

ISBN 0-374-23648-8

LC 2002-33882

"McManus went to Las Vegas in May 2000 on assignment for Harper's to cover the World Series of Poker. . . . He was to throw in coverage of the trial of Sandy Murphy, an ex-stripper, and her boyfriend, Rick Tabish, accused of murdering Ted Binion, the tournament's host. . . . To satisfy his own gambling urge, McManus enter the poker competition and spends 10 days immersed in the culture of Vegas and gambling, rendering a fast-paced, riveting account of his progress through the tournament. . . . A delicious inside look." Booklist

Includes bibliographical references

796   Athletic and outdoor sports and games

The **Best** American sports writing of the century; edited by David Halberstam. Houghton Mifflin 1999 776p $30; pa $18   **796**

1. Sports

ISBN 0-395-94513-5; 0-395-94514-3 pa

"Although there are pieces about mountain climbing, tennis and chess, fully half of the selections are about two sports: baseball and boxing. The book begins with a Best of the Best section led by Gay Talese's 1966 profile of Joe DiMaggio, 'The Silent Season of a Hero.'. . . The final section is a special six-piece tribute to a man who himself claimed to be the best of the best—Muhammad Ali." Publ Wkly

Clotfelter, Charles T.

Big-time sports in American universities. Cambridge University Press 2011 313p il $29   **796**

1. College sports 2. College sports -- United States

ISBN 1-107-00434-9; 978-1-107-00434-4

LC 2010-50331

This book presents "findings about the size, importance and effects of big-time college sports." (Publisher's note) Glossary. Index.

"Clotfelter sets himself an ambitious goal: using an analytical, data-rich approach to the questions of why many leading American universities embrace big-time, commercial athletics (while failing to fully acknowledge the size of its footprint), and whether the marriage is a good one for institutions and society as a whole. . . . He collects information on how much of The New York Times coverage of various universities focuses on their sports programs (much greater at institutions with big-time sports programs than at their peers without them), for instance, and mines a forthcoming study to show that undergraduates at one group of highly selective universities with commercial sports programs spend less time on academics than do their counterparts at institutions without top-level programs. In true economist's fashion, he asks: Do the benefits outweigh the costs? Clotfelter's answers, he acknowledges, are something less than fully satisfactory, and the book uncovers ample evidence for fanatics and haters of big-time sports alike." Inside Higher Ed

Includes bibliographical references

Cordes, Kelly

The **tower**; a chronicle of climbing and controversy on Cerro Torre. Kelly Cordes. Patagonia 2014 400 p. (hardcover : alk. paper) $27.95   **796**
    1. Mountaineering 2. Torre Mountain (Argentina)
    ISBN 1938340337; 9781938340338; 9781938340345
                                            LC 2014947861
This book by Kelly Cordes looks at "Patagonia's Cerro Torre, considered by many the most beautiful peak in the world. . . . controversy has swirled around this ice-capped peak since Cesare Maestri claimed first ascent in 1959. Since then a debate has raged, with world-class climbers attempting to retrace his route but finding only contradictions." (Publisher's note)

Dierker, Larry

This ain't brain surgery; how to win the pennant without losing your mind. Simon & Schuster 2003 289p il $25   **796**
    1. Baseball players 2. Houston Astros (Baseball team) 3. Sportscasters 4. Baseball managers
    ISBN 0-7432-0400-X
                                            LC 2003-52809
"Dierker, a pitcher and then radio commentator for the Houston Astros, stepped out of the announcer's booth to become the Astros' manager in 1997. . . . Baseball and the Houston Astros have been Dierker's professional adult life, but unlike many baseball lifers, he has a healthy perspective about the game and his role in it, as reflected in the title of this literate, humorous, and entertaining memoir." Booklist

Halberstam, David

The **teammates**. Hyperion 2003 217p il $22.95   **796**
    1. Baseball players 2. Sportscasters 3. Baseball managers 4. Baseball -- Biography 5. Boston Red Sox (Baseball team)
    ISBN 1-401-30057-X
                                            LC 2003-42334
"This account of good people living full lives and appreciating the experience will move readers." Booklist

Haskins, Don

★ **Glory** road; my story of the 1966 NCAA basketball championship and how one team triumphed against the odd and changed America forever. [by]

Don Haskins with Daniel Wetzel. Hyperion 2006 254p il pa $14.95   **796**
    1. Basketball coaches
    ISBN 1-4013-0791-4
                                            LC 2005-50349
"This is one of the best sports autobiographies in many years." Booklist

Kindred, Dave

Sound and fury; two powerful lives, one fateful friendship. Free Press 2006 368p il $27   **796**
    1. Lawyers 2. Television personalities 3. Sportscasters 4. Boxers (Persons)
    ISBN 0-7432-6211-5; 978-0-7432-6211-8
                                            LC 2005-55217
This is an account of the friendship of Muhammad Ali and Howard Cosell.
"Even if the shelves are sagging with books about Ali, room should be made for this approachable, touching, and altogether fascinating buddy comedy." Booklist

Includes bibliographical references

Miller, Stephen G.

Ancient Greek athletics. Yale University Press 2004 288p il map $35   **796**
    1. Athletics 2. Olympic games 3. Greece -- Civilization
    ISBN 0-300-10083-3
                                            LC 2003-16875
"Five chapters discuss the origins and history of the [Olympic] games and their sociopolitical significance, but at the core of the book are the 11 chapters that use archaeological and textual evidence . . . to reconstruct the physical reality of Greek athletics. Particularly valuable are the vivid reconstruction of the ancient Olympic program and the lucid discussion of the evidence for female athletic contests in ancient Greece." Choice

Includes bibliographical references

Rhoden, William C.

$40 million slaves; the rise, fall, and redemption of the Black athlete. Crown Publishers 2006 286p il $23.95   **796**
    1. Sports 2. Race discrimination 3. African American athletes
    ISBN 0-609-60120-2; 978-0-609-60120-4
                                            LC 2005-34952
"In his provocative, passionate, important and disturbing book—part memoir, part history, part journalism—William Rhoden . . . builds a historic framework that both accounts for the varieties of African-American athletic experience in the past and continues to explain them today." N Y Times Book Rev

Includes bibliographical references

Wertheim, L. Jon

This is your brain on sports; The Science of Underdogs, the Value of Rivalry & What We Can Learn From the T-Shirt Cannon. L. Jon Wertheim and Sam Sommers. Crown Archetype 2016 288 p. $26 **796**
    1. Sports -- Psychological aspects 2. Sports --

Miscellanea
ISBN 9780553447408

LC 2015021731

This book, by L. Jon Wertheim and Sam Sommers, "take[s] readers on a wild ride into the inner world of sports. Through the prism of behavioral economics, neuroscience, and psychology, they reveal the hidden influences and surprising cues that inspire and derail us—on the field and in the stands—and by extension, in corporate board rooms, office settings, and our daily lives." (Publisher's note)

"If sport s bring out the kooky, spooky, and creepy in us, Wertheim and Sommers give us a chance to understand ourselves and perhaps get a grip before we totally lose it." Kirkus

Includes bibliographical references

Winston, Wayne L.

Mathletics; how gamblers, managers, and sports enthusiasts use mathematics in baseball, basketball, and football. [by] Wayne Winston. Princeton University Press 2009 358p il $29.95   **796**
1. Mathematics 2. Sports -- Statistics
ISBN 978-0-691-13913-5; 0-691-13913-X

LC 2008-51678

"Sports fans will learn much from probability theory and statistical models. . . . A rare fusion of sports enthusiasm and numerical acumen." Booklist

Includes bibliographical references (p. 343-352)

Wong, Stephen

Smithsonian baseball; inside the world's finest private collections. photographs by Susan Einstein. HarperCollins 2005 il   **796**
1. Baseball -- Collectors and collecting. 2. Baseball -- Collectibles -- United States. 3. Baseball -- Collectibles -- United States -- Pictorial works.
ISBN 0-06-083851-5

"An oversized volume showcases 350 full-color photographs of twenty-one of the best private collections of baseball memorabilia, featuring numerous historical and previously unseen artifacts and providing eight expert essays on how to build a personal collection." (Publisher's note)

796.01   Sports--philosophy

Afremow, Jim

The **champion's** mind; how great athletes think, train, and thrive. Jim Afremow, PhD. Rodale Books 2014 269 p. (hardback) $24.99   **796.01**
1. Physical education 2. Sports -- Psychological aspects 3. Physical education and training
ISBN 1623361486; 9781623361488

LC 2013032605

In this book, by Jim Afremow, the author "offers the same advice he uses with Olympians, Heisman Trophy winners, and professional athletes, including: tips and techniques based on high-performance psychology research, such as how to get in a 'zone,' thrive on a team, and stay humble . . . , [and] how to progress within a sport and sustain excellence long-term." (Publisher's note)

Includes bibliographical references

Rotella, Bob

How champions think in sports and in life; Dr. Bob Rotella, with Bob Cullen. Simon & Schuster 2015 304 p. (Hardcover) $26   **796.01**
1. Success 2. Athletes 3. Sports -- Psychological aspects 4. Athletes -- Attitudes 5. Athletes -- Psychology 6. Success -- Psychological aspects
ISBN 1476788626; 9781476788623

LC 2014044600

This book, by sports psychologist Bob Rotella, is a "guide to success in all aspects of life-- not just sports-- from business to relationships to personal challenges of every variety. . . . It explores how to keep the mind from holding you back, whatever your physical gifts or other talents. It's about how to make a commitment, how to persevere, how to deal with failure-- and how to train your mind to create a self-image that promotes confidence and accomplishment." (Publisher's note)

"Rotella's liberal use of sports anecdotes and an effective piece on a coach's perspective (Kentucky basketball coach John Calipari) further underscore the importance of the core set of philosophies and behaviors he promotes, although his frequent and distractive allusions to faith and religion as one of the linchpins to an athlete's or a team's success may not appeal to more secular readers. A solid motivational text for the sports-minded and those interested in the bridging of athletics and exceptionalism." Kirkus

796.04   General kinds of sports and games

Nocera, Joe

Indentured; the inside story of the rebellion against the NCAA. Joe Nocera and Ben Strauss. Portfolio 2016 384 p. illustrations (hardcover) $30   **796.04**
1. Athletes 2. College sports 3. Sports -- Economic aspects 4. National Collegiate Athletic Association 5. College sports -- United States -- Management 6. College sports -- Economic aspects -- United States 7. College athletes -- United States -- Economic conditions 8. College sports -- Moral and ethical aspects -- United States
ISBN 9781591846321

LC 2015044500

This book, by Joe Nocera and Ben Strauss, "tells the story of a loose-knit group of rebels who decided to fight the hypocrisy of the NCAA, which blathers endlessly about the purity of its 'student-athletes' while exploiting many of them: The ones who get injured and drop out because their scholarships have been revoked. The ones who will neither graduate nor go pro. The ones who live in terror of accidentally violating some obscure rule in the four-hundred-page NCAA rulebook." (Publisher's note)

"Championship-level reporting on the boundaries of sport and business." Kirkus

Includes bibliographical references and index.

796.083   Boys--recreation--outdoor

Garlick, Hattie

Born to Be Wild; Hundreds of free nature activities for families. by Hattie Garlick. St. Martin's Press 2016 256 p. color illustrations $22   **796.083**
1. Creative activities
ISBN 147291533X; 9781472915337

This book, by Hattie Garlick, "contains easy-to-follow instructions for activities that require nothing more sophisticated than a child's imagination and access to a little outdoor space. Organized by season and then by material, it lets parents skip straight to . . . their present need. Everything you need to engage in all of its hundreds of activities can be found in your kitchen. No expensive art supplies or outward-bound kit required." (Publisher's note)

"Spring presents a wonderful opportunity to reconnect with the outdoors, and with this title nearby, even smartphone-obsessed kids will soon be clamoring to plan an outing." LJ

Includes bibliographical references and index.

796.087   People with disabilities and illnesses, gifted people

Shriver, Timothy

Fully alive; discovering what matters most. Timothy Shriver. Sarah Crichton Books 2014 304 p. 16 plates; illustrations (hardback) $27   **796.087**
1. Special Olympics 2. People with mental disabilities 3. Sports for people with mental disabilities
ISBN 0374280916; 9780374280918
LC 2014020245

In this memoir, author Timothy Shriver "shows how his teachers have been the world's most forgotten minority: people with intellectual disabilities. In these pages we meet the individuals who helped him come of age and find a deeper and more meaningful way to see the world." (Publisher's note)

"Sincere, profound and deeply satisfying." Kirkus

796.3   Ball games

Dawidoff, Nicholas

Collision Low Crossers; A Year Inside the Turbulent World of NFL Football. Nicholas Dawidoff. Little Brown & Co 2013 352 p. $87   **796.3**
1. Football 2. National Football League 3. Football -- United States 4. New York Jets (Football team)
ISBN 0316196797; 9780316196796
LC 2013030013

This book by Nicholas Dawidoff follows the football team the New York Jets throughout 2011, "operations, from the February scouting 'combine' of collegiate talent, through the May draft of college players, the torturous preseason of practices and games, and, finally, to the entire 16-game, regular season schedule and subsequent coaches' postmor-

tem. Head coach Rex Ryan and his staff receive the primary focus." (Booklist)

Includes bibliographical references and index

796.323   Basketball

Abrams, Jonathan

Boys among men; how the prep-to-pro generation redefined the NBA and sparked a basketball revolution. Jonathan Abrams. Crown Archetype 2015 336 p. color illustrations $28   **796.323**
1. High school students 2. National Basketball Association 3. Basketball draft 4. Basketball players -- Recruiting -- United States
ISBN 0804139253; 9780804139250
LC 2015027590

This book, by Jonathan Abrams, tells the "story of the prep-to-pro generation, those basketball prodigies who from 1995 to 2005 made the jump directly from high school to the [National Basketball Association]. 'Boys Among Men' goes behind the scenes and draws on hundreds of firsthand interviews to paint insightful and engaging portraits of the most pivotal figures and events during this time." (Publisher's note)

"Especially timely considering Kobe's recent retirement announcement, this essential, well-researched book will appeal to readers interested in basketball's business side as well as the factors that have helped shape the modern NBA." Library Journal

Blais, Madeleine

In these girls, hope is a muscle. Warner Bks. 1996 266p pa $13.95   **796.323**
1. Basketball 2. Cathedral High School (Springfield, Mass.)
ISBN 0-446-67210-6; 978-0-446-67210-8
First published 1995 by Atlantic Monthly Press

"Alternately funny, exciting and moving, the book should be enjoyed not only by girls and women who have played sports but also those who wanted to but let themselves be discouraged." Publ Wkly

Colton, Larry

Counting coup; a true story of basketball and honor on the Little Big Horn. Warner Bks. 2000 420p hardcover o.p. pa $14.95   **796.323**
1. Basketball 2. Women athletes 3. Native Americans -- Social conditions 4. Hardin High School (Hardin, Mont.) -- Basketball
ISBN 0-446-52683-5; 0-446-67755-8 pa
LC 00-24987

Conroy, Pat

My losing season. Talese 2002 402p hardcover o.p. pa $14.95   **796.323**
1. Authors 2. Novelists 3. Authors, American
ISBN 0-385-48912-9; 0-553-38190-3 pa
LC 2002-66212

"A wonderfully rich, informative, and well-researched reminiscence." Libr J

Davis, Seth

When March went mad; the game that transformed basketball. Henry Holt 2009 323p il $26 **796.323**

1. Basketball 2. Indiana State University 3. Michigan State University

ISBN 978-0-8050-8810-6; 0-8050-8810-5

LC 2008-47628

The author "chronicles the 1979 NCAA basketball championship game, which featured two future legends: Earvin 'Magic' Johnson and Larry Bird. The game was a pivotal moment in the development of the sport, leading to an explosion in popularity and a change in the way the game was played and promoted. . . . An essential primer for tournament junkies, and ideal reading material for TV timeouts." Kirkus

Includes bibliographical references

Dohrmann, George

★ **Play** their hearts out; a coach, his star recruit, and the youth basketball machine. Ballantine Books 2010 422p il $26 **796.323**

1. Basketball 2. Basketball coaches 3. Basketball players

ISBN 978-0-345-50860-7; 0-345-50860-2

LC 2010-15470

The author "follows California phenom Demetrius Walker through the cycle of Amateur Athletic Union (AAU) summer league hoops, from playing for ambitious hustler and coach Joe Keller to the face of grassroots basketball, longtime coach Pat Barrett. In a constant search for the next Lebron, just as before for the next Michael Jordan, AAU coaches, with support and financing from shoe giants Nike and Adidas, woo youngsters to their summer league basketball teams with gear, shoes, and promises of a college scholarship. . . . [Dohrmann's] insights into the seamy side of youth basketball are investigative journalism at its best." Libr J

Feinstein, John

★ **Last** dance; behind the scenes at the Final Four. John Feinstein. Little, Brown 2006 369p il $25.95 **796.323**

1. Basketball

ISBN 0-316-16030-X

LC 2005-28478

The author "employs the 2005 [Final Four] weekend as the catalyst to discuss the history of the event, the key people, and, most significantly, the effect that involvement in the Final Four has had on participants' lives. . . . The anecdotes are entertaining, and the insights into the tournament's logistics fascinating, but what will linger most are the remembrances of players, especially those who ended up on the losing side." Booklist

★ The **legends** club; Dean Smith, Mike Krzyzewski, Jim Valvano, and an Epic College Basketball Rivalry. John Feinstein. Doubleday 2016 416 p. illustrations (some color) (Hard cover) $27.95 **796.323**

1. College sports 2. Basketball teams 3. Basketball coaches 4. College basketball 5. Duke University -- Basketball -- History 6. Basketball teams -- North Carolina -- History 7. Sports rivalries -- North Carolina

-- History 8. Basketball coaches -- United States -- Biography 9. North Carolina State University -- Basketball -- History 10. University of North Carolina at Chapel Hill -- Basketball -- History

ISBN 9780385539418

LC 2015029890

This book, by John Feinstein, presents the "inside story of college basketball's fiercest rivalry among three coaching legends—University of North Carolina's Dean Smith, Duke's Mike Krzyzewski, and North Carolina State's Jim Valvano. . . . Feinstein pulls back the curtain on the recruiting wars, the intensely personal competition that wasn't always friendly, the enormous pressure and national stakes, and the battle for the very soul of college basketball allegiance in a hot-bed area." (Publisher's note)

"A text that will delight college basketball fans but also raises tacit questions about the effects of big-time athletics on a university's academic mission." Kirkus

A **march** to madness; the view from the floor in the Atlantic Coast Conference. Little, Brown 1997 464p il hardcover o.p. pa $14 **796.323**

1. Basketball 2. Atlantic Coast Conference

ISBN 0-316-27740-1; 0-316-27712-6 pa

LC 97-31060

Feinstein "covers one year with all of the teams in the perennially powerful Atlantic Coast Conference. After introducing each of the schools, their teams, their coaches, and their expectations for the 1996/97 basketball season, the book describes their progress week by week, culminating with Dean Smith's run to the NCAA Final Four. Such a detailed accounting of a sports season could seem interminable to readers, but Feinstein has again produced a narrative that is not only interesting but often exciting." Libr J

FreeDarko presents the macrophenomenal pro basketball almanac; styles, stats and stars in today's game. Bloomsbury USA 2008 219p il $23 **796.323**

1. Basketball 2. National Basketball Association

ISBN 978-1-59691-561-9; 1-59691-561-7

"This is a wonderful basketball book that blends a unique perspective, arresting presentation, and superior knowledge of its subject." Booklist

Fury, Shawn

Rise & fire; the origins, science, and evolution of the jump shot --- and how it transformed basketball forever. Shawn Fury. St. Martin's Press 2016 352 p. illustrations (hardback) $27.99 **796.323**

1. Basketball -- History

ISBN 9781250062161; 1250062160

LC 2015040454

This book, by Shawn Fury, "celebrates . . . [the jump shot in basketball] while tracing the history of how it revolutionized the game, shedding light on all corners of the basketball world, from NBA arenas to the playgrounds of New York City and the barns of Indiana. . . . [The author] obsesses over the jump shot, explores its fundamentals, puzzles over its complexities, marvels at its simplicity, and honors those who created some of basketball's greatest moments." (Publisher's note)

"Apart from Fury's historical account, ultimately we must return to the love letter, as it transports us back to the days when the world was just us, a basketball, and a hoop mounted in a driveway, an alley, a barn, or a deserted playground, and in our minds we became West or Robertson or Long, and it seemed we would be forever young." LJ

Includes bibliographical references and index.

Glockner, Andy

Chasing perfection; a behind-the-scenes look at the high-stakes game of creating an NBA champion. Andy Glockner. Da Capo Press 2016 288 p. illustrations (hardback) $25.99   **796.323**
1. Basketball teams 2. Sports -- Economic aspects 3. National Basketball Association 4. Basketball -- Philosophy 5. Basketball teams -- United States 6. Basketball -- Economic aspects -- United States 7. Basketball -- United States -- Statistical methods 8. National Basketball Association -- Forecasting -- Statistics
ISBN 0306824027; 9780306824029
    LC 2015043098
This book, by Andy Glockner, "goes behind the scenes of the multi-million dollar, high-stakes world of basketball player development, research and analysis, and the often secretive, cutting-edge methods that NBA franchises use to turn less-expensive, supporting players into vital parts of championship teams." (Publisher's note)

"Highly recommended for NBA junkies who scour box scores." LJ

Includes bibliographical references and index

McCallum, Jack

Dream team; how Michael, Magic, Larry, Charles, and the greatest team of all time conquered the world and changed the game of basketball forever. Jack McCallum. Ballantine Books 2012 xxix, 352 p.p col. ill. (hardback) $28   **796.323**
1. Olympic games 2. Basketball -- History 3. Basketball players -- United States -- Biography 4. Basketball -- United States -- History 5. Basketball teams -- United States -- History
ISBN 0345520483; 0345520505; 9780345520487; 9780345520500
    LC 2012006253
In this book "sports journalist Jack McCallum delivers the . . . story of . . . the 1992 U.S. Olympic Men's Basketball Team that captivated the world. . . . He offers a . . . look at the controversial selection process. . . . [a]nd he narrates . . . the legendary July 1992 intrasquad scrimmage that pitted the Dream Teamers against one another in what may have been the greatest pickup game--and the greatest exhibition of trash talk--in history." (Publisher's note)

"...[McCallum] effectively evokes the remarkable team while placing it within the larger historical context. Basketball and Olympics fans will welcome this nostalgic trip through the recent past." Kirkus

Merlino, Doug

The **hustle**; one team and ten lives in Black and White. Bloomsbury USA 2010 309p il $26 **796.323**
1. Basketball 2. School sports 3. Lakeside School

(Seattle, Wash.) 4. Washington (State) -- Race relations
ISBN 978-1-60819-215-1; 1-60819-215-6
    LC 2010-23030
"This book, both memoir and social analysis, is an essential read as a recent social history and personal story of America." Libr J

Reeder, Lydia

Dust bowl girls; a team's quest for basketball glory. Lydia Reeder. Algonquin Books of Chapel Hill 2017 304 p. (hardcover) $26.95   **796.323**
1. Basketball for women 2. Basketball coaches -- Oklahoma -- Biography 3. Basketball for women -- Oklahoma -- History 4. Women basketball players -- Oklahoma -- Biography 5. Oklahoma Presbyterian College -- Basketball -- History
ISBN 1616204664; 9781616204662
    LC 2016016234
This book, by Lydia Reeder, describes how "at the height of the Great Depression, Sam Babb, the charismatic basketball coach of tiny Oklahoma Presbyterian College, began dreaming. Like so many others, he wanted a reason to have hope. Traveling from farm to farm, he recruited talented, hardworking young women and offered them a chance at a better life: a free college education if they would come play for his basketball team, the Cardinals." (Publisher's note)

"Author Reeder, Babb's grandniece, had access to such primary materials as player diaries, which reveal the players' relationships to one another and their coach, and to a dustbowl era and region marked by serious hardship." Booklist

Includes bibliographical references

Reynolds, Bill

Hope; a school, a team, a dream. Bill Reynolds. St. Martin's Press 2016 256 p. color illustrations (hardback) $26.99   **796.323**
1. Basketball 2. High schools -- Rhode Island -- Providence
ISBN 9781250080691; 125008069X
    LC 2015037368
This book, by Bill Reynolds, profiles "Hope High School in Providence, Rhode Island . . . , once . . . known for its state championship basketball teams in the 1960s, but its 2012 team is much different. Disobedient, distracted, and overwhelmed by family troubles, with mismatched sneakers and a penchant for profanity and anger, these boys represent Coach Dave Nyblom's dream of a championship, however unlikely that might seem." (Publisher's note)

"A basketball book but also a candid look at inner-city life that should garner it a broad audience." Booklist

Simmons, Bill

The **book** of basketball; the NBA according to the sports guy. Ballantine/ESPN Books 2009 715p il $30; pa $18   **796.323**
1. Basketball 2. National Basketball Association
ISBN 978-0-345-51176-8; 0-345-51176-X; 978-0-345-52010-4 pa; 0-345-52010-6 pa
    LC 2009-36006
The author "summarizes the history of the league, discusses his personal fandom, includes a great 'what if?' chapter (what if Michael Jordan had been drafted second by Port-

land instead of third by Chicago?), analyzes Most Valuable Player choices through the years, and dissects the careers of the league's all-time best players. The true NBA fan will dive into this hefty volume and won't resurface for about a week, emerging from the man cave unshaven, smelling of beer and pizza, grinning, and armed with NBA history, insight, anecdotes, statistics, and a dozen new examples of Simmons' Unintentional Comedy Scale. This is just plain fun. Expect significant demand from hoops junkies." Booklist

Includes bibliographical references

Swidey, Neil

The **assist**; hoops, hope, and the game of their lives. PublicAffairs 2008 358p il $26   **796.323**
1. Basketball 2. School sports 3. Basketball coaches 4. Charlestown High School (Boston, Mass.)
ISBN 978-1-58648-469-9; 1-58648-469-9
LC 2007-35826
"This is a prodigiously reported, compulsively readable book that readers (sport fans or not) will savor." Publ Wkly

796.332 American football

Anderson, Lars

Carlisle vs. Army; Jim Thorpe, Dwight Eisenhower, Pop Warner, and the forgotten story of football's greatest battle. Random House 2007 349p il $24.95   **796.332**
1. Football 2. Generals 3. Presidents 4. Decathletes 5. Pentathletes 6. Football coaches 7. Olympic athletes 8. College presidents 9. United States Indian School (Carlisle, Pa.)
ISBN 978-1-4000-6600-1; 1-4000-6600-X
LC 2007-8410
"A forgotten football game in 1912, between Carlisle, led by Jim Thorpe and coached by the legendary Pop Warner, and Army, led by Dwight Eisenhower, becomes the launching point for a fascinating look at multiple levels of American popular culture." Booklist

Includes bibliographical references

The **Mannings**; The Fall and Rise of a Football Family. Lars Anderson. Ballantine Books 2016 368 p. color illustrations (hardcover : acid-free paper) $28   **796.332**
1. Football players 2. Football players -- United States -- Biography 3. Quarterbacks (Football) -- United States -- Biography
ISBN 1101883820; 9781101883822
LC 2016018007
This book, by Lars Anderson, is "a revealing portrait of the first family of American sports, . . . the Mannings. . . . Two generations have produced three NFL superstars: Archie Manning, the Ole Miss hero–turned–New Orleans Saint; his son Peyton, widely considered one of the greatest quarterbacks ever to play the game; and Peyton's younger brother, Eli, who won two Super Bowl rings of his own. And the oldest Manning child, Cooper—who was forced to quit playing sports." (Publisher's note)

"An expertly written impressionistic account of the first family of football that will be of wide interest." LJ
Includes bibliographical references and index

Benedict, Jeff

The **System**; The Glory and Scandal of Big-Time College Football. Jeff Benedict and Armen Keteyian. Random House Inc 2013 432 p. illustrations (chiefly color) (ebook) $50.85; $27.95   **796.332**
1. College football 2. College football coaches 3. Football 4. College sports -- United States 5. National Collegiate Athletic Association 6. Football -- Corrupt practices -- United States
ISBN 9780385536622; 0385536615; 9780385536615
LC 2013362311
In this book, by Jeff Benedict and Armen Keteyian, "NCAA football is big business. Every Saturday millions of people file into massive stadiums or tune in on television as 'athlete-students' give everything they've got to make their team a success. Billions of dollars now flow into the game. But what is the true cost? The players have no share in the oceans of money. And once the lights go down, the glitter doesn't shine so brightly." (Publisher's note)
"An overwhelming recommendation for all readers who love or hate college sports." LJ
Includes bibliographical references and index

Bissinger, H. G.

★ **Friday** night lights; a town, a team, and a dream. Da Capo Press 2000 367p il pa $15.95   **796.332**
1. Football 2. Permian High School (Odessa, Tex.)
ISBN 0-306-80990-7
LC 00-40510
First published 1990 by Addison-Wesley
"It is a tricky balancing act, but Mr. Bissinger carries it off: 'Friday Night Lights' offers a biting indictment of the sports craziness that grips not only Odessa but most of American society, while at the same time providing a moving evocation of its powerful allure." N Y Times Book Rev

Burke, Monte

Saban; the making of a coach. Monte Burke. Simon & Schuster 2015 352 p. (Hardcover) $27   **796.332**
1. College football coaches 2. University of Alabama -- Football -- History 3. Football coaches -- United States -- Biography
ISBN 1476789932; 9781476789934
LC 2015018182
Author Monte Burke presents a "biography of Nick Saban, the influential and polarizing University of Alabama football coach who not only transformed the college game but might also be the best ever at winning. Through unprecedented interviews with more than 250 friends, coworkers, rivals, former players, and others, Burke reveals the defining moments of the coach's life." (Publisher's note)
"With Saban's wins and losses over the years having been covered extensively in the media, Burke wisely focuses on the man rather than the play-by-play, and the result is a genuinely insightful look at a fierce competitor who nev-

ertheless seems to care for his players both on and off the field." Booklist

Includes bibliographical references

Cosell, Greg

The **games** that changed the game; the evolution of the NFL in seven Sundays. [by] Ron Jaworksi, with Greg Cosell and David Plaut. ESPN Books 2010 312p il $26; ebook $26 **796.332**
1. Football 2. National Football League
ISBN 978-0-345-51795-1; 978-0-345-51797-5 ebook
LC 2010-31008

"Filled with anecdotes, player recollections, and other wonderful details, this should be the most popular football book of the season. Terrific reading." Booklist

Dent, Jim

Courage beyond the game; Jim Dent. Thomas Dunne Books/St. Martin's Press 2011 xi, 333 p.p ill. **796.332**
1. Cancer patients 2. College football 3. Football players
ISBN 9780312652852; 9781250007001
LC 2011009348

This book, a 2011 "Kirkus Reviews" Best Nonfiction title, tells the story of "Freddie Steinmark [who] was an under-sized but scrappy young man when he arrived in Austin as a freshman at the University of Texas in 1967. Despite the pronouncement by many coaches that he was too small to play football at the college level, Freddie was a tenacious competitor who vowed to start every game as a varsity Longhorn. By the start of the 1969 season, Freddie was making his mark on the college gridiron and national stage as UT's star safety, but he'd also developed a crippling pain in his thigh that worried his high school sweetheart, Linda. Despite the increasingly debilitating pain, Freddie continued to play throughout the season, helping the Longhorns to rip through opponents like pulpwood. His final game was for the national championship at the end of 1969, when the Longhorns rallied to beat Arkansas in a legendary game that has become known as 'the Game of the Century.' Tragically, bone cancer took Freddie off the field when nothing else could." (Publisher's note)

Includes bibliographical references (p. [317]-318) and index.

Feinstein, John

Next man up; a year behind the lines in today's NFL. Little, Brown 2005 502p il $25.95 **796.332**
1. Football 2. Baltimore Ravens (Football team)
ISBN 0-316-00964-4

Feinstein's look at the current state of the National Football League (NFL) focuses on the 2004 Baltimore Ravens' season.

"Even those who are not fanatical football fans will find that, beyond the information provided on players and coaches, there are two other engaging topics in the book: Feinstein's ruminations on how reporting and writing about football are different from reporting and writing about other sports, and his portrayal of the business side of the game through conversations with Ravens owner Steve Bisciotti. . . . Professional football fans cannot lose by reading this book.

As for the rest of us, [it] provides interesting glimpses into a strange but popular cultural realm." Christ Sci Monit

Football's greatest stars; 3rd edition Firefly Books 2015 pbk $24.95 **796.332**
1. Football 2. Football players 3. National Football League
ISBN 9781770855953; 1770855955
LC 2015509094

"At the heart of Football's Greatest Stars is author Allan Maki's picks for the 50 greatest and most exciting players in the history of professional football. They're all here: from the pioneers of the game to the current stars to the legends headed to the Hall of Fame. Exciting photographs show these past and present superstars in action, and 32 franchise profiles chart the league's rise to the top of professional sports. This third edition also features a new chapter on the future greats currently rumbling on the field." (Publisher's note)

Includes bibliographical references (p. 241) and index

Gaul, Gilbert M., 1951-

Billion-Dollar Ball; a journey through the big-money culture of college football. Gilbert M. Gaul. Penguin Group USA 2015 272 p. (hardcover) $27.95 **796.332**
1. College football 2. Colleges and universities -- Finance
ISBN 9780670016730; 067001673X
LC 2015473475

This book, by Gilbert M. Gaul, "offers a . . . look inside the money culture of college football and how it has come to dominate a surprising number of colleges and universities. . . . College presidents have been unwilling or powerless to stop a system that has spawned a wildly profligate infrastructure of coaches, trainers, marketing gurus, and a growing cadre of bureaucrats whose sole purpose is to ensure that players remain academically eligible to play." (Publisher's note)

"Gaul's reporting is unassailable, but watch as his conclusions stir up a furor in the sports press. You don't even have to hate football to find this book valuable—and certainly worth reading." Kirkus

Gwynne, S. C.

The **Perfect** Pass; American genius and the reinvention of football. S. C. Gwynne. Scribner 2016 304 p. illustrations (ebook) $59.99; (hbk.) $27 **796.332**
1. Football coaches 2. Football -- History 3. Passing (Football) 4. Football -- Coaching 5. Football -- United States -- History
ISBN 9781508211761; 1501116193; 9781501116193
LC 2016012980

This book, by S. C. Gwynne, is the "story of how two unknown coaches revolutionized American football at every level, from high school to the NFL. Hal Mumme is one of a handful of authentic offensive geniuses in the history of American football. . . . Gwynne explores Mumme's leading role in changing football from a run-dominated sport to a pass-dominated one, the game that tens of millions of Americans now watch every fall weekend." (Publisher's note)

"That makes his subtitle all the more fitting, for undeniably, the two coaches changed the game—and brought glory to their institutions. A superb treat for all gridiron fans." Kirkus

Includes bibliographical references (pages 273-275) and index.

Parcells, Bill, 1941-

Parcells; A Football Life. Bill Parcells, Nunyo Demasio. Crown Archetype 2014 400 p. illustrations (some colored) (hardback) $30   **796.332**
1. Football coaches 2. New York Giants (Football team) 3. Football coaches -- United States -- Biography
ISBN 9780385346351; 0385346352

LC 2014027830

This book, by Bill Parcells, with Nunyo Demasio, presents an autobiography of the football coach Bill Parcells. "During his decades-long tenure as an NFL coach, he turned failing franchises into contenders. He led the ailing New York Giants to two Super Bowl victories, turned the New England Patriots into an NFL powerhouse, reinvigorated the New York Jets, brought the Dallas Cowboys back to life, and was most recently enshrined in the Pro Football Hall of Fame." (Publisher's note)

Includes bibliographical references and index

Roberts, Diane

Tribal; college football and the secret heart of America. by Diane Roberts. Harper 2015 256 p. illustration (hardback) $25.99   **796.332**
1. College sports 2. Football -- History 3. College football -- History 4. Football -- United States -- History 5. College sports -- United States -- History
ISBN 9780062342621

LC 2015025010

This book, by Diane Roberts, "tackles the controversies plaguing college athletics, tracing the dubious historical underpinnings of Americans' most popular sport. . . . Florida State's football team is always in the headlines, producing Heisman Trophy candidates, winning championships, and, at the same time, dealing with federal investigations into corruption and rape. Same as many big time collegiate sports programs. " (Publisher's note)

"This volume seems to be aimed at readers who already hate the sport." LJ

Ross, Charles K.

Mavericks, money, and men; the AFL, Black players, and the evolution of modern football. Charles Kenyatta Ross. Temple University Press 2016 200 p. illustrations (hardback : alk. paper) $84.5 **796.332**
1. Football -- History 2. African American athletes 3. African American football players 4. American Football League -- History 5. National Football League -- History 6. Discrimination in sports -- United States -- History
ISBN 9781439913062; 9781439913079

LC 2015031425

This book, by Charles Kenyatta Ross, "chronicles the [American Football League's] key events, including Buck Buchanan becoming the first overall draft pick in 1963, and the 1965 boycott led by black players who refused to play in the AFL-All Star game after experiencing blatant racism. He also recounts how the success of the AFL forced a merger

with the NFL in 1969, which arguably facilitated the evolution of modern professional football." (Publisher's note)

"An important chapter in U.S. racial history of the 1960s. Recommended for all collections." LJ

Includes bibliographical references and index

St. John, Warren

Rammer jammer yellow hammer; a journey into the heart of fan mania. Crown Publishers 2004 275p $24   **796.332**
1. Football 2. Alabama Crimson Tide (Football team)
ISBN 0-609-60708-1

LC 2003-24718

"Wearing a thin veneer of journalistic detachment, St. John followed his beloved Alabama Crimson Tide football team during the 1999 season. The result is a sharp, sneaky-funny, but loving portrait of the team and its incredibly loyal fans." Booklist

796.334   Soccer (Association football)

Anderson, Chris

The **numbers** game; why everything you know about soccer is wrong. Chris Anderson and David Sally. Penguin Books 2013 384 p. $16   **796.334**
1. Soccer 2. Mathematical analysis 3. Soccer -- Mathematical models 4. Soccer -- Statistical methods
ISBN 0143124560; 9780143124566

LC 2013011448

This book from Chris Anderson and David Sally is "about the use of analytics in soccer." Topics include "what percentage of possession determines victory," "whether it is best to focus on scoring goals or not conceding them," "how much coaches matter to a team's success," among others. (Kirkus Reviews)

Includes bibliographical references and index

Galeano, Eduardo, 1940-2015

Soccer in sun and shadow; by Eduardo Galeano; translated by Mark Fried. Perseus Books Group 2013 320 p. $16.99   **796.334**
1. Soccer
ISBN 1568584946; 9781568584942

LC 986769

This is a "revised and updated version" of Uruguayan author Eduardo Galeano's 1995 book about soccer. "Like so many children born in Latin America, Galeano . . . grew up wanting to play soccer. In his dreams, he was a star. During the day, however, he 'was the worst wooden leg ever to set foot on the little soccer fields of my country.' Nonetheless, his love affair with the sport continued." (Kirkus Reviews)

Honigstein, Raphael

Das Reboot; How German Soccer Reinvented Itself and Conquered the World. Raphael Honigstein. Nation Books 2015 276 p. $17.99   **796.334**
1. Germany 2. Soccer teams 3. World Cup (Soccer)
ISBN 1568585306; 9781568585307

Author "Raphael Honigstein charts the return of German soccer from the dreary functionality of the late 1990s to [Mario] Götze's moment of sublime, balletic genius and asks: How did this come about? The answer takes him from California to Stuttgart, from Munich to the Maracanã, via Dortmund and Amsterdam. Packed with exclusive interviews with key figures, including Jürgen Klinsmann, Thomas Müller, Oliver Bierhoff, and many more, Honigstein's book reveals the secrets of German soccer's success." (Publisher's note)

"Championship teams always have their books, but few are as thoughtful and edifying as this one." Booklist

Kirschbaum, Erik

Soccer without borders; Jürgen Klinsmann, Coaching the U.S. Men's National Soccer Team and the Quest for the World Cup. Erik Kirschbaum. Picador 2016 400 p. portrait (hardcover) $25 **796.334**
1. Soccer coaches 2. Soccer -- United States 3. Soccer teams -- United States 4. Soccer coaches -- Germany -- Biography
ISBN 9781250098313

LC 2016002387

This book, by Erik Kirschbaum, profiles "Jurgen Klinsmann, head coach of the U.S. men's national soccer team. . . . Erik Kirschbaum lays out Klinsmann's vision for making the U.S. men's soccer team a dominant world power for the first time in its history. . . . This book is a . . . road map for how to build a winning team in the most competitive professional sport on the globe." (Publisher's note)

"Kirschbaum provides a welcome sketch of Klinsmann, a thoughtful man of the world who has for years lived in California and who cannot be pigeonholed as merely a European trying to remake American soccer in the Old World image." Kirkus

Lloyd, Carli, 1982-

When nobody was watching; my hard-fought journey to the top of the soccer world. Carli Lloyd, with Wayne Coffey. Houghton Mifflin Harcourt 2016 256 p. color illustrations (hardcover) $26; (ebook) $26 **796.334**
1. Soccer players 2. Soccer -- United States -- History 3. Women soccer players -- United States -- Biography
ISBN 0544814622; 9780544814622; 9780544976801; 9780544814554

LC 2016036411

In this book, by soccer player Carli Lloyd, "there was a time when Carli almost quit the sport. In 2003 she was struggling, her soccer career at a crossroads. Then she found a trusted trainer, James Galanis, who saw in Carli a player with raw talent, skill, and a great dedication to the game. What Carli lacked were fitness, mental toughness, and character. Together they set to work, training day and night, fighting, grinding it out." (Publisher's note)

"This book is a remarkable portrait of the relentless drive and sacrifice required to truly be the best." Booklist

St. John, Warren

Outcasts united; a refugee team, an American town. Spiegel & Grau 2008 307p hardcover o.p. pa $15 **796.334**
1. Soccer 2. Refugees 3. Soccer coaches 4.

Maintenance services executives
ISBN 978-0-385-52203-8; 0-385-52203-7; 978-0-385-52204-5 pa; 0-385-52204-5 pa

LC 2008-40697

This is a "book about an unlikely soccer program in the outlying Atlanta burb of Clarkston, Georgia. . . . Clarkston's residents woke up one morning and found that the city's housing projects had become havens of resettlement for refugee families from war-ravaged locales including Liberia, Afghanistan and Bosnia. Soccer is a pastime like sandlot baseball or touch football to the often-traumatized boys on the Fugees, a ramshackle intramural team of nine to 17-year-olds that St. John follows, along with its Jordanian founder Luma Hassan Mufleh, a Smith-educated woman whose role as volunteer coach quickly expands to extended family member and social worker. St. John's aim is to draw a portrait of small-town America in transition, and his eye for detail is compelling from start to finish." Time Out N Y

Includes bibliographical references

Szymanski, Stefan

Money and Soccer; A Soccernomics Guide: Why Chievo Verona, Unterhaching, and Scunthorpe United Will Never Win the Champions League, Why Manchester City, Roma, and Paris. by Stefan Szymanski. Nation Books 2015 320 p. illustrations $16.99 **796.334**
1. Soccer 2. Soccer teams 3. Soccer players
ISBN 1568584768; 9781568584768

In this book, author Stefan Szymanski "tackles every soccer fan's burning questions. . . . From the abolition of the maximum wage in the 1960s, through to the impact of TV money both at home and abroad in the 1990s and 2000s, Szymanski explains how money, or lack of, affects your favorite club. Drawing on extensive research into financial records dating back to the 1970s, Szymanski provides clear analysis of the way that clubs have transformed in the modern era." (Publisher's note)

"A wonderful book for anyone with a slight interest in soccer or the business side of sports. The investigation is insightful and backed by strong statistics and evidence. For public libraries and academic collections serving business or sports management departments." LJ

Thompson, Teri

American huckster; How Chuck Blazer Got Rich From-and Sold Out-the Most Powerful Cabal in World Sports. Mary Papenfuss and Teresa Thompson. HarperCollins Publishers 2016 xiv, 255 p.p color illustrations (Hardcover) $26.99 **796.334**
1. Sports -- Corrupt practices 2. Soccer -- United States -- History 3. Soccer -- Management -- Corrupt practices 4. Fédération internationale de football association
ISBN 9780062449672

LC 2015050617

This book, by Mary Papenfuss and Teresa Thompson, is the "inside account of the international soccer scandal that rocked the world and the American at its center. . . . For years, Chuck Blazer skimmed over $20 million from FIFA, stashing his money in offshore accounts and real estate holdings that included a luxury apartment in Trump Tower, a

South Beach condo, and a hideaway in the Bahamas." (Publisher's note)

"This grim, always entertaining cautionary tale of greed and runaway ego is a worthy addition to any reader's collection of business fantasies gone awry." Pub Wkly

Includes bibliographical references

Vecsey, George

Eight world cups; my journey through the beauty and dark side of soccer. George Vecsey. Times Books 2014 304 p. illustrations (hardback) $28   **796.334**

1. Soccer 2. World Cup (Soccer)

ISBN 0805098488; 9780805098488

LC 2013042574

In this book, "sports columnist George Vecsey offers a personal perspective on the beautiful game. Blending witty travelogue with action on the field . . . Vecsey offers an . . . account of the last eight World Cups. He immerses himself in the great national leagues, historic clubs, and devoted fans and provides his up-close impressions of charismatic stars like Sócrates, Maradona, Baggio, and Zidane, while also chronicling the rise of the U.S. men's and women's teams." (Publisher's note)

"Vecsey's insights offer a unique look at the grace of the game as well as the underside of world soccer." LJ

Includes bibliographical references and index

Villoro, Juan

God Is Round; by Juan Villoro; illustrated by Thomas Bunstead. Simon & Schuster 2016 256 p. $16.99   **796.334**

1. Soccer 2. Soccer teams 3. Soccer players 4. World Cup (Soccer)

ISBN 1632060582; 9781632060587

This book, by Juan Villoro, illustrated by Thomas Bunstead, is an "exploration of the world's favorite sport and the passion, hopes, rivalries, superstitions, and global solidarity soccer inspires. . . . Villoro reports from the last World Cup of the twentieth century, paints portraits of contemporary soccer's most prominent stars (Lionel Messi, Cristiano Ronaldo, and Diego Armando Maradona), chats with Jorge Valdano, and teases out the contradictions of the Spanish league." (Publisher's note)

"For millions around the world, soccer is not just a game, but rather life itself and, as Villoro ably reveals, very much worth pursuing to the final whistle." Kirkus

796.34   Racket games

McPhee, John, 1931-

Levels of the game; [by] John McPhee. Farrar, Straus & Giroux 1969 149 p. $15   **796.34**

1. Tennis

ISBN 9780374515263

LC 76087219

This book, by John McPhee, is an "account of a tennis match played by Arthur Ashe against Clark Graebner at Forest Hills in 1968. [It] begins with the ball rising into the air for the initial serve and ends with the final point. McPhee provides a . . . stroke-by-stroke description while examining

the backgrounds and attitudes which have molded the players' games." (Publisher's note)

796.342   Tennis (Lawn tennis)

Fisher, Marshall

A **terrible** splendor; three extraordinary men, a world poised for war, and the greatest tennis match ever played. [by] Marshall Jon Fisher. Crown Publishers 2009 336p $25   **796.342**

1. Tennis 2. Davis Cup 3. National socialism 4. Davis cup 5. Tennis players

ISBN 978-0-307-39394-4; 0-307-39394-1

LC 2008-50527

"Richly detailed . . . the story moves from one nail-biting set to the next against a backdrop of improbably high personal and political stakes." Boston Globe

Includes bibliographical references

Gallwey, W. Timothy

The **inner** game of tennis; The Classic Guide to the Mental Side of Peak Performance. W. Timothy Gallwey. Random House Inc 1997 xx, 122 p.p illustrations $17; $51   **796.342**

1. Tennis 2. Tennis -- Psychological aspects

ISBN 0679778314; 9780679778318; 9780307758859

LC 97000895

This book on tennis, by W. Timothy Gallwey, "is a revolutionary program for overcoming the self-doubt, nervousness, and lapses of concentration that can keep a player from winning. Now available in a revised paperback edition, this classic bestseller can change the way the game of tennis is played." (Publisher's note)

McEnroe, John

You cannot be serious; {by} John McEnroe with Jams Kaplan. Putnam 2002 342p il $25.95; pa $14   **796.342**

1. Art dealers 2. Tennis players

ISBN 0-399-14858-2; 0-425-19008-0 pa

LC 2002-23875

Tennis star McEnroe's "recollections fall into three categories: accounts of key matches, life as a jet-setting celebrity, and reflections on the emotional roller coaster that has been his personal life." Booklist

Ryan, Mike

Tennis' greatest stars; Mike Ryan. Firefly Books Ltd 2014 216 p. illustrations, color portraits $35   **796.342**

1. Tennis players 2. Tennis -- Tournaments

ISBN 177085293X; 9781770852938

Author Mike Ryan's book on tennis "profiles the 50 greatest and most influential players of the game and presents a historical narrative of athletic prowess, popular culture and social responsibility. [It] is packed with action photographs that celebrate the game and thoughtful essays, which cover such topics as the birth of modern tennis, the major tournaments, international play, the various court surfaces and new technologies." (Publisher's note)

"This is a good purchase for any tennis collection and is recommended for the circulating collections of public libraries." Booklist

Wallace, David Foster, 1962-2008
  String theory; David Foster Wallace on tennis. by David Foster Wallace; introduction by John Jeremiah Sullivan. Library of America 2016 xv, 138 p.p illustrations $19.95   **796.342**
  1. Tennis 2. Tennis literature
  ISBN 1598534807; 9781598534801
                                        LC 2015951697
  This book collects "David Foster Wallace's legendary writings on tennis, five tour-de-force pieces written with a competitor's insight and a fan's obsessive enthusiasm." (Publisher's note)
  Includes bibliographical references

796.352   Golf

Cullen, Bob
  Golf is not a game of perfect; Bob Rotella with Bob Cullen. Simon & Schuster 1995 224 p. $24.99; (ebook) $18.99   **796.352**
  1. Golf 2. Golf -- Psychological aspects
  ISBN 068480364X; 9780684803647; 9781416563310
                                        LC 95001120
  This book, by Bob Rotella, is "filled with insightful stories about golf. . . . What Rotella does here . . . is to create an attitude and a mindset about all aspects of a golfer's game, from mental preparation to competition. . . . And, as some of the world's greatest golfers will attest, the results are spectacular. Golfers will improve their golf game and have more fun playing." (Publisher's note)

Feinstein, John
  A good walk spoiled; days and nights on the PGA tour. Little, Brown 1995 xx, 475p il hardcover o.p. pa $14.95   **796.352**
  1. Golf 2. PGA Tour Inc.
  ISBN 0-316-27737-1 pa
                                        LC 94-49552
  Along with "profiles of the game's big names—Norman, Price, Watson—Feinstein's sojourn through the 1994 PGA tour also offers remarkable glimpses of the marginal players who struggle to first qualify for the tour and then maintain their tenuous places on it. . . . Golfers of all ages simply won't be able to put this book down." Booklist

Frost, Mark
  The match; the day the game of golf changed forever. Mark Frost. 1st ed.; Hyperion 2007 p. cm.   **796.352**
  1. Golf -- California -- Pebble Beach -- History.
  ISBN 9781401302788
                                        LC 2007023325
  "A chronicle of a lesser-known 1956 golf match documents how Harvie Ward and Ken Venturi competed against the leading players as a result of a bet between sponsors Eddie Lowery and George Coleman, in a competition that

helped promote golf into a professional sport." (Publisher's note)
  "What makes this account so fresh and so exciting for golf fans is that—unlike any other re-creation of a great moment in sports history—Frost tells a story that, being virtually unknown, carries with it genuine suspense as to the outcome. Going well beyond the simple question of who will win, however, Frost makes us see this spur-of-the-moment match for what it was: the last hurrah of amateur golf. And, best of all, he captures one of those fleeting moments in sports when competing athletes reach a kind of transcendent perfection simultaneously. Superb narrative nonfiction." Booklist
  Includes bibliographical references..

Haney, Hank
  The big miss; my years coaching Tiger Woods. Hank Haney. 1st ed. Crown Archetype 2012 262 p. $26   **796.352**
  1. Haney, Hank 2. Golf -- Coaching 3. Golfers -- United States -- Biography 4. Golf coaches -- United States
  ISBN 0307985989; 9780307985989; 9780307985996
                                        LC 2012003092
  This memoir details Hank Haney's experiences as "American golfer [Tiger Woods's] former coach. . . . Haney assiduously monitored Woods's moods and frustrations, his silences and sulks. . . . This book is a[n] . . . account of an often-strained partnership as well as a . . . record of what it costs a man not only to dare to be the best of his generation but a champion for all the ages--until, that was, he suffered the biggest miss of all." (New Statesman)

Nicklaus, Jack
  Jack Nicklaus; my story. with Ken Bowden. Simon & Schuster 1997 505p il $30; pa $24.95   **796.352**
  1. Golf 2. Golfers
  ISBN 0-684-83628-9; 0-684-83870-2 pa
                                        LC 97-3824
  "What comes across most forcibly in this fine book is Nicklaus' respect for the complexity of golf and the never-ending challenges it affords players at every level." Booklist

Sampson, Curt
  Masters; golf, money, and power in Augusta, Georgia. Villard Bks. 1998 xxxiv, 263p il hardcover o.p. pa $14.95   **796.352**
  1. Golf 2. Augusta National Golf Club
  ISBN 0-375-75337-0 pa
                                        LC 97-49143
  This history of one of the PGA's most prestigious events "traces the tournament's history since 1933, revealing both the dramatic moments and the controversial secrets, most notably racism—certainly a book to raise eyebrows at the Augusta National Golf Club." Libr J

Wind, Herbert Warren

Five lessons; the modern fundamentals of golf. by Ben Hogan. NYT Special Services 1990 127 p. illustrations (some color) $24.99   **796.352**

1. Golf

ISBN 0671612972; 9780671723019

This book, by Ben Hogan, "outlines the building blocks of winning golf. . . . In each chapter, a different experience-tested fundamental is explained and demonstrated with clear illustrations—as though Hogan were giving you a personal lesson with the same skill and precision that made him a legend." (Publisher's note)

"The basics of hitting a ball with a club haven't changed much since this debuted, so this still offers valuable advice from one of the greats." LJ

796.357   Baseball

Barry, Dan

Bottom of the 33rd; hope and redemption in baseball's longest game. Harper 2011 255p il $26.99   **796.357**

1. Baseball 2. Baseball -- Records 3. Pawtucket Red Sox (Baseball team) 4. Rochester Red Wings (Baseball team) 5. Minor league baseball -- United States -- History

ISBN 978-0-06-201448-1; 0-06-201448-X

LC 2010-51656

"On a frigid evening in April 1981, 1,740 Pawtucket, R.I., Red Sox fans settled into their seats for a game with the Rochester Red Wings of the AAA International League. With the score tied 11 at the end of regulation, the teams played on. And on. On past 12:50 a.m., when the curfew provision, mysteriously missing from that year's edition of the rule book, would have suspended the contest; on past the 21st inning, when each team maddeningly scored a run; on past the 29th and record-tying inning; on past 4:00 a.m., the bottom of the 32nd, when the league president was finally reached and ordered the umpires to suspend the contest." Kirkus

Bissinger, H. G.

Three nights in August; strategy, heartbreak, and joy, inside the mind of a manager. [foreword by Tony La Russa] Houghton Mifflin 2005 xxi, 280p $25; pa $13.95   **796.357**

1. Baseball players 2. Baseball managers 3. St. Louis Cardinals (Baseball team)

ISBN 0-618-40544-5; 0-618-71053-1 pa

LC 2004-65134

For this book, the author "was given complete access to Tony La Russa and his St. Louis Cardinals. . . . La Russa collaborated fully, hid nothing, freely divulged his thoughts, notes, fears. The result is a fascinating look inside the day-to-day, game-by-game, inning by inning managing of a professional baseball team." N Y Times Book Rev

Includes bibliographical references

Clavin, Tom

The DiMaggios; Three Brothers, Their Passion for Baseball, Their Pursuit of the American Dream. Ecco 2013 320 p. $25.99   **796.357**

1. Baseball players -- United States 2. DiMaggio, Joe, 1914-1999

ISBN 006218377X; 9780062183774

This book looks at Vincent, Joe and Dominic DiMaggio. "Three brothers of 11 children born to Italian immigrants, the three boys excelled first in the Pacific Coast League for the local San Francisco Seals and then, one-by-one, they rose to play in the major leagues." Their careers during and after baseball and their personal relationships are explored. (Kirkus Reviews)

Cramer, Richard Ben

Joe DiMaggio; the hero's life. Simon & Schuster 2000 546p $28; pa $16   **796.357**

1. Baseball players

ISBN 0-684-85391-4; 0-684-86547-5 pa

LC 00-49232

In this biography of the baseball player, "Cramer taps every plank in the wall that DiMaggio erected around himself and that protected him from inquiry. In the wall's hollow spots, Cramer locates the girls, finds the Mob guys, and behind the legend of grace and elegance on and off the field discovers a legend who in reality was more often than not graceless and inelegant." New Yorker

Creamer, Robert W.

Stengel; his life and times. University of Neb. Press 1996 349p il pa $18.95   **796.357**

1. Baseball players 2. Baseball managers

ISBN 0-8032-6367-8

LC 95-40143

First published 1984 by Simon & Schuster

"Casey Stengel is remembered as either the shrewd, innovative New York Yankee manager who won 10 pennants and seven World Series from 1949 to 1960 or as the seemingly senile, aged master of malaprop who (mis)-managed the legendarily inept New York Mets in the early 1960s. Creamer . . . dissolves the apparently disparate images and melds them into an inclusive vision of an unexpectedly complex man." Booklist

Dykstra, Lenny, 1963-

House of nails; A Memoir of Life on the Edge. Lenny Dykstra. HarperCollins 2016 340 p. illustration, portraits (ebook) $26.99; (hardcover) $27.99   **796.357**

1. Businessmen 2. Baseball players

ISBN 0062407368; 9780062407382; 9780062407368

In this memoir by baseball player Lenny Dykstra, "Lenny tells all about his tumultuous career, from battling through crippling pain to steroid use and drug addiction, to a life of indulgence and excess, then, an epic plunge and the long road back to redemption. Was Lenny's hard-charging, risk-it-all nature responsible for his success in baseball and business and his precipitous fall from grace?" (Publisher's note)

"Dykstra makes no apologies, offering 'the real truth,' but readers' opinions of him will be harsh." Kirkus

Feinstein, John

Where nobody knows your name; life in the minor leagues of baseball. John Feinstein. Doubleday 2014 384 p. (hardcover) $26.95   **796.357**

1. Baseball players 2. Minor league baseball 3. Minor league baseball -- United States -- History

ISBN 0385535937; 9780385535939

LC 2013030645

This book, by John Feinstein, presents a " journey through the world of minor-league baseball. . . . Focusing exclusively on the Triple-A level, one step beneath Major League Baseball, Feinstein introduces readers to nine unique men: three pitchers, three position players, two managers, and an umpire. Through their compelling stories, Feinstein pulls back the veil on a league that is chock-full of gifted baseball players, managers, and umpires." (Publisher's note)

Geist, Bill

Little League confidential; one coach's completely unauthorized tale of survival. Dell Pub 1999 217p pa $15   **796.357**

1. Baseball 2. Little League Baseball, Inc.

ISBN 0-440-50877-0

First published 1992 by Macmillan

The author "relates his decade of service as a little-league baseball coach. He admittedly distills his experiences—and those of others—into a season-long 'docudrama' journal. He tells of pompous coaches lecturing their miniplayers on the subtleties of the infield fly rule; he addresses the question of positioning a player with a personal-injury lawyer for a dad. The book is a wonderful effort filled with empathy for kids, impatience for pushy parents, and a good sense of humor." Booklist

Goodwin, Doris Kearns

Wait till next year; a memoir. Simon & Schuster 1997 261p il hardcover o.p. pa $14   **796.357**

1. Authors 2. Historians 3. Biographers 4. Nonfiction writers 5. Political commentators 6. Brooklyn Dodgers (Baseball team)

ISBN 0-684-84795-7 pa

LC 97-39766

"For self-esteem-building female role models, for baseball lore and inning-by-inning action and for a lively trip into the recent American past, you could hardly do better." N Y Times Book Rev

Halberstam, David

Summer of '49. Morrow 1989 304p il hardcover o.p. pa $14.95   **796.357**

1. Boston Red Sox (Baseball team) 2. New York Yankees (Baseball team)

ISBN 978-0-06-088426-0; 0-06-088426-6

LC 89-2886

"This book is ostensibly about the pennant race between the Yankees and Red Sox {in 1949} and the 'rivalry' between Joe DiMaggio and Ted Williams. . . . It is a study of all the elements and personalities that influenced baseball that year and beyond. Halberstam brings them together in such an enjoyable, interesting, and informative manner that a reader needn't be a baseball fan to appreciate the book." Libr J

Hample, Zack

Watching baseball smarter; a professional fan's guide for beginners, semi-experts, and deeply serious geeks. Vintage 2007 254p il pa $13.95   **796.357**

1. Baseball

ISBN 978-0-307-28032-9; 0-307-28032-2

LC 2007-296737

The author "covers basics such as what to watch for in pitchers, catchers, hitters, fielders and base runners; he also provides answers to such nagging questions as why spectators stretch in the seventh inning and why most ballplayers grab their crotches. . . . Hample hits the equivalent of a reference book home run with his witty and loose style—taking a friendly for-a-fan-by-a-fan approach that doesn't hide his enormous depth of knowledge." Publ Wkly

Hogan, Lawrence D.

Shades of glory; the Negro Leagues and the story of African-American baseball. with a foreword by Jules Tygiel. National Geographic 2006 422p il $26   **796.357**

1. Baseball 2. Negro leagues 3. African American athletes

ISBN 0-7922-5306-X; 978-0-7922-5306-8

LC 2006-273216

This book "traces the history of black baseball from the 19th century to the first great teams, such as the Cuban Giants, and on to the era of the vibrant barnstorming teams from the East Coast, Chicago, and Cuba." Publisher's note

Jamieson, Dave

Mint condition; how baseball cards became an American obsession. Atlantic Monthly Press 2010 272p il $25   **796.357**

1. Baseball cards 2. Collectors and collecting

ISBN 978-0-8021-1939-1; 0-8021-1939-5

"For much of his book, Jamieson seems to be saying that greed and grownups have spoiled card collecting forever. But there's comfort in knowing that the cards have always appealed to baseball lovers and bottom-line business types for their own reasons. Even Jamieson holds out hope that they will find their proper place again in American kids' lives even if it's only in their closets." Minneapolis Star Tribune

Includes bibliographical references

Kenny, Brian

Ahead of the curve; Brian Kenny. Simon & Schuster 2016 368 p. $28   **796.357**

1. Baseball -- History 2. Baseball -- Statistics 3. Baseball -- United States -- Miscellanea

ISBN 1501106333; 9781501106330

LC 2015039474

In this book author Brian Kenny "uses stories from baseball's present and past to examine why we sometimes choose ignorance over information, and how tradition can trump logic, even when directly contradicted by evidence. Kenny wants fans to think critically, reject outmoded groupthink, and embrace the changes that have come with the 'sabermetric era.'" (Publisher's note)

"When Miguel Cabrera captured Major League Baseball's elusive Triple Crown in 2012, Kenny refused to join the adulatory journalists lauding his selection as the

American League's Most Valuable Player. Convinced that two-thirds of the Crown's jewels (namely, batting average and runs batted in) poorly measure a player's performance, Kenny argues that more-sophisticated metrics established Angels outfielder Mike Trout as a more deserving MVP. . . . Recognizing Oakland's Moneyball transformation as a harbinger of things to come, Kenny predicts that as managers grow increasingly data-savvy, they will throw off the restraints of tradition when shifting infielders, setting a batting order, and using the bullpen. Perhaps unwelcome among fans who love the myth and nostalgia of the diamond, this bolt of analytical lightning will make sports talk shows crackle." Booklist

Includes bibliographical references and index

Knight, Molly

The **best** team money can buy; how the Los Angeles Dodgers are fighting to become baseball's new superpower. Molly Knight. Simon & Schuster 2015 336 p. 8 plates; color illustrations (hardback) $26   **796.357**
1. Baseball teams 2. Baseball players 3. Los Angeles Dodgers (Baseball team)
ISBN 1476776296; 9781476776293
LC 2015017287
Author " Molly Knight tells the story of the Dodgers' 2013 and 2014 seasons with detailed, previously unreported revelations. She shares a behind-the-scenes account of the astonishing sale of the Dodgers, and why the team was not overpriced, as well as what the Dodgers actually knew in advance about rookie phenom and Cuban defector Yasiel Puig and how they and teammates handled him during his first two roller-coaster seasons. We learn how close manager Don Mattingly was to losing his job." (Publisher's note)
"A must-read for fans of the Dodgers and all Los Angeles sports teams. Knight's undercover work is like none other. Dodger fanatics, this book is for you." LJ

Kurkjian, Tim

I'm fascinated by sacrifice flies; inside the game we all love. Tim Kurkjian; foreword by George F. Will. St. Martin's Press 2016 256 p. (hardback) $26.99   **796.357**
1. Baseball 2. Baseball -- United States 3. Baseball -- United States -- Miscellanea
ISBN 9781250077936
LC 2015048747
In this book, "in the aftermath of the Steroid Era that stained the game of baseball, at a time when so many players are so rich and therefore have a sense of entitlement that they haven't earned, ESPN baseball commentator Tim Kurkjian shows readers how to love the game more than ever, with incredible insight and stories that are hilarious, heartbreaking, and revealing." (Publisher's note)
"Kurkjian's celebrity and the joyous contents within the covers merit the investment." Booklist

Kurlansky, Mark

The **Eastern** stars; how baseball changed the Dominican town of San Pedro de Macorís. Riverhead Books 2010 272p $25.95   **796.357**
1. Baseball 2. San Pedro de Macorís (Dominican

Republic)
ISBN 978-1-59448-750-7; 1-59448-750-2
LC 2009-41036
"In 1956, Ozzie (Osvaldo) Virgil played his first rookie season with the New York Giants, becoming the first Dominican baseball player to enter the major leagues in America. Over the next half a century, 471 Dominicans played in at least one major league game, and one in six of those players have come from the small sugar mill town of San Pedro de Macorís. . . . Kurlansky weaves a chronicle of the history of San Pedro de Macorís with the stories of young men seeking only to play baseball and escape the drudgery of working the sugarcane fields to produce a colorful social history of sport." Publ Wkly

Includes bibliographical references

Leavy, Jane

Sandy Koufax; a lefty's legacy. HarperCollins Pubs. 2002 xxii, 282p $23.95; pa $13.95 **796.357**
1. Baseball players 2. Baseball players -- United States -- Biography
ISBN 0-06-019533-9; 0-06-093329-1 pa
LC 2002-68722
Leavy discusses the career of Dodgers pitcher Sandy Koufax.
The author "delivers an honest and exquisitely detailed examination of a complex man." Publ Wkly

Leifer, Neil

Neil Leifer: Ballet in the dirt; the golden age of baseball. edited by Eric Kroll; introduction by Ron Shelton; captions by Gabriel Schechter. Taschen 2008 293p il $39.99   **796.357**
1. Baseball -- Pictorial works
ISBN 978-3-8228-4550-9; 3-8228-4550-7
"As a photographer for Sports Illustrated in the 1960s and 1970s, Neil Leifer captured many of baseball's defining moments. But it's the routine, workaday shots he took— Mickey Mantle beating a throw to first, Johnny Bench making a play at the plate or Casey Stengel scolding Yogi Berra during a pitching change—that make this collection fascinating. Here, in gorgeous black and white and Kodachrome color, is the game as it looked before the free-agency craze, before Moneyball, when every player pulled his socks to his knees and performance enhancement meant a big wad to chew." ForbesLife
Includes bibliographical references

Lewis, Michael

★ **Moneyball**; the art of winning an unfair game. Norton 2003 288p $23.95; pa $13.95 **796.357**
1. Baseball 2. Baseball executives
ISBN 0-393-05765-8; 0-393-32481-8 pa
LC 2003-5089
"With so many baseball books to choose from, it is difficult to single out a few as must-haves, but this one comes pretty close." Booklist

McGregor, Robert Kuhn, 1952-

A **Calculus** of Color; The Integration of Baseball's American League. Robert Kuhn McGregor.

McFarland Publishing 2015 277 p. illustrations, portraits $39.95 **796.357**
1. Baseball -- History 2. African American baseball players
ISBN 0786494409; 9780786494408

LC 2015005733

This book, by Robert Kuhn McGregor, "examines the integration of baseball--widely viewed as a triumph--through the experiences of the American League and finds only a limited shift in racial values. The teams accepted few black players and made no effort to alter management structures, and organized baseball remained an institution governed by tradition-bound owners." (Publisher's note)

"McGregor's account makes for a compelling read. A best sports book of 2015, and one that will stand the test of time." LJ

Miller, Sam

The **Only** Rule Is It Has to Work; Our Wild Experiment Building a New Kind of Baseball Team. by Ben Lindbergh and Sam Miller. Henry Holt & Co. 2016 368 p. color illustrations $30 **796.357**
1. Baseball 2. Sports -- Statistics
ISBN 1627795642; 9781627795647

LC 2016005561

This book, by Ben Lindbergh and Sam Miller, is "the ultimate in fantasy baseball. . . . Lindbergh and Miller apply their number-crunching insights to all aspects of assembling and running a team, following one cardinal rule for judging each innovation they try: it has to work. We meet colorful figures like general manager Theo Fightmaster and boundary-breakers like the first openly gay player in professional baseball. Even José Canseco makes a cameo appearance." (Publisher's note)

"With honest and captivating prose, the authors compel readers to care about players that don't make a lot of money yet still have big league dreams and aspirations." LJ

Passan, Jeff

The **Arm**; Inside the Billion-dollar Mystery of the Most Valuable Commodity in Sports. Jeff Passan. HarperCollins 2016 368 p. illustrations $26.99 **796.357**
1. Baseball pitchers
ISBN 0062400363; 9780062400369

This book focuses on baseball pitchers. "Every year, Major League Baseball spends more than $1.5 billion on pitchers. . . . For three years, Jeff Passan, the lead baseball columnist for Yahoo Sports, has traveled the world to better understand the mechanics of the arm and its place in the sport's past, present, and future." (Publisher's note)

"As Passan interviews professionals dealing with the problem—physicians, managers, trainers, pitchers, and even epidemiologists—he reports no magical breakthroughs. But he does give readers an insider's perspective on the threat hanging over every player who takes the mound." Booklist

Posnanski, Joe

The **soul** of baseball; a road trip through Buck O'Neil's America. Morrow 2007 276p $24.95 **796.357**
1. Baseball 2. Baseball players 3. Baseball coaches

4. Baseball managers 5. United States -- Description and travel
ISBN 978-0-06-085403-4; 0-06-085403-0

An account of how the author "spent a year on the road with the iconic Negro Leagues player and manager Buck O'Neil (1911-2006), recording the magnanimous 94-year-old's encounters with scores of fans and his vast repertoire of entertaining stories." Publ Wkly

Ripken, Cal

Play baseball the Ripken way; the complete illustrated guide to the fundamentals. [by] Cal Ripken, Jr. and Bill Ripken with Larry Burke. Random House 2004 236p il hardcover o.p. pa $15.95 **796.357**
1. Baseball
ISBN 1-4000-6122-9; 0-8129-7050-0 pa

LC 2003-66725

"This book is the next best thing to a personal lesson with the man who broke Lou Gehrig's record of playing in 2,632 consecutive games; it's a comprehensive look at all aspects of how to play baseball that will benefit young players and adult weekend warriors." Publ Wkly

Ruck, Rob

Raceball; how the Major Leagues colonized the Black and Latin game. Beacon Press 2010 273p il $25.95 **796.357**
1. Baseball 2. Race relations 3. African American athletes 4. Hispanic American athletes 5. Major League Baseball (Organization)
ISBN 978-0-8070-4805-4; 0-8070-4805-4

LC 2010-37079

The book "blends the intertwined histories of African American and Latin baseball, and their usually ill-fated interactions with Major League Baseball (MLB). . . . [It] recasts conventional notions of baseball history by showing how, in the decades before World War I, Havana became the hub of an international baseball culture. . . . Players in the Negro leagues banned from the major leagues commonly played winter ball in the Caribbean . . . until the early 1940s, along with many white big leaguers supplementing their incomes during the off-season. Cuban teams . . . beat the white major leaguers so frequently that MLB banned teams from playing under their own names, to avoid embarrassment." (Journal of American History)

The author "delves deeply into baseball history to explore the inextricable link between the two phenomena, starting with the struggles of black and Latin players in the segregated pre–Jackie Robinson era, continuing through the painful but inspirational period of integration and into the apex of African-American participation in the 1970s (when more than a quarter of players were black), before exploring the current state of a game dominated by Latin Americans. . . . Compellingly weaves together disparate threads of racial and sporting history." Kirkus

Includes bibliographical references

Sawchik, Travis

Big data baseball; math, miracles, and the end of a 20-year losing streak. Travis Sawchik. Flatiron Books 2015 256 p. (hardback) $26.99 **796.357**
1. Big data 2. Major League Baseball 3. Baseball

-- Statistics 4. Pittsburgh Pirates (Baseball team) 5. Baseball -- Economic aspects -- United States 6. Baseball players -- United States -- Statistics
ISBN 1250063507; 9781250063502

LC 2015011231

In this book on statistics in baseball, author Travis Sawchik presents "the story of how the 2013 Pirates, mired in the longest losing streak in North American pro sports history, adopted drastic big-data strategies to end the drought, make the playoffs, and turn around the franchise's fortunes. It is an entertaining and enlightening underdog story that uses the 2013 Pirates season as the perfect lens to examine the sport's burgeoning big-data movement." (Publisher's note)

"Casual and hard-core baseball fans alike who enjoyed Moneyball are sure to be entertained and informed by this sort-of sequel." LJ

Smith, Red

Red Smith on baseball; the game's greatest writer on the game's greatest years. with a foreword by Ira Berkow. Dee, I.R. 2000 363p il $24.95; pa $18.95 **796.357**
1. Baseball
ISBN 1-56663-289-7; 1-56663-415-6 pa

LC 99-53675

This volume contains columns written from the 1940s to the early 1980s. "Smith's essays on Bobby Thomson's 'shot heard 'round the world,' Mickey Mantle's first game and Don Larsen's no-hit pitching in the 1956 World Series are all worthy of memorization, and his trenchant views on the reserve clause and the night World Series games are strikes down the middle. As a bonus, the collection offers readers a fascinating look at how baseball writing has changed over the years, as have American attitudes." Publ Wkly

Stout, Glenn

Fenway 1912; the birth of a ballpark, a championship season, and Fenway's remarkable first year. Houghton Mifflin Harcourt 2011 xxii, 392p il $26 **796.357**
1. Fenway Park (Boston, Mass.) 2. Boston Red Sox (Baseball team)
ISBN 978-0-547-19562-9

LC 2011016068

"While some sports histories are bone-dry and distant, Stout imbues his account with a unique vibrancy and a razor-sharp intelligence. A wonderful sports book." Booklist

Stump, Al

Cobb; a biography. with a foreword by Jimmie Reese. Algonquin Bks. 1994 436p il hardcover o.p. pa $15.95 **796.357**
1. Baseball players
ISBN 1-56512-144-9 pa

LC 94-26122

The author, who collaborated with Cobb on his 1961 autobiography (My life in baseball), here presents his own version of the life and times of the baseball player

"Emphasizing Cobb's bitter final days, Stump's portrait of the splenetic Hall of Famer is both chilling and oddly moving." Am Libr

Includes bibliographical references

Svrluga, Barry

The **grind**; inside baseball's endless season. Barry Svrluga. Blue Rider Press 2015 192 p. illustrations (hardback) $23.95 **796.357**
1. Major League Baseball 2. Baseball -- Social aspects 3. Baseball -- United States 4. Baseball -- Psychological aspects
ISBN 0399176284; 9780399176289

LC 2015016056

This book, by Barry Svrluga, explores "what's it like to live through sports' longest season, the 162-game Major League Baseball schedule? . . . [This book] captures the frustration, impermanence, and glory felt by the players, the staff, and their families from the start of spring training to the final game of the year." (Publisher's note)

"A quick and enjoyable read for any baseball lover, not just Nationals fans." LJ

Includes bibliographical references and index

Tackett, Michael

The **Baseball** Whisperer; A Small-Town Coach Who Shaped Big League Dreams. Michael Tackett. Houghton Mifflin Harcourt 2016 272 p. illustrations (hardcover) $26 **796.357**
1. Baseball 2. Baseball coaches 3. Baseball -- Iowa -- Clarinda 4. Baseball coaches -- United States -- Biography
ISBN 9780544387645

LC 2015037778

This book, by Michael Tackett, "traces the . . . story of Merl Eberly and his Clarinda A's baseball team, which he tended over the course of five decades, transforming them from a town team to a collegiate summer league powerhouse. Along with Ozzie Smith, future manager Bud Black, and star player Von Hayes, Merl developed scores of major league players. . . . In the process, Merl taught them to be men, insisting on hard work, integrity, and responsibility." (Publisher's note)

"One of baseball's most humanizing backstories." Booklist

Thorn, John

Baseball in the Garden of Eden; the secret history of the early game. Simon & Schuster 2011 365p il $26; ebook $12.99 **796.357**
1. Baseball 2. Baseball -- United States -- History
ISBN 978-0-7432-9403-4; 0-7432-9403-3; 978-1-4391-7021-2 ebook

LC 2010045155

"Thorn writes with authority, precision and humor." Minneapolis Star Tribune

Includes bibliographical references

Tygiel, Jules

Baseball's great experiment; Jackie Robinson and his legacy. [with a new afterword] 25th anniversary ed, expanded ed; Oxford University Press 2008 415p il pa $19.95 **796.357**
1. Baseball 2. Baseball players 3. Army officers 4.

United States -- Race relations
ISBN 978-0-19-533928-4; 0-19-533928-2
LC 2008-273059
First published 1983
A history of the segregation and gradual integration of Afro-American athletes into major league baseball. In addition to Jackie Robinson, the author explores the careers of Larry Doby, Luke Easter, Satchel Paige, and others. Tygiel also notes the vast social and demographic changes wrought by WWII that made integration inevitable
Includes bibliographical references

796.4 Weight lifting, track and field, gymnastics

Hoffer, Richard
Something in the air; American passion and defiance in the 1968 Mexico City Olympics. Free Press 2009 258p il $26 **796.4**
1. Olympic games, 1968 (Mexico City, Mex.)
ISBN 978-1-4165-8894-8; 1-4165-8894-9
LC 2009-09045
"On Oct. 16, [Tommie] Smith won the gold and [John] Carlos the bronze in the 200-meter race. There they stood on the podium, heads hanging almost humbly and gloved fists raised in a defiant black power salute. Something in the Air, Richard Hoffer's skillfully told tale of the Mexico City Olympics, revolves around this arresting image. . . . There were many other dramas played out in Mexico City—involving George Foreman, the long jumper Bob Beamon and the high jumper Dick Fosbury, among others—and Hoffer gracefully brings them all into the same arena. More important, his jaunty but disciplined prose puts the wind at the reader's back and shows us how the leaps, lifts and dashes of 1968 made a significant impact on the civil rights movement and raised the political consciousness of athletes." N Y Times Book Rev
Includes bibliographical references

796.42 Track and field

Brown, Jeff
The **Runner's** Brain; How to Think Smarter to Run Better. Dr. Jeff Brown with Liz Neporent; foreword by Meb Keflezighi. St. Martin's Press 2015 240 p. $15.99 **796.42**
1. Performance 2. Mind and body 3. Running -- Psychological aspects
ISBN 1623363470; 9781623363475
LC 2015034962
This book, by Jeff Brown with Liz Neporent, "shows you how to unlock and capture the miraculous potential of the body's most mysterious and intriguing organ and rewire your mind for a lifetime of athletic success. The book is based on cutting-edge brain science and sports psychology that . . . [is used] in . . . private practice and as part of the medical team of several major road races including the Boston Marathon." (Publisher's note)
This accessible book is a result of Brown's own training and careful study of runners; he is intimately familiar with the considerations runners make, including the decision to compete, picking out "lucky" clothing, overcoming pre-race jitters and post-race blues, and "psych yourself up" for all types of weather. It will appeal to and aid runners of all levels and backgrounds, and perhaps those who aren't runners yet." Publisher's Weekly

Burfoot, Amby
Runner's world complete book of running; everything you need to run for weight loss, fitness, and competition. edited by Amby Burfoot. Rev. & updated ed.; Rodale; Distributed by Macmillan 2009 312p il pa $21.99 **796.42**
1. Running
ISBN 978-1-60529-579-4 pa
LC 2009-33150
First published 1997
Topics covered include: nutrition, injury prevention and treatment, shoe selection, mental readiness, and marathon preparation.

Caesar, Ed
Two hours; the quest to run the impossible marathon. Ed Caesar. Simon & Schuster 2015 256 p. maps (Hardcover) $26 **796.42**
1. Athletes 2. Marathon running 3. Marathon running -- Training
ISBN 145168584X; 9781451685848
LC 2014043224
This book, by Ed Caesar, is "about marathon running--including the current heated battle among the world's elite runners to reach the two-hour barrier--and how psychology, technology, economics, and the latest science affect the potential of human performance. . . . [The author] traces the history of the marathon as well as the science, physiology, and psychology involved in running so fast, for so long." (Publisher's note)
"Though the books are different in intent, readers might want to try David Epstein's The Sports Gene or Christopher McDougall's Born To Run." LJ

Dixon, Matt
The **well-**built triathlete; turning potential into performance. Matt Dixon. VeloPress 2014 368 p. illustrations (pbk. : alk. paper) $24.95 **796.42**
1. Triathletes
ISBN 1937715116; 9781937715113
LC 2014941073
In this book, "elite triathlon coach Matt Dixon reveals the approach he has used to turn age-group triathletes into elite professionals. . . . Dixon details the four pillars of performance that form the foundation of his highly successful purplepatch fitness program, showing triathletes of all abilities how they can become well-built triathletes and perform better year after year." (Publisher's note)

Douglas, Scott
Meb for mortals; how to run, think and eat like a champion marathoner. Meb Keflezighi with Scott Douglas. Rodale 2015 xi, 196 p.p illustrations $19.99; (ebook) $19.99 **796.42**
1. Marathon running 2. Marathon running -- Training

3. Long-distance running -- Training
ISBN 1623365473; 9781623365479; 9781623365486
LC 2016301845

This book, by Meb Keflezighi with Scott Douglas, "describes in unprecedented detail how three-time Olympian Keflezighi prepares to take on the best runners in the world. More important, the book shows everyday runners how to implement the training, nutritional, and mental principles that have guided him throughout his long career, which in addition to the 2014 Boston win includes an Olympic silver medal and the 2009 New York City Marathon title." (Publisher's note)

"The format is clean and the writing is simple and strong, all making this book a valuable tool for anyone with their sights set on running a marathon." Pub Wkly

Engle, Charlie

Running Man; A Memoir. Charlie Engle. Simon & Schuster 2016 304 p. (ebook) $19.99; (hardcover) $26　　　　　　　**796.42**
1. Marathon running 2. Long-distance runners
ISBN 9781476785806; 1476785783; 9781476785783

This memoir by ultra-marathon runner Charlie Engle chronicles "his globe-spanning races, his record-breaking run across the Sahara Desert, and how running helped him overcome drug addiction and an unjust stint in federal prison. After a decade-long addiction to crack cocaine and alcohol, Engle hit bottom with a near-fatal six-day binge that ended in a hail of bullets. As Engle got sober, he turned to running, which became his lifeline, his pastime, and his salvation." (Publisher's note)

"Similar to the journey of self-discovery chronicled in Rich Roll's Finding Ultra (2012), this is a fast-paced, well-written account of a man who accepts pain, pushes beyond imagined limits, and ultimately finds redemption and peace." Booklist

Finn, Adharanand

The **Way** of the Runner; A Journey into the Fabled World of Japanese Running. by Adharanand Finn. W W Norton & Co Inc 2016 326 p. $26.95　　**796.42**
1. Japan 2. Running 3. Marathon running
ISBN 1681771217; 9781681771212

This book, by Adharanand Finn, focuses on "Japan, the most running-obsessed nation on earth. . . . A 135-mile relay race, or "ekiden" is the country's biggest annual sporting event. Thousands of professional runners compete for corporate teams in some of the most competitive races in the world. The legendary "marathon monks" run a thousand marathons in a thousand days to reach spiritual enlightenment. Yet so much of Japan's running culture remains a mystery to the outside world." (Publisher's note)

"An elegant, well-written pleasure even for readers with no particular interest in foot racing." Kirkus

Heminsley, Alexandra

Running like a girl; notes on learning to run. Alexandra Heminsley. Scribner 2013 224 p. (ebook) $15.99; (trade paper) $15　　　　　**796.42**
1. Running 2. Running -- Anecdotes 3. Women runners -- United States -- Biography 4. Runners (Sports) --

United States -- Biography
ISBN 9781451697179; 1451697155; 9781451697124; 9781451697155
LC 2013018909

This memoir "tells the story of . . . how [author] Alexandra [Heminsley] makes running a part of her life, and reaps the rewards: not just the obvious things, like weight loss, health, and glowing skin; but self-confidence and immeasurable daily pleasure, along with a new closeness to her father—a marathon runner—and her brother, with whom she ultimately runs her first marathon." (Publisher's note)

Joyner-Kersee, Jackie

A **kind** of grace; the autobiography of the world's greatest female athlete. {by} Jackie Joyner-Kersee with Sonja Steptoe. Warner Bks. 1997 310p il $28　　　　　　　　　　　　**796.42**
1. African American athletes 2. Heptathletes 3. Olympic athletes 4. Child benefactors 5. Basketball players
ISBN 0-446-52248-1
LC 97-14966

"A competent account of an admirable life." Booklist

McDougall, Christopher

★ **Born** to run; a hidden tribe, superathletes, and the greatest race the world has never seen. Alfred A. Knopf 2009 287p $24.95　　　　　　**796.42**
1. Marathon running 2. Tarahumara Indians
ISBN 0-307-26630-3; 978-0-307-26630-9
LC 2009-922861

"Implausibly difficult marathons, hundreds of miles long, and the ultra-elite competitive runners who tackle them for fun. A hidden, almost mythical, tribe in Mexico untouched by modern disease. Shoe manufacturers driven by corporate greed to sustain an industry that has created modern running injuries. An anthropological study of homo sapiens physiology and the course we took to survive while Neanderthals died out. It may seem farfetched, but Born to Run entwines all those strands and even pop-culture references into an engaging and inspirational read." PopMatters

Robbins, Liz

A **race** like no other; 26.2 miles through the streets of New York. Harper 2008 336p il map $24.99　　　　　　　　　　　　　**796.42**
1. Marathon running
ISBN 978-0-06-137313-8; 0-06-137313-3
LC 2009-275043

A narrative account of the 2007 New York City marathon interweaves the stories of professional and amateur participants, from Great Britain's world-record holder Paula Radcliffe and Latvian two-time winner Jelena Prokopcuka to South African former champion Hendrick Ramaala and a young cancer survivor running his first race.

The author "allows readers to experience the event without ever putting on a pair of running shoes." Publ Wkly
Includes bibliographical references

Wade, Becky

Run the World; My 3,500-Mile Journey Through Running Cultures Around the Globe. Becky Wade.

HarperCollins 2016 288 p. illustrations (paperback) $15.99 **796.42**

1. Marathon running 2. Women athletes -- United States
ISBN 9780062416438; 006241643X

This book by Becky Wade tells "the story of her year-long exploration of diverse global running communities from England to Ethiopia—9 countries, 72 host families, and over 3,500 miles of running—investigating unique cultural approaches to the sport and revealing the secrets to the success of runners all over the world. . . . What she encountered far exceeded her expectations and changed her outlook into the sport she loved." (Publisher's note)

"Every so often a book comes along that becomes a cult classic for competitive runners but also has appeal to a broader audience... and this terrific debut is sure to join their ranks." Booklist

Includes bibliographical references (pages [267]-271).

796.425   Non-track races

Bede, Pam Nisevich

The **Runner's** world big book of marathon and half-marathon training; winning strategies, inpiring stories, and the ultimate training tools. Jennifer Van Allen ... [et.al.] Rodale 2012 xiii, 290 p.p illustrations $21.99; (ebook) $21.99 **796.425**

1. Marathon running 2. Marathon running -- Training
ISBN 1609616847; 9781609616847; 9781609619152; 9781609617080

LC 2012010217

This book, by Jennifer Van Allen, Bart Yasso, and Amby Burfoot, with Pam Nisevich Bede, "gives readers the core essentials of marathon training, nutrition, injury prevention, and more." (Publisher's note)

Includes bibliographical references (p. 273-278) and index

796.47   Tumbling, trampolining, acrobatics, contortion

Wall, Duncan

The **ordinary** acrobat; a journey into the wondrous world of the circus, past and present. Duncan Wall. Alfred A. Knopf 2013 336 p. (hardcover) $26.95 **796.47**

1. Circus 2. Acrobats and acrobatics 3. Circus -- History 4. Acrobats -- Biography 5. Circus performers -- Biography
ISBN 0307271722; 9780307271723

LC 2012038250

This book, by Duncan Wall, provides the "story of a young man's plunge into the . . . . world of the circus--taking readers deep into circus history and its renaissance as a contemporary art form, and behind the (tented) walls of France's most prestigious circus school. When Duncan Wall . . . applied on a whim to the training program at the École Nationale des Arts du Cirque . . . [he] was, to his surprise, accepted." (Publisher's note)

796.48   Olympic games

Goldblatt, David

The **Games**; A Global History of the Olympics. by David Goldblatt. W W Norton & Co Inc 2016 464 p. $29.95 **796.48**

1. Olympic games 2. Olympic athletes
ISBN 0393292770; 9780393292770

This book, by David Goldblatt, presents the "history of . . . the Olympics. He tells the epic story of the Games from their reinvention in Athens in 1896 to the present day, chronicling classic moments of sporting achievement. . . . He goes beyond the medal counts to explore how international conflicts have played out at the Olympics, including the role of the Games in Fascist Germany and Italy, the Cold War, and the struggles of the postcolonial world for recognition." (Publisher's note)

Spivey, Nigel Jonathan

The **ancient** Olympics; [by] Nigel Spivey. Oxford University Press 2004 xxi, 273p il $28; pa $14.95 **796.48**

1. Olympic games
ISBN 0-19-280433-2; 0-19-280604-1 pa

LC 2004-46147

This book "lets us imagine both the strangeness and the glory that surrounded sports in its infancy." Christ Sci Monit

Includes bibliographical references

796.5   Outdoor life

Citro, Asia

150 + screen-free activities for kids; The Very Best and Easiest Playtime Activities from FunAtHomeWithKids.com! Asia Citro, MEd, creator of Fun at Home with Kids. Adams Media 2014 255 p. color illustrations $18.99 **796.5**

1. Outdoor recreation 2. Creative activities 3. Outdoor recreation for children 4. Creative activities and seat work
ISBN 1440576157; 9781440576157

LC 2014021922

With this book, by Asia Citro, "your family will rediscover the spirit of imaginative play! These fun activities help develop your child's creativity and skills--all without a screen in sight. Featuring step-by-step instructions and beautiful photographs, each budget-friendly project will keep your child entertained, engaged, and learning all day long." (Publisher's note)

Includes bibliographical references and index

796.51   Walking

Berger, Karen

America's great hiking trails; Appalachian, Pacific Crest, Continental Divide, North Country, Ice Age, Potomac Heritage, Florida, Natchez Trace, Arizona, Pacific Northwest, New England. Karen Berger, Photography by Bart Smith. Rizzoli Interna-

tional Publications 2014 335 p. color ill., color maps (hardcover : alk. paper) $50   **796.51**
1. Hiking
ISBN 0789327414; 9780789327413

LC 2014936348

This book, by Karen Berger, is a "celebration of more than 50,000 miles of America's most iconic trails. . . . Each featured trail has its own section, complete with a map and photo gallery, and the reader explores what makes it one of the most magnificent hiking experiences anywhere in the world. Trail histories accompany detailed hiker-friendly descriptions that highlight the most scenic spots, with suggestions for shorter weekend and day hikes." (Publisher's note)

Includes bibliographical references (p. 334-335)

Solnit, Rebecca

Wanderlust; a history of walking. Viking 2000 326p il hardcover o.p. pa $15   **796.51**
1. Hiking 2. Walking 3. Voyages and travels
ISBN 0-14-028601-2 pa

LC 99-41153

The author presents a "look at how the act of walking . . . has influenced our history, our science, our literature, and the very way that we see ourselves as human beings. Drawing on a multitude of diverse disciplines, Solnit illustrates that walking has led to some of the best, and worst, incidents in all of history." Booklist

Includes bibliographical references

Spira, Timothy P.

Waterfalls and wildflowers in the Southern Appalachians; thirty great hikes. Timothy P. Spira. University of North Carolina Press 2015 304 p. illustrations, maps (pbk : alk. paper) $24   **796.51**
1. Waterfalls 2. Wild flowers 3. Appalachian Region 4. Appalachian Region, Southern -- Guidebooks 5. Hiking -- Appalachian Region, Southern -- Guidebooks 6. Trails -- Appalachian Region, Southern -- Guidebooks 7. Waterfalls -- Appalachian Region, Southern -- Guidebooks 8. Wild flowers -- Appalachian Region, Southern -- Guidebooks 9. Natural history -- Appalachian Region, Southern -- Guidebooks
ISBN 1469622645; 9781469622644

LC 2014044782

Author "Tim Spira's guidebook links waterfalls and wildflowers in a spectacularly beautiful region famous for both. Leading you to gorgeous waterfalls in Virginia, North Carolina, Tennessee, South Carolina, and Georgia, the book includes many hikes in the Great Smoky Mountains National Park and along the Blue Ridge Parkway." (Publisher's note)

"Biologist's will savor this handy hiking guide to a particularly beautiful region." LJ

796.52   Walking and exploring by kind of terrain

Denny, Glen

Valley walls; a memoir of climbing and living in yosemite. Glen Denny. Yosemite Conservancy 2016 240 p. (alk. paper) $18.95   **796.52**
1. Mountaineering 2. Yosemite National Park (Calif.)
ISBN 9781930238633

LC 2015956065

This memoir, by Glen Denny, "reveals a young man's coming of age and provides a vivid look at Yosemite's early climbing culture. He relates such precarious achievements as hauling water in glass gallon jugs up the east face of Washington Column, nailing the 750-foot Rostrum in a punishing heat wave, and dangling overnight on El Capitan's Dihedral Wall in a lightning storm." (Publisher's note)

"Climbing newcomers will benefit from the glossary, but the love Denny has for the climbs, climbers, and life during this era make this a must-have for outdoor enthusiasts." LJ

Isserman, Maurice

Continental divide; a history of American mountaineering. Maurice Isserman. W W Norton & Co Inc 2016 448 p. illustrations (hardcover) $28.95 **796.52**
1. Mountains 2. Mountaineering 3. Mountaineering -- United States -- History
ISBN 0393068501; 9780393068504

LC 2016000548

In this book author "Maurice Isserman tells the history of American mountaineering through four centuries of landmark climbs and first ascents. Mountains were originally seen as obstacles to civilization; over time they came to be viewed as places of redemption and renewal. Isserman traces the evolving social, cultural, and political roles mountains played in shaping the country." (Publisher's note)

"This broad sweep of American mountaineering history will satisfy general history readers and outdoor adventurers alike." LJ

Includes bibliographical references and index

Tabor, James M.

Blind descent; the quest to discover the deepest place on earth. Random House 2010 304p $26; ebook $26   **796.52**
1. Caves 2. Explorers 3. Spelunkers 4. Structural engineers
ISBN 978-1-4000-6767-1; 978-1-58836-994-9 ebook

LC 2009-33942

"The author examines the two polar opposites at the head of each of two major cave-diving expeditions: the win-at-all-costs, classic alpha-male, American Bill Stone, who led Mexican cave dives in Cheve and Huatula; and mild-mannered organization man, Ukrainian Alexander Klimchouk, who spearheaded the exploration of his country's notorious Krubera cave. Only one of these men came away with the distinction of having descended deeper into the earth's core than anyone else. Tabor expertly fashions a fly-on-the-wall narrative from the firsthand accounts of Stone, Klimchouk and their supporting casts of death-defying followers. . . . A fascinating and informative introduction to the sport of cave diving, as well as a dramatic portrayal of a significant man-vs.-nature conflict." Kirkus

Includes bibliographical references

Taylor, Joseph E.

Pilgrims of the vertical; Yosemite rock climbers and nature at risk. [by] Joseph E Taylor III. Harvard University Press 2010 368p il map $29.95 **796.52**

1. Mountaineering 2. Yosemite National Park (Calif.)
ISBN 978-0-674-05287-1; 0-674-05287-0

LC 2010-21578

Yosemite "has been a climber magnet for decades, and it was here that many of rock climbing's highly ritualized set of norms and mores evolved. . . . [This book] is at once a chronicle of how the sport evolved in Yosemite and a fascinating social history that considers climbing in the larger context of American life. . . . For the general reader, the book makes a fine introduction to the history of climbing and Yosemite's special place in its development. For climbers, 'Pilgrims of the Vertical' offers a somewhat idiosyncratic view of their sport." Wall Street J

Includes bibliographical references

796.522   Mountains, hills, rocks

Boukreev, Anatoli

The **climb**; tragic ambitions on Everest. [by] Anatoli Boukreev and G. Weston Dewalt. St. Martin's Press 1997 255p il hardcover o.p. pa $14.95 **796.522**

1. Mountaineering 2. Mount Everest Expedition (1996)
ISBN 0-312-20637-2 pa

LC 97-23194

"This is a first-person account of the tragic climbing experience in May 1996 on Mount Everest that left eight hikers dead and several others struggling to stay alive. . . . Fast-paced and easy to read, Boukreev's story of adventure and survival will remain in the reader's memory long after the book is finished." Libr J

Coburn, Broughton

Everest: mountain without mercy; introduction by Tim Cahill, afterword by David Breashears. National Geographic Soc. 1997 256p il maps hardcover o.p. pa $24 **796.522**

1. Mountaineering 2. Mount Everest Expedition (1996)
ISBN 0-7922-7014-2; 0-7922-6984-5 pa

LC 97-10765

"Bringing an understated yet powerful Buddhist/Sherpa ethical perspective to the tragedy on Everest chronicled in Jon Krakauer's Into Thin Air, Coburn reports on the IMAX film crew who participated in the rescue effort when the May 1996 expeditions led by guides Rob Hall and Scott Fischer ended in death and crippling injury." Publ Wkly

Conefrey, Mick

The **Ghosts** of K2; The Epic Saga of the First Ascent. by Mick Conefrey. Oneworld Publica-

tions 2015 336 p. 8 plates; illustrations; maps $27.99 **796.522**

1. Mountaineering 2. Mountains -- Pakistan
ISBN 1780745958; 9781780745954

This book on the mountain K2, by Mick Conefrey, "describes the early attempts to reach the summit and provides a fascinating exploration of the first ascent's complex legacy. From the drug-addicted occultist Aleister Crowley to Achille Compagnoni and Lindo Lacedelli, the Italian duo who finally made it to the summit, [it] charts how a slew of great men became fixated on this legendary mountain." (Publisher's note)

"An absorbing chronicle of K2's early history that all fans of mountaineering will enjoy." LJ

Jamling Tenzing Norgay

Touching my father's soul; a Sherpa's journey to the top of Everest. [by] Jamling Tenzing Norgay with Broughton Coburn. HarperSanFrancisco 2001 316p il map hardcover o.p. pa $15.95 **796.522**

1. Mountaineering 2. Mountaineers 3. Mount Everest Expedition (1996)
ISBN 0-06-251688-4 pa

LC 00-68723

This "work has considerably more depth than an exposition of the climb. . . . The son's climb is a pilgrimage exploring his relationship to his father, his Sherpa culture, and Buddhism. It is also a fascinating look into the world of climbers and their relationship to the Sherpas who risk their lives to assist them." Booklist

Krakauer, Jon, 1954-

★ **Into** thin air; a personal account of the Mount Everest disaster. Villard Bks. 1997 xx, 293p il $25.95; pa $14.95 **796.522**

1. Mountaineering 2. Mount Everest Expedition (1996)
3. Mountaineering -- Personal narratives
ISBN 0-679-45752-6; 0-385-49478-5 pa

LC 96-30031

This is an account of the author's May 1996 Mount Everest climbing expedition in which twelve fellow climbers died during a snow storm

"This tense, harrowing story is as mesmerizing and hard to put down as any well-written adventure novel." SLJ

Includes bibliographical references

Lewis-Jones, Huw

Conquest of Everest; George Lowe, Huw Lewis-Jones. Thames & Hudson Inc. 2013 240 p. (hardcover) $39.95 **796.522**

1. Mount Everest (China and Nepal)
ISBN 9780500544235

LC 2012947781

This book about Mount Everest "features a trove of original photographs and other rare materials from the George Lowe collection, many unpublished, complemented by classic images from the final ascent. Stunning landscapes, candid portraits, and action shots describe the day-by-day moments of the historic expedition as never before." (Publisher's note)

Trailside (Television program)

Rock climbing; a trailside guide. illustrations by Ron Hildebrand. Norton 2003 191p il (Trailside series guide) pa $18.95   **796.522**
1. Mountaineering
ISBN 0-393-31653-X
LC 96-52821

"Designed to be carried on the trail, this will ease beginners into the sport of rock climbing, with step-by-step illustrated tutorials, safety and first-aid tips, and more." Libr J

Includes bibliographical references

Zuckerman, Peter

Buried in the sky; the extraordinary story of the Sherpa climbers on K2's deadliest day. Peter Zuckerman and Amanda Padoan. W.W. Norton & Co. 2012 285 p. (hardcover) $26.95   **796.522**
1. Mountaineering 2. Mountains -- Pakistan 3. Sherpa (Nepalese people) 4. Outdoor life -- Accidents 5. Mountaineers -- Pakistan -- K2 (Mountain) 6. Mountaineering -- Pakistan -- K2 (Mountain) 7. Sherpa (Nepalese people) -- Social life and customs 8. Mountaineering accidents -- Pakistan -- K2 (Mountain)
ISBN 0393079880; 9780393079883
LC 2012008490

In this book, "Peter Zuckerman and Amanda Padoan explore the intersecting lives of [the Shirpas] Chhiring Dorje Sherpa and Pasang Lama, following them from their villages high in the Himalaya to the slums of Kathmandu, across the glaciers of Pakistan to K2 Base Camp. When disaster strikes in the Death Zone, Chhiring finds Pasang stranded on an ice wall, without an axe, waiting to die. The rescue that follows has become the stuff of mountaineering legend." (Publisher's note)

Includes bibliographical references and index.

796.54   Camping

White, Dan, 1967-

Under the stars; How America Fell in Love with Camping. Dan White. Henry Holt & Co. 2016 416 p. illustrations (hardback) $28   **796.54**
1. Camping 2. Outdoor life 3. Camping -- United States 4. Outdoor life -- United States
ISBN 9781627791953
LC 2015042691

In this book, author "Dan White travels the nation to experience firsthand—and sometimes face first—how the American wilderness transformed from the devil's playground into a source of adventure, relaxation, and renewal. Whether he's camping nude in cougar country, being attacked by wildlife while 'glamping,' or crashing a girls-only adventure for urban teens, . . . White seeks to animate the evolution of outdoor recreation." (Publisher's note)

"An adventurous, informative, and irreverent look at outdoor recreation." Booklist

Includes bibliographical references and index

796.6   Cycling and related activities

Bambrick, Yvonne

The **urban** cycling survival guide; need-to-know skills and strategies for biking in the city. by Yvonne Bambrick, illustrated by Marc Ngui. ECW Press 2015 208 p. illustrations (paperback) $16.95 **796.6**
1. Cycling 2. City and town life
ISBN 9781770412187; 1770412182

This book, by Yvonne Bambrick, illustrated by Marc Ngui, "is an accessible, straight-forward pocket guide that helps cyclists new to the urban environment negotiate all the challenges, obstacles, and rules--spoken and unspoken--that come with sharing the roads . . . , from picking the bike that's right for you to smart riding strategies, tips for drivers, and bike maintenance." (Publisher's note)

"This modern guide is filled with great advice that will help people become more confident and educated bike riders. For all libraries." LJ

Bike Snob

The **enlightened** cyclist; commuter angst, dangerous drivers, and other obstacles on the path to two-wheeled transcendence. Bike Snob NYC. Chronicle Books 2012 220 p. ill. (hardback) $16.95   **796.6**
1. Cycling 2. Transportation 3. Bicycle commuting
ISBN 1452105006; 9781452105000
LC 2011041747

This book, by the anonymous urban cyclist "BikeSnob-NYC," "takes on the trials and triumphs of bike commuting with snark, . . . asking the question: If we become better commuters, will that make us better people? From the deadly sins of biking to tactics for dealing with cars, pedestrians, and other cyclists, this primer on bike travel is . . . [written for] cyclists new and seasoned alike." (Publisher's note)

Byrne, David

Bicycle diaries. Viking 2009 297p il   **796.6**
1. Bicycle touring 2. Singers 3. Songwriters 4. Rock musicians 5. Urban transportation 6. Cycling -- Environmental aspects
ISBN 0670021148; 9780670021147
LC 2009-09390

This book contains accounts of Byrne's travels in New York and other cities, mainly by bicycle.

"In these random musings over many years while cycling through such places as Sydney, Australia; Manila, Philippines; San Francisco; or his home of New York, the former Talking Head, artist and author . . . offers his frank views on urban planning, art and postmodern civilization in general. . . . Candid and self-deprecating, Byrne offers a work that is as engaging as it is cerebral and informative." Publ Wkly

Moore, Tim

Gironimo! Riding the Very Terrible 1914 Tour of Italy. by Tim Moore. W.W. Norton & Co. Inc. 2015 368 p. illustrations $27.95   **796.6**
1. Bicycle racing 2. Bicycle touring 3. Bicycles -- History
ISBN 1605987786; 9781605987781

This book, by Tim Moore, focuses on the "1914 Giro d'Italia: The hardest bike race in history. Eighty-one riders started and only eight finished after enduring cataclysmic storms, roads strewn with nails, and even the loss of an eye by one competitor. . . . To truly capture the essence of what these riders endured a century ago, Tim acquires the ruined husk of a gear-less, wooden-wheeled 1914 road bike, some maps, and an alarming period outfit." (Publisher's note)

"Readers may tire of the repeated references to the state of his "intimate parts," but, as in his previous cycling book, French Revolutions (2002), Moore's patented combination of humor and travelogue proves thoroughly engaging." Booklist

Petersen, Grant

Just ride; a radically practical guide to riding your bike: equipment, health, safety, attitude. by Grant Petersen. Workman Pub. 2012 212 p. illustrations (alk. paper) $13.95   **796.6**
1. Cycling 2. Bicycles 3. Cycling -- Handbooks, manuals, etc 4. Bicycles -- Handbooks, manuals, etc
ISBN 0761155589; 9780761155584
LC 2012001429

This book, by Grant Petersen, encourages readers to "ride like you did when you were a kid-- just get on your bike and discover the pure joy of riding it. . . . Petersen shares a lifetime of unexpected facts, controversial opinions, expert techniques, and his own maverick philosophy. . . . Also includes chapters on Accessories, Upkeep, and Technicalities as well as a final chapter titled 'Velosophy' that includes the essential, memorable thought: Your Bike Is a Toy-- Have Fun with It." (Publisher's note)

"Smell what Petersen is cooking*. *Except for this funny idea he has that the poncho is the ultimate cycling garment." LJ

Weiss, Eben

The **ultimate** bicycle owner's manual; the universal guide to bikes, riding, and everything for beginner and seasoned cyclists. Eben Weiss. Black Dog & Leventhal 2016 240 p. color illustrations (paperback) $19.99   **796.6**
1. Cycling 2. Bicycles 3. Cycling -- Handbooks, manuals, etc 4. Bicycles -- Maintenance and repair -- Handbooks, manuals, etc
ISBN 9780316352673; 9780316352680
LC 2015041449

In this book, cyclist and author Eben Weiss "makes his vast experience and practical advice available to bike 'newbies' and veterans alike. Chapters cover Obtaining a Bike, Understanding Your Bike, Maintaining Your Bike, Operating Your Bike, Off-Road Riding, Coexisting with Drivers, Competitive Cycling, Bike Travel, Cycling with Kids, and What the Future Holds for Bikes in our Communities." (Publisher's note)

"A blogger and advocate of everything related to bicycling, Weiss (The Enlightened Cyclist; Bike Snob) uses passionate, smart, and witty prose to inspire and educate people interested in cycling." LJ

796.62   Bicycle racing

Hamilton, Tyler

The **Secret** Race; Inside the Hidden World of the Tour de France: Doping, Cover-ups, and Winning at All Costs. Bantam Books 2012 290 p. $28   **796.62**
1. Drug abuse 2. Bicycle racing 3. Sports -- Corrupt practices
ISBN 0345530411; 9780345530417

This book, by Tyler Hamilton and Daniel Coyle, winner of the 2012 William Hill Sports Book of the Year Award, offers a "look at the world of professional cycling--and the doping issue surrounding this sport and its most iconic rider, Lance Armstrong. . . . [The book] . . . takes us . . . inside a shadowy . . . world of unscrupulous doctors, . . . team directors, and athletes so relentlessly driven to succeed that they would do anything . . . to gain the edge they need to win." (Publisher's note)

Leonard, Max

Lanterne Rouge; The Last Man in the Tour de France. by Max Leonard. Yellow Jersey 2014 272 p. 13 plates; color illustrations $26.95   **796.62**
1. Tour de France (Bicycle race)
ISBN 0224091999; 1605987867; 9780224091992; 9781605987866

This book about the Tour de France, by Max Leonard, "tells the forgotten, often inspirational and occasionally absurd stories of the last-placed rider. We learn of stage winners and former yellow jerseys who tasted life at the other end of the bunch; the breakaway leader who stopped for a bottle of wine and then took a wrong turn; the doper whose drug cocktail accidentally slowed him down and the rider who was recognized as the most combative despite finishing at the back." (Publisher's note)

"Writer and amateur cyclist Leonard challenges what it means to achieve greatness through the mythos of the sport's underdogs. The author provides little information about the competitors we recognize as champions of the sport, instead populating the narrative with a strange sort of idol worship." Kirkus

796.7   Driving motor vehicles

Lyon, Danny

The **bikeriders**; by Danny Lyon. Chronicle Books Distributed in Canada by Raincoast Books 2003 121 p. ill. (some col.) $22.95   **796.7**
1. Photojournalism 2. Motorcyclists -- United States 3. Motorcycling -- United States -- Pictorial works 4. Motorcycling -- United States 5. Motorcyclists -- United States -- Portraits
ISBN 9780811841610; 081184160X; 0811841618
LC 2003055073

This book by Danny Lyon is "a seminal work of modern photojournalism, this landmark collection of photographs and interviews documents the abandon and risk implied in the name of the gang Lyon belonged to: the Chicago Outlaw Motorcycle Club. . . . This new edition includes . . .15 additional black-and-white photographs and 14 color prints-

-long thought missing--of works originally published in black-and-white." (Publisher's note)

"This Chronicle reprint includes all of the original material plus 15 new photos, and a new preface by the author." LJ

796.72   Automobile racing

Baime, A. J.

Go like hell; Ford, Ferrari, and their battle for speed and glory at Le Mans. Houghton Mifflin Harcourt 2009 304p il map $26   **796.72**

1. Sports cars 2. Automobile racing 3. Ferrari SpA 4. Ford Motor Co.

ISBN 978-0-618-82219-5; 0-618-82219-4

LC 2008-52948

"Baime tells an exciting story at a pace that manages to keep up with the drivers." Libr J

Includes bibliographical references

Busbee, Jay

Earnhardt Nation; The Full-throttle Saga of Nascar's First Family. Jay Busbee. HarperCollins 2016 352 p. illustrations (chiefly color) (hardcover) $26.99   **796.72**

ISBN 9780062367716; 0062367714

This book, by Jay Busbee, offers "portrait of the larger-than-life first family of NASCAR, the Earnhardts, and the rise of the world's fastest stock car racing organization. . . . Covering all the white-knuckle races, including the final lap at the Daytona 500 that claimed the life of the Intimidator, . . . [it] goes deep into the fast-paced world of NASCAR, its royal family's obsession with speed, and their struggle with celebrity." (Publisher's note)

"A smart look at an iconic but not necessarily admirable superstar and at what goes on behind the scenes in big-money sports."

Includes bibliographical references (pages 321-333).

Hawley, Samuel Jay

Speed duel; the inside story of the land speed record in the sixties. [by] Sam Hawley. Firefly Books 2010 360p il pa $24.95   **796.72**

1. Automobile racing 2. Automobile racing drivers

ISBN 978-1-55407-633-8

"Even readers who don't know a spark plug from a gear shift will be transfixed by Hawley's white-knuckled account of the ever-escalating competition to hold the Land Speed Record in the '60s and early '70s. Drawing from countless articles, profiles, documentaries, and interviews with the men and women who were there, Hawley traces the sport's evolution from its first four-wheeled record of 39mph in 1898, to today's jet-propelled 700mph-plus, recounting the creation, testing, and repair of legendary cars like the humble Green Monster and the charismatic Spirit of America." Publ Wkly

Includes filmography and bibliographical references

796.8   Combat sports

At the fights; American writers on boxing. edited by George Kimball & John Schulian; foreword by Colum McCann. Library of America 2011 517p $35   **796.8**

1. Boxing 2. Boxers (Sports)

ISBN 1-59853-092-5; 978-1-59853-092-6

This collection includes "work by the likes of Pete Hamill, Norman Mailer, Joyce Carol Oates, George Plimpton, David Remnick, Budd Schulberg and Gay Talese." (N Y Times Book Rev) Index.

"The book's editors accomplish several things in 'At the Fights.' They sample the work of devotees such as the incomparable A.J. Liebling and Gene Tunney on his defeat of Jack Dempsey, and of comparative outsiders such as James Baldwin and Joyce Carol Oates, whose novelistic fascination with violence, class and gender inevitably led her to ponder the boxing life. The collection plots a zigzag course through a century of boxing milestones, offering a striking range of approaches to the subject. It also throws open controversies racial, moral, legal and medical that have swirled around the sport since it first attained a sort of legitimacy. . . . [This anthology] presupposes an interest in writing as much as in boxing. Many of its contributors, such as Baldwin, Vic Ziegel, Pete Hamill, Bill Barich and Katherine Dunn, pay as much or more attention to stories tributary to fights as to the ring contests themselves. Observations in many different registers form an engrossing counterpoint as the book proceeds." San Francisco Chron

Cohen, Richard

By the sword; a history of gladiators, musketeers, samurai, swashbucklers, and Olympic champions. Random House 2002 xxiv, 519p il $29.95; pa $15.95   **796.8**

1. Fencing

ISBN 0-375-50417-6; 0-8129-6966-9 pa

LC 2002-21309

This is a worldwide history of sword fighting from Ancient Egypt to the present which considers its role in combat and sports, word origins and customs, and the fencing skills of politicians and actors

"A fascinating story told with literary verve and the pride of a longtime practitioner; highly recommended." Libr J

Includes bibliographical references

Hauser, Thomas

Boxing is-- reflections on the sweet science. The University of Arkansas Press 2010 270p pa $22.50   **796.8**

1. Boxing

ISBN 978-1-55728-942-1

LC 2010-15354

"The collection begins with a detailed biographical examination of the career of Sugar Ray Robinson, considered by many to be the greatest pound-for-pound fighter ever. It's a sadly familiar tale of poverty, ascendancy, fame, and decline, related in a respectful, objective style. The rest of the book is focused on the boxing events of 2009, from the high-profile career of Manny Pacquiao to the progress of several relatively unknown young fighters learning the trade in New

York's gyms. Hauser also explores the business end of boxing, especially its painful relationship with television, but above all, he is drawn to the people of the sport: the fighters, trainers, promoters, and hangers-on. Virtually every piece is notable for its carefully drawn characters who will linger on the edges of readers' minds long after the book has been shelved." Booklist

Includes bibliographical references

Howley, Kerry

Thrown; Kerry Howley. Sarabande Books 2014 paperback $15.95 **796.8**
1. Sports -- Fiction 2. Martial arts -- Fiction 3. Graduate students -- Fiction
ISBN 1936747928; 9781936747924

LC 2014010165

"A bookish young woman insinuates herself into the lives of two cage fighters--one a young prodigy, the other an aging journeyman.... Acclaimed essayist Kerry Howley follows these men for three years through the bloody world of mixed martial arts as they starve themselves, break bones, fail their families and form new ones in the quest to rise from remote Midwestern fairgrounds to packed Vegas arenas." (Publisher's note)

"Howley's brilliant prose is as dexterous and doughty as the fighters she trails, torquing into philosophy, parody, and sweat-soaked poetry. At times, the narrative is difficult to follow, while the contrast between her highbrow analysis and the aggressive MMA subculture can be disorienting. Her year-long immersion in the sport, however, proves as captivating as any blood-spattered spectacle." Pub Wkly

Margolick, David

Beyond glory; Joe Louis vs. Max Schmeling, and a world on the brink. Knopf 2005 423p il $26.95 **796.8**
1. Boxing 2. Soldiers 3. Boxers (Persons)
ISBN 0-375-41192-5

LC 2005-45141

The author discusses the historical significance of the fights between Joe Louis and German boxer Max Schmeling in 1936 and 1938.

This book "will be the definitive account of Louis versus Schmeling. And it's a hell of a good read besides." Booklist

Includes bibliographical references

796.83 Boxing

Assael, Shaun

The **murder** of Sonny Liston; Las Vegas, Heroin, and Heavyweights. Shaun Assael. Blue Rider Press 2016 320 p. illustrations (ebook) $65; (hardback) $27 **796.83**
1. Heroin abuse 2. Boxers (Sports) 3. African American athletes 4. Las Vegas (Nev.) -- History 5. African American boxers -- Biography 6. Las Vegas (Nev.) -- History -- 20th century 7. Boxers (Sports) -- United States -- Biography 8. Heroin -- Nevada -- Las Vegas -- History -- 20th century
ISBN 9780698156661; 9780399169755

LC 2016016232

This book, by Shaun Assael, is an "investigation into the mysterious death of Heavyweight Champion Sonny Liston, set against the dawn of the 1970s, when the mob was fighting to keep control of the Las Vegas Strip, Richard Nixon was launching America's first war on heroin, and boxing was in its glory days." (Publisher's note)

"Still, there is much here that will appeal to anyone interested in the intersection of crime and boxing." Booklist

Includes indexIncludes bibliographical references and index.

Butler, Brin-Jonathan

The **domino** diaries; my decade boxing with Olympic champions and chasing Hemingway's ghost in the last days of Castro's Cuba. by Brin-Jonathan Butler. Picador 2015 304 p. illustrations (hardback) $26 **796.83**
1. Boxing 2. Cuba -- Social life and customs 3. Boxing -- Cuba -- Anecdotes
ISBN 1250043700; 9781250043702

LC 2015012698

This book "is the culmination of [journalist Brin-Jonathan] Butler's decade spent in the trenches of Havana, trying to understand a culture perplexing to Westerners: one whose elite athletes regularly forgo multimillion-dollar opportunities to stay in Cuba and box for their country, while living in penury. Butler's fascination with this distinctly Cuban idealism sets him off on a remarkable journey, training with, befriending, and interviewing the champion boxers." (Publisher's note)

"Focusing on Dickensian characters as well as boxing, Butler's gonzo journalism should have broad appeal." LJ

Gildea, William

The **longest** fight; in the ring with Joe Gans, boxing's first African American champion. William Gildea. Farrar, Straus and Giroux 2012 245 p. ill. (hbk.) : $26.00 **796.83**
1. Boxing -- Biography 2. Gans, Joe, 1874-1910 3. African American boxers -- Biography 4. Boxers (Sports) -- United States -- Biography
ISBN 0374280975; 9780374280970

LC 2011040170

This book by William Gildea presents a biography of "Joe Gans, who in 1902 became the first African American boxing champion ... giving special attention to the fighter's ... championship bout against avowed racist Oscar 'Battling' Nelson.... Gildea gives full measure of Gans' remarkable accomplishments as an athlete ... while also showing Gans' equally remarkable poise in the face of horrific prejudice, officially sanctioned or not, during his entire career." (Booklist)

Includes bibliographical references and index.

Kram, Mark

The **ghosts** of Manila; the fateful, brutal blood feud between Muhammad Ali and Joe Frazier. HarperCollins Pubs. 2001 232p hardcover o.p. pa $12.95 **796.83**
1. Boxing 2. Boxers (Persons)
ISBN 0-06-095480-9 pa

LC 00-53934

This is "a fascinating blend of history and biography." Booklist

Liebling, A. J. (Abbott Joseph), 1904-1963

The **sweet** science; A.J. Liebling; with an introduction by Robert Anasi. North Point Press 2004 288 p. (ebook) $40; (pbk.) $16   **796.83**

1. Boxing 2. Boxers (Sports)

ISBN 9781466801868; 0374272271; 9780374272272

LC 2004049509

This book, by A.J. Liebling, "depicts the great events of boxing's American heyday: Sugar Ray Robinson's dramatic comeback, Rocky Marciano's rise to prominence, Joe Louis's unfortunate decline. Liebling never fails to find the human story behind the fight, and he evokes the atmosphere in the arena as distinctly as he does the goings-on in the ring." (Publisher's note)

Runstedtler, Theresa

Jack Johnson, rebel sojourner; boxing in the shadow of the global color line. Theresa Runstedtler. University of California Press 2012 xxii, 348 p.p (cloth : alk. paper) $34.95   **796.83**

1. Race relations 2. African American athletes 3. Racism in sports 4. Boxing -- United States -- History 5. African American boxers -- Biography 6. United States -- Race relations -- History 7. Boxers (Sports) -- United States -- Biography

ISBN 0520271602; 9780520271609

LC 2011027435

In this book, "[Theresa] Runstedtler . . . makes [boxer Jack] Johnson the centerpiece of what is also a study of global black-white relations during his era." The boxer "was given to living large, embarrassing white opponents, and consorting with white women at a time when Jim Crow flourished at home and the doctrine of the 'white man's burden' was encircling the globe. Therefore, even when he fled the United States after a Mann Act conviction, he couldn't escape racism." (Library Journal)

Includes bibliographical references and index.

Shanahan, Tim

Runnng with the champ; my heavyweight friendship with Muhammad Ali. by Tim Shanahan with Chuck Crisafulli. Simon & Schuster 2016 320 p. (hardcover) $27   **796.83**

1. Friendship 2. Boxers (Sports) 3. Boxers (Sports) -- United States -- Biography

ISBN 1501102303; 9781501102301

LC 2015034685

This book, by Tim Shanahan, is a "personal tribute to the remarkable friendship between [himself] and Muhammad Ali, including dozens of never-before-told stories about Ali, his family, his entourage, and various celebrities along the way—as well as never-before-published personal photos." (Publisher's note)

"Ali is the heart of the book, and Shanahan presents a complex but less bombastic person than is popularly associated with the name; generous to a fault, devoted to his religion and (despite four marriages) family, and a champion of the less fortunate." LJ

796.86   Fencing

Bennett, Alexander C.

Kendo; culture of the sword. Alexander C. Bennett. University of California Press 2015 328 p. illustrations (cloth : alk. paper) $32.95   **796.86**

1. Kendo 2. Swords 3. Swordplay -- Japan

ISBN 0520284372; 9780520284371

LC 2015004621

Author Alexander Bennett presents a "historical, cultural, and political account in English of the Japanese martial art of swordsmanship, from its beginnings in military training and arcane medieval schools to its widespread practice as a global sport today. Bennett shows how kendo evolved through a recurring process of 'inventing tradition,' which served the changing ideologies and needs of Japanese warriors and governments over the course of history." (Publisher's note)

"A highly recommended, useful resource for all readers interested in this popular sport." LJ

Includes bibliographical references and index

796.9   Ice and snow sports

Bennett, Jeff

The **complete** snowboarder; {by} Jeff Bennett, Scott Downey and Charles Arnell. 2nd ed; Ragged Mountain Press 2000 148p il pa $14.95   **796.9**

1. Snowboarding

ISBN 0-07-135787-4

LC 00-39059

First published 1994

This offers advice on getting started in snowboarding, equipment, techniques, snowboarding areas and trails, tricks, competitions, safety, and equipment maintenance.

796.935   Alpine skiing (Downhill skiing)

Vinton, Nathaniel

The **fall** line; how American ski racers conquered a sport on the edge. Nathaniel Vinton. W W Norton & Co Inc 2015 384 p. 16 plates; illustrations (hardcover) $26.95   **796.935**

1. Skiing 2. Winter sports -- United States 3. Skiers -- United States 4. Downhill skiing -- United States -- History

ISBN 0393244776; 9780393244779

LC 2014033594

This book, by Nathaniel Vinton, "is an authoritative portrait of a group of men and women taking mortal risks in a bid for sporting glory. A white-knuckled tour through skiing's deep traditions and least-accessible locales, . . . [The book] opens up the sexy, high-stakes world of downhill skiing-- its career-ending crashes, million-dollar sponsorship deals, international intrigue, and showdowns with nature itself." (Publisher's note)

"As the season progresses, Vinton adds rich historical context to each race venue, documenting course changes and rule revisions, while profiling past skiing greats, including

Austrians Franz Klammer and Hermann Maier. The subtitle is a bit of a misnomer as this is not simply a story of American skiers but, instead, a primer on the history and current state of Alpine skiing." Booklist

796.94 Snowmobiling

O'Brien, Keith
Catching the Sky; two brothers, one family, and our dream to fly. Colten Moore, with Keith O'Brien. Simon & Schuster 2016 272 p. color illustrations (Hardcover : alk. paper) $26 **796.94**
1. Extreme sports
ISBN 9781501117244; 9781501117251; 1501117246
LC 2015044662

This book, by Colten Moore, with Keith O'Brien, presents reflections of the author and his brother's careers in ATV and snowmobile extreme sports. The author offers a "look at extreme sports, what drives people to take wild chances, and how one man, Colten, couldn't stop even after the worst possible outcome." (Publisher's note)

"Moore's well-written memoir will enthrall fans of extreme sports, the X Games, and those trying to find their way after losing a loved one." LJ

Includes bibliographical references

796.962 Ice hockey

Hockey Hall of Fame Book of Players; edited by Steve Cameron. 2nd edition Firefly Books 2015 352 p. color illustrations pbk $29.95 **796.962**
1. Hockey players 2. Hockey -- History
ISBN 9781770855977; 1770855971
LC 2015509178

"Complete with more than 450 photos and over 70 artifacts--as well as stats, facts, quotes and other interesting stories and snapshots from each star's career--Hockey Hall of Fame Book of Players is the definitive book on the stars who have been awarded hockey's most prestigious honor." (Publisher's note)

McKinley, Michael
Hockey: a people's history. McClelland & Stewart 2006 346p il hardcover o.p. pa $37.50 **796.962**
1. Hockey
ISBN 0-7710-5769-5; 978-0-7710-5769-4; 0-7710-5771-7 pa; 978-0-7710-5771-7 pa
This history "chronicles hockey from its genesis as a winter substitute for lacrosse. A companion to a similarly titled CBC TV series, the lavishly illustrated book combines punchy boxed features celebrating individuals and hockey oddments and a detailed tracing of the game's development. . . . Essential for general sports as well as hockey-intensive collections." Booklist

Includes bibliographical references

797.1 Aquatic sports

American Canoe Association
Canoeing; outdoor adventures. editors, Pamela S. Dillon, Jeremy Oyen. Human Kinetics 2008 253p il (Outdoor adventures) pa $22.95 **797.1**
1. Canoes and canoeing
ISBN 978-0-7360-6715-7; 0-7360-6715-9
LC 2008-4392

The authors "discuss fitness basics, food and nutrition needs, and gear and equipment—from the canoe itself to life jackets, paddles, and clothing. They then cover . . . safety and survival guidelines, including weather, river hazards, capsizing, cold-water safety, and rescue protocols. . . [The DVD included contains] an introduction to paddle sports and basic safety and paddling techniques." Publisher's note

Kayaking; editors, Pamela S. Dillon, Jeremy Oyen. Human Kinetics 2009 237p il (Outdoor adventures) pa $22.95 **797.1**
1. Canoes and canoeing
ISBN 978-0-7360-6716-4; 0-7360-6716-7
LC 2008-32111

"Part I of Kayaking explains the background knowledge, fitness fundamentals, equipment and gear selection, nutritional needs, and safety and survival skills for a successful adventure. Part II helps build basic techniques, strokes, and maneuvers. . . [It includes] tips and instruction for the three most popular types of kayaking: sea, river, and whitewater. This book also includes the Quick-Start Your Kayak DVD to reinforce the paddling strokes and safety information found in the book. It features videos of kayaking maneuvers." Publisher's note

Includes bibliographical references

Fredston, Jill A.
Rowing to latitude; journeys along the Arctic's edge. [by] Jill Fredston. North Point Press 2001 289p il hardcover o.p. pa $15 **797.1**
1. Canoes and canoeing 2. Arctic regions -- Description and travel
ISBN 0-374-28180-7; 0-86547-655-1 pa
LC 2001-30049

The author and her husband, Doug Fesler "canoe the Arctic and sub-Arctic coastlines of Alaska, Canada, Greenland, Norway and Sweden for three months out of each year. . . . Fredston ably describes both the big picture—the coastline, encounters with polar bears, the high-stakes game of second-guessing storms and tides—and the details of their travels. . . . A must-read for armchair travelers, as well as a close and loving look at an intimate relationship." Publ Wkly

Halberstam, David, 1934-2007
The **amateurs**; The Story of Four Young Men and Their Quest for an Olympic Gold Medal. David Halberstam. Morrow 1985 221p il pbk $16; hbk o.p. **797.1**
1. Rowing 2. Olympic games
ISBN 0449910032; 9780449910030; 0688049486; 9780688049485
LC 85-2940

"Halberstam focuses on the quest of four oarsmen to become the United States's single sculler in the 1984 Olympics." (N Y Times Book Rev)

797.12   Types of vessels

Brown, Daniel James

★ The **Boys** in the Boat; Nine Americans and Their Epic Quest for Gold at the 1936 Berlin Olympics. Daniel James Brown. Penguin Group USA 2013 432 p. (hardcover) $28.95   **797.12**

1. Rowing 2. Olympic games, 1936 (Berlin, Ger.) 3. Rowing -- United States -- History 4. Rowers -- United States -- Biography 5. University of Washington -- Rowing -- History

ISBN 067002581X; 9780670025817

LC 2013001560

This book, by Daniel James Brown, "tells the story of the University of Washington's 1936 eight-oar crew and their . . . quest for an Olympic gold medal, a team that transformed the sport and grabbed the attention of millions of Americans. The sons of loggers, shipyard workers, and farmers, the boys defeated elite rivals first from eastern and British universities and finally the German crew rowing for Adolf Hitler in the Olympic games in Berlin, 1936." (Publisher's note)

Includes bibliographical references and index.

797.124   Sailing

Sleight, Steve

The **complete** sailing manual; Steve Sleight. DK Publishing 2012 448 p. color illustrations; maps (hc) $35   **797.124**

1. Sailing 2. Navigation 3. Sailing -- Handbooks, manuals, etc

ISBN 0756689694; 9780756689698

LC 2011534511

Written by Steve Sleight, "From learning the basics of sailing, to mastering navigation and boat care, 'The Complete Sailing Manual' is the most essential reference for sailing instructors and students. Revised and updated to include all of the latest developments in equipment and safety, and to reflect the current rules, regulations, and best practices, 'The Complete Sailing Manual' is . . . for anyone interested in sailing." (Publisher's note)

797.2   Swimming and diving

Beard, Amanda

In the water they can't see you cry; a memoir. Amanda Beard; with Rebecca Paley. 1st Touchstone hardcover ed. Simon & Schuster 2012 248 p. ill. (some col.) $24.99   **797.2**

1. Autobiographies 2. Olympic athletes 3. Depression (Psychology) 4. Swimmers -- United States -- Biography 5. Women swimmers -- United States -- Biography

ISBN 145164437X; 9781451644371

LC 2012006464

This book is a memoir by Olympic swimmer Amanda Beard, with Rebecca Paley. "[S]he competed in three more Olympic games . . . and enjoyed a lucrative modeling career on the side. . . . Unaware that she was suffering from clinical depression, she . . . expressed her emotions through self-destructive behavior. . . . Only when she met her future husband . . . did Amanda realize she needed help." (Publisher's note)

Checkoway, Julie

The **three**-year swim club; the untold story of Maui's sugar ditch kids and their quest for Olympic glory. by Julie Checkoway. Grand Central Pub 2015 432 p. 16 plates; illustrations $27   **797.2**

1. Swimming 2. Olympic games 3. Japanese Americans

ISBN 1455523445; 9781455523443

LC 2015947608

This book, by Julie Checkoway, is the "story of impoverished children who transformed themselves into world-class swimmers. In 1937, a schoolteacher on the island of Maui challenged a group of poverty-stricken sugar plantation kids to . . . become Olympians. . . . The children were Japanese-American, were malnourished and barefoot and had no pool. . . . In spite of everything . . . the children outraced Olympic athletes twice their size." (Publisher's note)

"Details about training, swim times, and the team's travels occasionally overwhelm Checkoway's tense, vivid, an d inspiring narrative. Not without its flaws, but a good choice for fans of David Halberstam's The Amateurs (1985), Daniel Boyne's The Red Rose Crew (2000), and similar books." Kirkus

Graver, Dennis

Scuba diving; Dennis Graver. 5th edition Human Kinetics 2016 illustrations pbk $29.95   **797.2**

1. Scuba diving

ISBN 1492525766; 9781492525769

LC 2016018110

"Scuba Diving offers step-by-step instruction on preparing for and managing a dive safely with information on the latest equipment, gear selection, recommended dive locations, technologies and techniques. Dennis Graver explains the basics of diving, including managing underwater emergencies, avoiding underwater hazards and equalizing pressure in the ears, sinuses and mask." (Publisher's note)

Mullen, P. H.

Gold in the water; the true story of ordinary men and their extraordinary dream of Olympic glory. Thomas Dunne Bks. 2001 326p il hardcover o.p. pa $14.95   **797.2**

1. Swimming 2. Olympic games, 2000 (Sydney, Australia)

ISBN 0-312-26595-6; 0-312-31116-8 pa

LC 2001-31955

"Mullen chronicles the U.S. Olympic swimming team on its journey to the 2000 Summer Games in Sydney. The text moves back and forth in time, giving a sense of the athletes as people and showing what motivates someone to structure his or her whole life toward a single goal." Booklist

Nestor, James

Deep; Freediving, Renegade Science, and What the Ocean Tells Us About Ourselves. James Nestor. Houghton Mifflin Harcourt 2014 272 p. illustrations (chiefly color) $27   **797.2**

1. Ocean 2. Skin diving

ISBN 0547985525; 9780547985527

LC 2014002593

"In 'Deep,' [author James] Nestor embeds with a gang of extreme athletes and renegade researchers who are transforming not only our knowledge of the planet and its creatures, but also our understanding of the human body and mind. . . . Most illuminating of all, Nestor unlocks his own freediving skills as he communes with the pioneers who are expanding our definition of what is possible in the natural world, and in ourselves." (Publisher's note)

"[B]rimming with vivid portraits, lucid scientific explanations, gripping (and funny) first-person accounts, and urgent facts about the ocean's endangerment, Nestor's Deep is galvanizing, enlightening, and invaluable." Booklist

Includes bibliographical references and index

Shapton, Leanne

Swimming studies; Leanne Shapton. Blue Rider Press 2012 320 p. (hbk.) $30   **797.2**

1. Swimming 2. Women swimmers -- Canada -- Biography

ISBN 0399158170; 9780399158179

LC 2012011506

This memoir by Leanne Shapton "explores the worlds of competitive and recreational swimming. From her training for the Olympic trials as a teenager to enjoying pools and beaches around the world as an adult, . . . Shapton offers a fascinating glimpse into the private, often solitary, realm of swimming. . . . [The book] reveals an intimate narrative of suburban adolescence, spent underwater in a discipline that continues to inspire Shapton's work as an artist and author." (Publisher's note)

Skolnick, Adam

One breath; death, freediving, and the quest to shatter human limits. by Adam Skolnick. Crown Archetype 2015 336 p. color illustrations $26 **797.2**

1. Scuba diving 2. Water safety 3. Divers -- United States -- Biography

ISBN 9780553447484; 9780553447491

LC 2015027589

In this book, by Adam Skolnick, "A handsome young American with an unmatched talent for the sport, Nick was among freediving's brightest stars. . . . So when Nick Mevoli arrived at Vertical Blue in 2013, the world's premier freediving competition, he was widely expected to challenge records and continue his meteoric rise to stardom. Instead, before the end of that fateful competition Nick Mevoli had died, a victim of the sport that had made him a star." (Publisher's note)

"A worthy addition to the growing body of literature on adventures that test the limits of nature and mankind." Kirkus

797.5 Air sports

Higgins, Matt

Bird dream; adventures at the extremes of human flight. Matt Higgins. The Penguin Press 2014 304 p. color illustrations $27.95   **797.5**

1. Flight 2. Aeronautical sports

ISBN 1594204659; 9781594204654

LC 2014005399

Written by Matt Higgins, "'Bird Dream' shows that recent decades have witnessed an unprecedented revolution in human flight. . . . Wingsuits were not new; they had fascinated men for centuries. Yet a modern design had improved safety and performance, allowing wingsuit pilots to leap from a helicopter or high cliff and soar for miles--using little more than their bodies--before deploying a parachute to reach the ground safely." (Publisher's note)

"A highflying, electrifying story of a treacherous sport in which every triumph is an eye blink away from becoming a disaster." Kirkus

Includes bibliographical references and index

798.2 Horsemanship

Letts, Elizabeth

The eighty-dollar champion; Snowman, the horse that inspired a nation. Ballantine Books 2011 352p $26   **798.2**

1. Horses

ISBN 978-0-345-52108-8; 978-0-345-52110-1 ebook

LC 2010050993

"In 1956, Harry De Leyer, a riding instructor at a Long Island girls' school, spent $80 on a horse that was bound for the slaughterhouse. He thought the animal might make a good horse for his students. But the horse, named Snowman by Harry's four-year-old daughter, turned out to be much more--a champion show-jumper." (Booklist)

Includes bibliographical references

798.4 Horse racing

Drape, Joe

American Pharoah; The Untold Story of the Triple Crown Winner's Legendary Rise. by Joe Drape. Hachette Books 2016 292 p. color illustrations $27   **798.4**

1. Horse racing

ISBN 0316268844; 9780316268844

This book about the racehorse American Pharoah, by Joe Drape, "is the definitive account not only of how the ethereal colt won the Kentucky Derby, Preakness, and Belmont Stakes, but how he changed lives. Through extensive interviews, Drape explores the making of an exceptional racehorse, chronicling key events en route to history." (Publisher's note)

"A captivating story woven with an affectionate yet honest portrayal of the sometimes seedy sport of kings, this work will appeal to horse-racing fans and anyone who enjoys athlete biographies." LJ

Includes bibliographical references (pages 275-278) and index.

Eisenberg, John

The **great** match race; when North met South in America's first sports spectacle. Houghton Mifflin Co. 2006 258p il $25   **798.4**

1. Horse racing

ISBN 978-0-618-55612-0; 0-618-55612-5

LC 2005-31540

The author "succeeds in creating a gripping yarn of sporting contest, portrayal of a historical moment and smart analysis of a country headed eventually for civil war." Publ Wkly

Includes bibliographical references

Hillenbrand, Laura

★ **Seabiscuit**; an American legend. Random House 2001 399p il $25.95; pa $15.95   **798.4**

1. Horse racing 2. Seabiscuit (Race horse)

ISBN 0-375-50291-2; 0-449-00561-5 pa

LC 2001-267852

"This is a remarkable tale well told by a writer who deftly blends history and sport." Economist

Includes bibliographical references

McGraw, Eliza

Here Comes Exterminator! the longshot horse, the Great War, and the making of an American hero. Eliza McGraw. St. Martin's Press 2016 336 p. illustrations (hardcover) $26.99   **798.4**

1. Horse racing -- United States -- History

ISBN 9781250065698; 1250065690

LC 2015048660

This book, by Eliza McGraw, "tells the story of how a gangling, long-shot Kentucky Derby winner named Exterminator became one of the most beloved racehorses of all time. . . . [The author] draws readers into the golden age of racing, with all its ups and downs, the ever-involving interplay of horses and people, and the beauty, grace, fear, and hope that are a daily part of life at the track." (Publisher's note)

"Unfolding without the fanfare of, say, a Seabiscuit or Man o' War, Exterminator's story, and that of the quietly competent and humane McDaniel, will still secure both horse and trainer a place in the hearts of animal lovers, and in horse racing's pantheon of champions." Booklist

Includes bibliographical references (pages [233]-314) and index.

Mitchell, Elizabeth

Three strides before the wire; the dark and beautiful world of horse racing. Hyperion 2002 403p $24.95; pa $14.95   **798.4**

1. Horse racing

ISBN 0-7868-6723-X; 0-7868-8622-6 pa

LC 2002-68817

The author "tells the story of Charismatic, who exploded out of the proletarian ranks of claiming horses to come within in a stone's throw of sweeping the Triple Crown in 1999 be-

fore suffering a career-ending injury in the Belmont Stakes. . . . Mitchell's book possesses an appeal that extends well beyond its subject." Booklist

Nack, William

Secretariat; the making of a champion. by William Nack. Da Capo Press 2002 xi, 367 p.p illustrations $16.99   **798.4**

1. Horse racing 2. Secretariat (Race horse) 3. Race horses -- United States -- Biography

ISBN 0306811332; 1401324010; 9780306811333; 9781401324018

LC 2007310325

This book, by William Nack, focuses on the horse Secretariat. "In 1973, Secretariat, the greatest champion in horse-racing history, won the Triple Crown. The only horse to ever grace the covers of Time, Newsweek, and Sports Illustrated in the same week, he also still holds the record for the fastest times in both the Kentucky Derby and the Belmont Stakes." (Publisher's note)

Ours, Dorothy

Man o' War; a legend like lightning. St Martin's Press 2006 342p il $24.95   **798.4**

1. Horse racing 2. Man o' War (Race horse)

ISBN 0-312-34099-0; 978-0-312-34099-5

LC 2006-41631

This is an account of the thoroughbred racehorse Man o' War, also known as Big Red.

This book "is clearly a labor of love, and it certifies Big Red's claim to immortality." N Y Times Book Rev

Includes bibliographical references

Squires, James D.

Horse of a different color; a tale of breeding geniuses, dominant females, and the fastest Derby winner since Secretariat. {by} Jim Squires. PublicAffairs 2002 300p il $26; pa $14   **798.4**

1. Horse racing 2. Kentucky Derby

ISBN 1-58648-117-7; 1-58648-180-0 pa

LC 2001-59602

This is the story of how the author, a former editor of the Chicago Tribune, became a breeder of thoroughbred race horses, including a horse named Monarchos, the champion of the 2001 Kentucky Derby

This "is fast paced and fun to read. It will appeal not only to horseracing fans but also to people making midlife career changes." Libr J

798.401 Betting

Ainslie, Tom

Ainslie's complete guide to thoroughbred racing; 3rd ed; Simon & Schuster 1986 349p il hardcover o.p. pa $14   **798.401**

1. Gambling 2. Horse racing

ISBN 0-671-65655-4 pa

LC 86-3879

First published 1968

A guide to the fundamentals of handicapping races including such topics as breeding, judging condition of the horses, calculating speed, track ratings and other tips for successful betting

798.8 Dog racing

Paulsen, Gary, 1939-

Winterdance; the fine madness of running the Iditarod. Harcourt Brace & Co. 1994 256p il $26; pa $15 **798.8**
1. Sled dog racing 2. Iditarod Trail Sled Dog Race, Alaska 3. Authors 4. Sledding 5. Sled dog racers 6. Children's authors 7. Short story writers 8. Young adult authors
ISBN 0-15-126227-6; 0-15-600145-4 pa
LC 93-42096

"The Alaskan Iditarod is an annual 1180-mile dogsled race from Anchorage to Nome that generally takes two to three weeks to complete. Paulsen . . . ran the race in 1983 and 1985 and was again in training when a heart condition forced him to retire. This book is primarily an account of Paulsen's first Iditarod." (Libr J)

"This book is primarily an account of Paulsen's first Iditarod and its frequent life-threatening disasters. . . . However, the book is more than a tabulation of tribulations; it is a meditation on the extraordinary attraction this race holds for some men and women." Libr J

799.1 Fishing

Bourne, Wade

Basic fishing; A Beginner's Guide. by Wade Bourne. Skyhorse Pub. 2011 159 p. color illustrations $12.99 **799.1**
1. Fishing
ISBN 1632203383; 9781616082109; 9781632203380
LC 2011017601

This book, by Wade Bourne, is a "beginner's guide for burgeoning fishermen. . . . Bourne was taught to fish by his father. In turn, Bourne taught his children how to fish. Now he brings his expertise to . . . a step-by-step guide that masterfully breaks down the art of fishing with diagrams, vivid photographs, and lessons." (Publisher's note)

Cermele, Joe

The **total** fishing manual; 317 Essential Fishing Skills. by Joe Cermele. Welden Owen 2013 256 p. color illustrations $29 **799.1**
1. Fishing
ISBN 1616284870; 1616286296; 9781616284879; 9781616286293

This book on fishing, by Joe Cermele, "is chock full of 317 field-tested tools, techniques and tactics. . . . Whether you're a beginner, a weekend angler or a serious sport fisher this book has the information you need to hook'em." (Publisher's note)

Rosenbauer, Tom

The **Orvis** guide to the essential American flies; how to tie the most successful freshwater and saltwater patterns. Universe 2011 208p il $35 **799.1**
1. Fishing 2. Artificial flies
ISBN 978-0-7893-2269-2
LC 2011-921540

This "resource features twenty quintessential fly patterns, including the Parachute Adams, Clouser Minnow, and Woolly Bugger. [Includes] detailed chapters exploring the history of and variations on each fly, interviews with fly originators, and step-by-step tying 'recipes' and instructions." Publisher's note

Talleur, Richard W.

L.L. Bean ultimate book of fly fishing. Lyons Press 2002 344p il hardcover o.p. pa $24.95 **799.1**
1. Fishing 2. Fly casting
ISBN 1-58574-632-0; 1-59228-891-X pa
LC 2002-73191

Each chapter also published separately

The topics discussed in this book include "assembly of fly tackle; the biology of fish; natural fish foods and how to imitate them; safety techniques; bass flies; where to find bass; the eleven habits of highly effective fly casters; the basic four-part cast; the roll cast; the basics of fly tying; types of flies; the top ten most popular and successful fly patterns; and . . . more." Publisher's note

799.12 Angling

Gierach, John

All Fishermen Are Liars; by John Gierach. Simon & Schuster 2014 224 p. illustrations $24 **799.12**
1. Fishing 2. Fly fishing -- Anecdotes
ISBN 145161831X; 9781451618310
LC 2013012784

In this book, author John Gierach "travels across North America from the Pacific Northwest to the Canadian Maritimes to seek out quintessential fishing experiences. Whether he's fishing a busy stream or a secluded lake amid snow-capped mountains, Gierach insists that fishing is always the answer--even when it's not clear what the question is." (Publisher's note)

"An engaging autobiographical introduction opens the book, which includes 22 perceptive and witty essays, recalling numerous fishing trips and offering insights on fly rods and fly patterns. . . . These lyrical essays explode with descriptions of beautiful places, big fish, and beautiful fish." Booklist

Includes bibliographical references and index

799.124 Fly fishing

Deeter, Kirk

The **little** red book of fly fishing; 250 tips to make you a better fisherman. Charlie Meyers and

Kirk Deeter. Skyhorse Pub. 2010 xv, 201 p.p color illustrations (alk. paper) $16.95 **799.124**

1. Fly casting 2. Fly fishing
ISBN 1602399816; 9781602399815

LC 2009046448

This book, by Charlie Meyers and Kirk Deeter, "offers a simple, digestible primer on the basic elements of fly fishing: the cast, presentation, reading water, and selecting flies. In the end, this collection of 240 tips is one of the most insightful, plainly spoken, and entertaining works on this sport—one that will serve both novices and experts alike in helping them reflect and hone in their approaches to fly fishing." (Publisher's note)

Includes bibliographical references and index

Rosenbauer, Tom

The **Orvis** fly-fishing guide; Tom Rosenbauer; photographs by Tom Rosenbauer & the Orvis Company; illustrations by Bob White. Lyons Press 2007 ix, 271 p.p color illustrations $24.95; (ebook) $30.99 **799.124**

1. Fly casting 2. Fly fishing
ISBN 1592288189; 9781592288182; 9780762762422

LC 2007274210

This book, by Tom Rosenbauer, "appears in a revised edition. . . . A best-selling, fully illustrated, and comprehensive book, this large-format volume has been required reading for every angler for the past two decades. Included here are instructions for tackle selection; casting and presentation; flies and their specific uses; successful techniques on stream, pond, or ocean; and the select tackle, flies, and methods for pursuing every major gamefish." (Publisher's note)

Includes bibliographical references (p. 261-263) and index.

Whitelaw, Ian

The **history** of fly fishing in fifty flies; Ian Whitelaw; illustration by Julie Spyropoulos. Stewart Tabori & Chang, an imprint of Abrams 2015 223 p. illustrations $22.50; (ebook) $22.50 **799.124**

1. Fly casting 2. Artificial flies 3. Fly fishing -- History 4. Flies, Artificial -- History
ISBN 1617691461; 9781617691461; 9781613127834

LC 2014942977

This book, by Ian Whitelaw, with illustration by Julie Spyropoulos, "recounts the history of a sport that dates back 2,000 years, focusing on milestone flies from the first feathered hook to contemporary patterns using cutting-edge materials. Among the countless fly patterns created over the centuries, these 50 have been carefully chosen to represent the development not only of the flies themselves, but also of fly-fishing techniques—and of rods, lines, and reels." (Publisher's note)

Includes bibliographical references (pages 218-219) and index

799.2 Hunting

Rinella, Steven

The **complete** guide to hunting, butchering, and cooking big game; Big Game. Steven Rinella. Spiegel & Grau 2014 416 p. illustrations (color), maps $25 **799.2**

1. Big game hunting 2. Cooking (Game) 3. Hunting -- United States 4. Game and game-birds, Dressing of 5. Big game hunting -- United States 6. Hunting -- United States -- Equipment and supplies
ISBN 081299406X; 9780812994063

LC 2014013333

This book, by Steven Rinella, is a "comprehensive big-game hunting guide for hunters ranging from first-time novices to seasoned experts, with more than 400 full-color photographs, including work by renowned outdoor photographer John Hafner." (Publisher's note)

"Rinella doesn't offer too many tips beyond the obvious grilled steaks and jerky, though wild pig hunters will appreciate his simple but flavorful recipe for smoked ham. It's a minor flaw in a book that's terrifically informative and is sure to inspire hunters to start poring over maps and readying themselves for their next hunt." Pub Wkly

The **Complete** Guide to Hunting, Butchering, and Cooking Wild Game; Small Game and Fowl. by Steven Rinella, photography by John Hafner. Random House Inc 2015 384 p. chiefly col. ill., maps (paperback) $25 **799.2**

1. Hunting 2. Cooking -- Game
ISBN 9780812987058; 0812987055

This book, by Steven Rinella with photography by John Hafner, is "a comprehensive small game hunting guide for hunters ranging from first-time novices to seasoned experts. . . . [Topics addressed include] recommendations on what equipment you will need . . . , basic and advanced hunting strategies for all North American small game . . . , instructions on how to field dress and butcher your own small game animals." (Publisher's note)

"The book stands well on its own, covering the requisite gear and skills... that hunters need to develop in order to ensure a successful hunt." Pub Wkly

799.29 History, geographic treatment, biography

Rinella, Steven

Meat eater; a natural history of an American hunter. Steven Rinella. Spiegel & Grau 2012 244 p. **799.29**

1. Hunting 2. Food of animal origin 3. Hunting stories, American 4. Hunting -- United States -- History 5. Hunters -- United States -- Biography
ISBN 0385529813; 9780385529815; 9780679645283

LC 2012018129

This book by Steven Rinella "chronicles Rinella's lifelong relationship with nature and hunting through the lens of ten hunts, beginning when he was an aspiring mountain man at age ten and ending as a thirty-seven-year-old Brooklyn father who hunts in the remotest corners of North America. . . . Rinella grapples with themes such as . . . the disappearance of the hunter himself as Americans lose their connection with the way their food finds its way to their tables." (Publisher's note)

800 LITERATURE, RHETORIC & CRITICISM

801 Philosophy and theory

Bloom, Harold, 1930-
The **anatomy** of influence. Yale University Press 2011 357p $32.50 **801**
1. Authors 2. Editors 3. Biographers 4. College teachers 5. Literary critics 6. Authors and readers 7. Literature -- Philosophy 8. Literature -- Appreciation 9. Literature -- History and criticism 10. Influence (Literary, artistic, etc.)
ISBN 978-0-300-16760-3; 0-300-16760-1
LC 2010-42456

It was the author's intention to "reveal . . . how writers struggle with the works of those who came before. He cites Shakespeare as the greatest writer in the English language. Moving forward chronologically from the 16th through the 20th centuries, [Harold] Bloom analyzes the works of such giants as John Milton, Samuel Johnson, Percy Bysshe Shelley, and Alfred, Lord Tennyson, illustrating their connections to Shakespeare. Bloom examines Walt Whitman's poetry in depth then considers James Joyce, D.H. Lawrence, Stephen Crane, and Wallace Stevens, as well as contemporary poets, e.g., A.R. Ammons, John Ashbery, and Mark Strand." (Libr J)

"The subtitle of Bloom's new book, 'Literature as a Way of Life,' is not an overstatement. For him, great authors don't merely imitate life or capture facets of being. They create 'heterocosms,' alternative but accessible worlds, open to us all. He had always been an esoteric populist, like his first subjects, Blake and Shelley." N Y Times Book Rev

Includes bibliographical references

Donoghue, Denis
Speaking of beauty. Yale University Press 2003 209p $24.95; pa $15 **801**
1. Aesthetics 2. English literature -- History and criticism
ISBN 0-300-09893-6; 0-300-10593-2 pa
LC 2002-12243

This book "is an eloquent reflection on the language beauty inspires and a careful critique of its place in literary criticism and cultural theory." N Y Times Book Rev

Includes bibliographical references

The **encyclopedia** of literary and cultural theory; general editor: Michael Ryan. Wiley-Blackwell 2011 3 v. **801**
1. Semiotics 2. Literature -- History and criticism
ISBN 9781405183123
LC 2010029411

This reference book "is . . . [a] multi-volume encyclopedia of literary and cultural theory. Arranged in three volumes covering Literary Theory from 1900 to 1966, Literary Theory from 1966 to the Present, and Cultural Theory, this encyclopedia provides . . . entries on the important concepts, theorists and trends in post-1900 literary and cultural theory. . . . [It includes] . . . over 300 entries of 1,000-7,000 words, . . . explanations of complex terms, important theoretical concepts, and tools for critical analysis and summaries of the work and ideas of key figures. (Publisher's note)

Includes bibliographical references and index.

Garber, Marjorie
The **use** and abuse of literature. Pantheon Books 2011 320p $28.95 **801**
1. Literature -- Philosophy
ISBN 978-0-375-42434-2; 0-375-42434-2
LC 2010-35417

Garber "examines classic texts like John Donne's 'The Canonization' and Ezra Pound's haiku-like poem 'In a Station of the Metro,' but she is equally happy to devote half a page to listing books with the phrase 'use and abuse' in their titles, and she spends what seems like an inordinate amount of time attacking a 30-year-old book called 'Metaphors We Live By' by George Lakoff and Mark Johnson, for its 'devaluation of the power and nature of words.' This variousness has been a hallmark of Garber's career — she is the author of books on Shakespeare, real estate, bisexuality, and pets — and it enlivens 'The Use and Abuse of Literature' with many incidental insights and pleasures. But the real justification for Garber's method is the way it enacts her central thesis: that literature is not so much a subject as an activity." Boston Globe

Gardner, John
On moral fiction. Basic Bks. 1978 214p hardcover o.p. pa $18 **801**
1. Literature -- Philosophy
ISBN 0-465-05226-6 pa
LC 77-20409

Gardner "submits that contemporary U.S. art, primarily that of fiction, is generally not of high quality because it is not moral, in that it strives to devalue rather than improve life. Furthermore, Gardner charges that critics have lost track of true, moral art and have failed to denounce that which is false or immoral." Booklist

Kermode, Frank
An **appetite** for poetry. Harvard Univ. Press 1989 242p $32 **801**
1. Blind 2. Poets 3. Authors 4. Lawyers 5. Criticism 6. Dramatists 7. Editors 8. Essayists 9. Literary critics 10. Insurance executives 11. Nobel laureates for literature 12. Poetry -- History and criticism 13. Literature -- History and criticism
ISBN 0-674-04093-7
LC 89-31725

This collection contains critical and textual readings of Milton, T. S. Eliot, Wallace Stevens, William Empson and the Bible

"Kermode is not simply a critic but also an artist. . . . In An Appetite for Poetry we encounter writing of balance and decorum, and reading of unflinching audacity." Commonweal

Includes bibliographical references

Kundera, Milan

★ The **curtain**; an essay in seven parts. translated from the French by Linda Asher. HarperCollins Publishers 2007 168p $22.95 **801**

1. Literature -- Philosophy 2. Fiction -- History and criticism

ISBN 978-0-06-084186-7; 0-06-084186-9

LC 2006-43420

"The immediacy of Kundera's evocative prose and the rich tapestry he weaves compel us to pick up and read, or reread, the bountiful literary treasures of Western literature. This could be a book from which to draw a summer reading list." Libr J

Mendelsohn, Daniel

Waiting for the barbarians; essays from the classics to pop culture. by Daniel Mendelsohn. New York Review Books 2012 423 p. (alk. paper) $24.95 **801**

1. Criticism 2. Classical literature 3. Popular culture -- United States 4. Literature -- History and criticism 5. Canon (Literature) 6. Literature -- Appreciation 7. Popular culture -- 21st century

ISBN 1590176073; 9781590176078

LC 2012012240

This book by Daniel Mendelsohn is a collection of his essays seen in "The New York Review of Books," "The New Yorker," and "The New York Times Book Review." This collection "brings together twenty-four of his recent essays . . . on a wide range of subjects. . . . Trained as a classicist, Mendelsohn moves easily from . . . considerations of the ways in which the classics continue to make themselves felt in contemporary life . . . to . . . takes on pop spectacles." (Publisher's note)

Moretti, Franco

Distant reading; Franco Moretti. Verso 2013 254 p. illustrations, maps (hardback : alk. paper) $95 **801**

1. Criticism 2. Literature -- History and criticism 3. Literature -- History and criticism -- Theory, etc

ISBN 1781681120; 9781781680841; 9781781681121

LC 2012047274

National Book Critics Circle Award Winner: Criticism (2013)

This collection of essays, by Franco Moretti, "challenges entrenched conceptions about world cultures and arts. In 'Modern European Literatu're: A Geographical Sketch,' he disputes the notion of a literature that reflects 'a European essence.' . . . In its companion piece, 'Conjectures on World Literature,' he similarly explodes the notion of a single contemporary literature that accommodates the writing of all nations." (Publishers weekly)

"Regardless of whether readers agree with Moretti's conclusions, they will find that his application of economic theory, network theory, and evolutionary models to literature

and culture shows these subjects from fresh and often provocative new perspectives." Pub Wkly

Includes bibliographical references and index

Weinstein, Arnold

A **scream** goes through the house; what literature teaches us about life. Random House 2003 xxxvii, 423p il $29.95; pa $14.95 **801**

1. Literature -- Philosophy

ISBN 0-375-50624-1; 0-8129-7243-0 pa

LC 2002-31719

"Blending the literary passion of Harold Bloom with the physiological insights of Antonio Damasio, Weinstein offers splendid readings of the creations of James Baldwin, Ingmar Bergman, Edvard Munch, Kafka, Faulkner, William Burroughs, and Toni Morrison." Booklist

Includes bibliographical references

803 Dictionaries, encyclopedias, concordances

Abrams, M. H. (Meyer Howard), 1912-2015

★ A **glossary** of literary terms; with contributions by Geoffrey Galt Harpham. 8th ed.; Thomson, Wadsworth 2005 370p pa $34.95 **803**

1. Reference books 2. Literature -- Dictionaries

ISBN 1-4130-0218-8; 978-1-4130-0218-8

LC 2004-111345

First published 1957

In a series of essays, the author discusses literary terms and definitions ranging from the traditional to the avant-garde. Subsidiary terms are included under major or generic terms.

Ayto, John

★ **Brewer's** dictionary of modern phrase & fable; by John Ayto & Ian Crofton. 2nd ed.; Chambers Harrap Pub. Ltd. 2010 853p $39.95 **803**

1. Allusions 2. Reference books 3. Literature -- Dictionaries

ISBN 978-0550-105-646

First published 2000 by Cassell

"Focusing on the 20th and 21st centuries, . . . [this book covers a] selection of buzzwords, catchphrases, slang, nicknames, fictional characters and . . . cultural phenomena from pop culture to politics, literature to technology." Publisher's note

★ **Benet's** reader's encyclopedia; edited by Bruce F. Murphy. 5th ed.; Collins 2008 1210p $60 **803**

1. Reference books 2. Literature -- Dictionaries

ISBN 978-0-06-089016-2

LC 2008-31430

First published 1948 under the editorship of William Rose Benet

This encyclopedia contains over 10,000 entries and covers world literature from early times to the present. Includes entries on authors, literary movements, principal characters, plot synopses, terms, awards, myths and legends, etc.

This is "an edifying staple for any literary library." Libr J

Cuddon, J. A.

The **Penguin** dictionary of literary terms and literary theory; 4th ed; Penguin 1999 1024p (Penguin reference) pa $29   **803**
1. Reference books 2. Literature -- Dictionaries
ISBN 0-14-051363-9; 978-0-14-051363-9
First published 1977 in the United Kingdom with title: A dictionary of literary terms; first United States edition published 1977 by Doubleday; this edition first published 1998 by Blackwell Publishers
"Comprehensive dictionary covering all literatures and time periods with basic definitions as currently used. Categories include technical terms, forms, genres, groups, movements, -isms, character types, phrases, motifs or themes, concepts, objects, and styles. Entries often indicate origin and cite examples. Numerous see and see also references." Guide to Ref Books. 11th edition

Cyclopedia of literary characters; rev ed; Salem Press 1998 5v set $368   **803**
1. Reference books 2. Characters and characteristics in literature 3. Literature -- Dictionaries
ISBN 0-89356-438-9
                   LC 97-45813
"Entries are arranged alphabetically by the title of the work. . . . {They} begin with the book's title, foreign title if originally published in a language other than English, author's name with birth and death years, date of first publication, genre, locale, time of action, and plot type. Characters are arranged in order of importance; major characters have 100- to 150-word write-ups. Volume 5 contains three indexes: title, author, and character." Booklist

★ **Oxford** dictionary of phrase and fable; edited by Elizabeth Knowles. 2nd ed.; Oxford University Press 2005 805p $40; pa $18.95   **803**
1. Allusions 2. Reference books 3. Literature -- Dictionaries
ISBN 978-0-19-860981-0; 978-0-19-920246-1 pa
First published 2000
This work seeks to define words and phrases of British cultural history.
This "is a highly useful tool to help understand what phrases mean and where they come from and should definitely be added to all reference collections." Booklist

Rockwood, Camilla

★ **Brewer's** dictionary of phrase & fable; edited by Camilla Rockwood. 18th ed.; Brewer's 2009 xxv, 1460p il $49.95   **803**
1. Allusions 2. Reference books 3. Mythology -- Dictionaries 4. Literature -- Dictionaries 5. English language -- Terms and phrases
ISBN 978-0-550-10411-3
              LC 2009-379960
First published 1870 under the editorship of Ebenezer Cobham Brewer
"Over 15,000 brief entries give the meanings and origins of a broad range of terms, expressions, and names of real, fictitious and mythical characters from world history, science, the arts and literature." N Y Public Libr. Ref Books for Child Collect. 2d edition

808   **Rhetoric and collections of literary texts from more than two literatures**

★ The **best** American essays 2012; David Brooks (editor), Robert Atwan (editor) Houghton Mifflin Harcourt 2012 310 p. $14.95   **808**
1. American essays
ISBN 0547840098; 9780547840093
"Edited by 'New York Times' columnist and best-selling author David Brooks, this . . . collection of the year's best includes thought-provoking essays from Marcia Angell, Miah Arnold, Mark Doty, Joseph Epstein, Jonathan Franzen, Malcolm Gladwell, Francine Prose, Lauren Slater, Sandra Tsing Loh, Jose Antonio Vargas, and others." (Publisher's note)

★ The **best** American travel writing 2012; William T. Vollman (editor), Jason WIlson (editor) Mariner Books 2012 256 p. $14.95   **808**
1. Travelers' writings, American
ISBN 0547808976; 9780547808970
This book, edited by Jason Wilson and William T. Vollman, is a collection of American travel writing featuring pieces including "including Monte Reel's look at how to explore the world like a Victorian gentleman and Elliott D. Woods' essay on the 'zabaleen,' or garbage pickers, in the Garbage City of Cairo." Other pieces include "Paul Theroux's short piece on the Maine coast and . . . Kimberly Meyer's essay on the elaborate Passion play performed each year in the Holy City of the Wichitas." (Kirkus)

Black nature; four centuries of African American nature poetry. edited by Camille T. Dungy. University of Georgia Press 2009 xxxv, 387p $69.95; pa $24.95   **808**
1. Nature poetry 2. American poetry -- African American authors
ISBN 978-0-8203-3277-2; 0-8203-3277-1; 978-0-8203-3431-8 pa; 0-8203-3431-6 pa
             LC 2009-18528
"Since Bryant, Longfellow, Whitman, and Dickinson, the image of 'nature poetry' has stayed traditionally white. This collection helps complete the picture, by including a people who were chained to a foreign land and yet sustained a love for it." Orion
Includes bibliographical references

Brewer, Robert Lee
Writer's Market; edited by Robert Lee Brewer. Writer's Digest various pagings   **808**
1. Publishers and publishing 2. Authorship -- Handbooks, manuals, etc.
Annual. First published 1922
"A guide for freelance writers, covering the practical side of writing for publication, including information about book publishers; consumer magazines; trade, technical and a few professional journals; scriptwriting; syndicates; greeting card and gift markets. Provides extensive lists of contests and awards and of relevant organizations and publications. Subject index of book publishers." Guide to Ref Books. 11th edition
Includes bibliographical references

Brown, Laura

How to write anything; a complete guide. Laura Brown. W W Norton & Co Inc 2014 608 p. illustrations (hardcover) $35 **808**

1. Writing 2. Rhetoric 3. Report writing 4. English language -- Rhetoric

ISBN 0393240142; 9780393240146

LC 2013045078

This book, by Laura Brown, is "a practical guide to everything you'll ever need to write—at work, at school, and in your personal life. With more than two hundred how-to entries and easy-to-use models organized into three comprehensive sections on work, school, and personal life, [it] covers a wide range of topics that make it an essential guide for the whole family." (Publisher's note)

"Comprehensive and accessible, the work guides users through just about any situation where the written word is necessary: social media for businesses, a plea to a professor for an extension, sympathy notes, wedding toasts, letters to the editor, and more." Booklist

Includes bibliographical references and index

★ The **Chicago** manual of style; 16th ed; The University of Chicago Press 2010 1026p **808**

1. Writing 2. Authorship 3. English language -- Usage 4. Printing -- Style manuals 5. Publishers and publishing 6. Authorship -- Style manuals 7. Authorship -- Handbooks, manuals, etc. 8. Publishers and publishing -- Handbooks, manuals, etc.

ISBN 0226104206; 9780226104201

LC 2009053612

First published 1906 with title: A manual of style

This style manual includes journals and electronic publications, descriptive headings on all numbered paragraphs, and chapters on grammar, usage, and documentation, including guidance on citing electronic sources.

Includes glossary and bibliographical references

Children's writer's & illustrator's market; edited by Alice Pope. Writer's Digest Books il **808**

1. Publishers and publishing 2. Authorship -- Handbooks, manuals, etc.

Annual. First published 1998

This reference includes listings of children's book publishers, magazines, agents, art reps, contests, clubs, conferences, awards, and grants with contact information, along with articles and interviews on a variety of subjects relating to children's writing, illustrating, and publishing

Includes bibliographical references

Conway, Jill K.

When memory speaks; reflections on autobiography. [by] Jill Ker Conway. Knopf 1998 205p hardcover o.p. pa $13 **808**

1. Autobiography 2. Biography as a literary form

ISBN 0-679-76645-6 pa

LC 97-49452

"Conway's small gem is a landmark in eliciting fresh contemplation of the inchoate complexity of memory's manifold voices." Publ Wkly

Includes bibliographical references

Garner, Bryan A.

Garner's Modern English Usage; by Bryan Garner. Oxford University Press 2016 1120 p. $50 **808**

1. English language -- Grammar

ISBN 0190491485; 9780190491482

This reference book, by Bryan Garner, "reflects usage lexicography at its finest. Garner explains the nuances of grammar and vocabulary with thoroughness, finesse, and wit. He discourages whatever is slovenly, pretentious, or pedantic." (Publisher's note)

Garvey, Mark

Stylized; a slightly obsessive history of Strunk & White's The elements of style. Simon & Schuster 2009 xxv, 208p il **808**

1. Poets 2. Authors 3. Rhetoric 4. Humorists 5. Novelists 6. Essayists 7. Satirists 8. College teachers 9. Children's authors 10. Nonfiction writers 11. English language -- Style 12. Authorship -- Style manuals 13. English language -- Rhetoric 14. Authorship -- Handbooks, manuals, etc.

ISBN 1-4165-9092-7; 978-1-4165-9092-7

LC 2009007166

This is a history of the composition and publication of William Strunk and E.B. White's The Elements of Style, which appeared in 1959.

"A fan's meticulously researched, bighearted tribute to a sturdy, perennial writing guide, this history of Elements of Style is complete and unreservedly affectionate." Publ Wkly

Includes bibliographical references

Glenn, Cheryl

Hodges' Harbrace handbook; [by] Cheryl Glenn ... [et al.] 16th ed; Thomson Wadsworth 2007 xxxi, 793p il $81.95 **808**

1. English language -- Grammar 2. English language -- Composition and exercises

ISBN 1-4130-1031-8

LC 2005-937964

First published 1941 under the authorship of John C. Hodges with title: Harbrace handbook of English. Frequently revised

A guide to the fundamentals of grammar, composition, and usage

Gutkind, Lee

You can't make this stuff up; the complete guide to writing creative nonfiction--from memoir to literary journalism and everything in between. Lee Gutkind. Da Capo Press/Lifelong Books 2012 xviii, 270 p.p **808**

1. Authorship 2. Creative writing 3. Creative nonfiction -- Technique 4. Exposition (Rhetoric) 5. Creative nonfiction -- Authorship 6. Reportage literature -- Technique

ISBN 9780738215549; 9780738215860

LC 2012018586

This book, by Lee Gutkind, offers advice for writing creative nonfiction. "From rags-to-riches-to-rags tell-alls to personal health sagas to literary journalism, everyone seems to want to try their hand at creative nonfiction. . . . Gutkind describes and illustrates each and every aspect of the genre, from defining a concept and establishing a writing process to the final product." (Publisher's note)

Includes bibliographical references (p. 255-259) and index

Hooks, Bell

Remembered rapture; the writer at work. Holt & Co. 1999 237p hardcover o.p. pa $13 **808**
1. Authorship 2. American literature -- African American authors

ISBN 0-8050-5910-5 pa

LC 98-7998

"The redoubtable Hooks offers a series of essays on writing, focusing on women, black writers (e.g., why there are so many black women novelists and so few in nonfiction), and what it was like to move to writer-saturated New York." Libr J

Lamott, Anne

Bird by bird; some instructions on writing and life. Pantheon Bks. 1994 xxxi, 239p $23; pa. $16 **808**
1. Authorship

ISBN 0-679-43520-4; 9780385480017

LC 94-5448

In this discussion of the craft of writing Lamott offers "examples and anecdotes that explain how she copes with self-doubt, writer's block, professional jealousy, and the discipline necessary to turn thoughts into words on a page. Her work is an honest appraisal of what it takes to be a writer and why it matters so much." Libr J

LaRocque, Paula, 1937-

The **book** on writing; the ultimate guide to writing well. Marion Street Press 2003 240p pa $18.95 **808**
1. Authorship

ISBN 0-9665176-9-5

LC 2003-13308

The author "organizes her book into three sections: mechanical and structural guidelines (i.e. sharpening accuracy and brevity), creative elements of storytelling (e.g., 'Let the Reader Do Some Work'), and style (grammar, usage and punctuation). LaRocque's advice is sane and sound: avoid pretension and over-complication, and stay away from jargon and clichés. . . . Beginning writers should find clear, useful advice here." Publ Wkly

★ **MLA** style manual and guide to scholarly publishing; 3rd ed.; Modern Language Association of America 2008 xxiv, 336p $32.50 **808**
1. Authorship -- Handbooks, manuals, etc.

ISBN 978-0-87352-297-7; 0-87352-297-4

LC 2008-2894

First published 1985 under authorship of Walter S. Achtert and Joseph Gibaldi

This book offers "guidance on writing scholarly texts, documenting research sources, submitting manuscripts to publishers, and dealing with legal issues surrounding publication." Publisher's note

Includes bibliographical references

Modern Language Association of America

★ **MLA** handbook for writers of research papers; 7th ed.; Modern Language Association of America 2009 xxi, 292p il pa $22 **808**
1. Report writing

ISBN 978-1-60329-024-1

LC 2008-47484

First published 1977 with title: MLA handbook for writers of research papers, theses, and dissertations

This manual discusses research strategies, formatting, documenting sources, writing basics and utilizing electronic sources.

Includes bibliographical references

Pinker, Steven, 1954-

The **sense** of style; the thinking person's guide to writing in the 21st century. Steven Pinker. Viking Adult 2014 368 p. illustrations (hardback) $27.95 **808**
1. Authorship 2. English language -- Grammar 3. English language -- Style

ISBN 0670025852; 9780670025855

LC 2014004509

In this writing guidebook, author Steven Pinker "shows how writing depends on imagination, empathy, coherence, grammatical knowhow, and an ability to savor and reverse engineer the good prose of others. He replaces dogma about usage with reason and evidence, allowing writers and editors to apply the guidelines judiciously, rather than robotically, being mindful of what they are designed to accomplish." (Publisher's note)

"A thoughtful addition for writing instruction collections; the chapter on "The Curse of Knowledge" should be mandatory reading for everyone." LJ

Includes bibliographical references and index

Plotnik, Arthur

Spunk & bite; a writer's guide to punchier, more engaging language & style. Random House 2005 263p hardcover o.p. pa $12.95 **808**
1. Rhetoric

ISBN 0-375-72115-0; 0-375-72227-0 pa

LC 2005-44934

The author "demonstrates how . . . unexpected humor, loquaciousness, and apt description can jolt a writer into engaged authorship. This primer is dotted with illustrative examples that range from Shakespeare and J.K. Rowling to Dave Barry and Maeve Binchy. . . . This is an entertaining and engaging choice for writers." Libr J

Pollack, John

Shortcut; how analogies reveal connections, spark innovation, and sell our greatest ideas. John Pollack. Gotham 2014 256 p. (hardback) $27 **808**
1. Analogy 2. Language and languages 3. Sociolinguistics 4. Creative thinking 5. Business communication 6. English language -- Business English

ISBN 1592408494; 9781592408498

LC 2014009895

Author John Pollack examines why "analogies are far more complex than their SAT stereotype and lie at the very core of human cognition and creativity. [Through] engaging stories, surprising examples, and a practical method to evaluate the truth or effectiveness of any analogy, 'Shortcut' will improve critical thinking, enhance creativity, and offer readers a fresh approach to resolving some of today's most intractable challenges." (Publisher's note)

"Perhaps not all readers will be fully persuaded to the impact of analogies but most, especially those with an interest in language and psychology, will come away entertained and informed." LJ

Prose, Francine

★ **Reading** like a writer; a guide for people who love books and for those who want to write them. HarperCollins Publishers 2006 273p **808**
1. Rhetoric 2. Creative writing 3. Books and reading 4. English language -- Rhetoric
ISBN 0-06-077704-4; 0-06-077705-2 pa; 978-0-06-077704-3; 978-0-06-077705-0 pa
LC 2005-58457

The author argues that "would-be writers should turn to the classics for inspiration." (N Y Times Book Rev)

This book "should be greatly appreciated in and out of the classroom. Like the great works of fiction, it's a wise and voluble companion." N Y Times Book Rev

Rabiner, Susan

Thinking like your editor; how to write serious nonfiction--and get it published. by Susan Rabiner and Alfred Fortunato. Norton 2002 284p $26.95; pa $14 **808**
1. Authorship
ISBN 0-393-03892-0; 0-393-32461-3 pa
LC 2001-44551

"In part one, on submissions, the authors discuss how to put together a book proposal and, . . . whether to work through an agent or go solo. In part two, they move to the writing process. . . . Part three discusses how authors and editors (both in-house and freelance) can work together well." Publ Wkly

Siegal, Allan

The **New** York times manual of style and usage; [by] Allan M. Siegal and William G. Connolly. rev and expanded ed; Times Bks. 1999 364p hardcover o.p. pa $15 **808**
1. Authorship -- Handbooks, manuals, etc.
ISBN 0-8129-6389-X pa
LC 99-10630

First published 1962 by McGraw-Hill under the editorship of Lewis Jordan with title: Style book for writers and editors

Rules and guidelines observed by The New York Times for consistency of spelling, capitalization, punctuation, abbreviation, and preferred usage

This work "contends with the AP stylebook in authority and usefulness." Columbia J Rev

Stein, Sol

Stein on writing; a master editor of some of the most successful writers of our century shares his craft

techniques and strategies. St. Martin's Press 1995 308p $24.95; pa $14.95 **808**
1. Authorship
ISBN 0-312-13608-0; 0-312-25421-0 pa
LC 95-31793

The author discusses the process of writing "fiction and nonfiction in terms of characterization, pacing, revision, evoking emotion, and 'liposuctioning flab.' Stein's own writing demonstrates the 'resonance' and 'particularities' he discusses, and his original checklists, writing exercises, and numerous examples encourage the reader/writer to see and do the same. A chapter of help sources and a glossary of terms provide the finishing touch." Libr J

Strunk, William

★ The **elements** of style; with revisions, an introduction, and a chapter on writing by E.B. White. 4th ed; Allyn & Bacon 1999 105p $14.95; pa $7.95 **808**
1. Rhetoric
ISBN 0-205-31342-6; 0-205-30902-X pa
LC 99-16419

First privately printed in 1918

This work provides guidelines for proper usage and composition. Misused expressions and commonly misspelled words are discussed. Includes examples.

This work is "prescriptive, conservative, and humorous; in sum, it is the best book available on how to write English prose." Nichols. Guide to Ref Books for Sch Media Cent. 4th edition

Turabian, Kate L.

Student's guide to writing college papers; 4th ed; The University of Chicago Press 2010 281p il (Chicago guides to writing, editing, and publishing) $39; pa $15; ebook $15 **808**
1. Dissertations 2. Report writing
ISBN 978-0-226-81630-2; 978-0-226-81631-9 pa; 978-0-226-81633-3 ebook
LC 2009-31583

First published 1963 with title: Student's guide for writing college papers

This guide covers selecting a topic, collecting material, planning and writing the paper, and preparing footnotes and bibliographies.

Includes bibliographical references

United States/Government Printing Office

★ **Style** manual; an official guide to the form and style of Federal Government printing 2008. U.S. Government Printing Office. [30th ed.]; U.S. G.P.O. 2008 453p pa $36 **808**
1. Printing -- Style manuals 2. Authorship -- Handbooks, manuals, etc. 3. Publishers and publishing -- Handbooks, manuals, etc.
ISBN 978-0-16-081812-7
LC 2009-376600

First published 1908 with title: Manual of style. Frequently revised

"A useful and extensive manual giving the practices of the Government Printing Office on copy preparation, with rules for capitalization, punctuation, abbreviations, etc., and information on foreign languages, including alphabets, with pronunciation, special rules, lists of numbers, etc." Guide to Ref Books. 11th edition

Walker, Janice R.

The **Columbia** guide to online style; [by] Janice R. Walker and Todd Taylor. 2nd ed.; Columbia University Press 2006 xxi, 288p il $45; pa $19.50 **808**
1. Bibliographical citations 2. Authorship -- Data processing -- Handbooks, manuals, etc.
ISBN 0-231-13210-7; 978-0-231-13210-7; 0-231-13211-5 pa; 978-0-231-13211-4 pa
LC 2006-24383
First published 1998
This is a "resource for citing electronic and electronically accessed sources. It is also a . . . style guide for creating documents electronically for submission for print or electronic publication." Publisher's note
Includes bibliographical references

The **Writer's** digest guide to good writing; edited by Thomas Clark {et al.} Writer's Digest Bks. 1994 338p hardcover o.p. pa $14.99 **808**
1. Authorship -- Handbooks, manuals, etc.
ISBN 1-58297-138-2 pa
LC 93-43554
This collection of articles culled from issues of Writer's Digest magazine contains "essays on how to write with simplicity, plot and pace a story, build suspense, create characters, and tackle certain genres, including mysteries, horror, romance, and various forms of nonfiction. The selections are organized by decades and include essays by Erle Stanley Gardner, Irving Wallace, Louis L'Amour {and} Allen Ginsberg," Booklist

Zinsser, William Knowlton

Writing to learn. Harper & Row 1988 256p hardcover o.p. pa $145 **808**
1. Rhetoric -- Study and teaching
ISBN 0-06-272040-6 pa
LC 87-45825
"Eschewing theory and philosophical breast-beating, Zinsser uses his own experience to reinforce the fact that clear, eloquent writing can be taught for every subject across the curriculum. A practical manual for teachers and a powerful reminder for everyone that good writing makes possible good thinking." Am Libr
Includes bibliographical referneces

808.02 Authorship techniques, plagiarism, editorial techniques

D'Agata, John

The **lifespan** of a fact; John D'Agata and Jim Fingal. W. W. Norton 2012 160p. **808.02**
1. E-mail 2. Journalists 3. Essay -- Authorship 4. Creative nonfiction -- Authorship
ISBN 9780393340730
LC 2011042637
In this book, "an essayist ([John] D'Agata) and his exasperated fact checker ([Jim] Fingal) debate the line between art and reality. . . . The text reproduces D'Agata's article about a teenager who leapt to his death from a Las Vegas Hotel, . . . Fingal's . . . fact-checking commentary, . . . and the authors' barbed e-exchanges on everything from the number of strip clubs in Vegas to the origins of tae kwon do and the existence of D'ata's mother's cat.' . . . D'Agata cheerfully admits to embroidering the story with factoids; meanwhile, Fingal's efforts to verify them . . . required seven years and the help of medical journals, academic linguists, satellite photos, and field research." (Publishers Weekly)
Includes bibliographical references.

Kidder, Tracy

Good prose; the art of nonfiction. Tracy Kidder and Richard Todd. Random House 2013 224 p. (acid-free paper) $26 **808.02**
1. Writing 2. Biography 3. Friendship 4. Authorship 5. Prose literature -- Authorship 6. Creative nonfiction -- Authorship
ISBN 1400069750; 9780679604723; 9781400069750
LC 2012021165
Author Tracy Kidder "explores three major nonfiction forms: narratives, essays, and memoirs." She looks at "the works of a wide range of writers, novelists as well as nonfiction writers, for models and instruction." Kidder writes "about narrative strategies (and about how to find a story, sometimes in surprising places), about the ethical challenges of nonfiction, and about the realities of making a living as a writer." (Publisher's book)
Includes bibliographical references and index.

Malcolm, Janet

Forty-one false starts; essays on artists and writers. Janet Malcolm. Farrar Straus & Giroux 2013 320 p. (hardcover : alk. paper) $27 **808.02**
1. Artists 2. Authors 3. Authorship
ISBN 0374157693; 9780374157692
LC 2012034570
This book by Janet Malcolm "brings together essays . . . that reflect her preoccupation with artists and their work. Her subjects are painters, photographers, writers, and critics. She explores Bloomsbury's obsessive desire to create things visual and literary; the 'passionate collaborations' behind Edward Weston's nudes; and the character of the German art photographer Thomas Struth, who is 'haunted by the Nazi past,' yet whose photographs have 'a lightness of spirit.'" (Publisher's note)
Includes bibliographical references

MFA vs NYC; the Two Cultures of American Fiction. edited by Chad Harbach. Faber and Faber, Inc. / n+1 Foundation, Inc. 2014 320 p. illustrations (pbk.) $16 **808.02**
1. Authorship 2. Creative writing 3. Vocational guidance 4. Authors and publishers 5. Fiction -- Authorship 6. Authorship -- Vocational guidance 7. Fiction -- Publishing -- United States 8. Authors and publishers -- United States 9. Creative writing (Higher education) -- United States
ISBN 0865478139; 9780865478138
LC 2013048115

This book, edited by Chad Harbach, describes and engages with how "the American literary scene has split into two cultures: New York publishing versus university MFA programs. This book brings together established writers, MFA professors and students, and New York editors, publicists, and agents to talk about these overlapping worlds, and the ways writers make (or fail to make) a living within them." (Publisher's note)

"Essential insights, masterfully assembled, on the precarious state of American publishing." Kirkus

Includes bibliographical references and index

808.06 Rhetoric of specific kinds of writing

Aiken, Joan

The **way** to write for children. St. Martin's Griffin 1999 97p pa $9.95 **808.06**
1. Authorship 2. Children's literature -- Technique
ISBN 0-312-20048-X

LC 99-166931

First published 1982 in the United Kingdom

"In this crisp, informative and often witty survey of 'the market' Aiken is also giving the customers—teachers, librarians, parents, every one concerned with children's literature of quality-a good general idea of what is available already and of what authors are trying to do." Times Lit Suppl

Jacob, Dianne

Will write for food; the complete guide to writing cookbooks, blogs, memoir, recipes, and more. Dianne Jacob. 3rd edition Da Capo Lifelong 2015 353 p. pbk $16.99 **808.06**
1. Food writing
ISBN 9780738218052; 0738218057

LC 2015003915

"The author "provides detailed, practical advice on such matters as recipe development; how to launch a blog and draw readers, pitch article and book ideas, and refine one's prose style; and where to go to network or study. Also included are writing exercises, extensive suggestions for further reading, lists of publications and websites that accept freelancers, and perspectives drawn from interviews with dozens of well-known food writers such as Mark Bittman, Deborah Madison, and Calvin Trillin. . . . An engaging, informative handbook for hobbyists and aspiring professionals." Libr J (review of 2nd edition)

Includes bibliographical references and index

Kephart, Beth

Handling the truth; on the writing of memoir. Beth Kephart. Gotham Books 2013 224 p. $16 **808.06**
1. Biography 2. Autobiography -- Authorship 3. Biography as a literary form
ISBN 159240815X; 9781592408153

LC 2012043517

In author Beth Kephart's book, "she thinks out loud about the form--on how it gets made, on what it means to make it, on the searing language of truth, on the thin line between remembering and imagining, and, finally, on the rights of memoirists. Drawing on proven writing lessons and

classic examples, on the work of her students and on her own memories of weather, landscape, color, and love, Kephart probes the wrenching and essential questions that lie at the heart of memoir." (Publisher's note)

Seuling, Barbara

How to write a children's book and get it published; 3rd ed; Wiley 2005 233p il pa $15.95 **808.06**
1. Authorship 2. Children's literature -- Technique
ISBN 0-471-67619-5

LC 2004-4691

First published 1984

Presents "five essential steps (from researching the current marketplace to submitting your manuscript) to publishing works for children." Libr J

Includes bibliographical references

Shulevitz, Uri

Writing with pictures; how to write and illustrate children's books. Watson-Guptill 1985 271p il hardcover o.p. pa $29.95 **808.06**
1. Picture books for children 2. Children's literature -- Technique
ISBN 0-8230-5935-9 pa

LC 85-15604

"With heavy emphasis on illustration, this detailed book guides aspiring authors/illustrators through telling the story and drawing the pictures to preparing artwork for the printer." Libr J

Includes bibliographical references

Turabian, Kate L.

★ A **manual** for writers of research papers, theses, and dissertations; Chicago Style for students and researchers. Kate L. Turabian; revised by Wayne C. Booth, Gregory G. Colomb, Joseph M. Williams, and the University of Chicago Press editorial staff. 8th edition University of Chicago Press 2013 xv, 448 p.p illustrations (Chicago guides to writing, editing, and publishing) (cloth : alkaline paper) $42.50 **808.06**
1. Dissertations 2. Report writing 3. Academic writing -- Handbooks, manuals, etc 4. Dissertations
ISBN 0226816370; 9780226816371; 9780226816388

LC 2012036981

This book, by Kate L. Turabian, "[begins] with an overview of the steps in the research and writing process . . . [and] provides an overview of citation practices with detailed information on the two main scholarly citation styles. . . . The final section treats all matters of editorial style, with advice on punctuation, capitalization, spelling, abbreviations, table formatting, and the use of quotations." (Publisher's note)

"This edition's new graphic design updates the look and feel of this resource and further develops rules and advice for the use and citation of online sources. In addition to featuring new templates for citing e-books, websites, blogs, social networks, discussion groups, online videos, and podcasts, the eighth edition offers new general advice to help students make good decisions about what information to include for online sources that may not have all the traditional elements useful in citing a print source." Choice

Includes bibliographical references (pages 409-433) and index

808.1 Rhetoric in specific literary forms

★ **2009** poet's market; Nancy Breen, editor. Writer's Digest Bks. 2008 572p pa $27.99 **808.1**
1. Poetry -- Marketing
ISBN 978-1-58297-544-3; 1-58297-544-2
Annual. First published 1989
"Useful for those aspiring to publish their poems in literary journals and magazines.... Entries include a brief journal profile, submission requirements, and contact information. Offers advice to beginning poets on getting published, brief articles by working poets/editors, grant information, contests and awards, poetry readings, writing colonies, organizations and publications useful to poets. Indexes for chapbook publishers, publishers by subject, publishers by state, and a general index." Guide to Ref Books. 11th edition
Includes bibliographical references

Abrams, M. H. (Meyer Howard), 1912-2015
The **fourth** dimension of a poem; and other essays. M.H. Abrams; foreword by Harold Bloom. W. W. Norton & Company 2012 240 p. (hardcover) $25.95 **808.1**
1. Poetics 2. American essays 3. Poetry -- History and criticism
ISBN 0393058301; 9780393058307
LC 2012020169
This book by M. H. Abrams presents "a collection of nine new and recent essays that challenge the reader to think about poetry in new ways. In these essays ... Abrams engages ... with pivotal figures in intellectual and literary history, among them Kant, Keats, and Hazlitt. The centerpiece of the volume is Abrams's ... essay 'The Fourth Dimension of a Poem' on the pleasure of reading poems aloud." (Publisher's note)
Includes bibliographical references and index.

Addonizio, Kim
The **poet's** companion; a guide to the pleasures of writing poetry. [by] Kim Addonizio and Dorianne Laux. Norton 1997 284p pa $14.95 **808.1**
1. Poetics
ISBN 0-393-31654-8
LC 96-40451
This work contains "three main sections: 'Subjects for Writing' (e.g. death, the erotic), 'The Poet's Craft' (metaphor, rhyme), and 'The Writing Life' (self-doubt, writer's block); four separate appendixes list other writing texts, anthologies, marketing tips, and electronic resources.... Both knowledgeable and practical in their approach, the authors offer everything a poet needs, including ... a gentle yet insistent lesson on grammar." Libr J
Includes bibliographical references

Deutsch, Babette
Poetry handbook: a dictionary of terms; 4th ed; HarperResource 2002 203p pa $14 **808.1**
1. Reference books 2. Poetry -- Terminology 3. Poetics -- Dictionaries
ISBN 0-06-463548-1
First published 1957 by Funk & Wagnalls

"The craft of verse described in dictionary form. Terms and techniques are defined and illustrated." N Y Public Libr. Ref Books for Child Collect. 2d edition

Higginson, William J.
The **haiku** handbook; how to write, teach, and appreciate haiku. [by] William J. Higginson and Penny Harter; foreword by Jane Reichhold. 25th anniversary ed.; Kodansha International 2009 331p pa $18 **808.1**
1. Haiku
ISBN 978-4-770-03113-6; 4-770-03113-0
LC 2009-36628
First published 1985 by McGraw-Hill
This book "presents haiku poets writing in English, Spanish, French, German, and five other languages on an equal footing with Japanese poets. Not only are the four great Japanese masters of the haiku represented (Bash'o, Buson, Issa, and Shiki) but also several major Western authors not commonly known to have written haiku. The book presents a ... history of the Japanese haiku, including the dynamic changes throughout the twentieth century as the haiku has been adapted to suburban and industrial settings. Full chapters are offered on form, the seasons in haiku, and haiku craft, plus background on the Japanese poetic tradition, and the effect of translation on our understanding of haiku." Publisher's note
Includes bibliographical references

Hirsch, Edward
How to read a poem; and fall in love with poetry. Harcourt Brace & Co. 1999 352p $23; pa $15 **808.1**
1. Poetics 2. Poetry -- History and criticism
ISBN 0-15-100419-6; 0-15-600566-2 pa
LC 98-50065
The author "has gathered an eclectic group of poems from many times and places, with selections as varied as postwar Polish poetry, works by Keats and Christopher Smart, and lyrics from African American work songs. A prolific, award-winning poet in his own right, Hirsch suggests helpful strategies for understanding and appreciating each poem. The book is scholarly but very readable and incorporates interesting anecdotes from the lives of the poets." Libr J
Includes bibliographical references

Hirsch, Edward, 1950-
A **Poet's** Glossary; by Edward Hirsch. Houghton Mifflin Harcourt 2014 736 p. $30 **808.1**
1. Poetry -- History and criticism 2. Poetics 3. Poetry -- Glossaries, vocabularies, etc
ISBN 0151011958; 9780151011957
LC 2014011675
In this book, author Edward Hirsch "has delved deeply into the poetic traditions of the world, returning with an inclusive, international compendium. Moving ... from the bards of ancient Greece to the revolutionaries of Latin America, from small formal elements to large mysteries, he provides thoughtful definitions for the most important poetic vocabulary, imbuing his work with a lifetime of schol-

arship and the warmth of a man devoted to his art." (Publisher's note)

"Offering definitions, a discussion of poetic techniques, and an unalloyed spiritual quality to his work, Hirsch's . . . alphabetically arranged glossary includes historical explanations, quotes, interpretative material, usage in various languages, and references to additional terms for even more clarification." LJ

Hirshfield, Jane, 1953-

Ten windows; how great poems transform the world. Jane Hirshfield. Alfred A. Knopf 2015 320 p. illustrations (hardcover) $24.95   **808.1**
1. Books and reading 2. Poetry -- History and criticism
ISBN 0385351054; 9780385351058
LC 2014025430

This book, by Jane Hirshfield, is a "collection of essays on how the best poems work. . . . Closely reading poems by Dickinson, Bashō, Szymborska, Cavafy, Heaney, Bishop, and Komunyakaa, among many others, Hirshfield reveals how poetry's world-making takes place: word by charged word." (Publisher's note)

"Hirshfield writes brilliantly of paradox in poetry, of what poets and stand-up comics have in common, and how poetry "counters isolation and meaninglessness." The profound pleasure Hirshfield takes in delineating poetry's efficacy makes for a beautifully enlightening volume." Booklist

Kooser, Ted

★ The **poetry** home repair manual; practical advice for beginning poets. University of Nebraska Press 2005 163p $19.95; pa $13.95   **808.1**
1. Poetics
ISBN 0-8032-2769-8; 0-8032-5978-6 pa
LC 2004-24700

"Among the many books offering advice on writing poetry, . . . [this book] stands out for its usefulness and, at the same time, for its inspiring view of the purposes of poetry." Midwest Quarterly

Includes bibliographical references

Oliver, Mary

A **poetry** handbook. Harcourt Brace & Co. 1994 130p pa $13   **808.1**
1. Poetics
ISBN 0-15-672400-6
LC 93-49676

A "handbook for young poets on the formal aspects and structure of poetry. Oliver excels at explaining the sound and sense of poetry—from scansion to imagery, diction to voice. She stresses the importance of reading poetry, since, in order to write well, 'it is entirely necessary to read widely and deeply.' Sage advice is given in an entire chapter dedicated to revision, wherein Oliver urges poets to consider their first draft 'an unfinished piece of work' that can be polished and improved later. Written in a pleasant and lucid style, this book is a wonderful resource." Libr J

Pinsky, Robert, 1940-

Singing School; Learning to Write (And Read) Poetry by Studying With the Masters. Robert Pinsky. W W Norton & Co Inc. 2013 160 p. $25.95   **808.1**
1. Poets 2. Poetry 3. Authorship 4. Poetics
ISBN 0393050688; 9780393050684
LC 2013022146

In this book, poet Robert Pinsky "focuses on how poets read poetry in order to learn how to write poetry, taking his instructive title from William Butler Yeats: 'Nor is there singing school but studying / Monuments of its own magnificence.' Pinsky has selected a . . . variety of salient poems and organized them into sections titled 'Freedom,' 'Listening,' 'Form,' and 'Dreaming Things Up.' He introduces each of the 80 selections with an illuminating bit of analysis." (Booklist)

Includes bibliographical references and index

The **Princeton** encyclopedia of poetry and poetics; Roland Greene, editor in chief; Stephen Cushman, general editor; Clare Cavanagh, Jahan Ramazani, Paul Rouzer, associate editors; Harris Feinsod, David Marno, Alexandra Slessarev, assistant editors. Princeton University Press 2012 xxxvi, 1639 p.p   **808.1**
1. Poetry -- Dictionaries 2. Poetics -- Dictionaries 3. Poetry -- History and criticism
ISBN 9780691133348; 9780691154916
LC 2012005602

Includes bibliographical references and index

808.2   Rhetoric of drama

Field, Syd

★ **Screenplay**; the foundations of screenwriting. Rev. ed.; Delta Trade Paperbacks 2005 320p il pa $16   **808.2**
1. Motion picture plays -- Technique
ISBN 0-385-33903-8
LC 2005-48491

First published 1979

This book covers the basics of writing a screenplay, including how to build a character, set up a scene, and what to do after the screenplay is written.

Hauge, Michael

Writing screenplays that sell. HarperReference 2011 349p pa $21   **808.2**
1. Motion picture plays -- Technique 2. Screenplays 3. Television scripts
ISBN 0-06-272500-9; 978-0-06-272500-4
LC 91-55005

First published 1988 by McGraw-Hill

"From renowned Hollywood story consultant Michael Hauge, considered "one of the most sought after lecturers and script consultants in the U.S." by Scriptwriter magazine, comes the ultimate concept-to-deal guide for writing and selling screenplays for movies and television—now fully revised and updated for the modern screenwriter in this all new

20th anniversary edition." (Publisher's note)
Includes bibliographical references

Inside the room; writing TV with the pros at UCLA Extension Writers' Program. edited by Linda Venis, Director, UCLA Extension Department of the Arts and Writers' Program. Gotham Books 2013 272 p. **808.2**
1. Television authorship 2. Television broadcasting 3. Television authorship -- Vocational guidance
ISBN 9781592408115

LC 2013004221

In this book, edited by Linda Venis, "accomplished writers from the . . . UCLA Extension Writers' Program provide a . . . how-to book for aspiring television writers. . . . Television writers . . . take aspiring writers through the process of writing their first spec script . . . and revising their scripts to meet pro standards. They also learn how to launch and sustain a writing career and get a rare look inside the process of creating, selling, and getting a TV show made." (Publisher's note)

"A practical guide to how TV is made, from bright idea to syndication. A raft of instructors from the UCLA Extension Writers' Program (including director Venis) and a pool of professional TV writers whose credits include such series as Mad Men, Frasier and The Simpsons guide aspiring TV writers through the process of joining the ranks of small-screen scribes, from drafting a first script to thriving in a writers' room to pitching an original series. The advice is clear and specific...An engaging and helpful how-to for hopeful TV writers or anyone interested in the nuts and bolts of this ephemeral art."

Now write! screenwriting; exercises by today's best writers and teachers. [by] Sherry Ellis with Laurie Lamson. Jeremy P. Tarcher/Penguin 2011 343p il pa $14.95 **808.2**
1. Motion picture plays -- Technique
ISBN 978-1-58542-851-9

LC 2010-29424

The editors "compile guidelines from successful screenwriters on all of the details of writing a screenplay, from choosing your story to structure to character development. Readers will be interested to hear the opinions of such estimated screenwriters as Linda Seger and Syd Field and their takes on what motivates them to write screenplays and how they cope with writer's block and revisions. . . . This guide stands out from the crowd by incorporating the techniques of a variety of different screenwriters rather than just one professional's approach. Highly recommended for readers interested in writing, screenwriting, film, and storytelling." Libr J

808.3 Rhetoric of fiction

Bingham, Harry
The **writers'** and artists' yearbook guide to how to write; the essential guide for authors. Bloomsbury 2012 xiv, 364 p.p (paperback) $22.95 **808.3**
1. Fiction -- Technique 2. Authorship -- Handbooks, manuals, etc.
ISBN 1408157179; 9781408157176

This book by Harry Bingham " is all about writing for publication. How to plan, create and edit work that will sell." It features "examples . . . from successful authors" and is designed "for writers of every genre: fiction and narrative non-fiction, literary and commercial, adults and children. The guide tells you how to . . . understand your market . . . deelop strong, empathetic characters [and] structure and maintain a compelling plot." (Publisher's note)

Butler, Robert Olen
From where you dream; the process of writing fiction. edited, with an introduction by Janet Burroway. Grove Press 2005 269p $24; pa $13 **808.3**
1. Authorship 2. Fiction -- Technique
ISBN 0-8021-1795-3; 0-8021-4257-5 pa

LC 2005-40251

This is a collection of lectures the author has given for his creative writing course at Florida State University.

This "is a remarkably candid, clarifying, and profoundly demanding how-to. . . . Incisive and provocative, Butler's tutorials are a must for anyone even thinking about writing fiction, and readers, too, will benefit from his passionate exhortations." Booklist

Eco, Umberto
Confessions of a young novelist. Harvard University Press 2011 231p il (The Richard Ellmann lectures in modern literature) $18.95 **808.3**
1. Authorship
ISBN 9780674058699; 0-674-05869-0

LC 2010-33172

"In the first three essays/lectures here, Eco addresses interesting questions: what is the boundary between fiction and nonfiction? How do novelists put together books? Why do we care about wholly fictional characters like Anna Karenina or Emma Bovary? His answer to the second question—on constructing a novel—is that he builds his novels by scrupulous attention to physical detail. The fourth essay, 'My Lists,' original to this collection, was not a lecture. It seems a throwaway but reflects Eco's pleasure in the detailed, serial listing of names as attempts to exhaust the plenitude of qualities and quiddities potentially attributable to any single object. . . . As always, Eco is diverting to read." Libr J
Includes bibliographical references

Gardner, John
The **art** of fiction; notes on craft for young writers. Knopf 1984 224p hardcover o.p. pa $12.95 **808.3**
1. Fiction -- Technique
ISBN 0-679-73403-1 pa

LC 83-47850

"This essay distills the late Gardner's ripest thoughts about what fiction is and how to go about learning to write it. The initial section deals with 'literary-aesthetic theory,' the second with 'the fictional process.' . . . The book concludes with two sets of exercises, one for class use and one for individual use. Recommended for any young writer or writing class, and for all readers who care about the craft of fiction." Booklist

On becoming a novelist; foreword by Raymond Carver. W.W. Norton 1999 xxv, 150p pa $14.95 **808.3**

1. Authorship 2. Fiction -- Technique

ISBN 0-393-32003-0

First published 1983 by Harper & Row

The author "explores the dynamic chemistry at the heart of the writer's creative process. Gardner's book is a superbly written, thoroughly original, eminently useful volume." Choice

Koch, Stephen

★ The **modern** library writer's workshop; a guide to the craft of fiction. Modern Library 2003 246p pa $12.95 **808.3**

1. Authorship 2. Fiction -- Technique

ISBN 0-375-75558-6

LC 2002-32593

"Koch's tone is both encouraging and forthright, and his accessible, friendly guide will be essential for aspiring writers." Booklist

Includes bibliographical references

Lukeman, Noah

The **plot** thickens; 8 ways to bring fiction to life. St. Martin's Press 2002 221p $19.95; pa $12.95 **808.3**

1. Fiction -- Technique

ISBN 0-312-28467-5; 0-312-30928-7 pa

LC 2001-58564

"Lukeman focuses on the mechanics of storytelling. He introduces budding writers to the techniques of characterization (ask yourself questions about the people you've created), the various ways of generating suspense (danger, a ticking clock), and the importance of conflict." Booklist

Maass, Donald

Writing the breakout novel; winning advice from a top agent and his bestselling client. foreword by Anne Perry. Writer's Digest Bks. 2001 264p hardcover o.p. pa $16.99 **808.3**

1. Fiction -- Technique

ISBN 1-58297-182-X pa

LC 2001-22036

"Using his own clients as case studies, Maass defines the most crucial elements of a breakout novel—a powerful sense of time and place, larger-than-life characters, a high degree of tension, good subplots, and universal themes—and shows the reader how to use these elements efficiently to write a novel that will generate interest and have the potential to hit the best sellers lists. Each section ends with checklists for review." Libr J

Morrell, Jessica Page

Thanks, but this isn't for us; a (sort of) compassionate guide to why your writing is being re-

jected. Jeremy P. Tarcher-Penguin 2009 357p pa $16.95 **808.3**

1. Authorship

ISBN 978-1-58542-721-5

LC 2009-23252

The author "explores several mistakes new authors make in their manuscripts among them lack of conflict, unbelievable dialogue, and details that lack specific sensory appeal. Each chapter begins with a lively overview of a common problem, then lists what Morrell calls 'deal breakers'—particular habits such as lack of subplots and one-dimensional bad guys—that deter an editor from accepting a manuscript for publication. She concludes each chapter with exercises designed to improve storytelling, and then lists book resources for those wanting to delve more deeply into studies of character, emotion, tension and plot. . . . Emerging and established writers alike will benefit from Morrell's shrewd observations." Writer

Includes bibliographical references

Nabokov, Vladimir Vladimirovich

Lectures on literature; {by} Vladimir Nabokov; edited by Fredson Bowers; introduction by John Updike. Harcourt Brace Jovanovich 1980 xxviii, 385p il hardcover o.p. pa $18 **808.3**

1. Poets 2. Authors 3. Novelists 4. Dramatists 5. Essayists 6. Travel writers 7. Literary critics 8. Short story writers 9. Fiction -- History and criticism

ISBN 978-0-15-602775-5; 0-15-602775-5

LC 79-3690

Companion volume to Lectures on Russian literature

In the early 1950s, before Nabokov became a famous writer, he taught literature at Wellesley and Cornell. The editor, with the help of Nabokov's wife and son, has collected seven lectures on "Mansfield Park," "Bleak House," "Madame Bovary," "The Strange Case of Dr. Jekyll and Mr. Hyde," "The Walk by Swann's Place," "The Metamorphosis" and "Ulysses." There are two additional lectures on other topics related to literature. The volume includes a sample examination for the course and pages of original manuscripts with maps and diagrams which the author used to illustrate his lectures

Piercy, Marge

So you want to write; how to master the craft of writing fiction and memoir. [by] Marge Piercy and Ira Wood. 2nd ed.; Leapfrog Press 2005 324p pa $16.95 **808.3**

1. Biography as a literary form 2. Fiction -- Technique

ISBN 0-9728984-5-X

First published 2001

This book "uses talks, exercises, anecdotes and examples proven in the classroom, to address: How to begin a piece by seducing your reader, How to create characters that embody the infinite contradictions of human behavior, How to master the elements of plotting fiction, How to create a strategy for telling the story of your life, How to learn to read critically, like a professional writer, How to write about painful personal material without coming off as a victim, [and] How to proceed if your work is continually rejected by publishers." Publisher's note

Includes bibliographical references

Roberts, Gillian

You can write a mystery. Writer's Digest Bks. 1999 124p il pa $12.99 **808.3**
1. Mystery fiction -- Technique
ISBN 0-89879-863-9

LC 99-19316

"Along with analysis of the literary aspects of mystery writing, Roberts also surveys such practical matters as grammar, punctuation, and how to submit the manuscript. If character and setting are what distinguish the best mysteries, failed plot mechanics are invariably what derail the worst. Roberts' basic but too-often-overlooked advice will help keep your story on track." Booklist

Includes bibliographical references

Stein, Sol

How to grow a novel; the most common mistakes writers make and how to overcome them. St. Martin's Press 1999 240p $25.95; pa $14.95 **808.3**
1. Fiction -- Technique
ISBN 0-312-20949-5; 0-312-26749-5 pa

LC 99-36922

"Stein states bluntly right from the beginning that 'liars say they write only for themselves' and that a 'lack of courtesy' toward the reader is one of the chief faults of unsuccessful writing. While this is perhaps a controversial notion, prospective writers will nonetheless be well rewarded by reading this collection of tips, methods, and numerous anecdotes." Libr J

Swain, Dwight V.

Creating characters; how to build story people. Writer's Digest Bks. 1990 195p hardcover o.p. pa $14.99 **808.3**
1. Characters and characteristics in literature 2. Fiction -- Technique
ISBN 0-89879-662-8 pa

LC 90-39640

"Swain talks to his readers in a conversational tone, suggesting techniques, giving examples to illuminate his points, and offering activities for sharpening character development skills. This is a book for those already committed to writing fiction and who want to think about the craft of writing." SLJ

Includes bibliographical references

Techniques of the selling writer. University of Okla. Press 1981 330p $24.95 **808.3**
1. Fiction -- Technique
ISBN 0-8061-1191-7

First published 1965 with title: Tricks & techniques of the selling writer

The author offers practical advice for creating and marketing publishable fiction

"Often called 'the bible of fiction writing,' this classic is dated slightly by references to such things as 'carbon copies.' But Swain's tried-and-true scene-and-sequel approach has generated many books and workshops." Libr J

Wheat, Carolyn

How to write killer fiction; the funhouse of mystery & the roller coaster of suspense. Perseverance Press 2003 191p il pa $13.95 **808.3**
1. Mystery fiction -- Technique 2. Suspense fiction -- Technique
ISBN 1-88028-462-6

LC 2002-15588

Wheat begins with a "discussion of the distinction between mystery and suspense . . . and then devotes a section to each genre. She offers up plenty of useful tips, such as how to dispense vital information in subtle ways and how to plant clues without being too obvious about it." Booklist

Includes bibliographical references

Wood, James

★ **How** fiction works. Farrar, Straus and Giroux 2008 265p $24 **808.3**
1. Fiction
ISBN 0-374-17340-0; 978-0-374-17340-1

LC 2008-10290

The author addresses such questions as "What is character, point of view, the value of metaphor and simile, and detail? Is it all artifice or realism, or could it be labeled imaginative truth? His engaging discussion covers narration in all its forms, the impersonal author, the tension that exists between an author's and a character's style, flat vs. round characters, irony, and more. Wood uses excerpts from works by notable authors, from Miguel Cervantes and Jane Austen to Saul Bellow and John Updike, to illustrate his statements with pinpoint precision. Whether he is commenting on a work's weakness or strength, he supports his opinion with reasoned scholarship." Libr J

Includes bibliographical references

808.5   Rhetoric of speech

Flaherty, Francis

The **elements** of story; field notes on nonfiction writing. Harper Collins 2009 xxi, 293p $24.99 **808.5**
1. Rhetoric 2. Storytelling
ISBN 978-0-06-168914-7; 0-06-168914-9

LC 2008-53946

The author offers 50 "tips on the many elements writers can convey in stories. Not a style guide, this is instead a nuts-and-bolts examination of the larger elements of a story. . . . This book can be read in one fell swoop to expose yourself to the full spectrum of story elements—such as theme, motion, artfulness, truth and fairness, leads, and titles—or it can be used as a guide during the process of writing nonfiction. An essential read for both freelance writers and students of journalism." Libr J

Includes bibliographical references

How to write & give a speech; a practical guide for anyone who has to make every word count. Joan Detz. 3rd edition St. Martin's Griffin 2014 224 p. pbk $16.99 **808.5**
1. Public speaking
ISBN 9781250041074; 1250041074

LC 2013032029

"This newly updated how to guide offers sound advice on every aspect of researching, writing, and delivering an effective speech. Filled with anecdotes, tips, examples, and practical advice, this accessible guide makes one of the most daunting tasks manageable-and even fun. . . . Updated to include new examples and the latest technology, as well as a section on social media, this is a must-have for anyone who writes and delivers speeches, whether novices or experienced veterans at the podium." (Publisher's note)

Includes bibliographical references and index

Linklater, Kristin

Freeing the natural voice; drawings by Douglas Florian. Drama Bk. Specialists 1976 210p il hardcover o.p. pa $19.95 **808.5**
1. Voice
ISBN 0-89676-071-5 pa

"Predicated on the basic assumptions that everyone has a voice capable of expressing a full range of emotions within a normal two- to four-octave scale and that daily stress compromises the voice's natural abilities and power {the author} presents a simple and clear narrative, as well as a full set of exercises to cultivate and strengthen the voice." Libr J

Meyers, Peter

As we speak; how to make your point and have it stick. by Peter Meyers and Shann Nix. Atria Books 2011 viii, 275 p.p ill. $25 **808.5**
1. Public speaking 2. Business communication 3. Communication in management 4. Interpersonal communication
ISBN 1439153051; 9781439153055

LC 2011015029

In this book, "Peter Meyers and Shann Nix offer a comprehensive approach for tackling the underlying obstacles that almost all of us experience when faced with speaking in public. In 'As We Speak,' you'll learn to master the three building blocks at the core of their approach: Content . . . Delivery . . . [and] State. . . . . Meyers and Nix also emphasize that effective communication is impossible without first becoming aware of your own true goals and personal beliefs." (Publisher's note)

Includes bibliographical references (p. 273-275)

Pinsky, Robert, 1940-

The **sounds** of poetry; a brief guide. Farrar, Straus & Giroux 1998 129p hardcover o.p. pa $13 **808.5**
1. Poetry
ISBN 0-374-52617-6

LC 98-18873

"By bringing his passion for the sound of language—so evident in his own poems—to his expert interpretations of the work of others, Pinsky cracks open the glass case that seems to separate poetry from everyday language, allowing the song of each poem to ring bright and clear." Booklist

Includes bibliographical references

808.8 Collections of literary texts from more than two literatures

The **Book** of eulogies; a collection of memorial tributes, poetry, essays, and letters of condolence. edited with commentary by Phyllis Theroux. Scribner 1997 400p $26 **808.8**
1. Eulogies 2. Bereavement
ISBN 0-684-82251-2

LC 97-2197

"Theroux has gathered over 100 eulogies delivered in the form of spoken tributes, editorials, letters of condolence, essays, and poetry. Many of these testimonials are eloquently penned by the well known to commemorate the well known (e.g., Thomas Merton on Flannery O'Connor, Robert F. Kennedy on Martin Luther King). Others are equally compelling memorials to unknown souls by everyday people. There are helpful commentaries by the author." Libr J

Into the garden; a wedding anthology: poetry and prose on love and marriage. edited by Robert Hass and Stephen Mitchell. HarperCollins Pubs. 1993 193p hardcover o.p. pa $13.95 **808.8**
1. Weddings 2. Poetry -- Collections
ISBN 0-06-092469-1 pa

LC 92-53339

This anthology of readings suitable for wedding ceremonies contains "American Indian, aboriginal Australian, ancient Egyptian, Buddhist, Hindu, and Sufi poetry and prose in addition to . . . biblical, classical Greek and Roman, European, and American passages. . . . {Also included are} traditional or tradition-respecting ceremonies." Booklist

Journalistas; 100 years of the best writing and reporting by women journalists. edited by Eleanor Mills with Kira Cochrane. Carroll & Graf 2005 xx, 364p pa $14.95 **808.8**
1. Women journalists 2. Literature -- Collections
ISBN 0-7867-1667-3

"From Djuna Barnes' 1914 account of being force-fed to end her hunger strike, to Eleanor Roosevelt's 1938 'My Day' column, to Rose George's 2004 article about gang rapes in France, this collection provides a broad and deep look at reporting by women in the past century." Booklist

The **Norton** book of modern war; edited by Paul Fussell. Norton 1991 830p $24.95 **808.8**
1. War in literature 2. Literature -- Collections
ISBN 0-393-02909-3

LC 90-36495

This anthology of 20th century prose and poetry about war covers World War I, the Spanish Civil War, World War II, the Korean War and Vietnam. Authors represented include Heinrich Böll, Marguerite Duras, Ernest Hemingway, Ron Kovic, Norman Mailer, Wilfred Owen and Siegfried Sassoon.

The **Paris** review book of heartbreak, madness, sex, love, betrayal, outsiders, intoxication, war, whimsy, horrors, God, death, dinner, baseball, travels, the art of writing, and everything else in the world

since 1953; by the editors of the Paris review; with an introduction by George Plimpton. Picador 2003 751p $30; pa $19 **808.8**
1. Literature -- Collections
ISBN 0-312-42238-5; 0-312-42239-3 pa
LC 2003-45971
This anthology includes works by "W.H. Auden, Ernest Hemingway, William Faulkner, Jack Kerouac, Elizabeth Bishop, Truman Capote, William Burroughs, Susan Sontag, Joyce Carol Oates, Toni Morrison, Jonathan Franzen, Ian McEwan and Alice Munro." Publ Wkly

Remembrances and celebrations; a book of eulogies, elegies, letters, and epitaphs. edited by Jill Werman Harris. Pantheon Bks. 1999 xxiii, 308p $25; pa $14 **808.8**
1. Eulogies 2. Bereavement
ISBN 0-375-40123-7; 0-375-70125-7 pa
LC 98-32149
"Comprised of eulogies from the 20th century, as well as, poetic elegies, condolence letters and tombstone epitaphs spanning from the 17th century to the present, this eclectic sourcebook offers inspiration for anyone seeking to memorialize a loved one. Since the mourners and the dead in each instance are well-known writers (Lillian Hellman eulogizes Dashiell Hammett) and public figures (Reverend Jesse Jackson lays Jackie Robinson to rest), the collection is a bonanza for the morbidly minded browser as well." Publ Wkly

808.81 Collections in specific forms

★ The **20th** Century in Poetry. W W Norton & Co Inc 2012 860 p. $35.00 **808.81**
1. Poetry -- Collections 2. Poetry -- History and criticism -- 20th century
ISBN 1605983640; 9781605983646
This poetry anthology, edited by Michael Hulse and Simon Rae, "presents in chronological order over four hundred poems written during the twentieth century. The authors, both published poets themselves, give an overview of each period of history, while notes to the poems place each one in its historical context and trace the century's poetic development. Concise biographies for each poet complete the anthology." (Publisher's note)

A **Book** of love poetry; edited and with an introduction by Jon Stallworthy. Oxford Univ. Press 1974 393p hardcover o.p. pa $18.95 **808.81**
1. Love poetry
ISBN 0-19-504232-8
First published 1973 in the United Kingdom with title: The Penguin book of love poetry
A collection of poems written during the past 2000 years arranged thematically from young love to the "long look back" of the aged
Includes indexes of poets, translators, titles and first lines

City lights pocket poets anthology; edited by Lawrence Ferlinghetti. City Lights Bks. 1995 259p $18.95 **808.81**
1. Poetry -- Collections
ISBN 0-87286-311-5
LC 95-31608
"Celebrating 40 years of publishing, this anthology contains selections from all 52 volumes of the 'Pocket Poets' series. Opening with Ferlinghetti's self-published 'Pictures of the Gone World,' the book {includes poems by} . . . Denise Levertov, Kenneth Patchen, Robert Duncan, . . . La Loca, Charles Upton, {and} Adam Cornford." (Libr J)
"Drawing from the 52 volumes published in the Pocket Poets series since 1956, this selection provides a handy sampler of many of the prominent avant-garde and leftist poets of the post-WW II era. . . . The series' extensive international scope is highlighted in poems culled from German, Russian, Italian, Dutch, Nicaraguan and Spanish poets." Publ Wkly

The **Columbia** Granger's dictionary of poetry quotations; edited by Edith P. Hazen. Columbia Univ. Press 1992 1132p $131 **808.81**
1. Quotations 2. Reference books
ISBN 0-231-07546-4
LC 91-42240
This work contains the "most memorable lines written by the greatest poets of English. Quotations are organized alphabetically by poet, and coded so one can find full text in hundreds of current anthologies. With keyword and subject indexing." Univ Press Books for Public and Second Sch Libr

★ The **Columbia** Granger's Index to poetry in collected and selected works; edited by Keith Newton. 2nd ed, completely rev; Columbia Univ. Press 2004 xxi, 1847p $225 **808.81**
1. Reference books 2. Poetry -- Indexes
ISBN 0-231-12528-3
LC 2003-51469
First published 1996
This "edition includes 315 works, by 266 different poets, locating more than 65,000 poems by title, first line, author, and subject. Included . . . are the works of many of the major American and British poets of the last thirty years, such as Robert Pinsky, Seamus Heaney, and Paul Muldoon; important twentieth-century American poets such as Langston Hughes, Dorothy Parker, and Robert Penn Warren; twentieth-century foreign poets in new translations, such as Eugenio Montale and Paul Celan; and diverse poets from all times and places, collected in new editions, such as Cold Mountain, Jones Very, and Guido Cavalcanti." Publisher's note

Favorite Poem Project
Americans' favorite poems; the Favorite Poem Project anthology. edited by Robert Pinsky and Maggie Dietz. Norton 1999 327p $27.50 **808.81**
1. Poetry -- Collections
ISBN 0-393-04820-9
LC 99-31979
"People across America, including many teens, share the poetry they love, and talk about what it means in their lives.

Their choices—from John Keats to Lucille Clifton—defy stereotypes, and their comments are heartfelt." Booklist

Granger, Edith

★ The **Columbia** Granger's index to poetry in anthologies; edited by Tessa Kale. 13th ed., completely rev., indexing anthologies published through May 31, 2006; Columbia University Press 2007 xxviii, 2376p $295   **808.81**
1. Reference books 2. Poetry -- Indexes
ISBN 0-231-13988-8; 978-0-231-13988-5
      LC 2006-14853
First edition, edited by Edith Granger, published 1904 by A. C. McClurg with title: Index to poetry and recitations. Fifth through eighth editions have title Granger's index to poetry

"The 400 total entries are organized alphabetically into three sections: 'Title, First Line, Last Line,' 'Author,' and 'Subject.' The anthologies referenced appear as abbreviations explained in a 14-page introductory list. An essential purchase for literature and poetry collections." Libr J
Includes bibliographical references

Language for a new century; contemporary poetry from the Middle East, Asia, and beyond. edited by Tina Chang, Nathalie Handal, and Ravi Shankar. W.W. Norton 2008 l, 734p il pa $27.95 **808.81**
1. Poetry -- Collections
ISBN 978-0-393-33238-4; 0-393-33238-1
      LC 2007-49424
"Even a diligent reader of contemporary poetry will leave this gathering feeling humbled by ignorance of the immense poetic energy of what used to be called the East." Booklist
Includes bibliographical references

Merwin, W. S. (William Stanley), 1927-

Selected translations 1948-2010; 1948-2011. [compiled by] W.S. Merwin. Copper Canyon Press 2012 407 p. (alk. paper) $40   **808.81**
1. Poetry 2. Translating and interpreting 3. Poetry -- Collections 4. Poetry -- Translations into English
ISBN 1556594097; 9781556594090
      LC 2012025545
This poetry collection, translated by W.S. Merwin, "is the lifework from one of America's greatest poets and translators. Dedicated to the art of translation since his undergraduate years at Princeton, Poet Laureate W.S. Merwin achieved an unmatched oeuvre of translated poems from every corner of the earth, from dozens of languages." (Publisher's note)

Milosz, Czeslaw

A **Book** of luminous things; an international anthology of poetry. edited and with an introduction by Czeslaw Milosz. Harcourt Brace & Co. 1996 xx, 320p hardcover o.p. pa $15   **808.81**
1. Poetry -- Collections
ISBN 0-15-600574-3
      LC 95-38060
"Nobel laureate Milosz states in his introduction that the purpose of this personal and eclectic collection is to pres-

ent poetry that is 'short, clear, readable, and . . . realistic, that is, loyal toward reality and attempting to describe it as concisely as possible.' . . . Most of the selections are from classical Chinese and 20th-century American and European (primarily Eastern European, Scandinavian, and French) poets." Libr J

Music of a distant drum; classical Arabic, Persian, Turkish, and Hebrew poems. translated and introduced by Bernard Lewis. Princeton Univ. Press 2001 222p il hardcover o.p. pa $17.95 **808.81**
1. Arabic poetry -- Collections 2. Hebrew poetry -- Collections 3. Persian poetry -- Collections 4. Turkish poetry -- Collections
ISBN 0-691-15010-9 pa; 0-691-08928-0
      LC 2001-19858
"Lewis, one of the foremost scholars of the Middle East, has devoted much of his career to the history of Islam; this volume collects his translations of poems—nearly all appearing in English for the first time—that span eleven centuries and four major Middle Eastern traditions. Many of the most striking works address, in spare, stirring lines, the twin demands of serving the self and serving God." New Yorker
Includes bibliographical references

The **Oxford** book of war poetry; chosen and edited by Jon Stallworthy. Oxford University Press 2008 xxxi, 358 p.p (paperback) $19.95 **808.81**
1. War poetry 2. Poetry -- Collections 3. War poetry/Collections
ISBN 0199554536; 9780199554539
      LC 8319303
This book is a collection of war poetry, arranged chronologically by conflict. The "250 poems in John Stallworthy's . . . anthology span centuries of human experience of war, from David's 'Lament for Saul and Jonathan,' and Homer's 'Iliad,' to the finest poems of the First and Second World Wars, and beyond." (Publisher's note)
Includes bibliographical references and indexes.

Poems to read; a new favorite poem project anthology. edited by Robert Pinsky and Maggie Dietz. Norton 2002 xxv, 352p $27.95   **808.81**
1. Poetry -- Collections
ISBN 0-393-01074-0
      LC 2002-321
"A graceful, sometimes jubilant, sometimes lyrical, sometimes brooding, but always welcoming and stirring collection." Booklist
Includes bibliographical references

The **Poetry** of our world; an international anthology of contemporary poetry. edited by Jeffrey Paine. HarperCollins Pubs. 2000 xxviii, 511p hardcover o.p. pa $18.95   **808.81**
1. Poetry -- Collections
ISBN 0-06-055369-3; 0-06-095193-1 pa
      LC 99-34921
In this global anthology "each section is preceded by a thoughtful introduction of several pages by the selector in that area. . . . A stunning and highly readable anthology." Libr J

Schiff, Hilda

Holocaust poetry; compiled and introduced by Hilda Schiff. St. Martin's Press 1995 xxiv, 234p hardcover o.p. pa $14.95 **808.81**

1. Poetry -- Collections 2. Holocaust, 1933-1945 -- Poetry

ISBN 0-312-13086-4; 0-312-14357-5 pa

LC 95-2708

"In English and in translation from many languages, more than 80 poets—including Wiesel, Fink, Brecht, Yevtushenko, Auden, and Sachs—give voice to what seems unspeakable. Schiff points out that compelling historical accounts document the facts and numbers, but a poem, like a story, makes us imagine how it felt for one person. These poems are stark and deceptively simple." Booklist

Includes bibliographical references

Till I end my song; a gathering of last poems. edited with commentaries by Harold Bloom. Harper 2010 xxviii, 377p $24.99 **808.81**

1. Poetics 2. Poetry -- History and criticism

ISBN 978-0-06-192305-0; 0-06-192305-2

LC 2010-20773

"These are poems that embrace change, time, life, the self, and death. Poems that have lasted and that will 'reverberate into the coming silence.' A collection of surpassing splendor and resonance." Booklist

University of California (System)

Poems for the millennium; the University of California book of modern and postmodern poetry. edited by Jerome Rothenberg and Pierre Joris. University of Calif. Press 1995 2v il v1 $70; v1 pa $29.95; v2 pa $29.95 **808.81**

1. Poetry -- Collections

ISBN 0-520-07225-1 v1; 0-520-07227-8 v1 pa; 0-520-20864-1 v2 pa

LC 93-49839

The poetry in this anthology is "often self-referential, certainly aware of its own artistry, embedded in political consciousness, and transgressive. It is the work of more than 100 poets, many little known in the U.S. Rothenberg and Joris see twentieth-century poetics as international and have postwar Japanese poet Fujii Sadakazu rubbing shoulders with Amiri Baraka and Andrei Voznesensky, Tomas Tranströmer and Diane di Prima." Booklist {review of v2}

The **Vintage** book of contemporary world poetry; edited and with an introduction by J.D. McClatchy. Vintage Bks. 1996 xxviii, 654p pa $16 **808.81**

1. Poetry -- Collections

ISBN 0-679-74115-1

LC 95-50628

A "varied collection of contemporary poetry from Europe, the Middle East, Africa, Asia, Latin America, and the Caribbean. Here readers will find Nobel laureates and other luminaries, such as Joseph Brodsky, Derek Walcott, Czeslaw Milosz, Octavio Paz, Wole Soyinka, Breyten Breytenbach, and Nguyen Chi Thien, as well as less well known poets. Editor McClatchy has chosen well, selecting poems that illuminate the personal as well as the universal." Booklist

Includes bibliographical references

World poetry; an anthology of verse from antiquity to our time. Katharine Washburn and John S. Major, editors; Clifton Fadiman, general editor. Norton 1998 xxii, 1338p $45 **808.81**

1. Poetry -- Collections

ISBN 0-393-04130-1

LC 97-10879

The anthology's "stated aim—'to surprise and delight the common reader'—may seem rather quaint; yet it is a worthy one, and is, on the whole, impressively fulfilled." Times Lit Suppl

Includes bibliographical references

808.82   Collections of drama

★ **2010**: the best women's stage monologues and scenes; edited and with a foreword by Lawrence Harbison. Smith & Kraus Book 2010 193p (Monologue and scene study series) pa $14.95 **808.82**

1. Acting 2. Monologues

ISBN 978-1-57525-774-7

Most recent edition: 2016

Annual. First published 1991 for the 1990 theater season under the editorship of Jocelyn Beard

This is a "selection of monologues and scenes from plays that were produced and/or published in the 2009-2010 theatrical season." Publisher's note

★ The **best** plays of 2006-2007; edited by Jeffrey Eric Jenkins; illustrated with production photographs. Limelight Eds. 2008 560p il (Best plays theater yearbook) $49.95 **808.82**

1. Drama -- Collections 2. Theater -- United States

ISBN 978-0-8791-0352-1

Annual. First published 1920. Variant titles: The Burns Mantle theater yearbook; The Applause/best plays theater yearbook

Some back volumes published by Dodd, Mead available from Applause Theatre Bk. Pubs.; reprints of older annuals available from Ayer; for full information on availability and price contact publishers.

The **best** stage scenes of 2007; edited by Lawrence Harbison; with a foreword by D.L. Lepidus. Smith & Kraus 2007 202p (Scene study series) pa $14.95 **808.82**

1. Drama 2. Acting

ISBN 978-1-57525-588-0; 1-57525-588-X

Annual. First published 1992 under the editorship of Jocelyn Beard

This title culls "selections from recent plays, divided among scenic groupings for men and women, men, and women. . . . The scenes vary in length and intensity, with each scene providing a setting, description, and the number of needed characters." Libr J

Nine plays of the modern theater; with an introduction by Harold Clurman. Grove Press 1981 896p
pa $21   **808.82**
1. Drama -- Collections
ISBN 0-8021-5032-2

LC 79-52121

"This comprehensive volume contains nine of the most important, most indispensable plays of the modern theatre. What Harold Clurman has done in this seminal collection is to create for us a portrait of the progress and turmoil of the twentieth century. Ranging from the eerie realism of Pinter's sinister "Birthday Party," to the absurd literalism of Ionesco's conformist city in "Rhinoceros," to the baroque fantasy world of Genet's brothel in "The Balcony," to the tragic hilarity of Stoppard's "Rosencrantz and Guildenstern Are Dead," these nine plays, each entirely distinct, together form an incisive, compelling, and sometimes heartbreaking mosaic of our time." (Publisher's note)

The **Ultimate** audition book; 222 monologues, 2 minutes & under. edited by Jocelyn A. Beard. Smith & Kraus 1997 2v + v4 (Monologue audition series) ea pa $19.95   **808.82**
1. Acting 2. Monologues
ISBN 1-57525-066-7 v1; 1-57525-270-8 v2;
1-57525-420-4 v4

LC 97-10471

This collection draws "upon lesser-known works from significant writers and those of contemporary favorites and reflects a wide range of tone, age, time period, and voice. Divided among female, male, and unisex categories, all meet the obligatory two minutes or less time limit imposed by most directors and auditions." Libr J [review of volume 2]
Includes bibliographical references

808.84   Collections of essays

The **Norton** book of personal essays; edited by Joseph Epstein. Norton 1997 477p $30   **808.84**
1. Essays
ISBN 0-393-03654-5

LC 96-26975

George Orwell, James Baldwin, Joan Didion, M. F. K. Fisher, Barbara Tuchman and Cynthia Ozick are among the authors chosen by Epstein for inclusion in this collection of "53 personal essays written in English by well-known authors during the past century. They were chosen because he 'found them interesting, touching, pleasing, amusing, delightful—above all, entertaining.' The result is a potpourri of selections that vary widely in subject and style. Topics range from music, racism, and traveling to fathers, children, and childhood." Libr J

Teachers & Writers Collaborative

The **Art** of the personal essay; an anthology from the classical era to the present. selected and with an introduction by Phillip Lopate. Anchor Bks. (NY) 1994 liv, 777p hardcover o.p. pa $17.95   **808.84**
1. Essays
ISBN 0-385-42339-X pa

LC 93-29708

"Not only are the selections a veritable feast, but Lopate's genre-defining introduction is not to be missed." Booklist
Includes bibliographical references

808.85   Collections of speeches

Sutton, Roberta Briggs

Speech index; an index to 259 collections of world famous orations and speeches for various occasions. 4th ed rev & enl; Scarecrow Press 1966 947p $85   **808.85**
1. Reference books 2. Speeches -- Indexes
ISBN 0-8108-0138-8
First published 1935 by the H.W. Wilson Company
"Speeches are indexed by orator, type of speech, and by subject, with a selected list of titles given in the appendix. Particularly useful for amateur speakers in locating examples to use in preparing a speech and models they can adapt to their needs." Ref Sources for Small & Medium-sized Libr. 6th edition

The **World's** great speeches; edited by Lewis Copeland, Lawrence W. Lamm, and Stephen J. McKenna. 4th enl 1999 ed; Dover Publs. 1999 xxii, 920p pa $17.95   **808.85**
1. Speeches
ISBN 0-486-40903-1

LC 99-32880

First published 1942 by Garden City Pub. Co.
An international collection of approximately 300 speeches by over 200 speakers arranged chronologically

808.86   Collections of letters

Mallon, Thomas

Yours ever; people and their letters. Pantheon Books 2009 338p $26.95   **808.86**
1. Letters
ISBN 978-0-679-44426-8; 0-679-44426-2

LC 2009-06315

Companion volume to A book of one's own (1984)
This is "an astute, exhilarating tour of the mailbag. . . . [It] is nuanced, informed, full-blooded, a vigorous literary salute." N Y Times Book Rev
Includes bibliographical references (p. 313-320)

808.88   Collections of miscellaneous writings

Boller, Paul F.

They never said it; a book of fake quotes, misquotes, and misleading attributions. [by] Paul F. Boller, Jr., and John George. Oxford Univ. Press 1989 xxv, 159p hardcover o.p. pa $15.95   **808.88**
1. Errors 2. Quotations 3. Literary forgeries
ISBN 0-19-506469-0 pa

LC 88-22115

In an alphabetical list of attributees' names or titles the authors expose the truth behind more than 200 phony quotations

Lend me your ears; Oxford dictionary of political quotations. edited by Sir Antony Jay. 4th ed; Oxford University Press 2010 xxv, 446p $24.95 **808.88**
1. Reference books 2. Political science -- Quotations
ISBN 978-0-19-957267-0

LC 2010-923325

First published 1996 with title: The Oxford dictionary of political quotations

Entries are organized "by speaker rather than by topic. Don't know the origin of a quotation? Fear not. Turn to the extensive keyword index or the briefer 'selective subject index' in the back of the volume. Helpful also are one-page special category quotes: epitaphs, misquotations, mottoes, slogans, etc. . . . [This is] a great value and an excellent choice for libraries lacking a current work in this area." Libr J

Nowlan, Robert A.
Born this day; a book of birthdays and quotations of prominent people through the centuries. 2nd ed.; McFarland & Co. 2007 511p $55 **808.88**
1. Birthdays 2. Quotations
ISBN 978-0-7864-2935-6; 0-7864-2935-6

LC 2007-3809

First published 1996

"Arranged chronologically by date of the month, the volume offers lists of 12 'significant' people born on each day, with a very brief biography and a representative or telling quotation uttered by the individual. In addition, each date lists the birthdays of a dozen or more lesser-known individuals, noting only name and year. . . . [This is] a fine ready-reference volume offering unique information." Booklist

O'Brien, Geoffrey
Bartlett's familiar quotations; a collection of passages, phrases, and proverbs traced to their sources in ancient and modern literature. by John Bartlett; Geoffrey O'Brien, general editor. 18th ed. Little, Brown, and Co. 2012 lxi, 1438 p.p (hardcover) $50.00 **808.88**
1. Quotations 2. Quotations, English
ISBN 0316017590; 9780316017596

LC 2012019870

This book, in its 18th edition, presents a collection of quotations "from the times of ancient Egyptians to the present day." (Publisher's note) It "includes 2500 new quotes and more than 800 newcomers, from Julia Child to David Foster Wallace. Quotes have been culled to bring in more foreigners and women and more material from fiction and poetry." (Library Journal)

The **Oxford** book of aphorisms; chosen by John Gross. Oxford University Press 2003 383p pa $19.95 **808.88**
1. Quotations
ISBN 0-19-280456-1

LC 2003-269712

First published 1983

"Contains a well-chosen collection of aphorisms, maxims, quotations, and pensees from ancient times to the present. Entries, arranged under 58 subject sections, are identified with name of aphorist, source, publication date, or approximate date of original statement. Headings include 'nature,' 'good and evil,' 'illusion and reality,' and 'secrets.' An introduction gives definitions of aphorisms and their use throughout history." Wynar. Guide to Ref Books for Sch Media Cent. 3d edition
Includes bibliographical references

The **Oxford** book of death; chosen and edited by D.J. Enright. Oxford University Press 2008 351p pa $19.95 **808.88**
1. Death -- Quotations
ISBN 978-0-19-955652-6

LC 2008-482099

First published 1983

"Much work has gone into this compilation, and the individual introductions to the component sections are, as we would expect, elegant, modest and very wise." Times Lit Suppl

★ **Oxford** dictionary of humorous quotations; edited by Ned Sherrin; with a foreword by Alistair Beaton. 4th ed; Oxford University Press 2008 536p hardcover o.p. pa $24.95 **808.88**
1. Quotations 2. Wit and humor 3. Reference books
ISBN 978-0-19-923716-6; 0-19-923716-6; 978-0-19-957006-5 pa; 0-19-957006-X pa

LC 2008-486673

First published 1995 with title: The Oxford book of humorous quotations

This dictionary "features 5,000 quotations organized into more than 200 subject categories. Quips are arranged by broad themes. . . . Coverage spans the centuries, and you are as likely to find lines by Johnny Depp, Ricky Gervais, and Eddie Izzard as you are those by Noel Coward, William Shakespeare, and George Bernard Shaw. . . . An amusing addition to the reference collection." Booklist

Oxford dictionary of modern quotations; edited by Elizabeth Knowles. 3rd ed.; Oxford University Press 2007 479p $39.95; pa $18.95 **808.88**
1. Quotations 2. Reference books
ISBN 978-0-19-920895-1; 0-19-920895-6; 978-0-19-954746-3 pa; 0-19-954746-7 pa

LC 2007-36871

First published 1991

"Containing more than 5,000 quotations from authors . . . [such] as Bertolt Brecht, George W. Bush, Homer Simpson, Carl Sagan, William Shatner, and Desmond Tutu, the dictionary is organized alphabetically by author, with . . . cross-referencing and keyword and thematic indexes." Publisher's note

Toasts; over 1,500 of the best toasts, sentiments, blessings, and graces. {compiled by} Paul Dickson; illustrated by Rollin McGrail. Crown 1991 256p il $19   **808.88**
1. Toasts 2. Wit and humor
ISBN 0-517-58412-3

LC 91-6967

"Covering traditional occasions such as anniversaries and weddings as well as a variety of other 'toastable' events, this book organizes 1,500 toasts under 75 alphabetically arranged subject headings. Included are ethnic, military, birthday, and holiday toasts. There are also toasts related to sports, aging, food, parents, and even cheese and champagne! The toasts have been gathered from a variety of toast books, many of which date from the late nineteenth and early twentieth centuries. An interesting history of toasting is included." Booklist

Includes bibliographical references

809   History, description, critical appraisal of more than two literatures

Atwood, Margaret, 1939-
In other worlds; SF and the human imagination. Nan A. Talese/Doubleday 2011 255p pa $24.95 **809**
1. Science fiction -- Authorship 2. Science fiction -- History and criticism
ISBN 978-0-385-53396-6

LC 2011013776

"Atwood is well known to sf readers for such novels as The Handmaid's Tale, Oryx and Crake, and The Year of the Flood. In this collection of essays and short fiction, she further explores the genre, beginning with her three previously unpublished Richard Ellman Lectures in Modern Literature, which she delivered at Emory University in 2010. . . . A clever, thoughtful investigation that will appeal to science fiction readers and Atwood's loyal fans." Libr J

Includes bibliographical references

Beacham's encyclopedia of popular fiction; edited by Kirk H. Beetz. Beacham Pub. 1996 19v **809**
1. Reference books 2. Fiction -- Bio-bibliography
ISBN 0-93383-338-5

LC 96-20771

This reference work consists of a three volume set of Biography series and sixteen volumes of Analyses series. Available separately or in sets. Apply to publisher for price

Bentley, Eric
The life of the drama. Applause Theatre Bk. Pubs. 1991 371p pa $12.95   **809**
1. Drama -- History and criticism
ISBN 1-55783-110-6

LC 91-28774

First published 1964 by Atheneum

The author discusses plot, character, dialogue, and action in various theatrical genres. Among the dramatists discussed are Aeschylus, Beckett, Brecht, Chekhov, Corneille, Goethe, Ibsen, Ben Jonson, Molière, Pirandello, Racine, Shakespeare, Shaw, and Sophocles

Includes bibliographical references

Black literature criticism; classic and emerging authors since 1950. Jelena O. Krstovic, project editor; forward by Howard Dodson. 2nd ed.; Gale Cengage Learning 2008 3v il set $459   **809**
1. Blacks in literature 2. English literature -- Black authors -- History and criticism 3. American literature -- African American authors -- History and criticism
ISBN 978-1-4144-3170-3; 1-4144-3170-8
First published 1992

"This work includes African American, Caribbean, and African writers who produce works in English. Authors range from relative newcomers . . . to classic authors. . . . [This is] a worthwhile purchase." Booklist

Includes bibliographical references

Bloom, Harold
The **Western** canon; the books and school of the ages. Riverhead Bks. 1995 546p pa $18   **809**
1. Blind 2. Poets 3. Judges 4. Authors 5. Diplomats 6. Novelists 7. Dramatists 8. Essayists 9. Translators 10. Lexicographers 11. Poets laureate 12. Psychoanalysts 13. Literary critics 14. Nonfiction writers 15. Writers on science 16. Short story writers 17. Writers on medicine 18. Writers on religion 19. Nobel laureates for peace 20. Nobel laureates for literature 21. Literature -- History and criticism
ISBN 1-57322-514-2; 978-1-57322-514-4
First published 1994 by Harcourt Brace & Co.

The "book succeeds not as a polemic but as a passionate, erudite and highly idiosyncratic series of essays about the literature dearest to one of America's most influential academics." Publ Wkly

Boyd, Brian
On the origin of stories; evolution, cognition, and fiction. Belknap Press of Harvard University Press 2009 540p il $35   **809**
1. Evolution 2. Authorship 3. Fiction -- Authorship 4. Fiction -- History and criticism
ISBN 978-0-674-03357-3; 0-674-03357-4

LC 2009-07642

The author "has created a compelling, erudite, and thoroughly original work about the nature of humanistic expression in art and literature. Beautifully written and wide-ranging, the book delves into social science, evolutionary biology, art, and literature to create a comprehensive account of the evolutionary origins of art and storytelling." Choice

Includes bibliographical references

Calvino, Italo
Why read the classics? translated from the Italian by Martin McLaughlin. Pantheon Bks. 1999 277p hardcover o.p. pa $13   **809**
1. Literature -- History and criticism
ISBN 0-679-74349-9 pa

LC 99-21535

Original Italian edition, 1991

"Calvino celebrates a wide range of great thinkers in these provocative essays. Here are writers from the ancient world, the Renaissance and recent times, and from the old and new worlds. . . . [These essays] are a reminder to us

that 'rereading' the classics can amuse as well as reward."
New Sci

Includes bibliographical references

Colby, Vineta

World authors, 1980-1985; editor, Vineta Colby. Wilson, H.W. 1990 938p il (Authors series) $140　　**809**
1. Reference books 2. Authors -- Dictionaries 3. Literature -- Bio-bibliography
ISBN 0-8242-0797-1

LC 90-49782

This volume covers 320 contemporary writers

World authors, 1985-1990; a volume in the Wilson authors series. editor, Vineta Colby. Wilson, H.W. 1995 970p il (Authors series) $140　　**809**
1. Reference books 2. Authors -- Dictionaries 3. Literature -- Bio-bibliography
ISBN 0-8242-0875-7

LC 95-41656

This volume covers 345 novelists, playwrights, poets, and other authors who have risen to prominence in the late 1980s

★ **Critical** survey of drama; edited by Carl Rollyson. 2nd rev ed; Salem Press 2003 8v set $499　　**809**
1. Reference books 2. Drama -- Dictionaries 3. English drama -- Dictionaries 4. American drama -- Dictionaries
ISBN 1-58765-102-5

LC 2003-2190

This set contains "about 630 essays, of which 570 discuss individual dramatists and 60 cover overview topics. . . . Each essay on a dramatist provides . . . material as birth and death dates, lists of the author's major dramatic works (with dates of first production and publication). Each essay opens with a brief survey of the author's publications in literary forms other than drama, a summary of the writer's professional achievements and awards, an extended biographical sketch that centers on the writer's development as a dramatist, and an extensive critical analysis of the writer's major dramatic works. Following this discussion is a list of major publications in fields other than drama and an annotated bibliography of critical works about the author." Publisher's note

Includes bibliographical references

Critical survey of mystery and detective fiction; editor, Carl Rollyson. Rev ed; Salem Press 2008 5v il set $399　　**809**
1. Mystery fiction -- History and criticism
ISBN 978-1-58765-397-1; 1-58765-397-4

LC 2007-40208

First published 1988 in four volumes under the editorship of Frank Northen Magill

This "is the most exhaustive and best-documented account of this genre available." Choice

Includes bibliographical references

★ **Cyclopedia** of literary places; consulting editor, R. Baird Shuman; editor, R. Kent Rasmussen; introduction by Brian Stableford. Salem Press 2003 3v set $305　　**809**
1. Reference books 2. Literary landmarks 3. Literature -- Encyclopedias
ISBN 1-58766-094-0

LC 2002-156159

"This three-volume set completes Salem's trilogy of reference works analyzing stories (Masterplots), characters (Cyclopedia of Literary Characters), and now settings in classic works of literature (mostly novels, though a few plays and poems are included). . . . Literary Places provides details of both real and imaginary geographic places that serve as settings for approximately 1300 titles covered in the previous works. . . . The entries are alphabetized by title, range in length from 300 to 1000 words, and feature author, type of work, type of plot, time of plot, and a brief synopsis. . . . Well written, easy to use, and fun to read, this set . . . is a valuable addition to all libraries." Libr J

Includes bibliographical references

Damrosch, David

The **buried** book; the loss and rediscovery of the great Epic of Gilgamesh. H. Holt 2007 315p il map hardcover o.p. pa $16.99　　**809**
1. Gilgamesh
ISBN 978-0-8050-8029-2; 0-8050-8029-5; 978-0-8050-8725-3 pa; 0-8050-8725-7 pa

LC 2006-49523

"Combining acuity about cultural contexts with wide-ranging knowledge, Damrosch's account is a superb and engrossing popular presentation." Booklist

Includes bibliographical references

Donoghue, Emma

Inseparable; desire between women in literature. Emma Donoghue. Alfred A. Knopf 2010 x, 271p ill. (hc : alk. paper) $27.95　　**809**
1. Female friendship 2. Women in literature 3. Lesbianism in literature
ISBN 9780307270948; 0307270947

LC 2009048368

Stonewall Book Awards: Israel Fisherman Non-Fiction Award (2011)

This book "explores the little-known literary tradition of love between women in Western literature, from Chaucer and Shakespeare to Charlotte Brontë, Dickens, Agatha Christie, and many more. . . . [It] examine[s] how desire between women in English literature has been portrayed, from schoolgirls and vampires to runaway wives, from cross-dressing knights to contemporary murder stories. [Author Emma] Donoghue looks at the work of those writers who have addressed the 'unspeakable subject,' examining whether such desire between women is freakish or omnipresent, holy or evil, heartwarming or ridiculous as she excavates a long-obscured tradition of (inseparable) friendship between women, one that is . . . central to our cultural history." (Publisher's note)

Includes bibliographical references (p. [207]-260) and index

Fraser, Kennedy

Ornament and silence; essays on women's lives. Knopf 1996 247p hardcover o.p. pa $13   **809**

1. Poets 2. Artists 3. Authors 4. Painters 5. Botanists 6. Novelists 7. Dramatists 8. Fashion designers 9. Essayists 10. Feminists 11. Biographers 12. Entomologists 13. College teachers 14. Literary critics 15. Magazine editors 16. Nonfiction writers 17. Writers on science 18. Short story writers 19. Writers on politics 20. New Yorker (Periodical)

ISBN 0-375-70112-5 pa

LC 96-11479

A collection of fourteen profiles, personal reminiscences and extended reviews of books.

"A 'daughter of the paternal old New Yorker' in her youth, Fraser . . . has moved on with time, taking for her more mature role models Nina Berberova, Edith Wharton, and Germaine Greer. Fraser's essays are quiet, thorough, and beautifully paced." Libr J

Ghosh, Amitav, 1956-

The **great** derangement; Climate Change and the Unthinkable. Amitav Ghosh. University of Chicago Press 2016 176 p. (cloth : alk. paper) $22   **809**

1. Climate change 2. Climatic changes in literature

ISBN 9780226323039

LC 2016018232

This book, by Amitav Ghosh, asks "are we deranged? . . . Ghosh argues that future generations may well think so. How else to explain our imaginative failure in the face of global warming? . . . Ghosh ends by suggesting that politics, much like literature, has become a matter of personal moral reckoning rather than an arena of collective action." (Publisher's note)

"A slim but certainly significant contribution to the climate crisis dialogue sure to provoke discussion and increased awareness about our imperiled planet." Kirkus

Includes bibliographical references (pages 165-196).

Hollands, Neil

Fellowship in a ring; a guide for science fiction and fantasy book groups. Libraries Unlimited 2010 300p pa $40   **809**

1. Books and reading 2. Book clubs (Discussion groups) 3. Fantasy fiction -- Bibliography 4. Science fiction -- Bibliography 5. Fantasy fiction -- History and criticism 6. Science fiction -- History and criticism

ISBN 978-1-59158-703-3; 1-59158-703-4

LC 2009-46456

This is "is an excellent resource for both novices looking to initiate groups, and veterans seeking to breathe new life into existing factions. The first chapter delineates the practical building blocks necessary to develop a thriving science fiction/fantasy book group, from suggestions of how to ward off potential problems and keep discussions interesting to creative ideas for preventing meetings from becoming stagnant. . . . Included is a list of fifty recommended science fiction and fantasy novels, with helpful information such as author background, plot summaries, a reading guide, and discussion questions. An especially thorough listing of

themes for discussion consists of resources, thematic questions, and suggested works." Voice Youth Advocates

Includes bibliographical references

Isherwood, Christopher, 1904-1986

Liberation; Diaries:1970-1983. HarperCollins 2012 928 p. $39.99   **809**

1. Gay men 2. Novelists

ISBN 0062084747; 9780062084743

This book is the "third and final volume of [Christopher] Isherwood's . . . diaries [and] concludes with a 136-page 'glossary' of names . . . . As the 1970's commence, lover Don Bachardy has just had his screenplay for 'Cabaret' . . . rejected. . . . The last diary entry dates to July 4, 1983, exactly two and a half years before Isherwood's death from cancer. In between, he regales readers with accounts of . . . dinners, parties, and foreign travels." (Publishers Weekly)

Iyer, Pico

The **man** within my head; Pico Iyer. Alfred A. Knopf 2012 241 p.   **809**

1. Travel 2. Self-realization 3. Fathers and sons 4. Novelists, English -- 20th century -- Biography

ISBN 030726761X; 9780307267610

LC 2011041285

In this book, author Pico "Iyer describes [writer Graham] Greene as constantly in his mind as a kind of imaginative touchstone. . . . In the second half . . . [Iyer] answers the question he poses in the first half. Why Greene? . . . His answer focuses on the ways that Greene's characters--Pyle and Fowler in 'The Quiet American,' for example - have a kind of father-and-son relationship to each other." (Washington Times)

James, Henry

Literary criticism. Library of Am. 1984 2v v1 ea $50   **809**

1. Literature -- History and criticism

ISBN 0-94050-023-2 v1; 0-94050-22-4 v2

LC 84-11241

"Grouped by nationality, alphabetically by author, and chronologically, the essays provide a kind of critical book within a book on such writers as Balzac, George Eliot, and Hawthorne. These groupings enable the reader to see how James approached a writer and to follow the development of his thinking about particular writers over the years." Publisher's note

Includes bibliographical references

Jarrell, Randall

No other book; selected essays, edited and introduced by Brad Leithauser. HarperCollins Pubs. 1999 xx, 376p hardcover o.p. pa $15   **809**

1. Poets 2. Authors 3. Lawyers 4. Novelists 5. Physicians 6. Essayists 7. Memoirists 8. Biographers 9. Translators 10. College teachers 11. Children's authors 12. Short story writers 13. Insurance executives 14. Nobel laureates for literature 15. Literature -- History and criticism 16. American poetry -- History and criticism

ISBN 0-06-095638-0 pa

LC 98-55353

"Jarrell taught his peers to appreciate first the young Robert Lowell and W. H. Auden, then Marianne Moore, William Carlos Williams, Elizabeth Bishop, Walt Whitman and Robert Frost. . . . The later Jarrell divided his prose between appreciations of poets, digressions on idiosyncratic passions, and funny or sad indictments of 1950s-style popular culture. . . . As a convincing, above all personal, guide to modern poets, and as a captivating writer of criticism Jarrell has no obvious 20th century equal." Publ Wkly

Kundera, Milan

Encounter; translated from the French by Linda Asher. Harper 2010 178p $23.99   **809**

1. Art appreciation 2. Music -- History and criticism 3. Literature -- History and criticism

ISBN 978-0-06-189441-1; 0-06-189441-9

LC 2010-04908

Original French edition, 2009

"Of specific interest are chapters comparing Francis Bacon to Samuel Beckett; Kundera's devilish mixing up of Roland Barthes with the dour theologian Karl Barth in a chance conversation; several discussions on the virtues of Rabelais as well as a restoration to prominence of Anatole France, who had been given the French intellectualist bum's rush; a powerful coupling of the bright birth of film with the sad death of Fellini; a scholar's relishing of Bertolt Brecht's body odor; the music of his fellow Czech Leos Janacek. Like the proverbial meal at the Chinese restaurant, the delicious musings of this book are filling at first. Two hours later, one craves more." Publ Wkly

Kurian, George Thomas

★ **Timetables** of world literature. Facts on File 2003 457p $65   **809**

1. Literature -- Chronology

ISBN 0-8160-4197-0

LC 2002-3891

Chronicles world literature from the Classical Age through the twentieth century, discussing literary developments and the relationship between literature and the political and social climate of each historical period

"This comprehensive reference . . . helps academic researchers place major works of literature from 58 countries in historical and cultural context." Libr J

Includes bibliographical references

Literary movements for students; presenting analysis, context, and criticism on literary movements. David Galens, project editor. Gale Group 2002 2v il set $185   **809**

1. Literature -- History and criticism

ISBN 0-7876-6517-7

LC 2002-10928

Entries provide "historical background information on each movement as well as modern critical interpretation of each movement's characteristic styles and themes. Approximately 25 movements are covered, including absurdism, Greek drama, modernism, science fiction/fantasy, surrealism and many others." Publisher's note

Includes bibliographical references

Literature and its times; profiles of 300 notable literary works and the historical events that influenced them. Gale Res. 1997 5v set $741   **809**

1. Literature -- History and criticism

ISBN 0-7876-0606-5

LC 97-34339

"The editors chose the selections (fiction, poetry, short stories, plays, biographies, and speeches) with the input of public libraries and secondary-school teachers. . . . Each volume covers a time range subdivided by dates and a general description . . . and begins with a brief overview of the historical events of the era, with a time-line providing a synopsis of each period." Libr J

★ **Magill's** survey of world literature; edited by Steven G. Kellman. Rev ed; Salem Press 2009 6v il set $499   **809**

1. Reference books 2. Literature -- Bio-bibliography 3. Literature -- History and criticism

ISBN 978-1-58765-431-2

LC 2008-46042

First published 1992 under the editorship of Frank Northen Magill

"A solid choice for anyone in need of an inexpensive, broad biocritical literary reference title on world literature." Libr J

Includes glossary and bibliographical references

Manguel, Alberto

The **dictionary** of imaginary places; {by} Alberto Manguel & Gianni Guadalupi; illustrated by Graham Greenfield; with additional illustrations by Eric Beddows; maps and charts by James Cook. Newly updated and expanded; Harcourt Brace & Co. 1999 755p il maps $40; pa $24   **809**

1. Reference books 2. Fantasy fiction -- Dictionaries

ISBN 0-15-100541-9; 0-15-600872-6 pa

LC 99-46994

First published 1980 by Macmillan

This resource "contains entries for more than 1,200 imaginary places from literature and folklore. Each entry describes the place, its locale, and history and provides citations to the source work or tale. More than 220 maps and illustrations are included." Booklist

Includes bibliographical references

★ **Masterplots** II, drama series; editor, Christian H. Moe. rev ed; Salem Press 2003 4v set $404 **809**

1. Drama -- Stories, plots, etc. 2. Drama -- History and criticism

ISBN 1-58765-116-5

LC 2003-12651

First published 1990

"This newest addition to a reference standard belongs in most public, academic, and secondary libraries." Booklist

Moore, Steven, 1978-

The **novel**; an alternative history: beginnings to 1600. Continuum 2010 698p $39.95 **809**

1. Fiction -- History and criticism

ISBN 9781441177049; 1-4411-7704-3

LC 2010-279268

"Reveling in the most innovative and daring creations, Moore energetically evaluates tales fantastic, chilling, hilarious, erotic, and tragic, comparing centuries-old novels to those of Barth, Gaddis, Pynchon, and Vollmann. Destined for controversy, Moore's erudite, gargantuan, kaleidoscopic, and venturesome alternative history will leave readers feeling as though they've been viewing literature with blinders on." Booklist

Includes bibliographical references

Mystery and suspense writers; the literature of crime, detection, and espionage. Robin W. Winks, editor in chief; Maureen Corrigan, associate editor. Scribner 1998 2v set $250 **809**

1. Reference books 2. Spies in literature 3. Mystery fiction -- Dictionaries

ISBN 0-684-80521-9

LC 98-36812

"Articles on 68 mystery writers ranging from Edgar Allen Poe to Sarah Paretsky run from ten to 20 pages and include information on the life and works as well as solid bibliographies for each author." Libr J

Niebuhr, Gary Warren

Make mine a mystery; a reader's guide to mystery and detective fiction. Libraries Unlimited 2003 605p $65 **809**

1. Reference books 2. Mystery fiction -- Bibliography 3. Mystery fiction -- History and criticism

ISBN 1-56308-784-7

LC 2003-271056

"The book is divided into two parts. In part 1, 'Introduction to Mystery Fiction,' Niebuhr devotes considerable space to background material: discussion of readers'-advisory service in general and the appeal of mystery fiction in particular and how to build and manage a mystery collection, followed by a history of the genre beginning in 1845. Part 2, 'The Literature,' annotates more than 2,500 titles by more than 200 authors.... Among guides to mystery fiction, this one stands out as being thorough and current. Essential for public libraries." Booklist

Nissley, Tom

A **reader's** book of days; true tales from the lives and works of writers for every day of the year. Tom Nissley; with illustrations by Joanna Neborsky. W.W. Norton & Co. Inc. 2014 464 p. (hardcover) $24.95 **809**

1. Authors 2. Anecdotes 3. Authorhip 4. Best books 5. Books and reading 6. Literature -- History and criticism

ISBN 0393239624; 9780393239621

LC 2013031250

This book, by Tom Nissley, "features bite- size accounts of events in the lives of great authors for every day of the year. Fictional events that take place within beloved books

are also included. {Authors featured include] Martin Amis, Jane Austen, James Baldwin, . . . [and] F.Scott Fitzgerald." (Publisher's note)

"The book itself is guaranteed to occupy plenty of pleasant hours, but Nissley's recommended reading lists are a bibliophilic bonus." Kirkus

Niven, Penelope, 1939-2014

★ **Thornton** Wilder; A Life. by Penelope Niven; forward by Edward Albee. HarperCollins 2012 xvi, 832 p.p (hardcover) $39.99; (ebook) $31.99 **809**

1. American authors -- Biography

ISBN 0060831367; 9780060831363; 9780062097774

This book by Penelope Niven presents a biography of "Pulitzer Prize-winning playwright and novelist Thornton Wilder. . . . Niven . . . combed through the author's many published and unpublished personal writings. . . . Through Wilder's own words, the reader is privy to his arrogant thrills and frequent bouts of self-doubt. Chronicling Wilder's successes and failures in various literary forms . . . . Niven includes brief criticism and reviews with each of his major works." (Publishers Weekly)

Ozick, Cynthia

★ The **din** in the head; essays. Houghton Mifflin Co. 2006 243p il $24 **809**

1. Literature -- History and criticism

ISBN 978-0-618-47050-1; 0-618-47050-6

LC 2005-16102

The author is "not only one of the finest novelists of our time but an essayist of startling spiritual verve and range." Christ Century

Poe, Edgar Allan

Essays and reviews. Library of Am. 1984 1544p $40 **809**

ISBN 0-940450-19-4

LC 83-19923

This volume is divided into six main divisions: Theory of poetry, Reviews of British and Continental authors; Reviews of American authors and American criticism; Magazines and criticism; The literary and social scene; and Articles and marginalia

Includes bibliographical references

★ **Reference** guide to world literature; editors, Sara Pendergast, Tom Pendergast. 3rd ed; St. James Press 2003 2v set $350 **809**

1. Reference books 2. Literature -- Bio-bibliography 3. Literature -- History and criticism

ISBN 1-55862-490-2

LC 2002-15410

First published 1984 by St. Martin's Press with title: Great foreign language writers

This work "contains 1,100 entries, about equally divided between entries on authors and on literary works. Each author entry in volume 1 includes a short biography, a signed critical essay, and selected lists of works by and about the author. Each literary work entry in volume 2 includes the author and date of publication (if known), a signed critical essay, and a selected list of critical studies. The scope of coverage is major works in languages other than English from the earliest known manuscripts to present day writers. . . . Because of its comprehensiveness and authority, this sturdily bound set is recommended for ready reference in libraries with large world literature sections and for smaller libraries needing more information in this area." Am Ref Books Annu, 2003

Includes bibliographical references

Roth, Philip

Shop talk; a writer and his colleagues and their work. Houghton Mifflin 2001 160p $23   **809**
   1. Authors 2. Literature -- History and criticism
   ISBN 0-618-15314-4

         LC 2001-24523

"In this collection of encounters with distinguished minds—unguarded interviews with Primo Levi and Aharon Appelfeld, among others; an odd exchange of letters with Mary McCarthy; fondly contentious portraits of Bernard Malamud and the painter Philip Guston—Roth manages to tease from his subjects the convictions that fuel their work and the vulnerabilities that make them human." N Y Times Book Rev

Short story writers; edited by Charles E. May. Rev. ed.; Salem Press 2008 3v il (Magill's choice) set $217   **809**
   1. Short stories -- History and criticism
   ISBN 978-1-58765-389-6

         LC 2007-32789

First published 1997

This set "covers writers from Giovanni Boccaccio and Geoffrey Chaucer to Anton Chekhov and Sandra Cisneros. . . . Readers, whether in need of a brief critical overview or in search of what to read next, will find this set extremely useful. Each entry includes a brief biography, a list of principal works, a note on other literary forms the author explored, and a concise list of achievements as well as brief essays . . . on particular stories." SLJ

Includes bibliographical references

Society for the Study of the Short Story

A **Reader's** companion to the short story in English; edited by Erin Fallon [et al.]; under the auspices of the Society for the Study of the Short Story. Greenwood Press 2001 xxxiv, 432p $105   **809**
   1. Short stories -- History and criticism
   ISBN 0-313-29104-7

         LC 00-25113

"Although most of the stories covered by Fallon's compilation were written in the later half of the 20th century, the scope is international. . . . Each chapter concisely profiles a writer and contains a biography, a brief review of criticism, a lengthier analysis of specific works, and a bibliography. A section covers the short story genre. This work is extremely important because of the popularity of the genre." Choice

Includes bibliographical references

The **story** about the story; great writers explore great literature. edited by J. C. Hallman. Tin House Books 2009 420p pa $18.95   **809**
   1. Literature -- History and criticism
   ISBN 978-0-9802436-9-7

         LC 2009-15717

In his introduction, "editor J.C. Hallman writes about what he calls a 'kind of personal literary analysis, criticism that contemplates rather than analyzes'. He goes on to make the case for writers writing about writing from an individual perspective as his ideal approach to critiquing literature and the inspiration behind his compiling these works by notable writers from Virginia Woolf and D.H. Lawrence to Susan Sontag and Milan Kundera. . . . The selections range from well-known essays like Vladimir Nabokov on The Metamorphosis (he tries to figure out exactly what kind of beetle Gregor Samsa had turned into) to quirkier pleasures like Salman Rushdie on The Wizard of Oz." PopMatters

★ **Supernatural** fiction writers; contemporary fantasy and horror. Richard Bleiler, editor. 2nd ed; Scribner 2003 1048p 2v (Scribner writers series) set $250   **809**
   1. Fantasy fiction -- History and criticism
   ISBN 0-684-31250-6

         LC 2002-11128

First published 1985

This edition "is organized alphabetically by writer. Articles range in length from 5 to 12 pages. There is some biographical information but emphasis is on the works, with analysis of important themes, types of work, and, in many cases, individual series and titles. Each article concludes with a selected bibliography of works by the author under discussion, critical and biographical studies, and Web sites if they are available." Booklist

Includes bibliographical references

Symons, Julian

Bloody murder; from the detective story to the crime novel. 3rd rev ed; Mysterious Press 1993 349p pa $30   **809**
   1. Mystery fiction -- History and criticism
   ISBN 0-89296-496-0

         LC 92-54127

First published 1972 in the United Kingdom. Present edition first published 1992 in the United Kingdom

A critical survey of crime fiction, including detective stories, psychological crime stories, thrillers, and espionage, covering authors from Poe to the 1990s

Thompson, Cliff

World authors, 1990-1995; editor, Clifford Thompson. Wilson, H.W. 1999 863p il (Authors series) $155   **809**
   1. Reference books 2. Authors -- Dictionaries 3. Literature -- Bio-bibliography
   ISBN 0-8242-0956-7

         LC 99-48161

This volume offers "articles on more than 300 poets, dramatists, essayists, novelists, and other writers." (Booklist)

Includes bibliographical references

World authors, 1995-2000; editors, Clifford Thompson, Mari Rich [et. al.] Wilson, H.W. 2003 872p il (Authors series) $160   **809**

1. Reference books 2. Authors -- Dictionaries 3. Literature -- Bio-bibliography

ISBN 0-8242-1032-8

LC 2003-45062

This reference includes 320 novelists, poets, dramatists, essayists, social scientists, and biographers who have published significant works from 1995 through 2000. Each profile details the author's life and career, the circumstances under which their works were produced, and their literary significance.

Includes bibliographical references

Yagoda, Ben

Memoir; a history. Riverhead Books 2009 291p $25.95   **809**

1. Autobiography

ISBN 1-59448-886-X; 978-1-59448-886-3

LC 2009-30859

"Yagoda traces the memoir from its birth in early Christian writings and Roman generals' journals . . . [through the] year of 2007." (Publisher's note) Index.

"With its mixture of literary criticism, cultural history and just enough trivia, Yagoda's survey is sure to appeal to scholars and bibliophiles alike." Publ Wkly

Includes bibliographical references

809.1   Literature in specific forms other than miscellaneous writings

Borges, Jorge Luis

This craft of verse; edited by Calin-Andrei Mihailescu. Harvard Univ. Press 2000 154p il (Charles Eliot Norton lectures) $25; pa $14.95   **809.1**

1. Poetry -- History and criticism

ISBN 0-674-00290-3; 0-674-00820-0 pa

LC 00-33541

This volume is based on the Argentine writer's "Charles Eliot Norton lectures [delivered] at Harvard in 1967-68. . . . [Borges] discusses some of his favorite texts, conducting a literary journey that began in his father's library in Buenos Aires." N Y Times Book Rev

Includes bibliographical references

Brodsky, Joseph

Less than one; selected essays. Farrar, Straus & Giroux 1986 501p hardcover o.p. pa $18   **809.1**

1. Poets 2. Authors 3. Essayists 4. College teachers

ISBN 0-374-52055-0 pa

LC 85-15900

The essays in this volume "begin and end with autobiographical pieces; in between there are alternate homages to favorite poets, both Russian and non-Russian, as well as substantial discussions of such topics as geography and

history, political force and ethical choice, and literary tradition." N Y Times Book Rev

Burt, Stephen

Close calls with nonsense; reading new poetry. Graywolf Press 2009 374p bibl f pa $19   **809.1**

1. Poetry -- History and criticism

ISBN 978-1-55597-521-0; 1-55597-521-6

LC 2008-935602

"This collection of 30 essays, many of which began as book reviews, confirms Stephen Burt's reputation as the leading poetry critic of his generation. Informative, matter-of-fact and abounding with an excited spirit more common to film and pop music reviews than to literary criticism, these essays will appeal to the unpracticed reader of contemporary poetry as well as the seasoned reader. . . . Burt comes to the poets he considers—including Rea Armantrout, Juan Felipe Herrera, Paul Muldoon and James Merrill—as both a scholar and a practitioner of the art, but he eschews the specialist's jargon as well as the indulgent lyricality that makes some poets' criticism more dazzling than illuminating." Publ Wkly

Includes bibliographical references

★ **Classic** writings on poetry; edited by William Harmon. Columbia University Press 2003 538p $79; pa $27.50   **809.1**

1. Poetry -- History and criticism

ISBN 0-231-12370-1; 0-231-12371-X pa

LC 2003-40917

This anthology contains "writing on poetry by such philosophical royalty as Plato, Aristotle, Milton, Sir Philip Sidney, Wordsworth, and Emily Dickinson. Readers are given a peek through the hole of history's fence into the lives and worlds of our poetic geniuses and reminded of the poem's matchless role in conveying reverence, remembering wars, recording history, entertaining, expressing deep emotion, and above all, allowing the finite mind, for one moment, to contain infinity." Libr J

Includes bibliographical references

Gioia, Dana

Can poetry matter? essays on poetry and American culture. Dana Gioia. 10th Anniversary ed; Graywolf Press 2002 231p pa $16   **809.1**

1. Poets 2. Artists 3. Authors 4. Lawyers 5. Painters 6. Criticism 7. Dramatists 8. Editors 9. Translators 10. Poets laureate 11. College teachers 12. Literary critics 13. Magazine editors 14. Writers on nature 15. Short story writers 16. Insurance executives 17. Poetry -- History and criticism

ISBN 1-55597-370-1

LC 2002-102971

First published 1992

In addition to addressing the business of being a poet and the new formalism, the author offers readings of Robinson Jeffers, Weldon Kees, Robert Bly and others.

"Gioia makes his case with erudition and skill, and the best essays bring attention to underappreciated poets like Ted Kooser." Libr J

Hirsch, Edward

Poet's choice; Edward Hirsch. Harcourt 2006 432p $25 **809.1**

1. Poetry -- History and criticism

ISBN 0-15-101356-X; 978-0-15-101356-2

LC 2005-26890

"Hirsch's aesthetic is unerring, and his interpretations are profound as he considers our 'collective destiny' and takes measure of poetry's encompassing vision." Booklist

Iron-Georges, Tracy

Masterplots II, poetry series; rev ed; Salem Press 2002 8v set $499 **809.1**

1. Poetry -- History and criticism

ISBN 1-58765-037-1

LC 2001-55059

"This set supersedes the six-volume Masterplots 2: Poetry Series (1992) and the three-volume Masterplots 2: Poetry Series Supplement (1998). It contains 1,385 signed entries written by scholars on individual poems, arranged alphabetically by poem title and ranging in length from three to five pages apiece." Booklist

Includes bibliographical references

Koch, Kenneth

Making your own days; the pleasures of reading and writing poetry. Simon & Schuster 1999 317p pa $15 **809.1**

1. Poetry -- Collections 2. Poetry -- History and criticism

ISBN 0-684-82438-8

LC 98-115810

First published 1998 by Scribner

"This book is divided into two parts: a series of essays on subjects such as meter, rhyme, and personification and an anthology of favorite poems. Most remarkably, non-English poems often appear with several translations, underscoring the flexibility of poetic language. Making Your Own Days will be most useful to writers already familiar with the basics." Libr J

Orr, David

Beautiful & pointless. HarperCollins 2011 200p $25.99 **809.1**

1. Poetry 2. Poetry -- History and criticism

ISBN 978-0-06-167345-0; 0-06-167345-5

LC 2011-11599

This book examines "why poetry seems especially personal and what it means to write 'in form.'" (Publisher's note)

This book presents a guide and cultural critique of the state of contemporary poetry by David Orr, an attorney, poet, and poetry reviewer for "The New York Times Book Review." The author looks at themes and influences of various modern poems, including the poem "Bush's War," by Robert Haas. He also explores his own history as an appreciator and writer of poetry. "[David Orr] takes a calisthenic view of poetry." (Nation)

What makes this book "different from thousands of other defenses of poetry is that, according to its author, poetry differs from music and stamp collecting in that people's love for poetry is measurably greater than their love for any other activity. Poetry fans don't just love poetry a little; they really love it." N Y Times Book Rev

Paglia, Camille

★ Break, blow, burn; Camille Paglia. Pantheon Books 2005 247p $20; pa $12.95 **809.1**

1. English poetry -- History and criticism 2. American poetry -- History and criticism

ISBN 0-375-42084-3; 0-375-72539-3 pa

LC 2004-56573

This work "is vintage Paglia: bracing, opinionated, and deliciously enjoyable." Natl Rev

Includes bibliographical references

★ Poetry in person; twenty-five years of conversation with America's poets. edited and with an introduction by Alexander Neubauer; postscript by Robert Polito. Alfred A. Knopf 2010 343p il $27.95 **809.1**

1. Poetics 2. Poetry -- Authorship 3. Poetry -- History and criticism

ISBN 978-0-307-26967-6

LC 2009-29277

"For almost 30 years, beginning in 1970, Pearl London taught a course at the New School called Works in Progress, to which she asked famous poets to come with drafts of new poems in hand. This book is a series of transcripts of discussions from those classes, taken from a series of previously unknown recordings found after London's death. . . . . Represented in these 23 conversations are such acknowledged masters of late 20th–century poetry as Robert Hass, Lucille Clifton, Amy Clampitt, and Charles Simic." Publ Wkly

809.3 Fiction--criticism

Brave new words; the Oxford dictionary of science fiction. edited by Jeffrey Prucher; introduction by Gene Wolfe. Oxford University Press 2007 xxxi, 342p $29.95 **809.3**

1. Reference books 2. Science fiction -- Dictionaries

ISBN 978-0-19-530567-8; 0-19-530567-1

LC 2006-37280

This is a "dictionary of the language of science fiction based on historical principles. . . . Entries include part of speech, etymology, definition with cross references to related terms, usage status (e.g., historical, jocular, derogatory, obsolete), variant forms, and . . . dated citations and quotations illustrating the usage of the word over time." Libr J

Includes bibliographical references

Ellis, Samantha

How to Be a Heroine; Or, what I've learned from reading too much. by Samantha Ellis. Chatto & Windus 2014 272 p. $14.95 **809.3**

1. Heroes and heroines 2. Characters and characteristics in literature

ISBN 0701187514; 1101872098; 9780701187514; 9781101872093

LC 2014021162

This book, by Samantha Ellis, is "a retrospective look at the literary ladies—the characters and the writers—whom she has loved since childhood. From early obsessions with the March sisters to her later idolization of Sylvia Plath, Ellis evaluates how her heroines stack up today. And, just as she excavates the stories of her favorite characters, Ellis also shares a frank, often humorous account of her own life growing up in a tight-knit Iraqi Jewish community in London." (Publisher's note)

"The book could equally be titled How to Be a Reader; Ellis is passionate and engaged, railing against writers who shortchange their creations and celebrating those whose characters represent their best selves. She is frank about times she has misread works, and she employs a rigorous feminist lens. Primarily, though, this is a rousing call for women to be the heroines in their own lives, and it's good fun, to boot." Booklist

809.889 Literature--Other ethnic and national groups

Kirsch, Adam

★ The **people** and the books; 18 Classics of Jewish Literature. Adam Kirsch. W W Norton & Co Inc 2016 432 p. map (ebook) $50; (hardcover) $28.95   **809.889**
1. Jewish literature 2. Bible. Old Testament 3. Jewish literature -- History and criticism 4. Bible. Old Testament -- Criticism, interpretation, etc
ISBN 9780393608311; 9780393241761
LC 2016024818

This book, by Adam Kirsch, is an "exploration of a rich literary tradition from the Bible to modern times. . . . [It] shows how central questions and themes of our history and culture are reflected in the Jewish literary canon: the nature of God, the right way to understand the Bible, the relationship of the Jews to their Promised Land, and the challenges of living as a minority in Diaspora." (Publisher's note)

"A fascinating, impeccably written, personal tour of the great books of Judaism." Kirkus

Includes bibliographical references and index
Eighteen classics of Jewish literature

810 Literatures of specific languages and language families

Acosta-Belen, Edna

The **Norton** anthology of Latino literature; Ilan Stavans, general editor; [editors], Edna Acosta-Belen [et al.] W.W. Norton & Co. 2010 2489p il map $59.95   **810**
1. American literature -- Hispanic American authors -- Collections
ISBN 978-0-393-08007-0; 0-393-08007-2
LC 2010-15108

"With a great array of writers celebrated and too little known, and invaluable supporting materials, this grand and affecting treasury of culturally rich and aesthetically dynam-

ic poems, fiction, drama, letters, diaries, and essays illuminates every aspect of Latino life." Booklist

Includes bibliographical references

★ **Baseball**: a literary anthology; edited by Nicholas Dawidoff. Library of Am. 2002 721p $35 **810**
1. Baseball 2. American literature -- Collections
ISBN 1-931082-09-X
LC 2001-38654

"Beginning with Thayer's Casey at the Bat and ending with Buster Olney, there are more than 700 pages of prose and poetry, fiction and sportswriting, writers and players. Scanning the table of contents, it almost seems like everybody wrote about baseball: Damon Runyon, Ring Lardner, James Weldon Johnson, William Carlos Williams, James Thurber. But so did Paul Gallico, Nelson Algren, Tallulah Bankhead, and Jacques Barzun. . . . Ineffable, indispensable, inimitable—just like baseball." Booklist

★ The **Beat** generation; a Gale critical companion. Lynn M. Zott, project editor. Gale 2003 3v (Gale critical companion collection) set $350 **810**
1. Beat generation 2. American literature -- History and criticism
ISBN 0-7876-7569-5
LC 2002-155786

"Volume 1 gathers a variety of sources that place the movement in cultural context. . . . Volumes 2-3 supply entries for 28 Beat authors. . . . Author entries include a brief biography, notes on major works and critical reception, a list of principal works, a selection of primary sources and secondary criticism, and further readings. . . . The selections include contributions by major Beat Generation scholars and provide a well-balanced, representative view of the Beats." Choice

Includes bibliographical references

Black women writers (1950-1980) a critical evaluation. edited by Mari Evans. Anchor Press 1984 xxviii, 543p hardcover o.p. pa $25   **810**
1. Poets 2. Actors 3. Authors 4. Singers 5. Novelists 6. Dramatists 7. Editors 8. Essayists 9. Columnists 10. Memoirists 11. College teachers 12. Literary critics 13. Social activists 14. Children's authors 15. Short story writers 16. Young adult authors 17. Theatrical directors 18. Motion picture directors 19. Nobel laureates for literature 20. American literature -- Women authors 21. American literature -- History and criticism 22. American literature -- African American authors
ISBN 0-385-17125-0 pa
LC 81-43914

Critical essays on Maya Angelou, Alice Childress, Toni Morisson, Lucille Clifton, and 11 other post World War II Afro-American women writers

"This important work, a tribute to the corpus of literature produced by black women, is an indispensable resource for any serious student, scholar or teacher desiring to probe the depths of the Afro-American literary tradition." Freedomways

Includes bibliographical references

The **Cambridge** handbook of American literature; edited by Jack Salzman. Cambridge Univ. Press 1986 286p $60 **810**
1. Reference books 2. American literature -- Dictionaries
ISBN 0-521-30703-1

LC 86-2587

This handbook's "750 entries, two thirds of them about authors, briefly describe the contents and contribution of key works, assess the careers of writers, and explain the tenets and characteristics of literary movements." Wilson Libr Bull

The **Cambridge** history of American literature; general editor, Sacvan Bercovitch; associate editor, Cyrus R.K. Patell. Cambridge Univ. Press 1994 8v set $1,050 **810**
1. American literature -- History and criticism
ISBN 0-521-85760-0

LC 92-42479

Scholars contribute essays assessing major authors, movements and trends in the development of American literature

Cheever, Susan
American Bloomsbury; Louisa May Alcott, Ralph Waldo Emerson, Margaret Fuller, Nathaniel Hawthorne, and Henry David Thoreau: their lives, their loves, their work. Simon & Schuster 2006 223p il $26 **810**
1. Authors, American 2. American literature -- History and criticism
ISBN 0-7432-6461-4; 978-0-7432-6461-7

LC 2006-45015

This book offers a "glimpse into life in Concord, MA, from about 1840 to the mid-1860s, when such luminaries as Louisa May Alcott, Ralph Waldo Emerson, Margaret Fuller, Nathaniel Hawthorne, and Henry David Thoreau lived, worked, and loved. . . . [This] volume examines the dynamic relationships among these remarkable men and women, who constituted what may be considered the first American literary community. . . . Essential reading for anyone with an interest in American letters." Libr J

Includes bibliographical references

★ The **Chronology** of American literature; America's literary achievements from the colonial era to modern times. edited by Daniel S. Burt. Houghton Mifflin 2004 805p il $40 **810**
1. American literature -- Collections
ISBN 0-618-16821-4

LC 2003-51142

"This chronology includes more than 8,400 literary works by more than 5,000 writers. Sections for each year are grouped in five chapters by period, from 1582 to 1999. Within each year, entries are grouped by genre, such as diaries and other personal writings, fiction, essays, literary criticism and scholarship, nonfiction, poetry, and drama. Within each genre, authors are listed alphabetically, generally with birth and death dates and short descriptions of named works for the year. . . . The Chronology of American

Literature is easy to browse and, for book lovers, difficult to put down." Booklist
Includes bibliographical references

Columbia literary history of the United States; Emory Elliott, general editor; associate editors, Martha Banta {et al.}; advisory editors, Houston A. Baker {et al.} Columbia Univ. Press 1988 xxviii, 1263p $119 **810**
1. American literature -- History and criticism
ISBN 0-231-05812-8

LC 87-14672

This anthology "expands the traditional subjects of literary history by incorporating current theoretical ideas and newly discovered writers. Includes treatment of recently explored subjects, such as the role of women and minorities in U.S. literature. No separate bibliography other than what is found in the text." N Y Public Libr Book of How & Where to Look it Up

★ The **Continuum** encyclopedia of British literature; Steven R. Serafin and Valerie Grosvenor Myer, editors. Continuum 2003 1184p $175 **810**
1. Reference books 2. English literature -- Encyclopedias
ISBN 0-8264-1456-7

LC 2002-9231

"This reference work provides a fascinating current take on the canon. . . . The historical/literary time line and the lists of prize titles alone will keep researchers happy." SLJ
Includes bibliographical references

Crossing the danger water; three hundred years of African-American writing. edited and with an introduction by Deirdre Mullane. Anchor Bks. (NY) 1993 xxii, 769p pa $20 **810**
1. American literature -- African American authors -- Collections
ISBN 0-385-42243-1

LC 93-17194

This anthology "includes fiction, autobiography, poetry, songs, and letters by such writers as Frederick Douglass, Sojourner Truth, W.E.B. Du Bois, Zora Neale Hurston, and Richard Wright. Many topics are covered, from slavery, education, the Civil War, Reconstruction, and political issues to spirituals, songs of the Civil Rights movement, and rap music." Libr J
Includes bibliographical references

Elie, Paul
The **life** you save may be your own; an American pilgrimage. Farrar, Straus and Giroux 2003 554p il hardcover o.p. pa $16 **810**
1. Monks 2. Poets 3. Authors 4. Novelists 5. Journalists 6. Reference books 7. Essayists 8. Social reformers 9. Newspaper editors 10. Nonfiction writers 11. Short story writers 12. Writers on religion 13. American literature -- Bio-bibliography 14. American literature -- History and criticism
ISBN 0-374-25680-2; 978-0-374-52921-5 pa; 0-374-52921-3 pa

LC 2002-192522

"This thoroughly researched and well-sourced work deserves attention from students of history, literature and religion, but it will be of special significance to Catholic readers interested in the expression of faith in the modern world." Publ Wkly

Encyclopedia of African-American writing; five centuries of contribution: trials & triumphs of writers, poets, publications and organizations. Shari Dorantes Hatch, editor. 2nd ed.; Grey House Pub. 2009 xxii, 863p il $165 **810**
1. Reference books 2. American literature -- African American authors -- Encyclopedias 3. American literature -- African American authors -- Bio-bibliography
ISBN 978-1-59237-291-1

First published 2000 by ABC-CLIO with title: African-American writers: a dictionary

"This voluminous and inclusive collection consists of 738 entries that cover authors and other topics related to African American writing, such as newspapers, magazines, journals, and publishers and figures such as educators, playwrights, journalists, academics, editors, and librarians from the past 500 years.... Although unsigned, the entries are highly accessible, very current, and chock-full of information for a range of audiences." Libr J
Includes bibliographical references

Encyclopedia of American Indian literature; [edited by] Jennifer McClinton-Temple, Alan Velie. Facts on File 2007 466p (Encyclopedia of American ethnic literature) $75 **810**
1. Reference books 2. Native American literature -- Encyclopedias 3. Native Americans in literature -- Encyclopedias
ISBN 0-8160-5656-0; 978-0-8160-5656-9

LC 2006-23762

"This book brings together solid information from scattered sources, facilitating research on an esoteric subject." Libr J
Includes bibliographical references

Facts on File, Inc.
★ **Encyclopedia** of American literature; 2nd ed; Facts on File 2008 4v il (Facts on File library of American literature) set $375 **810**
1. Reference books 2. American literature -- Encyclopedias
ISBN 978-0-8160-6476-2

LC 2007-25662

First published 2002

Entries in this encyclopedia cover works, writers, movements and other American literature-related topics from colonial times to the present. Each volume includes a chronology.
Includes bibliographical references

Hart, James David
★ The **Oxford** companion to American literature; [by] James D. Hart; with revisions and additions by Phillip W. Leininger. 6th ed; Oxford Univ. Press 1995 779p $49.95 **810**
1. Reference books 2. American literature -- Dictionaries
ISBN 0-19-506548-4

LC 94-45727

First published 1941

In addition to over 2000 entries for individual authors and more than 1,100 for important works this reference includes entries for literary movements, awards, magazines, printers, book collectors and newspapers. A chronological index of literary and social history is appended.

Jewish American literature; a Norton anthology. [compiled and edited by] Jules Chametzky [et al.] Norton 2000 xxiv, 1221p il $39.95 **810**
1. American literature -- Collections 2. American literature -- Jewish authors
ISBN 0-393-04809-8

LC 00-55393

The editors have attempted "to encompass Jewish literature from 1654 to the present in this collection of poems, cartoons, sermons, diaries, letters, stories, speeches, plays, prayers, novel excerpts, and critical writings either translated from Hebrew or Yiddish or written in English. Major sections group the literature chronologically to help identify large movements. . . . This great anthology is essential for Jewish studies and American literature collections." Libr J
Includes bibliographical references

Kazin, Alfred
An **American** procession. Harvard University Press 1996 408p pa $15.95 **810**
1. Poets 2. Authors 3. Humorists 4. Novelists 5. Dramatists 6. Historians 7. Naturalists 8. Philosophers 9. Editors 10. Essayists 11. Pacifists 12. Satirists 13. Memoirists 14. Screenwriters 15. Travel writers 16. Literary critics 17. Writers on nature 18. Nonfiction writers 19. Short story writers 20. Nobel laureates for literature 21. American literature -- History and criticism
ISBN 0-674-03143-1

LC 97-220259

First published 1984 by Knopf

"'An American Procession' is a refresher in the best sense: without any fundamental revision of our understanding of our classics, it vivaciously refreshes our awareness of them, and our gratitude for them." New Yorker

★ **Latino** and Latina writers; Alan West-Durán, editor. Charles Scribner's Sons 2004 1072p 2v (Scribner writers series) set $265 **810**
1. American literature -- Hispanic American authors
ISBN 0-684-31293-X

LC 2003-15728

This set "begins with five essays of social and historical commentary that focus on key elements of Latino culture in this country. What follows is a series of ten to 20-page biocritical essays on nearly 60 authors (e.g., Gary Soto, Pat Mora, Sandra Cisneros, Victor Villase or, Julia Alvarez, Richard Rodriguez, and Lorna Dee Cervantes). . . . One of the most comprehensive anthologies available of Latino writing in the United States." Libr J

Includes bibliographical references

★ **Magill's** survey of American literature; edited by Steven G. Kellman. Rev. ed; Salem Press 2007 6v il set $499 **810**
1. Reference books 2. Literature -- Bio-bibliography 3. Literature -- History and criticism
ISBN 978-1-58765-285-1; 1-58765-285-4

LC 2006-16503

First published 1992 with two volume supplement published 1996 under the editorship of Frank Northen Magill

"Examining selected works of 339 U.S. and Canadian writers, from Anne Bradstreet and Benjamin Franklin to Edward Bloor and Octavia E. Butler, this clearly written resource provides sturdy support for assignments, and will also be popular with discussion groups and with general readers of literature." SLJ

Includes bibliographical references

Matthiessen, F. O.

★ **American** renaissance; art and expression in the age of Emerson and Whitman. Oxford Univ. Press 1941 xxiv, 678p il hardcover o.p. pa $53 **810**
1. Poets 2. Artists 3. Authors 4. Novelists 5. Sculptors 6. Naturalists 7. Philosophers 8. Essayists 9. Pacifists 10. Writers on nature 11. Nonfiction writers 12. Short story writers 13. American literature -- History and criticism
ISBN 0-19-500759-X pa

A critical study of works by Emerson, Thoreau, Melville, Hawthorne and Whitman and their impact on American intellectual history.

Modern American memoirs; selected and edited by Annie Dillard and Cort Conley. HarperCollins Pubs. 1995 449p hardcover o.p. pa $16 **810**
1. Authors, American 2. American literature -- Collections
ISBN 0-06-092763-1 pa

LC 95-30755

The editors "have collected excerpts from the memoirs of 35 20th-century American authors. The selections represent the best in autobiographical writing published between 1917 and 1992. Included are nine women and 26 men, both black and white, some better known than others, all distinguished writers and wonderful storytellers. . . . The editors precede each entry with a biographical and contextual note. There's an opening essay on the art of the memoirist and an afterword listing additional classics in the genre." Libr J

Morgan, Bill

The **typewriter** is holy; the complete, uncensored history of the beat generation. Free Press 2010 291p il $28 **810**
1. Beat generation 2. American literature -- History and criticism 3. American literature -- 20th century -- History and criticism
ISBN 1-4165-9242-3; 978-1-4165-9242-6

LC 2009-42224

In this book, Bill Morgan "employs a wide focus to portray the remarkable group of writers and artists that became known as the Beat Generation. He suggests that Jack Kerouac, Lawrence Ferlinghetti, Gary Snyder, Gregory Corso, William Burroughs, and others had such divergent aims and styles that they cannot properly be considered a literary movement. Instead, he sees them as a circle of friends who loved literature and were united by [Allen] Ginsberg." (Library Journal)

"Morgan clearly loves his subjects, but he doesn't gloss over their erratic lifestyle, which involved amazing amounts of drugs and alcohol, and their consummate selfishness. . . . Morgan's own prose is straightforward, even pedestrian, but his ability to draw together so many events and personalities is astonishing." Providence J

Includes bibliographical references

National Story Project (U.S.)

I thought my father was God and other true tales from the National Story Project; edited and introduced by Paul Auster; Nelly Reifler, assistant editor. Holt & Co. 2001 xxi, 383p il hardcover o.p. pa $15 **810**
1. American literature -- Collections
ISBN 0-8050-6714-0; 0-312-42100-1 pa

LC 00-54397

"These are stop-you-in-your-tracks stories about hair-raising coincidences, miracles, tragedies, redemption, and moments of pure hilarity." Booklist

A **new** literary history of America; edited by Greil Marcus and Werner Sollors. Belknap Press of Harvard University Press 2009 1095p bibl f il (Harvard University Press reference library) $49.95 **810**
1. United States -- Civilization 2. American literature -- History and criticism
ISBN 978-0-674-03594-2; 0-674-03594-1

LC 2009014255

"This is an adventurous, jazzily choral, and kaleidoscopic book of interpretations, illuminations, and revitalized history." Booklist

Includes bibliographical references and index

★ The **Norton** anthology of African American literature; Henry Louis Gates, Jr., general editor, Nellie Y. McKay, general editor. 2nd ed; Norton 2003 2800p 2 computer laser optical discs pa $70.30 **810**
1. American literature -- African American authors -- Collections
ISBN 0-393-97778-1

LC 2003-66176

First published 1996

"The anthology is divided into seven sections, each with a separate introduction giving the sociopolitical factors that impacted on the material included therein. Featured are 120 writers, 52 of whom are women, richly representing African American vernacular literature, poetry, drama, short stories, novels, slave narratives, and autobiographies." Libr J [review of 1996 edition]

Includes bibliographical references

The **Oxford** book of the American South; testimony, memory, and fiction. edited by Edward L. Ayers, Bradley C. Mittendorf. Oxford Univ. Press 1997 597p hardcover o.p. pa $22   **810**
1. American literature -- Southern States -- Collections
ISBN 0-19-512493-6 pa

LC 96-45135

"Not limiting themselves to fiction (short stories and novels, either in full or in extract), the editors also gather memoirs, diaries, and essays. From both genders and races, from opposite poles on the economic scale, from an eighteenth-century naturalist to a former slave, from Thomas Jefferson to Eudora Welty, these writings give ringing voice to the experiences that have engendered a distinctive southern culture." Booklist

The **Oxford** book of women's writing in the United States; edited by Linda Wagner-Martin, Cathy N. Davidson. Oxford Univ. Press 1995 596p hardcover o.p. pa $27.50   **810**
1. American literature -- Women authors -- Collections
ISBN 0-19-513245-9 pa

LC 95-1499

This anthology provides "samples of the public and private work of 99 women of diverse racial and ethnic backgrounds who write in English and were born in or have lived in the United States over the past four centuries. They include short fiction (almost half of the book), poems, essays, plays, and speeches but have also gone beyond traditional genre categories to include performance pieces, erotica, diaries, letters, and recipes." Libr J

★ The **Oxford** encyclopedia of American literature; Jay Parini, editor-in-chief. Oxford University Press 2004 4v il set $495   **810**
1. Reference books 2. American literature -- Encyclopedias
ISBN 0-19-515653-6

LC 2002-156325

This set "provides a wealth of reliable information on standard bearers of American literature in an easy-on-the-eyes format for students and general readers." SLJ

Parini, Jay
Promised land; thirteen books that changed America. Doubleday 2008 385p il $24.95   **810**
1. American national characteristics 2. American literature -- History and criticism
ISBN 978-0-385-52276-2

LC 2008-9990

This is "a mind-expanding book of books guaranteed to provoke discussion and fuel reading groups." Booklist
Includes bibliographical references

Pierpont, Claudia Roth
Passionate minds; women rewriting the world. Knopf 2000 298p il hardcover o.p. pa $13   **810**
1. Poets 2. Actors 3. Authors 4. Lawyers 5. Novelists 6. Dramatists 7. Philosophers 8. Women authors 9. Diarists 10. Essayists 11. Feminists 12. Memoirists 13. Folklorists 14. Screenwriters 15. College teachers 16. Literary critics 17. Nonfiction writers 18. Short

story writers 19. Writers on politics 20. Political scientists 21. Nobel laureates for literature 22. Political and social philosophers 23. English literature -- Women authors -- History and criticism 24. American literature -- Women authors -- History and criticism
ISBN 0-679-43106-3; 0-679-75113-0 pa

LC 99-33349

"A scintillating collection of brief lives of women writers, a book that sparkles with intelligence, wit and human interest. . . . Unfolding with the dramatic élan of a novella, each one is exhaustively researched, sharply focused, convincingly opinionated." N Y Times Book Rev

The **Portable** beat reader; edited by Ann Charters. Viking 1992 xxxvi, 642p hardcover o.p. pa $17   **810**
1. Bohemianism 2. American literature -- Collections
ISBN 0-14-243753-0 pa

LC 91-16155

"Cutting through bohemian posturing and excess, Charters here reprints much of the most vital, readable and relevant material produced by the Beat generation." Publ Wkly
Includes bibliographical references

The **Portable** Harlem Renaissance reader; edited and with an introduction by David Levering Lewis. Viking 1994 xlvii, 766p hardcover o.p. pa $18   **810**
1. Harlem Renaissance 2. American literature -- African American authors -- Collections
ISBN 0-14-017036-7

LC 93-30233

"General categories include essay, memoir, fiction, poetry, and drama; specific writers include such expected names as Langston Hughes, Zora Neale Hurston, and Claude McKay, but lesser-known names are also represented. There is anger in these pages and also frustration, pride, pain, and elation, but above all there is incredible talent. Reading the collection straight through would be a wonderful education, but most readers will dip in here and there, and that is edifying, too." Booklist

The **Portable** sixties reader; edited by Ann Charters. Penguin Bks. 2003 xli, 628p il pa $16   **810**
1. American literature -- Collections 2. United States -- History -- 1961-1974
ISBN 0-14-200194-5

LC 2002-32266

This reader includes "essays, poetry, and fiction under thematic subjects, such as civil rights; women's rights; the sexual revolution; environmental issues; the antiwar, free-speech, and black-arts movements; and the use of drugs in pursuit of enlightenment. . . . [Includes works by] James Baldwin, Thomas Merton, Susan Sontag, Gary Snyder, Allen Ginsburg, Rachel Carson, Kate Millett, Nikki Giovanni, and many more." Booklist
Includes bibliographical references

The **Portable** Western reader; edited and with an introduction by William Kittredge. Penguin Bks. 1997 xxi, 600p pa $14.95 **810**

1. American literature -- West (U.S.) -- Collections
ISBN 0-14-023026-2

LC 96-47243

"Part 1, 'Ancient Stories,' shows the evolution of Native American storytelling from the early legends to contemporary stories and includes writings by Catherine McClellan, John Graves, and Louise Erdrich. Parts 2 and 3 contrast the mythology of the 19th-century 'Western' with the actual experience of living in the West. Most of these authors, from Walt Whitman to Larry McMurtry, will be familiar to readers. Part 4, 'Brilliant Possibilities,' showcases the new generation of Western writers, including Gretel Ehrlich, Jimmy Santiago Baca, and Sherman Alexie." Libr J

★ **Pushcart** Prize XXXVI: best of the small presses 2012; edited by Bill Henderson with the Pushcart Prize editors. Pushcart 2011 569p $35; pa $18.95 **810**

1. American literature -- Collections
ISBN 978-1-88888964-2; 978-1-8888864-5 pa

Annual. First published 1976

Each volume "consists of short stories, poems and essays; includes the work of established and beginning writers, and has a faintly subversive character. Its audience would seem to be primarily the young, yet among its contributors are many of the best writers in America. . . . Like all interesting literary journals, 'The Pushcart Prize' is eclectic and uneven. . . . The number and diversity of journals represented and the sheer length of it are impressive." Books of the Times

Includes bibliographical references

Salem Press Inc.

★ **Notable** Latino writers; from the editors of Salem Press. Salem Press 2005 3v il (Magill's choice) set $207 **810**

1. American literature -- Hispanic American authors -- History and criticism
ISBN 1-58765-243-9; 978-1-58765-243-1

LC 2005-17567

These volumes feature "122 essays about Latino novelists, short-story writers, poets, and playwrights of the Western Hemisphere who write in English, Spanish, or Portuguese. . . . This set may prove to be a useful research tool for students, teachers, and librarians." Libr J

Includes bibliographical references

Samet, Elizabeth D.

★ **Soldier's** heart; reading literature through peace and war at West Point. Farrar, Straus and Giroux 2007 259p $23 **810**

1. United States Military Academy 2. Soldiers -- United States 3. Literature -- Study and teaching
ISBN 978-0-374-18063-8; 0-374-18063-6

LC 2007-9159

"Like the best professors, Samet asks tough questions and offers no easy answers. Her book is filled with lively classroom discussions and poignant e-mails from former students now in Iraq, often writing about the books they're

reading there. . . . I know of no other new book that's a better choice for any reading group that loves to debate literature and politics." USA Today

Showalter, Elaine, 1941-

★ A **jury** of her peers; American women writers from Anne Bradstreet to Annie Proulx. Alfred A. Knopf 2009 586p $30 **810**

1. Women in literature 2. Literature -- Women authors 3. American literature -- Women authors 4. Women in literature -- United States 5. Women and literature -- United States -- History 6. American literature -- Women authors -- Bio-bibliography 7. American literature -- Women authors -- History and criticism
ISBN 978-1-4000-4123-7; 1-4000-4123-6

LC 2008-42312

"Showalter's writing is clear, lively, and authoritative; her research is impressive." Libr J

Includes bibliographical references

Taylor, Todd W.

★ The **Companion** to southern literature; themes, genres, places, people, movements, and motifs. edited by Joseph M. Flora and Lucinda H. MacKethan; associate editor, Todd Taylor. Louisiana State Univ. Press 2001 xxvi, 1054p $69.95 **810**

1. Reference books 2. Southern States -- Intellectual life 3. American literature -- Southern States -- Encyclopedias
ISBN 0-8071-2692-6

LC 2001-29959

"This unique compilation [is] . . . an excellent addition to libraries that support studies of Southern literature." Libr J

Includes bibliographical references

Transcendentalism; a reader. [edited by] Joel Myerson. Oxford Univ. Press 2001 xxxvii, 712p hardcover o.p. pa $32 **810**

1. New England -- Intellectual life 2. Transcendentalism -- Collections
ISBN 0-19-512212-7; 0-19-512213-5 pa

LC 00-21484

This reader "draws together in their entirety the essential writings of the Transcendentalist group during its most active period, 1836-1844. It includes the major publications of the Dial, the writings on democratic and social reform, the early poetry, nature writings, and all of Emerson's major essays, as well as an . . . introduction and annotations by Myerson." Publisher's note

Includes bibliographical references

Wall, Cheryl A.

Women of the Harlem Renaissance. Indiana Univ. Press 1995 246p il (Women of letters) hardcover o.p. pa $14.95 **810**

1. Nurses 2. Authors 3. Novelists 4. Dramatists 5. Harlem Renaissance 6. Editors 7. Essayists 8. Memoirists 9. Folklorists 10. Literary critics 11. Short story writers 12. American literature -- African American authors
ISBN 0-253-20980-3 pa

LC 95-3132

This study of women writers of the Harlem Renaissance begins with an overview: On being young—a woman—and colored, followed by critical and biographical studies of Jessie Redmond Fauset, Nella Larsen, and Zora Neale Hurston

"Wall offers strong critiques of these women's work, uncovering certain similarities, including, most importantly, the travel motif as not only a reflection of the mass migrations of the day but also a larger dislocation." Publ Wkly

Includes bibliographical references

Wilson, Edmund
Patriotic gore; studies in the literature of the American Civil War. Norton 1994 816p pa $19.95   **810**
1. Poets 2. Clergy 3. Judges 4. Authors 5. Lawyers 6. Generals 7. Pianists 8. Diplomats 9. Educators 10. Governors 11. Novelists 12. Presidents 13. Journalists 14. Abolitionists 15. Flutists 16. Essayists 17. Memoirists 18. Sociologists 19. Army officers 20. Political leaders 21. State legislators 22. Children's authors 23. Nonfiction writers 24. Secretaries of war 25. White supremacists 26. Members of Congress 27. Novelists, American 28. Short story writers 29. Writers on politics 30. Civil rights activists 31. Supreme Court justices 32. Spouses of prominent persons 33. American literature -- History and criticism 34. United States -- History -- 1861-1865, Civil War 35. United States -- History -- 1861-1865, Civil War -- Poetry 36. United States -- History -- 1861-1865, Civil War -- Biography
ISBN 978-0-393-31256-0; 0-393-31256-9
First published 1962 by Oxford University Press

"A collection of sixteen essays on writing related to the war including the memoirs of Union generals Grant and Sherman and Confederates Mosby and Lee, diaries, political writing, and fiction by writers such as Ambrose Bierce and John De Forest." Benet's Reader's Ency of Am Lit

810.8 American literature (English)--Collections

★ The **best** American science and nature writing 2012; edited by Dan Ariely and Tim Folger. Houghton Mifflin Harcourt 2012 325 p. $14.95   **810.8**
1. Science 2. Natural history
ISBN 0547799535; 9780547799537
This book, edited by Dan Ariely, "presents a smorgasbord of . . . science writing covering everything from the 1,000 species in the human gut to efforts to reverse-evolve a chicken into a dinosaur. The two dozen pieces reflect the conclusion that 'we are extraordinary yet flawed and predictably irrational creatures.' . . . Topics include allergies, marauder ants, lab-grown meat, airborne contaminants, the adolescent brain . . . and the sequencing of the Neanderthal genome." (Kirkus Reviews)

The **best** American science and nature writing 2014; edited by Deborah Blum and Tim Folger. Hough-

ton Mifflin Harcourt 2014 352 p. (paperback) $14.95   **810.8**
1. Nature 2. Science 3. Science and the humanities
ISBN 054400342X; 9780544003422
In this book, editors Deborah Blum and Tim Folger "[select for 2014] the year's top science and nature writing from writers who balance research with humanity and in the process uncover riveting stories of discovery across the disciplines." (Publisher's note)

"This carefully curated collection deserves a place on the shelves of libraries serving the scientifically curious public and fans of long-form, intellectual journalism." LJ

Bohemians, bootleggers, flappers, and swells; the best of early Vanity fair. introduction by Graydon Carter; edited by David Friend. The Penguin Press 2014 432 p. $29.95   **810.8**
1. Periodicals 2. World history -- 20th century 3. Literature, Modern -- 20th century 4. American literature -- 20th century 5. United States -- Civilization -- 20th century -- Literary collections
ISBN 1594205981; 9781594205989
          LC 2014009783
Edited by Graydon Carter "In honor of the 100th anniversary of Vanity Fair magazine, 'Bohemians, Bootleggers, Flappers, and Swells' celebrates the publication's astonishing early catalogue of writers, with works by Dorothy Parker, Noël Coward, P. G. Wodehouse, Jean Cocteau, Colette, Gertrude Stein, Edna St. Vincent Millay, Sherwood Anderson, Robert Benchley, Langston Hughes--and many others." (Publisher's note)

"These delightful period pieces reflecting the social mores of their time hold up in their innovation, style, and concern about modern life nearly a century later." Booklist

810.9 American literature (English)--History and criticism

African American literature; a guide to reading interests. edited by Alma Dawson and Connie Van Fleet. Libraries Unlimited 2004 xx, 470 p.p (alk. paper) $65   **810.9**
1. African Americans in literature 2. American literature -- African American authors 3. African Americans in literature -- Bibliography 4. African Americans -- Intellectual life -- Bibliography 5. African Americans in literature -- Handbooks, manuals, etc 6. American literature -- African American authors -- Bibliography 7. African Americans -- Intellectual life -- Handbooks, manuals, etc 8. American literature -- African American authors -- History and criticism -- Handbooks, manuals, etc
ISBN 1563089319; 9781563089312
          LC 2004048928
This book, edited by Alma Dawson and Connie Van Fleet, "is the first readers' advisory guide to focus specifically on African American literature. It is designed to help book professionals better serve not only African American readers, but all readers who enjoy works by African American authors. . . . Each chapter is further organized by sub-

genre and theme. Title-author and subject indexes provide additional access." (Publisher's note)

Includes bibliographical references (p. 419-431) and indexes

Bram, Christopher

Eminent outlaws; the gay writers who changed America. Christopher Bram. Twelve 2012 372 p. **810.9**

1. Social change 2. American authors 3. Gay men's writings 4. Gay men -- Biography 5. Homosexuality -- United States -- History 6. Gay authors -- United States 7. Authors, American -- 20th century 8. Gays' writings, American -- History and criticism

ISBN 9780446563130

LC 2011029910

"This book is a history, literary critique, and collective biography in one. Novelist [Christopher] Bram . . . discusses gay men . . . from Gore Vidal in the early postwar years up through the 1990s and close to the present. His main thesis, that 'good art can lay the groundwork for social change,' is demonstrated and contextualized in dozens of examples of how literature can be not just a reflection of the times but also a catalyst for change." (Library Journal)

Includes bibliographical references (p. 351-354) and index

Laing, Olivia

The **Trip** to Echo Spring; On Writers and Drinking. Olivia Laing. 1st U.S. ed. Picador 2014 352 p. illustrations, map (hbk.) $26 **810.9**

1. Alcoholism 2. Creation (Literary, artistic, etc.) 3. American literature -- History and criticism 4. Alcoholics in literature 5. Alcoholism in literature 6. Alcoholics -- United States 7. Authorship -- Psychological aspects 8. Creative ability -- Psychological aspects 9. Authors, American -- 20th century -- Alcohol use 10. American literature -- 20th century -- History and criticism

ISBN 1250039568; 9781250039569

LC 2013038323

In this book, "Olivia Laing examines the link between creativity and alcohol through the work and lives of six extraordinary men: F. Scott Fitzgerald, Ernest Hemingway, Tennessee Williams, John Berryman, John Cheever, and Raymond Carver. . . . Olivia Laing grew up in an alcoholic family herself. One spring, wanting to make sense of this ferocious, entangling disease, she took a journey across America that plunged her into the heart of these overlapping lives." (Publisher's note)

"Intently observant, curious, and empathetic, Laing, with shimmering detail and arresting insights, presents a beautifully elucidating and moving group portrait of writers enslaved by drink and redeemed by 'the capacity of literature to somehow . . . make one feel less flinchingly alone.' " Booklist

Includes bibliographical references

A **story** larger than my own; women writers look back on their lives and careers. edited by Janet Burroway. University of Chicago Press 2014 199 p. (cloth : alkaline paper) $55 **810.9**

1. Women poets 2. Women authors 3. Autobiographies 4. Women authors, American -- Literary collections

ISBN 022601407X; 9780226014074; 9780226014104

LC 2013032197

"In this engrossing volume edited by [Janet] Burroway . . ., 19 accomplished female authors reflect on their careers and offer insights on craft and life. The contributors, all of whom are 60 or older, came of professional age during second wave feminism, confronted the prejudice against women writers of the 1950's and 60's, and continue to publish in the digital age. The variety of voices and styles adds up to a mesmerizing tapestry of a generation, made up of both individual experiences and the commonalities between them." Pub Wkly

Writers of the Black Chicago renaissance; edited by Steven C. Tracy. University of Illinois Press 2011 vii, 523 p.p $50 **810.9**

1. African Americans -- Chicago (Ill.) 2. African Americans -- Political activity 3. American literature -- African American authors 4. Chicago (Ill.) -- Intellectual life -- 20th century 5. American literature -- 20th century -- History and criticism 6. American literature -- Illinois -- Chicago -- History and criticism 7. American literature -- African American authors -- History and criticism

ISBN 0252036395; 9780252036392

LC 2011029269

This book, edited by Steven C. Tracy, "explores the contours and content of the Black Chicago Renaissance, a creative movement that emerged from the crucible of rigid segregation in Chicago's 'Black Belt' from the 1930s through the 1960s. . . . The volume covers a vast collection of subjects, including many important writers such as Richard Wright, Gwendolyn Brooks, and Lorraine Hansberry as well as cultural products such as black newspapers, music, and theater." (Publisher's note)

Includes bibliographical references and index

811 American poetry

180 more; extraordinary poems for every day. selected and with an introduction by Billy Collins. Random House 2005 xxiii, 373p pa $14.95 **811**

1. American poetry -- Collections

ISBN 0-8129-7296-1

LC 2005-42798

Sequel to: Poetry 180

This is a second collection of 180 poems for each day of the school year, designed to expose high school students to poetry.

Ackerman, Diane, 1948-

Origami bridges; poems of psychoanalysis and fire. HarperCollins Pubs. 2002 147p $22.95; pa $11.95 **811**

1. Poetry -- By individual authors

ISBN 0-06-019988-1; 0-06-055529-7 pa

LC 2002-24685

"Sometimes addressed to herself and her personal history, at least as often addressed to 'Dr. B—,' Ackerman's passionate free verse (short, fluent and adorned by irregular rhyme) describes with nearly unmixed awe the relationship she created with her analyst, and the personal transformation she achieved." Publ Wkly

Adair, Virginia Hamilton

Ants on the melon; a collection of poems. Random House 1996 158p hardcover o.p. pa $15 **811**

1. Poetry -- By individual authors

ISBN 0-375-75229-3 pa

LC 95-25977

"The appearance of a first collection by a poet now blind and in her 83rd year must be accounted a triumph . . . {Adair} works with equal daring in free verse and more traditional forms; her subjects include social and religious commentary, but her principal theme is ordinary experience and its resistance to facile interpretation." Libr J

Beliefs and blasphemies; a collection of poems. Random House 1998 109p hardcover o.p. pa $15 **811**

1. Poetry -- By individual authors

ISBN 0-8129-9245-8 pa

LC 97-47403

"Adair's searching verses may not always have the ring of the contemporary, and they often stop short here of fully unfurling their insights. But at its best, this collection points the way back to an American tradition of religious poetry understood and cherished by the likes of Elizabeth Bishop and Louise Bogan." Publ Wkly

Adam, Helen

A **Helen** Adam reader; edited, with notes and an introduction by Kristin Prevallet. National Poetry Foundation 2007 492p il $59.95; $29.95 **811**

1. Poetry -- By individual authors

ISBN 978-0-943373-74-4; 0-943373-74-3; 978-0-943373-73-7 pa; 0-943373-73-5 pa

LC 2007-34740

In the Bay Area of the late 1940s Adam "found herself a member—some said godmother, witch or Nurse of Enchantment—of the interlocking Robert Duncan and Jack Spicer poetry circles, which, with the Beats, formed the avant-garde San Francisco Renaissance. . . . Adam combined the narrative economy of ballads—where each line is a discrete unit of information—with the lush sonic tapestry we associate with older Anglo-Saxon and Celtic strains of British verse. . . . On the page, Adam's intricate soundscapes compare with anything by Gerard Manley Hopkins and Dylan Thomas. But to see her sing her ballads—she chants 'Kiltory' on the Reader's accompanying DVD—is to appreciate how the language, trilling and seething by turns, possessed its acolyte." Nation

Includes bibliographical references

African-American poetry of the nineteenth century; an anthology. edited by Joan R. Sherman. University of Ill. Press 1992 506p hardcover o.p. pa $26.95 **811**

1. American poetry -- African American authors -- Collections

ISBN 0-252-06246-9 pa

LC 91-41709

"The introduction surveys the historical and cultural values of African American poetry. The poems themselves have historical as well as lyric value; unfamiliar as well as familiar poets are included. Though the poems are formal, the rhymes are generally unforced. . . . This anthology also includes an extensive bibliography to help researchers find other resources." Libr J

Alexander, Elizabeth, 1962-

Crave radiance; new and selected poems 1990-2010. Graywolf Press 2010 255p **811**

1. Poetry -- By individual authors

ISBN 9781555975685

LC 2010-922921

"This potent retrospective collection offers the best of Alexander's five previous books, including selections from her young-adult title, Miss Crandall's School for Young Girls and Little Misses of Color (2007), which hold their own as poems for adults of all ages here. . . . Alexander brings intellectual power, musicality, sensuousness, and vernacular immediacy to her lyrics, which entwine the personal with the social, the tactile with the imaginary, the past with the present." Booklist

Alexie, Sherman

Face. Hanging Loose Press 2009 159p $28; pa $15 **811**

1. Poetry -- By individual authors

ISBN 978-1-931236-71-3; 1-931236-71-2; 978-1-931236-70-6 pa; 1-931236-70-4 pa

LC 2008-46580

The author "has mastered both the metrical dance and fixed forms. A sequence of sonnets finds the Seven Deadly Sins in marriage, for instance; a villanelle begins with Mount Rushmore but eases into a consideration of America's Presidents, complemented by wry and smart footnotes. . . . There are a lot of serious undercurrents in his poetry, and they are always a pleasure to find." Libr J

Altman, Howard

In this house. Turtle Point Press 2010 81p pa $15.95 **811**

1. Poetry -- By individual authors

ISBN 978-1-933527-33-8

LC 2009-929505

A "collection of poems that look at the world with thought-provoking and elegantly bifurcated awareness: 'Inside every man is another man / He would like to leave behind.' At once sturdy and visionary, Altmann's work has won him a variety of fans that include not just poet John Ashbery but also actor Patricia Clarkson." Time Out N Y

Alvarez, Julia

The **woman** I kept to myself; poems. Algonquin Books of Chapel Hill 2004 155p hardcover o.p. pa $14.95 **811**

1. Poetry -- By individual authors

ISBN 1-56512-406-5; 1-61620-072-3 pa

LC 2003-70807

This "collection of 75 poems is divided into three sections, and each poem has three stanzas, exactly . . . The poet, who is from the Dominican Republic, writes about being raised with her sisters in New York. The subjects are personal—love, marriage, rejection, divorce, death, religion—but also universal." SLJ

★ **American** poetry, the twentieth century. Library of Am. 2000 2v ea $35 **811**
1. American poetry -- Collections
ISBN 1-88301-177-9 v1; 1-88301-178-7 v2
LC 99-43721
These volumes represent a "remarkable feat of assemblage, with excellent capsule biographies and explanatory notes at the end of each volume—the biographies, especially, are well worth reading." N Y Times Book Rev
Includes bibliographical references

★ **American** poetry: the seventeenth and eighteenth centuries; edited by David Shields. Library of America 2007 xxiii, 952p $40 **811**
1. American poetry -- Collections
ISBN 978-1-931082-90-7; 1-931082-90-1
LC 2007-929763
"Besides hefty helpings of the few figures meagerly represented in general American-lit surveys—Anne Bradstreet, Edward Taylor, John Trumbull, Timothy Dwight, Philip Freneau, Phyllis Wheatley—here are poems short and . . . long by dozens of others, most of them obscure to even thoroughgoing, historically minded poetry lovers. . . . The subject matter isn't all religion and politics. Work, family, leisure, and exceptional events and lives (one man recounts escape from the limited slavery that was indenture) are all written up. And, in regular rhymes and meters, it's all quite readable. Early-American history buffs as much as, if not more than, poetry readers may consider the book a gold mine." Booklist
Includes bibliographical references

American religious poems; an anthology by Harold Bloom. Harold Bloom and Jesse Zuba, editors. Library of America 2006 685p $40 **811**
1. Religious poetry 2. American poetry -- Collections
ISBN 1-931082-74-X
LC 2006-41031
An anthology of "verse on Christian, Jewish, Islamic, Buddhist, Native American spiritual, Transcendentalist and even agnostic themes, from 17th-century European colonists (one poet is Roger Williams, who founded Rhode Island) to up-and-comers in contemporary verse. Pious readers will have no trouble finding high-quality poetry that confirms their beliefs—from the monk Thomas Merton, the Anglican T.S. Eliot, the Jewish liturgical poet Esther Schor and the Louisiana-based Christian poet Martha Serpas. Yet from the 19th century to the present, from the decidedly heterodox Emily Dickinson forwards, the anthology often highlights the ways in which American spirituality has challenged all doctrines about who God is and what God does. . . . More than half of the book is taken up by 20th-century poets, who offer varied takes on what religion has come to mean in America." Publ Wkly

★ **American** war poetry; an anthology. edited by Lorrie Goldensohn. Columbia University Press 2006 413p $27.95 **811**
1. War poetry 2. American poetry -- Collections
ISBN 0-231-13310-3
LC 2005-54762
"Arranged by war, the book begins with the Colonial period and proceeds through Whitman admiring Civil War soldiers crossing a river to end with Brian Turner, who published his first book in 2005, beckoning a bullet in contemporary Iraq. Many voices, by turns elegiac, outraged, rhetorical and ecstatic are represented." Publ Wkly
Includes bibliographical references

American wits; an anthology of light verse. John Hollander, editor. Library of America 2003 xxv, 194p (American poets project) $20 **811**
1. American poetry -- Collections 2. Humorous poetry -- Collections
ISBN 978-1-931082-49-5; 1-931082-49-9
LC 2003-46636
This anthology "offers some exceptionally clever writing, much of which will be unfamiliar to many readers (and therefore all the more amusing). Hollander sensibly allots the most space to Ogden Nash and Dorothy Parker; the selections from both are solid. But Hollander's good judgment is best demonstrated by the third most represented poet here, the screenwriter Samuel Hoffenstein (1890-1947). . . . The poetry world currently has a surplus of writers who are eager, sometimes even desperate, to be funny, but we're suffering from a shortage of genuine wit." Poetry (Modern Poetry Association)

Angelou, Maya
★ The **complete** collected poems of Maya Angelou. Random House 1994 273p $24.95 **811**
1. Poetry -- By individual authors
ISBN 0-679-42895-X
LC 94-14501
This volume contains all of Angelou's published poems including her inaugural poem On the pulse of morning

I shall not be moved. Random House 1997 48p $15; pa $9.95 **811**
1. Poetry -- By individual authors
ISBN 0-679-45708-9; 0-553-35458-3 pa
First published 1990
"Angelou's themes include loss of love and youth, human oneness in diversity, the strength of blacks in the face of racism and adversity." Publ Wkly

Angles of ascent; a Norton anthology of contemporary African American poetry. edited by Charles Henry Rowell. W.W. Norton & Co. 2012 672 p. (pbk.) $24.95 **811**
1. American poetry -- African American authors 2. American poetry -- 21st century
ISBN 0393339408; 9780393339406
LC 2011042967
This poetry anthology, edited by Charles Henry Rowell, features "more than seventy [African American] poets. . . . These poets bear witness to the interior landscapes of their

own individual selves or examine the private or personal worlds of invented personae and, therefore, of human beings living in our modern and postmodern worlds. The anthology focuses on post-1960s poetry and includes such poets as Rita Dove, . . . Natasha Trethewey, . . . and Yusef Komunyakaa." (Publisher's note)

Armantrout, Rae
Versed. Wesleyan University Press 2009 121p (Wesleyan poetry) $22.95 **811**
1. Poetry -- By individual authors
ISBN 978-0-8195-6879-3; 0-8195-6879-1
LC 2008-43809
National Book Award Finalists (2009)
Pulitzer Prize (2010)
National Book Critics Award (2010)
Pulitzer Prize Finalist (2010)
This book "book comprises two sequences — 'Versed' and 'Dark Matter'— of loosely interlinked poems dealing with the prolific poet's usual subjects (the body, contemporary society, violence) as well as more personal explorations of illness and mortality, all relayed in Armantrout's concentrated, crystalline voice, with a predilection for skipping some steps along the way to sense." Publ Wkly

Ashbery, John
Collected poems 1956-1987; [edited by Mark Ford] Library of America 2008 1042p $40 **811**
1. Poetry -- By individual authors
ISBN 978-1-59853-028-5
"This major book, the first collection from Library of America by a living poet, offers a view of Ashbery's artistic development over many decades. . . . Watching Ashbery's art grow from the slippery romanticism and verbal hijinks of the early poems through the philosophical, if sideways, inquiry of the '70s, to the chattier, colloquial period inaugurated in the early '80s, is arresting. Though Ashbery has confounded and inspired in seemingly equal measure, he is, according to both his admirers and critics, the towering figure in contemporary American poetry." Publ Wkly

Notes from the air; selected later poems. Ecco 2007 364p $34.95 **811**
1. Poetry -- By individual authors
ISBN 978-0-06-136717-5; 0-06-136717-6
LC 2008-270813
This "volume—beginning with poems from April Galleons (1987) and ending with Where Shall I Wander (2005)—presents . . . [a] panoramic view of Ashbery's second phase, in which he explores, celebrates, sends up and revels in the American vernacular. . . . This is an essential book." Publ Wkly

Planisphere; new poems. Ecco 2009 143p $24.99 **811**
1. Poetry -- By individual authors
ISBN 978-0-06-191521-5; 0-06-191521-1
"In his rendering of American speech, slang, cliché, Ashbery has surpassed most of his contemporaries. But his persistent reach into the 'rut' of tradition should not be forgotten. He could say (with the great Nicaraguan poet Rubén Darío) that he is very 18th century and very archaic and very

modern, daring and cosmopolitan. When he becomes most serious, it is in the presence of either catastrophe or truth. His onslaughts of tragedy, emotional or physical, are of geological force while not relinquishing the vocabulary of iron." N Y Times Book Rev

Selected poems. Viking 1985 349p hardcover o.p. pa $17.95 **811**
1. Poetry -- By individual authors
ISBN 0-14-058553-2 pa
LC 85-40549
"Ashbery's work is seductive precisely because it alludes to shared traditions and assumptions about poetry. His poems attract us with their gestures of 'meaningful' discourse, the meditative pace of their syntax and the memories and expectations of meaningfulness that it evokes, the careful use of qualifiers, and the precisions and surprises of his diction." Benet's Reader's Ency of Am Lit

★ **Where** shall I wander; new poems. J. Ecco 2005 81p $22.95 **811**
1. Poetry -- By individual authors
ISBN 0-06-076529-1
LC 2004-53267
This collection of poetry features the poems "Ignorance of the Law Is No Excuse" and "A Visit to the House of Fools."
"Ashbery expresses a sly playfulness, a tender theatricality, a surreal sensibility, and an urbane wit. . . . Mercurial, elegant, funny, and magical, these mind-bending and beautifully haunting poems are the knowing work of a virtuoso." Booklist

★ A **worldly** country; new poems. Ecco Press 2007 76p $23.95 **811**
1. Poetry -- By individual authors
ISBN 0-06-117383-5; 978-0-06-117383-7
LC 2006-50279
This is a volume of poems by the author of Some Trees (1956); The Tennis Court Oath (1957); Rivers and Mountains (1966); Sunrise in Suburbia (1968); The Double Dream of Spring (1970); Self-portrait in a Convex Mirror (1975); Houseboat Days (1977); As We Know (1979); Shadow Trains (1981); Your Name Here (2000); and Where Shall I Wander (2006).
"Ashbery's syncopated lyrics are sheer pleasure in their music, collaged images, stabbing perceptions. Mysterious and truth-bearing poems that inspire us to 'flame on, flame on.'" Booklist

Auden, W. H.
Collected poems; edited by Edward Mendelson. Vintage Bks. 1991 xxvii, 926p pa $24 **811**
1. Poetry -- By individual authors
ISBN 0-679-73197-0
LC 91-158031
Originally published in hardcover in different form by Random House in 1976
A compilation of all the poems Auden wished to preserve, in his final revisions. Previous collected editions and later shorter poems are included. There is also an absurdist play written 1928: Paid on both sides

Baca, Jimmy Santiago

Spring poems along the Rio Grande. New Directions Pub. 2007 75p pa $12.95 **811**
1. Poetry -- By individual authors
ISBN 978-0-8112-1685-2; 0-8112-1685-3
LC 2006-101678

"The Rio Grande, as both setting and symbol of freedom and life, meanders through the poems, evoking a natural progression of time and the natural ebb and flow of feelings such as love, hope, and connection. The bosque along the river is home to birds both resident and migratory, trees, fish, bushes, insects, and encroaching urban life represented by power lines and interstate traffic noise. Jogging here, Baca evinces a love of his hometown of Albuquerque but, even more, reveals his well of poetic inspiration: Chicano, Catholic religiosity, Native American symbolism, and universal milestones. . . . With its highly accessible language and thoughtful reflections on the natural world, readers will find Baca's poetry extremely inviting." Booklist

Bang, Mary Jo

The **bride** of E; poems. Graywolf Press 2009 90p $22 **811**
1. Poetry -- By individual authors
ISBN 978-1-55597-539-5; 1-55597-539-9
LC 2009-926850

"The book takes the form of an abecedarian in which E stands for existence, with the engine of the alphabet overriding the entropy of emptiness, in which 'all action is in the mind, a cluster of notions/ in depravity's head independent of the dreadful/ invention of the magnetic temporary where/ a partition is positioned between right and wrong.' Many of these poems refer to the precariousness of human future, with Bang's medical background contributing convincing detail, and her sharp wit buoys the description with bleak meaning." Libr J

Elegy; poems. Graywolf 2007 92p $20 **811**
1. Poetry -- By individual authors
ISBN 978-1-55597-483-1; 1-55597-483-X
LC 2007-924768

The author "captures the complexity and courage of surviving the death of a child, an adult child, an imperfect child. The grief is multilayered, palpable. In this rendition of living in pain, in absence, in an altered reality, the reader never questions the authenticity of the work. . . . This is a book of exceptional grace and strength; it belongs in every library." Libr J

Barnett, Catherine

★ The **game** of boxes; poems. Catherine Barnett. Graywolf Press 2012 88 p. (alk. paper) $15.00 **811**
1. American poetry -- Collections
ISBN 1555976204; 9781555976200
LC 2012936220

This book of poetry by Catherine Barnett "is organized into three . . . sections; the first is called 'endless forms most beautiful.' Scattered amid poems about a mother and her son are pieces written from the first-person plural perspective of an amorphous chorus. . . . Fragmentary poems . . . [about] lust, sex, and sorrow form the book's second section, 'sweet

double, talk-talk.' . . . 'The modern period,' the book's last section is . . . the most lucidly personal." (Publishers Weekly)

Beat poets; selected and edited by Carmela Ciuraru. Knopf 2002 250p (Everyman's library pocket poets) $12.50 **811**
1. Beat generation 2. American poetry -- Collections
ISBN 978-0-375-41332-2; 0-375-41332-4
LC 2002-510236

"The defining work of Allen Ginsberg and Jack Kerouac provides the foundation for this collection, which also features statements on Beat poetics, selections from the alternately ardent, incendiary, and earnest correspondence of Beat Generation writers, and the improvisational verse of such Beat legends as Robert Creeley, Diane Di Prima, Gregory Corso, Denise Levertov, Lawrence Ferlinghetti, Philip Whalen, Bob Kaufman, and Peter Orlovsky, along with the work of other women writers and the lesser-known poets of this school." Publisher's note

Berkson, Bill

★ **Portrait** and dream; new and selected poems. Coffee House Press 2009 314p pa $22 **811**
1. Poetry -- By individual authors
ISBN 978-1-56689-229-2; 1-56689-206-6
LC 2008-52607

"There was always something of a mythical aura about Berkson, the collaborator of Frank O'Hara and one of the chiefs of the New York School whose friends included painters as well as poets. . . . Berkson's own poetry is subtle and demonstrably abstract in the manner of, let's say, DeKooning: it has an imagistic hardness and lushness that sweeps aside whatever you might have been thinking before." Exquisite Corpse

Bernstein, Charles, 1950-

All the whiskey in heaven; selected poems. Farrar, Straus and Giroux 2010 300p $26 **811**
1. Poetry -- By individual authors
ISBN 0-374-10344-5; 978-0-374-10344-6
LC 2009-10187

"This gathering of 30 years worth of work by the prominent L=A=N=G=U=A=G=E poet and essayist offers a . . . critique of the art of poetry itself, which means, among other things, a thorough investigation of language and the mind. Varied voices and genres are at play, from a colloquial letter of complaint to the manager of a Manhattan subway station to a fragmentary meditation on the forces that underlie the formation of knowledge." (Publishers Weekly)

"Bernstein takes his place in the mainstream of American poetry, the very 'Official Verse Culture' he's attacked entertainingly for years—a fate awaiting all our best outsiders. . . . Early Bernstein can be opaque, annoying those who see difficulty as elitist and who want poetry to be cuddly and educational. But everyone should love the later Bernstein, a writer who is accessible, enormously witty, often joyful—and even more evilly subversive." N Y Times Book Rev

Berrigan, Ted

★ The **collected** poems of Ted Berrigan; edited by Alice Notley, with Anselm Berrigan and Edmund Berrigan; introduction and notes by Alice Notley.

University of California Press 2005 749p $60; pa
$24.95   **811**

1. Poetry -- By individual authors
ISBN 978-0-520-23986-9; 0-520-23986-5; 978-0-520-
25155-7 pa; 0-520-25155-5 pa

LC 2005-42259

This volume collects the published and unpublished
works of a leading figure of the second-generation New York
School. Includes the first presentation of the Easter Monday
sequence in the order authorized by Berrigan shortly before
his death.

"More than 20 years in preparation, this is a major volume of 20th-century American poetry. . . . Berrigan was a
notoriously charismatic reader, teacher and participant in the
community that developed around the Poetry Project at St.
Mark's Church; his persona has been cited as often as his poems. This book closes the gap once and for all." Publ Wkly

Berry, Wendell

Collected poems, 1957-1982. North Point Press
1985 268p hardcover o.p. pa $17   **811**

1. Poetry -- By individual authors
ISBN 978-0-86547-197-9

LC 84-62305

"As a nature poet Berry has a grass-roots, homespun
quality that reminds one of Frost. He moves easily from witty lyrics and graceful elegies to moving love poems, philosophical odes and confessionals." Publ Wkly

Given; new poems. Shoemaker & Hoard 2005
152p $22   **811**

1. Poetry -- By individual authors
ISBN 1-59376-061-2

LC 2005-3762

"The latter half, 'Sabbaths 1998-2004,' . . . [contains]
the meditational poems Berry conceives on Sundays alone in
the woods on his farm. The other half's three parts contain,
respectively, short poems of observation, hortatory poems
varying in length from epigram to six-page public epistle,
and a brief verse play. . . . For those who believe that life
and the world are gifts, this is an invaluable book." Booklist

New collected poems. Counterpoint 2012 391 p.
$30.00   **811**

1. Haiku 2. Fathers -- Poetry 3. Poetry -- Collections
ISBN 1582438153; 9781582438153

This book "makes [poet Wendell] Berry's first Collected [volume] since 1987 and draws on volumes up through
'Leavings.'" It includes "a long elegy for Berry's father and
a set of haiku-sized poems. Benedictions and prayers coex-
ist with manifestos and georgic, the ancient genre of poems
about rural hard work." (Publishers Weekly)

A timbered choir; the sabbath poems, 1979-
1997. Counterpoint 1998 216p hardcover o.p. pa
$14.95   **811**

1. Poetry -- By individual authors
ISBN 978-15823-006-5

LC 98-4925

"Berry has continued periodically to write poems out-of-
doors on days of little other work. This book reprints Sabbaths, a collection of that writing, adding to it about one and

a half times as much new work. . . . Few other poets have
such chaste and precise diction or manage line and stanza
with such unaffected serenity." Booklist

Berryman, John

Collected poems, 1937-1971; edited and introduced by Charles Thornbury. Farrar, Straus & Giroux
1989 347p hardcover o.p. pa $25   **811**

1. Poetry -- By individual authors
ISBN 978-0-374-52281-0; 0-374-52281-2

LC 89-30944

"Berryman's poetry, sometimes mannered, elliptical,
and convoluted, is distinguished by precise technical control and continued experiments with style." Reader's Ency.
4th edition

★ The **dream** songs. Farrar, Straus & Giroux
1969 xx, 427p hardcover o.p. pa $18   **811**

1. Poetry -- By individual authors
ISBN 978-0-374-53066-2; 0-374-53066-1

This book contains the author's 385 'dream songs' that
originally appeared in various magazines, the Pulitzer Prize
winning 77 dream songs (1964) and His toy, his dream, his
rest (1968). The poet also provides a brief note about Henry,
the poems' central character

"Berryman makes brilliant use of his speaker's indiscriminately retentive perception—the patter of jukeboxes,
of cocktail parties, of the gutter and the cathedral—to drop
us dizzily into an original world where life is lived naked
and unashamed." Va Q Rev

The **best** American poetry; edited by Mark Doty.
Scribner Poetry 2012 240 p. (paperback)
$16   **811**

1. American poetry 2. Poetry -- Collections
ISBN 1439181527; 9781439181522

This is the 25th volume in the Best American Poetry series. This installment "runs the gamut of styles and positions,
from the experimentally mixed registers of Rae Armantrout
. . . to the unrelenting intensity of Frank Bidart . . . to an
extended meditation on art and family by Paisley Rekdal. .
. . [Mark] Doty, this year's guest editor . . . believes poetry
is available and useful to all who are willing to seek it out,
and so he has chosen poems that take the national pulse in
the midst of a tensed political moment." (Publishers Weekly)

★ **Best** of the Best American Poetry; 25th Anniversary. guest editor, Robert Pinsky; series editor,
David Lehman. Simon & Schuster 2013 xxviii,
322 p.p (hardcover) $35   **811**

1. American poetry 2. Poetry -- Collections
ISBN 1451658877; 9781451658873

This poetry anthology, edited by David Lehman, "celebrates twenty-five years of the 'Best American Poetry' series. . . . From its inception in 1988, it has been hotly debated, keenly monitored, ardently advocated (or denounced),
and obsessively scrutinized. . . . Out of the 1,875 poems that
have appeared in 'The Best American Poetry,' here are 100
that Robert Pinsky, the distinguished poet and man of letters,
has chosen for this milestone edition." (Publisher's note)

Bidart, Frank, 1939-

★ **Metaphysical** dog; Frank Bidart. Farrar, Straus and Giroux 2013 128 p. (hardcover) $24 **811**
1. Metaphysics -- Poetry 2. Poetry -- Collections
ISBN 0374173613; 9780374173616
LC 2012048069
National Book Award: Poetry Finalist (2013)
National Book Critics Circle Award (2013)
In this poetry collection by Frank Bidart, the author explores the themes of "words and sex, art and flesh." The book "reflects what the poet sees as fundamental in human feeling, what psychologists and mystics have called the 'hunger for the Absolute'--a hunger as fundamental as any physical hunger. This hunger must confront the elusiveness of the Absolute, our self-deluding, failed glimpses of it." (Publisher's note)
"There is a quiet, stirring grandeur here as Bidart contemplates the spectrum of existence, life's endless transformations, and our 'hunger for the absolute.'" Booklist
Includes bibliographical references and index

Star dust. Farrar, Straus and Giroux 2005 84p $20 **811**
1. Poetry -- By individual authors
ISBN 0-374-26973-4
LC 2004-56293
This is a collection of poetry by the author of Desire.
"The poems in this collection range from terribly lame confections questioning the appellation of 'poem' itself—to gracefully and powerfully moving lyrics. . . . The more formal Bidart gets, the stronger his work, like a living example of Richard Wilbur's dictum that the genie gains his strength from confinement in the bottle." Am Book Rev

Watching the spring festival. Farrar, Straus & Giroux 2008 61p $25 **811**
1. Poetry -- By individual authors
ISBN 978-0-374-28603-3; 0-374-28603-5
LC 2007-40513
This book is "a collection of masterful, carefully modulated lyrics, glimpses of the millennium's turn and dispatches from an ancient world." Antioch Rev

Bishop, Elizabeth

Edgar Allan Poe & the juke-box; uncollected poems, drafts, and fragments. edited and annotated by Alice Quinn. Farrar, Straus, and Giroux 2006 367p $30 **811**
1. Poetry -- By individual authors
ISBN 0-374-14645-4
LC 2005-11511
"The publication of 'Edgar Allan Poe & the Juke-Box,' which gathers for the first time Bishop's unpublished material, isn't just a significant event in our poetry; it's part of a continuing alteration in the scale of American life." N Y Times Book Rev
Includes bibliographical references

Blackburn, Paul

The **collected** poems of Paul Blackburn; edited, with an introduction, by Edith Jarolim. Persea Bks. 1985 xxxv, 667p il $55 **811**
1. Poetry -- By individual authors
ISBN 978-0-89255-086-9; 0-89255-086-4
LC 85-9309
"Much of Blackburn's poetry is an engaging mix of sharp, allusive adventuring, humor and wordplay, annotated fragments of musical speech, and a moderate but distinctive use of metaphor. Edith Jarolim's introduction provides a concise view of Blackburn's art and life." Choice

Blues poems; selected and edited by Kevin Young. Knopf 2003 256p (Everyman's library pocket poets) $12.50 **811**
1. Blues music -- Poetry 2. American poetry -- Collections
ISBN 978-0-375-41458-9; 0-375-41458-4
LC 2003-53149
A collection of "blues-influenced and blues-inflected poems from, among others, Gwendolyn Brooks, Allen Ginsberg, June Jordan, Richard Wright, Nikki Giovanni, Charles Wright, Yusef Komunyakaa, and Cornelius Eady. And here, too, are classic song lyrics—poems in their own right—from Bessie Smith, Robert Johnson, Ma Rainey, and Muddy Waters." Publisher's note

Bly, Robert

Eating the honey of words; new and selected poems. HarperFlamingo 1999 270p hardcover o.p. pa $14.95 **811**
1. Poetry -- By individual authors
ISBN 0-06-093069-1 pa
LC 98-51152
"Collecting over 200 poems from 1950 to 1998, this volume is an appealing poetic sampler, although the ten new poems are unexciting. The poems celebrating discoveries Bly makes when alone and silent are always striking, and his imaginative prose poems radiate witty delight." Libr J

The **night** Abraham called to the stars; poems. HarperCollins Pubs. 2001 95p hardcover o.p. pa $12.95 **811**
1. Poetry -- By individual authors
ISBN 0-06-093444-1 pa
LC 00-66360
"The book's 48 lyrics are written in a single (here terceted) form, the ghazal, used by such great Islamic poets as Ghalib, and harness high points of Western art and literature to draw general, biblically backed conclusions about the human condition out of the mire." Publ Wkly

Bonair-Agard, Roger

Bury my clothes; by Roger Bonair-Agard. Haymarket Books 2013 160 p. (pbk.) $16 **811**
1. Art 2. Race 3. Violence
ISBN 1608462692; 9781608462698
LC 2013006344
This book, by Roger Bonair-Agard, "is a meditation on violence, race, and the place in art at which they intersect. Art—specifically in oppressed communities—is about sur-

vival, . . . Bonair-Agard asserts, and establishing personhood in a world that says you have none. Through poetry, [he attempts to] transform both the world of art and the world itself." (Publisher's note)

Booth, Philip

Selves; new poems. by Philip Booth. Viking 1990 75p hardcover o.p. pa $9.95   **811**
    1. Poetry -- By individual authors
    ISBN 0-14-058646-6 pa

LC 89-40317

This collection "features contemplative poems born of the observant patience of North country life. The best are based on concrete observation. . . . Booth's strength is that he speaks of significant issues like the ultimate privacy of suffering, the painful hidden destruction of relationships, the coming of aging and death." Libr J

Bowers, Edgar

Collected poems. Knopf 1997 168p hardcover o.p. pa $15   **811**
    1. Poetry -- By individual authors
    ISBN 0-679-76607-3 pa

LC 96-38580

"Surety of rhythm, swiftness of thought, and deftness of phrase animate Bowers' triumphant poems about loss and the struggle to be whole. He is, above all, a delineator—vital, ironic, capable of panoramic sweep—of his transfiguring experiences in Germany during and after the Second World War. His roots are deep in Horace and Pindar, but amid all the eloquent austerity there are blessed moments of unexpected Mozartian lilt and wit." New Yorker

Brathwaite, Edward Kamau

Elegguas. Wesleyan University Press 2010 123p il (Wesleyan poetry) $22.50   **811**
    1. Poetry -- By individual authors
    ISBN 978-0-8195-6943-1; 0-8195-6943-7

LC 2009-35923

"This is a handsome, thoughtfully produced volume, shaped and sized to respect the poems' requirements for special graphic treatments, page formats, and line lengths. . . . The language varies as much, if not more or more dramatically in many ways, than the graphical treatments, from the intimate and colloquial diction of the work addressed to Zea Mexican [the poet's late wife], to the lyrical conventions of contemporary western poetry, to neologisms and invented forms, to the grammatical constructs of Caribbean speech. Brathwaite is equally adept and comfortable in all of these idioms." NewPages

Includes bibliographical references.

Brock-Broido, Lucie

Stay, Illusion; Poems. By Lucie Brock-Broido. Random House Inc 2013 112 p. (Hardcover) $26   **811**
    1. Bereavement 2. American poetry 3. Emotions -- Poetry
    ISBN 0307962024; 9780307962027

LC 2013023978

Author Lucie Brock-Broido presents a poetry collection designed to "spin, drape, and sculpt its virtuosic figures

around the ideas and emotions of mourning. Often Brock-Broido commemorates her father, remembering him on his own, in her family, in conjunction with her own past selves." (Publishers Weekly)

Includes bibliographical references

Bronk, William

Selected poems; selected by Henry Weinfield. New Directions 1995 80p pa $8.95   **811**
    1. Poetry -- By individual authors
    ISBN 978-0-8112-1314-1; 0-8112-1314-5

LC 95-290

"Bronk's poems are almost entirely abstract and disembodied . . . his language desiccated but also conversationally halting and embedded. There is no flesh, no world, precious little metaphor—as though every human attachment is cheating. If anything seems to work—such as cause and effect—it never adds up to anything. . . . Bronk is thinking and thinking, as purely as possible, about how we want—want not to be alone, want things to matter, want to feel that we are connected to reality. His poems are all about wanting and how there is no end to it." Poetry Foundation

Brooks, Gwendolyn

The essential Gwendolyn Brooks; Elizabeth Alexander, editor. Library of America 2005 148p il (American poets project) $20   **811**
    1. Poetry -- By individual authors
    ISBN 978-1-931082-87-7; 1-931082-87-1

LC 2005-44162

"A book like [this] can't make the statement that needs to be made: Gwendolyn Brooks is as important to twentieth-century American poetry as Robert Lowell. . . . Her best poems offer a curative, not only to the narcissistic gloom that we've inherited from the Confessionals, but to Eliot's over-aestheticized visions of social life. That Brooks's purposes were so different from Eliot's only strengthens the connection. It shows the vitality of true poetic inspiration, how it can cut across time, temperament, race, and even the motives of its own practitioners." Poetry (Modern Poetry Association)

In Montgomery, and other poems. Third World Press 2003 146p $22.95   **811**
    1. African Americans -- Poetry 2. Poetry -- By individual authors
    ISBN 0-88378-232-4

LC 2003-50749

This is a "posthumous collection consisting primarily of dramatic monologues in a stunning variety of voices, from those of urban children to Winnie Mandela's. Reading the title sequence resembles randomly tuning a radio dial to listen to the diverse voices of Montgomery, Alabama, a city of 'leaning and lostness, glazed paralysis.' . . . Especially moving are the children's monologues. . . . Brooks captures the fierce purity of these children's needs and desires. Her loving witness never sounded more clearly than in these late poems." Booklist

Budbill, David

Happy life. Copper Canyon Press 2011 117p pa
$16 **811**
1. Poetry -- By individual authors
ISBN 978-1-55659-374-1

LC 2011

The poems evoke "a recognizable immediacy and honesty, accompanied by an endearing wit. . . . Budbill's economical, brush-stroke approach . . . evinces a hard-won clarity, a pure, human tone." Libr J

Bukowski, Charles

★ The **pleasures** of the damned; poems, 1951-1993. edited by John Martin. Ecco 2007 556p
$29.95 **811**
1. Poetry -- By individual authors
ISBN 978-0-06-122843-8; 0-06-122843-5

LC 2007-282394

This book is "an insightful walk through the work of a poet by the man who knew him best, and it reveals Bukowski in the many, often conflicting dimensions that make him such a popular, accessible, and, yes, great artist. . . . This extraordinary collection establishes Bukowski as much more than just another West Coast Beat poet." Washington Post

Burnshaw, Stanley

The **collected** poems and selected prose; foreword by Thomas F Stanley. University of Texas Press 2002 487p il (Harry Ransom Humanities Research Center) $50 **811**
1. Poetry -- By individual authors
ISBN 978-0-292-70909-6; 0-292-70909-9

LC 2001-52226

"Stanley Burnshaw is one of those men of letters who are so variously productive, and for so long, that they can too easily be taken for granted as merely part of the climate. . . . Since any poet considers himself—and deserves to be considered—a poet first of all, it is wonderful news that Burnshaw's work has now been made available for a new generation of readers. The Collected Poems and Selected Prose . . . allows us to see Burnshaw as a genuine and very American heir of the Romantic tradition in poetry, who has pursued the highest themes over his long career." New Republic
Includes bibliographical references

Callow, Philip

From noon to starry night: a life of Walt Whitman. Dee, I.R. 1992 394p il $28.50; pa $14.95 **811**
1. Poets 2. Authors 3. Essayists
ISBN 0-929587-95-2; 1-56663-133-5 pa

LC 92-5311

"Infused with tenderness and respect, this fine biography deciphers the complexity of Whitman's sexuality and passionate creativity while celebrating his abiding compassion and grandeur of spirit." Booklist
Includes bibliographical references

Carr, Julie

100 notes on violence. Ahsahta Press, Boise State University 2010 109p pa $19 **811**
1. Violence -- Poetry 2. Poetry -- By individual authors
ISBN 978-1-934103-11-1; 1-934103-11-X

LC 2009-26057

"In evocative, powerfully disquieting knife thrusts of verse, Carr examines the human propensity to violence, displayed here in 'notes' that range from personal anecdote to news reports to a lullaby shouted down by the voice of a murderer." Libr J
Includes bibliographical references

Carruth, Hayden

★ Toward the distant islands; new & selected poems. edited and with an introduction by Sam Hamill. Copper Canyon Press 2006 181p pa
$17 **811**
1. Poetry -- By individual authors
ISBN 1-55659-236-1 pa

LC 2005-28705

Carruth's "books encompass Frostian tales of farm life with New England eccentrics, compilations of haiku, long and unguarded poems of erotic devotion, autobiographical laments, and sensitive odes to jazz greats. . . . All sides of Carruth's oeuvre find a place in this welcome volume. . . . The selection here gives just enough of everything Carruth has learned, and he has learned a lot, especially about the ways and landscapes of New England." Publ Wkly

Carson, Anne

Autobiography of red; a novel in verse. Knopf 1998 149p hardcover o.p. pa $12 **811**
1. Poetry -- By individual authors
ISBN 0-375-70129-X pa

LC 97-49472

"Is it poetry? Is it a novel in verse? A fable? A myth? However you define Carson's distinctive and wildly inventive new work, it is riveting reading. . . . Wistful yet whimsical, offhand yet intense, funky yet erudite . . . this is a reading experience like no other." Libr J

The **beauty** of the husband; a fictional essay in 29 tangos. Knopf 2001 147p $24; pa $12 **811**
1. Poetry -- By individual authors
ISBN 0-375-40804-5; 0-375-70757-3 pa

LC 00-62002

This poem is "at once the story of a failed marriage and an exploration of Romantic notions of beauty and truth. But Carson's idiosyncratic voice and her punchy declarative style—'You want a clean life I live a dirty one'—quickly make it clear that hers is a thoroughly modern take on the intimate cruelties of married life. And this is the primary pleasure of her writing: it is both entirely new and strangely familiar, like remembering a private language we thought we'd forgotten." New Yorker

Men in the off hours. Knopf 2000 166p il hardcover o.p. pa $12 **811**
1. Poetry -- By individual authors
ISBN 0-375-70756-5 pa

LC 00-267850

The author "makes bold references to everyone from Oedipus to Akhamatova, but the effect of these astute, gem-like little poems is less a history lesson than a challenging conversation in a sunlit garden." Libr J

Nox. New Directions 2010 un il $29.95   **811**
1. Poetry -- By individual authors
ISBN 978-0-8112-1870-2; 0-8112-1870-8
                LC 2009-01330
This "is an epitaph in the form of a book, a facsimile of a handmade book Carson wrote and created after the death of her brother." (N Y Times Book Rev)

The "book comes in a box the color of a rainy day, with a sliver of a family snapshot on the front. Inside is a Xerox-quality reproduction of a notebook, made after the death of her brother, including text and photographs and letters, pasted-in inkjet printouts, handwriting, paintings and collage. 'Nox' has no page numbers, and it's accordion-folded. It carries a whiff of visual art multiple or gift shop souvenir or 'Griffin & Sabine.' But trust me: it's an Anne Carson book. Maybe her best." N Y Times Book Rev

Red doc>; Anne Carson. 1st ed. Alfred A. Knopf 2013 167 p. (hardcover) $24.95; (ebook) $74.85   **811**
1. Epic poetry 2. Monsters -- Poetry 3. Literature -- Adaptations 4. Epic poetry, Greek -- Adaptations
ISBN 0307960587; 9780307960580; 9780307960597
                LC 2012032322
This book, by Anne Carson, is a mixed poetry-prose genre story following the author's character Geryon from her 1988 book "Autobiography of Red." The book "finds a way to push Geryon into new territories of dry, vaudevillian Americana. Whether she's talking war vets, flying cows, Latin etymology or Elvis, Carson once again blurs the lines of prose and poetry, and challenging both genres within a single poem." (American Poet)

Carver, Raymond
All of us; the collected poems. Knopf 1998 xxx, 386p hardcover o.p. pa $15   **811**
1. Poetry -- By individual authors
ISBN 978-0-375-70380-5; 0-375-70380-2
                LC 98-15880
"The great short story writer's poems are dark and funny, like the stories, and tell of domestic discord, crazy adventures and sweet intimacies, sometimes with sorrow but more often with thankfulness and affection." Booklist
Includes bibliographical references

A **new** path to the waterfall; poems. introduction by Tess Gallagher. Atlantic Monthly Press 1989 xxxi, 126p hardcover o.p. pa $14   **811**
1. Poetry -- By individual authors
ISBN 978-0-87113-374-8 pa; 0-87113-374-1 pa
                LC 88-34989
"In her moving introduction, Carver's widow, writer Tess Gallagher, notes how often a particular poem calls to mind a corresponding story, and the reverse is also true. Indeed, to know Carver by his prose is to know him only partially. Master at illuminating those often mundane moments that starkly dramatize entire lives, Carver was also master

at creating mood, and many of those poems have a striking lyrical intensity, especially when Carver unflinchingly faces death while celebrating life. A coda to a remarkable literary career." Libr J

Ciardi, John
The **collected** poems of John Ciardi; compiled and edited by Edward M. Cifelli. University of Ark. Press 1997 xxxii, 618p hardcover o.p. pa $34.95   **811**
1. Poetry -- By individual authors
ISBN 978-1-55728-449-5; 1-55728-449-0
                LC 96-46331
"This volume supersedes the earlier Selected Poems (1984) providing a vastly more comprehensive sampling of Ciardi's work: 450 poems culled from over 20 individual volumes published between 1940 and 1993. In it we find testimony to Ciardi's desire to achieve not 'a voice,' a style formed to forward an author's individuality, but 'voice'— one that is determined by the externals the poet addresses." Libr J

Clark, Tom
★ **Light** & shade; new and selected poems. introduction by Amy Gerstler. Coffee House Press 2006 338p pa $20   **811**
1. Poetry -- By individual authors
ISBN 1-56689-183-3
                LC 2005-35810
"Disarmingly casual yet saturated with loss, Clark's body of work revels in simplicities: lovers, friends, cities and landscapes (New York, Southern California, the Southwest), baseball, basketball, modern painters, sad weather, brief visions and ethereal promises. All make repeat appearances in a poetry rooted at once in spontaneity and in High Romantic aspiration." Publ Wkly

Clifton, Lucille, 1936-2010
★ The **collected** poems of Lucille Clifton 1965-2010; edited by Kevin Young and Michael S. Glaser; foreword by Toni Morrison; afterword by Kevin Young. BOA Editions 2012 xxxiv, 769 p.p   **811**
1. Women -- Poetry 2. Feminism -- Poetry 3. African Americans -- Poetry
ISBN 1934414905; 9781934414903
                LC 2012014244
This book, edited by Kevin Young and Michael S. Glaser, "combines all eleven of Lucille Clifton's published collections with more than fifty previously unpublished poems. The unpublished poems feature early poems from 1965-1969 . . . [and] a collection-in-progress titled the book of days (2008). . . . In the last year of her life, she was named the first African American woman to receive the . . . Ruth Lilly Poetry Prize . . . and was posthumously awarded the Robert Frost Medal." (Publisher's note)

Mercy; poems. 1st ed; BOA Editions 2004 79p (American poets continuum series) $22; pa $14.95   **811**
1. Poetry -- By individual authors
ISBN 1-929918-54-2; 1-929918-55-0 pa
                LC 2004-10396

"These are poems where great restraint mingles with disarming primal imagery to convey poems which hold tremendous emotional weight." Va Q Rev

Cloud, Abigail

Sylph; Poems. Abigail Cloud. Pleiades Press 2014 88 p. (pbk. : alk. paper) $17.95 **811**
1. Poetry -- Collections
ISBN 0807156930; 9780807156933
LC 2014931676

In this book of poems, Abigail Cloud "draws inspiration from nineteenth-century European Romantic ballets, which often portrayed scorned females as mystical spirits such as sylphs, shades, and wilis. Some of these creatures seduced men into dancing until they died punishment for inconstancy or lured them into love. For Cloud, the dark gravity that holds these enchanters to the earth is the same as our own and thus these demons are as everyday as air." (Publisher's note)

Cole, Henri

Middle earth; poems. Farrar, Straus & Giroux 2003 55p $23; pa $11 **811**
1. Poetry -- By individual authors
ISBN 0-374-20881-6; 0-374-52928-0 pa
LC 2002-29776

The author "examines the dichotomies between life and death, animal and human, and the lover and the beloved. Many of the poems, including, 'My Tea Ceremony' and 'Self-Portrait at the Red Princess,' show a marked Japanese influence; others record a grown son's grief over the death of his father. . . . Cole writes with clarity and an emotive resonance. These poems succeed as the best poems do: they transport the reader to other worlds, no less beautiful or complicated than our own. Highly recommended." Libr J

Collins, Billy

Nine horses; poems. Random House 2002 120p $21.95; pa $12.95 **811**
1. Poetry -- By individual authors
ISBN 1-4000-6177-6; 0-375-75520-9 pa
LC 2002-24868

Collins is "often able to proceed unburdened by many of the tools—assonance, alliteration, wordplay, complex metrics—that hang from the poet's belt; he makes his way in the world by being funny." N Y Times Book Rev

★ Sailing alone around the room; new and selected poems. Random House 2001 171p $21.95; pa $13.95 **811**
1. Poetry -- By individual authors
ISBN 0-375-50380-3; 0-375-75519-5 pa
LC 99-52861

"Collins will tackle any topic: his subject matter varies from snow days to Aristotle to forgetfulness. The results are accessible but not trite, comical but not laughable, and well crafted but not overly flamboyant. Collins relies heavily on

imagery, which becomes the cornerstone of the entire volume." Libr J

The **trouble** with poetry and other poems; Billy Collins. Random House 2005 88p $22.95 **811**
1. Poetry -- By individual authors
ISBN 0-375-50382-X
LC 2005-46562

"Skeptical of love and scornful of pretension, Collins is breathtaking in his appreciation of the earth's beauty and the precious daily routines that define life." Booklist

The **Columbia** history of American poetry; Jay Parini, editor; Brett C. Millier, associate editor. Columbia Univ. Press 1993 xxxi, 894p $86.50 **811**
1. Poetry -- By individual authors 2. American poetry -- History and criticism
ISBN 0-231-07836-6
LC 92-29399

"These 31 essays by various experts in the field interrogate, dismantle, and ultimately reassemble the history of poetry in the United States, from the work of the slave George Moses Horton . . . to the writings of Beat, Black Arts, and Marxist-oriented Language Poets of today. The great figures of the past—Whitman, Poe, Eliot, and so on—still loom, yet each time we are made to see them in some new way. . . . An essential volume that shows how poetry intersects with our lives and vice versa." Libr J

Includes bibliographical references

Conoley, Gillian

Peace; Gillian Conoley. Omnidawn Publishing 2014 112 p. (trade pbk. : alk. paper) $17.95 **811**
1. Poetry -- Collections
ISBN 1890650951; 9781890650957
LC 2013045789

Los Angeles Times Book Prize Finalist: Poetry (2014)

This collection of poems, by Gillian Conoley, "is haunted by personal and political history—by figures of Gandhi, Martin Luther King, Thoreau–by current senators and dead musicians, by speech and painting, by extraordinary and ordinary lives." (Publisher's note)

"Multi-award-winning poet Conoley (The Plot Genie) gives us objects (pears, violins, aircrafts, sky), people (presidents, poets, mothers, sons, Gandhi), and landscapes (Marksville, LA; a blueness sucking in the sun), as events spread unevenly across the page. The poet's spare language builds into scenes that stir understanding; they are careful so as not to disappoint: 'if time began we would do it again/ the lungs two oars in the middle of the ocean.'"

Corbett, William

The **Whalen** poem; drawings by Philip Guston. Hanging Loose Press 2011 61p pa $16 **811**
1. Poetry -- By individual authors
ISBN 978-1-934909-13-3
LC 2010-51639

"Corbett composed this book-length poem, he writes in his introduction, over the summer and autumn of 2007 while in Vermont reading an advanced copy of the collected poems of Philip Whalen (1923-2002). The result is truly a poem for summer, as flighty as a hummingbird, now pausing, now darting too fast to follow to the next luminous blooming. The poem's fluidity offers a delightful ride if one is willing to go along with it. Corbett's economy of language gives him the facility to flit between images, allusions and occurrences, be they personal or seasonal, and his wide ken allows him to track events on several planes at once. . . . Whalen seems to be a spiritual adviser for this poem, a teacher who proved that the paths of the mind, traced mindfully, can be poetry. . . . [The poem] displays an open-ended lyricism that resists closure with the awareness — the insistence — that nothing is ever over, life or a work of literature." Prague Post

Cording, Robert

Walking with Ruskin; poems. CavanKerry Press 2010 93p (Notable voices) pa $16 **811**

1. Poetry -- By individual authors

ISBN 978-1-933880-21-1; 1-933880-21-X

LC 2010-13639

These poems combine the "sacred and the mundane in unexpected ways. Even if you don't know much about poetry, Cording's poems tend to be fairly accessible because of their narrative approach, as well as their immersion in the everyday. The poems in this volume take as their subject matter a mother's grief for her child, looking though Czeslaw Milosz's glasses (literally), aging, taking a walk with a dog, and observing woodpeckers, swallows and starlings. . . . Above all, the poems in Walking with Ruskin celebrate the virtue of attentiveness to the created world around us." Christ and Pop Culture

Crane, Hart

★ **Complete** poems and selected letters. Library of America 2006 849p $40 **811**

1. Poetry -- By individual authors

ISBN 1-93108-299-5

LC 2006-40922

This volume "gathers all of the author's poetry and collected prose with a large sampling of his letters, some appearing in print for the first time. The correspondents include top writers William Carlos Williams, Marianne Moore, e.e. cummings, and Katherine Anne Porter. A good one-stop resource for Crane." Libr J

Creeley, Robert

The **collected** poems of Robert Creeley. University of California Press 1982 2v v1 o.p.; v1 pa $27.50; v2 $60; v2 pa $24.95 **811**

1. Poetry -- By individual authors

ISBN 0-520-04243-3 v1; 978-0-520-24158-9 v1 pa; 978-0-520-24159-6 v2; 978-0-520-25620-0 v2 pa

Creeley's style is "notably spare and laconic; his primary subject is love and the infinite incongruities that characterize love relationships. There is a distinct dearth of imagery in his poetry; the themes are rendered in a cerebral rather than sensual manner. For Creeley, the intent of the poem is definition, not description." Reader's Ency. 4th edition

Cronk, Laura

Having been an accomplice; Laura Cronk. 1st ed. Persea Books 2012 68 p. (original trade pbk. : alk. paper) $15 **811**

1. Love poetry 2. Poetry -- Collections 3. American

poetry -- Women authors -- Collections

ISBN 0892554134; 9780892554133

LC 2011042830

Lexi Rudnitsky First Prize: Poetry (2011)

This poetry collection, by Laura Cronk, winner of the 2011 Lexi Rudnitsky First Book Prize in Poetry, offers "love poems and interior monologues. . . . Within them, Laura Cronk writes, 'I want to blow up the Law with Language, having run my tongue around my mouth ten thousand times. Instead of not speaking, I want to speak.'" (Publisher's note)

Includes bibliographical references

Cummings, E. E.

★ **Complete** poems, 1904-1962; containing all the published poetry. edited by George J. Firmage. rev corr & expanded ed; Norton 1994 xxxii, 1102p $50 **811**

1. Poetry -- By individual authors

ISBN 978-0-87140-152-6; 0-87140-152-5

LC 91-29158

Expanded version of Complete poems, 1913-1962 (1972)

"This volume has been prepared directly from the poet's original manuscripts, preserving the original typography and format. It includes all the previously published works, from Tulips (1922) to Etcetera (1983), as well as 36 uncollected poems that originally appeared in little magazines or anthologies." Libr J

Dickinson, Emily, 1830-1886

★ The **poems** of Emily Dickinson; edited by R.W. Franklin. Reading ed; Belknap Press 1999 692p pa $18.50; $34.50 **811**

1. Poetry -- By individual authors

ISBN 0-674-01824-9 pa; 0-674-67624-6; 978-0-674-01824-2 pa; 978-0-674-67624-4

LC 99-11821

This work "includes a single version of each poem included in the 1998 Variorum. In this one-volume edition, Franklin selects the latest 'manifestation' of a poem in those not uncommon instances when Dickinson herself produced multiple copies." (Am Lit) Index.

"Within the guidelines Franklin has set himself, his choices of versions and of alternatives within versions are extremely sensible-and they are efficiently recorded at the end of the volume, making this the first time any volume of Dickinson's poems aimed at a general audience has offered information about the derivation of its texts." Raritan

Dickman, Michael

The **end** of the west. Copper Canyon Press 2009 89p pa $15 **811**

1. Poetry -- By individual authors

ISBN 978-1-55659-289-8; 1-556-59289-2

LC 2008-39990

"Some form of light—sunlight, moonlight, starlight, streetlight— appears in every one of the 18 poems in [this book.] . . . Slight and spare, the poems' frequent recurring themes accumulate beneficially, linking all the individual poems into one, more substantial, piece. Nothing grand takes place in these poems, but the quietness of the language and the creeping, sinister subject matter (heroin addiction, abusive fathers) make this . . . book captivating and very readable." Publ Wkly

Donnelly, Timothy

The **cloud** corporation. Wave Books 2010 153p **811**

1. Poetry -- By individual authors
ISBN 9781933517476

LC 2010-13946

This is a book of poems by Timothy Donnelly was the winner of the 2012 Kingsley Tufts Poetry Award. It includes "[p]rocedural poems, such as one that repurposes language from the Patriot Act . . . [and] a pair of . . . long poems [that] introduce a mind agoraphobicly trapped in its vast vocabulary." (Publishers Weekly) Topics include "finance and/ or capitalism . . . the political economy, [and] the environment". (Poetry)

"Timothy Donnelly pushes abstraction to the limits in this book—anything more, and the book would have collapsed. The book consists mostly of free-flowing tercets, lightly stressed, very much like the light feathery movement of clouds or water. The book is almost a manifesto against the utilization of images and making them the backbone of poetry. . . . This is a very existential, Sartrean project, a constant Sysiphian sifting of indispensable abstract thoughts, and a very challenging book to read." Huffington Post

Dorn, Edward

★ **Way** more West; new and selected poems. introduction by Dale Smith; edited by Michael Rothenberg. Penguin Books 2007 321p (Penguin poets) $20 **811**

1. Poetry -- By individual authors
ISBN 978-0-14-303869-6

LC 2006-50727

"Throughout his career, he was the least endearing, domesticated or predictable of poets, always determined to go his own way, no matter what anyone thought. And if he hadn't been that way, American poetry would be a lot less vital and interesting." N Y Times Book Rev

Includes bibliographical references

Doty, Mark, 1953-

Deep lane; poems. Mark Doty. W W Norton & Co Inc 2015 96 p. (hardcover) $25.95 **811**

1. Nature poetry 2. American poetry -- Collections
ISBN 9780224099837; 9780393070231

LC 2015000660

In this poetry collection, by Mark Doty, "these poems seek repair, finally, through the possibilities that sustain the speaker above ground: gardens and animals; the pleasure of seeing; the world tuned by the word. Time and again, an image of immolation and sacrifice is undercut by the fierce fortitude of nature: nature that is not just a solace but a potent antidote and cure." (Publisher's note)

"A somber, struggling, honest collection for Doty's many fans." LJ

Fire to fire; new and selected poems. Harper 2008 336p $22.95; pa $15.95 **811**

1. Poetry -- By individual authors
ISBN 978-0-06-075247-7; 0-06-075247-5; 978-0-06-

075251-4 pa; 0-06-075251-3 pa

LC 2007-44646

The author "combines new poems with the best of his previous volumes. His narrative style is expansive, filled with what has been described as a 'lyric glitter' that creates radiance around the ordinary." Libr J

Includes bibliographical references

Dove, Rita

American smooth; poems. W.W. Norton 2004 143p $22.95; pa $13.95 **811**

1. Poetry -- By individual authors
ISBN 0-393-05987-1; 0-393-32744-2 pa

LC 2004-11793

"In these free-verse poems, Dove speaks from her own perspective—as well as from that of biblical characters, black soldiers from World War I, a ten-year-old girl from Harlem, several musicians, and a pair of dancers. The selections work by lists, line breaks where ideas collide, and a juxtaposition of voices. Then using razor-sharp metaphors, Dove goes for the jugular and usually finds it. Although the book's sense of audience seems inconsistent, with some poems suitable for A Child's Garden of Verses and others for The Kama Sutra, the poems are evocative." Libr J

Collected poems; 1974-2004. Rita Dove. W W Norton & Co Inc 2016 448 p. (hardcover) $39.95; (ebook) $50 **811**

1. American poets 2. American poetry
ISBN 9780393285949; 9780393285956

LC 2016007501

National Book Award Finalist: Poetry (2016)

This book by Rita Dove presents "three decades of powerful lyric poetry. . . . This volume compiles Dove's fresh reflections on adolescence in 'The Yellow House on the Corner,' . . . the multifaceted gems of 'Grace Notes,' the exquisite reinvention of Greek myth in the sonnets of 'Mother Love,' . . . and the homage to America's kaleidoscopic cultural heritage in 'American Smooth," all celebrate Dove's mastery of narrative context with lyrical finesse." (Publisher's note)

"Through her alluring language, Dove has long made the exceedingly difficult seem effortless; each poem here is a testament to her brilliance." Pub Wkly

Includes bibliographical references and index.

On the bus with Rosa Parks; poems. Norton 1999 95p hardcover o.p. pa $12.95 **811**

1. Poetry -- By individual authors
ISBN 0-393-32026-X

LC 98-45057

Dove's "poems effortlessly suggest grand narratives and American myths, yet ground themselves tersely in localities, characters, practicalities and particulars. This seventh collection leads off with a Dove specialty, the historical sequence: her 'Cameos' lend broad, social relevance to an intermittently abandoned Depression-era wife and her family." Publ Wkly

Selected poems. Vintage Bks. 1993 xxvi, 210p
pa $13 **811**
  1. Poetry -- By individual authors
  ISBN 0-679-75080-0
                         LC 93-26112

"This volume places three previous collections under
one cover. . . . The selection begins with The Yellow House
on the Corner, Dove's first book, most notable for its poems
derived from slave narratives. Museum, her second book,
offers a potpourri of work that ranges over several continents
and many millenia; Dove's tirelessly exact language illuminates the lives of saints, contemporary lifestyles, and Greek
myths." Booklist

Downing, Brandon

Lake Antiquity; poems, 1996-2008. Fence
Books 2009 184p il pa $40 **811**
  1. Poetry -- By individual authors
  ISBN 978-1-934200-27-8; 1-934200-27-1

"Drawing on the tradition of fanciful collage practiced
by such poets as John Ashbery, David Shapiro, and Joe
Brainard, Brandon Downing wields his own scissors to
cut a distinctive patch within this New York School specialty. . . . Downing has sequenced his collages with cinematic pacing; you fly through these pages as you might in
a dream." Bookforum

Dugan, Alan

★ **Poems** seven; new and complete poetry. Seven Stories Press 2001 422p $35; pa $18.95 **811**
  1. Poetry -- By individual authors
  ISBN 1-58322-265-0; 1-58322-512-9 pa
                         LC 2001-41089

This collection documents "Dugan's project of comic,
bleak and formally varied commentary on a dirty, terminally
frayed and yet attractive America. . . . This carefully constructed, funny and sometimes unvarying volume combines
all six of Dugan's previous books with a decade's worth of
new verse." Publ Wkly

Duhamel, Denise

Ka-ching! University of Pittsburgh Press 2009
86p il (Pitt poetry series) $14.95 **811**
  1. Poetry -- By individual authors
  ISBN 978-0-8229-6021-8; 0-8229-6021-4 pa

"What better poetry for the current economic period
than Denise Duhamel's hymns to money, ATMs, her IRA
accounts, the Treasury, gambling. . .and Sean Penn? . . . Using prose poems, sonnets, sestinas, and other forms in Ka-Ching!, Duhamel is a wily technician, a touching humanist,
a poet deserving stardom." Entertainment Wkly

Duncan, Robert Edward

Selected poems; [by] Robert Duncan; edited by
Robert J. Bertholf. New Directions 1993 147p hardcover o.p. pa $12.95 **811**
  1. Poetry -- By individual authors
  ISBN 978-0-8112-1227-4; 0-8112-1227-0
                         LC 92-35812

Duncan "was one of the true masters of contemporary
American poetry. His oeuvre is by turns lyrical, experimental, archaic, visionary and political. . . . In Bertholf's brief,
insightful introduction, he makes necessary connections between the often-neglected early work and the later masterpieces." Publ Wkly

Dunn, Stephen

Different hours; poems. Norton 2000 121p
$22; pa $12.95 **811**
  1. Poetry -- By individual authors
  ISBN 0-393-04986-8; 0-393-32232-7 pa
                         LC 00-30556

"Stephen Dunn's poetry is strangely easy to like: philosophical but not arid, lyrical but rarely glib, his storytelling balanced effortlessly between the casual and the vivid.
But don't mistake that ease for lack of staying power." N Y
Times Book Rev

Local visitations; poems. Norton 2003 96p
$21.95 **811**
  1. Poetry -- By individual authors
  ISBN 0-393-05200-1
                         LC 2002-14204

"The opening section of poems recasts Dunn's average
American as the mythic Sisyphus, imprisoned by repetitive
work ('a repetition/which would never mean more/at the end
than at the start') and yet bereft without it ('But more often
he finds himself dreaming/of his rock, wishing it back, the
better/to defend himself against so many hours'). Nearly
half the collection transports 19th-century literary figures to
contemporary New Jersey towns ('Mary Shelley in Brigantine,' 'Hawthorne in Tuckerton'), a series of poems more attractive in concept than in practice, where the subjects often
fail to transcend the contrivance they inhabit." Libr J

Loosestrife. Norton 1996 96p $19; pa $12 **811**
  1. Poetry -- By individual authors
  ISBN 0-393-03982-X; 0-393-31683-1 pa
                         LC 96-1238

"Dunn understands that there is sorrow in beauty and a
'strange loneliness' even in pleasure, and he examines these
dichotomies in language and form as clear and chilling as
ice. We feel knocked off balance by the end of one line, then
steadied by the beginning of the next." Booklist

New & selected poems, 1974-1994. Norton 1994
296p hardcover o.p. pa $16.95 **811**
  1. Poetry -- By individual authors
  ISBN 978-0-393-31300-0; 0-393-31300-X
                         LC 93-33212

"Dunn might be called a Neo-Horatian poet. He is levelheaded, witty, conversational in his diction, and willing to
see in domestic life his means for attaining and imparting
wisdom. Yet Dunn's variations on Horatian odes and epodes are rarely the drab reportorial missives from the daily
grind which are found in so much contemporary poetry. He
knows that his first duty is to keep the quotidian life interesting, and this is no mean feat. . . . This is to say that Dunn's
a gifted talker, a kind of querulous raconteur, and even his
less successful poems are highly readable." Poetry (Modern
Poetry Association)

Eady, Cornelius

Brutal imagination; poems. Putnam 2001 108p
$24; pa $13   811

1. Poetry -- By individual authors

ISBN 0-399-14718-7; 0-399-14720-9 pa

LC 00-62674

In this "collection of poetry, Eady invokes a chorus of
fictional black characters, from Uncle Tom to the invented
criminal whom Susan Smith blamed for the kidnapping
of her children. A white woman's 'stray thought,' this man
haunts the best of these spare, stirring poems. If the poet's
premise—the personification of a black figment of the white
imagination—is complex, his verse is unsettingly direct."
New Yorker

Edson, Russell

The rooster's wife; poems. BOA Editions 2005
91p hardcover o.p. pa $14.95   811

1. Poetry -- By individual authors

ISBN 978-1-929918-63-8; 1-929918-63-1

LC 2004-24831

"Edson's prose poems are directly and indirectly concerned with feelings customarily suppressed during wake-
fulness, whose content is violent, scatological, and, especially, sexual. An Edson prose poem, however amusing and
ridiculous—however jokelike—it may be, is disturbing. . . .
Laughter never blunts the edges of Edson's elegantly macu-
late conceptions." Booklist

Eliot, T. S.

★ Collected poems, 1909-1962. Harcourt Brace
Jovanovich 1963 221p $23   811

1. Poetry -- By individual authors

ISBN 0-15-118978-1

This volume contains the complete text of 'Collected
poems, 1909-1935,' the 'Four quartets,' and several other
poems accompanied by brief prefatory notes

★ The complete poems and plays, 1909-1950.
Harcourt Brace & Co. 1952 392p $35   811

1. Poetry -- By individual authors

ISBN 0-15-121185-X

"This omnibus collection includes all of the author's early poetry as well as the Four Quartets, Old Possum's Book
of Practical Cats, and the plays Murder in the Cathedral, The
Family Reunion, and The Cocktail Party." (Publisher's note)

Inventions of the March Hare; poems 1909-1917.
edited by Christopher Ricks. Harcourt Brace & Co.
1997 xlii, 428p   811

1. Poetry -- By individual authors

ISBN 0151002746; 0156005875

LC 96-45399

"Though available in manuscript to scholars since 1968,
this is the first appearance—for all but five poems—of Eliot's 'lost' notebook of drafts and fragments." (Libr J) Indexes.

"Though available in manuscript to scholars since 1968,
this is the first appearance—for all but five poems—of Eliot's 'lost' notebook of drafts and fragments. Eliot never intended this unfinished work to see publication, but in page
after page his autumnal sensibility, his signature aura of

languid urban malaise—however tentative—surfaces unmistakably. . . . For scholars and devotees, Eliot's rehearsals
for immortality will yield a cornucopia of delights." Libr J

Ellis, Thomas Sayers, 1963-

Skin, Inc. identity repair poems. Graywolf Press
2010 181p il $23.00   811

1. Poetry -- By individual authors

ISBN 1555975674; 9781555975678

LC 2010-922920

This is a collection of poetry by the author of The Maverick Room (2005).

This collection of the author's poems "constitutes an impassioned argument for revitalizing America's calcified literary culture ('Flat, fixed and finished'), whose conventional
assumptions about the expression of racial identity severely
limit the aesthetic choices available to both writers and readers of color. . . . With honesty, eloquence, and precision, Ellis
calls for resistance to the outward imposition of social and
personal identity while acknowledging the difficulty of the
task. . . . Certain to ignite debate on campuses and blogs,
this work is the perfectly realized embodiment of its author's
intent, likely to inspire poets of all ethnic backgrounds for
some time to come." Libr J

Emerson, Ralph Waldo

★ Collected poems & translations. Library of
Am. 1994 637p $35   811

1. Poetry -- By individual authors

ISBN 0-940450-28-3

LC 93-40245

Contains Emerson's published poetry, plus selections of
his unpublished poetry from journals and notebooks, and
some of his translations of poetry from other languages, notably Dante's La vita nuova

Encyclopedia of American poetry, the twentieth century; edited by Eric L. Haralson. Fitzroy Dear-
born Pubs. 2001 846p $125   811

1. Reference books 2. Poets, American -- Dictionaries
3. American poetry -- Bio-bibliography

ISBN 1-57958-240-0

"The volume features more than 400 entries written by
academic contributors on individual poets, landmark poems,
and major topics. The poet entries are usually 1,000 to 2,000
words long and offer critical treatment of the poet's career
and major achievements along with a capsule biography. . .
. Approximately one-third of the poet entries include subentries for one or more landmark poems. The 'major topics' entries are longer (around 3,000 words) and include periods or
movements (Black Arts movement, Dada), verse traditions
(often ethnic, such as Asian American poetry), and styles
and themes (Confessional poetry, War and antiwar poetry)."
Booklist

Erdrich, Louise

Original fire; selected and new poems. Harper-
Collins Pubs. 2003 158p $23.95; pa $13.95   811

1. Poetry -- By individual authors

ISBN 0-06-620986-2; 0-06-093534-0 pa

LC 2003-40700

"With this volume, drawn from two previous collections and including 100 pages of new poems, {the author} presents her first collection in over a decade. . . . Poems from the first collection chronicle her Native American childhood and early schooling, while those from the second rework or invent Native American mythology. The new poems are more rooted in Catholicism and life as a middle-class American. . . . Essential reading for fans of Erdrich's fiction, this volume can be expected to draw poetry readers into the fold." Libr J

Estes, Angie

Tryst. Oberlin College Press 2009 75p (Field poetry series) pa $15.95 **811**

1. Poetry -- By individual authors
ISBN 9780932440358; 0-932440355

LC 2008-54661

"Gleeful and gorgeous, delighted by puns and other wordplay (including words from French, Latin and Italian), Estes's fast-paced free verse, rich with internal rhyme, takes rightful pride in the beauties it flaunts and explains. Her fourth collection finds, for recurrent motifs, saints' lives, medieval manuscripts, gold leaf and the alphabet. . . . Each deft poem weaves together multiple topics—some art-historical, others autobiographical—through chains of homonyms and knotty analogies." N Y Times Book Rev

Everson, Landis

Everything preserved: poems, 1955-2005; edited by Ben Mazer. Graywolf Press 2006 106p pa $15 **811**

1. Poetry -- By individual authors
ISBN 978-1-55597-453-4; 1-55597-453-8

LC 2006-924341

"Everson, who makes his book-length debut in his 70's as winner of the Poetry Foundation's Emily Dickinson first book award, swapped poems with a young Jack Spicer and John Ashbery, then stopped writing for 43 years until a recent creative outburst. This volume—divided into two sections, one for nine poems written between 1955 and 1960, and the other comprising the remaining 66, written since 2003—quickly establishes the charms of the playful early work. . . . The recent work is much more uneven—though much of it has been published in major literary magazines—and there are still plenty of pleasures to be found. Everson evokes the ordinary with a continually surprising touch." Publ Wkly

Every shut eye ain't asleep; an anthology of poetry by African Americans since 1945. edited by Michael Harper and Anthony Walton. Little, Brown 1994 327p hardcover o.p. pa $19 **811**

1. American poetry -- African American authors -- Collections
ISBN 0-316-34710-8 pa

LC 93-10788

"Using Robert Hayden and Gwendolyn Brooks's poetry as 'emblematic' successes, this anthology selects 35 African American poets (spanning three generations) who were born between 1913 and 1962 and came of age after 1945. Besides the well-known Imamu Baraka, Lucille Clifton, Rita Dove, and Etheridge Knight, the editors feature little-known or younger poets like Elizabeth Alexander, Gerald Barrax, Jayne Cortex, and Dolores Kendrick." Libr J

Fagan, Deirdre

Critical companion to Robert Frost; a literary reference to his life and work. Facts on File 2007 454p il $75 **811**

1. Poets 2. Authors
ISBN 0-8160-6182-3; 978-0-8160-6182-2

LC 2006-13269

"This encyclopedic guide offers critical entries on each of Frost's published poems, including such classics as 'The Road Not Taken,' 'Stopping By Woods on a Snowy Evening,' and 'The Death of the Hired Man.'" Publisher's note
Includes bibliographical references

Fay-LeBlanc, Gibson

Death of a ventriloquist; poems. by Gibson Fay-LeBlanc. University of North Texas Press 2012 x, 85 p.p **811**

1. Voice -- Poetry 2. Fatherhood -- Poetry 3. Poetry -- Collections 4. Ventriloquism -- Poetry 5. Ventriloquists -- Poetry
ISBN 157441447X; 9781574414479; 9781574414554

LC 2011042003

2011 Winner, Vassar Miller Prize in Poetry
In this poetry collection, "[Gibson] Fay-LeBlanc's lines . . . lure, guide, and yank us through poems in which 'a redstart in the boneset and spotted knapweed' and 'eel grass winding your ankles' are always waiting to dance upon the tongue. Whether he's overhearing a conversation in a tavern or the music stuck in his head, Fay-LeBlanc uses his ventriloquist to raise important questions about how we perform ourselves through language, creating a voice that locates its source in a 'Prayer of Glass' because it must hide its true source from us. . . . [I]n 'Notes on Colic,' where, in a dream, we suddenly see 'The foreman of the pity factory,/ where they produce the tiniest/ violins known to man//'that guy, / who can't stop itching his welts //'does a little jig /to make you feel better.'" (Publishers Weekly)
Includes bibliographical references

Fearing, Kenneth

Selected poems; Robert Polito, editor. Library of America 2004 xxi, 183p (American poets project) $20 **811**

1. Poetry -- By individual authors
ISBN 978-1-931082-57-0; 1-932082-57-X

LC 2003-60482

"Kenneth Fearing writes noir poetry, which is no surprise, considering that he also wrote several noir novels. . . . His poems flirt with narrative (but rarely commit), and they're written in a jittery free verse that sounds like the byproduct of a paranoid, slightly strung-out Whitman. . . . There are plenty of people currently writing variations on Fearing (possibly without being aware of it), but it's tough to beat the stylish chill of the original. These poems may be leaves the wind blows from one gutter to another, but sometimes the gutter's the only place to be." Poetry (Modern Poetry Association)

Fenton, James

Selected poems. Farrar, Straus & Giroux 2006 196p pa $14 **811**

1. Poetry -- By individual authors

ISBN 978-0-374-26065-1; 0-374-26065-6

LC 2006-2691

This "collection offers an introduction to the work of a leading British poet and former professor of poetry at Oxford. Love and menace are the principal muses for Fenton's dark wit. Whether describing how an ex is safe because she's no longer loved . . . or narrating war's awful arithmetic . . . the control behind these lines is often terrifying." Publ Wkly

Ferlinghetti, Lawrence

These are my rivers; new & selected poems, 1955-1993. New Directions 1993 308p il hardcover o.p. pa $13.95 **811**

1. Poetry -- By individual authors

ISBN 0-8112-1273-4

LC 93-10383

"Reading this hefty selection from 12 previous volumes, plus 50 pages of new poems, we realize how accurately the poet described himself in 1979: a man who 'thinks he's Dylan Thomas and Bob Dylan rolled together with Charlie Chaplin thrown in.' . . . His style is recognizable throughout—phlegmatic poems running several pages, often lacking stanza breaks, with short lines at the left margin or moving across the page as hand follows eye." Libr J

Ferry, David

Bewilderment; new poems and translations. David Ferry. University of Chicago Press 2012 xii, 113 p.p (paper : alkaline paper) $18 **811**

1. Death -- Poetry 2. Future life -- Poetry 3. Poetry -- Collections

ISBN 0226244881; 0226244903; 9780226244884; 9780226244907

LC 2011050366

National Book Award Finalist: Poetry (2012)

This is a collection of poems from 88-year-old poet David Ferry. The poems here "are concerned with personal memories, death, and life beyond corporeality. The translations that dot the book—of Catullus, Virgil, and Horace; Rilke, Montale, and Cavafy; and the Anglo-Saxon Genesis A ("The Offering of Isaac")—touch those themes, too." (Booklist)

Includes bibliographical references

Finney, Nikky

★ **Head** off & split; poems. TriQuarterly Books/ Northwestern University 2011 97p pa $15.95 **811**

1. Poetry -- By individual authors

ISBN 978-0-8101-5216-8; 0-8101-5216-9

LC 2010-28888

"Finney picks through the past selectively, and with flicks of the blade that are personal, political, poetic and always musical, gives us back the present moment with an intensity that makes a reader feel as if, until reading her volume, we have been unfed." Cleveland Plain Dealer

Flynn, Nick

The **captain** asks for a show of hands; poems. Graywolf Press 2011 94p $22 **811**

1. Poetry -- By individual authors

ISBN 978-1-55597-574-6

LC 2010-937512

In this poetry collection, the author "considers the quandary of soldiers trained never to question authority and the profound betrayal of trust encoded in orders to commit torture. His masterfully concise poems deploy lulling meter, evocative images, and shocking disclosures. . . . Each word is a lit match, a thrown stone, a howling blast, a choking torrent. Flynn has forged daringly intimate and clarion poems of conscience." Booklist

Forche, Carolyn

Blue hour. HarperCollins Pubs. 2003 73p hardcover o.p. pa $13.95 **811**

1. Poetry -- By individual authors

ISBN 0-06-009912-7; 978-0-06-009913-8 pa; 0-06-009013-5 pa

LC 2002-27270

This "gathering of elegiac meditations calls up ghostly memories both personal and universal as the poet mourns the terrible death of her grandmother, gives thanks for the blessing of her son's birth, and alludes with few words and deep feelings to the anguish of war and exile." Booklist

Ford, Katie

Blood lyrics; poems. Katie Ford. Graywolf Press 2014 80 p. (alk. paper) $16 **811**

1. Mothers -- Poetry 2. Poetry -- Collections

ISBN 1555976921; 9781555976927

LC 2014935705

Los Angeles Times Book Prizes Finalist: Poetry (2014)

This collection of poems by Katie Ford "is a mother's song, one seared with the knowledge that her country wages long, aching wars in which not all lives are equal. There is beauty imparted, too, but it arrives at a cost." (Publisher's note)

"Taken together, the poems become a meditation on the concurrence of abundance and peril, where sumptuous language expresses stark suffering and musical phrasing portrays a world of discord. Given these conditions, on the prospect 'That it is even possible to stay alive,' Ford posits, 'we should wake/ to each other and ransack/ this flushed skin of everything/ but praise.'" Pub Wkly

From totems to hip-hop; edited by Ishmael Reed. Thunder's Mouth Press 2003 xxx, 523p $34.95; pa $17.95 **811**

1. American poetry -- Collections

ISBN 1-56025-500-5; 1-56025-458-0 pa

LC 2002-75691

This is "a dynamic and original anthology, an unprecedented amalgam of poets representing many facets of American culture and society." Booklist

Frost, Robert

★ **Collected** poems, prose, & plays. Library of Am. 1995 1036p $35 **811**
1. Poetry -- By individual authors
ISBN 1-883011-06-X

LC 94-43693

This volume contains "all of the plays, a generous selection of prose, all collected poems, and 94 uncollected poems, as well as 17 poems that were previously unpublished." Libr J

Gallagher, Tess

Dear ghosts, poems. Graywolf Press 2006 140p $20 **811**
1. Poetry -- By individual authors
ISBN 1-55597-443-0

LC 2005-938149

"So compelling are Gallagher's graceful poems, they leave the reader feeling 'rearranged from the cells out.'" Booklist

Galvin, Brendan

★ **Habitat**; new and selected poems, 1965-2005. Brendan Galvin. Louisiana State University Press 2005 250p $49.95; pa $26.95 **811**
1. Poetry -- By individual authors
ISBN 0-8071-3046-X; 0-8071-3047-8 pa

LC 2004-22441

"Galvin's work is not only accessible, it turns the commonplace over into something new. A dory, a cormorant, a pack of dogs, a chickadee—all served up with the eye of someone who can take you on a trip of rediscovery into your own backyard." Cape Cod Voice

Gambito, Sarah Verdes

Delivered; poems. [by] Sarah Gambito. Persea Books 2009 64p pa $14 **811**
1. Poetry -- By individual authors
ISBN 978-0-89255-346-4

LC 2008-31269

The poems in this collection "are as much about language as they are about Gambito's Filipina heritage. . . . If disjunction is a way of talking about or recreating immigrant experience, these poems 'deliver'—that is, provide and lead us out of—the incoherences built into cultural transplantation. They are surrealistic, fierce, and playful." Libr J

Gander, Forrest

Core samples from the world; with photographs by Raymond Meeks, Graciela Iburtide and Lucas Foglia. New Directions 2011 95p il **811**
1. Poetry -- By individual authors
ISBN 0-8112-1887-2; 978-0-8112-1887-0

LC 2011-01154

"Gander is an experimental poet in the most literal sense of the word, in that each of his books attempts things that haven't been tried before, either by him or others. In this eighth collection, four sequences of poems respond to pictures by three photographers—Raymond Meeks, Graciela Iturbide, and Lucas Foglia—making of the images metaphors for people and places that are easy to see but difficult to penetrate. The poems don't describe the pictures so much

as work in chorus with them. . . . Concluding each section is a piece of jumpy prose, a kind of lyric essay, narrating one of four journeys-to Xinjiang, Mexico, Bosnia-Herzegovina, and Chile. . . . In these pieces, Gander gets as close as one can to the sensations of being an outsider straining toward empathy." Publ Wkly

★ **Eye** against eye; with ten photographs by Sally Mann. New Directions 2005 80p il pa $14.95 **811**
1. Poetry -- By individual authors
ISBN 0-8112-1635-7

LC 2005-14907

The "opener, 'Burning Towers, Standing Wall,' compares the building of a Mayan wall and its destruction–both from political and natural forces–to the collapse of the Twin Towers. In three long poems, linked with pieces that contrast a couple's relationship with a boy's budding adolescence, the reader is asked to regard the relationships between words and subjects. . . . Owing to the poems' placement and the near absence of punctuation, the reader is propelled through the verse, left with a sense of urgency and awe." Libr J

Torn awake. New Directions 2001 95p pa $13.95 **811**
1. Poetry -- By individual authors
ISBN 0-8112-1486-9

LC 2001-32657

"There is no solid ground in the world Forrest Gander conjures in his new book of poems, yet his tentativeness is one of this book's essential qualities. . . . The voices vary throughout this book's six highly speculative sequences, . . . yet again and again they call from their spectral airiness a single recurring image, an elemental configuration of man, woman and child." N Y Times Book Rev

Gerstler, Amy

Scattered at sea; Amy Gerstler. Penguin Books 2015 96 p. (Penguin poets) (paperback) $20 **811**
1. American poetry -- Collections 2. American poetry -- Women authors -- Collections
ISBN 014312689X; 9780143126898

LC 2015002411

NBA Longlist

This poetry collection by Amy Gerstler, long-listed for the 2015 National Book Award for Poetry, "evokes notions of dispersion, diaspora, sowing one's wild oats, having one's mind expanded or blown, losing one's wits, and mortality. Making use of dramatic monologue, elegy, humor, and collage, these poems explore hedonism, gender, ancestry, reincarnation, bereavement, and the nature of prayer." (Publisher's note)

"Accomplished and involving; for all poetry collections." LJ

Getty, Sarah

Bring me her heart; poems. Higganum Hill Books 2006 98p pa $12.95 **811**
1. Poetry -- By individual authors
ISBN 978-0-9741158-8-6; 0-9741158-8-6

LC 2005-23805

The author "makes meter, rhyme, and formal stanzas the vehicles of winning, natural expression." Booklist

Gibbons, Reginald

Creatures of a day; poems. Louisiana State University Press 2008 79p $45; pa $16.95 **811**
1. Poetry -- By individual authors
ISBN 978-0-8071-3317-0; 978-0-8071-3318-7 pa
LC 2007-34185
The author "presents intense encounters with everyday people amidst the historical and social contexts of everyday life. His poems are meditations on memory, obligation, love, death, celebration, and sorrow." Publisher's note
Includes bibliographical references

It's time: poems. Louisiana State Univ. Press 2002 64p $22.95; pa $15.95 **811**
1. Poetry -- By individual authors
ISBN 0-8071-2814-7; 0-8071-2815-5 pa
LC 2002-73076
"If the thoughtful poems in Gibbons' elegant seventh collection were pieces of music, they would be measured piano sonatas, each note, each word, carefully struck, precisely enunciated." Booklist

Gibran, Kahlil

★ The **Prophet**. Knopf 1923 107p il $15 **811**
1. Poetry -- By individual authors
ISBN 0-394-40428-9
A collection of poems by the mystical writer/artist, who was born in Lebanon and died in the United States, in which the prophet Almustafa deals with fundamental aspects of human life such as love, friendship, good and evil, self-knowledge, passion and reason, joy and sorrow, freedom, work, marriage and children, prayer and death

Gilbert, Jack

The **dance** most of all; poems. Alfred A. Knopf 2009 60p $25 **811**
1. Poetry -- By individual authors
ISBN 978-0-307-27076-4; 0-307-27076-9
LC 2008-44670
"These poems are deeply elegiac, looking back over a long life lived in the various modes one comes to associate with Gilbert: desire, love, longing and happiness. In short, Gilbert is as Romantic as ever, but that romance is tinged with a hard grief, a sense of loss, but ultimately one of acceptance. These are the poems of a man who realizes without reserve that his time is coming to an end. Death lingers in the background of these lines, reflected in the landscapes that close readers of Gilbert have come to know: Pittsburgh, Greece, Italy, Paris, the woods of Massachusetts where he now resides." Oregonian

★ **Refusing** heaven; poems. Knopf 2005 92p $25 **811**
1. Poetry -- By individual authors
ISBN 1-4000-4365-4
LC 2004-48844
"Jack Gilbert is a poet of reckless charisma and its aftermaths: a catch-as-catch-can Castiglione, consigned by the waywardness of his imagination to write his canon of manners and gestures in lyric poetry. The poems have the quality of brilliant, searching, addled talk after a wild night out. There's a sort of strung-out sprezzatura to this poet, as

he bobs and weaves among the memories of old loves in old, European cities. . . . These poems are the stream-of-consciousness work of a consciousness radically narrowed over time, practically armored against new experience. At their best, shuttling associatively between a few old obsessions, they attain claustrophobic beauty that sounds like nobody else." Poetry (Modern Poetry Association)

Gilbert, Jack, 1925-2012

Collected poems; by Jack Gilbert. Alfred A. Knopf 2012 408 p. **811**
1. Love poetry 2. Grief -- Poetry 3. Marriage -- Poetry 4. Poetry -- Collections
ISBN 9780307269683
LC 2011025743
This book is a collection of "poems about the joys and complexities of romantic love, about grief and about the power of experience deeply felt. . . . Here are also many and many kinds of poems about travel or life in farflung places, particularly Greece. Plentiful, too, are poems of marriage--its difficulties ("Eight years/ and her love for me quieted away"), its ecstasies, and its ending: divorce is memorably figured as "looking/ out at the bright moonlight on concrete." Gilbert is perhaps best known, however, for the grief-stricken poems that chart the dying of and then mourning over his wife, Michiko, of whom he writes, "The arches of her feet are like voices/ of children calling in the grove of lemon trees,/ where my heart is as helpless as crushed birds."" (Publishers Weekly)

Ginsberg, Allen

★ **Collected** poems, 1947-1997. HarperCollins Publishers 2006 xx, 1189p il hardcover o.p. pa $25.99 **811**
1. Poetry -- By individual authors
ISBN 978-0-06-113974-1; 0-06-113974-2; 978-0-06-113975-8 pa; 0-06-113975-0 pa
LC 2006-41191
First published 1984 with title: Collected poems, 1947-1980
This books "reprints the complete text of 1984's Collected Poems 1947-1980, along with the collections that followed: White Shroud, Cosmopolitan Greetings, and Death and Fame, including the original book attributes of each collection. A poet of extremes at times too trusting of his instincts, Ginsberg could be playful, angry, strident, obscene, graceful, and hilarious in the space of a page, and by now his readers know they are likely to encounter as many embarrassing poems as enlightening ones. Still, this compendium provides the most complete edition of Ginsberg available." Libr J

★ **Howl**, and other poems. City Lights Bks. 1956 44p pa $5.95 **811**
1. Poetry -- By individual authors
ISBN 0-87286-017-5
Howl "was widely regarded as the 'poetic manifesto' of the beat movement. The title poem consists of three sections and a footnote. The first section, a catalogue of nightmarish images, reflects a brutalized contemporary America. The second section is a diatribe against the forces and institutions which abet such dehumanization. The third section,

addressed to a mental hospital inmate, is an ironic commentary on society's diagnosis of 'madness.'" Reader's Ency. 4th edition

Spontaneous mind; selected interviews, 1958-1996. with a preface by Václav Havel; edited by David Carter. HarperCollins Pubs. 2001 601p hardcover o.p. pa $17.95   **811**
1. Poets 2. Authors 3. Beat generation
ISBN 0-06-093082-9 pa
    LC 00-40849
"The bulk of the collection [of interviews] dates from 1965-72, Ginsberg's years as countercultural symbol and spokesman: dialogues at demonstrations and on the road, transcripts from 'Firing Line' and the Chicago Seven trial." N Y Times Book Rev
Includes bibliographical references

Gioia, Dana
Disappearing ink; poetry at the end of print culture. Graywolf Press 2004 271p pa $16   **811**
1. Poetry -- By individual authors 2. American poetry -- History and criticism
ISBN 1-55597-410-4
    LC 2004-104190
In this collection of essays, the author discusses the current relevance of poetry and the ways in which it is evolving with the times.
The author "offers accessible, necessary criticism for lay and academic readers of serious poetry." Am Book Rev

Giovanni, Nikki
Bicycles; love poems. William Morrow 2009 109p $16.95   **811**
1. Poetry -- By individual authors
ISBN 978-0-06-172645-3
"Disarming, sly, sensual, and knowing, Giovanni's poems scan like the teasing and wise songs favored by Dinah Washington and Etta James." Booklist

Blues; for all the changes: new poems. Morrow 1999 100p $15   **811**
1. Poetry -- By individual authors
ISBN 0-688-15698-3
    LC 98-50996
"Giovanni never loses sight of the people in her work. In poems built with broken lines and paragraphs of prose, she spars with the ills that confront us, but every struggle has a human face." Libr J

Chasing Utopia; Nikki Giovanni. William Morrow 2013 160 p. $19.99   **811**
1. Poetry -- Collections
ISBN 0688156975; 9780688156978
    LC 2013008776
This collection of poems, by Nikki Giovanni, focuses on "the everyday where family and lovers gather, friends commune, and those no longer with us are remembered. And at every gathering there is food, food as sustenance, food as aphrodisiac, food as memory. A pot of beans are flavored with her mother's sighs, this sigh part cardamom, that one the essence of clove; a lover requests a banquet as an af-

firmation of ongoing passion; an homage is paid to the most time-honored appetizer, soup." (Publisher's note)
In Giovanni's "accessible, teasing, and poignant collection, she offers straightforward, plain-speaking, sneakily resonant poems, many in prose form." Booklist
Includes bibliographical references

The **collected** poetry of Nikki Giovanni, 1968-1998; chronology and notes by Virginia C. Fowler. William Morrow 2003 xliii, 452p $24.95   **811**
1. Poetry -- By individual authors
ISBN 0-06-054133-4
    LC 2004-302269
"Giovanni observes and embraces the world like few other poets; seize on these poems spanning three decades, and listen to her sing." Booklist
Includes bibliographical references

Quilting the black-eyed pea; poems and not quite poems. William Morrow 2002 110p $16.95   **811**
1. Poetry -- By individual authors
ISBN 978-0-06-009952-7; 0-06-009952-6
    LC 2002-66025
Giovanni "entwines the political and the personal and celebrates womanhood and black society and culture. Hers is an embracing, uplifting, and sustaining voice, one given to both anger and humor." Booklist

Gizzi, Peter
In defense of nothing; selected poems, 1987-2011. Peter Gizzi. Wesleyan University Press 2014 244 p. (Wesleyan Poetry Series) (cloth : alk. paper) $26.95   **811**
1. Poetry 2. Emotions -- Poetry
ISBN 0819574309; 9780819574305
    LC 2013041211
Los Angeles Times Book Prize Finalist: Poetry (2014)
The poems in this collection by Peter Gizzi "strike a dynamic balance of honesty, emotion, intellectual depth and otherworldly resonance--in Gizzi's work, poetry itself becomes a primary ground of human experience. Haunted, vibrant, and saturated with luminous detail, Gizzi's poetry enlists the American vernacular in a magical and complex music." (Publisher's note)
"Gizzi's poetry is 'silly with clarity,' infused with a restless vernacular that can elevate the mundane while making the impossible tangible." Pub Wkly

Gluck, Louise
Averno. Farrar, Straus and Giroux 2006 79p $22   **811**
1. Poetry -- By individual authors
ISBN 0-374-10742-4; 978-0-374-10742-0
    LC 2005-42658
"Empathic and unforgiving, the voice that unifies Persephone's despondent homelessness, Demeter's rageful mothering and Hades's smitten jealousy is unique in recent poetry, and reveals the flawed humanity of the divine." Publ Wkly

Glück, Louise, 1943-

★ **Faithful** and virtuous night; Louise Gluck. 1st ed. Farrar, Straus & Giroux 2014 80 p. (Hardcover) $23   **811**
1. American poetry
ISBN 0374152012; 9780374152017
LC 2013048984
National Book Award: Poetry (2014)

A poetry collection by Louise Glück, "This is a story of adventure, an encounter with the unknown, a knight's undaunted journey into the kingdom of death; this is a story of the world you've always known, that first primer where 'on page three a dog appeared, on page five a ball' and every familiar facet has been made to shimmer like the contours of a dream, 'the dog float[ing] into the sky to join the ball." (Publisher's note)

"Witty, philosophical, and sensuous, Glück embraces dichotomies . . . while gracefully posing provocative questions about the nexus between nature and art and the churning complexity of consciousness." Booklist

Poems 1962-2012; Louise Glück. Farrar, Straus and Giroux Ecco Press 2012 634 p. (alk. paper) $40   **811**
1. Free verse 2. Poetry -- Collections
ISBN 0374126089; 9780374126087
LC 2011051349

This book, by Louise Gluck, features selections from the American author's poetry published between 1962 and 2012. "With each successive book her drive to leave behind what came before has grown more fierce, . . . she invented a form to accommodate this need, the book-length sequence of poems, like a landscape seen from above, a novel with lacunae opening onto the unspeakable." (Publisher's note)

A **village** life. Farrar, Straus, and Giroux 2009 72p $23   **811**
1. Poetry -- By individual authors
ISBN 978-0-374-28374-2; 0-374-28374-5
LC 2008-49218

"Glück's achievement in this collection is to show, through the exigencies of the place she has chosen, how interpersonal relationships are formed, shaped and broken by the particular landscape in which they unfurl. Though the poems are intimate and deeply sympathetic, there remains the suggestion of a distance between Glück and the village life she writes about. When she declaims, 'No one really understands/ the savagery of this place,' it feels as though she is speaking less about her chosen subjects than about herself." Publ Wkly

Goldbarth, Albert

★ The **kitchen** sink; new and selected poems, 1972-2007. Graywolf Press 2007 345p $26   **811**
1. Poetry -- By individual authors
ISBN 978-1-55597-462-6; 1-55597-462-7
LC 2006-929502

"Albert Goldbarth just may be the American poet of his generation for the ages. Often humorous but always serious, Goldbarth combines erudite research, pop-culture fanaticism, and personal anecdote in ways that make his writings

among the most stylistically recognizable in the literary world." Georgia Rev

Good poems; selected and introduced by Garrison Keillor. Viking 2002 xxvi, 476p $25.95; pa $15   **811**
1. English poetry -- Collections 2. American poetry -- Collections
ISBN 0-670-03126-7; 0-14-200344-1 pa
LC 2002-16881

Keillor "has put together a collection of close to 300 poems he has read during . . . [the] PBS broadcast, The Writer's Almanac. . . . Poems are arranged by 19 general themes, such as 'Snow,' 'Failure,' and 'A Good Life.' Authors range from well-known oldies like Emily Dickinson and Robert Frost to unknowns like C.K. Williams. . . . An outstanding feature of this collection is that the selections are all so accessible—even folks who say they don't like poetry can find something here to enjoy." SLJ

Graber, Kathleen

The **eternal** city; poems. Princeton University Press 2010 78p (Princeton series of contemporary poets) $35; pa $16.95   **811**
1. Poetry -- By individual authors
ISBN 978-0-691-14609-6; 978-0-691-14610-2 pa
LC 2009-49321

"Graber's lengthy, long-lined, poems take in everything from St. Augustine to Pepperidge Farm Goldfish crackers to a rash of deaths in the poet's own family, and that's in just one poem. . . . Perhaps half the poems have an epigraph, from the likes of William Blake, Marcus Aurelius and Walter Benjamin. Those sources, as well as Graber's candid tone, set the poems in the midst of an ongoing conversation with the lessons of history and religion. But what makes Graber's poems so fresh and wild are the associative slips that happen between the distant past and the urgent present." Publ Wkly

Graham, Jorie

The **dream** of the unified field; selected poems, 1974-1994. Ecco Press 1995 199p hardcover o.p. pa $15   **811**
1. Poetry -- By individual authors
ISBN 0-88001-476-8 pa
LC 95-16572

"Combining great vision like Blake's, a Dickinsonian philosophical introspection, and a richly modern sensuality, this selection demonstrates the full range of Graham's poetic gifts." Booklist

From the New World; Poems 1976-2014. Jorie Graham. HarperCollins 2015 384 p. $29.99   **811**
1. Love 2. Poetry 3. Politics
ISBN 0062315404; 9780062315403
Los Angeles Times Book Prize: Poetry (2015)

This book is a "volume of poems, selected from almost four decades of work, that tracks the evolution of one of our most renowned contemporary poets, Pulitzer Prize-winner Jorie Graham. [Readers] can witness the unfolding of Graham's signature ethical and eco-political concerns, as well as her deft exploration of mythology, history, love and, increasingly, love of the world in a time of crisis." (Publisher's note)

"Although Graham never mentions the word Oversoul here, these difficult language poems are suggestive of transcendentalism in its truest sense. Graham may not visit Walden Pond, but she hangs clothes in her backyard, walks in the woods, and tends her garden (among the subjects of the poems here), using these occasions to mark the place where daily life meets the infinite." LJ

Overlord; poems. Ecco 2005 93p $22.95 **811**
1. Poetry -- By individual authors
ISBN 0-06-074565-7
LC 2004-53681

"In a distinctly forthright and empathic collection, Graham has constructed poems of lyrical steeliness and cauterizing beauty." Booklist

Greenbaum, Jessica

The **two** Yvonnes; poems. Jessica Greenbaum. Princeton University Press 2012 57 p. (pbk. : acid-free paper) $12.95 **811**
1. Motherhood -- Poetry 2. Poetry -- Collections
ISBN 0691156638; 9780691156620; 9780691156637
LC 2012020320

This book is Jessica Greenbaum's second poetry collection. "With fluent free verse broken up by sonnets, an abecedary and a pantoun, in allegories, comic anecdotes, and pivotal, confessional memories, Greenbaum lets us travel along with her as she grows from too-patient girl to agitated student, from the mother of a sick young child to all the sensations of being alive' after the child (to judge by the poems) has moved out." (Publishers Weekly)

Gregg, Linda

All of it singing. Graywolf Press 2008 224p $24 **811**
1. Poetry -- By individual authors
ISBN 978-1-55597-507-4; 1-55597-507-0
LC 2008-928247

This retrospective "selects from all of Gregg's published books—from her 1981 debut Too Bright to See to 2006's In the Middle Distance—including a group of new poems that show her ongoing investigations into the inner intensities of everyday brutality and grace. . . . The poems travel the globe, set in New England, California, Mexico, Greece and beyond, though wherever her poems go, Gregg never forgets that 'if paradise is to be here/ it will have to include her.' Gregg offers up poems of love lost and won, and of an average life lived with extraordinary force. . . . The poems always rejoice, however dark their subjects, in a powerful sense of simply being alive." Publ Wkly

Grossman, Allen R.

Descartes' loneliness; [by] Allen Grossman. New Directions 2007 64p il pa $16.95 **811**
1. Poetry -- By individual authors
ISBN 978-0-8112-1711-8; 0-8112-1711-6
LC 2007-26896

"Grossman once claimed poetry to be the historical enemy of human forgetfulness. This interest—or better, faith—in poetry's capacity to perform distinctly human acts of preservation has informed Grossman's writing from the beginning. This most recent book showcases some of Grossman's most affecting and memorable lyrics to date." Publ Wkly

Guest, Barbara

The **collected** poems of Barbara Guest; edited by Hadley Haden Guest. Wesleyan University Press 2008 525p (Wesleyan poetry) $39.95 **811**
1. Poetry -- By individual authors
ISBN 978-0-8195-6860-1; 0-8195-6860-0
LC 2008-20147

"It is impossible for a reader to leave The Collected Poems of Barbara Guest without appreciating the enormous spiritual gift her work has always offered in the form of an aesthetic and philosophical challenge." Boston Rev
Includes index. 'Works by Barbara Guest': p. xxvii-xxix

H. D.

Collected poems, 1912-1944; edited by Louis L. Martz. New Directions 1983 xxxvi, 629p hardcover o.p. pa $24.95 **811**
1. Poetry -- By individual authors
ISBN 978-0-8112-0971-7; 0-8112-0971-7
LC 83-6380

The editor's textual notes "offer valuable and illuminating scholarly commentary and present the most important of the textual variants. An informative and sensitively written introduction discusses aspects of the interpenetration of H.D.'s biography with her poetic sensibility. This volume is an impressive scholarly work." Choice

Hacker, Marilyn

Selected poems; 1965-1990. Norton 1994 250p $22; pa $13.95 **811**
1. Poetry -- By individual authors
ISBN 0-393-03675-8; 0-393-31349-2 pa
LC 94-27507

"Few poets have been as successful as Hacker in negotiating the boundary of the feminist and lesbian canon while generating a buzz around their early work. Iambic and readable, the pieces in Selected Poems—taken from five previous volumes—use unique inversions to explore self and other through changing situations between friends, lovers, family, and one's surroundings. . . . Often, these are poems of loss, of desire delayed, of pleasure deferred." Libr J

Squares and courtyards. Norton 2000 107p $21; pa $12 **811**
1. Poetry -- By individual authors
ISBN 0-393-04830-6; 0-393-32095-2 pa
LC 99-39110

"With customary fortitude and intelligence, Hacker confronts such sobering subjects as the trauma of her own chemotherapy and the loss of friends, in poems that are at once clear-sighted and emotionally full." New Yorker

Hacker, Marilyn, 1942-

A **stranger's** mirror; new and selected poems 1994/2014. by Marilyn Hacker. W W Norton & Co Inc 2015 320 p. (hardcover) $29.95 **811**
1. Poetry -- Collections
ISBN 0393244644; 9780393244649
LC 2014037031

This collection of poetry, by Marilyn Hacker, "include[s[work from four previous volumes along with twenty-five new poems. . . . Her poems belong to an urban world of cafés, bookshops, bridges, traffic, demonstrations, conversations, and solitudes. From there, Hacker reaches out to other sites and personas: a refugee camp on the Turkish/Syrian border; contrapuntal monologues of a Palestinian and an Israeli poet; intimate and international exchanges abbreviated on Skype." (Publisher's note)

"Hacker is an empathic, daring, and bracing poet of border-crossings and global conscience." Booklist

Halaby, Laila

My name on his tongue; poems. Laila Halaby. 1st ed. Syracuse University Press 2012 xi, 131 p.p (pbk. : alk. paper) $17.95 **811**
1. Arab Americans 2. Narrative poetry 3. Poetry -- Collections
ISBN 0815632940; 9780815632948
LC 2012006950

In this "poetry collection . . . [Laila] Halaby . . . narrates the need of Arab Americans to navigate new realities while giving voice to old ones. She writes about her personal feelings and daily experiences in a confessional mode. . . . She . . . interweaves insights about peace, war, family, nostalgia, exile, and sociopolitical conflicts, among other subjects, Halaby promotes poetry as both testimony and instrument of change." (Library Journal)

Hall, Donald

The **back** chamber. Houghton Mifflin Harcourt 2011 82p $22 **811**
1. Poetry -- By individual authors
ISBN 978-0-547-64585-8
LC 2011009152

This is "a mix of naughty, funny, sweet, and sad pieces about love, family, death, and the poignancy of things. The old rooms of his grandfather's farmhouse in New Hampshire, where Hall has lived since the 1970s, set the stage for recalled intimacies with his late wife, the poet Jane Kenyon, and recollections of the childhood that first brought him there. . . . Featuring moving, amusing, musical poems about love, aging, and baseball, this work will have broad appeal and is recommended for all collections." Libr J

White apples and the taste of stone; poems, 1946-2006. Houghton Mifflin Co. 2006 431p $30; pa $16.95 **811**
1. Poetry -- By individual authors
ISBN 978-0-618-53721-1; 0-618-53721-X; 978-0-618-91999-4 pa; 0-618-91999-6 pa
LC 2005-20047

"Given to formal short work in the '50s, to lengthy verse essays and verse memoirs later on, Hall shows consistent topics and moods: adult life among New Hampshire's farms and mountains, childhood in the Connecticut suburbs, equanimity and nostalgia, satire and self-satire, middle age and old age, regret and reserve. Most original in his long poems from the '80s and '90s, Hall achieved popular success in recent years,. . . collecting elegies and laments for his late wife, the poet Jane Kenyon." Publ Wkly

Harjo, Joy

A **map** to the next world; poetry and tales. Norton 2000 138p hardcover o.p. pa $13.95 **811**
1. Poetry -- By individual authors
ISBN 978-0-393-32096-1; 0-393-32096-0
LC 99-41099

"One of the most significant American Indian poets here expands her poetic practice to include what she calls tales but might as easily be considered prose poems. Harjo's verse has lately taken on a flowing, narrative quality; these tales, by contrast, take an imagistic, stream-of-consciousness form. . . . Written with authority and Harjo's trademark exploratory verve, this is fine, mature work." Booklist

Harper's anthology of 20th century Native American poetry; edited by Duane Niatum. Harper & Row 1988 xxxii, 396p hardcover o.p. pa $24.95 **811**
1. American poetry -- Native American authors
ISBN 0-06-250666-8 pa
LC 86-45023

This collection "contains the work of 36 native American poets, with hearty selections from each. Among the 36 are poets near the mainstream (Scott Momaday, James Welch, Louise Erdrich); those in academe (Gerald Vizenor, Linda Hogan, Jim Barnes); those writing in the tribal oral tradition (Barney Bush, Peter Blue Cloud, Wendy Rose); and those working in a modernist voice (Gladys Cardiff, Paula Gunn Allen). This book belongs in every collection that claims to represent the multiple voices of American literature today." Booklist

Includes bibliographical references

Harrington, Janice N.

Even the hollow my body made is gone; poems. foreword by Elizabeth Spires. BOA Editions, Ltd. 2007 85p (A. Poulin Jr. new poets of America series) pa $15.50 **811**
1. Poetry -- By individual authors
ISBN 978-1-929918-89-8; 1-929918-89-5
LC 2006-30823

The author "sets her first poetry collection mainly in Alabama during the civil-rights era. Her rich, colloquial poems, drawing on both folklore and science, are paeans to a weary but tenacious black family and their journey north through 'a night as wide as the River Jordan.' . . . When the poems themselves seem less pioneering than the spirit they evoke, their scope and empathy largely compensate." New Yorker

Harrison, Jim

In search of small gods. Copper Canyon Press 2009 120p $22 **811**
1. Poetry -- By individual authors
ISBN 978-155659-300-0; 1-55659-300-7
LC 2008-39992

Harrison "writes like a man reconciling the world at large with the natural world he knows well, one that still fascinates and inspires him. Many of his small gods are dogs, and many of them are fish or birds, that is, chickadees and hawks, willow flycatchers and hummingbirds. . . . He looks at them all with awe and ironic amusement. A group of prose poems centers this volume. Whether he imagines an Estonian World War II veteran who is fascinated by light or Vallejo in Paris, collecting empty wine bottles for small change, Harrison is heavily invested in narrative elements that range from the real to the surreal." Libr J

The **shape** of the journey; new & collected poems. Copper Canyon Press 1998 463p $30; pa $20 **811**

1. Poetry -- By individual authors

ISBN 1-55659-095-4; 1-55659-149-7 pa

LC 98-25501

"This large collection, which also includes a new grab bag of nature verse and prose poems called 'Geo-Bestiary,' has a meandering feel, although Harrison's concerns—aging, women, eating and drinking, hunting, the craft of writing and above all the spirit and rhythms of the natural world—are remarkably constant. . . . Harrison's writing is graceful, direct and muscular, even in those occasional places where the poems feel like dashed-off diary entries or, rarer still, when they hit a mawkish note." N Y Times Book Rev

Harrison, Jim, 1937-2016

Songs of unreason. Copper Canyon Press 2011 143p $22 **811**

1. Poetry -- By individual authors

ISBN 978-1-55659-389-5

LC 2011025560

"It wouldn't be a Harrison collection without the poet, novelist, and food critic's reverence for rivers, dogs, and women, but that's not to say Harrison has grown stale or uninteresting in his late poems. Often, as in 'A Part of My History,' which finds the poet tracking the ghost of García Lorca through Granada, his poems stun us simply, with the richness of the clarity, detail, and the immediacy of Harrison's voice. . . . Pushing his formal boundaries, Harrison closes the collection with the meditative 'Suite of Unreason,' a piece that boils down his sharp, epigrammatic lines into a sequence of fist-pumping short poems. But it also wouldn't be a Harrison poem without the hard melancholy that has come to define his voice." Publ Wkly

Hass, Robert

The **apple** trees at Olema; new and selected poems. Ecco 2010 352p $34.99 **811**

1. Poetry -- By individual authors

ISBN 978-0-06-192382-1; 0-06-192382-6

This "retrospective collection, drawn from five previous books, beginning with Field Guide (1973), opens with a generous selection of new poems redolent of Whitman and the blues. Narrative poems are droll and astringent in their musings over love's paradoxes and history's shifting claims, children's pleasures, poverty, and danger. . . . Hass distills experiences down to their essence as he limns landscapes, portrays friends and loved ones, and imagines the struggles of strangers. The ordinary is cracked open to reveal metaphysical riddles in poems that feel so natural, their formal complexities nearly elude our detection." Booklist

Time and materials; poems, 1997-2005. Ecco 2007 88p $22.95 **811**

1. Poetry -- By individual authors

ISBN 978-0-06-134960-7; 0-06-134960-7

LC 2007-30294

This collection of poetry by the former U.S. poet laureate "show a rare internal variety, even as they reflect his constant concerns. One is human impact on the planet at the century's end. . . . Another concern is biography and memory, not so much Hass's own life as the lives of family and friends. . . . Through it all runs a rare skill with long sentences, a light touch, a wish to make claims not just on our ears but on our hearts, and a willingness to wait—few poets wait longer, it seems—for just the right word." Publ Wkly

Includes bibliographical references

Haxton, Brooks

They lift their wings to cry; poems. Knopf 2008 78p $25 **811**

1. Poetry -- By individual authors

ISBN 978-0-307-26845-7; 0-307-26845-4

LC 2008-05766

"You could place Haxton in the Billy Collins school of poetry. His poems read readily, they are funny, smart, and so much more, as their blithe cleverness and charming humility lightly camouflage a spiritual dimension. But Haxton goes his own way, channels his sages of choice, and keeps it low-key, bemused, and philosophical. His emotional palette is warm. His frame of reference encompasses Heraclitus, Ovid, the Bible, a CAT scan. His fascination with the small creatures that make up the bulk of what we call nature—he writes of crickets, moths, birds, a mouse—has a scientific cast even as it springs from a freeflowing empathy with all of life." Booklist

Hayden, Robert Earl

Collected poems; edited by Frederick Glaysher. Liveright 1985 205p hardcover o.p. pa $15 **811**

1. Poetry -- By individual authors

ISBN 978-0-87140-159-5; 0-87140-159-2

LC 84-28880

"Hayden's poetry is a blend of unrivaled craftsmanship with a sharp, unrestrained vision. His subjects encompass the whole of human experience, from the extremely personal but never obscure ('Approximations') to the historical but never pedantic ('Belsen, Day of Liberation'). His technique is similarly varied. Hayden is as adept with haiku, imitations of Eskimo song-poems, or sonnets as he is with free verse. A particularly important addition to libraries with black literature collections." Booklist

Hayes, Terrance, 1971-

How to be drawn; Terrance Hayes. Penguin Books 2015 112 p. (pbk.) $20 **811**

1. Art -- Poetry 2. American poetry -- Collections

ISBN 9780143126881; 0143126881

LC 2014045785

NAACP Image Award: Outstanding Literary Work - Poetry (2016)

National Book Award Finalist: Poetry (2015)

National Book Critics Circle Award Finalist: Poetry (2015)

This poetry collection, by Terrance Hayes "explores how we see and are seen. While many of these poems bear the clearest imprint yet of Hayes's background as a visual artist, they do not strive to describe art so much as inhabit it. Thus, one poem contemplates the principle of blind contour drawing while others are inspired by maps, graphs, and assorted artists." (Publisher's note)

"Hayes writes far-reaching yet intimate monologues that are simultaneously subtle and hard-hitting; he unearths shards of shameful antebellum history and takes measure of the current state of moral and political paralysis." Booklist

Lighthead. Penguin Books 2010 95p (Penguin poets) pa $18   811
   1. Poetry -- By individual authors
   ISBN 978-0-14-311696-7; 0-14-311696-7
                   LC 2009-53319

This collection is a "celebration and castigation of American culture, one worthy of the term 'Americanist.' The title references the light of inspiration and the fire that pours from the heads of two teenage lynching victims in one of the opening poems. The fact that the title can do both inspiration and elegy is indicative of how meaning is contested terrain in Hayes' work. . . . [He] deftly quilts together different textures of language. Rants move into love poems and biting humor butts up against meditations. . . . Sound is of primary importance to Mr. Hayes. Throughout the book he borrows from hip-hop, jazz, slang, lists, and T-shirt slogans. Content aside, his poems are full of pure pleasure of sound in his startling and sonically dense images." Pittsburgh Post-Gazette

Healey, Steve
  10 Mississippi; poems. Coffee House Press 2010 113p pa $16   811
   1. Poetry -- By individual authors
   ISBN 978-1-56689-252-0; 1-56689-252-X
                   LC 2010-16259

"Steve Healey is one of our most promising young poets, and this collection is full of circumambulations around the same topics, in a skillful takeoff from Gertrude Stein's poetics. Healey quotes from Elizabeth Bishop 'Everything only connected by 'and' and 'and'' and from Steve Reich 'I discovered that the most interesting music of all was made by simply lining the loops up in unison, and letting them slowly shift out of phase with each other.' This seems to be his operative paradigm as well. The whole book is about the mendacity (and utter veracity) of connection; Healey's circling around the dead corpse of false consolations is extremely hypnotic and enchanting. The '10 Mississippi' sequence is particularly effective as a meditation on finality." Huffington Post

Hecht, Anthony
  Collected later poems. Knopf 2003 255p hardcover o.p. pa $16.95   811
   1. Poetry -- By individual authors
   ISBN 978-0-375-71030-8; 0-375-71030-2
                   LC 2003-44601

This volume contains: The transparent man (1990), Flight among the tombs (1996), and The darkness and the light (2001)

"From the outset a fastidious craftsman, Hecht developed out of the legacy of modernism a stately, intricate, rigorously formal poetry that slowly expanded in its range of tones and subject matter." Times Lit Suppl

Hicok, Bob, 1960-
  Elegy owed; Bob Hicok. Copper Canyon Press 2013 120 p. (hardcover : alk. paper) $22   811
   1. American poetry -- Collections
   ISBN 1556594364; 9781556594366
                 LC 2012043531

National Book Critics Circle Award Finalist: Poetry (2013)

This collection of poetry by Bob Hicok was a National Book Critics Circle Award finalist and won the Paterson Award for Literary Excellence. "In his seventh collection, Hicok builds startling images out of the everyday and the surreal, the comic and the sorrowful. . . . Intimate lyrics of love, fear, loss, and cosmic perplexity are matched by robust dissections and protests." (Booklist)

"Words have weight in Hicok's poems. They feel nailed in place, and the meter hits like the sure pounding of a hammer. Yet as heft, muscle, and precision draw you forward, Hicok evokes not solidity but, rather, shifting ground, flux, metamorphosis, and, most arrestingly, most unnervingly, death... This trenchant collection's got heart and soul." Booklist

Hillman, Brenda
  Cascadia. Wesleyan Univ. Press 2001 77p (Wesleyan poetry) $26; pa $13.95   811
   1. Poetry -- By individual authors
   ISBN 0-8195-6491-5; 0-8195-6492-3 pa
                 LC 2001-35504

"Geologists know 'Cascadia' as the name for the landmass that became the American West Coast: Hillman's serial mix of long and short poems links Californian geology, geography, history (a Gold Rush-era diarist named Shirley), continental philosophy, and personal experience. . . . Some poems are content with their lyrical verbal effects; others play with typography for effects that are energetic, familiar to readers of Susan Howe and Jorie Graham." Publ Wkly

  Pieces of air in the epic. Wesleyan Univ. Press 2005 87p $22.95; pa $14.95   811
   1. Poetry -- By individual authors
   ISBN 978-0-8195-6787-1; 0-8195-6787-6; 978-0-8195-6788-8 pa; 0-8195-6788-4 pa
                 LC 2005-18749

"The second in a tetralogy exploring the four elements, Hillman's expansive new work examines air not just as 'gusts & siroccos, chinooks, hamskin, whooshes' but as voice, song, and spirit. Were it not such a pun, one would be tempted to call this collection literally breathtaking; Hillman has pursued an ambitious program with remarkably fine-tuned language." Libr J

  Seasonal works with letters on fire; Brenda Hillman. Wesleyan University Press 2013 144 p. (Wesleyan poetry series) (cloth : alk. paper) $24.95   811
   1. Fire 2. Poetry -- Collections
   ISBN 0819574147; 9780819574145
                 LC 2013939069

This collection of poetry by Brenda Hillman focuses on "fire--its physical, symbolic, political, and spiritual forms. . . . Hillman evokes fire as metaphor and as event to chart subtle changes of seasons during financial breakdown, environmental crisis, and street movements for social justice; she gathers factual data, earthly rhythms, chants to the dead, journal entries, and lyric fragments in the service of a radical animism." (Publisher's note)

Hirsch, Edward

Earthly measures; poems. Knopf 1994 93p hardcover o.p. pa $18 **811**

1. Poetry -- By individual authors

ISBN 978-0-679-76566-0; 0-679-76566-2

LC 93-26410

"Hirsch contemplates manifestations of the divine in this set of ravishing poems infused with a deeply felt sense of place and history, seeking insights into how instances of spiritual revelation occur in the frequently brutal everyday world." Booklist

The **living** fire; new and selected poems, 1975-2010. Alfred A. Knopf 2010 237p $27 **811**

1. Poetry -- By individual authors

ISBN 978-0-375-41522-7; 0-375-41522-X

LC 2009-24452

In Hirsch's work, things are not always what they seem. Certainly, his poems work to dignify the everyday. But they do more than that. What makes Hirsch so singular in American poetry is the balance he strikes between the quotidian and something completely other an irrational counterforce, the living fire that gives its name to his new selected poems. . . . Literary and allusive, but also domestic and intimate, as it rises toward praise, Hirsch's voice resounds with both force and subtlety. One of the pleasures of reading the new selected poems is the chance to see that voice develop and then range freely and surprisingly. N Y Times Book Rev

On love; poems. Knopf 1998 86p hardcover o.p. pa $15 **811**

1. Poetry -- By individual authors

ISBN 978-0-375-70260-0; 0-375-70260-1

LC 97-49460

"The affirmation of On Love is its language, and the sense it gives that the language of love is inexhaustible. However conversant with the abyss, however true to the devastating logic of desire, the poems ultimately feel triumphant. They are held aloft by nothing but their own joyous artistry." Yale Rev

Special orders; poems. Alfred A. Knopf 2008 64p $25 **811**

1. Poetry -- By individual authors

ISBN 978-0-307-26681-1; 0-307-26681-8

LC 2007-40336

This collection "brings its demotic, heartfelt, autobiographical pieces together to form a picture of Hirsch's whole life, with sadness always visible, but joy in the foreground. He begins with his immigrant 'grandfather,/ an old man from the Old World'; remembers 'the second-story warehouse' where the young poet 'filled orders for the factory downstairs'; and moves on to his own life as a struggling, and then a successful, writer, teacher and father. Jewish and Yiddish heritage, in memory and on canvas (Chaim Soutine, Marc Chagall) pervades the first half of the volume. . . . The second half follows Hirsch as an adult, to Houston (where he

taught for many years) and back to New York City, where he now heads the Guggenheim Foundation." Publ Wkly

Hirshfield, Jane

After; poems. HarperCollins 2006 97p $23.95 **811**

1. Poetry -- By individual authors

ISBN 0-06-077916-0

LC 2005-50260

"These poems' topics range from global warming to insomnia, passion, cheese making, and sneezing. . . . [The author] engages historical figures from Rembrandt, Poe, and Tu Fu to Linnaeus, Roget, and Darwin. The beauty of these historically engaging poems, though, is that they remain firmly tied to our contemporary world." Va Q Rev

The **beauty**; poems. Jane Hirshfield. Alfred A. Knopf 2015 128 p. (hardback) $26 **811**

1. Poetry -- Collections 2. American poetry -- Collections

ISBN 0385351070; 9780385351072

LC 2014025831

NBA Longlist

This collection of poems, by Jane Hirshfield, "opens with a series of dappled, ranging 'My' poems--'My Skeleton,' 'My Corkboard,' 'My Species,' 'My Weather'--using materials sometimes familiar, sometimes unexpected, to explore the magnitude, singularity, and permeability of our shared existence." (Publisher's note)

"These open, approachable poems offer insights that ring true for anyone who's lived a little; they will appeal to a wide range of readers." LJ

Hix, H. L.

First fire, then birds; obsessionals 1985-2010. Etruscan Press 2010 291p $27.95 **811**

1. Poetry -- By individual authors

ISBN 978-0-9819687-4-2; 0-9819687-4-0

"Sometimes achingly beautiful in their accumulated details, sometimes grisly and violent, and sometimes tersely intellectual, Hix's collections have always been hard to forget: since his debut with the sonnets of Perfect Hell (1996), his books have differed greatly one from another, each with its signature long poem or sequence. . . . Formalists cherish Hix's frequent meter and rhyme; devotees of experiment enjoy the bizarre disjunctions and the philosophical demands. This retrospective shuffles individual poems and sequences from his first seven books to good effect, out of chronological order (along with aphorisms from a book of prose). Hix may make new readers' heads spin with his changes of focus, but he also gives them the chance to see his work whole." Publ Wkly

Hoagland, Tony

Unincorporated persons in the late Honda dynasty; poems. Graywolf Press 2010 90p pa $15 **811**

1. Poetry -- By individual authors

ISBN 978-1-55597-549-4; 1-55597-549-6

LC 2009-933818

"There are 15 or 20 better poets in America than Tony Hoagland, but few deliver more pure pleasure. His erudite comic poems are backloaded with heartache and longing, and they function, emotionally, like improvised explosive devices: the pain comes at you from the cruelest angles, on the sunniest of days. . . . On a superficial level Mr. Hoagland's poems — he writes in an alert, caffeinated, lightly accented free verse — resemble those of many writers in what one is tempted to call the Amiable School of American Poets, a group for which Billy Collins serves as both prom king and starting point guard. But Mr. Hoagland's verse is consistently, and crucially, bloodied by a sense of menace and by straight talk." N Y Times (Late N Y Ed)

What narcissism means to me. Graywolf Press 2003 78p pa $14 **811**
1. Poetry -- By individual authors
ISBN 1-55597-386-8 pa
LC 2003-101172

The author's "speaker devotes considerable energy to unmasking .... {his} vulnerable self, revealing its ugliness, hatred and social sensitivity. . . . In milder poems, which often revolve around eating dinner, drinking wine and hanging out with friends (typically other creative writing professors), he explores a more social self, slipping into a 'he said, she said' mode, and reporting at great length on friends' witticisms." Publ Wkly

Hodgen, John
Heaven & earth holding company. University of Pittsburgh Press 2010 73p (Pitt poetry series) pa $14.95 **811**
1. Poetry -- By individual authors
ISBN 978-0-8229-6114-7; 0-8229-6114-8

"Every writer wants to get the strange kaleidoscopic world of ten thousand things into their work; few succeed. But John Hodgen's Heaven and Earth Holding Company delivers that entirety in poem after poem —sun, rain, baseball, Frost and Shakespeare, the birth of a granddaughter, Abraham Lincoln, W.C Fields, saints, dogs, lovers, Viagra, Motel 6, those beeping airport carts. Hodgen's long-lined poems are propulsive, his sentences hypotactic, muscular, alliterative. . . . If these were just playful, wise-cracking poems they would give us pleasure enough; but Hodgen's poems fast-break from humor to sorrow and the mortal coils of our lives." On the Seawall

Hoffman, Daniel
Beyond silence; selected shorter poems, 1948-2003. Louisiana State Univ. Press 2003 226p $49.95; pa $26.95 **811**
1. Poetry -- By individual authors
ISBN 0-8071-2860-0; 0-8071-2861-9 pa
LC 2002-34090

The collection's "organization by theme brings poems from remote parts of his oeuvre into illuminating conversation with one another. And substantial recent poems such as 'Scott Nearing's Ninety-Eighth Year' and 'The Cape Racer' are as strong as anything he's written." NY Times Book Rev

Hollander, John
A draft of light; poems. Alfred A. Knopf 2008 109p $26 **811**
1. Poetry -- By individual authors
ISBN 978-0-307-26911-9; 0-307-26911-6
LC 2008-4751

"As one would expect of a poet whose work has been set to music, Hollander sees poetry as an oral art even though it is first written on paper. What one might not expect from this 78-year-old poet is the wordplay, lighthearted tone, and general mischievousness that seems to come trippingly from his pen. . . . This volume's title poem, for example, ends with a paraphrase of T.S. Eliot's 'Little Gidding.' Other poems paraphrase Percy Bysshe Shelley, Wallace Stevens, and Joyce Kilmer, to say nothing of William Shakespeare. Like Shakespeare, Hollander fuses a somber tone with comic conventions, resulting in the poetic equivalent of the problem play." Libr J

Includes bibliographical references

Figurehead & other poems. Knopf 1999 89p hardcover o.p. pa $15 **811**
1. Poetry -- By individual authors
ISBN 978-0-375-70433-8; 0-375-70433-7
LC 98-14208

Hollander's "justifiably confident in his skills, the solid grace of his constructions, and his ability to make both the light and dark sides of words, thoughts, and even life itself simultaneously visible. It's no wonder that among nimbly philosophic poems about Arachne, Cain, and a painting by Velázquez he disarms, charms, and intrigues his readers with a witty and imaginative tribute to the tabletop sculptures of Saul Steinberg and a bittersweet remembrance of George Moran, an old vaudevillian." Booklist

Hong, Cathy Park, 1976-
Engine empire; Cathy Park Hong. W.W. Norton & Co. 2012 95 p. **811**
1. Art -- Poetry 2. East Asian poetry 3. Computers -- Poetry 4. Poetry -- Collections 5. Frontier and pioneer life -- West (U.S.) -- Poetry
ISBN 0393082849; 9780393082845
LC 2012000596

"Engine Empire is a trilogy of lyric and narrative poems that evoke an array of genres and voices. . . . The first sequence, called 'Ballad of Our Jim,' draws inspiration from the Old West and follows a band of outlaw fortune seekers who travel to a California mining town during the 1800s. In the second sequence, 'Shangdu, My Artful Boomtown!' a fictional industrialized boomtown draws its inspiration from present-day Shenzhen, China. The third and last section, 'The World Cloud,' is set in the far future and tracks how individual consciousness breaks up when everything--books, our private memories--becomes immediately accessible data." (Publisher's note)

"The middle and final sections of this triptych are stronger than the first, where sound gets the better of sense, but much of this book is deliciously inventive. . . . A smart, disorienting look at our present-future set out in a rich hybrid language." LJ

Howard, Richard

★ **Inner** voices; selected poems, 1963-2003. Farrar, Straus and Giroux 2004 428p $35 **811**

1. Poetry -- By individual authors
ISBN 0-374-25862-7

LC 2004-40464

The author "chooses artists and art as the personae and subjects of many of his poems. . . . Besides artists, Howard often chooses writers as personae, including prominent Victorians (Whitman, Ruskin and Browning); correspondents with other writers and artists; and increasingly, himself as traveler, museumgoer, and engaged reader." Booklist

★ The **silent** treatment; new poems. Turtle Point Press 2005 114p pa $16.95 **811**

1. Poetry -- By individual authors
ISBN 1-885586-38-3

LC 2004-113837

Hannah Arendt, George Eliot, Cosima Wagner, and a boy in a photograph by Arkansas photographer Mike Disfarmer are among the speakers in this collection.

"In characterizing the poems of Richard Howard's latest collection, one is tempted to bypass 'golden' as a description and head straight on to platinum. Now in his eighth decade, Howard has long been–along with the late James Merrill, who jokingly coined the phrase–one of American poetry's 'Great Fancies.'" Wkly Stand

Without saying; new poems. Turtle Point Press 2008 108p pa $16.95 **811**

1. Poetry -- By individual authors
ISBN 978-1-933527-14-7 pa; 1-933527-14-5 pa

LC 2007-907229

"In this 14th collection of his own verse, [the author] returns to the kinds of poems that made him famous: elaborate dramatic monologues, impersonations and dialogues that are intricately alert to literary history and sexual desire. . . . In these thoughtful new poems, Howard offers, and excels in, sophisticated verbal comedy." Publ Wkly

Howe, Fanny, 1940-

Second childhood; Fanny Howe. Graywolf Press 2014 80 p. (alk. paper) $16 **811**

1. Chance 2. Poetry
ISBN 1555976824; 9781555976828

LC 2013958013

National Book Award Shortlist: Poetry (2014)

In this poetry collection by Fanny Howe "the observing poet is an impersonal figure who accompanies Howe in her encounters with chance and mystery. She is not one age or the other, in one time or another. Fanny Howe's poetry is known for its lyricism, fragmentation, experimentation, religious engagement, and commitment to social justice." (Publisher's note)

"Howe may occupy some familiar and traditional poetic spaces, but she populates them beautifully." Pub Wkly

Howe, Susan

Souls of the Labadie tract. New Directions Books 2007 127p pa $16.95 **811**

1. Poetry -- By individual authors
ISBN 978-0-8112-1718-7; 0-8112-1718-3

LC 2007-34255

"In her newest book, Howe stands in thrall to a 17th-century history of Deerfield, Mass., and then chases down an obscure reference to 'Labadist' in Wallace Stevens's family tree, which brings her to the story of a short-lived Utopian 'quietest sect,' followers of Jean de Labadie who established a community in Maryland in 1684 that vanished within 40 years. It is in these vast tracts of time made intimate by texts, by language, that Howe operates. . . . Beginning with a quote from Jonathan Edwards equating the silkworm to 'a type of Christ' and ending with a photograph of a fragment of the silk wedding dress of Edwards's wife, onto which Howe projects a text ('I have already shown that space is God'), this is intense stuff." Publ Wkly

That this. New Directions Pub. 2010 109p il pa $15.95 **811**

1. Poetry -- By individual authors
ISBN 978-0-8112-1918-1 pa; 0-8112-1918-6 pa

LC 2010-41791

"Death is one of the preeminent subjects of poetry, and Howe . . . approaches this topic with the gravitas of one who has endured loss. . . . [This] volume deals chiefly with the death of her husband, Peter Hare. The book juxtaposes Howe's personal recollections with excerpts from an assortment of documents, ranging from 18th-century diaries to an array of half-decayed ephemera, such as bits of Poussin prints and fragments of linguistic sculpture. . . . An intelligent and unorthodox treatment of grief, this title will appeal to poetry and visual arts enthusiasts." Libr J

Hughes, Langston

Selected poems of Langston Hughes; drawings by E. McKnight Kauffer. Knopf 1959 297p il hardcover o.p. pa $13.95 **811**

1. Poetry -- By individual authors
ISBN 0-679-72818-X; 978-0-679-72818-4

This collection represents Langston Hughes' own decisions as to which of his poems he wanted to preserve and reprint

Hugo, Richard, 1923-1982

Making certain it goes on; the collected poems of Richard Hugo. Norton 1983 xxi, 456p hardcover o.p. pa $19.95 **811**

1. Poetry -- By individual authors
ISBN 0-393-30784-0; 978-0-393-30784-9

LC 83-8016

This book gathers the verse of the American poet.

"Though he would never be a serene poet, his collected poems show Hugo turning toward a calm peace that would mark his best work in 'White Center' (1980) and 'The Right Madness On Skye' (1981), and in the 22 new poems in this volume. . . . Among the new poems included [here] Hugo was still driving, looking, and naming. If we had not noticed before that his great gift was the elegy, we see it now." N Y Times Book Rev

The **Hungry** Ear; poems of food & drink. edited by Kevin Young. St Martins Pr 2012 336 p. $25 **811**
1. Food -- Poetry 2. Poetry -- Collections
ISBN 1608195511; 9781608195510

This book, edited by Kevin Young, is a collection of poems related to food. "While some of the poems here are explicitly about the food itself: the blackberries, the butter, the barbecue--all are evocative of the experience of eating. Many of the poems are also about the everything else that accompanies food: the memories, the company, even the politics. . . . Poets include: Elizabeth Alexander, Elizabeth Bishop, Billy Collins, Mark Doty, Robert Frost, [and] Allen Ginsberg." (Publisher's note)

Huntington, Cynthia
Heavenly bodies; Cynthia Huntington. Southern Illinois University Press 2012 vii, 75 p.p (pbk. : alk. paper) $15.95 **811**
1. Nineteen sixties 2. Addiction -- Poetry 3. Sexual liberation -- Poetry
ISBN 0809330636; 0809330644; 9780809330638; 9780809330645
LC 2011022095

In this "collection of lyric poems, Cynthia Huntington gives an intimate view of the sexual revolution and rebellion in a time before the rise of feminism. 'Heavenly Bodies' is a testament to the duality of sex, the twin seductiveness and horror of drug addiction, and the social, political, and personal dramas of America in the 1960s." (Publisher's note)
Includes bibliographical references (p. 74-75)

Ignatow, David
I have a name. University Press of New England 1996 75p (Wesleyan poetry) hardcover o.p. pa $13.95 **811**
1. Poetry -- By individual authors
ISBN 978-0-8195-2240-5; 0-8195-2240-6
LC 96-19350

"Ignatow's words are spare and apparently casual, holding us riveted by the force of what is articulated but not spoken. . . . The subjects are timeless: loss, age, death, the joy of fleeting moments." Booklist

Shadowing the ground. Wesleyan Univ. Press 1991 68p (Wesleyan poetry) hardcover o.p. pa $13.95 **811**
1. Poetry -- By individual authors
ISBN 978-0-8195-1197-3; 0-8195-1197-8
LC 90-20872

"Here are sixty-five short, spare, untitled poems, their uniformity of appearance (two-thirds of them ten lines or fewer) belying the plural perspectives that David Ignatow brings to his considerations of age and death's imminence. . . . Shadowing the Ground celebrates contrary responses to unplanned obsolescence." World Lit Today

Jackson, Major
Holding company. W.W. Norton & Co. 2010 91p $24.95 **811**
1. Poetry -- By individual authors
ISBN 978-0-393-07080-4
LC 2010-17728

"The sonnet sequence has been a staple of love poetry; Major Jackson tries here a sequence of tenline poems, instead of the fourteen of the sonnet, and the form, as always, pressures the poet toward specific meanings. There is greater urgency to get to the point, and it makes the expression of love only more dire, more taut and almost unmanageable. The effect of these poems individually is a certain serenity, a distance toward public turmoil, but cumulatively they amount to a desperate rebellion, a willful declaration of immortality." Huffington Post

Hoops; poems. Norton 2006 125p $23.95 **811**
1. Poetry -- By individual authors
ISBN 0-393-05937-5; 978-0-393-05937-3
LC 2005-33320

The author's "poems are witty, musical, and intelligent; he is equally happy discussing the war on terror . . . or describing early crushes." New Yorker

Jacobsen, Josephine
In the crevice of time; new and collected poems. Johns Hopkins Univ. Press 1995 258p (Johns Hopkins, poetry and fiction) hardcover o.p. pa $25 **811**
1. Poetry -- By individual authors
ISBN 978-0-8018-6339-4; 0-8018-6339-2
LC 95-2798

"In this retrospective spanning nearly six decades of distinguished poetry, the best work comes at the beginning and the end. A contemporary of Robert Penn Warren and Elizabeth Bishop, Jacobsen continues to write stately poems informed by irony, fatalism, and an eloquent appreciation of strength in all its guises, physical and moral. An unabashed formalist, she carefully composes poems that are aggressively metrical . . . and whose surfaces are dense with metaphor, rhyme, assonance, alliteration, and omniscient authority." Libr J

Jarrell, Randall
★ The **complete** poems. Farrar, Straus & Giroux 1969 507p hardcover o.p. pa $22 **811**
1. Poetry -- By individual authors
ISBN 0-374-51305-8 pa

Collected here are the entire contents of three published volumes Selected poems (1955), The woman at the Washington Zoo (1960), and The Lost World (1965) plus poems published from 1934 to 1964 but never collected and some never before published

Jazz poems. Alfred A. Knopf 2006 256p (Everyman's library pocket poets) $12.50 **811**
1. Jazz music -- Poetry 2. American poetry -- Collections
ISBN 978-1-4000-4251-7; 1-4000-4251-8

A collection of poetry inspired by jazz music. Includes poems by Langston Hughes, E. E. Cummings, William Carlos Williams, Frank O'Hara, Gwendolyn Brooks, Yusef Komunyakaa, Charles Simic, Rita Dove, Ntozake Shange, Mark Doty, William Matthews, and C. D. Wright, among others.

Jeffers, Robinson

The **selected** poetry of Robinson Jeffers; edited by Tim Hunt. Stanford Univ. Press 2001 758p pa $34.95   **811**

1. Poetry -- By individual authors

ISBN 978-0-8047-4108-8; 0-8047-4108-5

LC 00-48490

"Hunt's edition strips the punctuation added by contemporary printers (which 'often obscures the rhythm and pacing of what Jeffers actually wrote, and at points even obscures meaning and nuance') and includes a carefully weighed choice of long and short works, as well as unpublished work. . . . This new selection will get readers closer than ever to the poems as Jeffers himself saw them." Publ Wkly

Johnson, James Weldon

Complete poems; edited with an introduction by Sondra Kathryn Wilson. Penguin Bks. 2000 xxxiii, 202p pa $14   **811**

1. Poetry -- By individual authors

ISBN 0-14-118545-7

LC 00-39969

This volume contains Fifty years and other poems (1917), God's trombones (1927), Saint Peter relates an incident of the resurrection day (1935), and a number of previously unpublished poems. The editor's introduction considers Johnson's achievements and influence

Includes bibliographical references

Johnson, Peter

Rants and raves; selected and new prose poems. White Pine Press 2010 107p pa $16   **811**

1. Poetry -- By individual authors

ISBN 978-1-935210-06-1; 1-935210-06-8

"In the course of reading and rereading his poems one may be reminded of a range of writers, ancient and modern, including Theophrastus, Baudelaire, John Berryman, James Thurber (oh yes!). Peter Johnson represents a big constituency, but always concretely. 'American Male, Acting Up' begins: 'They say your whole life flashes before you when you die, but I'm sure I'll witness the lives of others.' These pages swarm with the lives of others, most particularly 'Peter Johnson,' who rants and raves like any free-mouthed cynic of the good old empire. . . . Savage indignation aside, Johnson is a great poet of friendship and family life. His book brims with wild wisdom, aching longing, tenderness, and most importantly, laughter." Providence J

Johnson, Ronald

The **shrubberies**; edited by Peter O'Leary. Flood Editions 2001 136p pa $14   **811**

1. Poetry -- By individual authors

ISBN 0-9710059-0-7

LC 2002-279220

This "book consists of a loosely linked sequence written in the last years of the poet's life. With their brevity and almost microscopic wordplay, the poems resemble epigrams. But where epigrams click into place, these poems leave implications floating. . . . The pleasure and insight of these poems come from more than prosodic specifics. Unlike so many 'experimental poets,' Johnson writes from necessity. As Peter O'Leary explains in his eloquent afterword, Johnson had a 'sense that these poems completed his work as a poet.' Several of the poems address mortality with starkness and force." Poetry (Modern Poetry Association)

Johnston, Devin

★ **Traveler**. Farrar, Straus and Giroux 2011 67p $23   **811**

1. Poetry -- By individual authors

ISBN 978-0-374-27933-2; 0-374-27933-0

LC 2011-08457

This collection brings Johnston's "careful, graceful, almost neoclassical pen to scenes from all over the world—Japan, Shanghai, 'the Mongol steppes,' the Midwest 'when a thunderstorm/ trundles down the Wabash,' and the Scottish holy isle of Iona. . . . Sometimes sublime, more often astringent, Johnston's poems of places and things seen—they make up most of the volume—should please fans of that older world traveler, August Kleinzahler. Yet Johnston may be most original when his subjects turn up close to home: his cool temperament meets its fruitful complement when he writes of family and children, most of all his young daughter, who in the brief, fine triptych entitled 'Appetites' 'lies awake/ talking in confidential tones/ with one she calls/ my friend who eats me.' It would take a hard heart to resist such humor, such warmth, set amid such control as Johnston shows." Publ Wkly

Jones, Saeed

★ **Prelude** to bruise; Poetry. by Saeed Jones. First edition Coffee House Press 2014 124 p. (pbk.) $16   **811**

1. Poetry 2. American poetry -- 21st century

ISBN 1566893747; 9781566893749

LC 2014008086

Stonewall Book Award: Literature (2015)

In this poetry collection, by Saeed Jones, the author "has crafted a fever dream, something akin to magic. A dark night of the soul presented as the finest of evening gowns, these poems pulse with an elemental sensuality. . . . Using a personal symbology of femininity, violence, and the history of black America, Jones weaves a coming-of-age tale that is both terrible and revelatory." (Publishers' Weekly)

"In these searing, searching meditations on masculinity, race, and love, poet and Buzzfeed LGBT editor Jones peels back layers of beauty and pain." LJ

Jordan, June

★ **Directed** by desire; the collected poems of June Jordan. edited by Jan Heller Levi and Sara Miles. Copper Canyon Press 2005 649p $40   **811**

1. Poetry -- By individual authors

ISBN 1-55659-228-0

LC 2005-11701

Jordan's poems "consistently display a loving devotion to black English and pride in her femininity, race, and individuality. Directed by Desire is an important addition to African American or feminist poetry collections." Booklist

Justice, Donald Rodney

★ **Collected** poems. Knopf 2004 288p $25 **811**
1. Poetry -- By individual authors
ISBN 1-4000-4239-9

LC 2003-65735

"Though its primary subject is the past, his work as a whole is more extraordinarily present—more thrillingly contemporary—than most of the styles that have advertised their commitment to 'making it new' over the past half-century." N Y Times Book Rev

Kasischke, Laura

Space, in chains. Copper Canyon Press 2011 113p pa $16 **811**
1. Poetry -- By individual authors
ISBN 978-1-55659-333-8; 1-55659-333-3

LC 2010-40037

"Known for her representations of mothers and teenagers in her poems and in her many novels, Kasischke now takes equal interest in illness and old age: rightly celebrated for her irregular, spiky, and intricately rhyming lines, Kasischke has now extended her interest (begun with her last book, Lilies Without) in the prose poem, using its fragments for recollection. . . . For all its length and all its lists, the volume ends up tightly, almost wrenchingly focused on the omnipresence of suffering, the fact of mortality and the persistence of grief. Some readers might call it melodramatic; many more ought to call it symphonic, perceptive, profound." Publ Wkly

Kelly, Robert

Lapis; poems. Godine 2005 221p pa $18.95 **811**
1. Poetry -- By individual authors
ISBN 1-57423-186-3

LC 2004-16724

This collection "offers dream narratives, elegies, prayers, anecdotes, parables, dialogues, and folktales from a land that may not exist. . . . Kelly has done something remarkable. He has given magic back its dignity, finding it in human warmth." Bookforum

Red actions; selected poems, 1960-1993. Black Sparrow Press 1995 398p hardcover o.p. pa $18.95 **811**
1. Poetry -- By individual authors
ISBN 978-0-87685-977-3; 0-87685-977-5

LC 95-35351

"In more than 35 collections of poetry, Kelly has utterly failed at one thing: to pigeonhole himself into predictability. This rich selection from more than a quarter-century of work contains imagistic bits that seem like fragments of poetic tapestry, long surreal narratives, series poems, and sonorous chants. Whatever the form, they are marked by Kelly's erudition, which covers Greek archaeology as readily as twentieth-century music, Sumerian gods as well as contemporary painting. Yet his work is never merely academic, inspired as it is by a passionate intellect reminiscent of Wallace Stevens. This survey may draw him more of the readers he well deserves." Booklist

Kendall, Tim

The **art** of Robert Frost; Tim Kendall. Yale University Press 2012 xvi, 392 p.p (cloth : alk. paper) $35 **811**
ISBN 0300118139; 9780300118131

LC 2011041416

"This book presents a . . . selection of sixty-five poems from across [Robert] Frost's writing career, beginning in the 1890s and ending with . . . the 1940s. . . . In addition to close readings of the poems, 'The Art of Robert Frost' traces the development of Frost's writing career and relevant aspects of his life. The book also assesses . . . the poet's style, how it changes over time, and how it relates to the works of contemporary poets and movements, including Modernism." (Publisher's note)

Includes bibliographical references (p. 385-388) and index.

Kenner, Hugh

The **Pound** era. University of Calif. Press 1971 606p il hardcover o.p. pa $26.95 **811**
1. Poets 2. Authors 3. Literary critics 4. Poetry -- By individual authors
ISBN 978-0-520-02427-4; 0-520-02427-3

"As a reader of Pound, Kenner is superb. He moves with ease and authority through the most tangled passages of allusion, ideogram and fragments of Greek and Latin." N Y Times Book Rev

Includes bibliographical references

Kenyon, Jane

★ **Collected** poems. Graywolf Press 2005 357p $26 **811**
1. Poetry -- By individual authors
ISBN 1-55597-428-7

"This collected edition reproduces verbatim the four books Kenyon saw through to press; the poems from two posthumous collections, Otherwise and A Hundred White Daffodils; Kenyon's translations of Akhmatova; and four previously uncollected poems. . . . Taken as a whole, Kenyon's poems remain a sustaining record of a life staked out in very difficult terrain." Publ Wkly

Kerouac, Jack

Book of blues. Penguin Bks. 1995 273p (Penguin poets) pa $13.95 **811**
1. Poetry -- By individual authors
ISBN 0-14-058700-4

LC 94-45902

A "set of eight previously unpublished 'blues' poems written between 1954 and 1961. These long poems, series of 'choruses' or sketches, resemble, in form and avidity, Kerouac's amazing verse creation Mexico City Blues (1959). They are strongly tied to place and are, as the allusion to music implies, boldly improvisational." Booklist

★ **Book** of sketches, 1952-53; introduction by George Condo. Penguin Books 2006 413p (Penguin poets) pa $18 **811**
1. Poetry -- By individual authors
ISBN 978-0-14-200215-5; 0-14-200215-1

LC 2005-44535

"Somewhere between diary, verbal sketchbook and play-by-play account of whatever passed before his eyes, this collection of poems transcribed from notebooks Kerouac kept in his pocket between 1952 and 1954 turns out to rank with his most interesting work. . . . Kerouac hits all the notes for which he and his fellow beats are known. While not everything here is golden, the immediacy and unpretentiousness of this off-the-cuff writing makes it an intimate glimpse into the consciousness of a man who simply couldn't stop observing." Publ Wkly

Pomes all sizes; introduction by Allen Ginsberg. City Lights Bks. 1992 175p pa $13.95   **811**
1. Poetry -- By individual authors
ISBN 0-87286-269-0
LC 92-1204
"This book, which Kerouac prepared for publication before his death in 1969, collects poems written between 1954 and 1965. Most are playful—comments about friends, variations on the sounds of words. Yet a few extremely sensitive longer pieces appear, including 'Caritas,' in which the poet runs after a barefoot beggar boy to give him money for shoes and then begins to doubt the boy's veracity. Other intriguing poems reflect the poet's religious concerns of the moment, running the gamut of Eastern and Western religions." Libr J

Scattered poems. City Lights Bks. 1971 76p pa $7.95   **811**
1. Poetry -- By individual authors
ISBN 0-87286-064-7
This collection "contains poems that either have previously appeared in periodicals or have not appeared in print at all. The poems are delightfully representative of Kerouac: that free and easy style of writing from the music of the imagination, without a score to follow. Those familiar with the San Francisco school of poetry will readily see Kerouac's affinity in style and content with such writers as Rexroth, Everson, Snyder, Ferlinghetti, Ginsberg, et al. . . . Kerouac sings in the American language to an American tune." Libr J

Kinnell, Galway
A **new** selected poems. Houghton Mifflin 2000 173p hardcover o.p. pa $14   **811**
1. Poetry -- By individual authors
ISBN 978-0-618-15445-6; 0-618-15445-0
LC 99-48904
"New England resides in these pages. Kinnell is a native of America's first literary region. Cold snow and clear nights work their way into his poems. The sounds of the woods are everywhere. But these sounds do not echo Emerson. Like any good transcendentalist, Kinnell sees the spiritual in material things." Christ Sci Monit

Strong is your hold. Houghton Mifflin 2006 69p $25; pa $14.95   **811**
1. Poetry -- By individual authors
ISBN 978-0-618-22497-5; 0-618-22497-1; 978-0-547-05366-0 pa; 0-547-05366-5 pa
LC 2006-11292
"To many readers, the most appealing of these poems will be the half dozen in which the aging poet writes about

his wife: cuddling with her in sleep, making love with startling ferocity, waking to find they are holding hands, preparing to say goodbye if one dies before the other. Getting old, as we've heard, is not for sissies. The poet who once chased bears may have slowed a step, but here he's still making like Johnny Cash as he walks the line between sex and death, the odd and the normal, domesticity and wildness, this world and the next. . . . 'Strong Is Your Hold' comes with a CD of Kinnell reading his work in a steady, pleasant voice." N Y Times Book Rev

Kirby, David
Talking about movies with Jesus; poems. Louisiana State University Press 2011 70p (Southern messenger poets) $50; pa $17.95   **811**
1. Poetry -- By individual authors
ISBN 978-0-8071-3771-0; 0-8071-3771-5; 978-0-8071-3772-7 pa; 0-8071-3772-3 pa
LC 2010-24229
"David Kirby's poems will put you and your imagination on a jet plane and fly you both around the world. They'll take you to Italy and France or into conversations with Jesus and Elvis. They'll even force all of you serious critics to crack a smile." Flashpoint

Kizer, Carolyn
Cool, calm & collected; poems 1960-2000. Copper Canyon Press 2000 509p $30; pa $20   **811**
1. Poetry -- By individual authors
ISBN 1-55659-146-2; 1-55659-181-0 pa
LC 00-10243
Kizer "covers civil rights, women's rights and almost everything in between, but even when she's writing about more intimate matters, her underlying concern is freedom. . . . Despite her constant railing against the machine, however, Kizer's poetry remains fundamentally optimistic, perhaps because she seems to love existence almost in spite of herself." N Y Times Book Rev

Kleinzahler, August
Sleeping it off in Rapid City; poems, new and selected. Farrar, Straus and Giroux 2008 234p $26   **811**
1. Poetry -- By individual authors
ISBN 978-0-374-26583-0; 0-374-26583-6
LC 2007-41926
This is a collection of poetry by the author of Earthquake Weather (1989), Red Sauce, Whiskey, and Snow (1996), and Live from the Hong Kong Nile Club (2000).
The author "writes most often in a strongly accented free verse that is among the most articulate and alive sounds American poetry is currently making. He plays effortlessly with forms, voices, registers. And his range of cultural reference—from Catullus to Custer, from Lorca to Eric Dolphy—is wide and artfully deployed. Rarely does high, learned poetic art sound this casual." N Y Times (Late N Y Ed)

Klink, Joanna

Raptus. Penguin Books 2010 60p (Penguin poets) pa $18 **811**

1. Poetry -- By individual authors

ISBN 978-0-14-311772-8; 0-14-311772-6

LC 2010-08246

"What happens when a relationship fails? Klink gets into the nooks and crannies of that question in her third collection. She sinks into every aspect of the life past and present. . . . She has a rhythmic dedication, a sense that every last emotional corner will be examined in its own time and a keen focus aimed as much at herself as at others. As it cycles through need and loss, this book illuminates just how inextricable experiences can be from the people with whom they are shared." Publ Wkly

Includes bibliographical references

Knott, Bill

The **unsubscriber**. Farrar, Straus and Giroux 2004 122p $20; pa $13 **811**

1. Poetry -- By individual authors

ISBN 978-0-374-26415-4; 0-374-26415-5; 978-0-374-53014-3 pa; 0-374-53014-9 pa

LC 2004-41160

"Knott's talent for compression—his awareness of the physicality of language—has remained undiminished since his youth, surfacing in one poem after another. . . . Like a gifted composer also capable of brilliantly playing every instrument in the orchestra, Knott possesses talent beyond the average allotment. In all fairness, you are not likely to find a more imaginative and provocative book of poetry published in the last year than The Unsubscriber, but neither will you find one that can be more at odds with itself." Am Book Rev

Knox, Jennifer L.

The **mystery** of the hidden driveway. Bloof Books 2010 83p pa $15 **811**

1. Poetry -- By individual authors

ISBN 978-0-9826587-1-0

"If Jennifer L. Knox is a lot of 'fun,' she is also one of the bluntest, most cutting poets in the country. And one of the most consistent — The Mystery of the Hidden Driveway is her best book yet, full of ridiculous characters, speedy narratives of scotch-taped sex and drugs, of emotional instabilities that are likeable and addictive. This is a book of odd and unexpected pleasures, a reminder that if nothing is sacred, everything is." Coldfront

Koch, Kenneth

★ The **collected** poems of Kenneth Koch. Knopf 2005 761p $40 **811**

1. Poetry -- By individual authors

ISBN 1-4000-4499-5

LC 2004-63827

"The products of a lifetime of continual inventing are beautifully on display in this awe-inspiring banquet of a book." Publ Wkly

On the edge; collected long poems. Alfred A. Knopf 2007 411p $35 **811**

1. Poetry -- By individual authors

ISBN 978-0-307-26284-4; 0-307-26284-7

LC 2007-24041

"A principal force behind the New York School of poets that flourished at mid-century, Kenneth Koch never quite won the pride of place occupied by the likes of Frank O'Hara and John Ashbery. This volume compiles Koch's long poems, making an eloquent argument for his unique stature." New York

Koertge, Ron

The **ogre's** wife; poems. Ron Koertge. Red Hen Press 2013 80 p. $17.95 **811**

1. Poetry -- Collections

ISBN 1597097233; 9781597097239

LC 2013004265

In this collection of poems, Ronald Koertge "introduces readers to Little Red Riding Hood all grown up with a fondness for salsa and chips, explores the thorny relationship of Jackie Robinson and Pee Wee Reese, spies a Trojan pony and the children it bamboozles, and offers an alternate reading to the Icarus story. He meets Walt Whitman on the set of an X-rated movie, attends his gardener's funeral, and goes to his beloved race track." (Publisher's note)

Komunyakaa, Yusef

The **chameleon** couch; poems. Farrar, Straus and Giroux 2011 115p il $24 **811**

1. Poetry -- By individual authors

ISBN 978-0-374-12038-2; 0-374-12038-2

LC 2010-33148

In this collection, the author "shares unusually personal reflections steeped in his intimacy with ancestors, gods, and monsters. These finely formed lyrics are timeless in their shadows and wounds, and startlingly fresh in mood, metaphor, image, and such pairings as gargoyles and power lines, sugar and salt." Booklist

Talking dirty to the gods; poems. Farrar, Straus & Giroux 2000 134p hardcover o.p. pa $13 **811**

1. Poetry -- By individual authors

ISBN 0-374-52793-8 pa

LC 00-21277

"Komunyakaa's mournful surrealism seems to have found a perfect mathematical embodiment in this . . . collection, which comprises a hundred and thirty-two poems of four four-line stanzas. These are poems about the uncontrollable human and natural mysteries, and they are made sharper and more mysterious by the eternal recurrence of the stanzaic structure." New Yorker

Thieves of paradise. University Press of New England 1998 128p (Wesleyan poetry) $26; pa $14.95 **811**

1. Poetry -- By individual authors
ISBN 0-8195-6330-7; 0-8195-6422-2 pa

LC 97-40294

"The central subjects of Komunyakaa's poetry—his experiences in the Vietnam War and as an African-American male—have always been made compelling in his hands, and equally compelling has been the moodily energetic, jazz-inspired improvisatory technique that he employs with increasing mastery. But what is most gratifying about Komunyakaa's surrealist riffs, with their almost hallucinatory lushness, is their power to convince us that the individual imagination is more than equal to the most excruciating historical burden." New Yorker

Warhorses; poems. Farrar, Straus and Giroux 2008 86p $24 **811**

1. War poetry 2. Poetry -- By individual authors
ISBN 978-0-3742-8643-9; 0-3742-8643-4

LC 2007-51760

"The poems that comprise [this] new collection provide an astonishingly panoramic view of the totality of war. . . . Strongly recommended." Libr J

Kooser, Ted

Delights & shadows; poems. Copper Canyon Press 2004 87p pa $15 **811**

1. Poetry -- By individual authors
ISBN 1-55659-201-9

LC 2003-18447

These "poems reflect a joy for life through powerful human images and intimate observations of everyday things." Booklist

Flying at night; poems, 1965-1985. University of Pittsburgh Press 2005 142p (Pitt poetry series) $24.95; pa $14.95 **811**

1. Poetry -- By individual authors
ISBN 0-8229-4258-5; 0-8229-5877-5 pa

LC 2004-28397

"There is a simplicity to these poems, a healthy, peaceful spirit. . . . Kooser is a skilled craftsman, with a sharp eye and fine ear." Libr J

Kumin, Maxine

Connecting the dots; poems. Norton 1996 86p $18.95; pa $11.95 **811**

1. Poetry -- By individual authors
ISBN 0-393-03962-5; 0-393-31695-5 pa

LC 95-44441

"Kumin's is a poetry of wide sympathy and tact in which the ecumenical flavor is dominant, starting with the author's description of herself as a 'Jewish agnostic' educated at a convent school. Here both the odd and the even are at home: New Hampshire farm country as well as cosmopolitan Boston, Heidegger and Berlioz interwoven among depictions of spring training, Bosnia, and a New Year's Eve party. This

collection is full of generational severance and renewal." New Yorker

Jack and other new poems. W.W. Norton & Co 2005 112p hardcover o.p. pa $13.95 **811**

1. Poetry -- By individual authors
ISBN 978-0-393-32852-3; 0-393-32852-X

LC 2004-21762

This collection of poetry "focuses on three subjects the poet knows well: first, the fauna (wild and domestic) in and around her New Hampshire farm; second, the troubles and lessons of advancing age; third, large-scale political history, 'this century born in blood and bombs' as this Jewish-American poet has known it. . . . Most of her strongest work (the title poem included) concerns elderly or deceased animals, obvious analogues for Kumin's ill, deceased or grieving human beings." Publ Wkly

The **long** marriage; poems. Norton 2001 118p $21; pa $12 **811**

1. Poetry -- By individual authors
ISBN 0-393-04351-7; 0-393-32437-0 pa

LC 2001-34553

"Although several of the poems treat Kumin's 50-plus year marriage, one feels that the book's title may refer to 'marriage' as a kind of covenant between the poet and her environment. . . . Divided into seven sections, this collection also includes poems about sociopolitical situations (capital punishment, extinct wildlife, revolutions), considerations of aging and rehabilitation, and tributes to Hopkins, Wordsworth, Rukeyser, and Rilke." Libr J

Selected poems, 1960-1990. Norton 1997 294p $27.50; pa $17.95 **811**

1. Poetry -- By individual authors
ISBN 0-393-04073-9; 0-393-31836-2 pa

LC 96-42433

"A pastoral poet who was strongly influenced by friend and mentor Anne Sexton, Kumin is quite simply one of the very best poets writing today. The present collection represents a lifetime . . . of Kumin's work and includes selections from all her published volumes." Libr J

Kunitz, Stanley

★ The **collected** poems. Norton 2000 285p $27.95; pa $15.95 **811**

1. Poetry -- By individual authors
ISBN 0-393-05030-0; 0-393-32294-7 pa

LC 00-41130

"What makes this collection of a lifetime's work so valuable is the way it allows us to perceive the interconnectedness of all Kunitz has written. Each poem stands alone, but each also enriches the others." N Y Times Book Rev
Includes bibliographical references

Kyger, Joanne

About now; collected poems. National Poetry Foundation 2007 798p il $49.95; pa $34.95 **811**

1. Poetry -- By individual authors
ISBN 978-0-943373-72-0; 0-943373-72-7; 978-0-943373-71-3 pa; 0-943373-71-9 pa

LC 2006-48192

This volume "begins with poems of the 1950's, written when Kyger first came to San Francisco and joined the circle of poets around Robert Duncan and Jack Spicer, and ends with Night Palace, poems written in 2003 to 2004. . . . What is exciting about Kyger's poetry is the way she highlights moments which might seem mundane, but under her perceptive eye connect the individual with a greater reality, opening readers' awareness in the process. That immersion in the details of everyday life, quail crossing a yard, a phone call from a friend, or a retelling of last night's dream, is plumbed by Kyger to great depth and is epitomized by the collection's title." Jacket

Includes bibliographical references

Lang, Sarah

For Tamara; Sarah Lang. Anansi 2014 83 p. (pbk.) $19.95 **811**
1. Life skills 2. Motherhood -- Poetry
ISBN 1770893679; 9781770893672; 9781770893689; 9781770898097
LC 2013456916

This book, by Sarah Lang, "ostensibly intended as a document of essential practical and emotional advice, this handbook ultimately acts as a reassuring record of help and of hope. Anticipating her daughter's needs, from basic necessities and medical care to law and order, literature, science, and family, the mother provides her daughter with the means to persist in the face of adversity, disaster, and the everyday." (Publisher's note)

Larkin, Philip

The **complete** poems; Philip Larkin; edited by Archie Burnett. Farrar, Straus and Giroux 2012 729 p. **811**
1. English poetry 2. Poetry -- Collections 3. English poetry -- History and criticism
ISBN 0374126968; 9780374126964
LC 2011945978

This collection edited by Archie Burnett "brings together all of Philip Larkin's poems. In addition to those that appear in 'Collected Poems' (1988) and 'Early Poems and Juvenilia' (2005), some unpublished pieces from Larkin's typescripts and workbooks are included, as well as verse . . . that had been tucked away in his letters. . . . Larkin's poems are [also] given a comprehensive commentary. This . . . covers closely relevant historical contexts, persons and places, allusions and echoes, and linguistic usage. Prominence is given to the poet's comments on his own poems, which often outline the circumstances that gave rise to a poem or state what he was trying to achieve." (Publisher's note)

Laughlin, James

The **collected** poems of James Laughlin; with an introduction by Hayden Carruth. Moyer Bell 1994 xxxi, 574p il $34.95; pa $19.95 **811**
1. Poetry -- By individual authors
ISBN 978-1-559-21067-6; 1-559-21067-2; 978-1-559-21128-4 pa; 1-559-21128-8 pa
LC 91-32232

"These poems are the work of a man of keen intellectual and moral sophistication, who has read, thought, and lived deeply." Libr J

The **secret** room; poems. New Directions 1997 184p $22.95; pa $14.95 **811**
1. Poetry -- By individual authors
ISBN 0-8112-1343-9; 0-8112-1344-7 pa
LC 96-26188

Laughlin "shares his thoughts with humor and tenderness as he wades in the waters of his golden years. The speaker in many of these poems admires young women and thinks, 'I could see I was entirely out of/my depth.' He realizes he is not as strong as he once was, but he can still 'make old, sick words sound new.'" Libr J

Lauterbach, Ann

Or to begin again. Penguin Books 2009 115p (Penguin poets) pa $18 **811**
1. Poetry -- By individual authors
ISBN 978-0-14-311520-5; 0-14-311520-0
LC 2008-38414

"Intelligent but no less deeply feeling, this collection confirms Lauterbach's position as one of the most highly principled and tirelessly innovative poets writing today." Publ Wkly

Lax, Robert

Love had a compass; journals and poetry. edited by James J. Uebbing. Grove Press 1996 253p $22 **811**
1. Poetry -- By individual authors
ISBN 978-0-8021-1587-4; 0-8021-1587-X
LC 96-1255

The author has produced "some of the sparest imagist poetry in English with no thought about publishing where the literary high and mighty would read him. Lax dispenses with metaphor and largely with ego . . . to present what he sees with elemental forcefulness, as if in strong Mediterranean sunlight." Booklist

A **thing** that is; new poems. edited by Paul Spaeth. Overlook Press 1997 77p $25; pa $14.95 **811**
1. Poetry -- By individual authors
ISBN 978-0-87951-699-4; 0-8795-1699-2; 978-0-87951-885-1 pa; 0-87951-885-5 pa
LC 96-29264

"Given to short lines arranged in long columns, Lax's poems link the natural and personal in simple, direct, deadpan narration. The simplicity can be misleading, not in its initially unnoticed depth or metaphor but in its very purity, its almost ascetic singleness of purpose. . . . Lax has been working at the margins for a long time and has found a crisp and comfortable way of ordering and exploring his contemplations. This collection is not for everyone, but it is a essential for that special audience for truly avante-garde work." Libr J

Lazarus, Emma

Emma Lazarus; selected poems. John Hollander, editor. Library of America 2005 151p (American poets project) $20   **811**

1. Poetry -- By individual authors
ISBN 978-1-931082-77-8; 1-931082-77-4

                 LC 2004-61551

"At the age of eighteen [Lazarus] had written an impressive poem titled 'In the Jewish Synagogue at Newport,' which all readers recognized as a response to Longfellow's dignified and respectful poem about the Jewish cemetery there. . . . Lazarus became perhaps the most accomplished American writer of sonnets between the generations of Longfellow and Robert Frost. . . . [Her] remarkable 'Little Poems in Prose,' the title borrowed from Baudelaire, ranged with visionary power across centuries of Jewish experience." N Y Rev Books

Lee, Li-Young

Behind my eyes. W.W. Norton 2008 106p $24.95   **811**

1. Poetry -- By individual authors
ISBN 978-0-393-06542-8; 0-393-06542-1

"In this fourth collection by [the author], timely immigration issues drive such poems as 'Self-Help for Fellow Refugees,' but Lee swiftly folds them into broader inquiries about inheritance, memory and loss. . . . Lee's ringing clarity and his compelling life story have brought him uncommonly loyal readers: this volume should swell their ranks. A CD of Lee reading many of the poems is included." Publ Wkly

Leiter, Sharon

Critical companion to Emily Dickinson; a literary reference to her life and work. Facts on File 2006 448p il $75   **811**

1. Poets 2. Authors
ISBN 0-8160-5448-7; 978-0-8160-5448-0

                 LC 2005-28123

This book "opens with a foreword by poet and Dickinson scholar Gregory Orr and includes an introduction; an approximately 20-page biography of Dickinson; explications of 150 of her best-known poems (e.g., 'Because I Could Not Stop for Death'); an A-to-Z dictionary of relevant persons, places, and ideas illustrated with black-and-white photos; a chronology; bibliographies; and a comprehensive index." Libr J

Includes bibliographical references

Lerner, Ben

Angle of yaw. Copper Canyon Press 2006 127p pa $15   **811**

1. Poetry -- By individual authors
ISBN 1-55659-246-9

                 LC 2006-14260

"Employing the language of aphorism, advertising, parable, personal essay, political tirade, journalism and journal, the collage-like poems of Lerner's . . . collection express the ennui of American life in an era when even war feels like a television event." Publ Wkly

Levertov, Denise

Selected poems; with a preface by Robert Creeley; edited and with an afterword by Paul Lacey. New Directions 2002 220p hardcover o.p. pa $14.95 **811**

1. Poetry -- By individual authors
ISBN 978-0-8112-1554-1; 0-8112-1520-2

                 LC 2002-11891

This volume "endeavors to do what all 'selecteds' do: give readers a chance to see for themselves the development of a poetic sensibility. Editor Paul A. Lacey has brought together poems from nearly every collection of Levertov's oeuvre, producing a catalogue of the wildly diverse subjects that engaged her throughout her long career. Here are poems about love and war, about religion and art, about sorrow and joy, about political resistance and familial intimacy and, perhaps most significantly for Levertov's legacy, numerous poems about the practice of poetry itself." Harvard Rev

Levine, Philip

Breath; poems. Knopf 2004 82 p. $23   **811**

1. Poetry -- By individual authors
ISBN 1400042917

                 LC 2004040839

This is a collection of poetry by the author of Ashes, What Work Is, and The Simple Truth.

The author writes "free verse about American manliness, physical labor, simple pleasures and profound grief, often set in working-class Detroit (where Levine grew up) or in central California (where he now resides), sometimes tinged with reference to his Jewish heritage or to the Spanish poets of rapt simplicity (Machado, Lorca) who remain his most visible influence. Levine's 18th book will neither disappoint his devotees nor silence the doubters." Publ Wkly

The **mercy**; poems. Knopf 1999 81p hardcover o.p. pa $16   **811**

1. Poetry -- By individual authors
ISBN 978-0-375-70135-1; 0-375-70135-4

                 LC 98-43353

"Levine's poetry has been steadily moving to the front rank of American poetry for three decades. . . . If Walt Whitman's vision contained multitudes, and if Emerson's vision of nature transcended what it saw with its own eyes, Levine's poetic vision, nearly religious, transcends class, transcends natural boundaries, and transcends time." Atl Mon

New selected poems. Knopf 1991 292p hardcover o.p. pa $20   **811**

1. Poetry -- By individual authors
ISBN 978-0-679-74056-8; 0-679-74056-2

                 LC 90-53422

This selection contains poems Levine chose for his earlier Selected poems (1984), plus 15 new works

"This is a monumental work that somehow remains wonderfully accessible, largely because Levine has chosen pieces carefully, favoring shorter works and poems that address his staple themes of family (like 'Uncle' and 'My Son and I') and childhood ('Coming Home'). Many of the poems are powerfully imagistic." Libr J

News of the world; poems. Alfred A Knopf 2009 65p $25   **811**
1. Poetry -- By individual authors
ISBN 978-0-307-27223-2
LC 2009-16517

A volume of prose poems and formal verses includes pieces on breakfasting late-shift Detroit auto workers, a woman who sings with the Spanish dawn, and an Andorran communist black-market supplier.

The author's "flirtations with death in both prose poems and formal verse have a weightiness that remains long after you close the book, . . . These poems exude a certain melancholia, but Levine's ability to examine expertly the beauty in this sadness keeps them from veering toward the unnecessarily depressing. He can paint even the strange with simple, natural language in a way that's subtly moving, and the nostalgic glow he applies to his memories makes this work the perfect addition to the oeuvre that has come to define his life." Libr J

The **simple** truth; poems. Knopf 1994 69p hardcover o.p. pa $16   **811**
1. Poetry -- By individual authors
ISBN 978-0-679-76584-4; 0-679-76584-0
LC 94-14508

This "collection of poetry is largely about the past: friends lost, fates assigned, potatoes eaten, decisions made. . . . Levine's mingling of realism and romanticism, involving many near-meetings between them, produces fascinating, emotionally persuasive shifts and tonal modulations that closely approach a lived truth." Publ Wkly

What work is; poems. Knopf 1991 77p hardcover o.p. pa $15   **811**
1. Poetry -- By individual authors
ISBN 978-0-679-74058-2; 0-679-74058-9
LC 90-53421

"This collection amounts to a hymn of praise for all the workers of America. These proletarian heroes, with names like Lonnie, Loo, Sweet Pea, and Packy, work the furnaces, forges, slag heaps, assembly lines, and loading docks at places with unglamorous names like Brass Craft or Feinberg and Breslin's First-Rate Plumbing and Plating. . . . But Levine's characters are also significant for their inner lives, not merely their jobs." Libr J

Lewis, Robin Coste
★ **Voyage** of the Sable Venus and other poems; Robin Coste Lewis. Alfred A. Knopf 2016 160 p. (hardcover) $26   **811**
1. Feminism 2. Black women
ISBN 9781101875438; 9781101911204; 1101875437
LC 2014047762
National Book Award: Poetry (2015)

Poet Robin Coste Lewis presents " this meditation on the black female figure throughout time. Lewis's electrifying collection is a triptych that begins and ends with lyric poems considering the roles desire and race play in the construction of the self." (Publisher's note)

"Lacking a coherence across the sections, this title reads like two separate books." LJ

Limon, Ada
Bright dead things; Poems. by Ada Limon. Milkweed Editions 2015 128 p. (alk. paper) $16 **811**
1. Poetry -- Collections
ISBN 1571314717; 9781571314710
LC 2015000088
National Book Award Finalist: Poetry (2015)
National Book Critics Circle Award Finalist: Poetry (2015)

This book of poems, by Ada Limon, "examines the chaos that is life, the dangerous thrill of living in a world you know you have to leave one day, and the search to find something that is ultimately 'disorderly, and marvelous, and ours.'" (Publisher's note)

"Recurring instances of anxiety about mortality in Limón's poems complicate experiences so richly written and felt." Pub Wkly.

Lindsay, Sarah
Twigs & knucklebones. Copper Canyon Press 2008 117p $15   **811**
1. Poetry -- By individual authors
ISBN 9781556591648 pa
LC 2008-19578

This is a book of poems by the author of Primate Behavior (1997) and Mount Clutter (2002).

"Sarah Lindsay uses oddities and 'flukes' as a point of entry to broader questions regarding fate, bygone civilizations, and human nature. Written in finely crafted narrative verse, her poems take place in a diverse set of locales, both ancient and contemporary, and often explore the intersection of the unfamiliar with the everyday. . . . [This] is an enigmatic, evocative, and compelling book." Pedestal

Liu, Xiaobo, 1955-
★ **June** fourth elegies; [Nian nian liu si / Liu Xiaobo]; translated from the Chinese by Jeffrey Yang; foreword by Dalai Lama. Liu Xiaobo. Jonathan Cape 2012 xxv, 228 p.p   **811**
1. China -- Poetry 2. Political activists 3. Human rights -- Poetry 4. Chinese poetry -- Collections 5. Tiananmen Square Incident, Beijing (China), 1989 -- Poetry 6. China -- History -- Tiananmen Square Incident, 1989 -- Poetry
ISBN 1555976107; 9780224096812
LC 2012427497

This book is the "first publication of the poetry of 2010 Nobel Peace Prize Winner Liu Xiaobo . . . [who is] the foremost symbol of the struggle for human rights in China. . . . 'June Fourth Elegies' presents Liu's poems written across twenty years in memory of fellow protestors at Tiananmen Square, as well as poems addressed to his wife, Liu Xia. In this bilingual volume, Liu's poetry is . . . published . . . in both English translation and in the Chinese original." (Publisher's Note)

"Xiaobo rebukes his nation, 'used to memorializing tombs as palaces,' and his 'city of near perfect/ shamelessness.' He also casts a harsh eye on himself . . . 'Even if I have the courage/ to be jailed again,' Xiaobo writes, 'it

isn't courage enough/ to excavate memories of the dead.'"
(Publishers Weekly)

Nian nian liu si

Logan, William

Our savage art; poetry and the civil tongue. Columbia University Press 2009 346p bibl $29.50 **811**

1. American poetry -- History and criticism

ISBN 978-0-231-14732-3; 0-231-14732-5

LC 2008-36414

This collection is "the latest installment in William Logan's prolonged and rumbustious assault on the state of American poetry. . . . The most obvious advantage of Logan's Diogenes-like approach to much of the contemporary poetry he writes about is that it transforms the normally rather stultifying genre of the poetry review into something more akin to a blood sport. Logan's hounding and slashing, parodying and chastising, make for what editors call good copy." N Y Times Book Rev

Includes bibliographical references (p. [341]-344) and index

Longfellow, Henry Wadsworth

★ Poems and other writings. Library of Am. 2000 854p $35 **811**

1. Poetry -- By individual authors

ISBN 1-88301-185-X

LC 00-26678

This volume includes "Hiawatha, Evangeline, The Courtship of Miles Standish and 'The Midnight Ride of Paul Revere.' Here, too, are some surprisingly powerful lyric and meditative poems—well made, deeply felt, and not much like the schoolhouse favorites." Publ Wkly

Includes bibliographical references

Lorde, Audre

The collected poems of Audre Lorde. Norton 1997 489p $35; pa $17.95 **811**

1. Poetry -- By individual authors

ISBN 0-393-04090-9; 0-393-31972-5 pa

LC 97-10878

"Since her death in 1992, Lorde's reputation has continued to grow. In life a tough, eloquent crusader who demanded that we honor the varieties of human experience, she retained her hold on readers despite the unavailability of much of her work. This edition, then, should be welcomed wherever there is interest in women's, minority, and lesbian literature. It includes Lorde's passionately private early work as well as her later, more obviously political work." Booklist

Lowell, Amy

Selected poems; Honor Moore, editor. Library of America 2004 xxxi, 156p (American poets project) $20 **811**

1. Poetry -- By individual authors

ISBN 978-1-93108-270-9; 1-93108-270-7

LC 2004-48505

This volume contains "the 'cadenced verse' of [Lowell's] Imagist . . . works, her experiments in 'polyphonic prose,' her narrative poetry, and her adaptations from the classical Chinese." Publisher's note

Lowell, Robert

★ Collected poems; edited by Frank Bidart and David Gewanter, with the editorial assistance of DeSales Harrison. Farrar, Straus & Giroux 2003 1186p il $45 **811**

1. Poetry -- By individual authors

ISBN 0-374-12617-8

This collection includes "Lowell's first book, Land of Unlikeness (1944); and poems from his 11 ensuing collections, including Life Studies (1959) and The Dolphin (1973). . . . Substantial notes, a chronology, glossary, and critical essays make this an essential title. Readers who think they know Lowell's work will discover new facets, and readers just venturing into Lowell's potently rendered and ceaselessly evocative poetic universe will find much to contemplate." Booklist

Includes bibliographical references

Selected poems; rev ed; Farrar, Straus & Giroux 1977 255p hardcover o.p. **811**

1. Poetry -- By individual authors

LC 78-104855

First published 1976

A selection of over 200 poems tracing the development of one of the premier confessional poets of his generation

Lucas, Dave

Weather; poems. University of Georgia Press 2011 68p pa $16.95 **811**

1. Poetry -- By individual authors

ISBN 978-0-8203-3882-8; 0-8203-3882-6

LC 2010-44222

"The first thing one notices in 'Weather,' Dave Lucas' first poetry collection, is the almost shocking formality of the language not in vocabulary so much as in a theatrical phrasing no longer so common in poetry. Lucas frequently writes things like 'I am also seething / in my depths,' which might not be so interesting were it not for the fact that the book's main subject is the contemporary Midwest, most often Cleveland and its surrounding environs, which for Lucas, is a landscape as mythic as Troy. . . . If Lucas' almost oracular tone occasionally spills over into melodrama, he makes up for it by the absolute beauty of so many of his lines and descriptions. . . . This is a lovely, promising and powerful first book, even more so for readers who know its landscape." Cleveland Plain Dealer

Includes bibliographical references

MacGowan, Christopher J.

Twentieth-century American poetry; [by] Christopher MacGowan. Blackwell Pub 2004 331p (Blackwell guides to literature) $66.95; pa $27.95 **811**

1. Poetry -- By individual authors 2. American poetry -- History and criticism

ISBN 0-631-22025-9; 0-631-22026-7 pa

LC 2003-12196

This guide explores the historical and cultural contexts within which twentieth-century American poetry was created and includes a biographical dictionary of such key writers

as Robert Frost, Ezra Pound, T. S. Eliot, Langston Hughes, James Dickey, Adrienne Rich, and Rita Dove
Includes bibliographical references

Mackey, Nathaniel
Splay anthem. New Directions Book 2006 126p pa $15.95 **811**
1. Poetry -- By individual authors
ISBN 0-8112-1652-7
LC 2005-35051
"Often turning adversity to their advantage, the poems sing not of resurrection but repair, and Splay Anthem is the most delicate and delirious installment of Mackey's epic song of salvage. Its poems speak with a torn voice, a rasp punctuated by gasps of anguish and rumbling with the desire for rejuvenation." Nation

MacLeish, Archibald
Collected poems, 1917-1982; with a prefatory note to the newly collected poems by Richard B. McAdoo. Houghton Mifflin 1985 524p hardcover o.p. pa $19 **811**
1. Poetry -- By individual authors
ISBN 0-395-39569-0 pa
LC 85-14392
Collects all the known poetry of the author/public servant. As an expatriate in Paris his early work was heavily influenced by Pound and Eliot. After returning to the States his verse concerned itself more with America's political, social, and cultural heritage

Manning, Maurice
The common man. Houghton Mifflin Harcourt 2010 96p $22 **811**
1. Poetry -- By individual authors
ISBN 978-0-547-24961-2; 0-547-24961-6
LC 2009-29080
"The book balances our cynical, back-foot expectations as readers of contemporary poetry with its own unpretentious ambition incredibly well—the natural world becomes strange in Manning's hands, but not unrecognizably so." Sycamore Rev

Mariani, Paul L.
The broken tower: a life of Hart Crane; [by] Paul Mariani. Norton 1999 492p il hardcover o.p. pa $15.95 **811**
1. Poets 2. Authors 3. Short story writers
ISBN 0-393-32041-3 pa
LC 98-37726
"Using unpublished letters, manuscripts, and photographs [Mariani] pieces together the life and passions of this brilliant yet tormented man whose creative genius left us 'The Bridge' and whose influence still reverberates among poets today." Libr J
Includes bibliographical references

Lost puritan: a life of Robert Lowell. Norton 1994 527p il hardcover o.p. pa $15 **811**
1. Poets 2. Authors
ISBN 0-393-31374-3 pa
LC 93-48018

"Mariani, for all his moment-by-moment acuteness and lucidity, offers no radically new insights into Lowell's life or art, nor does he provide those powerfully developed thematic and narrative lines that distinguish the greatest literary biographies. Still, this remains an impressive piece of writing and documentation." Choice

Matthews, William
After all; last poems. Houghton Mifflin 1998 55p hardcover o.p. pa $13 **811**
1. Poetry -- By individual authors
ISBN 0-618-05685-8 pa
LC 98-22909
"Since Matthews was one of the few contemporary poets who really knew how to make the vernacular sing, it's sad to think that these are his last poems. Fittingly, some of them are autumnal, but they range widely and brightly from Prague in 1419 to a Caribbean island in 1967 to Martha Mitchell, Finn sheep, and a poetry reading at West Point. A lovely finale." Libr J

Selected poems and translations, 1969-1991. Houghton Mifflin 1992 200p hardcover o.p. pa $22.95 **811**
1. Poetry -- By individual authors
ISBN 978-0-395-66993-8; 0-395-66993-6
LC 91-45716
"Matthews has been widely praised for the solid grounding of his poems, and rightly so. His clear-cut metaphors illuminate the everyday world with the magic of semantic revelation and the grace of othermindedness." Booklist

May, Jamaal
Hum; Jamaal May. Alice James Books 2013 80 p. (pbk.) $15.95 **811**
1. Poetry -- Collections
ISBN 1938584023; 9781938584022
LC 2013022185
In this collection of poems, by Jamaal May, "poems buzz and purr like a well-oiled chassis. Grit, trial, and song thrum through tight syntax and deft prosody. From the resilient pulse of an abandoned machine to the sinuous lament of origami animals, here is the ever-changing hum that vibrates through us all, connecting one mind to the next." (Publisher's note)
"May, a teacher, seems acutely aware of the injustices in our current condition, but he seeks to educate rather than preach; his poems, exquisitely balanced by a sharp intelligence mixed with earnestness, makes his debut a marvel." Pub Wkly

Mayer, Bernadette
Scarlet tanager. New Directions 2005 117p pa $14.95 **811**
1. Poetry -- By individual authors
ISBN 0-8112-1582-2
LC 2005-5539
This collection demonstrates Mayer's "ease in many poetic forms, her attraction to New York City and to the Berkshires (where she now lives), her recovery from a recent stroke and her continued enthusiastic enmeshment with writing itself." Publ Wkly

McClure, Michael

★ **Of** indigo and saffron; new and selected poems. edited and with an introduction by Leslie Scalapino. University of California Press 2011 319p **811**

1. Poetry -- By individual authors

ISBN 0-520-26287-5; 978-0-520-26287-4

LC 2010-32585

"Scalapino includes those parts of McClure's oeuvre that focus on the questioning of identity, the uncertain position of the self, and the irrelevance of the traditional lyric 'I,' the bete noire of language poets. But Scalapino's selections do give a broad taste of McClure's perennial concerns with the body, alternative forms of consciousness and environmentalism. . . . McClure invented a new form for himself: the poem centered in the middle of the page, with occasional lines in capital letters (he has insisted that these are not meant to be shouted), with the phrase or line equivalent to Olson's notion of whatever encompasses a breath. McClure has been able to accommodate every thematic concern, every mood and temperament, within this form's versatile parameters." San Francisco Chron

McGrath, Thomas

Letter to an imaginary friend. Copper Canyon Press 1997 413p pa $20 **811**

1. Poetry -- By individual authors

ISBN 978-1-55659-078-8; 1-55659-078-4

LC 97-33929

"Although McGrath, who died in 1990 at 74, published the poem's four parts separately, it appears here complete for the first time. . . . A surprisingly accessible long poem in the Pound tradition of personal epics, Letter arrives 'helved, greaved, and garlanded' and compels our intimate attention." Publ Wkly

McHugh, Heather

★ **Upgraded** to serious. Copper Canyon Press 2009 85p $22 **811**

1. Poetry -- By individual authors

ISBN 978-1-55659-306-2

LC 2009-13347

This collection "offers exactingly ravishing poetry that digs deeply into big themes: free will, consciousness, ideas of language. . . . Thinking poems are often poems with lots of moving parts, and when reading (and rereading) this book one notes the elegance with which everything – perception, reflection, feeling – is held in play. And 'play' is the operative word: McHugh's method always involves some winning blend of precision and momentum." Globe and Mail

McLane, Maureen N., 1967-

My poets; Maureen N. McLane. Farrar, Straus and Giroux 2012 273 p. (hc : alk. paper) $25.00 **811**

1. Poets 2. Poetry -- History and criticism 3. Poetry -- Influence

ISBN 0374217491; 9780374217495

LC 2011041208

In this book, poet and critic Maureen N. McLane "presents an esoteric tour of her personal pantheon, the poets that have shaped her life." The text is a "mixture of prose criticism, memoir, anecdote, and imitative verse written in trib-

ute." The poets discussed include Geoffrey Chaucer, Elizabeth Bishop, H. D., and Gertrude Stein. (Publishers Weekly)

This Blue; Maureen N. McLane. Farrar Straus & Giroux 2014 128 p. (hardcover) $24 **811**

1. Nature 2. Poetry -- Collections

ISBN 0374275939; 9780374275938

LC 2013033882

National Book Award Shortlist: Poetry (2014)

In this poetry collection, author Maureen N. McLane presents "songs for and of a new century, poems both archaic and wholly now. In the middle of life, stationed in our common 'Terran Life,' the poet conjures urban pigeons, Adirondack mountains, Genoa, Andalucía, Belfast, Parma; here is a world sounded out, broken, possibly shareable, newly named." (Publisher's note)

"An exciting collection that celebrates the extraordinary in the ordinary: 'I've left words/ in woods the thrushes/ sing in refusing/ the extinction/ of the day.'" LJ

McMichael, James

Capacity. Farrar, Straus and Giroux 2006 74p $22 **811**

1. Poetry -- By individual authors

ISBN 978-0-374-11890-7; 0-374-11890-6

LC 2005-51628

"Better known for the infrastructural sweep of his work, McMichael is also a poet of the kind of centripetal force and barely contained emotional heat that we more often associate with the short lyric. What makes him unique in American poetry right now is the strength and subtlety with which he blends conceptual ambition with emotional power. It's very common these days to hear poets talking about their 'projects.' But in James McMichael we actually have a poet whose sustained investigation of a small set of obsessions has produced the most integral and surprising structures." Yale Rev

Melville, Herman

★ The **poems** of Herman Melville; edited by Douglas Robillard. rev ed; Kent State Univ. Press 2000 349p pa $29 **811**

1. Poetry -- By individual authors

ISBN 0-87338-660-4

LC 99-52872

First published 1976 by College and University Press Service

This volume "presents the complete texts of 'Battle-Pieces,' 'John Marr and Other Sailors,' and 'Timoleon,' as well as additional manuscript poems. Also presented are excerpts from the long narrative poem Clarel to give the reader a taste of the style and content of this work. The editor's introduction, as well as his notes at the end of each section, are informative as well as appreciative of Melville's status as a poet." Libr J

Includes bibliographical references

Menashe, Samuel

★ **New** and selected poems; Christopher Ricks, editor. Library of America 2005 191p (American poets project) $20 **811**

1. Poetry -- By individual authors

ISBN 1-931082-85-5

LC 2005-44161

"Menashe is a curious and meticulous writer, whose brief, sparsely punctuated poems depend on difficult rhyme and assonance schemes to relay his observations. A wry but basically optimistic poet, his best writing shows that the stylistic restrictions one selects rapidly cease to be restrictions, even when one identifies them as such." N Y Times Book Rev

Meredith, William

Effort at speech; new and selected poems. Tri-Quarterly Bks. 1997 231p $46; pa $17.95 **811**

1. Poetry -- By individual authors

ISBN 0-8101-5070-0; 0-8101-5071-9 pa

LC 97-9679

Meredith's early poems "are as subtle as aspirin. So easily digestible in their precise meter and perfectly tuned endrhyme, their power goes virtually unnoticed until the reader lifts his eyes from the page to find himself moved, affected. In work inspired by the poet's service at sea during WWII, devastation comes on the hushed waves of sonnets. . . . The poems in the book's latter half (1970-1987) find formalism surrendering some ground to free verse as Meredith attempts to salve not the sharp pains of war but the blunted ache of aging." Publ Wkly

Merrill, James

The **changing** light at Sandover; with the stage adaptation Voices from Sandover. edited by J.D. McClatchy and Stephen Yenser. 2nd Knopf hardcover ed.; Knopf 2006 627p il $40 **811**

1. Poetry -- By individual authors

ISBN 978-0-307-26321-6; 0-307-26321-5

LC 2006-273431

First published 1982 by Atheneum; 1992 by Knopf, without Voices from Sandover

This "is an arduous poem, steep and lofty, more than a little difficult to climb, explore, and comprehend, its intricate faceting of the serious and unserious, sacred and profane, vexing to many a reader; but it has, I believe, one controlling stratagem, Merrill's persistent use of doubling or 'entwinning.'. . . The trilogy (though it goes on far too long, gets periodically dizzy, has too much felix culpa and not enough mea culpa) is, surely, an astonishing performance." N Y Rev Books

★ The **collected** poems of James Merrill; edited by J.D. McClatchy and Stephen Yenser. Knopf 2001 xx, 885p $40; pa $27.50 **811**

1. Poetry -- By individual authors

ISBN 0-375-41139-9; 0-375-70941-X pa

LC 00-40542

"Excluded are some juvenilia and light verse, as well as Merrill's book-length poem The Changing Light at Sandover, in print as a separate volume. Merrill's sonnets, sapphics, longer sequences and sinuous sentences encompass

lyric pathos, ebullient comedy, rapt romance and acrid satire. Their formal sophistication can belie their depth of feeling, which is exactly what some readers love best about Merrill's work." Publ Wkly

Merton, Thomas

In the dark before dawn; new selected poems of Thomas Merton. edited with an introduction and notes by Lynn R. Szabo; preface by Kathleen Norris. New Directions 2005 253p pa $16.95 **811**

1. Poetry -- By individual authors

ISBN 978-0-8112-1613-5; 0-8112-1613-6

LC 2004-30957

"Szabo has drawn widely from the furious poetic writing of Merton's final years. This new spectrum of poems helps us tap into the complexity and mystery of Thomas Merton. Readers of Merton's journals will be aware of his shifting attitude to all sorts of things—being an American, being a monk at Gethsemani, being a writer, in particular a poet. Szabo helps us here by assembling the poems in eight thematic sections, so as to display the multiple Mertons. There was the contemplative, drawn to the silent beauties of Gethsemani Abbey, especially at night. There was the stinging and at times declamatory social critic, the admiring and painstaking translator, the avant garde experimentalist and, toward the end, the lovelorn monk." America

Merwin, W. S.

★ **Migration**; new & selected poems. Copper Canyon Press 2005 545p $40 **811**

1. Poetry -- By individual authors

ISBN 1-55659-218-3

LC 2004-17473

This volume contains poetry from sixteen of Merwin's collections.

"Complex, spiritual, and evocative, Merwin is a major poet, and this is a sublime measure of his achievements." Booklist

Middlebrook, Diane Wood

Anne Sexton; a biography. Vintage Bks. 1992 xxiii, 498p il pa $14 **811**

1. Poets 2. Authors 3. Dramatists 4. Poets, American

ISBN 0-679-74182-8

LC 92-50093

First published 1991 by Houghton Mifflin

"Ms. Middlebrook has written a wonderful book: just, balanced, insightful, complex in its sympathies and in its judgment of Sexton both as a person and as a writer." NY Times Book Rev

Includes bibliographical references

Millay, Edna St. Vincent

Collected poems; edited by Norma Millay. Harper & Row 1956 xxi, 738p hardcover o.p. pa $22.95 **811**

1. Poetry -- By individual authors

ISBN 0-06-090889-0 pa

The poems in this collection "are divided into two separate sections of lyrics and sonnets, arranged chronologically and printed in groups under the titles of the original volumes, ranging from 'Renascence' of 1917 to 'Mine the harvest,' published in 1954, four years after the poet's death." Booklist

★ **Selected** poems; J.D. McClatchy, editor. Library of Am. 2003 xxxiii, 231p (American poets project) $20 **811**

1. Poetry -- By individual authors

ISBN 1-931082-35-9

LC 2002-32126

This collection draws from all Millay's "verse books to display her career-long adroitness in her favorite form, the sonnet, and her variety by including even excerpts from an opera libretto. . . . Read occasionally and mixed with her saucy lyrics about erotic love, . . . [her sonnets] reveal their strengths—not of imagery, but of surprising attitudes expressed within strictly observed poetic conventions." Booklist

Moore, Marianne

★ The **poems** of Marianne Moore; edited by Grace Schulman. Viking 2003 449p hardcover o.p. pa $18 **811**

1. Poetry -- By individual authors

ISBN 0-14-303908-3 pa

LC 2003-50159

"The great modernist poet finally gets her due with this outstanding compilation." Libr J

Includes bibliographical references

Moten, Fred

The **Feel** Trio; by Fred Moten. University of Chicago Press 2014 104 p. $20 **811**

1. Poetry -- Collections 2. American poetry -- African American authors

ISBN 0988713713; 9780988713710

National Book Award Shortlist: Poetry (2014); Los Angeles Times Book Prize Finalist: Poetry (2014)

This book, by Fred Moten, "sets down three sets of lithe poem-series. . . . His references are contemporary as well as historical, steeped in jazz and black history, representing a cultural lexicon of the utmost accomplished chops filled with slang, humor, and critical acumen." (The Rumpus)

Murphy, Russell E.

Critical companion to T.S. Eliot; a literary reference to his life and work. [by] Russell Elliott Murphy. Facts on File 2007 614p il (Facts on File library of American literature) $75 **811**

1. Poets 2. Authors 3. Dramatists 4. Editors 5. Essayists 6. Literary critics 7. Nobel laureates for literature

ISBN 978-0-8160-6183-9; 0-8160-6183-1

LC 2006-34076

"This is an excellent and exhaustive resource and a good buy for most libraries." Booklist

Includes bibliographical references

Nadelberg, Amanda

Bright brave phenomena; poems. Amanda Nadelberg. Coffee House Press 2012 118 p. **811**

1. Emotions -- Poetry 2. Poetry -- Collections 3. Man-

woman relationship -- Poetry

ISBN 1566893038; 9781566893039

LC 2011029251

This collection of poetry "focus[es] on the ways life itself changes, depending on emotional shadings: 'I turned into a blanket and went everywhere. With him there was great purpose.' . . . A longer segmented poem chronicles various unhappinesses: 'And when her boyfriend walks to/ her, she looks like death, the/ face of death, big drapes/ in a tall room in France.' The boyfriend in this poem is just as mutable, taking the form of a blue door and a French vampire. Nadelberg's ebullient language captures the giddiness of love and youth. . . . But love can also deflate like 'two people and/ a broken thing/ as a road somewhere.' Her perspective is always staunchly feminine, unfolding like a present, her 'hysteria as a garden, a house/ the colors are beautiful.'" (Publishers Weekly)

Nemerov, Howard

★ The **selected** poems of Howard Nemerov; edited by Daniel Anderson; foreword by Wyatt Prunty. Swallow Press, Ohio University Press 2003 xxi, 154p $24.95; pa $16.95 **811**

1. Poetry -- By individual authors

ISBN 0-8040-1059-5; 0-8040-1060-9 pa

LC 2003-42380

The selections in this volume span Nemerov's entire poetic output

This volume "represents the broad spectrum of Nemerov's virtues as a poet—his intelligence, his wit, his compassion, and his irreverence. It stands as the retrospective collection of the best of what Nemerov left behind." Publisher's note

Niedecker, Lorine

Collected works; edited by Jenny Penberthy. University of Calif. Press 2002 xxiii, 471p $55; pa $25.95 **811**

1. Poetry -- By individual authors

ISBN 978-0-520-22433-9; 0-520-22433-7; 978-0-520-22434-6 pa; 0-520-22434-5 pa

LC 2001-5376

Niedecker "is often likened to Emily Dickinson. She, too, remained in the backwater where she was born. Large-scale interest in her work came only years after her death. Her characteristic poems are, like Dickinson's, short or in short stanzas, short-lined, and elliptical. But she wasn't reclusive; she connected with the Objectivists, New York poets 'led' by Louis Zukofsky. . . . Whereas Dickinson's poetry is metaphysical, Niedecker's mature work is profoundly physical, sparked by wry, class-conscious humor and usually rooted in her Black Lake Island, Wisconsin, neighborhood." Booklist

Includes bibliographical references

Norris, Kathleen

Journey: new and selected poems, 1969-1999. University of Pa. 2001 131p hardcover o.p. pa $16.95 **811**

1. Poetry -- By individual authors

ISBN 0-8229-5761-2 pa

A collection of Norris' "poetry spanning 30 years. Here are poems, arranged chronologically in four sections each beginning with a verse from the Song of Solomon, that tenderly describe an event or scene, examine it, and conclude with a flash of seemingly unrelated insight, leaving profound questions in the reader's heart. . . . Carrying her readers along on her deeply Christian journey, Norris avoids spiritual certainty and preachiness, remaining ever the seeker. Her poems are lyrical, accessible, and hauntingly touching to read and to reread." Libr J

Notley, Alice

★ **Grave** of light; new and selected poems, 1970-2005. Wesleyan University Press 2006 364p $29.95 **811**

1. Poetry -- By individual authors
ISBN 0-8195-6772-8

LC 2006-15712

"Experimental in every sense of the word, Alice Notley has produced an extensive body of work over 30 years in print. This new collection unites previously unpublished poems as well as those from both small-press chapbooks and more widely distributed volumes. Arranged in chronological order while maintaining poetic sequences, Notley's poems tell the story of her artistic development and bear witness to the multitude of styles and influences that Notley has explored. . . . Diversity is Notley's most consistent quality, and this makes her not only somewhat of an enigma aesthetically but also appealing to varying poetic tastes." Booklist

In the pines. Penguin Books 2007 131p (Penguin poets) pa $18 **811**

1. Poetry -- By individual authors
ISBN 978-0-14-311254-9; 0-14-311254-6

LC 2007-12076

"Notley takes the title of her 30-somethingth collection from a notorious American folk song: a man tries to get his lover to admit she's been unfaithful, asking her where she's slept, and her ambiguous answer—in the pines—only makes things worse. That menacing rhetorical moment informs the whole of this searing collection, which is part autobiography, part riposte to literary culture, and part lyrical reclamation of feminist territory. . . . This master poet continues to inspire and challenge." Publ Wkly

Nye, Naomi Shihab

You & yours: poems. BOA Editions 2005 87p (American poets continuum series) hardcover o.p. pa $15.50 **811**

1. Poetry -- By individual authors
ISBN 1-929918-68-2; 1-929918-69-0 pa

LC 2005-11360

"Tender yet forceful, funny and commonsensical, reflective and empathic, Nye writes radiant poems of nature and piercing poems of war, always touching base with homey details and radiant portraits of family and neighbors." Booklist

O'Hara, Frank

The **collected** poems of Frank O'Hara; edited by Donald Allen; with an introduction by John Ash-

bery. University of Calif. Press 1995 xxix, 586p pa $24.95 **811**

1. Poetry -- By individual authors
ISBN 0-520-20166-3

LC 94-24660

A reissue of the title first published 1971 by Knopf

The subjects of this collection "are lunch-time strolls past construction workers and bargains in wrist watches, the lives of artists (whether distant heroes or close friends), the distractions of city life, . . . homosexuality, . . . headlines glimpsed on newstands. . . . Some {are} . . . about friendships, occasional pieces written for a marriage or a departure." Newsweek

Includes bibliographical references

Olds, Sharon, 1942-

★ **Stag's** leap; by Sharon Olds. Alfred A. Knopf 2012 x, 89 p.p **811**

1. Divorced people -- Poetry
ISBN 0307959902; 9780307959904; 9780375712258

LC 2012004426

Pulitzer Prize: Poetry (2013)

This collection of poems by Sharon Olds "tells the story of a divorce, embracing strands of love, sex, sorrow, memory, and new freedom. . . . [Olds] shar[es] the feeling of invisibility that comes when we are no longer standing in love's sight; the surprising physical bond that still exists between a couple during parting; the loss of everything from her husband's smile to the set of his hip." (Publisher's note)

Oliver, Charles M.

Critical companion to Walt Whitman; a literary reference to his life and work. Facts on File 2005 408p il (Facts on File library of American literature) $65 **811**

1. Poets 2. Authors 3. Essayists
ISBN 0-8160-5768-0

LC 2005-4172

The author "begins this work with a biographical essay that includes several illustrations. A large portion of this book addresses Whitman's works, with entries for the individual poems and for the complete volumes. Each entry describes when and where the book was published and includes a brief account of the poem and its context. The third section of the volume covers people, places, publications, and topics related to Whitman's life and work." Choice

Includes bibliographical references

Oliver, Mary

★ **New** and selected poems. Beacon Press 2005 2v v1 $28.50; v1 pa $16; v2 $24.95; v2 pa $16 **811**

1. Poetry -- By individual authors
ISBN 0-8070-6878-0 v1; 0-8070-6877-2 v1 pa; 0-8070-6886-1 v2; 0-8070-6887-X v2 pa

Vol. 1 first published 1992; redesigned ed. to accompany the publication of vol. 2

Volume one contains poems written from 1965 to 1992. Volume two contains poems written from 1994 to 2005.

A **thousand** mornings; poems. Mary Oliver. Penguin Press 2012 82 p. $24.95   **811**
1. Nature poetry 2. Literature -- 21st century 3. American poetry -- Women authors
ISBN 1594204772; 9781594204777
LC 2012027310
In author Mary Oliver's book of poetry, she transports "us to the marshland and coastline of her beloved home, Provincetown, Massachusetts. In these pages, Oliver shares the wonder of dawn, the grace of animals, and the transformative power of attention. Whether studying the leaves of a tree or mourning her adored dog, Percy, she is ever patient in her observations and open to the teachings contained in the smallest of moments." (Publisher's note)

Olson, Charles
The **Maximus** poems; edited by George F. Butterick. University of Calif. Press 1985 652p hardcover o.p. pa $42   **811**
1. Poetry -- By individual authors
ISBN 978-520-05595-7; 0-520-05595-0
LC 79-65759
This edition contains the entire sequence of poems set in Gloucester, Massachusetts, whose protagonist is the mythical figure, Maximus
"It is impossible to describe in this small space the immensity of Charles Olson's achievement—as poet, theoretician and explorer of the 'human universe.' Just as Ezra Pound's writing energized Western poetry in the first half of this century, Olson in the 1950s redefined its direction and inspired the next generation of writers. . . . 'The Maximus Poems' are a complex far-ranging attempt to grasp the history of human thought." Christ Sci Monit

Oppen, George
★ **New** collected poems; edited with an introduction and notes by Michael Davidson; preface by Eliot Weinberger. New Directions 2002 xlv, 433p il $37.95   **811**
1. Poetry -- By individual authors
ISBN 0-8112-1488-5
LC 2001-44048
Replaces The collected poems of George Oppen (1975)
"Oppen, a Communist and an objectivist poet deeply influenced by Pound and Williams, believed that there were no ideas except in things, but he also believed, fiercely, that our relationship to things was inherently moral. . . . In 1934, he published a book of stunning, elliptical lyrics about 'big-Business' and American capitalism; he then fell silent for the next twenty-five years, during which he struggled to reconcile his fealty to social causes with the demands of aesthetic originality. The culmination of this struggle was his Pulitzer Prize-winning collection 'Of Being Numerous,' published in 1968, which, to a degree unmatched by any book of American poetry since, movingly portrays the individual in a collective world." New Yorker
Includes bibliographical references

Ostriker, Alicia
No heaven; [by] Alicia Suskin Ostriker. University of Pittsburgh Press 2005 136p (Pitt poetry series) pa $12.95   **811**
1. Poetry -- By individual authors
ISBN 0-8229-5875-9
In this "collection of clarion poems intimate and worldly, Ostriker writes about her life as a wife, mother, and grandmother with tenderness, but she is also edgy, erotic, funny, and ornery." Booklist

★ The **Oxford** anthology of African-American poetry; edited by Arnold Rampersad; associate editor, Hilary Herbold. Oxford University Press 2006 432p $32.50   **811**
1. American poetry -- African American authors -- Collections
ISBN 0-19-512563-0; 978-0-19-512563-4
LC 2005-15242
"Predicated on the fact that there is a vast body of poetry written by gifted black poets, this . . . anthology tells the story of African American culture and explicates its crucial role within the larger literary tradition. . . . There is much to admire about the artistry of the poems, and even more to discover about the African American experience." Booklist

★ The **Oxford** book of American poetry; chosen and edited by David Lehman; associate editor, John Brehm. Oxford University Press 2006 lvii, 1132p $35   **811**
1. American poetry -- Collections
ISBN 0-19-516251-X; 978-0-19-516251-6
LC 2005-36590
First published 1950 with title: The Oxford book of American verse
"The book is not only a sound historical survey, but also gives the reader a powerful taste of poetry's impact upon the wider world." Economist
Includes bibliographical references

Padgett, Ron, 1942-
Collected Poems; Ron Padgett. Coffee House Press 2013 810 p. (Trade Cloth) $44   **811**
1. American poetry -- Collections
ISBN 1566893429; 9781566893428
LC 2013017190
LA Times Book Prize Winner: Poetry (2013)
This collection of poems by Ron Padgett "gather[s] the work of more than fifty years. . . . Padgett's poems reverberate with his reading and friendships, from Andrew Marvell to Woody Guthrie and Kenneth Koch. Wry, insightful, and direct, they offer readers the rewards of his endless curiosity and generous spirit." (Publisher's note)
"That is Padgett at his most joyful. But this exemplar of the gloriously zany, this champion of comic-book characters, turns out also to be a fount of wisdom and good sense: 'It's not embarrassing to be sentimental/When the sentiment equals/ Seeing things just as they are here now.' David Lehman is the founder and editor of the Best American Poetry series and the author of the just-published New and Selected Poems (Scribner)." Pub Wkly

Page, P. K.

The **hidden** room; collected poems. {by} Patricia Kathleen Page. Porcupine's Quill 1997 2v ea $18.95 **811**
1. Poetry -- By individual authors
ISBN 0-88984-190-X v1; 0-88984-193-4 v2
LC 98-113870
These two volumes incude the majority of all of the poet's works published in volume form, from Unit of five to Hologram, along with some unpublished poems and poems hitherto published only in magazines

Pankey, Eric

The **pear** as one example; new & selected poems, 1984-2008. Ausable Press 2008 274p pa $16 **811**
1. Poetry -- By individual authors
ISBN 978-1-931337-39-7; 1-931337-39-X
LC 2007-49674
"Fans of an earlier generation of American poets, such as Elizabeth Bishop, A.R. Ammons, and Robert Bly, will find much to enjoy in this large volume of poetry that showcases an acute poetic prowess, capturing a range of heartfelt emotions and experiences. . . . For Pankey, each new dawn presents a multitude of poetic possibilities, and he incorporates both the ugly and the beautiful, pain and pleasure in his aesthetic vision." NewPages

Pankey, Eric, 1959-

Trace; poems. Eric Pankey. 1st ed. Milkweed Editions 2013 68 p. (paperback) $16 **811**
1. Belief and doubt -- Poetry 2. Depression (Psychology) -- Poetry
ISBN 1571314490; 9781571314499
LC 2012028097
This collection of poems, by Eric Pankey, "locates itself at a threshold between faith and doubt--between the visible and the invisible, the say-able and the ineffable, the physical and the metaphysical. Also a map of the poet's journey into a deep depression, these poems confront one man's struggle to overcome depression's smothering weight and presence." (Publisher's note)

Pardlo, Gregory, 1968-

Digest; Gregory Pardlo. Four Way Books 2014 75 p. (pbk. : alk. paper) $15.95 **811**
1. American poetry -- Collections
ISBN 1935536508; 9781935536505
LC 2014011291
Pulitzer Prize: Poetry (2015)
This collection of poems, by Gregory Pardlo, "draws from the present and the past to form an intellectual, American identity. In poems that forge their own styles and strategies, we experience dialogues between the written word and other art forms. Within this dialogue we hear Ben Jonson, we meet police K-9s, and we find children negotiating a sense of the world through a father's eyes and through their own." (Publisher's note)
Includes bibliographical references

Parini, Jay

Robert Frost; a life. Holt & Co. 1999 514p il $35; pa $16 **811**
1. Poets 2. Authors
ISBN 0-8050-3181-2; 0-8050-6341-2 pa
LC 98-26690
"Rarely has Frost's story been told this dexterously, or with a better understanding of the relation of Frost's personal crises to his accomplishment as a poet." Publ Wkly
Includes bibliographical references

★ The **Penguin** anthology of twentieth-century American poetry; edited with an introduction by Rita Dove. Penguin Books 2011 lii, 599 p.p **811**
1. American poetry -- Collections 2. American poetry -- 20th century
ISBN 9780143106432
LC 2011036342
The book provides an anthology of 20th century U.S. poetry. "Selecting from the canon of American poetry throughout the twentieth century, [Rita] Dove has created an anthology that represents the full spectrum of aesthetic sensibilities. . . . Featuring poems both classic and contemporary, this collection reflects both a dynamic and cohesive portrait of modern American poetry and outlines its trajectory over the past century." (Publisher's note)

Perillo, Lucia Maria

Inseminating the elephant; [by] Lucia Perillo. Copper Canyon Press 2009 93p $22 **811**
1. Poetry -- By individual authors
ISBN 978-1-55659-291-1; 1-55659-291-4
LC 2008-44772
Perillo "writes accessible, often funny poems that border on the profane. The title poem of this collection, her fifth, is about just what it says: zoologists tasked with helping impregnate an elephant (it's not easy). There's also an ode to bad smells, a middle-aged narrator's reluctant acceptance of cell phones and a meditation on a Viagra ad. Perillo has another rare power among versifiers: She is able to make dire, life-or-death concerns go down easy. . . . Physical decline is one of Perillo's major themes, one that she tackles with wry humor." Time Out N Y

Perillo, Lucia, 1958-2016

On the spectrum of possible deaths; Lucia Perillo. Copper Canyon Press 2012 81 p. **811**
1. Death -- Poetry 2. American poetry -- Collections 3. American poetry -- Women authors -- Collections
ISBN 155659397X; 9781556593970
LC 2011050110
This book is a poetry collection written by the 2009 Pulitzer Prize finalist author Lucia Perillo. "Perillo has long lived with, and written about, her struggle with debilitating multiple sclerosis. Her . . . sixth book of poems, published concurrently with her debut story collection, takes a . . . look at mortality." (Booklist)
"With subjects ranging from coyotes and Scotch broom to local elections and family history, . . . the mythic and mundane, of media and daily life, as she faces the treachery of illness." (Publisher's note)

Phillips, Patrick

Elegy for a broken machine; poems. by Patrick Phillips. Alfred A. Knopf 2015 80 p. (hardback) $26   **811**

1. Death 2. Poetry -- Collections 3. Father-son relationship

ISBN 0385353758; 9780385353755; 9780385353762

                 LC 2014026436

National Book Award Finalist: Poetry (2015)

This book of poems, by Patrick Phillips, "is at its core a son's lament for his father. This book of elegies takes us from the luminous world of childhood to the fluorescent glare of operating rooms and recovery wards, and into the twilight lives of those who must go on. . . . Phillips documents the unsung joys of midlife, the betrayals of the human body, and his realization that as the crowd of ghosts grows, we take our places, next in line." (Publisher's note)

"Phillips (Boy) examines masculinity and loss with a surgeon's precision in his elegiac third book... Phillips's careful language consciously breaks down these distinctions, fusing the roles men play throughout their lives, and connecting past to present... And Phillips ponders just what makes a human body different from any other relinquished object, imagining his mattress decaying at the dump 'as it sloughs its guts into the dirt.'" Pub Wkly

Phillips, Rowan Ricardo

Heaven; poems. Rowan Ricardo Phillips. Farrar, Straus & Giroux 2015 80 p. (hardback) $24   **811**

1. Heaven 2. Spiritual life

ISBN 9780374168520; 0374168520

                 LC 2014039377

NBA Longlist

In this poetry collection, author Rowan Ricardo Phillips "offers many answers, and none at all. Swerving elegantly from humor to heartbreak, from Colorado to Florida, from Dante's 'Paradise' to Homer's 'Iliad,' from knowledge to ignorance to awe, Phillips turns his gaze upward and outward, probing and upending notions of the beyond." (Publisher's note)

"Consistently smart and clearly talented, Phillips is one to read now and to watch for in the future." Booklist

Piercy, Marge

Colors passing through us; poems. Knopf 2003 157p $23; pa $15   **811**

1. Poetry -- By individual authors

ISBN 0-375-41537-8; 0-375-71005-1 pa

                 LC 2002-66145

The author "tempers 1960s politics and 1970s feminism with nostalgia for the world of her childhood. . . . Piercy celebrates daily life on Cape Cod, where she and her husband live, with poems about gardening, cats, cooking, canning, and sex after 60. While all of these poems are eminently readable, the best are angry and funny. . . . Piercy fans, of which there are many, will relish this collection." Libr J

Pinsky, Robert

Democracy, culture, and the voice of poetry. Princeton Univ. Press 2002 96p (University Center for Human Values series) $29.95; pa $12.95   **811**

1. Poetry -- By individual authors 2. American poetry

-- History and criticism

ISBN 0-691-09617-1; 0-691-12263-6 pa

                 LC 2002-25288

This is an "analysis of the way the intimate rhythms of American poetry invoke a social presence. Pinsky, a former poet laureate, passionately argues that American poetry is driven by the anxiety of being forgotten; the solitary poet makes us aware of the presence of others as he yearns for their approval while striving to preserve his uniqueness." N Y Times Book Rev

The **figured** wheel; new and collected poems, 1966-1996. Farrar, Straus & Giroux 1996 303p hardcover o.p. pa $17   **811**

1. Poetry -- By individual authors

ISBN 0-374-52506-4

                 LC 95-47617

"Brought together here are 16 new poems, the work of Pinsky's four original collections and a sampling of his fine translations, including a canto from his well-received version of the Inferno. Taken as a whole, this is the record of a poet who grows from highly competent to near-transcendent." Publ Wkly

Plath, Sylvia, 1932-1963

Ariel; the restored edition. foreword by Frieda Hughes. HarperCollins Publishers 2004 xxi, 211p $24.95   **811**

1. Poetry -- By individual authors

ISBN 0-06-073259-8

                 LC 2004-47703

First published 1955 in the United Kingdom

Sylvia Plath's posthumous volume of poetry, Ariel, was first published in the mid-1960s. "This facsimile edition restores, for the first time, the selection and arrangement of the poems as Sylvia Plath left them at the point of her death. In addition to the facsimile pages of Sylvia Plath's manuscript, this edition also includes in facsimile the complete working drafts of the title poem, 'Ariel,' in order to offer a sense of Plath's creative process as well as notes the author made for the BBC about some of the manuscript poems." (Publisher's note)

"Readers can see Plath's actual manuscript in this handsome facsimile, which provides a missing piece in the Plath annals and proves that there's nothing like going to the source." Booklist

★ The **collected** poems; edited by Ted Hughes. Harper & Row 1981 351p hardcover o.p. pa $17.95   **811**

1. Poetry -- By individual authors

ISBN 0-06-155889-3 pa

"Although her best poems deal with suffering and death, others are exhilarating and affectionate, and her tone is frequently witty as well as disturbing." Concise Oxford Companion to Engl Lit

Poe, Edgar Allan

Complete poems; edited by Thomas Ollive Mabbott. University of Ill. Press 2000 xxx, 627p il pa $25 **811**

1. Poetry -- By individual authors
ISBN 0-252-06921-8

LC 00-38639

This book contains 101 poems and their variants. In addition to classic poems such as The raven, The bells, and Annabel Lee, this volume contains previously uncollected poems, fragments, verses published in reviews, and poems attributed to Poe

Includes bibliographical references

Poems from the women's movement; edited by Honor Moore. Library of America 2009 238p (American poets project) $20 **811**

1. Women's movement 2. American poetry -- Women authors -- Collections
ISBN 978-1-59853-042-1

This is an anthology of poetry written by women during the women's movement of the late 1960s and 1970s.

"These direct, vibrant, potent, passionate, wild, strong, free, and freeing poems come less like a breath of fresh air than a strong wind." Booklist

Poetry 180; a turning back to poetry. selected and with an introduction by Billy Collins. Random House Trade Paperbacks 2003 xxiv, 323p pa $13.95 **811**

1. American poetry -- Collections
ISBN 0-8129-6887-5

LC 2002-36949

The editor "has collected 180 accessible modern poems: one for each day of the school year and together signifying a 180° turning back to poetry. These are poems, he says, you can 'get' the first time around, and he hopes that high schools will expose students to a poem a day via public address system or assemblies. A fine gathering of contemporary poets." Libr J

Includes bibliographical references

The **Poetry** anthology, 1912-2002; ninety years of America's most distinguished verse magazine. edited by Joseph Parisi & Stephen Young; with an introduction by Joseph Parisi. Ivan R. Dee 2002 lv, 509p $29.95; pa $16.95 **811**

1. American poetry -- Collections
ISBN 1-56663-468-7; 1-56663-604-3 pa

LC 2002-31178

A collection of 600 poems previously published in Poetry magazine, written by such poets as W.H. Auden, Elizabeth Bishop, Sylvia Plath, James Merrill, and Susan Hahn

This is a "comprehensive and thrilling anthology, a veritable history of twentieth-century poetry in English." Booklist

Poetry speaks expanded; hear poets from Tennyson to Plath read their own work. Elise Paschen & Rebekah Presson Mosby, editors; Charles Os-

good, narrator. [2nd ed.]; Sourcebooks 2007 384p il $49.95 **811**

1. English poetry -- Collections 2. American poetry -- Collections
ISBN 978-1-4022-1062-4; 1-4022-1062-0

LC 2007-37080

First published 2001 with title: Poetry speaks

"Reluctant poetry readers may find themselves drawn to the printed page by the spoken work, and poetry fans are likely to find much to love here." Publ Wkly

The **poets** laureate anthology; edited and with introductions by Elizabeth Hun Schmidt; foreword by Billy Collins. W.W. Norton & Co. 2010 liii, 762p $39.95 **811**

1. American poetry -- Collections
ISBN 978-0-393-06181-9

LC 2010-21692

Poems by each of the forty-three poets who have been named our nation's Poet Laureate since the post (originally called Consultant in Poetry to the Library of Congress) was established in 1937.

"A hefty and worthy read that everyone will want to savor. Essential for all contemporary poetry collections." Libr J

Poets of the Civil War; J.D. McClatchy, editor. Library of America 2005 211p il (American poets project) $20 **811**

1. American poetry -- Collections 2. United States -- History -- 1861-1865, Civil War -- Poetry
ISBN 978-1-93108-276-1; 1-93208-276-6

LC 2004-61552

"The poems wisely selected represent not only the main kinds of responses to the war but also the radically conflicting sympathies of the poets—with the Union cause or with the Confederacy—and the important postwar theme of reconciliation of North and South. McClatchy's selection has not only breadth of representation but fine choices within forms, causes, and poets." Sewanee Rev

★ **Poets** of World War II; Harvey Shapiro, editor. Library of Am. 2003 xxxii, 262p (American poets project) $20 **811**

1. World War, 1939-1945 -- Poetry
ISBN 1-931082-33-2

LC 2002-32125

The editor's "objective is to show that the American poets of the Second World War were as significant as their English counterparts in the first one, if different in tone. Even at their most biting, Siegfried Sassoon and Wilfred Owen struck a heroic note, penning anthems for 'doomed youth' and the destruction of innocence. . . . But those who survived battles of the second conflict to become important poets avoided the attempt to sound noble, or to celebrate fallen comrades. . . . Shapiro, a B-17 gunner, takes pains to show the spectrum of opinion that actually existed and how it evolved." New Leader

Includes bibliographical references

Postmodern American poetry; a Norton anthology. edited by Paul Hoover. 2nd ed. W W Norton & Co Inc 2013 lvii, 982 p.p (paperback) $39.95 **811**

1. Postmodernism 2. American poetry 3. American poetry -- 20th century 4. American poetry -- 21st century 5. Postmodernism (Literature) -- United States
ISBN 0393341860; 9780393341867

LC 2012039473

This book, edited by Paul Hoover, is a the second edition of an anthology of poems written after 1950, by such authors as "Robert Duncan, Denise Levertov, James Schuyler, Robert Creeley, Allen Ginsberg, Gary Snyder, Ted Berrigan, Clarence Major, Mei-Mei Berssenbrugge, and David Shapiro." (Booklist) It includes "important recent movements such as Newlipo, conceptual poetry, and Flarf." (Publisher's note)

Includes bibliographical references and index.

Pound, Ezra

★ The **cantos** of Ezra Pound. New Directions 1970 802p $42; pa $22.95 **811**

1. Poetry -- By individual authors
ISBN 0-8112-0350-6; 0-8112-1326-9 pa

"The first sections of the 'Cantos' were published in magazine form as early as 1917. Pound's conception of his epic changed several times during different phases of his life. Originally intended as a didactic treatise for 'philistine' Americans, it combined elements from classical myth, ancient Oriental poetry, Provençal ballads, and modern economic theory, to create a vast disjointed panorama of the growth of civilization. A monumental work of poetic enterprise." Reader's Ency. 4th edition

★ **Poems** and translations. Library of America 2003 1363p $45 **811**

1. Poetry -- By individual authors
ISBN 978-1-931082-41-9; 1-931082-41-3

LC 2003-40142

This volume "offers, in addition to the convenience of having Pound's shorter works compacted into a single volume, a useful chronology of his life and some very helpful, if at times overly terse, annotations to the poems' myriad foreign phrases and proper nouns. Richard Sieburth, an award-winning translator and the author of a previous book on Pound, is clearly at home with the material. . . . More important than all of this, however, what emerges from Poems and Translations is a personality, one of the strongest and strangest in modern poetry." Parnassus: Poetry in Review

Powell, D. A.

Useless landscape; or, a guide for boys. D. A. Powell. Graywolf Press 2012 80 p. (alk. paper) $22 **811**

1. Youth -- Poetry 2. Gay men -- Poetry 3. Diseases -- Poetry 4. Human body -- Poetry 5. Poetry -- Collections
ISBN 9781555976057

LC 2011942041

In this collection of poetry, D. A. Powell "revisits themes of body and illness, sacred space and seductive desecration. The first section is an examination of beauty divorced from utility; the second a . . . portrait of young people in acts of exploration." (Booklist) The poems vary in tone, . . . some based on life stories and others built on puns . . . the im-

poverished spaces of [Powell's] youth stand out among his backgrounds and metaphors for ecological disaster, for gay sexual awakening, for sex itself, for illness, and for love." (Publishers Weekly)

Powell, D. A., 1963-

Repast; tea, lunch, and cocktails. D. A. Powell. Graywolf Press 2014 224 p. (alk. paper) $20 **811**

1. Gay men -- Poetry 2. AIDS (Disease) -- Poetry
ISBN 1555976964; 9781555976965

LC 2014935838

This collection of poetry by D. A. Powell combines his books "Tea," "Lunch," and "Cocktails," with an introduction by novelist David Leavitt. Many of the poems are concerned with the AIDS epidemic among U.S. gay men in the late 20th century. "The trilogy's narrative arc, with its focus on survival, subverts the all-too-typical cliché of the gay man suffering and dying." (New Yorker)

Raab, Lawrence, 1946-

Mistaking each other for ghosts; poems. Lawrence Raab. Tupelo Press 2015 84 p. (pbk. : alk. paper) $16.95 **811**

1. American poetry
ISBN 1936797658; 9781936797653

LC 2015017797

NBA Longlist

The poems in this collection by Lawrence Raab feature "angels and human monsters, decades and generations, universities turned into ashes, the consolation of philosophy, despair in the middle of the night, a tutorial in lucid dreaming. Only his poetic humor gives away his American citizenship." (Publisher's note)

"With identifiable scenes that Raab has twisted for fresh insight, these are accessible poems most readers will appreciate." LJ

Rankine, Claudia, 1963-

★ **Citizen**; an American lyric. Claudia Rankine. Graywolf Press 2014 160 p. illustrations (some color) $20 **811**

1. American essays 2. Racism -- Poetry 3. United States -- Race relations
ISBN 1555976905; 9781555976903

LC 2014935702

National Book Critics Circle Award: Poetry (2014)
National Book Award Shortlist: Poetry (2014)
Los Angeles Times Book Prize Winner: Poetry (2014)

This book, by Claudia Rankine, "recounts mounting racial aggressions in ongoing encounters in twenty-first-century daily life and in the media. Some of these encounters are slights, seeming slips of the tongue, and some are intentional offensives in the classroom, at the supermarket, at home, on the tennis court with Serena Williams and the soccer field with Zinedine Zidane, online, on TV--everywhere, all the time." (Publisher's note)

"Combining poetry, essay, and images from media and contemporary art, Rankine's poetics capture the urgency of her subject matter." Pub Wkly

Includes bibliographical references

Rasmussen, Matt

Black aperture; poems. Matt Rasmussen. Louisiana State University Press 2013 64 p. (pbk. : alk. paper) $17.95 **811**

1. Suicide 2. Bereavement 3. Poetry -- Collections
ISBN 080715086X; 9780807150863

LC 2012038045

In this collection of poems, Matt Rasmussen "faces the tragedy of his brother's suicide, . . . blurring the edge between grief and humor. In Outgoing, the speaker erases his brother's answering machine message. . . . In other poems, once-ordinary objects become dreamlike. . . . Destructive and redemptive, [it] opens to the complicated entanglements of mourning: damage and healing, sorrow and laughter, and torment balanced with moments of relief." (Publisher's note)

Reed, Ishmael

New and collected poems, 1966-2006. Carroll & Graf 2006 xxi, 482p $25.95; pa $17.95 **811**

1. Poetry -- By individual authors
ISBN 978-0-7867-1788-0; 978-1-56858-341-9 pa

LC 2006-299409

"The mixture of humor and anger is . . . a hallmark of Ishmael Reed, whose strength as an editor, essayist, and novelist (and whose reputation as provocateur) has overshadowed his achievement as a poet. That achievement . . . is based in the vernacular, as well as in his use of folk materials, his fearlessness with form, and his 'irrational' tendency toward the spiritual, which stands as an indictment of the impoverished soul of a bottom-line age." Harvard Review

Rekdal, Paisley

Animal eye; Paisley Rekdal. University of Pittsburgh Press 2012 86 p. **811**

1. Love poetry 2. Poetry -- Collections 3. Loss (Psychology) -- Poetry 4. American poetry
ISBN 0822961792; 9780822961796

LC 2011277541

This book is a collection of poetry from Paisley Rekdal. "In poems long and short, Rekdal looks at paintings and wax models . . . , a stuffed fox . . . , a front-yard garden, a bouquet of flowers, all of which become harsh mirrors reflecting the painful lessons of lost love. 'What's the point of pain if it heals,' Rekdal asks, thinking of finding new love after divorce: these poems don't want to be let off easy. Even tango lessons aren't just for fun: 'The point is not to give yourself away but to connect/ as closely as you are able to// your partner's will in the embrace, so that intent/ slides seamlessly through two// sets of veins.' There's a bit of willful masochism in this dance--in any of life's various dances--when the goal is to join 'two separate hearts.'" (Publishers Weekly)

Revell, Donald

★ **Pennyweight** windows; new & selected poems. Alice James 2005 220p $26.95; pa $18.95 **811**

1. Poetry -- By individual authors
ISBN 1-882295-51-X; 1-882295-52-8 pa

LC 2004-26191

"Using history, mythology, and contemporary events as a backdrop . . . [the author] tries to balance a public, nearly didactic voice with a personal and revealing one. . . . This readable and well-edited collection—mostly culled from eight previous collections, with some new poems added—is a good representation of Revell's work." Libr J

Rexroth, Kenneth

★ The **complete** poems of Kenneth Rexroth; edited by Sam Hamill & Bradford Morrow. Copper Canyon Press 2003 xxxvi, 764p hardcover o.p. pa $24 **811**

1. Poetry -- By individual authors
ISBN 1-55659-217-5 pa

LC 2002-1706

"If you love looking things up and taking reading sidetrips, Rexroth is one of the most readable and rewarding twentieth-century American poets." Booklist

Reznikoff, Charles

★ The **poems** of Charles Reznikoff; 1918-1975. edited by Seamus Cooney. David R. Godine 2005 445p $45; pa $21.95 **811**

1. Poetry -- By individual authors
ISBN 1-57423-204-5; 1-57423-203-7 pa

LC 2005-21218

First published 1989 with title: Poems 1918-1975

This collection "of his poems . . . will be welcomed both by old and new readers of his work." Publ Wkly

Includes bibliographical references

Rich, Adrienne

Arts of the possible; essays and conversations. Norton 2001 190p $23.95; pa $13.95 **811**

1. Poetry 2. Feminism
ISBN 0-393-05045-9; 0-393-32312-9 pa

LC 00-51522

This volume "collects Rich's best-known prose from the 1970s and 1980s, with new writing that extends through the 1990s. In letters such as 'Why I Refused the National Medal for the Arts,' and through complaints about feminism as the cult of the personal and a renewed call for a collective global vision, she delights, and is by turns lyrical and polemical." Ms

Collected early poems, 1950-1970. Norton 1993 xxi, 435p hardcover o.p. pa $15 **811**

1. Poetry -- By individual authors
ISBN 0-393-31385-9 pa

LC 92-13150

This collection "contains all of the work included in Rich's first six books, and a few previously uncollected pieces as well. Her poetry of the 1950s stems from a strong, mostly male tradition, obviously and intentionally echoing the work of Frost, Williams, Dickinson and Stevens. . . . The poems written in the 1960s are pervaded by the poet's consciousness of the subversive nature of creativity, especially for women, a gift at risk of being suppressed or curtailed at any moment by the self, family or the male-dominated society. In the last poems of the period, Rich's voice is firm and brave, her language still searingly beautiful and individual."

This important volume charts the radical transformation of one of America's most significant poets." Publ Wkly

The **school** among the ruins: poems, 2000-2004. W.W. Norton 2004 113p $22.95　**811**
1. Poetry -- By individual authors
ISBN 0-393-05983-9

LC 2004-8370

"Rich, a clarion poet of conscience, gets the fractured timbre of our times just right in a collection of vigorous lyric poems about cell phones and television, terror and war, commercialization and 'social impotence.'" Booklist

Roethke, Theodore
The **collected** poems of Theodore Roethke. Doubleday 1966 279p hardcover o.p. pa $14.95　**811**
1. Poetry -- By individual authors
ISBN 0-385-08601-6 pa

Roethke's "refreshingly original rhythms are keenly articulated and often hypnotic. Although his work is uneven and he sometimes gives way to self-indulgence or to surprising naiveté, many of his best poems recreate disconcertingly intense psychic or mystical experience. He also had a flair for the seductively lyrical and the brashly irreverent. He ranks as one of the best poets of the first postmodern generation." Benet's Reader's Ency of Am Lit

Ronk, Martha
Transfer of Qualities; by Martha C. Ronk. University Press of New England　2013　88 p.　(pbk.) $17.95　**811**
1. Matter 2. Interpersonal relations
ISBN 9781890650827; 189065082X

National Book Awards: Poetry: Long List (2013)

This book, by Martha C. Ronk, "addresses the uncanny and myriad ways in which people and things, but also people and those around them, exchange qualities with one another, moving in on, unsettling: altering stance, attitude, mood, gesture. Each entry in the book probes the dissolving boundaries between those sharing space with one another; and the various cross-genres in the book--prose poem, creative non-fiction, personal essay--echo the theme of interdependence." (Publisher's note)

"Ronk's collection of "various objects," books, photograms, people and portraits dominate the collection, which moves from prose to lineated poems, to essays, to brief passages of nonfiction, seguing into topics of representation, death, mourning, love, and intimacy with the physical world." Pub Wkly
1. Objects. Various objects; The book; Photograms; Collecting -- 2. People. The unfamiliar; The familiar; Portaits -- 3. Transferred stories.

Ruefle, Mary
Selected poems. Wave Books 2010 154p $24　**811**
1. Poetry -- By individual authors
ISBN 978-1-933517-45-2; 1-933517-45-X

LC 2010-05808

"This first retrospective collection from Ruefle, which selects from her nine previous books of poetry, the earliest of which first appeared in 1982, shows her to be a poet of visionary imagination, abiding sensitivity, and melancholy humor." Publ Wkly

Rukeyser, Muriel
Selected poems; Adrienne Rich, editor. Library of America 2004 xxv, 180p (American poets project) $20　**811**
1. Poetry -- By individual authors
ISBN 978-1-931082-58-7; 1-931082-58-8

LC 2003-60484

"Rukeyser was born in 1913, which puts her in the generation of Bishop, Berryman, Lowell, and Jarrell. Her poems range from the sprawling to the epigrammatic; they often have a flat, documentary feel ('The tunnel is part of a huge water power project/begun, latter part of 1929'), and they're formally various (excerpted sections from a single long poem, 'Letter to the Front,' contain both a sonnet and a sestina). . . . At its best, Rukeyser's work can be open, energetic, and well constructed, if a little enamored of its own goody-goodness." Poetry (Modern Poetry Association)

Ryan, Kay
The **best** of it; new and selected poems. Grove Press 2010 288p $24　**811**
1. Poetry -- By individual authors
ISBN 978-0-8021-1914-8; 0-8021-1914-X

Ryan's "poems are as slim as runway models, so tiny you could almost tweet them. Their compact refinement, though, does not suggest ease or chic. Her voice is quizzical and impertinent, funny in uncomfortable ways, scuffed by failure and loss. Her mastery, like Emily Dickinson's, has some awkwardness in it, some essential gawkiness that draws you close. . . . [This] is a generous and nearly career-spanning collection of her verse." N Y Times Book Rev

Salah, Trish
Wanting in Arabic; poems. by Trish Salah. Mawenzi House Pub 2002 90 p. $19.95　**811**
1. Gender identity -- Poetry
ISBN 9781927494301; 9781894770002

LC 2003430842

Lambda Award: Transgender Fiction (2014)

This poetry collection, by Trish Salah, "dwells on the contradictions of a transsexual poetics, in its attendant disfigurations of lyric, ghazal, l'ecriture feminine, and, in particular, her own sexed voice. Without a memory of her father's language, the questions her poems ask are those for a home known through photographs, for a language lost with childhood." (Publisher's note)

Sandburg, Carl
★ The **complete** poems of Carl Sandburg; rev and expanded ed; Harcourt Brace Jovanovich 1970 xxxi, 797p $40　**811**
1. Poetry -- By individual authors
ISBN 0-15-100996-1

First published 1950

A collection of seven of the author's books: Chicago poems, 1916; Cornhuskers, 1918; Smoke and steel, 1920; Slabs of the sunburnt West, 1922; Good morning, America, 1925; The people, yes, 1936; Honey and salt, 1963

"Known for his free verse, written under the influence of Walt Whitman and celebrating industrial and agricultural America, American geography and landscape, figures in American history, and the American common people, {Sandburg} frequently makes use of contemporary American slang and colloquialisms." Herzberg. Reader's Ency of Am Lit

Sanders, Ed

Thirsting for peace in a raging century; selected poems, 1961-1985. [by] Edward Sanders. New and rev. ed.; Coffee House Press 2009 260p il pa $20
811
1. Poetry -- By individual authors
ISBN 978-1-56689-238-4 pa
LC 2009-28061

First published 1987; revised and updated with sixteen additional poems

This collection "restores Edward Sanders to his rightful place at the forefront of the poetry of his time, and reminds us that spending one's days in active pursuit of the betterment of all life on the planet isn't necessarily antithetical to the creation of first-rate writing." San Francisco Chron

Sarton, May

Selected poems of May Sarton; edited and with an introduction by Serena Sue Hilsinger and Lois Brynes. Norton 1978 206p hardcover o.p. pa $25
811
1. Poetry -- By individual authors
ISBN 978-0-393-04512-3; 0-393-04512-9
LC 78-14850

"What May Sarton does is to follow the round of a woman's life. Her verse is traditional, warm, ripe with the wisdom of her years as a poet, novelist, autobiographer. She draws on the artifacts of the past for images to live by in the here and now." Christ Sci Monit

Schulman, Grace

Days of wonder; new and selected poems. Houghton Mifflin 2002 189p $25; pa $14
811
1. Poetry -- By individual authors
ISBN 0-618-08623-4; 0-618-34082-3 pa
LC 2001-39531

"In a characteristic Schulman poem, large, difficult questions resonate in the small, singular moments of appreciation. . . . There are allusions to canonical painters and canonical poems, and a variety of religious references, which engender equal portions of reverence and lament. Many of the poems' small pleasures are found amid sometimes difficult sometimes serene backdrops." Publ Wkly

Schutt, Will

Westerly; Will Schutt; foreword by Carl Phillips. Yale University Press 2013 80 p. (Yale series of younger poets) (hardcover) $45.00; (paperback) $18
811
1. History -- Poetry 2. Poetry -- Collections
ISBN 030018851X; 9780300188509; 9780300188516
LC 2012033923

This poetry collection, by Will Schutt, is the winner of the 2012 "Yale Series of Younger Poets" award. "A young soldier dons Napoleon's hat. An out-of-work man wanders Berlin, dreaming he is Peter the Great. The famous exile Dante finally returns to his native city. . . . Familial and historical apparitions haunt this . . . collection of poems." (Publisher's note)

Schuyler, James

Collected poems. Farrar, Straus & Giroux 1993 429p hardcover o.p. pa $32
811
1. Poetry -- By individual authors
ISBN 978-0-374-52403-6; 0-374-52403-3
LC 92-40977

"Schuyler's subject is his life, and his poems often read like elegant journal entries. The book presents intimate and conversational accounts of life in the Eastern literary landscape—New York City, New England, Long Island. In urbane free verse, the poet recalls and meditates on music and painting, homosexuality, weekends with friends—John Ashbery and Fairfield Porter among them—deaths, a drive to the Hamptons. . . . Rarely has a poet imparted so much of his experience as honestly and engagingly as Schuyler does here." Publ Wkly

Seidel, Frederick

Poems 1959-2009. Farrar, Straus, and Giroux 2009 509p $40
811
1. Poetry -- By individual authors
ISBN 978-0-374-12655-1; 0-374-12655-0
LC 2008-47161

"Long regarded as a kind of elegant cult figure in poetry circles, Seidel has a reputation that precedes him into every room: decadent, name-dropper, sexual dalliant, Ducati enthusiast, son of privilege. This runs counter to the man himself. He doesn't do poetry readings and has, for the most part, shunned interviews. There is no doubt that Seidel is one of the best poets alive today, and now, with the release of 'Poems: 1959-2009,' his collected works can be taken at their measure: They are haughty, funny and terrifying, with plenty of delicious contention throughout." Los Angeles Times

Sendak, Maurice, 1928-2012

★ **My** brother's book; Maurice Sendak; [edited by] Michael di Capua. HarperCollins 2013 32 p. (hardcover bdg.) $18.95
811
1. Poetry 2. Poetry -- Collections
ISBN 0062234897; 9780062234896
LC 2012942549

In this book, "with influences from Shakespeare and William Blake, [Maurice] Sendak pays homage to his late brother, Jack, whom he credited for his passion for writing and drawing. Pairing Sendak's . . . poetry with his . . . artwork, . . . Sendak's tribute to his brother is an expression of both grief and love. . . . Pulitzer Prize--winning literary critic and Shakespearean scholar Stephen Greenblatt contributes a[n] . . . introduction." (Publisher's note)

Sexton, Anne
The **complete** poems; with a foreword by Maxine Kumin. Houghton Mifflin 1981 xxiv, 622p
hardcover o.p. pa $19 **811**
1. Poetry -- By individual authors
ISBN 0-395-95776-1 pa

LC 81-2482

"Even before her death in 1974, Sexton's work was the subject of critical controversy, often dismissed as mere confessionalism. But, as Maxine Kumin observes in an insightful introductory essay, Sexton 'delineated the problematic position of women—the neurotic reality of the time' and in so doing 'earned her place in the canon.'" Choice

Shapiro, Alan, 1952-
Reel to reel; Alan Shapiro. University of Chicago Press 2014 77 p. (pbk. : alk. paper) $18 **811**
1. American poetry -- Collections
ISBN 022611063X; 9780226110639

LC 2013016631

Pulitzer Prize Finalist: Poetry (2015)
This book, "Alan Shapiro's twelfth collection of poetry, moves outward from the intimate spaces of family and romantic life to embrace not only the human realm of politics and culture but also the natural world, and even the outer spaces of the cosmos itself. In language richly nuanced yet accessible, these poems inhabit and explore fundamental questions of existence, such as time, mortality, consciousness, and matter." (Publisher's note)

Shapiro, David
New and selected poems (1965-2006) Overlook Press 2007 267p $21.95 **811**
1. Poetry -- By individual authors
ISBN 978-1-58567-877-8; 1-58567-877-5

LC 2006-52718

"Shapiro is usually thought of as a New York School poet, but from the evidence of this selection it would probably be more accurate to call him a Greater New York School poet. His metropolis radiates outward to comprehend Weequahic Park and the Palisades, and his aleatory, portent-free sophistication seems confident enough to accommodate primitive, endearing, and frankly tender tropes and situations, as when a poet faces an ailing mother or a growing son. A perennial drama in this volume is that of an erudite and restlessly modernizing mind confronting pains and peculiarities that no amount of urbanity can assuage. . . . The effect is of unforeseen intimacy at the heart of abstraction." New Yorker

Shapiro, Karl Jay
★ **Selected** poems; [by] Karl Shapiro; John Updike, editor. Library of Am. 2003 xxxi, 197p il (American poets project) $20 **811**
1. Poetry -- By individual authors
ISBN 1-931082-34-0

LC 2002-32123

"Karl Shapiro, one of the more influential voices of the late 20th century, displayed complex and contrary tendencies in both his life and his poetry. Editor Updike notes that Shapiro's experimentation with voices and forms alienated

those who admired the metrical dexterity of his early poems." Libr J
Includes bibliographical references

Shaughnessy, Brenda
Human dark with sugar. Copper Canyon Press 2008 77p pa $15 **811**
1. Poetry -- By individual authors
ISBN 978-1-55659-276-8 pa; 1-55659-276-0 pa

LC 2007-52225

"The book's three sections contain nine, 11 and 10 poems, respectively, and that off-kilter triangulation . . . proves the right three-cornered lens for looking into the darkest corners of human relationships, including their embodiment. . . . This is a brilliant, beautiful and essential continuation of the metaphysical verse tradition." Publ Wkly

Shockley, Evie
The **new** black; poems. Wesleyan University Press 2011 104p il (Wesleyan poetry) **811**
1. Poetry -- By individual authors
ISBN 978-0-81957-140-3

LC 2010046345

In this book, the author "tells the reader not of some oversimplified and inaccurate version of 'the African-American experience' but of the plethora of experiences that inform the consciousness of one black woman in contemporary America. Shockley's work incorporates elements of myth without being patently 'mythical' and is personal without being self-indulgent, sentimental without being saccharine." Libr J

Simic, Charles, 1938-
The **Lunatic**; Poems. HarperCollins 2015 96 p. $22.99 **811**
1. Poetry -- Collections
ISBN 006236474X; 9780062364746

LC 2014450552

This book of poems, by Charles Simic, is "a dazzling collection of poems as original, meditative, and humorous as the legendary poet himself. . . . These seventy luminous poems range in subject from mortality to personal ads, from the simple wonders of nature to his childhood in war-torn Yugoslavia." (Publisher's note)
"Spiked with clues to larger mysteries, Simic's unnerving puzzle poems are works of insomniac witnessing and tempered love for our precious, haunted, rapturous, and dangerous world." Booklist

New and selected poems 1962-2012; Charles Simic. Houghton Mifflin Harcourt 2013 384 p. (hardcover) $30 **811**
1. Poetry -- Collections
ISBN 0547928289; 9780547928289

LC 2012042188

This poetry collection, by Pulitzer-prize winner and U.S poet laureate Charles Simic, "combin[es] for the first time the best of his early poems with his later works—including nearly three dozen revisions—along with seventeen new, never-before-published poems. Simic's body of work draws inspiration from a range of topics, from the inscrutability of ordinary life to American blues, from folktales to marriage and war." (Publisher's note)

★ The **voice** at 3:00 a.m; selected late & new poems. Harcourt 2003 177p $25   811
1. Poetry -- By individual authors
ISBN 0-15-100842-6
LC 2002-38715
"An important purchase for all libraries." Libr J

Simpson, Louis Aston Marantz
★ The **owner** of the house; new collected poems, 1940-2001. [by] Louis Simpson. BOA 2003 407p (American poets continuum series) $30.95; pa $19.95   811
1. Poetry -- By individual authors
ISBN 1-929918-38-0; 1-929918-39-9 pa
LC 2003-45241
The author "opens with 42 new poems and continues with selections from his 11 previous books, ending with There You Are. This work is filled with evocations of places like Jamaica, Manhattan, Paris, and Venice and range over time from tsarist Russia to World War II to the 1960s. Simpson's obsessive theme is the stultifying effect of middle-class suburban life. . . . The result is a collection both timely and accessible. . . . Highly recommended for all poetry collections." Libr J

Smith, Patricia
Shoulda been Jimi Savannah; Patricia Smith. Coffee House Press 2012 115 p. (alk. paper) $16.00   811
1. Women poets 2. African American women 3. Chicago (Ill.) -- Poetry
ISBN 1566892996; 9781566892995
LC 2011029282
[Patricia] Smith's mother bestowed on the poet a name fitting for a woman that would 'never idly throat the Lord's name or wear one/ of those thin, sparkled skirts that flirted with her knees./ She'd be a nurse or a third-grade teacher or a postal drone.' . . . But her father, though acquiescing, secretly called her Jimi Savannah, embodying 'the blues-bathed moniker of a ball breaker.' . . . This duality bursts forth in her poems about . . . growing up black and a woman during the 1960s." (Publishers Weekly)

Smith, Tracy K., 1972-
Life on Mars. Graywolf Press 2011 75p. pa $15   811
1. Poetry -- By individual authors
ISBN 1-55597-584-4; 978-1-55597-584-5
LC 2011920674
Pulitzer Prize: Poetry (2012)
"Smith shows herself to be a poet of extraordinary range and ambition. It's not easy to be so convincing in both the grand gesture and the reverent contemplation of a humble plate of eggs, and the early successes of this collection far outweigh its later missteps. As all the best poetry does, 'Life on Mars' first sends us out into the magnificent chill of the imagination and then returns us to ourselves, both changed and consoled." N Y Times Book Rev

Snodgrass, W. D.
★ **Not** for specialists; new and selected poems. BOA Editions 2006 251p (American poets continuum series) $27.95; pa $21.95   811
1. Poetry -- By individual authors
ISBN 1-92991-877-1; 1-92991-876-3 pa
LC 2005-54846
"If you think that writing primarily in rhyme and meter bespeaks equanimity, or sweetness of character, read Snodgrass. Oh, he mellows out in the face of nature, but he's prickly. . . . His many profoundly bemused and persuasive poems of love's tougher moments, his marvelous angry and denunciatory poems, and the chilling Fuehrer Bunker poems in the voices of the major Nazis during the war's last month—all these might have been impossible if Snodgrass was a nice, easygoing guy. He's not that sort, and his best work seems permanent because he isn't." Booklist

Snyder, Gary
No nature; new and selected poems. Pantheon Bks. 1992 390p hardcover o.p. pa $16   811
1. Poetry -- By individual authors
ISBN 978-0-679-74252-4
LC 92-54110
"There is an understated majesty about the ease with which Mr. Snyder puts the present into perspective." N Y Times Book Rev

Spicer, Jack
★ **My** vocabulary did this to me; the collected poetry of Jack Spicer. edited by Peter Gizzi and Kevin Killian. Wesleyan University Press 2008 496p il $35   811
1. Poetry -- By individual authors
ISBN 978-0-8195-6887-8
LC 2008-24997
"Impeccably edited, this collection gathers the remarkable output of a poet whose writing and person were too counter even for the counterculture of the late '50s and '60s. Spicer's work manages to combine heartbreak, hermeticism, and postwar disquiet in a way both completely of its time and still ahead of ours." Village Voice

Stafford, William Edgar
The **way** it is; new & selected poems. Graywolf Press 1998 xx, 268p $24.95; pa $16   811
1. Poetry -- By individual authors
ISBN 1-55597-269-1; 1-55597-284-5 pa
LC 97-80082
"Including 71 previously unpublished new poems, among them the poem Stafford wrote the day he died, this collection fully reacquaints us with a quiet, generous presence on the American poetic landscape." Publ Wkly

Stern, Gerald
This time; new and selected poems. Norton 1998 288p hardcover o.p. pa $15.95   811
1. Poetry -- By individual authors
ISBN 0-393-31909-1 pa
LC 97-43670

"At once self-involved and sympathetic, Stern catalogues with wry dexterity a vast range of sensory data and cultural detritus, always united by 'women and men of all sizes and all ages/living together, without satire.' This healthy collection of new poems and selections from his seven previous volumes . . . is remarkable for its generosity of spirit, manifested in a warm surrealism that is often turned with humor toward his own past." Publ Wkly

Stevens, Wallace

Collected poetry and prose. Library of Am. 1997 xxii, 1032p $35 **811**
  1. Poetry -- By individual authors
  ISBN 1-88301-145-0

LC 97-7023

Having all of Stevens' "poems—especially all the late poems—in one volume is a great thing (previously, one had to seek them out in three different books); the 'Adagia' and his replies to questionnaires are marvelous; and even in the somewhat turgid prose pieces, he sometimes expresses himself with exemplary force and concision." N Y Times Book Rev

Stone, Ruth

What love comes to; new & selected poems. foreword by Sharon Olds. Copper Canyon Press 2008 359p $32 **811**
  1. Poetry -- By individual authors
  ISBN 978-1-55659-271-3; 1-55659-271-X

LC 2007045832

Pulitzer Prize Finalist (2009)

"In a field in which collections of selected writings are constantly being released, this book stands out because Stone shows that simplicity can be a deceiving doorway into some of the most challenging poems written by an American poet. Stone's poems blend the personal with dimensions of the larger world in a manner reminiscent of the late William Stafford. Few poets have this gift for taking the workings of ordinary life and fusing them with a poetic process that sustains intense emotion, allowing human experience to be felt through the mysteries of language. . . . Ruth Stone belongs to every generation of poets who have taken the responsibility to give back to the world." Bloomsbury Rev

Strand, Mark, 1934-2014

Collected poems; by Mark Strand. Alfred A. Knopf 2014 520 p. (Hardcover) $30 **811**
  ISBN 0385352514; 9780385352512

LC 2013049034

"Gathered here is a half century's magnificent work by the former poet laureate of the United States and Pulitzer Prize winner whose haunting and exemplary style has influenced an entire generation of American poets." Publisher's Note

"For all the streamlined sadness of his dreamlike domain, Strand remains aware of other poets, which is particularly evident in his homages, translations, and elegies. His recent string of short sardonic prose poems are all quite distinct from one another, but all are instantly, recognizably Strand, 'erasing the world and leaving instead/ The invisible lines of its calling: Out there, out there.'" Pub Wkly

Swenson, May

Nature; poems old and new. Houghton Mifflin 1994 xxiii, 240p hardcover o.p. pa $15 **811**
  1. Poetry -- By individual authors
  ISBN 0-618-06408-7 pa

LC 93-45642

This collection of Swenson's poetry "brings together poems from several earlier books, as well as poems published only in magazines, and introduces us to nine splendid poems published here for the first time. This collection . . . is brought together with special attention to poems describing the environment; poems of tides and the sea, of birds and gardens, of moods and seasons, of self and others. . . . This is a collection to be treasured; it belongs in all libraries with even a modest selection of poetry." Libr J

Sze, Arthur

Compass Rose; Arthur Sze. Copper Canyon Press 2014 68 p. $16 **811**
  1. Poetry -- Collections
  ISBN 1556594674; 9781556594670

LC 2013025678

Pulitzer Prize Finalist: Poetry (2015)

This collection of poems by Arthur Sze features a "child playing a game, tea leaves resting in a bowl, an abandoned dog, a foot sticking out from a funeral pyre, an Afghan farmer pausing as mortars fire at the enemy." (Publisher's note)

"It's easy for readers to become lost in the intricacies, but the beauty of image and symmetry of ideas offer balance and direction." LJ

Includes bibliographical references

Szybist, Mary

★ **Incarnadine**; Mary Szybist. Graywolf Press 2013 72 p. (paperback) $15 **811**
  ISBN 1555976352; 9781555976354

LC 2012953979

This poetry anthology, by the National Book Critics Circle Award finalist Mary Szybist, is her second published collection. "One poem is presented as a diagrammed sentence. Another is an abecedarium made of lines of dialogue spoken by girls overheard while assembling a puzzle. Several poems arrive as a series of Annunciations, while others purport to give an update on Mary, who must finish the dishes before she will open herself to God." (Publisher's note)

Taggart, John

★ **Pastorelles**. Flood Editions 2004 104p pa $13.95 **811**
  1. Poetry -- By individual authors
  ISBN 0-974690-21-X

LC 2004-303826

"Among the small number of poets who have followed the difficult path of Zukofsky, George Oppen, Lorraine Niedecker, and William Bronk, John Taggart has kept more closely to the Objectivist trail than most, while at the same time developing his own signature style and deepening his explorations into the strata where vision, music, and language converge. Pastorelles may be his most consistent and fully realized collection, one that maintains and enlivens a literary movement that, even after decades, has still not been granted the degree of attention and critical analysis it deserves." Am Book Rev

Tarn, Nathaniel

Selected poems; 1950-2000. Wesleyan University Press 2002 335p (Wesleyan poetry) $45; pa $19.95   **811**

1. Poetry -- By individual authors

ISBN 978-0-8195-6541-9; 0-8195-6541-5; 978-0-8195-6542-6 pa; 0-8195-6542-3 pa

LC 2002-1701

"Arranged chronologically, [this volume] has reprints from nineteen of Tarn's thirty-five books. Here the literary reader can find reality hybrids and can experience the camaraderie of whole image systems from the twentieth century. No syllable is lonely or aloof. One is often reminded, by Tarn's references, his subjects, and his dedications, not only of Blake but of Yeats, Vallejo, Charles Olson, and Robert Duncan. Like those writers, his work brings together mythology, Western and Eastern philosophy (including Gnostic thought), political commentary, scientific investigations, naturalist descriptions and very personal love poetry." Jacket

Tate, James

Selected poems. Wesleyan Univ. Press 1991 239p hardcover o.p. pa $18.95   **811**

1. Poetry -- By individual authors

ISBN 978-0-8195-1192-8; 0-8195-1192-7

LC 90-50918

Tate has "created a voice and a kind of poem that no one else could have written. His comedy works not only to entertain, which it does marvelously—he has the rare ability to be very, very funny on the page—but partly to cover and partly to reveal underlying disorientation and angst." N Y Times Book Rev

Trinidad, David

Dear Prudence; new and selected poems. Turtle Point 2011 493p pa $19   **811**

1. Poetry -- By individual authors

ISBN 978-1-933527-47-5

A collection of poetry from gay poet Trinidad.

The author's "lucid, amusing, and sad journal poems, memoir poems, prose poems, couplets, elegies, sonnets, and impressive pantoums may seem to valorize trash, but that trash sustains a flawed yet invaluable soul aching for loving acceptance." Booklist

Troupe, Quincy

★ Transcircularities; new and selected poems. Coffee House Press 2002 368p $30; pa $17   **811**

1. Poetry -- By individual authors

ISBN 1-56689-137-X; 1-56689-135-3 pa

LC 2002-71277

Troupe's "verse returns continually to swing, bebop and free-jazz giants, imitating, commemorating or praising Coltrane, Duke, Bud Powell and others in a series of musicianly poems culminating in the recent 'Back to the Dream Time: Miles Speaks from the Dead.' Troupe's forms, driven by performability, range from ecstatic odes to overtly political expostulations." Publ Wkly

Twentieth-century American poetry; edited by Dana Gioia, David Mason, Meg Schoerke. McGraw Hill 2004 xlvi, 1143p il pa $79.69   **811**

1. American poetry -- Collections

ISBN 0-07-240019-6

LC 2003-61449

"The text is divided into sections like 'Realism and Naturalism' and 'The Harlem Renaissance,' with each section prefaced by a penetrating overview and each poet introduced by a biographical essay. Included are poets as diverse as Sherman Alexie, Ezra Pound, and Lucille Clifton, along with Nuyorican poets, New Formalists, Beats, imagists, and surrealists. Make room for this affordable, remarkable volume." Libr J

Includes bibliographical references

Twichell, Chase

Horses where the answers should have been; new and selected poems. Copper Canyon Press 2010 255p pa $19   **811**

1. Poetry -- By individual authors

ISBN 978-1-55659-318-5; 1-55659-318-X

LC 2009-48885

"To read a well done 'selected poems' is to follow a life, and we find that here as we watch the poet grow from one in love with thought and language to one who quietly yet intensely contemplates the world by leaning toward the essential. Hers is a world of wounded beauty which she confronts and records for us." N Y Journal of Books

Includes bibliographical references

Updike, John

Collected poems, 1953-1993. Knopf 1993 xxiv, 387p il hardcover o.p. pa $25   **811**

1. Poetry -- By individual authors

ISBN 978-0-679-76204-1; 0-679-76204-3

LC 92-28957

"From the outset Updike's poems are crisp and exact. There is a mock humbleness, ready wit, and divine concreteness to his subjects, an unrelenting curiosity behind his descriptions, and a prodding tension between the tactile and the abstract. . . . From the cocky exuberance of 'Midpoint,' a 1968 autobiographical cycle, to the wry, tender mischief of poems about domesticity, marriage, and aging, Updike's thrill over the unending discovery of poetry inspires images and metaphors of time-stopping perfection as well as humor rich in grace and knowingness." Booklist

Includes bibliographical references

Valentine, Jean

Door in the mountain; new and collected poems, 1965-2003. Wesleyan University Press 2004 285p (Wesleyan poetry) $29.95   **811**

1. Poetry -- By individual authors

ISBN 0-8195-6712-4

LC 2004-16019

"The defiant, angular, yet propulsively emotional recent poems that occupy the first and last parts of the book should please both fans of Valentine's earliest poetry and fans of her strongly feminist middle period." Publ Wkly

Includes bibliographical references

Van Duyn, Mona

★ **Selected** poems. Knopf 2002 218p $27.50;
pa $16   **811**
1. Poetry -- By individual authors
ISBN 0-375-41369-3; 0-375-70980-0 pa
LC 2001-50672

"Characterized by candor and compassion, Van Duyn's
poetry depicts the pleasures and drudgeries of middle-class
American life, an approach that at its best becomes an exploration of the spiritual and psychological dimensions of that
life. . . . The casually formal surfaces of Van Duyn's poems
often resemble those of her model, Elizabeth Bishop, and
like Bishop she excels at both formal and free verse." N Y
Times Book Rev

The **Vintage** book of African American poetry; edited and with an introduction by Michael S. Harper
and Anthony Walton. Vintage Bks. 2000 xxxiii,
403p pa $14.95   **811**
1. American poetry -- African American authors --
Collections
ISBN 0-375-70300-4
LC 99-39428

"Included in chronological order here are over two centuries of poets, from Jupitor Hammon (1720-1800) to Reginald Shepherd (b.1963). . . . The editors' eloquent, outspoken vision provides a springboard for further examination of
what constitutes the mainstream of American poetry." Libr J
Includes bibliographical references

Wakoski, Diane

The **diamond** dog. Anhinga Press 2010 110p
pa $15   **811**
1. Poetry -- By individual authors
ISBN 978-1-934695-15-9; 1-934695-15-7

Wakoski's "work is often associated with the Deep Image school, with its allegiance to the Jungian imagery said
to comprise the collective unconscious, as well as the Confessional and Beat movements in poetry. . . . All of these
– the Jungian images, the tendency to confess, the wild leaps
and unruly rhythms of the Beat poets, the theme of abandonment – figure in 'The Diamond Dog.' By now, though,
Wakoski is able to look back over her 22 books and connect these concerns in the essay called 'Creating a Personal
Mythology' that begins the book. Here she provides a career
perspective that her fans will welcome. Just as important,
she describes a way of writing that young poets will be able
to make their own. . . . Wakoski's rhythms are jazzy and
easygoing; they're accepting of the world in all its crunchy
variety, and they invite the reader to accept as well. The best
way to describe her poetics is to say that she asks the reader
to go for a walk with her." Christ Sci Monit

Walcott, Derek

Omeros. Farrar, Straus & Giroux 1990 325p
hardcover o.p. pa $16   **811**
1. Poetry -- By individual authors
ISBN 0-374-52350-9 pa
LC 90-33592

"No poet rivals Mr. Walcott in humor, emotional depth,
lavish inventiveness in language or in the ability to express
the thoughts of his characters and compel the reader to follow the swift mutations of ideas and images in their minds.
This wonderful story moves in a spiral, replicating human
thought." N Y Times Book Rev

Walcott, Derek, 1930-

The **Poetry** of Derek Walcott 1948-2013; Derek
Walcott; [selected by the poet Glyn Maxwell] Farrar,
Straus & Giroux 2014 640 p. (hardcover) $40 **811**
1. Poetry 2. Nature poetry 3. Identity (Psychology)
ISBN 0374125619; 9780374125615
LC 2013034997

This book of poetry by Derek Walcott, edited by Glyn
Maxwell, "draws from every stage of the poet's storied career. . . . Across sixty-five years, Walcott has grappled with
the themes that have defined his work as they have defined
his life. . . . This collection, . . . will prove as enduring as the
questions, the passions, that have driven Walcott to write for
more than half a century." (Publisher's note)

"A doorstop of a book, this collection reaches across Nobel laureate Walcott's career. A defining, definitive postcolonial poet, he writes of St. Lucia, the West, imperialism and
identity, and memory and pain." LJ

Waldman, Anne

In the room of never grieve; new and selected
poems, 1985-2003. Coffee House Press 2003 494p
il $30   **811**
1. Poetry -- By individual authors
ISBN 978-1-566-89145-5; 1-566-89145-0
LC 2003-55096

"If early work found [Waldman] most engaged with the
New York School, these later poems integrate her passions
for Buddhism and ethnopoetics into a unique style of vocal,
unabashedly current-event-laden, collagistic, wide-ranging
work. Waldman's quest to find forms appropriate to her shamanistic, didactic content is particularly compelling in Marriage: A Sentence, with its liquefied gender roles and synthesis of influences ranging from Stein to Corso. . . . Waldman's untiring efforts to link language, ritual and political
action come through clearly, urgently and often beautifully."
Publ Wkly
Includes bibliographical references and indexes

Waldrop, Keith

Transcendental studies; a trilogy. University of
California Press 2009 201p (New California poetry)
$50; pa $19.95   **811**
1. Poetry -- By individual authors
ISBN 978-0-520-25877-8; 978-0-520-25878-5 pa
LC 2008-25958

"Comprising three sequences—each almost a book in itself—plus an epilogue, it is an extended philosophical meditation on what are, broadly, the major themes of all poetry:
perception, the imagination, the body, and how the human
inner life interacts with the larger world. In mostly short, jagged free verse pieces, Waldrop goes at these lofty concepts
head-on in accessible, if cerebral, language." Publ Wkly

Waldrop, Rosmarie

Driven to abstraction. New Directions 2010
133p pa $16.95 **811**
　　1. Poetry -- By individual authors
　　ISBN 978-0-8112-1879-5; 0-8112-1879-1
　　　　　　　　　　　　　　LC 2010-14992
"Waldrop continues to actualize surprising poems.
Language is active and it enacts. In Driven to Abstraction,
questions are often answers—'Only God can create out of
nothing. But did he use up the void?'— and statements often questions. This specialized form of constructing prose
builds many lessons; sidling up against bigger and more layered themes, the book reads like a semester full of engaging
seminars." Coldfront

Walker, Alice

Hard times require furious dancing; new poems.
foreword and illustrations by Shiloh McCloud. New
World Library 2010 165p il $18 **811**
　　1. Poetry -- By individual authors
　　ISBN 978-1-57731-930-6
　　　　　　　　　　　　　　LC 2010-29972
In this poetry collection, the author "writes of loss and
disappointment, and the strength that rises from meeting
them unflinchingly. . . . These are powerful anthems of womanhood and age, although just as likely to be empowering to
men and to the not-yet-old." Booklist

Warren, Robert Penn

★ The **collected** poems of Robert Penn Warren; edited by John Burt; with a foreword by Harold
Bloom. Louisiana State Univ. Press 1998 xxvi, 830p
$44.95 **811**
　　1. Poetry -- By individual authors
　　ISBN 0-8071-2333-1
　　　　　　　　　　　　　　LC 98-26104
"This immense volume gathers 15 books of poetry—as
well as uncollected verse from the beginning and end of
his writing life—from a formidable American man of letters and our first poet laureate. . . . Scholars will especially
cherish the careful, copious textual and explanatory notes
provided by Warren's literary executor Burt . . . and fans of
American poetry and literary history alike should welcome
this opportunity to explore the prodigious oeuvre of one of
the New Criticism's most forceful, convincing proponents."
Publ Wkly

Wheatley, Phillis

The **poems** of Phillis Wheatley; edited with an
introduction by Julian D. Mason, Jr. rev & enl ed;
University of N.C. Press 1989 235p hardcover o.p.
pa $22.95 **811**
　　1. Poetry -- By individual authors
　　ISBN 0-8078-4245-1 pa
　　　　　　　　　　　　　　LC 88-23280
First published 1966
This volume contains all of the poems and letters known
to have been written by Wheatley, America's first significant
black woman writer

Whitman, Walt

★ **Complete** poetry and collected prose. Library
of Am. 1982 1380p $35; pa $17.95 **811**
　　1. Poetry -- By individual authors
　　ISBN 0-940450-02-X; 1-883011-35-3 pa
　　　　　　　　　　　　　　LC 81-20768
"Presented here is the great culminating edition of 1891-
92, the last supervised by Whitman himself. Whitman's
prose, no less extraordinary, includes reminiscences of 19th-
century New York City and notes on the Civil War, especially his service in Washington hospitals and glimpses of
President Lincoln." Publisher's Note

★ **Leaves** of grass; edited and with a new after-
word by David S. Reynolds. 150th anniversary ed.;
Oxford University Press 2005 167p $23 **811**
　　1. Poetry -- By individual authors
　　ISBN 0-19-518342-8
　　　　　　　　　　　　　　LC 2004-26509
First published 1855
"The book, radical in form and content, takes its title
from the themes of fertility, universality, and cyclical life. .
. . As he revised and added to the original edition, Whitman
arranged the poems in a significant autobiographical order."
Reader's Ency. 4th edition

★ **Selected** poems; Harold Bloom, editor. Library of Am. 2003 xxxi, 221p (American poets project) $20 **811**
　　1. Poetry -- By individual authors
　　ISBN 1-931082-32-4
　　　　　　　　　　　　　　LC 2002-32124
The editor "is concerned with Whitman's construction
of his all-encompassing persona, and he selects with that in
mind. . . . Bloom connects Whitman's project to the thesis
of his The American Religion (1992) that the tendency of
religion in America is to replace God with man, and with
the fragments, Bloom presents explicit evidence of the
attempt." Booklist
Includes bibliographical references

Whittier, John Greenleaf

Selected poems; Brenda Wineapple, editor. Library of America 2004 xxvii, 187p $20 **811**
　　1. Poetry -- By individual authors
　　ISBN 978-1-931082-59-4; 1-931082-59-6
　　　　　　　　　　　　　　LC 2003-60483
"Touching and effective as [many of] these poems are,
there is a longer one that ensures Whittier's place in our
canon. Of course I have 'SnowBound' in mind. This poem
of over nine hundred lines evokes a rural way of life, already
past when it was written, in its memories of a family isolated
in their farmhouse for a week by a blizzard. . . . This new selection may not restore Whittier to the schoolroom wall, but
surely it will help readers reassess the author of one major
long poem and a score of attractive lyrics and narratives that
deserve their place in our poetic tradition." Sewanee Rev

Wilbur, Richard, 1921-

Anterooms; new poems and translations. Houghton Mifflin Harcourt 2010 63p $20   **811**

1. Poetry -- By individual authors

ISBN 978-0-547-35811-6; 0-547-35811-3

LC 2010-05772

"The better work in Anterooms, however limited in quantity, is as good as anything Wilbur has ever written, and upholds certain virtues other poets would do well to acknowledge, even if they travel roads different from the relatively straight one Wilbur has followed." N Y Times Book Rev

★ **Collected** poems, 1943-2004. Harcourt 2004 608p il $35   **811**

1. Poetry -- By individual authors

ISBN 0-15-101105-2

LC 2004-9228

A comprehensive collection of works written throughout the course of the poet's more than sixty-year career includes "In Trackless Woods" and several new and previously unpublished pieces

"Technically, Wilbur remains assured and impressive; he is the premier American master of formal verse. His knowledge has expanded with his life, and his wit has grown in humor while mellowing linguistically. . . . He's indispensable." Booklist

Williams, C. K.

★ **Collected** poems. Farrar, Straus and Giroux 2006 682p $40   **811**

1. Poetry -- By individual authors

ISBN 978-0-374-12652-0; 0-374-12652-6

LC 2005-51867

"This weighty, even daunting, tome shows new and old readers the long arc of this Pulitzer Prize and National Book Award winner's career, from the morbid sanguinities of his apprentice work to the careful, moving, stanzaic focus evident in 21 new poems." Publ Wkly

Williams, Jonathan

★ **Jubilant** thicket; new & selected poems. Jonathan Williams. Copper Canyon Press 2005 pa $20   **811**

1. Poetry -- By individual authors

ISBN 1-55659-202-7

LC 2004-20436

"Pared down from 1,450 works over 55 years, this selection features jaunty dances through naughty woods . . ., jokes to and about Ezra Pound, selected listings from the Western Carolina Telephone Company phone book, limericks, 'metafours' (poems in which each line has four words), a poem for each Mahler symphony and acrostics using the names of friends like Guy Davenport. . . . By the end of the book, it becomes clear that Williams can make a verse out of whatever's at hand; the result is a kind of commonplace book for a life lived, with wry but inextinguishable enthusiasm, in the company of artists and arts." Publ Wkly

Williams, William Carlos

★ The **collected** poems of William Carlos Williams. New Directions 1986 2v v1 $40; v1 pa $23.95; v2 $38; v2 pa $22.95   **811**

1. Poetry -- By individual authors

ISBN 0-8112-0999-7 v1; 0-8112-1187-8 v1 pa; 0-8112-1063-4 v2; 0-8112-1188-6 v2 pa

"Williams's poetry is firmly rooted in the commonplace detail of everyday American life. He conceived of the poem as an object: a record of direct experience that deals with the local and the particular. He abandoned conventional rhyme and meter in an effort to reduce the barrier between the reader and his consciousness of his immediate surroundings. . . . Williams's original approach to poetry, his insistence on the importance of the ordinary, and his successful attempts at making his verse as 'tactile' as the spoken word had a far-reaching effect on American poetry." Reader's Ency. 4th edition

Paterson; prepared by Christopher MacGowan. rev ed; New Directions 1992 311p hardcover o.p. pa $15.95   **811**

1. Poetry -- By individual authors

ISBN 978-0-8112-1298-4; 0-8112-1298-X

LC 92-22956

First published 1963

"Set in Paterson, N.J., the poem is a statement on contemporary civilization. Williams uses one dominant metaphor throughout: the city is the human mind beside the river of time; the language of contemporary events (the waterfall) gives the only kind of meaning possible in the flux of time. The poem is composed of lyrics, narrative episodes, prose interludes, bits of letters, etc., to comprise an ecstatic statement on human life." Herzberg. Reader's Ency of Am Lit

Winder, Elizabeth

Pain, Parties, Work; Sylvia Plath in New York, Summer 1953. Elizabeth Winder. HarperCollins 2013 288 p. (hardcover) $25.99   **811**

1. New York (N.Y.)

ISBN 0062085492; 9780062085498

This biography, by Elizabeth Winder, follows "a young Sylvia Plath and the life-changing month that would lay the groundwork for her seminal novel, 'The Bell Jar.' In May of 1953, a twenty-one-year-old Plath arrived in New York City. . . . She was supposed to be having the time of her life. But what would follow was, in Plath's words, twenty-six days of pain, parties, and work, that ultimately changed the course of her life." (Publisher's note)

Words for the hour; a new anthology of American Civil War poetry. edited by Faith Barrett and Cristanne Miller. University of Massachusetts Press 2005 xxx, 401p il lib bdg $80; pa $27.95 **811**

1. War poetry 2. American poetry -- Collections 3. United States -- History -- 1861-1865, Civil War -- Poetry

ISBN 1-55849-510-X lib bdg; 1-55849-509-6 pa

LC 2005-18477

For this collection, the editors "limit their selection to work written between 1834 and 1891 by poets who lived through and often actively participated in antebellum, wartime, and aftermath events. . . . An interpretational, literary, and documentary monument." Booklist

Includes bibliographical references

Wright, C. D.

One with others; [a little book of her days] Copper Canyon Press 2010 168p pa $18   **811**

1. Poetry -- By individual authors 2. African Americans -- Civil rights -- Poetry

ISBN 978-1-55659-324-6; 1-55659-324-4

LC 2010-16789

"In August, 1969, a Memphis man known as Sweet Willie Wine led a group of black men on a four-day March Against Fear, from West Memphis to Little Rock, passing through the small towns of the Arkansas delta. . . . [This book] tells the story of the march, and of the only outsider to join it, a small-town white woman, Margaret Kaelin McHugh, whom Wright calls V. . . . [It] represents Wright's most audacious experiment yet in loading up lyric with evidentiary fact. . . . An affecting element of this book is the way its elegiac impulses accord with, even as they chafe against, the documentary impulses." New Yorker

★ **Steal** away; selected and new poems. Copper Canyon Press 2002 235p $25; pa $17   **811**

1. Poetry -- By individual authors

ISBN 1-55659-172-1; 1-55659-194-2 pa

LC 2001-7423

Wright's "poems are crazy quilts constructed out of bits of conversation, a to-do list, dreams, a treatment for a harrowing silent film, and a saxophone solo, but Wright also offers sophisticated readings of the routines and cycle of ordinary life, and ponders the amazing persistence of the everhungry body and the tricky mind. It's a boon to have such a wealth of her crackling, intelligent, erotic, 'painfully beautiful,' keep-you-on-your-toes poems in one place. New works accompany selections from nine previous, mostly out of print collections, and all are electrifying in their clear-eyed reports on desire, determination, and survival." Booklist

Wright, Charles

★ **Negative** blue; selected later poems. Farrar, Straus & Giroux 2000 206p $23; pa $15   **811**

1. Poetry -- By individual authors

ISBN 0-374-22020-4; 0-374-52773-3 pa

LC 99-36987

The author "collects a decade's worth of striking description and laid-back meditation in this sample of work from his last three books. . . . Wright's power lies less in whole poems than in lines within them: those linear strenghts owe something to Ezra Pound, and something more to the antiphonal balances of the Psalms. Wright ends the volume with seven new short poems." Publ Wkly

Wright, James Arlington

Above the river; the complete poems. [by] James Wright; with an introduction by Donald Hall. Farrar, Straus & Giroux 1990 xxxvii, 387p hardcover o.p. pa $20   **811**

1. Poetry -- By individual authors

ISBN 978-0-374-52282-7; 0-374-52282-0

LC 89-16538

"The narrowed range of Wright's characteristic subjects and format, the very delicacy of his instincts, confine him. But his best poems, with their grace and intelligence, not only stand as a rebuke to most of the glib work of his time, but remain among the finest examples of the midcentury American lyric." N Y Times Book Rev

Wright, Jay

★ **Transfigurations**; collected poems. Louisiana State Univ. Press 2000 619p $59.95; pa $24.95 **811**

1. Poetry -- By individual authors

ISBN 0-8071-2629-2; 0-8071-2630-6 pa

LC 00-40560

"Lyric poetry is a way of compressing experience into a heightened moment, but what happens when the experience is one of wanting not to be contained? Wright is an African-American poet who has contended with this dilemma for the last thirty years, and the result is a substantial collection of work. His forcefully musical rhythms drive even poems of everyday experience to a pleasingly contradictory transport. And the later, meditative poems are bound to the world by their attention to the sensual within the spiritual." New Yorker

Young, Kevin

Ardency; a chronicle of the Amistad rebels. compiled from authentic sources by Kevin Lowell Young. Alfred A. Knopf 2011 249p il map $27.95   **811**

1. Slavery -- Poetry 2. Amistad (Schooner) -- Poetry 3. Poetry -- By individual authors

ISBN 0307267644; 9780307267641

LC 2010-30007

"Young gathers here a chorus of voices that tells the story of the Africans who mutinied onboard the slave ship Amistad." (Publisher's note)

This poetry collection "chronicles the slave mutiny aboard the schooner Amistad in 1839. This three-part book focuses on the 53 Africans who rebelled against their would-be slave owners. Young expertly blends cultural and social history as well as religion to dramatize the lives of the rebels. His evocative use of language—punctuated with stunning metaphors—keeps the historical context clear while moving the gripping true story forward." Libr J

Zapruder, Matthew

Come on all you ghosts; Matthew Zapruder. Copper Canyon Press 2010 xi, 111p (alk. paper) $16   **811**

1. American poetry 2. Poetry -- Collections 3. Heroes and heroines -- Poetry 4. Poetry -- By individual authors

ISBN 1556593228; 9781556593222

LC 2010016787

This book of poetry is written by Matthew Zapruder, the winner of the William Carlos Williams Award. "The title poem is an elegy for heroes and mentors—from David Foster Wallace to Zapruder's father—and demonstrates a[n] . . . expansive range for the poet, highlighting as well a larger body of poetry that . . . wrestles with the desires to live rightly, to make art, and to confront the vast events of the day." (Publisher's note)

"Zapruder invokes a variety of second persons: sometimes it's a particular intimate, as in . . . 'Letter to a Lover' or . . . 'Poem for Hannah,' sometimes a recognizable public figure, as in . . . 'Poem for Ferlinghetti.'. . . . Greeting and address help the poet to escape the solitary confinement of consciousness." (LA Review of Books)

The poet "speaks 'with a voice that pretends to be shy/ and actually is, always in search of the question/ that might make you ask me one in return.' In his . . . signature, meandering style, he'll often begin with simple, even childlike observations ('Oh this Diet Coke is really good') that set off associative chains in search of subjects that resonate, psychologically or philosophically, with past personal experiences. . . . Seeming to discover themselves as they go, Zapruder's improvisations (or so they appear) enlist the reader as coexplorer, stumbling into candid self-revelations ('I am also/ always balancing/ on the smooth blade of not/ letting other people down') or surreal quips ('I feel like an elk getting a pelvic exam') with wide-eyed grace." Libr J

Zukofsky, Louis

Selected poems; Charles Bernstein, editor. Library of America 2006 xxvii, 172p $20   **811**

1. Poetry -- By individual authors
ISBN 978-1-93108-295-2

LC 2006-40808

"Contemporary poet Charles Bernstein uses these pages skillfully to present a compact but diverse selection of Zukofsky's writing, and he supplies a cogent introduction to both the biography and the poetics." Tikkun

811.54   American poetry--1945-1999

Gizzi, Peter

Archeophonics; Peter Gizzi. Wesleyan University Press 2016 108 p. (cloth : alk. paper) $24.95; (ebook) $18.99   **811.54**

1. Poetry -- Collections
ISBN 0819576808; 9780819576804; 9780819576811

LC 2016021168

National Book Award Finalist: Poetry (2016)

This book, by Peter Gizzi, "is a series of discrete poems that are linked by repeated phrases and words, and its themes and nothing less than joy, outrage, loss, transhistorical thought, and day-to-day life. It is a private book of public and civic concerns." (Publisher's note)

"Award-winning poet Gizzi here uses spare, focused language to reflect on language itself: its origins, structure, uses, and music." LJ

Hall, Donald, 1928-

The **selected** poems of Donald Hall; Donald Hall. Houghton Mifflin Harcourt 2015 160 p. (hardcover) $22; (ebook) $22   **811.54**

1. Poetry -- Collections
ISBN 9780544555600; 9780544555617

LC 2015004341

In this book, "former poet laureate Donald Hall selects [his] essential work. . . . Instead of creating new poems, he has looked back over his astonishingly rich body of work and hand-picked poems for this final, concise volume that will delight, and endure." (Publisher's note)

"Hall's best work combines these goals with a very dry humor, an almost too-mild regret; much of it stretches out over pages at an unrhymed, close-cut, dignified length." Pub Wkly

Mead, Jane

World of made and unmade; Jane Mead. Alice James Books 2016 100 p. (softcover : acid-free paper) $15.95   **811.54**

1. Death 2. Poetry -- Collections
ISBN 9781938584329

LC 2016011688

This book of poetry by Jane Mead "candidly and openly explores the long process that is death. These resonant poems discover what it means to live, die, and come home again. We're drawn in by sorrow and grief, but also the joys of celebrating a long life and how simple it is to find laughter and light in the quietest and darkest of moments." (Publisher's note)

"This accessible work will appeal to a wide range of readers." LJ

Stanford, Frank

What about this; the collected poems of Frank Stanford. Frank Stanford; edited by Michael Wiegers; introduction by Dean Young. Copper Canyon Press 2015 640 p. illustrations (hardcover) $40   **811.54**

1. American poetry -- Collections
ISBN 9781556594687

LC 2014045989

National Book Critics Circle Award Finalist: Poetry (2015)

This poetry collection, by Frank Stanford, edited by Michael Wiegers, is a posthumously-edited volume collecting a large selection of the literary works of Frank Stanford. It "includes hundreds of previously unpublished poems, a short story, an interview, and is richly illustrated with draft poems, photographs, and odd ephemera." (Publisher's note)

"Stanford demanded of poetry that it 'mean and sing,' and this is the definitive document of his uncanny ability to do just that." Pub Wkly

Young, Kevin

Blue laws; selected & uncollected poems, 1995-2015. Kevin Young. Alfred A. Knopf 2016 608 p. (ebook) $65; (hardcover) $30   **811.54**

1. American poetry 2. Poetry -- Collections
ISBN 9781101946947; 9780385351508

LC 2015017451

"'Blue Laws' gathers poems written over the past two decades, drawing from all nine of Kevin Young's previously published books of poetry and including a number of uncollected, often unpublished, poems. . . . This collection provides a grand tour of a poet whose personal poems and political poems are equally riveting." (Publisher's note)

"Young is an essential, dynamic, and resonant poet, and this commanding, 20-year retrospective belongs in libraries large and small." Booklist

Includes bibliographical references.

811.6 American poetry--2000-

Borzutzky, Daniel
★ The **performance** of becoming human; Daniel Borzutzky. Brooklyn Arts Press 2016 98 p. (pbk) $18   **811.6**
1. Globalization
ISBN 1936767465; 9781936767465
LC 2015028529
National Book Award: Poetry (2016)
In this book of poetry, author Daniel Borzutzky "returns to confront the various ways nation-states and their bureaucracies absorb and destroy communities and economies. . . . To become human is to navigate borders, including the fuzzy borders of institutions, the economies of privatization, overdevelopment, and underdevelopment, under which humans endure state-sanctioned and systemic abuses in cities, villages, deserts." (Publisher's note)

Gay, Ross, 1974-
Catalog of Unabashed Gratitude; by Ross Gay. University of Pittsburgh Press 2015 112 p. $15.95   **811.6**
1. Poetry -- Collections
ISBN 0822963310; 9780822963318
National Book Award Finalist: Poetry (2015)
NAACP Image Award Nominee: Outstanding Literary Work - Poetry (2016)
National Book Critics Circle Award Finalist: Poetry (2015)
This book of poems, by Ross Gay, "is a sustained meditation on that which goes away—loved ones, the seasons, the earth as we know it—that tries to find solace in the processes of the garden and the orchard. That is, this is a book that studies the wisdom of the garden and orchard, those places where all—death, sorrow, loss—is converted into what might, with patience, nourish us." (Publisher's note)
"Whether by contemplating the extraordinary within everyday acts (sleeping in clothes, drinking water, buttoning and unbuttoning a shirt), or by entwining past and present as he pays homage to parents, friends, even his former love, Gay embraces the natural cycles of life and death as only an introspective gardener and accomplished poet can." Booklist

Hopler, Jay
The **Abridged** History of Rainfall; by Jay Hopler. McSweeney's 2016 80 p. $22   **811.6**
1. Poetry -- Collections
ISBN 1944211268; 9781944211264
LC 2016050071
National Book Award Finalist: Poetry (2016)
This book of poetry, by Jay Hopler, "documents the struggle to live in the face of great loss, a task that sends him ranging through Florida's torrid subtropics, the mountains of the American West, the streets of Rome, and the Umbrian countryside." (Publisher's note)

Kaur, Rupi
Milk and honey; Rupi Kaur. Andrews McMeel Pub 2015 204 p. illustrations (paperback) $14.99; (ebook) $9.99   **811.6**
1. Healing 2. Poetry -- Collections
ISBN 9781449474256; 144947425X; 9781449478650
LC 2015946719
This book by Rupi Kaur "is a collection of poetry and prose about survival. About the experience of violence, abuse, love, loss, and femininity. The book is divided into four chapters, and each chapter serves a different purpose. Deals with a different pain. Heals a different heartache. . . . [It] takes readers through a journey of the most bitter moments in life and finds sweetness in them because there is sweetness everywhere if you are just willing to look." (Publisher's note)

Sharif, Solmaz
Look; Poems. by Solmaz Sharif. Farrar, Straus & Giroux 2016 96 p. (ebook) $20; $16   **811.6**
1. Poetry -- Collections
ISBN 9781555979409; 1555977448; 9781555977443
LC 2015953717
National Book Award Finalist: Poetry (2016)
This book of poetry, by Solmaz Sharif, "asks us to see the ongoing costs of war as the unbearable loss of human lives and also the insidious abuses against our everyday speech. In this virtuosic array of poems, lists, shards, and sequences, Sharif assembles her family's and her own fragmented narratives in the aftermath of warfare." (Publisher's note)
"In form, content, and execution, Sharif's debut is arguably the most noteworthy book of poetry yet about recent U.S.-led wars in Afghanistan, Iraq, and the greater Middle East." Pub Wkly

Sinclair, Safiya
Cannibal; Safiya Sinclair. University of Nebraska Press 2016 126 p. (paperback : alk. paper) $17.95   **811.6**
1. Jamaican poetry 2. Human body -- Poetry 3. Poetry -- Collections 4. Women -- Identity -- Poetry
ISBN 9780803290631; 9780803295384
LC 2016007774
"The poems in Safiya Sinclair's 'Cannibal' explore Jamaican childhood and history, race relations in America, womanhood, otherness, and exile. . . . Blooming with intense lyricism and fertile imagery, these full-blooded poems are elegant, mythic, and intricately woven. Here the female body is a dark landscape; the female body is cannibal. Sinclair shocks and delights her readers with her willingness to disorient and provoke." (Publisher's note)
"This is a tight, focused collection, and through her visceral language Sinclair paints the institution of white supremacy as not just an individualized phenomenon, but as a ruthless and menacing force." Pub Wkly

Youn, Monica

Blackacre; Poems. Monica Youn. Graywolf Press 2016 88 p. (ebook) $20; (alk. paper) $16   **811.6**

1. American poetry 2. American literature
ISBN 9781555979461; 9781555977504

LC 2016931136

This book, by Monica Youn, "is a centuries-old legal fiction—a placeholder name for a hypothetical estate. Treacherously lush or alluringly bleak, these poems reframe their subjects as landscape, as legacy—a bereavement, an intimacy, a racial identity. . . . With a surveyor's keenest tools, Youn marks the boundaries of the given, what we have been allotted: acreage that has been ruthlessly fenced, previously tenanted, ploughed and harvested, enriched and depleted." (Publisher's note)

"Youn's mesmerizing collection does the diligent work of presenting an aspect of death and loss from an entirely unique perspective." Booklist

Includes bibliographical references (page 83).

812   American drama in English

Abbotson, Susan C. W.

Critical companion to Arthur Miller; a literary reference to his life and work. Facts on File 2006 518p il (Facts on File library of American literature) $75   **812**

1. Authors 2. Dramatists 3. Screenwriters
ISBN 0-8160-6194-7; 978-0-8160-6194-5

LC 2006-22902

This book "covers Miller's entire canon, including plays, screenplays, fiction, short stories, and poetry, as well as many of his important essays and critical pieces. Also included are . . . entries on literary, theatrical, and personal figures important to Miller; key terms and topics connected to his work; and various theatrical companies and places with which he has been associated." Publisher's note

Includes bibliographical references

Adler, Stella

★ **Stella** Adler on America's master playwrights; Eugene O'Neill, Thornton Wilder, Clifford Odets, William Saroyan, Tennessee Williams, William Inge, Arthur Miller, Edward Albee. edited and with commentary by Barry Paris. Alfred A. Knopf 2012 xi, 385 p.p ill.   **812**

1. American drama 2. Drama -- Technique 3. American dramatists 4. Drama -- Explication 5. American drama -- 20th century -- History and criticism
ISBN 0679424431; 9780679424437

LC 2012018983

This book by Stella Adler, edited by Barry Paris "Brings together [Adler's] most important lectures on America's plays and playwrights, the giants of the twentieth century, men she knew, loved, and worked with. Adler considers, among them, Eugene O'Neill, . . . Tennessee Williams, . . . Clifford Odets, . . . [and] Arthur Miller." (Publisher's note)

Albee, Edward

★ **Who's** afraid of Virginia Woolf? Scribner Classics 2003 243p $24   **812**

1. College teachers -- Drama 2. Married people -- Drama 3. New England -- Drama
ISBN 0-7432-5525-9

LC 2003-54206

A reissue of the title first published 1962 by Atheneum Pubs.

Characters: 2 men, 2 women. 3 acts. First produced at the Billy Rose Theatre, New York City, October 13, 1962

"The play is a virulent unveiling of the relationship between George, a history professor, and his wife, Martha, the college president's daughter. Another couple, Nick and Honey, get caught in the crossfire of George and Martha's verbal and emotional lacerations, and it becomes clear that each character is engaged in an isolated struggle through a personal hell." Reader's Ency. 4th edition

Auburn, David

Proof; a play. Faber & Faber 2001 83p pa $13   **812**

1. Fathers -- Death -- Drama 2. Man-woman relationships -- Drama 3. Mathematicians -- Drama
ISBN 0-571-19997-6

LC 00-50284

Characters: 2 men, 2 women. 2 acts, 9 scenes. First produced by the Manhattan Theatre Club, New York City, May 23, 2000

"Twenty-five-year-old Catherine, who sacrificed college to care for her mentally ill father (once a brilliant, much-admired mathematician), is left in a kind of limbo after his death. Socially awkward and a bit of a shut-in, she is gruff with Hal, a former student who shows up even before the funeral wanting to root through the countless notebooks her father kept in the years of his decline, hoping to find mathematical gold. On the heels of his arrival comes Claire, Catherine's cosmopolitan, blandly successful, and pushy sister, with plans to sell their father's house and take Catherine . . . with her back to New York." SLJ

Includes bibliographical references and index

Baraka, Imamu Amiri

Dutchman, and The slave; two plays. [by] LeRoi Jones. Morrow 1964 88p hardcover o.p. pa $9.95   **812**

ISBN 978-0-688-21084-7; 0-688-21084-8

In Dutchman Baraka "explores the revolutionary potential of the educated black middle-class intellectual, represented by the protagonist, Clay, a would-be poet. When Clay is exposed as dangerous—that is, as a latent killer—by white society, seductively imaged as a beautiful white woman named Lula, he is summarily executed by that society. The Slave (1964), a fable set in a future of war between the races, continues the theme of black revolutionary militancy." Benet's Reader's Ency of Am Lit

The **Best** American short plays; edited by Howard Stein and Glenn Young. Applause Theatre Bk. Pubs.   **812**

1. One act plays 2. Drama -- Collections

This series of annual collections was begun in 1937 under the editorship of Margaret Mayorga with title: Best one-act plays, and published by Dodd, Mead through 1955 (starting in 1953 title changed to The best short plays). Beacon Press published the volumes from 1956 through 1961 when publication was suspended. Resumed 1968 under the editorship of Stanley Richards. From 1981 through 1989 edited by Ramon Delgado. Changed to current title and editors with 1990/1991 volume. Volumes prior to 1988 o.p. Apply to publisher for availability and price of retrospective annuals

In addition to the plays each annual contains brief biographical and bibliographical data about dramatists represented

Cervantes Saavedra, Miguel de

Man of La Mancha; a musical play. lyrics by Joe Darion; music by Mitch Leigh. Random House 1966 82p il hardcover o.p. pa $9.95 **812**
ISBN 0-394-40621-4; 0-394-40619-2 pa
Winner of the New York Drama Critics Circle award Best Musical 1966
Characters: 14 men, 5 women, extras. First produced at the ANTA Washington Square Theatre, New York City, November 22, 1965

Cruz, Nilo

Anna in the tropics. Theatre Communications Group 2003 84p pa $12.95 **812**
ISBN 1-55936-232-4
LC 2003-15859
Characters: 5 men, 3 women. 2 acts, 10 scenes. First produced at the New Theatre, Coral Gables, Florida, October 12, 2002
"Set in a cigar factory in Tampa, Florida, in 1929, where the Cuban-American employees have just hired a new 'lector' to read novels to them while they work, Anna and the Tropics is written in the lyrical, somewhat formalized parlance of a folktale. The play is both a piece of cultural history and a warm-spirited tribute to the transformative power of art." Time

Dowling, Robert M.

Critical companion to Eugene O'Neill; a literary reference to his life and work. Facts On File 2009 2v il (Facts on File library of American literature) set $150 **812**
1. Authors 2. Dramatists 3. Nobel laureates for literature
ISBN 978-0-8160-6675-9; 0-8160-6675-2
LC 2008-24135
"These volumes are wonderfully organized and very easy to use. . . . Entries are of a length to provide a good background of O'Neill's works and life." Booklist
Includes bibliographical references

Edson, Margaret

Wit; a play. Faber & Faber 1999 85p pa $13 **812**
ISBN 0-571-19877-5
LC 99-11921
Characters: 3 men, 3 women, extras. First produced at Long Wharf Theatre, New Haven, Connecticut, October 31, 1997

Foote, Horton

Beginnings; a memoir. Scribner 2001 270p il $24; pa $14 **812**
1. Actors 2. Authors 3. Novelists 4. Dramatists 5. Screenwriters 6. Television scriptwriters
ISBN 0-7432-1115-4; 0-7432-1116-2 pa
LC 2001-47088
Foote "chronicled his Wharton, TX, childhood in Farewell. . . . Now he continues his story where he left off, leaving Wharton at 17 to study to become an actor. He travels to theater school in Pasadena but eventually makes it to New York by way of Martha's Vineyard, where he soon discovers his talent for writing and hobnobs with the likes of Martha Graham, Tennessee Williams, and Agnes de Mille." Libr J

Collected plays. v2 Smith & Kraus 1996 216p v2 hardcover o.p. pa $19.95 **812**
ISBN 978-1-57525-019-9; 1-57525-019-5
"Foote's ear for naturalistic dialogue never fails him, and even in the midst of telling an exciting story . . . he never lets the potential for melodrama overwhelm things." Booklist

Gibson, William

★ The **miracle** worker. Scribner 2008 112p pa $12.99 **812**
1. Deaf 2. Blind 3. Authors 4. Memoirists 5. Humanitarians 6. Teachers of the deaf 7. Inspirational writers 8. Teachers of the blind 9. Social welfare leaders
ISBN 978-1-4165-9084-2; 1-4165-9084-6
LC 2008-275273
First published 1957
A text of the television play, intended for reading, of Anne Sullivan Macy's attempts to teach her pupil, Helen Keller, to communicate.
"The present text is meant for reading, and differs from the telecast version in that I have restored some passages that read better than they play and others omitted in performance for simple lack of time." Author's note

Goodrich, Frances

The **diary** of Anne Frank; by Frances Goodrich and Albert Hackett; newly adapted by Wendy Kesselman. Dramatists Play Service 2000 70p il pa $7.50 **812**
1. World War, 1939-1945 -- Jews -- Drama 2. Netherlands -- History -- 1940-1945, German occupation -- Drama
ISBN 0-8222-1718-X
LC 2006-455205
First published 1956 by Random House
Awarded the Pulitzer Prize and the New York Drama Critics Circle Award for 1956
Characters: 5 men, 5 women. 2 acts. First produced at the Cort Theatre, New York City, October 5, 1955.

Guare, John

Six degrees of separation; a play. Random House 1990 120p hardcover o.p. pa $12.95 **812**
ISBN 0-679-73481-3 pa
LC 90-53449

Characters: 13 men, 4 women. First produced at the Mitzi Newhouse Theater, New York City, June 1990

Gurney, A. R.

Love letters and two other plays: The golden age and What I did last summer; with an introduction by the playwright. Penguin Bks. 1990 209p pa $14   **812**

1. American drama -- 20th century

ISBN 978-0-452-26501-1; 0-452-16501-0

LC 90-34177

Love letters dramatizes the 30-year epistolary "exchange between an upper-class man and an upper-upper-class woman. . . . The Golden Age is an updated, romantic-comic variation upon Henry James' Aspern Papers in which a young academic locates an old woman who may possess a missing chapter of The Great Gatsby and schemes to get it from her. What I did Last Summer is about 14-year-old Charlie's bohemian season with Anna, the Pig Woman, who fosters his creativity as she once did his mother's." Booklist

Hansberry, Lorraine

★ **A raisin** in the sun. Modern Lib. 1995 xxvi, 135p $14.95; pa $6.50   **812**

ISBN 0-679-60172-4; 0-679-75533-0 pa

LC 95-16074

First published 1959

Awarded the New York Drama Critics Circle Award for the 1958-1959 season

Characters: 8 men, 3 women. 6 scenes in 3 acts. First produced at the Ethel Barrymore Theatre, New York City, March 11, 1959

"Hansberry's drama focuses on the Youngers, a 1950s African-American working-class family in Chicago striving to realize their individual dreams of prosperity and education, and their collective dream of a better life. It was the first play by an African-American woman to be produced on Broadway." Reader's Ency. 4th edition

Heintzelman, Greta

Critical companion to Tennessee Williams; [by] Greta Heintzelman, Alycia Smith Howard. Facts on File 2005 436p il (Facts on File library of American literature) $65; pa $19.95   **812**

1. Authors 2. Novelists 3. Dramatists 4. Short story writers

ISBN 0-8160-4888-6; 0-8160-6429-6 pa

LC 2004-7362

The authors "offer an excellent resource for those studying Williams's life and extensive body of work." Choice

Includes bibliographical references

Hughes, Langston

Five plays; edited with an introduction by Webster Smalley. Indiana Univ. Press 1963 258p hardcover o.p. pa $14.95   **812**

ISBN 0-253-32230-8; 0-253-20121-7 pa

Contents: Mulatto--Soul gone home--Little Ham--Simply heavenly--Tambourines to glory

Inge, William

4 plays. Grove Press 1979 304p pa $16   **812**

ISBN 0-8021-3209-X

LC 78-73032

First published 1958 by Random House

The author was awarded the Pulitzer Prize, 1953, for Picnic

Kushner, Tony

Angels in America; a gay fantasia on national themes. 1st combined pbk. ed.; Theatre Communications Group 2003 289p pa $15.95   **812**

1. Lawyers 2. Government officials

ISBN 1-55936-231-6

LC 2003-17904

Part one awarded the Pulitzer Prize, 1993

Millennium approaches first presented at the Eureka Theatre Company, San Francisco, May 1991. Perestroika first presented at the Mark Taper Forum, Los Angeles, November 1992.

Lawrence, Jerome

Inherit the wind; [by] Jerome Lawrence and Robert E. Lee. Ballantine Books trade pbk. ed.; Ballantine Books 2007 129p pa $9.95   **812**

1. Evolution -- Study and teaching -- Drama

ISBN 978-0-345-50103-5; 0-345-50103-9

LC 2007-281039

Characters: 23 men, 7 women. 3 acts 5 scenes. First produced at the National Theater, New York City, April 21, 1955

Mamet, David

Glengarry Glen Ross; a play. Grove Press 1984 108p pa $14   **812**

ISBN 978-0-8021-3091-4; 0-8021-3091-7

LC 83-49380

Awarded the Pulitzer Prize, 1984

Characters: 7 men. 2 acts, 4 scenes. First produced at The Cottlesoe Theatre, London, England, September 21, 1983

A "comedy is about smalltime, cutthroat real esate salesmen trying to grind out a living by pushing plots of land on reluctant buyers in a never-ending scramble for their fair share of the American dream." Publisher's note

Speed-the-plow. Grove Press 1988 82p (An Evergreen bk) pa $13   **812**

ISBN 978-0-8021-3046-4; 0-8021-3046-1

LC 87-7252

Characters: 2 men 1 woman. 3 acts. First produced on Broadway at the Royale Theater, May 3, 1988

"A brilliant black comedy, a dazzling dissection of Hollywood cupidity and another tone poem by our foremost master of the language of moral epilepsy. . . . On its deepest level it belongs with the darker disclosures of movie-biz pathology like Nathanael West's The Day of the Locust and F. Scott Fitzgerald's The Last Tycoon. In a sense Speed-the-Plow distills all of these to a stark quintessence: there's hardly a line in it that isn't somehow insanely funny or scarily insane." Newsweek

Miller, Arthur

★ **Collected** plays, 1944-1961. Library of America 2006 774p $35 **812**

ISBN 978-1-931082-91-4; 1-931082-91-X

LC 2005-49442

Norman, Marsha

Collected plays. v1 Smith & Kraus 1998 412p v1 (Contemporary playwrights series) pa $19.95 **812**

ISBN 1-57525-029-2

LC 97-7665

Norman's "characters, whether they be performers in a struggling two-bit circus, women in an all-night laundromat, or a Western outlaw, are ones we can easily identify with and understand." Libr J

O'Neil, Eugene

Complete plays; edited by Travis Bogard. Literary Classics of the United States 1988 3v (Library of America) v1 $40; v2 $40; v3 $35 **812**

ISBN 978-0-940450-48-6 v1; 978-0-940450-49-3 v2; 978-0-940450-50-9 v3

Parks, Suzan-Lori

Topdog /underdog. Theatre Communications Group 2001 110p pa $12.95 **812**

ISBN 1-55936-201-4

LC 2001-27316

Characters: 2 men. 6 scenes. First produced at The Joseph Papp Public Theater/New York Shakespeare Festival, New York City, July 22, 2001

This is "the story of Lincoln and Booth, two brothers whose names were given to them as a joke foretelling a lifetime of sibling rivalry and resentment. Haunted by the past, the brothers are forced to confront the shattering reality of their future." Publisher's note

The **play** that changed my life; America's foremost playwrights on the plays that influenced them. edited by Ben Hodges. Applause Theatre & Cinema Books 2009 173p il pa $18.99 **812**

1. Authorship 2. Drama -- Technique 3. Dramatists, American

ISBN 978-1-557837-40-0; 1-55783-740-6

LC 2009-32452

"Edited by Hodges, with a foreword by Paula Vogel, the book assembles 19 of the theater's usual suspects, many of them Pulitzer Prize winners, to explain what lured them into their line of work." Arts J

★ **Playwrights** at work; Paris review. edited by George Plimpton. Modern Lib. 2000 411p il pa $14.95 **812**

1. Poets 2. Actors 3. Authors 4. Novelists 5. Dramatists 6. Essayists 7. Memoirists 8. Screenwriters 9. Short story writers 10. Theatrical directors 11. Motion picture directors 12. Television scriptwriters 13. Nobel laureates for literature

ISBN 0-679-64021-5

LC 99-44064

"This is an excellent gathering of brilliant minds in the theater, and these interviews provide significant insight into the works of the writers." Libr J

Rose, Reginald

Twelve angry men; introduction by David Mamet. Penguin Books 2006 73p (Penguin classics) pa $11 **812**

ISBN 0-14-310440-3; 978-0-14-310440-7

LC 2006-46006

First published 1955 by Dramatic Pub.

Characters: 12 men. 3 acts. Original television broadcast on CBS program Studio One, September 20, 1954.

Shepard, Sam

Fool for love, and other plays; introduction by Ross Wetzsteon. Bantam Bks. 1984 307p pa $15 **812**

ISBN 978-0-553-34590-2; 0-553-34129-4

LC 84-45182

"Sam Shepard fills the role of professional playwright as a good ballet dancer or acrobat fulfills his role in performance. That is, he always delivers, he executes feats of dexterity and technical difficulty that an untrained person could not, and makes them seem easy." Village Voice

The **unseen** hand and other plays. Vintage Bks. 1996 383p pa $14.95 **812**

ISBN 978-0-679-76789-3; 0-679-76789-4

LC 95-47723

Simon, Neil

Brighton Beach memoirs. Plume 1995 130p pa $12 **812**

ISBN 0-452-27528-8

LC 95-21788

First published 1984 by Random House

Awarded the New York Drama Critics Circle Award for best play, 1983

"Sex and baseball are the primary preoccupations of 15-year-old Eugene Jerome, narrator of a seriocomic slice of lower-middle-class Jewish family life in Depression-era New York City. The several adolescent characters in the extended family add to the teenage appeal of Simon's . . . play." Booklist

★ The **collected** plays of Neil Simon; with an introduction by Neil Simon. Random House 1979 4v hardcover o.p. v1-2 each pa $25, v3 o.p., v4 pa $17 **812**

ISBN 978-0-452-25870-9 v1; 978-0-452-26358-1 v2; 978-0-679-40889-5 v3; 978-0-684-84785-6 v4

Lost in Yonkers. Plume 1993 120p (Plume drama) pa $12 **812**

ISBN 0-452-26883-4

LC 92-29111

First published 1991 by Random House

Awarded the Pulitzer Prize, 1991

Characters: 4 men, 3 women. 2 acts. First presented at the Stevens Center for the Performing Arts, Winston-Salem, December 31, 1990.

This play, "set in 1940s New York, is a sad-funny portrait of a dysfunctional family, headed by a woman who provided for her children but never showed them love." Booklist

The **play** goes on; a memoir. Simon & Schuster 1999 348p il hardcover o.p. pa $14 **812**
1. Authors 2. Dramatists 3. Screenwriters 4. Television scriptwriters
ISBN 0-684-86980-2 pa

LC 99-36449

Sequel to Rewrites

This memoir "recounts the second half of Simon's life, starting with the life-shattering impact of the death of his first wife, Joan, of cancer at 40, and proceeding through the ensuing 30 years, during which Simon had periods of incredible fertility and others in which his creativity dried up and he feared he would never write again." Booklist

Rewrites; a memoir. Simon & Schuster 1996 397p hardcover o.p. pa $14 **812**
1. Authors 2. Dramatists 3. Screenwriters 4. Television scriptwriters
ISBN 0-684-83562-2 pa

LC 96-13691

This first volume of the dramatist's memoirs focuses on his career as it evolved from writing high school skits to TV programs to Broadway

"This is a gentleman's autobiography, and Simon never stoops to dishing the dirt on his show biz cronies." Libr J

Wasserstein, Wendy

The **Heidi** chronicles and other plays. Vintage Bks. 1991 249p pa $13.95 **812**
ISBN 0-679-73499-6

LC 90-55681

First published 1990 by Harcourt Brace Jovanovich

This collection traces "three decades of changing styles, mores, life objectives, and intellectual challenges. Wasserstein examines her characters and their times with great good humor, complexity, depth of feeling, and a firm refusal to accept trite and easy images." Libr J

Wilder, Thornton

Collected plays & writings on theater. Library of America 2007 871p $40 **812**
1. Poetry -- By individual authors
ISBN 978-1-59853-003-2; 1-59853-003-8

LC 2006-48620

"Complementing the selection of plays is [a] . . . group of essays that captures Wilder's reflections on his plays and contains a revealing epistolary account of the film adaptation of Our Town, as well as evaluations of dramatists such as Sophocles, George Bernard Shaw, and the Austrian satirist Johann Nestroy (whose farce Einen Jux will er sich machen

Wilder . . . transformed into The Matchmaker)." Publisher's note

★ **Our** town; a play in three acts. foreword by Donald Margulies. HarperCollins Pubs. 2003 xx, 181p $19.95; pa $9.95 **812**
ISBN 0-06-053525-3; 0-06-051263-6 pa

A reissue with a new foreword of the title first published 1938 by Coward-McCann

Large mixed cast. First produced at McCarter's Theatre, Princeton, N.J., January 22, 1938.

"Presented without scenery of any kind, utilizing a narrator and loose episodic form, adventurous and imaginative in style, this unique play . . . is one of the most distinguished in the modern repertoire. It deals with the simplest and most touching aspects of life in a small town." HarperCollins Reader's Ency of Am Lit

Williams, Tennessee

★ **Plays,** 1937-1955. Library of America 2000 1054p $40 **812**
ISBN 978-1-883011-86-4; 1-883011-86-4

★ **Plays,** 1957-1980. Library of America 2000 999p $40 **812**
ISBN 978-1-883011-87-1; 1-883011-87-6

★ **A streetcar** named desire; with an introduction by Arthur Miller. New Directions 2004 192p pa $9.95 **812**
ISBN 0-8112-1602-0

LC 2004-11654

First published 1947

Characters: 6 women, 7 men. 11 scenes. First produced at the Barrymore Theatre, New York City, December 3, 1947

"A study of sexual frustration, violence, and aberration, set in New Orleans, in which Blanche Dubois' fantasies of refinement and grandeur are brutally destroyed by her brother-in-law, Stanley Kowalski, whose animal nature fascinates and repels her." Oxford Companion to Engl Lit. 5th edition

Wilson, August

Fences; a play. introduction by Lloyd Richards. New Am. Lib. 1986 101p pa $12 **812**
ISBN 978-0-452-26401-4

LC 86-5264

Awarded the Pulitzer Prize, 1987

Characters: 5 men, 1 woman, 1 girl. 2 acts, 9 scenes. First produced at the Yale Repertory Theatre, New Haven, Connecticut, April 30, 1985

Jitney. Overlook Press 2001 96p hardcover o.p. pa $14.95 **812**
ISBN 978-158567-370-4; 1-58567-370-6

LC 2001-33962

Winner of the New York Drama Critics Circle Award, 2000

Characters: 8 men, 1 woman. 2 acts, 8 scenes. This is a revised version of a play written 1979

Ma Rainey's black bottom; a play in two acts. New Am. Lib. 1985 111p pa $12 **812**

ISBN 978-0-452-26113-6; 0-452-26113-9

LC 84-27156

Characters: 8 men, 2 women. 2 acts. First produced at the Yale Repertory Theatre, New Haven, Connecticut, April 6, 1984

The **piano** lesson. New Am. Lib. 1990 108p hardcover o.p. pa $12 **812**

ISBN 978-0-452-26534-9; 0-452-26534-7

LC 90-38734

Awarded the Pulitzer Prize and the New York Drama Critics Circle Award, 1990

Characters: 5 men, 3 women. 2 acts, 7 scenes. First presented at the Yale Repertory Theatre, New Haven, November 26, 1987

Seven guitars. Dutton 1996 107p hardcover o.p. pa $12 **812**

ISBN 978-0-452-27692-5; 0-452-27692-6 pa

LC 95-50536

Winner of the New York Drama Critics Circle award, 1996

Characters: 4 men, 3 women. 2 acts, 9 scenes. First produced at the Goodman Theater, Chicago, January 21, 1995

"Pittsburgh, summer 1948. Five of his friends gather after the funeral of Floyd Barton, mysteriously murdered at 35, just as his first blues record had become a hit. The sixth play in Wilson's cycle concerned with twentieth-century African American lives is mostly a flashback. We learn what happened to Floyd, but before that horrifying climax, Wilson steeps us in the pathos that Floyd glimpsed a way to escape. . . As powerful as modern drama gets." Booklist

Two trains running; foreword by Laurence Fishburne. Theatre Communications Group 2007 99p $25 **812**

1. Nineteen sixties -- Drama. 2. African Americans -- Drama. 3. African American neighborhoods -- Drama. 4. Hill District (Pittsburgh, Pa.) -- Drama.

ISBN 978-1-55936-303-7

LC 2007-22095

First published 1992 by Dutton

Characters: 6 men, 1 woman. 2 acts 8 scenes. First produced at the Yale Repertory Theatre, New Haven, Ct., March 27, 1990

Wilson, Lanford

21 short plays. Smith & Kraus 1993 268p pa $19.95 **812**

ISBN 1-880399-31-8

LC 93-34434

"The plays range in form from finely crafted one-act plays to short 'skits' written for various benefits. They are arranged in chronological order and the collection spans the years from 1963 to 1991. Wilson's dramatic style has been characterized by such phrases as 'lyric realism' and 'poetic

realism,' but these short plays represent a far greater range of styles." Voice Youth Advocates

The **Talley** trilogy. Smith & Kraus 1999 272p (Collected works) hardcover o.p. **812**

"Wilson didn't begin what became, ultimately, a tetralogy with the idea of creating a play cycle. He just wanted to write a play set in the late 1970s that reflected in some way the post-Vietnam, post-Watergate letdown much of young America was feeling. . . . The resultant four-play cycle captures the Talley's foibles and follies as thoroughly—and as entertainingly—as J.D. Salinger's set of stories and short novels did the Glass family." Booklist

813   American fiction in English

Abbott, Alysia

Fairyland; a memoir of my father. by Alysia Abbott. 1st ed. W.W. Norton & Co. Inc. 2013 352 p. (hardcover) $25.95 **813**

1. Gay parents 2. Children of gay parents 3. Gay fathers -- Biography 4. Gay men -- California -- San Francisco -- Biography

ISBN 0393082520; 9780393082524

LC 2013011614

Lambda Literary Awards Finalist (2014)

Stonewall Book Awards: Nonfiction Honor Book (2014)

This book by Alysia Abbot recounts her relationship with her father, Steve Abbot, who "in the early 1970s . . . embraced his homosexuality and moved to San Francisco." The "memoir describes life with her poet-activist father and his openly gay lifestyle. . . . She watches as friends, and then her father, contract AIDS, and at age 21, she returns home to help care for him and is conflicted over feelings of duty and the desire to begin a life of her own." (Library Journal)

Includes bibliographical references.

Alice Walker; edited and with an introduction by Harold Bloom. New edition; Bloom's Literary Criticism; an imprint of Infobase Publishing 2007 223p (Modern critical views) $45 **813**

1. Poets 2. Authors 3. Novelists 4. Editors 5. Essayists 6. College teachers 7. Short story writers

ISBN 978-0-7910-9611-6

First published 1989

A collection of critical essays discussing the work of The Color Purple author Alice Walker.

Includes bibliographical references

Alice Walker's The color purple; edited and with an introduction by Harold Bloom. New ed.; Bloom's Literary Criticism 2008 191p (Modern critical interpretations) $45 **813**

1. Poets 2. Authors 3. Novelists 4. Editors 5. Essayists 6. College teachers 7. Short story writers

ISBN 978-0-7910-9614-7; 0-7910-9614-9

LC 2008-2775

First published 2000

A collection of ten essays providing international appraisal and interpretation of Walker's novel.

Includes bibliographical references

Atlas, James

Bellow; a biography. Random House 2000 686p il hardcover o.p. pa $29 **813**

1. Authors 2. Novelists 3. Dramatists 4. Authors, American 5. Short story writers 6. Nobel laureates for literature

ISBN 0-375-75958-1 pa

LC 00-42529

"Atlas shares his subject's devotion to literature, intimacy with Chicago (the city Bellow immortalized), and Jewishness, and he succeeds brilliantly in chronicling and interpreting Bellow's very full life, difficult personality, and powerful work." Booklist

Includes bibliographical references

Blume, Lesley M. M.

Everybody behaves badly; the true story behind Hemingway's masterpiece The Sun Also Rises. Lesley Blume. Eamon Dolan/Houghton Mifflin Harcourt 2016 352 p. illustrations, portraits (hardback) $27 **813**

ISBN 9780544276000

LC 2015037016

This book, by Lesley Blume, focuses on the "making of Ernest Hemingway's The Sun Also Rises, the outsize personalities who inspired it, and the vast changes it wrought on the literary world. . . . Blume resurrects the explosive, restless landscape of 1920s Paris and Spain and reveals how Hemingway helped create his own legend." (Publisher's note)

"Blume's reimagining of 1920s Paris and its scandalous denizens is vivid, spirited, and absorbing." Kirkus

Includes bibliographical references (pages 245-320) and index.

Boyd, Brian

Vladimir Nabokov: the American years. Princeton Univ. Press 1991 783p il hardcover o.p. pa $49 **813**

1. Poets 2. Authors 3. Novelists 4. Authors, Russian 5. Essayists 6. Memoirists 7. Translators 8. College teachers 9. Literary critics 10. Short story writers

ISBN 0-691-06797-X; 0-691-02471-5 pa

LC 90-26374

This volume, which completes the biography begun with Vladimir Nabokov: The Russian Years (1990), is an account of the writer's life from 1940, when he arrived in the United States.

Includes bibliographical references

Vladimir Nabokov: the Russian years. Princeton Univ. Press 1990 607p il hardcover o.p. pa $49 **813**

1. Poets 2. Authors 3. Novelists 4. Authors, Russian 5. Essayists 6. Memoirists 7. Translators 8. College teachers 9. Literary critics 10. Short story writers

ISBN 0-691-06794-5; 0-691-02470-7 pa

LC 90-8040

The author aims to "describe the liberal milieu of the aristocratic Nabokovs, their escape from Russia [after the Revolution], Nabokov's education at Cambridge, and the murder of his father in Berlin. Boyd then turns to the years

that Nabokov spent, impoverished, in Germany and France, until the coming of Hitler forced him to flee, with wife and son, to the United States." Publisher's note

Includes bibliographical references

Burroughs, Augusten

★ **Running** with scissors; a memoir. St. Martin's Press 2002 304p $23.95; pa $14 **813**

1. Authors 2. Novelists 3. Memoirists

ISBN 0-312-28370-9; 0-312-42227-X pa

LC 2001-58857

In this memoir the author recalls his youth with a mentally ill mother, living with his mother's psychiatrist in a chaotic household, and his early homosexual experiences

"Burroughs tempers the pathos with sharp, riotous humor in stories that are self-deprecating, raunchy, sexually explicit." Booklist

Burroughs, William S., 1914-1997

Rub out the words; the letters of William S. Burroughs 1959-1974. edited and with an introduction by Bill Morgan. Ecco 2012 xxxv, 444 p.p (hardcover) $35 **813**

1. Letters 2. Beat generation -- Correspondence 3. American authors -- Correspondence 4. Authors, American -- 20th century -- Correspondence

ISBN 006171142X; 9780061711428

LC 2012371022

This collection of correspondence by author William S. Burroughs "contains over 300 . . . letters written mostly to friends, family, and business associates between the publication of 'Naked Lunch' and Burroughs's return to New York City to teach at City College. While old friends like Allen Ginsberg are among the recipients, more of the letters are addressed to newer companions whom Burroughs met while living abroad, including Brion Gysin, Paul Bowles, and Alex Trocchi. Many letters evidence Burroughs's obsessions with the cut-up method, Scientology, and the effectiveness of apomorphine as a cure for addiction; others reveal a caring father concerned about his son's well-being and financial security. . . . [Editor Bill] Morgan includes helpful explanatory notes, a chronology, and a list of sources identifying the repositories holding the letters." (Libr J)

Includes bibliographical references and index

Cather, Willa, 1873-1947

The **selected** letters of Willa Cather; edited by Andrew Jewell and Janis Stout. 1st ed. Alfred A. Knopf 2013 752 p. (hardcover) $37.50; (ebook) $85.00 **813**

1. Authors -- Correspondence 2. Novelists, American -- 20th century -- Correspondence

ISBN 0307959309; 9780307959300; 9780307959317

LC 2012036882

This book is a collection of some of author Willa Cather's personal correspondence. "Beginning with a witty missive written in 1888 when she was only 14, the volume continues through her early years as a successful magazine editor for McLure's, into the 1910s and '20s, when she experienced success as a novelist, all the way through to her death in 1947." (Publishers Weekly)

★ The **Columbia** companion to the twentieth-century American short story; Blanche H. Gelfant, editor. Columbia Univ. Press 2000 660p $83.50; pa $24.50 **813**
1. Reference books 2. American fiction -- Bio-bibliography 3. Short stories -- History and criticism 4. American fiction -- History and criticism
ISBN 0-231-11098-7; 0-231-11099-5 pa
LC 00-31610
"The first 100 pages are devoted to thematic essays that focus on the form of the short story, the development of the genre, several distinct subject types (e.g., short stories of the Holocaust or of the working class), and four different ethnic groups (African American, Asian American, Chicano Latino American, and Native American). . . . The remainder of the book is devoted to over 100 individual author essays that focus on reading for pleasure and understanding rather than critical interpretation. Entries discuss the development of each author and the content and meaning of his or her major short stories." Libr J
Includes bibliographical references

Contemporary Jewish-American novelists; a bio-critical sourcebook. edited by Joel Shatzky and Michael Taub; with a foreword by Daniel Walden. Greenwood Press 1997 xxxi, 506p $105 **813**
1. Reference books 2. American fiction -- Jewish authors 3. American fiction -- Bio-bibliography
ISBN 0-313-29462-3
LC 96-37047
This "reference work 'includes alphabetically arranged entries for more than 75 Jewish-American novelists whose major works were largely written after World War II.' While major canonical figures such as Norman Mailer and Saul Bellow are profiled, lesser-known novelists—including Judith Katz, Lev Raphael, and Steve Stern—are covered as well. One of the editors' goals is to show the diversity of Jewish-American literature. . . . Each entry includes a biographical section, a cogent discussion of major works and themes, an overview of each novelist's critical reception, and a bibliography of both primary and secondary sources." Booklist

Crane, Stephen, 1871-1900
Prose and poetry. Library of Am. 1984 1379p $40; pa $15.95 **813**
1. Short stories
ISBN 0-940450-17-8; 1-883011-39-6 pa
LC 83-19908
"This collection also includes both Crane's collections of epigrammatic free verses—'The Black Riders' and 'War is kind'—and selections from his uncollected poems." Publisher's note

Dearborn, Mary V.
Mailer; a biography. Houghton Mifflin 1999 478p il hardcover o.p. pa $15 **813**
1. Authors 2. Novelists 3. Essayists 4. Authors, American
ISBN 0-395-73655-2; 0-618-15460-4 pa
LC 99-32214
"Dearborn supplies a close reading of one of the most controversial American writers of the postwar era. Mailer's

body of work, beginning with his career-defining first novel, The Naked and the Dead (1948), is analyzed with remarkable insight. Mailer's notorious personal life is also examined, as Dearborn sorts through the various preoccupations that have obsessed the writer over five decades in the literary spotlight." Booklist
Includes bibliographical references

Facts on File, Inc.
★ The **Facts** on File companion to the American novel; edited by Abby H.P. Werlock; assistant editor, James P. Werlock. Facts on File 2005 3v (Facts on File library of American literature) set $195 **813**
1. Reference books 2. American fiction -- Encyclopedias 3. American fiction -- Bio-bibliography
ISBN 0-8160-4528-3; 978-0-8160-4528-0
LC 2005-12437
"This A-to-Z reference contains 450 biographical overviews of American and foreign-born authors living in the United States and 500 signed analytical essays on their novels. . . . Libraries will value this compact set for including classics as well as hard-to-find contemporary authors." SLJ
Includes bibliographical references

Fargnoli, A. Nicholas
Critical companion to William Faulkner; a literary reference to his life and work. [by] A. Nicholas Fargnoli, Michael Golay, Robert W. Hamblin. Facts On File 2008 562p il (Facts on File library of American literature) $75 **813**
1. Authors 2. Novelists 3. Screenwriters 4. Short story writers 5. Nobel laureates for literature
ISBN 978-0-8160-6432-8
LC 2007-32361
First published 2001 with title: William Faulkner A to Z
"Coverage includes: Faulkner's major works, including novels, short stories, poetry, and nonfiction; descriptions of characters in Faulkner's fiction, such as Benjy and Quentin from The Sound and the Fury; details about Faulkner's family, friends, colleagues, and critics; real and fictional places important to Faulkner's life and literary development, from Yoknapatawpha County, Mississippi to Hollywood; interviews and speeches given by Faulkner; [and] ideas and events that influenced his life and works, including slavery, the Civil War, World War I, and civil rights." Publisher's note
Includes bibliographical references

Farrell, Susan Elizabeth
Critical companion to Kurt Vonnegut; a literary reference to his life and work. [by] Susan Farrell. Facts On File 2008 532p il (Facts on File library of American literature) $75 **813**
1. Authors 2. Novelists 3. Journalists 4. Biographers 5. Short story writers 6. Science fiction writers
ISBN 978-0-8160-6598-1
LC 2007-37900
This "book covers all his works, including his novels, such as the unforgettable Slaughterhouse-Five; his short stories, such as 'Harrison Bergeron'; and his lectures and essays. . . . Entries on his life, related people, places, and topics are also included." Publisher's note
Includes bibliographical references

Fitzgerald, F. Scott

A **life** in letters; edited by Matthew J. Bruccoli; with the assistance of Judith S. Baughman. Scribner 1994 xxiii, 503p hardcover o.p. pa $18   **813**
  1. Authors 2. Novelists 3. Screenwriters 4. Authors, American 5. Short story writers
  ISBN 0-684-19570-4; 0-684-80153-1 pa
                                                   LC 93-31011
"Essential reading for a full understanding of Fitzgerald as an artist and a man." Libr J

Gifford, Justin

Street poison; the life and times of Iceberg Slim. Justin Gifford. Doubleday 2015 288 p. 8 plates; ills.; portraits (hardcovers) $26.95   **813**
  1. African American authors -- Biography 2. Pimps -- Illinois -- Chicago -- Biography 3. African Americans -- Illinois -- Chicago -- Biography
  ISBN 0385538340; 9780385538343
                                                   LC 2014037252
This book, by Justin Gifford, is a "biography of one of America's bestselling, notorious, and influential writers of the twentieth century: Iceberg Slim, né Robert Beck. . . . From a career as a . . . ruthless pimp in the '40s and '50s, Iceberg Slim refashioned himself as the first and still the greatest of 'street lit' masters, whose vivid books have made him an icon . . . and a presiding spirit of 'blaxploitation' culture." (Publisher's note)
"Recommended for readers of popular fiction and African American literature." LJ

Gillespie, Carmen

Critical companion to Alice Walker; a literary reference to her life and work. Facts on File 2011 452p il (Facts on File library of American literature) $75   **813**
  1. Poets 2. Authors 3. Novelists 4. Editors 5. Essayists 6. College teachers 7. Short story writers
  ISBN 978-0-8160-7530-0; 978-1-4381-3488-8 ebook
                                                   LC 2010-18639
This book contains "entries on all of Walker's major works, including such novels as The Color Purple, Meridian, The Third Life of Grange Copeland, and Possessing the Secret of Joy; essay collections and essays, such as 'Beauty: When the Other Dancer Is the Self'; poetry collections and poems; and short stories. Each entry on a major work of fiction contains subentries on the work's main characters." Publisher's note
Includes bibliographical references

Critical companion to Toni Morrison; a literary reference to her life and work. Facts On File 2008 484p il (Facts on File library of American literature) $75   **813**
  1. Authors 2. Novelists 3. Dramatists 4. Essayists 5. College teachers 6. Literary critics 7. Nobel laureates for literature
  ISBN 978-0-8160-6276-8
                                                   LC 2006-38231
This book "examines Morrison's life and writing, featuring critical analyses of her work and themes, as well as . . .

. . . entries on related topics and relevant people, places, and influences." Publisher's note
Includes bibliographical references

Gunn, James E.

Isaac Asimov; the foundations of science fiction. by James Gunn. rev ed; Scarecrow Press 1996 276p hardcover o.p. pa $42   **813**
  1. Authors 2. Novelists 3. Biochemists 4. Children's authors 5. Writers on science 6. Short story writers 7. Young adult authors 8. Science fiction writers 9. Science fiction -- History and criticism
  ISBN 0-8108-3129-5; 0-8108-5420-1 pa; 978-0-8108-5420-8 pa
                                                   LC 96-21068
First published 1982 by Oxford Univ. Press
The author "focuses on Asimov's robots and on the Foundation trilogy, emphasizing throughout Asimov's limited use of background, style, and characterization, and his constantly recurring theme of the rational solution of a problem. The Lucky Starr juveniles get comparatively cursory treatment, but otherwise this is a very fine book indeed—well informed, clearly written, and judicious." Booklist {review of 1982 edition}
Includes bibliographical references

Haralson, Eric L.

Critical companion to Henry James; a literary reference to his life and work. [by] Eric Haralson and Kendall Johnson. Facts On File 2009 516p il (Facts on File library of American literature) $75   **813**
  1. Authors 2. Novelists
  ISBN 978-0-8160-6886-9
                                                   LC 2008-36451
This book "covers the life and works of Henry James as well as the related people, places, and topics that shaped his writing. Other features in this . . . title include a chronology of James's life, bibliographies of his works and of secondary sources, and black-and-white photographs and illustrations." Publisher's note
Includes bibliographical references

Hardwick, Elizabeth

Herman Melville. Viking 2000 161p (Penguin lives series) $19.95   **813**
  1. Authors 2. Novelists 3. Authors, American
  ISBN 0-670-89158-4
                                                   LC 00-36510
"Interweaving critical readings of his fiction and poetry with events in Melville's life, Hardwick offers glimpses into his tortured writing career, his sometimes difficult family life, and his ambivalent relationship with his friend Nathaniel Hawthorne." Libr J
Includes bibliographical references

Harrison, Kathryn, 1961-

The **kiss**; Kathryn Harrison. Random House 1997 207 p.   **813**
  1. Authors, American -- Biography 2. Novelists, American -- 20th century -- Biography
  ISBN 067944999X; 9780679449997
                                                   LC 97153826

In this memoir, Kathryn "Harrison here turns an un-flinching eye on the episode in her life that has most influenced those books: a secret, sexual affair with her father that began when she was 20. . . . Abandoned by her father as a child, neglected by an emotionally remote and impetuous mother, Harrison is raised by her grandparents. . . . A minister and amateur cameraman, her father visits Harrison after an absence of 10 years, when she is home from college on spring break. The boundary between flirtation and paternal affection is soon blurred. . . . Gradually consenting to his demands for sex, Harrison drops out of college and moves in with her father's new family, extricating herself from the affair only when her mother is stricken with metastatic breast cancer." (Publishers Weekly)

Herbert, Brian

★ **Dreamer** of Dune; the biography of Frank Herbert. TOR Bks. 2003 576p il $27.95; pa $16.95 **813**

1. Authors 2. Novelists 3. Science fiction writers

ISBN 0-7653-0646-8; 0-7653-0647-6 pa

LC 2002-42951

"This moving, sometimes painfully obsessive biography is an impressive testament of family loyalty and love. A must-read for Herbert fans (both senior and junior), it includes family photos and a bibliography." Publ Wkly

Hillerman, Tony

Seldom disappointed; a memoir. HarperCollins Pubs. 2001 341p il hardcover o.p. pa $13.95 **813**

1. Authors 2. Novelists 3. Journalists 4. Mystery writers 5. Authors, American

ISBN 0-06-050586-9 pa

LC 2001-24160

In this memoir Hillerman "relates his childhood in Oklahoma during the Depression, his service in World War II, his university education, his career in journalism and academia, and his eventual turn to writing mysteries. The entire book will appeal to his fans, but the first half is intensely gripping." Libr J

Includes bibliographical references

Hiney, Tom

Raymond Chandler; a biography. Atlantic Monthly Press 1997 310p il hardcover o.p. pa $14 **813**

1. Authors 2. Novelists 3. Screenwriters 4. Mystery writers

ISBN 0-8021-3637-0 pa

LC 97-264

"Hiney traces the writer's nomadic childhood from pre-Mafia Chicago to pre-telephone Nebraska, from Quaker Ireland and Edwardian England to his education south of London at Dulwich College and his 1913 arrival in the 'mean streets' of Los Angeles, the later setting for his crime fiction. . . . Living at over 100 addresses, he sustained no long friendships, and was 'variously rich, poor, drunk, teetotal, sacked, married and suicidal.'. . . No rough edges have been filed off for this revealing, well-written biography." Publ Wkly

Includes bibliographical references

Hurston, Zora Neale, 1891-1960

Novels and stories; Zora Neale Hurston. Library of Am. 1995 1041 p. $40 **813**

1. Short stories 2. African Americans 3. African Americans -- Fiction

ISBN 0940450836; 9780940450837

LC 94025757

This book "brings together for the first time all of [Zora Neale] Hurston's best works in one authoritative set. It features the acclaimed 1937 novel 'Their Eyes Were Watching God,' a lyrical masterpiece about a woman's struggle for love and independence. . . . A selection of short stories further displays Hurston's unique fusion of folk traditions and literary modernism--comic, ironic, and soaringly poetic." (Publisher's note)

"This two-volume set brings together for the first time all of Hurston's best works: four novels, two books of folklore, and the first complete edition of her famous autobiography, Dust Tracks on a Road." LJ

J.D. Salinger; edited with an introduction by Harold Bloom. New ed; Chelsea House 2008 254p (Modern critical views) $45 **813**

1. Authors 2. Novelists 3. Short story writers

ISBN 978-0-7910-9813-4

LC 2007-44662

First published 1987

This collection of nine essays provides a view of Salinger's critical reception. Among the contributors are David Galloway, Anthony Kaufman and Robert Coles.

Includes bibliographical references

John Steinbeck; edited and with an introduction by Harold Bloom. New ed; Bloom's Literary Criticism 2008 176p (Modern critical views) $45 **813**

1. Authors 2. Novelists 3. Screenwriters 4. Nobel laureates for literature

ISBN 978-0-7910-9787-8; 0-7910-9787-0

LC 2007-38676

First published 1987

A selection of criticism, arranged in chronological order of publication, devoted to the fiction of John Steinbeck.

Includes bibliographical references (p. 167-9)

Jones, Sharon L.

Critical companion to Zora Neale Hurston; a literary reference to her life and work. Facts On File 2008 288p il (Facts on File library of American literature) $75 **813**

1. Authors 2. Novelists 3. Dramatists 4. Memoirists 5. Folklorists 6. Short story writers

ISBN 978-0-8160-6885-2; 0-8160-6885-2

LC 2008-10052

This "covers all her writings, including Their Eyes Were Watching God; her landmark works of folklore and anthropology, such as Mules and Men; and shorter works." Publisher's note

Includes bibliographical references

Kerouac, Jack

Selected letters, 1957-1969; edited with an introduction and commentary by Ann Charters. Viking 1999 xxvii, 514p hardcover o.p. pa $17   **813**

1. Authors 2. Novelists

ISBN 0-14-029615-8 pa

LC 99-17374

This volume "starts with the publication of On the Road and continues almost to the day Kerouac died. The years 1957-1960, the height of Kerouac's career, occupy more than half the volume. Later letters record his struggle to care for his ailing mother, his efforts to finish his later books and his troubles with money and health. . . . Frequent addressees and subjects include Gary Snyder, Philip Whalen, Lawrence Ferlinghetti, William Burroughs and Allen Ginsberg." Publ Wkly

King, Stephen, 1947-

On writing; a memoir of the craft. Scribner 2000 288p hardcover o.p. pa $14.95; pa $17   **813**

1. Authors 2. Novelists 3. Authorship 4. Authors, American 5. Short story writers 6. Science fiction writers

ISBN 0-671-02425-6 pa; 9781439156810

LC 00-30105

The author recounts "his life from early childhood through the aftermath of the 1999 accident that nearly killed him. Along the way, King touts the writing philosophies of William Strunk and Ernest Hemingway, advocates a healthy appetite for reading, expounds upon the subject of grammar, critiques a number of popular writers, and offers the reader a chance to try out his theories. . . . Recommended for anyone who wants to write and everyone who loves to read." Libr J

Kirk, Connie Ann

Critical companion to Flannery O'Connor. Facts on File 2008 415p il (Facts on File library of American literature) $75   **813**

1. Authors 2. Novelists 3. Short story writers

ISBN 978-0-8160-6417-5

LC 2007-6512

This book examines O'Connor's "life and works, and includes critical analyses of some of the themes in her writing, as well as entries on related topics and relevant people, places, and influences." Publisher's note

Includes bibliographical references

Lardner, Ring

I'd hate myself in the morning; a memoir. {by} Ring Lardner, Jr. Thunder's Mouth Press 2000 198p il $22.95; pa $14.95   **813**

1. Novelists 2. Screenwriters

ISBN 1-56025-296-0; 1-56025-338-X pa

LC 00-44298

"Of interest to cultural historians as well as general readers, this book belongs in both academic and public libraries." Libr J

Levy, Andrew

Huck Finn's America; Mark Twain and the Era That Shaped His Masterpiece. Andrew Levy. Simon & Schuster 2014 368 p. $25   **813**

1. American literature -- History and criticism

ISBN 1439186960; 9781439186961

LC 2014040482

This book, by Andrew Levy, "shows how modern readers have been misunderstanding 'Huckleberry Finn' for decades. [Mark] Twain's masterpiece . . . is often discussed either as a carefree adventure story for children or a serious novel about race relations, yet Levy argues . . . it is neither. Instead, Huck Finn was written at a time when Americans were nervous about youth violence . . . and a debate was raging about education, popular culture, and responsible parenting." (Publisher's note)

"Delving deeply into 19th-century sources, generations of readers' responses and a wide range of Twain's writing, Levy complicates the possibilities of what the novel meant for its contemporaries and what it might mean for readers." Kirkus

Michaels, J. Ramsey

Passing by the dragon; the Biblical tales of Flannery O'Connor. by J. Ramsey Michaels. Cascade Books 2013 xii, 211 p.p (pbk.) $28   **813**

1. Christian fiction 2. American literature -- History and criticism 3. Christian fiction, American -- Criticism and interpretation

ISBN 1620322234; 9781620322239

LC 2012285239

This book, by J. Ramsey Michaels, "attempts a close reading of the fiction of Flannery O'Connor, story by story, with one eye on her use of the Bible, and her view of the Bible in relation to her own work. After introductory chapters on O'Connor's markings in her own Roman Catholic Bible, her book reviews in diocesan newspapers, and her impatience with her wayward readers, Michaels looks first at her two novels, 'Wise Blood' and 'The Violent Bear It Away,' and then at seventeen of her short stories." (Publisher's note)

Includes bibliographical references (p. 209-211)

Murphy, Mary McDonagh

Scout, Atticus, and Boo; a celebration of fifty years of To kill a mockingbird. Harper 2010 217p il $24.99   **813**

1. Authors 2. Novelists 3. Essayists 4. Short story writers

ISBN 978-0-06-192407-1; 0-06-192407-5

LC 2010-06739

The author tells the story of how the quiet, publicity-shy Southerner Harper Lee came to write her classic. She also conducts interviews (which will later be included in a documentary) with famous folks whose childhoods were transformed by the novel, such as Oprah, Tom Brokaw, and Scott Turow. Lee, now 84, didn't talk she never does, God bless herbut you come away from Murphy's book with a renewed amazement at what Lee was able to achieve with a single perfect novel. Entertaiment Wkly

Nabokov, Vladimir Vladimirovich

Speak, memory; an autobiography revisited. {by} Vladimir Nabokov; with an introduction by Brian Boyd. Knopf 1999 xxxv, 268p il map $17; pa $14 **813**

1. Poets 2. Authors 3. Novelists 4. Authors, Russian 5. Essayists 6. Memoirists 7. Translators 8. College teachers 9. Literary critics 10. Short story writers

ISBN 0-375-40553-4; 0-679-72339-0 pa

LC 98-49237

A revised version of the memoir first published 1951 in the United States with title: Conclusive evidence

These recollections of the author's youthful years give an account of a vanishing world. They offer a picture of the author's family, their flight from Russia, education in England, and émigré life in Paris and Berlin

Includes bibliographical references

Nadel, Ira Bruce

Critical companion to Philip Roth; a literary companion to his life and work. [by] Ira B. Nadel. Facts On File, Inc. 2011 356p il (Facts on File library of American literature) $75 **813**

1. Authors 2. Novelists 3. Short story writers

ISBN 978-0-8160-7795-3; 978-1-4381-3555-7 ebook

LC 2010022769

"Coverage includes: a . . . biography of Roth; entries on all of Roth's works; . . . entries on related people, places, and topics, such as anti-Semitism, Claire Bloom, Newark, satire, and . . . more; [and] appendixes, including a chronology, a bibliography of Roth's works, and a secondary-source bibliography." Publisher's note

Includes bibliographical references

Oliver, Charles M.

Critical companion to Ernest Hemingway; a literary reference to his life and work. Facts on File 2006 630p il (Facts on File library of American literature) $75 **813**

1. Poets 2. Authors 3. Novelists 4. Short story writers 5. Nobel laureates for literature

ISBN 0-8160-6418-0; 978-0-8160-6418-2

LC 2006-7970

First published 1999 with title: Ernest Hemingway A to Z

"This volume features entries on all of Hemingway's major and minor works, places and events related to his works, major figures in his life, and more. Appendixes include a complete list of Hemingway's works; a chronology; a genealogy; a . . . map for readers of Islands in the Stream; a list of film, stage, and radio adaptations; and a bibliography of secondary sources." Publisher's note

Includes filmography and bibliographical references

Parker, Hershel

Herman Melville; v1 a biography. Johns Hopkins Univ. Press 1996 942p v1 il maps $50; pa $29.95 **813**

1. Authors 2. Novelists 3. Authors, American 4.

Biography, Individual

ISBN 0-8018-5428-8; 0-8018-8185-4 pa

LC 96-18984

This, the first volume of a projected two-volume "biography of Melville, ends in 1851, when the author presented to his . . . friend Nathaniel Hawthorne an inscribed pre-publication copy of Moby-Dick." (Atl Mon) Index.

This, the first volume of a two-volume "biography of Melville, ends in 1851, when the author presented to his . . . friend Nathaniel Hawthorne an inscribed pre-publication copy of Moby-Dick." Atl Mon

Includes bibliographical references

Philbrick, Nathaniel

Why read Moby-Dick? Viking 2011 x, 131 p.p (hbk.) $25 **813**

1. Whaling -- Fiction 2. Shipwrecks -- Fiction 3. American literature -- History and criticism 4. Sea stories -- History and criticism

ISBN 0670022993; 9780670022991

LC 2011019766

This book attempts to offer Herman "Melville's [book 'Moby-Dick' a] . . . broad contemporary audience. . . . [Author] Nathaniel Philbrick . . . unpacked the story of the wreck of the whaleship Essex, the real-life incident that inspired Melville to write 'Moby-Dick.' Now, he sets his sights on the fiction itself, offering a . . . tour of . . . [the] novel. . . . Philbrick . . . navigates Melville's world and illuminates the book's humor and . . . characters-finding the thread that binds Ishmael and Ahab to our own time." (Publisher's note)

"In this cogent and passionate polemic for Melville's masterpiece, Philbrick . . . combines a critical eye and a reader's adoration to make a case for Moby-Dick. The plights of the Pequod, Ishmael and Ahab may seem irrelevant (or worse, quaint) compared to today's troubles, but Philbrick opines that within the pages of this American classic lie timeless archetypes whose relevance stretches across human history. . . . Less lit-crit and more readers' guide, this tome will remind fans why they loved the book in the first place, and whet the appetites of trepid potential readers." Publ Wkly

Includes bibliographical references

Phillips, Julie

James Tiptree, Jr. the double life of Alice B. Sheldon. St. Martin's Press 2006 469p il $27.95 **813**

1. Authors 2. Science fiction writers

ISBN 0-312-20385-3; 978-0-312-20385-6

LC 2006-40095

This is a biography of the American science fiction writer.

The author "has achieved a wonder: an evenhanded, scrupulously documented, objective yet sympathetic portrait of a deliberately elusive personality." Publ Wkly

Includes bibliographical references

Plimpton, George

Truman Capote; in which various friends, enemies, acquaintances, and detractors recall his turbulent career. Talese 1997 498p il hardcover o.p. pa $16.95 **813**

1. Authors 2. Novelists 3. Nonfiction writers 4. Short

story writers
ISBN 0-385-49173-5 pa

LC 97-14792

"The book is an intoxicating swirl of contradictory stories, serious analysis and rumors, adroitly edited in chapters arranged like those of a picaresque novel." Publ Wkly

Pritchard, William H.

Updike. University of Massachusetts Press 2005 350p pa $24.95   **813**

1. Poets 2. Authors 3. Novelists 4. Short story writers
ISBN 978-1-55849-507-4; 1-55849-507-X
First published 2000 by Steerforth Press

"All in all, Pritchard's book is a gentle and intelligent request for a little more thought and a little less cranky let'smoveon speed in judging the work of one of America's pre-eminent writers." N Y Times Book Rev
Includes bibliographical references

Rand, Ayn

Letters of Ayn Rand; edited by Michael S. Berliner; introduction by Leonard Peikoff. Dutton 1995 xxi, 681p il hardcover o.p. pa $20   **813**

1. Authors 2. Novelists 3. Philosophers 4. Nonfiction writers
ISBN 0-452-27404-4 pa

LC 94-23646

"Imbued with her fiercely held beliefs, the letters most devoted to politics and philosophy fairly blaze off the page. . . . Regardless of one's opinion of her thinking, her letters add greatly to our understanding of a most exceptional woman of letters." Booklist

Rehak, Melanie

Girl sleuth; Nancy Drew and the women who created her. Harcourt 2005 364p il $25; pa $14 **813**

1. Authors 2. Mystery writers 3. Children's authors 4. Young adult authors 5. Drew, Nancy (Fictitious character)
ISBN 0-15-101041-2; 0-15-603056-X pa

LC 2005-9129

"Packed with revealing anecdotes, Rehak's meticulously researched account of the publishing phenomenon that survived the Depression and WWII . . . will delight fans of the beloved gumshoe whose gumption guaranteed that every reprobate got his due." Booklist
Includes bibliographical references

Reynolds, David S., 1948-

Mightier than the sword; Uncle Tom's cabin and the battle for America. W. W. Norton & Co. 2011 351p il $27.95   **813**

1. Authors 2. Novelists 3. Abolitionists 4. Children's authors 5. Nonfiction writers 6. Short story writers
ISBN 978-0-393-08132-9; 0-393-08132-X

LC 2011-00702

"The powerful antislavery message of 'Uncle Tom's Cabin' fueled the flames leading to the Civil War, making it the most influential novel in American history. . . . Stowe claimed the novel came to her in a vision and God was its true author. Accordingly, her book is weighted with religious symbolism, which Reynolds interprets with typi-

cal English professor's zeal. He also examines its impacts not just on public attitudes toward slavery, but on women's rights, temperance, capitalism, minstrel shows, sexual customs and other aspects of mid-19th century American life. Reynolds dissects dozens of imitative novels, plays and minstrel shows — some against, others for slavery or segregation — and traces the influence of Stowe's novel into modern times, including film spin-offs. . . .[This is] not easy reading, but it offers virtually everything you ever wanted to know about 'Uncle Tom's Cabin' — and probably a lot more." Seattle Times

Roth, Philip

The **facts**; a novelist's autobiography. Vintage Bks. 1997 195p pa $14   **813**

1. Authors 2. Novelists 3. Authors, American 4. Short story writers
ISBN 0-679-74905-5; 978-0-679-74905-9

LC 96-28807

First published 1988 by Farrar, Straus & Giroux

"The Facts is a lively and serious version of a novelist's life, but it seems even more interesting as a new way of formulating the questions about the imagination that Roth has been pursuing with increasing complication in the Zuckerman novels." N Y Rev Books

Rowley, Hazel

Richard Wright; the life and times. Holt & Co. 2001 626p il hardcover o.p. pa $18   **813**

1. Authors 2. Novelists 3. Dramatists 4. Essayists 5. Nonfiction writers 6. Short story writers
ISBN 0-8050-7088-5 pa

LC 00-54249

"The strength of {this book} is {the} painstaking research. Rowley . . . has a daunting dedication to primary sources and her documentation is meticulous." N Y Times Book Rev
Includes bibliographical references

Sallis, James

Chester Himes; a life. Walker & Co. 2000 368p il $28; pa $18.95   **813**

1. Authors 2. Novelists 3. Mystery writers 4. Short story writers
ISBN 0-8027-1362-9; 0-8027-7639-6 pa

LC 00-63328

This is a biography of the African-American crime novelist. "Sentenced to 25 years in prison for armed robbery when he was 19, he turned to writing while behind bars and, when released after serving eight years, published two novels. Their poor reception by the white establishment only confirmed Himes's beliefs about racism in America. He eventually moved to Paris, spending most of the rest of his life abroad. . . . The author succeeds splendidly in fleshing Himes out in this riveting biography." Libr J
Includes bibliographical references

Savigneau, Josyane

Carson McCullers; a life. translated by Joan E. Howard. Houghton Mifflin 2001 370p il $30 **813**

1. Authors 2. Novelists 3. Dramatists 4. Short story

writers
ISBN 0-395-87820-9

LC 00-46547

This is a "heartfelt, honest portrait of one of the great novelists of the American South." Libr J
Includes bibliographical references

Schultz, Jeffrey D.
Critical companion to John Steinbeck; a literary reference to his life and work. [by] Jeffrey Schultz, Luchen Li. Facts on File 2005 406p il (Facts on File library of American literature) $65; pa $19.99 **813**
1. Authors 2. Novelists 3. Screenwriters 4. Nobel laureates for literature
ISBN 0-8160-4300-0; 0-8160-4301-9 pa

LC 2004-26100

"Useful, succinct, and reasonably priced, it packs an abundance of information into one compact resource." Libr J
Includes bibliographical references

Smiley, Jane
Thirteen ways of looking at the novel. Knopf 2005 591p $26.95 **813**
1. Authorship 2. Fiction -- History and criticism
ISBN 1-4000-4059-0

LC 2005-45181

"The book is roughly divided into three sections: the first classifies the novel, beginning with the most simple of definitions (e.g., it's long, in prose, has a protagonist), and adds moral and aesthetic complexity as it moves along. The second section consists of a primer for fledgling novelists. . . . The result is a thorough reflection on the art and craft of the novel from one of its best-known contemporary practitioners." Publ Wkly
Includes bibliographical references

Tate, Mary Jo
Critical companion to F. Scott Fitzgerald; a literary reference to his life and work. foreword by Matthew J. Bruccoli. Facts on File 2006 464p il (Facts on File library of American literature) $75 **813**
1. Authors 2. Novelists 3. Screenwriters 4. Short story writers
ISBN 0-8160-6433-4; 978-0-8160-6433-5

LC 2006-11393

First published 1998 with title: F. Scott Fitzgerald A to Z
This book "studies the legacy of this writer, highlighting significant themes and historical references of his various works." Publisher's note
Includes bibliographical references

★ A **Theodore** Dreiser encyclopedia; edited by Keith Newlin. Greenwood Press 2003 xxiii, 431p il $99.95 **813**
1. Authors 2. Novelists
ISBN 0-313-31680-5

LC 2003-40841

This is a "guide to the essential facts surrounding this prolific author's life and works. Dreiser's novels and short stories are covered, as are his plays, which are far less known. Front matter includes a list of entries, a chronology, and a preface that analyzes prior contributions to Dreiser

scholarship. Alphabetically arranged essays on his books, short stories, and magazine and newspaper pieces make up the book's core. . . . The book ends with a bibliography arranged by category (books by Dreiser, critical studies, biographies, etc.). Highly recommended." Choice
Includes bibliographical references and index

Turner, Frederick
Renegade; Henry Miller and the making of Tropic of Cancer. Frederick W. Turner. Yale University Press 2011 xi, 244 p.p (hardback) $24.95 **813**
1. United States -- History 2. Popular culture -- United States 3. Literature -- History and criticism 4. Censorship -- United States -- History -- 20th century 5. Authors and publishers -- United States -- History -- 20th century 6. Politics and literature -- United States -- History -- 20th century 7. Publishers and publishing -- United States -- History -- 20th century
ISBN 0300149492; 9780300149494

LC 2011019531

In this book, author Frederick W. Turner "reassesses [writer Henry Miller's book 'Tropic of Cancer']. . . . Turner's story traces Miller's mid-twentieth-century ramble back through the dark passages of US history . . . claiming that Miller (consciously or not) modeled himself and his books on the American-as-outlaw archetype. . . . Turner also argues that Miller's prose is part of a deep strain in American culture that mistrusts highbrow anything, literature especially, but celebrates talk, and loves big talk the best." (Bookforum)
Includes bibliographical references and index.

Vonnegut, Kurt, 1922-2007
Kurt Vonnegut; letters. edited by Dan Wakefield. Delacorte Press 2012 436 p. $35 **813**
1. American letters 2. Authors -- Correspondence
ISBN 0385343752; 9780345535399; 9780385343756

LC 2012001544

Author Kurt Vonnegut and editor Dan Wakefield present Vonnegut's "collection of personal correspondence." It includes "the letter a twenty-two-year-old Vonnegut wrote home immediately upon being freed from a German POW camp" and "wry dispatches from Vonnegut's years as a struggling writer slowly finding an audience and then dealing with sudden international fame in middle age." (Publisher's note)

Walker, Alice
The **same** river twice; honoring the difficult: a meditation on life, spirit, art, and the making of the film The color purple, ten years later. Scribner 1996 302p il hardcover o.p. pa $14 **813**
1. Poets 2. Authors 3. Novelists 4. Editors 5. Essayists 6. College teachers 7. Short story writers 8. Color purple (Motion picture)
ISBN 0-671-00377-1 pa

LC 95-30056

This "book finds the Pulitzer Prize-winning author still grappling with criticism of the film version of her novel The Color Purple. . . . Walker's memoir pieces together assorted journal entries, magazine clippings, occasional photographs and even her original screenplay to form an intimate scrapbook of the period." Publ Wkly

Includes bibliographical references

Wallace, David Foster, 1962-2008

The **David** Foster Wallace Reader; David Foster Wallace. Little, Brown & Co. 2014 963 p. (hardback) $35 **813**

ISBN 0316182397; 9780316182393

LC 2014032157

This book presents a collection of writings by David Foster Wallace. His "explorations of morality, self-consciousness, addiction, sports, love, and the many other subjects that occupied him are represented here in both fiction and nonfiction. . . . A dozen writers and critics, including Hari Kunzru, Anne Fadiman, and Nam Le, add afterwords to favorite pieces." (Publisher's note)

Walton, Jo, 1964-

What Makes This Book So Great; Re-reading the classics of science fiction and fantasy. Jo Walton. Tor 2014 448 p. (hardback) $26.99 **813**

1. Books and reading 2. Fantasy fiction -- History and criticism 3. Science fiction -- History and criticism 4. Books and reading -- United States 5. Fantasy fiction, American -- History and criticism 6. Science fiction, American -- History and criticism

ISBN 0765331934; 9780765331939

LC 2013028170

"This collection gathers 130 of [novelist Jo] Walton's blog posts from science fiction site Tor.com about her favorites works of sci-fi and fantasy. . . . The themes of the essays interweave . . . many are meditations on the genre as a whole more than reviews of specific works, and Walton often ties her points back to earlier posts." (Publishers Weekly)

"Walton shares not only her deep love for sf and fantasy in general and these novels in particular but the insights of a truly thoughtful reader." LJ

Weise, Jillian

The **book** of goodbyes; poems. by Jillian Weise. BOA Editions, Ltd. 2013 88 p. (pbk.) $16 **813**

1. American poetry

ISBN 1938160142; 9781938160141; 9781938160158

LC 2013013139

In this collection of poems, author Jillian Weise "forwards her . . . poetics by chronicling an affair with a man she names 'Big Logos.' These poems throw into question sex, the law, identity, sentiment, and power, shifting between lyric and narrative, hyper-realism and magical realism, fact and fiction." (Publisher's note)

"Throughout, Weise's masterfully balanced voice transforms even unique intricacies of her experience into a way to relate to—not alienate—the reader." Pub Wkly

White, Edmund

★ **My** lives. Ecco 2006 356p il $25.95 **813**

1. Authors 2. Novelists 3. Memoirists 4. Biographers 5. Short story writers

ISBN 0-06-621397-5; 978-0-06-621397-2

LC 2005-49506

First published 2005 in the United Kingdom

This is an autobiography by "an award-winning author and leader of the gay liberation movement of the 1960s. . . . The stories of his mother's egotism and incessant chatter, struggle to master the French language, obsession with European culture, literary associates, and work as a novelist, teacher, and essayist are largely overshadowed by graphic and explicit tales of the men in his life. . . . White's writing is amusing, descriptive, shocking, and, ultimately, thought-provoking." Libr J

Wideman, John Edgar

Hoop roots. Houghton Mifflin 2001 242p $24; pa $13 **813**

1. Authors 2. Novelists 3. Memoirists 4. College teachers 5. Nonfiction writers 6. Short story writers

ISBN 0-395-85731-7; 0-618-25775-6 pa

LC 2001-26455

Wideman "examines his lifelong relationship with basketball. He argues that basketball first allowed him to set his own standard in a white world that often imposes definitions of success on black people. A poignant, thought-provoking memoir." Booklist

Wiesel, Elie, 1928-2016

All rivers run to the sea; memoirs. Knopf 1995 432p il $35; pa $15 **813**

1. Authors 2. Novelists 3. Journalists 4. Holocaust survivors 5. Human rights activists 6. Nobel laureates for peace 7. Holocaust, 1933-1945 -- Personal narratives

ISBN 0-679-43916-1; 0-8052-1028-8 pa

LC 95-17607

Original French edition, 1994

"Wiesel's immensely moving, unforgettable memoir has the searing intensity of his novels and autobiographical tales." Publ Wkly

★ **And** the sea is never full; memoirs, 1969-translated from the French by Marion Wiesel. Knopf 1999 429p hardcover o.p. pa $15 **813**

1. Authors 2. Novelists 3. Journalists 4. Holocaust survivors 5. Human rights activists 6. Nobel laureates for peace 7. Holocaust, 1933-1945 -- Personal narratives

ISBN 0-8052-1029-6 pa

LC 99-15604

Continues the author's memoirs begun in All the rivers run to the sea

Original French edition, 1996

"This concluding volume begins when the author is age 40. He continues his travels . . . and he continues to write, his books including Souls on fire, Four Hasidic Masters, Twilight, and more. . . . Wiesel is the most significant writer to have made the Holocaust the major theme of his work, just as it has been of major importance to his life. The horror of the Holocaust can be felt in this memoir with an intensity beyond words." Booklist

William Faulkner; edited and with an introduction by Harold Bloom. New ed.; Bloom's Literary Criticism 2008 269p (Modern critical views) $45 **813**

1. Authors 2. Novelists 3. Screenwriters 4. Short

story writers 5. Nobel laureates for literature
ISBN 978-0-7910-9786-1

LC 2007-33754

First published 1986

"This volume of . . . critical essays examines The Sound and the Fury, Light in August, As I Lay Dying, Absalom, Absalom!, and other key works by this preeminent writer of the twentieth century." Publisher's note

Includes bibliographical references

Wright, Sarah Bird

Critical companion to Nathaniel Hawthorne; a literary reference to his life and work. Facts on File 2006 392p il (Facts on File library of American literature) $75 **813**

1. Authors 2. Novelists 3. Short story writers
ISBN 0-8160-5583-1; 978-0-8160-5583-8

LC 2005-34648

This book "offers critical entries on Hawthorne's novels, short stories, travel writing, criticism, and other works, as well as portraits of characters, including Hester Prynne and Roger Chillingworth. This . . . reference also provides entries on Hawthorne's family, friends—ranging from Herman Melville to President Franklin Pierce—publishers, and critics, as well as periodicals that published his work and important places and events in his life." Publisher's note

Includes bibliographical references

Zora Neale Hurston; edited and with an introduction by Harold Bloom. New ed; Chelsea House Publishers 2008 238p (Modern critical views) $45 **813**

1. Authors 2. Novelists 3. Dramatists 4. Memoirists 5. Folklorists 6. Short story writers
ISBN 978-0-7910-9610-9

LC 2007-49161

First published 1986

"Featuring supplemental material such as a chronology, a bibliography, and an index, [this book is a] critical look at Hurston's work and its influence on contemporary themes, such as race and gender in American society." Publisher's note

Includes bibliographical references

814   American essays in English

Als, Hilton, 1960-

★ White Girls; Hilton Als. McSweeney's 2013 300 p. $24 **814**

1. Race 2. Culture 3. Gender role
ISBN 1936365812; 9781936365814

Lambda Literary Awards Winner - LGBT Nonfiction (2014)

This book by Hilton Als presents a collection of essays. "His eponymous 'white girls' include Louise Brooks, Flannery O'Connor, Truman Capote, Richard Pryor, Malcolm X, Michael Jackson, Eminem, and others. Using his subjects as a springboard to analyze literature, photography, films, music, television, performance, race, gender, sexual orientation, and history, Als offers wry insights throughout." (Publishers Weekly)

"Whether his subject is his mother, himself, or seminal artists, Als is a fine, piercing observer and interpreter, a writer of lashing exactitude and veracity." Booklist

Angelou, Maya, 1928-2014

Wouldn't take nothing for my journey now. Random House 1993 141p hardcover o.p. pa $6.99 **814**

ISBN 0-679-42743-0; 0-553-56907-4 pa

LC 93-5904

The author "shares her thoughts about humankind: how to respect others of different cultures, opinions, and values as taught by universal philosophies. . . . Angelou's prose is brisk, fluid, and entrancing. This work will provide a taste of wisdom to all who read it." Libr J

Atwood, Margaret, 1939-

Writing with intent; essays, reviews, personal prose, 1983-2005. Carroll & Graf Publishers 2005 427p $26 **814**

ISBN 0-7867-1535-9

LC 2005-42086

Some of the essays in this volume were first published 2004 in Canada with title: Moving targets

In these essays, the author "comments on world events, fellow writers, and her own development. She reviews books by John Updike, Italo Calvino, Antonia Fraser, and Dashiell Hammett, as well as the lesser-known Robert Bringhurst, Hilary Mantel, and H. Rider Haggard. . . . This collection will not disappoint Atwood fans as her analyses both challenge and entertain." Libr J

Includes bibliographical references

Baker, Nicholson, 1957-

The way the world works; essays. Nicholson Baker. Simon & Schuster 2012 336 p. (hardcover) $25.00 **814**

1. American essays 2. Electronic books 3. Books and reading
ISBN 1416572473; 9781416572473

LC 2011052741

This book is a "collection of essays," in which "[Nicholson] Baker . . . poses important questions about our era of digital readership. As he notes in his essay on the Kindle 2, there is a distinction between a writer's work and its presentation in book form. Many essays staunchly defend the reading of print books and newspapers. . . . A proud defender of libraries and newspapers, Baker acknowledges the perception of him as 'a weirdo cultist, a ringleader' for books." (Publishers Weekly)

Baldwin, James

★ Collected essays. Library of Am. 1998 869p $35 **814**

ISBN 1-883011-52-3

LC 97-23496

The essays in this volume were selected by Toni Morrison. "Morrison has reprinted all of the material contained in Baldwin's previous collected essays, The Price of the Ticket (1985). She has added eleven pieces, the earliest of which dates from 1947—Baldwin's first published review, of a biography of Frederick Douglass, in the Nation—and the latest from 1984." Times Lit Suppl

The **beholder's** eye; a collection of America's finest personal journalism. edited and with an introduction by Walt Harrington. Grove Press 2005 xxii, 256p pa $14   **814**
ISBN 0-8021-4224-5

LC 2005-46242

"Each writer takes a unique approach to the subject, drawing the reader into the experience of pit-bull fighting or hunting with the Inuit. Among the collection: Harrington, who is married to a black woman, explores his evolving attitudes on race through the lens of his relationship with his in-laws, Pete Earley returns to his hometown in search of the meaning of a sister's death in their youth, Ron Rosenbaum explores his own outlook on life in a philosophical discourse with then-New York governor Mario Cuomo, Davis Miller is unabashedly starstruck in a comfortable and closeup look at Muhammad Ali at the home of Ali's mother, and Stephen S. Hall is personally probing in his exploration, via MRI, of his own brain and its functioning. These stories are amusing, insightful, and touching in a way that only something personal can be." Booklist

Berry, Wendell
Imagination in place; essays. Counterpoint 2010 196p $24   **814**
ISBN 978-1-58243-562-6; 1-58243-562-6

LC 2009-38104

"For those who've already come to admire Berry's moral clarity and closely argued critiques of contemporary society, 'Imagination in Place' is a welcome chance to continue the conversation." Christ Sci Monit
Includes bibliographical references

★ The **best** American essays 2010; edited with an introduction by Christopher Hitchens; Robert Atwan, series editor. Houghton Mifflin 2010 xxi, 272p (The best American series) pa $14.95 **814**
ISBN 978-0-547-39451-0
Annual. First published 1986
Editors select essays from general interest magazines that touch on topics political, scientific, historical, religious, and sociological, in addition to the personal and literary.

The **Best** American essays 2013; edited by Cheryl Strayed; series editor Robert Atwan. Houghton Mifflin Harcourt 2013 336 p. $14.95   **814**
1. American essays
ISBN 0544103882; 9780544103887;

In this book, editor Charyl Strayed presents her choices for the best essays written by American authors in 2013. "Zadie Smith muses at length about her coming to appreciate the artistry of Joni Mitchell, Steven Harvey provides a . . . recollection of his mother and her suicide, Jon Kerstetter writes of the pain of combat triage, and Vanessa Veselka presents a harrowing story of runaway girls who ride with truckers." (Publisher's note)

The "annual reprise of the venerable series takes a decidedly introspective turn. More than two dozen talented authors, selected by Strayed, write about themselves, more or less." Kirkus

The **best** American essays 2014; edited by John Jeremiah Sullivan and Robert Atwan. Houghton Mifflin Harcourt 2014 272 p. $14.95   **814**
1. American essays
ISBN 0544309901; 9780544309906

This collection of American essays is edited by John Jeremiah Sullivan and Robert Atwan. "Barry Lopez tells a harrowing tale of cruel molestation. Wells Tower brightly chronicles his visit to Burning Man with his father. Leslie Jamison describes victims of what seems to be an imaginary disease. Zadie Smith considers the rarity of true joy. Paul West presents a lighthearted piece on being introduced at a public lecture." (Kirkus Reviews)

"Good reading on a variety of topics by an observant band of essayists." Kirkus

★ The **Best** American essays of the century; Joyce Carol Oates, editor; Robert Atwan, coeditor; with an introduction by Joyce Carol Oates. Houghton Mifflin 2000 596p hardcover o.p. pa $18 **814**
ISBN 0-618-04370-5; 0-618-15587-2 pa

This anthology includes essays "that contemplate diverse worlds, from nature to courtrooms, war and family memories. Race is a pervasive theme, explored with candor and insight by many, including James Baldwin, Zora Neale Hurston, and, in a jolting 1912 condemnation of a Coatesville, Pennsylvania, lynching, John Jay Chapman." Booklist
Includes bibliographical references

The **Best** American Sports Writing 2014; edited by Christopher McDougall; series editor Glenn Stout. Houghton Mifflin Harcourt 2014 416 p. (paperback) $14.95   **814**
1. Sports journalism
ISBN 0544147006; 9780544147003

In this book, editor Christopher McDougall presents his choices for "the very best sports journalism of the past year." Selections include Paul Solotaroff and Ron Borges' "The Gangster in the Huddle," on football player Aaron Hernandez's criminal behavior, Amanda Ripley's "The Case Against High School Sports," and Jay Caspian Kang's "The End and Don King." (Publisher's note)

"Recommended for avid sports fans and readers of narrative nonfiction." LJ

Bradbury, Ray, 1920-2012
Bradbury speaks; too soon from the cave, too far from the stars. William Morrow 2005 243p hardcover o.p. pa $14.95   **814**
ISBN 0-06-058568-4; 0-06-058569-2 pa

LC 2005-41489

In this collection of essays, the author "weighs in on a medley of topics, including the allure of Paris, his enthusiasm for trains, the genesis of his most popular novels, and his reasons for remaining a diehard optimist. . . . By turns whimsical, insightful, and unabashedly metaphoric, his prose is immediately accessible as well as thought-provoking. Fans and nonfans alike should enjoy." Booklist

Burn this book; PEN writers speak out on the power of the word. edited by Toni Morrison. HarperStudio 2009 118p $16.99 **814**
1. Authorship 2. Censorship 3. Freedom of speech
ISBN 978-0-06-177400-3
"Published in conjunction with the PEN American Center, this slim collection of essays has an amazing list of contributors—Toni Morrison, John Updike, David Grossman, Francine Prose, Pico Iyer, Russell Banks, Paul Auster, Orhan Pamuk, Salman Rushdie, Ed Park, and Nadine Gordimer. . . . [They] discuss the importance of writing from various views, political and social. They illustrate the need for freedom of speech and human rights, and they emphasize the target writers become in a tyranny. . . . This is not an easy read, but it is a profound, absorbing, and moving collection of work." Libr J
Includes bibliographical references

Capote, Truman
★ **Portraits** and observations; the essays of Truman Capote. Random House 2007 518p $28.95 **814**
ISBN 978-1-4000-6661-2; 1-4000-6661-1
LC 2007-36624
This is a collection of 42 essays written by Capote from 1946 to 1984.
"The featured works cover the artist's interests in travel, celebrities, the arts—both visual and literary—crimes of passion, and himself. . . . This collection offers the highest quality of writing from a genuine American stylist." Libr J

Chabon, Michael
Maps and legends; reading and writing along the borderlands. McSweeney's 2008 222p $24 **814**
1. Authorship
ISBN 978-1-932416-89-3; 1-932416-89-7
"In 16 essays, Chabon maps his enthusiasms. . . . Although in part a fragmentary memoir—we receive revealing glimpses of Chabon's family, boyhood home of Columbia, Md., and personal history—'Maps and Legends' is also a manifesto, a declaration of literary principles that asserts the value, even necessity, of genre. Especially in the book's first half, Chabon makes this argument through example, by closely examining and celebrating Arthur Conan Doyle's Sherlock Holmes tales, Philip Pullman's 'His Dark Materials' series, M.R. James' ghost stories, and the comics of Howard Chaykin, Ben Katchor and Will Eisner. . . . However disparately engaging you find the ruminations on other writers, the book's concluding quintet of pieces on the inspirations behind Chabon's major work will prove an illuminating delight for those of us who have the same fannish devotion to his work as he does to Conan Doyle's." St. Louis Post-Dispatch

Codrescu, Andrei
New Orleans, mon amour; by Andrei Codrescu. Algonquin Books of Chapel Hill 2006 273p pa $14 **814**
1. New Orleans (La.) -- Social life and customs
ISBN 1-56512-505-3
LC 2005-53599
In this collection of short essays Codrescu sketches "portraits of a fabled city and its equally fabled inhabit-

ants. The author, who has called the Big Easy home for two decades, shows how, like some gigantic bohemian magnet, New Orleans attracts some of the world's most talented, self-indulgent freaks. Codrescu finds himself quite at home there. He expertly weaves pages of New Orleans history through his stories of personal discovery and debauchery. The last few essays, written post-Katrina, radiate simultaneous anger and clarity. Full of pride and defensiveness, Codrescu closes the collection ruminating about rebuilding the city and his longing to return to its rhythms and eccentricities. Despite Codrescu's frustrations, this collection is, in the end, gentle and sweet." Publ Wkly

Daum, Meghan
The **unspeakable**; and other subjects of discussion. Meghan Daum. Farrar, Straus & Giroux 2014 256 p. (hardback) $26 **814**
1. Social adjustment 2. Social conditions
ISBN 0374280444; 9780374280444
LC 2014014643
In this collection of essays, by Meghan Daum, "her old encounters with overdrawn bank accounts and oversized ambitions in the big city have given way to a new set of challenges. . . . She skewers the marriage-industrial complex and recounts a harrowing near-death experience following a sudden illness. Throughout, Daum pushes back against the false sentimentality and shrink-wrapped platitudes that surround so much of contemporary American experience." (Publisher's note)
"This book will appeal to memoir enthusiasts seeking an insightful reading experience that will entertain as well as challenge." LJ

Didion, Joan
We tell ourselves stories in order to live; collected nonfiction. with an introduction by John Leonard. Knopf 2006 1122p $30 **814**
ISBN 978-0-307-26487-9; 0-307-26487-4
LC 2006-41043
This volume "contains seven books of journalism—all of [Didion's] nonfiction except her 2005 memoir of new widowhood, 'The Year of Magical Thinking.' Didion's writing was from the beginning startlingly individual. . . . Say what you will about her somewhat self-centered style; America needs more courageous thinkers who will write about life as it is lived—not as elites on all sides seek to manufacture it." Nat Rev
Includes bibliographical references

Doctorow, E. L.
Creationists: selected essays, 1993-2006. Random House 2006 176p $24.95 **814**
1. Creation (Literary, artistic, etc.) 2. Literature -- History and criticism
ISBN 978-1-4000-6495-3; 1-4000-6495-3
"Doctorow chose his gallery with what may seem a generous dash of whimsy. Many of his writers and other 'creationists' are not exactly habitues of the canon. Standing alongside the likes of Mark Twain, Sinclair Lewis, Scott Fitzgerald and John Dos Passos are Harriet Beecher Stowe; W. G. Sebald; the anonymous translators of Genesis into the King James version; Harpo Marx; Albert Einstein; [and]

the makers of the atomic bomb. . . . And yet the writers assembled here efficiently serve the critic's intentions. Each yields in robustly illustrative ways to 'the voice of the book,' a voice more protean than the artist's own; a voice that soars into conjunction with the voice of the region, the nation, the times." N Y Times Book Rev

Du Bois, W. E. B.

★ **Writings**. Library of Am. 1986 1334p $40; pa $15.95　　　　**814**

ISBN 0-940450-33-X; 1-883011-31-0 pa

LC 86-10565

Includes bibliographical references

Ellison, Ralph

The **collected** essays of Ralph Ellison; edited with an introduction by John F. Callahan; preface by Saul Bellow. Modern Lib. 1995 xxix, 856p hardcover o.p. pa $18　　　　**814**

1. Artists 2. Authors 3. Pianists 4. Educators 5. Novelists 6. Dramatists 7. Economists 8. Journalists 9. Essayists 10. Screenwriters 11. Music teachers 12. Cabinet members 13. Newspaper editors 14. Nonfiction writers 15. Classical musicians 16. Short story writers 17. Civil rights activists 18. Jazz music -- History and criticism 19. International organization officials 20. Nobel laureates for economic sciences
ISBN 978-0-8129-6826-2 pa; 0-8129-6826-3 pa

LC 95-4719

This book "includes posthumously discovered reviews, criticism, and interviews, as well as the essay collections Shadow and Act (1964) . . . and Going to the Territory (1986), an exploration of literature and folklore, jazz and culture, and the nature and quality of lives that black Americans lead." Publisher's note

Ephron, Nora, 1941-2012

I feel bad about my neck; and other thoughts on being a woman. Knopf 2006 137p $21.95; pa $12.95　　　　**814**

1. Aging 2. Women
ISBN 0307264556; 0307276821; 9780307264558; 9780307276827

LC 2005-57780

In this collection of essays, Ephron looks "at women who are getting older and dealing with the tribulations of maintenance, menopause, empty nests, and life itself." (Publisher's note)

"While very little in the book is meant to be taken seriously, it is clever enough to qualify as more than just an assemblage of one-liners. Whether you agree with her observations or not, Ephron's perspective as an admittedly high-maintenance, New York-dwelling, successful screenwriter will keep you entertained." Christ Sci Monit

The **Most** of Nora Ephron; by Nora Ephron. Alfred A. Knopf 2013 576 p. (hardcover) $35　　**814**

1. Anthologies 2. Love stories 3. Women authors
ISBN 038535083X; 9780385350839

LC 2013016426

This posthumously-published book collects writings by Nora Ephron. Ephron and her editor "decided to structure

it around the subject matters she explored and the genres she used to explore them. As a result, the text of her novel Heartburn (1983) is included, as is the screenplay for Ephron's most beloved movie, When Harry Met Sally, and her late-in-life play, Lucky Guy. The remainder of the anthology consists of much briefer entries across a . . . diverse set of topics." (Kirkus Reviews)

"Whether Ephron is writing about politics or purses, sexism or soufflé, her appeal is her intelligent, incisive sense of humor." LJ

Fiedler, Leslie A.

Fiedler on the roof; essays on literature and Jewish identity. by Leslie Fiedler. Godine 1990 184p $19.95; pa $11.95　　　　**814**

1. Jews in literature
ISBN 0-87923-859-3; 0-87923-949-2 pa

LC 90-55282

"Disturbing, provocative, and brilliant." Libr J

Franzen, Jonathan, 1959-

★ **Farther** away; Jonathan Franzen. Farrar, Straus and Giroux 2012 321 p.　　　　**814**

1. American essays 2. Literature -- History and criticism 3. Interpersonal relations in literature
ISBN 0374153574; 9780374153571

LC 2011046067

The author presents "a collection of recent essays, speeches, and reviews, in which he lays out a view of literature in which storytelling and character development trump lyrical acrobatics, and unearths a few forgotten classics. . . . [Jonathan Franzen discusses] books that revel in the frustrations, despairs, and near-blisses of human relationships. . . . This intimate read is packed with provocative questions about technology, love, and the state of the contemporary novel." (Publishers Weekly)

The **Fun** of it; stories from The talk of the town, The New Yorker. edited by Lillian Ross; introduction by David Remnick. Modern Lib. 2001 xxi, 478p pa $16.95　　　　**814**

1. New Yorker (Periodical)
ISBN 0-375-75649-3

LC 00-68237

A "selection of stories from 'Talk' in chronologically arranged sections that begin with the 1920s and end in 2000. Many of the early contributions were unsigned, but through archival research Ross ferrets out and reveals the authors of many of those initial pieces. Included in this lively collection are pieces by writers—some of whom became New Yorker regulars—such as Robert Benchley, James Thurber, E. B. White, A. J. Liebling, John Updike, Garrison Keillor, Ann Beattie, Bill McKibben, Roger Angell, Steve Martin, and Susan Orlean." Libr J

Gay, Roxane

Bad Feminist; essays. Roxane Gay. HarperCollins 2014 336 p. $15.99　　　　**814**

1. Feminism 2. Feminist criticism
ISBN 0062282719; 9780062282712

This book, by Roxane Gay, is a "collection of essays spanning politics, criticism, and feminism. . . . Gay takes us through the journey of her evolution as a woman (Sweet Valley High) of color (The Help) while also taking readers on a ride through culture of the last few years (Girls, Django in Chains) and commenting on the state of feminism today (abortion, Chris Brown)." (Publisher's note)

"Writing about race, politics, gender, feminism, privilege, and popular media, [Gay] highlights how deeply misogyny is embedded in our culture, the careless language used to discuss sexual violence (seen in news reports of sexual assault), Hollywood's tokenistic treatment of race, the trivialization of literature written by women, and the many ways American society fails women and African-Americans." Pub Wkly

Ginsberg, Allen
★ **Deliberate** prose; selected essays, 1952-1995. HarperCollins Pubs. 2000 xxiv, 536p hardcover o.p. pa $17 **814**

ISBN 0-06-093081-0 pa

LC 99-41360

This collection of over 100 prose pieces "organizes the material under several general topics: 'Politics and Prophecies,' 'Drug Culture,' 'Manifestations and Spirituality,' 'Censorship and Sex Laws,' 'Autobiographical Fragments,' 'Literary Techniques and the Beat Generation,' 'Writer,' and 'Further Appreciations,' tributes to artistic collaborators and cultural heroes such as Robert Frank, Philip Glass, Andy Warhol, and the Beatles. . . . Taken together, they provide a rare glimpse into Ginsberg's creative practice, a key to sources and influences, and a good overview of his life and art." Libr J

Includes bibliographical references

Gottlieb, Robert Adams
★ **Lives** and letters. Farrar, Straus and Giroux 2011 426p $30 **814**
1. Persons 2. Celebrities

ISBN 978-0-374-29882-1; 0-374-29882-3

LC 2010-38530

"Having headed up two formidable cultural institutions, The New Yorker and the Alfred A. Knopf publishing house, Gottlieb is a fairly formidable cultural institution himself. When he passes judgment, we are inclined to listen. Befitting a man of letters, some of the essays meditate on literary figures and questions that attracted Gottlieb's curiosity. In one he examines the unlikely author-editor collaboration between Marjorie Kinnan Rawlings and Maxwell Perkins; in another he ponders how the 'wildly uneven' works of John Steinbeck have all managed to stay in print. The crowd-pleasing portion of the collection is provided by Gottlieb's critical reflections on biographies, many featuring celebrities who soared through life, egos ablaze. Discussing books about prima donnas as diverse as Margot Fonteyn and Judy Garland, Gottlieb is genteelly shocked by salacious revelations he considers an invasion of privacy, though not too shocked to give examples." Boston Globe

Hall, Donald, 1928-
Essays After Eighty; Donald Hall. Houghton Mifflin Harcourt 2014 144 p. (hardback) $22 **814**
1. Essays 2. Old age 3. Elderly men

ISBN 0544287045; 9780544287044

LC 2014016310

This book, by Donald Hall, presents a "collection of essays delivering . . . [an] unexpected view from the vantage point of very old age. . . . In . . . 'No Smoking,' he looks back over his lifetime, and several of his ancestors' lifetimes, of smoking unfiltered cigarettes, packs of them every day. Hall paints his past . . . [and], poignantly, often joyfully, he limns his present." (Publisher's note)

"America's 14th poet laureate and recipient of the National Medal of the Arts, among countless other honors, Hall offers essays that report meditatively from the 'unknown, unanticipated galaxy' of advanced age. He still lives to write, enjoying life at his ancestral Eagle Pond Farm." LJ

Hamid, Mohsin, 1971-
Discontent and its civilizations; dispatches from Lahore, New York, and London. Mohsin Hamid. Penguin Group USA 2015 240 p. (cloth) $27.95 **814**
1. Popular culture 2. Social conditions

ISBN 1594633657; 9781594633652; 9780241146323

LC 2014027668

This essay collection, by Mohsin Hamid, "brings together a wide variety of his work, a number of which appeared in print before, that touch on such subjects as international politics, the East-West divide, President Barack Obama's 2009 speech in Cairo, fundamentalism, and nationalism. Other more lighthearted topics: books and reading, the challenges the author faced moving back to Pakistan at a young age, and fatherhood, are also considered." (Library Journal)

"Hamid is an intelligent and impassioned writer whose work deserves a wide readership. Those interested in memoirs, world politics, and cultural and religious differences will enjoy these essays." LJ

Hemon, Aleksandar, 1964-
The **book** of my lives; Aleksandar Hemon. Farrar, Straus and Giroux 2013 214 p. (hardcover : alk. paper) $25 **814**
1. Sarajevo (Bosnia and Hercegovina)

ISBN 0374115737; 9780374115739

LC 2012034564

This collection of essays by Aleksandar Hemon focuses on "the war in the former Yugoslavia and its transformative effect on the material and metaphysical circumstances of Hemon's life. . . . In 'The Lives of a Flaneur,' in which he meditates on the loss of Sarajevo, he frames the story in geographical terms. . . . In 'Let There Be What Cannot Be,' by contrast, he frames the story of the war in literary terms: as a Serbian epic poem come to life." (The Nation)

Hitchens, Christopher, 1949-2011
Arguably; Essays by Christopher Hitchens. Christopher Hitchens. Twelve 2011 788p $30.00 **814**
1. American essays 2. Literature -- History and criticism 3. Criticism

ISBN 085789255X Atlantic Books; 9780857892553

Atlantic Books; 9781455502776; 9781455506781

LC 2011930917

This collection of essays by Christopher Hitchens "supplies fresh perceptions of such figures as varied as Charles Dickens, Karl Marx, Rebecca West, George Orwell, J.G. Ballard, and Philip Larkin . . . [and] pungent discussions and intrepid observations, gathered from a lifetime of traveling and reporting from such destinations as Iran, China, and Pakistan. . . . [This] volume is an intellectual self-portrait of a writer with . . . [a] vision of the human longing for reason and justice." (Publisher's note)

"Goading, brilliant, funny, and caring, Hitchens is a voice of enlightenment in a wilderness of cant." Booklist

Hustvedt, Siri

Living, thinking, looking; essays. Siri Hustvedt. Picador 2012 xiii, 384 p.p $18.00 **814**
1. Authorship 2. American essays 3. Psychologists -- Research 4. Hallucinations and illusions 5. Human beings
ISBN 1250009529; 9781250009524

LC 2011035714

In this essay collection, "[n]ovelist and essayist [Siri] Hustvedt . . . gathers 32 pieces (most previously published), written over the past six years, that she says are linked by an abiding curiosity about 'what it means to be human.'" Topics include a premigraine hallucination of Paul Bunyan, researching her novel "The Sorrows of an American," and the artist Louise Bourgeois. (Publishers Weekly)

Includes bibliographical references (p. [355]-380)

The **Inevitable**; contemporary writers confront death. edited by David Shields and Bradford Morrow; with an introduction by the editors. W. W. Norton & Co. 2011 332p $17.95 **814**
1. Death
ISBN 9780393339369 pa

LC 2010-43479

"Often poetic and at times funny or gruesome while exposing raw grief, the writers . . . tackle the subject of death with honesty and courage." Publ Wkly

Includes bibliographical references

Jamison, Leslie

★ The **empathy** exams; essays. Leslie Jamison. Graywolf Press 2014 256 p. (alk. paper) $15 **814**
1. Pain 2. Essays 3. Empathy
ISBN 1555976719; 9781555976712

LC 2013946927

"Beginning with her experience as a medical actor who was paid to act out symptoms for medical students to diagnose, Leslie Jamison's visceral and revealing essays ask essential questions about our basic understanding of others: How should we care about each other? How can we feel another's pain, especially when pain can be assumed, distorted, or performed? Is empathy a tool by which to test or even grade each other?" (Publisher's note)

"Jamison exhibits at once a journalist's courage to bear witness to acts and conditions that test human limits--incarceration, laboring in a silver mine, ultramarathoning, the loss of a child, devastating heartbreak, suffering from an unacknowledged illness--and a poet's skepticism at her own motives for doing so." Kirkus

Includes bibliographical references

Jones, Bill T., 1954-

Story/Time; the life of an idea. Bill T. Jones. Princeton University Press 2014 104 p. illustrations (some color) (The Toni Morrison Lecture Series) (hardcover : acid-free paper) $24.95 **814**
1. Choreographers 2. African American dancers 3. Literature, Experimental
ISBN 0691162700; 9780691162706

LC 2013050410

In this book, "African American dancer, choreographer, and director Bill T. Jones reflects on his art and life as he describes the genesis of Story/Time, a recent dance work produced by his company and inspired by the modernist composer and performer John Cage. . . . The book is filled with telling vignettes--about Jones's childhood as part of a large, poor, Southern family that migrated to upstate New York; about his struggles to find a place for himself in a white-dominated dance world." (Publisher's note)

"Derived from Jones' presentations at Princeton University for the Toni Morrison Lectures in 2012, the text is a hybrid. There is some introductory material explaining what follows. . . . The central--and largest--section is a series of 60 single-page narratives, each designed to consume a minute of dance and reading." Kirkus

Lethem, Jonathan

The **ecstasy** of influence; nonfictions, etc. Doubleday 2011 437p $27.95 **814**
ISBN 978-0-385-53495-6; 9780385534956

LC 2011016248

"Mr. Lethem's crowded pantheon, 'The Ecstasy of Influence' makes clear, includes Marvel comic books and misfit writers like Philip K. Dick, J. G. Ballard, Shirley Jackson and Charles Willeford. It includes improvisational filmmakers like John Cassavetes, little-known bands like the Go-Betweens and rumpled, bohemian critics like Manny Farber. Mr. Lethem is all about the underdogs, and he counts himself snug among their number. 'Most of my heroes,' he declares, 'are partly or entirely out of print.' Mailer gets a hall pass because he is, like Mr. Lethem, from Brooklyn, and because he took a grizzled interest in things like 'graffiti, underground film, marijuana and space travel.' Like almost everything Mr. Lethem has written, 'The Ecstasy of Influence' is a reflection of, and a pixelated homage to, those whose work he fetishizes. If this book has a thesis, it's this: For an artist, influence is everything." N Y Times (Late N Y Ed)

Martin, Steve

Pure drivel. Hyperion 1998 104p $19.95; pa $10.95 **814**
ISBN 0-7868-6467-2; 0-7868-8505-X pa

LC 98-28739

"The short essays, conversations, and proclamations collected here are relayed in a slyly deadpan Valley voice that belies the coiled craziness of their content. Martin also brings his gift for comedic timing to these creations, setting a quirky beat that perfectly sets off their ironic wiles." Booklist

Morris, Edmund, 1940-

This living hand; and other essays. Edmund Morris. Random House 2012 xx, 497 p.p ill. (acid-free paper) $32 **814**

1. Authorship 2. Literature 3. American essays 4. Literature -- History and criticism 5. Music 6. Biography 7. Biography -- Authorship 8. United States -- Biography 9. Presidents -- United States

ISBN 0812993128; 9780679644668; 9780812993127

LC 2012013612

This is a collection of essays by Pulitzer Prize and National Book Award winner Edmund Morris. He "begins with a 1972 essay . . . in which he recounts his time as a schoolboy in Kenya. . . . In other pieces, Morris laments the disappearance of snow on Mount Kilimanjaro; probes the psyche of South African writer Nadine Gordimer; explains his passion for writing biographies; . . . and bemoans the loss of the physical pleasure of writing with pen and ink or typewriter." (Kirkus)

Ozick, Cynthia

★ **Quarrel** & quandary; essays. Knopf 2000 247p hardcover o.p. pa $13 **814**

1. Authors 2. Children 3. Novelists 4. Diarists 5. Holocaust victims 6. Short story writers 7. Literature -- History and criticism

ISBN 0-375-72445-9 pa

LC 99-89889

Among the topics discussed in this collection of personal and literary essays are Henry James, Anne Frank, Kafka, poetry, and public intellectuals.

"All the essays collected here began life elsewhere as reviews and higher journalism. This kind of gathering of literary leftovers is usually not worth reprinting. Ozick's work is an exception. Her pieces have genuine durability. They are great essays." N Y Times Book Rev

Packer, George

Interesting times; writings from a turbulent decade. Farrar, Straus and Giroux 2009 409p $28 **814**

ISBN 978-0-3741-7572-6; 0-3741-7572-1

LC 2009-10186

A collection "essays chronicling global political and cultural tumult between 9/11 and the 2008 presidential election. . . . From Lagos to Myanmar, Tal Afar to Baghdad, the author reports on location and presents on-the-ground particulars that bring robust perspective to issues that are generally broadly reported. . . . In an era marked by the swift decline of well-researched, long-form journalism, these often heart-wrenching essays bring to life social, political and personal elements of far-flung crises in ways that elude more concise mediums." Kirkus

Paterniti, Michael

Love and Other Ways of Dying; Essays. Michael Paterniti. Random House Inc 2015 464 p. $28 **814**

1. Grief 2. Emotions

ISBN 0385337027; 9780385337021

LC 2014033162

In this essay collection, author "Michael Paterniti turns a keen eye on the full range of human experience, introducing us to an unforgettable cast of everyday people. He brings his full literary powers to bear, pondering happiness and grief, memory and the redemptive power of human connection." (Publisher's note)

"A wide variety of places and people are given Paterniti's trademark scrutiny here, and the resulting essays are illuminating and pleasantly verbose." LJ

Read Harder; edited by Ed Park and Heidi Julavits.

McSweeney's 2014 336 p. illustrations $18 **814**

1. Essays 2. Periodicals

ISBN 1940450187; 9781940450186

Editors Ed Park and Heidi Julavits present a collection of "essays from the second half of the Believer's decade-long (and counting) run. Featured articles include Nick Hornby on his first job, Rebecca Taylor on her time acting in no-budget horror movies, Francisco Goldman on the failings of memoir in dealing with personal tragedy, Megan Abbott and Sara Gran on V.C. Andrews." (Publisher's note)

"For fans of Eggers and McSweeny's publications, pop culture enthusiasts, and readers of literary magazines." LJ

Remnick, David

Reporting; writings from The New Yorker. Knopf 2006 483p $27.95 **814**

1. Journalism--United States 2. Essays

ISBN 0-307-26358-4; 978-0-307-26358-2

LC 2005-44709

The author "is an ideal reporter, combining erudition, curiosity, wit, an eye for the telling anecdote and empathy." Publ Wkly

Rich, Adrienne, 1929-2012

A **human** eye. W.W. Norton & Co. 2009 180p $24.95 **814**

1. Art and society 2. Poetry -- History and criticism

ISBN 978-0-393-07006-4; 0-393-07006-9

LC 2008049972

This book "collects ten years of [writer Adrienne Rich's] forewords, personal statements and reviews." (London Review of Books).

"Strong writing, Rich believes, is about 'how we are with each other,' and she finds this encompassing theme in the work of Muriel Rukeyser, whom Rich admires for her 'poetics of historical sensibility'; James Baldwin, who was 'uncanny' in his prescience; and June Jordan, who believed humor and pleasure are essential to social change. Rich deep-reads poetry written in the shadow of AIDS and during tyranny and war in Iraq, and argues that we must all be 'resistant to dogma.'" (Booklist)

This collection includes a "response to the anthology Iraqi Poetry Today, a critique of three classic socialist manifestos, and a rereading of The Dead Lecturer, an early volume of poems by LeRoi Jones. Rich engages the impulse to make art that both impels toward and interacts with social change, a theme she also traces through the letters of poets Robert Duncan and Denise Levertov, gay and lesbian politics and poetry, and influential texts on Zionism and the Jewish diaspora." Publisher's note

Includes bibliographical references

Richardson, Robert D.

Emerson; the mind on fire: a biography. by Robert D. Richardson, Jr.; with a frontispiece by Barry Moser. University of Calif. Press 1995 671p il $50; pa $21.95 **814**

1. Poets 2. Authors 3. Philosophers 4. Essayists

ISBN 0-520-08808-5; 0-520-20689-4 pa

LC 94-36008

"Richardson focuses principally on his subject's inner life, the life of his mind and spirit. But in this subtle portrayal of Emerson the thinker, the reader also sees the clearly limned portrait of Emerson the social activist. . . . A masterful work, this biography will attract the attention of scholars and serious general readers for decades." Booklist

Includes bibliographical references

Robinson, Marilynne, 1943-

When I was a child I read books; Marilynne Robinson. Farrar, Straus & Giroux 2012 xvi, 206 p **814**

1. Theology 2. Calvinism 3. American essays 4. Political science 5. United States -- Civilization 6. Philosophy, American 7. Theology -- United States 8. Calvinism -- United States 9. United States -- Civilization -- Philosophy 10. Political science -- United States -- Philosophy

ISBN 0374298785; 9780374298784

LC 2011041206

This collection of essays by Marilynne Robinson offers a critique of U.S. culture and politics. "Her enemies are many and varied -- militant atheists, scientists, . . . a political system that sees everything in terms of economic value, a government that commits the arch-crimes of closing libraries and filleting universities. . . . She observes that the idea of a public sector is now condemned by many Americans as 'socialism,' a stance at odds with the civic principles on which the country was founded." (New Statesman)

Includes bibliographical references.

Said, Edward W.

Reflections on exile and other essays. Harvard Univ. Press 2000 xxxv, 617p (Convergences) $36.95; pa $19.95 **814**

1. Authors 2. Criticism 3. Novelists 4. Nationalism 5. Philosophers 6. Psychologists 7. Palestinian Arabs 8. Politics in literature 9. Literary critics 10. Short story writers 11. Egypt -- Civilization 12. Motion picture directors 13. Literature -- History and criticism

ISBN 0-674-00302-0; 0-674-00997-5 pa

LC 00-44996

"Written between 1967 and the present by a literary critic and advocate for the Palestinian cause, these pieces often deal with the self-deceiving fictions of the colonizers about the people they oppress; others deplore some fashionable critical theories as unengaged with real life and history." N Y Times Book Rev

Includes bibliographical references

Sedaris, David

Dress your family in corduroy and denim. Little, Brown 2004 257p $24.95 **814**

ISBN 0-316-14346-4

LC 2003-65673

The author "has a unique ability to supply exactly the right details to bring every funny, awkward, ludicrous, painful, horrible real-life moment into harrowingly crisp focus." Booklist

Let's explore diabetes with owls; by David Sedaris. 1st ed. Little, Brown, and Co. 2013 ix, 275 p.p (hardcover) $27.00; (hardcover) $29.00 **814**

1. Swimming 2. Sea turtles 3. American essays

ISBN 0316154695; 9780316154697; 9780316233910 large print

LC 2013930473

This is an essay collection by David Sedaris. He draws on a "well of appalling childhood memories revolving around his mounting fears about being unlike other boys." He shares stories about his swimming competitions where "his irascible father vociferously championed his son's rival," his "courtship of a shy African American girl," and his "inept handling of captured baby sea turtles." (Booklist)

Me talk pretty one day. Little, Brown 2000 272p $22.95; pa $14.95 **814**

ISBN 0-316-77772-2; 0-316-77696-3 pa

LC 00-25052

"In this collection of 27 fairly short essays, some of which appeared in Esquire and The New Yorker, Sedaris gives the impression of ease and naturalness. Whether he is writing about overcoming a lisp, learning to play the guitar, trying to master French, or taking an IQ test, whether the locales are North Carolina, New York, or France, the author is both amused and amusing." Libr J

Shinner, Peggy

You feel so mortal; essays on the body. Peggy Shinner. University of Chicago Press 2014 199 p. (cloth : alkaline paper) $22 **814**

1. Body image 2. Human body 3. Human body -- Folklore 4. Human body -- Mythology

ISBN 022610527X; 9780226105277

LC 2013031722

Author Peggy Shinner presents this "collection of searing and witty essays about the body: her own body, female and Jewish; those of her parents, the bodies she came from; and the collective body, with all its historical, social, and political implications. What, she asks, does this whole mess of bones, muscles, organs, and soul mean? Searching for answers, she turns her keen narrative sense to body image, gender, ethnic history, and familial legacy." (Publisher's note)

Solnit, Rebecca

The **Faraway** Nearby; Rebecca Solnit. Penguin Group USA 2013 272 p. $25.95 **814**

1. Iceland 2. Dementia 3. American essays 4. Storytelling 5. Autobiography -- Authorship 6. Narration (Rhetoric) -- Psychological aspects

ISBN 0670025968; 9780670025961

LC 2013001563

In this essay collection, National Book Critics Circle Award-winner Rebecca Solnit offers a "study in empathy through these meandering reflections on subjects as diverse as her mother's descent into dementia, Che Guevara, and Solnit's own 'magical rescue' to Iceland for

some months as resident at the Library of Water museum."
(Publishers Weekly)

Sontag, Susan

★ **At** the same time; essays and speeches. edited by Paolo Dilonardo and Anne Jump; with a foreword by David Rieff. Farrar, Straus & Giroux 2007 235p $23   **814**

ISBN 0-374-10072-1; 978-0-374-10072-8

LC 2006-31179

This is a "collection of 16 essays written toward the end of . . . [Sontag's] life. . . . Every public and academic library should crave to own this." Libr J

Styron, William, 1925-2006

My generation; collected nonfiction. William Styron; edited by James L. W. West III. Random House Inc. 2015 656 p. illustrations (hardback) $35   **814**

1. Essays

ISBN 0812997050; 9780812997057; 9780812997064

LC 2014038029

This book, by William Styron, edited by James L. W. West III, "is the definitive gathering of William Styron's nonfiction. . . . Here are fifty years of Styron's essays, memoirs, reviews, op-eds, articles, eulogies, and speeches, reflecting the same brilliant style and informed thinking that he brought to his towering fiction and to a deeply committed public life." (Publisher's note)

"Elegant and entertaining, the writings in My Generation compose a definitive volume that will appeal to a broad audience. Summing Up: Highly recommended. Lower-division undergraduates through faculty; general readers." Choice

Tan, Amy

The **opposite** of fate; a book of musings. Putnam 2003 398p il $24.95; pa $15   **814**

1. Authors 2. Novelists 3. Essayists 4. Children's authors 5. Short story writers

ISBN 0-399-15074-9; 0-14-200489-8 pa

LC 2003-47190

"No matter how much readers already revere Tan, their appreciation for her will grow tenfold after experiencing these provocative and unforgettable revelations." Booklist

Tevis, Joni

The **world** is on fire; scrap, treasure, and songs of apocalypse. Joni Tevis. Milkweed Editions 2015 256 p. (softcover : acid-free paper) $16   **814**

1. American essays 2. End of the world

ISBN 1571313478; 9781571313478

LC 2014038727

In this book, by Joni Tevis, the author "reckons with her childhood fears by exploring the uniquely American fascination with apocalypse. From a haunted widow's wildly expanding mansion, to atomic test sites in the Nevada desert, her settings are often places of destruction and loss. And yet Tevis transforms these eerie destinations into sites of creation as well, uncovering powerful points of connection." (Publisher's note)

"Tevis's essays provide a travelog of her life. Her insights take readers from the steel of scissor blades and the cold waters of Alaska to the fire of atomic bomb testing grounds as seen through a View-Master." LJ

Trillin, Calvin

Too soon to tell. Farrar, Straus & Giroux 1995 292p hardcover o.p. pa $22   **814**

ISBN 0-374-27846-6; 978-0-374-52986-4 pa; 0-374-52986-8 pa

LC 94-24629

"In this collection of nearly 100 syndicated columns, Calvin Trillin holds forth on everything from the animal kingdom . . . to the possibility of being labeled a member of the cultural elite. . . . 'Too Soon to Tell' abounds with Mr. Trillin's self-deprecating humor and slyly acerbic insights, not to mention invaluable homespun wisdom." N Y Times Book Rev

Updike, John

Due considerations; essays and criticism. Alfred A. Knopf 2007 xxii, 703p il $40   **814**

ISBN 978-0-307-26640-8; 0-307-26640-0

LC 2007-18665

"A lush book to be savored over a long period of time." Booklist

Vidal, Gore

The **selected** essays of Gore Vidal; edited by Jay Parini. Doubleday 2008 458p $27.50   **814**

ISBN 978-0-385-52484-1; 0-385-52484-6

LC 2008-13517

"Regardless of what one thinks of Vidal, what Vidal thinks is never in doubt in these 24 essays, divided here into two groups: literary criticism and historical or cultural commentary. His writing is clear, sharp, and disciplined, and his approbation of William Dean Howells and Italo Calvino are as finely tuned as his excoriation of John Updike and Herman Wouk." Libr J

Includes bibliographical references

Vonnegut, Kurt

★ **A man** without a country; edited by Daniel Simon. Seven Stories Press 2005 146p il $23.95 **814**

ISBN 1-58322-713-X

LC 2005-14967

The author discusses politics, human nature, and other topics "in this collection of articles written over the last five years, many from the alternative magazine In These Times." Publ Wkly

Walker, Alice, 1944-

The **cushion** in the road; meditation and wandering as the whole world awakens to being in harm's way. Alice Walker. The New Press 2013 336 p. (hardcover) $26.95   **814**

1. Essays 2. Political science

ISBN 1595588728; 9781595588722

LC 2012041852

This book, by Alice Walker, offers a "collection of wide-ranging meditations. . . . [The book] revisits themes the . . . [author] has addressed throughout her career: racism, Africa, solidarity with the Palestinian people, the presidential campaign of Barack Obama, Cuba, healthcare, and the work of Aung San Suu Kyi. In doing so, Walker explores her conflicting impulses to retreat into inner contemplation and to remain deeply engaged with the world." (Publisher's note)

Wallace, David Foster

Consider the lobster; and other essays. Little, Brown 2005 343p il $25.95 **814**

ISBN 0-316-15611-6

LC 2005-10886

"Wallace's complex essays are written, and rightfully so, to be read more than once." Booklist

Includes bibliographical references

White, E. B.

Essays of E.B. White. Perennial Classics 1999 364p il pa $14.95 **814**

1. Ornithologists 2. Florida -- Description and travel 3. United States -- Politics and government 4. New York (N.Y.) -- Description and travel

ISBN 0-06-093223-6

LC 98-56019

First published 1977

Most of the essays first appeared in The New Yorker. "They range from a 1934 piece on the St. Nicholas Magazine 'League' and the distinguished writers who were members of it as children, to a 1975 report from Allen Cove, Maine, where White had retreated from the bedlam of the city." Publ Wkly

Williams, Terry Tempest

Finding beauty in a broken world. Pantheon Books 2008 419p $26 **814**

1. Aesthetics

ISBN 978-0-375-42078-8; 0-375-42078-9

LC 2008-7196

The naturalist author of Refuge and An Unspoken Hunger reflects on what it means to be human, the interconnection between the natural and human worlds, and how they combine to produce both tumult and peace, ugliness and beauty.

"Scientific in her exactitude, compassionate in her receptivity, and rhapsodic in expression, Williams has constructed a beautiful mosaic of loss and renewal that affirms, with striking lucidity, the need for reverence for all of life." Booklist

Includes bibliographical references

Wilson, Edmund

Literary essays and reviews of the 1920s & 30s. Library of America 2007 958p $40 **814**

1. Modernism (Aesthetics) 2. Literature -- History and criticism

ISBN 978-1-59853-013-1

LC 2007-928898

This volume collects The Shores of Light (1952), a collection of his early reviews and other writings; and Axel's Castle (1931), a book of literary criticism discussing modernism. It also includes several previously uncollected reviews.

"Anyone wishing to revisit the intellectual and literary passions of the period will be well advised to do so in the company of someone who could be a Virgil as well as recommend the reading of him. Edmund Wilson came as close

as anybody has to making the labor of criticism into an art." Atl Mon

Includes bibliographical references

Literary essays and reviews of the 1930s & 40s; [Lewis M. Dabney, editor] Library of America 2007 979p $40 **814**

1. Modernism (Aesthetics) 2. Literature -- History and criticism

ISBN 978-1-59853-014-8

LC 2007-928899

This volume gathers together The Triple Thinkers (1938, revised 1948), The Wound and The Bow (1941), Classics and Commercials (1950), along with a selection of uncollected reviews.

"This is a required purchase for all libraries, public and academic—even for those collections already having these texts in separate volumes." Libr J

Includes bibliographical references

814.54 American essays--1945-1999

Frazier, Ian

Hogs wild; selected reporting pieces. Ian Frazier. Farrar, Straus & Giroux 2016 384 p. (hardback) $26 **814.54**

1. Essays

ISBN 9780374298524

LC 2015036372

This book, by Ian Frazier, "assembles a decade's worth of his finest essays and reportage, and demonstrates the irrepressible passions and artful digressions that distinguish his enduring body of work. Part muckraker, part adventurer, and part raconteur, Frazier beholds, captures, and occasionally reimagines the spirit of the American experience." (Publisher's note)

"His celebrated humor glows rather than erupts in these more expository pieces. Pieces that show Frazier's ranging curiosity, lucent style, and capacious heart." Kirkus

Kinsley, Michael, 1951-

Old age; a beginner's guide. Michael Kinsley. Tim Duggan Books 2016 160 p. (hardback) $18 **814.54**

1. Life 2. Aging 3. Values 4. Parkinson's disease 5. Meaning (Psychology) 6. Aging -- United States 7. Authors, American -- Biography 8. Baby boom generation -- United States 9. Life change events -- Psychological aspects 10. Parkinson's disease -- Patients -- United States -- Biography

ISBN 9781101903766; 9781101903780

LC 2015038958

In this book, author "Michael Kinsley uses his own battle with Parkinson's disease to unearth answers to questions we are all at some time forced to confront. 'Sometimes,' he writes, 'I feel like a scout from my generation, sent out ahead to experience in my fifties what even the healthiest Boomers are going to experience in their sixties, seventies, or eighties.'" (Publisher's note)

"Kinsley's superb prose and well-judged tone—both frustrated and hopeful for the future—make this a valuable book for anyone interested in exploring ideas around life, death, and legacy." Pub Wkly

815 American speeches in English

★ **American** speeches. Library of America 2006
2v ea $35   **815**
1. American speeches
ISBN 1-931082-97-9 v1; 1-931082-98-7 v2
LC 2006-40928
This is a collection of over 120 historical speeches delivered between 1761 and 1997.
Includes bibliographical references

816 American letters in English

Letters of the century; America, 1900-1999. edited by Lisa Grunwald and Stephen J. Adler. Dial Press (NY) 1999 741p il hardcover o.p. pa $18   **816**
1. American letters 2. United States -- Civilization
ISBN 0-385-31590-2; 0-385-31593-7 pa
LC 99-16808
Among the letter writers gathered are "Carl Van Doren, Huey Long, Franklin D. Roosevelt, Lillian Hellman and a Vietnam soldier named Dusty. This is one of the most original literary tributes to the closing century." Publ Wkly
Includes bibliographical references

817 American humor and satire in English

Carlin, George
Napalm & silly putty. Hyperion 2001 269p
$22.95; pa $12.95   **817**
ISBN 0-7868-6413-3; 0-7868-8758-3 pa
LC 00-54055
The comedian "covers a wide range of issues from rape and religion to the homeless. . . . And any topic is fair game: abortion, airport security, cars, funerals, language, organ donors, sports, technology, TV and war. . . . Over 100 scintillating short pieces are interrupted by loony lists and hundreds of clever one-liners." Publ Wkly

Hull, Raymond
The **Peter** principle; why things always go wrong. [by] Laurence J. Peter and Raymond Hull. 1st Collins Business ed.; Collins Business 2009 xxvi, 161p il $19.99   **817**
1. Management -- Anecdotes
ISBN 978-0-06-169906-1
LC 2008-44122
First published 1969
"In a delightful spoof of administrative inefficiency in both public and private enterprise, the authors expound their theory known as the Peter Principle—'in a hierarchy every employee tends to rise to his level of incompetence.' From

this they develop their science of hierarchiology." Cincinnati Public Libr
Includes bibliographical references

Mirth of a nation; the best contemporary humor. edited by Michael J. Rosen. HarperPerennial 2000 619p pa $15.95   **817**
1. American wit and humor
ISBN 0-06-095321-7
LC 99-44293
An anthology of more than 50 contributors, "most represented by two or three short works. Included are veterans like Dave Barry, Roy Blount Jr., and Fran Lebowitz, and rising stars like David Sedaris, Sandra Tsing Loh, Patricia Marx, and David Rakoff. Though many of the pieces have been published or broadcast previously, some appear in this volume for the first time." Booklist

Trillin, Calvin, 1935-
Quite enough of Calvin Trillin; forty years of funny stuff. Calvin Trillin. Random House 2011 340 p. (hardcover) $27.00   **817**
1. American wit and humor 2. Politicians -- Humor
3. Civilization -- Humor 4. Authors, American -- 20th century -- Biography
ISBN 1400069823; 0812982215; 9780812982213; 9781400069828; 9780679604808
LC 2011004050
This is "a collection of author-selected excerpts from [Calvin Trillin's] memoirs, satires, and novels includes entries ranging from descriptions of untraditional holiday celebrations to observations about literary pop culture. . . . He addresses the horrors of witnessing a voodoo economics ceremony and the mystery of how his mother managed for thirty years to feed her family nothing but leftovers. . . . He even skewers deserving political figures in poetry." (Publisher's note)
The author "entertains with this collection of his song lyrics, comic verse, and more than 130 of the brief essays he originally wrote for the New Yorker, the New York Times, the Nation, and his syndicated King Features column. . . . Trillin dances around a subject, examines it from different angles, and often finds fun in the commonplace throughout this huge and hilarious comedic compendium." Publ Wkly

Twain, Mark, 1835-1910
Mark Twain's library of humor; illustrated by E.W. Kemble; Steve Martin, series ed.; introduction by Roy Blount. Modern Library 2000 xl, 560p il pa $17   **817**
1. American wit and humor
ISBN 978-0-679-64036-3
LC 00-25971
"Beginning with the piece that made Mark Twain famous—'The Notorious Jumping Frog of Calaveras County'—and ending with his fanciful 'How I Edited an Agricultural Paper,' this . . . anthology, an abridgment of the 1888 original, collects twenty of Twain's own pieces, in addition to tall tales, fables, and satires by forty-three of Twain's contemporaries, including Washington Irving, Harriet Beecher Stowe, Ambrose Bierce, William Dean Howells, Joel Chandler Harris, Artemus Ward, and Bret Harte." Publisher's note

818 American miscellaneous writings in English

Alcott, Louisa May

The **sketches** of Louisa May Alcott; with an introduction by Gregory Eiselein. Ironweed Press 2001
283p (Ironwood American classics) pa $22.95 **818**
ISBN 0-9655309-8-1

LC 00-57259

"Grouped into five categories ('Hospital sketches,' 'Letters from the Mountains,' 'Sketches of Europe,' 'Concord, Massachusetts,' and 'From The Youth's Companion and Merry's Museum,') these by turns frank, witty, ironic, charming and pensive pieces were almost all written when Alcott was between the ages of 28 and 43." Publ Wkly
Includes bibliographical references

Alvarez, Julia, 1950-

A **wedding** in Haiti; Julia Alvarez. Algonquin
Books of Chapel Hill 2012 287 p. **818**
1. Weddings 2. Friendship 3. Dominican Americans
4. Haiti Earthquake, Haiti, 2010 5. Haiti -- Description
and travel 6. Haitians -- Dominican Republic --
Biography
ISBN 9781616201302

LC 2012000452

This book by Julia Alvarez presents a memoir "about her pre- and post-earthquake travels around the island of Hispaniola and the Haitian boy who inspired them. The author met Piti, . . . in 2001, on a chance visit to a coffee farm [in] . . . the Dominican Republic. . . . In 2009, she received a surprise call from Piti telling her that she was invited to his wedding. . . . Eventually Piti called . . . to help him care for his extended family in the aftermath of the 2010 earthquake." (Kirkus)

Angelou, Maya, 1928-2014

Mom & me & mom; by Maya Angelou. 1st ed.
Random House 2012 224 p. (ebook) $66.00; (hardcover) $22.00 **818**
1. Mother-daughter relationship 2. African American authors -- Biography 3. Entertainers -- United States -- Biography 4. Authors, American -- 20th century -- Biography
ISBN 1400066115; 9780679645474; 9781400066117

LC 2012022257

This memoir, by Maya Angelou, "shares . . . her relationship with her mother. . . . Angelou reveals the triumphs and struggles of being the daughter of Vivian Baxter. . . . Vivian famously sent three-year-old Maya and her older brother away from their California home to live with their grandmother in Stamps, Arkansas. The subsequent feelings of abandonment stayed with Angelou for years, but their reunion, a decade later, began a story that has never before been told." (Publisher's note)

A **song** flung up to heaven. Random House 2002
212p $23.95; pa $13 **818**
1. Poets 2. Actors 3. Singers 4. Dramatists 5. Essayists 6. Memoirists 7. Children's authors
ISBN 0-375-50747-7; 0-553-38203-9 pa

LC 2001-34914

"This sixth installment in Angelou's autobiographical works begins in 1964 as Angelou returned to the U.S. from Ghana. . . . She worked in Watts at the time of the riots, and Malcolm X and Martin Luther King Jr. were both assassinated just before she was to begin working with them. . . . She moved to New York, where she rejoined a vibrant group of famous writers, intellectuals, and friends; worried about her young-adult son; and understood the humor and heartache of a painful love affair. . . . Spiced with her mother's aphorisms, her often-poetic prose is best at the end, as she muses on the condition of black women and sitting at her mother's table, begins to write I Know Why the Caged Bird Sings." Booklist

Baraka, Imamu Amiri

The **LeRoi** Jones/Amiri Baraka reader; by Amiri Baraka; edited by William Harris in collaboration with Amiri Baraka. 2nd ed; Thunder's Mouth Press 2000 xxxiii, 586p pa $16.95 **818**
1. Poets 2. Clergy 3. Mayors 4. Authors 5. Dramatists 6. Blues music 7. African American music 8. Television personalities 9. Cuba 10. Essayists 11. Talk show hosts 12. Political leaders 13. Members of Parliament 14. Civil rights activists 15. Presidential candidates
ISBN 1-56025-238-3

LC 99-32364

First published 1991

A collection of Baraka's poems, plays, and other writings. "The selections included are arranged chronologically in four distinct periods: The Beat Period (1957-62), The Transitional Period (1963-65), The Black Nationalist Period (1965-74), and The Third World Marxist Period (1974-present)." Libr J [review of 1991 edition]
Includes bibliographical references

Bishop, Elizabeth

Poems, prose, and letters; [selected and edited by Robert Giroux and Lloyd Schwartz] Library of America 2008 979p $40 **818**
1. Criticism 2. Poetry -- By individual authors
ISBN 978-1-59853-017-9; 1-59853-017-8

LC 2007-935885

"From the quietly riveting photograph on the dust jacket through the thorough index, the book is an elegant achievement that one imagines even the scrupulous and discriminating Elizabeth Bishop would approve. . . . This generous new collection lets us make connections across boundaries among many genres: poems, some hitherto uncollected and some mighty rough; translations over many years from ancient Greek, French, Spanish, and Portuguese; 'Personal Essays, Reminiscences, and Reporting;' 'Literary Statements and Reviews;' . . . and letters.' Yale Rev

Blount, Roy

Alphabetter juice, or, The joy of text; [by] Roy Blount, Jr. Farrar, Straus and Giroux 2011 283p $26; ebook $12.99 **818**
1. Vocabulary 2. American wit and humor 3. English language -- Dictionaries
ISBN 978-0-374-10370-5; 978-1-4299-2278-4 ebook

LC 2010-39937

This book "is almost a subgenre of its own, a reference book from a leading language expert that's also downright funny. . . . Anybody as eclectic as Blount is worth paying attention to; his passion for the sounds and senses of words makes this book infectiously fun reading for word lovers everywhere." Writer

Borich, Barrie Jean

Body geographic; Barrie Jean Borich. University of Nebraska Press 2013 272 p. (American lives) (paperback) $17.95   **818**

1. Minnesota 2. Chicago (Ill.) 3. Mind and body 4. Middle West -- Biography 5. Self-perception in women 6. Maps -- Psychological aspects 7. Lesbian authors -- United States -- Biography 8. Authors, American -- 20th century -- Biography 9. Middle West -- Geography -- Psychological aspects 10. Women -- Sexual behavior -- Psychological aspects

ISBN 0803239858; 9780803239852

LC 2012030607

Lambda Literary Awards Winner - Lesbian Memoir/Biography (2014)

This memoir, by Barrie Jean Borich, "turns personal history into an inspired reflection on the points where place and person intersect, where running away meets running toward, and where dislocation means finding oneself. One coordinate of Borich's story is Chicago . . . and the other is her own port of immigration, Minneapolis, the combined skylines of these two cities tattooed on Borich's own back." (Publisher's note)

Includes bibliographical references

Bryson, Bill, 1951-

I'm a stranger here myself; notes on returning to America after 20 years away. Broadway Bks. 1999 288p hardcover o.p. pa $14.95   **818**

1. United States -- Description and travel 2. United States -- Social life and customs

ISBN 0-7679-0382-X pa

LC 99-18074

The author collects "columns on America he wrote weekly, while living in New Hampshire in the mid-to-late 1990s, for a British Sunday newspaper. Although he happily describes himself as dazzled by American ease, friendliness and abundance, Bryson has no trouble finding comic targets, among them fast food, computer efficiency and, ironically, American friendliness and putative convenience." Publ Wkly

Capote, Truman

Music for chameleons; new writing. Random House 1980 262p hardcover o.p. pa $13   **818**

ISBN 0-679-74566-1 pa

LC 79-5532

"There are three sections: one of short stories, or something like; one consisting of the 'In cold blood'-like 'short novel, Handcarved coffins;' and one called 'Conversational portraits,' which is precisely that." Choice

Cather, Willa

★ **Stories,** poems, and other writings. Library of Am. 1992 1039p $35   **818**

1. Nebraska -- Literary collections

ISBN 0-940450-71-2

LC 91-62294

This volume contains the novels Alexander's bridge (1912) and My mortal enemy (1926); the poetry collection April twilights, and other poems (1923); the essay collection Not under forty (1936); and the following short story collections: Youth and the bright Medusa (1920); Obscure destinies (1932); The old beauty, and others (1948); and uncollected stories from 1892-1929

Dick, Philip K.

The **exegesis** of Philip K. Dick; edited by Pamela Jackson and Jonathan Lethem; Erik Davis, annotations editor. Houghton Mifflin Harcourt 2011 944p $40   **818**

1. Technology and civilization 2. Science fiction -- Authorship

ISBN 978-0-547-54925-5; 0-547-54925-3

LC 2011-28561

"'I sure have odd nights,' wrote Philip K. Dick in a July 1974 letter to a young woman writing her thesis on him. It's a tremendous understatement, and its inclusion in the early pages of The Exegesis — the long-awaited compendium of the sci-fi writer's papers — acts as a palate cleanser, a wry little weigh station wherein Dick pulls back from his own dense, circuitous investigation of his visions; laughs a little at himself; and then dives back in, allowing the reader to do the same. . . . Dick wrote more than eight thousand pages in the eight years leading up to his death in 1982, all in his attempts to decipher a series of visionary, multisensory experiences he had in February and March of '74 ('2-3-74') wherein he glimpsed a vast truth of the world." East Bay Express

Dillard, Annie

The **Annie** Dillard reader. HarperCollins Pubs. 1994 455p hardcover o.p. pa $15.95   **818**

ISBN 0-06-092660-0 pa

LC 94-19482

This reader includes Holy the firm; excerpts from Pilgrim at Tinker Creek, An American childhood, and Teaching a stone to talk; and a reworked version of the 1978 short story The living

"This selection of writings, chosen by Dillard herself, provides a perfect sampling of her incisive, versatile, and impeccable achievements." Booklist

Pilgrim at Tinker Creek. Harper & Row 1974 271p hardcover o.p. pa $14.95   **818**

1. Natural history -- Virginia

ISBN 0-06-123332-3 pa; 978-0-06-123332-6 pa

This work is "in an honored tradition of literature, not quite environmentalism and not the philosophy of science, it is rather the refraction of natural philosophy through the prismatic conscience of art. Highly recommended for the general reader—any general reader, anywhere—who wishes to deepen his awareness of his yard of world and to reflect upon it more profoundly." Choice

The **writing** life. Harper & Row 1989 111p hardcover o.p. pa $11   **818**
1. Poets 2. Authors 3. Essayists 4. Literary critics 5. Writers on nature 6. Biography, Individual 7. Creation (Literary, artistic, etc.)
ISBN 0-06-091988-4 pa

LC 89-45034

In this volume the author of Pilgrim at Tinker Creek (BRD 1974), Holy the Firm (BRD 1977, 1978), and An American Childhood (BRD 1987, 1988) discusses how she writes her books.

The author "probes the sorcery that levitates her own writing, discussing with clear eye and wry wit how, where and why she writes." Publ Wkly

Ellison, Ralph
★ **Going** to the territory. Random House 1986 338p hardcover o.p. pa $14.95   **818**
1. Artists 2. Authors 3. Composers 4. Novelists 5. Dramatists 6. Jazz musicians 7. Essayists 8. Band leaders 9. Nonfiction writers 10. Short story writers
ISBN 978-0-679-76001-6 pa; 0-679-76001-6 pa

LC 85-28117

"This collection of essays, addresses, and reviews deals with topics in literature, music, and race relations. . . . Ellison tries to view American culture as a cloth of one piece. His analysis of the growth of the culture, and of the dynamic interaction of the diverse elements within it, is perceptive and convincing." Libr J

Franklin, Benjamin
★ **Autobiography,** Poor Richard, and later writings; letters from London, 1757-1775, Paris, 1776-1785, Philadelphia, 1785-1790, Poor Richard's almanack, 1733-1758, The autobiography. Library of America 1997 816p $30   **818**
ISBN 1-883011-53-1

LC 97-21611

"This collection of Franklin's works begins with letters sent from London (1757-1775) describing the events and diplomacy preceding the Revolutionary War. The volume also contains political satires, bagatelles, pamphlets, and letters written in Paris (1776-1785), where he represented the revolutionary United States at the court of Louis XVI, as well as his speeches given in the Constitutional Convention and other works written in Philadelphia (1785-1790), including his last published article, a . . . satire against slavery. Also included are the . . . prefaces to Poor Richard's Almanack (1733-1758). . . . [The] Autobiography, Franklin's last word on his greatest literary creation—his own invented personality—is presented here in a new edition." Publisher's note
Includes bibliographical references

Gibran, Kahlil
The **collected** works; with eighty-four illustrations by the author. Everyman's Library 2007 880p il $27.50   **818**
ISBN 978-0-307-26707-8; 0-307-26707-5

LC 2007-28736

This anthology of writings by the Syrian poet includes The Madman, The Forerunner, The Prophet, Sand and Foam, Jesus the Son of Man, Earth Gods, The Wanderer, The Garden of the Prophet, Prose Poems, Spirits Rebellious, Nymphs of the Valley, and A Tear and a Smile.

Hogan, Linda
The **woman** who watches over the world; a native memoir. Norton 2001 224p $24.95; pa $13.95   **818**
1. Poets 2. Authors 3. Novelists 4. Dramatists 5. Native Americans 6. Essayists 7. Short story writers
ISBN 0-393-05018-1; 0-393-32305-6 pa

LC 00-49005

In this memoir the author chronicles "her difficult childhood, alcoholism, the anguish of her two psychologically damaged adopted children, and struggles with a neuromuscular disease. She also expresses a lacerating yet crucial vision of the tragic legacies of the U.S. government's brutal war on Native Americans." Booklist

Hughes, Langston
★ **I** wonder as I wander; an autobiographical journey. introd. by Arnold Rampersad. 2nd Hill and Wang ed; Hill & Wang 1993 xxii, 405p (American century series) pa $16   **818**
1. Poets 2. Authors 3. Novelists 4. Dramatists 5. African American authors 6. Poets, American 7. Short story writers 8. Young adult authors
ISBN 0-8090-1550-1

LC 92-39307

First published 1956 by Rinehart
Continuing the autobiography begun in The big sea (1940), this volume contains an account of Hughes' journeys through Russia, Spain, China, and Japan, as well as some incidents of his poetry readings in this country

Jackson, Shirley, 1916-1965
Let me tell you; new stories, essays, and other writings. Shirley Jackson; edited by Laurence Jackson Hyman and Sarah Hyman DeWitt. Random House Inc. 2015 432 p. (acid-free paper) $30 **818**
1. Essays 2. American short stories
ISBN 0812997662; 9780812997668

LC 2014036656

This book, edited by Laurence Hyman, Sarah Hyman DeWitt, and Ruth Frankling, "brings together the deliciously eerie short stories [Shirley] Jackson is best known for, along with frank, inspiring lectures on writing; comic essays about her large, boisterous family; and whimsical drawings. Jackson's landscape here is most frequently domestic: dinner parties and bridge, household budgets and homeward-bound commutes, children's games and neighborly gossip." (Publisher's note)
Includes bibliographical references

Jefferson, Thomas, 1743-1826
Writings. Library of Am. 1984 1600p $35 **818**
ISBN 0-940450-16-X

LC 83-19917

This is "the largest and most skillfully edited single-volume Jefferson ever published." N Y Times Book Rev
Includes bibliographical references

Johnson, James Weldon

The **essential** writings of James Weldon Johnson; edited and with an introduction by Rudolph P. Byrd; foreword by Charles Johnson. Modern Library 2008 xxx, 321p (Modern library classics) pa $15 **818**
ISBN 978-0-8129-7532-1; 0-8129-7532-4

"This collection of poetry, fiction, criticism, autobiography, political writing and two unpublished plays by James Weldon Johnson (1871-1938) spans 60 years of pure triumph over adversity. . . . [Johnson's] nobility, his inspiration shine forth from these pages, setting moral and artistic standards." Los Angeles Times Book Rev

Johnson, Joyce, 1935-

★ The **voice** is all; the lonely victory of Jack Kerouac. Joyce Johnson. Viking 2012 xx, 489 p.p $32.95 **818**
1. American authors -- Biography 2. Beat generation -- Biography 3. Authors, American -- 20th century -- Biography
ISBN 0670025100; 9780670025107
LC 2012000603

In this biography of Jack Kerouac, author Joyce Johnson "peels away layers of the Kerouac legend to show how, caught between two cultures and two languages, he forged a voice to contain his dualities. Looking . . . into how Kerouac's French Canadian background enriched his prose and gave him a unique outsider's vision of America, she tracks his development from boyhood through the phenomenal breakthroughs of 1951." (Publisher's note)
Includes bibliographical references (p 439-471) and index

Kaling, Mindy, 1979-

Is everyone hanging out without me? (and other concerns) Mindy Kaling. Crown Archetype 2011 ix, 222 p.p ill **818**
1. Actresses 2. American essays 3. American wit and humor
ISBN 9780307886262; 9780307886286
LC 2011033922

'In this book, author "Mindy Kaling . . . [offers thoughts about what she] thinks makes a great best friend (someone who will fill your prescription in the middle of the night), or what makes a great guy (one who is aware of all elderly people in any room at any time and acts accordingly), or what is the perfect amount of fame (so famous you can never get convicted of murder in a court of law), or how to maintain a trim figure (you will not find that information in these pages). . . . Mindy invites readers on a tour of her life and her unscientific observations on romance, friendship, and Hollywood." (Publisher's note)

Kiernan, Frances

Seeing Mary plain: a life of Mary McCarthy. Norton 2000 845p il $35; pa $25 **818**
1. Authors 2. Novelists 3. Essayists 4. Memoirists 5.

Literary critics 6. Short story writers
ISBN 0-393-03801-7; 0-393-32307-2 pa
LC 99-41098

Kiernan uses "her interviews with more than 200 sources to provide multiple points of view on McCarthy's life and work. McCarthy knew most of her generation's literary leading lights, from the Partisan Review crowd to anti-Vietnam activists. . . . Each chapter includes commentary by McCarthy, friends, ex-lovers, admirers, and adversaries." Booklist
Includes bibliographical references and index

Manguel, Alberto

A **reader** on reading. Yale University Press 2010 308p il $27.50 **818**
1. Books and reading
ISBN 978-0-300-15982-0; 0-300-15982-X
LC 2009-43719

"Lectures, columns, and other occasional writings are gathered here to form a meditation on 'the art of reading.' Thoughtful interrogations of the value of identity labels like 'Jewish fiction' or 'gay fiction' and the relationship between writers and editors mix with ruminations on the 'ideal reader' and the 'ideal library.' Several autobiographical essays detail a restless life that has taken Manguel from Buenos Aires to Tel Aviv, Canada, and, eventually, France, and an equally restless reading life. Predictable touchstones emerge—Dante and Homer, Shakespeare and Cervantes. Above all, there is Manguel's countryman Borges; he recalls reading aloud to the blind master as a young man in Argentina." New Yorker
Includes bibliographical references

McMurtry, Larry

Walter Benjamin at the Dairy Queen; reflections at sixty and beyond. Simon & Schuster 1999 204p il hardcover o.p. pa $12 **818**
1. Authors 2. Novelists 3. Essayists 4. Short story writers
ISBN 0-684-87019-3 pa
LC 99-19346

"When McMurtry recalls reading 'Don Quixote' as a thirteen-year-old on a Texas ranch and imagining himself as a character in the novel, other obsessional readers will immediately feel a kinship with this author. His appealing ruminations about his life and work as a reader, writer, and bookseller explore the differences between 'dense and empty, open and closed, new country and old cities, no society and old society'—the bare land in which he was reared and the crowded universe of literature." New Yorker

Mencken, H. L.

My life as author and editor; edited and with an introduction by Jonathan Yardley. Knopf 1993 xxi, 449p $30; pa $25 **818**
1. Authors 2. Essayists 3. Philologists 4. Social critics 5. Literary critics 6. Newspaper editors
ISBN 0-679-41315-4; 0-679-74102-X pa
LC 92-4496

An "absorbing memoir that anyone who cares about modern American literature will want to read." N Y Times Book Rev

Miller, Henry

Henry Miller on writing; selected by Thomas H. Moore from the published and unpublished works of Henry Miller. New Directions 1964 216p pa $11.95 **818**

ISBN 0-8112-0112-0

The author discusses the art and practice of writing with insights on how he set his goals, how he discovered the excitement of using words, how the books he read influenced him, and how he learned to draw on his own experiences

The **moment**; edited by Larry Smith. Harper Perennial 2012 344p. **818**

1. Autobiographies 2. American authors 3. American literature -- 21st century 4. Authors, American -- 21st century -- Biography

ISBN 9780061719653; 9780062099211

LC 2011033766

This book contains "stories of life-changing events from a cadre of ready, self-aware authors, each done in a page or two. A short selection of the contributors: A.J. Jacobs, Melissa Etheridge, Gregory Maguire, Dave Eggers, Elizabeth Gilbert, Jennifer Egan and Judy Collins. There are many 'wake-up calls,' some smiles and plenty of tears in these first-person explorations of a few eternal truths. Each of the 125 participants . . . tell of coming out and hiding, of seeking the light, the path, the truth, the way and/or the writers' inner selves. Those goals were achieved by aid of a word, sign, teacher, family road trip, some dope, an inner voice or, more than once, a Eurail pass." (Kirkus)

"Each author's ability to concisely describe such big moments pulls the reader in. Book and writing groups will have a lot to talk about after reading this first-rate collection." (Libr J)

★ The **Oxford** companion to Mark Twain; editor, Gregg Camfield. Oxford Univ. Press 2003 xxi, 767p il $75 **818**

1. Authors 2. Humorists 3. Novelists 4. Essayists 5. Satirists 6. Memoirists 7. Travel writers 8. Short story writers

ISBN 0-19-510710-1

LC 2002-151880

This volume "begins with 300 alphabetically arranged entries of varying lengths devoted to all [Twain's] works, places and people related to his life, and analyses of his views on a variety of topics, from animals to spiritualism. Next come a bibliography of his published works collated from other bibliographies, a chronology, and a general index." Choice

Includes bibliographical references

Parker, Dorothy

The **portable** Dorothy Parker; with a new introduction by Brendan Gill. rev and enl ed; Viking 1973 xxvii, 610p hardcover o.p. pa $18 **818**

ISBN 978-0-14-303953-2; 0-14-303953-9

First published 1944 with title: Dorothy Parker

This collection contains: thirty-two short stories; poems; drama reviews; book reviews, including the entire text of Constant reader; and miscellaneous articles

"It is hard to imagine a library that would not want this book." Choice

Plath, Sylvia

The **unabridged** journals of Sylvia Plath, 1950-1962; edited by Karen V. Kukil. Anchor Press 2000 732p il pa $18 **818**

1. Poets 2. Authors 3. Novelists

ISBN 0-385-72025-4

LC 00-42024

First published 2000 in the United Kingdom with title: Journals of Sylvia Plath, 1950-1962

"This is essential for anyone engaged in Plath studies." Libr J

Includes bibliographical references

Poe, Edgar Allan

★ **Poetry** and tales. Library of Am. 1984 1408p $37.50 **818**

1. Fantasy poetry 2. Horror fiction

ISBN 0-940450-18-6

LC 83-19931

This volume contains 70 stories and Poe's poetic work in its entirety

Includes bibliographical references

Rampersad, Arnold

★ The **life** of Langston Hughes Volume II: 1941-1967; I dream a world. 2nd ed; Oxford Univ. Press 2002 576p il hardcover o.p. pa $33 **818**

1. Poets 2. Authors 3. Novelists 4. Dramatists 5. African American authors 6. Poets, American 7. Short story writers 8. Young adult authors

ISBN 0-19-515161-5; 0-19-514643-3 pa

LC 2001-58766

First published 1988

This second volume of a two-volume biography of the Harlem Renaissance poet and author "finds Hughes rooting himself in Harlem, receiving stimulation from his rich cultural surroundings. Here he rethought his view of art and radicalism, and cultivated relationships with younger, more militant writers such as Richard Wright, Ralph Ellison, James Baldwin, and Amiri Bakara." Publisher's note

Includes bibliographical references

Rollyson, Carl E.

Susan Sontag; the making of an icon. {by} Carl Rollyson and Lisa Paddock. Norton 2000 370p il $29.95 **818**

1. Authors 2. Novelists 3. Essayists 4. Literary critics 5. Short story writers

ISBN 0-393-04928-0

LC 00-20402

The authors "have unearthed a deluge of information on Sontag's personal life—on her early years and family life, her lesbianism. . . her relationship with son David Rieff and her battles with breast cancer. While the authors provide an intelligent, though not strikingly original, analysis of her work, they are best at detailing how Sontag and her publishers have marketed her image as much as her thought." Publ Wkly

Includes bibliographical references

Silko, Leslie
Storyteller. Arcade Publishing 1989 278p pa
$17.95 **818**
ISBN 978-1-55970-005-4; 1-55970-005-X
First published 1981 by Seaver Books
This "consists of short stories, anecdotes, folktales, poems, historical and autobiographical notes, and photographs." N Y Times Book Rev

Sontag, Susan, 1933-2004
As consciousness is harnessed to flesh; journals and notebooks, 1964-1980. Susan Sontag; edited by David Rieff. Farrar, Straus and Giroux 2012 xii, 523 p.p **818**
1. Politics 2. Art criticism 3. American essays 4. American authors -- Biography 5. Authors, American -- 20th century -- Diaries
ISBN 0374100764; 9780374100766
LC 2011041210
This book, "the second of three volumes of Susan Sontag's journals and notebooks, begins where the first volume left off, in the middle of the 1960s. It traces and documents Sontag's evolution from fledgling participant in the artistic and intellectual world of New York City to world-renowned critic and dominant force in the world of ideas with the publication of the groundbreaking 'Against Interpretation' in 1966. 'As Consciousness is Harnessed to Flesh' follows Sontag through the turbulent years of the 1960s—from her trip to Hanoi at the peak of the Vietnam War to her time making films in Sweden—up to 1981 and the beginning of the Reagan era." (Publisher's note)

Sova, Dawn B.
Critical companion to Edgar Allan Poe; a literary reference to his life and work. Facts on File 2007 458p il (Facts on File library of American literature) $75 **818**
1. Poets 2. Authors 3. Essayists 4. Short story writers
ISBN 0-8160-6408-3; 978-0-8160-6408-3
LC 2006-29466
First published 2001 with title: Edgar Allan Poe, A-Z
"Biographical, historical, and critical material on Poe's life and work is presented in alphabetical order in three sections. The entries on Poe's works each provide a synopsis, a publication history, and character descriptions, while major works such as 'The Cask of Amontillado' and 'The Purloined Letter' have . . . [a] commentary and . . . further-reading suggestions." SLJ
Includes bibliographical references

Stein, Gertrude
Writings, 1903-1932. Library of Am. 1998 941p $40 **818**
ISBN 978-1-883011-40-6; 1-883011-40-X
LC 97-28915
In Stein's "early works, she sought a new kind of realism exemplified here by Q.E.D. (written 1903, published posthumously), a novel about lesbian entanglements at college, and the modern classic Three Lives (1909), a set of novellas about the lives of three ordinary women, described in the simplest and most direct of prose. In her . . . abstract 'portraits' Stein uses an extraordinary array of verbal techniques

to evoke those friends and collaborators—Matisse, Picasso, Apollinaire, Juan Gris, Satie, Mabel Dodge, Carl Van Vechten, Sherwood Anderson, Virgil Thomson—with whom she shared decades of revolutionary ferment in the arts. Her play Four Saints in Three Acts (1927), which became the basis for an opera by Virgil Thomson, is written for a freewheeling theater of the mind where everything becomes possible. In 'Lifting Belly' and other works she joyously celebrates her lifelong relationship with Alice B. Toklas, one of the most famous domestic partnerships of that century. The Autobiography of Alice B. Toklas (1933), Stein's oblique and playful memoir, became an immediate bestseller and sealed Stein's international celebrity." Publisher's note

★ **Writings,** 1932-1946. Library of Am. 1998 844p $40 **818**
ISBN 1-883011-41-8
LC 97-28916
In addition to theater pieces, fiction, and poetry "memoir, philosophical speculation, literary criticism and theory, all sorts of briefer forms that are hard to account for but easy to marvel at and even to delight in, pack these volumes, and constitute, as the editors surely intended us to discover, the most consistently achieved representation of new ways of responding to life and new possibilities of getting experience into words that American literature has to show." N Y Times Book Rev

Thompson, Hunter S.
The **great** shark hunt; strange tales from a strange time. Summit Bks. 1979 602p hardcover o.p. pa $16 **818**
ISBN 0-7432-5045-1 pa
LC 79-831
"A retrospective in journalistic theater, this gathers together excerpts from Thompson's 'Fear and Loathing in Las Vegas' and 'Fear and Loathing on the Campaign Trail,' plus his reportage from such diverse journals as 'Rolling Stone,' 'Playboy,' 'The New York Times,' etc., going back to 1962." Publ Wkly
Includes bibliographical references

Thoreau, Henry David
★ **Collected** essays and poems. Library of Am. 2001 703p $35 **818**
ISBN 1-883011-95-7
LC 00-46234
Among the 27 essays included are Civil disobedience, Walking, Martyrdom of John Brown, A Yankee in Canada, and Life without principle. Many of the poems were taken from Thoreau's journals and manuscripts
Includes bibliographical references

★ **Walden,** or, Life in the woods; with an introduction by Verlyn Klinkenborg. Knopf 1992 xxxi, 295p $19 **818**
ISBN 0-679-41896-2
LC 92-54444
First published 1854

"Philosophy of life and observations of nature drawn from the author's solitary sojourn of two years in a cabin on Walden Pond near Concord, Massachusetts." Pratt Alcove
Includes bibliographical references

A **week** on the Concord and Merrimack rivers; Walden, or, Life in the woods; The Maine woods; Cape Cod. Library of Am. 1985 1114p il $35 **818**
ISBN 0-940450-27-5

LC 85-5175

"Politically the most conscious of the Transcendentalists, an acute observer of natural and social facts, Thoreau was an outstanding prose stylist." Reader's Ency
Includes bibliographical references

Thursby, Jacqueline S.

Critical companion to Maya Angelou; a literary reference to her life and work. Facts On File 2011 430p il (Facts on File of American literature) $75 **818**
1. Poets 2. Actors 3. Singers 4. Dramatists 5. Essayists 6. Memoirists 7. Children's authors
ISBN 978-0-8160-8093-9; 978-1-4381-3610-3 ebook
LC 2010032716

Coverage includes a "biography of Angelou; entries on all of Angelou's major works, including all six of her book-length autobiographies, her major poems and poetry collections, her major essays and essay collections, her children's books, and more; entries on the autobiographical works contain subentries on the main figures in the work; entries on related people, places, and topics, such as Harlem, Michelle Obama, racism, San Francisco, and more; [and] appendixes, including chronologies, a bibliography of Angelou's works, and a secondary source bibliography." Publisher's note
Includes bibliographical references

Trethewey, Natasha D., 1966-

Beyond Katrina; a meditation on the Mississippi Gulf Coast. University of Georgia Press 2010 127p il **818**
1. Hurricane Katrina, 2005 2. African Americans -- Mississippi
ISBN 0-8203-3381-6; 978-0-8203-3381-6
LC 2010011417

A collection of essays, poems, and letters, chronicling the effects of Hurricane Katrina on the Mississippi Gulf Coast.

"By looking at the vast devastation with sober and poetic eyes, Trethewey has written a hauntingly beautiful book." Publ Wkly

Twain, Mark, 1835-1910

★ **Autobiography** of Mark Twain; Volume 3 The Complete and Authoritative Edition. by Mark Twain; edited by Harriet E. Smith, Benjamin Griffin, Victor Fischer, Michæl B. Frank, Amanda Gagel, Sharon K. Goetz, Leslie Diane Myrick, and Christopher M. Ohge. University of California Press 2015 792 p. illustrations $45 **818**
ISBN 0520279948; 9780520279940
LC 2009047700

"This third and final volume crowns and completes [Twain's] life's work. Like its companion volumes, it chronicles Twain's inner and outer life through a series of daily dictations that go wherever his fancy leads. Created from March 1907 to December 1909, these dictations present Mark Twain at the end of his life: receiving an honorary degree from Oxford University; railing against Theodore Roosevelt; founding numerous clubs." (Publisher's note)

The **wit** and wisdom of Mark Twain; edited by Alex Ayres. Harper & Row 1987 265p hardcover o.p. pa $13.95 **818**
ISBN 978-0-06-075104-3 pa; 0-06-075104-5 pa
LC 87-45020

The editor "provides systematic access to plenty of Twain's bon mots by arranging them in a dictionary of topics from Adam to youth. . . . Where background is needed, Ayres supplies it succinctly and, as an afterword, proffers 'What Mark Twain might say today' on such ponderables as communism, extraterrestrial intelligence, the national debt, terrorism, and the unborn. Much to Ayres' credit, many of these approximations sound markedly Twainian." Booklist
Includes bibliographical references

Updike, John, 1932-2009

Higher gossip; essays and criticism. edited by Christopher Carduff. 1st ed. Alfred A. Knopf 2011 528 p. ill. ebook $21.99; (hbk.) $40; (pbk.) $20 **818**
ISBN 9780307957177; 9780307957153; 9780812983685
LC 2011013586

This book is a "collection of miscellaneous prose [that] opens with a self-portrait of the writer in winter. . . . It concludes with a . . . meditation on a modern world robbed of imagination--a world without religion, without art--and on the difficulties of faith in a disbelieving age. In between are previously uncollected stories and poems, a pageant of scenes from seventeenth-century Massachusetts, five late 'golf dreams,' and several of Updike's commentaries on his own work. At the heart of the book are his . . . reviews--of John Cheever, Ann Patchett, Toni Morrison, William Maxwell, John le Carré, and essays on Aimee Semple McPherson, Max Factor, and Albert Einstein, among others. Also included are two decades of art criticism--on Chardin, El Greco, Blake, Turner, Van Gogh, Max Ernest, and more." (Publisher's note)

This is a compilation of "nearly 100 uncollected pieces by 'the preeminent literary journalist of our times.' Predominantly comprising literary and art criticism from a range of magazines, the volume also embraces poetry, fiction, memoir, and Updike's comments on his own work." Publ Wkly

Walsh, John Evangelist

Midnight dreary; the mysterious death of Edgar Allan Poe. St. Martin's Minotaur 2000 199p il pa $14.95 **818**
1. Poets 2. Authors 3. Essayists 4. Short story writers
ISBN 0-312-22732-9; 978-0-312-22732-6
LC 00-25571

First published 1998 by Rutgers Univ. Press

Walsh "has undertaken a superbly informed speculation on the week proceeding the mysterious death of Edgar Allan Poe 150 years ago." Libr J

Includes bibliographical references

Wayne, Tiffany K.

Critical companion to Ralph Waldo Emerson; a literary reference to his life and work. Facts On File 2010 444p il (Facts on File library of American literature) $75 **818**

1. Poets 2. Authors 3. Philosophers 4. Essayists

ISBN 978-0-8160-7358-0; 978-1-4381-3048-4 ebook

LC 2009-24809

"This reference book examines the life and works of a central thinker in American history. . . . It begins with Emerson's biography for context. Part 2 focuses on 140 significant (in the view of scholars) individual works, including 60 poems (most with one to three pages of synopses, critical commentary, and further reading). Part 3 covers related people, places, and topics. . . . The final appendixes offer a chronology of Emerson's life and times, bibliographies of both his works and relevant secondary sources." Choice

Includes bibliographical references. 'Bibliography of Emerson's works': p. 406-407. (BLCM)

Wilson, Ronaldo V.

Farther traveler; poetry, prose, other. Ronaldo V. Wilson. Counterpath 2014 157 p. (pbk. : alk. paper) $22 **818**

1. Poetry -- Collections 2. American prose literature

ISBN 1933996331; 9781933996332

LC 2014034097

This book, by Ronaldo V. Wilson, "is an expansive, complex hybrid of poetry, prose, and memoir that engages with contemporary culture, race and sexuality." (Publisher's note)

818.603 Authors--American literature--diaries

Faludi, Susan

In the Darkroom; by Susan Faludi. Henry Holt & Co. 2016 432 p. $32 **818.603**

1. Identity (Psychology) 2. Sex reassignment surgery 3. Father-daughter relationship

ISBN 080508908X; 9780805089080

LC 2016013605

This book, by Susan Faludi, is an "inquiry into the meaning of identity in the modern world. . . . When the feminist writer learned that her 76-year-old father—long estranged and living in Hungary—had undergone sex reassignment surgery, that investigation would turn personal and urgent." (Publisher's note)

"A moving and penetrating inquiry into manifold struggles for identity, community, a nd authenticity." Kirkus

819 American literatures in English not requiring local emphasis

Nafisi, Azar

★ The Republic of Imagination; America in Three Books. Azar Nafisi; illustrations by Peter Sis. Windmill Books 2015 352 p. illustrations (hardback) $28.95 **819**

1. Democracy 2. Imagination 3. Books and reading 4. American fiction 5. English teachers 6. Iranian American women 7. National characteristics in literature

ISBN 0670026069; 9780099558934; 0099558939; 9780670026067

LC 2014022287

This book, by Azar Nafisi, is an "original tribute to the vital importance of fiction in a democratic society. . . . [She blends] memoir and polemic with close readings of her favorite American novels--'The Adventures of Huckleberry Finn,' 'Babbitt,' and 'The Heart Is a Lonely Hunter,' among others." (Publisher's note)

"The author's literary exegesis lightly moves through her own experiences as a student,teacher, friend and new citizen. Touching on myriad literary examples, from L.Frank Baum to James Baldwin, her work is both poignant and informative." Kirkus

820 English and Old English (Anglo-Saxon) literatures

★ The Cambridge guide to literature in English; edited by Dominic Head. 3rd ed; Cambridge University Press 2006 xxiii, 1241p il $50 **820**

1. Reference books 2. English literature -- Dictionaries 3. American literature -- Dictionaries 4. English literature -- Bio-bibliography

ISBN 978-0-521-83179-6; 0-521-83179-2

LC 2006-271458

First published 1988 under the editorship of Ian Ousby

"The scope of material covered . . . extends to the literature of the United Kingdom and well beyond: Africa, Asia, Australia, Canada, the Caribbean, India, New Zealand, and the U.S. are all well represented. . . . Literary terms are explained, literary movements are summarized, and literary magazines are sketched in unsigned entries ranging in length from a few lines to a few paragraphs or more. . . . With its broad coverage, clearly written and accessible text, and relatively modest price, this is a must purchase for most reference collections." Booklist

Coles, Robert

Handing one another along; literature and social reflection. edited by Trevor Hall and Vicki Kennedy. Random House 2010 xxiv, 273p il $27; ebook $27 **820**

1. English literature -- History and criticism 2. American literature -- History and criticism

ISBN 978-1-4000-6203-4; 978-0-679-60403-7 ebook

LC 2009-47337

The author "adapts his undergraduate lectures on literature's contribution to the development of our moral character. . . . While less than comprehensive and eschewing more technical analyses, it delves into a generous handful of writers and artists—perennials like George Orwell, James Agee, Zora Neale Hurston, Tillie Olsen, Ralph Ellison, and Raymond Carver, among others—with uncommon insight and a personal touch, while offering excerpts of poetry and prose that often whet the appetite for more." Publ Wkly

Includes bibliographical references

Greer, Germaine

The **Cambridge** guide to women's writing in English; [edited by] Lorna Sage; advisory editors, Germaine Greer, Elaine Showalter. Cambridge Univ. Press 1999 696p il $80; pa $29   **820**
1. Reference books 2. English literature -- Women authors -- Dictionaries
ISBN 0-521-49525-3; 0-521-66813-1 pa
LC 98-50778

A "guide to women writers in the English language. The coverage is thorough, crossing historical, national, and generic boundaries as it ranges from Julian of Norwich to Terry Macmillan {sic}, from M.F.K. Fisher to Pauline Kael, from Ghanaian playwright Ama Ata Aidoo to Native American writer Mourning Dove. There are also articles on selected titles and themes. The entries, which range from 160 to 500 words, are informative, critical, and jargon-free." Libr J

The **history** of British women's writing; edited by Maroula Joannou. Palgrave Macmillan 2010 340 p. (hbk.) $90   **820**
1. English authors 2. English literature -- 20th century 3. English literature -- Women authors 4. Women and literature -- Great Britain -- History 5. English literature -- Women authors -- History and criticism
ISBN 0230282792; 9780230282797 (v. 8)
LC 2010026127

This book, edited by Maroula Joannou, examines British women authors who "do not fit into a recognized version of the modernist canon. Their complex and often troubled relationship to modernity—as readers, consumers, and travellers at home and abroad—requires new critical frameworks in which to discuss their writing as well as a revision of the territory that has been staked out as the preserve of Modernism by critical theory and practice." (Publisher's note)

Includes bibliographical references and indexes

Lee, Hermione

Virginia Woolf's nose; essays on biography. Princeton University Press 2005 141p $19.95 **820**
1. Poets 2. Authors 3. Novelists 4. Biography as a literary form 5. Diarists 6. Essayists 7. Military officials 8. Short story writers 9. Government officials 10. Members of Parliament
ISBN 0-691-12032-3
LC 2004-58457

"Lee's immensely enjoyable study will energize debate among thoughtful readers and should become essential reading for aficionados of literary biography." Publ Wkly

Includes bibliographical references

The **Norton** anthology of English literature; Stephen Greenblatt, general editor; M.H. Abrams, founding editor emeritus. 8th ed.; W.W. Norton 2006 2v il map   **820**
1. English literature -- Collections
ISBN 0-393-92713-X v1; 0-393-92531-5 v1 pa; 0-393-92715-6 v2; 0-393-92532-3 v2 pa
LC 2005-52313

First published 1962. Periodically revised

Contains representative writings of authors which convey the tone and trends of specific literary movements and periods. Both volumes contain explanatory footnotes, selected bibliographies, notes on literary forms and usage, an author-title index, and marginalia glossaries.

Includes bibliographical references

★ The **Oxford** companion to English literature; edited by Dinah Birch. 7th ed; Oxford University Press 2009 1164p $150   **820**
1. Reference books 2. English literature -- Dictionaries 3. American literature -- Dictionaries 4. English literature -- Bio-bibliography 5. American literature -- Bio-bibliography
ISBN 978-0-19-280687-1
LC 2009-455948

First published 1932 under the editorship of Sir Paul Harvey

"The subjects of the entries include literary works, authors, themes, archetypes, journals, and forms. . . . This companion is a highly authoritative resource, with clear, concise, and approachable entries on literary topics of high interest to students and scholars of English literature. An essential reference for most public, high school, and academic libraries." Libr J

★ The **Oxford** guide to literature in English translation; edited by Peter France. Oxford Univ. Press 2000 xxii, 656p hardcover o.p. pa $29.95 **820**
1. Translating and interpreting 2. Literature -- History and criticism
ISBN 0-19-924784-6 pa
LC 99-28791

This "guide emphasizes 'high-culture' books in translation that have had the most lasting impact on English-speaking culture since the Middle Ages. . . . The first 116 pages cover translation theory and history, while the heart of this guide is the 17 geographic sections that follow, starting with African languages, moving through Latin, and ending with the West Asian languages. There are excellent bibliographies and an author index." Libr J

Includes bibliographical references

Sanders, Andrew

The **short** Oxford history of English literature; 3rd ed; Oxford University Press 2004 756p pa $45   **820**
1. English literature -- History and criticism
ISBN 978-0-19-926338-7; 0-19-926338-8
LC 2004-49555

First published 1994

"The History provides detailed discussion of Old and Middle English literature, the Renaissance, Shakespeare, the seventeenth and eighteenth centuries, the Romantics, Victorian and Edwardian literature, Modernism, and postwar writing. Discussions of key writers and works are combined with analysis of the impact on literature of contemporary political, social, and intellectual developments. The book includes Scottish, Irish, and Welsh writers, and it asks about the future of the canon in the light of the fragmented condition of British writing in the post-imperial period." Publisher's note

Includes bibliographical references

Stewart, Bruce

The **Oxford** companion to Irish literature; edited by Robert Welch, assistant editor, Bruce Stewart. Oxford Univ. Press 1996 xxv, 614p maps $55 **820**
1. Reference books 2. Irish literature -- Dictionaries
ISBN 0-19-866158-4

LC 95-44943

Encompassing "Ireland's literary heritage from the bardic poets and Celtic sagas to twentieth-century authors like Brian Friel, Edna O'Brien, and Nuala Ni Dhomhnaill, the more than 2,000 unsigned entries cover writers, titles of major works, literary genres and motifs, folklore, mythology, periodicals, associations, and historical figures and events." Booklist

Vendler, Helen Hennessy

Coming of age as a poet; Milton, Keats, Eliot, Plath. [by] Helen Vendler. Harvard Univ. Press 2003 174p il $22.95 **820**
1. Blind 2. Poets 3. Authors 4. Novelists 5. Dramatists 6. Editors 7. Essayists 8. Literary critics 9. Writers on medicine 10. Nobel laureates for literature 11. English poetry -- History and criticism 12. American poetry -- History and criticism
ISBN 0-674-01024-8

LC 2002-27287

Vendler "succeeds in revealing the aesthetic power and technical beauty of great poetry." N Y Times Book Rev
Includes bibliographical references

821 English poetry

★ **100** essential modern poems; selected and introduced by Joseph Parisi. Ivan R. Dee 2005 305p $24.95 **821**
1. English poetry -- Collections 2. American poetry -- Collections
ISBN 1-56663-612-4

LC 2005-9897

"Preceded by wonderfully conversational and expertly appreciative biocritical essays about each poet, his choices are superb as he lingers over Yeats and Stevens and includes often-overlooked witty and satirical poets, among them Dorothy Parker, Ogden Nash, Kay Ryan, Frank O'Hara, and Billy Collins." Booklist

★ **100** great poems of the twentieth century; [edited by] Mark Strand. Norton 2005 320p $24.95 **821**
1. English poetry -- Collections 2. American poetry

-- Collections
ISBN 0-393-05894-8

LC 2005-2150

The editor "has selected works by poets of Europe and North and South America, and because there are so many gifted American poets, he restricted himself to those born before 1927. The result is a marvelously graceful, shimmering cosmos of poems by the likes of Anna Akhmatova, A. R. Ammons, Amy Clampit, Robert Desnos, Robert Frost, Nazim Hikmet, Kenneth Koch, Edna St. Vincent Millay, Gabriela Mistral, Eugenio Montale, Octavio Paz, and Derek Walcott." Booklist

Adamson, Robert

★ The **goldfinches** of Baghdad. Flood Editions 2006 103p pa $13.95 **821**
1. Poetry -- By individual authors
ISBN 0-9746902-8-7

Adamson "lives on the Hawksbury River in New South Wales. . . . To give an overview of his poetry is difficult, but it is largely concerned with where he is: the river, the natural environment and creatures, his life and history, his neighbours, love and death. It has little of the 'pastoral' feel about it, being obsessively attached to the present condition, and it never gives any sense of a contented settled existence free from urban cares, quite the reverse. There is indication indeed of a quite fraught personal existence, both past and present, without the poetry ever for a moment becoming 'confessional'. It is to objective for that and too poetic." Shearsman

Adcock, Fleur

★ **Poems** 1960-2000. Bloodaxe Books 2000 287p $54.95; pa $24.95 **821**
1. Poetry -- By individual authors
ISBN 1-85224-529-8; 1-85224-530-1 pa

Adcock's "imagination thrives on what threatens her peace of mind, and only when she is unguarded can these threats have their full creative effect. . . . Throughout her writing life, she has made a fine art from holding on to principles of orderliness and good clear sense; but she has made an even finer one from loosening her grip on them." Times Lit Suppl

An **anthology** of modern Irish poetry; edited by Wes Davis. Belknap Press of Harvard University Press 2010 976p $35 **821**
1. Irish poetry -- Collections 2. Irish poetry -- 20th century 3. English poetry -- Irish authors
ISBN 0-674-04951-9; 9780674049512

LC 2009-37231

Collected here is a "representation of Irish poetic achievement in the twentieth and twenty-first centuries, from poets such as Austin Clarke and Samuel Beckett who were writing while Yeats and Joyce were still living; to those who came of age in the turbulent '60s as sectarian violence escalated, including Seamus Heaney and Michael Longley; to a new generation of Irish writers, represented by such . . . voices as David Wheatley (born 1970) and Sinead Morrissey (born 1972). Editor Wes Davis has chosen work by more than fifty leading modern and contemporary Irish poets." (Publisher's note) Index.

This volume, "running to almost a thousand pages, comes from a country with a population roughly equal to that of Tennessee. The book includes upwards of 50 poets— and there's not a dull page in it. Editor Wes Davis's selection is judicious, while his introduction and notes are as informative as they are brief." Wall Street J

Auden, W. H.

★ **Collected** poems; edited by Edward Mendelson. Modern Library 2007 928p $40 **821**

1. Poetry -- By individual authors

ISBN 978-0-679-64350-0; 0-679-64350-8

LC 2006-47163

Originally published in different form by Random House in 1976

A compilation of all the poems Auden wished to preserve, in his final revisions. Previous collected editions and later shorter poems are included. There is also an absurdist play written 1928: Paid on both sides.

Bentley, G. E.

The **stranger** from paradise: a biography of William Blake. Yale Univ. Press 2001 xxvii, 532p il maps $39.95; pa $24.95 **821**

1. Poets 2. Artists 3. Authors 4. Engravers 5. Illustrators

ISBN 0-300-08939-2; 0-300-10030-2 pa

The author "traces Blake from his natal landscape, youth, marriage, and apprenticeship through to his later years as a working engraver, poet, and radical visionary. Bentley is academic and thorough, and this is more of a straight biography than an analysis." Libr J

Includes bibliographical references

★ The **Best** poems of the English language; from Chaucer through Robert Frost. selected and with commentary by Harold Bloom. HarperCollins Publishers 2004 xxviii, 972p $34.95; pa $19.95 **821**

1. English poetry -- Collections 2. American poetry -- Collections

ISBN 0-06-054041-9; 0-06-054042-7 pa

LC 2003-51104

"Arranged chronologically by author, the poems are preceded by commentaries that extol their specific virtues and place them in historical context. Taken together, they provide an overview of Bloom's own theories of writing, such as his notion that the greatest poems manifest an 'inevitability' of phrasing . . . Bloom rarely bores, and at his best he achieves a cogency . . . worthy of the poets he so deeply admires." Libr J

Includes bibliographical references

Blake, William

The **complete** poetry and prose of William Blake; edited by David V. Erdman; with a new foreword and commentary by Harold Bloom. Newly rev. ed., 1st Calif. ed.; University of California Press 2008 xxvi, 990p il $70 **821**

1. Poetry -- By individual authors

ISBN 978-0-520-04473-9

First published 1965 with title: Poetry and prose of William Blake

In addition to all of Blake's poetry, this volume also includes miscellaneous prose, marginalia, and letters

"The crucial preliminary problem [in establishing Blake's text] is simply to make out what Blake wrote. . . . Erdman has used modern aids such as infrared photography and microphotography. . . but his real achievement has been to look at Blake's text more closely and intelligently than any previous editor." N Y Rev Books

Boland, Eavan

New collected poems. W.W. Norton 2008 320p $27.95 **821**

1. Poetry -- By individual authors

ISBN 978-0-393-06579-4; 0-393-06579-0

LC 2007-42554

First published 2005 in the United Kingdom

"Boland's resilient braid of outspoken feminism with Irish identity has given her a following on both sides of the Atlantic. Here is the recent Boland whose rapid verse celebrates women's courage and women's work, both public (several poems acknowledge Mary Robinson, the former president of the Irish Republic) and unsung: the poet remembers herself, when young, asking a statue in Dublin to 'Make me a heroine.' Here is the poet who learned from Adrienne Rich, among others, how to tackle big topics of loyalty, rebellion, descent and dissent." Publ Wkly

A **woman** without a country; poems. Eavan Boland. W W Norton & Co Inc 2014 96 p. (hardcover) $24.95 **821**

1. Mothers 2. Daughters 3. Nationalism 4. Poetry -- Collections

ISBN 039324444X; 9780393244441

LC 2014030073

This collection of poems, by Eavan Boland, "looks at how we construct one another and how nationhood and history can weave through, reflect, and define the life of an individual. Themes of mother, daughter, and generation echo throughout these . . . poems, as they examine how--even without country or settled identity--a legacy of love can endure." (Publisher's note)

"A superb collection not to be missed, full of exquisite language, music, knowledge and emotion." LJ

British women poets of the Romantic era; an anthology. edited by Paula R. Feldman. Johns Hopkins Univ. Press 1997 xxxvi, 879p hardcover o.p. pa $29.95 **821**

1. English poetry -- Women authors -- Collections

ISBN 0-8018-6640-5 pa

LC 96-47417

An "anthology of works by 62 British women poets writing between 1770 and 1840. . . . The poets are presented in alphabetical order, with each entry including a brief biography with birth and death dates, sample poems, major works, selected works, and the source of the poetry. The result is a singular resource providing information found in no other reference work." Libr J

Includes bibliographical references

Bronte, Emily

The **complete** poems of Emily Jane Bronte; edited from the manuscripts by C. W. Hatfield. Columbia Univ. Press 1941 xxi, 262p $65; pa $20 **821**

1. Poetry -- By individual authors

ISBN 0-231-01222-5; 0-231-10347-6 pa

A re-editing of the complete poems of Emily Bronte, based on all the known manuscripts. About half of the 193 poems are those belonging to the so-called Gondal cycle

Brown, Terence

The **life** of W.B. Yeats; a critical biography. Blackwell 1999 410p il (Blackwell critical biographies) $66.95; pa $29.95 **821**

1. Poets 2. Authors 3. Dramatists 4. Poets, Irish 5. Memoirists 6. Nobel laureates for literature

ISBN 0-631-18298-5; 0-631-22851-9 pa

LC 99-28388

In this biography Brown places "Yeats's work as poet and dramatist in its political and social—as well as personal and erotic—context." N Y Times Book Rev

Includes bibliographical references

Browning, Elizabeth Barrett

★ **Sonnets** from the Portuguese; a celebration of love. St. Martin's Press 1986 [63] il $9.95 **821**

1. Poetry -- By individual authors

ISBN 0-312-74501-X

LC 86-13755

A series of sonnets which "were written during a period of seven years and are considered by some scholars to have been inspired by her love for her husband poet Robert Browning." New Century Handb of Engl Lit

Browning, Robert

Robert Browning; the major works. edited with notes by Adam Roberts; with an introduction by Daniel Karlin. Oxford University Press 2005 xxxii, 828p pa $18.95 **821**

1. Poetry -- By individual authors

ISBN 978-0-19-280626-0; 0-19-280626-2

LC 2006-277696

This "selection includes over eighty of [Browning's] shorter poems, amongst them his most famous and best-loved dramatic monologues, as well as the complete text of many of his longer poems. It contains three books from The Ring and the Book and Browning's critical writing, Essay on Shelley. This edition also selects generously from the love letters between Browning and Elizabeth Barrett." Publisher's note

Includes bibliographical references

★ **Robert** Browning's poetry; authoritative texts, criticism. selected and edited by James F. Loucks and Andrew M. Stauffer. 2nd ed.; W. W. Norton & Co. 2007 689p (A Norton critical edition) pa $14.50 **821**

1. Poetry -- By individual authors

ISBN 978-0-393-92600-2; 0-393-92600-1

LC 2006-47308

First published 1980

This collection of Browning's poetry, which includes Pauline, "reprints the texts of the seventeen-volume 'Fourth and complete edition' (Smith, Elder), of which all but the final volume were approved by Browning before his death. The poems are ordered chronologically according to their first appearance in book form." Publisher's note

Bunting, Basil

Complete poems; associate editor, Richard Caddel. New Directions Books 2003 239p pa $16.95 **821**

1. Poetry -- By individual authors

ISBN 978-0-8112-1563-3; 0-8112-1563-6

LC 2003-15465

This volume "offers adventure, a confident voice, neat takes on history (both recent and archaic), an attractively careworn secular ethics and an even more attractive combination of archaic and vernacular English models. It also offers superb verbal command, chiseling every stanza to the fewest, densest possible words, giving each an aural shape. Those shapes are not always mellifluous—sometimes they are harsh, a mouthful—but each demonstrates Bunting's mastery, proving itself on the page as well as in the ear, where all good poems find their place." Nation

Burns, Robert

Burns; poems. edited and introduced by Gerard Carruthers. Alfred A. Knopf 2007 255p (Everyman's library pocket poets) $12.50 **821**

1. Poetry -- By individual authors

ISBN 978-0-307-26616-3; 0-307-26616-8

LC 2006-47299

"A pioneer of the Romantic movement, Burns wrote in a light Scots dialect with brio, emotional directness, and wit, drawing on classical and English literary traditions as well as Scottish folklore. . . . All of his most famous lyrics and poems are here, from 'A Red, Red Rose,' 'To a Mouse,' and 'To a Louse' to Tam o'Shanter, 'Holy Willie's Prayer,' and 'Auld Lang Syne.'" Publisher's note

Byron, George Gordon Byron

Selected poetry of Lord Byron; edited by Leslie A. Marchand; introduction by Thomas Disch; notes by Jeffrey Vail. Modern Library 2001 745p (The Modern Library classics) pa $16 **821**

1. Poetry -- By individual authors

ISBN 978-0-375-75814-0; 0-375-75814-3

LC 2001-42771

"From 'Manfred,' with its evocation of the figure that came to be called the 'Byronic hero,' to the melancholy 'Childe Harold,' to the satirical masterpiece 'Don Juan' (presented here in judiciously selected form), this . . . [selection seeks to include] the essential Byron." Publisher's note

Chaucer, Geoffrey

★ The **complete** poetry and prose of Geoffrey Chaucer; edited by John H. Fisher. 2nd ed; Harcourt Brace & Co. 1989 1040p il $105.95 **821**

1. Poetry -- By individual authors

ISBN 0-03-028612-3

LC 88-29400

First published 1977
Includes bibliographical references

Christmas poems; selected and edited by John Hollander and J.D. McClatchy. Knopf 1999 254p (Everyman's library pocket poets) $12.50   **821**
1. Christmas -- Poetry 2. English poetry -- Collections 3. American poetry -- Collections
ISBN 0-375-40789-8

LC 99-36265

Contributors to this collection of Christmas poetry include Milton, Tennyson, Rossetti, Thackeray, Eliot, McGinley, Morris, Bishop and Geoffrey Hill

Coleridge, Samuel Taylor
The **complete** poems; edited by William Keach. Penguin 1997 xxx, 626p (Penguin classics) pa $18   **821**
1. Poetry -- By individual authors
ISBN 978-0-14-042353-2

This edition "contains the final texts of all the poems published in the poet's lifetime, together with a substantial selection from the verse still in manuscript on his death. William Keach's notes draw attention to significant variants, and important earlier versions of 'Monody on the Death of Chatterton', 'The Eolian Harp', 'The Rime of the Ancient Mariner' and 'Dejection: An Ode' are included in full. The poems are arranged in chronological order of composition." Publisher's note

The **Columbia** anthology of British poetry; edited by Carl Woodring and James Shapiro. Columbia Univ. Press 1995 xxxi, 891p $41   **821**
1. English poetry -- Collections
ISBN 0-231-10180-5

LC 94-46333

This anthology "contains major British poetry from Beowulf to the present day. Poets receive a short biographical introduction along with their poetry. . . . It includes more female poets than most comparable anthologies, and is conducive to browsing. Major poems such as Coleridge's 'Rime of the Ancient Mariner,' Britain's best-loved poems, and newly rediscovered poems are part of this collection." SLJ

Constantine, David
Collected poems. Bloodaxe Books 2005 384p pa $31.95   **821**
1. Poetry -- By individual authors
ISBN 1-85224-667-7

"From the first line on this book's first page ('As our bloods separate the clock resumes') to the first sentence on its last ('When the kingfisher flitted/ Under the hazels I entered again into boyhood') Constantine declares himself a Romantic, in almost all the loaded, unfashionable and daring senses that once-omnipresent term can bear. In his elaborate lines, intelligence and strong emotion are collaborators, not competitors; he knows how to let them spur each other on." Times Lit Suppl

★ **Contemporary** poets; editor, Thomas Riggs; with a preface by Diane Wakoski. 7th ed; St.

James Press 2001 xxiii, 1443p (Contemporary writers series) $230   **821**
1. Reference books 2. Poets, English -- Dictionaries 3. Poets, American -- Dictionaries 4. American poetry -- Bio-bibliography
ISBN 1-55862-349-3

LC 00-45882

First published 1970 with title: Contemporary poets of the English language

"A biographical handbook of contemporary poets, arranged alphabetically. Entries consist of a short biography, full bibliography, comments by many of the poets, and a signed critical essay." Ref Sources for Small & Medium-sized Libr. 6th edition
Includes bibliographical references

Davie, Donald
Collected poems; edited by Neil Powell. Carcanet 2002 xxi, 634p (Poetry pléiade) $49.95; pa $24.95   **821**
1. English poetry -- 20th century 2. Poetry -- By individual authors
ISBN 978-1-85754-579-1; 1-85754-579-6; 978-1-85754-406-0 pa; 1-85754-406-4 pa

"Davie's poetic output, which abundantly stretches from Hardyesque lyrics ('Bride of Reason,' 'A Winter Talent,' 'The Battered Wife') to cognitively powerful long poems ('Six Epistles to Eva Hesse,' 'The Forests of Lithuania'), from translations of Pasternak and Mandelstam to lyrically brutal political commentary ('August, 1968'), evinces a kind of wide sweep and committed imagination that doesn't necessarily close itself off to confrontation and experiential risk, nor resign itself to failure as the phenomenological and lyrical refusal of further inquiry. In this sense, Davie has always seemed to be a poet working in the very high art of his eighteenth-century forebears." Jacket

Davis, Dick
Belonging; poems. Swallow Press 2002 54p $24.95; pa $14.95   **821**
1. Poetry -- By individual authors
ISBN 0-8040-1042-0; 0-8040-1043-9 pa

LC 2002-17749

Davis' "poems are full of fine emotion, intelligence, wit, and multinational culture. He lithely celebrates the legendary rake Casanova; poignantly conjures 'Kipling's Kim, Thirty Years On'; economically reports a father's aching futility in comforting his child ('A Bit of Paternity'); deftly valorizes the power of art ('Just So'); and often muses on the shortness of life and the limitations of being human, so cogently that a single quatrain can take one's breath away." Booklist

Day Lewis, C.
The **complete** poems of C. Day Lewis; [edited by] Jill Balcon. Stanford Univ. Press 1992 745p hardcover o.p. pa $32.95   **821**
1. Poetry -- By individual authors
ISBN 978-0-8047-2585-9; 0-8047-2585-3

LC 91-68076

"The still lively fascination of his verse seems to depend on the variety of tones [Day Lewis] could pick up, change, and discard at will. . . . His modesty was genuine and profound, giving his verse texture its winning versatility, its air that 'tenure is not for me.' . . . Nothing that Day Lewis wrote is lacking its own sort of ephemeral though rediscoverable effectiveness. He was well aware of this, and it was a part of his modesty, as Jill Balcon points out in her thoughtful and sensitive introduction. . . . For anyone who likes poetry there is real interest here in [this] complete record." N Y Rev Books

Donne, John

★ The **complete** poetry and selected prose of John Donne; edited by Charles M. Coffin; introduction by Denis Donoghue; notes by W. T. Chmielewski. Modern Lib. 2001 xxxii, 697p pa $14.95   **821**
1. Poetry -- By individual authors
ISBN 0-375-75734-1
LC 2001-30077
A reissue of the Modern Library edition published 1994
This volume contains Donne's love poetry, satires, epigrams, verse letters and holy sonnets. Also includes selected prose and a sampling of private letters.

Poems and prose. A.A. Knopf 1995 256p (Everyman's library pocket poets) $12.50   **821**
1. Poetry -- By individual authors
ISBN 978-0-679-44467-1; 0-679-44467-X
LC 95-15330
"Contains Songs and Sonnets, Letters to the Countess of Bedford, The First Anniversary, Holy Sonnets, Divine Poems, excerpts from Paradoxes and Problems, Ignatius His Conclave, The Sermons, Essays and Devotions, and an index of first lines." Publisher's note

Dryden, John

John Dryden; the major works. edited with an introduction and notes by Keith Walker. Oxford University Press 2003 xviii, 967p pa $18.95   **821**
1. Poetry -- By individual authors
ISBN 978-0-19-284077-6; 0-19-284077-0
LC 2003-270051
This "edition brings together a unique combination of Dryden's poetry and prose—all the major poems in full, literary criticism, and translations—to give the essence of his work and thinking. The collection includes the poems, MacFlecknoe and Absalom and Achitophel as well as Dryden's classical translations; his versions of Homer, Horace, and Ovid are reproduced in full. There are also substantial selections from Dryden's Virgil, Juvenal, and other classical writers. Fables, Ancient and Modern, taken from Chaucer, Ovid, Boccaccio, and Homer, his last and possibly greatest work, also appears in full." Publisher's note
Includes bibliographical references

Feinstein, Elaine

Ted Hughes; the life of a poet. Norton 2001 273p il $29.95; pa $15.95   **821**
1. Poets 2. Authors 3. Poets laureate
ISBN 0-393-04967-1; 0-393-32362-5 pa
LC 2001-44925
This biography of the English poet examines Hughes's relationship with "his first wife, Sylvia Plath, who committed suicide in 1963 during the acrimonious breakup of their

marriage, . . . {and with} Assia Wevill, the woman for whom Hughes left Plath, and who later killed herself and their child." Economist
Includes bibliographical references

Fisher, Roy

★ **Selected** poems; edited by August Kleinzahler. Flood Editions 2011 158p pa $15.95   **821**
1. Poetry -- By individual authors
ISBN 978-0-9819520-6-2
"Fisher's texts have never been as well served on the page as they are here. The poems are given real space and the movement of Fisher's breath, rhythm and cadence is as clear as it possibly could be." Manchester Rev

Foster, R. F. (Robert Fitzroy), 1949-

W.B. Yeats: a life. v1 Oxford Univ. Press 1997 xxxi, 640p v1 il hardcover o.p. pa $29.95   **821**
1. Poets 2. Authors 3. Dramatists 4. Poets, Irish 5. Memoirists 6. Biography, Individual 7. Nobel laureates for literature
ISBN 0-19-211735-1; 0-19-288085-3 pa
LC 96-31671
This is the first installment of a two-volume biography of the Irish poet. Index.

W.B. Yeats: a life. v2 Oxford Univ. Press 2003 xxiv, 798p v2 il $47.50   **821**
1. Poets 2. Authors 3. Dramatists 4. Poets, Irish 5. Memoirists 6. Nobel laureates for literature
ISBN 0-19-818465-4
This second volume of a two-volume biography covers Yeats's final decades, from his 50th year to his death in 1939.
Includes bibliographical references

Foulds, Adam

The **broken** word; an epic poem of the British Empire in Kenya, and the Mau Mau uprising against it. Penguin 2011 60p (Penguin poets) pa $16 **821**
1. Kenya -- Poetry 2. Mau Mau -- Poetry
ISBN 978-0-14-311809-1
First published 2008 in the United Kingdom
Offers a lyrical poem about Tom, a young man who gets caught up in the violent 1950s Mau Mau Uprising in Kenya protesting the British colonial control of that country.
"A tour de force of a long narrative poem, rare in contemporary English poetry." Libr J

Geoffrey Chaucer's The Canterbury tales; edited and with an introduction by Harold Bloom. New ed; Chelsea House 2008 286p (Modern critical interpretations) $45   **821**
1. Poets 2. Authors 3. Poetry -- By individual authors
ISBN 978-0-7910-9618-5
LC 2007-49158
First published 1988 in three separate editions focusing on the Prologue, The knight's tale, and The pardoner's tale
A collection of eleven critical essays on Chaucer's well-known work, arranged in chronological order of their original publication.
Includes bibliographical references

Gunn, Thom

Boss Cupid. Farrar, Straus & Giroux 2000 111p hardcover o.p. pa $13 **821**

1. Poetry -- By individual authors

ISBN 0-374-52771-7 pa

LC 99-57739

"Boss Cupid offers a splendid introduction for the uninitiated. Almost all of Gunn's virtues are on display here: his playful, metrical dexterity, his unflinching celebration both of beauty and of transience. . . . Advancing age and the AIDS-related deaths of friends—'my everpresent dead'—figure prominently in these poems, but so does Gunn's humorous touch." Time

Collected poems. Farrar, Straus & Giroux 1994 495p pa $20 **821**

1. Poetry -- By individual authors

ISBN 978-0-374-52433-3; 0-374-52433-5

LC 93-74183

There is a "a unity of purpose that extends throughout the work, from the watchful early metrics through the syllabics, the reach and skill of the free verse and, in much of the latest work, a return to strong form that might be termed triumphant had it not been called into the service of matter so saddening." Times Lit Suppl

Hardy, Thomas

Thomas Hardy; the complete poems. edited by James Gibson. Palgrave 2001 xxxvi, 1003p il pa $33.95 **821**

1. Poetry -- By individual authors

ISBN 978-0-333-94929-0; 0-333-94929-3

LC 2001-32732

First published 1976

This collection "includes Hardy's more than 900 poems, complemented by detailed notes. Collected here are his eight books of verse, all the uncollected poems, Domicilium, and the songs from The Dynasts. This edition contains an additional poem, The Sound of Her." Publisher's note

Includes bibliographical references

Heaney, Seamus

District and circle. Farrar, Straus and Giroux 2006 78p $20 **821**

1. Poetry -- By individual authors

ISBN 0-374-14092-8; 978-0-374-14092-2

LC 2005-44687

This "collection of robust lyrics celebrates work, memory, and the physicality of existence. Brimming with anvils, hammers, shovels, and pumps, these poems are scored into the page with Heaney's signature accentual and alliterative force." Libr J

Electric light. Farrar, Straus & Giroux 2001 98p hardcover o.p. pa $13 **821**

1. Poetry -- By individual authors

ISBN 0-374-14683-7; 0-374-52841-1 pa

LC 00-67278

Heaney's "book of poems is a compendium of poetic genres set in an array of forms and tuned to many kinds of experience, the work of a mature poet and world citizen, aware of his cultural authority as a public man and of

the rights and responsibilities that go with it." N Y Times Book Rev

★ **Finders** keepers; selected prose 1971-2001. Farrar, Straus & Giroux 2002 452p $30; pa $15 **821**

1. Poets 2. Authors 3. Novelists 4. Dramatists 5. Librarians 6. Editors 7. Essayists 8. Memoirists 9. Translators 10. Poets laureate 11. College teachers 12. Literary critics 13. Nobel laureates for literature 14. Poetry -- History and criticism

ISBN 0-374-15496-1; 0-374-52878-0 pa

This collection "gathers Heaney's occasional prose from four decades, much of it meditating upon other poets who have moved him, including familiar members of the canon, such as Eliot and Yeats and Auden, and lesser-known and newer moderns, such as Hugh MacDiarmid, Thomas Kinsella, and Norman MacCaig, whose work draws his interest. Not surprisingly for a poet from a war-wracked land, Heaney comes back again and again to the question of how poetry can matter against human savagery." Booklist

Opened ground; selected poems, 1966-1996. Farrar, Straus & Giroux 1998 443p hardcover o.p. pa $16 **821**

1. Poetry -- By individual authors

ISBN 0-374-52678-8 pa

LC 98-4331

"The best of nobel laureate Heaney's poems, gathered from 12 previous collections, create a substantial volume that charts the course of one man's thoroughly examined personal life and reflects a volatile era in the life of his troubled country, Northern Ireland, though the particulars Heaney renders so vibrantly become archetypal and unbounded in their tragedy and bliss." Booklist

Heaney, Seamus, 1939-2013

Human chain. Farrar, Straus and Giroux 2010 85p $24 **821**

1. Poetry -- By individual authors

ISBN 978-0-374-17351-7

LC 2010-10274

This is the Irish poet and Nobel laureate's latest collection of verse.

"Nostalgia and memory, numinous visions and the earthy music of compound adjectives together control the short poems and sequences of the Irish Nobel laureate's 14th collection of verse. . . . Old teachers, schoolmates, farmhands, and even the employees of an 'Eelworks' arrive transfigured through Heaney's command of sound. . . . For all the variety of Heaney's framed glimpses, though, the standout poems grow from occasions neither trivial nor topical: Heaney in 2006 had a minor stroke, and the discreet analogies and glimpsed moments in poems such as 'Chanson d'Aventure' (about a ride in an ambulance) and 'In the Attic' ('As I age and blank on names') bring his characteristic warmth and subtlety to mortality, rehabilitation, recent trauma, and old age." Publ Wkly

Herbert, George

Herbert: poems. Alfred A. Knopf 2004 253p (Everyman's library pocket poets) $12.50 **821**

1. Poetry -- By individual authors 2. Christian poetry,

English -- Early modern, 1500-1700.
ISBN 978-1-4000-4329-3; 1-4000-4329-8

LC 2005-273574

Herbert experimented with a variety of forms, "from hymns and sonnets to 'pattern poems,' the shape of which reveal their subjects. Such technical agility never seems ostentatious, however, for precision of language and expression of genuine feeling were the primary concerns of this poet who admonished his readers to 'dare to be true.' An Anglican priest who took his calling with deep seriousness, he brought to his work a religious reverence richly allied with a playful wit and with literary and musical gifts of the highest order." Publisher's note

Hill, Geoffrey

★ The **orchards** of Syon. Counterpoint 2002 72p $24   **821**
1. Poetry -- By individual authors
ISBN 1-58243-166-3

LC 2001-47245

"Cast as a sequence of 72 uniform blank-verse soliloquies compounded out of a dissonant amalgam of demotic jabber and oracular utterance, 'The Orchards of Syon' confirms that Hill, for all his newfound volubility, can be as refractory as ever. . . . But for readers with the patience and stamina to stick with it, Hill's brooding meditations on his ancestral countryside's 'wintry swamp-thickets, brush-heaps of burnt light' or 'the burring air of the fell' carry the haunting force of a last will and testament." N Y Times Book Rev

Selected poems. Yale University Press 2009 276p   **821**
1. Poetry -- By individual authors
ISBN 978-0-300-12156-8

LC 2008-930384

First published 2006 in the United Kingdom
"After four decades with just five books, the past 10 years have seen Hill offer six more, including a trio of long works some liken to Dante and Blake. This first selected since 1994 . . . should get instant critical attention (and sustained academic adoption) even though it contains no new work. Here, entire, is Mercian Hymns, with its gorgeously medievalized evocation of a rural English upbringing. Here, complete, are all three recent long poems, with their erudite mix of elegy and jeremiad. . . . Here, too, are the descriptive beauties that sparkle through even Hill's most rebarbative works." Publ Wkly

The **triumph** of love. Houghton Mifflin 1998 82p hardcover o.p. pa $13   **821**
1. Poetry -- By individual authors
ISBN 0-618-00183-2 pa

LC 98-19502

This book-length poem "ends up so much more satisfying than much of Hill's recent work because there is so much more of Hill in it. . . . When we have read [the book] a few times (no one should read it just once) we know, more than we could from his previous work, what vexes and distresses,

what heartens and cheers Hill, what gives him his grim satisfactions and how." Yale Rev

Without title. Yale University Press 2007 81p $26; pa $16   **821**
1. Poetry -- By individual authors
ISBN 978-0-300-12176-6; 0-300-12176-8; 0-300-12157-1 pa; 978-0-300-12157-5 pa

LC 2006-926124

First published 2006 in the United Kingdom
"For much of Hill's five-decade career, his forbiddingly allusive and elliptical style, his sometimes peevish tone, his interest in English church history, and his rapt pastoralism have made him an unfashionable figure, but also a highly individual one. His latest collection exhibits typical erudition: who else would name-drop the Jesuit theologian Karl Rahner or describe Jimi Hendrix as an 'exquisite player of neumes' ('neumes' being an archaic form of musical notation)? Though the method is a magpie one, the impression that emerges is of absolute control and single-mindedness. And while Hill's outlook can seem willfully bleak . . . there is genuine grace in his descriptions of natural beauty." New Yorker

Hollis, Matthew

Now all roads lead to France; A Life of Edward Thomas. Matthew Hollis. Faber & Faber 2011 416 p. ill., maps   **821**
1. English poets -- Biography 2. World War, 1914-1918 -- Biography 3. Great Britain -- Armed forces -- Recruiting and enlistment -- Biography 4. Poets 5. Authors 6. Essayists 7. Writers on nature 8. Biography, Individual
ISBN 0571245994; 9780571245994

LC 2011505697

Costa Biography Award Winner (2011)
This book presents "a study of [poet Edward] Thomas's life and work from (roughly) the winter of 1913 onwards, with a strong emphasis on his poetic aspirations." (Times Literary Supplement). "[Matthew] Hollis gives a portrait of the artist as a man at work: shaping, revising, making poems. The biography . . . [is] a story of . . . the last four years of his life, during which he developed a close friendship with Robert Frost, decided to enlist in the army and fight in the First World War, and turned himself into a poet." (New Statesman)

Includes bibliographical references and index.

Hopkins, Gerard Manley

Poems and prose. Alfred A. Knopf 1995 256p (Everyman's library pocket poets) $13.50   **821**
1. Poetry -- By individual authors
ISBN 978-0-679-44469-5; 0-679-44469-6

LC 95-15331

This volume "contains a full selection of Hopkins's work, including selected verse, prose, and letters, and an index of first lines." Publisher's note

Housman, A. E.

★ The **collected** poems of A. E. Housman. Holt & Co. 1965 254p pa $16   **821**

1. Poetry -- By individual authors

ISBN 0-8050-0547-1

This anthology "constitutes the authorized canon of A. E. Housman's verse as established in 1939." Note on the text

Hughes, Ted, 1930-1998

Collected poems; edited by Paul Keegan. Farrar, Straus and Giroux 2003 1376p $50; pa $25   **821**

1. Poetry -- By individual authors

ISBN 978-0-374-12538-7; 0-374-12538-4; 978-0-374-52965-9 pa; 0-374-52965-5 pa

LC 2003-59938

"Paul Keegan has taken Hughes's New Selected Poems of 1995 as his model, and intercalated the expected and familiar Faber texts with uncollected or small press works like a Viennese layer cake—in astonishing quantity and quality." Poetry (Modern Poetry Association)

Johnston, Kenneth R.

The **hidden** Wordsworth; poet, lover, rebel, spy. Norton 1998 965 p. ill. $45; pa $24.95   **821**

1. Poets 2. Authors 3. Poets laureate 4. Spies -- Great Britain -- Biography 5. Poets, English -- 19th century -- Biography 6. Revolutionaries -- Great Britain -- Biography

ISBN 0393046230; 0393321592

LC 97-40317

The author seeks "to chronicle Wordsworth's life from 1770 to 1807." (Libr J) Bibliography. Index.

This "volume focuses on the poet's first thirty-six years, the tumultuous decades immortalized in 'The Prelude.' Johnston's spacious, absorbing argument—that Wordsworth's moments of emotion recollected in tranquillity were themselves rather less than tranquil—is amply supported by a thorough documentation of the multifarious life and times of the young poet, at Hawkshead, at Cambridge, in Grasmere, and abroad." New Yorker

Includes bibliographical references

Jonson, Ben

The **complete** poems; edited by George Parfitt. Penguin Books 1988 634p (Penguin classics) pa $17   **821**

1. Poetry -- By individual authors

ISBN 978-0-14-042277-1; 0-14-042277-3

LC 88-196178

"As well as the entire body of Jonson's nondramatic verse, extensively annotated, this edition contains many of the songs from his plays and masques and his translation of 'Horace, of the Art of Poetry'. His 'Conversations with Drummond', which adds much to our sense of the man, appears as an Appendix, as does 'Discoveries'; together they shed valuable light on Jonson's poetic theory and practice." Publisher's note

Keats, John

★ The **complete** poems of John Keats. Modern Lib. 1994 398p $19.95   **821**

1. Poetry -- By individual authors

ISBN 0-679-60108-2

LC 94-4339

The works in this compilation include Lamia, Isabella, The Eve of St. Agnes', Endymion, and La Belle Dame sans Merci

Poems. Knopf 1994 253p (Everyman's library pocket poets) $12.50   **821**

1. Poetry -- By individual authors

ISBN 0-679-43319-8

LC 94-2495

A representative collection by the influential English romantic.

Includes bibliographical references

Kipling, Rudyard, 1865-1936

Complete verse; definitive edition. Doubleday 1989 850p hardcover o.p. pa $20   **821**

1. Poetry -- By individual authors

ISBN 0-385-26089-X pa

LC 88-7364

Replaces Rudyard Kipling's verse: definitive edition, published 1940

This edition includes all of Kipling's published poetry and, in addition, more than 20 poems which have not previously appeared in the inclusive edition of his verse

Langland, William

Piers Plowman; the Donaldson translation, Middle English text, sources and backgrounds, criticism. edited by Elizabeth Robertson and Stephen H.A. Shepherd. Norton 2006 xxviii, 644p pa $15   **821**

1. Poetry -- By individual authors

ISBN 978-0-393-97559-8; 0-393-97559-2

LC 2004-57578

This Middle English poem is "written in 'Alliterative Verse' like Old English poetry and uses a deliberately rustic and archaic dialect. It is an allegorical moral and social satire, written as a 'vision' of the common medieval type." Reader's Ency. 4th edition

Larkin, Philip

★ **Collected** poems; edited and with an introduction by Anthony Thwaite. Farrar, Straus and Giroux 2004 218p pa $15   **821**

1. Poetry -- By individual authors

ISBN 978-0-374-52920-8; 0-374-52920-5

LC 2003-60846

First published 2003 in the United Kingdom

"Thwaite has gathered all the poems Larkin wrote between 1946 and 1985, the year of his death; he also includes a generous selection of work written earlier, before Larkin found his characteristic voice. In all, there are some 240 poems, 83 of them never published before. The unpublished work comes from every period of Larkin's career and increases by half the number of poems in his canon. The poet we now have is considerably more prolific than the one who issued only three small, mature collections in his lifetime.

With or without the new poems, Larkin is a major postwar British writer, and this is the best available collection of his poetry." Libr J

Lawrence, D. H.

The **complete** poems; collected and edited with an introduction and notes by Vivian de Sola Pinto and Warren Roberts. Penguin Books 1993 1079p (Penguin twentieth-century classics) pa $24.95   **821**

1. Poetry -- By individual authors
ISBN 978-0-14-018657-4; 0-14-018657-3
First published 1964 by Viking

This "collection of Lawrence's poems, with appendices containing juvenilia, variants, and early drafts, and Lawrence's own critical introductions to his poems, also includes full textual and explanatory notes, glossary, and index." Publisher's note

Lear, Edward

The **complete** verse and other nonsense; compiled and edited with an introduction and notes by Vivien Noakes. Penguin Bks. 2002 566p il pa $18   **821**

1. Nonsense verses 2. Poetry -- By individual authors
ISBN 0-14-200227-5

LC 2002-28998

This volume "presents all of Lear's verse and other nonsense writings, including stories, letters, and illustrated alphabets, as well as previously unpublished material, line drawings, and . . . [an] introduction by scholar Vivien Noakes." Publisher's note

Includes bibliographical references

MacDiarmid, Hugh

Selected poetry; introduction by Eliot Weinberger; edited by Alan Riach & Michael Grieve. New Directions 1993 289p $30.95   **821**

1. Poetry -- By individual authors
ISBN 978-0-8112-1248-9; 0-8112-1248-3

LC 93-5312

"The preface by the poet's son Michael Grieve, 'Recalling Hugh MacDiarmid,' includes major biographical facts which shaped the poet's work. . . . Alan Riach's 'Reading Hugh MacDiarmid' provides a scholarly look at MacDiarmid's importance to the Scottish Renaissance and the themes that informed his poetry. . . . In addition to the two introductory essays, the volume also contains a chronology of MacDiarmid's life, illustrating both his private maturation and the public events that influenced him. The real reason to purchase the volume, however, is for the exceptional overview and easy accessibility it provides to a major poetic voice not only in Scotland but in the world." World Lit Today

The **Making** of a poem; a Norton anthology of poetic forms. edited by Mark Strand and Eavan Boland. Norton 2000 xxxi, 366p hardcover o.p. pa $15.95   **821**

1. English poetry -- Collections 2. American poetry -- Collections
ISBN 0-393-32178-9 pa

LC 99-55233

A "collection of villanelles, sestinas, sonnets, elegies, pastorals, ballads, pantoums, odes, and other familiar structures that have shaped English poetry since Beowulf. Each chapter focuses on a single form. . . . Most useful are the selections themselves, which illustrate how particular forms have been employed over time, from canonical classics by Chaucer, Shelley, and Elizabeth Bishop through newer pieces by Hayden Carruth, Michael Palmer, and Thylias Moss." Libr J

Includes bibliographical references

Marvell, Andrew

Poems; [selected by Peter Washington] A. A. Knopf 2004 256p (Everyman's library pocket poets) $12.50   **821**

1. Poetry -- By individual authors
ISBN 978-1-4000-4252-4; 1-4000-4252-6

The "metaphysical poet Andrew Marvell was one of the chief wits and satirists of his time as well as a passionate defender of individual liberty. Today, however, he is known chiefly for his brilliant lyric poems, including 'The Garden,' 'The Definition of Love,' 'Bermudas,' 'To His Coy Mistress,' and the 'Horatian Ode' to Cromwell." Publisher's note

Maxwell, Glyn, 1962-

One thousand nights and counting; selected poems. Farrar, Straus and Giroux 2011 239p   **821**

1. Poetry -- By individual authors
ISBN 9780374226480

LC 2011005176

"The British poet Maxwell's first U.S. selected presents a conversational style that is a constant throughout, as is the setting of England and New England; otherwise, these often surreal and opaque poems range across moods and subjects. The best moments occur when readers can lose themselves in the very long poems, in particular the inventive re-imagining of the story of Noah's Ark, 'Out of the Rain,' and the elegiac 'Letters to Edward Thomas,' in which the speaker waits for a friend who never arrives. . . . Maxwell's poetry can be playful and inventive, beautiful and melancholic, but can also be self-aggrandizing . . . and even pretentious. . . . Yet Maxwell is one of stars of poetry across the pond and a rising presence here; this book should win him new fans." Publ Wkly

Morrissey, Sinéad

Parallax; and selected poems. Sinead Morrissey. Farrar, Straus & Giroux 2015 211 p. (hardcover) $26   **821**

1. Empiricism 2. Irish poetry
ISBN 0865478295; 9780865478299

LC 2014043835

National Book Critics Circle Award Finalist: Poetry (2015)

This poetry collection, by Sinead Morrissey, "which won the 2013 T. S. Eliot Prize, . . . explores what is captured, and what is lost, when houses and cityscapes, servants and saboteurs, are arrested in time by photography (or poetry), subjected to the authority of a particular perspective. Assured and disquieting, Morrisey's poems explore the paradoxes that result when we attempt to freeze our passing experience through art." (Publisher's note)

"An impressive collection showcasing an impressive career." Booklist

Motion, Andrew

Keats. University of Chicago Press 1999 636p il pa $18 **821**

1. Poets 2. Authors 3. Poets, English 4. Writers on medicine

ISBN 0-226-54240-8; 978-0-226-54240-9

LC 98-41014

First published 1997 in the United Kingdom

"Motion emphasizes that Keats was no otherworldly creature of exquisite sensibilities but a man whose liberal politics and commitment to medicine animated his aesthetics and enlightened his poetry." Booklist

Includes bibliographical references

Muldoon, Paul

★ **Horse** latitudes. Farrar, Straus and Giroux 2006 107p $22 **821**

1. Poetry -- By individual authors

ISBN 978-0-374-17305-0; 0-374-17305-2

LC 2006-306

"Beginning with a sequence of sonnets whose titles start with the letter B, to a series of instant messages formatted as haiku, to an ending that tributes rocker Warren Zevon, readers are in for a lively ride." Libr J

Maggot; poems. Farrar, Straus and Giroux 2010 134p $24 **821**

1. Poetry -- By individual authors

ISBN 978-0-374-20032-9; 0-374-20032-7

LC 2010-05700

"The play on the word maggot, which can also mean a whim or extravagant notion as well as the larva, tells us all we need to know about Paul Muldoon's poetics. So comfortable is he in both worlds, the debased and the ecstatic, that critics often willfully misunderstand him. . . . Everywhere in 'Maggot,' Mr. Muldoon chafes at the bit, belatedly, against duty and responsibility. He is most susceptible to the charge of triviality in his longer poems, and often in 'Maggot,' he does indeed flirt too closely with absurdity. . . . [He] barely squeaks by on the side of seriousness, but just barely! Credit him with continuing to walk that trapeze, with no net underneath him." Pittsburgh Post-Gazette

★ **Poems,** 1968-1998. Farrar, Straus & Giroux 2001 479p $35; pa $19 **821**

1. Poetry -- By individual authors

ISBN 0-374-12543-0; 0-374-52844-6 pa

LC 00-45607

"Language is heightened, experimental, and also utterly mundane, even coarse. His subjects match the language, what with trips on mescaline chockablock with bucolic landscapes. The luck of this collection is that it is long and dense enough to show the poet wrestling not only with craft—his intricate and often hidden rhymes show, right from the start, his obsession with form—but also with the reason for poetry in a technological age." Booklist

Murray, Les A.

The **biplane** houses. Farrar, Straus and Giroux 2007 99p $23 **821**

1. Poetry -- By individual authors

ISBN 978-0-374-11548-7; 0-374-11548-6

LC 2006-31763

First published 2006 in Australia

"Murray's poems, never exactly intimate and often patrolled by details and place-names nearly indecipherable to an outsider, reflect a life lived self-consciously and rather flamboyantly off the beaten track. . . . Pastoral is a sophisticated game pitting poets against earlier poets, like a chess match played across time. No poet writing about the natural world entirely opts out of the game, but Murray's poetry of elk and emus, bougainvillea and turmeric dust, comes close." New Yorker

★ **Conscious** and verbal; [by] Les Murray. Farrar, Straus & Giroux 2001 94p $23; pa $13 **821**

1. Poetry -- By individual authors

ISBN 0-374-12882-0; 0-374-52860-8 pa

LC 2001-40222

"The poet became a minor celebrity when he awoke from a three-week coma and was pronounced 'conscious and verbal,' but this new volume is more concerned with his familiar Australian topography: dead dogs, the 'Internationale,' oysters, soil, the color yellow. Murray sticks to the cheerfully formal lines that distinguish his work while letting his voice shift between chestnuts of local dialect and a brawny but humble standard English." New Yorker

Poems the size of photographs; [by] Les Murray. Farrar, Straus & Giroux 2003 128p $20 **821**

1. Poetry -- By individual authors

ISBN 0-374-23520-1

LC 2002-192520

First published in 2002 in the United Kingdom

"Murray concentrates his muscular style, passion for landscape, and satirical humor into short and pithy poems. Tightly framed, most can be taken in at a glance, and yet, like developing photographs, they fully disclose their finer details and nuances more slowly. Murray begins with a mischievous tribute to the 'new hieroglyphics,' the international symbols of airports and restaurants, pictographs of the forbidden and the required. The contrasts between words and images intrigue Murray and inform his sly, sometimes startling, always colorful and animated lyrics, yarns, and epigrams." Booklist

Taller when prone; poems. [by] Les Murray. Farrar, Straus and Giroux 2011 82p $24 **821**

1. Poetry -- By individual authors

ISBN 978-0-374-27237-1

First published 2010 in Australia

This "is Les Murray's first volume of new poems since The Biplane Houses, published five years ago." (Publisher's note)

The title of Murray's collection "plays with the notion of cutting self down to size. He uses humour to restore perspective (although the punchline to the wonderful and ludicrous 'A Frequent Flyer Proposes a Name', in which he suggests a name for a new London airport, does not qualify as a deflationary joke). There are many more serious and ambitious pieces here, too. There are elegies in the tradition of Gerard Manley Hopkins's 'Felix Randal' – 'Rugby Wheels', about a disabled rugby player, and 'Double Diamond', about a gauche octogenarian soldier at his wife's funeral. It is a collection filled with celebrations of ordinary people, extraordinary Australian birds and open endings. Murray has a gentle way with his poems, letting them go, never forcing a conclusion. One of his great gifts is that he is noninterventionist, never blocks a view – art in apparent artlessness." Guardian (UK)

★ The **New** Oxford book of Irish verse; edited, with translations, by Thomas Kinsella. Oxford Univ. Press 2001 xxx, 423p pa $16.95 **821**
1. Irish poetry -- Collections
ISBN 0-19-280192-9
LC 2001-278442
Replaces The Oxford Book of Irish verse, XVIIth century-XXth century, chosen by Donagh MacDonagh and Lennox Robinson (1958); this is a reissue of the 1986 edition

"This selection is divided into three parts. Book I opens with the earliest pre-Christian poetry in Old Irish and ends in the fourteenth century with the first Irish poetry in the English language. Book II covers the fourteenth to the eighteenth centuries and Book III the nineteenth and twentieth centuries." Publisher's note

★ The **Norton** anthology of modern and contemporary poetry; edited by Jahan Ramazani, Richard Ellmann, Robert O'Clair. 3rd ed; Norton 2003 2v pa set $75 **821**
1. English poetry -- Collections 2. American poetry -- Collections
ISBN 0-393-32429-X
LC 2002-37990
First published 1973 with title: The Norton anthology of modern poetry

This volume includes "1596 poems by 195 poets. . . . The anthology includes the works of such masters as Walt Whitman, Ezra Pound, Dylan Thomas, Langston Hughes, Gertrude Stein, Lucille Clifton, Louise Erdrich, and Allen Ginsberg. . . . Extensive, and beautifully composed introductions provide insight, observations, and historical context for the selections. . . . This ambitious, highly successful work is a veritable tribute to the enduring power of literature and language." SLJ
Includes bibliographical references

O'Driscoll, Dennis
Stepping stones; interviews with Seamus Heaney. Farrar, Straus, and Giroux 2008 xxx, 552p il map $32 **821**
1. Poets 2. Authors 3. Essayists 4. Translators 5. Nobel laureates for literature
ISBN 978-0-374-26983-8; 0-374-26983-1
LC 2008-41252
"The book is a collection of questions and answers, compiled, largely by correspondence, over a period of some seven years. The compiler, Dennis O'Driscoll a poet, senior tax inspector and strict questioner—persuades you that there will be no tolerance of arrears for Heaney here. The replies

are tantamount to, while not pre-empting, an autobiography, by someone who says he 'inclines to discretion' but is not a 'self-concealing person'. This is a forthright though not a confessional book, inclined both to 'elevated stuff' and to jokes." Times Lit Suppl
Includes bibliographical references

★ The **Oxford** book of comic verse; edited by John Gross. Oxford University Press 2009 xxxiv, 512p pa $19.95 **821**
1. English poetry -- Collections 2. American poetry -- Collections 3. Humorous poetry -- Collections
ISBN 978-0-19-956161-2
LC 2009-291577
First published 1994
The editor "defines comic verse as primarily meant to amuse. From this bland definition he delves his principles of inclusion: funny poems that do not exceed the boundaries of good taste. No bawdy lyrics, no skewering satire here. Within these limits, he surveys the field from Chaucer to Glyn Maxwell (1962)." Publ Wkly
Includes bibliographical references

★ The **Oxford** book of English verse; edited by Christopher Ricks. Oxford Univ. Press 1999 xxxii, 690p $39.95 **821**
1. English poetry -- Collections
ISBN 0-19-214182-1
LC 99-20831
First published 1900 under the editorship of Sir Arthur Quiller-Couch with title: The Oxford book of English verse, 1250-1900. Present edition replaces The New Oxford book of English verse, 1250-1950, edited by Helen Gardner published 1972

This collection "starts with anonymous 13th-century lyric and ends with Seamus Heaney; in between are seven centuries' worth of poems in English from Britain and Ireland. . . . Ricks brings in plenty of dialect verse, excerpts from long poems and verse plays, and a few translations into English. . . . Long after reviewers stop debating how Ricks chose each item, readers will keep returning to these pages to find yet another good poem they've not before seen." Publ Wkly

The **Oxford** book of sonnets; edited by John Fuller. Oxford Univ. Press 2000 xxxiv, 362p $25; pa $15.95 **821**
1. English poetry -- Collections 2. American poetry -- Collections
ISBN 0-19-214267-4; 0-19-280389-1 pa
LC 00-36757
"Indisputable masterpieces appear plentifully, but Fuller's determination to present a large number of distinguished practitioners assures that there are also many superb poems by virtual unknowns. And Fuller's introduction is a sharp-witted miracle of concise comprehensiveness." Booklist
Includes bibliographical references

The **Oxford** companion to Chaucer; edited by Douglas Gray. Oxford University Press 2003 xxiii, 526p il map $95 **821**

1. Poets 2. Authors 3. Poetry -- By individual authors
ISBN 0-19-811765-5

LC 2004-270323

This reference includes "more than 2,000 signed entries on various aspects of Chaucer and his works as well as their larger cultural and literary context." Choice

Includes bibliographical references

Paterson, Don

Rain. Farrar, Straus, and Giroux 2010 61p $24; pa $13 **821**

1. Poetry -- By individual authors
ISBN 978-0-374-24629-7; 978-0-374-53268-0 pa

LC 2009-938696

"There's something of the shadow puppeteer in Don Paterson — reading his poems, you don't know what's real and what's illusion; they play with the reader's perceptions and sense of perspective, so that you aren't quite sure whether what you're looking at are the moving figures themselves or the backlit projection screen. At their best, this gives them a curiously disorienting quality, like looking at a photographic negative, in which the world or its representation has been turned inside out." Guardian (London)

The **Penguin** book of the sonnet; 500 years of a classic tradition in English. edited by Phillis Levin. Penguin Bks. 2001 419p pa $18 **821**

1. English poetry -- Collections 2. American poetry -- Collections
ISBN 0-14-058929-5

LC 00-62350

In an introductory essay, Levin "discusses the sonnet's origins, history, traditions, and possibilities. . . . Interwoven with the history are approaches to interpreting and criticizing this poetic form. The bulk of the text is an anthology of over 600 sonnets composed by more than 230 poets. Over 150 of the poets represented wrote during the 20th century." Libr J

Includes bibliographical references

Pickard, Tom

★ **Hole** in the wall; new & selected poems. Flood Editions 2004 139p pa $15 **821**

1. Poetry -- By individual authors
ISBN 0-9710059-3-1

"In the Objectivist tradition, paring words down to broaden their sound and register meaning, Pickard's work here is of compact, dazzling, Bunting-esque musicality. It also bursts with a fluid sensual appeal reminiscent of D.H. Lawrence." Skanky Possum

Pope, Alexander

Selected poetry; edited with an introduction and notes by Pat Rogers. Oxford University Press 1998 xxiii, 226p (Oxford world's classics) pa $12.95 **821**

1. Verse satire, English. 2. Poetry -- By individual authors
ISBN 978-0-19-283494-2; 0-19-283494-0

LC 98-230887

Pope achieved "success with his first published work at the age of twenty-one. A succession of brilliant poems followed, including An Essay on Criticism (1711), Windsor Forest (1715), and his masterpiece, The Rape of the Lock. A second period of great poetry was begun in 1728 with the appearance of the first Dunciad. All these works . . . are included in this selection of his poetry." Publisher's note

Includes bibliographical references

Presley, Frances

Myne; new & selected poems and prose 1976-2005. Shearsman Books 2006 199p $20 **821**

1. Poetry -- By individual authors
ISBN 0-907562-87-6 pa

"Myne is a survey of Frances Presley's career to date, as well as a new collection of her poems. It begins with two recent cycles: the title sequence inspired by the Somerset landscape, and 'Stone Settings' which retraces the enigmatic patterns of prehistoric stones on Exmoor. Also here are the entire Somerset Letters, and Linocut, both originally published by Oasis Books, plus substantial selections from the author's first two books, The Sex of Art and Hula Hoop." Publisher's note

Raine, Kathleen, 1908-2003

The **collected** poems of Kathleen Raine. Counterpoint 2001 368p $30 **821**

1. Imagination -- Poetry 2. Poetry -- By individual authors
ISBN 1-58243-135-3; 978-1-58243-135-2

LC 00-64448

"Raine's poetry asks us to notice the divine in nature and thereby to walk a path of mindfulness. The Collected Poems draws from more than fifty years of published work, including some nineteen previously uncollected poems." (Women's Rev Books)

"Here is a signature collection of [Raine's] work that will delight many and introduce her to many others. She deserves a very wide audience, as she has much to teach us. . . . Her personal religious journey was from a strict Protestant upbringing through conversion to Roman Catholicism to Eastern Vedic belief. From first to last, her poetry is unified by a tone of transcendental belief in visions, presence, angels, and oracles rooted in her Scottish mother's experience of nature." World Lit Today

Robinson, Edwin Arlington

Poems; selected and edited by Scott Donaldson. A. A. Knopf 2007 553p (Everyman's library pocket poets) $12.50 **821**

1. Poetry -- By individual authors
ISBN 978-0-307-26576-0; 0-307-26576-5

LC 2006-48269

"Wisely concentrating on poems of short and middling length, Donaldson . . . admits extracts only from Captain Craig and the ending of Lancelot. . . . [He] gives us whole texts of 'Rembrandt to Rembrandt,' 'Isaac and Archibald,' 'Aunt Imogen,' 'John Brown,' and 'Ben Jonson Entertains a Man from Stratford'— major poems all. For texts, he draws entirely from the Collected Poems, save for 'Romance' and four poems given as they appeared in magazines." New Criterion

Ross, David A.

Critical companion to William Butler Yeats; a literary reference to his life and work. Facts On File 2008 652p il (Facts on File library of world literature) $75　　　**821**

1. Poets 2. Authors 3. Dramatists 4. Memoirists 5. Nobel laureates for literature

ISBN 978-0-8160-5895-2

LC 2008-13642

"Coverage includes: all of Yeats's . . . poems, as well as all his volumes of poetry; all his plays and important drama-related topics, including Dublin's Abbey Theatre, which he helped establish; his critical and other nonfiction writing, including his . . . autobiographies; important themes in his work; [and] friends and literary influences, including Maud Gonne and James Joyce." Publisher's note

Includes bibliographical references

Rossetti, Christina Georgina

Christina Rossetti; the complete poems. text [edited] by R.W. Crump; notes and introduction by Betty S. Flowers. Penguin 2001 lv, 1221p (Penguin Classics) pa $20　　　**821**

1. Poetry -- By individual authors

ISBN 978-0-14-042366-2; 0-14-042366-4

LC 2002-281810

This "fully annotated collection, based on the definitive texts, brings together fantasy poems such as 'Goblin Market,' terrifyingly vivid verses for children, love lyrics, sonnets, hymns, and ballads, as well as the vast body of her devotional poetry. . . . [This edition] incorporates contextual notes as well as notes on the text and language, an introduction, and a chronology of Rossetti's life and work." Publisher's note

Includes bibliographical references

Rossignol, Rosalyn

Critical companion to Chaucer; a literary reference to his life and work. Facts on File 2006 648p il $85　　　**821**

1. Poets 2. Authors

ISBN 0-8160-6193-9; 978-0-8160-6193-8

LC 2006-99

First published 1999 with title: Chaucer A to Z

This book on the works of Chaucer includes a biography of Chaucer, synopses and critical commentary on his works (including the Canterbury Tales), and lists of related people, places and topics.

Includes bibliographical references

Satyamurti, Carole

Mahabharata; a modern retelling. by Carole Satyamurti. W W Norton & Co Inc 2015 1200 p. 32 plates; color illustrations (hardcover) $39.95　　　**821**

1. Indian poetry 2. Sanskrit language 3. India -- History -- To 324 B.C. -- Poetry

ISBN 9780393081756; 0393081753

LC 2014033595

In this book, author "Carole Satyamurti's English retelling covers all eighteen books of the Mahabharata. This new version masterfully captures the beauty, excitement, and profundity of the original Sanskrit poem as well as its magnificent architecture and extraordinary scope." (Publisher's note)

"Satyamurti's exquisitely lucid and involving retelling is bookended with expert commentary by Wendy Doniger (The Hindus: An Alternative History, 2009) and translator and scholar Vinay Dharwadker." Booklist

Includes bibliographical references

Schmidt, Michael

★ Lives of the poets. Knopf 1999 975p hardcover o.p. pa $20　　　**821**

1. Poets, English -- Biography 2. Poetry -- By individual authors 3. English poetry -- History and criticism 4. American poetry -- History and criticism

ISBN 0-375-70604-6 pa

LC 98-51913

First published 1998 in the United Kingdom

In this "survey of poetry in English, Schmidt . . . enthuses about more than 250 poets whose work dates from the 14th century to 1998. More than a critical essay, this friendly and accessible history embodies the life of poetry and conveys its changeable, subjective beauty." Libr J

Includes bibliographical references

Shelley, Percy Bysshe, 1792-1822

Poems. Knopf 1993 250p (Everyman's library pocket poets) $12.50　　　**821**

1. Poetry -- By individual authors

ISBN 978-0-679-42909-8; 0-679-42909-3

LC 93-78335

"Among the English Romantics, [Shelley] has recovered his position as an undoubted major figure: the poet of volcanic hope for a better world, of fiery inspirations shot upward through bitter gloom." Oxford Companion to Engl Lit. 6th edition rev.

Shelley's poetry and prose; authoritative texts, criticism. selected and edited by Donald H. Reiman and Neil Fraistat. 2nd ed; Norton 2002 xxii, 786p il pa $18.75　　　**821**

1. Poetry -- By individual authors

ISBN 0-393-97752-8

LC 2001-30903

First published 1977

"This edition includes all of Shelley's greatest poetry and other poems frequently taught or discussed . . . as well as three of his most important prose works." Preface

Includes bibliographical references

Sisson, C. H.

Selected poems; foreword by M.L. Rosenthal. New Directions 1996 94p pa $9.95　　　**821**

1. Poetry -- By individual authors

ISBN 978-0-8112-1327-1; 0-8112-1327-7

LC 95-47599

"C.H. Sisson's Christianity is an austere, rural form that forbids pity for a newborn duckling that will obviously not survive. Yet Sisson, like Frost, sees death and old age as part of a design, not so much insidious as inexorable and thus no occasion for tears. Like Donne, whom he commemorates in 'A Letter to John Donne,' Sisson understands probably better than any contemporary poet the struggle between the call of the flesh and the love of God, and he knows, like Donne, that their reconciliation can only occur in art. . . . The poems [collected here] are sardonic, elegiac, but not despairing." World Lit Today

Smith, Stevie

Collected poems; edited with a preface by James MacGibbon. New Directions 1983 591p il pa $19.95   **821**

1. Poetry -- By individual authors
   ISBN 0-8112-0882-6

LC 83-43008

First published 1975 in the United Kingdom

Smith "wrote three novels, but has been more widely recognized for her witty, caustic, and enigmatic verse, much of it illustrated by her own comic drawings." Concise Oxford Companion to Engl Lit

Spark, Muriel, 1918-2006

All the poems of Muriel Spark. New Directions 2004 130p pa $13.95   **821**

1. Poetry -- By individual authors
   ISBN 0-8112-1576-8; 978-0-8112-1576-3

LC 2004-948

This volume collects the poems of the author of Memento Mori (1959) and The Prime of Miss Jean Brodie (1961).

"As one might expect from a novelist who has always made use of the full range of fictional genres and devices, All the Poems does not come in a straightforward, chronological package or arrangement; from the outset, the book, like so much else written by Spark, is amusingly perverse. Beginning with 'A Tour of London' (c1950-51), it then immediately skips, in terms of both time and place, to 'The Dark Music of the Rue du Cherche-Midi' (2000), comes right up to date with 'The Creative Writing Class' (2003), travels back to 'The Victoria Falls' (c1948) and 'Shipton-under-Wychwood' (c1950), before regressing finally to a series of translations from Latin (c1949). The reader is therefore encouraged to search for the persistent themes and obvious connections. There is clearly a concern and interest in certain technical forms; there is a ballad, an ode, a couple of villanelles. There's the sharp intelligence and wry wit demonstrated in poems that function mainly as conundrums, unanswered questions and, possibly, as skipping rhymes. . . . But the most memorable parts of the book are those that give some clue to Spark's lifelong determination and dedication to her craft." Guardian (UK)

Spencer, Bernard, 1909-1963

Complete poetry: translations & selected prose; edited by Peter Robinson. Bloodaxe Books 2011 351p pa $33.95   **821**

1. Poetry -- By individual authors
   ISBN 978-1-85224-891-8 pa; 1-85224-891-2 pa

Spencer "was not a natural self-promoter, publishing sparely and modestly; moreover, his semi-expatriate status and the adventurousness of his reading all but excluded him from narrower and more familiar English traditions. . . . This new edition by Peter Robinson, who has worked extensively with the Spencer archive at Reading University, is the first to appear since Roger Bowen's Collected Poems of 1981, and

aims to stir new interest in the work. As well as Spencer's two published collections, Aegean Islands and Other Poems (1946) and With Luck Lasting (1963), and the later poems collected by Bowen, Robinson includes previously uncollected and unpublished drafts, prose drawn from interviews, lectures and notes, and Spencer's pioneering translations of George Seferis, Odysseus Elytis and Eugenio Montale. Reading these alongside his own poems, it becomes clearer than ever how much Spencer drew on Greek and Latin traditions, blending them with the green-grass Englishness of Edward Thomas, and the civilised anguish of MacNeice to make what Robinson's excellent introduction calls 'a European poetry in English'." Guardian (UK)

Spenser, Edmund

★ The **faerie** queene; edited by Thomas P. Roche, Jr., with the assistance of C. Patrick O'Donnell, Jr. Penguin Books 1987 1246p (Penguin classics) pa $20   **821**

1. Poetry -- By individual authors
   ISBN 978-0-14-043307-8; 0-14-042207-2

"The greatest work of Spenser, of which the first three books were entrusted to the printer in Nov. 1589, and the second three were published in 1596." Oxford Companion to Engl Lit

Stevenson, Anne

★ **Poems,** 1955-2005. Bloodaxe Books 2005 413p $64.95; pa $29.95   **821**

1. Poetry -- By individual authors
   ISBN 1-85224-721-5; 1-85224-699-5 pa

"While Anne Stevenson is most certainly, and rightly, regarded as one of the major poets of our period, it has never been by virtue of this or that much anthologised poem, but by the work or mind as a whole. It is not so much a matter of the odd lightning-struck tree as of an entire landscape, and that landscape is always humane, intelligent and sane, composed of both natural and rational elements, and amply furnished with patches of wit and fury, which only serve to bring out the humanity." London Magazine

Swift, Daniel

Bomber County; the poetry of a lost pilot's war. Farrar, Straus and Giroux 2010 269p il $26   **821**

1. World War, 1939-1945 -- Poetry 2. Great Britain -- Royal Air Force 3. English poetry -- History and criticism 4. War poetry, English -- History and criticism 5. World War, 1939-1945 -- Literature and the war 6. English poetry -- 20th century -- History and criticism 7. World War, 1939-1945 -- Great Britain -- Literature and the war
   ISBN 0374273316; 9780374273316

LC 2010-23402

'Bomber County' narrates the story of Daniel Swift's grandfather, "a pilot with the 83rd Squadron of the Royal Air Force, who on June 12, 1943, climbed aboard a Lancaster bomber, along with six other men for a raid on Münster, Germany. His plane never returned." (N Y Times (Late N Y Ed))

"Swift has found an ingeniously oblique way to throw fresh light on history. His main achievement here is not new facts but what is done with them, in a subtle exercise in traversing genres." Times Lit Suppl

Includes bibliographical references

Tennyson, Alfred Tennyson

Poems. A. A. Knopf 2004 255p (Everyman's library pocket poets) $12.50 **821**

1. Poetry -- By individual authors

ISBN 978-1-4000-4187-9; 1-4000-4187-2

LC 2003-49505

"This collection includes such famous poems as 'The Lady of Shalott' and 'The Charge of the Light Brigade.' There are extracts from all the major masterpieces—Idylls of the King, The Princess, In Memoriam—and several complete long poems, such as 'Ulysses' and 'Demeter and Persephone,' that demonstrate his narrative grace. Finally, there are many of the short lyrical poems, such as 'Come into the Garden, Maud' and 'Break, Break, Break,' for which he is justly celebrated." Publisher's note

Thomas, Dylan

The **poems** of Dylan Thomas; edited with an introduction and notes by Daniel Jones; with a preface by Dylan Thomas. rev ed; New Directions 2003 xxix, 320p il $34.95 **821**

1. Poetry -- By individual authors

ISBN 978-0-8112-1541-1; 0-8112-1541-5

LC 2002-155790

First published 1971

"To the 90 poems Thomas published in Collected Poems, 1934-1952 Jones has added 102 and placed the total, as far as he could determine, in the chronological order of their composition. Some of the poems were still in manuscript form when Thomas died; others had been published in periodicals and anthologies. In an appendix, Jones offers Thomas' early poems—including one written when the poet was 12." Libr J [review of 1971 edition]

Includes bibliographical references

Tomlinson, Charles

Selected poems; 1955-1997. New Directions 1997 226p pa $13.95 **821**

1. Poetry -- By individual authors

ISBN 978-0-8112-1369-1; 0-8112-1369-2

LC 97-25373

"These poems are a fine achievement; they are the work of a consciousness mostly at ease with its dwelling in this world, and unabashed by a lack of inclination to dwell unduly on shadows rather than light. The sunniness of disposition, both geographically and psychologically, combined with Tomlinson's canny ability to metrically heighten what still sounds to the ear like the language of common day, give a tone that might be rationally described as Tomlinsonian. This . . . [is] a book essential to any collection of the best poetry of the postwar years." Am Book Rev

Skywriting and other poems. Ivan R. Dee 2003 96p $18.95 **821**

1. Poetry -- By individual authors

ISBN 978-1-566-63541-7; 1-556-63541-1

LC 2003-55504

"Mr Tomlinson is an eloquent poet of place—in this collection he moves through Mexico, Italy, Japan, and his home county of Gloucestershire—whose work combines visual exactitude with an uncommon gracefulness of expression." Economist

Turnbull, Gael

★ **There** are words; collected poems. Shearsman Books 2006 495p pa $30 **821**

1. Poetry -- By individual authors

ISBN 0-90756-289-2

"Restlessly experimental—but never for its own sake—Turnbull was constantly doing what Ezra Pound asked of poets at the beginning of the twentieth century, namely to make it new. His range is very wide. He employed the long line before C.K. Williams or Ciaran Carson; he experimented with prose-poems, found-poems; he wrote ballads, poems meant to be read out loud, poems that deftly rhyme and ones that deftly don't; he shaped poems on the page with varying line-lengths and indentings; he used the spaces between lines and verses functionally; the touch is sometimes light, sometimes profoundly earnest. . . . In the almost 500pp of this superb Collected Poems there isn't one dud piece, one poem that doesn't have genuine poetic power and resonance." Stride (UK)

West, Richard

Chaucer, 1340-1400; the life and times of the first English poet. Carroll & Graf Pubs. 2000 302p il map hardcover o.p. pa $14 **821**

1. Poets 2. Authors 3. Great Britain -- History -- 1154-1399, Plantagenets

ISBN 0-7867-0925-1 pa

LC 00-712752

West's biography "combines history and literary criticism. He places Chaucer within his historical context and examines his life and writings." Libr J

Wordsworth, William

★ **Selected** poetry of William Wordsworth; edited by Mark Van Doren; introduction by David Bromwich. Modern Lib. 2001 xxii, 687p $24.95; pa $11.95 **821**

1. Poetry -- By individual authors

ISBN 0-679-64224-2; 0-375-75941-7 pa

LC 00-66444

This collection "represents Wordsworth's prolific output, from the poems first published in Lyrical Ballads in 1798 . . . to the late 'Yarrow Revisited.' Wordsworth's poetry is celebrated for its deep feeling, its use of ordinary speech, the love of nature it expresses, and its representation of commonplace things and events." Publisher's note

Yeats, W. B.

The **collected** poems of W.B. Yeats; edited by Richard J. Finneran. Rev. 2nd ed.; Scribner Paperback Poetry 1996 xxv, 544p pa $20 **821**

1. Poetry -- By individual authors

ISBN 978-0-684-80731-7; 0-684-80731-9

LC 96-23314

First published 1989 by Collier Books

This volume "includes all of the poems authorized by Yeats for inclusion in his standard canon. . . . Revised and corrected, this edition includes Yeats's own notes on his poetry, complemented by explanatory notes from . . .Yeats scholar Richard J. Finneran." Publisher's note

822 English drama

Bennett, Alan

The **history** boys. Faber and Faber 2006 xxvii, 109p pa $13 **822**
1. England -- Drama. 2. Education -- Drama. 3. Boarding schools -- Drama. 4. Teacher-student relationships -- Drama.
ISBN 978-0-571-22464-7; 0-571-22464-4
LC 2005-936593
First published 2004 in the United Kingdom
Characters: 11 men, 1 woman extras. First produced at the Lyttleton Theatre, London, May 18, 2004
"Nothing could diminish the incendiary achievement of this subtle, deep-wrought and immensely funny play about the value and meaning of education. . . . In short, a superb, life-enhancing play." Guardian

Bolt, Robert

A **man** for all seasons; a play in two acts. Random House 1962 xxv, 163p il hardcover o.p. pa $9.50 **822**
1. Saints 2. Authors 3. Statesmen 4. Writers on law 5. Writers on religion 6. Great Britain -- History -- 1485-1603, Tudors -- Drama
ISBN 0-679-72822-8 pa
Characters: 11 men, 2 women. First produced in the United States at the ANTA Theatre, New York City, November 22, 1961

Christie, Agatha

The **mousetrap** and other plays. New American Library 2000 742p hardcover o.p. pa $7.99 **822**
1. English drama -- Collections
ISBN 0-451-20118-3; 0-451-20114-0 pa
LC 00-64727
First published 1978 by Dodd, Mead
"The noted mystery writer composed adaptations of seven novels and stories into arresting plays as well as creating one original theater piece ('Verdict'). . . . All are as delightful to read for pleasure as Christie's mystery novels, especially since some that earlier appeared in the latter form have been intriguingly altered." Booklist

Churchill, Caryl

Mad forest; a play from Romania. Theatre Communications Group 1996 87p pa $13.95 **822**
ISBN 1-55936-114-X; 978-1-55936-114-9
LC 96-12875
First published 1991 in the United Kingdom
Large mixed cast. 3 acts. First performed at the New York Theater Workshop, New York, December 4, 1991
This play "explores the reactions of two ordinary families to the confused events of the Romanian revolution: the dreadful damage done to people's lives by years of repression, and the painful difficulties of sudden but lasting change." Publisher's note

Coward, Noel

Three plays; Blithe spirit, Hay fever, Private lives. introduction by Philip Hoare. Vintage Bks. 1999 254p $13 **822**
ISBN 0-679-78179-X
LC 98-47414
First published 1965 by Dell

Dryden, John

★ **All** for love; edited by David M. Vieth. University of Neb. Press 1972 xxxiv, 146p (Regents Restoration drama series) hardcover o.p. pa $24.95 **822**
1. Queens
ISBN 0-8032-5379-6 pa
An English Restoration tragedy which is an adaptation of Shakespeare's "Antony and Cleopatra" done in blank verse

Everyman, and medieval miracle plays; edited by A. C. Cawley; with a new preface and bibliography by Anne Rooney. Tuttle 1993 256p hardcover o.p. pa $6.95 **822**
1. Mysteries and miracle plays
ISBN 0-460-87280-X pa
First Everyman's library edition published 1909 with title: Everyman, with other interludes including eight miracle plays
In addition to Everyman, this collection includes plays from the Towneley, Coventry, York and Chester cycles.
Includes bibliographical references

Fugard, Athol

Blood knot and other plays. Theatre Communications Group 1991 202p hardcover o.p. pa $15 **822**
ISBN 978-1-55936-019-7; 1-55936-019-4
LC 90-29029
"The brothers of Blood Knot—one dark-skinned, one light—betray their dream of a better future with the impossible wish of passing for white. In Hello and Goodbye, a poor white brother and sister churn through their once-promising past to comprehend their bleak present. Boesman and Lena, black husband and wife, tramp homelessly through a severe and unforgiving landscape, discovering strength and delivering devotion through an encounter with a mysterious old African." Publisher's note

★ **Master** Harold-- and the boys. Vintage Books 2009 60p pa $12.95 **822**
1. South Africa -- Race relations -- Drama
ISBN 978-0-307-47520-6; 0-307-47520-4
LC 2010-292381
First published 1982 by Random House
Characters: 3 men. 1 act. First produced at the Yale Repertory theatre, New Haven, Connecticut, 1982.

Gay, John

The **beggar's** opera; edited by Edgar V. Roberts; music edited by Edward Smith. University of Neb.

Press 1969 xxix, 238p music (Regents Restoration drama series) hardcover o.p. pa $21.95 **822**
ISBN 978-0-8032-5361-2 pa; 0-8032-5361-3 pa
First published 1728
A ballad opera, this is a rogues' comedy satirizing corrupt politics in 18th century England

Heaney, Seamus
The **burial** at Thebes; a version of Sophocles' Antigone. Farrar, Straus and Giroux 2004 79p $18 **822**
ISBN 0-374-11721-7

LC 2004-43986
"There are many translations of Sophocles' Antigone but few with the understated power and spare beauty of . . . Heaney's version. . . . Written in a muscular but lively style, the translation, like Heaney's best poetry, finds music in the language of the streets and reveals the raw, primal power in the most carefully constructed rhetorical tropes." Booklist

Jonson, Ben
Volpone and other plays; edited by Michael Jamieson. Penguin 2004 496p (Penguin classics) pa $12 **822**
ISBN 978-0-14-144118-4; 0-14-144118-6

LC 2004-275516
First published 1966 in the United Kingdom with title: Three comedies
"Ben Jonson created in Volpone and The Alchemist hilarious portraits of cupidity and chicanery, while in Bartholomew Fair he portrays his fellow Londoners at their most festive—and most bawdy." Publisher's note

Marlowe, Christopher, 1564-1593
The **complete** plays; edited by Frank Romany and Robert Lindsey. Penguin Books 2003 xliv, 702p (Penguin classics) pa $15 **822**
ISBN 978-0-14-043633-4; 0-14-043633-2

LC 2004-268858
Includes bibliographical references

Osborne, John
Look back in anger. Penguin 1982 96p (Penguin Plays) pa $12 **822**
ISBN 0-14-048-175-3; 978-0-14-048-175-4

LC 82-9144
First published 1957 by Criterion Books
Characters: 3 men, 2 women. First produced at the Royal Court Theatre, London, May 8, 1956
This play "introduced a new strain of realism to British theatre and set the tone for the generation of anti-Establishment writers who became known as the Angry Young Men. Osborne described his own parents as 'impoverished middle class,' but his play deals with the frustrations, crude language, and squalid conditions of working-class life." Reader's Ency. 4th edition

Peters, Sally
Bernard Shaw; the ascent of the superman. Yale Univ. Press 1996 328p il hardcover o.p. pa $22 **822**
1. Authors 2. Novelists 3. Dramatists 4. Dramatists,

English 5. Essayists 6. Nonfiction writers 7. Nobel laureates for literature
ISBN 0-300-06097-1; 0-300-07500-6 pa

LC 95-37248
An "exploration of the ambiguities and passions that formed this great playwright and thinker. Shaw's sexuality, always a good topic of speculation, is studied here, but one wishes for more insights and in-depth analysis. Peters does devote a chapter to Shaw's close relationship with the actor and playwright Harley Granville Barker, mainly from Shaw's point of view. One may not agree with Peter's conclusions, but they will prove to be of interest to anyone studying Shaw." Libr J
Includes bibliographical references

Pinter, Harold
Complete works; with an introduction, Writing for the theatre. Grove Weidenfeld 1990 4v v1 pa $14.50; v2 pa $13.50; v3 pa $14; v4 pa $13.50 **822**
ISBN 0-8021-5096-9 v1; 0-8021-3237-5 v2; 0-8021-5049-7 v3; 0-8021-5050-0 v4

LC 90-13933
First Grove Press edition published 1977-1981

Shaffer, Peter
★ **Equus**. Scribner 2005 112p pa $12 **822**
ISBN 0-7432-8730-4; 978-0-7432-8730-2

LC 2005-51600
First published 1973 in the United Kingdom
Characters: 5 men, 4 women. 1 act, 35 scenes. First produced by the National Theater, London, July 26, 1973
Drama about "a jolting confrontation between a psychiatrist and a 17-year-old boy who has blinded six horses from the stable where he is employed. As the probe into the boy's attitudes and behavior deepens, this criminal act is revealed to have been a result of his notions of a sexual/religious spirit in horses." Booklist

★ **Peter** Shaffer's Amadeus; with an introduction by the director Sir Peter Hall and a wholly new preface by the author. Perennial Bks. 2001 xxxiv, 124p pa $15 **822**
1. Composers
ISBN 0-06-093549-9

LC 2001-278382
First published 1980 in the United Kingdom
Characters: 9 men, 1 woman, extras. 2 acts. First produced at the National Theater of Great Britain, November 1979

Shaw, Bernard, 1856-1950
Arms and the man; a pleasant play. [by] Bernard Shaw; introduction by Rodelle Weintraub; definitive text under the editorial supervision of Dan H. Laurence. Penguin Books 2006 xxvi 73 (Penguin classics) pa $9 **822**
ISBN 978-0-14-303976-1; 0-14-303976-8

LC 2005-56724

First produced 1894. Comedy set in Bulgaria satirizing romantic attitudes about war.

Heartbreak House; a fantasia in the Russian manner on English themes. definitive text under the editorial supervision of Dan H. Laurence; with an introduction by David Hare. Penguin Books 2000 160p il (Penguin Classics) pa $10   **822**

ISBN 978-0-14-043787-4; 0-14-043787-8

LC 2001-266517

Written in 1913, first produced 1920

"A complex allegorical work in which Shaw indicts apathy, confusion, and lack of purpose as the causes of the world's problems. The characters—all larger than life and with symbolic names—are gathered at the home of an eccentric sea captain; they each represent an evil in the modern world. Into their midst comes young Ellie Dunn, whose search for a husband Shaw treats as a new generation searching for a way of life." Benet's Reader's Ency. 4th edition

Includes bibliographical references

Major Barbara; definitive text under the editorial supervision of Dan H. Laurence; with an introduction by Margery Morgan. Penguin Books 2000 156p (Penguin classics) pa $11   **822**

1. Crime 2. Salvation Army 3. Father-daughter relationship

ISBN 978-0-14-043790-4; 0-14-043790-8

LC 2002-275028

In this "comedy, originally staged in 1905, Andrew Undershaft, a millionaire armaments dealer, loves money and despises poverty. His energetic daughter Barbara, however, is a devout major in the Salvation Army. She sees her father as just another soul to be saved. But when the Salvation Army needs funds to keep going, it is Undershaft who saves the day." Publisher's note

Man and Superman; a comedy and a philosophy. definitive text under the editorial supervision of Dan H. Laurence; introduced by Stanley Weintraub. Penguin 2000 264p (Penguin classics) pa $11   **822**

ISBN 978-0-14-043788-1; 0-14-043788-6

"In Man and Superman, Shaw combined seriousness with comedy to create a satirical and buoyant exposé of the eternal struggle between the sexes. . . . This volume includes Shaw's Preface of 1903 and his appendix, 'The Revolutionist's Handbook', the cast list from the first production of Man and Superman and a list of his principal works." Publisher's note

★ **Pygmalion** . . . and My fair lady; [Pygmalion] by George Bernard Shaw; and My fair lady/based on Shaw's Pygmalion; adaptation and lyrics by Alan Jay Lerner; music by Frederick Loewe. 50th anniversary ed.; Signet Classic 2006 219p pa $5.95   **822**

ISBN 0-451-53009-8

My fair lady was awarded the New York Drama Critics Circle Award for 1956

This volume includes the complete texts of Shaw's Pygmalion and Lerner's musical adaptation My fair lady.

Saint Joan; a chronicle play in six scenes and an epilogue. definitive text under the editorial supervision of Dan H. Laurence; with 'On playing Joan' by Imogen Stubbs; and an introduction by Joley Wood. Penguin 2003 xx, 168p (Penguin classics) pa $12   **822**

1. Saints

ISBN 978-0-14-043791-6; 0-14-04379-1

First produced 1923

Chronicle play in "which Joan of Arc, the young girl who led France to victory over the English, emerges as an unlettered country girl gifted with masterful will and innate intelligence." McGraw-Hill Ency World Drama

Sheridan, Richard Brinsley

The **school** for scandal and other plays; edited with an introduction by Eric S. Rump. New ed; Penguin 2004 288p (Penguin classics) pa $12   **822**

1. Great Britain -- Social life and customs

ISBN 978-0-14-043240-4

First published 1988

"In The Rivals, Captain Absolute becomes his own rival for the hand of Lydia Languish wooing her under another name, while her aunt, the verbally inept Mrs Malaprop, wishes her to marry the real Captain. The Critic, featuring the pompous Puff and the arrogant Sneer, is a mocking depiction of the theatre, playwrights and, of course, critics. And The School for Scandal continues the theme of imposture when Sir Oliver Surface tests his nephews by appearing before them in disguise, and learns that reputation and the approval of society are of little value. In his introduction, Eric S. Rump places the plays in their historical and dramatic context and examines their enduring popularity." Publisher's note

Stoppard, Tom

Arcadia. Faber & Faber 1993 97p hardcover o.p. pa $14   **822**

ISBN 0-571-16934-1 pa

LC 94-103754

Characters: 8 men, 3 women. 2 acts, 7 scenes. First produced at the Royal National Theatre, London, 1993. In the U.S., first produced at the Lincoln Center Theater, New York City, March 30, 1995

The **invention** of love. Grove Press 1998 102p pa $12   **822**

1. Poets 2. Authors

ISBN 0-8021-3581-1

LC 98-28331

Characters: 19 men, 1 woman, extras. 2 acts. First performed at the American Conservatory Theater, San Francisco, January 14, 2000

★ **Rosencrantz** and Guildenstern are dead. Grove Press 1967 126p hardcover o.p. pa $12 **822**

1. Poets 2. Authors 3. Dramatists

ISBN 0-8021-3275-8 pa

Characters: 13 men, 2 women, extras. First produced in this form April 11, 1967 in London

This play "took the theatre world on both sides of the Atlantic by storm. The originality of the idea which put Hamlet's two insignificant friends centerstage was matched by the brilliance of the dialogue between these bewildered nonentities." Reader's Ency. 4th edition

Travesties. Grove Press 1975 99p pa $13 **822**
ISBN 0-8021-5089-6

Characters: 5 men, 2 women. Prologue, 2 acts. First produced at the Aldwych Theatre, London, June 10, 1974

Synge, J. M.
The **complete** plays. Vintage Bks. 1960 268p pa $10 **822**
ISBN 0-394-70178-X

Thomas, Dylan
Under milk wood; a play for voices. New Directions 1954 107p music pa $8.95 **822**
ISBN 0-8112-0209-7

"A radio play for voices. Written in poetic, inventive prose, this play is full of humor, a joyful sense of the goodness of life and love, and a strong Welsh flavor. It is an impression of a spring day in the lives of the people of Llareggub, a Welsh village situated under Milk Wood. It has no plot, but a wealth of characters who dream aloud, converse with one another, and speak in choruses of alternating voices." Reader's Ency. 4th edition

Wilde, Oscar
★ The **importance** of being earnest and other plays; introduction by Terrence McNally; notes by Michael F. Davis. Modern Library 2003 257p pa $9.95 **822**
ISBN 0-8129-6714-3

LC 2003-44566

The title play, written in 1895, is a drawing room comedy exposing quirks and foibles of Victorian society with plot revolving around amorous pursuits of two men who face social obstacles when they woo young ladies of quality. The book also features Lady Windermere's fan (1893), a four act comedy about a woman who has an affair when she suspects her husband of adultery, and An ideal husband (1895), a comedy about a blackmail scheme involving a lord's investment in the Suez Canal days before the British government's purchase of it, and his wife's reaction to her husband's past misdeeds.

822.3 Drama of Elizabethan period, 1558-1625

Baker, William
The **facts** on file companion to Shakespeare; William Baker and Kenneth Womack. Facts On File 2011 5 v. (acid-free paper) $375.00 **822.3**
1. English drama -- History and criticism
ISBN 0816078203; 9780816078202

LC 2010054012

This book focuses on the author William Shakespeare. "Volume 1 is made up of background essays and more on Shakespeare's times and texts. Poems and sonnets are covered in volume 2, offering for each analysis and a bibliography. In volumes 3, 4, and 5, plays are covered in a 'complete works' fashion designed for use as a textbook. . . . These are followed by an overview essay and excerpts from 'classic criticism.'"(Booklist)

Includes bibliographical references and index

Bate, Jonathan
Soul of the age; a biography of the mind of William Shakespeare. Random House 2009 471p il map $35 **822.3**
1. Poets 2. Authors 3. Dramatists
ISBN 978-1-4000-6206-5

LC 2008-16561

In this biography of Shakespeare, the author uses "the Bard's own 'Seven Ages of Man' speech from As You Like It to envision him as an infant, a school boy, a lover, a soldier, a justice, a pantaloon, and an old man entering 'oblivion.' The result is a fresh new way to look at Shakespeare and a welcome reminder of what literary biography can still do." Libr J

Includes bibliographical references

Bloom, Harold
Hamlet: poem unlimited. Riverhead Bks. 2003 154p hardcover o.p. pa $13 **822.3**
1. Poets 2. Authors 3. Dramatists
ISBN 1-57322-233-X; 1-57322-377-8 pa

LC 2002-31691

"Far superior to existing theories of performance and worth yards of criticism for each well-wrought page." Libr J

Shakespeare: the invention of the human. Riverhead Bks. 1998 xx, 745p hardcover o.p. pa $18 **822.3**
1. Poets 2. Authors 3. Dramatists
ISBN 1-57322-751-X pa

LC 98-21325

"The passion and obsessiveness of Bloom's approach are its greatest recommendation." N Y Rev Books

Boyce, Charles
Critical companion to William Shakespeare; a literary reference to his life and work. Rev. ed; Facts on File 2005 2v il (Facts on File library of world literature) set $104.50 **822.3**
1. Poets 2. Authors 3. Dramatists
ISBN 0-8160-5373-1

LC 2004-25769

First published 1990 with title: Shakespeare A to Z

"The first two-thirds [of this set] covers the plays. Arranged alphabetically by title, the 3000 entries generally consist of a scene-by-scene summary, a commentary, sources, theatrical history, and character sketches. The last one-third features entries for actors, composers, musicians, places that figured in the plays, and miscellaneous items." Libr J

Includes bibliographical references

Bryson, Bill, 1951-

Shakespeare; the world as stage. Atlas Books/
HarperCollins   2007   199p   (Eminent lives)
$19.95   **822.3**
1. Poets 2. Authors 3. Dramatists
ISBN 978-0-06-074022-1; 0-06-074022-1
LC 2007-21647

In this biography, the author marshals "the usual little
facts that others might overlook—for example, that in
Shakespeare's day perhaps 40% of women were pregnant
when they got married—to paint a portrait of the world in
which the Bard lived and prospered. . . . Bryson is a pleasant
and funny guide to a subject at once overexposed and elusive—as Bryson puts it, he is a kind of literary equivalent of
an electron—forever there and not there." Publ Wkly

Includes bibliographical references

Butler, Colin

The **practical** Shakespeare; the plays in practice
and on the page. Ohio University Press 2005 205p
$39.95; pa $19.95   **822.3**
1. Poets 2. Authors 3. Dramatists
ISBN 0-8214-1621-9; 0-8214-1622-7 pa
LC 2004-30580

"Notes on staging, acting behaviors, scenes not shown,
entrances, exits, characterizations, prologues, choruses, and
staging are each featured in the text. References to specific
scenes in the plays are used to illustrate and support the material. Any group preparing a production of one of the plays
should find this a useful reference." Univ Press Books for
Public and Second Sch Libr, 2006

Includes bibliographical references

Collins, Paul

★ The **book** of William; how Shakespeare's
first folio conquered the world. Bloomsbury 2009
246p $25   **822.3**
1. Poets 2. Authors 3. Dramatists 4. Rare books
ISBN 978-1-59691-195-6; 1-59691-195-6
LC 2009-6722

"Witty, detailed, and highly entertaining, . . . [this book]
will be appreciated by fans of Shakespeare, history, or human folly." Libr J

Includes bibliographical references

Falk, Dan

The **Science** of Shakespeare; a New Look at the
Playwright's Universe. Dan Falk. Thomas Dunne
Books/St. Martin's Press 2014 384 p. illustrations
(hardback) $27.99   **822.3**
1. Science -- History 2. Literature and science 3.
Literature and science -- England -- History -- 17th
century
ISBN 1250008778; 9781250008770
LC 2013046842

This book by Dan Falk "explores the connections between the famous playwright and the beginnings of the
Scientific Revolution---and how, together, they changed the
world forever. We meet a colorful cast of Renaissance thinkers, including Thomas Digges, who . . . lived in the same
neighborhood as Shakespeare; Thomas Harriot--'England's
Galileo--who aimed a telescope at the night sky months

ahead of his Italian counterpart; and Danish astronomer Tycho Brahe." (Publisher's note)

"This eminently readable book should prove fascinating
to both lovers of science and bardolators." LJ

Includes bibliographical references and index

Frye, Northrop

Northrop Frye on Shakespeare; edited by Robert
Sandler. Yale Univ. Press 1986 186p hardcover o.p.
pa $17   **822.3**
1. Poets 2. Authors 3. Dramatists
ISBN 0-300-04208-6 pa
LC 86-50485

Shakespeare scholar Frye provides in-depth analyses of
ten plays.

"Frye's work is completely accessible, its style crisp and
engaging. Most of all, it is full of basic 'good sense' about
our most abused literary figure." Libr J

Garber, Marjorie

Shakespeare after all. Pantheon Books 2004
989p hardcover o.p. pa $20   **822.3**
1. Poets 2. Authors 3. Dramatists
ISBN 0-375-42190-4; 0-385-72214-1 pa
LC 2004-40063

The author "provides a handbook on Shakespeare's
plays. After an introduction supplying standard overviews
of the Renaissance theater and Shakespeare's life, she offers
a critical essay on each play, complete with bibliographies
and filmographies. The strength of this work is that Garber
shows how the plays are interrelated by recurring language,
characters, and themes, how each era has interpreted Shakespeare for itself, and how Shakespeare continues to shape
today's culture." Libr J

Includes bibliographical references

Shakespeare and modern culture. Pantheon
Books 2008 326p il $30   **822.3**
1. Poets 2. Authors 3. Dramatists
ISBN 978-0-307-37767-8; 0-307-37767-9
LC 2008-26802

"Writing on ten plays, [Garber] offers examples of their
'uncanny' anticipation of present-day phenomena and our
own appropriations of them, as in the now fashionable use of
'Henry V' as a blueprint for success in business. (She quotes
one manual that calls Bardolph's hanging the 'ultimate
pink slip.') Garber's approach is eclectic, spanning Freud
and evolutionary biology; occasionally, she gets caught
up in secondary concerns, but she is an inspiring reader."
New Yorker

Includes bibliographical references

Greenblatt, Stephen J.

Will in the world; how Shakespeare became
Shakespeare. [by] Stephen Greenblatt. Norton 2004
430p il $26.95   **822.3**
1. Poets 2. Authors 3. Dramatists
ISBN 0-393-05057-2
LC 2004-11512

"Greenblatt is at his best when he merges his gifts as a
literary critic and scholar with his instincts as a biographer.
He writes with real subtlety and skill about the sonnets. . . .

He also writes very well about the climate of fear and the use of public punishment and torture in Elizabethan and early Jacobean England, and how this enters into the very spirit of Shakespeare's work." N Y Times Book Rev

Includes bibliographical references

★ The **Greenwood** companion to Shakespeare; a comprehensive guide to students. edited by Joseph Rosenblum. Greenwood Press 2005 4v set $299.95 **822.3**

1. Poets 2. Authors 3. Dramatists
ISBN 0-313-32779-3

LC 2004-28690

"Each of the set's four volumes relates to a specific genre—Overviews and the History Plays (Vol. 1), The Comedies (Vol. 2), The Tragedies (Vol. 3), and The Romances and Poetry (Vol. 4)—and is organized in 'Cliff Notes' fashion, devoting each entry to a single play, long poem, sonnet, or sonnet pair. . . . A great introduction to the Bard." Libr J

Includes bibliographical references

Heylin, Clinton

So long as men can breathe; the untold story of Shakespeare's Sonnets. Da Capo Press 2009 280p $24 **822.3**

1. Poets 2. Authors 3. Dramatists
ISBN 978-0-306-81805-9; 0-306-81805-1

LC 2009-08999

An account of the publication of Shakespeare's Sonnets. The author "introduces us to the 'unholy alliance' involved in this precarious enterprise: Thomas Thorpe, the publisher, a self-described 'well wishing adventurer;' George Eld, the printer, heavily embroiled in large-scale pirating; William Aspley, the prestigious bookseller, who mysteriously ended his association with Thorpe soon after. Leaving the calamitous world of Elizabethan publishing, Heylin goes on to chart the many editions of the Sonnets through the years and the editorial decisions that led to their present configuration." Publisher's note

Includes bibliographical references

Kenji Yoshino

A **thousand** times more fair; what Shakespeare can teach us about justice. Ecco 2011 305p $26.99; ebook $12.99 **822.3**

1. Poets 2. Authors 3. Dramatists 4. Law in literature
ISBN 0-06-176910-X; 0-06-208772-X ebook; 978-0-06-176910-8; 978-0-06-208772-0 ebook

Looks at the roles of justice and law in the lives of modern-day people through the lens of Shakespeare's plays.

"Readers will find Yoshino provocative, often controversial, and Shakespeare, as always, entertaining." Publ Wkly

Includes bibliographical references

Kermode, Frank

Shakespeare's language. Farrar, Straus & Giroux 2000 324p hardcover o.p. pa $15 **822.3**

1. Poets 2. Authors 3. Dramatists
ISBN 0-374-52774-1 pa

LC 99-55846

Kermode "devotes particular attention to the four great tragedies written at the height of Shakespeare's powers:

Hamlet, Othello, King Lear and Macbeth. While Kermode's concern is with the Bard's verse, he betrays no simplistic notions about literary language operating in a vacuum. A careful, close analysis of passages in each play is informed by a breathtaking knowledge of Elizabethan history and culture, as well as by the entire history of Shakespeare criticism from Coleridge to Eliot and the new historicists." Publ Wkly

Includes bibliographical references

Lamb, Charles

Tales from Shakespeare; by Charles & Mary Lamb; with an introduction by Marina Warner. Penguin Books 2007 304p (Penguin classics) pa $12 **822.3**

1. Poets 2. Authors 3. Dramatists
ISBN 978-0-14-144162-7; 0-14-144162-3
First published 1807

A now classic collection of twenty plays by Shakespeare adapted as prose stories—the comedies by Mary Lamb, the tragedies by Charles Lamb

"The Tales were the first version of 'Shakespeare' to be published specifically for children. They are written in a clear, vigorous style, not often encumbered by the attempt to make the language resemble that of the original. A lot is left out. . . . But the literary quality of the Tales makes them outshine almost every other English children's book of this period, and they proved an immediate and lasting success." Oxford Companion to Child Lit

★ **Living** with Shakespeare; essays by writers, actors, and directors. Edited by Susannah Carson; Foreword by Harold Bloom. Vintage Books, A Division of Random House, Inc. 2013 xxviii, 500 p.p ill. (paperback) $16 **822.3**
ISBN 0307742911; 9780307742919

LC 2012039745

This book, edited by Susanna Carson, presents collected essays reflecting on the works and influence of playwright William Shakespeare. "Carson invites forty actors, directors, scholars, and writers to reflect on why his work is still such a vital part of our culture. We hear from James Earl Jones on reclaiming Othello as a tragic hero, Julie Taymor on turning Prospero into Prospera, Camille Paglia on teaching the plays to actors, . . . [and] Germaine Greer on the playwright's home life." (Publisher's note)

"Editor Carson's eclecticism aims to break down the usual disciplinary borders and reduce the intimidating distance that often yawns between Shakespeare experts and general readers... The essays include much justified reverence, but also some healthy questioning, as well as limited forays into cross-cultural dialogues... [A] consistently stimulating read..." Pub Wkly.

Norwich, John Julius

Shakespeare's kings; the great plays and the history of England in the Middle Ages, 1337-1485. Scribner 2000 401p il hardcover o.p. pa $16 **822.3**

1. Poets 2. Authors 3. Dramatists
ISBN 0-7432-0031-4 pa

LC 99-58271

The author offers "overviews of Edward III; Richard II; Henry IV, parts 1 and 2; Henry V; Henry VI, parts 1, 2, and

3; and Richard III, examining each play through the lens of history. In addition to providing the necessary historical commentary, he also fills in the gaps between the plays, enabling readers to thoroughly comprehend the entire series in the proper historical context." Booklist

Nuttall, A. D.

Shakespeare the thinker. Yale University Press 2007 428p $30   **822.3**
  1. England -- Intellectual life -- 16th century 2. England -- Intellectual life -- 17th century
  ISBN 978-0-300-11928-2; 0-300-11928-3
                                              LC 2006-35179
The author "traces ideas about motivation, identity, speech, and symbol in Shakespeare's plays. His study is rich in unexpected juxtapositions: Hippolyta, of 'A Midsummer Night's Dream,' finds herself in casual conversation with David Hume, and Titus Andronicus is seen in the context of 'Goodfellas.' The analysis never pulls too far away from the action onstage; indeed, Nuttall painstakingly shows Shakespeare's skill at negotiating abstract ideas through suspense, conflict, and character." New Yorker
  Includes bibliographical references

★ The **Oxford** companion to Shakespeare; general editor, Michael Dobson; associate general editor, Stanley Wells. Oxford Univ. Press 2001 xxix, 541p il maps hardcover o.p. pa $39.95   **822.3**
  1. Poets 2. Authors 3. Dramatists 4. Reference books
  ISBN 0-19-280614-9 pa; 0-19-811735-3
                                              LC 2001-277478
This volume "illuminates not only Shakespeare's life and works but also the many forms that interpretation of Shakespeare has taken in the centuries since his death." Booklist
  Includes bibliographical references

Rasmussen, Eric

The **Shakespeare** thefts; in search of the first folios. Palgrave Macmillan 2011 212p il   **822.3**
  1. Poets 2. Theft 3. Authors 4. Dramatists 5. Rare books 6. Book collecting
  ISBN 9780230109414; 9780230341203 ebook
                                              LC 2011028287
This book discusses "the known surviving copies of the 1623 First Folio, which published 36 of [William] Shakespeare's plays. Of the 232 recorded surviving copies, the majority are in public institutions rather than private hands. [Eric] Rasmussen . . . and his team of researchers were part of the global quest to catalog every extant copy." (Library Journal)
  "Part literary history and part detective story, this is an engaging book about the known surviving copies of the 1623 First Folio, which published 36 of Shakespeare's plays. Of the 232 recorded surviving copies, the majority are in public institutions rather than private hands. Rasmussen . . . and his team of researchers were part of the global quest to catalog every extant copy. Rasmussen uses a lively, nonacademic style and engrossing anecdotes to tell us about one of history's most fascinating books." Libr J
  Includes bibliographical references

Rosenbaum, Ron

The **Shakespeare** wars; clashing scholars, public fiascoes, palace coups. Random House 2006 601p $35   **822.3**
  1. Poets 2. Authors 3. Dramatists
  ISBN 0-375-50339-0; 978-0-375-50339-9
                                              LC 2006-42541
The author "conveys the impassioned arguments of leading directors and scholars concerning how Shakespeare should be printed and performed. . . . Balancing academic reportage with his own lively observations, Rosenbaum wrestles with the weightiest issues of Shakespeare studies in a down-to-earth manner that readers will applaud." Publ Wkly
  Includes bibliographical references

Shakespeare, William, 1564-1616

★ The **complete** works; general editors, Stanley Wells and Gary Taylor; editors, Stanley Wells . . . . [et al.]; with introductions by Stanley Wells. 2nd ed.; Clarendon Press; Oxford University Press 2005 lxxv, 1344p il $40   **822.3**
  ISBN 0-19-926717-0
                                              LC 2005-47272
  First published 1986
This anthology "features a brief introduction to each work as well as [a] General Introduction. . . . [The volume includes] essay on language, a list of contemporary allusions to Shakespeare, an index of Shakespearean characters, a glossary, a consolidated bibliography, and an index of first lines of the Sonnets." Publisher's note

Shapiro, James

Contested Will; who wrote Shakespeare? James Shapiro. Simon & Schuster 2010 339 p. $26 **822.3**
  1. Poets 2. Authors 3. Dramatists
  ISBN 978-1-4165-4162-2; 1-4165-4162-4;
  1416541624; 9781416541622
                                              LC 2009032710
"A thorough, engaging work whose arguments would prove more persuasive were we not living in an era of such fierce anti-intellectualism and pervasive conspiracy theory." Kirkus
  Includes bibliographical references and index

A **year** in the life of William Shakespeare, 1599. HarperCollins Publishers 2005 394p il map $27.95   **822.3**
  1. Poets 2. Authors 3. Dramatists 4. Biography, Individual
  ISBN 0-571-21448-0
                                              LC 2005-43342
Shapiro discusses the year 1599 in the life of William Shakespeare, the year when he wrote Henry the Fifth, Julius Caesar, As You Like It, and Hamlet, and became involved with the new Globe theatre. Index.
  The author "offers a critical examination of four plays Shakespeare wrote in the seminal year of 1599—Henry V, Julius Caesar, As You Like It, and Hamlet—and of the events that influenced the Bard at the time of their writing. . . . This work gives the reader a realistic sense of the multilayered and complex political, social, and literary pressures that

influenced Shakespeare as a citizen of England, as a business partner in the Globe Theatre, and as a writer." Libr J

Includes bibliographical references

Wells, Stanley W.

★ **Shakespeare**: for all time; [by] Stanley Wells. Oxford Univ. Press 2003 xxi, 442p il $40   **822.3**
1. Poets 2. Authors 3. Dramatists
ISBN 0-19-516093-2

LC 2002-27412

First published 2002 in the United Kingdom

"Chapters on Shakespeare's life in Stratford and in London offer a . . . view of the development of the writer's career and personality. At the core of the book lies a . . . study of the writings themselves—how Shakespeare set about writing a play, his relationships with the company of actors with whom he worked, his developing mastery of the literary and rhetorical skills that he learned at the Stratford grammar school, the essentially theatrical quality of the structure and language of his plays. Subsequent chapters trace the fluctuating fortunes of his reputation and influence." Publisher's note

Includes bibliographical references

Wills, Garry

Verdi's Shakespeare; man of the theater. Viking 2011 220p $25.95   **822.3**
1. Opera 2. Poets 3. Authors 4. Composers 5. Dramatists 6. Italy -- History -- 19th century
ISBN 978-0-670-02304-2

LC 2011019768

Includes bibliographical references

822.33   William Shakespeare

Mays, Andrea E.

The **millionaire** and the bard; Henry Folger's obsessive hunt for Shakespeare's first folio. by Andrea E. Mays. Simon & Schuster 2015 368 p. illustrations, portraits (trade paperback) $16   **822.33**
1. Book collecting 2. Publishers and publishing -- History 3. New York (N.Y.) -- Intellectual life 4. New York (N.Y.) -- Commerce -- History 5. London (England) -- Intellectual life -- 17th century 6. Millionaires -- New York (State) -- New York -- Biography 7. Book collectors -- New York (State) -- New York -- Biography 8. Publishers and publishing -- England -- London -- History -- 17th century
ISBN 9781439118238; 9781439118252

LC 2015001458

This book, by Andrea E. Mays, "tells the . . . story of the making of the First Folio. . . . When Shakespeare died in 1616 half of his plays died with him. No one—not even their author—believed that his writings would last. . . . Seven years later, in 1623, Shakespeare's business partners, companions, and fellow actors, John Heminges and Henry Condell, gathered copies of the plays and manuscripts, edited and published thirty-six of them." (Publisher's note)

Includes bibliographical references and index

823   English fiction

Achebe, Chinua, 1930-2013

Home and exile. Anchor Bks. 2001 115p pa $11   **823**
1. Africa -- Civilization
ISBN 978-0-385-72133-2; 0-385-72133-1

LC 2001-22599

First published 2000 by Oxford University Press

"This slim volume—told in Achebe's subtle, witty and gracious style—is one of those small gems of literary and historical analysis that readers will treasure and reread over the years." Publ Wkly

Includes bibliographical references

There was a country; a personal history of Biafra. Chinua Achebe. Penguin Press 2012 352 p. $27.95   **823**
1. Autobiographies 2. Nigeria -- History -- Civil War, 1967-1970 3. Authors, Nigerian -- 20th century -- Biography 4. Nigeria -- History -- Civil War, 1967-1970 -- Personal narratives
ISBN 1594204829; 9781594204821

LC 2012005603

This memoir recounts author Chinua Achebe's experience of "the Nigerian civil war, also known as the Biafran War, of 1967-1970. The conflict was infamous for its savage impact on the Biafran people, Chinua Achebe's people, many of whom were starved to death after the Nigerian government blockaded their borders. . . . [Achebe] took the Biafran side in the conflict and served his government as a roving cultural ambassador, from which vantage he absorbed the war's full horror." (Publisher's note)

Includes bibliographical references and index.

Attwell, David

J. M. Coetzee and the Life of Writing; Face-to-Face With Time. Prof David Attwell. Penguin Group USA 2015 272 p. illustrations, map, portraits (hbk.) $27.95; (pbk.) $17.00   **823**
ISBN 9780525429616; 9780143128816; 9780198746331; 0198746334; 0525429611; 0143128817

In this book author "David Attwell explores the extraordinary creative processes behind [J.M.] Coetzee's novels. Using Coetzee's manuscripts, notebooks and research papers--recently deposited at the Harry Ransom Center of the University of Texas at Austin--Attwell produces a fascinating story. He shows convincingly that Coetzee's work is strongly autobiographical, the memoirs being continuous with the fictions, and that his writing proceeds with never-ending self-reflection." (Publisher's note)

"This accessible, nonacademic study doesn't reveal much in the way of deep biography yet provides a valuable examination of the Nobel laureate's fiction that will appeal to students and fans of Coetzee and anyone interested in the process and work of writing." LJ

Baker, William

Critical companion to Jane Austen; a literary reference to her life and work. Facts on File 2008 644p il (Facts on File library of world literature) $75 **823**

1. Authors 2. Novelists

ISBN 978-0-8160-6416-8

LC 2006-102848

This book examines Jane Austen's "life and works, and includes critical analyses of the themes within her writing, as well as entries on related topics and relevant people, places, and influences." Publisher's note

Includes bibliographical references

Ballard, J. G., 1930-2009

Miracles of life; Shanghai to Shepperton : an autobiography. J.G. Ballard. Liveright Pub. Corporation 2013 272 p. il (hardcover) $25.95   **823**

1. Authorship 2. World War, 1939-1945 -- Influence 3. Novelists, English -- 20th century -- Biography

ISBN 0871404206; 9780871404206

LC 2012033865

This book presents an autobiography by the English novelist and short story writer J. G. Ballard. "the first half of the book portrays Ballard's experiences in the Lunghua internment camp near Shanghai during World War II and sheds light on his relationship with his parents. He also describes the tragic death of his wife, just after he started to establish himself as a writer, and to a lesser degree his unconventional relationship with lifelong partner Claire Walsh." (Kirkus Reviews)

Barnes, Julian, 1946-

Levels of life; by Julian Barnes. Alfred A. Knopf 2013 144 p. (hardcover) $22.95   **823**

1. Grief 2. Bereavement

ISBN 0385350775; 9780345806581; 9780385350778

LC 2013004601

In this book author Julian Barnes presents his thoughts on the subject of grief "beginning in the nineteenth century and leading . . . into an entirely personal account of loss." (Publisher's note) "It is divided into three . . . parts: a . . . discussion of ballooning; a . . . short story about the fictional romance of a real English adventurer named Fred Burnaby and the celebrated actress Sarah Bernhardt; and a . . . consideration of grief." (New York Review of Books)

Bayley, John

Elegy for Iris. St. Martin's Press 1999 275p il hardcover o.p. pa $13   **823**

1. Authors 2. Novelists 3. Philosophers 4. Alzheimer's disease 5. Essayists 6. College teachers 7. Literary critics

ISBN 0-312-42111-7 pa

LC 98-40895

"This splendid book enlarges our imagination of the range and possibilities of love." N Y Times Book Rev

Bowker, Gordon, 1934-

★ James Joyce; a new biography. Gordon Bowker. Farrar, Straus and Giroux 2012 608 p. ill. (hbk. : alk. paper) $35.00   **823**

1. Authors, Irish 2. Authors, Irish -- 20th century -- Biography

ISBN 0374178720; 9780374178727

LC 2011045954

This biography of James Joyce "show[s] the complexities and contradictions of the man. . . . The author charts . . . his struggle to survive in the early days of his adulthood and marriage, the sad madness of his daughter, . . . and his difficulty finding publishers for 'Dubliners' and the more controversial works that followed. . . . We see Joyce, too, as a prodigious worker." (Kirkus Reviews)

Includes bibliographical references and index

The **Cambridge** companion to Jane Austen; edited by Edward Copeland and Juliet McMaster. Cambridge Univ. Press 1997 251p (Cambridge companions to literature)   **823**

1. Authors 2. Novelists

ISBN 0-521-49517-2; 0-521-49867-8 pa

LC 96-23387

This volume contains a selection of critical essays on the English novelist. "Deirdre Le Faye provides an Austen chronology; Jan Fergus outlines the situation of professional women writers; other essays deal with the novels and letters, and with . . . 'themes' (class, money, religion and politics)." (Times Lit Suppl) Bibliography. Index.

Scholars assess "Jane Austen's works in the contexts of her contemporary world, and of present-day critical discourse. Besides discussions of Austen's novels and letters, there are essays on religion, politics, class consciousness, publishing practices, domestic economy, style in the novels and the significance of her juvenile works. A chronology provides biographical information." Publisher's note

The **Columbia** history of the British novel; John Richetti, editor; John Bender, Deirdre David, Michael Seidel, associate editors. Columbia Univ. Press 1994 xxix, 1064p $95   **823**

1. English fiction -- History and criticism

ISBN 0-231-07858-7

LC 92-35749

In this chronologically arranged volume, scholars provide 39 essays surveying the history of the British novel. "Some essays are devoted to individual authors (e.g., Austen, Dickens), others to several authors (e.g., Amis, Snow, and Wilson), and still others to such topics as 'The Gothic Novel, 1764-1824.' Each essay has a brief selected bibliography; an appendix includes thumbnail sketches of 100 of the British novelists discussed." Libr J

Conradi, Peter

Iris Murdoch; a life. {by} Peter J. Conradi. Norton 2001 xxix, 706p il $35; pa $19.95   **823**

1. Authors 2. Novelists 3. Philosophers 4. Essayists

ISBN 0-393-04875-6; 0-393-32401-X pa

LC 2001-32972

"Rich footnoting leads the reader to expansions on the narrative as well as to the authority behind the biographer's statements. Scholars need this text, but it will also intrigue lay readers." Libr J

Includes bibliographical references

Cusk, Rachel, 1967-
★ **Aftermath**; on marriage and separation. Rachel Cusk. Farrar, Straus and Giroux 2012 146 p. (alk. paper) $20.00 **823**
1. Marriage 2. Biography 3. Family life 4. Divorce -- Psychological aspects 5. Marriage -- Psychological aspects 6. Authors, English -- 20th century -- Biography
ISBN 0374102139; 9780374102135

LC 2012003807

Author Rachel Cusk looks at "the breakdown of her domestic life. [The book tells the traditional story of] man meets woman . . . [and] create a family . . . [then the] family falls apart . . . [and the] man, woman and children grieve . . . [S]he weaves in figures from ancient Greek drama (Oedipus, Antigone, Agamemnon, Clytemnestra) . . . The last and most unorthodox chapter is told, by Cusk, from the perspective of her au pair Sonia, a scared, scarred girl whom the author abruptly fired when her husband left." (Kirkus)

Davis, Paul B.
★ **Critical** companion to Charles Dickens; a literary reference to his life and work. Rev ed; Facts on File 2007 676p il (Facts on File library of world literature) $75 **823**
1. Authors 2. Novelists
ISBN 0-8160-6407-5; 978-0-8160-6407-6

LC 2006-3026

First published 1998 with title: Charles Dickens A-Z

This "reference contains entries on this writer's works, including the characters in each work, . . . historical and thematic information, and critical discussion. It also includes entries on related people, places, themes, topics, and influences. Additional features include 116 illustrations, a chronology, a bibliography of primary and secondary sources, and much more." Publisher's note

Includes bibliographical references

Dirda, Michael
On Conan Doyle; or, The whole art of storytelling. Princeton University Press 2011 210p (Writers on writers) $19.95 **823**
1. Authors 2. Novelists 3. Mystery writers
ISBN 978-0-691-15135-9; 0-691-15135-0

LC 2011-20674

"Dirda is at his best in his sensitive appreciation of Doyle's style, direct, fluent, and surprisingly flexible as he moves from genre to genre, and in his account of manly civic inspiration as the value Doyle aimed above all to inculcate in his writing . . . . An endearing, well-balanced introduction to a writer the Strand Magazine called 'the greatest natural storyteller of his age.'" Kirkus

Includes bibliographical references

★ The **Facts** on File companion to the British novel. Facts on File 2005 2v (Facts on File library of world literature) set $140 **823**
1. English fiction -- History and criticism
ISBN 0-8160-6377-X; 978-0-8160-6377-2

LC 2004-20914

"With more than one thousand entries, each with a selected bibliography and a set of very usable appendixes, this work accomplishes much in a compact set." Ref & User Services Quarterly

Includes bibliographical references

Fargnoli, A. Nicholas
Critical companion to James Joyce; a literary companion to his life and work. [by] A. Nicholas Fargnoli, Michael Patrick Gillespie. Rev ed; Facts On File 2006 450p il (Facts on File library of world literature) $65; pa $19.95 **823**
1. Poets 2. Authors 3. Novelists 4. Dramatists 5. Short story writers
ISBN 0-8160-6232-3; 978-0-8160-6232-4; 0-8160-6689-2 pa; 978-0-8160-6689-6 pa

LC 2005-15721

First published 1995 with title: James Joyce A to Z

The authors "divide this reference to the writer's life and work into four parts. Part 1 is a brief biography. Part 2 focuses on individual works (e.g., Dubliners), including its publication date, a brief history, a synopsis, early critical reception, contemporary perspectives, and one or two recommended titles for further reading. The entries in Part 3 cover people (including friends and relatives), places, and ideas related to Joyce. Part 4 contains an appendix, a bibliography of the writer's work, a bibliography of secondary sources, chronologies, family trees, and more. . . . [This is] a great primer for those needing a detailed introduction into Joyce's world." Libr J

Includes bibliographical references

Ford, Paul F.
Companion to Narnia; a complete guide to the magical world of C.S. Lewis's The chronicles of Narnia. foreword by Madeleine L'Engle; illustrated by Lorinda Bryan Cauley. Rev and expanded; HarperSanFrancisco 2005 xxvi, 530p il map pa $16.95 **823**
1. Authors 2. Novelists 3. Theologians 4. Essayists 5. Satirists 6. Literary critics 7. Children's authors
ISBN 0-06-079127-6

First published 1980

C. S. Lewis wrote seven books of fantasy that are collectively called The Chronicles of Narnia. This book "is an encyclopedia of Narnian names and terms and related matters, with . . . footnoted articles, page references to American and British hardcover editions, cross-references, and a running footline for quick location of materials in the alphabet." Choice

Includes bibliographical references

Frank, Katherine

Crusoe; Daniel Defoe, Robert Knox and the creation of a myth. Katherine Frank. Bodley Head 2011 338 p.   **823**

1. Castaways in literature 2. Crusoe, Robinson (Fictitious character)

ISBN 0224073095; 9780224073097

LC 2011486701

This book "introduces Robert Knox, once a true captive, who survived on his wits and the English practice of making your environment adapt to your needs rather than adjusting to it. . . . As Defoe cherry-picked incidents from different lives, he adapted them to reflect disasters he had suffered. . . . Frank parallels the lives and adventures of Defoe, Knox and Crusoe, illustrating a deep relationship between author and models. This side-by-side biography of the two men shows similarities between their lives and their attitudes toward disaster, although their personalities and moralities were markedly different. Many have said that Crusoe is much more a self-help book than a novel, while Knox's story is a treatise rather than a travel book." (Kirkus)

Includes bibliographical references and index.

Gordimer, Nadine

Conversations with Nadine Gordimer; edited by Nancy Topping Bazin and Marilyn Dallman Seymour. University Press of Miss. 1990 xxiv, 321p (Literary conversations series) $46   **823**

1. Authors 2. Novelists 3. Dramatists 4. Essayists 5. Short story writers 6. Nobel laureates for literature

ISBN 0-87805-444-8

LC 90-12556

This is a collection of interviews in which Gordimer talks "about her life as a white South African, about her fiction, and about writers she admires." Booklist

Includes bibliographical references

Hardy, Thomas, 1840-1928

The **Collected** Letters of Thomas Hardy; Further Letters 1861-1927. edited by Michael Millgate and Keith Wilson. Oxford University Press 2012 320 p. $160   **823**

1. Letters

ISBN 0199607753; 9780199607754

LC 77030355

This book, edited by Michael Millgate and Keith Wilson, "contains previously unpublished letters from all periods of [poet Thomas] Hardy's career, his earliest known letter among them. It introduces important new correspondents, throws fresh light on existing correspondences, and richly enhances the reader's understanding of both familiar and hitherto unfamiliar aspects of Hardy's life and work and of the times in which he lived." (Publisher's note)

Head, Dominic

★ The **Cambridge** introduction to modern British fiction, 1950-2000. Cambridge Univ. Press 2002 307p $65; pa $22   **823**

1. English fiction -- History and criticism

ISBN 0-521-66014-9; 0-521-66966-9 pa

LC 2001-43261

"Anyone with an interest in the contemporary novel, not just British fiction, will appreciate this outstanding survey and analysis. . . . The quality of discussion is admirably consistent within and between each chapter, the prose as carefully crafted as the judgments are measured. . . . This book should become a standard reference work for its subject." Choice

Includes bibliographical references

★ **Horror**: another 100 best books; edited by Stephen Jones and Kim Newman; with a foreword by Peter Straub. Carroll & Graf Publishers 2005 456p pa $16.95   **823**

1. Best books 2. Horror fiction -- History and criticism

ISBN 0-7867-1577-4

First published 1988

"Horror fans seeking what to read next will not only find out here; they'll also have their taste and appreciative capacity refined by the intelligent, passionate commentary of the 100 writers who selected these 100 books." Booklist

Hughes, Kathryn

George Eliot; the last Victorian. Cooper Square Press 2001 383p il pa $19.95   **823**

1. Authors 2. Novelists 3. Essayists 4. Authors, English

ISBN 0-8154-1121-9; 978-0-8154-1121-5

LC 2001-28024

First published 1998 in the United Kingdom

In this biography Hughes "shows how George Eliot (nee Mary Anne Evans, 1819-80), in spite of her outwardly anti-Victorian lifestyle, was in fact a true Victorian. . . . A solitary, ascetic child and young woman, she was raised in an upwardly mobile country family. . . . In 1852 she met the married writer and editor George Henry Lewes, with whom she lived until his death in 1878." Libr J

Includes bibliographical references

James, P. D., 1920-2014

Talking about detective fiction. Alfred A. Knopf 2009 198p il $22   **823**

1. Mystery fiction -- History and criticism 2. Detective and mystery stories, English -- History and criticism

ISBN 978-0-307-59282-8

LC 2009-38501

P. D. James offers a "book-length essay on the roots, ethics and methods of the detective story." (N Y Times (Late N Y Ed))

"For crime fiction fans, this master class from one of the leading practitioners of the art will be a real treat." Publ Wkly

Includes bibliographical references

Time to be in earnest; a fragment of autobiography. Knopf 2000 269p hardcover o.p. pa $12.95   **823**

1. Authors 2. Novelists 3. Mystery writers

ISBN 0-345-44212-1 pa

LC 99-57603

"In 1997, on the eve of her 77th birthday noted mystery novelist James . . . decided to keep a diary for the first time ever, recording one year in her life. The result is this 'fragment of autobiography,' a mix of memoir, ruminations on everything from her writing career to Princess Diana's death, and literary criticism." Libr J

Kermode, Frank

Concerning E.M. Forster. Farrar, Straus and Giroux 2009 180p $24   **823**

1. Authors 2. Novelists 3. Essayists 4. Literary critics 5. Short story writers

ISBN 978-0-374-29899-9; 0-374-29899-8

LC 2009-39143

"Overall, Kermode's occasional exasperation with his subject enlivens rather than distorts his eminently fair assessment. Like all good criticism, Concerning EM Forster makes one want to read the books under discussion once more, and it ends on an appropriately affectionate note." Times (London)

Includes bibliographical references

Kiberd, Declan

Ulysses and us; the art of everyday life in Joyce's masterpiece. W.W. Norton & Co. 2009 399p $28.95   **823**

1. Poets 2. Authors 3. Novelists 4. Dramatists 5. Short story writers

ISBN 978-0-393-07099-6; 0-393-07099-9

LC 2009014101

This "is an ideal introduction [to Ulysses] for the uninitiated—accessible, richly argued, funny and, in a kind of devil's advocacy fashion, begging for rebuttal." Publ Wkly

Includes bibliographical references

King, Dean

Patrick O'Brian; a life revealed. Holt & Co. 2000 397p il hardcover o.p. pa $15   **823**

1. Authors 2. Novelists 3. Biographers 4. Writers on the sea 5. Short story writers

ISBN 0-8050-5977-6 pa

LC 99-48495

"This is exactly the sort of literary biography that O'Brian, the author of the celebrated Aubrey/Maturin naval novels, hoped to avoid. Reluctant to provide facts about himself, and often untruthful when he did so, O'Brian . . . had much in his past that he wanted buried. He walked away from his first marriage, changed his name from Russ to O'Brian, and pretended Anglo-Irish ancestry. King's diligent research yields pleasing details." New Yorker

Includes bibliographical references

Le Carré, John, 1931-

★ The **Pigeon** Tunnel; Stories from My Life. by John le Carré. Penguin Group USA 2016 320 p. $30   **823**

1. Authors 2. Espionage 3. Autobiographies 4. Intelligence service

ISBN 0735220778; 9780735220775

In this memoir, author John le Carré is "writing about . . . visiting Rwanda's museums of the unburied dead in the aftermath of the genocide, celebrating New Year's Eve 1982 with Yasser Arafat and his high command, interviewing a German woman terrorist in her desert prison in the Negev, listening to the wisdoms of the great physicist, dissident, and

Nobel Prize winner Andrei Sakharov, [and] meeting with two former heads of the KGB." (Publisher's note)

"Always insightful, frequently charming, and sometimes sobering, the memorable tales told by master storyteller le Carré (A Delicate Truth) about his life will surely delight both longtime fans and newcomers. Le Carré's stories take readers around the world, covering his posting as a young intelligence officer in post-WWII Germany, his time in Gorbachev's Russia, and research trips for his novels. . . . But his self-deprecating humor and wit are never far away, and he proves a most elegant and genial host on this tour of his life and work." PW

Lee, Hermione

★ **Virginia** Woolf. Knopf 1997 893p il hardcover o.p. pa $20   **823**

1. Authors 2. Novelists 3. Women authors 4. Essayists 5. Authors, English 6. Short story writers

ISBN 0-375-70136-2 pa

LC 97-71155

First published 1996 in the United Kingdom

Lee "re-creates the world Woolf was born into in 1882, a maze of formalities and reticences, and then leads us through changes that, slow in coming but shocking in effect, made all that seem light-years away by the time Woolf was 50. She convinces us that Woolf, contrary to previous assumptions, reveled in a deep intimacy with her husband, Leonard. Finally, she makes a persuasive case for the underlying sanity of this woman as she battled her own madness and shows the brilliant literary uses she made of her instability." N Y Times Book Rev

Includes bibliographical references

Maunder, Andrew

The **Facts** on File companion to the British short story. Facts on File 2006 528p (Facts on File library of world literature) $75   **823**

1. Short stories -- History and criticism

ISBN 0-8160-5990-X; 978-0-8160-5990-4

LC 2006-6897

More than 450 alphabetically arranged entries cover authors, characters, and major short stories. Literary terms, themes, and motifs are covered. Winners of prizes and awards are noted.

Includes glossary and bibliographical references

Mead, Rebecca

★ **My** life in Middlemarch; Rebecca Mead. CrownCrown Publishers 2014 304 p. $25   **823**

1. Creation (Literary, artistic, etc.)

ISBN 0307984761; 9780307984760

LC 2013011477

In this "hybrid work of literary criticism, biography, and memoir," author Rebecca Mead discusses her relationship with the book "Middlemarch" by George Eliot. She "identifies strongly with aspects of Eliot's life and that of the characters in Middlemarch, [and] returns to the novel during various stages of her life: as a young Englishwoman finding her way in New York; in relationships with difficult men; as a stepmother and wife; and eventually as the mother of a son." (Publishers Weekly)

"A rare and remarkable fusion of techniques that draws two women together across time and space." Kirkus

Includes bibliographical references

Miller, Laura

The **magician's** book; a skeptic's adventures in Narnia. Little, Brown and Co. 2008 311p $25.99 **823**

1. Authors 2. Novelists 3. Theologians 4. Essayists 5. Satirists 6. Literary critics 7. Children's authors 8. Children's literature -- History and criticism

ISBN 978-0-316-01763-3; 0-316-01763-9

LC 2008-20629

The author explores the meaning and influence of C.S. Lewis' Chronicles of Narnia series while revealing how Lewis's troubled childhood, unconventional love life, and friendship with J. R. R. Tolkien affected his writing.

"Miller's book is itself a welcome bit of magic: part reader's log, part biography, part literary criticism." N Y Times Book Rev

Montillo, Roseanne

★ The **lady** and her monsters; a tale of dissections, attempts to reanimate dead tissue, and the writing of Mary Shelley's Frankenstein. Roseanne Montillo. 1st ed. William Morrow 2013 322 p. ill. (hardcover) $26.99; (ebook) $21.99 **823**

1. Women and literature -- England -- History -- 19th century

ISBN 9780062025814; 9780062025838; 9780062235886

LC 2012021509

This book, by Roseanne Motillo, "brings to life the . . . science, and real-life horrors behind Mary Shelley's gothic masterpiece, 'Frankenstein.' Montillo recounts how--at the intersection of the Romantic Age and the Industrial Revolution--Shelley's Victor Frankenstein was inspired by actual scientists of the period: curious and daring iconoclasts who were obsessed with the inner workings of the human body and how it might be reanimated after death." (Publisher's note)

"Fraught with suicides, superstitions, natural disasters, and love affairs, the life of Mary Shelley shares much emotionally with the harrowing tale of her great protagonist, Victor Frankenstein. A delicious and enticing journey into the origins of a masterpiece." Pub Wkly

Includes bibliographical references (p. 305-310) and index.

Moore, Wendy

★ **How** to create the perfect wife; Britain's most ineligible bachelor and his enlightened quest to train the ideal mate. Wendy Moore. Basic Books 2013 360 p. (hardcover) $27.99 **823**

1. Wives 2. Marriage 3. Authors, English -- 18th century 4. Marriage -- Great Britain -- History -- 18th century

ISBN 0465065740; 9780465065745

LC 2012048149

This book, by Wendy Moore, tells "tale of one man's mission to groom his ideal mate. [18th-century British writer Thomas] Day adopted two young orphans from the Foundling Hospital and, guided by the writings of Jean-Jacques

Rousseau and the principles of the Enlightenment, attempted to teach them to be model wives. His peculiar experiment inevitably backfired--though not before he had taken his theories about marriage, education, and femininity to shocking extremes." (Publisher's note)

Includes bibliographical references and index

Naipaul, V. S.

Between father and son; selected correspondence of V.S. Naipaul and his family, 1949-1953. edited by Gillon Aitken. Knopf 2000 297p $26; pa $13 **823**

1. Authors 2. Novelists 3. Journalists 4. Essayists 5. Travel writers 6. Radio reporters 7. Nonfiction writers 8. Short story writers 9. Nobel laureates for literature

ISBN 0-375-40730-8; 0-375-70726-3 pa

LC 99-31089

"In 1950, at the age of 17, famous-writer-in-the-making V. S. Naipaul ventured to Oxford University in England on a scholarship supplied by the government of his native Trinidad. He and his father maintained a rich, full correspondence during his time away, and these letters fortunately have been gathered into book form." Booklist

Include bibliographical references

Ngugi wa Thiong'o, 1938-

In the house of the interpreter; a memoir. Ngugi wa'Thiong'o. Pantheon Books 2012 240 p. (hardback) $25.95 **823**

1. Revolutionaries -- Kenya -- Biography 2. Authors, Kenyan -- 20th century -- Biography

ISBN 0307907694; 9780307907691

LC 2012013986

The book by author Ngugi wa Thiong'o presents a collection of his writings. It focuses on the "author's life and times at boarding school--the first secondary educational institution in British-ruled Kenya--in the 1950s, against the backdrop of the tumultuous Mau Mau Uprising for independence and Kenyan sovereignty." Throughout his journey, "he falls victim to the forces of colonialism in the person of a police officer encountered on a bus journey, and he is thrown into jail for six days." (Publisher's note)

Nokes, David

Jane Austen; a life. University of Calif. Press 1998 577p il pa $24.95 **823**

1. Authors 2. Novelists 3. Women authors 4. Authors, English

ISBN 0-520-21606-7; 978-0-520-21606-8

LC 98-15785

First published 1997 by Farrar, Straus & Giroux

"Eschewing the biographer's usual perspective of omniscient foreknowledge in favor of a novelistic perspective of ambiguous immediacy, Nokes allows us to see Austen's talent as a mystery unfolding, not a fact explained. We thus witness the emergence of a personality sufficiently subtle and complex to produce Sense and Sensibility, Pride and Prejudice, and Emma. Readers of Austen's fiction will rejoice at having a biography so carefully nuanced, so refreshingly candid." Booklist

Includes bibliographical references

O'Brien, Edna

James Joyce. Viking 1999 179p (Penguin lives series) $19.95   **823**

1. Poets 2. Authors 3. Novelists 4. Dramatists 5. Short story writers
ISBN 0-670-88230-5

LC 99-23214

O'Brien "tells the story of the aspiring young writer and his downwardly mobile family, his escape to Europe, the constant struggle to scrape together enough money to live on, and finally his relative comfort, thanks to patrons, once Ulysses was published. She also provides thoughtful appreciations of Joyce's major works." Booklist

Includes bibliographical references

Olsen, Kirstin

All things Austen; an encyclopedia of Austen's world. Greenwood Press 2005 2v il maps set $157.95   **823**

1. Authors 2. Novelists 3. Reference books
ISBN 0-313-33032-8

LC 2004-28664

"This well-written and meticulously researched work provides a convenient means for general readers, students, and scholars to gain a better understanding of the social, cultural, and political climate of Austen's time." Booklist

Saler, Michael

As if; modern enchantment and the literary prehistory of virtual reality. Michael Saler. Oxford University Press 2012 x, 283 p.p (pbk. : acid-free paper) $27.95   **823**

1. Virtual reality 2. Imaginary places 3. Books and reading 4. Fantastic, The, in literature 5. Marvelous, The, in literature 6. Virtual reality in literature 7. Imaginary societies in literature
ISBN 0195343174; 9780195343168; 9780195343175

LC 2011010276

This book by Michael Saler was "named one of the 'Best Books of 2012' by the editors of 'The Huffington Post.' . . . It explains how, "beginning in the late nineteenth century, when Sherlock Holmes became the world's first 'virtual reality' character, readers began to colonize imaginary worlds. . . . From Lovecraft's Cthulhu Mythos and Tolkien's Middle-earth to the World of Warcraft and Second Life, 'As If' provides a cultural history that reveals how we can remain enchanted but not deluded in an age where fantasy and reality increasingly intertwine." (Publisher's note)

Includes bibliographical references and index.

Shakespeare, Nicholas

Bruce Chatwin. Talese 2000 618p il $35; pa $18   **823**

1. Authors 2. Novelists 3. Memoirists 4. Travel writers
ISBN 0-385-49829-2; 0-385-49830-6 pa

LC 99-36474

"This life of the author of 'The Songlines', who died of AIDS in 1989, portrays a man, beset with an almost biological lust for loneliness, whose singular genius was for passionate transitory connection." N Y Times Book Rev

Includes bibliographical references

Shields, Carol

Jane Austen. Viking 2001 185p (Penguin lives series) hardcover o.p. pa $13   **823**

1. Authors 2. Novelists 3. Women authors 4. Authors, English
ISBN 0-670-89488-5; 0-14-303516-9 pa

LC 00-43807

"In chronicling her subject's life and personality, Shields emphasizes Austen's keen ability to listen, observe, and capture clearly the social mores of her time and explore human nature in her writing. Shields contends that historical references are behind many of the scenes and characters in Austen's novels, and as a way of more clearly personalizing Austen's experiences or feelings, she interjects commentary regarding writing and publishing that is presumably based on personal experience." Libr J

Smiley, Jane

Charles Dickens. Viking 2002 212p (Penguin lives series) $19.95   **823**

1. Authors 2. Novelists 3. Authors, English
ISBN 0-670-03077-5

LC 2001-45607

This "biography examines Dickens' life through his work, starting not with his birth but rather the beginnings of his literary career. After writing short essays for a monthly magazine, Dickens began the serialization of his first novel, The Pickwick Papers. Dickens quickly became both a bestselling novelist and a famous man, who had to contend with both the envy of other authors and, much later on, the very public dissolution of his marriage. . . . Smiley's superb and thoughtful analysis should appeal to anyone familiar with the great author's work." Booklist

Swift, Jonathan

A tale of a tub, and other work; edited with an introduction by Angus Ross and David Woolley. Oxford Univ. Press 1986 xxviii, 237p (The World's classics) pa $8.95   **823**

ISBN 0-19-283593-9

LC 85-5072

A tale of a tub, The battle of the books, and A discourse concerning the mechanical operation of the spirit, were first published together in 1704. The first is an allegorical satire ridiculing the corruptions of religion and learning by extremists and pedants. The second is a mock heroic satire on squabbles concerning the relative merits of ancient and modern authors presented as an account of the battle between ancient and modern books in St James Library. The third ridicules the manner of worship and preaching of religious enthusiasts of the period

Tomalin, Claire

Jane Austen; a life. Knopf 1997 341p il hardcover o.p. pa $14   **823**

1. Authors 2. Novelists 3. Women authors 4. Authors, English
ISBN 0-679-76676-6 pa

LC 97-36887

The author "has produced a portrait of remarkable subtlety. The light Ms. Tomalin casts on her subject is strong but oblique: the profile of the novelist appears surrounded by her friends and neighbours and by her energetic and beloved family." Economist

A **truth** universally acknowledged; 33 great writers on why we read Jane Austen. edited by Susannah Carson; foreword by Harold Bloom. Random House 2009 295p $25   **823**
1. Authors 2. Novelists
ISBN 978-1-4000-6805-0; 1-4000-6805-3
   LC 2009-12904
"A collection for both newcomers to the charms of Jane Austen and those longtime 'Janeites'. . . . The writers in this volume explain their own relationship with Austen and together are a kind of invitation for us, whether we're Janeites or not, to understand why we are so in her thrall." Chicago Trib
Includes bibliographical references

Wainaina, Binyavanga, 1971-
One day I will write about this place. Graywolf Press 2011 256p   **823**
1. Authors 2. Novelists 3. Journalists 4. College teachers 5. Short story writers 6. Biography, Individual
ISBN 1555975917; 9781555975913
   LC 2011923190
In this memoir, the Kenyan writer describes "his school days, his mother's religious period, his failed attempt to study in South Africa as a computer programmer, a moving family reunion in Uganda, and his travels around Kenya. The landscape in front of him always claims his main attention, but he also evokes the shifting political scene that unsettles his views on family, tribe, and nationhood. Throughout, reading is his refuge and his solace. And when, in 2002, a writing prize comes through, the door is opened for him to pursue the career that perhaps had been beckoning all along." (Publisher's note)

Weldon, Fay
Auto da Fay. Grove Press 2003 366p il $25; pa $14   **823**
1. Authors 2. Novelists 3. Dramatists 4. Short story writers
ISBN 0-8021-1750-3; 0-8021-4142-0 pa
   LC 2002-44685
First published 2002 in the United Kingdom
This "autobiography primarily focuses on her peripatetic childhood and difficult years of single parenthood, concluding in the 1960s with her second marriage and the beginning of her writing career. . . . Filled with warmth, wit, and her trademark irreverence, Weldon's memoir is a vivid and engaging account of a brave and brainy 'lost girl' who found her way." Booklist

Wilson, A. N., 1950-
C.S. Lewis; a biography. Norton 1990 334p il hardcover o.p. pa $15.95   **823**
1. Authors 2. Novelists 3. Theologians 4. Essayists 5. Satirists 6. Literary critics 7. Children's authors 8. Biography, Individual
ISBN 0-393-32340-4 pa
   LC 89-27361

This is a biography of the English scholar, novelist, and Christian apologist. Bibliography. Index.
"The mixture presented in Wilson's biography of the life of learning, the college life at Magdalen where he taught, of domestic drama and bad temper, religion, and sex, is irresistible." N Y Rev Books
Includes bibliographical references

Winterson, Jeanette, 1959-
Why be happy when you could be normal? Jeanette Winterson. Jonathan Cape 2011 230 p. $25   **823**
1. Novelists 2. Autobiographies 3. Adopted children 4. Mother-daughter relationship 5. Women authors -- Biography 6. Authors, English -- 20th century -- Biography
ISBN 0224093452; 0802120105; 9780224093453; 9780802120106
   LC 2011507186
Guardian Best Book of 2011
In this book, "author [Jeanette Winterson] ponders her youth and examines how those challenging years changed and shaped her as an adult. Frequently locked out on the doorstep by her abusive, Pentecostal, adoptive mother or often told she was 'a fault to heaven, a fault against the dead, and a fault to nature,' Winterson wondered if she had ever been wanted, by her biological or adoptive mother. . . . At age 16, she was kicked out of the house and forced to live in her car. Books and words brought comfort and led Winterson to Oxford and writing, but she descended into a deep depression when her lover left her. The search for her true identity and her birth mother helped bring her back from the darkness." (Kirkus)

Woolf, Virginia
Moments of being; edited, with an introduction and notes, by Jeanne Schulkind. 2nd ed; Harcourt Brace Jovanovich 1985 230p pa $14   **823**
1. Authors 2. Novelists 3. Women authors 4. Essayists 5. Authors, English 6. Short story writers
ISBN 0-15-661918-0
   LC 85-8521
First published 1976
This volume consists of unpublished autobiographical writings, including several "Reminiscences" written at the start of Woolf's career, a piece entitled "A sketch of the past" written shortly before her suicide, and papers read to the Memoir Club.
Includes bibliographical references

823.8   English fiction--1837-1899

Skal, David J.
★ **Something** in the Blood; The Untold Story of Bram Stoker, the Man Who Wrote Dracula. by David J. Skal. W W Norton & Co Inc 2016 672 p. illustrations (some color) $35   **823.8**
ISBN 1631490109; 9781631490101
   LC 2016028093
This book, by David J. Skal, is a biography of Bram Stoker. "Skal exhumes the inner world and strange genius of

the writer who birthed an undying cultural icon, painting an astonishing portrait of the age in which Stoker was born— a time when death was no metaphor but a constant threat easily imagined as a character existing in flesh and blood." (Publisher's note)

"An engagingly written, well-documented biography of a famous writer we all think we know, even if we really don't." Booklist

Includes bibliographical references and index.

824 English essays

Carlyle, Thomas

Sartor resartus; edited with an introduction and notes by Kerry McSweeney and Peter Sabor. Oxford Univ. Press 1987 xlii, 273p (The World's classics) pa $11.95 **824**

ISBN 0-19-283673-0

LC 87-5753

First published 1833-1834, Sartor resartus contains the germ of Carlyle's philosophy. It purports to be an interpretation of the work of an erudite German professor but is really the story of Carlyle's own fierce spiritual conflict between doubt and faith. It presents a philosophy of clothes, or the outward forms of things

Includes bibliographical references

De Quincey, Thomas

The **confessions** of an English opium-eater and other writings. Penguin Books 2003 xliv, 296p pa $14 **824**

1. Drug abuse

ISBN 978-0-14-043901-4; 0-14-043901-3

"Confessions forged a link between artistic self-expression and addiction, paving the way for later generations of literary drug-users from Baudelaire to Burroughs, and anticipating psychoanalysis with its insights into the subconscious. This edition is based on the original serial version of 1821, and reproduces the two 'sequels', 'Suspiria de Profundis' (1845) and 'The English Mail-Coach' (1849). It also includes a critical introduction discussing the romantic figure of the addict and the tradition of confessional literature, and an appendix on opium in the nineteenth century." Publisher's note

Dyer, Geoff

Otherwise known as the human condition; selected essays and reviews, 1989-2010. Graywolf Press 2011 421p il **824**

1. Criticism

ISBN 1-555-97579-8; 978-1-55597-579-1

LC 2010-937517

This book of essays covers "a broad territory stretching from photographers such as Richard Avedon and William Gedney. . .musicians Miles Davis and Def Leppard; writers like D.H. Lawrence, Ian McEwan, and Richard Ford; as well as personal ruminations on, say, reader's block." (Publishers Weekly)

"A grab-bag of critical essays, reportage and personal stories from the irrepressibly curious Dyer. . . . The title of this hefty tome, featuring pieces published in two

United Kingdom—only collections, suggests ponderous philosophizing. But though Dyer takes his art seriously, his prose is as relaxed and self-effacing as it is informed. . . . Though the book is wide-ranging, his command is consistent, whether he's writing about Richard Avedon or model airplanes." Kirkus

Includes bibliographical references

Gaiman, Neil, 1960-

The **view** from the cheap seats; Selected Nonfiction. Neil Gaiman. William Morrow 2016 544 p. (hardback) $26.99 **824**

1. Essays

ISBN 0062262262; 9780062262264

LC 2015046480

This book, by Neil Gaiman, is a "collection of nonfiction essays. . . . [It] explores a broad range of interests and topics, including (but not limited to): authors past and present; music; storytelling; comics; bookshops; travel; fairy tales; America; inspiration; libraries; ghosts; and the title piece, . . . which recounts the author's experiences at the 2010 Academy Awards in Hollywood." (Publisher's note)

"With this volume, Gaiman has shown that his nonfiction rivals his much-lauded fiction." Pub Wkly

James, Clive

As of this writing; the essential essays, 1968-2002. Norton 2003 619p $35 **824**

1. Literature -- History and criticism

ISBN 0-393-05180-3

"James writes with fluent wit, remarkable warmth, deep knowledge, and an exhilarating sense of mission." Booklist

Kermode, Frank

★ **Pieces** of my mind; essays and criticism, 1958-2002. Farrar, Straus & Giroux 2003 466p $26; pa $16 **824**

ISBN 0-8090-7601-2; 0-374-52936-1 pa

LC 2003-54727

The author "parses complicated, even esoteric aspects of story and text, metaphysics and poetry, and the link between social change and the evolution of the novel, yet he is unfailingly clear and cheerfully engaging, classy, and stimulating." Booklist

Includes bibliographical references

O'Faolain, Nuala

A **radiant** life; Nuala O'Faolain; [introduction by Fintan O'Toole; note by Sheridan Hay]. Abrams Image 2011 302p pa $18.95 **824**

1. Women -- Ireland 2. Catholic Church -- Ireland

ISBN 978-0-8109-9806-3; 0-8109-9806-8

LC 2010-37687

"The collection spans two decades and runs the gamut, from feminism to social justice, from pop culture to the elusive fruits of progress. It makes little difference that they spring from a quintessentially Irish voice; they are universal in their appeal. Read more: Book review: Nuala O'Faolain's Irish prose holds universal appeal." Denver Post

Orwell, George, 1903-1950

Essays; selected and introduced by John Carey. Alfred A. Knopf 2002 xlv, 1369p (Everyman's library) $35   **824**

ISBN 978-0-375-41503-6; 0-375-41503-3

"The real reason we read Orwell is because his own fault-line, his fundamental schism, his hybridity, left him exceptionally sensitive to the fissure—which is everywhere apparent–between what ought to be the case and what actually is the case. He says the unsayable." Financial Times

Pratchett, Terry, 1948-2015

★ A **slip** of the keyboard; collected nonfiction. Terry Pratchett. Doubleday 2014 336 p. (hardback) $26.95   **824**

1. Wit and humor
ISBN 0385538308; 9780385538305; 9780804169226
LC 2014011949

This book, by Terry Pratchett, is a collection of the author's "nonfiction work, and it brings together the finest examples of his extraordinary wit and his persuasive prose. Whether in short opinion pieces (on death and taxes), or in long essays, speeches, and interviews (covering a range of topics from mushrooms to orangutans), this collection is a fascinating look inside an extraordinary writer's mind." (Publisher's note)

"The essays, letters, speeches, and articles feature all the wit and charm of his beloved novels and allow readers a more personal look at Pratchett's life and beliefs. In a mere 336 pages, Pratchett ruminates on the underappreciated role of fantasy fiction and its importance in the literary world; the trick to becoming a successful author (hint: there isn't one); the care and feeding of authors while on book tours; and his work with fellow writer and friend Neil Gaiman." Booklist

Smith, Zadie, 1975-

Changing my mind; occasional essays. Penguin Press 2009 306p $26.95   **824**

ISBN 978-1-59420-237-7; 1-59420-237-0
LC 2009-23419

The author has organized this collection of "essays into sections on reading, being, seeing, feeling, and remembering to create a strong and piquant collection. As the title implies, Smith's thinking evolves before our eyes as she articulates her responses to art and life. . . . Smith is a superb essayist of skill, candor, and caring." Booklist

Includes bibliographical references

Wilde, Oscar

The **artist** as critic; critical writings of Oscar Wilde. edited by Richard Ellmann. University of Chicago Press 1982 xxviii, 446p pa $36.50   **824**

1. Criticism 2. Literature -- History and criticism
ISBN 978-0-226-89764-6; 0-226-89764-8
LC 82-13361

Wilde's "book reviews and occasional pieces prove that while Wilde could be superbly malicious with fatheads, he was a generous and painstaking critic, quick to find merit and delighted to announce the discovery. It is easy to damn a book amusingly. Wilde could praise amusingly, a rare and difficult trick." Atlantic

827   English humor and satire

The **Oxford** book of humorous prose; William Caxton to P.G. Wodehouse: a conducted tour. [chosen and edited] by Frank Muir. Oxford Univ. Press 1990 xxxiv, 1162p hardcover o.p. pa $21.50 **827**

1. English wit and humor 2. American wit and humor
ISBN 0-19-280379-4 pa

LC 89-9242

"Selections are generally very short, with bridges, often fairly humorous of themselves, by Muir. The humor ranges from the broad to the subtle and, in fact, in any other way that humor might range; there's something in here for everyone." Libr J

828   English miscellaneous writings

Angel, Katherine

Unmastered; a book on desire, most difficult to tell. by Katherine Angel. Farrar, Straus and Giroux 2013 368 p. (alk. paper) $26   **828**

1. Sex 2. Women -- Sexual behavior 3. Desire
ISBN 0374280401; 9780374280406

LC 2012048072

Author Katherine Angel presents a "personal meditation on sex, power, and female desire. It is also a powerful reckoning with our contradictory and deeply entrenched notions of sexuality. Angel embraces the highly charged oppositions—dominance versus submission, liberation versus dependence—and probes the porousness between masculine and feminine, thought and sensation, self and culture, power and pliancy, always reveling in the elusiveness of easy answers." (Publisher's note)

Includes bibliographical references and index

DeGategno, Paul J.

Critical companion to Jonathan Swift; a literary reference to his life and works. [by] Paul J. DeGategno, R. Jay Stubblefield. Facts on File 2006 474p il (Facts on File library of world literature) $75 **828**

1. Poets 2. Clergy 3. Authors 4. Satirists 5. Pamphleteers 6. Writers on politics
ISBN 0-8160-5093-7; 978-0-8160-5093-2

LC 2005-25470

This "work is divided into five parts. These parts consist of a ten-page biography of satirist Jonathan Swift (1667-1745); a 'Works A-Z' section that includes synopses and commentaries that generally run to several hundred words on virtually all of Swift's poems, essays, and books; a 'Related Entries' section with similar brief articles on persons, topics, and places relevant to Swift studies; appendixes that include a chronology of Swift's life; a . . . bibliography of primary and secondary works; and an index." Libr J

Includes bibliographical references

Huxley, Elspeth

The **flame** trees of Thika; memories of an African childhood. Penguin Bks. 2000 280p pa $15 **828**
1. Authors 2. Novelists 3. Kenya 4. Memoirists
ISBN 0-14-118378-0; 978-0-14-118378-7

LC 99-47965

First published 1959 by Morrow

This is an account of the author's childhood on a coffee plantation in Kenya. She describes the landscape, the Kikuya peoples, the European settlers and the difficulties her parents faced adjusting to life in the bush.

James, Clive, 1939-

Latest readings; Clive James. Yale University Press 2015 192 p. (cloth : alk. paper) $25 **828**
1. Critics 2. Books and reading
ISBN 0300213190; 9780300213195

LC 2014958943

This memoir, by Clive James, "contains his reflections on what may well be his last reading list. A look at some of James's old favorites as well as some of his recent discoveries, this book also offers a revealing look at the author himself, sharing his evocative musings on literature and family, and on living and dying." (Publisher's note)

"James relishes the limited reading time he has and makes no bones about it, providing sparkling commentary on his old favorites and new discoveries." Pub Wkly

Johnson, Samuel, 1709-1784

Samuel Johnson; the major works. edited with an introduction and notes by Donald Greene. Oxford University Press 2000 xxvii, 840p (Oxford world's classics) pa $18.95 **828**
ISBN 978-0-19-284042-4; 0-19-284042-8

LC 83-17280

"This volume celebrates Johnson's astonishing talent by selecting widely across the full range of his work. It includes 'London' and 'The Vanity of Human Wishes' among other poems, and many of his essays for the Rambler and Idler. The prefaces to his edition of Shakespeare and his famous Dictionary, together with samples from the texts, are given, as well as selections from A Journey to the Western Islands of Scotland, the Lives of the Poets, and Rasselas in its entirety. There is also a substantial representation of lesser-known prose, and of his poetry, letters, and journals." Publisher's note
Includes bibliographical references

Ker, Ian

G. K. Chesterton; a biography. Ian Ker. Oxford University Press 2011 747 p. ill. $65.00 **828**
1. Intellectuals 2. English authors -- Biography 3. Poets 4. Authors 5. Essayists 6. Novelists 7. Biographers 8. Travel writers 9. Literary critics 10. Short story writers 11. Biography -- Individual
ISBN 0199601283; 9780199601288

LC 2010940318

This book, by Ian Ker, offers a biography of the author G. K. Chesterton. "Remembered as a brilliant creator of nonsense and satirical verse, author of the Father Brown stories, . . . and yet today he is not counted among the major English novelists and poets. However, this . . . biography argues that

Chesterton should be seen as the successor of the great Victorian prose writers, Carlyle, Arnold, Ruskin, and above all Newman." (Publisher's note)
Includes bibliographical references and index

Martin, Peter

★ A **life** of James Boswell. Yale Univ. Press 2000 613p $35; pa $18.95 **828**
1. Authors 2. Lawyers 3. Biographers
ISBN 0-300-08489-7; 0-300-09312-8 pa

This is a biography of the diarist and author of The life of Samuel Johnson

"Martin has written the best biography of the greatest biographer in the English language. . . . One of the many virtues of Martin's work is his successful synthesis of Boswell's life story with a keen analysis of Boswell's artistry." Atl Mon
Includes bibliographical references

Mda, Zakes

Sometimes there is a void; memoirs of an outsider. Zakes Mda. Farrar, Straus and Giroux 2012 561 p. **828**
1. Authors, South African 2. South Africa -- Politics and government 3. Authors, South African -- 20th century -- Biography
ISBN 9780374280949

LC 2011020817

In this book, "South African novelist, playwright and poet [Zakes] Mda . . . pens a memoir setting his experiences against the backdrop of a country in turmoil. . . . Although he spent his early years in Soweto, Mda was forced to escape to Lesotho after his father was exiled because of his activism against apartheid. . . . Mda's . . . journeys of romance, rebellion and his search for an artistic calling often kept him feeling like an outsider, a theme repeated throughout the memoir." (Kirkus Reviews)

Meyers, Jeffrey

Orwell; wintry conscience of a generation. Norton 2000 380p il maps hardcover o.p. pa $16.95 **828**
1. Authors 2. Novelists 3. Essayists
ISBN 0-393-32263-7 pa

LC 00-38020

"With wit and acumen, Meyers portrays a complex, eccentric, intelligent, and unbending man hard on family and friends, a writer of singular gifts, and a 'prophetic moralist' whose vision continues to illuminate society's dark side." Booklist
Includes bibliographical references

★ The **New** Oxford book of literary anecdotes. Oxford University Press 2006 385p il hardcover o.p. pa $16.95 **828**
1. Authors, English -- Anecdotes 2. Authors, American -- Anecdotes 3. English literature -- Anecdotes
ISBN 0-19-280468-5; 978-0-19-280468-6; 0-19-954341-0 pa; 978-0-19-954341-0 pa

LC 2005-33698

First published 1975 under the editorship of James Sutherland with title: The Oxford book of literary anecdotes

The editor "has compiled more than 700 anecdotes about English-language writers, from Geoffrey Chaucer to J.K. Rowling. The brief, chronologically-arranged (by subject's birth date) entries offer a glimpse into the personalities and times of these authors." Libr J

Includes bibliographical references

Orwell, George, 1903-1950

★ Diaries; George Orwell; edited by Peter Davison; introduction by Christopher Hitchens. 1st American ed. Liveright 2012 597 p. **828**

1. Diaries 2. English authors 3. English novelists 4. English literature 5. Authors 6. Essayists 7. Novelists 8. Biography, Individual

ISBN 0871404109; 9780871404107

LC 2012009895

This book, edited by Peter Davison, offers the personal writings of the British author George Orwell. "Written as individual books throughout his career, the eleven surviving diaries collected here record Orwell's youthful travels among miners and itinerant laborers, the fearsome rise of totalitarianism, the horrific drama of World War II, and the feverish composition of his great masterpieces 'Animal Farm' and '1984.'" (Publisher's note)

Includes bibliographical references and index.

Quinn, Edward

Critical companion to George Orwell; a literary reference to his life and work. Facts On File 2009 450p il (Facts on File library of world literature) $75 **828**

1. Authors 2. Novelists 3. Essayists

ISBN 978-0-8160-7091-6

LC 2008-26727

This volume provides a "review of Orwell's life and covers all his novels, nonfiction, and other writings. . . . It is a superb resource for those desiring an introduction to George Orwell, the man and the writer." Booklist

Includes bibliographical references

Sisman, Adam

Boswell's presumptuous task; the making of the life of Dr. Johnson. Penguin 2002 351p il pa $15 **828**

1. Authors 2. Lawyers 3. Biographers

ISBN 978-0-14-200175-2; 0-14-200175-9

First published 2000 in the United Kingdom

James Boswell's The Life of Samuel Johnson was published in 1791, six years after the death of its subject. In this book, Sisman chronicles Boswell's motives for writing his biography and the techniques he adopted.

"Mr. Sisman's book is illuminating both of Boswell's character and of all aspects of his authorship." Economist

Includes bibliographical references

Swift, Graham

Making an elephant; writing from within. Alfred A. Knopf 2009 400p il $26.95 **828**

ISBN 978-0-307-27099-3

LC 2009-14052

"Out from behind the scrim of fiction, Swift is highly entertaining, at once welcoming and teasing, clever and probing." Booklist

Includes bibliographical references

Thomas, Dylan

A child's Christmas in Wales; with woodcuts by Ellen Raskin. New Directions 2007 51p il pa $9.95 **828**

1. Christmas -- Wales

ISBN 978-0-8112-1731-6; 0-8112-1731-0

LC 2007-24727

First published 1954

The Welsh poet Dylan Thomas recalls the celebration of Christmas with his family and the feelings it evoked in him as a child.

For any season of the year "the language is enchanting and the poetry shines with an unearthly radiance." N Y Times Book Rev

Woolf, Virginia

The Virginia Woolf reader; edited by Mitchell A. Leaska. Harcourt Brace Jovanovich 1984 371p hardcover o.p. pa $16 **828**

ISBN 0-15-693590-2 pa

LC 84-4478

Excerpts from Woolf's "novels form less than 20 percent of a reader whose selections of short stories, essays, letters, and diary entries are excellent. This collection will be useful to those already familiar with Woolf's novels and seeking an introductory selection of her other writings." Libr J

Zaretsky, Robert

Boswell's enlightenment; Robert Zaretsky. Belknap Press of Harvard University Press 2015 288 p. **828**

1. Enlightenment -- Scotland 2. Europe -- Description and travel 3. Scots -- Europe -- History -- 18th century 4. Authors, Scottish -- 18th century -- Biography 5. Travelers -- Europe -- History -- 18th century 6. Philosophy and religion -- Scotland -- History -- 18th century

ISBN 9780674368231

LC 2014037309

Includes bibliographical references and index

830 German literature and literatures of related languages

★ Encyclopedia of German literature; Matthias Konzett, editor. Fitzroy Dearborn Pubs. 2000 2v set $175 **830**

1. Reference books 2. German literature -- Encyclopedias 3. German literature -- Bio-bibliography

ISBN 1-57958-138-2

"Essay-like entries cover three main categories: authors, works (novels, books of poetry, and essays), and topics, the last encompassing everything from literary terms and movements, artistic forums, cities, and historical eras to the key legacy of the Frankfurt School and its members. Rather lengthy lists for further reading are provided with each essay." Libr J

Includes bibliographical references

831 German poetry

Celan, Paul

Breathturn into timestead; the collected later poetry: a bilingual edition. Paul Celan; translated by Pierre Joris. Farrar Straus & Giroux 2014 736 p. (hardback) $40 **831**

1. German poetry 2. Europe -- History -- 20th century
ISBN 0374125988; 9780374125981

LC 2014020543

Translator Pierre Joris presents the "first appearance in English of the complete late volumes [of poet Paul Celan]. The later poems--six books, three of them posthumous--comprise new compounds, alienated images, hauntingly crystallized phrases that sound like nobody's native tongue." (Publishers Weekly)

"Celan's poetry focuses on a new (and very ancient) kind of light: the light of 'the other's Other,' the dark, invisible light beyond all fictions of the abyssal non-origin of being, time, and space. Poetry suffers from what Celan calls Lichtzwang, "light duress," which has prevented poetry from 'darkening over' to its essence. Summing Up: Highly recommended. Upper-division undergraduates through faculty." Choice

Includes bibliographical references and index

★ **Poems** of Paul Celan; translated by Michael Hamburger. Rev and expanded; Persea Bks. 2002 xxxiv, 366p $35; pa $18.95 **831**

1. Poetry -- By individual authors
ISBN 0-89255-275-1; 0-89255-276-X pa

LC 2001-59341

First published 1980 with title: Paul Celan: poems

"This bilingual German-English selection culled from [the poet's] nine collections reveals that his is a poetry of darkness: anguish over what life offers and denies; the ever-present shadow of death that shades each breath. . . . Yet it also expresses an undefined, perhaps undefinable, joy." Booklist [review of 1989 edition]

Goethe, Johann Wolfgang von

Selected poetry; translated with an introduction and notes by David Luke. Penguin Books 2005 xliv, 283p (Penguin classics) pa $16 **831**

1. Poetry -- By individual authors
ISBN 978-0-14-042456-0; 0-14-042456-3

First published 1999 in the United Kingdom

"The introduction gives a thoughtful summary of Goethe's fascinating and problematic life. . . . What Luke triumphantly does is not only to stay close to the original, but also to create a total structure that gives a convincing sense of the overall movement of the poem. . . . Goethe made no secret of his huge debt to Shakespeare; perhaps the English tradition might celebrate the new millennium by learning something from him in return. David Luke's selection makes an excellent starting point." Times Lit Suppl

Morike, Eduard Friedrich

Mozart's journey to Prague and a selection of poems; [by] Eduard Mörike; translated and with an introduction and notes by David Luke; Scots translations by Gilbert McKay. rev ed; Penguin Books 2003 xl, 216p (Penguin Classics) pa $14 **831**

1. Poetry -- By individual authors
ISBN 978-0-14-044737-8; 0-14-044737-7

LC 2004-298957

First published 1997 in the United Kingdom

A selection of Mörike's most popular romantic and classical folk and fairy-tale poems. Also includes the 1855 novella Mozart's journey to Prague, an imaginary recreation of the journey Mozart made from Vienna to Prague in 1787 to conduct the first performance of Don Giovanni.

Includes bibliographical references

Rilke, Rainer Maria

★ **Duino** elegies; translated by David Young; with an introduction and commentary. W. W. Norton 2006 202p pa $13.95 **831**

1. Poetry -- By individual authors
ISBN 978-0-393-32884-4; 0-393-32884-8

LC 2006-9872

First English translation published 1939; this translation was originally published in Field, Contemporary Poetry and Poetics, issues 5 through 9 and as a Norton paperback edition in 1992

"These elegies, the last great work of the poet, were named for the castle of Duino on the Adriatic, where they were first conceived." New Statesman (1913)

New poems; selected and translated by Edward Snow. rev bilingual ed; North Point Press 2001 329p pa $15 **831**

1. Poetry -- By individual authors
ISBN 0-86547-612-8

LC 2001-42714

In this "translation, Edward Snow renders into believable English the complete text of Rilke's work of early maturity. . . Maintaining fidelity to Rilke's idiosyncratic and problematic German, Snow does not reproduce his formal structures but does capture the rhythms, tone shifts, and overall feel of the poems to an admirable degree. Bilingual edition." Booklist [review of 1984 edition of New poems (1907)]

★ **Sonnets** to Orpheus; translated by M.D. Herter Norton. W. W. Norton 2006 160p pa $13.95 **831**

1. Poetry -- By individual authors
ISBN 0-393-32885-6

First English translation 1936 in the United Kingdom; this translation first published 1942

"Deeply rooted in the symbolist tradition, the 'Sonnets' collapse the barriers that exist between the inner and the outer world and celebrate the inherently musical quality of language. In his masterful translation of the 'Sonnets',

Young captures the fluidity of the original with sensitivity and precision." Libr J

Uncollected poems; selected and translated by Edward Snow. Bilingual ed; North Point Press 1995 265p hardcover o.p. pa $15   **831**
1. Poetry -- By individual authors
ISBN 0-86547-513-X pa

LC 94-24438

"Snow is particularly adept at capturing what one might call the non-Orphic side of Rilke's voice. Even in the most complex and rhetorically charged pieces, however, Snow is careful never to simplify Rilke. . . . Most important of all, these translations . . . let us get beyond the simplifications of the Rilke legend with its cycles of transcendent inspiration and imaginative paralysis." New Repub

Sebald, Winfried Georg, 1944-2001

Across the land and the water; new and selected poems, 1964-2001. W.G. Sebald; [translated from the German by Iain Galbraith] Random House 2012 166 p.   **831**
1. Authors, German 2. German poetry -- Collections 3. World War, 1939-1945 -- Germany -- Poetry
ISBN 9781400068906

LC 2011025272

The book "compiles [W. G. Sebald's] . . . poetic output from his student days through to the last years of his life. . . . Sebald's poems engage . . . with the private archives of Germany's memory of the war. . . . Each poem, in its way, reaches towards the irreducible truth of a large number of individuals, Jewish and non-Jewish, brutally transported from home and out of recognition and existence." (New Statesman)

Includes bibliographical references

832   German drama

Durrenmatt, Friedrich

The **visit**; a tragi-comedy. translated from the German by Patrick Bowles. Grove Press 1962 109p pa $12   **832**
ISBN 0-8021-3066-6

Characters: 28 men, 6 women, extras. 3 acts. First produced in the United States at the Lunt-Fontaine Theatre, New York City, May 5, 1958

This play "concerns millionaire Claire Zachanassian's return to her small home town where, in her youth, she was seduced and abandoned by III. She seeks revenge and, to get it, she bribes the entire population: every man, woman and child will be rich for the rest of their lives if they agree to put III to death. After a feeble moral struggle and a travesty of a trial, the people of Güllen condemn and execute the erstwhile lover. In so doing they condemn themselves and Dürrenmatt condemns society as a whole." Cambridge Guide to World Theatre

Goethe, Johann Wolfgang von

★ **Goethe's** Faust; the original German and a new tr. and introduction by Walter Kaufmann; part

one and sections from part two. Anchor Books 1962 503p pa $10.95   **832**
ISBN 978-0-385-03114-1; 0-385-03114-9
Part I first published 1808; Part II 1832

In this epic drama "Mephistopheles makes a bargain with the aged Faust. If Faust is granted one moment of complete contentment, he loses his soul. Faust regains his youth and with Mephistopheles he travels about enjoying every form of earthly pleasure." Haydn. Thesaurus of Book Dig

Lessing, Gotthold Ephraim

Nathan the Wise, Minna von Barnhelm, and other plays and writings; edited by Peter Demetz; foreword by Hannah Arendt. Continuum 1991 xxvii, 335p (German library) hardcover o.p. pa $29.95   **832**
ISBN 0-8264-0706-4; 0-8264-0707-2 pa

LC 91-19344

Schiller, Friedrich

Don Carlos and Mary Stuart; translated with notes by Hilary Collier Sy-Quia; adapted in verse drama by Peter Oswald; with an introduction by Lesley Sharpe. Oxford University Press 2008 xxx, 359p il pa $13.95   **832**
1. Queens 2. Princes
ISBN 978-0-19-954074-7

LC 2008-275155

First published 1996

This volume contains Don Carlos and Mary Stuart, two German historical dramas. "Dating from 1787 and 1800 respectively, one play was written immediately before the French Revolution, the other in its aftermath. These new translations into blank verse are accurate, elegant, and playable. The Introduction, Notes, and Chronology set the plays in their cultural and intellectual background, while a family tree explains the historical relationship between Don Carlos and Mary Stuart." Publisher's note

Includes bibliographical references

The **robbers** [and] Wallenstein; translated with an introduction by F. J. Lamport. Penguin Books 1979 472p (Penguin classics) pa $16   **832**
ISBN 978-0-14-044368-4; 0-14-044368-1

In The robbers (1782) a man, cheated out of his inheritance by his brother, forms a band of thieves. The Wallenstein trilogy, based on the fall of the German general Count Albrecht von Wallenstein, is comprised of: Wallenstein's camp (1798), The Piccolominis (1799), and Wallenstein's death (1799).

833   German fiction

Sebald, Winfried Georg

★ **On** the natural history of destruction; with essays on Alfred Andersch, Jean Amery, and Peter Weiss. {by} W.G. Sebald; translated by Anthea Bell. Random House 2003 202p $23.95; pa $12.95 **833**
1. Artists 2. Authors 3. Painters 4. Novelists 5. Dramatists 6. Philosophers 7. Essayists 8. Nonfiction writers 9. Short story writers 10. German literature

-- History and criticism 11. World War, 1939-1945 --
Literature and the war
ISBN 0-375-50484-2; 0-375-75657-4 pa
LC 2002-75187
Original German edition, 1999

Stach, Reiner
★ **Kafka,** the years of insight; Reiner Stach;
translated by Shelley Frisch. Princeton University
Press 2013 720 p. (hardcover) $35 **833**
1. Tuberculosis 2. Authors, Austrian -- 20th century
-- Biography
ISBN 0691147515; 9780691147512
LC 2012042048
This book is part of Reiner Stach's three-part biography
of author Franz Kafka. This volume "covers the period from
1916 to 1924, his terminal years." Topics include "his fa-
ther's disapprobation, his job at the Worker's Accident In-
surance Institute, his turbulent courtships with Felice Bauer,
Milena Jesenská, and Dora Diamant, and finally his encounter with malignant and fatal tuberculosis." (Library Journal)
Includes bibliographical references and index.

838 German miscellaneous writings

Kleist, Heinrich von
Selected writings; edited and translated by David
Constantine. Hackett Pub. 2004 xxvii, 442p $44;
pa $14.95 **838**
ISBN 978-0-87220-744-8; 0-87220-744-7; 978-0-
87220-743-1 pa; 0-87220-743-9 pa
LC 2004-54378
"This volume includes the majority of Kleist's writings
in English translation. An outstanding representation of his
work, this selection offers three plays, eight short stories,
five anecdotes, and three essays. Kleist's dramas and stories
resonate with complex circumstances and obscure consequences that the characters struggle to sail through. Things
are not always what they seem to be; intriguingly, the guilty
can look innocent and the innocent guilty. The play The
Broken Jug, as well as the stories 'Michael Kohlhaas' and
'The Chilean Earthquake,' depict predicaments of the falsely accused who are denied justice. Constantine . . . does an
outstanding job of conveying the beauty of Kleist's literary
style while allowing himself some liberties in translation."
Libr J
Includes bibliographical references

839 Other Germanic literatures

★ **The Sagas** of Icelanders; a selection. preface
by Jane Smiley; introduction by Robert Kellogg.
Viking 2000 lxvi, 782p il maps (World of the
sagas) hardcover o.p. pa $20 **839**
1. Sagas 2. Old Norse literature
ISBN 0-14-100003-1 pa
LC 99-44111
"The Icelandic Sagas are among the masterpieces of
world literature whose composition stretches from about the
year 1000 to 1500. Presenting the adventures of Norse and

Viking heroes, the sagas are told with ritual simplicity and a
realism that anticipate the modern novel." Libr J
Includes bibliographical references

Singer, Isaac Bashevis
More stories from my father's court; translated
by Curt Leviant. Farrar, Straus & Giroux 2000 216p
hardcover o.p. pa $12 **839**
1. Authors 2. Novelists 3. Journalists 4. Essayists
5. Jews -- Poland 6. Children's authors 7. Short story
writers 8. Nobel laureates for literature
ISBN 0-374-52798-9 pa
LC 00-37583
Sequel to In my father's court
These pieces were first published in Yiddish in the Jewish daily Forward from 1955-1960
These autobiographical sketches depict the workings of
the beth din, the rabbinical court that met in the Singer's
Warsaw home
"This book is a portrait of the artist as a voyeuristic ye-
shiva boy, someone who assimilated into his soul the weird
contradictions of modern Jewish life and, half chronicler
and half creator, spun them into lasting stories." N Y Times
Book Rev

839.3 Netherlandish literatures

Prose, Francine
Anne Frank; the book, the life, the afterlife.
HarperCollins 2009 322p $24.99 **839.3**
1. Children 2. Creative writing 3. Diarists 4. Holocaust
victims 5. Holocaust, 1933-1945 -- Personal narratives
ISBN 978-0-06-143079-4; 0-06-143079-X
LC 2009-17703
"In this definitive, deeply moving inquiry into the life of
the young, imperiled artist, and masterful literary exegesis
of The Diary of a Young Girl, Prose tells the crushing story
of the Frank family, performs a revelatory analysis of Anne's
exacting revision of her coming-of-age memoir, and assesses her father's editorial decisions as he edited his murdered
daughter's manuscript for publication. . . . Extraordinary testimony to the power of literature and compassion." Booklist
Includes bibliographical references

839.7 Swedish literature

Hammarskjold, Dag
Markings; translated from the Swedish by Leif
Sjöberg & W. H. Auden; with a foreword by W. H.
Auden. Knopf 1964 xxiii, 221p hardcover o.p. pa
$13.95 **839.7**
1. Spiritual life
ISBN 0-394-43532-X; 0-307-27742-9 pa; 978-0-307-
27742-8 pa
Original Swedish edition, 1963
The author described this account as a sort of white book
concerning his negotiations with himself and with God. A
record of his inner life, it opens with a poem he wrote around
1925; most of the entries were made during the nineteen for-

ties and fifties—and the book ends with a poem written only a few weeks before his plane crashed.

Prideaux, Sue

Strindberg; a life. Sue Prideaux. Yale University Press 2012 371 p. (cl : alk. paper) $40.00 **839.7**

1. Dramatists -- Biography 2. Authors, Swedish -- 19th century -- Biography

ISBN 0300136935; 9780300136937

LC 2011038050

This book is a biography of the Swedish playwright August Strindberg. "Strindberg (1849-1912) had a miserable childhood and became the devoted father of five children. . . . His plays, murderously claustrophobic scorpion dances of marriage, portray extreme psychological states. He also painted Turneresque pictures, was an expert photographer and gardener, and dabbled fruitlessly in alchemy and the occult." (Booklist)

Includes bibliographical references and index.

Strindberg, August

Strindberg: five plays; translated, with an introduction by Harry G. Carlson. University of Calif. Press 1983 297p hardcover o.p. pa $21.95 **839.7**

ISBN 978-0-520-04698-6 pa

LC 82-15882

Tranströmer, Tomas, 1931-2015

The **great** enigma. New Directions 2006 xxi, 262p pa $16.95 **839.7**

ISBN 978-0-8112-1672-2; 0-8112-1672-1

LC 2006-22551

This volume "offers the most generous collection of Tranströmer's poems to date. . . . Lean and uncluttered, Fulton's translations in The Great Enigma neither preach nor moralize. They refuse staged psychology and let interiority take shape as mysterious judgments, made by the selection of detail and the juxtaposition of things and times and experiences." Boston Rev

839.8　Danish and Norwegian literatures

Ibsen, Henrik

★ The **complete** major prose plays; translated [from the Norwegian] and introduced by Rolf Fjelde. New American Library 1978 1143p pa $28 **839.8**

ISBN 978-0-452-26205-8; 0-452-26205-4

LC 78-50714

First published 1978 by Farrar, Straus & Giroux

Contents: Pillars of society; A doll house; Ghosts; An enemy of the people; The wild duck; Rosmersholm; The lady from the sea; Hedda Gabler; The master builder; Little Eyolf; John Gabriel Borkman; When we dead awaken

Includes bibliographical references

Jacobsen, Rolf

The **roads** have come to an end now; selected and last poems of Rolf Jacobsen. translated by Rob-

ert Bly, Roger Greenwald, and Robert Hedin. Copper Canyon Press 2001 168p pa $16 **839.8**

ISBN 1-55659-165-9

LC 2001-4488

"This bilingual (Norwegian-English) edition of 73 poems demonstrates a poet whose vision of the natural world and humanity's place in it is cosmically penetrative. Jacobsen regards the world as filled with an essential energy, animated by what must be God, and reading his work induces a certain calm ecstasy about everyday existence." Booklist

Wullschlager, Jackie

Hans Christian Andersen; the life of a story teller. University of Chicago Press 2002 489p il map pa $19 **839.8**

1. Authors 2. Novelists 3. Dramatists 4. Authors, Danish 5. Children's authors 6. Short story writers

ISBN 0-226-91747-9; 978-0-226-91747-4

LC 2002-18010

First published 2000 in the United Kingdom

"Wullschlager succeeds brilliantly at portraying Andersens inner mind and uncovering his hopes and fears and details the historical context that served to produce such a grand body of literature. . . . [This biography] will be a standard study for years to come." Libr J

Includes bibliographical references

840.9　French literature--history and criticism

Becker, Daniel Levin

Many subtle channels; in praise of potential literature. Daniel Levin Becker. Harvard University Press 2012 x, 338 p.p (alk. paper) $27.95 **840.9**

1. Authorship 2. Intellectuals 3. Literary style 4. Oulipo (Association) 5. Literary form 6. Authors, American -- 21st century -- Biography

ISBN 0674065778; 9780674065772

LC 2011044577

This book centers on the achievements of "Ouvroir de Littérature Potentielle, or Oulipo, a collective of writers and mathematicians. . . . Since the group's formation in 1960, members of the Oulipo . . . have been concocting . . . intricate [literary] challenges. . . . 'Many Subtle Channels' is Levin Becker's personal history of this literature and his tribute to the people who helped create it, including [Georges] Perec, Jacques Roubaud, Italo Calvino, and Marcel Duchamp." (Bookforum)

841　French poetry

Baudelaire, Charles

Les fleurs du mal; the complete text of The flowers of evil. in a new translation by Richard Howard; illustrated with nine original monotypes by Michael Mazur. Godine 1982 xxxii, 365p il hardcover o.p. pa $18.95 **841**

1. Poetry -- By individual authors

ISBN 978-0-87923-462-1 pa; 0-87923-462-8 pa

LC 81-13283

Original French edition, 1857

"Howard puts the original's rhymed alexandrines primarily into iambic pentameter blank verse, which allows him to capture the immediate, concrete, visceral quality of Baudelaire's imagery." Choice

Poems. Knopf 1993 256p (Everyman's library pocket poets) $12.50 **841**
1. Poetry -- By individual authors
ISBN 0-679-42910-7

LC 93-14363

A representative selection of poetry by the French symbolist.

Beckett, Samuel

Collected poems in English and French. Grove Press 1977 147p hardcover o.p. pa $13.95 **841**
1. Poetry -- By individual authors
ISBN 978-0-8021-3096-9 pa

LC 77-77855

This work contains poems written by Beckett in English and French along with his translations and bilingual versions of poems by Eluard, Rimbaud, Apollinaire, and Chamfort

Chanson de Roland

★ The **song** of Roland; translated, with an introduction, by W.S. Merwin. Modern Library 2001 137p pa $11.95 **841**
1. Roland (Legendary character)
ISBN 0-375-75711-2

LC 00-48989

"This heroic poem celebrates the mighty feats of Roland, the great French hero in the time of Charlemagne. The medieval legend has replaced and transformed the actual facts of history to a great extent but the epic poem has continued in popularity." Bookman's Manual

Includes bibliographical references

French poetry, 1820-1950, with prose translations; selected, translated, and introduced by William Rees. Penguin Books 1994 xli, 854p (Penguin classics) pa $22 **841**
1. French poetry -- Collections
ISBN 978-0-14-042385-3; 0-14-042385-0

LC 91-127343

First published 1990 in the United Kingdom

"While this anthology contains . . . generous selections from the established giants—Baudelaire, Rimbaud, Mallarmé, Valéry, Apollinaire, Michaux—it also draws attention to interesting 'minor' poets, such as Claudel or Cendrars, whose writing has been vital to the evolution of poetry in France. William Rees gives us an introduction to each poet, his or her life, affinities and aesthetics, and the significant literary movements Romanticism, the Parnassian Movement, Symbolism, Cubism, Surrealism and 'Négritude' are signposted and discussed." Publisher's note

Mallarme, Stephane

Collected poems and other verse; translated with notes by E.H. and A.M. Blackmore; with an intro-

duction by Elizabeth McCombie. Oxford University Press 2006 xxxvii, 282p pa $15.95 **841**
1. Poetry -- By individual authors
ISBN 978-0-19-280362-7; 0-19-280362-X

This collection presents Mallarme's "Poesies in the last arrangement known to have been approved by the author. Prose poems, uncollected verse, and the unique, unclassifiable Un Coup de des. . . (A Dice Throw. . .) are also present, including over 20 items that have never previously been translated. Original spelling, punctuation, and lineation have been preserved throughout." Publisher's note

The **Random** House book of twentieth-century French poetry; with translations by American and British poets; edited by Paul Auster. Random House 1982 xlix, 635p hardcover o.p. pa $26 **841**
1. French poetry -- Collections
ISBN 978-0-394-71748-7 pa; 0-394-71748-1 pa

LC 82-280

This bilingual edition collects the verse of forty-eight poets as translated by eighty-four poets. The volume opens with a section of poems by Guillaume Apollinaire and closes with a group of poems by Philippe Denis. The original and translation appear on facing pages

"This excellent anthology undertakes a double task: to provide a comprehensive view of French poetry in the twentieth century and to show, in the range of translators it offers, the influences of that poetry on American and British poets. . . . Paul Auster has done an excellent job of matching poets and translators." Nation

Includes bibliographical references

Rimbaud, Arthur

Poems; [selected by Peter Washington] Knopf 1994 288p (Everyman's library pocket poets) $12.50 **841**
1. Poetry -- By individual authors
ISBN 978-0-679-43321-7; 0-679-43321-X

LC 94-2496

A collection of work by the French Symbolist known for his daring images and pioneering prose poems

Verlaine, Paul

Selected poems; translated by C. F. MacIntyre. University of Calif. Press 1948 xx, 228p il pa $15.95 **841**
1. Poetry -- By individual authors
ISBN 0-520-01298-4

Eighty poems, chosen from Verlaine's first six books. French originals and translations are on facing pages. Contains a preface by the translator

The translator "has done Verlaine a gracious courtesy, and American readers a great kindness. The charm, verbal fireworks, sympathy and nostalgia of this major French poet are Englished with color and convictions." Chicago Sunday Trib

Includes bibliographical references

842   French drama

Beckett, Samuel

Dramatic works; Paul Auster, series editor; introduction by Edward Albee. Grove Press 2006 509p (Samuel Beckett: the Grove centenary edition) $24.95   **842**

ISBN 978-0-8021-1819-0; 0-8021-1819-4

LC 2005-55078

Contents: Waiting for Godot; Endgame; All that fall; Act without words I; Embers; Act without words II; Krapp's last tape; Rough for theatre I; Rough for theatre II; The old tune; Happy days; Rough for radio I; Rough for radio II; Words and music; Cascando; Play; Film; Come and go; Eh Joe; Breath; Not I; That time; Footfalls; Ghost trio; . . . but the clouds . . . ; A piece of monologue; Rockaby; Ohio impromptu; Quad; Catastrophe; Nacht und Träume; What where

Camus, Albert

Caligula & three other plays; translated from the French by Stuart Gilbert; with a preface written specially for this edition and translated by Justin O'Brien. Knopf 1958 302p hardcover o.p. pa $13   **842**

ISBN 978-0-394-70207-0 pa; 0-394-70207-7 pa

"Four of the author's best-known plays, written between 1938 and 1950. 'Caligula,' about the infamous emperor's self-destroying rebellion against fate; 'The Misunderstanding,' about the murder of a man by his ghoulish mother and sister,' 'The Just Assassins,' on the self-questionings of terrorists; and 'State of Siege,' an allegory about the refusal of one individual in a plague-stricken city to compromise with evil." Publ Wkly

Genet, Jean

The **blacks**: a clown show; translated from the French by Bernard Frechtman. Grove Press 1960 128p pa $13   **842**

ISBN 0-8021-5028-4

Original French edition, 1958

"Using the framework of a play within a play, [the production] exposes racial prejudice and stereotypes while exploring black identity. As a troupe of black actors re-enact the trial and ensuing murder of a white woman before a kangaroo court, the Queen and her entourage look on and comment. Five of the 13 black actors white up to play the establishment figures." (The Independent)

The **maids** [and] Deathwatch; two plays. with an introduction by Jean-Paul Sartre; translated from the French by Bernard Frechtman. Grove Press 1954 166p hardcover o.p. pa $14   **842**

ISBN 978-0-8021-5056-1 pa; 0-8021-5056-X pa

Deathwatch, a one-act play written 1947 and first produced 1949 "deals with an insignificant criminal who tries to assume the highly desirable and prestigious role of murderer. . . . In 'The Maids (Les bonnes),' produced in 1947, . . . two servant girls have created an elaborate ritual in which they impersonate their mistress and finally murder her symbolically." McGraw-Hill Ency of World Drama

Goldsby, Robert W.

Molière on stage; what's so funny? Robert W. Goldsby. Anthem Press 2012 xx, 202 p.p (pbk. : alk. paper) $39.95   **842**

ISBN 0857284428; 0857284444; 9780857284426; 9780857284440

LC 2012001708

This book by Robert W. Goldsby "takes the reader onstage, backstage and into the audience of Molière's plays, analyzing the performance of his works in both his own time and in ours. . . . This text . . . investigates four key topics. . . : Molière's early experiences that lead to his later theater experiences; his central great plays of love and lust; his comedic genius and his passion for the stage; and the final words and performances of his life." (Publisher's note)

Includes bibliographical references (p. [191]-196) and index

Ionesco, Eugene

Rhinoceros, and other plays; translated by Derek Prouse. Grove Press 1960 141p pa $10   **842**

ISBN 0-8021-3098-4

Three satirical comedies by a leading dramatist of the "theater of the absurd." In Rhinoceros, one man resists the pressure to conform as everyone about him accepts their transformation into rhinoceroses and he finds himself socially isolated. In The future is in eggs, a couple must produce eggs destined to become intellectuals. The leader is a satire on the mass adulation of political figures in which the leader turns out to be a headless figure

Moliere

The **misanthrope** and other plays. Signet Classics 2005 524p pa $7.95   **842**

ISBN 0-451-52987-1; 978-0-451-52987-9

LC 2006-276841

"Written during the triumphant final years of Molière's career, these seven works represent the mature flowering of his artistry and the most profound development of his vision of humanity." (Publisher's note)

★ **Tartuffe** and other plays. Signet Classics 2007 xxiv, 408p pa $7.95   **842**

ISBN 978-0-451-53033-2

LC 2007-275593

"Including The Ridiculous Precieuses, The School for Husbands, The School for Wives,Don Juan, The Versailles Impromptu, and The Critique of the School for Wives, this collection showcases the talent of perhaps the greatest and best-loved French playwright." (Publisher's note)

Includes bibliographical references

Rostand, Edmond

Cyrano de Bergerac; translated and adapted for the modern stage by Anthony Burgess. Applause Theatre & Cinema Bks. 1998 175p pa $6.95   **842**

1. Poets 2. Authors 3. Soldiers

ISBN 1-55783-230-7

LC 96-2545

A reissue of the title first published 1971 by Knopf

This version was commissioned for production at the Tyrone Guthrie Theater in Minneapolis. It is adapted and translated from the French play originally produced in 1897. Cyrano, the hero, a Gascon poet and swordsman notorious for his long nose, is in love with Roxana

Samuel Beckett's Waiting for Godot; edited and with an introduction by Harold Bloom. New ed; Chelsea House 2008 172p (Modern critical interpretations) $45 **842**
1. Poets 2. Authors 3. Novelists 4. Dramatists 5. Short story writers 6. Nobel laureates for literature
ISBN 978-0-7910-9793-9

LC 2007-49864

First published 1987
Critical interpretations of Beckett's classic tragicomedy illustrating the apparent meaninglessness of life.
Includes bibliographical references

Sartre, Jean Paul, 1905-1980
★ **No** exit, and three other plays. Vintage Bks. 1989 275p pa $12 **842**
ISBN 0-679-72516-4

LC 89-40097

No exit is a modern morality play; The flies is a reworking of the Orestes-Electra story. The third play concerns a young Communist intellectual's attempt to maintain his integrity as party line changes and personal relationships alter perceptions of his murder of a party boss who had fallen out of favor, but whose memory is later rehabilitated. The last play concerns a prostitute's involvement in false charges of rape against a murdered black man and his companion in a town in the American South

843 French fiction

Carter, William C.
Marcel Proust; a life. Yale Univ. Press 2000 946p $45; pa $18.95 **843**
1. Authors 2. Novelists 3. Essayists 4. Literary critics
ISBN 0-300-08145-6; 0-300-09400-0 pa

LC 99-53701

"Excavating biographic details out of such material as untranslated memoirs and recently collected letters, Carter . . . accounts for the daily affairs of this social butterfly-turned-hypochondriac and shut-in. Proust's romances and infatuations, his political action during the Dreyfus affair, and his literary runs-ins with Anatole France and André Gide, as well as larger issues such as his homosexuality, all receive lengthy treatment." Publ Wkly
Includes bibliographical references

Jack, Belinda Elizabeth
George Sand; a woman's life writ large. {by} Belinda Jack. Knopf 2000 395p il hardcover o.p. pa $16 **843**
1. Authors 2. Novelists 3. Dramatists
ISBN 0-679-77918-3 pa

LC 99-40857

"Prodigious author, cross-dresser, lover of Chopin and Alfred de Musset, intimate of (among others) Liszt, Balzac, Dumas (père and fils), Turgenev, and Flaubert (who cried twice at her funeral), Sand was both before her time and

quintessentially of it. Jack's nuanced, moving assessment of the writer's early years . . . is the strongest section of this packed life. When Sand moves onto a larger stage, Jack's style becomes breathless, as if she could barely keep up with her flamboyant subject." New Yorker

Severson, Marilyn S.
★ **Masterpieces** of French literature. Greenwood Press 2004 186p (Greenwood introduces literary masterpieces) $45 **843**
1. French literature -- History and criticism
ISBN 0-313-31484-5

LC 2003-59635

Among the novels discussed are Albert Camus's The stranger and The plague, Gustave Flaubert's Madame Bovary, Victor Hugo's The hunchback of Notre Dame and Les Miserables, and Alexander Dumas's The three musketeers
"Students and general readers seeking a thorough understanding of these influential novels will benefit greatly from this outstanding guide." Libr J
Includes bibliographical references

Shattuck, Roger
Proust's way; a field guide to In search of lost time. Norton 2000 xxiv, 290p hardcover o.p. pa $16.95 **843**
1. Authors 2. Novelists 3. Essayists 4. Literary critics
ISBN 0-393-32180-0 pa

LC 99-58472

Shattuck "explains the major settings of the work, summarizes character and plot, and discusses central themes. Shattuck acknowledges that there is no one right interpretation of In Search of Lost Time but succeeds in providing a framework to help readers get through it. He addresses readers coming to the work for the first time." Libr J
Includes bibliographical references

844 French essays

Camus, Albert
★ The **myth** of Sisyphus, and other essays; translated from the French by Justin O'Brien. Knopf 1955 212p hardcover o.p. pa $12.95 **844**
ISBN 0-679-73373-6 pa
Personal reflections on the meaning of life and the philosophical questions surrounding suicide

Resistance, rebellion, and death; translated from the French and with an introduction by Justin O'Brien. Knopf 1961 271p hardcover o.p. pa $13.95 **844**
ISBN 978-0-679-76401-4 pa; 0679764011 pa
"A selection of forthright essays on contemporary world politics, on capital punishment and the relations of the state and the individual, and on art, chosen from the three volumes of 'Actuelles,' published in France between 1950 and 1958." Publ Wkly

Frampton, Saul
When I am playing with my cat, how do I know she is not playing with me? Montaigne and being in

touch with life. Pantheon Books 2011 300p $26;
ebook $12.99   **844**
  1. Judges 2. Authors 3. Essayists
  ISBN 978-0-375-42471-7; 978-0-307-37959-7 ebook
LC 2010-43642

The author "renders a rigorous history of ideas in this
engaging account of the life and the work of Michel de Montaigne (1533–1592). . . . Frampton tucks a good deal of biography into his tour of the evolution of the essays and the
events that inspired them—but his extraordinary achievement is in conveying—and inviting the reader to commune
with—Montaigne's unique sensibility and his take on death,
sex, travel, friendship, kidney stones, the human thumb, and
above all, 'the power of the ordinary and the unremarkable,
the value of the here-and-now.' This scholarly romp through
the Renaissance is a jewel." Publ Wkly

Includes bibliographical references

848   French miscellaneous writings

Bair, Deirdre
  Simone de Beauvoir; a biography. Summit Bks.
1990 718p il hardcover o.p. pa $31.95   **848**
  1. Authors 2. Novelists 3. Dramatists 4. Philosophers
5. Essayists 6. Feminists 7. Biographers 8. Nonfiction
writers 9. Short story writers 10. Nobel laureates for
literature
  ISBN 0-671-74180-2 pa
LC 89-22029

"Bair's biography of the French author, philosopher,
and feminist aims to restore the balance between interest
in de Beauvoir's personal life—as the lifelong companion of Jean-Paul Sartre and sometime lover of Nelson Algren—and the question of her achievements as a writer and
thinker." Booklist

Includes bibliographical references

Damrosch, Leo
  ★ **Jean**-Jacques Rousseau; restless genius. Leo
Damrosch. Houghton Mifflin Co. 2005 x, 566 p.p
ill., map o.p.; (pbk.) $12.00; o.p.   **848**
  1. Philosophers 2. Authors 3. Novelists 4. Memoirists
5. Political and social philosophers
  ISBN 9780618446964; 9780618872022; 0618446966
LC 2005013579

L.L. Winship/PEN New England Award: Nonfiction
(2006)

This book "is [a] . . . single-volume biography of [Jean-
Jacques] Rousseau, . . . published in English for the general
reader. It . . . illuminate[s] the last decade of his life, a time
when his psychological complexity and strangeness came
to the fore yet his intellect and creative powers triumphed
over his difficult, paranoid temperament. During those ten
years, he finished the 'Confessions,' wrote the 'Dialogues,'
or 'Rousseau Judge of Jean-Jacques,' which he tried in vain
to place in the Notre-Dame cathedral for safekeeping, and
began writing 'Reveries of the Solitary Walker.'" (Publisher's note)

"A delight to read, Damrosch comes as close to Rousseau's authentic self as we are likely to get." N Y Times
Book Rev
  Includes bibliographical references (p. [499]-549)
and index.

Gordon, Lois G.
  The **world** of Samuel Beckett, 1906-1946; {by}
Lois Gordon. Yale Univ. Press 1996 250p il $50;
pa $16.95   **848**
  1. Poets 2. Authors 3. Novelists 4. Dramatists 5.
Short story writers 6. Nobel laureates for literature
  ISBN 0-300-06409-8; 0-300-07495-6 pa
LC 95-22851

Gordon "examines the first 40 years of the playwright/
novelist's 83-year life, which includes periods in Ireland,
where he was born; in Paris, where he spent much of his
life; and in London, Germany, and other parts of France. . . .
Gordon has been thorough in her research and careful in her
presentation." Choice
  Includes bibliographical references

Kaplan, Alice
  The **collaborator**: the trial & execution of Robert
Brasillach; {by} Alice Kaplan. University of Chicago Press 2000 308p $25; pa $15   **848**
  1. Authors 2. Novelists 3. Journalists 4.
Collaborationists 5. Fascism — France 6. World
War, 1939-1945 — France 7. France — Intellectual life
— 20th century 8. Authors, French — 20th century —
Biography 9. Intellectuals — France — Political activity
10. France — History — 1940-1945, German occupation
11. World War, 1939-1945 — Collaborationists — France
12. Fascism and literature — France — History — 20th
century
  ISBN 0-226-42414-6; 0-226-42415-4 pa
LC 99-48291

The author considers the trial of French author Robert
Brasillach, a Nazi collaborator, who was executed by firing
squad in 1945. She explores "the questions posed by the
prosecution . . . during the trial. What responsibility do writers bear for their work? When do words become crimes?"
(N Y Times Book Rev) Index.

Kaplan details "the life of Robert Brasillach, a prolific
and controversial French critic who was executed for treason, at age 35, after France's liberation from the Nazis. A
fascist-leaning writer known for his defense of Nazi crimes
. . . Brasillach was the only distinguished writer put to death
by the postwar French government." Publ Wkly

  Includes bibliographical references

Mabanckou, Alain
  The **lights** of Pointe-Noire; a memoir. Alain
Mabanckou; translated by Helen Stevenson. The
New Press 2016 208 p. illustrations (hardback)
$23.95   **848**
  1. Authors 2. Congo (Republic) 3. Authors, Congolese
(Brazzaville) — Biography
  ISBN 9781620971901
LC 2015032791

In this memoir, "Alain Mabanckou left Congo in 1989,
at the age of twenty-two, not to return until a quarter of a

century later. When he finally came back to Pointe-Noire, a bustling port town on Congo's southeastern coast, he found a country that in some ways had changed beyond recognition: the cinema where, as a child, Mabanckou gorged on glamorous American culture had become a Pentecostal temple, and his secondary school has been renamed in honor of a previously despised colonial ruler." (Publisher's note)

"Mabanckou blurs past and present further with a subtle writing style that involves a variety of techniques. It's no wonder he has won multiple awards. He is an artist—even of the memoir form." LJ

Rimbaud, Arthur

Rimbaud; complete works, selected letters: a bilingual edition. translated with an introduction and notes by Wallace Fowlie; updated, revised and with a foreword by Seth Whidden. University of Chicago Press 2005 xxxvi, 458p il $50; pa $19 **848**
ISBN 978-0-226-71976-4; 0-226-71976-6; 978-0-226-71977-1 pa; 0226719774 pa
LC 2005-41859

First published 1966
In this bilingual edition of Rimbaud's work the original French texts are accompanied by English prose translations. In addition to the complete poetic works there are two prose fragments, a short story in the form of a seminarian's journal, and a selection of letters chosen to illustrate biographical details and Rimbaud's credo as a poet.

Includes bibliographical references

Sartre, Jean-Paul, 1905-1980

We Have Only This Life to Live; Selected Essays, 1939-1975. by Jean-Paul Sartre; edited by Ronald Aronson and Adrian van den Hoven. Random House Inc 2013 600 p. (paperback) $22.95 **848**
1. Life 2. Literature 3. Modern philosophy
ISBN 1590174941; 9781590174937
LC 2013001043

This collection, by Jean-Paul Sartre, edited by Adrian van den Hoven and Ronald Aronson, presents essays by the author collected between 1939 and 1975. "Here Sartre writes about Faulkner, Bataille, Giacometti, Fanon, the liberation of France, torture in Algeria, existentialism and Marxism, friends lost and found, and much else." (Publisher's note)

Todd, Olivier

Albert Camus; a life. translated by Benjamin Ivry. abr & ed English version; Knopf 1997 434p il $30 **848**
1. Authors 2. Novelists 3. Dramatists 4. Authors, French 5. Essayists 6. Nobel laureates for literature
ISBN 0-679-42855-0
LC 97-2991

Original French edition, 1996
This is a biography of the French novelist, playwright, literary editor, and philosopher.

"Todd's exhaustive biography, which aims—and succeeds—in presenting 'the man' and not just the writer, has been shortened for its English translation, which refers readers to the French edition for notes, sources and bibliography." Publ Wkly

Valery, Paul

Selected writings. New Directions 1950 256p hardcover o.p. pa $12.95 **848**
ISBN 0-8112-0213-5 pa

"Seventeen poems are translated by eighteen translators, including Denis Devlin, Léonie Adams, and C. Day Lewis. . . . The rest of the book is composed of the French love miscellanies, essays, dialogues, and critiques." New Yorker

Voltaire

The portable Voltaire; edited, and with an introduction by Ben Ray Redmen. Viking 1949 569p hardcover o.p. pa $17 **848**
ISBN 0-14-015041-2 pa

The selections from Voltaire's works include: Candide, part one; Three stories: Zadig, Micromegas, and Story of a good Brahmin; Letters, and selections from the Philosophical Dictionary and other works. The editor's introduction gives a biographical sketch of Voltaire.

849 Occitan, Catalan, Franco-Provençal literatures

Pla, Josep

The Gray Notebook; Josep Pla; translated from the Catalan by Peter Bush; introduction by Valentí Puig. New York Review Books 2013 656 p. (New York Review Books Classics) (alk. paper) $19.95 **849**
1. Diaries 2. Authors, Spanish 3. Authors, Catalan -- 20th century -- Biography
ISBN 1590176715; 9781590176719
LC 2013028497

This book presents the diary of author Joseph Pla, translated by Peter Bush. "Aspiring to be a writer, not a lawyer, he resolved to hone his style by keeping a journal. In it he wrote about his family, local characters, . . . the quips, quarrels, ambitions, and amours of his friends; writers he liked and writers he didn't; and the long . . . walks he would take in the countryside under magnificent skies." (Publisher's note)

"Pla . . . is considered one of the greatest writers of Catalan language, and this beautiful translation lets English readers glory in the quiet strength of his words." Kirkus

850 Literatures of Italian, Dalmatian, Romanian, Rhaetian, Sardinian, Corsican languages

★ The Oxford companion to Italian literature; edited by Peter Hainsworth and David Robey. Oxford Univ. Press 2002 xli, 644p maps $95 **850**
1. Reference books 2. Italian literature -- Dictionaries 3. Italian literature -- Bio-bibliography
ISBN 0-19-818332-1
LC 2001-59301

"A magisterial addition to the Oxford companions to literature, this volume goes far beyond its core subject of Italian literature to cover its substrate and context. . . . An excellent ready-reference companion for readers seeking less an introduction to the summits of the literature . . . but a reminder of relevant details." Choice

Includes bibliographical references

Ruud, Jay

Critical companion to Dante; a literary reference to his life and work. Facts on File 2008 566p il (Facts on File library of world literature) $75   **850**

1. Poets 2. Authors

ISBN 978-0-8160-6521-9

LC 2007-33473

This title covers the works of Dante, including The Divine Comedy, La Vita Nuova, and his philosophical works.

"Ruud has written a useful introductory resource that students and lay readers alike can enjoy." Booklist

Includes bibliographical references

851   Italian poetry

Ariosto, Lodovico

Orlando Furioso/The frenzy of Orlando, part 1; a romantic epic. by Ludovico Ariosto; translated with an introduction by Barbara Reynolds. Penguin Books 1975 827p map (Penguin classics) pa $18   **851**

1. Poetry -- By individual authors

ISBN 978-0-14-044311-0; 0-14-044311-8

LC 75-327748

An English verse translation in the original meter of the epic poem by the sixteenth-century Italian poet, courtier, and statesman, which is based on the adventures of Roland and other knights of Charlemagne in the wars against the Saracens

This translation is "lucid, lively, and eminently readable. . . . The first volume contains one-half (23) of the cantos plus invaluable aids for the reader: a lengthy, informative introduction, a list of characters and devices, maps and genealogical tables, notes for each canto and an index of proper names." Choice

Orlando Furioso/The frenzy of Orlando, part 2; a romantic epic. [by] Ludovico Ariosto; translated with an introduction by Barbara Reynolds. Penguin Books 1977 794p (Penguin Classics) pa $18   **851**

1. Poetry -- By individual authors

ISBN 978-0-14-044310-3; 0-14-044310-X

"The value of this faithful translation is primarily that it helps you with the Italian. It lets you make your way painlessly into the poem. . . . It does not . . . draw attention to itself. Modestly, it points across, to the things going on in the original." Times Lit Suppl

Dante Alighieri

The **divine** comedy; translated by Allen Mandelbaum; with an introduction by Eugenio Montale; and notes by Peter Armour. Alfred A. Knopf 1995 798p il (Everyman's library) $25   **851**

1. Poetry -- By individual authors

ISBN 978-0-679-43313-2; 0-679-43313-9

LC 95-75206

An epic poem, completed in 1321, in which the poet describes his visionary spiritual journey through Hell, Purgatory and Paradise—guided first by the classical poet Vergil and then by his beloved Beatrice—which results in a purification of his religious faith.

The **Inferno**; translated by Robert Hollander and Jean Hollander; introduction & notes by Robert Hollander. Doubleday 2000 704p hardcover o.p. pa $16.95   **851**

1. Poetry -- By individual authors

ISBN 978-0-385-49698-8 pa; 0-385-49698-2 pa

LC 00-34531

A translation of Dante's poem, in which the Roman poet Virgil guides Dante through the underworld.

"The heart of the Hollanders' edition is the translation itself, which nicely balances the precision required for a much-interpreted allegory and the poetic qualities that draw most readers to the work. The result is a terse, lean Dante with its own kind of beauty. . . . The Hollanders' lines will satisfy both the poetry lover and scholar; they are at once literary, accessible and possessed of the seeming transparence that often characterizes great translations. The Italian text is included on the facing page for easy reference, along with notes drawing on some 60 Dante scholars, several indexes, a list of works cited and an introduction by Robert Hollander." Publ Wkly

Includes bibliographical references

Paradiso; a verse translation by Robert & Jean Hollander; introduction & notes by Robert Hollander. Doubleday 2007 915p $40; pa $19.95   **851**

1. Poetry -- By individual authors

ISBN 978-0-385-50678-6; 0-385-50678-3; 978-1-4000-3115-3 pa; 1-4000-3115-X pa

LC 2007-18070

This is a verse translation of the third volume of Dante's Divine Comedy with the original Italian text on facing pages and an introduction and notes.

"Dante's terza rima is impossible to recreate satisfactorily in English, but the Hollanders have produced a fine verse substitute. . . . Splendid as this new translation is, the endlessly valuable notes are what make this edition supplant all others. The commentary here has evolved not only from extensive research but also from the famous Dante Seminar Hollander has taught at Princeton for many years." Natl Rev

The **portable** Dante; translated, edited, and with an introduction and notes by Mark Musa. Penguin Bks. 1995 xliii, 654p pa $17   **851**

1. Poetry -- By individual authors

ISBN 0-14-243754-9

LC 94-15988

First published 1947

Contains complete verse translations of The Divine comedy and La vita nuova

This book "contains complete verse translations of Dante's two masterworks, The Divine Comedy and La Vita

Nuova, as well as a bibliography, notes, and an introduction by . . . Mark Musa." Publisher's note

Includes bibliographical references

Purgatorio; a verse translation by Jean and Robert Hollander; introduction and notes by Robert Hollander. Doubleday 2003 xxiv, 742p hardcover o.p. pa $18.95 **851**

1. Poetry -- By individual authors

ISBN 978-0-385-49700-8 pa

LC 2002-67100

"To enter Dante's Purgatorio is to step into a charmed world, balanced by the rhythmic interplay of sleep, dreams, light, shadows, smiles, tears, and the reverberations of both solo and choral song. This is the most aesthetically vibrant of Dante's three realms, the one in which the artisanal gestures of poet, painter, and musician prevail. . . . The Hollanders have rendered both the supple lyricism and the rich imagery of the Purgatorio with an admirably informed expertise, preserving the stately economy of Dante's Italian throughout." Literary Rev (Madison, N. J.)

Includes bibliographical references

Montale, Eugenio

The **collected** poems of Eugenio Montale 1925-1977; translated by William Arrowsmith; edited by Rosanna Warren. W. W. Norton & Co. 2012 793 p. **851**

1. Italian poetry 2. Poetry -- Collections 3. Modernism in literature

ISBN 0393080633; 9780393080636

LC 2011034993

This poetry collection features works of the 20th-century Nobel Prize-winning writer Eugenio Montale, edited by Rosanna Warren and translated by William Arrowsmith. "Hailed as one of the key poets of the modern era, Eugenio Montale . . . helped to create international Modernism. . . . His poems chart [a] . . . response to the shocks of modernity, fascism, and two world wars." Publisher's note)

Includes bibliographical references and index.

★ **Collected** poems, 1920-1954; translated and annotated by Jonathan Galassi. rev ed; Farrar, Straus & Giroux 2000 625p pa $18 **851**

1. Poetry -- By individual authors

ISBN 0-374-52625-7

LC 00-35456

First published 1997

"It is generally agreed that the core of Montale's work consists of three major collections: Cuttlefish Bones (1925), The Occasions (1939), and The Storm, etc. (1956). Galassi chooses to publish all three together, separating them from a body of work of almost equal length that came later. He defends this decision in a brilliant afterword that offers the best short account I have yet come across of the nature, import, and elusive content of Montale's work." N Y Rev Books {review of 1997 edition}

Includes bibliographical references

Saba, Umberto

Songbook; the selected poems of Umberto Saba. translated by George Hochfield and Leonard Nathan;

introduction, notes, and commentary by George Hochfield. Yale University Press 2009 562p $35 **851**

1. Poetry -- By individual authors

ISBN 978-0-300-13603-6; 0-300-13603-X

LC 2008-17685

"The author of more than fifteen individual books of poetry and a thousand pages of prose, Saba is best known for his Il Canzoniere (The Songbook), a continually revised and augmented collection in poems of his life's work. . . . [This volume] has been handsomely produced by Yale University Press; not among the least of its attractions is how well it fits in the hand. The edition includes, among other work, a generous number of Saba's earliest poems; all fifteen sonnets of his important Autobiografia (1924); several of his experimental works of 1928-29, titled Preludes and Fugues; and a sampling of his late-life poems, including his beautiful sequence Uccelli (Birds) from 1948. . . . Clearly a labor of love, these collaborative versions, presented with the Italian on facing pages, occupied Hochfield and Nathan for more than a decade." Nation

854 Italian essays

Calvino, Italo, 1923-1985

★ **Collection** of Sand; essays. Italo Calvino; translated by Martin McLaughlin. First U.S. Edition Houghton Mifflin Harcourt Mariner Books 2014 288 p. $13.95 **854**

1. Essays

ISBN 0544146468; 9780544146464

LC 2014001373

This collection of essays, by Italo Calvino, is "the last of his works published during his lifetime. Here he applies his graceful intellect to the delights of the visual world, in essays on subjects ranging from cuneiform and antique maps to Mexican temples and Japanese gardens." (Publisher's note)

"The book offers a delectable array of cognitive insights, ancient history, and Calvino's indispensable voice." Pub Wkly

Eco, Umberto

How to travel with a salmon & other essays; translated from the Italian by William Weaver. Harcourt Brace & Co. 1994 248p il hardcover o.p. pa $15 **854**

ISBN 978-0-15-600125-0 pa; 0-15-600125-X pa

LC 94-10340

"In this collection of parodies, satires and whimsical mini-essays written over the last 30 years, Italian novelist/critic Eco . . . takes readers on a delightful romp through the absurdities of modern life." Publ Wkly

858 Italian miscellaneous writings

Hughes-Hallett, Lucy

Gabriele d'Annunzio; poet, seducer and preacher of war. by Lucy Hughes-Hallett. Alfred A. Knopf 2013 608 p. $35 **858**

1. Nationalists -- Italy -- Biography 2. Fascism --

Italy -- History -- 20th century 3. Poets, Italian -- 20th century -- Biography 4. Rijeka (Croatia) -- History -- 20th century 5. Italy -- Politics and government -- 1914-1945 6. Militarism -- Italy -- History -- 20th century 7. Politics and literature -- Italy -- History -- 20th century 8. World War, 1914-1918 -- Territorial questions -- Croatia -- Rijeka

ISBN 0307263932; 9780307263933

LC 2012033943

This book by Lucy Hughes Hallett presents a biography of "the Italian modernist writer and demagogue" Gabriele d'Annunzio. "He was a brilliant, scandalous literary celebrity . . . a ruthless seducer of women; an avowed Nietzschean superman and an effeminate voluptuary who loved fashion, furnishings, and flowers; and a blood-thirsty militarist who helped propel Italy into World War I with his pro-war oratory and reveled in the carnage he witnessed at the front." (Publishers Weekly)

Includes bibliographical references and index

860 Literatures of Spanish, Portuguese, Galician languages

The **Cambridge** history of Latin American literature; edited by Roberto González Echevarría and Enrique Pupo-Walker. Cambridge Univ. Press 1996 3v ea $180 **860**

1. Latin American literature -- History and criticism
ISBN 0-521-34069-1 v1; 0-521-34070-5 v2; 0-521-41035-5 v3

LC 93-37750

"The editors have added an interdisciplinary dimension to their work by incorporating the materials and methodologies proper to history. . . . [This] will become a classic in the field." Choice

★ The **Cambridge** history of Spanish literature; edited by David T. Gies. Cambridge University Press 2004 863p $160 **860**

1. Spanish literature -- History and criticism
ISBN 0-521-80618-6

LC 2004-45601

"The classics of the canon of eleven centuries of Spanish literature are covered, from Berceo, Cervantes and Calderón to García Lorca and Martín Gaite, but attention is also paid to lesser-known writers and works. . . . The volume concludes with a consideration of the influences of film and new media on modern Spanish literature." Publisher's note

Includes bibliographical references

★ **Concise** encyclopedia of Latin American literature; editor, Verity Smith. Fitzroy Dearborn Pubs. 2000 xxi, 678p $75 **860**

1. Reference books 2. Latin American literature -- Encyclopedias 3. Latin American literature -- Bio-bibliography
ISBN 1-57958-252-4

Based on the Encyclopedia of Latin American literature (1997)

Contains entries on 50 leading writers and 50 important works of Latin American and Caribbean literature. Also in-

cludes survey articles on the literature of individual countries and topical essays. Bibliographies of primary and secondary sources are listed

Includes bibliographical references

861 Spanish poetry

Aleixandre, Vicente

A **longing** for the light; selected poems of Vicente Aleixandre. edited by Lewis Hyde. 2nd ed; Copper Canyon Press 2007 xxi, 279p pa $18 **861**

1. Poetry -- By individual authors
ISBN 978-1-55659-254-6; 1-55659-254-X

LC 2007-992

First published 1979 by Harper & Row

This "is the only available bilingual Spanish-English translation of the poetry of Nobel Laureate Vicente Aleixandre. The collection spans the entirety of Aleixandre's career—from early surrealist work to his complex and fascinating 'dialogues.' It also contains prose interludes, an introduction by editor Lewis Hyde, and a descriptive bibliography." Publisher's note

Borges, Jorge Luis

★ **Selected** poems; edited by Alexander Coleman. Viking 1999 477p hardcover o.p. pa $20 **861**

1. Poetry -- By individual authors
ISBN 0-14-058721-7 pa

LC 99-10318

"Poetry is the heart of Borges' metaphysical, mythical, and cosmopolitan oeuvre. . . . Editor Coleman commissioned a wealth of new translations for this unprecedented and invaluable collection, and the roster of translators includes such luminaries as Robert S. Fitzgerald, W.S. Merwin, Mark Strand, and John Updike." Booklist

Cardenal, Ernesto

Pluriverse; new and selected poems. edited by Jonathan Cohen; with a foreword by Lawrence Ferlinghetti; translations from the Spanish by Jonathan Cohen [et al.] New Directions Pub. 2009 249p pa $17.95 **861**

1. Poetry -- By individual authors
ISBN 978-0-8112-1809-2 pa; 0-8112-1809-0 pa

LC 2008-40582

"Cardenal, now in his 80s, is a Roman Catholic priest and was a leading light of the Nicaraguan Sandinistas. One of his country's most revered figures, Cardenal is these days being persecuted by President Daniel Ortega, the leader whose legend Cardenal did much to create and who has slid now into authoritarian rule. Such tends to be the fate of the revolutionary writer. Cardenal is political, of course, and much of the work presented here (translated by many illustrious hands, including Jonathan Cohen, Thomas Merton and Kenneth Rexroth) deals with the struggle and history of his country and Latin America at large. But he can sing lyrically too. . . . Beautiful." Los Angeles Times Book Rev

Cid

The **poem** of the Cid; translated by Rita Hamilton and Janet Perry; with an introduction and notes by Ian Michael. Penguin 1984 242p map pa $14 **861**
1. Poetry -- By individual authors
ISBN 0-14-044446-7

"The poem is based on the exploits of Rodrigo or Ruy Diaz de Bivar (c.1043-1099), who was known as 'el Cid.' . . . Similar in form to the 'Chanson de Roland,' the poem is notable for its simplicity and directness and for its exact, picturesque detail. Despite the inclusion of much legendary material, the figure of the Cid who is depicted as the model Castilian warrior, is not idealized to an extravagant degree." Reader's Ency. 4th edition

Garcia Lorca, Federico

Collected poems; edited and with an introduction and notes by Christopher Maurer; translated by Francisco Aragon [et al.] Farrar, Straus & Giroux 1991 893p (Poetical works) hardcover o.p. pa $25 **861**
1. Poetry -- By individual authors
ISBN 978-0-374-52691-7; 0-374-52691-5 pa

This bilingual edition of Garcia Lorca's poetry, "which modestly claims not to be 'definitive,' includes every poem written by the acclaimed Spanish poet except Poet in New York. Assembled in the light of recent scholarship, its contents have been rendered into English by newer translators such as Alan S. Trueblood, Catherine Brown, Will Kirkland, and Greg Simon; older translators such as Stephen Spender, Langston Hughes, and Ben Belitt are not represented. Generally, rhyme and assonance are sacrificed to the 'silent counterpoint of poetic meaning,' and old-fashioned diction is avoided." Libr J

Poet in New York; edited and with an introduction and notes by Christopher Maurer; translated by Greg Simon and Steven F. White. Farrar, Straus & Giroux 1988 xxx, 275p il pa $18 **861**
1. New York (N.Y.) -- Poetry
ISBN 978-0-374-52540-8; 0-374-52083-4
LC 87-33154

This "is one of the perplexing classics of twentieth-century poetry. It is a difficult, sometimes bewildered, often hermetic work. It is elusive and enigmatic, mysterious, tortured—a book, to borrow one of the poet's own phrases, 'that can baptize in dark water all who look at it.' Reading it in [this] convincing new translation, . . . one feels the anguished authority and the demonic force and impact of the original. For all its strangeness, Lorca's testament may well be one of the greatest books of poems ever written about New York City." New Yorker
Includes bibliographical references

Neruda, Pablo

★ The **poetry** of Pablo Neruda; edited and with an introduction by Ilan Stavans. Farrar, Straus and Giroux 2003 996p hardcover o.p. pa $20 **861**
1. Poetry -- By individual authors
ISBN 0-374-29995-1; 0-374-52960-4 pa
LC 2002-32548

"Stavans has assembled the most complete anthology of Neruda yet available in English, drawing evenhandedly from the various stages of the poet's long and complex career. Neruda was, it seems, at least half a dozen poets, many of them in competition with the others. Needless to say, there are wonders in these pages that will delight readers unfamiliar with the tumultuously varied planet known as Neruda." Nation
Includes bibliographical references

Paz, Octavio

★ The **collected** poems of Octavio Paz, 1957-1987; edited & translated by Eliot Weinberger; with additional translations by Elizabeth Bishop [et al.] New Directions 1987 669p il hardcover o.p. pa $26.95 **861**
1. Poetry -- By individual authors
ISBN 978-0-8112-1173-4 pa; 0-8112-1173-8 pa
LC 87-23989

"Dense, weighty, and miraculous, this bilingual edition compresses into one volume all the poems published in book form since 1957. Nearly 200 poems, some newly translated, many new to an English-language edition, conclusively demonstrate Paz's power." Libr J
Includes bibliographical references

The **poems** of Octavio Paz; edited and translated by Eliot Weinberger with additional translations by Elizabeth Bishop, Paul Blackburn, Denise Levertov, Muriel Rukeyser, and Charles Tomlinson. New Directions 2012 606 p. (cloth : acid-free paper) $39.95 **861**
1. Mexican poetry 2. Poetry -- Collections
ISBN 0811220435; 9780811220439
LC 2012016228

This book edited and translated by Eliot Weinberger is "the first retrospective collection of [Octavio] Paz's poetry to span his entire writing career. . . . This edition includes many poems that have never been translated into English before, new translations based on Paz's final revisions, and a . . . capsule biography of Paz by Weinberger, as well as notes on the poems in Paz's own words, taken from various interviews he gave throughout his life." (Publisher's note)
Includes bibliographical references and index.

The **Penguin** book of Spanish verse; introduced and edited by J.M. Cohen; with plain prose translations of each poem. 3rd ed; Penguin 1988 xliii, 596p pa $18 **861**
1. Spanish poetry -- Collections
ISBN 978-0-14-058570-4; 0-14-058570-2
LC 88-166999

First published 1956
More than 300 works by 100 poets reflect nine centuries of poetry in Spain.

Then come back; the lost Neruda. Pablo Neruda; translated by Forrest Gander. Copper Canyon

Press 2016 160 p. color ill., facimilies (hardback) $23 **861**
1. Poetry -- Collections
ISBN 9781556594946

LC 2015048546

This book, translated by Forrest Gander, presents "Pablo Neruda's lost poems. . . . Originally composed on napkins, playbills, receipts, and notebooks, Neruda's lost poems are full of eros and heartache, complex wordplay and deep wonder. Presented with the Spanish text, full-color reproductions of handwritten poems, and dynamic English translations, [it] simultaneously completes and advances the oeuvre of the world's most beloved poet." (Publisher's note)
Includes bibliographical references.

Torre, Monica de la

Reversible monuments; contemporary Mexican poetry. edited by Mónica de la Torre and Michael Wiegers. Copper Canyon Press 2002 675p pa $20 **861**
1. Mexican poetry -- Collections
ISBN 1-55659-159-4

LC 2002-6189

This bilingual anthology includes 31 contributors, "most writing in Spanish but some in indigenous languages. Spacious and accommodating, this work presents a generous number of gracefully translated poems by each poet, a felicitous in-depth approach that makes this much more than a sampler, and a sound decision given the poet's propensity for long, dreamy poems. Sensuality is ever-present, as is an intimate connection with nature. . . . This is without doubt a landmark volume." Booklist

Twentieth century Latin American poetry; a bilingual anthology. edited by Stephen Tapscott. University of Tex. Press 1996 xxii, 418p il (Texas Pan American series) hardcover o.p. pa $26.95 **861**
1. Latin American poetry -- Collections
ISBN 0-292-78140-7 pa

LC 95-40288

This anthology "samples the works of more than 75 poets, including such giants as Neruda, Dario, Reyes, Vallejo, Borges and Paz. With original-language versions and translations set side by side, the collection is arranged in order of the poets' dates of birth from José Marti, born in Cuba in 1853, to Marjorie Agosin, born in the U.S. 102 years later. Tapscott's well-conceived and lucid introduction is expanded in concise individual introductions that provide basic information and some evaluation." Publ Wkly
Includes bibliographical references

862 Spanish drama

Calderon de la Barca, Pedro

Life's a dream; a prose translation and critical introduction by Michael Kidd. University Press of Colorado 2004 159p hardcover o.p. pa $13.95 **862**
ISBN 978-0-87081-777-9 pa

LC 2004-10260

17th century Spanish verse play in prose translation. King of Poland tests son, imprisoned from birth because of prophecy, to see if he will become tyrant. Savage at first, Prince later shows true nobility, exposing actual meaning of prophecy.
"Michael Kidd advances the work of two often-exclusive camps of comediantes: scholarship and performance. While his introduction provides ample criticism for the scholar, he successfully presents an accessible script for theatre practitioners looking to enact the story of the play." Bulletin of Hispanic Studies
Includes bibliographical references

Vega, Lope de

Three major plays; translated with an introduction and notes by Gwynne Edwards. Oxford University Press 2008 xli, 300p (Oxford world's classics) pa $14.95 **862**
ISBN 978-0-19-954017-4; 0-19-954017-9

LC 98-26991

Reissue of a title first published 1999
"Fuente Ovejuna , based on Spanish history, and revealing how tyranny leads to rebellion, is perhaps [Vega's] best-known play. The Knight from Olmedo is a moving dramatization of impetuous and youthful passion which ends in death. Punishment without Revenge, Lope's most powerful tragedy, centres on the illicit relationship of a young wife with her stepson and the revenge of a dishonoured husband." Publisher's note
Includes bibliographical references

863 Spanish fiction

Allende, Isabel

My invented country; a nostalgic journey through Chile. translated from the Spanish by Margaret Sayers Peden. HarperCollins Pubs. 2003 199p map $23.95; pa $13.95 **863**
1. Authors 2. Novelists 3. Dramatists 4. Journalists 5. Authors, Chilean 6. Chile 7. Children's authors
ISBN 0-06-054564-X; 0-06-054567-4 pa

LC 2002-191267

"In this memoir-cum-study of her 'home ground,' the author delves into the history, social mores and idiosyncrasies of Chile, where she was raised, showing, in the process, how that land has served as her muse. . . . This is a reflective book, lacking the pull of Allende's fiction but unearthing intriguing elements of the author's captivating history." Publ Wkly

864 Spanish essays

Borges, Jorge Luis

★ **Selected** non-fictions; edited by Eliot Weinberger; translated by Esther Allen, Suzanne Jill Levine & Eliot Weinberger. Viking 1999 559p hardcover o.p. pa $20 **864**
ISBN 978-0-14-029011-0 pa; 0-14-029011-7 pa

LC 99-12386

"Shifting effortlessly from Homer to Hitler, from Kafka to King Kong, these hundred and sixty-one essays, appreciations, prologues, and philosophical investigations are dizzying in scope and dazzling in execution. But it is Borges's dogged pursuit of familiar themes—infinity and eternity, reflexivity and recurrence—which gives this collection its unusual unity and depth." New Yorker

Includes bibliographical references

Fuentes, Carlos

Myself with others; selected essays. Farrar, Straus & Giroux 1988 214p $19.95; pa $18 **864**

ISBN 0-374-21750-5; 0-374-52237-5 pa

LC 87-7448

Essays by the Mexican writer on subjects ranging from the cinema of Buñuel to the literary output of Cervantes, Borges and Garcia Marquez

Paz, Octavio

★ The **labyrinth** of solitude; The other Mexico, Return to the labyrinth of solitude, Mexico and the United States, The philanthropic ogre. Grove Press 1985 398p hardcover o.p. pa $14.50 **864**

1. Mexican national characteristics 2. Mexico -- Civilization

ISBN 978-0-8021-5042-4 pa; 0-8021-5042-X pa

LC 82-47999

The labyrinth of solitude and The other Mexico were first published 1961 and 1972 respectively

In this collection of essays and one interview, Paz explorers the cultural and historical influences on the social behavior of his countrymen

Vargas Llosa, Mario

The **language** of passion; translated by Natasha Wimmer. Farrar, Straus & Giroux 2003 292p $24; pa $14 **864**

ISBN 0-374-18326-0; 0-312-42254-7 pa

LC 2002-37909

"This collection focuses on the essays that appeared during the 1990s, most of which are imbued with a wit and an intellect that make them instantly engaging." Libr J

Includes bibliographical references

868 Spanish miscellaneous writings

Abad, Hector

Oblivion; a memoir. Héctor Abad; translated from the Spanish by Anne McLean and Rosalind Harvey. Farrar, Straus and Giroux 2012 263 p. **868**

1. Biography 2. Political activists 3. Father-son relationship 4. Physicians -- Colombia -- Biography 5. Political activists -- Crimes against 6. Colombia -- Politics and government -- 1974- 7. Political activists -- Colombia -- Biography 8. Authors, Colombian -- 20th century -- Biography

ISBN 0374223971; 9780374223977

LC 2011045885

This memoir by Héctor Abad describes the life and work of the author's father "Héctor Abad Gómez, a professor and doctor devoted to his family . . . and committed to a better Colombia. The latter aspiration cost him his life when he was assassinated in 1987." Topics include "Gómez's public health and human rights projects" such as founding "the Colombian Institute of Family Wellbeing, which built aqueducts and sewer systems in villages, rural districts, and cities." (Publishers Weekly)

Biron, Rebecca E.

Elena Garro and Mexico's modern dreams; Rebecca E. Biron. Bucknell University Press 2012 294 p. (Buckell studies in Latin American literature and theory) (cloth : alk. paper) $90 **868**

1. Mexico -- Civilization 2. Modernism in literature 3. Modernism (Literature) -- Mexico 4. National characteristics, Mexican, in literature

ISBN 1611484707; 9781611484700

LC 2012042552

Author Rebecca E. Biron's book focuses on Elena Garro. "The famously scandalous first wife of Nobel Prize winner poet Octavio Paz, and an award-winning author in her own right, Garro constructed a mysterious and often contradictory persona through her very public participation in Mexican political conflicts. . . . Garro's public persona and critical perspective expose the anxieties regarding ethnicity, gender, economic class, and professional identity that define Mexican modernity." (Publisher's note)

Includes bibliographical references and index

869 Literatures of Portuguese and Galician languages

Antunes, Antonio Lobo

The **fat** man and infinity; and other writings. translated with an introduction by Margaret Jull Costa. W. W. Norton & Company 2009 396p il $26.95 **869**

ISBN 978-0-393-06198-7; 0-393-06198-1

LC 2008-41551

This volume "collects the short, impressionistic newspaper columns, or 'cronicas,' that [Antunes] has written for various publications, notably the Portuguese newspaper O Público. Mr. Antunes has played down these columns, referring to them as 'divertissments' written to earn pocket money. But as this book's translator, Margaret Jull Costa, points out, in Portugal these collections 'have enjoyed the kind of popular success his novels never have.' (This book also contains a selection of Mr. Antunes's short stories. . .). Mr. Antunes makes for an unusual newspaper columnist. Jimmy Breslin he's not. His bite-size essays contain no political ruminations and almost nothing about sports, or popular culture, or literary criticism or run-ins with the great and good. Instead they are interior diaries of a kind, most of them imbued with a deep nostalgia for the author's youth." N Y Times Book Rev

Camoes, Luis de

★ **Selected** sonnets; edited and translated by William Baer. Bilingual ed; University of Chicago Press 2005 199p il $26   **869**

1. Poetry -- By individual authors

ISBN 0-226-09266-6

LC 2004-58521

Camões "is Portugal's great sonneteer. He published only one sonnet in his lifetime, and many of doubtful authorship crept into the canon during their first century of great popularity. Baer presents 70 in Portuguese and his own English versions, formally faithful to the originals except that in the octaves Baer uses four (abba, cddc) rather than Camoes' two (abba, abba) rhymes. A sketch of Camoes' amazingly adventurous and colorful life, his works, and his reputation precedes the poems." Booklist

---

870   Latin literature and literatures of related Italic languages

The **Portable** Roman reader; edited, and with an introduction by Basil Davenport. Viking 1951 656p hardcover o.p. pa $18   **870**

1. Latin literature -- Collections

ISBN 0-14-015056-0 pa

This anthology includes selections from Plautus, Terence, Caesar, Virgil, Seneca, Juvenal as well as complete plays by Plautus and Terence and the anonymous poem Vigil of Venus

---

871   Latin poetry

Horace

The **epistles** of Horace; [translated by] David Ferry. Farrar, Straus, and Giroux 2001 203p hardcover o.p. pa $19   **871**

1. Poetry -- By individual authors

ISBN 978-0-374-52852-7 pa; 0-374-52852-7 pa

LC 00-52746

"Ferry takes his bearings from the great blank verse poets of the last two hundred years, especially Frost, and while he manages to be faithful to the meaning, substance and shades, of the Latin original, Ferry achieves through his historical, cultural, and linguistic cross-pollination something more important and lasting than mere translation: he brings to life new as well as old possibilities for poetry in America now." Harvard Rev

Includes bibliographical references

Virgil

The **eclogues** of Virgil; a translation by David Ferry. Farrar, Straus & Giroux 1999 101p hardcover o.p. pa $14   **871**

1. Poetry -- By individual authors

ISBN 978-0-374-52696-2 pa; 0-374-52696-6 pa

LC 98-52547

The Eclogues "comprise not much more than 800 lines in total, but they may be the most influential collection of short poems by one author ever written. . . . It is a conspicu-

ous merit of Ferry's translations that they have a kind of transparency; he does not intrude his style or his personality between the reader and himself. His versions are rather plain, unfussy, and usually of a quiet dignity." New Republic

---

872   Latin dramatic poetry and drama

Plautus, Titus Maccius

The **pot** of gold, and other plays; [by] Plautus; tr. by E. F. Watling. Penguin Books 1965 267p (Penguin Classics) pa $12   **872**

ISBN 978-0-14-044149-9; 0-14-044149-2

LC 65-8577

Plautus "romanized many of the plots and characters of New Greek Comedy. Through his plays, he introduced to the non-Greek world characters which have since become part of traditional western European comedy, among them the braggard soldier (in his Miles Gloriosus) and the sly servant (in his Pseudolus)." Benet's Reader's Ency. 4th edition

The **rope**, and other plays; [by] Plautus; tr. by E. F. Watling. Penguin Books 1964 284p (Penguin Classics) pa $12   **872**

ISBN 978-0-14-044136-9; 0-14-044136-0

LC 63-2117

Terence

Terence, the comedies; translations by Palmer Bovie, Constance Carrier, and Douglass Parker; edited by Palmer Bovie. Johns Hopkins Univ. Press 1992 xxi, 398p (Complete Roman drama in translation) hardcover o.p. pa $25   **872**

ISBN 978-0-8018-4354-9 pa; 0-8018-4354-5 pa

LC 91-33984

First published 1974 by Rutgers University Press with title: The complete comedies of Terence

Virgil

The **Georgics** of Virgil; a translation. a translation [translated] by David Ferry. Farrar, Straus and Giroux 2005 xx, 202p hardcover o.p. pa $14 **872**

ISBN 978-0-374-16131-0 pa; 0-374-16131-9 pa

LC 2004-20023

"Ferry shows tremendous skill with his taut yet pliant pentameter. He also employs demotic and high lyrical diction with equal finesse. His version contains all the freshness of American speech and all the classical poise of the original: it comes across neither as a curatorial act of conservation nor as a modish remake. . . . This is the best poetry of Ancient Rome, rendered by the best translator of modern America." Poetry (Modern Poetry Association)

---

873   Latin epic poetry and fiction

Ovid

★ **Metamorphoses**; [by] Ovid; translated and with notes by Charles Martin; introduction by Bernard Knox. W.W. Norton & Co 2004 xxvi, 597p $57; pa $17.95 **873**

ISBN 0-393-05810-7; 0-393-32642-X pa

LC 2003-14491

"A series of tales in Latin verse. . . . Dealing with mythological, legendary, and historical figures, they are written in hexameters, in fifteen books, beginning with the creation of the world and ending with the deification of Caesar and the reign of Augustus." Reader's Ency. 4th edition

Includes bibliographical references

Tales from Ovid; [translated by] Ted Hughes. Farrar, Straus & Giroux 1997 257p hardcover o.p. pa $14 **873**

1. Poetry -- By individual authors

ISBN 0-374-52587-0 pa

LC 97-36061

Hughes retells 24 Greco-Roman myths from Ovid's Latin epic Metamorphoses.

This is "an inspired act of translation that stands as vigorous poetry in its own right." N Y Times Book Rev

Includes bibliographical references

Virgil

The **Aeneid**; translated by Robert Fitzgerald. Knopf 1992 xxvii,483 (Everyman's library) $20 **873**

1. Poetry -- By individual authors

ISBN 978-0-679-41335-6; 0-679-41335-9

LC 91-58698

This translation first published 1983 by Random House

"Fitzgerald's is so decisively the best modern Aeneid that it is unthinkable anyone will want to use any other version for a long time to come. Latinists, as they read it, will be led to consider their original afresh. Those without Latin are going to find, to their surprise, and I hope their pleasure, that the poem is still as good as anyone ever said it was." N Y Rev Books

874 Latin lyric poetry

Catullus, Gaius Valerius

The **poems** of Catullus; translated by Charles Martin. Johns Hopkins Univ. Press 1990 181p hardcover o.p. pa $19.95 **874**

1. Poetry -- By individual authors

ISBN 978-0-8018-3926-9 pa; 0-8018-3926-2 pa

LC 89-45486

First published 1979 in limited edition by Abattoir Editions, the University of Nebraska at Omaha

"The introduction ranges through Martin's observations on Catullus' place among Roman lyricists, his virtuosity, acuity, irony, and appeal to modern poets. The translations themselves, while open to inevitable quibbling among Latinists, are remarkably true to the versification, denotations, and connotations of the original texts. Martin is particularly adept at shaping the English into approximations of the Latin meters." Choice

Horace

The **odes** of Horace; a translation by David Ferry. Farrar, Straus & Giroux 1997 343p hardcover o.p. pa $28 **874**

1. Poetry -- By individual authors

ISBN 978-0-374-52572-9 pa; 0-374-52572-2 pa

LC 97-9483

Ferry "wisely does not try to reproduce Horace's meters in English. . . . And he often rearranges Horace's material to fit the run of his own verse, sometimes to stunning effect. . . . This is a Horace for our times." N Y Rev Books

875 Latin speeches

Cicero, Marcus Tullius

Political speeches; [by] Cicero; translated with introductions and notes by D.H. Berry. Oxford University Press 2006 xl, 345p map pa $13.95 **875**

1. Speeches 2. Rome -- History

ISBN 978-0-19-283266-5; 0-19-283266-2

LC 2005-20919

"Cicero (106-43 BC) was the greatest orator of the ancient world and a leading politician of the closing era of the Roman republic. This book presents nine speeches which reflect the development, variety, and drama of his political career,among them two speeches from his prosecution of Verres, a corrupt and cruel governor of Sicily; four speeches against the conspirator Catiline; and the Second Philippic , the famous denunciation of Mark Antony which cost Cicero his life. Also included are On the Command of Gnaeus Pompeius , in which he praises the military successes of Pompey, and For Marcellus , a panegyric in praise of the dictator Julius Caesar." Publisher's note

Includes bibliographical references

877 Latin humor and satire

Erasmus, Desiderius

Praise of folly; and, Letter to Maarten Van Dorp, 1515. [by] Erasmus of Rotterdam; translated by Betty Radice; with an introduction and notes by A.H.T. Levi. Penguin Books 1993 lvi, 188p (Penguin classics) pa $13 **877**

ISBN 978-014-044608-1; 0-14-044608-7

LC 94-142502

A "satirical monologue in Latin. . . . Folly praises herself and proclaims her superiority over Wisdom. The author's argument, of course, is 'that it is folly not to see things as they really are; scholars should not abandon ideals just because they cannot be fully realized but should apply their learning and reason as best they can to daily living.'" Reader's Adviser

Juvenal

The **sixteen** satires; translated with an introduction and notes by Peter Green. 3rd ed; Penguin Books 1999 lxviii, 252p (Penguin classics) pa $13 **877**

ISBN 978-0-14-044704-0; 0-14-044704-0

LC 99-987049

First published 1967

"The sixteen 'Satires' of Juvenal, which contain a vivid picture of contemporary Rome under the Empire, have seldom been equalled as biting diatribes. . . . Juvenal's invectives in powerful hexameters, exact and epigrammatic, were aimed at lax and luxurious society, tyranny, criminal excesses, and the immorality of women." Reader's Adviser

878 Latin miscellaneous writings

Caesar, Julius

The **Gallic** War; with an English translation by H. J. Edwards. Harvard Univ. Press 1958 xxii, 616p il maps $21.50 **878**

1. Rome -- History
ISBN 0-674-99080-3

Caesar's account of his campaign (58-50 B.C.) to bring the province of Gaul (France) under his control.

Cicero, Marcus Tullius

On the good life; translated with an introduction by Michael Grant. Penguin Books 1971 382p map (Penguin classics) pa $16 **878**

1. Ethics
ISBN 978-0-14-044244-1; 0-14-044244-8

LC 77-30399

For "Roman orator and statesman Cicero, 'the good life' was at once a life of contentment and one of moral virtue and the two were inescapably intertwined. This volume brings together a wide range of his reflections upon the importance of moral integrity in the search for happiness. . . . Cicero presents his views upon the significance of friendship and duty to state and family, and outlines a clear system of practical ethics." Publisher's note

Martial

Epigrams; selected and translated by James Michie; introduction by Shadi Bartsch. Modern Library 2002 xxxiv, 199p (Modern Library classics) pa $14.95 **878**

1. Epigrams
ISBN 978-0-375-76042-6; 0-375-76042-3

LC 2002-22343

First published 1972

Michie "has translated a selection of the epigrams—about one tenth of what Martial wrote. He has the text on the facing page—a great advantage if you can read Latin—an Introduction [and] Notes. . . . [He] uses rhyme, and makes his Martial much more like the English idea of an epigram than like the epigrams in the Greek Anthology. There isn't much pure humor in Latin literature (as opposed to waspishness and scurrility) but Martial is often very funny." Encounter (London, England)

Includes bibliographical references

Suetonius Tranquillus, C.

★ The **twelve** Caesars; {by} Gaius Suetonius Tranquillus; translated by Robert Graves; revised

with an introduction by Michael Grant. Penguin Bks. 2003 363p maps pa $14 **878**

1. Emperors 2. Rome -- History 3. Emperors -- Rome
ISBN 0-14-044921-3

LC 2003-267782

A reissue with new Chronology and updated further reading of the translation published 1957

"A detailed account of the life and times of the first twelve emperors from Caesar to Domitian." Reader's Ency. 4th edition

Includes bibliographical references

Tacitus, Cornelius

Complete works of Tacitus; translated from the Latin by Alfred John Church and William Jackson Brodribb; edited and with an introduction by Moses Hadas. McGraw-Hill 1964 773p il pa $14.75 **878**

1. Generals 2. Rome -- History 3. Colonial administrators 4. Germany -- History -- 0-1517
ISBN 0-07-553639-0; 978-0-07-553639-0

First published 1942 by Modern Lib.

880 Classical Greek literature and literatures of related Hellenic languages

Jenkyns, Richard

★ **Classical** literature; an epic journey from homer to virgil and beyond. Richard Jenkyns. Basic Books 2015 288 p. (hardcover) $27.99 **880**

1. Epic poetry 2. Romance literature
ISBN 0465097979; 9780465097975

LC 2015953494

In this book, author "Richard Jenkyns explores a thousand years of classical civilization, carrying readers from the depths of the Greek dark ages through the glittering heights of Rome's empire. Jenkyns begins with Homer and the birth of epic poetry before exploring the hypnotic poetry of Pindar, Sappho, and others from the Greek dark ages." (Publisher's note)

"A rich, witty, perceptive, and brief account of the Greek and Latin classics and their importance, both in themselves and in their enduring influence on the Western world. One of the best introductions available to the general reader." LJ

Includes bibliographical references (pages 247-259) and index.

The **Norton** book of classical literature; edited by Bernard Knox. Norton 1993 866p $29.95 **880**

1. Greek literature -- Collections
ISBN 0-393-03426-7

LC 92-10378

"A comprehensive volume of more than 300 pieces of classical literature, primarily Greek but also some Roman." Booklist

★ The **Oxford** companion to classical literature; edited by M.C. Howatson. 3rd ed.; Oxford University Press 2011 un map $65 **880**

1. Reference books 2. Classical literature -- Dictionaries
ISBN 978-0-19-954854-5

First published 1937 under the editorship of Sir Paul Harvey

This work "covers classical literature from the appearance of the Greeks, around 2200 B.C., to the close of the Athenian philosophy schools in A.D. 529. It includes articles on authors, major works, historical notables, mythological figures, and topics of literary significance. Short summaries of major works, chronologies, charts, and maps are special features." Nichols. Guide to Ref Books for Sch Media Cent. 4th edition

Thorburn, John E.

★ The **Facts** on File companion to classical drama. Facts on File 2005 680p map (Facts on File library of world literature) $71.50   **880**

1. Reference books 2. Classical drama -- Encyclopedias
ISBN 0-8160-5202-6

LC 2004-16803

"It is difficult to think of any other resource quite this thorough that combines all of Greek and Roman drama into a convenient single-volume publication." Libr J

Includes bibliographical references

881   Classical Greek poetry

7 Greeks; translations by Guy Davenport. New Directions 1995 241p pa $16.95   **881**

1. Greek literature -- Collections
ISBN 978-0-8112-1288-5; 0-8112-1288-2

LC 95-4227

Davenport has translated a sampling of seventh- to third-century B.C.E. Greek poetry. "Included among the poems and fragments are lyrics by Archilochos, Sappho, Alkman, and Anakreon; philosophical verse by Herakleitos and Diogenes; and comic dramatic verse by Herondas. Arguing that no translation is final and occasionally offering several versions of the same work, Davenport attempts to capture the tone of the original rather than offering a literal or formal rendition." Libr J

Apollonius

The **voyage** of Argo: the Argonautica; translated with an introd. by E.V. Rieu. 2nd ed; Penguin Books 1971 213p map (Penguin Classics) pa $14   **881**

1. Argonauts (Greek mythology) 2. Poetry -- By individual authors
ISBN 978-0-14-044085-0; 0-14-044085-0
This translation first published 1959

An epic account of Jason's voyage in quest of the Golden Fleece written in the third century B.C.

882   Classical Greek dramatic poetry and drama

Aeschylus

Aeschylus; edited by David Grene and Richmond Lattimore. University of Chicago Press 1992 352p (Complete Greek tragedies) $55   **882**

ISBN 978-0-226-30764-0; 0-226-30764-6

The **Oresteia**; translated by Alan Shapiro and Peter Burian. Oxford University Press 2003 285p (The Greek tragedy in new translations) hardcover o.p. pa $11.95   **882**

ISBN 978-0-19-513592-3 pa; 0-19-513592-X pa

LC 2002-66272

"The collaboration of poet and scholar . . . produces a language that is easy to read and easy to speak." Libr J

Includes bibliographical references

Aristophanes

The **complete** plays; the new translations by Paul Roche. New American Library 2005 715p pa $17   **882**

1. Athens (Greece) -- Drama.
ISBN 978-0-451-21409-6; 0-451-21409-9

LC 2004-56681

Euripides

Euripides; edited by David Grene and Richmond Lattimore. University of Chicago Press 1992 665p (Complete Greek tragedies) $65   **882**

ISBN 978-0-226-30766-4; 0-226-30766-2
First published 1942

Euripides [2] edited by David Grene and Richmond Lattimore. University of Chicago Press 1992 314p (Complete Greek tragedies) $44   **882**

ISBN 978-0-226-30767-1; 0-226-30767-0
First published 1958

Seneca, Lucius Annaeus

Four tragedies, and Octavia; [by] Seneca; tr. with an introduction by E. F. Watling. Penguin Books 1966 318p (Penguin Classics) pa $14   **882**

ISBN 978-0-14-044174-1; 0-12-044174-3

LC 66-8618

"Although their themes are borrowed from Greek drama, these exuberant and often macabre plays focus on action rather than moral concerns and are strikingly different in style from Seneca's prose writing." Publisher's note

Sophocles

Sophocles; edited by David Grene and Richmond Lattimore. University of Chicago Press 1992 466p (Complete Greek tragedies) $50 **882**

ISBN 978-0-226-30765-7; 0-226-30765-4

The **Theban** plays of Sophocles; translated by David R. Slavitt. Yale University Press 2007 237p $28 **882**

ISBN 978-0-300-11776-9; 0-300-11776-0

LC 2006-26965

"This version is meant to be an updated one, and the easy currency of its diction is a great virtue. The natural cadences of its free verse slide smoothly and sometimes beautifully into the ear." Claremont Rev Books

Includes bibliographical references

883 Classical Greek epic poetry and fiction

Alexander, Caroline

The **war** that killed Achilles; the true story of Homer's Iliad and the Trojan War. Viking 2009 296p map $26.95 **883**

1. Poets 2. Authors 3. Trojan War 4. War in literature
ISBN 978-0-670-02112-3; 0-670-02112-1

LC 2009-20160

"In its bones and sinews, the book is a nobly bold, even rousing, venture, a read-through of the 'Iliad,' from beginning to end, always with a sharp eye to half a century of revealing scholarship, by great Hellenists like Gregory Nagy, Jasper Griffin, M.L. West and many others. The book's best ideas won't be new to readers versed in this work, but it would be hard to find a faster, livelier, more compact introduction to such a great range of recent Iliadic explorations." N Y Times Book Rev

Includes bibliographical references

Homer

The **Iliad**; translated by Robert Fitzgerald. Knopf 1992 xxi, 594p (Everyman's library) $22 **883**

1. Poetry -- By individual authors
ISBN 978-0-679-41075-1; 0-679-41075-9

LC 91-53222

This translation first published 1974 by Anchor Press/ Doubleday

Homer's epic of the Trojan War in blank verse

"Fitzgerald has solved virtually every problem that has plagued translators of Homer. The narrative runs, the dialogue speaks, the military action is clear, and the repetitive epithets become useful text rather than exotic relics. Aside from the ability to write poetry, which is basic to the undertaking, Mr. Fitzgerald's success derives from the use of a predominantly Anglo-Saxon vocabulary, a concentration on

specific meanings, and an occasional arbitrary, but highly effective, substitution of implication for literal sense." Atlantic

Iliad; translated by Stanley Lombardo; introduction by Sheila Murnaghan. Hackett 1997 516p $37.95; pa $12.95 **883**

1. Poetry -- By individual authors
ISBN 978-0-87220-353-2; 0-87220-353-0; 978-0-87220-352-5 pa; 0-87220-352-2 pa

LC 96-53368

This is a translation from the Greek of the epic poem on the Trojan War

"Lombardo manages to be respectful of Homer's dire spirit while providing on nearly every page some wonderfully fresh refashioning of his Greek. The result is a vivid and sometimes disarmingly hard-bitten reworking of a great classic. . . . Not all of Lombardo's gambles pay off, and his attention-grabbing colloquialisms sometimes undermine the force of the original. . . . Still, the success of so many of Lombardo's choices more than makes up for the false notes." N Y Times Book Rev

Odyssey; translated by Stanley Lombardo; introduction by Sheila Murnaghan. Hackett 2000 414p il $37.95; pa $12.95 **883**

1. Poetry -- By individual authors
ISBN 978-0-87220-485-0; 0-87220-485-5; 978-0-87220-484-3 pa; 0-87220-484-7 pa

LC 99-54175

A retelling of Homer's epic that describes the wanderings of Odysseus after the fall of Troy.

Lombardo "has brought his laconic wit and love of the ribald, as well as his clever use of idiomatic American slang, to his version of the 'Odyssey.' His carefully honed syntax gives the narrative energy and a whirlwind pace. The lines, rhythmic and clipped, have the tautness and force of Odysseus' bow." N Y Times Book Rev

Includes bibliographical references

The **Odyssey**; translated by Robert Fagles; introduction and notes by Bernard Knox. Viking 1996 541p $35; pa $16 **883**

1. Poetry -- By individual authors
ISBN 978-0-670-82162-4; 978-0-14-026886-7 pa

LC 96-17280

This is a verse translation of Homer's epic poem

"Fagles' Odyssey is the one to put into the hands of younger, first-time readers, not least because of its paucity of notes, which, though sometimes frustrating, is a sign that translation has been used to do the work of explanation. Altogether, an outstanding piece of work." Booklist

Includes bibliographical references

The **Odyssey**; translated by Robert Fitzgerald; with an introduction by Seamus Heaney. Knopf 1992 xxvii, 509p (Everyman's library) $21 **883**

1. Poetry -- By individual authors
ISBN 978-0-679-41047-8; 0-679-41047-3

LC 92-52903

This translation first published 1961 by Anchor Press/ Doubleday

"Fitzgerald's new Odyssey . . . deserves to be singled out for what it is—a masterpiece." Nation

Includes bibliographical references

The **Odyssey**; Homer; translated, with an introduction and notes, by Stephen Mitchell. Atria Books 2013 xlv, 375 p.p map (hdbk.) $35   **883**
1. Greek literature
   ISBN 1451674171; 9781451674170
                 LC 2012050572

This version of Homer's work, translated by Stephen Mitchell, "brings Odysseus and his adventures vividly to life. . . . One-eyed maneating giants; irresistibly seductive sirens; shipwrecks and narrow escapes; princesses and monsters; ghosts sipping blood at the Underworld's portal, desperate for a chance to speak to the living; and the final destruction of all Odysseus's enemies in the banquet hall." (Publisher's note)

"Employing the five-beat, minimally iambic line he used for his translation of The Iliad (2011), Mitchell retells the first, still greatest adventure story in Western literature with the same clarity, sweep, and force." Booklist

Includes bibliographical references

Manguel, Alberto

Homer's The Iliad and The Odyssey; a biography. Atlantic Monthly Press 2008 285p (Books that changed the world) $19.95   **883**
1. Poets 2. Authors 3. Epic poetry
   ISBN 978-0-87113-976-4; 0-87113-976-6
   First published 2007 in the United Kingdom

A "study of the influence of The Iliad and The Odyssey on Western literature. First describing the two epics and the Homer question, Manguel then compares various translations in English, Spanish, French, and German, a move that brings out the complexities and richness of Homer's language. Does the poet sing of the rage, wrath, anger, rancor, or mania of Achilles? Then, following a more or less chronological progression, Manguel surveys the various shifting interpretations of the epics from Plato and Virgil to the present, including extended discussions of Derek Walcott, Timothy Findley, and Jorge Luis Borges. Highly recommended for general readers." Libr J

Nicolson, Adam

Why Homer matters; by Adam Nicolson. Henry Holt & Co 2014 320 p. 8 plates; color ills., maps (hardcover) $30   **883**
1. Epic poetry 2. Greek poetry -- History and criticism 3. Landscapes -- Europe 4. Europe -- Description and travel 5. Epic poetry, Greek -- History and criticism
   ISBN 1627791795; 9781627791793
                 LC 2014006763

In this book, author Adam Nicolson, "sees the Iliad and the Odyssey as the foundation myths of Greek-- and our-- consciousness, collapsing the passage of 4,000 years and making the distant past of the Mediterranean world as immediate to us as the events of our own time. . . . [The book] is a magical journey of discovery across wide stretches of the past, sewn together by the poems themselves and their metaphors of life and trouble." (Publisher's note)

"Nicholson writes in a clear, fluid prose with apparently effortless ease; his vivid descriptions of landscapes and archaeological remains and his passionate engagement with history make this book a page-turner. Classicists will no doubt find fault with some of Nicholson's statements, but they will also be grateful to the author for explaining to the larger public in such an appealing fashion why Homer is not only unique but also relevant and necessary today. Summing Up: Highly recommended. General readers." Choice

Includes bibliographical references and index

884   Classical Greek lyric poetry

Pindar

★ The **complete** odes of Pindar; translated by Anthony Verity; with an introduction and notes by Stephen Instone. Oxford University Press 2007 xxvii, 186p (Oxford world's classics) pa $15.95   **884**
1. Poetry -- By individual authors
   ISBN 978-0-19-280553-9; 0-19-280553-3
                 LC 2006-39673

The Odes (Epinicia) celebrated victories in the great national games, and were accompanied by music, which is lost to us. The fragments represent almost every kind of lyric poem.

"Since Pindar's Epinicia are generally concerned with mythical subjects, reserving praise of the mortal victor for the end of the ode, his works are a fine source of legend." Reader's Ency. 4th edition

Sappho

★ **If** not, winter; fragments of Sappho. translated by Anne Carson. Knopf 2002 397p $27.50; pa $14   **884**
1. Poetry -- By individual authors
   ISBN 0-375-41067-8; 0-375-72451-6 pa
                 LC 2001-50247

"Carson's translation follows Sappho's diction and form . . . closely and includes the Greek original on the facing page. Much of what survives of Sappho are fragments, often just a stray word, phrase, or even a few letters. Like many modern poets, Carson deploys these on the blank page, letting their suggestiveness fill the gaps and create whole lyrics in the imagination of the readers." Libr J

Includes bibliographical references

888   Classical Greek miscellaneous writings

Aristotle

★ The **basic** works of Aristotle; edited, and with an introduction by Richard McKeon. Random House 1941 xxxix, 1487p $49.95; pa $19.95   **888**
   ISBN 0-394-41610-4; 0-375-75799-6 pa

Contains entire texts of the following: Physica; De generatione et corruptione; De anima; Parva naturalia; Metaphysica; Ethica Nicomachea; Politica; De poetica

Includes bibliographical references

Plato

The **collected** dialogues of Plato, including the letters; edited by Edith Hamilton and Huntington Cairns. With introd. and prefatory notes. Princeton University Press 1961 xxv, 1743p (Bollingen series) $49.50   **888**

ISBN 978-0-691-09718-3; 0-691-09718-6

"This elegant edition contains many of the best and most readable English translations of the Dialogues and Letters. . . . Judiciously edited, beautifully printed." Rev of Metaphysics

The **republic**; edited by G.R.F. Ferrari; translated by Tom Griffith. Cambridge Univ. Press 2000 xl-viii, 382p (Cambridge texts in the history of political thought) $38; pa $11   **888**

1. Utopias 2. Political science
ISBN 0-521-48173-2; 0-521-48443-X pa

LC 00-24471

Griffith's "aim was to translate the Greek text as if it were a conversation, and he has succeeded admirably. The text does indeed flow like a conversation, with the entire back-and-forth interaction that such exchanges involve. . . . [He] has also written a very useful introduction that places the work in a historical context and provides a glossary that will help readers identify individuals and places mentioned in the work." Libr J

Includes bibliographical references

889   Modern Greek literature

Cavafy, Constantine P.

★ **Collected** poems; [by] C.P. Cavafy; translated, with introduction and commentary, by Daniel Mendelsohn. Alfred A. Knopf 2009 547p $35 **889**

1. Poetry -- By individual authors
ISBN 978-0-375-40096-4; 0-375-40096-6

LC 2008-34718

"Mendelsohn drew together his interests in ancient history, literature, gay life and culture, and beautiful language to produce the finest, most readable version of the modern Greek poet Cavafy (1863-1933) to come along in decades." Publ Wkly

★ The **unfinished** poems; [by] C.P. Cavafy; the first English translation, with introduction and commentary, by Daniel Mendelsohn. Alfred A. Knopf 2009 121p $30   **889**

1. Poetry -- By individual authors
ISBN 978-0-307-26546-3; 0-307-26546-3

LC 2008-34717

Original Greek edition, 1994

This book "contains the first English versions of 30 poems that Cavafy had not finished entirely to his satisfaction when he died. All are in his most developed manner, in which apprehension of the past is so rich and powerful as to expunge mere nostalgia. They are historical vignettes of the declines of Alexander's Hellenistic hegemony, imperial Rome, and the Byzantine Empire; and glowing memories, triggered by news items, drink, or moonlight, of decades-old homosexual rapture. . . . One could become well informed about centuries of seldom-taught history just by reading the notes, though yet more so by absorbing the poems, as well." Booklist

Elytes, Odysseus

The **collected** poems of Odysseus Elytis; translated by Jeffrey Carson and Nikos Sarris; introduction and notes by Jeffrey Carson. Rev and expanded ed; Johns Hopkins University Press 2005 $60   **889**

1. Poetry -- By individual authors
ISBN 0-8018-8045-9

LC 2004-13496

First published 1997

"The work of 1979 Nobel Prize winner Elytis (1911-96) has the quality of a cathedral or epic—vast in scope yet richly decorated. This excellent 'complete' collected edition (it omits unpublished poems) testifies to the bountiful, sincere nature of Elytis's voice as patriot and poet. . . . Containing informative annotations, a chronology, an autobiographical essay, and the author's Nobel address, this work is a valuable resource on international poetry." Libr J

Includes bibliographical references

891   East Indo-European and Celtic literatures

Barks, Coleman

Rumi: the big red book; the great masterpiece celebrating mystical love and friendship. the collected translations of Coleman Barks, based on the work of John Moyne ... [et al.] HarperOne 2010 492p $29.95; ebook $14.99   **891**

1. Poetry -- By individual authors
ISBN 978-0-06-190582-7; 978-0-06-202078-9 ebook

LC 2010-7895

This is "a vast collection centering on Shams Tabrizi, a wandering mystic who transformed Rumi's life. Rumi was already renowned when Shams arrived in Konya, in today's Turkey, having wandered for years searching for someone with a soul as profound as his own with whom to share 'sobbet,' a mystical conversation about God and love. Rumi and Shams inspired each other for several years, until Shams mysteriously disappeared. He lives on in Rumi's searching poems. . . . Richly sensual yet never flowery, Barks' language emphasizes Rumi's embodied spirituality in a book to savor." Booklist

Includes bibliographical references

Firdawsi

★ **Shahnameh**; the Persian book of kings. [by] Abolqasem Ferdowsi; translated by Dick Davis; with a foreword by Azar Nafisi. Viking 2006 xxxvii, 886p il $45   **891**

ISBN 0-670-03485-1

LC 2005-42352

"Unlike Western epics that grasp the events of a single generation, whether of men or angels, Persia's Book of Kings encompasses whole ages of the world, chronicling the stratagems of Kings and heroes as real as Alexander the Great and as legendary as Rostam. . . . Action, myth, and history fairly fly off the page, for Davis renders Ferdowsi's 50,000 sesquipedalian lines of poetry as a prose narrative that here and there erupts into sonnet-sized snatches of verse. The scheme works brilliantly. Repeated for pages on end, Ferdowsi's lines, each longer than an heroic couplet, breed longueurs, but Davis's carefully rendered snatches of the best classic Farsi poetry illuminate the English text like so many Persian miniatures." New Criterion

Hafiz

The **gift**; poems by the great Sufi master. translated by Daniel James Ladinsky. Penguin/Arkana 1999 333p pa $16   **891**
  1. Poetry -- By individual authors
  ISBN 978-0-14-019581-1; 0-14-019581-5

                      LC 99-10920
"Less well known in the U.S. than his Sufi predecessor, Rumi, Hafiz (Shams-ud-din Muhammad) is also worthy of attention, and Ladinsky's free translations should help see that he gets it. Hafiz is so beloved in Iran that he outsells the Koran. Many know his verses by heart and recite them with gusto. And gusto is appropriate to this passionate, earthy poet who melds mind, spirit, and body in each of his usually brief pensees. Ladinsky has deliberately chosen a loose and colloquial tone for this collection, which might grate on the nerves of purists but makes Hafiz come vividly alive for the average reader." Booklist

I am the beggar of the world; landays from contemporary Afghanistan. translated and presented by Eliza Griswold; photographs by Seamus Murphy. Farrar Straus & Giroux 2014 160 p. illustrations (hardcover) $24   **891**
  1. Afghan literature 2. Poetry -- Collections 3. Poetry -- Women authors -- Collections 4. Folk poetry, Pushto -- Translations into English 5. Pushto poetry -- 20th century -- Translations into English 6. Pushto poetry -- Women authors -- Translations into English
  ISBN 0374191875; 9780374191870

                   LC 2013035179
Translated by Eliza Griswold, with photographs by Seamus Murphy, this book is a "collection of clandestine poems by Afghan women. . . . War, separation, homeland, love-- these are the subjects of landays, which are brutal and spare, can be remixed like rap, and are powerful in that they make no attempts to be literary." (Publisher's note)

"Griswold's selections illustrate the rich potential of this poetic form, at once contemporary and timeless. Murphy's stunning photographs complement the text perfectly." Booklist

Jalal al-Din Rumi

The **essential** Rumi; translated by Coleman Barks, with John Moyne, A.A. Arberry, Reynold Nicholson. Harper 1995 302p $23.95; pa $14.95   **891**
  1. Poetry -- By individual authors
  ISBN 978-0-06-250958-1; 0-06-250958-6; 978-0-06-250959-8 pa; 0-06-250959-4 pa

                   LC 94-44995
A collection of ecstatic verse by the 13th-century Sufi mystic

Narayan, R. K.

★ The **Ramayana**; a shortened modern prose version of the Indian epic (suggested by the Tamil version of Kamban) introduction by Pankaj Mishra. Penguin Books 2006 157p (Penguin classics) pa $13   **891**
  ISBN 0-14-303967-9

                  LC 2006-45201
First published 1972
A retelling of Prince Rama's courtship of the fourteen-year-old Sita, their exile, Sita's abduction, the search, and the great battle with her abductor Ravana, involving a pantheon of gods, heroes, and evil spirits.

Persian poets; selected and edited by Peter Washington. Knopf 2000 254p (Everyman's library pocket poets) $12.50   **891**
  1. Persian poetry -- Collections
  ISBN 978-0-375-41126-7
Includes works by Omar, Sanai, Attar, Rumi, Saadi, Hafez, and Jami

Tagore, Rabindranath

Selected poems; translated by William Radice. Penguin Books 2005 202p (Penguin classics) pa $14   **891**
  1. Poetry -- By individual authors
  ISBN 978-0-14-044988-4
"This collection offers a wide array of Tagore's poems from 1882 to 1941, plus textual notes and other scholarly extras." Libr J

891.6   Celtic literatures

Tain bo Cuailnge

The **Tain**; translated from the Irish epic Tain Bo Cuailnge. [translated] by Thomas Kinsella; with brush drawings by Louis le Brocquy. Oxford University Press 2002 282p il map pa $19.95   **891.6**
  ISBN 0-19-280373-5

                  LC 2002-726950
This translation first published 1969
This Irish epic is the "centerpiece of the eighth-century Ulster cycle of heroic tales. . . . [This] translation is based on the partial texts in two medieval manuscripts, with elements from other versions. This edition includes a group of related stories which prepare for the action of the Tain." Publisher's note
Includes bibliographical references

891.7   Russian literature and related East Slavic literatures

Bartlett, Rosamund

★ **Tolstoy**; 1st U.S. ed. Houghton Mifflin Harcourt 2011 544 p.   **891.7**
  1. Biography 2. Novelists 3. Dramatists 4. Authors, Russian 5. Authors 6. Short story writers 7. Writers

on religion 8. Biography, Individual
ISBN 9781846681387 Profile Books; 1846681383
Profile Books; 9780151014385

LC 2010050015

This book presents a biography of writer Leo Tolstoy which draws primarily upon Russian scholarship, as well as Tolstoy's "memoirs and correspondences," to narrate his life. "As a cultural historian, Bartlett strives to place the man within his time and milieu. Her Tolstoy in his incarnations as aristocrat, muzhik, czar and other roles is thoroughly Russian, and she uses him to introduce her anglophone readers to sometimes exotic details of Russian life and history. . . . She offers, for instance, a brief history of the family of Tolstoy's wife, the Behrses, who came from a different order of Russian society than the counts and princes from whom Tolstoy descended. . . . There are similar . . . digressions about the Caucasus, Russian Orthodoxy, peasant life, Tolstoyans and other matters." (The Globe and Mail)

Batuman, Elif

The **possessed**; adventures with Russian books and the people who read them. Farrar, Straus and Giroux 2010 296p pa $15   **891.7**
  1. Russian literature -- History and criticism
  ISBN 978-0-374-53218-5; 0-374-53218-4

LC 2009-25416

In this book, the author "makes you look at Russian literature from a fresh perspective, using an unusual blend of memoir and travelogue as she delves into the lives and personalities of such Russian literary giants as Isaac Babel, Fyodor Dostoevsky and Leo Tolstoy. Many of the chapters are extensions of pieces Batuman first wrote for The New Yorker and n+1 and range geographically from Palo Alto, Calif., where Batuman managed to lose one of Babel's daughters at the local airport, to Uzbekistan, where Batuman spent a few months studying Uzbek. In a sense, the details of Batuman's essays are less significant than the tone. She cruises through minor crises with an air of detached amusement, eye focused on the little absurdities that make travel—and people—fun." Cleveland Plain Dealer

Includes bibliographical references

Brodsky, Joseph

★ **Collected** poems in English, 1972-1999; edited by Ann Kjellberg. Farrar, Straus & Giroux 2000 539p $30; pa $18   **891.7**
  1. Poetry -- By individual authors
  ISBN 0-374-12545-7; 0-374-52838-1 pa

LC 00-21059

This volume "gathers all the poetry in English Brodsky originally saw through to press in books (or had earmarked for eventual publication), including Russian poems he translated or co-translated. Originally Russian verse from the '60s and '70s gives way to the later, sometimes lighter, work of his last two decades, when he found a second home in the speech of his adoptive country." Publ Wkly

Callow, Philip

Chekhov, the hidden ground; a biography. Dee, I.R. 1998 428p il $30; pa $18.95   **891.7**
  1. Authors 2. Dramatists 3. Physicians 4. Short story

writers
ISBN 1-56663-187-4; 1-56663-395-8 pa

LC 97-46679

"Callow sees Chekhov as distant in virtually all his relationships, with romantic disillusionment and the search for intimacy recurring themes in his writing. He argues persuasively that while Chekhov's art is resplendent with human emotion, his own life was strangely cold and remote. . . . Not strictly a literary biography, this book is particularly effective in discussing Chekhov's work as it relates to his life." Libr J

Includes bibliographical references

The **Cambridge** history of Russian literature; edited by Charles A. Moser. rev ed; Cambridge Univ. Press 1992 709p hardcover o.p. pa $55   **891.7**
  1. Russian literature -- History and criticism
  ISBN 0-521-42567-0 pa

LC 91-38275

This volume presents "a survey of Russian literature from the beginnings to this decade, in sufficient but not overwhelming detail.' Ten chapters by specialists elucidate this history from 988 to approximately 1980, with a lengthy bibliography at the end of the volume." Sheehy. Guide to Ref Books. 10th edition. suppl

Chekhov, Anton Pavlovich

Chekhov; the four major plays. in new translations by Curt Columbus. Ivan R. Dee 2005 294p pa $15.95   **891.7**
  ISBN 978-1-56663-626-1; 1-56663-626-4

LC 2004-48612

"Columbus's translation triumphs through its clarity and consistent use of the active voice." Chicago Reader

The **complete** plays; [by] Anton Chekhov; translated, edited, and annotated by Laurence Senelick. W. W. Norton 2006 lx, 1060p pa $22.95   **891.7**
  ISBN 978-0-393-04885-8; 0-393-04885-3; 978-0-393-33069-4 pa; 0-393-33069-9 pa

LC 2005-24362

"This volume contains work never previously translated, including the newly discovered farce The Power of Hypnotism, the first version of Ivanov, Chekhov's early humorous dialogues, and a description of lost plays and those Chekhov intended to write but never did." Publisher's note

The **portable** Chekhov; edited and with an introduction by Avrahm Yarmolinsky. Viking 1947 631p hardcover o.p. pa $17   **891.7**
  ISBN 0-14-015035-8 pa

This collection contains "two plays, 'The Cherry Orchard' and 'The Boor,' 28 short stories and selections from Chekhov's letters." Publ Wkly

Malcolm, Janet

Reading Chekhov; a critical journey. Random House 2001 209p hardcover o.p. pa $13.95 **891.7**
  1. Authors 2. Dramatists 3. Physicians 4. Short story writers
ISBN 0-375-50668-3; 0-375-76106-3 pa

LC 2001-19585

"The author's pilgrimage to Chekhov's Russia—Moscow, St. Petersburg, the gardens of his villa in Yalta—is a reunion with this most reticent of literary fathers. Malcolm analyzes the transformations that Chekhov grants his redeemable roués and guileless heroines, and illuminates the hidden surreality and waywardness of his realism." New Yorker

Includes bibliographical references

Mandelstam, Osip

The **selected** poems of Osip Mandelstam; translated by Clarence Brown and W.S. Merwin. New York Review Books 2004 167p (New York Review Books classics) pa $14.95   **891.7**

1. Poetry -- By individual authors

ISBN 978-1-59017-091-1; 1-59017-091-1

LC 2004-14656

First published 1974 by Atheneum

"The Brown/Merwin versions represent a sensitive and sensible selection of Mandelstam's poetry. The translations do not attempt to imitate Mandelstam's fluid syntax or subtle sound play. But they are honest representations of Mandelstam's themes and recurrent imagery and many of them, particularly certain of the poems in the section 'Poems of the Thirties,' come across as fine English poems." Libr J

Mayakovsky, Vladimir

Listen! early poems. translated by Maria Enzensberger; with a foreward [sic] by Elaine Feinstein. City Lights Bks. 1991 60p pa $9.95   **891.7**

1. Poetry -- By individual authors

ISBN 978-0-87286-255-5; 0-87286-255-0

LC 91-10330

First published 1987 in the United Kingdom

This collection of the Russian poet's early work has parallel text in Russian and English and is illustrated with some of Mayakovsky's art.

Nabokov, Vladimir Vladimirovich

Lectures on Russian literature; edited with an introduction by Fredson Bowers. Harcourt Brace Jovanovich 1981 324p il hardcover o.p. pa $16 **891.7**

1. Authors 2. Novelists 3. Dramatists 4. Physicians 5. Communism and literature 6. Memoirists 7. Short story writers 8. Writers on religion 9. Russian literature -- History and criticism

ISBN 0-15-602776-3 pa

Companion volume Lectures on literature

This book is "derived from notes Nabokov made for his literature classes at Wellesley and Cornell. Included are chapters on Gogol, Turgenev, Dostoevsky, Tolstoy, Chekhov, and Gorki, as well as several miscellaneous essays on censorship and the art of translation." Libr J

Popoff, Alexandra

The **wives**; The Women Behind Russia's Literary Giants. Alexandra Popoff. Pegasus Books 2012 332p. $27.95   **891.7**

1. Wives 2. Authorship 3. Authors, Russian

ISBN 1605983667; 9781605983660

This book, by Alexandra Popoff, explores the "women behind the greatest works of Russian literature. . . . From Sophia Tolstoy to Vera Nabokov, . . . Anna Dostevsky, and

Natalya Solzhenitsyn, these women ranged from stenographers and typists to editors, researchers, translators, and even publishers. Living under restrictive regimes, many of these women battled censorship and preserved the writers' illicit archives, often risking their own lives to do so." (Publisher's note)

Pushkin, Aleksandr Sergeevich

Eugene Onegin and other poems; translated by Charles Johnston. Knopf 1999 240p (Everyman's library pocket poets) $12.50   **891.7**

1. Poetry -- By individual authors

ISBN 978-0-375-40672-0; 0-375-40672-7

Tale in verse of a rich, bored young man who rather offhandedly destroys his chance at love by killing a friend in a duel and alienating his would-be beloved

Reference guide to Russian literature; editor, Neil Cornwell; associate editor, Nicole Christian. Fitzroy Dearborn Pubs. 1998 xl, 972p $160 **891.7**

1. Reference books 2. Russian literature -- Dictionaries 3. Russian literature -- Bio-bibliography

ISBN 1-88496-410-9

LC 97-169924

A guide to approximately 270 writers and their works "author entries include telegraphic biographical sketches, detailed bibliographies of Russian- and English-language sources and critical studies, and, in many cases, 1000-word entries for specific novels, plays, and stories. There are alphabetical and chronological lists, 13 introductory essays on various aspects of Russian literature, and a Russian/English title index." Libr J

Includes bibliographical references

Terras, Victor

A **history** of Russian literature. Yale Univ. Press 1991 654p $37   **891.7**

1. Russian literature -- History and criticism

ISBN 978-0-300-04971-8; 0-300-04971-4

LC 91-13337

This history of Russian literature begins with a chapter on folklore and then presents a chronological account covering Old Russian literature (eleventh to sixteenth centuries); the seventeenth century; the eighteenth century; the Romantic period; the age of the novel; the Silver Age, and the Soviet period

"The book's minor shortcomings are overshadowed by its numerous merits; its accuracy, keenness of observation, subtle comments, vivid quotations, erudition. . . . Almost every page of the book invites one to read and re-read Russian literature." Times Lit Suppl

Includes bibliographical references

Tolstaia, Tat'iana

Pushkin's children; writings on Russia and Russians. [by] Tatyana Tolstaya; translated by Jamey Gambrell. Houghton Mifflin 2003 242p pa $15   **891.7**

1. Poets 2. Authors 3. Novelists 4. Presidents 5. Prime ministers 6. Political prisoners 7. Cabinet members 8. Communist leaders 9. Nonfiction writers 10. Short story writers 11. Writers on politics 12.

Nobel laureates for peace 13. Nobel laureates for literature 14. Russia -- Politics and government
ISBN 0-618-12500-0

LC 2002-27610

"Tolstaya's essays in this compact, historically significant volume offer a fascinating, highly intelligent analysis of Russian society and politics." Publ Wkly

Tsvetaeva, Marina Ivanovna

Selected poems; [by] Marina Tsvetayeva; translated and introduced by Elaine Feinstein; with literal versions provided by Angela Livingstone .... [et al.] Penguin Books 1994 131p (Penguin twentieth-century classics) pa $15   **891.7**
ISBN 978-0-14-018759-5; 0-14-018759-6

First published 1971 by Oxford Univ. Press

"As a poet Tsvetaeva impresses with her psychic energy, she is on fire with poetry, and nothing is put in perspective, everything is immediate, emotional in the best sense." N Y Times Book Rev

Volkov, Solomon

Romanov riches; Russian writers and artists under the tsars. translated from the Russian by Antonina W. Bouis. Alfred A. Knopf 2011 285p il $30 **891.7**
1. Emperors 2. Empresses 3. Russian arts 4. Authors, Russian 5. Arts, Russian 6. Artists -- Russia 7. Russia -- History 8. Composers -- Russia 9. Russia -- Kings and rulers 10. Russia -- Intellectual life 11. Russian literature -- History and criticism
ISBN 0-307-27063-7; 978-0-307-27063-4

LC 2010-45132

This is a "cultural history of Russia from the rise of the house of Romanov in 1613 to its downfall at the hands of the Bolsheviks in 1917." (Publisher's note) Index.

"Volkov revitalizes our understanding of rebellious poet Pushkin and offers fresh insights into Tchaikovsky, Dostoevsky, and Turgenev. A thrillingly anecdotal and incisive look at the paradigmatic and paradoxical Romanov world of politics, patronage, and the quest for artistic freedom." Booklist

Includes bibliographical references

Yevtushenko, Yevgeny Aleksandrovich

Selected poems; [by] Yevgeni Yevtushenko; translated by Robin Milner-Gulland and Peter Levi; with an introduction by Robin Milner-Gulland. Penguin Books 2008 90p il (Penguin Classics) pa $14   **891.7**
1. Poetry -- By individual authors
ISBN 978-0-14-042477-5; 0-14-042477-6

First published 1961

"These poems beat and tumble and thrash with life." Daily Telegraph

891.71   Russian poetry

Akhmatova, Anna Andreevna

The **complete** poems of Anna Akhmatova; {by} Anna Akhmatova; translated by Judith Hemschemey-

er; edited and with an introduction by Roberta Reeder. Zephyr Press (Somerville) 1990 2v il hardcover o.p. pa $29   **891.71**
1. Poetry -- By individual authors
ISBN 0-939010-27-5 pa

LC 88-51831

"Anna Akhmatova—the high priestess of Russian poetry—saw her husband shot, her son imprisoned twice by Stalin, her work banned in the 1930's and late 40's. . . . Sonorous, calm, deliberate in movement, her Russian has no English equivalent, but in this admirably restrained and accurate translation, sense and message strike with all the weight of the original." N Y Times Book Rev

Poems; [by] Akhmatova; translated by D.M. Thomas. New expanded ed.; Knopf 2006 6p (Everyman's library pocket poets) $12.50   **891.7**
1. Poetry -- By individual authors
ISBN 978-0-307-26424-4; 0-307-26424-6

LC 2006-297217

First published 1985 in the United Kingdom with title: You will hear thunder

A representative selection of material from all her major works—including "Requiem" commemorating the victims of Stalin's terror.

Mandelstam, Nadezhda

Hope against hope; a memoir. translated from the Russian by Max Hayward; with an introduction by Clarence Brown and: Nadezhda Mandelstaum (1899-1980): an obituary, by Joseph Brodsky. Modern Lib. 1999 442p pa $23   **891.71**
1. Authors 2. Memoirists 3. Translators
ISBN 978-0-375-75316-9; 0-375-75316-8

LC 98-47833

"Mandelstam tells the story of her family's experiences of hardship in Soviet Russia under Stalin. What is remarkable about the book is not just its content but also its authorial voice, which, in Max Hayward's deft translation, is so unique and consistent that the reader can get a sense of it by opening the book at random and reading almost any paragraph. Although Hope Against Hope is a painful book to read, one of the things that makes it bearable, apart from its sheer beauty, is a kind of unquenchable spirit and optimism that keeps rising to the surface, compounding the more mysterious consolations of art." Harper's

891.73   Russian fiction

Finn, Peter

The **Zhivago** affair; the Kremlin, the CIA, and the battle over a forbidden book. Peter Finn and Petra Couvee. Pantheon Books 2013 368 p. (hard cover : alkaline paper) $26.95   **891.73**
1. Cold war 2. Books -- Censorship 3. Dissenters -- Soviet Union -- Biography 4. Prohibited books -- Soviet Union -- History 5. Authors, Russian -- 20th century -- Biography 6. Politics and literature -- Soviet Union -- History 7. Soviet Union -- Foreign relations -- United States 8. United States -- Foreign relations -- Soviet

Union 9. Soviet Union -- Politics and government -- 1953-1985 10. United States. Central Intelligence Agency -- History -- 20th century
ISBN 0307908003; 9780307908001

LC 2013033875

This book, by Peter Finn and Petra Couvele, offers "the dramatic story of how a forbidden book in the Soviet Union became a secret CIA weapon in the ideological battle between East and West. ., , The CIA . . . published a Russian-language edition of 'Doctor Zhivago' and smuggled it into the Soviet Union. Copies were devoured in Moscow and Leningrad, sold on the black market, and passed surreptitiously from friend to friend." (Publisher's note)

"Drawing on recently declassified CIA documents, Finn and Couvée present an engaging thriller, in which bureaucratic obstructions and Cold War politics threaten the publication of a controversial masterpiece of world literature." Booklist

Includes bibliographical references and index

Pitzer, Andrea

★ The **Secret** History of Vladimir Nabokov; Andrea Pitzer. W W Norton & Co Inc 2013 352 p. (hardcover) $29.95   **891.73**
1. Authors, Russian -- 20th century -- Biography. 2. Authors, American -- 20th century -- Biography. 3. Nabokov, Vladimir Vladimirovich, 1899-1977 -- Criticism and interpretation.
ISBN 1605984116; 9781605984117

This book, by Andrea Pitzer, discusses the life and work of the Russian novelist Vladimir Nabokov, who "witnessed the horrors of his century, escaping Revolutionary Russia then Germany under Hitler. . . . He repeatedly faced accusations of turning a blind eye to human suffering to write artful tales of depravity. But does one of the greatest writers in the English language really deserve the label of amoral aesthete bestowed on him by so many critics?" (Publisher's note)

"Drawing on new biographical material and her sharp critical senses, Pitzer reveals the tightly woven subtext of the novels, always keen to shine a light where the deception is not obvious. . . . Though no substitute for Brian Boyd's definitive two-volume biography, this is a brilliant examination that adds to the understanding of an inspiring and enigmatic life." Kirkus

891.8   Slavic (Slavonic) literatures

Capek, Karel

R.U.R. and The insect play; by the Brothers Capek. Oxford Univ. Press 1961 179p pa $15.95 **891.8**
ISBN 0-19-281010-3

"R.U.R." is a fantasy in which robots revolt against their human masters. In "The insect play," a dying tramp dreams about insect life

Dimkovska, Lidija

PH neutral history; Lidija Dimkovska; translated from the Macedonian by Ljubica Arsovska and Peggy Reid. Copper Canyon Press 2012 120 p. (pbk. : alk. paper) $16.00   **891.8**
1. Suicide -- Poetry 2. Nostalgia -- Poetry 3. Macedonia

(Republic) -- Folklore -- Poetry
ISBN 1556593759; 9781556593758

LC 2011044017

In this, the "sixth collection of poetry" by "Macedonian poet and novelist Lidija Dimkovska," the author "scrutinizes life's customary and trivial details in a quest for greater meaning." Topics referenced include "religious tenents," "native folklore," and "nostalgia for her youth." Her brother's suicide offers her "reflections on death and its neutralization: life." (Publisher's note)

Havel, Vaclav

The **garden** party and other plays. Grove Press 1993 273p $13.00; pa $14   **891.8**
ISBN 978-0-8021-3307-6; 0-8021-3307-X

LC 93-8656

"Gathered together here for the first time are seven plays that span Havel's career from his early days at the Theater of the Balustrade through the Prague Spring, Charter 77, and the repeated imprisonments that made Havel's name into a rallying cry and propelled him to the leadership of his country." Publisher's note

Herbert, Zbigniew

The **collected** poems, 1956-1998; translated and edited by Alissa Valles; with additional translations by Czesaw Milosz and Peter Dale Scott; introduction by Adam Zagajewski. Ecco Press 2007 600p $34.95   **891.8**
1. Poetry -- By individual authors
ISBN 978-0-06-078390-7; 0-06-078390-7

LC 2006-40856

Herbert is a "titan of not only Polish poetry, but of twentieth-century European poetry. His celebrated alter ego, Mr. Cogito, ranks as the one of the most original characters in modern poetry. . . . Herbert lived through the Nazi occupation of 1941 and the Soviet occupations of 1939 and 1944 and was an active member of Poland's underground resistance. Decades later, after marshal law was declared in Poland in 1981, Herbert supported the underground opposition to communism and was an important figure in the Solidarity movement. . . . If Herbert is a political poet, he's political in the way Don Quixote is political. He doesn't make us more aware. He makes us more human." Brooklyn Rail

Milosz, Czeslaw

Legends of modernity; essays and letters from occupied Poland, 1942-1943. translated from the Polish by Madeline G. Levine; introduction by Jaroslaw Anders. Farrar, Straus and Giroux 2005 266p $25   **891.8**
1. Miłosz, Czesław -- Correspondence. 2. Andrzejewski, Jerzy, 1909-1983 -- Correspondence. 3. Authors, Polish -- 20th century -- Correspondence.
ISBN 0-374-18499-2

LC 2005-40950

Original Polish edition, 1996

"Written to the young intellectual Jerzy Andrejewski, the letters reveal Milosz's concern about the political climate of the era and the deterioration of religious influence owing to the chaos all across Europe and the rest of the world. . . . The essays explore the ideas of William James, André Gide,

Stendhal (Henri Beyle), Honoré de Balzac, and others as they relate to religious faith, reason and rationalism, contradictions, doubting, and believing in a civilized world and its religious institutions. . . . Reading Milosz is a demanding, rewarding, and ultimately powerful experience for the mind and the soul." Libr J

★ **Milosz's** ABCs; translated from the Polish by Madeline G. Levine. Farrar, Straus & Giroux 2001 313p hardcover o.p. pa $14   **891.8**
    ISBN 0-374-52795-4 pa
                       LC 00-42176

"The short prose entries in this quiet book take note of some of the people and places and ideas that contributed to the making of Milosz. The subjects of his sketches range from Alchemy and Curiosity to Rimbaud and Whitman, from childhood friends to Polish intellectuals little known in the West. But what could have been no more than a light memory work becomes almost a registry of gratitude: a meditation on the obligations of having lived a life and the responsibilities inherent in its particulars." New Yorker

Includes bibliographical references

★ **New** and collected poems 1931-2001. HarperCollins Pubs. 2001 xxi, 776p $45; pa $19.95 **891.8**
    1. Poetry -- By individual authors
    ISBN 0-06-019667-X; 0-06-051448-5 pa
                       LC 2001-50123

"Milosz has stated repeatedly in his poems his belief in the power of language to rescue from the void all he has seen and all the people he has known in a long life. But beneath this belief, it now appears, was the deeper belief that none of this was possible because of the inadequacy of language to capture reality, though he maintains this always has to be the poet's goal. . . . Throughout his career and throughout this vast collection, Milosz argues with himself about his poetics." N Y Times Book Rev

A **roadside** dog. Farrar, Straus & Giroux 1998 208p hardcover o.p. pa $14   **891.8**
    ISBN 0-374-52623-0 pa
                       LC 98-14026

"Milosz makes a wise, wryly humane fin de siècle companion." Publ Wkly

To begin where I am; selected essays. edited and with an introduction by Bogdana Carpenter and Madeline G. Levine. Farrar, Straus & Giroux 2001 462p hardcover o.p. pa $15   **891.8**
    1. Poets 2. Authors 3. Novelists 4. Dramatists 5. Philosophers 6. Political prisoners 7. Editors 8. Essayists 9. Translators 10. College teachers 11. Literary critics 12. Short story writers 13. Vilnius (Lithuania) 14. Nobel laureates for literature 15. Political and social philosophers
    ISBN 0-374-52859-4 pa
                       LC 2001-33356

A retrospective of Milosz's "prose works, in which he weaves autobiography and portraits of people, famous and otherwise, who have influenced him into graceful and pro-

vocative musings on time, history, religion, science, and art." Booklist

Includes bibliographical references

★ **Monologue** of a dog; new poems. translated from the Polish by Clare Cavanagh and Stanislaw Baranczak; [foreword by Billy Collins] Harcourt 2005 96p $22   **891.8**
    1. Poetry -- By individual authors
    ISBN 0-15-101220-2
                       LC 2005-16084

Original Polish edition, 2002

This is a collection of poems by the author of Miracle Fair (2001).

In this volume, Nobel laureate Szymborska "invites readers to linger over moments small, earthly, and sometimes life-altering. With characteristically simple language and imagery, wit and irony, she shows us how life can change at any moment. Hers are the politics of the everyday, little observations on the value of life." Libr J

Sosnowski, Andrzej

    Lodgings; selected poems, 1987-2010. translated from the Polish by Benjamin Paloff. Open Letter 2011 163p pa $13.95   **891.8**
    1. Poetry -- By individual authors
    ISBN 978-1-934824-32-0; 1-934824-32-1
                       LC 2010-52054

With this volume, "translator Benjamin Paloff has made an important contribution to the body of Polish poetry currently available to readers in English. Complete with a translator's note, a conversation between Sosnowski and Paloff, and poems that span Sosnowski's entire career to date (1987-2010), Lodgings offers an unusual glimpse into a polyphonous, expansive, and chameleonic strain of Polish poetry. The poems included are pulled from nine of Sosnowski's collections . . . , and they are presented, with two exceptions, in their original order." Words without Borders

Szymborska, Wislawa, 1923-2012

    Map; Collected and Last Poems. Houghton Mifflin Harcourt 2015 464 p. $32   **891.8**
    ISBN 0544126025; 9780544126022
                       LC 2015297265

This collection of poems by Wislawa Szymborska, translated by Clare Cavanaugh and Stanislaw Baranczak, "trace Szymborska's work until her death in 2012. Of the approximately two hundred and fifty poems included here, nearly forty are newly translated; thirteen represent the entirety of the poet's last Polish collection, Enough, never before published in English." (Publisher's note)

"Throughout, Szymborska considers loss and fragility, as when former lovers walk past each other and an aging professor is no longer allowed his vodka and cigarettes. She writes, too, of the imprecision of memory, and in the title poem, the discovery that maps 'give no access to the vicious truth.' This is a brilliant and important collection." Booklist

Poems, new and collected, 1957-1997; translated from the Polish by Stanisaw Baranczak and Clare Cavanagh.

Harcourt Brace & Co. 1998 273p $27; pa $17 **891.8**
ISBN 0-15-100353-X; 0-15-601146-8 pa
LC 97-32277

This career-spanning collection by the 1996 Nobel Prize winner includes her Nobel lecture

Szymborska's "work is ultimately wisdom literature, written in a first person that expresses a universal humanity that American poets—lockstep individualists all—haven't dared essay since early in this century." Booklist

Zagajewski, Adam

★ **Without** end; new and selected poems. translations by Clare Cavanagh [et al.] Farrar, Straus & Giroux 2002 285p $30; pa $15 **891.8**
ISBN 0-374-22096-4; 0-374-52861-6 pa
LC 2001-40252

"Zagajewski's poetic evolution is clearly charted in 'Without End,' a new anthology of his work that is made up of his three English-language collections—'Tremor' (1985), 'Canvas' (1991) and 'Mysticism for Beginners' (1997)—as well as his most recent work and new translations of some early poems. . . . Zagajewski's poems pull us from whatever routine threatens to dull our senses, from whatever might lull us into mere existence. This is an astonishing book." N Y Times Book Rev

Zagajewski, Adam, 1945-

Eternal enemies; translated from the Polish by Clare Cavanagh. Farrar, Straus and Giroux 2008 116p **891.8**
1. Poetry -- By individual authors
ISBN 0-374-21634-7; 978-0-374-21634-4
LC 2007-42855

This is a collection of poetry by the author of Two Cities (1995), Without End (2002), and A Defense of Ardor (2004).

"Cavanagh's supple translations let the verse sing in American English without making this Polish poet sound too American." Publ Wkly

Unseen hand; translated from the Polish by Clare Cavanagh. Farrar, Straus and Giroux 2011 107p $23 **891.8**
1. Poetry -- By individual authors
ISBN 978-0-374-28089-5; 0-374-28089-4
LC 2010-46274

Original Polish edition, 2009

The book "is Adam Zagajewski's sixth book of poetry translated into English. . . . . If Szymborska is a poet of imaginary journeys, Zagajewski is a real traveler with a ticket and a suitcase. He even has a poem called 'Self-Portrait in an Airplane.' Many of his poems are about towns and cities in Europe and the United States that he had either lived in or visited. Poetry and travel are allied, Czeslaw Milosz once claimed, since poetry is an expression of wondering at things, landscapes, people, their habits and mores. . . . He compares the impassive river Garonne, flowing in silence, to an Indian brave in plumes of sun; a plane taking off from an airport to a zealous pupil who believes what the old masters told him; the light bulbs hissing in gray hallways at night to the signals of sinking ships." (New York Review of Books)

"The collective calm of these poems creates an odd tension: Within [Zagajewski's] clear, contemplative lines, the indifference of time can always be felt drifting unstoppably by, even as we attempt to scaffold it with history or cage it with memory. . . . [The poems,] translated by the admirably consistent Clare Cavanagh, move through the various locales of Zagajewski's life; from his Polish upbringing in Lvov and the provincial garrison town of Gliwice (to which his family was forced to move shortly after his birth in 1945), to various stints in Krakow, Paris, and Chicago. Markers of place and time are everywhere, but Zagajewski is especially perceptive of the ways the past is channeled through the present — his 'now' tends to carry the authority of an 'always.'" Boston Globe

892 Afro-Asiatic literatures

Amichai, Yehuda

Poems of Jerusalem; and, Love poems; a bilingual edition. Sheep Meadow Press 1992 265p pa $16.95 **892**
1. Poetry -- By individual authors
ISBN 1-87881-819-8
LC 92-31558

Poems of Jerusalem first published 1988 by Perennial Lib.; Love poems first published 1981 by Harper & Row

This work is "actually drawn from eight previous works and boasts an even larger array of translators (including Stephen Mitchell, David Rosenberg, Ted Hughes, and the poet himself). The thematic arrangement deftly emphasizes the Israeli poet's constant preoccupation with both Jerusalem and love." Libr J

The **selected** poetry of Yehuda Amichai; edited and translated from the Hebrew by Chana Bloch and Stephen Mitchell. newly rev & expanded ed; University of Calif. Press 1996 195p pa $16.95 **892**
1. Poetry -- By individual authors
ISBN 0-520-20538-3
LC 96-18580

First published 1986

"Although much of Amichai's poetry focuses on war, he is able to describe its horrors by maintaining a clear distance between himself and his subject. The result is a finely controlled emotional pitch that allows the poet to convey his sense of pain and outrage without pathos or sentimentality. He writes colloquially, in language that is always commensurate with emotional experience." Reader's Ency. 4th edition

Gilgamesh

★ **Gilgamesh**; a new English version [by] Stephen Mitchell. Free Press 2004 290p $25; pa $14 **892**
ISBN 0-7432-6164-X; 0-7432-6169-0 pa
LC 2004-50072

"Relying on existing translations (and in places where there are gaps, on his own imagination), Mitchell seeks language that is as swift and strong as the story itself. . . . This wonderful new version of the story of Gilgamesh shows how the story came to achieve literary immortality—not because it is a rare ancient artifact, but because reading it can make

people in the here and now feel more completely alive."
Publ Wkly

Includes bibliographical references

892.4 Hebrew literature

Amichai, Yehuda

Open closed open; poems. translated from the
Hebrew by Chana Bloch and Chana Kronfeld. Harcourt Brace & Co. 2000 184p $25 **892.4**
   1. Poetry -- By individual authors
   ISBN 0-15-100378-5

                  LC 00-23537

Original Hebrew edition, 1998

Amichai "writes with the casual wisdom and generous
humor of a master." Booklist

Shabtai, Aharon

War & love, love & war; new and selected poems. translated by Peter Cole. New Directions 2010
175p pa $15.95 **892.4**
   1. Poetry -- By individual authors
   ISBN 978-0-8112-1890-0; 0-8112-1890-2

                 LC 2010-10440

"Gritty, controversial and intensely lyrical, this is an excellent collection from one of Israel's most important contemporary poets. Spanning more than three-anda-half decades of writing, it exhibits a wealth of experimentation with
various styles, and a multitude of yearnings and obsessions.
As the title implies, engagement with the Israeli-Palestinian
conflict is one of the book's chief subjects. The real gem,
though, is the closing cycle of poems, which mourns the
passing of Shabtai's wife, Tanya Reinhart." Forward

Includes bibliographical references

892.7 Arabic and Maltese literatures

Anthology of modern Palestinian literature; edited
and introduced by Salma Khadra Jayyusi. Columbia Univ. Press 1992 xxxiii, 744p hardcover o.p.
pa $30.50 **892.7**
   1. Arabic literature -- Collections
   ISBN 0-231-07508-1; 0-231-07509-X pa

                 LC 92-5189

"Presented here are translations of poems, stories, and
excerpts from novels, as well as works by Palestinian poets
who write in English. Also included are personal narratives
by Palestinian writers depicting the varied aspects of Palestinian life from the turn of the century to the present. . . .
Biographical sketches introduce the authors, and a chronology of modern Palestinian history provides background for
some of the events and places referred to in the selections.
The introduction by the editor provides a concise but comprehensive political history of Palestinian literature during
the twentieth century." Publisher's note

Includes bibliographical references

Darwish, Mahmud

If I were another; translated from the Arabic by
Fady Joudah. Farrar, Straus and Giroux 2009 201p
$28 **892.7**
   1. Poetry -- By individual authors
   ISBN 978-0-374-17429-3; 0-374-17429-6

                 LC 2009-11521

This volume "comprises four nonconsecutive books of
longer poems spanning 1990 to 2005. These works follow
Darwish's poetic development from a historically focused
middle period to the devastatingly personal lyric-epic of
his late style. Formally varied—Rubaiyats alternate with
sprawling freeform poems, in which prose paragraphs meet
both long and short verse lines—Darwish's Sufi-inspired
poetry probes, admires, describes, longs for and questions."
Publ Wkly

Includes bibliographical references

Night and horses and the desert; an anthology of
   classical Arabic literature. edited by Robert Irwin. Anchor Books 2001 462p pa $16 **892.7**
   1. Arabic literature -- Collections 2. Arabic literature
   -- History and criticism
   ISBN 0-385-72155-2

                 LC 2001-53721

First published 2000 by Overlook Press

"The chapter on the Qur'an is perhaps the most essential
as it examines just how vital the dogma of Islam has been
for the Arabic understanding of culture and art. . . . This persuasive work will surely fill in the gap in the study of Arabic
literature in this country." Publ Wkly

Includes bibliographical references

The **Poetry** of Arab women; a contemporary anthology. edited by Nathalie Handal. Interlink Bks.
   2000 xxi, 355p pa $22 **892.7**
   1. Arabic poetry -- Collections
   ISBN 978-1-56656-374-1; 1-56656-374-7

                 LC 00-58054

"Handal deserves high praise for producing an anthology that mirrors faithfully Arab women's creative role
throughout the last century." Multicultural Rev

Tales of the Marvellous and News of the Strange;
   translated by Malcolm C. Lyons; introduced by
   Robert Irwin. Penguin Group USA 2015 496 p.
   (hbk.) $30 **892.7**
   1. Short stories 2. Arabic literature
   ISBN 0141395036; 9780141395036

                 LC 2014472568

This book, translated by Malcolm C. Lyons and illustrated by Coralie Bickford-Smith, is "a great cache of ancient, magical stories in the same tradition as 'The Arabian
Nights.'. . . Dating from at least a millennium ago, these are
the earliest-known Arabic short stories, which survived in
a single, ragged manuscript in a library in Istanbul." (Publisher's note)

"Coupled with an informative introduction by Robert Irwin, author of The Arabian Nights: A Companion, this book
is a welcome and recommended addition to those who enjoy
the Arabian Nights." LJ

Includes bibliographical references.

894 Literatures of Altaic, Uralic, Hyperborean, Dravidian languages; literatures of miscellaneous languages of south Asia

Pamuk, Orhan

Other colors; essays and a story. translated from the Turkish by Maureen Freely. Alfred A. Knopf 2007 433p il $27.95   **894**

ISBN 978-0-307-26675-0; 0-307-26675-3

LC 2007-21132

Original Turkish edition, 1999

"Whether he's writing wistfully about Andre Gide as the hero of Turkish intellectuals . . . or recalling how he used to collect Coca-Cola cans as a boy, from the trash cans of expat Americans, Pamuk is taking the world we thought we knew and making it fresh and alive." N Y Times Book Rev

895.1 Chinese literature

An **Anthology** of Chinese literature; beginnings to 1911. edited and translated by Stephen Owen. Norton 1996 xlviii, 1212p hardcover o.p. pa $59.65   **895.1**

1. Chinese literature -- Collections
ISBN 0-393-97106-6 pa

LC 95-11409

"In a book that moves roughly chronologically through the tradition, Owen gathers texts according to genres, themes, forms, and other groupings to show the way essential texts build off each other and how the tradition echoes itself. Included are a range of forms . . . presented . . . {with} commentary to provide a . . . view of the interplay between Chinese literature, culture, and history." Publisher's note

Includes bibliographical references

Anthology of modern Chinese poetry; edited and translated by Michelle Yeh. Yale Univ. Press 1993 245p hardcover o.p. pa $21   **895.1**

1. Chinese poetry -- Collections
ISBN 0-300-05947-7 pa

LC 92-16322

"Arranged chronologically, this selection of twentieth-century poetry from China and Taiwan offers a few poems by each of 67 poets born between 1891 and 1963. Its scope is enormous, its range impressive. Editor Yeh's translations are accessible and fluid; her introduction and notes are helpful without being overbearingly scholarly." Booklist

Includes bibliographical references

The **Columbia** book of Chinese poetry; from early times to the thirteenth century. translated and edited by Burton Watson. Columbia Univ. Press 1984 385p il (Translations from the Oriental classics) $69; pa $27   **895.1**

1. Chinese poetry -- Collections
ISBN 0-231-05682-6; 0-231-05683-4 pa

LC 83-26182

This anthology's "arrangement is historical, beginning with selections from a first millenium BC collection of Chinese verse (the Shih ching), and ending with tz'u lyrics from the Sung period (AD 960-1279). The 12 selections [are] each prefaced with a two- or three-page introduction." Choice

Includes bibliographical references

The **Columbia** history of Chinese literature; Victor H. Mair, editor. Columbia Univ. Press 2001 xx, 1342p $78   **895.1**

1. Chinese literature -- History and criticism
ISBN 0-231-10984-9

LC 2001-28236

This "history explores a wide range of Chinese literature, from the classics to humor to folk tales to oral traditions, and moves from ancient times to the end of the 20th century. . . . Mair has overseen a host of excellent scholars writing on a vast subject." Libr J

Includes bibliographical references

Mountain home; the wilderness poetry of ancient China. selected and translated by David Hinton. New Directions Pub. 2005 xxi, 295p map pa $17.95   **895.1**

1. Chinese poetry -- Collections
ISBN 978-0-8112-1624-1

LC 2005-869

First published 2002 by Counterpoint

"Translator and scholar Hinton ensures that Western readers will experience this supreme collection of Chinese rivers-and-mountains (shan-shui) poetry at the deepest possible level by succinctly explaining the cosmology inherent in this vital and profoundly influential tradition. The keys to understanding the elegant poetry of such masters as T'ao Ch'ien (365-427), Li Po (701-762), and Lu Yu (1125-1210) are realizing that they perceive no divide between the human and what we call nature, or between being and nonbeing. . . . Oneness with life at its purest is the desired mode for these thoughtful, yet often playful, poets, and dwelling within these meditative pages is the first step on the way there." Booklist

The **New** Directions anthology of classical chinese poetry; edited by Eliot Weinberger; translations by William Carlos Williams . . . [et al.] New Directions 2003 xxvii, 242p $24.95; pa $16.95   **895.1**

1. Chinese poetry -- Collections
ISBN 978-0-8112-1540-4; 0-8112-1540-7; 978-0-8112-1605-0 pa; 0-8112-1605-5 pa

LC 2002-156731

The poems are "translated into English by four of the best-known American poets of the 20th century—Ezra Pound, William Carlos Williams, Kenneth Rexroth and Gary Snyder—and an academic scholar/translator called David Hinton, who deserves to be as well known as the others. It is not often that an anthology really demands attention. . . . This poetry means what it says. It feels companionable, and even sexy. It is not excessively—or confusingly—metaphorical. It is not foggy with abstract philosophising. It lacks the shriek of rhetoric; it seems to move, so often, at an agreeable walking pace. It feels spacious. In fact, there seems to be space between the words themselves. It mixes the high and the low with seeming ease. Its temper suggests

that there is no unsuitable subject matter for poetry at all."
New Statesman

895.6   Japanese literature

Haiku before haiku; from the Renga masters to Basho. translated, with an introduction, by Steven D. Carter. Columbia University Press 2011 163p (Translations from the Asian classics) $69.50; pa $22.50; ebook $9.99   **895.6**
1. Haiku 2. Renga 3. Japanese poetry
ISBN 978-0-231-15648-6; 978-0-231-15647-9 pa; 978-0-231-52706-4 ebook

LC 2010-37030

"While the rise of the charmingly simple, brilliantly evocative haiku is often associated with the seventeenth-century Japanese poet Matsuo Basho, the form had already flourished for more than four hundred years before Basho even began to write. These early poems, known as hokku, are identical to haiku in syllable count and structure but function differently as a genre. Whereas each haiku is its own constellation of image and meaning, a hokku opens a series of linked, collaborative stanzas in a sequence called renga. . . . [This anthology] presents 320 hokku composed between the thirteenth and early eighteenth centuries, from the poems of the courtier Nijo Yoshimoto to those of the genre's first 'professional' master, Sogi, and his disciples. It features 20 masterpieces by Basho himself." Publisher's note
Includes bibliographical references

Keene, Donald

Five modern Japanese novelists. Columbia Univ. Press 2002 113p $26   **895.6**
1. Japanese literature -- History and criticism
ISBN 0-231-12610-7

LC 2002-73412

The author's essays, "part memoir and part literary evaluation, are ideal introductions to their subjects." Booklist
Includes bibliographical references

The **pleasures** of Japanese literature. Columbia Univ. Press 1988 133p il (Companion to Asian studies) $60; pa $19.50   **895.6**
1. Aesthetics 2. Theater -- Japan 3. Japanese literature -- History and criticism
ISBN 0-231-06736-4; 0-231-06737-2 pa

LC 88-18069

The author discusses Japanese aesthetics, poetry, fiction and drama, focusing on works of the premodern period
"If your library has no other introduction to the Japanese classics, nor any need for another, this is the one it ought to include." Booklist
Includes bibliographical references

Seeds in the heart; Japanese literature from earliest times to the late sixteenth century. with a new preface by the author, Donald Keene. Columbia University Press 1999 1265p (History of Japanese literature) pa $37   **895.6**
1. Japanese literature -- History and criticism
ISBN 0-231-11441-9

LC 99-25990

First published 1993 by Holt & Co.
This volume completes the author's history of Japanese literature begun with: World within walls (1977) and Dawn to the West (1984).
"The first half of 'Seeds in the Heart' encompasses everything from the myths, legends, songs and poems of the eighth-century 'Kojiki' ('Record of Ancient Matters') and 'Manyoshu,' a collection of 4,500 poems, to the 'The Tale of Genji' and later works of fiction. . . . During Japan's middle ages (1185-1600), Buddhism and popular (rather than aristocratic) forms of storytelling and theater generated a repertory of characters and genres that would eventually form the country's first broadly based, national culture. The literature of these centuries has rarely attracted the scholarly attention paid to the earlier 'high' classical tradition. So Mr. Keene's attention to this period makes the second half of 'Seeds in the Heart' especially valuable." N Y Times Book Rev
Includes bibliographical references

Modern Japanese writers; Jay Rubin, editor. Scribner 2000 434p $130   **895.6**
1. Authors, Japanese 2. Japanese literature -- History and criticism
ISBN 0-684-80598-7

LC 00-63505

"This handbook is a collection of alphabetically arranged articles on 23 twentieth-century Japanese writers and one literary genre, written by noted scholars in the field. Entries are generally around 18 pages in length. Each author entry treats a writer's life and work and is accompanied by a selected bibliography of primary and secondary sources. Most of the writers included have been translated into English, and two of them, Kawabata Yasunari and Oe Kenzaburo, are Nobel Prize winners." Booklist
Includes bibliographical references

One hundred poems from the Japanese; {edited and translated} by Kenneth Rexroth. New Directions 1956 143p hardcover o.p. pa $11.95   **895.6**
1. Japanese poetry -- Collections
ISBN 0-8112-0181-3 pa

A bilingual collection of poems drawn chiefly from the traditional Manoshu, Kokinshu, and Hyakunin Isshu collections and also containing examples of haiku and other later forms. The translator's introduction provides background information on the history and nature of Japanese poetry
Includes bibliographical references

Waley, Arthur

The **No** plays of Japan; an anthology. Dover Publications 1998 270p pa $12.95   **895.6**
1. No plays
ISBN 978-0-486-40156-0

LC 97-46053

First published 1921 in the United Kingdom; first United States edition published 1922 by Knopf

Contains translation of 20 No plays and summaries of 16 more. In his introduction Mr. Waley gives a brief history of the No drama, its origin, the text of the plays, and the chief playwrights. He also tells about the stage settings, costumes and properties used in the production of these plays. The greatest representation is given to the works of Seami and Zenchiku Ujinobu

896   African literatures

The **Penguin** book of modern African poetry; edited by Gerald Moore and Ulli Beier. 4th ed.; Penguin Books 2007 xxvi, 448p pa $17   **896**
1. African poetry -- Collections
ISBN 978-0-14-042472-0; 0-14-042472-5
First published 1963 in the United Kingdom with title: Modern poetry from Africa
This anthology includes over 200 poems by 67 poets from 23 countries.
Includes bibliographical references

897   Literatures of North American native languages

The **Cambridge** companion to Native American literature; edited by Joy Porter and Kenneth M. Roemer. Cambridge University Press 2005 343p il map hardcover o.p. pa $26.95   **897**
1. Native American literature -- History and criticism
ISBN 978-0-521-52979-2 pa; 0-521-52979-4 pa
LC 2005-44298
Essays organized "by historical and cultural context, by genre, and according to individual authors. Particularly insightful and informative are the tightly written essays on the eight currently best-known Indian writers. Also included are maps, a time line, suggested readings, and a brief series of 40 biobibliographies of notable Native American writers. . . . Readers of this volume should probably already have a working knowledge of the main figures in this increasingly important and respected segment of American literature." Libr J

900   HISTORY

900   History, geography, and auxiliary disciplines

Black, Jeremy
Other pasts, different presents, alternative futures; Jeremy Black. Indiana University Press 2015 252 p. (paperback : alkaline paper) $30   **900**
1. Alternative histories 2. History -- Philosophy 3. Agent (Philosophy) 4. Imaginary histories 5. History -- Methodology 6. Contingency (Philosophy)
ISBN 9780253016973; 9780253017048
LC 2015006248

This book, by Jeremy Black, "offers a short guide to [counterfactualism], one that is designed to argue its value as a tool for public and academe alike. Black focuses on the role of counterfactualism in demonstrating the part of contingency, and thus human agency, in history, and the salutary critique the approach offers to determinist accounts of past, present, and future." (Publisher's note)
"For those interested in this fascinating subject, Black's book is indispensable." Pub Wkly
Includes bibliographical references and index

Báez, Fernando
A **universal** history of the destruction of books; from ancient Sumer to modern-day Iraq. translated by Alfred MacAdam. Atlas & Co. 2008 354p il map $25   **900**
1. Censorship 2. Books -- Censorship 3. Books and reading -- History 4. Libraries -- Destruction and pillage
ISBN 978-1-934633-01-4
LC 2008-932321
Original Spanish edition, 2004
This is a "horrific chronicle of the centuries-long assault on human memory. . . . A sobering reminder of just how deep-seated is the instinct to destroy other people's truths." Kirkus
Includes bibliographical references

Schweitzer, Albert, 1875-1965
Out of my life and thought; an autobiography. Albert Schweitzer; foreword by Jimmy Carter; new foreword by Lachlan Forrow; translated by Antje Bultmann Lemke. Johns Hopkins University Press 2009 xx, 272 p.p ill. (paperback) $27   **900**
ISBN 0801894123; 9780801894121
LC 2009925674
This book presents Albert Schweitzer's "autobiography, first published in 1933" in which he "discusses his research into primitive Christianity and his search for the historical Jesus; his love of Bach, 'poet and painter in sound'; his fancy for rebuilding old church organs. His philosophy, which he called 'Reverence for Life,' blends mysticism and rationalism, with an impulse to release the 'active ethic' he sees latent in Christianity." (Publishers Weekly)
Includes bibliographical references (p. 257-260) and index

901   Philosophy and theory of history

Hobsbawm, E. J.
On history. New Press (NY) 1997 305p $25; pa $15.95   **901**
1. Historiography
ISBN 1-56584-393-2; 1-56584-468-8 pa
"In these collected pieces—articles, lectures and reviews—Eric Hobsbawm surveys the writings of modern historians with the magisterial gaze of a man who has seen both the rise of Hitler and the fall of Communism. He notes how the discipline has changed in the last century: how social history and economic history have come of age, how modern historians speak of change and forces where Victorians spoke of ideas and progress. He rejects postmodernist claims

that history can be freely revised because all facts are merely intellectual constructions." N Y Times Book Rev

MacMillan, Margaret

Dangerous games; the uses and abuses of history. Modern Library 2009 188p $22   **901**

1. Historiography 2. History -- Philosophy

ISBN 978-0-679-64358-6; 0-679-64358-3

First published 2008 in Canada with title: The uses and abuses of history

Explores the ways in which history has been used to influence people and government, focusing on how reportage of past events has been manipulated to justify religious movements and political campaigns. Based on the Joanne Goodman lecture series of the University of Western Ontario.

"This is a must read for anyone who wants to understand the importance of correctly understanding the past." Publ Wkly

Includes bibliographical references

Ortega, Jose

The **revolt** of the masses; translated, annotated, and with an introduction by Anthony Kerrigan; edited by Kenneth Moore; with a foreword by Saul Bellow. University of Notre Dame Press 1985 xxxi, 192p hardcover o.p. pa $13.95   **901**

1. Proletariat 2. Civilization 3. Europe -- Civilization

ISBN 0-393-31095-7

LC 81-40457

Original Spanish edition, 1930; first English translation, 1932

This work argues for the "leveling out of outstanding qualities in men and culture, as it traces the development of the 'mediocre soul' out of 19th-century bourgeois culture to the advent of the new totalitarian democracy in which none are nor aspire to be superior to others but rather to be 'just like everybody else.' The masses are not the impoverished or politically oppressed proletariat but span the classes marked by a 'qualitative determinant': 'the mass is the average man.'" (Libr J) First published in Spain in 1929. For an earlier English translation see BRD 1932.

Spengler, Oswald

The **decline** of the West, volume one; Form and actuality. authorized translation with notes by Charles Frances Atkinson. A. Knopf 1996 various paging $45   **901**

1. History -- Philosophy 2. Civilization -- History

ISBN 0-394-42179-5

First published 1926

The first volume of a work that "reflects the pessimistic atmosphere in Germany after World War I. Spengler maintained that history has a natural development, in which every culture is a distinct organic form that grows, matures, and decays." Reader's Ency. 4th edition

Includes bibliographical references

902 Miscellany of history

Grafton, Anthony

Cartographies of time; a history of the timeline. [by] Daniel Rosenberg and Anthony Grafton. Princeton Architectural Press 2010 272p il $50   **902**

1. Historical chronology 2. History -- Philosophy

ISBN 978-1-56898-763-7; 1-56898-763-3

LC 2008-52892

The authors "aim to provide the first full account of the development of the modern timeline, from its inauspicious beginnings in crude lists and tables, to the glorious, colorful artworks that convey the sweep of time with arresting visual drama. There's more to this story, however. The story of the timeline is also the story of how humanity's perception of time has evolved, and how the various representations of time can tell us much about the personality and proclivity of the era in which it was designed. . . . Rosenberg and Grafton's text is crisp and informative, but the true stars of Cartographies of Time are the numerous illustrations and photographs of the chronologies themselves." PopMatters

Includes bibliographical references.

Grun, Bernard

★ The **timetables** of history; a historical linkage of people and events. 4th ed.; Simon & Schuster 2005 835p $25   **902**

1. Historical chronology

ISBN 0-7432-7003-7; 978-0-7432-7003-8

LC 2005-49766

Original German edition, 1946; first published in the United States 1975

This chronology "includes material from 4500 BCE to 2004. . . . The information is listed by year in seven columns labeled 'History, Politics', 'Literature, Theater', 'Religion, Philosophy, Learning', 'Visual Arts', 'Music', 'Science, Technology, Growth', and 'Daily Life.' . . . This work is an excellent chronological tool, and should be found in all libraries." Choice

The **timetables** of American history; Laurence Urdang, editor; with an introduction by Henry Steele Commager and a new foreword by Arthur Schlesinger, Jr. Simon & Schuster 2001 534p il pa $24   **902**

1. Historical chronology

ISBN 0-7432-0261-9

First published 1982

Presents information chronologically in tabular form. Each double-page spread has columns for history and politics, the arts, science and technology, and miscellaneous.

902.2 Illustrations, models, miniatures

National Geographic Society (U.S.)

National Geographic visual history of the world; [authors, Klaus Berndl . . . et al.]. National Geographic Society 2005 656p il $35   **902.2**

1. World history

ISBN 0-7922-3695-5

LC 2005-541553

"Over 4,000 illustrations and photographs cover individuals and events from prehistory (the beginning to ca. 4000 BCE) to the contemporary world (1945 to the present). . . . This educational and entertaining volume of social, cultural, and military history will appeal to a wide readership." Choice

Terra Maxima; The Records of Humankind. edited by Wolfgang Kunth. Firefly Books Ltd 2013 576 p. color illustrations $49.95   **902.2**

1. World records 2. Technological innovations

ISBN 1770852425; 9781770852426

LC 2013456556

This book, edited by Wolfgang Kunth, "is comprised of more than 3,000 full-color photographs . . . that showcase the biggest and the best religious, cultural, and technological marvels of the world. The work is broken down into 10 sections: 'Countries and Nations,' 'Languages and Scripts,' 'Faith and Religion,' 'Cities and Metropolises,' 'Urban Megastructures,' 'Transportation and Traffic,' 'Aviation and Space Travel,' 'Art and Culture,' 'Science and Research,' and 'Sports and Leisure.'" (Booklist)

"The emphasis is on the visual, with sumptuous color photographs printed on heavy stock, many appearing on full spreads. The text, while minimal, is nevertheless informative, pointing out interesting historical, architectural, and other details about the structures pictured." LJ

904 Collected accounts of events

Davis, Lee Allyn

Man-made catastrophes; [by] Lee Davis. rev ed; Facts on File 2002 402p il $60   **904**

1. Disasters

ISBN 0-8160-4418-X

LC 2001-54324

First published 1993

This describes man-made disasters "from the burning of Babylon in 538B.C. to the 2001 terrorist attack on the World Trade Center in New York City. . . . [The entries] are organized by disaster type: air crashes, civil unrest and terrorism, explosions, maritime disasters, nuclear and industrial accidents, railway disasters, and space disasters." Publisher's note

Includes bibliographical references

Hanson, Victor Davis

Carnage and culture; landmark battles in the rise of Western power. Doubleday 2001 492p il hardcover o.p. pa $16   **904**

1. Battles 2. Military history

ISBN 0-385-72038-6 pa

LC 00-65582

"This provocative work is likely to engender controversy." Booklist

Includes bibliographical references

907 Education, research, related topics of history

Hamilton, Nigel

★ **Biography;** a brief history. Harvard University Press 2007 345p il $21.95   **907**

1. Biography as a literary form

ISBN 978-0-674-02466-3; 0-674-02466-4

LC 2006-51132

"Hamilton has given readers a thoughtprovoking look at biography in its various forms; a fascinating and handy reference book for anyone wishing to know more about the history and art of biography." Libr J

Includes bibliographical references (p. 315-21)

Mills, Elizabeth S.

Evidence explained; citing history sources from artifacts to cyberspace. [by] Elizabeth Shown Mills. 2nd ed; Genealogical Pub. Co. 2009 885p $59.95   **907**

1. History -- Sources 2. History -- Research

ISBN 978-0-8063-1806-6

LC 2009-934128

First published 2007

This resource is "indispensable for scholars and accessible enough to meet the needs of amateur genealogists and students." Libr J

Includes bibliographical references

Tuchman, Barbara Wertheim

Practicing history; selected essays. by Barbara W. Tuchman. Knopf 1981 306p hardcover o.p. pa $14.95   **907**

1. Diplomats 2. Governors 3. Presidents 4. Historiography 5. Modern history 6. Executive power 7. Vietnam War, 1961-1975 8. Israel 9. Financiers 10. College presidents 11. Nobel laureates for peace 12. World War, 1914-1918 -- United States 13. China -- Foreign relations -- United States 14. United States -- Foreign relations -- China

ISBN 0-345-30363-6 pa

LC 81-47509

A collection of essays on the nature, methodology and writing of history

907.2 Historical research

Bailyn, Bernard

Sometimes an art, never a science, always a craft; on history. by Bernard Bailyn. Alfred A. Knopf 2015 320 p. $28   **907.2**

1. Modern history 2. History -- Philosophy 3. Historiography -- Philosophy 4. United States -- Historiography 5. Great Britain -- Colonies --

Historiography
ISBN 1101874473; 9781101874479

LC 2014022229

Author "Bernard Bailyn argues in this . . . collection of essays, history always combines approximations based on incomplete data with empathic imagination, interweaving strands of knowledge into a narrative that also explains. This is a stirring and insightful work drawing on the wisdom and perspective of a career spanning more than five decades." (Publisher's note)

"Another theme is the role of creativity in historical inquiry, and in one of this selection's more personal (yet unfailingly scholarly) essays, Bailyn pays tribute to historians whose innovative methods revealed 'hitherto submerged worlds' while also acknowledging the limitations inherent to such disruptions. Essays on Loyalists in the American Revolution and Thomas Hutchinson, the Royalist governor of Massachusetts, circle back to Bailyn's colonial bailiwick." Booklist

Includes bibliographical references and index

909 World history

★ **Africana**: the encyclopedia of the African and African American experience; editors, Kwame Anthony Appiah, Henry Louis Gates, Jr. 2nd ed; Oxford University Press 2005 5v set $550 **909**
1. Reference books 2. Africa -- Encyclopedias 3. Blacks -- Encyclopedias 4. African diaspora -- Encyclopedias 5. African Americans -- Encyclopedias
ISBN 978-0-19-517055-9; 0-19-517055-5

LC 2004-20222

First published 1999 by Basic Civitas Bks.

This encyclopedia covers "prominent individuals, events, trends, places, political movements, art forms, business and trade, religions, ethnic groups, organizations, and countries on both sides of the ocean. . . . There are articles on contemporary nations of sub-Saharan Africa, ethnic groups from various regions of Africa, African American Academy award winners, Caribbean musical styles, African religions in Brazil, and European colonial powers." Booklist [review of 1999 edition]

Includes bibliographical references

Aries, Philippe

A **History** of private life; v2 [Philippe Ariès and Georges Duby, general editors; translated by] Arthur Goldhammer. Belknap Press 1988 650p v2 il hardcover o.p. pa $28 **909**
1. Family life 2. Manners and customs 3. Medieval civilization
ISBN 0-674-40001-1

LC 86-18286

"Spanning the period from the 11th century to the Renaissance and focusing on France and Tuscan Italy, this [second volume] continues the . . . five-volume history of private life from the Roman world to the present. 'Private' is here defined as what medieval people considered intimate, familial, domestic." Libr J

Includes bibliographical references

Boorstin, Daniel J.

The **creators**. Random House 1992 811p il hardcover o.p. pa $18.95 **909**
1. Arts 2. Civilization 3. Creation (Literary, artistic, etc.)
ISBN 0-394-54395-5; 0-679-74375-8 pa

LC 91-39948

In this volume "Boorstin undertakes an interpretive history of creativity in Western civilization. Packed with shrewd, entertaining profiles of Dante, Goethe, Benjamin Franklin and dozens of others, this stimulating synthesis sets the achievements of individual geniuses into a coherent narrative of humanity's advance from ignorance." Publ Wkly

Includes bibliographical references

Brendon, Piers

★ The **decline** and fall of the British Empire, 1781-1997. Alfred A. Knopf 2008 xxii, 786p il map $37.50 **909**
1. Great Britain -- History 2. Great Britain -- Colonies 3. Great Britain -- Civilization 4. Commonwealth countries -- History
ISBN 978-0-307-26829-7; 0-307-26829-2

LC 2008-14192

First published 2007 in the United Kingdom

"A richly detailed, lucid account of how the British Empire grew and grew—and then, not quite inexorably, fell apart." Kirkus

Includes bibliographical references

Brenner, Frederic

Diaspora: homelands in exile. HarperCollins 2003 2v il map set $100 **909**
1. Jews -- Pictorial works
ISBN 0-06-008778-1

LC 2003-42328

This is a "collection of photographs, taken over the course of 25 years, chronicling Jewish lives, often in declining communities, in every corner of the world, from Azerbaijan and Uzbekistan to Ethiopia and Las Vegas. For anyone, Jewish or otherwise, who generally thinks of Jews in terms of Israel and the United States, the book will be a revelation." Publ Wkly

Includes bibliographical references

Brown, Cynthia Stokes

A **big** history; from the Big Bang to the present. Distributed by W.W. Norton 2007 288p il map $25.95 **909**
1. Human ecology 2. World history
ISBN 978-1-59558-196-9; 1-59558-196-0

LC 2007-6741

"In a multidisciplinary narrative subtly emphasizing the mutual impact of people and planet, Brown covers Earth's history from the big bang through the development of life and the growth of civilization. . . . This exciting saga crosses space and time to illustrate how humans, born of stardust, were shaped—and how they in turn shaped the world we know today." Publ Wkly

Cahill, Thomas

The **gifts** of the Jews; how a tribe of desert nomads changed the way everyone thinks and feels. Talese 1998 291p (Hinges of history) $23.50; pa $14 **909**

1. Jews -- History 2. Judaism -- History 3. Bible -- O.T. -- History of Biblical events

ISBN 0-385-48248-5; 0-385-48249-3 pa

LC 97-45139

In this colloquial look at the influence of the Hebrew Bible on civilization, the author gives "the Jews credit for revolutionizing the concepts of democracy, universal law, monotheism, linear time, personal vocation, destiny, self-improvement and the belief in the equality of all humans. He stumbles on the odd aside and occasionally is surprisingly insensitive... Still, his passion and breadth of knowledge are admirable." N Y Times Book Rev

Includes bibliographical references

Sailing the wine-dark sea; why the Greeks matter. Talese 2003 304p (Hinges of history) $27.50; pa $14.95 **909**

1. Greece -- Civilization

ISBN 0-385-49553-6; 0-385-49554-4 pa

LC 2003-50725

This author "begins with a discussion of Homer's Iliad and Odyssey and how these two epic poems relate to the history of Greece. He then focuses on such themes as the Greek alphabet, literature, and political system, and its playwrights, philosophers, and artists. A final chapter examines the effects that Greco-Roman and Judeo-Christian traditions had on each other." Booklist

Includes bibliographical references

The **Cambridge** illustrated history of the Islamic world; edited by Francis Robinson. Cambridge Univ. Press 1996 xxiii, 328p map (Cambridge illustrated history) hardcover o.p. pa $36.99 **909**

1. Islamic countries -- History

ISBN 0-521-43510-2; 0-521-66993-6 pa

LC 95-37562

"Facts about Islam's history and practice are presented, along with its economic, societal, and intellectual structures. Excellent graphics support the text. Maps are extensive and exact." SLJ

Includes bibliographical references

Cliff, Nigel

Holy war. Harper 2011 x, 547 p.p col. ill., maps (chiefly col) **909**

1. Muslims 2. Explorers 3. Christians 4. Trade routes 5. World history -- 15th century

ISBN 978-0-06-173512-7

LC 2011021331

This book presents an historical "interpretation of Vasco da Gama's groundbreaking voyages, seen as a turning point in the struggle between Christianity and Islam." It was the author's intent to demonstrate "that both Vasco da Gama and his archrival, Christopher Columbus, set sail with the clear purpose of launching a Crusade whose objective was to reach the Indies; seize control of its markets in spices, silks, and precious gems from Muslim traders; and claim for Portugal or Spain, respectively, all the territories they discovered. Vasco da Gama triumphed in his mission and drew a dividing line between the Muslim and Christian eras of history -- what we in the West call the medieval and the modern ages." (Publisher's note)

Includes bibliographical references and index.

Cole, Juan

The **New** Arabs; How the Wired and Global Youth of the Middle East Is Transforming It. Juan Cole. Simon & Schuster 2014 384 p. (hardback) $26 **909**

1. Arab Spring, 2010- 2. Youth -- Political activity 3. Arab countries -- Politics and government

ISBN 9781451690392; 1451690398

LC 2014005627

This book, by Juan Cole, "illuminates the role of today's Arab youth--who they are, what they want, and how they will affect world politics. Beginning in January 2011, the revolutionary wave of demonstrations and protests, riots, and civil wars that comprised what many call 'the Arab Spring' shook the world. These upheavals were spearheaded by youth movements, and yet the crucial role they played is relatively unknown." (Publisher's note)

"Cole's deep, nuanced exploration of political and social currents underneath the uprisings shines; he shows Westerners who think the Arab world is divided between corrupt despots and Islamist zealots just how strong and pervasive the tendencies towards liberalism and democracy are." Pub Wkly

Includes bibliographical references and index

Crowley, Roger

Conquerors; how Portugal forged the first global empire. by Roger Crowley. Random House Inc 2015 416 p. illustrations, maps $30 **909**

1. Imperialism 2. Portugal -- History 3. Imperialism -- History 4. Portugal -- Colonies -- History -- 16th century

ISBN 0812994000; 9780812994001

LC 2015008152

This book, by Roger Crowley, focuses on "the history of Portuguese exploration. . . . Drawing on extensive first-hand accounts, it brings to life the exploits of an extraordinary band of conquerors - men such as Afonso de Albuquerque, the first European since Alexander the Great to found an Asian empire - who set in motion five hundred years of European colonisation and unleashed the forces of globalisation." (Publisher's note)

"In a riveting narrative, Crowley (City of Fortune: How Venice Ruled the Seas, 2012, etc.) chronicles Portugal's horrifically violent trajectory from 'impoverished, marginal' nation to European power, vying with Spain and Venice to dominate the spice trade... An impressive history of global clashes, religious zealotry, and economic triumph." Kirkus

Includes bibliographical references and index

Culbertson, Shelly

The **fires** of spring; a post-Arab Spring journey through the turbulent new Middle East. Shelly Culbertson. St. Martin's Press 2016 384 p. map (hardback) $29.99 **909**

1. Arab Spring, 2010- 2. Arab countries -- Politics and government 3. Arab countries -- Politics and government -- 21st century
ISBN 9781250067043; 9781466874954

LC 2015043186

This book, by Shelly Culbertson, "bring[s] the post Arab Spring world to light in a holistic context. . . . Culbertson strives to answer the questions 'what led to the Arab Spring,' 'what is it like there now,' and 'what trends after the Arab Spring are shaping the future of the Middle East?' . . . It delves into what Arab Spring optimism was about, and at the same time sheds light on the pain and dysfunction that continues to plague some parts of the region." (Publisher's note)

"A book rich in invaluable information about both current conditions and possible future trends in Middle Eastern life and politics." Booklist

Includes bibliographical references (pages 315-355) and index.

★ **Cultures** of the Jews; a new history. edited with an introduction by David Biale. Schocken Bks. 2002 xxxiii, 1196p il $45 **909**

1. Jewish civilization 2. Jews -- History
ISBN 0-8052-4131-0

LC 2002-23008

"The book is truly one of the most important works on the subject ever published." Booklist

Includes bibliographical references

Daily life through world history in primary documents; Lawrence Morris, general editor. Greenwood Press 2009 3v il set $299.95 **909**

1. Reference books 2. Civilization -- History -- Sources 3. Manners and customs -- History -- Sources
ISBN 978-0-313-33898-4

LC 2008-8925

"Each of the three volumes . . . begins with a chronology of the era covered as well as a clear, concise historical overview that provides readers with core knowledge of the cultures discussed. The more than 530 entries are grouped into seven categories: domestic, economic, intellectual, material, political, recreational, and religious life." Booklist

Includes bibliographical references

Encyclopedia of Islam and the Muslim world; edited by Richard C. Martin. Macmillan Reference USA 2004 2v il map set $295 **909**

1. Reference books 2. Islam -- Encyclopedias
ISBN 0-02-865603-2

LC 2003-9964

"A solid choice for libraries needing a general treatment of Islam in sufficient detail." Choice

Includes bibliographical references

Encyclopedia of the developing world; Thomas M. Leonard, editor. Routledge 2005 3v set $625 **909**

1. Reference books 2. Developing countries --

Encyclopedias
ISBN 1-57958-388-1

LC 2005-49976

The entries "detail developments from 1945 forward. In addition to basic statistical and geographical information, country-focused entries detail history, economy, and political situation. Thematic entries cover people (e.g., Jomo Kenyatta), historical topics (e.g., colonialism), economic and government models (e.g., communism), the environment (e.g., water) and organizations (e.g., WTO)." Libr J

Includes bibliographical references

Fargues, Philippe

The **atlas** of the Arab world; [by] Philippe Fargues & Rafic Boustani. Facts on File 1991 144p il maps $55 **909**

1. Arab countries
ISBN 0-8160-2346-8

LC 89-675447

"A wealth of information presented in colorful maps, graphs, diagrams, and charts. Arranged by broad cultural topics such as ethnic groups and religions, society, cities, oil and industry, facts not readily available in standard resources are presented and compared." SLJ

Includes bibliographical references

Ferguson, Niall

Empire: the rise and demise of the British world order and the lessons for global power. Basic Books 2003 392p il map hardcover o.p. pa $17.95 **909**

1. Imperialism 2. Commonwealth countries 3. Great Britain -- Colonies 4. Great Britain -- Foreign relations
ISBN 0-465-02329-0 pa

LC 2003-41469

First published 2002 in the United Kingdom

This book "is ambitious, provocative, and entertaining—a rare hat trick in the genre of historical writing—in its meticulous charting of the rise and fall of the world's largest empire. . . . Ferguson makes a subtle, but impressive, argument that free trade, the English language, and superior education helped improve the lot of those under colonial rule." Natl Rev

Includes bibliographical references

Frankopan, Peter

The **Silk** Roads; a new history of the world. by Peter Frankopan. Alfred A. Knopf 2016 656 p. ill. (some col.), maps **909**

1. Imperialism 2. Acculturation 3. East and West 4. World history 5. Culture conflict 6. Silk Road -- History 7. Trade routes -- Central Asia 8. Imperialism -- History 9. Trade routes -- History 10. Acculturation -- History 11. East and West -- History 12. Culture conflict -- History
ISBN 9781101946329

LC 2015013264

In this book, author Peter Frankopan "realigns our understanding of the world, pointing us eastward. He vividly re-creates the emergence of the first cities in Mesopotamia and the birth of empires in Persia, Rome and Constantinople, as well as the depredations by the Mongols, the transmission of the Black Death and the violent struggles over Western imperialism. Throughout the millennia, it was the appetite for foreign goods that brought East and West together." (Publisher's note)

"A timely challenge to conventional thinking about a pivotal part of the globe." Booklist

Includes bibliographical references and index.

Freeman, Charles

★ **Egypt,** Greece, and Rome; civilizations of the ancient Mediterranean. 2nd ed; Oxford Univ. Press 2004 688p $29.95   **909**

1. Mediterranean civilization
ISBN 0-19-926364-7

LC 2004-41505

First published 1996

Freeman's "introduction to the ancient Mediterranean adds Egypt to the standard Greco-Roman nexus. Covering an immense variety of material with competence and sensitivity to nuance, Freeman relates the familiar parts of the classical story, but his is no mere rehash of the Persian War or the fall of the Roman Republic. He analytically recounts political events, religious movements, and society, with steady awareness of the fragmented character of the surviving evidence." Booklist [review of 1996 edition]

Includes bibliographical references

Galeano, Eduardo H.

Mirrors; stories of almost everyone. [by] Eduardo Galeano; English translation by Mark Fried. Nation Books 2009 391p il $26.95   **909**

1. History -- Miscellanea
ISBN 978-1-56858-423-2; 1-56858-423-7

LC 2009-004518

This book contains some 600 meditations on events or persons in history.

"Each entry is an avatar of outrage over the depredations of power against its multifarious victims, those rendered helpless by poverty, religion, race, sexual identity or—as in the vignettes about Galileo and Isaac Babel—the simple accident of being right when the truth defined by the prevailing authority was wrong. . . . As in his previous books, [Galeano] succeeds in capturing the bottomless horror of the state's capacity to inflict pain on the individual, offering as effective an act of political dissent as exists anywhere in contemporary literature." N Y Times Book Rev

Great events from history, The 17th century, 1601-1700; editor, Larissa Juliet Taylor. Salem Press 2005 2v il map set $160   **909**

1. Reference books 2. World history -- 17th century
ISBN 1-58765-225-0; 978-1-58765-225-7

LC 2005-17362

Companion volume to Great lives from history, The 17th century, 1601-1700

Some of the essays in this work were originally published in Chronology of European history, 15,000 B.C. to 1997 (1997) and Great events from history: North American series. Rev. ed. (1997)

This set "offers two to three-page essays that detail the major milestones of the century as well as social developments that were reflective of daily life during the period. The perspective here is international and spans a variety of

categories, including religion and theology, cultural and intellectual history, expansion and land acquisition, and natural disasters. A list of key figures involved in each event is provided." SLJ

Includes bibliographical references

Great events from history, The Renaissance & early modern era, 1454-1600; editor, Christina J. Moose. Salem Press 2005 2v il map set $160   **909**

1. Renaissance 2. Reference books 3. World history -- 15th century 4. World history -- 16th century
ISBN 1-58765-214-5; 978-1-58765-214-1

LC 2004-28878

Companion volume to Great lives from history, The Renaissance & early modern era, 1454-1600

Some of the essays were previously published in various works

This collection of essays covers events in the scientific, intellectual, literary, sociological, political and military disciplines that happened worldwide during the Renaissance.

Includes bibliographical references

Harari, Yuval Noah

Sapiens; A Brief History of Humankind. Yuval Noah Harari. HarperCollins 2015 464 p. illustrations, maps $29.99   **909**

1. Evolution 2. Human beings
ISBN 0062316095; 9780062316097

LC 2014028418

This book, by Yuval Noah Harari, offers a "narrative of humanity's creation and evolution . . . that explores the ways in which biology and history have defined us and enhanced our understanding of what it means to be 'human.' . . . Dr. Harari also compels us to look ahead, because over the last few decades humans have begun to bend laws of natural selection that have governed life for the past four billion years." (Publisher's note)

"Although Harari's ideas may be controversial for some readers, those who are interested in history, anthropology, and evolution will find his work a fascinating, hearty read." LJ

★ A **Historical** atlas of the Jewish people; from the time of the patriarchs to the present. general editor, Eli Barnavi; English edition editor, Miriam Eliav-Feldon; cartography, Michel Opatowski; new edition revised by Denis Charbit. new ed; Schocken Bks. 2002 321p il maps $45   **909**

1. Jews -- History -- Maps
ISBN 0-8052-4226-0

LC 2003-279553

First published 1992 by Knopf

"Covering three millennia of Jewish history and culture through a combination of concise text, accurate and well-drawn maps, and a sumptuous array of photographs, diagrams, and reproductions of paintings, this atlas succeeds in covering all the main themes of the Jewish experience. The material is arranged chronologically and systematically. . . . The result is a reference that will profit both scholars and lay readers." Libr J [review of 1992 edition]

History; the definitive visual guide : from the dawn
of civilization to the present day. editorial consultant, Adam Hart-Davis. Dorling Kindersley Limited, a Penguin Random House Company 2015
620 p. ill. (some color), color maps $50   **909**
1. World history 2. Civilization -- History 3. World
history -- Pictorial works
ISBN 1465437975; 9781465437976
LC 2015451995
This book, edited by Adam Hart-Davis, "tells the story of
mankind from prehistory to the present day using a unique
visual approach, filled with timelines, images of artifacts,
photography, graphics, and more. Now in its third edition,
. . . [it] has been revised and updated to bring today's current events into wider context and includes all new material
on the global recession, green technologies, and the Internet
and social media." (Publisher's note)

The **history** book; contributors, Reg Grant, consultant editor, Fiona Coward, Thomas Cussans, Joel
Levy, Philip Parker, Sally Regan, Philip Wilkinson. DK Publishing 2016 352 p. illustrations
(some color) $25   **909**
1. World history -- Juvenile literature 2. World history
-- Juvenile literature
ISBN 1465445102; 9781465445100
LC 2016429085
This book "is a fascinating journey through the most significant events in history and the big ideas behind each one,
from the dawn of civilization to the lightning-paced culture
of today. One hundred crystal-clear articles explore the Law
Code of Hammurabi, the Renaissance, the American Revolution, World War II, and much, much more, bringing the
events and people of history to life." (Publisher's note)
Includes bibliographical references and index

History of the world in 1,000 objects; DK Publishing Inc. 2014 480 p. illustrations, color maps
$50   **909**
1. World history 2. Material culture 3. History --
Sources 4. World history -- Sources 5. Material culture
-- History
ISBN 1409354660; 1465422897; 9781409354666;
9781465422897
LC 2014497752
This reference book, published by Dorling Kindersley,
overviews world history through the examination of 1,000
objects exhibited through the U.S. Smithsonian Museums.
"With objects revealing how our ancestors lived, what they
believed and valued, and how these items helped shape civilization, . . . [the book] contains a treasure trove of human
creativity from earliest cultures to the present day." (Publisher's note)

Hourani, Albert Habib
A **history** of the Arab peoples; with a new af-
terword by Malise Ruthven. 2nd ed; Belknap Press
2002 xx, 565p il maps hardcover o.p. pa $18.95 **909**
1. Arab civilization 2. Arab countries -- History
ISBN 0-674-01017-5; 0-674-05819-4 pa
LC 2003-269357
First published 1991

This history of the Arab peoples is divided into five
parts: The making of a world (seventh-tenth century); Arab
Muslim societies (eleventh-fifteenth century); The Ottoman
age (sixteenth-eighteenth century); The age of European
empires (1800-1939); The age of nation-states (since 1939).
Includes a 2002 afterword, genealogies and dynasties
Includes bibliographical references

Johnson, Paul, 1928-
A **history** of the Jews. Harper & Row 1987
644p hardcover o.p. pa $17   **909**
1. Jews -- History
ISBN 0-06-091533-1 pa
LC 85-42575
This "is an absorbing, provocative, well-written, often
moving book, an insightful and impassioned blend of history
and myth, story and interpretation." Christ Sci Monit
Includes bibliographical references

Kennedy, Hugh
★ The **great** Arab conquests; how the spread of
Islam changed the world we live in. Da Capo 2007
421p $27.95   **909**
1. Islamic civilization 2. Islam -- History
ISBN 0-306-81585-0; 978-0-306-81585-0
LC 2008-297360
The author "has produced an extremely readable work
chronicling the early Arab conquests to 750 CE. In the flowing narrative style for which he has become known, Kennedy brings together Arab, Byzantine, Armenian, Coptic, and
Persian histories, legends, and anecdotes related to Arab expansion into the lands stretching from the Iberian Peninsula
to the Sind. . . . Each chapter details the conquest of a given
region, intertwining historic reality with legendary tales to
provide for very colorful reading." Choice
Includes bibliographical references

Kwarteng, Kwasi
Ghosts of empire; Britain's legacies in the modern world. Kwasi Kwarteng. Perseus Books Group
2012 480 p. (hardcover) $29.99   **909**
1. Colonization 2. Modern history 3. Great Britain --
Colonies 4. Imperialism -- History 5. Decolonization
-- History 6. Great Britain -- Colonies -- History
ISBN 1610391209; 9781610391207
LC 2011935845
Author Kwasi Kwarteng presents "a narrative history of
the British Empire, one that . . . sees the Empire for what it
was: a series of local fiefdoms administered in varying degrees of competence or brutality by a cast of characters as
outsized and eccentric as anything conjured by Gilbert and
Sullivan. The truth, as Kwarteng reveals, is that there was
no such thing as a model for imperial administration . . .
The idiosyncracies of viceroys and soldier-diplomats who
ran the colonial enterprise continues to impact the world,
from Kashmir to Sudan, Baghdad to Hong Kong." (Publisher's note)
Includes bibliographical references (p. [433]-446)
and index

Lamb, David

★ The **Arabs**; journeys beyond the mirage. 2nd Vintage Books ed, rev and updated; Vintage Bks. 2002 348p map pa $15 **909**

1. Arab countries

ISBN 1-4000-3041-2

LC 2002-524048

First published 1987 by Random House

"Intelligent and incisive . . . Mr. Lamb has the first-rate reporter's tools, and he uses them to relate, with compelling detail, who the Arabs are." N Y Times Book Rev

Includes bibliographical references

Mann, Charles C.

1493; uncovering the new world Columbus created. Knopf 2011 535p il map $30.50; ebook $14.99 **909**

1. Explorers 2. Modern history 3. Economic conditions 4. Industrial revolution 5. Economic history 6. Ecology -- History 7. Commerce -- History 8. Agriculture -- History 9. America -- Exploration 10. America -- Discovery and exploration

ISBN 978-0-307-26572-2; 0-307-26572-2; 978-0-307-59672-7 ebook

LC 2011003408

"Mann traces the subtle, epochal influences of the intercontinental 'Columbian Exchange' of flora, fauna, commodities, and peoples, showing how European honeybees and earthworms remade New World landscapes; how New World corn, potatoes, and fertilizer ignited Eurasian population booms; how Old World diseases prompted an eruption of slavery in the Western Hemisphere; . . . how Latin American silver undermined China's Ming Dynasty; and how the decimation of Indian peoples changed the world's climate. . . . Brilliantly assembling colorful details into big-picture insights, Mann's fresh, challenge to Eurocentric histories puts interdependence at the origin of modernity." Publ Wkly

Includes bibliographical references

Morris, Ian

Why the West rules--for now; the patterns of history, and what they reveal about the future. Farrar, Straus and Giroux 2010 750p il map **909**

1. East and West 2. Modern civilization 3. Western civilization 4. Comparative civilization

ISBN 0374290024; 9780374290023

LC 2010005702

Morris argues that Western dominance is largely "the result of geography on the everyday efforts of ordinary people as they deal with crises of resources, disease, migration, and climate." (Publisher's note) Bibliography. Index.

"It may seem at first sight a little odd to recommend a history book as a guide to the future. But Morris' new book illustrates perfectly why one really scholarly book about the past is worth a hundred fanciful works of futurology." Foreign Affairs

Includes bibliographical references

National Geographic concise history of the world; an illustrated timeline. edited by Neil Kagan. Revised edition National Geographic Society 2013 416 p. ill. (some col.), maps $40 **909**

1. World history 2. Historical chronology

ISBN 1426211783; 9781426211782

LC 2015430064

"For readers of all ages, world history is easily accessible, depicted as never before—so that events occurring simultaneously around the world can be viewed at-a-glance together. . . . The book's innovative time line truly sets it apart, allowing readers to scan across a spread and explore a single area or compare contemporary societies across the globe." (Publisher's note)

Includes bibliographical references (pages 405-406) and index

Pagden, Anthony

★ **Peoples** and empires; a short history of European migration, exploration, and conquest from Greece to the present. Modern library ed; Modern Lib. 2001 xxv, 206p hardcover o.p. pa $10.95 **909**

1. Colonies 2. World history 3. Immigration and emigration

ISBN 0-679-64096-7; 0-8129-6761-5 pa

LC 00-66204

This "overview of European empire building and colonization commences with the diffusion of Greek civilization and traces the subsequent evolution of the ensuing Roman, Spanish, French, and British empires. More interesting than how those empires physically expanded is the insightful discussion on what motivated individual men and entire nations to migrate and conquer." Booklist

Includes bibliographical references

Parker, Geoffrey

Global crisis; war, climate change and catastrophe in the seventeenth century. Geoffrey Parker. Yale University Press 2012 871 p. (cloth : alkaline paper) $40 **909**

1. World history -- 17th century 2. Climate change -- History -- 17th century 3. History, Modern -- 17th century 4. Military history -- 17th century 5. Civil war -- History -- 17th century 6. Disasters -- History -- 17th century 7. Revolutions -- History -- 17th century 8. Climatic changes -- Social aspects -- History -- 17th century

ISBN 0300153236; 9780300153231

LC 2012039448

This book "presents a history of the 17th century. . . . Focusing on climate-driven unrest around the world, [Geoffrey] Parker illustrates how events such as drought can drive disease, war, and social change. . . . He traces connections between climate and population and war, factors further influencing attitudes toward education and consumption." (Publishers Weekly)

Includes bibliographical references

Roberts, Callum

The **unnatural** history of the sea. Island Press/Shearwater Books 2007 435p il map $28 **909**

1. Ocean 2. Commercial fishing 3. Human influence

on nature
ISBN 978-1-59726-102-9; 1-59726-102-5

LC 2007-1841

"Starting with the eighteenth-century voyages of Vitus Bering, Roberts leads the reader through a wealth of maritime history revealing countless examples of overfishing. . . . Thoughtful, inspiring, devastating, and powerful, Roberts' comprehensive, welcoming, and compelling approach to an urgent subject conveys large problems in a succinct and involving manner. Readers won't be able to put it down." Booklist

Includes bibliographical references

Roberts, J. M.

The **new** history of the world; 4th rev ed; Oxford Univ. Press 2003 1232p il map $40   **909**

1. World history
ISBN 0-19-521927-9

LC 2003-270110

First published 1976 in the United Kingdom with title: The Hutchinson history of the world; first published 1976 in the United States in a slightly different form by Knopf with title: History of the world; this edition first published 2002 in the United Kingdom with title: The New Penguin history of the world

This overview of history from prehistoric times to the effects of the September 11, 2001 attacks is divided into eight sections: Before history--beginnings; The first civilizations; The classical Mediterranean; The age of diverging traditions; The making of the European age; The great acceleration; The end of the Europeans' world; The latest age

Rogan, Eugene

The **Arabs**; a history. Basic Books 2009 553p il map   **909**

1. Arab civilization 2. Imperialism -- History 3. Arab countries -- History 4. Nationalism -- Arab countries -- History 5. Arab countries -- Politics and government
ISBN 0465071007; 9780465071005

LC 2009-28575

"Eugene Rogan traces five centuries of Arab history, from the Ottoman conquests through the British and French colonial periods and up to the present age." (Publisher's note) Index.

This "is not a particularly happy story, but it is a fascinating one, and exceedingly well told. [Eugene] Rogan manoeuvres with skilful assurance, maintaining a steady pace through time, and keeping the wider horizon in view even as he makes use of a broad range of judiciously chosen primary sources to enrich the narrative." Economist

Includes bibliographical references

Sachar, Howard Morley

A **history** of the Jews in the modern world; [by] Howard M. Sachar. Knopf 2005 831p hardcover o.p. pa $23   **909**

1. Jews -- History
ISBN 0-375-41497-5; 1-4000-3097-8 pa

LC 2004-48814

This book "relates an immensely complex story with precision and learning." N Y Times Book Rev

Includes bibliographical references

Schama, Simon, 1945-

★ The **story** of the Jews; finding the words : 1000 BC-1492 AD. by Simon Schama. HarperCollins 2014 512 p. ill. (chiefly col.), maps $39.99 **909**

1. Jews -- History
ISBN 0060539186; 9780060539184

This book, by Simon Schama, "details the story of the Jewish experience, tracing it across three millennia, from their beginnings as an ancient tribal people to the opening of the New World in 1492. . . . It takes you to . . . a Jewish kingdom in the mountains of southern Arabia; a Syrian synagogue glowing with . . . wall paintings; [and] the palm groves of the Jewish dead in the Roman catacombs." (Publisher's note)

"Schama has written an unconventional but masterful and deeply felt history of his people, which seamlessly integrates themes of art, religion, and ethnicity as he illustrates how Jews both influenced and were influenced by the other people they lived among for more than 1,500 years." Booklist

Includes bibliographical references (pages 431-465) and index

Tinniswood, Adrian

Pirates of Barbary; corsairs, conquests, and captivity in the seventeenth-century Mediterranean. Riverhead Books 2010 xx, 343p il map $26.95   **909**

1. Pirates 2. North Africa -- History 3. Mediterranean region -- History
ISBN 978-1-59448-774-3

LC 2010-23421

Tinniswood "demonstrates an excellent grasp of obscure sources in crafting a comprehensive synthesis. . . . Throughout, the writing is precise and mordant but also witty, allowing the reader to feel empathy for the rough and absurd lives of these long-ago mariners, and agree with the author's conclusion that whatever the corsairs' faults, a lack of courage was not among them." Kirkus

Includes bibliographical references

Treuer, Anton

Everything you wanted to know about Indians but were afraid to ask; Anton Treuer. Borealis Books 2012 190 p. (pbk. : alk. paper) $15.95   **909**

1. Native Americans 2. Native Americans -- History 3. Native Americans -- Social life and customs
ISBN 0873518616; 0873518624; 9780873518611; 9780873518628

LC 2011053026

In this book Anton Treuer "endeavors to address misconceptions held by non-natives about the American Indian experience in the United States. He accomplishes his task by posing and answering approximately 125 questions divided into ten categories: 'Terminology,' 'History,' 'Religion, Culture & Identity,' 'Powwow,' 'Tribal Languages,' 'Politics,' 'Economics,' 'Education,' 'Perspectives: Coming to Terms and Future Directions,' and 'Finding Ways to Make a Difference.'" (Library Journal)

Includes bibliographical references and index

Watson, Peter, 1943-

★ The **great** divide; nature and human nature in the old world and the new. Peter Watson. Harper 2012 610 p. $31.99 **909**

1. World history 2. America -- History 3. America -- Civilization 4. Eastern hemisphere -- History 5. Eastern hemisphere -- Civilization

ISBN 0061672459; 9780061672453

This book by Peter Watson "compares the development of humankind in the Old World and the New between 15,000 BC and AD 1500. Watson identifies three major differences between the two worlds -- climate, domesticable mammals, and hallucinogenic plants -- that combined to produce very different trajectories of civilization in the two hemispheres." The author draws on "knowledge in archaeology, anthropology, geology, meteorology, cosmology, and mythology." (Publisher's note)

Includes bibliographical references and index.

Ideas; a history of thought and invention, from fire to Freud. Peter Watson. HarperCollins 2005 xix, 822 p.p $19.99 **909**

1. Civilization -- History 2. Intellectual life -- History

ISBN 0060935642; 006621064X; 9780060935641

LC 2005050255

This book by Peter Watson presents an "overview of the intellectual development of humans from the discovery of fire up to the beginning of the twentieth century." Topics include "the emergence of language . . . the exploration of the physical world with the Atomists, mathematics, astronomy, literature . . . the rise of Christianity, [and] the rise of the Arabs." (Institute of Public Affairs Review)

Includes bibliographical references (p. [747]-804) and indexes

Winchester, Simon

Pacific; Silicon Chips and Surfboards, Coral Reefs and Atom Bombs, Brutal Dictators, Fading Empires, and the Coming Collision of the World's Superpowers. Simon Winchester. HarperCollins 2015 480 p. illustrations, maps $28.99 **909**

1. Pacific Ocean 2. Pacific region 3. Pacific Coast (North America)

ISBN 0062315412; 9780062315410

LC 2015020468

"Simon Winchester offers an enthralling biography of the Pacific Ocean and its role in the modern world, exploring our relationship with this imposing force of nature. Winchester takes us from the Bering Strait to Cape Horn, the Yangtze River to the Panama Canal, and to the many small islands and archipelagos that lie in between. He observes the fall of a dictator in Manila, visits aboriginals in northern Queensland, and is jailed in Tierra del Fuego, the land at the end of the world. " (Publisher's note)

"Winchester . . . does not do the expected: there is no chapter about the geological history of the ocean, followed by a slow chronology. Instead, realizing the difficulty of his own task, the author focuses on 10 aspects of the ocean and its inhabitants--islanders, those on the shores--and uses them to illustrate some historical points." Kirkus

Includes bibliographical references and index

Worth, Robert F.

A **rage** for order; the Middle East in turmoil, from Tahrir Square to ISIS. Robert F. Worth. Farrar, Straus & Giroux 2016 272 p. (hardback) $26 **909**

1. Arab Spring, 2010- 2. Middle East -- Politics and government 3. Arab countries -- Politics and government -- 21st century

ISBN 9780374252946; 9780374710712; 0374252947

LC 2015041559

This book, by Robert F. Worth, is "the first work of literary journalism to track the tormented legacy of . . . the Arab Spring. We meet a Libyan rebel who must decide whether to kill the Qaddafi-regime torturer who murdered his brother; a Yemeni farmer who lives in servitude to a poetry-writing, dungeon-operating chieftain; and an Egyptian doctor who is caught between his loyalty to the Muslim Brotherhood and his hopes for a new, tolerant democracy." (Publisher's note)

General readers and policymakers will find this timely volume enlightening." Library Journal

909.07 General historical periods

Andrea, Alfred J.

Encyclopedia of the crusades. Greenwood Press 2003 xxiii, 356p il, maps $75 **909.07**

1. Reference books 2. Crusades -- Encyclopedias 3. Europe -- Church history -- Encyclopedias

ISBN 0-313-31659-7

LC 2003-48544

This encyclopedia includes "more than 200 entries, each one between approximately 10 lines and four pages in length. . . . The introduction gives the entries some historical context and defines the term crusade for the reader. The entries are in alphabetical order and include cross-references in bold type to other entries in the book. Many entries also include suggested readings, both primary sources and historical studies. At the end of the work, the author has included a chronology of important dates and events, a 'Basic Crusade Library' of further readings in bibliographic essay style, and a general index. . . . This encyclopedia is recommended for high-school, undergraduate, and public libraries." Booklist

Includes bibliographical references

Asbridge, Thomas

★ The **crusades**; the authoritative history of the war for the Holy Land. [by] Thomas Asbridge. Ecco Press 2010 767p il map **909.07**

1. Crusades 2. Medieval civilization 3. Christianity and other religions 4. Religion and civilization 5. Church history -- 600-1500, Middle Ages

ISBN 9780060787288

Asbridge sets out to "uncover what drove Muslims and Christians alike to embrace the ideals of 'jihad' and crusade, and considers how these holy wars reshaped the medieval world and why they continue to influence events today." (Publisher's note) Index.

"Covering the 200-year period of the Crusades in a single volume is a monumental task, but Asbridge . . . handles it well, presenting an evenhanded view of the actions of Christian and Muslim forces and paying particular attention to the larger-than-life figures of Richard the Lionheart and

Saladin. In addition to relating the facts of the expeditions, he explores both the motivations of the Crusaders . . . and the reasons that Christians eventually failed to retain any hold on conquered territory." Libr J

Includes bibliographical references

Burns, Thomas S.

A **history** of the Ostrogoths. Indiana Univ. Press 1984 299p il hardcover o.p. pa $19.95   **909.07**
1. Teutonic peoples 2. Medieval civilization
ISBN 0-253-20600-6 pa

LC 83-49286

This "study of the Ostrogoths . . . explores the interaction between Rome and her eastern Germanic neighbors with the focus on the Ostrogothic experience. Traditional literary sources are looked at with a fresh eye, and new archaeological materials are thoroughly explored." Libr J

Includes bibliographical references

Catlos, Brian A.

Infidel kings and unholy warriors; faith, power, and violence in the age of crusade and jihad. Brian A. Catlos. Farrar, Straus and Giroux 2014 416 p. illustrations, maps (hardback) $28   **909.07**
1. Crusades 2. Crusades -- Influence 3. Mediterranean region -- History -- 476-1517
ISBN 0809058375; 9780809058372

LC 2013043160

In this history of the Crusades, author Brian A. Catlos "puts us on the ground in the Mediterranean world of 1050-1200. We experience the sights and sounds of the region just as enlightened Islamic empires and primitive Christendom began to contest it. We learn about the siege tactics, theological disputes, and poetry of this enthralling time. And we see that people of different faiths coexisted far more frequently than we are commonly told." (Publisher's note)

Includes bibliographical references and index

Cobb, Paul M.

The **race** for paradise; an Islamic history of the crusades. Paul M. Cobb. Oxford University Press 2014 360 p. illustrations, maps (hardback) $29.95   **909.07**
1. Crusades 2. Muslims -- History 3. Muslims -- Mediterranean Region -- History -- To 15000 4. Islam -- Relations -- Christianity -- History -- To 1500 5. Christianity and other religions -- Islam -- History -- To 1500
ISBN 0199358117; 9780199358113

LC 2013040040

This book, by Paul M. Cobb, "offers a new history of the confrontations between Muslims and Franks we now call the 'Crusades,' one that emphasizes the diversity of Muslim experiences of the European holy war. . . . Cobb considers the Arab perspective on all shores of the Muslim Mediterranean, from Spain to Syria." (Publisher's note)

"Cobb's multidisciplinary approach illuminates the experience of invaded societies in their chaotic and climactic contacts with the Other." Pub Wkly

Includes bibliographical references and index

★ The **Crusades**; an encyclopedia. Alan V. Murray, editor. ABC-CLIO 2006 4v il map set $385   **909.07**
1. Reference books 2. Crusades -- Encyclopedias
ISBN 1-57607-862-0; 978-1-57607-862-4

LC 2006-19410

This encyclopedia "surveys all aspects of the crusading movement from its origins in the 11th century to its decline in the 16th century." Publisher's note

Includes bibliographical references

Dictionary of the Middle Ages; Joseph R. Strayer, editor in chief. Scribner 1982 12v + index il maps set $1,625   **909.07**
1. Reference books 2. Middle Ages -- Dictionaries
ISBN 0-684-19073-7

LC 82-5904

ALA RUSA Dartmouth Medal honorable mention (1990)

"Authoritative and modern, this interdisciplinary dictionary spans the years from A.D. 500 to 1500, taking cognizance of the Byzantine, Islamic, and Jewish contributions to medieval life as well as the European. . . . The contents are in alphabetical sequence, some articles providing brief definitions or identifications, others offering extensive background and analysis." Ref Sources: a brief guide

Great events from history, The Middle Ages, 477-1453; editor, Brian A. Pavlac; consulting editors, Byron Cannon, . . . [et al.] Salem Press 2005 2v il map set $160   **909.07**
1. Middle Ages 2. Reference books 3. Medieval civilization
ISBN 1-58765-167-X; 978-1-58765-167-0

LC 2004-16640

Companion volume to Great lives from history, The Middle Ages, 477-1453

Some essays were previously published in Great events from history (1972-1980), Chronology of European history: 15,000 B.C. to 1997 (1997), Great events from history: North American series, revised edition (1997), Great events from history: ancient and medieval series (1972), and Great events from history: modern European series (1973)

This set "offers 322 essays, beginning with Confucianism arrives in Japan (fifth or sixth century) and ending with Fall of Constantinople (May 29, 1453)." Booklist

Includes bibliographical references

The **Oxford** illustrated history of the Crusades; edited by Jonathan Riley-Smith. Oxford Univ. Press 1995 436p il maps hardcover o.p. pa $26.50   **909.07**
1. Crusades
ISBN 0-19-820435-3; 0-19-285428-3 pa

LC 94-24229

Scholars explore the complex religious, economic, and military aspects of the Crusades.

Includes bibliographical references

Phillips, Jonathan

Holy warriors; a modern history of the Crusades. Random House 2010 434p il map $30 **909.07**

1. Crusades 2. Middle East -- History 3. Europe -- Church history 4. Church history -- 600-1500, Middle Ages

ISBN 978-1-4000-6580-6; 1-4000-6580-1

LC 2009-33153

The author "superbly condenses the four centuries of the Crusades into a single, easily accessible volume. . . . The narrative weaves a tragic tapestry, beginning with the bloodily successful First Crusade, through the establishment of the Crusader states, to the failure of subsequent Crusades, the victories of the Muslim 'counter-Crusade,' and the continuing legacy of religious and cultural hatred that permeates the Holy Land. . . . This is an outstanding summary of centuries of religious strife." Publ Wkly

Includes bibliographical references

909.08   Modern history, 1450/1500-

Aaronovitch, David

Voodoo histories; the role of the conspiracy theory in shaping modern history. Riverhead Books 2010 388p il $26.95 **909.08**

1. Conspiracies

ISBN 978-1-59448-895-5

LC 2009-37018

First published 2009 in the United Kingdom

"The book is an evenhanded, lively, and fascinating look not just at the people who believe these theories but also at the people who promote them: the evidence manipulators, the liars, the con artists, and the almost pathetically gullible and uninformed." Booklist

Includes bibliographical references

Garton Ash, Timothy

★ Free world; America, Europe, and the surprising future of the West. Random House 2004 286p il map $24.95; pa $14.95 **909.08**

1. World politics -- 1991-

ISBN 1-400-06219-5; 1-400-07646-3 pa

LC 2004-53862

The author "traces the gradual unravelling of the Atlantic alliance back through the destruction of the Twin Towers in 2001, America's 9/11, to the fall of the Berlin Wall on November 9, 1989, Europe's 9/11. He writes with great insight, balance and yet with passion, too." Times Lit Suppl

Includes bibliographical references

Herman, Arthur

The idea of decline in Western history. Free Press 1996 521p pa $23.95 **909.08**

1. Historians 2. Philosophers 3. Western civilization

ISBN 0-684-82791-3; 978-1-4165-7633-4 pa; 1-4165-7633-9 pa

LC 96-36285

"Herman recaps the two-century-long tradition of criticism of Western civilization. . . . He covers two historians most closely identified with predicting decline, Oswald Spengler and Arnold Toynbee, and also brings forth less fa-

mous prognosticators of the doom of the West. . . . An accessible survey for the serious nonacademic." Booklist

Includes bibliographical references

Jasanoff, Maya

Edge of empire; lives, culture, and conquest in the East, 1750-1850. Knopf 2005 404p il $27.95 **909.08**

1. Collectors and collecting 2. Great Britain -- Colonies

ISBN 1-4000-4167-8

LC 2004-60221

"In graceful prose and with evocative illustrations, Jasanoff scores her points about conquest, collecting, and cultural crossing, offering a thoughtful and highly subtle study." Libr J

Includes bibliographical references

Kennedy, Paul M., 1945-

The rise and fall of the great powers; economic change and military conflict from 1500 to 2000. by Paul Kennedy. Vintage Books 1989 xxv, 677 p.p hardcover o.p. pa $17 **909.08**

1. Modern history 2. Balance of power 3. Economic conditions 4. Economic history 5. Military history, Modern 6. Military readiness -- Economic aspects

ISBN 0-679-72019-7 pa; 0679720197 pa

LC 88040123

"Kennedy's great achievement is that he makes us see our current international problems against a background of empires that have gone under because they were unable to sustain the material cost of greatness; and he does so in a universal historical perspective." N Y Rev Books

Bibliography: p. 625-662

Tuchman, Barbara Wertheim

The march of folly; from Troy to Vietnam. [by] Barbara W. Tuchman. Knopf 1984 447p il hardcover o.p. pa $16.95 **909.08**

1. Popes 2. Trojan War 3. Reformation 4. Modern history 5. Vietnam War, 1961-1975 6. Great Britain -- Colonies -- America 7. United States -- History -- 1600-1775, Colonial period

ISBN 0-345-30823-9 pa

LC 83-22206

The author analyzes examples of governmental bumbling including the Trojan horse, the U.S. involvement in Vietnam, and the British loss of the American colonies.

Includes bibliographical references

909.7   Specific historical periods since 1700

Great events from history, The 18th century, 1701-1800; editor John Powell. Salem Press 2006 2v il map set $160 **909.7**

1. Reference books 2. World history -- 18th century

ISBN 978-1-58765-279-0; 1-58765-279-X

LC 2006-5406

Companion volume to Great lives from history, The 18th century, 1701-1800

Some essays previously published in Great events from history: North American series (1997) and Chronology of European history (1997)

"Topics include geopolitical events, social and intellectual issues, scientific developments, philosophy, and the arts. The global coverage emphasizes turning points that redirected and shaped history and helped create the modern world. Essays have an average length of 1600 words. Each one begins with a short summary of the topic and includes dates, locales, categories, key figures, text, significance, further reading, see-also references, and cross-referencing to other essays in this set and in the rest of the series. . . . An informative resource." SLJ

Includes bibliographical references

Winik, Jay

★ The **great** upheaval; America and the birth of the modern world, 1788-1800. Harper 2007 xx, 659p il map $29.95; pa $17.95   **909.7**
1. Modern history 2. Modern civilization 3. United States -- History -- 1783-1809
ISBN 0-06-008313-1; 978-0-06-008313-7; 0-06-008314-X pa; 978-0-06-008314-4 pa
"An outstandingly wide-ranging account of this vital era in world history." Booklist
Includes bibliographical references

909.8   World history--1800-

Getty Images Inc.

History of the world in photographs; [by] Getty Images; Encyclopedia Britannica. Black Dog & Leventhal 2008 559p il $50   **909.8**
1. Modern history -- Pictorial works
ISBN 978-1-57912-583-7; 1-57912-583-2
This "volume would entice just about anyone to learn about history." Libr J

909.81   World history--19th century, 1800-1899

Great events from history, The 19th century, 1801-1900; editor, John Powell. Salem Press 2006 4v il map set $360   **909.81**
1. Reference books 2. World history -- 19th century
ISBN 978-1-58765-297-4; 1-58765-297-8
LC 2006-19789
Companion volume to Great lives from history, The 19th century, 1801-1900
Some of the essays in this work appeared in various other Salem Press sets
"These volumes cover the world's most important events and developments from 1801 through 1900. . . . Essays address important social and cultural developments in daily life: major literary movements, significant developments in art and music, trends in immigration, and progressive social legislation." Publisher's note
Includes bibliographical references

909.82   World history--20th century, 1900-1999

Cold War; the essential reference guide. James R. Arnold and Roberta Wiener, editors. ABC-CLIO 2012 xxxii, 443 p.p (hardcopy : alk. paper) $89.00   **909.82**
1. International relations 2. Cold war -- Encyclopedias 3. World politics -- 1945-1991 -- Encyclopedias
ISBN 1610690036; 1610690044; 9781610690034; 9781610690041
LC 2011028418
This reference book, edited by James R. Arnold and Roberta Wiener, provides "85 signed alphabetical entries, along with 6 essays discussing the causes and consequences of the Cold War, the growth of technology, evolving East-West relations, proxy wars and military aid, and Ronald Regan and the Cold War. . . . The chronology begins in February 1945 with the Yalta Conference . . . and ends with the official dissolution of the Soviet Union, in December 1991." (Booklist)
Includes bibliographical references and index.

The **Columbia** history of the 20th century; {edited by} Richard W. Bulliet. Columbia Univ. Press 1998 651p $62; pa $29   **909.82**
1. World history -- 20th century
ISBN 0-231-07628-2; 0-231-07629-0 pa
LC 97-39426
Scholars contribute chapters on topics ranging "from 'Ethnicity and Racism,' to 'Nationalism,' 'Communications,' 'Industry and Business,' and others. The idea is for readers to peruse those chapters that appeal to them. Articles average under 25 pages, so content is quite broad. While the level of scholarship varies a bit, overall quality is good." Libr J
Includes bibliographical references

Dallek, Robert

The **lost** peace; leadership in a time of horror and hope, 1945-1953. Harper 2010 420p il $28.99; ebook $22.99   **909.82**
1. Cold war 2. World politics -- 1945- 3. World War, 1939-1945 -- Peace
ISBN 978-0-06-162866-5; 978-0-06-201671-3 ebook
LC 2010-05727
The author's "interpretation of the thinking and actions of American, Chinese, European, and Soviet leaders is worth the book's reasonable price. This is solid historical scholarship from a master." Libr J
Includes bibliographical references

Emmerson, Charles

1913; in search of the world before the great war. Charles Emmerson. PublicAffairs 2013 544 p. (hardcover) $30   **909.82**
1. World history -- 19th century 2. World War, 1914-1918 -- Causes 3. Nineteen thirteen, A.D
ISBN 1610392566; 9781610392563; 9781610392570
LC 2013935895
In this book, author Charles Emmerson "surveys a selection of cities around the world as they appeared in 1913. Portraying the European capitals of the next year's belligerent countries, Emmerson strikes a cosmopolitan tone by

noting social interconnections linking London to Paris to Berlin to Constantinople. Diarists and travelers populate his narratives, their descriptions lending eyewitness immediacy to his delineation of streetscapes, new architecture, and political issues." (Booklist)

"By staying so tightly focused on this single year, Emmerson is able to reveal causal mechanisms while simultaneously making readers wonder what could have been." Pub Wkly

Includes bibliographical references (p. [495]-501) and index

Nineteen-thirteen

Encyclopedia of conflicts since World War II; edited by James Ciment. 2nd ed; M.E. Sharpe 2007 4v set $439   **909.82**
1. Reference books 2. World politics -- 1945- -- Encyclopedias
ISBN 978-0-7656-8005-1; 0-7656-8005-X

LC 2006-14011

First published 1999

"The illustrations are strong and the maps helpful, and the thumbnail biographies and glossary are useful. A valuable resource for most school and public libraries." SLJ

Includes bibliographical references

Encyclopedia of the Cold War; a political, social, and military history. Spencer C. Tucker, editor. ABC-CLIO 2007 5v il map set $495   **909.82**
1. Reference books 2. Cold war -- Encyclopedias 3. World politics -- 1945- -- Encyclopedias
ISBN 978-1-85109-701-2

LC 2007-9681

"The content gives a broad global view of an anxious period and provides useful background for some of today's conflicts." Booklist

Includes bibliographical references

Gilbert, Martin
  History of the twentieth century. Morrow 2001 783p maps hardcover o.p. pa $19.95   **909.82**
1. World history -- 20th century
ISBN 0-06-050594-X pa

LC 2001-32612

Condensed version of the three-volume work first published 1997-1999

The author "chronicles world events year by year, from the dawn of aviation to the flourishing technology age, taking us through World War I to the inauguration of Franklin Roosevelt as president of the United States and Hitler as chancellor of Germany. He continues on to document wars in South Africa, China, Ethiopia, Spain, Korea, Vietnam, and Bosnia, as well as apartheid, the arms race, the moon landing, and the beginnings of the computer age, while interspersing the influence of art, literature, music, and religion." Publisher's note

Great events from history: The 20th century, 1901-1940; editor, Robert F. Gorman. Salem Press 2007 6v il map set $495   **909.82**
1. Reference books 2. World history -- 20th century
ISBN 978-1-58765-324-7; 1-58765-324-9

LC 2007-1930

Some of the essays in this work originally appeared in various Salem Press publications

This work "identifies key events that helped to shape the course of the history of the world from 1901 to 1940. In more than 1,000 essays, a plethora of topics are presented, including Canada claiming the Arctic Islands (1901); the plague killing 1.2 million in India (1907); Gertrude Ederle swimming the English Channel (1926); Stalin beginning the Purge Trials (1934); and Germany hosting the 1936 Olympics." Booklist

Includes bibliographical references

Great events from history: The 20th century, 1941-1970; editor, Robert F. Gorman. Salem Press 2008 6v il map set $495   **909.82**
1. Reference books 2. World history -- 20th century
ISBN 978-1-58765-331-5; 1-58765-331-1

LC 2007-37204

Some of the essays in this work originally appeared in various Salem Press publications

The articles in this set "cover everything from the bombing of Pearl Harbor to the celebration of the First Earth Day. Each article lists a locale, key figures, categories, and a summary of events; readers can search for additional information based on categories or key figures. The sixth volume contains a bibliography, personage, subject, category, and geographical indexes and a chronological list of entries. . . . An excellent cross-reference tool." Libr J

Includes bibliographical references

Great events from history: The 20th century, 1971-2000; editor, Robert F. Gorman. Salem Press 2008 6v il map set $495   **909.82**
1. Reference books 2. World history -- 20th century
ISBN 978-1-58765-338-4; 1-58765-338-9

LC 2007-51351

Some of the essays originally appeared in other Salem Press sets

This set "provides extended coverage of 1,083 major events between 1971 and 2000." Publisher's note

Includes bibliographical references

Hillstrom, Kevin
  ★ The **Cold** War; foreward by Christian Ostermann. Omnigraphics 2006 xx, 536p il (Primary sourcebook series) $65   **909.82**
1. Cold war 2. World politics -- 1945-1991
ISBN 0-7808-0934-3; 978-0-7808-0934-5

LC 2006-15330

"The wide-ranging scope of documents compiled in this volume will provide AP history and social studies classes with a wealth of information for research and analysis." Libr Media Connect

Includes glossary and bibliographical references

Huntington, Samuel P.

The **clash** of civilizations and the remaking of world order. Simon & Schuster 1996 367p il maps hardcover o.p. pa $17   **909.82**

1. World politics -- 1965- 2. Modern civilization -- 1950-

ISBN 0-684-84441-9 pa

LC 96-31492

"The Huntington argument that the West should stop intervening in civilizational conflicts it doesn't understand makes a powerful claim that internationalists cannot easily ignore." N Y Times Book Rev

Jeffery, Keith

1916; A Global History. by Keith Jeffery. St. Martin's Press 2016 448 p. 16 plates; illustrations; maps $30   **909.82**

1. World War, 1914-1918

ISBN 1620402696; 9781620402696

In this book, "blood-soaked trenches of the Low Countries and North-Eastern Europe were essential battlegrounds during the First World War, but the war reached many other corners of the globe, and events elsewhere significantly affected its course. Covering the twelve months of 1916, eminent historian Keith Jeffery uses twelve moments from a range of locations and shows how they reverberated around the world." (Publisher's note)

"A brilliant compendium of everything-you-didn't-know-about World War I, which, for many readers, will be a great deal." Kirkus

Judt, Tony

Reappraisals; reflections on the forgotten twentieth century. Penguin Press 2008 448p bibl f $29.95   **909.82**

1. Modern history 2. World history -- 20th century

ISBN 978-1-59420-136-3; 1-59420-136-6

LC 2007-30297

The author "writes informatively about Manes Sperber, tenderly about Primo Levi, enthusiastically about Hannah Arendt. . . . [Tony Judt is] not only a historian of the first rank but (in a word we need an equivalent for) a politico-logue who gives engagement a good name." N Y Times Book Rev

Includes bibliographical references and index

Junger, Sebastian

Fire. Norton 2001 224p $24.95   **909.82**

1. War 2. Disasters 3. Terrorism 4. World politics -- 1991-

ISBN 0-393-01046-5

LC 2001-45236

The stories are "all told with Junger's unfailing eye for detail, which often lends the pieces a disturbing authenticity." Libr J

Knauer, Kelly

TIME History's Greatest Images; the World's 100 Most Influential Photographs. Time Home Entertainment 2012 154 p. $29.95   **909.82**

1. World history 2. Photojournalism

ISBN 1603201971; 9781603201971

This book is a compilation of photographs that "TIME" magazine considers the "most significant and influential photos in history." Here are "scientific breakthroughs, political upheavals and social revolutions, from the first photographs of an embryo in a human womb to the indelible images of America's Civil Rights movement. Here are sailors kissing nurses, a single man defying a Chinese tank, firefighters raising the American flag over the ruins of the World Trade Center." (Publisher's note)

Kurlansky, Mark

1968; the year that rocked the world. Ballantine 2004 xx, 441p il $26.95   **909.82**

1. Insurgency 2. Radicalism 3. World history -- 1945-

ISBN 0-345-45581-9

LC 2004-299128

This is an account "of the global, social, and political upheaval, warfare, and assassinations that define one year in a tumultuous decade." Booklist

Includes bibliographical references

Lukacs, John, 1924-

A **short** history of the twentieth century; by John Lukacs. The Belknap Press of Harvard University Press 2013 220 p. (hardcover) $24.95   **909.82**

1. World War, 1939-1945 2. World history -- 20th century 3. History, Modern -- 20th century

ISBN 9780674725362; 0674725360

LC 2013007948

This book, written by historian John Luckacs, offers a concise history of the twentieth century--its two world wars and cold war, its nations and leaders. The great themes woven through this spirited narrative are . . . the fading of liberalism, the rise of populism and nationalism, the achievements and dangers of technology, and the continuing democratization of the globe." (Publisher's note)

Includes bibliographical references and index.

Milo, Paul

Your flying car awaits; robot butlers, lunar vacations, and other dead-wrong predictions from the twentieth century. Harper 2009 280p pa $14.99   **909.82**

1. Forecasting 2. Modern civilization

ISBN 978-0-06-172460-2

LC 2009-19710

"The book is broken into little sections that are quick and concise but never lacking in detail or depth." PopMatters

National Geographic Society (U.S.)

National Geographic eyewitness to the 20th century. National Geographic Soc. 1998 400p il hardcover o.p. pa $22.95 **909.82**
1. World history -- 20th century
ISBN 0-7922-8063-6 pa

LC 98-22756
"Chapters are arranged thematically by decade and open with a six-page essay discussing each era. . . . Most useful of all are the double-page spreads for each year presenting events, people, and themes in short paragraph entries. Brief trends and trivia are listed vertically. A time line appears along the bottom of the pages. Photographs bring the discussions to life and sidebars present interesting developments and people." SLJ

The **Oxford** history of the twentieth century; edited by Michael Howard and Wm. Roger Louis. Oxford Univ. Press 1998 xxii, 458p il hardcover o.p. pa $26.50 **909.82**
1. World history -- 20th century
ISBN 978-0-19-280378-8 pa; 0-19-280378-6 pa
LC 98-12861
"Besides global wars hot and cold, population explosion and urbanization impacted the entire century, as one of 27 articles in Twentieth Century underscores. Embracing nonpolitical topics in areas such as physics, modernism in art, and international economics, this work exposes the interested reader to developments that have affected most people." Booklist
Includes bibliographical references

Reynolds, David

Summits; six meetings that shaped the twentieth century. Basic Books 2007 544p il map $35 **909.82**
1. Diplomacy 2. World politics 3. World history -- 20th century
ISBN 978-0-465-06904-0; 0-465-06904-5
"The author's thorough mastery of his subject is reflected in the fluency and assurance of the writing." Publ Wkly
Includes bibliographical references

Schwartz, Richard Alan

The **1990s**; [by] Richard A. Schwartz. Facts on File 2006 496p il (Eyewitness history) $75 **909.82**
1. United States -- History -- 1989- 2. United States -- Politics and government -- 1989-
ISBN 0-8160-5696-X

LC 2004-28884
This book "provides hundreds of firsthand accounts of the 1990s—including diary entries, letters, speeches, and newspaper accounts—that illustrate how historical events appeared to those who lived through them. Each chapter provides an introductory essay and a chronology of events." Publisher's note
Includes bibliographical references

Sebestyen, Victor

1946; The Making of the Modern World. by Victor Sebestyen. Random House Inc 2015 464 p. 16 plates; illustrations; maps $30 **909.82**
1. World politics -- 1945-1991 2. World history -- 20th century
ISBN 1101870427; 9781101870426
LC 2015014902
This book is "about the year that would signal the beginning of the Cold War, the end of the British Empire, and the beginning of the rivalry between the United States and the USSR. Victor Sebestyen reveals the events of 1946 by chronologically framing what was taking place in Europe, the Middle East, and Asia, with seminal decisions made by heads of state that would profoundly change the old order forever." (Publisher's note)
"Highly recommended for anyone interested in world history or for those seeking to understand why the world is as it is today." LJ

Service, Robert, 1947-

The **End** of the Cold War, 1985-1991; Robert Service. PublicAffairs 2015 xxii, 643 p.p illustrations (HC) $35 **909.82**
1. Cold war 2. United States -- Foreign relations -- Soviet Union 3. Disarmament 4. World politics -- 1945-1989 5. Cold War -- Diplomatic history 6. Germany -- History -- Unification, 1990 7. Soviet Union -- Foreign relations -- 1985-1991 8. United States -- Foreign relations -- 1981-1989 9. Soviet Union -- Foreign relations -- United States
ISBN 9781610394994; 9781610395007
LC 2015942161
Author Robert Service's book is an "investigation of the final years of the Cold War. [It] opens a window onto the dramatic years that would irrevocably alter the world's geopolitical landscape, and the men at their fore. 'The End of the Cold War' captures the astonishing relationship between [Ronald] Reagan and [Mikhail] Gorbachev, two exceptional politicians who cooperated against all odds during extraordinary times." (Publisher's note)
"A wholly satisfying, likely definitive, but not triumphalist account of the end of an era." Kirkus
Includes bibliographical references (pages 501-518) and index

Tuchman, Barbara Wertheim

The **proud** tower; a portrait of the world before the war, 1890-1914. [by] Barbara W. Tuchman. 1st Ballantine Books ed; Ballantine Books 1996 528p il pa $15.95 **909.82**
1. Composers 2. Socialism 3. Anarchism and anarchists 4. Army officers 5. Europe -- Social conditions 6. World history -- 19th century 7. World history -- 20th century 8. United States -- Social conditions
ISBN 0-345-40501-3

LC 96-96511
First published 1966 by Macmillan
The author describes prewar social conditions in the U.S., France, England and Germany.
Includes bibliographical references

909.826   World history--1960-1969

The **60s**; the story of a decade. The New Yorker; edited by Henry Finder; introduction by David Remnick. Random House Inc. 2016 752 p. $35   **909.826**

1. Nineteen sixties 2. New York (N.Y.) -- History 3. United States -- Civilization -- 1945-

ISBN 9780679644835

         LC 2016013617

"The third installment of a fascinating decade-by-decade series, this anthology collects historic New Yorker pieces from the most tumultuous years of the twentieth century—including work by James Baldwin, Pauline Kael, Sylvia Plath, Roger Angell, Muriel Spark, and John Updike—alongside new assessments of the 1960s by some of today's finest writers." (Publisher's note)

"Collectively, the essays provide a keen intellectual view of the 1960s while reintroducing readers to some of the best writers of the decade." LJ

909.83   World history--21st century, 2000-2099

Bergen, Peter L.

The **longest** war; the enduring conflict between America and al-Qaeda. Free Press 2011 xx, 473p il map   **909.83**

1. Terrorism 2. Iraq War, 2003-2011 3. Iraq War, 2003-4. War on terrorism 5. Al Qaeda (Organization) 6. War on Terrorism, 2001- 7. Terrorism -- United States -- Prevention

ISBN 0743278933; 1439160597; 9780743278935; 9781439160596

         LC 2010-15268

"Most histories of the war on terror have been written largely from the American perspective, while this book [aims to] fold into the narrative the perspective of al-Qaeda and allied jihadist groups. . . . This book is first a narrative history of the 'war on terror' based upon a synthesis of . . . available open-source materials, together with my own interviewing and reporting. . . . The book also aspires to provide an analytic net assessment of the 'war on terror' to see what conclusions might now be drawn about what al-Qaeda and its allied groups accomplished in the first decade of the twenty-first century and where the United States and her partners have succeeded and failed." (Author's note) Bibliography. Index.

This is "a broad, almost stereoscopic account that brings an array of sources together into an illuminating synthesis. . . . If you want a solid, readable history of the Long War, this is a great place to start." Washington Monthly

Includes bibliographical references

Khan, Mahvish Rukhsana

My Guantanamo diary; the detainees and the stories they told me. Public Affairs 2008 302p il $25.95   **909.83**

1. Prisoners of war 2. Afghan War, 2001- 3. War on terrorism 4. Guantánamo Bay Naval Base (Cuba)

ISBN 978-1-58648-498-9

         LC 2008-274233

This book "provides a valuable account of what we can now recognize as one of the most shameful episodes in the war on terror. It is hard to read this book without a growing sense of embarrassment and indignation." N Y Times Book Rev

Includes bibliographical references

Klosterman, Chuck, 1972-

 ★ **But** What If We're Wrong? Thinking About the Present As If It Were the Past. Chuck Klosterman. Penguin Group USA 2016 288 p. (ebook) $85.50; (hardback) $26   **909.83**

1. Forecasting 2. Future life 3. Popular culture -- United States 4. United States -- Civilization -- 1970-

ISBN 9780451484901; 9780399184123; 0399184120

         LC 2016023103

This book, by Chuck Klosterman, "visualizes the contemporary world as it will appear to those who'll perceive it as the distant past. Chuck Klosterman asks questions that are profound in their simplicity: How certain are we about our understanding of gravity? How certain are we about our understanding of time? What will be the defining memory of rock music, five hundred years from today? How seriously should we view the content of our dreams?" (Publisher's note)

"Replete with lots of nifty, whimsical footnotes, this clever, speculative book challenges our beliefs with jocularity and perspicacity." Kirkus

Includes bibliographical references and index.

Reuters; our world now. Reuters. 5th ed. Thames & Hudson 2012 352 p. col. ill. (pbk.) $24.95   **909.83**

1. Journalism 2. Photojournalism 3. History, Modern -- 21st century -- Pictorial works 4. Civilization, Modern -- 21st century -- Pictorial works

ISBN 0500289867 2012 edition; 9780500289860 2012 edition

         LC 2011933209

This fifth volume in the Our World series from news agency Reuters "captures 2011 in over 350 powerful photos covering the full range of news reporting—politics, commerce, conflict, accidents and disasters, the environment, faith and festivities, entertainment, celebrity and lifestyle. . . . [C]aptions summarize the story behind each image." (Publisher's note)

910   Geography and travel

Allaby, Michael

The **encyclopedia** of Earth; a complete visual guide. [authors, Michael Allaby ... [et al.]] University of California Press 2008 608p il map $39.95 **910**

1. Reference books 2. Earth sciences -- Encyclopedias

ISBN 978-0-520-25471-8; 0-520-25471-6

         LC 2008-6956

This "source includes six main sections. 'Birth' is an overview of Earth's history and evolution; 'Fire' covers its inner workings, structure, and landscape; 'Land' covers rocks, minerals, and habitats; 'Air' covers weather; 'Water' includes information on oceans, rivers, and lakes; and 'Humans' is about humankind's relationship with Earth, including management of its resources. . . . This is a stunning, reasonably priced resource, especially useful for those in need of illustrations or a visual representation of a phenomenon or concept." Choice

Fuller, Gary

The **trivia** lover's guide to the world; geography for the lost and found. Gary Fuller. Rowman & Littlefield Publishers, Inc. 2012 270 p. (pbk. : alk. paper) $16.95 **910**

1. Geography -- Miscellanea
ISBN 1442214031; 9781442214033; 9781442214040
LC 2011051863

In this book on geography for general-interest readers, "using a game-show format and trivia questions, [Gary] Fuller goes beyond short answers to expound on a wide variety of geographic topics. . . . The chapters are arranged around particular themes, which include state capitals, the why and where of various cities, and the links between religion and geography." (Booklist)

Points unknown; a century of great exploration. edited by David Roberts. Norton 2000 608p $29.95 **910**

1. Explorers 2. Voyages and travels 3. Adventure and adventurers
ISBN 0-393-05000-9
LC 00-32915

"A mesmerizing display of the pull adventure exerts." Booklist

Thomas, Nicholas

Cook; the extraordinary voyages of Captain James Cook. Walker & Company 2003 xxxvii, 467p il map $28; pa $18.95 **910**

1. Explorers 2. Naval officers 3. Travel writers
ISBN 0-8027-1412-9; 0-8027-7711-2 pa
LC 2003-57648

"Rich, vivid and deeply provocative, Thomas's work combines premiere adventure story with thorough history and intensive sociology." Publ Wkly

Includes bibliographical references

910.2   Geography--Miscellany; world travel guides

Stellin, Susan

How to travel practically anywhere; the ultimate travel guide. Houghton Mifflin Co. 2006 321p pa $15.95 **910.2**

1. Travel
ISBN 978-0-618-60753-2; 0-618-60753-6
LC 2005-22728

This "guide to travel planning that covers the ins and outs (and ups and downs) of do-it-yourself travel. . . . [The author] offers information and advice on topics that traditional travel guides discuss only minimally: solo travel, travel insurance, last-minute planning, government travel advisories, web fares, home-exchange information, and

more; she also includes a helpful section on what to do in an emergency—when you need a doctor or have lost your passport. . . . This comprehensive and well-researched guide is useful for both new and seasoned travelers and is highly recommended for all libraries with travel collections." Libr J

Ultimate travel; our list of the 500 best places to see... ranked. by Lonely Planet (Author) Lonely Planet 2015 328 p. color illustrations $24.99 **910.2**

1. Travel 2. Voyages and travels
ISBN 1760342777; 9781760342777

This travel guide published by Lonely Planet, "is a compilation of the 500 most unmissable sights and attractions in the world. . . . Ranked by Lonely Planet's global community of travel experts, . . . big name mega-sights such as the Eiffel Tower and the Taj Mahal battle it out with lesser-known hidden gems for a prized place in the top 10, making this the only bucket list you'll ever need." (Publisher's note)

"Travelers with a competitive edge will savor this work as they plan their next excursions." LJ

The **World**; a traveller's guide to the planet. Lonely Planet 2014 959 p. color illustrations; maps $29.99 **910.2**

1. Travel
ISBN 1743600658; 9781743600658

This book has "taken the highlights from the world's best guidebooks and put them together into one 960-page whopper to create the ultimate guide to Earth. This user-friendly A-Z gives a flavour of each country in the world, including a map, travel highlights, info on where to go and how to get around, as well as some quirkier details to bring each place to life." (Publisher's note)

"This first edition was produced by the Australia-based office of the publisher; readers may find that the work's focus differs from their own perception of what is best in a given country. An excellent guide for the world's least-visited destinations." LJ

World Heritage sites; a complete guide to 981 UNESCO World Heritage sites. by UNESCO. Firefly Books Ltd 2014 896 p. illustrations, maps; portraits $29.95 **910.2**

1. Historic sites 2. Historic buildings
ISBN 1770852530; 9781770852532

This book "presents the complete and most up-to-date list of 981 World Heritage sites, including the 26 sites inscribed in 2012 and the 19 sites inscribed in 2013. Some of these newly inscripted sites are Red Basque Bay Whaling Station, Canada; Historic Centre of Agadez, Niger; Medici Villas and Gardens, Tuscany, Italy; Mount Etna, also in Italy; and the Nabib Sand Sea in Namibia." (Publisher's note)

910.285   Computer applications

Bray, Hiawatha

You are here; from the compass to GPS, the history and future of how we find ourselves. Hiawatha Bray. Basic Books 2014 272 p. (hardback) $27.99 **910.285**

1. Navigation 2. Global Positioning System 3.

Technological innovations -- Social aspects 4. Geospatial data 5. Electronics in navigation -- History 6. Geographic information systems -- History ISBN 0465032850; 9780465032853

LC 2014002731

This book, by Hiawatha Bray, "examines the rise of our technologically aided era of navigational omniscience--or how we came to know exactly where we are at all times. In a sweeping history of the development of location technology in the past century, Bray shows how . . . humankind ingeniously solved one of its oldest and toughest problems--only to herald a new era in which it's impossible to hide." (Publisher's note)

Includes bibliographical references and index

910.3 Geography--Dictionaries, encyclopedias, concordances, gazetteers

★ The **Columbia** gazetteer of the world; edited by Saul B. Cohen. 2nd ed.; Columbia University Press 2008 3v set $595   910.3
1. Gazetteers 2. Reference books
ISBN 978-0-231-14554-1

LC 2008-9181

First published 1952 with title: The Columbia Lippincott gazetteer of the world

"The 170,000-plus entries cover political, physical, and special places, including monuments and historic sites. . . . Historically accurate, this title can be considered a reference standard." Libr J

The **Oxford** companion to world exploration; David Buisseret, editor in chief. Oxford University Press 2007 2v il map set $250   910.3
1. Exploration
ISBN 0-19-514922-X; 978-0-19-514922-7

LC 2006-27968

"The entries are presented in alphabetical order and cover not only individual explorers, but also some geographic regions, wars, commercial operations, and religious organizations. . . . This work will become the first stop for students and general readers who seek either basic information or a starting point for further reading." Sci Books Films

Includes bibliographical references

Waldman, Carl

Encyclopedia of exploration; [by] Carl Waldman and Alan Wexler. Facts on File 2004 2v il map (Facts on File library of world history) set $225 **910.3**
1. Explorers 2. Exploration 3. Voyages and travels
ISBN 0-8160-4678-6

LC 2004-10625

"The first volume is all biographical entries with accompanying appendixes that list explorers by occupation, area(s) explored, chronology, and the respective explorers' nationality. The second volume has topical entries about all things related to exploration, such as specific areas, technologies, and routes." Am Ref Books Annu, 2005

Includes bibliographical references

910.4 Accounts of travel and facilities for travelers

Baggett, Jennifer

The **lost** girls; three friends, four continents, one unconventional detour around the world. [by] Jennifer Baggett, Holly C. Corbett, Amanda Pressner. HarperCollins 2010 542p map $24.99; ebook $11.99   **910.4**
1. Backpacking 2. Voyages and travels 3. Women -- Travel
ISBN 978-0-06-168906-2; 978-0-06-199347-3 ebook

LC 2009-54294

"Friends Pressner, Baggett, and Corbett were all busy climbing the corporate ladder of Manhattan media when they realized that, in their late twenties, they weren't sure they wanted the golden handcuffs of New York success. Reprioritizing, they decide on a rebellious, extreme course of action: quit their jobs, abandon their boyfriends, and take a yearlong trip around the world. In this group memoir, the three take turns chronicling a journey from Peru to Kenya to Vietnam to Australia, and everywhere in between. . . . [The authors] provide passionate, vivid descriptions of their far-flung travels, bolstered by thoughtful insights and genuine intentions, making this an intensely enjoyable read for fans of travel writing." Publ Wkly

Bathurst, Bella

The **wreckers**; a story of killing seas and plundered shipwrecks, from the eighteenth century to the present day. Houghton Mifflin 2005 326p il maps $25   **910.4**
1. Shipwrecks 2. Great Britain -- Local history
ISBN 0-618-41677-3

LC 2005-45951

The author "explains that 'wreckers' were people who watched for a ship in distress and stole everything on board of any value, sometimes also drowning the crew and burning the boats. . . . Bathurst traveled to eight wrecking 'hot spots' in Britain in researching the history of wrecking over the last 300 years, its heyday occurring in the eighteenth and nineteenth centuries. . . . The result is an exceptional chronicle of knavery." Booklist

Includes bibliographical references (p. 309-19)

Bellec, Francois

Unknown lands; the log books of the great explorers. translated by Lisa Davidson and Elizabeth Ayre. Overlook Press 2002 213p il map $55 **910.4**
1. Explorers 2. Voyages and travels
ISBN 1-58567-201-7

LC 2001-36800

"Weaving together logs, correspondence, and stories of the 'ordinary and extraordinary men' who explored the oceans and unknown lands over five centuries, Bellec offers a . . . . snapshot of the cultural and political circumstances that set the stage for maritime adventures and New World discoveries. Eyewitness accounts retold alongside maps and drawings contribute to an enlightening view of the minds, hearts, and talents of adventurers such as Columbus, Vasco de Gama, and James Cook. . . . This is simply a stunning book." Libr J

Includes bibliographical references

Bergreen, Laurence

Over the edge of the world; Magellan's terrifying circumnavigation of the globe. Morrow 2003 458p il maps hardcover o.p. pa $15.95 **910.4**

1. Explorers 2. Voyages around the world

ISBN 0-06-621173-5; 0-06-093638-X pa; 978-0-06-093638-9 pa

LC 2003-50143

The author "tells a well-rounded story of Magellan, not just that of the romanticized hero but also that of the explorer's darker side. . . . Fascinating reading for history buffs, and a great story that rivals any seagoing adventure." Booklist

Includes bibliographical references

Brandt, Anthony

The **man** who ate his boots; the tragic history of the search for the Northwest Passage. Alfred A. Knopf 2010 441p il map $28.95 **910.4**

1. Explorers 2. Northwest Passage 3. Arctic regions -- Exploration

ISBN 978-0-307-26392-6; 0-307-26392-4

LC 2009-38835

The author tells the story of the search for the Northwest Passage, from its beginnings early in the age of exploration through its development into a British national obsession to the final sordid, terrible descent into scurvy, starvation, and cannibalism.

"Often witty in his approach, Brandt makes the absurdity of Arctic exploration and the quest for the Northwest Passage entertaining for the general reader. Highly recommended for fans of British or Arctic exploration history." Libr J

Includes bibliographical references

Burgin, Robert

Going places; a reader's guide to travel narratives. Robert Burgin. Libraries Unlimited 2013 xxx, 572 p.p (Real stories series) (hardcopy : alk. paper) $70 **910.4**

1. Travel writing

ISBN 1598849727; 9781598849721

LC 2012035744

This book, by Robert Burgin, "examines the subgenres of the travel narrative genre in its seven chapters, categorizing and describing approximately 600 titles according to genres and broad reading interests, and identifying hundreds of other fiction and nonfiction titles as read-alikes and related reads by shared key topics. The author has also identified award-winning titles and spotlighted further resources on travel lit." (Publisher's note)

"Each chapter has a section on classics and ends with lists of books for readers to consider starting with, 'Fiction Read-Alikes,' notes, and footnotes. The excellent definitions and annotations will help librarians and readers understand and find books on this popular subject." Booklist

Includes bibliographical references and indexes

Chaplin, Joyce E.

★ **Round** about the earth; circumnavigation from Magellan to orbit. Joyce E. Chaplin. Simon & Schuster 2012 535 p. (hardcover) $35 **910.4**

1. Travel -- History 2. Transportation -- History 3. Voyages around the world -- History

ISBN 1416596194; 9781416596196; 9781416596202; 9781439100066

LC 2012016459

This book, by Joyce E. Chaplin, offers a "full history of . . . circumnavigation. . . . For almost five hundred years, human beings have been finding ways to circle the Earth. . . . The story begins with the first centuries of circumnavigation, when few survived the attempt. . . . Once continental railroads were built, circumnavigators could traverse sea and land. . . . Finally humans took to the skies to circle the globe in airplanes. Not much later, . . . in orbit." (Publisher's note)

Includes bibliographical references and index.

Cordingly, David

Under the black flag; the romance and the reality of life among the pirates. Random House 1996 296p maps hardcover o.p. pa $15 **910.4**

1. Pirates

ISBN 0-679-42560-8; 978-0-8129-7722-6 pa; 0-8129-7722-X pa

LC 95-41414

"This succinct history is full of unexpected revelations about the facts and myths of piracy; a typical seventeenth-century Western pirate vessel, for example, was run democratically long before the French Revolution, and one of the most successful pirates of all time was a nineteenth-century Chinese woman who controlled some fifty thousand seagoing outlaws." New Yorker

Includes bibliographical references

Women sailors and sailors' women; an untold maritime history. Random House 2001 286p il hardcover o.p. pa $14.95 **910.4**

1. Women 2. Voyages and travels 3. Adventure and adventurers

ISBN 0-375-75872-0 pa

LC 00-62762

A look at "the lives of the intrepid women who went to sea during the great age of sail. Countless females set sail for reasons of adventure, romance, or duty in the seventeenth, eighteenth, and nineteenth centuries. Included among their numbers were the wives or mistresses of ships' officers, prostitutes, female pirates, and women disguised as male sailors. . . . A significant contribution to both women's history and maritime scholarship." Booklist

Includes bibliographical references

Dana, Richard Henry

Two years before the mast; a personal narrative of life at sea. introduction by Gary Kinder; notes by Duncan Hasell. Modern Library 2001 xxiv, 516p il pa $12.95 **910.4**

1. Seafaring life 2. Voyages and travels

ISBN 0-375-75794-5

LC 2001-31243

First published anonymously in 1840

The author "shipped out of Boston in 1834 on the Pilgrim and sailed around the Horn to California on a hide-trading expedition. The book is based on the journal he kept during the voyage. Horrified by the brutal captain's mistreatment of the sailors, and shocked by their lack of legal redress, Dana wrote with a burning indignation that did much to rouse the public to the mariners' plight." HarperCollins Reader's Ency of Am Lit. 2d edition

Eat Pray Love Made Me Do It; Life Journeys Inspired by Elizabeth Gilbert's Bestselling Memoir. introduction by Elizabeth Gilbert. Penguin Group USA 2016 240 p. (pbk) $16   **910.4**
1. Self 2. Autobiographies
ISBN 0399576770; 9780399576775
LC 2016002749
This collection of essays, edited by Michelle Koufopoulos, shows how the memoir "'Eat Pray Love' helped one writer to embrace motherhood, another to come to terms with the loss of her mother, and yet another to find peace with not wanting to become a mother at all. One writer, reeling from a difficult divorce, finds new love overseas; another, a lifelong caregiver, is inspired to take an annual road trip, solo." (Publisher's note)

"More than one contributor mentions being given a copy of Eat Pray Love by a concerned mother or friend; such readers will relish this work. It will also appeal to those whose lives were similarly changed, or those who hope to be so." LJ

Fagan, Brian
Beyond the blue horizon; how the earliest mariners unlocked the secrets of the oceans. Brian Fagan. New York 2012 313 p. ill., maps $28   **910.4**
1. Exploration 2. Ocean travels -- History 3. Seafaring life -- History 4. Sea peoples -- History 5. Navigation, Prehistoric 6. Ocean travel -- History
ISBN 1608190056; 9781608190058
LC 2011045758
In this book, "historian Brian Fagan tackles . . . the enduring quest to master the oceans, the planet's most mysterious terrain. . . . From the moment when ancient Polynesians first dared to sail beyond the horizon, Fagan . . . explains how our mastery of the oceans changed the course of human history. . . . Fagan reveals how seafaring evolved so that the forbidding realms of the sea gods were transformed from barriers into a nexus of commerce and cultural exchange." (Publisher's note)

Includes bibliographical references and index

Garcia Marquez, Gabriel
The **story** of a shipwrecked sailor; who drifted on a life raft for ten days . . . translated from the Spanish by Randolph Hogan. Knopf 1986 106p hardcover o.p. pa $11   **910.4**
1. Survival after airplane accidents, shipwrecks, etc.
ISBN 0-679-72205-X pa
LC 85-45673
Original Spanish edition, 1970
"In 1955 Garcia Marquez was working as a reporter in Colombia. One of his stories was a serialized account of a sailor who was swept overboard with seven other crew

members of a Colombian destroyer and who was the only one to survive. This book presents Garcia Marquez' version of the sailor's first-person narrative." Booklist

Heat-Moon, William Least
Here, there, elsewhere; stories from the road. William Least Heat-Moon. Little, Brown and Co. 2013 402 p. $29.99   **910.4**
1. Travel
ISBN 0316110248; 9780316110242
LC 2012953180
This book is a collection of short writings from travel writer William Least Heat-Moon. "Culled from 30 years of magazine articles, these pieces roam across terrain both familiar and exotic. Many find magic in mundane patches of America, from improbably delicious fried-fish stands on Minnesota's Lake Superior shore to oddly idyllic Gulf Coast industrial canals and Seattle's rebel micro-breweries." (Publishers Weekly)

Henion, Leigh Ann
Phenomenal; a hesitant adventurer's search for wonder in the natural world. Leigh Ann Henion. Penguin Press 2015 276 p. map (hardcover) $26.95   **910.4**
1. Spiritual life 2. Voyages and travels 3. Spiritual biography 4. Women shamans -- Biography
ISBN 1594204713; 9780143108030; 9781594204715
LC 2014036661
This memoir, by Leigh Ann Henion, "begins in hardship: with Henion deeply shaken by the birth of her beloved son, shocked at the adversity a young mother faces with a newborn. . . . Convinced that the greatest key to happiness—both her own and that of her family—lies in periodically venturing into the wider world beyond home, Henion sets out on a global trek to rekindle her sense of wonder." (Publisher's note)

Heyerdahl, Thor
Kon-Tiki; across the Pacific by raft. translated by F.H. Lyon. Washington Square Press 1984 240p map (Enriched classics series) pa $5.99   **910.4**
1. Pacific Ocean 2. Ethnology -- Polynesia 3. Kon-Tiki Expedition (1947)
ISBN 0-671-72652-8
LC 84-42785
Original Norwegian edition, 1948
The "story of the six men who crossed the Pacific from Peru to the Polynesians on a primitive balsa-log raft such as Peruvian natives of the fifth century used, to prove that it was possible that the legendary race that came to Easter Island and the Polynesians could have come from Peru." Wis Libr Bull

Hoffman, Carl
The **lunatic** express; discovering the world -- via its most dangerous buses, boats, trains, and planes. Broadway Books 2010 286p map $24.99   **910.4**
1. Transportation 2. Voyages and travels
ISBN 0-7679-2980-2; 978-0-7679-2980-6
LC 2009-21477

Hoffman "manages to be both brave and compassionate as he lurches on his near-interminable journey from his home turf in the Adams Morgan neighborhood of Washington to the Gobi Desert and back again. He learns enough about himself en route to satisfy the travel-writing theorists, true, and this can be a little tedious. But—more important—he learns along the way a great deal about the habits of the world's peripatetic poor, and he writes about both the process and the people with verve and charity, making this book both extraordinary and extraordinarily valuable." Wall Street J

An Innocent Abroad; Dave Eggers, Richard Ford, Pico Iyer, John Berendt, Alexander McCall Smith and Jane Smiley. Lonely Planet 2014 320 p. $15.99   **910.4**
1. Travel 2. Authors 3. Celebrities
ISBN 1743603606; 9781743603604

In this book "more than 20 well-known writers and celebrities share the travel experiences that shaped their personalities and changed their lives. Contributors include Dave Eggers, Richard Ford, Pico Iyer, John Berendt, Alexander McCall Smith and Jane Smiley." (Publisher's note)

"Most but not all of these vignettes effectively convey the sense of novelty, and sometimes wide-eyed wonder, that youthful travelers are often fortunate to experience." Booklist

Junger, Sebastian
★ The **perfect** storm; a true story of men against the sea. Norton 1997 226p il map $23.95; pa $14.95   **910.4**
1. Storms 2. Shipwrecks
ISBN 0-393-04016-X; 0-393-33701-4 pa

LC 96-42412

"With waves as high as a hundred feet and winds so strong that anemometers were torn from their moorings, the storm of the title struck unsuspecting mariners off the coast of Nova Scotia in October, 1991. Junger traces the last voyage of the Andrea Gail—a commercial swordfishing boat that was lost, with all six hands, in the storm—and his account is relentlessly suspenseful." New Yorker

Konstam, Angus
The **history** of pirates. Lyons Press 1999 192p il maps hardcover o.p. pa $19.95   **910.4**
1. Pirates
ISBN 1-58574-516-2 pa

The author "chronicles the evolution of piracy from antiquity to the present. . . . Konstam profiles individual pirates, explores infamous vessels, and compares and contrasts various pirate regions and eras. He does a commendable job of separating fact from fiction." Booklist

Literature of travel and exploration; an encyclopedia. Jennifer Speake, editor. Fitzroy Dearborn 2003 3v il map set $495   **910.4**
1. Voyages and travels
ISBN 1-57958-247-8

LC 2003-5352

"This is a rich introduction to primary sources . . . and an excellent source for further research." Booklist
Includes bibliographical references

Lord, Walter
★ A **night** to remember. Holt & Co. 1955 209p il hardcover o.p. pa $14   **910.4**
1. Shipwrecks 2. Titanic (Steamship)
ISBN 0-03-027615-2; 0-8050-7764-2 pa

A detailed account of "the tragic drama of that terrible night—April 4, 1912—when the 'Titanic,' the unsinkable ship, struck an iceberg and went down in the icy waters of the Atlantic." Libr J

Macleod, Alasdair
Explorers; great tales of adventure and endurance. Royal Geographical Society; [written by Alasdair Macleod] DK in association with the Smithsonian Institution 2010 360p il $40   **910.4**
1. Explorers 2. Exploration
ISBN 978-0-7566-6737-5

"The book covers the history of exploration from the discovery of the ancient Egyptians in Nubia to the exploration of space by the Soviet Union and the United States in the 20th century. . . . [It] is a wonderful introduction to the various personalities who, over a period of several thousand years, devoted themselves to studying the world and revealing its fascinatingly diverse landscapes, conditions, and cultures." Sci Books Films

McPhee, John A.
Looking for a ship. Farrar, Straus & Giroux 1990 241p $18.95; pa $15   **910.4**
1. Seafaring life 2. Stella Lykes (Freighter)
ISBN 0-374-19077-1; 0-374-52319-3 pa

LC 90-3311

In this book McPhee focuses on the "plight of the U.S. merchant marine. Accompanying Second Mate Andy Chase on a 42-day run down the west coast of South America aboard the S.S. Stella Lykes, McPhee provides the reader with stories and tales of modern seafaring life and the problems of making a living as a merchant mariner. . . . An engrossing tale of the sea, with excellent detail and humanity." Libr J

Morris, Jan
Contact! a book of encounters. W. W. Norton & Co. 2010 202p $23.95   **910.4**
1. Voyages and travels
ISBN 978-0-393-07640-0

LC 2009-52193

The author "collects vignettes of encounters with and observations of people from her numerous adventures and assignments. Varying from a few sentences to a few paragraphs, each vignette paints a picture or tells a story that brings a personal touch to the narrative of Morris's life and travels. They range from the humorous to the enchanting and tell us as much about Morris as she tells us of people around the world. This is not a typical travelog that one reads essay by essay but something to pick up and put down as time allows. Readers will appreciate the diversity of the people, from the famous to the relatively unremarkable, from six continents." Libr J

Nooteboom, Cees

Nomad's hotel; travels in time and space. translated from the Dutch by Ann Kelland; [introduction by Alberto Manguel] Houghton Mifflin Harcourt 2009 242p il pa $13.95 **910.4**

1. Voyages and travels

ISBN 978-0-15-603535-4

LC 2008-20813

First published 2006 in the United Kingdom

The author "surrounds his reader with the sounds, sights, and smells of his wanderings in this lyrical collection written over three decades. From the bone-chilling dampness of winter in the Aran Islands and the insistent bells marking time in the labyrinth of Venice to the endless dry and empty lands of Gambia and Mali, whose people struggle to find their future, Nooteboom weaves a compelling, perceptive, and yet wondering view of the places he visits. . . . Armchair traveling at its best." Libr J

Podell, Albert

Around the World in 50 Years; My Adventure to Every Country on Earth. Albert Podell. St. Martin's Press 2015 384 p. illustrations $26.99 **910.4**

1. Travel 2. Automobile travel

ISBN 1250051983; 9781250051981

LC 2014033858

In this book author Albert Podell describes how he "achieved two great goals that others had told him were impossible. First, he set a record for the longest automobile journey ever made around the world. After that--although it took him forty-seven more years--Albert Podell set another record by going to every country on Earth." (Publisher's note)

Read, Piers Paul

★ **Alive**; sixteen men, seventy-two days, and insurmountable odds--the classic adventure of survival in the Andes. Harper Perennial 2005 398p il pa $13.95 **910.4**

1. Survival after airplane accidents, shipwrecks, etc. 2. Andes

ISBN 0-06-077866-0

First published 1974 by Lippincott

The author describes the extraordinary hardships endured by the survivors of a horrific plane crash in the Andes.

Sides, Hampton

★ **In** the kingdom of ice; the grand and terrible polar voyage of the U.S.S. Jeannette. Hampton Sides. Doubleday 2014 480 p. illustrations, maps $28.95 **910.4**

1. Arctic regions -- Exploration 2. United States -- Exploring expeditions 3. Jeannette (Steamer) -- History 4. Shipwrecks -- Arctic Ocean -- History -- 19th century

ISBN 0385535376; 9780385535373

LC 2014004367

This book by Hampton Sides recounts how "James Gordon Bennett . . . funded an official U.S. naval expedition to reach the Pole, choosing as its captain a young officer named George Washington De Long, who had gained fame for a rescue operation off the coast of Greenland. . . . De Long led a team of 32 men deep into uncharted Arctic waters. . . . On July 8, 1879, the USS Jeannette set sail from San Francisco to cheering crowds." (Publisher's note)

"Sides . . . tapped amazing archival material, including diaries, letters, and the ship logs, to render a completely thrilling saga of survival in unbelievably harsh conditions." Booklist

Includes bibliographical references

Turner, Steve

The **band** that played on; the extraordinary story of the 8 musicians who went down with the Titanic. Thomas Nelson 2011 259p $24.99 **910.4**

1. Titanic (Steamship) 2. Musicians -- Biography

ISBN 978-1-59555-219-8; 1-59555-219-7

LC 2010-47182

This is the "first book since the great ship went down to examine the lives of the eight musicians who were employed by the Titanic. What these men did -- standing calmly on deck playing throughout the disaster -- achieved global recognition. But their individual stories, until now, have been largely unknown. What Turner has uncovered is a narrow but unique slice of history -- one more chapter of compelling Titanic lore." Christ Sci Monit

Includes bibliographical references

Wheeler, Sara

The **magnetic** north; notes from the Arctic circle. Farrar, Straus and Giroux 2011 315p il map $26; ebook $12.99 **910.4**

1. Arctic regions -- Description and travel

ISBN 9780374200138; 0374200130; 9781429991940 ebook

LC 2010-14576

"With wry humor and extensive research, Wheeler captures a swiftly transforming region with which we all have a symbiotic relationship." N Y Times Book Rev

Includes bibliographical references (p. [297]-302) and index.

Williams, Glyndwr

Arctic labyrinth; the quest for the Northwest Passage. [by] Glyn Williams. University of California Press 2010 439p il map $34.95 **910.4**

1. Explorers 2. Northwest Passage 3. Arctic regions -- Exploration

ISBN 978-0-5202-6627-8

LC 2009-35546

First published 2009 in the United Kingdom

"If you read one book on the history of the mythic Northwest Passage, read this one. . . . Williams deftly weaves together explorers' logbooks and diaries (published and unpublished) with a lifetime of research, and the result is a masterpiece." Libr J

Includes bibliographical references

Wilson, Penny

Lusitania; triumph, tragedy, and the end of the Edwardian age. Greg King and Penny Wilson. St. Martin's Press 2015 370 p. 8 plates; illustrations (hardback) $27.99 **910.4**

1. Shipwreck victims 2. Lusitania (Steamship) 3.

Upper class -- United States -- Biography 4. Ocean travel -- North Atlantic Ocean -- Anecdotes 5. Shipwreck victims -- North Atlantic Ocean -- Anecdotes 6. Upper class -- Social life and customs -- 20th century
ISBN 1250052548; 9781250052544

LC 2014040843

In this book on the Lusitania, "the authors tell the grim tale of the titular doomed passenger liner, which was torpedoed by a German U-boat in the early stages of World War I. The ship sank within 18 minutes; sending nearly 1,200 people of all ages, nationalities, and social classes to terrible deaths in the Irish Sea and setting off a political firestorm that would eventually culminate in the United States joining the war." (Library Journal)

"The authors devote inordinate portions of the text to biographies of passengers and still more to the lives of the survivors, but their exploration of the facts surrounding the mystery is the primary pleasure of the book. Those who relish tales of the rich and famous will appreciate this book, but the real joy is in the authors' detective work and attention to detail." Kirkus

World's best travel experiences; 400 extraordinary places with recollections by Bill Bryson, Anna Quindlen, and more. by National Geographic. National Geographic 2012 319 p. col. ill., col. map (hardcover : alk. paper) $40   **910.4**
1. Voyages and travels
ISBN 1426209592; 9781426209598

LC 2012016594

This travel guide offers "400 awe-inspiring destinations chosen by National Geographic's family of globe-trotting contributors; dozens of fun, 'Best of the World' themed lists; illuminating sidebars, several by travel and literary luminaries such as Anna Quindlen, Bill Bryson, Gore Vidal, and Pico Iyer; and hundreds of . . . images to bring to life a wide variety of location categories--from entire countries to mountaintop villages to pristine lakes to ancient wonders." (Publisher's note)

"Readers will dip into this book for inspiration for future travel as well as for fuel for beautiful daydreams." LJ

910.41   Trips around the world

Foer, Joshua
  Atlas Obscura; An Explorer's Guide to the World's Hidden Wonders. Joshua Foer; Dylan Thuras; Ella Morton. Workman Pub Co 2016 480 p. $35   **910.41**
1. Adventure travel 2. Exploration -- Atlases 3. Curiosities and wonders
ISBN 0761169083; 9780761169086

LC 2016041548

This book by Joshua Foer, Dylan Thuras and Ella Morton "celebrates over 700 of the strangest and most curious places in the world. Talk about a bucket list: here are natural wonders—the dazzling glowworm caves in New Zealand, or a baobob tree in South Africa that's so large it has a pub inside. . . . Architectural marvels, including the M.C. Escher-like stepwells in India, . . . [and] mind-boggling events, like the Baby Jumping Festival in Spain." (Publisher's note)

"Featuring full-color illustrations, this hefty and gorgeously produced tome will be eagerly pored over by readers of many ages and fans of the original website." Booklist

910.9   History, geographic treatment, biography

Winter, Kathleen
  Boundless; tracing land and dream in a new Northwest Passage. Kathleen Winter. Counterpoint Press 2015 272 p. 16 plates; illustrations; map (hardcover) $27   **910.9**
1. Northwest Passage 2. Inuit -- Canada -- Social conditions 3. Northwest Passage -- Description and travel
ISBN 1619025671; 9781619025677

LC 2015022219

This book describes how "author Kathleen Winter took a journey across the legendary Northwest Passage--connecting the Pacific and Atlantic Oceans--alongside marine scientists, historians, archaeologists, anthropologists, and curious passengers. From Greenland to Baffin Island and all along this arctic passage, Winter witnesses the new mathematics of the melting North. . . . Throughout the journey she also learns much from her fellow travellers." (Publisher's note)

"Perceptive and thoughtful, Winter's ruminations on Arctic life and its continuous clashes with modern civilization are compelling and thought-provoking. The north is a place rarely visited and little understood, but it looms ever larger in our collective future, and to ignore it and its people would be an act of global arrogance." Booklist

910.91   Geography of and travel in areas, regions, places in general

Franklin, Jonathan
  438 days; an extraordinary true story of survival at sea. Jonathan Franklin. Atria Books 2015 288 p. color illustrations, maps (ebook) $16.99; (hardcover) $26   **910.91**
1. Survival at sea -- Pacific Ocean 2. Chiapas (Mexico) -- Biography 3. Shipwrecks -- Marshall Islands 4. Fishing boats -- Mexico -- Chiapas 5. Illegal aliens -- Mexico -- Biography 6. Fisheries -- Mexico -- Chiapas -- History 7. Fishers -- Mexico -- Chiapas -- Biography 8. Salvadorans -- Mexico -- Chiapas -- Biography 9. Fishing villages -- Mexico -- Chiapas -- Social life and customs
ISBN 9781501116315; 9781501116292

LC 2015030740

This book by Jonathan Franklin tells the story of Salvador Alvarenga, "the fisherman who survived fourteen months in a small boat seven thousand miles across the Pacific Ocean. On November 17, 2012, a pair of fishermen left the coast of Mexico, . . . a violent storm ambushed them as they were fishing eighty miles offshore. . . . On January 30, 2014, Alvarenga, . . . wild-bearded and half-mad castaway, washed ashore on a nearly deserted island on the far side of the Pacific." (Publisher's note)

"Franklin sprinkles the story with expert opinions to give it depth and context, but the most striking details are those offered by Alvarenga himself about the challenges he faced day in and day out. A spectacular triumph of grit over adversity, 438 Days is an intense, immensely absorbing read." Booklist

Kurson, Robert

Pirate hunters; the search for the Golden Fleece. Robert Kurson. Random House Inc 2014 304 p. color illustrations (hardcover) $28 **910.91**
1. Adventure fiction 2. Shipwrecks -- Fiction 3. Buried treasure -- Fiction 4. Deep diving 5. Treasure troves 6. Pirates -- History 7. Golden Fleece (Ship) 8. Shipwrecks -- Dominican Republic
ISBN 9781400063369; 9780804194662; 1400063361
LC 2014020225

In this book by Robert Kurson, "John Chatterton and John Mattera are willing to risk everything to find . . . the ship of the infamous pirate Joseph Bannister. . . . They must travel the globe in search of historic documents and accounts of the great pirate's exploits, face down dangerous rivals, battle the tides of nations and governments and experts. But it's only when they learn to think and act like pirates . . . that they become able to go where no pirate hunters have gone before." (Publisher's note)

"An enjoyable read, especially if you've got a thing for pirates." Kirkus

Lewis, Matt

Last man off; a true story of disaster and survival on the Antarctic seas. Matt Lewis. Plume 2015 256 p. illustrations (some color) (paperback) $17 **910.91**
1. Rescues -- Antarctic Ocean 2. Sudur Havid (Fishing boat) 3. Shipwrecks -- Antarctic Ocean 4. Severe storms -- Antarctic Ocean 5. Survival at sea -- Antarctic Ocean
ISBN 0147515343; 9780147515346
LC 2015004920

On June 6, 1998, twenty-three-year-old Matt Lewis had just started his dream job as a scientific observer aboard a deep-sea fishing boat in the waters off Antarctica. As the crew haul in the line for the day, a storm begins to brew. When the captain vanishes and they are forced to abandon ship, Lewis leads the escape onto three life rafts, where the battle for survival begins." Publisher's note.

A darkly exhilarating memoir of tragedy at sea." Kirkus
Includes bibliographical references

O'Neill, Zora

All strangers are kin; adventures in Arabic and the Arab world. Zora O'Neill. Houghton Mifflin Harcourt 2016 336 p. (hardcover) $25 **910.91**
1. Arabic language 2. Middle East -- Description and travel 3. Arab countries -- Description and travel 4. O'Neill, Zora -- Travel -- Arab countries 5. Travel writers -- United States -- Biography 6. Women journalists -- United States -- Biography 7. Arabic language -- Study and teaching -- Foreign speakers
ISBN 9780547853185
LC 2015020508

In this book, readers join author Zora O'Neill "for a grand tour through the Middle East. You will laugh with her in Egypt, delight in the stories she passes on from the United Arab Emirates, and find yourself transformed by her experiences in Lebanon and Morocco. She's packed her dictionaries, her unsinkable sense of humor, and her talent for making fast friends of strangers." (Publisher's note)

"What emerges is the idea of language as a connection, passion, and a reflection of the lives and history of diverse Arab peoples, a view which is lacking in the general news coverage of Middle Eastern conflict. Glimpses of daily life, particularly of Arab women, are intriguing and sometimes unexpected, including the rich assortment of Lebanese cursing while driving." LJ

Includes bibliographical references

Seaman, Camille

Melting away; a ten-year journey through our endangered Polar Regions. Camille Seaman. Princeton Architectural Press 2015 156 p. color illustrations (alk. paper) $55 **910.91**
1. Icebergs 2. Polar regions -- Pictorial works 3. Animals -- Polar regions -- Pictorial works 4. Icebergs -- Polar regions -- Pictorial works 5. Natural history -- Polar regions -- Pictorial works 6. Climatic changes -- Environmental aspects -- Polar regions -- Pictorial works
ISBN 9781616892609
LC 2014018830

This book, written and illustrated by Camille Seaman, presents photography of the polar regions, documenting climate change. "As an expedition photographer aboard small ships in the Arctic and Antarctic, she has chronicled the accelerating effects of global warming on the jagged face of nearly fifty thousand icebergs." (Publisher's note)

"In her inimitable way, Seaman writes that she was 'recording the voice of these places with my cameras.' That voice is quiet and deeply affecting—a relief from the shouted rhetoric that so often accompanies conversation on climate change. A sterling addition to all photography collections." LJ

Wilkinson, Alec

The ice balloon; S.A. Andrée and the heroic age of arctic exploration. by Alec Wilkinson. Alfred A. Knopf 2011 239 p. **910.91**
1. Balloons 2. Explorers -- Sweden 3. Polar regions -- Exploration 4. Arctic regions -- Exploration 5. Explorers -- Sweden -- Biography 6. Balloon ascensions -- Arctic regions 7. Polar regions -- Discovery and exploration 8. Arctic regions -- Discovery and exploration
ISBN 9780307594808
LC 2011025434

This book explores a 1897 voyage, when "Swedish national S.A. Andrée and a crew of two attempted to fly from Spitsbergen to the North Pole and back via hydrogen balloon. [Alec] Wilkinson . . . describes this little-known Arctic expedition and provides details about late 19th-century ballooning. After being aloft for nearly 66 hours while traveling 517 miles, the balloon landed 300 miles short of the pole. Thus Andrée, Nils Strindberg, and Knut Fraenkel began the hard work of crossing the Arctic to find land. . . . Andrée's journal abruptly ends with his landing on White Island after nearly three months of sledging. No one knows exactly how or when the men died, a fact that lends greater mystery to this unusual Arctic expedition." (Libr J)

Includes bibliographical references (p. [237]-239)

911 Historical geography

Atlas of exploration; cartography by Philip's; foreword by John Hemming. Oxford University Press 2008 256p il map $50 **911**
1. Reference books 2. Exploration -- Atlases
ISBN 978-0-19-534318-2

LC 2008-626565

First published 1998 with title: Oxford atlas of exploration

"This atlas describes many of the explorations and participants that changed history and enhanced man's knowledge and perception of the world. . . . The volume is a visual delight, festooned with more than 100 specially drawn maps and 300 b&w and color photographs, period paintings, and illustrations on the various explorations." Libr Media Connect

Beck, Warren A.

Historical atlas of the American West; by Warren A. Beck and Ynez D. Haase. University of Okla. Press 1989 xlii, 78p maps hardcover o.p. pa $24.95 **911**
1. Reference books 2. Historical atlases 3. West (U.S.) -- Historical geography
ISBN 0-8061-2456-3

LC 88-40540

"Defining the West as that part of the United States lying west of the 100th meridian, Beck and Haase provide a cartographic survey of the history of the region. In addition to maps illustrating such standard themes as natural resources, exploration and travel routes, the growth of the transportation network, and Indian tribal lands, the authors have included detailed maps on such topics as the Spanish-Mexican land grants and the Mt. St. Helens's eruption. . . . This atlas is an essential purchase for most libraries." Libr J

Hayes, Derek

★ **Historical** atlas of the American West; with original maps. University of California Press 2009 288p il map **911**
1. Reference books 2. Historical atlases 3. West (U.S.) -- Historical geography 4. Western states -- Historical geography -- Maps
ISBN 9780520256521

LC 20090279536

"The West, for the purpose of this atlas, is defined as the Dakotas, Nebraska, Kansas, Oklahoma, Texas, and all states west of them, including Alaska, but not Hawai'i. More than 600 maps have been carefully selected and beautifully reproduced in full color. They provide the primary-source documentation for the historical narrative, written for the general reader, tracing the development of the Western United States from its indigenous inhabitants to European exploration, the migration of settlers, and 20th-century events. . . . A high quality publication at an amazingly low price, this atlas is

highly recommended for all public and academic libraries, history buffs, and map enthusiasts." Libr J

Includes bibliographical references

Historical atlas of the United States; with original maps. University of California Press 2007 280p il map $45 **911**
1. Atlases 2. Reference books 3. United States -- Historical geography -- Maps
ISBN 978-0-520-25036-9; 0-520-25036-2

LC 2006-42405

"Hayes has produced an excellent visual history of the land that became the US. The work includes 535 maps gathered from a variety of international collections, coupled with more than 60 other illustrations to chronicle the expansion and development of the nation over the last 500 years." Choice

Includes bibliographical references

Hellmann, Paul T.

★ **Historical** gazetteer of the United States. Routledge 2005 865p $150 **911**
1. Reference books 2. United States -- Gazetteers 3. United States -- Local history -- Dictionaries 4. United States -- Historical geography -- Dictionaries
ISBN 0-415-93948-8

LC 2004-11421

This reference provides "historical records of U.S. cities and towns. Arrangement is alphabetical by state, including the District of Columbia. Each state chapter contains a brief description of major cities, date of incorporation into the U.S., the number of counties, and a rough breakdown of how the state categorizes municipalities, towns, townships, and cities. This is followed by alphabetical entries for significant places. Inclusion is determined more by historical importance (national or regional) than by population. All county seats are included. Entries are in paragraph form and typically begin by noting the country and the part of the state in which the place is located as well as its approximate distance from the state's most important city. Events are listed chronologically ." Booklist

Magocsi, Paul R.

Historical atlas of Central Europe; [by] Paul Robert Magocsi. rev and expanded ed; University of Wash. Press 2002 274p maps (History of East Central Europe) hardcover o.p. pa $45 **911**
1. Atlases 2. Reference books 3. Central Europe -- Historical geography -- Maps
ISBN 0-295-98146-6

LC 2001-27907

First published 1993 with title: Historical atlas of East Central Europe

"The volume is arranged chronologically, with coverage beginning about A.D. 400 (roughly the time of the demise of the Roman Empire) and continuing through the end of the 20th century. The maps and tables provide information on military affairs; population and population movements; economy; ethnolinguistic distributions; and religious, cultural, and educational institutions. All are extremely well done." SLJ

Thubron, Colin

   Shadow of the Silk Road. Harper Collins 2007 363p map $25.95   **911**

   1. Asia -- Description and travel

   ISBN 978-0-06-123172-8; 0-06-123172-X

                      LC 2006-52142

   First published 2006 in the United Kingdom

   "An illuminating account of a breathtaking journey." Booklist

912   Graphic representations of surface of earth and of extraterrestrial worlds

Aczel, Amir D.

   The riddle of the compass; the invention that changed the world. Harcourt 2001 178p il maps hardcover o.p. pa $13   **912**

   1. Compass

   ISBN 0-15-100506-0; 0-15-600753-3 pa

                      LC 00-47153

   This book tracks "down the roots of the compass and tells the story of navigation through the ages." Publisher's note

   Includes bibliographical references

Atlas A-Z. DK 2012 432 p. $11.95   **912**

   1. Atlases 2. Geography

   ISBN 0756689775; 9780756689773

                      LC 2012587235

   This book is the updated fifth edition of Dorling Kindersley Publishing's pocket atlas. Readers can "[c]arry the world in [their] pocket[s] with this . . . . global guide combining maps, facts, and statistics" about world geography. (Publisher's note)

Atlas of the World; [prepared by National Geographic Maps for the Book Division] Random House Inc 2014 448 p. 1 atlas; color maps; color ils $195   **912**

   1. Atlases

   ISBN 1426213549; 9781426213540

                      LC 200445002

   This book presents "illustrated maps and informational graphics [that] chart rapidly changing global themes such as population trends, urbanization, health and longevity, human migration, climate change, communications, and the world economy. The core of any atlas is the reference mapping section and the 10th Edition boasts the largest and most comprehensive collection of political maps ever published by National Geographic." (Publisher's note)

Knox, Paul

   The atlas of cities; mapping the urban world. Paul Knox. Columbia University Press 2014 256 p. color illustrations, maps (cloth) $49.50   **912**

   1. Atlases 2. Cities and towns

   ISBN 0691157812; 9780691157818

                      LC 2013954981

   This atlas by Paul Knox focuses on cities. "Each of the 13 chapters addresses a specific type of city, including those that are typically discussed (imperial, industrial, and megac-

ity), as well as other types of cities (e.g., celebrity, green, and creative). Each chapter focuses on a core city with secondary cities as supporting documentation for the subtopic discussion." (Choice: Current Reviews for Academic Libraries)

   "This fascinating survey effectively complemented and enriched by color maps, charts, and illustrations, celebrates the urban landscape's past, present, and potential for the future. Intended for the general reader, Knox's reference is recommended to anyone interested in urban studies and geography." LJ

Lavin, Stephen J.

   Atlas of the great plains; Stephen J. Lavin, Fred M. Shelley, and J. Clark Archer; foreword by David J. Wishart; introduction by John C. Hudson. University of Nebraska Press 2011 335p il $39.95   **912**

   1. Atlases 2. Reference books 3. Great Plains -- History -- Maps

   ISBN 978-0-8032-1536-8

Lester, Toby

   The fourth part of the world; the race to the ends of the Earth, and the epic story of the map that gave America its name. Free Press 2009 462p il map $30   **912**

   1. Map drawing 2. World maps 3. Cartographers 4. America -- Maps 5. Cartography -- History 6. Voyages and travels -- History 7. Discoveries in geography -- History

   ISBN 1416535314; 9781416535317

                      LC 2009-1230

   This "chronicle of the early 16th-century creation of the Waldseemüller map offers insight into how monks, classicists, merchants and other contributors from earlier periods shaped the map's creation and subsequently informed modern worldviews." (Publisher's note)

   The book is "history of the centuries-long European fascination with depicting the world in two dimensions." (Reviews in American History).

   "In 2003, the Library of Congress paid $10 million for a 1507 map of the world that first used the name 'America' for lands in the New World. It was touted as America's birth certificate. Lester . . . traces the fascinating background to the creation of this map, as Europeans tried to assimilate the discoveries of Columbus, Vespucci, and other explorers into their worldview. . . . Lester provides an engrossing adventure for both general and informed lay readers." Libr J

   Includes bibliographical references

A **Map** of the World; According to Illustrators & Storytellers. edited by Antonis Antoniou, Robert Klanten, Sven Ehmann, and Hendrik Hellige. Prestel Pub 2013 224 p. chiefly color illustrations $60   **912**

   1. Maps 2. Map drawing 3. Cartography 4. Thematic maps 5. Artists as cartographers

   ISBN 3899554698; 9783899554694

                      LC 2013482415

   This book, edited by Antonis Antoniou, R. Klanten, H. Ehmann, H. Hellige, "features the most original and sought-after map illustrators whose work is in line with the zeitgeist. [It] is a compelling collection of their work--from accurate and surprisingly detailed representations to personal, naïve, and modernistic interpretations. The featured projects from around the world range from maps and atlases inspired by classic forms to cartographic experiments and editorial illustrations." (Publisher's note)

★ **National** Geographic visual atlas of the world. National Geographic Society 2009 416p il map $100   **912**
1. Atlases 2. Reference books
ISBN 978-1-4262-0332-9
                                     LC 2008-627044
This atlas "has the usual atlas features but emphasizes the more than 850 UNESCO World Heritage Sites. . . . Double-page spreads of regional maps are framed with four to six color photographs of the heritage sites that are indicated on the map. . . . Beautiful color photography and clear topical material combined with detailed maps of areas not covered as well in other world atlases make the Visual Atlas a recommended purchase. This is a first choice for any library needing a new medium-priced atlas." Booklist
Includes bibliographical references

The **new** atlas of the Arab world. American University in Cairo Press 2010 144p il map $39.50 **912**
1. Atlases 2. Reference books 3. Arab countries -- Maps
ISBN 978-977-416-419-4
This atlas contains maps of the Arab world "showing physical features, political boundaries, towns, and communication networks. In addition, each of the twenty-two countries is the subject of an illustrated essay, with notes and . . . statistics on the geography, population, history and politics, and economy of the country. The countries covered are: Algeria, Bahrain, Comoros, Djibouti, Egypt, Iraq, Jordan, Kuwait, Lebanon, Libya, Mauritania, Morocco, Oman, Palestine, Qatar, Saudi Arabia, Somalia, Sudan, Syria, Tunisia, United Arab Emirates, Yemen." Publisher's note

New Concise World Atlas; by Oxford University Press. Oxford University Press 2013 288 p. illustrations, color maps $39.95   **912**
1. Atlases 2. Population
ISBN 0199829810; 9780199829811
This book, in its fourth edition, presents "over 100 pages of the most up-to-date topographic and political maps. . . . Recent changes to the world's geography are thoroughly captured in this edition; fully updated tables and world statistics provide data on climate, population, area, and physical dimensions. Finally, an index with over 58,000 items make searching for lesser-known locales quick and easy." (Publisher's note)

★ **Oxford** Atlas of the world; [cartography by Philip's] 19th ed. Oxford University Press 2012 448 p. il map (hardcover) $89.95   **912**
1. Atlases 2. Earth -- Maps 3. Physical geography 4. Reference books
ISBN 0199937826; 9780199937820
                                     LC 20100594813
First published 1992. Frequently revised. Variant title: Atlas of the world

This world atlas offers "new census information, dozens of city maps . . . satellite images of Earth, and a geographical glossary." It " provides details on such topics as climate, the greenhouse effect, employment and industry, standards of living, agriculture, population and migration, and global conflicts." (Publisher's note)
"...[U]pdated annually, this large-format resource continues to earn pride of place on the atlas case's top shelf for its combination of currency and eye-widening graphics. The physical, political, and country and regional maps that make up the volume's core are works of art-brilliantly designed for easy comprehension, rendered in bright colors and sharp detail... Atlases are among the quickest reference sources to age, so for classroom or library collections in which students search in vain...this makes a first-rate replacement." SLJ

Rand McNally Goodes World Atlas; edited by Howard Veregin. Rand McNally 2009 400 p. $45   **912**
1. Maps 2. Atlases
ISBN 0528877542; 9780528877544
This book, edited by Howard Veregin, "features over 250 pages of maps, from definitive physical and political maps to important thematic maps that illustrate the spatial aspects of many important topics. [It] includes 160 pages of new, digitally produced reference maps, as well as new thematic maps on global climate change, sea level rise, CO_2 emissions, polar ice fluctuations, deforestation, extreme weather events, infectious diseases, water resources, and energy production." (Publisher's note)

Riffenburgh, Beau
Mapping the world; the story of cartography. Beau Riffenburgh. Carlton Books 2014 160 p. illustrations, maps hbk $29.95   **912**
1. Maps 2. Historical geography
ISBN 9780233004396; 0233004394
Previously published 2011 as The Men Who Mapped the World
"Containing numerous maps from the archives of the Royal Geographical Society, Mapping the World tells the story of the philosophers, explorers, artists, and scientists who brought together their skills to produce some of the most intriguing artifacts ever created." (Publisher's note)

The **Times** comprehensive atlas of the world; by The Times UK. 14th edition Trafalgar Square 2014 544 p. illustrations, maps $200   **912**
1. Atlases
ISBN 0007551401; 9780007551408
                                     LC 2012358515
This book is a "prestigious and authoritative world atlas. . . . New features include a double page map of the Arctic Ocean, new maps of sub-ice features in the Antarctic Ocean and the Antarctic, and physical maps of all the continents. Major updates include 5,000 place name changes; . . . a beautifully illustrated section on current issues from climate to economy; updated national parks and conserved areas; . . . and towns and populations in Brazil and Japan." (Publisher's note)

912.09 History and biography of maps and map making

Atlas of Yellowstone; senior editor, W. Andrew Marcus; cartographic editor, James E. Meacham; Yellowstone editor, Ann W. Rodman; production manager, Alethea Y. Steingisser; consulting editor, Stuart Allan; text editor, Ross West. University of California Press University of Oregon 2012 1 atlas (xxi, 274 p.)p ill. (some col.), chiefly col. (cloth : alk. paper) $65 **912.09**
  1. Yellowstone National Park -- Atlases 2. Physical geography -- Yellowstone National Park -- Maps
  ISBN 0520271556; 9780520271555
  LC 2011037533

This book by W. Andrew Marcus presents an atlas of Yellowstone National Park. "Material ranges from broad overviews to specific details. The 524 maps are presented in five sections: 'Geographic Setting' . . . 'Human Geography' . . . 'Physical Geography' . . . 'Wildlife' . . . and 'Reference Maps.' . . . The atlas also includes 50 color illustrations and more than 260 line illustrations." (Library Journal)

Includes bibliographical references (p. 262-267) and index

Brotton, Jerry

Great maps; Jerry Brotton. DK Publishing 2014 256 p. illustrations (some color) $25 **912.09**
  1. Maps 2. Map drawing 3. Cartography 4. Cartography -- History
  ISBN 1465424636; 9781465424631
  LC 2012278182

In this book, by Jerry Brotton, "[t]he world's finest maps [are] explored and explained, . . . [f]rom Ptolemy's world map to the Hereford's Mappa Mundi, through Mercator's map of the world to the latest maps of the Moon and Google Earth. . . . Revealing the stories behind 55 historical maps by analyzing graphic close-ups, [it] also profiles key cartographers and explorers to look why each map was commissioned, who it was for and how they influenced navigation." (Publisher's note)

"The thematic maps are particularly interesting, including a "Cholera Map" from 1854, a map depicting the slave population of the Southern states, and Dr. Livingstone's map of Africa. Booklist

Janes, Andrew

Maps; Their Untold Stories. Rose Mitchell and Andrew Janes. St. Martin's Press 2014 256 p. color illustrations; maps $50 **912.09**
  1. Maps 2. Map drawing
  ISBN 1408189674; 9781408189672

This book by Rose Mitchell and Andrew Janes "drawn from seven centuries of maps held in the National Archives at Kew, looks at a variety of maps, from those found in 14th Century manuscripts, through early estate maps, to sea charts, maps used in military campaigns, and maps from treaties." (Publisher's note)

913 Geography of and travel in ancient world

Grant, Michael, 1954-

A **guide** to the ancient world; a dictionary of classical place names. Wilson, H.W. 1986 728p maps $105 **913**
  1. Reference books 2. Classical dictionaries 3. Mediterranean region -- Gazetteers
  ISBN 0-8242-0742-4
  LC 86-15785

"This dictionary provides background for about nine hundred places important to an understanding of the cultures of the ancient Greeks, Etruscans, and Romans. . . . The time period covered is from the first millennium B.C. until the fall of the Roman empire in the fifth century A.D. Depending on the subject, a typical entry includes information about history, geography, archaeology, and sometimes art and mythology." Am Ref Books Annu, 1987

914 Geography of and travel in Europe

Baxter, John

The **most** beautiful walk in the world; a pedestrian in Paris. Harper Perennial 2011 298p il pa $14.99 **914**
  1. Walking 2. Paris (France) -- Description and travel
  ISBN 978-0-06-199854-6; 0-06-199854-0
  LC 2010-46259

The author "knows Paris, both the modern, cosmopolitan city of today as well as the 1920s cultural mecca of expat American authors like Ernest Hemingway and F. Scott Fitzgerald. Baxter, in fact, lives in the same Paris building that once was a Jazz Age hangout for literary greats like James Joyce, Ezra Pound, Hemingway, and others. It's also the site of Sylvia Beach's famous bookstore, Shakespeare and Company. . . . [He] takes us on a tour of the city's outdoor cafes, amazing restaurants, cabarets, and gorgeous architecture; he tells us about its history and its unique passion for art. Baxter gives us a Paris that is not just a place but an idea." Boston Globe

Boswell, James

The **journal** of a tour to the Hebrides with Samuel Johnson. Kessinger Publishing 2004 277p pa $28.95 **914**
  1. Lexicographers 2. Literary critics 3. Hebrides (Scotland) -- Description
  ISBN 978-1-4191-6794-2; 1-4191-6794-4
  First published 1785

The renowned biographer here recounts the daily events of a tour which he took in 1773 with Johnson

Bryson, Bill, 1951-

Notes from a small island. Morrow 1996 324p hardcover o.p. pa $14 **914**
  1. Great Britain -- Civilization 2. Great Britain -- Description and travel
  ISBN 0-380-72750-1 pa
  LC 95-43437

"Before his return to the U.S. after a 20-year residence in England, journalist Bryson . . . embarked on a farewell tour of his adopted homeland. His trenchant, witty and detailed observations of life in a variety of towns and villages will delight Anglophiles." Publ Wkly

★ The **road** to Little Dribbling; adventures of an American in Britain. by Bill Bryson. Doubleday, an Imprint of Penguin Random House 2016 400 p. illustrations, map (hardcover) $28.95 **914**
  1. Great Britain -- Description and travel 2. Great Britain -- Civilization -- 21st century
  ISBN 9780385539289
LC 2015027450
In this book travel writer and humorist Bill Bryson revisits England after having lived there as an expatriate 20 years earlier. "Bryson rediscovers the wondrously beautiful, magnificently eccentric, endearingly singular country that he both celebrates and, when called for, twits. . . . He offers acute and perceptive insights into all that is best and worst about Britain today." (Publisher's note)

"Anglophiles will find Bryson's field notes equally entertaining and educational." Kirkus

Caro, Ina
  Paris to the past; traveling through French history by train. W.W. Norton & Co. 2011 381p map $27.95 **914**
  1. Historic sites 2. Railroads -- France 3. France -- Description and travel 4. Paris (France) -- Description and travel
  ISBN 978-0-393-07894-7; 0-393-07894-9
LC 2011-03060
"One single Paris Metro line can take you through a dazzling panoply of history: the Chateau de Vincennes, Charles V's 14th-century fortress; Francis I's Hotel de Ville; the Place de la Concorde, constructed by Louis V in the mid-18th century; the Palais-Royal, fashioned by Philippe Egalite in the late 18th century; and the 21st-century neighborhood of La Defense. Take another Metro line, Caro discovered gleefully, and you can descend to the period of the Romans, on the Ile-de-la-Cite, then arrive glamorously in the 19th century, at the Opera Garnier. Moreover, you can manage day trips to sites as far away as Tours (90 minutes by TGV) in one day, returning to Paris. In this cheerful, logical, easy-to-follow narrative (which includes favorite restaurants and hotels), Caro builds on previous trips to France and presents her timeline through history chronologically, from the 12th-century Basilica of Saint-Denis, where nearly all of the French kings and queen are buried, to the Gare d'Orsay, now fabulously converted into a museum of 19th-century art." Kirkus

Includes bibliographical references

Kerkeling, Hape
  I'm off then; my journey along the Camino de Santiago. translated from the German by Shelley Frisch. Free Press 2009 333p il pa $15 **914**
  1. Spain -- Description and travel
  ISBN 978-1-416-55387-8; 1-416-55387-8
LC 2008-51464
Original German edition, 2006

"Hape Kerkeling, a popular TV talk-show host and cabaret star in his native Germany, cuts loose from the comforts of Düsseldorf and sets off on a hike across the Pyrenees to the grave of St. James at the Cathedral of Santiago de Compostela. Searching for spiritual meaning, this self-described 'couch potato' follows a 1,000-year-old pilgrimage route that lures 100,000 trekkers each year, experiencing almost insufferable heat and physical agony in the process. . . . He skips some of the hardest stretches to hitch rides with local farmers or hop aboard trains, and he avoids fetid pilgrims' hostels whenever possible in favor of the best hotel in town (often not much better). Despite such tactics, this gregarious traveler soon gets into the spirit of things, and his encounters with fellow pilgrims, including a Peruvian shaman with a creepy fondness for 'Mein Kampf,' can be both funny and moving." N Y Times Book Rev

Macfarlane, Robert, 1976-
  The **wild** places. Penguin Books 2008 340p map pa $15 **914**
  1. Wilderness areas 2. Ireland -- Description and travel 3. Great Britain -- Description and travel
  ISBN 978-0-14-311393-5; 0-14-311393-3
LC 2008-17162
First published 2007 in the United Kingdom
"Evocative and well-written, a delight for nature and travel buffs." Kirkus
Includes bibliographical references

Mayes, Frances
  A **year** in the world; journeys of a passionate traveller. Broadway Books 2006 xx, 420p map hardcover o.p. pa $15 **914**
  1. Europe -- Description and travel
  ISBN 0-7679-1005-2; 978-0-7679-1005-7; 978-0-7679-1006-4 pa; 0-7679-1006-0 pa
LC 2005-50831
"Befitting her gifts as a poet, Mayes' prose shines with evocative imagery, bringing life to every subject she encounters across her peripatetic year." Booklist
Includes bibliographical references

McGregor, James H. S.
  Paris from the ground up. Belknap Press of Harvard University Press 2009 327p il map $29.95 **914**
  1. Paris (France) -- History 2. Paris (France) -- Description and travel
  ISBN 978-0-674-03316-0; 0-674-03316-7
LC 2008-43696
"Readers can use this as a well-researched but accessible history of Paris, tracing the story of the City of Light from its earliest residents, the Gauls and the Parisii, to the present day. Travelers will use chapters on churches, cathedrals, museums, and neighborhoods; those interested in the history of a particular area or landmark will find the index excellent. The many illustrations enhance the text, and the ten historical and contemporary maps help pinpoint attractions both ancient and modern." Libr J
Includes bibliographical references

Rumiz, Paolo

The **fault** line; traveling the other Europe, from Finland to Ukraine. Paolo Rumiz. Rizzoli Ex Libris 2015 256 p. map (alk. paper) $27.95   **914**

1. Eastern Europe 2. Europe -- Description and travel
ISBN 0847845427; 9780847845422

LC 2014944522

In this book, author Paolo Rumiz "traces the path that has twice cut Europe in two-- first by the Iron Curtain and then by the artificial scaffolding of the EU-- moving through vibrant cities and abandoned villages, some places still gloomy under the ghost of these imposing borders, some that have sought to erase all memory of it and jump with both feet into the West (if only the West would have them)." (Publisher's note)

"Exploring the border between Russia and the European Union, Rumiz realized that he was traveling "a seismic fault that's only apparently dormant" because Russia, under Putin, is becoming a renewed threat. A richly detailed journey into Europe's dark past and vulnerable present." Kirkus

Starr, William W.

Whisky, kilts, and the Loch Ness Monster; traveling through Scotland with Boswell and Johnson. University of South Carolina Press 2011 223p map $29.95   **914**

1. Authors 2. Lawyers 3. Biographers 4. Lexicographers 5. Literary critics 6. Scotland -- Description and travel
ISBN 978-1-57003-948-5

LC 2010020165

The author "is a Samuel Johnson and James Boswell fanatic. He here relates meeting Scots along his travels who drew a blank when asked about Johnson and Boswell, despite the men's whirlwind journey through Scotland in 1773. . . . Starr traces their trek in reverse via car, using their own words as guides and inspiration as he tours the great Scottish sites (and partakes in the great Scottish beverage). . . . Scottish history and travel buffs and Johnson and Boswell enthusiasts will find this fun and inspiring." Libr J

Includes bibliographical references

914.1   British Isles--geography

Macfarlane, Robert, 1976-

Landmarks; Robert Macfarlane. Penguin Group USA 2016 448 p. illustrations (paperback) $18   **914.1**

1. Great Britain 2. English language 3. English literature
ISBN 0241967872; 9780241967874; 9780241146538
Includes additional glossary.

This book, by Robert Macfarlane, shortlisted for the 2015 Samuel Johnson prize for non-fiction, "explores the linguistic and literary terrain of the British archipelago, from the Shetlands to Cornwall and from Cumbria to Suffolk, offering themed glossaries of hundreds of these rare, deeply local, poetical terms, organized by . . . geographical terrains." (Publisher's note)

Includes bibliographical references and index.

914.2   England--geography

Macfarlane, Robert, 1976-

The **old** ways; a journey on foot. Robert Macfarlane. Viking 2012 432 p.   **914.2**

1. Trails 2. Walking 3. Landscapes 4. Natural history 5. Voyages and travels 6. England -- Description and travel 7. Scotland -- Description and travel
ISBN 9780670025114

LC 2012005887

This book of nature writing by Robert Macfarlane recounts his travels on "the old ways -- the footpaths and tracks, the sea lanes and ghost roads -- that criss-cross the planet. . . . The central subject matter of 'The Old Ways' . . . is the land immediately around us, a land we too readily take for granted, and so fail to see as holy. Here the author's guides are the spirits of such former saunterers as Edward Thomas and Eric Ravilious, as well as the many nameless others who revered and cherished that land." (New Statesman)

Includes bibliographical references and index

914.3   Germany--geography

Fodor's Germany; Fodor's Travel Publications, Inc. Random House Inc 2016 896 p. (paperback) $24.99   **914.3**

1. Travel 2. Germany -- Description and travel
ISBN 110187970X; 9781101879702

LC 2016015119

This travel guidebook, published by the Fodor's Travel Publications company, "covers the best Germany has to offer. This full-color guide will help travelers plan the perfect trip, from scenic drives through quaint half-timber towns to wine tasting in the country's top wine regions." (Publisher's note)

Egert-Romanowska, Joanna

Germany; Joanna Egert-Romanowska and Malgorzata Omilanowska. DK Pub 2016 584 p. color ill., color map (paperback) $30   **914.3**

1. Germany -- Description and travel
ISBN 9781465440181; 1465440186

It "takes you by the hand, leading you straight to the best attractions [that Germany] . . . has to offer, from its beautiful castles and cathedrals to its popular beer halls, festivals, and Christmas markets to walks and hikes through the countryside." (Publisher's note)

Galicka, Izabella

Dk Eyewitness Munich & the Bavarian Alps; Izabella Galicka and Katarzyna Michalska. DK Pub 2016 336 p. color ill., color maps (paperback) $25   **914.3**

1. Munich (Germany) -- Description and travel 2. Bavaria (Germany) -- Description and travel
ISBN 9781465440198; 1465440194

LC 2001047748

This book, by Izabella Galicka and Katarzyna Michalska, part of the publisher's "Eyewitness Travel Guide" series, "is your go-to guide to this beautiful region. Discover the best that Munich and the Bavarian Alps have to offer, from local festivals and markets to all the must-see sights. Experience Oktoberfest, ski down the Alps, and tour Neuschwanstein Castle." (Publisher's note)

914.4 France--geography

Baxter, John, 1939-

Five nights in Paris; after dark in the City of Light. John Baxter. William Morrow 2015 352 p. illustrations (paperback) $14.99   **914.4**
1. Autobiographies 2. Paris (France) -- Description and travel 3. Paris (France) -- Tours 4. Paris (France) -- Intellectual life 5. Walking -- France -- Paris -- Guidebooks 6. Paris (France) -- Social life and customs 7. Nightlife -- France -- Paris -- Guidebooks 8. Neighborhoods -- France -- Paris -- Guidebooks
ISBN 0062296256; 9780062296252

LC 2015000100

This memoir by John Baxter "takes [readers] on a nocturnal stroll through five iconic Parisian neighborhoods and his own memories. As he takes you through five of the city's greatest neighborhoods-- Montmartre, Montparnasse, the Marais, and more-- Baxter shares pithy anecdotes about his life in France, as well as fascinating knowledge he has gleaned from leading literary tours of the city by dark." (Publisher's note)

"In closing, Baxter writes, "each of us must, in our own way, as with a new lover, seduce, or allow ourselves to be seduced by the Paris night." This is not a walking guide to Paris, but it is most certainly a guide to seeing and knowing Paris, one no Francophile should be without." Kirkus

France; edited by Rosemary Bailey. DK Pub 2016 672 p. illustrations (paperback) $30   **914.4**
1. France -- Description and travel
ISBN 9781465440174; 1465440178

This book, printed by Dorling Kindersley, edited by Rosemary Bailey, is part of the publisher's "Eyewitness Travel Guides" series. It presents "the best attractions . . . [that France] has to offer. Discover France region-by-region, from Champagne in the north to the sun-blessed corner of Provence and the Côte d'Azur. Stand in awe of the châteaux of the Loire, lie on the beautiful beaches of Corsica, and climb to the top of the Eiffel Tower." (Publisher's note)

Wells, Patricia

The **Food** Lover's Guide to Paris; The Best Restaurants, Bistros, Cafés, Markets, Bakeries, and More. by Patricia Wells; with Emily Buchanan; assisted by Susan Herrmann Loomis; photographs by Gianluca Tamorri. Workman Pub Co 2014 454 p. illustrations $16.95   **914.4**
1. Restaurants 2. French cooking 3. Paris (France) -- Description and travel
ISBN 0761173382; 9780761173380

LC 2014003074

This book, by Patricia Wells, "offers an elegantly written go-to guide to the very best restaurants, cafés, wine bars, and bistros in Paris, as well as where to find the flakiest crois-

sants, earthiest charcuteries, sublimest cheese, most ethereal macarons, and impeccable outdoor markets. . . . Included are 40 recipes from some of her favorite chefs and purveyors and . . .all the practical information: addresses, websites, email, hours, closest métro stop, specialties, and more." (Publisher's note)

"The short and to the point but completely enticing entries are sprinkled with the author's experiences and preferences." LJ

Includes bibliographical references (pages 427-436) and index

914.504 Italy--travel

The **rough** guide to Italy; edited by Amanda Tomlin and Claire Saunders. Rough Guides 2016 1038 p. (paperback) $26.99   **914.504**
1. Travel 2. Italy -- Description and travel
ISBN 0241216222; 9780241216224

LC 2006204291

This book, edited by Amanda Tomlin and Claire Saunders, part of the publisher's "Rough Guides" series, offers a "travel guide to [Rome, Italy.] . . . From the top draws of Rome and Florence to the hidden corners of Friuli and Liguria, this guide will help you make the most of your trip to Italy. You will find all the detailed information you need, from vaporetto routes in Venice to hole-in-the-wall pizza joints in Naples to the best spot to watch the sunset on the Amalfi Coast." (Publisher's note)

914.6 Spain--geography

Dk Eyewitness Back Roads Spain; edited by Anna Ghose. DK Pub 2016 264 p. color ill., color maps (paperback) $25   **914.6**
1. Spain -- Description and travel
ISBN 9781465440433; 1465440437

This book, printed by Dorling Kindersley, edited by Anna Ghose, is part of the publisher's "Eyewitness Travel Back Roads" series. It presents "scenic routes to discover charming villages, local restaurants, and intimate places to stay [in Spain]. Twenty-five themed drives, each lasting one to seven days, reveal breathtaking views, hidden gems, and authentic local experiences that can only be discovered by road." (Publisher's note)

914.7 Russia--geography

Eichar, Donnie

Dead Mountain; the true story of the Dyatlov Pass incident. by Donnie Eichar. Chronicle Books 2013 288 p. illustrations, map (hardback) $24.95 **914.7**
1. Mountaineering 2. Mysterious deaths 3. Hiking -- Russia (Federation) -- Ural Mountains Region 4. Ural Mountains Region (Russia) -- History -- 20th century 5. Mountaineering accidents -- Russia (Federation) -- Ural

Mountains Region -- 20th century
ISBN 1452112746; 9781452112749

LC 2013014843

This book, by Donnie Eichar, focuses on how "in February 1959, a group of nine experienced hikers in the Russian Ural Mountains died mysteriously on an elevation known as Dead Mountain. Eerie aspects of the incident--unexplained violent injuries, signs that they cut open and fled the tent without proper clothing or shoes, a strange final photograph taken by one of the hikers, and elevated levels of radiation found on some of their clothes--have led to decades of speculation over what really happened." (Publisher's note)

"Eichar marries the short story of the students' lives with the procedural tale of the official investigation and then integrates his own amateur investigation. . . . [A] well-told and accurate whodunit." Kirkus

Greene, David

Midnight in Siberia; A Journey into the Heart of Russia. David Greene. W W Norton & Co Inc 2014 320 p. illustrations, map $26.95   **914.7**
1. Russia 2. Social change 3. Railroad travel 4. Russia (Federation) -- Biography 5. Interviews -- Russia (Federation) 6. Social change -- Russia (Federation) 7. Railroad travel -- Russia (Federation) 8. Social problems -- Russia (Federation) 9. Russia (Federation) -- Social conditions 10. Russia (Federation) -- Description and travel 11. Russia (Federation) -- Social life and customs 12. Velikaia Sibirskaia magistral
ISBN 0393239950; 9780393239959

LC 2014029382

This book "chronicles David Greene's journey on the Trans-Siberian Railway, a 6,000-mile cross-country trip from Moscow to the Pacific port of Vladivostok. In quadruple-bunked cabins and stopover towns sprinkled across the country's snowy landscape, Greene speaks with ordinary Russians about how their lives have changed in the post-Soviet years." (Publisher's note)

"With abundant interpersonal detail, Greene delivers a lively, tangible feeling of meeting modern Russians on one of the world's famous railroads." Booklist

914.94 Switzerland -- geography

Bewes, DicconSlow

Train to Switzerland; One Tour, Two Trips, 150 Years-and a World of Change Apart. by Diccon Bewes. Nicholas Brealey Publishing 2014 320 p. il-lustrations, map, portraits (hardcover) $29.95   **914.94**
1. Locomotives 2. Switzerland -- Description and travel
ISBN 9781857886092; 9781857886252; 1857886097

LC 2015451055

This book, by Diccon Bewes, describes train travel throughout Europe. It "follows Thomas Cook's groundbreaking tour from England to the Swiss Alps. Bewes uses traveler Jemima Morell's diary from 1863 to retrace the trip and explore the revolutionary affect the journey had on both Britain and Switzerland." (Publisher's note)

"Covering the development of tourism, rail travel, and hospitality, this account informs while providing an entertaining read for lovers of history and travel." LJ

915   Geography of and travel in Asia

Belliveau, Denis

In the footsteps of Marco Polo; [by] Denis Belliveau and Francis O'Donnell. Rowman & Littlefield Publishers 2008 280p il map $29.95   **915**
1. Travelers 2. Travel writers 3. Asia -- Description and travel
ISBN 978-0-7425-5683-6; 0-7425-5683-2

LC 2008-23411

"The stunning photographs in this elegant book should please even the most casual reader, while the authors' unpretentious observations will satisfy those who want to know more about a still alien world. A travel/adventure book rather than a study of Marco Polo the man or a history of his travels, this volume deserves many readers. Warmly recommended." Libr J

Includes bibliographical references

Elliot, Jason

Mirrors of the unseen; journeys in Iran. St. Martin's Press 2006 415p il $26.95   **915**
1. Iran -- Description and travel
ISBN 978-0-312-30191-0; 0-312-30191-X

LC 2006-42918

The author discusses his travels in Iran.

"With Iran so central in the news, this is a good read for the armchair traveler and amateur geopolitical strategist alike." Publ Wkly

Feiler, Bruce S.

Walking the Bible; a journey by land through the five books of Moses. by Bruce Feiler. Morrow 2001 451p $26; pa $14.95   **915**
1. Middle East -- Description 2. Bible -- O.T. -- Pentateuch -- Geography
ISBN 0-380-97775-3; 0-380-80731-9 pa

LC 00-56076

"Determined to connect more deeply with his religious roots, Feiler joined an archaeologist in a trek through the Middle East, visiting the sites mentioned in the Pentateuch, the first five books of the Hebrew Bible. A book full of wonder and awe and personal enlightenment." Booklist

Includes bibliographical references

Gargan, Edward A.

A **river's** tale; a year on the Mekong. Knopf 2002 332p il maps hardcover o.p. pa $14.95   **915**
1. Southeast Asia -- Description and travel
ISBN 0-375-70559-7 pa

LC 2001-38056

"A chronicle of a year-long journey along the nearly 3,000 miles of the Mekong River as it descends from the Tibetan plateau through southern Asia, Gargan's book is a vivid look at the disparate peoples [that] settled the length of the river's path." Publ Wkly

Includes bibliographical references

Grange, Kevin

Beneath blossom rain; discovering Bhutan on the toughest trek in the world. University of Nebraska Press 2011 336p il map (Outdoor lives) pa $19.95 **915**

1. Mountaineering 2. Bhutan -- Description and travel
ISBN 978-0-8032-3433-8; 0-8032-3433-3

LC 2010-28970

"For the armchair traveler, Grange does a fine job of showing readers the nature, history, and landscape of Bhutan, as well as taking us to remote villages and monasteries. . . He is equally open about what is essentially a personal search for meaning." Seattle Post-Intelligencer

Includes bibliographical references.

Horwitz, Tony

Baghdad without a map, and other misadventures in Arabia. Dutton 1991 276p map hardcover o.p. pa $16 **915**

1. Middle East -- Description and travel
ISBN 0-452-26745-5 pa

LC 90-46653

"Horwitz mixes insight and humor in these observations that illustrate on an everyday level both the contradictions and the idiosyncrasies of the Arab world." Booklist

Jubber, Nicholas

Drinking arak off an ayatollah's beard; a journey through the inside-out worlds of Iran and Afghanistan. Da Capo Press 2010 327p il map pa $15.95 **915**

1. Shahnameh (Epic poem) 2. Iran -- Social conditions 3. Iran -- Description and travel 4. Afghanistan -- Social conditions 5. Afghanistan -- Description and travel
ISBN 978-0-306-81884-4

LC 2009-48191

"Jubber's account offers a full and satisfying panorama of the region with its rich paradoxes and complexities intact." Publ Wkly

Includes bibliographical references

MacLean, Rory

Magic bus; on the hippie trail from Istanbul to India. Ig Pub. 2009 280p pa $14.95 **915**

1. Hippies 2. India -- Description and travel 3. Middle East -- Description and travel 4. Central Asia -- Description and travel
ISBN 978-0-9788431-9-9; 0-9788431-9-3

LC 2008-45918

First published 2006 in the United Kingdom

"For a certain breed of independent travelers in the 1960s and '70s, Asia was the Promised Land. For nearly 20 years during those iconic decades, flower children, beat philosophers, and Western wanderers took to the road for the roughly 6,000-mile journey from Turkey to India. Hundreds of thousands may have made the trek, though no one has an exact count. For years after, the trip was nearly impossible to make through this war-torn area — especially for Westerners. So after parts of the trail reopened in 2002, UK-based Canadian travel writer Rory MacLean set his sights east. . . . He recounts his eight-month journey along this epic route. The book strings together a series of vignettes from his trip that en masse form a well-rounded and insightful look into the region." Boston Globe

Man, John

Marco Polo; The Journey That Changed the World. John Man. HarperCollins 2014 400 p. 16 plates; ills.; maps; plans $15.99 **915**

1. Exploration
ISBN 0062375075; 9780062375070

Author John Man presents the "story of the world's most famous traveler, retracing his legendary journey from Venice to China, the moment East first met West. Man traveled in Marco Polo's footsteps to Xanadu then on to Beijing and through modern China in search of the history behind the legend. [He] draws on his own journey, new archaeological findings, and deep archival study to paint a vivid picture of Marco Polo and the great court of Kublai Khan." (Publisher's note)

Morris-Suzuki, Tessa

To the Diamond Mountains; a hundred-year journey through China and Korea. Rowman & Littlefield Publishers 2010 201p il map $34.95 **915**

1. Artists 2. Authors 3. Adventurers 4. China -- Description and travel 5. China -- Social life and customs 6. Korea (North) -- Description and travel 7. Korea (South) -- Description and travel 8. Korea (North) -- Social life and customs 9. Korea (South) -- Social life and customs
ISBN 978-1-4422-0503-1; 978-1-4422-0505-5 ebook

LC 2010023685

"Morris-Suzuki, an Australian professor, recently traveled through northeast China and the two Koreas; she was retracing the route of Emily Kemp, an extraordinary writer, artist, and intrepid adventurer who wrote about her experiences a century ago. Morris-Suzuki, like her predecessor, is a keen observer and a fine writer; she has combined the disciplines of history and travel writing in an absorbing analysis of the past, present, and future of this volatile region." Booklist

Includes bibliographical references

Polo, Marco, 1254-1323?

The **travels** of Marco Polo; the illustrated edition. Marco Polo, edited by Morris Rossabi, translated by Henry Yule. Sterling Signature 2012 377 p. $40 **915**

1. Exploration 2. Mongols -- Hsitory 3. Voyages and travels 4. Asia -- Description and travel -- Early works to 1800
ISBN 1402796307; 9781402796302

LC 2011051047

This book, written by Marco Polo and edited by Morris Rossabi, "offers the complete text of Polo's travelogue, enhanced with more than 200 images--including illuminated manuscripts, paintings, photographs, and maps. Sidebars and dozens of informative footnotes combine to present Polo and his travels." (Publisher's note)

Rose, Daniel Asa

Larry's kidney; being the true story of how I found myself in China with my black sheep cousin and his mail-order bride, skirting the law to get him

a transplant and save his life. William Morrow 2009
305p $25.99 **915**
1. Kidneys 2. Transplantation of organs, tissues, etc. 3.
China -- Description and travel
ISBN 978-0-06-170870-1

LC 2009-517312

"A satisfying, hysterical page-turner, this will captivate
fans of travel writing and family narratives, with special interest for anyone who's helped a love one through serious
illness." Publ Wkly

Theroux, Paul

The **great** railway bazaar; by train through Asia.
Houghton Mifflin 1975 342p hardcover o.p. pa
$14.95 **915**
1. Railroads -- Asia 2. Asia -- Description and travel
ISBN 0-618-65894-7 pa

The author "took a four-month solitary lecture tour of
Asia in 1973, traveling by train wherever possible. His route
was through Turkey, Iran, India, Southeast Asia, Japan, and
back to London via the Soviet Union. He writes of conversations and impressions of the people encountered." Libr J

Riding the iron rooster; by train through China.
Paul Theroux. 1st Mariner Books ed.; Houghton
Mifflin 2006 480p map pa $7.50 **915**
1. Railroads 2. China -- Description and travel
ISBN 978-0-6186-5897-8

LC 2006028745

First published 1988 by Putnam's

This is an account of the author's yearlong rail journey
through China. "For Theroux, traveling is both about people—their thoughts, customs, and peculiarities-and a form
of autobiography, and here we learn as much about his own
quirks and fancies as we do about the intriguing world of
contemporary China." Libr J

Thubron, Colin

To a mountain in Tibet. Harper 2011 227p map
$24.99; ebook $19.99 **915**
1. Tibet (China) -- Description and travel
ISBN 978-0-06-176826-2; 978-0-06-206605-3 ebook

LC 2010-43013

"Emotional subtlety and vivid evocations of the people
and places are only part of what makes the book so enjoyable. The present-tense narration allows readers make discoveries alongside Thubron, which adds immeasurably to
the intimacy and immediacy of the reading experience. A
powerful and hauntingly elegiac hybrid of travelogue and
memoir." Kirkus

Winchester, Simon

The **river** at the center of the world; a journey
up the Yangtze and back in Chinese time. Holt & Co.
1996 xx, 410p maps hardcover o.p. **915**
1. Yangtze River valley (China)

LC 96-12399

In 1994, the author followed the Yangtze's "course from
the East China Sea to Tibet by boat, car, train, plane, bus and
foot; but this is more than an ordinary account of a traveler's
pilgrimage, although it is a must for any visitor to China.
Wryly humorous, gently skeptical, immensely knowledge-

able as he wends his way along the 3900 miles of the great
river, Winchester provides an irresistible feast of detail about
the character of the river itself, the landscape, the cities, villages and people along its banks." Publ Wkly
Includes bibliographical references

915.6 Middle East--geography

Taseer, Aatish

★ **Stranger** to history; a son's journey through
Islamic lands. by Aatish Taseer. Canongate 2009
323 p. ill., map $16 **915.6**
1. Islam 2. Islamic civilization 3. Middle East --
Description and travel 4. Fathers and sons 5. Islam
-- Middle East
ISBN 155597628X; 1847670717; 9781555976286;
9781847670717

LC 2009483559

This book, by Aatish Taseer, "is the story of the journey
[which the author] made to try to understand what it means
to be Muslim in the twenty-first century. Starting from Istanbul, Islam's once greatest city, he travels to Mecca, its most
holy, and then home through Iran and Pakistan. Ending in
Lahore, at his estranged father's home, on the night Benazir Bhutto was killed, it is also the story of Taseer's divided
family over the past fifty years." (Publisher's note)

915.9 Southeast Asia--geography

DK Eyewitness Travel Cambodia & Laos. DK Publishing 2016 288 p. col. ill., col. maps $25 **915.9**
1. Cambodia 2. Laos -- Description and travel
ISBN 1465440062; 9781465440068

LC 2011205904

This travel guide from DK Publishing explains how
"whether you want to explore the temples of Angkor Wat,
take a boat trip through the famous Tham Kong Lo caves, or
sunbathe on stunning white beaches in southern Cambodia,
Cambodia and Laos offer exhilarating options for visitors."
(Publisher's note)

"For readers who intend to go to Cambodia and/or Laos,
this guide provides a nice snapshot of the countries' look,
history, and culture with some specifics for planning purposes and a compact size for portability." LJ

Eyewitness Travel Malaysia & Singapore; edited by
Aruna Ghose. DK Publishing 2016 356 p. col.
ill., col. maps (paperback) $25 **915.9**
1. Malaysia -- Description and travel 2. Singapore --
Description and travel
ISBN 1465440054; 9781465440051

This book, edited by Aruna Ghose and the staff of Dorling Kindersley Eyewitness Travel, presents a travel guide
for Malaysia and Singapore. "Whether you want to discover
the best places to spot colorful fish and jungle-dwelling animals like orangutans, or are looking to sample the incredible
food in the ultra-modern metropolises of Kuala Lumpur and
Singapore, this region offers an astounding range of experiences." (Publisher's note)

"This inclusive photographic treat will make even 'stay at home' travelers feel like they are actually there." LJ

Houton, Jody

A **geek** in Thailand; discovering the land of golden buddhas, pad thai and kickboxing. Jody Houton. Tuttle Publishing 2016 160 p. illustrations (chiefly color) (pbk.) $18.95 **915.9**

1. Asia -- Description and travel 2. Thailand -- Social life and customs
ISBN 0804844488; 9780804844482
LC 2015949992

This book, by Jody Houton, "offers a concise but insightful take on Thailand for tourists, expats, would-be expats, and others--anyone, in fact, with an interest in visiting or learning about the Land of Smiles. Subjects range from the touchstones of Thai culture and history, such as its politics and economy, Buddhism and folklore, to chapters on traditional Thai design and craftsmanship, including its highly acclaimed architecture and fine silk textiles." (Publisher's note)

"Warning: after reading this alluring book, you will have to travel to Thailand." Library Journal

916   Geography of and travel in Africa

Benanav, Michael

Men of salt; across the Sahara with the caravan of white gold. Lyons Press 2006 220p il map $23.95 **916**

1. Salt 2. Sahara Desert -- Description and travel
ISBN 1-59228-772-7; 978-1-59228-772-7
LC 2005-23205

"Even if readers don't find the idea of spending 40 harrowing days with a caravan crossing some of the world's most unforgiving desert as enticing as Benanav does, that doesn't mean they won't quickly devour his thrilling account of that otherworldly journey." Publ Wkly

Includes bibliographical references

Butcher, Tim

Chasing the Devil; a journey through sub-Saharan Africa in the footsteps of Graham Greene. Atlas & Co. 2011 325p il map $26.95 **916**

1. Authors 2. Novelists 3. Essayists 4. Travel writers 5. Short story writers 6. Motion picture critics 7. Liberia -- Description and travel 8. Sierra Leone -- Description and travel
ISBN 978-1-935633-29-7; 1-935633-29-5
First published 2010 in the United Kingdom

"Butcher used Graham Greene's little-known 1935 travel book, Journey Without Maps, as his guide on the 350-mile trek from Freetown, on the coast of Sierra Leone, to the coast of Liberia." Publ Wkly

Includes bibliographical references

Campbell, James T.

Middle passages; African American journeys to Africa, 1787-2005. [by] James Campbell. Penguin Press 2006 513p il (The Penguin history of American life) $29.95 **916**

1. Africa -- Description and travel
ISBN 1-59420-083-1; 978-1-59420-083-0
LC 2005-58672

"From the repatriation of former slaves in the early years of the United States to the recent heritage tourism featuring Goree Island and other slave-trading sites, Campbell provides an artful reconstruction of the often bittersweet experience of return and reunion." N Y Times Book Rev

Grant, Richard

Crazy river; a journey to the source of the Nile. Free Press 2011 336p pa $15; ebook $9.99 **916**

1. Explorers 2. Travel writers 3. Asian studies specialists 4. Tanzania -- Social conditions 5. East Africa -- Social conditions 6. Middle Eastern studies specialists 7. Tanzania -- Description and travel 8. East Africa -- Description and travel
ISBN 978-1-4391-5414-4 pa; 978-1-4391-5764-0 ebook
LC 2011012168

"The Malagarasi River in Tanzania had not been fully traveled by either Westerners or Africans. So, the tradition of 19th-century British explorers, first and foremost Richard Burton, who became his spectral travel companion, Grant set out to do so. But his adventures on the river—disease and disappointment, danger from crocs, hippos and bandits—became but part of his larger story about what Africa is and how to make sense of it. . . . Dyspeptic, disturbing and brilliantly realized, Grant's account of Africa is literally unforgettable." Kirkus

Langewiesche, William

Sahara unveiled; a journey across the desert. Pantheon Bks. 1996 301p il hardcover o.p. pa $14 **916**

1. Sahara Desert
ISBN 0-679-75006-1 pa
LC 95-48864

"Besides evoking the Sahara's power, majesty, emptiness, heat, beauty and terrors and describing its ecology and meteorology, Langewiesche adds details that may astonish armchair travelers who still think of the desert as populated by camels and Bedouins. . . . He is knowledgeable about the imprint of French colonialism on North African economy and politics, and about Muslim beliefs in practice. Throughout this vivid account, he scatters many charming native folktales." Publ Wkly

Matthiessen, Peter

African silences. Random House 1991 225p maps hardcover o.p. pa $13 **916**

1. Africa -- Description 2. Natural history -- Africa
ISBN 0-679-73102-4 pa
LC 90-52893

"In this account of three trips to Central and Western Africa, Matthiessen reports on the almost total devastation of wildlife in Senegal, Gambia, and the Ivory Coast and describes an expedition searching for the rare Congo peacock and gorillas in the Virunga Mountains of Zaire." Libr J

Tayler, Jeffrey

Angry wind; through Muslim Black Africa by truck, bus, boat, and camel. Houghton Mifflin 2005 252p map $25   **916**
1. Sahel -- Description and travel
ISBN 0-618-33467-X

LC 2004-54066

"This substantial and informative work is no mere travel tale—it is a firsthand account of the author's deeply personal quest for knowledge and understanding of a people and a region that continues to struggle with extreme poverty and unrest." Libr J

Theroux, Paul

Dark star safari; overland from Cairo to Cape Town. Houghton Mifflin 2003 472p maps $28 **916**
1. Africa -- Description and travel
ISBN 0-618-13424-7

LC 2002-32710

First published 2002 in the United Kingdom
"Where Theroux sees Africa uncluttered by preconceived notions, his writing can be brilliant. . . . But where Theroux has traveled before—40 years ago, as first a Peace Corps teacher, then a lecturer at Uganda's Makerere University in the golden years just after the country's independence—he sees Africa not for what it is, but for what it might have been." Christ Sci Monit

★ **Last** train to Zona Verde; my ultimate African safari. Paul Theroux. Houghton Mifflin Harcourt 2013 368 p. $27   **916**
1. Angola -- Description and travel 2. South Africa -- Description and travel 3. Namibia -- Description and travel
ISBN 061883933X; 9780618839339

LC 2013000388

In this book, by Paul Theroux, the author "sets out on a new journey through the continent he knows and loves best. Theroux first came to Africa as a twenty-two-year-old Peace Corps volunteer. . . . Now he returns, after fifty years on the road, to explore the little-traveled territory of western Africa and to take stock both of the place and of himself." (Publisher's note)

"The acclaimed travel writer and novelist chronicles his journey through Africa as tourist, adventure-seeker, thinker and hopeful critic... Reading this enlightening book won't only open a window into Theroux's mind, it will also impart a deeper understanding of Africa and travel in general." Kirkus

916.2   Egypt--geography

Wood, Levison

Walking the Nile; by Levison Wood. Atlantic Monthly Press 2016 352 p. color ill., map, portraits $26   **916.2**
1. Nile River -- Description and travel
ISBN 0802124496; 9780802124494

This book, by Levison Wood, "is a captivating account of a remarkable and unparalleled Nile journey. Starting in November 2013 in a forest in Rwanda, . . . Wood set forth

on foot, aiming to become the first person to walk the entire length of the fabled river. He followed the Nile for nine months, over 4,000 miles, through six nations—Rwanda, Tanzania, Uganda, South Sudan, the Republic of Sudan, and Egypt—to the Mediterranean coast." (Publisher's note)

Armchair travelers and those looking for a side of Africa not generally seen will find adventure sprinkled with culture and history in this narrative that circumvents the colonial pomp while following in the shadow of the original British explorers of Africa.

Includes index (p. [328] - 338).

917   Geography of and travel in North America

Ambrose, Stephen E., 1936-2002

★ **Undaunted** courage; Meriwether Lewis, Thomas Jefferson, and the opening of the American West. Simon & Schuster 1996 511p il maps $30; pa $17   **917**
1. Explorers 2. Lewis and Clark Expedition (1804-1806) 3. Biography, Individual 4. Territorial governors 5. West (U.S.) -- Exploration
ISBN 0-684-81107-3; 0-684-82697-6 pa

LC 95-37146

This is a "portrait of Meriwether Lewis, the co-leader with William Clark of the . . . {1804-1806} expedition across the North American continent." (America) Bibliography. Index.

This treatment of the Lewis and Clark Expedition "is essentially a biography of Lewis, although the bulk of it is a lively retelling of the journey of the two captains—together with their party of soldiers and frontiersmen, Clark's black slave, York, and the legendary Shoshone Indian woman, Sacagawea, and her infant son—conveyed with passionate enthusiasm by Mr. Ambrose and sprinkled liberally with some of the most famous and vivid passages from the travelers' journals." N Y Times Book Rev

Includes bibliographical references

Beatty, Michael A.

County name origins of the United States. McFarland & Co. 2001 665p $195   **917**
1. United States -- Local history 2. Geographic names -- United States
ISBN 0-7864-1025-6

LC 2001-18034

Arranged alphabetically by state, this study shows "how each county in the United States was named. Dates and circumstances under which counties were named or renamed are provided, including brief biographical, geographical, and other relevant historical information. In cases where name derivations are unknown or disputed, an informed discussion gives probable origins." Libr J

Includes bibliographical references

Bryson, Bill, 1951-

A **walk** in the woods; rediscovering America on the Appalachian Trail. Broadway Bks. 1998 276p hardcover o.p. pa $14.95 **917**

1. Appalachian region -- Description and travel

ISBN 0-7679-0251-3; 0-7679-0252-1 pa

LC 97-32627

"Bryson's breezy, self-mocking tone may turn off readers who hanker for another 'Into Thin Air' or 'Seven Years in Tibet.' Others, however, may find themselves turning the pages with increasing amusement and anticipation as they discover that they're in the hands of a satirist of the first rank, one who writes (and walks) with Chaucerian brio." N Y Times Book Rev

Includes bibliographical references

The **Columbia** gazetteer of North America; edited by Saul B. Cohen. Columbia Univ. Press 2000 1157p il $156 **917**

1. North America -- Gazetteers

ISBN 0-231-11990-9

LC 00-27512

"This work includes more than 50,000 entries covering every incorporated place and country in the United States, along with many unincorporated places and physical features throughout North America. Arranged alphabetically, each entry includes a pronunciation guide, location information, and longitude and latitude where appropriate. If the listing is a municipality, brief population figures are provided as well. . . . Color maps of the physical regions of North America, along with political maps of the region, are included as reference points." Am Ref Books Annu, 2001

Cronkite, Walter, 1916-2009

Around America; a tour of our magnificent coastline. drawings by David Canright. Norton 2001 211p il maps $23.95; pa $13.95 **917**

1. United States -- Local history 2. United States -- Description and travel

ISBN 0-393-04083-6; 0-393-32335-8 pa

LC 00-69563

In this "rumination on the people and places along America's seashores, Cronkite shows his reverence for the country's coastal means of travel. Starting in the Northeast, working south, then circling around to the West Coast, the book reads like a lively but laid-back cruise." Publ Wkly

Duncan, Dayton

Lewis & Clark; the journey of the Corps of Discovery. based on a documentary film by Ken Burns, written by Dayton Duncan; with a preface by Ken Burns and conributions by Stephen E. Ambrose, Erica Funkhouser, William Least Heat-Moon. Knopf 1997 248p il maps $45 **917**

1. Lewis and Clark Expedition (1804-1806) 2. West (U.S.) -- Exploration

ISBN 0-679-45450-0

LC 97-73823

This is a companion volume to PBS television film "Lewis and Clark: The journey of the Corps of Discovery," by Ken Burns.

An "attractive book with a well-written text and an excellent presentation of historic paintings, photographs, maps, and original quotations from various of Lewis and Clark's journals." Sci Books Films

Ferris, Gary W.

Presidential places; a guide to the historic sites of U.S. presidents. [by] Gary Ferris. Blair 1999 284p il pa $15.95 **917**

1. Historic sites 2. Presidents -- United States -- Homes 3. United States -- Description and travel

ISBN 0-89587-176-9

LC 98-50395

This is a "guide to historic places of interest relating to all the American presidents. Included are, among other things, presidential birthplaces, where they lived, where they went to school, the churches they attended, where they are buried, and the monuments, museums, and libraries dedicated to their lives and administrations." Libr J

Includes bibliographical references

Fletcher, Colin

The **man** who walked through time. Vintage Bks. 1989 247p il pa $14.95 **917**

1. Grand Canyon (Ariz.)

ISBN 0-679-72306-4; 978-0-679-72306-6

LC 72-4082

First published 1967 by Knopf

An account of the author's journey on foot through the Grand Canyon National Park.

Frazier, Ian

Great Plains. Farrar, Straus & Giroux 1989 290p il maps hardcover o.p. pa $13 **917**

1. West (U.S.) -- Description 2. Great Plains -- Description 3. West (U.S.) -- Social life and customs 4. Great Plains -- Social life and customs

ISBN 0-312-27850-0 pa

LC 88-31106

The author recounts his experiences and observations traveling in the Western United States.

"This is a colorful and engaging blend of travelogue, local color, geography and folklore." Publ Wkly

Gimlette, John

Theatre of fish; travels through Newfoundland and Labrador. Alfred A. Knopf 2005 xxii, 360p il map $25 **917**

1. Atlantic Coast (North America)

ISBN 1-4000-4322-0

LC 2005-44149

"Readers will be fascinated by Newfoundland's and Labrador's bizarre, often tragic pasts and equally strange presents, and they will be glad it was the eloquent Gimlette who made the trip so they don't have to." Publ Wkly

Includes bibliographical references

Heat Moon, William Least

Blue highways; a journey into America. photographs by the author; with a new afterword by the

author. Back Bay Bks. 1999 429p il $29.95; pa
$14.95 **917**
1. United States -- Description and travel
ISBN 0-316-35391-4; 0-316-35329-9 pa
LC 00-265444
A reissue of the title first published 1982 by Little, Brown
An account of the author's journey across the U.S. in a
van taking only secondary roads

Roads to Quoz; an American mosey. Little,
Brown and Co. 2008 581p il map $27.99 **917**
1. United States -- Description and travel
ISBN 978-0-316-11025-9; 0-316-11025-6
LC 2008-19375
The author's "journey is as meandering as the Ouachita
itself, and readers will relish the experiences he and . . . [his
wife] describe along their trip." Libr J

Home ground; language for an American landscape.
Barry Lopez, editor; Debra Gwartney, managing
editor. Trinity University Press 2006 xxiv, 449p
il $29.95 **917**
1. Reference books 2. Americanisms -- Encyclopedias
3. Geographic names -- Encyclopedias
ISBN 978-1-59534-024-5; 1-59534-024-6
LC 2006-19942
This is a "collection of geographical terms from every
region of the United States. The 45 contributors, among
them Jon Krakauer and Barbara Kingsolver, chose words
that Americans use to describe landscape features where
they live, then enriched their definitions with literary quotes,
comments, irony, and humor. The result is a readable A-to-Z
geological and geographical dictionary that surpasses other
dictionaries in both scope and coverage." Libr J
Includes bibliographical references

Jenkins, Peter
A **walk** across America. Morrow 1979 288p il
maps hardcover o.p. pa $6.99 **917**
1. United States -- Description and travel
ISBN 0-06-095955-X pa
LC 78-10320
This book chronicles the author's journey with his dog
from New York to the Gulf of Mexico

Krakauer, Jon, 1954-
Into the wild; Jon Krakauer. Villard Bks. 1996
xi, 207 p.p maps hardcover o.p. (pbk.) $12.95;
(hbk.) $26 **917**
1. Alaska -- Description and travel 2. Alaska --
Biography 3. Biography, Individual 4. West (U.S.)
-- Biography
ISBN 0385486804; 067942850X; 9780679428503
LC 95020008
This book, by Jon Krakauer, is the "story of a young man
on a quest for knowledge and experience. . . . Chris Mc-
Candless loved the road, the unadorned life, the Tolstoyan
call to asceticism. After graduating college, he took off on
another of his long destinationless journeys, this time cut-
ting all contact with his family and changing his name to
Alex Supertramp. . . . Ultimately, in 1992, his terms got him

into mortal trouble when he ran up against something--the
Alaskan wild." (Kirkus Reviews)

McMurtry, Larry
Roads; driving America's great highways. Simon
& Schuster 2000 206p hardcover o.p. pa $13 **917**
1. Roads 2. United States -- Description and travel
ISBN 0-684-86885-7 pa
LC 00-27889
In this volume McMurtry provides "reminiscence and
commentary on whatever pops up in the windows or in his
mind as he crisscrosses the country: enigmatic glances at the
Western past, salutes to hundreds of literary and historical
figures." N Y Times Book Rev

National Geographic Society (U.S.)
★ **National** Geographic guide to the national
parks of the United States; [project manger, Caroline
Hickey] 8th ed. National Geographic 2016 480p il
pa $28 **917**
1. National parks and reserves -- United States
ISBN 9781426216510
Updated periodically
This guide provides information on each of the fifty-
eight national parks, including things to do, campgrounds
and accommodations, and facilities for the disabled.
"You can't do better than this guide. . . . Highly detailed
and beautiful, this one is a must for all collections." Libr J

The **official** guide to America's national parks; editor: Molly Moker. 13th ed; Fodors Travel Pub.
2009 xxxix, 488p il map pa $18.95 **917**
1. National parks and reserves -- United States
ISBN 978-1-4000-1628-0
First published 1979 with title: The complete guide
to America's national parks. Periodically revised.
Publisher varies
This park visitors' guide also covers national monuments, military parks, seashores and lakeshores, historic
sites, and battlefields. Entries are listed by State, and include
contact information, activities and facilities, travel directories, and nearby attractions and points of interest.
Includes bibliographical references

Sandoval-Strausz, A. K.
★ **Hotel**; an American history. Yale University
Press 2007 375p il map $37.50 **917**
1. Hotels and motels
ISBN 978-0-300-10616-9; 0-300-10616-5
LC 2007-10239
The author "develops social, moral, economic, legal and
political connections with originality and insight. His impas-
sioned reading of our 'built environment' is fascinating, his
research prodigious. And the subject merits his talent as a
historian." N Y Times Book Rev
Includes bibliographical references

Stone, Nathaniel
On the water; discovering America in a rowboat.
illustrations by Elizabeth Stone. Broadway Bks.
2002 323p il $21.95; pa $12.95 **917**
1. Boats and boating 2. United States -- Description

and travel

ISBN 0-7679-0841-4; 0-7679-0842-2 pa

LC 2002-18489

"Pushing off from New York City's Hudson River, {the author} rowed to the Erie Canal, down to Ohio, onward to the Mississippi, across the Gulf to Key West, and back up along the coastline of the Atlantic to Maine. It was a 6,000-mile journey, and it took him 10 months to complete. This is the chronicle of his adventure, his voyage into and around America, the story of the people he met and the places he saw. . . . It's a straightforward, crisply written memoir." Booklist

Thoreau, Henry David

★ **Cape** Cod; photographs by Scot Miller. Ill. ed. of the American classic.; Houghton Mifflin Co. 2008 255p il $35   **917**

1. Cape Cod (Mass.) -- Description and travel

ISBN 978-0-618-75845-6; 0-618-75845-3

LC 2007-42952

First published 1865

This "account is based on the author's experiences during the three short visits to Cape Cod (Oct. 1849; June 1850; July 1855), and includes ten essays on the history and character of the inhabitants, 'The Highland Light,' Nantucket, the sea, the beach, and other aspects of the Cape." Oxford Companion to Am Lit

The **Maine** woods; introduction by Edward Hoagland. Penguin Books 1988 xxxiii, 442p (Penguin nature library) pa $16   **917**

1. Maine -- Description and travel

ISBN 0-14-017013-8

LC 88-3644

First published 1864 by Ticknor & Fields

This account of the author's rambles around the lakes and woods of Maine "records three different excursions: Thoreau's trip to Mount Katahdin (which he called 'Ktaadn'), published in the 'Union Magazine' in 1848; 'Chesuncook,' which appeared in the 'Atlantic Monthly' in the same year; and 'The Allegash and the East Branch,' which is a marvel of precise observation." Herzberg. Reader's Ency of Am Lit

Wallis, Michael

Route 66: the mother road. St. Martin's Griffin 2001 276p il maps $35; pa $19.95   **917**

1. West (U.S.) -- Description and travel

ISBN 0-312-28167-6; 0-312-28161-7 pa

LC 2001-31944

This is a reissue of the title first published 1990

The author examines the highway's history, roadside diners, towns, motels, and people

Includes bibliographical references

Woodger, Elin

Encyclopedia of the Lewis and Clark Expedition; [by] Elin Woodger, Brandon Toropov; foreword by Ned Blackhawk. Facts on File 2004 xxv, 438p il (Facts on File library of American history) $65.00; pa $21.95   **917**

1. Lewis and Clark Expedition (1804-1806) 2. West

(U.S.) -- Exploration

ISBN 0-8160-4781-2; 0-8160-4782-0 pa

LC 2003-6120

"This is a complete, authoritative overview of a fascinating landmark in American history and will be a first purchase for most libraries." SLJ

Includes bibliographical references

917.104   Canada--travel

Canada; edited by Rebecca Miles. DK Pub 2016 440 p. color ill., color maps (paperback) $25   **917.104**

1. Canada -- Description and travel

ISBN 9781465440211; 1465440216

LC 2016013497

This book, printed by Dorling Kindersley, edited by Rebecca Miles, is part of the publisher's "Eyewitness Travel Guides" series. It presents "the best attractions . . . [that Canada] has to offer, from the rich historical and cultural treasures of its cities to the stunning scenery of its landscapes and coastlines. Visit the Citadelle of Quebec, eat world-class cuisine in Vancouver, take in the beauty of Niagara Falls, and go whale watching on the coasts." (Publisher's note)

917.2   Mexico--geography

Craig, William

Yankee come home; on the road from San Juan Hill to Guantánamo. William Craig. Walker & Co. 2012 437 p. $28.00   **917.2**

1. Spanish-American War, 1898 2. Guantanamo Bay Detention Camp 3. United States -- Foreign relations -- Cuba

ISBN 080271093X; 9780802710932

In this book, "based on his trip to Cuba in 2005, [William] Craig's multipronged account shifts among the events of his journey, thoughts on Cuban culture, an ancestor whom family lore had charging up San Juan Hill in 1898, and his critical views of the history of American-Cuban relations. The Spanish-American War holds these parts together as Craig summarizes Cuban insurrections against the Spanish and the destruction of the 'Maine,' which furnished the American casus belli." (Booklist)

Includes bibliographical references and index.

917.28   Central America

Hely, Steve

The **wonder** trail; true stories from Los Angeles to the end of the world. Steve Hely. Dutton 2016 336 p. illustrations, map (hardcover) $27   **917.28**

1. Travel writing 2. South America -- Description and travel 3. Central America -- Description and travel 4. Curiosities and wonders -- South America 5. South America -- Social life and customs 6. Central America -- Social life and customs 7. Curiosities and wonders

-- Central America
ISBN 9780525955016

LC 2015038442

This book, by Steve Hely, "is the story of a trip from Los Angeles to the bottom of South America. . . . From Mexico City to Oaxaca; into ancient Mayan ruins; the jungles, coffee plantations, and remote beaches of Central America; across the Panama Canal; by sea to Colombia; to the wild Easter celebration of Popayán; to the Amazon rainforest; the Inca sites of Cuzco and Machu Picchu; to the Galápagos Islands; the Atacama Desert of Chile; and down to wind-worn Patagonia." (Publisher's note)

"Hely's hilarious descriptions of the stunning sights and quirky people he encounters along the way will delight experienced globetrotters and armchair travelers alike." LJ

917.3   Geography of and travel in United States

Abroad at home; the best international travel in North America. National Geographic. National Geographic Books 2015 288 p. color illustrations (pbk. : alk. paper) $24.95   **917.3**
1. Travel 2. North America 3. Canada -- Description and travel 4. United States -- Description and travel
ISBN 1426214995; 9781426214998

LC 2014037548

This book from National Geographic "presents a potpourri of international experiences in the United States and Canada. Discover the villages, neighborhoods, and regions that cover the breadth of North America's great global diversity--Chinatowns and Little Italys, of course, but also Polish, German, French, Russian, and Japanese enclaves." (Publisher's note)

"Recommended for those seeking an international flavor in their hometown or nearby cities, or travelers planning a trip with a singular flair to North American regions." LJ

Gill, A. A.
    To America with love; A.A. Gill. Simon & Schuster 2013 256 p. (hardback) $25   **917.3**
1. Cultural critique 2. United States -- Description and travel 3. United States -- Social life and customs
ISBN 1416596216; 9781416596219; 9781439100448

LC 2013019543

This book is Scottish-born A.A. Gill's tribute to America. He "devotes his . . . to defending the country's earnest belief in government by the people, as well as its brashness of character, frank celebration of success, sublime sense of nature, and childish delight in speechifying and hucksterism, among other things." (Publishers Weekly)

National Geographic Guide to the State Parks of the United States; 4th edition National Geographic Society 2012 384 p. illustrations, maps $25   **917.3**
1. Parks -- United States 2. United States -- Guidebooks
ISBN 1426208898; 9781426208898

"Of the state parks' 25,000 miles of trails and recreation, the authors have selected favorites for hiking and biking, horseback riding, and wildflower gazing as well as ample opportunities for the birdwatcher or rock climber, the wild-

life observer or the amateur archaeologist. The guide features more than 200 gorgeous, color photographs that capture the spendor of the parks, insider tips from state parks staff that are invaluable planning tools, and 32 easy-to-use maps that highlight sites, trails and campgrounds, as well as information on recreational activities, camping, and lodging." (Publisher's note)

Savoy, Lauret
    Trace; a journey through memory, history, and the American land. Lauren Edith Savoy. Counterpoint Press 2015 240 p. (hardback) $25   **917.3**
1. United States -- Race relations 2. United States -- Social conditions
ISBN 1619025736; 9781619025738

LC 2015009588

Author Lauret Savoy "explores how the country's still unfolding history, and ideas of "race," have marked her and the land. From twisted terrain within the San Andreas Fault zone to a South Carolina plantation, from national parks to burial grounds, from 'Indian Territory' and the U.S.-Mexico Border to the U.S. capital, 'Trace' grapples with a searing national history to reveal the often unvoiced presence of the past." (Publisher's note)

"Springing from the literal Earth to metaphor, Savoy demonstrates the power of narrative to erase as easily as it reveals, yielding a provocative, eclectic exposé of the palimpsest historically defining the U.S. as much as any natural or man-made boundary." Kirkus

917.4   Northeastern States

Grossinger, Tania
    Growing up at Grossinger's; Tania Grossinger. Skyhorse Pub. 2008 187 p. 16 plates; illustrations (alk. paper) $14.95   **917.4**
1. Grossinger (N.Y.)
ISBN 1602392056; 9781602392052

LC 2007045847

"'To be devoured in one non-stop gulp...fascinating reading.' The New York Post From 1919 to 1986, Grossinger's Catskill Resort Hotel provided a summer retreat from the city heat for New York's Jews, and entertained the great, the near-great, and the not so great, Jews and Gentiles alike. A melting pot of the Borscht Belt, sports, and showbiz worlds, loyal visitors included Red Buttons, Rocky Marciano, Eddie Fisher, and Jackie Robinson. Tania Grossinger grew up there. In her fascinating insider's account of life in the hospitality industry, she sheds light on how hotel children keep up with the frenetic pace of life, and how they come to grips with the outside world (which intrudes now and again), sex (happening in every room), and, occasionally, their intellectual interests. Growing Up at Grossinger's is both a wonderful coming-of-age story and a sentimental reading of a chapter of the Jewish experience in America that has now closed. 25 b/w photographs." Publisher's Note

917.47 New York

Freudenheim, Ellen

The **Brooklyn** experience; the ultimate guide to neighborhoods & noshes, culture & the cutting edge. Ellen Freudenheim. Rutgers University Press 2016 360 p. (paperback : alkaline paper) $23.95 **917.47**
1. Brooklyn (New York, N.Y.) 2. New York (N.Y.) -- Description and travel 3. New York (N.Y.) -- Guidebooks 4. Brooklyn (New York, N.Y.) -- Guidebooks
ISBN 9780813577432

LC 2015035672

This book, by Ellen Freudenheim, is a "comprehensive Brooklyn guidebook. . . . Walk over the Brooklyn Bridge at dawn or sunset, discover thirty-eight unique Brooklyn neighborhoods, and experience the borough like a native. Find out where to go to the beach and to eat great pizza, what to do with the kids, how to enjoy free and cheap activities, and where to savor Brooklyn's famous cuisines." (Publisher's note)

"Even those readers who think they know everything about this New York City borough will probably find a surprising tidbit in these pages." LJ

Includes bibliographical references and index

918 Geography of and travel in South America

Chatwin, Bruce

In Patagonia; introduction by Nicholas Shakespeare. Penguin Books 2003 204p il map (Penguin classics) pa $15 **918**
1. Patagonia (Argentina and Chile) -- Description and travel
ISBN 0-14-243719-0; 978-0-14-243719-3

LC 2002-45038

First published 1977 in the United Kingdom

This travelogue "captures the exotic characters and scenery Chatwin encountered in the southern tip of South America on a search for an important prehistoric artifact." Booklist

Grann, David

The **lost** city of Z; a tale of deadly obsession in the Amazon. Doubleday 2009 339p il map $27.50 **918**
1. Explorers 2. Amazon River valley
ISBN 978-0-385-51353-1; 0-385-51353-4

LC 2008-17432

Interweaves the story of British explorer Percy Fawcett, who vanished during a 1925 expedition into the Amazon, with the author's own quest to uncover the mysteries surrounding Fawcett's final journey and the secrets of what lies deep in the Amazon jungle.

"A colorful tale of true adventure, marked by satisfyingly unexpected twists, turns and plenty of dark portents." Kirkus

Includes bibliographical references (p. 315-326)

Insight Guide Explore Rio; Insight Guides. Insight Guides 2016 128 p. $12.99 **918**
1. Rio de Janeiro (Brazil) -- Description and travel
ISBN 1780055536; 9781780055534

This travel guide for Rio de Janeiro, Brazil, "is the ideal pocket companion when discovering this exciting city: a full-colour guide containing 14 easy-to-follow routes through the city's many fascinating neighbourhoods, from the Centro Histórico and the charming Santa Teresa district to the fabled beaches of Copacabana to Ipanema and beyond to the Costa Verde." (Publisher's note)

"In time for the Summer Games, this focused and travel-friendly (5.9" x 0.9" x 8.3") guide to Rio is filled with the clear, beautiful photographs for which the 'Insight' series is so well known." LJ

Theroux, Paul

The **old** Patagonian express; by train through the Americas. Houghton Mifflin 1979 404p hardcover o.p. pa $15 **918**
1. America -- Description 2. Railroads -- Latin America
ISBN 0-395-52105-X pa

LC 79-15353

The author describes his journey from Boston to Patagonia by train

918.1 Brazil--geography

Brazil; DK Publishing. DK Publishing 2016 448 p. ill. (chiefly col.), col. maps $30 **918.1**
1. Brazil -- Description and travel
ISBN 1465439595; 9781465439598

This book "is your in-depth guide to the very best of [Brazil]. . . . Whether you want to explore the streets of Rio de Janeiro or lounge on its beaches, celebrate the culture of Carnaval and discover the best places to hear the sounds of bossa nova and samba, or explore the vast Amazon rain forest in the north, Brazil proves to be an extraordinarily diverse country of modern cities, verdant landscapes, and rich heritage." (Publisher's note)

"With lots of color photos and easy-to-read descriptions, these guides also serve as a good reference source and aide-mémoire when patrons return home and need to identify locations in photos." LJ

Stafford, Ed

Walking the Amazon; 860 days. one step at a time. Ed Stafford. Plume Books 2012 319 p. $16.00 **918.1**
1. Hiking 2. Amazon River 3. Autobiographies 4. Amazon River valley 5. Hiking -- Amazon River Region 6. Amazon River Region -- Description and travel
ISBN 0452298261; 9780452298262

LC 2012010986

In this "memoir . . . about becoming the first person to perambulate the Amazon's entire length, [Ed] Stafford chronicles the countless obstacles he faced, including canoes of armed indigenous peoples, dehydration, sickness, lack of sleep . . . . and overwhelming swarms of insects. In addition . . . the author explores his friendship with the longest lasting of his many walking companions, Gadiel 'Cho' Sanchez Rivera." (Kirkus Reviews)

918.15 Rio de Janeiro

De Vries, Alexandra

Frommer's Rio de Janeiro day By day; by Alexandra deVries. FrommerMedia 2014 192 p. $13.95 **918.15**

1. Rio de Janeiro (Brazil) -- Description and travel
ISBN 1628871547; 9781628871548

In this travel guidebook, by Alexandra deVries, "Rio de Janeiro is currently the hottest of all the world's pleasure capitals. . . . In compact handy form, and featuring four-color photos of the city's major sights, these remarkable guides have shown millions how to schedule their time -- and they do that now for Rio de Janeiro." (Publisher's note)

"Written by translator and Rio resident de Vries, this compact (0.8" x 4.2" x 7.5", ten ounces) guide includes a pull-out map. These packable guides travel well." LJ

Dk Eyewitness Top 10 Rio De Janeiro; DK Publishing. DK Publishing 2016 128 p. col. ill.; col. maps. $14 **918.15**

1. Rio de Janeiro (Brazil) -- Description and travel
ISBN 1465440925; 9781465440921

This book is a "newly updated pocket travel guide for Rio de Janeiro. [It] will lead you straight to the best attractions the city has to offer, from visiting the iconic Cristo Redentor statue to experiencing the Carnival parade at the Sambodromo to soaking up the atmosphere on the famous Copacabana Beach." (Publisher's note)

"This trim 128-page, 13-ounce handy guide is an impressive package. It essentially lists top-ten sites by category: beaches, Carnival, shopping, tours/excursions, museums and galleries, children's activities, restaurants, bars/nightclubs, sports, and insider tips." LJ

Lonely Planet Rio De Janeiro; by Lonely Planet. Lonely Planet 2016 263 p. color ill., color maps $21.99 **918.15**

1. Rio de Janeiro (Brazil) -- Description and travel
ISBN 1743217676; 9781743217672

This travel guide for Rio de Janeiro, Brazil, "is your passport to all the most relevant and up-to-date advice on what to see, what to skip, and what hidden discoveries await you. Stroll barefoot on Ipanema beach, take in the view from Pao de Acucar (Sugarloaf), or shake your hips at an old-fashioned samba club; all with your trusted travel companion. Get to the heart of Rio de Janeiro and begin your journey now!" (Publisher's note)

Rigby, Claire

Fodor's Rio de Janeiro & Sao Paulo; by Fodor's Travel Guides. Random House Inc 2015 275 p. illustrations $19.99 **918.15**

1. Brazil -- Description and travel 2. Rio de Janeiro (Brazil) -- Description and travel
ISBN 1101878355; 9781101878354

LC 2008215092

In this book, "As host of the 2016 Summer Olympics, Rio de Janeiro will see an influx of visitors in upcoming years, and this colorful city, along with the equally vibrant metropolis of São Paulo, will not disappoint. Whether travelers want to soak in the sun on Rio's glamorous Copacabana Beach, shop in São Paulo's cutting-edge fashion boutiques, or indulge in Latin American's most innovative cuisine, [this book] . . . ensures they get the most out of these two exciting cities." (Publisher's note)

"An updated third edition of a reliable guide, with special attention given to the 2016 Summer Olympic Games." LJ

Sommers, Michael

Moon Rio De Janeiro; by Michael Sommers. Avalon Travel Publishing 2015 100 p. $9.99 **918.15**

1. Rio de Janeiro (Brazil) -- Description and travel
ISBN 1612389368; 9781612389363

LC 2016024893

This book on Rio de Janeiro, Brazil, by Michael Sommers, "is a 100-page compact guide to the colorful squares, sultry nightlife, and fabulous white sand beaches of this Brazilian metropolis and surrounding areas. . . . Sommers offers his seasoned advice on must-see attractions, and includes maps with sightseeing highlights so you can make the most of your time." (Publisher's note)

"An excerpt of the publisher's larger Moon Brazil guide by Texas-born Sommers, who now lives in the Brazilian city of Salvador. Readers will enjoy his personal, expat perspective." LJ

Includes bibliographical references (pages 290-302) and index.

919 Geography of and travel in Australasia, Pacific Ocean islands, Atlantic Ocean islands, Arctic islands, Antarctica and on extraterrestrial worlds

Bell, Jim, 1965-

The **interstellar** age; inside the forty-year Voyager mission. Jim Bell. Dutton 2015 336 p. 8 plates; color illustrations (hardback) $27.95 **919**

1. Project Voyager 2. Planets -- Exploration 3. Outer space -- Exploration 4. Astronautics -- United States 5. Voyager Project
ISBN 0525954325; 9780525954323

LC 2014031706

This book, by planetary scientist Jim Bell, presents the "story of the men and women who drove the Voyager spacecraft mission. . . . Bell reveals what drove and continues to drive the members of this extraordinary team, including Ed Stone, Voyager's chief scientist and the one-time head of NASA's Jet Propulsion Lab; [and] Charley Kohlhase, an orbital dynamics engineer who helped to design many of the critical slingshot maneuvers around planets that enabled the Voyagers to travel so far." (Publisher's note)

"A highly enjoyable read for anyone with an interest in popular science." LJ

Bryson, Bill

In a sunburned country. Broadway Bks. 2000 307p il maps hardcover o.p. pa $14.95 **919**

1. Australia -- Description and travel
ISBN 0-7679-0386-2 pa

LC 00-25566

In this book, Bryson "chronicles his exploration of Australia, he introduces us to a town that went without electricity until the early 1990s, a former high-ranking politician who hawks his own autobiography to passersby, an assortment of coffee shops and restaurants, . . . a type of giant worm, and the world's most poisonous creature, the box jellyfish." Booklist

Includes bibliographical references

Chatwin, Bruce

The **songlines**. Viking 1987 293p hardcover o.p. pa $13.95   **919**
1. Australian aborigines 2. Australia -- Description
ISBN 0-14-009429-6 pa

LC 86-40512

"This is an important book and a challenging one. . . . It is full of odd characters, bizarre incidents, moments of poetry—some of them comic—that spring as much from the writer's own generosity of spirit as from the richness of things." Times Lit Suppl

Cookman, Scott

★ **Ice** blink; the mysterious fate of Sir John Franklin's lost polar expedition. Wiley 2000 244p il maps $24.95; pa $15.95   **919**
1. Explorers 2. Northwest Passage 3. Naval officers 4. Travel writers 5. Arctic regions -- Exploration
ISBN 0-471-37790-2; 0-471-40420-9 pa

LC 99-47620

In this "account of the fabled 1845 Franklin expedition in search of the Northwest Passage, Cookman inculpates a novel malefactor in the tragedy: botulism. In the 1980s, three frozen corpses of expedition members were found and exhumed. . . . Autopsies revealed lead, fingering lead-soldered cans from the provisions. . . . Adventure readers will flock to this fine regaling of the enduring mystery surrounding the best-known disaster in Arctic exploration." Booklist

Includes bibliographical references

Fleming, Fergus

Ninety degrees North; the quest for the North Pole. Grove Press 2002 xxi, 470p il maps $26; pa $15   **919**
1. North Pole 2. Arctic regions -- Exploration
ISBN 0-8021-1725-2; 0-8021-4036-X pa

LC 2002-21469

Companion volume to Barrow's boys (2000)

First published 2001 in the United Kingdom

"The book is fascinating for how Fleming renders the haughty, post-Enlightenment brio of the principal adventurers and the extreme, often fatal ends toward which it pushed them." Publ Wkly

Includes bibliographical references

Geiger, John

Frozen in time; the fate of the Franklin expedition. Owen Beattie & John Geiger. Greystone Books 1998 xi, 185 p.p ill. (some col.), maps $17.95 **919**
1. Northwest Passage
ISBN 1550546163; 1771640790; 9781771640794

LC 00688217

This book, by Owen Beattie and John Geiger, "tells the dramatic story of how Sir John Franklin's elite naval forces came within sight of the Northwest Passage, only to suc-

cumb to unimaginable horrors. . . . It shows how the excavation of three sailors from the 1845-48 Franklin expedition, buried for 138 years on the Arctic headland of Beechey Island, has shed new light on what has been one of the world's great maritime mysteries." (Publisher's note)

"The authors present a richly researched history of the expedition and the following relief expeditions and seamlessly merge the worlds of forensic anthropology and 19th-century history. Reading almost like a whodunit page-turner, Beattie and Geiger capture the thrill of making new scientific discoveries and finding important clues to solve a haunting mystery." Pub Wkly

Includes bibliographical references (p. 169-174) and index

Larson, Edward J. (Edward John), 1953-

★ An **empire** of ice; Scott, Shackleton, and the heroic age of Antarctic science. Edward J. Larson. Yale University Press 2011 xiv, 326 p.p ill., maps   **919**
1. Explorers 2. Scientific expeditions 3. Antarctica -- Exploration 4. Antarctic regions -- Discovery and exploration 5. Antarctica -- Discovery and exploration -- British
ISBN 0300154089; 9780300154085

LC 2010044396

This book, by Edward J. Larson, "presents a . . . new take on Antarctic exploration. Retold with added information, [it] . . . place[s] the famed voyages of Norwegian explorer Roald Amundsen, his British rivals Robert Scott and Ernest Shackleton, and others in a larger scientific, social, and geopolitical context." (Publisher's note)

Includes bibliographical references (p. 295-315) and index

Preston, Diana

A **first** rate tragedy; Robert Falcon Scott and the race to the South Pole. Houghton Mifflin 1998 269p il map hardcover o.p. pa $14   **919**
1. Explorers 2. South Pole 3. Antarctica -- Exploration 4. British Antarctic ("Terra Nova") Expedition (1910-1913)
ISBN 0-618-00201-4 pa

LC 98-47411

"A whole generation was brought up on the legend of Scott of the Antarctic. Diana Preston successfully explains why and how this came about. . . . {She} has written a first-rate book retelling the familiar tale in compulsive terms and adding a thoughtful twist of her own." Times Lit Suppl

Includes bibliographical references

Pyne, Stephen J.

★ **Voyager**; seeking newer worlds in the third great age of discovery. Viking 2010 444p il $29.95   **919**
1. Project Voyager 2. Planets -- Exploration 3. Astronautics -- United States
ISBN 978-0-670-02183-3; 0-670-02183-0

LC 2009-46305

"By looking at the mission of Voyager 1 and Voyager 2 and comparing it with past voyages of discovery on Earth, Pyne offers a unique and engrossing history of the Western world's love affair with such journeys. . . . [The author] calls the Voyager mission the hallmark of a 'Third Great Age of Discovery,' similar to ambitious seagoing expeditions in the 16th and 18th centuries. . . . Pyne captures the Western passion for exploration and the lure of the unknown, while relating the fascinating story of two fragile spacecraft continuing after three decades their brave quest across space and time." Publ Wkly.

Includes bibliographical references

Roberts, David, 1943-

Alone on the ice; the greatest survival story in the history of exploration. David Roberts. W. W. Norton & Company 2013 256 p. (hardcover) $27.95   **919**
1. Wilderness survival 2. Antarctica -- Exploration 3. Antarctica -- Discovery and exploration
ISBN 0393083713; 9780393083712

LC 2012037677

This book by David Roberts presents a "portrait of Aussie explorer Douglas Mawson and his arduous trek through some of the most treacherous icy Antarctic terrain. . . . Roberts parallels the courageous achievements of Mawson's team on the 1911-1913 journey along the previously uncharted regions of the landscape with those of his acclaimed peers . . . battling the bitter cold, starvation, and peril to the limits of human endurance." (Publishers Weekly)

Includes bibliographical references and index

Solomon, Susan

The **coldest** March. Yale Univ. Press 2001 xxii, 383p il maps hardcover o.p. pa $16.95   **919**
1. Explorers 2. South Pole 3. Antarctica -- Exploration 4. British Antarctic ("Terra Nova") Expedition (1910-1913)
ISBN 0-300-08967-8; 0-300-09921-5 pa

LC 00-54996

"In November 1911, Capt. Robert Falcon Scott and his British team set out to be the first to reach the South Pole. Battling the brutal weather of Antarctica, they reached the pole in January 1912 only to discover that a Norwegian team had beat them there by nearly a month. On their return from the Pole, Scott and four of his companions died in harsh conditions. Ever since, history has not known whether to label them heroes or bunglers. Solomon . . . analyzes all the factors present during Scott's expedition in an attempt to explain that his failure was due not to incompetence but to a combination of unpredictable weather, erroneous choices and bad luck." Libr J

Includes bibliographical references

Theroux, Paul

The **happy** isles of Oceania; paddling the Pacific. Houghton Mifflin Co. 2006 528p map pa $15.95   **919**
1. Oceania -- Description and travel
ISBN 978-0-618-65898-5; 0-618-65898-X

LC 2006-28742

First published 1992 by Putnam

The author "spent 18 months in a one-man collapsible kayak exploring such exotic Pacific islands as New Zealand, Australia, the Soloman and Cook Islands, Fiji, Samoa, Tahiti, Easter Island, and Hawaii. . . . A brilliant storyteller with an eye for the absurd, Theroux takes the reader to little-known places where time seems to have stood still and people lead simple lives totally unrelated to 20th-century America." Libr J

92   Biography

Aaron, Hank, 1934-

Bryant, Howard. The **last** hero; a life of Henry Aaron. Pantheon Books 2010 600p il $29.95   **92**
1. Baseball players 2. African American athletes 3. Baseball -- Biography
ISBN 978-0-375-42485-4; 0-375-42485-7

LC 2009-40573

This biography of the baseball player "reveals a multifaceted man, a great American, and an accomplished athlete, in that order. . . . Bryant evokes the apparently distant world marked by cruel segregation, racism, and poverty of the soul, as well as reliving some of the greatest moments of baseball. A most welcome book, most highly recommended." Libr J

Includes bibliographical references

Abdul-Jabbar, Kareem, 1947-

★ Abdul-Jabbar, Kareem. **On** the shoulders of giants; my journey through the Harlem Renaissance. [by] Kareem Abdul-Jabbar with Raymond Obstfeld. Simon & Schuster 2007 274p il hardcover o.p. pa $18.99   **92**
1. Harlem Renaissance 2. Basketball players 3. Nonfiction writers 4. African Americans -- Biography
ISBN 1-4165-3488-1; 978-1-4165-3488-4; 1-4165-3489-X pa; 978-1-4165-3489-1 pa

LC 2006-51776

"By mixing personal anecdotes with traditional research and reporting, . . . [Abdul-Jabbar] acts as a knowledgeable, passionate tour guide through the artistic and social history of one America's most dynamic creative eras." N Y Times Book Rev

Includes bibliographical references

Abdullahi, Asad

Steinberg, Jonny. A **man** of good hope; by Jonny Steinberg. Alfred A. Knopf 2014 336 p. illustrations, maps (hardcover : alk. paper) $26.95   **92**
1. African Refugees 2. Somalia -- Social conditions 3. Refugees -- Somalia 4. Somalia -- Biography 5. Somalis -- South Africa -- Biography 6. Somalis -- United States -- Biography
ISBN 0385352727; 9780385352727; 9780385352734; 9780804171045

LC 2013046388

This biography by Jonny Steinberg tells how "In January 1991, when civil war came to Mogadishu, the capital of Somalia, two-thirds of the city's population fled. Among them was eight-year-old Asad Abdullahi. . . . Serially betrayed by the people who promised to care for him, Asad lived his childhood at a skeptical remove from the adult world, his relation to others wary and tactical. . . . By the time he reached the cusp of adulthood, Asad had honed an array of wily talents." (Publisher's note)

"Steinberg's solid prose is perfect for the task of sharing Asad's history. He probes the darkest moments of his subject's life without ever becoming maudlin, telling the story starkly and bluntly. He ably demonstrates to readers Asad's absolute refusal to give up while reminding them that, despite his tribulations, in many ways, his path was his own to form. For truly capturing the power of dreams and the resilience of human nature, this book deserves a wide audience." Kirkus

Abu-Jaber, Diana

Abu-Jaber, Diana, 1960- **Life** Without a Recipe; A Memoir of Food and Family. Diana Abu-Jaber. W W Norton & Co Inc 2016 256 p. $26.95   92
1. Food 2. Family
ISBN 0393249093; 9780393249095
LC 2016000543
This memoir, by Diana Abu-Jaber, is the author's "celebration . . . . of escaping family and making family on one's own terms. As Diana discovers, however, building confidence in one's own path sometimes takes a mistaken marriage or two—or in her case, three: to a longhaired boy-poet, to a dashing deconstructionist literary scholar, and finally to her steadfast, outdoors-loving Scott. It also takes a good deal of angst . . . and even when she knew what she wanted . . . the nerve to pursue it." (Publisher's note)

"Abu-Jaber renders her relationships to both food and family in rich, joyful detail." Booklist

Achebe, Chinua, 1930-2013

Achebe, Chinua, 1930-2013. The **education** of a British-protected child; essays. A.A. Knopf 2009 172p $24.95; pa $14.95   92
1. Poets 2. Racism 3. Authors 4. Novelists 5. Authors, Nigerian 6. Nigeria 7. Essayists 8. Short story writers 9. Nigeria -- Colonization 10. African literature -- History and criticism
ISBN 978-0-3072-7255-3; 9780307473677
LC 2009017480
This is a collection of essays by the author of Things Fall Apart. In the title piece, Achebe discusses "growing up in colonial Nigeria and inhabiting its 'middle ground,' recalling both his happy memories of reading novels in secondary school and the harsher truths of colonial rule. . . . Politics and history figure in 'What Is Nigeria to Me?,' 'Africa's Tarnished Name,' and 'Politics of the Politicians of Language.' And Achebe's . . . family comes into view in 'My Dad and Me' and 'My Daughters.'" (Publisher's note)

"With African literature emerging as a world force, it's good to have Achebe back after more than 20 years, offering 17 sterling essays." (Library Journal)
Includes bibliographical references

Acheson, Dean, 1893-1971

Chace, James. **Acheson**; the Secretary of State who created the American world. Simon & Schuster 1998 512p hardcover o.p. pa $20   92
1. Authors 2. Nonfiction writers 3. Secretaries of state 4. United States -- Foreign relations
ISBN 978-1-416-54865-2; 1-416-54865-3
LC 98-3801

"Dean Acheson was Truman's Secretary of State from 1949 to 1953, and today's world, as Chace shows in this lucid biography, was shaped in no small degree by his efforts." New Yorker
Includes bibliographical references

Adams, Abigail, 1744-1818

★ Adams, John. **My** dearest friend; letters of Abigail and John Adams. edited by Margaret A. Hogan and C. James Taylor. Belknap Press of Harvard University Press 2007 508p il map $35   92
1. Presidents 2. Vice-presidents 3. Parents of presidents 4. Spouses of presidents 5. Presidents -- United States 6. Presidents' spouses -- United States
ISBN 978-0-674-02606-3; 0-674-02606-3
LC 2007-4380
This collection of correspondence between John and Abigail Adams includes "selection from the entire body of the Adams' correspondence, from their courtship . . . until Abigail left the White House near the end of John's presidential term, reminding him, 'I want to see the list of judges.' . . . This is a treasure, for general readers and scholars alike." Booklist

Holton, Woody. **Abigail** Adams; a life. Free Press 2009 483p il map $30   92
1. Presidents 2. Vice-presidents 3. Biography, Individual 4. Parents of presidents 5. Spouses of presidents 6. Presidents' spouses -- United States 7. Women in politics -- United States -- History -- 18th century
ISBN 978-1-4165-4680-1; 1-4165-4680-4
LC 2009016288
This is a "reinterpretation of Adams's life story and of women's roles in the creation of the republic." (Publisher's note) Index.

"Holton's superb biography shows us a three-dimensional Adams as a forward-thinking woman with a mind of her own." Publ Wkly
Includes bibliographical references

Adams, Ansel, 1902-1984

Alinder, Mary Street. **Ansel** Adams; a biography. Holt & Co. 1996 xx, 489p il hardcover o.p. pa $17.95   92
1. Photographers
ISBN 0-8050-5835-4 pa
LC 95-44741
"As Alinder traces the straightforward course of Adams' dazzling career . . . she emphasizes the connection between his stunning landscape photography and his zealous work with the Sierra Club. Alinder is as lucid on the topic of Adams' technical mastery as on his environmentalism and aesthetics, and she also tackles the muddle of his contentious private life with aplomb and candor." Booklist
Includes bibliographical references

Adams, Henry, 1838-1918

Adams, Henry. The **education** of Henry Adams; an autobiography. with a new introduction by Donald Hall. Houghton Mifflin 2000 517p pa $12   **92**

1. Authors 2. Novelists 3. Historians 4. Essayists

ISBN 0-618-05666-1

LC 00-26235

First published 1918

"The book omits any mention of the thirteen years of Adams's marriage and the seven years following his wife's suicide. It does, however, present a vivid picture of the people and places the author knew." Reader's Ency. 4th edition

Adams, John Quincy, 1767-1848

Giles Unger, Harlow. **John** Quincy Adams; Harlow Giles Unger. Da Capo Press 2012 xv, 364 p.p ill., map (hardcover : alk. paper) $27.50   **92**

1. Statesmen -- United States -- Biography 2. Presidents -- United States -- Biography 3. United States -- Politics and government -- 1789-1815 4. United States -- Politics and government -- 1825-1829

ISBN 030682129X; 9780306821295; 9780306821301

LC 2012009399

This book, by Harlow Giles Unger, offers a biography of the U.S. president John Quincy Adams. "He fought for Washington, served with Lincoln, witnessed Bunker Hill, and sounded the clarion against slavery on the eve of the Civil War. He negotiated an end to the War of 1812, . . . and won the Supreme Court decision that freed the African captives of 'The Amistad.' He served his nation as minister to six countries, secretary of state, senator, congressman, and president." (Publisher's note)

Includes bibliographical references (p. 339-348) and index.

Kaplan, Fred, 1937- **John** Quincy Adams; American visionary. Fred Kaplan. HarperCollins Publishers 2014 672 p. ill. (some col.), col. map $29.99 **92**

1. Presidents -- United States 2. Presidents -- United States -- Biography

ISBN 0061915416; 9780061915413

LC 2013035334

This book, by Fred Kaplan, "brings into focus the . . . life of John Quincy Adams--the little known . . . sixth president of the United States and the first son of John and Abigail Adams. . . . Kaplan draws on a trove of unpublished archival material to trace Adams's evolution from his childhood during the Revolutionary War to his brilliant years as Secretary of State to his time in the White House and beyond." (Publisher's note)

"Kaplan sees not an inadequate man in a position he could not manage. He sees instead a 'visionary,' who stood for a united American republic free of the divisiveness of slavery." Booklist

Includes bibliographical references and index

Nagel, Paul C. **John** Quincy Adams; a public life, a private life. Harvard University Press 1999 432p il map pa $18.95   **92**

1. Presidents 2. Senators 3. Members of Congress 4. Secretaries of state 5. Presidents -- United States

ISBN 0-674-47940-8

First published 1997 by Knopf

The author traces the life and career of the sixth president of the United States "utilizing diary entries to provide keen insight into this extraordinary man, who often suffered from severe depression. The result is a fascinating psycho-biography." Libr J

Includes bibliographical references

Remini, Robert Vincent. **John** Quincy Adams; [by] Robert V. Remini. Times Bks. 2002 172p (American presidents series) $20   **92**

1. Presidents 2. Senators 3. Members of Congress 4. Secretaries of state 5. Presidents -- United States 6. United States -- Politics and government -- 1783-1865

ISBN 0-8050-6939-9

LC 2002-24210

The author's "judicious, eloquent survey of the sixth president's life and career intends not to proffer new and explosive ideas but to fashion recent scholarship into a highly readable overview for the general reader." Booklist

Includes bibliographical references

Thomas, Louisa. **Louisa**; The Extraordinary Life of Mrs. Adams. by Louisa Thomas. Penguin Group USA 2016 512 p. portrait $30   **92**

1. Presidents' spouses -- United States

ISBN 1594204632; 9781594204630

In this biography, author Louisa Thomas, "unfolds the portrait of Louisa Catherine Adams, the wife of John Quincy Adams who witnessed firsthand the greatest transformations of her time. Born in London to an American father and a British mother . . . Louisa Catherine Johnson was raised in circumstances very different from the New England upbringing of the future president John Quincy Adams. . . . Their often tempestuous but deeply close marriage lasted half a century." (Publisher's note)

"Thomas has written an excellent account of the life of this woman, who certainly merits greater attention and praise." Booklist

Traub, James. **John** Quincy Adams; militant spirit. James Traub. Basic Books, a member of the Perseus Books Group 2016 640 p. (hardcover) $35   **92**

1. Presidents -- United States -- Biography 2. United States -- Politics and government 3. United States -- History -- 1783-1865 4. United States -- Foreign relations -- 1783-1865 5. United States -- Politics and government -- 1783-1865

ISBN 9780465028276

LC 2015030745

In this book, by James Traub, "[John Quincy] Adams surfaces as an ambitious intellectual with deeply held convictions striving to hold his family together through illness, tragedy, and financial woes while relentlessly promoting a strong, active federal government as the young but rapidly expanding and diversifying nation grappled with geographic sectionalism and political partisanship." (Library Journal)

"An impassioned biography of 'a coherent and consistent thinker who adhered to his core political convictions across his decades of public service.' " Kirkus

Includes bibliographical references and index

Adams, John, 1735-1826

★ Adams, John. **My** dearest friend; letters of Abigail and John Adams. edited by Margaret A. Hogan and C. James Taylor. Belknap Press of Harvard University Press 2007 508p il map $35 **92**
1. Presidents 2. Vice-presidents 3. Parents of presidents 4. Spouses of presidents 5. Presidents -- United States 6. Presidents' spouses -- United States
ISBN 978-0-674-02606-3; 0-674-02606-3
LC 2007-4380

This collection of correspondence between John and Abigail Adams includes "selection from the entire body of the Adams' correspondence, from their courtship . . . until Abigail left the White House near the end of John's presidential term, reminding him, 'I want to see the list of judges.' . . . This is a treasure, for general readers and scholars alike." Booklist

★ Grant, James. **John** Adams; party of one. [by] James L. Grant. Farrar, Straus and Giroux 2005 530p il $30 **92**
1. Presidents 2. Vice-presidents 3. Presidents -- United States
ISBN 0-374-11314-9
LC 2004-10863

The author "is excellent at developing Adams' devotion to liberty, honed by British policies that affronted him and turned him into a revolutionary. In Grant's fine synthesis, Adams on the page is the pious, ambitious, and loving man he was in life." Booklist
Includes bibliographical references

Holton, Woody. **Abigail** Adams; a life. Free Press 2009 483p il map $30 **92**
1. Presidents 2. Vice-presidents 3. Biography, Individual 4. Parents of presidents 5. Spouses of presidents 6. Presidents' spouses -- United States 7. Women in politics -- United States -- History -- 18th century
ISBN 978-1-4165-4680-1; 1-4165-4680-4
LC 2009016288

This is a "reinterpretation of Adams's life story and of women's roles in the creation of the republic." (Publisher's note) Index.
"Holton's superb biography shows us a three-dimensional Adams as a forward-thinking woman with a mind of her own." Publ Wkly
Includes bibliographical references

McCullough, David G., 1933- **John** Adams; {by} David McCullough. Simon & Schuster 2001 751p il maps $35; pa $18.95 **92**
1. Presidents 2. Vice-presidents 3. Large print books 4. Presidents -- United States 5. United States -- Politics and government -- 1775-1783 6. United States -- Politics and government -- 1783-1809 7. United States -- Politics and government -- 1797-1801 8. United States -- Politics and government -- 1775-1783, Revolution
ISBN 0-684-81363-7; 0-7432-2313-6 pa
LC 2001-27010

This is a biography of the second president of the United States. Index.
"This is a wonderfully stirring biography; to read it is to feel as if you are witnessing the birth of a country firsthand." Booklist
Includes bibliographical references

Adams, John, 1947-

Adams, John. **Hallelujah** junction; composing an American life. Farrar, Straus and Giroux 2008 340p il $26 **92**
1. Composers
ISBN 978-0-374-28115-1; 0-374-28115-7
LC 2008-17922

An eminent composer shares the story of his life, from his childhood and early studies in classical composition to his minimalist and "docu-opera" achievements, in an account that evaluates his professional relationships and the social movements that inspired his creative process
"Readers will enjoy the candor and completeness of the book, which serves as a gateway to an accomplished body of work. Like the author's music: carefully considered, deliberate and often exciting, gathering together many disparate elements of American life." Kirkus

Adams, Louisa Catherine, 1775-1852.

Thomas, Louisa. **Louisa**; The Extraordinary Life of Mrs. Adams. by Louisa Thomas. Penguin Group USA 2016 512 p. portrait $30 **92**
1. Presidents' spouses -- United States
ISBN 1594204632; 9781594204630

In this biography, author Louisa Thomas, "unfolds the portrait of Louisa Catherine Adams, the wife of John Quincy Adams who witnessed firsthand the greatest transformations of her time. Born in London to an American father and a British mother . . . Louisa Catherine Johnson was raised in circumstances very different from the New England upbringing of the future president John Quincy Adams. . . . Their often tempestuous but deeply close marriage lasted half a century." (Publisher's note)
"Thomas has written an excellent account of the life of this woman, who certainly merits greater attention and praise." Booklist

Adams, Rachel, 1968-

Adams, Rachel. **Raising** Henry; a memoir of motherhood, disability, and discovery. Rachel Adams. Yale University Press 2013 272 p. (cloth : alk. paper) $26 **92**
1. Down syndrome 2. Mother-son relationship 3. Children with disabilities 4. Parents of children with disabilities
ISBN 0300180004; 9780300180008
LC 2013002096

In this memoir on her experiences raising a child with Down syndrome, author Rachel Adams "chronicles the first three years of Henry's life and her own transformative experience of unexpectedly becoming the mother of a disabled child. . . . Adams untangles the contradictions of living in a society that is more enlightened and supportive of people with disabilities than ever before, yet is racing to perfect pre-

natal tests to prevent children like Henry from being born."
(Publisher's note)

"The author's clear, precise memoir offers an account of
her feelings, which run the gamut from shocked dismay to
unequivocal acceptance, and the process by which she and
her husband arrived at a place of profound love and gratitude
for Henry and his differences." Kirkus

Includes bibliographical references

Addams, Jane, 1860-1935

Knight, Louise W. **Jane** Addams; spirit in action.
W. W. Norton 2010 334p il $28.95   **92**
1. Authors 2. Philanthropists 3. Hull House (Chicago,
Ill.) 4. Essayists 5. Pacifists 6. Social welfare leaders
7. Nobel laureates for peace 8. Chicago (Ill.) -- Social
conditions
ISBN 978-0-393-07165-8

LC 2010-20648

"Knight, the author of Citizen (2006), provides the first
full-length biography of Jane Addams in 35 years. She carefully traces Addams' philosophical progression as she Addams evolvedfrom a passive reformer into an active collaborator, who tirelessly worked with, not for, others to usher in a
new era of democracy and social justice." (Booklist)

Includes bibliographical references

Addario, Lynsey

Addario, Lynsey. **It's** What I Do; A Photographer's Life of Love and War. Lynsey Addario. Penguin Group USA 2015 384 p. illustrations (chiefly
color) $29.95   **92**
1. Photographers 2. Photojournalism 3. Afghan War,
2001- 4. War photography -- 20th century 5. War
photographers -- United States -- Biography 6. Women
photographers -- United States -- Biography
ISBN 159420537X; 9781594205378

LC 2014036653

Author Lysey Addario's memoir explores "the last 10
years of global war and strife while candidly portraying the
intimate life of a female photojournalist. The award-winning
photographer brings an incredible sense of humanity to all
the battlefields of her life" and explores "the role of gender
and how being a woman has impacted every aspect of her
personal and professional lives." (Kirkus Reviews)

"A brutally real and unrelentingly raw memoir that is as
inspiring as it is horrific." Kirkus

Agassi, Andre, 1970-

Agassi, Andre, 1970- **Open**; an autobiography.
A. Knopf 2009 385p il $28.95   **92**
1. Tennis 2. Tennis players 3. Tennis -- Biography 4.
Biography, Individual
ISBN 0-307-26819-5; 978-0-307-26819-8

LC 2009-24004

This is a memoir by the eight-time Grand Slam championship winner who founded the Andre Agassi Charitable
Foundation and the Andre Agassi College Preparatory
Academy for underprivileged children in Las Vegas. Agassi
discusses his childhood, his relationship with his father, his
tennis matches, his addiction in 1997 to crystal meth and
his recovery, his rivalries with other players such as Pete
Sampras, his fall out of the top 100 ranked players and his

return to become the oldest man ever ranked number one,
and the final match of his career at the U.S. Open on September 3, 2006.

"By sharing an unvarnished, at times inspiring story in
an arresting, muscular style, Agassi may have just penned
one of the best sports autobiographies of all time. Check—
it's one of the better memoirs out there, period. . . . Fans will
devour Agassi's juicy revelations about both himself and
other tennis luminaries." Time

Agassiz, Louis, 1807-1873

Irmscher, Christoph. **Louis** Agassiz; creator of
American science. Christoph Irmscher. Houghton
Mifflin Harcourt 2013 448 p. $35   **92**
1. Naturalists -- United States -- Biography 2. Natural
history -- United States -- History -- 19th century
ISBN 0547577672; 9780547577678

LC 2012014225

This book, by Christoph Irmscher, is a biography of the
scientist Louis Agassiz, sometimes called the "founding father of American science. . . . The irrepressible Louis Agassiz, . . . focused his prodigious energies on the fauna of the
New World. Invited to deliver a series of lectures in Boston,
he never left, becoming the most famous scientist of his
time." (Publisher's note)

"A masterful portrait illuminating the tangled human dynamics of science." Booklist

Includes bibliographical references and index

Agee, James, 1909-1955

Wranovics, John. **Chaplin** and Agee; the untold
story of the tramp, the writer, and the lost screenplay.
Palgrave Macmillan 2005 256p il $24.95   **92**
1. Poets 2. Actors 3. Authors 4. Novelists 5.
Screenwriters 6. Nonfiction writers 7. Motion picture
critics 8. Motion picture directors 9. Motion picture
producers
ISBN 1-403-96866-7

LC 2004-62807

A "double biography of two of the 20th century's most
talented artists. Wranovic's hook is a lost screenplay titled
The Tramp's New World, which Agee wrote for Chaplin after the detonation of the atomic bomb over Hiroshima. . . .
Using personal correspondence and critical reviews, Wranovics re-creates the fascinating historical backdrop of the
Agee/Chaplin friendship, interweaving into the stunning
tapestry the colorful lives of such luminaries as Brecht,
Auden, Ed Sullivan, and John Huston." Choice

Aitkenhead, Decca

Aitkenhead, Decca. **All** at sea; A Memoir. Decca
Aitkenhead. Nan A. Talese/Doubleday 2016 240 p.
(hardback) $25   **92**
1. Bereavement 2. Journalists -- Biography 3.
Journalists -- Great Britain -- Biography
ISBN 9780385540650

LC 2016006847

In this memoir, "on a hot, still morning on a beautiful
beach in Jamaica, Decca Aitkenhead's life changed forever.
Her four-year-old son was paddling peacefully at the water's
edge when a wave pulled him out to sea. Her partner, Tony,

swam out and saved their son's life—then drowned before her eyes." (Publisher's note)

"While her grief is nearly incapacitating, readers will appreciate the frank manner in which she shares it. Intense and surprising from start to finish." Booklist

Akhmatova, Anna Andreevna, 1889-1966

★ Feinstein, Elaine. **Anna** of all the Russias; the life of Anna Akhmatova. Knopf 2006 331p il $27.50 **92**

1. Poets 2. Authors
ISBN 1-4000-4089-2; 978-1-4000-4089-6

LC 2005-44542

First published 2005 in the United Kingdom

"In her superb and concise biography, Feinstein brings to life the complex interplay between poetic truth and the ordinary truth of experience in the poet's life and work. . . . Feinstein's poetic sensibility gives her book a distinctive quality, setting it apart from previous biographies." N Y Rev Books

Includes bibliographical references

Al Jundi, Sami, 1962-

Al Jundi, Sami. The **hour** of sunlight; one Palestinian's journey from prisoner to peacemaker. by Sami al Jundi and Jen Marlowe. Nation Books 2010 344p il pa $16.99 **92**

1. Prisoners 2. Palestinian Arabs 3. Israel-Arab conflicts 4. Pacifists
ISBN 978-1-56858-448-5

LC 2010-29340

The authors "trace al Jundi's evolution from Palestinian militant to peacemaker. As teenagers, al Jundi and two friends joined the PLO, but when a bomb exploded as they were building it, one boy was killed, and the other two badly injured—and on the receiving end of Israeli interrogations and torture. Sentenced to a decade in prison, al Jundi dedicates himself to an extensive education program maintained by the prisoners themselves, ultimately committing himself to nonviolence and to bridging the Israeli-Palestinian divide." Publ Wkly

Includes bibliographical references

Al-Maria, Sophia

Al-Maria, Sophia. The **Girl** Who Fell to Earth; A Memoir. HarperCollins 2012 288 p. (paperback) $14.99 **92**

1. Arab Americans 2. Culture conflict
ISBN 006199975X; 9780061999758

In this memoir, "when Sophia Al-Maria's mother sends her away from rainy Washington State to stay with her husband's desert-dwelling Bedouin family in Qatar, she intends it to be a sort of teenage cultural boot camp. What her mother doesn't know is that there are some things about growing up that are universal. In Qatar, Sophia is faced with a new world she'd only imagined as a child. She sets out to find her freedom, even in the most unlikely of places." (Publisher's note)

Albee, Edward, 1928-2016

Gussow, Mel. **Edward** Albee; a singular journey: a biography. Applause 2001 448p il pa $16.95 **92**

1. Authors 2. Dramatists 3. Dramatists, American
ISBN 978-1-55783-447-8; 1-55783-447-4

First published 1999 by Simon & Schuster

"Albee regained his position as one of America's greatest playwrights with the 1994 production of 'Three Tall Women,' achieving a level of theatrical mastery and critical acclaim that he hadn't seen since 'Who's Afraid of Virginia Woolf' and 'A Delicate Balance,' almost two decades earlier. The years in between were marked by excessive drinking, outrageous behavior, inferior work, and a diminished career, but Gussow, with a light and generous touch, shows us the strengths of an artist whose core of resilience ultimately insured his survival." New Yorker

Includes bibliographical references

Albertine, Viv, 1954-

Albertine, Viv. **Clothes,** Clothes, Clothes. Music, Music, Music. Boys, Boys, Boys; A Memoir. Viv Albertine. St. Martins Press 2014 432 p. illustrations (hbk.) $27.99 **92**

1. Guitarists 2. Punk rock music 3. Women rock musicians 4. Slits (Musical group) 5. Punk rock musicians -- Great Britain -- Biography
ISBN 1250065992; 9781250065995

LC 2014029971

In this memoir, punk rock musician Viv Albertine presents a "look at a traditionally male-dominated scene. . . . The author recalls rebelling from conformity and patriarchal society ever since her days as an adolescent girl in the same London suburb of Muswell Hill where the Kinks formed. With brash honesty . . . Albertine writes of immersing herself into punk culture among the likes of the Sex Pistols." (Publisher's note)

"This pioneer and pivotal punk rocker discusses her relationships/friendships with fellow musicians Joe Strummer, Johnny Rotten, Sid Vicious, and Johnny Thunders in this fascinating insider's look at the punk scene from a female perspective." Booklist

Alcott, Amos Bronson, 1799-1888

Matteson, John. **Eden's** outcasts; the story of Louisa May Alcott and her father. W.W. Norton 2007 497p il $29.95 **92**

1. Authors 2. Educators 3. Novelists 4. Philosophers 5. Authors, American 6. Nonfiction writers 7. Young adult authors
ISBN 978-0-393-05964-9

LC 2007-13707

"Matteson's lucid, commanding biography casts new light on an unusual father-daughter bond and a new land at war with itself." Booklist

Includes bibliographical references

Alcott, Louisa May, 1832-1888

Matteson, John. **Eden's** outcasts; the story of Louisa May Alcott and her father. W.W. Norton 2007 497p il $29.95 **92**

1. Authors 2. Educators 3. Novelists 4. Philosophers 5. Authors, American 6. Nonfiction writers 7. Young adult authors
ISBN 978-0-393-05964-9

LC 2007-13707

"Matteson's lucid, commanding biography casts new light on an unusual father-daughter bond and a new land at war with itself." Booklist

Includes bibliographical references

Reisen, Harriet. **Louisa** May Alcott; the woman behind Little women. Henry Holt 2009 362p $26 **92**
1. Authors 2. Novelists 3. Authors, American 4. Young adult authors
ISBN 978-0-8050-8299-9; 0-8050-8299-9
LC 2009-10637

In this biography of the American author, "Reisen analyzes Louisa's great pleasure in writing lucrative pulp fiction, her sacrifices, adventures, and brilliant career. Here . . . is Alcott whole, a trailblazing woman grasping freedom in a time of sexual inequality and war, a survivor of cruel tragedies, a quintessential American writer." Booklist

Includes bibliographical references

Alden, Ginger

Alden, Ginger. **Elvis** and Ginger; Ginger Alden. Ace Books 2014 400 p. illustrations (chiefly color) (hardcover) $26.95 **92**
1. Actresses -- United States -- Biography 2. Rock musicians -- United States -- Biography
ISBN 0425266338; 9780425266335
LC 2014009089

In this memoir Ginger Alden discusses her " whirlwind romance [with Elvis Presley] from first kiss to his stunning proposal of marriage. She details his exploration of Eastern religions, his perception of being a 'legend,' his devotion to family and friends, and her attempt to know the insular group surrounding Elvis. And for the very first time she talks about the devastating end of it all, and the 50,000 mourners and reporters who descended on Graceland in 1977." (Publisher's note)

"It's an outpouring of affection for a man who has stayed in the author's mind all these years, a way for her to show the world the Elvis she knew. The book has a pretty much guaranteed readership, as many Elvis fans will read anything and everything that appears in print about their idol." Booklist

Alderson, Sandy

Kettmann, Steve. **Baseball** maverick; How Sandy Alderson Revolutionized Baseball and Revived the Mets. by Steve Kettmann. Atlantic Monthly Press 2015 320 p. illustrations (hardcover) $26 **92**
1. Baseball -- Coaching
ISBN 0802119980; 9780802119988

This book, by Steve Kettmann, describes how "In 2010, the New York Mets were in trouble. . . . They had recently suffered an embarrassing September collapse and two bitter losing seasons. . . . And their principle owners were embroiled in the largest financial scam in American history. To whom did they turn? Sandy Alderson, a former marine who served in Vietnam and graduated from Harvard Law." (Publisher's note)

"Kettmann has written a worthy biography of a compelling figure, but the author's desire to produce his own version of Moneyball has caused him to overstate his case." Kirkus

Aldrin, Buzz, 1930-

Aldrin, Buzz, 1930- **No** dream is too high; life lessons from a man who walked on the Moon. Buzz Aldrin with Ken Abraham. National Geographic 2016 224 p. illustrations (chiefly color) (hardback) $22 **92**
1. Astronauts 2. Scientists 3. Conduct of life 4. Space flight to the moon 5. Conduct of life -- Philosophy 6. Astronauts -- United States -- Biography
ISBN 9781426216497
LC 2015037069

In this book, astronaut Buzz Aldrin "reflects on the wisdom, guiding principles, and irreverent anecdotes he's gathered through his event-filled life—both in outer space and on earth—in this inspiring guide-to-life for the next generation. Everywhere he goes, crowds gather to meet Buzz Aldrin. . . . Best known for a generation of astronauts whose achievements surged in just a few years from the first man in space to first men on the moon." (Publisher's note)

"Aldrin's journey will engage space exploration enthusiasts, and his motivational advice will connect especially well with young adults." LJ

Alexander, Elizabeth, 1962-

Alexander, Elizabeth, 1962- The **light** of the world; a memoir. Elizabeth Alexander. Grand Central Publishing 2015 224 p. (hardback) $26 **92**
1. Marriage 2. Bereavement 3. Loss (Psychology) 4. Women poets, American -- Biography
ISBN 9781455599875
LC 2014020884

NAACP Image Award Nominee: Outstanding Literary Work- Nonfiction (2016)

National Book Critics Circle Award Finalist: Autobiography (2015)

Pulitzer Prize Finalist: Biography (2016).

In this memoir, by Elizabeth Alexander, named Best Book of 2015 by several venues including the "New York Times," "NPR," and "Library Journal," the author "finds herself at an existential crossroads after the sudden death of her husband. . . . She reflects on the beauty of her married life, the trauma resulting from her husband's death, and the solace found in caring for her two teenage sons." (Publisher's note)

"Fashioning her mellifluous narrative around the beauty she found in Ghebreyesus, Alexander is grateful, patient, and willing to pursue a fit of magical thinking that he might just return." Pub Wkly

Alexandra, Empress, consort of Nicholas II, Emperor of Russia, 1872-1918

Massie, Robert K., 1929- **Nicholas** and Alexandra. Ballantine Books 2000 613p il map pa $18.95 **92**
1. Monks 2. Emperors 3. Empresses 4. Courtiers 5. Russia -- History 6. Russia -- Kings and rulers
ISBN 0-345-43831-0; 978-0-345-43831-7
LC 99-91507

First published 1967 by Atheneum

This study provides an intimate account of the Romanov family and the coming of the Russian Revolution. Kerensky, Lenin and Rasputin are among the personalities profiled.

This book, "solid with research, reads as lightly as a novel, as authoritatively as a textbook. Dialogue and lively description lend a sense of immediacy, but his notes, discreetly relegated to the back of the book, show how carefully he has avoided slipping into fiction." Christ Sci Monit

Includes bibliographical references

Ali, Khaliah

Ali, Khaliah. **Fighting** weight; how I achieved healthy weight loss with banding, a new procedure that eliminates hunger--forever. [by] Khaliah Ali; George Fielding, Christine Ren, Lawrence Lindner. HarperCollins 2007 241p il $22.95   **92**
1. Weight loss 2. Fashion designers 3. Memoirists 4. Talk show hosts 5. Models (Persons) 6. Stomach -- Surgery 7. Children of prominent persons
ISBN 0-06-117094-1; 978-0-06-117094-2
LC 2007-60870
The author "describes her own lifelong battle with obesity and the effect of her own gastric-banding surgery.... Coauthor George Fielding, M.D., who performed Ali's surgery, explains the process and how it differs from other bariatric surgeries.... A good combination of scientific information and personal narrative, this title belongs in all public libraries." Libr J

Ali, Muhammad, 1942-2016

Remnick, David. **King** of the world: Muhammad Ali and the rise of an American hero. Random House 1998 326p il hardcover o.p. pa $14   **92**
1. African American athletes 2. Boxers (Persons)
ISBN 0-375-50065-0; 0-375-70229-6 pa
LC 98-24539
"This is the best book ever on Muhammad Ali and one of the best on America in the 1960s." Booklist

Includes bibliographical references

★ Smith, Johnny. **Blood** brothers; the fatal friendship of Muhammad Ali and Malcolm X. Randy Roberts and Johnny Smith. Basic Books 2016 392 p. illustrations (hardcover : alk. paper) $28.99   **92**
1. African Americans -- Biography 2. Black Muslims -- Biography
ISBN 9780465079704
LC 2015043982
In this book, historians Randy Roberts and Johnny Smith "reveal how Malcolm [X] molded Cassius Clay into Muhammad Ali, helping him become an international symbol of black pride and black independence.... Malcolm's death marked the end of a critical phase of the civil rights movement, but the legacy of his friendship with Ali has endured. We inhabit a new era where the roles of entertainer and activist, of sports and politics, are more entwined than ever before." (Publisher's note)

"A page-turning tale from the 1960s about politics and sports and two proud, extraordinary men whose legacies endure." Kirkus

Includes bibliographical references and index

Ali, Nujood

Ali, Nujood. **I** am Nujood, age 10 and divorced; [by] Nujood Ali, with Delphine Minoui; translated by Linda Coverdale. Three Rivers Press 2010 188p pa $12   **92**
1. Children 2. Child marriage 3. Yemen 4. Abused persons
ISBN 978-0-307-58967-5; 0-307-58967-6
LC 2009-33063
"One of 16 children living in squalor in Yemen, Nujood was married off at about age 10. Though her husband vowed he'd wait for sex until she reached puberty, he rapes her on their first night together. After months of abuse, Nujood goes to the courthouse, where with heartbreaking naiveté, she tells a judge she wants a divorce. Supported by the legal system, Nujood gets her wish." People

Includes bibliographical references

Ali, Taha Muhammad

★ Hoffman, Adina. **My** happiness bears no relation to happiness; a poet's life in the Palestinian century. Yale University Press 2009 454p il map $27.50   **92**
1. Poets 2. Authors
ISBN 978-0-300-14150-4
LC 2008-37298
"An exceptional introduction to a literary world that has, until now, been little known to English-language readers, this is highly recommended for all libraries." Libr J

Includes bibliographical references

Alison, Jane

Alison, Jane. The **sisters** antipodes. Houghton Mifflin Harcourt 2009 276p $23   **92**
1. Authors 2. Novelists
ISBN 978-0-15-101280-0; 0-15-101280-6
LC 2008-14747
The author describes "the strangely definitive reconfiguration of her family when her parents broke up and switched partners and children with another couple they met in Australia. ... [This is] a truly unusual, harrowing journey of identity." Publ Wkly

Allen, Richard, 1760-1831

Newman, Richard S. **Freedom's** prophet; Bishop Richard Allen, the AME Church, and the Black founding fathers. New York University Press 2008 359p il $34.95   **92**
1. Slaves 2. Bishops 3. African Methodist Episcopal Church
ISBN 978-0-8147-5826-7; 0-8147-5826-6
LC 2007-43259
"Newman's beautifully written study is not only a first-rate social history of the early Republic and African-American culture and religion, it provides a detailed sketch of Allen that is sure to become the definitive biography of the leader." Publ Wkly

Includes bibliographical references

Allende family

★ Allende, Isabel. **Paula**; translated from the Spanish by Margaret Sayers Peden. HarperPerennial 2008 330, 23p pa $14.99   **92**
1. Authors 2. Novelists 3. Dramatists 4. Journalists

5. Authors, Chilean 6. Children's authors
ISBN 978-0-06-156490-1
First published 1995
Allende "interweaves the story of her own life with the slow dying of her 28-year-old daughter, Paula." Publ Wkly

Allende, Isabel

★ Allende, Isabel. **Paula**; translated from the Spanish by Margaret Sayers Peden. HarperPerennial 2008 330, 23p pa $14.99   **92**
1. Authors 2. Novelists 3. Dramatists 4. Journalists 5. Authors, Chilean 6. Children's authors
ISBN 978-0-06-156490-1
First published 1995
Allende "interweaves the story of her own life with the slow dying of her 28-year-old daughter, Paula." Publ Wkly

Allende, Isabel. The **sum** of our days; translated from the Spanish by Margaret Sayers Peden. Harper-Collins 2008 320p $26.95   **92**
1. Authors 2. Novelists 3. Dramatists 4. Journalists 5. Authors, Chilean 6. Children's authors
ISBN 978-0-06-155183-3; 0-06-155183-X
    LC 2007-33251
"In this sequel to her memoir Paula (1995), about the yearlong coma suffered by her daughter, Chilean novelist Allende tells of the difficult years following Paula's death. . . Surprisingly candid, frequently funny, and highly aware of her own failings, Allende is a person fully engaged in life, and readers will find her eloquent memoir inspirational reading." Booklist

Allilueva, Svetlana, 1926-2011

★ Sullivan, Rosemary. **Stalin's** daughter; the extraordinary and tumultuous life of Svetlana Alliluyeva. Rosemary Sullivan. Harper 2015 752 p. illustrations (hardback) $35   **92**
1. Defectors -- United States -- Biography 2. Immigrants -- United States -- Biography 3. Soviet Union -- History -- 1925-1953 -- Biography 4. Children of heads of state -- Soviet Union -- Biography
ISBN 0062206109; 9780062206107; 9780062206121
    LC 2014045982
National Book Critics Circle Award Finalist: Biography (2015)
This book, by Rosemary Sullivan, offers a "biography of Svetlana Stalin, a woman fated to live her life in the shadow of one of history's most monstrous dictators--her father, Josef Stalin. . . . Svetlana Stalin spent her youth inside the walls of the Kremlin . . . , but she did not escape tragedy. . . As she gradually learned about the extent of her father's brutality after his death, Svetlana . . . in 1967 shocked the world by defecting to the United States." (Publisher's note)
"Svetlana's letters and family photographs enhance the portrait of a woman tortured by the secrets, lies, and intrigues at the center of her early life as a Kremlin princess and in later years as the object of fascination and scorn as the daughter of the feared Russian dictator." Booklist
Includes bibliographical references

Altman, Robert, 1925-2006

Zuckoff, Mitchell. **Robert** Altman; the oral biography. Alfred A. Knopf 2009 560p il   **92**
1. Motion picture producers and directors 2. Television directors 3. Biography, Individual 4. Motion picture directors 5. Motion picture producers
ISBN 0-307-26768-7; 978-0-307-26768-9
    LC 2009-19847
This is a biography of the director of such films as MASH (1970), Nashville (1975), The Player (1992), and Gosford Park (2001). Filmography. Index.
This "is a smart, amusing, lively book, full of anecdotes and a generous step toward perceiving the glorious and perverse ways of Altman himself." New Repub
Includes filmography

Ames, Robert, 1934-1983

Bird, Kai, 1951- The **Good** Spy; The Life and Death of Robert Ames. by Kai Bird. Random House Inc 2014 448 p. illustrations $26   **92**
1. Intelligence service -- United States 2. United States. Central Intelligence Agency
ISBN 0307889750; 9780307889751
    LC 2013049480
This book, by Kai Bird, is a biography "of CIA agent Robert Ames, one of America's most important assets in the [Middle East] until his life was cut short by the bomb that exploded outside the American Embassy in Beirut in April 1983." (Library Journal)
"A low-key, respectful life of a decent American officer whose quietly significant work helped lead to the Oslo Accords." Kirkus
Includes bibliographical references (pages 403-410) and index

Amis, Kingsley, 1922-1995

Amis, Martin. **Experience**. Hyperion 2000 406p il $23.95; pa $14   **92**
1. Poets 2. Authors 3. Humorists 4. Novelists 5. Essayists 6. Literary critics 7. Short story writers
ISBN 0-7868-6652-7; 0-375-72683-7 pa
    LC 00-699777
This is a "portmanteau of personal history, ancestor worship and promiscuous opinionizing, and a piñata of literary gossip that Amis beats with a stick, causing many names to drop. . . . And if we stay put till the last 100 pages, it will break our heart." N Y Times Book Rev

Bradford, Richard. **Lucky** him: the life of Kingsley Amis. Owen, P. 2001 432p il $44.95   **92**
1. Poets 2. Authors 3. Humorists 4. Novelists 5. Essayists 6. Literary critics 7. Short story writers
ISBN 0-7206-1117-2
    LC 2001-431013
This is a biography of the English novelist, best known for such works as Lucky Jim, The old devils, and Difficulties with girls

"The writing is consistently clear and the insights—literary and biographical—are formidable." Publ Wkly

Includes bibliographical references

Leader, Zachary. The **life** of Kingsley Amis. Pantheon Books 2007 996p $39.95　　　　**92**

1. Poets 2. Authors 3. Humorists 4. Novelists 5. Essayists 6. Literary critics 7. Short story writers

ISBN 978-0-375-42498-4; 0-375-42498-9

LC 2006-35012

First published 2006 in the United Kingdom

The "great virtue of Leader's biography of Amis is that you do not have to share his high opinion of the subject to benefit from the book's prodigious research and wealth of information so well presented." San Francisco Chronicle

Includes bibliographical references

Amis, Martin

Amis, Martin. **Experience**. Hyperion 2000 406p il $23.95; pa $14　　　　**92**

1. Poets 2. Authors 3. Humorists 4. Novelists 5. Essayists 6. Literary critics 7. Short story writers

ISBN 0-7868-6652-7; 0-375-72683-7 pa

LC 00-699777

This is a "portmanteau of personal history, ancestor worship and promiscuous opinionizing, and a piñata of literary gossip that Amis beats with a stick, causing many names to drop. . . . And if we stay put till the last 100 pages, it will break our heart." N Y Times Book Rev

Amundsen, Roald, 1872-1928

Bown, Stephen R. The **last** Viking; the life of Roald Amundsen. Stephen R. Bown. Da Capo Press 2012 xxii, 357 p.p ill., maps (hardcover : alk. paper) $27.50　　　　**92**

1. Explorers -- Norway -- Biography 2. North Pole -- Discovery and exploration -- Norweigian 3. Arctic regions -- Discovery and exploration -- Norweigian

ISBN 0306820676; 9780306820670; 9780306821622

LC 2012012126

This book by Stephen R. Bown is a biography of Roald Amundsen, "a legend of the heroic age of exploration. . . . In 1900, the four great geographical mysteries--the Northwest Passage, the Northeast Passage, the South Pole, and the North Pole--remained blank spots on the globe. Within twenty years Roald Amundsen would claim all four prizes. . . . Féted in his lifetime as an international celebrity, pursued by women and creditors, he died in the Arctic on a rescue mission." (Publisher's note)

Includes bibliographical references and index

Andalibian, Rahimeh

The **rose** hotel; a memoir of secrets, loss, and love from Iran to America. Rahimeh Andalibian. National Geographic 2015 336 p. (hardback) $26 **92**

1. Iranian Americans 2. Iran -- History -- 1941-1979 3. Iranian American women -- Biography 4. Political refugees -- Iran -- Biography 5. Political refugees -- United States -- Biography 6. Iran -- History -- Revolution, 1979 -- Personal narratives

ISBN 1426214790; 9781426214790

LC 2014037952

"In this . . . memoir, Iranian-born author Rahimeh Andalibian tells the story of her family: how they survived the 1979 revolution; their move to California; and their attempts to adapt in the face of addiction, teenage rebellion, and new traditions. Andalibian struggles to make sense of two brutal crimes: a rape, avenged by her father, and a murder, of which her beloved oldest brother stands accused." (Publisher's note)

"A powerful and uplifting memoir of tragedy and healing." Kirkus

Andersen, Hans Christian, 1805-1875

Andersen, Jens. **Hans** Christian Andersen: a new life; translated from the Danish by Tiina Nunnally. Overlook Press 2005 624p il hardcover o.p. pa $22.95　　　　**92**

1. Authors 2. Novelists 3. Dramatists 4. Authors, Danish 5. Children's authors 6. Short story writers

ISBN 1-58567-642-X; 1-58567-737-X pa

LC 2004-65985

The author examines Andersen's "considerable gifts as an oral storyteller; his eccentric, often annoying public habits; his ambivalent sexuality; his bouts of narcissism; his painfully slow transformation from rough-hewn provincial and awkward melodramatist into brilliant, internationally famous writer-celebrity. The biography is best and most moving when it is frank about formerly suppressed aspects of Andersen's life." Booklist

Includes bibliographical references

Anderson, Clayton C., 1959-

Anderson, Clayton, 1959- The **ordinary** spaceman; from boyhood dreams to astronaut. Clayton C. Anderson; foreword by Nevada Barr. University of Nebraska Press 2015 400 p. (cloth : alkaline paper) $29.95　　　　**92**

1. nternational Space Station 2. Astronauts -- United States -- Biography 3. Extravehicular activity (Manned space flight) 4. United States. National Aeronautics and Space Administration -- Biography

ISBN 0803262825; 9780803262829

LC 2014048858

This memoir, by Clayton C. Anderson, describes the author's experiences as an astronaut "from the application process to launch aboard the space shuttle Atlantis, from serving as a family escort for the ill-fated Columbia crew in 2003 to his own daily struggles--family separation, competitive battles to win coveted flight assignments, the stress of a highly visible job, and the ever-present risk of having to make the ultimate sacrifice." (Publisher's note)

Anderson, Marian, 1897-1993

Keiler, Allan. **Marian** Anderson; a singer's journey. University of Illinois Press 2002 447p hardcover o.p. pa $21.95　　　　**92**

1. African American singers 2. Opera singers 3. African American women -- Biography

ISBN 0-684-80711-4; 0-252-07067-4 pa

LC 99-43319

First published 2000 by Scribner

The author's "clear, succinct prose, initially lacking narrative coherence, gains strength and momentum as his subject matures from a young and struggling artist into one of the enduring voices of our century." Publ Wkly

Includes discography and bibliographical references

Anderson, Terry A., 1949-

Anderson, Sulome. The **Hostage's** Daughter; A Story of Family, Madness, and the Middle East. by Sulome Anderson. HarperCollins 2016 288 p. $25.99 **92**

1. Hostages 2. Lebanese 3. Father-daughter relationship 4. Middle East -- Social conditions
ISBN 0062385496; 9780062385499

In this book, Sulome Anderson, "a journalist and daughter of one of the world's most famous hostages, Terry Anderson, takes an intimate look at her father's captivity during the Lebanese Hostage Crisis and the ensuing political firestorm on both her family and the United States—as well as the far-reaching implications of those events on Middle Eastern politics today." (Publisher's note)

"Through these dual narratives, Anderson creates a compelling depiction of the collateral damage of terrorism and a remarkable piece of investigative journalism with a surprise twist." Pub Wkly

Anderson, Tim, 1972-

Anderson, Tim. **Sweet** Tooth; a memoir. Tim Anderson. Lake Union Pr 2014 334 p. $14.95 **92**

1. Gay teenagers 2. Autobiographies
ISBN 1477818073; 9781477818077

LC 2013919514

"'Sweet Tooth' is Tim Anderson's . . . memoir of life after his hormones and blood sugar both went berserk at the age of fifteen. With Morrissey and The Smiths as the soundtrack, Anderson self-deprecatingly recalls love affairs with vests and donuts, first crushes, coming out, and inaugural trips to gay bars. What emerges is the story of a young man trying to build a future that won't involve crippling loneliness or losing a foot to his disease." (Publisher's note)

"Staying true to his experiences, Anderson evokes the juvenile tendency toward self-destruction in a way that is simultaneously funny and frustrating. The combination gives readers a visceral taste of the rollercoaster ride that was his young adulthood." Pub Wkly

Andoe, Joe

Andoe, Joe. **Jubilee** city; a memoir at full speed. William Morrow 2007 207p il $22.95 **92**

1. Artists 2. Painters
ISBN 978-0-06-124031-7; 0-06-124031-1

In this "memoir, Andoe narrates his journey from his Tulsa childhood through redneck, hard-partying teen years to a highly successful career as a (hard-partying redneck) painter in New York City. While Andoe may not be a professional writer, his humor and offbeat artistic sensibility make up for any lack of prose-writing chops. Through discrete anecdotes that seldom run longer than two pages, Andoe assembles vivid portraits of his family and friends and of the various environments he inhabited-the working-class Tulsa neighborhoods of the 1960s, the high school and college drug culture at the end of the hippie era, and the New York art scene of the 1980s." Publ Wkly

Andrews, Julie

Andrews, Julie. **Home**; a memoir of my early years. Hyperion 2008 339p il $26.95 **92**

1. Actors 2. Singers 3. Children's authors
ISBN 978-0-7868-6565-9; 0-7868-6565-2

LC 2007-48830

"Spanning events from her 1935 birth to the early 1960s, . . . [the author] covers her rise to fame and ends with Walt Disney casting her in Mary Poppins (1963). . . . The heart of her book documents the rehearsals, tryouts and smash 1956 opening of My Fair Lady. Readers will rejoice, since Andrews is an accomplished writer who holds back nothing while adding a patina of poetry to the antics and anecdotes throughout this memoir of bittersweet backstage encounters and theatrical triumphs." Publ Wkly

Angell, Roger, 1920-

Angell, Roger, 1920- **This** old man; all in pieces. Roger Angell. Doubleday 2015 320 p. illustrations (hardback) $26.95 **92**

1. Criticism 2. Popular culture
ISBN 0385541139; 9780385541138

LC 2015018255

This book, by Roger Angell, offers "a selection of writings that celebrate a view from the tenth decade of an engaged, vibrant life. . . . Angell won the 2015 American Society of Magazine Editors' Best Essay award for 'This Old Man,' which forms a centerpiece for this book. . . . The book gathers essays, letters, light verse, book reviews, Talk of the Town stories, farewells, haikus, Profiles, Christmas greetings, late thoughts on the costs of war." (Publisher's note)

"While essays such as the titular "This Old Man" and "Over the Wall" grab and hold tighter than others, fans of The New Yorker (and of baseball, one of Angell's most beloved subjects), will take pleasure in digging into this rich collection culled from an extraordinary career." Library Journal

Angelou, Maya, 1928-2014

★ Angelou, Maya. **I** know why the caged bird sings. Random House 2002 281p $21.95 **92**

1. Poets 2. Actors 3. Singers 4. Dramatists 5. Women authors 6. African American authors 7. Essayists 8. Memoirists 9. Children's authors
ISBN 0-375-50789-2

LC 2001-41914

First published 1969

The first volume in the author's autobiographical series covers her childhood and adolescence in rural Arkansas, St. Louis, and San Francisco.

"Angelou is a skillful writer; her language ranges from beautifully lyrical prose to earthy metaphor, and her descriptions have power and sensitivity." Libr J

Followed by Gather together in my name (1974); Singin' and swingin' and gettin' merry like Christmas (1976); The heart of a woman (1981); All God's children need traveling shoes (1986); A song flung up to heaven (2002)

Angelou, Maya, 1928-2014. **Letter** to my daughter. Random House 2008 166p $25 **92**

1. Poets 2. Actors 3. Singers 4. Dramatists 5. Women authors 6. African American authors 7. Essayists 8.

Memoirists 9. Children's authors
ISBN 978-1-4000-6612-4

LC 2008-28843

"A slim volume packed with nourishing nuggets of wisdom." Kirkus

Gillespie, Marcia Ann. **Maya** Angelou; a glorious celebration. [by] Marcia Ann Gillespie, Rosa Johnson Butler and Richard A. Long; foreword by Oprah Winfrey. Doubleday 2008 191p il $30 **92**
1. Poets 2. Actors 3. Singers 4. Dramatists 5. Women authors 6. African American authors 7. Essayists 8. Memoirists 9. Children's authors
ISBN 978-0-385-51108-7

LC 2007-31301

This look at Maya Angelou's life as well as her myriad interests and accomplishments by the people who know her best (longtime friends Marcia Ann Gillespie and Richard Long and niece Rosa Johnson Butler) features over 150 sepia portraits, family photographs, and letters. Includes a bibliography of her works.

"A loving tribute to one of the most renowned authors today, this work is highly recommended." Libr J

Anne Boleyn, Queen, consort of Henry VIII, King of England, 1507-1536

Weir, Alison. The **lady** in the tower; the fall of Anne Boleyn. Ballantine Books 2009 434p il $28 **92**
1. Queens 2. Great Britain -- History -- 1485-1603, Tudors
ISBN 978-0-345-45321-1; 0-345-45321-2

LC 2009-42748

Historian Weir is "well equipped to parse the evidence, ferret out the misconceptions and arrive at sturdy hypotheses about what actually befell Anne. Her command of minutiae is impressive, as is her enthusiasm for even the most minor aspects of Anne's frequently distorted story." N Y Times Book Rev

Includes bibliographical references

Anne, Queen of Great Britain, 1665-1714

Somerset, Anne. **Queen** Anne; the politics of passion. Anne Somerset. Alfred A. Knopf 2013 621 p. illustrations, portraits $35 **92**
1. Great Britain -- Kings and rulers 2. Queens -- Great Britain -- Biography 3. Great Britain -- History -- Anne, 1702-1714
ISBN 0307962881; 9780307962881

LC 2012035334

This book, by Anne Somerset, is a biography of British Queen Anne. "She ascended the thrones of England, Scotland and Ireland in 1702, at age thirty-seven, . . . and five years later united two of her realms, England and Scotland, as a sovereign state, creating the Kingdom of Great Britain. She had a history of personal misfortune, overcoming ill health . . . and living through seventeen miscarriages, stillbirths, and premature births in seventeen years." (Publisher's note)

"Anne's natural reserve and her instinct for discretion has led historians to believe that she was weak and dominated by women of stronger character. Somerset's impressive

scholarship debunks that belief and shows Anne as a masterful, even authoritative, queen who survived the influence of her 'friends.'" Kirkus

Includes bibliographical references and index

Anthony, Susan B., 1820-1906

Anthony, Susan B. **Failure** is impossible; Susan B. Anthony in her own words. [edited by] Lynn Sherr. Times Bks. 1995 xxviii, 384p il hardcover o.p. pa $23 **92**
1. Feminism 2. Suffragists 3. Abolitionists
ISBN 0-8129-2718-4

LC 94-29913

This is a collection of Susan B. Anthony's journal entries, correspondence, speeches, interviews, and published writings. The author has arranged the selections by topic and chronologically within topics

Includes bibliographical references

Antonia, Mother

Jordan, Mary. The **prison** angel; Mother Antonia's journey from Beverly Hills to a life of service in a Mexican jail. [by] Mary Jordan and Kevin Sullivan. Penguin Press 2005 237p il $24.95 **92**
1. Nuns
ISBN 1-59420-056-4

LC 2004-60238

The authors describe the "journey of a woman who, at the age of 50, left the comforts of suburban L.A. to begin a charity mission in Mexico. . . . This is an inspiring story of one woman's compassion and her own journey of spiritual growth." Booklist

Antonius, Marcus, ca. 83-30 B.C.

Goldsworthy, Adrian Keith. **Antony** and Cleopatra; [by] Adrian Goldsworthy. Yale University Press 2010 470p il map $35 **92**
1. Queens 2. Generals 3. Statesmen 4. Orators 5. Rome -- History 6. Egypt -- History
ISBN 978-0-300-16534-0

LC 2010-929122

"Narrating [Antony] and Cleopatra's parts in the tumultuous end of the Roman Republic, Goldsworthy skillfully integrates the partial and partisan source material into an accessible presentation of a classic tale from classical times." Booklist

Includes bibliographical references

Apana, Chang, 1871-1933

Yunte Huang. **Charlie** Chan; the untold story of the honorable detective and his rendezvous with American history. W.W. Norton 2010 354p il map **92**
1. Detectives 2. Biography, Individual 3. Chan, Charlie (Fictional character) 4. Chan, Charlie (Fictitious character)
ISBN 0393069621; 9780393069624

LC 2010016653

This is a history of Charlie Chan, the detective feaured in six novels and 47 movies. Huang contends that Charlie

Chan is based upon Chang Apana, a real-life Chinese detective on the Honolulu police force. Bibliography. Index.

This "is a terrifically enjoyable and informative book, one that should appeal to both students of racial history and to fans of one of cinema's greatest detectives." Washington Post Book World

Includes bibliographical references

Apess, William, 1798-1839

Gura, Philip F., 1950- The **life** of William Apess, Pequot; Philip F. Gura. University of North Carolina Press 2014 216 p. (cloth : alk. paper) $26   **92**
1. Pequot Indians 2. Pequot Indians -- Biography 3. Indians, Treatment of -- New England -- History 4. Methodist Church -- New England -- Clergy -- Biography
ISBN 1469619989; 9781469619989

LC 2014026609

In this book, author Philip F. Gura "offers the first book-length chronicle of [Pequot Indian preacher William] Apess's fascinating and consequential life. After an impoverished childhood marked by abuse, Apess soldiered with American troops during the War of 1812, converted to Methodism, and rose to fame as a lecturer who lifted a powerful voice of protest against the plight of Native Americans in New England and beyond." (Publisher's note)

"This outstanding biography is essential reading for those interested in either Native American studies or American literature. LJ

Includes bibliographical references and index

Appleseed, Johnny, 1774-1845

Means, Howard B. **Johnny** Appleseed; the man, the myth, the American story. [by] Howard Means. Simon & Schuster 2011 320p il map $26; ebook $12.99   **92**
1. Apples 2. Frontier and pioneer life 3. Pioneers 4. Fruit growers
ISBN 978-1-4391-7825-6; 978-1-4391-7827-0 ebook

LC 2011-665

"Delightfully wry and perceptive, Means' quest to understand Chapman/Appleseed is a captivating achievement in Americana." Booklist

Arana, Marie

Arana, Marie. **American** chica; two worlds, one childhood. Dial Press (NY) 2001 309p hardcover o.p. pa $12.95   **92**
1. Authors 2. Novelists 3. Editors 4. Memoirists 5. Literary critics
ISBN 0-385-31963-0 pa

LC 00-47529

The author, born to a Peruvian father and an American mother, writes of her childhood in Peru

Arana "blends a journalist's dedication to research with a style that sings with humor. Her memoir is an outstanding contribution to the growing shelf of Latina literature." Publ Wkly

Arbus, Diane, 1923-1971

Lubow, Arthur. **Diane** Arbus; Portrait of a Photographer. Arthur Lubow. HarperCollins 2016 752 p. illustrations $35   **92**
1. Photography 2. Women photographers -- Biography
ISBN 0062234323; 9780062234322

LC 2016015617

This book, by Arthur Lubow, is a "biography of . . . Diane Arbus, one of the most influential and important photographers of the twentieth century. He deftly traces Arbus's development from a wealthy, sexually precocious free spirit into first, a successful New York fashion photographer and then, a singular artist who coaxed secrets from her subjects. Lubow reveals that Arbus's profound need not only to see her subjects but to be seen by them drove her to forge unusually close bonds with these people." (Publisher's note)

"Lubow's portrait is the most sharply focused, encompassing, and incisive to date." Booklist

Includes bibliographical references (pages 619-714) and index.

Archimedes, ca. 287-212 B.C.

Hirshfeld, Alan. **Eureka** man; the life and legacy of Archimedes. Walker 2009 242p il map $26   **92**
1. Scientists 2. Mathematicians 3. Writers on science 4. Science -- Greece -- History
ISBN 978-0-8027-1618-7; 0-8027-1618-0

LC 2009-05608

"Thoroughly enjoyable look at the tumultuous life and resounding influence of a genius of antiquity. . . . Hirshfeld writes clearly and with enthusiasm, navigating even the occasional dense mathematical concept with easy-to-understand language and accompanying diagrams." Kirkus

Includes bibliographical references

Arkin, Alan, 1934-

Arkin, Alan. An **improvised** life; a memoir. Da Capo Press 2011 201p $17   **92**
1. Actors 2. Theatrical directors
ISBN 978-0-306-81966-7

LC 2010-45034

"Arkin looks back on his career as an actor, but this memoir forgoes the backstage gossip and star-studded anecdotes readers might expect. In fact, the author largely ignores his accomplishments in favor of charting his inner evolution as an artist, focusing on intellectual and spiritual epiphanies that have shaped his approach to acting. . . . Earnest, intelligent and well-observed—less a celebrity memoir than a serious consideration of the principles of acting and improvisation. " Kirkus

Armstrong, Karen, 1944-

Armstrong, Karen. The **spiral** staircase; my climb out of darkness. Knopf 2004 xxii, 305p hardcover o.p. pa $14   **92**
1. Nuns 2. Religious scholars
ISBN 0-375-41318-9; 0-385-72127-7 pa

LC 2003-47550

This "is the story of Armstrong's personal spiritual quest, which led her at age 17 to join a convent. However, she found that her own skeptical nature and the physical constraints of convent life crippled her intellectually and spiritually. . . . After seven years, Armstrong left the convent." SLJ

Armstrong, Lance

Strickland, Bill. **Tour** de Lance; the extraordinary story of Lance Armstrong's fight to reclaim the Tour De France. Harmony Books 2010 300p il map $25.99 **92**

1. Athletes 2. Cyclists 3. Olympic athletes
ISBN 978-0-307-58984-2

LC 2010-4504

This is "the story of Lance Armstrong's return in 2009, after a three-year absence, to the Tour de France. . . . Strickland, who had access to Armstrong's inner circle, enhances it with an eye for detail and an understanding of its importance in the context of cycling's own physical demands and singular history. He reminds readers, as if they need it, of Armstrong's supremacy and laser dedication in the sport. . . . An irresistible account of a story that needed telling." Booklist

Armstrong, Louis, 1900-1971

Armstrong, Louis. **Louis** Armstrong, in his own words; selected writings. edited and with an introduction by Thomas Brothers; annotated index by Charles Kinzer. Oxford Univ. Press 1999 xxvii, 255p il hardcover o.p. pa $14.95 **92**

1. Singers 2. Jazz musicians 3. Band leaders 4. Trumpet players
ISBN 0-19-514046-X

LC 99-17040

In this collection Armstrong "recounts episodes from his childhood in New Orleans, pays tribute to other musicians, and extolls the virtues of marijuana, laxatives, and rice and beans while speaking candidly about race relations, the music business, and his extramarital affairs. The joy he took in expressing himself on paper is abundantly evident." New Yorker

Includes bibliographical references

Teachout, Terry. **Pops**; a life of Louis Armstrong. Houghton Mifflin Harcourt 2009 475p il $30 **92**

1. Jazz musicians 2. Biography, Individual 3. Jazz -- History and criticism
ISBN 978-0-15-101089-9; 0-15-101089-7

LC 2009-6035

"The author makes an eloquent case for Armstrong's status as a pioneer, not just in jazz but in the broader context of 20th-century art. A rewarding jazz biography and a revealing look at a broad swath of American cultural history." Kirkus

Includes discography and bibliographical references

Armstrong, Louis, 1901-1971

★ Brothers, Thomas. **Louis** Armstrong, master of modernism; by Thomas Brothers. W.W. Norton & Co. Inc. 2014 608 p. illustrations (hardcover) $39.95 **92**

1. Jazz musicians -- Biography
ISBN 0393065820; 9780393065824

LC 2013037726

Pulitzer Prize Finalist: Biography or Autobiography (2015)

Author Thomas Brothers presents an "account of [jazz musician] Louis Armstrong--his life and legacy--during the most creative period of his career . . . in the 1920s and early 1930s, when Armstrong created not one but two modern musical styles. [The book] blends cultural history, musical scholarship, and personal accounts from Armstrong's contemporaries to reveal his enduring contributions to jazz and popular music." (Publisher's note)

A "monumental follow-up to Louis Armstrong's New Orleans (2006). . . . Brothers' work, covering an astonishingly creative decade, is comprehensive and firmly grounded in musicology and in the racial and cultural climate of the 1920s. It is voluminously researched, compellingly written, and supported by a valuable discography and bibliography." Booklist

Includes bibliographical references, discography, and index

Armstrong, Neil, 1930-2012

Barbree, Jay. **Neil** Armstrong; A Life of Flight. Jay Barbree. St. Martin's Press 2014 320 p. illustrations $27.99 **92**

1. Astronauts 2. Air pilots -- Biography 3. Project Apollo (U.S.) -- History 4. Space flight to the moon -- History 5. Astronauts -- United States -- Biography
ISBN 125004071X; 9781250040718

LC 2014008696

"Working from 50 years of conversations he had with [astronaut] Neil [Armstrong] . . . , [author Jay] Barbree writes about Neil's three passions--flight, family, and friends. This is the inside story of Neil Armstrong from the time he flew . . . in the Korean War and then flew a rocket plane called the X-15 to the edge of space, to when he saved his Gemini 8 by flying the first emergency return from Earth orbit and then flew Apollo-Eleven to the moon's Sea of Tranquility." (Publisher's note)

"The author paints a detailed and colorful picture of his subject and an unbiased depiction of the period in which he lived, while also demonstrating reverence for Armstrong as a confidant." LJ

Aron, Wendy

Aron, Wendy. **Hide** & seek; how I laughed at depression, conquered my fears and found happiness. Kunati 2008 235p pa $14.95 **92**

1. Authors 2. Dramatists 3. Journalists 4. Depression (Psychology) 5. Memoirists 6. Television scriptwriters
ISBN 978-1-60164-158-8

LC 2008-14008

"In her efforts to subdue raging depression, TV and stage writer Aron tried to no avail virtually every mainstream and alternative remedy. Her adventures among the lunatic fringe are laugh-out-loud funny. . . . Anyone who has overcome recurring bouts with the blues will relish this comic self-help tale." Libr J

Includes bibliographical references

Astaire, Adele

Riley, Kathleen, 1974- The **Astaires**; Fred & Adele. Kathleen Riley. Oxford University Press 2012 xxiii, 241 p.p (alk. paper) $27.95 **92**

1. Actors -- United States -- Biography 2. Dancers --

United States -- Biography 3. Actresses -- United States
-- Biography

ISBN 0199738416; 9780199738410

LC 2011018462

This book, by Kathleen Riley, offers a biography of the
sibling-entertainers Fred and Adele Astaire. "Kathleen Riley
traces the Astaires' rise to fame from . . . child performers
on small-time vaudeville stages . . . to their 1917 debut on
Broadway to star billings on both sides of the Atlantic. . . .
Ultimately, Fred's dancing expertise surpassed his sister's,
and their paths diverged: Adele married into British aristocracy, and Fred headed for Hollywood." (Publisher's note)

Includes bibliographical references and index.

Astaire, Fred

Riley, Kathleen, 1974- The **Astaires**; Fred &
Adele. Kathleen Riley. Oxford University Press
2012 xxiii, 241 p.p (alk. paper) $27.95　　　**92**
1. Actors -- United States -- Biography 2. Dancers --
United States -- Biography 3. Actresses -- United States
-- Biography

ISBN 0199738416; 9780199738410

LC 2011018462

This book, by Kathleen Riley, offers a biography of the
sibling-entertainers Fred and Adele Astaire. "Kathleen Riley
traces the Astaires' rise to fame from . . . child performers
on small-time vaudeville stages . . . to their 1917 debut on
Broadway to star billings on both sides of the Atlantic. . . .
Ultimately, Fred's dancing expertise surpassed his sister's,
and their paths diverged: Adele married into British aristocracy, and Fred headed for Hollywood." (Publisher's note)

Includes bibliographical references and index.

Atanasoff, John V.

Smiley, Jane. The **man** who invented the computer; the biography of John Atanasoff, digital pioneer. Doubleday 2010 246p il $25.95　　　**92**
1. Inventors 2. Physicists 3. Mathematicians 4.
Computer scientists

ISBN 978-0-385-52713-2; 0-385-52713-6

LC 2010-18887

"Engrossing. Smiley takes science history and injects it
with a touch of noir and an exciting clash of vanities." Kirkus

Includes bibliographical references

Athill, Diana

Athill, Diana. **Somewhere** towards the end.
W.W. Norton 2009 182p $24.95; pa $13.95　　　**92**
1. Aging 2. Authors 3. Old age 4. Editors 5.
Memoirists 6. Translators 7. Short story writers

ISBN 978-0-393-06770-5; 0-393-06770-X; 978-0-
393-33800-3 pa; 0-393-33800-2 pa

LC 2008-41533

First published 2008 in the United Kingdom

The author "offers a spry dispatch on the condition of
being elderly. . . . Her perspective is both remorseless and
tender as she considers the waning of her sexual desire, the
sharpening of her atheist resolve, her increasing preference
for nonfiction rather than novels . . . and the truth that, even
in her advanced state, much of her time is taken up with caring for those still older. The achievement of Athill's work is

its refusal to reduce the specificities of her captivating life to
homilies about wisdom." New Yorker

Atkins, Vera, 1908-2000

Helm, Sarah. A **life** in secrets; Vera Atkins and
the missing agents of WWII. Nan A. Talese 2006
493p il map hardcover o.p. pa $16　　　**92**
1. Intelligence service agents 2. World War, 1939-1945
-- Secret service 3. Great Britain -- Special Operations
Executive

ISBN 0-385-50845-X; 978-1-4000-3140-5 pa;
1-4000-3140-0 pa

LC 2005-56870

First published 2005 in the United Kingdom

This is a biography of "the highest-ranking female official in the French section of a WWII British intelligence
unit that aided the resistance. Atkins sent 400 agents into
France, including 39 women she'd personally recruited and
supervised. . . . Helm has produced a memorable portrait of
a woman who knowingly sent other women to their deaths
and a searing history of female courage and suffering during
WWII." Publ Wkly

Includes bibliographical references

Atlas, Teddy

Atlas, Teddy. **Atlas**; from the streets to the ring: a
son's struggle to become a man. [by] Teddy Atlas and
Peter Alson. Ecco 2006 278p il $24.95　　　**92**
1. Sports trainers

ISBN 0-06-054240-3; 978-0-06-054240-5

LC 2005-52104

The author "traces his circuitous route from Staten Island street thug, emotionally ignored by his doctor father, to
renowned [boxing] trainer. . . . It's all here—the good, the
bad and the ugly of Teddy Atlas, often rendered in a crude
but convincing street language, captured so faithfully and
so forcefully by his collaborator, Peter Alson." N Y Times
Book Rev

Attila, King of the Huns, d. 453

Kelly, Christopher. The **end** of empire; Attila the
Hun and the fall of Rome. W.W. Norton 2009 350p
il map $26.95　　　**92**
1. Huns 2. Tribal leaders 3. Rome -- History

ISBN 978-0-393-06196-3

LC 2009-009072

First published 2008 in the United Kingdom with
title: Attila the Hun: barbarian terror and the fall of the
Roman Empire

The author "paints an engaging portrait of Attila the
Hun's rise to prominence and places the feared warlord in
the context of his own time." Libr J

Includes bibliographical references

Audibert-Boulloche, Christiane

Kaiser, Charles. The **cost** of courage; by Charles
Kaiser. Other Press 2015 288 p. illustrations (hardcover) $26.95　　　**92**
1. World War, 1939-1945 -- Biography 2. World War,
1939-1945 -- Underground movements -- France 3.
Guerrillas -- France -- Biography 4. France -- History --
German occupation, 1940-1945 -- Biography 5. World

War, 1939-1945 -- Underground movements -- France -- Biography

ISBN 1590516141; 9781590516140

LC 2015008560

This book, by Charles Kaiser, tells the "heroic true story of the three youngest children of a . . . family who worked together in the French Resistance. . . . In the autumn of 1943, André Boulloche . . . coordinat[ed] all the Resistance movements in the nine northern regions of France only to be betrayed by one of his associates . . . and taken prisoner. His sisters carried on the fight without him until the end of the war." (Publisher's note)

"Kaiser's account of a family's devotion and resilience in the face of horrific tyranny tells a highly recommended story of resolve and bravery that can't help but feel romantic in its selfless and profound obligation, but this is not gloss nor ungrounded canonization." LJ

Audubon, John James, 1785-1851

Rhodes, Richard. **John** James Audubon; the making of an American. Knopf 2004 528p il $30; pa $16 **92**

1. Artists 2. Painters 3. Naturalists 4. Ornithologists 5. Writers on science 6. Biography, Individual 7. Artists -- United States

ISBN 0-375-41412-6; 0-375-71393-X pa

LC 2003-69489

This is a biography of the American ornithologist and painter.

The author "chronicles Audubon's ineluctable sense of mission, phenomenal skills, and triumph over adversity. . . . Rhodes sets Audubon's engrossing tale within the context of the War of 1812, the Louisiana Purchase, the wars against Native Americans (whom Audubon profoundly admired), and the rapid decimation of the American wilderness. . . . Full of passion and discovery, hardship and transcendence, Audubon's story is at once intimate and mythic, and Rhodes' fresh, comprehensive biography will capture the imagination of readers everywhere." Booklist

Includes bibliographical references

Augustus, Emperor of Rome, 63 B.C.-14 A.D.

★ Everitt, Anthony. **Augustus**; the life of Rome's first emperor. Random House 2006 377p il map $26.95 **92**

1. Emperors 2. Rome -- History

ISBN 1-4000-6128-8; 978-1-4000-6128-0

LC 2006-41735

The author's "writing is so crisp and so lively he brings both Rome and Augustus to life in this magnificent work, a must-read for anyone interested in classical times." Booklist

Includes bibliographical references

Goldsworthy, Adrian. **Augustus**; first Emperor of Rome. Adrian Goldsworthy. Yale University Press 2014 624 p. illustrations $35 **92**

1. Rome -- History 2. Emperors -- Rome 3. Emperors -- Rome -- Biography 4. Rome -- History -- Augustus, 30 B.C.-14 A.D

ISBN 0300178727; 9780300178722

LC 2014940657

This biography, by Adrian Goldsworthy, focuses on "Caesar Augustus. . . . began as a teenage warlord, whose only claim to power was as the heir of the murdered Julius Caesar. . . . Over the next half century he reinvented himself as a servant of the state who gave Rome peace and stability, and created a new system of government-- the Principate or rule of an emperor." (Publisher's note)

"Goldsworthy tells the story well. A commendable book. Summing Up: Highly recommended. General and undergraduate readers." Choice

Includes bibliographical references (pages [522]-586) and index

Aung San Suu Kyi

Wintle, Justin. **Perfect** hostage; a life of Aung San Suu Kyi, Burma's prisoner of conscience. Skyhorse Pub. 2008 464p il map $27.95 **92**

1. Political prisoners 2. Women political activists 3. Dissenters 4. Political leaders 5. Nonfiction writers 6. Human rights activists 7. Nobel laureates for peace 8. Myanmar -- Politics and government 9. National League for Democracy (Burma)

ISBN 978-1-60239-266-3; 1-60239-266-8

LC 2007-51031

This is a biography of the Burmese human rights activist.

The author "writes with a snarling wit, firm grasp of Burma's horrors, and penetrating respect for this tenacious and composed prisoner of conscience, detailing her genius for connecting with people, the threats against her life, and her devotion to peace." Booklist

Includes bibliographical references (p. 432-9)

Austen, Jane, 1775-1817

Harman, Claire. **Jane's** fame; how Jane Austen conquered the world. Henry Holt and Co. 2010 277p il $26 **92**

1. Authors 2. Novelists 3. Women authors 4. Authors, English

ISBN 978-0-8050-8258-6; 0-8050-8258-1

LC 2009-22291

First published 2009 in the United Kingdom

"Engagingly written and full of fascinating bits of information as well as valuable insights, this is a must for any serious Austen reader." Booklist

Includes bibliographical references

Auster, Paul, 1947-

Auster, Paul, 1947- **Report** from the interior; Paul Auster. Henry Holt and Company 2013 352 p. (hardback) $27 **92**

1. Letters 2. Adolescence 3. Authors, American -- 20th century -- Biography

ISBN 0805098577; 9780805098570

LC 2013002417

Author Paul Auster has divided this book into four parts. The "first is a childhood psychobiography, to the age of 12, recognizing the distortions and holes in memory while discovering the magic of literature. . . . The second consists of exhaustively detailed synopses of two movies that he saw in his midteens, The Incredible Shrinking Man (1957) and was a Fugitive from a Chain Gang (1932)." The third and fourth parts include letters to his wife and a scrapbook. (Kirkus Reviews)

Austin, Paul, 1955-

Austin, Paul. **Beautiful** eyes; a father transformed. Paul Austin. W.W. Norton & Company 2014 288 p. (hardcover) $25.95   **92**
1. Father and child 2. Down syndrome -- Patients -- Biography 3. Parents of children with disabilities -- Biography 4. Children with mental disabilities -- United States -- Biography
ISBN 039308244X; 9780393082449
LC 2014025600
This book, by Paul Austin, "is the story of a father's journey toward acceptance of a child who is different. . . . [The author] chronicles his life with his daughter [with Down syndrome]: watching her learn to walk and talk and form her own opinions, making decisions about her future, and navigating cultural assumptions and prejudices—all the while confronting, with poignancy and moving candor, his own limitations as her father." (Publisher's note)
"This tender, bright and flawed child showed how being different enhanced her humanity rather than detracted from it. A poignant and candid father's memoir." Kirkus

Autry, Gene, 1907-1998

George-Warren, Holly. **Public** cowboy no. 1; the life and times of Gene Autry. Oxford University Press 2007 406p il $28   **92**
1. Actors 2. Singers 3. Country musicians 4. Cowboys 5. Baseball executives 6. Broadcasting executives
ISBN 978-0-19-517746-6; 0-19-517746-0
LC 2006-36369
This is a biography of the radio performer, singer and actor who performed in rodeos and appeared in such movies as Public Cowboy No.1 (1937) and The Phantom Empire (1935).
"This colorful study is much more than a biography of Autry; it also tells the story of country-western music, singing cowboys, radio and early television, and celebrity." Choice
Includes filmography, discography, and bibliographical references

Avonmore, William Charles Yelverton, Viscount, 1824-1883

Schama, Chloe. **Wild** romance; a Victorian story of a marriage, a trial, and a self-made woman. Walker & Co. 2010 249p il map $24   **92**
1. Authors 2. Novelists 3. Army officers 4. Great Britain -- Social life and customs
ISBN 978-0-8027-1736-8; 0-8027-1736-5
LC 2009-44758
Schama details the "bigamy trial of William Charles Yelverton, which dominated the front pages of Irish, Scottish, and British newspapers in 1861. Although the story of Yelverton and his first wife, Theresa Longworth, practically tells itself through court documents, letters, and public opinion, Schama adds a journalist's touch in her story development. The latter part of the book deals with Theresa's later life in America as a self-made woman still haunted by her past." Libr J
Includes bibliographical references

Axelrod, David, 1955-

Axelrod, David, 1955- **Believer**; My Forty Years in Politics. David Axelrod. Penguin Group USA 2015 416 p. illustrations $35   **92**
1. United States -- Politics and government -- 1989-
ISBN 1594205876; 9781594205873
LC 2015302608
This memoir, by David Axelrod, focuses on his "twenty-year friendship with Barack Obama, a warm partnership that inspired both men even as it propelled each to great heights. Taking a chance on an unlikely candidate for the U.S. Senate, Axelrod ultimately collaborated closely with Obama on his political campaigns, and served as the invaluable strategist who contributed to the tremendous victories of 2008 and 2012." (Publisher's note)
"Axelrod's careful connection of the dots provides an illuminating study in how political power moves from generation to generation. The book-closing call to remake politics would sound like so much cheerleading in other hands, but Axelrod's connecting of Obama to JFK makes it work. Obama has been profiled many times but seldom with so practical an outlook. An excellent view of politics from the inside." Kirkus

Axelrod, Howard, 1973-

Axelrod, Howard. The **point** of vanishing; a memoir of two years in solitude. Howard Axelrod. Beacon Press 2015 224 p. (hardback : acid-free paper) $16   **92**
1. Vision disorders 2. Self-perception 3. Visual perception 4. Vermont -- Biography 5. Solitude -- Psychological aspects 6. Young men -- United States -- Biography 7. Vision, Monocular -- Psychological aspects 8. People with visual disabilities -- United States -- Biography 9. Eye -- Wounds and injuries -- Patients -- United States -- Biography
ISBN 9780807075463
LC 2015004216
This memoir, by Howard Axelrod, named a Best Book by several journals including "Slate," "Chicago Tribune," and "Entropy Magazine," follows the author's life after an accident which blinded his right eye. "Desperate for a sense of orientation he could trust, he retreated to a jerry-rigged house in the Vermont woods, where he lived without a computer or television, and largely without human contact, for two years." (Publisher's note)
"This memoir is a keeper, touching and eloquent, full of hard lessons learned. Readers will hope for more from first-time-author Axelrod." Booklist

Ayers, Nathaniel Anthony

★ Lopez, Steve. The **soloist**; a lost dream, an unlikely friendship, and the redemptive power of music. G. P. Putnam's Sons 2008 273p hardcover o.p. pa $15   **92**
1. Violinists 2. Homeless persons 3. Homeless 4. Schizophrenics 5. Street entertainers
ISBN 978-0-399-15506-2; 0-399-15506-6; 978-0-425-23836-3 pa; 0-425-23836-9 pa
LC 2007-46314
The true story of Nathaniel Ayers, a musician who becomes schizophrenic and homeless, and his friendship with

Steve Lopez, the Los Angeles columnist who discovers and writes about him in the newspaper.

"With self-effacing humor, fast-paced yet elegant prose and unsparing honesty, Lopez tells an inspiring story of heartbreak and hope." Publ Wkly

Baartman, Saartjie

Crais, Clifton C. **Sara** Baartman and the Hottentot Venus; a ghost story and a biography. [by] Clifton Crais and Pamela Scully. Princeton University Press 2009 232p il map $29.95 **92**

1. Biography, Individual 2. Racism in museum exhibits 3. Museum exhibits -- Moral and ethical aspects
ISBN 9780691135809; 0-691-13580-0

LC 2008-14918

"A member of a small indigenous tribe of herdsmen dubbed the Hottentots by Dutch colonists (but known today by their name Khoikhoi), Baartman was captured in the course of ongoing colonial warfare that effected a genocidal destruction of this peaceful people. Having been enslaved, she was taken to Europe by a member of the family that 'owned' and exhibited her much as an exotic animal might be. . . . [The authors] have done an excellent job not only of telling this rebarbative story but of putting it into the context of its time. This enables them to explain what permitted such an exhibition while at the same time viewing it through our (thankfully) more humane and enlightened lens." Los Angeles Times Book Rev

Includes bibliographical references

★ Holmes, Rachel. **African** queen; the real life of the Hottentot Venus. Random House 2007 161p il $23.95 **92**

1. Entertainers
ISBN 978-1-4000-6136-5; 1-4000-6136-9

LC 2006-45166

"This is a probing look at historical racism and sexual exploitation presented through the life of an extraordinary woman." Booklist

Includes bibliographical references

Babbage, Charles, 1791-1871

Essinger, James. **Ada's** algorithm; how Lord Byron's daughter Ada Lovelace launched the digital age. James Essinger. Melville House 2014 272 p. illustrations (hardback) $25.95 **92**

1. Computers -- History 2. Women mathematicians 3. Mathematicians -- Biography 4. Computers -- History -- 19th century 5. Mathematicians -- Great Britain -- Biography 6. Women mathematicians -- Great Britain -- Biography
ISBN 1612194087; 9781612194080

LC 2014021837

In this book, author James Essinger "makes the case that the computer age could have started two centuries ago if [Ada] Lovelace's contemporaries had recognized her research and fully grasped its implications. . . . [S]tarting with the outrageous behavior of her father [Lord Byron], which made Ada instantly famous upon birth. Ada would go on to overcome numerous obstacles to obtain a level of education typically forbidden to women of her day." (Publisher's note)

"Essinger (Spellbound: The Surprising Origins and Astonishing Secrets of English Spelling, 2007, etc.) presents Ada's story with great enthusiasm and rich detail, painting her life as one that was rich with opportunity and access but stifled by sexism. Ada continues to inspire, and by using her own voice via letters and research, the author brings her to life for a new generation of intrepid female innovators. A robust, engaging and exciting biography." Kirkus

Includes bibliographical references and index

Bacall, Lauren, 1924-

Bacall, Lauren. **By** myself and then some. HarperEntertainment 2005 506p il $26.95 **92**

1. Actors
ISBN 0-06-075535-0

LC 2005-40256

First published 1979 by Knopf with title: Lauren Bacall by myself

In this memoir, the actress describes how she got her start in acting and her relationships with other actors, including Humphrey Bogart.

"Certainly more intelligently written than your average celebrity autobiography, this memoir tells a fascinating story of one woman's journey through life with an intimacy that's sure to engage legions of readers." Booklist

Bach, Johann Sebastian, 1685-1750

Gardiner, John Eliot. **Bach**; music in the castle of heaven. by John Eliot Gardiner. Alfred A. Knopf 2013 672 p. il. (chiefly col.), map, music (hardback) $35 **92**

1. Composers, German 2. Composers -- Biography 3. Composers -- Germany -- Biography
ISBN 0375415297; 9780375415296

LC 2013030398

"Originally published in Great Britain as Music in the castle of heaven, by Allen Lane"--Title page verso

National Book Critics Circle Award Finalist: Biography (2013)

In this book, author John Eliot Gardiner, "takes us . . . into [German composer Johann Sebastian] Bach's works and mind . . . explaining in . . . detail the ideas on which Bach drew, how he worked, how his music is constructed, how it achieves its effects--and what it can tell us about Bach the man." (Publisher's note)

"Although Gardiner celebrates Bach's accomplishments through this dense, demanding but rewarding work, he reminds readers continually that the composer was no saint. . . . [T]he author's focus is not so much on the man but on the music." Kirkus

Includes bibliographical references and index

★ Geck, Martin. **Johann** Sebastian Bach; life and work. translated from the German by John Hargraves. Harcourt 2006 738p il $40 **92**

1. Composers
ISBN 978-0-15-100648-9; 0-15-100648-2

LC 2006-12390

This book "adds original scholarship to an exhaustive study of other studies of Bach. And although it is often dense with information, it is just as often entertaining: rich in anecdotes and scintillating in its conjectures." N Y Times (Late N Y Ed)

Includes bibliographical references

Wolff, Christoph. **Johann** Sebastian Bach; the learned musician. Norton 2000 599p il hardcover o.p. $21.95   **92**
1. Composers
ISBN 9780393322569; 0393322564

LC 99-54364

This work "is likely to be the standard one-volume Bach biography for some time to come. It is a solid, richly informative treatment, presenting the copious details of Bach's life in a coherent, readable narrative." N Y Rev Books

Includes bibliographical references

Baer, Max, 1909-1959

Schaap, Jeremy. **Cinderella** Man; James J. Braddock, Max Baer, and the greatest upset in boxing history. Houghton Mifflin 2005 324p il hardcover o.p. pa $13.95   **92**
1. Boxers (Persons) 2. Boxing -- Biography
ISBN 0-618-55117-4; 0-618-71190-2 pa

LC 2004-66085

The author goes into "detail on the brawny, reserved Braddock, who, at his lowest moments, was reduced to living off government relief and doing grueling work on the Hoboken, N.J., docks. But the story is as much about Max Baer, the lovably clownish and handsome heavyweight Braddock defeated as a 10-to-one underdog. . . . Boxing enthusiasts will be more than satisfied by Schaap's meticulous account, which includes round-by-round details of the fight, as well as profiles of other fighters of the era." Publ Wkly

Includes bibliographical references

Bailey, Blake, 1963-

Bailey, Blake. The **Splendid** Things We Planned; A Family Portrait. by Blake Bailey. W.W. Norton & Co. Inc 2014 288 p. illustrations $25.95   **92**
1. Alcoholism 2. Drug abuse 3. Family life 4. Mental illness 5. Authors, American -- Biography 6. Biographers -- United States -- Biography
ISBN 0393239578; 9780393239577

LC 2013039720

In this book, "biographer [Blake] Bailey tells the story of his own life by chronicling his brother Scott's alcoholism and drug addiction, which causes him to descend into violence and madness. Told in chronological order, starting with the marriage of his straight-laced lawyer father to his bohemian, German-immigrant mother, Bailey's story captures the contradictions and tensions that simmer just below the surface of the family, as they try to live a normal suburban life in Oklahoma." (Publishers Weekly)

A "haunting portrait of more than one tortured soul and a heartfelt probing of the limits of brotherly love." Booklist

Bailey, Elisabeth Tova

Bailey, Elisabeth Tova. The **sound** of a wild snail eating. Algonquin Books of Chapel Hill 2010 190p il $18.95   **92**
1. Snails 2. Authors 3. Essayists 4. Short story writers

5. Biography, Individual
ISBN 978-1-56512-606-0

LC 2010-18603

"A small, short book filled with an enormous amount of natural history and science about snails; also, an acknowledgment of an individual's determination to recover and regain life with humor and insight. Highly recommended." Libr J

Includes bibliographical references

Baker, Russell, 1925-

Baker, Russell, 1925- **Growing** up. New American Library 1983 278p pa $15   **92**
1. Authors 2. Humorists 3. Journalists 4. Essayists 5. Satirists 6. Memoirists
ISBN 0-452-25550-3
First published 1982 by Congdon & Weed

This book "recounts the first 24 years of [Baker's] life as the son of an independent and deep-rooted Virginian family." Natl Rev

Balanchine, George, 1904-1983

Gottlieb, Robert Adams. **George** Balanchine: the ballet maker. HarperCollins\Atlas Books 2004 224p (Eminent lives) $19.95; pa. $13.99   **92**
1. Ballet 2. Dancers 3. Choreographers
ISBN 0-06-075070-7; 9780060750718

LC 2004-48856

"This loving tribute captures Balanchine's legacy: his energy, confidence, lack of pretension and, most important, his joy in creation." Publ Wkly

Includes bibliographical references

★ Teachout, Terry. **All** in the dances: a brief life of George Balanchine. Harcourt 2004 208p $22 **92**
1. Ballet 2. Dancers 3. Choreographers
ISBN 0-15-101088-9

LC 2004-9226

"Balanchine's ballets are modern masterpieces, and Teachout, moving chronologically from work to work, uses them as stepping stones to tell Balanchine's own story. This is highly recommended as a first book on the life and art of George Balanchine for students and the general reader." Publ Wkly

Includes bibliographical references

Balbirer, Nancy

Balbirer, Nancy. **Take** your shirt off and cry; a memoir of near-fame experiences. Bloomsbury 2009 231p pa $16   **92**
1. Actors 2. Memoirists
ISBN 978-1-59691-478-0; 1-59691-478-5

LC 2008-45397

"It is a fact of life seldom discussed in our celebrity-mad media: most actors do not become either rich or famous. Balbirer revels in her failure in this witty, poignant, exceedingly well-written memoir chronicling the ups and downs (mostly downs) of a trained, hardworking actress who always seems on the cusp of greatness but who nevertheless always fails to make the grade." Booklist

Ball, Lucille, 1911-1989

Ball, Lucille. **Love,** Lucy; {by} Lucille Ball with Betty Hannah Hoffman; foreword by Lucie Arnaz. Putnam 1996 286p il pors $24.95 **92**

1. Entertainers -- United States -- Biography

ISBN 0-399-14205-3

LC 96-20751

Lucille Ball's autobiography is "the story of the ingenue from Jamestown, New York, determined to go to Broadway, destined to make a big splash, bound to marry her Valentino, Desi Arnaz. It tells of their life together - both storybook and turbulent: intimate stories of their children and friends; wonderful backstage anecdotes; the creation of the most popular show on TV; the production empire they founded; the dissolution of their marriage. And, with a heartfelt happy ending, her enduring marriage to Gary Morton." (Publisher's note)

Balzac, Honoré de, 1799-1850

Robb, Graham. **Balzac;** a life. Norton 1994 521p il hardcover o.p. pa $15 **92**

1. Authors 2. Novelists 3. Short story writers

ISBN 0-393-31387-5 pa

LC 94-18614

"Balzac's life was more cause for incredulity than anything he wrote, and Robb compellingly sets out the documentable facts against and within the world Balzac created from them.... The result is nearly a novel, although Robb does not fictionalize with re-created dialogs and hypothetical events. He has in fact produced an extensive traditional biography . . . not a critical reassessment." Libr J

Includes bibliographical references

Bard, Elizabeth

Bard, Elizabeth. **Lunch** in Paris; a love story, with recipes. Little, Brown and Co. 2010 324p $23.99 **92**

1. Journalists 2. French cooking 3. Art historians 4. Americans -- France 5. Paris (France) -- Description and travel

ISBN 978-0-316-04279-6; 0-316-04279-X

LC 2009-22064

"Falling in love with a Frenchman was not in Elizabeth Bard's master plan, but then he took her to a local canteen: 'Not to minimize Gwendal's many charms, but he was halfway to home base as soon as I cut into that marvelous steak,' she writes. Culture shock set in as she learned to shop and cook in Paris, standing in line here for the best green beans, going there for the best walnuts. I thought the recipes were a cutesy touch until I made a few of them: chicken tagine with two kinds of lemon, spiced apricots, chouquettes. Forget the narrative — you could just buy this as a cookbook." Entertainment Wkly

Baret, Jeanne, 1740-1807

Ridley, Glynis. The **discovery** of Jeanne Baret; a story of science, the high seas, and the first woman to circumnavigate the globe. Crown Publishers 2010 288p il $25; ebook $25 **92**

1. Botanists 2. Explorers 3. Women scientists 4. Voyages around the world

ISBN 978-0-307-46352-4; 978-0-307-46354-8 ebook

LC 2010-16778

This is a biography "of Jeanne Baret. Born in 1740 in France's Loire valley, Baret became an expert 'herb woman' who proved to be indispensable to the ambitious botanist Philibert Commerson, accompanying him as his assistant when Commerson was appointed naturalist for France's first expedition to circumnavigate the globe. But women were forbidden, so Baret dressed as a man. . . . Woven throughout this gripping story are Ridley's piquant insights into eighteenth-century exploration, botany, taxonomy, biopiracy, and sexism. Baret could not have asked for a more exacting and expressive champion. Ridley is incandescent in her passion for the truth." Booklist

Includes bibliographical references

Barnes, Jane, 1942-

Barnes, Jane. **Falling** in love with Joseph Smith; my search for the real prophet. Jane Barnes. Jeremy P. Tarcher/Penguin 2012 294 p. $25.95 **92**

1. Faith 2. Mormons 3. Mormon Church 4. Conversion -- Mormon Church

ISBN 1585429252; 9781585429257

LC 2012018119

This book is an "account of a female intellectual's passion for Mormon prophet Joseph Smith and her near-conversion to the faith." Jane Barnes "developed an especially profound fascination with Smith. Her interest manifested first as a treatment for a PBS documentary about Smith's life, then evolved into a full-blown love for the man and his work." She explored the Mormon faith and learned of her family's connections to it. (Kirkus Reviews)

Barnes, Julian, 1946-

Barnes, Julian. **Nothing** to be frightened of. Alfred A. Knopf 2008 243p $24 **92**

1. Death 2. Authors 3. Novelists 4. Essayists 5. Authors, English 6. Television critics 7. Short story writers

ISBN 978-0-307-26963-8; 0-307-26963-9

LC 2008-19603

This is "an elegant memoir and meditation, a deep seismic tremor of a book that keeps rumbling and grumbling in the mind for weeks thereafter." N Y Times Book Rev

Barr, Nevada

Barr, Nevada. **Seeking** enlightenment--hat by hat; a skeptic's path to religion. Putnam 2003 222p $21.95; pa $13 **92**

1. Authors 2. Park rangers 3. Mystery writers

ISBN 0-399-15057-9; 0-425-19603-8 pa

LC 2003-43101

The author "charts the course of her spiritual evolution, how she sought to understand the many aspects of spiritual life, from forgiveness ('a sigh of relief on which the memory of evil is breathed out') to pain ('it is a duty to relieve our own pain') to commitment ('not a contract with the world but with the self'). Barr's account of her transformation from nonbeliever to committed churchgoer—but one who maintains a healthy sense of doubt even as she prays and attends Bible studies—is moving but never saccharine." Booklist

Barthelme, Donald

Daugherty, Tracy. **Hiding** man; a biography of Donald Barthelme. St. Martin's Press 2008 581p il $35   92

1. Authors 2. Novelists 3. Authors, American 4. Short story writers

ISBN 978-0-312-37868-4; 0-312-37868-8

LC 2008-29881

"Not dwelling on Barthelme's dark soul or his uneven work, Daugherty has created a convincing narrative from a life that was engaged, passionate and maybe even fulfilled." N Y Times Book Rev

Includes bibliographical references (p. 549-556)

Basie, Count, 1904-1984

Basie, Count. **Good** morning blues: the autobiography of Count Basie; as told to Albert Murray. Da Capo Press 1995 399p il pa $17.95   92

1. Pianists 2. Jazz musicians 3. African American musicians 4. Band leaders

ISBN 0-306-81107-3

LC 94-44697

"Basie pays tribute to his colleagues and managers (and to John Hammond for 'discovering' him), but does not hesitate to discuss their weaknesses and short-comings; his language is direct and earthy. Although some of the book reads more like a catalogue or itinerary than an autobiography, it will have strong appeal for jazz buffs and fans of the late bandleader." Publ Wkly

Bass, Rick, 1958-

Bass, Rick. **Why** I came West. Houghton Mifflin Co. 2008 238p $24; pa $14.95   92

1. Authors 2. Novelists 3. Geologists 4. Conservationists 5. Literary landmarks 6. Essayists 7. West (U.S.) 8. Authors, American 9. Writers on nature 10. Short story writers

ISBN 978-0-618-59675-1; 0-618-59675-5; 978-0-5472-3771-8 pa; 0-5472-3771-5 pa

LC 2007-30660

Bass "tells the tale of his apprenticeship to literature and the place that has defined his life for the past two decades, Montana's Yaak Valley. Bass looks back to his Houston childhood, Utah college years, and work as an oil geologist in Mississippi, searching for clues to his love-at-first sight response to the Yaak. As he describes his deep immersion in this bountiful land as a hunter, hiker, artist, and environmentalist, he . . . shares his anguish over the clear-cutting of woods, and chronicles the hard work of wilderness advocacy and the virulent hatred it arouses. Versed in paradox, Bass is bracing in his candor about how difficult it will be to change our destructive ways, and incandescent in his reasoned call to preserve the few remaining unspoiled places." Booklist

Baszile, Jennifer, 1969-

Baszile, Jennifer. The **Black** girl next door; a memoir. Simon & Schuster 2009 310p il $25 92

1. Historians 2. Memoirists 3. College teachers

ISBN 978-1-4165-4327-5; 1-4165-4327-9

LC 2008-12867

"The Baszile family's move to an exclusive white suburb in Palos Verde, California, was the culmination of the parents' striving for a racially integrated, middle-class life. For their daughters, it meant isolation and coping with the occasional racial slurs that went along with the advantages of suburban life. Their parents veered between an aggressive integration strategy and an equally aggressive strategy to keep their daughters socially connected to other black teens. . . . This is an absorbing look behind the facade of one black family's striving for integration and the American dream." Booklist

Bauman, Jeff

Witter, Bret. **Stronger**; Jeff Bauman, with Bret Witter. Grand Central Publishing 2014 244 p. illustrations (hardcover) $26   92

1. Terrorism victims 2. Amputees -- Rehabilitation 3. Boston Marathon Bombing, Boston, Mass., 2013

ISBN 1455584371; 9781455584376

LC 2013050788

Jeff Bauman was next to the bomb when it exploded at the Boston Marathon on April 15, 2013. Pictures of him flooded the media as he became the iconic image of the tragedy: Bauman in a wheel chair, legs missing from the knees down. The following weeks of speculation and the eventual police shootout with the Tsarnaev brothers is well documented. Bauman and co-author Bret Witter are telling a different story, a personal story. . . . Bauman does not sugar coat the heroism of his situation. He's upfront about the difficulties of amputation, of his family adjusting to new realities, [and] of being a sudden media personality." (Publishers Weekly)

"Only a misanthrope would fail to be moved by Bauman's guileless narration of the horrors of rehabilitation or his frustration with learning to live with his new prosthetic legs. This is the simple story of one decent guy who fights hard to stay strong in the face of adversity." LJ

Beach, Sylvia

The **letters** of Sylvia Beach; edited by Keri Walsh; with a foreword by Noël Riley Fitch. Columbia University Press 2010 347p il $29.95   92

1. Booksellers and bookselling 2. Memoirists 3. Booksellers 4. Shakespeare and Company 5. Booksellers and bookselling -- France -- Paris 6. Paris (France) -- Intellectual life -- 20th century

ISBN 978-0-231-14536-7; 0-231-14535-5

LC 2009-45434

"Beach's story has been told before. . . . [But these letters] have an unvarnished charm all their own. Written to friends, writers, customers and family members, they depict a witty and resourceful woman struggling to keep her business, her writers and her precarious existence afloat." N Y Times Book Rev

Includes bibliographical references

Beah, Ishmael

★ Beah, Ishmael, 1980- A **long** way gone; memoirs of a boy soldier. Farrar, Straus & Giroux 2007 229p map pa $12; $22   92

1. Refugees 2. Soldiers 3. Children and war 4. Memoirists 5. Social activists 6. Sierra Leone -- History -- Civil War, 1991- 7. Sierra Leone -- History -- Civil War, 1991-2002

ISBN 0-374-53126-9 pa; 0-374-95191-8; 978-0-374-

10523-5; 978-0-374-53126-3 pa
LC 2006-17101
The author writes about his experiences as a recruit in the Sierra Leone Army.

"In 1993, when the author was twelve, rebel forces attacked his home town, in Sierra Leone, and he was separated from his parents. For months, he straggled through the war-torn countryside, starving and terrified, until he was taken under the wing of a Shakespeare-spouting lieutenant in the government army. Soon, he was being fed amphetamines and trained to shoot an AK-47. . . . Beah's memoir documents his transformation from a child into a hardened, brutally efficient soldier who high-fived his fellow-recruits after they slaughtered their enemies—often boys their own age—and who 'felt no pity for anyone.'" New Yorker

Beasley, Sandra

Beasley, Sandra. **Don't** kill the birthday girl; tales from an allergic life. Crown Publishers 2011 229p il $23; ebook $11.99   **92**
1. Poets 2. Authors 3. Food allergy
ISBN 978-0-307-58811-1; 978-0-307-58813-5 ebook
LC 2010043724
"If you didn't have sympathy for this relatively new generation of sufferers, you will after Beasley's book. . . . The emotional stuff is the best—from worrying about kissing boys who may have eaten forbidden foods, to considering the implications of having kids who'll have to wash their hands before hugging their mother." Maclean's

Beatty, Warren, 1937-

Biskind, Peter. **Star**; how Warren Beatty seduced America. Simon & Schuster 2010 627p il $30 **92**
1. Actors 2. Motion picture directors 3. Motion picture producers
ISBN 978-0-7432-4658-3; 0-7432-4658--6
LC 2009-22225
"Biskind brings his historian's acumen to bear on the production of era-defining triumphs like Bonnie and Clyde (1967), Shampoo (1975) and Reds (1981), as well as notorious flops like Ishtar (1987), Love Affair (1994) and Town & Country (2001), and his accounts are full of juicy gossip and intriguing insights into the actor's psychology. . . . A gripping portrait of a difficult talent." Kirkus
Includes bibliographical references

Beaumarchais, Pierre Augustin Caron de, 1732-1799

Lever, Maurice. **Beaumarchais**; a biography. Farrar, Straus and Giroux 2008 411p $35 **92**
1. Authors 2. Dramatists 3. Dramatists, French
ISBN 9780374113285; 0-374-11328-9
LC 2008-55449
"Best known as the author of the comedies that became Mozart's 'The Marriage of Figaro' and Rossini's 'The Barber of Seville,' Beaumarchais was a high-spirited adventurer for whom writing plays was only an 'honest relaxation.' This erudite and wry biography covers the full range of his occupations, including watchmaking, espionage, pamphleteering, and transatlantic trade." New Yorker
Includes bibliographical references

Becker, Suzy

Becker, Suzy. **I** had brain surgery, what's your excuse? an illustrated memoir. Workman Pub 2003 282p il $19.95   **92**
1. Authors 2. Humorists 3. Cartoonists 4. Illustrators 5. Memoirists 6. AIDS activists 7. Social activists 8. Nonfiction writers
ISBN 0-7611-2478-0
LC 2003-60039
Becker "was suffering seizures but didn't tell anyone until a friend witnessed an incident. Eventually, she was scheduled for brain surgery to remove a tumor. Writing with the dry sense of humor that some of us rely on to make it through situations, Becker recalls her reactions to her medical problems, from liking the first doctor who gave her no bad news ('just stress') to the terror of the eventual diagnosis. Her descriptions of the surgery and its dreadful, but temporary, effects on her ability to speak, read, write, and draw make for especially compelling reading. . . . Becker has turned one person's experience into a universal story of family, healing, and the return to creativity." Libr J

Beecher, Henry Ward, 1813-1887

★ Applegate, Debby. The **most** famous man in America; the biography of Henry Ward Beecher. Doubleday 2006 529p il map $27.95 **92**
1. Clergy 2. Nonfiction writers
ISBN 0-385-51396-8; 978-0-385-51396-8
LC 2005-54842
This is a biography of the American clergyman.
"By illuminating Beecher's position in history, Applegate has produced a biography worthy of its subject." N Y Times Book Rev
Includes bibliographical references

Beethoven, Ludwig van, 1770-1827

Morris, Edmund, 1940- **Beethoven**: the universal composer. HarperCollins Publishers 2005 243p (Eminent lives) $21.95; pa $13.99 **92**
1. Composers
ISBN 0-06-075974-7; 978-0-06-075974-2; 9780060759759
LC 2006-274925
This is a biography of the German composer.
The author "clearly admires his subject not only for the work but also for his constant fight against the odds, and he has written an ideal biography for the general reader." Publ Wkly
Includes bibliographical references

Suchet, John. **Beethoven**; the man revealed. John Suchet. Grove Press 2013 xiii, 273 p.p illustrations (chiefly color) (hbk.) $30 **92**
1. Composers, German 2. Composers -- Biography 3. Composers -- Germany -- Biography
ISBN 080212206X; 9780802122063
LC 2012518710
This book, by John Suchet, is a biography of composer Ludwig von Beethoven. "Suchet illuminates the composer's difficult childhood, his struggle to maintain friendships and romances, his ungovernable temper, his obsessive efforts to control his nephew's life, and the excruciating decline

of his hearing." It also discusses "the landmark events in Beethoven's career--from his competitive encounters with Mozart to the circumstances surrounding the creation of the well-known 'Fur Elise' and 'Moonlight Sonata.'" (Publisher's note)

"For the many readers lacking the proper background in musical theory, British broadcaster and Beethoven authority Suchet's explanations of Beethoven's music sing to us almost as if we could hear it." Kirkus

Includes bibliographical references and index

★ Swafford, Jan. **Beethoven**; anguish and triumph : a biography. Jan Swafford. Houghton Mifflin Harcourt 2014 1104 p. illustrations $40   **92**
1. Composers, German 2. Composers -- Biography 3. Composers -- Germany -- Biography
ISBN 061805474X; 9780618054749
LC 2014011681
In this book, music historian Jan Swafford "mines sources never before used in English-language biographies to reanimate the revolutionary ferment of Enlightenment-era Bonn, where Beethoven grew up and imbibed the ideas that would shape all of his future work. Swafford then tracks his subject to Vienna, capital of European music, where Beethoven built his career in the face of critical incomprehension, crippling ill health, romantic rejection, and . . . his ever-encroaching deafness." (Publisher's note)

"Rich in biographical detail, the volume contains revealing excerpts from many of Beethoven's letters and from the written observations of his visitors and family; it also contains detailed analyses of many of his most notable works." Kirkus

Includes bibliographical references and index

Belafonte, Harry

Belafonte, Harry. **My** song; a memoir. with Michael Shnayerson. Alfred A. Knopf 2011 469p il   **92**
1. Actors 2. Singers 3. African American singers 4. Social activists
ISBN 9780307272263; 9780307700483
LC 2011014602
The popular singer and former UNICEF Goodwill Ambassador shares the story of his life and career, from his impoverished childhood in Harlem and Jamaica and his racial barrier-breaking career to his commitment to numerous civil causes.

The author "covers his public career as an American entertainment icon (which solidified with his 1956 album, Calypso) and his interactions with many politicians and celebrities, e.g., Paul Robeson, Poitier, Marlon Brando, and Robert Kennedy, among many others. How these different strands interweave—the anger generated by the poverty and racial discrimination of his early years, the socially conscious reformer, and the well-respected entertainer—make for a potent memoir of our times." Libr J

Belafonte, Henry

Becoming Belafonte; black artist, public radical. by Judith E. Smith. University of Texas Press 2014 368 p. (Discovering America) (cloth : alkaline paper) $35   **92**
1. Black musicians 2. Actors, Black -- United States -- Biography 3. Musicians, Black -- United States -- Biography 4. African American civil rights workers -- Biography
ISBN 0292729146; 9780292729148
LC 2014006424
This book, by Judith E. Smith, part of the "Discovering America" series, is a biography of the African American musician Henry Belafonte. The author "sets Belafonte's compelling story within a history of American race relations, black theater and film history, McCarthy-era hysteria, and the challenges of introducing multifaceted black culture in a moment of expanding media possibilities and constrained political expression." (Publisher's note)

Smith gives us plenty of detail about his movies (the good, bad and ugly), his recordings, his relationships with women, and his battles with the ugly racial status quo in 1950s and '60s America. So engaging that readers will crave a sequel: Belafonte since the '70s?"

Includes bibliographical references and index

Bell, Alexander Graham, 1847-1922

★ Gray, Charlotte. **Reluctant** genius; Alexander Graham Bell and the passion for invention. Arcade Pub. 2006 466p il map $29.95   **92**
1. Inventors 2. Teachers of the deaf 3. Telecommunications executives
ISBN 1-55970-809-3; 978-1-55970-809-8
LC 2005-29609
The author "recounts both the inventor of the telephone's creation of the device and the projects he pursued once his future was secured. . . . Combining the household history of the Bells with that of Alexander's successive enthusiasms (Helen Keller, kites, airplanes, hydrocraft), Gray fairly portrays the attractions and exasperations of Bell's life." Booklist

Includes bibliographical references

Bell, Gertrude Margaret Lowthian, 1868-1926

Howell, Georgina. **Gertrude** Bell; queen of the desert, shaper of nations. Farrar, Straus and Giroux 2007 481p il map hardcover o.p. pa $16   **92**
1. Explorers 2. Travelers 3. Archeologists 4. Archaeologists 5. Women -- Travel 6. Biography, Individual 7. Middle East -- History -- 20th century 8. Great Britain -- Colonies -- Administration -- History -- 20th century
ISBN 0-374-16162-3; 0-374-53135-8 pa; 978-0-374-16162-0; 978-0-374-53135-5 pa
LC 2006-29994
First published 2006 in the United Kingdom with title: Daughter of the desert

This is a biography of the British archaeologist and author of Desert and the Sown (1907) and Persian Pictures (1928). Bell "advised the Viceroy of India; then, as an army major, she traveled to the front lines in Mesopotamia. There she supported the creation of an autonomous Arab nation for Iraq, promoting and manipulating the election of King Faisal to the throne and helping to draw the borders of the fledgling state." (Publisher's note) Index.

"Bell's role in the creation of Iraq and the placement of Faisal upon the throne, is fully detailed. . . . But the strength and delight of Howell's superb biography is in the fullness with which Bell's character is drawn." Publ Wkly

Includes bibliographical references

Bell, Laura, 1954-

Bell, Laura. **Claiming** ground. Alfred A. Knopf 2010 241p $24.95   **92**

1. Shepherds 2. Ranch life 3. Conservationists 4. Wyoming 5. Memoirists

ISBN 978-0-307-27288-1

LC 2009-29644

"After college, a Kentucky girl spends a summer in Wyoming to find herself and regroup. Thirty years later, she's still there. In this memoir, Bell vividly depicts her life out West, starting with her first job herding sheep—an occupation usually done by men. She goes on to write about her life as a ranch hand, masseuse, housewife, stepmother, and forest ranger, mixing work experiences with touching and poignant accounts of family and friends. . . . Bell here turns in satisfying reading for ranching enthusiasts, memoir fanatics, and anyone who likes to get lost in stories about rural life and nature's beauty." Libr J

Bellamy, Richard

Stein, Judith E. **Eye** of the sixties; Richard Bellamy and the Transformation of Modern Art. Judith E. Stein. Farrar, Straus & Giroux 2016 384 p. (hardback) $27   **92**

1. Art dealers 2. Art -- 20th century 3. Art dealers -- United States -- Biography 4. Art and society -- United States -- History -- 20th century

ISBN 9780374151324; 9780374715205

LC 2015036468

This book, by Judith E. Stein, focuses on "Richard Bellamy . . . one of the first advocates of pop art, minimalism, and conceptual art. Based on decades of research and hundreds of interviews with artists, friends, dealers, and lovers, . . . 'Eye of the Sixties' recovers the elusive Bellamy and tells the story of a counterculture that became the mainstream." (Publisher's note)

"This is an endearing and illuminating work of biography. A shadowy figure of the 1960s art world is gloriously revealed." Kirkus

Includes bibliographical references and index

Belle, Dido Elizabeth, 1761-1804

Byrne, Paula. **Belle**; the slave daughter and the Lord Chief Justice. Paula Byrne. Harper Perennial 2014 304 p. illustrations (paperback) $14.99   **92**

1. Racially mixed people 2. Great Britain -- Race relations 3. Great Britain -- History -- 18th century 4. Slaves -- England -- Biography 5. Nobility -- England -- Biography

ISBN 0062310771; 9780062310774

LC 2014007447

"From . . . biographer Paula Byrne, the . . . tale that inspired the major motion picture 'Belle' (May 2014) starring Tom Wilkinson, Miranda Richardson, Emily Watson, Penelope Wilton, and Matthew Goode--a stunning story of the first mixed-race girl introduced to high society England and

raised as a lady. . . . Growing up in his lavish estate, Dido was raised as a sister and companion to her white cousin, Elizabeth." (Publisher's note)

"Byrne brings to this brief history an eye for telling details of daily life, slaveholders' unthinkable cruelty, and the fervent work of a few good men and women who changed their world." Kirkus

Includes bibliographical references

Bellow, Saul, 1915-2005

Bellow, Saul, 1915-2005. **Saul** Bellow; letters. edited by Benjamin Taylor. Viking 2010 571p il $35   **92**

1. Authors 2. Novelists 3. Dramatists 4. Authors, American 5. Short story writers 6. Biography, Individual 7. Nobel laureates for literature

ISBN 978-0-670-02221-2; 0-670-02221-7

LC 2010-22395

"Collected for the first time, Bellow's letters offer an alluring backstory to the Chicago-bred imagination that created The Adventures of Augie March, Herzog, Humboldt's Gift and won the Nobel Prize. Like the fiction, the missives can be brilliant, glistening, scathing, boring, funny, generous, probing and always genuinely human. . . . The correspondents throughout are friends, lovers, wives, agents and publishers. Among the dozens of major literary figures with whom Bellow corresponded were William Faulkner, Bernard Malamud, Edmund Wilson, John Berryman, Ralph Ellison, Robert Penn Warren, Philip Roth and Martin Amis. While nothing can substitute for a Bellow novel, Letters offers a strong salve to those who miss his familiar voice. The range of interests, battles fought and art created reflected here is Olympian. Yet the cauldron for much of it was the everyday streets of Chicago." Chicago Sun-Times

The **Life** of Saul Bellow; to fame and fortune, 1915-1964. by Zachary Leader. Alfred A. Knopf 2015 832 p. 24 plates; illustrations (hardback) $40   **92**

1. American authors -- Biography 2. Novelists, American -- 20th century -- Biography

ISBN 0307268837; 9780307268839; 9780307388933

LC 2014020092

This book, by Zachary Leader, is the first of a two-volume biography of the writer Saul Bellow. This volume "traces Bellow's Russian roots; his birth and early childhood in Quebec; his years in Chicago; his travels in Mexico, Europe, and Israel; the first three of his five marriages; and the novels from 'Dangling Man' and 'The Adventures of Augie March' to the best-selling 'Herzog.'" (Publisher's note)

"To be sure, offended friends and former wives have interpreted Bellow's literary treatment of their life facts as mean-spirited and vindictive. But millions of appreciative readers recognize in Bellow's work the grit of a James T. Farrell and the exuberance of a Charles Dickens. A must-read for students of American literature." Booklist

Includes bibliographical references and index

Belzoni, Giovanni Battista, 1778-1823

Noël Hume, Ivor. **Belzoni**; the giant archaeologists love to hate. Ivor Noel Hume. University of

Virginia Press 2011 301 p. ill. (some col.), maps $34.95 **92**

1. Archeologists -- Biography 2. Egypt -- Antiquities 3. Egyptologists -- Biography 4. Egypt -- Description and travel 5. Excavations (Archaeology) -- Egypt 6. Archaeologists -- Egypt -- Biography 7. Archaeologists -- Italy -- Biography

ISBN 0813931401; 9780813931401

LC 2011000693

This book by Ivor Noel Hume presents a biography of "Giovanni Belzoni (1778-1824) . . . one of the most controversial figures in in the history of Egyptian archaeology. . . . The book includes . . . accounts of Belzoni's . . . productive, and physically brutal, expeditions, as well as a . . . portrait of his wife, Sarah, who suffered the hardships of the Egyptian deserts and later bore the brunt of the disillusionment that came with the declining popular perception of her husband." (Publisher's note)

Includes bibliographical references (p. [289]-292) and index

Benga, Ota

Newkirk, Pamela. **Spectacle**; the astonishing life of Ota Benga. Pamela Newkirk. HarperCollins 2015 320 p. illustrations (hardcover) $25.99 **92**

1. Pygmies -- United States -- Biography 2. Human zoos -- United States -- History -- 20th century

ISBN 006220100X; 9780062201003

NAACP Image Award: Outstanding Literary Work-Nonfiction (2016)

In this book, by Pamela Newkirk, "an award-winning journalist reveals a little-known and shameful episode in American history, when an African man was used as a human zoo exhibit--a shocking story of racial prejudice, science, and tragedy in the early years of the twentieth century." (Publisher's note)

"Newkirk gives us more than the tragic story of one Congolese man. She offers a look into the history of American eugenics and the concepts of racial anthropology that have served as the foundation for racial intolerance for generations. Benga's story is one part of a bigger problem--a problem that continues to exist--and Newkirk doesn't allow us to forget him. Nor should she." LJ

Benton, Thomas Hart, 1889-1975

Adams, Henry. **Tom** and Jack; the intertwined lives of Thomas Hart Benton and Jackson Pollock. Bloomsbury Press 2009 405p il $35 **92**

1. Artists 2. Painters 3. Illustrators 4. Lithographers 5. Artists -- United States

ISBN 1-59691-420-3; 978-1-59691-420-9

LC 2009-12309

"In this absorbing, carefully reasoned inquiry into a profound relationship between two painters, Adams reclaims the wrongfully maligned Benton and recalibrates our perception of Pollock and his masterpieces." Booklist

Includes bibliographical references (p. 375-390)

Bergen, Candice, 1946-

Bergen, Candice, 1946- A **fine** romance; Candice Bergen. Simon & Schuster 2015 368 p. 16 plates; illustrations (hardcover) $28 **92**

1. Marriage 2. Actresses 3. Actors -- United States -- Biography

ISBN 1476746095; 9780684808277; 9781476746098

LC 2014029293

In this memoir, actress Candice Bergen "describes her first marriage at age thirty-four to famous French director Louis Malle; her overpowering love for her daughter, Chloe; the unleashing of her inner comic with 'Murphy Brown'; her trauma over Malle's death; her joy at finding new love; and her pride at watching Chloe blossom." (Publisher's note)

"Witty and poignant and touching upon the many phases and challenges of daily existence, this book will appeal to a wide audience, especially those who are familiar with Bergen's work. For circulating libraries and entertainment collections." Library Journal

Bergman, Ingrid, 1915-1982

Spoto, Donald. **Notorious**; the life of Ingrid Bergman. Da Capo Press 2001 474p il pa $22 **92**

1. Actors

ISBN 978-0-306-81030-5; 0-306-81030-1

First published 1997 by HarperCollins

The author's "perceptions about Bergman personally and professionally are keen, and the narrative reads like a full-bodied story, not just a listing of professional credits and personal landmarks." Booklist

Includes bibliographical references

Thomson, David, 1941- **Ingrid** Bergman; photo research by Lucy Gray. Faber and Faber, Inc. 2010 113p il (Great stars) pa $14 **92**

1. Actors

ISBN 978-0-86547-934-0

LC 2009-41757

First published 2009 in the United Kingdom

In this biography, the author describes Bergman's "Hollywood-like rise, seemingly both unexpected and preordained, from talented Swedish actress to Hollywood goddess. . . . He reserves his harshest criticism not for her increasingly chaotic private life but for how, after her brilliance in the 1940s—Casablanca, Gaslight, and the Hitchcock masterpieces Spellbound and Notorious, and more—she settled into a kind of unsatisfying mediocrity in the 1950s and 1960s. Thomson speculates that her fortunes faded with her legendary beauty." Booklist

Bernanke, Ben, 1953-

Bernanke, Ben, 1953- The **Courage** to Act; A Memoir of a Crisis and Its Aftermath. by Ben S. Bernanke. W W Norton & Co Inc. 2015 448 p. 32 plates; ills; portraits $35 **92**

1. Global Financial Crisis, 2008-2009 2. United States -- Economic conditions

ISBN 039324721X; 9780393247213

This memoir, by former chair of the Federal Reserve Ben S. Bernanke, is an "unrivaled look at the fight to save the American economy. . . . Working with two U.S. presidents, and under fire from a fractious Congress and a public incensed by behavior on Wall Street, the Fed—alongside colleagues in the Treasury Department—successfully stabilized a teetering financial system." (Publisher's note)

"One of the finest memoirs on the financial crisis to date, this title belongs in all libraries with holdings in economic and social history. Readers desiring further readings on the economic crisis might consult Alan S. Blinder's After the Music Stopped." LJ

Bernard, Pierre, 1875-1955

Love, Robert. The **Great** Oom; the improbable birth of yoga in America. Viking 2010 402p il **92**

1. Yoga 2. Yogis 3. United States -- Religion
ISBN 067002175X; 9780670021758

LC 2009044784

This book focuses on Pierre Bernard's involvement in the popularization of Yoga in the United States. Bibliography. Index.

A "history of yoga's early days in America. The spiritual discipline that has colonized America's gyms and trendy loft spaces was once a fringe practice, its advocates treated as charlatans and, occasionally, criminals. Yoga's cultural rise is a story of scandal, financial shenanigans, bodily discipline, oversize egos and bizarre love triangles, with a few performing elephants thrown in for good measure. Mr. Love tells his story through the life of one of yoga's earliest promoters, Pierre Bernard—known as the 'Great Oom'—a zany man whose talent for self-invention rivaled that of P.T. Barnum." Wall Street J

Includes bibliographical references

Bernini, Gian Lorenzo, 1598-1680

Mormando, Franco. **Bernini**; his life and his Rome. University of Chicago Press 2011 429p il map pa $35 **92**

1. Artists 2. Sculptors 3. Architects 4. Artists, Italian
ISBN 978-0-226-53852-5; 0-226-53852-4

LC 2011023774

In this biography "of Baroque sculptor Gian Lorenzo Bernini since his death in 1680, . . . Mormando constructs a comprehensive, extraordinarily vivid portrait of the sculptor known as 'the Michelangelo of his age.' . . . Of great interest to general readers seeking a well-researched, highly readable portrait of the sculptor and those interested in the cultural history of baroque Rome." Publ Wkly

Includes bibliographical references

Bernstein, Leonard, 1918-1990

★ Bernstein, Burton. **Leonard** Bernstein; American original; how a modern renaissance man transformed music and the world during his New York Philharmonic years, 1943-1976. [by] Burton Bernstein and Barbara B. Haws. HarperCollins 2008 223p il $29.95 **92**

1. Composers 2. Musicians 3. Conductors (Music) 4. New York Philharmonic 5. Composers -- United States
ISBN 978-0-06-153786-8; 0-06-153786-1

LC 2008-13702

"A flat-out wonderful book." Booklist

Leonard Bernstein; An American Musician. Allen Shawn. Yale University Press 2014 360 p. (Jewish lives) (cloth : alk. paper) $25 **92**

1. Composers -- United States 2. Musicians -- United States
ISBN 0300144288; 9780300144284

LC 2014941713

This book, by Allen Shawn, is a biography on musician Leonard Bernstein. "[T]he breadth of Bernstein's musical composition is explored, through the spectacular range of music he composed-from 'West Side Story' to 'Kaddish' to 'A Quiet Place' and beyond-and through his intensely public role as an internationally celebrated conductor." Publisher's note

"Shawn gives some space to Bernstein's critics, as well, and he does not neglect the composer's final sad slide. A nearly impossible task, recording this lush life, but Shawn helps us comprehend the magic." Kirkus

Berra, Yogi, 1925-2015

★ Barra, Allen. **Yogi** Berra; eternal Yankee. W. W. Norton & Co. 2009 451p il $27.95 **92**

1. Baseball players 2. Baseball coaches 3. Baseball managers 4. Baseball -- Biography 5. New York Yankees (Baseball team)
ISBN 978-0-393-06233-5; 0-393-06233-3

LC 2008-45799

"Barra brings to his sporting version of the Everyman story an encyclopedic knowledge and warm understanding of the game of baseball; meticulous research into business, sociology, and history; and a fluid writing style. . . . Baseball biography taken to a higher level." Booklist

Includes bibliographical references

Berrigan, Sandy

Berrigan, Ted. **Dear** Sandy, hello; letters from Ted to Sandy Berrigan. edited by Sandy Berrigan and Ron Padgett. Coffee House Press 2010 310p il pa $19.95 **92**

1. Poets 2. Authors 3. Poets, American
ISBN 978-1-56689-249-0; 1-56689-249-X

LC 2010-16258

"In addition to the letters, this collection contains never-before-published reproductions from A Book of Poetry for Sandy, featuring Berrigan's cutouts, drawings, photographs of fellow poets and artists, and excerpts from poems that eventually became The Sonnets." Publisher's note

Berrigan, Ted, 1934-1983

Berrigan, Ted. **Dear** Sandy, hello; letters from Ted to Sandy Berrigan. edited by Sandy Berrigan and Ron Padgett. Coffee House Press 2010 310p il pa $19.95 **92**

1. Poets 2. Authors 3. Poets, American
ISBN 978-1-56689-249-0; 1-56689-249-X

LC 2010-16258

"In addition to the letters, this collection contains never-before-published reproductions from A Book of Poetry for Sandy, featuring Berrigan's cutouts, drawings, photographs of fellow poets and artists, and excerpts from poems that eventually became The Sonnets." Publisher's note

Betjeman, John Sir, 1906-1984

Wilson, A. N. **Betjeman**; a life. Farrar, Straus & Giroux 2006 375p il $27   **92**
1. Poets 2. Authors 3. Satirists 4. Poets laureate 5. Architectural historians 6. Historic preservationists
ISBN 978-0-374-11198-4; 0-374-11198-7
LC 2006-930677
Wilson's biography of the British Poet Laureate "is a sharp-edged triumph of honest hero worship. Amazingly, he has found a real-life character whom he can love and admire. . . . Brushing aside hundreds of chatty anecdotes and conversations that might have happened, Wilson has tied his primary source material around a subtle analysis of the ultimate first sources, the poems themselves. This, it is safe to say, should be the final biography." Times Lit Suppl

Bewick, Thomas, 1753-1828

Uglow, Jennifer S. **Nature's** engraver; a life of Thomas Bewick. Farrar, Straus and Giroux 2007 458p il map $30   **92**
1. Artists 2. Woodcuts 3. Illustrators 4. Woodcut artists
ISBN 978-0-374-11236-3; 0-374-11236-3
LC 2006-31878
First published 2006 in the United Kingdom
"Biographies rarely afford a glimpse behind the office door, and it is the image of Bewick at work that is so valuable here. . . . It is hard to imagine a better biographer for this subject than Uglow, with her background in publishing and her knowledge of the North of England and the eighteenth century. It is also hard to imagine a more beautifully produced and illustrated book: scores of Bewick's frameless vignettes float frame-free and captionless throughout, appearing as they would have done in his own time, tale pieces every one." Times Lit Suppl
Includes bibliographical references

Bhutto, Benazir

★ Bhutto, Benazir. **Reconciliation**; Islam, democracy, and the West. HarperCollins 2008 328p $27.95   **92**
1. Prime ministers 2. Islam and politics 3. Political leaders 4. Prime ministers -- Pakistan 5. Pakistan -- Politics and government
ISBN 978-0-06-156758-2; 0-06-156758-2
This "is a book of enormous intelligence, courage and clarity. . . . Washington should arrange to have the portions of the book about Islam republished as a separate volume and translated into several languages. It would do more to win the battle of ideas within Islam than anything an American president could ever say." N Y Times Book Rev
Includes bibliographical references

Bierce, Ambrose, 1842-1914?

Morris, Roy. **Ambrose** Bierce; alone in bad company. Oxford University Press 1998 306p pa $19.95   **92**
1. Authors 2. Journalists 3. Essayists 4. Authors,

American 5. Short story writers
ISBN 0-19-512628-9
LC 98-33467
First published 1995 by Crown
"Mr. Morris's disturbing, vividly realized biography brings to life a haunted writer whose private torments mirrored a turbulent era." NY Times Book Rev
Includes bibliographical references

Bilal, Wafaa, 1966-

Bilal, Wafaa. **Shoot** an Iraqi; art, life and resistance under the gun. by Wafaa Bilal and Kari Lydersen. City Lights 2008 177p il pa $16.95   **92**
1. Artists 2. Video artists 3. Performance artists 4. Iraq War, 2003- -- Art and the war
ISBN 978-0-8728-6491-7; 0-8728-6491-X
LC 2008-20487
The creator of 'Domestic Tension,' an unsettling interactive performance piece that speaks to the horrors of life in a conflict zone, reveals his experiences growing up under Saddam Hussein's rule.
"A powerful and demanding read, that is, frankly, a literary punch to the gut." Booklist

Billy, the Kid

Gardner, Mark L. **To** hell on a fast horse; Billy the Kid, Pat Garrett, and the epic chase to justice in the Old West. William Morrow 2010 325p il $26.99   **92**
1. Outlaws 2. Sheriffs
ISBN 978-0-06-136827-1; 0-06-136827-X
LC 2009025467
A "double biography of the iconic western outlaw Billy the Kid and Sheriff Pat Garrett. Maintaining an objective perspective on both men in a narrative closely tied to historic source materials, Gardner's quick-moving story follows events of the civil war in Lincoln County, New Mexico Territory in 1877–78, and the Kid's death-by-shooting at the hands of Garrett in 1881. . . . The final chapters describing Garrett as an old-style lawman in a postfrontier society, with interactions with President Theodore Roosevelt, serve to distinguish this book from other recent Kid biographies." Libr J
Includes bibligraphical references

★ Wallis, Michael. **Billy** the Kid; the endless ride. W.W. Norton & Co. 2007 328p il map $25.95   **92**
1. Outlaws
ISBN 978-0-393-06068-3; 0-393-06068-3
LC 2006-101364
"Drawing on archival sources and interviews as well as documents and secondary works, Wallis digs beneath the surface, clearly identifying what is known or probable and presenting the reasonable alternatives for what is conjecture." Libr J
Includes bibliographical references

Bingham, Hiram, 1875-1956

Heaney, Christopher. **Cradle** of gold; the story of Hiram Bingham, a real-life Indiana Jones, and the

search for Machu Picchu. Palgrave Macmillan 2010
285p il $27   **92**
   1. Incas 2. Explorers 3. Governors 4. Historians 5.
Senators 6. Machu Picchu (Peru) 7. Peru -- Antiquities
   ISBN 0-230-61169-9; 978-0-230-61169-6
                     LC 2009-38535
"On an archaeological trip to Peru on July 24, 1911, Hiram Bingham, an American explorer and history professor at Yale, happened upon the ruins of the Inca city of Machu Picchu. Although the site was already known to the local native people, Bingham made the Machu Picchu ruins famous and received acclaim as their 'discoverer.' Heaney presents a well-researched and very readable biography of Bingham from his childhood in Hawaii as the son of missionaries, through his education and careers as historian, educator, explorer, and finally politician. He probes the depths of Bingham's work and character, examining setbacks, scandals, and achievements and skillfully unraveling Bingham's role in the controversy that still exists today between the government of Peru and Yale University over the ownership of the Machu Picchu burials and artifacts." Libr J
   Includes bibliographical references

Bismarck, Otto, Furst von, 1815-1898

   Steinberg, Jonathan. **Bismarck**; Jonathan Steinberg. Oxford University Press 2011 x, 577 p., [16] p. of platesp $34.95   **92**
   1. Statesmen -- Germany -- Biography 2. Germany -- Politics and government -- 1866-1918
   ISBN 978-0-19-978252-9; 0-19-978252-0;
9780199782529
                     LC 2010045387
The author of this biography of German Chancellor Otto von Bismarck argues that his subject "remains 'the most remarkable and complex political leader of the nineteenth century' . . . [Jonathan] Steinberg sets out to understand how the man with 'an extraordinary, gigantic self' did it. He reminds readers that Bismarck succeeded only as long as he was indispensable to his royal master and ultimately he fell when Wilhelm II had had enough. Prof. Steinberg also uses his knowledge of nineteenth-century European history . . . to describe the stage on which Bismarck acted. In addition he pays great attention to original sources and Bismarck's collected works." (Contemporary Review) Index.
   "This is a beautifully written book that provides a stimulating and enjoyable introduction to the history of modern Europe." New Statesman
   Includes bibliographical references (p. [528]-537) and index

Bizet, Georges, 1838-1875

   MacDonald, Hugh. **Bizet**; Hugh Macdonald. Oxford University Press 2014 xi, 300 p.p illustrations, music (hardback : alk. paper) $36.95   **92**
   1. Composers 2. Composers -- France -- Biography
   ISBN 9780199781560; 0199781567
                     LC 2013041576
This biography of Georges Bizet, by Hugh Macdonald, "goes beyond the composer's most famous opera to take an in-depth look at his entire life and oeuvre. In so doing, Macdonald identifies a number of previously unknown pieces by

Bizet, assembling the first comprehensive catalogue of the composer's work." (Publisher's note)
   "Macdonald includes numerous musical examples of Bizet's lesser-known compositions, and these are extremely useful... this book is an important addition to the English-language literature on French music." Choice
   Includes bibliographical references (pages 277-283) and index

Black Elk, 1863-1950

   Black Elk. **Black** Elk speaks; being the life story of a holy man of the Oglala Sioux. [as told through] John G. Neihardt; foreword by Vine Deloria, Jr.; with illustrations by Standing Bear; essays by Alexis N. Petri and Lori Utecht. University of Nebraska Press 2004 xxix, 270p il map pa $19.95; pa $14.95 **92**
   1. Shamans 2. Oglala Indians 3. Native Americans -- Biography
   ISBN 9780803283916; 0-8032-8385-7
                     LC 2004-12692
   A reprint of the title first published 1932 by Morrow
   The Indian whose life story this is, was born in 1863. He was a famous warrior and hunter in his youth, and became a practicing medicine man among his people. Of him Neihardt says, "As an indubitable seer, he seemed to represent the consciousness of the Plains Indian more fully than any other I had ever known."
   This "is about as near as you can get to seeing life and death, war and religion, through an Indian's eyes." Outlook

   Steltenkamp, Michael F. **Black** Elk, holy man of the Oglala. University of Okla. Press 1993 xxiii, 211p il maps hardcover o.p. pa $17.95   **92**
   1. Shamans 2. Oglala Indians 3. Indian leaders
   ISBN 0-8061-2988-3 pa
                     LC 93-22089
This "is the story of Black Elk's later years, when the holy man converted to Roman Catholicism and worked actively as a catechist, converting the Lakota to his new religion." Antioch Rev
   Includes bibliographical references

Blackburn, Lucie, d. 1895

   ★ Smardz Frost, Karolyn. **I've** got a home in glory land; a lost tale of the Underground Railroad. Farrar, Straus & Giroux 2006 450p il map $30 **92**
   1. Slaves 2. Underground railroad 3. Coach drivers
   ISBN 978-0-374-16481-2; 0-374-16481-9
                     LC 2006-64
The author's "fascination with her subject and love of detailed historical documentation are evident in this engrossing look at a couple who defied slavery with their escape and their assistance to other fugitive slaves." Booklist
   Includes bibliographical references

Blackburn, Thornton, 1813 or 14-1890

★ Smardz Frost, Karolyn. **I've** got a home in glory land; a lost tale of the Underground Railroad. Farrar, Straus & Giroux 2006 450p il map $30　**92**

1. Slaves 2. Underground railroad 3. Coach drivers
ISBN 978-0-374-16481-2; 0-374-16481-9

LC 2006-64

The author's "fascination with her subject and love of detailed historical documentation are evident in this engrossing look at a couple who defied slavery with their escape and their assistance to other fugitive slaves." Booklist

Includes bibliographical references

Blackjack, Ada, 1898-1983

Niven, Jennifer. **Ada** Blackjack; a true story of survival in the Arctic. Hyperion 2003 431p il map $24.95　**92**

1. Explorers 2. Arctic regions -- Exploration 3. Wrangel Island (Russia) -- Exploration
ISBN 0-7868-6863-5

LC 2003-50826

The book "is exhilarating reading." Booklist
Includes bibliographical references

Blackmun, Harry A.

Greenhouse, Linda. **Becoming** Justice Blackmun; Harry Blackmun's Supreme Court journey. Times Books 2005 268p il $25　**92**

1. Supreme Court justices 2. United States -- Supreme Court
ISBN 0-8050-7791-X

LC 2004-63772

The author's "achievement in her meticulous narrative history is to provide new ammunition for Justice Blackmun's critics as well as his admirers. And readers who are unfamiliar with the inner workings of the court could not hope for a more engrossing introduction." N Y Times (Late N Y Ed)

Blagojevich, Rod R., 1956-

Brackett, Elizabeth. **Pay** to play; how Rod Blagojevich turned political corruption into a national sideshow. Ivan R. Dee 2009 247p il $24.95　**92**

1. Governors 2. Political corruption 3. State legislators 4. Members of Congress
ISBN 978-1-56663-834-0

LC 2009-10566

"Blagojevich, the well-coiffed, Elvis-loving former Illinois governor, gained national disrepute for his alleged attempts to sell the vacated U.S. Senate seat of President Barack Obama. . . . Brackett details the long and rocky road that brought Blagojevich to infamy. . . . A thorough and concise look at political corruption and the brazen man behind the scandal." Booklist

Blair, Tony

Blair, Tony. A **journey**; my political life. Alfred A. Knopf 2010 699p il $35; ebook $35　**92**

1. Prime ministers 2. Political leaders 3. Members of Parliament 4. Prime ministers -- Great Britain
ISBN 978-0-307-26983-6; 978-0-307-59487-7 ebook

LC 2010-28262

These are the memoirs of the British Labour Party politician who served as the prime minister of the United Kingdom from 1997 to 2007.

"Without delving too deeply into his personal life, . . . [Blair] gives the reader a good sense of his role not just as a public figure but also as a son, husband, and father. . . . Particulars of British party politics might elude some American readers, but the narrative keeps flowing. Essential for readers of current British politics." Libr J

Includes bibliographical references

Blanco, Richard, 1968-

Blanco, Richard, 1968- The **Prince** of Los Cocuyos; A Miami Childhood. Richard Blanco. HarperCollins 2014 272 p. $25.99　**92**

1. Poets 2. Gay men 3. Cuban Americans
ISBN 0062313762; 9780062313768

LC 2014501685

Author Richard Blaco offers his "inspiring memoir from the first Latino and openly gay inaugural poet, which explores his coming-of-age as the child of Cuban immigrants and his attempts to understand his place in America while grappling with his burgeoning artistic and sexual identities. (Publisher's note)

"Filled with colorful characters, often poignant and sometimes melancholy, Blanco's episodic memoir is a meditation on belonging, on self-acceptance, and on his family's almost mystical connection to Cuba." Booklist

Blunt, Anthony, 1907-1983

Carter, Miranda. **Anthony** Blunt: his lives. Farrar, Straus & Giroux 2001 590p il $30; pa $18 **92**

1. Spies 2. Art historians 3. Museum administrators
ISBN 0-374-10531-6; 0-312-42146-X pa

LC 2001-50135

"Thoroughly researched and carefully crafted, this is sure to be the definitive biography." Publ Wkly

Blunt, Judy, 1954-

Blunt, Judy. **Breaking** clean. Knopf 2002 303p hardcover o.p. pa $13　**92**

1. Authors 2. Ranchers 3. Memoirists
ISBN 0-375-70130-3 pa

LC 2001-29861

The author chronicles the hardships she endured as a ranch wife, mother, and laborer in rural Montana, and how she left it all, including her marriage, to get herself a college education and become a writer

Blunt has a "keen and poetic awareness, steely candor, and commanding storytelling skills." Booklist

Boeheim, Jim, 1944-

Boeheim, Jim, 1944- **Bleeding** Orange; Fifty Years of Blind Referees, Screaming Fans, Beasts of the East, and Syracuse Basketball. by Jim Boeheim, with Jack McCallum. HarperCollins 2014 320 p. 8 plates; color illustrations $27.99　**92**

1. College basketball 2. Coaching (Athletics)
ISBN 0062316648; 9780062316646

In this autobiography, Syracuse basketball coach Jim Boeheim "reflects on his life, his teachers, and the game he loves. . . . Boeheim has experienced it all triumph, despair, redemption; controversy, heartbreak, and scandal; championships, epic disappointments, colorful personalities, NCAA investigations. His combative personality helped ignite what was arguably the most competitive college basketball conference ever: the Big East of the 1980s." (Publisher's note)

"The tales from the Big East in its heyday mark some of the highlights of the book, as do his coaching insights. Sometimes accused of being a complainer on the court, Boeheim comes across as likable in this readable, thoughtful book about coaching college basketball." Kirkus

Bogart, Humphrey, 1899-1957

Thomson, David, 1941- **Humphrey** Bogart; photo research by Lucy Gray. Faber and Faber, Inc. 2010 127p il (Great stars) pa $14   92
1. Actors
ISBN 978-0-86547-933-3

LC 2009-41758

First published 2009 in the United Kingdom

In this biography, the author "focuses on how long it took the well-bred and educated Bogart to develop his trademark style as the rough-hewn, disillusioned, world-weary, wisecracking, fallen romantic of Casablanca and The Maltese Falcon. He charts Bogart's progress from New York stage performer to featured player in 1930s Hollywood, where he was often cast as a certain kind of feral street rat, to star." Booklist

Bolick, Kate

Bolick, Kate. **Spinster**; a life of one's own. Kate Bolick. Crown 2015 336 p. illustrations, portraits (hardback) $26   92
1. Single women 2. Single women -- History
ISBN 0385347138; 9780385347136

LC 2014037871

This book examines "the pleasures and possibilities of remaining single. Using her own experiences as a starting point, journalist and cultural critic Kate Bolick invites us into her carefully considered, passionately lived life, weaving together the past and present to examine why she--along with over 100 million American women, whose ranks keep growing--remains unmarried." (Publisher's note)

"Smartly written, intimate, and heartfelt, Spinster challenges readers to reconsider what a successful life feels like for women and gifts them with a wondrous group of historic figures to immerse themselves in. A brilliant and timely narrative for twenty-first-century bluestockings, and book groups shall rejoice from all the wonders it has to offer." Booklist

Bolivar, Simon, 1783-1830

Arana, Marie. **Bolivar**; American liberator. Marie Arana. Simon & Schuster 2013 603 p. ill. (chiefly col.), maps (hardcover) $35   92
1. Venezuela -- History -- 1810-1830 2. Heads of state -- South America -- Biography 3. South America -- History -- Wars of Independence, 1806-1830
ISBN 1439110190; 9781439110195; 9781439124956

LC 2012034661

In this book, "Peruvian journalist [Marie] Arana . . . chronicles Gen. Simón Bolívar's struggle against the Spanish Empire in the 1810s and '20s through several dizzying cycles of battlefield victory, triumphal procession, demoralizing reversal, and squalid exile, before he finally drove imperial forces out of Venezuela, Colombia, Ecuador, and Peru." (Publishers Weekly)

"Drawing on Bolívar's voluminous correspondence and political writings, Arana assembles a chronological narrative that does justice to both Bolívar's august achievements and his human imperfections. This well-rounded work reveals not just an accomplished military tactician but also an able statesman." LJ

Includes bibliographical references and index

Bolkovac, Kathryn

Bolkovac, Kathryn. The **whistleblower**; sex trafficking, military contractors, and one woman's fight for justice. [by] Kathryn Bolkovac with Cari Lynn. Palgrave Macmillan 2011 240p il map $25; pa $16; ebook $11.99   92
1. Whistle blowing 2. Juvenile prostitution 3. Bosnia and Hercegovina 4. Human rights activists 5. United Nations employees
ISBN 978-0-230-10802-8; 978-0-230-11522-4 pa; 978-0-230-11563-7 ebook

LC 2010-23196

This story "bristles with disturbing details and heartfelt compassion." Publ Wkly

Bonaparte, Paolina, 1780-1825

Fraser, Flora. **Pauline** Bonaparte; Venus of Empire. Alfred A. Knopf 2009 287p il $28.95   92
1. Princesses 2. Patrons of the arts
ISBN 978-0-307-26544-9; 0-307-26544-7

LC 2008-28639

This "narrative by British biographer Fraser . . . fleshes out the privileged and politically unstable world of Pauline, who both commissioned and modeled nearly nude for Canova's symbolic marble statue Venus Victorious as a testament to herself. Pauline's raison d'être was the joyful pursuit of astonishing variety in her love affairs, which Fraser asserts may have been a source of her invalidism throughout her adult life. But her life showcased the dangers in Napoleonic France as well as its pleasures: she faced death from yellow fever and insurrection in French colonial Haiti. Fraser's narrative provides insight into the permissive culture of the French Empire and glimpses into Napoleon as a protective and exasperated older brother while simultaneously engaged in politics, invasions and his eventual fall from power." Publ Wkly

Includes bibliographical references

Bonhoeffer, Dietrich, 1906-1945

Marsh, Charles. **Strange** glory; a life of Dietrich Bonhoeffer. by Charles Marsh. Alfred A. Knopf 2014 528 p. illustrations (hardcover) $35   92
1. Clergy 2. Theologians 3. Germany -- History -- 1933-1945
ISBN 0307269817; 9780307269812; 9780307390387

LC 2013045873

This book, by Charles Marsh, offers a biography of "Dietrich Bonhoeffer, the German pastor, theologian, and anti-Hitler conspirator. . . . [I]t was the Nuremberg laws that set Bonhoeffer's earthly life on an ineluctable path toward destruction. His denunciation of the race statutes as heresy and his insistence on the church's moral obligation to defend all victims of state violence, regardless of race or religion, alienated him from what would become the Reich church." (Publisher's note)

"Marsh's portrait is of a spoiled, materialistic, and selfish young man who develops, over time, into a German hero. The writing is clear and concise, the endnotes extensive, and the index generous." LJ

Includes bibliographical references and index

Metaxas, Eric. **Bonhoeffer**; pastor, martyr, prophet, spy: a Righteous Gentile vs. the Third Reich. Thomas Nelson 2010 591p il   **92**
1. Spies 2. Clergy 3. Theologians 4. Dissenters 5. Writers on religion 6. Biography, Individual 7. Germany -- History -- 1933-1945
ISBN 1595551387; 1595552464; 9781595551382; 9781595552464 pa

LC 2009013944

This is a biography of the German Lutheran pastor and theologian executed by the Nazis for plotting to overthrow Hitler.

"Insightful and illuminating, this tome makes a powerful contribution to biography, history and theology." Publ Wkly
Includes bibliographical references

Boone, Daniel, 1734-1820

Faragher, John Mack. **Daniel** Boone; the life and legend of an American pioneer. Holt & Co. 1992 429p il maps hardcover o.p. pa $18   **92**
1. Frontier and pioneer life 2. Scouts 3. Pioneers
ISBN 0-8050-3007-7 pa

LC 92-21873

"The popular image of Daniel Boone is that of an unlettered backwoodsman, skilled hunter and Indian fighter. But evidence argues that he was reasonably well educated for his time and place, that he was a landowner, businessman and a respected leader of frontier society. Faragher . . . has sifted through folklore and fact to reconstruct a realistic portrait of Boone and the expanding frontier. . . . Faragher has written an absorbing, definitive biography." Publ Wkly
Includes bibliographical references

Morgan, Robert. **Boone**; a biography. Algonquin Books of Chapel Hill 2007 538p il map $29.95 **92**
1. Frontier and pioneer life 2. Scouts 3. Pioneers 4. Biography, Individual 5. Frontier and pioneer life -- Kentucky
ISBN 1-56512-455-3; 978-1-56512-455-4

LC 2007-14204

This is a biography of the frontiersman. Index.
This is an "absorbing and stirring chronicle of the great frontiersman." Booklist
Includes bibliographical references

Booth, John Wilkes, 1838-1865

Alford, Terry. **Fortune's** Fool; The Life of John Wilkes Booth. Terry Alford. Oxford University Press 2015 416 p. illustrations $29.95   **92**
1. Actors -- United States -- Biography 2. United States -- History -- 1861-1865, Civil War
ISBN 0195054121; 9780195054125

LC 2014040917

National Book Critics Circle Award Finalist: Biography (2015)

In this biography of John Wilkes Booth, author "Terry Alford provides the first comprehensive look at the life of an enigmatic figure whose life has been overshadowed by his final, infamous act. Tracing Booth's story from his uncertain childhood in Maryland, characterized by a difficult relationship with his famous actor father, to his successful acting career on stages across the country, Alford offers a nuanced picture of Booth as a public figure, performer, and deeply troubled man." (Publisher's note)

Borges, Jorge Luis, 1899-1986

Williamson, Edwin. **Borges**, a life. Viking 2004 416p $34.95   **92**
1. Poets 2. Authors 3. Novelists 4. Essayists 5. Translators 6. Literary critics 7. Short story writers
ISBN 0-670-88579-7

LC 2004-41290

This "is a richly psychological, dynamically intellectual, and deeply affecting portrait of an often anguished and inhibited man who, through heroic perserverance and spiritual conviction, found salvation in writing and transformed literature for all time." Booklist
Includes bibliographical references

Borgia, Lucrezia, 1480-1519

Bradford, Sarah. **Lucrezia** Borgia; life, love, and death in Renaissance Italy. Viking 2004 xxiv, 421p il map $27.95; pa $16   **92**
1. Patrons of the arts
ISBN 0-670-03353-7; 0-14-303595-9 pa

LC 2004-54881

The author "presents Lucrezia as an intelligent noblewoman, powerless to defy her family's patriarchal order, yet an enlightened ruler in her own right as Duchess of Ferrara. . . . As a project designed to distinguish the historical Lucrezia Borgia from the legend, Bradford's readable biography resoundingly succeeds." Publ Wkly
Includes bibliographical references

Born, Max, 1882-1970

Greenspan, Nancy Thorndike. The **end** of the certain world; the Nobel physicist who ignited the quantum revolution. Basic Books 2005 374p il $26.95   **92**
1. Physicists 2. Nobel laureates for physics
ISBN 0-7382-0693-8

LC 2004-21809

"This empathetic work . . . lifts a deserving figure out of semi-obscurity and adds a valuable perspective on the origin of modern physics." Publ Wkly
Includes bibliographical references

Boswell, James, 1740-1795

Boswell's enlightenment; Robert Zaretsky. Belknap Press of Harvard University Press 2015 288 p. (cloth : alkaline paper) $26.95   92

1. Travelers 2. Enlightenment 3. Philosophy and religion 4. Enlightenment -- Scotland 5. Europe -- Description and travel 6. Scots -- Europe -- History -- 18th century 7. Authors, Scottish -- 18th century -- Biography 8. Travelers -- Europe -- History -- 18th century 9. Philosophy and religion -- Scotland -- History -- 18th century

ISBN 0674368231; 9780674368231

LC 2014037309

This book, by Robert Zaretsky, "examines the conflicting credos of reason and faith, progress and tradition that pulled [James] Boswell, like so many eighteenth-century Europeans, in opposing directions. . . . In his relentless quizzing of Voltaire and Rousseau, Hume and Johnson, Paoli and Wilkes on topics concerning faith, the soul, and death, he was not merely a celebrity-seeker but-- for want of a better term-- a truth-seeker." (Publisher's note)

"A fascinating character study, Boswell's Enlightenment helps readers understand what that something was. It is also the story of Boswell's struggle to reconcile his strict Calvinist upbringing with the ideas of the Enlightenment and with his tempestuous impulses and literary ambition. Summing Up: Essential. Lower-division undergraduates through faculty; general readers." Choice

Includes bibliographical references and index

Boulloche, André

Kaiser, Charles. The cost of courage; by Charles Kaiser. Other Press 2015 288 p. illustrations (hardcover) $26.95   92

1. World War, 1939-1945 -- Biography 2. World War, 1939-1945 -- Underground movements -- France 3. Guerrillas -- France -- Biography 4. France -- History -- German occupation, 1940-1945 -- Biography 5. World War, 1939-1945 -- Underground movements -- France -- Biography

ISBN 1590516141; 9781590516140

LC 2015008560

This book, by Charles Kaiser, tells the "heroic true story of the three youngest children of a . . . family who worked together in the French Resistance. . . . In the autumn of 1943, André Boulloche . . . coordinat[ed] all the Resistance movements in the nine northern regions of France only to be betrayed by one of his associates . . . and taken prisoner. His sisters carried on the fight without him until the end of the war." (Publisher's note)

"Kaiser's account of a family's devotion and resilience in the face of horrific tyranny tells a highly recommended story of resolve and bravery that can't help but feel romantic in its selfless and profound obligation, but this is not gloss nor ungrounded canonization." LJ

Bourdain, Anthony

Bourdain, Anthony. Kitchen confidential; adventures in the culinary underbelly. Updated ed; Harper Perennial 2007 312, 22p pa $15.99   92

1. Cooks 2. Authors 3. Novelists 4. Television

personalities 5. Memoirists

ISBN 978-0-06-089922-6; 0-06-089922-0

LC 2007-280057

First published 2000

"This is one bitter, nasty, searing, hard-to-swallow piece of work. But if you can choke the thing down, you'll probably wake up grinning in the middle of the night. . . . In a style partaking of Hunter S. Thompson, Iggy Pop and a little Jonathan Swift, Bourdain gleefully rips through the scenery to reveal private backstage horrors little dreamed of by the trusting public. . . . To a world infested with synthesized romance, candlelit illusions and sentimental piety, 'Kitchen Confidential' offers a nice palate-clearing taste of poison." N Y Times Book Rev

Bourdain, Anthony. Medium raw; a bloody valentine to the world of food and the people who cook. Ecco Press 2010 281p $26.99   92

1. Cooks 2. Authors 3. Novelists 4. Television personalities 5. Memoirists

ISBN 978-0-06-171894-6; 0-06-171894-7

This book mixes personal memoir with travelogues and ruminations on such matters as the degradation of the American hamburger, the dumbing down of the Food Network, the tedium of multicourse tasting menus and the rise of food gurus such as David Chang. . . . Mr. Bourdain is a vivid, bawdy and often foul-mouthed writer. He thrills in the attack, but he is also an enthusiast who writes well about things he holds dear. His detailed reporting on the backroom lives of restaurant employees is terrific. Wall Street J

Bowie, David

Bowie on Bowie; interviews and encounters with David Bowie. edited by Sean Egan. Chicago Review Press 2015 432 p. (hardback) $28.95   92

1. Rock musicians -- England 2. Rock musicians -- England -- Interviews

ISBN 9781569769775

LC 2014042080

This book, edited by Sean Egan, "presents some of the best interviews [rock musician David] Bowie has granted in his near five-decade career. Each interview traces a new step in his unique journey, successively freezing him in time as young novelty hit-maker, hairy hippie, Ziggy Stardust, Aladdin Sane, the Thin White Duke, . . . and, finally, . . . beloved elder statesman of challenging popular music. In all of these iterations he is remarkably articulate." (Publisher's note)

" Egan's curation places each interview in context, though the editorial language is choppy, giving helpful social reference points and highlighting the musician's notable remarks. Documented identities include Bowie as the brassy, bright-eyed newcomer, the rakish bisexual glam star, the evocative ambient artist using music as rehab, well into his later years as the reserved family man who has little use for the press. . . . this is a fascinating journey through the mind of a musician many people claim to "know" but who proves time and again that his own essence is often foreign to himself. An asset for Bowie fans." LJ

Includes bibliographical references and index

Morley, Paul. The age of Bowie; how David Bowie made a world of difference. by Paul Morley.

Simon & Schuster 2016 483 p. illustrations (some color) $30 **92**

1. Rock musicians -- England -- Biography
ISBN 1501151150; 9781501151156

In this book, author Paul Morley "constructs a definitive story of Bowie that explores how he worked, played, aged, structured his ideas, influenced others, invented the future, and entered history as someone who could and would never be forgotten. Morley captures the greatest moments from across Bowie's life and career." (Publisher's note)

There is a great deal of cultural history to enjoy in this personal, engaged and slyly scholarly biography. Morley's triumph is to know there is no such thing as the definitive story: new generations of fans will continue to make it up as they go along." New Statesman

Boyd, Gerald

Boyd, Gerald M. **My** Times in black and white; race and power at the New York Times. [by] Gerald M. Boyd; afterword by Robin D. Stone. Lawrence Hill Books 2010 402p il **92**

1. Journalists 2. New York times 3. Newspaper editors 4. Biography, Individual 5. United States -- Race relations
ISBN 1-55652-952-X; 978-1-55652-952-8
LC 2009-35506

This is a memoir of Boyd's experiences as a reporter and editor at The St. Louis Post-Dispatch and The New York Times. Index.

The author "has written a good book filled with ill feeling toward the Times, many of its editors, and a variety of colleagues who turned against him under pressure or simply because they wanted him to fail and be damned. . . . Lovers of newspaper gossip will find it delightfully indiscreet about self-serving treacheries hatched in the newsroom by people simultaneously engaged in high-minded pursuit of all the news that's fit to print." N Y Rev Books

Boylan, Jennifer Finney, 1958-

Boylan, Jennifer Finney. **I'm** looking through you; growing up haunted. Broadway Books 2008 270p il $23.95 **92**

1. Ghosts 2. Authors 3. Novelists 4. Transsexualism 5. Transsexuals 6. Authors, American 7. Short story writers 8. Young adult authors
ISBN 978-0-7679-2174-9; 0-7679-2174-7
LC 2007-19199

The author, a male-to-female transgendered person, "uses the metaphor of 'being haunted' throughout to illustrate not only her boyhood experiences but also the memories that have shaped her as a person as she struggled with her gender identity throughout most of her life. . . . Her writing style is witty, self-deprecating, entertaining, and often poignant, especially when describing family and friends who have passed away. An adventure to read, this is highly recommended for all libraries." Libr J

Boyle, Robert, 1627-1691

Hunter, Michael. **Boyle**; between God and science. Yale University Press 2009 366p il **92**

1. Chemists 2. Physicists 3. Scientists 4. Religion and science 5. Nonfiction writers 6. Writers on science 7. Biography, Individual 8. Religion and science -- England -- History -- 17th century
ISBN 0-300-12381-7; 9780300123814
LC 2009-13997

This is a biography of the seventeenth-century natural philosopher and scientist. Index.

"This painstakingly researched biography of the seventeenth-century scientist Robert Boyle outlines a life in which 'science and theology were truly complementary' but not always in harmony. Best known for Boyle's law, which established a constant relationship between air's volume and its pressure, Boyle was a moralist from a privileged upbringing whose conception of science—both of its empirical basis and of its transformative potential for mankind—was far ahead of its time." New Yorker

Includes bibliographical references

Bradbury, Ray, 1920-2012

Eller, Jonathan R. **Becoming** Ray Bradbury. University of Illinois Press 2011 324p il $34.95 **92**

1. Authors 2. Novelists 3. Screenwriters 4. Authors, American 5. Children's authors 6. Short story writers 7. Science fiction writers
ISBN 978-0-252-03629-3
LC 2011008562

The author "provides a detailed account of the experiences that shaped Ray Bradbury's life and writing career from his childhood until he embarked on the screenplay for John Huston's Moby Dick in late 1953. . . . Eller's work is thorough and enlightening on the subject of one of science fiction's greatest minds. Highly recommended not just for Bradbury fans but for all students of science fiction." Libr J

Includes bibliographical references

Weller, Sam. The **Bradbury** chronicles; the life of Ray Bradbury. William Morrow 2005 384p il $26.95; pa $15.95 **92**

1. Authors 2. Novelists 3. Screenwriters 4. Authors, American 5. Children's authors 6. Short story writers 7. Science fiction writers
ISBN 0-06-054581-X; 0-06-054584-4 pa
LC 2004-59491

"Weller's research—based on interviews with Bradbury as well as family members and colleagues—is almost exhaustive in its detail, and he does a fine job of presenting the facts of his subject's unique life. The lively, conversational prose brings out the writer's winning personality and turns his struggles and successes into a highly readable story." SLJ

Includes bibliographical references

Braddock, James J., 1906-1974

Schaap, Jeremy. **Cinderella** Man; James J. Braddock, Max Baer, and the greatest upset in boxing history. Houghton Mifflin 2005 324p il hardcover o.p. pa $13.95 **92**

1. Boxers (Persons) 2. Boxing -- Biography
ISBN 0-618-55117-4; 0-618-71190-2 pa
LC 2004-66085

The author goes into "detail on the brawny, reserved Braddock, who, at his lowest moments, was reduced to living off government relief and doing grueling work on the Hoboken, N.J., docks. But the story is as much about Max

Baer, the lovably clownish and handsome heavyweight Braddock defeated as a 10-to-one underdog. . . . Boxing enthusiasts will be more than satisfied by Schaap's meticulous account, which includes round-by-round details of the fight, as well as profiles of other fighters of the era." Publ Wkly

Includes bibliographical references

Bradstreet, Anne, 1612?-1672

Gordon, Charlotte. **Mistress** Bradstreet; the untold life of America's first poet. Little, Brown and Co. 2005 337p il map $27.95   **92**

1. Poets 2. Authors 3. Women poets 4. Colonists
ISBN 0-316-16904-8

LC 2004-22702

This is a biography of the colonial poet.

"Written with maximal clarity and communicativeness, this is a vibrant, engaging, realistic portrayal of early colonial Massachusetts and of its fascinating biographical subject." Booklist

Includes bibliographical references

Brady, Tom, 1977-

Myers, Gary. **Brady** vs Manning; the untold story of the rivalry that transformed the NFL. Gary Myers. Crown Archtype 2015 264 p. 8 unnumbered pages of plates (hbk.) $26   **92**

1. National Football League 2. Sports rivalries -- United States 3. Football -- United States -- History 4. Football players -- United States -- Biography 5. Quarterbacks (Football) -- United States -- Biography
ISBN 0804139377; 9780804139373

LC 2015027579

Author Gary Meyer presents this "inside account of the greatest rivalry in NFL history. Myers tackles this subject from every angle and with unprecedented access and insight, drawing on a huge number of never-before-heard interviews with [Tom] Brady and [Peyton] Manning, their coaches, their families, and those who have played with them and against them." (Publisher's note)

"Myers is a thorough professional with impeccable contacts to successfully tell this account, which will be of interest to all football fans." Library Journal

Includes bibliographical references and index

Bragg, Rick

Bragg, Rick. The **prince** of Frogtown. Alfred A. Knopf 2008 255p $24   **92**

1. Authors 2. Journalists 3. Stepfathers 4. Father-son relationship 5. Memoirists
ISBN 978-1-4000-4040-7; 1-4000-4040-X

LC 2007-38884

The author "merges his father's history of severe hardships and simple joys with a tale from the present: his own relationship with his 10-year-old stepson. . . . [This book] is lush with narratives about manhood, fathers and sons, families and the changing face of the rural South." Publ Wkly

Braverman, Blair

Welcome to the Goddamn Ice Cube; Chasing Fear and Finding Home in the Great White North.

Brahms, Johannes, 1833-1897

Swafford, Jan. **Johannes** Brahms; a biography. Knopf 1997 xxii, 699p il hardcover o.p. $20 **92**

1. Composers
ISBN 978-0-679-74582-2; 0-679-74582-3

LC 97-29308

"Swafford's study, clearly a labor of profound affection, is a model biography: eloquent, clear-sighted and often moving." Publ Wkly

Includes bibliographical references

Brandeis, Louis Dembitz, 1856-1941

Urofsky, Melvin I. **Louis** D. Brandeis; a life. Pantheon Books 2009 955p il   **92**

1. Judges 2. Lawyers 3. Biography, Individual 4. Supreme Court justices 5. United States -- Supreme Court 6. Law -- United States -- History
ISBN 9780375423666

LC 200903992

This is a biography of the American lawyer who was nominated to the Supreme Court in 1916 and served as a justice until his retirement in 1939. Index.

This is a "monumental, authoritative and appreciative biography of the man Franklin D. Roosevelt called 'Isaiah.'" N Y Times Book Rev

Includes bibliographical references

Braun, Eva

Gortemaker, Heike B. **Eva** Braun; life with Hitler. by Heike B. Görtemaker; translated from the German by Damion Searls. Alfred A. Knopf 2011 324 p. $27.95; ebook $13.99   **92**

1. Women -- Germany -- Biography 2. Mistresses -- Germany -- Biography 3. Germany -- History -- 1933-1945 -- Biography 4. Spouses of heads of state -- Germany -- Biography
ISBN 978-0-307-59582-9; 978-0-307-70139-8 ebook; 9780307595829

LC 2011009551

This book offers a biography of Adolf Hilter's mistress Eva Braun. "Although by the early-to-mid-Thirties Eva Braun thought that her relationship with Hitler was now on a more established footing, she was soon disillusioned by even longer absences. . . . Görtemaker writes of Eva Braun's 'practically unassailable position at Hitler's side,' even if in the dangerous and byzantine world of the Nazi hierarchy nothing was guaranteed. . . . Hitler . . . appreciate[d] her unquestioning loyalty. . . . Eva Braun . . . probably knew little of the sadism, the squalor, and the horror of the camps. As an impressionable young woman, she had been molded in her opinions during her time in Hitler's presence." (New York Review of Books)

The author "coaxes from history's shadows the woman who for 14 years was the companion, lover and, near the end, wife of Adolf Hitler." Kirkus

Includes bibliographical references

by Blair Braverman. HarperCollins 2016 288 p.
$25.99 **92**

1. Young women 2. Arctic regions
ISBN 0062311565; 9780062311566

This book, by Blair Braverman, is a "memoir of a young woman reclaiming her courage in the stark landscapes of the north. By the time Blair Braverman was eighteen, she had left her home in California, moved to arctic Norway to learn to drive sled dogs, and found work as a tour guide on a glacier in Alaska. Determined to carve out a life as a 'tough girl' . . . she slowly developed the strength and resilience the landscape demanded of her." (Publisher's note)

"Her external experiences are extraordinary in the frigid north that so few have experienced, but it's what happens internally that both sets this memoir apart and gives it universal resonance. Indelible characters, adventurous spirit, and acute psychological insight combine in this multilayered debut." Kirkus

Bray, Willie Reginald, 1879-1939

Tingey, John. The **Englishman** who posted himself and other curious objects. Princeton Architectural Press 2010 175p il $24.95 **92**

1. Autographs 2. Collectors 3. Eccentrics 4. Postal service -- Great Britain
ISBN 978-1-56898-872-6

LC 2009-48612

"The disposition of Bray's collection and how Tingey discovered it add further interest to an already fascinating account. Equally engaging as the narrative are the illustrations." Fine Books & Collections

Includes bibliographical references.

Brecht, Bertolt, 1898-1956

Fuegi, John. **Brecht** and company; sex, politics, and the making of the modern drama. Grove Press 1994 xx, 732p il hardcover o.p. pa $20 **92**

1. Poets 2. Authors 3. Novelists 4. Dramatists 5. Theatrical directors
ISBN 0-8021-3910-8 pa

LC 93-23051

The author "believes Brecht wrote very little in the dramas that made him famous; rather, he systematically plagiarized and 'collaborated' with lovers and colleagues by signing his name to plays they essentially wrote. . . . Fuegi's massive effort examines every aspect of Brecht's career and personality, and ranges from his childhood in Augsburg through his early successes and his exile to his return to East Germany." Booklist

Includes bibliographical references

Brenner, Carl

Brenner, Marie. **Apples** and oranges; my brother and me, lost and found. Farrar, Straus & Giroux 2008 268p il $24; pa $15 **92**

1. Cancer 2. Lawyers 3. Journalists 4. Fruit growers
ISBN 978-0-374-17352-4; 0-374-17352-4; 978-0-312-42880-8 pa; 0-312-42880-4 pa

LC 2008-08929

"In this elegiac memoir, the author, a reporter, applies the same investigative skills that led to her exposé of the tobacco industry and Enron to a more intimate subject: her

contentious relationship with her late brother. From an eccentric Jewish Texan family of compulsive record keepers—their father maintained a four-page list of his life's achievements—Marie became a New York liberal, Carl a diehard conservative who abandoned a legal career to farm apples. As a teenager, he smashed his sister's Joan Baez records; as an adult, given a diagnosis of terminal cancer, he informed her via FedEx. Her attempts to smooth over their differences by mastering the language of fruit (Carl often started conversations, 'I am going to give you a quiz') are at once comic and tinged with regret." New Yorker

Brenner, Marie

Brenner, Marie. **Apples** and oranges; my brother and me, lost and found. Farrar, Straus & Giroux 2008 268p il $24; pa $15 **92**

1. Cancer 2. Lawyers 3. Journalists 4. Fruit growers
ISBN 978-0-374-17352-4; 0-374-17352-4; 978-0-312-42880-8 pa; 0-312-42880-4 pa

LC 2008-08929

"In this elegiac memoir, the author, a reporter, applies the same investigative skills that led to her exposé of the tobacco industry and Enron to a more intimate subject: her contentious relationship with her late brother. From an eccentric Jewish Texan family of compulsive record keepers—their father maintained a four-page list of his life's achievements—Marie became a New York liberal, Carl a diehard conservative who abandoned a legal career to farm apples. As a teenager, he smashed his sister's Joan Baez records; as an adult, given a diagnosis of terminal cancer, he informed her via FedEx. Her attempts to smooth over their differences by mastering the language of fruit (Carl often started conversations, 'I am going to give you a quiz') are at once comic and tinged with regret." New Yorker

Breslin, Ed

Breslin, Ed. **Drinking** with Miss Dutchie; a memoir. Thomas Dunne Books 2011 274p $23.99 **92**

1. Dogs 2. Alcoholism 3. Editors 4. Memoirists 5. Publishing executives
ISBN 978-0-312-61975-6

LC 2010-39302

"Breslin writes about the death of his cherished dog, Miss Dutchie, and how, with her help, he succeeded in overcoming alcoholism. While not a dog-lover himself, in 1994 he bought Dutchie sight-unseen, as a surprise birthday gift for his wife. However, he freely admits that his motives were not entirely pure. 'I got Miss Dutchie to get Lynn off my back about my drinking,' he writes. Breslin had recently quit a decades-long career in publishing in an attempt to write a novel, and he did not expect to be spending his valuable time with a dog. . . . The story revolves around the dog who became the center of the childless couple's life, but the author also writes affectingly about his efforts to overcome addiction to alcohol and nicotine." Kirkus

Breslin, Jimmy

Breslin, Jimmy. **I** want to thank my brain for remembering me; a memoir. Little, Brown 1996 219p hardcover o.p. pa $12.95 **92**

1. Authors 2. Novelists 3. Columnists 4. Nonfiction

writers
ISBN 0-316-11879-6 pa
LC 96-10488

"Confronting the possibility of death just past age 65 . . . Breslin memory-surfs through a troubled childhood and a lifetime in various journalistic trenches, from copyboy to columnist. . . . The book is full of family stories, political stories, and classic Breslin street stories, plus lots of details about brain operations from both patient's and surgeon's point of view." Booklist

Brierley, Saroo

Brierley, Saroo. A **long** way home; a memoir. Saroo Brierley with Larry Buttrose. G.P. Putnam's Sons 2014 272 p. illustrations, maps (paperback) $16   **92**
1. Adopted children 2. Missing children 3. International adoption 4. Hobart (Tas.) -- Biography 5. Kolkata (India) -- Biography 6. Intercountry adoption -- India 7. East Indians -- Australia -- Biography 8. Birthparents -- India -- Identification 9. Intercountry adoption -- Australia -- Tasmania 10. Adopted children -- Australia -- Tasmania -- Biography
ISBN 0425276198; 9780399169281; 9780425276198
LC 2014003745

This memoir by Saroo Brierley with Larry Buttrose narrates how Brierley, as a child, "got lost on a train in India. . . . He survived alone for weeks on the rough streets of Calcutta before ultimately being transferred to an agency and adopted by a couple in Australia. . . . With the advent of Google Earth, he had the opportunity to look for the needle in a haystack he once called home. . . . After years of searching, he . . . set off to find his family." (Publisher's note)

Brinckle, Gordon, 1915-2007

Messick, Kendall. The **projectionist**. Princeton Architectural Press 2010 159p il $40   **92**
1. Motion picture theaters 2. Motion picture projectionists
ISBN 978-1-56898-933-4
LC 2010-08864

"Marveling at this amazing creation, Kendall knew that he had to photograph not only the theater, but the theater's owner and creator. And fortunately, the timing was perfect. Mr. Brinckle, a very elderly man, was extremely concerned about what would happen to his masterpiece after his passing. Their collaboration has resulted into something quite remarkable." Lenscratch

Brinkley, John Richard, 1885-1942

Brock, Pope. **Charlatan**; America's most dangerous huckster, the man who pursued him, and the age of flimflam. Crown Publishers 2008 324p il   **92**
1. Physicians 2. Quacks and quackery 3. Swindlers 4. Broadcasters 5. Biography, Individual 6. Quacks and quackery -- United States
ISBN 0307339882; 9780307339881
LC 2007-10074

This is a biography of John Richard Brinkley. In 1917, Brinkley arrived in "Milford, Kansas. He set up a medical practice and introduced . . . [a] surgical method of using goat glands to restore the fading virility of local farmers.

. . . Thousands of paying customers quickly turned 'Dr.' Brinkley into America's richest and most famous surgeon." (Publisher's note)

"Presentation is everything in telling this elaborate, many-faceted story. And Mr. Brock's has three outstanding virtues. First of all, he has a terrific ear for singling out quotations. . . . Second, he is selective. This fast-moving, light-stepping book takes care not to throw in extraneous detail. Third, his own voice is wry enough to compete with the actual Brinkley material, which is saying a great deal." N Y Times (Late N Y Ed)

Includes bibliographical references

Britten, Benjamin, 1913-1976

Powell, Neil, 1948- **Benjamin** Britten; a life for music. by Neil Powell. Henry Holt and Company 2013 528 p. $37   **92**
1. Composers -- Biography 2. Composers -- England -- Biography
ISBN 0805097740; 9780805097740
LC 2012051536

In this biography of "Benjamin Britten, the celebrated British composer . . . [Neil] Powell . . . traces the development of Britten's musical gifts from his childhood and youth in England to his travels to America, his meetings and lifelong friendship with W.H. Auden, and his crucial role in helping to establish the Alderburgh Festival. . . . He probes the genius of Britten's compositions from Sinfonietta . . . to the triptych of Peter Grimes . . . Billy Budd, and Death in Venice." (Publishers Weekly)

Includes bibliographical references and index

Brokaw, Tom, 1940-

Brokaw, Tom, 1940- A **Lucky** Life Interrupted; A Memoir of Hope. Tom Brokaw. Random House Inc. 2015 240 p. $27   **92**
1. Journalists 2. Cancer patients 3. Physician and patient 4. Multiple myeloma -- Treatment 5. Multiple myeloma -- Patients -- United States -- Biography
ISBN 1400069696; 9781400069699
LC 2015008653

In this memoir, journalist Tom Brokaw reflects on his diagnosis with "multiple myeloma, a treatable but incurable blood cancer. Brokaw takes us through all the seasons and stages of this surprising year, the emotions, discoveries, setbacks, and struggles--times of denial, acceptance, turning points, and courage. After his diagnosis, Brokaw began to keep a journal, approaching this new stage of his life in a familiar role: as a journalist." (Publisher's note)

"Brokaw's account lacks the depth and fire of Christopher Hitchens' Mortality (2013), but it belongs on the same shelf as a wise and oddly comforting look at the toughest news of all." Kirkus

Brontë, Charlotte, 1816-1855

Gaskell, Elizabeth Cleghorn. The **life** of Charlotte Bronte; [by] Elizabeth Gaskell; edited with an introduction and notes by Angus Eason. Oxford University Press 2001 xxxvi, 587p (Oxford world's classics) pa $13.95   **92**
1. Poets 2. Authors 3. Novelists 4. Women authors

5. Authors, English
ISBN 0-19-283805-9
First published 1857
"Mrs. Gaskell was herself a popular novelist, who commanded a very wide audience. She brought to bear upon the biography of Charlotte Bronte all those literary gifts which had made the charm of her seven volumes of romance. . . . It is quite certain that Charlotte Bronte would not stand on so splendid a pedestal today but for the single-minded devotion of her accomplished biographer." Clement K. Shorter

Includes bibliographical references

Gordon, Lyndall. **Charlotte** Bronte; a passionate life. Norton 1995 418p il hardcover o.p. pa $17 **92**
1. Poets 2. Authors 3. Novelists 4. Women authors 5. Authors, English
ISBN 0-393-31448-0 pa
First published 1994 in the United Kingdom
The author "dismantles once and for all the image of Charlotte Brontë as a figure of pathos and presents, instead, a courageous survivor, a determined writer, and a woman of volcanic emotion. . . . Gordon, as skilled at literary analysis as at chronicling a life, approaches Brontë's tragic and enduringly relevant story from several angles, carefully identifying all the autobiographical elements of her novels and contrasting her commitment to writing and her independent spirit to her era's strict and pitiless code of behavior for women." Booklist

Includes bibliographical references

Brookhiser, Richard

Brookhiser, Richard. **Right** time, right place; coming of age with William F. Buckley, Jr. and the conservative movement. Basic Books 2009 262p $27.50 **92**
1. Authors 2. Novelists 3. Historians 4. Journalists 5. Conservatism 6. Columnists 7. Biographers 8. National review 9. Magazine editors
ISBN 978-0-465-01355-5; 0-465-01355-4
LC 2009-03073
"Think of a cause you care about deeply. Who's the figure you most admire in that movement? Now picture that person taking you to lunch, when you're 23, and declaring that you—you!—will be his successor. Such was the fantasy that Richard Brookhiser lived as a protégé of National Review editor William F. Buckley Jr., conservatism's standard-bearer for a half-century. Brookhiser was, to put it mildly, a prodigy. He wrote his first magazine cover story at 14. Steep falls often follow such precocious rises. But when Buckley changed his mind and sought a different heir, Brookhiser didn't self-destruct; he just rejiggered his career. Such equanimity means Right Time, Right Place is refreshingly free of spicy score settling and juicy revelations. Instead, readers get tasty morsels of candor caramelized in the searing heat of self-reflection. The result is a psychologically rich personal narrative." Christ Sci Monit

Brown, Carolyn

★ Brown, Carolyn. **Chance** and circumstance; twenty years with Cage and Cunningham. Alfred A. Knopf 2007 645p il $37.50 **92**
1. Poets 2. Authors 3. Dancers 4. Composers 5.

Choreographers 6. Essayists
ISBN 978-0-394-40191-1; 0-394-40191-3
LC 2006-48799
The author "traces the trajectory of her modern dance career with that organization during its crawling stages in the 1950s and 1960s, when composer John Cage was musical director and artist Robert Rauschenberg was set and costume designer. Brown documents the company's early struggles for acceptance (it was considered avant-garde), various tours, and eventual world recognition. . . . This book will appeal to modern dance buffs and memoir readers." Libr J

Brown, Claude, 1937-2002

Brown, Claude. **Manchild** in the promised land. Touchstone 1999 415p pa $19.95; pa $14.95 **92**
1. Authors 2. Journalists 3. Essayists 4. Memoirists 5. African Americans -- Biography 6. African Americans -- Harlem (New York, N.Y.)
ISBN 9781451626674; 0-684-86418-5
First published 1965 by Macmillan
This is "the autobiography of a young black man raised in Harlem. It is a realistic description of life in the ghetto. . . . The core of the book concerns the 'plague' of heroin addiction that swept through Harlem in the 1950s taking the lives of many of Brown's contemporaries." Publ Wkly

Brown, Helen Gurley

Hauser, Brooke. **Enter** Helen; The Invention of Helen Gurley Brown and the Rise of the Modern Single Woman. Brooke Hauser. Harper 2016 480 p. illustrations (hardback) $28.99 **92**
1. Single women 2. Women -- Social conditions 3. Women -- New York (State) -- New York -- Biography 4. Single women -- New York (State) -- New York -- Biography
ISBN 9780062342669; 9780062342676
LC 2015038742
This book, by Brooke Hauser, is "about legendary Cosmopolitan editor and champion of the single girl Helen Gurley Brown. . . . At a time when women's magazines taught housewives how to make the perfect casserole, Helen spoke directly to the single girl next door, cheekily advising her on how to pursue men, money, power, pleasure, and, most of all, personal happiness." (Publisher's note)

Includes bibliographical references (pages 395-445) and index.

Hirshey, Gerri. **Not** pretty enough; The Unlikely Triumph of Helen Gurley Brown. Gerri Hirshey. Sarah Crichton Books; Farrar, Straus & Giroux 2016 528 p. illustrations (Hardback) $27 **92**
1. Women authors 2. Periodicals -- United States 3. Editors -- United States -- Biography 4. Periodical editors -- United States -- Biography
ISBN 9780374169176; 9780374712235
LC 2016007143
This book, by Gerri Hirshey, is a biography of Helen Gurley Brown. "Her life story is astonishing, from her roots in the Ozark Mountains of Arkansas, to her single-girl decade as a Mad Men-era copywriter in Los Angeles, which informed her first bestseller, to her years at the helm of Cosmopolitan. Helen Gurley Brown told her own story

many times, but coyly, with plenty of camouflage." (Publisher's note)

"This account sheds light on a complex woman whose controversial personality helped form both second-wave feminism and the magazine industry." LJ

Includes bibliographical references and index

Scanlon, Jennifer. **Bad** girls go everywhere: the life of Helen Gurley Brown. Oxford University Press 2009 270p il $27.95　　　　　　　**92**
1. Columnists 2. Magazine editors 3. Nonfiction writers

ISBN 978-0-19-534205-5; 0-19-534205-4

LC 2008-30466

This is a biography of Helen Gurley Brown, former editor of Cosmopolitan magazine and author of Sex and the Single Girl (1962), Sex and the Office (1964), and Single Girl's Cookbook (1969).

"Jennifer Scanlon delivers Helen Gurley Brown's 'delightfully knotty life story' in a neat and satisfying package. . . . This is not chick lit but cultural history, the first serious biography of the woman who, in Scanlon's view, 'ushered in and has long continued to define the feminist mainstream.'" Natl Rev

Includes bibliographical references

Brown, James, 1933-2006

Brown, James. **James** Brown, the godfather of soul; by James Brown with Bruce Tucker; new introduction by Bruce Tucker; epilogue by Dave Marsh. Thunder's Mouth Press 1997 352p il pa $14.95 **92**
1. Singers 2. African American singers 3. Soul musicians

ISBN 978-1-56025-115-6; 1-56025-115-8

LC 90-31961

First published 1986 by Macmillan

This "is a solid, informative autobiography, and fans will welcome its vast discography." N Y Times Book Rev

Includes discography

Sullivan, James. The **hardest** working man; how James Brown saved the soul of America: live at the Boston Garden, 1968. Gotham Books 2008 244p il $25　　　　　　　**92**
1. Singers 2. African American singers 3. Soul musicians

ISBN 978-1-592-40390-5; 1-592-40390-5

LC 2008-13670

"Sullivan examines James Brown's role in saving Boston from the fires and riots that swept the U.S. after Martin Luther King Jr.'s assassination. Booked into Boston Garden the night of April 5, 1968, Brown agreed to put the show on live local TV to give would-be rioters reason to stay home. Garden management wanted to cancel, doubtless to avoid rioting in the Garden, but Brown and Boston's first black city councillor interceded with Mayor Kevin White to prevent cancellation. Sullivan goes further in crediting Brown for keeping the peace than others have, and so doing, he also examines the Godfather of Soul's life and career in the context

of the Civil Rights movement. . . . A good record of a pivotal event and a serviceable Brown bio, to boot." Booklist

Includes bibliographical references

★ McBride, James, 1957- **Kill** 'em and leave; searching for the real James Brown. James McBride. Spiegel & Grau 2016 256 p. $28　　　　**92**
1. Musicians -- United States 2. Soul musicians -- United States -- Biography

ISBN 9780679645627; 9780812993509

LC 2015026358

This book, by James McBride, "is more than a book about James Brown. Brown's rough-and-tumble life, through McBride's lens, is an unsettling metaphor for American life: the tension between North and South, black and white, rich and poor. McBride's travels take him to forgotten corners of Brown's never-before-revealed history." (Publisher's note)

"An unconventional and fascinating portrait of Soul Brother No. 1 and the significance of his rise and fall i n American culture." Kirkus

Smith, R. J. The **one**; the life and music of James Brown. RJ Smith. Gotham Books 2012 455 p. $18　　　　　　　　　　　　　**92**
1. Funk (Music) 2. Soul musicians -- United States -- Biography

ISBN 1592406572; 1592407420; 9781592406579; 9781592407422

LC 2011028536

This is R.J. Smith's "look at the life and times of the late, great James Brown, self-proclaimed Soul Brother Number One and Hardest Working Man in Show Business and leading inspiration to a generation of singers like [Mitch] Ryder. . . . Smith considers Brown's life and career story, right down to brushes with the law, including his incarcerations at both and early age and later in life, when age and substance abuse overcame Brown's legendary control of his image and lifestyle." (Booklist)

Includes bibliographical references and index

Brown, James, 1957-

Brown, James. The **Los** Angeles diaries; a memoir. Morrow 2003 200p $21.95; pa $12.95　　　**92**
1. Authors 2. Novelists 3. Short story writers

ISBN 0-06-052151-1; 0-06-052152-X pa

LC 2003-48779

"Brown's revelations have no smugness or self-congratulation; they reek of remorse and desire, passion and futility. . . . The result is a grimly exquisite memoir that reads like a noir novel but grips unrelentingly like the hand of a homeless drunk begging for help." Publ Wkly

Brown, John, 1800-1859

★ Horwitz, Tony. **Midnight** rising; John Brown and raid that sparked the Civil War. Henry Holt and Co. 2011 365p il map $29; ebook $12.99　　　**92**
1. Abolitionists 2. Pioneers 3. Harpers Ferry (W. Va.) -- History -- John Brown's Raid, 1859

ISBN 978-0-8050-9153-3; 0-8050-9153-X; 978-1-4299-9698-3 ebook; 1-4299-9698-6 ebook

LC 2011015659

The author presents a "narrative of Brown and the raid on Harpers Ferry that in many ways set the stage for Southern secession and civil war. . . . Horwitz's Brown did not die in vain. By recalling the drama that fired the imagination and fears of Brown's time, Midnight Rising calls readers to account for complacency about social injustices today. This is a book for our time." Libr J

Includes bibliographical references

Reynolds, David S. **John** Brown, abolitionist; the man who killed slavery, sparked the Civil War, and seeded civil rights. Alfred A. Knopf 2005 578p il $35 **92**

1. Abolitionists

ISBN 0-375-41188-7

LC 2004-48864

"Almost every page forces you to think hard, and in new ways, about American violence, American history, and what used to be called the American character." New Yorker

Includes bibliographical references

Brownfield, Christopher J.

Brownfield, Christopher J. **My** nuclear family; a coming-of-age in America's twenty-first century military. Alfred A. Knopf 2010 314p il $26.95; ebook $26.95 **92**

1. Nuclear submarines 2. Memoirists 3. Naval officers 4. Political scientists 5. Iraq War, 2003- -- Personal narratives

ISBN 978-0-307-27169-3; 978-0-307-59428-0 ebook

LC 2010-11833

This "is not the best book written by an insider about America's post-9/11 military, but it's certainly the most entertaining. It's got a cocky, star-spangled, wide-angle feel, as if a subversive young novelist had decided to rewrite a Tom Clancy thriller after first piloting some nuclear submarines as a gonzo practice drill. . . . This is a book that's going to rattle some cages." N Y Times Book Rev

Includes bibliographical references

Brownstein, Carrie, 1974-

Brownstein, Carrie, 1974- **Hunger** Makes Me a Modern Girl; A Memoir. Carrie Brownstein. Riverhead Books 2015 244 p. illustrations $27.95 **92**

1. Women -- Biography 2. Riot grrrl movement 3. Singers -- Biography 4. Women rock musicians 5. Rock musicians -- United States -- Biography 6. Singers -- United States -- Biography 7. Women singers -- United States -- Biography 8. Women rock musicians -- United States -- Biography

ISBN 1594486638; 9781594486630

LC 2015024629

This memoir, by Carrie Brownstein, is "a narrative of her escape from a turbulent family life into a world where music was the means toward self-invention, community, and rescue. . . . Brownstein chronicles the excitement and contradictions within the era's flourishing and fiercely independent music subculture, including experiences that sowed the seeds for the observational satire of the popular television series Portlandia years later." (Publisher's note)

"A strong, engaging pop culture memoir: personal detail, a little dish, and a well-written look at what made the music, and the culture that spawned it, matter." LJ

Bruni, Frank, 1964-

Bruni, Frank. **Born** round; the secret history of a full-time eater. Penguin Press 2009 354p il $25.95; pa $16 **92**

1. Obesity 2. Food critics

ISBN 978-1-59420-231-5; 1-59420-231-1; 978-0-14-311767-4 pa; 0-14-311767-X pa

LC 2009-09532

"The book does not contain paeans to the glories of localvorism. It's not a tale of bawdy kitchen exploits, or of finding your true self over a bowl of pasta in Rome . . . His memoir tells a story of food addiction, eating disorders, and a lifelong struggle with his voracious appetite . . . Born Round makes for a breezy read. Even at its darkest, it goes down easy." Village Voice

Bryan, William Jennings, 1860-1925

Kazin, Michael. A **godly** hero; the life of William Jennings Bryan. Knopf 2006 374p il hardcover o.p. pa $16.95 **92**

1. Authors 2. Lawyers 3. Political leaders 4. Secretaries of state 5. Presidential candidates

ISBN 0-375-41135-6; 978-0-385-72056-4 pa; 0-385-72056-4 pa

LC 2005-44105

"Kazin is not the first biographer to tackle the Great Commoner, but he is definitely the best writer among them. 'A Godly Hero' is a richly textured narrative with an excellent pace." Christ Sci Monit

Includes bibliographical references

Bryson, Bill, 1951-

Bryson, Bill, 1951- The **life** and times of the thunderbolt kid; a memoir. Broadway Books 2006 270p il $25 **92**

1. Authors 2. Journalists 3. Essayists 4. Linguists 5. Lexicographers 6. Travel writers 7. Nonfiction writers 8. Biography, Individual

ISBN 0-7679-1936-X; 978-0-7679-1936-4

LC 2006-43859

In this book, Bill Bryson "recounts his childhood and teen years. When he was very young, he ran about his town with a towel for a cape, declaring himself the superhero, Thunderbolt Kid. His father wrote for the local paper, his mother worked there as well, leaving their home rather free from 'the domestic arts' (i.e. rather dirty). As he grew up, some of his friends were demonically destructive, while others were skilled at liberating boxcar loads of beer." (Voice of Youth Advocates)

The author "recounts the world of his younger self, buried in comic books in the Kiddie Corral at the local supermarket, resisting civil defense drills at school, and fruitlessly trying to unravel the mysteries of sex. . . . The larger world of 1950s America emerges through the lens of 'Billy's' world, including the dark underbelly of racism, the fight against communism, and the advent of the nuclear age." Libr J

Includes bibliographical references

Buber, Martin, 1878-1965

Friedman, Maurice S. **Encounter** on the narrow ridge: a life of Martin Buber; {by} Maurice Friedman. Paragon House 1991 496p il $22.95; pa $18.95   **92**

1. Authors 2. Zionism 3. Novelists 4. Philosophers 5. Jewish philosophy 6. Essayists 7. Translators 8. Writers on religion

ISBN 1-55778-453-1; 1-55778-596-1 pa

LC 90-44502

This biography (based on the author's three volume Martin Buber's life and work) "traces Buber's career showing the pivotal events in his life as well as the influences of Judaism, Christianity, general philosophical thought, and linguistics on his writings and lectures. Friedman analyzes succinctly, but with great care, Buber's responses to the important events of the 20th century." Libr J

Includes bibliographical references

Buck, Pearl S. (Pearl Sydenstricker), 1892-1973

Spurling, Hilary. **Pearl** Buck in China; journey to The Good Earth. Simon & Schuster 2010 304p il map $27; ebook $12.99   **92**

1. Authors 2. Novelists 3. Short 4. Essayists 5. Memoirists 6. Biographers 7. Authors, American 8. Biography, Individual 9. Nobel laureates for literature

ISBN 978-1-4165-4042-7; 1-4165-4042-3; 978-1-4391-8044-0 ebook; 1-4391-8044-X ebook

LC 2010-07712

Published in the United Kingdom with title: Burying the bones

This is a biography of the American author of The Good Earth (1931).

The author's "account of Buck's 'rootless and fractured existence' provides a fascinating dissection of the tortured relationships between a man of God, the hapless wife sucked into supporting his mission and their increasingly sceptical daughter, Pearl, who, in 1933, publicly turned her back on her late father's church. It is also just as revealing about the no less tortured relationship between the West and China in the early part of the last century." Economist

Includes bibliographical references

Buckley, Bryan

Sielski, Mike. **Fading** echoes; a true story of rivalry and brotherhood from the football field to the fields of honor. Berkley Books 2009 342p il $24.95   **92**

1. School sports 2. Iraq War, 2003-2011 3. Marines 4. Army officers 5. Iraq War, 2003- 6. Football -- Biography 7. Soldiers -- United States

ISBN 978-0-425-22974-3

LC 2009-17001

"Bryan Buckley was the captain of Central Bucks West and [Colby] Umbrell was one of the leaders of Central Bucks East when their teams clashed in their senior year of 1998. Eight years later, both were officers leading men in combat in Iraq, Buckley as a marine and Umbrell as an army ranger. Both were proudly fighting for ideals in which they believed, and only one would come home alive. Sielski . . . chronicles the lives of these two athletes and illustrates how their personalities and values were formed from inter-

actions with family, friends, coaches, and community. In the process, he writes of much broader topics in contemporary American life: dreams, competition, resolve, war, honor, sacrifice, and true heartbreak." Libr J

Includes bibliographical references

Buckley, Christopher Taylor, 1952-

Buckley, Christopher Taylor. **Losing** Mum and Pup; a memoir. [by] Christopher Buckley. Twelve 2009 251p il $24.99; pa $13.99   **92**

1. Authors 2. Humorists 3. Novelists 4. Philanthropists 5. Columnists 6. Socialites 7. Speechwriters 8. Magazine editors 9. Authors, American 10. Spouses of prominent persons

ISBN 978-0-446-54094-0; 0-446-54094-3; 978-0-446-54095-7 pa; 0-446-54095-1 pa

LC 2008-43532

"Christopher Buckley has not written a 'Mommie Dearest' for the Evelyn Waugh set. 'Losing Mum and Pup' is a subtle, fond and, above all, honest chronicle of his celebrated parents. . . . Buckley has pulled off what eludes many writers: he has written candidly but not unkindly about people whose vices and virtues he sees clearly." Newsweek

Buckley, Gail Lumet, 1937-

★ Buckley, Gail Lumet, 1937- The **Black** Calhouns; From Civil War to Civil Rights With One African American Family. by Gail Lumet Buckley. Atlantic Monthly Press 2016 336 p. 8 plts; ills; gen tbls; ports $26   **92**

1. African Americans -- Biography

ISBN 0802124542; 9780802124548

In this book, author "Gail Lumet Buckley—daughter of actress Lena Horne—delves deep into her family history, detailing the experiences of an extraordinary African-American family from Civil War to Civil Rights. Beginning with her great-great grandfather Moses Calhoun, a house slave who used the rare advantage of his education to become a successful businessman in post-war Atlanta, Buckley follows her family's two branches: one that stayed in the South, and the other that settled in Brooklyn." (Publisher's note)

"This personal and historical account covers much of the same ground as Buckley's previous book, The Hornes; fans of Lena Horne will enjoy. " LJ

Buckley, Pat

Buckley, Christopher Taylor. **Losing** Mum and Pup; a memoir. [by] Christopher Buckley. Twelve 2009 251p il $24.99; pa $13.99   **92**

1. Authors 2. Humorists 3. Novelists 4. Philanthropists 5. Columnists 6. Socialites 7. Speechwriters 8. Magazine editors 9. Authors, American 10. Spouses of prominent persons

ISBN 978-0-446-54094-0; 0-446-54094-3; 978-0-446-54095-7 pa; 0-446-54095-1 pa

LC 2008-43532

"Christopher Buckley has not written a 'Mommie Dearest' for the Evelyn Waugh set. 'Losing Mum and Pup' is a subtle, fond and, above all, honest chronicle of his celebrated parents. . . . Buckley has pulled off what eludes many writers: he has written candidly but not unkindly about people whose vices and virtues he sees clearly." Newsweek

Buckley, William F. (William Frank), 1925-2008

★ Bogus, Carl T. **Buckley**; William F. Buckley Jr. and the rise of American Conservatism. Carl T. Bogus. Bloomsbury 2011 416 p. $30.00	**92**

1. Conservatism -- United States -- History 2. United States -- Politics and government 3. Journalists -- United States -- Biography 4. Conservatism -- United States -- Biography

ISBN 1596915803; 9781596915800

LC 2011012734

This book is not only a biography of publisher William F. Buckley; it also looks at "the story of the conservative movement's origins" in the U.S. during the 20th century. Author Carl T. Bogus "explains the competing philosophies of different conservative sects—Burkean conservatism, libertarianism, Ayn Rand's objectivism." (Library Journal)

Includes bibliographical references and index.

Brookhiser, Richard. Right time, right place; coming of age with William F. Buckley, Jr. and the conservative movement. Basic Books 2009 262p $27.50	**92**

1. Authors 2. Novelists 3. Historians 4. Journalists 5. Conservatism 6. Columnists 7. Biographers 8. National review 9. Magazine editors

ISBN 978-0-465-01355-5; 0-465-01355-4

LC 2009-03073

"Think of a cause you care about deeply. Who's the figure you most admire in that movement? Now picture that person taking you to lunch, when you're 23, and declaring that you – you! – will be his successor. Such was the fantasy that Richard Brookhiser lived as a protégé of National Review editor William F. Buckley Jr., conservatism's standard-bearer for a half-century. Brookhiser was, to put it mildly, a prodigy. He wrote his first magazine cover story at 14. Steep falls often follow such precocious rises. But when Buckley changed his mind and sought a different heir, Brookhiser didn't self-destruct; he just rejiggered his career. Such equanimity means Right Time, Right Place is refreshingly free of spicy score settling and juicy revelations. Instead, readers get tasty morsels of candor caramelized in the searing heat of self-reflection. The result is a psychologically rich personal narrative." Christ Sci Monit

Buckley, Christopher Taylor. Losing Mum and Pup; a memoir. [by] Christopher Buckley. Twelve 2009 251p il $24.99; pa $13.99	**92**

1. Authors 2. Humorists 3. Novelists 4. Philanthropists 5. Columnists 6. Socialites 7. Speechwriters 8. Magazine editors 9. Authors, American 10. Spouses of prominent persons

ISBN 978-0-446-54094-0; 0-446-54094-3; 978-0-446-54095-7 pa; 0-446-54095-1 pa

LC 2008-43532

"Christopher Buckley has not written a 'Mommie Dearest' for the Evelyn Waugh set. 'Losing Mum and Pup' is a subtle, fond and, above all, honest chronicle of his celebrated parents. . . . Buckley has pulled off what eludes many writers: he has written candidly but not unkindly about people whose vices and virtues he sees clearly." Newsweek

Buckley, William F. Miles gone by; a literary autobiography. [by] William F. Buckley Jr. Regnery Pub. 2004 594p il $29.95; pa $18.95	**92**

1. Authors 2. Novelists 3. Columnists 4. Magazine editors

ISBN 0-89526-089-1; 0-89526-004-2 pa

LC 2004-7170

This "is an elegant book, one of Buckley's best, and the man the reader meets in these pages is the Platonic ideal of a dinner companion, a raconteur whose pomposity is calculated and whose self-deprecation charms." N Y Times Book Rev

Buffalo Bill, 1846-1917

Warren, Louis S. **Buffalo** Bill's America; William Cody and the Wild West Show. Alfred A. Knopf 2005 652p il $30	**92**

1. Entertainers 2. Frontier and pioneer life 3. Scouts 4. Hunters 5. Circus executives 6. Circus performers

ISBN 0-375-41216-6

LC 2004-63280

This is a biography of the American showman.

This book "is well written and exhaustively researched, the weightiest and surely the most ambitious book ever published about Cody and his times." N Y Times Book Rev

Includes bibliographical references

Buffett, Warren E.

Schroeder, Alice D. The **snowball**: Warren Buffett and the business of life; [by] Alice Schroeder. Bantam Books 2008 960p il $35	**92**

1. Capitalists and financiers 2. Financiers

ISBN 978-0-553-80509-3; 0-553-80509-6

LC 2008-17338

A portrait of the life and career of investment guru Warren Buffett

"In a book that is dominated by unstinting descriptions of Buffett's appetites—for profit, women (particularly nurturing maternal types), food (Buffett maintained his and his family's weight by 'dangling money')—it is refreshing that Schroeder keeps her tone free of judgment or awe; Buffett's plain-speaking suffuses the book and renders his public and private successes and failures wonderfully human and universal. . . . Inspiring managerial advice abounds and competes with gossipy tidbits . . . in this rich, surprisingly affecting biography." Publ Wkly

Includes bibliographical references

Bullock-Prado, Gesine, 1970-

Bullock-Prado, Gesine. **Confections** of a closet master baker; one woman's sweet journey from unhappy Hollywood executive to contented country baker. illustrations by Raymond G. Prado. Broadway Books 2009 226p il $24	**92**

1. Baking 2. Bakers 3. Motion picture executives

ISBN 978-0-7679-3268-4

LC 2009-945

The author "chronicles her career change from schmoozing Hollywood production company executive to running a bakery in Montpelier, VT. . . . . Memoir lovers will find this a lighthearted, entertaining read filled with humor and acerbic wit; foodies will enjoy the insider's view of running a bakery." Libr J

Bunch, Robert, 1820-

Dickey, Christopher. **Our** Man in Charleston; Britain's Secret Agent in the Civil War South. Christopher Dickey. Crown 2015 368 p. illustrations, map (hardback) $27   92

1. Diplomats -- Great Britain -- Biography 2. United States -- History -- 1861-1865, Civil War 3. Spies -- Great Britain -- History -- 19th century 4. Great Britain -- Foreign relations -- United States 5. United States -- Foreign relations -- Great Britain 6. Espionage -- Great Britain -- History -- 19th century 7. Confederate States of America -- Foreign relations -- Great Britain 8. Great Britain -- Foreign relations -- Confederate States of America 9. Diplomatic and consular service, British -- Confederate States of America 10. Diplomatic and consular service, British -- United States -- History -- 19th century

ISBN 9780307887276; 0307887278

LC 2015016637

This book, by Christopher Dickey, profiles the career of Robert Bunch, the British consul officer assigned to Charleston, South Carolina in 1853, who acted as an influential figure regarding the British official position on the U.S. Civil War. "Between the Confederacy and recognition by Great Britain stood one unlikely Englishman who hated the slave trade. His actions helped determine the fate of a nation." (Publisher's note)

"A great book explaining the workings of what Dickey calls an erratic, cobbled-together coalition of ferociously independent states. It should be in the library of any student of diplomacy, as well as Civil War buffs." Kirkus

Bundy, Ted

Rule, Ann. The **stranger** beside me; Updated 20th anniversary ed; Signet 2001 548p il pa $7.99   92

1. Criminals 2. Murderers

ISBN 0-451-20326-7; 978-0-451-20326-7

First published 1980 by Norton

This is a biography of Ted Bundy, written by someone who "worked a suicide hotline in Seattle with Ted Bundy, not knowing he was a serial killer." Libr J

Burana, Lily

Burana, Lily. **I** love a man in uniform; a memoir of love, war and other battles. Weinstein Books 2009 352p $23.95   92

1. Authors 2. Military spouses 3. Editors 4. Essayists 5. Memoirists 6. Stripteasers

ISBN 978-1-60286-083-4; 1-60286-083-1

This "is a humorous, moving and surprising account of married life in today's military." N Y Times Book Rev

Burbank, Luther, 1849-1926

Smith, Jane S. The **garden** of invention; Luther Burbank and the business of breeding plants. Penguin Press 2009 354p il $25.95   92

1. Plant breeding 2. Horticulturists

ISBN 978-1-59420-209-4

LC 2009-1822

"An accessible introduction to an agricultural innovator that gives equal weight to his life of experimentation and what it has meant for society." Kirkus

Includes bibliographical references

Burke, Edmund, 1729-1797

Norman, Jesse. **Edmund** Burke; the first conservative. by Jesse Norman. Basic Books, A Member of the Perseus Books Group 2013 325 p. ill. ports, maps (hardcover) $27.99   92

1. Political philosophy 2. Orators -- Great Britain -- Biography 3. Statesmen -- Great Britain -- Biography 4. Political scientists -- Great Britain -- Biography 5. Great Britain -- Politics and government -- 1760-1820

ISBN 0465058973; 9780465058976

LC 2013935334

This book, written by Jesse Norman, presents a biography of Edmund Burke "an 18th-century Irish philosopher and statesman [and] champion of human rights and the Anglo-American constitutional tradition, and a lifelong campaigner against arbitrary power. As Norman reveals, Burke was often ahead of his time, anticipating the abolition of slavery and arguing for free markets, equality for Catholics in Ireland, and responsible government in India." (Publisher's note)

Includes bibliographical references (p. [299]-305) and index.

Burns, Robert, 1759-1796

Crawford, Robert. The **bard**; Robert Burns, a biography. Princeton University Press 2009 465p $35   92

1. Poets 2. Authors

ISBN 978-0-691-14171-8; 0-691-14171-1

LC 2008-937561

"Crawford's Burns, merrily mixing high and low culture, seems eerily contemporary. He shares with great hip-hop artists a genius for catchy, sexy, and memorable rhymes gloriously liberated from the hegemony of standard English." New Yorker

Includes bibliographical references

Burroughs, Augusten

Burroughs, Augusten. **Lust** and Wonder; Augusten Burroughs. St. Martin's Press 2016 298 p. $26.99   92

1. Love 2. Dating (Social customs) 3. Interpersonal relations

ISBN 0312342039; 9780312342036

LC 2015041615

In this memoir "chronicling the development and demise of the different relationships he's had while living in New York, [author] Augusten Burroughs examines what it means to be in love, what it means to be in lust, and what it means to be figuring it all out." (Publisher's note)

"His brutal honesty about himself—and others—is as sharp and surprising as ever, and how Burroughs manages to effortlessly convey so much of his complicated histories, such as a lifelong need to bury his fears in the purchase of jewelry, is a lesson in the elegant use of narrative as a vehicle for truth." Booklist

Burroughs, William S., 1914-1997

Miles, Barry. **Call** Me Burroughs; A Life. Barry Miles. Twelve 2014 736 p. illustrations (hardback) $32   **92**

1. Beat generation 2. American authors 3. Novelists, American -- 20th century -- Biography
ISBN 1455511951; 9781455511952

LC 2013032565

Writer William "Burroughs was the original cult figure of the Beat Movement, and with the publication of his novel 'Naked Lunch,' which was originally banned for obscenity, he became a guru to the 60s youth counterculture. In 'Call Me Burroughs,' biographer and Beat historian Barry Miles presents the first full-length biography of Burroughs to be published in a quarter century." (Publisher's note)

A "dense, detailed, yet wonderfully readable and entertaining narrative that illuminates, without sensationalizing, Burroughs's manifold peculiarities." Pub Wkly

Includes bibliographical references and index

Burton, Isabel, Lady, 1831-1896

Lovell, Mary S. A **rage** to live: a biography of Richard and Isabel Burton. Norton 1998 910p il hardcover o.p. pa $19.95   **92**

1. Authors 2. Explorers 3. Travel writers 4. Asian studies specialists 5. Middle Eastern studies specialists
ISBN 0-393-32039-1 pa

LC 98-29886

This is "a readable narrative of great verve and passion." N Y Rev Books

Includes bibliographical references

Burton, Richard Francis Sir, 1821-1890

Lovell, Mary S. A **rage** to live: a biography of Richard and Isabel Burton. Norton 1998 910p il hardcover o.p. pa $19.95   **92**

1. Authors 2. Explorers 3. Travel writers 4. Asian studies specialists 5. Middle Eastern studies specialists
ISBN 0-393-32039-1 pa

LC 98-29886

This is "a readable narrative of great verve and passion." N Y Rev Books

Includes bibliographical references

Burton, Richard, 1925-1984

Kashner, Sam. **Furious** love; Elizabeth Taylor, Richard Burton, and the marriage of the century. [by] Sam Kashner and Nancy Schoenberger. Harper 2010 500p il $27.99   **92**

1. Actors
ISBN 978-0-06-156284-6; 0-06-156284-X

LC 2010-06732

"In this dual biography of the two legendary film stars, the authors draw upon new information, including interviews with Elizabeth Taylor and with the Burton family, to capture the famously passionate and tumultuous relationship between the legendary couple. . . . It's a mesmerizing tale, but it's also sad, and sometimes ugly, as the two stars engaged in vicious fights, nursed their jealousies and insecurities, and descended into alcoholism while outwardly living a life of glamour and sophistication." Booklist

Includes bibliographical references

Busch, Benjamin

Busch, Benjamin, 1968- **Dust** to dust; a memoir. Benjamin Busch. HarperCollins Publishers 2012 309 p. ill. (alk. paper) $26.99   **92**

1. Autobiographies 2. Iraq War, 2003-2011 3. Iraq War, 2003-2011 -- Biography 4. Madison County (N.Y.) -- Biography 5. Actors -- United States -- Biography 6. Iraq War, 2003-2011 -- Personal narratives, American 7. United States. Marine Corps -- Officers -- Biography
ISBN 0062014846; 9780062014849

LC 2012009518

In this memoir, Benjamin Busch, son of the novelist Frederick Busch, "intersperses stories of growing up in North Carolina, rural New York, and California with his harrowing and life-defining experiences on the sports field and on the battlefields of Iraq. While his father experienced the world through language and had an intellectual relationship with the physical universe, Busch gains comprehension of his environment by throwing himself against it." (Publishers Weekly)

Bush, George W.

Bush, George W. (George Walker), 1946- **Decision** points. Crown Publishers 2010 497p il $35; ebook $14.99   **92**

1. Governors 2. Presidents 3. Biography, Individual 4. Children of presidents 5. Presidents -- United States
ISBN 978-0-307-59061-9; 0-307-59061-5; 978-0-307-59062-6 ebook

"Critics on both the left and right are challenged to walk in his shoes, and may come away with a new view of the former president—or at least an appreciation of the hard and often ambiguous choices he was forced to make. . . . Honest, of course, but also surprisingly approachable and engaging." Kirkus

Bush, George, 1924-

Bush, George. **All** the best, George Bush; my life in letters and other writings. Scribner 1999 640p il $30; pa $16   **92**

1. Diplomats 2. Presidents 3. Vice-presidents 4. Members of Congress 5. Parents of presidents 6. United Nations officials 7. Presidents -- United States
ISBN 0-684-83958-X; 0-7432-0041-1 pa

LC 99-40440

The former president presents his autobiography in the form of annotated letters, memos, journal entries, and speeches written between 1942 and March 1999

This work "is refreshing and, in many ways, will shed more light on the man's personal character and public persona than any memoir or biography could. It offers an intrigu-

ing picture of a man who takes fierce pride in his modesty."
Publ Wkly

Bush, George W. (George Walker), 1946- **41**; a
portrait of my father. by George W. Bush. Random
House Inc 2014 304 p. portraits (chiefly color)
$28 **92**
1. Presidents -- United States -- Biography
ISBN 0553447785; 9780553447781
LC 2014469972
In this book, by George W. Bush, "the 43rd President
of the United States [offers] . . . a personal biography of his
father, George H. W. Bush, the 41st President. . . . The book
covers the entire scope of . . . [his father's] life and career,
including his service in the Pacific during World War II, his
pioneering work in the Texas oil business, and his political
rise as a Congressman, U.S. Representative to China and
the United Nations, CIA Director, Vice President, and President." (Publisher's note)

Destiny and Power; The American Odyssey of
George Herbert Walker Bush. by Jon Meacham. Random House Inc. 2015 848 p. color illustrations, map $35
1. Presidents -- United States -- Biography
ISBN 1400067650; 9781400067657
LC 2015016550
First edition
This biography, by Jon Meacham, "chronicles the life of
George Herbert Walker Bush. Drawing on President Bush's
candid personal diaries; on the diaries of his wife, Barbara;
and on extraordinary access to the forty-first president and to
his family, Meacham paints an intimate and surprising portrait of an intensely private man who led the nation through
tumultuous times." (Publisher's note)
"In Zelig-like fashion, George H. W. Bush was present at
many of the most important events of the last 65-plus years,
and the remarkable story of his life and times comes vividly
alive in the words of this highly skilled writer." Booklist

Parmet, Herbert S. **George** Bush; the life of a
Lone Star Yankee. with a new introduction by the
author. Transaction Pubs. 2001 576p il (American
presidents) pa $29.95 **92**
1. Diplomats 2. Presidents 3. Vice-presidents 4.
Members of Congress 5. Parents of presidents 6.
United Nations officials 7. Presidents -- United States
ISBN 0-7658-0730-0; 978-0-7658-0730-4
LC 00-42597
First published 1997 by Scribner
This biography of the forty-first president of the United
States details his "climb up the business and political ladder
in Texas . . . [then focuses on his] first runs for office, in
1964, when he faced a problem that dogged him his entire
career: convincing right-wing Republicans that he was a
true-blue Goldwater conservative. But he wasn't, and Par-
met astutely analyzes both the contributors to and the forces
within the Republican Party with which the unideological
Bush had to contend." Booklist
Includes bibliographical references

Byrnes, Thomas, 1842-1910
Conway, J. North. The **big** policeman; the rise
and fall of America's first, most ruthless, and greatest
detective. Lyons Press 2010 323p il $24.95 **92**
1. Detectives 2. Police officials 3. Police -- New York
(N.Y.)
ISBN 978-1-59921-965-3
This is a biography of "Thomas Byrnes, a New York
City law enforcer whose career peaked in the 1890s as su-
perintendent of the police force. Impressed by Byrnes' ascent, which began with street-patrol courageousness in the
city's 1863 antidraft, antiblack riots, Conway proceeds to
Byrnes' successes as a detective, which form the core of the
biography. Going case-by-case, . . . Conway combines narrative with explanation of Byrnes' methods of investigation
and interrogation. . . . Creating period atmosphere by quoting extensively from newspaper accounts of the sensational
crimes Byrnes solved, Conway portrays his subject's cleverness and excesses with a flawed-hero flavor that should draw
in true-crime fans." Booklist
Includes bibliographical references

**Byron, Anne Isabella Milbanke Byron, Baroness,
1792-1860**
Lady Byron and Her Daughters; Julia Markus. W
W Norton & Co Inc 2015 384 p. illustrations $28.95
1. Single parents
ISBN 0393082687; 9780393082685
LC 2015022540
This biography by Julia Markus is a "reevaluation of
Lady Byron's marriage and the untold story of her complex
life as single mother and progressive force. The center of
public attention after her tumultuous marriage to Lord Byron, Annabella Milbanke transformed herself from a neglected wife into a figure of incredible resilience and social
vision." (Publisher's note)
"While stilted writing and complex literary allusions
may weaken the appeal of this narrative for general readers,
it is recommended for fans of biography, history, literature,
and women's studies." LJ

**Byron, George Gordon Byron, 6th Baron, 1788-
1824**
Eisler, Benita. **Byron**--child of passion, fool
of fame. Knopf 1999 837p il hardcover o.p. pa
$18 **92**
1. Poets 2. Authors
ISBN 0-679-74085-6 pa
LC 98-35261
"This is a splendidly readable biography of a perpetually
fascinating genius." Atl Mon
Includes bibliographical references

Bystrolëtov, D. A., 1901-1975
Draitser, Emil. **Stalin's** Romeo spy; the remarkable rise and fall of the KGB's most daring operative:
the true life of Dmitri Bystrolyotov. Northwestern
University Press 2010 420p il map $35.00 **92**
1. Spies 2. Novelists 3. Russian espionage 4.
Translators 5. Political prisoners -- Soviet Union 6.

Intelligence service -- Soviet Union -- History
ISBN 0810126648; 9780810126640

LC 2009-44637

This book presents a "biography of one of Soviet Russia's most flamboyant and successful illegals, Dmitry Bystrolyotov." Author Emil Draitser chronicles Bystrolyotov's life from his "youthful adventures around the Black Sea coast, to his pre-WWII travels back and forth across Europe as a 'night of cloak and dagger,' to his term in Norillag, one of the worst of [Joseph] Stalin's slave labor camps." (Russian Life)

"In the 1930s, Dmitri Bystrolyotov moved effortlessly through European capitals, seducing women and collecting secrets for Stalin's Russia—until he was caught in one of Stalin's purges and sent to the Gulag. Emil Draitser tells Bystrolyotov's story." Wall Street J

Includes bibliographical references (p. 407-412) and index.

Cadillac Man

Cadillac Man. **Land** of the lost souls; my life on the streets. Bloomsbury 2009 288p $25   **92**
1. Veterans 2. Homeless persons 3. Homeless
ISBN 978-1-596-914063; 1-596-91406-8

LC 2008-41111

Memoir of a man who became homeless at age 44. Describes his adventures and daily experiences that he recorded in a series of spiral notebooks over fourteen years. He writes about the "indelible characters" who share his New York City streets, including Penny, a young runaway whom he eventually reunites with her family

"A surprising find, Cadillac lets readers in on a rarely seen community, revealing the compassionate hearts that beat even in the most despairing circumstances." Publ Wkly

Caesar, Julius, 100-44 B.C.

★ Goldsworthy, Adrian Keith. **Caesar**; life of a colossus. [by] Adrian Goldsworthy. Yale University Press 2006 583p il map $35   **92**
1. Statesmen 2. Historians 3. Rome -- History
ISBN 978-0-300-12048-6; 0-300-12048-6

LC 2006-922060

This biography draws "together Julius Caesar's personal, political, and military history into a single volume. . . . This is an engaging and well-drawn resource for those who wish to be introduced to the man who was Caesar." Libr J

Includes bibliographical references

Cage, John

★ Brown, Carolyn. **Chance** and circumstance; twenty years with Cage and Cunningham. Alfred A. Knopf 2007 645p il $37.50   **92**
1. Poets 2. Authors 3. Dancers 4. Composers 5. Choreographers 6. Essayists
ISBN 978-0-394-40191-1; 0-394-40191-3

LC 2006-48799

The author "traces the trajectory of her modern dance career with that organization during its crawling stages in the 1950s and 1960s, when composer John Cage was musical director and artist Robert Rauschenberg was set and costume designer. Brown documents the company's early struggles for acceptance (it was considered avant-garde), various

tours, and eventual world recognition. . . . This book will appeal to modern dance buffs and memoir readers." Libr J

Silverman, Kenneth. **Begin** again; a biography of John Cage. Alfred A. Knopf 2010 483p il $40. **92**
1. Poets 2. Authors 3. Composers 4. Essayists 5. Biography, Individual
ISBN 1-4000-4437-5; 978-1-4000-4437-5

LC 2010-09525

This is a biography of the American "musician, inventor, composer, poet." (Publisher's note) Index.

In this biography of "one of the most influential composers of the 20th century . . . [the author traces Cage's] innovations chronologically—his breakthrough years as a composer of experimental dance and percussion music, his definitive decade inventing chance-derived music as a member of the New York School of artists and musicians in the '50s, and his later development of indeterminate music, the content of which could be created by the performer. . . . Not just an exemplary biography, but a significant contribution to the cultural history of American music." Kirkus

Includes bibliographical references

Cagney, James, 1899-1986

McCabe, John. **Cagney.** Carroll & Graf Pub. 1999 439p il pa $18.95   **92**
1. Actors
ISBN 978-0-7867-0580-1; 0-7867-0580-9
First published 1997 by Knopf

This work "exceeds the typical standards of celebrity biography because McCabe is fully attentive to the many dimensions of his subject's artistry." Commonweal

Includes filmography and bibliographical references

Calcaterra, Regina

Calcaterra, Regina. **Etched** in Sand; A True Story of Five Siblings Who Survived an Unspeakable Childhood on Long Island. HarperCollins 2013 320 p. $15.99   **92**
1. Child abuse 2. Foster children
ISBN 0062218832; 9780062218834

This memoir presents the "true story of a woman surviving domestic abuse as a child, emancipating herself as a teenager, and then becoming a successful attorney. . . . Her story begins with an account of life among 'a scrappy pack of homeless siblings' and narrows to [Regina] Calcaterra's rise to executive director of the New York State Moreland Commission on Utility Preparation and Response." (Publishers Weekly)

Caldwell, Gail, 1951-

★ Caldwell, Gail. **Let's** take the long way home; a memoir of friendship. Random House 2010 190p $23   **92**
1. Friendship 2. Journalists 3. Columnists 4. Memoirists 5. Literary critics
ISBN 978-1-4000-6738-1; 1-4000-6738-3

LC 2009-29384

"This is a book you'll want to share with your own 'necessary pillars of life,' as Caldwell refers to her nearest and dearest. . . . Her memoir, a tribute to the enduring power of friendship, is a lovely gift to readers." Washington Post

Caldwell, Gail. **New** life, no instructions; a memoir. by Gail Caldwell. Random House 2014 176 p. (alk. paper) $23   **92**

1. Journalists -- United States -- Biography 2. Critics -- United States -- Biography 3. Total hip replacement -- Patients -- Biography

ISBN 1400069548; 9781400069545

LC 2013015486

In this memoir, author Gail Caldwell "confronts . . . the hurdles that life throws her way—in this case, hip surgery while tending to a new pet Samoyed. . . . After the death of her beloved Clementine, in 2008, she tracked down a Samoyed breeder . . . and procured a new puppy, Tula. However, at age 57 and with a 'bum leg,' . . . Caldwell wondered at the wisdom of getting a very muscular, high-octane dog when her leg strength seemed to be diminishing." (Publishers Weekly)

"Readers will enjoy Caldwell's thoughtful, wide-eyed view of the world around her and her musings on how we get our bearings in midlife." Kirkus

Includes bibliographical references and index

Campanella, Roy, 1921-1993

Kashatus, William C. **Jackie** and Campy; the untold story of their rocky relationship and the breaking of baseball's color line. William C. Kashatus. University of Nebraska Press 2014 248 p. illustrations, map (cloth : alk. paper) $24.95   **92**

1. African American baseball players 2. Race discrimination in sports -- History 3. Male friendship -- United States 4. Racism in sports -- United States 5. Discrimination in sports -- United States 6. African American baseball players -- Biography 7. Baseball players -- United States -- Biography

ISBN 0803246331; 9780803246331

LC 2013033133

This book, by William C. Kashatus, focuses on "the first black players to be candidates to break professional baseball's color barrier, Jackie Robinson and Roy Campanella. . . . The two men were divided by . . . [their] differing beliefs about the fight for civil rights. Robinson, the more aggressive and intense of the two, thought Jim Crow should be attacked head-on; Campanella, more passive and easygoing, believed that ability, not militancy, was the key to racial equality." (Publisher's note)

"Kashatus has written a superb narrative of sports, race, and politics in the 1950s and '60s, and also tells of the bittersweet consequences in Jackie and Campy's lives." Pub Wkly

Includes bibliographical references and index

Campbell, William, 1730?-1778

Harris, J. William. The **hanging** of Thomas Jeremiah; a free Black man's encounter with liberty. Yale University Press 2009 223p il map $27.50   **92**

1. Diplomats 2. Merchants 3. Ship captains 4. Colonial leaders 5. Plantation owners 6. Government officials 7. Colonial administrators 8. Slavery -- United States 9. South Carolina -- Race relations 10. African

Americans -- Social conditions

ISBN 978-0-300-15214-2; 0-300-15214-0

LC 2009-15233

This is an "account of nebulous historical figure Thomas Jeremiah. . . . Owner of a fishing company and worth $200,000 in 2009 dollars, . . . [Jeremiah] was probably the richest black man in North America; he was also a slaveowner. That didn't stop him from becoming a scapegoat, accused by patriot leader Henry Laurens—a wealthy plantation owner with hundreds of slaves—of secretly leading a British-sponsored slave insurrection. Though Governor William Campbell, aggrieved by the unlawfulness of Jeremiah's trial, interceded, it didn't stop those determined to hang Jeremiah. . . . Readers will learn much about the darker side of American institutions; students of American history and civil rights will appreciate Harris's impassive approach and thorough standards." Publ Wkly

Includes bibliographical references

Capone, Al, 1899-1947

Balsamo, William. **Young** Al Capone; the untold story of Scarface in New York, 1899-1925. [by] William Balsamo and John Balsamo. Skyhorse Pub. 2010 270p il $24.95   **92**

1. Mafia 2. Criminals 3. Mobsters 4. Bootleggers

ISBN 978-1-616-08085-3

LC 2010-34682

"Before he became the mythical untouchable 'Scarface,' Alphonse Capone (1899-1947) was a young, cunningly brutal thug schooled by hardboiled criminal minds in pre-Depression Brooklyn, N.Y. . . . [The authors] revisit Capone's apprenticeship years in the violent Brooklyn Navy Yard street gangs and his transformation from a wayward youth to polished, cold-blooded gangster under the tutelage of two master mobsters, Johnny Torrio and 'Frankie Yale' Ioele. . . . With insider facts and spare narrative, the authors show us not only how Capone got his scarred face; they deliver a scathing portrait of a power-mad predator coming up through the criminal ranks." Publ Wkly

Eig, Jonathan. **Get** Capone; the real story of America's legendary gangster. Simon & Schuster 2010 468p il $28   **92**

1. Criminals 2. Organized crime 3. Mobsters 4. Bootleggers

ISBN 978-1-4165-8059-1; 1-4165-8059-X

LC 2009-33949

The author "rescues the narrative of Al Capone from the realm of pop melodrama, offering vibrant historical storytelling and a nuanced, enigmatic portrait of Capone and his Chicago milieu. . . . An impressive, accessible history of a troubled time." Kirkus

Includes bibliographical references

Capote, Truman, 1924-1984

★ Capote, Truman. **Too** brief a treat; the letters of Truman Capote. edited by Gerald Clarke. Random House 2004 487p il $27.95; pa $16   **92**

1. Authors 2. Novelists 3. Nonfiction writers 4. Short story writers

ISBN 0-375-50133-9; 0-375-70241-5 pa

LC 2004-50313

"Capote's untrammeled personality fairly falls off the pages of these letters, and rather than being irritating, his disregard of reticence is especially poignant in this day of sterile e-mailing. Ideal for devotees to dip into here and there instead of reading from start to finish." Booklist

Includes bibliographical references

Long, Robert Emmet. **Truman** Capote, enfant terrible. Continuum 2008 130p $24.95 **92**
1. Authors 2. Novelists 3. Authors, American 4. Nonfiction writers 5. Short story writers
ISBN 978-0-8264-2763-2; 0-8264-2763-4
LC 2008-4957

Long recounts "Capote's early life, highlighting his tragic childhood and the relationships the eccentric author maintained with various members of New York's elite. Long draws heavily from Capote's unpublished papers and from Gerald Clarke's Capote: A Biography. This brief sketch, however, sets the stage for a compelling analysis of the effect of the author's tragic life on the gothic nature of his prose. Long brilliantly places each piece in the context of the author's life and of the culture at the time of its release. The book ends with a retrospective contemplation of Capote's influence and place in American letters. Each chapter represents a cogent and concise snapshot of Capote's genius in a specific period, while the entire book becomes a journey through Capote's life, work, and demons placed within the context of American literary culture." Libr J

Includes bibliographical references

Caravaggio, Michelangelo Merisi da, 1573-1610

Ebert-Schifferer, Sybille. **Caravaggio**; the artist and his work. Sybille Ebert-Schifferer. J. Paul Getty Museum 2012 319 p. (hardback) $59.95 **92**
1. Painters 2. Art -- History
ISBN 1606060953; 9781606060957
LC 2011045619

This book is a biography of painter Michelangelo Merisi da Caravaggio. "Rather than accept the stories of the artist as merely an uneducated troublemaker (albeit a wildly talented one), . . . [Sybille] Ebert-Schifferer instead strictly focuses her attention on historical documents and technical research. Beholden to incontrovertible evidence, and taking advantage of X-ray examinations of the paintings, the author finds her way to frequent insight." (Publishers Weekly)

Includes bibliographical references and index.

Graham-Dixon, Andrew. **Caravaggio**; a life sacred and profane. Andrew Graham-Dixon. Allen Lane 2010 544p ill. (chiefly col.), maps (hbk.) $39.95; pbk $24.95 **92**
1. Artists 2. Painters 3. Painting, Italian 4. Biography, Individual
ISBN 0713996749; 9780713996746; 9780393343434; 039334343X
LC 2010497954

This book presents a biography of "Michelangelo Merisi, known as Caravaggio (1571-1610), . . . contextualizing the artist's early life in the town of Caravaggio and in Milan. . . . The author then chronicles Caravaggio's artistic success in Rome. . . . He created many masterpieces there, but the rejection of The Death of the Virgin by its ecclesiastical

commissioners, the author argues, may have prompted Caravaggio to commit murder." (Publishers Weekly)

Prose, Francine. **Caravaggio**; painter of miracles. Atlas Books/HarperCollins 2005 149p il (Eminent lives) $21.95 **92**
1. Artists 2. Painters 3. Artists, Italian
ISBN 0-06-057560-3
LC 2005-40203

"A contemporary of Shakespeare, Caravaggio was 'belligerent, contemptuous, and competitive,' a revered artist and a notorious street fighter wanted for murder who died at 39 under tragic circumstances. Much has been written about Caravaggio and his dramatic paintings, especially his daringly earthy depictions of biblical scenes, but somehow Prose's concentrated interpretation has a stronger impact. Not only does she cover all the biographical essentials but she also more clearly and descriptively explicates the pioneering painter's unique perception of the miraculous in everyday life. Prose also reveals, with both subtlety and flourish, how Caravaggio's frank interpretations of violence and pain, fear and grief, dignity and transcendence are matched with a brilliant subversion of our sense of reality." Booklist

Carlin, Kelly, 1963-

Carlin, Kelly. A **Carlin** Home Companion; Growing Up With George. Kelly Carlin. St. Martin's Press 2015 336 p. $26.99 **92**
1. Comedians -- Family relationships
ISBN 1250058252; 9781250058256
LC 2015017795

This book by Kelly Carlin offers a glimpse of the inner life of her father, comedian George Carlin. Kelly was "born at the very beginning of his decades-long career in comedy. . . . She witnessed his transformation in the '70s, as he fought back against---and talked back to---the establishment. . . . Kelly not only watched her father constantly reinvent himself and his comedy, but also had a front row seat to the roller coaster turmoil of her family's inner life." (Publisher's note)

"A funny, honest, and compassionate account of growing up with a master of comedy." Kirkus

Carnegie, Andrew, 1835-1919

Nasaw, David. **Andrew** Carnegie. Penguin Press 2006 878p il $35; pa $20 **92**
1. Philanthropists 2. Metal industry executives
ISBN 1-59420-104-8; 0-14-311244-9 pa
LC 2006-44840

This is a biography of the Scottish-born businessman and philanthropist. Carnegie was the founder of the Carnegie Steel Company which later became U.S. Steel.

"Highly readable despite it's length, 'Andrew Carnegie' shows signs of prodigious original research on almost every page." N Y Times (Late N Y Ed)

Includes bibliographical references

Wall, Joseph Frazier. **Andrew** Carnegie. University of Pittsburgh Press 1989 1137p il hardcover o.p. pa $22.50 **92**

1. Philanthropists 2. Metal industry executives

ISBN 0-8229-5904-6 pa

LC 88-38160

A reissue of the title first published 1970 by Oxford University Press

This biography follows Carnegie from his boyhood in Scotland through his emigration to America, his rise in the business world, and his early ventures in oil, railroads, telegraphy, and the iron and steel industries

Includes bibliographical references

Carnegie, Dale, 1888-1955

Watts, Steven. **Self**-help Messiah; Dale Carnegie and success in modern America. by Steven Watts. Other Press 2013 32 p. $29.95 **92**

1. Self-help techniques 2. Success 3. Conduct of life 4. Orators -- United States -- Biography 5. Teachers -- United States -- Biography 6. Authors, American -- 20th century -- Biography

ISBN 1590515021; 9781590515020

LC 2013003227

This book, by Steven Watts, "tells the story of [Dale] Carnegie's personal journey and how it gave rise to the movement of self-help and personal reinvention. His book, 'How to Win Friends and Influence People,' became a best seller worldwide. Carnegie conceived his book to help people learn to relate to one another and enrich their lives through effective communication. His success was extraordinary, so hungry was 1920s America for a little psychological insight." (Publisher's note)

"A fascinating portrait of the father of self-help and incisive analysis of the mercurial era that produced him." Kirkus

Caro, Helga Gerda

★ Seth, Vikram, 1952- **Two** lives; Vikram Seth. HarperCollins 2005 503p ill. (pbk.) $15.95; o.p. **92**

1. Poets 2. Authors 3. Dentists 4. Novelists 5. London (England) -- Biography" 6. East Indians -- England -- London 7. Interracial marriage -- England -- London 8. Authors, English -- 20th century -- Biography 9. Authors, Indic -- Homes and haunts -- England -- London 10. London (England) -- Social life and customs -- 20th century

ISBN 9780060599676; 0060599669

LC 2005052694

In this book, the author presents biographies of "his Shanti Uncle and Aunty Henny. . . . Shanti was Seth's grandfather's brother, a dentist who studied in Berlin, lodging with Fau Caro, whose daughter, Henny was in love with someone else. He left for Britain in 1936. . . . [I]n 1940, as war broke out, he enlisted, served throughout and lost his right arm in combat. . . . Meanwhile, Henny, a German Jew, arrived in Britain weeks before war was declared, leaving her beloved mother and sister behind to death camp murder. . . . Part two

of his narrative focuses on Shanti. Part three, Henny's story . . . is based on a trove of remarkable letters she received and wrote. . . . Part four examines their marriage (they didn't marry until seven years after the war), and part five details a family mystery about Shanti's will and Seth's . . . research into these lives." (Publishers Weekly)

"In clear and elegant writing, Seth explores the macrocosm through the microcosm, resulting in a most unusual, worthwhile book." Publ Wkly

Carr, David

Carr, David. The **night** of the gun; a reporter investigates the darkest story of his life, his own. Simon & Schuster 2008 389p il $26; pa $15 **92**

1. Journalists 2. Drug addicts 3. Columnists 4. Memoirists

ISBN 978-1-4165-4152-3; 1-4165-4152-7; 978-1-4165-4153-0 pa; 1-4165-4153-5 pa

LC 2008-12178

Carr "takes a detailed inventory of his years of drug addiction, chronicling the slide from drinking and marijuana use during his teen years in Minneapolis to shooting cocaine and smoking crack while trying to maintain his life as a reporter and the father of twin girls. Carr is meticulous in the investigation of his past, reconstructing events with the aid of police reports, magazine rejection letters, and more than sixty interviews with friends, former dealers, and fellow-addicts. His journalistic skills are on full display as he works to excavate the truth from his often hazy memories. He evinces genuine remorse for his frequently reprehensible behavior and succeeds in creating something more than merely another entry in what he terms the 'growing pile of junkie memoirs.'" New Yorker

Carroll, Diahann

Carroll, Diahann. The **legs** are the last to go; aging, acting, marrying, and other things I learned the hard way. Amistad 2008 271p il $24.95 **92**

1. Actors 2. Singers 3. African American actors 4. African American singers

ISBN 978-0-06-076326-8; 0-06-076326-4

"Carroll looks back on a groundbreaking career: the first black actress to star in her own television show and, more recently, the first black actress to play the role of Norma Desmond in Sunset Boulevard. In between, Carroll has racked up a breathtaking list of achievements on stage, in film, and on television. She's also racked up four failed marriages and a life full of the kind of mistakes a driven woman will make climbing to the top of a show-business career during a period when women and African Americans had few opportunities. Carroll is candid about the trials and tribulations—as well as the joys and triumphs—in her public and private life." Booklist

Carroll, James

Carroll, James. **Practicing** Catholic. Houghton Mifflin Harcourt 2009 385p $28 **92**

1. Authors 2. Priests 3. Novelists 4. Catholic Church 5. Memoirists

ISBN 978-0-618-67018-5; 0-618-67018-1

LC 2008-37386

"This book is both a memoir of former priest and writer Carroll's life and a keen analysis of American Catholicism in the late 20th century. . . . Brilliant prose, historically insightful, and sincere passion remain hallmarks of the author's work." Libr J

Includes bibliographical references

Carroll, Lewis, 1832-1898

Cohen, Morton Norton. **Lewis** Carroll; a biography. by Morton N. Cohen. Knopf 1995 xxiii, 577p il hardcover o.p. pa $14.36 **92**
1. Authors 2. Novelists 3. Mathematicians 4. Children's authors 5. Writers on science
ISBN 0-679-74562-9 pa

LC 95-2663

"Delightfully illustrated with photographs and Carroll's drawings woven throughout, this extraordinary, meticulous biography gives us a sharper and deeper picture of Carroll than any before, presenting a many-sided man." Publ Wkly

Carson, Rachel, 1907-1964

Lytle, Mark Hamilton. The **gentle** subversive; Rachel Carson, Silent spring, and the rise of the environmental movement. Oxford University Press 2007 277p il $23; $12.95 **92**
1. Authors 2. Conservationists 3. Environmental movement 4. College teachers 5. Marine biologists 6. Writers on nature 7. Writers on science 8. Biography, Individual 9. Environmentalism -- History
ISBN 0-19-517246-9; 0-19-517247-7 pa; 978-0-19-517246-1; 978-0-19-517247-8 pa

LC 2006-49350

This book, by Mark Hamilton Lytle, presents a biography of Rachel Carson, an "accomplished marine biologist who worked for many years for the US Fish and Wildlife Service. In mid-career she gained wide fame as a lyrical popular science writer specializing in studies of the ocean and seashore life. 'Silent Spring' (1962), her final work, won acclaim as a breakthrough book that transformed people's conceptions of the place of science in the natural world." (Choice: Current Reviews for Academic Libraries)

The author "examines the life of Rachel Carson, founder of today's environmental movement and antithesis of the stereotypical 1950s woman. Carson was educated in the sciences, worked full time, and was her family's primary provider and caregiver. Genteel in appearance, she was firmly committed to her goal of preserving nature. Using a lyrical, narrative style, Lytle probes Carson's interests and her purposes in writing a series of wellknown books that include The Sea Around Usand her most famous, Silent Spring." Libr J

Includes bibliographical references

Souder, William. **On** a farther shore; the life and legacy of Rachel Carson. William Souder. 1st ed. Crown Publishing Group 2012 496 p. ill. (hardcover) $30.00; (ebook) $85.00 **92**
1. Biology 2. Women authors 3. Carson, Rachel, 1907-1964 4. Naturalists -- United States -- Biography 5. Environmentalism -- United States -- History 6. Science writers -- United States -- Biography 7. Environmentalists -- United States -- Biography 8.

Marine biologists -- United States -- Biography 9. Environmental ethics -- United States -- History 10. Pesticides -- Environmental aspects -- United States -- History
ISBN 030746220X; 9780307462206; 9780307462213; 9780307462220

LC 2012003077

In "this . . . biography, [William] Souder . . . portrays [Rachel] Carson as a woman passionate in friendship, poetic and innovative in her books about the sea, gentle but ambitious, assiduously keeping tabs on her publisher's promotion of her work. A writer since childhood, Carson, inspired by a college professor, developed a love for biology and combined her two passions in a career that included three best-selling books." (Publishers Weekly)

Includes bibliographical references (p. 477-486) and index.

Carter, Jimmy, 1924-

Carter, Jimmy. **Everything** to gain; making the most of the rest of your life. [by] Jimmy and Rosalynn Carter. University of Arkansas Press 1995 176p pa $21.95 **92**
1. Governors 2. Presidents 3. Nobel laureates for peace 4. Presidents -- United States
ISBN 978-1-55728-388-7; 1-55728-388-5
First published 1987 by Random House

"The former president and First Lady alternate first-person reminiscences with sections written jointly to tell the story of their lives after leaving the White House in 1980. Frankly acknowledging the trauma of the lost election, the Carters record their efforts to overcome the difficulties of making a fresh start while deeply in debt, adjusting to life in a small house in Plains, Ga., and other challenges." Publ Wkly

Carter, Jimmy, 1924- A **full** life; reflections at ninety. Jimmy Carter. Simon & Schuster 2015 272 p. illustrations (chiefly color) (hardcover : alk. paper) $28 **92**
1. Presidents -- United States -- Biography 2. United States -- Politics and government -- 1977-1981
ISBN 1501115634; 9781501115639; 9781501115646

LC 2015007489

In this memoir, by Jimmy Carter, "Jimmy Carter, thirty-ninth President, Nobel Peace Prize winner, international humanitarian, fisherman, reflects on his full and happy life with pride, humor, and a few second thoughts. . . . Carter tells what he is proud of and what he might do differently. He discusses his regret at losing his re-election, but how he and Rosalynn pushed on and made a new life and second and third rewarding careers." (Publisher's note)

"The drawings and poems by the author add even more of a personal touch, though crises in his marriage and his "estrangement" from the Obama presidency offer the most noteworthy revelations. A memoir that reads like an epilogue to a life of accomplishment." Kirkus

Carter, Jimmy. An **hour** before daylight; memories of my rural boyhood. Simon & Schuster 2001 284p il hardcover o.p. pa $15 **92**
1. Governors 2. Presidents 3. Nobel laureates for

peace 4. Presidents -- United States 5. Georgia -- Social life and customs
ISBN 0-7432-1193-6; 0-7432-1199-5 pa
LC 00-48248
In this memoir, the thirty-ninth president of the United States remembers his childhood in rural Georgia.

This "is social and agricultural history as plain and honest as one of the tables the author makes in his workshop—an American classic." New Yorker

Carter, Jimmy. **Keeping** faith: memoirs of a president. University of Ark. Press 1995 633p il pa $34.95
92
1. Governors 2. Presidents 3. Nobel laureates for peace 4. Presidents -- United States
ISBN 1-55728-330-3
LC 95-9691
A reissue of the title first published 1982 by Bantam Bks.

These memoirs treat such matters as "improving relations with China; enacting energy legislation; negotiating the second Strategic Arms Limitation treaty (SALT II); concluding the Panama Canal treaties; and convincing Menachem Begin and Anwar Sadat to reach agreement at Camp David. Carter also devotes more than a quarter of the book to the frustrations arising from the capture of hostages in Tehran." N Y Rev Books

Carter, Jimmy. **Sharing** good times. Simon & Schuster 2004 174p $21; pa $13
92
1. Governors 2. Presidents 3. Nobel laureates for peace 4. Presidents -- United States
ISBN 0-7432-7033-9; 0-7432-7068-1 pa
LC 2004-51351
The author "recalls various occasions in his life that became 'lasting sources of pleasure.' . . . [These remembrances] include his personal reasons for seeing his father as a hero, watching minor and major-league baseball games growing up, his days in the navy, road trips with his wife and children, his entry into politics, taking vacations while in the White House, his famous volunteer work, and even his hobbies." Booklist

Carter, Jimmy, 1924- **White** House diary. Farrar, Straus and Giroux 2010 570p il $30; ebook $14.99
92
1. Biography, Individual 2. Presidents -- United States 3. United States -- Politics and government -- 1974-1989 4. United States -- Politics and government -- 1977-1981
ISBN 978-0-374-28099-4; 978-1-4299-9065-3 ebook
LC 2010-15544
Jimmy Carter, the 39th president of the United States, presents an edited and annotated version of a diary he kept during his term in office.

"That the language is blunt and occasionally a little un-Christian may come as a surprise. . . . But the writings here reflect the Mr. Carter we know: boastful and painfully confessional, sanctimonious and callous, insightful and unself-aware. These are the thoughts of a secular preacher and calculating politician, surrounded by friends and yet often alone." N Y Times (Late N Y Ed)

Carter, Robert, 1728-1804
Levy, Andrew. The **first** emancipator; the forgotten story of Robert Carter, the founding father who freed his slaves. Random House 2005 310p hardcover o.p. pa $15.95
92
1. Plantation owners 2. Biography, Individual 3. Slavery -- United States
ISBN 0-375-50865-1; 0-375-76104-7 pa
LC 2004-54054
"In 1791, [Robert] Carter began a manumission process that would eventually free some 450 people on his northern Virginia plantations and beyond. . . . [Levy focuses] on Carter's psychic and religious struggles as he progressed haltingly toward the act of manumission." (N Y Times Book Rev) Index.

"This well-written and thoroughly engaging book will certainly appeal to readers interested in the history of 18th- and 19th-century Virginia, but also to those interested in the history of slavery and racism in America and in historical biography." Publ Wkly

Includes bibliographical references

Carver, Raymond
Sklenicka, Carol. **Raymond** Carver; a writer's life. Scribner 2009 578p il $35
92
1. Poets 2. Authors 3. Authors, American 4. Short story writers
ISBN 978-0-7432-6245-3; 0-7432-6245-X
LC 2009-27291
This is a biography of the American short-story writer and poet.

The author "spoke with nearly everyone in Carver's orbit, making the book a kind of history of American fiction in the '70s and '80s, capturing the crucial writers (Richard Ford, Tobias Wolff, John Cheever) and sea changes in the publishing industry that made Carver such a powerful influence on writers today. The epic biography that Carver deserves." Kirkus

Includes bibliographical references

Cash, Johnny
Hilburn, Robert. **Johnny** Cash; the life. by Robert Hilburn. Little, Brown and Co. 2013 608 p. $32
92
1. Musicians -- United States
ISBN 0316194751; 9780316194754
LC 2013941828
In this biography, "drawing upon his personal experience with [musician Johnny] Cash and a trove of never-before-seen material from the singer's inner circle, [author Robert] Hilburn creates [a] . . . deeply human portrait of one of the most iconic figures in modern popular culture - not only a towering figure in country music, but also a seminal influence in rock, whose personal life was far more troubled, and whose musical and lyrical artistry much more profound." (Publisher's note)

"The personal knowledge aided by extensive archival research and always compelling, accessible writing make this an instant-classic music biography with something to offer all generations of listeners." Kirkus

★ Kleist, Reinhard. **Johnny** Cash; I see a darkness: a graphic novel. [translated from the German edition by Michael Waaler] Abrams ComicArts 2009 221p il pa $17.95　　　　　　　　　　　　**92**

1. Singers 2. Graphic novels 3. Country musicians 4. Biographical graphic novels 5. Songwriters 6. Country musicians -- Graphic novels

ISBN 978-0-8109-8463-9

LC 2010-279149

Original German edition, 2006

The author "presents a biography (with seemingly invented dialog that stays true to the facts) focusing on Cash's turning points: from his poor family's 1935 relocation to a New Deal-created cotton farming community, through his troubled first marriage, endless touring, the amphetamine abuse of his early musical career, and climaxing with a famous, highly charged 1968 concert at California's Folsom Prison. Kleist also dramatizes several of Cash's songs and relates the tragic story of Glen Sherley, a Folsom inmate who sent Cash a song he had written hoping Cash would play it in the show. The ruggedness of Kleist's black-and-white illustrations suits their subject, as the stark portrayal of Cash's withdrawal from drugs is inventive and harrowing... . This thoughtful and compelling portrait of a towering talent with a tortured soul is recommended for all teen and adult music fans." Libr J

Includes bibliographical references

Streissguth, Michael. **Johnny** Cash; the biography. Da Capo Press 2006 334p il hardcover o.p. pa $15.95　　　　　　　　　　　　　　　　　　**92**

1. Singers 2. Country musicians 3. Songwriters

ISBN 0-306-81368-8; 0-306-81565-6 pa

LC 2006-101191

This is a biography of the country singer and songwriter.

The author "leaves us mightily impressed with the volume of Cash's work and the convictions that animate it, and perhaps even more impressed by Cash's endurance of his own self-destructiveness. . . . Streissguth gives everyone interested in Cash a very satisfying book about him." Booklist

Includes bibliographical references

Cash, Rosanne, 1955-

★ Cash, Rosanne. **Composed**; a memoir. Viking 2010 343p $26.95　　　　　　　　　　　　**92**

1. Singers 2. Country musicians 3. Songwriters

ISBN 978-0-670-02196-3

LC 2010-10327

"The moving chapters about Roseanne Cash's glorious career—and the moments of great tenderness and tension with her legendary family—are like exquisite album tracks: Individually they are great reads, but together they add up to something cohesive and powerful. Composed provides no bombshell confessions about her failed marriage to Rodney Crowell or her wonderfully complicated relationship with her dad, Johnny. (Though she does dismiss the biopic Walk the Line as 'an egregious oversimplification of our family's private pain.') Instead, Cash delivers writerly meditations on what it means to be an artist and a public person and, yes, a

daughter. Rare is the celebrity memoir that is so full of self-awareness and dignity." Entertainment Wkly

Cassady, Neal

★ Sandison, David. **Neal** Cassady; the fast life of a beat hero. [by] David Sandison and Graham Vickers. Chicago Review Press 2006 340p il $24.95　　　　　　　　　　　　　　　　**92**

1. Authors 2. Beat generation 3. Memoirists

ISBN 978-1-55652-615-2; 1-55652-615-6

LC 2006-9112

"Drawing on Cassady's correspondence, interviews with those who knew him, and previous works by memoirist Carolyn Cassady (the subject's widow), biographer Tom Christopher, and others, Sandison and Vickers portray Cassady as all too human—a desperate, lost soul who was plagued by contradictions and sought personal fulfillment and spiritual salvation. Debunking the mythology that grew up around Cassady as a result of his appearance in works by Kerouac, Ken Kesey, and Tom Wolfe, the authors attempt to separate the life from the legend. They present Cassady as someone who wanted to be a good husband and father but was unable to conquer his demons, which included sex, drugs, gambling, and an innate restlessness. Ironically, it was these very demons that ensured Cassady's place in American literature." Libr J

Includes bibliographical references

Casso, Gaspipe, 1942-

Carlo, Philip. **Gaspipe**; confessions of a Mafia boss. William Morrow 2008 346p il $25.95　　**92**

1. Mafia 2. Criminals 3. Organized crime 4. Mobsters 5. Informers

ISBN 978-0-06-142984-2

LC 2008-2683

"This powerful story is required reading for anyone with a yen for the Mafia, the criminal underworld and a law enforcement system struggling to keep up." Publ Wkly

Castelli, Leo, 1907-1999

Cohen-Solal, Annie. **Leo** & his circle; the life of Leo Castelli. Alfred A. Knopf 2010 540p il $35　**92**

1. Art dealers

ISBN 978-1-4000-4427-6; 1-4000-4427-8

LC 2009-34454

First published 2009 in France

This is a biography of the art dealer from Trieste who came to New York in 1941 and opened his first New York gallery in 1957. Castelli displayed early work by Andy Warhol, Jasper Johns, Roy Lichtenstein, and Cy Twombly.

This "biography fleshes out not only a fascinating portrait of Castelli but also the excitement of the developing American art world to which he was so central." Publ Wkly

Includes bibliographical references

Castro, Fidel, 1926-2016

★ Castro, Fidel. **Fidel** Castro: my life; a spoken autobiography. [by] Fidel Castro and Ignacio Ramonet; translated by Andrew Hurley. Scribner 2008 723p il map $40　　　　　　　　　　　　**92**

1. Presidents 2. Communist leaders 3. Cuba -- Politics

and government

ISBN 978-1-4165-5328-1; 1-4165-5328-2

Original Spanish edition, 2006

Ramonet "sat down with Castro over the course of many hours, engaging him in long, involved discussions about his revolutionary life (and little about his personal life). The result is, in the words of the interviewer, Castro's 'political testament, an oral summoning-up of Fidel Castro's life by Fidel himself at almost eighty.' That rather simple description does not begin to cover the magnitude and significance of this major document. . . . By itself an incomplete history of the Cuban Revolution, to be sure, but an important—the ultimate insider view—contribution to the complete picture." Booklist

Includes bibliographical references

Coltman, Leycester. The **real** Fidel Castro; with a foreword by Julia E. Sweig. Yale Univ. Press 2003 335p il map $30; pa $20   **92**

1. Presidents 2. Communist leaders 3. Cuba -- Politics and government

ISBN 0-300-10188-0; 0-300-10760-9 pa

LC 2003-12942

This biography "offers a fresh assessment of the revolutionary leader. . . . It chronicles the events of Castro's extraordinary life and explores the contradiction between the private character and the public reputation." Univ Press Books for Public and Second Sch Libr, 2004

Includes bibliographical references

Szulc, Tad. **Fidel**; a critical portrait. Post Road Press 2000 703p map pa $18.95   **92**

1. Presidents 2. Communist leaders 3. Cuba -- Politics and government

ISBN 978-0-380-80888-5; 0-380-80888-9

First published 1986 by Morrow

The author "devotes the greater part of this book to Castro's early, formative years and the forging and triumph of his revolutionary movement. The years of Castro's rule after the Bay of Pigs invasion receive briefer treatment. Well written and very readable." Choice

Includes bibliographical references

Catharine Parr, Queen, consort of Henry VIII, King of England, 1512-1548

Porter, Linda. **Katherine** the queen; the remarkable life of Katherine Parr, the last wife of Henry VIII. St. Martin's Press 2010 383p il $27.99   **92**

1. Queens 2. Biography, Individual 3. Great Britain -- History -- 1485-1603, Tudors 4. Great Britain -- History -- Henry VIII, 1509-1547

ISBN 9780312384388

LC 2010035251

In this biography of Katherine Parr, Porter argues that "Henry VIII's last queen was a more human, complex and modern figure than has hitherto been realized." (Publisher's note) Index.

"Although often depicted by the Victorians as a matronly nurse to an elderly king, Katherine Parr (1512–1548), according to Porter, was a stylish trendsetter of 30, sensual, confident, dynamic, exceptionally educated and cultured, and able to perform with aplomb on both an English and in-ternational stage. . . . Rich, perceptive, nuanced and creative, this first full-scale biography gives one of Britain's best but least-known queens her due." Publ Wkly

Includes bibliographical references

Cather, Willa, 1873-1947

Lee, Hermione. **Willa** Cather; double lives. Pantheon Bks. 1989 410p il hardcover o.p. pa $23 **92**

1. Authors 2. Novelists 3. Western writers 4. Short story writers

ISBN 0-679-73649-2 pa

LC 89-43233

The author's "discussion of Cather's 12 novels and numerous stories is so absorbing that it provokes a rereading of the work, which makes it a valuable critical study." N Y Times Book Rev

Includes bibliographical references

Woodress, James Leslie. **Willa** Cather; a literary life. {by} James Woodress. University of Neb. Press 1987 xx, 583p il hardcover o.p. pa $29.95 **92**

1. Authors 2. Novelists 3. Western writers 4. Short story writers

ISBN 0-8032-9708-4 pa

LC 86-30894

The author "does a fine job of describing Willa Cather's colorful public life and of piecing together the puzzle of her unconventional private life. . . . Mr. Woodress does not try to superimpose on Cather's life any theories—feminist, Freudian, Lacanian, or otherwise. Instead, he recounts in straightforward and lively prose the life of a remarkable woman." N Y Times Book Rev

Includes bibliographical references

Catherine II, the Great, Empress of Russia, 1729-1796

★ Catherine. The **memoirs** of Catherine the Great; a new translation by Mark Cruse and Hilde Hoogenboom. Modern Library 2005 xc, 247p il map $26.95 **92**

1. Empresses 2. Russia -- History 3. Russia -- Kings and rulers

ISBN 0-679-64299-4

LC 2004-61107

Original French edition, 1859

This is "a source of major importance and every serious library should own it." Choice

Jaques, Susan. The **Empress** of Art; Catherine the Great and the Transformation of Russia. by Susan Jaques. W W Norton & Co Inc 2016 384 p. color illustrations $35   **92**

1. Russia -- History

ISBN 160598972X; 9781605989723

This book, by Susan Jaques, is an "art-oriented biography of . . . Catherine the Great. . . . A German princess who married a decadent and lazy Russian prince, Catherine mobilized support amongst the Russian nobles, playing off of her husband's increasing corruption and abuse of power. She then staged a coup that ended with him being strangled with his own scarf in the halls of the palace, and she being crowned the Empress of Russia." (Publisher's note)

"An absorbing account of a fascinating figure and her legacy." Booklist

Includes bibliographical references (pages 407-447) and index.

Rounding, Virginia. **Catherine** the Great; love, sex and power. St. Martin's Press 2007 566p il $29.95 **92**

1. Empresses 2. Russia -- History 3. Russia -- Kings and rulers

ISBN 978-0-312-32887-0; 0-312-32887-7

LC 2006-47084

First published 2006 in the United Kingdom

The author "relies on memoirs, private letters and previous monographs as she details how, after dissolution of the unhappy marriage that brought Catherine (1729-1798) to Russia from Germany, the empress juggled her relationships with men as she attempted to thrust Russia into the modern era and make it a European power. . . . [This] work will appeal to Catherine-philes and those interested in women's history." Publ Wkly

Includes bibliographical references

Catlin, George, 1796-1872

Eisler, Benita. The **Red** Man's Bones; George Catlin, Artist and Showman. Benita Eisler. W W Norton & Co Inc 2013 432 p. (hardcover) $29.95 **92**

1. Native Americans in art 2. West (U.S.) -- In art 3. Painters -- United States -- Biography

ISBN 0393066169; 9780393066166

LC 2013013973

"The first biography in over sixty years of a great American artist whose paintings are more famous than the man who made them." (Publisher's note)

"A welcome new evaluation of a significant American artist honed by the Wild West spirit and hucksterism of the age. Biographer of Byron, Chopin, George Sand and others (Naked in the Marketplace: The Lives of George Sand, 2007, etc.), Eisler now turns her considerable research talents to fleshing out the life and work of Pennsylvania-born artist George Catlin (1796-1892), whose sympathetic portraits of the Native Americans he sought out and lived among render an incalculable record of (and tribute to) a vanished people." Kirkus

Includes bibliographical references and index

Catto, Octavius V., 1839-1871

Biddle, Daniel R. **Tasting** freedom; Octavius Catto and the battle for equality in Civil War America. [by] Daniel R. Biddle [and] Murray Dubin. Temple University Press 2010 616p il $35; e-book $35 **92**

1. Political activists 2. African American athletes 3. African American educators 4. Baseball -- Biography 5. Biography, Individual 6. African Americans -- Biography 7. Pennsylvania -- Race relations 8. Philadelphia (Pa.) -- Race relations -- History 9. Civil rights movements -- Pennsylvania -- Philadelphia 10. African Americans -- Civil rights -- Pennsylvania -- Philadelphia

ISBN 978-1-59213-465-6; 978-1-59213-467-0 e-book

LC 2009049276

This is a biography of 19th-century civil rights activist and baseball player "Octavius Catto of Philadelphia. Catto was a part of the city's black intelligentsia and a vigorous proponent of equal rights. . . . Catto became a martyr to his cause when, at age 32, he was gunned down in Philadelphia's 1871 election-day riot. . . . [The authors] present a clear and compelling portrait of this significant early civil rights activist; they also present a thoughtful assessment of how Catto's efforts relate to the modern black civil rights movement." Choice

Includes bibliographical references

Cayce, Edgar, 1877-1945

Kirkpatrick, Sidney. **Edgar** Cayce; an American prophet. Riverhead Bks. 2000 564p il hardcover o.p. pa $16 **92**

1. Psychics

ISBN 1-57322-896-6 pa

LC 00-27975

This is a "fair, fascinating, and well-researched biography of one of 20th-century America's most famous psychics." Libr J

Chabon, Michael

Chabon, Michael. **Manhood** for amateurs; the pleasures and regrets of a husband, father, and son. Harper 2009 306p $25.99 **92**

1. Authors 2. Fathers 3. Novelists 4. Men -- Psychology 5. Short story writers

ISBN 978-0-06-149018-7; 0-06-149018-0

LC 2009-4749

"For the most part in these pages [Chabon] manages to write about himself, his family and his generation with humor and introspective wisdom. As in his novels, he shifts gears easily between the comic and the melancholy, the whimsical and the serious, demonstrating once again his ability to write about the big subjects of love and memory and regret without falling prey to the Scylla and Charybdis of cynicism and sentimentality." N Y Times (Late N Y Ed)

Chagall, Marc, 1887-1985

★ Wullschlager, Jackie. **Chagall**; a biography. Alfred A. Knopf 2008 582p il $40 **92**

1. Artists 2. Painters 3. Artists, Russian

ISBN 978-0-375-41455-8; 0-375-41455-X

LC 2008-6162

This is a biography of the Russian artist and author of Lithographs (1960), My Life (1960), and The Jerusalem Windows (1962).

"This biography presents Chagall's moving portraits of a vanished age in colors as glowing and haunting as his own canvases." Washington Post Book World

Includes bibliographical references

Chaloner, William, d. 1699

Levenson, Thomas. **Newton** and the counterfeiter; the unknown detective career of the world's greatest scientist. Houghton Mifflin Harcourt 2009 318p $25; pa $14.95 **92**

1. Physicists 2. Mathematicians 3. Counterfeits and counterfeiting 4. Counterfeiters 5. Writers on science

ISBN 978-0-15-101278-7; 0-15-101278-4; 978-0-547-

33604-6 pa; 0-547-33604-7 pa

LC 2008-53511

"Levenson demonstrates a surpassing felicity in his brisk treatment of this late-17th-century true-crime adventure. . . . Swift, agile treatment of a little known but highly entertaining episode in a legendary life." Kirkus

Includes bibliographical references

Chambers, Whittaker

Chambers, Whittaker. **Witness**; forewords by William F. Buckley and Robert D. Novak. 50th annivesary ed; Regnery Pub. 2001 808p pa $19.95 **92**

1. Authors 2. Journalists 3. Memoirists 4. Communism -- United States

ISBN 978-0-89526-789-4; 0-89526-789-6

First published 1952 by Random House

Whittaker Chambers' own account of his life, his connection with the Communist Party and his repudiation of it, and his role in the Hiss-Chambers trial.

Champlain, Samuel de, 1567-1635

★ Fischer, David Hackett. **Champlain's** dream. Simon & Schuster 2008 834p il map $40 **92**

1. Explorers 2. America -- Exploration

ISBN 978-1-4165-9332-4; 1-4165-9332-2

LC 2008-16286

The author "offers the definitive biography of an extraordinary and flawed man: Samuel de Champlain (1567-1635): spy, explorer, courtier, soldier and founder and governor of New France (today's Quebec)." Publ Wkly

Includes bibliographical references

Chanel, Coco, 1883-1971

Garelick, Rhonda K. **Mademoiselle**; Coco Chanel and the pulse of history. Rhonda Garelick. Random House 2014 608 p. illustrations (hardback) $35 **92**

1. Fashion design 2. Fashion designers 3. Fashion designers -- France -- Biography 4. Fashion design -- History -- 20th century

ISBN 1400069521; 9781400069521

LC 2014006844

This book, by Rhonda Garelick, is a biography of fashion designer Coco Chanel. "Raised in rural poverty and orphaned early, the young Chanel supported herself as best she could. Then, as an uneducated nineteen-year-old café singer, she attracted the attention of a wealthy and powerful admirer and parlayed his support into her own hat design business. For the rest of Chanel's life, the professional, personal, and political were interwoven." (Publisher's note)

"Garelick pursues the catalog of Chanel's subsequent ill-fated lovers, her work with the Ballets Russes, her vast earnings from Chanel No. 5 and her fraught partnership with the Wertheimer brothers while frankly discussing her relentless, social-climbing attraction to right-wing, reactionary and racist elements.Certainly a definitive portrait, especially considering Garelick's intriguing venture into modern 'branding.'" Kirkus

Includes bibliographical references and index

Vaughan, Hal. **Sleeping** with the enemy; Coco Chanel's secret war. Knopf 2011 279p il $27.95; ebook $13.99 **92**

1. Fashion designers 2. Perfumers 3. German espionage 4. Biography, Individual 5. Cosmetics industry executives 6. World War, 1939-1945 -- Secret service

ISBN 978-0-307-59263-7; 978-0-307-95703-0 ebook; 0-7011-8500-7 Chatto & Windus; 978-0-7011-8500-8 Chatto & Windus

LC 2011020430

The author argues "that there were two sides to the elegant Coco Chanel. Using information from French counterintelligence sources as well as other documents hidden for years in French, German, Italian, Soviet, and U.S. archives, he unmasks her activities during the war years; she embarked on a romance with a senior German officer in occupied Paris and cooperated with German military intelligence agents. . . . Engrossing and accessible, this is recommended for general readers interested in fashion celebrity, espionage, or World War II." Libr J

Includes bibliographical references and index

Chaplin, Charlie, 1889-1977

Ackroyd, Peter, 1949- **Charlie** Chaplin; Peter Ackroyd. Nan A. Talese/Doubleday 2014 272 p. illustrations (Ackroyd's brief lives) (alk. paper) $25.95 **92**

1. Comedians -- Biography 2. Actors -- United States 3. Comedians -- United States -- Biography 4. Motion picture actors and actresses -- United States -- Biography

ISBN 0385537379; 9780385537377

LC 2014013009

This book, by Peter Ackroyd, is a biography of silent film actor Charlie Chaplin. It "turns the spotlight on Chaplin's life as well as his work, from his humble theatrical beginnings in music halls to winning an honorary Academy Award. Everything is here, from the glamor of his golden age to the murky scandals of the 1940s and eventual exile to Switzerland." (Publisher's note)

"Readers are left with an understanding of Chaplin's background, the biographical details of his long and troubled life, and some idea of the hellish conditions on the exacting filmmaker's sets, but conclusions about his significance as an artist, his work's relationship to the culture at large, and the internal forces that engendered such personal misery and creative transcendence fail to cohere. A comprehensive look at Chaplin the man but lacking as a portrait of the artist and his legacy." Kirkus

Includes bibliographical references and index

The **essential** Chaplin; perspectives on the life and art of the great comedian. edited with an introduction by Richard Schickel. I.R. Dee 2006 315p $27.50; pa $16.95 **92**

1. Actors 2. Motion picture directors 3. Motion picture producers 4. Motion picture producers and directors --

Biography
ISBN 978-1-56663-682-7; 1-56663-682-5; 978-1-56663-701-5 pa; 1-56663-701-5 pa

LC 2005-37250

"The book's best feature is its organized cacophony, its trace of this astonishingly long and rich body of work and personal travail . . . in some several dozen voices of fading or lasting memory, and with countless aesthetic and ideological grudges beyond the narrow province of the movies. There is much to savor in these essays; and the book might also serve as a worthy companion to a reader's return to Chaplin's films themselves." Va Q Rev

Wranovics, John. **Chaplin** and Agee; the untold story of the tramp, the writer, and the lost screenplay. Palgrave Macmillan 2005 256p il $24.95 **92**
1. Poets 2. Actors 3. Authors 4. Novelists 5. Screenwriters 6. Nonfiction writers 7. Motion picture critics 8. Motion picture directors 9. Motion picture producers
ISBN 1-403-96866-7

LC 2004-62807

A "double biography of two of the 20th century's most talented artists. Wranovic's hook is a lost screenplay titled The Tramp's New World, which Agee wrote for Chaplin after the detonation of the atomic bomb over Hiroshima. . . . Using personal correspondence and critical reviews, Wranovics re-creates the fascinating historical backdrop of the Agee/Chaplin friendship, interweaving into the stunning tapestry the colorful lives of such luminaries as Brecht, Auden, Ed Sullivan, and John Huston." Choice

Chapman, Eddie, 1914-1997

Macintyre, Ben, 1963- **Agent** Zigzag; a true story of Nazi espionage, love, and betrayal. Harmony Books 2007 364p il $25.95 **92**
1. Thieves 2. Intelligence service agents 3. World War, 1939-1945 -- Secret service
ISBN 978-0-307-35340-5

LC 2006-101603

This is a biography of Eddie Chapman, a British double agent during World War II.

"Meticulously researched—relying extensively on recently released wartime files of Britain's Secret Intelligence Service—Macintyre's biography often reads like a spy thriller." Publ Wkly

Includes bibliographical references

Chapman, Eunice, 1778-1863

Woo, Ilyon. The **great** divorce; a nineteenth-century mother's extraordinary fight against her husband, the Shakers, and her times. Atlantic Monthly Press 2010 404p $25 **92**
1. Divorce 2. Shakers 3. Child custody 4. Parental kidnapping 5. Converts 6. Feminists 7. Abusive persons 8. Shakers -- New York (State)
ISBN 0-8021-1946-8; 978-0-8021-1946-9

This is an account of the divorce, in the early 19th century, of James and Eunice Chapman, and the involvement of the Shaker community in the proceedings. "In 1818, Eunice gained her legislative divorce—the only one ever granted in New York. She also regained her children." (N Y Times Book Rev)

"Both Eunice's struggle and the Shakers' story fascinate equally while dispelling romanticized myths of utopian societies in the tumultuous postrevolutionary period." Publ Wkly

Includes bibliographical references

Chapman, James, 1763-1852

Woo, Ilyon. The **great** divorce; a nineteenth-century mother's extraordinary fight against her husband, the Shakers, and her times. Atlantic Monthly Press 2010 404p $25 **92**
1. Divorce 2. Shakers 3. Child custody 4. Parental kidnapping 5. Converts 6. Feminists 7. Abusive persons 8. Shakers -- New York (State)
ISBN 0-8021-1946-8; 978-0-8021-1946-9

This is an account of the divorce, in the early 19th century, of James and Eunice Chapman, and the involvement of the Shaker community in the proceedings. "In 1818, Eunice gained her legislative divorce—the only one ever granted in New York. She also regained her children." (N Y Times Book Rev)

"Both Eunice's struggle and the Shakers' story fascinate equally while dispelling romanticized myths of utopian societies in the tumultuous postrevolutionary period." Publ Wkly

Includes bibliographical references

Charlemagne, Emperor, 742-814

Wilson, Derek A. **Charlemagne**. Doubleday 2006 226p il map $26; pa $14.95 **92**
1. Emperors 2. Kings and rulers
ISBN 0-385-51670-3; 0-307-27480-2 pa

LC 2005-48483

The author "writes with clarity and passion, and his thesis is food for thought for both general readers and students." Libr J

Includes bibliographical references

Charles, Prince of Wales, 1948-

Born to be king; Prince Charles on planet Windsor. Catherine Mayer. Henry Holt & Co. 2015 258 p. 8 plates; color illustrations (hardcover) $28 **92**
1. Princes 2. Princes -- Great Britain -- Biography
ISBN 1627794387; 9781627794381

LC 2014042418

This book, by Catherine Mayer, offers a "portrait of Charles, Prince of Wales. . . . Now sixty-six, Prince Charles has spent his entire life preparing to be king while insisting on being his own man. In this brilliant portrait, he emerges as a complex character driven by a painful past, a questing intellect, and a powerful impulse not only to reshape the monarchy but to use the long wait for the throne to work toward high ideals." (Publisher's note)

"Though far from comprehensive, Mayer's intriguing snapshot of Prince Charles reveals the often overlooked intricacies of his personality." Kirkus

Includes bibliographical references and index

Charles II, King of Great Britain, 1630-1685

Uglow, Jennifer S. A **gambling** man; Charles II's Restoration game. [by] Jenny Uglow. Farrar, Straus and Giroux 2009 580p il map $35   **92**

1. Kings 2. Great Britain -- History -- 1660-1688, Restoration

ISBN 978-0-374-28137-3; 0-374-28137-8

LC 2009-25469

"When Charles II became King of England, in 1660, his task was daunting: to restore the authority of the monarchy while courting a fractious parliament. Uglow's vivid history of the first decade of his reign shows how boldly Charles embraced the openness and experimentation of the Age of Reason." New Yorker

Includes bibliographical references

Charlotte Augusta, Princess of Great Britain, 1796-1817

Williams, Kate. **Becoming** Queen Victoria; the tragic death of Princess Charlotte and the unexpected rise of Britain's greatest monarch. Ballantine Books 2010 448p il $30; ebook $30   **92**

1. Queens 2. Princesses 3. Great Britain -- Kings and rulers

ISBN 978-0-345-46195-7; 978-0-345-52193-4 ebook

LC 2010-13227

First published 2008 in the United Kingdom with title: Becoming queen

"A lively, juicy read, full of the sordid details of the debauched rule of kings and princes that led to the moralistic rule of a queen focused on creating a royal family that embodied the ideals of a nation. Perfect for fans of royal histories and historical television shows or armchair historians interested in a swift and enjoyable read." Libr J

Includes bibliographical references

Chase, Salmon P. (Salmon Portland), 1808-1873

American queen; the rise and fall of Kate Chase Sprague, Civil War "Belle of the North" and gilded age woman of scandal. John Oller. Da Capo Press, A Member of the Perseus Books Group 2014 416 p. illustrations (hardcover) $25.99

1. Chase, Salmon P. (Salmon Portland), 1808-1873 2. United States -- Politics and government -- 19th century 3. Socialites -- United States -- Biography

ISBN 0306822806; 9780306822803; 9780306822810

LC 2014012054

This book, by John Oller, focuses on the "daughter of Salmon P. Chase, Lincoln's treasury secretary, Kate Chase. As her widowed father's hostess, she . . . [had] hopes of making her father president and herself his First Lady. To facilitate that goal, she married one of the richest men in the country, the . . . governor of Rhode Island. . . . But when William Sprague turned out to be less of a prince as a husband, Kate found comfort in the arms of a powerful married senator." (Publisher's note)

"Oller's work is less the story of a woman's political rise and fall and more one that reveals how the social limitations of the past created tragic outcomes for talented females. A well-researched, thoughtful biography of a woman who 'became entirely her own person, a rare feat for women of her day.'" Kirkus

Includes bibliographical references and index

Chatwin Bruce

Under the sun; the letters of Bruce Chatwin. selected and edited by Elizabeth Chatwin and Nicholas Shakespeare. Viking 2011 554p il $35   **92**

1. Authors 2. Novelists 3. Memoirists 4. Travel writers 5. Authors, English 6. Biography, Individual

ISBN 0670022462; 9780670022465

LC 2010-33591

First published 2010 in the United Kingdom

This is a collection of letters by the author of In Patagonia (1977) and The Songlines (1987). "'Under the Sun' contains letters written across four decades, from the time Chatwin was a boy in an English boarding school to letters dictated from his deathbed." (N Y Times (Late N Y Ed)) Index.

"Chatwin's many appreciators will see the compilation in its overall significance as a personal visit with one of their literary heroes, as much as that is possible now." Booklist

Chaucer, Geoffrey, d. 1400

Ackroyd, Peter. **Chaucer**; Peter Ackroyd. 1st ed in the U.S.A; Nan A. Talese/Doubleday 2005 188p il (Ackroyd's brief lives) $19.95   **92**

1. Poets 2. Authors

ISBN 0-385-50797-6

LC 2004-49796

This "account of the life of Geoffrey Chaucer (1343?-1400) [is also] a consideration of his role in shaping England's national identity. The poet is hailed as the 'progenitor of a national style,' and deft literary analysis explicates Chaucer's innovations while acknowledging the influence of other poets. . . . Much is made of Chaucer's position in the royal court, which provided the financial means to live comfortably while writing his verse." Publ Wkly

Includes bibliographical references

Chavez, Cesar, 1927-1993.

Pawel, Miriam. The **Crusades** of Cesar Chavez; a biography. Miriam Pawel. St. Martin's Press 2014 560 p. ill (some col), map $35   **92**

1. Hispanic Americans -- History 2. Hispanic Americans -- Biography 3. Labor movement -- United States

ISBN 1608197107; 9781608197101

This book by Miriam Pawel presents a "biography of the innovative, daring, and persevering activist" Cesar Chavez. "Chavez (1927-93) dropped out of school to work in the fields to support his destitute, homeless family, joining the ranks of California's exploited Mexican American migrant workers. Driven by his social conscience, pragmatic genius, and motivational ardor . . . Chavez created a scrappy and revolutionary labor union for 'the poorest, most powerless workers in the country.'" (Booklist)

"Pawel's clear, accessible prose befits a subject famous for his plain rhetoric, ensuring a broad readership can appreciate this valuable exploration of Chavez's unique legacy." Pub Wkly

Includes bibliographical references and index.

Cheever, John, 1912-1982

Bailey, Blake. **Cheever**; a life. Alfred A. Knopf 2009 770p il $35 **92**

1. Authors 2. Novelists 3. Authors, American 4. Short story writers

ISBN 978-1-4000-4394-1; 1-4000-4394-8

LC 2008-42277

The author "plunges deeply into the murky, sometimes fetid stew of John Cheever's life (1912-82). Beginning with his 1982 appearance at Carnegie Hall to receive the National Medal for Literature (more details appear some 650 pages later), the author proceeds in chronological fashion to tell the story of a deeply needy, difficult man.... [This is a] superb work that shows Cheever wrestling with dark angels, but wresting from those encounters some celestial prose." Kirkus

Includes bibliographical references

Chekhov, Anton Pavlovich, 1860-1904

Chekhov, Anton Pavlovich. **Anton** Chekhov's life and thought; selected letters and commentary. translated from the Russian by Michael Henry Heim, in collaboration with Simon Karlinsky; selection, introduction, and commentary by Simon Karlinsky. Northwestern Univ. Press 1997 494p pa $39.95 **92**

1. Authors 2. Dramatists 3. Physicians 4. Short story writers

ISBN 978-0-8101-1460-9; 0-8101-1460-7

LC 96-41240

First published 1973 by Harper & Row with title: Letters of Anton Chekhov

"Karlinsky's extended commentary and detailed notes amount to a first-rate critical biography, with much unfamiliar information and arrows pointing us toward further investigation." Newsweek

Chen, Da, 1962-

Chen, Da. **Colors** of the mountain. Random House 1999 310p hardcover o.p. pa $13 **92**

1. Lawyers 2. Linguists 3. Calligraphers 4. China -- History -- 1949-

ISBN 0-385-72060-2 pa

"Despite the devastating circumstances of his childhood and adolescence, Chen recounts his coming of age with arresting simplicity." Publ Wkly

Chen, Pauline W.

★ Chen, Pauline W. **Final** exam; a surgeon's reflections on mortality. Alfred A. Knopf 2007 267p $23.95 **92**

1. Surgeons 2. Terminal care -- Ethical aspects

ISBN 978-0-307-26353-7; 0-307-26353-3

LC 2006-49361

"A graceful, precise, and empathetic writer enthralled by her work, Chen imparts much about medical schooling and surgery, too." Booklist

Includes bibliographical references

Cheng, Nien, 1915-2009

Cheng, Nien. **Life** and death in Shanghai. Grove Press 1987 547p hardcover o.p. pa $16 **92**

1. Political prisoners 2. Memoirists 3. China -- History -- 1949-

ISBN 0-14-010870-X pa

LC 86-45254

First published 1986 in the United Kingdom

This "is a volume that belongs on the shelf alongside the writings of Primo Levi, Elie Wiesel, Dith Pran, and other chroniclers of ideological fanaticism, its dehumanizing consequences, and its all too rare resisters." Christ Sci Monit

Chiang, Kai-shek, 1887-1975

Taylor, Jay. The **generalissimo**; Chiang Kai-shek and the struggle for modern China. Belknap Press of Harvard University Press 2009 722p il map $35 **92**

1. Generals 2. Presidents 3. Presidents -- China 4. Presidents -- Taiwan 5. China -- History -- 1912-1949

ISBN 978-0-674-03338-2

LC 2008-40492

This is a biography of the Chinese president who was forced into exile in Taiwan in 1949.

"Taylor's fact-based chronological presentation of Chiang should temper the preexisting opinions of him that history readers may take into reading the book.... An important biography, essential to the Chinese history shelves." Booklist

Includes bibliographical references

Chiang, Mei-ling, 1898-2003

Li, Laura Tyson. **Madame** Chiang Kai-Shek; China's eternal first lady. Atlantic Monthly 2006 557p il map $30 **92**

1. Spouses of presidents

ISBN 0-87113-933-2; 978-0-87113-933-7

LC 2005-58858

This is a biography of the wife of former Chinese president Chiang Kai-Shek.

"With access to newly opened files, fluent insights into China's convulsive transformation, and a phenomenal gift for elucidating intricate politics and complicated psyches, Li brilliantly analyzes a fearless and profoundly conflicted woman of extraordinary force." Booklist

Includes bibliographical references

Pakula, Hannah. The **last** empress; Madame Chiang Kai-Shek and the birth of modern China. Simon & Schuster 2009 787p il map $35 **92**

1. Spouses of presidents 2. China -- History -- 1912-1949

ISBN 978-1-4391-4893-8; 1-4391-4893-7

LC 2009-17576

This is a biography of Soong Mei-ling, who became the wife of the Chinese Nationalist leader Chiang Kai-shek.

"A winning combination of measured, balanced research and critical evaluation—the definitive account of an important figure in 20th-century Chinese politics." Kirkus

Includes bibliographical references

Child, Julia

As always, Julia; the letters of Julia Child and Avis DeVoto: food, friendship, and the making of a masterpiece. selected and edited by Joan Reardon. Houghton Mifflin Harcourt Pub. Co. 2010 416p il $26 **92**

1. Cooks 2. Television personalities 3. Editors 4. Cookbook writers 5. Literary critics 6. Biography, Individual

ISBN 9780547417714

LC 2010-25840

This volume presents "the previously unpublished correspondence between the American chef and her unofficial literary agent from 1952 to 1965, offering insight into such events as Julia's early experiences as a new bride in Paris, her support of her diplomat husband and her views on period politics." (Publisher's note) Index.

"Their letters span a wide range of topics, from cookbooks, menus, recipes, and restaurants to Balzac, sex, goose stuffing, gardening, learning languages, the political climate, Sunday afternoon cocktail parties, and proofreading. Witty, enlightening and entertaining." Publ Wkly

Child, Julia. **My** life in France; [by] Julia Child with Alex Prud'homme. Knopf 2006 317p il $25.95 **92**

1. Cooks 2. Television personalities 3. Cookbook writers

ISBN 1-4000-4346-8; 978-1-4000-4346-0

LC 2005-44727

This is a "memoir of the famous chef's first, formative sojourn in France with her new husband, Paul Child, in 1949. . . . This is a valuable record of gorgeous meals in bygone Parisian restaurants, and the secret arts of a culinary genius." Publ Wkly

Fitch, Noel Riley. **Appetite** for life; the biography of Julia Child. Doubleday 1997 569p il hardcover o.p. pa $16.95 **92**

1. Cooks 2. Television personalities 3. Cookbook writers

ISBN 0-385-49383-5 pa

LC 97-11061

This biography details the private life and professional career of PBS' The French chef, whose Mastering the art of French cooking (1961) revolutionized the American kitchen

"Fitch not only richly details Child's personal life but also effectively places her writing and television shows within the context of work by other cooking luminaries of the time. Entertaining and informative." Libr J

Includes bibliographical references

★ Spitz, Bob. **Dearie**; the remarkable life of Julia Child. Bob Spitz. A.A. Knopf 2012 viii, 557 p.p ill. **92**

1. French cooking 2. Cooks -- Biography 3. Cooks -- France -- Biography 4. Cooks -- United States -- Biography

ISBN 0307272222; 9780307272225

LC 2012019632

This book, by Bob Spitz, offers a biography of the television cooking personality Julia Child. "At its heart, [the book]

is a story about a woman's search for her own unique expression. . . . Julia Child was a directionless . . . woman who ran off halfway around the world to join a spy agency during World War II. She eventually settled in Paris, where she learned to cook and collaborated on . . . a book that changed the food culture of America." (Publisher's note)

"An engrossing biography of a woman worthy of iconic status." Kirkus

Includes index.

Chopin, Frédéric, 1810-1849

Eisler, Benita. **Chopin's** funeral. Knopf 2003 230p il $23; pa $13.95 **92**

1. Pianists 2. Composers 3. Classical musicians

ISBN 0-375-40945-9; 0-375-70868-5 pa

LC 2002-73097

"Eisler is a compelling storyteller, sweeping the reader into the exhilarating milieu of Paris in the 1820s and 1830s." Libr J

Includes bibliographical references

Christensen, Kate, 1962-

Christensen, Kate. **Blue** plate special; an autobiography of my appetites. Kate Christensen. Doubleday 2013 368 p. (hardcover : alkaline paper) $26.95 **92**

1. Food -- Psychological aspects 2. Appetite -- Psychological aspects 3. Mothers and daughters -- United States 4. Authors, American -- 21st century -- Biography 5. Women authors, American -- 21st century -- Biography

ISBN 0385536267; 9780385536264

LC 2012048556

In this memoir, "food--eating it, cooking it, reflecting on it--becomes the vehicle for unpacking a life. [Kate] Christensen explores her history of hunger--not just for food but for love and confidence and a sense of belonging . . . starting with her unorthodox childhood in 1960s Berkeley. . . . After a whirlwind adolescent awakening, Christensen strikes out to chart her own destiny within the literary world and the world of men, both equally alluring and dangerous." (Publisher's note)

Christgau, Robert

Christgau, Robert. **Going** Into the City; Portrait of a Critic As a Young Man. Robert Christgau. HarperCollins 2015 384 p. $27.99 **92**

1. New York (N.Y.) 2. Popular culture

ISBN 0062238795; 9780062238795

This memoir by Robert Christgau "is a look back at the upbringing that grounded him, the history that transformed him, and the music, books, and films that showed him the way. It is a loving portrait of a lost New York. It's an homage to the city of Christgau's youth from Queens to the Lower East Side--a city that exists mostly in memory today. And it's a love story about the Greenwich Village girl who roamed this realm of possibility with him." (Publisher's note)

"Christgau is a critic's critic and a music aficionado. This one is a must-have for those interested in music, journalism, pop culture, and U.S. history." LJ

Churchill, Clementine, 1885-1977

Clementine; The Life of Mrs. Winston Churchill. by Sonia Purnell. Penguin Group USA 2015 448 p. 16 plates; ills; portraits $30   **92**
ISBN 0525429778; 9780525429777

LC 2015373202

This book, by Sonia Purnell, presents an overview of the wife of British Prime Minister Winston Churchill. "Born into impecunious aristocracy, the young Clementine was the target of cruel snobbery. Many wondered why Winston married her, but their marriage proved to be an exceptional partnership. Beautiful and intelligent, but driven by her own insecurities, she made her career her mission." (Publisher's note)

"Purnell is sympathetic to the strains of Clementine's life but unapologetic about her maternal shortcomings. A riveting, illuminating life of a remarkable woman."

Churchill, Winston Sir, 1874-1965

D'Este, Carlo. **Warlord**; a life of Winston Churchill at war, 1874-1945. Harper 2008 845p il map $39.95   **92**
1. Statesmen 2. Historians 3. Prime ministers 4. Memoirists 5. Cabinet members 6. Members of Parliament 7. Nobel laureates for literature 8. Prime ministers -- Great Britain
ISBN 978-0-06-057573-1; 0-06-057573-5

LC 2008-9272

A biography of Winston Churchill's military career from his youth through World War II.

"D'Este has produced an outstanding work that should take its rightful place alongside the dozens of other studies of this most remarkable statesman." Libr J
Includes bibliographical references

Johnson, Paul. **Churchill**. Viking 2009 181p il $24.95   **92**
1. Statesmen 2. Historians 3. Prime ministers 4. Memoirists 5. Cabinet members 6. Members of Parliament 7. Nobel laureates for literature 8. Prime ministers -- Great Britain 9. Great Britain -- Politics and government -- 20th century
ISBN 978-0-670-02105-5; 0-670-02105-9

LC 2009-08326

"From his beginnings as a youthful war correspondent, to his mature political career, to his hobbies of landscape painting and bricklaying, no aspect of Churchill's life is ignored. . . . An overview of Churchill's life that instructs rather than awes is Johnson's great achievement." New Criterion
Includes bibliographical references

★ Manchester, William. The **last** lion, Winston Spencer Churchill; defender of the realm, 1940-1965. by William Manchester. Little, Brown 2012 1183 p. ill., [32] p. of plates, maps $40   **92**
1. Great Britain -- History 2. World War, 1939-1945 -- Great Britain 3. Great Britain -- Foreign relations -- 20th century 4. Great Britain -- Politics and government -- 20th century
ISBN 9780316547703 (v. 3)

LC 82024972

This book, by William Manchester and Paul Reid, "picks up shortly after Winston Churchill became Prime Minister. . . . Churchill organized his nation's military response and defense; compelled [Franklin Delano Roosevelt] into supporting America's beleaguered cousins, and personified the . . . ethos that helped the Allies win the war, while at the same time adapting . . . his country to the . . . shift of world power from the British Empire to the United States." (Publisher's note)
Includes bibliographies and indexes

Manchester, William. The **last** lion, Winston Spencer Churchill; visions of glory, 1874-1932. Little, Brown 1983 973p il maps $50   **92**
1. Statesmen 2. Historians 3. Prime ministers 4. Memoirists 5. Cabinet members 6. Biography, Individual 7. Members of Parliament 8. Nobel laureates for literature 9. Prime ministers -- Great Britain 10. Great Britain -- Politics and government -- 20th century
ISBN 0-316-54503-1

LC 82-24972

This first volume of a projected three-volume biography of Churchill covers the life of the British statesman from his birth up to his split with the Conservative party over its policy regarding Indian self-rule.
Includes bibliographical references

Manchester, William. The **last** lion, Winston Spencer Churchill; alone, 1932-1940. Little, Brown 1988 xxvi, 756p il map $50   **92**
1. Statesmen 2. Historians 3. Prime ministers 4. Memoirists 5. Cabinet members 6. Biography, Individual 7. Members of Parliament 8. Nobel laureates for literature 9. Prime ministers -- Great Britain 10. Great Britain -- Foreign relations 11. Great Britain -- Politics and government -- 20th century
ISBN 0-316-54512-0

LC 82-24972

This second volume of a projected three-volume biography of the British statesman "covers the years leading up to the outbreak of World War II." (Time)
Includes bibliographical references

Toye, Richard. **Churchill's** empire; the world that made him and the world he made. Henry Holt 2010 xx, 423p il $32   **92**
1. Statesmen 2. Historians 3. Prime ministers 4. Memoirists 5. Cabinet members 6. Members of Parliament 7. Great Britain -- Colonies 8. Nobel laureates for literature 9. Prime ministers -- Great Britain
ISBN 978-0-8050-8795-6

LC 2010-1427

In this biography, the author "stresses that Churchill (1874-1965), a Victorian aristocrat, assumed white superiority but regularly proclaimed that nonwhites deserved equal rights and, eventually, independence once they discarded their primitive ways and achieved European levels of culture. . . . This work is a valuable contribution to greater understanding of a historical icon." Booklist
Includes bibliographical reference

Cicero, Marcus Tullius, 106-43 B.C.

Everitt, Anthony. **Cicero**; the life and times of Rome's greatest politician. Random House 2002 359p il maps hardcover o.p. pa $14.95 **92**

1. Statesmen 2. Philosophers 3. Orators 4. Rome -- History

ISBN 0-375-75895-X pa

LC 2001-48531

This "masterful biography draws on Cicero's letters to his friend Atticus to give a clear picture of the famous Roman orator, noting both his brilliance and his faults." Booklist

Includes bibliographical references

Ciezadlo, Annia

Ciezadlo, Annia. **Day** of honey; a memoir of food, love, and war. Free Press 2011 382p $26; pa $12.99 **92**

1. Journalists 2. Women journalists 3. Memoirists 4. Food -- Social aspects 5. Lebanon -- Social life and customs 6. Baghdad (Iraq) -- Social life and customs

ISBN 978-1-4165-8393-6; 1-4165-8393-9; 978-1-4165-8422-3 pa; 1-4165-8422-6 pa

LC 2010-19739

"There are many good reasons to read 'Day of Honey.' It's a carefully researched tour through the history of Middle Eastern food. It's filled with adrenalized scenes from war zones, scenes of narrow escapes and clandestine phone calls and frightening cultural misunderstandings. . . . These things wouldn't matter much, though, if her sentences didn't make such a sensual, smart, wired-up sound on the page." N Y Times Book Rev

Includes bibliographical references

Cixi, Empress dowager of China, 1835-1908

Jung Chang, 1952- **Empress** Dowager Cixi; the concubine who launched modern China. by Jung Chang. Alfred A. Knopf 2013 480 p. ill (some color), map (hardcover) $30 **92**

1. Empresses 2. China -- History -- 19th century 3. China -- History -- 1861-1912 4. Empresses -- China -- Biography 5. China -- Politics and government -- 19th century

ISBN 0307271609; 9780307271600; 9780307456700

LC 2013020766

Author Jung Chang "provides a revisionist biography of a controversial concubine who rose through the ranks to become a long-reigning, power-wielding dowager empress during the delicate era when China emerged from its isolationist cocoon to become a legitimate player on the international stage. [He shows how] as Cixi's power and influence grew . . . she radically shifted official attitudes toward Western thoughts, ideas, trade, and technology." (Booklist)

Chang "uses the work of revisionist scholars to paint a largely plausible portrait of a ruthless, farsighted politician who welcomed change and restructured the state." LJ

Includes bibliographical references and index

Clapton, Eric

Clapton, Eric, 1945- **Clapton**; the autobiography. Broadway Books 2007 343p il $26 **92**

1. Singers 2. Guitarists 3. Rock musicians 4.

Biography, Individual

ISBN 978-0-385-51851-2; 0-385-51851-X

LC 2007-15482

"As he retraces every step of his career, from the early stints with the Yardbirds and Cream to his solo successes, Clapton also devotes copious detail to his drug and alcohol addictions, particularly how they intersected with his romantic obsession with Pattie Boyd. . . . Both the youthful excesses and the current calm state are narrated with an engaging tone that nudges Clapton's story ahead of other rock 'n' roll memoirs." Publ Wkly

Schumacher, Michael. **Crossroads**; the life and music of Eric Clapton. Citadel Press 2003 420p il pa $15.95 **92**

1. Singers 2. Guitarists 3. Rock musicians

ISBN 978-0-8065-2466-5; 0-8065-2466-9

First published 1995 by Hyperion

The author "chronicles the life and career of the reclusive British blues performer. . . . Schumacher covers a tale of unhappy personal relationships, a failed marriage, drug and alcohol addiction and the tragic death of the performer's infant son, while giving full account of Clapton's significant accomplishments as guitarist and vocalist, his forays into rock and his performances and recordings." Publ Wkly

Clare, John, 1793-1864

Bate, Jonathan. **John** Clare: a biography. Farrar, Straus & Giroux 2003 648p il map $40 **92**

1. Poets 2. Authors

ISBN 0-374-17990-5

LC 2003-44063

This biography "succeeds splendidly . . . not only making generous use of Clare's own wonderful prose and verse but adding historical perspective and a constant, intelligent probing which amount almost to a dialogue with Clare's view of himself." Times Lit Suppl

Includes bibliographical references

Clark, Huguette, 1906-2011

Dedman, Bill, 1960- **Empty** mansions; the mysterious life of Huguette Clark and the spending of a great American fortune. Bill Dedman and Paul Clark Newell, Jr. Ballantine Books 2013 496 p. illustrations (some color) (hardback : acid-free paper) $28 **92**

1. Wealth 2. Mansions -- United States -- History 3. Recluses -- United States -- Biography 4. Heiresses -- United States -- Biography 5. Eccentrics -- United States -- Biography 6. Collectors and collecting -- United States -- Biography

ISBN 0345534522; 9780345534521

LC 2013023933

This book by Bill Dedman and Paul Clark Newell, Jr. is about "wealth and loss, connecting the Gilded Age opulence of the nineteenth century with a twenty-first-century battle over a $300 million inheritance. At its heart is a reclusive heiress named Huguette Clark, a woman so secretive that, at the time of her death at age 104, no new photograph of her had been seen in decades." (Publisher's note)

"Although William Mangam's The Clarks: An American Phenomenon (1941) examined Huguette's father, Gilded

Age millionaire W.A. Clark, and C.B. Glasscock's The War of the Copper Kings includes him, this is the first book on Huguette. An enlightening read for those interested in the opulent lifestyles afforded the offspring of the Gilded Age magnates and the mysterious ways of wealth." LJ

Includes bibliographical references and index

Clay, Henry, 1777-1852

Heidler, David Stephen. **Henry** Clay; the essential American. [by] David S. Heidler and Jeanne T. Heidler. Random House 2010 595p il $30 **92**

1. Statesmen 2. Senators 3. Members of Congress 4. Secretaries of state 5. Speakers of the House 6. United States -- Congress 7. Statesmen -- United States 8. United States -- Politics and government -- 1815-1861
ISBN 978-1-4000-6726-8; 1-4000-6726-X

LC 2009-27872

"Anyone wanting to understand political, economic, and social life in the early republic will appreciate the Heidlers' command of sources and balanced treatment of a man too long in the shadow of Andrew Jackson and very much a metaphor for his era." Libr J

Includes bibliographical references

Cleage, Pearl

Cleage, Pearl. **Things** I Should Have Told My Daughter; Lies, Lessons & Love Affairs. Pearl Cleage. Atria Books 2014 320 p. (hardback) $23.99 **92**

1. Motherhood 2. Women authors 3. Self-realization 4. Self-realization in women 5. Women authors, American -- Biography
ISBN 1451664699; 9781451664690; 9781451664706

LC 2013034164

This book, by Pearl Cleage, "reprints journal entries chronicling her tumultuous life in the 1970s and '80s . . . the decades in which she discovered her vocation as a playwright, poet and novelist while remaining deeply engaged in political activism, as a speechwriter for the first black mayor of Atlanta, and as a feminist grappling with marriage, motherhood, divorce and subsequent sexual freedom." (Kirkus Reviews)

Includes bibliographical references and index

Cleese, John

Cleese, John, 1939- **So,** anyway... John Cleese. Crown Archetype 2014 392 p. 24 plates; illustrations (cloth) $28 **92**

1. Comedians -- Biography 2. Actors -- Great Britain -- Biography 3. Comedians -- Great Britain -- Biography 4. Motion picture actors and actresses -- Great Britain -- Biography
ISBN 038534824X; 9780385348249

LC 2014037869

In this book, actor and comedian John Cleese "takes readers on a Grand Tour of his ascent in the entertainment world, from his humble beginnings in a sleepy English town and his early comedic days at Cambridge University (with future Python partner Graham Chapman), to the founding of the landmark comedy troupe that would propel him to worldwide renown." (Publisher's note)

Cleland, Max, 1942-

Cleland, Max. **Heart** of a patriot; how I found the courage to survive Vietnam, Walter Reed and Karl Rove. [by] Max Cleland, with Ben Raines. Simon & Schuster 2009 259p il $26 **92**

1. Amputees 2. Veterans 3. Senators 4. Government officials 5. Veterans -- United States 6. State government officials 7. United States -- Congress -- Senate
ISBN 978-1-4391-2605-9

LC 2009-11620

"This heartrending memoir is aimed at former soldiers who have struggled with the trauma of war and at those of us who haven't served in the military but need to understand the personal cost to those who have." Booklist

Includes bibliographical references

Clemente, Roberto, 1934-1972

Maraniss, David. **Clemente**; the passion and grace of baseball's last hero. Simon & Schuster 2006 401p il maps hardcover o.p. pa $15 **92**

1. Baseball players 2. Baseball -- Biography
ISBN 0-7432-1781-0; 978-0-7432-1781-1; 0-7432-9999-X; 978-0-7432-9999-2 pa

LC 2006-42235

The author "has produced a baseball-savvy book sensitive to the social context that made Clemente, a black Puerto Rican, a leading indicator of baseball's future." N Y Times Book Rev

Includes bibliographical references

Santiago, Wilfred. **21**; the story of Roberto Clemente : a graphic novel. Wilfred Santiago. Fantagraphics 2011 148p. chiefly ill. $22.99 **92**

1. Graphic novels 2. Baseball players -- Graphic novels 3. Baseball -- Graphic novels
ISBN 978-1-56097-892-3

"Santiago opens his dazzlingly drawn comics biography of the pioneering Puerto Rican ballplayer on the final game of the 1972 season, with Clemente just one hit shy of joining the 3,000-hit club. Fans will know, of course, that 3,000 would also be his final tally, as he would die in a plane crash delivering relief supplies to the earthquake-rocked Nicaragua that winter. Santiago skitters around formative scenes from Clemente's childhood—striking a complex chord of family, homeland, and a driving passion for baseball—before tracing significant moments from his professional career: staring down racism with the same resolute demeanor with which he faced a high heater, snagging batting championships and fans' hearts many times over, and always looking for ways to honor his heritage." Booklist

Includes bibliographic references.

Cleopatra, Queen of Egypt, d. 30 B.C.

Fletcher, Joann. **Cleopatra** the great; the woman behind the legend. Harpercollins 2011 454p map $27.99 **92**

1. Queens 2. Egypt -- History
ISBN 978-0-06-058558-7

First published 2008 in the United Kingdom

In this biography, the author "argues that Cleopatra's genius as a strategist, which allowed her to restore a fading

Egypt to its former glory, is what makes her the 'true heir' to her ancestor Alexander the Great. . . . Those interested in Cleopatra, ancient history, or a well-written and academically sound biography will enjoy this authentic look at a queen of Egypt who managed to be all things to all people—mother, queen, goddess, and whore." Libr J

Includes bibliographical references

Goldsworthy, Adrian Keith. **Antony** and Cleopatra; [by] Adrian Goldsworthy. Yale University Press 2010 470p il map $35   **92**

1. Queens 2. Generals 3. Statesmen 4. Orators 5. Rome -- History 6. Egypt -- History
ISBN 978-0-300-16534-0

LC 2010-929122

"Narrating [Antony] and Cleopatra's parts in the tumultuous end of the Roman Republic, Goldsworthy skillfully integrates the partial and partisan source material into an accessible presentation of a classic tale from classical times." Booklist

Includes bibliographical references

★ Schiff, Stacy, 1961- **Cleopatra**; a life. Little, Brown and Co. 2010 368p il map $29.99; ebook $14.99   **92**

1. Queens 2. Egypt -- History 3. Biography, Individual
ISBN 978-0-316-00192-2; 0-316-00192-9; 978-0-316-12180-4 ebook

LC 2010-06988

"It's dizzying to contemplate the thicket of prejudices, personalities and propaganda Schiff penetrated to reconstruct a woman whose style, ambition and audacity make her a subject worthy of her latest biographer. After all, Stacy Schiff's writing is distinguished by those very same virtues." N Y Times Book Rev

Includes bibliographical references

Cleveland, Grover, 1837-1908

Graff, Henry F. **Grover** Cleveland. Times Bks. 2002 154p il (American presidents series) $20 **92**

1. Mayors 2. Governors 3. Presidents 4. District attorneys 5. Presidents -- United States
ISBN 0-8050-6923-2

LC 2002-20315

A biography of the only American president to serve two nonconsecutive terms

This "volume is a valuable addition to the literature on the Presidency and is a compelling argument for taking Cleveland seriously as a President." Libr J

Includes bibliographical references

Cleveland, Pat

Cleveland, Pat. **Walking** with the muses; A Memoir. by Pat Cleveland (with Lorraine Glennon) 37 INK 2016 352 p. illustrations (some color) (hardcover : alk. paper) $26.99; (ebook) $18.99 **92**

1. Fashion models 2. African American women -- Biography 3. Fashion -- United States 4. Fashion designers -- United States 5. African American models -- Biography
ISBN 9781501108228; 9781501108235;

9781501108242

LC 2015041692

This memoir is an "account of the international adventures of fashion model Pat Cleveland—one of the first black supermodels during the wild sixties and seventies. . . . Ranging from the streets of New York to the jet-set beaches of Mexico, from the designer retailers of Paris to the offices of Diana Vreeland, here is Cleveland's larger-than-life story." (Publisher's note)

"Some readers will be particularly interested in her discussion of Bill Cosby, but Cleveland is the real star of her own story of passion, strength, and elegance above all." Pub Wkly

Includes bibliographical references and index

Clinton, Bill, 1946-

Branch, Taylor. The **Clinton** tapes; wrestling history with the president. Simon & Schuster 2009 707p $35; pa $20   **92**

1. Governors 2. Presidents 3. Presidents -- United States 4. United States -- Politics and government -- 1989-
ISBN 978-1-4165-4333-6; 1-4165-4333-3; 978-1-4165-4334-3 pa; 1-4165-4334-1 pa

"Not everyone who begins it will finish Branch's book, yet Clinton's remarks . . . contribute critically to the historical record and accordingly merit a place in most library collections." Booklist

Clinton, Bill. **My** life. Knopf 2004 957p il $35   **92**

1. Governors 2. Presidents 3. Presidents -- United States 4. United States -- Politics and government -- 1989-
ISBN 0-375-41457-6

LC 2004-107564

In this memoir the former president traces his life from his childhood in Arkansas through his time as governor of Arkansas and then focuses on his White House years

"Clinton's memoir has the raw material for a blockbuster book." Publ Wkly

Clinton, Hillary Rodham, 1947-

Bernstein, Carl. A **woman** in charge; the life of Hillary Rodham Clinton. Alfred A. Knopf 2007 628p il $27.95   **92**

1. Lawyers 2. Senators 3. Secretaries of state 4. Spouses of presidents 5. Presidential candidates
ISBN 978-0-375-40766-6; 0-375-40766-9

LC 2007-17472

The author "offers a three-dimensional portrait of a person with enduring strengths (discipline, tenacity, a sustaining religious faith) and weaknesses (excessive secrecy, a tendency to self-righteousness and a habit of nursing grudges). . . . Bernstein almost always finds new facts and telling details. [His] account benefits enormously from remarkably candid on-the-record assessments of both Clintons by intimates such as close friend Jim Blair and Betsey Wright,

Clinton's gubernatorial chief of staff in Arkansas." Los Angeles Times Book Rev

Includes bibliographical references

Clinton, Hillary Rodham, 1947- **Hard** choices; Hillary Rodham Clinton. Simon & Schuster 2014 656 p. ill. (chiefly color), maps $35　　　**92**
1. Autobiographies 2. Women politicians 3. United States -- Foreign relations
ISBN 1476751447; 9781476751443

LC 2014407811

This book by Hillary Rodham Clinton discusses how "to her surprise, her former rival for the Democratic Party nomination, newly elected President Barack Obama, asked her to serve in his administration as Secretary of State. This memoir is the story of the four . . . years that followed, and the hard choices that she and her colleagues confronted." (Publisher's note)

"Hillary Clinton follows the well-trod path of possible presidential candidates: a few years out, write a book. Unlike the authors of a lot of these tomes, Clinton actually has an interesting story to tell, beginning with the loss of the 2008 presidential election and how she was convinced to become part of Barack Obama's team of rivals when she took the job as Secretary of State. . . . Clinton goes into deep detail about her work in Asia, Iraq and Afghanistan, Latin America, and other hot spots around the globe. She details her vision for U.S. foreign policy and the role of diplomacy. Along the way, she introduces readers to a who's who of world leaders and gives insight into the way they think and do business. Written engagingly (and some will say with calculation), the book also offers Clinton the opportunity to get certain issues out of the way (not that her apologies about her Iraq vote and Benghazi will placate her critics)." Booklist

Clinton, Hillary Rodham. **Living** history. Simon & Schuster 2003 562p il $28; pa $16　　　**92**
1. Lawyers 2. Senators 3. Secretaries of state 4. Spouses of presidents 5. Presidential candidates
ISBN 0-7432-2224-5; 0-7432-2225-3 pa

LC 2003-276264

"This book is important not because of the history Senator Clinton records, but because of the history she doesn't record, and what that airbrushing tells us about the history she aspires to shape." N Y Times Book Rev

Close, Chuck, 1940-
Finch, Christopher. **Chuck** Close; life. Prestel 2010 350p il $34.95　　　**92**
1. Artists 2. Painters 3. Artists -- United States
ISBN 978-3-7913-3677-0

"Focusing on Close's paradigm-altering approaches to portraiture, the author offers an astounding and inspiring story of an artist of uncommon powers." Booklist
Includes bibliographical references

Cobain, Kurt, 1967-1994
Cross, Charles R. **Heavier** than heaven: a biography of Kurt Cobain. Hyperion 2001 381p il $24.95; pa $14.95　　　**92**
1. Singers 2. Guitarists 3. Rock musicians 4. Nirvana

(Musical group)
ISBN 0-7868-6505-9; 0-7868-8402-9 pa

LC 2001-24187

This is a biography of Kurt Cobain, the lead singer of the rock group Nirvana, who committed suicide in 1994 at the age of 27

"Cross followed the Nirvana juggernaut from the beginning, and though he nearly bludgeons the reader with tales of Cobain's debauched excesses, one is still drawn to the artist's foreceful personality." Libr J

Cross, Charles R. **Here** we are now; the lasting impact of Kurt Cobain. Charles R. Cross. It Books 2014 192 p. illustration (hardcover) $22.99　　　**92**
1. Popular culture -- United States 2. Rock musicians -- United States -- Biography 3. Nirvana (Musical group) 4. Rock music -- 1991-2000 -- History and criticism
ISBN 0062308211; 9780062308214; 9780062308221

LC 2013045769

"In 'Here We Are Now: The Lasting Impact of Kurt Cobain,' [author] Charles R. Cross . . . examines the legacy of the Nirvana front man and takes on the question: why does Kurt Cobain still matter so much, 20 years after his death? Kurt Cobain is the icon born of the 90s, a man whose legacy continues to influence pop culture and music. Cross explores the impact Cobain has had on music, fashion, film, and culture, and attempts to explain his lasting and looming legacy." (Publisher's note)

"This short but intriguing book explores the troubled musician as a kind of muse for seemingly unrelated fields (modern hip-hop, medical studies, high-end fashion) as well as a champion for gay and women's rights and racial equality." LJ

Cobb, Ty, 1886-1961
Leerhsen, Charles. **Ty** Cobb; a terrible beauty. Charles Leerhsen. Simon & Schuster 2015 352 p. 8 plates; illustrations (hardback) $27.50　　　**92**
1. Baseball players -- Biography 2. Baseball players -- United States -- Biography
ISBN 1451645767; 9781451645767

LC 2014041478

This book, by Charles Leerhsen, is an "authoritative biography of [baseball player] Ty Cobb. . . . [W]hen he retired in 1928, after twenty-one years with the Detroit Tigers and two with the Philadelphia Athletics, he held more than ninety records. . . . But Cobb was also one of the game's most controversial characters. He got in a lot of fights, on and off the field, and was often accused of being overly aggressive." (Publisher's note)

"This is an important work for baseball and American historians as Cobb was one of the country's first true superstars. How he dealt with fame, a new byproduct of the modern age, serves as a useful social history." LJ
Includes bibliographical references and index

Cockburn, Henry, 1982-
Cockburn, Henry. **Henry's** demons; living with schizophrenia: a father and son's story. [by] Patrick Cockburn and Henry Cockburn. Scribner 2011 238p il $25; ebook $11.99　　　**92**
1. Artists 2. Painters 3. Schizophrenia 4. Father-son

relationship 5. Schizophrenics
ISBN 978-1-4391-5470-0; 1-4391-5470-8; 978-1-4391-6035-0 ebook; 1-4391-6035-X ebook
LC 2010-17760
"This straightforward, unsentimental book, is a bold plea for more research and cutting-edge therapies to combat mental illness." Publ Wkly

Cohen, Leonard, 1934-2016

Leonard Cohen on Leonard Cohen; interviews and encounters. edited by Jeff Burger. Chicago Review Press 2014 624 p. illustrations (Musicians in Their Own Words) (cloth) $29.95 **92**
1. Singers 2. Composers 3. Singers -- Canada -- Interviews 4. Composers -- Canada -- Interviews 5. Poets, Canadian -- 20th century -- Interviews
ISBN 1613747586; 9781613747582
LC 2013034568
This book, edited by Jeff Burger, "collects interviews from various sources to present the singular Leonard Cohen in his own voice. The earliest piece is an interview on Canadian television in 1966; the most recent is an article in the Guardian from January of [2014]. Editor Burger divides the book into four parts: the 1960s and 1970s . . . the 1980s . . . the 1990s . . . and the new millennium." (Booklist)
"Burger's discerning editorial hand selects those conversations with Cohen that offer insights into his music." Pub Wkly

★ Simmons, Sylvie. **I'm** your man; the life of Leonard Cohen. Sylvie Simmons. Ecco 2012 570 p. **92**
ISBN 0061994987; 9780061994982
Author Sylvie Simmons' biography of Leonard Cohen, "[t]he legend behind such songs as 'Suzanne,' 'Bird on the Wire' and 'Hallelujah' and the poet and novelist behind such groundbreaking literary works as 'Beautiful Losers' and 'Book of Mercy,' . . . traces the arc of his prodigious achievements to his remarkable retreat in the mid-nineties -- when . . . he entered a monastery on a rocky mountaintop above Los Angeles -- and finally to his reemergence for a sold-out world tour." (Publisher's note)

Colby, William Egan, 1920-1996

★ Woods, Randall B. **Shadow** warrior; William Egan Colby and the CIA. Randall B. Woods. Basic Books 2013 576 p. (hbk. : alk. paper) $29.99 **92**
1. United States. Central Intelligence Agency 2. Intelligence officers -- United States -- Biography 3. United States. Central Intelligence Agency -- Biography 4. World War, 1939-1945 -- Secret service -- United States 5. Vietnam War, 1961-1975 -- Secret service -- United States
ISBN 0465021948; 9780465021949; 9780465037889
LC 2012040332
This book by Randall B. Woods presents a biography of "World War II commando, Cold War spy, and CIA director under presidents [Richard] Nixon and [Gerald] Ford, William Egan Colby. Drawing on multiple new sources, including interviews with members of Colby's family, Woods has crafted a . . . biography of one of the most fascinating

and controversial figures of the twentieth century." (Publisher's note)
Includes bibliographical references and index

Cole, Nat King, 1919?-1965

★ Epstein, Daniel Mark. **Nat** King Cole. Northeastern University Press 2000 437p il pa $20 **92**
1. Singers 2. Pianists 3. Jazz musicians 4. African American singers
ISBN 1-555-53469-4; 978-1-555-53469-1
LC 00-42727
First published 1999 by Farrar, Straus & Giroux
"The biographer sometimes digs too deep into esoterica, spending pages analyzing the lyrics of Straighten Up and Fly Right, for example. But when he recounts the singer's personal struggles, including a shocking 1956 onstage kidnapping attempt by Alabama racists, the human drama is, well unforgettable." Time
Includes bibliographical references

Cole, Natalie

Cole, Natalie. **Angel** on my shoulder; an autobiography. written with Digby Diehl. Warner Bks. 2000 353p il $38 **92**
1. Singers 2. Pop musicians
ISBN 978-0-446-52746-0; 0-446-52746-7
LC 00-61455
In this memoir by the daughter of the late Nat King Cole, the Grammy Award-winning songstress recalls her childhood, her personal battle and victory over drugs and alcohol, and the legal battles with her mother and siblings over her father's estate
"Although she concentrates mostly on the good times, Cole isn't shy about the bad times, which makes this intriguing, engaging, and inspirational life story worthy of attention." Booklist

Colette, 1873-1954

Thurman, Judith. **Secrets** of the flesh: a life of Colette. Knopf 1999 592p il hardcover o.p. pa $18.95 **92**
1. Authors 2. Novelists 3. Biographers
ISBN 0-345-37103-8 pa
LC 99-18959
Thurman focuses on the "morally subversive Colette in the social milieu of early-20th-century Paris. . . . {She} does not hesitate to expose the dishonest, selfish, exploitive facets of the feminist icon who wrote articles for Occupation newspapers and sometimes behaved heartlessly toward lovers. Nevertheless, her Colette comes off as an appealing, even heroic, figure." Publ Wkly
Includes bibliographical references

Collins, Lauren

Collins, Lauren. **When** in French; Love in a Second Language. Lauren Collins. Penguin Press 2016 256 p. (hardback) $27; (ebook) $65 **92**
1. Love 2. Man-woman relationship 3. French as a second language
ISBN 9781594206443; 9780698191075
LC 2016017611

In this book, by Lauren Collins, "a language barrier is no match for love. . . . Collins discovered this firsthand when, in her early thirties, she moved to London and fell for a Frenchman named Olivier. . . . In learning French, Collins must wrestle with the very nature of French identity and society—which, it turns out, is a far cry from life back home in North Carolina." (Publisher's note)

"Throughout, the author ably weaves together the personal and the historical. A memoir filled with pleasing passages in every chapter." Kirkus

Coltrane, John, 1926-1967

Ratliff, Ben. **Coltrane**; the story of a sound. Farrar, Straus & Giroux 2007 xxi, 250p il hardcover o.p. pa $16 **92**

1. Jazz musicians 2. African American musicians 3. Saxophonists

ISBN 978-0-374-12606-3; 0-374-12606-2; 978-0-312-42778-8 pa; 0-312-42778-6 pa

LC 2007-4362

This is a biography of the jazz musician.

This is an "engaging study of the jazz saxophonist's artistic influence. . . . Ratliff patiently explicates Coltrane's legend, writing in short, aphoristic bursts, often as elliptically as his subject played tenor saxophone, but never less than lucidly." N Y Times Book Rev

Includes bibliographical references

Columbus, Christopher

Morison, Samuel Eliot. **Admiral** of the ocean sea: a life of Christopher Columbus; maps by Erwin Raisz; drawings by Bertram Greene. Little, Brown 1942 xx, 680p il maps hardcover o.p. pa $28.99 92

1. Explorers

ISBN 0-316-58478-9 pa

A condensation of the author's two-volume work with same title also published in 1942 but now o.p.

"An authoritative . . . biography of Columbus which is also decidedly original in its emphasis on the ability of Columbus as seaman and navigator and in the amount of space given to tracing the routes of the voyages and landings." Libr J

Commerson, Philibert, 1727-1773

Ridley, Glynis. The **discovery** of Jeanne Baret; a story of science, the high seas, and the first woman to circumnavigate the globe. Crown Publishers 2010 288p il $25; ebook $25 **92**

1. Botanists 2. Explorers 3. Women scientists 4. Voyages around the world

ISBN 978-0-307-46352-4; 978-0-307-46354-8 ebook

LC 2010-16778

This is a biography "of Jeanne Baret. Born in 1740 in France's Loire valley, Baret became an expert 'herb woman' who proved to be indispensable to the ambitious botanist Philibert Commerson, accompanying him as his assistant when Commerson was appointed naturalist for France's first expedition to circumnavigate the globe. But women were forbidden, so Baret dressed as a man. . . . Woven throughout this gripping story are Ridley's piquant insights into eighteenth-century exploration, botany, taxonomy, biopiracy, and sexism. Baret could not have asked for a more exacting

and expressive champion. Ridley is incandescent in her passion for the truth." Booklist

Includes bibliographical references

Common (Musician)

Common. **One** day it'll all make sense; a memoir. by Common with Adam Bradley. 1st Atria Books hardcover ed.; Atria Books 2011 305 p. ill. (chiefly col.) $25 **92**

1. Fame 2. Gangs 3. Rap music 4. African Americans -- Chicago (Ill.) 5. African American entertainers -- Biography 6. Rap musicians -- United States -- Biography

ISBN 9781451625875; 9781451625882 pa; 9781451625905

LC 2011021691

Street Lit Book Award Medal: Adult Non-Fiction (2012)

The author of the book, the hip-hop musician Common, "discusses fame and the deeper meanings of his life. . . . He portrays himself as an openhearted, curious kid, trying to understand the tumult of Chicago's African-American South Side. . . . Common writes frankly about his youthful involvement with gang culture, portrayed as an inevitable rite of passage that became increasingly violent. . . . By 1989, his early demos as Common Sense were drawing industry attention, and he dropped out of college to pursue this calling, over his mother's objections. Much of what follows is a . . . showbiz narrative, moving from hip-hop to film acting." (Kirkus)

Includes bibliographical references and index

Connolly, Kevin Michael, 1985-

Connolly, Kevin Michael. **Double** take; a memoir. HarperStudio 2009 227p il $19.99; pa $14.99 **92**

1. Skiing 2. Athletes 3. Photographers 4. Skateboarding 5. People with disabilities 6. Skiers 7. Athletes with disabilities

ISBN 978-0-06-179153-6; 978-0-06-179152-9 pa

LC 2009-30496

"An X Games competitive skier and photographer recounts an extraordinary life spent overcoming immense physical limitations. Connolly was born without legs in the summer of 1985, in Helena, Mont. . . . A courageous, immensely rewarding chronicle expressed in arresting words and pictures." Kirkus

Conway, Jill K., 1934-

Conway, Jill K. **True** north; a memoir. Knopf 1994 250p hardcover o.p. pa $13 **92**

1. Historians 2. College teachers 3. College presidents

ISBN 0-679-74461-4 pa

LC 93-45302

"Conway analyzes her own experiences in the U.S. and Canada just as thoughtfully and penetratingly as her academic work investigates the lives of several previous generations of American women." Booklist

Cook, James, 1728-1779

Blainey, Geoffrey. **Sea** of dangers; Captain Cook and his rivals in the South Pacific. Ivan R. Dee 2009 322p il map $27.50 **92**
1. Explorers 2. Voyages around the world 3. Ship captains 4. Naval officers 5. Travel writers 6. Oceania -- Exploration
ISBN 978-1-56663-825-8; 1-56663-825-9
LC 2008-52623

"An excellent work of popular history that recounts the exploits of men who dramatically expanded our knowledge of the globe." Booklist
Includes bibliographical references

Hough, Richard Alexander, 1922-1999. **Captain** James Cook; {by} Richard Hough. Norton 1995 398p il hardcover o.p. pa $18.95 **92**
1. Explorers 2. Naval officers 3. Travel writers
ISBN 0-393-31519-3 pa
LC 94-35998

First published 1994 in the United Kingdom
"Hough's easygoing, thorough treatment . . . spotlights a proud, determined man." Booklist
Includes bibliographical references

Cooke, Sam

★ Guralnick, Peter. **Dream** boogie; the triumph of Sam Cooke. Little, Brown 2005 750p il $27.95 **92**
1. Singers 2. Soul musicians
ISBN 0-316-37794-5
LC 2005-77

This is a biography of the American singer.
"For those who only know the singer through his pop hits—'You Send Me'; 'Twistin' the Night Away'—the extensive account of his childhood background in gospel music will prove fascinating, and the evocation of the harsh realities faced by African-American musicians touring the South a powerful reminder of just how explosive this music could be." Publ Wkly
Includes discography and bibliographical references

Coolidge, Calvin, 1872-1933

Shlaes, Amity. **Coolidge**; Amity Shlaes. Harper 2013 viii, 565 p., [14] p. of platesp ill, $35 **92**
1. United States -- History -- 1919-1933 2. United States -- Economic conditions -- 1919-1933 3. Presidents -- United States -- Biography 4. United States -- Politics and government -- 1923-1929
ISBN 0061967556; 9780061967559
LC 2012032098

In this biography of U.S. President Calvin Coolidge, "[Amity] Shlaes shows that the mid-1920s was . . . a triumphant period that established our modern way of life. . . . Coolidge's discipline and composure, Shlaes reveals, represented not weakness but strength. . . . Coolidge proved unafraid to take on the divisive issues of this crucial period: reining in public-sector unions, unrelentingly curtailing spending, and rejecting funding for new interest groups." (Publisher's note)
Includes bibliographical references and index

Cooper, Alex, 1994-

Cooper, Alex. **Saving** Alex; when I was fifteen I told my Mormon parents I was gay, and that's when my nightmare began. Alex Cooper and Joanna Brooks. HarperOne 2016 256 p. (hardcover) $24.99 **92**
1. Mormons 2. Lesbians 3. LGBT youth 4. United States -- Biography 5. Mormon gays -- United States -- Biography
ISBN 9780062374608; 9780062374622; 9780062455291
LC 2015031520

In this memoir, author Alex Cooper "told her parents that she was gay, and the nightmare began. She was driven from her home in Southern California to Utah, where, against her will, her parents handed her over to fellow Mormons who promised to save Alex from her homosexuality. For eight harrowing months, Alex was held captive in an unlicensed 'residential treatment program' modeled on the many 'therapeutic' boot camps scattered across Utah." (Publisher's note)
"Alex's horrifying story is one that needs to be heard, and her book is an eloquent testament to that. It is encouraging proof that, as Alex is told, things do get better." Booklist

Cooper, Anderson

Cooper, Anderson, 1967- The **rainbow** comes and goes; a mother and son talk about life, love, and loss. Anderson Cooper and Gloria Vanderbilt. HarperCollins 2016 290 p. illustrations (hardback) $27.99 **92**
1. Mother-son relationship 2. Celebrities -- Biography 3. Journalists -- Biography 4. Celebrities -- United States -- Biography 5. Mothers and sons -- United States -- Correspondence 6. Television journalists -- United States -- Biography
ISBN 0062454943; 9780062454942; 9780062454966; 9780062466730
LC 2016000369

This book, by Anderson Cooper and Gloria Vanderbilt, "offers a rare window into their close relationship and fascinating life stories, including their tragedies and triumphs. In these often humorous and moving exchanges, they share their most private thoughts and the hard-earned truths they've learned along the way. In their words their distinctive personalities shine through—Anderson's journalistic outlook on the world is a sharp contrast to his mother's idealism and unwavering optimism." (Publisher's note)
"Vanderbilt and her son, Cooper, relate the touching story of how an epistolary exchange created new emotional intimacy between them." Pub Wkly

Cooper, Anderson, 1967- The **rainbow** comes and goes; a mother and son talk about life, love, and loss. Anderson Cooper and Gloria Vanderbilt. HarperCollins 2016 290 p. illustrations (hardback) $27.99 **92**
1. Mother-son relationship 2. Celebrities -- Biography 3. Journalists -- Biography 4. Celebrities -- United States -- Biography 5. Mothers and sons -- United States -- Correspondence 6. Television journalists --

United States -- Biography
ISBN 0062454943; 9780062454942; 9780062454966; 9780062466730

LC 2016000369

This book, by Anderson Cooper and Gloria Vanderbilt, "offers a rare window into their close relationship and fascinating life stories, including their tragedies and triumphs. In these often humorous and moving exchanges, they share their most private thoughts and the hard-earned truths they've learned along the way. In their words their distinctive personalities shine through—Anderson's journalistic outlook on the world is a sharp contrast to his mother's idealism and unwavering optimism." (Publisher's note)

"Vanderbilt and her son, Cooper, relate the touching story of how an epistolary exchange created new emotional intimacy between them." Pub Wkly

Cooper, Douglas, 1911-1984

Richardson, John. The **sorcerer's** apprentice; Picasso, Provence, and Douglas Cooper. University of Chicago Press 2001 318p il pa $17 **92**

1. Art critics 2. Biographers 3. Art historians
ISBN 0-226-71245-1

First published 1999 by Knopf

Picasso biographer John Richardson "has written a concise account of the first half of his own life and notably of his long relationship as a young man with the Cubist art historian and collector Douglas Cooper. The account concentrates on the dozen years, from early 1949 to the end of 1960, when Richardson lived with Cooper, visiting museums and monuments all over Europe, meeting the great artists and other personalities of the day, and restoring the colonnaded Chateau de Castille in the south of France." NY Times Book Rev

Includes bibliographical references

Cooper, Gary, 1901-1961

Thomson, David, 1941- **Gary** Cooper; photo research by Lucy Gray. Faber and Faber 2010 129p il (Great stars) pa $14 **92**

1. Actors
ISBN 978-0-86547-932-6

LC 2009-41759

First published 2009 in the United Kingdom

In this biography of the actor, "Cooper is presented as a hapless, weak-willed adulterer whose lean body, rugged handsomeness and preternatural stillness translated on camera as a quintessentially American rectitude and heroic stoicism. . . . Thomson is wickedly funny and startlingly poetic in his observations." Kirkus

Cooper, Helene

Cooper, Helene. The **house** at Sugar Beach; in search of a lost African childhood. Simon & Schuster 2008 354p il map $25 **92**

1. Journalists 2. Liberia
ISBN 0-7432-6624-2; 978-0-7432-6624-6

The author traces her childhood in wartorn Liberia and her reunion with a foster sister who had been left behind when her family fled the region.

"A coming-of-age story told with unremitting honesty. With her pedigree and her freedom from internalized racism, Cooper is liberated to enjoy a social universe that is a fluid mix of all things American and African. . . . While Cooper's memoir is mesmerizing in its portrayal of a Liberia rarely witnessed, its description of the psychological devastation—and coping mechanisms—brought on by profound loss is equally captivating." N Y Times Book Rev

Cooper, James Fenimore, 1789-1851

Franklin, Wayne. **James** Fenimore Cooper; the early years. Yale University Press 2007 708p il map $40 **92**

1. Authors 2. Novelists 3. Authors, American
ISBN 978-0-300-10805-7; 0-300-10805-2

LC 2006-31247

"This volume profoundly enriches our understanding of how the young writer helped forge our national mythology in works such as The Last of The Mohicans and The Pioneers." Booklist

Includes bibliographical references

Copeland, Misty

Copeland, Misty, 1982- **Life** in motion; an unlikely ballerina. by Misty Copeland with Charisse Jones. Touchstone Books 2014 288 p. (hardcover) $24.99 **92**

1. Ballet 2. Ballet dancers 3. African American dancers -- Biography 4. Ballerinas -- United States -- Biography 5. Ballet dancers -- United States -- Biography
ISBN 1476737983; 9781476737980

LC 2014002922

This book presents a memoir by Misty Copeland, an African American soloist for the American Ballet Theatre. "When a teacher encouraged I 3-year-old Misty to take ballet at the Boys and Girls Club of Los Angeles, she discovered a hidden talent. Her natural flexibility and grace had her on pointe within two months, something other ballerinas work years to achieve. She was offered lead roles before finishing high school." (Booklist)

"The ballet world, replete with "Balanchine" bodies—tall, thin, and white—may not seem like a place for a dancer who is five-foot, two-inches, curvy (by ballet standards), and black. But Copeland, despite her late start to ballet at age 13, became the third African American soloist in the history of the American Ballet Theater. Her memoir describes her childhood flitting around to the houses of her mother's different boyfriends until the coach on her drill team encourages her to try a ballet class at the local Boys and Girls Club... Instead of rags to riches, Copeland goes from baggy shorts to leotards as she navigates the whitewashed world of ballet." (Library Journal)

Copernicus, Nicolaus, 1473-1543

Repcheck, Jack. **Copernicus'** secret; how the scientific revolution began. Simon & Schuster 2007 239p il map $25 **92**

1. Astronomers
ISBN 978-0-7432-8951-1; 0-7432-8951-X

LC 2007-24649

"The book is fascinating reading, even to those who may be familiar with much of its contents." Choice

Includes bibliographical references

Vollmann, William T. **Uncentering** the Earth; Copernicus and The Revolutions of the Heavenly Spheres. Norton 2006 295p il (Great discoveries) $22.95 **92**

1. Astronomers

ISBN 0-393-05969-3

LC 2005-25864

"Readers who want to understand the significance of Copernicus's book in both his own time and ours will find this the next best thing to reading it." Publ Wkly

Coronado, Rodney A., 1966-

Kuipers, Dean. **Operation** Bite Back; Rod Coronado's war to save American wilderness. Bloomsbury 2009 309p il $25 **92**

1. Environmentalists 2. Animal rights movement 3. Animal rights activists

ISBN 1-59691-458-0; 978-1-59691-458-2

LC 2009-6600

This "account of animal rights activist Rod Coronado follows the charismatic Coronado from his introduction to animal protection in the 1980s to his campaign of sabotage against the fur industry, his life in the underground and on reservations among fellow Native Americans, and ultimately his arrests and incarcerations. . . . An important book that will appeal to readers interested in environmental and social issues." Libr J

Corrigan, Kelly, 1967-

Corrigan, Kelly. **Glitter** and Glue; A Memoir. by Kelly Corrigan. Random House Inc 2014 240 p. ill. $26 **92**

1. Travel 2. Nannies 3. Mother-daughter relationship 4. Motherhood 5. Mothers and daughters 6. Sydney (N.S.W.) -- Biography 7. Americans -- Australia -- Sydney (N.S.W.) -- Biography

ISBN 034553283X; 9780345532831

LC 2013041936

This memoir, by Kelly Corrigan, "examines the bond . . . between mothers and daughters. . . . After college, . . . [Corrigan] took off for Australia to see things and do things. . . . In a matter of months, her savings shot, she had a choice: get a job or go home. That's how Kelly met John Tanner, a newly widowed father of two looking for a live-in nanny. . . . Every day she spent with the Tanner kids was a day spent reconsidering her relationship with her mother." (Publisher's note)

"Written in a breezy style with humor and heart, the book reminds us how rewarding it can be to see a parent outside the context of our own needs." Kirkus

Corrigan, Kelly. The **middle** place. Voice/Hyperion 2008 266p il $23.95; pa $14.95 **92**

1. Breast cancer 2. Columnists 3. Cancer patients

ISBN 978-1-4013-0336-5; 978-1-4013-4093-3 pa

LC 2007-15316

The author "was a happily married mother of two young daughters when she discovered a cancerous lump in her breast. She was still undergoing treatment when she learned that her beloved father, who'd already survived prostate cancer, now had bladder cancer. Corrigan's story could have been unbearably depressing had she not made it clear from the start that she came from sturdy stock. . . . Those learning to accept their own adulthood might find strength—and humor—in Corrigan's feisty memoir." Publ Wkly

Cosell, Howard, 1918-1995

Ribowsky, Mark. **Howard** Cosell. W.W. Norton & Co. 2011 477p il $29.95 **92**

1. Sports 2. Lawyers 3. Television personalities 4. Sportscasters

ISBN 978-0-393-08017-9; 0-393-08017-X

LC 2011-27501

This book offers a biography of "Howard Cosell, of ABC, who died in 1995, [and] was [a] . . . . famous television sports announcer. . . . He was a star for three decades, and during his early-1970s heyday, which coincided with the maximum reach of network television, he was a ubiquitous figure in American culture. . . . [The book attempts to elucidate] the interplay among Cosell's life story, the stories he covered, and the institutional rise of televised sports . . . [and larger claims] about American culture. . . . [The author examines how] Cosell became a star by covering a bigger star, Muhammad Ali, the great heavyweight boxer, [as well as other aspects of his career.]" (N Y Review of Books)

"The sportscaster Howard Cosell erupted onto the national stage in the 1960s and quickly became a pop-culture icon. His raspy, heavily New York-accented voice, a sharp mind, an expansive vocabulary and a photographic memory were packaged into a larger-than-life and sometimes abrasive figure. Whether his audience loved him, hated him or loved to hate him, they tuned in, and he turned them on. He was impossible to ignore. . . . Mr. Ribowsky's book is an entertaining read and a thought-provoking portrayal of the multifaceted Howard Cosell in all his glory and enmity. It is based on voluminous, well-sourced research into print and electronic material, coupled with numerous interviews with Cosell's contemporaries." Wall Street J

Includes bibliographical references

Costello, Elvis.

Costello, Elvis, 1954- **Unfaithful** Music & Disappearing Ink; by Elvis Costello. Penguin Group USA 2015 352 p. illustrations, portraits (ebook) $32.50; $30 **92**

1. Musicians -- Biography

ISBN 9780698140653; 0399167250; 9780399167256

LC 2015032865

This memoir, by Elvis Costello, "offers his unique view of his unlikely and sometimes comical rise to international success, with diversions through the previously undocumented emotional foundations of some of his best-known songs and the hits of tomorrow. It features many stories and observations about his renowned cowriters and co-conspirators, though Costello also pauses along the way for considerations of the less appealing side of fame." (Publisher's note)

"Costello comes across as the perennial outsider, as someone who is surprised that he has been invited to the party. A must for Costello fans everywhere." Booklist

Cousteau, Jacques Yves, 1910-1997

Matsen, Bradford. **Jacques** Cousteau; the sea king. [by] Brad Matsen. Pantheon Books 2009 296p il $27.95   **92**

1. Authors 2. Oceanography 3. Divers 4. Naval officers 5. Oceanographers 6. Nonfiction writers
ISBN 978-0-375-42413-7; 0-375-42413-X

LC 2009-11640

This biography "places Cousteau's films, books, and fame into the context of the rest of his life—ambitions, childhood, family relationships, friendships, and disagreements. . . . Readers who dive, who are interested in ecology or the oceans, or who simply recognize the name Cousteau, will want to read this full, well-rounded portrait of one of the world's greatest explorers and conservationists. Highly recommended." Libr J

Includes bibliographical references

Coutts, Marion

Coutts, Marion. The **Iceberg**. Black Cat 2016 304 p. $16   **92**

1. Brain -- Tumors 2. Families of terminally ill
ISBN 9780802124609

Originally published 2014 in Great Britain

This memoir recounts how "in 2008, Marion Coutts' husband, the art critic Tom Lubbock, was diagnosed with a brain tumour, and told that he had not more than two years to live. . . . Tom was 53 when he died, leaving Marion and their son Eugene, just two years old, alone. . . . Coutts describes the eighteen months leading up to her partner's death; an account of a family unit under assault, and how the three of them fought to keep it intact." (Publisher's note)

"A poetic and moving chronicle of loss." Kirkus

Cox, Lynne

Cox, Lynne. **Swimming** to Antarctica; tales of a long-distance swimmer. Knopf 2004 323p $24.95   **92**

1. Women athletes 2. Swimmers
ISBN 0-375-41507-6

LC 2003-47577

"Cox is a pleasure. . . . Many passages are grip-the-page exciting, whether she's dodging Antarctic icebergs or Nile River sewage." Booklist

Coxeter, H. S. M. (Harold Scott Macdonald), 1907-2003

★ Roberts, Siobhan. **King** of infinite space; Donald Coxeter, the man who saved geometry. Walker & Co. 2006 399p il $27.95   **92**

1. Mathematicians 2. College teachers
ISBN 0-8027-1499-4; 978-0-8027-1499-2

LC 2006-497355

This is the story of geometer H. S. M. "Donald" Coxeter's "life, his work, and his interactions with mathematicians, scientists, and artists of his time. . . . The author carefully weaves a lot of mathematical details into her work, but not so much that it becomes burdensome to the historical focus of the book." Sci Books Films

Includes bibliographical references

Crabapple, Molly

Crabapple, Molly. **Drawing** Blood; by Molly Crabapple. HarperCollins 2015 336 p. color illustrations $29.99   **92**

1. Artists 2. Young women 3. Culture conflict
ISBN 0062323644; 9780062323644

In this memoir, "Molly Crabapple had the eye of an artist and the spirit of a radical. After a restless childhood on New York's Long Island, she left America to see Europe and the Near East, a young artist plunging into unfamiliar cultures. . . . Returning to New York City after 9/11 to study art, she posed nude for sketch artists and sketchy photographers, danced burlesque, and modeled for the world famous Suicide Girls." (Publisher's note)

"Lavishly illustrated, the book offers a candid portrayal of an artist's journey to self-knowledge and fulfillment." Kirkus

Craddock, Ida C., 1857-1902

Schmidt, Leigh Eric. **Heaven's** bride; the unprintable life of Ida C. Craddock, American mystic, scholar, sexologist, martyr, and madwoman. Basic Books 2010 335p il   **92**

1. Mysticism 2. Occultists 3. Sex researchers 4. Biography, Individual
ISBN 9780465002986

LC 2010-929343

This is a biography of the American freethinker. Index.

The author "delineates the life of Philadelphia-born self-styled religion scholar and sexologist Ida Craddock (1857–1902), who navigated two important currents in late-19th-century America: the campaign for 'moral purity' waged by a righteous Protestant majority, and a spirit of liberalism and spiritualism as advocated by women's-rights activists, intellectuals and free-thinkers. . . . A colorful contextual study of Craddock and her teeming era." Kirkus

Includes bibliographical references

Crais, Clifton C.

Crais, Clifton. **History** lessons; a memoir of madness, memory, and the brain. Clifton Crais. The Overlook Press 2014 272 p. (alk. paper) $26.95 **92**

1. Amnesia 2. Autobiographies 3. Collective memory 4. Autobiographical memory 5. New Orleans (La.) -- Biography 6. Historians -- United States -- Biography
ISBN 1468303686; 9781468303681

LC 2014002373

"Born in Louisiana to a soon-to-be absent father and an alcoholic mother--who tried to drown him in a bathtub when he was three--[author] Clifton Crais spent his childhood . . . living with relatives too old or infirmed to care for him, or rambling on his own through New Orleans. . . . Crais examines the science of memory and forgetting, from the ways in which experience shapes the developing brain to . . . chronic childhood amnesia . . . from which he suffers." (Publisher's note)

"The ambiguities of a life only half recalled are fully illuminated in this chronicle of trying to understand what has been forgotten." LJ

Crane, Kathleen, 1951-

Crane, Kathleen. **Sea** legs; tales of a woman oceanographer. Westview Press 2003 318p il map hardcover o.p. pa $16 **92**
1. Oceanography 2. Women scientists 3. Oceanographers
ISBN 0-8133-4004-7; 0-8133-4285-6 pa
LC 2003-1690

"Crane chronicles the relentless adversity she faced in becoming a world-class oceanographer with a modest matter-of-factness that almost camouflages the high caliber of her achievements. . . . She was the first to postulate the existence of the now famous deep-sea hot springs. . . . Crane's experiences are diverse, dramatic, and important; her understanding of international affairs and environmental realities laudable and moving; and her triumphs over personal sorrows and illness impressive and inspiring." Booklist

Includes bibliographical references

Crazy Horse, Sioux Chief, ca. 1842-1877

McMurtry, Larry. **Crazy** Horse. Viking 1999 148p (Penguin lives series) hardcover o.p. pa $14 **92**
1. Oglala Indians 2. Indian chiefs 3. Native Americans -- Biography
ISBN 0-670-88234-8; 0-14-303480-4 pa
LC 98-26644

"Though essentially a loner and devoid of political ambition, Crazy Horse was a respected military tactician, equally feared and admired for the strength and the intensity of his convictions. Rather than merely attempting to sort out fact from fiction, McMurtry incorporates conjecture and legend into this philosophical portrait of both the man and the myth." Booklist

Powers, Thomas. The **killing** of Crazy Horse. Alfred A. Knopf 2010 568p il map $30 **92**
1. Oglala Indians 2. Indian chiefs 3. Biography, Individual 4. Dakota Indians -- Wars
ISBN 978-0-375-41446-6; 0-375-41446-0
LC 2010-16842

"With the Great Sioux War as background and context, . . . Powers recounts the final months and days of Crazy Horse's life." (Publisher's note) Bibliography. Index.

"Despite the title, this beautifully written and absorbing work is less about the death of Crazy Horse and more about the personality and life of the Native American icon. It is also an insightful and scrupulously fair examination of the culture of Plains Indian bands and their interaction with advancing white civilization in the nineteenth century." Booklist

Includes bibliographical references

Crick, Francis, 1916-2004

Ridley, Matt. **Francis** Crick; discoverer of the genetic code. Atlas Books 2006 213p (Eminent lives) $19.95 **92**
1. Genetics 2. Scientists 3. Biochemists 4. Nobel laureates for physiology or medicine
ISBN 0-06-082333-X; 978-0-06-082333-7
LC 2005-55878

"A briskly written essential for the DNA shelf." Booklist
Includes bibliographical references

Cromwell, Thomas, Earl of Essex, 1485?-1540

Borman, Tracy. **Thomas** Cromwell; The Untold Story of Henry Viii's Most Faithful Servant. Tracy Borman. Atlantic Monthly Press 2015 336 p. 16 plates; illustrations; maps $30 **92**
1. Great Britain -- History -- 1485-1603, Tudors
ISBN 0802123171; 9780802123176

This biography by Tracy Borman profiles Thomas Cromwell. "As Henry VIII's right-hand man, Cromwell was the architect of the English Reformation, secured Henry's divorce from Catherine of Aragon and plotted the downfall of Anne Boleyn. Borman reveals a different side of one of the most notorious figures in history: that of a caring husband and father, a fiercely loyal servant and friend, and a revolutionary who helped make medieval England into a modern state." (Publisher's note)

"Neglecting neither the public persona nor the private man, Borman provides an insightful biography of a much-maligned historical figure." Booklist

Cronkite, Walter

★ Brinkley, Douglas. **Cronkite**; Douglas Brinkley. Harper, an imprint of HarperCollins Publishers 2012 xi, 819 p.p illustrations (hardback) $34.99 **92**
1. Television broadcasting of news 2. Journalists -- United States -- Biography 3. Television journalists -- United States -- Biography
ISBN 0061374261; 9780061374265
LC 2011051467

This book, by Douglas Brinkley, is a biography of Walter Cronkite. "For decades, Walter Cronkite was known as 'the most trusted man in America'. . . . Brinkley traces Cronkite's story from his roots in Missouri and Texas through the Great Depression, . . . to World War II [and later]. . . . [H]e covered presidential elections, the space program, Vietnam, and the first televised broadcasts of the Olympic Games, as both a reporter and later as an anchor for the evening news." (Publisher's note)

Crosby, Bing, 1904-1977

Giddins, Gary. **Bing** Crosby: a pocketful of dreams: the early years, 1903-1940. Little, Brown 2001 728p il $30; pa $17.95 **92**
1. Actors 2. Singers
ISBN 0-316-88188-0; 0-316-88645-9 pa
LC 00-44403

"Giddins has contributed a landmark study of popular singing in the first half of the twentieth century." Booklist
Includes bibliographical references

Crowell, Rodney, 1950-

★ Crowell, Rodney. **Chinaberry** sidewalks. Alfred A. Knopf 2011 259p il $24.95 **92**
1. Singers 2. Country musicians 3. Songwriters
ISBN 978-0-307-59420-4
LC 2010-35996

"Crowell is among the best storytellers to emerge from Nashville. Up to now, he told his stories in song, but with this heartfelt memoir, he can now be called a writer of the first order. Houston, where Crowell grew up in the 1950s and early 1960s, was a city full of characters found in stereotypical country songs: hard-drinking fathers and longsuffering mothers singing along to the beer-soaked ballads of Hank Williams. But this is not fiction; Crowell actually lived the life, soaking up its exhilarating and disturbing atmosphere. Crowell is unsparingly honest, yet there is an admirable restraint here, too." Booklist

Crystal, Billy

Crystal, Billy, 1948- **Still** foolin' 'em; where i've been, where i'm going, and where the hell are my keys? by Billy Crystal. Henry Holt and Company 2013 288 p. (hardback) $28 **92**
1. Aging 2. American wit and humor 3. Comedians -- United States -- Biography
ISBN 0805098208; 9780805098204

LC 2013012238

Author and comedian Billy Crystal "outlines the absurdities and challenges that come with growing old, from insomnia to memory loss to leaving dinners with half your meal on your shirt. Crystal not only catalogues his physical gripes, but offers a road map to his 77 million fellow baby boomers who are arriving at this milestone age with him. He also looks back at the most powerful and memorable moments of his long and storied life." (Publisher's note)

"Avoiding the trappings—excess schmaltz, laundry list of famous friends, boozy party log—of so many celebrity memoirs, Crystal delivers a funny and genuinely moving chronicle of his life inside and outside Hollywood." Pub Wkly

Culkin, Jennifer

Culkin, Jennifer. A **final** arc of sky; a memoir of critical care. Beacon Press 2009 237p $24.95 **92**
1. Nurses 2. Authors 3. Nursing 4. Essayists
ISBN 978-0-8070-7285-1

LC 2008-46810

"It's clear that Culkin has little use for cheap sentiment. However, this memoir time and again shares with us her efforts to make meaning of the pain and fear and loss that is intrinsic to her line of work. . . . The author gets even more personal when she shares stories from her own family. With unflinching honesty, she talks about how she coped with the decline of her father's health; what she did at the deathbed of her mother; and how she came to terms with her own MS diagnosis. 'A Final Arc of Sky' tackles that toughest of subjects—our own mortality—with grit, compassion, and humor." Bellingham Herald
Includes bibliographical references

Cummings, E. E. (Edward Estlin), 1894-1962

★ Sawyer-Laucanno, Christopher. **E.E.** Cummings; a biography. Sourcebooks 2004 606p il $29.95; pa $16.95 **92**
1. Poets 2. Authors
ISBN 1-570-71775-3; 1-4022-0594-5 pa

LC 2004-12234

This biography of poet and artist e.e. cummings draws parallels between cummings' private life and his work.

This "is a responsible, adept, and necessary contribution to the body of secondary work about one of America's greatest poets." Christ Sci Monit

Cunningham, Merce

★ Brown, Carolyn. **Chance** and circumstance; twenty years with Cage and Cunningham. Alfred A. Knopf 2007 645p il $37.50 **92**
1. Poets 2. Authors 3. Dancers 4. Composers 5. Choreographers 6. Essayists
ISBN 978-0-394-40191-1; 0-394-40191-3

LC 2006-48799

The author "traces the trajectory of her modern dance career with that organization during its crawling stages in the 1950s and 1960s, when composer John Cage was musical director and artist Robert Rauschenberg was set and costume designer. Brown documents the company's early struggles for acceptance (it was considered avant-garde), various tours, and eventual world recognition. . . . This book will appeal to modern dance buffs and memoir readers." Libr J

Curie, Marie, 1867-1934

Brian, Denis. The **Curies**; a biography of the most controversial family in science. Wiley 2005 438p il $30 **92**
1. Chemists 2. Physicists 3. Nobel laureates for physics
ISBN 0-471-27391-0

LC 2005-7001

This book "follows five generations of the Sklodowska-Curie-Joliot family. Beginning before Marie Sklodowska and Pierre Curie meet, Brian details their courtship and 11-year marriage, bringing the reader to the Curie dinner table and into the converted garden shed (replete with a leaking roof) where the Curies' work on polonium and radium transformed physics and won them two Nobel prizes. . . . Extremely well-done and highly recommended." Publ Wkly
Includes bibliographical references

Dry, Sarah. **Curie**; with an essay by Sabine Seifert. Haus 2003 170p il (Life & times) pa $15.95 **92**
1. Chemists 2. Physicists 3. Women scientists 4. Chemists -- France 5. Chemists -- Poland 6. Women chemists -- France 7. Women chemists -- Poland 8. Nobel laureates for physics
ISBN 1-904341-29-2

This is a biography of the first woman to win two Nobel Prizes, one for physics and the other for chemistry

"Concise and engaging, this amply illustrated history of Madame Curie . . . makes an excellent introduction to the feminist icon and scientific pioneer. Dry does an excellent job of delineating the major events of Curie's life, including her early education in the underground schools of the 19th-century Polish resistance movement, her heady intellectual courtship with Pierre Curie in France, and later their discovery of radioactivity in 1898. Sidebars on topics such as the invention of the laboratory, and the inclusion of Seifert's essay on Irène Joliot-Curie, Marie Curie's less famous daughter and co-worker, make this pocket sized book especially comprehensive, and a wonderful introduction to a fascinating and inspiring career." Publ Wkly
Includes bibliographical references

Curie, Pierre, 1859-1906

Brian, Denis. The **Curies**; a biography of the most controversial family in science. Wiley 2005 438p il $30 **92**

1. Chemists 2. Physicists 3. Nobel laureates for physics

ISBN 0-471-27391-0

LC 2005-7001

This book "follows five generations of the Sklodowska-Curie-Joliot family. Beginning before Marie Sklodowska and Pierre Curie meet, Brian details their courtship and 11-year marriage, bringing the reader to the Curie dinner table and into the converted garden shed (replete with a leaking roof) where the Curies' work on polonium and radium transformed physics and won them two Nobel prizes. . . . Extremely well-done and highly recommended." Publ Wkly

Includes bibliographical references

Custer, George A. (George Armstrong), 1839-1876

McMurtry, Larry, 1936- **Custer**; Larry McMurtry. Simon & Schuster 2012 178 p. (hardcover) $35 **92**

1. Little Bighorn, Battle of the, 1876 2. Native Americans -- Wars 3. United States. Army -- Biography 4. Generals -- United States -- Biography 5. Little Bighorn, Battle of the, Mont., 1876 6. United States -- History -- Civil War, 1861-1865

ISBN 9781451626209; 1451626207

LC 2012012374

Author Larry McMurtry presents a biography of George Armstrong Custer. "On June 25, 1876, General George Armstrong Custer and his 7th Cavalry attacked a large Lakota Cheyenne village on the Little Bighorn River in Montana Territory. He lost not only the battle but his life--and the lives of his entire cavalry. 'Custer's Last Stand' was a spectacular defeat that shocked the country and grew quickly into a legend that has reverberated in our national consciousness to this day." (Publisher's note)

Includes bibliographical references.

Stiles, T. J. **Custer's** trials; a life on the frontier of a new America. T. J. Stiles. Alfred A. Knopf 2015 592 p. illustrations (hardcover) $30 **92**

1. Native Americans -- Wars 2. United States. Army -- Biography 3. Generals -- United States -- Biography 4. Little Bighorn, Battle of the, Mont., 1876 5. United States -- History -- Civil War, 1861-1865

ISBN 0307592642; 9780307592644

LC 2015002070

National Book Critics Circle Award Finalist: Biography (2015)

Pulitzer Prize Finalist: Biography (2016)

This biography of George Armstrong Custer, by T. J. Stiles, "paints a portrait of Custer both deeply personal and sweeping in scope, proving how much of Custer's legacy has been ignored. . . . The key to understanding Custer, Stiles writes, is keeping in mind that he lived on a frontier in time. In the Civil War, the West, and many areas overlooked in previous biographies, Custer helped to create modern America, but he could never adapt to it." (Publisher's note)

"Stiles ably points out [Custer's] many defining flaws: his heroic style didn't work in an era of tact and skill, and there is no doubt that he was self-serving, generally assuming that rules weren't made for him and never showing remorse. In addition to examining Custer's life, the author also introduces his cook, the fascinating Eliza Brown, an escaped slave who deserves a biography of her own." Kirkus

Includes bibliographical references and index

Wert, Jeffry D. **Custer**; the controversial life of George Armstrong Custer. Simon & Schuster 1996 462p il maps hardcover o.p. pa $20 **92**

1. Generals 2. Army officers

ISBN 0-684-81043-3; 0-684-83275-5 pa

LC 96-7290

"Focusing on Custer's Civil War actions, Wert methodically examines a man often considered an enigma in American history. Clear writing and excellent use of primary source materials demonstrate how history should be written." Booklist

Dahl, Roald

Sturrock, Donald. **Storyteller**; the authorized biography of Roald Dahl. Simon & Schuster 2010 655p il $30 **92**

1. Authors 2. Authors, English 3. Children's authors 4. Short story writers

ISBN 978-1-4165-5082-2; 1-4165-5082-8

LC 2010-07175

"In this authorized biography of Dahl, Sturrock, the artistic director of the Roald Dahl Foundation, reveals a life marked by tragedy: the early deaths of Dahl's father and sister, his son's tragic accident, the death of a daughter at seven, and the debilitating stroke of his wife, Patricia Neal, at age 39...This carefully researched and unflinching portrait of an immensely complicated and talented writer will appeal to Dahl's fans and other serious readers of biography." (Library Journal)

Includes bibliographical references

Dalai Lama II, 1476-1542.

Mullin, Glenn H. The **second** Dalai Lama; his life and teachings. translated, edited, introduced, and annotated by Glenn H. Mullin. Snow Lion Publications 2005 270p pa $16.95 **92**

ISBN 1-55939-233-9

LC 2005-281580

Dalai Lama XIV, 1935-

★ Bstan-'dzin-rgya-mtsho, Dalai Lama XIV, 1935- **Freedom** in exile; the autobiography of the Dalai Lama. HarperCollins Pubs. 1990 288p il maps hardcover o.p. pa $15 **92**

1. Buddhism 2. Tibet (China) 3. Buddhist leaders 4. Political leaders 5. Nobel laureates for peace

ISBN 0-06-098701-4

LC 89-46523

"The Dalai Lama's story is, in part, a chapter in the 2,500-year history of Buddhism as well as a testament to the 'mendacity and barbarity' of Communist China. He shares the details of his amazing life, a glimpse at some of the mysteries of Tibetan Buddhism, and his unshakable belief in the basic good of humanity." Booklist

★ Iyer, Pico. The **open** road; the global journey of the fourteenth Dalai Lama. Bloomsbury 2008 288p $24   92
1. Buddhist leaders 2. Political leaders 3. Nobel laureates for peace
ISBN 978-0-307-26760-3; 0-307-26760-1
LC 2007-43991

"The combination of Iyer's exacting observations, incisive analysis, and frank respect for the unknowable results in a uniquely internalized, even empathic portrait of one of the world's most embraced and least understood guiding lights." Booklist
Includes bibliographical references

Danticat, Edwidge, 1969-
★ Danticat, Edwidge, 1969- **Brother,** I'm dying. Alfred A. Knopf 2007 272p hardcover o.p. pa $15   92
1. Authors 2. Novelists 3. Dramatists 4. Women authors 5. Editors 6. Essayists 7. Children's authors 8. Short story writers 9. Biography, Individual
ISBN 1-4000-3430-2 pa; 1-4000-4115-5; 978-1-4000-3430-7 pa; 978-1-4000-4115-2
LC 2007-06887

This family memoir by the author of The Dew Breaker (2004) centers on the experiences of "her father, Mira, and his older brother, Joseph." (Publisher's note)
The author "has written a fierce, haunting book about exile and loss and family love, and how that love can survive distance and separation, loss and abandonment and somehow endure, undented and robust." N Y Times (Late NY Ed)

Danticat, Edwidge, 1969- **Create** dangerously; the immigrant artist at work. Princeton University Press 2010 189p (Toni Morrison lecture series) $19.95   92
1. Authors 2. Novelists 3. Dramatists 4. Women authors 5. Editors 6. Essayists 7. Children's authors 8. Short story writers 9. Biography, Individual 10. Haiti -- Social conditions
ISBN 0-691-14018-9; 978-0-691-14018-6
LC 2010-10302

This is Danticat's "new collection of essays, adapted and updated from the Toni Morrison Lecture she gave in 2008 at Princeton University, and expanded with her writing for The New Yorker, The Progressive and other publications." (N Y Times Book Rev) Index.
This "tender . . . book about loss and the unquenchable passion for homeland makes us remember the powerful material from which most fiction is wrought: it comes from childhood, and place. No matter her geographic and temporal distance from these, Danticat writes about them with the immediacy of love." N Y Times Book Rev
Includes bibliographical references

Danton, Georges Jacques, 1759-1794
Lawday, David. The **giant** of the French Revolution; Danton, a life. Grove Press 2010 294p il map $27.50   92
1. Revolutionaries 2. France -- History -- 1789-1799, Revolution
ISBN 978-0-8021-1933-9

"This is the best biography of Danton to be written since Hilaire Belloc's over 100 years ago. Both the scholar and the general reader will find this biography an informative and lively read." Libr J
Includes bibliographical references

Darling, Ron, 1960-
Darling, Ron. The **complete** game; reflections on baseball, pitching, and life on the mound. by Ron Darling, with Daniel Paisner. Alfred A. Knopf 2009 272p $24.95   92
1. Baseball players 2. Baseball -- Biography
ISBN 978-0-307-26984-3; 0-307-26984-1
LC 2008-55706

Darling, "the stalwart ex-Mets starter and incumbent Mets broadcaster . . . offers pitches and outcomes (but no box scores) from ten selected games in his career, including a successful World Series start against the Red Sox at Fenway Park in 1986, a gruesome windy-day thumping suffered at Wrigley Field, and his celebrated extra-inning near-no-hitter back when he was pitching for Yale. Among them are enough oddities and thrilling turns of baseball to make a reader glad to be here and—well, not out there." New Yorker

Darnley, Henry Stewart, Lord, 1545-1567
Weir, Alison. **Mary,** Queen of Scots, and the murder of Lord Darnley. Ballantine Bks. 2003 670p il map $27.95; pa $16.95   92
1. Queens 2. Princes 3. Scotland -- History -- 16th century
ISBN 0-345-43658-X; 0-8129-7151-5 pa
LC 2002-34467

"No stone is left unturned in {Weir's} investigation, and despite its detail, her book is as dramatic as witnessing firsthand the most riveting court case." Booklist

Darrow, Clarence, 1857-1938
Farrell, John A. **Clarence** Darrow; attorney for the damned. Doubleday 2011 561p il $32.50; ebook $15.99   92
1. Lawyers 2. Memoirists 3. Writers on law 4. State legislators
ISBN 978-0-385-52258-8; 0-385-52258-4; 978-0-385-53451-2 ebook
LC 2010-46273

This is a biography of the American lawyer who defended John Scopes, Nathan Leopold and Richard Loeb.
"Farrell gleans from previously undisclosed material to offer a completely engaging portrait of a flawed man of noble ideals." Booklist
Includes bibliographical references

Darwin, Charles, 1809-1882

Browne, Janet. **Charles** Darwin; v1 a biography. Princeton Univ. Press 1996 605p v1 il pa $25.95   **92**
1. Naturalists 2. Travel writers 3. Writers on science
ISBN 0-691-02606-8

LC 95-53319

First published 1995 by Knopf

This first volume of a two-part biography of Darwin focuses on his early years, leading up to his marriage and his moving out of London to the countryside of Kent.

The author "captures the spirit of a quietly revolutionary scientist whose ingrained Victorian prejudices were at odds with his radical ideas." Publ Wkly

Includes bibliographical references

Followed by Charles Darwin: The power of place (2002)

Browne, Janet. **Charles** Darwin. v2 Knopf 2002 591p v2 il $37.50   **92**
1. Naturalists 2. Travel writers 3. Writers on science
ISBN 0-679-42932-8

This second volume of Browne's biography of Darwin begins "a year before the publication of On the Origin of Species, with the arrival of a package from Alfred Russel Wallace, whose own ideas on natural selection virtually mirrored Darwin's, forcing him to go public. . . . Browne's subject is monumental, but her writing style is never overburdened by the weight. Rather, her prose is elegant in its clarity of thought, her craftsmanship impeccable in the way it weaves a coherent whole from the innumerable threads of thought, experience and persona that comprised this colossal life." Publ Wkly

Includes bibliographical references

David, King of Israel

Pinsky, Robert. The **life** of David. Schocken 2005 209p (Jewish encounters) $19.95   **92**
1. Kings
ISBN 0-8052-4203-1

LC 2005-41696

The author "considers the peculiarities, paradoxes, and timeless significance of David's often baffling story from his golden days as a handsome upstart confronting King Saul in 'gangsterish' encounters to David's wild years as a desert Robin Hood and ascension to the throne. . . . Witty, frank, skeptical, and clearly moved by mercurial David's chutzpah and losses, Pinsky brings remarkable lucidity, depth, and creativity to his dynamic and poetic reading of a legendary figure who has become emblematic of both destructive and heroic aspects of human nature." Booklist

Davidman, Joy

Joy; poet, seeker, and the woman who captivated C. S. Lewis. Abigail Santamaria. Houghton Mifflin Harcourt 2015 416 p. 16 plates; illustrations (hardback) $28   **92**
1. Women poets 2. Women poets, American -- Biography 3. Authors' spouses -- Great Britain -- Biography 4. Christian converts from Judaism -- United States -- Biography
ISBN 0151013713; 9780151013715

LC 2014034506

This book, by Abigail Santamaria, offers a "biography of Joy Davidman [that] brings her out from C. S. Lewis's shadow. . . . A poet and radical, Davidman was a frequent contributor to the communist vehicle New Masses and an active member of New York literary circles in the 1930s and 40s. . . . A mother, a novelist, a vibrant and difficult and intelligent woman, she set off for England in 1952, determined to captivate the man whose work had changed her life." (Publisher's note)

"With access to unpublished documents and family papers, Santamaria has fashioned a compelling narrative, remaining cleareyed about her subject's many personal failings." Kirkus

Includes bibliographical references and index

Davis, Bette, 1908-1989

Thomson, David, 1941- **Bette** Davis; photo research by Lucy Gray. Faber and Faber 2010 128p il (Great stars) pa $14   **92**
1. Actors
ISBN 978-0-86547-931-9

LC 2009-41760

First published 2009 in the United Kingdom

"Chronicling Davis' life and evolution in Hollywood, Thomson illustrates how changes in her often-disappointing private life (she had a habit of marrying the wrong men) influenced and often deepened her onscreen persona. Reading of how Davis bounced from one bad movie to the next in the early years of her career, it's hard not to share Thomson's enthusiasm for her talent, drive, and will. And it is hard not to feel Thomson's disappointment when Davis' major, artistic breakthroughs (The Little Foxes, All About Eve) are followed by lapses into forgettable mediocrity (The Man Who Came to Dinner, Payment on Demand)." Booklist

Includes filmography and bibliographical references

Davis, Jefferson, 1808-1889

Cooper, William J. **Jefferson** Davis, American. Knopf 2000 757p il maps $35; pa $18   **92**
1. Statesmen 2. Senators 3. Political leaders 4. Secretaries of war 5. Confederate States of America 6. United States -- History -- 1861-1865, Civil War
ISBN 0-394-56916-4; 0-375-72542-3 pa

LC 00-62006

In this biography of the president of the Confederacy, the author traces Davis' political career and personal life, including his days at West Point, as Secretary of War in the Mexican War, and as U.S. senator from Mississippi

"In the already cluttered field of Civil War history, Cooper's is the definitive biography; readers will be particularly pleased to discover the compelling power of his narrative." Publ Wkly

Includes bibliographical references

Davis, Jennifer Pharr

Davis, Jennifer Pharr. **Called** again; a story of love and triumph. by Jennifer Pharr Davis. Beaufort Books 2013 298 p. (ebook) $15.95; pbk $15.95 **92**
1. Hikers -- United States -- Biography
ISBN 9780825306532; 0825307457; 9780825306938; 9780825307454

LC 2014036228

"In 2011, Jennifer Pharr Davis became the overall record holder on the Appalachian Trail. By hiking 2,181 miles in 46 days - an average of 47 miles per day - she became the first female to ever set that mark. . . . This is Jennifer's story, in her own words, about how she started this journey with a love for hiking and more significantly a love for her husband Brew." (Publisher's note)

"A serviceably written yet inspired exploration of the meaning of commitment." Kirkus

Davis, Miles

Cook, Richard. **It's** about that time; Miles Davis on and off record. Oxford University Press 2007 373p il $27   92
   1. Jazz musicians 2. African American musicians 3. Band leaders 4. Flugelhornists 5. Trumpet players
   ISBN 978-0-19-532266-8; 0-19-532266-5
                          LC 2006-50694
"Cook's thoughtful, illuminating criticism and boundless knowledge of his subject make this a rich and satisfying read for jazz aficionados and novices alike." Publ Wkly
  Includes discography and bibliographical references

Davis, Miles. **Miles,** the autobiography; {by} Miles Davis with Quincy Troupe. Simon & Schuster 1989 431p il hardcover o.p. pa $15   92
   1. Jazz musicians 2. African American musicians 3. Band leaders 4. Flugelhornists 5. Trumpet players
   ISBN 0-671-72582-3 pa
                             LC 89-19652
"The legendary jazz musician Miles Davis . . . takes us on a historical journey that begins with his growing up in the mid-1920s in East St. Louis, then moves on to New York City in the 1940s, where he was a student at the Julliard School of Music, and to his encounters with other jazz greats like Charlie Parker, Dizzy Gillespie, Billie Holiday, Herbie Hancock, and George Duke." Libr J

Dawkins, Richard, 1941-

Dawkins, Richard, 1941- An **Appetite** for Wonder; The Making of a Scientist. HarperCollins 2013 304 p. $27.99   92
   1. Atheism 2. Scientists -- Biography
   ISBN 0062225790; 9780062225795
"In the first volume of a projected two-volume memoir, evolutionary biologist and ethologist [Richard] Dawkins . . . looks back on his life from childhood through the publication of his first and most famous book, 'The Selfish Gene,' in 1976. . . . Ultimately, this is a self-portrait of a . . . man whose radical positions are the logical outgrowth of his skeptical, science-based approach. . . . . His memoir is more about science than atheism, although both topics crop up." (Library Journal)

Day, Doris, 1924-

Kaufman, David. **Doris** Day; the untold story of the girl next door. Virgin Books 2008 626p il $29.95; pa $19.95   92
   1. Actors 2. Singers
   ISBN 978-1-90526-430-8; 1-90526-430-5; 978-0-75351-809-0 pa; 0-75351-809-0 pa
                           LC 2008-9410

This is a biography of the actor who starred in such films as Love Me or Leave Me (1955), The Man Who Knew Too Much (1956), and Pillow Talk (1959).

"Readers, especially fans of the star, will thoroughly enjoy this meaty, well-written, entertaining look at the surprisingly tumultuous life of an American icon." Booklist
  Includes bibliographical references

De Kooning, Willem, 1904-1997

Swan, Annalyn. **De** Kooning: an American master; [by] Mark Stevens and Annalyn Swan. Knopf 2004 731p il $35   92
   1. Artists 2. Painters
   ISBN 1-4000-4175-9
                         LC 2004-48297
This is a biography of the twentieth-century painter and a study of his work

This is a "sweeping, authoritative biography. . . . . The elusiveness of its subject makes the achievements of 'De Kooning' that much more dazzling. This is a book that traces de Kooning's history, puts him on Freud's couch, plumbs the mysteries of his cryptic and ever-changing work and follows the arc of modern art through much of the 20th century, fusing all these elements into a remarkably lucid narrative." N Y Times (Late N Y ed)
  Includes bibliographical references

De Mille, Cecil B., 1881-1959

★ Eyman, Scott. **Empire** of dreams; the epic life of Cecil B. DeMille. Simon & Schuster 2010 579p il $35; ebook $16.99   92
   1. Motion picture producers and directors 2. Motion picture directors 3. Motion picture producers
   ISBN 978-0-7432-8955-9; 0-7432-8955-2; 978-1-4391-8041-9 ebook; 1-4391-8041-5 ebook
                         LC 2010-27710
This is a biography of the film director and producer Cecil B. DeMille, whose movies include King of Kings and The Ten Commandments.

"Eyman's evocative prose and exhaustive research makes this an engaging and authoritative biography." Publ Wkly
  Includes bibliographical references

De Voto, Avis

As always, Julia; the letters of Julia Child and Avis DeVoto: food, friendship, and the making of a masterpiece. selected and edited by Joan Reardon. Houghton Mifflin Harcourt Pub. Co. 2010 416p il $26   92
   1. Cooks 2. Television personalities 3. Editors 4. Cookbook writers 5. Literary critics 6. Biography, Individual
   ISBN 9780547417714
                         LC 2010-25840
This volume presents "the previously unpublished correspondence between the American chef and her unofficial literary agent from 1952 to 1965, offering insight into such events as Julia's early experiences as a new bride in Paris, her support of her diplomat husband and her views on period politics." (Publisher's note) Index.

"Their letters span a wide range of topics, from cookbooks, menus, recipes, and restaurants to Balzac, sex, goose stuffing, gardening, learning languages, the political climate, Sunday afternoon cocktail parties, and proofreading. Witty, enlightening and entertaining." Publ Wkly

DeVita, Vincent T., Jr., 1935-

★ DeVita-Raeburn, Elizabeth, 1966- The **death** of cancer; after fifty years on the front lines of medicine, a pioneering oncologist reveals why the war on cancer is winnable--and how we can get there. Vincent T. DeVita, Jr., M.D., Elizabeth DeVita-Raeburn. Sarah Crichton Books/Farrar, Straus & Giroux 2015 336 p. 16 plates; illustrations (hardback) $28 **92**
    1. Cancer 2. Cancer -- History 3. Cancer -- Chemotherapy 4. Oncologists -- United States -- Biography
    ISBN 0374135606; 9780374135607

LC 2015011104

This book on cancer, by Vincent T. DeVita and Elizabeth DeVita-Raeburn, is an "illuminating and deeply personal look at the science and the history of one of the world's most formidable diseases. . . . DeVita believes that we're well on our way to curing cancer but that there are things we need to change in order to get there." (Publisher's note)

"Highly recommended for all readers interested in cancer or medical research. Those seeking a more comprehensive and a less intimate chronicle should check out Siddhartha Mukherjee's The Emperor of All Maladies." Library Journal

Dean, James, 1931-1955

★ Gehring, Wes D. **James** Dean: rebel with a cause. Indiana Historical Society Press 2005 303p il (Indiana biography series) $19.95 **92**
    1. Actors
    ISBN 0-87195-181-9

LC 2005-41440

This is a "study of Dean's entire life and an appreciation of his rightful place in film history. Gehring makes the point that audiences have confused the actor with his troubled-teenager roles, and he counters that misimpression with a fuller portrait." Booklist

Includes filmography and bibliographical references

Deford, Frank, 1938-

Deford, Frank. **Over** time; my life as a sportswriter. Frank Deford. Atlantic Monthly Press 2012 354 p. $25 **92**
    1. Autobiographies 2. Sports journalism
    ISBN 0802120156; 9780802120151

In this autobiography sportswriter Frank Deford describes how he "joined 'Sports Illustrated' in 1962. . . . In 1990, he was Editor-in-Chief of 'The National Sports Daily,' one of the most ambitious--and ill-fated--projects in the history of American print journalism. But then, he's endured: writing ten novels, winning an Emmy . . . , [and reading] commentary on NPR's 'Morning Edition.'" (Publisher's note)

Delany family

Delany, Sadie. **Having** our say; the Delany sisters' first 100 years. [by] Sarah and A. Elizabeth Delany; with Amy Hill Hearth. Kodansha Int. 1993 210p il pa $17; $20 **92**
    1. Dentists 2. Centenarians 3. Science teachers 4. Nonfiction writers 5. United States -- Race relations 6. African American women -- Biography
    ISBN 9780385312523; 1-56836-010-X

LC 93-23890

"The combination of the two voices, beautifully blended by Ms. Hearth, evokes an epic history, often cruel and brutal, but always deeply humane in their spirited telling of it." N Y Times Book Rev

Delany, Bessie

Delany, Sadie. **Having** our say; the Delany sisters' first 100 years. [by] Sarah and A. Elizabeth Delany; with Amy Hill Hearth. Kodansha Int. 1993 210p il pa $17; $20 **92**
    1. Dentists 2. Centenarians 3. Science teachers 4. Nonfiction writers 5. United States -- Race relations 6. African American women -- Biography
    ISBN 9780385312523; 1-56836-010-X

LC 93-23890

"The combination of the two voices, beautifully blended by Ms. Hearth, evokes an epic history, often cruel and brutal, but always deeply humane in their spirited telling of it." N Y Times Book Rev

Delany, Mary Granville Pendarves, 1700-1788

Peacock, Molly, 1947- The **paper** garden; an artist begins her life's work at 72. Bloomsbury USA 2010 397p il $30 **92**
    1. Artists 2. Collage 3. Women artists 4. Flowers in art 5. Artists, British 6. Creation (Literary, artistic, etc.) 7. Biography, Individual 8. Creative ability in old age
    ISBN 978-1-60819-523-7; 1-60819-523-6

"The author entwines the story of Delany with private reflections on her own life as an artist and a woman. As Peacock undertook her eccentric quest to discover the life of the woman who created the beautiful paper mosaics that she so admired, she discovered resonant parallels. . . . A lyrical, meditative rumination on art and the blossoming beauty of self that can be the gift of age and love." Kirkus

Includes bibliographical references

Delany, Sadie

Delany, Sadie. **Having** our say; the Delany sisters' first 100 years. [by] Sarah and A. Elizabeth Delany; with Amy Hill Hearth. Kodansha Int. 1993 210p il pa $17; $20 **92**
    1. Dentists 2. Centenarians 3. Science teachers 4. Nonfiction writers 5. United States -- Race relations 6. African American women -- Biography
    ISBN 9780385312523; 1-56836-010-X

LC 93-23890

"The combination of the two voices, beautifully blended by Ms. Hearth, evokes an epic history, often cruel and brutal, but always deeply humane in their spirited telling of it." N Y Times Book Rev

Dempsey, Jack, 1895-1983

Kahn, Roger. A **flame** of pure fire: Jack Dempsey and the roaring '20s. Harcourt Brace & Co. 1999 474p il hardcover o.p. pa $15 **92**

1. Boxers (Persons)

ISBN 0-15-601414-9 pa

LC 99-15382

This biography details the life and career of heavyweight boxer William Harrison "Jack" Dempsey

"In graceful and fluid prose, Kahn presents the con men, gangsters, prostitutes and starlets who inhabited the turbulent, Prohibition-era story of Jack Dempsey." Publ Wkly

Includes bibliographical references

Denevi, Timothy

Denevi, Timothy. **Hyper**; a personal history of ADHD. Timothy Denevi. Simon & Schuster 2014 304 p. (hardback) $26 **92**

1. Attention deficit disorder 2. Attention-deficit-disordered adults -- Biography 3. Attention-deficit hyperactivity disorder -- Complications

ISBN 1476702578; 9781476702575; 9781476702582

LC 2013042085

This book, by Timothy Denevi, is a "memoir about what it's like to be a child with ADHD. . . . [U]sing his own experience as a springboard, Denevi also reveals the origins of ADHD, from the late nineteenth century when hyperactivity was attributed to defective moral conscience, demons, or head trauma, through the twentieth century when food additives, bad parenting, and even government conspiracies were blamed, to the most recent genetic research." (Publisher's note)

"A well-written, easy-to-read journey of one man's experience living with ADHD and the history of the disorder. Parents may see their children in Denevi's story, and adults may see themselves in the childhood accounts that are shared here. A great addition to a large developmental disabilities collection." LJ

Includes bibliographical references (pages 261-274)

Descartes, René, 1596-1650

★ Watson, Richard A. **Cogito** ergo sum: the life of Rene Descartes; {by} Richard Watson. Godine 2002 375p $35 **92**

1. Authors 2. Philosophers 3. Mathematicians

ISBN 1-56792-184-1

LC 2001-40858

"For all of his puckish delight in a juicy anecdote, Watson recognizes and carefully explicates the cultural centrality of Descartes' intellectual legacy. That legacy ensures numerous readers sure to praise a biographer who delivers both the philosopher's cerebral doctrines and his unmistakably human conduct." Booklist

Includes bibliographical references

Devonshire, Deborah Vivien Freeman-Mitford Cavendish, Duchess of, 1920-2014

Thompson, Laura. The **six**; The Lives of the Mitford Sisters. Laura Thompson. St. Martin's Press 2016 400 p. ill., genealogical table (hardcover) $29.99 **92**

1. Sisters 2. Women authors 3. Great Britain -- Biography 4. Sisters -- Great Britain -- Biography 5. Authors, English -- 20th century -- Biography 6. Women authors, English -- 20th century -- Biography

ISBN 9781250099532

LC 2016024061

This book, by Laura Thompson, focuses on "the Mitford sisters: Nancy, Pamela, Diana, Unity, Jessica, and Deborah. Born into country-house privilege in the early years of the 20th century, they became prominent as 'bright young things' in the high society of interwar London. Then, as the shadows crept over 1930s Europe, the stark—and very public—differences in their outlooks came to symbolize the political polarities of a dangerous decade." (Publisher's note)

"Appreciators of biography and social history will find much to engage their interest here." Booklist

Includes bibliographical references and index

DiMaggio, Joe

Kennedy, Kostya. **56**; Joe DiMaggio and the last magic number in sports. Sports Illustrated Books 2011 367p il por $26.95 **92**

1. Baseball players 2. Baseball -- Biography 3. New York Yankees (Baseball team)

ISBN 9781603201773; 1603201777

Recounts Joe DiMaggio's streak during the summer of 1941 and how it found its way into countless lives.

"From the private world inhabited only by DiMaggio and his new bride to Newark barbershops, the playgrounds of Queens, and the streets of DiMaggio's hometown, San Francisco, Kennedy humanizes an immortal accomplishment." Publ Wkly

Includes bibliographical references (p. 351-357) and index.

Diaghilev, Serge, 1872-1929

Scheijen, Sjeng. **Diaghilev**; a life. translated by Jane Hedley-Prôle and S.J. Leinbach. Oxford University Press 2010 552p il **92**

1. Ballet dancers 2. Theatrical producers 3. Biography, Individual

ISBN 0199751498; 9780199751495

LC 2010-02205

Original Dutch edition, 2009; first English translation published 2009 in the United Kingdom

This is a "biography of Serge Diaghilev, founder and impresario of the Ballets Russes." (Publisher's note) Bibliography. Index.

"The parade of great dancers, composers, and artists through Diaghilev's life give this book the sweep of a Russian novel with a fascinating, brilliant, and complex protagonist who, according to the author, lived a very public life, but kept his most intimate feelings hidden." Publ Wkly

Includes bibliographical references

Diana, Princess of Wales, 1961-1997

★ Brown, Tina. The **Diana** chronicles. Doubleday 2007 542p $27.50 **92**

1. Princesses

ISBN 978-0-385-51708-9; 0-385-51708-4

This is a biography of Diana, Princess of Wales.

"Like scraping barnacles off an old hulk, Tina Brown has taken the story of Princess Diana, hosed off layers of hearsay and myth, sifted through tons of accumulated legend, and presented us with a fresh and vividly perceptive portrait." Times Lit Suppl

Includes bibliographical references

Dickens, Charles, 1812-1870

★ Slater, Michael. **Charles** Dickens. Yale University Press 2009 696p il $35   **92**
    1. Authors 2. Novelists 3. Authors, English
    ISBN 978-0-300-11207-8; 0-300-11207-6
               LC 2009-26834

This "biography actually feels somewhat austere: Slater sticks to the known Gradgrindian facts, emphasizes the writing and public performances, seldom goes in for much scene-painting or gratuitous anecdote, and refuses to speculate unduly without evidence. . . . For anybody who wants to know more about this dynamo of Victorian letters, Michael Slater's superb biography is the one to read." Washington Post Book World

Includes bibliographical references (p. 624-626)

Tomalin, Claire. **Charles** Dickens; a life. Claire Tomalin. Penguin Press 2011 527 p. ill., maps $35   **92**
    ISBN 978-1-59420-309-1; 1-59420-309-1
               LC 2011031466

The book presents a biography of author Charles Dickens, with topics including "the familiar story of the idyllic childhood years in Kent . . . the terrible experience of being forced to work in a blacking factory rather than go to school . . . a rapid, improbable journey from obscure clerk to diligent reporter and sketch-writer . . . [and] Dickens' moral and physical decline as he abandoned his wife . . . to pursue and ultimately seduce [actress Nelly Ternan]." (History Today)

Dickinson, Amy

Dickinson, Amy. The **mighty** queens of Freeville; a mother, a daughter, and the town that raised them. Hyperion Books 2009 225p $22.99   **92**
    1. Authors 2. Journalists 3. Advice columnists
    ISBN 978-1-4013-2285-4; 1-4013-2285-9
               LC 2008-26525

"In the summertime of 2002, after spending months living off of her credit cards between freelance writing jobs, Dickinson sent in an audition column to the Chicago Tribune and became the paper's replacement for the late Ann Landers. Here, Dickinson traces her own personal history, as well as the history of her mother's family whose members make up the Mighty Queens of Freeville, N.Y., the small town where Dickinson was raised, and where she raised her own daughter between stints in London; New York City; Washington, D.C.; and Chicago. Dickinson writes with an honesty that is at once folksy and intelligent, and brings to life all of the struggles of raising a child (Dickinson was a single mother) and the challenges and rewards of having a supportive extended family." Publ Wkly

Dickinson, Emily, 1830-1886

★ Gordon, Lyndall. **Lives** like loaded guns; Emily Dickinson and her family's feuds. Viking 2010 491p il $32.95   **92**
    1. Poets 2. Authors 3. Poets, American
    ISBN 978-0-670-02193-2; 0-670-02193-8
               LC 2009-46311

The author argues that "it wasn't heartbreak that kept the poet sequestered, . . . it was epilepsy, a then-uncontrollable and shameful malady. With one stroke, Gordon recasts Dickinson's entire oeuvre. She then reveals the outrageous treachery of the poet's esteemed brother, Austin, who held his unmarried sisters, wife Susan, and their children hostage to his passion for his ambitious mistress, Mabel Loomis Todd, whose scheming husband encouraged the affair. . . . A jolting and utterly intriguing watershed achievement." Booklist

Includes bibliographical references

Didion, Joan

Daugherty, Tracy. The **Last** Love Song; A Biography of Joan Didion. by Tracy Daugherty. St. Martin's Press 2015 672 p. 8 plates; ills.; portraits (hardcover) $35   **92**
    1. American authors
    ISBN 9781250010025; 1250010020
               LC 2015017162

This book, by Tracy Daugherty, "delves deep into the life of distinguished American author and journalist Joan Didion. . . . Daugherty takes readers on a journey back through time, following a young Didion in Sacramento, through to her adult life as a writer interviewing those who know and knew her personally, while maintaining a respectful distance from the reclusive literary great." (Publisher's note)

"A strong biography. Who won't want to read this "hot" book?" LJ

★ Didion, Joan, 1934- The **year** of magical thinking. Knopf 2005 227p $23.95   **92**
    1. Authors 2. Novelists 3. Journalists 4. Essayists 5. Screenwriters 6. Nonfiction writers 7. Biography, Individual
    ISBN 1-4000-4314-X
               LC 2005-45132

"Several days before Christmas 2003, John Gregory Dunne and Joan Didion saw their only daughter, Quintana, fall ill with what seemed at first flu, then pneumonia, then complete septic shock. She was put into an induced coma and placed on life support. Days later—the night before New Year's Eve—the Dunnes were just sitting down to dinner after visiting the hospital when John Gregory Dunne suffered a massive and fatal coronary. In a second, [a] . . . partnership of forty years was over. Four weeks later, their daughter pulled through. Two months after that, arriving at LAX, she collapsed and underwent six hours of brain surgery at UCLA Medical Center to relieve a massive hematoma. This book is Didion's attempt to make sense of the 'weeks and then months that cut loose any fixed idea I ever had about death, about illness . . . about marriage and children and memory . . . about the shallowness of sanity, about life itself.'" (Publisher's note)

The author "chronicles the year following the death of her husband, fellow writer John Gregory Dunne, from a massive heart attack on December 30, 2003, while the couple's only daughter, Quintana, lay unconscious in a nearby hospital suffering from pneumonia and septic shock. . . . This is an indispensable addition to Didion's body of work and a lyrical, disciplined entry in the annals of mourning literature." Publ Wkly

Dillard, Annie

Dillard, Annie. An **American** childhood. Harper & Row 1987 255p hardcover o.p. pa $14   **92**

1. Poets 2. Authors 3. Essayists 4. Literary critics 5. Writers on nature

ISBN 0-06-091518-8 pa

LC 87-45042

In this autobiography, Dillard presents as account of her life from her childhood in Pittsburgh until her entrance into college

"Dillard's luminous prose painlessly captures the pain of growing up in this wonderful evocation of childhood. . . . The events of childhood often loom larger than life; the magic of Dillard's writing is that she sets down typical childhood happenings with their original immediacy and force." Publ Wkly

Diller, Phyllis, 1917-2012

Diller, Phyllis. **Like** a lampshade in a whorehouse; my life in comedy. [by] Phyllis Diller with Richard Buskin. J.P. TarcherPenguin 2005 266p il $24.95; pa $14.95   **92**

1. Comedians

ISBN 1-585-42396-3; 1-585-42476-5 pa

LC 2004-58520

This is an autobiography by the American comedian.

"Brash comedy and a surprising bitterness fuel this unsparing account of Diller's drive to make it big." Publ Wkly

Dinesen, Isak, 1885-1962

★ Thurman, Judith. **Isak** Dinesen; the life of a storyteller. St. Martin's Press 1982 495p il hardcover o.p. pa $18   **92**

1. Authors 2. Novelists 3. Memoirists 4. Short story writers

ISBN 0-312-13525-4 pa

LC 82-5573

This biography traces Dinesen's life from her childhood in Denmark through her years in Kenya and her return to Denmark to focus on her literary career

"With great insight and a novelist's gift for nuance and narrative sweep, Thurman shows the extraordinary degree to which Dinesen's life and art meshed. In addition, Thurman's sensitive criticism of Dinesen's work reveals exceptional artistry in its own right." Booklist

Includes bibliographical references

Disney, Walt, 1901-1966

Gabler, Neal. **Walt** Disney; the triumph of the American imagination. Neal Gabler. Alfred A. Knopf 2006 xx, 851 p.p 32 plates : illustrations $23   **92**

1. Walt Disney Company 2. Disney, Walt, 1901-1966 3. Animators -- United States -- Biography

ISBN 067943822X; 0679757473; 9780679438229;

9780679757474

LC 2006045257

This book, by Neal Gabler, presents a biography of the American entertainer Walt Disney. "Gabler shows us the young Walt Disney breaking free of a heartland childhood of discipline and deprivation and making his way to Hollywood. We see the visionary, whose desire for escape . . . led him to the reinvention of animation. . . . Gabler also reveals a wounded, lonely, and often disappointed man, who, despite worldwide success, was plagued with financial problems much of his life." (Publisher's note)

"Although Gabler focuses on corporate matters at the expense of critical treatment of the films, he presents a balanced treatment of the man and his achievements, realistically assessing Disney's considerable impact and offering insight into the hidden, restless soul who constantly challenged himself, risking the financial stability of his empire more than once in his unceasing pursuit of his dreams." Booklist

Includes bibliographical references (p. [805]-815) and index

Dixon, Willie

Inaba, Mitsutoshi, 1964- **Willie** Dixon; preacher of the blues. Scarecrow Press 2011 xxxi, 445p il (African American cultural theory and heritage) $55; ebook $57.99   **92**

1. Singers 2. Blues musicians 3. African American musicians 4. Blues music -- History and criticism

ISBN 978-0-8108-6993-6; 978-0-8108-6994-3 ebook

LC 2009033237

"This exhaustive biography and analysis of Dixon's music, the most comprehensive study of Dixon's life and work available, features extensive references, many details drawn from interviews, an analysis of Dixon's composition and studio methods, and a complete discography. Inaba . . . tells the story of Dixon's life, from his 1915 birth in Vicksburg, Mississippi, through his childhood in an impoverished area blemished further by racism, to his adulthood in Chicago as a boxer and musician. . . . From the Big Three Trio to Dixon's highly productive years with Chess Records to finally, his own Blues Factory studio, Inaba traces and comments on the significance of Dixon's lasting imprint on music." Publ Wkly

Includes discography and bibliographical references

Dolan, Timothy Michael

Boyle, Christina. An **American** Cardinal; the biography of Cardinal Timothy Dolan. Christina Boyle. St. Martin's Press 2014 304 p. illustrations (hardcover) $27.99   **92**

1. Cardinals 2. Cardinals -- United States -- Biography

ISBN 1250032873; 9781250032874

LC 2014028470

Author Christina Boyle presents "a book about power and the Roman Catholic church today framed by the life of a man who might someday become the first American pope. Timothy Michael Dolan was born in Maplewood, Missouri in 1950. In 2009, he was made Archbishop of New York. Several months later he was elevated to cardinal. There were clear signs that the ailing Pope Benedict XVI saw him as a bright hope for the future." (Publisher's note)

"All readers, not just Roman Catholics, will be inspired by this story of a Midwestern boy-turned-prominent figure and leaders can learn a lot from his handling of opposition, conflict, and the press." LJ

Domino, Fats, 1928-

Coleman, Rick. **Blue** Monday; Fats Domino and the lost dawn of rock 'n' roll. Da Capo 2006 364p il map hardcover o.p. pa $15.95   **92**

1. Singers 2. Pianists 3. Rock musicians 4. African American musicians

ISBN 0-306-81491-9; 978-0-306-81531-7 pa; 0-306-81531-1 pa

Coleman has crafted a "biography of Fats Domino, drawing on new interviews with the pianist himself. From his childhood in New Orleans through the early days of rock'n'roll, when he endured travel difficulties in the segregated South and frequent riots at his concerts, Fats remained a shy but demanding performer and personality. A homesick father who seemed to cherish his family, Fats was also a hard-drinking womanizer, and Coleman tells his story with compassion and honesty up to Fats's survival of Hurricane Katrina in his Ninth Ward home. His argument that rock'n'roll sprung from Fats and the New Orleans sound is hard to dispute, as Fats was playing long before others now credited with starting the revolution. Despite the occasional slips into fandom, this is an essential purchase for any library collecting the history of rock'n'roll." Libr J

Includes bibliographical references

Dostoyevsky, Fyodor, 1821-1881

★ Frank, Joseph. **Dostoevsky**; a writer in his time. edited by Mary Petrusewicz. Princeton University Press 2009 959p il $35   **92**

1. Authors 2. Novelists 3. Authors, Russian 4. Short story writers

ISBN 978-0-691-12819-1

LC 2009-1418

An abridged edition of the author's five volume work published 1976-2002

"Frank displays a brilliant command of Dostoyevsky's heroic endeavors, and his biography reads readily, especially for such a scholarly work." Libr J

Includes bibliographical references and index

Doty, James R.

Doty, James R. **Into** the Magic Shop; A Neurosurgeon's Quest to Discover the Mysteries of the Brain and the Secrets of the Heart. by James R. Doty MD (Author) Penguin Group USA 2016 288 p. illustrations $26   **92**

1. Altruism 2. Surgeons 3. Compassion 4. Mind and body 5. Nervous system

ISBN 1594632987; 9781594632983

In this memoir, by James R. Doty, "Growing up in the high desert of California, Jim Doty was poor, with an alcoholic father and a mother chronically depressed. . . . Today he is the director of the . . . (CCARE) at Stanford University. But back then his life was at a dead end until at twelve he wandered into a magic shop looking for a plastic thumb. Instead, he met Ruth, a woman who taught him a series of

exercises to ease his own suffering and manifest his greatest desires." (Publisher's note)

"An optimistic and engagingly well-told life story that incorporates scientific investigation into its altruistic message." Kirkus

Doty, Mark

Doty, Mark, 1953- **Dog** years; a memoir. HarperCollins Publishers 2007 215p $23.95   **92**

1. Poets 2. Authors 3. Dogs 4. Essayists

ISBN 0-06-117100-X; 978-0-06-117100-0

LC 2006-46491

"In a memoir, the poet Mark Doty meditates on grief and the death of his dogs." (N Y Times Book Rev)

The author "celebrates the 16 lovely years his two beloved 70-pound Labs, Beau and Arden, gave him. . . . Against a backdrop of devastating human loss, both personal (the death of his partner) and public (9/11), Doty bears witness to the inexorable decline of his beloved retrievers. . . . Poignant, intelligent, and quite simply superb." Libr J

Doughty, Caitlin

Doughty, Caitlin. **Smoke** gets in your eyes; and other lessons from the crematory. Caitlin Doughty. W W Norton & Co Inc. 2014 272 p. (hardcover) $24.95   **92**

1. Cremation 2. Autobiographies 3. Undertakers and undertaking 4. Undertakers and undertaking -- Anecdotes 5. Undertakers and undertaking -- United States -- Biography

ISBN 0393240231; 9780393240238

LC 2014017294

This book describes how author Caitlin Doughty "took a job at a crematory, turning morbid curiosity into her life's work. Thrown into a profession of gallows humor and vivid characters (both living and very dead), Caitlin learned to navigate the secretive culture of those who care for the deceased. 'Smoke Gets in Your Eyes' tells an unusual coming-of-age story full of bizarre encounters and unforgettable scenes." (Publisher's note)

"Not shying away from candid descriptions of corpses, cremation, and putrefaction, Doughty— . . . details postmortem proceedings not to repulse but to reveal our modern society's 'death denial.'" Booklist

Includes bibliographical references

Douglas, Marjory Stoneman

Davis, Jack E. An **Everglades** providence; Marjory Stoneman Douglas and the American environmental century. University of Georgia Press 2009 758p il map $34.95   **92**

1. Authors 2. Novelists 3. Conservationists 4. Nature conservation 5. Centenarians 6. Everglades (Fla.) 7. Writers on nature 8. Short story writers 9. Biography, Individual 10. Everglades (Fla.) -- Environmental conditions

ISBN 0-8203-3071-X; 978-0-8203-3071-6

LC 2008-49073

This book presents a biography of Marjory Stoneman Douglas, "a suffragist, a lifetime feminist and supporter of the ERA, a champion of social justice, and an author of diverse literary talent. She came of age literally and professionally during the American environmental century, the century in which Americans mobilized an unprecedented popular movement to counter the equally unprecedented liberties they had taken in exploiting, polluting, and destroying the natural world." (Publisher's note)

This is "both a portrait of one of the 20th century's most important environmental figures and a history of Florida's Everglades. The long-lived Douglas (1890-1998) is best known for the classic The Everglades: River of Grass and her tireless efforts to preserve that region. But she was also a lifelong feminist and social activist who worked to advance human rights. . . . In addition to the rich detail and documentation of Douglas's life, Davis offers an impressive look at America during Douglas's lifetime and the growth of America's environmental movement." Libr J

Includes bibliographical references

Douglass, Frederick, 1817?-1895

★ Douglass, Frederick, 1818-1895. **Autobiographies**. Library of Am. 1994 1126p $35; pa $13.95 **92**

1. Slaves 2. Authors 3. Abolitionists 4. Memoirists 5. African Americans -- Biography
ISBN 0-940450-79-8; 1-883011-30-2 pa

LC 93-24168

"This one volume containing Douglass's seminal works is highly recommended for black history collections." Libr J

Includes bibliographical references

Douglass, Frederick, 1818-1895. **My** bondage and my freedom; edited with an introduction and notes by John David Smith. Penguin Bks. 2003 lx, 366p (Penguin Classics) pa $12 **92**

1. Slaves 2. Authors 3. Abolitionists 4. Memoirists 5. African Americans -- Biography
ISBN 0-14-043918-8

LC 2002-28992

First published 1855 by Orton & Mulligan

In this autobiography Douglass tells of his life as a slave and his early years in the abolitionist movement.

Includes bibliographical references

Douglass, Frederick, 1818-1895. **Narrative** of the life of Frederick Douglass, an American slave; written by himself; edited with an introduction by Houston A. Baker, Jr. Penguin Bks 1982 159p il pa $10 **92**

1. Slaves 2. Authors 3. Abolitionists 4. Memoirists 5. African Americans -- Biography
ISBN 0-14-039012-X

LC 82-5371

Originally published 1845 by the Boston Anti-slavery office

"Frederick Douglass became famous as a slave who escaped to the North and spent his lifetime in the abolitionist movement. His 'Narrative,' one of three autobiographical works written by the self-taught slave, is the story of his life up to his escape to freedom." Libr J

Includes bibliographical references

Picturing Frederick Douglass; An Illustrated Biography of the Nineteenth Century's Most Photo-

graphed American. John Stauffer, Zoe Trodd, and Celeste-Marie Bernier. W W Norton & Co Inc 2015 320 p. illustrations (some color) $49.95 **92**

1. Abolitionists -- Biography 2. Abolitionists -- United States -- Biography 3. African American abolitionists -- Biography
ISBN 0871404680; 9780871404688

LC 2015020546

This biography, by John Stauffer, Zoe Trodd, and Celeste-Marie Bernier, focuses on "Frederick Douglass (1818-1895), the ex-slave turned leading abolitionist, eloquent orator, and seminal writer whose fiery speeches transformed him into one of the most renowned and popular agitators of his age. Now, . . . Douglass emerges as a leading pioneer in photography, both as a stately subject and as a prescient theorist." (Publisher's note)

"The authors have pieced together an illuminating life portrait without extraneous biographical material, focusing intensely on their subject's belief in the strength of photographs." Kirkus

Includes bibliographical references and index

Downs, Paul

Downs, Paul. **Boss** Life; Surviving My Own Small Business. Paul Downs. Penguin Group USA 2015 368 p. black and white illustrations $26.95 **92**

1. New business enterprises 2. Cabinetmakers -- United States 3. Small business -- United States -- Management 4. New business enterprises -- United States -- Management
ISBN 0399172335; 9780399172335

LC 2015016068

This book, by Paul Downs, "paints an honest portrait of a real business, with a real boss, a real set of employees, and the real challenges they face. Fresh out of college in 1986, Downs opened his first business, a small company that builds custom furniture. In 1987, he hired his first employee. That's when things got complicated. As his enterprise began to grow, he had to learn about management, cash flow, taxes, and so much more." (Publisher's note)

"This is an invaluable look into operational details for anyone considering starting a business or caught up in the struggle of owning and running one." Booklist

Doyle, Arthur Conan Sir, 1859-1930

★ Doyle, Arthur Conan. **Arthur** Conan Doyle; his life in letters. edited by Jon Lellenberg, Daniel Stashower & Charles Foley. Harper Press 2007 706p il $37.95 **92**

1. Authors 2. Novelists 3. Authors, Scottish 4. Mystery writers
ISBN 978-1-59420-135-6; 1-59420-135-8

LC 2007-14692

This volume presents the selected correspondence of the British author at various points during his life.

"This will be essential reading for all fans of Conan Doyle and his sleuth." Publ Wkly

Jaher, David. The **witch** of lime street; séance, seduction, and Houdini in the spirit world. David

Jaher. Crown Publishers 2015 448 p. illustrations (alk. paper) $28 **92**

1. Spiritualism 2. Spiritualists -- United States -- Biography 3. Women mediums -- United States -- Biography 4. Spiritualism -- United States -- History -- 20th century

ISBN 0307451062; 9780307451064

LC 2015009392

In this book, by David Jaher, "in 1924, the pretty wife of a distinguished Boston surgeon came to embody the raging national debate over Spiritualism. . . . Reporters dubbed her the blonde Witch of Lime Street, but she was known to her followers simply as Margery. . . . Margery was the best hope for the psychic practice to be empirically verified. Her supernatural gifts beguiled four of the judges. There was only one left to convince...the acclaimed escape artist, Harry Houdini." (Publisher's note)

"Through a combination of feminine seduction and illusionist skill that even Houdini admired, Crandon became the one psychic to almost win the respect of the scientific community and outshine Houdini as an entertainer. Jaher's narrative style is as engaging as his character portraits are colorful. Together, they bring a bygone age and its defining spiritual obsessions roaring to life. Fascinating, sometimes thrilling, reading." Kirkus

Includes bibliographical references and index

Du Bois, W. E. B. (William Edward Burghardt), 1868-1963

★ Lewis, David Levering. **W.E.B.** Du Bois; a biography. Henry Holt and Co. 2009 893p hardcover o.p. pa $25 **92**

1. Authors 2. Novelists 3. Historians 4. Editors 5. Essayists 6. Sociologists 7. Nonfiction writers 8. Civil rights activists 9. African Americans -- Biography 10. African Americans -- Civil rights

ISBN 978-0-8050-8769-7; 0-8050-8769-9; 978-0-8050-8805-2 pa; 0-8050-8805-9 pa

LC 2008-696

Condensed and updated edition of a 2 volume set, first published 1993-2000

This is a biography of the African American scholar who helped bring forth the civil rights movement.

Includes bibliographical references

Dubus, Andre, 1959-

Dubus, Andre, 1959- **Townie**; a memoir. [by] Andre Dubus III. W. W. Norton & Co. 2011 387p $25.95 **92**

1. Authors 2. Novelists 3. Authors, American 4. Short story writers 5. Biography, Individual

ISBN 978-0-393-06466-7; 0-393-06466-2

LC 2010038029

This is a memoir by the author of Bluesman (1993) and The Garden of Last Days (2008). "Young Andre and his siblings, two sisters and a brother, grew up in a series of Massachusetts mill towns after their father left their mother for one of his . . . young students." (N Y Times (Late N Y Ed))

"The author grew up poor in Massachusetts mill towns, the oldest of four children of the celebrated short-story writer Andre Dubus (1936-1999), who abandoned the family in 1968 to pursue a young student. Beautifully written and

bursting with life, the book tells the story of a boy struggling to express his 'hurt and rage,' first through violence aimed at school and barroom bullies and ultimately through the power of words." Kirkus

Dulles, Allen Welsh, 1893-1969

Grose, Peter. **Gentleman** spy; the life of Allen Dulles. University of Mass. Press 1996 641p il pa $19.95 **92**

1. Lawyers 2. Diplomats 3. Government officials 4. Intelligence service officials 5. United States -- Central Intelligence Agency

ISBN 1-55849-044-2; 978-1-55849-044-4

LC 96-19010

First published 1994 by Houghton Mifflin

This biography of the CIA director under Eisenhower and Kennedy "renders the interplay of person and public event and allows readers to enter the dark world of US-sponsored terror and covert paramilitary operations. . . . Grose sets forth in fascinating and often unfamiliar detail the spectacular CIA covert operations: in Iran, Guatemala, Indonesia; the U2 incident; the Bay of Pigs." Choice

Talbot, David. The **Devil's** Chessboard; Allen Dulles and the Rise of America's Secret Government. by David Talbot. HarperCollins 2015 704 p. illustrations $29.99 **92**

1. United States. Central Intelligence Agency

ISBN 0062276166; 9780062276162

LC 2015487367

This book, by David Talbot, is a "portrait of Allen Dulles, the man who transformed the CIA into the most powerful--and secretive--colossus in Washington. . . . Drawing on . . . U.S. government documents, U.S. and European intelligence sources, the personal correspondence and journals of Allen Dulles's wife and mistress, and exclusive interviews with the children of prominent CIA officials . . . Talbot reveals the underside of one of America's most powerful and influential figures." (Publisher's note)

Includes bibliographical references and index

Duncan, Isadora, 1877-1927

Duncan, Isadora, 1877-1927. **My** life; Isadora Duncan; introduction by Joan Acocella; with a prefatory essay by Doree Duncan. Liveright paperback ed. Liveright Publishing Corporation, a division of W. W. Norton & Company 2013 368 p. (paperback) $17.95 **92**

1. Dance 2. Women dancers -- Biography

ISBN 0871403188; 9780871403186

LC 2012049575

This book, by Isadora Duncan, presents the autobiography of "the choreographer and dancer . . . [who] not only revolutionized dance in the twentieth century but blazed a path for other visionaries who would follow in her wake. . . . From her early enchantment with classical music and poetry to her great successes abroad, to her sensational love affairs and headline-grabbing personal tragedies, Duncan's story is a dramatic one." (Publisher's note)

Dunne, John Gregory, 1932-2003

★ Didion, Joan, 1934- The **year** of magical thinking. Knopf 2005 227p $23.95 **92**
1. Authors 2. Novelists 3. Journalists 4. Essayists 5. Screenwriters 6. Nonfiction writers 7. Biography, Individual
ISBN 1-4000-4314-X

LC 2005-45132

"Several days before Christmas 2003, John Gregory Dunne and Joan Didion saw their only daughter, Quintana, fall ill with what seemed at first flu, then pneumonia, then complete septic shock. She was put into an induced coma and placed on life support. Days later—the night before New Year's Eve—the Dunnes were just sitting down to dinner after visiting the hospital when John Gregory Dunne suffered a massive and fatal coronary. In a second, [a] . . . partnership of forty years was over. Four weeks later, their daughter pulled through. Two months after that, arriving at LAX, she collapsed and underwent six hours of brain surgery at UCLA Medical Center to relieve a massive hematoma. This book is Didion's attempt to make sense of the 'weeks and then months that cut loose any fixed idea I ever had about death, about illness . . . about marriage and children and memory . . . about the shallowness of sanity, about life itself.'" (Publisher's note)

The author "chronicles the year following the death of her husband, fellow writer John Gregory Dunne, from a massive heart attack on December 30, 2003, while the couple's only daughter, Quintana, lay unconscious in a nearby hospital suffering from pneumonia and septic shock. . . . This is an indispensable addition to Didion's body of work and a lyrical, disciplined entry in the annals of mourning literature." Publ Wkly

Dylan, Bob, 1941-

Bell, Ian. **Once** upon a time; the lives of Bob Dylan. Ian Bell. Pegasus 2013 590 p. $35; $17.95 **92**
1. Musicians -- United States 2. Singers -- United States -- Biography
ISBN 1605984817; 1605986275; 1780574568; 1780575734; 9781605984810; 9781605986272; 9781780574561; 9781780575735

LC 2012545195

"In Once upon a time, award-winning writer Ian Bell draws together the tangled strands of the many lives of Bob Dylan in all their contradictory brilliance. For the first time, the laureate of modern America is set in his entire context: musical, historical, literary, political and personal." (Publisher description)

"This is best described as a fully formed emotional biography, a fascinating read about an artist who, to this day, defends his right of 'artistic autonomy,' refusing to be anyone but himself, whoever that may be." Booklist

Lives of Bob Dylan

Dylan, Bob, 1941- **Chronicles**. v1 Simon & Schuster 2004 293p v1 il $24 **92**
1. Singers 2. Folk musicians 3. Rock musicians 4. Songwriters 5. Biography, Individual
ISBN 0-7432-2815-4

LC 2004-564

This is the first installment of a projected three-volume autobiography by the American singer and songwriter.

"This book will stand as a record of a young man's self-education, as contagious in its frank excitement as the letters of John Keats and as sincere in its ramble as Jack Kerouac's On the Road, to which Dylan frequently refers. A person of Dylan's stature could have gotten away with far less; that he has been so thoughtful in the creation of this book is a measure of his talents, and a gift to his fans." Publ Wkly

Brown, Donald. **Bob** Dylan; American troubadour. Donald Brown. Rowman & Littlefield Publishers, Inc. 2014 308 p. (Tempo : a Rowman & Littlefield music series on rock, pop, and culture) (cloth : alk. paper) $40 **92**
1. Musicians -- United States
ISBN 0810884208; 9780810884205; 9780810884212

LC 2013044394

This biography, by Daniel Brown, "follows [Bob] Dylan chronologically through his career, from young troubadour in Greenwich Village who unwittingly became the spokesman of a generation through his controversial electric transformation to the 'rural glory' of the Basement Tapes to his richly creative Blood on the Tracks period to his born-again phase to his current renaissance as a rock elder and cultural force." (Booklist)

"While it covers familiar territory, the book's strength is a thorough assessment of Dylan's career, album by album, song by song." LJ

Includes bibliographical references, discography, and index

Dyson, Freeman J.

Schewe, Phillip F. **Maverick** Genius; The Pioneering Odyssey of Freeman Dyson. Phillip F. Schewe. St Martins Pr 2013 352 p. $27.99 **92**
1. Physicists -- Biography 2. Mathematicians -- Biography
ISBN 0312642350; 9780312642358

Author Phillip F. Schewe presents a biography of Freeman J. Dyson. "Schewe examines the life of a man whose accomplishments have shaped our world in many ways," focusing on theoretical physics "from quantum physics to national defense, from space to biotechnology . . . Many of his [Dyson's] colleagues, including Nobelists Steven Weinberg and Frank Wilczek, as well as his wives and his children, Esther and George Dyson, have been interviewed for this book." (Publisher's note)

Earhart, Amelia, 1898-1937

Winters, Kathleen C. **Amelia** Earhart; the turbulent life of an American icon. Palgrave Macmillan 2010 242p il map $25 **92**
1. Air pilots 2. Missing persons 3. Women air pilots 4. Memoirists
ISBN 978-0-230-61669-1

LC 2010-20026

"With erudite analysis of everything from Earhart's flying to her marriage and longtime financial support of her parents and sister, Winters proves there is still much to learn about this American icon." Booklist

Includes bibliographical references

Earp, Wyatt, 1848-1929

Barra, Allen. **Inventing** Wyatt Earp; his life and many legends. Carroll & Graf Pubs. 1998 432p hardcover o.p. pa $15.95   **92**
1. Sheriffs
ISBN 0-7867-0685-6 pa
"Barra is at his best in describing the efforts of assorted Hollywood icons, including John Ford, John Sturges, and Kevin Costner, to depict the 'real' Earp." Booklist

Tefertiller, Casey. **Wyatt** Earp; the life behind the legend. Wiley 1997 403p $45; pa $19.95   **92**
1. Sheriffs
ISBN 0-471-18967-7; 0-471-28362-2 pa
LC 97-2932
"An engrossing, satisfying inspection of a quintessential figure in American popular culture." Booklist
Includes bibliographical references

Ebadi, Shririn, 1947-

Ebadi, Shirin, 1947- **Until** We Are Free; My Fight for Human Rights in Iran. by Shirin Ebadi. Random House Inc 2016 304 p. $27   **92**
1. Human rights 2. Women -- Iran 3. Women lawyers 4. Human rights advocacy 5. Iran -- Social conditions
ISBN 0812998871; 9780812998870
LC 2015027147
In this book, Iranian human rights lawyer Shirin Ebadi "tells her story of courage and defiance in the face of a government out to destroy her, her family, and her mission: to bring justice to the people and the country she loves. For years the Islamic Republic tried to intimidate Ebadi. . . . Despite finding herself living under circumstances reminiscent of a spy novel, nothing could keep Ebadi from speaking out and standing up for human dignity." (Publisher's note)
"The captivating and candid story of a woman who took on the Iranian government and survived, despite every attempt to make her fail." Kirkus

Ebert, Roger

Ebert, Roger, 1942-2013. **Life** itself; a memoir. Grand Central Pub. 2011 436p il $27.99; ebook $12.99   **92**
1. Autobiographies 2. Motion picture industry 3. Motion pictures -- History and criticism 4. Writers on film 5. Motion picture critics
ISBN 978-0-446-58497-5; 978-0-446-58498-2 ebook
LC 2011022442
The book presents an autobiography by newspaper film reviewer Roger Ebert. It is "an episodic tour of Ebert's memory cabinet, one three-or-four page jot at a time, from his upbringing and his college opportunities to his days as a cub reporter in Chicago, his decision to quit drinking and join AA in 1979, [and] his screenwriting with Russ Meyer. . . . [Ebert] spends many chapters recalling the dinners and interviews he had with Martin Scorsese, Werner Horzog, Robert Mitchum, Woody Allen etc. Naturally, he also ruminates at length about his testy relationship with TV co-host Gene Siskel." (Sight & Sound)
"Ebert illuminates and assesses his life with the same insight and clarity that mark his acclaimed movie reviews." Booklist

Eckford, Elizabeth, 1942-

Margolick, David. **Elizabeth** and Hazel; two women of Little Rock. Yale University Press 2011 310p il $26   **92**
1. School integration 2. Arkansas -- Race relations 3. Little Rock (Ark.) -- Race relations 4. Central High School (Little Rock, Ark.) 5. School integration -- Arkansas -- Little Rock -- History -- 20th century
ISBN 978-0-300-14193-1; 0-300-14193-9
LC 2011-14101
"When Elizabeth Eckford braved the gauntlet of white hecklers leading to the newly desegregated Central High School in Little Rock, Arkansas, in 1957, photographers captured her image and that of the angry young white woman behind her. Elizabeth, the stoic, and Hazel Bryan, the tormentor, were frozen as icons. Elizabeth was part of the Little Rock Nine, the black teens who became the targets of race hatred as well as national and international inspirations. . . . Margolick draws on interviews and press reports of the time to present a very nuanced analysis of how Elizabeth and Hazel were affected by the scene that made them famous. . . . A complex look at two women at the center of a historic moment." Booklist
Includes bibliographical references

Edelman, Marian Wright, 1939-

Edelman, Marian Wright. **Lanterns**; a memoir of mentors. HarperPerennial 2000 xxi, 208p il pa $14   **92**
1. Mentoring 2. Social welfare leaders 3. Children's rights advocates
ISBN 0-06-095859-6
LC 00-33430
First published 1999 by Beacon Press
"Throughout this absorbing memoir, Edelman's voice resounds with spirituality, a reliance on her faith, and a belief in equality." Booklist
Includes bibliographical references

Edge, Rosalie

Furmansky, Dyana Z. **Rosalie** Edge, hawk of mercy; the activist who saved nature from the conservationists. [by] Dyana Z. Furmansky; with a foreword by Bill McKibben & an afterword by Roland C. Clement. University of Georgia Press 2009 312p il $28.95   **92**
1. Suffragists 2. Conservationists 3. Feminists
ISBN 978-0-8203-3341-0; 0-8203-3341-7
LC 2009-8551
The book discusses "Mabel Rosalie Barrow Edge (1877–1962) [who was] . . . a conservation activist . . . [and t]he founder of the Emergency Conservation Committee (ECC). . . . Using previously unavailable primary sources, Dyana Z. Furmansky offers an engaging portrait of Edge as activist while piecing together the story of Edge as a daughter, wife, mother, friend, and colleague. . . . Furmansky notes that Edge's writings, public testimony, and sometimes-assertive personal style inspired others to see and care about nature as she did. Furmansky looks for clues to Edge's commitment to nature in her privileged New York childhood, in her experiences abroad, and in her engagement with the suffrage movement. Edge's activism began after she read a 1929

pamphlet called 'Crisis in Conservation,' written in part by Willard Van Name, who would become Edge's mentor and financial backer. This pamphlet inspired Edge to found the ECC." (Journal of American History)

A biography of the conservationist and suffragette who "founded the Hawk Mountain Sanctuary and fought hard for the Olympic National Park. Clearly relishing every moment of Edge's remarkable life, Furmansky vividly enriches environmental history with her inspiring portrait of this indomitable champion of the wild." Booklist

Includes bibliographical references

Edison, Thomas A. (Thomas Alva), 1847-1931

Degraaf, Leonard. **Edison** and the rise of innovation; Leonard DeGraaf; foreword by Bill Gates. Sterling Signature 2013 xxvii, 244 p.p color illustrations; map $29.95 **92**
1. Inventions -- History 2. Inventors -- United States -- Biography
ISBN 1402767366; 9781402767364
LC 2013443854

This book, by Leonard DeGraaf, "presents, in intimate detail, the man who helped engineer the modern world. One of history's most prolific inventors, and perhaps America's first celebrity, Thomas Alva Edison did more than bring incandescent light into every household and industry; he created a world-renowned brand, raised capital to support research and business, and pursued patents for his 1,000+ inventions." (Publisher's note)

"A worthy and visually pleasing mid-length biography recommended for those who prefer Edison the businessman and social phenomenon to the scientist. With a foreword by Bill Gates." LJ

Includes bibliographical references and index

★ Israel, Paul. **Edison**; a life of invention. Wiley 1998 552p il $50; pa $18.95 **92**
1. Inventors
ISBN 0-471-52942-7; 0-471-36270-0 pa
LC 98-10105

This biography focuses on Edison's technical work, experiments, and business dealings

"Dozens of facsimiles of his original drawings are reproduced, which fortify the impression of Edison's meticulousness, as do Israel's accounts of his business ventures." Booklist

Includes bibliographical references

Edmundson, Mark, 1952-

Edmundson, Mark. **Why** football matters; my education in the game. Mark Edmundson. The Penguin Press 2014 240 p. $26.95 **92**
1. Football players 2. Father-son relationship 3. Fathers and sons 4. Football players -- United States -- Biography
ISBN 1594205752; 9781594205750
LC 2014009726

"When Mark Edmundson's son began to play organized football, and proved to be very good at it, Edmundson had to come to terms with just what he thought about the game. Doing so took him back to his own childhood, when as a shy, soft boy growing up in a blue-collar Boston suburb in the

sixties, he went out for the high school football team. 'Why Football Matters' is the story of what happened to Edmundson when he tried to make himself into a football player." (Publisher's note)

"Beautifully written and impressively thought out, this smart memoir should appeal to a wide audience." LJ

Edward I, King of England, 1272-1307

A **Great** & Terrible King; Edward I and the Forging of Britain. by Marc Morris. W W Norton & Co Inc 2015 480 p. 8 plates; color ills., maps $29.95 **92**
1. Great Britain -- Kings and rulers 2. Great Britain -- History -- 0-1066 3. Biography, Individual 4. Great Britain -- History -- Edward I, 1272-1307
ISBN 1605986844; 9781605986845

This biography, by Marc Morris, depicts the life of the English king known as "Longshanks." Edward I "defeated and killed the famous Simon de Montfort in battle; travelled across Europe to the Holy Land on crusade; conquered Wales, extinguishing forever its native rulers, and constructed [castles] at Conwy, Harlech, Beaumaris and Caernarfon." (Publisher's note)

"Highly recommended for scholars and generalists alike interested in the Middle Ages." LJ

Edward III, King of England, 1312-1377

Ormrod, W. Mark. **Edward** III; W. Mark Ormrod. Yale University Press 2012 xx, 721 p.p (cl : alk. paper) $45.00 **92**
1. Great Britain -- Kings and rulers -- Biography 2. Great Britain -- History -- Edward III, 1327-1377 3. Great Britain -- Politics and government -- 1327-1377
ISBN 0300119100; 9780300119107
LC 2011013536

In this biography of Edward III of England, it was the author's intent to demonstrate "that Edward's personality and ambitions remained absolutely at the heart of English royal policy for at least forty years, and that his skills as a politician shaped a unique political culture that brought about a long period of domestic stability within England." (Times Literary Supplement)

Includes bibliographical references and index.

Edward VII, King of Great Britain, 1841-1910

★ Ridley, Jane. The **heir** apparent; a life of Edward VII, the playboy prince. Jane Ridley. Random House Inc 2013 752 p. (alk. paper) $35 **92**
1. Great Britain -- Kings and rulers 2. Great Britain -- Kings and rulers -- Biography 3. Great Britain -- History -- Edward VII, 1901-1910
ISBN 1400062551; 9780812994759; 9781400062553
LC 2013002597

This biography, by Jane Ridley, "chronicles the . . . life of Queen Victoria's firstborn son. . . . Born Prince Albert Edward . . . the future King Edward VII had a . . . reputation for debauchery. . . . Yet by the time he died . . . he had proven himself a deft diplomat, hardworking head of state, and the architect of Britain's modern constitutional monarchy." (Publisher's note)

Includes bibliographical references and index

Edwards, Jonathan, 1703-1758

Marsden, George M. **Jonathan** Edwards; a life. Yale Univ. Press 2003 xx, 615p $35; pa $19.95 **92**
1. Clergy 2. Theologians 3. Congregationalism 4. College presidents 5. Writers on religion
ISBN 0-300-09693-3; 0-300-10596-7 pa
LC 2002-013611

"Clearly sympathetic to his subject without ever becoming an outright apologist for either his character or his theology, Marsden . . . writes with such verve that he has given us not only the definitive biography but also a narrative that reads like a novel—that most appropriate art form for examining the interior drama of the soul." Commonweal
Includes bibliographical references

Eichmann, Adolf, 1906-1962

Stangneth, Bettina. **Eichmann** before Jerusalem; the unexamined life of a mass murderer. by Bettina Stangneth; translated from the German by Ruth Martin. Alfred A. Knopf 2014 608 p. (hardback) $35 **92**
1. War criminals 2. Holocaust, Jewish (1939-1945) 3. War criminals -- Germany -- Biography
ISBN 0307959678; 9780307959676
LC 2014001031

National Jewish Book Awards Finalist: Holocaust (2014)
This book, by Bettina Stangneth, translated by Ruth Martin, offers a "reassessment of the life of Adolf Eichmann--a . . work . . . that reveals his activities and notoriety among a global network of National Socialists following the collapse of the Third Reich and that permanently challenges Hannah Arendt's notion of the 'banality of evil.'" (Publisher's note)

"Stangneth masterfully sifts through the information from these lively social gatherings conducted at journalist Sassen's home three years before Eichmann's kidnapping by Israeli agents. A rigorously documented, essential work not only about Eichmann's masterly masquerade, but also about how we come to accept appearances as truth." Kirkus
Includes bibliographical references (pages 535-555) and index

Einstein, Albert, 1879-1955

Einstein, Albert. **Einstein** on politics; his private thoughts and public stands on nationalism, Zionism, war, peace, and the bomb. edited by David E. Rowe and Robert Schulmann. Princeton University Press 2007 xxxiv, 523p il $29.95 **92**
1. Politics 2. Physicists 3. Nobel laureates for physics
ISBN 978-0-691-12094-2; 0-691-12094-3
LC 2006-100303

This is a collection of excerpts from Albert Einstein's writings on politics and other social topics.

"Powerful in its personal and political disclosures, this is an essential primary source." Booklist
Includes bibliographical references

★ Isaacson, Walter. **Einstein**: his life and universe. Simon & Schuster 2007 xxii, 675p il hardcover o.p. pa $17.95 **92**
1. Physicists 2. Nobel laureates for physics
ISBN 978-0-7432-6473-0; 0-7432-6473-8; 978-0-7432-6474-7 pa; 0-7432-6474-6 pa
LC 2006-51264

This book tells the story of the German-American physicist's life.

"This is a warm, insightful, affectionate portrait with a human and immensely charming Einstein at its core." N Y Times (Late N Y Ed)
Includes bibliographical references

Eire, Carlos M. N.

Eire, Carlos M. N., 1951- **Learning** to die in Miami; confessions of a refugee boy. [by] Carlos Eire. Free Press 2010 307p $26 **92**
1. Cuban refugees 2. Cuban Americans 3. Memoirists 4. Miami (Fla.) 5. College teachers 6. Religious scholars 7. Writers on religion 8. Biography, Individual
ISBN 978-1-4391-8190-4; 1-4391-8190-X
LC 2009052286

Continues Waiting for snow in Havana (2003)
The author, a professor of history and religious studies at Yale, continues the memoir begun with Waiting for Snow in Havana (2003). In the present volume he writes about his introduction to America in 1962, when he was eleven.

The author "takes readers on his personal journey, beginning in 1962 when he and his brother arrived in Florida as part of Operation Peter Pan—an evacuation of 14,000 Cuban children whose parents arranged for their relocation to the United States, away from Castro. Eire's prose engages us throughout as we learn of the challenges he faced as he assimilated to his new world. . . . Readers of memoir and immigrant stories will appreciate Eire's journey and celebrate his accomplishments." Libr J

Eire, Carlos M. N., 1951- **Waiting** for snow in Havana; confessions of a Cuban boy. {by} Carlos Eire. Free Press 2003 383p il hardcover o.p. pa $15 **92**
1. Memoirists 2. Havana (Cuba) 3. College teachers 4. Religious scholars 5. Operation Peter Pan 6. Writers on religion 7. Havana (Cuba) -- Biography 8. Chicago (Ill.) -- Biography 9. Cuban Americans -- Biography 10. Refugee children -- United States -- Biography
ISBN 0-7432-1965-1; 0-7432-4641-1 pa; 978-0-7432-4641-5
LC 2002-73875

"From 1960 through 1962, some fourteen thousand Cuban children were airlifted—unaccompanied—to the United States by Operation Pedro (Peter) Pan. Once here, they were farmed out to CIA-funded refugee camps, then to foster homes. Many never saw their island parents again. Carlos Eire, now a Yale professor of history and religious studies, was a Peter Pan. {This memoir} tells mostly of Eire's privileged boyhood during the pre-Castro 1950s." Commonweal

Eisenhower, Dwight D. (Dwight David), 1890-1969

Ambrose, Stephen E. **Eisenhower**; soldier and president. Simon & Schuster 1990 635p il hardcover o.p. pa $18 **92**
1. Generals 2. Presidents 3. College presidents 4. Presidents -- United States
ISBN 0-671-74758-4 pa
LC 90-9701

Condensed version of a two volume work published 1983-1984

"Tracing Eisenhower's family background, education, military and political careers, and influence as elder statesman, the author chronicles Eisenhower's triumphs and failures and at the same time provides a vivid picture of the off-duty Ike. . . . This is the definitive one-volume biography of Eisenhower." Publ Wkly

Includes bibliographical references

Johnson, Paul, 1928- **Eisenhower**; a life. Paul Johnson. Viking 2014 144 p. $25.95   **92**
1. Presidents -- United States 2. Generals -- United States -- Biography 3. Presidents -- United States -- Biography
ISBN 0670016829; 9780670016822

LC 2014005313

In this biography, author Paul "Johnson chronicles President Eisenhower's modest childhood in Kansas, his college years at West Point, and his rapid ascent through the military ranks, culminating in his appointment as Supreme Commander of the Allied Forces in Europe during World War II. . . . Johnson notes that when Eisenhower left the White House at age 70 . . . he feared for the country's future and prophetically warned of the looming military-industrial complex." (Publisher's note)

"Johnson views Eisenhower positively and asserts that Eisenhower not being a combat general but a staff officer for most of his career contributed to his success as president. Johnson's contribution will serve as a great introduction to 'Ike' the man, but anyone interested in the details of WWII generalship or the politics of the Eisenhower administration will have to look elsewhere."

Includes bibliographical references and index

Eisner, Will, 1917-2005

Schumacher, Michael. **Will** Eisner; a dreamer's life in comics. Bloomsbury 2010 359p il $28   **92**
1. Authors 2. Cartoonists 3. Comic book writers 4. Publishing executives
ISBN 978-1-60819-013-3

LC 2010-11283

"Born in 1917, Will Eisner, now known as the father of the graphic novel, grew up in the Bronx poor but resourceful. . . . [The author] zeroes in on the essence of Eisner's success: his rare ability to unite art (he inherited his phenomenal gift for drawing from his immigrant artist father) with practicality (his mother's specialty). . . . Propelled by Eisner's geyserlike energy and output, Schumacher keenly chronicles Eisner's brilliant career within a lively history of American comics and creates an inspiring portrait of a perpetually diligent and innovative artist whose belief in comics as fine art fueled a new and fertile creative universe." Booklist

Includes bibliographical references

Eleanor, of Aquitaine, Queen, consort of Henry II, King of England, 1122?-1204

Weir, Alison. **Eleanor** of Aquitaine; a life. Ballantine Bks. 2000 xxi, 441p il maps $28; pa $15.95   **92**
1. Queens
ISBN 0-345-40540-4; 0-345-43487-0 pa

LC 99-54785

First published 1999 in the United Kingdom with title Eleanor of Aquitaine: by the wrath of God, Queen of England

A biography of the twelfth-century queen, first of France, then of England, the consort of Henry II and mother of Richard the Lionhearted

"In approaching as complex a subject as feudalism, Weir wears her learning lightly and has a pleasant habit of anticipating all the questions of a curious reader." Publ Wkly

Includes bibliographical references

Eliot, T. S. (Thomas Stearns), 1888-1965

Crawford, Robert, 1959- **Young** Eliot; from St. Louis to The Waste Land. Robert Crawford. Farrar, Straus & Giroux 2015 512 p. 16 plates; illustrations (hardback) $35   **92**
1. Poets 2. Eliot, T. S. (Thomas Stearns), 1888-1965 3. Poets, American -- 20th century -- Biography
ISBN 0374279446; 9780374279448

LC 2014047118

In this book on poet T.S. Eliot, "biographer Robert Crawford presents us with the first volume of a comprehensive account of this poetic genius. 'Young Eliot' traces the life of the twentieth century's most important poet from his childhood in St. Louis to the publication of his revolutionary poem 'The Waste Land.'" (Publisher's note)

"It's hard to imagine a literary biography of greater merit being published this year." Booklist

Includes bibliographical references and index

★ Gordon, Lyndall. **T.S.** Eliot; an imperfect life. Norton 1999 721p $35; pa $18.95   **92**
1. Poets 2. Authors 3. Dramatists 4. Editors 5. Essayists 6. Literary critics 7. Nobel laureates for literature
ISBN 0-393-04728-8; 0-393-32093-6 pa

LC 98-46864

First published 1998 in the United Kingdom

"Gordon's book is the most authoritative life of Eliot thus far, and is certain to spark new controversies." Publ Wkly

Includes bibliographical references

Elizabeth I, Queen of England, 1533-1603

Guy, John. **Elizabeth**; The Forgotten Years. John Guy. Penguin Group USA 2016 512 p. ill., facimiles, map, portrait (hardcover) $35   **92**
1. Great Britain -- History -- 1558-1603, Elizabeth
ISBN 9780670786022; 0670786020

This book, by John Guy, offers a biography of Queen Elizabeth I of England, focusing on her struggles in establishing her power. "For twenty-five years she had struggled to assert her authority over advisers who pressed her to marry and settle the succession; now, she was determined not only to reign but also to rule. . . . John Guy introduces us to a woman who is refreshingly unfamiliar: at once powerful and vulnerable, willful and afraid." (Publisher's note)

"Near the end, Guy's comparisons to Richard II, the usurped king, the usurper Bolingbroke, and Shakespeare's play take your breath away. One of the best biographies of Elizabeth ever." Kirkus

Includes bibliographical references and index.

Hilton, Lisa. **Elizabeth**; Renaissance Prince. Lisa Hilton. Houghton Mifflin Harcourt 2015 384 p. 16 unnumbered pages of plates $27   92

1. Great Britain -- History -- 1558-1603, Elizabeth
ISBN 0544577841; 9780544577848

LC 2015004340

This biography of Queen Elizabeth I of England, by Lisa Hilton, is a "fresh interpretation . . . of a queen who saw herself primarily as a Renaissance prince and used Machiavellian statecraft to secure that position. A decade since the last major biography, this 'Elizabeth' breaks new ground and depicts a queen who was much less constrained by her femininity than most treatments claim." (Publisher's note)

"Those who enjoyed Hilton's previous books will most likely want to read this one, as will die-hard fans of Elizabeth. Readers seeking a more nuanced look at the queen and Tudor politics should turn instead to works by Antonia Fraser or Alison Weir." LJ

Norton, Elizabeth. The **Temptation** of Elizabeth Tudor; Elizabeth I, Thomas Seymour, and the Making of a Virgin Queen. by Elizabeth Norton. W W Norton & Co Inc 2016 416 p. $28.95   92

1. Queens -- Great Britain 2. Great Britain -- History -- 1485-1603, Tudors
ISBN 1605989487; 9781605989488

In this book, by Elizabeth Norton, the "Tudor court in the wake of Henry VIII's death had never been more perilous for the young Elizabeth. . . . Elizabeth is living with the king's widow, Catherine Parr, and her new husband, Thomas Seymour. . . . Ambitious and dangerous, Seymour begins an overt flirtation with Elizabeth that ends with Catherine sending her away. When Catherine dies a year later and Seymour is arrested for treason soon after, a scandal explodes." (Publisher's note)

"Highly recommended for readers interested in British history and the Tudor dynasty. Fans of historical fiction such as Philippa Gregory's "Tudor Court" series will also find themselves invested in the real-life scandal that befell one of England's most famous queens" LJ

Includes bibliographical references and index.

Ellington, Duke, 1899-1974

Teachout, Terry. **Duke**; a life of Duke Ellington. Terry Teachout. Gotham Books 2013 496 p. $30 **92**

1. Jazz musicians -- United States -- Biography
ISBN 1592407498; 9781592407491

LC 2013011138

This book presents a biography of musician Duke Ellington. "The grandson of a slave, he dropped out of high school to become one of the world's most famous musicians, a showman of incomparable suavity who was as comfortable in Carnegie Hall as in the nightclubs where he honed his style. He wrote some fifteen hundred compositions, many of which . . . remain beloved standards, and he sought inspiration in an endless string of transient lovers." (Publisher's note)

Ellis, William Henry, 1864-1923

Jacoby, Karl. The **strange** career of William Ellis; the Texas slave who became a Mexican millionaire. Karl Jacoby. W W Norton & Co Inc 2016 336 p. illustrations, map (hardcover) $27.95   **92**

1. Slaves -- Emancipation 2. Businessmen -- Biograpy 3. Reconstruction (1865-1876) 4. African Americans -- Biography 5. Slaves -- Texas -- Biography 6. Businessmen -- Mexico -- Biography 7. Millionaires -- Mexico -- Biography 8. United States -- Race relations -- History 9. Mexican-American Border Region -- Biography 10. Passing (Identity) -- United States -- History 11. African Americans -- Texas -- Politics and government 12. Reconstruction (U.S. history, 1865-1877) -- Biography
ISBN 9780393239256

LC 2016007019

In this book, by Karl Jacoby, "Guillermo Eliseo was a fantastically wealthy Mexican. . . . But for all his obvious riches and his elegant appearance, Eliseo was also the possessor of a devastating secret: he was not, in fact, from Mexico at all. Rather, he had begun life as a slave named William Ellis, born on a cotton plantation in southern Texas during the waning years of King Cotton." (Publisher's note)

"Jacoby's masterly writing places race and its meaning at the center of this essential work. Readers will gain fresh insight into life during Reconstruction as well as the riddle of racial identities." LJ

Includes bibliographical references and index

Ellison, Ralph

★ Rampersad, Arnold. **Ralph** Ellison; a biography. Alfred A. Knopf 2007 657p il $35   **92**

1. Authors 2. Novelists 3. Essayists 4. Literary critics 5. Short story writers
ISBN 978-0-375-40827-4; 0-375-40827-4

LC 2006-26464

"As the first scholar granted complete access to the Ellison papers, Rampersad introduces us to people and places that reveal the total range of Ellison's sensibilities. . . . Through elegant and lively prose, Rampersad reveals sides of Ellison that are disturbing and instructive." Charlotte Observer

Includes bibliographical references

Engels, Friedrich, 1820-1895

Hunt, Tristram. **Marx's** general; the revolutionary life of Friedrich Engels. Metropolitan Books 2009 430p il $32   **92**

1. Political and social philosophers
ISBN 978-0-8050-8025-4; 0-8050-8025-2

LC 2009-03845

"A useful and well-done study of Engels and the radical epoch he helped create." Booklist

Includes bibliographical references

Equiano, Olaudah, 1745-1797

★ Carretta, Vincent. **Equiano,** the African; biography of a self-made man. University of Georgia Press 2005 xxiv, 436p il map $29.95 **92**
1. Slaves 2. Abolitionists 3. Memoirists
ISBN 0-8203-2571-6

LC 2005-11898

"This is a thoroughly rich, engrossing, and well-researched portrait of an exceptional man and the cause he championed." Booklist

Includes bibliographical references

Erdrich, Louise

Erdrich, Louise. **Books** and islands in Ojibwe country. National Geographic Soc. 2003 143p il map (National Geographic directions) $20 **92**
1. Poets 2. Authors 3. Novelists 4. Ojibwa Indians 5. Essayists 6. Children's authors 7. Short story writers
ISBN 0-7922-5719-7

LC 2003-45906

"Fans of Erdrich's bestselling fiction will recognize her signature combination of the sacred and the ordinary in this lively traveler's memoir, and many will enjoy the rare glimpse of her personal life as well as the physical facts of her journey from her home in Minneapolis to the lakes and islands of her Ojibwe ancestors in Ontario and Minnesota." Booklist

Esfandiari, Haleh, 1940-

Esfandiari, Haleh. **My** prison, my home; one woman's story of captivity in Iran. Ecco/HarperCollins 2009 230p il $25.99 **92**
1. Political prisoners 2. Middle Eastern studies specialists 3. Iran -- Foreign relations -- United States 4. United States -- Foreign relations -- Iran
ISBN 978-0-06-158327-8; 0-06-158327-8

"Esfandiari, born in Tehran in 1940, had been living in the U.S. with her Jewish husband since 1980 when she returned to Tehran in December 2006 to visit her aging mother. On the eve of her departure for the U.S. she was picked up for interrogation—and ended up spending four months in solitary confinement in the dreaded Evin Prison, drawing worldwide attention. In her remarkable memoir, Esfandiari tells the story of her education, her evolution from an apolitical student to an ardent feminist and staunch supporter for the rights of Iranian women, and her many accomplishments, including serving as director of the Woodrow Wilson Center's Middle East Program." Booklist

Eteraz, Ali

Eteraz, Ali. **Children** of dust; a memoir of Pakistan. HarperOne 2009 337p $25.99 **92**
1. Muslims 2. Radicalism 3. Journalists 4. Islamic fundamentalism 5. Bloggers 6. Memoirists 7. Writers on politics 8. Writers on religion
ISBN 978-0-06-156708-7

LC 2009-9666

The author "opens his memoir with a vivid description of his father promising Allah that if God bestowed him with a son, that boy 'will become a great leader and servant of Islam.' The rest of the book finds Eteraz, whose given name is Abir ul Islam (which translates as 'Perfume of Islam') try-

ing to come to terms with his father's mannat, or covenant, and understand the role that Islam will play in his life as well as the role he will play for Islam. . . . A gifted writer and scholar, Eteraz is able to create a true-life Islamic bildungsroman as he effortlessly conveys his coming-of-age tale while educating the reader. When his religious awakening finally occurs, his catharsis transcends the page." Publ Wkly

Evers, Medgar Wiley, 1925-1963

Evers, Medgar Wiley. The **autobiography** of Medgar Evers: a hero's life and legacy revealed through his writings, letters, and speeches; edited by Myrlie Evers-Williams and Manning Marable. Basic Civitas Books 2005 xxiv, 352p il $26; pa $14 **92**
1. Civil rights activists
ISBN 0-465-02177-8; 0-465-02178-6 pa

LC 2006-296327

This is a collection of "Evers's unpublished papers and personal collections as well as [his widow] Evers-Williams's recollections. The resulting text resurrects the life, intellectual output, and creative legacy of the slain civil rights hero." Libr J

Includes bibliographical references

Evert, Chris

Howard, Johnette. The **rivals**; Chris Evert vs. Martina Navratilova: their epic duels and extraordinary friendship. Broadway Books 2005 296p il $24.95 **92**
1. Tennis players 2. Tennis -- Biography
ISBN 0-7679-1884-3

LC 2004-61918

"This work makes a fine contribution to the history of women in sports." Publ Wkly

Exmouth, Edward Pellew, Viscount, 1757-1833

Taylor, Stephen. **Commander**; the life and exploits of Britain's greatest frigate captain. Stephen Taylor. W.W. Norton 2012 320 p. **92**
1. War 2. Biography 3. Military personnel 4. Great Britain -- History, Naval -- 18th century 5. Great Britain -- History, Naval -- 19th century 6. Great Britain. Royal Navy. Officers -- Biography 7. Frigates -- Great Britain -- History -- 18th century 8. Frigates -- Great Britain -- History -- 19th century
ISBN 9780393071641

LC 2012027783

This book by Stephen Taylor presents a biography of British naval commander Edward Pellew. He discusses "Pellew's meteoric rise to midshipman within four years and his first command by age 25. Rare in a seaman, he could swim and more than once dove into the sea to save a crewmember, and his physical prowess . . . was the stuff of legend." In addition, Taylor describes "life at sea during wars in America, the English Channel, the Indian Ocean and the Mediterranean." (Kirkus Reviews)

Includes bibliographical references and index

Fairbanks, Douglas, 1883-1939

Goessel, Tracey. The **first** king of Hollywood; the life of Douglas Fairbanks. Tracey Goessel. Chicago Review Press 2015 560 p. 24 plates; illustrations (hardback) $34.95 **92**

1. Actors -- United States -- Biography 2. Motion picture producer and directors -- United States -- Biography

ISBN 9781613734049

LC 2015018526

This book, by Tracey Goessel, presents a biography of the film actor Douglas Fairbanks. "Irrepressibly vivacious, he spent his life leaping over and into things, from his early Broadway successes to his marriage to the great screen actress Mary Pickford to the way he made Hollywood his very own town. . . . And in founding United Artists with Pickford, Charlie Chaplin, and D. W. Griffith, he challenged the studio system." (Publisher's note)

"The author draws on the actor's voluminous speeches and public statements, as well as a cache of love letters between Doug and Mary. Sadly, many Fairbanks films have been lost, but this highly recommended book illuminates a vanished era of American film." LJ

Includes bibliographical references and index

Fanon, Frantz, 1925-1961

Macey, David. **Frantz** Fanon; a biography. Picador 2001 640p maps $40; pa $20 **92**

1. Diplomats 2. Psychiatrists 3. Revolutionaries 4. Algeria -- History 5. Writers on medicine 6. Algeria -- Biography 7. Political and social philosophers 8. Intellectuals -- Algeria -- Biography 9. Psychiatrists -- Algeria -- Biography 10. Revolutionaries -- Algeria -- Biography

ISBN 0-312-27550-1; 0-312-30042-5 pa

LC 2001-21807

"Based on extensive research and original research, an objective look at the author of one of the most unsettling books of the 1960s, The Wretched of the Earth, reveals Frantz Fanon to be a complex figure--writer, psychiatrist, propagandist, and ambassador." (Publisher's note)

"Macey's writing and research is rich with historical context and personal information that both Fanon loyalists and general readers will appreciate." Libr J

Includes bibliographical references

Faraday, Michael, 1791-1867

Hirshfeld, Alan. The **electric** life of Michael Faraday. Walker & Co. 2006 258p il $24 **92**

1. Chemists 2. Physicists 3. Writers on science

ISBN 0-8027-1470-6

LC 2005-25533

In this biography of the English scientist, the author "explains Faraday's status as one of the most inspirational and significant figures of science. . . . A vibrant portrayal that emphasizes Faraday's qualities of wonder, acuity, and diligence, which propelled him to greatness." Booklist

Includes bibliographical references

Faulkner, William, 1897-1962

★ Parini, Jay. **One** matchless time; a life of William Faulkner. HarperCollins Publishers 2004 492p il $29.95; pa $14.95 **92**

1. Authors 2. Novelists 3. Screenwriters 4. Short

story writers 5. Nobel laureates for literature

ISBN 0-06-621072-0; 0-06-093555-3 pa

LC 2004-42891

The author "offers a portrait of a man always trying to invent a new mask for himself as well as the portrait of an artist consumed by a desire to tell about the South and its class struggles, its depravity, and its captivity to the double bonds of land and history. Parini examines each of Faulkner's novels, from Soldier's Pay to The Reivers, and connects the Snopses, Sutpens, and Compsons of Faulkner's mythic Yoknapatawpha County foibles, his insecurities, and his inestimable literary achievement." Libr J

Includes bibliographical references

Feiffer, Jules

Feiffer, Jules. **Backing** into forward; a memoir. Nan A. Talese-Doubleday 2010 440p il $30 **92**

1. Artists 2. Authors 3. Novelists 4. Dramatists 5. Cartoonists 6. Illustrators 7. Satirists 8. Authors, American 9. Children's authors

ISBN 978-0-385-53158-0

LC 2009-21933

This is an autobiography by the American syndicated cartoonist.

"Feiffer is masterful at self-analyzing the skinny Jewish kid from the Bronx who grew up during the Depression, whose sister was a Communist, and whose distant cousin Roy Cohn was a Red-baiter, while he himself was full of insecurities but fortunate enough to 'luck into the zeitgeist.' . . . He offers social commentary and memorable moments from career and family life as he moved from cartooning to screen and playwriting, to authoring children's books, all the while maintaining a wry perspective that shows in the cartoons interspersed throughout this wonderful memoir." Booklist

Feinstein, Michael

Feinstein, Michael, 1956- The **Gershwins** and me; a personal history in twelve songs. by Michael Feinstein with Ian Jackman. Simon & Schuster 2012 351 p. illustrations (some color) (hc : alk. paper) $45 **92**

1. Popular music -- Writing and publishing -- United States

ISBN 1451645309; 9781451645309; 9781451645316; 9781451645323; 9781451645330

LC 2012006833

Here, author Michael Feinstein "begins with a swift account of how he met Ira Gershwin, the lyricist of the celebrated duo, and how he subsequently went to work for him for six years. . . . Although he tells the Gershwins' stories, childhood to grave, he also . . . discusses the Gershwins' love lives, the significant performers of their work (from Fred Astaire to Ethel Merman), their successes and flops, their experiences in Hollywood and the devastation of George's shocking death at 38 (brain tumor)." (Kirkus)

Includes bibliographical references and index

Feldman, Deborah, 1986-

Feldman, Deborah. **Exodus**; a memoir. by Deborah Feldman. Blue Rider Press 2014 304 p. **92**

1. Hasidism 2. Jews -- New York (N.Y.) 3. New York (N.Y.) -- Biography 4. Jews -- New York (State) -- New

York -- Identity 5. Jews -- New York (State) -- New York -- Biography

ISBN 9780399162770

LC 2013046263

"In 2009, at the age of twenty-three, Deborah Feldman packed up her young son and their few possessions and walked away from her insular Hasidic roots. She was determined to forge a better life for herself, away from the rampant oppression, abuse, and isolation of her Satmar upbringing in Williamsburg, Brooklyn. Out of her experience came the incendiary, bestselling memoir Unorthodox, and now, just a few years later, Feldman has embarked on a triumphant journey of self-discovery—a journey in which she begins life anew as a single mother, an independent woman, and a religious refugee." Publisher's Note

"The overall effect is captivating, entertaining and informative, providing readers with an honest assessment of the strength of one's convictions and the effect a strict religious background can have on a person. An enthralling account of how one Orthodox Jewish woman turned her back on her religion and found genuineness and validity in her new life." Kirkus

Feldman, Deborah. **Unorthodox**; the scandalous rejection of my Hasidic roots. Deborah Feldman. Simon & Schuster 2012 p. cm. illustrations   92

1. Hasidim 2. Jews -- New York (N.Y.) 3. Jews -- New York (State) -- New York -- Biography 4. Hasidim -- New York (State) -- New York -- Biography 5. Hasidim -- New York (State) -- New York -- Social conditions

ISBN 9781439187005; 9781439187012; 9781439187029

LC 2011001386

"In her bestselling memoir, . . . Deborah Feldman recounts the story of her apostasy from the Satmar community of Hasidic Jews in which she was raised. . . . As often happens for those who eventually leave the ultra-Orthodox fold, secular books become the portal through which one comes to see a larger world. The teenage Feldman revels in the freedom of the public library. . . . She provides a litany of abuse stories to explain her growing disillusionment with the Satmar." (Commentary)

"Born into the insular and exclusionary Hasidic community of Satmar in Brooklyn to a mentally disabled father and a mother who fled the sect, Feldman, as she recounts in this nicely written memoir, seemed doomed to be an outsider from the start. Raised by devout grandparents who forbade her to read in English, the ever-curious child craved books outside the synagogue teaching. Feldman's spark of rebellion started with sneaking off to the library and hiding paperback novels under her bed. . . . She starts to experience panic attacks and the stirrings of her final break with being Hasidic. It's when she finally does get pregnant and wants something more for her child that the full force of her uprising takes hold and she plots her escape. Feldman, who now attends Sarah Lawrence College, offers this engaging and at times gripping insight into Brooklyn's Hasidic community." Pub Wkly

Ferlinghetti, Lawrence

Ferlinghetti, Lawrence, 1919- **Writing** Across the Landscape; Travel Journals 1950-2013. by Lawrence Ferlinghetti; edited by Giada Diana and Mat-

thew Gleeson. W W Norton & Co Inc 2015 496 p. illustrations $35   92

1. Travel writing

ISBN 163149001X; 9781631490019

LC 2015026292

This book, edited by Giada Diana and Matthew Gleeson, "present[s] a Lawrence Ferlinghetti never before encountered, an elegant prose stylist and tireless political activist who was warning against the pernicious sins of our ever-expansive corporate culture long before such thoughts ever seeped into mainstream consciousness. . . . Evoking each journey with a mixture of travelogue and poetry as well as his own hand-drawn sketches, Ferlinghetti adopts the role of an American bard." (Publisher's note)

"Avid readers of Ferlinghetti's work will welcome this collection as the 100th anniversary of his birth in 2019 draws ever nearer. It may also provide grist for future biographers." LJ

Fey, Tina, 1970-

Fey, Tina, 1970- **Bossypants**. Little, Brown and Co. 2011 277p il $26.99   92

1. Actors 2. Comedians 3. Autobiographies 4. American wit and humor 5. Screenwriters 6. Biography, Individual 7. Television scriptwriters

ISBN 978-0-316-05686-1

LC 2011002415

In this book, comedian "Tina Fey's story can be told. From her youthful days as a vicious nerd to her tour of duty on 'Saturday Night Live'; from her passionately halfhearted pursuit of physical beauty to her life as a mother eating things off the floor; from her one-sided college romance to her nearly fatal honeymoon -- from the beginning of this paragraph to this final sentence. Tina Fey reveals all, and proves what we've all suspected: you're no one until someone calls you bossy." (Publisher's note)

"Perhaps best known to mass audiences for her writing and performances on Saturday Night Live, Fey's most inventive work is likely her writing for the critically acclaimed TV show 30 Rock, in which she stars alongside Alec Baldwin and fellow SNL alum Tracy Morgan. In typical self-deprecating style, the author traces her awkward childhood and adolescence, rise within the improv ranks of Second City and career on the sets of SNL and 30 Rock." Kirkus

Feynman, Richard Phillips, 1918-1988

Krauss, Lawrence Maxwell. **Quantum** man; Richard Feynman's life in science. [by] Lawrence M. Krauss. W.W. Norton 2011 350p il (Great discoveries) $24.95   92

1. Authors 2. Physicists 3. Writers on science 4. Nobel laureates for physics

ISBN 978-0-393-06471-1; 0-393-06471-9

LC 2010-45512

"This book is highly recommended for readers who want to get to know one of the preeminent scientists of the 20th century." Publ Wkly

Includes bibliographical references

Ottaviani, Jim. **Feynman**; written by Jim Ottaviani; art by Leland Myrick; coloring by Hilary Sycamore. 1st ed. First Second 2011 262 p. chiefly ill. (some col.) (hardcover) $29.99; (paperback) $19.99; (prebind) $33.99 **92**

1. Atomic bomb 2. Nobel Prizes 3. Musicians -- Biography 4. Biography, Individual 5. Physicists -- Graphic novels

ISBN 1596432594; 9781596432598; 9781596438279; 9781451722406

LC 2010036260

Author Jim Ottaviani presents a "graphic novel biography . . . [of] Nobel-winning quantum physicist, adventurer, musician, world-class raconteur, and one of the greatest minds of the twentieth century: Richard Feynman . . . . [The book] tells the story of the great man's life from his childhood in Long Island to his work on the Manhattan Project and the Challenger disaster." (Publisher's note)

"This is a fascinating look at the life of an eccentric genius, a man who worked on the Manhattan Project, won a Nobel Prize, was the first great physicist to teach freshmen classes, and was the investigator into the cause of the Challenger explosion who discovered the problem was the 0-rings. This work was so entertaining it was difficult to put down." Voice Youth Advocates

Fillmore, Millard, 1800-1874

Finkelman, Paul. **Millard** Fillmore. Times Books 2011 171p (American presidents series) $23; ebook $10.99 **92**

1. Presidents 2. Vice-presidents 3. Members of Congress 4. Presidents -- United States 5. United States -- Politics and government -- 1815-1861

ISBN 978-0-8050-8715-4; 978-1-4299-2301-9 ebook

LC 2010-47174

The author "describes Millard Fillmore's nearly forgotten presidency by rigidly contrasting him with Abraham Lincoln, another self-made man who wrestled with racial and regional tensions as president. . . . This book is an enlightening view into the often overlooked beginnings of the Civil War, which history buffs and students alike will find enjoyable." Publ Wkly

Includes bibliographical references

Finnegan, William

Finnegan, William. **Barbarian** Days; A Surfing Life. by William Finnegan. Penguin Group USA 2015 464 p. illustrations (hardcover) $27.95 **92**

1. Surfing

ISBN 1594203474; 9781594203473

Pulitzer Prize: Biography (2016)

This memoir, by William Finnegan, is a "self-portrait of a lifelong surfer. . . . Raised in California and Hawaii, Finnegan started surfing as a child. He has chased waves all over the world, wandering for years through the South Pacific, Australia, Asia, Africa. A bookish boy, and then an excessively adventurous young man, he went on to become a distinguished writer and war reporter." (Publisher's note)

"The constants flowing through this part coming-of-age story and part travelog are the ocean and the waves that the author tries to better understand. The result is an up-close and personal homage to the surfing lifestyle through the author's journey as a lifelong surfer." LJ

Fischer, Bobby, 1943-2008

Brady, Frank. **Endgame**; Bobby Fischer's remarkable rise and fall--from America's brightest prodigy to the edge of madness. Crown 2010 402p il $25.99 **92**

1. Chess 2. Chess players

ISBN 978-0-307-46390-6; 0-307-46390-7

LC 2010-33840

"Brady's insightful biography of the legendary chess player focuses more on Fischer's life as a chess champion than on his much-publicized legal troubles and alleged psychological breakdowns. Brady first became friends with Fischer at a chess tournament when they were both children, and he combines a traditional biography with a personal memoir. . . . Brady is uniquely qualified to write this book. Not only is he a seasoned biographer and someone who knew Fischer on a personal level; he's also an accomplished chess player himself, able to convey the game's intricacies to the reader in a clear, uncomplicated manner." Booklist

Fisher, Carrie, 1956-2016

Fisher, Carrie, 1956-2016 **Wishful** drinking. Simon & Schuster 2008 163p il $21 **92**

1. Actors 2. Authors 3. Novelists 4. Memoirists 5. Short story writers 6. Biography, Individual

ISBN 1-439-10225-2; 978-1-439-10225-1

This is a memoir by the author of Postcards From the Edge (1987), which became a film in 1990.

In this "memoir, Carrie Fisher—actress, novelist and self-described daughter of 'Hollywood inbreeding'—writes about her tumultuous life as showbiz royalty. In Wishful Drinking, Fisher discusses her bipolar disorder, addictions and divorce—and still manages to laugh." NPR

Fisk, Carlton, 1947-

Wilson, Doug. **Pudge**; the biography of Carlton Fisk. Doug Wilson. Thomas Dunne Books 2015 368 p. 8 plates; illustrations (hardcover : alk. paper) $26.99 **92**

1. Baseball players 2. Catchers (Baseball) -- United States -- Biography

ISBN 1250065437; 9781250065438

LC 2015027529

In this biography of baseball player Carlton Risk, author Doug Wilson "uses his own extensive research and interviews with childhood friends and major league teammates to examine the life and career of a leader who followed a strict code and played with fierce determination. Fisk retired having played in more games and hit more home runs than any other catcher before him. A baseball superstar in the 1970s and 80s, Fisk was known not just for his dedication to the sport and tremendous plays but for the respect with which he treated the game." (Publisher's note)

"A well-researched account of a legendary ball player." LJ

Includes bibliographical references and index

Flaubert, Gustave, 1821-1880

Brown, Frederick. **Flaubert**; a biography. Little, Brown 2006 628p il $35 **92**

1. Authors 2. Novelists 3. Short story writers

ISBN 0-316-11878-8

LC 2005-17036

This is a biography of the nineteenth-century French novelist.

The author "has put together a judicious work that sticks to the record and relies on expertly chosen passages from Flaubert's brilliant letters and the works of his contemporaries to develop a convincing portrait, brushstroke by brushstroke." N Y Times (Late N Y Ed)

Includes bibliographical references

Fleming, Victor, 1883-1949

Sragow, Michael. **Victor** Fleming; an American movie master. Pantheon 2008 645p il $40 **92**

1. Motion picture directors 2. Motion picture producers and directors -- Biography

ISBN 978-0-375-40748-2; 0-375-40748-0

LC 2008-15255

Fleming "was the director MGM tapped to take over two thorny, unwieldy and expensive projects—'The Wizard of Oz' and 'Gone With the Wind'—and make them into enormous successes. Had he never completed those two epics, Fleming's other cinematic triumphs had already sealed his reputation. They included 'The Virginian,' 'Red Dust,' 'Mantrap,' 'Bombshell' and 'Captains Courageous.' . . . Mr. Sragow deftly takes us through the twists and turns of Fleming's life, with a vital sense of time and place. We learn much not only about Fleming, but also about his contemporaries and the Hollywood they lived in." Washington Times

Includes bibliographical references and filmography

Flynn, Nick, 1960-

Flynn, Nick. **Another** bullshit night in Suck City; a memoir. W.W. Norton & Co 2004 347p il $23.95 **92**

1. Poets 2. Authors

ISBN 0-393-05139-0

LC 2004-11796

This "memoir describes the years poet Flynn . . . spent, in his late 20s, working at one of the city's homeless shelters, where his path crisscrossed with his down-and-out father's. . . . Although it's depressing, the book never seems hopeless, because readers know the author has succeeded at doing what his father only pretended to do: write, and write well." Publ Wkly

Fogerty, John, 1945-

Fogerty, John. **Fortunate** son; my life, my music. John Fogerty. Little, Brown & Co. 2015 416 p. 16 plates; illustrations (hc) $30 **92**

1. Musicians 2. Bands (Music)

ISBN 0316244570; 9780316244572

LC 2015943212

This book is the "memoir from John Fogerty, the legendary singer-songwriter and creative force behind Creedence Clearwater Revival. He reveals how he brought CCR to number one in the world, eclipsing even the Beatles in 1969. By the next year, though, Creedence was falling apart; their amazing, enduring success exploded and faded in just a few short years." (Publisher's note)

"This isn't just an account of one musician's ups and downs with art and life; Fogerty has created a solid study of popular music over the past 50 years." Pub Wkly

Foner, Moe, 1915-2002

Foner, Moe. **Not** for bread alone; a memoir. by Moe Foner with Dan North; foreword by Ossie Davis. Cornell Univ. Press 2002 142p $25 **92**

1. Labor leaders 2. Health care personnel

ISBN 0-8014-4061-0

LC 2002-5100

Foner's "memoir is a unique window into the evolution of 1199 SEIU from its origins as a tiny conglomeration of drugstore employees into the country's largest healthcare union." Libr J

Includes bibliographical references

Ford, Henry, 1863-1947

Watts, Steven. The **people's** tycoon; Henry Ford and the American century. Knopf 2005 614p il $30 **92**

1. Antisemitism 2. Philanthropists 3. Automobile executives

ISBN 0-375-40735-9

LC 2004-48594

"Steven Watts is intelligent, thorough and engaging . . . in telling the story of an American who not only was influential but remains unavoidable to this day." N Y Times Book Rev

Includes bibliographical references

Foreman, Tom

Foreman, Tom. **My** year of running dangerously; a dad, a daughter, and a ridiculous plan. Tom Foreman. Blue Rider Press, an imprint of Penguin Random House 2015 288 p. illustrations (hardback) $25.95 **92**

1. Father-daughter relationship 2. Marathon running -- Training 3. Aging -- Psychological aspects 4. Marathon running -- United States 5. Fathers and daughters -- United States 6. Journalists -- United States -- Biography 7. Marathon running -- Psychological aspects 8. Middle-aged men -- United States -- Biography 9. Long-distance runners -- United States -- Biography

ISBN 0399175474; 9780399175473

LC 2015017237

This memoir is author Tom Foreman's "journey through four half-marathons, three marathons, and one 55-mile race. What started as an innocent request from his daughter quickly turned into a rekindled passion for long-distance running--for the training, the camaraderie, the defeats, and the victories. Told with honesty and humor, Foreman's account captures the universal fears of aging and failure alongside the hard-won moments of triumph." (Publisher's note)

"Even the author's long-suffering family had to admit at the end of the season that he was happier, and readers will enjoy running alongside him." Kirkus

Forster, E. M. (Edward Morgan), 1879-1970

Moffat, Wendy. A **great** unrecorded history; a new life of E.M. Forster. Farrar, Straus and Giroux 2010 480p il $32.50   **92**

1. Authors 2. Novelists 3. Essayists 4. Authors, English 5. Literary critics 6. Short story writers

ISBN 978-0-374-16678-6; 0-374-16678-1

LC 2009-29504

In this "well-written, intelligent and perceptive biography of Forster . . . [the author attemps] to draw a picture of a figure who was sensitive, sensuous and kind, an artist who possessed a keen, plain sort of wisdom and lightness of touch that make him, to this day, an immensely influential novelist, almost a prophet. She uses the sources for our knowledge of Forster's sexuality, including letters and diaries, without reducing the mystery and sheer individuality of Forster, without making his sexuality explain everything." N Y Times Book Rev

Includes bibliographical references

Fort, Charles, 1874-1932

Steinmeyer, Jim. **Charles** Fort; the man who invented the supernatural. J. P. Tarcher/Penguin 2008 332p il $24.95   **92**

1. Supernatural 2. Parapsychology 3. Curiosities and wonders 4. Parapsychologists 5. Writers on science

ISBN 978-1-58542-640-9; 1-58542-640-7

LC 2008-5961

"Steinmeyer is an elegant and unobtrusive author who shows us an entirely fascinating, shy, and witty man. . . . This book is not to be missed." Libr J

Includes bibliographical references

Fosdick, Sarah Graves, 1825-1871

Brown, Daniel. The **indifferent** stars above; the harrowing saga of a Donner Party bride. [by] Daniel James Brown. William Morrow 2009 337p il $25.99   **92**

1. Donner party 2. Overland journeys to the Pacific 3. Pioneers 4. Frontier and pioneer life -- California

ISBN 978-0-06-134810-5; 0-06-134810-4

LC 2008-40646

"In April 1846, as young newlywed Sarah Graves departed her Illinois home on a journey to California, she could not foresee the misery and horror that awaited her. After numerous delays on their difficult westward path, she and her family found themselves dangerously behind schedule as winter loomed, and they decided to join an ill-fated wagon train under the leadership of George Donner. Ending up snowbound and starving in the Sierra Nevada range, the Donner party descended into cannibalism. . . . Never melodramatic or maudlin, Brown's work gracefully balances graphic depictions of extreme privation with humanizing glimpses of the emigrants' everyday hopes and fears." Libr J

Includes bibliographical references

Fosse, Bob, 1927-1987

★ Wasson, Sam. **Fosse**; by Sam Wasson. Houghton Mifflin Harcourt 2013 672 p. $32   **92**

1. Choreographers 2. Choreographers -- United States

-- Biography

ISBN 0547553293; 9780547553290

LC 2013026082

This book, by Sam Wasson, presents a biography of choreographer and director Bob Fosse. "Fosse revolutionized nearly every facet of American entertainment, forever marking Broadway and Hollywood with his iconic style--hat tilted, fingers splayed--that would influence generations of performing artists. Yet in spite of Fosse's innumerable achievements, no accomplishment ever seemed to satisfy him, and offstage his life was shadowed in turmoil and anxiety." (Publisher's note)

Foster, Stephen Collins, 1826-1864

Emerson, Ken. **Doo**-dah!: Stephen Foster and the rise of American popular culture. Da Capo Press 1998 400p il pa $16.50   **92**

1. Composers 2. Songwriters

ISBN 0-306-80852-8

LC 98-15480

First published 1997 by Simon & Schuster

The author "explores the roots of early popular music while tracing the tragic life of composer Stephen Collins Foster. . . . He also aims his spotlight at other musical personalities of the period, and provides further illumination of how Foster's songs have been incorporated into popular contemporary melodies. . . . Emerson's exhaustive research . . . has been meticulously worked into a vivid portrait of 19th-century America." Publ Wkly

Includes discography and bibliographical references

Fox, Michael J.

Fox, Michael J. **Always** looking up; the adventures of an incurable optimist. Hyperion 2009 279p il $25.99   **92**

1. Actors 2. Parkinson's disease -- Personal narratives

ISBN 978-1-4013-0338-9

LC 2008-55129

An autobiography of the actor and Parkinson's disease sufferer.

Fox, Michael J. **Lucky** man; a memoir. Hyperion 2002 304p $22.95; pa $12.95   **92**

1. Actors 2. Parkinson's disease -- Personal narratives

ISBN 0-7868-6764-7; 0-7868-8874-1 pa

In this autobiography the actor discusses his professional career in feature films and television. He also "writes of the last 10 years, during which--with the unswerving support of his wife, family, and friends--he has dealt with his illness. He talks about what Parkinson's has given him: the chance to appreciate a wonderful life and career, and the opportunity to help search for a cure and spread public awareness of the disease." Publisher's note

Francis, Pope, 1936-

Cool, Michel. **Francis**, a new world pope; Michel Cool; translated by Regan Kramer. William B. Eerdmans Publishing Company 2013 viii, 120 p.p illustrations (pbk. : alk. paper) $14   **92**

ISBN 0802871003; 9780802871008

LC 2013020717

Author Michel Cool "surveys Pope Francis's journey to the papacy, his convictions, his personality, his writings, and the challenges he faces in his new office--governance of the church, new evangelization in secularized societies, and poverty, among many others." (Publisher's note)

"An intelligent and prudent guide to the new pope, Cool's book urges a modest optimism about Francis's leadership." LJ

Includes bibliographical references and index

Vallely, Paul. **Pope** Francis; the struggle for the soul of Catholicism. Paul Vallely. St. Martin's Press 2015 496 p. 8 plates; illustrations $30
1. Catholic Church
ISBN 1632861151; 9781632861153

In this book author "Paul Vallely reexamines the complex past of Jorge Mario Bertoglio and adds nine new chapters, revealing many untold, behind-the-scenes stories from his first years in office that explain this Pope of paradoxes. Vallely lays bare the intrigue and in-fighting surrounding Francis's attempt to cleanse the scandal-ridden Vatican Bank. He unveils the ambition and arrogance of top bureaucrats resisting the Pope's reform of the Roman Curia." (Publisher's note)

"A well-written, balanced portrait of a man leading the church in a new direction. This title will appeal to anyone who seeks a well-rounded study of the current Pope." LJ

Francis, of Assisi, Saint, 1182-1226
Martin, Valerie. **Salvation**: scenes from the life of St. Francis. Knopf 2001 268p hardcover o.p. pa $13 **92**
1. Saints 2. Writers on religion
ISBN 0-375-70883-9 pa
LC 00-44361

"This portrait will be most interesting to readers who are already familiar with the basic facts of Francis's life and remain open to exploring a new, gritty interpretation of them." Publ Wkly

Includes bibliographical references

Frank family
Gies, Miep. **Anne** Frank remembered; the story of the woman who helped to hide the Frank family. [by] Miep Gies and Alison Leslie Gold. Simon & Schuster trade pbk. ed.; Simon and Schuster Paperbacks 2009 264p il pa $15 **92**
1. Holocaust, 1933-1945 2. Amsterdam (Netherlands) 3. Netherlands -- History -- 1940-1945, German occupation
ISBN 978-1-4165-9885-5; 1-4165-9885-5
LC 2009294295
First published 1987

"A memoir by the courageous Dutch woman who helped hide the Frank family, this book augments the Anne Frank story. Perceptive characterizations, with insight into life in Amsterdam during the Nazi occupation." SLJ

Frank, Anne, 1929-1945
Barnouw, David. The **diary** of Anne Frank: the critical edition; rev Critical ed; Doubleday 2003 851p il $75 **92**
1. Children 2. Diarists 3. Holocaust victims 4. Jews -- Netherlands 5. Holocaust, 1933-1945 6. World War, 1939-1945 -- Jews 7. Netherlands -- History -- 1940-1945, German occupation
ISBN 0-385-50847-6
LC 2003-269527
First published 1989

This volume brings together "the three known versions of Frank's diary—the original, a self-edited version . . . {and} another edited by her father. It also contains . . . handwriting and paper analyses, new documentation regarding the Frank family's arrest, and . . . information about the diary's troubled publication history." Libr J {review of 1989 edition}

Includes bibliographical references

★ Frank, Anne. The **diary** of a young girl: the definitive edition; edited by Otto H. Frank and Mirjam Pressler; translated by Susan Massotty. Bantam 1997 340p $29.95; pa $7.99 **92**
1. Children 2. Diarists 3. Holocaust victims 4. Jews -- Netherlands 5. Holocaust, 1933-1945 6. World War, 1939-1945 -- Jews 7. Netherlands -- History -- 1940-1945, German occupation
ISBN 0-385-47378-8; 9780553577129
LC 94-41379

"This new translation of Frank's famous diary includes material about her emerging sexuality and her relationship with her mother that was originally excised by Frank's father, the only family member to survive the Holocaust." Libr J

Jacobson, Sidney. **Anne** Frank; the Anne Frank House authorized graphic biography. [by] Sid Jacobson and Ernie Colón. Hill and Wang 2010 152p il $30; pa $16.95 **92**
1. Children 2. Graphic novels 3. Biographical graphic novels 4. Diarists 5. Holocaust victims 6. Jews -- Netherlands -- Graphic novels 7. Holocaust, 1933-1945 -- Graphic novels 8. World War, 1939-1945 -- Jews -- Graphic novels
ISBN 978-0-8090-2684-5; 978-0-8090-2685-2 pa
LC 2010-5776

"Panel arrangements effectively show simultaneous events happening in the life of the family and in the world, while brief 'snapshots' provide enough historical information to make motives, fears, and expectations sensible to anyone unfamiliar with the Holocaust's machinery. More than simply poignant, this biography elucidates the complex emotional aspects of living a sequestered adolescence as a brilliant, budding writer." Booklist

Includes bibliographical references

Müller, Melissa, 1967- **Anne** Frank; the biography. by Melissa Muller; translated by Rita and Robert Kimber. 2nd U.S. ed. Metropolitan Books/

Henry Holt and Company 2013 480 p. hardcover o.p. (hardcover) $35   **92**
1. Children 2. Amsterdam (Netherlands) -- Biography 3. Jewish children in the Holocaust -- Biography 4. Jews -- Netherlands -- Amsterdam -- Biography 5. Holocaust, Jewish (1939-1945) -- Netherlands -- Amsterdam -- Biography

ISBN 0805087311; 9780805087314

LC 2013000297

This biography of Anne Frank "was originally published in 1998, but this expanded edition takes into account diary entries that had previously been redacted by Anne's father [Otto], as well as recently discovered letters from Otto to relatives in the United States and unpublished documents provided to [Melissa] Müller during interviews with those who knew Anne and her family." (Publishers Weekly)

"Müller includes a family tree; a family history; and considerable insight into the character, personality, and quality of life of Anne's parents, relatives, and friends. Interviews with many of these surviving people give a clearer idea of the situation and Anne's reactions to it." SLJ

Frank, Barney, 1940-

★ Frank, Barney, 1940- **Frank**; A Life in Politics from the Great Society to Same-Sex Marriage. by Barney Frank. Farrar, Straus & Giroux 2015 400 p. 16 plates; illustrations (hardback) $28   **92**
1. Politicians -- United States 2. United States. Congress. House 3. Legislators -- United States -- Biography 4. United States -- Politics and government -- 20th century 5. United States -- Politics and government -- 21st century 6. Politicians -- Massachusetts -- Biography 7. United States. Congress. House -- Biography 8. Gay legislators -- United States -- Biography 9. United States -- Politics and government -- 1989- 10. United States -- Politics and government -- 1945-1989

ISBN 9780374280307

LC 2014040383

In this memoir, politician Barney Frank "discusses the satisfactions, fears, and grudges that come with elected office. He recalls the emotional toll of living in the closet and how his public crusade against homophobia conflicted with his private accommodation of it. He discusses his painful quarrels with allies; his friendships with public figures; . . . and how he found love with his husband, Jim Ready, becoming the first sitting member of Congress to enter a same-sex marriage." (Publisher's note)

"Anyone interested in contemporary history or politics will definitely want to read this highly accessible memoir." LJ

Frankl, Viktor E.

★ Frankl, Viktor E. (Viktor Emil), 1905-1997. **Man's** search for meaning; part one translated by Ilse Lasch; foreword by Harold S. Kushner; afterword by William J. Winslade. Beacon Press 2006 165p pa $13   **92**
1. Psychologists 2. Holocaust, 1933-1945 -- Personal narratives

ISBN 0-8070-1427-3; 978-0-8070-1427-1

LC 2006-287144

Original German edition, 1946

"Between 1942 and 1945 Frankl labored in four different camps, including Auschwitz, while his parents, brother, and pregnant wife perished. Based on his own experience and the experiences of others he treated later in his practice, Frankl argues that we cannot avoid suffering but we can choose how to cope with it, find meaning in it, and move forward with renewed purpose. Frankl's theory—known as logotherapy, from the Greek word logos ('meaning')—holds that our primary drive in life is not pleasure, as Freud maintained, but the discovery and pursuit of what we personally find meaningful." Publisher's note

Franklin, Aretha

★ Ritz, David. **Respect**; the life of Aretha Franklin. David Ritz. 1st edition Little, Brown & Co. 2014 528 p. illustrations (hardcover) $30   **92**
1. African American singers -- Biography 2. Singers 3. Soul musicians

ISBN 0316196835; 9780316196833

LC 2014018985

This biography by David Ritz describes how "it was not until 1967, when a white Jewish producer insisted [singer Aretha Franklin] return to her gospel-soul roots, that fame and fortune finally came via 'Respect' and a rapidfire string of hits. She has evolved ever since, amidst personal tragedy, surprise Grammy performances, and career reinventions." (Publisher's note)

"[C]ommendable for its depth, much of which comes from interviews with key figures and family members, as well as Ritz's highly readable, captivating style. It's a compelling record of the life of a musical titan and a fascinating picture of the process of recording some of the seminal popular music of our time." LJ

Includes bibliographical references, discography, filmography and index

Franklin, Benjamin, 1706-1790

★ Franklin, Benjamin. The **autobiography** of Benjamin Franklin; introduction by Lewis Leary. Simon & Schuster 2004 143p pa $10.95   **92**
1. Authors 2. Diplomats 3. Inventors 4. Statesmen 5. Scientists 6. Writers on science 7. Members of Congress 8. Statesmen -- United States

ISBN 0-7432-5506-2

LC 2003-54477

Written between 1771 and 1788

"Franklin's account of his life, written for his son William. . . . During the Revolutionary War, the manuscript was put aside. . . . Franklin later more than doubled the length . . . but still took the story only to 1757-1759, ending before the period of his greatest public service. Still, the book remains the first undisputed classic of American literature and one of the most interesting autobiographies in English." Benet's Reader's Ency of Am Lit

Isaacson, Walter. **Benjamin** Franklin; an American life. Simon & Schuster 2003 590p il $30; pa $16.95   **92**
1. Authors 2. Diplomats 3. Inventors 4. Statesmen 5. Scientists 6. Writers on science 7. Members of

Congress 8. Statesmen -- United States
ISBN 0-684-80761-0; 0-7432-5807-X pa

LC 2003-50463

This "is a thoroughly researched, crisply written, convincingly argued chronicle that is also studded with little nuggets of fresh information." N Y Times Book Rev

Includes bibliographical references

★ Lepore, Jill. **Book** of ages; the life and opinions of Jane Franklin. Jill Lepore. Alfred A. Knopf 2013 464 p. $27.95   **92**

1. Boston (Mass.) -- Biography 2. Women -- United States -- Social conditions -- 18th century
ISBN 0307958345; 9780307958341

LC 2013001012

This book on Jane Franklin Mecom by Jill Lepore tells "the story of Benjamin Franklin's youngest sister . . . using only a few of her letters and a small archive of births and deaths." (Kirkus Reviews) "Jane's surviving letters are . . . the correspondence of a smart, witty, hardworking woman who 'loved best books about ideas,' reveled in gossip, expressed 'impolite' opinions on religion and politics, and shared piquant observations of the struggle for American independence." (Booklist)

Includes bibliographical references

Franklin, Rosalind, 1920-1958

Maddox, Brenda. **Rosalind** Franklin: the dark lady of DNA. HarperCollins Pubs. 2002 380p il $29.95; pa $15.95   **92**

1. DNA 2. Chemists 3. Biologists 4. Geochemists
ISBN 0-06-018407-8; 0-06-098508-9 pa

LC 2002-68898

The author "does an excellent job of revisiting Franklin's scientific contributions . . . while revealing Franklin's complicated personality." Libr J

Includes bibliographical references

Franzen, Jonathan

Franzen, Jonathan. The **discomfort** zone; a personal history. Farrar, Straus & Giroux 2006 195p $22   **92**

1. Authors 2. Novelists
ISBN 978-0-374-29919-4; 0-374-29919-6

LC 2006-2700

This is a memoir by the author of The Corrections.

"For those who admire the razor-sharp jabs Franzen makes at himself and anyone else standing too close, 'The Discomfort Zone' is both a delicious read and a clever showcase for Franzen's talents." Christ Sci Monit

Frederick II, King of Prussia, 1712-1786

Blanning, Tim. **Frederick** the Great; king of Prussia. Tim Blanning. Random House Inc 2016 688 p. chiefly ill. (some col.), maps (acid-free paper) $35   **92**

1. Prussia -- Kings and rulers 2. Seven Years' War, 1756-1763 3. Enlightenment -- Germany -- Prussia 4. Prussia (Germany) -- Kings and rulers -- Biography 5. Prussia (Germany) -- Intellectual life -- 18th century 6. Prussia (Germany) -- History -- Frederick II, 1740-1786 7. Social change -- Germany -- Prussia -- History -- 18th

century
ISBN 1400068126; 9781400068128

LC 2015030616

Author Tim Blanning presents this biography of Frederick the Great, "the legendary autocrat whose enlightened rule transformed the map of Europe and changed the course of history. In examining Frederick's private life, Blanning also carefully considers the long-debated question of Frederick's sexuality, finding evidence that Frederick lavished gifts on his male friends and maintained homosexual relationships throughout his life, while limiting contact with his estranged, unloved queen to visits that were few and far between." (Publisher's note)

"Readers both casual and scholarly will enjoy this profile for the in-depth examination of its subject, his placement in the historical events of the time, and his future in German history." LJ

Includes bibliographical references and index

Freud, Sigmund, 1856-1939

Gay, Peter. **Freud**; a life for our time. with a new foreword. Norton 2006 810p il pa $21.95   **92**

1. Psychoanalysts 2. Writers on medicine
ISBN 0-393-32861-9

LC 2006-283026

First published 1988

"The book is beautifully written. Gay's approach is to try to understand Freud and his alliances and environment rather than to worship or challenge him." Choice

Includes bibliographical references

Friedan, Betty, 1921-2006

Friedan, Betty. **Life** so far. Simon & Schuster 2000 399p il hardcover o.p. pa $17   **92**

1. Authors 2. Feminism 3. Feminists 4. Nonfiction writers 5. Organization officials
ISBN 0-684-80789-0; 978-0-7432-9986-2 pa; 0-7432-9986-8 pa

LC 00-23920

In this memoir, "Friedan reminisces over a life of social activism that has included helping to found the National Organization for Women, the National Abortion and Reproductive Rights Action League, and the National Women's Political Caucus, as well as writing the pivotal The Feminine Mystique." Libr J

Fu, Ping, 1958-

Ping Fu. **Bend,** not break; a life in two worlds. Ping Fu with MeiMei Fox. Portfolio/Penguin 2013 288 p. $27.95   **92**

1. Resilience (Personality trait) 2. Geomagic (Firm) 3. Young women -- China -- Biography 4. Chinese American women -- Biography 5. Businesswomen -- United States -- Biography 6. Entrepreneurship -- United States -- Biography 7. Nanjing hang kong hang tian da xue -- Biography 8. Political refugees -- United States -- Biography 9. Women computer scientists -- United States -- Biography 10. China -- History -- Cultural Revolution, 1966-1976 -- Personal narratives
ISBN 1591845521; 9781591845522

LC 2012035389

This book, by Ping Fu with MeiMei Fox, is the autobiography of a Chinese immigrant. "Born on the eve of China's Cultural Revolution, Ping . . . grew up fighting hunger . . . and shielding her younger sister from the teenagers in Mao's Red Guard. At twenty-five, she found her way to the United States." This book "depicts a journey from . . . the dogmatic anticapitalism of Mao's China to the high-stakes, take-no-prisoners world of technology start-ups in the United States." (Publisher's note)

Fuller, Alexandra, 1969-

Fuller, Alexandra. **Don't** let's go to the dogs tonight; an African childhood. Random House 2002 301p il hardcover o.p. pa $13.95   **92**
1. Authors 2. Zimbabwe 3. Memoirists
ISBN 0-375-50750-7; 0-375-75899-2 pa
LC 2001-41752
"Fuller grew up in Rhodesia (now Zimbabwe) during the civil war, and she watched her parents fight against the local Africans to keep their farm. In a memoir powerful in its frank straightforwardness, she neither apologizes for nor champions her family's views and actions. Instead she gives us an honest, moving portrait of one family struggling to survive tumultuous times." Booklist

Followed by Cocktail hour under the tree of forgetfulness (2011)

Fuller, Margaret, 1810-1850

Von Mehren, Joan. **Minerva** and the muse: a life of Margaret Fuller. University of Mass. Press 1995 398p il $40; pa $20.95   **92**
1. Feminists 2. Biographers 3. Social reformers
ISBN 0-87023-941-4; 1-55849-015-9 pa
LC 94-18663
"Von Mehren is sympathetic to Fuller's lifelong struggle to achieve fame and public acclamation for her views on Transcendentalism and feminism, but she balances her sympathy with objectivity and distance." Libr J
Includes bibliographical references

Gaiman, Neil

Campbell, Hayley. The **art** of Neil Gaiman; by Hayley Campbell. Harper Design Intl 2014 320 p. illustrations (some color) $39.99   **92**
1. English authors
ISBN 0062248561; 9780062248565

In this book, author Hayley Campbell "gives an insider's glimpse into the artistic inspirations and musings of . . . Neil Gaiman. . . . A master of several genres, including, but not limited to, bestselling novels, children's books, groundbreaking comics, and graphic novels, . . . Gaiman has been called a rock star of the literary world. Now, for the first time, Gaiman reveals the inspiration behind his signature artistic motifs." (Publisher's note)

"Campbell has clearly taken great care to construct such a lavish and detailed offering and fans will be hanging on every word and illustration for a deeper insight into Gaiman's eccentric genius. Highly recommended for anyone who has dearly loved any of his many works." LJ

Galilei, Galileo, 1564-1642

Heilbron, J. L. **Galileo**. Oxford University Press 2010 508p il $34.95   **92**
1. Astronomers 2. Writers on science 3. Astronomy -- History 4. Biography, Individual 5. Italy -- Intellectual life 6. Science -- Italy -- History
ISBN 978-0-19-958352-2; 0-19-958352-8
This "will no doubt become the standard, comprehensive biography. . . . In one of his most inventive sections, [Heilbron] creates a Galilean dialogue on issues of algebra and geometry. Though not easy to read, it brilliantly expresses the ambiguities and blind alleys as Galileo wrestled with the conceptual difficulty of introducing a nongeometrical quantity—time itself— into the proportions." N Y Times Book Rev
Includes bibliographical references

Sobel, Dava. **Galileo's** daughter; a historical memoir of science, faith, and love. Walker & Co. 1999 420p $27   **92**
1. Nuns 2. Astronomers 3. Writers on science 4. Children of prominent persons
ISBN 0-8027-1343-2
LC 99-23885
"Sobel has a remarkable ability to explain technical subjects without being simplistic or pedantic. There is a tremendous amount of fascinating detail in this work, and yet it reads as smoothly and compellingly as fiction." Libr J
Includes bibliographical references

Galliano, John

Thomas, Dana. **Gods** and Kings; The Rise and Fall of Alexander Mcqueen and John Galliano. Dana Thomas. Penguin Group USA 2015 432 p. 32 plates; portraits $29.95   **92**
1. Fashion designers
ISBN 1594204942; 9781594204944
LC 2015460559
In this book, author Dana Thomas "tells the true story of [Alexander] McQueen and [John] Galliano. In so doing, she reveals the revolution in high fashion in the last two decades--and the price it demanded of the very ones who saved it. They had similar backgrounds: sensitive, shy gay men raised in tough London neighborhoods, their love of fashion nurtured by their doting mothers. Both struggled to get their businesses off the ground, despite early critical success." (Publisher's note)

"This is a dark story about excess, commerce, aristocracy and fashion as high theater that is as operatic as the dizzying shows it describes. A deep dive into the provocative art of creation and the toll it exacts from those touched by its gifts."

Gandhi, Mahatma, 1869-1948

Gandhi, Mahatma. An **autobiography;** the story of my experiments with truth. translated from the original in Gujarati by Mahadev Desai; with a foreword by Sissela Bok. Beacon Press 1993 528p $10.95   **92**
ISBN 0-8070-5909-9
LC 93-19758

"In [Gandhi's] classic autobiography he recounts the story of his life and how he developed his concept of active nonviolent resistance, which propelled the Indian struggle for independence and countless other nonviolent struggles of the twentieth century." (Publisher's note)

★ Guha, Ramachandra, 1958- **Gandhi** before India; Ramachandra Guha. Alfred A. Knopf 2014 672 p. illustrations, maps $35 **92**
1. India -- History -- 20th century 2. Statesmen -- India -- Biography 3. South Africa -- Politics and government -- 1836-1909 4. East Indians -- South Africa -- Politics and government
ISBN 0385532296; 9780385532297
LC 2013025014
This biography "takes us from Mohandas Gandhi's birth in 1869 through his upbringing in Gujarat, his two years as a student in London, and his two decades as a lawyer and community organizer in South Africa." Author Ramachandra Guha "makes clear that Gandhi's work in South Africa--far from being a mere prelude to his accomplishments in India--was profoundly influential on his evolution as a political thinker, social reformer, and beloved leader." (Publisher's note)
"This first volume in a two-part biography of Gandhi from Guha . . . proves itself an essential work for its bold purpose, extensive research, and engaging prose." Pub Wkly
Includes bibliographical references and index

Lelyveld, Joseph. **Great** soul; Mahatma Gandhi and his struggle with India. Alfred A. Knopf 2011 425p il map $28.95; ebook $14.99 **92**
1. Authors 2. Journalists 3. Essayists 4. Pacifists 5. Memoirists 6. Political leaders 7. Statesmen -- India 8. Writers on politics 9. Biography, Individual 10. India -- Politics and government 11. India -- Politics and government -- 1919-1947
ISBN 978-0-307-26958-4; 978-0-307-59536-2 ebook
LC 2010-34252
"Mr. Lelyveld has restored human depth to the Mahatma, the plaster saint, allowing his flawed human readers to feel a little closer to his lofty ideals of nonviolence and universal brotherhood." N Y Times (Late N Y Ed)
Includes bibliographical references

Mohandas. **Gandhi**; the man, his people, and the empire. University of California Press 2008 xv, 738p il map $34.95 **92**
1. Authors 2. Journalists 3. Essayists 4. Pacifists 5. Memoirists 6. Political leaders 7. Writers on politics 8. India -- Politics and government
ISBN 978-0-520-25570-8; 0-520-25570-4
LC 2007-40986
First published 2006 in India with title: Mohandas: a true story of a man, his people, and an empire
The author exhibits a deep "understanding of the social and political landscape of India, of the cleavages of caste and religion, and of the dynamics of the dominant Congress Party (to which Gandhi had a lifelong allegiance). Rajmohan takes us at a leisurely pace through the broad sweep of Gandhi's personal and public life." Times Lit Suppl
Includes bibliographical references (p. 703-708)

Garcia, Jerry
Jackson, Blair. **Garcia**; an American life. Viking 1999 497p hardcover o.p. $18 **92**
1. Singers 2. Guitarists 3. Rock musicians 4. Grateful Dead (Musical group)
ISBN 978-0-14-029199-5; 0-14-029199-7
LC 99-28775
"Jackson has written a wonderful account of the beginnings of the band . . . in the mid-1960's, their relationship with Ken Kesey and his Merry Pranksters, their embrace of psychedelic drugs and the adoration and obsession of Deadheads throughout the country." N Y Times Book Rev
Includes bibliographical references

García Lorca, Federico, 1898-1936
Gibson, Ian. **Federico** Garcia Lorca: a life. Pantheon Bks. 1989 xxii, 551p il hardcover o.p. pa $18 **92**
1. Poets 2. Authors 3. Dramatists 4. Theatrical directors
ISBN 0-679-77401-7 pa
LC 88-28871
Loosely based on the two-volume Spanish work published 1985-1987
This is a biography of the Spanish writer who was assassinated during the Spanish Civil War
"Gibson's sense of place is equalled by his sense of person. His re-creation of the teeming artistic talent and the café life of Spain in the 1930s is superb. So effective is Gibson's account of Lorca's vitality and fecundity that along with admiration for the poet's opulent talent, he provokes a fierce outrage at his ultimate fate." Times Lit Suppl
Includes bibliographical references

García Márquez, Gabriel, 1928-
Garcia Marquez, Gabriel. **Living** to tell the tale; translated by Edith Grossman. Knopf 2003 483p maps $26.95; pa $14.95 **92**
1. Authors 2. Novelists 3. Journalists 4. Short story writers 5. Nobel laureates for literature
ISBN 1-4000-4134-1; 1-4000-3454-X pa
LC 2003-58924
"Garcia Márquez tells the entrancing story of his remarkable family, chronicles the turbulence of his troubled country, Colombia, and offers a piquant portrait of himself as a struggling young writer. A resplendent memoir written with compassion and artistry." Booklist

★ Martin, Gerald. **Gabriel** Garcia Marquez; a life. Alfred A. Knopf 2009 642p il map **92**
1. Authors 2. Novelists 3. Journalists 4. Authors, Colombian 5. Short story writers 6. Nobel laureates for literature
ISBN 978-0-307-27177-8
LC 200903806
First published 2008 in the United Kingdom
This is a biography of the Colombian novelist and author of One Hundred Years of Solitude (1967) and Love in the Time of Cholera (1985).
"This superbly researched biography is nothing short of a tour de force. . . . This work not only details the life of a

great writer but also provides considerable insight into life in Latin America." Libr J

Includes bibliographical references

Gardner, Chris

Gardner, Chris. The **pursuit** of happyness; [by] Chris Gardner with Quincy Troupe and Mim Eichler Rivas. Amistad 2006 302p il map $25.95   92

1. Securities brokers

ISBN 978-0-06-074486-1; 0-06-074486-3

LC 2005-57203

The author "recounts his 'long walk to Wall Street,' a journey that took him from a childhood in the ghettos of Milwaukee to an enormously successful career as a stockbroker in New York city." Libr J

Garland, Judy

Clarke, Gerald. **Get** happy: the life of Judy Garland. Random House 2000 510p il hardcover o.p. pa $15.95   92

1. Actors 2. Singers

ISBN 0-385-33515-6 pa

LC 99-36285

"This exhaustively researched and illuminating biography . . . is as compassionate as it is wrenching." Publ Wkly

Includes bibliographical references

Garrett, Pat F. (Pat Floyd), 1850-1908

Gardner, Mark L. **To** hell on a fast horse; Billy the Kid, Pat Garrett, and the epic chase to justice in the Old West. William Morrow 2010 325p il $26.99   92

1. Outlaws 2. Sheriffs

ISBN 978-0-06-136827-1; 0-06-136827-X

LC 2009025467

A "double biography of the iconic western outlaw Billy the Kid and Sheriff Pat Garrett. Maintaining an objective perspective on both men in a narrative closely tied to historic source materials, Gardner's quick-moving story follows events of the civil war in Lincoln County, New Mexico Territory in 1877–78, and the Kid's death-by-shooting at the hands of Garrett in 1881. . . . The final chapters describing Garrett as an old-style lawman in a postfrontier society, with interactions with President Theodore Roosevelt, serve to distinguish this book from other recent Kid biographies." Libr J

Includes bibliographical references

Gates, Henry Louis

Gates, Henry Louis. **Colored** people; a memoir. [by] Henry Louis Gates, Jr. Knopf 1994 216p hardcover o.p. pa $13   92

1. Authors 2. Philologists 3. College teachers 4. Literary critics 5. Social scientists 6. Nonfiction writers

ISBN 0-679-73919-X pa

LC 93-12256

"As Gates traces his evolution from 'Negro' to Afro-wearing 'black,' he also traces the evolution of Piedmont (and, by extension, of much of America) at a time when the relationship between the races was being redefined." Newsweek

Gates, Robert Michael, 1943-

Gates, Robert Michael, 1943- A **passion** for leadership; lessons on change and reform from fifty years of public service. Robert M. Gates. Alfred A. Knopf 2016 256 p. $27.95   92

1. Leadership 2. Civil service 3. Leadership -- United States 4. Organizational change -- United States 5. United States -- Politics and government 6. Texas A & M University System -- Biography 7. Cabinet officers -- United States -- Biography 8. Public administration -- United States -- Anecdotes 9. Administrative agencies -- United States -- Reorganization 10. United States. Department of Defense -- Officials and employees -- Biography 11. United States. Central Intelligence Agency -- Officials and employees -- Biography

ISBN 030795949X; 9780307959492

LC 2015010209

Author Robert Gates presents this "assessment of why big institutions are failing us and how smart, committed leadership can effect real improvement regardless of scale. He offers us the ultimate insider's look at how major bureaus, organizations, and companies can be transformed, which is by turns heartening and inspiring and always instructive." (Publisher's note)

"Solid advice that should be passed on to leaders at any season of life and particularly helpful to those new to such responsibility. Highly recommended for public and academic leadership collections." Library Journal

Gazzaniga, Michael S.

Gazzaniga, Michael S. **Tales** from Both Sides of the Brain; a life in neuroscience. Michael S. Gazzaniga. HarperCollins 2015 432 p. illustrations, portraits $28.99   92

1. Brain 2. Neurosciences

ISBN 0062228803; 9780062228802

This book, by Michael S. Gazzaniga, "tells the impassioned story of his life in science and his decades-long journey to understand how the separate spheres of our brains communicate and miscommunicate with their separate agendas. . . . He paints a vivid portrait not only of his discovery of split-brain theory, but also of his comrades in arms--the many patients, friends, and family who have accompanied him on this wild ride of intellectual discovery." (Publisher's note)

"For those familiar with the groundbreaking studies that make up the field's backbone, however, the book is a rare opportunity to relive the history of cognitive neuroscience through Gazzaniga's knowledgeable and relatable perspective. Summing Up: Recommended. Upper-division undergraduates and above." Choice

Gehrig, Lou, 1903-1941

Robinson, Ray. **Iron** horse: Lou Gehrig in his time. Norton 1990 300p il pa $14.95   92

1. Baseball players 2. Baseball -- Biography

ISBN 978-0-393-32882-0 pa; 0-393-32882-1 pa

LC 89-29272

"Playing in the considerable shadow of Babe Ruth, Lou Gehrig's accomplishments as baseball's 'Iron Horse' include a legendary record of 2,130 consecutive games played. . . . Robinson's narrative not only traces Gehrig's life and career but also provides an insightful look at baseball in the 1920s and the Depression years." Libr J

Gehry, Frank O., 1929-

Goldberger, Paul. **Building** art; the life and work of Frank Gehry. by Paul Goldberger. Alfred A. Knopf 2015 528 p. 8 plates; illustrations (hardback) $35   **92**

1. Architecture -- United States 2. Architects -- United States -- Biography

ISBN 0307701530; 9780307701534

LC 2015026562

This book, by Paul Goldberger, is "an engaging, nuanced exploration of the life and work of Frank Gehry, undoubtedly the most famous architect of our time. This . . . critical biography presents and evaluates the work of a man who has almost single-handedly transformed contemporary architecture in his innovative use of materials, design, and form, and who is among the very few architects in history to be both respected by critics . . . and embraced by the general public." (Publisher's note)

"With avid precision and invaluable insight, Goldberger charts the complicated, punishing battles Gehry waged to construct his ambitious, dreamworld buildings, from private homes to Guggenheim Bilbao, the Walt Disney Concert Hall, Facebook headquarters, and beyond. The result is an involving work of significant architectural history and a discerning and affecting portrait of a daring and original master builder." Booklist

Isenberg, Barbara. **Conversations** with Frank Gehry. Alfred A. Knopf 2009 290p il map $40 **92**

1. Architects

ISBN 978-0-307-26800-6; 0-307-26800-4

LC 2008-47616

This book "brings together in one book a series of candid interviews that the accomplished Isenberg recorded between 2004 and 2008, embracing Gehry's entire life and career, comprising a kind of verbal autobiography. . . . This very accessible, readable volume will be a gold mine for scholars and the general public for generations." Libr J

Gelb, Arthur, 1924-

Gelb, Arthur. **City** room. Putnam 2003 664p $29.95; pa $17.95   **92**

1. Newspaper editors 2. New York Times Company

ISBN 0-399-15075-7; 0-425-19831-6 pa

LC 2003-43154

This is a "memoir of life at The New York Times by one who spent nearly 50 years there, rising from copy boy to managing editor; {the author} has the power to evoke whole generations of change in the news business, reaching back to the glorious postwar years of manual typewriters, chain smokers, and all-nighters." N Y Times Book Rev

Genghis Khan, 1162-1227

Weatherford, J. McIver. **Genghis** Khan and the making of the modern world; [by] Jack Weatherford. Crown 2004 320p   **92**

ISBN 0-609-61062-7

LC 2003-20659

"When the Mongols, led by Genghis Khan, exploded out of the central Asian steppes in the early thirteenth century, they began the acquisition of the largest land empire in history. Eventually, the Mongol Empire extended from the Pacific to the Mediterranean and from northern Siberia to Southeast Asia. Yet the West focuses primarily on Mongol savagery. In his revisionist history of the empire, anthropology professor Weatherford uses the so-called Secret History, a long-suppressed Mongol text, to balance the scales." (Booklist)

George III, King of Great Britain, 1738-1820

Hadlow, Janice. A **royal** experiment; the private life of King George III. Janice Hadlow. Henry Holt & Co 2014 704 p. 16 plates; ills.; gen. table (hardback) $40   **92**

1. Great Britain -- Kings and rulers 2. Great Britain -- Kings and rulers -- Biography 3. Great Britain -- History -- George III, 1760-1820

ISBN 0805096566; 9780805096569; 9780805096576

LC 2014024707

In this book, author Janice Hadlow examines the "story of King George III's radical pursuit of happiness in his private life with Queen Charlotte and their 15 children. Against his irresistibly awful family background--of brutal royal intrigue, infidelity, and betrayal--George fervently pursued a radical domestic dream: he would have a faithful marriage and raise loving, educated, and resilient children." (Publisher's note)

"Extended forays into the king's periods of madness, which began in 1788 and finally incapacitated him for good in 1811, also diffuse the narrative focus. Unconvincing as revisionist history but enjoyable for its vivid depiction of several varieties of royal lifestyles - and plenty of royal gossip." Kirkus

Includes bibliographical references and index

Georges, Nicole J.

Georges, Nicole J. **Calling** Dr. Laura; a graphic memoir. Nicole J. Georges. Houghton Mifflin Harcourt 2013 260 p. illustrations pbk $16.95   **92**

1. Lesbians' writings 2. Autobiographical graphic novels 3. Family secrets -- Comic books, strips, etc 4. Identity (Psychology) -- Comic books, strips, etc

ISBN 0547615590; 9780547615592

LC 2012022389

Lambda Award: Graphic Novel (2014)

This graphic novel by Nicole J. Georges tells how when she "was two years old, her family told her that her father was dead. When she was twenty-three, a psychic told her he was alive. Her sister, saddled with guilt, admits that the psychic is right and that the whole family has conspired to keep him a secret. Sent into a tailspin about her identity, Nicole turns to radio talk-show host Dr. Laura Schlessinger for advice." (Publisher's note)

"Georges' quirky, big-faced, and evocative drawings, tempered by a variety of panel sizes, show the bespectacled author as she comes to terms with her mother's lies to her as a child about her father being dead. . . . An excellent graphic memoir offering engaging insights for those who share--or don't share any of Georges' worries and traits." Booklist

Geronimo, 1829-1909

★ Utley, Robert Marshall, 1929- **Geronimo**; Robert M. Utley. Yale University Press 2012 348 p. (clothbound : alk. paper) $30 **92**

1. Apache Indians -- History 2. Apache Indians -- Wars, 1883-1886 3. Apache Indians -- Kings and rulers -- Biography

ISBN 9780300126389; 0300126387

LC 2012019521

This book by Robert M. Utley is a biography of "the Apache fighter Geronimo. . . . Utley unfolds the story through the alternating perspectives of whites and Apaches. . . . What it was like to be an Apache fighter-in-training, why Indians as well as whites feared Geronimo, how Geronimo maintained his freedom, and why he finally surrendered--the answers to these questions and many more fill the pages of this . . . volume." (Publisher's note)

Includes bibliographical references and index

Gershwin, George, 1898-1937

Feinstein, Michael, 1956- The **Gershwins** and me; a personal history in twelve songs. by Michael Feinstein with Ian Jackman. Simon & Schuster 2012 351 p. illustrations (some color) (hc : alk. paper) $45 **92**

1. Popular music -- Writing and publishing -- United States

ISBN 1451645309; 9781451645309; 9781451645316; 9781451645323; 9781451645330

LC 2012006833

Here, author Michael Feinstein "begins with a swift account of how he met Ira Gershwin, the lyricist of the celebrated duo, and how he subsequently went to work for him for six years. . . . Although he tells the Gershwins' stories, childhood to grave, he also . . . discusses the Gershwins' love lives, the significant performers of their work (from Fred Astaire to Ethel Merman), their successes and flops, their experiences in Hollywood and the devastation of George's shocking death at 38 (brain tumor)." (Kirkus)

Includes bibliographical references and index

Hyland, William G. **George** Gershwin; a new biography. Praeger Pubs. 2003 312p il $39.95 **92**

1. Composers

ISBN 0-275-98111-8

LC 2003-46303

"This fresh and well-researched biography of one of America's great composers is highly recommended for all libraries." Libr J

Includes bibliographical references

★ Pollack, Howard. **George** Gershwin; his life and work. University of California Press 2006 884p il $39.95 **92**

1. Composers

ISBN 978-0-520-24864-9; 0-520-24864-3

LC 2006-17926

"This engaging biography is also a tour de force of scholarship." Booklist

Includes bibliographical references

Gershwin, Ira, 1896-1983

Feinstein, Michael, 1956- The **Gershwins** and me; a personal history in twelve songs. by Michael Feinstein with Ian Jackman. Simon & Schuster 2012 351 p. illustrations (some color) (hc : alk. paper) $45 **92**

1. Popular music -- Writing and publishing -- United States

ISBN 1451645309; 9781451645309; 9781451645316; 9781451645323; 9781451645330

LC 2012006833

Here, author Michael Feinstein "begins with a swift account of how he met Ira Gershwin, the lyricist of the celebrated duo, and how he subsequently went to work for him for six years. . . . Although he tells the Gershwins' stories, childhood to grave, he also . . . discusses the Gershwins' love lives, the significant performers of their work (from Fred Astaire to Ethel Merman), their successes and flops, their experiences in Hollywood and the devastation of George's shocking death at 38 (brain tumor)." (Kirkus)

Includes bibliographical references and index

Gevisser, Mark

Gevisser, Mark. **Lost** and Found in Johannesburg, a memoir; Lost and Found in Johannesburg, a memoir. Mark Gevisser. Farrar, Straus & Giroux 2014 328 p. illustrations, maps (hardback) $27 **92**

1. Africa -- Social conditions 2. South Africa -- Race relations 3. Johannesburg (South Africa) -- Biography 4. Authors, South African -- 20th century -- Biography

ISBN 0374176760; 9780374176761

LC 2013033018

In this memoir Mark Gevisser "remembers his privileged childhood in a walled white world. Then, in the mid-1990s, visiting Johannesburg . . . Gevisser is held hostage at gunpoint, bound and gagged with two women friends when three brutal robbers break into their home. Is his assailant a prisoner from the apartheid war? The honest blend of sympathy and fury drives the story: his guilt now about his privilege, but also relief and sadness." (Booklist)

"With lots of photos that show the people and places, including the mountains of yellow mine dumps from Jo'burg's gold, this is a must for those who want to experience the personal reality of apartheid and its aftermath." Booklist

Includes bibliographical references

Gielgud, John Sir, 1904-2000

Gielgud, John. An **actor** and his time. Applause Theatre Bk. Pubs. 1997 333p $21.95; pa $16.95 **92**

1. Actors 2. Theatrical directors 3. Theatrical producers

ISBN 1-55783-299-4; 1-55783-415-6 pa

LC 97-31701

First published 1979 in the United Kingdom

This autobiography chronicles Gielgud's work in the theatre and motion pictures. Includes his personal reminiscences of Ellen Terry, Sarah Bernhardt, Mrs. Patrick Campbell, Bernard Shaw and Ralph Richardson, among others

Gielgud "proves himself to be a storyteller of the highest order, making this essential reading for theater lovers." Libr J

Gilbert, Elizabeth, 1969-

Gilbert, Elizabeth, 1969- **Eat,** pray, love; one woman's search for everything across Italy, India and Indonesia. Viking 2006 334p $24.95 **92**

1. Authors 2. Novelists 3. Journalists 4. Short story writers 5. Biography, Individual
ISBN 0-670-03471-1

LC 2005-42435

"In order to give herself the time and space to find out who she really was and what she really wanted, [the author] got rid of her belongings, quit her job, and undertook a year-long journey around the world—all alone. Eat, Pray, Love is the . . . chronicle of that year." (Publisher's note)

"A probing, thoughtful title with a free and easy style, this work seamlessly blends history and travel for a very enjoyable read." Libr J

Ginsberg, Allen, 1926-1997

Ginsberg, Allen. The **letters** of Allen Ginsberg; edited by Bill Morgan. DaCapo Press 2008 468p $30 **92**

1. Poets 2. Authors 3. Poets, American
ISBN 978-0-30681-463-1; 0-30681-463-3

LC 2008-11054

"Morgan, Ginsberg's biographer (I Celebrate Myself) and archivist, studied 3700 letters left behind by the poet, selecting 165 of the most significant for this edition; over 125 appear here for the first time. Always intelligent, sometimes gossipy, and occasionally cranky and impatient, Ginsberg is accurately reflected in these letters taken together. Correspondents include Ginsberg's father, Louis, and brother, Eugene; the poet's longtime companion, Peter Orlovsky; fellow Beat writers Jack Kerouac, William Burroughs, and Gregory Corso; and a host of friends and acquaintances." Libr J

Includes bibliographical references

Morgan, Bill. **I** celebrate myself; the somewhat private life of Allen Ginsberg. Viking 2006 702p il $29.95 **92**

1. Poets 2. Authors 3. Beat generation
ISBN 0-670-03796-6

LC 2006-50045

"Relying heavily on Ginsberg's journals and letters, as well as interviews with close friends, [Morgan] creates here a detailed, revealing portrait of Ginsberg as a gifted poet and flawed human being driven by a fierce hunger for love and an insatiable thirst for fame. This most exhaustive biography to date chronicles Ginsberg's life from cradle to grave, but a major theme is Ginsberg's love life especially his relationship with Peter Orlovsky. Although he became an icon for gay liberation, Ginsberg tended to fall in love with straight men like Jack Kerouac, Neal Cassady, and Orlovsky, which, of course, led to a good deal of rejection and frustration. Morgan's is the first life of Ginsberg to explore this curious paradox in any depth. Cleverly designed, his book includes marginal references to the poems Ginsberg was working on at the time. A monumental work." Libr J

Gionfriddo, Tim

Gionfriddo, Paul. **Losing** Tim; How our health and education systems failed my son with schizophre-

nia. Paul Gionfriddo. Columbia University Press 2014 264 p. (cloth : alk. paper) $24.95 **92**

1. Schizophrenia 2. Education -- United States 3. Mental health services -- United States 4. Mental health policy -- United States 5. Schizophrenia in children -- Patients -- United States -- Biography
ISBN 9780231168281

LC 2014008507

This book, by Paul Gionfriddo, "describes how [the author's son] Tim and others like him come to live on the street. Gionfriddo takes stock of the numerous injustices that kept his son from realizing his potential from the time Tim first began to show symptoms of schizophrenia to the inadequate educational supports he received growing up, . . . and his frequent encounters with the . . . criminal-justice system and its substandard mental health care." (Publisher's note)

Includes bibliographical references

Giraldi, William

Giraldi, William. The **Hero's** Body; A Memoir. by William Giraldi. Liveright Pub Corp 2016 288 p. illustrations, portraits $25.95 **92**

1. Death 2. Masculinity 3. Father-son relationship
ISBN 0871406667; 9780871406668

This book, by William Giraldi, is a "memoir of motorcycles and muscles, of obsession and grief, and of a young man who learned how to stay alive through literature. At just forty-seven years old, William Giraldi's father was killed in a horrific motorcycle crash while racing on a country road. . . . Giraldi writes . . . about the fragility and might of the American male." (Publisher's note)

"A hearty, bittersweet familial chronicle of masculinity drawing on the underappreciated bond between fathers and sons." Kirkus

Giuliani, Rudolph W.

Siegel, Frederick F. The **prince** of the city; Giuliani, New York, and the genius of American life. [by] Fred Siegel, with Harry Siegel. Encounter Books 2005 386p $26.95 **92**

1. Mayors 2. Lawyers 3. District attorneys 4. Presidential candidates 5. New York (N.Y.) -- Politics and government
ISBN 1-594-03084-7

LC 2005-40127

This is a "narrative of Giuliani's eight years (1994-2001) as New York's chief elected executive. The account engagingly portrays how Giuliani made things happen, ranging from Giuliani the man to Giuliani the politician to Giuliani the policy innovator." Choice

Includes bibliographical references

Glass, Philip

Glass, Philip, 1937- **Words** Without Music; A Memoir. W W Norton & Co Inc 2015 288 p. illustrations $29.95 **92**

1. Composers -- Biography 2. Musicians -- Biography
ISBN 0871404389; 9780871404381

LC 2015000421

"In this episodic narrative of intellectual and artistic development, famed American composer [Philip] Glass describes his involvement in the avant-garde music and art scenes in New York in the 1950s through the 1980s. . . . He recounts touring the Indian subcontinent in search of a guru and eventually winning fame for repetitive compositions like 'Einstein on the Beach' and 'Koyaanisqatsi,' which delighted some listeners and enraged others." (Publishers Weekly)

"Aspiring musicians and artists will learn much from Glass, as will general readers, musical or not, who will discover an artistic life exceptionally well lived." Booklist

Goddard, Robert Hutchings, 1882-1945

★ Clary, David A. **Rocket** man; Robert H. Goddard and the birth of the space age. Hyperion 2003 324p il $24.95 **92**

1. Rocketry 2. Physicists 3. Aerospace engineers 4. Aeronautical engineers
ISBN 0-7868-6817-1

LC 2002-27321

In this biography Goddard emerges "as a paradoxical man who relentlessly promoted his work, winning hundreds of thousands of dollars in Guggenheim grants, while shunning offers to collaborate with other scientists. Clary presents a clear and relatively straightforward narrative of his subject's life. . . . Readers who come to this generally well-written biography with some knowledge of Goddard's significance will find much of interest to fill out their knowledge of this complex and fascinating scientist for whom NASA's Goddard Space Center is named." Publ Wkly

Includes bibliographical references

Goebbels, Joseph, 1897-1945

Longerich, Peter. **Goebbels**; a biography. Peter Longerich; translated by Alan Bance, Jeremy Noakes and Lesley Sharpe. Random House 2014 1024 p. illustrations (hardback) $40 **92**

1. National socialism -- History 2. Germany -- History -- 1933-1945 3. World War, 1939-1945 -- Germany 4. Nazis -- Biography 5. Germany -- History -- 1918-1933
ISBN 1400067510; 9781400067510

LC 2014004828

This biography, by historian Peter Longerich, focuses on "Joseph Goebbels . . . one of Adolf Hitler's most loyal acolytes. . . . [It] documents Goebbels's ascent through the ranks of the Nazi Party, where he became a member of the Führer's inner circle and launched a brutal campaign of anti-Semitic propaganda. Though endowed with near-dictatorial control of the media . . . Goebbels is a man dogged by insecurities and beset by bureaucratic infighting." (Publisher's note)

"As Longerich acknowledges, his reliance on Goebbels' diaries as a primary source is problematic, since Goebbels' accounts of events and personalities seem designed to impress himself. Still Longerich's efforts to glean the truth from exaggerations and distortions are credible, and this is an outstanding contribution to our understanding of the Nazi regime." Booklist

Includes bibliographical references and index

Goethe, Johann Wolfgang von, 1749-1832

Armstrong, John. **Love**, life, Goethe; lessons of the imagination from the great German poet. 1st American ed.; Farrar, Straus and Giroux 2007 482p il $30 **92**

1. Poets 2. Authors 3. Novelists 4. Dramatists 5.

Essayists 6. Nonfiction writers 7. Writers on science
ISBN 978-0-374-29968-2; 0-374-29968-4

LC 2006-34072

First published 2006 in the United Kingdom

"Armstrong's thoughtful analysis of Goethe's life and works enables readers to fully appreciate the great German poet as an eminently human genius striving for growth and wholeness." Booklist

Includes bibliographical references

Gogh, Vincent van, 1853-1890

Naifeh, Steven. **Van** Gogh; [by] Steven Naifeh and Gregory White Smith. Random House 2011 xiii, 953 p.p some colored ill, maps **92**

1. Painters 2. Mental illness 3. Biography, Individual
ISBN 9781588360472; 9780375507489; 0375507485

LC 2010053005

This book offers a biography of Vincent van Gogh. The book explores "his early struggles to find his place in the world; his intense relationship with his brother Theo; his impetus for turning to brush and canvas; and his move to Provence, where in a brief burst of . . . productivity he painted some of the best-loved works in Western art. The authors also shed . . . light on . . . Van Gogh's inner world: his deep immersion in literature and art; his erratic and tumultuous romantic life; and his bouts of depression and mental illness." (Publisher's note)

Includes bibliographical references and index.

Gooch, Brad, 1952-

Gooch, Brad. **Smash** Cut; Brad Gooch. HarperCollins 2015 256 p. illustrations $27.99 **92**

1. New York (N.Y.) 2. Art -- 20th century
ISBN 0062354957; 9780062354952

LC 2015460361

Written by Brad Gooch, this book is a "memoir of life in 1980s New York City--a colorful and atmospheric tale of wild bohemians, glamorous celebrity, and complicated passions--with cameo appearances by Madonna, Robert Mapplethorpe, William Burroughs, and a host of other legendary artists. . . . At its center is his love affair with film director Howard Brookner, pieced together from fragments of memory and fueled by a panoply of emotions." (Publisher's note)

"This candid memoir lovingly evokes a life, and a world, lost." Kirkus

Goodall, Jane, 1934-

★ Goodall, Jane. **Beyond** innocence; an autobiography in letters: the later years. edited by Dale Peterson. Houghton Mifflin 2001 418p il $28; pa $15 **92**

1. Women scientists 2. Primatologists 3. Writers on nature 4. Nonfiction writers
ISBN 0-618-12520-5; 0-618-25734-9 pa

LC 00-54124

In this "volume of Goodall's letters, a lively portrait is formed through her missives as the young woman rose to the height of her scientific contributions and fame. She became a mother, divorced her first husband, married her second, and lost him to cancer. She was also the first to observe cannibalism in chimps, lost many of her study troop during a polio epidemic, and weathered the kidnapping of a group of her students. . . . . This illuminating glimpse into the mind, emotions, and philosophy of an important scientist who also happens to be a celebrated figure will be requested in all libraries." Booklist

Peterson, Dale. **Jane** Goodall: the woman who redefined man. Houghton Mifflin 2006 740p il $24.95; pa $17.95 **92**

1. Women scientists 2. Primatologists 3. Writers on nature 4. Nonfiction writers
ISBN 978-0-395-85405-1; 0-395-85405-9; 978-0-547-05356-1 pa; 0-547-05356-8 pa

LC 2006-6050

Peterson "vividly and significantly enriches our understanding of Goodall as a scientist, spiritual thinker, and humanist." Booklist
Includes bibliographical references

Gore, Al, 1948-

Zelnick, Bob. **Gore**: a political life. Regnery Pub. 1999 384p $29.95; pa $16.95 **92**

1. Vice-presidents 2. Conservationists 3. Senators 4. Members of Congress 5. Presidential candidates 6. Nobel laureates for peace
ISBN 0-89526-326-2; 0-89526-241-X pa

LC 99-194035

Zelnick examines the life and career of Al Gore, the former senator from Tennessee and Vice President of the United States

The author provides "a useful and comprehensive survey of the highs and lows of Gore's political career." NY Times Book Rev

Gould, Glenn, 1932-1982

Hafner, Katie. A **romance** on three legs; Glenn Gould's obsessive quest for the perfect piano. Bloomsbury 2008 259p il $24.99; pa $16 **92**

1. Pianos 2. Pianists 3. Composers 4. Steinway & Sons
ISBN 978-1-59691-524-4; 1-59691-524-2; 978-1-59691-525-1 pa; 1-59691-525-0 pa

LC 2007-48808

"When Gould was paired with the right composer, Bach especially, he could make you wonder if he was altogether human. And reading Hafner on Gould is sometimes as much fun as listening to him play. And that's saying a lot." Newsweek
Includes bibliographical references

Goya, Francisco, 1746-1828

Blackburn, Julia. **Old** man Goya. Pantheon Bks. 2002 239p il $23; pa $13 **92**

1. Artists 2. Etchers 3. Painters 4. Printmakers
ISBN 0-375-40611-5; 0-375-70579-1 pa

LC 2002-280534

The author "focuses on the second half of Goya's long and amazingly productive life, beginning with the devastating illness that left him deaf at age 47. . . . {She} not only empathetically imagines the sea change caused by Goya's abrupt sensory loss, and convincingly assesses its impact on his work, she also conjures up the artists's mise-en-scène, from the frenetic streets of Madrid to the sanctuary of the studio, the bizarreness of the court of Charles IV, the horrors of famine and war, Goya's long marriage, and, after his wife's death, late-life relationship with a much younger woman. . . . {This is a} vital, inventively participatory portrait of a master portraitist and observer of life." Booklist
Includes bibliographical references

Graham, Billy, 1918-

Graham, Billy. **Just** as I am; the autobiography of Billy Graham. HarperSanFrancisco 1997 xxiii, 760p il maps hardcover o.p. pa $18 **92**

1. Clergy 2. Evangelists 3. Inspirational writers
ISBN 0-06-063387-5; 0-06-063392-1 pa

LC 97-605

"In this memoir, Graham looks back at age 78 on his lifetime of personal relationships, ministry, leadership, and experiences. He chronicles such events and stories as his boyhood in North Carolina, his first steps in ministry, details of evangelistic trips and revivals, and meetings with world and local leaders. . . . All libraries would do well to stock this readable title by an important national figure." Libr J

Wacker, Grant. **America's** pastor; Billy Graham and the shaping of a nation. Grant Wacker. The Belknap Press of Harvard University Press 2014 448 p. illustrations (alk. paper) $27.95

1. Christianity -- United States 2. Christianity and culture -- United States -- History -- 20th century
ISBN 0674052188; 9780674052185

LC 2014014155

This book, by Grant Wacker, "is an appraisal of the roles [Billy] Graham, the great evangelist, played during a career spanning from the late 1930s to his last crusade in 2005. Wacker examines not so much what Graham did as how he did it--a matter of manners and management as much as of vision and talent." (Booklist)

"Wacker doesn't shrink, however, from showing how Graham's fascination with presidential politics led him astray repeatedly while allowing that he was a genuine spiritual counselor to the presidents—Lyndon Johnson, in particular. If a great subject deserves a great book, Billy Graham has one." Booklist
Includes bibliographical references and index

Graham, Mark (Mark A.)

Dreazen, Yochi. The **invisible** front; a story of loss and love. Yochi Dreazen. Crown 2014 320 p. 8 plates; illustrations (hardback) $26 **92**

1. Suicide -- United States 2. War -- Psychological aspects 3. Sons -- United States -- Death 4. United States. Army -- Biography 5. Sociology, Military -- United States 6. Generals -- United States -- Biography 7. Soldiers -- Mental health -- United States 8. Post-traumatic stress disorder -- United States
ISBN 0385347839; 9780385347839

LC 2014007360

This book by Yochi Dreazen is "is the story of how one family tries to set aside their grief and find purpose in almost unimaginable loss. The Grahams work to change how the Army treats those with PTSD and to erase the stigma that prevents suicidal troops from getting the help they need before making the darkest of choices." (Publisher's note)

"Mental health care workers, sociologists, and military historians will find this book a useful first step in a much larger conversation. Readers dealing with mental health issues can take comfort in knowing they are not alone, and others may find motivation in the stories Dreazen relates to help generate change." LJ

Grande, Reyna

Grande, Reyna. The **distance** between us; a memoir. Reyna Grande. Atria Books 2012 336 p. (hardcover) $25.00   92
1. Poor 2. Novelists 3. Immigrants -- United States 4. Mexican Americans -- Biography 5. Los Angeles (Calif.) -- Biography 6. Immigrants -- United States -- Biography 7. Mexican American women authors -- Biography 8. Abused children -- United States -- Biography 9. Mexico -- Emigration and immigration -- Social aspects 10. United States -- Emigration and immigration -- Social aspects
ISBN 1451661770; 9781451661774; 9781451661781; 9781451661804
                                              LC 2012001634
This book presents a memoir by "award-winning novelist . . . [Reyna] Grande. . . . Four-year-old Grande and her two siblings lived with their cruel grandmother after both parents departed for the U.S. in search of work. . . . Eight years later her father returned and reluctantly agreed to take his children to the States. . . . Surrounded by family turmoil, Grande discovered a love of writing . . . and went on to become the first person in her family to graduate from college." (Publishers Weekly)

Grandmaster Flash, 1958-

Grandmaster Flash. The **adventures** of Grandmaster Flash; my life, my beats. by Grandmaster Flash with David Ritz. Broadway Books 2008 258p il $22.95   92
1. Hip-hop 2. Musicians 3. Rap musicians 4. Disc jockeys (Club)
ISBN 978-0-7679-2475-7; 0-7679-2475-4
                                              LC 2007-48224
"Grandmaster Flash is best known in conjunction with the Furious Five, the first hip-hop artists inducted into the Rock and Roll Hall of Fame. But before the fame, Joseph Robert Saddler was born into an abusive family in the Bronx. His evolution from a kid spinning records in the streets to hip-hop stardom is an inspiring story filled with heartbreak, determination, and perseverance." Libr J
Includes discography and bibliographical references

Grant, Ulysses S. (Ulysses Simpson), 1822-1885

Bunting, Josiah. **Ulysses** S. Grant; [by] Josiah Bunting III. Times Books 2004 xx, 180p (American presidents series) $20   92
1. Generals 2. Presidents 3. United States -- History -- 1861-1865, Civil War
ISBN 0-8050-6949-6
                                              LC 2004-47889

"This superb book should support those who are gradually moving Grant from the lower to the upper half of rankings of chief executives." Publ Wkly
Includes bibliographical references

Korda, Michael. **Ulysses** S. Grant: the unlikely hero. Atlas Books\HarperCollins 2004 161p (Eminent lives) $19.95   92
1. Generals 2. Presidents 3. United States -- History -- 1861-1865, Civil War
ISBN 0-06-059015-7
                                              LC 2004-46125
The author "freshly characterizes his man without psychologizing an unpromising subject. . . . This is a highly readable, accurate study of the man." Publ Wkly
Includes bibliographical references

Smith, Jean Edward. **Grant**. Simon & Schuster 2001 781p il $35; pa $20   92
1. Generals 2. Presidents 3. United States -- History -- 1861-1865, Civil War
ISBN 0-684-84926-7; 0-684-84927-5 pa
                                              LC 00-53794
This biography surveys the career and achievements of the 18th U.S. president, from his days at West Point to the Civil War campaigns and his subsequent elevation to the presidency
"While he acknowledges Grant's failure to rein in his 'friends' and cabinet members as president, Smith convincingly illustrates how Grant's backbone and political skills were used to advance the cause of former slaves in the South. This is an outstanding and long overdue reevaluation of the life and career of a great American." Booklist
Includes bibliographical references

★ White, Ronald C. **American** Ulysses; A Life of Ulysses S. Grant. Ronald C. White. Random House 2016 880 p. illustrations, maps $35   92
1. Generals -- United States -- Biography 2. Presidents -- United States -- Biography 3. United States -- Politics and government -- 1869-1877 4. United States -- History -- Civil War, 1861-1865 -- Biography
ISBN 9781400069026
                                              LC 2015044513
This biography of Ulysses S. Grant by Ronald C. White "shows Grant to be a generous, curious, introspective man and leader. . . . Grant was not only a brilliant general but also a passionate defender of equal rights in post-Civil War America. . . . He used the power of the federal government to battle the Ku Klux Klan. He was the first president to state that the government's policy toward American Indians was immoral, and the first ex-president to embark on a world tour." (Publisher's note)
"The author portrays a humble, gentle, independent soul—a writer, in the end, who found his voice writing his extraordinary memoirs just before his death in 1885. An engaging resurrection of Grant featuring excellent maps and character sketches." Kirkus
Includes bibliographical references and index

Grealy, Lucy, 1963-2002

Patchett, Ann. **Truth** & beauty; a friendship. HarperCollins Publishers 2004 257p hardcover o.p. pa $13.95   **92**

1. Poets 2. Authors 3. Novelists 4. Women authors 5. Memoirists

ISBN 0-06-057214-0; 0-06-057215-9 pa

LC 2003-67586

"As young writers. Patchett and Lucy Grealy began an intense friendship that lasted until Grealy's tragic death. With intimacy, gracy, and humor, Patchett's memoir captures Lucy's exuberance and her roller-coaster struggles with disfigurement and depression." Booklist

Greene, Graham, 1904-1991

Greene, Graham, 1904-1991. **Graham** Greene; a life in letters. edited by Richard Greene. W. W. Norton & Company 2008 446p il $35   **92**

1. Authors 2. Novelists 3. Essayists 4. Travel writers 5. Short story writers 6. Motion picture critics

ISBN 978-0-393-06642-5; 0-393-06642-8

LC 2008-40452

First published 2007 in the United Kingdom

"Greene is presented in these letters through the five main preoccupations of his life: Roman Catholicism, politics, love, travel and . . . the processes of writing and publishing. . . . This well-thought-out collection newly reveals a remarkable activist-writer." Publ Wkly

Includes bibliographical references

Greenspan, Alan

Greenspan, Alan, 1926- The **age** of turbulence; adventures in a new world. Penguin Press 2007 531p il $35   **92**

1. Economists 2. Bankers 3. Government officials 4. Biography, Individual 5. Presidential advisers 6. Regulatory agency officials 7. United States -- Economic conditions -- 1945-

ISBN 978-1-59420-131-8

LC 2007-13169

This is a memoir by the American economist who served as "Chairman of the Federal Reserve Board, from 1987 to 2006." (Publisher's note) Index.

"The former U. S. Federal Reserve Board chair relates his life story, focusing on lessons learned in government service, particularly post-9/11. He also includes political anecdotes, asserts his faith in market capitalism, and shares his predictions for the world of 2030." Libr J

Includes bibliographical references

Gregorian, Vartan

Gregorian, Vartan. The **road** to home; my life and times. Simon & Schuster 2003 354p il hardcover o.p. pa $15   **92**

1. Library directors 2. College presidents 3. Foundation officials

ISBN 0-684-80834-X; 978-0-7432-5565-3; 0-7432-5565-8 pa

LC 2003-45566

In this "memoir, Gregorian explains how he went from a childhood in a poor section of Tabriz, Iran, to become president of the New York Public Library and, later, the president of Brown University." Publ Wkly

Grescoe, Taras

Shanghai grand; forbidden love and international intrigue in a doomed world. Taras Grescoe. St. Martin's Press 2016 480 p. illustrations, map (hardcover) $28.99   **92**

1. Shanghai (China) -- History 2. Shanghai (China) -- Biography 3. Aliens -- China -- Shanhai -- Biography 4. Cathay Hotel (Shanghai, China) -- History 5. Americans -- China -- Shanhai -- Biography 6. Adventure and adventurers -- China -- Shanhai -- Biography 7. Shanghai (China) -- Social life and customs -- 20th century 8. Sino-Japanese War, 1937-1945 -- Social aspects -- China -- Shangahi

ISBN 9781250049711; 9781466850675

LC 2016001124

This book, by Taras Grescoe, offers a biography of American journalist Emily Hahn "in free-wheeling 1930s Shanghai. . . . New Yorker writer Emily Hahn arrived there in 1935, intending to stay for two weeks. She fled, along with other expatriates, in 1943. Those eight years were filled with adventure, danger, love, and sex." (Kirkus Reviews)

"Grescoe (Straphanger, 2012) interweaves a cast of intriguing international characters into this seductive biography of a time, a place, a poet, and a girl." Booklist

Includes bibliographical references and index.

Grey, Zane, 1872-1939

Pauly, Thomas H. **Zane** Grey; his life, his adventures, his women. University of Illinois Press 2005 385p il map $34.95   **92**

1. Authors 2. Novelists 3. Western writers 4. Biography, Individual

ISBN 0-252-03044-3; 978-0-252-03044-4

LC 2005-9413

This is a biography of the "author of westerns like 'Riders of the Purple Sage,' 'The Light of Western Stars' and 'Code of the West.'" (N Y Times Book Rev) Index.

The author "offers an honest exploration of the complex author. . . . A solid, entertaining read." Choice

Includes bibliographical references

Grove, Andrew S., 1936-

Tedlow, Richard S. **Andy** Grove; the life and times of an American. Portfolio 2006 512p $29.95   **92**

1. Intel Corp. 2. College teachers 3. Electronics industry executives

ISBN 978-1-591-84139-5; 1-591-84139-9

LC 2006-49829

The author "presents the story of Andy Grove, a penniless Hungarian immigrant who became an icon of twentieth-century corporate America. Grove joined Intel in 1968 at its founding, and while he was CEO from 1987 to 1998, 'market capitalization increased from $4.3 billion to $197.6 billion, a compound annual growth rate of 42% and a total increase of almost 4,500%.' Grove led the company with Intel's 386 microprocessor, which became the industry standard. Tedlow describes Grove, Time magazine's 1997 man of the year, as an extraordinary manager, author, and significant player in the fights against prostate cancer and Parkinson's disease. With unique access to Grove and Intel's internal resources and documents, Tedlow claims objectivity, telling the truth as he sees it in this laudatory narrative, although he also confirms his close ties to the subject." Booklist

Groves, Leslie R., 1896-1970

Norris, Robert S. **Racing** for the bomb: General Leslie R. Groves, the Manhattan Project's indispensable man. Steerforth Press 2002 xxi, 722p hardcover o.p. pa $24.95 **92**
1. Generals 2. Manhattan Project 3. Computer industry executives
ISBN 1-58642-067-4 pa
LC 2001-57629

This is a biography of the military engineer in charge of the Manhattan Project, which developed the atomic bomb.

This "work will not only serve scholars and general readers equally well but also take its place among the handful of best books about the birth of the atomic age." Booklist
Includes bibliographical references

Grymes, James A.

Grymes, James A. **Violins** of hope; violins of the Holocaust, instruments of hope and liberation in mankind's darkest hour. James A. Grymes. Harper Perennial 2014 336 p. illustrations (paperback) $15.99 **92**
1. Violins 2. Holocaust, 1939-1945 3. Holocaust victims -- Biography 4. Violinists -- Europe -- Biography 5. Jewish musicians -- Europe -- Biography 6. Musical instruments -- Maintenance and repair -- History -- 20th century
ISBN 0062246836; 9780062246837; 9780062246844
LC 2013050151

National Jewish Book Award Winner: Holocaust (2014)

This book by James A Grymes "tells the remarkable stories of violins played by Jewish musicians during the Holocaust, and the Israeli violin maker dedicated to bringing these inspirational instruments back to life. Today, these instruments serve as . . . memorials to those who perished and testaments to those who survived. In this spirit, renowned Israeli violinmaker Amnon Weinstein has devoted the past twenty years to restoring the violins of the Holocaust." (Publisher's note)

"This book does not provide scientific background as does Justin Gregg's Are Dolphins Really that Smart? but will interest general and YA readers, as well as nature lovers, who will lose their eagerness to visit dolphin shows and may be motivated toward further reading on the subject." LJ

Guevara, Che, 1928-1967

Anderson, Jon Lee. **Che** Guevara; a revolutionary life. Grove Press 1997 814p il maps hardcover o.p. pa $20 **92**
1. Physicians 2. Revolutionaries
ISBN 0-8021-3558-7 pa
LC 97-3993

This is a "biography of the life and death of the larger-than-life revolutionary Ernesto 'Che' Guevara, the Argentine doctor who joined with Castro to overturn Fulgencio Batista's reign in Cuba. . . . This book, with its 89 photo-

graphs, will be an invaluable addition to the literature of American revolutionaries." Booklist
Includes bibliographical references

Guevara, Ernesto Che. **Diary** of a combatant; from the Sierra Maestra to Santa Clara, Cuba, 1956-58. Ernesto Che Guevara; edited by María del Carmen Ariet. Ocean Press 2011 368 p. ill., map, facsim. $23.95 **92**
1. Diaries 2. Cuba -- History -- 1958-1959, Revolution
ISBN 0987077945; 9780987077943
LC 2011943989

This book is a translation of the diary "Ernesto Che Guevara kept during the guerrilla war in Cuba when he joined the struggle to overthrow the Batista dictatorship that led to the 1959 revolution. . . . [It was] meticulously transcribed by his widow, Aleida March. . . . Other features of this new book are fifty-eight unpublished photos from Che's personal archive and unpublished letters (including correspondence between Che and Fidel)." (Publisher's note)

"Editor Ariet has included a useful chronology and a most helpful biographical glossary, detailing many of the names Che introduces in these diaries." LJ
Includes bibliographical references

Guggenheim, Peggy, 1898-1979

★ Gill, Anton. **Art** lover; a biography of Peggy Guggenheim. HarperCollins Pubs. 2002 480p il $29.95; pa $15.95 **92**
1. Art collectors 2. Patrons of the arts
ISBN 0-06-019697-1; 0-06-095681-X pa
LC 2001-51731

Guggenheim "was known as much for her sexual exploits as for her championing of modern art, a fact Gill . . . examines with candor, sensitivity, and mellifluous grace." Booklist
Includes bibliographical references

Prose, Francine. **Peggy** Guggenheim; The Shock of the Modern. Francine Prose. Yale University Press 2015 240 p. 10 plates; illustrations $25 **92**
1. Jewish women 2. Art -- Collectors and collecting
ISBN 0300203489; 9780300203486
LC 2015932202

Author Francine Prose "offers a singular reading of [Peggy] Guggenheim's life that will enthrall enthusiasts of twentieth-century art, as well as anyone interested in American and European culture and the interrelationships between them. The lively and insightful narrative follows Guggenheim through virtually every aspect of her extraordinary life, from her unique collecting habits and paradigm-changing discoveries, to her celebrity friendships, failed marriages, and scandalous affairs." (Publisher's note)

"This finely researched and well-written work honestly examines the often disturbing world of an acclaimed figure. Readers who are interested in modern art and its background will find this of particular interest. For large arts and circulating collections." LJ

Guppy, Joe

Guppy, Joe. **My** fluorescent God; a psychotherapist confronts his most challenging case--his own. by

Joe Guppy. Booktrope Editions 2014 197 p. illustrations $14.95   **92**

1. Paranoia 2. Mental health 3. Mentally ill -- Washington (State) -- Seattle -- Biography 4. Psychotherapists -- Washington (State) -- Seattle -- Biography 5. Paranoia -- Patients -- Washington (State) -- Seattle -- Biography 6. Psychoses -- Patients -- Washington (State) -- Seattle -- Biography

ISBN 1620154412; 9781620154410

LC 2014912378

This book by Joe Guppy, "recreated from journal entries and the notes of mental-health professionals, [is] the story of the author's struggle to rebuild his sanity. Joe Guppy's life derailed in 1979. The 23-year-old was dealing with a bad breakup and existential angst, but it was a few stomach pills he took in Mexico that pushed him over the edge into paranoid psychosis." (Publisher's note)

"Beautifully written, honest, enlightening, hope-giving and valuable - essential for anyone interested in or struggling with mental health issues." Kirkus

Includes bibliographical references (page [200])

Guthrie, Woody, 1912-1967

Klein, Joe. **Woody** Guthrie; a life. Knopf 1980 475p il pa $17   **92**

1. Singers 2. Folk musicians 3. Memoirists 4. Songwriters 5. Musicians -- United States

ISBN 0-385-33385-4 pa

LC 80-7634

"The author incorporates into his text a great deal of information sifted from Guthrie's voluminous unpublished writings. . . . He also uses information from historical sources, published works, and hundreds of interviews to place Guthrie in a social and historical perspective. The result of all this research is . . . a very interesting and personal biography." Libr J

Gödel, Kurt

Goldstein, Rebecca. **Incompleteness**; the proof and paradox of Kurt Godel. Rebecca Goldstein. W.W. Norton 2005 296p il (Great discoveries) $22.95   **92**

1. Mathematicians

ISBN 0-393-05169-2

LC 2004-23052

This "is a stimulating exploration of both the power and the limitations of the human intellect." Publ Wkly

Includes bibliographical references

Hadfield, Chris, 1959-

Hadfield, Chris, 1959- An **astronaut's** guide to life on earth; what going to space taught me about ingenuity, determination, and being prepared for anything. Col. Chris Hadfield. Little, Brown and Co. 2013 304 p. ill. (some col.) $28   **92**

1. Astronauts 2. Outer space -- Exploration

ISBN 0316253014; 9780316253017

LC 2013943519

Author and astronaut Chris Hadfield "takes readers deep into his years of training and space exploration to show how to make the impossible possible. Through eye-opening, entertaining stories filled with the adrenaline of launch, the mesmerizing wonder of spacewalks, and the measured, calm responses mandated by crises, he explains how conventional wisdom can get in the way of achievement-and happiness." (Publisher's note)

"The author emphasizes that becoming an astronaut involved developing physical capabilities and technical skills through tireless practice and a fanatic attention to detail. . . . A page-turning memoir of life as a decorated astronaut." Kirkus

Hadrian, Emperor of Rome, 76-138

Everitt, Anthony. **Hadrian** and the triumph of Rome. Random House 2009 xxix, 392p il map $30   **92**

1. Emperors 2. Rome -- History 3. Emperors -- Rome

ISBN 978-1-4000-6662-9; 1-4000-6662-X

LC 2009-05683

"Emperor from 117 to 138 A.D., Hadrian styled himself princeps, or first among equals, and his reversal of his predecessors' expansionist policies contributed to an era of prosperity and relative calm. He was unapologetically Hellenic, a poet and a dabbler in magic, and he kept in his retinue a young male lover whom he later deified. If Hadrian is indeed an enigma, it's because so few accounts of his life have survived, and this is where Everitt—whose books rely heavily on primary sources—runs into difficulty. One gets a clear and compelling sense of Hadrian's times, but the Emperor himself remains tantalizingly unknowable." New Yorker

Includes bibliographical references

Halbreich, Betty, 1927-

Halbreich, Betty. **I'll** drink to that; a life in fashion, straight, no chaser. Betty Halbreich. The Penguin Press 2014 304 p. $27.95   **92**

1. Fashion 2. Clothing and dress 3. Personal appearance 4. Beauty, Personal 5. Image consultants -- United States -- Biography

ISBN 1594205701; 9781594205705

LC 2014009695

This memoir is by "Betty Halbreich, [who] has spent nearly forty years as the legendary personal shopper at Bergdorf Goodman. . . . She has helped many find their true selves through clothes, frank advice, and her own brand of wisdom. She is trusted by the most discriminating persons--including Hollywood's top stylists--to tell them what looks best. But Halbreich's personal transformation from a cosseted young girl to a fearless truth teller is the greatest makeover of her career." (Publisher's note)

"Names are dropped and stories are told in Halbreich's distinctive voice. Fashion mavens will enjoy the industry gossip while mere mortals may benefit from the closet organization tips." LJ

Hale, Robert (Robert Allen), 1941-2008

Kizzia, Tom. **Pilgrim's** wilderness; a true story of faith and madness on the Alaska Frontier. by Tom Kizzia; edited by Kevin Doughten. Crown 2013 336 p. illustrations, map $25   **92**

1. Alaska 2. Dysfunctional families 3. Cults -- Alaska -- McCarthy 4. Incest -- Alaska -- McCarthy 5. McCarthy (Alaska) -- Biography 6. Pioneers -- Alaska -- McCarthy -- Biography 7. Criminals -- Alaska

-- McCarthy -- Biography 8. Dysfunctional families -- Alaska -- McCarthy 9. Abusive men -- Alaska -- McCarthy -- Biography 10. Fundamentalists -- Alaska -- McCarthy -- Biography
ISBN 0307587827; 9780307587824; 9780307587848
LC 2012016502

This book, by Tom Kizzia, edited by Kevin Doughten, presents the "true story of a modern-day homesteading family in the deepest reaches of the Alaskan wilderness--and of the chilling secrets of its maniacal, spellbinding patriarch. . . . [The book] unfolds the . . . story of a charismatic spinner of American myths who was not what he seemed, the townspeople caught in his thrall, and the family he brought to the brink of ruin." (Publisher's note)

"The horror at the heart of this story about religious extremism on the fringes of the last American frontier is slow to reveal itself, but when that horror fully emerges, it will swallow most readers. Provocative and disturbing." Kirkus

Includes bibliographical references

Haley, Alex

Norrell, Robert J. **Alex** Haley and the books that changed a nation; by Robert J. Norrell. Palgrave Macmillan 2015 272 p. 8 plates; illustrations (hardback) $26.99   92
1. African American authors 2. African American journalists -- Biography 3. Authors, American -- 20th century -- Biography
ISBN 1137279605; 9781137279606
LC 2015016043

This biography on Alex Haley, by Robert J. Norrell, "follows him from his childhood in relative privilege in deeply segregated small town Tennessee to fame and fortune in high powered New York City. It was in the Navy, that Haley discovered himself as a writer, which eventually led his rise as a star journalist in the heyday of magazine personality profiles." (Publisher's note)

"With such a strong focus on the writing of Haley's two major works, this book will appeal primarily to readers who enjoyed or were inspired by The Autobiography of Malcolm X and Roots and wish to learn their backstories." LJ

Hamilton, Alexander, 1757-1804

★ Chernow, Ron. **Alexander** Hamilton. Penguin Press 2004 818p il $35   92
1. Statesmen 2. Secretaries of the treasury 3. United States -- Politics and government -- 1783-1809
ISBN 1-594-20009-2
LC 2003-65641

"Chernow makes fresh contributions to Hamiltoniana: no one has discovered so much about Hamilton's illegitimate origins and harrowed youth; few have been so taken by Hamilton's long-suffering, loving wife, Eliza. . . . This is a fine work that captures Hamilton's life with judiciousness and verve." Publ Wkly

Includes bibliographical references

Hamilton, Gabrielle, 1965-

Hamilton, Gabrielle. **Blood,** bones & butter; the inadvertent education of a reluctant chef. Random House 2011 291p $26   92
1. Cooks 2. Restaurateurs 3. Biography, Individual
ISBN 978-1-4000-6872-2; 1-4000-6872-X; 978-1-58836-931-4 ebook; 1-58836-931-5 ebook
LC 2010-17518

This book recounts how "when [Gabrielle] Hamilton was growing up, her parents would throw enormous parties for their friends and neighbors. Cooking for more than one hundred people was a common event in her family life. As she grew up, she sought to recreate the challenge and joy of feeding all those people and, unsurprisingly, she became a world-class chef. Her journey to owning her own New York City restaurant was not smooth, and took her all over the world." (Voice of Youth Advocates)

Though this book "is rhapsodic about food—in every variety, from the humble egg-on-a-roll sandwich served by Greek delis in New York to more esoteric things like 'fried zucchini agrodolce with fresh mint and hot chili flakes'— the book is hardly just for foodies. Ms. Hamilton . . . is as evocative writing about people and places as she is at writing about cooking." N Y Times (Late N Y Ed)

Hamilton, Jeremiah G., -1875

White, Shane. **Prince** of darkness; the untold story of Jeremiah G. Hamilton, Wall Street's first black millionaire. Shane White. Palgrave Macmillan 2015 360 p. $27.99   92
1. Finance -- United States 2. African Americans -- Biography 3. African American businesspeople 4. United States -- Social conditions 5. United States -- Race relations -- History 6. Millionaires -- United States -- Biography 7. United States -- Social conditions -- 19th century 8. Finance -- United States -- History -- 19th century 9. African Americans -- Social conditions -- 19th century 10. African American capitalists and financiers -- Biography 11. United States -- Race relations -- History -- 19th century
ISBN 9781250070562
LC 2015011416

In this book, author Shane White "reveals the larger than life story of [Jeremiah G. Hamilton] who defied every convention of his time. He wheeled and dealt in the lily white business world, he married a white woman, he bought a mansion in rural New Jersey, he owned railroad stock on trains he was not legally allowed to ride, and generally set his white contemporaries teeth on edge when he wasn't just plain outsmarting them." (Publisher's note)

"Superb scholarship and a sprightly style recover an unaccountably overlooked life in our history." Kirkus

Includes bibliographical references (pages 325-354) and index.

Hanagarne, Joshua, 1977-

Hanagarne, Josh. The **world's** strongest librarian; a memoir of Tourette's, faith, strength, and the power of family. Joshua Hanagarne. Gotham Books 2013 288 p. (hardcover) $26   92
1. Tourette syndrome 2. Public libraries -- Utah -- Salt Lake City 3. Librarians -- Utah -- Salt Lake City --

Biography

ISBN 1592407870; 9781592407873

LC 2012037713

This memoir, by Josh Hanagarne, is the story of a Mormon with Tourette Syndrome. "By the time [Josh Hanagarne] was twenty, . . . his Tourette's tics escalated to nightmarish levels. Determined to conquer his affliction, Josh underwent everything from quack remedies to lethargy-inducing drug regimes. . . . At last, an eccentric, autistic strongman . . . taught Josh how to 'throttle' his tics into submission through strength-training." (Publisher's note)

Handel, George Frideric, 1685-1759

Harris, Ellen T. **George** Frideric Handel; a life with friends. Ellen T. Harris. W. W. Norton & Company 2014 496 p. illustrations (hardcover) $37.95   92

1. Composers -- Biography

ISBN 0393088952; 9780393088953

LC 2014008148

This book, by Ellen T. Harris, is "[a]n intimate portrait of [George Frideric] Handel's life and inner circle. . . . Harris has spent years tracking down the letters, diaries, personal accounts, legal cases, and other documents connected to these bequests. The result is a tightly woven tapestry of London in the first half of the eighteenth century, one that interlaces vibrant descriptions of Handel's music with stories of loyalty, cunning, and betrayal." (Publisher's note)

A "readable tale of one of the world's most enigmatic musicians and composers." Pub Wkly

Includes bibliographical references, discography, and index

Handwerker, Nathan, 1892-1974

Handwerker, Lloyd. **Famous** Nathan; a family saga of Coney Island, the American dream, and the search for the perfect hot dog. Lloyd Handwerker and Gil Reavill. Flatiron Books 2016 320 p. illustrations (hardback) $26.99   92

1. Hot dogs 2. Coney Island (New York, N.Y.) 3. Family-owned business enterprises 4. Nathan's Famous 5. Coney Island (New York, N.Y.) -- History 6. Frankfurters -- New York (State) -- History 7. Hot dog stands -- New York (State) -- History 8. Fast food restaurants -- New York (State) -- History

ISBN 9781250074546; 1250074541

LC 2016001605

In this book, written with Gil Reavill, author Lloyd Handwerker "relates every knowable detail about Nathan's Famous: employee tensions, how the potatoes were sourced, even who painted the signed. He also nestles his grandfather's story in the greater context of family struggles, Coney Island, the history of hot dogs, and the evolving American landscape." (Publishers Weekly)

"It's an American Dream tale with a captivating central character, served with the same delicious snap as an authentic Nathan's hot dog." Booklist

Includes bibliographical references.

Handy, W. C. (William Christopher), 1873-1958

Robertson, David. **W.C.** Handy; the life and times of the man who made the blues. Alfred A. Knopf 2009 286p il $27.95   92

1. Composers 2. Blues music 3. Blues musicians 4. Music publishers

ISBN 978-0-307-26609-5; 0-307-26609-5

LC 2008-45983

The author "casts overdue light on Handy's essential role in establishing the blues as a popular art, and he does this, much to his credit, without resorting to dubious claims that Handy was the first or the best of the blues' multiple progenitors. A mark of both the evenhandedness of his scholarship and the delicacy of his writing is Robertson's resistance to the idea of Handy as the Father of the Blues — a notion that Handy himself advanced and exploited deftly during his lifetime." N Y Times Book Rev

Includes bibliographical references

Hansberry, Lorraine, 1930-1965

Hansberry, Lorraine. **To** be young, gifted, and Black; Lorraine Hansberry in her own words. adapted by Robert Nemiroff; with drawings and art by Lorraine Hansberry; introduction by James Baldwin; and a new preface by Jewell Handy Gresham Nemiroff. 1st Vintage Books ed; Vintage Books 1995 xxx, 261p il pa $8.95; pa $13.95   92

1. Authors 2. Dramatists 3. Essayists 4. Newspaper editors 5. Nonfiction writers 6. Dramatists, American 7. African American women -- Biography

ISBN 9780451531780; 0-679-76415-1

LC 96-119999

First published 1969 by Prentice-Hall

Work on this book and on the script for the play of the same title, which was presented at New York's Cherry Lane Theatre in 1969, "proceeded concurrently, each drawing upon the experiences and creative discoveries of the other, but ultimately diverging quite drastically." Postscript

Hardy, Thomas, 1840-1928

Tomalin, Claire. **Thomas** Hardy. Penguin Group 2006 xxv, 486p il map $35   92

1. Poets 2. Authors 3. Novelists 4. Short story writers

ISBN 1-59420-118-8; 978-1-59420-118-9

LC 2007-295886

"A priceless resource for the general reader and the Victorian scholar." Booklist

Includes bibliographical references

Hari, Daoud

Hari, Daoud. The **translator**; a tribesman's memoir of Darfur. Random House 2008 204p hardcover o.p. pa $13   92

1. Refugees 2. Memoirists 3. Guides (Persons) 4. Sudan -- History -- Darfur conflict, 2003-

ISBN 978-1-4000-6744-2; 1-4000-6744-8; 978-0-8129-7917-6 pa; 0-8129-7917-6 pa

LC 2007-42308

In this memoir, the author recounts his life in Darfur, Sudan before and after the conflict in 2003.

"Those with the courage to join Hari's odyssey may find this a life-changing read." Publ Wkly

Harris, Neil Patrick, 1973-

Harris, Neil Patrick, 1973- **Neil** Patrick Harris; choose your own autobiography. by Neil Patrick Harris; as unshredded and pasted back together by David Javerbaum. Crown Archetype 2014 ix, 294 p.p 8 plates; color illustrations (hardcover) $26 **92**

1. Plot-your-own stories 2. Actors -- United States -- Biography

ISBN 0385346999; 9780385346993

LC 2014016637

In this book, by Neil Patrick Harris, edited by David Javerbaum, a "Joycean experiment in light celebrity narrative, actor/personality/carbon-based-life-form Neil Patrick Harris lets you, the reader, live his life. You will be born to New Mexico. You will get your big break at an acting camp. You will get into a bizarre confrontation outside a nightclub with actor Scott Caan. Even better, at each critical juncture of your life you will choose how to proceed." (Publisher's note)

Harrison, Benjamin, 1833-1901

Calhoun, Charles W. **Benjamin** Harrison. Times Books 2005 206p il (American presidents series) $20 **92**

1. Presidents 2. Senators 3. Presidents -- United States

ISBN 0-8050-6952-6; 978-0-8050-6952-5

LC 2004-63778

The author "dusts off an almost thoroughly forgotten chief executive, known primarily for serving between Cleveland's two terms, to disclose a harbinger of the modern, activist president. . . . One of the most revelatory entries in the American Presidents series." Booklist

Includes bibliographical references

Harrison, George, 1943-2001

Thomson, Graeme. **George** Harrison; Behind the Locked Door. Graeme Thomson. Overlook Books 2015 464 p. 8 plates; ills.; portraits $29.95 **92**

1. Beatles 2. Musicians

ISBN 1468310658; 9781468310658

In this biography, author Graeme Thompson "challenges the image of George Harrison as 'the quiet Beatle,' portraying the guitarist as a complex person trying to navigate a middle course between materiality and spirituality, and fame and reclusivity. . . . Thomson chronicles Harrison's life from his rather run-of-the mill childhood and his early days of making music with The Quarrymen to the beginnings of The Beatles, their rapid ascent to fame and their just as speedy descent." (Publishers Weekly)

"Thomson is especially compelling in his illumination of Harrison's inner life, his robust spirituality, and his deep love of Indian culture." Booklist

Harrison, William Henry, 1773-1841

Collins, Gail. **William** Henry Harrison; Gail Collins. Times Books/Henry Holt and Co. 2012 xviii, 153 p.p **92**

1. War of 1812 2. Presidents -- United States -- Biography 3. Governors -- Indiana -- Biography 4.

United States -- History -- 1783-1865 5. Presidents -- United States -- Election -- 1840 6. United States -- Politics and government -- 1841-1845

ISBN 9780805091182

LC 2011018976

This book offers a biography of U.S. former president William Henry Harrison. "Despite the legendary 1840 campaign featuring a 'log cabin, hard cider' frontiersman with humble origins, Harrison was born on a Virginia plantation, built himself a mansion as governor of the rough Indiana frontier territory, and avoided alcohol. His fame rested on two victories: the 1811 battle of Tippecanoe against the Shawnee Indians, and the 1813 Battle of the Thames during the War of 1812, in which the Indian leader Tecumseh was killed. For decades afterward, he struggled as a farmer and Ohio politician; he lost the 1836 presidential election but won four years later." (Publishers Weekly)

Includes bibliographical references and index

Hatshepsut, Queen of Egypt

Cooney, Kara, 1972- The **woman** who would be king; Hatshepsut's Rise to Power in Ancient Egypt. Kara Cooney. Crown Publishers 2014 384 p. 8 plates; ills; plans; maps $28 **92**

1. Queens 2. Egypt -- Kings and rulers 3. Pharaohs -- Biography 4. Queens -- Egypt -- Biography 5. Egypt -- Kings and rulers -- Biography 6. Egypt -- History -- Eighteenth dynasty, ca. 1570-1320 B.C

ISBN 0307956768; 9780307956767

LC 2014000243

This book, by Kara Cooney, is a "biography of the longest-reigning female pharaoh in Ancient Egypt. . . . Hatshepsut--the daughter of a general who usurped Egypt's throne and a mother with ties to the previous dynasty--was born into a privileged position in the royal household. . . . Her failure to produce a male heir was ultimately the twist of fate that paved the way for her improbable rule as a cross-dressing king." (Publisher's note)

"By examining her subject within the context of the stringent gender restrictions of her time and place, [Cooney] attempts to explain the motivations and the thought processes of one of the most successful female leaders of the ancient world." Booklist

Ryan, Donald P. **Beneath** the sands of Egypt; adventures of an unconventional archaeologist. William Morrow 2010 286p il $26.99; ebook $12.99 **92**

1. Queens 2. Archeologists 3. Archaeologists 4. College teachers 5. Egypt -- Antiquities 6. Excavations (Archeology) -- Egypt

ISBN 978-0-06-173282-9; 0-06-173282-6; 978-0-06-200280-8 ebook; 0-06-200280-5 ebook

LC 2010-20355

"Ryan, the archaeologist who rediscovered tomb KV 60 in the Valley of the Kings (later identified as the final resting place of the pharoah Hatshepsut), takes us through his life, career, and numerous expeditions. It's a thrilling book, not because it's full of Indiana Jones heroics but because Ryan's enthusiasm for what he does (more dirt-sifting than bullwhip-wielding) is manifested on every page; and . . . he catches us up in his excitement, makes us wish we weren't just reading about this stuff but were actually doing it. . . . This wonderful adventure story should be must reading for anyone aspiring to become an archaeologist, but even those of us who harbor no such dreams will be aching to get a little dirt under our fingernails." Booklist

Havel, Václav, 1936-2011

Havel, Vaclav. **To** the castle and back; translated from the Czech by Paul Wilson. Knopf 2007 383p $27.95; pa $15.95 **92**

1. Authors 2. Dramatists 3. Presidents 4. Essayists 5. Dissenters 6. Czech Republic -- Politics and government 7. Czechoslovakia -- Politics and government

ISBN 978-0-307-26641-5; 0-307-26641-9; 978-0-307-33845-2 pa; 0-307-38845-X pa

LC 2007-4413

Original Czech edition, 2006

The book "gives Havel's account of his journey from dissident-in-chief to head of state during the Velvet Revolution of 1989—and the turmoil that followed. Hardly a conventional memoir, its three intermixed narratives are at first as disorienting as his role reversal—which dismayed his wife Olga as much as himself. . . . These selections are by turns obscure, funny, insightful, poignant, and peevish. . . . Living in truth was what [Havel] preached as a dissident, and it is what he preached as president. . . . Whatever his political shortcomings in office, at least in this, the Czechs were privileged to have Havel as president." Commonweal

Hawa Abdi, 1947-

Abdi, Hawa. **Keeping** hope alive; one woman, 90,000 lives changed. Hawa Abdi with Sarah J. Robbins. Grand Central Pub. 2013 272 p. (hardcover) $26.99 **92**

1. Refugees -- Somalia 2. Somalia -- Biography 3. Gynecologists -- Somalia -- Biography 4. Women gynecologists -- Somalia -- Biography 5. Human rights workers -- Somalia -- Biography 6. Women human rights workers -- Somalia -- Biography

ISBN 1455503762; 9781455503766; 9781619696389

LC 2012041781

This book presents a memoir by physician Haw Abdi, "who, along with her daughters, has kept 90,000 of her fellow citizens safe, healthy, and educated for over 20 years in Somalia." The author "is the founder of a massive camp for internally displaced people located a few miles from wartorn Mogadishu, Somalia. Since 1991, when the Somali government collapsed . . . she has dedicated herself to providing help for people whose lives have been shattered by violence and poverty." (Publisher's note)

Hawking, Stephen, 1942-

Hawking, Stephen, 1942- **My** brief history; Stephen Hawking. Bantam Books 2013 144 p. illustrations $22 **92**

1. Cosmology 2. Black holes (Astronomy) 3. Physicists -- Biography

ISBN 0345535286; 9780345535283

LC 2013027938

In this autobiography, Stephen Hawking "opens up about the challenges that confronted him following his diagnosis of ALS at age twenty-one. Tracing his development as a thinker, he explains how the prospect of an early death urged him onward through numerous intellectual break-throughs, and talks about the genesis of his masterpiece 'A Brief History of Time'". (Publisher's note)

"Hawking says it all with charm, intermingling his personal life with abstruse theoretical physics in nontechnical language. Revealing the power of mind over body, this is an enjoyable, entertaining, and inspiring work." Choice

Hawthorne, Nathaniel, 1804-1864

★ Wineapple, Brenda. **Hawthorne**: a life. Alfred A. Knopf 2003 xii, 509 p.p il $30 **92**

1. Authors 2. Novelists 3. Short story writers

ISBN 0-375-40044-3; 9780812972917

LC 2002-192485

In this biography Wineapple discusses the "public controversies that shaped [Hawthorne's] world: the Whig triumphs that cost him his customhouse job and forced him into writing; the critical exchanges that heartened him with praise for his work . . . and wounded him with disparagement; and the Civil War battles that drove him to despair— and into political disrepute as a copperhead." Booklist

Includes bibliographical references (p. 473-486) and index.

Haydn, Joseph, 1732-1809

Haydn; edited by David Wyn Jones; consultant editor Otto Biba. Oxford Univ. Press 2002 xxi, 515p il map (Oxford composer companions) $75 **92**

1. Composers

ISBN 0-19-866216-5

LC 2002-510033

"This volume will be useful to persons who need quick, specific information about Haydn, his works, and 18th-century style." Choice

Hazan, Marcella

Hazan, Marcella. **Amarcord,** Marcella remembers; the remarkable life story of the woman who started out teaching science in a small town in Italy, but ended up teaching America how to cook Italian. Gotham Books 2008 307p il $27.50 **92**

1. Cooks 2. Italian cooking 3. Cookbook writers 4. Cooking teachers

ISBN 978-1-59240-388-2; 1-59240-388-3

LC 2007-46197

This is a memoir by the author of The Classic Italian Cook Book (1973) and More Classic Italian Cooking (1978).

"Hazan has selected the best stories from her own life to present Amarcord with all the warmth and humor of a long meal in famiglia made from the choicest ingredients. . . . If you've never been [to] Italy, the time spent with Hazan will have you planning your next vacation faster than you can say manicotti." Christ Sci Monit

Hearst, William Randolph, 1863-1951

Whyte, Kenneth. The **uncrowned** king; the sensational rise of William Randolph Hearst. Counterpoint 2009 546p il $30 **92**

1. Publishers and publishing 2. Newspaper editors 3. Newspaper executives

ISBN 978-1-58243-467-4; 1-58243-467-0

LC 2008-47442

"A very worthwhile reexamination of the rise of a flawed but accomplished man." Booklist

Includes bibliographical references (p. 505-511)

Hefner, Hugh

Watts, Steven. **Mr.** Playboy; Hugh Hefner and the American dream. Wiley 2008 529p il $29.95 **92**

1. Magazine executives

ISBN 9780471690597; 0-4716-9059-7

LC 2008-9572

"This is not a gossip book but a well-documented biography written with access to Hefner's over 1800 scrapbooks, the company archives, and interviews. Watts finds Hefner comparable to the subjects of his other books about Henry Ford and Walt Disney in that all were major contributors to aspects of the American dream." Libr J

Includes bibliographical references

Heisenberg, Werner, 1901-1976

Cassidy, David C., 1945- **Beyond** uncertainty; Heisenberg, quantum physics, and the bomb. David C. Cassidy. Bellevue Literary Press 2009 480 p. $27 **92**

1. Physicists 2. Biography, Individual 3. Nobel laureates for physics 4. Physicists -- Germany -- Biography 5. World War, 1939-1945 -- Science -- Germany 6. Atomic bomb -- Germany -- History -- 20th century

ISBN 978-1-934137-13-0; 1-934137-13-8; 1934137138; 9781934137130

LC 2008039885

This is a biography "of the German wunderkind Werner Heisenberg (1901–1976), who won the 1932 Nobel Prize in physics for revolutionizing the nascent field of quantum physics, first with his matrix interpretation of quantum mechanics, then with his famous uncertainty principle. . . . Exhaustively detailed yet eminently readable, this is an important book." Publ Wkly

Includes bibliographical references (p. [411]-456) and index

Heller, Joseph

Daugherty, Tracy. **Just** one catch; a biography of Joseph Heller. St. Martin's Press 2011 548p il $35 **92**

1. Authors 2. Novelists 3. Authors, American 4. Short story writers 5. Biography, Individual

ISBN 978-0-312-59685-9; 0-312-59685-5

LC 2011-20749

This biography offers "countless insightful, amusing anecdotes from Heller's childhood, military service and postpublication notoriety as a celebrated literary figure. But the writing, publishing and ensuing aftermath of Catch-22 is the clear focal point of Daugherty's book. Lacking the self-assured swagger of Norman Mailer and the countercultural sway of the Beats, Heller was a long-frustrated and surprising emergent on the literary scene. A reluctant participant in the burgeoning Madison Avenue advertising world of the 1950s, Heller seemed a figure unlikely to publish a work of such unimpeachable influence. Published when Heller was 39, Catch-22 represents the high-water mark of his career and to some extent his personal life—it is as if everything prepublication was prologue and everything that followed was postscript. Heller wrote copiously throughout the remainder of his life but never attained those heights again, critically or commercially. Nonetheless, Daugherty persuasively endorses the view of Heller as a pivotal figure in American letters." Time Out N Y

Includes bibliographical references

Hellman, Lillian, 1906-1984

Hellman, Lillian. **Pentimento**. Little, Brown 1973 297p hardcover o.p. pa $14.95 **92**

1. Authors 2. Dramatists 3. Memoirists 4. Dramatists, American

ISBN 0-316-35288-8 pa

This continuation of An unfinished woman—a memoir (1969) offers sketches of events and people from the author's past. She reminisces about her childhood in the South, some of her eccentric relatives including Cousin Bethe and Uncle Willy, Julia, her childhood friend who was trapped by the Nazis, Dashiell Hammett, who was her lover, and her experiences in the theater

"Pentimento is valuable as a picture of a woman and writer in the making." New Repub

Martinson, Deborah. **Lillian** Hellman; a life with foxes and scoundrels. Counterpoint 2005 448p il $27.95 **92**

1. Authors 2. Dramatists 3. Memoirists 4. Dramatists, American

ISBN 1-58243-315-1

LC 2005-16616

This is "a richly thorough, sometimes somber, and fairly objective portrait of an enigmatic individual." Libr J

Includes bibliographical references

Hemingway, Ernest, 1899-1961

Lynn, Kenneth S. **Hemingway**. Harvard University Press 1995 702p il pa $27 **92**

1. Poets 2. Authors 3. Novelists 4. Journalists 5. Authors, American 6. Short story writers 7. Nobel laureates for literature

ISBN 0-674-38732-5; 978-0-674-38732-4

LC 95-129513

First published 1987 by Simon and Schuster

"Taking as his premise Hemingway's glib assertion that the only analyst he relied upon was his 'portable Corona Number 3,' Lynn tracks the exploration of a disordered inner world as Hemingway sought to find some sort of resolution to the agony of his personal conflicts through 'his cunningly wrought fiction.' The man who emerges from Lynn's biography is a vastly more complex and compelling figure than the white-bearded, pontificating 'Papa' of myth." Publ Wkly

Includes bibliographical references

Reynolds, Michael S. **Hemingway**: the Paris years; [by] Michael Reynolds. W.W. Norton 1999 402p il map pa $18.95 **92**

1. Poets 2. Authors 3. Novelists 4. Journalists 5. Authors, American 6. Short story writers 7. Nobel laureates for literature

ISBN 0-393-31879-6

First published 1989 by Blackwell

In this second volume of a five-volume biography of Hemingway begun with The young Hemingway (1998), the author "locates Hemingway in an American sociocultural context wherein he rejects middle-class restraints and aspires to identity as hero and self-reliant frontiersman (soldier, bullfighter, hunter, lover). The genius of the book lies in a graceful and informative linkage between literary creation and biographical incident." Libr J

Includes bibliographical references

Hendrix, Jimi

★ Cross, Charles R. **Room** full of mirrors; a biography of Jimi Hendrix. Hyperion 2005 384p il $24.95; pa $15.99   **92**

1. Singers 2. Guitarists 3. Rock musicians
ISBN 1-401-30028-6; 0-7868-8841-5 pa

LC 2005-46362

"Admirably comprehensive and well referenced, this is the Hendrix biography to acquire if you can acquire only one." Booklist

Includes bibliographical references

Henry VIII, King of England, 1491-1547

Weir, Alison. The **lost** Tudor princess; the life of Margaret Douglas of Scotland. Alison Weir. Ballantine Books 2016 576 p. illustrations, maps (hardcover : alk. paper) $30   **92**

1. Great Britain -- History -- 1485-1603, Tudors 2. Nobility -- Great Britain -- Biography 3. Nobility -- Great Britain -- History -- 16th century 4. Great Britain -- History -- Tudors, 1485-1603 -- Biography
ISBN 9780345521392

LC 2015037958

This book, by Alison Weir, offers a "biography of Margaret Douglas, the beautiful, cunning niece of Henry VIII of England who used her sharp intelligence and covert power to influence the succession after the death of Elizabeth I. . . . Lady Margaret Douglas, Countess of Lennox, was an important figure in Tudor England, yet today, while her contemporaries—Anne Boleyn, Mary, Queen of Scots, Elizabeth I—have achieved celebrity status, she is largely forgotten." (Publisher's note)

"An abundantly detailed history from an author steeped in England's past." Kirkus

Includes bibliographical references and index

Hensley, William L., 1941-

Hensley, William L. **Fifty** miles from tomorrow; a memoir of Alaska and the real people. [by] William L. Iggiagruk Hensley. Farrar, Straus and Giroux 2008 256p il map $24   **92**

1. Inupiat 2. Eskimo leaders 3. State legislators
ISBN 978-0-374-15484-4; 0-374-15484-8

LC 2008-31409

The author "manages to make fresh an old narrative of people who arise just as their culture is being erased—be they 'Braveheart' Scotsmen or outback Aborigines. His book is also bright and detailed, moving along at a clip most sled dogs would have trouble keeping up with." N Y Times Book Rev

Henson, Jim

Jones, Brian Jay. **Jim** Henson; the biography. Brian Jay Jones. Ballantine Books 2013 608 p. (hbk.) $35; (pbk.) $20   **92**

1. Muppet show (Television program) 2. Sesame Street (Television program) 3. Puppeteers -- United States -- Biography 4. Television producers and directors -- United States -- Biography
ISBN 0345526112; 9780345526113; 9780345526120; 0345526112

LC 2013024039

This book explores "the life of Muppets creator Jim Henson (1936-1990) . . . explaining how Henson grew up to become a daring puppeteer and scriptwriter, how he managed to attract so much remarkable talent to his side, and how his stressful business relationship with the Disney Company might have aggravated the bacterial infection that weakened the normally healthy Henson, who died at age 53 while trying to negotiate the planned Disney purchase of the franchise." (Kirkus Reviews)

Includes bibliographical references and index

Hepburn, Audrey, 1929-1993

Walker, Alexander. **Audrey**; her real story. St. Martin's Press 1995 319p il hardcover o.p. pa $16.95   **92**

1. Actors
ISBN 0-312-18046-2 pa

LC 94-33716

The author "recounts his subject's childhood in war-torn Europe and her early stage and film career. . . . Both the narrative and the writing itself become more lively as he discusses the heyday of her career, her sometimes turbulent love life and her work with Third World children for UNICEF." Publ Wkly

Hepburn, Katharine, 1907-2003

Berg, A. Scott. **Kate** remembered. Putnam 2003 370p il $25.95; pa $15   **92**

1. Actors
ISBN 0-399-15164-8; 0-425-19909-6 pa

LC 2003-545232

In this posthumous biography, the author reveals "details about such pivotal events as the death of her brother by hanging, her relationships with powerful men like Howard Hughes and John Ford, and her slow, sad decline. . . . Berg's writing is so intimate that readers may feel they are hiding behind a curtain as they listen to the stories he elicits from his subject. Kate herself comes across pretty much the way she did on screen: bossy, courageous, and self-involved." Booklist

Hepburn, Katharine. **Me**; stories of my life. Knopf 1991 420p il hardcover o.p. pa $15.95 **92**

1. Actors
ISBN 0-345-41009-2

LC 90-50805

This book "sounds just like its author—lots of cropped sentences, dashes, Hepburnian phrasing. But it's not a full-dress autobiography; as the subtitle proclaims, this is a collection of stories. . . . Still, fans will not be disappointed. Beginning with her early years . . . and concluding with her relationship with Tracy, Hepburn delivers all kinds of wry moments and, of course, a most interesting cast of characters." Booklist

Mann, William J. **Kate**: the woman who was Hepburn. H. Holt 2006 xxviii, 621p il $30   92
  1. Actors
  ISBN 978-0-8050-7625-7; 0-8050-7625-5
This is a biography of the American actress.
"This will surely be the definitive version of Hepburn's life for decades to come, as it is an outstanding example of painstaking research matched with splendid writing." Publ Wkly
  Includes bibliographical references

Herriot, James

Herriot, James. **All** creatures great and small; 20th anniversary ed; St. Martin's Press 1992 442p $21.95; pa $13.95   92
  1. Authors 2. Veterinarians 3. Veterinary medicine 4. Memoirists
  ISBN 0-312-08498-6; 0-312-33085-5 pa
                                       LC 92-18975
  First published 1972
The first volume of Herriot's autobiographical account of the practice of veterinary medicine in Yorkshire, England in the 1930s
  Followed by All things bright and beautiful (1974), All things wise and wonderful (1977), and The Lord God made them all (1981)

Hersh, Seymour M.

Miraldi, Robert. **Seymour** Hersh; scoop artist. Robert Miraldi. Potomac Books, An Imprint of the University of Nebraska Press 2013 415 p. (cloth : alk. paper) $34.95   92
  1. Journalism -- United States 2. Journalists -- United States -- Biography 3. United States -- Foreign relations -- 1989- 4. United States -- Foreign relations -- 1945-1989 5. United States -- Politics and government -- 1989- 6. United States -- Politics and government -- 1945-1989
  ISBN 1612344755; 9781612344751
                                       LC 2013023619
This book, by Robert Miraldi, offers a biography of the investigative reporter Seymour Hersh. "From his exposé of the My Lai massacre in 1969 to his revelations about torture at Abu Ghraib prison in 2004, Hersh has consistently captured the public imagination, spurred policymakers to reform, and drawn the ire of presidents. . . . This . . . biography captures a . . . successful career of important exposés and outstanding accomplishments." (Publisher's note)
"A deep biographical treatment of the Pulitzer Prize-winning journalist who is the scourge of those in power. . . . Hersh comes across as a good guy of limited patience when approached by fellow journalists and as a bulldog with sharp teeth when in his reporter mode." Kirkus
  Includes bibliographical references and index

Higashida, Naoki, 1992-

Naoki Higashida. The **reason** I jump; the inner voice of a thirteen-year-old boy with autism. by Na-

oki Higashida; translated by KA Yoshida and David Mitchell. Random House 2013 176 p. illustrations (acid-free paper) $22   92
  1. Autism 2. Autistic children 3. Autistic people -- Psychology 4. Autistic people -- Japan -- Biography
  ISBN 0812994868; 9780812994865
                                       LC 2012045703
In this book, "a 13-year-old Japanese author illuminates his autism from within. . . . The book takes the form of a series of straightforward questions followed by answers. . . . He describes the difficulty of expressing through words what the brain wants to say, the challenge of focusing and ordering experience, the obsessiveness of repetition, the comfort found in actions that others might find odd, and the frustration of being the source of others' frustration." (Kirkus Reviews)
A "a mixture of invaluable anecdotal information, practical advice and whimsical self-expression." Pub Wkly

Highsmith, Patricia, 1921-1995

Schenkar, Joan. The **talented** Miss Highsmith; the secret life and serious art of Patricia Highsmith. St. Martin's Press 2009 684p il $40   92
  1. Authors 2. Novelists 3. Mystery writers 4. Authors, American
  ISBN 978-0-312-30375-4
                                       LC 2009-18363
"It is hard to imagine a more thoroughly fact-filled or energetic biography than 'The Talented Miss Highsmith' or one more determined to examine the deepest recesses of its complicated subject. Ms. Schenkar's presentation is cubist, off-putting at first, featuring separated essays that isolate various topics. The dislocation can be confusing, yet one soon comes to accept the method as a way of mining the many veins of a very strange life." Wall Street J
  Includes bibliographical references

Hilfiger, Tommy

Hilfiger, Tommy, 1951- **American** dreamer; My Life in Fashion & Business. Tommy Hilfiger with Peter Knobler; foreword by Quincy Jones. Ballantine Books 2016 352 p. (hardcover : alk. paper) $30 92
  1. Fashion designers 2. Fashion designers -- United States -- Biography
  ISBN 9781101886212
                                       LC 2016023113
In this memoir, fashion designer "Tommy Hilfiger shares his . . . life story for the first time. . . . [It] brims with anecdotes that cover Tommy's years as a club kid and scrappy entrepreneur in 1970s New York as well as unique insights into the exclusive A-list personalities with whom he's collaborated and interacted. . . . Tommy takes us behind the scenes of every decision—and every mistake—he's ever made, offering advice on leadership, business, team-building, and creativity." (Publisher's note)
"An honest, straightforward, mostly entertaining autobiography of the man who created a classic yet hip line of clothing." Kirkus

Hill, Joe, 1879-1915

Adler, William M. The **man** who never died; the life, times, and legacy of Joe Hill, American labor icon. Bloomsbury 2011 435p il $30 **92**

1. Poets 2. Authors 3. Folk musicians 4. Songwriters 5. Revolutionaries 6. Biography, Individual 7. Industrial Workers of the World

ISBN 978-1-59691-696-8; 1-59691-696-6

LC 2011009821

This is a biography of the poet, songwriter and labor activist who was executed in 1915. Index.

"Presenting Hill as man and symbol, Adler contributes vitally to labor history." Booklist

Includes bibliographical references

Hilleman, Maurice R., 1919-2005

Offit, Paul A. **Vaccinated**; one man's quest to defeat the world's deadliest diseases. Smithsonian Books/Collins 2007 254p $26.95 **92**

1. Biologists 2. Vaccination 3. Microbiologists

ISBN 978-0-06-122795-0; 0-06-122795-1

LC 2006-53054

"This book leaves one with a great appreciation for the work of the Salks and Sabins of the world, and it makes one want to lead a movement to enshrine Maurice Hilleman in the pantheon of American pop heroes." Choice

Includes bibliographical references

Himmler, Heinrich, 1900-1945

Breitman, Richard. The **architect** of genocide; Himmler and the final solution. University Press of New England 1992 335p (The Tauber Institute for the Study of European Jewry) pa $30 **92**

1. Heads of state 2. National socialism 3. Nazi leaders 4. Germany -- Politics and government -- 1933-1945

ISBN 0-87451-596-3; 978-0-87451-596-1

LC 92-53857

First published 1991 by Knopf

"This engrossing, detailed study constitutes a powerful refutation of revisionist scholars who claim that Hitler did not plan the Final Solution in advance but instead improvised it out of either military or political frustration." Publ Wkly

Includes bibliographical references

Hines, Richard, 1945-

Hines, Richard. **No** Way but Gentlenesse; A Memoir of How Kes, My Kestrel, Changed My Life. Richard Hines. St. Martin's Press 2016 288 p. (hardcover) $26 **92**

1. Falconry

ISBN 9781632865021; 1632865025

This memoir, by Richard Hines, describes "how catching and training a kestrel changed the life of a young British boy. . . . Always a naturalist at heart, Hines soon was reading all he could find regarding falconry. It was near Tankersley Old Hall that he took his first kestrel, called Kes, and began training her." (Kirkus Reviews)

"A delightful story of a boy, his birds, and his pursuit of knowledge in spite of society's dictates." Kirkus

Hirohito, Emperor of Japan, 1901-1989

★ Bix, Herbert P. **Hirohito** and the making of modern Japan. HarperCollins Pubs. 2000 800p il maps hardcover o.p. pa $18 **92**

1. Emperors 2. Japan -- Politics and government

ISBN 0-06-093130-2 pa

LC 99-89427

"In 1945, fearing that the Japanese would resist American occupation unless the Emperor ordered them to obey, General MacArthur colluded with Hirohito in maintaining that the sovereign had been powerless to control Japan's military leaders. . . . {Bix}, uses newly available sources to argue that Hirohito was a war criminal. An imperialist whose policies reflected his belief in the racial superiority of the Japanese, Hirohito governed by manipulation for almost two decades, and used the threat of Soviet Communism to justify domestic repression and soaring military budgets. The author's virtuoso scholarship and accessible narrative invite us into Hirohito's world." New Yorker

Includes bibliographical references

Hirsi Ali, Ayaan, 1969-

Hirsi Ali, Ayaan. **Infidel**. Free Press 2007 353p il $26; pa $15 **92**

1. Refugees 2. Muslim women 3. Feminists 4. Memoirists 5. Members of Parliament

ISBN 0-7432-8968-4; 978-0-7432-8968-9; 0-7432-8969-2 pa; 978-0-7432-8969-6 pa

LC 2006-49762

"A Somali by birth and a recently elected member of the Dutch Parliament, Ms. Hirsi Ali had waged a personal crusade to improve the lot of Muslim women. Her warnings about the dangers posed to the Netherlands by unassimilated Muslims made her Public Enemy No. 1 for Muslim extremists, a feminist counterpart to Salman Rushdie. The circuitous, violence-filled path that led Ms. Hirsi Ali from Somalia to the Netherlands is the subject of 'Infidel,' her brave, inspiring and beautifully written memoir." N Y Times (Late N Y Ed)

Hitchcock, Alfred, 1899-1980

Chandler, Charlotte. **It's** only a movie; Alfred Hitchcock, a personal biography. Simon & Schuster 2005 349p il $26 **92**

1. Motion picture directors

ISBN 0-7432-4508-3

LC 2004-52559

The author reveals "several insights into Hitchcock's technical genius, creative worldview and personality. . . . Chandler allows her sources to reminisce at great length, and they tend to tell fascinating stories." Publ Wkly

Includes filmography

Hitchens, Christopher, 1949-2011

Hitchens, Christopher, 1949-2011. **Hitch-22**; a memoir. Twelve 2010 435p il $26.99 **92**

1. Authors 2. Journalists 3. Essayists 4. Writers on politics 5. Biography, Individual

ISBN 978-0-446-54033-9

LC 2009051959

This is an autobiography by the British journalist. Christopher Hitchens is the author of For the Sake of Argument:

Essays and Minority Reports (1993); Blood, Class, and Nostalgia (1990); Blood, Class, and Empire (2004), and God is Not Great (2007). Index.

Few authors can rile as easily as Hitchens does, but even his detractors might find it difficult to put down a book so witty, so piercing, so spoiling for a fight. He makes you want to be as good a reader as he is a writer. Booklist

Hitler, Adolf, 1889-1945

Breitman, Richard. The **architect** of genocide; Himmler and the final solution. University Press of New England 1992 335p (The Tauber Institute for the Study of European Jewry) pa $30   92
1. Heads of state 2. National socialism 3. Nazi leaders 4. Germany -- Politics and government -- 1933-1945
ISBN 0-87451-596-3; 978-0-87451-596-1
LC 92-53857
First published 1991 by Knopf
"This engrossing, detailed study constitutes a powerful refutation of revisionist scholars who claim that Hitler did not plan the Final Solution in advance but instead improvised it out of either military or political frustration." Publ Wkly
Includes bibliographical references

Cornwell, John. **Hitler's** pope: the secret history of Pius XII. Viking 1999 430p il hardcover o.p. pa $15   92
1. Popes 2. Heads of state 3. Nazi leaders
ISBN 0-14-029627-1 pa
LC 99-28311
"Relying on exclusive access to Vatican and Jesuit archives, . . . {the author} argues that through a 1933 Concordat with Hitler, Pope Pius XII facilitated the dictator's rise—and, ultimately, the Holocaust." Libr J
Includes bibliographical references

★ Hitler, Adolf. **Mein** Kampf; translated by Ralph Manheim. Houghton Mifflin 1943 xxi, 694p $40; pa $22   92
1. Heads of state 2. National socialism 3. Nazi leaders 4. Germany -- Politics and government -- 1918-1933
ISBN 0-395-95105-4; 0-395-92503-7 pa
"Hitler's steady rise to power was interrupted only by the Beer Hall Putsch (1923), an unsuccessful attempt to overthrow the Weimar Republic. . . . During the nine months of imprisonment that followed he wrote 'Mein Kampf' (1924; tr. 'My struggle,' 1940). This book contained autobiographical and reflective passages, rife with hysterical anti-Semitism and paranoia, as well as the program he intended to implement; for the West it was a warning that went unheeded." Reader's Ency. 3d edition

Kershaw, Ian. **Hitler**; a biography. W.W. Norton 2008 1029p il map $39.95   92
1. Heads of state 2. Nazi leaders
ISBN 978-0-393-06757-6; 0-393-06757-2
LC 2008-37294
This abridgment of the author's two-volume biography on Hitler "retains two themes of Kershaw's full-scale original: analyzing the political support the demagogue mustered from the populace and key institutional centers of Germany

on his ascent to and exercise of power; and the decisive personal role of Hitler in instigating World War II and genocide. The narrative Kershaw constructs on this foundation is a superb organization and expression of Hitler's chronological arc that plummeted the world into catastrophe and moral trauma, a trajectory informed by Kershaw's attention to rationalizations by which people in and outside Germany, whether leaders or led, buried doubts about Hitler until his power was unrestrained, impossible to stop but by war or assassination. Manifestly, Kershaw constitutes core-collection material." Booklist
Includes bibliographical references

Ullrich, Volker. **Hitler**; ascent, 1889-1939. Volker Ullrich; translated from the German by Jefferson Chase. Alfred A. Knopf 2016 1008 p. (hardcover) $40   92
1. Dictators 2. National socialism 3. Personality -- Case studies 4. Germany -- History -- 1933-1945 5. Dictators -- Germany -- Biography 6. Heads of state -- Germany -- Biography 7. Germany -- Politics and government -- 1933-1945
ISBN 038535438X; 9780385354387
LC 2015047202
This biography of Adolf Hitler, by Volker Ullrich, "reveals the man behind the public persona, from Hitler's childhood to his failures as a young man in Vienna to his experiences during the First World War to his rise as a far-right party leader. Ullrich deftly captures Hitler's intelligence, instinctive grasp of politics, and gift for oratory as well as his megalomania, deep insecurity, and repulsive worldview." (Publisher's note)
"Above all, in this long but skillfully narrated study, Ullrich reveals Hitler to have been an eminently practical politician—and frighteningly so... one of the best works on Hitler and the origins of the Third Reich to appear in recent years." Kirkus

Hockney, David

Sykes, Chrisopher Simon. **David** Hockney; the biography, 1937-1975. Christopher Simon Sykes. Doubleday 2012 384 p. $35   92
1. Artists -- Great Britain -- Biography
ISBN 9780385531443; 0385531443
LC 2011041629
This book is the first volume of "the ever-evolving English artist. . . . A friend of the artist, photographer Sykes . . . , provides [a] . . . sense of what has fed the artist's fertile, restless imagination. . . . His attendance at the Royal College of Art in London in 1959 drew out the tremendous talents of this awkward provincial kid, exposing him to modern art for the first time . . . , and shaping his sense as a gay artist. . . . His work attracted the attention of hot young London dealer John Kasmin, and he visited New York City and resolved to go blonde after watching a TV commercial. . . . Considered bright, witty and inventive, Hockney spent the transformative years of 1963-5 in Los Angeles, creating his early iconic work." (Kirkus)
Includes bibliographical references and index

Sykes, Christopher Simon. **David** Hockney; The Biography, 1975-2012. Christopher Simon Sykes.

Random House Inc 2014 448 p. 16 plates; illustrations $40 **92**
1. British art 2. Artists, British
ISBN 0385535902; 9780385535908

LC 2011041629

In this biography, Christopher Simon Sykes "explores the life and work of . . . [British artist] David Hockney. . . . His career has spanned and epitomized the art movements of the past five decades. Picking up Hockney's story in 1975, this book finds him flitting between Notting Hill and California, where he took inspiration for the swimming pool series of paintings; creating acclaimed set designs for operas around the world; and embracing emerging technologies." (Publisher's note)

Rich with archival detail and the insight of family, friends, and the artist himself, the book is an engaging read." LJ

Hoffa, Jimmy, b. 1913

Russell, Thaddeus. **Out** of the jungle; Jimmy Hoffa and the remaking of the American working class. Temple University Press 2003 272p il (Labor in crisis) pa $21.95 **92**
1. Missing persons 2. Labor leaders 3. Trucking executives 4. International Brotherhood of Teamsters, Chauffeurs, Warehousemen and Helpers of America
ISBN 1-592-13027-5; 978-1-592-13027-6

LC 2002-43556

First published 2001 by Knopf

"Russell makes good use of a range of primary-source materials plus period newspaper accounts and other materials to highlight this story." Libr J
Includes bibliographical references

Hoffman, Claire

Hoffman, Claire. **Greetings** from Utopia Park; Claire Hoffman. HarperCollins 2016 288 p. illustrations $25.99 **92**
1. Iowa 2. Women journalists 3. Transcendental meditation
ISBN 0062338846; 9780062338846

In this memoir, Claire Hoffman "reflects on her childhood in the heartland, growing up in an increasingly isolated meditation community in the 1980s and '90s. When Claire Hoffman's alcoholic father abandons his family, his desperate wife, Liz, tells five-year-old Claire and her seven-year-old brother, Stacey, that they are going to heaven--Iowa--to live in Maharishi's national headquarters for Heaven on Earth." (Publisher's note)

"With honesty and sincerity, this account of coming of age within the ostensible confines of an alternative lifestyle delivers valuable knowledge of another phenomenon of cultural divergence." LJ

Holiday, Billie, 1915-1959

★ Holiday, Billie. **Lady** sings the blues; [Billie Holiday with William Dufty] 50th anniversary ed.; Harlem Moon 2006 231p il pa $15.95 **92**
1. Singers 2. Blues musicians 3. African American singers
ISBN 978-0-7679-2386-6; 0-7679-2386-3

LC 2007-271682

First published 1956 by Doubleday

"A hard, bitter and unsentimental book, written with brutal honesty and having much to say not only about Billie Holiday, the person, but about what it means to be poor and black in America." N Y Her Trib Books
Includes discography

Holman, James, 1786-1857

Roberts, Jason. A **sense** of the world; how a blind man became history's greatest traveler. HarperCollins Publishers 2006 382p il $26.95; pa $14.95 **92**
1. Blind 2. Naval officers 3. Travel writers
ISBN 0-00-716106-9; 978-0-00-716106-5; 0-00-716126-3 pa; 978-0-00-716126-3 pa

LC 2005-58166

The author "narrates the life of a 19th-century British naval officer who was mysteriously blinded at 25, but nevertheless became the greatest traveler of his time. . . . Roberts does Holman justice, evoking with grace and wit the tale of this man once lionized as 'The Blind Traveler.'" Publ Wkly
Includes bibliographical references

Hooks, Bell

Hooks, Bell. **Belonging**; a culture of place. Routledge 2008 230p $95; pa $19.95 **92**
1. Home 2. Poets 3. Authors 4. Dramatists 5. Women authors 6. African American authors 7. Kentucky 8. Essayists 9. Feminists 10. Memoirists 11. Social critics 12. College teachers 13. Children's authors 14. Nonfiction writers
ISBN 978-0-415-96815-7; 978-0-415-96816-4 pa

LC 2008-21846

The author "writes about the solace she found as a girl in the hills of Kentucky, her long years away, and her return, which has inspired a fresh look at the self-reliant communities of black Appalachians and their nurturing connection to the land." Booklist
Includes bibliographical references

Hooks, Bell. **Wounds** of passion; a writing life. Holt & Co. 1997 xxiii, 260p hardcover o.p. pa $13 **92**
1. Poets 2. Authors 3. Dramatists 4. Essayists 5. Feminists 6. Memoirists 7. Social critics 8. College teachers 9. Children's authors 10. Nonfiction writers
ISBN 0-8050-5722-6 pa

LC 97-23506

In this continuation of the author's autobiography, Hooks chronicles "her rigorous education, both in a long, complicated relationship with a fellow writer and as a college and graduate student, experiences that led her away from poetry (her first literary love) to groundbreaking prose that expressed her feminist convictions and views on the status of black women in America." Booklist

Hoover, Herbert, 1874-1964

Rappleye, Charles. **Herbert** Hoover in the White House; the ordeal of the presidency. Charles Rappleye. Simon & Schuster 2016 576 p. illustrations (hardcover) $32.50 **92**
1. United States -- Politics and government -- 1929-

1933 2. Presidents -- United States -- Biography
ISBN 9781451648676; 9781451648683
LC 2015027333
This book, by Charles Rappleye, offers an alternative "portrait of [the] Depression-era president Herbert Hoover [that] reveals a very different figure than the usual Hoover, engaged and active but loathe to experiment and conscious of his inability to convey hope to the country. . . . The Hoover we see here—bright, well meaning, energetic—lacked the single critical element to succeed as president. He had a first-class mind and a second-class temperament." (Publisher's note)
"A fair, fresh, and fantastic reappraisal of a forgotten figure." LJ
Includes bibliographical references and index

Hope, Bob, 1903-2003

Quirk, Lawrence J. **Bob** Hope: the road well-traveled. Applause Theatre Bk. Pubs. 1998 327p il hardcover o.p. pa $14.95 **92**
1. Actors 2. Comedians
ISBN 1-55783-353-2; 1-55783-450-4 pa
LC 98-87957
"Quirk recaps Hope's life and surveys his relationships with myriad entertainment personalities. . . . This is a good, solid Hollywood bio by a veteran Tinseltown observer." Booklist
Includes filmography and bibliographical references

Zoglin, Richard. **Hope**; entertainer of the century. Richard Zoglin. Simon & Schuster 2014 576 p. 16 plates; illustrations (hardcover) $30 **92**
1. Comedians -- United States -- Biography
ISBN 1439140278; 9781439140277; 9781439140284
LC 2014014371
This book, by Richard Zoglin, presents a biography of Bob Hope, "born in 1903, and until his death in 2003, . . . [he was] the only entertainer to achieve top-rated success in every major mass-entertainment medium, from vaudeville to television and everything in between. . . . [This book] is both a celebration of an entertainer whose vast contribution has never been properly appreciated, and a complex portrait of a gifted but flawed man." (Publisher's note)
"Not just for Hope fans, Zoglin's work will also appeal to readers interested in the colorful history of American entertainment, in which Hope played a prominent role." Booklist
Includes bibliographical references and index

Hopkins, Lightnin', 1912-1982

Govenar, Alan B. **Lightnin'** Hopkins; his life and blues. Chicago Review Press 2010 334p il $28.95 **92**
1. Singers 2. Guitarists 3. Blues music 4. Blues musicians 5. African American musicians 6. Songwriters
ISBN 978-1-55652-962-7
LC 2009-48798
In this "biography of the prolific and influential blues icon Sam 'Lightnin' Hopkins, . . . [the author] presents important new research and employs neglected primary sources to offer an accessible critical analysis of Hopkins's artistic achievement buttressed by generous quotations from

his lyrics. . . . [This] biography of an important figure in blues history is an essential purchase for anyone interested in American popular music or African American culture." Libr J
Includes discography and bibliographical references

Hopper, Grace, 1906-1992

★ Beyer, Kurt W. **Grace** Hopper and the invention of the information age. MIT Press 2009 398p il (Lemelson Center studies in invention and innovation) $27.95 **92**
1. Admirals 2. Computer scientists 3. Computer programming 4. Biography, Individual 5. COBOL (Computer program language)
ISBN 978-0-262-01310-9
LC 2008-44229
This is a biography of the computer programmer who "abandoned academia to serve her country in the Navy after Pearl Harbor. . . . Hopper made herself 'one of the boys' in Howard Aiken's wartime Computation Laboratory at Harvard, then moved on to the Eckert and Mauchly Computer Corporation. . . . Hopper's greatest technical achievement was to create the tools that would allow humans to communicate with computers in terms other than ones and zeroes." (Publisher's note) Index.
"In Beyer's fascinating mix of biography and technological history, Grace Hopper comes vividly to life as a navy admiral who launched the art of computer programming." Booklist
Includes bibliographical references

Hopwood, Shon

Burke, Dennis. **Law** man; Shon Hopwood with Dennis Burke. Crown Publishers 2012 308 p. col. ill. $25.00 **92**
1. Lawyers -- Biography 2. Prisoners -- Biography 3. Jailhouse lawyers -- Nebraska -- Biography
ISBN 0307887839; 9780307887832; 9780307887856
LC 2011035313
This book, by Shon Hopwood with Dennis Burke, offers a memoir of a man who reformed after being imprisoned for bank robbery into a successful jailhouse lawyer. "By the time Shon walked out of Pekin Prison he'd pulled off a series of legal miracles, earned the undying gratitude of numerous inmates, won the woman of his dreams, and built a new life for himself far greater than anything he could have imagined." (Publisher's note)
"Hopwood's prison memoir and long journey back into society are told with brutal and riveting honesty." LJ

Horne, Lena

Gavin, James. **Stormy** weather; the life of Lena Horne. Atria 2009 598p il $27; pa $16 **92**
1. Actors 2. Singers 3. African American women 4. African American singers
ISBN 978-0-7432-7143-1; 0-7432-7143-2; 978-0-7432-7144-8 pa; 0-7432-7144-0 pa
LC 2009-08170
This is a biography of the American singer who has appeared in the films Stormy Weather and Cabin in the Sky (both 1943) and on Broadway in Jamaica (1957) and The Lady and Her Music (1981).

Horne "has had a life so rich in ups and downs as to make page after page eventful and suspenseful. This all the more so since the book is also two books in one: a thorough and fluent biography and a history of the slow social rise of black people despite crippling discrimination and stinging humiliations—a history in which Horne's story is embedded." N Y Times Book Rev

Includes discography, filmography, and bibliographic references

Houdini, Harry, 1874-1926

Jaher, David. The **witch** of lime street; séance, seduction, and Houdini in the spirit world. David Jaher. Crown Publishers 2015 448 p. illustrations (alk. paper) $28   **92**
1. Spiritualism 2. Spiritualists -- United States -- Biography 3. Women mediums -- United States -- Biography 4. Spiritualism -- United States -- History -- 20th century
ISBN 0307451062; 9780307451064

LC 2015009392

In this book, by David Jaher, "in 1924, the pretty wife of a distinguished Boston surgeon came to embody the raging national debate over Spiritualism. . . . Reporters dubbed her the blonde Witch of Lime Street, but she was known to her followers simply as Margery. . . . Margery was the best hope for the psychic practice to be empirically verified. Her supernatural gifts beguiled four of the judges. There was only one left to convince...the acclaimed escape artist, Harry Houdini." (Publisher's note)

"Through a combination of feminine seduction and illusionist skill that even Houdini admired, Crandon became the one psychic to almost win the respect of the scientific community and outshine Houdini as an entertainer. Jaher's narrative style is as engaging as his character portraits are colorful. Together, they bring a bygone age and its defining spiritual obsessions roaring to life. Fascinating, sometimes thrilling, reading." Kirkus

Includes bibliographical references and index

House, Callie, 1861-1928

Berry, Mary Frances. **My** face is black is true; Callie House and the struggle for ex-slave reparations. Knopf 2006 314p il pa $14.95; $26.95 **92**
1. Needleworkers 2. Laundry workers 3. Social activists 4. Biography, Individual 5. African Americans -- Reparations 6. African American women -- Biography
ISBN 0-307-27705-4 pa, Vintage; 1-4000-4003-5 Knopf; 978-0-307-27705-3 pa, Vintage

LC 2004-51330

This is a biography of Carrie House, an African American washerwoman and former slave. House was a leader of the National Ex-Slave Mutual Relief, Bounty, and Pension Association (ESMRBPA). Index.

The author "unearths the intriguing story of Callie House (1861–1928), a Tennessee washerwoman and seamstress become activist, and the organization she led, the National Ex-Slave Mutual Relief, Bounty and Pension Association. . . . Students and scholars of African-American history, as well as those engaged in the current reparations debates, will be

deeply informed by the rise and fall of the Ex-Slave Association." Publ Wkly

Includes bibliographical references

House, Edward Mandell, 1858-1938

Neu, Charles E. **Colonel** House; a biography of Woodrow Wilson's silent partner. Charles E. Neu. Oxford University Press 2015 720 p. 16 plates $34.95   **92**
1. American diplomatic and consular service 2. Treaty of Versailles (1919) 3. World War, 1914-1918 -- Peace 4. Statesmen -- United States -- Biography 5. United States -- Foreign relations -- 1913-1921 6. United States -- Politics and government -- 1913-1921
ISBN 0195045505; 9780195045505

LC 2014015227

Author Charles E. Neu presents a biography of Edward M. House "who rose to become one of the century's greatest political operators. Ambitious and persuasive, House worked largely behind the scenes, developing ties of loyalty and using patronage to rally party workers behind his candidates. In 1911 he met Woodrow Wilson, and almost immediately the two formed what would become one of the most famous friendships in American political history." (Publisher's note)

"Neu deems House a 'patient, crafty, and sometimes cynical' infighter and 'a shrewd observer of human foibles,' widely admired but faulted by some at the height of his fame for developing an exaggerate d sense of his own importance. A significant, brightly written American story." Kirkus

Includes bibliographical references and index

Howe, Ben Ryder

Howe, Ben Ryder. **My** Korean deli; risking it all for a convenience store. Henry Holt and Co. 2010 304p $25   **92**
1. Korean Americans 2. Convenience stores 3. Editors 4. Small business owners
ISBN 978-0-8050-9343-8; 0-8050-9343-5

LC 2010-24962

The author's "wife Gab bought (with the money the couple had saved for a down payment on their first house) her hardworking Korean parents a deli in Brooklyn as a gesture of thanks for all their self-sacrifice. What follows is a series of both comic and tragic vignettes that will leave the reader as surprised as the author about how emotionally invested you can get in a deli. . . . [Howe] delivers a smartly written narrative about love, literature, and the lengths one goes to for family, which turns out to be epically far." Maclean's

Howe, Gordie, 1928-2016

Howe, Gordie, 1928-2016. **Mr.** Hockey; My Story. Gordie Howe. Penguin Group USA 2014 320 p. 16 plates; color illustrations $27.95   **92**
1. Hockey players 2. Autobiographies
ISBN 0399172912; 9780399172915

LC 2015410204

In this autobiography, former hockey player Gordie Howe "takes us through it all, from his Depression-era childhood and early obstacles through the ups and downs of his spectacular career, to his enduring marriage and close relationship with his children, to his thoughts on the game of hockey today." (Publisher's note)

"The author intersperses portions of personal letters he sent to and received from family members. Lots of action, a bit of rumination and few regrets in this unremarkable work by a most remarkable athlete." Kirkus

Hughes, Langston, 1902-1967

Marshall, Paule. **Triangular** road; a memoir. BasicCivitas Books 2009 165p il $23   **92**
1. Poets 2. Authors 3. Novelists 4. Dramatists 5. African American authors 6. Essayists 7. Short story writers 8. Young adult authors 9. African Americans -- Intellectual life
ISBN 978-0-465-01359-3
LC 2008-36671
This is a memoir by the author of Praisesong for the widow (1983).
"Though fiction may have pride of place in . . . [the author's] heart, 'Triangular Road' reveals a strong gift for self-scrutiny made all the more revealing by quiet humor and what appears to be complete honesty." Washington Post

Rampersad, Arnold. The **life** of Langston Hughes Volume I: 1902-1941; I, too, sing America. 2nd ed; Oxford University Press 2002 478p il hardcover o.p. pa $33   **92**
1. Poets 2. Authors 3. Novelists 4. Dramatists 5. African American authors 6. Poets, American 7. Short story writers 8. Young adult authors
ISBN 0-19-515160-7; 0-19-514642-5 pa
First published 1986
This is the first volume of a two-volume set chronicling the life of the Harlem Renaissance poet and author.
Includes bibliographical references

Humbert, Agnès, 1894-1963

Humbert, Agnes. **Resistance**; a woman's journal of struggle and defiance in occupied France. Bloomsbury 2008 370p il $26   **92**
1. Art historians 2. Underground leaders 3. World War, 1939-1945 -- Personal narratives 4. World War, 1939-1945 -- Prisoners and prisons 5. World War, 1939-1945 -- Underground movements 6. France -- History -- 1940-1945, German occupation
ISBN 978-1-59691-559-6; 1-59691-559-5
LC 2008-16603
Original French edition, 1946
"Humbert's firsthand account of her work for the resistance in occupied Paris and her subsequent arrest and deportation to a forced-labor camp in Germany is an invaluable addition to works highlighting the role of women during wartime." Publ Wkly
Includes bibliographical references

Humboldt, Alexander von, 1769-1859

★ Wulf, Andrea. The **invention** of nature; Alexander von Humboldt's new world. by Andrea Wulf. Alfred A. Knopf 2015 496 p. ill. (some col.), maps (hardcover) $30   **92**
1. Scientists -- Biography 2. Naturalists -- Biography 3. Scientists -- Germany -- Biography 4. Naturalists -- Germany -- Biography
ISBN 038535066X; 9780385350662
LC 2015017505
Carnegie Medal Shortlist: Nonfiction (2016)
Los Angeles Times Book Prize: Science & Technology (2015)
This book, by Andrea Wulf, "reveals the forgotten life of Alexander von Humboldt, the visionary German naturalist whose ideas changed the way we see the natural world--and in the process created modern environmentalism. . . . She . . . discusses his prediction of human-induced climate change, his remarkable ability to fashion poetic narrative out of scientific observation, and his relationships with iconic figures such as Simón Bolívar and Thomas Jefferson." (Publisher's note)
Wulf "presents with zest and eloquence the full story of Humboldt's adventurous life and extraordinary achievements, from making science 'accessible and popular' to his early warnings about how deforestation, monoculture agriculture, and industrialization would engender disastrous climate change." Booklist
Includes bibliographical references and index

Hurston, Zora Neale, 1891-1960

Boyd, Valerie. **Wrapped** in rainbows; the life of Zora Neale Hurston. Scribner 2003 527p il $30 **92**
1. Authors 2. Novelists 3. Dramatists 4. African American authors 5. Memoirists 6. Folklorists 7. Short story writers 8. African American women -- Biography
ISBN 0-684-84230-0
LC 2002-17011
This is a biography of the folklorist and author of Their Eyes Were Watching God (1937), Tell My Horse (1938), Dust Tracks on a Road (1942) and Seraph on the Suwanee (1948)
"As the author adeptly and passionately analyzes Hurston's revolutionary books, intense spirituality, and myriad adventures, Hurston emerges in all her splendor—not only smarter, tougher, and more dazzlingly alive than most people but also freer." Booklist
Includes bibliographical references

★ Hurston, Zora Neale. **Dust** tracks on a road; an autobiography. with a foreword by Maya Angelou. 1st Harper Perennial Modern Classic ed; Harper Perennial Modern Classics 2006 308p il pa $13.95 **92**
1. Authors 2. Novelists 3. Dramatists 4. African American authors 5. Memoirists 6. Folklorists 7. Short story writers 8. African American women -- Biography
ISBN 0-06-085408-1; 978-0-06-085408-9
LC 2005-52616
First published 1942 by Lippincott

The author describes her wanderings in and out of schools and jobs as a young girl, finishing her course work at Barnard, and beginning her life's work.

Includes bibliographical references

Hurston, Zora Neale. **Zora** Neale Hurston: a life in letters; collected and edited by Carla Kaplan. Doubleday 2002 880p il $40; pa $19.95   **92**
1. Authors 2. Novelists 3. Dramatists 4. African American authors 5. Memoirists 6. Folklorists 7. Short story writers 8. African American women -- Biography
ISBN 0-385-49035-6; 0-385-49036-4 pa
LC 00-65671
A collection of over 500 letters by the Harlem Renaissance author
These letters reveal "a gifted yet complex personality at once humorous, cynical, and analytical." Libr J
Includes bibliographical references

Hussein, King of Jordan, 1935-1999
Ashton, Nigel. **King** Hussein of Jordan; a political life. [by] Nigel Ashton. Yale University Press 2008 431p il map $35   **92**
1. Kings 2. Jordan -- History 3. Biography, Individual 4. Jordan -- Kings and rulers 5. Jordan -- Politics and government 6. Jordan -- Politics and government -- 1952-1999
ISBN 0-300-09167-2; 978-0-300-09167-0
LC 2008-10803
This is a biography of King Hussein of Jordan, who "reigned for nearly half a century, from his grandfather's assassination in 1953 to his own death in 1999." (Publisher's note) Bibliography. Index.
With "unprecedented access to the late king's entire correspondence and more than two dozen interviews . . . Ashton reveals Hussein's longstanding covert contact with Israel and his clandestine communications with Israelis in the immediate aftermath of the 1967 war to suggest the possibilities and missed opportunities (including by the U.S.) for a peaceful settlement in the Palestinian-Israeli conflict." Publ Wkly
Includes bibliographical references (p. 371-378)

Huston, Anjelica
Huston, Anjelica, 1951- **Watch** me; a memoir. by Anjelica Huston. Scribner 2014 400 p. illustrations (some color) (hardback) $27.99   **92**
1. Actresses -- Biography 2. Motion picture actors and actresses -- United States -- Biography
ISBN 1476760349; 9781476760346; 9781476760360
LC 2014029235
This memoir, by actress Anjelica Huston, is an "account of her seventeen-year love affair with Jack Nicholson, her rise to stardom, and her mastery of the craft of acting. . . . She writes about . . . her Academy Award-winning portrayal of Maerose Prizzi in Prizzi's Honor; about her collaborations with many of the greatest directors in Hollywood. . . . She movingly and beautifully describes the death of her father John Huston and her marriage to sculptor Robert Graham." (Publisher's note)

"This memoir with both substance and flair is a must-read for Huston fans, those who enjoy film, and anyone who wishes to be inspired by a richly textured life well presented. For all entertainment collections." LJ
Includes bibliographical references and index

Huston, John, 1906-1987
Meyers, Jeffrey. **John** Huston; courage and art. Crown Archetype 2011 475p il $30; ebook $14.99   **92**
1. Motion picture producers and directors 2. Screenwriters 3. Motion picture directors
ISBN 978-0-307-59067-1; 978-0-307-59069-5 ebook
LC 2010047642
"By balancing the flamboyant life with the landmark works of legendary movie director John Huston, . . . Meyers reveals how a flawed man produced nearly flawless and indelible films." Booklist
Includes filmography and bibliographical references

Hynde, Chrissie.
Hynde, Chrissie, 1951- **Reckless**; My Life as a Pretender. by Chrissie Hynde. Random House Inc 2015 352 p. 32 plates; color illustrations $26.95 **92**
1. Rock musicians -- United States -- Biography
ISBN 0385540612; 9780385540612
LC 2015027449
This memoir, by musician Chrissie Hynde, "tells her life story in full and utterly fascinating detail, from her all-American Ohio fifties childhood to her classic baby-boomer seduction by the rock of the sixties to her sojourn in the crucible of punk that was seventies London to her instant emergence with her band, The Pretenders, in 1980 into stardom as a frontwoman and songwriter." (Publisher's note)

Ian, Janis, 1951-
Ian, Janis. **Society's** child; my autobiography. Jeremy P. Tarcher/Penguin 2008 xxii, 361p il $26.95   **92**
1. Singers
ISBN 9781585426751
LC 2008-17130
This is a memoir by the American folk singer.
"Fans will love the book, of course, but many nonfans, too, should find this painfully candid memoir hard to put down." Booklist
Includes bibliographical references

Ice-T
Ice-T. **Ice**; a memoir of gangster life and redemption--from South Central to Hollywood. [by] Ice-T and Douglas Century. One World Books 2011 251p il $25; ebook $12.99   **92**
1. Actors 2. Rap music 3. African American musicians 4. Rap musicians
ISBN 978-0-345-52328-0; 978-0-345-52330-3 ebook
LC 2010-41069
"A fascinating and inspiring story about an African American orphan who beat the odds to become successful, this memoir will appeal to fans of hip-hop and popular culture." Booklist

Isabella I, Queen of Spain, 1451-1504

Downey, Kirstin. **Isabella**; the warrior queen. Kirstin Downey. Nan A. Talese/Doubleday 2014 544 p. 16 plates; illustrations; maps (alk. paper) $35 **92**

1. Spain -- History 2. Queens -- Spain -- Biography 3. Spain -- History -- Ferdinand and Isabella, 1479-1516
ISBN 0385534116; 9780385534116

LC 2014003895

Los Angeles Times Book Prize Finalist: Biography (2014)

Author Kirstin Downey presents a"biography of Isabella of Castile, the controversial Queen of Spain who sponsored Christopher Columbus's journey to the New World, established the Spanish Inquisition, and became one of the most influential female rulers in history." (Publisher's note)

"As one of the most influential political players of the transitional era bridging the Middle Ages and the Renaissance, Isabella has earned her place in the spotlight." Booklist

Includes bibliographical references and index

Ishi

★ Kroeber, Theodora. **Ishi** in two worlds; a biography of the last wild Indian in North America. University of Calif. Press 1976 262p il $50; pa $16.95 **92**

1. Yana Indians 2. Linguistic informants
ISBN 0-520-00674-7; 0-520-22940-1 pa
First published 1961

An account "of the life of the sole survivor of a California Indian tribe. The author, wife of the famed anthropologist, reconstructs the decimation of Ishi's {Yana} people and his reluctant entry in 1911 into the world of his conquerors." Booklist

Ivan IV, the Terrible, Czar of Russia, 1530-1584

De Madariaga, Isabel. **Ivan** the Terrible; first tsar of Russia. Yale University Press 2005 xxi, 484p il map $35 **92**

1. Emperors
ISBN 0-300-09757-3

LC 2004-29807

This is a biography of the Russian tsar.

This "is a persuasively argued, widely researched and impressively authoritative work that casts new light on the Tsar, his reign, and Russia in the sixteenth century." Times Lit Suppl

Includes bibliographical references

Ives, Charles Edward, 1874-1954

Swafford, Jan. **Charles** Ives; a life with music. Norton 1996 525p il hardcover o.p. $18.95 **92**

1. Composers
ISBN 978-0-393-31719-0; 0-393-31719-6

LC 95-22549

"Ives was a professional organist, a successful insurance executive, a political idealist, and an immensely prolific composer. The author believes that Ives's transcendentalism was central to his identity, ceaselessly inspiring him while also spurring him on to an inevitable physical collapse. Swafford—a composer himself—intersperses his biography with valuable 'entr'actes' of approachable musical analysis,

and ends with a ringing endorsement of Ives as an ideal composer for a democratic society." New Yorker

Includes bibliographical references

Jackson, Andrew, 1767-1845

★ Brands, H. W. **Andrew** Jackson; his life and times. Doubleday 2005 620p il map $35 **92**

1. Generals 2. Presidents 3. Presidents -- United States
ISBN 0-385-50738-0; 978-0-385-50738-7

LC 2005-42178

This is a biography of the seventh president of the United States.

This book "is a bracing, human portrait of both a remarkable man and of American democracy as it was transformed from a 'government of the people' into a 'government by the people.'" Publ Wkly

Includes bibliographical references

Meacham, Jon. **American** lion; Andrew Jackson in the White House. Random House 2008 483p il $30 **92**

1. Generals 2. Presidents 3. Presidents -- United States
ISBN 978-1-4000-6325-3; 1-4000-6325-6

LC 2008-23466

The author "looks past the theatrics and posturing to the essential elements of Jackson's many showdowns. Mr. Meacham . . . dispenses with the usual view of Jackson as a Tennessee hothead and instead sees a cannily ambitious figure determined to reshape the power of the presidency during his time in office (1829 to 1837). Case by case, Mr. Meacham dissects Jackson's battles and reinterprets them in a revealing new light." N Y Times (Late N Y Ed)

Includes bibliographical references

Remini, Robert Vincent. **Andrew** Jackson; [by] Robert V. Remini; foreword by General Wesley K. Clark. Palgrave Macmillan 2008 204p il map (Great generals series) $21.95 **92**

1. Generals 2. Presidents 3. Presidents -- United States
ISBN 0-230-60015-8; 978-0-230-60015-7

LC 2008-394

This is a "study of Jackson from a military perspective. Remini maintains a birth-to-death narrative while keeping the focus on Jackson's fundamental existence as a soldier. The result is a fine introduction based on years of advanced knowledge on the subject, distilled by Remini into a very good read." Libr J

Includes bibliographical references

Wilentz, Sean. **Andrew** Jackson. Times Books 2005 195p (American presidents series) $20 **92**

1. Generals 2. Presidents 3. Presidents -- United States
ISBN 0-8050-6925-9

LC 2005-52857

The author "shows that our complicated seventh president was a central figure in the development of American democracy. . . . It is rare that historians manage both Wilentz's deep interpretation and lively narrative." Publ Wkly

Includes bibliographical references

Jackson, Michael, 1958-2009

★ Greenburg, Zack O'Malley, 1985- **Michael** Jackson, Inc; the rise, fall and rebirth of a billion-dollar empire. Zack O'Malley Greenburg. Atria Books 2014 293 p. $26 **92**

1. Music industry 2. Musicians -- United States 3. Popular music -- Economic aspects -- United States
ISBN 1476705968; 9781476705965

LC 2013045449

"'Michael Jackson, Inc.' reveals the incredible rise, fall, and rise again of Michael Jackson's fortune--driven by the unmatched perfectionism of the King of Pop. 'Forbes' senior editor Zack O'Malley Greenburg uncovers never-before-told stories from interviews with more than 100 people, including music industry veterans Berry Gordy, John Branca, and Walter Yetnikoff; artists 50 Cent, Sheryl Crow, and Jon Bon Jovi; and members of the Jackson family." (Publisher's note)

"A quick-moving yet comprehensive narrative of the singer's career, downfall and unlikely post-mortem second act." Kirkus

Includes bibliographical references and index

Jackson, Shirley, 1916-1965

★ Franklin, Ruth. **Shirley** Jackson; A Rather Haunted Life. by Ruth Franklin. W W Norton & Co Inc 2016 656 p. (ebook) $50; $35 **92**

1. Women authors -- Biography
ISBN 9781631492129; 0871403137; 9780871403131

LC 2016014711

This biography, by Ruth Franklin, "establishes Shirley Jackson as a towering figure in American literature. . . . Placing Jackson within an American Gothic tradition that stretches back to Hawthorne and Poe, Franklin demonstrates how her unique contribution to this genre came from her focus on 'domestic horror.'" (Publisher's note)

"A consistently interesting biography that deftly captures the many selves and multiple struggles of a true American original." Kirkus

Includes bibliographical references (pages 503-580) and index.

Jackson, Stonewall, 1824-1863

Gwynne, S. C. **Rebel** Yell; The Violence, Passion, and Redemption of Stonewall Jackson. S. C. Gwynne. Simon & Schuster 2014 688 p. illustrations, maps, portraits $35 **92**

1. Confederate States of America -- History 2. United States -- History -- 1861-1865, Civil War
ISBN 1451673280; 9781451673289

LC 2014010046

This book, by S. C. Gwynne, is an "account of how Civil War general Thomas 'Stonewall' Jackson became a great and tragic American hero. . . . In April 1862 Jackson was merely another Confederate general in an army fighting what seemed to be a losing cause. By June he had engineered perhaps the greatest military campaign in American history and was one of the most famous men in the Western world. He had, moreover, given the Confederate cause what it had recently lacked--hope." (Publisher's note)

"Gwynne presents Jackson's eccentric personality in biographical episodes that he injects into the arc of Jackson's Civil War campaigns and battles. . . . [The] technique succeeds, thanks to his spry prose and cogent insight, in revealing Jackson's character." Booklist

Includes bibliographical references (pages 577-634) and index

Robertson, James I. **Stonewall** Jackson; James I. Robertson, Jr. Macmillan 1997 xxiii, 950 p.p illustrations, maps $63 **92**

1. Confederate States of America -- History 2. United States -- History -- 1861-1865, Civil War 3. Biography, Individual 4. Confederate States of America -- Army
ISBN 9780028646855; 0028646851

LC 96017042

In this biography of Stonewall Jackson, author James Robertson "traces his life from his humble beginnings, through his military career, to his untimely death in 1863, discussing his military campaigns and strategies, religious beliefs, personal eccentricities, and more." (Publisher's note)

"Robertson's bibliography, which runs to 25 pages of fine print, reveals the solid bedrock on which this work is built; his documentation is a model of thoroughness. The book is illustrated with rare photographs. A highly readable, remarkably interesting study of Jackson as both man and military leader." Choice

Includes bibliographical references (p. 793-787) and index

Jacobs, Harriet A., 1813-1897

Yellin, Jean Fagan. **Harriet** Jacobs: a life. Basic Civitas Books 2004 394p il map $27.50; pa $16.95 **92**

1. Slaves 2. Authors 3. Domestics 4. Memoirists
ISBN 0-465-09288-8; 0-465-09289-6 pa

LC 2003-17256

"This scholarly account, woven in a reader friendly fashion, restores 'an heroic woman who lived in an heroic time' to history and to us." Publ Wkly

Includes bibliographical references

Jacobs, Jane, 1916-2006

Kanigel, Robert. **Eyes** on the street; The Life of Jane Jacobs. by Robert Kanigel. Alfred A. Knopf 2016 512 p. illustrations, map (hardcover) $35 **92**

1. City planning 2. Urban renewal 3. Women authors -- Biography 4. Sociology, Urban -- Philosophy 5. City planners -- Canada -- Biography 6. City planners -- United States -- Biography 7. City planning -- Canada -- History -- 20th century 8. Urban renewal -- Canada -- History -- 20th century 9. City planning -- United States -- History -- 20th century 10. Urban renewal -- United States -- History -- 20th century
ISBN 9780307961907

LC 2015050758

This biography of Jane Jacobs by Robert Kanigel tells the story of the "woman who raised three children, wrote seven groundbreaking books, saved neighborhoods, stopped expressways, was arrested twice, and engaged at home and on the streets in thousands of debates--all of which she won." (Publisher's note)

Includes bibliographical references and index

Jaffrey, Madhur

Jaffrey, Madhur. **Climbing** the mango trees; a memoir of a childhood in India. Knopf 2006 297p il $25   **92**
1. Actors 2. Cookbook writers
ISBN 1-4000-4295-X; 978-1-4000-4295-1
LC 2006-45255
First published 2005 in the United Kingdom
This is the memoir by the Indian actress and cookbook author.
The author's "taste memories sparkle with enthusiasm, and her talent for conveying them makes the book relentlessly appetizing." N Y Times Book Rev

Jahren, Hope

★ Jahren, Hope, 1969- **Lab** girl; Hope Jahren. Alfred A. Knopf 2016 304 p. (hardcover) $26.95 **92**
1. Biologists 2. Friendship 3. Geobiology -- Research -- Anecdotes 4. Biologists -- United States -- Biography
ISBN 9781101874936; 1101874937
LC 2015024305
This memoir, by Hope Jahren, is "about work, love, and the mountains that can be moved when those two things come together. It is told through Jahren's remarkable stories: about her childhood in rural Minnesota with an uncompromising mother and a father who encouraged hours of play in his classroom's labs; about how she found a sanctuary in science, and learned to perform lab work done . . . and about the inevitable disappointments, but also the triumphs and exhilarating discoveries, of scientific work." (Publisher's note)
"Jahren's forthright, beautifully expressed, and galvanizing chronicle deserves the widest possible readership." Booklist
Includes bibliographical references

James, Eloisa

★ James, Eloisa. **Paris** in love; a memoir. Eloisa James. Random House 2012 x, 260 p.p **92**
1. Autobiographies 2. Women -- Biography 3. Americans -- France 4. Paris (France) -- Description and travel 5. Life change events 6. Authors, American -- Biography 7. Cancer -- Patients -- Biography 8. Self-actualization (Psychology) 9. Quality of life -- France -- Paris 10. Women authors, American -- Biography 11. Americans -- France -- Paris -- Biography
ISBN 9780679604440; 9781400069569; 0679604448; 1400069564
LC 2011040662
This expatriate memoir by Eloisa James tells how "in 2009, [the] . . . author . . . sold her house, took a sabbatical from her job as a Shakespeare professor, and moved her family to Paris. [The story} chronicles her joyful year . . . [w]ith no classes to teach, no committee meetings to attend, no lawn to mow or cars to park, Eloisa revels in the ordinary pleasures of life . . . She copes with her Italian husband's notions of quality time; her two hilarious children, ages eleven and fifteen, as they navigate schools—not to mention puberty—in a foreign language; and her mother-in-law Marina's raised eyebrow in the kitchen (even as Marina overfeeds Milo, the family dog)." (Publisher's note)

James, Etta, 1938-2012

James, Etta. **Rage** to survive; the Etta James story. [by] Etta James with David Ritz. Da Capo Press 2003 288p il pa $18   **92**
1. Singers 2. Blues musicians 3. Songwriters 4. Soul musicians 5. Singers -- United States
ISBN 0-306-81262-2; 978-0-306-81262-0
First published 1995 by Villard Books
"With a supporting cast resembling the roster of the Rock Hall of Fame, this autobiography reads as its author sings-rough, gritty, and brutally honest." Libr J
Discography

James, William, 1842-1910

Richardson, Robert D. **William** James; in the maelstrom of American modernism: a biography. Houghton Mifflin 2006 622p il $30   **92**
1. Philosophers 2. Psychologists 3. Writers on science
ISBN 978-0-618-43325-4; 0-618-43325-2
LC 2005-37776
This is a biography of the psychologist and philosopher.
The author's "enthusiasm for what he calls 'the matchless incandescent spirit' of William James is contagious." Publ Wkly
Includes bibliographical references (p. 586-9)

Jamison, Kay R.

Jamison, Kay R. **Nothing** was the same; a memoir. by Kay Redfield Jamison. Alfred A. Knopf 2009 208p $25   **92**
1. Bereavement 2. Psychiatrists 3. Psychologists 4. Hodgkin's disease 5. Manic-depressive illness 6. College teachers
ISBN 978-0-307-26537-1; 0-307-26537-4
LC 2009-11096
"The great gift Jamison offers here, beyond her honesty and the beauty of her writing, is perspective: a clear-eyed view of illness and death, sanity and insanity, love and grief. . . . Jamison seems to be telling the truth, no matter how difficult it may be, in a way that avoids self-pity and inspires courage." Washington Post Book World

Jang, Jin-sung

Jang Jin-sung. **Dear** Leader; poet, spy, escapee?: a look inside North Korea. Jang Jin-sung; translated by Shirley Lee. 37 Ink/Atria Books 2014 368 p. (hardback) $27.99   **92**
1. Poets 2. Korea (North) 3. Autobiographies 4. Korea (North) -- Biography 5. Propaganda -- Korea (North) 6. Poets -- Korea (North) -- Biography 7. Political refugees -- Korea (North) -- Biography 8. Korea (North) -- Politics and government -- 1994-2011
ISBN 147676655X; 9781476766553
LC 2014010236
This memoir tells how "[a]s North Korea's State Poet Laureate, Jang Jin-sung led a charmed life. With food provisions . . . , a travel pass, access to strictly censored information, and audiences with Kim Jong-il himself, his life in Pyongyang seemed safe and secure. But this privileged existence was about to be shattered. When a strictly forbidden magazine he lent to a friend goes missing, Jang Jin-sung must flee for his life." (Publisher's note)

"A defector of Kim Jong-il's rarefied inner circle reveals the desperate, despicable machinations of North Korea's police state." Kirkus

Jang, Lucia

McClelland, Susan. **Stars** Between the Sun and Moon; One Woman's Life in North Korea and Escape to Freedom. Lucia Jang and Susan McClelland. Douglas & McIntyre 2014 288 p. $26.95   **92**
   1. Refugees 2. Korea (North) -- Politics and government
ISBN 0393249220; 1771620358; 9780393249224; 9781771620352

LC 2015019384

This book by Lucia Jang and Susan McClelland is Jang's "memoir by a North Korean woman who defied the government to keep her family alive. Happy to serve her country, Jang worked in a factory as a young woman. There, a man she thought was courting her raped her. Forced to marry him when she found herself pregnant, she continued to be abused by him. She knew that, to keep the child, she had to leave North Korea. In a dramatic escape, she was smuggled with her newborn to China, fled to Mongolia . . . before eventually settling in Canada." (Publisher's note)

"An emotional and engrossing work that sheds light on daily life in this opaque country. Highly recommended for readers interested in North Korea as well as those who enjoy inspirational stories. Fans of Barbara Demick's Nothing To Envy will especially appreciate this work." LJ

Janowitz, Tama

Janowitz, Tama. **Scream**; A Memoir of Glamour and Dysfunction. Tama Janowitz. HarperCollins 2016 304 p. illustrations hardcover $25.99   **92**
   1. Women authors
ISBN 9780062391322; 0062391321

This memoir by Tama Janowitz "recalls the quirky literary world of young downtown New York in the go-go 1980s and reflects on her life today far away from the city indelible to her work. . . . Janowitz . . . [recounts] the vagaries of fame and fortune as a writer devoted to her art. Here, too, is Tama as daughter, wife, and mother, wrestling with aging, loss, and angst, both adolescent (her daughter) and middle aged (her own)." (Publisher's note)

"Sniping, scathing, grim, and hilarious, Janowitz's primal scream exposes the poisoned wellspring that gave rise to the gritty and canny ludicrousness of her novels, the highs and lows of her writing life, and the boons and traumas of fame and love." Booklist

Jauhar, Sandeep, 1968-

Jauhar, Sandeep. **Doctored**; the disillusionment of an American physician. Sandeep Jauhar. Farrar, Straus and Giroux 2014 288 p. (hardback) $26 **92**
   1. Physicians 2. Medical care -- United States 3. Physicians -- United States -- Autobiography 4. Delivery of Health Care -- trends -- United States
ISBN 0374141398; 9780374141394

LC 2013041344

This memoir, by Sandeep Jauhar, "observes the crisis of American medicine through the eyes of an attending cardiologist. . . . With a decade's worth of elite medical training behind him, he is eager to settle down and reap the rewards

of countless sleepless nights. Instead, he is confronted with sobering truths. . . . Provoked by his unsettling experiences, [the author] . . . has written an introspective memoir that is also an impassioned plea for reform." (Publisher's note)

"At times whiny, Jauhar's narrative provides a grim picture of modern medicine and the plight of contemporary physicians. And do not forget the domino effect: 'Unhappy doctors make for unhappy patients.'" Booklist

Jefferson, Margo, 1947-

★ Jefferson, Margo. **Negroland**; A Memoir. Margo Jefferson. Random House Inc 2015 240 p. illustrations $25   **92**
   1. Aristocracy 2. African Americans 3. United States -- Social conditions 4. African Americans -- Race identity 5. Chicago Region (Ill.) -- Biography 6. Elite (Social sciences) -- Illinois -- Chicago Region 7. African American women -- Illinois -- Chicago -- Biography 8. Chicago (Ill.) -- Race relations -- History -- 20th century -- Anecdotes 9. Chicago Region (Ill.) -- Social life and customs -- 20th century -- Anecdotes 10. African Americans -- Illinois -- Chicago -- Social life and customs -- 20th century 11. African American girls -- Illinois -- Chicago Region -- Social conditions -- 20th century
ISBN 0307378454; 9780307378453

LC 2015006843

National Book Critics Circle Award Finalist: Autobiography (2015)

This memoir by Margo Jefferson is a "meditation on race, sex, and American culture through the prism of the author's rarefied upbringing and education among a black elite concerned with distancing itself from whites and the black generality. Jefferson has spent most of her life among (call them what you will) the colored aristocracy, . . . inhabitants of Negroland, 'a small region of Negro America where residents were sheltered by a certain amount of privilege.'" (Publisher's note)

"Jefferson swings the narrative back and forth through her life, exploring the tides of racism, opportunity, and dignity while also provocatively exploring the inherent contradictions for Jefferson and her family members in working so tirelessly to differentiate themselves." Kirkus

Includes bibliographical references (pages [243]-248)

Jefferson, Thomas, 1743-1826

Bernstein, Richard B. **Thomas** Jefferson; [by] R.B. Bernstein. Oxford University Press 2003 253p il hardcover o.p. pa $15.95   **92**
   1. Architects 2. Presidents 3. Vice-presidents 4. Essayists 5. Presidents -- United States
ISBN 0-19-516911-5; 978-0-19-518130-2 pa; 0-19-518130-1 pa

LC 2003-5556

The author "provides a . . . view not of Jefferson the politician, but of the man whose ideas changed the world and provided the US with a sense of purpose. This short biography provides a judicious synthesis of the prevailing scholarship on the third president and explores more deeply his views on government and union, slavery (revealing what is known about the Sally Hemings affair and what cannot yet be determined), and debt. . . . Its concise form, limited notes,

and evenhanded style will appeal to general readers seeking insight into an incredibly complex historical figure." Choice
Includes bibliographical references

Ellis, Joseph J. **American** sphinx: the character of Thomas Jefferson. Knopf 1997 365p $29.95; pa $15   **92**
1. Architects 2. Presidents 3. Vice-presidents 4. Essayists
ISBN 0-679-44490-4; 0-679-76441-0 pa
LC 96-26171
"Penetrating Jefferson's placid, elegant facade, this extraordinary biography brings the sage of Monticello down to earth without either condemning or idolizing him." Publ Wkly

★ Gordon-Reed, Annette. **Most** Blessed of the Patriarchs; Thomas Jefferson and the Empire of the Imagination. Annette Gordon-Reed and Peter S. Onuf. Liveright 2016 320 p. illustrations, maps $27.95   **92**
1. Christianity 2. United States -- History -- 1775-1783, Revolution
ISBN 0871404427; 9780871404428
LC 2016000927
This biography of Thomas Jefferson, by Annette Gordon-Reed and Peter S. Onuf, "present[s] an absorbing and revealing character study that dispels the many clichés that have accrued over the years about our third president. Tracing Jefferson's philosophical development from youth to old age, the authors explore what they call the 'empire' of Jefferson's imagination—an expansive state of mind born of his origins in a slave society, his intellectual influences, and the vaulting ambition that propelled him into public life." (Publisher's note)
"An elegant, astute study that is both readable and thematically rich." Kirkus
Includes bibliographical references and index.

Hitchens, Christopher. **Thomas** Jefferson: author of America. HarperCollins Publishers 2005 188p (Eminent lives) $19.95   **92**
1. Architects 2. Presidents 3. Vice-presidents 4. Essayists 5. Presidents -- United States
ISBN 0-06-059896-4
LC 2005-296593
"Beginning with his aristocratic upbringing, . . . this biography explores both the private and public aspects of Jefferson's life, from his political philosophies to his affair with his slave Sally Hemings. . . . This opinionated, lively narrative sheds light not only on Jefferson's complex personality but on the politics of his time, making it both a fascinating character study and an excellent review of early American history." Publ Wkly

★ Meacham, Jon. **Thomas** Jefferson; the art of power. Jon Meacham. 1st ed. Random House 2012 448 p. (acid-free paper) $35   **92**
1. Presidents -- United States -- Biography 2. United States -- Politics and government -- 1783-1809
ISBN 1400067669; 9780679645368; 9781400067664
LC 2012013700

In this book, author Jon Meacham "claims that previous . . . scholars have not grasped the authentic [Thomas] Jefferson . . . a power-hungry, masterful, pragmatic leader who was not above being manipulative to achieve his goal: an enduring, democratic republic defined by him. A brilliant philosopher whose lofty principles were sometimes sidelined for more realistic goals, Meacham's Jefferson, neither idol nor rogue, is a complex mortal with serious flaws and contradictions." (Library Journal)
Includes bibliographical references and index.

Jeremiah, Thomas, d. 1775
Harris, J. William. The **hanging** of Thomas Jeremiah; a free Black man's encounter with liberty. Yale University Press 2009 223p il map $27.50   **92**
1. Diplomats 2. Merchants 3. Ship captains 4. Colonial leaders 5. Plantation owners 6. Government officials 7. Colonial administrators 8. Slavery -- United States 9. South Carolina -- Race relations 10. African Americans -- Social conditions
ISBN 978-0-300-15214-2; 0-300-15214-0
LC 2009-15233
This is an "account of nebulous historical figure Thomas Jeremiah. . . . Owner of a fishing company and worth $200,000 in 2009 dollars, . . . [Jeremiah] was probably the richest black man in North America; he was also a slaveowner. That didn't stop him from becoming a scapegoat, accused by patriot leader Henry Laurens—a wealthy plantation owner with hundreds of slaves—of secretly leading a British-sponsored slave insurrection. Though Governor William Campbell, aggrieved by the unlawfulness of Jeremiah's trial, interceded, it didn't stop those determined to hang Jeremiah. . . . Readers will learn much about the darker side of American institutions; students of American history and civil rights will appreciate Harris's impassive approach and thorough standards." Publ Wkly
Includes bibliographical references

Jewel, 1974-
Jewel, 1974- **Never** broken; songs are only half the story. Jewel. Blue Rider Press 2015 384 p. illustrations (some color) (ebook) $48; $27.50   **92**
1. Singers -- Biography 2. Singers -- United States -- Biography
ISBN 9780698192102; 9780399174339
LC 2015024911
This book, by musician Jewel, "tells the story of her life, and the lessons learned from her experience and her music. Living on a homestead in Alaska, Jewel learned to yodel at age five, and joined her parents' entertainment act, working in hotels, honky-tonks, and biker bars. Behind a strong-willed family life with an emphasis on music and artistic talent, however, there was also instability, abuse, and trauma." (Publisher's note)
"Jewel's lyrics, generously included throughout, reflect her authenticity and generosity. This is a solidly good read." Pub Wkly

Joan, of Arc, Saint, 1412-1431

Castor, Helen. **Joan** of Arc; a history. by Helen Castor. Harper 2015 352 p. color illustrations; map (hardcover) $27.99   **92**
1. Medieval civilization 2. Hundred Years' War, 1339-1453 3. Soldiers -- France -- Biography 4. Women heroes -- France -- Biography 5. Women soldiers -- France -- Biography 6. France -- History -- Charles VII, 1422-1461 7. Christian women saints -- France -- Biography
ISBN 0062384392; 9780062384393; 9780062384409
LC 2014029053
In this biography of Joan of Arc, author "Helen Castor tells afresh the gripping story of the peasant girl from Domremy who hears voices from God, leads the French army to victory, is burned at the stake for heresy, and eventually becomes a saint. Instead of an icon, she gives us a living, breathing woman confronting the challenges of faith and doubt, a roaring girl who, in fighting the English, was also taking sides in a bloody civil war." (Publisher's note)
"Castor carefully combs the record of her interrogation then and rehabilitation 25 years later. An unorthodox yet erudite and elegant biography of this 'massive star.'" Kirkus
Includes bibliographical references and index

Pernoud, Regine. **Joan** of Arc: her story; Régine Pernoud, Marie-Véronique Clin; translated and revised by Jeremy duQuesnay Adams; edited by Bonnie Wheeler. St. Martin's Griffin 1999 xxii, 304p il map hardcover o.p. pa $16.95   **92**
1. Saints 2. Christian saints 3. France -- History -- 1328-1589, House of Valois
ISBN 0-312-21442-1; 0-312-22730-2 pa
LC 98-45059
Original French edition, 1986
This work "traces the appearance of Joan as a documented historical character rather than adhering to a standard chronological sequence. Informing the narrative is a novel interpretation of Joan as a political prisoner. Moving beyond the narrative, the American translator . . . has added a series of appendixes containing valuable contextual material. . . . These materials discuss key historical events, provide biographical information on Joan's contemporaries, and discuss Joan's afterlife in history, literature, folklore, art, and iconography." Libr J
Includes bibliographical references

Jobrani, Maziyar, 1972-

Jobrani, Maz, 1972- **I'm** not a terrorist, but I've played one on tv; memoirs of a Middle Eastern funny man. Maz Jobrani. Simon & Schuster 2014 240 p. (hardcover) $24   **92**
1. Actors 2. Iranian Americans 3. Stereotype (Social psychology) 4. Iranian Americans -- Biography 5. Actors -- United States -- Biography 6. Comedians -- United States -- Biography 7. Stereotypes (Social psychology) -- United States
ISBN 9781476749983; 1476749981
LC 2014015012
Author Maz Jobrani presents this "memoir of growing up Iranian in America, and the quest to make it in Hollywood. Maz shares his struggle to build an acting career in post-9/11

Hollywood. But finally, through patience, determination, and only the occasional unequivocal compromising of his principles, he found a path to stardom." (Publisher's note)
"A funny and occasionally insightful memoir of an Iranian-American comedian finding a voice in showbiz." Kirkus

Jobs, Steve, 1955-2011

★ Isaacson, Walter. **Steve** Jobs. Simon & Schuster 2011 656p il por   **92**
1. Executives 2. Biography, Individual 3. Apple Computer, Inc. -- History 4. Businesspeople -- United States -- Biography 5. Computer engineers -- United States -- Biography
ISBN 9781451648546; 1451648537; 9781451648539; 9781451648553; 1451648553 ebook
LC 2011045006
This is a biography of the former CEO of Apple, Inc.
This book discusses the "basic outlines of [Steve] Jobs' career. . . . He was the co-creator of the personal computer. . . . [A]gainst the backdrop of [Jobs's] abrasive personality, [Walter] Isaacson's book offers an overriding message . . . he was a creative genius whose profound understanding of consumer appetites allowed him to create technology that no one else imagined or even thought feasible." (Commentary)
This "is an encyclopedic survey of all that Mr. Jobs accomplished, replete with the passion and excitement that it deserves." N Y Times Book Rev
Includes bibliographical references and index.

Tetzeli, Rick. **Becoming** Steve Jobs; the evolution of a reckless upstart into a visionary leader. Brent Schlender and Rick Tetzeli. Crown Business 2015 447 p. 16 plates; color illustrations (hardback) $30   **92**
1. Apple Inc. 2. Leadership 3. Apple Computer, Inc. -- Management 4. Businesspeople -- United States -- Biography 5. Computer engineers -- United States -- Biography
ISBN 0385347405; 9780385347402; 9780804138369
LC 2014031660
In this book, authors Brent Schlender and Rick Tezeli "focus on the years after Jobs's 1985 ouster from Apple and then on his 1997 return to guide the company's resurgence with a string of hit iProducts. They depict a spiritual journey . . . where he learned the art of not interfering with talented subordinates; he emerged a more patient man with a tempered strategic outlook and an ability to listen to underlings when they screamed back at him." (Publishers Weekly)
"Schlender and Tetzeli's account is unusually intimate thanks to voluminous interviews and Schlender's many personal encounters with Jobs over decades of covering him, and a reverential tone sometimes surfaces -- as when Jobs's lieutenant Tim Cook offered Jobs his own liver for a transplant -- in this corrective to Walter Isaacson's more jaundiced biography. But the authors are clear-eyed about Jobs's flaws and give lucid, detailed analyses of his maneuverings and product initiatives; theirs is one of the most nuanced and revealing assessments of Jobs's controversial career." Pub Wkly

John Paul II, Pope, 1920-2005

Flynn, Raymond. **John** Paul II; a personal portrait of the pope and the man. St. Martin's Press 2001 204p il hardcover o.p. pa $14.95   **92**
  1. Popes
  ISBN 0-312-28328-8 pa

                    LC 00-45965

Flynn, the "former mayor of Boston and ex-ambassador to the Vatican, tells us . . . what his book is not: It is not a biography, or an analysis. . . . Flynn views it, rather, as a profile based on his own experiences with Pope John Paul II, dating back to a 1969 visit to Boston of then-Cardinal Karol Wojtyla." Natl Rev

O'Connor, Garry. **Universal** Father: a life of John Paul II. Bloomsbury 2005 436p il map $24.95 **92**
  1. Popes
  ISBN 1-59691-096-8

"The text is divided into four distinct phases of Pope John Paul II's life: '1920-1946,' '1946-1978,' '1978-1990,' and '1990-2005.' Each phase balances fact with anecdotal evidence, which lends the biography both credibility and charm. . . . This timely and remarkable biography will be sought after by serious readers." Libr J

John, King of England, 1167-1216

Morris, Marc. **King** John; Treachery and Tyranny in Medieval England: the Road to Magna Carta. Marc Morris. W.W. Norton & Co. Inc. 2015 400 p. 8 plates; color ills., maps $29.95   **92**
  1. Middle Ages 2. Great Britain -- Kings and rulers
  ISBN 1605988855; 9781605988856

                    LC 2015452049

This book on England's King John by Marc Morris "offers a compelling portrait of an extraordinary man, whose reign marked a momentous turning point in the history of Britain and Europe. Morris draws on contemporary chronicles and the king's own letters to bring the real King John vividly to life." (Publisher's note)

"Describing the king's exactions, Morris shows how they provoked opposition from England's magnates. Despite Magna Carta's subsequent renown as the foundation of constitutional law, at the time it was a truce surrounded by civil war. That the war ended quickly after John died in 1216 points, suggests Morris, to his personal shortcomings as significant causes of the disasters of his reign. Balanced and dramatic, Morris' riveting account will effortlessly attract history readers." Booklist

Johnson, Andrew, 1808-1875

Gordon-Reed, Annette. **Andrew** Johnson. Times Books/Henry Holt and Company 2011 166p il (American presidents series) $23   **92**
  1. Governors 2. Presidents 3. Vice-presidents 4. Members of Congress 5. Presidents -- United States 6. United States -- Politics and government -- 1865-1898
  ISBN 978-0-8050-6948-8

                    LC 2010-32595

"Andrew Johnson rose from humble beginnings in the South to serve as Lincoln's second vice president, thus becoming President just as the Civil War was ending. He showed none of his predecessor's political finesse and is of-

ten viewed as among the worst to hold the office. . . . [The author] argues that the nation went from the best President to the worst during this most crucial period of its history. This slim study does cover Johnson from birth to death (1808–75), but the focus is assuredly on his presidency." Libr J
  Includes bibliographical references

Johnson, Harriet McBryde

Johnson, Harriet McBryde. **Too** late to die young; nearly true tales from a life. Henry Holt and Co. 2005 261p $23; pa $14   **92**
  1. Lawyers 2. Human rights activists
  ISBN 0-8050-7594-1; 0-312-42571-6 pa

                    LC 2004-54007

In this memoir, the wheelchair-bound lawyer and activist describes her battles for disability rights.

"From her first demonstration against the MDA telethon to her celebrated debate with Peter Singer of Harvard, who has stated that killing a disabled infant is not morally equivalent to killing a person, this lady pulls no punches. An entertaining look at an activist who insists on living life her way, disability or no." Libr J

Johnson, Jack, 1878-1946

★ Ward, Geoffrey C. **Unforgivable** blackness; the rise and fall of Jack Johnson. Knopf 2004 492p il $26.95   **92**
  1. Boxers (Persons)
  ISBN 0-375-41532-7

                    LC 2004-48524

The author "brings us back into Johnson's life and times with exquisitely rendered details, and the fight scenes themselves are gripping: fights so bloody that referees have to change shirts midbout, for instance, and a manager who pulls a gun on his fighter to keep him from quitting. The authoritative biography of Johnson for sure, but also one of the best boxing books in recent memory." Booklist
  Includes bibliographical references

Johnson, Lady Bird, 1912-2007

Caroli, Betty Boyd. **Lady** Bird and Lyndon; the hidden story of a marriage that made a president. Betty Boyd Caroli. Simon & Schuster 2015 464 p. 16 plates; illustrations (hardcover) $29.99   **92**
  1. Presidents -- United States -- Biography 2. Married people -- United States -- Biography 3. Presidents' spouses -- United States -- Biography
  ISBN 1439191220; 9781439191224; 9781439191231
                    LC 2015011027

This biography of the marriage of U.S. President Lyndon B. Johnson, by Betty Boyd Caroli, offers "a fresh look at Lady Bird Johnson that upends her image as a plain Jane who was married for her money and mistreated by Lyndon. This Lady Bird worked quietly behind the scenes through every campaign, every illness, and a trying presidency as a key strategist, fundraiser, barnstormer, peacemaker, and indispensable therapist." (Publisher's note)

"Caroli's suggestion and amplification of a virtual pact teased out of Lyndon and Bird's correspondence during a very brief courtship frames the story of this alliance.

Recommended for history buffs and devotees of human behavior." LJ

Includes bibliographical references and index

Gillette, Michael L. **Lady** Bird Johnson; an oral history. Michael L. Gillette. Oxford University Press 2012 400 p. illustrations (hardback : alk. paper) $29.95 **92**

1. United States -- History 2. Presidents' spouses -- United States -- Biography 3. United States -- Politics and government -- 1945-1989
ISBN 0199908087; 9780199908080

LC 2012011580

For this book, Michael L. Gillette, "former director of the LBJ Library's oral history program, has selected and edited these interviews" with former U.S. First Lady Lady Bird Johnson. The histories "cover the first lady's life from her birth in 1912 through [Lyndon B.] Johnson's presidency, thus throwing light on a more than half a century of American history." (Publishers Weekly)

Includes bibliographical references and index

Johnson, Lyndon B. (Lyndon Baines), 1908-1973

Caro, Robert A. The **path** to power. Knopf 1982 xxiii, 882p il (The years of Lyndon Johnson) $49.95; pa $19.95 **92**

1. Presidents 2. Vice-presidents 3. Senators 4. Members of Congress 5. Presidents -- United States 6. United States -- Politics and government -- 20th century
ISBN 0-394-49973-5; 0-679-72945-3 pa

LC 90-201781

This volume, the first volume of a projected four-volume biography of Lyndon B. Johnson, "follows him from the Hill Country to New Deal Washington, from his boyhood through the years of the Depression to his debut as Congressman, his . . . defeat in his first race for the Senate, and his attainment, nonetheless, at age 31, of the national power for which he hungered." Publisher's note

Includes bibliographical references

★ Caro, Robert A., 1935- The **passage** of power; Robert A. Caro. Alfred A. Knopf 2012 xix, 712 p.p **92**

1. Biography 2. Presidents -- United States -- Biography 3. United States -- Politics and government -- 1945- 4. United States -- Politics and government -- 1963-1969
ISBN 0679405070; 9780679405078

LC 2012010752

This fourth book of Robert A. Caro's series on Lyndon Baines Johnson (LBJ) "chronicles LBJ's life from 1958 to the passage of the Civil Rights Act, in July 1964. It follows Johnson as he . . . seeks the Democratic presidential nomination in 1960; as he is outmaneuvered by John F. Kennedy; as he" cultivates himself to be the "most powerful Senate majority leader in American history" and finally "as he has the presidency thrust upon him following Kennedy's murder." (Atlantic Monthly)

Includes bibliographical references and index.

Gillette, Michael L. **Lady** Bird Johnson; an oral history. Michael L. Gillette. Oxford University Press 2012 400 p. illustrations (hardback : alk. paper) $29.95 **92**

1. United States -- History 2. Presidents' spouses -- United States -- Biography 3. United States -- Politics and government -- 1945-1989
ISBN 0199908087; 9780199908080

LC 2012011580

For this book, Michael L. Gillette, "former director of the LBJ Library's oral history program, has selected and edited these interviews" with former U.S. First Lady Lady Bird Johnson. The histories "cover the first lady's life from her birth in 1912 through [Lyndon B.] Johnson's presidency, thus throwing light on a more than half a century of American history." (Publishers Weekly)

Includes bibliographical references and index

Peters, Charles. **Lyndon** B. Johnson. Times Books 2010 199p (American presidents series) $23 **92**

1. Presidents 2. Vice-presidents 3. Senators 4. Members of Congress 5. Presidents -- United States 6. United States -- Politics and government -- 1945-
ISBN 978-0-8050-8239-5

LC 2009-45612

"Peters describes Johnson's Texas childhood, his years in Congress, his frustrating years as Kennedy's vice president, and the triumphs and failures of his presidency (1963-68). . . . This book is aimed at general readers who want a brief account of this controversial President. . . . Its intended audience will not be disappointed with this fast-moving story." Libr J

Includes bibliographical references

Johnson, Robert, 1911-1938

★ Wald, Elijah. **Escaping** the delta; Robert Johnson and the invention of the blues. Amistad 2004 342p $24.95; pa $14.95 **92**

1. Singers 2. Guitarists 3. Blues music 4. Blues musicians 5. African American musicians 6. Songwriters
ISBN 0-06-052423-5; 0-06-052427-8 pa

LC 2003-52287

The author "writes better than anyone else ever has about the blues. If you read only one book about blues—maybe ever—read this one." Booklist

Includes bibliographical references

Johnson, Samuel, 1709-1784

Boswell, James. The **life** of Samuel Johnson; with an introduction by Claude Rawson. Random House 1992 liii, 127p il (Everyman's library) $30 **92**

1. Lexicographers 2. Literary critics
ISBN 0-679-41717-6

LC 92-52915

First published 1791

"The most famous biography in the English language. It is an intimate and minute delineation of the great lexicographer's life, character and person, enlivened with small-talk, gossip and bits of familiar correspondence. It is also an admirable portrayal of the society of which Johnson was the outstanding figure." Pratt Alcove

Includes bibliographical references

Martin, Peter. **Samuel** Johnson; a biography. Harvard University Press 2008 608p il $35   92
1. Lexicographers 2. Literary critics
ISBN 978-0-674-03160-9; 0-674-03160-1
LC 2008-11327

This "biography of the English essayist, lexicographer, and literary personality . . . emphasizes aspects of Johnson not covered by any previously published biographies . . . notably Johnson's deep depressions; his liberal views on women writers, slavery, and poverty (he was not the complete Tory that others have painted him); and Johnson as a writer whose works deserve to be better known by the general public. Martin covers all the well-known facts and accomplishments of Johnson's life, and he emphasizes the turbulent times in which Johnson lived and the intriguing people he knew. Scholarly but written in an engaging manner and featuring many quotations from Johnson and his friends and acquaintances, this [is a] new portrait of a complex, multi-faceted writer and thinker." Libr J

Includes bibliographical references (p. 565-572)

Meyers, Jeffrey. **Samuel** Johnson; the struggle. Basic Books 2008 528p il $35   92
1. Lexicographers 2. Authors, English 3. Literary critics
ISBN 978-0-465-04571-6; 0-465-04571-5
LC 2008-12302

This biography "departs from a strict chronology to narrate significant events and their meaning for Johnson. A central concern involves one of Johnson's darkest secrets, which Meyers says other biographers have evaded: his masochistic sexuality at the hands of his confidante Mrs. Hester Thrale. The biography also speculates on other aspects of Johnson's sex life, both during his marriage to a much older woman and after her death. But Meyers's book is balanced and accomplishes much else." Publ Wkly

Includes bibliographical references

Jones, John Paul, 1747-1792

Morison, Samuel Eliot. **John** Paul Jones; a sailor's biography. with an introduction by James C. Bradford; charts and diagrams by Erwin Raisz. Naval Inst. Press 1989 xxvi, 537p il (Classics of naval literature) hardcover o.p. pa $24.95   92
1. Naval officers 2. United States -- Naval history
ISBN 1-55750-410-5 pa
LC 89-13423

A reissue with a new introduction of the title first published 1959 by Little, Brown

"Morison has destroyed the myth of John Paul Jones but has left us a more human, more understandable character." Best Sellers

Includes bibliographical references

★ Thomas, Evan. **John** Paul Jones; sailor, hero, father of the American Navy. Simon & Schuster 2003 383p il hardcover o.p. pa $16   92
1. Naval officers 2. United States -- Naval history
ISBN 0-7432-0583-9; 978-0-7432-5804-3; 0-7432-5804-5 pa
LC 2003-42411

"The complex portrait is rendered with nautical precision—the author knows his topsail from his topgallant—and a lively eye for such details as the Enlightenment virtues espoused by Freemasonry or the proper way to kiss a French lady in the eighteenth century." Publ Wkly

Includes bibliographical references

Jones, Malcolm, 1952-

Jones, Malcolm. **Little** boy blues; a crash course in growing up. Pantheon Books 2010 228p il map $24.95   92
1. Journalists 2. Magazine editors
ISBN 978-0-307-37772-2; 0-307-37772-5
LC 2009-17838

"In the background of this memoir, the South also complicates the child's horizon, with its own coded vocabulary, reprimanding glances and generations clinging to a crumbling way of life. . . . With all the hype, marketing and lying that the genre's been subjected to in recent years, I had forgotten that it is also the most vulnerable, intimate form a writer can employ. Often, this gets covered over in supportspeak: the way a writer's memories turn into a way to help alleviate the pain of others suffering from similar memories. Jones is far too good a writer to indulge in messianic messages." PopMatters

Jones, Quincy, 1933-

Jones, Quincy. **Q**: the autobiography of Quincy Jones. Doubleday 2001 412p il $26; pa $15.95 92
1. Composers 2. Conductors (Music) 3. Music arrangers 4. Recording producers
ISBN 0-385-48896-3; 0-7679-0510-5 pa
LC 2001-28151

"With some chapters written by Jones, and others by his family and friends . . . this (auto)biography full of behind-the-scenes anecdotes has an improvisational feel that suits its subject: a jazz musician and superstar composer. . . . Jones has composed a life story that gives much more than the typical celebrity memoir." Publ Wkly

Includes discography and filmography

Joplin, Janis

Cooke, John Byrne. **On** the road with Janis Joplin; John Byrne Cooke. Berkley Books 2014 432 p. 8 plates; illustrations (hardcover) $27.95   92
1. Rock music -- United States 2. Rock musicians -- United States -- Biography
ISBN 9780425274118
LC 2014034647

This book, by John Byrne Cooke, is the memoir of the road manager of the Rock musician Janis Joplin. "In 1967, as the new sound of rock and roll was taking over popular music, John Byrne Cooke was at the center of it all. . . . He witnessed the astonishing breakout performances of Janis Joplin and Jimi Hendrix at the Monterey Pop Festival that June. Less than six months later, he was on a plane to San Francisco, taking a job as road manager for Janis and her band." (Publisher's note)

"Rock music fans will love reading this up-close view of Joplin. The end of the book feels like losing her all over again." LJ

Joplin, Scott, 1868-1917

Berlin, Edward A. **King** of ragtime: Scott Joplin and his era. Oxford Univ. Press 1994 334p il hardcover o.p. pa $21.50   92
1. Pianists 2. Composers 3. Jazz musicians
ISBN 0-19-510108-1 pa

LC 93-28318

"Essential in any library concerned with American music." Booklist
Includes bibliographical references

Jordan, Michael, 1963-

Lazenby, Roland. **Michael** Jordan; the life. Roland Lazenby. Little Brown & Co 2014 720 p. ill. (some col.) $30   92
1. African American baseball players 2. Basketball players -- United States -- Biography
ISBN 0316194778; 9780316194778

LC 2014932746

In this biography about basketball player Michael Jordan, "basketball journalist Roland Lazenby. . .draws on his personal relationships with Jordan's coaches; countless interviews with Jordan's friends, teammates, and family members; and interviews with Jordan himself to provide the first truly definitive study of Michael Jordan: the player, the icon, and the man." (Publisher's note)

"Lazenby's thoroughly enjoyable biography is an impressive portrait of a man consumed by his competitive ambitions." LJ
Includes bibliographical references and index

Josephine, Empress, consort of Napoleon I, Emperor of the French, 1763-1814

Williams, Kate. **Ambition** and desire; the dangerous life of Josephine Bonaparte. Kate Williams. Ballantine Books 2015 400 p. 16 plates; color illustrations (hardback : alkaline paper) $30   92
1. Empresses 2. Empresses -- France -- Biography
ISBN 0345522834; 9780345522832

LC 2014030438

This book, by Kate Williams, focuses on "Napoleon Bonaparte['s] wife, Josephine. . . . Born Marie-Josèphe-Rose de Tascher de La Pagerie on the Caribbean island of Martinique, the woman Napoleon would later call Josephine was the ultimate survivor. She endured a loveless marriage to a French aristocrat-- executed during the Reign of Terror-- then barely escaped the guillotine blade herself. Her near-death experience only fueled [her] ambition. . . . In 1795, she met Napoleon." (Publisher's note)

"Meeting her match in Napoléon Bonaparte, Josephine and he embarked on a doomed marital odyssey characterized by personal jealousies and political obsessions. An in-depth portrait of the substantive woman behind the throne." Booklist
Includes bibliographical references and index

Joyce, James, 1882-1941

Ellmann, Richard. **James** Joyce; new and rev ed; Oxford Univ. Press 1982 887p il hardcover o.p. pa $27.50   92
1. Poets 2. Authors 3. Novelists 4. Dramatists 5. Short story writers
ISBN 0-19-503381-7 pa

LC 81-22455

First published 1959

This "is a vast undertaking and continuing achievement—massive, masterly, and definitive, rich in anecdote and detail. It is also extremely readable; the easy, often sympathetic style communicates gracefully not only facts but analysis." Choice
Includes bibliographical references

Judas Iscariot

★ Gubar, Susan. **Judas**; a biography. W. W. Norton & Co. 2009 453p il $27.95   92
1. Apostles
ISBN 978-0-393-06483-4; 0-393-06483-2

LC 2008-42967

An account of the story of the New Testament's archvillain and his history over the past 2000 years in which Gubar links Christian anti-Semitism with Christianity's attempt to grapple with transcendent evil.

"An exhaustive, beautifully written cultural history of our favorite wrongdoer, Gubar's work is an immensely rewarding and crucially important book." Libr J
Includes bibliographical references

Kael, Pauline, 1919-2001

Kellow, Brian. **Pauline** Kael; a life in the dark. Viking 2011 417p il $27.95   92
1. Motion pictures 2. Writers on film 3. Motion picture critics
ISBN 978-0-670-02312-7; 0-670-02312-4

LC 2011-21798

This book by Brian Kellow presents a biography of film critic Pauline Kael. "She first came to some prominence as a movie maven in San Francisco, where she selected programs for an art house and opined on films for listener-supported radio. She was already 50 when she began writing for the New Yorker, but those two decades of her life take up roughly 75 percent of Kellow's book," which "tell[s] her story mostly through her most famous (and notorious) reviews." (Kirkus Reviews)

"During her glory years at The New Yorker from 1968 to 1991, Pauline Kael enlivened the quiet art of analyzing movies with a lusty noise that echoes in certain movie-festival hallways a decade after her death. . . . [Kellow] brings two unassailable strengths to a bio that's bound to be catnip for both Kael's fans and her naysayers. First, he is impressively thorough in his research. He ferrets out illuminating information about Kael's childhood as the daughter of Polish

Jewish chicken farmers in California, her never-quite-satisfactory romantic relationships with men, her dependence on the daughter she raised as a single mother, her financial struggles, and (most juicily) her oil-and-water clashes with The New Yorker's painfully genteel editor William Shawn. As for Kellow's second strength, it's an elegantly simple one: He's a movie lover but not a professional critic. Kael had many axes to grind, but Kellow appears to have none." Entertainment Wkly

Kafka, Franz, 1883-1924

★ Kafka, die Jahre der Entscheidungen/English. **Kafka,** the decisive years; the decisive years. translated from the German by Shelley Frisch. 1st U.S. ed.; Harcourt 2005 581p il $35   **92**
1. Poets 2. Authors 3. Novelists 4. Short story writers
ISBN 0-15-100752-7
LC 2005-14554
Original German edition, 2002
This first of a projected three-volume biography focuses on Kafka's life from 1910 to 1915, during which he wrote "The Metamorphosis" and The Trial.
"Essential reading for all Kafka devotees." Booklist
Includes bibliographical references

Murray, Nicholas. **Kafka.** Yale University Press 2004 440p il $30   **92**
1. Poets 2. Authors 3. Novelists 4. Short story writers
ISBN 0-300-10631-9
LC 2004-107048
This biography "relates Kafka's brief life, trying valiantly to depict a more normal Kafka, a man who lived in society with good friends, enjoyed sex, had wide-ranging intellectual interests and became enamored of Judaism. In Murray's account, Kafka's employer valued him highly, and under the imprint of no less a figure than Kurt Wolff, he experienced some literary success. Despite Murray's best efforts to contain Kafka's idiosyncrasies, though, the writer remains the tormented soul who created out of his personal anxieties and agonies some of the most acclaimed works of the 20th century." Publ Wkly
Includes bibliographical references

Kaganovich family

Laskin, David. The **Family**; Three Journeys into the Heart of the Twentieth Century. David Laskin. Viking Adult 2013 400 p. $32   **92**
1. Jews 2. Genealogy 3. World history -- 20th century 4. Jews -- Belarus -- Biography 5. Valozhyn (Belarus) -- Biography 6. Jews, Belarusian -- Palestine -- Biography 7. Jews, Belarusian -- United States -- Biography
ISBN 067002547X; 9780670025473
LC 2013017047
Author David Laskin presents a "work of twentieth century history through the riveting story of one extraordinary Jewish family. In tracing the roots of . . . his own family . . . Laskin honors the traditions, the lives, and the choices of his ancestors: revolutionaries and entrepreneurs, scholars and farmers, tycoons and truck drivers." (Publisher's note)
Includes bibliographical references (pages 341-371) and index

Kahlo, Frida, 1907-1954

Kahlo, Frida. The **diary** of Frida Kahlo; an intimate self-portrait. introduction by Carlos Fuentes; essay and commentaries by Sarah M. Lowe; [project director, Claudia Madrazo; editor, Phyllis Freeman; translators, Barbara Crow de Toledo and Ricardo Pohlenz] 2005 ed.; Harry N. Abrams 2005 295p il $24.95   **92**
1. Artists 2. Painters 3. Artists, Mexican
ISBN 0-8109-5954-2
LC 2006-284768
First published 1995
"Sprinkled with irony, black humor, even gaiety . . . this volume is a testament to Kahlo's resilience and courage." Publ Wkly
Includes bibliographical references

Kaling, Mindy

Kaling, Mindy, 1979- **Why** not me? Mindy Kaling. Crown Archetype 2015 228 p. illustrations (hardcover) $25   **92**
1. Actresses 2. Adulthood 3. Adulthood -- Humor 4. Conduct of life -- Humor 5. Actors -- Unted States -- Biography
ISBN 9780804138147; 0804138141
LC 2015020444
In this collection of essays, author Mindy Kaling "shares her ongoing journey to find contentment and excitement in her adult life, whether it's falling in love at work, seeking new friendships in lonely places, attempting to be the first person in history to lose weight without any behavior modification whatsoever, or most important, believing that you have a place in Hollywood when you're constantly reminded that no one looks like you." (Publisher's note)
"Photos and subheadings divide chapters for zippy reading. There are thoughtful lessons, too: entitlement can be good, if it comes from confidence and hard work—hence the book's title. And having confidence, for that matter, if you're not a certain color, size, or gender is a wonderful kind of subversion. Booklist

Kambalu, Samson, 1975-

Kambalu, Samson. The **jive** talker; an artist's genesis: a memoir. Free Press 2008 320p $24   **92**
1. Artists
ISBN 978-1-4165-5931-3; 1-4165-5931-0
LC 2008-26784
"Artist Kambalu recounts his long journey from poverty in Malawi to fame in the London art world. The 'jive talker' was his father, a hospital administrator whose career ups and downs set the mood for the entire family even as they endured the political fortunes of Malawi under Life President Hastings Banda. Kambalu senior died of AIDS in 1995, bequeathing his family memories of his odd assortment of books and love of words." Booklist

Kamkwamba, William, 1987-

Kamkwamba, William. The **boy** who harnessed the wind; William Kamkwamba and Bryan Mealer.

William Morrow 2009 273 p. (hbk.) $25.99; pa $14.99 **92**

1. Windmills -- Malawi 2. Malawi -- Rural conditions 3. Water-supply, Rural -- Malawi 4. Rural electrification -- Malawi 5. Electric power production -- Malawi 6. Mechanical engineers -- Malawi -- Biography
ISBN 0-06-173032-7; 0-06-173033-5 pa; 0061730327; 978-0-06-173032-0; 978-0-06-173033-7 pa; 9780061730320

LC 2010275963

Autobiography of a teenager in Malawi who builds a windmill and brings electricity to his village.

"This exquisite tale strips life down to its barest essentials, and once there finds reason for hopes and dreams, and is especially resonant for Americans given the economy and increasingly heated debates over health care and energy policy." Publ Wkly

Kane, Elisha Kent, 1820-1857

McGoogan, Kenneth. **Race** to the Polar Sea; the heroic adventures of Elisha Kent Kane. [by] Ken McGoogan. Counterpoint 2008 380p il map $28 **92**

1. Explorers 2. Physicians 3. Travel writers 4. Arctic regions -- Exploration
ISBN 978-1-58243-440-7; 1-58243-440-9

LC 2008-12045

This is a biography of the American explorer who discovered the Humboldt Glacier.

"With his access to previously unknown Kane logbooks, McGoogan makes an impressive case for the bravery and importance of the explorer who first identified the Greenland ice sheet." Publ Wkly

Includes bibliographical references

Karajan, Herbert von

Osborne, Richard. **Herbert** von Karajan; a life in music. Northeastern Univ. Press 2000 851p il $37.50 **92**

1. Conductors (Music)
ISBN 1-55553-425-2

LC 99-59108

First published 1998 in the United Kingdom

"Because Karajan's career developed in Nazi Germany, Osborne dwells at length . . . on Karajan's involvement with the regime and his postwar exoneration. Drawing on a vast variety of source materials and quoting some in full, Osborne takes us on the enthralling musical journey that was the life of one of the greatest of conductors." Booklist

Includes bibliographical references

Karp, Brianna, 1985-

Karp, Brianna. The **girl's** guide to homelessness; a memoir. Harlequin 2011 344p pa $16.95 **92**

1. Office workers 2. Homeless persons 3. Homeless
ISBN 978-0-373-89235-8

LC 2010044201

"Sexually and emotionally abused by her parents, Karp left home ASAP. Self-sufficiency delighted her; she adored her job and beach cottage. She lost both to the recession and moved into a trailer she parked in a Walmart lot while using free Starbucks wi-fi and her laptop to apply for jobs. She began blogging about her situation, documenting her struggles with homelessness and trying to regain stability. Candidly humorous, Karp's memoir is sharp and insightful, reminding readers just how perilous the security of a permanent address can be and offering tips on what to do if it is lost." Libr J

Karr, Mary

Karr, Mary. **Lit**; a memoir. Harper 2009 386p $25.99; pa $14.95 **92**

1. Poets 2. Authors 3. Alcoholics 4. Essayists 5. Memoirists 6. Poets, American 7. College teachers
ISBN 978-0-06-059698-9; 0-06-059698-8; 978-0-06-059699-6 pa; 0-06-059699-6 pa

LC 2009-24810

The author reveals how, shortly after giving birth to a child she adored, she drank herself into the same numbness that nearly devoured her charismatic but troubled mother, reaching the brink of suicide before a spiritual awakening led her to sobriety.

Karr "has written a book that lassos you, hogties your emotions and won't let you go. It's a memoir that . . . explores the subjectivity of memory even as it chronicles with searching intelligence, humor and grace the author's slow, sometimes exhilarating, sometimes painful discovery of her vocation." N Y Times (Late N Y Ed)

Katlama, Jacqueline Boulloche, 1918-1994

Kaiser, Charles. The **cost** of courage; by Charles Kaiser. Other Press 2015 288 p. illustrations (hardcover) $26.95 **92**

1. World War, 1939-1945 -- Biography 2. World War, 1939-1945 -- Underground movements -- France 3. Guerrillas -- France -- Biography 4. France -- History -- German occupation, 1940-1945 -- Biography 5. World War, 1939-1945 -- Underground movements -- France -- Biography
ISBN 1590516141; 9781590516140

LC 2015008560

This book, by Charles Kaiser, tells the "heroic true story of the three youngest children of a . . . family who worked together in the French Resistance. . . . In the autumn of 1943, André Boulloche . . . coordinat[ed] all the Resistance movements in the nine northern regions of France only to be betrayed by one of his associates . . . and taken prisoner. His sisters carried on the fight without him until the end of the war." (Publisher's note)

"Kaiser's account of a family's devotion and resilience in the face of horrific tyranny tells a highly recommended story of resolve and bravery that can't help but feel romantic in its selfless and profound obligation, but this is not gloss nor ungrounded canonization." LJ

Kazan, Elia

Schickel, Richard. **Elia** Kazan; a biography. HarperCollins 2005 xxxi, 510p il $29.95 **92**

1. Authors 2. Novelists 3. Memoirists 4. Theatrical directors 5. Motion picture directors
ISBN 0-06-019579-7

LC 2005-43344

This is "the life story of the distinguished stage and screen director. No mere page turner, this is a page devourer, generating the kind of suspense that is usually the province of the playwright or novelist." N Y Times Book Rev

Includes bibliographical references

Kazin, Alfred, 1915-1998

Cook, Richard M., 1941- **Alfred** Kazin's journals; selected and edited by Richard M. Cook. Yale University Press 2011 598p $45   92

1. Biography, Individual

ISBN 978-0-300-14203-7; 0-300-14203-X

LC 2010-45254

The literary critic's "passions — for sex, for novels, for ideas, for talk, for city life — spill from 'Alfred Kazin's Journals,' edited by his biographer, Richard M. Cook. This is a remarkable book, easily one of the great diaries and moral documents of the past American century. What it lacks in cohesiveness it makes up in its frankness, its quick-pivoting angularities. Kazin dismisses his journal at one point as a 'disorderly pile of shavings.' That disorder only adds to its amplitude." N Y Times Book Rev

Includes bibliographical references

Keaton, Buster, 1895-1966

Meade, Marion. **Buster** Keaton; cut to the chase. 1st Da Capo Press ed.; Da Capo Press 1997 440p il pa $18   92

1. Actors 2. Motion picture directors

ISBN 0-306-80802-1

LC 97-17745

First published 1995 by HarperCollins

The author "paints a moving and loving portrait of a comic genius, mechanical thinker, and superb athlete. The book provides the context of family and friends, (including Charlie Chaplin and Fatty Arbuckle) behind Keaton's career, and in doing so adds flesh and humanity to the funny bones and gags that have entertained and marveled audiences for decades. A remarkably gentle and insightful story of a silent comic riddle." Choice

Includes filmography and bibliographical references

Keller, Helen, 1880-1968

Herrmann, Dorothy. **Helen** Keller; a life. University of Chicago Press 1999 394p il pa $22   92

1. Deaf 2. Blind 3. Authors 4. Memoirists 5. Humanitarians 6. Inspirational writers 7. Social welfare leaders

ISBN 0-226-32763-9; 978-0-226-32763-1

LC 99-23242

First published 1998 by Knopf

The author "takes us beyond the image of Helen Keller portrayed in The Miracle Worker to unearth a passionate, politically radical woman whose inspiration and teacher, Annie Sullivan, is equally fiery and brilliant. Herrmann brings us into the every day lives of the famous pair, but the story is hardly mundane. . . . Herrmann gives us fascinating details via archives and unpublished memoirs to show how society's view of disabled people was greatly shaped by Keller and Sullivan." Libr J

Includes bibliographical references

Keller, Helen. **Helen** Keller: selected writings; edited by Kim E. Nielsen; consulting editor, Harvey

J. Kaye. New York University Press 2005 317p il (History of disability series) $35   92

1. Deaf 2. Blind 3. Authors 4. Memoirists 5. Humanitarians 6. Inspirational writers 7. Social welfare leaders

ISBN 0-8147-5829-0

LC 2004-28974

This is a collection "of Keller's personal letters, political writings, speeches, and excerpts of her published materials from 1887 to 1968." Univ Press Books for Public and Second Sch Libr, 2006

Includes bibliographical references

★ Keller, Helen. The **story** of my life; edited and with a preface by James Berger. The restored ed.; Modern Library 2003 xlvi, 343p il hardcover o.p. pa $9.95   92

1. Deaf 2. Blind 3. Authors 4. Memoirists 5. Humanitarians 6. Inspirational writers 7. Social welfare leaders

ISBN 0-679-64287-0; 0-8129-6886-7 pa

LC 2002-40971

First published 1903

This biography of the inspirational Keller contains accounts of her home life and her relationship with her devoted teacher Anne Sullivan.

Includes bibliographical references

Kennan, George Frost, 1904-2005

Kennan, George Frost. **Sketches** from a life. W. W. Norton 2000 365p pa $14.95   92

1. Authors 2. Diplomats 3. Historians 4. Centenarians 5. Nonfiction writers 6. United States -- Foreign relations

ISBN 978-0-393-32139-5; 0-393-32139-8

First published 1989 by Pantheon

"This is a collection of very private reflections spanning some 60 years of foreign service in Nazi Germany, the Baltic states, the Low Countries, the Soviet Union, as well as nonofficial travels covering the entire globe. Kennan has marvelous insight into his ever-changing surroundings—an insight that is always sharp, sometimes melancholy, and punctuated frequently by dry, Midwestern wit." Libr J

Includes bibliographical references

Thompson, Nicholas. The **hawk** and the dove; Paul Nitze, George Kennan, and the history of the Cold War. Henry Holt 2009 403p il $27.50   92

1. Authors 2. Cold war 3. Diplomats 4. Statesmen 5. Historians 6. Centenarians 7. Nonfiction writers 8. Government officials 9. Biography, Individual 10. Secretaries of the navy 11. United States -- Officials and employees 12. United States -- Foreign relations -- 1945-1989 13. National security -- United States -- History -- 20th century 14. Anti-communist movements -- United States -- History -- 20th century

ISBN 0805081429; 9780805081428

LC 2009-09225

This biography of Nitze and Kennan focuses on their "careers as statesmen, policy makers and public intellectuals." (N Y Times Book Rev) Index.

This book "does an inspired job of telling the story of the Cold War through the careers of two of its most interesting and important figures." Washington Monthly

Includes bibliographical references

Kennedy, Edward Moore, 1932-2009

English, Bella. **Last** lion; the fall and rise of Ted Kennedy. Simon & Schuster 2009 464p il $28 **92**

1. Senators 2. Siblings of presidents 3. Presidential candidates 4. United States -- Congress -- Senate

ISBN 978-1-4391-3817-5; 1-4391-3817-6

LC 2008-50491

"A respectful but not stuffy . . . [biography] of Edward Kennedy, the playboy of legendary appetites turned senior statesman. . . . A balanced, nuanced, warts-and-all portrait." Kirkus

Includes bibliographical references

★ Kennedy, Edward Moore. **True** compass; a memoir. [by] Edward M. Kennedy. Twelve 2009 532p il $35 **92**

1. Senators 2. Siblings of presidents 3. Presidential candidates 4. United States -- Congress -- Senate

ISBN 978-0-446-53925-8; 0-446-53925-2

This autobiography by the former senator from Massachusetts was published posthumously.

"Mr. Kennedy's conversational gifts as a storyteller and his sense of humor . . . shine through here, as does his old-school sense of public service and his hard-won knowledge, in his son Teddy Jr.'s words, that 'even our most profound losses are survivable.'" N Y Times (Late N Y Ed)

Includes bibliographical references

Kennedy, John F. (John Fitzgerald), 1917-1963

Brinkley, Alan. **John** F. Kennedy; Alan Brinkley. 1st ed. Times Books 2012 xviii, 202 p.p $23 **92**

1. Biography 2. Kennedy family 3. United States -- Politics and government 4. Presidents -- United States -- Biography 5. United States -- Politics and government -- 1961-1963

ISBN 0805083499; 9780805083491

LC 2011043747

Author Alan Brinkley discusses John F. Kennedy, suggesting that "he left an enormous legacy as a charismatic leader and a glamorous symbol of hope and purpose long after his death." Brinkley describes Kennedy as "the handsome, unscholarly, self-indulgent son of Joseph Kennedy, whose enormous wealth and ambition cleared his path through Massachusetts and then national politics." The book features Kennedy's experiences "as a [president,] congressman and senator, [describing his views on] . . . military spending . . . [and] civil rights." (Kirkus Reviews)

Includes bibliographical references and index

Clarke, Thurston. **JFK's** last hundred days; the transformation of a man and the emergence of a great president. Thurston Clarke. The Penguin Press 2013 448 p. (hardcover) $29.95 **92**

1. United States -- Politics and government -- 1961-1974 2. Change (Psychology) -- Case studies 3. Presidents -- United States -- Biography 4. Political leadership -- United States -- Case studies 5. United States -- Politics

and government -- 1961-1963

ISBN 159420425X; 9781594204258

LC 2012047456

"This . . . look at J.F.K.'s last 100 days makes the case that had he survived that fateful November afternoon, his political star would've only continued to rise in a seemingly assured second term. [Thurston] Clarke . . . contends that Kennedy's successful resolution of the Cuban Missile Crisis, as well as his popular stances on civil rights, lunar exploration, arms reduction, and tax cuts would've overshadowed his romantic scandals, [and] tensions relating to Vietnam." (Publishers Weekly)

Includes bibliographical references and index

Dallek, Robert. **Let** every nation know; John F. Kennedy in his own words. [by] Robert Dallek and Terry Golway. Sourcebooks MediaFusion 2006 289p il $29.95; pa $19.95 **92**

1. Presidents 2. Senators 3. Members of Congress 4. Presidents -- United States 5. United States -- Politics and government -- 1961-1974

ISBN 1-4022-0647-X; 978-1-4022-0647-4; 1-4022-0922-3 pa; 978-1-4022-0922-2 pa

LC 2005-37973

"The voice of John F. Kennedy is burned into the brains of people of a certain age. But younger citizens may not be familiar with his ideas and the distinctive way in which he expressed himself. There have been past recordings of JFK's presidential speeches, but this unique package pairs a CD of the speeches with a collection of essays on them by historians Golway and Dallek (the latter wrote his own JFK book, An Unfinished Life, 2003). The result is nothing short of terrific..." (Booklist)

Includes bibliographical references

Dallek, Robert. An **unfinished** life: John F. Kennedy, 1917-1963. Little, Brown 2003 838p il $30; pa $17.95 **92**

1. Presidents 2. Senators 3. Members of Congress 4. Presidents -- United States 5. United States -- Politics and government -- 1961-1974

ISBN 0-316-17238-3; 0-316-90792-8 pa

LC 2002-116388

This is a biography of the thirty-fifth president of the United States

The author "has written the most accessible, balanced, and scholarly biography yet of JFK. . . . It is the Kennedy biography against which others will be measured." Libr J

Includes bibliographical references

Mahoney, Richard D. **Sons** and brothers: the days of Jack and Bobby Kennedy. Arcade Pub. 1999 441p il $27.95; pa $14.95 **92**

1. Diplomats 2. Presidents 3. Senators 4. Financiers 5. Attorneys general 6. Members of Congress 7. Parents of presidents 8. Siblings of presidents 9. Presidential candidates 10. Regulatory agency officials 11. United States -- Politics and government -- 1961-1974

ISBN 1-55970-480-2; 1-55970-534-5 pa

LC 99-25681

"Writing in a steady, almost relentlessly elegiac tone, Mahoney proves that the lives and deaths of John F. and

Robert F. Kennedy remain as compelling now as they were throughout the turbulent 1960s." Publ Wkly

Includes bibliographical references

Sorensen, Theodore C., 1928-2010. **Counselor**; a life at the edge of history. [by] Ted Sorensen. HarperCollins 2008 556p il $27.95   **92**

1. Lawyers 2. Presidents 3. Senators 4. Members of Congress 5. Government officials 6. Biography, Individual 7. Presidential advisers 8. United States -- Politics and government -- 20th century

ISBN 0-06-079871-8; 978-0-06-079871-0

LC 2007-47328

This is a memoir by President Kennedy's advisor and speechwriter. Index.

"This book is instantly essential for any student of the period. It fills gaps in the historical record; it vividly conveys life inside the administration; and it generously dishes anecdotes." Washington Post Book World

Kennedy, John F. Jr., 1960-1999

Anderson, Christopher. The **good** son; JFK Jr. and the mother he loved. Christopher Andersen. Gallery Books 2014 368 p. 16 plates; illustrations $27   **92**

1. Children of presidents -- United States -- Biography

ISBN 1476775567; 9781476775562; 9781476775579

LC 2014024249

This book, by Christopher Andersen, presents a biography of John F. Kennedy, Jr. and his mother Jacqueline Kennedy. The author "explores his reactions to his mother's post-Dallas suicidal depression and growing dependence on prescription drugs (as well as men); how Jackie felt about the women in her son's life ... to his turbulent marriage; the senseless plane crash that took his life; the aftermath of shock, loss, grief, and confusion; and much more." (Publisher's note)

"Sensitive and astute, Andersen's book offers an intriguing look at a fraught mother-son dynamic that, years after the deaths of both Jackie and John Jr., still has the power to mesmerize. An intimate and compelling look at 'the most brilliant star in the Kennedy firmament.'" Kirkus

Kennedy, Joseph P., 1888-1969

Mahoney, Richard D. **Sons** and brothers: the days of Jack and Bobby Kennedy. Arcade Pub. 1999 441p il $27.95; pa $14.95   **92**

1. Diplomats 2. Presidents 3. Senators 4. Financiers 5. Attorneys general 6. Members of Congress 7. Parents of presidents 8. Siblings of presidents 9. Presidential candidates 10. Regulatory agency officials 11. United States -- Politics and government -- 1961-1974

ISBN 1-55970-480-2; 1-55970-534-5 pa

LC 99-25681

"Writing in a steady, almost relentlessly elegiac tone, Mahoney proves that the lives and deaths of John F. and Robert F. Kennedy remain as compelling now as they were throughout the turbulent 1960s." Publ Wkly

Includes bibliographical references

★ Nasaw, David. The **patriarch**; the remarkable life and turbulent times of Joseph P. Kennedy.

David Nasaw. Penguin Press 2012 xxiv, 868 p.p ill. $40   **92**

1. Presidents -- United States -- Family 2. Ambassadors -- United States -- Biography 3. Politicians -- United States -- Biography 4. Businesspeople -- United States -- Biography

ISBN 1594203768; 9781594203763

LC 2012027315

In this biography, "[David] Nasaw takes on Joseph P. Kennedy, businessman, Hollywood mogul, founding chair of the Securities and Exchange Commission, U.S. ambassador to Britain, and, of course, father to our 35th President. He had exclusive access to Kennedy's papers and addresses some longstanding questions." (Library Journal)

Includes bibliographical references (p. [793]-834) and index

Kennedy, Kathleen, 1920-1948

Byrne, Paula. **Kick**; The True Story of JFK's Sister and the Heir to Chatsworth. Paula Byrne. Harper 2016 352 p. illustrations (hardcover) $29.99   **92**

1. Kennedy family 2. Aristocracy -- Great Britain 3. Americans -- England -- Biography 4. Young women -- England -- Biography 5. Socialites -- United States -- Biography 6. Young women -- United States -- Biography 7. Aristocracy (Social class) -- Great Britain -- Biography 8. Great Britain -- Social life and customs -- 20th century 9. United States -- Social life and customs -- 20th century 10. Presidents -- United States -- Brothers and sisters -- Biography

ISBN 9780062296276

LC 2016008270

This book, by Paula Byrne, is a "biography of the ... young Kennedy sister who charmed American society and the English aristocracy, and would break with her family for love. .... The fourth Kennedy child, the irrepressible Kathleen, stood out. ... [She] shock[ed] and alienate[d] her devout family by falling in love and marrying the scion of a virulently anti-Catholic family—William Cavendish, the heir apparent of the Duke of Devonshire and Chatsworth." (Publisher's note)

"At first, the book is less a biography and more a society report of England's upper class, but it evolves into an exciting, heartbreakingly tense love story." Kirkus

Includes bibliographical references and index

True story of Kick Kennedy, JFK's forgotten sister and the heir to Chatsworth

Leaming, Barbara. **Kick** Kennedy; the charmed life and tragic death of the favorite Kennedy daughter. Barbara Leaming. Thomas Dunne Books, an imprint of St. Martin's 2016 304 p. illustrations (hardcover) $27.99   **92**

1. Kennedy family 2. Aristocracy -- Great Britain 3. Catholics -- England -- Biography 4. Socialites -- United States -- Biography 5. Young women -- United States -- Biography 6. Americans -- England -- London -- Biography 7. Young women -- England -- London -- Biography 8. Aristocracy (Social class) -- Great Britain -- Biography 9. Great Britain -- Social life and customs -- 20th century 10. Presidents -- United States

-- Brothers and sisters -- Biography
ISBN 9781250071316

LC 2016007364

This book, by Barbara Leaming, is a biography of "Kathleen 'Kick' Kennedy. . . . The daughter of the American ambassador to the Court of St James's, Kick swept into Britain's aristocracy like a fresh wind on a sweltering summer day. In a decaying world where everything was based on stultifying sameness and similarity, she was gloriously, exhilaratingly different. Kick was the girl whom all the boys fell in love with, the girl who remained painfully out of reach for most of them." (Publisher's note)

"Leaming candidly demystifies the life of one of the least-known Kennedys and vividly illuminates the complex world of British aristocracy." Booklist

Includes bibliographical references and index.

Kennedy, Robert F., 1925-1968

Clarke, Thurston. The **last** campaign; Robert F. Kennedy and 82 days that inspired America. Thurston Clarke. Henry Holt 2008 321p il $25; pa $15   **92**

1. Senators 2. Attorneys general 3. Siblings of presidents 4. Presidential candidates 5. United States -- Politics and government -- 20th century
ISBN 978-0-8050-7792-6; 0-8050-7792-8; 978-0-8050-9022-2 pa; 0-8050-9022-3 pa

LC 2007-45880

In this account of Robert F. Kennedy's run for president, Clarke "follows on Bobby's heels as he plunged headlong into his campaign, from Kansas and Indiana to Oregon and California, throwing off his brother's mantle and becoming at last his own man. He spoke passionately, almost recklessly, inciting crowds to frenzy with his idealistic speeches about the moral shame of Vietnam, the needs of the poor and minorities and the responsibility of each American. Incorporating accounts by a gamut of reporters, politicians, family and 'Honorary Kennedys,' as well as extracts from Bobby's own stunning stump speeches, Clarke compellingly recreates this 'huge, joyous adenture.'" Kirkus

Includes bibliographical references

Mahoney, Richard D. **Sons** and brothers: the days of Jack and Bobby Kennedy. Arcade Pub. 1999 441p il $27.95; pa $14.95   **92**

1. Diplomats 2. Presidents 3. Senators 4. Financiers 5. Attorneys general 6. Members of Congress 7. Parents of presidents 8. Siblings of presidents 9. Presidential candidates 10. Regulatory agency officials 11. United States -- Politics and government -- 1961-1974
ISBN 1-55970-480-2; 1-55970-534-5 pa

LC 99-25681

"Writing in a steady, almost relentlessly elegiac tone, Mahoney proves that the lives and deaths of John F. and Robert F. Kennedy remain as compelling now as they were throughout the turbulent 1960s." Publ Wkly

Includes bibliographical references

Schlesinger, Arthur M. (Arthur Meier), 1917-2007. **Robert** Kennedy and his times; {by} Arthur

M. Schlesinger, Jr. Houghton Mifflin 1978 1066p il hardcover o.p. pa $17.95   **92**

1. Senators 2. Attorneys general 3. Siblings of presidents 4. Presidential candidates 5. United States -- Politics and government -- 20th century
ISBN 978-0-618-21928-5 pa; 0-618-21928-5 pa

LC 78-8469

"A highly sympathetic and readable political biography covering in depth Robert Kennedy's tenure in public life. At times extremely partisan, at times dispassionate, Schlesinger's study effectively captures Kennedy's impact on national politics and the main currents of American politics during the 1950s and 1960s." Choice

Includes bibliographical references

★ Thomas, Evan. **Robert** Kennedy; his life. Simon & Schuster 2000 509p il hardcover o.p. pa $15   **92**

1. Senators 2. Attorneys general 3. Siblings of presidents 4. Presidential candidates 5. United States -- Politics and government -- 20th century
ISBN 0-7432-0329-1 pa

LC 00-41995

"A solid, judicious life of a politician whose tragic death inspired a generation of what-if history." Booklist

Includes bibliographical references

Tye, Larry. **Bobby** Kennedy; the making of a liberal icon. Larry Tye. Random House Inc 2016 608 p. $32   **92**

1. Legislators -- United States -- Biography 2. United States. Congress. Senate -- Biography 3. United States -- Politics and government -- 1945-1989
ISBN 0812993349; 9780812993349

LC 2016004991

This biography of Robert F. Kennedy by Larry Tye "draws on unpublished memoirs, unreleased government files, and fifty-eight boxes of papers that had been under lock and key for the past forty years. He conducted hundreds of interviews with RFK intimates--including Bobby's widow, Ethel, his sister Jean, and his aide John Siegenthaler--many of whom have never spoken to another biographer." (Publisher's note)

"The author chides RFK for such things as slanting his account of the Bay of Pigs, his perhaps excessive pursuit of Jimmy Hoffa, and his early hawkishness on Vietnam. But the contrary image is clear: a good, if not great man; an unspeakable loss. Kirkus

Includes bibliographical references and index

Kennedy, Rosemary

Larson, Kate Clifford. **Rosemary**; The Hidden Kennedy Daughter. Kate Clifford Larson. Houghton Mifflin Harcourt 2015 320 p. 16 plates; illustrations $27   **92**

1. Kennedy family
ISBN 0547250258; 9780547250250

LC 2015028793

In this biography by Kate Clifford Larson "major new sources -- Rose Kennedy's diaries and correspondence, school and doctors' letters, and exclusive family interviews -- bring Rosemary alive as a girl adored but left far behind by her competitive siblings. Larson reveals both the sensitive care Rose and Joe gave to Rosemary and then . . . the often desperate and duplicitous arrangements the Kennedys made to keep her away from home as she became increasingly intractable." (Publisher's note)

"This expertly researched work offers a candid examination of a once-forgotten member of one of America's most famous families. It will appeal to Kennedy devotees and readers interested in society's evolving understanding of the intellectually and physically disabled."

Kenney, David Ngaruri, 1973-

Kenney, David Ngaruri. **Asylum** denied; a refugee's struggle for safety in America. [by] David Ngaruri Kenney and Philip G. Schrag. University of California Press 2008 352p il map $40; pa $17.95 **92**

1. Refugees 2. Political refugees 3. Kenya 4. Immigrants -- United States

ISBN 978-0-520-25510-4; 0-520-25510-0; 978-0-520-26159-4 pa; 0-520-26159-3 pa

LC 2007-48703

"One cannot read this book without experiencing rage, disbelief, and an overwhelming sense of sadness over the inhumanity Kenney suffered, both in Kenya and in this country. Still, it is also an inspiring story of human courage, heartfelt friendships, and unrelenting devotion to fighting the good fight. . . . This account should be required reading for anyone who has contact with immigrants in America. It should also be on the reading list of anyone who cares about the preservation of human rights and human dignity in our world." Calif Lawyer

Includes bibliographical references

Kerouac, Jack, 1922-1969

Kerouac, Jack. **Selected** letters, 1940-1956; edited with an introduction and commentary by Ann Charters. Viking 1995 xxvi, 629p hardcover o.p. pa $16.95 **92**

1. Authors 2. Novelists

ISBN 0-14-023444-6 pa

LC 94-12911

The editor "made two very wise decisions here: she supplied continuity and context for the letters, and she included significant letters from the correspondents. The frustration of the long-rejected writer is doubly felt by the reader, since this selection ends on the eve of the big Beat breakthrough." Choice

Includes bibliographical references

Keynes, John Maynard, 1883-1946

Davenport-Hines, R. P. T. (Richard Peter Treadwell), 1953- **Universal** Man; The Lives of John Maynard Keynes. Richard Davenport-Hines. Basic Books 2015 432 p. illustration $29.99 **92**

1. Economists -- Biography

ISBN 0465060676; 9780465060672

LC 2015934354

In this book author "Richard Davenport-Hines revives our understanding of John Maynard Keynes (1883-1946), the twentieth century's most charismatic and revolutionary economist. Keynes helped FDR launch the New Deal,

saved Britain from financial crisis twice over the course of two World Wars, and instructed Western nations on how to protect themselves from revolutionary unrest, economic instability, high unemployment, and social dissolution." (Publisher's note)

"Although this approach necessitates recovering some chronological ground—obviously he was a pundit and lover most of his life—the author is quite successful in avoiding redundancy. The result is that the intellectual, social, professional, and personal aspects of Keynes are described and analyzed both independently and as they interrelated to create a complex and brilliant thinker. This is a splendid biography that will fascinate the general reader and give new insight to the scholar. Summing Up: Highly recommended. Undergraduates through faculty; two-year technical students; general readers." Choice

Khrushchev, Nikita Sergeevich, 1894-1971

Nikita Khrushchev; edited by William Taubman, Sergei Khrushchev, and Abbott Gleason; translated by David Gehrenbeck, Eileen Kane, and Alla Bashenko. Yale Univ. Press 2000 391p $45 **92**

1. Heads of state 2. Communist leaders 3. Political leaders 4. Soviet Union -- Politics and government

ISBN 0-300-07635-6

LC 99-51323

A collection of essays re-evaluating aspects of Khrushchev's political career. Topics include his rise to power and his domestic, foreign, and military policy. Two essays compare Khrushchev and Gorbachev

Includes bibliographical references and index

Taubman, William. **Khrushchev**; the man and his era. Norton 2003 p. cm **92**

1. Heads of state 2. Communist leaders 3. Political leaders 4. Heads of state -- Soviet Union -- Biography

ISBN 0-393-05144-7

LC 2002-26404

Includes bibliographical references and index

Kilgore, Bernard, 1908-1967

Tofel, Richard J. **Restless** genius; Barney Kilgore, The Wall Street journal, and the invention of modern journalism. St. Martin's Press 2009 271p il $25.95 **92**

1. Journalists 2. Wall Street journal 3. Newspaper executives

ISBN 978-0-312-53674-9; 0-312-53674-7

LC 2008-29880

"What makes this work especially appealing is the incorporation of the many letters Kilgore wrote to his father, giving the reader a glimpse into this esteemed newsman's way of thinking about his newspaper and the news of the day." Libr J

Includes bibliographical references

Kim, Eunsun, 1986-

Kim, Eunsun, 1986- A **Thousand** Miles to Freedom; My Escape from North Korea. by Eunsun Kim,

Sébastien Falletti, translated by David Tian. St. Martin's Press 2015 240 p. (hardcover) $24.99 **92**
1. Refugees 2. Korea (North)
ISBN 1250064643; 9781250064646

LC 2015015581

In this book, by Eunsun Kim, Sébastien Falletti, and translated by David Tian, the author describes how "her mother decided to escape North Korea with [her] and her sister, not knowing that they were embarking on a journey that would take them nine long years to complete. Before finally reaching South Korea and freedom, Eunsun and her family would live homeless, fall into the hands of Chinese human traffickers, survive a North Korean labor camp, and cross the deserts of Mongolia on foot." (Publisher's note)

"An urgent cry for compassion for the author's fellow North Koreans, trapped and strangled of liberty and life." Kirkus

Kim, Jong-il, 1942-2011

Harden, Blaine. The **Great** Leader and the Fighter Pilot; The True Story of the Tyrant Who Created North Korea and the Young Lieutenant Who Stole His Way to Freedom. by Blaine Harden. Penguin Group USA 2015 288 p. 16 plates; illustrations; maps $27.95 **92**
1. United States -- Foreign relations -- Korea (North)
ISBN 0670016578; 9780670016570

LC 2014038542

In this book, author Blaine Harden "tells the . . . story of how Kim Il Sung grabbed power and plunged his country into war against the United States while the youngest fighter pilot in his air force was playing a high-risk game of deception--and escape. As Kim ascended from Soviet puppet to godlike ruler, No Kum Sok noisily pretended to love his Great Leader. That is, until he swiped a Soviet MiG-15 and delivered it to the Americans." (Publisher's note)

"An enjoyable read that is highly recommended for those interested in Cold War or North Korean history, or for anyone who likes a strong narrative. Readers who enjoy this book might also appreciate No Kum-Sok's A MiG-15 to Freedom." LJ

Jang Jin-sung. **Dear** Leader; poet, spy, escapee?: a look inside North Korea. Jang Jin-sung; translated by Shirley Lee. 37 Ink/Atria Books 2014 368 p. (hardback) $27.99 **92**
1. Poets 2. Korea (North) 3. Autobiographies 4. Korea (North) -- Biography 5. Propaganda -- Korea (North) 6. Poets -- Korea (North) -- Biography 7. Political refugees -- Korea (North) -- Biography 8. Korea (North) -- Politics and government -- 1994-2011
ISBN 147676655X; 9781476766553

LC 2014010236

This memoir tells how "[a]s North Korea's State Poet Laureate, Jang Jin-sung led a charmed life. With food provisions . . . , a travel pass, access to strictly censored information, and audiences with Kim Jong-il himself, his life in Pyongyang seemed safe and secure. But this privileged existence was about to be shattered. When a strictly forbidden magazine he lent to a friend goes missing, Jang Jin-sung must flee for his life." (Publisher's note)

"A defector of Kim Jong-il's rarefied inner circle reveals the desperate, despicable machinations of North Korea's police state." Kirkus

Kim, Joseph

Kim, Joseph. **Under** the same sky; from starvation in North Korea to salvation in America. by Joseph Kim; contributions by Stephan Talty. Houghton Mifflin Harcourt 2015 288 p. (hardback) $28 **92**
1. Famines 2. Refugees 3. Human rights 4. Christian ethics 5. Immigrants -- United States 6. Rescue work -- China 7. Christian ethics -- China 8. Human rights -- Korea (North) 9. Victims of famine -- Korea (North) 10. Refugees -- Korea (North) -- Biography 11. Immigrants -- United States -- Biography
ISBN 0544373170; 9780544373174

LC 2014039686

This book, by Joseph Kim, is a "searing story of starvation and survival in North Korea, followed by a dramatic escape, rescue by activists and Christian missionaries, and success in the United States thanks to newfound faith and courage." (Publisher's note)

"Both volumes put a human face to an often misunderstood country and will appeal to a wide range of readers." LJ

Kimball, Kristin

Kimball, Kristin. The **dirty** life; on farming, food, and love. Scribner 2010 276p $25; ebook $11.99 **92**
1. Authors 2. Farmers 3. Journalists 4. Organic farming 5. Farm life -- New York (State)
ISBN 978-1-4165-5160-7; 978-1-4391-8714-2 ebook

"A hearty, chromatic account of a meaningful accomplishment in farming, 'that dirty concupiscent art.'" Kirkus

King, Clarence, 1842-1901

Sandweiss, Martha A. **Passing** strange; a Gilded Age tale of love and deception across the color line. Penguin Press 2009 370p il $27.95 **92**
1. Geologists 2. Travel writers 3. Passing (Identity) 4. Writers on science 5. Government officials 6. Biography, Individual 7. United States -- Race relations 8. African Americans -- Race identity 9. Racially mixed people -- Race identity
ISBN 978-1-59420-200-1

LC 2008-34886

The book tells the story of "Clarence King (1842–1901), the eminent nineteenth-century geologist . . . [and] mapper of the American West . . . [who] successfully avoided military service in the Civil War and chose instead to cultivate his manliness in the rugged life of a western explorer." In particular the book looks at his travels across the color line in the U.S. and how "for the last thirteen years of his life he led a double life in Brooklyn as James Todd, a light-skinned African American Pullman porter." (Journal of American History)

Sandweiss's "great accomplishment is to have explored not only how the 19th-century explorer and scientist Clarence King reinvented himself but also why that reinvention was so singularly American. Best of all are Ms. Sandweiss's insights into what King's deception and its consequences really mean." N Y Times (Late N Y Ed)

Includes bibliographical references

King, Martin Luther, Jr., 1929-1968

Burns, Rebecca. **Burial** for a King; Martin Luther King Jr.'s funeral and the week that transformed Atlanta and rocked the nation. Scribner 2011 244p il $25; ebook $11.99   **92**
1. Clergy 2. Nonfiction writers 3. Civil rights activists 4. Nobel laureates for peace 5. Atlanta (Ga.) -- Race relations 6. United States -- Race relations
ISBN 978-1-4391-3054-4; 978-1-4391-4309-4 ebook
LC 2010-29980

This is a "recreation of the aftermath of Martin Luther King Jr.'s assassination. . . . [The author] provides a snapshot of a still-segregated nation poised between uneasy reconciliation and violent chaos. Using terse language and precise, straightforward descriptions . . . she views the crisis and aftermath of King's death in Memphis through multiple points of view, beginning with the traumatic center of his family and closest associates in Atlanta. . . . A pertinent, you-are-there historical page-turner with a strong moral message." Kirkus

Flowers, Arthur. **I** see the promised land; a life of Martin Luther King Jr. [text by] Arthur Flowers, [illustrations by] Manu Chitrakar, [design by] Guglielmo Rossi. Groundwood Books/House of Anansi Press 2013 154 p. il $16.95   **92**
1. Clergy 2. Graphic novels 3. Biographical graphic novels 4. Nonfiction writers 5. Civil rights activists 6. Nobel laureates for peace 7. African Americans -- Civil rights -- Graphic novels
ISBN 1554983282; 9781554983285

This book is an illustrated biography of civil rights activist Martin Luther King Jr. by African American novelist and performance poet Arthur Flowers. "He weaves the entire history of the enslavement of black Americans into King's story, refers to unspecified gods taking an interest in affairs, and comments on King's speeches." (School Library Journal)

"A myth-making take on King's life that has both emotional and intellectual impact, the Flowers/Chitrakar collaboration supplies fresh color and richness to the oft-told history of this game-changer." Libr J

Jackson, Troy. **Becoming** King; Martin Luther King, Jr. and the making of a national leader. introduction by Clayborne Carson. University Press of Kentucky 2008 248p (Civil rights and the struggle for Black equality in the twentieth century) $35   **92**
1. Clergy 2. Nonfiction writers 3. Civil rights activists 4. Nobel laureates for peace 5. African Americans -- Civil rights
ISBN 978-0-8131-2520-6; 0-8131-2520-0
LC 2008-25041

"The author's comprehensive analysis of King's sermons before, during and after the boycott artfully depicts a man in transition, from naive do-gooder to world-changer. Jackson's treatment of Montgomery in the post-boycott era offers new insight into the void in leadership and the fractious infighting among the movement's luminaries after King departed

the scene. An informed investigation of the struggles that defined a time and place-and the man who gave them a voice." Kirkus

Includes bibliographical references (p. 229-239) and index.

Young, Andrew. An **easy** burden; the civil rights movement and the transformation of America. foreword by Quincy Jones. Baylor University Press 2008 550p il pa $29.95   **92**
1. Clergy 2. Mayors 3. Nonfiction writers 4. Members of Congress 5. Civil rights activists 6. United Nations officials 7. Nobel laureates for peace 8. United States -- Race relations 9. African Americans -- Civil rights
ISBN 978-1-602580-73-2
LC 2007-49679
First published 1996 by HarperCollins Pubs.

This memoir focuses on Young's early life as a middle-class African American growing up in segregated New Orleans, his call to the ministry, and his years working with Dr. King and the Southern Christian Leadership Conference.

Kingston, Maxine Hong

Kingston, Maxine Hong, 1940- The **woman** warrior; China men. Maxine Hong Kingston; with an introduction by Mary Gordon. Everyman's Library 2005 xxix, 541 p.p $25   **92**
1. Chinese Americans -- History 2. California -- Biography 3. Chinese Americans -- California -- Biography 4. Authors, American -- 20th century -- Biography 5. Chinese Americans -- California -- Social life and customs
ISBN 1400043840; 9781400043842
LC 2004061143
National Book Critics Circle Award for General Nonfiction (1976)

This volume, by Maxine Hong Kingston, reprints of her award winning books "The Woman Warrior" and "China Men." The first work "is Kingston's disturbing and fiercely beautiful account of growing up Chinese-American in California." The second is "Kingston's unforgettable imaginative journey into the hearts and minds of generations of Chinese men in America, from those who worked on the transcontinental railroad in the 1840s to those who fought in Vietnam." (Publisher's note)

Kipling, Rudyard, 1865-1936

Gilmour, David. The **long** recessional: the imperial life of Rudyard Kipling. Farrar, Straus & Giroux 2002 351p il maps $26; pa $15   **92**
1. Poets 2. Authors 3. Novelists 4. Memoirists 5. Children's authors 6. Short story writers 7. Nobel laureates for literature
ISBN 0-374-18702-9; 0-374-52896-9 pa
LC 2002-100585

This biography focuses on Kipling's social and political views in relation to the British Empire, especially as expressed in his fiction and poetry

The author "offers a brief, sympathetic, well-informed, and highly readable account of Kipling." Libr J

Includes bibliographical references

Ricketts, Harry. **Rudyard** Kipling; a life. Carroll & Graf Pubs. 2000 434p il hardcover o.p. pa $16   **92**

1. Poets 2. Authors 3. Novelists 4. Memoirists 5. Children's authors 6. Short story writers 7. Nobel laureates for literature

ISBN 0-7867-0830-1 pa

First published 1999 in the United Kingdom with title: The unforgiving minute: a life of Rudyard Kipling

This work "succeeds in disentangling some of the political muddle of Kipling's life. Ricketts' literary analysis is competent, if unsophisticated. Most valuably, he traces the debt to Browning and the many other resonant literary allusions in Kipling's work, thus undermining the charges of philistinism . . . levelled against it." New Statesman (Engl)

Kirshenblatt, Mayer, 1916-

Kirshenblatt, Mayer. **They** called me Mayer July; painted memories of a Jewish childhood in Poland before the Holocaust. [by] Mayer Kirshenblatt, Barbara Kirshenblatt-Gimblett. University of California Press 2007 411p il (S. Mark Taper Foundation imprint in Jewish studies) $39.95   **92**

1. Artists 2. Painters 3. Holocaust survivors 4. Memoirists 5. Jews -- Poland

ISBN 978-0-520-24961-5

LC 2006-36182

"Kirshenblatt's illustrated memoir of growing up as a Jew in pre-World War II Poland reads like an episodic novel as he introduces the reader to village life and the myriad of unusual and interesting characters." Univ Press Books for Public and Second Sch Libr, 2008

Includes bibliographical references

Kissinger, Henry, 1923-

Dallek, Robert. **Nixon** and Kissinger; partners in power. HarperCollins Publishers 2007 740p il $32.50   **92**

1. Presidents 2. Vice-presidents 3. Senators 4. College teachers 5. Nonfiction writers 6. Members of Congress 7. Writers on politics 8. Secretaries of state 9. Presidential advisers 10. Nobel laureates for peace 11. United States -- Foreign relations 12. International relations specialists

ISBN 978-0-06-072230-2; 0-06-072230-4

LC 2006-52100

A look "behind the scenes at this quintessential pair of power brokers and their lasting influence, for good and ill, on the political stage." Bookmarks Magazine

Includes bibliographical references

Ferguson, Niall, 1964- **Kissinger**; The Idealist, 1923-1968. Penguin Group USA 2015 656 p. 32 plates : illustrations $36   **92**

1. Diplomacy

ISBN 1594206538; 9781594206535

Author "Niall Ferguson shows in this magisterial two-volume biography, drawing not only on [Henry] Kissinger's hitherto closed private papers but also on documents from more than a hundred archives around the world, the idea of Kissinger as the ruthless arch-realist is based on a profound misunderstanding." (Publisher's note)

"It will surprise many readers how quickly Kissinger finds his principles incompatible with the Kennedy-Johnson policy in Vietnam, and how reluctant he is to serve under the devious Nixon. A sophisticated portrait, certain to stir debate--and to heighten expectations for the sequel." Booklist

Knapp, Caroline

★ Caldwell, Gail. **Let's** take the long way home; a memoir of friendship. Random House 2010 190p $23   **92**

1. Friendship 2. Journalists 3. Columnists 4. Memoirists 5. Literary critics

ISBN 978-1-4000-6738-1; 1-4000-6738-3

LC 2009-29384

"This is a book you'll want to share with your own 'necessary pillars of life,' as Caldwell refers to her nearest and dearest. . . . Her memoir, a tribute to the enduring power of friendship, is a lovely gift to readers." Washington Post

Knight, Bobby

Knight, Bobby. **Knight**: my story; [by] Bob Knight with Bob Hammel. Thomas Dunne Bks. 2002 387p il $25.95; pa $14.95   **92**

1. Basketball coaches 2. Basketball -- Biography

ISBN 0-312-28257-5; 0-312-31117-6 pa

LC 2001-48990

"College hoops fans can learn more about the game from this book than from most instructional guides." Publ Wkly

Knight, Philip H., 1938-

Knight, Philip H., 1938- **Shoe** dog; Phil Knight. Scribner, an imprint of Simon & Schuster, Inc. 2016 386 p. (hardback) $29   **92**

1. Nike (Firm) 2. Businesspeople -- United States -- Biography 3. Sporting goods industry -- United States -- History

ISBN 1501135910; 9781501135910; 9781501150111

LC 2016010080

In this memoir, "Nike founder and board chairman Phil Knight shares the inside story of the company's early days as an intrepid start-up and its evolution into one of the world's most iconic, game-changing, and profitable brands. . . . In this age of start-ups, Knight's Nike is the gold standard, and its swoosh is more than a logo. A symbol of grace and greatness, it's one of the few icons instantly recognized in every corner of the world." (Publisher's note)

"Has anyone else ever written as evocatively about selling shoes? Well, George Pelecanos wrote a crime novel called Shoedog, and there's a character in it who sells shoes with a definite flair, but that's really something very different. And, yet, maybe not. Pelecanos brings his street characters to vivid life and makes us care about them. Remarkably, Knight does the same thing for a giant corporation—certainly an even more formidable task." Booklist

Koenigswarter, Pannonica de, Baroness, 1913-

1988

Kastin, David. **Nica's** dream; the life and legend of the jazz baroness. W. W. Norton 2011 336p il $26.95 **92**

1. Patrons of the arts 2. Jazz music -- History and criticism

ISBN 978-0-393-06940-2

LC 2011013213

"Kastin succeeds in bringing the surprisingly selfeffacing Nica to blazing life while also capturing the transcendent synergy among now-iconic jazz musicians, beat writers, and abstract painters, a creative cosmos profoundly enriched by the passion, largesse, and daring of the incomparable baroness." Booklist

Includes discography and bibliographical references

Koestler, Arthur, 1905-1983

Scammell, Michael. **Koestler**; the literary and political odyssey of a twentieth-century skeptic. Random House 2009 xxi, 689p il **92**

1. Authors 2. Novelists 3. Journalists 4. Essayists 5. Authors, English

ISBN 0-394-57630-6; 978-0-394-57630-5

LC 2008-51108

"Although he wrote more than 30 books, Koestler is today known primarily, perhaps exclusively, as the author of 'Darkness at Noon,' his gripping short novel of Stalinist coercion. The biographer Michael Scammell wants to put Koestler's multifaceted intelligence back on display and to show that something more than frivolity or opportunism lay behind his ever-shifting preoccupations and allegiances. As a source of information, 'Koestler,' the work of two decades, will never be surpassed. As an argument for the man's importance, however, it must contend with the eccentricity of Koestler's preoccupations and—although Scammell does not always seem to realize it—his vices."

Koppel, Ted, 1940-

Koppel, Ted. **Off** camera; private thoughts made public. Knopf 2000 320p hardcover o.p. pa $14 **92**

1. Television moderators 2. Television news anchors

ISBN 0-375-72708-6 pa

LC 00-34919

The television journalist of Nightline presents a daily diary for 1999 chronicling "the controversial events from the century's last year, such as the Clinton impeachment trial and the Columbine High School shootings. . . . The subtitle of the book may lead some readers to expect a bit of muckraking, but they will be disappointed. . . . Yet one does not get the sense that Koppel is restraining himself or hiding anything, merely that this is a person who lives his life with integrity so that his private thoughts are full of the same." Libr J

Koretz, Leo, 1879-1925

Jobb, Dean. **Empire** of deception; the incredible story of a master swindler who seduced a city and captivated the nation. by Dean Jobb. Algonquin Books of Chapel Hill 2015 352 p. illustrations (paperback) $16.95 **92**

1. Swindlers and swindling -- United States -- History 2. Chicago (Ill.) -- Biography 3. Lawyers -- Illinois

-- Chicago -- Biography 4. Chicago (Ill.) -- Social conditions -- 20th century 5. Chicago (Ill.) -- Economic conditions -- 20th century 6. Swindlers and swindling -- Illinois -- Chicago -- Biography 7. Fugitives from justice -- Nova Scotia -- Halifax -- Biography 8. Capitalists and financiers -- Illinois -- Chicago -- Biography 9. Ponzi schemes -- Illinois -- Chicago -- History -- 20th century 10. Commercial crimes -- Illinois -- Chicago -- History -- 20th century

ISBN 1616205350; 9781616205355; 9781616201753

LC 2014042711

This book, by Dean Jobb, describes how in 1920s Chicago, Illinois, "a slick, smooth-talking, charismatic lawyer named Leo Koretz [sought] to entice hundreds of people to invest as much as $30 million--upwards of $400 million today--in phantom timberland and nonexistent oil wells in Panama." (Publisher's note)

"The author keeps readers on edge following the scam's collapse and the worldwide manhunt, as they wait to see if Koretz might just get away with it. A highly readable, entertaining story offering a solid education for anyone lacking scruples and wanting to make money. Surely Bernie Madoff studied Koretz's methods." Kirkus

Includes bibliographical references and index

Kozol, Jonathan, 1936-

Kozol, Jonathan, 1936- The **theft** of memory; losing my father one day at a time. Jonathan Kozol. Crown Publishers 2015 320 p. (hardback) $26 **92**

1. Brain 2. Father-son relationship 3. Alzheimer's disease patients 4. Neurologists -- Biography 5. Fathers and sons -- Biography 6. Alzheimer's disease -- Biography

ISBN 0804140979; 9780804140973; 9780804140997

LC 2014041699

In this memoir, author Jonathan Kozol tells "the story of his father's life and work as a nationally noted specialist in disorders of the brain and his astonishing ability, at the onset of Alzheimer's disease, to explain the causes of his sickness and then to narrate, step-by-step, his slow descent into dementia." (Publisher's note)

"The author's approach is shrewd yet warmly empathetic; he is curious about how the mind's gradual breakdown exposes its machinery, and raptly attuned to the emotional effects of these changes on his parents and himself. The result is a clear-eyed and deeply felt meditation on the aspects of family that age does not ravage." Pub Wkly

Includes bibliographical references and index

Kramer, Clara, 1927-

Kramer, Clara. **Clara's** war; one girl's story of survival. [by] Clara Kramer with Stephen Glantz. Ecco 2009 339p il $25.99 **92**

1. Holocaust survivors 2. Memoirists 3. Jews -- Poland 4. Holocaust, 1933-1945 -- Personal narratives

ISBN 978-0-06-172860-0; 0-06-172860-8

First published 2008 in the United Kingdom

ALA RUSA Sophie Brody Award Honor Book (2010)

"Based on her wartime diary, which she kept while hiding in a basement in Poland, Kramer's book vividly recalls the tensions within her hidden community after the Nazis overtook the town of Zolkiew in 1942. Of particular interest are revelations about the family who hid the Kramers, particularly how an anti-Semitic Polish householder demonstrated great courage in shielding Jews in his basement." Libr J

Krasner, Lee, 1908-1984

Levin, Gail, 1948- **Lee** Krasner; a biography. William Morrow 2011 546p il $30; ebook $23.99   **92**

1. Artists 2. Painters 3. Women artists 4. Biography, Individual 5. Artists -- United States

ISBN 978-0-06-184525-3; 0-06-184525-6; 978-0-06-207462-1 ebook; 0-06-207462-8 ebook

LC 2010-46347

This is a "full-length treatment of the talented and tenacious painter. . . . Levin piles up adequate evidence to assure Krasner's place in the American abstract expressionist pantheon. Detailed and meticulously researched, this is essential reading for those who want to know more about protofeminist artist Krasner, New York-based action/abstract expressionist painting, and the postwar NYC art scene." Libr J

Kreuger, Ivar, 1880-1932

Partnoy, Frank. The **match** king; Ivar Kreuger, the financial genius behind a century of Wall Street scandals. PublicAffairs 2009 272p $26.95; pa $15.95   **92**

1. Swindlers and swindling 2. Capitalists and financiers 3. Financiers 4. Kreuger & Toll, Inc. 5. Manufacturing executives

ISBN 978-1-58648-743-0; 1-58648-743-4; 978-1-58648-812-3 pa; 1-58648-812-0 pa

The author "delivers a thrilling account of the grandfather of all Ponzi and Madoff schemes—Ivar Kreuger (1880-1932), who made his fortune in the 1920s by raising money from American investors to lend to European governments in exchange for match monopolies. . . . A fascinating depiction of a man and his era." Publ Wkly

Includes bibliographical references (p. 230-235)

Kubrick, Stanley

LoBrutto, Vincent. **Stanley** Kubrick; a biography. Da Capo Press 1999 579p pa $20   **92**

1. Motion picture directors 2. Motion picture producers and directors -- Biography

ISBN 0-306-80906-0

LC 98-47434

First published 1996 by Fine, D.I.

"For the true film buff, there's an astonishing amount of technical information, but there's also a good deal of illuminating backstage human interest." Publ Wkly

Includes filmography and bibliographical references

Kumin, Maxine, 1925-2014

Kumin, Maxine. The **Pawnbroker's** Daughter; A Memoir. W W Norton & Co Inc. 2015 160 p. illustrations $25.95   **92**

1. Poets 2. Women authors

ISBN 0393246337; 9780393246339

LC 2015009312

This memoir by Maxine Kumin "charts her journey from a childhood in a Jewish community in Depression-era Philadelphia, where [her] father was a pawnbroker, to Radcliffe College, where she comes into her own as an intellectual and

meets the soldier-turned-Los Alamos scientist who would become her husband; to her metamorphosis from a poet of 'light verse' to a 'poet of witness'; to her farm in rural New England, the subject and setting of much of her later work." (Publisher's note)

"The real joy of this book is the author's love of all things country and New England. Kumin and her husband experienced an idyllic life on their 200-acre horse farm in New Hampshire, 'living a wide-open lifestyle.' Happily, she shared that life with the rest of us through her writing." Kirkus

Kurosawa, Akira, 1910-1998

Kurosawa, Akira. **Something** like an autobiography; translated by Audie E. Bock. Knopf 1982 205p il hardcover o.p. pa $15   **92**

1. Motion picture industry 2. Motion picture directors

ISBN 0-394-71439-3 pa

LC 81-48100

These are the memoirs of the Japanese filmmaker, covering his life up to 1951-52, when his film Rashomon won international awards

This "is a fascinating, moving record of one man's pursuit of excellence in a single art." N Y Times Book Rev

Kurson, Robert, 1963-

Kurson, Robert. **Crashing** through; a story of risk, adventure, and the man who dared to see. Random House 2007 306p il $25.95   **92**

1. Authors 2. Journalists 3. Nonfiction writers

ISBN 978-1-4000-6335-2; 1-4000-6335-3

LC 2007-3092

The book "becomes most interesting when the flaws in Mr. May's new eyesight become apparent. He makes wondrous discoveries of things blind people never hear about—shadows, freckles, the movement and transparency of running water—but has more difficulty with the cognitive aspects of pattern recognition. He can see facial features but cannot decipher facial expressions. . . . Eventually the joy of sight fades for him and the investigatory challenges begin." N Y Times (Late N Y Ed)

Kurzweil, Allen

Whipping Boy; The Forty-year Search for My Twelve-year-old Bully. HarperCollins 2015 384 p. 16 plates; illustrations; maps $27.99   **92**

1. Bullies

ISBN 0062269488; 9780062269485

LC 2014027555

This book "chronicles Allen Kurzweil's search for his twelve-year-old nemesis, a bully named Cesar Augustus. The obsessive inquiry, which spans some forty years, takes Kurzweil all over the world, from a Swiss boarding school (where he endures horrifying cruelty) to the slums of Manila, from the Park Avenue boardroom of the world's largest law firm to a federal prison camp in Southern California." (Publisher's note)

"More important than even the scam and the man Cesar became, however, is the poignant way that Kurzweil strives to get an explanation for the bully's bad behavior in order to heal the wounds he's carried since school. The story will resonate with anyone who had a Cesar growing up, as so many did." Booklist

La Tour du Pin Gouvernet, Henriette Lucie Dillon, marquise de, 1770-1853

Moorehead, Caroline. **Dancing** to the precipice: Lucie de la Tour du Pin and the French Revolution. HarperCollins 2009 480p il $27.99   **92**

  1. Memoirists 2. France -- Social life and customs 3. United States -- Social life and customs

  ISBN 978-0-7011-7904-5; 0-7011-7904-X

"In 1820, at the age of forty-nine, Lucie Dillon, the Marquise de la Tour du Pin, started writing her memoirs, an endeavor that went on for thirty years and produced one of the great monuments of French history. Lucie began life as an aristocrat, débuting at Versailles at the age of eleven; at the beginning of the Terror, as friends and relatives fell to the guillotine, she fled France with her husband and children. Resilient and resourceful, the family thrived on a farm in upstate New York, where Lucie churned butter, traded with Indians, and played hostess to Talleyrand. A return to France brought Lucie and her husband into Napoleon's inner circle; in later years, following an exile in London, they found favor with the restored Bourbon monarchy. Moorehead's biography, drawing on a trove of previously unpublished correspondence, captures the rhythm of the radical contrasts in her subject's life." New Yorker

  Includes bibliographical references

LaMarche, Una

Lamarche, Una. **Unabrow**; misadventures of a late bloomer. Una LaMarche. Plume 2015 272 p. illustrations (paperback) $16   **92**

  1. Mothers 2. Young women 3. Bildungsromans 4. Conduct of life 5. Popular culture -- United States 6. Coming of age -- United States 7. Mothers -- United States -- Biography 8. Young women -- United States -- Biography 9. Popular culture -- United States -- Miscellanea

  ISBN 9780142181447

        LC 2014021212

In this memoir, author Una LaMarche "shares the cringe-inducing lessons she's learned from a life as a late bloomer, including the seven deadly sins of DIY bangs, how not to make your own jorts, and how to handle pregnancy, plucking, and the rites of passage during which your own body is your worst frenemy." (Publisher's note)

"LaMarche is entertaining and fresh; readers will want to savor this sassy, offbeat commentary." Pub Wkly

Lacks, Henrietta

★ Skloot, Rebecca, 1972- The **immortal** life of Henrietta Lacks. Crown Publishers 2010 369p il $26   **92**

  1. Cancer 2. Homemakers 3. Human experimentation in medicine 4. Cancer patients 5. African American women -- Biography

  ISBN 978-1-4000-5217-2

        LC 2009-31785

"A thorny and provocative book about cancer, racism, scientific ethics and crippling poverty, 'The Immortal Life of Henrietta Lacks' also floods over you like a narrative dam

break, as if someone had managed to distill and purify the more addictive qualities of 'Erin Brockovich,' 'Midnight in the Garden of Good and Evil' and 'The Andromeda Strain.' More than 10 years in the making, it feels like the book Ms. Skloot was born to write." N Y Times Book Rev

  Includes bibliographical references

Lafayette, Marie Joseph Paul Yves Roch Gilbert Du Motier, marquis de, 1757-1834

Auricchio, Laura. The **marquis**; Lafayette reconsidered. Laura Auricchio. Alfred A. Knopf 2014 416 p. illustrations, maps (harcover : alk. paper) $30   **92**

  1. Generals -- France -- Biography 2. France. Armée -- Biography 3. Statesmen -- France -- Biography 4. Generals -- United States -- Biography 5. United States -- History -- Revolution, 1775-1783 -- Biography 6. United States -- History -- Revolution, 1775-1783 -- Participation, French

  ISBN 0307267555; 9780307267559; 9780307387455

        LC 2013046386

This book, by Laura Auricchio, offers "a major biography of the Marquis de Lafayette, French hero of the American Revolution, who, at age nineteen, volunteered to fight under George Washington; a biography that looks past the storybook hero and selfless champion of righteous causes who cast aside family and fortune to advance the transcendent aims of liberty and justice commemorated in America." (Publishera's note)

"A first-rate work that should appeal to history readers of all kinds." LJ

  Includes bibliographical references

Gaines, James R. **For** liberty and glory; Washington, Lafayette, and their revolutions. W.W. Norton & Co. 2007 533p il map $29.95   **92**

  1. Generals 2. Statesmen 3. Presidents 4. France -- History -- 1789-1799, Revolution 5. United States -- History -- 1775-1783, Revolution

  ISBN 0-393-06138-8; 978-0-393-06138-3

        LC 2007-22449

Gaines examines the relationship between George Washington and the Marquis de Lafayette.

This is a "fresh and engaging new look at the pair. . . . Gaines has a dry sense of humor and an appreciation for human foibles. . . . The American founding fathers, in particular, come across as extraordinary men with ordinary obsessions and—surprise!—senses of humor." Christ Sci Monit

  Includes bibliographical references

Lakshmi, Padma.

Lakshmi, Padma, 1970- **Love,** loss, and what we ate; Padma Lakshmi. HarperCollins 2016 325 p. (hardcover) $26.99   **92**

  1. Cooking

  ISBN 0062202618; 9780062202611

This book, by Padma Lakshmi, is a "memoir of food and family, survival and triumph . . . [that] traces the arc of Padma Lakshmi's unlikely path from an immigrant childhood to a complicated life in front of the camera. . . . [It shares] Lakshmi's extraordinary account of her journey from that humble kitchen, ruled by ferocious and unforgettable women, to the judges' table of Top Chef and beyond." (Publisher's note)

Lamarr, Hedy, 1913-2000

Rhodes, Richard. **Hedy's** folly; the life and breakthrough inventions of Hedy Lamarr, the most beautiful woman in the world. Doubleday 2011 261p il $26.95; ebook $13.99　　　　**92**
1. Actors
ISBN 978-0-385-53438-3; 978-0-385-53439-0 ebook
　　　　　　　　　　　　　　LC 2011021746

"Here's a recipe that might surprise you: take a silverscreen sex goddess (Hedy Lamarr), an avant-garde composer (George Antheil), a Hollywood friendship, and mutual technological curiosity, and mix well. What results is a patent for spread-spectrum radio, which has impacted the development of everything from torpedoes to cell phones and GPS technologies. This surprising and long-forgotten story is brought to life . . . [by Rhodes,] who deftly moves between Nazi secrets, scandalous films, engineering breakthroughs, and musical flops to weave a taut story that straddles two very different worlds—the entertainment industry and wartime weaponry—and yet somehow manages to remain a delectable read." Libr J

Includes bibliographical references

Shearer, Stephen Michael. **Beautiful**; the life of Hedy Lamarr. Thomas Dunne Books 2010 464p il $29.99　　　　**92**
1. Actors
ISBN 978-0-312-55098-1; 0-312-55098-7
　　　　　　　　　　　　　　LC 2010-13058

This biography chronicles "the life of Hollywood legend Hedy Lamarr, from her cosseted childhood in an assimilated Jewish family in Austria to her early breaks in Max Reinhardt's internationally famous theater company; her scandalous, career-launching nude scene in the Czech film Ecstasy; her tortured first marriage to Jewish Nazi arms manufacturer Friedrich Mandl (dubbed an 'honorary Aryan' by the Third Reich); and her daring escape from the sadistic Mandl and Nazi Germany to Los Angeles and MGM. . . . One finishes the book feeling that one has read a complete portrait of Hedy Lamarr, actor and inventor, a biography that reveals, with drama and wit, how much more there was to this complex, brilliant woman than her ethereal natural beauty." Booklist

Includes bibliographical references

Lancaster, Burt, 1913-1994

Buford, Kate. **Burt** Lancaster; an American life. Da Capo Press 2001 447p il pa $20　　　　**92**
1. Actors 2. Motion picture producers
ISBN 978-0-306-81019-0; 0-306-81019-0
First published 2000 by Knopf

"Lancaster's decades-long political involvement with liberal causes (and his constant run-ins with the House Un-American Activities Committee in the 1950s) are a central theme in this well-researched and engaging biography, which also details the artist's acting career, his turns as a producer and his personal life." Publ Wkly

Includes filmography and bibliographical references

Landry, Tom

Ribowsky, Mark. The **last** cowboy; a life of Tom Landry. Mark Ribowsky. Liveright Publishing Corporation 2014 720 p. (hardcover) $29.95　　**92**
1. Football coaches 2. Dallas Cowboys (Football team) 3. Dallas Cowboys (Football team) -- History 4. Football coaches -- United States -- Biography
ISBN 9780871403339
　　　　　　　　　　　　　　LC 2013034731

Author Mark Ribowsky presents a biography of professional football coach Tom Landry. He "begins amid the dusty roads of Mission, Texas, where Tom Landry's childhood played out like a homespun American fable. It then takes us to the war-torn skies over western Europe, where the straight-A student and high school football star piloted a B-17 through thirty harrowing, at times near-fatal, missions. And finally back to a booming Texas, where he continued his faithful march toward gridiron immortality." (Publisher's note)

"Tom Landry spent 40 years in professional football, most notably 29 years as the original coach of the oft-celebrated Dallas Cowboys. Landry was one of the most innovative and influential coaches in NFL history, essentially inventing his own offensive and defensive systems that spread throughout the league...Although Ribowsky (Howard Cosell) is gratuitously snarky about Landry's religious and political beliefs at times, he recounts Landry's life honestly, avoiding both distortion and hagiography while portraying a stoic, flawed man of honor... Nonetheless, this is a triumph of extensive research and interviews. It will be welcomed by all football fans." (Library Journal)

Includes bibliographical references and index

Lange, Dorothea, 1895-1965

Gordon, Linda. **Dorothea** Lange; a life beyond limits. W.W. Norton 2009 xxiii, 536p il $35　　**92**
1. Women photographers 2. Biography, Individual 3. Photography -- History -- United States
ISBN 978-0-393-05730-0; 0-393-05730-5
　　　　　　　　　　　　　　LC 2009-19639

This is a biography of the American photographer who worked for the Historical Section of the Farm Security Administration (FSA) during the Depression.

"Gordon's elegant biography is testament to Lange's gift for challenging her country to open its eyes." N Y Times Book Rev

Includes bibliographical references

Larsen, Nella

Hutchinson, George. **In** search of Nella Larsen; a biography of the color line. Belknap Press of Harvard University Press 2006 611p il $39.95　　**92**
1. Nurses 2. Authors 3. Novelists 4. Short story writers
ISBN 0-674-02180-0; 978-0-674-02180-8
　　　　　　　　　　　　　　LC 2005-58129

This is a biography of the author of Quicksand (1928) and Passing (1929).

The author "has produced what must be the definitive biography of Larsen. It's hard to think of a stone he hasn't looked under in his quest to establish the facts, correct mistakes and trace her private life. But Hutchinson's biography also manages to be an insightful reconsideration of a much-studied period in American literature and black cultural history." Nation

Includes bibliographical references

Laskin, David, 1953-

Laskin, David. The **Family**; Three Journeys into the Heart of the Twentieth Century. David Laskin. Viking Adult 2013 400 p. $32   92
1. Jews 2. Genealogy 3. World history -- 20th century 4. Jews -- Belarus -- Biography 5. Valozhyn (Belarus) -- Biography 6. Jews, Belarusian -- Palestine -- Biography 7. Jews, Belarusian -- United States -- Biography
ISBN 067002547X; 9780670025473

LC 2013017047

Author David Laskin presents a "work of twentieth century history through the riveting story of one extraordinary Jewish family. In tracing the roots of . . . his own family . . . Laskin honors the traditions, the lives, and the choices of his ancestors: revolutionaries and entrepreneurs, scholars and farmers, tycoons and truck drivers." (Publisher's note)

Includes bibliographical references (pages 341-371) and index

Latus, Amy, 1965-2002

Latus, Janine. **If** I am missing or dead. Simon & Schuster 2007 309p il $25   92
1. Journalists 2. Abused women 3. Memoirists 4. Abused persons 5. Murder victims 6. Social activists
ISBN 978-0-7432-9653-3; 0-7432-9653-2

LC 2006-52313

"When journalist Latus's younger sister Amy vanishes at age 37 in 2002, authorities find a chiller of a note in Amy's desk: 'If I am missing or dead . . . question Ron.' Ron Ball is Amy's ex-con boyfriend, and when Amy's body is found, something shatters in Latus. A victim of abuse herself, Latus tunnels back to her difficult suburban childhood to decode why two smart, talented sisters might be so starving for love that they would risk their lives to get it. Latus's book unfolds like a gripping novel, getting at the brutal heart of darkness that underscores domestic violence." People

Latus, Janine, 1959-

Latus, Janine. **If** I am missing or dead. Simon & Schuster 2007 309p il $25   92
1. Journalists 2. Abused women 3. Memoirists 4. Abused persons 5. Murder victims 6. Social activists
ISBN 978-0-7432-9653-3; 0-7432-9653-2

LC 2006-52313

"When journalist Latus's younger sister Amy vanishes at age 37 in 2002, authorities find a chiller of a note in Amy's desk: 'If I am missing or dead . . . question Ron.' Ron Ball is Amy's ex-con boyfriend, and when Amy's body is found, something shatters in Latus. A victim of abuse herself, Latus tunnels back to her difficult suburban childhood to decode why two smart, talented sisters might be so starving for love that they would risk their lives to get it. Latus's book unfolds like a gripping novel, getting at the brutal heart of darkness that underscores domestic violence." People

Lauper, Cyndi, 1953-

Lauper, Cyndi, 1953- **Cyndi** Lauper; a memoir. Cyndi Lauper with Jancee Dunn. Atria Books 2012 338 p. 16 unnumbered pages of plates $26   92
1. Women rock musicians 2. Singers -- United States -- Biography
ISBN 143914785X; 9781439147856

LC 2013560375

Author Cyndi Lauper "left her home in Ozone Park, Queens, at age 17 to escape a sexually abusive stepfather and the limitations on life—especially for women—imposed by a hardscrabble working-class neighborhood and male-dominated family culture. . . . Her life changed in 1983, however, with the release of She's So Unusual, which . . . made Lauper an instant star. . . . Inevitably, her superstar aura faded, but her eclectic musical output did not." (Kirkus)

Laurens, Henry, 1724-1792

Harris, J. William. The **hanging** of Thomas Jeremiah; a free Black man's encounter with liberty. Yale University Press 2009 223p il map $27.50   92
1. Diplomats 2. Merchants 3. Ship captains 4. Colonial leaders 5. Plantation owners 6. Government officials 7. Colonial administrators 8. Slavery -- United States 9. South Carolina -- Race relations 10. African Americans -- Social conditions
ISBN 978-0-300-15214-2; 0-300-15214-0

LC 2009-15233

This is an "account of nebulous historical figure Thomas Jeremiah. . . . Owner of a fishing company and worth $200,000 in 2009 dollars, . . . [Jeremiah] was probably the richest black man in North America; he was also a slaveowner. That didn't stop him from becoming a scapegoat, accused by patriot leader Henry Laurens—a wealthy plantation owner with hundreds of slaves—of secretly leading a British-sponsored slave insurrection. Though Governor William Campbell, aggrieved by the unlawfulness of Jeremiah's trial, interceded, it didn't stop those determined to hang Jeremiah. . . . Readers will learn much about the darker side of American institutions; students of American history and civil rights will appreciate Harris's impassive approach and thorough standards." Publ Wkly

Includes bibliographical references

Laveau, Marie, 1794-1881

Ward, Martha Coonfield. **Voodoo** queen; the spirited lives of Marie Laveau. by Martha Ward. University Press of Mississippi 2004 246p il map $26   92
1. Witches 2. Voodooism
ISBN 1-578-06629-8

LC 2003-18292

"Spiritual leaders Marie Laveau, mother and daughter, reigned in New Orleans between the 1820s and 1880s. Through their story, Ward offers fresh perspective on Creole culture and voodoo." Booklist

Including bibliographical references

Lawrence, D. H. (David Herbert), 1885-1930

Worthen, John. **D.H.** Lawrence; the life of an outsider. Counterpoint 2005 xxvi, 518p il $29.95 92
1. Poets 2. Authors 3. Novelists 4. Dramatists 5.

Essayists 6. Short story writers
ISBN 1-58243-341-0
"Using as a unifying theme Lawrence's perpetual status as an outsider, both in working-class Nottinghamshire and in the English literary world, Worthen gives us the full sweep of this groundbreaking writer's utterly unconventional, often torturous, and occasionally rhapsodic life." Booklist
Includes bibliographical references

Worthen, John. **D.H.** Lawrence, the early years, 1885-1912. Cambridge Univ. Press 1991 626p il (The Cambridge biography D.H. Lawrence, 1885-1930) hardcover o.p. pa $30   **92**
1. Poets 2. Authors 3. Novelists 4. Dramatists 5. Essayists 6. Short story writers
ISBN 0-521-43772-5 pa
LC 90-23423
This "first volume of Cambridge's three-volume life of Lawrence, . . . takes the young writer through his elopement with Frieda. . . . This persuasive biography is compulsive good reading from cover to cover. A major event in modern literary studies." Libr J
Includes bibliographical references

Lawrence, Sarahlee

Lawrence, Sarahlee. **River** house; a memoir. Tin House Books 2010 272p pa $16.95   **92**
1. Farmers 2. Rafting (Sports) 3. Adventure and adventurers
ISBN 978-0-9825691-3-9
LC 2010-7702
"Handy with tools and rafts, a good neighbor, and a mighty fine horsewoman, Lawrence is also adept with language, writing with arresting lucidity and a driving need to understand her father, her legacy, the land, community, work, and herself. A true adventure story of rare dimension." Booklist

Lawrence, T. E. (Thomas Edward), 1888-1935

★ Brown, Malcolm. **T.E.** Lawrence. New York University Press 2003 160p il map (Historic lives) $21.95   **92**
1. Authors 2. Soldiers 3. Archaeologists 4. Travel writers
ISBN 0-8147-9920-5
LC 2003-51387
"The book is a major literary work." Publ Wkly
Includes bibliographical references

Korda, Michael, 1933- **Hero**; the life and legend of Lawrence of Arabia. Harper 2010 762p il map $34.99   **92**
1. Authors 2. Soldiers 3. Archaeologists 4. Travel writers 5. Biography, Individual 6. Soldiers -- Great Britain 7. World War, 1914-1918 -- Middle East 8. World War, 1914-1918 -- Campaigns -- Turkey 9. World War, 1914-1918 -- Campaigns -- Middle East
ISBN 978-0-06-171261-6
LC 2010-33189
This is a biography of T. E. Lawrence, the "British scholar, adventurer, soldier, and hero who became a myth in his lifetime." (Publisher's note) Index.

"This magisterial biography of British soldier and adventurer T.E. Lawrence celebrates a life spent subverting authority in the most glamorous—and bizarre—ways. . . . [The author] gives a rousing, lucid account of Lawrence's leadership of the Arab revolt against the Ottoman Empire during WWI and his diplomatic championing of Arab nationalism. But it's Lawrence's artistic bent . . . and his magnetic but tortured soul that take center stage." Publ Wkly
Includes bibliographical references

Sattin, Anthony. The **Young** T. E. Lawrence; Anthony Sattin. W W Norton & Co Inc 2015 352 p. illustrations, maps $28.95   **92**
1. Middle East -- History 2. Soldiers -- Great Britain -- Biography 3. Archaeologists -- Great Britain -- Biography 4. World War, 1914-1918 -- Campaigns -- Arab countries
ISBN 0393242668; 9780393242669
LC 2014032063
This book, by Anthony Sattin, profiles "the years that turned T. E. Lawrence into Lawrence of Arabia. . . . This intimate biography is the first to focus on Lawrence in his twenties, the untold story of the awkward archaeologist from Oxford who, on first visiting 'The East,' fell in love with Arab culture and found his life's mission." (Publisher's note)
"Recommended as an insightful, gracefully written, and sensitive account that explains how a shy, private young man developed into a widely known and revered 'hero' who was never comfortable with his fame." LJ
Includes bibliographical references and index

Lawson, Jenny, 1979-

Lawson, Jenny. **Furiously** happy; a funny book about horrible things. Jenny Lawson. Flatiron Books 2015 352 p. illustrations (hardback) $26.99   **92**
1. Mental illness -- Humor 2. Journalists -- United States -- Biography 3. Humorists, American -- 21st century -- Biography
ISBN 1250077001; 9781250077004
LC 2015022196
In this book, by Jenny Lawson, the author "pokes fun at herself as she addresses the serious nature of her mental and physical illnesses. . . . Rather than hiding the facts, she openly divulges, in a darkly humorous way, how she copes with rheumatoid arthritis, depression, panic attacks, anxiety, and the days when she is driven to pull her hair out or cut herself." (Kirkus Reviews)
"Lawson's goal is not to offend, although that might happen to some readers, but to lay bare the truth about her struggles in life so that others can benefit. She does a solid job exposing the hidden nature of mental illness by putting a direct spotlight on her own issues, thereby illuminating an often taboo subject. Her amusing essays open up a not-so-funny topic: mental illness in its many guises. Kudos to Lawson for being a flagrant and witty spokesperson for this dark subject matter." Kirkus

LeMieux, Richard

LeMieux, Richard. **Breakfast** at Sally's; one homeless man's inspirational journey. Skyhorse 2008 433p il $24.95 **92**

1. Homeless persons 2. Homeless 3. Memoirists
ISBN 978-1-60239-293-9; 1-60239-293-5

LC 2008-24420

"Former successful businessman Richard LeMieux has lived better than the average American, but descended, through economic and personal failures, to homelessness for almost two years. Writing of life on the streets with his dog, Willow, he introduces a cast of characters from his experiences. . . . This inspirational political and social memoir can offer readers hope for a renewal of faith—in God and humanity. All public libraries will want this book for their collections." Libr J

Leadbelly, 1885-1949

Wolfe, Charles K. The **life** and legend of Leadbelly; [by] Charles Wolfe and Kip Lornell. Da Capo Press 1999 333p il pa $16.95 **92**

1. Singers 2. Guitarists 3. Blues music 4. African American musicians 5. Songwriters 6. Accordionists
ISBN 978-0-306-80896-8; 0-306-80896-X
First published 1992 by HarperCollins

"Drawing on a variety of primary and secondary sources, including numerous interviews, Wolfe and Lornell attempt to separate fact from fiction. . . . Photographs, informative notes, and a full discography are valuable additions." Choice

Includes discography and bibliographical references

Lear, Norman

Lear, Norman, 1922- **Even** This I Get to Experience; Norman Lear. Penguin Group USA 2014 448 p. illustrations, portraits $32.95 **92**

1. Autobiographies 2. Comedy television programs
ISBN 1594205728; 9781594205729

LC 2014032903

This memoir by Norman Lear describes how "Lear led a charmed life throughout postwar Hollywood's golden years, befriending the likes of Carl Reiner and Mel Brooks; writing and directing Frank Sinatra, Robert Redford, Dick Van Dyke, and Martha Raye; becoming the highest paid comic writer in the country while working for Jerry Lewis and Dean Martin. Not to mention, Lear flew some fifty bombing missions over Germany with the Fifteenth Air Force." (Publisher's note)

"A big-hearted, richly detailed chronicle of comedy, commitment and a long life lived fully." Kirkus

Leary, Timothy, 1920-1996

Greenfield, Robert. **Timothy** Leary; a biography. Harcourt, Inc. 2006 689p il $28 **92**

1. Psychologists 2. College teachers 3. Social reformers
ISBN 0-15-100500-1; 978-0-15-100500-0

LC 2005-30154

This is a biography of LSD guru and counterculture icon Timothy Leary.

"A veritable who's who of the age of Aquarius and a real page-turner, Greenfield's cornerstone portrait of the acidhead who would be king brilliantly illuminates the paradoxes of the psychedelic age." Booklist

Leavitt, Henrietta Swan, 1868-1921

Johnson, George. **Miss** Leavitt's stars; the untold story of the woman who discovered how to measure the universe. W. W. Norton 2005 162p il (Great discoveries) $22.95 **92**

1. Astronomers 2. Photometrists
ISBN 0-393-05128-5

LC 2005-02823

This is a biography of the American astronomer whose research concerned the measuring of distance in space.

This book is "a fine tribute to a remarkable woman of science." Publ Wkly

Includes bibliographical references

Ledyard, John, 1751-1789

Gifford, Bill. **Ledyard**; in search of the first American explorer. Harcourt 2007 331p il map $25 **92**

1. Explorers 2. Travel writers
ISBN 978-0-15-101218-3; 0-15-101218-0

LC 2006-17064

This book "makes an important contribution to the existing literature through its personal approach to Ledyard's life. Few of Ledyard's letters and journals remain . . . but, by using most of what's available and tracking down details through his own travels, the author paints a fascinating portrait of the man he calls the 'archetype of the restless American wanderer.'" N Y Times Book Rev

Lee, Gypsy Rose, 1914-1970

Abbott, Karen. **American** rose; a nation laid bare: the life and times of Gypsy Rose Lee. Random House 2010 422p il $26; ebook $12.99 **92**

1. Actors 2. Novelists 3. Striptease 4. Stripteasers
ISBN 978-1-4000-6691-9; 978-0-679-60456-3 ebook

LC 2010-15081

"Imaginative and engaging, Abbott's biography of the celebrated stripper, who died in 1970 at age 59, also proves a well-informed look at the evolution of musical theater in the early 20th century." Publ Wkly

Includes bibliographical references

Lee, Harper

Mills, Marja. The **Mockingbird** Next Door; Life with Harper Lee. Marja Mills. The Penguin Press 2014 288 p. illustrations (hardback) $27.95 **92**

1. Alabama 2. American authors 3. Alabama -- Biography 4. Authors, American -- 20th century -- Biography
ISBN 1594205191; 9781594205194

LC 2013039938

This book, by Marja Mills, is a memoir recounting her friendship with "To Kill a Mockingbird" author Harper Lee. "Journalists have trekked to her hometown of Monroeville, Alabama, where . . . Lee, known to her friends as Nelle, has lived with her sister, Alice, for decades, trying and failing to get an interview with the author. But in 2001, the Lee sisters opened their door to Chicago Tribune journalist Marja

Mills. It was the beginning of a long conversation--and a great friendship." (Publisher's note)

Lee, Robert E. (Robert Edward), 1807-1870

★ Blount, Roy. **Robert** E. Lee; a Penguin life. [by] Roy Blount, Jr. Lipper/Viking Bk. 2003 210p (Penguin lives series) $19.95; pa $13   92
    1. Generals 2. College presidents 3. Confederate States of America -- Army 4. United States -- History -- 1861-1865, Civil War
    ISBN 0-670-03220-4; 0-14-303866-4 pa
                        LC 2002-32423
    This is a biography of "the famous Southern general admired for his military leadership but also scorned for defending the Confederacy. Blount's concise writing keeps his biography trim and succinct, and his admiration for the subject allows for enjoyable reading." Booklist
    Includes bibliographical references

    Fellman, Michael. The **making** of Robert E. Lee. Johns Hopkins Univ. Press 2003 360p il pa $19.95   92
    1. Generals 2. College presidents 3. United States -- History -- 1861-1865, Civil War
    ISBN 0-8018-7411-4
                        LC 2002-43290
    First published 2000 by Random House
    "Struggling to subdue his ambitions and passions in a peacetime military career whose monotony was only momentarily breached by the Mexican American War and at Harpers Ferry, Lee found in the Civil War a chance to express himself fully. In a study rich with discussions of Lee's religious beliefs and political opinions, the author skewers previous efforts to detach Lee from slavery, racism, and the mentality of the Lost Cause. Sure to arouse debate, this book challenges and delights." Libr J
    Includes bibliographical references

    Freeman, Douglas Southall, 1886-1953. **Lee**; an abridgment in one volume, by Richard Harwell, of the four-volume R. E. Lee. with a new foreword by James M. McPherson. Scribner 1991 xxiii, 601p il maps hardcover o.p. pa $18   92
    1. Generals 2. College presidents 3. United States -- History -- 1861-1865, Civil War
    ISBN 0-684-82953-3 pa
                        LC 91-20088
    First published 1961
    "Students of history will continue to want and to use the original four-volume work but most general readers will find this abridgment more convenient and adequate to their interest. All footnotes and all of the appendix have been omitted as well as details of Civil War action that are not necessary to show the main course of Lee's life and action." Booklist

    Horn, Jonathan. The **Man** Who Would Not Be Washington; Robert E. Lee's Civil War and His Decision That Changed American History. Jonathan Horn. Simon & Schuster 2015 384 p. illustrations, maps $28   92
    1. United States -- History -- 1861-1865, Civil War --

Biography
    ISBN 147674856X; 9781476748566
                       LC 2014029702
    This book, by Jonathan Horn, offers the "true story of Robert E. Lee, the brilliant soldier bound by marriage to George Washington's family but turned by war against Washington's crowning achievement, the Union. . . . This . . . biography follows Lee through married life, military glory, and misfortune. The story that emerges is more complicated, more tragic, and more illuminating than the familiar tale." (Publisher's note)
    "In tracing Lee's biography, Horn establishes the powerful connection that both Lee and Washington had to slavery and the complex meaning of both states' rights and the Founding Fathers to white Southerners of Lee's generation. Historians will find little that is new, but undergraduates will consider it informative. Summing Up: Recommended. Public and undergraduate libraries." Choice

    Korda, Michael, 1933- **Clouds** of Glory; The Life and Legend of Robert E. Lee. Michael Korda. HarperCollins 2014 640 p. illustrations, maps $40   92
    1. Command of troops 2. United States -- History -- 1861-1865, Civil War
    ISBN 0062116290; 9780062116291
                       LC 2014415636
    This book, by Michael Korda, is a "historical biography of General Robert E. Lee. . . . [It] analyzes Lee's command during the Civil War and explores his responsibility for the fatal stalemate at Antietam, his defeat at Gettysburg . . . and ultimately, his failed strategy for winning the war. As Korda shows, Lee's dignity, courage, leadership, and modesty made him a hero on both sides of the Mason-Dixon Line." (Publisher's note)
    Korda "examines the life of Robert E. Lee from start to finish, illuminating not just the man, but his extended family and the society which produced him." Pub Wkly
    Includes bibliographical references and index

    Thomas, Emory M. **Robert** E. Lee; a biography. Norton 1995 472p il maps pa $17.95   92
    1. Generals 2. College presidents 3. United States -- History -- 1861-1865, Civil War
    ISBN 0-393-31631-9 pa
                       LC 95-10522
    "Civil War historian Thomas presents Lee as neither an icon nor a flawed figure, but rather as a man who made the best of his lot, whose comic vision of life ultimately shaped him into an individual who was both more and less than his legend." Publ Wkly
    Includes bibliographical references

Leiber, Jerry, 1933-2011

    Leiber, Jerry. **Hound** dog; the Leiber & Stoller autobiography. [by] Jerry Leiber and Mike Stoller with David Ritz. Simon & Schuster 2009 322p il $25   92
    1. Composers 2. Lyricists 3. Songwriters 4. Rock music -- History and criticism
    ISBN 978-1-4165-5938-2; 1-4165-5938-8
                       LC 2008-47821

"Collaboration is a messy business. So is autobiography. But it shouldn't be forgotten that Leiber and Stoller were among the pioneers who helped bring black and white musical forms together. It has been a historically fraught process, but the collision of cultures is probably what has given such energy and tension to American music. Hound Dog is an important part of that story." N Y Times Book Rev

Includes bibliographical references

Lenin, Vladimir Ilich, 1870-1924

Pomper, Philip. **Lenin's** brother; the origins of the October Revolution. W.W. Norton & Co. 2010 276p il $24.95　　　　　　　　　　　　　　　　**92**

1. Heads of state 2. Revolutionaries 3. Communist leaders 4. Political leaders 5. Soviet Union -- History -- 1917-1921, Revolution

ISBN 978-0-393-07079-8

LC 2009-27390

"In 1887, the future leader of the Russian revolution, Vladimir Ulyanov (later Lenin), was 17 when his 21-year-old brother was hanged for his role in a bungled attempt to assassinate Czar Alexander III. Historians consider this the seminal event that launched Lenin's career as a revolutionary. . . . [The author] delivers an absorbing and surprisingly detailed account of Alexander Ulyanov's short life and even shorter career (four months) as a terrorist." Publ Wkly

Includes bibliographical references

Lennon, John, 1940-1980

Greenberg, Keith Elliot. **December** 8, 1980; the day John Lennon died. Backbeat Books 2010 240p il $24.99　　　　　　　　　　　　　　　　　　　**92**

1. Singers 2. Rock musicians 3. Songwriters

ISBN 978-0-87930-963-3

LC 2010-31425

"Greenberg's definitive and unforgettable inquiry into John Lennon's death illuminates the cruel mysteries of madness, and, more resonantly, all the qualities that made Lennon such an exceptional and compelling artist." Booklist

Includes bibliographical references

Norman, Philip. **John** Lennon; the life. Ecco HarperCollins 2008 851p il $34.95; pa $19.99 **92**

1. Singers 2. Rock musicians 3. Songwriters

ISBN 978-0-06-075401-3; 0-06-075401-X; 978-0-06-075402-0 pa; 0-06-075402-8 pa

LC 2008-4684

This is a biography of the singer-songwriter and author of In His Own Write (1964), A Spaniard in the Works (1965), and Lennon Remembers (1971).

This work's "ambitious range proves to be its strength, enveloping you in ways that a quicker read could not. . . . [This] is a gift of a book, heartfelt and heart-rending." Christ Sci Monit

Riley, Tim. **Lennon**; the man, the myth, the music--the definitive life. Hyperion 2011 765p il $35　　　　　　　　　　　　　　　　　　　**92**

1. Singers 2. Rock musicians 3. Songwriters 4. Biography, Individual

ISBN 978-1-4013-2452-0; 1-4013-2452-5

LC 2011-15657

"Here is Lennon in the fullness of his diffracted personality, across the spectrum of his phases and faces. Leather John, mugging sailors in Hamburg — 'A Lennon punch felled him to his knees' — is superseded by Beatle John, mugging for the world's press. . . . Beatle John contains both 'Ed Sullivan' John, yodeling harmonies and bending his knees in awkward demi-pliés, and 'Revolver' John, acid-head, sleepyhead, drug dormouse, singing in that cold little cocoon voice (Riley calls it 'timefrozen') about floating downstream and not wanting to be woken up. Then there's 'Imagine' John, the drooping sage. And finally, of course, John the martyr." N Y Times Book Rev

Includes bibliographical references and discography

Lennox, Margaret Douglas, Countess of, 1515-1578

Weir, Alison. The **lost** Tudor princess; the life of Margaret Douglas of Scotland. Alison Weir. Ballantine Books 2016 576 p. illustrations, maps (hardcover : alk. paper) $30　　　　　　　　　**92**

1. Great Britain -- History -- 1485-1603, Tudors 2. Nobility -- Great Britain -- Biography 3. Nobility -- Great Britain -- History -- 16th century 4. Great Britain -- History -- Tudors, 1485-1603 -- Biography

ISBN 9780345521392

LC 2015037958

This book, by Alison Weir, offers a "biography of Margaret Douglas, the beautiful, cunning niece of Henry VIII of England who used her sharp intelligence and covert power to influence the succession after the death of Elizabeth I. . . . Lady Margaret Douglas, Countess of Lennox, was an important figure in Tudor England, yet today, while her contemporaries—Anne Boleyn, Mary, Queen of Scots, Elizabeth I—have achieved celebrity status, she is largely forgotten." (Publisher's note)

"An abundantly detailed history from an author steeped in England's past." Kirkus

Includes bibliographical references and index

Lenz, Frank, d. 1894

Herlihy, David V. The **lost** cyclist; the epic tale of an American adventurer and his mysterious disappearance. [by] David V. Herlihy. Houghton Mifflin Harcourt 2010 326p il map　　　　　　　　**92**

1. Cycling 2. Photographers 3. Cyclists 4. Murder victims 5. Retail personnel 6. Biography, Individual

ISBN 0-547-19557-5; 0-547-52198-7 pa; 978-0-547-19557-5; 978-0-547-52198-5 pa

LC 2009-28857

This is a biography of "Frank Lenz, a 24-year-old wheelman [who] departed New York in 1892 to round the globe. . . . [Lenz disappeared in] eastern Turkey, in the midst of a Turkish and Kurdish campaign that would kill some 10,000 Armenian civilians." (N Y Times Book Rev) Index.

"This well-researched and stylishly written book puts Lenz back in the public eye as well as offering readers a look at the very early days of modern cycling." Booklist

Leonardo, da Vinci, 1452-1519

Aquino, Lucia. **Leonardo** Da Vinci; preface by Mario Pomilio; [translation, Miriam Hurley] Rizzoli 2005 173p il (Art classics) pa $9.95 **92**

1. Artists 2. Painters 3. Scientists 4. Artists, Italian 5. Writers on science

ISBN 978-0-8478-2677-3; 0-8478-2677-5

LC 2004-099908

This book "features a literary introduction and . . . . description of a selection of the artist's masterpieces. . . . [It also includes] a visual chart with captions as to the whereabouts of each painting and a . . . bibliography." Publisher's note

Includes bibliographical references

White, Michael. **Leonardo**; the first scientist. St. Martin's Press 2000 370p il $27.95; pa $16.95 **92**

1. Artists 2. Painters 3. Scientists 4. Artists, Italian 5. Writers on science

ISBN 0-312-20333-0; 0-312-27026-7 pa

The author "focuses on the scientific creations of da Vinci, emphasizing his notebooks, which had been lost for 200 years and only portions of which have been recovered. White describes how da Vinci's personal life affected his scientific discoveries and predictions, and vice versa." Booklist

Leonowens, Anna Harriette, 1831-1915

Landon, Margaret. **Anna** and the King of Siam; illustrated by Margaret Ayer. Harper & Row 1944 391p il map hardcover o.p. pa $14.95 **92**

1. Kings 2. Governesses 3. Thailand -- Social life and customs

ISBN 0-06-095488-4 pa

Anna Leonowens' experiences at the Siamese court in the 1860's. From her experiences she wrote two books, "The English governess at the Siamese court," and "The romance of the harem." The author has put these two books into one story with additions to make a complete tale.

Lerner, Betsy

Lerner, Betsy. The **bridge** ladies; a memoir. Betsy Lerner. Harper Wave 2016 320 p. (hardback) $25.99 **92**

1. Bridge (Game) 2. Female friendship 3. Intergenerational relations 4. Mother-daughter relationship 5. Female friendship -- United States 6. Women bridge players -- United States 7. Mothers and daughters -- United States 8. Intergenerational relations -- United States 9. Literary agents -- United States -- Biography 10. Bridge clubs -- Social aspects -- United States 11. Older women -- United States -- Social life and customs

ISBN 9780062354464; 9780062467164

LC 2015043022

In this memoir, by Betsy Lerner, "a fifty-year-old Bridge game provides an unexpected way to cross the generational divide between a daughter and her mother. . . . Lerner finds herself back in her childhood home, not five miles from the mother she spent decades avoiding. When Roz needs help after surgery, it falls to Betsy to take care of her. She expected a week of tense civility; what she got instead were the Bridge Ladies." (Publisher's note)

"This beautifully written, bittersweet story of ladies of a certain age and era will have wide appeal." Pub Wkly

Lessing, Doris May, 1919-

★ Lessing, Doris May. **Under** my skin; volume one of my autobiography, to 1949. {by} Doris Lessing. HarperCollins Pubs. 1994 419p il hardcover o.p. pa $15 **92**

1. Authors 2. Novelists 3. Dramatists 4. Essayists 5. Short story writers 6. Nobel laureates for literature

ISBN 0-06-092664-3 pa

LC 94-20051

"In this immediate, vivid, beautifully paced memoir, Doris Lessing sets the individual against history, the personal against the general, and shows, by the example of her own life set down honestly, how biography and fiction mesh, how fiction transmutes the personal to the general, how the particular experience illuminates the universe." London Rev Books

Levi, Primo, 1919-1987

Angier, Carole. The **double** bond: Primo Levi, a biography. Farrar, Straus & Giroux 2002 xxvi, 898p il $40; pa $20 **92**

1. Poets 2. Authors 3. Chemists 4. Novelists 5. Holocaust survivors 6. Essayists 7. Memoirists 8. Short story writers

ISBN 0-374-11315-7; 0-374-52898-5 pa

This is a biography of the Italian Jewish chemist and writer. Levi was the author of The Periodic Table, Survival in Auschwitz, The Drowned and the Saved and Other People's Trades

"Angier's long, gripping narrative of Levi's time in Auschwitz synthesizes the best of his memoirs, poetry, fiction, essays, and scientific writing. . . . A compelling biography and a must for all Holocaust collections." Booklist

Includes bibliographical references

Levi, Primo, 1919-1987. The **periodic** table; translated from the Italian by Raymond Rosenthal. Schocken Bks. 1984 233p hardcover o.p. pa $12 **92**

1. Poets 2. Authors 3. Chemists 4. Novelists 5. Holocaust survivors 6. Essayists 7. Memoirists 8. Short story writers

ISBN 0805210415 pa; 0-8052-1041-5 pa

LC 84-5453

Original Italian edition, 1975

"This curious memoir, organized in 21 chapters from Argon to Zinc, ransacks the periodic table of the elements for strained metaphors as it traces one adolescent's search for identity. Levi ironically portrays himself as a young aspiring chemist eager to fathom nature's secrets."

"This curious memoir, organized in 21 chapters from Argon to Zinc, ransacks the periodic table of the elements for strained metaphors as it traces one adolescent's search for identity. Levi ironically portrays himself as a young aspiring chemist eager to fathom nature's secrets." Publ Wkly

Lewin, W. H. G. (Walter H. G.)

★ Goldstein, Warren. **For** the love of physics; from the end of the rainbow to the edge of time--a journey through the wonders of physics. [by] Walter

Lewin and Warren Goldstein. Free Press 2011 302p il $26; ebook $12.99   **92**

1. Physicists 2. Physics -- Study and teaching 3. Colleges and universities -- Faculty

ISBN 978-1-4391-0827-7; 978-1-4391-2354-6 ebook

LC 2010-47737

"MIT's Lewin is deservedly popular for his memorable physics lectures . . . and this quick-paced autobiography-cum-physics intro fully captures his candor and lively teaching style. . . . [This text] glows with energy and should please a wide range of readers." Publ Wkly

Lewis, C. S. (Clive Staples), 1898-1963

McGrath, Alister E., 1953- **C.** S. Lewis; a life : eccentric genius, reluctant prophet. Alister McGrath. Tyndale House Publishers 2013 350 p. (hc) $24.99   **92**

1. Authors -- Biography 2. Christian literature 3. Authors, English -- 20th century -- Biography

ISBN 9781414339351; 1414339356

LC 2012033140

This book, by Alister McGrath, is a biography of the 20th century Christian author and apologist Clive Staples Lewis. "After thoroughly examining recently published Lewis correspondence, Alister challenges some of the previously held beliefs about the exact timing of Lewis's shift from atheism to theism and then to Christianity. [The author] paints a portrait of an eccentric thinker who became an inspiring, though reluctant, prophet for our times." (Publisher's note)

Includes bibliographical references and index

Lewis, Jerry, 1926-

Lewis, Jerry. **Dean** & me; a love story. Doubleday 2005 340p il $26.95   **92**

1. Actors 2. Singers 3. Comedians 4. Television personalities 5. Motion picture directors

ISBN 0-7679-2086-4

LC 2005-49682

"This is a wild, joyous book, but also a heartbreaking one." N Y Times Book Rev

Lewis, John, 1940-

★ Lewis, John. **March**; Book Three. by John Lewis and Andrew Aydin; illustrated by Nate Powell. Top Shelf Productions 2016 256 p. chiefly illustrations pbk $19.99   **92**

1. Civil rights -- United States

ISBN 9781603094023; 1603094024

National Book Award: Young People's Literature (2016)

This book is the "conclusion of the award-winning and best-selling March trilogy. Congressman John Lewis, an American icon and one of the key figures of the civil rights movement, joins co-writer Andrew Aydin and artist Nate Powell to bring the lessons of history to vivid life for a new generation, urgently relevant for today's world." (Publisher's note)

"Though Lewis and Aydin throw a lot at readers in this volume, their message, helped along seamlessly and splendidly by Powell's fantastic, cinematic artwork, is abundantly clear: the victories of the civil rights movement, symbolized in particular by Barack Obama's inauguration, are hard-won

and only succeeded through the dogged dedication of a wide variety of people." Booklist

★ Lewis, John. **March**; Book Two. by John Lewis and Andrew Aydin; illustrated by Nate Powell. Top Shelf Productions 2015 192 p. chiefly ill. (pbk) $19.95   **92**

1. African Americans -- Civil rights -- Graphic novels 2. Civil rights movements 3. African American legislators 4. Legislators -- United States 5. African Americans -- Civil rights 6. African American civil rights workers 7. Civil rights workers -- United States 8. Autobiographical comic books, strips, etc.

ISBN 9781603094009; 1603094008

LC bl2015004150

Eisner Award: Best Reality-Based Work (2016)

Eisner Nominee: Best Publication for Teens (2016)

This graphic novel, by John Lewis and Andrew Aydin, illustrated by Nate Powell, "takes us behind the scenes of some of the most pivotal moments of the Civil Rights Movement. . . . After the success of the Nashville sit-in campaign, John Lewis is more committed than ever to changing the world through nonviolence -- but as he and his fellow Freedom Riders board a bus into the vicious heart of the deep south, they will be tested like never before." (Publisher's note)

"Heroism and steadiness of purpose continue to light up Lewis' frank, harrowing account of the civil rights movement's climactic days. . . . The contrast between the dignified marchers and the vicious, hate-filled actions and expressions of their tormentors will leave a deep impression on readers." Kirkus

★ Lewis, John R., 1940- **March**; Book One. John Lewis; [co-written by] Andrew Aydin; [art by] Nate Powell. Top Shelf Productions 2013 121 p. chiefly ill. (acid-free paper) $14.95   **92**

1. African Americans -- Civil rights -- Graphic novels 2. Civil rights movements -- United States -- Comic books, strips, etc

ISBN 9781603093002

LC 2013218903

Coretta Scott King (Author) Honor Book (2014)

This graphic novel, by U.S. congressman John Lewis, "in collaboration with co-writer Andrew Aydin and New York Times best-selling artist Nate Powell . . . spans John Lewis' youth in rural Alabama, his life-changing meeting with Martin Luther King, Jr., the birth of the Nashville Student Movement, and their battle to tear down segregation through nonviolent lunch counter sit-ins, building to a . . . climax on the steps of City Hall." (Publisher's note)

"This is superb visual storytelling that establishes a convincing, definitive record of a key eyewitness to significant social change." SLJ

Li, Charles N., 1940-

Li, Charles N. The **bitter** sea; coming of age in a China before Mao. HarperCollins Publishers 2008 283p il hardcover o.p. pa $14.99   **92**

1. Anthropologists 2. Linguists 3. College teachers 4. China -- History -- 1949-

ISBN 978-0-06-134664-4; 0-06-134664-0; 978-0-06-

170954-8 pa; 0-06-170954-9 pa

LC 2007-25697

The author, "who had an extraordinary life growing up in pre-Communist China, shares his story of betrayal, loss, hope, and triumph in this lyrical account. . . . This brilliant memoir is as much about modern Chinese history as it is about familial relationships." Libr J

Li, Leslie, 1945-

Li, Leslie. **Daughter** of heaven; a memoir with earthly recipes. Arcade Pub. 2005 274p $25; pa $13.95   92

1. Chinese cooking

ISBN 1-55970-768-2; 1-55970-800-X pa

LC 2004-23452

The book centers on the author's "relationship with both her father and Nai-nai, her grandmother, who lands in New York City for an extended visit. . . . In stories and in the nearly 20 recipes (including Drunken Chicken and Cantonese Fried Rice), Li reveals the tale of an Asian woman caught between many different worlds and times and places." Booklist

Liddell, Eric, 1902-1945.

Hamilton, Duncan. **For** the Glory; Eric Liddell's Journey from Olympic Champion to Modern Martyr. Duncan Hamilton. Penguin Group USA 2016 400 p. illustrations (hardcover) $28   92

1. Christian biography

ISBN 9781594206207; 1594206201

This book, by Duncan Hamilton, offers the "inspiring story of Eric Liddell, hero of [The film] 'Chariots of Fire,' from his Olympic medal to his missionary work in China to his last, brave years in a Japanese work camp during WWII. . . . Liddell ran--and lived--for the glory of his God. After winning gold, he dedicated himself to missionary work. He travelled to China to work in a local school and as a missionary." (Publisher's note)

"Poignant and tragic yet stimulating, Liddell's personality leaps off the pages and will draw in all readers, from history and sports enthusiasts to casual fans of nonfiction." LJ

Includes bibliographical references (pages 359-376) and index.

Lightman, Alan P., 1948-

Screening room; a memoir. Alan Lightman. Pantheon Books 2014 272 p. illustrations (hard cover : alk. paper) $25.95   92

1. Family life 2. Memphis (Tenn.) -- History

ISBN 9780307379399; 0307379396

LC 2013049341

In this memoir, by Alan P. Lightman, describes life in "Memphis[, Tennessee] from the 1930s through the 1960s that includes the early days of the movies and a powerful grandfather whose ghost remains an ever-present force in the lives of his descendants. . . . At the heart of it all is a family haunted by the memory of its domineering patriarch and the author's struggle to understand his conflicted loyalties." (Publisher's note)

"The cumulative effect of Lightman's memories is wrenching: Loss and illness and death wander freely in his pages, reminding us of the evanescence of youth and prom-

ise. The author shows us many small moments, igniting each with sparks of passion, memory and intelligence." Kirkus

Lincoln, Abraham, 1809-1865

Blumenthal, Sidney, 1948- A **self**-made man; the political life of Abraham Lincoln, 1809-1849. Sidney Blumenthal. Simon & Schuster 2016 576 p. illustrations (hardback) $35   92

1. Politicians -- United States 2. Presidents -- United States -- Biography 3. United States -- Politics and government -- 1815-1861

ISBN 147677725X; 9781476777252; 9781476777269

LC 2015027339

This biography of Abraham Lincoln by Sideny Blumenthanl "describes a socially awkward suitor. His marriage to the upper class Mary Todd was crucial to his social aspirations and his political career. Blumenthal's robust portrayal is based on prodigious research of Lincoln's record and of the period and its main players. It reflects both Lincoln's time and the struggle that consumes our own political debate." (Publisher's note)

"In this engrossing life-and-times study of the formative years of Abraham Lincoln (1809-65), before he became a national figure, political journalist and historian Blumenthal (The Strange Death of Republican America) takes the reader deep into Illinois and national politics to locate the character and content of Lincoln's ideas, interests, and identity, and to understand his driving ambition to succeed in law and politics. In doing so, the author makes the important point that Lincoln gained empathy and understanding of "the people" from his own self-awareness and need to escape his own origins of relative poverty and hard struggle. . . . If Blumenthal sometimes loses Lincoln in his detailed accounting of patronage, politicking, and personalities, great and small, he effectively shows that the president's Illinois was a proving ground for the politics of expansion, economic development, nativism, anti-Mormonism, and slavery that both reflected and affected national concerns. Lincoln, the self-made man, is revealed as tried-and-true, ready for the troubled times that came in the years leading up to the Civil War." LJ

Includes bibliographical references and index

Brookhiser, Richard. **Founders'** son; a life of Abraham Lincoln. Richard Brookhiser. Basic Books 2014 376 p. 8 plates; color illustrations (hardcover) $27.99   92

1. Presidents -- United States 2. United States -- Politics and government -- 1861-1865 3. Presidents -- United States -- Biography

ISBN 046503294X; 9780465032945

LC 2014021173

In this book, "historian Richard Brookhiser presents a compelling new biography of Abraham Lincoln that highlights his lifelong struggle to carry on the work of the Founding Fathers. Following Lincoln from his humble origins in Kentucky to his assassination in Washington, D.C., Brookhiser shows us every side of the man: laborer, lawyer, congressman, president; storyteller, wit, lover of ribald jokes; depressive, poet, friend, visionary." (Publisher's note)

"This highly accessible read will appeal most to readers who desire to learn more about Lincoln and especially the ideas, dogmas, and dreams that moved him to his public career and life in the White House." LJ

Includes bibliographical references and index

Burlingame, Michael. **Abraham** Lincoln; a life. Johns Hopkins University Press 2008 2v il set $125   **92**
1. Lawyers 2. Presidents 3. State legislators 4. Members of Congress 5. Biography, Individual 6. Presidents -- United States
ISBN 0-8018-8993-6; 978-0-8018-8993-6
LC 2007-52919

In this 2-volume set on U.S. President Abraham Lincoln, "volume 1 covers Lincoln's early childhood, his experiences as a farm boy in Indiana and Illinois, his legal training, and the political ambition that led to a term in Congress in the 1840s. In volume 2, [Michael] Burlingame examines Lincoln's life during his presidency and the Civil War, narrating . . . the crisis over Fort Sumter and Lincoln's own battles with relentless office seekers, hostile newspaper editors, and incompetent field commanders." (Publisher's note)

The author "has produced the finest Lincoln biography in more than 60 years. . . . Future Lincoln books cannot be written without it, and from no other book can a general reader learn so much about Abraham Lincoln." Publ Wkly

Includes bibliographical references

Carwardine, Richard. **Lincoln**: a life of purpose and power. Knopf 2006 394p il map $27.50   **92**
1. Lawyers 2. Presidents 3. State legislators 4. Members of Congress 5. Presidents -- United States 6. United States -- History -- 1861-1865, Civil War
ISBN 1-4000-4456-1
LC 2005047230

First published 2003 in the United Kingdom

This book "is not only analytical and smart, it's also delightfully readable—and it will surely emerge as one of the most important Lincoln books to be published this decade." Publ Wkly

Includes bibliographical references

Donald, David Herbert. **Lincoln**. Simon & Schuster 1995 714p il maps hardcover o.p. pa $20   **92**
1. Lawyers 2. Presidents 3. State legislators 4. Members of Congress 5. Presidents -- United States
ISBN 0-684-80846-3; 0-684-82535-X pa
LC 95-4782

This biography examines: "Lincoln's relationship with his father; his romance with Ann Rutledge; his bouts of 'hypo,' which amounted at times almost to clinical depression; his marriage; his political ambition; his attitudes toward slavery and black people; his relations with radical Republicans during the Civil War; the mistakes and successes of his wartime leadership." Atl Mon

Includes bibliographical references

★ Goodwin, Doris Kearns, 1943- **Team** of rivals; the political genius of Abraham Lincoln. Simon & Schuster 2005 916p il map $35   **92**
1. Lawyers 2. Governors 3. Presidents 4. Senators 5. Attorneys general 6. State legislators 7. Members

of Congress 8. Secretaries of state 9. Biography, Individual 10. Supreme Court justices 11. Presidential candidates 12. Presidents -- United States 13. Secretaries of the treasury 14. United States -- Politics and government -- 1861-1865
ISBN 0-684-82490-6
LC 2005-44615

"The knowledge gained here about these three significant figures who well attended Lincoln gain for the reader an even keener appreciation of the rare individual that he was." Booklist

Includes bibliographical references

Holzer, Harold. **Lincoln** president-elect; Abraham Lincoln and the great secession winter 1860-1861. Simon & Schuster 2008 623p il $30   **92**
1. Lawyers 2. Presidents 3. State legislators 4. Members of Congress 5. Presidents -- United States
ISBN 978-0-7432-8947-4; 0-7432-8947-1
LC 2008-21520

"This excellent study fills a gap about which not much has been written in Lincoln's presidential career." Choice

Includes bibliographical references

Keneally, Thomas. **Abraham** Lincoln. Viking 2003 183p (Penguin lives series) hardcover o.p. pa $14   **92**
1. Lawyers 2. Presidents 3. State legislators 4. Members of Congress 5. Presidents -- United States 6. United States -- History -- 1861-1865, Civil War
ISBN 0-670-03175-5; 0-14-311475-1 pa
LC 2003-268078

"Keneally's Lincoln is a self-actuated farm boy made good by self-discipline, savvy instincts, wit, the wisdom acquired from courtrooms, friendships, and political huckstering—and luck . . . [The author] recounts Lincoln's early missteps in romance, business, and politics and his self-doubts and depression as his star dimmed several times, and he concedes Lincoln's erratic course toward emancipation and a successful strategy for Union victory during the Civil War . . . This is an epic compressed into a tightly written biography that all Americans might read with profit. Keneally's occasional tendency to let folklore stand as fact notwithstanding, there is no better brief introduction to Lincoln and his American dream." Libr J

Kunhardt, Philip B. **Looking** for Lincoln; the making of an American icon. [by] Philip B. Kunhardt III, Peter W. Kunhardt and Peter W. Kunhardt, Jr.; foreword by David Herbert Donald; introduction by Doris Kearns Goodwin. Alfred A. Knopf 2008 494p il $50   **92**
1. Lawyers 2. Presidents 3. State legislators 4. Members of Congress 5. Presidents -- United States
ISBN 978-0-307-26713-9; 0-307-26713-X
LC 2008-14193

Sequel to: Lincoln: an illustrated biography

"The Kunhardts' book represents a visual and literary feast for all devotees of the sacred national idol that is Lincoln." Publ Wkly

Includes bibliographical references

The **Lincoln** anthology; great writers on his life and legacy from 1860 to now. edited by Harold Holzer. Library of America 2009 964p il $40   **92**

1. Lawyers 2. Presidents 3. State legislators 4. Members of Congress 5. Presidents -- United States
ISBN 978-1-59853-033-9; 1-59853-033-X

LC 2008-934337

This "is a solid compilation of work on Abraham Lincoln from a diverse selection of writers in various genres, celebrating his extensive legacy and providing insight from a number of angles and time periods." Publ Wkly

Includes bibliographical references

Lind, Michael. **What** Lincoln believed; the values and convictions of America's greatest president. Doubleday 2005 358p $27.95   **92**

1. Lawyers 2. Presidents 3. State legislators 4. Members of Congress 5. Presidents -- United States
ISBN 0-385-50739-9

LC 2004-41333

"Some readers may not recognize their own cherished Lincoln in Lind's well-researched and reasoned book. Yet it adds a valuable perspective to the vast arena of Lincoln scholarship." Christ Sci Monit

Includes bibliographical references

★ McPherson, James M. **Abraham** Lincoln. Oxford University Press 2009 79p $12.95   **92**

1. Lawyers 2. Presidents 3. State legislators 4. Members of Congress 5. Presidents -- United States
ISBN 978-0-19-537452-0; 0-19-537452-5

LC 2008-35623

"McPherson, America's leading authority on Lincoln and his times, demonstrates his complete command of his subject in this concise but remarkably rich and perceptive biography. . . . This little book is bigger than its pages and should be in every library, schoolhouse, and home." Libr J

Includes bibliographical references

★ McPherson, James M., 1936- **Tried** by war; Abraham Lincoln as commander in chief. Penguin Press 2008 329p il map hardcover o.p. pa $17 **92**

1. Lawyers 2. Presidents 3. State legislators 4. Members of Congress 5. Presidents -- United States 6. Executive power -- United States -- History 7. United States -- History -- 1861-1865, Civil War 8. United States -- History -- Civil War, 1861-1865 9. United States -- Politics and government -- 1861-1865
ISBN 0-14-311614-2 pa; 1-594-20191-9; 978-0-14-311614-1 pa; 978-1-594-20191-2

LC 2008-25229

This is an account of the ways in which Lincoln "worked with, or against, his senior commanders to defeat the Confederacy and reshape the presidential role." (Publisher's note) Index.

This book "is a perfect primer, not just for Civil War buffs or fans of Abraham Lincoln, but for anyone who wishes to understand the evolution of the president's role as commander in chief." N Y Times Book Rev

Includes bibliographical references

★ Our **Lincoln**; new perspectives on Lincoln and his world. edited by Eric Foner. W.W. Norton 2008 336p il   **92**

1. Lawyers 2. Presidents 3. State legislators 4. Members of Congress 5. Presidents -- United States 6. United States -- History -- 19th century 7. United States -- History -- Civil War, 1861-1865 8. United States -- Politics and government -- 1861-1865
ISBN 0-393-06756-4; 9780393067569

LC 2008-17096

"Twelve essays present the ideas of recent historians on Lincoln's evolving views on race, religion, and civil liberties, his military leadership, his family, photographs and portraits of Lincoln, and the use of his memory in the 21st century." (Publisher's note) Index.

Historians "collectively situate Lincoln's ideas, interests, and policies and the meanings various people from abolitionists to neo-Confederates have found in Lincoln, from the microscopic to a wider historical context of politics, culture, and memory. Essays explore such topics as presidential leadership, civil liberties, citizenship and rights, democratic politics, mass-produced imagery, African colonization, antislavery, race, religion, family life, writing sensibilities and style, and the need to claim Lincoln for one's own cause. The eloquent and compelling results show how and why Lincoln was both a man of his time and a man for all time." Libr J

Includes bibliographical references

Pinsker, Matthew. **Lincoln's** sanctuary; Abraham Lincoln and the Soldiers' Home. Oxford University Press 2003 256p il maps hardcover o.p. pa $17.95   **92**

1. Lawyers 2. Presidents 3. State legislators 4. Members of Congress 5. Presidents -- United States 6. United States Soldiers' and Airmen's Home (Washington, D.C.)
ISBN 0-19-516206-4; 978-0-19-517985-9 pa; 0-19-517985-4 pa

LC 2003-1215

The author "follows the War President to his 'retreat' at the Soldiers' Home away from the daily noise, posturing, and politicking of the capital and finds there a serenity that allowed Lincoln to relax with his family, think through issues, conduct secret meetings with allies and enemies, and reinvigorate his resolve. . . . Through Pinsker's probing inquiry into sources heretofore surprisingly underused, the ever elusive private Lincoln comes into new light. A book for our time and for all libraries." Libr J

Sandburg, Carl. **Abraham** Lincoln: The prairie years and The war years; illustrated ed; Harcourt Brace Jovanovich 1970 640p il maps hardcover o.p. pa $26   **92**

1. Lawyers 2. Presidents 3. Frontier and pioneer life 4. State legislators 5. Members of Congress 6. Presidents -- United States 7. United States -- History -- 1861-1865, Civil War
ISBN 0-15-602752-6 pa
First published 1954

A condensation of the two volumes of "The prairie years" (1926) and the four volumes of "The war years" (1939). The author has taken advantage of material made available since the original volumes were published to include in this edition of his lifetime study of Lincoln

"A biography that as a whole is superior to the longer life. This one volume has a form which the six lacked. It is a tighter and tidier book. It retains the superb qualities of the original work without the faults of the latter." Saturday Rev

Includes bibliographical references

Shenk, Joshua Wolf. **Lincoln's** melancholy; how depression challenged a president and fueled his greatness. Houghton Mifflin 2005 350p $25 **92**
1. Lawyers 2. Presidents 3. State legislators 4. Members of Congress 5. Presidents -- United States
ISBN 0-618-55116-6
LC 2005-9653
"An estimable contribution to the Lincoln literature." Booklist
Includes bibliographical references

Symonds, Craig L. **Lincoln** and his admirals; Abraham Lincoln, the U.S. Navy, and the Civil War. Oxford University Press 2008 430p il $27.95 **92**
1. Lawyers 2. Presidents 3. State legislators 4. Military officials 5. Members of Congress 6. Government officials 7. Newspaper executives 8. United States -- Navy 9. Secretaries of the navy 10. State government officials 11. Presidents -- United States 12. United States -- History -- 1861-1865, Civil War -- Naval operations
ISBN 978-0-19-531022-1; 0-19-531022-5
LC 2008-4251
"For scholars and the general reader alike, an insightful and highly readable treatment of a neglected dimension of Lincoln's wartime leadership." Kirkus
Includes bibliographical references (p. 407-416)

★ Van Sciver, Noah. The **Hypo**; The Melancholic Young Lincoln. Noah Van Sciver. Fantagraphics 2012 192 p. chiefly ill. $24.99 **92**
1. Depression (Psychology) 2. Biographical graphic novels
ISBN 1606996193; 9781606996195
This graphic novel, by Noah Van Sciver, "is based on [Abraham] Lincoln's battle with depression. . . . [It] follows the twenty-something Abraham Lincoln as . . . a rising Whig in the state's legislature as he arrives in Springfield, IL to practice law. . . . But, as time passes and uncertainty creeps in, young Lincoln is forced to battle a dark cloud of depression brought on by a chain of defeats and failures culminating into a nervous breakdown that threatens his life and sanity." (Publisher's note)
"A thoroughly engaging graphic novel that seamlessly balances investigation and imagination." Pub Wkly

White, Ronald C. **A.** Lincoln; a biography. Random House Pub. Group 2009 796p il map $35 **92**
1. Lawyers 2. Presidents 3. State legislators 4. Members of Congress 5. Presidents -- United States 6. United States -- Politics and government -- 1861-1865
ISBN 978-1-4000-6499-1
LC 2008-28840

In this biography, the author "follows the familiar trajectory of the 16th President's life; what's unique is his insight into the moral and intellectual framework of Lincoln's thinking. . . . An exceptional work that belongs in every public and academic library." Libr J
Includes bibliographical references (p. [745]-764) and index.

White, Ronald C. The **eloquent** president: a portrait of Lincoln through his words; [by] Ronald C. White, Jr. Random House 2005 xxiii, 448p il $26.95; pa $15.95 **92**
1. Lawyers 2. Presidents 3. State legislators 4. Members of Congress 5. Presidents -- United States
ISBN 1-400-06119-9; 0-8129-7046-2 pa
LC 2004-50766
The author "traces Lincoln's evolving rhetoric over the course of his presidency in a series of highly detailed critical essays. He follows Lincoln from the cautious, lawyerly text of the First Inaugural to the soaring, triumphant poetics of the Gettysburg Address." Publ Wkly
Includes bibliographical references

Lincoln, Mary Todd, 1818-1882

Baker, Jean H. **Mary** Todd Lincoln; a biography. Norton 1987 429p il hardcover o.p. pa $17.95 **92**
1. Spouses of the presidents 2. Spouses of presidents
ISBN 0-393-30586-4 pa
LC 86-23757
The author "portrays Mrs. Lincoln as a woman tortured by a series of family bereavements and thwarted from developing her natural talents by a patriarchal society that branded as 'unwomanly' her involvement in her husband's political career. Ms. Baker establishes her first argument with a lengthy investigation of Mary Todd's early family history in Lexington, Ky., and sustains the second by enlarging upon such topics as 19th-century domesticity, childbirth, mourning customs, spiritualism and America's deplorable insanity laws." NY Times Book Rev
Includes bibliographical references

Clinton, Catherine. **Mrs.** Lincoln; a life. HarperCollins 2009 415p il $26.99 **92**
1. Spouses of presidents 2. Presidents' spouses -- United States
ISBN 978-0-06-076040-3; 0-06-076040-0
The author "sifts through the many criticisms of Mary Lincoln to offer a sensitive reassessment that debunks unjust attacks and reveals Mrs. Lincoln's many strengths—charitableness, devotion to family and nation, unwavering love and encouragement for her beleaguered husband—alongside the mental illness and flaws of temperament for which she is better known. . . . Written in a style that will appeal to the general reader, Clinton's book features sufficient nuance to satisfy scholars looking for a greater interpretation of the life of this controversial historical figure." Libr J
Includes bibliographical references

Lindbergh, Anne Morrow, 1906-2001

Hertog, Susan. **Anne** Morrow Lindbergh; a biography. Talese 1999 561p il hardcover o.p. pa $17   **92**

1. Poets 2. Authors 3. Novelists 4. Diarists 5. Essayists 6. Memoirists 7. Spouses of prominent persons

ISBN 0-385-72007-6 pa

LC 99-28759

After her marriage to Charles Lindbergh, Anne Morrow "soon recognized the difficulty of reconciling her literary ambitions with accompanying her husband as copilot, navigator and radio operator. After the tragic kidnapping and death of their first child, which they blamed in part on dogged press coverage of their personal life, the Lindberghs moved abroad. They became embroiled with the leaders of Nazi Germany, according to Hertog, because Charles believed that the democratic system was weak and ineffectual. . . . This sympathetic portrayal of Anne as a wife, mother, poet and feminist may well find a readership more interested in a talented woman's creative struggle than in the oft-told Lindbergh story." Publ Wkly

Includes bibliographical references

Lindbergh, Reeve. **Under** a wing; a memoir. Delta Trade Paperbacks 1999 223p il pa $15   **92**

1. Poets 2. Authors 3. Generals 4. Novelists 5. Air pilots 6. Diarists 7. Essayists 8. Memoirists 9. Air force officers 10. Children's authors 11. Spouses of prominent persons 12. Children of prominent persons

ISBN 978-0-385-33444-0; 0-385-33444-3

First published 1998 by Simon & Schuster

"A rare memoir whose goal is not to expose but finally to understand." Libr J

Winters, Kathleen C. **Anne** Morrow Lindbergh; first lady of the air. Palgrave Macmillan 2006 241p il map $24.95   **92**

1. Poets 2. Authors 3. Novelists 4. Diarists 5. Essayists 6. Memoirists 7. Spouses of prominent persons

ISBN 978-1-4039-6932-3; 1-4039-6932-9

LC 2006-43290

This book focuses on Anne Morrow Lindbergh's career as an aviator. "She was one of the earliest female pilots, as well as the first American female glider pilot, and a radio operator. . . . Winters shows in great detail that Lindbergh accomplished this under the glare of an unremitting spotlight, and in the company of an often-demanding spouse. That the author is able to bring something new to the Lindbergh story is impressive, and she does it through both technical explanations of Lindbergh's accomplishments and Anne's own words about her flying exploits, marriage, and writing." Booklist

Includes bibliographical references

Lindbergh, Charles, 1902-1974

Kessner, Thomas. The **flight** of the century; Charles Lindbergh & the rise of American aviation. Oxford University Press 2010 313p il map (Pivotal moments in American history)   **92**

1. Generals 2. Air pilots 3. Memoirists 4. Air force

officers 5. Biography, Individual 6. Aeronautics -- United States -- History

ISBN 0-19-532019-0; 978-0-19-532019-0

LC 2010-06082

Thomas Kessner's book examines "how and why Lindbergh elicited so much popular excitement and what his status as an international hero meant for the development of aviation." (J Am Hist) Index.

"In May 1927 at the age of 25, the 'Lone Eagle' flew from New York to Paris, a startling accomplishment that made the awkward, reticent aviator the world's best-known person. But Lindbergh lived until 1974, and two elements were added to his legacy — he was the father whose tiny son was kidnapped and slain by Bruno Hauptmann, and, much worse for his reputation, he was the fascist-tinged advocate of U.S. neutrality before World War II. . . . [Kessner's book] aims to balance the equation. His book recaps Lindbergh's epochal flight and carries it forward, discussing his subsequent role in the aviation boom that followed. While there is nothing particularly earth-shattering about what he has written, Kessner's fresh perspective breathes new life into Lindbergh's tale." Philadelphia Inquirer

Includes bibliographical references and index

Lindbergh, Reeve. **Under** a wing; a memoir. Delta Trade Paperbacks 1999 223p il pa $15   **92**

1. Poets 2. Authors 3. Generals 4. Novelists 5. Air pilots 6. Diarists 7. Essayists 8. Memoirists 9. Air force officers 10. Children's authors 11. Spouses of prominent persons 12. Children of prominent persons

ISBN 978-0-385-33444-0; 0-385-33444-3

First published 1998 by Simon & Schuster

"A rare memoir whose goal is not to expose but finally to understand." Libr J

Lindbergh, Reeve

Lindbergh, Reeve. **Under** a wing; a memoir. Delta Trade Paperbacks 1999 223p il pa $15   **92**

1. Poets 2. Authors 3. Generals 4. Novelists 5. Air pilots 6. Diarists 7. Essayists 8. Memoirists 9. Air force officers 10. Children's authors 11. Spouses of prominent persons 12. Children of prominent persons

ISBN 978-0-385-33444-0; 0-385-33444-3

First published 1998 by Simon & Schuster

"A rare memoir whose goal is not to expose but finally to understand." Libr J

Lindhout, Amanda

★ Corbett, Sara. A **house** in the sky; a memoir. Amanda Lindhout, Sara Corbett. Scribner 2013 373 p. (paperback) $16   **92**

1. Somalia 2. Hostages 3. Somalia -- History -- 1991- 4. Hostages -- Somalia -- Biography 5. Journalists -- Canada -- Biography

ISBN 1451645619; 9781451645606; 9781451645613

LC 2013016015

In this book, "Canadian journalist [Amanda] Lindhout gives . . . [an] account of her 459-day captivity at the hands of Somali Islamist rebels. . . . Convinced war-torn Somalia would be the 'hurricane' to make her career, in August 2008, at age 25, she . . . set off to view a displaced-persons' camp but was instead carjacked by a group of kidnappers. . . . Her captors moved her frequently from hideout to hideout, and she . . . was raped and tortured." (Publishers Weekly)

Includes bibliographical references and index

Linné, Carl von, 1707-1778

Blunt, Wilfrid. **Linnaeus,** the compleat naturalist; with an introduction by William T. Stearn. Princeton Univ. Press 2002 264p il maps $35   **92**

1. Botanists 2. Writers on science

ISBN 0-691-09636-8

First published 1971 by Viking with title: The compleat naturalist: a life of Linnaeus

This biography traces the Swedish scientist's life from his days as a poor student at Lund University through his scientific achievements and academic career at Uppsala

Includes bibliographical references

Link, Mardi

Bootstrapper; from broke to badass on a northern Michigan farm. Mardi Jo Link. Alfred A. Knopf 2013 272 p. (hardback) $24.95   **92**

1. Farmers 2. Divorced women 3. Autobiographies

ISBN 0307596915; 9780307596918; 9780307743589

LC 2012042425

First edition

In this memoir, author Mardi Jo Link details how following her divorce, "more broke than ever, [she] makes a seemingly impossible resolution: to hang on to her century-old farmhouse in northern Michigan and continue to raise her three boys on well water and wood chopping and dirt. Armed with an unfailing sense of humor and three resolute accomplices, Link . . . withstands any blow to her pride in order to preserve the life she wants." (Publisher's note)

"Link's pride in her sons and the life they have made shines throughout the book and is obviously well deserved. Neither sugarcoated nor wallowing in self-pity, Link's storytelling is as tough, honest, and unyielding as one would expect from a Michigan farmer. Her account, told with humor and panache, of pulling oneself up after disappointment and loss will appeal to the bootstrapper in all of us." Booklist

The **Drummond** Girls; A Story of Fierce Friendship Beyond Time and Chance. Mardi Link. Grand Central Publishing 2015 272 p. illustrations, map (hardcover) $26   **92**

1. Women 2. Female friendship

ISBN 145555474X; 9781455554744

LC 2015010926

This book, by Mardi Jo Link, is a "memoir about the friendship between eight women forged over two decades. The eight Drummond Girls first met in 1991. . . . At the time, they were all waitresses, bartenders, or regular customers. When one of them got engaged, they celebrated with a trip to Drummond Island. . . . They've made this voyage every year since then as a way to retain a piece of their wild youth, despite the taming influence of marriage, motherhood, and management." (Publisher's note)

"Link ably portrays her initial sense of isolation and need for friendship, providing descriptions of the wilderness she has found on the island and her increasing allegiance to these women as they all gradually grow older and experience life events that change them forever. A moving,

honest, and laughter-filled account of eight women who gather one weekend every year and enjoy themselves to the fullest." Kirkus

Lispector, Clarice, 1925-1977

Moser, Benjamin. **Why** this world; a biography of Clarice Lispector. Oxford University Press 2009 479p il $29.95   **92**

1. Authors 2. Novelists 3. Journalists 4. Women authors 5. Short story writers 6. Biography, Individual

ISBN 0-19-538556-X; 978-0-19-538556-4

LC 2008-55639

This is a biography of the Brazilian novelist.

"Lispector makes a difficult, often lurid subject, and Moser's account of her life is riveting—he draws extensively on previously untranslated letters and criticism (he does the translations himself, from Yiddish, German, French and Portuguese); at times the book reads like a gothic horror story." Nation

Includes bibliographical references

Lithgow, John, 1945-

Lithgow, John, 1945- **Drama**; an actor's education. John Lithgow. Harper 2011 $26.99; $12.99 **92**

1. Actors -- United States -- Biography

ISBN 978-0-06-173497-7; 978-0-06-209773-6 ebook; 9780061734977

LC 2011008172

"More than the run-of-the-mill 'And then I met . . . And then I was in . . . ' actor's autobiography, this is both a memoir full of emotion and a cautionary tale." Libr J

Little Richard

White, Charles. The **life** and times of Little Richard; the quasar of rock. Updated ed; Da Capo Press 1994 282p il pa $16   **92**

1. Singers 2. Rock musicians 3. African American musicians

ISBN 0-306-80552-9; 978-0-306-80552-3

LC 93-48054

First published 1984 by Harmony Bks.

This biography of the American singer discusses "his flamboyant stage antics; his blatant flaunting of racial taboos; his sexual experiences; his bewildering career that careened between show business and the church; and exactly how he created the music that would become a symbol of rebellion for kids all over the world." Publisher's note

Includes discography and filmography

Lively, Penelope, 1933-

Lively, Penelope. A **house** unlocked. Grove Press 2002 225p il $23; pa $13   **92**

1. Authors 2. Novelists 3. Children's authors 4. Short story writers

ISBN 0-8021-1712-0; 0-8021-4007-6 pa

LC 2001-55745

First published 2001 in the United Kingdom

"The British novelist Penelope Lively spent her early childhood in Egypt, but it was her school holidays at Golsoncott—a manor house that her grandparents bought in the wilds of Somerset, in 1923—that shaped her life. In this slim, beguiling book, Lively describes the contents and customs of the house. . . . By meticulously tracing the provenance of these objects, she re-creates the life they once furnished." New Yorker

Includes bibliographical references

Lobdell, William

Lobdell, William. **Losing** my religion; how I lost my faith reporting on religion in America--and found unexpected peace. Collins 2009 291p $25.99   92

1. Journalists 2. Bloggers

ISBN 978-0-06-162681-4; 0-06-162681-3

LC 2008-24010

"Lobdell's spiritual journey fascinates, not least on account of the irony of his trajectory from agnosticism to belief to atheism while covering religion. It's a story that may raise eyebrows among believers and nonbelievers alike." Booklist

Includes bibliographical references

Lobo, Julio, 1898-1983

Rathbone, John Paul. The **sugar** king of Havana; the rise and fall of Julio Lobo, Cuba's last tycoon. Penguin Press 2010 304p il map $27.95   92

1. Sugar 2. Businessmen 3. Cuba -- History 4. Agribusiness executives

ISBN 978-1-59420-258-2; 1594202583

LC 2010-13790

"An exceptionally rich portrait not only of an empire and its progenitor but Cuba itself, and the economic legacy of Castro's revolution, the loss of capital, and the end of Cuba's 'great age of sugar.'" Publ Wkly

Includes bibliographical references

Lockwood, Belva Ann, 1830-1917

Norgren, Jill. **Belva** Lockwood; the woman who would be president. New York University Press 2007 311p il $40; pa $22   92

1. Lawyers 2. Suffragists 3. Lecturers 4. Biography, Individual 5. Presidential candidates 6. Women in politics -- United States

ISBN 0-8147-5834-7; 0-8147-5851-7 pa; 978-0-8147-5834-2; 978-0-8147-5851-9 pa

LC 2006-34486

This is a biography of Belva Lockwood, a lawyer and suffragist who twice ran for president. Index.

"Those with interests in women's, political, social, and cultural history will enjoy Lockwood." Choice

Includes bibliographical references

Lomax, Alan, 1915-2002

Szwed, John F. **Alan** Lomax; the man who recorded the world. Viking 2010 438p $29.95   92

1. Authors 2. Folk music 3. Folklorists 4. Musicologists 5. Writers on music 6. Biography, Individual

ISBN 978-0-670-02199-4

LC 2010-15332

This is a biography of the American folklorist and ethnomusicologist.

This "biography is a worthy testament to Lomax's passions and ideals, which gifted the world some of the most important American recordings ever made." New Statesman

Includes bibliographical references

Lombardi, Vince

Maraniss, David. **When** pride still mattered: a life of Vince Lombardi. Simon & Schuster 1999 541p il hardcover o.p. pa $16   92

1. Football coaches 2. Green Bay Packers (Football team)

ISBN 0-684-77018-5 pa

LC 99-37859

"From Lombardi's formative years as a player and coach at Fordham University through assistantships with West Point and the Giants and, finally, to his tenure as head coach of the Packers, Maraniss presents a portrait of a complicated human being who was a great teacher but a mediocre listener, an effective psychologist despite being rife with flaws." Publ Wkly

Includes bibliographical references

London, Jack, 1876-1916

Adam, Philip. **Jack** London, photographer; [by] Jeanne Campbell Reesman, Sara S. Hodson, & Philip Adam. University of Georgia Press 2010 271p il $49.95   92

1. Authors 2. Novelists 3. Photographers 4. Authors, American 5. Short story writers

ISBN 978-0-8203-2967-3

LC 2010005973

"This book will be of great appeal to a broad range of audiences interested in history, American literature, and photography." Libr J

Includes bibliographical references

Labor, Earle. **Jack** London; an American life. Earle Labor. Farrar Straus & Giroux 2013 480 p. (hardback) $30   92

1. American authors -- Biography 2. Authors, American -- 19th century -- Biography 3. Authors, American -- 20th century -- Biography

ISBN 0374178488; 9780374178482

LC 2012050948

This book presents a biography of writer Jack London. "Born in San Francisco in 1876 to an impoverished single mother, London . . . took up factory work to support his household while still a child, and by age 18 had worked as an oyster pirate, sailor, and rail-riding hobo. Omnivorous reading and sporadic education fueled his desire to write, and a year spent surviving the Yukon Gold Rush (1897-1898) provided him with inspiration for his earliest nonfiction and fiction." (Publishers Weekly)

Includes bibliographical references and index

Long, Huey Pierce, 1893-1935

Hair, William Ivy. The **Kingfish** and his realm: the life and times of Huey P. Long. Louisiana State Univ. Press 1991 406p il map hardcover o.p. pa $21.95   92

1. Governors 2. Senators 3. State government officials 4. Louisiana -- Politics and government

ISBN 0-8071-2124-X pa

LC 91-18546

This is a biography of the man who was governor of Louisiana from 1928 to 1932 and senator from 1932 until his assassination in 1935

"Written with passion and mordant wit, the book is literally hard to put down; the Kingfish seems to stimulate good writing. Overall, {this} is one of the more convincing negative biographies of recent years." Rev Am Hist

Includes bibliographical references

Longworth, Alice Roosevelt, 1884-1980

Cordery, Stacy A. **Alice**; Alice Roosevelt Longworth, from White House princess to Washington power broker. Viking 2007 590p il $32.95 **92**
1. Socialites 2. Children of presidents
ISBN 978-0-670-01833-8

LC 2006-103087

This is a biography of Alice Roosevelt Longworth, the Washington hostess and author of Crowded Hours (1933).

The author "pens an authoritative, intriguing portrait of a first daughter who broke the mold." Publ Wkly

Includes bibliographical references (p. [555]-572) and index.

Louis XIV, King of France, 1638-1715

Fraser, Antonia. **Love** and Louis XIV; the women in the life of the Sun King. Nan A. Talese/Doubleday 2006 xxviii, 388p il $32.50 **92**
1. Kings
ISBN 978-0-38550984-8; 0-385-50984-7

LC 2006-44674

This is an account of Louis XIV's relationships with his wife and his mistresses.

"One of the most enveloping popular histories of the current publishing season." Booklist

Includes bibliographical references

Louis, Joe, 1914-1981

Roberts, Randy. **Joe** Louis; hard times man. Yale University Press 2010 308p il $27.50 **92**
1. African American athletes 2. Boxing -- History 3. Boxing -- Biography 4. Biography, Individual
ISBN 978-0-300-12222-0

LC 2010-15422

In this biography of the American boxer, "Roberts handles the boxing action with professional aplomb, and he knows when to cut away to tell us something of consequence and when to return to the ring. The author ably chronicles Louis's rise from Alabama cotton fields to the cavernous Yankee Stadium, where celebrities glittered in the ringside seats for his big fights; the development of the mass media (boxing was enormously popular on radio); Louis's career in the U.S. Army; and his sad decline, amid unpayable debts and mental illness. All legendary athletes should hope for treatment by such capable, compassionate hands." Kirkus

Includes bibliographical references and index

Lovelace, Ada King, Countess of, 1815-1852

Essinger, James. **Ada's** algorithm; how Lord Byron's daughter Ada Lovelace launched the digital age. James Essinger. Melville House 2014 272 p. illustrations (hardback) $25.95 **92**
1. Computers -- History 2. Women mathematicians 3.

Mathematicians -- Biography 4. Computers -- History -- 19th century 5. Mathematicians -- Great Britain -- Biography 6. Women mathematicians -- Great Britain -- Biography
ISBN 1612194087; 9781612194080

LC 2014021837

In this book, author James Essinger "makes the case that the computer age could have started two centuries ago if [Ada] Lovelace's contemporaries had recognized her research and fully grasped its implications. . . . [S]tarting with the outrageous behavior of her father [Lord Byron], which made Ada instantly famous upon birth. Ada would go on to overcome numerous obstacles to obtain a level of education typically forbidden to women of her day." (Publisher's note)

"Essinger (Spellbound: The Surprising Origins and Astonishing Secrets of English Spelling, 2007, etc.) presents Ada's story with great enthusiasm and rich detail, painting her life as one that was rich with opportunity and access but stifled by sexism. Ada continues to inspire, and by using her own voice via letters and research, the author brings her to life for a new generation of intrepid female innovators. A robust, engaging and exciting biography." Kirkus

Includes bibliographical references and index

Loy, Myrna

Leider, Emily W. **Myrna** Loy; the only good girl in Hollywood. [by] Emily W. Leider. University of California Press 2011 411p il $34.95 **92**
1. Actors
ISBN 978-0-520-25320-9; 0-520-25320-5

LC 2011-11571

"Loy's gifts are easy to enjoy, hard to describe. She's been lucky in attracting an even-tempered sympathetic biographer like Ms. Leider, whose book, like the best of its genre, sends you back to the films." Wall Street J

Includes bibliographical references

Luce, Clare Boothe, 1903-1987

Morris, Sylvia Jukes. **Rage** for fame: the ascent of Clare Boothe Luce. Random House 1997 561p il hardcover o.p. pa $27 **92**
1. Authors 2. Diplomats 3. Dramatists 4. Members of Congress 5. Writers on politics
ISBN 0-8129-9249-0 pa

LC 96-43084

This first of a projected two-volume biography "describes how the future congresswoman and second wife of Time magazine founder Henry Luce, bedded her way upward while career-climbing in New York journalism and writing a stage mega-hit, The Women. . . . By 1942—at age 39—she turned to politics and was elected a Republican representative from Connecticut." Publ Wkly

Includes bibliographical references

Luce, Henry Robinson, 1898-1967

★ Brinkley, Alan. The **publisher**; Henry Luce and his American century. Alfred A. Knopf 2010 531p il $35 **92**
1. Journalists 2. Publishers and publishing 3. Magazine editors 4. Magazine executives
ISBN 978-0-679-41444-5; 0-679-41444-4

LC 2009-38834

"In this superb biography Alan Brinkley . . . has told the curiously depressing story of a brilliant man who got everything wrong, including so many of the things that mattered most to him. Mr Brinkley has an eye for both the telling detail and the broad sweep of Luce's role as the man who saw the need for a national news magazine and foresaw the American century." Economist

Includes bibliographical references

Luther, Martin, 1483-1546

Bainton, Roland Herbert. **Here** I stand: a life of Martin Luther. Abingdon Press 1950 422p il music hardcover o.p. pa $7   **92**
1. Reformation 2. Theologians 3. Social reformers 4. Religious leaders 5. Writers on religion 6. Europe -- Church history
ISBN 0-687-16895-3 pa
This biography of Martin Luther interprets his work, writings, and lasting contributions. It recreates the spiritual setting of the sixteenth century and shows Luther's place within it

Includes bibliographical references

Erikson, Erik H. **Young** man Luther; a study in psychoanalysis and history. Norton 1958 288p hardcover o.p. pa $13.95   **92**
1. Reformation 2. Theologians 3. Social reformers 4. Religious leaders 5. Writers on religion 6. Europe -- Church history
ISBN 0-393-31036-1 pa
"This study of Martin Luther as a young man was planned as a chapter in a book on emotional crises in late adolescence and early adulthood. But Luther proved too bulky a man to be merely a chapter." Preface

Hendrix, Scott H. **Martin** Luther; visionary reformer. Scott H. Hendrix. Yale University Press 2015 368 p. illustrations, maps (cl : alk. paper) $35   **92**
1. Reformation 2. Reformation -- Germany -- Biography
ISBN 9780300166699; 0300166699
LC 2015017636
This book, by Scott H. Hendrix, is an "account of the life of Martin Luther [that] provides a new perspective on one of the most important religious figures in history, focusing on Luther's entire life, his personal relationships and political motivations, rather than on his theology alone. Relying on the latest research and quoting extensively from Luther's correspondence, Hendrix paints a richly detailed portrait of an extraordinary man who, while devout and courageous, had a dark side as well." (Publisher's note)

"This carefully documented, fast-paced telling will delight readers of biography, history, and fiction; historians, theologians, and psychologists may gain deeper insights into how flaws in personality and the zeitgeist itself often prejudice the pursuit of truth." LJ

Includes bibliographical references and index.

Oberman, Heiko Augustinus. **Luther**: man between God and the Devil; {by} Heiko A. Oberman; translated by Eileen Walliser-Schwarzbart. Yale

Univ. Press 1990 xx, 380p il hardcover o.p. pa $20   **92**
1. Reformation 2. Theologians 3. Social reformers 4. Religious leaders 5. Writers on religion 6. Europe -- Church history
ISBN 978-0-300-10313-7 pa; 0-300-10313-1 pa
LC 89-5747
Original German edition, 1982
The author "posits that to understand Luther the reformer is to first realize he was a medieval man for whom Satan was as real as God and human. By placing Luther back into the context of his own age, Oberman strips away any simplistic, post-Enlightenment notions of Luther as the savior of humanity from the darkest obscurantism of the Catholic Church. . . . A triumph of scholarship that brings Luther to life in all of his furious, outspoken, and violent passion." Booklist

Includes bibliographical references

Wilson, Derek A. **Out** of the storm; the life and legacy of Martin Luther. [by] Derek Wilson. St. Martin's Press 2008 399p il $29.95   **92**
1. Reformation 2. Theologians 3. Social reformers 4. Religious leaders 5. Writers on religion 6. Europe -- Church history
ISBN 978-0-312-37588-1; 0-312-37588-3
LC 2007-39331
"A nuanced portrait of a perplexing titan." Booklist
Includes bibliographical references

Luttrell, Marcus, 1975-

Lone survivor; the eyewitness account of Operation Redwing and the lost heroes of SEAL Team 10. Marcus Luttrell; with Patrick Robinson. 1st ed.; Little, Brown & Co. 2007 390 p. ill., maps $28 **92**
1. Afghan War, 2001- 2. United States. Navy. SEALs 3. Afghan War, 2001- -- Campaigns 4. United States. Navy. SEALs -- Officers 5. Afghan War, 2001- -- Personal narratives, American
ISBN 0316067598; 9780316067591
LC 2007921207
This memoir by Marcus Luttrell, with Patrick Robinson, recalls how "in late June 2005, four U.S. Navy SEALs left their base in northern Afghanistan for the mountainous Pakistani border. Their mission was to capture or kill a notorious al Qaeda leader known to be ensconced in a Taliban stronghold surrounded by a small but heavily armed force. Less then twenty-four hours later, only one of those Navy SEALs remained alive." (Publisher's note)

Luxenberg, Steve

Luxenberg, Steve. **Annie's** ghosts; a journey into a family secret. Hyperion Books 2009 401p il $24.99   **92**
1. Newspaper editors
ISBN 978-1-4013-2247-2; 1-4013-2247-6
LC 2008-55661
"Part memoir, part mystery, part history of the mental-health movement, . . . [this] is a fascinating account of a life lived in the shadows." Booklist
Includes bibliographical references

Lynn, Loretta

Lynn, Loretta. **Still** woman enough; a memoir. {by} Loretta Lynn with Patsi Bale Cox. Hyperion 2002 244p il $24.95; pa $7.99 **92**

1. Singers 2. Country musicians 3. Songwriters
ISBN 0-7868-6650-0; 0-7868-8987-X pa

In this sequel to Coal miner's daughter, "Lynn mostly focuses on her marriage and the trials and pleasures of Nashville stardom, including fond recollections of friends like Conway Twitty and Tammy Wynette. . . . Though her grammar may make purists flinch . . . Lynn's literary voice is as natural and endearing as her songs." Publ Wkly

Maathai, Wangari, 1940-2001

Maathai, Wangari. **Unbowed**; a memoir. [by] Wangari Muta Maathai. Knopf 2006 314p il hardcover o.p. pa $15 **92**

1. Biologists 2. Conservationists 3. Environmentalists 4. Kenya 5. Nobel laureates for peace 6. Green Belt Movement (Kenya)
ISBN 0-307-26348-7; 978-0-307-26348-3; 0-307-27520-5 pa; 978-0-307-27520-2 pa

LC 2006-44729

"Nobel Peace Prize winner Maathai tells the unforgettable story of her Kenya girlhood, struggles as a biologist and professor, and founding of the Green Belt Movement to restore Kenya's decimated forests and provide women with work." Booklist

MacArthur, Douglas, 1880-1964

Frank, Richard B. **MacArthur**; foreword by Wesley K. Clark. Palgrave Macmillan 2007 224p (Great generals series) hardcover o.p. pa $12.95 **92**

1. Generals
ISBN 1-4039-7658-9; 978-1-4039-7658-1; 0-230-61397-7 pa; 978-0-230-61397-3 pa

This biography of the World War II general is an "assessment of both the man and the soldier, covering the failures and triumphs in an assured and dispassionate tone. . . . A good starting point for generalists." Libr J

★ Herman, Arthur. **Douglas** MacArthur; American warrior. Arthur Herman. Random House 2016 912 p. illustrations, maps (ebook) $65; $40 **92**

1. Generals -- United States -- Biography 2. United States. Army -- Biography 3. United States -- History, Military -- 20th century
ISBN 9780812994896; 9780812994889

LC 2015039817

This book, by Arthur Herman, is a biography of Douglas MacArthur. "MacArthur's life spans the emergence of the United States Army as a global fighting force. Its history is to a great degree his story. The son of a Civil War hero, he led American troops in three monumental conflicts—World War I, World War II, and the Korean War. Born four years after Little Bighorn, he died just as American forces began deploying in Vietnam." (Publisher's note)

"Herman presents a superb reexamination of MacArthur and his role in American history." Booklist
Includes bibliographical references and index

Perry, Mark. The **most** dangerous man in America; the making of Douglas MacArthur. Mark Perry. Basic Books 2014 416 p. illustrations (hardcover) $29.99 **92**

1. Generals 2. United States -- Military history 3. United States. Army -- Biography 4. Generals -- United States -- Biography 5. United States -- History, Military -- 20th century
ISBN 0465013287; 9780465013289; 9780465080670

LC 2014004629

"At times, even his admirers seemed unsure of what to do with General Douglas MacArthur. . . . In 'The Most Dangerous Man in America,' celebrated historian Mark Perry examines how this paradox of a man overcame personal and professional challenges to lead his countrymen in their darkest hour. As Perry shows, Franklin Roosevelt and a handful of MacArthur's subordinates made this feat possible, taming MacArthur, making him useful, and finally making him victorious." (Publisher's note)

"While much has been written on the general topic, Perry is strong on discussing MacArthur's relationship with FDR as well as his fellow officers in the Pacific." LJ
Includes bibliographical references and index

MacArthur, Douglas, 1880-1964.

Borneman, Walter R., 1952- **Macarthur** at war; world war II in the Pacific. Walter R. Borneman. Little, Brown & Co. 2016 608 p. illustrations, maps (hc) $30 **92**

1. World War, 1939-1945
ISBN 0316405329; 9780316405324

LC 2016931808

This book, by Walter R. Borneman, is the "definitive account of General Douglas MacArthur's rise during World War II. . . . Architect of stunning triumphs and inexplicable defeats, General MacArthur is the most intriguing military leader of the twentieth century. There was never any middle ground with MacArthur. This in-depth study of the most critical period of his career shows how MacArthur's influence spread far beyond the war-torn Pacific." (Publisher's note)

"An able researcher and fluent writer, Borneman holds solid appeal for the military history audience." Booklist
Includes bibliographical references (pages 561-577) and index.

MacLaine, Shirley, 1934-

MacLaine, Shirley, 1934- **Above** the line; my Wild oats adventure. Shirley MacLaine. Atria Books 2016 224 p. $24 **92**

1. Actresses 2. Motion pictures -- Production and direction 3. Wild oats (Motion picture) 4. Entertainers -- United States -- Biography 5. Spiritualists -- United States -- Biography
ISBN 1501136410; 9781501136412

LC 2015040061

This memoir by Shirley MacClaine chronicles her "experiences filming 'Wild Oats' in the Canary Islands and the extraordinary memories her time there brought forth of a past life on the lost continent of Atlantis. As the movie set descends into pandemonium, Shirley finds fascinating corollaries between the island's cataclysmic fate and our own dangerous trajectory." (Publisher's note)

"MacLaine is wickedly honest about moviemaking, sincere and enthusiastic in describing her beliefs, and welcoming in the skepticism of others—it's all refreshing and fun." Kirkus

MacLeish, Archibald, 1892-1982

MacLeish, Archibald. **Archibald** MacLeish: reflections; edited by Bernard A. Drabeck and Helen E. Ellis; foreword by Richard Wilbur. University of Mass. Press 1986 291p il $40; pa $18.95   **92**

1. Poets 2. Authors 3. Essayists 4. Librarians of Congress

ISBN 0-87023-511-7; 0-87023-623-7 pa

LC 85-28912

"In this genial, relaxed book we have a golden view of the candidly retrospective statesman-poet in his old age as he really was, with most pretension and all rhetoric abandoned." N Y Times Book Rev

Includes bibliographical references

Machiavelli, Niccolo, 1469-1527

Unger, Miles J. **Machiavelli**; a biography. Miles J. Unger. 1st Simon & Schuster hc. ed. Simon & Schuster 2011 x, 400 p.p ill. (some col.) , map (hardcover) $28   **92**

1. Authors 2. Statesmen 3. Dramatists 4. Philosophers 5. Authors, Italian -- Biography 6. Statesmen -- Italy -- Biography 7. Intellectuals -- Italy -- Biography 8. Italy -- History -- 1492-1559 -- Biography 9. Political scientists -- Italy -- Biography 10. Florence (Italy) -- History -- 1421-1737 -- Biography

ISBN 1416556281; 9781416556282

LC 2010054130

This book is Miles J. Unger's biography of Machiavelli. "Unger utilizes Machiavelli's correspondence to present a complex portrait, showing his subject in the varied public roles he played: civil servant, diplomat, political philosopher, and playwright. All of Machiavelli's writings are discussed and analyzed here." (Library Journal)

Includes bibliographical references (p. [353]-386) and index.

Viroli, Maurizio. **Niccolo's** smile: a biography of Machiavelli; translated from the Italian by Antony Shugaar. Farrar, Straus & Giroux 2000 271p maps hardcover o.p. pa $13   **92**

1. Authors 2. Statesmen 3. Dramatists 4. Writers on politics 5. Political and social philosophers

ISBN 0-374-52800-4 pa

LC 00-29380

This biography of the Italian political philosopher traces his life "from respected secretary of the Florentine republic, dispatched on crucial diplomatic missions to Europe's most illustrious courts, to forgotten commoner. . . . Viroli provides a detailed, historical background for Machiavelli's personal triumphs and woes. But the strength of this work lies in his

ceaseless concentration on Machiavelli the man, who comes alive on each page." Publ Wkly

Includes bibliographical references

Madison, Dolley, 1768-1849

Allgor, Catherine. A **perfect** union; Dolley Madison and the creation of the American nation. Henry Holt & Co. 2006 493p il $30   **92**

1. Biography, Individual 2. Spouses of presidents

ISBN 0-8050-7327-2; 978-0-8050-7327-0

LC 2005-55127

This is a biography of the First Lady. Allgor argues that while Dolley Madison's "gender prevented her from openly playing politics, those very constraints of womanhood allowed her to construct an American democratic ruling style, and to achieve her husband [James's] political goals." (Publisher's note) Index.

"In this evocative study a remarkable woman, creator of the 'first lady' role, comes vividly to life. " N Y Times Book Rev

Includes bibliographical references

Madison, James, 1751-1836

Broadwater, Jeff. **James** Madison; a son of Virginia & a founder of the nation. Jeff Broadwater. University of North Carolina Press 2012 xvi, 266 p.p   **92**

1. Presidents -- United States 2. Founding Fathers of the United States 3. Statesmen -- United States -- Biography 4. Presidents -- United States -- Biography 5. United States -- Politics and government -- 1789-1815 6. United States -- Politics and government -- 1809-1817

ISBN 9780807835302

LC 2011035946

In this biography of U.S. President James Madison, professor "[Jeff] Broadwater specifically provides readers with a detailed account of Madison's attempts to secure religious freedom in his native Virginia, his relationship with his charismatic wife Dolley Madison (sometimes referred to as 'Lady Presidentess'), and his ongoing struggle with his ideas about slavery." (Publishers Weekly)

Includes bibliographical references and index.

Cheney, Lynne V., 1941- **James** Madison; a life reconsidered. Lynne Cheney. Viking Adult 2014 576 p. illustrations (hardback) $36   **92**

1. Presidents -- United States 2. Statesmen -- United States -- Biography 3. United States -- Politics and government -- 1783-1865

ISBN 0670025194; 9780670025190

LC 2013047837

This biography of U.S. president James Madison, by Lynne Cheney, "explores the astonishing story of a man of vaunted modesty. . . . Among the Founding Fathers, Madison was a true genius of the early republic. Outwardly reserved, Madison was the intellectual driving force behind the Constitution and crucial to its ratification. His visionary political philosophy and rationale for the union of states--so eloquently presented in The Federalist papers--helped shape . . . America." (Publisher's note)

"Cheney conclusively demonstrates through the historical record that Madison, in word and deed, was a primary figure in shaping early American development." Pub Wkly

Includes bibliographical references and index

Signer, Michael. **Becoming** Madison; the extraordinary origins of the least likely founding father. Michael Signer. Public Affairs 2015 384 p. (hardcover : alk. paper) $28.99   **92**

1. Founding Fathers of the United States 2. Presidents -- United States -- Biography 3. United States -- Politics and government -- 1783-1809

ISBN 1610392957; 9781610392952

LC 2014038885

This book offers the "story of James Madison's coming of age, providing . . . insight into the Founding Father. Michael Signer takes a fresh look at the life of our fourth president. His focus is on Madison before he turned thirty-six, the years in which he did his most enduring work: battling with Patrick Henry . . . over religious freedom; introducing his framework for a strong central government; becoming the intellectual godfather of the Constitution." (Publisher's note)

"The author offers some dramatic set pieces demonstrating Madison's method in action—the 1784 fight against religious assessments in Virginia, the Constitutional Convention, the Virginia ratification battle, etc.—illustrating its effectiveness against more conventional tactics and politicians. He's particularly good at showing how Madison's discipline, relentless logic and faith in reason allowed him to triumph over his in-state antagonist, Patrick Henry. A perfect introduction to a deeply private and immensely important man." Kirkus

Includes bibliographical references and index

Stewart, David O. **Madison's** Gift; Five Partnerships That Built America. David O. Stewart. Simon & Schuster 2015 432 p. 24 plates; illustrations $28   **92**

1. Founding Fathers of the United States 2. Statesmen -- United States -- Biography 3. Presidents -- United States -- Biography 4. United States -- Politics and government -- 1775-1783 5. United States -- Politics and government -- 1783-1865 6. Friendship -- Political aspects -- United States -- History

ISBN 145168858X; 9781451688580

LC 2014021393

In this book, author David O. Stewart "examines [James Madison] from a fresh angle, looking at the ways in which Madison's associations with George Washington, Alexander Hamilton, Thomas Jefferson, James Monroe, and his wife, Dolley, helped create the United States. Stewart illuminates much about the history-making relationships among these celebrated figures." (Publisher's Weekly)

"The book is well-grounded in primary sources but relies on only a handful of secondary works and ignores much of the recent scholarship on the early republic and its political culture. A well-written and pleasurable read, but students of the era won't find anything new here. Summing Up:

Recommended. General and undergraduate readers; public libraries." Choice

Includes bibliographical references and index

Wills, Garry. **James** Madison. Times Bks. 2002 xx, 184p (American presidents series) $20   **92**

1. Presidents 2. Members of Congress 3. Secretaries of state 4. Presidents -- United States

ISBN 0-8050-6905-4

LC 2002-19692

The author "maintains that Madison possessed qualities that served him well early in his career but proved to be a handicap during his Presidency. . . . Written with flair, this clear and balanced account is based on a sure handling of the material." Libr J

Includes bibliographical references

Mahler, Gustav, 1860-1911

Lebrecht, Norman. **Why** Mahler? how one man and ten symphonies changed our world. Pantheon Books 2010 326p $27.95   **92**

1. Composers 2. Conductors (Music)

ISBN 978-0-375-42381-9; 0-375-42381-8

LC 2010-06034

"This is music history, criticism, and biography at its best. A treasure trove for Mahler fans, this is also likely to convert even the most obstinate detractor. Highly recommended for all music lovers." Libr J

Includes bibliographical references

Mailer, Norman, 1923-2007

Lennon, J. Michael. **Norman** Mailer; a double life. J. Michael Lennon. Simon & Schuster 2013 928 p. $40   **92**

1. American novelists 2. Journalists -- United States -- Biography 3. Authors, American -- 20th century -- Biography

ISBN 1439150192; 9781439150191

LC 2013005097

In this biography of Norman Mailer, author J. Michael Lennon depicts his subject "as a dual-natured personality: a passive observer and an activist, a family man and a philanderer,. . . . While Lennon treats readers to accounts of Mailer's celebrity and his relations with stars such as Muhammad Ali . . . he also explores the writer's seamier side, including his stabbing of Adele Morales, his second wife, and his support of Jack Abbott, who committed murder after being paroled." (Library Journal)

"Detailed and anecdotal without being gossipy . . . and a must-read for students and admirers of Mailer's work." Kirkus

Includes bibliographical references and index

Mailer, Norris Church. A **ticket** to the circus; a memoir. Random House 2010 416p il $26   **92**

1. Artists 2. Authors 3. Novelists 4. Essayists 5. Authors, American 6. Spouses of prominent persons

ISBN 978-1-4000-6794-7; 1-4000-6794-4

LC 2009-33941

This memoir by Norris Church Mailer focuses on her marriage of thirty-three years to Norman Mailer.

The author adds "a fat new sheaf to the public dossier on her late husband, Norman Mailer, and tells an involving coming-of-age story to boot. . . . The book will be of interest to anyone who works in a university marriage lab. It also shows that Norman wasn't the only talented raconteur in the family." N Y Times Book Rev

Mailer, Norris Church

Mailer, Norris Church. A **ticket** to the circus; a memoir. Random House 2010 416p il $26   **92**
1. Artists 2. Authors 3. Novelists 4. Essayists 5. Authors, American 6. Spouses of prominent persons
ISBN 978-1-4000-6794-7; 1-4000-6794-4
LC 2009-33941

This memoir by Norris Church Mailer focuses on her marriage of thirty-three years to Norman Mailer.

The author adds "a fat new sheaf to the public dossier on her late husband, Norman Mailer, and tells an involving coming-of-age story to boot. . . . The book will be of interest to anyone who works in a university marriage lab. It also shows that Norman wasn't the only talented raconteur in the family." N Y Times Book Rev

Mainardi, Diogo

Mainardi, Diogo. The **fall**; a father's memoir in 424 steps. by Diogo Mainardi; translated from the Portuguese by Margaret Jull Costa. Other Press 2014 176 p. illustrations (hardback) $20   **92**
1. Cerebral palsy 2. Father-son relationship 3. Fathers and sons -- Biography 4. Paralysis, Spastic, in children -- Biography
ISBN 1590517008; 9781590517000; 9781590517017
LC 2014005571

This memoir by Diogo Mainardi is "424 short passages [that] match the number of steps taken by [his] son Tito as he walks, with great difficulty, alongside his father through the streets of Venice, the city where a medical mishap during Tito's birth left him with Cerebral Palsy. Mainairdi begins to draw on his knowledge of art and history, seeking to better explain a tragedy that was entirely avoidable." (Publisher's note)

"Tito emerges as collaborator in the book—not as a cause or a type or a symbol but as a happy, well-adjusted, well-loved individual with a life well worth living. A singularly compelling memoir." Kirkus

Majorana, Ettore

Magueijo, Joao. A **brilliant** darkness; the extraordinary life and disappearance of Ettore Majorana, the troubled genius of the nuclear age. Basic Books 2009 280p il $27.50   **92**
1. Physicists 2. Nuclear physics
ISBN 978-0-465-00903-9; 0-465-00903-4
LC 2009-37678

The author "paints the life of a twenty something math prodigy who joined Enrico Fermi, Emilio Segre, and the other 'Via Panisperna Boys' who in 1934 discovered nuclear fusion. The author could have easily fallen into the jargon of his profession to describe the work of a fellow scientist, but he does not. His clear explanation of Majorana's insight

into nuclear physics, often accompanied with drawings and illustrations, will appeal to a wide audience." Libr J
Includes bibliographical references

Malamud, Bernard, 1914-1986

Smith, Janna Malamud. **My** father is a book; a memoir of Bernard Malamud. Houghton Mifflin 2006 292p $24   **92**
1. Authors 2. Novelists 3. Short story writers 4. Biography, Individual
ISBN 0-618-69166-9; 978-0-618-69166-1
LC 2005-24736

"On the twentieth anniversary of Bernard Malamud's death, Janna Malamud Smith explores her father's private, unpublished letters and journals to remember the life of [the writer]." (Publisher's note)

"Analytical without being acrimonious, honest without wallowing in self-preening exposure, this is a wise, generous book full of insights on what it's like to be a writer and to be a writer's daughter." Christ Sci Monit
Includes bibliographical references

Malcolm X, 1925-1965

Carson, Clayborne. **Malcolm** X: the FBI file; introduction by Spike Lee; edited by David Gallen. Carroll & Graf Pubs. 1991 514p il hardcover o.p. pa $13.95   **92**
1. Black Muslim leaders 2. Civil rights activists 3. United States -- Federal Bureau of Investigation
ISBN 0-88184-758-5 pa
LC 91-26697

"This is a collection of declassified documents from the FBI surveillance of the orator and religious (later political) leader that, with historian Carson's studious commentary, focuses less on Malcolm's relation to the FBI and more on that to the larger civil rights movement. These excerpts . . . follow his travels and speeches, media interviews and FBI interviews, oftentimes including transcripts as written or summarized by Gallen and Carson." Booklist

★ Malcolm X. The **autobiography** of Malcolm X; with the assistance of Alex Haley; introduction by M. S. Handler; epilogue by Alex Haley; afterword by Ossie Davis. Ballantine Bks. 1992 500p $25; pa $15   **92**
1. Black Muslims 2. Black Muslim leaders 3. Civil rights activists 4. African Americans -- Biography
ISBN 0-345-37975-6; 0-345-37671-4 pa
LC 92-52659

First published 1965 by Grove Press

Based on tape-recorded conversations with Alex Haley, this account of the life of the Black Muslim leader was completed shortly before his murder

Alex Haley "did his job with sensitivity and with devotion. . . . {The book} will have a permanent place in the literature of the Afro-American struggle." N Y Rev Books

★ Marable, Manning. **Malcolm** X; a life of reinvention. Manning Marable. Viking 2011 594 p., [16] p. of platesp ill. $30   **92**
1. Black Muslims 2. Black Muslim leaders 3. Civil

rights activists 4. African Americans -- Biography 5. African Americans -- Civil rights

ISBN 978-0-670-02220-5; 0-670-02220-9

LC 2010025768

Pulitzer Prize: History (2012)

This "biography of Malcolm X draws on new research to trace his life from his troubled youth through his involvement in the Nation of Islam, his activism in the world of Black Nationalism, and his assassination." (Publisher's note) Glossary. Bibliography. Index.

This is an "account of the 'lives' of Malcolm X (1925-65), including his years as a street hustler in Boston and Harlem, his time in prison where voracious reading led to his transformation into the devout follower of Elijah Muhammad's Nation of Islam (NOI), his rise as the NOI's chief minister, and, finally, his split from Elijah Muhammad and his acceptance of all people who would work for African American human and economic rights." Libr J

Perry, Bruce. **Malcolm**; the life of a man who changed black America. Station Hill Press 1991 542p il hardcover o.p. pa $14.95   **92**
  1. Black Muslim leaders 2. Civil rights activists

ISBN 0-88268-121-4 pa

LC 90-23350

"Perry traces Malcolm X's footsteps from birth in 1925 to death in 1965, using several hundred interviews to fill in detail and correct the autobiography Alex Haley edited. Probing what he labels as the deep-seated and hidden causes that made Malcolm who and what he was, Perry produces a portrait of an emotionally abused and abandoned boy who grew to manipulate his fearful helplessness into emotional and political power." Libr J

Includes bibliographical references

★ Smith, Johnny. **Blood** brothers; the fatal friendship of Muhammad Ali and Malcolm X. Randy Roberts and Johnny Smith. Basic Books 2016 392 p. illustrations (hardcover : alk. paper) $28.99   **92**
  1. African Americans -- Biography 2. Black Muslims -- Biography

ISBN 9780465079704

LC 2015043982

In this book, historians Randy Roberts and Johnny Smith "reveal how Malcolm [X] molded Cassius Clay into Muhammad Ali, helping him become an international symbol of black pride and black independence. . . . Malcolm's death marked the end of a critical phase of the civil rights movement, but the legacy of his friendship with Ali has endured. We inhabit a new era where the roles of entertainer and activist, of sports and politics, are more entwined than ever before." (Publisher's note)

"A page-turning tale from the 1960s about politics and sports and two proud, extraordinary men whose legacies endure." Kirkus

Includes bibliographical references and index

Mandela, Nelson

Jones, Barbara. **Mandela**; My Prisoner, My Friend. Christo Brand, with Barbara Jones. Thomas

Dunne Books/St. Martin's Press 2014 288 p. 16 plates; ills; portraits $26.99   **92**
  1. Political prisoners 2. African National Congress -- Biography 3. Robben Island (South Africa) -- Anecdotes 4. South Africa -- Race relations -- Anecdotes 5. Pollsmoor Prison (South Africa) -- Anecdotes 6. Political prisoners -- South Africa -- Biography 7. Correctional personnel -- South Africa -- Biography 8. South Africa -- Politics and government -- Anecdotes

ISBN 1250055261; 9781250055262

LC 2014026586

In this book by Christo Brand and Barbara Jones, Nelson Mandela's "life's sacrifices [are] recounted in vivid detail by the prison guard with whom he became lifelong friends. For 12 years Brand watched Mandela scrub floors, empty his toilet bucket, grieve over the deaths of family and friends yet remain as strong as any freedom fighter in history. Won over by Madiba's charm and authentic concern for the well-being of others, Brand became Mandela's confidant and at times accomplice." (Publisher's note)

"The author quickly recounts Mandela's general biography, including the Rivonia trial for sabotage that landed him in prison, but this is really a tale of two men and their shared humanity in an inhumane place. A worthy addition to the canon of Mandela literature that details a relationship that many knew about but few truly understood." Kirkus

Mandela, Nelson. **Long** walk to freedom: the autobiography of Nelson Mandela. Little, Brown 1994 558p il hardcover o.p. pa $16.95   **92**
  1. Presidents 2. Political prisoners 3. Political leaders 4. Human rights activists 5. Nobel laureates for peace 6. South Africa -- Race relations 7. South Africa -- Politics and government

ISBN 0-316-54818-9 pa

LC 94-79980

This book "provides important new evidence to the forty-year story of apartheid, as seen by its most formidable opponent. And there is enough candour to provide insights into the nature of leadership." Times Lit Suppl

Mandela, Nelson, 1918-2013. **Conversations** with myself. Farrar Straus & Giroux 2010 454p il map $28   **92**
  1. Presidents 2. Political prisoners 3. Political leaders 4. Biography, Individual 5. Human rights activists 6. Apartheid -- South Africa 7. Nobel laureates for peace 8. Presidents -- South Africa 9. South Africa -- Race relations 10. South Africa -- Politics and government 11. South Africa -- Politics and government -- 20th century

ISBN 978-0-374-12895-1; 0-374-12895-2

LC 2010-933174

This "is a moving account of Mandela's struggle and a testament to his triumph." Publ Wkly

Includes bibliographical references

Mandela, Nelson, 1918-2013. **In** his own words; edited by Kader Asmal, David Chidester, [and] Wilmot James. Little, Brown 2003 558p il $28.95   **92**
  1. Presidents 2. Political prisoners 3. Political leaders 4. Human rights activists 5. Nobel laureates for peace

6. South Africa -- Race relations 7. South Africa -- Politics and government
ISBN 0-316-11019-1

LC 2004-107807

"This collection of Mandela's speeches shows why he remains a universal hero. . . . This volume will be in great demand for the personal drama, the history, and, yes, for the inspiring moral values." Booklist

Sampson, Anthony. **Nelson** Mandela; the authorized biography. Knopf 1999 xxvi, 672p hardcover o.p. pa $19   **92**
1. Presidents 2. Political prisoners 3. Political leaders 4. Human rights activists 5. Nobel laureates for peace 6. South Africa -- Race relations 7. South Africa -- Politics and government
ISBN 0-679-78178-1 pa

LC 99-18498

"While not neglecting the personality of the man, Mr. Sampson has concentrated on the politics, and, for an authorised life, it can be treated as definitive." Economist
Includes bibliographical references

Smith, David James. **Young** Mandela. Little, Brown 2010 405p il   **92**
1. Apartheid 2. Presidents 3. Political prisoners 4. Anti-apartheid movement 5. Political leaders 6. Biography, Individual 7. Human rights activists 8. African National Congress 9. Nobel laureates for peace 10. South Africa -- Politics and government
ISBN 0-316-03548-3; 978-0-316-03548-4

LC 2010-31883

This is an account of Mandela's life from boyhood through the early 1960s. Bibliography. Index.
"No hagiography, Smith's measured study qualifies, lends nuance to, and even contradicts the mythology around Mandela's background and formative influences." Publ Wkly
Includes bibliographical references

Manet, Édouard, 1832-1883

Brombert, Beth Archer. **Edouard** Manet; rebel in a frock coat. University of Chicago Press 1997 505p il pa $19.95   **92**
1. Artists 2. Painters 3. Artists, French
ISBN 0-226-07544-3; 978-0-226-07544-0

LC 97-3321

First published 1996 by Little, Brown
"To recount Manet's life, as Brombert has done in this elegant biography, is to tell the story of an enormously influential artist struggling to paint what he called 'the spirit of contemporaneity' while remaining committed to the conservative institutions of civil life—the very same institutions that shunned him." New Yorker
Includes bibliographical references

Mankiller, Wilma

Mankiller, Wilma. **Mankiller**: a chief and her people; {by} Wilma Mankiller and Michael Wallis.

St. Martin's Press 1993 xxiv, 292p il hardcover o.p. pa $14.95   **92**
1. Cherokee Indians 2. Indian chiefs
ISBN 0-312-20662-3 pa

LC 93-25698

"A must-read for everyone interested in, specifically, the history of Native Americans and women and, in general, tales of exceptional people." Booklist

Mankoff, Bob

Mankoff, Bob. **How** about never--is never good for you? my life in cartoons. Bob Mankoff. Henry Holt & Co. 2014 304 p. illustrations (hardback) $32.50   **92**
1. Illustrators 2. Cartoons and caricatures 3. New Yorker (New York, N.Y. : 1925) 4. Cartoonists -- United States -- Biography 5. Periodical editors -- United States -- Biography
ISBN 080509590X; 9780805095906

LC 2013021129

In this memoir, cartoonist and editor Bob Mankoff "allows us into the hallowed halls of 'The New Yorker' to show us the soup-to-nuts process of cartoon creation, giving us a detailed look not only at his own work, but that of the other talented cartoonists who keep us laughing week after week. For desert, he reveals the secrets to winning the magazine's caption contest." (Publisher's note)
"... How About Never serves up not only a mini-collection of great cartoons but also as a look at the shift in styles through the editorships of legendary William Shawn, Tina Brown, and current editor David Remnick. Mankoff also provides a very funny and insightful look at how to win the New Yorker cartoon caption contest."

Mann, Sally, 1951-

★ Mann, Sally, 1951- **Hold** Still; A Memoir With Photographs. by Sally Mann. Little, Brown & Co. 2015 496 p. illustrations (some color) $32 **92**
1. Genealogy 2. Southern States
ISBN 0316247766; 9780316247764

LC 2014959584

National Book Award Finalist: Nonfiction (2015)
Carnegie Medal: Nonfiction (2016)
This book, by Sally Mann, is a "revealing . . . memoir and family history. . . . Mann's preoccupation with family, race, mortality, and the storied landscape of the American South are revealed as almost genetically predetermined, written into her DNA by the family history that precedes her. Sorting through boxes of family papers and yellowed photographs she finds more than she bargained for." (Publisher's note)
"Here photographer Mann chronicles her rich and eccentric family history, told through the exploration of old documents and images stored away in her attic. . . . Raw and darkly humorous, Mann's writing is consistently honest and poignant as she depicts her beloved Virginia farm, her childhood, her parents, and her children." LJ
Includes bibliographical references (page 478)

Mann, Thomas, 1875-1955

Kurzke, Hermann. **Thomas** Mann; life as a work of art: a biography. translated by Leslie Willson. Princeton Univ. Press 2002 581p il $35   **92**

1. Authors 2. Novelists 3. Essayists 4. Short story writers 5. Nobel laureates for literature
ISBN 0-691-07069-5

LC 2002-23665

"A major achievement in literary biography." Booklist

Manning, Peyton

Myers, Gary. **Brady** vs Manning; the untold story of the rivalry that transformed the NFL. Gary Myers. Crown Archtype 2015 264 p. 8 unnumbered pages of plates (hbk.) $26   **92**

1. National Football League 2. Sports rivalries -- United States 3. Football -- United States -- History 4. Football players -- United States -- Biography 5. Quarterbacks (Football) -- United States -- Biography
ISBN 0804139377; 9780804139373

LC 2015027579

Author Gary Meyer presents this "inside account of the greatest rivalry in NFL history. Myers tackles this subject from every angle and with unprecedented access and insight, drawing on a huge number of never-before-heard interviews with [Tom] Brady and [Peyton] Manning, their coaches, their families, and those who have played with them and against them." (Publisher's note)

"Myers is a thorough professional with impeccable contacts to successfully tell this account, which will be of interest to all football fans." Library Journal

Includes bibliographical references and index

Mansfield, William Murray, Earl of, 1705-1793

Byrne, Paula. **Belle**; the slave daughter and the Lord Chief Justice. Paula Byrne. Harper Perennial 2014 304 p. illustrations (paperback) $14.99   **92**

1. Racially mixed people 2. Great Britain -- Race relations 3. Great Britain -- History -- 18th century 4. Slaves -- England -- Biography 5. Nobility -- England -- Biography
ISBN 0062310771; 9780062310774

LC 2014007447

"From . . . biographer Paula Byrne, the . . . tale that inspired the major motion picture 'Belle' (May 2014) starring Tom Wilkinson, Miranda Richardson, Emily Watson, Penelope Wilton, and Matthew Goode--a stunning story of the first mixed-race girl introduced to high society England and raised as a lady. . . . Growing up in his lavish estate, Dido was raised as a sister and companion to her white cousin, Elizabeth." (Publisher's note)

"Byrne brings to this brief history an eye for telling details of daily life, slaveholders' unthinkable cruelty, and the fervent work of a few good men and women who changed their world." Kirkus

Includes bibliographical references

Mantle, Mickey, 1931-1995

★ Leavy, Jane. The **last** boy; Mickey Mantle and the end of America's childhood. HarperCollins Publishers 2010 456p il $27.99   **92**

1. Baseball players 2. Baseball -- History 3. Baseball -- Biography 4. Biography, Individual 5. New York Yankees (Baseball team)
ISBN 978-0-06-088352-2; 0-06-088352-9

This is a biography of the New York Yankees center fielder. Bibliography. Index.

"This is unlike any biography on the sports shelf. Leavy, in exploring her own ambivalent feelings toward Mantle, permits readers to experience the same confusing emotions that many of those around him felt: proud to bask in his reflected glory but too intimidated to confront him. . . . A masterpiece of sports biography." Booklist

Mao Zedong, 1893-1976

Chang, Jung. **Mao**: the unknown story; [by] Jung Chang, Jon Halliday. Knopf 2005 814p il $35   **92**

1. Heads of state 2. Communist leaders 3. Political leaders 4. China -- Politics and government
ISBN 0-679-42271-4

LC 2004-63826

"This is a magisterial work. . . . This biography supplies substantial . . . information and presents it all in a stylish way that will put it on bedside tables around the world." N Y Times Book Rev

Includes bibliographical references

Mapplethorpe, Robert

★ Smith, Patti, 1946- **Just** kids. Ecco 2010 278p il $27; pa $16   **92**

1. Rock musicians 2. Poets, American 3. Biography, Individual
ISBN 978-0-06-621131-2; 0-06-621131-X; 978-0-06-093622-8 pa; 0-06-093622-3 pa

The author writes about her relationship with the photographer Robert Mapplethorpe in the late 1960s and 1970s.

This "is one of the best books ever written on becoming an artist—not the race for online celebrity and corporate sponsorship that often passes for artistic success these days, but the far more powerful, often difficult journey toward the ecstatic experience of capturing radiance of imagination on a page or stage or photographic paper." Washington Post

Maraniss, David

Maraniss, David. **Into** the story; a writer's journey through life, politics, sports and loss. Simon & Schuster 2010 283p il $26   **92**

1. Journalists 2. Biographers
ISBN 978-1-4391-6002-2; 1-4391-6002-3

LC 2009-42338

"In this collection of previously published articles and excerpts from his books, . . . [the author] ranges over topics from the death of his sister and the deaths of strangers on September 11 to the political fortunes of Barack Obama, Bill Clinton, and Al Gore and the timeless contributions to sports of legendary figures like Vince Lombardi, Muhammad Ali, and Roberto Clemente. . . . Maraniss's lively sketches illuminate the lives of significant cultural and political figures and intimately capture various moments that define modern American cultural history." Publ Wkly

Maravich, Pete, 1947-1988

★ Kriegel, Mark. **Pistol**; the life of Pete Maravich. Free Press 2007 381p il $27; pa $15   **92**

1. Basketball players

ISBN 978-0-7432-8497-4; 0-7432-8497-6; 978-0-7432-8498-1 pa; 0-7432-8498-4 pa

LC 2006-51526

This is a biography of the basketball player who played at Louisiana State University before joining the N.B.A.

The author "skillfully pulls off the balancing act required of good sports biography. It plays large historical forces (segregation, the rise of televised sports) against the individual magic of its subject." New York

Includes bibliographical references

Marconi, Guglielmo, 1874-1937

Raboy, Marc. **Marconi**; The Man Who Networked the World. Marc Raboy. Oxford University Press 2016 872 p. illustrations, map $39.95   **92**

1. Inventors -- Biography 2. Telecommunication -- History 3. Radio -- Italy -- History 4. Telegraph, Wireless -- History 5. Inventors -- Italy -- Biography 6. Telegraph, Wireless -- Marconi system 7. Electrical engineers -- Italy -- Biography

ISBN 9780199313587

LC 2015042075

This biography of Guglielmo Marconi by Marc Raboy narrates how "Marconi popularized-and, more critically, patented-the use of radio waves. . . . [After] a demonstration of his wireless apparatus in London at the age of 22 in 1896, he established his Wireless Telegraph & Signal Company and seemed unstoppable. He was decorated by the Czar of Russia, named an Italian Senator, knighted by King George V of England, and awarded the Nobel Prize for Physics-all before the age of 40." (Publisher's note)

"A comprehensive portrait of a complicated man, Raboy's meticulous, judicious work merits anchorage on science-history shelves." Booklist

Includes bibliographical references and index

Margery, 1888-1941

Jaher, David. The **witch** of Lime Street; séance, seduction, and Houdini in the spirit world. David Jaher. Crown Publishers 2015 448 p. illustrations (alk. paper) $28   **92**

1. Spiritualism 2. Spiritualists -- United States -- Biography 3. Women mediums -- United States -- Biography 4. Spiritualism -- United States -- History -- 20th century

ISBN 0307451062; 9780307451064

LC 2015009392

In this book, by David Jaher, "in 1924, the pretty wife of a distinguished Boston surgeon came to embody the raging national debate over Spiritualism. . . . Reporters dubbed her the blonde Witch of Lime Street, but she was known to her followers simply as Margery. . . . Margery was the best hope for the psychic practice to be empirically verified. Her supernatural gifts beguiled four of the judges. There was only one left to convince...the acclaimed escape artist, Harry Houdini." (Publisher's note)

"Through a combination of feminine seduction and illusionist skill that even Houdini admired, Crandon became the one psychic to almost win the respect of the scientific community and outshine Houdini as an entertainer. Jaher's narrative style is as engaging as his character portraits are colorful. Together, they bring a bygone age and its defining spiritual obsessions roaring to life. Fascinating, sometimes thrilling, reading." Kirkus

Includes bibliographical references and index

Maria Celeste, 1600-1634

Sobel, Dava. **Galileo's** daughter; a historical memoir of science, faith, and love. Walker & Co. 1999 420p $27   **92**

1. Nuns 2. Astronomers 3. Writers on science 4. Children of prominent persons

ISBN 0-8027-1343-2

LC 99-23885

"Sobel has a remarkable ability to explain technical subjects without being simplistic or pedantic. There is a tremendous amount of fascinating detail in this work, and yet it reads as smoothly and compellingly as fiction." Libr J

Includes bibliographical references

Marie Antoinette, Queen, consort of Louis XVI, King of France, 1755-1793

Lever, Evelyne. **Marie** Antoinette; the last queen of France. translated from the French by Catherine Temerson. Farrar, Straus & Giroux 2000 357p il hardcover o.p. pa $16.95   **92**

1. Queens 2. France -- History -- 1589-1789, Bourbons

ISBN 0-312-28333-4 pa

LC 00-28763

The author examines "the opulent Versailles subculture and the queen whose royal excesses served as a major catalyst for the revolutionary upheaval of 1789. Through the skillful use of memoirs and other primary documents, Lever creates an empathic picture of Louis XVI's headstrong wife." Libr J

Includes bibliographical references

Marion, Robert

Marion, Robert. **Genetic** rounds; a doctor's encounters in the field that has revolutionized medicine. Kaplan Pub. 2009 275p $24.95   **92**

1. Physicians 2. Medical genetics 3. Pediatricians

ISBN 978-1-60714-460-1

LC 2009-19110

This is "a straightforward, and often poignant, collection of true stories. Particularly compelling are several stories that describe the pain and pathos of life for some individuals with genetic disorders." Am J Human Genetics

Maris, Roger, 1934-1985

Clavin, Thomas. **Roger** Maris; baseball's reluctant hero. [by] Tom Clavin and Danny Peary. Simon & Schuster 2010 422p il $26.99   **92**

1. Baseball players 2. Baseball -- Biography 3. New York Yankees (Baseball team)

ISBN 978-1-4165-8928-0; 1-4165-8928-7

LC 2009-39722

The authors "trace the dramatic arc of Maris's life, from his boyhood in Fargo through his early pro career in the

Cleveland Indians farm program, to his World Series championship years in New York and beyond. At the center is the exciting story of the 1961 season and the ordeal Maris endured as an outsider in Yankee pinstripes, unloved by fans who compared him unfavorably to their heroes Ruth and Mantle, relentlessly attacked by an aggressive press corps who found him cold and inaccessible, and treated miserably by the organization." Publisher's note

Includes bibliographical references

Markham, Beryl, 1902-1986

West with the night; Beryl Markham; illustrated by Alan Phillips. Easton Press 1989 261 p. illustrations $16   **92**

1. Autobiographies 2. Women air pilots 3. Women air pilots -- Africa -- Biography 4. Women air pilots -- Great Britain -- Biography

ISBN 0865477639; 9780865477636

LC 91228442

In this memoir, author Beryl Markham discusses how "she and her father moved to Kenya when she was a girl, and she grew up with a zebra for a pet; horses for friends; baboons, lions, and gazelles for neighbors. She made money by scouting elephants from a tiny plane. And she would spend most of the rest of her life in East Africa as an adventurer, a racehorse trainer, and an aviatrix--she became the first person to fly nonstop from Europe to America." (Publisher's note)

Marlowe, Christopher, 1564-1593

★ Honan, Park. **Christopher** Marlowe; poet & spy. Oxford University Press 2005 421p il $32.50   **92**

1. Authors 2. Dramatists 3. Dramatists, English 4. Great Britain -- History -- 1485-1603, Tudors

ISBN 0-19-818695-9

LC 2005-19761

This is a biography of the sixteenth-century English dramatist.

The author "sheds light on the much-speculated (and previously erroneously reported) aspects of Marlowe's life without neglecting its more ordinary features (his stable two-parent upbringing, his diligent scholarship at Cambridge) or destroying the poet's aura of intrigue." Publ Wkly

Includes bibliographical references

Nicholl, Charles. The **reckoning**; the murder of Christopher Marlowe. University of Chicago Press 1995 413p il pa $33   **92**

1. Authors 2. Dramatists 3. Dramatists, English 4. Great Britain -- History -- 1485-1603, Tudors

ISBN 0-226-58024-5; 978-0-226-58024-1

First published 1992 in the United Kingdom

The author argues that the Elizabethan playwright, who is believed to have been stabbed in a dispute over the bill ('recknynge') at Eleanor Bull's victualling house in 1593, was in fact murdered with government complicity as part of a plot against Sir Walter Raleigh.

"A remarkable piece of scholarship, this work carefully reconstructs the events leading up to the murder with all the excitement and suspense of a modern mystery novel; at the same time it vividly conveys the energy and color of Elizabethan England." Libr J

Includes bibliographical references

Marsh, Henry, 1954-

Do No Harm; Stories of Life, Death and Brain Surgery. Henry Marsh. St. Martin's Press 2015 304 p. $25.99   **92**

1. Surgeons 2. Brain -- Surgery

ISBN 125006581X; 9781250065810

LC 2015002573

This book by Henry Marsh "provides unforgettable insight into the countless human dramas that take place in a busy modern hospital. Above all, it is a lesson in the need for hope when faced with life's most difficult decisions. Marsh reveals the fierce joy of operating, the profoundly moving triumphs, the harrowing disasters, the haunting regrets, and the moments of black humor that characterize a brain surgeon's life." (Publisher's note)

"One of the best books ever about a life in medicine, Do No Harm boldly and gracefully exposes the vulnerability and painful privilege of being a physician." Booklist

Marshal, William

Asbridge, Thomas. The **Greatest** Knight; the remarkable life of William Marshal, the power behind five English thrones. Thomas Asbridge. HarperCollins 2014 256 p. illustrations (color), maps $27.99   **92**

1. Knights and knighthood

ISBN 006226205X; 9780062262059

LC 2015431306

This book, by Thomas Asbridge, presents a "portrait of one of history's most illustrious knights--William Marshal. . . . Historian Thomas Asbridge draws upon the thirteenth-century biography and an array of other contemporary evidence to present a compelling account of William Marshal's life and times. Asbridge follows Marshal on his journey from rural England onto the battlefields of France, to the desert castles of the Holy Land and the verdant shores of Ireland." (Publisher's note)

"Matters did not improve after Henry's death, so Marshal's career comes across as a relentless series of intrigues, battles, atrocities, truces quickly broken, internal revolts and treason that often included Marshal for reasons the author must guess because historical evidence is lacking. A valuable biography of an important figure in a distant, violent, barely comprehensible era." Kirkus

Marshall, Dan

Marshall, Dan. **Home** is burning; a memoir. Dan Marshall. Flatiron Books 2015 320 p. (hardback) $27.99   **92**

1. Family life 2. Children of cancer patients 3. Fathers and sons -- United States 4. Mothers and sons -- United States 5. Fathers and daughters -- United States 6. Mothers and daughters -- United States 7. Cancer -- Patients -- Family relationships 8. Cancer -- Patients -- United States -- Biography

ISBN 9781250068828

LC 2015022200

This memoir, by Dan Marshall, named best book of the year for 2015 by "Entertainment Weekly," follows "Dan Marshall. 25, good job, great girlfriend, and living the dream life in sunny Los Angeles without a care in the world. Until his mother calls. . . . It turns out his mom's cancer . . . is back. And to add insult to injury, his loving father has been diagnosed with ALS. Sayonara L.A., Dan is headed home to Salt Lake City, Utah." (Publisher's note)

"Home Is Burning packs a wallop. Marshall doesn't hold back in his descriptions of how a horrific illness wreaks havoc on his dad's body, and he takes an unflinching look at how real families fall apart—and pull together—in their own ways."

Marshall, John, 1755-1835

Unger, Harlow Giles. **John** Marshall; the chief justice who saved the nation. Harlow Giles Unger. Da Capo Press 2014 384 p. illustrations (hardback) $27.99   **92**

1. Judges -- Biography 2. Judges -- United States -- Biography 3. United States. Supreme Court -- Biography

ISBN 0306822202; 9780306822209; 9780306822216
    LC 2014008405

This biography, by Harlow Giles Unger, "reveals how Virginia-born John Marshall emerged from the Revolutionary War's bloodiest battlefields to become one of the nation's most important Founding Fathers: America's greatest Chief Justice. Marshall served his country as an officer, Congressman, diplomat, and Secretary of State before President John Adams named him the nation's fourth Chief Justice, the longest-serving in American history." (Publisher's note)

"Roughly half of the book covers Marshall's earlier career as a soldier and politician as well as his family life. But Unger is at his best covering the history-altering judicial activities of the court under Marshall, especially as the court clashed with the executive power of the Jefferson and Jackson administration. Unger's admiration for Marshall sometimes leads him to unfairly demean his opponents, especially Jefferson. Still, this is a well-done tribute to the man who made the judiciary a truly coequal branch of the national government." Booklist

Includes bibliographical references and index

Marshall, George C. (George Catlett), 1880-1959

Unger, Irwin. **George** Marshall; a biography. by Debi Unger and Irwin Unger, with Stanley Hirshson. Harper 2014 552 p. ill. (hbk.) $35   **92**

1. World War, 1939-1945 -- United States 2. United States -- Politics and government -- 20th century 3. United States. Army -- Biography 4. Generals -- United States -- Biography 5. Statesmen -- United States -- Biography 6. Cabinet officers -- United States -- Biography 7. United States. Department of State -- Officials and employees -- Biography

ISBN 0060577193; 9780060577193
    LC 2015413285

This book, by Debi Unger and Irwin Unger, is a "major historical biography of George C. Marshall-- the general who ran the U.S. campaign during the Second World War, the Secretary of State who oversaw the successful rebuilding of post-war Europe, and the winner of the Nobel Peace

Prize. . . . [It] follows his life from his childhood in Western Pennsylvania and his military training at the Virginia Military Institute to his role during and after World War II and his death in 1959." (Publisher's note)

"The authors praise him [Marshall] for his management of the vast military expansion and his ability to cope with the difficulties inherent in controlling a giant military coalition. His decisions regarding the implementation of D-Day and the planned invasion of Japan are justifiably questioned, as are his choices as the Cold War commenced. This is an excellent reexamination of Marshall's career that is ideal for general readers." Booklist

Includes bibliographical references (pages 519-526) and index

Marshall, Paule, 1929-

Marshall, Paule. **Triangular** road; a memoir. BasicCivitas Books 2009 165p il $23   **92**

1. Poets 2. Authors 3. Novelists 4. Dramatists 5. African American authors 6. Essayists 7. Short story writers 8. Young adult authors 9. African Americans -- Intellectual life

ISBN 978-0-465-01359-3
    LC 2008-36671

This is a memoir by the author of Praisesong for the widow (1983).

"Though fiction may have pride of place in . . . [the author's] heart, 'Triangular Road' reveals a strong gift for self-scrutiny made all the more revealing by quiet humor and what appears to be complete honesty." Washington Post

Marshall, Thurgood, 1908-1993

Rowan, Carl Thomas. **Dream** makers, dream breakers; the world of Justice Thurgood Marshall. [by] Carl T. Rowan. Welcome Rain 2002 475p il pa $18.95   **92**

1. Judges 2. Lawyers 3. Solicitors general 4. Civil rights activists 5. Supreme Court justices 6. United States -- Supreme Court 7. National Association for the Advancement of Colored People

ISBN 978-1-56649-235-5; 1-56649-235-1

First published 1993 by Little, Brown

The author "offers a no-holds barred account of one of the most influential and controversial figures in American law and jurisprudence of this century. His work brings to life Marshall, the Surpreme Court, U.S. law and modern America itself. Particularly effective is Rowan's account of the innovative legal arguments Marshall and his colleagues employed to win the now-famous Brown v. Board of Education case of 1954." Libr J

Includes bibliographical references

Williams, Juan. **Thurgood** Marshall; American revolutionary. Times Bks. 1998 459p il hardcover o.p. pa $16   **92**

1. Lawyers 2. Solicitors general 3. Civil rights activists 4. Supreme Court justices 5. African Americans -- Biography 6. United States -- Supreme Court 7. African Americans -- Civil rights

ISBN 0-8129-3299-4 pa
    LC 98-9735

"Williams presents Marshall as a revolutionary 'of grand vision,' but this well-rounded portrait of the man also addresses his vanities and warts, from his ascension to his deflation and subsequent redemption. This is a must read for all Americans concerned with the struggle for civil and individual rights." Booklist

Includes bibliographical references

Martin, Billy, 1928-1989

Pennington, Bill. **Billy** Martin; baseball's flawed genius. Bill Pennington. Houghton Mifflin Harcourt 2015 604 p. illustratioins (hardback) $30   **92**
1. Baseball -- Coaching 2. New York Yankees (Baseball team) 3. New York Yankees (Baseball team) -- History 4. Baseball players -- New York (State) -- New York -- Biography 5. Baseball managers -- New York (State) -- New York -- Biography
ISBN 0544022092; 9780544022096; 9780544022942
                                                LC 2014039677

Author Bill Pennignton presents this biography of former New York Yankees baseball player and manager Billy Martin. "Drawing on exhaustive interviews with friends, family, teammates, and countless adversaries, Pennington paints an indelible portrait of a man who never backed down for the game he loved. From his shantytown upbringing in a broken home; to his days playing for the Yankees when he almost always helped his team find a way to win; through sixteen years of managing" (Publisher's note)

"Pennington analyzes the ongoing conflict that was Billy Martin—including his relationships with equally complex individuals such as George Steinbrenner and Reggie Jackson—from all sides (Billy's varied career is covered chronologically, but it's the Yankee years, however sporadic, that matter) and with balance and impressive depth. He thus provides what is likely to be the definitive profile, which, as such, belongs in most library sports collections, especially those where Yankee fans cluster." Booklist

Martin, Dean

Lewis, Jerry. **Dean** & me; a love story. Doubleday 2005 340p il $26.95   **92**
1. Actors 2. Singers 3. Comedians 4. Television personalities 5. Motion picture directors
ISBN 0-7679-2086-4
                                                LC 2005-49682
"This is a wild, joyous book, but also a heartbreaking one." N Y Times Book Rev

Martin, Luther, 1744-1826

Kauffman, Bill. **Forgotten** founder, drunken prophet; the life of Luther Martin. ISI Books 2008 202p $25   **92**
1. Lawyers 2. Members of Congress 3. Law enforcement officials 4. State government officials 5. United States -- Constitutional Convention (1787) 6. United States -- Politics and government -- 1783-1809
ISBN 978-1-933859-73-6; 1-933859-73-3
                                                LC 2008-928223
Kauffman "tells the story of Luther Martin, one of America's less-remembered founding fathers. A livid Anti-Federalist, Martin has gone down in the annals of 18th century America as little more than a footnote. He was accused

of being an absolute boor, drinking to excess, rambling in speech with incessant monotony, and having an altogether prickly disposition. Kauffman takes up the cross of giving Martin a fair shake, not by defending the man but just by telling his story. . . .. Never the explicit apologist, Kauffman delicately and humorously weaves a more complete portrait of Martin. Furthermore, Kauffman's writing is well-founded upon a towering bibliography that Kauffman adroitly parses." PopMatters

Includes bibliographical references

Martin, Mary, 1913-1990

Kaufman, David. **Some** enchanted evenings; The Glittering Life and Times of Mary Martin. David Kaufman. St. Martin's Press 2016 432 p. illustrations (hardcover) $29.99   **92**
1. Singers -- Biography 2. Singers -- United States -- Biography
ISBN 9781250031754; 9781250031761
                                                LC 2015047863

This biography, by David Kaufman, "is the delectable story of the one and only Mary Martin, a woman who described herself as a chicken farmer from Texas only to become Peter Pan and capture America's heart." (Publisher's note)

"A warm and well-researched... appreciation of one of the stage's most beloved performers and, on the evidence here, least interesting legends." Kirkus

Includes bibliographical references

Martin, Roger H., 1943-

Martin, Roger H. **Racing** Odysseus; a college president becomes a freshman again. University of California Press 2008 262p $24.95   **92**
1. Higher education 2. Biography, Individual 3. Education, Higher -- United States 4. St. John's College (Annapolis, Md.)
ISBN 978-0-520-25541-8; 0-520-25541-0
                                                LC 2007-51017

Martin "examines a number of experiences uncommon to 61-year-old college presidents. On a sabbatical after horrific treatments for cancer, he enrolled as a freshman at St. John's College in Maryland, studied classics, joined the crew team, prepared for a major race, and learned to connect with his 18-year-old classmates. He notes the follies of the students, as well as his own, and offers perceptive and affectionate insights into the challenges of growing up in today's complicated world. Education is his profession, and as he carefully observes the impact of the Great Books curriculum at St. John's, he sees the relevance of the Greek classics to our own time." Libr J

Includes bibliographical references

Martin, Sasha

Life from scratch; a memoir of food, family, and forgiveness. Sasha Martin. National Geographic 2015 336 p. (hardback) $25   **92**
1. Cooking 2. Family life 3. Cooks -- United States -- Biography 4. Cooks -- United States -- Family relationships
ISBN 1426213743; 9781426213748
                                                LC 2014033548

In this memoir, "food writer and blogger Sasha Martin set out to cook-- and eat-- a meal from every country in the world. As cooking unlocked the memories of her rough-and-tumble childhood and the loss and heartbreak that came with it, Martin became more determined than ever to find peace and elevate her life through the prism of food and world cultures." (Publisher's note)

"Along the way, Martin learned how to cope with ever-changing circumstances and to cook, even while her brother succumbed to tragically self-destructive behaviors. Martin peppers this memoir with recipes reflective of her life's circumstances of the moment, from stuffed artichokes to apple pie. Her assured prose endows this narrative of an atypical upbringing with both immediacy and poignancy."

Martin, Steve, 1945-

Martin, Steve. **Born** standing up; a comic's life. Scribner 2007 209p il $25   **92**

1. Actors 2. Comedians 3. Novelists 4. Dramatists 5. Memoirists 6. Screenwriters

ISBN 978-1-4165-5364-9; 1-4165-5364-9

LC 2007-27143

This is an autobiography by the comedian and author of Shopgirl (2000).

This book "does a sharp-witted job of breaking down the step-by-step process that brought [the author] from Disneyland, where he spent his version of a Dickensian childhood as a schoolboy employee, to both the pinnacle of stardom and the brink of disaster. . . . Even for readers already familiar with Mr. Martin's solemn side, [this] is a surprising book: smart, serious, heartfelt and confessional without being maudlin." N Y Times (Late NY Ed)

Marton, Endre, 1910-2005

Marton, Kati. **Enemies** of the people; my family's journey to America. Simon & Schuster 2009 272p il $26   **92**

1. Authors 2. Journalists 3. Political prisoners 4. Hungary -- History 5. Nonfiction writers

ISBN 978-1-4165-8612-8; 1-4165-8612-1

LC 2009-14480

"An American journalist trolls the archives of the Hungarian secret police (AVO) to piece together her parents' imprisonment in and flight from Hungary in the mid-1950s. . . . The author's probing work effectively renders an enormously unsettled, painful time of shifting allegiances and political treachery. . . . A dark, compelling narrative of secrecy and betrayal." Kirkus

Includes bibliographical references

Marton, Ilona, 1912-2004

Marton, Kati. **Enemies** of the people; my family's journey to America. Simon & Schuster 2009 272p il $26   **92**

1. Authors 2. Journalists 3. Political prisoners 4. Hungary -- History 5. Nonfiction writers

ISBN 978-1-4165-8612-8; 1-4165-8612-1

LC 2009-14480

"An American journalist trolls the archives of the Hungarian secret police (AVO) to piece together her parents' imprisonment in and flight from Hungary in the mid-1950s. . . . The author's probing work effectively renders an enormous-

ly unsettled, painful time of shifting allegiances and political treachery. . . . A dark, compelling narrative of secrecy and betrayal." Kirkus

Includes bibliographical references

Marton, Kati

Marton, Kati. **Enemies** of the people; my family's journey to America. Simon & Schuster 2009 272p il $26   **92**

1. Authors 2. Journalists 3. Political prisoners 4. Hungary -- History 5. Nonfiction writers

ISBN 978-1-4165-8612-8; 1-4165-8612-1

LC 2009-14480

"An American journalist trolls the archives of the Hungarian secret police (AVO) to piece together her parents' imprisonment in and flight from Hungary in the mid-1950s. . . . The author's probing work effectively renders an enormously unsettled, painful time of shifting allegiances and political treachery. . . . A dark, compelling narrative of secrecy and betrayal." Kirkus

Includes bibliographical references

Marx, Groucho, 1891-1977

Kanfer, Stefan. **Groucho**: the life and times of Julius Henry Marx. Knopf 2000 465p il hardcover o.p. pa $15   **92**

1. Comedians 2. Television personalities 3. Game show hosts

ISBN 0-375-70207-5 pa

LC 99-54002

"Plagued by nagging financial insecurities, partly realized literary ambitions, and difficult, unsatisfying relations with his wives, lovers, and daughters, Groucho was a 'depressive clown,' notes Kanter. . . . The book also details Groucho's ambivalent relations with his son, Arthur; his brothers; New Deal liberals; intellectuals and collaborators like S. J. Perelman; and his custodian, Erin Fleming." Libr J

Includes bibliographical references

Marx, Jenny

Gabriel, Mary. **Love** and capital; Karl and Jennie Marx and the birth of a revolution. Little, Brown and Company 2011 lviii, 707p il   **92**

1. Marxism 2. Writers on politics 3. Spouses of prominent persons 4. Political and social philosophers

ISBN 0-316-06611-7; 978-0-316-06611-2

LC 2010-44021

An "account of the lives of Karl Marx and his wife, Jenny von Westphalen. . . . Tracing their tumultuous lives from Prussia, via Paris to Brussels and finally London, Gabriel tells the story of a woman who forswore the comforts of her noble upbringing to raise a family in often very straitened circumstances with a man committed in both his life and letters to social justice and the emancipation of the working class. Equally at home with the details of Marxist theory and revolutionary Europe as she is with the private lives of Karl and Jenny, the author dazzles most with her fascinating accounts of the lives of the Marx children." Publ Wkly

Includes bibliographical references

Marx, Karl, 1818-1883

Gabriel, Mary. **Love** and capital; Karl and Jennie Marx and the birth of a revolution. Little, Brown and Company 2011 lviii, 707p il **92**

1. Marxism 2. Writers on politics 3. Spouses of prominent persons 4. Political and social philosophers
ISBN 0-316-06611-7; 978-0-316-06611-2
LC 2010-44021

An "account of the lives of Karl Marx and his wife, Jenny von Westphalen. . . . Tracing their tumultuous lives from Prussia, via Paris to Brussels and finally London, Gabriel tells the story of a woman who forswore the comforts of her noble upbringing to raise a family in often very straitened circumstances with a man committed in both his life and letters to social justice and the emancipation of the working class. Equally at home with the details of Marxist theory and revolutionary Europe as she is with the private lives of Karl and Jenny, the author dazzles most with her fascinating accounts of the lives of the Marx children." Publ Wkly

Includes bibliographical references

Sperber, Jonathan. **Karl** Marx; a nineteenth-century life. Jonathan Sperber. W W Norton & Co Inc 2013 512 p. (hardcover) $35 **92**

1. Communists -- Germany -- Biography 2. Philosophers -- Germany -- Biography
ISBN 0871404672; 9780871404671
LC 2012044951

This book by Jonathan Sperber is a biography of "Karl Marx, the German philosopher and political firebrand turned London émigré journalist. . . . Sperber demonstrates that Marx had more in common with Robespierre than with twentieth-century Communists. Using the complete Marx and Engels database . . . Sperber juxtaposes the private man against the public agitator who helped foment the 1848-49 Revolution and whose incendiary books inflamed the dissident world of Europe." (Publisher's note)

Includes bibliographical references (p.   ) and index

Mary, Blessed Virgin, Saint

Hazleton, Lesley. **Mary:** a flesh-and-blood biography of the Virgin Mother. Bloomsbury 2004 246p $24.95 **92**

1. Saints
ISBN 1-582-34236-9
LC 2003-17403

Hazleton "takes readers through an impressive array of historical, cultural, literary, and spiritual topics. . . . This book is an easy read, and Hazleton's stream-of-consciousness style is intriguing." Libr J

Includes bibliographical references

Mary, Queen of Scots, 1542-1587

Fraser, Antonia. **Mary** Queen of Scots; illustrated abridged ed; Delacorte Press 1978 208p il hardcover o.p. pa $19.95 **92**

1. Queens 2. Scotland -- History -- 16th century 3. Great Britain -- History -- 1485-1603, Tudors
ISBN 0-380-31129-X pa
LC 78-703

A condensation of the title first published 1969

A look at the tragic life of Mary Stuart, the 16th century Catholic ruler of Protestant Scotland, and her incessant struggle with political and religious opponents

Includes bibliographical references

Weir, Alison. **Mary,** Queen of Scots, and the murder of Lord Darnley. Ballantine Bks. 2003 670p il map $27.95; pa $16.95 **92**

1. Queens 2. Princes 3. Scotland -- History -- 16th century
ISBN 0-345-43658-X; 0-8129-7151-5 pa
LC 2002-34467

"No stone is left unturned in {Weir's} investigation, and despite its detail, her book is as dramatic as witnessing first-hand the most riveting court case." Booklist

Weir, Alison. The **lost** Tudor princess; the life of Margaret Douglas of Scotland. Alison Weir. Ballantine Books 2016 576 p. illustrations, maps (hardcover : alk. paper) $30 **92**

1. Great Britain -- History -- 1485-1603, Tudors 2. Nobility -- Great Britain -- Biography 3. Nobility -- Great Britain -- History -- 16th century 4. Great Britain -- History -- Tudors, 1485-1603 -- Biography
ISBN 9780345521392
LC 2015037958

This book, by Alison Weir, offers a "biography of Margaret Douglas, the beautiful, cunning niece of Henry VIII of England who used her sharp intelligence and covert power to influence the succession after the death of Elizabeth I. . . . Lady Margaret Douglas, Countess of Lennox, was an important figure in Tudor England, yet today, while her contemporaries—Anne Boleyn, Mary, Queen of Scots, Elizabeth I—have achieved celebrity status, she is largely forgotten." (Publisher's note)

"An abundantly detailed history from an author steeped in England's past." Kirkus

Includes bibliographical references and index

Maryam Jameelah, 1934-2012

Baker, Deborah. The **convert**; a tale of exile and extremism. Graywolf Press 2011 246p il $23 **92**

1. Converts 2. Muslim women 3. Biography, Individual
ISBN 1-55597-582-8; 978-1-55597-582-1

This is a biography of the Islamic polemicist Maryam Jameelah. Jameelah was "born as Margaret Marcus in 1934 in New Rochelle, N.Y." (N Y Times Book Rev)

This "is a cogent, thought-provoking look at a radical life and its rippling consequences." Publ Wkly

Includes bibliographical references

Mason, George, 1725-1792

★ Broadwater, Jeff. **George** Mason, forgotten founder. University of North Carolina Press 2006 329p il $34.95 **92**

1. Statesmen 2. Essayists 3. Colonial leaders 4. Plantation owners
ISBN 978-0-8078-3053-6; 0-8078-3053-4
LC 2006-10729

"Because Mason left little evidence of his private life, there are blurred edges in the portrait that Broadwater paints, but overall this is an exemplary biography: sympathetic but dispassionate, thorough but not cluttered, convincing in its interpretations and arguments. It leaves no doubt that Mason deserves to be returned to the esteem and reputation he enjoyed during his lifetime, but in no way is it hagiography." Washington Post Book World

Includes bibliographical references

Massery, Hazel Bryan, 1942-

Margolick, David. **Elizabeth** and Hazel; two women of Little Rock. Yale University Press 2011 310p il $26 **92**

1. School integration 2. Arkansas -- Race relations 3. Little Rock (Ark.) -- Race relations 4. Central High School (Little Rock, Ark.) 5. School integration -- Arkansas -- Little Rock -- History -- 20th century
ISBN 978-0-300-14193-1; 0-300-14193-9

LC 2011-14101

"When Elizabeth Eckford braved the gauntlet of white hecklers leading to the newly desegregated Central High School in Little Rock, Arkansas, in 1957, photographers captured her image and that of the angry young white woman behind her. Elizabeth, the stoic, and Hazel Bryan, the tormentor, were frozen as icons. Elizabeth was part of the Little Rock Nine, the black teens who became the targets of race hatred as well as national and international inspirations. . . . Margolick draws on interviews and press reports of the time to present a very nuanced analysis of how Elizabeth and Hazel were affected by the scene that made them famous. . . . A complex look at two women at the center of a historic moment." Booklist

Includes bibliographical references

Massimino, Mike, 1962-

Massimino, Mike. **Spaceman**; An Astronaut's Unlikely Journey to Unlock the Secrets of the Universe. Mike Massimino. Crown 2016 336 p. color illustrations (hardcover) $28 **92**

1. Astronauts 2. Space flight 3. Astronauts -- United States -- Biography 4. Space flights -- United States -- History 5. Hubble Space Telescope (Spacecraft) -- Maintenance and repair -- History
ISBN 9781101903544

LC 2016011667

In this book, astronaut Mike Massimino "puts you inside the suit, with all the zip and buoyancy of life in microgravity. . . . Taking us through the surreal wonder and beauty of his first spacewalk, the tragedy of losing friends in the Columbia shuttle accident, and the development of his enduring love for the Hubble Telescope . . . Massimino has written an ode to never giving up and the power of teamwork to make anything possible." (Publisher's note)

"This is an engaging and uplifting memoir that's sure to give readers a deeper appreciation for the U.S. space program and inspire some future astronauts." Pub Wkly

Masters, Jarvis

Masters, Jarvis. **That** bird has my wings; the autobiography of an innocent man on death row.

[by] Jarvis Jay Masters. HarperOne 2009 281p $24.99 **92**

1. Prisoners 2. African Americans -- Biography
ISBN 978-0-06-173045-0; 0-06-173045-9

LC 2009-22124

"A heartbreaking memoir; the brutal conditions of Masters's boyhood will be difficult for some readers to take, but his ultimate message of hope and reconciliation is moving and inspiring." Libr J

Matisse, Henri

Spurling, Hilary. **Matisse** the master; a life of Henri Matisse, the conquest of colour, 1909-1954. Knopf 2005 xxi, 511p il $40 **92**

1. Artists 2. Painters
ISBN 0-679-43429-1

LC 2004-51074

Companion volume to The unknown Matisse

"Spurling's rich, flexible style is well attuned to the rigors and flights of Matisse's creative life." Publ Wkly

Includes bibliographical references

Spurling, Hilary. The **unknown** Matisse; v1 a life of Henri Matisse. Knopf 1998 xxv, 480p v1 il $40 **92**

1. Artists 2. Painters
ISBN 0-679-43428-3

LC 97-46816

In this first volume of the author's biography of the French artist, Spurling focuses on Matisse's training as an art student in Paris

This volume "makes for a gripping read and reveals much about the artist's early development." Publ Wkly

Includes bibliographical references

Maugham, W. Somerset (William Somerset), 1874-1965

Hastings, Selina. The **secret** lives of Somerset Maugham; a biography. Random House 2010 626p il **92**

1. Authors 2. Novelists 3. Dramatists 4. Travel writers 5. Authors, English 6. Short story writers 7. Biography, Individual
ISBN 978-1-4000-6141-9

LC 2009-35797

This is a biography of the English novelist and playwright.

"This steady-eyed biography of an extraordinary, extravagant, generous and bitter artist will not only fascinate its readers but encourage some to go to his work for the first time." Times Lit Suppl

Includes bibliographical references (p. 599-602)

Mauldin, Bill, 1921-2003

DePastino, Todd. **Bill** Mauldin; a life up front. W.W. Norton 2008 370p il $27.95 **92**

1. Cartoonists
ISBN 978-0-393-06183-3; 0-393-06183-3

LC 2007-40494

This is a biography of the author of What's Got Your Back Up? (1961), I've Decided I Want My Seat Back (1965), and The Brass Ring (1971). During World War II, Mauldin was a cartoonist who depicted the daily lives of soldiers for the G.I. newspaper Stars and Stripes.

"Thoroughly researched and sprightly written, DePastino's balanced biography is a solid introduction to an American original. Classic Mauldin cartoons are an entertaining bonus." Publ Wkly

Includes bibliographical references

Maxwell, William, 1908-2000

What there is to say we have said; the correspondence of Eudora Welty and William Maxwell. edited by Suzanne Marrs. Houghton Mifflin Harcourt 2011 499p il $35   **92**

1. Authors 2. Novelists 3. Magazine editors 4. Short story writers

ISBN 0547376499; 9780547376493; 978-0-547-37649-3; 0-547-37649-9

LC 2010-42105

"Letters between writers often have a lot of shop talk of interest to other writers and literary cultists, but this collection yields broader pleasures, too. In addition to being stellar writers, Welty and Maxwell were also accomplished critics, and one of the joys of the book is eavesdropping on their assessments of authors as varied as John Updike and Virginia Woolf, Anton Chekhov and Charles Dickens, William Faulkner and E. M. Forster. Welty and Maxwell also shared an intense love of gardening – so much so that Marrs was forced, in the book's index, to include an extensive listing of various varieties of roses. . . . As these letters show, Welty and Maxwell regarded domestic life not as a tedious distraction from the writing desk, but as a crucial source of insight. . . . The title of the collection comes from Maxwell's conclusion, as he and Welty faced their mortality, that 'what there is to say we have said, in one way or the other. You know how much we love you.' That love, a source of sustenance and strength between two great writers, is also a bright tonic for the readers of this volume." Christ Sci Monit

Includes bibliographical references

Mayakovsky, Vladimir, 1893-1930

Night wraps the sky; writings by and about Mayakovsky. edited by Michael Almereyda. Farrar, Straus and Giroux 2008 xxvii, 272p il $27   **92**

1. Poets 2. Authors 3. Dramatists

ISBN 978-0-374-28135-9; 0-374-28135-1

LC 2007-46662

"The book further explores Mayakovsky's relationships with Lili Brik and Tatiana Yakovleva, explains his propaganda work, and addresses his mixture of the surreal, the lyric, and the sarcastic; the text is generously illustrated with photographs of Mayakovsky's friends and contemporaries and artworks of the times." Libr J

Mayer, Louis B. (Louis Burt), 1885-1957

★ Eyman, Scott. **Lion** of Hollywood; the life and legend of Louis B. Mayer. Simon & Schuster 2005 596p il $35   **92**

1. Motion picture executives

ISBN 0-7432-0481-6

LC 2005-42472

"Eyman's extensive knowledge of old Hollywood, his scrupulous research and his refusal to indict the often-pillo-

ried Mayer make this biography an often revelatory delight." Publ Wkly

Includes bibliographical references

Mayes, Frances

Mayes, Frances. **Under** magnolia; a Southern memoir. Frances Mayes. Crown Publishers 2014 336 p. illustrations (hardback) $26   **92**

1. Bildungsromans 2. Autobiographies 3. Southern States 4. Authors, American -- 20th century -- Biography

ISBN 0307885917; 9780307885913

LC 2013042448

"'Under Magnolia' is a . . . moving ode to family and place, and a . . . meditation on the ways they define us. . . . With acute sensory language, [author Frances] Mayes relishes the sweetness of the South, the smells and tastes at her family table, the fragrance of her hometown trees, and writes an unforgettable story of a girl whose perspicacity and dawning self-knowledge lead her out of the South and into the rest of the world, and then to a profound return home." (Publisher's note)

"With her trademark skill for capturing the essence of place and time, Mayes candidly reveals a youth riddled with psychological abuse and parental neglect that, nevertheless, ignited a fiery passion for adventure and self-discovery." Booklist

Includes bibliographical references

Mayfield, Kate

The **undertaker's** daughter; Kate Mayfield. Gallery Books 2015 368 p. (hardback) $24.99 **92**

1. Undertakers and undertaking 2. Authors -- United States -- Biography

ISBN 1476757283; 9781476757285; 9781476757292

LC 2014006727

In this memoir, by Kate Mayfield, the author "explores what it meant to be the daughter of a small-town undertaker. . . . After Kate Mayfield was born, she was taken directly to a funeral home. Her father was an undertaker, and for thirteen years the family resided in a place nearly synonymous with death. . . . In a memoir that reads like a Harper Lee novel, Mayfield draws the reader into a world of Southern mystique and ghosts." (Publisher's note)

"Mayfield's "secret life" forced her to lie and sneak around, and her teenage angst was only compounded by the brutal revelation from her sister Evelyn, a thoroughly unpleasant bully, that her father was a serial philanderer and a drunk. Mayfield fashions a poignant send-off to Jubilee in this thoughtfully rendered work." Pub Wkly

Mays, Willie, 1931-

Hirsch, James S. **Willie** Mays; the life, the legend. authorized by Willie Mays. Scribner 2010 628p il $30   **92**

1. Baseball players 2. Baseball -- History 3. Baseball -- Biography 4. Biography, Individual 5. New York Giants (Baseball team)

ISBN 978-1-4165-4790-7; 1-4165-4790-8

LC 2009-49214

"This is a superb baseball book, but it's also a riveting narrative of Mays' life and times, ranging from his penchant for fancy suits to urban development in New York City to the giddy cult of celebrity. In the mid-1950s, Willie Mays was as famous as anyone in the country, gracing the cover of Time and other magazines and appearing on numerous television shows. More impressive — and what distinguishes this book from the run-of-the-mill sports biography — is Hirsch's extensive and cogent take on race relations and the civil-rights movement both within and outside of baseball." Seattle Times

Includes bibliographical references

Mbeki, Thabo, 1942-

Gevisser, Mark. A **legacy** of liberation; Thabo Mbeki and the future of the South African dream. Palgrave Macmillan 2009 376p il $29.95   92

1. Presidents 2. Political leaders 3. Government officials 4. South Africa -- Politics and government
ISBN 978-0-230-61100-9; 0-230-61100-1

LC 2008-50763

Abridged version of a book first published 2007 in South Africa with title: Thabo Mbeki: the dream deferred

This is a biography of South Africa's second president. Gevisser "traces Mbeki's family back several generations, from colonial disposession through the struggle for liberation. . . . Mbeki's life story has the makings of a gripping tale. . . . Gevisser writes well, particularly when he is witness to an event, when his narrative leaps off the page." N Y Times Book Rev

Includes bibliographical references (p. [346]-365) and index

McBee, Thomas Page

Man alive; a true story of violence, forgiveness and becoming a man. Thomas Page McBee. City Lights Publishers 2014 172 p. (City lights/sister spit) (paperback) $15.95   92

1. Violence 2. Masculinity 3. Transsexualism 4. Gender identity -- United States 5. Transsexuals -- United States -- Biography 6. Transgender people -- United States -- Biography 7. Female-to-male transsexuals -- United States -- Biography
ISBN 0872866246; 9780872866249

LC 2014022173

Author "Thomas Page McBee attempts to answer [What does it really mean to be a man?] by focusing on two of the men who most impacted his life; one, his otherwise ordinary father who abused him as a child, and the other, a mugger who almost killed him. Standing at the brink of the life-changing decision to transition from female to male, McBee seeks to understand these examples of flawed manhood." (Publisher's note)

"Full of bravery and clear, far-sighted compassion and devoid of sentiment, victimization, and cliché, McBee's meditations bring him a hard-won sense of self—one that is bound to inspire any reader who has struggled with internal dissonance." Pub Wkly

McBride, James

McBride, James. The **color** of water; a black man's tribute to his white mother. Riverhead Bks. 1996 228p il pa $14; $23.95   92

1. Authors 2. Novelists 3. Journalists 4. Memoirists

5. Parents of prominent persons
ISBN 1-57322-578-9 pa; 1-57322-022-1

LC 95-37243

"Told with humor and clear-eyed grace, McBride's memoir is not only a terrific story, it's a subtle contribution to the current debates on race and identity. . . . The sheer strength of spirit, pain and humor of McBride and his mother as they wrestled with different aspects of race and identity is vividly told." Nation

McCain, John S., 1936-

McCain, John S. **Faith** of my fathers; {by} John McCain with Mark Salter. Random House 1999 349p $25   92

1. Prisoners of war 2. Senators 3. Members of Congress 4. Presidential candidates
ISBN 0-375-50191-6

LC 99-13496

This is a "serious, utterly engrossing account of faith, fathers and military tradition." Publ Wkly

McCarthy, Joseph, 1908-1957

Wicker, Tom. **Shooting** star: the brief arc of Joe McCarthy. Harcourt 2006 212p $22   92

1. Senators
ISBN 978-0-15-101082-0; 0-15-101082-X

LC 2005-20990

This is a biography of the Senator from Wisconsin who led the House Committee on Un-American Activities and was censured by the Senate in 1954.

"This perceptive, well-written book should have wide appeal." Choice

Includes bibliographical references

McCartney, Paul

Sounes, Howard. **Fab**; an intimate life of Paul McCartney. Da Capo Press 2010 634p il $29.95 92

1. Singers 2. Rock musicians 3. Beatles 4. Songwriters
ISBN 978-0-306-81783-0

LC 2010-936124

"Divided into two equally large sections—'With the Beatles' and 'After the Beatles'—Fab covers all the highlights of McCartney's life and long career: his early days in Liverpool; his meeting with John Lennon; the craziness of Beatlemania; his solo albums; the creation and collapse of his post-Beatles band, Wings; his marriage to Linda Eastman; his last meetings with Lennon; his drug bust in Japan; his forays into classical music; his disastrous second marriage to Heather Mills. . . . Sounes is often brutally honest, offering a full portrait—warts and all—of one of the most famous men of the modern era. A must for Beatles and McCartney fans." Booklist

Includes bibliographical references

McClellan, George Brinton, 1826-1885

Sears, Stephen W. **George** B. McClellan; the young Napoleon. Da Capo Press 1999 482p il map pa $16.95   92

1. Generals 2. Governors 3. Presidential candidates 4. United States -- History -- 1861-1865, Civil War
ISBN 0-306-80913-3

LC 98-33277

First published 1988 by Ticknor & Fields

This biography of the Civil War general "covers both the awkward character traits that led to McClellan's incompetence and the battlefield actions that he regularly bungled. In addition to its merit as Civil War history, the book is of great interest as the portrait of an intelligent man working at what he failed to realize was the wrong profession." Atlantic

Includes bibliographical references

McClelland, Mac

Irritable hearts; a PTSD love story. Mac McClelland. Flatiron Books 2015 320 p. (hardback) $27.99   **92**

1. Haiti Earthquake, Haiti, 2010 2. Post-traumatic stress disorder 3. Man-woman relationships 4. Earthquakes -- Psychological aspects 5. Journalists -- United States -- Biography 6. Post-traumatic stress disorder -- Patients -- United States -- Biography

ISBN 1250052890; 9781250052896

LC 2014034163

Author Mac McClelland presents her memoir "investigating the damage in her own mind and repairing her broken psyche. She begins to probe the depths of her illness, exploring our culture's history with PTSD, delving into the latest research. When . . . McClelland left Haiti after reporting on the devastating earthquake of 2010, she never imagined how the assignment would irrevocably affect her own life." (Publisher's note)

"The author takes a maximalist approach, focusing exhaustively on her own experiences and grim sensations (as well as those of the people she encounters), so the narrative feels progressively less focused while remaining compassionate and perceptive regarding this elusive malady. McClelland's candor and empathy are admirable, but this would have benefited from more editorial shaping." Kirkus

McCourt family

★ McCourt, Frank, 1930-2009. **Angela's** ashes; a memoir. Scribner 1996 364p il pa $14; $25 **92**

1. Authors 2. Irish Americans 3. Memoirists 4. High school teachers 5. Biography, Individual

ISBN 0-684-84267-X pa; 0-684-87435-0

LC 96-5335

This is a memoir by a New York City high school teacher. "Born to Irish immigrants in Depression-era Brooklyn, McCourt's mother (Angela) and father . . . return to family in Ireland. . . . A baby sister dies in Brooklyn, and two more brothers die in Ireland. . . . {McCourt suffers from} afflictions brought on by the starvation and squalor in his family's . . . Limerick slum, including a bout of typhoid." (Commonweal)

"Frank McCourt, a teacher, grandfather and occasional actor, was born in New York City, but grew up in the Irish town of Limerick during the grim 1930's and 40's before he came back here as a teen-ager. His recollections of childhood are mournful and humorous, angry and forgiving." N Y Times Book Rev

McCourt, Alphie

McCourt, Alphie. A **long** stone's throw. Sterling & Ross Publishers 2008 267p $24.95   **92**

1. Irish Americans 2. Memoirists 3. Restaurateurs 4.

Business managers 5. Immigrants -- United States

ISBN 978-0-9814535-5-2; 0-9814535-5-4

LC 2008-32672

"Alphie is the youngest of the four McCourt brothers and the third—after Frank and Malachy—to pen a memoir about his life in Ireland and the U.S. . . . McCourt always finds irony in life and his tales of the bar and restaurant business and its clientele are laugh-out-loud funny. Sensitive, lyrical, funny, stubborn, impetuous, McCourt writes with a steady hand, a joyful heart, and an Irishman's sense of life's absurdities." Publ WKly

McCourt, Frank

McCourt, Frank. **Teacher** man; a memoir. Scribner 2005 258p $26   **92**

1. Authors 2. Irish Americans 3. Memoirists 4. High school teachers

ISBN 0-7432-4377-3

LC 2005-54113

"Full of gritty specifics, never preachy, often hilarious, McCourt's . . . book thrusts you right into the hormones-and-catcalls chaos of the classroom—where learning is not just a mystery but a flat-out miracle." Newsweek

McCourt, Frank. **'Tis**; a memoir. Scribner 1999 367p hardcover o.p. pa $14   **92**

1. Authors 2. Irish Americans 3. Memoirists 4. High school teachers

ISBN 0-684-86574-2 pa

LC 99-31280

Sequel to Angela's ashes

This volume "takes McCourt from his arrival in America and subsequent service in the Korean War through the mid-1980s. . . . This memoir features a mesmerizing narrative fraught with sufferings. It triumphs by effecting a genuinely comic meditation upon human frailty, grace and possibility." Publ Wkly

★ McCourt, Frank, 1930-2009. **Angela's** ashes; a memoir. Scribner 1996 364p il pa $14; $25 **92**

1. Authors 2. Irish Americans 3. Memoirists 4. High school teachers 5. Biography, Individual

ISBN 0-684-84267-X pa; 0-684-87435-0

LC 96-5335

This is a memoir by a New York City high school teacher. "Born to Irish immigrants in Depression-era Brooklyn, McCourt's mother (Angela) and father . . . return to family in Ireland. . . . A baby sister dies in Brooklyn, and two more brothers die in Ireland. . . . {McCourt suffers from} afflictions brought on by the starvation and squalor in his family's . . . Limerick slum, including a bout of typhoid." (Commonweal)

"Frank McCourt, a teacher, grandfather and occasional actor, was born in New York City, but grew up in the Irish town of Limerick during the grim 1930's and 40's before he came back here as a teen-ager. His recollections of childhood are mournful and humorous, angry and forgiving." N Y Times Book Rev

McCourt, James, 1941-

McCourt, James. **Lasting** City; the Anatomy of Nostalgia. James McCourt. Liveright Pub. Corporation 2013 336 p. (hardcover) $26.95	**92**
1. Autobiographies 2. Irish Americans 3. New York (N.Y.) -- 20th century
ISBN 0871404583; 9780871404589
LC 2013031496

This memoir by James McCourt is "an operatic recollection that braids a nostalgic portrait of old-Irish New York with a boy's funny, gutter-snipe precocity and hardly innocent coming-of-age in the 1940s and '50s. . . . Mating fact with fantasy, or fantasy with fact, McCourt takes us from his deeply moving bedside account of his mother Catherine's death to its traumatic aftermaths." (Publisher's note)

"[L]ess autobiography than a powerful work of creative nonfiction. . . . Intensely personal, unabashedly playful, and brilliantly inventive in its own gorgeous spotlight." Booklist

McCracken, Elizabeth

McCracken, Elizabeth. An **exact** replica of a figment of my imagination; a memoir. Little, Brown and Co. 2008 184p $19.99	**92**
1. Authors 2. Novelists 3. Librarians 4. Bereavement 5. Miscarriage 6. Essayists 7. Short story writers 8. Biography, Individual
ISBN 978-0-316-02767-0; 0-316-02767-7
LC 2008-5032

This is a memoir by the American novelist. "Two years ago [Elizabeth McCracken] was living in a remote part of France, working on her novel, and waiting for the birth of her first child. This book is about what happened next. In her ninth month of pregnancy, she learned that her baby boy had died. How do you deal with and recover from this kind of loss? . . . McCracken considers the nature of love and grief [here]." (Publisher's note)

"McCracken has succeeded in writing a beautiful, precise and heartbreaking account without sentimentality or pity." Publ Wkly

McCurley, T. Mark

Maurer, Kevin. **Hunter** Killer; Inside America's Unmanned Air War. T. Mark McCurley and Kevein Maurer. Penguin Group USA 2014 352 p. illustrations $27.95	**92**
1. Drone aircraft 2. Military art and science
ISBN 0525954430; 9780525954439
LC 2015016824

Authors T. Mark McCurley and Kevin Maurer offer a "look at the US military's secretive Remotely Piloted Aircraft program. McCurley provides an unprecedented look at the aviators and aircraft that forever changed modern warfare. This is the first account by an RPA pilot, told from his unique-in-history vantage point supporting and executing Tier One counterterrorism missions." (Publisher's note)

"The author ably chronicles the tedious, routine work involving 'days drenched in blood,' and he gives a good sense of the evolution of the RPA since the 1990s and the intensive human element necessary to command it. An illuminating tale of a pilot on the cutting edge." Kirkus

McDaniel, Hattie, 1895-1952

Jackson, Carlton. **Hattie**: the life of Hattie McDaniel. Madison Bks. 1989 220p il hardcover o.p. pa $12.95	**92**
1. Actors
ISBN 1-56833-004-9 pa
LC 89-30903

"For those of us who knew her only as 'Mammy' in Gone with the Wind, Hattie McDaniel's life story holds lots of surprises. She was also a singer, songwriter, and radio, stage, and TV performer. With an anecdotal style, the author clears up a lot of errors concerning her career." Booklist
Includes bibliographical references

Watts, Jill. **Hattie** McDaniel; black ambition, white Hollywood. Amistad 2005 352p il hardcover o.p. pa $14.95	**92**
1. Actors
ISBN 0-06-051490-6; 0-06-051491-4 pa
LC 2005-42126

"Watts is both sympathetic and honest: we pity McDaniel and her unenviable position, but at the same time, see how her intense careerism drove her often to accommodate rather than challenge film industry racism. . . . Watts' research is extensive, her writing clear and accessible, and her book a thorough, engaging, intelligent piece of historical scholarship." Women's Rev of Books

McKean, Thomas, 1734-1817

McKean, David. **Suspected** of independence; the revolutionary life of Thomas McKean. David McKean. PublicAffairs, a Member of the Perseus Books Group 2016 320 p. illustrations (hardcover) $27.99	**92**
1. Governors 2. Statesmen -- United States 3. United States. Continental Congress, 1774 4. United States -- History -- 1775-1783, Revolution 5. Governors -- Pennsylvania -- Biography 6. Statesmen -- United States -- Biography 7. United States. Continental Congress -- Biography 8. United States -- History -- Revolution, 1775-1783 -- Biography 9. United States. Declaration of Independence -- Signers -- Biography
ISBN 9781610392211
LC 2016005686

In this book, by David McKean, "Thomas McKean lived a radical, boisterous, politically intriguing life and was one of the most influential and enduring of America's Founding Fathers. . . . His life uniquely intersected with the many centers of power in the still-formative country during its most vulnerable years, and shows the degree of uncertainty that characterized newly independent America, unsure of its future or its identity." (Publisher's note)

"His story has been long in coming and worth the wait. For students of the Revolutionary era, the author delivers a useful biography of a significant player in the birth pangs of the new nation." Kirkus
Includes bibliographical references and index

McKenney, Eileen, d. 1940

Meade, Marion. **Lonelyhearts**; the screwball world of Nathanael West and Eileen McKenney.

Houghton Mifflin Harcourt 2010 392p il map
$28   92
1. Authors 2. Novelists 3. Screenwriters 4. Authors,
American 5. Spouses of prominent persons
ISBN 978-0-15-101149-0
LC 2009-13285
"West and McKenney died young in a car crash in
1940—too soon for him to know that his lacerating novels,
especially The Day of the Locust (1939), would become
American classics; too soon for his new wife, Eileen, to
claim her life for her own after her sister, Ruth, co-opted it
to write her best-seller, My Sister Eileen (1938). . . . [The
author] tells the trenchant and secret-laden life stories of
West (born Nathan Weinstein in New York) and Ohioan
McKenney in a ravishingly atmospheric yet propulsive
narrative." Booklist
Includes bibliographical references

McKinley, William, 1843-1901
★ Phillips, Kevin P. **William** McKinley; {by}
Kevin Phillips. Times Bks. 2003 188p (American
presidents series) $20   92
1. Governors 2. Presidents 3. Members of Congress 4.
United States -- Politics and government -- 1898-1919
ISBN 0-8050-6953-4
LC 2003-50701
"This little work of rehabilitation should help set McKin-
ley's reputation right." Publ Wkly
Includes bibliographical references

McLuhan, Marshall, 1911-1980
Coupland, Douglas. **Marshall** McLuhan; you
know nothing of my work! Atlas & Co. 2010 216p
$24   92
1. Authors 2. Mass media 3. Sociologists 4. Literary
critics 5. Nonfiction writers 6. Television critics
ISBN 978-1-935633-16-7
This is a biography of the Canadian mass media specialist.
"The book rewards by refusing to slip into the numbing
vortex of academic discourse, taking a fizzy, pop-culture approach to explaining a deep thinker, one who ended up popularized almost in spite of himself." N Y Times Book Rev

McMullen, William, 1824-1901
Biddle, Daniel R. **Tasting** freedom; Octavius
Catto and the battle for equality in Civil War America.
[by] Daniel R. Biddle [and] Murray Dubin. Temple
University Press 2010 616p il $35; e-book $35 92
1. Political activists 2. African American athletes 3.
African American educators 4. Baseball -- Biography
5. Biography, Individual 6. African Americans
-- Biography 7. Pennsylvania -- Race relations 8.
Philadelphia (Pa.) -- Race relations -- History 9. Civil
rights movements -- Pennsylvania -- Philadelphia 10.
African Americans -- Civil rights -- Pennsylvania --
Philadelphia
ISBN 978-1-59213-465-6; 978-1-59213-467-0 e-book
LC 2009049276
This is a biography of 19th-century civil rights activist
and baseball player "Octavius Catto of Philadelphia. Catto
was a part of the city's black intelligentsia and a vigorous
proponent of equal rights. . . . Catto became a martyr to his

cause when, at age 32, he was gunned down in Philadelphia's 1871 election-day riot. . . . [The authors] present a
clear and compelling portrait of this significant early civil
rights activist; they also present a thoughtful assessment of
how Catto's efforts relate to the modern black civil rights
movement." Choice
Includes bibliographical references

McMurtry, Larry
McMurtry, Larry. **Books**; a memoir. Simon &
Schuster 2008 259p $24   92
1. Authors 2. Novelists 3. Booksellers and bookselling
4. Essayists 5. Authors, American 6. Short story
writers
ISBN 978-1-416-58334-9; 1-416-58334-3
LC 2008-10565
"A pleasant amble in Bookland and a treat for the book-
ishly inclined." Kirkus

McPartland, Marian
De Barros, Paul. **Shall** we play that one together?
the life and art of jazz piano legend Marian McPartland. Paul de Barros. St. Martin's Press 2012 496 p.
(hardcover) $35.00   92
1. Pianists -- United States -- Biography 2. Jazz
musicians -- United States -- Biography
ISBN 0312558031; 9780312558031; 9781250019011
LC 2012028242
This biography of Marian McPartland, by Paul de Barros, is "[t]he story of the distinguished female jazz pianist
who devoted herself to her art and won popularity, the respect of her colleagues and just about every honor the profession bestows. . . . De Barros tells us about her albums . . .
[and] McPartland's versatility and success with Piano Jazz,
her NPR show that began in 1978. . . . The author also charts
her fierce devotion to jazz education and, sadly, her physical
decline." (Kirkus)
Includes bibliographical references

McPherson, Aimee Semple, 1890-1944
Epstein, Daniel Mark. **Sister** Aimee: the life of
Aimee Semple McPherson. 1993 475p il hardcover
o.p. pa $18   92
1. Evangelists
ISBN 0-15-600093-8 pa
LC 92-23324
This is a biography of the American evangelist and
faith healer
"Any secular treatment of a subject who claims divine
inspiration must sooner or later confront The Question: did
God actually speak to her? Epstein's hedge is that Sister Aimee believed He did. . . . On the whole, however, the book is
a lively read. That it is neither hagiography nor exposé is its
strength as well as its weakness. Sister Aimee emerges as an
unlikely yet compelling heroine." Natl Rev
Includes bibliographical references

McQueen, Alexander
Thomas, Dana. **Gods** and Kings; The Rise and
Fall of Alexander Mcqueen and John Galliano. Dana

Thomas. Penguin Group USA 2015 432 p. 32 plates; portraits $29.95 **92**

1. Fashion designers
ISBN 1594204942; 9781594204944

LC 2015460559

In this book, author Dana Thomas "tells the true story of [Alexander] McQueen and [John] Galliano. In so doing, she reveals the revolution in high fashion in the last two decades--and the price it demanded of the very ones who saved it. They had similar backgrounds: sensitive, shy gay men raised in tough London neighborhoods, their love of fashion nurtured by their doting mothers. Both struggled to get their businesses off the ground, despite early critical success." (Publisher's note)

"This is a dark story about excess, commerce, aristocracy and fashion as high theater that is as operatic as the dizzying shows it describes. A deep dive into the provocative art of creation and the toll it exacts from those touched by its gifts."

McTell, Blind Willie, 1898?-1959

Gray, Michael. **Hand** me my travelin' shoes; in search of Blind Willie McTell. Chicago Review Press 2009 432p il $26.95 **92**

1. Blind 2. Singers 3. Guitarists 4. Blues music 5. Blues musicians 6. Songwriters
ISBN 978-1-55652-975-7

LC 2009-22329

First published 2007 in the United Kingdom

"Less a conventional biography than a mixture of history, travelogue and detective story, Gray paints an evocative portrait of an artist who defied blues stereotypes." Kirkus

Includes bibliographical references

McWilliam, Candia

McWilliam, Candia. **What** to look for in winter. HarperCollins 2012 464p **92**

1. Blind 2. Alcoholism 3. Autobiographies
ISBN 0062094505; 9780062094506

This book is a memoir of "novelist Candia McWilliam [who] began losing her sight, a gradual onset of blindness that seemed like an assault cruelly tailored for someone whose life consisted of reading and writing. Propelled to look inward and into the past, McWilliam embarked on a painful personal voyage through a waste of snows punctuated by shards of ice as she attempted to write her life back. What followed was a flow of memory: her childhood in Edinburgh, her devastating alcoholism, finding and losing her bearings in Cambridge and London, her marriages, her children, and, overshadowing it all, her mother's suicide." (Publisher's note)

Mead, Margaret, 1901-1978

Mead, Margaret. **Blackberry** winter; my earlier years. with a new introduction by Nancy Lutkehaus. Kodansha International 1995 305p il (Kodansha globe) pa $15 **92**

1. Anthropologists 2. Curators 3. Writers on science
ISBN 1-568-36069-X; 978-1-568-36069-0

LC 95-13302

First published 1972 by Morrow

"About one-third of Mead's autobiography covers the years before she became an anthropologist and another third her field work in Samoa, in New Guinea, among the Omaha Indians, and in Bali. . . . The concluding chapters . . . describe in subjective detail her role as mother and grandmother." Choice

Includes bibliographical references

Meagher, Thomas Francis, 1823-1867

★ Egan, Timothy. The **immortal** Irishman; the Irish revolutionary who became an American hero. Timothy Egan. Houghton Mifflin Harcourt 2016 384 p. (hardcover) $28; (ebook) $28 **92**

1. Revolutionaries 2. Irish -- United States 3. Ireland -- History -- Famine, 1845-1852 4. Irish Americans -- Biography 5. Governors -- Montana -- Biography 6. Prisoners -- Tasmania -- Biography 7. Heroes -- United States -- Biography 8. Generals -- United States -- Biography 9. Revolutionaries -- Ireland -- Biography 10. United States. Army -- Officers -- Biography 11. United States. Army of the Potomac. Irish Brigade 12. United States -- History -- Civil War, 1861-1865 -- Biography
ISBN 9780544272880; 9780544272477

LC 2015037256

In this book, by Timothy Egan, the "Irish-American story, with all its twists and triumphs, is told through the improbable life of one man. A dashing young orator during the Great Famine of the 1840s, . . . Thomas Francis Meagher led a failed uprising against British rule, for which he was banished to a Tasmanian prison colony. He escaped and six months later was heralded in the streets of New York—the revolutionary hero, back from the dead." (Publisher's note)

"A fascinating, well-told story by an author fully committed to his subject. Egan's impeccable research, uncomplicated readability, and flowing narrative reflect his deep knowledge of a difficult and complex man." Kirkus

Includes bib and index

Mecom, Jane, 1712-1794

★ Lepore, Jill. **Book** of ages; the life and opinions of Jane Franklin. Jill Lepore. Alfred A. Knopf 2013 464 p. $27.95 **92**

1. Boston (Mass.) -- Biography 2. Women -- United States -- Social conditions -- 18th century
ISBN 0307958345; 9780307958341

LC 2013001012

This book on Jane Franklin Mecom by Jill Lepore tells "the story of Benjamin Franklin's youngest sister . . . using only a few of her letters and a small archive of births and deaths." (Kirkus Reviews) "Jane's surviving letters are . . . the correspondence of a smart, witty, hardworking woman who 'loved best books about ideas,' reveled in gossip, expressed 'impolite' opinions on religion and politics, and shared piquant observations of the struggle for American independence." (Booklist)

Includes bibliographical references

Meeink, Frank, 1975-

Meeink, Frank. **Autobiography** of a recovering skinhead; Frank Meeink's story. as told to Jody M. Roy. Hawthorne Books 2010 350p pa $10   **92**

1. White supremacy movements 2. Memoirists 3. Gang members 4. Social activists 5. White supremacists 6. Motivational speakers

ISBN 978-0-9790188-2-4

LC 2009-27527

"Before he was out of his teens, Meeink, a member of a group of white supremacists, was behind prison bars. But by the time he was released on parole, he was a changed man, having cast off his hatred; he became a public speaker, sharing his experiences, helping others to understand the nature of hatred and to find ways to combat it. . . . Stories of personal redemption don't get much more interesting than this one, and the gritty first-person narrative . . . draws the reader into Meeink's story, giving it an immediacy and a visceral intensity that makes us feel as though we've lived a bit of his life. Readers should be warned that the book is unflinchingly straightforward: some of the language is quite raw, and some of the imagery quite graphic." Booklist

Melendez, Benjy

Voloj, Julian. **Ghetto** Brother; Warrior to Peacemaker. Julian Voloj; illustrated by Claudia Ahlering. NBM Publishing 2015 128 p. chiefly b&w ill. $12.99   **92**

1. Peace movements 2. Gangs -- Graphic novels 3. Puerto Ricans -- New York (N.Y.)

ISBN 1561639486; 9781561639489

This graphic novel by Julian Voloj, illustrated by Claudia Ahlering, "tells the true story of Benjy Melendez, a Bronx legend, son of Puerto-Rican immigrants, who founded, at the end of the 1960s, the notorious Ghetto Brothers gang. From the seemingly bombed-out ravages of his neighborhood, wracked by drugs, poverty, and violence, he managed to extract an incredibly positive energy from this riot ridden era: his multiracial gang promoted peace rather than violence." (Publisher's note)

"Using Melendez as narrator-protagonist, Voloj places the seminal events of November and December 1971 in the contexts of post—WWII Puerto Rican immigration and difficult assimilation to New York, and of Melendez's personal development as he learned of and adopted his Jewish heritage. Ahlering bases her artwork partly on news and documentary photography, although she doesn't incorporate or copy photos but draws on them for detail, composition, and tonal variety." Booklist

Mellon, Andrew William, 1855-1937

★ Cannadine, David. **Mellon**; an American life. A.A. Knopf 2006 779p il $35   **92**

1. Philanthropists 2. Financiers 3. Art collectors 4. Secretaries of the treasury

ISBN 0-679-45032-7; 978-0-679-45032-0

LC 2006-45116

This is a "biography of Andrew Mellon, the powerful American financier, secretary of the treasury, and art collector. . . . Cannadine's recounting of Mellon's public career

make this a worthy contribution to our understanding of the man and his era." Booklist

Includes bibliographical references

Melton, Glennon Doyle

Melton, Glennon Doyle. **Love** warrior; A Memoir. Glennon Doyle Melton. Flatiron Books 2016 272 p. (hardcover) $25.99; (ebook) $60   **92**

1. Women authors 2. Divorced women 3. American authors 4. Divorced women -- United States -- Biography

ISBN 9781250075727; 9781250110152; 9781250075741

LC 2016016415

In this memoir, "just when Glennon Doyle Melton was beginning to feel she had it all figured out—three happy children, a doting spouse, and a writing career so successful . . . . —her husband revealed his infidelity and she was forced to realize that nothing was as it seemed. . . . [This book] is the story of one marriage, . . . [and] the healing that is possible for any of us when we refuse to settle for good enough and begin to face pain and love head-on." (Publisher's note)

"Though the memoir sometimes reads like a self-help book rather than a narrative, it nevertheless tells a compelling story about self-discovery and the nature of mature love. Candid, brave, and generous." Kirkus

Melville, Herman, 1819-1891

Delbanco, Andrew. **Melville**; his world and work. Knopf 2005 xxiii, 415p il map $30   **92**

1. Authors 2. Novelists 3. Authors, American

ISBN 0-375-40314-0

LC 2005-40919

"This is sure to elicit new appreciation for Melville's work and could well be the best one-volume biography for some time to come." Libr J

Includes bibliographical references

Mencken, H. L. (Henry Louis), 1880-1956

Rodgers, Marion Elizabeth. **Mencken**; the American iconoclast. Oxford University Press 2005 662p il $35   **92**

1. Authors 2. Essayists 3. Philologists 4. Social critics 5. Literary critics 6. Newspaper editors

ISBN 0-19-507238-3

LC 2005-47786

"This is a meticulous portrait of one of the most original and complicated men in American letters." Publ Wkly

Includes bibliographical references

Teachout, Terry. The **skeptic**: the life of H.L. Mencken. HarperCollins Pubs. 2002 410p il $29.95; pa $15.95   **92**

1. Authors 2. Essayists 3. Philologists 4. Social critics 5. Literary critics 6. Newspaper editors

ISBN 0-06-050528-1; 0-06-050529-X pa

LC 2002-24953

This is "an engrossing, sympathetic biography." Booklist

Includes bibliograpical references

Mendeleev, Dmitri I.

★ Gordin, Michael D. A **well**-ordered thing: Dmitrii Mendeleev and the shadow of the periodic table. Basic Books 2004 364p il $30   **92**

1. Chemists 2. Periodic law
ISBN 0-465-02775-X

LC 2003-25533

"This is not a chronological biography of the man; rather, it is a work that shows Mendeleev as an important part of the changes that occurred in Russia during the days between the freeing of the serfs in 1861 and the crumbling of tsarist power in 1905." Sci Books & Films

Includes bibliographical references

Mendelsohn, Daniel, 1960-

Mendelsohn, Daniel. The **lost**; a search for six of six million. photographs by Matt Mendelsohn. HarperCollins Publishers 2006 512p il $27.95   **92**

1. Journalists 2. Classicists 3. College teachers 4. Literary critics 5. Holocaust, 1933-1945
ISBN 0-06-054297-7

LC 2006-41096

The author describes his efforts to find out what happened to his uncle Shmiel Jager, his wife and four daughters, who lived in the Polish town of Bolechow, and perished during the Holocaust.

"Mr. Mendelsohn, an evocative, ruminative writer, brings to life the vanished world not just of prewar Poland but also of his childhood and his extended family." N Y Times (Late N Y Ed)

Mendelssohn, Felix, 1809-1847

Mercer-Taylor, Peter Jameson. The **life** of Mendelssohn; [by] Peter Mercer-Taylor. Cambridge Univ. Press 2000 238p il (Musical lives) hardcover o.p. pa $34.99   **92**

1. Composers
ISBN 0-521-63025-8; 0-521-63972-7 pa

LC 99-58441

"The book is well written, carefully produced, and a pleasure to read." Choice

Merman, Ethel, 1908 or 9-1984

Flinn, Caryl. **Brass** diva; the life and legends of Ethel Merman. University of California Press 2007 542p il $34.95; pa $18.95   **92**

1. Actors 2. Singers
ISBN 978-0-520-22942-6; 0-520-22942-8; 978-0-520-26022-1 pa; 0-520-26022-8 pa

LC 2007-29515

This is a biography of the singer and musical comedy star who appeared in the shows Girl Crazy (1930), Annie Get Your Gun (1946), and Gypsy (1959).

"A definitive all-inclusive piece of work that has been masterfully put together." Univ Press Books for Public and Second Sch Libr, 2008

Includes bibliographical references, discography, and filmography

Merrill, James, 1926-1995

Hammer, Langdon. **James** Merrill; life and art. Langdon Hammer. Alfred A. Knopf 2015 912 p. 32 plates; illustrations (hardback) $40   **92**

1. American poets 2. Gay men -- United States -- Biography 3. Gay authors -- United States -- Biography 4. Poets, American -- 20th century -- Biography
ISBN 0375413332; 9780375413339

LC 2014029325

Lambda Literary Awards: Gay Memoir/Biography (2016)

This book by Langdon Hammer is a biography of poet James Merrill. "The objective seems to look at the line between art and life in Merrill's poetry--not the least of which is seen in the intersection between Merrill's obsession with the Ouija board as literary starter and some of his experimental long poems . . . and the influence of poets Oscar Wilde and Rainer Maria Rilke. Hammer points to Merrill's need to define his own masculinity as a gay man." (Library Journal)

"While certainly organized for readers who adore biographies and life dramas, this will strongly appeal to those who love to discover where art springs from life." Library Journal

Merton, Thomas, 1915-1968

★ Merton, Thomas, 1915-1968. The **seven** storey mountain; Fiftieth anniversary edition; Harcourt Brace & Co. 1998 467p $35; pa $16   **92**

1. Monks 2. Poets 3. Authors 4. Nonfiction writers 5. Writers on religion
ISBN 0-15-100413-7; 0-15-601086-0 pa

LC 98-198169

First published 1948. This edition "includes an introduction by Merton's editor, Robert Giroux, and a reader's note by biographer and Thomas Merton Society Founder Fr. William Shannon." Libr J

"The autobiography of a poet who became a convert to Catholicism and at the age of 26 after a full and traveled world career as student and teacher, entered a Trappist monastery." Publ Wkly

Micheaux, Oscar, 1884-1951

McGilligan, Patrick. **Oscar** Micheaux; the great and only; the life of America's first great Black filmmaker. HarperCollins Publishers 2007 402p il $29.95   **92**

1. Authors 2. Novelists 3. Screenwriters 4. Motion picture directors
ISBN 978-0-06-073139-7; 0-06-073130-7

LC 2007-60735

"One of the fascinating side streets in American film is the history of 'race pictures,' celluloid productions by black artists for black audiences during those decades when Jim Crow laws enforced segregation. The mainstay of race pictures was Oscar Micheaux (18841951), an intrepid filmmaker-novelist-entrepreneur whose career spanned four decades and who made more than 40 movies. . . . McGilligan's prose style may be pedestrian, but he organizes his biographical materials into a lively, readable tale." N Y Times Book Rev

Michelangelo Buonarroti, 1475-1564

Unger, Miles J. **Michelangelo**; a life in six masterpieces. Miles J. Unger. Simon & Schuster 2014 416 p. illustrations, map (hardback) $29.95 **92**

1. Artists, Italian 2. Artists -- Biography

ISBN 9781451678741; 1451678746

LC 2013045778

In this biography of the artist Michelangelo, author "Miles Unger narrates the astonishing life of this driven and difficult man through six of his greatest masterpieces. Each work expanded the expressive range of the medium, from the Pietà Michelangelo carved as a brash young man, to the apocalyptic Last Judgment, the work of an old man tested by personal trials." (Publisher's note)

"Unger highlights Michelangelo's singular achievement without glossing over the defects in his mercurial character—or obscuring the corruption and violence pervading his Renaissance world. A masterful portrait of a dauntingly complex figure." Booklist

Includes bibliographical references and index

Miletich, Patrick Jay, 1968-

Wertheim, L. Jon. **Blood** in the cage; mixed martial arts, Pat Miletich, and the furious rise of the UFC. Houghton Mifflin Harcourt 2009 251p il $25 **92**

1. Martial arts 2. Sportswriters 3. Ultimate Fighting Championship (Organization)

ISBN 978-0-618-98261-5; 0-618-98261-2

LC 2008-36764

"MMA has yet to find its great scribe, its Liebling, Pierce Egan or Norman Mailer, but it is young. Until that new bard of bloodshed comes along, 'Blood in the Cage' will stand as a worthy introduction to the birth of something both awful and beautiful." Salon

Mill, John Stuart, 1806-1873

Mill, John Stuart. **Autobiography**; edited with an introduction by John M. Robson. Penguin Bks. 1989 234p pa $8.95 **92**

1. Economists 2. Philosophers 3. Essayists 4. Writers on politics

ISBN 0-14-043316-3

LC 91-103446

Written 1873

"A human document of unusual interest. Mill, a noble spirit educated by a narrow-minded pedant, shut off from all normal contact, developed an egotism that makes this book so completely an autobiography that besides his father and [his] wife he seems to exist alone in a world of which he has both center and circumference." Pratt Alcove

Includes bibliographical references

Millay, Edna St. Vincent, 1892-1950

Milford, Nancy. **Savage** beauty: the life of Edna St. Vincent Millay. Random House 2001 550p il $29.95; pa $14.95 **92**

1. Poets 2. Authors 3. Dramatists

ISBN 0-394-57589-X; 0-375-76081-4 pa

LC 2001-18598

"In 1923, Edna St. Vincent Millay became the first woman to win the Pulitzer Prize for poetry. To write her biography, Milford . . . persuaded Millay's younger sister and sole heir, Norma, to give her access to hundreds of Millay's personal papers, letters, and notebooks. Selecting from 'this extraordinary collection,' Milford meticulously integrates Millay's major poems, letters received and sent, reactions of friends, and comments from extensive interviews with Norma into an orderly and affecting narrative." Libr J

Includes bibliographical references

Miller, Arthur, 1915-2005

Bigsby, Christopher. **Arthur** Miller; 1915-1962. [by] Christopher Bigsby. Harvard University Press 2009 739p il $35 **92**

1. Authors 2. Dramatists 3. Screenwriters 4. Dramatists, American

ISBN 978-0-674-03505-8; 0-674-03505-4

LC 2009-2489

First published 2008 in the United Kingdom

This is a biography of the American playwright.

"A richly detailed, revealing look at the making of a playwright and a man." Kirkus

Includes bibliographical references

Gottfried, Martin. **Arthur** Miller; his life and work. Da Capo Press 2003 484p il hardcover o.p. pa $18 **92**

1. Authors 2. Dramatists 3. Screenwriters

ISBN 0-306812-14-2; 0-306813-77-7 pa

LC 2004-298989

This is "an uncomfortable, challenging work, forbidding us any bien-pensant ease, and we should be grateful for it." Times Lit Suppl

Includes bibliographical references

Miller, Donald, 1971-

Blue like jazz; nonreligious thoughts on Christian spirituality. Donald Miller. Thomas Nelson 2008 ix, 243 p.p illustrations $16.99 **92**

1. Christian life 2. Spiritual life 3. Christian biography -- United States

ISBN 0785263705; 1400204585; 9781400204588

LC 2003002223

This spiritual memoir, by Donald Miller, describes how "when [the author] came to know Jesus Christ, he pursued the Christian life with great zeal. Within a few years he had a successful ministry that ultimately left him feeling empty, burned out, and, once again, far away from God. In this intimate, soul-searching account, Miller describes his remarkable journey back to a culturally relevant, infinitely loving God." (Publisher's note)

Miller, Kimberly Rae

Miller, Kimberly Rae. **Coming** clean; Kimberly Rae Miller. New Harvest/Houghton Mifflin Harcourt 2013 272 p. (hardback) $25 **92**

1. Compulsive hoarding 2. Parent-child relationship 3. Authors -- United States -- Biography

ISBN 9780544025837

LC 2013010483

In this memoir, author Kim Miller relates the story of a childhood lived "behind the closed doors of her family's idyllic Long Island house, navigating between teetering stacks of aging newspapers, broken computers, and boxes upon boxes of unused junk festering in every room--the product of her father's painful and unending struggle with hoarding." (Publisher's note)

"An engrossing, sympathetic exploration of living with hoarder parents." Kirkus

Miller, Lee, 1907-1977

★ Burke, Carolyn. **Lee** Miller; a life. Knopf 2005 426p il $35   **92**

1. Photographers 2. Models (Persons)

ISBN 0-375-40147-4

LC 2004-43844

This is a biography of the model and photographer.

This "sympathetic tribute sheds further light on the lives of this highly original, often misunderstood woman." Economist

Includes bibliographical references

Miller, Sue

Miller, Sue. The **story** of my father; a memoir. Knopf 2003 173p il $22.50; pa $12.95   **92**

1. Authors 2. Novelists 3. Memoirists 4. Short story writers

ISBN 0-375-41479-7; 0-345-45544-4 pa

LC 2002-69460

"A familiar but still touching story of a parent's descent into Alzheimer's disease; the deeper Miller's father sinks into confusion, the more powerfully candid her writing becomes." N Y Times Book Rev

Mills, Marja

Mills, Marja. The **Mockingbird** Next Door; Life with Harper Lee. Marja Mills. The Penguin Press 2014 288 p. illustrations (hardback) $27.95   **92**

1. Alabama 2. American authors 3. Alabama -- Biography 4. Authors, American -- 20th century -- Biography

ISBN 1594205191; 9781594205194

LC 2013039938

This book, by Marja Mills, is a memoir recounting her friendship with "To Kill a Mockingbird" author Harper Lee. "Journalists have trekked to her hometown of Monroeville, Alabama, where . . . Lee, known to her friends as Nelle, has lived with her sister, Alice, for decades, trying and failing to get an interview with the author. But in 2001, the Lee sisters opened their door to Chicago Tribune journalist Marja Mills. It was the beginning of a long conversation--and a great friendship." (Publisher's note)

Milton, John, 1608-1674

Campbell, Gordon. **John** Milton; life, work, and thought. [by] Gordon Campbell [and] Thomas N. Corns. Oxford University Press 2008 488p il map $39.95   **92**

1. Blind 2. Poets 3. Authors 4. Essayists 5. Great Britain -- History -- 1603-1714, Stuarts

ISBN 978-0-19-928984-4; 0-19-928984-0

LC 2008-300712

This biography "draws chiefly on documentary evidence and an easy familiarity with the 17th-century English scene. As a prodigy scholar, pamphleteer, government translator on the international stage and the blind . . . bard of the Bible,

Milton found himself astride a world of hardening views, as it spiraled in political and spiritual transition. . . . The authors set Milton's imaginative life against this backdrop, stretching from Shakespeare, to whom Milton's father may have been loosely connected, to Dryden's ingenious staging of Paradise Lost in couplets. With nearly 100 pages of notes and bibliography, this is a no-nonsense contribution to our understanding of a genius who, in many ways, is hardly remote from our times." Publ Wkly

Includes bibliographical references (p. 446-472)

Hawkes, David. **John** Milton; a hero for our time. Counterpoint 2010 354p $28   **92**

1. Blind 2. Poets 3. Authors 4. Poets, English 5. Essayists

ISBN 978-1-58243-437-7; 1-58243-437-9

LC 2009-53998

"Hawkes writes with little academic jargon, and his style is lively and entertaining. Political and religious history enthusiasts will find this excellent and challenging." Libr J

Includes bibliographical references

Min, Anchee, 1957-

Min, Anchee. **Red** Azalea. Anchor Books 2006 306p pa $13   **92**

1. Actors 2. Artists 3. Authors 4. Novelists 5. Photographers 6. Memoirists 7. China -- History -- 1949-

ISBN 978-1-4000-9698-5; 1-4000-9698-7

LC 2006-271433

First published 1994 by Pantheon Bks.

"In this memoir of growing up in China during the Cultural Revolution, sexual freedom becomes a powerful political as well as literary statement." N Y Times Book Rev

★ Min, Anchee, 1957- The **Cooked** Seed; A Memoir. Anchee Min. St. Martin's Press 2013 368 p. $26   **92**

1. Immigrants -- United States 2. China -- History -- 1949-1976 3. Chinese -- United States -- Biography 4. Chinese American authors -- Biography 5. Immigrants -- United States -- Biography

ISBN 1596916982; 9781596916982

LC 2013015953

This book is an "examination of the legacy of Mao Zedong's Cultural Revolution," in which author Anchee Min offers a "contrast between American and Chinese attitudes about human worth and dignity. Raised in Shanghai in a hardscrabble family of four children and educated parents who were denounced as 'bourgeois,' Min was plucked as a teenager from a labor camp in 1974" to appear in propaganda films. At 27, she came to the U.S. (Publishers Weekly)

Includes bibliographical references and index

Minnelli, Vincente, 1910-1986

Levy, Emanuel. **Vincente** Minnelli; Hollywood's dark dreamer. St. Martin's Press 2009 448p il $35   **92**

1. Motion picture producers and directors 2. Motion picture directors

ISBN 978-0-312-32925-9; 0-312-32925-3

LC 2008-28751

"Relying mostly on secondary sources, Levy traces [Minnelli's] career from early days as a stage designer in New York to arrival at MGM and his most fruitful period, the 1950s, when his films were box office and critical successes, to his frustrating final decades after the collapse of the studio system. . . . Levy provides some valuable insight into the life of a genuine artist who struggled—frequently successfully—to inject a higher aesthetic into popular entertainment." Booklist

Includes bibliographical references

Miskjian, Stepan, 1886-1974

MacKeen, Dawn Anahid. The **hundred**-year walk; an Armenian odyssey. Dawn Anahid MacKeen. Houghton Mifflin Harcourt 2016 352 p. illustrations, map (hardcover) $24 **92**
1. Genocide -- Armenia 2. Armenian massacres, 1915-1923 3. World War, 1914-1918 -- Armenia 4. Armenian massacres survivors -- Biography 5. Young men -- Armenia -- History -- Biography 6. Escapes -- Armenia -- History -- 20th century 7. Desert survival -- Syria -- History -- 20th century
ISBN 9780618982660
LC 2015016713

In this book, by Dawn Anahid MacKeen, "in the heart of the Ottoman Empire as World War I rages, Stepan Miskjian's world becomes undone. He is separated from his family as they are swept up in the government's mass deportation of Armenians into internment camps. . . . [The book] alternates between Stepan's saga and another journey that takes place a century later, after his family discovers his long-lost journals." (Publisher's note)

"Powerful, terrible stories about what people are willing to do to other people—but leavened with hope and, ultimately, forgiveness." Kirkus

Includes bibliographical references

Mitchell, Joan

Albers, Patricia. **Joan** Mitchell; lady painter: a life. Alfred A. Knopf 2011 xxi, 514p il ebook $21.99; $40 **92**
1. Artists 2. Painters 3. Women artists 4. Abstract expressionism 5. Biography, Individual 6. Artists -- United States
ISBN 978-0-307-59598-0 ebook; 978-0-375-41437-4
LC 2011-00457

This is a "biography of the abstract expressionist painter who came of age in the 1950s, '60s, and '70s." (Publisher's note) Index.

This is a "biography of Joan Mitchell (1925–92), a major 20th-century American artist. . . . This significant biography covers all aspects of Mitchell's life, including her synesthesia, eidetic memory, alcoholism, troubled relationships, and art. Filled with intimate details of her complex personality and unconventional lifestyle, this is a conscientiously objective yet sympathetic portrait of the 'lady painter' and the social and cultural contexts in which she became a successful artist in the male-dominated Parisian and New York art worlds." Libr J

Includes bibliographical references

Mitford family

Thompson, Laura. The **six**; The Lives of the Mitford Sisters. Laura Thompson. St. Martin's Press 2016 400 p. ill., genealogical table (hardcover) $29.99 **92**
1. Sisters 2. Women authors 3. Great Britain -- Biography 4. Sisters -- Great Britain -- Biography 5. Authors, English -- 20th century -- Biography 6. Women authors, English -- 20th century -- Biography
ISBN 9781250099532
LC 2016024061

This book, by Laura Thompson, focuses on "the Mitford sisters: Nancy, Pamela, Diana, Unity, Jessica, and Deborah. Born into country-house privilege in the early years of the 20th century, they became prominent as 'bright young things' in the high society of interwar London. Then, as the shadows crept over 1930s Europe, the stark—and very public—differences in their outlooks came to symbolize the political polarities of a dangerous decade." (Publisher's note)

"Appreciators of biography and social history will find much to engage their interest here." Booklist

Includes bibliographical references and index

Mitford, Jessica, 1917-1996

Thompson, Laura. The **six**; The Lives of the Mitford Sisters. Laura Thompson. St. Martin's Press 2016 400 p. ill., genealogical table (hardcover) $29.99 **92**
1. Sisters 2. Women authors 3. Great Britain -- Biography 4. Sisters -- Great Britain -- Biography 5. Authors, English -- 20th century -- Biography 6. Women authors, English -- 20th century -- Biography
ISBN 9781250099532
LC 2016024061

This book, by Laura Thompson, focuses on "the Mitford sisters: Nancy, Pamela, Diana, Unity, Jessica, and Deborah. Born into country-house privilege in the early years of the 20th century, they became prominent as 'bright young things' in the high society of interwar London. Then, as the shadows crept over 1930s Europe, the stark—and very public—differences in their outlooks came to symbolize the political polarities of a dangerous decade." (Publisher's note)

"Appreciators of biography and social history will find much to engage their interest here." Booklist

Includes bibliographical references and index

Mitford, Nancy, 1904-1973

Thompson, Laura. The **six**; The Lives of the Mitford Sisters. Laura Thompson. St. Martin's Press 2016 400 p. ill., genealogical table (hardcover) $29.99 **92**
1. Sisters 2. Women authors 3. Great Britain -- Biography 4. Sisters -- Great Britain -- Biography 5. Authors, English -- 20th century -- Biography 6. Women authors, English -- 20th century -- Biography
ISBN 9781250099532
LC 2016024061

This book, by Laura Thompson, focuses on "the Mitford sisters: Nancy, Pamela, Diana, Unity, Jessica, and Deborah. Born into country-house privilege in the early years of the 20th century, they became prominent as 'bright young things' in the high society of interwar London. Then, as the shadows crept over 1930s Europe, the stark—and very public—differences in their outlooks came to symbolize the political polarities of a dangerous decade." (Publisher's note)

"Appreciators of biography and social history will find much to engage their interest here." Booklist

Includes bibliographical references and index

Mitford, Pamela, 1907-1994

Thompson, Laura. The **six**; The Lives of the Mitford Sisters. Laura Thompson. St. Martin's Press 2016 400 p. ill., genealogical table (hardcover) $29.99　　　　　　　　　　　　　　　　　**92**

1. Sisters 2. Women authors 3. Great Britain -- Biography 4. Sisters -- Great Britain -- Biography 5. Authors, English -- 20th century -- Biography 6. Women authors, English -- 20th century -- Biography
ISBN 9781250099532

LC 2016024061

This book, by Laura Thompson, focuses on "the Mitford sisters: Nancy, Pamela, Diana, Unity, Jessica, and Deborah. Born into country-house privilege in the early years of the 20th century, they became prominent as 'bright young things' in the high society of interwar London. Then, as the shadows crept over 1930s Europe, the stark—and very public—differences in their outlooks came to symbolize the political polarities of a dangerous decade." (Publisher's note)

"Appreciators of biography and social history will find much to engage their interest here." Booklist

Includes bibliographical references and index

Mitford, Unity, 1914-1948

Thompson, Laura. The **six**; The Lives of the Mitford Sisters. Laura Thompson. St. Martin's Press 2016 400 p. ill., genealogical table (hardcover) $29.99　　　　　　　　　　　　　　　　　**92**

1. Sisters 2. Women authors 3. Great Britain -- Biography 4. Sisters -- Great Britain -- Biography 5. Authors, English -- 20th century -- Biography 6. Women authors, English -- 20th century -- Biography
ISBN 9781250099532

LC 2016024061

This book, by Laura Thompson, focuses on "the Mitford sisters: Nancy, Pamela, Diana, Unity, Jessica, and Deborah. Born into country-house privilege in the early years of the 20th century, they became prominent as 'bright young things' in the high society of interwar London. Then, as the shadows crept over 1930s Europe, the stark—and very public—differences in their outlooks came to symbolize the political polarities of a dangerous decade." (Publisher's note)

"Appreciators of biography and social history will find much to engage their interest here." Booklist

Includes bibliographical references and index

Mithridates VI Eupator, King of Pontus, ca. 132-63 B.C.

Mayor, Adrienne. The **Poison** King; the life and legend of Mithridates, Rome's deadliest enemy. Princeton University Press 2009 448p il map $29.95　　　　　　　　　　　　　　　　　**92**

1. Kings and rulers 2. Kings 3. Rome -- History 4. Black Sea region -- History 5. Mediterranean region

-- History
ISBN 9780691126838

LC 2009-15050

This is "a reappraisal of Mithradates's character and a detailed account of his scientific pursuits, notably his in-depth studies of poison. . . . [The author places] him in his proper context as a Greco-Persian ruler following in the footsteps of his purported ancestor Alexander the Great. The most compelling aspect of this book is Mayor's engaging style. A true storyteller, she makes Mithradates's world come alive." Libr J

Includes bibliographical references

Moaveni, Azadeh, 1976-

Moaveni, Azadeh. **Honeymoon** in Tehran; two years of love and danger in Iran. Random House 2009 340p $26　　　　　　　　　　　　　　　　　**92**

1. Authors 2. Journalists 3. Iranian Americans 4. Women journalists 5. Memoirists
ISBN 978-1-4000-6645-2; 1-4000-6645-X

The Iranian-American author describes her return to Iran as a reporter for 'Time' magazine, her marriage to an Iranian man, the repressive Iranian society and its impact, and her family's decision to leave Iran.

"This perfect blend of political commentary and social observation is an excellent choice for readers interested in going beyond the headlines to gain an in-depth understanding of twenty-first-century Iran." Booklist

Includes bibliographical references

Moaveni, Azadeh. **Lipstick** jihad; a memoir of growing up Iranian in America and American in Iran. Public Affairs 2005 249p $25; pa $13　　　　**92**

1. Authors 2. Journalists 3. Iran 4. Memoirists
ISBN 1-58648-193-2; 1-58648-378-1 pa

LC 2004-43184

"Moaveni, an Iranian-American who grew up in California, decided to embark on a journey in spring 2000 to rediscover her Iranian heritage. In this account, she . . . conveys the tensions she observed between the fundamentalist mullahs and younger Iranians, who are pushing for a more Westernized, modern Iran. . . . A charming and informative memoir." Libr J

Modigliani, Amedeo, 1884-1920

Secrest, Meryle. **Modigliani**; a life. Alfred A. Knopf 2011 387p il $35; ebook $17.99　　　　**92**

1. Artists, Italian 2. Biography, Individual
ISBN 978-0-307-26368-1; 978-0-307-59547-8 ebook

LC 2010-45357

This "is an enjoyable read for all, and a most welcome contribution to Modigliani scholarship." Publ Wkly

Molina, Bengie

Molina; the story of the father who raised an unlikely baseball dynasty. Bengie Molina with Joan Ryan. Simon & Schuster 2015 272 p. color illustrations (hardback) $25　　　　　　　　　　　　**92**

1. Baseball 2. Father-son relationship 3. Fathers and sons 4. Fathers -- Puerto Rico 5. Baseball -- Puerto

Rico
ISBN 1451641044; 9781451641042; 9781451641059
LC 2014043223

This book, by Bengie Molina with Joan Ryan, is a "memoir about his father, who through baseball taught his three sons about loyalty, humility, courage, and the true meaning of success. Bengie and his two brothers--Jose and six-time All-Star Yadier--became famous catchers in the Major Leagues and have six World Series championships among them." (Publisher's note)

"This memoir will appeal to any baseball fan as well as patrons from Puerto Rican communities." LJ

Mongkut, King of Siam, 1804-1868

Landon, Margaret. **Anna** and the King of Siam; illustrated by Margaret Ayer. Harper & Row 1944 391p il map hardcover o.p. pa $14.95 **92**

1. Kings 2. Governesses 3. Thailand -- Social life and customs

ISBN 0-06-095488-4 pa

Anna Leonowens' experiences at the Siamese court in the 1860's. From her experiences she wrote two books, "The English governess at the Siamese court," and "The romance of the harem." The author has put these two books into one story with additions to make a complete tale.

Monk, Thelonious, 1917-1982

★ Kelley, Robin D. G., 1962- **Thelonious** Monk; the life and times of an American original. Free Press 2009 588p il $30 **92**

1. Pianists 2. Jazz musicians 3. African American musicians 4. Jazz 5. Biography, Individual

ISBN 0-684-83190-2; 978-0-684-83190-9
LC 2009-08526

This is a biography of the jazz musician and composer. Discography. Videography. Index.

The author "knows music, especially Monk's music, and his descriptions of assorted studio and live dates, along with what Monk is up to musically throughout, are handled expertly. . . . Likewise, the characters in Monk's life and career are well served. . . . The 'genius of modern music' has gotten the passionate, and compassionate, advocate he deserves." N Y Times Book Rev

Includes discography, videography, and bibliographical references

Monroe, James, 1758-1831

Unger, Harlow G. The **last** founding father; James Monroe and a nation's call to greatness. [by] Harlow Giles Unger. Da Capo Press 2009 388p il map $26 **92**

1. Presidents 2. Secretaries of state 3. Presidents -- United States 4. United States -- Politics and government -- 1783-1865

ISBN 978-0-306-81808-0
LC 2009-26195

"A worthy attempt to rescue Monroe from obscurity for a mainstream audience." Kirkus

Includes bibliographical references (p. 371-376)

Monroe, Marilyn, 1926-1962

★ Taraborrelli, J. Randy. The **secret** life of Marilyn Monroe. Grand Central Pub. 2009 560p il $26.99 **92**

1. Actors

ISBN 978-0-446-58082-3
LC 2008-44704

For this biography, the author "delves beneath the legend of Marilyn Monroe to uncover the stark facts of the life and times of a singularly vulnerable woman woefully unequipped to deal with the quotidian business of 'normal' life, much less the pressures of a Hollywood career and international celebrity. . . . A painful and engrossing account of the profoundly damaged personality at the heart of the world's greatest sex symbol." Kirkus

Includes filmography

Montaigne, Michel de, 1533-1592

Bakewell, Sarah. **How** to live, or, A life of Montaigne in one question and twenty attempts at an answer. Other Press 2010 389p il map $25; ebook $19.99 **92**

1. Judges 2. Authors 3. Authors, French 4. Essayists

ISBN 978-1-59051-425-2; 978-1-59051-426-9 ebook
LC 2010-26896

"In a wide-ranging intellectual career, Michel de Montaigne found no knowledge so hard to acquire as the knowledge of how to live this life well. By casting her biography of the writer as 20 chapters, each focused on a different answer to the question How to live? Bakewell limns Montaigne's ceaseless pursuit of this most elusive knowledge. Embedded in the 20 life-knowledge responses, readers will find essential facts—when and where Montaigne was born, how and whom he married, how he became mayor of Bordeaux, how he managed a public life in a time of lethal religious and political passions. . . . Because Montaigne's capacious mirror still captivates many, this insightful life study will win high praise from both scholars and general readers." Booklist

Includes bibliographical references

Montana, Joe, 1956-

Dunnavant, Keith. **Montana**; the biography of football's Joe Cool. Keith Dunnavant. Thomas Dunne Books 2015 336 p. illustrations (chiefly color) (hardcover) $26.99 **92**

1. Football players 2. Football players -- United States -- Biography 3. Quarterbacks (Football) -- United States -- Biography

ISBN 9781250017840; 125001784X
LC 2015019171

Author Keith Dunnavant "builds his portrait through research and dozens of personal interviews with those who have known [Joe] Montana. This . . . volume also tells the less familiar story of Montana's early career and his battles with his high-school and college coaches, both of whom were slow to recognize Montana's talent. That changed in San Francisco, where Montana and coach Bill Walsh were the perfect match." (Booklist)

"Well written and researched, this title will be of interest to a wide range of sports fans." LJ

Montross, Christine

Falling into the fire; a psychiatrist's encounters with the mind in crisis. Christine Montross. Penguin Press 2013 256 p. $16 **92**

1. Mentally ill 2. Human behavior 3. Mental illness 4. Medical personnel 5. Physician-patient relationship 6. Behavior -- Personal Narratives 7. Mental Disorders -- therapy -- Personal Narratives 8. Physician-Patient Relations -- Personal Narratives 9. Attitude of Health Personnel -- Personal Narratives 10. Mental Disorders -- psychology -- Personal Narratives 11. Mentally Ill Persons -- psychology -- Personal Narratives

ISBN 0143125710; 9780143125716; 9781594203930

LC 2013007699

This book "is psychiatrist Christine Montross's thoughtful investigation of the gripping patient encounters that have challenged and deepened her practice. . . . Each case study presents its own line of inquiry, leading Montross to seek relevant psychiatric knowledge from diverse sources. A doctor of uncommon curiosity and compassion, Montross discovers lessons in medieval dancing plagues, in leading forensic and neurological research, and in moments from her own life." (Publisher's note)

"Diagnoses rest upon a physician's knowledge and judgment but also clinical intuition. We are all fragile and vulnerable creatures. Compassion counts." Booklist

Includes bibliographical references and index

Mooney, Jonathan

Mooney, Jonathan. The **short** bus; a journey beyond normal. H. Holt 2007 272p hardcover o.p. pa $14.99 **92**

1. Students with disabilities 2. Memoirists 3. Social activists 4. Motivational speakers

ISBN 978-0-8050-7427-7; 0-8050-7427-9; 978-0-8050-8804-5 pa; 0-8050-8804-0 pa

LC 2006-52588

The author's "target audience is not policy makers but his fellow misfits, and his boundless empathy will surely console those who also face the worst that cruel schoolchildren and the educational bureaucracy have to offer." N Y Times Book Rev

Mooney, Paul

Mooney, Paul. **Black** is the new white; a memoir. Simon Spotlight Entertainment 2009 264p il $24.99 **92**

1. Actors 2. Comedians 3. Screenwriters 4. Television scriptwriters 5. United States -- Race relations

ISBN 978-1-4165-8795-8; 1-4165-8795-0

LC 2009-19572

"Paul Mooney recalls the day he became Richard Pryor's shadow partner. It was 1968, and the two young comics were sitting in a Hollywood greasy spoon, with Pryor nursing another hangover, so Mooney lightened the mood with an off-the-cuff, X-rated one-liner that made his buddy convulse. . . . [This book] is Mooney's unvarnished memoir of that friendship. At a time when comedians—even African American icons such as Bill Cosby—never talked about race, Pryor (aided and abetted by Mooney) dared to confront the elephant in the room. Mooney, who has also written for 'In Living Color' and 'Chappelle's Show,' also traces his own path from humble Deep South roots to a comedy elder statesman known for his incisive riffs on racism." Los Angeles Times book Rev

Moore, Marianne, 1887-1972

Leavell, Linda. **Holding** on upside down; the life and work of Marianne Moore. Linda Leavell. Farrar Straus & Giroux 2013 480 p. 16 plates; illustrations (hardcover) $30 **92**

1. Women poets 2. Mother-daughter relationship

ISBN 0374107297; 9780374107291

LC 2013006521

National Book Critics Circle Award Finalist: Biography (2013)

In this book, author Linda Leavell "draws from the archive and private estate of American poet Marianne Moore (1887-1972) to illustrate how the modernist poet evolved from writing carefully crafted, cutting-edge poetry to producing the more prolific poems of her later years. Correspondence reveals that Moore's mother, Mary, used emotional manipulation, money, and a secret family vernacular to control both her son, Warner (John), and Marianne." (Library Journal)

"Recommended for students of poetry and readers of Moore. For more formative details of Moore's life, see Susan Forward's Toxic Parents." LJ

Includes bibliographical references and index

Molesworth, Charles. **Marianne** Moore; a literary life. Northeastern University Press 1991 xxii, 472p il pa $16.95 **92**

1. Poets 2. Authors 3. Essayists 4. Poets, American

ISBN 1-555-53115-6

LC 91-13570

First published 1990 by Atheneum Pubs.

"Molesworth charts the growth of a major modernist through careful critical readings of her poetry and prose, her work as an editor of the Dial, and an examination of Moore as an active, social New York literary figure whose colleagues and admirers included T.S. Eliot and Ezra Pound." Publ Wkly

Includes bibliographical references

Moore, Mary Tyler

Moore, Mary Tyler. **Growing** up again; life, love, and oh yeah, diabetes. St. Martin's Press 2009 216p il $24.95 **92**

1. Actors 2. Diabetes

ISBN 978-0-312-37631-4; 0-312-37631-6

LC 2008-37579

"While working on The Dick Van Dyke Show, . . . [the author] was diagnosed with juvenile (Type 1) diabetes and quickly discovered that managing the disease is a full-time job. . . . Moore details the daily challenges she faces to maintain healthy blood sugar levels. . . . Moore's humor, authoritative information, and honest evaluation of her own experiences with diabetes make this work essential for diabetes and consumer health collections." Libr J

Moore, Michael

Rapoport, Roger. **Citizen** Moore; the life and times of an American iconoclast. RDR 2006 310p il $15.95 **92**

1. Screenwriters 2. Social critics 3. Magazine editors 4. Nonfiction writers 5. Motion picture directors 6. Motion picture producers and directors -- Biography

ISBN 1-57143-163-2; 9781571431639 pa

In this biography of the controversial filmmaker, the author "compares Moore to Upton Sinclair and Ralph Nader, chronicling the filmmaker's early activism, community organizing, radio and theater career, and involvement in alternative journalism. . . . In this engaging profile, Rapoport portrays the quirks and complexities of a man whose life is as fascinating as his films." Booklist

Moore, Wes, 1975-

Moore, Wes, The **other** Wes Moore; the story of one name and two fates. [by] Wes Moore; afterword by Tavis Smiley. Spiegel & Grau 2010 233p il $25 **92**

1. Prisoners 2. Murderers 3. Memoirists 4. Army officers 5. Baltimore (Md.) 6. African Americans -- Biography

ISBN 978-0-385-52819-1

LC 2009-41663

"In 2000, Wes Moore had recently been named a Rhodes Scholar in his final year of college at Johns Hopkins University when he read a newspaper article about another Wes Moore who was on his way to prison. It turned out that the two of them had much in common, both young black men raised in inner-city neighborhoods by single mothers. Stunned by the similarities in their names and backgrounds and the differences in their ultimate fates, the author eventually contacted the other Wes Moore and began a long relationship. . . . The author examines eight years in the lives of both Wes Moores to explore the factors and choices that led one to a Rhodes scholarship, military service, and a White House fellowship, and the other to drug dealing, prison, and eventual conversion to the Muslim faith, with both sharing a gritty sense of realism about their pasts." Booklist

The **work**; creating success in new and meaningful ways. Wes Moore. Spiegel & Grau 2014 272 p. (hardback) $25 **92**

1. African Americans -- Biography 2. Military personnel -- United States 3. Baltimore (Md.) -- Biography 4. African American men -- Biography

ISBN 9780679646013; 9780812993578

LC 2013038679

This book by Wes Moore is "the story of how one young man traced a path through the world to find his life's purpose. Moore graduated from a difficult childhood in the Bronx and Baltimore to an adult life that would find him at some of the most critical moments in our recent history: as a combat officer in Afghanistan; a White House fellow in a time of wars abroad and disasters at home; and a Wall Street banker during the financial crisis." (Publisher's note)

"This is a beautifully philosophical look at the expectation that work should bring meaning to our lives through service to others." Booklist

Moore, Westley W.

Moore, Wes, 1978- The **other** Wes Moore; the story of one name and two fates. [by] Wes Moore; afterword by Tavis Smiley. Spiegel & Grau 2010 233p il $25 **92**

1. Prisoners 2. Murderers 3. Memoirists 4. Army officers 5. Baltimore (Md.) 6. African Americans -- Biography

ISBN 978-0-385-52819-1

LC 2009-41663

"In 2000, Wes Moore had recently been named a Rhodes Scholar in his final year of college at Johns Hopkins University when he read a newspaper article about another Wes Moore who was on his way to prison. It turned out that the two of them had much in common, both young black men raised in inner-city neighborhoods by single mothers. Stunned by the similarities in their names and backgrounds and the differences in their ultimate fates, the author eventually contacted the other Wes Moore and began a long relationship. . . . The author examines eight years in the lives of both Wes Moores to explore the factors and choices that led one to a Rhodes scholarship, military service, and a White House fellowship, and the other to drug dealing, prison, and eventual conversion to the Muslim faith, with both sharing a gritty sense of realism about their pasts." Booklist

Moran, Caitlin, 1975-

★ Moran, Caitlin. **How** to be a woman; Caitlin Moran. Harper Perennial 2011 305 p. (pbk.) $15.99 **92**

1. Feminism 2. Women -- Great Britain 3. Journalists -- England -- Biography 4. Women journalists -- England -- Biography 5. Women -- Great Britain -- Social conditions -- Humor

ISBN 0062124293; 9780062124296

LC 2012372347

Originally published: London : Ebury Press, 2011.

This book is "part memoir, part postmodern feminist rant" from British TV critic Caitlin Moran. "Moran's journey into womanhood begins on her 13th birthday when boys throw rocks at her 182-pound body, and her only friend, her sister Caz, hands her a homemade card reminding her to please turn 18 or die soon so Caz can inherit her bedroom." Moran "embarrasses herself often enough to become an authority on how to masturbate; name one's breasts; and forgo a Brazilian bikini wax." (Publishers Weekly)

Morante, Elsa, d. 1985

Tuck, Lily. **Woman** of Rome: a life of Elsa Morante. HarperCollins 2008 263p il $25.95 **92**

1. Poets 2. Authors 3. Novelists 4. Women authors 5. Italian authors 6. Authors, Italian 7. Short story writers

ISBN 978-0-06-147256-5; 0-06-147256-5

LC 2007-44647

"Written with a charming personal touch . . . that warms the narrative to a fine glow, this is a vital biography bringing to American audiences a writer most will have previously known little about." Booklist

Includes bibliographical references (p. 245-246)

Morgan, J. Pierpont (John Pierpont), 1837-1913

Strouse, Jean. **Morgan**; American financier. HarperPerennial 2000 796p il pa $18   **92**

1. Businesspeople 2. Bankers 3. Financiers 4. Book collectors

ISBN 0-06-095589-9; 978-0-06-095589-2

LC 99-87598

First published 1999 by Random House

"Strouse is in full command of Pierpont Morgan's personal life, his financial operations, his collecting, and his benefactions, and presents a rich, vivid picture of the background against which they took place. . . . She has written a magnificent biography, which illuminates her subject and his world." N Y Rev Books

Includes bibliographical references

Morgan, William, 1928-1961

Weiss, Mitch. The **Yankee** comandante; the untold story of courage, passion, and one American's fight to liberate Cuba. Michael Sallah and Mitch Weiss. Lyons Press 2015 288 p. illustrations, map (hardcover : alk. paper) $26.95   **92**

1. Cuba -- History -- 1958-1959, Revolution 2. Revolutionaries -- Cuba -- History -- 20th century 3. Revolutionaries -- United States -- History -- 20th century 4. Cuba -- History -- Revolution, 1959 -- Participation, American

ISBN 0762792876; 9780762792870

LC 2014033720

This book by Michael Sallah and Mitch Weiss is the story of "William Morgan, a tough-talking ex-paratrooper, [who[stunned family and friends when in 1957 he left Ohio to join freedom fighters in the mountains of Cuba. He led one band of guerrillas, and Che Guevara another, and together they swept through the country, ultimately forcing corrupt dictator Fulgencio Batista from power." (Publisher's note)

"Olga lives today in the U.S., and Sallah and Weiss interviewed her extensively. They also make clear Morgan's flaws: he had at least three wives and several children by them; was court martialed by the U.S. Army, serving time in prison; and was employed by and associated with known mobsters. Though the tale does not end happily, it's a romantic and entertaining read." Pub Wkly

Includes bibliographical references and index

Morris, Tom, 1821-1908

Cook, Kevin. **Tommy's** honor; the story of old Tom Morris and young Tom Morris, golf's founding father and son. Gotham Books 2007 327p il $27.50   **92**

1. Golf 2. Golfers

ISBN 978-1-59240-297-7; 1-59240-297-6

LC 2007-8165

"In Cook's telling, the story of Tom Morris, winner of golf's first Open Championship in 1860, and his son, Tommy, who won the Open three years in a row, becomes a compelling saga of near-Homeric proportions." Booklist

Includes bibliographical references

Morris, Tom, 1851-1875

Cook, Kevin. **Tommy's** honor; the story of old Tom Morris and young Tom Morris, golf's found-ing father and son. Gotham Books 2007 327p il $27.50   **92**

1. Golf 2. Golfers

ISBN 978-1-59240-297-7; 1-59240-297-6

LC 2007-8165

"In Cook's telling, the story of Tom Morris, winner of golf's first Open Championship in 1860, and his son, Tommy, who won the Open three years in a row, becomes a compelling saga of near-Homeric proportions." Booklist

Includes bibliographical references

Morrison, Jim, 1943-1971

Hopkins, Jerry. **No** one here gets out alive; by Jerry Hopkins and Daniel Sugerman. Warner Bks. 1980 387p il hardcover o.p. pa $7.99   **92**

1. Singers 2. Rock musicians 3. Songwriters 4. Doors (Musical group)

ISBN 0-446-60228-0 pa

LC 79-26611

This biography of rock musician Jim Morrison gives "an idea of how profoundly Morrison, as lyricist and lead singer of the Doors, affected the youth of America in the late 1960s. . . . The book includes a list of the Doors' records, books, and films." Booklist

Riordan, James. **Break** on through: the life and death of Jim Morrison; [by] James Riordan and Jerry Prochnicky. Morrow 1991 544p il hardcover o.p. pa $15   **92**

1. Singers 2. Rock musicians 3. Songwriters 4. Doors (Musical group)

ISBN 0-688-11915-8 pa

LC 90-26580

This look at the life and work of Jim Morrison is "well documented and avoids unfounded speculation and unnecessary tales of debauchery common to many other rock 'n' roll biographies. . . . An excellent biography of a true rock icon." Choice

Includes discography and bibliographical references

Moses, Robert, 1888-1981

Caro, Robert A. The **power** broker: Robert Moses and the fall of New York. Knopf 1974 1246, xxxivp il $50; pa $21.95   **92**

1. Urban planners 2. Local government officials 3. State government officials

ISBN 0-394-48076-7; 0-394-72024-5 pa

This is a biographical critique of the man who in four decades as a public official "built most of the parks, bridges and highways in and around New York City." Newsweek

Includes bibliographical references

Mosler, Layne

Driving hungry; a memoir. Layne Mosler. Pantheon Books 2015 320 p. (hardback) $24.95   **92**

1. Restaurants 2. Voyages and travels 3. Restaurants -- Anecdotes 4. Taxicab drivers -- Anecdotes 5. Food writers -- Germany -- Biography 6. Food writers -- United States -- Biography

ISBN 1101870311; 9781101870310

LC 2014043506

This book is a memoir "by food journalist and blogger (taxigourmet.com) [Layne] Mosler, whose journey starts in Buenos Aires, where the author asks her taxi driver to take her to his favorite eatery, and jumps back and forth across time and place (including New York, where she drives a cab herself, and Berlin), in search of the perfect bite." (Library Journal)

"Mosler's lively and accessible writing style joyfully captures the satisfaction gained by trusting your instincts and seeking out new places, food, and people." Kirkus

Mosley, Diana, 1910-2003

Thompson, Laura. The **six**; The Lives of the Mitford Sisters. Laura Thompson. St. Martin's Press 2016 400 p. ill., genealogical table (hardcover) $29.99 **92**
1. Sisters 2. Women authors 3. Great Britain -- Biography 4. Sisters -- Great Britain -- Biography 5. Authors, English -- 20th century -- Biography 6. Women authors, English -- 20th century -- Biography
ISBN 9781250099532
LC 2016024061
This book, by Laura Thompson, focuses on "the Mitford sisters: Nancy, Pamela, Diana, Unity, Jessica, and Deborah. Born into country-house privilege in the early years of the 20th century, they became prominent as 'bright young things' in the high society of interwar London. Then, as the shadows crept over 1930s Europe, the stark—and very public—differences in their outlooks came to symbolize the political polarities of a dangerous decade." (Publisher's note)

"Appreciators of biography and social history will find much to engage their interest here." Booklist

Includes bibliographical references and index

Mowat, Farley

King, James. **Farley**: the life of Farley Mowat. Steerforth Press 2002 397p il $27.95 **92**
1. Authors 2. Historians 3. Ethnologists 4. Children's authors 5. Nonfiction writers
ISBN 1-58642-055-0
LC 2002-151149
The author "recounts Mowat's life from his experience in college to his service in World War II and his work in the Northwest Territories as a student biologist. The emerging portrait is of a man whose evolution as both an environmentalist and an artist was profound, an activist who has never backed away from a controversy. The exploration of Mowat's life is detailed but never boring." Libr J

Includes bibliographical references

Mowat, Farley. **Born** naked. Houghton Mifflin 1994 256p il maps hardcover o.p. pa $13 **92**
1. Authors 2. Historians 3. Naturalists 4. Canadian authors 5. Ethnologists 6. Authors, Canadian 7. Children's authors 8. Nonfiction writers
ISBN 0-395-73528-9
LC 93-23702
First published 1993 in Canada
"There are no dull pages here; every man, woman, child, and animal mentioned even casually makes an impression. . . . Highly recommended to all those who like good writing." Libr J

Moyers, William C.

Moyers, William C. **Broken**: my story of addiction and redemption; [by] William Cope Moyers with Katherine Ketcham. Viking 2006 372p il $25.95 **92**
1. Journalists
ISBN 0-670-03789-3; 978-0-670-03789-6
LC 2006-41378
The author's "gripping account of his struggles with alcohol and crack addiction will have readers rooting for him from the very beginning." Libr J

Mozart, Wolfgang Amadeus, 1756-1791

Einstein, Alfred. **Mozart**; his character, his work. translated by Arthur Mendel and Nathan Broder. Oxford Univ. Press 1945 492p il music hardcover o.p. pa $22.50 **92**
1. Composers
ISBN 0-19-500732-8 pa
The author's "examination of the events of Mozart's life in relation to his character, and even more, his analysis of the sources, models, and methods of the musician's creative processes are penetrating and illuminating." Christ Sci Monit

Gutman, Robert W. **Mozart**; a cultural biography. Harcourt Brace & Co. 1999 839p hardcover o.p. pa $25 **92**
1. Composers
ISBN 978-0-15-601171-6 pa; 0-15-601171-9 pa
LC 99-31953
The author interweaves "the chronology of Mozart's life and musical compositions with essays on the social, political, and religious fabrics of the 18th century, offering extended discourses on the Enlightenment, Sturm und Drang, Freemasonry, and other movements that influenced the composer both personally and in his works." Libr J

Includes bibliographical references

Solomon, Maynard. **Mozart**; a life. HarperCollins Pubs. 1995 640p il hardcover o.p. pa $22.95 **92**
1. Composers
ISBN 0-06-019046-9; 978-0-06-088344-7 pa; 0-06-088344-8 pa
LC 94-42277
"The author explores Mozart's life and works with a wealth of facts that were culled from 18th-century sources as well as from the most recent scholarship. Mozart and his family emerge in a new light from this mass of well-chosen detail through Solomon's own convincing interpretation of events and relationships. Appropriate musical and pictorial examples, which will appeal to both scholarly and casual readers, accompany the text." Libr J

Includes bibliographical references

Muir, John, 1838-1914

★ Heacox, Kim. **John** Muir and the ice that started a fire; how a visionary and the glaciers of Alaska changed America. Kim Heacox. Lyons Press 2014 264 p. illustrations, map (hardback) $25.95 **92**
1. Alaska 2. Glaciers 3. Nature conservation 4. Glaciers -- Alaska 5. Climatic changes -- Alaska 6.

Nature conservation -- Alaska
ISBN 0762792426; 9780762792429

LC 2013050235

This book, by Kim Heacox, "takes two of the most compelling elements in the narrative of wild America, John Muir and Alaska, and combines them into a brisk and engaging biography. . . . The book also offers an environmental caveat on global climate change and the glaciers' retreat alongside a beacon of hope: Muir shows us how one person changed America, helped it embrace its wilderness, and in turn, gave us a better world." (Publisher's note)

"The book is an engaging and informative look at Muir and his life's work, as well as a timely call to action that poses difficult questions to the reader and the philosophies that underpin modern life." Pub Wkly

Includes bibliographical references and index

Muir, John. The **story** of my boyhood and youth; with a foreword by Vernon Carstensen. University of Wisconsin Press 1965 227p hardcover o.p. pa $17.95 **92**

1. Authors 2. Naturalists 3. Writers on nature
ISBN 0-299-03654-5 pa

LC 65-14539

First published 1913 by Houghton Mifflin
"The naturalist's childhood in a strict Presbyterian home in Scotland, his boyhood experiences of the privations and out-of-door delights of pioneer life on a Wisconsin farm, and his shifts and contrivances while earning his way through the state university." Cleveland Public Libr

Wilkins, Thurman. **John** Muir; apostle of nature. University of Okla. Press 1995 xxvii, 302p il maps (Oklahoma western biographies) hardcover o.p. pa $21.95 **92**

1. Authors 2. Naturalists 3. Writers on nature
ISBN 0-8061-2797-X pa

LC 95-11426

"Wilkins follows Muir from his Scottish boyhood, clouded by a harsh, fundamentalist father, to an adolescence of arduous farmwork in Wisconsin to a lifelong career of exploration and study of wildernesses, particularly those of the western U.S., and vividly relates some of Muir's more perilous adventures on cliffside and snowfield. . . . An affectionate, uncluttered tale of an American folk hero." Booklist

Includes bibliographical references

Worster, Donald. A **passion** for nature; the life of John Muir. Oxford University Press 2008 535p il map $34.95 **92**

1. Authors 2. Naturalists 3. Writers on nature
ISBN 978-0-19-516682-8; 0-19-516682-5

LC 2008-1441

The author "draws on John Muir's (1838-1914) correspondence and writings to offer an enlightening biography of the influential naturalist. . . . Competently documented, this all-inclusive biography explains the life and times of a figure known to all who love nature and will appeal to general readers and anyone interested in the early roots of today's green movement and its founding fathers." Libr J

Includes bibliographical references (p. 494-508)

Munch, Edvard, 1863-1944

Prideaux, Sue. **Edvard** Munch; behind the Scream. Yale University Press 2005 391p il map $35 **92**

1. Artists 2. Painters
ISBN 0-300-11024-3

LC 2005-12040

Prideaux's "treatment is very effective and her writing, cohesive, clear, and often compelling." Libr J

Includes bibliographical references

Murakami, Haruki, 1949-

Murakami, Haruki, 1949- **What** I talk about when I talk about running; a memoir. translated from the Japanese by Philip Gabriel. Alfred A. Knopf 2008 179p $21 **92**

1. Authors 2. Novelists 3. Marathon running 4. Nonfiction writers 5. Short story writers 6. Biography, Individual
ISBN 0-307-26919-1; 978-0-307-26919-5

LC 2008-17774

First published 2007 in Japan
This memoir covers Murakami's "four-month preparation for the 2005 New York City Marathon." (Publisher's note)

Murdoch, Rupert

Wolff, Michael. The **man** who owns the news; inside the secret world of Rupert Murdoch. Broadway Books 2008 446p $29.95 **92**

1. Mass media 2. Businessmen 3. Newspaper executives 4. Publishing executives 5. Broadcasting executives 6. Motion picture executives
ISBN 978-0-385-52612-8; 0-385-52612-1

LC 2008-37414

This biography of the Australian media entrepreneur describes how Rupert Murdoch came to own various companies, including The Wall Street Journal as well as its parent company, Dow Jones.

"There's lots of good material. . . . Perhaps most instructive, Wolff has melded interview and observation into what might be called a plausible theory of Murdoch." LA Times

Includes bibliographical references (p. 430-434)

Murray, Liz

Murray, Liz. **Breaking** night; a memoir of forgiveness, survival, and my journey from homeless to Harvard. Hyperion 2010 334p il $24.99 **92**

1. Students 2. Homeless persons 3. Children of drug addicts 4. Homeless 5. Motivational speakers
ISBN 978-0-7868-6891-9; 0-7868-6891-0

LC 2010-13679

"Neither sensationalizing nor soliciting pity, Murray's generous account of and caring attitude toward her past are not only uplifting, but also a fascinating lesson in the value of dedication." Booklist

Murray, Pauli, 1910-1985

★ Bell-Scott, Patricia. The **firebrand** and the First Lady; portrait of a friendship : Pauli Murray, Eleanor Roosevelt, and the struggle for social justice.

Patricia Bell-Scott. Alfred A. Knopf 2016 480 p. illustrations (hardcover : alk. paper) $30   **92**
1. Female friendship -- United States 2. African American feminists -- Biography 3. Episcopal Church -- Clergy -- Biography 4. African American intellectuals -- Biography 5. Presidents' spouses -- United States -- Biography 6. Women social reformers -- United States -- Biography 7. African American women civil rights workers -- Biography
ISBN 9780679446521
                     LC 2015014872
This book, by Patricia Bell-Scott, profiles the figures of Pauli Murray and Eleanor Roosevelt. It "tells the story of how a brilliant writer-turned-activist, granddaughter of a mulatto slave, and the first lady of the United States, whose ancestry gave her membership in the Daughters of the American Revolution, forged an enduring friendship that changed each of their lives and helped to alter the course of race and racism in America." (Publisher's note)
"Bell-Scott's groundbreaking portrait of these two tireless and innovative champions of human dignity adds an essential and edifying facet to American history." Booklist
Includes bibliographical references and index.

Murrow, Edward R.
Edwards, Bob. **Edward** R. Murrow and the birth of broadcast journalism; {by} Robert A. Edwards. Wiley 2004 174p (Turning points) $19.95   **92**
1. Journalists 2. Radio reporters 3. Government officials 4. Television reporters 5. Television news anchors
ISBN 0-471-47753-2
                     LC 2003-21223
"The author chronicles Murrow's innovations in radio and television broadcasting, including live radio reports of the war in progress in Europe in 1940; exposure of the despotism of Senator Joseph McCarthy on CBS in 1953; the powerful television documentary Harvest of Shame on the deplorable conditions of migrant workers in the U.S.; and the first in-depth television news program, See It Now. . . . Edwards brings to life the early days of radio and television and the innovations that Murrow sparked. . . . Readers interested in journalism will enjoy this slim book." Booklist
Includes bibliographical references

Sperber, Ann M. **Murrow,** his life and times; {by} A. M. Sperber; with a preface by Neil Hickey. Fordham Univ. Press 1998 xxvi, 795p il $35; pa $25   **92**
1. Journalists 2. Radio reporters 3. Government officials 4. Television reporters 5. Television news anchors
ISBN 0-8232-1881-3; 0-8232-1882-1 pa
                     LC 98-52507
A reissue of the title first published 1986 by Freundlich Bks.
This "ambitious exploration of Murrow's life places his story in the foreground of what is, as well, a panorama of the years 1935-65." N Y Times Book Rev
Includes bibliographical references

Mutch, Maria
Know the night; a memoir. Maria Mutch. Simon & Schuster 2014 224 p. (hardcover) $25   **92**
1. Autobiographies 2. Autistic children 3. Parents of children with disabilities 4. Insomnia -- Biography 5. Down syndrome -- Biography 6. Mothers and sons -- Biography 7. Books and reading -- Psychological aspects
ISBN 1476702748; 9781476702742; 9781476702759
                     LC 2013008363
In this memoir "Maria Mutch explores the miraculous power that care and communication have in the face of the deep, personal isolation that often comes with disability. A chronicle of the witching hours between midnight and six a.m., this meditative book takes place during the twoyear period in which Mutch's son Gabriel, who is autistic and also has Down syndrome, rarely slept through the night." (Publisher's note)
"Canadian Mutch is already a triple-threat author, having published poems, essays, and short fiction. Here she draws on her evident writing talents to discuss the nights she spent exploring the universe with son Gabriel, an autistic child with Down syndrome who suffered through a bad period of sleeplessness. In-house enthusiasm for this affecting, lyrical tale." LJ
Includes bibliographical references (page 202)

Mutter, Thomas D. (Thomas Dent), 1811-1859
★ Aptowicz, Cristin O'Keefe. **Dr.** Mütter's Marvels; A True Tale of Intrigue and Innovation at the Dawn of Modern Medicine. by Cristin O'Keefe Aptowicz. Gotham Books 2014 384 p. ill (hardcover) $27.50   **92**
1. Surgery -- History 2. Physicians -- Biography 3. Mutter Museum 4. Museums -- History -- Pennsylvania 5. Pathology -- History -- Pennsylvania 6. History, 19th Century -- Pennsylvania 7. Physicians -- Pennsylvania -- Biography 8. General Surgery -- History -- Pennsylvania 9. General Surgery -- Pennsylvania -- Biography
ISBN 1592408702; 9781592408702
                     LC 2014014747
This book, by Cristin O'Keefe Aptowicz, is a biography of surgeon Thomas Dent Mütter. "Mütter was . . . [a] medical innovator who pioneered the use of ether as anesthesia, the sterilization of surgical tools, and a compassion-based vision for helping the severely deformed, which clashed spectacularly with the sentiments of his time. . . . He . . . amassed an immense collection of medical oddities that would later form the basis of Philadelphia's Mütter Museum." (Publisher's note)
"In her deftly crafted narrative, the author provides an absorbing account of the charismatic surgeon's life and career as well as a vivid look at the medical practices and prejudices of his time." Kirkus
Includes bibliographical references and index

Nafisi, Azar
Nafisi, Azar. **Reading** Lolita in Tehran; a memoir in books. Random House 2003 347p $23.95; pa $11.16   **92**
1. Books and reading 2. Memoirists 3. Women -- Iran

4. College teachers 5. Literary critics
ISBN 0-375-50490-7; 0-8129-7106-X pa

LC 2002-36724

"In 1997 Iran, Nafisi formed an illicit book group whose syllabus provided the perfect framework for appraising life before and after the Islamic Revolution—and afforded her female students what little freedom they knew. Through impassioned discussions of Nabokov, James, and Fitzgerald, she details her teaching career and the obstacles her students faced. Her seamless blend of literary criticism and memoir begets a whole new genre." Libr J

★ Nafisi, Azar. **Things** I've been silent about; memories. Random House 2008 336p il $27   **92**
1. Memoirists 2. Women -- Iran 3. College teachers 4. Literary critics
ISBN 978-1-4000-6361-1; 1-4000-6361-2

LC 2008-482096

This is the author's "account of growing up under a chilly, tyrannical parent in a changing Iran. . . . An immensely rewarding and beautifully written act of courage, by turns amusing, tender and obsessively dogged." Kirkus

Naipaul, V. S. (Vidiadhar Surajprasad), 1932-
French, Patrick. The **world** is what it is; the authorized biography of V.S. Naipaul. Knopf 2008 554p il $30   **92**
1. Authors 2. Novelists 3. Journalists 4. Essayists 5. Travel writers 6. Radio reporters 7. Nonfiction writers 8. Short story writers 9. Nobel laureates for literature
ISBN 978-1-4000-4405-4; 1-4000-4405-7

LC 2008-6988

This authorized study of Nobel laureate V.S. Naipaul examines his difficult early life as a child of Indian parents in colonial Trinidad, his Oxford education, the depression that marked his life in England, his complex personal life and romantic relationships, and his pursuit of becoming a great writer.

This book "is a prodigious achievement, a wonderful biography, a justification for the art of biography itself." Times Lit Suppl

Includes bibliographical references

Naipaul, V. S. **Reading** & writing; a personal account. New York Review of Bks. 2000 64p $16.95   **92**
1. Authors 2. Novelists 3. Journalists 4. Essayists 5. Travel writers 6. Radio reporters 7. Nonfiction writers 8. Short story writers 9. Nobel laureates for literature
ISBN 0-940322-38-2

LC 99-49615

Naipaul writes about his experiences growing up as an Indian living in Trinidad, his travels in India, his education at Oxford, and his struggles as a young writer in London

The author "elegantly expresses hard-earned wisdom about literature and culture, the political stakes of history and the relationship between the writer and the world." N Y Times Book Rev

Napoleon I, Emperor of the French, 1769-1821
Broers, Michael. **Napoleon**; Soldier of Destiny. Michael Broers. W W Norton & Co Inc 2015 608 p. 8 plates; ills.; ports.; maps (hardcover) $35   **92**
ISBN 1605988723; 9781605988726

This biography, by Michael Broers, "is the first life of Napoleon, in any language, that makes full use of his newly released personal correspondence compiled by the Napoléon Foundation in Paris. All previous lives of Napoleon have relied more on the memoirs of others than on his own uncensored words." (Publisher's note)

"Highly recommended for general readers and scholars alike." LJ

Gueniffey, Patrice. **Bonaparte**; 1769-1802. Patrice Gueniffey; translated by Steven Rendall. The Belknap Press ofHarvard University Press 2015 1024 p. (alk. paper) $39.95   **92**
1. France -- History -- 1799-1815 2. Emperors -- France -- Biography 3. Heads of state -- France -- Biography 4. France -- History -- Consulate and First Empire, 1799-1815
ISBN 0674368355; 9780674368354

LC 2014034162

This book, by Patrice Gueniffey, translated by Steven Rendall, "takes up the epic narrative . . . of Napoleon himself. . . . Gueniffey follows Bonaparte from his obscure boyhood in Corsica, to his meteoric rise during the Italian and Egyptian campaigns of the Revolutionary wars, to his proclamation as Consul for Life in 1802. Bonaparte is the story of how Napoleon became Napoleon." (Publisher's note)

Includes bibliographical references and index

★ Roberts, Andrew, 1963- **Napoleon**; a life. Andrew Roberts. Viking 2014 926 p. ill. (chiefly col.), maps hbk $45   **92**
1. Napoleonic Wars, 1800-1815
ISBN 0670025321; 9780670025329

LC 2013497791

Los Angeles Times Book Prizes Winner: Biography (2014)

Author Andrew Roberts presents "the first one-volume biography to take advantage of the recent publication of Napoleon's thirty-three thousand letters, which radically transform our understanding of his character and motivation. Roberts traveled to fifty-three of Napoleon's sixty battle sites, discovered crucial new documents in archives, and even made the long trip by boat to St. Helena. " (Publisher's note)

"Other opinionated observers . . . consider Napoleon a self-absorbed opportunist plagued by his incompetent economics, pugnacious foreign policy, totalitarian government and massive propaganda, but Roberts offers a solid reconsideration." Kirkus

Includes bibliographical references and index

Schom, Alan. **Napoleon** Bonaparte; a life. HarperCollins Pubs. 1997 xxii, 888p hardcover o.p. pa $23.95   **92**
1. Emperors 2. France -- Kings and rulers
ISBN 0-06-092958-8 pa

LC 97-5805

"Schom's judgments have all the more impact for being brief and infrequent. What really interests him is telling the story of the man who made universal rules for others but recognized none for himself. He tells it straightforwardly and well; and not, thankfully, at the multi-volume length he believes the subject still really requires." Times Lit Suppl

Includes bibliographical references

Nash, Ogden, 1902-1971

Parker, Douglas M. **Ogden** Nash; the life and work of America's laureate of light verse. with a foreword by Dana Gioia. Ivan R. Dee 2005 316p il $27.50 **92**

1. Poets 2. Authors 3. Humorists 4. Children's authors
ISBN 1-566-63637-X

LC 2004-59912

"Parker's is a useful, highly readable biography of one of America's best-loved poets." Publ Wkly

Includes bibliographical references

Navratilova, Martina, 1956-

Howard, Johnette. The **rivals**; Chris Evert vs. Martina Navratilova: their epic duels and extraordinary friendship. Broadway Books 2005 296p il $24.95 **92**

1. Tennis players 2. Tennis -- Biography
ISBN 0-7679-1884-3

LC 2004-61918

"This work makes a fine contribution to the history of women in sports." Publ Wkly

Nawaz, Zarqa.

Nawaz, Zarqa. **Laughing** All the Way to the Mosque; The Misadventures of a Muslim Woman. Zarqa Nawaz. Little, Brown & Co. 2016 240 p. (paperback) $18.99 **92**

1. Wit and humor 2. Islam -- Customs and practices
ISBN 0349005931; 9780349005935

In this book, Muslim writer and humorist Zarqa Nawaz describes how "being a practicing Muslim in the West is sometimes challenging, sometimes rewarding and sometimes downright absurd. How do you explain why Eid never falls on the same date each year; why it is that Halal butchers also sell teapots and alarm clocks; how do you make clear to the plumber that it's essential the toilet is installed within sitting-arm's reach of the tap?" (Publisher's note)

"Nawaz's self-deprecating wit is endearing, and her simple, factual tone provides education without ever being boring. This memoir provides an important glimpse into the everyday life of a Western Muslim family, but, even better, it is a laugh-out-loud story that everyone can enjoy." Pub Wkly

Needham, Joseph, 1900-1995

Winchester, Simon. The **man** who loved China; the fantastic story of the eccentric scientist who unlocked the mysteries of the Middle Kingdom. HarperCollins Publishers 2008 316p il map $27.95 **92**

1. Scientists 2. Biochemists 3. Science historians 4. Writers on science 5. Biography, Individual 6. Science

-- China -- History
ISBN 978-0-06-088459-8; 0-06-088459-2

LC 2007-40516

The author "explores Needham's fascinating and sometimes controversial personal life, his travels to China, and especially the significance and topicality of his scholarship on the early accomplishments of Chinese science and technology. . . . Essential for all libraries." Libr J

Includes bibliographical references

Neel, Alice, 1900-1984

Hoban, Phoebe. **Alice** Neel; the art of not sitting pretty. St. Martin's Press 2010 500p il $35 **92**

1. Artists 2. Painters 3. Women artists
ISBN 978-0-312-60748-7; 0-312-60748-7

LC 2010-35781

"Judicious and ardent, Hoban has created a galvanizing portrait of a 'rebel artist' who remained true to her humanist convictions." Booklist

Includes bibliographical references

Nehru, Jawaharlal, 1889-1964

Brown, Judith M. **Nehru**; a political life. Yale University Press 2003 407p il $35 **92**

1. Prime ministers 2. Nonfiction writers 3. Prime ministers -- India
ISBN 0-300-09279-2

LC 2003-5807

"This compelling biography, the most complete and penetrating account of Nehru yet written, casts new light on both the public and private man. It also offers insights into the history of India's nationalist movement and the complexities of constructing a new nation state in the aftermath of imperial rule." Univ Press Books for Public and Second Sch Libr, 2004

Includes bibliographical references

Nelson, Horatio Nelson, Viscount, 1758-1805

Hibbert, Christopher. **Nelson**; a personal history. Addison-Wesley 1994 472p il hardcover o.p. pa $22 **92**

1. Admirals
ISBN 0-201-40800-7 pa

LC 94-39545

The book "succeeds admirably in presenting a vivid and intimate picture of Nelson and Lady Hamilton together, helped by numerous and apt illustrations, half of them in colour. . . . The result is essentially a book of domestic detail, told with charm and perception." Times Lit Suppl

Includes bibliographical references

Sugden, John. **Nelson**: a dream of glory, 1758-1797. Henry Holt 2004 943p il map $35 **92**

1. Admirals
ISBN 0-8050-7757-X

LC 2004-54057

"This first of a projected two-volume study covers the least familiar period of Nelson's life, from childhood through his rise to international fame in 1797. . . . Sugden's account of Nelson's early career certainly bids fair to fill the gaps,

ranging from the future admiral's first years to the disastrous action off Tenerife. . . . Sugden has done well here." Libr J
Includes bibliographical references (p. 883-906)

Nelson, Paul

Avery, Kevin. **Everything** is an afterthought; the life and writings of Paul Nelson. Fantagraphics Books 2011 xxvi, 497p il $29.99   **92**
1. Journalists 2. Music critics 3. Writers on music 4. Rock music -- History and criticism
ISBN 978-1-60699-475-7
"Seamlessly incorporating the perspectives of Nick Tosches, Robert Christgau, and Jann Wenner, Avery has crafted both a cautionary tale and a celebration of a noir-influenced writer who deserves a place alongside Lester Bangs for his ability to live, always, in the music. Devotees of folk, establishment rock 'n' roll, and pulp fiction will rue not having discovered Nelson sooner." Libr J
Includes bibliographical references

Nelson, Willie

★ Patoski, Joe Nick. **Willie** Nelson; an epic life. Little, Brown 2008 567p il $27.99; pa $16.99 **92**
1. Singers 2. Country musicians 3. Songwriters
ISBN 978-0-316-01778-7; 0-316-01778-7; 978-0-316-01779-4 pa; 0-316-01779-5 pa
LC 2007-44984
A biography of the country music singer and songwriter.
"This impressive, entertaining chronicle of Willie Nelson's life is replete with exactly what you'd expect—honky-tonk, long nights on the open road, whiskey, womanizing and weed—but . . . [the author] looks beyond country music trappings to find the funny, talented, determined man who became an unlikely icon." Publ Wkly
Includes discography and bibliographical references

Nemat, Marina

Nemat, Marina. **Prisoner** of Tehran; a memoir. Free Press 2007 306p $26   **92**
1. Political prisoners 2. Memoirists 3. Iran -- History -- 1979-
ISBN 1-4165-3742-2; 978-1-4165-3742-7
LC 2006-50191
Nemat was sixteen when she was arrested in Iran in early 1982 for political protests against the new fundamentalist regime. This is an account of her prison experiences.
The author's "story is not so much a political history lesson than it is a memoir of faith and love, a protest against violence that cannot be silenced. . . . Her persistence in standing for goodness is a lesson for us all." Christ Sci Monit

Neruda, Pablo, 1904-1973

★ Feinstein, Adam. **Pablo** Neruda; a passion for life. Bloomsbury 2004 497p il $32.50; pa $18.95   **92**
1. Poets 2. Authors 3. Diplomats 4. Novelists 5. Nobel laureates for peace 6. Nobel laureates for literature
ISBN 1-582-34410-8; 1-582-34594-5 pa
LC 2004-715
"Feinstein undoubtedly researched every existent source and found new ones, and the result is a detailed and accurate

biography. . . . This is a necessary book, with many beautiful photos." Publ Wkly
Includes bibliographical references

Urrutia, Matilde. **My** life with Pablo Neruda; {translated by} Alexandria Giardino. Stanford University Press 2004 318p $27.95   **92**
1. Poets 2. Authors 3. Diplomats 4. Novelists 5. Nobel laureates for peace 6. Nobel laureates for literature
ISBN 0-8047-5009-2
LC 2004-8535
Original Spanish edition, 1986
"Urrutia, Neruda's third wife, provides a . . . biography from her particular vantage. Her purpose is twofold: to present her Pablo as the exuberant, warm, and loving individual he was and to inform readers of the menace imposed by Chilean dictator Pinochet, who was responsible for the assassination of elected president Allende, Neruda's close friend. Urrutia's account is highly selective but well worth reading for another perspective on this great man." Libr J

Newman, Paul, 1925-2008

Levy, Shawn. **Paul** Newman; a life. Harmony Books 2009 490p il $29.99; pa $16   **92**
1. Actors 2. Motion picture directors 3. Automobile racing drivers
ISBN 978-0-307-35375-7; 0-307-35375-3; 978-0-307-35376-4 pa; 0-307-35376-1 pa
LC 2009-11220
This is a behind-the-scenes examination of the actor's life, from his merry pranks on the set to his lasting romance with Joanne Woodward to the devastating impact of his son's death from a drug overdose
"An illuminating look at one of the true greats, full of humor and intelligent analysis—highly recommended." Kirkus
Includes bibliographical references

Newton, Isaac Sir, 1642-1727

Fara, Patricia. **Newton**: the making of genius. Columbia Univ. Press 2002 347p il $83.50; pa $23   **92**
1. Physicists 2. Scientists 3. Mathematicians 4. Writers on science
ISBN 0-231-12806-1; 0-231-12807-X pa
LC 2003-265510
This "social history examines the reasons behind Isaac Newton's canonization as scientific genius. . . . Fara contributes to Newton's biography by focusing on the roots of Newton's apotheosis. She examines how idealized portraits propagated Newton's public image, and how the marketing of Newtonian images outside academic circles commercialized science in the same way Einstein's face sells today. Throughout, Fara, . . . effectively employs the words and imagery of religious discourse to characterize the idealization and commercialization of Newton in the service of emerging secular politics and culture." Publ Wkly
Includes bibliographical references

Gleick, James. **Isaac** Newton. Pantheon Bks. 2003 272p il hardcover o.p. pa $13   **92**
1. Physicists 2. Scientists 3. Mathematicians 4.

Writers on science
ISBN 0-375-42233-1; 1-4000-3295-4 pa
LC 2002-192696

This "is now the biography of choice for the interested layman. Gleick copes with the complex tapestry of Newton's interests by teasing them apart into individual chapters, assembled into a smooth chronological flow. . . . Newton the man emerges from the shadows." N Y Times Book Rev

Includes bibliographical references

Levenson, Thomas. **Newton** and the counterfeiter; the unknown detective career of the world's greatest scientist. Houghton Mifflin Harcourt 2009 318p $25; pa $14.95   **92**
1. Physicists 2. Mathematicians 3. Counterfeits and counterfeiting 4. Counterfeiters 5. Writers on science
ISBN 978-0-15-101278-7; 0-15-101278-4; 978-0-547-33604-6 pa; 0-547-33604-7 pa
LC 2008-53511

"Levenson demonstrates a surpassing felicity in his brisk treatment of this late-17th-century true-crime adventure. . . . Swift, agile treatment of a little known but highly entertaining episode in a legendary life." Kirkus

Includes bibliographical references

Westfall, Richard S. The **life** of Isaac Newton. Cambridge Univ. Press 1993 328p il hardcover o.p. pa $16   **92**
1. Physicists 2. Scientists 3. Mathematicians 4. Writers on science 5. Biography, Individual
ISBN 0-521-47737-9 pa
LC 92-33777

"The life that I here present is a reduced version of the full-scale biography Never at Rest {BRD 1981, 1982}. . . . In reducing the work in length, I have attempted to make it more accessible to a general audience by also reducing its technical content. . . . To facilitate consultation, I have retained the titles of the original chapters; and the contents of the chapters, as condensations, follow the same patterns of organization." (Preface) Annotated bibliography. Index.

In this book the author has "reduced his longer 1980 biography of Newton (Never at Rest) to a size that is more suitable for general audiences. The result is a work whose faults lie only in the paucity of source materials that all Newton biographers face. . . . Westfall's book comes as close to presenting the man as the impersonal evidence allows without undue extrapolation." Sci Books Films

Includes bibliographical references

Nicholas II, Emperor of Russia, 1868-1918

Ferro, Marc. **Nicholas** II; the last of the tsars. translated by Brian Pearce. Oxford Univ. Press 1993 305p il map hardcover o.p. pa $19.95   **92**
1. Emperors 2. Russia -- History 3. Russia -- Kings and rulers
ISBN 0-19-509382-8 pa
LC 92-41440

"The last Tsar, as this fluently written biography makes abundantly clear, was largely to blame for the demise of the monarchy. Ferro is concerned to illuminate the personality of the Tsar, his relationship with his wife and Rasputin and

to look again at the circumstances surrounding his death." Hist Today

Includes bibliographical references

Massie, Robert K., 1929- **Nicholas** and Alexandra. Ballantine Books 2000 613p il map pa $18.95   **92**
1. Monks 2. Emperors 3. Empresses 4. Courtiers 5. Russia -- History 6. Russia -- Kings and rulers
ISBN 0-345-43831-0; 978-0-345-43831-7
LC 99-91507

First published 1967 by Atheneum

This study provides an intimate account of the Romanov family and the coming of the Russian Revolution. Kerensky, Lenin and Rasputin are among the personalities profiled.

This book, "solid with research, reads as lightly as a novel, as authoritatively as a textbook. Dialogue and lively description lend a sense of immediacy, but his notes, discreetly relegated to the back of the book, show how carefully he has avoided slipping into fiction." Christ Sci Monit

Includes bibliographical references

Nightingale, Florence, 1820-1910

Bostridge, Mark. **Florence** Nightingale; the making of an icon. Farrar, Straus and Giroux 2008 646p il $35   **92**
1. Nurses 2. Nonfiction writers
ISBN 978-0-374-15665-7; 0-374-15665-4
LC 2008-31424

Bostridge presents a "well-researched, and comprehensive biography of Nightingale, drawing heavily on letters, diaries, and other primary sources in a successful effort to create a balanced and authentic portrait of the woman, not the myth. Beginning with moving depictions of Nightingale's struggles to be allowed to pursue her calling despite her family's objections, Bostridge skillfully illuminates the spiritual and philosophical motivations that drove Nightingale's impassioned and lifelong dedication to the causes of nursing and public health reform." Libr J

Includes bibliographical references

Nitze, Paul H.

Thompson, Nicholas. The **hawk** and the dove; Paul Nitze, George Kennan, and the history of the Cold War. Henry Holt 2009 403p il $27.50   **92**
1. Authors 2. Cold war 3. Diplomats 4. Statesmen 5. Historians 6. Centenarians 7. Nonfiction writers 8. Government officials 9. Biography, Individual 10. Secretaries of the navy 11. United States -- Officials and employees 12. United States -- Foreign relations -- 1945-1989 13. National security -- United States -- History -- 20th century 14. Anti-communist movements -- United States -- History -- 20th century
ISBN 0805081429; 9780805081428
LC 2009-09225

This biography of Nitze and Kennan focuses on their "careers as statesmen, policy makers and public intellectuals." (N Y Times Book Rev) Index.

This book "does an inspired job of telling the story of the Cold War through the careers of two of its most interesting and important figures." Washington Monthly

Includes bibliographical references

Nixon, Richard M. (Richard Milhous), 1913-1994

Black, Conrad M. **Richard** M. Nixon; a life in full. [by] Conrad Black. PublicAffairs 2007 1152p il $40 **92**

1. Presidents 2. Vice-presidents 3. Senators 4. Nonfiction writers 5. Members of Congress 6. Presidents -- United States

ISBN 978-1-58648-519-1; 1-58648-519-9

LC 2007-34530

This is a biography of the thirty-seventh president.

"Black's superb volume, incorporating much new research, is an important and worthy addition to the literature." Publ Wkly

Includes bibliographical references

Dallek, Robert. **Nixon** and Kissinger; partners in power. HarperCollins Publishers 2007 740p il $32.50 **92**

1. Presidents 2. Vice-presidents 3. Senators 4. College teachers 5. Nonfiction writers 6. Members of Congress 7. Writers on politics 8. Secretaries of state 9. Presidential advisers 10. Nobel laureates for peace 11. United States -- Foreign relations 12. International relations specialists

ISBN 978-0-06-072230-2; 0-06-072230-4

LC 2006-52100

A look "behind the scenes at this quintessential pair of power brokers and their lasting influence, for good and ill, on the political stage." Bookmarks Magazine

Includes bibliographical references

Thomas, Evan. **Being** Nixon; the fears and hopes of an American president. Evan Thomas. Random House Inc. 2015 656 p. illustrations $35 **92**

1. Presidents -- United States 2. Nixon, Richard M. (Richard Milhous), 1913-1994 3. Presidents -- United States -- Biography 4. United States -- Politics and government -- 1969-1974

ISBN 0812995368; 9780812995367

LC 2015009669

Author Evan Thomas presents this "biography of Richard Nixon, . . . a complicated figure who was both determinedly optimistic and tragically flawed. Thomas reveals the contradictions of a leader whose vision and foresight led him to achieve détente with the Soviet Union and reestablish relations with communist China, but whose underhanded political tactics tainted his reputation long before the Watergate scandal." (Publisher's note)

"Thomas doesn't shy away from showing Nixon at his worst, acknowledging Nixon's penchant for the "maudlin," his "self-pity," his fear of confrontation, and his often poisonous rivalry with Henry Kissinger. Thomas is generous to his subject, contextualizing Nixon and often teasing out his well-concealed desire to do the right thing." Pub Wkly

Includes bibliographical references and index

Niyizonkiza, Deogratias, 1970-

Kidder, Tracy. **Strength** in what remains. Random House 2009 277p $26; pa $16 **92**

1. Genocide 2. Refugees 3. Students 4. Burundi

ISBN 978-1-4000-6621-6; 1-4000-6621-2; 978-0-

8129-7761-5 pa; 0-8121-7761-0 pa

LC 2008-44865

"This profoundly gripping, hopeful and crucial testament is a work of the utmost skill, sympathy and moral clarity." Publ Wkly

Includes bibliographical references

Noguchi, Isamu, 1904-1988

Herrera, Hayden. **Listening** to stone; the art and life of Isamu Noguchi. Hayden Herrera. Farrar Straus & Giroux 2015 592 p. illustrations (hardback) $40 **92**

1. Sculptors -- United States -- Biography 2. Japanese American sculptors -- Biography

ISBN 0374281165; 9780374281168

LC 2014031274

Los Angeles Times Book Prize: Biography (2015)

This book, by Hayden Herrera, is a biography of the American artist Isamu Noguchi. "Combining the personal correspondence of and interviews with Noguchi and those closest to him--from artists, patrons, assistants, and lovers--[Hayden] Herrera has created an authoritative biography of one of the twentieth century's most important sculptors." (Publisher's note)

"Herrera adroitly shows that Noguchi was more than just a sculptor--he was a skilled craftsman, a heartbreaker, and a philosopher of design." Pub Wkly

Includes bibliographical references and index

Norris, Gloria

Norris, Gloria. **Kookooland**; Gloria Norris. Regan Arts 2015 355 p. illustrations $27 **92**

1. Family life 2. Autobiographies

ISBN 1941393608; 9781941393604

LC 2015930624

This memoir by Gloria Norris is a "profound portrait of how violence echoes through a family, and through a community. From the tragedy, Gloria finds a way to carve out a future on her own terms and ends up just where she wants to be. " (Publisher's note)

"A tumble through a tumultuous time, in which the heroine inexplicably, beautifully lands on her feet." Booklist

Norris, Kathleen, 1947-

Norris, Kathleen. **Acedia** & me; a marriage, monks, and a writer's life. Riverhead Books 2008 334p $25.95 **92**

1. Poets 2. Apathy 3. Authors 4. Melancholy 5. Monasticism and religious orders 6. Inspirational writers

ISBN 978-1-59448-996-9

LC 2008-10150

"The result of Norris's decades-long meditation on acedia is peaceful, graceful prose, amplified by word histories and gentle humor." Christ Today

Includes bibliographical references

Norris, Michele, 1961-

Norris, Michele. The **grace** of silence; a memoir. Pantheon Books 2010 185p il $24.95; ebook $24.95 **92**

1. Journalists 2. Women journalists 3. Radio reporters

4. Television reporters 5. United States -- Race relations
6. African American women -- Biography
ISBN 978-0-307-37876-7; 978-0-307-37946-7 ebook
LC 2010-19285
"In examining her personal roots for this memoir, African American Norris . . . found some skeletons in her family's closet. For example, she discovered that in the early 20th century her grandmother had dressed as Aunt Jemina to pitch pancake flour to the wives of white farmers in the Midwest. Using her skills as an investigative reporter, Norris also pieces together details of an incident in 1946 when her father was shot by a white policeman in Birmingham, AL. . . . Norris's family history offers Americans of all races a moving and revealing account of the obstacles facing several generations of middle-class African Americans in the pre-Civil Rights era." Libr J
Includes bibliographical references

Northup, Solomon, 1808-1863

★ Northup, Solomon. **Twelve** years a slave; Solomon Northup; introduction by Ira Berlin; general editor Henry Louis Gates, Jr. Penguin Books 2012 xxxvi, 240 p.p ill., music (Penguin Classics) (pbk.) $16 92
1. Slaves -- United States -- 19th century 2. Slaves' writings, American 3. African Americans -- Biography 4. Slaves -- United States -- Biography 5. Slavery -- Louisiana -- History -- 19th century 6. Plantation life -- Louisiana -- History -- 19th century
ISBN 0143106708; 9780143106708
LC 2012012550
This autobiographical book "recounts how Solomon Northup, born a free man in New York, was lured to Washington, D.C., in 1841 with the promise of fast money, then drugged and beaten and sold into slavery. He spent the next twelve years of his life in captivity on a Louisiana cotton plantation. After his rescue, Northup published this . . . detailed account of slave life." (Publisher's note)
Includes bibliographical references and index

Nostradamus, 1503-1566

Gerson, Stéphane. **Nostradamus**; how an obscure Renaissance astrologer became the modern prophet of doom. Stephane Gerson. St. Martins Press 2012 368 p. (hardcover) $29.99 92
1. Prophecies 2. Prophecies (Occultism) 3. Twentieth century -- Forecasts
ISBN 0312613687; 9780312613686
LC 2012031001
In this book, "historian Stéphane Gerson takes readers on a journey back in time to explore the life and afterlife of Michel de Nostredame, the astrologer whose 'Prophecies' have been interpreted, adopted by successive media, and eventually transformed into the Gospel of Doom for the modern age. . . . Gerson shows that Nostradamus . . . tells us more about our past and our present than about our future." (Publisher's note)

Novacek, Michael J.

Novacek, Michael J. **Time** traveler; in search of dinosaurs and ancient mammals from Montana to

Mongolia. {by} Michael Novacek. Farrar, Straus & Giroux 2002 368p il $26; pa $15 92
1. Curators 2. Paleontologists
ISBN 0-374-27880-6; 0-374-52876-4 pa
LC 2001-40438
"The author first describes the youthful experiences that inspired him to become a paleontologist. . . . Then Novacek launches into his various expeditions. . . . Interweaving his adventures with explanations of where his finds fit into the geologic past, Novacek has combined the comedic with the informative in this entertaining survey of his career." Booklist
Includes bibliographical references

Nudelman, Meyer

Nuland, Sherwin B. **Lost** in America; a journey with my father. Knopf 2003 209p $24; pa $12 92
1. Authors 2. Surgeons 3. Factory workers 4. Writers on medicine
ISBN 0-375-41294-8; 0-375-75722-1 pa
LC 2002-40795
"Written with enormous empathy, yet without a hint of sentimentality, Nuland's memoir is both heartbreaking and breathtaking." Publ Wkly

Nuland, Sherwin B.

Nuland, Sherwin B. **Lost** in America; a journey with my father. Knopf 2003 209p $24; pa $12 92
1. Authors 2. Surgeons 3. Factory workers 4. Writers on medicine
ISBN 0-375-41294-8; 0-375-75722-1 pa
LC 2002-40795
"Written with enormous empathy, yet without a hint of sentimentality, Nuland's memoir is both heartbreaking and breathtaking." Publ Wkly

Nureyev, Rudolf, 1938-1993

★ Kavanagh, Julie. **Nureyev**; the life. Pantheon Books 2007 782p il $37.50 92
1. Ballet dancers
ISBN 978-0-375-40513-6; 0-375-40513-5
LC 2006-38137
In this biography of the Russian ballet dancer, the author "chronicles Nureyev's many tempestuous relationships, including his legendary work with Margot Fonteyn and his formative affair with the outstanding Danish dancer Erik Bruhn. . . . Kavanagh's consummate biography will stand as a pillar in dance history." Booklist
Includes bibliographical references

Nusseibeh, Sari

David, Anthony. **Once** upon a country; a Palestinian life. [by] Sari Nusseibeh, with Anthony David. Farrar, Straus and Giroux 2007 542p il $27.50 92
1. Philosophers 2. Palestinian Arabs 3. Israel-Arab conflicts 4. Political leaders 5. College presidents 6. Biography, Individual
ISBN 0-374-29950-1; 978-0-374-29950-7
LC 2006-13272
This is an autobiography by "Sari Nusseibeh, a Palestinian intellectual and public figure." (N Y Times (Late N Y Ed))

"This is a rare book, one written by a partisan in the struggle over Palestine who nevertheless recognizes—and bravely records—the moral and political failures of his own people." Los Angeles Times

Includes bibliographical references

Nyad, Diana

Nyad, Diana, 1949- **Find** a way; one wild and precious life. Diana Nyad. Alfred A. Knopf 2015 304 p. 16 plates; illustrations; map (hardback) $26.95 **92**

1. Success 2. Swimmers -- United States -- Biography
ISBN 0385353618; 9780385353618

LC 2015009932

"At 64, celebrated long-distance swimmer Nyad accomplished a feat that had eluded her at 28--making the first solo swim from Cuba to Florida without a shark cage. While Cuba to the Keys is 94 miles for the proverbial crow, Nyad lacked wings and ultimately covered 110 miles through the powerful Gulf current, navigating hazards that included toxic jellyfish and peckish sharks, as well as severe nausea and dehydration. As Nyad narrates the financial and physical demands of her odyssey, which she undertook after a three-decade break from swimming, she also reviews her career as a television journalist and talk show host." (Publishers Weekly)

"Particularly effective in its ability to portray the complex psychology of an extreme endurance athlete, Nyad's moving account is well suited for readers interested in open-water swimming, endurance sports, athletes' memoirs, or age-defying adventures." LJ

O'Brien, Edna

O'Brien, Edna, 1930- **Country** Girl; A Memoir. by Edna O'Brien. Little, Brown and Co. 2013 x, 357 p.p ill. (hardcover) $27.99 **92**

1. Authors 2. Women authors -- Biography 3. Women authors, Irish -- 20th century -- Biography
ISBN 031612270X; 9780316122702

LC 2012047510

This memoir, written by Edna O'Brien, starts "with [her] birth in a grand but deteriorating house in Ireland, [and] moves through convent school to elopement, divorce, single-motherhood, the wild parties of the [1960s] in London, and encounters with Hollywood giants, pop stars, and literary titans. There is love and unrequited love, and the glamour of trips to America as an acclaimed writer hosted by Jackie Onassis and Hillary Clinton." (Publisher's note)

"While O'Brien overly devotes her time to cataloguing the notable actors, writers, and politicians of her acquaintance, the accounts of her childhood and her descriptions of Ireland soar with a lyricism reminiscent of Joyce." LJ

O'Brien, Jack, 1939-

O'Brien, Jack. **Jack** be nimble; the accidental education of an unintentional director. Jack O'Brien. Farrar, Straus & Giroux 2013 368 p. (hardback) $35 **92**

1. Theatrical producers and directors 2. Television producers and directors -- United States -- Biography 3. Theatrical producers and directors -- United States

-- Biography
ISBN 0865478988; 9780865478985

LC 2012048077

This book presents a memoir by director Jack O'Brien. "Following a fairly normal Midwestern childhood, O'Brien hoped to make his mark by writing lyrics for Broadway but was instead pulled into the growing American regional theater movement by the likes of John Houseman, Helen Hayes, Ellis Rabb, and Eva Le Gallienne. He didn't intend to become a director, or to direct some of the most brilliant . . . personalities of the age, but . . . that's what happened." (Publisher's note)

"Highly recommended for lovers of the theater and those interested in acting and directing." LJ

Includes bibliographical references and index

O'Connor, Flannery

Cash, Jean W. **Flannery** O'Connor: a life. University of Tenn. Press 2002 356p il $30; pa $24.95 **92**

1. Authors 2. Novelists 3. Short story writers
ISBN 1-572-33192-5; 1-572-33305-7 pa

LC 2002-250

"Cash analyzes the woman behind the myth, introducing an extraordinarily intelligent human being noted for her keen sense of humor, intellectual versatility, and tremendous capacity for friendship. This intimate chronicle of a major literary talent will appeal to both students and scholars." Booklist

Includes bibliographical references

★ Gooch, Brad. **Flannery**; a life of Flannery O'Connor. Little, Brown and Co. 2009 448p il $30 **92**

1. Authors 2. Novelists 3. Women authors 4. Authors, American 5. Short story writers 6. Biography, Individual
ISBN 978-0-316-00066-6; 0-316-00066-3

LC 2008-28504

This biography of writer Flannery O'Connor, by Brad Gooch, focuses on "O'Connor's significant friendships--with Robert Lowell, Elizabeth Hardwick, Walker Percy, and James Dickey among others--and her deeply felt convictions, as expressed in her communications with Thomas Merton, Elizabeth Bishop, and Betty Hester. . . . O'Connor's capacity to live fully--despite the chronic disease that eventually confined her to her mother's farm in Georgia" is also discussed. (Publisher's note)

"Gooch comfortably traces her fiction to its real-life roots in a meticulous yet seemingly effortless writing style, resulting in the definitive biography as well as providing the impetus for general readers to return to O'Connor's timeless fiction." Booklist

Includes bibliographical references

O'Connor, Flannery. The **habit** of being; letters. edited and with an introduction by Sally Fitzgerald. Farrar, Straus & Giroux 1979 617p hardcover o.p. pa $20 **92**

1. Authors 2. Novelists 3. Short story writers
ISBN 0-374-52104-2 pa

LC 78-11559

This collection includes letters to friends in the literary establishment: Robert Lowell and Elizabeth Hardwick, Caroline Gordon Tate, Robert and Sally Fitzgerald and others

O'Connor, Sandra Day

Biskupic, Joan. **Sandra** Day O'Connor; how the first woman on the Supreme Court became its most influential justice. Ecco 2005 419p il $26.95 **92**
1. Supreme Court justices
ISBN 0-06-059018-1
LC 2005-52103
The author "offers an insightful biography of perhaps the most influential associate justice in recent history." Libr J
Includes bibliographical references

O'Dell, Chris, 1947-

O'Dell, Chris. **Miss** O'Dell; my hard days and long nights with the Beatles, the Stones, Bob Dylan, Eric Clapton, and the women they loved. [by] Chris O'Dell with Katherine Ketcham. Touchstone 2009 403p il $26 **92**
1. Music industry 2. Hypnotists 3. Memoirists 4. Drug abuse counselors 5. Rock musicians -- Anecdotes
ISBN 978-1-416-59093-4; 1-416-59093-5
LC 2009-14555
"An irresistible memoir of one of the lesser lights of a major constellation of rock stars and their satellites." Kirkus

O'Keeffe, Georgia, 1887-1986

Drohojowska-Philp, Hunter. **Full** bloom; the art and life of Georgia O'Keeffe. W.W. Norton 2004 630p hardcover o.p. pa $21.95 **92**
1. Artists 2. Painters 3. Biography, Individual
ISBN 0-393-05853-0; 0-393-32741-8 pa
LC 2003-26071
This is a biography of the American painter.
"O'Keeffe lived a long, adventurous, and profoundly productive life, and Drohojowska-Philp charts her triumphs over adversity in an involving, revelatory biography that attains the grand scope and depth her subject deserves." Booklist
Includes bibliographical references

O'Malley, Walter Francis, 1903-1979

D'Antonio, Michael. **Forever** blue; the true story of Walter O'Malley, baseball's most controversial owner, and the Dodgers of Brooklyn and Los Angeles. Riverhead Books 2009 355p il $25.95 **92**
1. Baseball executives 2. Baseball -- Biography 3. Brooklyn Dodgers (Baseball team) 4. Los Angeles Dodgers (Baseball team)
ISBN 978-1-59448-856-6; 1-59448-856-8
LC 2008-46311
"This is a wonderfully readable, insightful, and—for anyone interested in baseball history—important biography of the man who forever changed the course of the game in America." Booklist
Includes bibliographical references

O'Neill, Eugene, 1888-1953

Dowling, Robert M. **Eugene** O'Neill; a life in four acts. Robert M. Dowling. Yale University Press 2014 584 p. illustrations (hardback) $35 **92**
1. American dramatists 2. Dramatists, American -- 20th century -- Biography
ISBN 0300170335; 9780300170337
LC 2014014634
Los Angeles Times Book Prize Finalist: Biography (2014)
This biography, by Robert M. Dowling, focuses on playwright Eugene O'Neill. "Dowling traces the trajectory of O'Neill's career: his two semesters in George Baker's noted playwriting seminar at Harvard; his professional growth with the Provincetown Players; the production of his first full-length play, Beyond the Horizon (1920), which won a Pulitzer Prize; and his prolific output for the next two decades." (Kirkus Reviews)
"A well-rounded portrait of the playwright that can serve as a comprehensive introduction while also considering previously unknown facets of O'Neill's life and work." LJ
Includes bibliographical references and index

O'Reilly, Bill

O'Reilly, Bill. A **bold** fresh piece of humanity. Broadway Books 2008 256p il $26 **92**
1. Journalists 2. Talk show hosts 3. Television reporters 4. Television moderators
ISBN 978-0-7679-2882-3; 0-7679-2882-2
LC 2008-25510
This is a memoir by the broadcaster and author of The O'Reilly Factor (2000), The No Spin Zone (2001), and Who's Looking Out For You? (2003).

O'Rourke, Barbara Kelly, d. 2008

O'Rourke, Meghan. The **long** goodbye; a memoir. Riverhead Books 2011 306p $25.95 **92**
1. Poets 2. Authors 3. Bereavement 4. Mother-daughter relationship 5. Essayists 6. Cancer patients 7. Poets, American 8. Magazine editors 9. Biography, Individual 10. Mothers and daughters
ISBN 978-1-59448-798-9
LC 2010047948
"The raw feelings, the inevitable self-pity over each person's own loss, and their futile wishes to somehow make Mother's last days not be her last days will likely feel all too close to home for many who have suffered similarly. . . . Every tear-stained page is not a road map, but rather a lovely gift from a fellow traveler." Booklist
Includes bibliographical references

O'Rourke, Meghan

O'Rourke, Meghan. The **long** goodbye; a memoir. Riverhead Books 2011 306p $25.95 **92**
1. Poets 2. Authors 3. Bereavement 4. Mother-daughter relationship 5. Essayists 6. Cancer patients 7. Poets, American 8. Magazine editors 9. Biography, Individual 10. Mothers and daughters
ISBN 978-1-59448-798-9
LC 2010047948
"The raw feelings, the inevitable self-pity over each person's own loss, and their futile wishes to somehow make

Mother's last days not be her last days will likely feel all too close to home for many who have suffered similarly. . . . Every tear-stained page is not a road map, but rather a lovely gift from a fellow traveler." Booklist

Includes bibliographical references

O'Shea, James

O'Shea, James. The **deal** from hell; how moguls and Wall Street plundered great American newspapers. PublicAffairs 2011 395p $28.99   **92**
1. Journalists 2. Los Angeles times 3. Newspaper editors 4. Newspaper executives 5. Newspapers -- United States 6. Cooperative organization administrators
ISBN 978-1-58648-791-1; 978-1-58648-865-9 ebook
LC 2011009204

In this book, James O'Shea "details the development, events, and aftermath of the Tribune Company's 2007 purchase by investor Sam Zell. . . . O'Shea suggests the 'deal from hell' resulted from executive malpractice that unnecessarily jeopardized the financial and journalistic status quo of a declining--but profitable--mass-media conglomerate." (Choice: Current Reviews for Academic Libraries)

The author "recounts the events leading to the dissolution of several major American newspapers in this gripping story of a troubled industry. Told from the 'front-row,' O'Shea shows how ill-advised mergers, mismanagement, acquisitive Wall Street execs, and the Tribune Company's eventual bankruptcy filing crippled an industry. . . . For those who want an inside look at what makes American journalism work (and not work), O'Shea offers a unique and valuable perspective." Publ Wkly

Includes bibliographical references

Oakley, Annie, 1860-1926

Kasper, Shirl. **Annie** Oakley. University of Okla. Press 1992 288p il $29.95; pa $19.95   **92**
1. Marksmen 2. Frontier and pioneer life -- West (U.S.)
ISBN 0-8061-2418-0; 0-8061-3244-2 pa
LC 91-50864

This biography of the legendary sharpshooter "not only paints a picture of a woman with an unusual occupation for her time; it also colors the whole era of Wild West performers from Buffalo Bill to Will Rogers." Booklist

Includes bibliographical references

Oates, Joyce Carol, 1938-

★ Oates, Joyce Carol. The **journal** of Joyce Carol Oates: 1973-1982; edited by Greg Johnson. Ecco 2007 509p il $29.95   **92**
1. Poets 2. Authors 3. Novelists 4. Women authors 5. Essayists 6. Authors, American 7. Children's authors 8. Short story writers
ISBN 978-0-06-122798-1; 0-06-122798-6
LC 2007-29378

This is a collection of diaries from the period when Oates published Do With Me What You Will (1973), Bellefleur (1980), and other works.

"This journal immerses the reader in a complex, searching, imaginative personality—an artist who continues to refine her search for literary expression." Publ Wkly

Includes bibliographical references

The **Lost** Landscape; A Writer's Coming of Age. HarperCollins 2015 288 p. 8 plates; ills.; portraits $27.99   **92**
1. Women authors 2. Authors -- Family life
ISBN 0062408674; 9780062408679

In this autobiography, author Joyce Carol Oates "re-creates the early years of her life in western New York State. . . . From early memories of her relatives to remembrances of a particularly poignant friendship with a red hen, from her first friendships to her first experiences with death," the book shows "the ways in which Oates's life (and her life as a writer) was shaped by early childhood and how her later work was influenced by a hardscrabble rural upbringing." (Publisher's note)

"Given the popularity of Oates' previous memoir, this spellbinding coming-of-age narrative, backed by an author tour and an extensive media campaign, will be a veritable readers' magnet." Booklist

Oates, Joyce Carol, 1938- A **widow's** story; a memoir. Ecco 2011 415p il $27.99   **92**
1. Poets 2. Widows 3. Authors 4. Novelists 5. Bereavement 6. Loss (Psychology) 7. Essayists 8. Biographers 9. Magazine editors 10. Authors, American 11. Children's authors 12. Short story writers 13. Biography, Individual 14. Spouses of prominent persons
ISBN 9780062015532

This is an account of the novelist's loss of her "husband of 47 years, Raymond J. Smith. . . . He collaborated with his wife in founding The Ontario Review as well as Ontario Review Books." (N Y Times (Late N Y Ed))

"In a narrative as searing as the best of her fiction, Oates describes the aftermath of her husband Ray's unexpected death from pneumonia. Scattershot moments stand out — the day she cancels their 30-year subscription to The New York Times, unable to bear the sight of his favorite paper; her fury at the tulips, harbingers of spring, pushing through the snow ('Too soon! This is too soon!'); the night she weans herself from Lorazepam. A Widow's Story is the painful, scorchingly angry journey of a woman struggling to live in a house 'from which meaning has departed, like air leaking from a balloon.' " Entertainment Wkly

Obama, Barack, 1961-

Alter, Jonathan. The **promise**; President Obama, year one. Simon & Schuster 2010 458p il $28; ebook $12.99   **92**
1. Lawyers 2. Presidents 3. Senators 4. State legislators 5. Nobel laureates for peace 6. Presidents -- United States 7. United States -- Politics and government -- 2001- 8. United States -- Politics and government -- 2009-
ISBN 978-1-4391-0119-3; 978-1-4391-5408-3 ebook
LC 2010-20438

"Alter's writing is sharp. His tone is breezy and engaging but appropriate to the subject matter. No deep, dark secrets are revealed, but readers will come away from this book with a good idea of how the Obama administration understands itself." Commonweal

Includes bibliographical references

★ Maraniss, David. **Barack** Obama; the story. David Maraniss. Simon & Schuster 2012 xxiii, 641 p.p $32.50   **92**

1. Children -- Travel 2. Presidents -- United States 3. Hawaii -- Biography 4. Presidents -- United States -- Biography

ISBN 1439160406; 9781439160404; 9781439160411; 9781439167533

LC 2011052983

This book offers a biography of Barack Obama, "the 44th president [of the United States,] through the age of 27." Topics include the "confluence of Kenya and Kansas in Obama's veins," "the legacy of his father's keen intellect, his mother's self-possession, social conscience, and anthropologist's neutrality, and Obama's cosmopolitan childhood spent bouncing between Hawaii and Indonesia." (Publishers Weekly)

Includes bibliographical references (p. 607-609) and index

Mendell, David. **Obama**; from promise to power. Amistad 2007 406p il $25.95; pa $14.95   **92**

1. Lawyers 2. Presidents 3. Racially mixed people 4. Senators 5. State legislators 6. Nobel laureates for peace 7. Presidents -- United States 8. African Americans -- Biography 9. United States -- Congress -- Senate

ISBN 978-0-06-085820-9; 0-06-085820-6; 978-0-06-085821-6 pa; 0-06-085821-4 pa

This is a biography of President Barack Obama

The author "draws on interviews with Obama, his wife, family, friends, aides, and rivals, as well as his own extensive coverage since Obama's days in the Illinois Senate, to offer a nuanced, compelling look at a man of idealism and ambition intent on making history." Booklist

Includes bibliographical references

★ Obama, Barack. **Dreams** from my father; a story of race and inheritance. Crown Publishers 2007 442p $25.95   **92**

1. Lawyers 2. Presidents 3. Racially mixed people 4. Senators 5. State legislators 6. Nobel laureates for peace 7. Presidents -- United States 8. African Americans -- Biography

ISBN 978-0-307-38341-9

LC 2007-271892

First published 1995 by Times Books

This is the autobiography of the Illinois senator who would later become the 44th president of the United States.

The author "offers an account of his life's journey that reflects brilliantly on the power of race consciousness in America. . . . Obama writes well; his account is sensitive, probing, and compelling." Choice [review of 1995 edition]

★ Remnick, David, 1958- The **bridge**; the life and rise of Barack Obama. Alfred A. Knopf 2010 656p il $29.95   **92**

1. Lawyers 2. Presidents 3. Racially mixed people 4.

Senators 5. State legislators 6. Biography, Individual 7. Nobel laureates for peace 8. Presidents -- United States 9. African Americans -- Biography 10. United States -- Politics and government -- 2001-2009

ISBN 978-1-4000-4360-6; 1-4000-4360-3

LC 2010-922697

This is a biography of the 44th president of the United States.

Writing with emotional precision and a sure knowledge of politics, Mr. Remnick situates Mr. Obama's career firmly within a historical context. He puts Mr. Obama's life and political philosophy in perspective with the civil rights movement that shaped his imagination, as well as the power politics of Chicago, and the politics of race as it has been played out, often nastily, on the state and national stages. N Y Times (Late N Y Ed)

Includes bibliographical references (p. [617]-623) and index

Obama, Michelle, 1964-

Slevin, Peter. **Michelle** Obama; a life. Peter B. Slevin. Alfred A. Knopf 2015 432 p. 16 plates; illustrations $27.95   **92**

1. Women lawyers 2. Presidents' spouses -- United States 3. African American lawyers -- Biography 4. African American women lawyers -- Biography 5. Presidents' spouses -- United States -- Biography

ISBN 9780307958822; 0307958825

LC 2014041100

This book, by Peter Slevin, is an "account of the life and times of Michelle Obama. Slevin follows Michelle to the White House from her working-class childhood on Chicago's largely segregated South Side. He illuminates her tribulations at Princeton University and Harvard Law School during the racially charged 1980s and the dilemmas she faced in Chicago while building a high-powered career, raising a family and helping . . . Barack Obama become president of the United States." (Publisher's note)

"She is one of his greatest assets in public office and an important foil to criticism that he is not "black enough." Slevin delivers a somewhat fawning portrait, but when necessary, he is willing to criticize and reveal his subject's missteps." Kirkus

★ Swarns, Rachel L. **American** tapestry; the story of the black, white, and multiracial ancestors of Michelle Obama. Rachel L. Swarns. Amistad 2012 391 p., [8] p. of platesp ill. (some col.) $27.99   **92**

1. Genealogy 2. United States -- Race relations 3. African American families 4. African Americans -- Biography 5. Racially mixed people -- United States -- Biography

ISBN 0061999865; 9780061999864

LC 2012454035

This book traces the ancestry of U.S. First Lady Michelle Obama. "'New York Times' reporter [Rachel L.] Swarns traces the threads, some not previously known to Michelle Obama herself . . . to black, white, Native American, and multiracial family members. . . . Swarns presents the complicated story of race in the U.S. through the prism of one family's history. . . . A central figure is Melvinia, a

young slave girl who gave birth to mixed-race children."
(Publishers Weekly)

Includes bibliographical references (p. [357]-367)
and index

Oher, Michael, 1986-

★ Lewis, Michael. The **blind** side; evolution of
a game. W.W. Norton 2006 299p $24.95   92
1. College sports 2. Football players 3. Biography,
Individual 4. Football -- Biography 5. College sports
-- United States
ISBN 0-393-06123-X; 978-0-393-06123-9

                          LC 2006-23509

Michael Oher, the young man at the center of this story,
"will one day be among the most highly paid athletes in the
National Football League. When we first meet him, he is
one of thirteen children by a mother addicted to crack; he
does not know his real name, his father, his birthday, or any
of the things a child might learn in school—such as, say,
how to read or write. Nor has he ever touched a football.
What changes? He takes up football, and school, after a
rich, Evangelical, Republican family plucks him from the
. . . streets. Their love is the first great force that alters the
world's perception of the boy, whom they adopt. The second
force is the evolution of professional football itself into a
game where the quarterback must be protected at any cost.
Our protagonist turns out to be the priceless combination of
size, speed, and agility necessary to guard the quarterback's
greatest vulnerability: his blind side." (Publisher's note)

The author "describes the NFL's ever-growing obsession
with left tackles as a means to counter defenders who seem
to grow bigger, stronger, and more vicious each season. He
juxtaposes that narrative with the unlikely story of [football
player] Michael Oher. . . . The book works on three levels.
First as a shrewd analysis of the NFL; second, as an expose
of the insanity of big-time college football recruiting; and,
third, as a moving portrait of the positive effect that love,
family, and education can have in reversing the path of a life
that was destined to be lived unhappily and, most likely, end
badly." Booklist

Ol' Dirty Bastard, 1969-2004

Lowe, Jaime. **Digging** for dirt; the life and death
of ODB. Faber and Faber 2008 273p $25   92
1. Rap music 2. African American musicians 3. Rap
musicians
ISBN 978-0-8654-7969-2; 0-8654-7969-0

                          LC 2008-29144

"As one of Wu Tang Clan, Russell Jones became known
for his off-kilter raps and odd stage mannerisms. Like band-
mates Method Man and Ghostface Killah, he also had a solo
career as Ol' Dirty Bastard (ODB) that placed two number-
one albums on the rap charts, and his duet with Mariah
Carey, 'Fantasy,' brought mainstream success. Simply put,
life was good. As time went by, though, he devolved into a
more and more disturbed state, and some of his entertaining
traits came to suggest mental-health issues. . . . Seemingly
unable to avoid incarceration for a variety of offenses, he
died of 'heart failure after cerebral hemorrhaging,' arguably
caused by years of drug and other abuse. Lowe tells ODB's
tale admirably thoroughly, making this a must-have profile
of a singular personality and another sad casualty in rap
history." Booklist

Ollestad, Norman, 1968-

Ollestad, Norman. **Crazy** for the storm; a memoir of survival. Ecco 2009 272p il $25.99   92
1. Aircraft accidents 2. Father-son relationship 3.
Memoirists
ISBN 978-0-06-176672-5; 0-061-76672-0

                          LC 2008-53675

"In the winter of 1979, the 11-year-old Ollestad survived
a plane crash in which his father and his father's girlfriend
were killed. Alternating with young Norman's nine-hour
trek to safety are scenes from the year preceding the crash,
when the boy took a surfing trip with his father through the
jungle along Mexico's Pacific coast. The flashbacks sections
are the most fascinating parts of the book, and Ollestad ably
captures the contrast between his charismatically cool father,
Norman Sr., and his bullying stepfather-to-be, Nick. . . . [He]
presents a captivating account of high-altitude disaster that
nicely dovetails with his coming-of-age story in '70s California. Deep and resonant." Kirkus

Onassis, Jacqueline Kennedy, 1929-1994

Anderson, Christopher. The **good** son; JFK
Jr. and the mother he loved. Christopher Andersen.
Gallery Books 2014 368 p. 16 plates; illustrations
$27   92
1. Children of presidents -- United States -- Biography
ISBN 1476775567; 9781476775562; 9781476775579

                          LC 2014024249

This book, by Christopher Andersen, presents a biography of John F. Kennedy, Jr. and his mother Jacqueline
Kennedy. The author "explores his reactions to his mother's
post-Dallas suicidal depression and growing dependence on
prescription drugs (as well as men); how Jackie felt about
the women in her son's life . . to his turbulent marriage;
the senseless plane crash that took his life; the aftermath of
shock, loss, grief, and confusion; and much more." (Publisher's note)

"Sensitive and astute, Andersen's book offers an intriguing look at a fraught mother-son dynamic that, years after
the deaths of both Jackie and John Jr., still has the power to
mesmerize. An intimate and compelling look at 'the most
brilliant star in the Kennedy firmament.'" Kirkus

Bowles, Hamish. **Jacqueline** Kennedy; the
White House Years: selections from the John F. Ken-
nedy Library and Museum. {compiled and edited by}
Hamish Bowles; with essays by Arthur Schlesinger,
Jr., Hamish Bowles, and James Wagner. Bulfinch
Press 2001 198p il $50   92
1. Editors 2. Socialites 3. Spouses of presidents
ISBN 0-8212-2745-9

                          LC 00-66237

The selections "examine in detail different aspects of
Jackie's life, including the inauguration, her White House
style, her travels, and her hats, as well as other topics. . . .
Viewers can expect a sense of nostalgia, a swelling of pride,

and a tightening of the throat. A time line of Jackie's life is appended." Booklist

Davis, John H. **Jacqueline** Bouvier; an intimate memoir. [by] John Davis. Wiley 1996 208p il $24.95; pa $14.95   **92**
   1. Editors 2. Socialites 3. Spouses of presidents
   ISBN 0-471-12945-3; 0-471-24944-0 pa
                        LC 96-4332
"Davis is an engaging writer, and although many of the facts of his story will be known by Kennedy aficionados, there is a wistful sweetness to his writing that captures both the woman and the era of privileged upbringings." Booklist

Leaming, Barbara. **Jacqueline** Bouvier Kennedy Onassis; the untold story. by Barbara Leaming. Thomas Dunne Books/St. Martin's Press 2014 368 p. 8 plates; color illustrations (hardcover) $27.99
   1. Widows 2. Celebrities -- United States -- Biography 3. Presidents' spouses -- United States -- Biography 4. Post-traumatic stress disorder -- Patients -- Biography
   ISBN 1250017645; 9781250017642
                   LC 2014026768
This book, by Barbara Leaming, "document[s] Jacqueline Kennedy Onassis' brutal, lonely and valiant thirty-one year struggle with post-traumatic stress disorder (PTSD) that followed JFK's assassination. We see how a spirited young woman's rejection of a predictable life led her to John F. Kennedy and the White House, how she sought to reconcile the conflicts of her marriage . . . and how the trauma of her husband's murder . . . led her to seek a very different kind of life." (Publisher's note)
"Leaming tells a heart-wrenching story of a woman who not only endured a horrific event but also struggled to recover and was often misunderstood as she eventually carved out a life of her own making." Booklist
   Includes bibliographical references and index

Oppenheimer, Frank, 1912-1985
Cole, K. C. **Something** incredibly wonderful happens; Frank Oppenheimer and the world he made up. Houghton Mifflin Harcourt 2009 396p il $27   **92**
   1. Physicists 2. College teachers 3. Biography, Individual 4. Museum administrators
   ISBN 978-0-15-100822-3; 0-15-100822-1
                   LC 2008052954
This is a biography of the physicist and young brother of J. Robert Oppenheimer.
"In a thought-provoking and pleasant manner, Cole's much-welcomed book shines a new light on a remarkable man and scientist. Readers interested in good popular science biographies will enjoy this." Libr J
   Includes bibliographical references

Oppenheimer, J. Robert, 1904-1967
Bernstein, Jeremy. **Oppenheimer**; portrait of an enigma. Dee, I.R. 2004 223p il $25   **92**
   1. Physicists 2. College teachers 3. Government officials
   ISBN 1-566-63569-1
                   LC 2003-66652

The author "recounts Oppenheimer's eclectic life as it evolved in the US through his education and service at several prestigious institutions. . . . The book is not a review of Oppenheimer's contributions to physics or the development of the atomic bomb; rather, it provides insight into the human side of a brilliant individual, all things considered. Of course, his leadership of the Manhattan Project, and his persecution by Congress for alleged communist sympathies, defined Oppenheimer's career. Bernstein provides personalized insights into both." Choice
   Includes bibliographical references

★ Bird, Kai. **American** Prometheus; the triumph and tragedy of J. Robert Oppenheimer. [by] Kai Bird and Martin J. Sherwin. Knopf 2005 721p il hardcover o.p. pa $18.95   **92**
   1. Physicists 2. College teachers 3. Government officials
   ISBN 0-375-41202-6; 0-375-72626-8 pa
                   LC 2004-61535
The authors explore Oppenheimer's life "from his youth as a child prodigy through his radical political activities in the 1930s, and on to the Manhattan Project and its political fallout. The humanity of the troubled man behind the porkpie hat emerges on every page of this unquestionably definitive account." Booklist
   Includes bibliographical references

★ Monk, Ray. **Robert** Oppenheimer; a life inside the center. Ray Monk. 1st American ed. Doubleday 2013 xvi, 825 p.p (hardback) $37.50   **92**
   1. Atomic bomb -- History 2. Physicists -- Biography 3. Physicists -- United States -- Biography 4. Atomic bomb -- United States -- History -- 20th century 5. Physicists -- United States -- Intellectual life -- 20th century
   ISBN 0385504071; 9780385504072
                   LC 2012046045
This book by Ray Monk is a biography of physicist Robert Oppenheimer. "As a young professor at Berkeley, the wealthy, cultured Oppenheimer finally came into his own as a physicist and also began a period of support for Communist activities. . . . He was chosen to lead the Manhattan Project and develop . . . the atomic bomb. Upon its creation, Oppenheimer . . . refused to help create the far more powerful hydrogen bomb, bringing the wrath of McCarthyite suspicion upon him." (Publisher's note)
   Includes bibliographical references and index

Orwell, George, 1903-1950
★ Taylor, David J. **Orwell**: the life; {by} D.J. Taylor. Holt & Co. 2003 466p il $30; pa $17 **92**
   1. Authors 2. Novelists 3. Essayists
   ISBN 0-8050-7473-2; 0-8050-7693-X pa
                   LC 2003-41747
"Starting with a . . . . description of Orwell's funeral in 1950, Taylor . . . presents the years in India, the 'down and out' adventures, fighting in Spain, Orwell's work with the BBC during the war, and his final great novels. Taylor breaks the chronological flow with nine brief, interpretive essays (e.g., on Orwell's face, voice, and paranoia). . . . Taylor's

book is a fresh and compelling life of the man he calls 'a light glinting in the darkness.'" Libr J

Includes bibliographical references

Osama bin Laden

Randal, Jonathan C. **Osama**: the making of a terrorist; {by} Jonathan Randal. Knopf 2004 339p $26.95   **92**

1. Terrorism 2. Terrorists
ISBN 0-375-40901-7

LC 2004-46522

The author's "meticulous account of the emergence and spread of the terror virus is less a biography of the strange, desiccated Saudi Arabian terrorist who heads Al Qaeda than a map of the world that produced him and his fellow Islamists. This is the biography of a hatred: deep, detailed, and depressing." N Y Times Book Rev

Includes bibliographical references

Scheuer, Michael. **Osama** bin Laden; [by] Michael Scheuer. Oxford University Press 2011 278p $19.95   **92**

1. Terrorists 2. Biography, Individual
ISBN 978-0-19-973866-3; 0-19-973866-1

LC 2010-21715

The author "offers a serious and nonideological treatment and analysis of bin Laden's thinking. Unlike many Western analysts who dismiss bin Laden as simplistic, uncouth, and incompetent, Scheuer portrays him as a patient, devout, and talented, albeit ruthless, leader who remains a formidable enemy of the West. . . . This informative book is one of the most detailed biographical sketches of bin Laden available in the West and is useful for both the general public and specialists." Libr J

Includes bibliographical references

Osborne, John, 1929-1994

Heilpern, John. **John** Osborne; the many lives of the angry young man. Alfred A. Knopf 2007 527p il $35   **92**

1. Authors 2. Dramatists
ISBN 978-0-375-40315-6; 0-375-40315-9

LC 2006-46575

First published 2006 in the United Kingdom

"Heilpern draws on Osborne's bleak private notebooks to generate acute readings of his often autobiographical plays. Sympathy for the man and admiration for the work don't blind Heilpern to his subject's outsized flaws. Osborne had a talent for invective and could be cruelly intolerant in matters large and small. He threatened theatre critics with physical violence by way of anonymous seaside postcards. Stung by his teenage daughter's indifference to high culture, he damned her as 'criminally commonplace' and never spoke to her again. Without excusing such 'breathtaking abuse,' Heilpern makes a compelling case for Osborne as a necessary 'truthteller' and 'unyielding advocate of individualism in conformist times.'" New Yorker

Includes bibliographical references

Osborne, Steve

The **job**; true tales from the life of a New York City cop. by Steve Osborne. Doubleday 2015 272 p. (hardcover) $25.95   **92**

1. Police -- New York (State) -- New York 2. Police -- New York (State) -- New York -- Biography 3. New York (N.Y.). Police Department -- Officials and employees -- Biography
ISBN 0385539622; 9780385539623

LC 2014032375

In this memoir, author and police officer Steve Osborne "has seen a thing or two in his twenty years in the NYPD--some harmless things, some definitely not. . . . From his days as a rookie cop to the time spent patrolling in the Anti-Crime Unit--and his visceral, harrowing recollections of working during 9/11--Steve Osborne's stories capture both the absurdity of police work and the bravery of those who do it." (Publisher's note)

"Osborne's personal life is described only obliquely in the book, including his reasons for leaving the NYPD (although the chapter on 9/11 provides clues), but this is a solid insider's account of what life is like on the force." Pub Wkly

Osbourne, Ozzy

Osbourne, Ozzy. **I** am Ozzy; [by] Ozzy Osbourne with Chris Ayres. Grand Central Publishing 2010 391p $26.99   **92**

1. Singers 2. Rock musicians 3. Black Sabbath (Musical group)
ISBN 978-0-446-56989-7

LC 2009-937230

"Osbourne offers the most detail about growing up and the Black Sabbath years – no surprise as you'd expect decades of drug use have nearly wiped clean those later years. He discusses his youth in England, his brief stint in jail, how a flier posted in a music store – 'Ozzy Zig Needs a Gig' – led to the eventual formation of Black Sabbath, his relationship with his wives and children, his own health scares, and The Osbournes television show. The book is written with Osbourne's wit and sense of humor as he shares laugh-out-loud tales of practical jokes while touring around the world and recording inside a castle. There's even a look at the sensitive side when he discusses the death of guitarist Randy Rhodes and his wife's (Sharon's) battle with cancer." Creative Loafing

Owens, Jesse, 1913-1980

Schaap, Jeremy. **Triumph**; the untold story of Jesse Owens and Hitler's Olympics. Houghton Mifflin 2007 272p il $24; pa $14.95   **92**

1. African American athletes 2. Olympic games, 1936 (Berlin, Ger.) 3. Olympic athletes 4. Runners (Athletes)
ISBN 978-0-618-68822-7; 0-618-68822-6; 978-0-618-91910-9 pa; 0-618-91910-4 pa

LC 2006-26926

"Schaap's chronicle of Jesse Owens's journey to and glorious triumph at the 1936 Berlin Olympics is snappy and dramatic, with an eye for the rousing climax." Publ Wkly

Includes bibliographical references

Oz, Amos

Oz, Amos. A **tale** of love and darkness; translated from the Hebrew by Nicholas de Lange. Harcourt 2004 538p $26 **92**

1. Authors 2. Novelists 3. Essayists 4. Short story writers

ISBN 0-15-100878-7; 9780156032520

LC 2004-7302

"A powerful story of the making of a writer . . . Oz's panoramic memoir enhances the history of literature and of Israel, and the literature of examined lives." Booklist

Padilla Peralta, Dan-el

Padilla Peralta, Dan-el. **Undocumented**; A Dominican Boy's Odyssey from a Homeless Shelter to the Ivy League. by Dan-el Padilla Peralta. Penguin Group USA 2015 320 p. illustrations $27.95 **92**

1. Homeless persons 2. Dominican Americans 3. Unauthorized immigrants 4. United States -- Immigration and emigration

ISBN 159420652X; 9781594206528

Alex Award (2016)

This book, by Dan-el Padilla Peralta, is an "undocumented immigrant's journey from a New York City homeless shelter to the top of his Princeton class. . . . As a boy, he came here legally with his family. Together they left Santo Domingo behind, but life in New York City was harder than they imagined. Their visas lapsed. . . . Without papers, [they] faced tremendous obstacles." (Publisher's note)

Padilla Peralta "writes candidly about hard times including a period spent in a dangerous homeless shelter, breaking through the harsh immigrant clichés to a pure humanistic level that any reader can embrace." Pub Wkly

Paige, Satchel, 1906-1982

Fox, William Price. **Satchel** Paige's America. University of Alabama Press 2005 142p pa $16.95 **92**

1. Baseball players 2. Baseball -- Biography

ISBN 0-8173-5189-2

LC 2004-18911

This biography is based upon the author's conversations with the legendary baseball pitcher as he spent a week following him around Kansas City, MO, in 1970.

This is "a lively, moving, and often hilarious tale of an encounter 30 years ago and of a life richly led." Libr J

Tye, Larry. **Satchel**; the life and times of an American legend. Random House 2009 392p il **92**

1. Baseball players 2. African American athletes 3. Baseball -- Biography 4. Biography, Individual 5. Negro leagues -- History

ISBN 0812977971; 1400066514; 9780812977974; 9781400066513

LC 2008-44858

A biography of the Negro League pitcher Satchel Paige "evaluates the role of discrimination in limiting his career, covering such topics as his near-defeat of a young Joe DiMaggio, the Jim Crow biases that prevented his signing with the big leagues until he was in his forties, and his [legacy]." (Publisher's note)

This is a "discerning, empathetic and hype-free [biography]. . . . While Paige's life has become the stuff of legend, its particulars are not easily verified. . . . Yet 'Satchel' makes a cool, clear, tenacious effort to find the real Paige behind all [the] hyperbole." N Y Times (Late N Y Ed)

Includes bibliographical references

Paine, Thomas, 1737-1809

Collins, Paul. The **trouble** with Tom: the strange afterlife and times of Thomas Paine. Bloomsbury 2005 278p map hardcover o.p. pa $15 **92**

1. Essayists 2. Pamphleteers 3. Writers on politics 4. Writers on religion 5. Political and social philosophers

ISBN 1-58234-502-3; 1-58234-613-5 pa

LC 2005-45240

The author "traces the bizarre story of Thomas Paine's remains through nearly two centuries of American and English history. . . . Part travelogue, part memoir and part historical mystery, this book reads like a wry, witty novel and offers a delicious twist at the end." Publ Wkly

Includes bibliographical references

Palin, Michael

Palin, Michael, 1943- **Halfway** to Hollywood; diaries 1980-1988. Thomas Dunne Books 2011 622p il $32.50 **92**

1. Actors 2. Authors 3. Comedians 4. Humorists 5. Screenwriters 6. Biography, Individual 7. Television scriptwriters 8. Monty Python (Comedy troupe)

ISBN 0312682026; 9780312682026

First published 2009 in the United Kingdom

This second volume of diaries by the Monty Python comedian traces the years during which the troupe completed their final performances together. Index.

Palmer, Arnold, 1929-2016

Palmer, Arnold. A **golfer's** life; {by} Arnold Palmer with James Dodson. Ballantine Bks. 1999 420p il hardcover o.p. pa $15 **92**

1. Golfers

ISBN 0-345-41482-9 pa

LC 98-51681

Palmer's "immense popularity is widely credited with rescuing professional golf in the late 1950s and 1960s. Written with humor and candor, the book recounts Palmer's friendships and rivalries with the greats of the game, his enduring marriage to Winnie Palmer, his legendary triumphs and disasters, and his battle against cancer." Libr J

Palmer, Arnold, 1929-2016. A **life** well played; My Stories. Arnold Palmer. St. Martin's Press 2016 272 p. (hardcover) $22.99; (ebook) $60 **92**

1. Conduct of life 2. Golfers -- United States -- Biography

ISBN 9781250085948; 9781250085955

LC 2016013252

In this book, golfer Arnold Palmer "takes stock of the many experiences of his life, bringing new details and insights to some familiar stories and sharing new ones. . . . Gracious, fair, and a true gentleman, 'Arnie' was the gold standard of how to conduct yourself in your career, life, and relationships. . . . [His] book offers advice . . . , sharing personal stories of his career on the course, success in business, and . . . relationships that gave meaning to his life." (Publisher's note)

"A heartfelt, sincere, mini-self-portrait by a man who epitomizes class." Kirkus

Papp, Joseph

★ Turan, Kenneth. **Free** for all; Joe Papp, the Public, and the greatest theater story ever told. [by] Kenneth Turan and Joseph Papp; with the assistance of Gail Merrifield Papp. Doubleday 2009 592p il $39.95   **92**

1. Theatrical producers and directors 2. Theatrical directors 3. Theatrical producers 4. Joseph Papp Public Theater (New York, N.Y.)

ISBN 978-0-7679-3168-7

LC 2008-50887

"A wonderful book that clearly and powerfully shows that Papp's own story was the most enduring drama he ever produced." Kirkus

Paracelsus, 1493-1541

Webster, Charles. **Paracelsus**; medicine, magic and mission at the end of time. Yale University Press 2008 326p il $40   **92**

1. Alchemy 2. Physicians 3. Alchemists 4. Writers on science

ISBN 978-0-300-13911-2; 0-300-13911-X

LC 2008-27973

In this consideration of the "Renaissance doctor, alchemist, and theologian, Webster draws on nonscientific writings by Paracelsus that have been made widely available only in the past few decades. . . . [Paracelsus] orbited a wealthy and powerful class of physicians, but his unorthodox views made him a virtual 'vagrant' among his peers. He broke from the millennia-old theory of the humors, developing new medical theories based upon a mystical vision of man as a microcosm of the universe, and an alchemically informed notion of the intrinsic properties of certain metals. Webster paints Paracelsus as a 'religious and social controversialist,' and argues that the diverse strands of his thought were unified by his belief that the end of time was near, when, he imagined, the demise of physical suffering would obviate the need for medical intervention." New Yorker

Includes bibliographical references and index.

Parker, Charlie, 1920-1955

Crouch, Stanley, 1945- **Kansas** City lightning; the rise and times of Charlie Parker. by Stanley Crouch. Harper 2013 384 p. $27.99   **92**

1. Jazz musicians 2. Jazz musicians -- United States -- Biography

ISBN 0062005596; 9780062005595

LC 2013015773

This book, by Stanley Crouch, "is the first installment in . . . [a] portrait of one of the most talented and influential musicians of the twentieth century, from Stanley Crouch, one of the foremost authorities on jazz and culture in America. Drawing on interviews with peers, collaborators, and family members, 'Kansas City Lightning' recreates Parker's Depression-era childhood; his early days navigating the Kansas City nightlife." (Publisher's note)

Parker, Dorothy, 1893-1967

Meade, Marion. **Dorothy** Parker; what fresh hell is this? Penguin 1989 459p il pa $20   **92**

1. Poets 2. Authors 3. Humorists 4. Dramatists 5. Essayists 6. Screenwriters 7. Authors, American 8. Short story writers

ISBN 0-14-011616-8; 978-0-14-011616-8

LC 88-23782

First published 1988 by Villard Books

"The author has written a disturbing story of a writer whose life was marked by endless disturbances and self-depreciation, and who left behind no correspondence, manuscripts, or private papers. Under the circumstances, Ms. Meade has brilliantly reconstructed her subject's life. . . . The book is a tribute to a woman who left her mark on the literary history of her times and whose coruscating wit is still remembered." West Coast Rev Books

Includes bibliographical references

Parker, Quanah, Comanche Chief, 1845?-1911

Gwynne, S. C. **Empire** of the summer moon; Quanah Parker and the rise and fall of the Comanches, the most powerful Indian tribe in American history. Scribner 2010 371p il map $27.50   **92**

1. Comanche Indians 2. Indian chiefs 3. West (U.S.) -- History 4. Comanche Indians -- Wars 5. Western States -- History 6. Comanche Indians -- History 7. Frontier and pioneer life -- West (U.S.) 8. Frontier and pioneer life -- Western States

ISBN 978-1-4165-9105-4; 1-4165-9105-2

LC 2009049747

"A welcome contribution to the history of Texas, Westward expansion and Native America." Kirkus

Includes bibliographical references

Parks, Rosa, 1913-2005

Brinkley, Douglas. **Rosa** Parks. Viking 2000 246p (Penguin lives series) hardcover o.p. pa $13   **92**

1. Civil rights activists 2. African Americans -- Civil rights 3. African American women -- Biography

ISBN 0-670-89160-6; 0-14-303600-9 pa

LC 00-35916

"Rosa Parks' story takes readers from rural Alabama to the Montgomery Industrial School for Girls, marriage to barber Raymond Parks, quiet activism in the '30s and '40s, a first experience of integration at the Highlander Folk School, arrest in 1955 and the bus boycott, a move to Detroit, and more than 20 years on the staff of Rep. John Conyers (D-Mich.)." Booklist

Includes bibliographical references

Theoharis, Jeanne. The **rebellious** life of Mrs. Rosa Parks; Jeanne Theoharis. Beacon Press 2012 360 p. (hardcover : alk. paper) $27.95   **92**

1. Montgomery (Ala.) -- Biography 2. Montgomery (Ala.) -- Race relations 3. Civil rights workers -- Alabama -- Montgomery -- Biography 4. African American women civil rights workers -- Alabama -- Montgomery -- Biography 5. Segregation in transportation -- Alabama -- Montgomery -- History -- 20th century 6. African Americans -- Civil rights --

Alabama -- Montgomery -- History -- 20th century
ISBN 0807050474; 9780807050477; 9780807050484
LC 2012031992

This book by Jeanne Theoharis is a "political biography of Rosa Parks [that] examines her six decades of activism, challenging perceptions of her as an accidental actor in the civil rights movement. . . . [Theoharis] shows readers how this civil rights movement radical sought--for more than a half a century--to expose and eradicate the American racial-caste system in jobs, schools, public services, and criminal justice." (Publisher's note)

Includes bibliographical references and index

Parravani, Cara

Parravani, Christa, 1978- **Her**; a memoir. Christa Parravani. Henry Holt & Co 2013 320 p. $26 **92**
1. Twins 2. Sisters 3. Rape victims 4. Loss (Psychology) 5. Twins -- United States -- Biography 6. Sisters -- United States -- Biography
ISBN 0805096531; 9780805096538
LC 2012029499

In this memoir, author Christa Parravani "deconstructs the intense bonds between identical twins, the trauma of her sister's death and her battle against similar self-destruction. . . . Plagued by unstable and abusive father figures and poverty, [Christa and Cara] still managed to attend prestigious colleges, begin careers as artists and embark on marriages. But following a rape while out walking her dog, [Cara] began a terrifying descent into drugs and self-destruction." (Kirkus Reviews)

A "finely wrought achievement of grace, emotional honesty, and self-possession." Pub Wkly

Parravani, Christa

Parravani, Christa, 1978- **Her**; a memoir. Christa Parravani. Henry Holt & Co 2013 320 p. $26 **92**
1. Twins 2. Sisters 3. Rape victims 4. Loss (Psychology) 5. Twins -- United States -- Biography 6. Sisters -- United States -- Biography
ISBN 0805096531; 9780805096538
LC 2012029499

In this memoir, author Christa Parravani "deconstructs the intense bonds between identical twins, the trauma of her sister's death and her battle against similar self-destruction. . . . Plagued by unstable and abusive father figures and poverty, [Christa and Cara] still managed to attend prestigious colleges, begin careers as artists and embark on marriages. But following a rape while out walking her dog, [Cara] began a terrifying descent into drugs and self-destruction." (Kirkus Reviews)

A "finely wrought achievement of grace, emotional honesty, and self-possession." Pub Wkly

Parsons, Jack, 1914-1952

Pendle, George. **Strange** angel; the otherworldly life of rocket scientist John Whiteside Parsons. Harcourt 2005 350p il $25; pa $15 **92**
1. Scientists
ISBN 0-15-100997-X; 0-15-603179-5 pa
LC 2004-10666

"Marshaling a cast of characters ranging from Robert Millikan to L. Ron Hubbard, Pendle offers a fascinating glimpse into a world long past, a story that would make a compelling work of fiction if it weren't so astonishingly true." Publ Wkly

Includes bibliographical references

Pascal, Blaise, 1623-1662

Connor, James A. **Pascal's** wager; the man who played with God. HarperSanFrancisco 2006 224p il $24.95 **92**
1. Theologians 2. Mathematicians 3. Writers on religion
ISBN 978-0-06-076691-7; 0-06-076691-3
LC 2006-43489

This biography of the mathematician and theologian focuses on his Jansenist religious beliefs.

This book "should interest readers drawn to the crossroads of religion and science." Booklist

Includes bibliographical references

Patchett, Ann

Patchett, Ann, 1963- **This** Is the Story of a Happy Marriage; Ann Patchett. HarperCollins 2013 320 p. $27.99 **92**
1. Opera 2. Divorce 3. Human-animal relationship
ISBN 0062236679; 9780062236678

This is an essay collection from award-winning author Ann Patchett. She explores "some of the milestones of her life, such as her deep love for her dog, Rose (not to be confused with the desire for a baby), learning from scratch how to love opera in order to write her bestseller 'Bel Canto,' preparing with her ex-cop father's guidance for the grueling L.A. Police Academy exams ('The Wall'), . . . and her painful but merciful segue from divorce to remarriage." (Publishers Weekly)

Patel, Eboo, 1975-

Patel, Eboo. **Acts** of faith; the story of an American Muslim, the struggle for the soul of a generation. Beacon Press 2010 195p pa $14 **92**
1. Multiculturalism 2. Sociologists 3. Youth leaders 4. Religious leaders 5. Writers on religion 6. Organization officials 7. Muslims -- United States
ISBN 978-0-8070-0622-1; 0-8070-0622-X
LC 2010-537438

First published 2007

The author, "a founder of the Interfaith Youth Core, traces the personal journey that led to the group's formation and introduces readers to its philosophy." Kirkus

Includes bibliographical references

Paterson, Katherine

Paterson, Katherine. **Stories** of my life; by Katherine Paterson. Dial Books for Young Readers 2014 320 p. illustrations (hardcover) $17.99 **92**
1. Autobiographies 2. Women authors -- Biography 3. Children's stories -- Authorship 4. Authors, American -- 20th century -- Biography
ISBN 0803740433; 9780803740433
LC 2013042628

Author Katherine "Paterson's tales reveal details about her life from her childhood with missionary parents, to living as a single woman in Japan, to raising four children in suburban Maryland with her minister husband. . . . Filled with personal photos and letters, this . . . history from a legendary writer lets fans in on the making of literary classics." (Publisher's note)

"Written in a conversational style, these 'kitchen sink stories' will perhaps be received best by professional adults and readers who grew up with her books; much of what she recounts is about the distant past, courtship, and motherhood. What absolutely shines through is Paterson's warm, self-effacing humor, and the extraordinary humility of a writer who has won two National Book Awards, two Newbery Medals, and the Hans Christian Andersen Medal." Pub Wkly

Patterson, Floyd

Levy, Alan Howard. **Floyd** Patterson; a boxer and a gentleman. [by] Alan H. Levy. McFarland & Co. 2008 289p il pa $35 **92**
1. African American athletes 2. Boxers (Persons) 3. Boxing -- Biography
ISBN 978-0-7864-3950-8; 0-7864-3950-5
LC 2008-32250
This is a "biography of the man who was the youngest world heavyweight champion in boxing history as well as the first boxer to regain the championship after losing it. . . . This book is not only an excellent study of Patterson but a superior source on professional boxing from the mid-1950s through the mid-1970s." Libr J
Includes bibliographical references

★ Stratton, W. K. **Floyd** Patterson; the fighting life of boxing's invisible champion. W. K. Stratton. Houghton Mifflin Harcourt 2012 xiv, 269 p.p ill. (hardback) $25.00 **92**
1. Boxers (Sports) 2. African Americans -- Civil rights 3. African American boxers -- Biography 4. Boxers (Sports) -- United States -- Biography
ISBN 0151014302; 9780151014309
LC 2012017319
This biography "examines one of the most complex fighters ever to wear the heavyweight crown," boxer Floyd Patterson. "Patterson started boxing [in high school] and . . . caught the eye of trainer Cus D'Amato . . . . By focusing on historical context, Stratton clarifies how Patterson could be trumpeted as a hero of the civil rights movement, then labeled an 'Uncle Tom' a few years later." (Publishers Weekly)
Includes bibliographical references and index.

Patterson, Pat, 1941-

Patterson, Pat. **Accepted**; by Pat Patterson. ECW Press 2016 320 p. illustrations (some color) $25.95 **92**
1. Wrestling
ISBN 177041293X; 9781770412934
In this memoir, professional wrestler Pat Patterson "recalls the trials and tribulations of climbing to the upper ranks of sports-entertainment—as a performer and, later, as a backstage creative force." (Publisher's note)
"Patterson is a very good storyteller, and his tales from the road about well-known personalities such as the fun-seeking Andre the Giant and the forever-young-at-heart Ray Stevens are wonderfully told, and many of the wrestlers' time-killing pranks are laugh-out-loud funny." Pub Wkly

Patton, George S. (George Smith), 1885-1945

Hirshson, Stanley P. **General** Patton: a soldier's life. HarperCollins Pubs. 2002 xxii, 826p il maps $34.95; pa $18.95 **92**
1. Generals 2. Army officers
ISBN 0-06-000982-9; 0-06-000983-7 pa
LC 2002-68881
The author attempts "to round out the unknown familial aspects of Patton's life and {provide a} . . . context for understanding the enigmatic commander. . . . Those interested in Patton will find Hirshson's book valuable reading." Libr J
Includes bibliographical references

★ Showalter, Dennis E. **Patton** and Rommel; men of war in the twentieth century. [by] Dennis Showalter. Berkley Caliber 2005 441p $24.95 **92**
1. Generals 2. World War, 1939-1945 3. Marshals 4. Army officers
ISBN 0-425-19346-2
LC 2004-57464
This is a "parallel biography of George Patton and Erwin Rommel. The research is thorough, the quality of the writing superb. . . . [The author] ranks as a scholar who has done them justice, making two complex men and a vast panorama of military history remarkably accessible for experts and lay readers alike." Publ Wkly

Payne, Ethel, 1911-1991

Morris, James McGrath. **Eye** on the Struggle; Ethel Payne, the First Lady of the Black Press. James McGrath Morris. HarperCollins 2015 480 p. 16 plates; illustrations $27.99
1. Journalists 2. African Americans -- Civil rights
ISBN 0062198858; 9780062198853
LC 2015296496
This book examines the life of "Ethel Payne (1911-91), a pioneering journalist, [who] covered the civil rights movement for The Chicago Defender, a premier black newspaper. Biographer [James McGrath] Morris . . . details Payne's work, preserving her legacy and filling in part of the missing history of the fight for equality." (Library Journal)
"Morris' straight-ahead chronicle of Payne's extraordinary front-line life reveals how invincible and incisive she was as she forthrightly "combined journalism with advocacy" and made the most of the "box seat on history" she fought so ardently and courageously to occupy." Booklist

Peace, Robert, 1980-2010

★ Hobbs, Jeff. The **short** and tragic life of Robert Peace; a brilliant young man who left Newark for the Ivy League but did not survive. Jeff Hobbs. Scribner 2014 416 p. illustrations (hardcover) $27 **92**
1. African Americans -- Social conditions 2. Drug dealers 3. Working class African Americans 4. African American college graduates 5. Yale University --

Alumni and alumnae

ISBN 147673190X; 9781476731919; 9781476731902

LC 2014001213

Los Angeles Times Book Prize: Current Interest (2014)

This book, by Jeff Hobbs, is a "biography of the short life of a talented young African-American man who escapes the slums of Newark for Yale University only to succumb to the dangers of the streets--and of one's own nature--when he returns home. . . . [The book] encompasses the most enduring conflicts in America: race, class, drugs, community, imprisonment, education, family, friendship, and love." (Publisher's note)

"Writing with novelistic detail and deep insight, Hobbs, who was Peace's roommate at Yale, registers the disadvantages his friend faced while avoiding hackneyed fatalism and sociology. Hobbs reveals a man whose singular experience and charisma made him simultaneously an outsider and a leader in both New Haven and Newark." Pub Wkly

Includes bibliographical references

Pelosi, Nancy, 1940-

Pelosi, Nancy. **Know** your power; a message to America's daughters. with Amy Hill Hearth. Doubleday 2008 180p $23.95; pa $14.95   **92**

1. Women politicians 2. Members of Congress 3. Speakers of the House 4. Politicians -- United States

ISBN 978-0-385-52586-2; 0-385-52586-9; 978-0-7679-2944-8 pa; 0-7679-2944-6 pa

LC 2008-20607

"In this graceful personal and political history, Pelosi describes growing up as the daughter of a congressman in an Italian-American Catholic world . . . and her burgeoning political interest. . . . Pelosi's book is a simply crafted acknowledgment of the support of her family, mentors and helpful colleagues without rhetorical flourishes, insider scandal or intimate revelations—a gentle account from a tough politician." Publ Wkly

Perelman, Grigori

Gessen, Masha. **Perfect** rigor; a genius and the mathematical breakthrough of the century. Houghton Mifflin Harcourt 2009 242p $26   **92**

1. Mathematicians

ISBN 978-0-15-101406-4; 0-15-101406-X

LC 2009-14742

"The story of Russian mathematical prodigy Grigory Perelman, who solved a problem that had stumped everyone for a century—then walked away from his chosen field. . . . [The author] paints a fascinating picture of the Soviet math establishment and of the mind of one of its most singular products. An engrossing examination of an enigmatic genius." Kirkus

Includes bibliographical references

Perkins, Frances, 1882-1965

Downey, Kirstin. The **woman** behind the New Deal; the life of Frances Perkins, FDR's Secretary of Labor and his moral conscience. Nan A. Talese 2009 458p il $35   **92**

1. Cabinet officers 2. College teachers 3. Secretaries of labor 4. State government officials 5. United States

-- Dept. of Labor

ISBN 978-0-385-51365-4; 0-385-51365-8

LC 2008-23208

A biography of "one of FDR's confidants and the first female secretary of labor in U.S. history. . . . Like many biographers, Downey . . . is enamored of her subject. But her fascination serves her well, allowing her to construct an intriguing catalog of Perkins's achievements and explore the influences that held sway in her life, a psychological approach lacking in previous Perkins biographies. Here Perkins's triumphs and tragedies are compiled into a compelling narrative that never loses its scholarly touch." Libr J

Includes bibliographical references

Peter, Jason, 1974-

Peter, Jason. **Hero** of the underground; a memoir. [by] Jason Peter with Tony O'Neill. St. Martin's Press 2008 289p $24.95; pa $14.95   **92**

1. Heroin 2. Drug abuse 3. Football players 4. Football -- Biography

ISBN 978-0-312-37576-8; 0-312-37576-X; 978-0-312-56103-1 pa; 0-312-56103-2 pa

LC 2008-12364

A former NFL player traces his journey from professional athlete to drug addict after injuries ended his career, describing the range of physical, psychological, and legal dilemmas that affected his perception of reality and nearly ended his life.

"Avoiding self-help urgings and self-congratulations, Peter (who is now clean) and O'Neill have crafted an unflinching look at the dark side of a life devoted to pleasure." Publ Wkly

Pham, Thong Van

★ Pham, Andrew X. The **eaves** of heaven; a life in three wars. by Andrew X. Pham, on behalf of my father, Thong Van Pham. Harmony Books 2008 301p $24.95   **92**

1. Refugees 2. Vietnamese Americans 3. Vietnam -- History

ISBN 978-0-307-38120-0; 0-307-38120-X

LC 2007-33894

"In a narrative set between the years of 1940 and 1976, Pham . . . recounts the story of his once wealthy father, Thong Van Pham, who lived through the French occupation of Indochina, the Japanese invasion during WWII, and the Vietnam War. . . . For those not familiar with Vietnamese history, Pham does an admirable job of recounting the complex cast of characters and the political machinations of the various groups vying for power over the years. In the end, he also gracefully delivers a heartfelt family history." Publ Wkly

Includes bibliographical references

Phillips, Sam, 1923-2003

★ Guralnick, Peter. **Sam** Phillips; the man who invented rock 'n' roll. Peter Guralnick. Little, Brown & Co. 2015 752 p. illustrations (hc) $32   **92**

1. Record producers 2. Rock music -- History and criticism 3. Sound recording executives and producers

-- United States -- Biography
ISBN 9780316042741

LC 2015024690

In this book, author Peter Guralnick "brings us the life of Sam Phillips, the visionary genius who singlehandedly steered the revolutionary path of Sun Records. The music that he shaped in his tiny Memphis studio with artists as diverse as Elvis Presley, Ike Turner, Howlin' Wolf, Jerry Lee Lewis, and Johnny Cash, introduced a sound that had never been heard before. " (Publisher's note)

"The author emphasizes Phillips's contributions to rock and roll's 1950s emergence in the racially charged South and his personal and professional relationships with not only the many famous singers and musicians who benefited commercially and artistically from his vision, encouragement, and technical skills but also the obscure rockabilly, blues, country, and pop artists who were given an opportunity to express themselves on vinyl. . . . This long but consistently engaging book offers a more detailed and intimate account than Kevin and Tanja Crouch's Sun King and is recommended to fans of early American popular music." LJ

Includes bibliographical references and index

Piaf, Édith, 1915-1963

Burke, Carolyn. **No** regrets; the life of Edith Piaf. Alfred A. Knopf 2011 282p il $27.95   **92**

1. Singers

ISBN 978-0-307-26801-3; 0-307-26801-2

LC 2010-35229

The author "focuses on the internationally renowned French vocalist and lyricist best known for the song 'La Vie en Rose.' Piaf is commonly associated with la chanson réaliste, realistic songs that speak to the underprivileged. . . . Burke's contextual detail and attention to research will appeal to scholars, and her masterful storytelling will engage readers." Libr J

Includes bibliographical references

Pickford, Mary, 1893-1979

Whitfield, Eileen. **Pickford**; the woman who made Hollywood. University Press of Ky. 1997 441p il $27.50   **92**

1. Actors

ISBN 0-8131-2045-4

LC 97-29312

"Silent screen star Mary Pickford was 'America's Sweetheart,' capturing the imagination of the public as 'Little Mary,' the adolescent with spunk. She married swashbuckler Douglas Fairbanks, and with Charlie Chaplin and D.W. Griffith they formed United Artists, the first production company run by people who acted and directed. . . . Though it does include delicious anecdotes from those who were there, this is not simply a typical celebrity biography but a 'biography' of the times." Libr J

Includes bibliographical references

Pinter, Harold, 1930-2008

Fraser, Antonia. **Must** you go? my life with Harold Pinter. Nan A. Talese/Doubleday 2010 328p il $28.95; ebook $28.95   **92**

1. Authors 2. Dramatists 3. Dramatists, English 4. Screenwriters 5. Authors, English 6. Nobel laureates

for literature

ISBN 978-0-385-53250-1; 978-0-385-53251-8 ebook

LC 2010-7374

Harold Pinter's widow, the biographer, historian and novelist Antonia Fraser, recalls their years together from 1975 until the playwright's death of cancer on Christmas Eve in 2008.

The author "simultaneously creates a tender portrait of an exciting marriage, and a deliciously detailed account of living in the thick of creativity and fame." Entertainment Wkly

Pirsig, Robert M., 1928-

Pirsig, Robert M. **Zen** and the art of motorcycle maintenance; an inquiry into values. Morrow 1974 412p $26; pa $13.95   **92**

1. Authors 2. Novelists 3. Essayists

ISBN 0-688-00230-7; 0-06-083987-2 pa

A collection of the author's philosophical musings inspired by a motorcycle trip with his son

Pius XII, Pope, 1876-1958

Cornwell, John. **Hitler's** pope: the secret history of Pius XII. Viking 1999 430p il hardcover o.p. pa $15   **92**

1. Popes 2. Heads of state 3. Nazi leaders

ISBN 0-14-029627-1 pa

LC 99-28311

"Relying on exclusive access to Vatican and Jesuit archives, . . . {the author} argues that through a 1933 Concordat with Hitler, Pope Pius XII facilitated the dictator's rise—and, ultimately, the Holocaust." Libr J

Includes bibliographical references

Plimpton, George, 1927-2003

George, being George; George Plimpton's life as told, admired, deplored, and envied by 200 friends, relatives, lovers, acquaintances, rivals, and a few unappreciative observers. edited by Nelson W. Aldrich, Jr. Random House 2008 423p il $30   **92**

1. Authors 2. Journalists 3. Essayists 4. Sportswriters 5. Magazine editors

ISBN 978-1-4000-6398-7; 1-4000-6398-1

LC 2007-46215

"George Plimpton (1927–2003) wore many hats: writer, Paris Review editor, actor, boxing fanatic, toastmaster, prankster, fireworks enthusiast, urban cyclist. In the oral history George, Being George, Nelson W. Aldrich Jr. skillfully weaves together more than 200 voices into a coherent account of Plimpton's prismatic existence. . . . The contributors—who include literary luminaries Norman Mailer, Gore Vidal and Peter Matthiessen—report on Plimpton's life with varying degrees of grandiosity and nuance." Time Out N Y

Plummer, Christopher

Plummer, Christopher. **In** spite of myself; a memoir. Knopf 2009 648p il $29.95   **92**

1. Actors

ISBN 978-0-679-42162-7; 0-679-42162-9

LC 2008-31229

The author is "an enchanting observer of the showbiz cavalcade, drawing vivid thumbnails of everyone from Laurence Olivier to Lenny Bruce and tossing off witty anecdotes

. . . like the most effortless ad libs. The result is a sparkling star turn from a born raconteur for whom all the world is indeed a stage." Publ Wkly

Poe, Edgar Allan, 1809-1849

Ackroyd, Peter. **Poe**; a life cut short. Nan A. Talese/Doubleday 2008 205p il (Ackroyd's brief lives) $21.95   **92**
1. Poets 2. Authors 3. Essayists 4. Authors, American 5. Short story writers
ISBN 978-0-385-50800-1; 0-385-50800-X
    LC 2008-18244
Explores Poe's literary accomplishments and legacy against the background of his erratic, dramatic, and sometimes sordid life, including his marriage to his thirteen-year-old cousin and his much-written-about problems with gambling and alcohol.
This "readable account should appeal to Poe devotees and newcomers alike." Publ Wkly
Includes bibliographical references

Collins, Paul. **Edgar** Allan Poe; the fever called living. Paul Collins. New Harvest/Houghton Mifflin Harcourt 2014 144 p. $20   **92**
1. Authors -- Biography 2. Authors, American -- 19th century -- Biography
ISBN 0544261879; 9780544261877
    LC 2013024777
This biography of Edgar Allan Poe by Paul Collins "illuminates Poe's huge successes and greatest flop (a 143-page prose poem titled Eureka), and even tracks down what may be Poe's first published fiction." (Publisher's note)
"Although Collins doesn't provide much new information, the clean, crisp narrative presents the puzzling Poe as a deeply troubled and toweringly talented artist." Kirkus
Includes bibliographical references and index

Silverman, Kenneth. **Edgar** A. Poe; mournful and never-ending remembrance. HarperCollins Pubs. 1991 564p il hardcover o.p. pa $18   **92**
1. Poets 2. Authors 3. Essayists 4. Short story writers
ISBN 0-06-092331-8 pa
    LC 90-56397
The author explains "how Poe's early life influenced his work. He details Poe's turbulent career as poet, short story writer, and editor . . . and traces his literary development through bouts of alcoholism and hallucinations and disputes with literary rivals. An excellent addition to the literature that furthers understanding of America's gothic tale-teller." Libr J
Includes bibliographical references

Poehler, Amy, 1971-

Yes please. HarperCollins 2014 352 p. illustrations (chiefly color) $28.99   **92**
1. Wit and humor 2. Autobiographies
ISBN 0062268341; 9780062268341
    LC 2014469870
"A collection of stories, thoughts, ideas, lists, and haikus from the mind of one of our most beloved entertainers, 'Yes Please' offers Amy's thoughts on everything from her 'too safe' childhood outside of Boston to her early days in

New York City, her ideas about Hollywood and 'the biz,' the demon that looks back at all of us in the mirror, and her joy at being told she has a 'face for wigs.'" (Publisher's note)
"These quibbles aside, the book is well worth reading for Poehler's fans and anyone who enjoyed Tina Fey's Bossypants or Mindy Kaling's Is Everyone Hanging Out Without Me?" LJ

Poitier, Sidney

Goudsouzian, Aram. **Sidney** Poitier; man, actor, icon. University of North Carolina Press 2004 480p il $29.95   **92**
1. Actors 2. Motion picture directors
ISBN 0-8078-2843-2
    LC 2003-19372
The author "traces Poitier's journey from life as the son of a poor Bahamian farmer to celebrity status in the States as a trailblazing actor who has received as much criticism as praise for his portrayal of dignified and stoical black men." Booklist
Includes bibliographical references

★ Poitier, Sidney. The **measure** of a man; a spiritual autobiography. HarperSanFrancisco 2007 299p il $25.95; pa $14.95   **92**
1. Actors 2. Motion picture directors 3. Actors -- United States -- Biography
ISBN 978-0-06-135791-6; 0-06-135791-X; 978-0-06-135790-9 pa; 0-06-135790-1 pa
A reissue of the title first published 2000
"Poitier attempts to unravel for himself his own remarkable life story, looking at early life experiences, his family, and various themes that he believes have contributed to his success. Measure is not a chronological autobiography; the book emphasizes themes that have shaped his life. . . . Poitier's tale is an affirmation of the value of morality and personal integrity in leading a successful, fulfilling life." Booklist

Polk, James K. (James Knox), 1795-1849

Borneman, Walter R. **Polk**; the man who transformed the presidency and America. Random House 2008 422p il map $30   **92**
1. Governors 2. Presidents 3. Members of Congress 4. Speakers of the House 5. Presidents -- United States
ISBN 978-1-4000-6560-8
    LC 2007-14040
The author "presents a birth-death biography of Polk. . . . Borneman has a pleasing style and makes fine use of primary sources that all demonstrate why Polk is habitually ranked as one of the ten best presidents by historians." Libr J
Includes bibliographical references

Merry, Robert W., 1946- A **country** of vast designs; James K. Polk, the Mexican War, and the conquest of the American continent. Simon & Schuster 2009 576p il map   **92**
1. Governors 2. Presidents 3. Members of Congress 4. Biography, Individual 5. Speakers of the House 6. Presidents -- United States 7. United States -- Territorial expansion 8. United States -- Territorial expansion -- History 9. United States -- Politics and government --

1815-1861 10. United States -- Politics and government -- 1841-1845 11. United States -- Politics and government -- 1845-1849 12. United States -- Politics and government -- 1845-1861
ISBN 0743297431; 9780743297431

LC 2009024131

This is a biography of the eleventh president of the United States. Bibliography. Index.

"Merry's chronicle is filled with excellent insights into the critical events and fine portrayals of a cast of statesmen, warriors, and scheming rogues. . . . [This is] an outstanding addition to American history collections." Booklist

Includes bibliographical references (p. 543-550)

Pollock, Jackson, 1912-1956

Adams, Henry. **Tom** and Jack; the intertwined lives of Thomas Hart Benton and Jackson Pollock. Bloomsbury Press 2009 405p il $35   **92**
1. Artists 2. Painters 3. Illustrators 4. Lithographers 5. Artists -- United States
ISBN 1-59691-420-3; 978-1-59691-420-9

LC 2009-12309

"In this absorbing, carefully reasoned inquiry into a profound relationship between two painters, Adams reclaims the wrongfully maligned Benton and recalibrates our perception of Pollock and his masterpieces." Booklist

Includes bibliographical references (p. 375-390)

Solomon, Deborah. **Jackson** Pollock; a biography. Cooper Square Press 2001 287p il pa $17.95   **92**
1. Artists 2. Painters 3. Abstract expressionism 4. Artists -- United States
ISBN 978-0-8154-1182-6; 0-8154-1182-0

LC 2001-28915

First published 1987 by Simon and Schuster

A biography of the American abstract expressionist painter.

"A concisely written biography; the footnotes indicate solid research." Libr J

Includes bibliographical references

Polo, Marco, 1254-1323?

Bergreen, Laurence. **Marco** Polo; from Venice to Xanadu. Knopf 2007 415p il map $28.95; pa $16.95   **92**
1. Explorers 2. Travelers 3. Voyages and travels 4. Travel writers 5. China -- Description and travel
ISBN 978-1-4000-4345-3; 1-4000-4345-3; 978-1-4000-7880-6 pa; 1-4000-7880-6 pa

LC 2007-21860

This is a biography of the Venetian explorer.

The author "gives a full-blooded rendition of Polo's astonishing journey. It is richly researched and vividly conveyed." Washington Post Book World

Includes bibliographical references (p. 383-391)

Pop, Iggy, 1947-

Trynka, Paul. **Iggy** Pop; open up and bleed. Broadway Books 2007 371p il $23.95; pa $14.95   **92**
1. Singers 2. Rock musicians 3. Punk rock music 4.

Songwriters
ISBN 978-0-7679-2319-4; 978-0-7679-2320-0 pa

LC 2006-30216

"Drawing from original interviews with Iggy (né James Newell Osterberg Jr.) and his countless accomplices over the years, Trynka . . . has constructed a comprehensive portrait of the seemingly indestructible rock provocateur, one that touches all the familiar bases in recounting Iggy's riotous ascent from suburban Michigan schoolboy to frontman of the Stooges to solo artist with an intermittently transcendent career to composer of a drug-inspired hit song that became the jingle for a luxury cruise line." N Y Times Book Rev

Includes bibliographical references

Porter, Cole, 1891-1964

McBrien, William. **Cole** Porter; a biography. Knopf 1998 459p il hardcover o.p. $16   **92**
1. Composers 2. Lyricists
ISBN 978-0-679-72792-7; 0-679-72792-2

LC 97-46116

In this biography of the American songwriter, the author "weaves a complex and groundbreaking portrait of Porter, interspersed with lyrics and 72 illustrations, recounting his affluent upbringing in Peru, Ind., and his emergence in the 1930s as the musical theater's reigning sophisticate. . . . This astute biography will help to create a standard-setting portrait of Porter as a homosexual artist in a heterosexual world." Publ Wkly

Includes bibliographical references

Posner, Jessica

Find Me Unafraid; Love, Loss, and Hope in an African Slum. by Kennedy Odede and Jessica Posner. HarperCollins 2015 272 p. color illustrations $27.99   **92**
1. Volunteer work 2. Youth -- Africa 3. Love -- Social aspects
ISBN 0062292854; 9780062292858

This book "is the story of two young people from completely different worlds: Kennedy Odede from Kibera, the largest slum in Africa, and Jessica Posner from Denver, Colorado. . . . Kennedy . . . started a youth empowerment group he called Shining Hope for Communities (SHOFCO). Then in 2007, Wesleyan undergraduate Jessica Posner spent a semester abroad in Kenya working with SHOFCO. Breaking all convention, she decided to live in Kibera with Kennedy, and they fell in love." (Publisher's note)

"It's exciting and inspiring to see how much Kennedy and Jessica are able to accomplish, and how many lives they're changing for the better with SHOFCO, which started with Kennedy's purchase of a twenty-cent soccer ball." Booklist

Potter, Beatrix, 1866-1943

★ Lear, Linda J. **Beatrix** Potter; a life in nature. [by] Linda Lear. Allen Lane/Penguin 2007 583p il $30   **92**
1. Artists 2. Authors 3. Illustrators 4. Children's authors
ISBN 9780312369347; 0-312-36934-4

LC 2006-51245

This is a biography of the children's author.

This "is a meticulously researched and brilliantly recreated life that . . . is endlessly fascinating and often illuminating. It is altogether a remarkable achievement." Booklist
Includes bibliographical references (p. 541-544)

Pouillon, Nora

My organic life; how a pioneering chef helped shape the way we eat today. Nora Pouillon. Alfred A. Knopf 2015 272 p. illustrations (hardback) $26.95 **92**
1. Women cooks 2. Organic farming 3. Cooking -- Natural foods 4. Organic living 5. Cooking (Natural foods) 6. Cooks -- United States -- Biography 7. Women cooks -- United States -- Biography
ISBN 0385350759; 9780385350754
LC 2014036931
This book, by Nora Pouillon, "is the story of an unheralded culinary pioneer. . . . First as a cooking teacher, then as a restaurant owner, and eventually as the country's premier organic restaurateur, she charted a path that forever changed our relationship with what we eat. . . . Along the way, Nora redefined what food could be, forging close relationships with local producers and launching initiatives to take the organic movement mainstream." (Publisher's note)
"This autobiography is a good choice for those interested in a restaurateur's life or those wishing to know more about the field of organics. Unfortunately, there are no recipes included. Look to the author's other books Cooking with Nora and Cooking in a Healthy Way, for those." LJ

Pound, Ezra, 1885-1972

Tytell, John. **Ezra** Pound; the solitary volcano. Anchor Press 1987 368p il hardcover o.p. pa $19 **92**
1. Poets 2. Authors 3. Literary critics
ISBN 0-385-19870-1 pa
LC 86-25912
"In this incisive interpretative biography, based on interviews with those who knew him and a mass of published and unpublished Poundiana, Tytell examines the circumstances behind the poems and thereby generates new understanding of the man." Publ Wkly
Includes bibliographical references

Powell, Colin L., 1937-

De Young, Karen. **Soldier**: the life of Colin Powell. Knopf 2006 610p il $28.95 **92**
1. Generals 2. Secretaries of state 3. Statesmen -- United States
ISBN 1-400-04170-8
LC 2006-45288
This is a "diligent, sympathetic, but not uncritical full-scale biography." N Y Rev Books
Includes bibliographical references

★ Koltz, Tony. **It** worked for me; in life and leadership. Colin Powell with Tony Koltz. 1st ed. Harper 2012 xii, 283 p.p (hardback) $27.99; (paperback) $27.99; (ebook) $21.99 **92**
1. Leadership 2. Iraq War, 2003-2011 3. African American generals -- Biography 4. Leadership -- United States 5. United States -- Politics and government --

1993-2001 -- Quotations, maxims, etc
ISBN 0062135120; 9780062135124; 9780062184061; 9780062135148
LC 2012002970
This autobiography continues the life story of Colin Powell. "The author rose in the military to become 'the first black Army officer to have a four-star troop command.' . . . He describes how . . . his military training also prepared him for his role in government. . . . Powell reviews his profound disagreements with Defense Secretary Donald Rumsfeld and Vice President Dick Cheney on the handling of the war in Iraq, while taking full responsibility for mistakes made on his watch." (Kirkus Reviews)

Powell, Colin L. **My** American journey; [by] Colin L. Powell, with Joseph E. Persico. Random House 1995 643p il $26.95; pa $14.95 **92**
1. Generals 2. Secretaries of state 3. Statesmen -- United States
ISBN 0-679-43296-5; 0-345-46641-1 pa
LC 95-17119
This "is an endearing and well-written book. It will make you like Colin Powell." N Y Times Book Rev

Powers, J. F.

Suitable accommodations; an autobiographical story of family life : the letters of J. F. Powers, 1942-1963. edited by Katherine A. Powers. Fararr, Straus & Giroux 2013 480 p. illustrations (hardcover) $35 **92**
1. Letters 2. American authors 3. Authors, American -- 20th century -- Correspondence
ISBN 0374268061; 9780374268060
LC 2013010997
This book, edited by Katherine A. Powers, presents a "collection of letters from the late J. F. Powers. . . . Beginning in prison, where Powers spent more than a year as a conscientious objector, the letters move on to his courtship, marriage, comically unsuccessful attempt to live in the woods, life in the Midwest and in Ireland, an unorthodox view of the Catholic Church, and an increasingly bizarre search for 'suitable accommodations,' which included three full-scale emigrations to Ireland." (Publisher's note)

Presley, Elvis, 1935-1977

Alden, Ginger. **Elvis** and Ginger; Ginger Alden. Ace Books 2014 400 p. illustrations (chiefly color) (hardcover) $26.95 **92**
1. Actresses -- United States -- Biography 2. Rock musicians -- United States -- Biography
ISBN 0425266338; 9780425266335
LC 2014009089
In this memoir Ginger Alden discusses her " whirlwind romance [with Elvis Presley] from first kiss to his stunning proposal of marriage. She details his exploration of Eastern religions, his perception of being a 'legend,' his devotion to family and friends, and her attempt to know the insular group surrounding Elvis. And for the very first time she talks about the devastating end of it all, and the 50,000 mourners and reporters who descended on Graceland in 1977." (Publisher's note)

"It's an outpouring of affection for a man who has stayed in the author's mind all these years, a way for her to show the world the Elvis she knew. The book has a pretty much guaranteed readership, as many Elvis fans will read anything and everything that appears in print about their idol." Booklist

★ Guralnick, Peter. **Careless** love: the unmaking of Elvis Presley. Little, Brown 1999 767p il $27.95; pa $17.95   **92**

1. Actors 2. Singers 3. Rock musicians
ISBN 0-316-33222-4; 0-316-33297-6 pa

LC 98-25778

This second and concluding volume of Guralnick's biography of the rock star covers "Elvis's hitch in the army through his death in 1977. . . . The breadth of Guralnick's research is nothing short of amazing, and his lyrical narrative presents an empathetic portrait of a man struggling with drugs, sex, family, personal eccentricities, money, and the delicate web of relationships surrounding any famous figure." Libr J

Includes bibliographical references

Mason, Bobbie Ann. **Elvis** Presley. Viking 2002 178p (Penguin lives series) hardcover o.p. pa $13   **92**

1. Actors 2. Singers 3. Rock musicians
ISBN 0-670-03174-7; 0-14-303889-3 pa

LC 2002-28873

The author "chronicles Elvis' sad story: humble origins, 1954 breakthrough, adoption by 'the Colonel' (manager Tom Parker), early TV appearances, army hitch, the death of his mother, marriage to Priscilla, Hollywood, 1968 'comeback', Las Vegas headliner, prescription drug abuse, meeting with Nixon, and death at 42 in 1977." Booklist

Includes discography, filmography and bibliographical references

Preston, Katherine, 1984-

Preston, Katherine. **Out** with it; how stuttering helped me find my voice. Katherine Preston. Atria Books 2013 244 p. (hardback) $24   **92**

1. Stutterers 2. Speech disorders 3. Stutterers -- Biography
ISBN 1451676581; 9781451676587; 9781451676594

LC 2012048984

This book is a memoir by Katherine Preston about her "struggle to come to terms with her stuttering." She began stuttering around the age of 7, and the book starts there, . . . capturing the mix of abject terror and curious observation that childhood stuttering can create. . . . She chronicles her many interviews with fellow stutterers--people bullied, people strengthened, and people driven from those they care about." (Kirkus Reviews)

Price, Reynolds, 1933-2011

Price, Reynolds. **Ardent** spirits; leaving home, coming back. Scribner 2009 408p il $35   **92**

1. Authors 2. Novelists 3. Essayists 4. College teachers 5. Short story writers
ISBN 978-0-7432-9189-7; 0-7432-9189-1

LC 2009-2376

In this memoir, Price "takes up where his 1989 Clear Pictures left off—with a young Price heading for England on a Rhodes scholarship, a young man lighting into new and unfamiliar territories and the lessons he learns about literature, life and love. Covering the years 1955 to 1961, Price chronicles the challenges of living in a strange place, his emotional insecurities and his anxieties about his ability to complete the thesis on Milton, his adventures in Europe with a close friend and his eventual return to his alma mater, Duke University, to teach writing and literature. Along the way, Price recalls his friendships with Stephen Spender, Cyril Connolly, W.H. Auden and his brief encounters with Jean-Paul Sartre and J.R.R. Tolkien. . . . [Price] powerfully articulates the strength of memory in shaping our lives and gracefully draws us into a literary life lived fully." Publ Wkly

Priestley, Joseph, 1733-1804

Johnson, Steven, 1968- The **invention** of air; a story of science, faith, revolution, and the birth of America. Riverhead Books 2008 254p il $25.95 **92**

1. Clergy 2. Chemists 3. Scientists 4. Writers on science 5. Biography, Individual
ISBN 1-59448-852-5; 978-1-59448-852-8

LC 2008-46101

This "portrait of scientist and theologian Joseph Priestley evaluates his friendships with such Founding Fathers as Benjamin Franklin and Thomas Jefferson while citing his role in the nation's intellectual development and the founding of the Unitarian Church." (Publisher's note) Bibliography. Index.

"What enlivens the book is that Johnson does not simply describe the system within which Priestley and his contemporaries hashed out the features of classical science; he sets it against other, later systems for comprehending physical reality, showing laymen how far we have come from the classical age of science." N Y Times Book Rev

Includes bibliographical references

Pritchett, V. S. (Victor Sawdon), 1900-1997

Treglown, Jeremy. **V.S.** Pritchett: a working life. Random House 2005 334p $25.95   **92**

1. Authors 2. Novelists 3. Literary critics 4. Short story writers
ISBN 0-375-50853-8

LC 2004-53857

This biography follows the life and career of the English writer, who for most of the century ennobled the ordinary and whose two tumultuous marriages fueled his art

"Treglown's genial and sympathetic biography effectively expands . . . awareness of the life and career of this greatly accessible and warmhearted writer of fiction, travel literature, and criticism. . . . This is a biography as open-minded and unpretentious as Pritchett's own writing." Booklist

Includes bibliographical references

Prokofiev, Sergey, 1891-1953

★ Nice, David. **Prokofiev**: from Russia to the West, 1891-1935. Yale Univ. Press 2003 390p il music $35   **92**

1. Composers
ISBN 0-300-09914-2

"Part 1 chronicles Prokofiev's childhood, family relationships, and training at the St. Petersburg Conservatoire, while Part 2 covers his concert tours in America, France, and Germany and prodigious compositional output, beginning with the fairy tale opera, The Love of Three Oranges. . . . Nice embeds many musical examples in the body of the text and writes cogently about them. . . . Overall, the writing is fluid and unencumbered by excessive analytical detail, and at times witty. . . . Throughout, the composer's outsized personality and compositional brilliance shine through." Libr J

Includes discography and bibliographical references

Proulx, Annie

Proulx, Annie, 1935- **Bird** cloud; a memoir. Scribner 2011 234p il map $26; ebook $12.99 **92**

1. Authors 2. Novelists 3. Journalists 4. Women authors 5. Editors 6. Nonfiction writers 7. Short story writers 8. Biography, Individual 9. Natural history -- Wyoming 10. Wyoming -- Description and travel

ISBN 978-0-7432-8880-4; 978-1-4391-7171-4 ebook

"'Bird Cloud' is the name Annie Proulx gave to 640 acres of Wyoming wetlands and prairie and four-hundred-foot cliffs plunging down to the North Platte River. On the day she first visited, a cloud in the shape of a bird hung in the evening sky. Proulx also saw pelicans, bald eagles, golden eagles, great blue herons, ravens, scores of bluebirds, harriers, kestrels, elk, deer and a dozen antelope. She fell in love with the land, then owned by the Nature Conservancy, and she knew what she wanted to build on it—a house in harmony with her work, her appetites and her character, a library surrounded by bedrooms and a kitchen. . . . Bird Cloud is the story of designing and constructing that house—with its solar panels, Japanese soak tub, concrete floor and elk horn handles on kitchen cabinets. It is also a . . . natural history and archaeology of the region—inhabited for millennia by Ute, Arapaho and Shoshone Indians—and a family history, going back to nineteenth-century Mississippi riverboat captains and Canadian settlers." (Publisher's note)

"Proulx bought a 640-acre nature preserve by the North Platte River in Wyoming and started building her dream house, a project that took years and went hundreds of thousands of dollars over budget. In her bustling account, Proulx salivates over the prospect of a Japanese soak tub, polished concrete floor, solar panels, and luxe furnishings that often turn into pricey engineering fiascoes. . . . [This] is a fine evocation of place that becomes a meditation on the importance of a home, however harsh and evanescent." Publ Wkly

Includes bibliographical references

Pryor, Richard, 1940-2005

Henry, David. **Furious** cool; Richard Pryor and the world that made him. by David Henry and Joe Henry. Algonquin Books 2013 400 p. $25.95 **92**

1. Comedians -- Biography 2. Comedians -- United States -- Biography 3. Motion picture actors and actresses -- United States -- Biography

ISBN 1616200782; 9781616200787

LC 2013019665

In this biography of Richard Pryor, authors David Henry and Joe Henry "bring him to life both as a man and as an artist, providing an in-depth appreciation of his talent and his lasting influence, as well as an . . . examination of the world

he lived in and the influences that shaped both his persona and his art." (Publisher's note)

"A beautifully written account of the troubled life of a manic genius." Booklist

Includes bibliographical references

Mooney, Paul. **Black** is the new white; a memoir. Simon Spotlight Entertainment 2009 264p il $24.99 **92**

1. Actors 2. Comedians 3. Screenwriters 4. Television scriptwriters 5. United States -- Race relations

ISBN 978-1-4165-8795-8; 1-4165-8795-0

LC 2009-19572

"Paul Mooney recalls the day he became Richard Pryor's shadow partner. It was 1968, and the two young comics were sitting in a Hollywood greasy spoon, with Pryor nursing another hangover, so Mooney lightened the mood with an off-the-cuff, X-rated one-liner that made his buddy convulse. . . . [This book] is Mooney's unvarnished memoir of that friendship. At a time when comedians—even African American icons such as Bill Cosby—never talked about race, Pryor (aided and abetted by Mooney) dared to confront the elephant in the room. Mooney, who has also written for 'In Living Color' and 'Chappelle's Show,' also traces his own path from humble Deep South roots to a comedy elder statesman known for his incisive riffs on racism." Los Angeles Times book Rev

Puccini, Giacomo, 1858-1924

Berger, William. **Puccini** without excuses; a refreshing reassessment of the world's most popular composer. Vintage Books 2005 471p pa $16 **92**

1. Opera 2. Composers

ISBN 978-1-4000-7778-6; 1-4000-7778-8

LC 2005-46157

The author "sets Puccini within his times before discussing the circumstances of each opera's premiere and famous interpreters of the roles, providing character lists and synopses and fleshing all this out with musical commentary. Chapters on opera production and the genre's relation to film are useful. . . . Berger's lucid yet hardly dispassionate views are designed to elicit strong reactions, so this is not the first place one should go for an unbiased introduction to the composer's oeuvre. But the author's grounding information is helpful for the novice, and he refers to some of the current authoritative sources." Libr J

Pulitzer, Joseph, 1847-1911

Morris, James McGrath. **Pulitzer**; a life in politics, print, and power. Harper 2010 558p il $29.99 **92**

1. Journalists 2. Members of Congress 3. Newspaper executives

ISBN 978-0-06-079869-7; 0-06-079869-6

LC 2009-27501

This is an "excellent book: a thorough, possibly definitive biography of the man who shaped the modern newspaper more than anyone else." Washington Post

Includes bibliographical references

Pushkin, Aleksandr Sergeevich, 1799-1837

★ Binyon, T. J. **Pushkin**: a biography. Knopf 2003 xxix, 727p il maps $35; pa $20   **92**

1. Poets 2. Authors 3. Novelists 4. Short story writers

ISBN 1-4000-4110-4; 1-4000-7652-8 pa

LC 2003-112113

The author argues that Pushkin's "political views and rebellious temper were a continual source of trouble, inviting criticism and condemnation his entire life and eventually ending it in 1837 when he was fatally wounded in a duel with George D'Anthes. . . . A stunning achievement, this thorough biography is sure to become the definitive account of Pushkin's life for years to come and will appeal to the scholar and general reader alike." Libr J

Includes bibliographical references

Putin, Vladimir

Putin, Vladimir. **First** person: an astonishingly frank self-portrait; by Russia's president Vladimir Putin with Nataliya Gevorkyan, Natalya Timakova, and Andrei Kolesnikov; translated by Catherine A. Fitzpatrick. PublicAffairs 2000 206p il pa $15 **92**

1. Presidents 2. Prime ministers

ISBN 1-58648-018-9

LC 00-132549

This volume is "the product of some 24 hours of interviews with Putin conducted by three Russian journalists, with brief comments from other sources, including Putin's family, friends, teachers, and some associates. . . . The approach is chronological , describing Putin as son, schoolboy, university student, young intelligence specialist, spy, democrat, bureaucrat, family man, and politician." Booklist

Qazwini, Hassan

Qazwini, Hassan. **American** crescent; A Muslim cleric on the power of his faith, the struggle against prejudice, and the future of Islam and America. Random House 2007 282p il $26.95 **92**

1. Islamic leaders 2. Muslims -- United States

ISBN 978-1-4000-6454-0; 1-4000-6454-0

LC 2007-10345

This "a useful book, especially for American readers who are unfamiliar with Islam or who wonder how Muslim Americans and Arab-Americans can be integrated into American life." N Y Times Book Rev

Includes bibliographical references

Queller, Jessica, 1969-

Queller, Jessica. **Pretty** is what changes; impossible choices, the breast cancer gene, and how I defied my destiny. Spiegel & Grau 2008 247p $24.95 **92**

1. Breast cancer 2. Surgical patients 3. Television scriptwriters 4. Cancer -- Genetic aspects

ISBN 978-0-385-52040-9; 0-385-52040-9

LC 2008-4303

The author tells her story—from her mother's death from ovarian cancer and her positive testing for the breast cancer gene BRCA-1 to her decision to have a double mastectomy and remove her ovaries.

This "story is seamless and gripping; readers will be rooting for Queller and her heroic decision to confront her genetic destiny." Publ Wkly

Questlove

Greenman, Ben. **Mo'** meta blues; the world according to Questlove. by Ahmir "Questlove" Thompson and Ben Greenman. Grand Central Pub. 2013 288 p. (hardcover) $26   **92**

1. Musicians

ISBN 1455501352; 9781455501359

LC 2013932326

This book is a memoir by "Questlove" Thompson, the cofounder and drummer of the band the Roots. Here, he "tells of his work as a DJ and producer with some of the biggest names in the music business, such as Jay-Z and Common, and Dave Chappelle," His "recollections touch on everything from drumming at age five in his father's professional doo-wop and soul band to roller-skating as an adult with Eddie Murphy at a bizarre party hosted by Prince." (Publishers Weekly)

Quiñones-Hinojosa, Alfredo

Quiñones-Hinojosa, Alfredo. **Becoming** Dr. Q; my journey from migrant farm worker to brain surgeon. with Mim Eichler Rivas. University of California Press 2011 317p il $27.50   **92**

1. Surgeons 2. Migrant labor 3. Mexican Americans 4. Neurologists 5. Neurosurgeons

ISBN 978-0-520-27118-0; 0-520-27118-1

LC 2011011531

"When the callow Quiñones-Hinojosa, or Dr. Q, made up his mind to pursue a better life and, especially, an education in the U.S., no border or barrier could have kept him from his destiny: a fate that led eventually to his becoming a Johns Hopkins University neurosurgeon, professor, and brain-cancer research scientist. Indeed, the brash teenager left all that was familiar in his native Mexico and, with less than $70 in his pocket, climbed the fence. In fact, he scaled it twice because he was caught the first time and sent back. . . Quiñones-Hinojosa's story is gripping, inspiring, and just plain awesome." Booklist

Rabin, Yitzhak, 1922-1995

Shalom, friend: the life and legacy of Yitzhak Rabin; the Jerusalem Report staff; edited by David Horovitz; prologue by Hirsch Goodman. Newmarket Press 1996 314p il maps $24.95   **92**

1. Prime ministers 2. Cabinet members 3. Political leaders 4. Nobel laureates for peace

ISBN 1-55704-287-X

LC 96-5146

"This is a collaborative effort by more than a dozen writers and editors of the Jerusalem Report, a prestigious Israeli newsmagazine, all of whom had close personal and professional knowledge of the former prime minister, assassinated in November 1995. Their views are supplemented by numerous, interviews with knowledgeable people." Libr J

Includes bibliographical references

Rackley, Adam

Salt, sweat, tears; the men who rowed the oceans. Adam Rackley. Penguin Books 2014 272 p. 16 plates; illustrations; map (paperback) $16 **92**
1. Rowing 2. Ocean travel 3. Atlantic Ocean 4. Rowers -- Biography
ISBN 0143126660; 9780143126669
LC 2014010916

Author Adam Rackley presents "his story of adventure, endurance, and self-discovery. For more than seventy days, Adam Rackley and his rowing partner ate, slept and rowed in a boat seven meters long by two meters wide, in one of the world's most extreme environments." (Publisher's note)

"Told in an earnest and captivating style by first-time author Rackley will delight both armchair enthusiasts and real-life adventurers when they discover another sport for their dreams." LJ

Rand, Ayn, 1905-1982

Heller, Anne Conover. **Ayn** Rand and the world she made; [by] Anne C. Heller. Nan A. Talese/Doubleday 2008 567p il $35 **92**
1. Authors 2. Novelists 3. Philosophers 4. Women authors 5. Authors, American 6. Nonfiction writers 7. Objectivism (Philosophy)
ISBN 978-0-385-51399-9
LC 2008-27638

This is a biography of the author of Atlas Shrugged and The Fountainhead.

The author "has delivered a thoughtful, flesh-and-blood portrait of an extremely complicated and self-contradictory woman, coupling this character study with literary analysis and plumbing the quirkier depths of Rand's prodigious imagination." N Y Times (Late N Y Ed)

Includes bibliographical references

Rand, Ayn. **Journals** of Ayn Rand; edited by David Harriman; foreword by Leonard Peikoff. Dutton 1997 727p il hardcover o.p. pa $22 **92**
1. Authors 2. Novelists 3. Philosophers 4. Nonfiction writers
ISBN 0-452-27887-2 pa
LC 97-12737

"This work offers almost everything the author ever wrote to herself. As intriguing yet sometimes numbing as her fiction, the book, which covers the years from 1927 to the mid-1970s, contains her first philosophical stabs, notes on her novels, HUAC testimony against alleged Hollywood communists, and her unfinished projects." Publ Wkly

Rankin, Lissa, 1969-

Rankin, Lissa. The **anatomy** of a calling; a road map for awakening to your life's purpose. Lissa Rankin. Rodale 2015 288 p. (trade hardcover) $24.99 **92**
1. Vocation 2. Conduct of life 3. Holistic medicine -- United States 4. Physicians -- United States -- Biography
ISBN 9781623365745
LC 2015040863

In this book, physician Lissa Rankin "shares her story [through the lens of Joseph Campbell's "Hero's Journey"

paradigm.] She encourages you to find out where you are on your own journey, offering inspiring guideposts and practices along the way. With compelling lessons on trusting intuition, surrendering to love, and learning to see adversity as an opportunity for soul growth . . . [she] invites you to make a powerful shift in consciousness and reach your highest destiny." (Publisher's note)

"Readers who seek more information and methodology regarding mind/body healing and health through diverse spiritual practices will find Rankin's story fascinating." Pub Wkly

Rao, Cheeni

Rao, Cheeni. **In** Hanuman's hands; a memoir of recovery and redemption. HarperOne 2009 399p $25.99 **92**
1. Authors 2. Dramatists 3. Drug addicts 4. East Indian Americans 5. Editors 6. Memoirists 7. Short story writers
ISBN 978-0-06-073662-0; 0-06-073662-3
LC 2008-55421

"It is the rapture of . . . [the author's] language; his hallucinatory, world-bridging storytelling; and his high-wire variations on the timeless struggles between truth and deception, good and evil, that make this journey to hell and back all-consuming and profound." Booklist

Rasputin, Grigori Efimovich, 1871-1916

Massie, Robert K., 1929- **Nicholas** and Alexandra. Ballantine Books 2000 613p il map pa $18.95 **92**
1. Monks 2. Emperors 3. Empresses 4. Courtiers 5. Russia -- History 6. Russia -- Kings and rulers
ISBN 0-345-43831-0; 978-0-345-43831-7
LC 99-91507

First published 1967 by Atheneum

This study provides an intimate account of the Romanov family and the coming of the Russian Revolution. Kerensky, Lenin and Rasputin are among the personalities profiled.

This book, "solid with research, reads as lightly as a novel, as authoritatively as a textbook. Dialogue and lively description lend a sense of immediacy, but his notes, discreetly relegated to the back of the book, show how carefully he has avoided slipping into fiction." Christ Sci Monit

Includes bibliographical references

Rather, Dan

Diehl, Digby. **Rather** outspoken; my life in the news. Dan Rather with Digby Diehl. Grand Central Pub. 2012 vi, 309 p.p (regular edition) $27.99 **92**
1. CBS Inc. 2. Television broadcasting of news 3. Television journalists -- United States -- Biography
ISBN 1455502413; 9781455502417; 9781455513468
LC 2011052227

This book by Dan Rather presents an "investigation of how the news media has become dangerously intertwined with politics and corporate interests." It focuses on "the circumstances behind his firing from CBS News, where he had worked as a reporter since 1962. . . . In between, he provides . . . portraits of the presidents he has interviewed . . . and expresses concern for the future of independent media in an industry that is increasingly kowtowing to the almighty bottom line." (Kirkus Reviews)

Reagan, Ronald, 1911-2004

Brands, H. W. **Reagan**; the life. H.W. Brands. Doubleday 2015 816 p. 16 plates; color illustrations (hardback) $35   **92**

1. Presidents -- United States -- Biography 2. United States -- Politics and government -- 1981-1989
ISBN 0385536399; 9780385536394
LC 2014038054

This biography by H.W. Brands "establishes Ronald Reagan as one of the two great presidents of the twentieth century, a true peer to Franklin Roosevelt. 'Reagan' conveys . . . how the confident force of Reagan's personality and the unwavering nature of his beliefs enabled him to engineer a conservative revolution in American politics and play a crucial role in ending communism in the Soviet Union." (Publishers' note)

"This is a detailed look at a president who sparked much controversy and affection and it belongs in most collections of presidential biography." Booklist

Buckley, William F. The **Reagan** I knew; [by] William F. Buckley, Jr. Basic Books 2008 279p il $25   **92**

1. Actors 2. Governors 3. Presidents 4. Presidents -- United States
ISBN 978-0-465-00926-8; 0-465-00926-3
LC 2008-32557

"The correspondence, which spans the period 1965–98 (with one final letter, written in 2005), seems on the surface to be concerned almost entirely with mundane matters: thank-you letters written after a get-together, apologies for missed birthdays, etc. But look beneath the surface, and you'll find a revealing portrait of two men: Reagan, a driven political contender who never gave up his decency or his sense of family, and Buckley, a tireless Reagan booster who used his many public forums to promote Reagan's political agenda." Booklist

Reagan, Ron. **My** father at 100. Viking 2011 228p il $25.95   **92**

1. Actors 2. Governors 3. Presidents 4. Presidents -- United States
ISBN 978-0-670-02259-5; 0-670-02259-4
LC 2010-45833

The son of Ronald and Nancy Reagan presents an assessment of his father's life that features his childhood observations of the qualities that rendered the future fortieth president a powerful leader.

A "nuanced and satisfying portrait is provided by Ron Reagan in My Father at 100. . . . [This work] is most poignant in its description of the author's search for his father's approval, forever just out of reach." Time

★ Reagan, Ronald. **Reagan**; a life in letters. edited, with an introduction and commentary by Kiron K. Skinner, Annelise Anderson, {and} Martin Anderson; with a foreword by George P. Shultz. Free Press 2003 934p $35; pa $18.95   **92**

1. Actors 2. Governors 3. Presidents 4. Presidents -- United States
ISBN 0-7432-1966-X; 0-7432-1967-8 pa
LC 2003-49249

"This volume consists of a sampling of the former president's copious outpouring of personal letters, from his childhood to the onset of Alzheimer's after the presidency. The editors . . . arrange the letters thematically, introduce each chapter with a brief commentary, and introduce each letter with a sentence or two of explanation. The editors have done an admirable job in compiling these documents. Their commentary is exactly as it might have been had Ronald Reagan been able to produce this volume himself." Choice

Includes bibliographical references

Reagan, Ronald, 1911-2004. The **Reagan** diaries; edited by Douglas Brinkley. HarperCollins 2007 767p il $35; pa $19.99   **92**

1. Biography, Individual 2. Presidents -- United States 3. United States -- Politics and government -- 1974-1989 4. United States -- Politics and government -- 1981-1989
ISBN 978-0-06-087600-5; 0-06-087600-X; 978-0-06-155833-7 pa; 0-06-155833-8 pa

"There is a kind of touching banality to many of the entries, as though Reagan were just another CEO writing about corporate life at the top, albeit corporate life that revolved around nuclear and hostage negotiations. Edited by Douglas Brinkley . . . , the book shows a Reagan almost sweetly amazed by small trappings of office. . . . Reading these diaries, Americans will find it easier to understand how Reagan did what he did for so long: by steady work, and a steadfast commitment to the job at hand." Newsweek

Rebanks, James

The **shepherd's** life; modern dispatches from an ancient landscape. James Rebanks. Flatiron Books 2015 293 p. illustrations (hardcover) $25.99   **92**

1. Shepherds 2. Country life 3. Livestock industry 4. Sheep -- England -- Lake District 5. Farm life -- England -- Lake District 6. Farmers -- England -- Lake District -- Biography 7. Shepherds -- England -- Lake District -- Biography
ISBN 1250060249; 9781250060242
LC 2015011233

This book, by James Rebanks, "takes us through a shepherd's year, offering a unique account of rural life and a fundamental connection with the land that most of us have lost. It is a story of working lives, the people around him, his childhood, his parents and grandparents, a people who exist and endure even as the culture--of the Lake District, and of farming--changes around them." (Publisher's note)

Red Cloud, 1822-1909

Drury, Bob. The **heart** of everything that is; the untold story of Red Cloud, an American legend. Bob Drury and Tom Clavin. Simon & Schuster 2013 400 p. illustrations, maps (hardcover) $30   **92**

1. Oglala Indians 2. Red Cloud's War, 1866-1867
ISBN 1451654669; 9781451654660; 9781451654684
LC 2013003200

"Drawing on a wealth of evidence, including Red Cloud's biography, which was lost for nearly a hundred years, this never-before-told story of the great Oglala Sioux chief - the only Plains Indian to defeat the United States Army in a war - places readers at the center of the conflict over western expansion." (Publisher's note)

The authors "offer a battle-and-skirmish account of Sioux leader Red Cloud's war on the whites who invaded the Great Plains, though their narrative is strong on ethno-historical matters as well. . . . A well-researched and -written account of an often overlooked figure in the history of the Indian Wars." Kirkus

Includes bibliographical references and index

Redding, Otis, 1941-1967

Ribowsky, Mark. **Dreams** to remember; Otis Redding, Stax Records, and the transformation of Southern soul. Mark Ribowsky. Liveright Publishing Corp., A Division of W.W. Norton & Co. 2015 336 p. 8 plates; illustrations (hardcover) $27.95 **92**
1. Soul music 2. Soul music -- History and criticism 3. Soul musicians -- United States -- Biography
ISBN 0871408732; 9780871408730

LC 2015009097

This biography, by Mark Ribowsky, describes how, "when he died in one of rock's string of tragic plane crashes, Otis Redding was only twenty-six, yet already the avatar of a new kind of soul music. The beating heart of Memphis-based Stax Records, he had risen to fame belting out gospel-flecked blues in stage performances that seemed to ignite not only a room but an entire generation." (Publisher's note)

"Unlike other performers who died far too young, Redding's death did not come out of abuse, and though he suffered, it was a universal human suffering--a pain in the heart that, partnered with unerring musical instinct, personal strength, and a little tenderness, he transformed into art. Ribowsky goes into the seamy side of the record business but also the sheer beauty and magic of the sixties soul music that Redding epitomized." Booklist

Includes bibliographical references and index

Reeve, Christopher, 1952-2004

Reeve, Christopher. **Still** me. Random House 1998 309p il hardcover o.p. pa $7.99 **92**
1. Actors 2. People with disabilities 3. People with physical disabilities
ISBN 0-345-43241-X pa

LC 98-10223

This autobiography begins with Reeve's "riding accident and relates in almost slow-motion detail what happened before and after the near-fatal spill in 1995. His remembrances then move back and forth in time. Reeve's early life, his complex relationships, and his career are juxtaposed against the life he leads now as filmmaker, husband and father, and spokesman for those with spinal-cord injuries." Booklist

Reichl, Ruth

Reichl, Ruth. **Comfort** me with apples; more adventures at the table. Random House 2001 302p $24.95; pa $13.95 **92**
1. Memoirists 2. Food critics 3. Magazine editors
ISBN 0-375-50195-9; 0-375-75873-9 pa

LC 00-53355

Sequel to Tender at the bone (1998)

"In this second installment of her memoirs, {Reichl} retraces her route from married life on a commune in late-seventies Berkeley to her first job as a food critic, dining at expensive restaurants in Los Angeles with her glamorous editor. . . . Reichl writes with gusto, and her story has all the ingredients of a modern fairy tale: hard work, weird food, and endless curiosity." New Yorker

Reichl, Ruth. **Garlic** and sapphires. Penguin Press 2005 333p $24.95 **92**
1. Memoirists 2. Food critics 3. Magazine editors
ISBN 1-594-20031-9

LC 2004-51362

"Reichl's ability to experience meals in such a dramatic way brings an infectious passion to her memoir. Reading this work . . . , ensures that the next time readers sit down in a restaurant, they'll notice things they've never noticed before." Publ Wkly

Reiner, Jon

Reiner, Jon. The **man** who couldn't eat; a memoir. Gallery 2011 313p $25; ebook $11.99 **92**
1. Sick 2. Inflammatory bowel diseases
ISBN 978-1-4391-9246-7; 1-4391-9246-4; 978-1-4391-9254-2 ebook; 1-4391-9254-5 ebook

LC 2011005441

"Reiner's self-pitiless account stands out for the irony of a foodie being unable to eat, the sheer magnitude of the torment endured, the courage to stare down unrelenting pain, the honest introspection into how suffering made the author insufferable and rocked his family and, above all, his refreshingly snide attitude toward his disease. . . . An inspiring, incredible tale. " Kirkus

Reinhardt, Django, 1910-1953

Dregni, Michael. **Django**: the life and music of a Gypsy legend. Oxford University Press 2004 326p il $35; pa $16.95 **92**
1. Guitarists 2. Jazz musicians
ISBN 0-19-516752-X; 0-19-530448-9 pa

LC 2004-6214

This "biography does its complex subject justice. And even when Dregni dallies overlong on some byways, his immersion in the period's history enriches his storytelling and our understanding. The panoramic results present Django Reinhardt as he has never been seen." N Y Times Book Rev

Includes bibliographical references

Rembrandt Harmenszoon van Rijn, 1606-1669

Schama, Simon. **Rembrandt's** eyes. Knopf 1999 640p il $50; pa $35 **92**
1. Artists 2. Etchers 3. Painters 4. Drafters
ISBN 0-679-40256-X; 0-375-70981-9 pa

LC 99-19971

Schama's prose unfurls the life of Rembrandt in all its pathos. From prodigy to pauper, the troubled genius of 17th century Dutch painting is intricately conceived as he rises and falls in a world of war, plague and stolid bourgeois comfort. . . . Schama's book is a marvel of storytelling: sometimes heart pounding, always sympathetic and coolly reasoned. Seamlessly joining social history and art, what a triumph of scholarship and imagination." Time

Reynolds, Debbie, 1932-2016

Reynolds, Debbie, 1932- **Make** 'em Laugh; Short-term Memories of Longtime Friends. Debbie Reynolds and Dorian Hannaway. William Morrow 2015 288 p. 16 plates; ills; portraits $25.99 **92**

1. Actresses 2. Performing arts 3. Motion picture industry

ISBN 0062416634; 9780062416636

In this memoir author Debbie Reynolds, written with Dorian Hannaway, "continues her intimate chat with fans in this entertaining collection of anecdotes, stories, jokes, and random musings. Debbie shares memories of late night pals and some of the greatest comedians of all time, stories from the big screen and small, and tales of marriage, motherhood, and children." (Publisher's note)

"Reynolds, who refers to herself as a comic (hence the book's title), has done some outstanding film work—with Singin' in the Rain at the forefront—but what's most impressive here is her (almost always) upbeat outlook and her fond regard for the deep friendships she has forged throughout her life. This isn't exactly a showbiz memoir; it's more of a memory book by a woman who has lived a rich life that happened to involve Hollywood." Booklist

Rhodes, William Reginald

Rhodes, William R. **Banker** to the world; leadership lessons from the front lines of global finance. [by] William R. Rhodes. McGraw-Hill 2011 xxxiii, 249p $25; ebook $25 **92**

1. Leadership 2. Decision making 3. Banks and banking 4. International finance 5. Bankers 6. Biography, Individual 7. Banks and banking, International

ISBN 978-0-07-170425-0; 0-07-170425-6; 978-0-07-170424-3 ebook; 0-07-170424-8 ebook

LC 2010032040

This book "should be required reading not only for other bankers, but also for Washington's would-be reformers of Wall Street, and most of all for the ordinary lay citizen dismayed by the persisting panic that has gripped us since 2007." Am Spectator

Includes bibliographical references

Rice, Anne, 1941-

Rice, Anne. **Called** out of darkness; a spiritual confession. Alfred A. Knopf 2008 245p $24 **92**

1. Authors 2. Novelists 3. Women authors 4. Spiritual life 5. Catholic Church 6. Authors, American

ISBN 0-307-26827-6; 978-0-307-26827-3

LC 2008-20192

This memoir by the author of Interview With the Vampire (1976) focuses on Rice's return to Catholicism.

"As plainly written as a Quaker spiritual journal, Rice's confession of faith will impress many who wouldn't think of reading vampire romances—and possibly many who read little else." Booklist

Includes bibliographical references

Rice, Condoleezza, 1954-

Rice, Condoleezza, 1954- **Extraordinary,** ordinary people; a memoir of family. Crown Publishers 2010 342p il **92**

1. College teachers 2. Government officials 3.

Political scientists 4. Secretaries of state 5. Biography, Individual 6. Presidential advisers 7. College administrators 8. Statesmen -- United States 9. African American women -- Biography

ISBN 978-0-307-58787-9; 978-0-307-71960-7 ebook

LC 2010-21645

"The personal story of the former Secretary of State traces her childhood in segregated Alabama, describes the influence of people who shaped her life, and pays tribute to her parents' characters and sacrifices." (Publisher's note) Index.

"Rice's graceful memoir is a personal, multigenerational look into her own, and our country's, past. With vivid and heartfelt writing, Rice, U.S. secretary of state under George W. Bush, looks back on her grandparents and parents, then moves forward through her own life up to the 2000 election. . . . Readers will perceive Rice's emotion in relating her story, yet her portrayal seems fair and unbiased." Libr J

Richards, Keith

★ Richards, Keith. **Life**; [by] Keith Richards with James Fox. Little, Brown 2010 564p il $29.99; ebook $14.99 **92**

1. Guitarists 2. Rock musicians 3. Rolling Stones

ISBN 978-0-316-03438-8; 978-0-316-12856-8 ebook

This autobiography of the Rolling Stones guitarist "is way more than a revealing showbiz memoir. It is also a high-def, high-velocity portrait of the era when rock 'n' roll came of age, a raw report from deep inside the counterculture maelstrom of how that music swept like a tsunami over Britain and the United States. It's an eye-opening all-nighter in the studio with a master craftsman disclosing the alchemical secrets of his art. And it's the intimate and moving story of one man's long strange trip over the decades, told in dead-on, visceral prose without any of the pretense, caution or self-consciousness that usually attend great artists sitting for their self-portraits." N Y Times Book Rev

Richardson, John, 1924-

Richardson, John. The **sorcerer's** apprentice; Picasso, Provence, and Douglas Cooper. University of Chicago Press 2001 318p il pa $17 **92**

1. Art critics 2. Biographers 3. Art historians

ISBN 0-226-71245-1

First published 1999 by Knopf

Picasso biographer John Richardson "has written a concise account of the first half of his own life and notably of his long relationship as a young man with the Cubist art historian and collector Douglas Cooper. The account concentrates on the dozen years, from early 1949 to the end of 1960, when Richardson lived with Cooper, visiting museums and monuments all over Europe, meeting the great artists and other personalities of the day, and restoring the colonnaded Chateau de Castille in the south of France." NY Times Book Rev

Includes bibliographical references

Richter, Charles F., 1900-1985

Hough, Susan Elizabeth. **Richter's** scale; measure of an earthquake, measure of a man. Princeton University Press 2007 335p il $27.95   **92**
1. Scientists 2. Seismologists 3. College teachers
ISBN 978-0-691-12807-8; 0-691-12807-3
LC 2006-16480

"The discussions of the effects of earthquakes on land, structures, and people and the intense search for an understanding of the complex, underlying science will be of interest to many. Readers with substantially different levels of scientific knowledge will find the book comprehensible and interesting." Sci Books Films

Includes bibliographical references (p. 231-240)

Rickey, Branch, 1881-1965

Breslin, Jimmy. **Branch** Rickey. Viking 2010 147p (Penguin lives series) $19.95   **92**
1. Baseball managers 2. Baseball executives 3. Baseball -- Biography 4. Biography, Individual 5. Brooklyn Dodgers (Baseball team)
ISBN 0-670-02249-7; 978-0-670-02249-6
LC 2010-35008

This is a biography of Branch Rickey, the president and general manager of the Brooklyn Dodgers, who, in 1947, brought Jackie Robinson to the team.

"Breslin reveals much about the development of baseball, the Dodgers' last years in Brooklyn, and the struggle to overcome the national pastime's racism while tracing the life, deeds, and some (but not all) of Branch Rickey's warts. A breezy read, this 'Penguin Life' is nonetheless insightful, humorous, and biting at times as it traces how the man dubbed 'the Mahatma' by sportswriters emerged from obscurity as an Idaho lawyer to develop the baseball farm system, multiple MLB winners, Vero Beach spring training, the scientific teaching of skills, and the MLB expansion that brought New York the Mets." Libr J

Includes bibliographical references

Ride, Sally

Sherr, Lynn. **Sally** Ride; America's first woman in space. Lynn Sherr. Simon & Schuster 2014 400 p. illustrations (hardcover) $28   **92**
1. Women astronauts 2. Women -- Biography 3. Astronauts -- United States -- Biography
ISBN 1476725764; 9781476725765; 9781476725772
LC 2013039647

This book is "The definitive biography of Sally Ride, America's first woman in space, with exclusive insights from Ride's family and partner, by [journalist Lynn Sherr] who covered NASA during its transformation from a test-pilot boys' club to a more inclusive elite. . . . Sally Ride made history as the first American woman in space." (Publisher's note)

"This is an intimate and enormously appealing biography of a fascinating woman, a triumph of research and sensitivity that lives up to its subject." Booklist

Includes bibliographical references and index

Rideau, Wilbert

Rideau, Wilbert. **In** the place of justice; a story of punishment and deliverance. Alfred A. Knopf 2010 366p il map $26.95   **92**
1. Thieves 2. Prisoners 3. Journalists 4. Murderers 5. Louisiana State Penitentiary
ISBN 978-0-307-26481-7; 0-307-26481-5
LC 2009038526

"In 1961, after a bungled bank robbery, Rideau was convicted of murder at the age of 19 and received a death sentence that was later commuted to life in prison at Louisiana's Angola penitentiary, then the most violent in the nation. Against all expectations, his own included, he turned his up-to-then cursed life around, becoming editor of the prison newsmagazine, the Angolite, and an NPR correspondent who published nationally acclaimed articles on prison violence, rape and sexual slavery, and the cruelty of the electric chair. Rideau frames his 44-year fight to get his conviction reduced to manslaughter and win parole (he succeeded in 2005) as a black man's struggle against a racist criminal justice establishment. . . . Rideau's story is a compelling reminder that rehabilitation should be the focus of a penal system." Publ Wkly

Riefenstahl, Leni, 1902-2003

Bach, Steven. **Leni:** the life and work of Leni Riefenstahl. A.A. Knopf 2007 368p il $30   **92**
1. Actors 2. Centenarians 3. Motion picture directors 4. Motion picture producers
ISBN 978-0-375-40400-9; 0-375-40400-7
LC 2006-49323

This is a biography of the filmmaker.

This "is a lively, incisive look at a compelling and somewhat appalling figure who demonstrated that beauty isn't always truth." Publ Wkly

Includes bibliographical references

Trimborn, Jurgen. **Leni** Riefenstahl; translated from the German by Edna McCown. Faber & Faber 2007 351p il $30   **92**
1. Actors 2. Centenarians 3. Motion picture directors 4. Motion picture producers
ISBN 978-0-374-18493-3; 0-374-18493-3
LC 2006-13263

Original German edition, 2002

This is a biography of the German filmmaker whose work includes Triumph of the Will, a propaganda film for Hitler, and Olympia, a documentary of the 1936 Olympics in Berlin

Trimborn "interviewed Riefenstahl in 1997, when he was twenty-five, having already spent six years of 'intensive labor' on the project, and he briefly entertained the quixotic hope of writing a definitive book with her blessing and collaboration. Unwilling to misrepresent himself as a hagiographer, he was doomed to fail, though his disappointment does not seem to have warped his fair-mindedness. . . . [The author's] aim was to correct the murky published record and the 'attitudes' of his compatriots. One has to admire the sniperlike precision with which he takes out fugitive falsehoods that have lived under cover for a century." New Yorker

Riis, Jacob A. (Jacob August), 1849-1914

Buk-Swienty, Tom. The **other** half; the life of Jacob Riis and the world of immigrant America. translated from the Danish by Annette Buk-Swienty. W.W. Norton & Co. 2008 331p il $27.95   **92**
1. Journalists 2. Memoirists 3. Photojournalists 4. Social reformers
ISBN 978-0-393-06023-2; 0-393-06023-3
LC 2008-22853

This "biography is superb—not only as an instructive tale for today's journalists, but as a remarkable immigrant saga for readers from all vocations." Columbia J Rev
Includes bibliographical references and index

Ripert, Eric

Chambers, Veronica. **32** yolks; from my mother's table to working the line. Eric Ripert, with Veronica Chambers. Random House 2016 256 p. (hardback : acid-free paper) $28   **92**
1. Cooks 2. Restaurants 3. Cooking, French 4. Coming of age -- France -- Paris 5. Cooks -- France -- Paris -- Biography 6. Restaurateurs -- France -- Paris -- Biography
ISBN 9780812992984
LC 2015050280

This memoir, by Eric Ripert, is a "coming-of-age story about the making of a French chef, from the culinary icon behind the renowned New York City restaurant Le Bernardin. Taking us from Eric Ripert's childhood in the south of France and the mountains of Andorra into the demanding kitchens of such legendary Parisian chefs as Joël Robuchon and Dominique Bouchet, . . . '32 Yolks' is the . . . story of how one of our greatest living chefs found himself . . . in the kitchen." (Publisher's note)

"Readers may know Ripert as the meditative host of the PBS series Avec Eric; a fan-favorite judge on Bravo's Top Chef; and the owner of Le Bernardin, a French seafood restaurant in New York. His roots, however, are far from that calm and thoughtful adult. This memoir tells of Ripert's tumultuous childhood in France where a love of excellent food was instilled in him early on. . . . Although the loving descriptions of flavors and cooking techniques will make some long for recipes, this narrative sheds light on the carefully controlled chaos behind the scenes at several top restaurants in the 1970s and 1980s. It will appeal to fans of Anthony Bourdain's Kitchen Confidential and Joe Bastianich and Mario Batali's Restaurant Man." LJ
Thirty-two yolks

Ripken, Cal, Jr.

Ripken, Cal. The **only** way I know; [by] Cal Ripken, Jr., and Mike Bryan. Viking 1997 326p il hardcover o.p. pa $12.95   **92**
1. Baseball players 2. Baseball -- Biography 3. Baltimore Orioles (Baseball team)
ISBN 0-670-87193-1; 0-14-026626-7 pa
LC 97-9159

"Cal Junior chronicles his moves through the minor leagues and into the majors in great detail, always pointing out what he learned at each step of the journey and who taught it to him. There are some great baseball anecdotes—

especially involving fiery Oriole skipper Earl Weaver—and plenty of the behind-the-scenes detail." Booklist

Rivera, Diego, 1886-1957

Marnham, Patrick. **Dreaming** with his eyes open; a life of Diego Rivera. University of California Press 2000 350p il pa $29.95   **92**
1. Artists 2. Painters 3. Artists, Mexican
ISBN 0-520-22408-6; 978-0-520-22408-7
LC 99-44964

First published 1998 by Knopf
"For the browsing public as well as specialists in European, Latin American, and American modern art, this book is not to be overlooked." Libr J
Includes bibliographical references

Rivera, Mariano, 1969-

Rivera, Mariano, 1969- The **closer**; Mariano Rivera, Wayne Coffey. Little, Brown & Co. 2014 280 p. ill. (some col.) (hardcover) $28   **92**
1. Baseball pitchers
ISBN 0316400734; 9780316400732; 9780316405621; 9780316277617
LC 2014934754

In this memoir, relief pitcher Mariano Rivera "his extraordinary story of survival, love, and baseball. . . . The thirteen-time All-Star discusses his drive to win; the secrets behind his legendary composure; the story of how he discovered his cut fastball; the untold, pitch-by-pitch account of the ninth inning of Game 7 in the 2001 World Series; and why the lowest moment of his career became one of his greatest blessings." (Publisher's note)

"[I]n this entertaining, admirably subdued autobiography, the glory is God's: Rivera's story brims with examples of his faith." Pub Wkly

Robbins, Jerome

★ Vaill, Amanda. **Somewhere**; the life of Jerome Robbins. Broadway Books 2006 675p il $40   **92**
1. Dancers 2. Choreographers 3. Theatrical directors
ISBN 0-7679-0420-6; 978-0-7679-0420-9
LC 2006-48960

This is a biography of the choreographer of such works as Afternoon of a Faun, On the Town, Gypsy, West Side Story, and Fiddler on the Roof.

"The book is essential reading for lovers of theater and dance." Publ Wkly
Includes bibliographical references

Robbins, Tom, 1932-

Robbins, Tom, 1932- **Tibetan** Peach Pie; A True Account of an Imaginative Life. Tom Robbins. HarperCollins 2014 28 p. $27.99   **92**
1. Autobiographies 2. American authors
ISBN 006226740X; 9780062267405

In this memoir by Tom Robbins, "we travel with Tommy Rotten--his mother's pet name for him--from his birth in Statesville, N.C., through his youth in Virginia--including a stint at Hargrave Military Academy--his meteorological training in the military, and his peripatetic pursuit of language and wonder. . . . Along the way, Robbins offers flashes of enlightenment into the writing of each of his novels." (Publishers Weekly)

"Each piece stands on its own, but when read side by side they develop into a powerful argument about magic and the necessity of imaginative, interior worlds." LJ

Robert I, King of Scots, 1274-1329

Penman, Michael. **Robert** the Bruce; King of Scots. Michael Penman. Yale University Press 2014 456 p. 16 unnumbered pages of plates (cl : alk. paper) $45   **92**
  1. Kings and rulers 2. Scotland -- History 3. Scotland -- Kings and rulers -- Biography 4. Scotland -- History -- Robert I, 1306-1329
  ISBN 0300148720; 9780300148725
                                        LC 2014007172
This biography, by Michael Penman, is about "Robert the Bruce (1274-1329) [who] famously defeated the English at Bannockburn and became the hero king responsible for Scottish independence. . . . Penman investigates Robert's resettlement of lands and offices, the development of Scotland's parliaments, his handling of plots to overthrow him, his relations with his family and allies, his piety and court ethos, and his conscious development of an image of kingship." (Publisher's note)

"Penman details the social forces Robert faced at the time, from the reconfiguring of aristocratic and ecclesiastical interests to the development of a parliament, from the establishment of a national identity to creation of the symbols and ceremonies of the monarchy. Dense with research, Penman's look at Scotland's King Robert the Bruce fascinates." Booklist
Includes bibliographical references and index

Roberts, Deborah, 1960-

Roberts, Deborah. **Been** there, done that; family wisdom for modern times. Al Roker, Deborah Roberts with Laura Morton. New American Library 2016 288 p. (hardback) $27   **92**
  1. Parenting 2. Family life 3. Parenting -- Anecdotes 4. Family life -- Anecdotes 5. African American television journalists -- United States -- Anecdotes
  ISBN 0451466365; 9780451466365
                                        LC 2015031342
Authors Al Roker and Deborah Roberts presents this "collection of life lessons, hard-won wisdom, and instructive family anecdotes from [their] lives, from their parents and grandparents, and from dear friends, famous and not. Here, Al and Deborah candidly share childhood obstacles like obesity and growing up in the segregated south; the challenges and blessings that come from raising very different kids; hard-won truths about marriage and career." (Publisher's note)

"Despite Roker's tendency toward hackneyed 'dad jokes' and sometimes trite observations (e.g., technology can get in the way of genuine interactions), this is an entertaining, encouraging read and a sweet testament to the couple's devotion to their marriage and family." Publisher's Weekly

Robeson, Eslanda Goode, 1896-1965

Ransby, Barbara. **Eslanda**; the large and unconventional life of Mrs. Paul Robeson. Barbara Ransby.

Yale University Press 2013 424 p. (cloth : alk. paper) $35   **92**
  1. Harlem Renaissance 2. African American anthropologists -- Biography 3. Women anthropologists -- United States -- Biography
  ISBN 0300124341; 9780300124347
                                        LC 2012022359
In this book, Barbara Ransby "details the accomplishments, struggles and impact of Eslanda Cardozo Goode Robeson. . . . Ransby outlines Essie's early life and family history, delves into the high points of her married life in Harlem, and recounts her growing awareness and tenacious engagement in the numerous political causes she supported." (Kirkus)
Includes bibliographical references and index

Robeson, Paul, 1898-1976

Ransby, Barbara. **Eslanda**; the large and unconventional life of Mrs. Paul Robeson. Barbara Ransby. Yale University Press 2013 424 p. (cloth : alk. paper) $35   **92**
  1. Harlem Renaissance 2. African American anthropologists -- Biography 3. Women anthropologists -- United States -- Biography
  ISBN 0300124341; 9780300124347
                                        LC 2012022359
In this book, Barbara Ransby "details the accomplishments, struggles and impact of Eslanda Cardozo Goode Robeson. . . . Ransby outlines Essie's early life and family history, delves into the high points of her married life in Harlem, and recounts her growing awareness and tenacious engagement in the numerous political causes she supported." (Kirkus)
Includes bibliographical references and index

Robeson, Paul. **Here** I stand; with a preface by Lloyd L. Brown and a new introduction by Sterling Stuckey. Beacon Press 1988 xxxvi, 121p hardcover o.p. pa $14   **92**
  1. Actors 2. Singers 3. Football players 4. Civil rights activists 5. African Americans -- Civil rights
  ISBN 0-8070-6445-9 pa
                                        LC 87-47882
First published 1958 by Othello Associates

"Combining a narrative of his life and travels with commentary on history and the events of his time, [the author] relates the fight against segregation to social progress for all Americans, white and black, claiming that 'white supremacy' disenfranchises and impoverishes white workers and white farmers as well as black." Libr J

Robeson, Paul. The **undiscovered** Paul Robeson; the early years (1898-1939) Wiley 2001 383p il $30   **92**
  1. Actors 2. Singers 3. Football players 4. Civil rights activists 5. African Americans -- Biography
  ISBN 0-471-24265-9
                                        LC 2001-17656
This is the first volume of a biography of the African American actor, singer and political activist by his son. It covers the years from Robeson's birth in Princeton, N.J., through the 1930s

"Extensively illustrated with personal photographs, this is a unique account of a brilliant but troubled man." Libr J

Includes bibliographical references

Robespierre, Maximilien, 1758-1794

McPhee, Peter. **Robespierre**; a revolutionary life. Peter McPhee. Yale University Press 2012 299 p. (cloth : alk. paper) $40   **92**
1. Statesmen -- France -- Biography 2. Revolutionaries -- France -- Biography 3. France -- History -- Revolution, 1789-1799 4. France -- Politics and government -- 1789-1799 5. France -- History -- Reign of Terror, 1793-1794
ISBN 0300118112; 9780300118117

LC 2011027640

This book provides a "treatise on the life of one of France's most notorious revolutionaries. Maximilien Robespierre (1758-1794) . . . [became] a leader of the leftist Jacobins in the revolutionary National Convention. . . . Robespierre began his career as an opponent of capital punishment but ended it obsessed with omnipresent treasonous conspiracies and meting out death without trial to perceived enemies of the state . . . . [Author Peter] McPhee . . . strives to rehabilitate Robespierre somewhat, arguing that the sanguinary excesses of the period were necessary to sustain the revolution against attacks from without and within, and that Robespierre's role in them was later exaggerated by other deputies seeking to minimize their own culpability." (Kirkus)

Includes bibliographical references

Robinson, Jackie, 1919-1972

Falkner, David. **Great** time coming: the life of Jackie Robinson, from baseball to Birmingham. Simon & Schuster 1995 382p il hardcover o.p. pa $18.95   **92**
1. Baseball players 2. Army officers
ISBN 0-684-82348-9 pa

LC 94-44876

This is a biography of the baseball player and civil rights activist. In addition to covering Robinson's professional career, the book focuses attention on his life after baseball

"Falkner has written a very balanced account—neither muckraking nor fawning—of a fascinating and complex figure, one whose importance and interest reaches well beyond his exploits as an athlete." Christ Sci Monit

Includes bibliographical references

Kashatus, William C. **Jackie** and Campy; the untold story of their rocky relationship and the breaking of baseball's color line. William C. Kashatus. University of Nebraska Press 2014 248 p. illustrations, map (cloth : alk. paper) $24.95   **92**
1. African American baseball players 2. Race discrimination in sports -- History 3. Male friendship -- United States 4. Racism in sports -- United States 5. Discrimination in sports -- United States 6. African American baseball players -- Biography 7. Baseball players -- United States -- Biography
ISBN 0803246331; 9780803246331

LC 2013033133

This book, by William C. Kashatus, focuses on "the first black players to be candidates to break professional base-ball's color barrier, Jackie Robinson and Roy Campanella. . . . The two men were divided by . . . [their] differing beliefs about the fight for civil rights. Robinson, the more aggressive and intense of the two, thought Jim Crow should be attacked head-on; Campanella, more passive and easygoing, believed that ability, not militancy, was the key to racial equality." (Publisher's note)

"Kashatus has written a superb narrative of sports, race, and politics in the 1950s and '60s, and also tells of the bittersweet consequences in Jackie and Campy's lives." Pub Wkly

Includes bibliographical references and index

Robinson, Jackie. **I** never had it made; an autobiography. by Jackie Robinson as told to Alfred Duckett; foreword by Cornel West; introduction by Hank Aaron. Ecco Press 1995 xxii, 275p il hardcover o.p. pa $13.95   **92**
1. Baseball players 2. African American athletes 3. Army officers 4. Baseball -- Biography
ISBN 0-06-055597-1

LC 94-45279

Robinson, Sugar Ray, 1921-1989

★ Haygood, Wil. **Sweet** thunder; the life and times of Sugar Ray Robinson. Alfred A. Knopf 2009 461p il $27.95   **92**
1. Boxers (Persons) 2. Boxing -- Biography
ISBN 978-1-4000-4497-9

LC 2009-5534

This "book is certainly one of the best biographies of a boxer ever written . . . [and] an important contribution to both sports literature and African American studies." Washington Post Book World

Includes bibliographical references

Robison, John Elder, 1957-

Robison, John Elder. **Look** me in the eye; my life with Asperger's. Crown Publishers 2007 288p $25.95   **92**
1. Photographers 2. Asperger's syndrome 3. Mechanics (Persons) 4. Restorers 5. Memoirists
ISBN 978-0-307-39598-6; 0-307-39598-7

LC 2007-13139

In this memoir, the author describes growing up with Asperger's syndrome (which went undiagnosed until he was 40 years old), dealing with an alcoholic father and a mentally unstable mother, and developing an affinity for machines that would eventually lead him to a career restoring classic cars.

"Robison's memoir is must reading for its unblinking (as only an Aspergian can) glimpse into the life of a person who had to wait decades for the medical community to catch up with him." Booklist

Includes bibliographical references

Rockefeller, John D. (John Davison), 1839-1937

Chernow, Ron. **Titan**: the life of John D. Rockefeller, Sr. Random House 1998 xxii, 774p il $30; pa $18   **92**
1. Philanthropists 2. Energy industry executives
ISBN 0-679-43808-4; 0-679-75703-1 pa

LC 97-33117

"This book is a triumph of the art of biography. Unflaggingly interesting, it brings John D. Rockefeller Sr. ... to life through sustained narrative portraiture of the large-scale, 19th-century kind." N Y Times Book Rev

Includes bibliographical references

Rockne, Knute, 1888-1931

Robinson, Ray. **Rockne** of Notre Dame; the making of a football legend. Oxford Univ. Press 1999 290p il hardcover o.p. pa $16.95   **92**

1. Football coaches   2. Notre Dame Fighting Irish (Football team)

ISBN 0-19-515792-3 pa

LC 99-13712

"After a childhood sketch, Robinson briefly touches on Rockne's playing career before devoting most of the book to a game-by-game description of Rockne's 12 years as coach, during which his Notre Dame teams, with the help of Rockne's motivational techniques and coaching tactics, won an astounding 105 games while losing only 12. To Robinson's credit, the book is cleanly written and mainly free of sports jargon." Publ Wkly

Rockwell, Norman

Solomon, Deborah, 1957- **American** mirror; the life and art of Norman Rockwell. Deborah Solomon. Farrar Straus & Giroux 2013 512 p. illustrations (some color) (hardback) $28   **92**

1. Illustrators -- United States   2. Painters -- United States -- Biography   3. Illustrators -- United States -- Biography

ISBN 0374113092; 9780374113094

LC 2013021682

LA Times Book Prize Finalist: Biography (2013)

This biography of Norman Rockwell "reveals an enormously complicated man whose wholesome vision of America was not merely commercial kitsch, but art that sprung from an emotional life fraught with anxiety, depression, and self-doubt. This sympathetic portrait depicts a repressed and humble Rockwell. . . . Thrice married and an apathetic husband, he clearly preferred the companionship of male friends and was likely a closeted homosexual." (Publishers Weekly)

"Praised for her biographies of Jackson Pollock and Joseph Cornell, noted art critic Solomon makes a surprise leap to rock-solid Americana artist Norman Rockwell. But as she says, Rockwell painted "a history of the American people that had never happened," and she goes on to detail his not-so-apple-pie personality." LJ

Includes bibliographical references (pages 443-468) and index

Rodgers, Jimmie, 1897-1933

Mazor, Barry. **Meeting** Jimmie Rodgers; how America's original roots music hero changed the pop sounds of a century. Oxford University Press 2009 376p il $27.95   **92**

1. Singers   2. Country musicians   3. Songwriters   4. Country music -- History and criticism

ISBN 978-0-19-532762-5

LC 2008-41924

"This is a fine addition to the literature on Rodgers. . . . [The author] traces Rodgers's influence through the 20th

century and into the 21st not only on country music but also on popular music of many other genres and on media such as film. Whereas Rodgers's influence on country artists could be expected, his influence on people as diverse as Rick Nelson, George Harrison, and Louis Armstrong might not. A book for both music researchers and fans." Choice

Includes bibliographical references

Rodriguez, Daniel

Rise; a soldier, a dream, and a promise kept. Daniel Rodriguez; contributions by Joe Layden. Houghton Mifflin Harcourt 2014 256 p. 8 plates; illustrations (hardback) $26   **92**

1. College football   2. Afghan War, 2001-   3. Military personnel -- United States   4. Layden, Joseph, 1959-   5. Clemson Tigers (Football team)   6. United States. Army -- Biography   7. Soldiers -- United States -- Biography   8. Afghan War, 2001- -- Personal narratives, American   9. Iraq War, 2003-2011 -- Personal narratives, American

ISBN 0544365607; 9780544365605

LC 2014016742

Author Daniel Rodriguez presents this memoir, a "narrative of a young soldier, his unlikely dream, and how he found his way out of darkness. He fought in the infamous Battle of Kamdesh and for his bravery he was awarded a Purple Heart and the Bronze Star. Daniel returned home . . . in the clutches of PTSD. He embarked on a grueling training regimen and . . . earned a spot on the Clemson University football team." (Publisher's note)

"This is an uncommonly solid memoir. Recommended for all readers, particularly those interested in sports and military books." LJ

A soldier, a dream, and a promise kept

Rodriguez, Richard, 1944-

Rodriguez, Richard. **Hunger** of memory; the education of Richard Rodriguez: an autobiography. Bantam trade pbk. ed.; Bantam Books 2004 212p pa $15   **92**

1. Poets   2. Authors   3. Television personalities   4. Essayists   5. Memoirists   6. Mexican Americans -- Biography

ISBN 0-553-38251-9

LC 2004-269979

First published 1982 by Godine

An account "of the coming of age of a person of Mexican descent and culture in American society and the inevitable transition in the private life of his family. Rodriguez focuses on his educational experiences, from his parochial elementary school . . . to his university years and subsequent experience as an educator." Libr J

Rodríguez, Richard. **Darling**; a spiritual autobiography. by Richard Rodriguez. Viking 2013 256 p. illustrations $26.95   **92**

1. Sex   2. Religion   3. Autobiographies   4. United States -- Religion   5. Christian pilgrims and pilgrimages -- Israel   6. Catholic Church -- United States -- Biography

ISBN 0670025305; 9780670025305

LC 2013017046

In this book, author Richard Rodriguez "examin[es] his continuing belief in God and in the Catholic Church in the context of his life as a gay man in the early years of the twenty-first century, years, he says, that have been defined by religious extremism, rising public atheism, and what he calls 'digital distraction.' And, yet, in the wake of September 11, Rodriguez found himself searching for commonality rather than difference between the 'religions of the desert'." (Booklist)

"With compassion and profundity of vision, Rodriguez offers a compelling view of modern spirituality that is as multifaceted as it is provocative." Kirkus

Rogers, Jimmy

Goins, Wayne Everett. **Blues** all day long; the Jimmy Rogers story. Wayne Everett Goins; foreword by Kim Wilson. University of Illinois Press 2014 416 p. 16 plates (Music in American life) (pbk. : alk. paper) $29   **92**
1. Guitarists 2. Blues musicians 3. Guitarists -- United States -- Biography 4. Jazz musicians -- United States -- Biography
ISBN 0252080173; 9780252038570; 9780252080173; 9780252096495
LC 2014007477

In this biography of musician Jimmy Rogers author "Wayne Everett Goins mines seventy-five hours of interviews with Rogers' family, collaborators, and peers to follow a life spent in the blues. Goins' account takes Rogers from recording Chess classics and barnstorming across the South to a late-in-life renaissance that included new music, entry into the Blues Hall of Fame, and high profile tours with Eric Clapton and the Rolling Stones." (Publisher's note)

"Goins enthusiastically tracks Rogers' early years playing in the juke-joint South and his arrival in Chicago in 1945, where he began his dynamic, downright telepathic collaboration with Muddy Waters. Fluent in the blues vernacular, Goins gleans fresh facts and vivid memories from dozens of lively interviews to capture the energy and struggles of the Chicago blues scene, from Maxwell Street to the Chess Records studios, as he tracks the ups and downs of devoted family man Rogers' career with Waters, Little Walter, Howlin' Wolf, and many others. Rogers' story, including his retreat from music during the 1960s, triumphant return, and international stardom, is engrossing, and Goins' zeal and nimble expressiveness are thrilling as he praises Rogers' "special brand of lyrics," his "irresistible, buttery-smooth vocal quality," and his "highly sophisticated melodic, harmonic, and rhythmic style" while celebrating Rogers' "timeless passion and conviction." Booklist

Includes bibliographical references, discography, and index

Rogers, Robbie

Marcus, Eric. **Coming** out to play; Robbie Rogers with Eric Marcus. Penguin Books 2014 240 p. color illustrations $17   **92**
1. Gay men 2. Soccer players 3. Gay athletes -- United States -- Biography 4. Soccer players -- United States -- Biography
ISBN 014312661X; 9780143126614
LC 2014011229

In this book, professional soccer player Robbie Rogers " takes readers on his incredible journey from terrified

teenager to a trailblazing out and proud professional soccer player for the L.A. Galaxy, who has embraced his new identity as a role model and champion for those still struggling with the secrets that keep them from living their dreams." (Publisher's note)

"Rogers's debut is great inspiration for people of all ages struggling with shame and grappling with identity issues with regard to sexuality or otherwise. Those who enjoy memoir and stories of people who overcome difficulty will embrace this account." LJ

Roiphe, Anne Richardson, 1935-

Roiphe, Anne Richardson. **Art** and madness; a memoir of lust without reason. [by] Anne Roiphe. Nan A. Talese/Doubleday 2011 220p il $24.95 **92**
1. Authors 2. Novelists 3. Women authors 4. Essayists 5. Authors, American 6. Biography, Individual
ISBN 9780385531641
LC 2010-28051

This book recounts the lost years of Anne Roiphe's twenties, when the author put her dreams of becoming a writer on hold to devote herself to the magnetic but coercive male artists of the period.

"Roiphe's narrative moves in punchy, spare episodes, nonchronologically and erratically, veering from past to present tense, and requiring effort on the part of the reader. Yet she is a masterly writer: her work presents vivid, priceless snapshots of the roiling era of Communist hysteria, faddish homosexuality, male privilege, and the heartbreaking fragility of talented men and their dreams of fame." Publ Wkly

Roiphe, Anne Richardson. **Epilogue**; a memoir. [by] Anne Roiphe. Harper 2008 214p il $24.95 **92**
1. Widows 2. Authors 3. Novelists 4. Bereavement 5. Women authors 6. Essayists 7. Authors, American
ISBN 978-0-06-125462-8; 0-06-125462-2
LC 2008-34530

The author "tells an unflinching and unsentimental story of widowhood's stupefying disquiet, of surviving love and living on." Publ Wkly

Roker, Al, 1954-

Roberts, Deborah. **Been** there, done that; family wisdom for modern times. Al Roker, Deborah Roberts with Laura Morton. New American Library 2016 288 p. (hardback) $27   **92**
1. Parenting 2. Family life 3. Parenting -- Anecdotes 4. Family life -- Anecdotes 5. African American television journalists -- United States -- Anecdotes
ISBN 0451466365; 9780451466365
LC 2015031342

Authors Al Roker and Deborah Roberts presents this "collection of life lessons, hard-won wisdom, and instructive family anecdotes from [their] lives, from their parents and grandparents, and from dear friends, famous and not. Here, Al and Deborah candidly share childhood obstacles like obesity and growing up in the segregated south; the challenges and blessings that come from raising very different kids; hard-won truths about marriage and career." (Publisher's note)

"Despite Roker's tendency toward hackneyed 'dad jokes' and sometimes trite observations (e.g., technology can get in the way of genuine interactions), this is an entertaining, encouraging read and a sweet testament to the couple's devotion to their marriage and family." Publisher's Weekly

Rommel, Erwin, 1891-1944

★ Showalter, Dennis E. **Patton** and Rommel; men of war in the twentieth century. [by] Dennis Showalter. Berkley Caliber 2005 441p $24.95 **92**
1. Generals 2. World War, 1939-1945 3. Marshals 4. Army officers
ISBN 0-425-19346-2
LC 2004-57464

This is a "parallel biography of George Patton and Erwin Rommel. The research is thorough, the quality of the writing superb. . . . [The author] ranks as a scholar who has done them justice, making two complex men and a vast panorama of military history remarkably accessible for experts and lay readers alike." Publ Wkly

Roosevelt family

McCullough, David G. **Mornings** on horseback; {by} David McCullough. Simon & Schuster 1981 445p il hardcover o.p. pa $16 **92**
1. Governors 2. Presidents 3. Vice-presidents 4. Nobel laureates for peace 5. Presidents -- United States
ISBN 0-671-44754-8 pa
LC 81-1697

This biography follows Theodore Roosevelt from his childhood to his defeat for mayor of New York and marriage to Edith Carow in 1886.

"Based on diligent and thorough research, with emphasis on family, physical ailments, and friends, and written with verve and color, this is a stimulating book that will appeal to the general reader." Libr J

Includes bibliographical references

Peyser, Marc. **Hissing** cousins; the untold story of Eleanor Roosevelt and Alice Roosevelt Longworth. Marc Peyser and Timothy Dwyer. Nan A. Talese/Doubleday 2015 352 p. 8 plates; illustrations (alk. paper) $28.95 **92**
1. Cousins 2. Presidents' spouses -- United States 3. Cousins -- United States -- Biography 4. Presidents' spouses -- United States -- Biography
ISBN 0385536011; 9780385536011
LC 2014026766

This book, by Marc Peyser and Timothy Dwyer, is a "double biography of first cousins Eleanor Roosevelt and Alice Roosevelt Longworth. . . . Do-gooder Eleanor was committed to social justice but hated the limelight; acid-tongued Alice, who became the wife of philandering Republican congressman Nicholas Longworth, was an opponent of big government who gained notoriety for her cutting remarks." (Publisher's note)

"Peyser and Dwyer's detailed and witty double biography is hard to put down, a fascinating look at an era and two exceptionally strong, intelligent women." Booklist

Includes bibliographical references and index

Untold story of Eleanor Roosevelt and Alice Roosevelt Longworth

Roosevelt, Curtis

Roosevelt, Curtis. **Too** close to the sun; growing up in the shadow of my grandparents, Franklin and Eleanor. PublicAffairs 2008 302p il $29.95 **92**
1. Diplomats 2. Governors 3. Presidents 4. People with disabilities 5. Grandparent-grandchild relationship 6. Columnists 7. Philatelists 8. Humanitarians 9. Social activists 10. Spouses of presidents 11. College administrators 12. United Nations officials 13. Presidents -- United States 14. Presidents' spouses -- United States
ISBN 9781586485542
LC 2008-33994

Offers a portrait of this celebrated president and his wife as experienced by the grandson of FDR, who recounts what it was like to come of age under constant media attention and public scrutiny in their formidable shadows

"No one alive today knew Franklin and Eleanor quite as well as Curtis, their eldest grandson, and his sister. Thus this splendid, intimate memoir represents an invaluable addition to the literature of the Roosevelt era." Publ Wkly

Includes bibliographical references

Roosevelt, Eleanor, 1884-1962

★ Bell-Scott, Patricia. The **firebrand** and the First Lady; portrait of a friendship : Pauli Murray, Eleanor Roosevelt, and the struggle for social justice. Patricia Bell-Scott. Alfred A. Knopf 2016 480 p. illustrations (hardcover : alk. paper) $30 **92**
1. Female friendship -- United States 2. African American feminists -- Biography 3. Episcopal Church -- Clergy -- Biography 4. African American intellectuals -- Biography 5. Presidents' spouses -- United States -- Biography 6. Women social reformers -- United States -- Biography 7. African American women civil rights workers -- Biography
ISBN 9780679446521
LC 2015014872

This book, by Patricia Bell-Scott, profiles the figures of Pauli Murray and Eleanor Roosevelt. It "tells the story of how a brilliant writer-turned-activist, granddaughter of a mulatto slave, and the first lady of the United States, whose ancestry gave her membership in the Daughters of the American Revolution, forged an enduring friendship that changed each of their lives and helped to alter the course of race and racism in America." (Publisher's note)

"Bell-Scott's groundbreaking portrait of these two tireless and innovative champions of human dignity adds an essential and edifying facet to American history." Booklist

Includes bibliographical references and index.

Cook, Blanche Wiesen. **Eleanor** Roosevelt. v2 Viking 1999 686p v2 hardcover o.p. pa $20 **92**
1. Diplomats 2. Columnists 3. Humanitarians 4. Social activists 5. Spouses of presidents 6. United Nations officials 7. Presidents' spouses -- United States
ISBN 0-14-017894-5 pa

"Cook is unafraid to take on difficult issues . . . thus rendering the biography not simply a riveting read but also a profoundly moving and wise account of how history has been shaped by the intricacies of the human heart, mind and spirit." Publ Wkly

Includes bibliographical references

Goodwin, Doris Kearns. **No** ordinary time; Franklin and Eleanor Roosevelt: the home front in World War II. Simon & Schuster 1994 759p il hardcover o.p. pa $18   **92**

1. Diplomats 2. Governors 3. Presidents 4. People with disabilities 5. Columnists 6. Philatelists 7. Humanitarians 8. Social activists 9. Spouses of presidents 10. United Nations officials 11. United States -- History -- 1933-1945 12. World War, 1939-1945 -- United States

ISBN 0-684-80448-4 pa

LC 94-28565

"This is a nearly day-by-day account of the doings of Franklin and Eleanor Roosevelt during the Second World War. While Eleanor was championing the rights of female munitions workers and of Negroes in segregated Army barracks, her husband was making and breaking policy." New Yorker

Includes bibliographical references

Quinn, Susan. **Eleanor** and Hick; The Love Affair That Shaped a First Lady. Susan Quinn. Penguin Group USA 2016 416 p. illustrations, portraits (hardcover) $30; (ebook) $95   **92**

1. Female friendship 2. Presidents' spouses -- United States

ISBN 9781594205408; 9780735289413; 159420540X

LC 2016303873

This book by Susan Quinn offers an "intimate account of the love between Eleanor Roosevelt and reporter Lorena Hickok—a relationship that, over more than three decades, transformed both women's lives and empowered them to play significant roles in one of the most tumultuous periods in American history. . . . The bond these women shared was grounded in their determination to better their troubled world." (Publisher's note)

"A relentlessly captivating study of two remarkable individuals who helped extend the roles of American women in the public policy realm." Kirkus

Includes bibliographical references (pages 363-389) and index.

Roosevelt, Curtis. **Too** close to the sun; growing up in the shadow of my grandparents, Franklin and Eleanor. PublicAffairs 2008 302p il $29.95   **92**

1. Diplomats 2. Governors 3. Presidents 4. People with disabilities 5. Grandparent-grandchild relationship 6. Columnists 7. Philatelists 8. Humanitarians 9. Social activists 10. Spouses of presidents 11. College administrators 12. United Nations officials 13. Presidents -- United States 14. Presidents' spouses -- United States

ISBN 9781586485542

LC 2008-33994

Offers a portrait of this celebrated president and his wife as experienced by the grandson of FDR, who recounts what it was like to come of age under constant media attention and public scrutiny in their formidable shadows

"No one alive today knew Franklin and Eleanor quite as well as Curtis, their eldest grandson, and his sister. Thus this splendid, intimate memoir represents an invaluable addition to the literature of the Roosevelt era." Publ Wkly

Includes bibliographical references

Roosevelt, Franklin D. (Franklin Delano), 1882-1945

Brands, H. W. **Traitor** to his class; the privileged life and radical presidency of Franklin Delano Roosevelt. Doubleday 2008 888p il $35   **92**

1. Governors 2. Presidents 3. People with disabilities 4. Philatelists 5. Presidents -- United States

ISBN 978-0-385-51958-8; 0-385-51958-3

LC 2008-15164

This is a study of Franklin D. Roosevelt's life and career.

"A thoroughly readable, scrupulously fair assessment of the one president who could inspire a Mt. Rushmore makeover." Kirkus

Includes bibliographical references

Brinkley, Douglas. **Rightful** heritage; Franklin D. Roosevelt and the land of America. Douglas Brinkley. HarperCollins 2016 768 p. charts, illustrations, maps (hardcover) $35   **92**

1. Environmental protection -- United States

ISBN 9780062089236; 0062089234

This book, by Douglas Brinkley, is a political profile of "Franklin Delano Roosevelt, chronicling his essential yet under-sung legacy as the founder of the Civilian Conservation Corps (CCC) and premier protector of America's public lands. FDR built from scratch dozens of State Park systems and scenic roadways." (Publisher's note)

"Brinkley vividly tracks Roosevelt's 'political know-how, legislative muscle, and fearlessness' from a unique and important perspective in this engrossing and richly illuminating portrait of one of the American environment's most ardent and effective champions." Booklist

Includes bibliographical references and index.

Fried, Albert. **F.D.R.** and his enemies. St. Martin's Press 1999 261p hardcover o.p. pa $15.95 **92**

1. Governors 2. Presidents 3. People with disabilities 4. Philatelists 5. People with disabilities 6. Presidents -- United States 7. United States -- Politics and government -- 1933-1945

ISBN 0-312-23827-4 pa

LC 98-56141

The author "examines Roosevelt's conflict with and victory over varied critics, including Al Smith, Huey Long, Charles Lindbergh, and Charles Coughlin. Fried convincingly asserts that Roosevelt defeated his critics primarily because he was a superb pragmatist who refused to be hindered by an ideological straightjacket." Booklist

Includes bibliographical references

Goodwin, Doris Kearns. **No** ordinary time; Franklin and Eleanor Roosevelt: the home front in World War II. Simon & Schuster 1994 759p il hardcover o.p. pa $18   **92**

1. Diplomats 2. Governors 3. Presidents 4. People with disabilities 5. Columnists 6. Philatelists 7.

Humanitarians 8. Social activists 9. Spouses of presidents 10. United Nations officials 11. United States -- History -- 1933-1945 12. World War, 1939-1945 -- United States

ISBN 0-684-80448-4 pa

LC 94-28565

"This is a nearly day-by-day account of the doings of Franklin and Eleanor Roosevelt during the Second World War. While Eleanor was championing the rights of female munitions workers and of Negroes in segregated Army barracks, her husband was making and breaking policy." New Yorker

Includes bibliographical references

Lelyveld, Joseph. **His** final battle; Franklin Roosevelt in the last months. Joseph Lelyveld. Alfred A. Knopf 2016 416 p. (hardcover) $30   **92**

1. Presidents -- United States -- Health 2. Presidents -- United States -- Biography 3. United States -- Foreign relations -- 1933-1945 4. United States -- Politics and government -- 1933-1945

ISBN 0385350791; 9780385350792

LC 2015050730

This book, by Joseph Lelyveld, examines the "narrative threads of [Franklin] Roosevelt's final months, showing how he juggled the strategic, political, and personal choices he faced as the war, his presidency, and his life raced in tandem to their climax. Lelyveld examines the choices Roosevelt faced, shining new light on his state of mind, preoccupations, and motives, both as leader of the wartime alliance and in his personal life." (Publisher's note)

"An elegant, affecting work that offers fresh insights on a much-mythologized president." Kirkus

Includes bibliographical references and index

Roosevelt, Curtis. **Too** close to the sun; growing up in the shadow of my grandparents, Franklin and Eleanor. PublicAffairs 2008 302p il $29.95   **92**

1. Diplomats 2. Governors 3. Presidents 4. People with disabilities 5. Grandparent-grandchild relationship 6. Columnists 7. Philatelists 8. Humanitarians 9. Social activists 10. Spouses of presidents 11. College administrators 12. United Nations officials 13. Presidents -- United States 14. Presidents' spouses -- United States

ISBN 9781586485542

LC 2008-33994

Offers a portrait of this celebrated president and his wife as experienced by the grandson of FDR, who recounts what it was like to come of age under constant media attention and public scrutiny in their formidable shadows

"No one alive today knew Franklin and Eleanor quite as well as Curtis, their eldest grandson, and his sister. Thus this splendid, intimate memoir represents an invaluable addition to the literature of the Roosevelt era." Publ Wkly

Includes bibliographical references

Smith, Jean Edward. **FDR**. Random House 2007 858p il $35   **92**

1. Governors 2. Presidents 3. People with disabilities

4. Philatelists 5. Presidents -- United States

ISBN 978-1-4000-6121-1; 1-4000-6121-0

LC 2006-43087

Smith's "FDR is at once a careful, intelligent synopsis of the existing Roosevelt scholarship (the sheer bulk of which is huge) and a meticulous reinterpretation of the man and his record. Smith pays more attention to Roosevelt's personal life than have most previous biographers. He is openly sympathetic yet ready to criticize when that is warranted, and to do so in sharp terms; he conveys the full flavor and import of Roosevelt's career without ever bogging down in detail." Washington Post Book World

Includes bibliographical references

Roosevelt, Quentin, 1897-1918.

Burns, Eric. The **Golden** Lad; The Haunting Story of Quentin and Theodore Roosevelt. by Eric Burns. W W Norton & Co Inc 2016 300 p. illustrations $26.95   **92**

1. Father-son relationship 2. Presidents -- United States -- Children

ISBN 1605989517; 9781605989518

This book, by Eric Burns, is a biography of Theodore Roosevelt and his youngest son Quentin. "How does looking at Theodore's relationship with his son, and understanding him as a father, tell us something new about this larger-than-life-man? Does it reveal a more human side? A more hypocritical side? Or simply, if tragically, a nature so surprisingly sensitive, despite the bluster, that he would die of a broken heart?" (Publisher's note)

"Burns's unique, stirring account of America's most colorful president allows Teddy Roosevelt, the man and father, to step off the page." Pub Wkly

Includes bibliographical references (pages 181-184) and index.

Roosevelt, Theodore, 1858-1919

Brinkley, Douglas. The **wilderness** warrior; Theodore Roosevelt and the crusade for America. Harper 2009 940p il map $34.99   **92**

1. Nature conservation 2. Conservation of natural resources 3. Biography, Individual 4. Presidents -- United States 5. Wilderness areas -- United States 6. Conservation of natural resources -- United States -- History -- 20th century

ISBN 978-0-06-056528-2; 0-06-056528-4

This biography of the 26th president of the United States focuses on his interests and activities on behalf of conservation and nature.

The author "has absorbed a huge amount of research, but encyclopedic inclusiveness and repetition occasionally mar narrative movement. . . . But this book has Rooseveltian energy. It is largehearted, full of the vitality of its subject and a palpable love for the landscape it describes." N Y Times Book Rev

Includes bibliographical references

Burns, Eric. The **Golden** Lad; The Haunting Story of Quentin and Theodore Roosevelt. by Eric Burns. W W Norton & Co Inc 2016 300 p. illustrations $26.95   **92**

1. Father-son relationship 2. Presidents -- United States

-- Children

ISBN 1605989517; 9781605989518

This book, by Eric Burns, is a biography of Theodore Roosevelt and his youngest son Quentin. "How does looking at Theodore's relationship with his son, and understanding him as a father, tell us something new about this larger-than-life-man? Does it reveal a more human side? A more hypocritical side? Or simply, if tragically, a nature so surprisingly sensitive, despite the bluster, that he would die of a broken heart?" (Publisher's note)

"Burns's unique, stirring account of America's most colorful president allows Teddy Roosevelt, the man and father, to step off the page." Pub Wkly

Includes bibliographical references (pages 181-184) and index.

Cooper, John Milton. The **warrior** and the priest; Woodrow Wilson and Theodore Roosevelt; [by] John Milton Cooper, Jr. Belknap Press 1983 442p il hardcover o.p. pa $20.95   **92**

1. Governors 2. Presidents 3. Vice-presidents 4. College presidents 5. Nobel laureates for peace 6. Presidents -- United States 7. United States -- Politics and government -- 1898-1919

ISBN 0-674-94751-7 pa

LC 83-6021

The author's "distinctions are sharp, his insights original, his judgments balanced and his narrative unfailingly graceful." N Y Times Book Rev

Includes bibliographical references

DiSilvestro, Roger L. **Theodore** Roosevelt in the Badlands; a young politician's quest for recovery in the American West. Walker & Co. 2011 352p il map $27   **92**

1. Governors 2. Presidents 3. Ranch life 4. Vice-presidents 5. Nobel laureates for peace 6. Presidents -- United States 7. Frontier and pioneer life -- North Dakota

ISBN 978-0-8027-1721-4

LC 2010-44297

"Focused on TR in his twenties, DiSilvestro's work elaborates on the future president's days devoted to hunting and ranching in the Dakota Territory. . . . With its sources fully researched and capably integrated, DiSilvestro's account definitively fills in this part of TR's story." Booklist

Includes bibliographical references

McCullough, David G. **Mornings** on horseback; {by} David McCullough. Simon & Schuster 1981 445p il hardcover o.p. pa $16   **92**

1. Governors 2. Presidents 3. Vice-presidents 4. Nobel laureates for peace 5. Presidents -- United States

ISBN 0-671-44754-8 pa

LC 81-1697

This biography follows Theodore Roosevelt from his childhood to his defeat for mayor of New York and marriage to Edith Carow in 1886.

"Based on diligent and thorough research, with emphasis on family, physical ailments, and friends, and written with verve and color, this is a stimulating book that will appeal to the general reader." Libr J

Includes bibliographical references

★ Morris, Edmund. The **rise** of Theodore Roosevelt; Modern Library pa. ed; Modern Lib. 2001 xxxiv, 920p il pa $17.95   **92**

1. Governors 2. Presidents 3. Vice-presidents 4. Nobel laureates for peace 5. Presidents -- United States

ISBN 0-375-75678-7

LC 2001-30520

A reissue of the title first published 1979 by Coward, McCann & Geoghegan

This first volume of a three volume study of the life and times of Theodore Roosevelt "covers Roosevelt's life up to the age of 42, when an assassin's bullet elected him the youngest president in the nation's history." Booklist

Includes bibliographical references

Followed by Theodore Rex (2001) and Colonel Roosevelt (2010)

★ Morris, Edmund. **Theodore** Rex. Random House 2001 772p il map $35; pa $16.95   **92**

1. Governors 2. Presidents 3. Vice-presidents 4. Nobel laureates for peace 5. Presidents -- United States

ISBN 0-394-55509-0; 0-8129-6600-7 pa

LC 2001-19366

"The second entry in Morris's . . . three-volume life of Theodore Roosevelt focuses on the presidential years 1901 through early 1909." Publ Wkly

Includes bibliographical references

Followed by Colonel Roosevelt (2010)

★ Morris, Edmund, 1940- **Colonel** Roosevelt. Random House 2010 766p il map $35; ebook $35   **92**

1. Biography, Individual 2. Presidents -- United States 3. United States -- Politics and government -- 1909-1913 4. United States -- Politics and government -- 1913-1921

ISBN 978-0-375-50487-7; 0-375-50487-7; 978-0-679-60415-0 ebook; 0-679-60415-4 ebook

LC 2010-5890

Sequel to Theodore Rex (2001)

"Mr. Morris has addressed the toughest and most frustrating part of Roosevelt's life with the same care and precision that he brought to the two earlier installments. And if this story of a lifetime is his own life's work, he has reason to be immensely proud." N Y Times (Late N Y Ed)

Includes bibliographical references

O'Toole, Patricia. **When** trumpets call; Theodore Roosevelt after the White House. Simon & Schuster 2005 494p il hardcover o.p. pa $16   **92**

1. Governors 2. Presidents 3. Vice-presidents 4. Nobel laureates for peace 5. Presidents -- United States

ISBN 0-684-86477-0; 0-684-86478-9 pa

LC 2004-62590

The author "adeptly revisits this story, uncovering previously unexploited material and presenting a fuller and more sympathetic account. . . . O'Toole has written the definitive account of TR's postpresidential years." Libr J

Includes bibliographical references

Rose, Pete, 1941-

Kennedy, Kostya. **Pete** Rose; An American Dilemma. Kostya Kennedy. Time Home Entertainment Inc. 2014 352 p. illustrations $26.95 **92**

1. Sports betting 2. Rose, Pete, 1941- 3. Major League Baseball 4. Baseball players -- Biography

ISBN 1618930966; 9781618930965

LC 2013949234

This book on former professional baseball player Pete Rose presents a "consideration of Rose's place in baseball history 25 years after his ban from Major League Baseball (MLB) and from Hall of Fame consideration because he bet on baseball games. The narrative shifts between Rose's past--with anecdotes from family, friends, and former teammates--to his present life working the autograph circuit and filming a reality show with his young fiancée." (Library Journal)

"This is a wonderful biography as well as a thoughtful examination of a moral quandary." Booklist

Includes bibliographical references and index

Rosenblatt, Roger

Rosenblatt, Roger. **Making** toast; a family story. Ecco 2010 166p $21.99 **92**

1. Authors 2. Bereavement 3. Journalists 4. Grandparent-grandchild relationship 5. Essayists 6. Authors, American 7. Nonfiction writers 8. Political commentators

ISBN 978-0-06-182593-4; 0-06-182593-X

"A 38-year-old pediatrician named Amy Solomon collapsed on her treadmill at home. She died of what was discovered to be a rare, undiagnosed heart defect. The day she died, Amy's parents—Roger and Ginny Rosenblatt—drove from their house on Long Island to their daughter's home in Bethesda, Md. The Rosenblatts have been there ever since, helping their son-in-law take care of three children, who were 6, 4, and 1 when their mother died. Now, Roger Rosenblatt has written about this reconfigured family in an exquisite, restrained little memoir filled with both hurt and humor." NPR

Ross, Barney, 1909-1967

Century, Douglas. **Barney** Ross. Schocken Books 2006 215p il (Jewish encounters) $19.95 **92**

1. Boxers (Persons)

ISBN 0-8052-4223-6; 978-0-8052-4223-2

LC 2005-49939

This is a biography of the American boxer.

"This is an excellent story of a man and his times. And proof positive that time does not relinquish its hold over men or monuments." N Y Times Book Rev

Includes bibliographical references

Ross, Betsy, 1752-1836

Miller, Marla R. **Betsy** Ross and the making of America. Henry Holt 2010 467p il map $30 **92**

1. Dressmakers 2. Needleworkers 3. Biography, Individual 4. Flags -- United States 5. Philadelphia (Pa.) -- History -- 18th century 6. Philadelphia (Pa.)

-- History -- 19th century 7. United States -- History -- 1775-1783, Revolution

ISBN 0-8050-8297-2; 978-0-8050-8297-5

LC 2009-35385

This is a biography of the flag-maker Betsy Ross and a portrait of Revolutionary War-era Philadelphia. Index.

"This first-rate biography of Ross (1752–1836) is authoritative and engrossing and goes a long way toward recovering the history of early American women and work." Publ Wkly

Includes bibliographical references

Rossi, Chef

Rossi, Chef. The **Raging** Skillet; the true life story of Chef Rossi. by Rossi. Feminist Press 2015 220 p. illustrations (pbk.) $15.95 **92**

1. Cookbooks 2. Cooks -- Biography 3. Jewish cooking 4. Raging Skillet (Catering service) 5. Cooks -- United States -- Biography

ISBN 155861902X; 9781558619029

LC 2015012151

This cookbook and memoir, by Chef Rossi, "is one woman's story of cooking her way through some of the most unlikely kitchens in New York City—at a 'beach' in Tribeca, an East Village supper club, and a makeshift grill at ground zero in the days immediately following 9/11. Forever writing her own rules, Rossi ends up becoming the owner of one of the most sought-after catering companies in the city." (Publisher's note)

"The inclusion of numerous recipes related to each narrative is an added garnish to an already satisfying meal. A humorous and witty chronicle of a woman's pulling-herself-up-by-her-bootstraps rise through the culinary ranks." Kirkus

Rossini, Gioacchino, 1792-1868

Servadio, Gaia. **Rossini**; a life. Carroll & Graf Publishers 2003 244p il $26 **92**

1. Composers

ISBN 0-7867-1195-7

LC 2003-43563

"This is a deeply rewarding book, written with real personality and much scholarship." Publ Wkly

Includes bibliographical references

Roth, Henry, 1906-1995

Kellman, Steven G. **Redemption**: the life of Henry Roth. W.W. Norton 2005 371p il $25.95 **92**

1. Authors 2. Novelists 3. Essayists 4. Short story writers

ISBN 0-393-05779-8

LC 2005-11979

The author "traces Roth's fascinating career from his birth in Galicia, Austria-Hungary, to his final years in New Mexico. He focuses on his experience of New York's Lower East Side and Jewish and Irish Harlem. . . . This biography should be included in all public library and academic collections." Libr J

Includes bibliographical references

Roth, Joseph, 1894-1939

Roth, Joseph, 1894-1939. **Joseph** Roth; Joseph Roth; translated and edited by Michael Hofmann. W. W. Norton 2012 xvii, 551p $39.95   **92**
1. Authors 2. Novelists 3. Journalists 4. Authors, Austrian 5. Short story writers
ISBN 978-0-393-06064-5
LC 2011032677

This book "contains 457 letters [by writer Joseph Roth], only a small number of which are to family or close friends or comment on his novels as he was writing them. Most are to fellow writers . . . or to translators and colleagues at The Frankfurter Zeitung and other newspapers for which Roth wrote essays, reviews, and sketches." He discusses "his personal affairs, . . . and, most of all, his unending financial woes." Other topics include "Nazism, . . . Jewishness, . . . [and] the Soviet Union." (New York Times)

Includes bibliographical references

Rothschild, Charlotte, 1819-1884

Weintraub, Stanley. **Charlotte** and Lionel; a Rothschild love story. Free Press 2003 316p il hardcover o.p. pa $22.95   **92**
1. Bankers 2. Members of Parliament 3. Spouses of prominent persons
ISBN 0-7432-2686-0; 978-1-4165-7332-6; 1-4165-7332-1 pa
LC 2002-29994

The author profiles one of the Victorian era's "oddly (given their Jewishness and British anti-Semitism) quintessential couples. Lionel Rothschild, scion of the British branch of the famed banking family, married his beautiful German wife, Charlotte, in 1836, when she was 16 (he was a decade older). The bride was, following family custom, also Lionel's cousin and would mature into a sparkling saloniste and hostess whose dinner invitations, Weintraub notes, were preferred over those from Buckingham Palace. . . . Weintraub offers an enticing inside look at a storied family that played a central public role in Victorian England." Publ Wkly

Includes bibliographical references

Rothschild, Lionel Nathan, Baron, 1808-1879

Weintraub, Stanley. **Charlotte** and Lionel; a Rothschild love story. Free Press 2003 316p il hardcover o.p. pa $22.95   **92**
1. Bankers 2. Members of Parliament 3. Spouses of prominent persons
ISBN 0-7432-2686-0; 978-1-4165-7332-6; 1-4165-7332-1 pa
LC 2002-29994

The author profiles one of the Victorian era's "oddly (given their Jewishness and British anti-Semitism) quintessential couples. Lionel Rothschild, scion of the British branch of the famed banking family, married his beautiful German wife, Charlotte, in 1836, when she was 16 (he was a decade older). The bride was, following family custom, also Lionel's cousin and would mature into a sparkling saloniste and hostess whose dinner invitations, Weintraub notes, were preferred over those from Buckingham Palace. . . . Weintraub offers an enticing inside look at a storied fam-

ily that played a central public role in Victorian England." Publ Wkly

Includes bibliographical references

Rousey, Ronda, 1987-

My fight / your fight; Ronda Rousey. Regan Arts 2015 301 p. illustrations $27.95   **92**
1. Mixed martial arts 2. Women athletes -- Biography
ISBN 1941393268; 9781941393260
LC 2015930623

In this memoir, by Ronda Rousey, with Maria Burns Ortiz, "marked by her signature charm, barbed wit, and undeniable power, ... [mixed martial artist Ronda Rousey describes] the toughest fights of her life--in and outside the Octagon--reveals the painful loss of her father when she was eight years old, the intensity of her judo training, her battles with love, her meteoric rise to fame, the secret behind her undefeated UFC record, and what it takes to become the toughest woman on Earth." (Publisher's note)

"The book is just too long; it could have been more than 50 pages shorter, and Rousey would still have inspired her readers. But her warrior mentality is always evident, and one of her more helpful pieces of advice is to feel angry, not sad, after a loss. She urges would-be elite athletes—and really, anyone—to set goals, then become obsessed with elevating them. Plainspoken, often repetitive, and always fiery. Rousey is a fierce yet endearing role model—and a woman possessed." Kirkus

Rousseau, Jean-Jacques, 1712-1778

Cranston, Maurice. **Jean**-Jacques: the early life and work of Jean-Jacques Rousseau, 1712-1754. University of Chicago Press 1991 382p il map pa $23   **92**
1. Authors 2. Novelists 3. Memoirists 4. Political and social philosophers
ISBN 0-226-11862-2
LC 90-45994

First published 1983 by Norton

"Cranston presents Rousseau's work in the context of his life. He proceeds impartially but not dispassionately; his scholarship is impeccable but not obtrusive. The result is a most readable narrative that has something for readers at all levels of sophistication." Choice

Includes bibliographical references

Cranston, Maurice. The **solitary** self: Jean-Jacques Rousseau in exile and adversity; with a foreword by Sanford Lakoff. University of Chicago Press 1997 247p il $35; pa $20   **92**
1. Authors 2. Novelists 3. Memoirists 4. Political and social philosophers
ISBN 0-226-11865-7; 0-226-11866-5 pa
LC 96-12922

"This final volume in Cranston's definitive trilogy chronicles Rousseau's last turbulent years as an outcast in England and Neuchatel, after the burning of %Emile and the order for his arrest. . . . This is a scholarly yet ingratiating portrayal of a man whose last years found him battling sciatica and Voltaire, enjoying botany and Boswell. Cranston's authoritative work has given us an invaluable account of the paradoxical life of an emotionally devoted yet tactlessly demanding man." Booklist

Includes bibliographical references

Rousseau, Jean-Jacques. **Confessions**; edited and introduced by P. N. Furbank. Knopf 1992 2v in 1 $20   **92**
1. Authors 2. Novelists 3. Memoirists 4. Political and social philosophers
ISBN 0-679-40998-X
LC 91-53194

First Everyman's library edition, 1931

"An autobiography by Jean-Jacques Rousseau. The twelve volumes, written between 1766 and 1770, were published posthumously (I-VI, 1781; VII-XII, 1788). In this work, Rousseau 'frankly and sincerely' reveals the details of his erratic and rebellious life. Scholars find, however, that his unconscious motivation was to justify himself in the eyes of his supposedly numerous persecutors." Reader's Ency. 4th edition

Routledge, Katherine, 1866-1935
Van Tilburg, JoAnne. **Among** stone giants; the life of Katherine Routledge and her remarkable expedition to Easter Island. foreword by Andrew Tatham. Scribner 2003 351p il $26   **92**
1. Easter Island 2. Archaeologists
ISBN 0-7432-4480-X
LC 2002-42751

This is a "biography of Katherine Routledge, an Englishwoman who was the first to attempt a methodical archaeological study of Easter Island." N Y Times Book Rev

Includes bibliographical references

Rozelle, Pete
Izenberg, Jerry. **Rozelle**; a biography. Jerry Izenberg; foreword by David Stern. University of Nebraska Press 2014 312 p. 10 unnumbered pages of plates (hardback) $29.95   **92**
1. National Football League 2. Football commissioners -- United States -- Biography
ISBN 0803255748; 9780803255746; 9780803266988
LC 2014016577

This book by Jerry Izenberg "chronicles the life and times of the architect of the modern National Football League, Pete Rozelle, who transformed football into arguably the most successful sports league in the world. When he became commissioner in 1960, the league . . . was mired in an outdated business model. Rozelle introduced revenue and television profit sharing to guarantee the success of small-market teams and brought every NFL game to national television." (Publisher's note)

"All professional football fans will enjoy this well-reported biography of a seminal figure in NFL history." LJ

Includes bibliographical references and index

Rudd, Mark, 1947-
Rudd, Mark. **Underground**; my life with SDS and the Weathermen. William Morrow 2009 324p il map $25.99   **92**
1. Teachers 2. Radicalism 3. Youth leaders 4. Revolutionaries 5. Weathermen (Organization) 6.

Students for a Democratic Society
ISBN 978-0-06-147275-6; 0-06-147275-1

"Even those who condemn Rudd's work in history can be grateful for Rudd's work of history. 'Underground' is honest and funny, passionate and contrite, meticulously researched and deeply philosophical: an essential document on the '60s." Washington Post Book World

Rudnick, Paul
Rudnick, Paul. **I** shudder; and other reactions to life, death, and New Jersey. Harper 2009 318p $23.99   **92**
1. Authors 2. Humorists 3. Novelists 4. Dramatists 5. Screenwriters 6. Dramatists, American
ISBN 978-0-06-178018-9; 0-06-178018-9
LC 2009-36459

This is the author's "collection of uproariously self-deprecating essays about being gay and Jewish in suburban New Jersey and downtown Manhattan, and about his career as a playwright and script doctor in Hollywood and on Broadway." N Y Times Book Rev

Rufus, Rob
Rufus, Robert. **Die** young with me; by Rob Rufus. Touchstone Books 2016 400 p. (hardcover) $25   **92**
1. Cancer patients 2. Cancer -- Patients -- Biography 3. Punk rock musicians -- United States -- Biography
ISBN 1501142615; 9781501142611; 9781501142628
LC 2016005363

This memoir, by Rob Rufus, tells "true story of a teenager diagnosed with cancer and how music was the one thing that helped him get through his darkest days. . . . [Punk rock] blares constantly from the basement of Rob and Nat Rufus—identical twin brothers. . . . When Rob is diagnosed with a rare form of cancer that has already progressed to Stage Four, not only are his dreams of punk rock stardom completely shredded, there is a very real threat that this is one battle that can't be won." (Publisher's note)

"By refusing to abandon hope, easy though it would have been to do so, Rufus' memoir makes a valuable contribution to the literature of healing and recovery." Kirkus

Rupert, Prince, Count Palatine, 1619-1682
Spencer, Charles Edward Maurice Spencer. **Prince** Rupert; the last cavalier. [by] Charles Spencer. Weidenfeld and Nicolson 2007 430p il $37.95; pa $19.95   **92**
1. Princes 2. Admirals 3. Generals 4. Great Britain -- History -- 1642-1660, Civil War and Commonwealth
ISBN 978-0-297-84610-9; 0-297-84610-8; 978-0-7538-2401-6 pa; 0-7538-2401-9 pa

"This delightful book could change the nonspecialist reader's perception of the English Civil War era as tedious while impressing those already familiar with it. . . . highly recommended for any college, high school, or public library." Libr J

Includes bibliographical references

Rushdie, Salman

★ Rushdie, Salman, 1947- **Joseph** Anton; a memoir. Salman Rushdie. Random House 2012 xii, 636 p.p (acid-free paper) $30   **92**
1. Protective custody 2. Freedom of the press 3. Islam and literature 4. Fatwas -- Personal narratives 5. Authors, Indic -- Great Britain -- Biography 6. Blasphemy (Islam) -- History -- 20th century
ISBN 0812992784; 9780679643883; 9780812992786
LC 2012372283

This memoir describes author Salman Rushdie's time under police protection after Iranian leader Ayatollah Khomeini issued a death sentence against the author following the publication of his novel "The Satanic Verses." The book answers questions like "How do a writer and his family live with the threat of murder for more than nine years? How does he go on working? . . . How does despair shape his thoughts and actions, . . . how does he learn to fight back?" (Publisher's note)

Russo, Frank

The **Cooperstown** chronicles; baseball's colorful characters, unusual lives, and strange demises. Frank Russo. Rowman & Littlefield Pub Inc 2015 304 p. illustrations (cloth : alk. paper) $40   **92**
1. Baseball -- History 2. Baseball teams -- History 3. Baseball players -- Biography 4. Baseball -- United States -- History 5. Baseball players -- United States -- Death 6. Baseball players -- United States -- Biography 7. Baseball players -- United States -- Social life and customs
ISBN 1442236396; 9781442236394
LC 2014019500

This book, by Frank Russo, "takes an entertaining look at the unusual lives, strange demises, and downright rowdy habits of some of the most colorful personalities in the history of baseball. Chapters profile the game's well-known tough-guys, the hard-drinking revelers, head-hunting pitchers, players who took their own lives, and those who died far too young from accidents or diseases." (Publisher's note)

"Fans of baseball, in particular baseball history, will enjoy this work for the multitude of players (various teams, various years) that are documented in its pages." LJ
Includes bibliographical references and index

Russo, Richard, 1949-

Russo, Richard, 1949- **Elsewhere**; Richard Russo. Alfred A. Knopf 2012 246 p. $25.95   **92**
1. Biography 2. Authors -- Family life 3. Parent-child relationship 4. Gloversville (N.Y.) -- Biography 5. Novelists, American -- Biography
ISBN 0307959538; 9780307959539
LC 2012016354

Author Richard Russo presents a book that chronicles his life. When he went to college, "his mother joined him as they drove to Arizona, and she'd rarely be far from him in the decades that followed. Russo describes how his life decisions were often limited by the need to accommodate his mother's particular needs and, later, debilitating illness . . . He explores how her options were limited as a single mother in the '60s, as a product of a manufacturing culture

that collapsed before her eyes, and as a woman who needed to define herself through other men." (Kirkus Reviews)

Russo, Vito, 1946-1990

Schiavi, Michael. **Celluloid** activist; the life and times of Vito Russo. [by] Michael Schiavi. University of Wisconsin Press 2011 361p il $29.95; e-book $14.95   **92**
1. Gay activists 2. Film historians 3. Gay rights activists 4. ACT UP (Organization) 5. Motion picture critics 6. Homosexuality in motion pictures 7. Gay and Lesbian Alliance Against Defamation
ISBN 978-0-299-28230-1; 978-0-299-28233-2 e-book
LC 2010-44627

"Conventionally academic but complex portrait of an undeservedly obscure gay author and activist." Kirkus
Includes bibliographical references

Ruth, Babe, 1895-1948

Creamer, Robert W. **Babe**; the legend comes to life. Simon & Schuster 1974 443p il hardcover o.p. pa $14   **92**
1. Baseball players 2. Baseball -- Biography
ISBN 0-671-76070-X pa
This biography covers Babe Ruth's personal life and his sports career.

Rutherford, Ernest, 1871-1937

Reeves, Richard. A **force** of nature; the frontier genius of Ernest Rutherford. W. W. Norton & Co. 2008 207p il (Great discoveries) $23.95   **92**
1. Physicists 2. Nobel laureates for chemistry
ISBN 978-0-393-05750-8; 0-393-05750-X
LC 2007-33184

The author "re-introduces Ernest Rutherford, one of the founding geniuses of nuclear physics. . . . This biography does an outstanding job of capturing the excitement and almost breathless pace of physics research in the 20th century's first four decades." Publ Wkly
Includes bibliographical references

Ryan, Donald P., 1957-

Ryan, Donald P. **Beneath** the sands of Egypt; adventures of an unconventional archaeologist. William Morrow 2010 286p il $26.99; ebook $12.99   **92**
1. Queens 2. Archeologists 3. Archaeologists 4. College teachers 5. Egypt -- Antiquities 6. Excavations (Archeology) -- Egypt
ISBN 978-0-06-173282-9; 0-06-173282-6; 978-0-06-200280-8 ebook; 0-06-200280-5 ebook
LC 2010-20355

"Ryan, the archaeologist who rediscovered tomb KV 60 in the Valley of the Kings (later identified as the final resting place of the pharoah Hatshepsut), takes us through his life, career, and numerous expeditions. It's a thrilling book, not because it's full of Indiana Jones heroics but because Ryan's enthusiasm for what he does (more dirt-sifting than bullwhip-wielding) is manifested on every page; and . . . he catches us up in his excitement, makes us wish we weren't just reading about this stuff but were actually doing it. . . . This wonderful adventure story should be must reading for anyone aspiring to become an archaeologist, but even those of us who harbor no such dreams will be aching to get a little dirt under our fingernails." Booklist

Sabbag, Robert

Sabbag, Robert. **Down** around midnight; a memoir of crash and survival. Viking 2009 214p $25.95 **92**

1. Journalists 2. Aircraft accidents 3. Survival after airplane accidents, shipwrecks, etc. 4. Authors, American

ISBN 978-0-670-02102-4

LC 2008-46688

"A remarkably powerful, human story not merely of a plane crash but of the impact that one brief moment can have on an entire life." Booklist

Sacagawea, b. 1786

★ Clark, Ella Elizabeth. **Sacagawea** of the Lewis and Clark expedition; {by} Ella E. Clark and Margot Edmonds. University of Calif. Press 1979 171p il hardcover o.p. pa $16.95 **92**

1. Lewis and Clark Expedition (1804-1806) 2. Interpreters 3. Guides (Persons)

ISBN 0-520-05060-6 pa

LC 78-65466

"Sacagawea, the Shoshone Indian woman who accompanied the Lewis and Clark expedition, has been a regional heroine and a feminist celebrity for most of this century. But, as these writers show, her role as 'the guide' was more fictive than actual. . . . Based on careful interpretation of the explorer's journals, this revisionist study does a good job of redefining her actual contributions." Booklist

Includes bibliographical references

Sacks, Oliver, 1933-2015

On the move; a memoir. by Oliver Sacks. Alfred A. Knopf 2015 416 p. 32 plates : illustrations (hardcover : alk. paper) $27.95 **92**

1. Drug addicts 2. Scientists -- Biography 3. Neurologists -- England -- Biography 4. Neurologists -- United States -- Biography

ISBN 0385352549; 9780385352543

LC 2015001870

In this autobiography by Olvier Sacks, "as he recounts his experiences as a young neurologist in the early 1960s, first in California, where he struggled with drug addiction, and then in New York, where he discovered a long-forgotten illness in the back wards of a chronic hospital, we see how his engagement with patients comes to define his life." (Publisher's note)

"On the Move is an engaging and candid introduction to a man who transcended the life of a clinical practitioner to become a medical storyteller and humanitarian. Sacks's prose reflects his intelligence, drive, enthusiasm, and, most especially, curiosity about the world. This book is a striking tale of an unorthodox individual and a pleasure to read. Summing Up: Highly recommended. All readership levels." Choice

Sackville-West, Vita

Dennison, Matthew. **Behind** the Mask; The Life of Vita Sackville-west. Matthew Dennison. St. Mar-

tin's Press 2015 416 p. 16 plates; color illustrations $29.99 **92**

1. Women -- Great Britain 2. Celebrities -- Biography

ISBN 1250033942; 9781250033949

LC 2015002466

Author Matthew Dennison presents this "biography of Vita Sackville-West, the 20th century aristocrat, literary celebrity, devoted wife, famous lover of Virginia Woolf, recluse, and iconoclast who defied categorization. His narrative charts a fascinating course from Vita's lonely childhood at Knole, through her affectionate but 'open' marriage to Harold Nicolson, . . . and through Vita's literary successes and disappointments." (Publisher's note)

"Dennison downplays Vita's relationship with Woolf as a smoldering and significant writerly friendship. His narrative is utterly absorbing in its attention to the minutiae of property, inheritance, houses, clothing, and letters. All the while, the author extracts from Vita's writing rich autobiographical detail. A lively, vigorously written biography of a singular character that beckons readers urgently back to Sackville-West's writing." Kirkus

Sagan, Carl, 1934-1996

Poundstone, William. **Carl** Sagan; a life in the cosmos. Holt & Co. 1999 473p il $30 **92**

1. Authors 2. Novelists 3. Astronomers 4. Essayists 5. Astrophysicists 6. Writers on science 7. Science fiction writers

ISBN 0-8050-5766-8; 9780805057676

LC 99-14615

This is an "exhaustive and detailed account, especially when discussing Sagan's original scientific work and influences." Libr J

Includes bibliographical references

Said, Edward W.

Said, Edward W. **Out** of place; a memoir. Knopf 1999 295p il $26.95; pa $14 **92**

1. Authors 2. Essayists 3. Social critics 4. Literary critics 5. Writers on politics

ISBN 0-394-58739-1; 0-679-73067-2 pa

LC 99-31106

In this memoir Said offers an "account of his intellectual and moral development. At the heart of Said's story is the sense of dislocation experienced by a boy whose father was a Palestinian-born American citizen, whose mother was Lebanese, and who was raised in Egypt under the colonial rule of the British. This is the moving tale of a man who is always an outsider." Publ Wkly

Said, Kurban, 1905-1942

Reiss, Tom. The **Orientalist**; solving the mystery of a strange and a dangerous life. Random House 2005 xxvii, 433p il $25.95; pa $14.95 **92**

1. Authors 2. Novelists 3. Historians 4. Biographers

ISBN 1-4000-6265-9; 0-8129-7276-7 pa

LC 2004-50928

This is a biography of Lev Nussimbaum, a Jew from Baku who wrote in Germany under the pseudonyms Essad Bey and Kurban Said.

The author "takes the reader through his own search for the truth; through the twists of 20th-century history in Rus-

sia and Germany, and hence though the life-story itself. This would be hard work if the interweaving of biography, investigation and geopolitics were not so elegant." Economist
Includes bibliographical references

Saks, Elyn R.

The **center** cannot hold; my journey through madness. Hyperion 2008 351 p. $16   **92**
1. Autobiographies 2. Schizophrenia 3. Biography, Individual
ISBN 1401309445; 9781401309442

This book "is the . . . story of [author] Elyn [R. Saks]'s life, from the first time that she heard voices speaking to her as a young teenager, to attempted suicides in college, through learning to live on her own as an adult in an often terrifying world. Saks discusses frankly the paranoia . . . , the voices in her head telling her to kill herself . . . as well the . . . obstacles she overcame to become a highly respected professional." (Publisher's note)

Saldana, Stephanie

Saldana, Stephanie. The **bread** of angels; a journey to love and faith. Doubleday 2010 309p $24.95; pa $15   **92**
1. Christianity and other religions 2. Spiritual biography 3. Biography, Individual 4. Islam -- Relations -- Christianity 5. Christianity and other religions -- Islam 6. Damascus (Syria) -- Description and travel
ISBN 978-0-385-52200-7; 0-385-52200-2; 978-0-307-28046-6 pa; 0-307-28046-2 pa
     LC 2009-16852

This book "operates on several levels: as a spiritual testament and journey of faith; as a Western woman's positive encounter with Islam; as a writer's successful quest to find poetry and beauty even in the midst of war; and as a love story, told with novelistic suspense and a refreshing humor that keeps the romanticism of her story as grounded in reality as possible. . . . This is the type of memoir, recounting a journey to the depths of the soul, that makes the personal universal." America

Salinger, J. D. (Jerome David), 1919-2010

Beller, Thomas. **J.D.** Salinger; the escape artist. Thomas Beller. New Harvest 2014 160 p. (Icons) (hardback) $20   **92**
1. American authors -- Biography 2. Authors, American -- 20th century -- Biography
ISBN 0544261992; 9780544261990
     LC 2013045583

In this book, author Thomas Beller "gives us a sense of life at 'The New Yorker' . . . and a portrait of editor Gus Lobrano, whose relationship with [writer J. D.] Salinger has rarely been written about. He visits Salinger's summer camp and the apartment buildings where the author lived. He reads the famous works with obsessive attention, finding in them an image of his own life experience." (Publisher's note)

★ Slawenski, Kenneth. **J.D.** Salinger; a life. Random House 2011 450p il $27; ebook $27   **92**
1. Authors 2. Novelists 3. Authors, American 4. Short story writers
ISBN 978-1-4000-6951-4; 978-0-679-60479-2 ebook
     LC 201008926
First published 2010 in the United Kingdom

This biography is "a highly informative effort to assess the arc of Salinger's career, the themes of his fiction, and his influence on 20th-century American literature. . . . Slawenski describes Salinger's three marriages, records his contentious relationships with his publishers, his special relationship with the New Yorker, and Slawenski's assiduous research allows him to identify and assess many obscure and unpublished stories. In total, an invaluable work that sheds fascinating light on the willfully elusive author." Publ Wkly
Includes bibliographical references

Salk, Jonas, 1914-1995

Jacobs, Charlotte DeCroes. **Jonas** Salk; a life. Charlotte DeCroes Jacobs. Oxford University Press 2015 576 p. 16 plates; illustrations (hardback) $34.95   **92**
1. Poliomyelitis vaccine 2. AIDS vaccines 3. Influenza vaccines -- History 4. Poliomyelitis vaccine -- History 5. Poliomyelitis -- United States -- History 6. Virologists -- United States -- Biography 7. Poliomyelitis -- Vaccination -- United States -- History
ISBN 0199334412; 9780199334414
     LC 2014040267

This book, by Charlotte DeCroes Jacobs, is a "complete biography of Jonas Salk, . . . [which] unravels Salk's story to reveal an unconventional scientist and a misunderstood and vulnerable man. Despite his incredible success in developing the polio vaccine, Salk was ostracized by his fellow scientists, who accused him of failing to give proper credit to other researchers and scorned his taste for media attention." (Publisher's note)

"Throughout, the author demonstrates a deep understanding of the character and the nature of science in the latter half of the 20th century. Jacobs makes a convincing case that Salk was a shy man who never succeeded in making the scientific or personal connections that could bring happiness, but his idealism proved a boon to mankind." Kirkus
Includes bibliographical references and index

Kluger, Jeffrey. **Splendid** solution: Jonas Salk and the conquest of polio. G.P. Putnam's Sons 2004 373p il hardcover o.p. pa $15   **92**
1. Physicians 2. Poliomyelitis 3. Microbiologists 4. Writers on medicine
ISBN 0-399-15216-4; 0-425-20570-3 pa
     LC 2004-50527
"Can't-put-it-down medical-science history." Booklist
Includes bibliographical references

Sampson, Deborah, 1760-1827

★ Young, Alfred Fabian. **Masquerade**: the life and times of Deborah Sampson, Continental soldier; [by] Alfred F. Young. Knopf 2004 417p il map $26.95; pa $16   92

1. Soldiers 2. Women soldiers 3. Memoirists 4. United States -- History -- 1775-1783, Revolution
ISBN 0-679-44165-4; 0-679-76185-3 pa
LC 2003-47549

This book "makes a valuable contribution to American women's history. It offers nuggets of insight about an array of historical topics. . . . What's more, it tells a terrific story." Rev Am Hist

Includes bibliographical references

Samuelsson, Marcus

Chambers, Veronica. **Yes**, chef; a memoir. Marcus Samuelsson. Random House Inc 2012 319 p. ill. (pbk) $16   92

1. Cooks 2. Family life 3. Swedish Americans -- Biography 4. Cooks -- United States -- Biography 5. African American cooks -- United States -- Biography
ISBN 9780385342612; 0385342616; 9780385342605; 9780440338819
LC 2011042220

James Beard Foundation Award: Writing and Literature (2013)

In this memoir, the author Marcus Samuelsson, was "born in Ethiopia, . . . placed in an orphanage after his mother died from tuberculosis, and the Samuelsson family adopted him and his sister. After becoming a famous chef, the author sought out his roots in multiple visits to his birth country. During one of those visits, he reconnected with his father, and he has kept in touch with his birth family since then. In rich detail, the author tracks his rise as a chef." (Kirkus Reviews)

"This distinctive and compelling memoir has all the elements of a good story: humor, travel, and a young individual overcoming obstacles via a passionate calling." LJ

Sand, George, 1804-1876

Eisler, Benita. **Naked** in the marketplace; the lives of George Sand. Counterpoint 2006 308p $26.95   92

1. Authors 2. Novelists 3. Dramatists
ISBN 978-1-58243-349-3; 1-58243-349-6
LC 2006-21684

This is a biography of the French writer.

"Eisler's portrait of this woman of many firsts brings Sand and her boldly improvised life forward more vividly than ever before." Booklist

Includes bibliographical references

Harlan, Elizabeth. **George** Sand. Yale University Press 2004 376p il $35   92

1. Authors 2. Novelists 3. Dramatists
ISBN 0-300-10417-0
LC 2004-10315

"Sand, née, Aurore Dupin, left her husband and two children in provincial France and successfully launched herself as a self-supporting writer in Paris, donning men's clothing to ease passage into the professional world and taking a pseudonym to protect her aristocratic family's name. Sand took on many lovers, among them poet Alfred de Musset and composer Frédéric Chopin. Yet despite Sand's outward daring, as Harlan shows, she obsessed over her identity, as both a woman and an aristocrat. . . . Harlan sensitively analyzes the gaps and idiosyncrasies in her subject's heavily self-edited correspondence, autobiography and novels to uncover a fresh portrait of this volatile, imaginative woman of letters." Publ Wkly

Includes bibliographical references

Sanders, Bernard

Rall, Ted. **Bernie**; by Ted Rall. Random House Inc 2016 192 p. color illustrations (paperback) $16.95   92

1. Biographical graphic novels
ISBN 9781609806989; 1609806980
LC 2015046626

This graphic novel, by Ted Rall, presents a profile of U.S. politician Bernie Sanders and "offers a clear and condensed assessment of the rightward-drifting evolution of the Democratic Party. . . . Most political biographies depict the evolution of a politician. Bernie Sanders, on the other hand, has been politically consistent for half a century. What happened is that the country caught up with him." (Publisher's note)

Sanders, Bernard, 1941- **Outsider** in the White House; Bernie Sanders with Huck Gutman; afterword by John Nichols. Verso Books 2015 368 p. illustrations $16.95   92

1. Politicians -- United States 2. United States. Congress. Senate 3. Presidential candidates -- United States -- Biography 4. Legislators -- United States -- Biography 5. United States. Congress. House -- Biography 6. United States -- Politics and government -- 1989-
ISBN 9781784784188; 9781784784195; 9781784784201
LC 2015031867

In this biography, written with Huck Gutman, Bernie Sanders "tells the story of a passionate and principled political life. He describes how, after cutting his teeth in the Civil Rights movement, he helped build a grassroots political movement in Vermont, making it possible for him to become the first independent elected to the US House of Representatives in forty years. The story continues into the US Senate and through the dramatic launch of his presidential campaign." (Publisher's note)

Sanders, Scott R. (Scott Russell), 1945-

Sanders, Scott R. A **private** history of awe; [by] Scott Russell Sanders. North Point Press 2006 322p hardcover o.p. pa $15   92

1. Authors 2. Novelists 3. Essayists 4. College teachers 5. Children's authors 6. Short story writers
ISBN 0-86547-693-4; 978-0-86547-693-6; 978-0-86547-734-6 pa; 0-86547-734-5 pa
LC 2005-14236

The author "uses autobiography as a vehicle for far-reaching reflections on nature and humankind. . . . Sanders' thoughtful reflections on the cycles of life, the flashpoints of awe, and our quest for meaning are quietly revelatory." Booklist

Includes bibliographical references

Sanger, Margaret, 1879-1966

Baker, Jean H. **Margaret** Sanger. Hill and Wang 2011 349p il $35   **92**
1. Nurses 2. Birth control 3. Women's rights 4. Essayists 5. Feminists 6. Memoirists 7. Social activists 8. Family planning advocates
ISBN 978-0-8090-9498-1

LC 2011008439

This biography of Margaret Sanger "seeks to clear the noted birth-control pioneer's name of the charges of elitism and racism, which have darkened her reputation in recent years. . . . It was the death of a young woman from a self-induced abortion that impelled her to take up the cause of women's rights to contraception. . . . [The author] acknowledges Sanger's support of eugenics but asserts that Sanger was being pragmatic, requiring allies and finding many in the then-popular eugenics movement." (Kirkus Reviews)

"Baker relates Sanger's crusade with unfailing precision as she recounts Sanger's years as a nurse, when she mended the damage caused by self-induced abortions and listened to the pitiful plights of young women enchained by the relentless cycle of childbirth. Sanger distributed pamphlets on contraception, risking imprisonment on account of their legally designated obscenity; opened the first legal family planning clinic in 1940; and at the culmination of her career, in the 1960s, promoted use of the birth control pill. Connecting the details of each battle Sanger won and lost, Baker recreates the train of events in an arduous, iconic, and controversial journey. A moving biography chronicling the hard-fought struggle for women to gain control of their reproductive destiny." Booklist

Santana, Carlos

Santana, Carlos, 1986- The **universal** tone; my life. Carlos Santana. Little, Brown & Co. 2014 544 p. 32 plates; color illustrations (hardcover) $30 **92**
ISBN 0316244929; 9780316244923

LC 2014940685

This memoir, by Carlos Santana with Ashley Kahn and Hal Miller, "offers a page-turning tale of musical self-determination and inner self-discovery, with personal stories filled with colorful detail and life-affirming lessons. The . . . [book] traces his journey from his earliest days playing the strip bars in Tijuana . . . and brings to light the establishment of his signature guitar sound; his roles as husband, father, recording legend, and rock guitar star." (Publisher's note)

"An appreciative and unpretentious chronicle, this is required reading for Santana fans and devotees of classic rock legends." Kirkus

Saperstein, Jesse A.

Getting a life with Asperger's; lessons learned on the bumpy road to adulthood. Jesse A. Saperstein. Penguin Group 2014 220 p. (paperback) $15   **92**
1. Asperger's syndrome 2. Saperstein, Jesse A. -- Mental health 3. Asperger's syndrome -- Patients -- Life skills guides 4. Asperger's syndrome -- Patients

-- United States -- Biography
ISBN 0399166688; 9780399166686

LC 2014011613

This book, by Jesse A. Saperstein, is a memoir of growing up with Asperger's syndrome. The author, "diagnosed at the age of 14, . . . has struggled, triumphed, flubbed, soared, educated, and inspired. Along the road to adulthood, he has learned many lessons the hard way. In this honest and engaging book, he offers a guided tour of what he's learned about getting along with others, managing emotions, succeeding in school and work, building relationships, and more." (Publisher's note)

Sartre, Jean Paul, 1905-1980

Sartre, Jean Paul. The **words**; translated from the French by Bernard Frechtman. Vintage 1981 255p pa $11.95   **92**
1. Authors 2. Novelists 3. Dramatists 4. Philosophers 5. Authors, French 6. Essayists 7. Nonfiction writers 8. Short story writers 9. Nobel laureates for literature
ISBN 0-394-74709-7; 978-0-394-74709-5
First published 1964 by Braziller

The French existentialist writer "examines the formation of his character during his childhood years, which were passed in a completely adult world between his widowed mother and her parents. The central event of his childhood was the discovery of the world of words, of language." Libr J

Sattouf, Riad

Sattouf, Riad, 1978- The **Arab** of the Future; A Graphic Memoir. by Riad Sattouf. Metropolitan Books 2015 160 p. chiefly ill. $26   **92**
1. Arabs 2. Nomads
ISBN 1627793445; 9781627793445

LC 2014041152

LA Times Book Prize: Graphic Novel/Comics (2015)
Eisner Nominee: Best Reality-Based Work (2016)

In this graphic memoir, author Riad Sattouf "recounts his nomadic childhood growing up in rural France, [Muammar] Gaddafi's Libya, and [Hafez] Assad's Syria--but always under the roof of his father, a Syrian Pan-Arabist who drags his family along in his pursuit of grandiose dreams for the Arab nation." (Publisher's note)

"Caught between his parents, Sattouf makes the best of his situation by becoming a master observer and interpreter, his clean, cartoonish art making a social and personal document of wit and understanding." Pub Wkly

Sattouf, Riad, 1978- The **Arab** of the Future 2; A Childhood in the Middle East, 1984-1985: a Graphic Memoir. Riad Sattouf; translated by Sam Taylor. Metropolitan Books 2016 160 p. chiefly illustrations $26   **92**
1. Autobiographies 2. Middle East -- Social conditions
ISBN 1627793518; 9781627793513

The second volume of Riad Sattouf's graphic memoir "takes in the sweep of politics, religion, and poverty, but is steered by acutely observed small moments: the daily sadism of his schoolteacher, the lure of the black market, with its menu of shame and subsistence, and the obsequiousness of his father in the company of those close to the regime." (Publisher's note)

"Rather than being incongruous with the oppressive society and grim events he depicts, Sattouf's broadly cartoonish drawing style imparts a level of attachment that makes his story bearable." Booklist

Scalia, Antonin

Murphy, Bruce Allen. **Scalia**; a court of one. Bruce Allen Murphy. Simon & Schuster 2014 736 p. illustrations $35   **92**

1. Constitutional law -- United States 2. Judges -- United States -- Biography 3. United States. Supreme Court -- Biography

ISBN 0743296494; 9780743296496

LC 2013042971

This biography by Bruce Allen Murphy describes how "Antonin Scalia knew only success in the first fifty years of his life. . . . Scalia's evident legal brilliance . . . led everyone to predict he would unite a new conservative majority. . . . Instead he became a Court of One. Rather than bringing the conservatives together, Scalia drove them apart. . . . 'Scalia: A Court of One' is the . . . story of one of the most polarizing figures ever . . . on the nation's highest court." (Publisher's note)

"Murphy details Scalia's behind-the-scenes angling to push himself as the leading advocate for originalism and to get on the Supreme Court. But his scathing critiques set him at odds with conservatives, most notably Sandra Day O'Connor, pushing many to the center. Murphy offers a highly engaged, well-researched analysis of a brash justice whose single-mindedness may ultimately reduce his legacy." Booklist

Includes bibliographical references and index

Schaap, Rosie

Drinking with men; a memoir. Rosie Schaap. Riverhead Hardcover 2013 272 p. (hardback) $26.95   **92**

1. Bars 2. Alcoholics 3. Women -- Alcohol use 4. Women alcoholics -- Biography 5. Bars (Drinking establishments)

ISBN 1594487111; 9781594487118

LC 2012030405

In this memoir, Rosie Schaap "shares her unending quest for the perfect local haunt, which takes her from a dive outside Los Angeles to a Dublin pub full of poets, and from small-town New England taverns to a character-filled bar in Manhattan's TriBeCa. Drinking alongside artists and expats, ironworkers and soccer fanatics, she finds these places offer a safe haven, a respite, and a place to feel most like herself." (Publisher's note)

"Early passages can seem a bit naive, as when she suggests bars' negative depiction in popular culture (what about Cheers?) or when she just can't understand what her friends and family have against her new pals from the bar. But, as her remembered self ages, deeper and richer insights emerge. Ultimately, this is as much about growing up in bars as it is growing out of them." Booklist

Schön, Jan Hendrik

Reich, Eugenie Samuel. **Plastic** fantastic; how the biggest fraud in physics shook the scientific world. Palgrave Macmillan 2009 266p $26.95   **92**

1. Physicists 2. Fraud in science 3. Biography, Individual

ISBN 0230224679; 9780230224674; 0-230-22467-9; 978-0-230-22467-4

LC 2008-51801

This is the story of Bell Laboratories "physicist Jan Hdnrik Schön who faked the discovery of a new superconductor made from plastic." (Publisher's note) Index.

"A compelling look inside big science at one of its least admirable moments." Kirkus

Includes bibliographical references

Schiaparelli, Elsa, 1890-1973

Elsa Schiaparelli; A Biography. by Meryle Secrest. Random House Inc 2014 400 p. illustrations $35   **92**

1. Fashion designers

ISBN 030770159X; 9780307701596

LC 2014025820

This biography, by Meryle Secrest, focuses on French fashion designer Elsa Schiaparelli. "She was known as the Queen of Fashion; a headline attraction in the international glitter-glamour show of the late twenties and thirties. . . . Secrest writes of Schiaparelli's keen instincts-- an astute businesswoman, she launched herself into hats, hose, soaps, shoes, handbags, in the space of a few years. By 1930, her company was grossing millions of francs a year." (Publisher's note)

"Richly illustrated and endlessly intriguing, Secrest's biography illuminates the 'daredevil swagger' of Schiaparelli's clothes and the oft-besieged couturier's inexhaustible tenacity and dazzling creativity." Booklist

Volk, Patricia. **Shocked**; my mother, Schiaparelli, and me. Patricia Volk. Alfred A. Knopf 2013 304 p. ill. (some col.) (hardcover) $26.95   **92**

1. Femininity 2. Beauty, Personal 3. Mothers and daughters -- United States 4. Fashion designers -- France -- Paris -- Biography

ISBN 9780307962102; 0307962105

LC 2012034922

This book by Patricia Volk presents a "study of two very different but very glamorous women--her mother, Audrey, an upper-class New York domestic goddess with the looks and manners of Grace Kelly, and genius haute couture European artist Elsa Schiaparelli, whose book, art, and (yes) perfume forever change the course of young Volk's life." (Library Journal)

"[T]he narrative that emerges from Volk's deft interweaving of lives is as sharp-eyed as it is wickedly funny." Kirkus

Includes bibliographical references

Schiff, Dorothy, 1903-1989

Nissenson, Marilyn. The **lady** upstairs; Dorothy Schiff and the New York Post. St. Martin's Press 2007 500p il $29.95 **92**

1. New York post 2. Newspaper executives

ISBN 978-0-312-31310-4; 0-312-31310-1

LC 2006-53087

This "is Marilyn Nissenson's carefully documented and revealing account of Schiff's nearly four decades of ownership. It's an admiring but not uncritical story of a woman who at her best 'was feisty rather than cowed, personally diffident but professionally forceful,' and who, although married four times, ended up wedded mainly to the paper itself." Columbia J Rev

Includes bibliographical references

Schindler, Oskar, 1908-1974

Crowe, David. **Oskar** Schindler; the untold account of his life, wartime activities, and the true story behind the list. [by] David M. Crowe. Westview Press 2004 766p il $30 **92**

1. Humanitarians 2. Manufacturing executives

ISBN 0-8133-3375-X

LC 2004-13879

This book "is essential in understanding one of the most extraordinary figures from the Holocaust." Booklist

Includes bibliographical references

Schlesinger, Arthur M., 1917-2007

Schlesinger, Arthur M. (Arthur Meier), 1917-2007. **Journals**: 1952-2000; edited by Andrew Schlesinger and Stephen Schlesinger. Penguin Press 2007 894p $40 **92**

1. Authors 2. Historians 3. Biographers 4. Nonfiction writers 5. Government officials 6. Historians -- United States 7. United States -- History -- 1945-

ISBN 978-1-594-20142-4

The distinguished political historian's journals provide an intimate history of postwar America, the writer's contributions to multiple presidential administrations, and his relationships with numerous cultural and intellectual figures.

This book "contains juicy morsels on every one of its [pages]. . . . The book contains not just his witty apercus, but those of hundreds of A-list friends, some of whom are still alive and will blanch at seeing private lunches in print. The presidential scuttlebutt is prime. . . . The private scoresettling is fun reading." Newsweek

Schlesinger, Arthur M. (Arthur Meier), 1917-2007. A **life** in the twentieth century; innocent beginnings, 1917-1950. [by] Arthur M. Schlesinger, Jr. Houghton Mifflin 2000 557p il $28.95; pa $15 **92**

1. Authors 2. Historians 3. Biographers 4. Nonfiction writers 5. Government officials 6. Historians -- United States

ISBN 0-395-70752-8; 0-618-21925-0 pa

LC 00-61322

This first volume of Schlesinger's autobiography covers the author's life through the publication of The Age of Jackson and The Vital Center.

Schlesinger's "autobiography, skillfully interweaving the personal and the historical, is elegantly simple and marvellously clear. Complex thoughts are set forth with a lucidity that conceals the depth of the intellectual analysis. Wit, humour and the resources of a natural storyteller sweep the reader along." Economist

Schneerson, Menachem Mendel, 1902-1994

Telushkin, Joseph, 1948- **Rebbe**; The Life and Teachings of Menachem M. Schneerson, the Most Influential Rabbi in Modern History. Joseph Telushkin. HarperCollins 2014 640 p. illustrations, portraits $29.99 **92**

1. Rabbis 2. Biography 3. Chabad-Lubavitch

ISBN 0062318985; 9780062318985

National Jewish Book Award Finalist: Biography, Autobiography, Memoir (2014)

"In this . . . biography, Joseph Telushkin offers a . . . portrait of the late Rabbi Menachem Mendel Schneerson, a towering figure who saw beyond conventional boundaries to turn his movement, Chabad-Lubavitch, into one of the most dynamic and widespread organizations ever seen in the Jewish world." (Publisher's note)

"The book is rich with accounts of encounters with the Rebbe, including, besides his own followers, Jews of many denominations, secular Israeli leaders, American politicians, students of philosophy, and non-Jews. What stands out is Schneerson's engagement with the principles by which he managed to wield a considerable and controversial influence upon the American cultural scene and the Jewish world." Pub Wkly

Schriever, Bernard A., 1910-2005

Sheehan, Neil. A **fiery** peace in a cold war; Bernard Schriever and the ultimate weapon. Random House 2009 534p il $32 **92**

1. Cold war 2. Generals 3. Nuclear weapons 4. Ballistic missiles 5. Air force officers

ISBN 978-0-679-42284-6

LC 2009-02247

The author "has written the best kind of biography, one that tells history through a central character. . . . The real story is of the bureaucratic hand-to-hand combat that let to . . . [the ICBM] finally taking flight. . . . Crafting an engrossing five-hundred-page account of a bureaucratic tussle is no easy task. Yet Sheehan makes it work." Columbia J Rev

Includes bibliographical references (p. [501]-509) and index.

Schultz, Philip, 1945-

Schultz, Philip. **My** dyslexia. W. W. Norton & Co. 2011 120p $21.95 **92**

1. Poets 2. Authors 3. Dyslexia 4. Poets, American 5. College teachers

ISBN 978-0-393-07964-7

LC 2011015859

The author "tackles his struggle with dyslexia—a condition he only learned he had when his son was diagnosed. Schultz paints a precise and compelling picture of how his brain works, how he sees himself, and how he thinks others have seen him throughout his life. . . . His affecting prose will inspire compassion and leave readers with an understanding not only of dyslexia, but of the lifelong challenges that someone with disabilities may face." Publ Wkly

Schulz, Charles M.

★ Michaelis, David. **Schulz** and Peanuts; a biography. Harper 2007 655p il $34.95 **92**
1. Cartoonists 2. Peanuts (Comic strip)
ISBN 978-0-06-621393-4; 0-06-621393-2

This is a biography of the cartoonist and author of Happiness is a Warm Puppy (1962), The Charlie Brown Dictionary (1973), Peanuts Jubilee (1975), Snoopy's Tennis Book (1979), and Things I Learned After It Was Too Late (1981).

"It is Mr. Michaelis's achievement in these pages that he leaves us with both a shrewd appreciation of Schulz's minimalist art and a sympathetic understanding of Schulz the man." N Y Times (Late N Y Ed)

Includes bibliographical references

Schumann, Robert, 1810-1856

Geck, Martin. **Robert** Schumann; the life and work of a romantic composer. Martin Geck; translated by Stewart Spencer. The University of Chicago Press 2012 320 p. $35 **92**
1. Composers -- Germany -- Biography
ISBN 9780226284699; 0226284697

LC 2012007981

This book by Martin Geck is a biography of Robert Schumann, "one of the most important and representative composers of the Romantic era. . . . Geck shows Schumann to be not only a major composer and music critic . . . but also a political activist, the father of eight children, and an addict of mind-altering drugs. . . . Schumann was able to control his demons and channel the tensions that seethed within him into music that mixes the popular and esoteric." (Publisher's note)

Includes bibliographical references and index

Scott, Dred, ca. 1795-1858

VanderVelde, Lea. **Mrs.** Dred Scott; a life on slavery's frontier. Oxford University Press 2009 480p il map $34.95 **92**
1. Slaves 2. Biography, Individual 3. Slavery -- United States 4. Spouses of prominent persons 5. United States -- Supreme Court 6. Slaves -- Legal status, laws, etc. 7. Slaves -- United States -- Biography
ISBN 0-19-536656-5; 978-0-19-536656-3

LC 2008-27920

This is a "biography of Harriet Scott, wife of Dred Scott, and the story of the family's flight for freedom." (Publisher's note) Bibliography. Index.

"Through Harriet Scott's life, the author is able to create a valuable portrait of the development of slavery on the U.S. frontier during an era in which that scourge was leading the country toward civil war. Despite the wealth of historical knowledge presented, the heart of this well-researched work is the tragic tale of how a loving family's effort to gain their freedom was brutally rejected by Supreme Court justices bent on maintaining the institution of slavery at all costs." Libr J

Includes bibliographical references (p. 443-466)

Scott, Harriet Robinson

VanderVelde, Lea. **Mrs.** Dred Scott; a life on slavery's frontier. Oxford University Press 2009 480p il map $34.95 **92**
1. Slaves 2. Biography, Individual 3. Slavery -- United States 4. Spouses of prominent persons 5. United States -- Supreme Court 6. Slaves -- Legal status, laws, etc. 7. Slaves -- United States -- Biography
ISBN 0-19-536656-5; 978-0-19-536656-3

LC 2008-27920

This is a "biography of Harriet Scott, wife of Dred Scott, and the story of the family's flight for freedom." (Publisher's note) Bibliography. Index.

"Through Harriet Scott's life, the author is able to create a valuable portrait of the development of slavery on the U.S. frontier during an era in which that scourge was leading the country toward civil war. Despite the wealth of historical knowledge presented, the heart of this well-researched work is the tragic tale of how a loving family's effort to gain their freedom was brutally rejected by Supreme Court justices bent on maintaining the institution of slavery at all costs." Libr J

Includes bibliographical references (p. 443-466)

Scott, Wendell, 1921-1990

Donovan, Brian. **Hard** driving: the Wendell Scott story; the odyssey of NASCAR'S first Black driver. Steerfort Press 2008 311p il hardcover o.p. pa $16.99 **92**
1. Automobile racing 2. African American athletes 3. Automobile racing drivers
ISBN 978-1-58642-144-1; 978-1-58642-160-1 pa

LC 2008-24287

For this biography, the author "interviewed Scott extensively over the last 14 months of his life. He also interviewed more than 200 other individuals, including Scott's widow and children. The result is the gripping story of a fascinating, brave man who deserves serious recognition for his solitary accomplishment. . . . A must-read for NASCAR fans." Booklist

Includes bibliographical references

Sediqi, Kamela, 1977-

Lemmon, Gayle Tzemach. The **dressmaker** of Khair Khana; five sisters, one remarkable family, and the woman who risked everything to keep them safe. Harper 2011 256p **92**
1. Dressmaking 2. Businesswomen 3. Taliban 4. Afghanistan 5. Dressmakers
ISBN 978-0-06-173237-9

LC 2010-20774

This book "is a fascinating window on Afghan life under the Taliban and a celebration of women the world over who support their loved ones with tenacity, inventiveness and sheer guts." People

Includes bibliographical references

Seek, Amy

God and Jetfire; confessions of a birth mother. Amy Seek. Farrar, Straus & Giroux 2015 352 p. (hardback) $27   **92**

1. Adoption 2. Motherhood 3. Families 4. Open adoption

ISBN 0374164452; 9780374164454; 9780374713829

LC 2014044643

This book, by Amy Seek, "is a mother's account of her decision to surrender her son in an open adoption and of their relationship over the twelve years that follow. Facing an unplanned pregnancy at twenty-two, Amy Seek and her ex-boyfriend begin an exhaustive search for a family to raise their child. . . . For decades, closed adoptions were commonplace. Now, new laws are guaranteeing adoptees' access to birth records, and open adoption is on the rise." (Publisher's note)

"Seek's prose is lyrical, at times heart-wrenching, as she deeply explores her pain, regret, and longing. The author provides an informative view of open adoption (its advantages as well as its drawbacks). There is nothing prescriptive or commonplace about this true story of a mother who has to learn—as all parents must—both how to embrace, and how to let go." Pub Wkly

Seeger, Pete

★ Dunaway, David King. **How** can I keep from singing? the ballad of Pete Seeger. Trade paperback ed.; Villard 2008 xxx, 512p il pa $18   **92**

1. Singers 2. Folk musicians 3. Songwriters

ISBN 978-0-345-50608-5

LC 2007-41814

A reprint of the title first published 1981 by McGraw-Hill

"The focus of Seeger's life has been on using music as a force for social change. . . . But he is perhaps best known as the major banjo-playing folksinger who pioneered the folk music revival that flowered in the 1960s. This excellent book provides a well-written and extensively researched account, not only of Seeger's life, but also of the social and political movements of the times in which he lived. An extensive bibliography and discography add to the book's usefulness." Libr J

Includes discography and bibliographical references

Wilkinson, Alec. The **protest** singer; an intimate portrait of Pete Seeger. Alfred A. Knopf 2009 151p il $22.95; pa $14   **92**

1. Singers 2. Folk musicians 3. Songwriters

ISBN 978-0-307-26995-9; 978-0-307-39098-1 pa

LC 2008-54387

The author "draws on interviews with Seeger and others to present a seamless chronicle of his life and music, vivifying his passion for humanity, love of the environment, and deep curiosity about music." Libr J

Semmelweis, Ignác Fülöp, 1818-1865

Nuland, Sherwin B., 1930-2014. The **doctors'** plague; germs, childbed fever, and the strange story of Ignac Semmelweis. Norton 2003 191p il (Great discoveries) $21.95; pa $13.95   **92**

1. Physicians 2. Writers on medicine 3. Puerperal septicemia

ISBN 0-393-05299-0; 0-393-32625-X pa

LC 2003-11412

This is an account of the work of the 19th-century obstetrician Ignas Semmelweis. "Semmelweis is remembered for the now-commonplace notion that doctors must wash their hands before examining patients. . . . With deaths from childbed fever exploding, Semmelweis discovered that doctors themselves were spreading the disease. While his simple reforms worked immediately, they also threatened the medical establishment." (Publisher's note)

Seth, Shanti Behari

★ Seth, Vikram, 1952- **Two** lives; Vikram Seth. HarperCollins 2005 503p ill. (pbk.) $15.95; o.p. **92**

1. Poets 2. Authors 3. Dentists 4. Novelists 5. London (England) -- Biography" 6. East Indians -- England -- London 7. Interracial marriage -- England -- London 8. Authors, English -- 20th century -- Biography 9. Authors, Indic -- Homes and haunts -- England -- London 10. London (England) -- Social life and customs -- 20th century

ISBN 9780060599676; 0060599669

LC 2005052694

In this book, the author presents biographies of "his Shanti Uncle and Aunty Henny. . . . Shanti was Seth's grandfather's brother, a dentist who studied in Berlin, lodging with Fau Caro, whose daughter, Henny was in love with someone else. He left for Britain in 1936. . . . [I]n 1940, as war broke out, he enlisted, served throughout and lost his right arm in combat. . . . Meanwhile, Henny, a German Jew, arrived in Britain weeks before war was declared, leaving her beloved mother and sister behind to death camp murder. . . . Part two of his narrative focuses on Shanti. Part three, Henny's story . . . is based on a trove of remarkable letters she received and wrote. . . . Part four examines their marriage (they didn't marry until seven years after the war), and part five details a family mystery about Shanti's will and Seth's . . . research into these lives." (Publishers Weekly)

"In clear and elegant writing, Seth explores the macrocosm through the microcosm, resulting in a most unusual, worthwhile book." Publ Wkly

Seton, Elizabeth Ann, Saint, 1774-1821

Barthel, Joan. **American** saint; the life of Elizabeth Seton. Joan Barthel. Thomas Dunne Books 2014 304 p. illustrations (hardback) $26.99   **92**

1. Religious biography 2. Christian saints -- Biography 3. Christian saints -- United States -- Biography

ISBN 0312571623; 9780312571627

LC 2013030995

In this biography of Elizabeth Seton, author Joan Barthel "tells the . . . story of a woman whose life featured wealth and poverty, passion and sorrow, love and loss. Elizabeth was born into a prominent New York City family in 1774. . . . When Elizabeth and her wealthy husband Will sailed to Italy in a doomed attempt to cure his tuberculosis, she and her family were quarantined. . . . And when Elizabeth later became a Catholic, she was so scorned that people talked of burning down her house." (Publisher's note)

"A biography of the first American saint. . . offering a rounded portrait of an ambitious woman who struggled mightily to fulfill the tenets of her faith: to be obedient, merciful and good." Kirkus

Includes bibliographical references and index

Seuss, Dr.

Morgan, Judith. **Dr.** Seuss & Mr. Geisel; a biography. [by] Judith & Neil Morgan. Da Capo Press 1996 345p il pa $18.50   **92**

1. Artists 2. Authors 3. Humorists 4. Illustrators 5. Authors, American 6. Children's authors

ISBN 0-306-80736-X; 978-0-306-80736-7

LC 96-19313

First published 1995 by Random House

"Fans of The Cat in the Hat, The Grinch Who Stole Christmas and other classics may be surprised to learn that Dr. Seuss was terrified of children and had none of his own, and that writing verse was a supreme effort for him. While children's literature is Ted Geisel's principal claim to fame, his creative life was multifarious, including an apprenticeship with film director and army major Frank Capra during WWII and stints in advertising. The authors deftly evoke the settings where Geisel lived and worked." Publ Wkly

Sewall, Samuel, 1652-1730

LaPlante, Eve. **Salem** witch judge; the life and repentance of Samuel Sewall. HarperSanFrancisco 2007 352p il map $25.95   **92**

1. Judges 2. Diarists 3. Colonial leaders 4. Massachusetts -- History -- 1600-1775, Colonial period

ISBN 978-0-06-078661-8; 0-06-078661-2

LC 2007-18392

"In 1692, Salem magistrate Samuel Sewall (1652-1730), along with several others, presided over the conviction and execution of 20 people accused of witchcraft. Five years and much soul-searching later, Sewall publicly repented of his part in the witch trials. . . . [The author] richly narrates his life in its cultural and religious setting." Publ Wkly

Includes bibliographical references

Seward, William Henry, 1801-1872

Stahr, Walter. **Seward**; Lincoln's indispensable man. by Walter Stahr. Simon & Schuster 2012 720 p. $32.50; (hardcover) $32.50   **92**

1. Legislators 2. Statesmen -- United States 3. Statesmen -- United States -- Biography 4. United States. Dept. of State -- Biography 5. Cabinet officers -- United States -- Biography 6. United States -- Foreign relations -- 1861-1865 7. United States -- Politics and government -- 1861-1865

ISBN 9781439127940; 1439121168; 9781439121160; 9781439121184

LC 2011052984

This book presents a biography of William Henry Seward, U.S. Secretary of State under President Abraham Lincoln. "Seward was New York governor and senator, then a rival for Lincoln's place on the 1860 presidential ticket, finally senior cabinet officer. . . . Among other things, he kept Britain out of the Civil War, then negotiated the acquisition of Alaska for the U.S." (Publishers Weekly)

Includes bibliographical references and index

Shabazz, Betty

Rickford, Russell John. **Betty** Shabazz: a remarkable story of survival and faith before and after Malcolm X; foreword by Myrlie Evers-Williams. Sourcebooks 2003 xxii, 633p il $35   **92**

1. Civil rights activists 2. Spouses of prominent persons 3. African Americans -- Civil rights

ISBN 1-4022-0171-0

LC 2002-003447

"Just as the achievements of her husband, Malcolm X, were overshadowed by those of Martin Luther King Jr., Betty Shabazz's accomplishments have been overshadowed by those of King's widow. {The author} corrects that imbalance with this penetrating biography." Booklist

Includes bibliographical references

Shackleton, Ernest Henry Sir, 1874-1922

Smith, Michael. **Shackleton**; By Endurance We Conquer. Michael Smith. Oneworld Publications 2014 464 p. illustrations; maps; portraits $30   **92**

1. Antarctica -- Exploration

ISBN 1780745729; 9781780745725

Author Michael Smith offers "a fresh perspective to the Heroic Age of Polar Exploration that was dominated by [Ernest] Shackleton's enduringly fascinating story. His incredible adventures on four expeditions to the Antarctic have captivated generations. But Shackleton was a flawed character whose chaotic private life, marked by romantic affairs, unfulfilled ambitions, and failed business ventures, contrasted with his celebrity status as the leading explorer." (Publisher's note)

"Shackleton is admired for his leadership skills while his repeated off-ice failures are overlooked or unknown. Smith offers a fascinating assessment of his subject, one that will be enjoyed by readers of biographies, polar literature, and adventure stories." LJ

Shakur, Tupac

Dyson, Michael Eric. **Holler** if you hear me: searching for Tupac Shakur. Basic Bks. 2001 292p il hardcover o.p. pa $15   **92**

1. Poets 2. Actors 3. Hip-hop 4. Rap music 5. African American musicians 6. Rap musicians

ISBN 0-465-01755-X; 0-465-01728-2 pa

LC 2001-36564

"Dyson's discussion goes beyond slogans and poses to the actualities of 'thug life' and the consequences of Shakur's passions and allegiances. Piquant and analytical." Booklist

Includes bibliographical references

Sharon, Ariel

Landau, David. **Arik**; the life of Ariel Sharon. by David Landau. Alfred A. Knopf 2014 656 p. illustrations, map hbk $35   **92**

1. Israel -- History 2. Israel -- Politics and government 3. Generals -- Israel 4. Arab-Israeli conflict 5. Prime ministers -- Israel

ISBN 1400042410; 9781400042418

LC 2012049631

Author David Landau presents a biography of Ariel Sharon, a "man who is considered by many to be Israel's greatest military leader and political statesman, illustrating how

Sharon's leadership transformed Israel, and how his views were shaped by the changing nature of Israeli society." (Publisher's note)

"Splendid reporting, comprehensive research and probing analysis inform this unblinking view of a complicated man and a sanguinary geography." Kirkus

Includes bibliographical references and index

Shaw, Artie, 1910-2004

Nolan, Tom. **Three** chords for beauty's sake: the life of Artie Shaw. W.W. Norton 2010 430p il $29.95   **92**
1. Jazz musicians 2. Band leaders 3. Clarinetists
ISBN 978-0-393-06201-4; 0-393-06201-5
       LC 2010-06301

In this biography of the swing clarinetist-bandleader Nolan, "who interviewed Shaw and many of his band mates and intimates, appraises his difficult subject with a cool eye. His briskly written work lauds the musician's instrumental virtuosity and ambitious conceptions, but the author cuts Shaw no slack about his many personal failings—his arrogance, anger, selfishness, egocentricity and his horrific relationships with parents, wives and children. It's a multidimensional portrait of a brilliant yet self-absorbed autodidact who could never find happiness or satisfaction, even when his greatest fantasies of fame and success were realized. An exemplary work of jazz biography." Kirkus

Includes bibliographical references

Shawn, Allen

Shawn, Allen. **Wish** I could be there; notes from a phobic life. Viking 2007 267p $24.95   **92**
1. Composers 2. Agoraphobia
ISBN 0-670-03842-3; 978-0-670-03842-8
       LC 2006-41368

The author "probes the causes of his long struggle with agoraphobia—a fear of certain spaces which makes it difficult to 'move forward in the world without knowing already what lies ahead'—in this vividly written combination of memoir and scientific inquiry." New Yorker

Includes bibliographical references

Sheehan, Jason

★ Sheehan, Jason. **Cooking** dirty; a story of life, sex, love and death in the kitchen. Farrar, Straus and Giroux 2009 355p $26; pa $15   **92**
1. Cooks 2. Food critics
ISBN 978-0-374-28921-8; 0-374-28921-2; 978-0-374-53227-7 pa; 0-374-53227-3 pa
       LC 2008-47158

"Sheehan's memoir is emphatically not about 'the glam end of cooking' or celebrity chefs, but about 'a straight blue-collar gig,' where the kitchens are staffed by the kind of guys who get off on the fact that the work is insanely grueling. . . . The war stories are as profane and outrageous as you'd expect, and Sheehan finds just the right balance between bravado and humility." Publ Wkly

Sheehy, Gail

Sheehy, Gail, 1937- **Daring**; My Passages: a Memoir. Gail Sheehy. William Morrow 2014 416 p. illustrations (some color) $29.99   **92**
1. Women journalists 2. Journalism -- United States -- History 3. Journalists -- United States -- Biography
ISBN 0062291696; 9780062291691
       LC 2014034090

This memoir, by Gail Sheehy, is "a chronicle of her trials and triumphs as a groundbreaking 'girl' journalist in the 1960s. . . . [It] is the story of the unconventional life of a writer who dared . . . to walk New York City streets with hookers and pimps to expose violent prostitution; to march with civil rights protesters in Northern Ireland as British paratroopers opened fire; to seek out Egypt's president Anwar Sadat when he was targeted for death after making peace with Israel." (Publisher's note)

"Sheehy gives readers a distinct glimpse into some of the most important events of the last 40 years. . . . Her perspective on the women's movement and the decline of print journalism is especially compelling." LJ

Shelley, Mary Wollstonecraft, 1797-1851

Gordon, Charlotte. **Romantic** outlaws; the extraordinary lives of Mary Wollstonecraft and her daughter Mary Shelley. Charlotte Gordon. Random House Inc 2015 672 p. illustrations (hardback) $30; (paperback) $18.00   **92**
ISBN 9781400068425; 1400068428; 9780812980479; 0812980476
       LC 2014014841

National Book Critics Circle Award Finalist: Biography (2015)

In this biography of Mary Wollstonecraft and Mary Shelley author Charlotte Gordon "reunites the trailblazing author who wrote 'A Vindication of the Rights of Woman' and the Romantic visionary who gave the world 'Frankenstein'--two courageous women who should have shared their lives, but instead shared a powerful literary and feminist legacy." (Publisher's note)

"Gordon's prose is compelling and her scholarship meticulous; her contention that both women led 'lives as memorable as the words they left behind' is brilliantly supported." LJ

Includes bibliographical references and index

Seymour, Miranda. **Mary** Shelley. Grove Press 2001 655p il $35; pa $20   **92**
1. Authors 2. Novelists 3. Women authors 4. Authors, English
ISBN 0-8021-1702-3; 0-8021-3948-5 pa
       LC 2001-35094

First published 2000 in the United Kingdom

"A convincing and memorable portrait." Booklist

Includes bibliographical references

Shen, Aisling Juanjuan, 1974-

Shen, Aisling Juanjuan. A **tiger's** heart; the story of a modern Chinese woman. Soho Press 2009 309p $24   **92**
1. Memoirists 2. Financial analysts 3. Immigrants -- United States 4. Yangtze River valley (China) 5.

Chinese Americans -- Biography
ISBN 978-1-56947-586-7; 1-56947-586-5

LC 2009-5426

"Like a suspense novel, this book is impossible to put down. All readers interested in China, as well as memoir fans (especially of success stories), must read this astonishing title." Libr J

Shepard, Sadia

Shepard, Sadia. The **girl** from foreign; a search for shipwrecked ancestors, forgotten histories, and a sense of home. Penguin Press 2008 364p il map $25.95; pa $16 **92**
1. Memoirists 2. Jews -- India 3. Motion picture directors
ISBN 978-1-59420-151-6; 978-0-14-311577-9 pa

LC 2008-3912

A young Muslim-Christian woman travels to an insular Jewish community in India to unlock her family's secret history.

"A readable account that gives a vivid taste of life in present-day India as well as a poignant glimpse of complicated family relations." Kirkus

Includes bibliographical references

Sherman, William T. (William Tecumseh), 1820-1891

Fellman, Michael. **Citizen** Sherman; a life of William Tecumseh Sherman. University Press of Kansas 1997 486p il pa $19.95 **92**
1. Generals 2. Memoirists 3. Secretaries of war 4. United States -- History -- 1861-1865, Civil War
ISBN 978-0-7006-0840-9; 0-7006-0840-0
First published 1995 by Random House

"This superb biography gives as full a portrait of nineteenth-century family dynamics as of the dynamics of the battlefield. Fellman's Sherman is not a lovable man, but he is a complete one." New Yorker

Includes bibliographical references

Kennett, Lee B. **Sherman**; a soldier's life. [by] Lee Kennett. HarperCollins Pubs. 2001 426p il maps hardcover o.p. pa $14.95 **92**
1. Generals 2. Memoirists 3. Secretaries of war 4. United States -- History -- 1861-1865, Civil War
ISBN 0-06-093074-8 pa

LC 2001-16687

This is a "well-balanced analytical biography." Publ Wkly

Includes bibliographical references

Woodworth, Steven E. **Sherman**; [foreword by Wesley K. Clark] Palgrave Macmillan 2009 198p il map (Great generals series) $21.95 **92**
1. Generals 2. Memoirists 3. Secretaries of war 4. United States -- History -- 1861-1865, Civil War
ISBN 0-230-61024-2; 978-0-230-61024-8

LC 2008-22060

This is a biography of the Civil War general.

"An excellent brief life of a major and controversial figure." Booklist

Includes bibliographical references

Short, Martin, 1950-

I must say; my life as a humble comedy legend. Martin Short; with David Kamp. Harper 2014 336 p. 16 plates; illustrations $26.99 **92**
1. Comedians 2. Television actors and actresses -- Canada -- Biography
ISBN 0062309528; 9780062309525

LC 2014028617

In this memoir author "Martin Short takes you on a rich, hilarious, and occasionally heartbreaking ride through his life and times, from his early years in Toronto as a member of the fabled improvisational troupe Second City to the all-American comic big time of Saturday Night Live and memorable roles in movies." (Publisher's note)

"A true vaudevillian, Short is always on as he delivers funny anecdotes from a diffuse and storied career." Kirkus

Shteyngart, Gary, 1972-

★ Shteyngart, Gary. **Little** failure; a memoir. Gary Shteyngart. Random House Inc 2014 368 p. illustrations hbk $27 **92**
1. Autobiographies 2. Russian Americans 3. Children of immigrants
ISBN 0679643753; 9780679643753

LC 2013013217

National Jewish Book Award Finalist: Biography, Autobiography, Memoir (2014)

"After three acclaimed novels, Gary Shteyngart turns to memoir in a candid, witty, deeply poignant account of his life so far. Shteyngart shares his American immigrant experience, . . . with self-deprecating humor, moving insights, and literary bravado. . . . Swinging between a Soviet home life and American aspirations, Shteyngart found himself living in two contradictory worlds, all the while wishing that he could find a real home in one." (Publisher's note)

"An immigrant's memoir like few others, with as sharp an edge and as much stylistic audacity as the author's well-received novels." Kirkus

Shulman, Alix Kates

Shulman, Alix Kates. **To** love what is; a marriage transformed. Farrar, Straus and Giroux 2008 160p $22 **92**
1. Love 2. Authors 3. Marriage 4. Novelists 5. Feminists
ISBN 978-0-374-27815-1; 0-374-27815-6

LC 2008-21504

"A fall from a loft bed left author Shulman's 75-year-old husband with traumatic brain injury and utterly dependent on his wife, as she recounts in this deeply affecting memoir of their ordeal together. . . . Carving out time for herself and her writing kept her from having a nervous breakdown, and while her hope at times flagged, Shulman's devotion never faltered, as demonstrated by her candid account." Publ Wkly

Shuster, Joe

Ricca, Brad. **Super** boys; the amazing adventures of Jerry Siegel and Joe Shuster: the creators of Superman. Brad Ricca. St Martins Pr 2013 432 p. $27.99 **92**
1. Superman (Fictitious character) 2. Cartoonists -- United States -- Biography 3. Comic books, strips, etc.

-- United States -- History and criticism
ISBN 0312643802; 9780312643805

LC 2013004046

This biography of Superman creators Jerry Siegel and
Joe Shuster, by Brad Ricca, "reveals the real-life model for
Lois Lane . . . and the model for Superman himself (Johnny
Weissmuller, who played Tarzan). At the center of the story,
of course, is Siegel and Shuster's decision to sell the Superman rights to Action Comics for a pittance--a choice they
lamented the rest of their lives. The pair endured poverty,
bad marriages, bad health, and a lack of recognition for their
work." (Publishers Weekly)

"Ricca's comprehensive biography reveals the turmoil
and creative genius that led to our most enduring superhero,
the Man of Steel." Pub Wkly

Includes bibliographical references (pages 403-406)
and index

Sickles, Daniel E., 1825-1914

★ Keneally, Thomas. **American** scoundrel: the
life of the notorious Civil War General Dan Sickles.
Talese 2002 397p $27.50; pa $15   **92**
1. Generals 2. Diplomats 3. Members of Congress
ISBN 0-385-50139-0; 0-385-72225-7 pa

LC 2001-43078

"A frequently spellbinding recitation of the career of a
totally awful politician, crook, adulterer and murderer who
was no good as a general either." N Y Times Book Rev

Sieberson, Steve

The **naked** mountaineer; misadventures of an
Alpine traveler. Steve Sieberson; foreword by Lou
Whittaker. University of Nebraska Press 2014 272
p. (paperback : alk. paper) $19.95   **92**
1. Mountaineering 2. Voyages and travels 3.
Mountaineering -- Anecdotes 4. Mountaineers -- United
States -- Biography
ISBN 0803248792; 9780803248793

LC 2014009140

This book, by Steve Sieberson, "recounts a series of solo
journeys to some of the world's most exotic peaks in places
such as Switzerland, Japan, and Borneo. However, it is far
from the typical heroic mountain-expedition book. Although
Steve Sieberson did reach many summits, in most cases his
travels were more memorable for what he encountered along
the way than for the actual climbing." (Publisher's note)

"Fans of Bill Bryson and anyone who has thought about
climbing a mountain will enjoy this charming account of one
man's trek to various parts of the world, though it is unlikely
to impress anyone who is a professional climber." LJ

Siegel, Jerry, 1914-1996

Ricca, Brad. **Super** boys; the amazing adven-
tures of Jerry Siegel and Joe Shuster: the creators of
Superman. Brad Ricca. St Martins Pr 2013 432 p.
$27.99   **92**
1. Superman (Fictitious character) 2. Cartoonists --
United States -- Biography 3. Comic books, strips, etc.
-- United States -- History and criticism
ISBN 0312643802; 9780312643805

LC 2013004046

This biography of Superman creators Jerry Siegel and
Joe Shuster, by Brad Ricca, "reveals the real-life model for
Lois Lane . . . and the model for Superman himself (Johnny
Weissmuller, who played Tarzan). At the center of the story,
of course, is Siegel and Shuster's decision to sell the Superman rights to Action Comics for a pittance--a choice they
lamented the rest of their lives. The pair endured poverty,
bad marriages, bad health, and a lack of recognition for their
work." (Publishers Weekly)

"Ricca's comprehensive biography reveals the turmoil
and creative genius that led to our most enduring superhero,
the Man of Steel." Pub Wkly

Includes bibliographical references (pages 403-406)
and index

Simon, Carly

Simon, Carly, 1945- **Boys** in the trees; a memoir.
Carly Simon. Flatiron Books 2015 384 p. illustra-
tions (hardcover) $28.99   **92**
1. Youth 2. Singers 3. Singers -- United States --
Biography
ISBN 1250095891; 9781250095893; 9781250095909

LC 2015038193

This memoir by Carly Simon "reveals her remarkable
life, beginning with her storied childhood as the third daughter of Richard L. Simon, the co-founder of publishing giant
Simon & Schuster, her musical debut as half of The Simon
Sisters performing folk songs with her sister Lucy in Greenwich Village, to a meteoric solo career that would result in
13 top 40 hits, including the #1 song 'You're So Vain.' The
memoir recalls a childhood enriched by music and culture,
but also one shrouded in secrets that would eventually tear
her family apart." (Publisher's note)

"Memoirs by rock icons of the 1960s and '70s are flying
fast and furious these days. This is one of the best, lively
and memorable. Check the new album that accompanies the
book, too." Kirkus

Simon, Scott

Simon, Scott. **Unforgettable**; a son, a mother,
and the lessons of a lifetime. Scott Simon. Flatiron
Books 2015 256 p. (hardback) $24.99   **92**
1. Death 2. Twitter (Web site) 3. Mother-son
relationship 4. Journalists -- United States -- Biography
ISBN 125006113X; 9781250061133

LC 2015002582

This book " is a son's spirited, affecting, and inspiring
tribute to his remarkable mother and the love between parent
and child. When NPR's Scott Simon began tweeting from
his mother's hospital room in July 2013, he didn't know that
his missives would soon spread well beyond his 1.2 million
Twitter followers. . . . Over the course of a few days, Simon
chronicled his mother's death and reminisced about her life,
revealing her humor and strength, and celebrating familial
love." (Publisher's note)

"Simon appreciates how generously Patti is treated by
the staff at the hospital, which brings up memories of the
'lovely' men who courted her. He takes his quirky, devoted,
gracious mother on her own terms, and his work shimmers
as a touching tribute." Pub Wkly

Simone, Nina

Cohodas, Nadine. **Princess** Noire; the tumultuous reign of Nina Simone. Pantheon Books 2010 449p il $30 **92**

1. Singers 2. Pianists 3. Jazz musicians 4. African American singers 5. African American musicians 6. Songwriters 7. Soul musicians 8. Biography, Individual
ISBN 0-307-37899-3 ebook; 0-375-42401-6; 978-0-307-37899-6 ebook; 978-0-375-42401-4

LC 2009-22252

This is a biography of the singer. Discography. Bibliography. Index.

"Looking at every aspect of Simone's work, from stage decorum to audience interaction, the author offers many rich insights into her subject's conflicted emotional world. Throughout, she nurtures the reader's empathy for the artist but takes care to avoid unfounded speculation on racism or gender bias. In fact, this is a 360-degree profile of Simone, offering solid critical insights at every turn." Choice

Includes discography and bibliographical references

Sinatra, Frank, 1915-1998

★ Friedwald, Will. **Sinatra!** the song is you; a singer's art. Da Capo Press 1997 559p il pa $18.50 **92**

1. Actors 2. Singers
ISBN 0-306-80742-4

LC 96-43855

A reprint of the title first published 1995 by Scribner
Friedwald's "commentary is alert and perceptive, and even more valuable is the wealth of pointed reminiscence drawn from interviews he has done with musicians who worked closely with Mr. Sinatra." N Y Times Book Rev

Includes discography and bibliographical references

Kaplan, James, 1951- **Frank**; the voice. Doubleday 2010 786p il $35; ebook $35 **92**

1. Actors 2. Singers 3. Biography, Individual
ISBN 0-385-51804-8; 0-385-53364-0 ebook; 978-0-385-51804-8; 978-0-385-53364-5 ebook

LC 2009-31046

This biography covers the life of the American singer and actor from his birth in 1915 to his comeback in 1954 in the film From Here to Eternity. Index.

"Kaplan's enthralling tale of an American icon serves as an introduction of 'old blue eyes' to a new generation of listeners while winning the hearts of Sinatra's diehard fans." Publ Wkly

Includes bibliographical references

★ Kaplan, James, 1951- **Sinatra**; the chairman. by James Kaplan. Doubleday 2015 992 p. illustrations (hardcover) $35 **92**

1. Singers -- United States -- Biography
ISBN 9780307946935; 9780385535397; 9780385535403

LC 2015008973

"Just in time for the Chairman's centennial, the . . . sequel to James Kaplan's bestselling 'Frank: The Voice.' . . . Like Peter Guralnick on Elvis, Kaplan goes behind the legend to give us the man in full, in his many guises and aspects: peerless singer, (sometimes) accomplished actor,

business mogul, tireless lover, and associate of the powerful and infamous." (Publisher's note)

"An appropriately big book for an oversized artistic presence." Kirkus

Includes bibliographical references (pages 936-940) and index.

Santopietro, Tom. **Sinatra** in Hollywood. Thomas Dunne Books 2008 530p il $29.95 **92**

1. Actors 2. Singers
ISBN 978-0-312-36226-3; 0-312-36226-9

LC 2008-24941

"Striving for honest critiques and a witty, encyclopedic coverage, Santopietro begins with Sinatra's 1935 short subjects; dances through the grandiose 1940s MGM musicals; documents Sinatra's professional and personal despair and decline in such giant turkey disasters as The Kissing Bandit (1948); and analyzes his Oscar-winning comeback in From Here to Eternity (1953). . . . This mammoth movie compendium, filled with forgotten facts, 53 b&w photos and a detailed filmography, is certain to satisfy Sinatra's legions of fans." Publ Wkly

Includes bibliographical references

Singh, Sophia Duleep, 1876-1948

Anand, Anita. **Sophia**; Princess, Suffragette, Revolutionary. Anita Anand. St. Martin's Press 2015 432 p. 24 plates; illustrations $30 **92**

1. Suffragists
ISBN 1632860813; 9781632860811

Author Anita Anand present a biography of "Sophia Duleep Singh, [who] was born into Indian royalty. Sophia, goddaughter of Queen Victoria, was raised a genteel aristocratic Englishwoman. But when, in secret defiance of the British government, she travelled to India, she returned a revolutionary. Her causes were the struggle for Indian Independence, the fate of the lascars, the welfare of Indian soldiers in the First World War -- and, above all, the fight for female suffrage." (Publisher's note)

"Anand writes with a journalist's sense for a solid story and a historian's eye for fascinating anecdotes. Filled with rich detail and walks through little-known avenues of the past, this work is bound to enchant history lovers, those interested in women's studies, Anglophiles, and anyone who enjoys biographies." LJ

Sirhan, Kamilah, d. 2001

Hikayati sharhun yatul./English. The **locust** and the bird; my mother's story. translated from the Arabic by Roger Allen. Pantheon Books 2009 302p il $24.95 **92**

1. Muslim women 2. Parents of prominent persons
ISBN 978-0-307-37820-0; 0-307-37820-9

LC 2008-54683

"Al-Shaykh's poignant family history, narrated in the voice of her mother, Kamila, transports us to Beirut in the nineteen-thirties. At eleven, the beautiful and strong-willed Kamila is illiterate, her family penniless. She falls in love with the handsome Muhammad, but at fourteen is married off to an older man. . . . Later, Kamila runs away with Muhammad, abandoning her daughters. Al-Shaykh writes in the prologue that this book is largely an attempt to come to terms with that decision. Through telling her mother's story, she learns to appreciate the sacrifices demanded of so many Arab women in their bid for freedom." New Yorker

Sitting Bull, Dakota Chief, 1831-1890

Utley, Robert Marshall. **Sitting** Bull: the life and times of an American patriot; by Robert M. Utley. Henry Holt 2008 464p il pa $18 **92**

1. Indian chiefs
ISBN 978-0-8050-8830-4; 0-8050-8830-X

A reissue with a new preface by the author of the title first published 1993

"This book is well written, strongly documented, and fairly reasoned to satisfy even specialists within the field. It surpasses all previous biographies of Sitting Bull." Choice

Includes bibliographical references

Yenne, Bill. **Sitting** Bull. Westholme 2008 379p il map $29.95 **92**

1. Dakota Indians 2. Indian chiefs
ISBN 978-1-59416-060-8; 1-59416-060-0

In this biography, the author "captures the extraordinary life of Plains Indian leader Sitting Bull while providing new insight into the nomadic culture of the Lakota." Publ Wkly

Includes bibliographical references

Skinner, B. F. (Burrhus Frederic), 1904-1990

Bjork, Daniel W. **B.F.** Skinner; a life. American Psychological Assn. 1997 298p il pa $19.95 **92**

1. Psychologists
ISBN 1-55798-416-6

LC 96-40385

A reissue of the title first published 1993 by Basic Bks.

This is a biography of the psychologist known for his utopian novel Walden Two, his book Beyond freedom and dignity, and his behaviorist theories

"Bjork places Skinner squarely in the context of the US social, technological, and political history. . . . Although heavily documented, Bjork's book is very readable because documentation is in endnotes. A handsome, well-indexed work, with an excellent bibliography." Choice

Slowinski, Joseph, 1962-2001

James, Jamie. The **snake** charmer; a life and death in pursuit of knowledge. Hyperion 2008 260p il $24.95 **92**

1. Snakes 2. Curators 3. Herpetologists
ISBN 978-1-4013-0213-9; 1-4013-0213-0

LC 2007-48987

James recounts "the gritty and sad story of Joe Slowinski, a flamboyant and well-known herpetologist who died in Burma in 2001, aged 38, from the poisonous bite of a krait snake. . . . This book is both a tribute to Slowinski's spirit and scientific accomplishments, and a cautionary tale about the dangers of an overly passionate ambition." Publ Wkly

Smith Rakoff, Joanna, 1972-

My Salinger year; by Joanna Smith Rakoff. Alfred A. Knopf 2014 272 p. (hardcover) $25.95 **92**

1. Publishers and publishing -- History -- 20th century
2. Authors, American -- 21st century -- Biography 3. Literature publishing -- United States -- History -- 21st

century
ISBN 0307958000; 9780307947987; 9780307958006

LC 2013026931

This book, by Joanna Smith Rakoff, is a "memoir about literary New York in the late nineties, a pre-digital world on the cusp of vanishing, where a young woman finds herself entangled with one of the last great figures of the century. At twenty-three, after leaving graduate school to pursue her dreams of becoming a poet, Joanna Rakoff moves to New York City and takes a job as assistant to the storied literary agent for J. D. Salinger." (Publisher's note)

"As Rakoff recounts her funny and wrenching personal predicaments, she also charts the quiet battle of attrition between the values of the old publishing world, personal and impassioned, and the aggressively invasive corporate imperative. An intriguing look at the ever-fascinating Salinger and a gracefully incisive tale of love and literature, creativity and survival." Booklist

Smith, Alfred Emanuel, 1873-1944

Finan, Christopher M. **Alfred** E. Smith, the happy warrior. Hill & Wang 2002 396p il $26; pa $16 **92**

1. Governors 2. Political leaders 3. State legislators 4. Presidential candidates 5. United States -- Politics and government
ISBN 0-8090-3033-0; 0-8090-1632-X pa

LC 2002-19476

"Finan writes well, but for an occasional lapse into anachronism." NY Times Book Rev

Includes bibliographical references

Smith, Joseph, 1805-1844

Barnes, Jane. **Falling** in love with Joseph Smith; my search for the real prophet. Jane Barnes. Jeremy P. Tarcher/Penguin 2012 294 p. $25.95 **92**

1. Faith 2. Mormons 3. Mormon Church 4. Conversion -- Mormon Church
ISBN 1585429252; 9781585429257

LC 2012018119

This book is an "account of a female intellectual's passion for Mormon prophet Joseph Smith and her near-conversion to the faith." Jane Barnes "developed an especially profound fascination with Smith. Her interest manifested first as a treatment for a PBS documentary about Smith's life, then evolved into a full-blown love for the man and his work." She explored the Mormon faith and learned of her family's connections to it. (Kirkus Reviews)

Bushman, Richard L. **Joseph** Smith; rough stone rolling. [by] Richard Lyman Bushman, with the assistance of Jed Woodworth. Knopf 2005 740p il map $35; pa $18.95 **92**

1. Mormons 2. Mormon leaders
ISBN 1-4000-4270-4; 1-4000-7753-2 pa

LC 2004-61613

In this biography of the founder of the Mormon church, the author "stresses the boy seer's thoroughly ordinary origins—born to a hard-pressed New England farm family and denied all but the rudiments of a formal education—to emphasize the marvel of the religious revolution he brought about.. . . . A deft portrait of a deeply controversial figure." Booklist

Includes bibliographical references

Remini, Robert Vincent. **Joseph** Smith. Viking 2002 190p (Penguin lives series) $19.95 **92**
1. Mormons 2. Mormon leaders
ISBN 0-670-03083-X
LC 2001-56762
"A masterful evenhanded précis that will engross history and religion readers alike." Booklist

Includes bibliographical references

Smith, Julian
Smokejumper; A Memoir by One of America's Most Select Airborne Firefighters. James A. Ramos, Julian Smith. HarperCollins 2015 336 p. illustrations (color), map $27.99 **92**
1. Wildfires 2. Fire fighters
ISBN 0062319620; 9780062319623
LC 2015007015
This memoir, written by Jason A. Ramos with Julian Smith, presents an "inside look at the thrilling world of smokejumpers, the airborne firefighters who parachute into the most remote and rugged areas of the United States, confronting the growing threat of nature's blazes. Ramos takes readers into his exhilarating and dangerous world, explores smokejumping's remarkable history, and explains why their services are more essential than ever before." (Publisher's note)

"Most of us avoid jumping from the frying pan into the fire, but as an elite smokejumper with the Department of the Interior Ramos does it regularly, often alone or with just one partner." LJ

Smith, Lee, 1944-
Smith, Lee. **Dimestore**; a writer's life. Lee Smith. Algonquin Books 2016 224 p. $24.95 **92**
1. Women authors 2. Appalachian Region 3. Grundy (Va.) -- Biography 4. Grundy (Va.) -- Social life and customs
ISBN 1616205024; 9781616205027
LC 2015023739
This memoir describes how, "set deep in the mountains of Virginia, the Grundy of [author] Lee Smith's youth was a place of coal miners, tent revivals, mountain music, drive-in theaters, and her daddy's dimestore. It was in that dimestore . . . that she became a storyteller. Even when she was sent off to college to earn some 'culture,' she understood that perhaps the richest culture she might ever know was the one she was driving away from." (Publisher's note)

"In this candid, wistful, appreciative, and beguiling memoir, Smith offers a distinctive and intimate look at one writer's beginnings." Booklist

Smith, Patti, 1946-
★ Smith, Patti, 1946- **Just** kids. Ecco 2010 278p il $27; pa $16 **92**
1. Rock musicians 2. Poets, American 3. Biography, Individual
ISBN 978-0-06-621131-2; 0-06-621131-X; 978-0-06-093622-8 pa; 0-06-093622-3 pa

The author writes about her relationship with the photographer Robert Mapplethorpe in the late 1960s and 1970s.

This "is one of the best books ever written on becoming an artist—not the race for online celebrity and corporate sponsorship that often passes for artistic success these days, but the far more powerful, often difficult journey toward the ecstatic experience of capturing radiance of imagination on a page or stage or photographic paper." Washington Post

M train; Patti Smith. Alfred A. Knopf 2015 272 p. illustrations (hardcover : alk. paper) $25 **92**
1. Women authors 2. Autobiographies 3. Rock musicians -- United States -- Biography 4. Women rock musicians -- United States -- Biography
ISBN 1101875100; 9781101875100; 9781101875117
LC 2015012904
This memoir by Patti Smith is "a meditation on travel, detective shows, literature, and coffee. Through prose that shifts fluidly between dreams and reality, past and present, and across a landscape of creative aspirations and inspirations, we travel to Frida Kahlo's Casa Azul in Mexico; to a meeting of an Arctic explorer's society in Berlin; to a ramshackle seaside bungalow in New York's Far Rockaway that Smith acquires just before Hurricane Sandy hits; and to the graves of Genet, Plath, Rimbaud, and Mishima." (Publisher's note)

"In many ways, this book defies categorizing, and that is one of its many charms. It is absorbing and lingers long after its end. Fans of Smith will enjoy this as will writers, artists, and all those inspired by a creative mind. For circulating collections." LJ

Smith, Raymond J.
Oates, Joyce Carol, 1938- A **widow's** story; a memoir. Ecco 2011 415p il $27.99 **92**
1. Poets 2. Widows 3. Authors 4. Novelists 5. Bereavement 6. Loss (Psychology) 7. Essayists 8. Biographers 9. Magazine editors 10. Authors, American 11. Children's authors 12. Short story writers 13. Biography, Individual 14. Spouses of prominent persons
ISBN 9780062015532
This is an account of the novelist's loss of her "husband of 47 years, Raymond J. Smith. . . . He collaborated with his wife in founding The Ontario Review as well as Ontario Review Books." (N Y Times (Late N Y Ed))

"In a narrative as searing as the best of her fiction, Oates describes the aftermath of her husband Ray's unexpected death from pneumonia. Scattershot moments stand out — the day she cancels their 30-year subscription to The New York Times, unable to bear the sight of his favorite paper; her fury at the tulips, harbingers of spring, pushing through the snow ('Too soon! This is too soon!'); the night she weans herself from Lorazepam. A Widow's Story is the painful, scorchingly angry journey of a woman struggling to live in a house 'from which meaning has departed, like air leaking from a balloon.'" Entertainment Wkly

Smith, Tracy K.

Smith, Tracy K., 1972- **Ordinary** light; a memoir. Tracy K. Smith. Alfred A. Knopf 2015 368 p. (hardback) $25.95   **92**

1. Authors 2. Poets -- Psychology 3. Home -- Psychological aspects 4. Coming of age -- United States 5. Mothers -- United States -- Death 6. African Americans -- Race identity 7. Identity (Psychology) -- United States 8. Mothers and daughters -- United States 9. African American women authors -- Biography

ISBN 0307962660; 9780307962669

                LC 2014026185

National Book Award Finalist: Nonfiction (2015)

Tracy K. Smith "interrogates her childhood in suburban California, her first collision with independence at Harvard, and her Alabama-born parents' recollections of their own youth in the Civil Rights era. These dizzying juxtapositions . . . will in due course compel Tracy to act on her passions for love and 'ecstatic possibility,' and her desire to become a writer." (Publisher's note)

"Smith holds our intellectual and emotional attention ever so tightly as she charts her evolving thoughts on the divides between races, generations, economic classes, and religion and science and celebrates her lifesaving discovery of poetry as 'soul language.'" Booklist

Smithson, James, 1765-1829

Ewing, Heather P. The **lost** world of James Smithson; science, revolution, and the birth of the Smithsonian. [by] Heather Ewing. Bloomsbury 2007 432p il map $29.95   **92**

1. Chemists 2. Geologists 3. Scientists 4. Philanthropists 5. Smithsonian Institution -- History

ISBN 978-1-59691-029-4; 1-59691-029-1

This is a biography of the British chemist who founded the Smithsonian Institution in Washington, DC.

The author "provides a readable and informative perspective on late Enlightenment chemistry, backing it up with extensive archival research and forays into secondary literature on science." Times Lit Suppl

Includes bibliographical references

Snetsinger, Phoebe, 1931-1999

★ Gentile, Olivia. **Life** list; a woman's quest for the world's most amazing birds. Bloomsbury USA 2008 345p il $26   **92**

1. Bird watching 2. Bird watchers 3. Biography, Individual

ISBN 1-59691-169-7; 978-1-59691-169-7

                LC 2008-27036

This is a biography of birder Phoebe Snetsinger. Index.

Gentile describes Phoebe Snetsinger as a "frustrated stay-at-home wife and mother during the 1950s and 1960s who began birding to escape the boredom of suburban life. When she was diagnosed with terminal cancer at age 49, she decided to travel the world in search of birds while her health allowed. Each trip became a short-term goal for Phoebe and let her focus on birds instead of the cancer. She did this for 18 years, traveling between two and ten months a year, despite two cancer recurrences, injuries, assaults, kidnapping, and other difficulties. Phoebe eventually amassed

a life list of 8,674 species, or 85 percent of living birds then known." Libr J

Includes bibliographical references

Sneum, Thomas, 1917-2007

Ryan, Mark. **Hornet's** sting; the amazing untold story of World War II spy Thomas Sneum. Skyhorse Pub. 2009 386p il map $24.95   **92**

1. Spies 2. World War, 1939-1945 -- Secret service

ISBN 978-1-6023-9710-1

                LC 2009-6210

Sneum's "real-life exploits include all the key elements of any good spy story: sex, danger, and intrigue. . . . Readers will find the book hard to put down." Libr J

Includes bibliographical references

Snyder, John

★ Snyder, John. **Hill** of Beans; coming of age in the last days of the Old South. John Snyder. Natl Book Network 2011 256 p. $24.00   **92**

1. Family life 2. Southern States -- History 3. Great Depression, 1929-1939

ISBN 098306220X; 9780983062202

In this memoir, "[John] Snyder documents growing up in the Carolinas during the Great Depression . . . . Presenting remembrances from three geographic locations that shaped his young life, Snyder explores Cedar Mountain, N.C. . . . Greenville, S.C. . . . and the Snyder family farm in Walhalla, S.C. . . . Snyder also . . . profiles a wide range of family and friends—most notably his father, a hard man given to arcane phrases . . . and his Aunt Bess." (Publishers Weekly)

Includes bibliographical references and index.

Socrates

★ Hughes, Bettany. The **hemlock** cup; Socrates, Athens, and the search for the good life. Alfred A. Knopf 2011 484p il map $35   **92**

1. Philosophers 2. Athens (Greece) -- History

ISBN 978-1-4000-4179-4; 1-4000-4179-1

                LC 2010-45486

"For decades, while his city underwent war and hardship and defeat and civil war and political restructuring, Socrates settled himself in the agora and talked of inner things, the essence of things. Some of his words were taken down by acolytes such as Plato and Xenophon; some of his mannerisms were mocked by playwrights such as Aristophanes; the master himself, a man Hughes claims 'we can all benefit from getting to know a little better,' wrote nothing, but his recorded dialogues, his 'Socratic method' of relentless questioning, have become indispensable pieces of our Western mental furniture. Hughes revisits all of this with the panache of a born explainer, enthusiastically filling out the world of ancient Athens. . . . She takes readers through the torturous birth and early crises of Athenian democracy, and she's refreshingly evenhanded about the resentment such a democracy might feel toward somebody like Socrates." Washington Post

Includes bibliographical (p. 438-472) references

Johnson, Paul, 1928- **Socrates**; a man for our times. Viking 2011 208p $25.95   **92**

1. Philosophers

ISBN 978-0-670-02303-5

LC 2011019767

"A succinct, useful exploration of life in ancient Athens and of the great philosopher's essential beliefs." Kirkus

Includes bibliographical references

Sonnenberg, Susanna

Sonnenberg, Susanna. **Her** last death; a memoir. Scribner 2008 273p $24   **92**

1. Authors 2. Journalists 3. Columnists

ISBN 978-0-7432-9108-8; 0-7432-9108-5

LC 2007-3515

Sonnenberg's memoir illuminates her resolve to forge her independence, to become a woman capable of trust and to be a good mother to her own children after being raised by a mother who was a compulsive liar and a drug user.

"A heartbreaking yet wickedly entertaining portrait of a magically seductive, immensely flawed mother who fails dramatically as a parent and of a daughter who learns to trust and love others despite an orphanlike upbringing marked by disillusion." Libr J

Sontag, Susan, 1933-2004

Sontag, Susan. **Reborn**; journals and notebooks, 1947-1963. edited by David Rieff. Farrar, Straus and Giroux 2008 318p $24   **92**

1. Authors 2. Novelists 3. Women authors 4. Essayists 5. Literary critics 6. Authors, American 7. Short story writers

ISBN 978-0-374-10074-2; 0-374-10074-8

LC 2008-34247

"As a psychic collage, Reborn is far more fascinating than the sum of its parts: lists of errands, scraps of dialogue, notes on the breakup of a marriage. An essential tension animates almost every page. Sontag's theoretical mind always wants to be totalizing—to sum up, distill, command. But journal entries are, like the lives they document, provisional, incomplete, ragged. The resulting clash—with its canceled insights, non sequiturs, and self-critical marginalia—often reads like a brilliant pomo bildungsroman: A Portrait of the Theorist As a Young Woman." New York

Sorensen, Theodore C., 1928-2010

Sorensen, Theodore C., 1928-2010. **Counselor**; a life at the edge of history. [by] Ted Sorensen. HarperCollins 2008 556p il $27.95   **92**

1. Lawyers 2. Presidents 3. Senators 4. Members of Congress 5. Government officials 6. Biography, Individual 7. Presidential advisers 8. United States -- Politics and government -- 20th century

ISBN 0-06-079871-8; 978-0-06-079871-0

LC 2007-47328

This is a memoir by President Kennedy's advisor and speechwriter. Index.

"This book is instantly essential for any student of the period. It fills gaps in the historical record; it vividly conveys life inside the administration; and it generously dishes anecdotes." Washington Post Book World

Soto, Jock

Marshall, Leslie. **Every** step you take; a memoir. with Leslie Marshall. Harper 2011 271p il $24.99; ebook $11.99   **92**

1. Ballet dancers

ISBN 978-0-06-173238-6; 978-0-06-209798-9 ebook

LC 2011012725

"Acclaimed dancer Soto—a principal for the New York City Ballet for 20 years (1985–2005)—writes about his career, his Native American heritage, his homosexuality, his passion for cooking, his struggles to find a family and his discovery of love. . . . A powerful story, affectionately told, about the demands and dimensions of personal and professional success." Kirkus

Sotomayor, Sonia, 1954-

★ Sotomayor, Sonia, 1954- **My** beloved world; Sonia Sotomayor. Knopf 2013 ix, 315 p., [16] p. of platesp ill. (hardback) $27.95   **92**

1. Hispanic American women 2. Hispanic American women -- Biography 3. Judges -- United States -- Biography 4. Hispanic American judges -- Biography 5. United States. Supreme Court -- Officials and employees -- Biography

ISBN 0307594882; 9780307594884

LC 2012031797

Author Sonia Sotomayor presents an autobiography as "the first Hispanic and third woman appointed to the United States Supreme Court . . . She determined to become a lawyer, . . . from valedictorian of her high school class to the highest honors at Princeton, Yale Law School, the New York County District Attorney's office, private practice, and appointment to the Federal District Court before the age of forty." (Publisher's note)

"Graceful, authoritative memoir from the country's first Hispanic Supreme Court justice. . . . The author vividly narrates her scholarly adventures at Princeton, where she advocated for Latino faculty, and Yale Law School, where she dealt with smaller cases in preparation for the complexities of work in the district attorney's office. In 1992, she received an appointment to the U.S. District Court for the Southern District of New York. The author's text forms a cultural patchwork of memories and reflections as she mines the nuances of her parents' tumultuous relationship, fondly recalls family visits in Puerto Rico and offers insight on a judicial career that's just beginning when the memoir ends. . . . Mature, life-affirmative musings from a venerable life shaped by tenacity and pride." Kirkus

Soyinka, Wole

★ Soyinka, Wole. **You** must set forth at dawn; a memoir. Random House 2006 499p map $26.95 **92**

1. Poets 2. Authors 3. Novelists 4. Dramatists 5. Essayists 6. Memoirists 7. Nobel laureates for literature

ISBN 0-375-50365-X; 978-0-375-50365-8

"By turns panoramic and intimate, ruminative and politically resolute, Soyinka's memoir is a dense but intriguing conversation between a writer and his times." Publ Wkly

Spark, Muriel

Stannard, Martin. **Muriel** Spark; the biography. W.W. Norton & Co. 2010 xxvi, 627p il $35   92
1. Authors 2. Novelists 3. Women authors 4. Authors, Scottish 5. Biographers 6. Short story writers
ISBN 978-0-393-05174-2

LC 2009-47982

First published 2009 in the United Kingdom
This is "among the richest and most satisfying literary biographies of our time: not only a portrait of the artist herself but also a rendering of her literary and social context and a judicious examination of her works." Wall Street J
Includes bibliographical references

Speaker, Tris, 1888-1958

Gay, Timothy M. **Tris** Speaker; the rough-and-tumble life of a baseball legend. University of Nebraska Press 2005 314p il $27.95   92
1. Baseball players 2. Baseball managers
ISBN 0-8032-2206-8

LC 2005-16975

This is a "look at the Hall of Fame center fielder, whose colorful personality and remarkable talent were overshadowed by contemporaries like Ty Cobb and Cy Young. . . . Gay has insured the righting of history with this biography. A worthwhile read for any sports fan." Publ Wkly

Spector, Phil

★ Brown, Mick. **Tearing** down the wall of sound; the rise and fall of Phil Spector. Knopf 2007 452p il $26.95; pa $16.95   92
1. Record producers 2. Songwriters 3. Music arrangers 4. Recording producers
ISBN 978-1-4000-4219-7; 1-400-04219-4; 978-1-4000-7661-1 pa; 1-4000-7661-7 pa

LC 2007-4819

This is a biography of the record producer and songwriter.
"Stacked with incredible anecdotes, Brown's entertaining and nuanced portrait lifts the fog of myth and outright falsehood (including Spector's own) that have obscured the celebrity producer (like an enormous, gravity-defying wig) through the years." Publ Wkly
Includes bibliographical references

Speer, Albert, 1905-1981

Fest, Joachim C. **Speer**: the final verdict; {by} Joachim Fest; translated from the German by Ewald Osers and Alexandra Dring. Harcourt 2002 419p il $30; pa $15   92
1. Architects 2. War criminals 3. National socialism 4. Memoirists 5. Nazi leaders 6. Germany -- Politics and government -- 1933-1945
ISBN 0-15-100556-7; 0-15-602874-3 pa

LC 2002-6074

"This is a valuable, important biography, but perhaps it is an effort to explain the unexplainable." Booklist
Includes bibliographical references

Sereny, Gitta. **Albert** Speer; his battle with truth. Knopf 1995 757p il hardcover o.p. pa $25   92
1. Architects 2. War criminals 3. National socialism 4. Memoirists 5. Nazi leaders 6. Germany -- Politics and government -- 1933-1945
ISBN 0-679-76812-2 pa

LC 94-19764

The author of this biography of the Nazi war criminal "conducted intensive and protracted interviews with Speer . . . and many of the people who were close to him. Along with the interviews and analysis are good descriptions of what was happening in Germany throughout the Third Reich. Sereny's clear and concise prose makes this book suitable for both the scholar and the lay reader. She has produced what will become one of the standard works in Holocaust studies." Libr J
Includes bibliographical references

Spender, Stephen, 1909-1995

Sutherland, John. **Stephen** Spender; a literary life. Oxford University Press 2005 627p il $40 92
1. Poets 2. Authors 3. Novelists 4. Essayists 5. Memoirists 6. Biographers 7. Literary critics 8. Short story writers
ISBN 0-19517-816-5

LC 2004-09727

"Stephen Spender was one of a generation of Oxford-educated English writers, including W. H. Auden and Christopher Isherwood, who sought to revolutionize literature in the 1930s. In this official account of his life . . . emphasis is appropriately placed on the 1930s, when Spender came to prominence writing prose, short stories, criticism, and journalism in addition to his politically charged poetry. He was as experimental in life as in art, as evidenced by his bisexuality and his loyalty to left-wing Socialist causes." Libr J

Spiker, Ted

Down size; 12 truths for turning pants-splitting frustration into pants-fitting success. Ted Spiker; foreword by Mehmet C. Oz, MD. Hudson Street Press 2014 288 p. (hardback) $25.95   92
1. Weight loss 2. Overweight persons -- United States -- Biography
ISBN 1594631913; 9781594631917

LC 2014015115

In this book, author Ted Spiker "takes readers on an inspiring, candid, and comical journey, exploring the art and science of weight loss through his own struggles as a pear-shaped man in a not-so-pear-shaped world, with research about food, exercise, and the psychology of losing weight. He reveals twelve truths about successful weight loss, in areas such as temptation, frustration, nutrition, and inspiration." (Publisher's note)
"Most importantly, Spiker advocates personalized diets over a one-size-fits-all approach. Throughout the book, he gently nudges and encourages readers, winning their trust by sharing personal moments from his own weight-loss story." Pub Wkly

Sprague, Kate Chase, 1840-1899

Oller, John. **American** queen; the rise and fall of Kate Chase Sprague, Civil War "Belle of the North" and gilded age woman of scandal. John Oller. Da Capo Press, A Member of the Perseus Books Group 2014 416 p. illustrations (hardcover) $25.99 **92**
1. Chase, Salmon P. (Salmon Portland), 1808-1873 2. United States -- Politics and government -- 19th century 3. Socialites -- United States -- Biography
ISBN 0306822806; 9780306822803; 9780306822810
LC 2014012054

This book, by John Oller, focuses on the "daughter of Salmon P. Chase, Lincoln's treasury secretary, Kate Chase. As her widowed father's hostess, she . . . [had] hopes of making her father president and herself his First Lady. To facilitate that goal, she married one of the richest men in the country, the . . . governor of Rhode Island. . . . But when William Sprague turned out to be less of a prince as a husband, Kate found comfort in the arms of a powerful married senator." (Publisher's note)

"Oller's work is less the story of a woman's political rise and fall and more one that reveals how the social limitations of the past created tragic outcomes for talented females. A well-researched, thoughtful biography of a woman who 'became entirely her own person, a rare feat for women of her day.'" Kirkus

Includes bibliographical references and index

Springsteen, Bruce

Carlin, Peter Ames. **Bruce**; Peter Ames Carlin. Simon & Schuster 2012 xi, 494 p.p ill. **92**
1. Rock musicians -- Biography 2. Rock musicians -- United States -- Biography
ISBN 9781439191828; 9781439191835; 9781439191842
LC 2012020890

This book describes how, "For more than four decades, Bruce Springsteen has reflected the heart and soul of America with a career that includes twenty Grammy Awards, more than 120 million albums sold, two Golden Globes, and an Academy Award. [Author] Peter Ames Carlin . . . encompasses the breadth of Springsteen's astonishing career and explores the inner workings of a man who managed to redefine generations of music." (Publisher's note)

"The author presents his subject as a supremely gifted musician and truly heroic figure, albeit one with a lot on his troubled mind." Kirkus

Includes bibliographical references and index.

Stalin, Joseph, 1879-1953

Conquest, Robert. **Stalin**; breaker of nations. Viking 1991 346p il hardcover o.p. pa $14.95 **92**
1. Dictators 2. Heads of state 3. Communist leaders 4. Political leaders 5. Soviet Union -- Politics and government
ISBN 0-14-016953-9 pa
LC 91-28782

"Intended for the general reader, [this work] provides a superb portrait of the man who terrorized his country for 30 years. . . . Briskly written, authoritative yet not pedantic,

filled with interesting incidents and anecdotes, [it] makes for fascinating reading." N Y Times Book Rev

Includes bibliographical references

Khlevniuk, Oleg V. **Stalin**; new biography of a dictator. Oleg V. Khlevniuk; translated by Nora S. Favorov. Yale University Press 2015 408 p. 16 plates; illustrations (cloth : alk. paper) $35 **92**
1. Russia -- History -- 1917-1991, Soviet Union 2. Dictators -- Soviet Union -- Biography 3. Heads of state -- Soviet Union -- Biography 4. Soviet Union -- Politics and government -- 1936-1953
ISBN 0300163886; 9780300163889
LC 2014039237

This book, by Oleg V. Khlevniuk, translated by Nora S. Favorov, "offers an unprecedented, fine-grained portrait of [Joseph] Stalin the man and dictator. Without mythologizing Stalin as either benevolent or an evil genius, Khlevniuk resolves numerous controversies about specific events in the dictator's life while assembling many hundreds of previously unknown letters, memos, reports, and diaries into a . . . narrative of a life that altered the course of world history." (Publisher's note)

"Readers with an interest in Soviet history, and those who can't wait for the next two volumes of Kotkin's Stalin, will appreciate this well-documented portrayal of a man whose despotic rule reverberates in Russia to this day." LJ

Includes bibliographical references and index

★ Kotkin, Stephen. **Stalin**; Volume 1 Paradoxes of Power, 1878-1928. Stephen Kotkin. Penguin Group USA 2014 912 p. illustrations, maps hbk $40 **92**
1. Russia -- History -- 1917-1991, Soviet Union 2. Soviet Union -- History -- 1925-1953 3. Dictators -- Soviet Union -- Biography 4. Heads of state -- Soviet Union -- Biography 5. Political culture -- Soviet Union -- History 6. Soviet Union -- Politics and government -- 1917-1936 7. Soviet Union -- Politics and government -- 1936-1953
ISBN 9781594203794; 1594203792
LC 2014032906

Los Angeles Times Book Prizes Finalist: Biography (2014)

Pulitzer Prize Finalist: Biography or Autobiography (2015)

In this biography on Joseph Stalin, author Stephen Kotkin "gives an intimate view of the Bolshevik regime's inner geography of power. . . . Kotkin rejects the inherited wisdom about Stalin's psychological makeup, showing us instead how Stalin's near paranoia was fundamentally political, and closely tracks the Bolshevik revolution's structural paranoia, the predicament of a Communist regime in an overwhelmingly capitalist world, surrounded and penetrated by enemies." (Publisher's note)

"In this first volume of a planned three-volume biography, Kotkin . . . begins unraveling Stalin's strange, monstrous life. This is an epic, thoroughly researched account that presents a broad vision of Stalin, from his birth to his rise to absolute power." Pub Wkly

Includes bibliographical references and index

★ Montefiore, Sebag. **Stalin**: the court of the red tsar; by Simon Sebag Montefiore. Knopf 2004 xxvii, 785p il map $30   **92**

1. Dictators 2. Heads of state 3. Communist leaders 4. Political leaders 5. Soviet Union -- History

ISBN 1-400-04230-5

LC 2003-27390

First published 2003 in the United Kingdom

"In the relentless detail, the mood-setting descriptions of the leader's surroundings, the sketches of the people around him and in Stalin's own words, pranks and tempers, Montefiore gives us not only the most intimate view of the general secretary that we have to date but a rounded and complex portrait of a man who could go from charming to lethal in the space of a few seconds." Nation

Includes bibliographical references

★ Montefiore, Sebag. **Young** Stalin; [by] Simon Sebag Montefiore. Knopf 2007 xxxii, 460p il map $30   **92**

1. Dictators 2. Heads of state 3. Communist leaders 4. Political leaders 5. Soviet Union -- History

ISBN 1-4000-4465-0; 978-1-4000-4465-8

LC 2007-29220

Stalin "is brilliantly brought to life in this superb biography." Hist Today

Includes bibliographical references

Pringle, Peter. The **murder** of Nikolai Vavilov; the story of Stalin's persecution of one of the great scientists of the twentieth century. Simon & Schuster 2008 370p il $26   **92**

1. Botanists 2. Heads of state 3. Communist leaders 4. Plant geneticists 5. Political leaders

ISBN 978-0-7432-6498-3; 0-7432-6498-3

LC 2008-03510

This is a biography of the Russian botanist and geneticist who was starved to death in a Soviet prison in 1943.

This "is a must-read to grasp the ultimate, disasterous effect of politics trumping science." Sci Books Films

Includes bibliographical references

Radzinsky, Edvard. **Stalin**; the first in-depth biography based on explosive new documents from Russia's secret archives. translated by H.T. Willetts. Doubleday 1996 607p il hardcover o.p. pa $16.95   **92**

1. Dictators 2. Heads of state 3. Soviet Union 4. Communist leaders 5. Political leaders

ISBN 0-385-47954-9 pa

LC 95-4495

For this biography of the Soviet ruler the author "has examined mountains of rare archival sources and interviewed many who lived through decades of Stalinist (mis)rule. The result is the best general biography of Stalin to date. Radzinsky strips away layer after layer of myth, falsehood, and

enigma to produce a riveting portrait of a man whose primary role model was Ivan the Terrible." Libr J

Includes bibliographical references

Service, Robert. **Stalin**; a biography. Belknap Press of Harvard University Press 2005 715p il map $29.95   **92**

1. Dictators 2. Heads of state 3. Communist leaders 4. Political leaders 5. Soviet Union -- History

ISBN 0-674-01697-1

LC 2004-61115

This book covers Stalin's life "from his early, troubled years in a small town in Georgia to the pinnacle of power in the Kremlin. . . . By providing such a rich and complex portrait of the dictator and the Soviet system, Service humanizes Stalin without ever diminishing the extent of the atrocities he unleashed upon the Soviet population." Publ Wkly

Includes bibliographical references

Stanley, Henry M. (Henry Morton), 1841-1904

Jeal, Tim. **Stanley**; the impossible life of Africa's greatest explorer. Yale University Press 2007 570p il map $38   **92**

1. Explorers 2. Journalists 3. Travel writers

ISBN 978-0-300-12625-9; 0-300-12625-5

LC 2007-923548

This is a biography of the explorer.

"There have been many biographies of Stanley, but Jeal's is the most felicitous, the best informed, the most complete and readable and exhaustive." N Y Times Book Rev

Includes bibliographical references

Stanley, Ralph, 1927-2016

Stanley, Ralph. **Man** of constant sorrow; my life and times. [by] Ralph Stanley with Eddie Dean. Gotham Books 2009 452p $27.50   **92**

1. Bluegrass music 2. Banjo players 3. Bluegrass musicians

ISBN 978-1-592-40425-4

LC 2009-21920

A memoir by the bluegrass singer and banjo player.

"Unashamedly old-fashioned, opinionated and prickly, . . . [the author is] at his best recalling his backwoods upbringing, the vicissitudes of the bluegrass road, the murder of one of his lead singers, regional Democratic politics, the power of gospel music and old-time religion and the fast-vanishing South of his boyhood. An often tart yet affecting music memoir." Kirkus

Stanton, Edwin M. (Edwin McMasters), 1814-1869

Marvel, William. **Lincoln's** autocrat; the life of Edwin Stanton. William Marvel. University of North Carolina Press 2015 632 p. illustrations (Civil War America) (cloth : alk. paper) $35   **92**

1. Reconstruction (1865-1876) 2. Statesmen -- United States -- Biography 3. United States -- Politics and government -- 19th century 4. United States -- History -- 1861-1865, Civil War -- Biography 5. United States. War Department -- Biography 6. Cabinet officers -- United States -- Biography 7. Reconstruction (U.S. history, 1865-1877) -- Biography 8. United States --

Politics and government -- 1861-1865 9. United States -- Politics and government -- 1865-1869 10. United States -- History -- Civil War, 1861-1865 -- Biography
ISBN 1469622491; 9781469622491

LC 2014032690

This biography, by William Marvel, focuses on "Edwin M. Stanton, . . . Lincoln's Secretary of War during most of the Civil War and under Johnson during the early years of Reconstruction. . . . Climbing from a difficult youth to the pinnacle of power, Stanton used his authority--and the public coffers--to pursue political vendettas, and he exercised sweeping wartime powers with a cavalier disregard for civil liberties." (Publisher's note)

"A complex work that will appeal to Civil War scholars and general readers who want a deeper treatment of Stanton than found in Doris Kearns Goodwin's Team of Rivals." LJ

Includes bibliographical references and index

Life of Edwin M. Stanton

Stanton, Elizabeth Cady, 1815-1902

Ginzberg, Lori D. **Elizabeth** Cady Stanton; an American life. Hill and Wang 2009 254p il $25 **92**
1. Feminism 2. Suffragists 3. Women -- Suffrage 4. Biography, Individual 5. Women -- Suffrage -- History
ISBN 0-8090-9493-2; 978-0-8090-9493-6

LC 2008-54395

This is a biography of the women's rights activist and author of Eighty Years and More (1898). Bibliography. Index.

The author "makes a convincing case for Stanton as the founding philosopher of the American women's rights movement in a lively voice that enhances her eccentric subject. . . . Ginzberg has created a vibrant portrait of a key, often misrepresented figure in American history." Am Hist

Includes bibliographical references

Stanton, Tom

Stanton, Tom. **Road** to Cooperstown; a father, two sons, and the journey of a lifetime. Thomas Dunne Bks. 2003 260p il $24.95; pa $13.95 **92**
1. Artists 2. Painters 3. Baseball -- Biography 4. National Baseball Hall of Fame and Museum
ISBN 0-312-30350-5; 0-312-33118-5 pa

LC 2003-40862

Companion volume to The final season

The author "examines family, fatherhood, life and, of course, baseball while on a road trip that was a lifetime in the making." Publ Wkly

Staples, Mavis

Kot, Greg. **I'll** take you there; Mavis Staples, the Staple Singers, and the march up freedom's highway. Greg Kot. Scribner 2014 320 p. illustrations (hardback) $26 **92**
1. Staple Singers 2. Gospel musicians -- United States -- Biography
ISBN 1451647859; 9781451647853; 9781451647860

LC 2013032633

This book, by Greg Kot, is a biography of "Mavis Staples--lead singer of the Staple Singers and a major figure in the music that shaped the civil rights era. From her love affair with Bob Dylan, to her creative collaborations with Prince, to her recent revival alongside Wilco's Jeff Tweedy,

this . . . account shows Mavis as you've never seen her before. . . . Readers will also hear from Prince, Bonnie Raitt, David Byrne, Marty Stuart, Ry Cooder, Steve Cropper, and many other individuals." (Publisher's note)

"Kot's effort remains clear and respectful and takes us deep into the golden age of Mavis and her marvelously talented group." Pub Wkly

Includes bibliographical references, discography, and index

Stapp, John P. (John Paul), 1910-1999

Ryan, Craig. **Sonic** wind; the story of John Paul Stapp and how a renegade doctor became the fastest man on Earth. by Craig Ryan. Liveright Publishing Corp., A Division of W.W. Norton & Co. 2015 384 p. illustrations (hardcover) $27.95 **92**
1. Aeronautics 2. Biophysicists -- United States -- Biography 3. United States. Air Force -- Officers -- Biography 4. Aeronautics -- Safety measures -- Research -- United States -- History -- 20th century 5. Motor vehicles -- Safety appliances -- Research -- United States -- History -- 20th century
ISBN 0871406772; 9780871406774

LC 2015013245

This book, by Craig Ryan, is the "untold story of an eccentric, scientific visionary whose death-defying research has saved millions of lives. . . . The exploits of John Paul Stapp (1910-1999) come to thrilling life in this biography of a Renaissance man who was once blasted . . . across the desert in his Sonic Wind rocket sled, only to be slammed to a stop in barely a second. The experiment . . . revolutionize[d] automobile and aircraft design." (Publisher's note)

"A fine, groundbreaking biography of one of aeromedical sciences' more legendary figures." LJ

Includes bibliographical references and index

Steffens, Lincoln, 1866-1936

Steffens, Lincoln. The **autobiography** of Lincoln Steffens; foreword by Thomas C. Leonard. Heyday Books 2005 882p il (California legacy book) pa $21.95 **92**
1. Authors 2. Journalists 3. Essayists 4. Biographers 5. Social reformers 6. Writers on politics
ISBN 1-59714-016-3

LC 2005-27009

First published 1931 by Harcourt Brace & Co.

The life of an American reporter, journalist, student of ethics and politics.

"Here is a textbook on journalism; a treasure house for the historian of that wave of social idealism that shook the United States from 1900 to 1917; a casebook for the psychologist of political types. Above all it is the vivid diary of a bold and humane pilgrim." Survey

Stein, Gertrude, 1874-1946

Malcolm, Janet. **Two** lives; Gertrude and Alice. Yale University Press 2007 229p il $25 **92**
1. Poets 2. Authors 3. Novelists 4. Essayists 5. Memoirists 6. Literary critics 7. Authors, American 8. Private secretaries
ISBN 978-0-300-12551-1; 0-300-12551-8

LC 2007-12085

"This is a vital addition to Stein criticism as well as an important work that critiques the political responsibility of the artist (even a genius) to the larger world." Publ Wkly

Includes bibliographical references

Stein, Gertrude. The **autobiography** of Alice B. Toklas. Modern Lib. 1993 342p hardcover o.p. pa $13　　　　　　　　　　　　　　　　　　　**92**

1. Poets 2. Authors 3. Novelists 4. Essayists 5. Memoirists 6. Literary critics 7. Authors, American 8. Private secretaries 9. Paris (France) -- Intellectual life

ISBN 0-679-60081-7; 0-679-72463-X pa

LC 93-15339

First published 1933 by Harcourt Brace & Co.

"The book is really Stein's autobiography, presented as though written by her secretary, Alice Toklas. The book provoked a rejoinder from various Parisian artists and writers, Testimony Against Gertrude Stein (1935). . . . For the average reader, however, Stein's book holds much fascination in its views of Parisian life and personalities, and the whole is offered in a genuinely witty style." Benet's Reader's Ency of Am Lit

Steinberg, Neil

Steinberg, Neil. **Drunkard**; a hard-drinking life. Dutton 2008 270p $24.95; pa $15　　　　　　**92**

1. Journalists 2. Nonfiction writers 3. Alcoholics -- Rehabilitation

ISBN 978-0-5259-5065-3; 0-5259-5065-6; 978-0-4522-9543-8 pa

LC 2007-51603

"Forced by the court into rehab, Steinberg chronicles his journey to sobriety, following a circuitous route that included plenty of stops in local watering holes along the way. . . . Frank, funny, and insightful, Steinberg writes the book of his life." Booklist

Steinem, Gloria

Heilbrun, Carolyn G. The **education** of a woman; the life of Gloria Steinem. Ballantine Books 1996 450p il pa $23　　　　　　　　　　　**92**

1. Authors 2. Feminism 3. Journalists 4. Feminists 5. Memoirists 6. Magazine editors

ISBN 0-345-40621-4; 978-0-345-40621-7

First published 1995 by Dial Press

"The portrait that results is nuanced and thoughtful. . . . Heilbrun's goal is at once to understand how Steinem became the woman she is, and what her life can teach us about childhood and family, self and society. Slow at the start, but Heilbrun soon captures readers' interest and imagination." Booklist

Includes bibliographical references

My life on the road; Gloria Steinem. Random House Inc 2015 304 p. illustrations (hardback) $28　　　　　　　　　　　　　　　　　　　**92**

1. Feminism 2. Women's rights 3. Feminism -- United States 4. Feminists -- United States -- Biography

ISBN 0679456201; 9780679456209

LC 2015010718

This memoir by Gloria Steinem is "the moving, funny, and profound story of Gloria's growth and also the growth

of a revolutionary movement for equality-- and the story of how surprising encounters on the road shaped both. From her first experience of social activism among women in India to her work as a journalist in the 1960s; from the whirlwind of political campaigns to the founding of Ms. magazine." (Publisher's note)

"Illuminating and inspiring, this book presents a distinguished woman's exhilarating vision of what it means to live with openness, honesty, and a willingness to grow beyond the apparent confinement of seemingly irreconcilable polarities. An invigoratingly candid memoir from a giant of women's rights." Kirkus

Stern, Jessica, 1958-

Stern, Jessica. **Denial**; a memoir of terror. Ecco Press 2010 300p $24.99; ebook $11.99　　　　**92**

ISBN 978-0-06-162665-4; 978-0-06-200011-8 ebook

A scientist and expert on terrorism and post-traumatic stress disorder describes her own journey through trauma and its lingering effects after repressing and disassociating her own ordeal as the victim of an unsolved sexual assault as a teenager.

"Though the narrative continually threatens to spiral into stream-of-consciousness ramblings, Stern always manages to hold it together, thus lending a sense of the floating dissociation she often feels while still holding the narrative together as a cohesive whole. She successfully unearths difficult emotional terrain without sinking into utter subjectivity and maintains an orderly progression without becoming clinical. A disturbing, captivating memoir." Kirkus

Includes bibliographical references

Steward, Samuel M., 1909-1993

Spring, Justin. **Secret** historian; the life and times of Samuel Steward, professor, tattoo artist, and sexual renegade. Farrar, Straus and Giroux 2010 478p il $32.50; ebook $16.99　　　　　　　　　　　　**92**

1. Authors 2. Novelists 3. Tattoo artists 4. College teachers 5. Authors, American 6. Short story writers 7. Biography, Individual

ISBN 0-374-28134-3; 1-4299-3294-5 ebook; 978-0-374-28134-2; 978-1-4299-3294-3 ebook

LC 2009-43086

This book is "drawn from the secret diaries and journals of novelist, poet, and university professor Samuel M. Steward." (Publisher's note) Index.

"This is a rich and exuberant biography of a man who deserves to be better known, as well as a rare window on gay life in an era known mostly for its furtiveness and repression." Economist

Includes bibliographical references

Stoller, Mike, 1933-

Leiber, Jerry. **Hound** dog; the Leiber & Stoller autobiography. [by] Jerry Leiber and Mike Stoller with David Ritz. Simon & Schuster 2009 322p il $25　　　　　　　　　　　　　　　　　　　**92**

1. Composers 2. Lyricists 3. Songwriters 4. Rock music -- History and criticism

ISBN 978-1-4165-5938-2; 1-4165-5938-8

LC 2008-47821

"Collaboration is a messy business. So is autobiography. But it shouldn't be forgotten that Leiber and Stoller were among the pioneers who helped bring black and white musical forms together. It has been a historically fraught process, but the collision of cultures is probably what has given such energy and tension to American music. Hound Dog is an important part of that story." N Y Times Book Rev

Includes bibliographical references

Stone, I. F. (Isidor Feinstein), 1907-1989

Guttenplan, D. D. **American** radical; the life and times of I. F. Stone. Farrar, Straus and Giroux 2009 570p il $35   **92**

1. Authors 2. Journalists 3. Magazine editors
ISBN 978-0-374-18393-6; 0-374-18393-7
     LC 2009-09667

This is a biography of the American journalist who published I.F. Stone's Weekly from 1953 until 1971.

"Guttenplan's lively biography brings back to life a man whose work has often been forgotten but whose writing and life provide a model for the kind of freethinking journalism missing in society today." Publ Wkly

Includes bibliographical references (p. [483]-538) and index. (BLCM)

★ MacPherson, Myra. **All** governments lie; the life and times of rebel journalist I.F. Stone. Scribner 2006 564p il hardcover o.p. pa $20   **92**

1. Authors 2. Journalists 3. Magazine editors
ISBN 978-0-684-80713-3; 0-684-80713-0; 978-1-4165-5679-4 pa; 1-4165-5679-6 pa
     LC 2006-42389

"This biography interweaves his life and journalism within the context of the social and political era, providing an engaging overview of a complex man who challenged his contemporaries. Many of the political issues Stone confronted will resonate with today's readers." Libr J

Includes bibliographical references

Stone, Robert, 1937-

Stone, Robert. **Prime** green; remembering the sixties. Ecco 2007 229p il $25.95   **92**

1. Authors 2. Novelists 3. Screenwriters 4. United States -- History -- 1961-1974
ISBN 0-06-019816-8; 978-0-06-019816-9
     LC 2006-46351

The author "is a born storyteller, with a wonderful feel for place and character that vividly evokes the cultural gulf America crossed in that decade." Publ Wkly

Stowe, Harriet Beecher, 1811-1896

Hedrick, Joan D. **Harriet** Beecher Stowe; a life. Oxford Univ. Press 1994 507p il hardcover o.p. pa $19.95   **92**

1. Authors 2. Novelists 3. Abolitionists 4. Children's authors 5. Nonfiction writers 6. Short story writers
ISBN 0-19-509639-8 pa
     LC 93-16610

This biography "brings to life not just the complex and fascinating woman and writer but also the 19th-century America that shaped her and was in turn shaped by her. Hedrick manages to weave into her immensely readable biogra-

phy a history teeming with the domestic detail of the famous Beecher clan, the settling of the West, and the impact of the Civil War and the abolition movement." Libr J

Includes bibliographical references

Stravinsky, Igor, 1882-1971

Joseph, Charles M. **Stravinsky** inside out. Yale Univ. Press 2001 xx, 320p il $29.95   **92**

1. Composers
ISBN 0-300-07537-5
     LC 2001-913

This study "reveals a . . . flawed and fragile human being, who craved approval, dealt ungenerously with colleagues, loved James Bond movies, and tried hard to further his son's musical career. Although the aged Stravinsky's eagerness to play the role of celebrity composer for the golden age of television . . . was an embarrassment, most of these episodes testify to the protean survival skills of an artist whose sense of identity was always in flux and whose cunning was commensurate with his talent." New Yorker

Includes bibliographical references and index

Joseph, Charles M. **Stravinsky** inside out. Yale Univ. Press 2001 xx, 320p il $29.95   **92**

1. Composers
ISBN 0-300-07537-5
     LC 2001-913

This study "reveals a . . . flawed and fragile human being, who craved approval, dealt ungenerously with colleagues, loved James Bond movies, and tried hard to further his son's musical career. Although the aged Stravinsky's eagerness to play the role of celebrity composer for the golden age of television . . . was an embarrassment, most of these episodes testify to the protean survival skills of an artist whose sense of identity was always in flux and whose cunning was commensurate with his talent." New Yorker

Includes bibliographical references

Walsh, Stephen. **Stravinsky**: a creative spring; Russia and France, 1882-1934. University of California Press 2002 698p il pa $25.95   **92**

1. Composers
ISBN 978-0-520-22749-1; 0-520-22749-2
     LC 2002-23256

First published 1999 by Knopf

"In this reference-oriented biography, Walsh uses diaries, press clippings, and other materials to probe in detail the life of a man kept very busy with effectively dividing his time between performance, composition, family, and mistress." Booklist

Includes bibliographical references

Walsh, Stephen. **Stravinsky**: the second exile; France and America, 1934-1971. Stephen Walsh. Alfred A. Knopf 2006 709p il $40   **92**

1. Composers
ISBN 0-375-40752-9
     LC 2005-47231

Sequel to Stravinsky: a creative spring

"This is essential reading for musicologists and other music enthusiasts who wish to delve into the life and mind of perhaps the greatest composer of the 20th century." Libr J

Includes bibliographical references

Strayed, Cheryl, 1968-

Strayed, Cheryl. **Wild**; from lost to found on the Pacific Crest Trail. Cheryl Strayed. Alfred A. Knopf 2012 315 p. map **92**

1. Hiking 2. Bereavement 3. Pacific Crest Trail 4. Mountains -- North America 5. Women authors -- Biography 6. Pacific Crest Trail -- Description and travel 7. Authors, American -- 21st century -- Biography

ISBN 9780307592736; 0307592731

LC 2011033752

The author "recounts her experience hiking the Pacific Crest Trail (PCT) in 1995 after her mother's death and her own subsequent divorce. Designated a National Scenic Trail in 1968 but not completed until 1993, the PCT runs from Mexico to Canada, and [Cheryl] Strayed hiked sections of it two summers after it was officially declared finished. She takes readers with her on the trail, and the transformation she experiences on its course is significant: she goes from feeling out of her element with a too-big backpack and too-small boots to finding a sense of home in the wilderness and with the allies she meets along the way. . . . [She includes] descriptions of the natural wonders near the PCT, particularly Mount Hood, Crater Lake, and the Sierras--what John Muir proclaimed the 'Range of Light.'" (Libr J)

Streb, Elizabeth

Streb, Elizabeth. **Streb**; how to become an extreme action hero. foreword by Anna Deavere Smith & introduction by Peggy Phelan. Feminist Press 2010 201p il pa $18.95 **92**

1. Dance 2. Dancers 3. Choreographers 4. Human locomotion 5. Biography, Individual 6. Movement, Psychology of 7. Human beings -- Attitude and movement

ISBN 978-1-55861-656-1

LC 2009-52614

"Elizabeth Streb has been testing the potential of the human body since childhood. Can she fly? Can she run up walls? Can she break through glass? How fast can she go? Combining memoir and theory, Streb [aims to] convey how she became an extreme action choreographer, developing a form of movement that's more NASCAR than modern dance, more boxing than ballet." (Publisher's note) Index.

"In this dizzying, inspirational self-help memoir, choreographer and performer Streb details her lifelong exploration of movement, the body, and time while providing brief lessons in math and practical philosophy. . . . In her explanations and experiments, including an unprotected and unrehearsed dive through glass, Streb gives readers news ways to consider the body and its movement, from 'the mechanical measurement of the legs, arms, torso, neck, hips, feet, shoulders, ankles, and knees' to 'the alchemic processes of the neurological systems.' Accompanied by full-color and black-and-white photographs, Streb's riveting prose should provoke and inspire philosophy students, dancers, and athletes of all kinds." Publ Wkly

Includes bibliographical references

Streisand, Barbra

Mann, William J. **Hello,** gorgeous; becoming Barbra Streisand. William J. Mann. Houghton Mifflin Harcourt 2012 576 p. (hardback) $30.00 **92**

1. Fame 2. Singers 3. Singers -- United States -- Biography

ISBN 0547368925; 9780547368924

LC 2012016364

In this book, "[b]estselling biographer [William J.] Mann . . . chronicles the . . . series of events as [Barbra] Streisand 'gate-crashed her way to fame.' Mann tightens the focus in this . . . volume to just the early, formative years of her career, choosing 1964 as his cutoff point. . . . The marketing of Streisand and the men in her life are key themes throughout." (Publishers Weekly)

Includes bibliographical references and index.

Strouse, Charles

Strouse, Charles. **Put** on a happy face; a Broadway memoir. Union Square Press 2008 326p il $19.95 **92**

1. Composers 2. Musicians 3. Composers -- United States

ISBN 978-1-4027-5889-8; 1-4027-5889-8

LC 2008-300247

"Three-time Tony Award–winning composer Strouse is best known for the musical Annie and his All in the Family theme, 'Those Were the Days.' While wary of the ghosts that appear, he summons up memories of a career that spans decades, beginning with his Manhattan boyhood, study at Rochester's Eastman School of Music, touring the South with Butterfly McQueen and early collaborations with lyricist Lee Adams. . . . Although he covers his film scores and music for TV commercials, the book's best chapters center on the staging struggles of Annie and Applause, plus breaking racial barriers with Sammy Davis Jr. in Golden Boy. . . . Detailing desperate rewrites, insecurities of theater people, footlight failures and humiliations, as well as theatrical triumphs, Strouse's superb backstage memoir deserves a standing ovation." Publ Wkly

Stuart, Granville, 1834-1918

Milner, Clyde A. **As** big as the West; the pioneer life of Granville Stuart. [by] Clyde A. Milner II and Carol A. O'Connor. Oxford University Press 2009 430p il map $34.95 **92**

1. Miners 2. Diplomats 3. Merchants 4. Frontier and pioneer life 5. Montana 6. Pioneers 7. Ranchers

ISBN 978-0-19-512709-6; 0-19-512709-9

"In fully revealing Stuart's fascinating and complex life, Milner and O'Connor illuminate the conflicting realities of the frontier." Libr J

Includes bibliographical references and index

Stuart, Jeb, 1833-1864

Wert, Jeffry D. **Cavalryman** of the lost cause; a biography of J.E.B. Stuart. Simon & Schuster 2008 496p il map $32; pa $18 **92**

1. Generals 2. Confederate States of America -- Army 3. United States -- History -- 1861-1865, Civil War

ISBN 978-0-7432-7819-5; 0-7432-7819-4; 978-0-

7432-7824-9 pa; 0-7432-7824-0 pa

LC 2007-51552

This is a chronicle of the life of "the controversial cavalry leader of the Army of Northern Virginia until his death in combat in 1864. Wert's thoughtful account of Stuart's role at Gettysburg eventuates in a balanced analysis of a well-conceived reconnaissance-in-force. . . . This is a portrait of a Stuart more complex and, indeed, more attractive than either his friends or his enemies have painted in at least a generation." Booklist

Includes bibliographical references

Stuart, Sarah Payne

Stuart, Sarah Payne. **Perfectly** miserable; guilt, God and real estate in a small town. Sarah Payne Stuart. Riverhead Hardcover 2014 320 p. illustrations (hardback) $27.95 **92**

1. Autobiographies 2. Mother-daughter relationship 3. American literature -- New England 4. Authors, American -- 20th century -- Biography 5. Authors, American -- 21st century -- Biography

ISBN 1594631816; 9781594631818

LC 2013048095

"At eighteen, Sarah Payne Stuart fled her mother and all the other disapproving mothers of her too perfect hometown of Concord, Massachusetts, only to return years later when she had children of her own. Whether to defy the previous generation or finally earn their approval and enter their ranks, she hurled herself into upper-crust domesticity. . . . When Stuart's own mother dies, she realizes that there is no one left to approve or disapprove." (Publisher's note)

Sullivan, Ed, 1902-1974

Maguire, James. **Impresario**; the life and times of Ed Sullivan. Billboard Books 2006 344p il $24.95 **92**

1. Television personalities 2. Columnists

ISBN 0-8230-7962-7; 978-0-8230-7962-9 ISBN-13

The author "has written a fascinating biography and meticulously recorded the birth of TV, the heyday of newspaper columnists and the glamour of New York." Publ Wkly

Surville, Jean Francois de, 1717-1770

Blainey, Geoffrey. **Sea** of dangers; Captain Cook and his rivals in the South Pacific. Ivan R. Dee 2009 322p il map $27.50 **92**

1. Explorers 2. Voyages around the world 3. Ship captains 4. Naval officers 5. Travel writers 6. Oceania -- Exploration

ISBN 978-1-56663-825-8; 1-56663-825-9

LC 2008-52623

"An excellent work of popular history that recounts the exploits of men who dramatically expanded our knowledge of the globe." Booklist

Includes bibliographical references

Swift, Jonathan, 1667-1745

★ Damrosch, Leo. **Jonathan** Swift; his life and his world. Leo Damrosch. Yale University Press 2013 573 p. illustrations, maps (The Lewis Walpole Series in Eighteenth-Century Culture and History) (clothbound : alk. paper) $35 **92**

1. Authors, Irish 2. Authors, Irish -- 18th century -- Biography

ISBN 0300164998; 9780300164992

LC 2013013063

Pulitzer Prize Finalist: Biography or Autobiography (2014)

"In this . . . biography, Leo Damrosch draws on discoveries made over the past thirty years to tell the story of [Jonathan] Swift's life anew. Probing holes in the existing evidence, he takes seriously some daring speculations about Swift's parentage, love life, and various personal relationships and shows how Swift's public version of his life--the one accepted until recently--was deliberately misleading." (Publisher's note)

"A rich and rewarding portrait of an irreplaceable genius." Kirkus

Includes bibliographical references and index

Sylvester II, Pope, ca. 945-1003

Brown, Nancy Marie. The **abacus** and the cross; the story of the pope who brought the light of science to the Dark Ages. Basic Books 2010 310p il map $27.95 **92**

1. Popes 2. Religion and science 3. Biography, Individual

ISBN 9780465009503; 0465009506

LC 2010-36361

"As readably knowledgeable about Gerbert's political fortunes as about his intellectual influence, Brown is a lively narrator and interesting interpreter of Gerbert's life and world. This portrait gives both the science and the history audiences something to talk about." Booklist

Includes bibliographical references and index.

Taft, Helen Herron, 1861-1943

Anthony, Carl Sferrazza. **Nellie** Taft; the unconventional first lady of the ragtime era. 1st ed; William Morrow 2005 534p il $29.95; pa $15.95 **92**

1. Spouses of presidents

ISBN 0-06-051382-9; 0-06-051383-7 pa

LC 2004-52553

"This lively biography provides an illuminating glimpse into the life of an until-now underappreciated First Lady." Booklist

Includes bibliographical references

Tallchief, Maria

Tallchief, Maria. **Maria** Tallchief; America's prima ballerina. [by] Maria Tallchief with Larry Kaplan. University Press of Florida 2005 368p pa $19.95 **92**

1. Ballet dancers 2. Dance teachers 3. Ballerinas -- United States -- Biography. 4. Osage Indians -- United States -- Biography. 5. Indian ballerinas -- United States -- Biography.

ISBN 0-8130-2846-9; 978-0-8130-2846-0

LC 2005-42211

First published 1997 by Henry Holt

In this memoir Tallchief focuses "on her remembrances of her years with choreographer George Balanchine. . . . She met Balanchine at the start of her career, when she was with the Ballet Russe de Monte Carlo and Balanchine was about to form a company that would become a precursor to the New York City Ballet. Tallchief subsequently became Balanchine's wife, muse, and prima ballerina, and, though the marriage was short-lived, their artistic partnership endures in Balanchine's works created for Tallchief. She also writes about other stars, but the memoir sparkles when she recalls the subtlety and detail of a movement or the beauty of a musical phrase." Libr J

Tammet, Daniel, 1979-

Tammet, Daniel. **Born** on a blue day; inside the extraordinary mind of an autistic savant: a memoir. Free Press 2007 226p il $24; pa $14   **92**
1. Autism 2. Asperger's syndrome 3. Savants (Savant syndrome) 4. Mental calculators
ISBN 1-4165-3507-1; 978-1-4165-3507-2; 1-4165-4901-3 pa; 978-1-4165-4901-7 pa

LC 2006-41331
First published 2006 in the United Kingdom
This "autobiography is as fascinating as Benjamin Franklin's and John Stuart Mill's, both of which are, like his, about the growth of a mind." Booklist

Taylor, Barbara Brown

Taylor, Barbara Brown. An **altar** in the world; a geography of faith. HarperOne 2008 216p $24.99 **92**
1. Clergy 2. Spiritual life 3. Religious scholars 4. Writers on religion
ISBN 978-0-06-137046-5

LC 2008-18303
"Taylor is one of those rare people who truly can see the holy in everything. Since everyone should know such a person, those who don't can—no, must—read this book, with its friendly reminders of everyday sacred." Publ Wkly

Taylor, Elizabeth, 1932-2011

Kashner, Sam. **Furious** love; Elizabeth Taylor, Richard Burton, and the marriage of the century. [by] Sam Kashner and Nancy Schoenberger. Harper 2010 500p il $27.99   **92**
1. Actors
ISBN 978-0-06-156284-6; 0-06-156284-X

LC 2010-06732
"In this dual biography of the two legendary film stars, the authors draw upon new information, including interviews with Elizabeth Taylor and with the Burton family, to capture the famously passionate and tumultuous relationship between the legendary couple. . . . It's a mesmerizing tale, but it's also sad, and sometimes ugly, as the two stars engaged in vicious fights, nursed their jealousies and insecurities, and descended into alcoholism while outwardly living a life of glamour and sophistication." Booklist
Includes bibliographical references

Taylor, Major, 1878-1932

Balf, Todd. **Major**; a Black athlete, a White era, and the fight to be the world's fastest human being. Crown Publishers 2008 306p il $24; pa $13.95 **92**
1. Bicycle racing 2. African American athletes 3.

Cyclists
ISBN 978-0-307-23658-6; 0-307-23658-7; 978-0-307-23659-3 pa; 0-307-23659-5 pa

LC 2007-20747
The author "chronicles the life of the unlikeliest of stars in the early years of cycling: Marshall 'Major' Taylor. Taylor was an incomparable athlete, poet and celebrity, but he was also a black man living during a time when the scars of the Civil War and slavery were still fresh in the minds of Americans. Balf . . . does great work presenting the complex nature of Taylor's life, including his upbringing in poverty in Indianapolis, the years he was treated as a son by a rich white family, the fans who both worshipped and vilified him and his close relationships with his white trainer and promoter." Publ Wkly
Includes bibliographical references

Teffi, N. A. (Nadezhda Aleksandrovna), 1872-1952

Teffi, N. A. (Nadezhda Aleksandrovna), 1872-1952. **Memories**; from Moscow to the Black Sea. by Teffi; translated by Robert and Elizabeth Chandler, Anne-Marie Jackson and Irina Steinberg; introduction by Edythe Haber. New York Review Books 2016 240 p. illustration (alk. paper) $16.95 **92**
1. Women authors 2. Russia -- History -- 1917-1921, Revolution 3. Women authors, Russian -- 20th century -- Biography 4. Soviet Union -- History -- Revolution, 1917-1921 -- Personal narratives
ISBN 9781590179512

LC 2015043142
This book, by Teffi, is a "personal account of the author's last months in Russia and Ukraine. . . . In 1918, in the immediate aftermath of the Russian Revolution, Teffi, who stories and journalism had made her a celebrity in Moscow, was invited to read from her work in Ukraine. She accepted the invitation eagerly, though she had every intention of returning home. As it happened, her trip ended four years later in Paris, where she would spend the rest of her life in exile." (Publisher's note)

Teller, Edward, 1908-2003

★ Goodchild, Peter. **Edward** Teller, the real Dr Strangelove. Harvard University Press 2004 xxv, 469p il $29.95   **92**
1. Physicists 2. Writers on science
ISBN 0-674-01669-6

LC 2004-54257
This is a biography of "the 'father of the hydrogen bomb,' a witness against J. Robert Oppenheimer in the latter's security hearing, and, finally, an ardent promoter of the Cold War arms race. . . . {The author} studied a wide range of primary and secondary sources and interviewed many people on both sides of the controversies that swirled around Teller. The result is a remarkably well-balanced study of a notoriously prickly and opinionated person." Libr J
Includes bibliographical references

Teller, Edward. **Memoirs**; a twentieth-century journey in science and politics. {by} Edward Teller with Judith Shoolery. Perseus Bks. 2001 628p il hardcover o.p. pa $18.95   **92**

1. Physicists 2. Writers on science

ISBN 0-7382-0778-0 pa

This memoir, by the nuclear physicist who worked to develop the hydrogen bomb, recounts his origins in the scientific community in Germany prior to the Nazi takeover and describes his "work on safe proliferation of nuclear energy, the so-called Stars Wars defense system and the early detection of earth-crossing objects. . . . Readers can enjoy these panoramic and beautifully written recollections of one of the great scientific, if controversial, figures of all time." Publ Wkly

Includes bibliographical references

Teresa, Mother, 1910-1997

Spink, Kathryn. **Mother** Teresa; a complete authorized biography. by Kathryn Spink. HarperOne 2011 336 p. ill. $15.99   **92**

1. Nuns 2. Nobel Prizes 3. Missions -- India 4. Christian missionaries 5. Biography, Individual 6. Missionaries of Charity

ISBN 0062026143; 9780062026149

LC 2011001621

"Spink's biography benefits from her own 18-year involvement with the work of the Missionaries of Charity Order as well as from the intimate relationship she developed over the years with Mother Teresa. . . . A final chapter in the book provides glimpses of Mother Teresa's affection for Princess Diana, a brief description of Mother Teresa's funeral and a short account of the election of Sister Nirmal as her successor." (Publ Wkly)

Terkel, Studs, 1912-2008

Terkel, Studs, 1912-2008. **Touch** and go; a memoir. [by] Studs Terkel, with Sydney Lewis. New Press 2007 269p il $24.95   **92**

1. Authors 2. Historians 3. Talk show hosts 4. Authors, American 5. Television moderators

ISBN 978-1-59558-043-6; 1-59558-043-3

LC 2007-18673

"Terkel's memoir is . . . a medley of all the extraordinary characters he's encountered through his career, from the adult loners of his youth in Chicago's Wells-Grand Hotel, to New Deal politicians. Terkel details his long journey through law school, the air force, theater, radio, early television, sports commentary, jazz criticism and oral history. . . . Americans might get to know their collective past a lot better if all history lessons were as absorbing and entertaining as this one." Publ Wkly

Tesla, Nikola, 1856-1943

Carlson, W. Bernard. **Tesla**; inventor of the electrical age. W. Bernard Carlson. Princeton University Press 2013 xiii, 500 p.p ill. (hardcover) $29.95 **92**

1. Electricity -- History 2. Inventors -- United States -- Biography 3. Electrical engineers -- United States -- Biography

ISBN 0691057761; 9780691057767

LC 2012049608

This book, by W. Bernard Carlson, presents a biography of the inventor Nikola Tesla, "a major contributor to the electrical revolution . . . at the turn of the twentieth century. His inventions, patents, and theoretical work formed the basis of modern AC electricity, and contributed to the development of radio and television. . . . An astute self-promoter and gifted showman, he cultivated a public image of the eccentric genius." (Publisher's note)

"Carlson provides not only a more detailed explanation of Tesla's science but also a . . . focused psychological account of Tesla's inventive process." Booklist

Includes bibliographical references and index

Thatcher, Margaret

Moore, Charles. **Margaret** Thatcher; At Her Zenith: In London, Washington and Moscow. Charles Moore. Alfred A. Knopf 2013 821 p. illustrations (v. 2 : hardcover) $35   **92**

1. Prime ministers -- Great Britain 2. Great Britain -- Politics and government 3. Prime ministers -- Great Britain -- Biography 4. Conservative Party (Great Britain) -- Biography 5. Women prime ministers -- Great Britain -- Biography 6. Great Britain -- Politics and government -- 1979-1997

ISBN 9780307958969; 0307958965

LC 2013020670

In this biographical book, author Charles Moore, "reveals as never before how Mrs. [Margaret] Thatcher transformed relations with Europe, privatized the commanding heights of British industry. . . . It describes her role on the world stage with dramatic immediacy, identifying Mikhail Gorbachev as 'a man to do business with' before he became a leader of the Soviet Union . . . and Ronald Reagan, her great ideological soul mate, to order world affairs according to her vision." (Publisher's note)

"A chronology of world events, copious notes, and an extensive bibliography enhance an exhaustive narrative that will fascinate students of contemporary British history and politics." Booklist

Includes bibliographical references and index

★ Moore, Charles. **Margaret** Thatcher; The Authorized Biography: From Grantham to the Falklands. Charles Moore. Knopf 2013 896 p. (v. 1 : hardcover) $35   **92**

1. Prime ministers -- Great Britain -- Biography 2. Conservative Party (Great Britain) -- Biography 3. Women prime ministers -- Great Britain -- Biography 4. Great Britain -- Politics and government -- 1979-1997

ISBN 9780307958945; 0307958949

LC 2013020670

This "authorized biography of Margaret Thatcher reveals . . . the early life, rise to power, and first years as prime minister of the woman who transformed Britain and the world in the late twentieth century. [Author Charles] Moore has had unique access to all of Thatcher's private and governmental papers, and interviewed her and her family extensively for this book." (Publisher's note)

Includes bibliographical references and index

Thomas, Abigail, 1941-

Thomas, Abigail. A **three** dog life. Harcourt 2006 182p $22   **92**

1. Authors 2. Novelists 3. Short story writers
ISBN 978-0-15-101211-4; 0-15-101211-3

LC 2005-33782

"Thomas has elevated what could be, at best, an over-emotional sermon or, at worst, a grim romp in self-pity to a high plain of true inspiration." Booklist

What Comes Next and How to Like It; A Memoir. Abigail Thomas. Simon & Schuster 2015 240 p. $24   **92**

1. Widows 2. Adjustment (Psychology)
ISBN 1476785058; 9781476785059

LC 2015295750

This book is a "memoir about many things, but at the center is a steadfast friendship between [author] Abigail Thomas and a man she met thirty-five years ago. Through marriages, child-raising, the vicissitudes and tragedies of life, it is this deep, rich bond that has sustained her." (Publisher's note)

"This episodic memoir is full of love and life. Readers will identify with the feelings and the people even as they realize how different they are, how wondrous." Booklist

Thomas, Dylan, 1914-1953

Lycett, Andrew. **Dylan** Thomas: a new life. Overlook Press 2004 434p il $35   **92**

1. Poets 2. Authors
ISBN 1-58567-541-5

First published 2003 in the United Kingdom

"Other biographies . . . have ably recounted the essential details of Thomas's life, but Lycett here provides a wealth of useful detail, bringing the Welsh poet's life story up to date." Libr J

Includes bibliographical references

Thomas, Becket, Saint, 1118?-1170

Guy, John. **Thomas** Becket; warrior, priest, rebel : a nine-hundred-year-old story retold. John Guy. Random House 2011 424 p.   **92**

1. Biography 2. Christian saints 3. Christianity and politics 4. Great Britain -- History -- 1066-1154, Norman period 5. Statesmen -- Great Britain -- Biography 6. Christian saints -- England -- Biography 7. Christian martyrs -- England -- Biography 8. Great Britain -- History -- Henry II, 1154-1189 -- Biography
ISBN 1400069076; 9780679603412; 9781400069071

LC 2011042794

This book by John Guy presents a biography "of Thomas Becket (1118-1170), the man who refused to subordinate the power of the church to the power of the state, and was martyred for it. . . . Distilling and disputing materials from several previous Becket biographies, Guy traces his subject's development from a handsome, superficial, and socially ambitious youth to a mature man who rose intellectually, morally, and politically to become lord chancellor to Henry II. In 1162, he was named archbishop of Canterbury, a position he accepted reluctantly, knowing that his honest exercise of the office as a defender of liberty and as one who would assert the church's power to cancel unjust state laws would bring him into conflict with Henry." (Publishers Weekly)

Includes bibliographical references and index.

Thompson, Hunter S., 1937-2005

McKeen, William. **Outlaw** journalist; the life and times of Hunter S. Thompson. W. W. Norton 2008 428p il $27.95; pa $16.95   **92**

1. Authors 2. Novelists 3. Journalists 4. Satirists 5. Columnists 6. Nonfiction writers
ISBN 978-0-393-06192-5; 0-393-06192-2; 978-0-393-33545-3 pa; 0-393-33545-3 pa

LC 2008-13214

This is a biography of the journalist and author of Hell's Angels (1967), Fear and Loathing in Las Vegas (1972), The Great Shark Hunt (1979) and Generation of Swine (1988).

"The book does justice to the legend that was Thompson. The thorough reporting lends insight to a writer who was as much a personality as a scribe." Am Journalism

Includes bibliographical references

Thompson, Hunter S. The **kingdom** of fear; loathsome secrets of a star-crossed child in the final days of the American century. Simon & Schuster 2003 xx, 354p il hardcover o.p. pa $16   **92**

1. Authors 2. Novelists 3. Journalists 4. Satirists 5. Columnists 6. Nonfiction writers
ISBN 0-684-87323-0; 978-0-684-87324-4; 0-684-87324-9 pa

LC 2002-191228

In this book the American journalist writes about his life and career experiences

"Just as Thompson paved his own way in writing about politics, sports, news and culture throughout the 1960s and '70s, he now offers an autobiography that is typically unorthodox in style but still revealing previously unknown facts about its subject. Wavering between the uproarious and the lunatic, it's vintage Thompson through and through." Publ Wkly

★ Wenner, Jann S. **Gonzo**; the life of Hunter S. Thompson. by Jann S. Wenner & Corey Seymour; introduction by Johnny Depp. Little, Brown 2007 467p il $28.99   **92**

1. Authors 2. Novelists 3. Journalists 4. Satirists 5. Columnists 6. Nonfiction writers
ISBN 978-0-316-00527-2; 0-316-00527-4

LC 2007-11693

This oral biography is a "look at the turbulent life of Gonzo journalism pioneer Hunter S. Thompson (1937-2005). . . . This fine, fond biography amuses, inspires, outrages and haunts at all the right moments—and sometimes all at once." Publ Wkly

Thomson, David, 1941-

Thomson, David, 1941- **Try** to tell the story; a memoir. Alfred A. Knopf 2009 214p $23.95   **92**

1. Authors 2. Novelists 3. Father-son relationship 4. Biographers 5. Film historians 6. World War, 1939-1945 -- Personal narratives
ISBN 978-0-375-41213-4; 0-375-41213-1

LC 2008-19605

"In the heart of this haunting, eloquent memoir, as might be expected, [Thomson] gets rhapsodic when recalling the films that left an indelible impression on him: Red River, Meet Me in St. Louis, Citizen Kane, East of Eden. While following a film critic in the making, we also see the changing cultural landscape of the 1940s and 1950s through his eyes." Publ Wkly

Thoreau, Henry David, 1817-1862

Sullivan, Robert. The **Thoreau** you don't know; what the prophet of environmentalism really meant. Collins 2009 354p $25.99   **92**

1. Authors 2. Naturalists 3. Essayists 4. Pacifists 5. Authors, American 6. Writers on nature 7. Nonfiction writers

ISBN 978-0-06-171031-5; 0-06-171031-8

LC 2008-34495

The author "endeavors to free Henry David Thoreau from his calcified reputation as a cantankerous hermit and nature worshipper. Sounding like your favorite teacher who manages to make history fun and relevant, Sullivan vibrantly portrays the sage of Walden as a geeky, curious, compassionate fellow of high intelligence and deep feelings who loved company, music, and long walks." Booklist

Thorndike, Joseph Jacobs, 1913-2005

Thorndike, John. The **last** of his mind; a year in the shadow of Alzheimer's. Swallow Press 2009 243p il $24.95   **92**

1. Alzheimer's disease 2. Magazine editors

ISBN 978-0-8040-1122-8; 0-8040-1122-2

LC 2009-26118

"A brave, moving story of a son's devotion to his dying father . . . Thorndike's prose is serenely beautiful and his patience in caring for an Alzheimer's patient is extremely admirable. An affecting work of emotional honesty and forgiveness." Kirkus

Thorpe, Jim, 1888-1953

Buford, Kate. **Native** American son; the life and sporting legend of Jim Thorpe. Alfred A. Knopf 2010 479p il $35   **92**

1. Athletes 2. Biography, Individual 3. Native Americans -- Biography

ISBN 978-0-375-41324-7; 0-375-41324-3

LC 2010012815

This biography of the Native American athlete covers topics ranging "from the disastrous divvying up of Native American land that young Jim witnessed in 1890s Oklahoma; to Thorpe's stellar performances in football, baseball, and track and field; to the stripping of his 1912 Olympics medals because he was paid to play baseball for two summers; and, finally, to the makeshift life he cobbled together after his playing days ended. Buford imparts a sense of the incandescent skills Thorpe applied to his sports, and the dis-

crimination and self-destruction that shadowed him throughout his life." Booklist

Includes bibliographical references

★ Crawford, Bill. **All** American; the rise and fall of Jim Thorpe. John Wiley & Sons, Inc 2004 284p il $24.95   **92**

1. Athletes 2. Decathletes 3. Pentathletes 4. Olympic athletes 5. Native Americans -- Biography

ISBN 0-471-55732-3

LC 2004-14376

This "terse, punchy biography of sports legend Thorpe (1888–1953) illuminates the current debate over the exploitation of unpaid college athletes by moneymaking, headline-grabbing educational institutions." Publ Wkly

Includes bibliographical references

Timerman, Jacobo, 1923-1999

Timerman, Jacobo. **Prisoner** without a name, cell without a number; translated from the Spanish by Toby Talbot. University of Wisconsin Press 2002 164p (The Americas) pa $17.95   **92**

1. Journalists 2. Political prisoners 3. Newspaper executives

ISBN 978-0-299-18244-1; 0-299-18244-4

First published 1981 by Knopf

The author, "an outspoken Zionist and formerly a newspaper publisher in Buenos Aires, relates his 30-month political incarceration—torture and isolation in a clandestine prison, then detention in an official penal institution—which preceded his expulsion from Argentina in 1979." Publ Wkly

Tirone Smith, Mary-Ann, 1944-

★ Tirone Smith, Mary-Ann. **Girls** of tender age; a memoir. Free Press 2006 285p il map $24   **92**

1. Authors 2. Novelists 3. Memoirists 4. Young adult authors

ISBN 0-7432-7977-8

LC 2005-51376

This memoir, an "unsentimental view of life in a post-World War II working-class family, is interspersed with the story of Bob Malm, a serial pedophile who brutally murdered a fifth-grade classmate of hers in December 1953. . . This poignant memoir belongs in all collections." Libr J

Includes bibliographical references

Titian, approximately 1488-1576

Hale, Sheila. **Titian**; His Life. Sheila Hale. HarperCollins 2012   **92**

1. Painters -- Biography 2. Venice (Italy) -- History

ISBN 006059876X; 9780060598761

This book by Sheila Hale presents a "biography of [painter] Tiziano Vecellio (c.1480-1576), better known as Titian. . . . Hale examines Titian's life and career within the cultural, economic, political, and social contexts of 16th-century Venice and Italy. As she details his ambitious rise through Venetian society, she also tells the broader story

of the artist's stylistic evolution and the world he lived in."
(Library Journal)

Hudson, Mark. **Titian**; the last days. Walker
2009 304p il $27   **92**
   1. Artists 2. Painters 3. Artists, French
   ISBN 978-0-8027-1076-5; 0-8027-1076-X
   "At the time of his death—from plague, in Venice in
1576—Titian had been one of the most celebrated artists in
Europe for most of the century, the revered portrait painter
of popes, emperors, and kings. But in his final works, as
plague swept Venice, Titian, then in his mid-eighties, began confronting darker themes, including his own mortality.
Hudson focusses his book on this group of paintings, now
largely lost, and discusses Titian's career with humor, enlivening a potentially staid subject." New Yorker

Tocqueville, Alexis de

Epstein, Joseph. **Alexis** De Tocqueville; democracy's guide. Atlas Books 2006 208p (Eminent
lives) $21.95   **92**
   1. Statesmen 2. Writers on politics 3. Political
scientists
   ISBN 0-06-059898-0; 978-0-06-059898-3
               LC 2006-47175
   The author provides an "examination of the man, his
works, his influence, his times and what we can learn from
Democracy in America. . . . As an introduction to the man
and a primer for his works, Epstein's book is admirable."
Publ Wkly

Toklas, Alice B.

Malcolm, Janet. **Two** lives; Gertrude and Alice.
Yale University Press 2007 229p il $25   **92**
   1. Poets 2. Authors 3. Novelists 4. Essayists 5.
Memoirists 6. Literary critics 7. Authors, American 8.
Private secretaries
   ISBN 978-0-300-12551-1; 0-300-12551-8
               LC 2007-12085
   "This is a vital addition to Stein criticism as well as an
important work that critiques the political responsibility of
the artist (even a genius) to the larger world." Publ Wkly
   Includes bibliographical references

Stein, Gertrude. The **autobiography** of Alice B.
Toklas. Modern Lib. 1993 342p hardcover o.p. pa
$13   **92**
   1. Poets 2. Authors 3. Novelists 4. Essayists 5.
Memoirists 6. Literary critics 7. Authors, American 8.
Private secretaries 9. Paris (France) -- Intellectual life
   ISBN 0-679-60081-7; 0-679-72463-X pa
               LC 93-15339
   First published 1933 by Harcourt Brace & Co.
   "The book is really Stein's autobiography, presented as
though written by her secretary, Alice Toklas. The book provoked a rejoinder from various Parisian artists and writers,
Testimony Against Gertrude Stein (1935). . . . For the average reader, however, Stein's book holds much fascination in
its views of Parisian life and personalities, and the whole is
offered in a genuinely witty style." Benet's Reader's Ency
of Am Lit

Toorpakai, Maria, 1990-

Holstein, Katharine. A **Different** Kind of Daughter; The Girl Who Hid from the Taliban in Plain Sight.
Maria Toorpakai with Katharine Holstein. Twelve
2016 368 p. 8 plates; illustrations; map $27   **92**
   1. Taliban 2. Sports for women 3. Women -- Pakistan
   ISBN 1455591416; 9781455591411
   This memoir, by Maria Toorpaki with Katharine Holstein, "tells of Maria's harrowing journey to play the sport
she knew was her destiny, first living as a boy and roaming
the violent back alleys of the frontier city of Peshawar, rising
to become the number one female squash player in Pakistan.
But it was also a death sentence, thrusting her into the national spotlight and the crosshairs of the Taliban, who wanted Maria and her family dead. Maria knew her only chance
of survival was to flee the country." (Publisher's note)
   "This astonishing and inspirational memoir chronicles
more than Maria's life; it also relates the story of her parents,
an incredible couple, who, despite the odds, fought for the
betterment and education of themselves, their children, and
the Pakistani people." Library Journal

Torre, Joe, 1940-

Torre, Joe. The **Yankee** years; [by] Joe Torre and
Tom Verducci. Doubleday 2009 502p il $26.95 **92**
   1. Baseball players 2. Baseball managers 3. Baseball
-- Biography 4. New York Yankees (Baseball team)
   ISBN 978-0-385-52740-8; 0-385-52740-3
               LC 2008-52628
   Joe Torre, who was manager of the New York Yankees
from 1996 to 2007, focuses on the team's circumstances
beginning with their loss of the seventh game of the 2001
World Series.
   "This is an interesting and fast read and, for those who
are not aficionados of baseball, the clash of powerful personalities and drama are more than sufficient to merit attention.
Baseball enthusiasts, while undoubtedly familiar with the
characters and events, will find the quick review of 12 years
of Yankee history enjoyable for its details, particularly as the
men's words flesh out the drama behind the sports pages."
USA Today

Toulouse-Lautrec, Henri de, 1864-1901

Frey, Julia. **Toulouse**-Lautrec; a life. Phoenix
1995 597p il pa $27.50   **92**
   1. Artists 2. Painters 3. Lithographers 4. Artists,
French
   ISBN 1-85799-363-2; 978-1-85799-363-9
   First published 1994 by Viking
   "The author chronicles Toulouse-Lautrec's transforma-
tion from a pampered invalid into one of the most radical
of the fin de siecle artists. . . . Her sensitive, eloquent, and
richly illustrated biography has brought the real Toulouse-
Lautrec out from behind the scrim of myth." Booklist
   Includes bibliographical references

Toussaint Louverture, 1743?-1803

★ Bell, Madison Smartt. **Toussaint** Louverture; a biography. Pantheon Books 2007 333p map $27 **92**

1. Generals 2. Revolutionaries
ISBN 978-0-375-42337-6; 0-375-42337-0
LC 2006-45848

This is a biography of the Haitian leader.

"This is the best biography of Toussaint yet, in large part because Bell does not shy away from the man's contradictions." N Y Times Book Rev

Includes bibliographical references

Tracy, Spencer, 1900-1967

Curtis, James. **Spencer** Tracy; a biography. Alfred A. Knopf 2011 1001p il $39.95; ebook $19.99 **92**

1. Actors 2. Biography, Individual
ISBN 978-0-307-26289-9; 978-0-307-59522-5 ebook
LC 2011014719

This is a biography of the actor. Bibliography. Index.

The author "presents an exhaustive and exhausting biography of the legendary Hollywood star, famed for his uncanny naturalism and authority on camera and best remembered for the series of films he made with longtime companion Katharine Hepburn. . . . A monumental, definitive biography of one the finest film actors in the history of the medium." Kirkus

Includes bibliographical references and index

Trebincevic, Kenan, 1980-

Shapiro, Susan. The **Bosnia** list; a memoir of war, exile, and return. Kenan Trebincevic and Susan Shapiro. Penguin Books 2014 336 p. illustrations, map (paperback) $16 **92**

1. Muslims 2. Bosnia and Hercegovina 3. Yugoslav War, 1991-1995 4. Bosnian Americans -- Biography 5. Brčko (Bosnia and Hercegovina) -- Biography 6. Escapes -- Bosnia and Hercegovina -- History -- 20th century 7. Bosnia and Hercegovina -- Ethnic relations -- History -- 20th century 8. Yugoslav War, 1991-1995 -- Bosnia and Hercegovina -- Personal narratives
ISBN 0143124579; 9780143124573
LC 2013035345

In this memoir, author Kenan Trebincevic "blends his childhood experience of Bosnia's tragedy with a return to his original home in Brcko after nearly 20 years in the United States. The titular list is of goals the author intends to accomplish. They include seeking out surviving friends and relatives as well as confronting Serbs guilty of crimes against Trebincevi's defenceless Muslim family." (Library Journal)

"An engaging memoir of war trauma and the redemption to be found in confronting it." Kirkus

Includes bibliographical references and index

Trebing, Katie, 2002-

Whitehouse, Beth. The **match**; savior siblings and one family's battle to heal their daughter. Beacon Press 2010 255p $24.95; pa $16 **92**

1. Sick 2. Fertilization in vitro 3. Procurement of organs, tissues, etc. 4. Bone marrow -- Transplantation
ISBN 978-0-8070-7286-8; 0-8070-7286-9; 978-0-

8070-0121-9 pa; 0-8070-0121-X pa
LC 2009035949

The author "tracks Stacy and Steve Trebing and their decision to create a baby boy selected as an embryo as a genetic match for a sister suffering from Diamond-Blackfan anemia, a rare and fatal disease." Publ Wkly

Trillin, Alice, 1938-2001

Trillin, Calvin. **About** Alice. Random House 2007 78p $14.95 **92**

1. Television producers
ISBN 1-4000-6615-8; 978-1-4000-6615-5
LC 2006-45573

"This succinct account of Alice's upbringing, their meeting, their romance, their family, and her career beyond that of Trillin's helpmeet, offers glimpses into a multifaceted character." Booklist

Trotsky, Leon, 1879-1940

★ Service, Robert, 1947- **Trotsky**; a biography. Belknap Press of Harvard University Press 2009 600p il map $35 **92**

1. Revolutionaries 2. Communist leaders 3. Political leaders 4. Nonfiction writers 5. Biography, Individual 6. Soviet Union -- History 7. Communism -- Soviet Union 8. Soviet Union -- Foreign relations
ISBN 0-674-03615-8; 978-0-674-03615-4
LC 2009-25417

This biography discusses Trotsky's "relations with the leaders he was trying to unify; his attempt to disguise his political closeness to Stalin; and his role in the early 1920s as the progenitor of political and cultural Stalinism." (Publisher's note) Index.

"Thick and intensely researched but a pleasure to read, . . . [this] should remain the definitive work for some time. . . . This is a thoughtful, rewarding and essential contribution to 20th-century history." Publ Wkly

Includes bibliographical references

Truman, Harry S., 1884-1972

Dallek, Robert. **Harry** S. Truman; Robert Dallek. Times Books 2008 xviii, 183p.p (American presidents series) $22 **92**

1. Presidents 2. Vice-presidents 3. Senators 4. Presidents -- United States
ISBN 978-0-8050-6938-9
LC 2008-10193

This is a biography of the 33rd president.

This book is "the best starting point for knowledge of Truman's life and for an astute assessment of his career." Publ Wkly

Includes bibliographical references

Donald, Aida D. **Citizen** soldier; a life of Harry S. Truman. Aida D. Donald. Basic Books 2012 xvi, 265 p.p (hardcover : alk. paper) $26.99 **92**

1. Soldiers -- United States -- Biography 2. Presidents -- United States -- Biography 3. United States -- Politics and government -- 1945-1953
ISBN 046503120X; 9780465031207
LC 2012025583

This book by Aida D. Donald is a biography of former U.S. President Harry S. Truman. "When Franklin Roosevelt passed away in April 1945, Truman unexpectedly found himself at the helm of the American war effort--and in command of the atomic bomb, the most lethal weapon humanity had ever seen. Truman's decisive leadership during the remainder of World War II and the period that followed reshaped American politics, economics, and foreign relations." (Publisher's note)

Includes bibliographical references and index

McCullough, David G., 1933- **Truman**; {by} David McCullough. Simon & Schuster 1992 1117p il $40; pa $22   92
1. Senators 2. Presidents 3. Vice-presidents
ISBN 0-671-45654-7; 0-671-86920-5 pa
LC 92-5245

This is a biography of the thirty-third president of the United States. Bibliography. Index.

This biography of the 33rd president "not only conveys in rich detail Truman's accomplishments as a politician and statesman, but also reveals the character and personality of this constantly-surprising man—as schoolboy, farmer, soldier, merchant, county judge, senator, vice president and chief executive. The book relates how Truman overcame the stigma of business failure and debt . . . and acquired a reputation for honesty, reliability and common sense." Publ Wkly

Includes bibliographical references

Trump, Donald J., 1946-
Slater, Robert. **No** such thing as over-exposure; inside the life and celebrity of Donald Trump. Prentice Hall 2005 xxiv, 247p $24.95   92
1. Hotel executives 2. Airline executives 3. Real estate developers 4. Construction industry executives
ISBN 0-13-149734-0
LC 2004-116294

Donald Trump "is not so easily understood, but this book goes a long way toward defining him." Booklist

Includes bibliographical references

Tubman, Harriet, 1820?-1913
Clinton, Catherine. **Harriet** Tubman: the road to freedom. Little, Brown 2004 272p hardcover o.p. pa $14.95   92
1. Abolitionists 2. Underground railroad 3. African American women -- Biography
ISBN 0-316-14492-4; 0-316-15594-2 pa
LC 2003-56185

"Clinton turns sobriquets into meaningful descriptors of a unique person. In her hands, a familiar legend acquires human dimension with no diminution of its majesty and power." Publ Wkly

Includes bibliographical references

Humez, Jean McMahon. **Harriet** Tubman; the life and the life stories. [by] Jean M. Humez. University of Wisconsin Press 2004 471p il (Wisconsin studies in autobiography) hardcover o.p. pa $21.95   92
1. Abolitionists 2. Underground railroad 3. African

American women -- Biography
ISBN 0-299-19120-6; 0-299-19124-9 pa
LC 2003-5676

In this volume the author "includes a collection of Tubman's autobiographical stories culled from rare early publications and manuscript sources. This book will become an important resource for scholars, historians, and general readers interested in slavery, the Underground Railroad, the Civil War, and African American women." Univ Press Books for Public and Second Sch Libr, 2004

Includes bibliographical references

Larson, Kate Clifford. **Bound** for the promised land; Harriet Tubman, portrait of an American hero. Ballantine Bks. 2003 xxi, 402p il map $26.95; pa $14.95   92
1. Abolitionists 2. Underground railroad 3. African American women -- Biography
ISBN 0-345-45627-0; 0-345-45628-9 pa
LC 2004-297886

"Using a clear writing style, Larson does an excellent job of placing Tubman in the context of her times." SLJ

Includes bibliographical references

Turing, Alan Mathison, 1912-1954
Copeland, B. Jack. **Turing**; Pioneer of the Information Age. by Jack Copeland. Oxford Univ Press 2013 224 p. $21.95   92
1. Mathematicians -- Biography 2. Turing, Alan Mathison, 1912-1954 3. Mathematicians -- Great Britain -- Biography
ISBN 0199639795; 9780199639793
LC 2012289154

Author Jack Copeland presents an "introduction to . . scientist [Alan Turing] and his work. Copeland describes Alan Turing's revolutionary ideas about Artificial Intelligence and his pioneering work on Artificial Life, his all-important code-breaking work during World War II, and his contributions to mathematics, philosophy, and the foundations of computer science." (Publisher's note)

Includes bibliographical references and index

Leavitt, David. The **man** who knew too much; Alan Turing and the invention of the computer. W. W. Norton 2006 319p il (Great discoveries) $22.95 92
1. Mathematicians
ISBN 0-393-05236-2
LC 2005-18034

This is a biography of the British mathematician.

The author "succeeds in drawing a wonderfully vivid picture of his shy, dry, brilliant hero." Natl Rev

Includes bibliographical references

Turner, Ted, 1938-
Auletta, Ken. **Media** man; Ted Turner's improbable empire. Norton 2004 205p il $22.95   92
1. Philanthropists 2. Boat racers 3. Baseball executives 4. Broadcasting executives
ISBN 0-393-05168-4
LC 2004-12215

The author "describes how Turner's upbringing by a domineering father and his marriage to and later divorce from actress and radical Jane Fonda influenced his life and career. He also shows how Turner revolutionized TV by turning a tiny Atlanta station into a national cable powerhouse." Libr J

Includes bibliographical references

Turner, Tina

Turner, Tina. **I, Tina**; {by} Tina Turner, with Kurt Loder. Morrow 1986 236p il pa $6.99   **92**

1. Singers 2. Rhythm and blues musicians

ISBN 0-380-70097-2 pa

LC 86-16455

"Kurt Loder has edited I, Tina nicely, letting {Turner's} narrative take center stage, punctuating it with the voices of friends, colleagues, and family." Nation

Twain, Mark, 1835-1910

Loving, Jerome. **Mark** Twain; the adventures of Samuel L. Clemens. University of California Press 2010 491p il $34.95   **92**

1. Authors 2. Humorists 3. Novelists 4. Essayists 5. Satirists 6. Memoirists 7. Travel writers 8. Authors, American 9. Short story writers 10. Biography, Individual

ISBN 978-0-520-25257-8

LC 2009-15366

The author "serves up a balanced literary biography of a crowded life—'to renew our acquaintance with this familiar stranger in our literature and culture.' Many of the best chapters include sensitive appraisals of The Adventures of Huckleberry Finn, The Tragedy of Pudd'nhead Wilson, and the anonymously published Personal Recollections of Joan of Arc, with The Adventures of Tom Sawyer put in a different context as possibly the most overrated work of American fiction when considered as adult literature. . . . [This] is a solid contribution to literary interpretation of the man who infused American literature with what has been called 'tragic laughter.'" Publ Wkly

Includes bibliographical references

Powers, Ron. **Mark** Twain; a life. Free Press 2005 722p il $35   **92**

1. Authors 2. Humorists 3. Novelists 4. Essayists 5. Satirists 6. Memoirists 7. Travel writers 8. Short story writers

ISBN 0-7432-4899-6

LC 2005-48816

"A masterful biography of interest to both general readers and academics." Booklist

Includes bibliographical references

Shelden, Michael. **Mark** Twain; man in white: the grand adventure of his final years. Random House 2010 xxxix, 484p il $30   **92**

1. Authors 2. Humorists 3. Novelists 4. Essayists 5. Satirists 6. Memoirists 7. Travel writers 8. Authors, American 9. Short story writers

ISBN 978-0-679-44800-6; 0-679-44800-4

LC 2009-19719

The author "tells the story of Twain's last 40 months, richly detailing fresh facts new to most readers and fleshing out the conventional Twain biography to make the man's life complete. . . . This superb biography, told in a nonacademic tone, is saturated with sadness, but every reader will be grateful that, finally, Mark Twain appears before us, warts and all." Libr J

Includes bibliographical references

★ Twain, Mark, 1835-1910. **Autobiography** of Mark Twain; v1 The Complete and Authoritative Edition. Harriet Elinor Smith, editor; associate editors: Benjamin Griffin, Victor Fischer, Michael B. Frank, Sharon K. Goetz, Leslie Myrick. University of California Press 2010 736 p. ill. (The Mark Twain papers) (hbk.) $45.00   **92**

1. Autobiographies 2. Authors, American -- 19th century -- Biography

ISBN 0520267192; 9780520267190 (alk. paper)

LC 2009047700

This is "the first of a projected three-volume edition of the complete, uncensored autobiography. The book became an immediate bestseller and was hailed as the capstone of the life's work of America's favorite author." It includes text that was not to be published until the 100th anniversary of Twain's death. (Publisher's note)

"Laced with Twain's unique blend of humor and vitriol, the haphazard narrative is engrossing, hugely funny, and deeply revealing of its author's mind." Pub Wkly

Includes bibliographical references (p. 681-712) and index

Tweedy, Damon

Black Man in a White Coat; A Doctor's Reflections on Race and Medicine. Damon Tweedy. St. Martin's Press 2015 304 p. $26   **92**

1. Physicians 2. Medicine -- United States 3. African Americans -- Health and hygiene

ISBN 1250044634; 9781250044631

LC 2015018599

Author Damon Tweedy presents this "memoir of his experience grappling with race, bias, and the unique health problems of black Americans. [It] examines the complex ways in which both black doctors and patients must navigate the difficult and often contradictory terrain of race and medicine. As Tweedy transforms from student to practicing physician, he discovers how often race influences his encounters with patients." (Publisher's note)

"Clearly at odds with the racial and class-stratified machinations of the medical industry, the author writes with dignified authority on the imbalances in opportunities and available social and medical service platforms to the many African-American patients seeking clinical care and of his pivotal role in making a difference. In this unsparingly honest chronic l e, Tweedy cohesively illuminates the experiences of black doctors and black patients and reiterates the need for improved understanding of racial differences within global medical communities." Kirkus

Tye, Laurene, 1931-1989

Tye, Diane. **Baking** as biography; a life story in recipes. McGill-Queen's University Press 2010 268p il   **92**

1. Baking 2. Homemakers 3. Eating customs 4. Women -- Canada 5. Biography, Individual 6. Food

-- Social aspects 7. Canada -- Social life and customs
ISBN 978-0-7735-3724-8; 978-0-7735-3725-5 pa
Diane Tye uses her mother's recipe collection as a focus
for this memoir and study of Maritime culture. Index

"Using her mother's recipes as a framework, Tye . . . explores Canadian women's roles from 1930 to 1980. She recalls her mother as a minister's wife who didn't care for baking yet consistently produced an abundance of sweets for her family, church, and community. Her succinct recipes range from simple (biscuits and oatcakes) to 'exotic' (anything involving JELL-O, Dream Whip, or canned pie filling). . . . Because this book blends memoir, biography, culinary history, and research, it should appeal to both scholars and readers who enjoy historical or intellectual food writing." Libr J
Includes bibliographical references

Tyler, John, 1790-1862

★ Crapol, Edward P. **John** Tyler; the accidental president. University of North Carolina Press 2006 332p il map $37.50 **92**
1. Governors 2. Presidents 3. Vice-presidents 4. Senators 5. Members of Congress
ISBN 978-0-8078-3041-3; 0-8078-3041-0
LC 2005-37963
In this biography of the former U.S. president, the author "argues that Tyler was in fact a terrifically strong president who helped strengthen the executive branch. . . . This balanced, fascinating volume will introduce a new generation of readers to an oft-ignored president." Publ Wkly
Includes bibliographical references

May, Gary. **John** Tyler. Times Books/Henry Holt and Co. 2008 183p (American presidents series) $22 **92**
1. Governors 2. Presidents 3. Vice-presidents 4. Senators 5. Members of Congress 6. Presidents -- United States
ISBN 978-0-8050-8238-8; 0-8050-8238-7
LC 2008-18131
This biography of the American president focuses on "Tyler's controversial presidency, which saw him set aside his dedication to the Constitution to gain his two great ambitions: Texas and a place in history." Publisher's note
Includes bibliographical references

Tynan, Tracy

Tynan, Tracy. **Wear** and tear; The Threads of My Life. Tracy Tynan. Scribner 2016 320 p. illustrations (hardcover : alk. paper) $26 **92**
1. Fashion designers 2. Fashion designers -- United States -- Biography 3. Women fashion designers -- United States -- Biography
ISBN 9781501123689; 9781501123696
LC 2015031108
This book, by Tracy Tynan, is a "candid . . . memoir told through clothes. . . . When Tracy started writing about her life she found that clothing was the focus of many of her stories. She recalls her father's dandy attire and her mother's Pucci dresses, as well as her parents' rancorous marriage and divorce, her father's prodigious talents and celebrity lifestyle, and her mother's lifelong struggle with addiction.

She tackles issues big and small using clothes as an entrée." (Publisher's note)
"Each of the three-dozen gemlike chapters cover an episode built around a specific piece of clothing, from a designer crepe de chine gown to a maroon plaid dress to a tiny pink knitted cap, a gift of love for Tynan's premature baby. The sum total is an absorbing memoir well-told from a singular perspective." LJ

Uhlberg, Myron

Uhlberg, Myron. **Hands** of my father; a hearing boy, his deaf parents, and the language of love. Bantam Books 2009 232p il $23 **92**
1. Deaf 2. Authors 3. Children's authors
ISBN 978-0-553-80688-5; 0-553-80688-2
LC 2008-25628
A memoir about growing up the son of deaf parents in 1940s Brooklyn
"Uhlberg's emotions toward his family, and especially his father, run the gamut from embarrassment to anger to a deep and abiding love. Sections titled 'Memorabilia' pepper the narrative, and many black-and-white photographs are scattered throughout this rich, textured portrait of the deaf community on Coney Island at a turbulent time in U.S. history." SLJ

Ulianov, Aleksandr, 1886-1887

Pomper, Philip. **Lenin's** brother; the origins of the October Revolution. W.W. Norton & Co. 2010 276p il $24.95 **92**
1. Heads of state 2. Revolutionaries 3. Communist leaders 4. Political leaders 5. Soviet Union -- History -- 1917-1921, Revolution
ISBN 978-0-393-07079-8
LC 2009-27390
"In 1887, the future leader of the Russian revolution, Vladimir Ulyanov (later Lenin), was 17 when his 21-year-old brother was hanged for his role in a bungled attempt to assassinate Czar Alexander III. Historians consider this the seminal event that launched Lenin's career as a revolutionary. . . . [The author] delivers an absorbing and surprisingly detailed account of Alexander Ulyanov's short life and even shorter career (four months) as a terrorist." Publ Wkly
Includes bibliographical references

Umbrell, Colby, 1981-2007

Sielski, Mike. **Fading** echoes; a true story of rivalry and brotherhood from the football field to the fields of honor. Berkley Books 2009 342p il $24.95 **92**
1. School sports 2. Iraq War, 2003-2011 3. Marines 4. Army officers 5. Iraq War, 2003- 6. Football -- Biography 7. Soldiers -- United States
ISBN 978-0-425-22974-3
LC 2009-17001
"Bryan Buckley was the captain of Central Bucks West and [Colby] Umbrell was one of the leaders of Central Bucks East when their teams clashed in their senior year of 1998. Eight years later, both were officers leading men in combat in Iraq, Buckley as a marine and Umbrell as an army ranger. Both were proudly fighting for ideals in which they believed, and only one would come home alive. Sielski

... chronicles the lives of these two athletes and illustrates how their personalities and values were formed from interactions with family, friends, coaches, and community. In the process, he writes of much broader topics in contemporary American life: dreams, competition, resolve, war, honor, sacrifice, and true heartbreak." Libr J

Includes bibliographical references

Ung, Chou

★ Ung, Loung. **Lucky** child; a daughter of Cambodia reunites with the sister she left behind. HarperCollins Publishers 2005 268p il $24.95; pa $13.95 **92**

1. Homemakers 2. Cambodian Americans 3. Memoirists 4. Social activists 5. Cambodia -- History -- 1975-

ISBN 0-06-073394-2; 0-06-073395-0 pa

LC 2004-54346

Sequel to First they killed my father

In this "memoir, Ung picks up where her first . . . left off, with the author escaping a devastated Cambodia in 1980 at age 10 and flying to her new home in Vermont. . . . She and her eldest brother, with whom she escaped, left behind their three other siblings. This book is alternately heart-wrenching and heartwarming, as it follows the parallel lives of Loung Ung and her closest sister, Chou, during the 15 years it took for them to reunite." Publ Wkly

Includes bibliographical references

Ung, Loung, 1970-

★ Ung, Loung. **Lucky** child; a daughter of Cambodia reunites with the sister she left behind. HarperCollins Publishers 2005 268p il $24.95; pa $13.95 **92**

1. Homemakers 2. Cambodian Americans 3. Memoirists 4. Social activists 5. Cambodia -- History -- 1975-

ISBN 0-06-073394-2; 0-06-073395-0 pa

LC 2004-54346

Sequel to First they killed my father

In this "memoir, Ung picks up where her first . . . left off, with the author escaping a devastated Cambodia in 1980 at age 10 and flying to her new home in Vermont. . . . She and her eldest brother, with whom she escaped, left behind their three other siblings. This book is alternately heart-wrenching and heartwarming, as it follows the parallel lives of Loung Ung and her closest sister, Chou, during the 15 years it took for them to reunite." Publ Wkly

Includes bibliographical references

Ungern-Sternberg, Roman, 1885-1921

Palmer, James. The **bloody** white baron; the extraordinary story of the Russian nobleman who became the last khan of Mongolia. Basic Books 2009 274p $26.95 **92**

1. Generals 2. Soviet Union -- History -- 1917-1921, Revolution

ISBN 978-0-465-01448-4; 0-465-01448-8

LC 2008-937254

First published 2008 in the United Kingdom

"What makes 'The Bloody White Baron' so exceptional is Palmer's lucid scholarship, his ability to make perfect sense of the maelstrom of a forgotten war. This is a brilliant book." N Y Times Book Rev

Includes bibliographical references

Updike, John

★ Begley, Adam. **Updike**; Adam Begley. Harper 2014 576 p. illustrations (hardback) $29.99 **92**

1. American authors 2. American literature -- History and criticism 3. Authors, American -- 20th century -- Biography

ISBN 0061896454; 9780061896453

LC 2013039246

Los Angeles Times Book Prize Finalist: Biography (2014)

This biography of John Updike "explores the stages of the writer's pilgrim's progress: his beloved home turf of Berks County, Pennsylvania; his escape to Harvard; his brief, busy working life as the golden boy at The New Yorker; his family years in suburban Ipswich, Massachusetts; his extensive travel abroad; and his retreat to another Massachusetts town, Beverly Farms, where he remained until his death in 2009." (Publisher's note)

"Begley draws on deep research and interviews with the author and his circle to chart his early influences—in particular his ambitious mother, Linda—and rigorously explore the heavily autobiographical dimensions of his fiction and poetry." Pub Wkly

Includes bibliographical references and index

Valenti, Jessica.

Valenti, Jessica, 1978- **Sex** object; a memoir. Jessica Valenti. HarperCollins 2016 288 p. (hardback) $25.99 **92**

1. Feminism

ISBN 9780062435088; 9780062435095; 0062435086

LC 2016017749

In this memoir, Jessica Valenti "explores the toll that sexism takes on women's lives, from the everyday to the existential. From subway gropings and imposter syndrome to sexual awakenings and motherhood, . . . [it] reveals the painful, embarrassing, and sometimes illegal moments that shaped Valenti's adolescence and young adulthood in New York City." (Publisher's note)

"An entertaining and shocking memoir from a leading feminist writer." Booklist

Vampira, 1921-2008

Poole, W. Scott. **Vampira**; dark goddess of horror. W. Scott Poole. Soft Skull Press Distributed by Publishers Group West 2014 320 p. illustrations (paperback) $16.95 **92**

1. Actresses -- Biography 2. Popular culture -- United States 3. Actresses -- United States -- Biography 4. Entertainers -- United States -- Biography

ISBN 1593765436; 9781593765439

LC 2014014147

This book, by W. Scott Poole, "detail[s] the story of cult horror figure Vampira that actually tells the much wider story of 1950s America and its treatment of women and sex, as well as capturing a fascinating swath of Los Angeles history. . . . Poole gives us the eclectic life of the dancer, stripper, actress, and artist Maila Nurmi, who would reinvent herself as Vampira during the backdrop of 1950s America." (Publisher's note)

"Before there was Dr. Morgus, Svengoolie, and Elvira, there was the titular Vampira. This stone-cold winner belongs in every American studies collection." LJ

Van Buren, Martin, 1782-1862

Widmer, Edward L. **Martin** Van Buren; [by] Ted Widmer. Times Bks. 2005 189p (American presidents series) $20   92

1. Presidents 2. Vice-presidents 3. Secretaries of state 4. Presidents -- United States
ISBN 0-8050-6922-4

LC 2004-53652

The author "keenly evokes the environment that enabled Van Buren to thrive. . . . Widmer also lends a certain dignity to Van Buren's post-presidential attempts to resolve the sectional crisis." N Y Times Book Rev
Includes bibliographical references

Van Gogh, Vincent, 1853-1890

Bell, Julian. **Van** Gogh; A Power Seething. Julian Bell. New Harvest 2015 176 p. 8 plates; color illustrations $20   92

1. Painters
ISBN 0544343735; 9780544343733

Author Julian Bell presents this book on painter Vincent Van Gogh. "He was a great writer as well. In his six hundred—plus letters to [his brother] Theo he chronicled with heartbreaking urgency his mental breakdowns, acrimonious family relations, and struggles with art dealers. Shading this dark story is the artist's acquaintance with prostitutes and penury, stormy scenes with his friend Paul Gauguin, and dissipated Parisian nights with Henri de Toulouse-Lautrec." (Publisher's note)

"Bell describes with glorious acuity the rapid artistic evolution of this self-taught genius propelled by a 'peculiar inner seething,' celebrating with unique fluency Van Gogh's 'rapturous vision' and the 'visual electricity' of his masterpieces. A vividly illuminating portrait both for readers versed in Van Gogh and those who are newly curious." Booklist

Van Vechten, Carl, 1880-1964

Bernard, Emily. **Carl** Van Vechten and the Harlem Renaissance; a portrait in black and white. Emily Bernard. Yale University Press 2012 xiii, 358 p.p (cloth : alk. paper) : $30.00   92

1. Harlem Renaissance 2. African Americans in literature 3. Harlem (New York, N.Y.) -- Intellectual life -- 20th century 4. African Americans -- New York (State) -- New York -- Intellectual life
ISBN 0300121997; 9780300121995

LC 2011034190

This book presents a "biographical treatment of a significant figure in the explosion of black arts that was centered in Harlem in New York City in the 1920s and 1930s . . . As the author posits, Carl Van Vechten was a 'white man with a passion for blackness.' Movie critic, novelist, and photographer Van Vechten possessed enough of his own fame and influence that he could provide struggling black artists not only with emotional sustenance but also lead them to exposure to a wider commercial arena than they might have been able

to enter on their own. [Emily] Bernard . . . interprets Van Vechten's life in terms of just how 'messy' was the 'tangle' of white-black relations within the structure of the Harlem Renaissance." (Booklist)
Includes bibliographical references and index.

★ White, Edward. The **Tastemaker**; Carl Van Vechten and the Birth of Modern America. Edward White. Farrar, Straus & Giroux 2014 400 p. illustrations (hardback) $30   92

1. Photographers -- Biography 2. American authors -- Biography 3. Photographers -- United States -- Biography 4. Authors, American -- 20th century -- Biography
ISBN 0374201579; 9780374201579

LC 2013034003

A biography by Edward White, "'The Tastemaker' explores the many lives of Carl Van Vechten, the most influential cultural impresario of the early twentieth century: a patron and dealmaker of the Harlem Renaissance, a photographer who captured the era's icons, and a novelist who created some of the Jazz Age's most salacious stories." (Publisher's note)

"In orderly chapters, White tackles this complicated, multifaceted, tremendously fascinating and contradictory subject. . . . A vigorous, fully fleshed biography of an important contributor to American culture." Kirkus
Includes bibliographical references and index

Van Zandt, Townes, 1944-1997

Kruth, John. **To** live's to fly; the ballad of the late, great Townes Van Zandt. Da Capo 2007 326p il $26   92

1. Singers 2. Guitarists 3. Folk musicians 4. Country musicians 5. Songwriters
ISBN 978-0-306-81553-9; 0-306-81553-2

This is "the first biography of legendary Texas singer/songwriter Townes Van Zandt (1944-97). In his struggle for recognition among a wider public, Van Zandt wrestled for years with depression and alcoholism while writing songs—e.g., 'Pancho and Lefty' and 'Be Here To Love Me'—that today are revered by the elite of Texas and Nashville songwriters as well as by a cult group of fans. Through access to Van Zandt's friends, family members, and fellow musicians, Kruth provides an intimate and unflinching look at the singer's life." Libr J

Vance, J. D.

Vance, J. D. **Hillbilly** elegy; A Memoir of a Family and Culture in Crisis. J. D. Vance. HarperCollins 2016 272 p. $27.99   92

1. Family life 2. Working class 3. Social mobility 4. Lawyers -- Biography
ISBN 0062300547; 9780062300546

LC 2016017254

This book by J. D. Vance is a "personal analysis of a culture in crisis—that of white working-class Americans. . . . The Vance family story begins . . . in postwar America. J. D.'s grandparents were 'dirt poor and in love,' and moved north from Kentucky's Appalachia region to Ohio. . . . They raised a middle-class family, and eventually their grandchild (the author) would graduate from Yale Law School, a . . .

marker of their success in achieving generational upward mobility." (Publisher's note)

"Both heartbreaking and heartwarming, this memoir is akin to investigative journalism." LJ

Includes bibliographical references (pages 263-264).

Vanderbilt, Cornelius, 1794-1877

Renehan, Edward J. **Commodore**; the life of Cornelius Vanderbilt. [by] Edward J. Renehan Jr. Basic Books 2007 xx, 364p il $27.50   **92**

1. Businessmen 2. Financiers 3. Railroad executives 4. Shipping executives

ISBN 978-0-465-00255-9; 0-465-00255-2

LC 2007-22392

"A warts and more warts portrait of a brilliantly successful, genuinely despicable man." Kirkus

Includes bibliographical references

★ Stiles, T. J. The **first** tycoon; the epic life of Cornelius Vanderbilt. Alfred A. Knopf 2009 719p $37.50   **92**

1. Businessmen 2. Railroads -- History 3. Biography, Individual 4. Steamboats -- History

ISBN 978-0-375-41542-5; 0-375-41542-4

LC 2008-47879

National Book Award Finalists (2009)

This is a biography of the American steamship and railroad magnate.

"This is a mighty—and mighty confident—work, one that moves with force and conviction and imperious wit through Vanderbilt's noisy life and times. . . . This is state-of-the-art biography, crisper and more piquant than a 600-page book has any right to be." N Y Times (Late N Y Ed)

Includes bibliographical references

Vanderbilt, Gloria, 1924-

Cooper, Anderson, 1967- The **rainbow** comes and goes; a mother and son talk about life, love, and loss. Anderson Cooper and Gloria Vanderbilt. HarperCollins 2016 290 p. illustrations (hardback) $27.99   **92**

1. Mother-son relationship 2. Celebrities -- Biography 3. Journalists -- Biography 4. Celebrities -- United States -- Biography 5. Mothers and sons -- United States -- Correspondence 6. Television journalists -- United States -- Biography

ISBN 0062454943; 9780062454942; 9780062454966; 9780062466730

LC 2016000369

This book, by Anderson Cooper and Gloria Vanderbilt, "offers a rare window into their close relationship and fascinating life stories, including their tragedies and triumphs. In these often humorous and moving exchanges, they share their most private thoughts and the hard-earned truths they've learned along the way. In their words their distinctive personalities shine through—Anderson's journalistic outlook on the world is a sharp contrast to his mother's idealism and unwavering optimism." (Publisher's note)

"Vanderbilt and her son, Cooper, relate the touching story of how an epistolary exchange created new emotional intimacy between them." Pub Wkly

Cooper, Anderson, 1967- The **rainbow** comes and goes; a mother and son talk about life, love, and loss. Anderson Cooper and Gloria Vanderbilt. HarperCollins 2016 290 p. illustrations (hardback) $27.99   **92**

1. Mother-son relationship 2. Celebrities -- Biography 3. Journalists -- Biography 4. Celebrities -- United States -- Biography 5. Mothers and sons -- United States -- Correspondence 6. Television journalists -- United States -- Biography

ISBN 0062454943; 9780062454942; 9780062454966; 9780062466730

LC 2016000369

This book, by Anderson Cooper and Gloria Vanderbilt, "offers a rare window into their close relationship and fascinating life stories, including their tragedies and triumphs. In these often humorous and moving exchanges, they share their most private thoughts and the hard-earned truths they've learned along the way. In their words their distinctive personalities shine through—Anderson's journalistic outlook on the world is a sharp contrast to his mother's idealism and unwavering optimism." (Publisher's note)

"Vanderbilt and her son, Cooper, relate the touching story of how an epistolary exchange created new emotional intimacy between them." Pub Wkly

Varmus, Harold

Varmus, Harold. The **art** and politics of science. W.W. Norton 2009 315p il $24.95   **92**

1. Scientists 2. Nobel Prizes 3. Microbiologists 4. College teachers 5. Government officials 6. Public health officials 7. National Institutes of Health (U.S.) 8. Nobel laureates for physiology or medicine

ISBN 978-0-393-06128-4; 0-393-06128-0

LC 2008-42963

"Varmus offers a plain-spoken and fascinating story of his path from graduate student in English literature to the forefront of biomedical research. His journey to the highest echelons of the scientific establishment is as interesting for its incidental details as for its glimpse into the process of modern biomedical science." Washington Post

Includes bibliographical references

Vavilov, N. I. (Nikola Ivanovich), 1887-1943

Pringle, Peter. The **murder** of Nikolai Vavilov; the story of Stalin's persecution of one of the great scientists of the twentieth century. Simon & Schuster 2008 370p il $26   **92**

1. Botanists 2. Heads of state 3. Communist leaders 4. Plant geneticists 5. Political leaders

ISBN 978-0-7432-6498-3; 0-7432-6498-3

LC 2008-03510

This is a biography of the Russian botanist and geneticist who was starved to death in a Soviet prison in 1943.

This "is a must-read to grasp the ultimate, disasterous effect of politics trumping science." Sci Books Films

Includes bibliographical references

Vespucci, Amerigo, 1451-1512

★ Fernandez-Armesto, Felipe. **Amerigo**; the man who gave his name to America. Random House 2007 231p il map $24.95; pa $15   **92**

1. Explorers 2. America -- Exploration
ISBN 978-1-4000-6281-2; 1-4000-6281-0; 978-0-8129-7298-6 pa; 0-8129-7298-8 pa
LC 2006-51739

First published 2006 in the United Kingdom

The author chronicles the life and times of the explorer and navigator Amerigo Vespucci

"A well-connected Florentine wheeler-dealer who settled in Seville, Vespucci began by outfitting Columbus's ships and later made voyages of his own. . . . Fernandez-Armesto accepts that Amerigo Vespucci made two voyages to north eastern South America, one in 1499 and another in 1501-02. But the evidence is maddeningly vague on exactly where he went, what he did, and even in what capacity he served (he is unlikely to have been the commander, as he claimed). Faced by such unreliable sources, Fernandez-Armesto sticks to what can be said of Vespucci with confidence, and wisely opts to paint a rich portrait of the times rather than speculate about details that may never be known." Times Lit Suppl

Includes bibliographical references

Victoria, Queen of Great Britain, 1819-1901

Baird, Julia. **Victoria**; The Queen: An Intimate Biography of the Woman Who Ruled an Empire. Julia Baird. Random House 2016 720 p.   **92**

1. Queens -- Great Britain -- Biography 2. Great Britain -- History -- Victoria, 1837-1901
ISBN 9781400069880
LC 2015025297

In this biography of Queen Victoria, historian Julia Baird "reveals the real woman behind the myth: a bold, glamorous, unbreakable queen—a Victoria for our times. Drawing on previously unpublished papers, this . . . is a story of love and heartbreak, of devotion and grief. . . . Baird brings . . . to life the fascinating story of a woman who struggled with . . . balancing work and family, raising children, . . . finding an identity, searching for meaning." (Publisher's note)

"Baird does not turn a blind eye on Victoria's darker sides, including her willfulness, selfishness, and self-pity. But that simply adds dimensions to a significant character." Booklist

Includes bibliographical references and index

Erickson, Carolly. **Her** little majesty: the life of Queen Victoria. Simon & Schuster 1997 304p il hardcover o.p. pa $19.95   **92**

1. Queens 2. Great Britain -- History -- 19th century
ISBN 0-7432-3657-2 pa
LC 96-35041

This is a biography of the British monarch

"Erickson has a knack for plucking pithy quotes, and the essentials of the queen's life are often deftly set out." Publ Wkly

Includes bibliographical references

Hibbert, Christopher. **Queen** Victoria; a personal history. Basic Bks. 2000 557p il hardcover o.p. pa $21   **92**

1. Queens 2. Great Britain -- History -- 19th century
ISBN 0-306-81085-9 pa
LC 2001-269136

Hibbert explores the life and reign of the British monarch based on "primary sources, particularly the 60 million words of Victoria's letters and journals. As a result, he renders Victoria and her familial and political relationships with deliciously gossipy and often touching intimacy." N Y Times Book Rev

Includes bibliographical references

Williams, Kate. **Becoming** Queen Victoria; the tragic death of Princess Charlotte and the unexpected rise of Britain's greatest monarch. Ballantine Books 2010 448p il $30; ebook $30   **92**

1. Queens 2. Princesses 3. Great Britain -- Kings and rulers
ISBN 978-0-345-46195-7; 978-0-345-52193-4 ebook
LC 2010-13227

First published 2008 in the United Kingdom with title: Becoming queen

"A lively, juicy read, full of the sordid details of the debauched rule of kings and princes that led to the moralistic rule of a queen focused on creating a royal family that embodied the ideals of a nation. Perfect for fans of royal histories and historical television shows or armchair historians interested in a swift and enjoyable read." Libr J

Includes bibliographical references

★ Wilson, A. N., 1950- **Victoria**; a life. A. N. Wilson. Penguin Press 2014 624 p. ill, port, genealogical table hbk $36   **92**

1. Queens -- Great Britain 2. Great Britain -- Kings and rulers 3. Great Britain -- History -- Victoria, 1837-1901
ISBN 159420599X; 9781594205996
LC 2014013973

This biography, by A. N. Wilson, "includes a wealth of new material from previously unseen sources to show us Queen Victoria as she's never been seen before. Wilson explores the curious set of circumstances that led to Victoria's coronation, her strange and isolated childhood, her passionate marriage to Prince Albert and his pivotal influence even after death and her widowhood and subsequent intimate friendship with her Highland servant John Brown." (Publisher's note)

"[F]ew if any previous biographers have viewed her as incisively and absorbingly as Wilson does in his lengthy but smoothly flowing treatment of the queen's long life. . . . [He] sees Victoria as a woman who battled demons and emerged from her various darknesses victorious as a functioning woman and monarch." Booklist

Includes bibliographical references and index

Vidal, Gore, 1925-2012

Parini, Jay. **Empire** of self; a life of Gore Vidal. by Jay Parini. Doubleday 2015 480 p. 32 plates : illustrations (hardback) $35 **92**
1. American authors 2. Authors, American -- 20th century -- Biography
ISBN 0385537565; 9780385537568
LC 2015004719

This book, by Jay Parini, is an "authorized yet frank biography of Gore Vidal. . . . Parini crafts Vidal's life into an accessible, entertaining story that puts the experience of one of the great American figures of the postwar era into context; introduces the author and his works to a generation who may not know him; and looks behind the scenes at the man and his work in ways never possible before his death." (Publisher's note)

"It's difficult to paint an appealing picture of a narcissist, but Parini has produced a balanced account of a man of immense talent who sometimes used it wisely and other times didn't. Lively and insightful, this book should find favor among lovers of literature and biography. It's got heart." LJ

Vidal, Gore. **Point** to point navigation; a memoir, 1964 to 2006. Doubleday 2006 277p il $26 **92**
1. Authors 2. Novelists 3. Dramatists 4. Essayists 5. Screenwriters
ISBN 0-385-51721-1; 978-0-385-51721-8
LC 2006-11644

"The memoir is a perfect encapsulation of Vidal's outsized personality—and readers' reactions will be determined by how they already feel about him." Publ Wkly

Villani, Cédric

Birth of a theorem; a mathematical adventure. Cédric Villani; illustrations by Claude Gondard. Faber & Faber, Inc. an affiliate of Farrar, Straus & Giroux 2015 272 p. illustrations (hardback) $26 **92**
1. Mathematicians -- Biography 2. Mathematicians -- France -- Biography
ISBN 0865477671; 9780865477674
LC 2014031268

"In 2010, French mathematician Cédric Villani received the Fields Medal, the most coveted prize in mathematics, in recognition of a proof which he devised with his close collaborator Clément Mouhot to explain one of the most surprising theories in classical physics. 'Birth of a Theorem' is Villani's own account of the years leading up to the award. It invites readers inside the mind of a great mathematician as he wrestles with the most important work of his career." (Publisher's note)

"And though readers will marvel at his remarkable genius, they will also recognize how much Villani depends on loving family ties, congenial friendships, and supportive institutions to nurture that genius. A rare portal into stratospheric mathematics." Booklist

Volk, Audrey Morgen

Volk, Patricia. **Shocked**; my mother, Schiaparelli, and me. Patricia Volk. Alfred A. Knopf 2013 304 p. ill. (some col.) (hardcover) $26.95 **92**
1. Femininity 2. Beauty, Personal 3. Mothers and daughters -- United States 4. Fashion designers --

France -- Paris -- Biography
ISBN 9780307962102; 0307962105
LC 2012034922

This book by Patricia Volk presents a "study of two very different but very glamorous women--her mother, Audrey, an upper-class New York domestic goddess with the looks and manners of Grace Kelly, and genius haute couture European artist Elsa Schiaparelli, whose book, art, and (yes) perfume forever change the course of young Volk's life." (Library Journal)

"[T]he narrative that emerges from Volk's deft interweaving of lives is as sharp-eyed as it is wickedly funny." Kirkus
Includes bibliographical references

Volk, Patricia

Volk, Patricia. **Shocked**; my mother, Schiaparelli, and me. Patricia Volk. Alfred A. Knopf 2013 304 p. ill. (some col.) (hardcover) $26.95 **92**
1. Femininity 2. Beauty, Personal 3. Mothers and daughters -- United States 4. Fashion designers -- France -- Paris -- Biography
ISBN 9780307962102; 0307962105
LC 2012034922

This book by Patricia Volk presents a "study of two very different but very glamorous women--her mother, Audrey, an upper-class New York domestic goddess with the looks and manners of Grace Kelly, and genius haute couture European artist Elsa Schiaparelli, whose book, art, and (yes) perfume forever change the course of young Volk's life." (Library Journal)

"[T]he narrative that emerges from Volk's deft interweaving of lives is as sharp-eyed as it is wickedly funny." Kirkus
Includes bibliographical references

Volpe, Joseph

Volpe, Joseph. The **toughest** show on earth; my rise and reign at the Metropolitan Opera. [by] Joseph Volpe with Charles Michener. Knopf 2006 304p il $25.95 **92**
1. Music administrators 2. Metropolitan Opera (New York, N.Y.)
ISBN 0-307-26285-5; 978-0-307-26285-1
LC 2005-57932

This is a memoir by the "general manager of New York's Metropolitan Opera since 1990. . . . This enthralling book provides an insider's view of a complex and fascinating institution." Libr J
Includes bibliographical references

Volpe, Lou

Sokolove, Michael. **Drama** high; the incredible true story of a brilliant teacher, a struggling town, and the magic of theater. by Michael Sokolove. Riverhead Hardcover 2013 352 p. ill (hardback) $27.95 **92**
1. College and school drama 2. Performing arts -- Study and teaching 3. English teachers -- Pennsylvania -- Levittown -- Biography 4. High school teachers -- Pennsylvania -- Levittown -- Biography 5. Theater -- Producers and directors -- Pennsylvania -- Levittown

-- Biography
ISBN 1594488223; 9781594488221
LC 2013019393

In this book, author Michael Sokolove "chronicles the [Harry S Truman High School] drama director [Lou Volpe's] last school years and follows a group of student actors as they work through riveting dramas both on and off the stage. This is a story of an economically depressed but proud town finding hope in a gifted teacher and the magic of theater." (Publisher's note)

"During the season Sokolove spends at Truman, Volpe and his kids put on the play Good Boys and True and the musical Spring Awakening—both of which address teen sexuality, angst, and reckless behavior. Volpe pushes his student actors hard, but for most of them, being in one of his productions is transformative. Many alums go on to pursue careers in theater or the arts. A powerful look at the way a dynamic and dedicated teacher can change lives." (Booklist)

Voltaire, 1694-1778

★ Pearson, Roger. **Voltaire** almighty; a life in pursuit of freedom. Bloomsbury 2005 xxxii, 447p il $35   92

1. Poets 2. Authors 3. Novelists 4. Dramatists 5. Philosophers 6. Essayists
ISBN 978-1-58234-630-4; 1-58234-630-5
LC 2005-53027

This is a biography of the French philosopher.

The author "has composed a lively and thorough account of the illustrious philosophe's chaotic life." Choice

Includes bibliographical references

Von Braun, Wernher, 1912-1977

Biddle, Wayne. **Dark** side of the moon; Wernher von Braun, the Third Reich, and the space race. W.W. Norton 2009 220p il map $25.95   92

1. Rocketry 2. Scientists 3. Aerospace engineers 4. NASA officials
ISBN 978-0-393-05910-6; 0-393-05910-3
LC 2009-15572

"A stern, prosecutorial portrait of the famous German American rocketeer." Booklist

Includes bibliographical references

★ Neufeld, Michael J. **Von** Braun; dreamer of space, engineer of war. A.A. Knopf 2007 587p il $35; pa $19.95   92

1. Rocketry 2. Scientists 3. Aerospace engineers 4. NASA officials
ISBN 978-0-307-26292-9; 0-307-26292-8; 978-0-307-38937-4 pa; 0-307-38937-5 pa
LC 2007-5711

This "is a meticulously researched and technically accurate biography of von Braun." N Y Rev Books

Includes bibliographical references

Von Furstenberg, Diane, 1946-

The **woman** I wanted to be; Diane von Furstenberg. Simon & Schuster 2014 256 p. 24 plates; color illustrations (hardback) $26   92

1. Cancer patients 2. Fashion designers 3. Women -- Identity 4. Women philanthropists -- Biography

5. Fashion designers -- United States -- Biography 6. Cancer -- Patients -- United States -- Biography 7. Women philanthropists -- United States -- Biography 8. Women fashion designers -- United States -- Biography
ISBN 1451651546; 9781451651546; 9781451651553
LC 2014033232

In this book, fashion designer Diane von Furstenberg "reflects on her extraordinary life-- from childhood in Brussels to her days as a young, jet-set princess, to creating the dress that came to symbolize independence and power for an entire generation of women. . . . She opens up about her family and career, overcoming cancer, building a global brand, and devoting herself to empowering other women." (Publisher's note)

"This is a fascinating glimpse into the life of one of the fashion world's most enduring stars that will fascinate fashionistas and fans of strong, creative women." Pub Wkly

Vonnegut, Kurt, 1922-2007

Shields, Charles J. **And** so it goes: Kurt Vonnegut: a life. Henry Holt and Co. 2011 513p il $30 92

1. Authors 2. Novelists 3. Journalists 4. Biographers 5. Authors, American 6. Short story writers 7. Science fiction writers
ISBN 978-0-8050-8693-5
LC 2010-45173

"Kurt Vonnegut had a chip on his shoulder when it came to the critics. Despite being one of the most popular writers of his generation, he routinely complained that his work was overlooked, or miscast as high-concept, middle-brow fiction. The publication of Charles J. Shields's fascinating new biography . . . probably won't put this beef to rest, at least among his loyalists. But it does provide a definitive and disturbing account of the late author, whose ambition and talent transformed him from an obscure science fiction writer to a countercultural icon." Boston Globe

Includes bibliographical references

Vreeland, Diana

Stuart, Amanda Mackenzie. **Empress** of Fashion; A Life of Diana Vreeland. Amanda Mackenzie Stuart. HarperCollins 2012 419 p. ill. (some col.) $35   92

1. Fashion
ISBN 0061691747; 9780061691744

This book is a biography of fashion editor Diana Vreeland by Amanda Mackenzie Stuart. Mackenzie describes how Vreeland's "creation of an idealized image she called the Girl, coupled with a creative flair 'and the development of an idiosyncratic way with words,' propelled Vreeland into becoming one of the most influential tastemakers in American fashion." (Publishers Weekly)

Waits, Tom, 1949-

Hoskyns, Barney. **Lowside** of the road; a life of Tom Waits. Broadway Books 2009 xxix, 609p il $29.95   92

1. Actors 2. Singers 3. Rock musicians 4. Blues musicians 5. Songwriters
ISBN 978-0-7679-2708-6; 0-7679-2708-7

This "book lights up and whirls like one of the greasy carnival rides in Mr. Waits's own sprawling oeuvre . . . Mr.

Hoskyns rummaged through Mr. Waits's interviews, pored through the historical record and talked to those who were willing to speak. Thus his unauthorized biography mirrors, in some ways, Mr. Waits's own junkyard aesthetic. Mr. Hoskyns picks up what shards of Mr. Waits's life he can find and holds them to the light, turning them eagerly in his hands." N Y Times Book Rev

Wallace, Alfred Russel, 1823-1913

Slotten, Ross A. The **heretic** in Darwin's court; the life of Alfred Russel Wallace. Columbia University Press 2004 602p il maps $77.50; pa $25 **92**

1. Naturalists 2. Writers on science

ISBN 0-231-13010-4; 0-231-13011-2 pa

LC 2003-68833

"With a narrative of almost 500 pages, the biography was clearly a labor of love for the author, who is a medical doctor and a Wallace enthusiast. Although some readers may find the amount of material overwhelming, it is quite accessible to general audiences." Sci Books Films

Includes bibliographical references

Wallace, David Foster

Max, D. T., ca. 1962- **Every** love story is a ghost story; a life of David Foster Wallace. D.T. Max. Viking 2012 356 p. $27.95 **92**

1. Suicide 2. Literary style 3. Depression (Psychology) 4. Novelists, American -- 20th century -- Biography

ISBN 0670025925; 9780670025923

LC 2012008488

Author D. T. Max's "book begins with [author David Foster] Wallace's childhood and ends with his suicide, detailing both the highs (his marriage to Karen Green) and lows (his string of breakdowns that began in college). There is the mutating public and critical opinion of his work, his troubled history with women, and his tendency to roam for much of his life while he struggled to balance writing and relationships, and writing and well-being." (Publishers Weekly)

Includes bibliographical references and index.

Wallace, Perry

Maraniss, Andrew. **Strong** inside; Perry Wallace and the collision of race and sports in the South. Andrew Maraniss. Vanderbilt University Press 2014 472 p. illustrations (hardback) $35 **92**

1. African American baseball players 2. Southern States -- Race relations 3. Vanderbilt University -- Basketball -- History 4. Basketball players -- United States -- Biography 5. Vanderbilt Commodores (Basketball team) -- History 6. Civil rights -- History -- Southern States -- 20th century 7. Racism in sports -- Southern States -- History -- 20 century

ISBN 0826520235; 9780826520234; 9780826520241

LC 2014015257

This book, by Andrew Maraniss, offers a "detailed biography of Perry Wallace, the first African American basketball player in the SEC. . . . [It] digs deep beneath the surface to reveal a more complicated and profound story of sports pioneering than we've come to expect from the genre. Perry Wallace's unusually insightful and honest introspection reveals his inner thoughts throughout his journey." (Publisher's note)

"Nuanced and complex, Strong Inside is an invaluable resource for studying the state of race relations in the US, both past and present. Summing Up: Highly recommended. Lower-division undergraduates through faculty and professionals; general readers." Choice

Includes bibliographical references and index

Wallach, Eli, 1915-

Wallach, Eli. The **good,** the bad, and me; in my anecdotage. Harcourt 2005 312p il $25; pa $16 **92**

1. Actors

ISBN 0-15-101189-3; 0-15-603169-8 pa

LC 2004-23121

The author "tells his story, from a Brooklyn childhood as the only Jew in an Italian neighborhood, through Actors Studio days with Brando and others, and on to his long and illustrious career on both stage and screen. . . . This compelling memoir shows the full range of a remarkable actor's life." Booklist

Walls, Jeannette

★ Walls, Jeannette. The **glass** castle; a memoir. Scribner 2005 288p $25; pa $14 **92**

1. Authors 2. Novelists 3. Memoirists 4. Gossip columnists

ISBN 0-7432-4753-1; 0-7432-4754-X pa

LC 2004-58907

"Shocking, sad, and occasionally bitter, this gracefully written account speaks candidly, yet with surprising affection, about parents and about the strength of family ties—for both good and ill." Booklist

Walsh, Bill, 1931-2007

Harris, David. The **genius;** how Bill Walsh reinvented football and created an NFL dynasty. Random House 2008 385p il $26 **92**

1. Football coaches 2. Football -- Biography 3. San Francisco 49ers (Football team)

ISBN 978-1-4000-6665-0; 1-4000-6665-4

LC 2008-16566

"Walsh was one of the NFL's greatest coaches, and Harris' book does him justice." Booklist

Includes bibliographical references

Walsh, Mikey

Walsh, Mikey. **Gypsy** boy; my life in the secret world of the Romany Gypsies. Mikey Walsh. Thomas Dunne Books/St. Martin's Press 2012 278 p. **92**

1. Gay men -- Biography 2. England -- Ethnic relations 3. Gypsies -- England -- Biography 4. England -- Social life and customs 5. Romanies -- England 6. Young gay men -- England -- Biography

ISBN 9780312622084; 9781250011978

LC 2011038168

This memoir, a "number-one best-seller in the UK following its 2009 release," was written "under a pseudonym to protect . . . [author Mikey] Walsh [who] has ongoing concerns for his safety after leaving the highly secretive Romany Gypsy community 15 years ago. . . . He claims his ultraviolet father once put a contract out on his life. He was born into a roving caravan of outsiders, brutally abused as a child (both physically by his father and sexually by an uncle), and never received any formal education growing up. He is also gay." (Booklist)

Walters, Barbara, 1931-

Walters, Barbara. **Audition**; a memoir. Alfred A. Knopf 2008 612p il $29.95   **92**

1. Women journalists 2. Talk show hosts 3. Television news anchors

ISBN 978-0-307-26646-0; 0-307-26646-X

LC 2008-05843

This is a memoir by the television newscaster.

"Alternating between tales of her personal struggles, professional achievements and insider anecdotes about the celebrities and world leaders she's interviewed, this mammoth memoir's energy never flags." Publ Wkly

Walton, Bill, 1952-

Walton, Bill, 1952- **Back** from the dead; Bill Walton. Simon & Schuster 2016 336 p. 24 plates; illustrations (hardcover) $27   **92**

1. Broadcasting 2. Wounds and injuries 3. Basketball players -- United States -- Biography 4. Sportscasters -- United States -- Biography

ISBN 1476716862; 9781476716862

LC 2015031712

This "memoir from sports and cultural icon Bill Walton recounts his devastating injuries and amazing recoveries, set in the context of his UCLA triumphs under John Wooden, his storied NBA career, and his affinity for music and the Grateful Dead. In his own words, 'Back from the Dead' shares this dramatic story, including his basketball and broadcasting careers, his many setbacks and rebounds, and his ultimate triumph as the toughest of champions." (Publisher's note)

"This memoir is defined by trials as much as successes and will appeal to readers who appreciated Walton as player and commentator." Library Journal

Walton, Sam

Walton, Sam. **Sam** Walton, made in America; my story. by Sam Walton with John Huey. Bantam Books 1992 346p il pa $7.99   **92**

1. Businessmen 2. Retail executives 3. Wal-Mart Stores, Inc.

ISBN 0-553-56283-5; 978-0-553-56283-5

First published 1992 by Doubleday

The founder of Wal-Mart Stores, the largest retail chain in the world, recounts how he made his fortune.

"Readers will enjoy the folksy narrative of the small-town millionaire who revolutionized retail distribution. . . . Coauthor Huey does a fine job of incorporating candid testimonials from family members and associates." Libr J

Wambach, Abby, 1980-

Wambach, Abby, 1980- **Forward**; a memoir. Abby Wambach. Dey Street Books 2016 230 p. (hardback) $26.99   **92**

1. Soccer players 2. Women athletes 3. Soccer players -- United States -- Biography 4. Women soccer players -- United States -- Biography

ISBN 0062466984; 9780062466983; 9780062467003

LC 2016037369

In this memoir, professional soccer player Abby Wambach "shares her inspiring and often brutal journey from girl in Rochester, New York, to world-class athlete. Far more than a sports memoir, [it is a] tale of resilience and redemption—and a reminder that heroism is, above all, about embracing life's challenges with fearlessness and heart." (Publisher's note)

"A cut above the standard sports memoir." Booklist

Warburg, Siegmund George Sir, 1902-1982

Ferguson, Niall, 1964- **High** financier; the lives and time of Siegmund Warburg. Penguin Press 2010 548p il pa $22; $35   **92**

1. Banks and banking 2. Bankers 3. SBC Warburg (Firm) 4. Biography, Individual 5. Banks and banking -- Great Britain -- History -- 20th century

ISBN 978-0-14-311940-1 pa; 978-1-59420-246-9

LC 2010-18353

This is a biography of the founder of the investment bank S. G. Warburg and Company. Index.

"Ferguson draws a richly vivid portrait of this unusual banker, an intellectual who read the Latin and Greek classics in the original and preferred Nietzsche to newspapers." N Y Times Book Rev

Includes bibliographical references

Ward, Jesmyn

Ward, Jesmyn. **Men** We Reaped; A Memoir. by Jesmyn Ward. Bloomsbury USA 2013 272 p. $26   **92**

1. Death 2. Grief 3. Poverty -- United States 4. African American men -- Mississippi 5. Rural poor -- Mississippi -- Biography 6. African American women authors -- Biography

ISBN 160819521X; 9781608195213

LC 2013013600

In this memoir, author Jesmyn Ward tells how she "grew up in poverty in rural Mississippi. She writes powerfully about the pressures this brings, on the men who can do no right and the women who stand in for family in a society where the men are often absent. She bravely tells her story, revisiting the agonizing losses of her only brother and her friends." (Publisher's note)

Includes bibliographical references and index

Ward, Samuel, 1814-1884

Jacob, Kathryn Allamong. **King** of the lobby; the life and times of Sam Ward, man-about-Washington in the Gilded Age. Johns Hopkins University Press 2010 212p il $40   **92**

1. Lobbying 2. Lobbyists 3. United States -- Politics and government -- 1861-1865 4. United States -- Politics and government -- 1865-1898

ISBN 978-0-8018-9397-1; 0-8018-9397-6

LC 2009-9807

The author's "trim and surprising biography of Sam Ward . . . will not change most people's view of what is essentially a hustler's profession. But she brilliantly shows how, in the hands of a master, lobbying can be lifted to the level of art." Wall Street J

Includes bibliographical references

Wareham, Dean

Wareham, Dean. **Black** postcards; a rock & roll romance. Penguin Press 2008 324p il $25.95 **92**

1. Singers 2. Guitarists 3. Rock musicians 4. Luna (Musical group) 5. Galaxie 500 (Musical group)

ISBN 978-1-59420-155-4; 1-59420-155-2

LC 2007-35280

"In this collection of over 50 sequential autobiographical essays, . . . [the author] takes us from his childhood in New Zealand, through his formative years exploring New York City's punk scene, to his adult life in Cambridge, MA, where he becomes a notable figure in the alternative music scene. Wareham documents in great detail the history of his two bands, Galaxy 500 and Luna. . . . Fans of Wareham's bands and such bands as Bongwater, Cocteau Twins, R.E.M., and the Velvet Underground, as well as anyone with an interest in American and European alternative music, will find this to be an insightful and entertaining read." Libr J

Warhol, Andy, 1928?-1987

★ Scherman, Tony. **Pop**; the genius of Andy Warhol. [by] Tony Scherman and David Dalton. HarperCollins 2009 509p il $40 **92**

1. Artists 2. Pop art 3. Artists -- United States 4. Motion picture directors

ISBN 978-0-06-621243-2; 0-06-621243-X

LC 2009-24815

This biography covers the artist's career and personal life through 1968.

"Not only is . . . [this book] well written and researched, it manages to unearth details that reframe the debate about Warhol's real importance as an artist." Bookforum

Includes bibliographical references

Wariner, Ruth.

Wariner, Ruth. The **sound** of gravel; a memoir. Ruth Wariner. Flatiron Books 2016 352 p. illustrations (hardcover) $27.99 **92**

1. Mormons 2. Polygamy 3. Wariner, Ruth

ISBN 9781250077691

LC 2015037663

This book, by Ruth Wariner, is "the true story of one girl's coming-of-age in a polygamist family. . . . Growing up on a farm in rural Mexico, where authorities turn a blind eye to the practices of her community, Ruth lives in a ramshackle house. . . . At church, preachers teach that God will punish the wicked by destroying the world. . . . As she begins to doubt her family's beliefs and question her mother's choices, she struggles to . . . forge a better life for herself. " (Publisher's note)

"With power and insight, Wariner's tale shows a road to escape from the most confining circumstances." Booklist

Warren, Elizabeth

Warren, Elizabeth, 1949- A **fighting** chance; Elizabeth Warren. Metropolitan, Henry Holt & Co. 2014 384 p. illustrations (chiefly color) (hardcover) $28 **92**

1. Autobiographies 2. Politicians' writings 3. Middle class -- United States 4. Legislators -- United States -- Biography 5. United States. Congress. Senate -- Biography 6. Women legislators -- United States -- Biography 7. United States -- Politics and government -- 2009-

ISBN 1627790527; 9781627790529

LC 2014000776

This book by Elizabeth Warren tells the "story of the two-decade journey that taught her how Washington really works--and really doesn't. . . . She fought for better bankruptcy laws for ten years and lost. She tried to hold the federal government accountable during the financial crisis but became a target of the big banks. . . . Finally, at age 62, she decided to run for elective office and won the most competitive--and watched--Senate race in the country." (Publisher's note)

"Warren emerges as a committed advocate with real world sensibility, who tasted tough economic times at an early age and did not forget its bitterness." Pub Wkly

Includes bibliographical references and index

Washington, Booker T., 1856-1915

Harlan, Louis R. **Booker** T. Washington: the making of a black leader, 1856-1901. Oxford Univ. Press 1972 379p il hardcover o.p. pa $21.50 **92**

1. Slaves 2. Authors 3. Educators 4. African American educators 5. Memoirists 6. Nonfiction writers 7. Tuskegee Institute 8. Civil rights activists 9. African Americans -- Biography

ISBN 0-19-501915-6 pa

This book "covers Washington's life from his birth as a slave in western Virginia up to [the year 1901, when he dined] with Theodore Roosevelt at the White House, an event signifying white recognition of Washington as the chief spokesman for black interests in the period before World War I." Libr J

Harlan, Louis R. **Booker** T. Washington: the wizard of Tuskegee, 1901-1915. Oxford Univ. Press 1983 548p il hardcover o.p. pa $24.95 **92**

1. Slaves 2. Authors 3. Educators 4. African American educators 5. Memoirists 6. Nonfiction writers 7. Tuskegee Institute 8. Civil rights activists 9. African Americans -- Biography

ISBN 0-19-504229-8 pa

LC 82-14547

This is the second and concluding volume of a life of the black educator and founder of Tuskegee Institute.

"Having avoided the pitfalls of white guilt and black rage and the temptation to judge the past by standards of the present, Mr. Harlan deserves honors for his remarkable achievement." N Y Times Book Rev

Includes bibliographical references

Norrell, Robert J. **Up** from history; the life of Booker T. Washington. Belknap Press of Harvard University Press 2009 508p il $35 **92**

1. Slaves 2. Authors 3. Educators 4. African American educators 5. Memoirists 6. Nonfiction writers 7. Tuskegee Institute 8. Biography, Individual 9. Civil rights activists 10. African Americans -- Biography 11. Race discrimination -- History

ISBN 067403211X; 9780674032118; 978-0-674-03211-8; 0-674-03211-X

LC 2008-32599

This is a biography of the educator who founded the Tuskegee Institute and wrote the memoir Up From Slavery (1901). Index.

This "is in all respects an exemplary book, scrupulously fair to its subject and thus to the reader as well." Washington Post Book World

Includes bibliographical references

Smock, Raymond W. **Booker** T. Washington; black leadership in the age of Jim Crow. [by] Raymond W. Smock. Ivan R. Dee 2009 223p il (Library of African-American biography) $26   **92**
1. Slaves 2. Authors 3. Educators 4. African American educators 5. Memoirists 6. Nonfiction writers 7. Tuskegee Institute 8. Civil rights activists 9. African Americans -- Biography
ISBN 978-1-56663-725-1; 1-56663-725-2
LC 2009-3277

The author "examines Washington's legacy and how he came to be alternately lauded and lambasted for his practical approach to racism following Reconstruction: to build a school to prepare blacks to occupy the unchallenged place set aside for them in the Jim Crow South. . . . This is a nuanced portrait of an enigmatic man of enduring contribution to black leadership." Booklist

Includes bibliographical references

★ Washington, Booker T. **Up** from slavery; edited with an introduction and notes by William L. Andrews. Oxford University Press 2008 xxvii, 196p (Oxford world's classics) pa $9.95   **92**
1. Slaves 2. Authors 3. Educators 4. African American educators 5. Memoirists 6. Nonfiction writers 7. Tuskegee Institute 8. Civil rights activists 9. African Americans -- Biography
ISBN 978-0-19-955239-9
LC 2008-279129

First published 1901

"The classic autobiography of the man who, though born in slavery, educated himself and went on to found Tuskegee Institute." N Y Public Libr

Includes bibliographical references

Washington, George, 1732-1799

Breen, T. H. **George** Washington's journey; the president forges a new nation. T.H. Breen. Simon & Schuster 2015 320 p. illustrations, maps (hardcover) $28   **92**
1. Presidents -- United States -- Travel 2. United States -- Politics and government -- 1789-1797 3. Presidents -- Travel -- United States -- History -- 18th century
ISBN 9781451675429; 9781451675436
LC 2015007283

This book, by T. H. Breen, "introduces us to a George Washington we rarely meet. By nature shy and reserved, the brand new president decided that he would visit the new citizens in their own states, that only by showing himself could he make them feel part of a new nation. He displayed himself as victorious general . . . and as President. . . . Washington drew on his immense popularity, even hero worship, to send a powerful and lasting message—that America was now a nation." (Publisher's note)

"Breen's superb chronicle offers glimpses into Washington's love of his country and its people, and his willingness to meet them on their own terms to secure the unity of the new republic." Pub Wkly

Includes bibliographical references and index

Brookhiser, Richard. **Founding** father: rediscovering George Washington. Free Press 1996 230p hardcover o.p. pa $14   **92**
1. Generals 2. Presidents 3. Presidents -- United States
ISBN 0-684-83142-2 pa
LC 95-50650

"Brookhiser's slim, graceful volume is readable in one sitting. His style is muscular and discursive, yet unaffectedly erudite." Christ Sci Monit

Includes bibliographical references

Chernow, Ron. **Washington**; a life. Penguin Press 2010 xxi, 904p il $40   **92**
1. Biography, Individual 2. Presidents -- United States 3. United States -- Politics and government -- 1775-1783 4. United States -- Politics and government -- 1783-1809
ISBN 978-1-59420-266-7
LC 2010-19154

Chernow "has done justice to the solid flesh, the human frailty and the dental miseries of his subject—and also to his immense historical importance. . . . This is a magnificently fair, full-scale biography. Its judgments are lapidary." Economist

Includes bibliographical references

★ Ellis, Joseph J. **His** Excellency; George Washington. Knopf 2004 320p il hardcover o.p. pa $15   **92**
1. Generals 2. Presidents 3. Presidents -- United States
ISBN 1-4000-4031-0; 1-4000-3253-9 pa
LC 2004-46576

The author "offers a magisterial account of the life and times of George Washington, celebrating the heroic image of the president whom peers like Jefferson and Madison recognized as 'their unquestioned superior' while acknowledging his all-too-human qualities." Publ Wkly

Includes bibliographical references

Flexner, James Thomas. **George** Washington and the new nation, 1783-1793. Little, Brown 1969 466p il map (His George Washington) $42   **92**
1. Generals 2. Presidents 3. Presidents -- United States
ISBN 0-316-28600-1
LC 78-117042

This third volume of a four-volume biography of Washington focuses on the period between the end of the Revolutionary War through his first term as president.

Includes bibliographical references

Flexner, James Thomas. **George** Washington: anguish and farewell 1793-1799. Little, Brown 1972 554p il (His George Washington) $45   **92**
1. Generals 2. Presidents 3. Presidents -- United States
ISBN 0-316-28602-8
LC 72-6875

This final volume of a four-volume biography of Washington covers his second term as president, his retirement, and death.

Includes bibliographical references

Flexner, James Thomas. **George** Washington: the forge of experience, 1732-1775. Little 1965 390p il map (His George Washington) $40   **92**
1. Generals 2. Presidents 3. Presidents -- United States
ISBN 0-316-28597-8

LC 65-21361

The author "covers forty-three years of Washington's life in this volume, the first in a series of four . . . [that carries] Washington through the Revolutionary War and on to the end of his life." Publisher's note

Includes bibliographical references

Fraser, Flora. The **Washingtons**; join'd by friendship, crown'd by love. Flora Fraser. Alfred A. Knopf 2015 448 p. 24 plates; color illustrations (hardcover : alk. paper) $30   **92**
1. United States -- Biography 2. Generals -- United States -- Biography 3. Presidents -- United States -- Biography 4. Generals' spouses -- United States -- Biography 5. Presidents' spouses -- United States -- Biography 6. United States -- History -- Revolution, 1775-1783 -- Biography
ISBN 0307272788; 9780307272782; 9780307474438

LC 2014045521

This book, by Flora Fraser, presents a portrait of the lives and marriage of George and Martha Washington, the first family of the U.S. It "begins in colonial Virginia in 1759, when George Washington woos and weds Martha Dandridge Parke Custis. . . . [The book describes] the public Washington and of the war he waged, and gives us, as well, the domestic Washingtons, whether at Mount Vernon before and during the war or in New York and Philadelphia during his presidency." (Publisher's note)

"Fraser's prose flows well with the voices of her 18th-century subjects. However, the impression that emerges from the copious details of plantation management, children's tutoring, and relatives born and dying is of two busy lives on parallel courses; their devotion to each other is clearly evident, but so are several potential sources of sharp conflict between them. Fraser provides no sense of how these shoals were negotiated or how these formidable individuals actually got on with each other when they could be together. A difficult task crowned with mixed success." Kirkus

Includes bibliographical references and index

Gaines, James R. **For** liberty and glory; Washington, Lafayette, and their revolutions. W.W. Norton & Co. 2007 533p il map $29.95   **92**
1. Generals 2. Statesmen 3. Presidents 4. France -- History -- 1789-1799, Revolution 5. United States -- History -- 1775-1783, Revolution
ISBN 0-393-06138-8; 978-0-393-06138-3

LC 2007-22449

Gaines examines the relationship between George Washington and the Marquis de Lafayette.

This is a "fresh and engaging new look at the pair. . . . Gaines has a dry sense of humor and an appreciation for hu-man foibles. . . . The American founding fathers, in particular, come across as extraordinary men with ordinary obsessions and—surprise!—senses of humor." Christ Sci Monit

Includes bibliographical references

Johnson, Paul. **George** Washington: the Founding Father. HarperCollins Publishers 2005 126p (Eminent lives) $19.95   **92**
1. Generals 2. Presidents 3. Presidents -- United States
ISBN 0-06-075365-X

LC 2004-52907

This is a biography of the first president of the United States.

The author "submits a beautifully cogent, enthrallingly perceptive, and . . . startlingly fresh take on the ultimate American icon." Booklist

Includes bibliographical references

Larson, Edward. The **Return** of George Washington; How the United States Was Reborn. Edward Larson. HarperCollins 2014 400 p. 8 plates; color illustrations $29.99   **92**
1. United States -- Politics and government -- 1783-1865
ISBN 0062248677; 9780062248671

LC 2014037147

In this book, historian Edward Larson "[reveals] how [George] Washington saved the United States by coming out of retirement to lead the Constitutional Convention and serve as our first president. After leading the Continental Army to victory in the Revolutionary War, George Washington shocked the world: he retired. . . . Yet as Washington contentedly grew his estate, the fledgling American experiment floundered." (Publisher's note)

"Larson identifies Washington's three goals—'respect abroad, prosperity at home, and development westward'—and includes an account of an inaugural dish that makes turducken seem unambitious. Profound, even affectionate, scholarship infuses every graceful sentence." Kirkus

Randall, Willard Sterne. **George** Washington; a life. Holt & Co. 1997 548p hardcover o.p. pa $18   **92**
1. Generals 2. Presidents 3. United States -- History 4. Presidents -- United States
ISBN 0-8050-5992-X pa

LC 97-19125

"Chronicling less the adaptive leader of the struggling rebellion or the persuasive conciliator of the infant republic, Randall . . . portrays instead the vain, restless, ambitious provincial who got 'tremendously lucky'. . . . Altogether human, Randall's demythologized Washington comes vividly to life." Publ Wkly

Includes bibliographical references

Washington, Martha, 1731-1802

Brady, Patricia. **Martha** Washington; an American life. Viking 2005 276p il $24.95; pa $15 **92**
1. Spouses of presidents 2. Presidents' spouses -- United States
ISBN 0-670-03430-4; 0-14-303713-7 pa

LC 2004-61242

"Brady's splendid biography offers a compelling new portrait of this passionate, committed founding mother who has unjustly been obscured by others, such as Abigail Adams." Publ Wkly

Includes bibliographical references

Fraser, Flora. The **Washingtons**; join'd by friendship, crown'd by love. Flora Fraser. Alfred A. Knopf 2015 448 p. 24 plates; color illustrations (hardcover : alk. paper) $30   92

1. United States -- Biography 2. Generals -- United States -- Biography 3. Presidents -- United States -- Biography 4. Generals' spouses -- United States -- Biography 5. Presidents' spouses -- United States -- Biography 6. United States -- History -- Revolution, 1775-1783 -- Biography

ISBN 0307272788; 9780307272782; 9780307474438
LC 2014045521

This book, by Flora Fraser, presents a portrait of the lives and marriage of George and Martha Washington, the first family of the U.S. It "begins in colonial Virginia in 1759, when George Washington woos and weds Martha Dandridge Parke Custis. . . . [The book describes] the public Washington and of the war he waged, and gives us, as well, the domestic Washingtons, whether at Mount Vernon before and during the war or in New York and Philadelphia during his presidency." (Publisher's note)

"Fraser's prose flows well with the voices of her 18th-century subjects. However, the impression that emerges from the copious details of plantation management, children's tutoring, and relatives born and dying is of two busy lives on parallel courses; their devotion to each other is clearly evident, but so are several potential sources of sharp conflict between them. Fraser provides no sense of how these shoals were negotiated or how these formidable individuals actually got on with each other when they could be together. A difficult task crowned with mixed success." Kirkus

Includes bibliographical references and index

Waters, Ethel, 1896-1977

Bogle, Donald. **Heat** wave; the life and career of Ethel Waters. HarperCollins 2011 624p il $26.99   92

1. Actors 2. Singers 3. African American singers 4. Biography, Individual

ISBN 0-06-124173-3; 978-0-06-124173-4
LC 2010-29230

This is a biography of the actress and singer Ethel Waters, who starred in the film Cabin in the Sky (1943). Bibliography. Index.

"In this powerful biography, Bogle recovers the rich fullness of singer Ethel Waters's life (1896–1977). In vivid though often exhausting detail, Bogle traces Waters's rise from the poverty of her surroundings in Chester, Pa., through her early musical successes in Harlem in the 1920s and 1930s to her film and Broadway career and her later religious conversion as her health declined." Publ Wkly

Includes bibliographical references

Waters, John, 1946-

Waters, John. **Role** models. Farrar, Straus and Giroux 2010 304p il $25   92

1. Motion picture producers and directors 2. Screenwriters 3. Motion picture directors

ISBN 978-0-374-25147-5; 0-374-25147-9
LC 2009-42211

"The famed cult-film director recalls the famous—and not-so-famous—people he has idolized over the years. . . . In this consistently charming and witty collection of essays, he fondly remembers the many artists he has admired throughout his life, from stars, such as Little Richard, to such near-unknown figures as the 1960s Baltimore stripper Lady Zorro. . . . An impressive, heartfelt collection by a true American iconoclast." Kirkus

Includes bibliographical references

Waters, John. **Carsick**; John Waters. Farrar Straus & Giroux 2014 336 p. illustrations (hardcover) $26   92

1. Hitchhiking 2. Autobiographies 3. Hitchhiking -- United States 4. United States -- Description and travel 5. United States -- Social life and customs -- 21st century -- Humor 6. Motion picture producers and directors -- United States -- Biography

ISBN 0374298637; 9780374298630
LC 2013034093

In this book, author "John Waters is putting his life on the line. Armed with wit, a pencil-thin mustache, and a cardboard sign that reads 'I'm Not Psycho,' he hitchhikes across America from Baltimore to San Francisco, braving lonely roads and treacherous drivers. But who should we be more worried about, the delicate film director with genteel manners or the unsuspecting travelers transporting the Pope of Trash?" (Publisher's note)

"For more than half of this account of his 2012 cross-country journey . . . [Waters] imagines what lies in store, with dueling full-length novellas that spin best and worst case scenarios. . . . [A] sweet and funny ride." Kirkus

Watson, James D., 1928-

Watson, James D. **Avoid** boring people; lessons from a life in science. Alfred A. Knopf 2007 347p il $26.95   92

1. Scientists 2. College teachers 3. Molecular biologists 4. Nobel laureates for physiology or medicine

ISBN 978-0-375-41284-4; 0-375-41284-0
LC 2007-15675

"In this memoir, Watson shows by example how to get to the top and stay there. Spanning his boyhood interest in birds to his resignation from Harvard University in 1976 to his leadership of Cold Spring Harbor Laboratory, Watson's reminiscences encompass his claim to fame—cocredit for deducing DNA's structure in 1953—but focus on his ambition and his conduct of academic politics. . . . In angular and opinionated prose, Watson proves as engaging as ever." Booklist

Includes bibliographical references

Watson, James D. **Genes,** girls, and Gamow; after the double helix. Knopf 2002 xxix, 259p il $26; pa $14   92

1. College teachers 2. Molecular biologists 3. Nobel laureates for physiology or medicine

ISBN 0-375-41283-2; 0-375-72715-9 pa

LC 2001-38543

"In 1953, Watson, then 25, and colleague Francis Crick discovered the structure of DNA. . . . Here Watson . . . gives a detailed, journal-writer's account of the aftermath, recalling . . . his younger self's professional and—equally pressing—amorous ambitions. . . . Reading Watson is a delight, an opportunity to breathe the rarefied air of his generation's greatest scientists and to crash a faculty cocktail party or two along the way." Publ Wkly

Wayne, John, 1907-1979

Eliot, Marc. **American** titan; searching for John Wayne. Marc Eliot. Dey Street Books 2014 432 p. 16 plates; illustrations (hardcover) $28.99   92

1. Actors 2. Motion picture actors and actresses -- United States -- Biography

ISBN 0062269003; 9780062269003; 9780062269027

LC 2014014183

In this book on actor John Wayne, "Marc Eliot digs deep beneath the myth in this revealing look at the most legendary Western film hero of all time; the man with the distinctive voice, walk, and demeanor who was an inspiration to many and a symbol of American masculinity, power, and patriotism. Eliot pays tribute to the man and the myth, identifying and analyzing the many interesting contradictions that made John Wayne who he was." (Publisher's note)

"But given that it tells the same story without any unique insights, the book can't help coming across as a bit been there, done that. Still, it's a solidly written account of Wayne's life and does a credible job with the question of how the legend affected Wayne, the person. Libraries with room on the shelves for two new Wayne biographies should slide this one in beside Eyman's work." Booklist

Includes bibliographical references and index

Eyman, Scott. **John** Wayne: the life and legend; the life and legend. Scott Eyman. Simon & Schuster 2014 672 p. illustrations (hardback) $32.50   92

1. Actors -- United States -- Biography 2. Motion picture actors and actresses -- United States -- Biography

ISBN 1439199582; 9781439199589

LC 2013032604

Author Scott Eyman "interviewed [John] Wayne, as well as many family members, and he has drawn on previously unpublished reminiscences from friends and associates of the Duke in this biography, as well as documents from his production company that shed light on Wayne's business affairs. He traces Wayne from his childhood to his stardom in Stagecoach and dozens of films after that." (Publisher's note)

"Insightful, exhaustive and engrossing—a definitive portrait of the man and the legend." Kirkus

Includes bibliographical references and index

Weill, Kurt, 1900-1950

Schebera, Jurgen. **Kurt** Weill; an illustrated life. translated by Caroline Murphy. Yale Univ. Press 1995 381p il $55; pa $38   92

1. Composers

ISBN 0-300-06055-6; 0-300-07284-8 pa

LC 94-41444

Original German edition, 1990

"Schebera makes wonderful use of archival illustrations: concert programs, advertisements, photos, even a few record labels from the Twenties and Thirties. This is a scholarly work, but the appealing subject, complete with the drama of Nazi persecution and flight from prewar Germany, makes it a good choice for most music collections." Libr J

Includes discography and bibliographical references

Weiner, Jennifer

Weiner, Jennifer, 1970- **Hungry** heart; Adventures in Life, Love, and Writing. Jennifer Weiner. Atria Books 2016 432 p. (ebook) $13.99; (hardback) $27   92

1. American authors -- Biography 2. Authors, American -- 20th century -- Biography

ISBN 9781476723440; 9781476723402

LC 2016022112

In this collection of stories, by Jennifer Weiner, "no subject is off-limits: . . . sex, weight, envy, money, her mother's coming out of the closet, her estranged father's death. From lonely adolescence to modern childbirth to hearing her six-year-old daughter say the f-word—fat—for the first time, Jen dives deep into the heart of female experience." (Publisher's note)

"Like her enormously popular commercial fiction, from its very first page this memoir will enthusiastically reach out to female readers and swiftly draw them close." Pub Wkly

Weisskopf, Michael

Weisskopf, Michael. **Blood** brothers; among the soldiers of Ward 57. H. Holt 2006 301p il hardcover o.p. pa $15   92

1. Journalists 2. Iraq War, 2003- -- Personal narratives

ISBN 978-0-8050-7860-2; 0-8050-7860-6; 978-0-8050-8660-7 pa; 0-8050-8660-9 pa

LC 2006-43382

"Weisskopf recognizes his own experience in that of the soldiers, making for a wonderful story of tragedy and recovery." Libr J

Includes bibliographical references

Welles, Orson, 1915-1985

Callow, Simon. **Orson** Welles; the road to Xanadu. Simon Callow. Penguin Bks. 1997 640p illustrations pa $14.95; $20   92

1. Motion picture producers and directors -- Biography

ISBN 0-14-025456-0; 0140254560; 9780140254563

LC 95037138

This biography, by Simon Callow, covers actor and director Orson Welles's "prodigious childhood; his youth in New York, with its fraught partnership with John Houseman and the groundbreaking triumph of his all-black Macbeth; the pioneering radio work that culminated in the notorious

1938 broadcast of War of the Worlds; and finally, his work in Hollywood, including an authoritative account of the making of Citizen Kane." (Publisher's note)

"His research is effortlessly vast, and Callow corrects many of the myths and dissemblings surrounding Welles, some of them put out by Welles himself." Kirkus

Includes filmography. Includes bibliographical references and index.

Callow, Simon. **Orson** Welles; Volume 2 hello Americans. Simon Callow. Penguin Books 2007 513 p. illustrations, portraits $20 **92**

1. Motion picture producers and directors
ISBN 0140275177; 9780140275179

This biography, by Simon Callow, on actor and director Orson Welles "examines the years following Citizen Kane up to the time of Macbeth, in which Welles's Hollywood film career unraveled. In close and colorful detail, Callow offers a scrupulous analysis of the factors involved, revealing the immense and sometimes self-defeating complexities of Welles's temperament as well as some of the monstrous personalities with whom he had to contend." (Publisher's note)

"Destined to be the definitive word. Highly recommended." LJ

Includes lists of stage productions, radio broadcasts, films, writings, and sound recordings (pages 445-463).

Includes bibliographical references (pages 465-493) and index.

Callow, Simon. **Orson** Welles; One-man Band. Simon Callow. Penguin Group USA 2016 624 p. $40 **92**

1. Motion picture producers and directors
ISBN 0670024910; 9780670024919

This biography of Orson Welles, by Simon Callow, "begins with Welles's self-exile from America, and his realization that he could function only to his own satisfaction as an independent film maker, a one-man band, in fact, which committed him to a perpetual cycle of money raising. The book reveals what it was like to be around Welles, and . . ., what it was like to be him, answering the riddle that has long fascinated film scholars and lovers alike: Whatever happened to Orson Welles?" (Publisher's note)

"Welles rightly imagined that people would never stop writing about him after he died. Callow continues to set the standard in this increasingly crowded field." Kirkus

McGilligan, Patrick. **Young** Orson; The Years of Luck and Genius on the Path to Citizen Kane. by Patrick McGilligan. HarperCollins 2015 832 p. illustrations $40; (ebook) $37.99 **92**

1. Actors -- United States -- Biography 2. Authors -- United States -- Biography
ISBN 0062112481; 9780062112484; 9780062112507
LC 2016297780

In this biography, author Patrick McGilligan "brings young Orson [Welles] into focus as never before. He chronicles Welles's early life growing up in Wisconsin and Illinois as the son of an alcoholic industrialist and a radical suffragist and classical musician, and the magical early years of his career, including his marriage and affairs, his influential friendships, and his artistic collaborations." (Publisher's note)

"Exhaustively researched but well-paced and stuffed with beguiling detail, this is a vivid, sympathetic portrait of Welles's youthful promise and achievement, before the misfires and compromises of his later years." Pub Wkly

Includes bibliographical references and index.

Wellington, Arthur Wellesley, Duke of, 1769-1852

Hibbert, Christopher. **Wellington**; a personal history. Perseus Books 1999 460p il map pa $22 **92**

1. Generals 2. Statesmen 3. Prime ministers 4. Great Britain -- History -- 19th century
ISBN 0-7382-0148-0; 978-0-7382-0148-1

First published 1997 in the United Kingdom by HarperCollins

"Altogether, Wellington does not quite pass the 'niceness' test. . . . He was a difficult man, a major military figure, a minor Prime Minister and in sum a historically important legend. Hibbert skillfully brings out all these characteristics." N Y Times Book Rev

Includes bibliographical references

Wells-Barnett, Ida B., 1862-1931

★ Giddings, Paula. **Ida**: a sword among lions; Ida B. Wells and the campaign against lynching. Amistad 2008 800p il $35 **92**

1. Authors 2. Lynching 3. Journalists 4. Women political activists 5. Essayists 6. Nonfiction writers 7. Newspaper executives 8. Civil rights activists 9. African Americans -- Civil rights 10. African American women -- Biography
ISBN 978-0-06-051921-6; 0-06-051921-5

"An iconic figure in American history, Wells was not always celebrated by her contemporaries for her groundbreaking activism because of her assertive politics and difficult personality. . . . Giddings offers a look at how Wells' own self-assertion affected her relationships with family, friends, colleagues, and the broader American public as she evolved as a woman and an activist. . . . With meticulous research, including Wells' own diary, Giddings brings to life one of the most fascinating women in American history, giving readers a real feel for the texture and context of Wells' life." Booklist

Includes bibliographical references

Welty, Eudora, 1909-2001

Marrs, Suzanne. **Eudora** Welty: a biography. Harcourt 2005 652p il $28 **92**

1. Authors 2. Novelists 3. Authors, American 4. Short story writers
ISBN 0-15-100914-7
LC 2004-30490

This book "belongs on the shelf beside its subject's own work. Neither hagiography nor pathography, it is, you feel, the thoroughly respectful and straightforward biography its honest, modest, intensely private subject would have wanted." N Y Times Book Rev

Includes bibliographical references

Waldron, Ann. **Eudora**; a writer's life. Doubleday 1998 398p il hardcover o.p. pa $23 **92**

1. Authors 2. Novelists 3. Authors, American 4. Short

story writers
ISBN 0-385-47648-5 pa

LC 98-5708

This is a biography of the writer from Mississippi
"Waldron's biography of Welty is the first to be written and, until the definitive treatment arrives, will satisfy readers curious to know details about the life of this much loved figure." Booklist

Includes bibliographical references

Welty, Eudora. **One** writer's beginnings. Harvard Univ. Press 1984 104p il (William E. Massey, Sr. lectures in the history of American civilization) hardcover o.p. pa $12   **92**
   1. Authors 2. Novelists 3. Authors, American 4. Short story writers
ISBN 0-674-63925-1; 0-674-63927-8 pa

LC 83-18638

A series of lectures in which the author reflects on her Southern heritage and her early artistic influences.

Meanwhile there are letters; the correspondence of Eudora Welty and Ross Macdonald. edited and with an introduction by Suzanne Marrs and Tom Nolan. Arcade Publishing 2015 568 p. illustrations (some color) (hardback) $35   **92**
   1. Authors -- Correspondence 2. Authors, American -- 20th century -- Correspondence
ISBN 1628725273; 9781628725278

LC 2015005957

This book, edited by by Suzanne Marrs and Tom Nolan, presents correspondence between authors Ross Macdonald and Eudora Welty. "They brought their literary talents to bear on a wide range of topics, discussing each others' publications, the process of translating life into fiction, the nature of the writer's block each encountered, books they were reading, and friends and colleagues they cherished." (Publisher's note)
   "An intimate, luminous portrait of a friendship." Kirkus
Includes bibliographical references and index

What there is to say we have said; the correspondence of Eudora Welty and William Maxwell. edited by Suzanne Marrs. Houghton Mifflin Harcourt 2011 499p il $35   **92**
   1. Authors 2. Novelists 3. Magazine editors 4. Short story writers
ISBN 0547376499; 9780547376493; 978-0-547-37649-3; 0-547-37649-9

LC 2010-42105

"Letters between writers often have a lot of shop talk of interest to other writers and literary cultists, but this collection yields broader pleasures, too. In addition to being stellar writers, Welty and Maxwell were also accomplished critics, and one of the joys of the book is eavesdropping on their assessments of authors as varied as John Updike and Virginia Woolf, Anton Chekhov and Charles Dickens, William Faulkner and E. M. Forster. Welty and Maxwell also shared an intense love of gardening – so much so that Marrs was forced, in the book's index, to include an extensive listing of various varieties of roses. . . . As these letters show, Welty and Maxwell regarded domestic life not as a tedious distrac-

tion from the writing desk, but as a crucial source of insight. . . . The title of the collection comes from Maxwell's conclusion, as he and Welty faced their mortality, that 'what there is to say we have said, in one way or the other. You know how much we love you.' That love, a source of sustenance and strength between two great writers, is also a bright tonic for the readers of this volume." Christ Sci Monit

Includes bibliographical references

West, Jerry, 1938-
Lazenby, Roland. **Jerry** West; the life and legend of a basketball icon. ESPN Books; Ballantine Books 2010 xxi, 422p il $28   **92**
   1. Basketball players 2. Basketball executives 3. Basketball -- Biography 4. Los Angeles Lakers (Basketball team)
ISBN 978-0-345-51083-9; 0-345-51083-6

LC 2009-43777

The life of the basketball great from his hardscrabble West Virginia youth to his pro career with the Los Angeles Lakers from 1960 to 1974

"Sports biographies tend to careen between breathless hagiography and the slyly salacious. Lazenby . . . has produced something of a different order — a first-rate piece of narrative nonfiction whose subject happens to be a star athlete. His biography of West is, by turns, smart, beautifully reported, well-written and psychologically shrewd. It also manages to put both the NBA and individual players in a telling social and historical context without straying into didacticism." PopMatters

Includes bibliographical references

West, Nathanael, 1903-1940
Meade, Marion. **Lonelyhearts**; the screwball world of Nathanael West and Eileen McKenney. Houghton Mifflin Harcourt 2010 392p il map $28   **92**
   1. Authors 2. Novelists 3. Screenwriters 4. Authors, American 5. Spouses of prominent persons
ISBN 978-0-15-101149-0

LC 2009-13285

"West and McKenney died young in a car crash in 1940—too soon for him to know that his lacerating novels, especially The Day of the Locust (1939), would become American classics; too soon for his new wife, Eileen, to claim her life for her own after her sister, Ruth, co-opted it to write her best-seller, My Sister Eileen (1938). . . . [The author] tells the trenchant and secret-laden life stories of West (born Nathan Weinstein in New York) and Ohioan McKenney in a ravishingly atmospheric yet propulsive narrative." Booklist

Includes bibliographical references

Wharton, Edith, 1862-1937
Lee, Hermione. **Edith** Wharton. Alfred A. Knopf 2007 869p il $35   **92**
   1. Authors 2. Novelists 3. Nonfiction writers 4. Short story writers
ISBN 978-0-375-40004-9; 0-375-40004-4

LC 2006-48795

"Marked by an elegant literary style that does justice to its subject and a clear, compassionate eye for detail, [this]

is not only the best book on its subject, but one of the finest literary biographies to appear in recent years." Atlanta Journal-Constitution

Includes bibliographical references

White, Ashley, 1987-2011

Lemmon, Gayle Tzemach. **Ashley's** war; the untold story of a team of women soldiers on the Special Ops battlefield. Gayle Tzemach Lemmon. Harper-Collins 2015 320 p. illustrations (hbk.) $26.99 **92**

1. Afghan War, 2001- 2. Women in the military 3. Special forces (Military science) -- United States

ISBN 006233381X; 9780062333810

LC 2015460337

This book, by Gayle Tzemach Lemmon, tells the "story of a groundbreaking team of female American warriors who served alongside Special Operations soldiers on the battlefield in Afghanistan—including Ashley White, a beloved soldier who died serving her country's cause. . . .The idea was that women could access places and people that had remained out of reach, and could build relationships—woman to woman—in ways that male soldiers in a conservative, traditional country could not." (Publisher's note)

"This compassionate and intimate exposé addressing the female battlefield experience will resonate with readers interested in the woman warriors of today's military." LJ

White, Bill

White, Bill. **Uppity**; my untold story about the games people play. [by] Bill White with Gordon Dillow; foreword by Willie Mays. Grand Central Pub. 2011 303p il $26.99   **92**

1. Baseball players 2. African American athletes 3. Sportscasters 4. Baseball executives 5. Baseball -- Biography 6. Sport association executives 7. United States -- Race relations

ISBN 9780446555258; 0446555258

LC 2010-38025

"During his 13 years as a player, [Bill White] won All-Star recognition and frequent Gold Gloves as a slick-fielding, power-hitting first baseman, though he was never the flamboyant type who would call attention to himself. Then he embarked on an 18-year career as a broadcaster, memorably providing a balance to the more unpredictable Phil Rizzuto as announcers for the New York Yankees. He capped his career by serving five years as president of the National League. . . . Whatever his level of involvement, White approached baseball as a career through which he made his living rather than a sport he loved, an attitude that is likely to ruffle sentimentalists. . . . He describes the abuse he took from redneck fans during minor league days when he was one of the few black players on a team, through his battles with the white tycoons who exerted increasing control over the industry before he resigned as league president. Yet his account is otherwise color blind as it separates the heroes of White's life (Willie Mays, Bing Devine, Johnny Keane and others in addition to Rizzuto) from the villains." Kirkus

White, E. B. (Elwyn Brooks), 1899-1985

Elledge, Scott. **E.** B. White; a biography. Norton 1984 400p il hardcover o.p. pa $21.95   **92**

1. Poets 2. Authors 3. Humorists 4. Novelists

5. Essayists 6. Satirists 7. Authors, American 8. Children's authors

ISBN 0-393-30305-5 pa

LC 83-4032

The author is "fair, respectful, thorough, entertaining, skillful and unpedantic. He has performed a splendid exercise in scholarship and literary analysis, and the result is fun." N Y Times Book Rev

Includes bibliographical references

White, E. B. **Letters** of E.B. White; originally collected and edited by Dorothy Lobrano Guth. Rev. ed.; Harper Collins 2006 713p il $35   **92**

1. Poets 2. Authors 3. Humorists 4. Novelists 5. Essayists 6. Satirists 7. Authors, American 8. Children's authors

ISBN 978-0-06-075708-3; 0-06-075708-6

LC 2006-43490

First published 1976

This collection of letters by the essayist, poet, novelist and author of several classic children's books is chronologically arranged. Written between the years 1908 when White was nine and 1985 when he died, they concern his relationships with his wife, Katherine White and his family and friends, which include Harold Ross, James Thurber, Robert Benchley, Alexander Woollcott and others.

White, Edmund, 1940-

White, Edmund. **City** boy; my life in New York during the 1960s and 70s. Bloomsbury USA 2009 297p $26   **92**

1. Authors 2. Gay men 3. Novelists 4. Memoirists 5. Biographers 6. Authors, American 7. Short story writers 8. New York (N.Y.) -- Intellectual life

ISBN 978-1-596-91402-5; 1-596-91402-5

LC 2009-12493

The author "weaves erotic encounters and long-ago literati into a vast tapestry of Manhattan memories. . . . This is a brilliant recreation of an era, rich in revels, revolutions and 'leather boys leading the human tidal wave.'" Publ Wkly

White, Michael

Travels in Vermeer; a memoir. Michael White. Persea Books 2015 178 p. (alk. paper) $17.95 **92**

1. Divorce 2. Art appreciation

ISBN 0892554371; 9780892554379

LC 2014016180

NBA Longlist

This memoir by Michael White is his "account of how a poet, in the midst of a bad divorce, finds consolation and grace through viewing the paintings of Vermeer, in six world cities. Through these travels and his encounters with Vermeer's radiant vision, White finds grace and personal transformation." (Publisher's note)

"An enchanting book about the transformative power of art." Kirkus

Whitman, Walt

Martin, Justin. **Rebel** Souls; Walt Whitman and America's First Bohemians. Justin Martin. Da Capo

Press 2014 368 p. 16 plates; illustrations (A Merloyd Lawrence book) (hardback) $27.99 **92**
1. Bohemianism -- New York (N.Y.) 2. New York (N.Y.) -- Intellectual life -- 19th century 3. Bohemianism -- New York (State) -- New York -- History -- 19th century 4. Bars (Drinking establishments) -- New York (State) -- New York -- History -- 19th century
ISBN 0306822261; 9780306822261; 9780306822278
LC 2014008822
This book, by Justin Martin, is "about the colorful group of artists--regulars at Pfaff's Saloon in Manhattan--rightly considered America's original Bohemians. Besides a young [Walt] Whitman, the circle included actor Edwin Booth; trailblazing stand-up comic Artemus Ward; psychedelic drug pioneer and author Fitz Hugh Ludlow; and brazen performer Adah Menken, famous for her Naked Lady routine." (Publisher's note)
"This book is a lively and entertaining read for students of American literature, history, and culture. Summing Up: Essential. All readers." Choice
Includes bibliographical references and index

Wiesel, Elie
★ Wiesel, Elie. **Night**; translated from the French by Marion Wiesel; [with a new preface by the author; foreword by Francoise Mauriac] Hill and Wang 2006 xxi, 120p $19.95; pa $9 **92**
1. Authors 2. Novelists 3. Journalists 4. Holocaust survivors 5. Human rights activists 6. Nobel laureates for peace 7. Holocaust, 1933-1945 -- Personal narratives
ISBN 0-374-39997-2; 978-0-374-39997-9; 0-374-50001-0 pa; 978-0-374-50001-6 pa
LC 2005-936797

Wiesenthal, Simon
Segev, Tom. **Simon** Wiesenthal; the life and legends. Doubleday 2010 482p il $35; ebook $35 **92**
1. Authors 2. Architects 3. Holocaust survivors 4. Nazi 5. Essayists 6. Memoirists 7. Nazi hunters 8. Jewish leaders 9. Jews -- Austria 10. Biography, Individual
ISBN 978-0-385-51946-5; 978-0-385-53371-3 ebook
LC 2009-53480
The book is a biography about "Simon Wiesenthal, . . . the survivor of a succession of concentration camps, . . . [and] the Nazi hunter who tracked down Adolf Eichmann and brought to justice such [war criminals] . . . as Franz Stangl, the commandant of Treblinka, . . . and Hermine Braunsteiner." The author recounts how Wiesenthal "talked his way into jobs with the American military—an army war crimes unit and the local bureau of the counterintelligence corps—and became the head of local refugee groups, . . . as well as a representative of the Joint Distribution Committee, a Jewish relief organization working with DPs. The American connection, which involved identifying and apprehending war criminals, led directly to his life's work: creating a database of Nazi criminals, tracking them down, and bringing them to justice." (New York Review of Books)
"The man who emerges from this text is ultimately more complex, and indeed likable, than the mythologized figure. Segev's study should be the standard for many years." Libr J
Includes bibliographical references

Wilberforce, William, 1759-1833
Hague, William Jefferson. **William** Wilberforce; the life of the great anti-slave trade campaigner. HarperCollins 2008 582p il $35 **92**
1. Abolitionists 2. Philanthropists 3. Essayists 4. Writers on religion 5. Members of Parliament
ISBN 978-0-15-101267-1; 0-15-101267-9
LC 2007-45981
First published 2007 in the United Kingdom
Hague describes how Wilberforce, "dedicating his political life to moral causes . . . decided on two: 'the reformation of manners,' as he confided to his diary, and the abolition of African slavery. Wilberforce's campaign against vice had scant historical effect, but that against slavery in British realms arguably prodded the Western world toward abolition. Why Wilberforce's effort (trade in slaves was banned in 1807; abolition occurred in 1834) followed a tortuous path becomes understandable as Hague explains the parliamentary practicalities that Wilberforce faced. Incorporating Wilberforce's domestic life, Hague's effort is a well-rounded portrait of the pioneering British abolitionist." Booklist

Wilde, Oscar, 1854-1900
Ellmann, Richard. **Oscar** Wilde. Knopf 1988 680p il hardcover o.p. pa $19.95 **92**
1. Poets 2. Authors 3. Novelists 4. Dramatists 5. Lecturers
ISBN 0-394-75984-2 pa
LC 87-45354
First published 1987 in the United Kingdom
"Wilde's life epitomizes the classic formula for a tragic history, the man who, by hubris, falls from greatness. In Mr. Ellmann's hands, the story becomes as compelling as fiction while never deviating from the facts. Humour and elegance illuminate the accounts of Wilde's family, his friends and the enemies he earned." Economist
Includes bibliographical references

Wilder, Billy, 1906-2002
It's the pictures that got small; Charles Brackett on Billy Wilder and Hollywood's golden age. edited by Anthony Slide. Columbia University Press 2014 448 p. 16 unnumbered pages of plates (cloth : alk. paper) $34.95 **92**
1. Motion pictures -- Production and direction 2. Screenwriters -- United States -- Diaries 3. Motion picture producers and directors -- United States -- Diaries 4. Motion pictures -- Production and direction -- United States -- History -- 20th century
ISBN 9780231167086
LC 2014015801
This book, edited by Anthony Slide, offers an "annotated collection of writings taken from dozens of [screenwriter Charles] Brackett's unpublished diaries . . . [and] clarifies Brackett's critical contribution to [director Billy] Wilder's films and Hollywood history while enriching our knowledge of Wilder's achievements in writing, direction, and style." (Publisher's note)
"Though the diary format is not for all readers, anyone interested in the golden age of film should enjoy this very

entertaining and illustrative look at the film industry of the 1930s and 1940s." LJ

Includes bibliographical references and index

Sikov, Ed. **On** Sunset Boulevard: the life and times of Billy Wilder. Hyperion 1998 675p il hardcover o.p. pa $17.95 **92**

1. Screenwriters 2. Motion picture directors

ISBN 0-7868-8503-3 pa

LC 98-23504

"Sikov has painted as good a portrait of Billy Wilder, the man, the artist, the showman, the self-promoter, the profitably prescient art collector and the successful businessman, as we are likely to get from the outside." N Y Times Book Rev

Includes filmography

Wilder, Laura Ingalls, 1867-1957

Anderson, William T. **Laura** Ingalls Wilder country; text by William Anderson; color photography by Leslie A. Kelly. HarperPerennial 1990 119p il hardcover o.p. pa $24.95 **92**

1. Authors 2. Novelists 3. Western writers 4. Children's authors 5. Young adult authors 6. Literary landmarks -- United States

ISBN 0-06-097346-3 pa

LC 89-46512

"Contemporary and period photographs of the places in the Laura Ingalls Wilder books have been combined with a narrative about the actual historical settings." Horn Book

Wilder, Laura Ingalls, 1867-1957. **Pioneer** girl; the annotated autobiography. Laura Ingalls Wilder; Pamela Smith Hill, editor. South Dakota Historical Society Press 2014 365 p. illustrations, maps (alk. paper) $39.95 **92**

1. Frontier and pioneer life 2. Frontier and pioneer life -- United States 3. Women pioneers -- United States -- Biography 4. Women authors, American -- 20th century -- Biography

ISBN 0984504176; 9780984504176

LC 2014027174

This autobiography, by Laura Ingalls Wilder, edited by Pamela Smith Hill, "hidden away since the 1930s, . . . reveals the true stories of her pioneering life. Some of her experiences will be familiar; some will be a surprise. . . . [This text] re-introduces readers to the woman who defined the pioneer experience for millions of people around the world." (Publisher's note)

"Lengthy footnotes make the manuscript somewhat tricky to navigate, but Hill's comments are cogent and her arguments strong, and this will be welcomed wherever there are Wilder fans. Illustrated with maps, photos, and artwork, and appended with additional manuscripts and an extensive bibliography." Booklist

Includes bibliographical references and index

Wilkinson, James, 1757-1825

Linklater, Andro. An **artist** in treason; the extraordinary double life of General James Wilkinson. Walker 2009 392p il map $27 **92**

1. Spies 2. Generals 3. Territorial governors 4. United States -- Politics and government -- 1783-1865

ISBN 978-0-8027-1720-7

LC 2009-19184

A profile of the Continental Army general explores his career with the Spanish secret service, his protection by four presidents in spite of his treasonous acts, and his role in foiling Aaron Burr's conspiracy to break up the Union.

The author "lucidly details the general's often tangled affairs, but he also uses his story to illuminate the personal feuds, political struggles, and international entanglements that helped shape the young United States. He manages to tell this story of skullduggery and self-interest without wagging his finger in high moral dudgeon at Wilkinson's betrayals. In fact, at times the wily double-crosser almost comes across as sympathetic—but never as someone to trust." Am Heritage

Includes bibliographical references and index.

Willan, Anne

Friedman, Amy. **One** souffle at a time; a memoir of food and France. Anne Willan; with Amy Friedman. St. Martin's Press 2013 320 p. ill. (hardcover) $27.99 **92**

1. Cooks 2. French cooking 3. Cooking, French

ISBN 0312642172; 9780312642174; 9781466837027

LC 2013004043

IACP Cookbook Award (2014)

In this book, chef Anne Willan "tells her story and the story of the food-world greats--including Julia Child, James Beard, Simone Beck, Craig Claiborne, Richard Olney, and others--who changed how the world eats and who made cooking fun. She writes about how a sturdy English girl from Yorkshire made it not only to the stove, but to France, and how she overcame the exceptionally closed male world of French cuisine to found and run her school." (Publisher's note)

"A charming, if not revelatory, portrait of a woman determined to bring French cuisine to a wider audience, with emphasis on traditional, accessible recipes that respect the intellectual side of cookery." Kirkus

Williams, Art, Jr.

Kersten, Jason. The **art** of making money; the story of a master counterfeiter. Gotham Books 2009 292p $26 **92**

1. Criminals 2. Counterfeits and counterfeiting 3. Counterfeiters

ISBN 978-1-59240-446-9

LC 2009-9407

This "absorbing account reads like crime fiction, offering an understanding of modern counterfeiting that will appeal to readers of that genre as well as those who like true crime." Libr J

Williams, Hank, 1923-1953

Escott, Colin. **Hank** Williams; the biography. {by} Colin Escott with George Merritt and William

MacEwen. Little, Brown 1994 307p il hardcover o.p. pa $19.99   **92**

1. Singers 2. Country musicians 3. Songwriters

ISBN 0-316-24938-6 pa

LC 93-48092

A look at the career of the influential country singer/songwriter. Williams' self-destructive behavior and turbulent personal life are also examined

Includes discography and bibliographical references

★ Hemphill, Paul. **Lovesick** blues; the life of Hank Williams. Viking 2005 207p $23.95   **92**

1. Singers 2. Country musicians 3. Songwriters

ISBN 0-670-03414-2

LC 2004-65113

This is a biography of the country singer.

"This is the finest work of literature about Williams yet written." Booklist

Williams, Jay, 1981-

Williams, Jay. **Life** is not an accident; a memoir of reinvention. Jay Williams. Harper 2015 272 p. color illustrations (hardcover) $26.99   **92**

1. National Basketball Association 2. Television broadcasting of sports 3. Basketball players -- United States -- Biography 4. Sportscasters -- United States -- Biography

ISBN 9780062327987

LC 2015050965

In this memoir, author Jay Williams, "details his rise to NBA stardom, the terrible accident that ended his career and plunged him into a life-altering depression, and how he ultimately found his way out of the darkness. . . . Williams talks about the accident that transformed him. . . . He tells it straight about the scandalous recruiting process and his decision to return to Duke and Coach K. . . . He also speaks out about corruption . . . and about his time in the NBA." (Publisher's note)

"Recommended for anyone interested in a behind-the-scenes look at the lives of college basketball and NBA players." LJ

Williams, Roger, 1604?-1683

Gaustad, Edwin Scott. **Roger** Williams; [by] Edwin S. Gaustad. Oxford University Press 2005 150p il (Lives and legacies) $17.95   **92**

1. Clergy 2. Puritans 3. Colonial leaders 4. Writers on religion 5. United States -- History -- 1600-1775, Colonial period

ISBN 0-19-518369-X

LC 2004-25246

The author "provides not just an excellent introduction to the man but a deep analysis of his largely unacknowledged influence on our political and cultural life." Reason

Williams, Ted, 1918-2002

Bradlee, Benjamin C., 1921-2014. The **kid**; the immortal life of Ted Williams. Ben Bradlee, Jr. Little Brown & Co 2013 864 p. illustrations $35   **92**

1. Baseball -- United States 2. Baseball players --

United States -- Biography

ISBN 0316614351; 9780316614351

LC 2013028253

This book, by Ben Bradlee, Jr., offers a biography of the baseball player Ted Williams. "Born in 1918 in San Diego, Ted would spend most of his life disguising his Mexican heritage. During his 22 years with the Boston Red Sox, Williams electrified crowds across America--and shocked them, too: His notorious clashes with the press and fans threatened his reputation. Yet while he was a God in the batter's box, he was profoundly human once he stepped away from the plate." (Publisher's note)

"Sprawling, entertaining life of the baseball great, renowned as a sports hero while leading a life as checkered as Babe Ruth's or Ty Cobb's." Kirkus

Includes bibliographical references and index

Linn, Edward. **Hitter**: the life and turmoils of Ted Williams; {by} Ed Linn. 1993 437p il hardcover o.p. pa $16   **92**

1. Baseball players 2. Baseball managers 3. Boston Red Sox (Baseball team)

ISBN 0-15-600091-1 pa

LC 92-41870

"Linn's book is not a typical game-by-game baseball biography, but a series of snapshots of Williams's career. The {author} . . . touches on the many high points, but does not neglect Williams's warts, including his constant battle with Boston baseball writers. The product of an unhappy childhood, Williams formed close friendships with the 'underdogs,' and gave unsparingly of himself to a charity for combatting cancer in children." Libr J

Williams, Tennessee, 1911-1983

★ Lahr, John. **Tennessee** Williams; Mad Pilgrimage of the Flesh. John Lahr. W W Norton & Co Inc 2014 736 p. illustrations hc $39.95   **92**

1. American dramatists

ISBN 9780393021240; 0393021246

LC 2014022281

National Book Critics Circle Award: Biography (2014)

National Book Award Shortlist: Nonfiction (2014)

Written by John Lahr, "'Tennessee Williams: Mad Pilgrimage of the Flesh' gives intimate access to the mind of one of the most brilliant dramatists of his century, whose plays reshaped the American theater and the nation's sense of itself. This . . . biography sheds a light on Tennessee Williams's warring family, his guilt, his creative triumphs and failures, his sexuality and numerous affairs, his misreported death, even the shenanigans surrounding his estate." (Publisher's note)

"Drawing on vast archival sources and unpublished manuscripts, as well as interviews, memoirs and theater history, he fashions a sweeping, riveting narrative. There is only one word for this biography: superb." Kirkus

Includes bibliographical references (pages 725-730) and index

Leverich, Lyle. **Tom**; the unknown Tennessee Williams. Norton 2007 644p il pa $35   **92**

1. Authors 2. Novelists 3. Dramatists 4. Short story

writers 5. Dramatists, American
ISBN 978-0-393-31663-6; 0-393-31663-7
First published 1995 by Crown

This is the first installment of a projected two-volume biography of the American dramatist. Coverage begins with Williams' birth in 1911 and extends to the opening of The Glass Menagerie in 1945.

"The book is a tremendous accomplishment, and Leverich is an appealing biographer: modest, thorough, balanced, and passionate. In prose that is clear—if not scintillating—he bushwhacks a path through a morass of gossip and myth, and prepares the way for a more subtle interpretation of the man and his plays." New Yorker

Spoto, Donald. The **kindness** of strangers: the life of Tennessee Williams. Da Capo Press 1997 409p il pa $18.50   **92**
1. Authors 2. Novelists 3. Dramatists 4. Short story writers
ISBN 0-306-80805-6

LC 97-8428

First published 1985 by Little, Brown

"Based on hundreds of interviews with those who knew him and on other previously unpublished material, {the author} presents a portrait of Tennessee Williams which is both respectful and sensitive." Wilson Libr Bull
Includes bibliographical references

Williams, William Carlos, 1883-1963

Leibowitz, Herbert A. **Something** urgent I have to say to you: the life and works of William Carlos Williams; [by] Herbert Leibowitz. Farrar, Straus and Giroux 2011 496p il $40   **92**
1. Poets 2. Authors 3. Physicians 4. Essayists 5. Short story writers
ISBN 978-0-374-11329-2; 0-374-11329-7

LC 2010-46548

"In the 50s when Williams first became popular, convention said critics did not cross boundaries to conjecture on psychological motivations. This book is very much a product of a new century where all is transparent; and if Williams broke taboos in writing, Leibowitz does in reporting. . . . Leibowitz is quick to attribute Williams's writing to his tortured sexuality. The poet's pull between duty and a libidinous fantasy world is well known but never before used so relentlessly as capital. This also makes the book as readable as fiction, something bound to get it off the shelf and into the reader's hands. Leibowitz tackles the poetry through the man, not the other way around. . . . In the second half of the book, Leibowitz's comparison of Williams's book Spring and All to T.S. Eliot's The Waste Land is a brilliant analysis. Also, the careful reasoning behind Williams's In the American Grain is a contribution to literary thought. Another real bonus is that this biography tracks the Little Magazine movement in America nicely." Washington Independent Rev of Books
Includes bibliographical references

Wills, Garry, 1934-

Wills, Garry. **Outside** looking in; adventures of an observer. Viking 2010 195p $25.95   **92**
1. Authors 2. Historians 3. Journalists 4. Essayists 5.

Social critics 6. College teachers
ISBN 978-0-670-02214-4

LC 2010-05323

"Wills's curiosity and personal integrity shine through this intellectual memoir that is both intimate and journalistic. Readers who have followed Wills's writing career will welcome these reflections on his life and the world around him." Libr J
Includes bibliographical references

Wilson, Brian, 1942-

Wilson, Brian, 1942- **I** am Brian Wilson; A Memoir. Brian Wilson. Da Capo Press 2016 336 p. illustrations (hardcover : alk. paper) $26.99 **92**
1. Rock musicians -- United States -- Biography
ISBN 9780306823060; 9780306823077

LC 2016030071

This memoir, by Brian Wilson, "reveals as never before the man who fought his way back to stability and creative relevance, who became a mesmerizing live artist, who forced himself to reckon with his own complex legacy, and who finally completed Smile, the legendary unfinished Beach Boys record that had become synonymous with both his genius and its destabilization. Today Brian Wilson is older, calmer, and filled with perspective and forgiveness." (Publisher's note)

"Wilson's emotional authenticity is beguiling as he takes readers deeply into his mind, voices and all, to describe his unique manifestation of musical genius." Pub Wkly
Includes bibliographical references and index

Wilson, Diane

Wilson, Diane. An **unreasonable** woman; a true story of shrimpers, politicos, polluters and the fight for Seadrift, Texas. foreword by Kenny Ausubel. Chelsea Green 2005 400p map $27.50; pa $18 **92**
1. Conservationists 2. Environmental protection 3. Fishermen
ISBN 1-931498-88-1; 978-1-931498-88-3; 1-933392-27-4 pa; 978-1-933392-27-1 pa

LC 2005-9894

"With the discovery that her 'piddlin' little county on the Gulf Coast' led the nation in toxic emissions, shrimper Wilson, a mother of five, found herself embarking on a voyage of discovery and activism that would strain her marriage and stretch her horizons. A David up against big-time chemical Goliaths, Wilson is a gifted storyteller, rendering dialogue and pacing plot turns as a novelist might." Publ Wkly

Wilson, Woodrow, 1856-1924

★ Berg, A. Scott. **Wilson**; A. Scott Berg. G.P. Putnam's Sons 2013 832 p. $40   **92**
1. Presidents -- United States 2. Presidents -- United States -- Biography 3. United States -- Politics and government -- 1913-1921
ISBN 0399159215; 9780399159213

LC 2013009339

This book is a biography of the United States' 28th president, Woodrow Wilson. Author A. Scott Berg "is generally sympathetic to the man (he puts much emphasis on Wilson's love for his two wives and characterizes him as a passionate lover as well as a determined leader), while taking a more critical stand against his racial views and policies, his handling of the League of Nations, and of the secrecy that surrounded his late-presidency illness." (Publishers Weekly)

★ Brands, H. W. **Woodrow** Wilson. Times Books 2003 169p il (American presidents series) $20   **92**
1. Governors 2. Presidents 3. College presidents 4. Nobel laureates for peace 5. Presidents -- United States
ISBN 0-8050-6955-0

LC 2002-41393

The author "presents Wilson as a moralistic, idealistic intellectual who came to the presidency well versed in domestic policy but sadly lacking in knowledge and experience of international affairs, a leader who ultimately sacrificed his health and his presidential legacy in a doomed battle with Sen. Henry Cabot Lodge to have the League of Nations ratified. . . . Brands's brief, skillful life of the President is recommended for all public libraries." Libr J
Includes bibliographical references

Cooper, John Milton. The **warrior** and the priest: Woodrow Wilson and Theodore Roosevelt; [by] John Milton Cooper, Jr. Belknap Press 1983 442p il hardcover o.p. pa $20.95   **92**
1. Governors 2. Presidents 3. Vice-presidents 4. College presidents 5. Nobel laureates for peace 6. Presidents -- United States 7. United States -- Politics and government -- 1898-1919
ISBN 0-674-94751-7 pa

LC 83-6021

The author's "distinctions are sharp, his insights original, his judgments balanced and his narrative unfailingly graceful." N Y Times Book Rev
Includes bibliographical references

Cooper, John Milton. **Woodrow** Wilson; a biography. Alfred A. Knopf 2009 702p il $35   **92**
1. Governors 2. Presidents 3. College presidents 4. Biography, Individual 5. Nobel laureates for peace 6. Presidents -- United States 7. United States -- Politics and government -- 1898-1919 8. United States -- Politics and government -- 1913-1921 9. United States -- Politics and government -- 1919-1933
ISBN 978-0-307-26541-8

LC 2009-19097

This is a biography of the twenty-eighth president of the United States. Index.
"Cooper exhibits complete command of his materials, a sure knowledge of the man and a nuanced understanding of a presidency almost Shakespearean in its dimensions." Kirkus
Includes bibliographical references (p. [601]-668) and index.

Winkfield, Jimmy, 1882-1974
Drape, Joe. **Black** maestro; the epic life of an American legend. Morrow 2006 280p il $24.95 **92**
1. Jockeys
ISBN 0-06-053729-9; 978-0-06-053759-6

LC 2006-41939

This is a biography of "Jimmy Winkfield, the last black jockey to win the Kentucky Derby. . . . This well-researched

biography of Jimmy Winkfield and the larger chapter of America his life highlights is a valuable and entertaining read." Publ Wkly

Winters, Richard
Alexander, Larry. **Biggest** brother; the life of Major D. Winters, the man who led the Band of Brothers. NAL Caliber 2005 287p il $24.95   **92**
1. Veterans 2. World War, 1939-1945 3. Army officers
ISBN 0-451-21510-9

LC 2004-27330

This is "the story of what distinguished Easy Company from other first-class field units: its leadership, in the person of Major Richard Winters, its commander. . . . Alexander is especially good at showing how Winters' sense of responsibility developed as a student, an enlistee, in OCS, and as an officer. He also gives a detailed picture of the army of 60-plus years ago, and the process that turned thousands of young civilians into the men who beat the Germans." Booklist

Wizenberg, Molly
Wizenberg, Molly. A **homemade** life; stories and recipes from my kitchen table. illustrations by Camilla Engman. Simon & Schuster 2009 320p il $25   **92**
1. Cooking 2. Women authors 3. Cookery 4. Bloggers 5. Food critics
ISBN 1-4165-5105-0; 978-1-4165-5105-8

LC 2008-36430

"When Molly Wizenberg's father died of cancer, everyone told her to go easy on herself, to hold off on making any major decisions for a while. But when she tried going back to her apartment in Seattle and returning to graduate school, she knew it wasn't possible to resume life as though nothing had happened. So she went to Paris, a city that held vivid memories of a childhood trip with her father. . . . She was supposed to be doing research for her dissertation, but more often, she found herself peering through the windows of chocolate shops. . . . Molly's blog Orangette started out merely as a pleasant pastime. But it wasn't long before her writing and recipes developed [a following]. . . . In A Homemade Life: Stories and Recipes from My Kitchen Table, Molly Wizenberg recounts a life with the kitchen at its center." (Publisher's note) Recipe index.
This "delightful . . . book will undoubtedly be gobbled up like a tin of Christmas cookies." Libr J

Wodehouse, P. G. (Pelham Grenville), 1881-1975
McCrum, Robert. **Wodehouse**; a life. Norton 2004 530p il $27.95   **92**
1. Authors 2. Humorists 3. Novelists 4. Dramatists 5. Short story writers
ISBN 0-393-05159-5

LC 2004-18562

The author "takes the reader from Wodehouse's school days at Dulwich to his successful work as a Broadway lyricist and a master storyteller of Edwardian times who gave us Bertie Wooster and Jeeves to his darkest hour during World War II and final years of semi-exile in America. He offers his most spirited and convincing analysis in countering accusations that Wodehouse knowingly collaborated with the Nazis. . . . This work is thoroughly researched and well written; it will please Wodehouse aficionados and general readers alike." Libr J

Includes bibliographical references

Wolff, Tobias, 1945-

★ Wolff, Tobias. **This** boy's life: a memoir. Atlantic Monthly Press 1989 288p hardcover o.p. pa $14 **92**

1. Authors 2. Novelists 3. Memoirists 4. College teachers 5. Authors, American 6. Nonfiction writers 7. Short story writers

ISBN 0-871-13248-6; 0-8021-3668-0 pa

LC 88-17600

The novelist and short story writer "offers an engrossing and candid look into his childhood and adolescence in his first book of nonfiction. In unaffected prose he recreates scenes from his life that sparkle with the immediacy of narrative fiction. The result is an intriguingly guileless book, distinct from the usual reflective commentary of autobiography." Libr J

Wollstonecraft, Mary, 1759-1797

Gordon, Charlotte. **Romantic** outlaws; the extraordinary lives of Mary Wollstonecraft and her daughter Mary Shelley. Charlotte Gordon. Random House Inc 2015 672 p. illustrations (hardback) $30; (paperback) $18.00 **92**

ISBN 9781400068425; 1400068428; 9780812980479; 0812980476

LC 2014014841

National Book Critics Circle Award Finalist: Biography (2015)

In this biography of Mary Wollstonecraft and Mary Shelley author Charlotte Gordon "reunites the trailblazing author who wrote 'A Vindication of the Rights of Woman' and the Romantic visionary who gave the world 'Frankenstein'--two courageous women who should have shared their lives, but instead shared a powerful literary and feminist legacy." (Publisher's note)

"Gordon's prose is compelling and her scholarship meticulous; her contention that both women led 'lives as memorable as the words they left behind' is brilliantly supported." LJ

Includes bibliographical references and index

Gordon, Lyndall. **Vindication**; a life of Mary Wollstonecraft. HarperCollins 2005 562p il $29.95 **92**

1. Authors 2. Novelists 3. Essayists 4. Feminists 5. Writers on politics

ISBN 0-06-019802-8

LC 2005-40237

The author "tackles this formidable woman with grace, clarity and much new research. . . . Gordon relates Wollstonecraft's story with the same potent mixture of passion and reason her subject personified." N Y Times Book Rev

Includes bibliographical references

Wood, Grant, 1891-1942

Evans, R. Tripp. **Grant** Wood; a life. Alfred A. Knopf 2010 402p il $37.50; ebook $37.50 **92**

1. Artists 2. Painters 3. Artists -- United States

ISBN 978-0-307-26629-3; 978-0-307-59433-4 ebook

LC 2010-18019

"Evans transforms our view of painter Grant Wood and his all-American paintings, including American Gothic, in a revelatory and heartrending biography of an artist forced to conceal his homosexuality." Booklist

Includes bibliographical references

Wooden, John, 1910-2010

Davis, Seth. **Wooden**; a coach's life. Seth Davis. Times Books 2014 608 p. illustrations (hardback) $35 **92**

1. College basketball 2. Basketball coaches -- United States -- Biography

ISBN 0805092803; 9780805092806

LC 2013020209

This book, by Seth Davis, offers a biography of the University of California, Los Angeles basketball coach John Wooden. "His UCLA teams reached unprecedented heights in the 1960s and '70s capped by a run of ten NCAA championships in twelve seasons and an eighty-eight-game winning streak. . . . Davis shows how hard Wooden strove for success, . . . only to discover that reaching new heights brought new burdens and frustrations." (Publisher's note)

"Davis has avoided stultifying, game-by-game detail (but does offer genuinely exciting accounts of several key games) and has provided a multidimensional, nearly cradle-to-grave portrait of a highly successful and revered coach and teacher, in the process delivering a history of the evolution of college basketball and profiles of many of its stars." Booklist

Includes bibliographical references (pages 327-565) index

Woodhull, Victoria C., 1838-1927

Goldsmith, Barbara. **Other** powers; the age of suffrage, spiritualism, and the scandalous Victoria Woodhull. HarperPerennial 1999 531p il pa $16 **92**

1. Feminism 2. Suffragists 3. Spiritualism 4. Feminists 5. Women -- Suffrage 6. Presidential candidates

ISBN 0-06-095332-2

LC 98-33315

First published 1998 by Knopf

"Victoria Woodhull was a charismatic and notorious figure in the struggle for women's rights in the years following the Civil War. She was the first woman to address Congress and the first woman to run for president. Goldsmith . . . has successfully woven together a history of Woodhull's life with the lives of the powerful she touched." Libr J

Includes bibliographical references

Woods, Tiger, 1975-

Callahan, Tom. **In** search of Tiger; a journey through golf with Tiger Woods. Crown 2003 245p il $23.95; pa $14   **92**
1. Golfers
ISBN 0-609-60943-2; 1-4000-5140-1 pa
LC 2002-11350

The author "examines Tiger's early years, how he got to the top of his game and his vision for the future. Anecdotes and insider insights highlight portraits of major Tiger victories. . . . This is a comprehensive examination of the man, his talent, his competition and the world of professional golf, a must-read for fans and players alike." Publ Wkly

Woolf, Leonard, 1880-1969

★ Glendinning, Victoria. **Leonard** Woolf; a biography. Simon & Schuster 2006 498p il $30 **92**
1. Authors 2. Editors 3. Essayists 4. Memoirists 5. Writers on politics 6. Publishing executives
ISBN 978-0-7432-4653-8; 0-7432-4653-5
LC 2006-49784

This is a biography of the publisher and author of Empire and Commerce in Africa (1920), Village in the Jungle (1926), After the Deluge (1931), Quack, Quack! (1935), Barbarians Within and Without (1939), Sowing (1960), Growing (1961), Beginning Again (1964), Downhill All the Way (1967), and The Journey Not the Arrival Matters (1969).

"Glendinning's generous biography does not ignore that Woolf could be grumpy and was too often cheeseparing, but her account does justice to his range of passions, his literary and political contributions and, above all, his human goodness—he was a man who knew how to live." New Statesman

Includes bibliographical references

Woolf, Virginia, 1882-1941

Briggs, Julia. **Virginia** Woolf: an inner life. Harcourt 2005 527p il $30   **92**
1. Authors 2. Novelists 3. Women authors 4. Essayists 5. Authors, English 6. Short story writers
ISBN 0-15-101143-5
LC 2005-16048

"That this book is a must for Woolf fans goes without saying, but it is also a must for anyone interested in the nature of female consciousness at its most self-aware and the workings of artistic sensibility at their most illuminating." Publ Wkly

Includes bibliographical references

Woolf, Virginia. A **moment's** liberty: the shorter diary; abridged and edited by Anne Olivier Bell; introduction by Quentin Bell. Harcourt Brace Jovanovich 1990 516p hardcover o.p. pa $20 **92**
1. Authors 2. Novelists 3. Essayists 4. Authors, English 5. Short story writers
ISBN 0-15-161894-1; 0-15-661912-1 pa
LC 90-33428

An abridged edition of the five volumes of Woolf's Diary, published 1977-1984

"The diaries here may appeal to a larger audience, not least because each year represented is prefaced by a wonderfully succinct overview. Here are Woolf's superbly drawn portraits of Max Beerbohm, T.S. Eliot, John Maynard Keynes, Katherine Mansfield—and her occasionally acerbic remarks on what they said and did. But the diaries are also a repository for luminous thoughts on birds and weather, the pleasures of walking or listening to music." Publ Wkly

Woolman, John, 1720-1772

Slaughter, Thomas P. The **beautiful** soul of John Woolman, apostle of abolition. Hill and Wang 2008 464p il map   **92**
1. Clergy 2. Authors 3. Abolitionists 4. Diarists 5. Essayists 6. Quaker leaders 7. Biography, Individual 8. Slavery and the church -- Society of Friends
ISBN 0-8090-9514-9; 978-0-8090-9514-8
LC 2008-22765

This is a biography of the New Jersey Quaker abolitionist. Index.

"Any understanding of the history of social reform in America begins with Woolman, and understanding Woolman begins here." Kirkus

Includes bibliographical references and index

Worden, Alfred M., 1932-

Worden, Al, 1932- **Falling** to Earth; an Apollo 15 astronaut's journey. [by] Al Worden with Francis French. Smithsonian Books 2011 300p il **92**
1. Astronauts 2. Apollo project 3. Space flight to the moon 4. Air force officers 5. Biography, Individual 6. Apollo 15 (Spacecraft)
ISBN 1-58834-309-X; 978-1-58834-309-3
LC 2011003440

"Worden is eloquent, witty, and brutally honest, still in awe of the company he kept and the history he belongs to. A solid addition to space-literature collections."

"Worden is eloquent, witty, and brutally honest, still in awe of the company he kept and the history he belongs to. A solid addition to space-literature collections." Booklist

Includes bibliographical references

Wordsworth, Dorothy, 1771-1855

Wilson, Frances. The **ballad** of Dorothy Wordsworth; a life. Farrar, Straus and Giroux 2009 316p il map $30   **92**
1. Poets 2. Authors 3. Diarists 4. Poets laureate 5. Travel writers 6. Authors, English
ISBN 978-0-374-10867-0; 0-374-10867-6
LC 2008-41263

First published 2008 in the United Kingdom

"Ms. Wilson focuses primarily on the years 1800-3, when Dorothy, then in her late 20s and early 30s, lived with her brother in the Lake District of England and kept her famous Grasmere Journals, which were not published in full until 1958. They were crucial years, not just for her but also for her brother, who was still writing some of his most important poems, and for Samuel Coleridge, who moves in and out of this book like the third magpie in a bustling nest. Ms. Wilson's decision to limit her scope was a small bit of genius. She's written a succinct yet roomy book, one that moves along with novelistic buoyancy and grace." N Y Times Book Rev

Includes bibliographical references

Wordsworth, William, 1770-1850

Wilson, Frances. The **ballad** of Dorothy Wordsworth: a life. Farrar, Straus and Giroux 2009 316p il map $30   **92**

1. Poets 2. Authors 3. Diarists 4. Poets laureate 5. Travel writers 6. Authors, English

ISBN 978-0-374-10867-0; 0-374-10867-6

LC 2008-41263

First published 2008 in the United Kingdom

"Ms. Wilson focuses primarily on the years 1800-3, when Dorothy, then in her late 20s and early 30s, lived with her brother in the Lake District of England and kept her famous Grasmere Journals, which were not published in full until 1958. They were crucial years, not just for her but also for her brother, who was still writing some of his most important poems, and for Samuel Coleridge, who moves in and out of this book like the third magpie in a bustling nest. Ms. Wilson's decision to limit her scope was a small bit of genius. She's written a succinct yet roomy book, one that moves along with novelistic buoyancy and grace." N Y Times Book Rev

Includes bibliographical references

Wright, Frank Lloyd, 1867-1959

★ Huxtable, Ada Louise. **Frank** Lloyd Wright. Lipper\Viking 2004 251p il (Penguin lives series) $19.95   **92**

1. Architects 2. Nonfiction writers

ISBN 0-670-03342-1

LC 2004-46477

"The eventfulness of the extraordinary life and the refreshing intelligence and craft of the author make this book a pleasure to read. That I found myself on occasion arguing with the text only proves the provocative quality of Huxtable's exploration." N Y Times Book Rev

Secrest, Meryle. **Frank** Lloyd Wright; a biography. University of Chicago Press 1998 634p il pa $20   **92**

1. Architects 2. Nonfiction writers

ISBN 0-226-74414-0

LC 97-51590

First published 1992 in the United Kingdom; first United States edition published 1993 by Knopf

A portrait of a "complex, often contradictory architect. . . . Secrest writes with authority and compassion about Wright's long and turbulent career. Her exhaustive scholarship provides fresh insights into Wright's personality." Libr J

Includes bibliographical references

Wright, IO Tillett, 1985-

Wright, IO Tillett, 1985- **Darling** Days; A Memoir. iO Tillett Wright. HarperCollins 2016 400 p. $26.99   **92**

1. Culture 2. Identity (Psychology)

ISBN 0062368206; 9780062368201

This memoir, by iO Tillett Wright, is an "examination of culture and identity, of the instincts that shape us and the norms that deform us, and of the courage and resilience of a child listening closely to her deepest self. When a group of boys refuse to let six-year-old iO play ball, she instantly adopts a new persona, becoming a boy named Ricky, a

choice her parents support and celebrate. It is the start of a profound exploration of gender and identity." (Publisher's note)

" It's unclear how this engagingly reckless soul found the poise to launch a publishing, acting, and writing career; she just seemed to be doing it by her late teens. If Wright can pull it off, there's hope for just about everybody. An earnest and heartfelt memoir cloaked under a battle-toughened exterior." Kirkus

Wright, Orville, 1871-1948

★ McCullough, David. The **Wright** brothers; by David McCullough. Simon & Schuster 2015 320 p. illustrations, maps $30   **92**

1. Aeronautics 2. Aeronautics -- United States -- Biography 3. Aeronautics -- United States -- History -- 20th century

ISBN 1476728747; 9781476728742

LC 2014046049

In this book, author David McCullough "tells the dramatic story-behind-the-story about the courageous brothers who taught the world how to fly: Wilbur and Orville Wright. On a winter day in 1903, in the Outer Banks of North Carolina, two unknown brothers from Ohio changed history. But it would take the world some time to believe what had happened: the age of flight had begun, with the first heavier-than-air, powered machine carrying a pilot." (Publisher's note)

"McCullough's usual warm, evocative prose makes for an absorbing narrative; he conveys both the drama of the birth of flight and the homespun genius of America's golden age of innovation." Pub Wkly

Includes bibliographical references and index

Wright, Orville. **How** we invented the airplane; an illustrated history, edited with an introduction and commentary by Fred C. Kelly; additional text by Alan Weissman. Dover Publs. 1988 87p il pa $9.95 **92**

1. Inventors 2. Aeronautics -- History 3. Aircraft industry executives

ISBN 0-486-25662-6

LC 87-33037

First published 1953 by D. McKay

This "account by the two inventors . . . covers experiments, discovery of aeronautical principles, construction of planes and motors, first flights, and much more. Also included is a later account written by both brothers." Publisher's note

Includes bibliographical references

Wright, Richard, 1908-1960

★ Wright, Richard. **Black** boy; (American hunger): a record of childhood and youth. foreword by Edward P. Jones. 60th anniversary ed., 1st ed.; HarperCollinsPublishers 2005 419p $24.95; pa $14.95   **92**

1. Authors 2. Novelists 3. Dramatists 4. African American authors 5. Essayists 6. Nonfiction writers 7. Short story writers 8. African Americans -- Social conditions

ISBN 0-06-083400-5; 978-0-06-083400-5; 0-06-

113024-9 pa; 978-0-06-113024-3 pa
LC 2005-52698
First published 1945 by World Publishing Company
This autobiographical work concludes with Wright "newly arrived in Chicago in 1927 as a fugitive from the white South that never knew him. [It] relates his nomadic life in Tennessee, Arkansas, and Mississippi, abandoned by his father and with his mother working at menial jobs or incapacitated by illness." Benet's Reader's Ency of Am Lit
Includes bibliographical references

Wright, Wilbur, 1867-1912

★ McCullough, David. The **Wright** brothers; by David McCullough. Simon & Schuster 2015 320 p. illustrations, maps $30 **92**
1. Aeronautics 2. Aeronautics -- United States -- Biography 3. Aeronautics -- United States -- History -- 20th century
ISBN 1476728747; 9781476728742
LC 2014046049
In this book, author David McCullough "tells the dramatic story-behind-the-story about the courageous brothers who taught the world how to fly: Wilbur and Orville Wright. On a winter day in 1903, in the Outer Banks of North Carolina, two unknown brothers from Ohio changed history. But it would take the world some time to believe what had happened: the age of flight had begun, with the first heavier-than-air, powered machine carrying a pilot." (Publisher's note)
"McCullough's usual warm, evocative prose makes for an absorbing narrative; he conveys both the drama of the birth of flight and the homespun genius of America's golden age of innovation." Pub Wkly
Includes bibliographical references and index

Wright, Orville. **How** we invented the airplane; an illustrated history. edited with an introduction and commentary by Fred C. Kelly; additional text by Alan Weissman. Dover Publs. 1988 87p il pa $9.95 **92**
1. Inventors 2. Aeronautics -- History 3. Aircraft industry executives
ISBN 0-486-25662-6
LC 87-33037
First published 1953 by D. McKay
This "account by the two inventors . . . covers experiments, discovery of aeronautical principles, construction of planes and motors, first flights, and much more. Also included is a later account written by both brothers." Publisher's note
Includes bibliographical references

Wyatt, Richard Jed, 1939-2002

Jamison, Kay R. **Nothing** was the same; a memoir. by Kay Redfield Jamison. Alfred A. Knopf 2009 208p $25 **92**
1. Bereavement 2. Psychiatrists 3. Psychologists 4. Hodgkin's disease 5. Manic-depressive illness 6. College teachers
ISBN 978-0-307-26537-1; 0-307-26537-4
LC 2009-11096
"The great gift Jamison offers here, beyond her honesty and the beauty of her writing, is perspective: a clear-eyed

view of illness and death, sanity and insanity, love and grief. . . . Jamison seems to be telling the truth, no matter how difficult it may be, in a way that avoids self-pity and inspires courage." Washington Post Book World

Wyeth, Andrew, 1917-2009

Wyeth, Andrew. **Andrew** Wyeth; autobiography. [by] Andrew Wyeth and Thomas Hoving. Bulfinch Press 1999 168p il $29.99 **92**
1. Artists 2. Painters 3. Artists -- United States
ISBN 978-0-8212-2569-1; 0-8212-2569-3
First published 1995
"Each painting is accompanied by commentary from the artist that lends insight into his life and character. Several nude studies are included." Booklist [review of 1995 edition]
Includes bibliographical references

Wyeth, N. C. (Newell Convers), 1882-1945

Michaelis, David. **N.C.** Wyeth; a biography. Perennial 2003 555p il pa $27.95 **92**
1. Artists 2. Painters 3. Illustrators 4. Artists -- United States
ISBN 0-06-008926-1; 978-0-06-008926-9
LC 2003-42876
First published 1998 by Knopf
"Michaelis's work is an outstanding example of the biographer's art. Integrating Wyeth's complex personal and psychological life with his artistic oeuvre, Michaelis creates a portrait of both the artist and the man." Libr J
Includes bibliographical references

Wynette, Tammy, 1942-1998

McDonough, Jimmy. **Tammy** Wynette; tragic country queen. Viking 2010 432p il $27.95 **92**
1. Singers 2. Country musicians
ISBN 978-0-670-02153-6; 0-670-02153-9
LC 2009-42565
"Mr. McDonough is crazy about Wynette but also detached enough to see her clearly, writing with obvious respect for both her life and art. . . . You 'bookish types,' as Mr. McDonough describes his readers, will surely want to listen to her sing on the basis of this book's recommendations. With an emphatic sense of her place in country music—at the top of the heap, casting a shadow big enough to obscure today's woefully synthetic assembly-line singers—he combines a love of her overlooked and minor classics with a compelling big-picture life story. His opinions are often corroborated by the colorfully authentic voices of those who knew her well and marveled at her moxie." N Y Times (Late N Y Ed)
Includes bibliographical references

Yelverton, Thérèse, Viscountess Avonmore, 1832?-1881

Schama, Chloe. **Wild** romance; a Victorian story of a marriage, a trial, and a self-made woman. Walker & Co. 2010 249p il map $24 **92**
1. Authors 2. Novelists 3. Army officers 4. Great Britain -- Social life and customs
ISBN 978-0-8027-1736-8; 0-8027-1736-5
LC 2009-44758

Schama details the "bigamy trial of William Charles Yelverton, which dominated the front pages of Irish, Scottish, and British newspapers in 1861. Although the story of Yelverton and his first wife, Theresa Longworth, practically tells itself through court documents, letters, and public opinion, Schama adds a journalist's touch in her story development. The latter part of the book deals with Theresa's later life in America as a self-made woman still haunted by her past." Libr J

Includes bibliographical references

Young, Andrew, 1932-

Young, Andrew. An **easy** burden; the civil rights movement and the transformation of America. foreword by Quincy Jones. Baylor University Press 2008 550p il pa $29.95 **92**
1. Clergy 2. Mayors 3. Nonfiction writers 4. Members of Congress 5. Civil rights activists 6. United Nations officials 7. Nobel laureates for peace 8. United States -- Race relations 9. African Americans -- Civil rights
ISBN 978-1-602580-73-2

LC 2007-49679

First published 1996 by HarperCollins Pubs.

This memoir focuses on Young's early life as a middle-class African American growing up in segregated New Orleans, his call to the ministry, and his years working with Dr. King and the Southern Christian Leadership Conference.

Young, Steve, 1961-

Benedict, Jeff. **QB**; My Life Behind the Spiral. Steve Young with Jeff Benedict. Houghton Mifflin Harcourt 2016 384 p. (hardcover) $30 **92**
1. Football players 2. San Francisco 49ers (Football team) 3. Football players -- United States -- Biography
ISBN 9780544845763

LC 2016024863

In this sports memoir, "former San Francisco 49er, Super Bowl champion, NFL MVP, and Hall of Famer Steve Young gives readers an unprecedented . . . inside look at what it takes to become a super-elite professional quarterback." (Publisher's note)

Yousafzai, Malala, 1997-

Lamb, Christina. **I** am Malala; The Girl Who Stood Up for Education and Was Shot by the Taliban. Malala Yousafzai. Little, Brown and Co. 2013 viii, 327 p.p (hardcover) $26.00 **92**
1. Terrorism 2. Women -- Pakistan 3. Girls -- Education
ISBN 0316322407; 9780316322409

LC 2013941811

Amelia Bloomer Project (2014)

This memoir, by Malala Yousafzai, "is the . . . tale of a family uprooted by global terrorism, of the fight for girls' education, of a father who, himself a school owner, championed and encouraged his daughter to write and attend school, and of . . . parents who have a . . . love for their daughter in a society that prizes sons." (Publisher's note)

"On October 9, 2012, the teenaged Yousafzai was very nearly assassinated by members of the Taliban who objected to her education and women's rights activism in Pakistan. Currently, she lives in England, under threat of execution by the Taliban if she returns home. Lamb, who has been re-ported from Pakistan for 26 years and was named Foreign Correspondent of the Year five times, helps Yousafzai tell her hugely significant story." (Library Journal)

Zantovsky, Michael

Havel; A Life. Michael Zantovsky. Grove Press 2014 512 p. illustrations $30 **92**
1. Czech authors
ISBN 0802123155; 9780802123152

LC 2015430681

This book by Michael Zantovsky is a biography of "Václav Havel . . . one of the most prominent figures of the twentieth century: iconoclast and intellectual, renowned playwright turned political dissident, president of a united then divided nation, and dedicated human rights activist. Written by Michael Zantovsky--Havel's former press secretary, advisor, and longtime friend--[it] presents a revelatory portrait of this giant among men." (Publisher's note)

"antovský lends a more impartial eye to Havel's subsequent 10-year term as president of the newly formed Czech Republic, when he was no longer at Havel's side, and to the travails of his last years. This moving, perceptive chronicle succeeds in showing the many dimensions of a towering 20th-century figure." Pub Wkly

Zappa, Frank

Zappa, Frank. The **real** Frank Zappa book; [by] Frank Zappa, with Peter Occhiogrosso. Poseidon Press 1989 352p il hardcover o.p. pa $14 **92**
1. Composers 2. Guitarists 3. Rock musicians 4. Songwriters 5. Recording producers
ISBN 0-671-70572-5 pa

LC 89-3470

"The outspoken Zappa, one of the most inventive and controversial artists of the past 20 years, is frank, often disgusting, and always entertaining in describing his life. . . . Zappa also relates his opinions about the music performing and recording industries, but then rattles on about a myriad of things: church, drugs, yuppies, politics." Libr J

Zeitoun, Abdulrahman

Eggers, Dave, 1970- **Zeitoun**. McSweeney's 2009 351p il $24 **92**
1. Hurricane Katrina, 2005 2. Contractors 3. House painters 4. New Orleans (La.) 5. Muslims -- United States 6. New Orleans (La.) -- History 7. Arab Americans -- Social conditions 8. Hurricane Katrina, 2005 -- Social aspects
ISBN 978-1-934781-63-0; 1-934781-63-0

This book is a more powerful indictment of America's dystopia in the Bush era than any number of well-written polemics. N Y Times Book Rev

Includes bibliographical references

Zellner, Robert, 1939-

Zellner, Robert. The **wrong** side of Murder Creek; a White southerner in the freedom movement. [by] Bob Zellner, with Constance Curry; foreword by Julian Bond. NewSouth Books 2008 351p il $27.95 **92**
1. Historians 2. Civil rights demonstrations 3. College teachers 4. Civil rights activists 5. Southern States

-- Race relations 6. Student Nonviolent Coordinating Committee

ISBN 978-1-58838-222-1; 1-58838-222-2

LC 2008-25962

"Zellner's memoir focuses on his experiences as a civil rights activist from 1960 to 1967. He tells a story that is sometimes horrific, always interesting, and ultimately inspirational about a white Southerner's commitment to racial justice. . . . This powerful portrait of a courageous man is highly recommended." Libr J

Zevon, Warren

Zevon, Crystal. **I'll** sleep when I'm dead; the dirty life and times of Warren Zevon. foreword by Carl Hiassen. Ecco Press 2007 452p il $26.95; pa $15.95
92

1. Singers 2. Rock musicians 3. Songwriters

ISBN 978-0-06-076345-9; 0-06-076345-0; 978-0-06-076349-7 pa; 0-06-076349-3 pa

LC 2006-52138

"Interweaving the remembrances of Zevon's many friends with entries from his own journals, Crystal, his widow, presents an intimate look at Zevon's wild life of drugs, women, and music. Among others, Jackson Browne, Linda Ronstadt, Bruce Springsteen, Carl Hiaasen, Stephen King, and the Everly Brothers, with whom Zevon got his start, share reminiscences. . . . All pop music collections need this book." Libr J

Zhao Ziyang

Prisoner of the state; the secret journal of premier Zhao Ziyang. translated and edited by Bao Pu, Renee Chiang and Adi Ignatius; foreword by Roderick MacFarquhar. Simon and Schuster 2009 306p il $26 **92**

1. Prime ministers 2. Cabinet members 3. Communist leaders 4. Biography, Individual 5. China -- Politics and government 6. China -- Politics and government -- 1976-2002 7. China -- History -- Tiananmen Square Incident, 1989

ISBN 1-4391-4938-0; 978-1-4391-4938-6

This "memoir produced from tapes the former Chinese premier recorded in secrecy during his sixteen years of house arrest discusses his efforts to stop the Tiananmen Square massacre and the need for China to adopt democratic reforms." (Publisher's note)

"Until the appearance of this posthumous work, not a single voice of dissent had ever emerged from the [Chinese Communist] party's inner circle. . . . Fascinating." Economist

Ziegesar, Peter von

Von Ziegesar, Peter. The **looking** glass brother; Peter von Ziegesar. St. Martin's Press 2013 336 p. (hardback) $25.99
92

1. Brothers 2. Mentally ill 3. Authors -- United States -- Biography

ISBN 0312592981; 9780312592981

LC 2013004049

In this memoir, Peter von Ziegesar describes his relationship with his mentally ill stepbrother, also named [Little] Peter. They had been out of touch for decades "when Little Peter surfaced in New York City just before Big Peter's first child was born. As Big Peter tried to figure out how to help

recalcitrant and homeless Little Peter, he began facing his own fraught past." (Booklist)

Ziegfeld, Florenz, 1869-1932

Mordden, Ethan. **Ziegfeld**; the man who invented show business. St. Martin's Press 2008 335p il **92**

1. Theatrical producers and directors 2. Theatrical producers 3. Biography, Individual

ISBN 0312375433; 9780312375430

LC 2008028746

This is a biography of the impresario whose Ziegfeld Follies showcased such performers as Fanny Brice, Will Rogers, Eddie Cantor, W.C. Fields, and Marilyn Miller. Index.

"In his witty, well-researched biography of the great producer Florenz Ziegfeld, Mordden discusses Ziegfeld's extraordinary eye for talent and transforming approach to staging musicals." Booklist

Includes bibliographical references

Zierman, Addie

Zierman, Addie. **When** we were on fire; a memoir of obsessive faith. Addie Zierman. Convergent Books 2013 256 p. $14.99
92

1. Christians 2. Christian life 3. Autobiographies 4. Christian biography -- United States

ISBN 1601425457; 9781601425454

LC 2013022552

In this memoir, author Addie Zierman "grows up in an average, Bible-studying, Christian family but as a teenager, her zeal for being the perfect, evangelical Christian girl reaches a new level, one that disturbs even her parents. Falling in love with a rigid, similarly zealous, boy named Chris who is bound for mission work doesn't hurt these faith pursuits, and is in fact the reason behind her newfound obsessions with purity and perfect devotion to Jesus." (Publishers Weekly)

Zine, Edward E.

Murphy, Terry Weible. **Life** in rewind; the story of a young courageous man who persevered over OCD and the Harvard doctor who broke all the rules to help him. with Michael A. Jenike and Edward E. Zine. HarperCollins 2009 242p il $24.99
92

1. Mentally ill 2. Obsessive-compulsive disorder

ISBN 978-0-06-156153-5; 0-06-156153-3

LC 2008-51240

"Murphy, mother of an OCD patient, recounts the . . . tale of Ed Zine, a man so mired in obsessive-compulsive behavior that he was trapped for six years in his squalid basement, compelled to perform an endless series of rituals meant to stop time and the inevitability of death. . . . Murphy traces Zine's illness from its roots in childhood trauma (his mother's death from cancer) through its full flower, shortly after high school graduation, when it began to take over his life. Unable to get Zine out of his house, leading OCD expert Jenike made the three-hour trip from his Boston office to Zine's Cape Cod home once a week. The bond between them developed slowly and with difficulty, but ultimately proved deeper than either suspected. . . . A passionate, faithful narrative from a reporter who understands the stakes and the people behind them, this is a fascinating, hopeful read." Publ Wkly

Zinn, Howard, 1922-2010

Duberman, Martin. **Howard** Zinn; a life on the left. Martin Duberman. New Press 2012 **92**

1. Historians -- United States -- Biography
ISBN 9781595586780

LC 2012017592

This biography of historian Howard Zinn by Martin Duberman, a "bestselling author . . . political activist . . . lecturer, and one of America's most recognizable and admired progressive voices," details Zinn's life "from the battlefields of World War II to the McCarthy era, the civil rights and the antiwar movements, and beyond." (Publisher's note)

Includes bibliographical references and index

Zombory-Moldován, Bela

The **burning** of the world; a memoir of 1914. by Béla Zombory-Moldován; translated from the Hungarian by Peter Zombory-Moldovan. New York Review Books 2014 184 p. illustrations, maps (New York Review Books classics) (paperback) $16.95 **92**

1. Hungary -- History 2. World War, 1914-1918 -- Personal narratives 3. Artists -- Hungary -- Biography 4. Soldiers -- Hungary -- Biography 5. Veterans -- Hungary -- Biography 6. Hungary -- History -- 1867-1918 -- Biography 7. World War, 1914-1918 -- Social aspects -- Hungary 8. World War, 1914-1918 -- Personal narratives, Hungarian
ISBN 1590178092; 9781590178096

LC 2014013207

In this memoir, "Hungarian artist Béla Zombory-Moldován was on holiday when the First World War broke out in July 1914. Called up by the army, he soon found himself hundreds of miles away, advancing on Russian lines and facing relentless rifle and artillery fire. Badly wounded, he returned to normal life, which now struck him as unspeakably strange. He had witnessed, he realized, the end of a way of life, of a whole world." (Publisher's note)

"This book is recommended for anyone interested in World War I, war memoirs, and the history of eastern Europe." LJ

Zumwalt, Elmo R., 1920-2000

Berman, Larry. **Zumwalt**; the life and times of Admiral Elmo Russell "Bud" Zumwalt, Jr. Larry Berman. Harper 2012 528 p. **92**

1. United States. Navy 2. Vietnam War, 1961-1975 -- Naval operations 3. Admirals -- United States -- Biography 4. United States. Navy -- Officers -- Biography 5. Vietnam War, 1961-1975 -- Naval operations, American 6. United States. Office of the Chief of Naval Operations -- History -- 20th century
ISBN 0061691305; 9780061691300

LC 2012032320

This book, by Larry Berman, offers a biography of "Admiral Elmo Russell Zumwalt, Jr. . . . In a career spanning forty years, he rose to the top echelon of the U.S. Navy as a commander of all navy forces in Vietnam and then as CNO from 1970 to 1974. His tenure came at a time of scandal and tumult, from the Soviets' challenge to the U.S. for naval supremacy and a duplicitous endgame in Vietnam to Watergate and an admirals' spy ring." (Publisher's note)

Includes bibliographical references

Zweig, Stefan, 1881-1942

Prochnik, George. The **Impossible** Exile; Stefan Zweig at the end of the world. George Prochnik. Other Press 2014 408 p. illustrations (hardcover) $27.95 **92**

1. Jewish authors -- 20th century -- Biography 2. Authors, Austrian -- 20th century -- Biography 3. Europe -- History -- 20th century -- Biography
ISBN 1590516125; 9781590516126

LC 2013025383

National Jewish Book Award: Biography, Autobiography, Memoir (2014)

In this book, George Prochnik "examines the life of exiled Austrian writer Stefan Zweig (1881-1942) to shed light on the affliction of exile that redefined the lives and works of many intellectuals during WWII. Perhaps best known for his novellas, Zweig, who was Jewish, fled from his native Vienna and spent time abroad (New York, Rio de Janeiro), but was never able to adjust." (Publishers Weekly)

"Intelligent, reflective and deeply sad portrait of a man tragically cut adrift by history." Kirkus

Includes bibliographical references

920 Collective biography

Abdul-Jabbar, Kareem

Black profiles in courage; a legacy of African American achievement. [by] Kareem Abdul-Jabbar and Alan Steinberg; foreword by Henry Louis Gates, Jr. Morrow 1996 xxiv, 232p il hardcover o.p. pa $13 **920**

1. Slaves 2. Authors 3. Children 4. Explorers 5. Inventors 6. Abolitionists 7. Sheriffs 8. Colonists 9. Dissenters 10. Memoirists 11. Murder victims 12. Revolutionaries 13. Writers on science 14. Civil rights activists 15. African Americans -- Biography
ISBN 0-688-13097-6; 0-380-81341-6 pa

LC 96-26245

The authors have provided "interesting and nuanced accounts of heroic African Americans whose accomplishments changed U.S. history. . . . Although Abdul-Jabbar is highly critical of past and present racism in the U.S., he gives credit to the abolitionist movement and leaders such as William Lloyd Garrison for their efforts toward ending slavery." Publ Wkly

Includes bibliographical references

Acocella, Joan Ross

Twenty-eight artists and two saints; essays. [by] Joan Acocella. Pantheon Books 2007 524p il $30 **920**

1. Artists 2. Art -- 20th century
ISBN 978-0-375-42416-8; 0-375-42416-4

LC 2006-47266

"Like every great critic, Acocella is subjective, uncompromising. She has a distinct point of view, a refreshingly not-fashionable one—she salutes Sunday-school virtues!—and writes from her conviction that beneath its hectic, irresponsible, even intoxicated surface, art makes singularly unglamorous demands: integrity, sacrifice, discipline." N Y Times Book Rev

Adams, Maureen B.

Shaggy muses; the dogs who inspired Virginia Woolf, Emily Dickinson, Edith Wharton, Elizabeth Barrett Browning, and Emily Bronte. Ballantine Books 2007 299p il $24.95 **920**

    1. Dogs 2. Poets 3. Authors 4. Novelists 5. Essayists 6. Nonfiction writers 7. Short story writers

    ISBN 978-0-345-48406-2; 0-345-48406-1

                            LC 2006-101291

"Despite their different personalities and backgrounds, these writers all had in common dogs that provided stability and consistency in their lives. Each chapter is a minibiography of an author emphasizing and offering anecdotes about the deep bond she shared with her dog. By using diaries, letters, illustrations, and sometimes passages from these women's writings, Adams provides a unique perspective of her subjects as pet owners. A recurrent theme is the comfort the dogs provided. . . . From this unusual vantage point, Adams succeeds in linking these writers' lives in various ways." Libr J

    Includes bibliographical references

African American lives; edited by Henry Louis Gates, Jr. and Evelyn Brooks Higginbotham. Oxford University Press 2004 xxvi, 1025p $55 **920**

    1. African Americans -- Biography

    ISBN 0-19-516024-X

                            LC 2003-23640

"This work opens multiple fresh vistas on proper African American history. . . . Essential for any serious African American collection." Libr J

    Includes bibliographical references

Almanac of Famous People; A Comprehensive Reference Guide to More Than 40,000 Famous and Infamous Newsmakers from Biblical Times to the Present. edited by Kristin Mallegg. 10th ed. Gale / Cengage Learning 2011 2887 p. (hardcover) $280 **920**

    1. Celebrities -- Encyclopedias

    ISBN 1414445482; 9781414445489

This reference book offers "biographical information on more than 30,000 famous individuals and groups." Entries provide the "subject's best-known name, complete name, nickname, [and] name of group," "dates and places of birth and death," and "nationality and occupation. Most entries include citations to sources that provide additional biographical information." (Publisher's note)

Angelo, Bonnie

    ★ **First** families; the impact of the White House on their lives. Morrow 2005 336p il hardcover o.p. pa $15.95 **920**

    1. White House (Washington, D.C.) 2. Presidents -- United States -- Family

    ISBN 0-06-056356-7; 0-06-056358-3 pa

                        LC 2005-41474

"Relying heavily on the recollections and memoirs of presidential family members, White House staff, and D.C. journalists, this chatty slice of Americana is chock-full of fun First Family facts." Booklist

    Includes bibliographical references

Anthony, Carl Sferrazza

America's first families; an inside view of 200 years of private life in the White House. Touchstone 2000 411p il hardcover o.p. pa $18 **920**

    1. White House (Washington, D.C.) 2. Presidents -- United States -- Family

    ISBN 0-684-86442-8 pa

                        LC 00-64936

"This close-up look at the lives of White House residents offers an intimate and objective perspective on the fish-bowl life most First Families have experienced." Libr J

    Includes bibliographical references

Baker, John F.

The **Washingtons** of Wessyngton Plantation; stories of my family's generational journey to freedom. Atria 2009 419p il $26; (pa) $16 **920**

    1. Slavery 2. Plantation life

    ISBN 978-1-4165-6740-0; 1-4165-6740-2; 9781416567417

                        LC 2008-18742

"When Baker was in a seventh-grade social studies class, he saw a photograph of four African Americans in a textbook. Baker later learned from his grandmother that the three men and one woman were ancestors, former slaves of the Washington family of Tennessee. . . . Based on the papers of the Washington family, U.S. census records, period newspaper accounts, interviews with 11 family members, and DNA evidence, Baker's book traces his family from its origin in West Africa through enslavement in Virginia and Tennessee, the Civil War, emancipation and sharecropping, and departure from the rural South for the urban North. He also provides a detailed account of life on the Wessyngton Plantation, once the largest tobacco plantation in the United States. Historians will find this book useful for its examination of rural life in the 19th-century South, and general readers will find a moving story of a family achieving freedom." Libr J

    Includes bibliographical references

Ball, Edward

The **sweet** hell inside; the rise of an elite Black family in the segregated South. Perennial 2002 384p il pa $13.95 **920**

    1. African Americans -- Biography

    ISBN 978-0-06-050590-5; 0-06-050590-7

    First published 2001 by Morrow

"The Harlestons of South Carolina were descended from a slave woman and her master, the start of a line of fair-skinned blacks who rose to prominence in the state through commerce, social service, and the arts. . . . [The author] was approached by Edwina Harleston Whitlock, a distant black relative (a sixth cousin, twice removed), to take a storehouse of genealogical material she had about her family and to write its history. The result is a stunning look at a fascinating family and the history of blacks in the U.S. from the 1800s to the 1960s." Booklist

Includes bibliographical references

Barrett, Paul M.

American Islam; the struggle for the soul of a religion. Farrar, Straus & Giroux 2006 304p $25 **920**

1. Islam 2. Biography, Collective 3. Muslims -- United States 4. United States -- Ethnic relations

ISBN 0-374-10423-9; 978-0-374-10423-8

LC 2006-11404

The author presents profiles of seven American Muslims. They include Khaled Abou El Fadi, an Egyptian-born law professor and Islamic scholar at UCLA; Osama Siblani, a secular Lebanese Shiite who publishes a weekly newspaper in Dearborn, Mich.; Siraj Wahhaj, an African American prayer leader, formerly a member of the Nation of Islam, now a Sunni; and "Asra Nomani, a colleague of Mr. Barrett's from The Wall Street Journal, who . . . [criticized] the way American mosques demean women." (N Y Times (Late N Y Ed)) Bibliography. Index.

"In the post-9/11 world Muslims have frequently been stereotyped as monolithically murderous. . . . The heated debates among Muslims themselves about violence committed under the banner of Islam are often drowned out in the fray. Paul M. Barrett's timely and engaging new book brings some of those voices in the United States to life." N Y Times (Late N Y Ed)

Includes bibliographical references

Bell, Eric Temple

★ **Men** of mathematics; [by] E. T. Bell. Simon & Schuster 1937 xxi, 592p il hardcover o.p. pa $18 **920**

1. Authors 2. Physicists 3. Astronomers 4. Theologians 5. Philosophers 6. Mathematicians 7. Essayists 8. Logicians 9. Memoirists 10. College teachers 11. Writers on science 12. Writers on religion

ISBN 0-671-62818-6 pa

This volume looks at the lives and contributions of 35 pioneers of modern mathematics.

Benfey, Christopher E. G.

A **summer** of hummingbirds; love, art, and scandal in the intersecting worlds of Emily Dickinson, Mark Twain, Harriet Beecher Stowe, and Martin Johnson Heade. [by] Christopher Benfey. Penguin Press 2008 287p il $25.95 **920**

1. Poets 2. Artists 3. Authors 4. Painters 5. Humorists 6. Novelists 7. Abolitionists 8. Women in literature 9. Essayists 10. Satirists 11. Memoirists 12. Travel writers 13. Children's authors 14. Nonfiction writers 15. Short story writers 16. United States -- History -- 1865-1898 17. American literature -- History and criticism

ISBN 978-1-594-20160-8; 1-594-20160-9

LC 2007-36512

"Benfey's subtitle neatly conveys the fascinating and sometimes tortuous complexities of this literary/historical snapshot of post–Civil War America. . . . Benfey finds a common connection among these diverse characters through, improbably, hummingbirds, an intense interest in which

seems to have taken hold of artists and writers throughout the late nineteenth century. Benfey's eclectic and original approach brings this period and these personalities vividly to life. He presents sensitive critiques of literature and art alongside tales of illicit love and broken, bent, or triumphant lives, all of which makes for compelling reading for specialist and nonspecialist alike." Booklist

Berkin, Carol

Civil War wives; the lives and times of Angelina Grimke Weld, Varina Howell Davis, and Julia Dent Grant. Alfred A. Knopf 2009 361p il $28.95 **920**

1. Authors 2. Abolitionists 3. Feminists 4. Nonfiction writers 5. Spouses of presidents 6. Spouses of prominent persons 7. Women -- United States -- Biography 8. Married women -- United States -- History 9. United States -- History -- 1861-1865, Civil War -- Women 10. United States -- History -- Civil War, 1861-1865 -- Women 11. Women -- United States -- Social conditions -- 19th century

ISBN 978-1-4000-4446-7

LC 2009-19476

This joint biography of First Lady Julia Dent Grant, Varena Davis, the wife of Confederate President Jefferson Davis, and Angelina Grimké, the abolitionist and feminist who married fellow abolitionist Theodore Weld, contends that "their personal beliefs were overshadowed by the supporting roles they played to their high-profile husbands before unique wartime and personal challenges brought their characters to the foreground." (Publisher's note) Bibliography. Index.

"This finely nuanced, absorbing account makes an important contribution to both Civil War literature and the history of American women." Booklist

Includes bibliographical references (p. 317-345)

Black Firsts: 4,000 Ground-breaking and Pioneering Historical Events; 4,000 ground-breaking and pioneering historical events. edited by Jessie Carney Smith. 3rd ed. Visible Ink Press 2013 833 p. $24.95 **920**

1. World records 2. African Americans -- History 3. African Americans -- History -- Miscellanea. 4. World records -- United States -- Miscellanea.

ISBN 9781578593699

LC 2012034407

"Achievements, pride, and accomplishments involving people, places, and events in black history are gathered in Black Firsts: 4,000 Ground-Breaking and Pioneering Events. This new edition collects and celebrates the thousands of world-moving people and hard-to-find facts and accomplishments that have helped shape society and culture. It recognizes and honors both renowned and lesser-known barrier-breaking trailblazers in all fields - arts, entertainment, business, civil rights, education, government, invention, journalism, religion, science, sports, music, and more." (Publisher's note)

"The third edition of this invaluable resource of African American achievements updates the previous edition, from 2003 to the present day. Events are arranged into categories such as arts and entertainment; government (local, state, and federal); science and medicine; and education, with subheadings within each category. These firsts are listed in chronological order and range from a couple of sentences to almost a full page. Contemporary achievements are included as well as previously undiscovered firsts from the pre-Revolutionary War era. More than 350 photos are included. Recommended for anyone from elementary-school age to adults who are interested in African American history." (Booklist)

Boller, Paul F.

Presidential wives; {by} Paul F. Boller, Jr. 2nd, rev ed; Oxford Univ. Press 1998 553p pa $17.95 **920**

1. Presidents' spouses -- United States
ISBN 0-19-512142-2

LC 98-3480

First published 1988

This collection covers every First Lady from Martha Washington to Hillary Rodham Clinton. The author devotes a chapter to each of his subjects featuring a biographical essay followed by anecdotes

Includes bibliographical references (p. 491-542) and index

Bond, Jenny

Who the hell is Pansy O'Hara? the fascinating stories behind 50 of the world's best-loved books. [by] Jenny Bond & Chris Sheedy. Penguin Books 2008 318p pa $13 **920**

1. Authorship 2. Authors, English 3. Authors, American
ISBN 978-0-14-311364-5; 0-14-311364-X

LC 2007-39840

"From Stephen King's childhood fascination with gruesome comics to the famous family name behind Peter Benchley, . . . Bond and Sheedy light up some intriguing angles on many popular authors. Journalists in Australia, the authors deliver their 50 profiles with reportorial vigor, moving quickly through each profile while highlighting the salient and salacious details of, for example, the role played by Mary Shelley's literary legacy (daughter of two leading British writers) and her free-love husband (poet Percy Shelley) in the genesis of Frankenstein. . . . Between the engaging information and the range of popular texts (Pride and Prejudice, The Origin of Species, The War of the Worlds, In Cold Blood, Lolita, Roots, The Cat in the Hat, The Da Vinci Code), this affectionate literary history should appeal to many readers." Publ Wkly

Includes bibliographical references

Booknotes (Television program)

Booknotes: life stories; notable biographers on the people who shaped America. {complied by} Brian Lamb. Times Bks. 1999 xxiii, 471p il hardcover o.p. pa $16.95 **920**

1. Biography
ISBN 0-8129-3339-7 pa

LC 98-41374

"Lamb, host of C-SPAN's Booknotes, has compiled an anthology of interviews focusing on the lives of 75 prominent people from the 1700s to the present. The result is chatty and informal." Libr J

Borneman, Walter R., 1952-

The **admirals**; Nimitz, Halsey, Leahy, and King--the five-star admirals who won the war at sea. Walter R. Borneman. Little, Brown and Co. 2012 559 p. ill., maps $29.99 **920**

1. World War, 1939-1945 -- Naval operations 2. United States. Navy -- Biography 3. World War, 1939-1945 -- Biography 4. Admirals -- United States -- Biography 5. United States. Navy -- History -- 20th century 6. Naval art and science -- History -- 20th century 7. World War, 1939-1945 -- Naval operations, American
ISBN 0316097845; 9780316097840

LC 2011032394

This book, by historian Walter R. Borneman, tells the story of the "[o]nly four men in American history [who] have been promoted to the five-star rank of Admiral of the Fleet: William Leahy, Ernest King, Chester Nimitz, and William Halsey. . . . Drawing upon journals, ship logs, and other primary sources, he brings an incredible historical moment to life, showing us how the four admirals revolutionized naval warfare forever with submarines and aircraft carriers." (Publisher's note)

"Borneman deftly manipulates multiple narrative strands and a wealth of detail. He vividly fleshes out the numerous vain, ambitious men vying for power at the top and examines their important decisions and lasting ramifications." Kirkus

Includes bibliographical references and index

Brightman, Carol

Sweet chaos; the Grateful Dead's American adventure. Pocket 1999 356p il pa $17 **920**

1. Singers 2. Guitarists 3. Rock musicians 4. Grateful Dead (Musical group)
ISBN 0-671-01117-0

First published 1998 by Clarkson Potter

"Brightman's is an engrossing treatment of the Dead and their times. . . . She offers fresh perspectives and insights and captures the flavor of the band." Booklist

Includes bibliographical references

Brighton, Terry

Patton, Montgomery, Rommel; masters of war. Crown Forum 2009 426p il map $30 **920**

1. Generals 2. Marshals 3. Army officers 4. World War, 1939-1945 -- Biography
ISBN 978-0-307-46154-4

First published 2008 in the United Kingdom with title: Masters of battle

"Brighton shows how during the period between the wars, each refined his skills, which included reading one another's published treatises on the subject of mobile warfare. The author pulls no punches in revealing their flaws as well. Very highly recommended." Libr J

Includes bibliographical references

Brower, Kate Andersen

First women; the grace and power of America's modern first ladies. Kate Andersen Brower. HarperCollins 2016 380 p. illustrations (chiefly color) (hardcover) $28.99 **920**

1. Women -- United States -- Biography 2. Presidents'

spouses -- United States

ISBN 0062439650; 9780062439666; 9780062439659

This book, by Kate Andersen Brower, presents "an intimate, news-making look at the true modern power brokers at 1600 Pennsylvania Avenue: the First Ladies, from Jackie Kennedy to Michelle Obama. One of the most underestimated—and challenging—positions in the world, the First Lady of the United States must be many things." (Publisher's note)

"Brower writes with grace and ease and finely outlines the lives of these influential figures, providing deep insights into the experiences of each." LJ

Includes bibliographical references (pages [337]-363) and index.

Burns, Ken, 1953-

★ The **Roosevelts**; An Intimate History. by Geoffrey C. Ward and Ken Burns. Random House Inc 2014 576 p. illustrations $60   **920**

ISBN 0307700232; 9780307700230

LC 2014019251

In this companion book to the PBS series, authors Geoffrey C. Ward and Ken Burns "present an intimate history of three extraordinary individuals from the same extraordinary family--Theodore, Eleanor, and Franklin Delano Roosevelt. . . . All the history the Roosevelts made is here, but this is primarily an intimate account, the story of three people who overcame obstacles that would have undone less forceful personalities." (Publisher's note)

"Starting with Teddy's asthma-plagued youth and ending with Eleanor's death in 1962, every aspect of their lives and legacies is touched upon. Hundreds of photos, newspaper clippings, and accompanying captions flesh out the story, which expands to cover their friends and family, enemies, and (alleged) lovers." Pub Wkly

Includes bibliographical references and index

Cannon, John

The **kings** & queens of Britain; [by] John Cannon and Anne Hargreaves. 2nd ed., rev; Oxford University Press 2009 404p il map (Oxford paperback reference) pa $19.99   **920**

1. Reference books 2. Great Britain -- History 3. Great Britain -- Kings and rulers

ISBN 978-0-19-955922-0; 0-19-955922-8

LC 2009-278738

First published 2001

This book "details the pedigree, birth order, and political legacies of 600 English, Irish, and Welsh regents. . . . Studded with informative black-and-white artifact illustrations, maps, portraits, and family trees, this [is an] extensive quick-reference." Libr J

Includes bibliographical references

Carey, Charles W.

American inventors, entrepreneurs & business visionaries; [by] Charles W. Carey, Jr. Rev. ed; Facts On File 2010 xxi, 455p il (Facts on File library of American history) $95   **920**

1. Inventors 2. Businesspeople 3. Reference books 4.

United States -- Biography

ISBN 978-0-8160-8146-2; 978-1-4381-3336-2 ebook

LC 2009-54269

First published 2002

"This biographical dictionary includes profiles of more than 300 individuals who have made significant and lasting contributions to American industry dating from the Colonial era to the present. Each entry addresses the subject chronologically through his or her life, focusing on major professional achievements as well as personal triumphs and tragedies. . . . The book paints a fascinating portrait of American ingenuity. A well-written biographical dictionary that will appeal to anyone interested in the history of American invention and entrepreneurialism." Libr J

Includes bibliographical references

Caroli, Betty Boyd

First ladies; from Martha Washington to Michelle Obama. Rev. and updated ed.; Oxford University Press 2010 xxii, 437p il pa $17.95   **920**

1. Presidents' spouses -- United States

ISBN 978-0-19-539285-2; 0-19-539285-X

LC 2010-14673

First published 1987

In addition to profiling each woman who has served as First Lady the author examines the ways the role has evolved over the years.

Includes bibliographical references

Carr, Jonathan

The **Wagner** clan; the saga of Germany's most illustrious and infamous family. Grove Atlantic 2007 409p $27.50; pa $16.95   **920**

ISBN 978-0-87113-975-7; 0-87113-975-8; 978-0-8021-4399-0 pa; 0-8021-4399-7 pa

"Carr's sprightly, fluent narrative places the family in its historical and intellectual context without reducing it to the symbolic effigy it has often become." Publ Wkly

Includes bibliographical references

Carroll, Sean B.

★ **Brave** genius; two remarkable friends and their unlikely journey from the French resistance to the Nobel prize. Sean B. Carroll. Crown Publishers 2013 576 p. $28   **920**

1. World War, 1939-1945 -- France 2. Nobel Prize winners -- France -- Biography 3. France -- Intellectual life -- 20th century 4. Molecular biologists -- France -- Biography 5. Authors, French -- 20th century -- Biography 6. Authors, Algerian -- 20th century -- Biography 7. World War, 1939-1945 -- Underground movements -- France 8. Politics and culture -- France -- History -- 20th century

ISBN 0307952339; 9780307952332; 9780307952349

LC 2012050707

Author Sean B. Carroll tells how "writer Albert Camus and budding scientist Jacques Monod were quietly pursuing ordinary, separate lives in Paris. After the German invasion and occupation of France, each joined the Resistance to help liberate the country [and] after the war . . . they became friends. [He] tells the story of how each man endured the most terrible episode of the twentieth century and then blossomed into extraordinarily creative and engaged individuals." (Publisher's note)

"A rare chronicle of valiant thinkers fighting political oppression and transcending professional boundaries." Booklist

Includes bibliographical references

Castor, Helen

She-wolves; the women who ruled England before Elizabeth. Harper/Collins 2011 480p il map $27.99; ebook $19.99   **920**

1. Queens 2. Great Britain -- Kings and rulers 3. Monarchy -- Great Britain -- History 4. Great Britain -- History -- Elizabeth, 1558-1603

ISBN 978-0-06-143076-3; 978-0-06-206578-0 ebook

LC 2010013263

The author "recounts the lives of six women who exercised—or tried to exercise—political power in England prior to Elizabeth I: Matilda, granddaughter of William the Conqueror; Eleanor of Aquitaine; Isabella of France; Margaret of Anjou; Jane Grey; and Mary Tudor. . . . Readers of popular history of British royals will enjoy their immensely human stories and applaud the indomitable will of these strong protofeminists." Libr J

Includes bibliographical references

Chernow, Ron

The Warburgs; the twentieth-century odyssey of a remarkable Jewish family. Random House 1993 820p il hardcover o.p. pa $21   **920**

1. Bankers

ISBN 0-679-74359-6 pa

LC 93-16599

The author "chronicles the saga of {one} of the world's most powerful and oldest banking families. In telling this monumental tale of the Warburgs, Chernow offers a panoramic view of nearly 500 years of world history, concentrating on the role of Jews in German business, culture, and politics from the time of Kaiser Wilhelm to that of Adolf Hitler. He also explains how the Warburgs extended their influence to America by marrying into two influential families." Booklist

Includes bibliographical references

Clay, Catrine

King, Kaiser, Tsar; three royal cousins who led the world to war. Walker & Company 2007 416p il $26.95; pa $16.99   **920**

1. Emperors 2. Kings and rulers 3. World War, 1914-1918 4. Kings

ISBN 0-8027-1623-7; 978-0-8027-1623-1; 0-8027-1677-6 pa; 978-0-8027-1677-4 pa

This is a "biography of not one but three significant men. King George V of England, Kaiser Wilhelm II of Germany, and Tsar Nicholas II of Russia (familiarly known as Georgie, Willy, and Nicky) were more than just the leaders of three of the most powerful countries in the world in the early 20th century—they were cousins who had grown up together, played together, and attended family functions together. . . . [The author] provides an intimate look inside the lives of these boys as they grew into manhood and became king,

kaiser, and tsar, bringing new pleasures and details to a well-known subject." Libr J

Includes bibliographical references

Cohen, Rich

Sweet and low; a family story. Farrar, Straus and Giroux 2006 272p il $25   **920**

1. Food industry executives 2. Cumberland Packing Corporation

ISBN 0-374-27229-8; 978-0-374-27229-6

LC 2005-15730

This "is a story peopled with eccentrics and naifs and scoundrels, and a story recounted with uncommon acuity and wit." N Y Times (Late N Y Ed)

Coll, Steve

The Bin Ladens; an Arabian family in the American century. Penguin Press 2008 671p il $35 **920**

1. Saudi Arabia -- History

ISBN 978-1-59420-164-6

LC 2007-42748

This "book not only gives us the most psychologically detailed portrait of the brutal 9/11 mastermind yet, but in telling the epic story of Osama bin Laden's extended family, it also reveals the crucial role that his relatives and their relationship with the royal house of Saud played in shaping his thinking, his ambitions, his technological expertise and his tactics." N Y Times (Late N Y Ed)

Includes bibliographical references

Contemporary black biography, v68; profiles from the international black community. Gale Res. 2008 275p il $124   **920**

1. African Americans -- Biography

ISBN 978-1-4144-3275-5; 1-4144-3275-5

Started publication 1992. Editors vary

"Included in each volume are biographies of innovators in the black global community who are currently living and/or who have had a lasting impact on society. Every field of endeavor imaginable is represented, from science, politics, and creative arts to sports. . . . This . . . title will be useful for its coverage of current people in the news who are not as easy to find elsewhere." Booklist

Dance, Stanley

The world of Count Basie. Da Capo Press 1985 xxi, 399p il pa $18   **920**

1. Singers 2. Pianists 3. Guitarists 4. Jazz musicians 5. Drummers 6. Flutists 7. Trombonists 8. Band leaders 9. Clarinetists 10. Saxophonists 11. Trumpet players

ISBN 0-306-80245-7

LC 85-12901

A reprint of the title first published 1980 by Scribner

This book "consists of numerous tape-recorded and edited interviews with musicians and vocalists associated with Basie, and each gets to tell his own story. Many overlap and there are interesting confirmations and disputes over details. The language has been polished (and no doubt in some cases cleaned up), but Dance does not noticeably impose his own views on others. There are good photographs." Choice

Includes discography and bibliographical references

Davis, Peter G.

The **American** opera singer; the lives and adventures of America's great singers in opera and concert, from 1825 to the present. Doubleday 1997 626p il hardcover o.p. pa $19.95 **920**

1. Singers

ISBN 0-385-42174-5 pa

LC 97-9123

"Davis tells anecdotes and presents essential details of his subjects' personal lives in biographical sketches ranging from a paragraph to several pages in length." Booklist

Includes bibliographical references

Davis, William C.

Crucible of commmand; Ulysses S. Grant and Rober E. Lee -- the war they fought, the peace they forged. William C. Davis. Da Capo Press, a Member of the Perseus Books Group 2014 xxi, 629 p.p 16 plates; illustrations; maps (hardcover) $32.50 **920**

1. United States -- History -- 1861-1865, Civil War 2. United States. Army -- Biography 3. Generals -- United States -- Biography 4. Confederate States of America. Army -- Biography 5. Generals -- Confederate States of America -- Biography 6. United States -- History -- Civil War, 1861-1865 -- Biography

ISBN 0306822458; 9780306822452

LC 2013497767

This book by William C. Davis examines the lives of Ulysses S. Grant and Robert E. Lee. Exploring their personalities, their characters, their ethical and moral compasses, and their political and military worlds, ... Davis, one of America's preeminent historians, uses substantial, newly discovered evidence on both men to find surprising similarities between them, as well as new insights and unique interpretations on how their lives prepared them for the war." (Publisher's note)

Includes bibliographical references (pages 593-607) and index

De Lisle, Leanda

The **sisters** who would be queen; Mary, Katherine, and Lady Jane Grey: a Tudor tragedy. Ballantine Books 2009 xxx, 350p il $30 **920**

1. Queens 2. Courtiers 3. Great Britain -- Kings and rulers 4. Great Britain -- History -- 1485-1603, Tudors

ISBN 978-0-345-49135-0

LC 2009-31074

First published 2008 in the United Kingdom

This is a biography of the Grey sisters, "who were victimized in the notoriously vicious Tudor power struggle and whose heirs would otherwise probably be ruling England today." Publisher's note

Includes bibliographical references

De Waal, Edmund

The **hare** with amber eyes; a family's century of art and loss. Farrar, Straus and Giroux 2010 354p il map $26 **920**

1. Art collections 2. Bankers 3. Art collectors 4. Magazine executives 5. Patrons of the arts

ISBN 978-0-374-10597-6

LC 2010-25539

"From a hard and vast archival mass of journals, memoirs, newspaper clippings and art-history books, Mr de Waal has fashioned, stroke by minuscule stroke, a book as fresh with detail as if it had been written from life, and as full of beauty and whimsy as a netsuke from the hands of a master carver." Economist

Denlinger, Elizabeth Campbell

Before Victoria; extraordinary women of the British Romantic era. by Elizabeth Campbell Denlinger; foreword by Lyndall Gordon. Columbia University Press 2005 188p il $41.50 **920**

1. Women -- Great Britain 2. Great Britain -- History -- 19th century

ISBN 0-231-13630-7

LC 2004-59267

This book "offers portraits of a group of women who were scientists, artists, writers, poets, philanthropists and reformers during the Romantic Era and details how their accomplishments changed the social and economic landscape for women." Univ Press Books for Public and Second Sch Libr, 2006

Includes bibliographical references

Dinnage, Rosemary

★ **Alone!** alone!: lives of some outsider women. New York Review Books 2004 296p $24.95 **920**

1. Women authors 2. Women -- Biography

ISBN 1-590-17069-5

LC 2003-27805

The subjects of this volume of biographical essays include: Gwen John, Stevie Smith, Barbara Pym, Simone Weil, Clementine Churchill, Ottoline Morrell, Dora Russell, Giuseppina Verdi, Olive Schreiner, Helena Blavatsky and Annie Besant; Marie Stopes, Enid Blyton, Angela Brazil, Isak Dinesen, Rebecca West, Margaret Oliphant, Alice James and Katherine Mansfield

"The book is dutifully footnoted and academically solid yet is also beautifully written, marked with great feeling and vivid flashes of insight. It cannot fail to enrich a collection." Libr J

Dray, Philip

Capitol men; the epic story of Reconstruction through the lives of the first Black congressmen. Houghton Mifflin Co. 2008 463p il $30 **920**

1. Reconstruction (1865-1876) 2. African Americans -- Biography 3. United States -- Congress -- House 4. United States -- Politics and government -- 1865-1898

ISBN 978-0-618-56370-8; 0-618-56370-9

LC 2008-11292

"A welcome addition to the literature of the Civil War and Reconstruction Era, and important for students of the civil-rights movement and its origins." Kirkus

Includes bibliographical references

Duberman, Martin B., 1930-

★ **Hold** tight gently; Michael Callen, Essex Hemphill, and the Battlefield of AIDS. Martin Duberman. New Press, The 2014 368 p. illustrations (hardback) $27.95 **920**

1. Gay men 2. AIDS (Disease) 3. Gay artists -- United States -- Biography 4. Gay singers -- United States -- Biography 5. HIV-positive persons -- United States -- Biography 6. AIDS (Disease) -- Patients -- United States -- Biography

ISBN 1595589457; 9781595589453

LC 2013039158

Stonewall Honor Book - Nonfiction (2015)

In this book, historian Martin Duberman "attempts to revive AIDS awareness by detailing the early years of the epidemic, particularly the period of 1981-1995. He sets the details within a framework constructed around the experiences of two men: white singer/activist Michael Callen and black poet/cultural worker Essex Hemphill, both of whom lived with AIDS for years and died at age 38." (Publishers Weekly)

"This combination of cautionary tale, history, and dual biography of compelling, if obscure, artist-activists is fluidly written." LJ

Includes bibliographical references and index

Emling, Shelley

Marie Curie and her daughters; the private lives of science's first family. Shelley Emling. 1st ed. Palgrave Macmillan 2012 xx, 219 p.p ill. (hardback) $26.00 **920**

1. Mothers and daughters 2. Women chemists -- Biography 3. Women journalists -- Biography 4. Women philanthropists -- Biography 5. Women scientists -- Family relationships

ISBN 0230115713; 9780230115712

LC 2012005625

In this book, Shelley Emling "tells the story of science icon Marie Sklodowska Curie . . . . Emling writes here of Curie's later years and of her relationships with her daughters . . . . Curie's trips to the United States and her relationship with magazine editor and socialite Missy Meloney, who started a fund to buy radium for Curie, are covered here in both personal and professional terms." (Library Journal)

Includes bibliographical references and index.

Englehart, Murray

AC /DC; maximum rock and roll. [by] Murray Englehart with Arnaud Durieux. Morrow 2007 488p il $25.95 **920**

1. Rock musicians 2. AC\DC (Musical group)

ISBN 0-06-113391-4; 978-0-06-113391-6

LC 2007-295661

This is a "biography of the wildly successful Australian rockers. Covering everything from guitarist Angus Young's first record purchase (Club A Go-Go by the Yardbirds) to the band's induction into the Rock and Roll Hall of Fame and all points in between, this book is a godsend for fans." Publ Wkly

Includes discography

Evans, Harold

They made America; [by] Harold Evans, with Gail Buckland and David Lefer. Little, Brown 2004 496p $40; pa $18.95 **920**

1. Inventors 2. Inventions

ISBN 0-316-27766-5; 0-316-01385-4 pa

LC 2003-65954

The author "profiles 70 of America's leading inventors, entrepreneurs and innovators, some better known than others. Along with such obvious choices as Henry Ford, Thomas Edison and the Wright brothers, Evans profiles Lewis Tappan (an abolitionist who dreamed up the idea of credit ratings), Gen. Georges Doriot (pioneer of venture capital) and Joan Ganz Cooney, of the Children's Television Workshop." Publ Wkly

Farris, Scott

Almost president; the men who lost the race but changed the nation. Lyons Press 2012 339p il $24.95 **920**

1. Presidents -- United States -- Election 2. United States -- Politics and government

ISBN 978-0-7627-6378-8

LC 2011033001

When the author "lost a 1998 race for Wyoming's at-large congressional district, he was prompted to examine the role losers play in democracy. Farris notes that some unsuccessful White House aspirants have had a far greater impact on American history than many who became president. . . . Moving chronologically through 184 years, he finds past/present linkages as he profiles Henry Clay, Stephen Douglas, William Jennings Bryan, Al Smith, Thomas E. Dewey, Barry Goldwater, George McGovern, Ross Perot, Al Gore, John Kerry, and John McCain. . . . Documenting changes in the face of America and the impact of such issues as race, religion, and workplace reform on elections, Farris writes with a lively flair, skillfully illustrating his solid historical research with revelatory anecdotes and facts." Publ Wkly

Includes bibliographical references

Feather, Leonard

From Satchmo to Miles; new foreword by the author. Da Capo Press 1984 258p il (Roots of jazz) hardcover o.p. pa $16 **920**

1. Blind 2. Singers 3. Pianists 4. Composers 5. Jazz musicians 6. Blues musicians 7. African American musicians 8. Band leaders 9. Saxophonists 10. Pop musicians 11. Flugelhornists 12. Trumpet players 13. Recording producers

ISBN 0-306-80302-X pa

LC 83-15223

First published 1972 by Stein & Day

A collection of profiles of jazz musicians including Count Basie, Lester Young, Oscar Peterson, Ray Charles, Don Ellis, Duke Ellington, Billie Holiday, Ella Fitzgerald, Louis Armstrong, Dizzy Gillespie, Norman Granz, Miles Davis and Charlie Parker.

Feldman, Burton

112 Mercer Street; Einstein, Russell, Godel, Pauli, and the end of innocence in science. edited and

completed by Katherine Williams. Arcade Pub. 2007
243p $26   **920**
1. Physicists 2. Scientists 3. Philosophers 4.
Mathematicians 5. Essayists 6. Logicians 7.
Nonfiction writers 8. Nobel laureates for physics 9.
Nobel laureates for literature
ISBN 978-1-55970-704-6; 1-55970-704-6
                                        LC 2007-1194
"During the winter of 1943–1944, Albert Einstein met
weekly with three other aging geniuses—philosopher Ber-
trand Russell, mathematician Kurt Gödel and physicist
Wolfgang Pauli—in the study of his home at 112 Mercer
Street in Princeton, N.J. . . . What the authors present are
illuminating biographical sketches of these men and their
earlier, groundbreaking work." Publ Wkly
Includes bibliographical references

Feldman, Noah
Scorpions; the battles and triumphs of FDR's
great Supreme Court justices. Twelve 2010 513p il
$30   **920**
1. Judges 2. Lawyers 3. Governors 4. Presidents
5. People with disabilities 6. Senators 7. Philatelists
8. Attorneys general 9. Government officials 10.
Biography, Collective 11. Presidential advisers 12.
Supreme Court justice 13. Supreme Court justices 14.
Judges -- United States 15. Regulatory agency officials
16. United States -- Supreme Court
ISBN 978-0-446-58057-1; 0-446-58057-0
                                        LC 2010-07788
The book discusses the period of U.S. Supreme Court
history in which "FDR had promised the next Supreme
Court seat to Joe Robinson, the Senate majority leader who
led the fight for the court-packing bill in Congress. As the
plan was collapsing in the Senate, the exhausted Robinson
died of a heart attack. Roosevelt nominated Senator Hugo
Black for the seat. He was able to appoint eight more justices, including Felix Frankfurter, William O. Douglas, and
Robert Jackson, who with Black are generally recognized
to be among the Court's greatest judges. These four are the
subjects of Noah Feldman's 'Scorpions.' . . . Feldman's .
. . book is . . . focused on the members of the Court and
their decisions; . . . but also takes more time to explain each
judge's distinctive theories of the Constitution and the role
of judges in interpreting it." (New York Review of Books)
The author argues "that the 'distinctive constitutional
theories' of Roosevelt's four greatest justices, all of whom
began as New Deal liberals—Hugo Black, William O. Douglas, Felix Frankfurter, and Robert Jackson—have continued
to 'cover the whole field of constitutional thought' up to the
present day. . . . This is a first-rate work of narrative history
that succeeds in bringing the intellectual and political battles
of the post-Roosevelt Court vividly to life." Publ Wkly
Includes bibliographical references

Fenn, Lisa
Carry on; A Story of Resilience, Redemption,
and an Unlikely Family. Lisa Fenn. HarperCollins
2016 256 p. $25.99   **920**
1. Journalists 2. At risk students 3. People with
disabilities
ISBN 0062427830; 9780062427830

This memoir, by Lisa Fenn, is "about [the] ESPN producer's unexpected relationship with two disabled wrestlers
from inner city Cleveland, and how these bonds--blossom-
ing, ultimately, into a most unorthodox family--would transform their lives. Dartanyon Crockett was legally blind as a
result of Leber's disease; Leroy Sutton lost both his legs at
eleven, when he was run over by a train. Fenn dedicated herself to ensuring their success long after the reporting was
finished." (Publisher's note)
"When she filmed the story of two talented high school
wrestlers in her hometown, Cleveland, multi-award-winning
ESPN producer Fenn didn't just end up with a proclaimed
feature (also called Carry On). She also became, in effect,
family to the two closely bonded young men, both disabled:
Leroy Sutton lost his legs at 11 when he was run over by
a train and Dartanyon Crockett, who eventually became a
member of the U.S. Judo team at the London Olympics and
is gearing up for Brazil, is legally blind." LJ

Flanders, Judith
A circle of sisters; Alice Kipling, Georgiana
Burne-Jones, Agnes Poynter and Louisa Baldwin.
W.W. Norton & Co. 2005 xxiii, 392p $27.95   **920**
1. Poets 2. Authors 3. Novelists 4. Short story
writers 5. Parents of prominent persons 6. Spouses of
prominent persons
ISBN 0-393-05210-9
                                        LC 2004-65415
This is a collective biography of the McDonald sisters,
two of whom grew up to marry Edward Burne-Jones and
Edward Poynter, while the other two became the mothers of
Rudyard Kipling and prime minister Stanley Baldwin.
"Offering perceptive commentary on the prescribed role
of women in Victorian society to be mere helpmeets, Flanders' attentive, scholarly accuracy is enhanced by piquant
observations that demonstrate both her professional talent
and personal take on the lives of these remarkable, but unremarked upon, women." Booklist
Includes bibliographical references

Fraser, Antonia
The wives of Henry VIII. Knopf 1993 479p il
hardcover o.p. pa $18.95   **920**
1. Queens 2. Kings 3. Great Britain -- History -- 1485-
1603, Tudors
ISBN 978-0-394-58538-3; 978-0-679-73001-9 pa;
0-679-73001-X pa
                                        LC 92-52950
First published 1992 in the United Kingdom with title:
The six wives of Henry VIII
This work examines the lives of the six women—Catherine of Aragon, Anne Boleyn, Jane Seymour, Anna of Cleves, Katherine Howard, and Catherine Parr—who became
Queens of England between 1509 and 1547. The author discusses their marriages to Henry VIII
"Fraser's readable style, empathy for her subjects, and
piquant use of historical details and anecdotes make this a
satisfying addition to the history shelves." Libr J
Includes bibliographical references

Fraser, Flora

Princesses; the six daughters of George III. Knopf 2005 478p il hardcover o.p. pa $16.95 **920**

1. Queens 2. Princesses 3. Kings 4. Great Britain -- Kings and rulers

ISBN 0-679-45118-8; 1-4000-9669-5 pa

First published 2002 in the United Kingdom

This "is a rich and richly hued Regency tale. . . . Fraser is splendidly at home in the 18th century, adroit at teasing history out from between guarded lines." N Y Times Book Rev

Includes bibliographical references

Gigante, Denise

The **Keats** brothers; Denise Gigante. Belknap Press of Harvard University Press 2011 ix, 499p.p ill., maps **920**

1. Brothers 2. Poets, English

ISBN 9780674048560

LC 2011014487

This book examines the impact of "George [Keats]'s 1818 move to the western frontier of the United States," which "created in John [Keats] an abysm of alienation and loneliness that would inspire the poet's most plangent and sublime poetry. [Author] Denise Gigante's account of this emigration places John's life and work in a transatlantic context . . . while revealing the emotional turmoil at the heart of some of the most lasting verse in English." (Publisher's note)

Gordon-Reed, Annette

★ The **Hemingses** of Monticello; an American family. W.W. Norton & Co. 2008 798p il map $35 **920**

1. Slaves 2. Architects 3. Presidents 4. Vice-presidents 5. Essayists 6. Mistresses 7. African Americans -- Biography

ISBN 978-0-393-06477-3

LC 2008-14642

The author tells the story of the Hemingses, an American slave family and their close blood ties to Thomas Jefferson.

"This is a masterpiece brimming with decades of dedicated research and dexterous writing." Libr J

Includes bibliographical references

Gould, Jonathan

Can't buy me love; the Beatles, Britain, and America. Harmony Books 2007 661p il $27.50 **920**

1. Rock musicians 2. Beatles

ISBN 978-0-307-35337-5; 0-307-35337-0

LC 2007-13240

"Gould's combination group biography, cultural history, and musical criticism artfully places the Beatles in their time and social context while examining with great skill how they became an international phenomenon comparable only to themselves." Booklist

Includes bibliographical references

Grant, Colin

The **natural** mystics; Marley, Tosh, and Wailer. W. W. Norton 2011 305p il $26.95 **920**

1. Singers 2. Reggae music 3. Songwriters 4. Percussionists 5. Reggae musicians 6. Wailers

(Musical group)

ISBN 0-393-08117-6; 9780393081176

LC 2011-12323

This is a history of the Jamaican reggae group, the Wailers. Bibliography. Index.

"This history of the Wailers, among the first acts to bring reggae to a worldwide audience in the 1970s, doesn't function like most music biographies. Grant . . . resists assembling detailed family trees for the band's prime movers, Bob Marley, Peter Tosh and Bunny Wailer. Nor does he obsess over discography or even dwell much on the musical shifts the trio made as it evolved from playful, syncopated ska to emotionally intense Rastafarian reggae. Instead of writing from a critical remove, Grant freely injects the story with first-person asides about his experiences with interviewees. All these tactics are assets, because they help the author avoid stock band-history patter and instead drill into the broader cultural life of 20th-century Jamaica." Kirkus

Includes bibliographical references

Grant, Gail Milissa

At the elbows of my elders; one family's journey toward civil rights. Missouri History Museum 2008 251p il $24.95 **920**

1. Undertakers 2. African Americans -- Biography 3. United States -- Race relations 4. African Americans -- Civil rights

ISBN 978-1-8839-8266-9; 1-8839-8266-9

LC 2008-24219

"Grant's father, a lawyer and civil rights activist in St. Louis in the 1950s, was among the less well known resisters of segregation, eventually working with more prominent figures, from Thurgood Marshall to Ralph Bunche and A. Phillip Randolph, to fight racial inequities in St. Louis. Grant recalls a long line of family resisters, middle-class business owners who were always on the forefront of the racial divide, challenging Jim Crow laws and practices while sustaining the social and economic underpinnings of the segregated black community. . . . This is a fascinating look at the struggles of one black family that mirrored the national struggle for civil rights." Booklist

Includes bibliographical references

Groom, Winston

The **aviators**; Eddie Rickenbacker, Jimmy Doolittle, Charles Lindbergh, and the epic age of flight. Winston Groom. National Geographic 2013 464 p. (hardback : alkaline paper) $30 **920**

1. Air pilots -- Biography 2. World War, 1939-1945 -- Aerial operations 3. Heroes -- United States -- Biography 4. Air pilots -- United States -- Biography 5. Air pilots, Military -- United States -- Biography 6. United States -- History, Military -- 20th century 7. Adventure and adventurers -- United States -- Biography 8. Aeronautics -- United States -- History -- 20th century 9. Aeronautics, Military -- United States -- History -- 20th century

ISBN 1426211562; 9781426211560

LC 2013015171

This book, by Winston Groom, "tells the saga of three . . . aviators--Charles Lindbergh, Eddie Rickenbacker, and Jimmy Doolittle. . . . [Their] adventures take us from . . .

World War I through . . . World War II and beyond, including . . . military raids and survival-at-sea. . . . Groom's . . . narrative tells their intertwined stories--from broken homes to Medals of Honor." (Publisher's note)

"A gripping document of a brilliant era in our history and a few of the men who helped make it so." Kirkus

Includes bibliographical references and index

Gross, Michael
Rogues' gallery; the secret history of the moguls and the money that made the Metropolitan Museum. Broadway Books 2009 545p $29.95 **920**
1. Art -- Collectors and collecting 2. Metropolitan Museum of Art (New York, N.Y.) -- History
ISBN 978-0-7679-2488-7; 0-76792488-6
LC 2008-41480
"A deft rendering of the down-and-dirty politics of the art world." Kirkus
Includes bibliographical references

The **Grove** book of opera singers; edited by Laura Macy. Oxford University Press 2008 626p il $39.95 **920**
1. Opera 2. Singers
ISBN 978-0-19-533765-5; 0-19-533765-4
LC 2008-17065
"A useful and comprehensive tool for novice and experienced opera researchers alike." Libr J

Haley, Alex
★ **Roots**; the saga of an American family: the 30th anniversary edition. Vanguard Books 2007 899p pa $15.95 **920**
1. African American families. 2. African Americans -- Biography.
ISBN 978-1-59315-449-3; 1-59315-449-6
LC 2007-8822
First published 1976 by Doubleday
This book details Haley's "search for the genealogical history of his family. He describes his trip to Gambia, the African homeland of his ancestors, and recounts the lives of his forebears." Benet's Reader's Ency of Am Lit

Hardesty, Von
Black wings; courageous stories of African Americans in aviation and space history. HarperCollins Publishers 2007 180p il $21.95 **920**
1. African American pilots 2. African American astronauts
ISBN 978-0-06-126138-1
LC 2007-21270
"This book companion to the Smithsonian National Air and Space Museum exhibit of the same name offers a look at the little-known and long-neglected history of black pioneers in aviation. . . . [Along with] the Tuskegee Airmen, Hardesty profiles barnstormers, including the Blackbirds; William J. Powell, founder of an aviation club; military flyers, including Benjamin O. Davis Jr.; and astronauts Guy Bluford, Ronald McNair, and Mae Jemison. This is an inspiring look at the adventurous individuals who pushed against the limits of racial discrimination to realize their passion for flying." Booklist
Includes bibliographical references

Hargittai, Istvan
The **Martians** of science; five physicists who changed the twentieth century. Oxford University Press 2006 xxiv, 313p il map $34.50 **920**
1. Physicists 2. Mathematicians 3. College teachers 4. Writers on science 5. Mathematics teachers 6. Aeronautical engineers 7. Nobel laureates for physics
ISBN 978-0-19-517845-6; 0-19-517845-9
LC 2005-29427
This is a "presentation of the lives of five scientists (physicists and engineers) from Hungary who went to Germany and then to the United States. They . . . [are] Theodore von Karman, Leo Szilard, Eugene P. Wigner, John von Neumann, and Edward Teller. . . . [This book is an] extremely valuable account of the lives of these five brilliant and interesting Hungarian physicists." Sci Books Films
Includes bibliographical references

Haskins, James
African American religious leaders; [by] Jim Haskins and Kathleen Benson. Wiley 2008 162p il (Black stars) lib bdg $24.95 **920**
1. African Americans -- Religion 2. African Americans -- Biography
ISBN 978-0-471-73632-5; 0-471-73632-5
LC 2007-27347
"It's great to have all these figures between two covers, and even a sampling of the entries captures the importance of religion, and its leaders, in African American life." Booklist
Includes bibliographical references

Heller, Nancy
Women artists; an illustrated history. 4th ed.; Abbeville Press 2003 312p il $39.95 **920**
1. Women artists
ISBN 978-0-7892-0768-5; 0-7892-0768-0
LC 2004-269241
First published 1987
"Organized in six chapters by century, the survey provides brief biographical information, some critical analysis and context, and at least one color plate of the work of 125 women artists who lived and worked in Europe or North America. . . . An excellent resource." SLJ
Includes bibliographical references

Hibbert, Christopher
The **House** of Medici; its rise and fall. Morrow 1975 364p il maps hardcover o.p. pa $16 **920**
1. Bankers 2. Political leaders 3. Florence (Italy) -- History
ISBN 0-688-05339-4 pa
First published 1974 in the United Kingdom with title: The rise and fall of the House of Medici
This book is concerned with "heads of the Medici family {who} directed the government of the Florentine state from 1434, with Cosimo's return from exile, until the death of the Grand Duke Giovanni Gastone in 1737." Times Lit Suppl
Includes bibliographical references

Hutchison, Kay Bailey

American heroines; the spirited women who shaped our country. 1st ed; William Morrow 2004 384p il $24.95; pa $14.95 **920**

1. Women -- United States -- Biography

ISBN 0-06-056635-3; 0-06-056636-1 pa

LC 2004-56677

"Hutchinson's lively, personal writing makes this an accessible and important volume." Booklist

James, Clive

Cultural amnesia; necessary memories from history and the arts. W.W. Norton & Co. 2007 xxxii, 876p il $35 **920**

1. Artists 2. Musicians 3. Philosophers 4. Intellectuals 5. Intellectual life 6. Western civilization

ISBN 978-0-393-06116-1; 0-393-06116-7

LC 2006-36398

The author "not only preserves culture and nurtures humanism but also revitalizes the beauty and power of the English language." Booklist

Kane, Joseph Nathan

★ Facts about the presidents; a compilation of biographical and historical information. Joseph Nathan Kane, Janet Podell [editors] 8th ed; Wilson, H.W. 2009 720p $150 **920**

1. Reference books 2. Presidents -- United States

ISBN 9780824210878

LC 2008056016

First published 1959

The main part of this work provides an individual chapter on each President, from Washington through Barack Obama, presenting such information as family, education, election, Vice President, main events and accomplishments of his administration, and First Lady. Part two contains tables and lists presenting comparative data on all the Presidents

Kennedy, John F.

★ Profiles in courage. HarperCollins Pubs. 2003 xxii, 245p $19.95; pa $13.95 **920**

1. Judges 2. Courage 3. Lawyers 4. Governors 5. Statesmen 6. Presidents 7. Senators 8. Army officers 9. Political leaders 10. State legislators 11. Members of Congress 12. Newspaper executives 13. Secretaries of state 14. Territorial governors 15. Supreme Court justices 16. Presidential candidates 17. Secretaries of the interior 18. Politicians -- United States

ISBN 0-06-053062-6; 0-06-085493-6 pa

LC 2003-40676

A reissue of the title first published 1956

This series of profiles of Americans who took courageous stands at crucial moments in public life includes John Quincy Adams, Daniel Webster, Thomas Hart Benton, Sam Houston, Edmund G. Ross, Lucius Q. C. Lamar, George Norris, Robert A. Taft and others.

Includes bibliographical references

Kimball, George

Four kings; Leonard, Hagler, Hearns, Duran, and the last great era of boxing. [foreword by Pete Hamill] McBooks Press 2008 339p il $22.95; pa $16.95 **920**

1. Boxers (Persons) 2. Olympic athletes 3. Boxing -- Biography

ISBN 978-1-59013-162-6; 1-59013-162-2; 978-1-59013-238-8 pa; 1-59013-238-6 pa

LC 2008-13825

The author "resurrects Sugar Ray Leonard, Marvin Hagler, Thomas Hearns, and Roberto Duran from the mists of memory, re-creating the nine bouts the middleweights fought against one another in the 1980s. A great boxing book." Booklist

Includes bibliographical references

Kingston, Maxine Hong

China men. Knopf 1980 308p hardcover o.p. pa $13.95 **920**

1. Chinese Americans -- Biography

ISBN 0-679-72328-5 pa

LC 79-3469

This book "paints a rich picture of the writer's male family members, but those portraits of her grandfathers, father, and brothers are interspersed with fascinating bits of historical data. . . . The whole is held together by pieces of folklore that one feels compelled to go back to and reread." Libr J

Kreisler, Harry

Political awakenings; conversations with history. New Press; distributed by Perseus Distribution 2010 286p pa $17.95 **920**

1. Political activists 2. World history -- 1945- 3. World politics -- 1945-

ISBN 978-1-59558-340-6

LC 2009-36808

"As the director of the Institute of International Studies at the University of California at Berkeley, Kreisler has spent 25 years interviewing hundreds of well-regarded economists, politicians, activists, and artists. In this fascinating collection, he offers 20 of those interviews, focusing on the common theme of how their ideas and perspectives were formulated. . . . Interviews are organized under topical headings, including protest and change, environmental issues, imperialism, resistance through the arts, and human rights." Booklist

Laskin, David

The long way home; an American journey from Ellis Island to the Great War. Harper 2010 xxiv, 386p il $26.99 **920**

1. Soldiers -- United States 2. Immigrants -- United States 3. World War, 1914-1918 -- Biography

ISBN 978-0-06-123333-3

LC 2009-28191

The author follows "the lives of 12 American doughboys who had been born in Europe and who then returned there to fight for their adopted country in World War I. It's an imaginative concept, and Laskin mines family legends and official documents to tell the stories of these ordinary foot soldiers from Italy and Ireland, Poland and Russia, Slovakia and Norway." Washington Post

Includes bibliographical references

Lattin, Don

The **Harvard** Psychedelic Club; how Timothy Leary, Ram Dass, Huston Smith, and Andrew Weil killed the fifties and ushered in a new age for America. HarperCollins Publishers 2010 256p il $24.99 **920**

1. Physicians 2. Hallucinogens 3. Psychologists 4. Counter culture 5. Yogis 6. College teachers 7. Social reformers 8. Harvard University 9. Nonfiction writers 10. Religious scholars 11. Writers on medicine 12. Writers on religion 13. Alternative medicine practitioners

ISBN 978-0-06-165593-7; 0-06-165593-7

LC 2009-26323

"Mr. Lattin does a lovely, gently humorous job of setting the scene and bringing these men together. . . . This groovy story unfurls . . . like a ready-made treatment for a sprawling, elegiac and crisply comic movie, let's say Robert Altman by way of Wes Anderson." N Y Times (Late N Y Ed)

Includes bibliographical references

Leamer, Laurence

The **Kennedy** men; 1901-1963: the laws of the father. Perennial 2002 882p il pa $19.95 **920**

1. Diplomats 2. Presidents 3. Senators 4. Financiers 5. Political leaders 6. Members of Congress 7. Parents of presidents 8. Regulatory agency officials

ISBN 978-0-06-050288-1; 0-06-050288-6

First published 2001 by Morrow

This is a biography of Joseph P. Kennedy and his sons from the beginning of the last century through the assassination of John F. Kennedy.

"Leamer's writing is impressive throughout, regularly catching the reader up with a felicitous phrase or a surprising insight." Booklist

Includes bibliographical references

Life stories; profiles from The New Yorker. edited by David Remnick. Random House 2000 480p hardcover o.p. pa $15.95 **920**

1. Poets 2. Actors 3. Authors 4. Dancers 5. Comedians 6. Novelists 7. Homemakers 8. Journalists 9. Ballet dancers 10. Choreographers 11. Mathematicians 12. Baseball players 13. Television personalities 14. Essayists 15. Memoirists 16. Screenwriters 17. Sportscasters 18. Game show hosts 19. Mystery writers 20. Talk show hosts 21. Boxers (Persons) 22. College teachers 23. Literary critics 24. Magazine editors 25. Writers on crime 26. Advice columnists 27. Children's authors 28. Magazine executives 29. Short story writers 30. Television producers 31. Television scriptwriters 32. United States -- Biography 33. Spouses of prominent persons 34. Nobel laureates for literature

ISBN 0-375-50355-2; 0-375-75751-1 pa

LC 99-53712

An assemblage of 25 biographical profiles spanning the years 1927 to 1999 "with subjects ranging from Ernest Hemingway and Marlon Brando to a fake prince, a pair of eccentric mathematicians, and Biff the show dog." Booklist

Louvin, Charlie, 1927-2011

Satan is real; the ballad of the Louvin Brothers. Charlie Louvin and Benjamin Whitmer. itBooks 2012 297 p. $22.99 **920**

1. Brothers 2. Musicians

ISBN 0062069039; 9780062069030

This book tells "[t]he tempestuous history of country music's Louvin Brothers, recalled by the younger musical sibling [Charlie]. . . . Here, Charlie . . . recounts the twosome's rise from hardscrabble beginnings in Alabama's cotton country to national fame. Basically self-taught, the brothers were reared on church singing before they launched an uphill professional career in the '40s. Louvin maps the pair's arduous journey through small-town radio gigs and endless regional touring." (Kirkus)

Louvish, Simon

Monkey business; the lives and legends of the Marx brothers: Groucho, Chico, Harpo, Zeppo with added Gummo. St. Martin's Press 2000 471p il hardcover o.p. pa $13.95 **920**

1. Comedians

ISBN 0-312-28382-2 pa

LC 00-302623

First published 1999 in the United Kingdom

In addition to Groucho, the author "expands the canvas to appraise the contributions of the other brothers, plus Margaret Dumont, a regular target of the brothers' mayhem. . . . Louvish does a solid job of separating fact from fiction and includes a family tree and a discussion of the FBI's file on the group." Libr J

Mackrell, Judith

Flappers; Six Women of a Dangerous Generation. Judith Mackrell. Sarah Crichton Books 2014 480 p. illustrations $28 **920**

1. Women's movement 2. Nineteen twenties 3. Women -- United States -- Biography 4. Sex role -- United States -- History -- 20th century 5. Sex customs -- United States -- History -- 20th century 6. Popular culture -- United States -- History -- 20th century

ISBN 0374156085; 9780374156084

LC 2013035397

Originally published: Great Britain : Macmillan, 2013

This book by Judith Mackrell profiles "six women, Zelda Fitzgerald, Diana Cooper, Nancy Cunard, Tallulah Bankhead, Josephine Baker and Tamara de Lempicka, whose careers as drinking, smoking, jazzing party creatures reached their critical mass in 1925. . . . Mackrell draws an analogy between the experimental freedoms of the Roaring Twenties and those of the Swinging Sixties." (Times Literary Supplement)

"Avidly researched and deeply inquisitive, Mackrell's prodigious group portrait is spectacularly dramatic and thought-provoking." Booklist

Includes bibliographical references and index

MacMillan, Margaret

History's People; Personalities and the Past. Margaret MacMillan. House of Anansi Press 2015 304 p. $24.95 **920**

1. Historians 2. Modern history
ISBN 1487000057; 9781487000059

In this book, author and "historian Margaret MacMillan gives her own personal selection of figures of the past, women and men, some famous and some little-known, who stand out for her. Some have changed the course of history and even directed the currents of their times. Others are memorable for being risk-takers, adventurers, or observers." (Publisher's note)

"Although some of the people MacMillan has chosen are not well-known, their accomplishments are no less important than those well-recognized by first or last name. Her prose is succinct and informative, and even when her transitions from one person to another are not the smoothest, the information imparted is solid. A concise, educational overview of some of the men and women who have carved out spots in the annals of history and why they should be remembered. Fans of the author are in for another treat." Kirkus

Malone, John Williams

It doesn't take a rocket scientist; great amateurs of science. {by} John Malone. Wiley 2002 232p $24.95 **920**

1. Clergy 2. Authors 3. Chemists 4. Novelists 5. Architects 6. Physicists 7. Presidents 8. Scientists 9. Astronomers 10. Vice-presidents 11. Essayists 12. Geneticists 13. Photometrists 14. Microbiologists 15. Writers on science 16. Short story writers 17. Science fiction writers
ISBN 0-471-41431-X

LC 2003-269159

This examines the lives and work of ten amateur scientists, including Gregor Mendel, David H. Levy, Henrietta Swan Leavitt, Joseph Priestley, Michael Faraday, Grote Reber, Arthur C. Clarke, Thomas Jefferson, Susan Hendrickson, and Felix d'Herelle

Includes bibliographical references

Martin, James

My life with the saints. Loyola Press 2006 411p $22.95 **920**

1. Christian saints 2. Priests 3. Spiritual life 4. Biography, Individual
ISBN 0-8294-2001-0

LC 2005-28466

James Martin, SJ, presents his reflections on various saints and also on Dorothy Day and Thomas Merton.

The author "relates how he discovered various 'saints' and how each has affected his life. . . . Despite a theme built on a particular facet of Catholic belief, Martin's animated style and wide-ranging experiences make this a book readers of diverse backgrounds will enjoy." Publ Wkly

Includes bibliographical references

Marton, Kati

The **great** escape; nine Jews who fled Hitler and changed the world. Simon & Schuster 2006 271p il $27 **920**

1. Authors 2. Novelists 3. Physicists 4. Journalists 5. Photographers 6. Mathematicians 7. Jewish refugees 8. Essayists 9. Jews -- Hungary 10. College teachers 11. Photojournalists 12. Writers on science 13. Mathematics teachers 14. Motion picture directors 15. Motion picture producers 16. Nobel laureates for physics
ISBN 978-0-7432-6115-9; 0-7432-6115-1

LC 2006-49162

"By looking at these nine lives—salvaged, and crucial—Marton provides a moving measure of how much was lost." New Yorker

Includes bibliographical references

Hidden power; presidential marriages that shaped our recent history. Pantheon Bks. 2001 414p il hardcover o.p. pa $14 **920**

1. Presidents -- United States 2. Presidents' spouses -- United States
ISBN 0-385-72188-9 pa

This book provides a "survey of a dozen First Couples, from Edith and Woodrow Wilson to Laura and George Bush. Marton mixes some good history with a lot of pop marriage psychology to show the part that patience, tolerance, insight, determination, sex and occasionally even love have played in the pursuit and exercise of presidential power." Time

Includes bibliographical references

Matteson, John

The **lives** of Margaret Fuller; John Matteson. W. W. Norton & Co. 2012 384p. **920**

1. Feminism 2. Women authors 3. Feminists -- United States -- Biography 4. Women authors, American -- 19th century -- Biography
ISBN 9780393068054

LC 2011040432

This book offers a biography of "writer and a fiery social critic, Margaret Fuller (1810-1850). . . . She became the leading female figure in the transcendentalist movement, wrote a celebrated column of literary and social commentary for Horace Greeley's newspaper, and served as the first foreign correspondent for an American newspaper. . . . , In 1848 she joined the fight for Italian independence and, the following year, reported on the struggle." (Publisher's note)

Includes bibliographical references and index.

Matuz, Roger

Reconstruction era: biographies; Lawrence W. Baker, project editor. UXL 2004 xxiv, 246p il (Reconstruction Era reference library) $60 **920**

1. Reconstruction (1865-1876)
ISBN 0-7876-9218-2

LC 2004-17300

This "volume covers political and military leaders as well as activists, artists, writers, and more. Among them are Louisa May Alcott, Frederick Douglass, Ulysses S. Grant, and Zebulon Vance. Within each biographical entry are cross-references to other individuals covered in this volume." Booklist

Includes bibliographical references

McBrien, Richard P.

Lives of the popes; the pontiffs from St. Peter to John Paul II. HarperOne 2006 522p il pa $19.95 **920**

1. Popes 2. Papacy

ISBN 978-0-06-087807-8; 0-06-087807-X

A reissue of the title first published 1997

McBrien offers "plenty of historical facts and sobering, valuable judgments." N Y Times Book Rev

Includes bibliographical references

The **Mitfords**; letters between six sisters. edited by Charlotte Mosley. Harper 2007 xxi, 834p il $39.95 **920**

1. Eccentrics

ISBN 978-0-06-137364-0; 0-06-137364-8

"The lost art of letter writing is splendidly portrayed in this massive volume of correspondence among the six Mitford sisters: Nancy, Pamela, Diana, Unity, Jessica, and Deborah. . . . Arranged chronologically covering the years 1925-2002, they include footnotes identifying people, places, and activities. In introductions to each of the nine sections of letters, Mosley provides a synopsis of the major events in each sister's life as well as thoughtful commentary and analysis." Libr J

Includes bibliographical references

Mordden, Ethan

Love song; the lives of Kurt Weill and Lotte Lenya. Ethan Mordden. St. Martin's Press 2012 x, 334 p.p (hardcover) $29.99 **920**

1. Singers -- Biography 2. Composers -- Biography

ISBN 0312676573; 9780312676575; 9781250017574

LC 2012028287

This book by Ethan Mordden is "a dual biography [of composer Kurt Weill and actress Lotte Lenya] that unfolds against the background of the tumultuous twentieth century. . . . The romance of Weill, the Jewish cantor's son, and Lenya, the Viennese coachman's daughter, changed the history of Western music. With Bertolt Brecht, they created one of the definitive works of the twentieth century, The Threepenny Opera, a smash that would live on in musical theatre history." (Publisher's note)

Morgan, Edmund Sears

★ **American** heroes; profiles of men and women who shaped early America. [by] Edmund S. Morgan. W.W. Norton & Co. 2009 278p il $27.95 **920**

1. Heroes and heroines 2. United States -- History -- 1783-1809 3. United States -- History -- 1775-1783, Revolution 4. United States -- History -- 1600-1775, Colonial period

ISBN 978-0-393-07010-1; 0-393-07010-7

LC 2009-714

"This book is a perfect gem. . . . Both specialists and general readers will find this book both authoritative and fun to read." Libr J

Morgan, Robert, 1944-

Lions of the West; heroes and villains of the westward expansion. Algonquin Books of Chapel Hill 2011 xxiii, 497p il map $29.95; ebook $28.95 **920**

1. West (U.S.) -- History 2. West (U.S.) -- Biography 3. United States -- Territorial expansion

ISBN 978-1-56512-626-8; 978-1-61620-119-7 ebook

LC 2011023832

This is a "collection of biographical sketches of 10 men largely limited to the pivotal roles each played in America's westward expansion. Included are four U.S. presidents, Thomas Jefferson, Andrew Jackson, James K. Polk, and John Quincy Adams; orchardist and naturalist John 'Johnny Appleseed' Chapman; frontier legends Davy Crockett and Kit Carson; statesmen Sam Houston and Nicholas Trist; and General Winfield Scott. . . . This collective biography provides a digestible introduction to American expansion, Manifest Destiny, and the larger-than-life men who led the inexorable charge westward." Booklist

Includes bibliographical references

Morrow, Lance

The **best** year of their lives; Kennedy, Johnson, and Nixon in 1948: learning the secrets of power. Basic Books 2005 xl, 312p $26 **920**

1. Presidents 2. Vice-presidents 3. Senators 4. Nonfiction writers 5. Members of Congress 6. United States -- Politics and government -- 1945-1953

ISBN 0-465-04723-8

LC 2005-1836

"The book succeeds in drawing together three fascinating characters into an illuminating historical intersection. You don't have to agree with all of Morrow's interpretations to be entertained by his lively treatment of three crucial figures during an important time in American history." N Y Times Book Rev

Includes bibliographical references

Mortimer, Gavin

The **great** swim. Walker & Company 2008 325p il map $24.95 **920**

1. Women athletes 2. Marathon swimming 3. United States -- History -- 1919-1933

ISBN 978-0-8027-1595-1; 0-8027-1595-8

LC 2008-256

Draws on primary sources, diaries, and family interviews to document the story of four American athletes who in 1926 became the first women to swim the English Channel, in an account that also cites the media frenzy that surrounded their achievement.

"The book can be read as the story of a sporting competition or as an exploration of our timeless fascination with celebrity. Either way, it's an absorbing and inspirational saga in the Seabiscuit mold." Booklist

Includes bibliographical references

Nelson, James Carl

The **remains** of Company D; a story of the Great War. St. Martin's Press 2009 363p il map $25.99 **920**

1. Soldiers 2. Veterans 3. Centenarians 4. Soldiers -- United States 5. World War, 1914-1918 -- Personal

narratives 6. United States -- Army -- Infantry Regiment, 28th
ISBN 978-0-312-55100-1; 0-312-55100-2

LC 2009-16931

"This outstanding book paints the portrait of a small military unit, in this case, Company D of the Twenty-eighth Infantry Regiment in World War I. . . . Nelson orients the narrative around his grandfather, who lived to 101 despite serious wounds and awakened Nelson's interest in WWI by what he did not say about his experiences. Nelson set out to tell the Company D story from official records and the documents and reminiscences left behind by dozens of other veterans. . . . [The author] writes so clearly about the background, especially trench warfare, that even readers with minimal WWI knowledge will feel educated as well as fascinated." Booklist

Includes bibliographical references

The **Norton** book of American autobiography; edited and introduced by Jay Parini and with a preface by Gore Vidal. Norton 1999 711p $32.50 **920**
1. Autobiography 2. United States -- Biography
ISBN 0-393-04677-X

LC 98-43398

"Parini has compiled over 60 selections from autobiographies and memoirs published since the 17th century. . . . {He} includes works by such diverse writers as Henry David Thoreau, U.S. Grant, Gertrude Stein, Malcom X, Mary McCarthy, and Richard Rodriguez. . . . The selections are arranged chronologically, and each is prefaced by an introduction on its author and its merit." Libr J

Includes bibliographical references

Paul, Richard

We could not fail; the first African Americans in the Space Program. by Richard Paul and Steven Moss. University of Texas Press 2015 274 p. illustrations (cloth : alk. paper) $30 **920**
1. African American astronauts 2. United States. National Aeronautics and Space Administration 3. African American engineers -- Biography 4. African American astronauts -- Biography 5. African American professional employees -- Biography 6. Race discrimination -- United States -- History -- 20th century 7. Discrimination in employment -- United States -- History -- 20th century 8. United States. National Aeronautics and Space Administration -- Rules and practice -- History 9. United States. National Aeronautics and Space Administration -- Officials and employees -- History 10. United States. National Aeronautics and Space Administration -- Officials and employees -- Biography
ISBN 0292772491; 9780292772496

LC 2014030513

In this book, authors Richard Paul and Steven Moss "profile ten pioneer African American space workers whose stories illustrate the role NASA and the space program played in promoting civil rights. They recount how these technicians, mathematicians, engineers, and an astronaut candidate surmounted barriers to move, in some cases literally, from the cotton fields to the launching pad." (Publisher's note)

"Vital and of interest to all Americans, from history and space buffs to students, researchers, and casual readers." LJ

Includes bibliographical references and index

First African Americans in the Space Program

Persico, Joseph E.

Franklin and Lucy; President Roosevelt, Mrs. Rutherfurd, and the other remarkable women in his life. Random House 2008 443p il $28; pa $18 **920**
1. Diplomats 2. Governors 3. Presidents 4. People with disabilities 5. Archivists 6. Columnists 7. Philatelists 8. Humanitarians 9. Social activists 10. Private secretaries 11. Parents of presidents 12. Spouses of presidents 13. United Nations officials 14. Presidents -- United States 15. Spouses of prominent persons 16. Presidents' spouses -- United States
ISBN 978-1-4000-6442-7; 1-4000-6442-2; 978-0-8129-7496-6 pa; 0-8129-7496-4 pa

LC 2007-36851

The author "engagingly and eloquently narrates the tangled relationships between Franklin and the various women to whom he became close. . . . Persico offers what will prove an important, lasting addition to the literature of the Roosevelts." Publ Wkly

Includes bibliographical references

Plutarch

Plutarch: the lives of the noble Grecians and Romans; the Dryden translation; edited and revised by Arthur Hugh Clough. Modern Lib. 1992 2v ea $23.95 **920**
1. Rome -- Biography 2. Greece -- Biography
ISBN 0-679-60008-6 v1; 0-679-60009-4 v2

LC 92-50223

First Modern Library edition published 1932

This work is "arranged mainly in pairs in which a Greek and a Roman are contrasted. His subjects, who include Demosthenes and Cicero, were statesmen or generals. In the process of writing about them, he invents dialogue and describes the emotions of the personages involved." Reader's Ency. 4th edition

Poulter, Ian

No Limits; My Autobiography. Trafalgar Square Books 2014 320 p. $32.95 **920**
1. Golfers
ISBN 1782066888; 9781782066880

This book by golf player Ian Poulter details his career "from his early rejection as a Spurs youth player, right through to his match-winning contributions to successive European Ryder Cup Triumphs. Poulter went from an assistant professional staffing the club shop to a global superstar, turning pro when he still had a handicap of 4 but the drive and self-belief to make it to the top." (Publisher's note)

Povey, Glenn

Echoes: the complete history of Pink Floyd. Chicago Review Press 2010 388p il $39.95 **920**
1. Rock musicians 2. Pink Floyd (Musical group)
ISBN 978-1-56976-313-1; 1-56976-313-5
First published 2007 in the United Kingdom

"Long time fans will find Echoes a pleasure to read as well as to look at. For the most part, the book has the knowing and reverential feeling of liner notes. But occasionally some mordant humor comes through. . . . A congenital defect of tribute volumes is that they tend to recite band lore that you already know about. For the most part, Povey avoids this tendency and digs up some of the strange bypaths of the band's long history." PopMatters

Includes discography and bibliographical references

Rappaport, Helen

The **Romanov** sisters; the lost lives of the daughters of Nicholas and Alexandra. Helen Rappaport. St. Martin's Press 2014 448 p. illustrations (hardback) $27.99   **920**

1. Princesses -- Russia -- Biography -- Sources 2. Sisters

ISBN 1250020204; 9781250020208

LC 2014003159

This book, by Helen Rappaport, presents biographical material on "the four captivating Russian Grand Duchesses--Olga, Tatiana, Maria and Anastasia Romanov. . . . [The book] sets out to capture the joy as well as the insecurities and poignancy of those young lives against the backdrop of the dying days of late Imperial Russia, World War I and the Russian Revolution." (Publisher's note)

"A gossipy, revealing story of the doomed Russian family's fairy tale life told by an expert in the field." Kirkus

Includes bibliographical references and index

Ritter, Lawrence S.

The **glory** of their times; the story of the early days of baseball told by the men who played it. new enl ed; Morrow 1984 360p il hardcover o.p. pa $14.95   **920**

1. Baseball -- Biography

ISBN 0688112730 pa

LC 84-221549

First published 1966 by Macmillan

A collection of 26 oral histories of baseball's early days by veteran players

Roberts, Cokie

★ **Founding** mothers; the women who raised our nation. William Morrow 2004 xx, 359p il $24.95; pa $14.95   **920**

1. Women -- United States -- History

ISBN 0-06-009025-1; 0-06-009026-X pa

LC 2004-042873

"In addition to telling wonderful stories, Roberts also presents a very readable, serviceable account of politics—male and female—in early America. If only our standard history textbooks were written with such flair!" Publ Wkly

Ladies of liberty; the women who shaped our nation. William Morrow 2008 481p il $26.95; pa $15.99   **920**

1. Women -- United States -- History 2. Women -- United States -- Biography 3. United States -- History -- 1783-1865

ISBN 978-0-06-078234-4; 0-06-078234-X; 978-0-06-078235-1 pa; 0-06-078235-8 pa

"While Roberts' aim is to see the period from her subjects' point of view, she is not uncritical; for instance, Roberts casts blame on Mrs. Adams's uncompromising partisanship 'in the undoing of her husband.' With a little-seen perspective and fascinating insight into the culture of the day, this is popular history done right." Publ Wkly

Roiphe, Katie

Uncommon arrangements; seven portraits of married life in London literary circles, 1910-1939. Dial Press 2007 343p il $26   **920**

1. Marriage 2. Women authors 3. Authors, English

ISBN 978-0-385-33937-7; 0-385-33937-2

LC 2007-11798

"Roiphe is at her most insightful—and funniest—in showing us where the declared credo of her characters collides with reality. . . . Often these unorthodox unions endured only because someone was willing to knuckle under." N Y Times Book Rev

Rubin, Louis Decimus

My father's people; a family of Southern Jews. {by} Louis D. Rubin Jr. Louisiana State Univ. Press 2002 139p il $22.50   **920**

ISBN 0-8071-2808-2

LC 2002-454

The author "tells the stories of Hyman and Fannie Rubin, his grandparents, and their seven children. . . . Rubin's descriptions are affectionate, yet he doesn't gloss over their flaws, and as a result, those he knows best come alive for readers." Publ Wkly

Salley, Columbus

The **black** 100; a ranking of the most influential African-Americans, past and present. Columbus Salley. rev ed; Kensington Publishing Corp. 1999 384p il pa $18.95   **920**

1. African Americans -- Biography

ISBN 978-0-8065-1550-2; 0-8065-1550-3

LC 98-47713

A reprint of the title first published 1993 by Carol Publishing Group

The author profiles 100 black men and women and ranks them, based upon his subjective evaluation of their contributions to black American society. They include Dr. Martin Luther King, Jr., Malcolm X, Zora Neale Hurston, Paul Robeson, Muhammad Ali, Arthur Ashe, Toni Morrison, Oprah Winfrey, and August Wilson

Includes bibliographical references

Schiff, Karenna Gore

Lighting the way; nine women who changed modern America. Miramax Books/Hyperion 2006 528p il $25.95; pa $17.95   **920**

1. Women -- United States -- Biography

ISBN 1-4013-5218-9; 1-4013-6015-7 pa

LC 2005-56247

"This is an inspirational collection of biographies of women of various social, ethnic, and racial backgrounds fighting for social justice." Booklist

Includes bibliographical references

Schonberg, Harold C.

The **great** pianists; rev and updated; Simon & Schuster 1987 525p il hardcover o.p. pa $18 **920**
1. Pianists 2. Composers 3. Musicians 4. Statesmen 5. Prime ministers 6. Conductors (Music) 7. Classical musicians

ISBN 0-671-63837-8 pa

LC 87-341

First published 1963

Beginning with the Bach family, the author describes the personal lives and careers of outstanding pianists from the eighteenth century to the present

Scott-Heron, Gil, 1949-2011

The **last** holiday; Gil Scott Heron. Grove Press 2012 384p. **920**
1. Music industry 2. Autobiographies 3. African American musicians

LC 97808802129017

"This [book, a posthumously published memoir,] is a . . . testament to the career and achievements of [African-American musician and writer] Gil Scott-Heron. But it is also a . . . personal account of his growing up in the South, a . . . portrait of Stevie Wonder, and a . . . narrative vehicle for Scott-Heron's . . . insights into the music industry, the civil rights movement, modern America, governmental hypocrisy, and our wider place in the world." (Publisher's note)

Sebag Montefiore, Simon, 1965-

★ The **Romanovs**; 1613-1918, by Simon Sebag Montefiore. Alfred A. Knopf 2016 784 p. illustrations $35 **920**
1. Russia -- Kings and rulers 2. Russia -- History -- 0-1917 3. Russia -- History -- 1613-1917 4. Russia -- Kings and rulers -- Biography

ISBN 9780307266521

LC 2015046026

This book, by Simon Sebag Montefiore, "is the intimate story of twenty tsars and tsarinas, some touched by genius, some by madness, but all inspired by holy autocracy and imperial ambition. . . . Montefiore's . . . chronicle reveals their secret world of unlimited power and ruthless empire-building, overshadowed by palace conspiracy, family rivalries, sexual decadence and wild extravagance, with a global cast of adventurers, courtesans, revolutionaries and poets." (Publisher's note)

"Montefiore's compassionate and incisive portraits of the Romanov rulers and their retinues, his liberal usage of contemporary diaries and correspondence, and his flair for the dramatic produce a narrative that effortlessly holds the reader's interest and attention despite its imposing length." Pub Wkly

Includes bibliographical references

Sifters: Native American women's lives; edited by Theda Perdue. Oxford Univ. Press 2001 260p (Viewpoints on American culture) $55; pa $19.95 **920**
1. Native American women

ISBN 0-19-513080-4; 0-19-513081-2 pa

LC 00-39950

"From Pocahontas, a Powhatan woman of the seventeenth century, to Ada Deer, the Menominee woman who headed the Bureau of Indian Affairs in the 1990s, the essays span four centuries. Each one recounts the experiences of women from vastly different cultural traditions. . . . Contributors focus on the ways in which different women have fashioned lives that remain firmly rooted in their identity as Native women." Publisher's note

Includes bibliographical references

Singer, Mark

Character studies; encounters with the curiously obsessed. Houghton Mifflin 2005 256p hardcover o.p. pa $13.95 **920**
1. Actors 2. Educators 3. Magicians 4. Eccentrics and eccentricities 5. Collectors 6. Book collectors 7. Hotel executives 8. Airline executives 9. Purchasing managers 10. Real estate developers 11. Motion picture directors 12. Construction industry executives

ISBN 0-618-77363-0 pa

LC 2004-62757

This is a "mix of . . . [the author's] portraits from The New Yorker, gathered in book form for the first time. In the essays he trains his skills on the likes of Martin Scorsese and Donald Trump; The Wednesday Group, the self-selected intelligentsia of El Paso; well-known bibliophile Michael Zinman; high-powered women who decide to quit the fast track; and Richard Seiverling, a Tom Mix fan determined to preserve the memory of the movie cowboy. It's quite a cast of characters, and Singer lavishly gives them all their due." Libr J

Smith, Andrew

Moondust; in search of the men who fell to earth. Fourth Estate 2005 372p il $24.95; pa $14.95 **920**
1. Astronauts 2. Apollo project

ISBN 0-00-71554-17; 978-0-00-715541-5; 0-00-715542-5 pa; 978-0-00-715542-2 pa

LC 2005-40081

This book describes the lives of nine astronauts after they walked on the moon.

"In an artful blend of memoir and popular history, Smith makes flesh-and-blood people out of icons and reveals the tenderness of his own heart." Publ Wkly

Includes bibliographical references

Spera, Keith

Groove interrupted; loss, renewal, and the music of New Orleans. St. Martin's Press 2011 260p $26.99 **920**
1. Musicians 2. Hurricane Katrina, 2005 3. Music -- New Orleans (La.)

ISBN 978-0-312-55225-1; 0-312-55225-4

LC 2011-10122

This look at the music community "of New Orleans is a collection of profiles of individual musicians who all had their ability to make music threatened after Hurricane Katrina in 2005. . . . many of the stories presented here had their origin in Spera's articles written before and after Katrina. All of them show how artists as varied as blues guitarist Clarence 'Gatemouth' Brown, jazz trumpeter Terence Blanchard, heavy metal singer Phil Anselmo of Pantera, and New Orleans legends Fats Domino and Allen Toussaint tried 'to make sense of the storm through music, comforting themselves and uplifting those around them.' Some of the finest profiles—and there is no weak one in the book—detail a combination of sadness and joy, such as Aaron Neville's triumphant return to the city after the death of his wife to close out the 2008 New Orleans Jazz & Heritage Festival." Publ Wkly

Spitz, Bob

★ The **Beatles**: the biography. Little, Brown 2005 983p il hardcover o.p. pa $17.99 **920**

1. Rock musicians 2. Beatles

ISBN 0-316-80352-9; 0-316-01331-5 pa

LC 2005-3838

This "beautifully written chronicle breathes new life into the familiar story of the Liverpool boys who conquered the world and became . . . the most influential entertainers of the past century. The author's passion for his subject, and for every nuance of every scene, electrifies even the most familiar moments in the legend." N Y Times Book Rev

Includes discography and bibliographical references

Stark, Steven D.

Meet the Beatles; a cultural history of the band that shook youth, gender, and the world. HarperEntertainment 2005 344p il $26.95; pa $14.95 **920**

1. Rock musicians 2. Beatles

ISBN 0-06-000892-X; 0-06-000893-8 pa

LC 2004-59794

In this biography of the Beatles, the author focuses "as much on the cultural trends that produced the Beatles—and the trends they created—as on the Fab Four themselves. . . . Throughout, Stark is sharp and insightful, even when he wades into the psychoanalytic waters of the John/Yoko and Paul/Linda relationships." Publ Wkly

Stolen voices; young people's war diaries from World War I to Iraq. edited with commentaries by Zlata Filipovic and Melanie Challenger; foreword by Olara A. Otunnu. Penguin 2007 xxiii, 293p il pa $14 **920**

1. Children and war

ISBN 978-0-14-303871-9; 0-14-303871-0

The editors have "compiled 14 diaries that were kept by children during wartime, from World War I to Iraq. Their poignant voices will break your heart." Libr J

Strathern, Paul

The **artist,** the philosopher, and the warrior; the intersecting lives of da Vinci, Machiavelli, and Borgia and the world they shaped. Bantam Books 2009 xxiii, 456p il map $30 **920**

1. Artists 2. Authors 3. Painters 4. Statesmen 5. Dramatists 6. Scientists 7. Renaissance 8. Heads of state 9. Writers on science 10. Writers on politics 11. Italy -- History -- 0-1559 12. Political and social philosophers

ISBN 978-0-553-80752-3

LC 2009-6950

Strathern "does for Machiavelli and da Vinci what he does for Borgia: creates a flesh-and-blood portrait for each

that defies historical stereotype. Using his novelist's eye and a historian's sweep, Strathern conveys the emotional subtleties that animated their lives. It's no small feat that he makes you care deeply for these complex figures who lived half a millennium ago." Washington Post

Includes bibliographical references

Strauss, Neil

Everyone loves you when you're dead; journeys into fame and madness. It Books 2011 507p il pa $16.99 **920**

1. Celebrities 2. Rock musicians

ISBN 978-0-06-154367-8

LC 2010-52255

"By his own count, the author has conducted some 3,000 interviews with the famous, not-so-famous, used-to-be-famous and ought-to-be-famous denizens of popular culture. Here he brings together the best of these interviews in loosely and at times bizarrely connected chapters. All the well-knowns are here, including Madonna, Lady Gaga, David Bowie, The Who, Kenny G, Led Zeppelin, Puffy Combs and Bo Diddley. . . . Gonzo interviewing at its best." Kirkus

Szegedy-Maszák, Marianne

I kiss your hands many times; hearts, souls, and wars in Hungary. Marianne Szegedy-Maszak. Spiegel & Grau, an imprint of The Random House Publishing Group 2013 400 p. $27 **920**

1. Holocaust, 1939-1945 2. World War, 1939-1945 -- Hungary 3. Hungary -- Biography 4. Jews -- Hungary -- Biography 5. Holocaust, Jewish (1939-1945) -- Hungary 6. Hungarians -- United States -- Biography

ISBN 0385524854; 9780385524858; 9780679645221

LC 2012043179

"This . . . family history weaves together the lives of journalist [Marianne] Szegedy-Maszák's parents . . . with the fate of their native Hungary during and after WWII. The author's father, Aladár, was a Gentile civil servant in the Hungarian Foreign Ministry, whereas her mother, Hanna, came from a family of Jewish industrialists who converted to Christianity. Aladár and Hanna's romance . . . continues to grow even after Aladár is shipped off to the Dachau concentration camp." (Publishers Weekly)

Includes bibliographical references

Taraborrelli, J. Randy

After Camelot; an intimate history of the Kennedy family, 1968 to the present. J. Randy Taraborrelli. Grand Central Pub. 2012 602 p. **920**

1. Kennedy family 2. Presidents' spouses -- United States 3. Presidents -- United States -- Family

ISBN 9780446553902

LC 2011029518

For this book, which "document[s] America's "royal family," . . . [J. Randy Taraborrelli] conducted interviews with [Kennedy] family members and their intimates, such people as Eunice Kennedy Shriver, Oleg Cassini, Robert McNamara, Pierre Salinger, Arthur Schlesinger Jr., and numerous confidential sources. He also relied heavily on the 40 years of personal correspondence between Jackie Kennedy and Lady Bird Johnson. . . . [The book offers] a . . . view of family dynamics in crises both public and private: financial negotiations before Jackie's marriage to Onassis; family interference in Pat Kennedy and Peter Lawford's troubled marriage; Ted Kennedy's bad behavior at Chappaquiddick, and his support of Caroline's abortive Senate run to carry on the 'family dynasty.'" (Publishers Weekly)

Includes bibliographical references and index

Terkel, Studs, 1912-2008

My American century. New Press 1997 xxiii, 532p hardcover o.p. pa $14.95 **920**
1. United States -- Biography
ISBN 1-56584-469-6 pa
LC 96-52779

This volume gathers "the introductions Terkel wrote for his eight oral-history books (and the fiftieth anniversary edition of Steinbeck's The Grapes of Wrath) with 40-odd interviews: Terkel's conversations with gangsters and grandmothers, authors and executives, photographers and farmers, cabbies and crusaders. . . . A superb introduction to Terkel's work (or to oral history) and a trip down memory lane for his fans." Booklist

Thomas, Robert McG.

52 McGs; the best obituaries from legendary New York Times writer Robert McG. Thomas Jr. edited by Chris Calhoun; foreword by Thomas Mallon. Scribner 2001 192p il hardcover o.p. pa $14.95 **920**
1. Obituaries
ISBN 1-4165-9827-8 pa
LC 2001-42952

"This highly browsable collection of 52 obits shows Thomas at his deadline best." Publ Wkly

Tillyard, Stella K.

A royal affair; George III and his scandalous siblings. [by] Stella Tillyard. Random House 2006 xxiv, 352p il $26.95 **920**
1. Kings 2. Great Britain -- Kings and rulers
ISBN 978-1-4000-6371-0; 1-4000-6371-X
LC 2006-45130

This biography examines the life of King George III of Great Britain and his siblings.

"This riveting account reminds us that in the past, the misdemeanors of royals had serious, not simply gossip-rag, implications." Booklist

Includes bibliographical references

Tinniswood, Adrian

The Verneys; a true story of love, war, and madness in seventeenth-century England. Riverhead Books 2007 569p il map $35 **920**
1. Great Britain -- History -- 1603-1714, Stuarts
ISBN 978-1-59448-948-8; 1-59448-948-3
LC 2007-911

"The letters of the Verney family survive as the largest and most continuous collection of personal correspondence from seventeenth-century Britain, and Tinniswood draws on them to produce a lively, almost novelistic account of an aristocratic family. . . Their stories range from the outrageous—Sir Francis Verney, who 'turned Turk' and became a pirate along the Barbary Coast; 'Mad' Mary Verney, whose husband's philandering drove her to zelotypia, or morbid

jealousy—to the more familiar and heartrending: a father and son separated by political allegiances during civil war; a patriarch who worries about his children's financial security. Tinniswood's portraits are intimate, compelling, and deftly situated within the broader historical period, so that the turbulence of the seventeenth century is rendered as a human drama." New Yorker

Includes bibliographical references

Tomkins, Calvin

Lives of the artists. Henry Holt 2008 254p $26 **920**
1. Art -- 20th century 2. Artists -- Biography
ISBN 978-0-8050-8872-4; 0-8050-8872-5
LC 2008-13121

"Tomkins is a ruthless observer. . . . Books that trade on content that originally appeared in the New Yorker have become a small industry, but not all are as intimate as this one." Publ Wkly

Unferth, Deb Olin

Revolution; Deb Olin Unferth. Henry Holt 2011 208p. **920**
1. Authors 2. Novelists 3. Revolutions 4. Autobiographies 5. Nicaragua -- Politics and government 6. College teachers 7. Short story writers 8. Biography, Individual
ISBN 978-0-8050-9323-0; 0-8050-9323-0
LC 201023471

The author writes about "the year she ran away from college with her . . . boyfriend and followed him to Nicaragua to join the Sandinistas." (Publisher's note)

Waller, Maureen

Sovereign ladies; the six reigning queens of England. St. Martin's Press 2007 554p il $29.95; pa $19.95 **920**
1. Queens 2. Great Britain -- Kings and rulers
ISBN 978-0-312-33801-5; 0-312-33801-5; 978-0-312-38608-5 pa; 0-312-38608-7 pa
LC 2007-16181

First published 2006 in the United Kingdom

This is a "glossy, deeply detailed . . . comparative examination of the six queens who have ruled England in their own right." Kirkus

Includes bibliographical references

Walsh, Jim

The Replacements; all over but the shouting; an oral history. MBI Pub. Co. and Voyageur Press 2007 304p il $21.95 **920**
1. Rock musicians 2. Replacements (Musical group)
ISBN 978-0-7603-3062-3; 0-7603-3062-X
LC 2007-22576

"In this loving, appropriately ramshackle tribute to one of the most beloved rock-and-roll bands of the 1980s, Walsh gives his subjects the oral history treatment, assembling a wide range of associates, friends and famous fans to put their memories on the record." Publ Wkly

Includes bibliographical references

Ward-Royster, Willa

How I got over; Clara Ward and the world-famous Ward Singers. {by} Willa Ward-Royster; as told to Toni Rose; foreword by Horace Clarence Boyer. Temple Univ. Press 1997 263p hardcover o.p. pa $24.95   **920**

1. Gospel music 2. Clara Ward Singers
ISBN 1-56639-489-9; 978-1-56639-490-1 pa;
1-56639-490-2 pa

LC 96-5943

"Ward-Royster relates the rise of her family's world-renowned gospel group, formed by her mother and headlined by her sister. . . . The book contains details on everything from successful performances on the stage of the Apollo, major TV variety shows, and international tours to top sales of hit recordings and friendships with such luminaries as Mahalia Jackson." Libr J

Warner, Ezra J.

Generals in blue; lives of the Union commanders. Louisiana State Univ. Press 1964 xxiv, 679p il $39.95   **920**

1. Generals 2. United States -- History -- 1861-1865, Civil War -- Biography
ISBN 0-8071-0822-7

This book contains biographical sketches of the 583 men who attained the rank of general during the Civil War years. A photograph of each man is also included

Includes bibliographical references

Generals in gray; lives of the Confederate commanders. Louisiana State Univ. Press 1959 xxvii, 420p il $39.95   **920**

1. Generals 2. Confederate States of America -- Biography 3. United States -- History -- 1861-1865, Civil War -- Biography
ISBN 0-8071-0823-5

"Biographical sketches of the Confederate generals; concise outlines of their military careers, also giving dates of birth and death and places of burial. The product of ten years of research, much of it done in interviews with descendants. Illustrated with 425 portraits." Publ Wkly

Includes bibliographical references

Waugh, Alexander

Fathers and sons; the autobiography of a family. Nan A. Talese 2007 472p il $27.50   **920**

1. Authors 2. Authors, English
ISBN 978-0-385-52150-5; 0-385-52150-2

LC 2007-5239

First published 2004 in the United Kingdom

"The scion of an illustrious—and fabulously eccentric—English literary dynasty referees four generations of father-son antagonisms in this scintillating family memoir. Waugh . . . focuses on the fraught relationship between his great-grandfather, prominent critic and publisher Arthur Waugh, and Arthur's son, the famous novelist Evelyn. . . . If this tome were merely an excuse to reprint some of Evelyn's hilarious jottings, it would be well worth the price, but it's also

an absorbing study of how writers process their most painfully formative experiences." Publ Wkly

Includes bibliographical references

The House of Wittgenstein; a family at war. Doubleday 2009 333p il $28.95   **920**

1. Metal industry executives
ISBN 978-0-385-52060-7; 0-385-52060-3

LC 2008-33312

Waugh "tells the story of the downfall of the wealthy Wittgenstein family. He follows the intellectually and musically gifted Wittgenstein children as history conspires to rob them of one of Europe's largest fortunes. Waugh weaves the family's story around that of the fourth son, Paul: losing his arm in the Great War, Paul gained international acclaim as a left-handed concert pianist; at that time, his brother Ludwig's notoriety was limited to a small circle at Cambridge. With the rise of the Nazis, the Wittgenstein siblings were declared racially Jewish and held hostage for their wealth—a peril that ratchets up the book's tension and contributes to the already tragic atmosphere haunting the family. Waugh sifted through letters and journals held in archives and private collections for this masterfully researched work that brings the characters of this previously untold story to life. He moves seamlessly among historical circumstance, personal relations, and the world of classical composition and performance." Libr J

Includes bibliographical references (p. 315-21)

Waxman, Sharon

Rebels on the backlot; six maverick directors and how they conquered the Hollywood studio system. 1st ed; W. Morrow 2005 386p il $25.95; pa $14.95   **920**

1. Actors 2. Screenwriters 3. Video directors 4. Motion picture directors 5. Motion pictures -- Production and direction
ISBN 0-06-054017-6; 0-06-054018-4 pa

LC 2004-59269

This is the author's "study of six boundary-breaking young directors who revolutionized 1990s filmmaking and still represent a refreshing alternative to 'cookie cutter scripts and cheap MTV imagery.' Her full-blooded profiles introduce Quentin Tarantino (Pulp Fiction), Paul Thomas Anderson (Boogie Nights), David Fincher (Fight Club), Steven Soderbergh (Traffic), David O. Russell (Three Kings) and Spike Jonze (Being John Malkovich). . . . Their stories make for compelling reading." Publ Wkly

Includes bibliographical references

Weber, Nicholas Fox, 1947-

The Bauhaus group; six masters of modernism. Alfred A. Knopf 2009 521p il $40   **920**

1. Artists 2. Painters 3. Architects 4. Artists, German 5. Avant-garde (Aesthetics) 6. Bauhaus 7. Weavers 8. Printmakers 9. Art teachers 10. Textile artists 11. Furniture designers 12. Biography, Collective 13. Avant-garde (Aesthetics) -- Germany -- History -- 20th century
ISBN 978-0-307-26836-5; 0-307-26836-5

LC 2009-28729

"A rigorously researched and often fascinating history that morphs into memoir." Kirkus

Includes bibliographical references

Weintraub, Stanley

15 stars; Eisenhower, MacArthur, Marshall: three generals who saved the American century. Free Press 2007 541p il $30 **920**

1. Generals 2. Statesmen 3. Presidents 4. College presidents 5. Secretaries of state 6. Secretaries of defense 7. Nobel laureates for peace

ISBN 978-0-7432-7527-9; 0-7432-7527-6

LC 2007-16018

The author "provides a detailed and absorbing gloss on the relationships among three extraordinary leaders." Libr J

Includes bibliographical references

Weller, Sheila

Girls like us; Carole King, Joni Mitchell, and Carly Simon--and the journey of a generation. Atria Books 2008 584p il $27.95; pa $17 **920**

1. Singers 2. Folk musicians 3. Rock musicians 4. Women musicians 5. Songwriters

ISBN 978-0-743-49147-1; 0-743-49147-5; 978-0-743-49148-8 pa; 0-743-49148-3 pa

LC 2007-43445

This is a biography of the singer-songwriters Carole King, Joni Mitchell, and Carly Simon.

"A must-read for any fan of these artists, this bio will prove an absorbing, eye-opening tour of rock (and American) history for anyone who's appreciated a female musician in the past thirty years." Publ Wkly

West, Cornel, 1953-

Cornel West on Black prophetic fire; in dialogue with and edited by Christa Buschendorf. Beacon Press 2014 248 p. illustrations (hardback : acid-free paper) $25.95 **920**

1. African Americans -- Biography 2. Prophets -- United States -- Biography 3. Revolutionaries -- United States -- Biography

ISBN 0807003522; 9780807003527

LC 2014010359

This book, by Cornel West and edited by Christa Buschendorf, is a "look at nineteenth- and twentieth-century African American leaders and their visionary legacies. . . . [It] provides a fresh perspective on six revolutionary African American leaders: Frederick Douglass, W. E. B. Du Bois, Martin Luther King Jr., Ella Baker, Malcolm X, and Ida B. Wells." (Publisher's note)

"West bemoans the "deodoriz[ing]" of these radical figures—e.g., shying away from W.E.B. Du Bois' communist sympathies and the turn toward complicity with the white mainstream. The concluding section, "Last Words on the Black Prophetic Tradition in the Age of Obama," however, is lacking, as West aims his vitriol against the "cowardly capitulation of Black leadership to Obama's neoliberal policies," without a chance for vigorous rebuttal. Lively, heated, fighting words—self-serious but never dull." Kirkus

Includes bibliographical references and index

Black prophetic fire

Wiencek, Henry

The Hairstons; an American family in black and white. St. Martin's Press 1999 xx, 361p il map hardcover o.p. pa $14.95 **920**

1. Slavery -- United States 2. United States -- Race relations 3. African Americans -- Southern States

ISBN 0-312-25393-1 pa

LC 98-44014

Wiencek tells the "story of the Hairston family, the largest slaveholders in the South and one of the wealthiest families in the U.S. Wiencek details the race mixing that occured between master and slave and the family's efforts to keep its dark-skinned members enslaved and to maintain wealth only for its white members. A fascinating book that explores the complexity of family and racial relationships in the U.S." Booklist

Includes bibliographical references

Wolff, Daniel

★ How Lincoln learned to read; twelve great Americans and the educations that made them. Bloomsbury 2009 345p $26 **920**

1. United States -- Biography 2. Education -- United States -- History

ISBN 978-1-59691-290-8; 1-59691-290-1

LC 2008-24695

"This provocative book is not only an important addition to the history of education in America, but also a valuable contribution to the history and understanding of the country's ideas and culture." SLJ

Includes bibliographical references

Xinran

China witness; voices from a silent generation. translated from Chinese by Nicky Harman, Julia Lovell and Esther Tyldesley. Pantheon Books 2009 434p il map $28.95 **920**

1. China -- Biography

ISBN 978-0-375-42547-9; 0-375-42547-0

LC 2008-35840

First published 2008 in the United Kingdom

The author, "traveling across the expanse of the Chinese Republic over the years, sought out those who had witnessed the rise of communism more than half a century ago. The result is this stirring, startlingly honest account of life under Chairman Mao and the current reformers revamping the socialist state." Publ Wkly

920.003 Dictionaries, encyclopedias, concordances of biography as a discipline

★ The African American national biography; editors in chief, Henry Louis Gates, Jr., Evelyn Brooks-Higginbotham. Oxford University Press 2008 8v il set $995 **920.003**

1. Reference books 2. African Americans -- Biography -- Dictionaries

ISBN 978-0-19-516019-2

LC 2007-44671

"A supplement to the 24-volume American National Biography . . . [this biographical encyclopedia] records the contributions of more than 4,000 African Americans—slaves, architects, entertainers, dentists, political leaders, artists, poets, and activists. . . . [This] is a major . . . standard reference work that most libraries of any size will want to have." Booklist

Includes bibliographical references

American statesmen; secretaries of state from John Jay to Colin Powell. edited by Edward S. Mihalkanin. Greenwood Press 2004 xxxv, 571p $99.95   **920.003**
1. Reference books 2. Statesmen -- United States -- Dictionaries
ISBN 0-313-30828-4

LC 2004-10871

For a fuller review, see: Booklist, Feb. 15, 2005

This biographical dictionary features "65 biographical essays on each of the secretaries of state plus two important interim secretaries. . . . Each essay blends biographical information, early life, education, and influences; career information, appointment, and relations with the president and Congress; and a review of the major issues and accomplishments during the secretary's tenure in office." Am Ref Books Annu, 2005

Includes bibliographical references

American writers; a collection of literary biographies. Leonard Unger, editor in chief. Scribner 1974 4v + supplement I-IV set $1845   **920.003**
1. Reference books 2. Authors, American -- Dictionaries 3. American literature -- History and criticism
ISBN 0-684-80586-3

"Signed essays on the life and works of selected American authors; selective bibliographies by and about each author. The basic set (1974. 4 v.) contains 97 essays originally published in the University of Minnesota pamphlets on American writers series; some have been revised and updated. Each of the 2-v. supplements covers 29 writers not included in the parent series; the supplements give greater attention to women and minorities." Guide to Ref Books. 11th edition

American writers: selected authors; a three volume set containing sixty-four essays from the parent publication is available $325 (ISBN 0-684-80604-5)

Ancell, R. Manning
The **biographical** dictionary of World War II generals and flag officers; the U.S. Armed Forces. {by} R. Manning Ancell with Christine M. Miller. Greenwood Press 1996 706p $130.95   **920.003**
1. World War, 1939-1945 -- Biography
ISBN 0-313-29546-8

LC 95-50450

"The nearly 2,400 entries, which, according to the preface, represent 99 percent of the total number who served, are listed in alphabetical order in six chapters: 'Army,' 'Army Air Force,' 'National Guard,' 'Navy,' 'Marine Corps,' and 'Coast Guard.' . . . The volume concludes with two appendixes (state-by-state and service-by-service summary of birthplaces and birth dates; generals and flag officers who died during World War II) and an alphabetical index to all biographees." Booklist

Includes bibliographical references

Attwater, Donald
The **Penguin** dictionary of saints; {by} Donald Attwater, with Catherine Rachel John. 3rd ed; Penguin Bks. 1995 381p pa $15.95   **920.003**
1. Reference books 2. Christian saints -- Dictionaries
ISBN 0-14-051312-4

LC 96-165638

First published 1965

"Information includes classification of saints (martyr, confessor, and so on); date of existence; their circumstances in becoming a saint; and their feast day. It also provides a glossary and lists of further reading, some patron saints, some emblems that identify specific saints, and feast days in the order that they arrive within the calendar year." Am Ref Books Annu, 1997

Bader, Philip
★ **African**-American writers; revised by Catherine Reef. Rev. ed; Facts On File 2010 340p il (A to Z of African Americans) $49.50   **920.003**
1. Reference books 2. African American authors -- Dictionaries 3. American literature -- African American authors -- Bio-bibliography
ISBN 978-0-8160-8141-7

LC 2010-05463

First published 2004

This book "profiles popular and prominent African-American writers across many genres of literature. Each entry in this . . . resource provides a biographical profile, concentrating on the major literary works and accomplishments of each author as well as an outline of his or her contributions to American literature." Publisher's note

Includes bibliographical references

★ **Biographical** encyclopedia of artists; Sir Lawrence Gowing, general editor. Facts on File 2005 4v il set $260   **920.003**
1. Reference books 2. Artists -- Biography -- Encyclopedias
ISBN 0-8160-5803-2

LC 2005-40500

First published 1983 by Prentice-Hall as volume two of Encyclopedia of visual art

"The artists covered include Laurie Anderson, Frank Gehry, Anselm Kiefer, Jan Vermeer, and Andy Warhol. . . . A visual chronology of artists by country and era functions as an index to artists, and an alphabetical artist/subject index concludes the work." Libr J

Includes bibliographical references

★ **Black** women in America; Darlene Clark Hine, editor in chief. 2nd ed; Oxford University Press 2005 3v il set $325   **920.003**
1. Reference books 2. African American women -- Dictionaries
ISBN 0-19-515677-3

LC 2005-1532

First published 1993 by Carlson Pub.

"The essays offer fascinating glimpses into black women's economic, social, and political contributions, even at the grassroots level, and explore issues such as spirituality, domestic servitude, and mixed-race identity in terms of how they have shaped history." SLJ

Includes bibliographical references

Butler, Alban

★ **Butler's** Lives of the saints. Christian Classics 1956 4v set $149.95; pa set $109.95 **920.003**

1. Reference books 2. Christian saints -- Dictionaries

ISBN 0-87061-045-7; 0-87061-137-2 pa

A reprint of the four volume set published 1956 by Kenedy; New edition of a work first published 1756-1759. The calendar arrangement is retained, but the number of entries has almost doubled and many of the entries have been rewritten in whole or part

"The biographies of the saints and beati are arranged by their feast days with each of the four volumes containing three months. . . . Each volume has a table of contents arranged by the days of the month with a list of the feasts for each day." Booklist

Colby, Vineta

World authors, 1975-1980; editor, Vineta Colby. Wilson, H.W. 1985 829p il (Authors series) $140 **920.003**

1. Reference books 2. Authors -- Dictionaries 3. Literature -- Bio-bibliography

ISBN 0-8242-0715-7

LC 85-10045

This work profiles the lives and works of 379 writers

Contemporary women artists; editors, Laurie Collier Hillstrom, Kevin Hillstrom; with a preface by Lucy R. Lippard. St. James Press 1999 760p $175 **920.003**

1. Reference books 2. Women artists -- Dictionaries

ISBN 1-558-62372-8

LC 99-10053

This work "covers 350 women artists, mostly US painters and sculptors. Entries are helpfully indexed by nationality and medium and include photographers, performance and video artists, ceramicists, filmmakers, textile artists, and weavers from countries in Latin America and western and eastern Europe." Choice

Includes bibliographical references

Drew, Bernard A.

100 most popular nonfiction authors; biographical sketches and bibliographies. Libraries Unlimited 2007 438p il (Popular authors series) $65 **920.003**

1. Reference books 2. Authors -- Dictionaries 3. Literature -- Bio-bibliography

ISBN 978-1-59158-487-2

LC 2007-19949

"The authors, chosen by means of consultations with librarians, are those whose impact has been seen mostly in the last half century, among them Diane Ackerman, John Krakauer, David McCullough, and Cornel West. Entries are headed by author's birth year and birthplace, and, if ap-

plicable, date of death, and by signature work and primary genres." Booklist

Includes bibliographical references

Encyclopedia of women's autobiography; edited by Victoria Boynton and Jo Malin; Emmanuel S. Nelson, advisory editor. Greenwood Press 2005 2v set $249.95 **920.003**

1. Autobiography 2. Reference books 3. Women -- Biography -- Encyclopedias

ISBN 0-313-32737-8

LC 2005-8526

This set's "encyclopedic and culturally diverse nature should appeal to a wide audience and provide a valuable starting point for further research." Libr J

Includes bibliographical references

Farmer, David Hugh

The **Oxford** dictionary of saints; 5th ed; Oxford University Press 2004 xxiv, 579p map pa $16.95 **920.003**

1. Reference books 2. Christian saints -- Dictionaries

ISBN 978-0-19-860949-0; 0-19-860949-3 pa

LC 2005-272790

A reissue of the title first published 1978

This biographical dictionary profiles the lives, cults, and artistic associations of over 1,000 saints, from the famous to the obscure. An appendix on pilgrimage sights in Europe is also included

"Even those who do not believe in the saints . . . will be able to enjoy and to profit from this splendid book." Economist

Includes bibliographical references

Friedman, Ian C.

Latino athletes. Facts on File 2007 278p il (A to Z of Latino Americans) $44 **920.003**

1. Reference books 2. Athletes -- Dictionaries 3. Hispanic Americans -- Dictionaries

ISBN 978-0-8160-6384-0; 0-8160-6384-2

LC 2006-16901

"Gymnast Trent Dimas, mountain biker Juli Furtado, and speed skater Derek Parra are among the 176 athletes profiled in this volume. . . . Following the entries, athletes are listed by sport, year of birth, and ethnicity or country of origin." Booklist

Includes bibliographical references

Friedwald, Will

A **biographical** guide to the great jazz and pop singers. Pantheon Books 2010 811p $45 **920.003**

1. Reference books 2. Singers -- Dictionaries 3. Jazz music -- Dictionaries 4. Popular music -- Dictionaries 5. Jazz music -- Bio-bibliography 6. Popular music -- Bio-bibliography

ISBN 978-0-375-42149-5; 0-375-42149-1

LC 2009-44405

The author "celebrates 200-odd performers of jazz and pop standards, from the mid-20th-century titans—Louis Armstrong, Bing Crosby, Ella Fitzgerald, Frank Sinatra—to latter-day acolytes like Diana Krall and Harry Connick Jr., with a raft of unjustly obscure singers in between. . . .

Friedwald is all about the music; he primly shies away from his subjects' scandal-prone personal lives, but accords each a substantial career retrospective, selected discography and wonderfully pithy interpretive essay. . . . Friedwald's exuberant medley is that rarest of things: music criticism that actually makes you sit up and listen." Publ Wkly

Garraty, John Arthur

★ **American** national biography; general editors, John A. Garraty, Mark C. Carnes. Oxford Univ. Press 1999 24v set $2,095 **920.003**
1. Reference books 2. United States -- Biography -- Dictionaries
ISBN 0-19-520635-5
LC 98-20826
ALA RUSA Dartmouth Medal (1999)

"ANB defines 'American' broadly as a person whose significance, achievement, fame, or influence occurred during residence within what is now the US, or whose life or career directly influenced the course of US history. Subjects must have died before 1996. . . . Subjects are arranged alphabetically. The typical entry, 750 to 7,500 words in length, proceeds chronologically, following the major personal and professional events of the subject's life, birth to death. The concluding paragraph attempts to assess the subject's contributions from today's perspective. A brief bibliography after each entry, not meant to be comprehensive, lists major sources, including locations of archives and collections of personal papers." Choice

Includes bibliographical references

Gates, Alexander E.

A to Z of earth scientists. Facts on File 2002 336p il (Notable scientists) $45 **920.003**
1. Earth sciences 2. Reference books 3. Scientists -- Dictionaries
ISBN 0-8160-4580-1
LC 2002-14616

This "profiles the lives of 192 people who devoted their careers to the disciplines and subdisciplines of the earth sciences during the 18th century to the present. . . . Entries appear in alphabetic order under the name by which the scientist is most commonly known. Also included are birth date, date of death (if applicable), nationality, and earth science specialty. An essay containing more personal data, including an emphasis on the scientist's main work and contributions to the field follows this information." Am Ref Books Annu, 2003

Includes bibliographical references

Great lives from history, The 17th century, 1601-1700; editor, Larissa Juliet Taylor. Salem Press 2005 2v il set $160 **920.003**
1. Reference books 2. Biography -- Dictionaries 3. World history -- 17th century
ISBN 1-58765-222-6; 978-1-58765-222-6
LC 2005-17804

Companion volume to Great events from history, The 17th century, 1601-1700

First published as part of the Great lives from history series, published 1987-1995 under the editorship of Frank N.

Magill; previously published as half of volume 4 of Dictionary of world biography, published 1998-1999

This "is a collection of biographical essays, ranging from three to five pages in length and documenting the lives of those individuals who helped to shape the history of the 17th century. The coverage is also global and includes both well-known and lesser-known figures." SLJ

Includes bibliographical references

Great lives from history, The 19th century, 1801-1900; editor, John Powell. Salem Press 2006 4v il map set $360 **920.003**
1. Reference books 2. Biography -- Dictionaries 3. World history -- 19th century
ISBN 978-1-58765-292-9; 1-58765-292-7
LC 2006-20187

Companion volume to Great events from history, The 19th century, 1801-1900

First published as part of the Great lives from history series, published 1987-1995 under the editorship of Frank N. Magill; previously published as volumes 5 and 6 of Dictionary of world biography, published 1998-1999

"A total of 737 essays covering 757 major figures including 123 on women make up the set. . . . Major world leaders appear here, as well as the giants of religious faith who dominated the century: monarchs, presidents, popes, philosophers, writers, social reformers, educators, and military leaders who left their imprint on political as well as spiritual institutions." Publisher's note

Includes bibliographical references

Great lives from history, The ancient world, prehistory-476 C.E; editor, Christina A. Salowey. Salem Press 2004 2v il, maps set $160 **920.003**
1. Ancient history 2. Reference books 3. Biography -- Dictionaries
ISBN 1-587-65152-1; 978-1-58765-164-9
LC 2004-705

Companion volume to Great events from history, The ancient world, prehistory-476 C.E

First published as part of the Great lives from history series, published 1987-1995 under the editorship of Frank N. Magill; previously published as volume 1 of Dictionary of world biography, published 1998-1999

This "set provides three-to-six-page biographies on major personages from the ancient world. Arranged alphabetically, each article gives basic information such as when and where the individual was born and also where and when he or she died, a description of his or her early life and life's work, the significance of the individual, an annotated bibliography, and related entries in both this set and in the . . . [Great events from history] set." Ref & User Services Quarterly

Includes bibliographical references

Great lives from history, the Middle Ages, 477-1453; editor, Shelley Wolbrink. Salem Press 2005 2v il map set $160 **920.003**
1. Reference books 2. Middle ages -- Biography 3. Biography -- Dictionaries
ISBN 1-58765-164-5; 978-1-58765-164-9
LC 2004-16696

Companion volume to Great events from history, the Middle Ages, 477-1453

First published as part of the Great lives from history series, published 1987-1995 under the editorship of Frank N. Magill; previously published as volume 2 of Dictionary of world biography, published 1998-1999

These "volumes focus on the people throughout the world from after the Fall of Rome, in 476 C.E., to 1453. Coverage is worldwide. . . . Each entry begins with ready-reference information, followed by a summary of the person's life, a paragraph or two on 'Significance,' a list of further readings, and cross-references to entries both within the set and within the [Great events in history] companion set." Booklist

Includes bibliographical references

Great lives from history, the Renaissance & early modern era, 1454-1600; editor, Christina J. Moose. Salem Press 2005 2v il map set $160   **920.003**
1. Renaissance 2. Reference books 3. Biography -- Dictionaries
ISBN 1-58765-211-0; 978-1-58765-211-0
LC 2004-28875
Companion volume to Great events from history, the Renaissance & early modern era, 1454-1600

First published as part of the Great lives from history series, published 1987-1995 under the editorship of Frank N. Magill; previously published as volume 3 of Dictionary of world biography, published 1998-1999

"This two-volume work offers biographies of 338 historical figures in entries that range from two to five pages in length. A publisher's note in volume 1 explains the set's format and use. All the biographies include name, nationality or ethnicity, historical role, dates, and area(s) of achievement; description of early life, work, and significance; an annotated bibliography; and cross-references." Choice

Includes bibliographical references

Great lives from history: Notorious lives; editor, Carl L. Bankston III. Salem Press 2007 3v il set $252   **920.003**
1. Criminals 2. Dictators 3. Terrorists 4. War criminals 5. Reference books 6. Political corruption 7. Biography -- Dictionaries
ISBN 978-1-58765-320-9
LC 2006-32935
"The scope and depth of coverage make it a valuable resource for not just biographies but for criminal justice and popular culture as well." Booklist

Includes bibliographical references

Great lives from history: the 20th century, 1901-2000; editor, Robert F. Gorman. Salem Press 2008 10v il set $795   **920.003**
1. Reference books 2. Biography -- Dictionaries 3. World history -- 20th century
ISBN 978-1-58765-345-2
LC 2008-17125
First published as part of the Great lives from history series, published 1987-1995 under the editorship of Frank N.

Magill; previously published as volumes 7-9 of Dictionary of world biography, published 1998-1999

"This ten-volume set offers 1,330 . . . biographies of major personages in world history (many still living) from 1901-2000. . . . The personages covered are identified with one or more of the following regions: Africa, Asia, Australia, Caribbean, Europe, Latin America, Middle East, North America, South America, and Southeast Asia." Publisher's note

Includes bibliographical references

Hamilton, Neil A.
Presidents; a biographical dictionary. Ian C. Friedman, reviser. 3rd ed; Facts on File 2010 496p il (Facts on File library of American history) $85; pa $19.95   **920.003**
1. Reference books 2. Presidents -- United States -- Dictionaries
ISBN 978-0-8160-7708-3; 978-0-8160-8247-6 pa
LC 2009-10191
First published 2001

This book "contains biographies and portraits of all presidents, a . . . chronology of the life of each president, and suggested further reading about each president." Publisher's note

Includes bibliographical references

Havlice, Patricia Pate
Index to artistic biography. Scarecrow Press 1973 2v set $135   **920.003**
1. Reference books 2. Artists -- Biography 3. Biography -- Indexes
ISBN 0-8108-0540-5
The first two volumes list some 70,000 artists' biographies found in sixty-four reference works. The first supplement covers seventy titles and lists around 47,000 names. The second supplement covers 131 titles published from 1980 through 1999

★ **Holy** people of the world; a cross-cultural encyclopedia. Phyllis G. Jestice, editor. ABC-CLIO 2004 3v il set $285   **920.003**
1. Reference books 2. Religious biography -- Encyclopedias
ISBN 1-576-07355-6
LC 2004-22606
"This edition deserves to become well-worn by the time a second appears." Libr J

Includes bibliographical references

Jaques Cattell Press
Who's who in American politics 2007-2008; [prepared by Marquis Who's Who] 21st ed.; Marquis Who's Who 2007 xxxvi, 1960p $314.10 **920.003**
1. Reference books 2. Politicians -- United States -- Dictionaries
ISBN 978-0-8379-6918-3
Biennial. First published 1967 by Bowker

"Biographical directory of political leaders in the Congress, the executive branch of the federal government, state legislatures, state executive branches, mayors of cities with populations over 50,000, national and state party chairs, national party committee members, county chairs, and state supreme court justices. Entries are arranged by state, then alphabetically by name. Indexed by name." Ref Sources for Small & Medium-sized Libr. 6th edition

Kelly, J. N. D.

The **Oxford** dictionary of Popes; with new material by Michael Walsh. Updated [ed]; Oxford University Press 2006 349p pa $21.43 **920.003**

1. Reference books 2. Popes -- Dictionaries

ISBN 978-0-19-861433-3; 0-19-861433-0

LC 2006-277841

First published 1986

"An excellent source of information, arranged chronologically with an alphabetical index. Includes popes, antipopes, and an appendix on Pope Joan." Ref Sources for Small & Medium-sized Libr. 6th edition

Includes bibliographical references

Krismann, Carol

★ **Encyclopedia** of American women in business; from colonial times to the present. [by] Carol H. Krisman. Greenwood Press 2004 692p 2v set $175 **920.003**

1. Reference books 2. Businesswomen -- Encyclopedias 3. Women executives -- Encyclopedias

ISBN 0-313-32757-2

LC 2004-56065

The author "presents the stories of 327 businesswomen who have succeeded as entrepreneurs, executives, or business owners in profit-making enterprises from Colonial times to this day. . . . In addition to the biographies, the book contains entries for work-related issues like old-boys network, office romance, and diversity as well as profiles of agencies related to women. . . . This excellent reference book is wonderfully readable and should encourage readers to conduct further research of the women profiled." Libr J

Includes bibliographical references

Kuhlman, Erika A.

A to Z of women in world history; [by] Erika Kuhlman. Facts on File 2002 452p il (Facts on File library of world history) $49.50 **920.003**

1. Reference books 2. Women -- Biography -- Dictionaries

ISBN 0-8160-4334-5

LC 2001-54327

"The 260 women who are profiled here have not only made a mark on their own cultures but have also 'influenced other women from diverse cultures and different historical periods pursuing the same goals.'. . . Entries are organized first under 14 areas of accomplishment, from 'Adventurers and Athletes' to 'Writers.'. . . Entries are generally around two pages in length, and each offers suggestions for further reading. . . . A to Z of Women in World History is a good place to start for researchers who are taking a sphere-of-activity approach to women's history. This highly readable volume is recommended." Booklist

Includes bibliographical references

Mandel, David

Who's who in the Jewish Bible. Jewish Publication Society 2007 xx, 422p pa $30 **920.003**

1. Reference books 2. Bible -- O.T. -- Biography -- Dictionaries

ISBN 978-0-8276-0863-4; 0-8276-0863-2

LC 2007-27288

"Using only the Bible as its basis, this encyclopedia catalogues 3,000 characters from A to Z. General readers and students interested in past Jewish life will find this work most useful as a quick reference for information and a starting point for research." Booklist

Includes bibliographical references

Martinez Wood, Jamie

Latino writers and journalists. Facts on File 2007 294p il (A to Z of Latino Americans) $44 **920.003**

1. Reference books 2. Hispanic Americans -- Dictionaries 3. American literature -- Hispanic American authors -- Bio-bibliography

ISBN 0-8160-6422-9; 978-0-8160-6422-9

LC 2006-17394

This book "brings together 150 writers identified as Latino Americans. Approximately one-third of the profiles are accompanied by photographs." Booklist

Includes bibliographical references

Millar, David

★ The **Cambridge** dictionary of scientists; [by] David Millar [et al.] 2nd ed; Cambridge Univ. Press 2002 464p il hardcover o.p. $99; pa $34.99 **920.003**

1. Reference books 2. Scientists -- Dictionaries

ISBN 0-521-80602-X; 0-521-00062-9 pa

LC 2002-512240

First published 1996 as a revision of: Chambers concise dictionary of scientists

"The alphabetically organized, illustrated biographical dictionary . . . [covers] over 1,500 key scientists . . . from 40 countries. Physics, chemistry, biology, geology, astronomy, mathematics, medicine, meteorology and technology are all represented and special attention is paid to pioneer women." Publisher's note

Monush, Barry

★ **Screen** world presents the encyclopedia of Hollywood film actors; v1 edited by Barry Monush. Applause Theatre and Cinema Bks. 2003 1200p v1 il $35 **920.003**

1. Reference books 2. Actors -- Dictionaries 3. Motion pictures -- Biography -- Dictionaries

ISBN 1-557-83551-9

LC 2002-152728

"The first of a projected two-volume set, this encyclopedia provides biographical profiles of actors who worked in Hollywood between 1915 and 1965 . . . . [The author] includes all Oscar-winning actors as well as performers who became prominent in film before the late 1960s. . . . Entries are arranged in alphabetical order (Bud Abbott and Lou Costello to George Zucco), include vital statistics, and note any higher-education institution the actor attended. . . . This is an item that academic libraries and specialized film libraries will want to add. It would also no doubt find an audience in public libraries." Booklist

Musicians & composers of the 20th century; editor Alfred W. Cramer. Salem Press 2009 5v il set $399 **920.003**
1. Reference books 2. Music -- Bio-bibliography 3. Musicians -- Dictionaries
ISBN 978-1-58765-512-8

LC 2009-2980

"The work covers 614 composers, performers, and teachers, chosen for musical influence as well as fame. All major genres are covered, from classical to rap, along with many subgenres, such as rockabilly, atonal, and funk. . . . This work provides valuable, basic information on the topic as well as multiple, easy-access routes to it. Highly recommended." Libr J

Includes bibliographical references

New dictionary of scientific biography; Noretta Koertge, editor in chief. Scribner's 2008 8v il set $995 **920.003**
1. Reference books 2. Scientists -- Dictionaries
ISBN 978-0-684-31320-7

LC 2007-31384

First published 1970-1980 in 16 volumes with title: Dictionary of scientific biography

This biographical dictionary "contains thousands of biographies of mathematicians and natural scientists from all countries and from all historical periods." Publisher's note

Includes bibliographical references

Newton, David E.
Latinos in science, math, and professions. Facts on File 2007 274p il (A to Z of Latino Americans) $44 **920.003**
1. Reference books 2. Scientists -- Dictionaries 3. Mathematicians -- Dictionaries 4. Hispanic Americans -- Dictionaries
ISBN 978-0-8160-6385-7; 0-8160-6385-0

LC 2006-16769

Among the figures profiled in this biographical dictionary "are sociology expert Maxine Baca Zinn; Ellen Ochoa, the first Latina in space; and research entomologist Fernando E. Vega." Libr J

Includes bibliographical references

Notable American women: the modern period; a biographical dictionary. edited by Barbara Sicherman {et al.} Harvard Univ. Press 1980 xxii, 773p hardcover o.p. pa $41.50 **920.003**
1. Reference books 2. Women -- United States -- Biography 3. United States -- Biography -- Dictionaries
ISBN 0-674-62733-4 pa

LC 80-18402

This set provides "1 1/2- to 2-page biographies and references for 442 American women. Women were chosen from science, business, and engineering as well as from such traditional fields as education, entertainment, and social work, with a wide variety of @career patterns, philosophical outlooks and personal styles' represented. . . . Entries describe the life and personality of the individual, evaluate

her career, and place it in an historical context. Special emphasis is given to the conflicting demands of her public and personal lives." Choice

Notable black American men, book I; Jessie Carney Smith, editor. Gale Res. 1998 xxxiv, 1365p il $150 **920.003**
1. Reference books 2. United States -- Biography -- Dictionaries 3. African Americans -- Biography -- Dictionaries
ISBN 0-7876-0763-0

LC 98-38166

Companion to Notable black American women

This work, the first volume of a two-volume biographical dictionary, "profiles 500 men, from poet Jupiter Hammon (b. 1711) to Tiger Woods. . . . Each entry begins with birth and death dates and a few words describing the subject's major fields of endeavor, followed by a biographical essay, a list of references, and, in some cases, a note on collections of source material." Booklist

Includes bibliographical references

Notable black American men, book II; Jessie Carney Smith, editor. Thomson Gale 2007 xxiv, 827p il $193 **920.003**
1. Reference books 2. United States -- Biography -- Dictionaries 3. African Americans -- Biography -- Dictionaries
ISBN 0-7876-6493-6; 978-0-7876-6493-0

LC 2006-21193

Covering "prominent newsmakers as well as lesser-known individuals, . . . [this second volume of a two-volume work] offers full biographical entries, portraits, addresses for living listees and recommended sources for further study." Publisher's note

Includes bibliographical references

Notable black American women, book I; Jessie Carney Smith, editor. Gale Res. 1992 xlvii, 1334p il $203 **920.003**
1. Reference books 2. African American women -- Dictionaries 3. United States -- Biography -- Dictionaries
ISBN 0-8103-4749-0

LC 91-35074

This first volume of a three-volume biographical encyclopedia "documents the achievements of 500 African-American women who have made significant contributions to American culture from the colonial era to the present. . . . Subjects include women active in all fields of endeavor, from education, science, and the arts, to business, law and politics. . . . Authoritative and entertaining at the same time." Am Libr

Notable black American women, Book III; Jessie Carney Smith, editor. Gale 2003 lxxviii, 881p il $165 **920.003**
1. Reference books 2. African American women -- Dictionaries 3. United States -- Biography -- Dictionaries
ISBN 0-7876-6494-4

In this third volume of a three-volume biographical dictionary, "narrative biographical essays . . . discuss each woman's significant achievements and the public response to those achievements. . . . [This book] features 300 contemporary and historical women, including Sarah Allen, Alicia Keys, Ruth Simmons and . . . more." Publisher's note

Includes bibliographical references

Notable native Americans; Sharon Malinowski, editor; George H.J. Abrams, consulting editor and author of foreword. Gale Res. 1995 xliv, 492p il $105   **920.003**

1. Reference books 2. Native Americans -- Dictionaries
ISBN 0-8103-9638-6

LC 94-36202

This is a "compilation of biographical and bibliographical information on more than two hundred and sixty-five notable Native North American men and women throughout history, from all fields of endeavor. . . . Approximately thirty percent of the entries focus on historical figures and seventy percent on contemporary or twentieth-century individuals. Signed narrative essays, ranging from one to three pages in length, include Indian names and their English translations as well as name variants." Preface

Oakes, Elizabeth H.

★ **A to Z of chemists.** Facts on File 2002 276p il $45   **920.003**

1. Chemists 2. Reference books 3. Scientists -- Dictionaries
ISBN 0-8160-4579-8

LC 2002-68685

"This title includes 152 biographies of chemists, including 23 women. . . . The entries run between 750 and 1200 words (one to one and one-half pages apiece). They all begin with a summary of the subject's major contribution, followed by a chronological biography of their personal and professional life. Appendixes list the birthplace and country of activity of the chemists as well as a chart of their life spans." Libr J

Includes bibliographical references

American writers. Facts on File 2004 430p il (American biographies) $65   **920.003**

1. Reference books 2. Authors, American -- Dictionaries 3. American literature -- Bio-bibliography
ISBN 0-8160-5158-5

LC 2003-15743

"The volume has alphabetically arranged entries for approximately 260 authors from a variety of genres—poetry, fiction, drama, essay, and autobiography. Each . . . entry contains a short biography, critical analysis, and a bibliography of works about the author in both printed and Web formats. . . . [This book] offers a convenient introduction and is a worthwhile purchase." Booklist

Includes bibliographical references

Otfinoski, Steven

Latinos in the arts. Facts on File 2007 277p il (A to Z of Latino Americans) $44   **920.003**

1. Reference books 2. Actors -- Dictionaries 3. Artists -- Dictionaries 4. Musicians -- Dictionaries 5. Hispanic

Americans -- Dictionaries
ISBN 978-0-8160-6394-9; 0-8160-6394-X

LC 2006-16900

"This volume profiles more than 178 individuals in the performing and visual arts 'who were born in the United States or who settled here permanently,' among them Marc Anthony, Cameron Diaz, Carmen Miranda, Tito Punete, and Shakira. Each entry concludes with a list of 'Further Reading' . . . and, in many cases, 'Further Listening' and 'Further Viewing.'" Booklist

Includes bibliographical references

Powell, John

Great lives from history, The 18th century, 1701-1800; editor, John Powell; editor, first edition, Frank N. Magill. Salem Press 2006 2v il map set $160   **920.003**

1. Reference books 2. Biography -- Dictionaries 3. World history -- 18th century
ISBN 978-1-58765-276-9; 1-58765-276-5

LC 2006-5336

Companion volume to Great events from history, The 18th century, 1701-1800

First published as part of the Great lives from history series, published 1987-1995 under the editorship of Frank N. Magill; previously published as half of volume 4 of Dictionary of world biography, published 1998-1999

"The alphabetically listed subjects encompass 36 areas of expertise and include John Newbery, Pontiac, Qianlong, Hannah More, Pius IV, Paul Revere, and Shah Wali Allah, among others. Each article is approximately three pages long and lists the subject's major accomplishments, important dates, and areas of achievement. . . . A well-written, useful set." SLJ

Includes bibliographical references

Rich, Mari

★ **World** authors, 2000-2005; editors, Jennifer Curry, David Ramm, Mari Rich, Albert Rolls. Wilson, H. W. 2007 800p il (Authors series) $170 **920.003**

1. Reference books 2. Authors -- Dictionaries 3. Literature -- Bio-bibliography
ISBN 978-0-8242-1077-9

This book "covers some 300 novelists, poets, dramatists, essayists, scientists, biographers, and other authors whose books [were] published 2000 through 2005." Publisher's note

Schneider, Dorothy

★ **First** ladies; a biographical dictionary. [by] Dorothy Schneider, Carl J. Schneider. 3rd ed; Facts on File 2010 436p il (Facts on File library of American history) $85   **920.003**

1. Reference books 2. Presidents' spouses -- United States -- Dictionaries
ISBN 978-0-8160-7724-3

LC 2009-9047

First published 2001

This book "covers all the women who have held this esteemed 'office' since the founding of the United States. . . . Arranged chronologically by term of presidency, each biographical entry includes a . . . biography emphasizing each first lady's life during the presidency, as well as a chronology, appendixes, and suggestions for further reading." Publisher's note

Includes bibliographical references

The **Scribner** encyclopedia of American lives; Kenneth T. Jackson, editor in chief; Karen Markoe, general editor; Arnold Markoe, executive editor. Scribner 1998 8v il set $768   **920.003**
1. Reference books 2. United States -- Biography -- Dictionaries
ISBN 0-684-31292-1

LC 98-33793

"Scribner envisions SEAL as the continuation of the Dictionary of American Biography (DAB). . . . Selection criteria are that the biographees made significant contributions to American life and culture. . . . An appreciable number of women and people of color are recognized. All biographies are signed contributions by 332 scholars." Libr J [review of first two volumes]

The **Scribner** encyclopedia of American lives, The 1960s; William L. O'Neill, volume editor. Scribner 2003 2v il set $250   **920.003**
1. Reference books 2. United States -- Biography -- Dictionaries
ISBN 0-684-80666-5

LC 2002-12581

"The two alphabetically arranged volumes in SEAL 1960s contain biographical sketches, usually between 1,000 and 2,000 words, of 647 figures who 'defined the decade, or who were influential at the time.' Americans from different races, socioeconomic groups, classes, and regions of the U.S. are included, along with the occasional person of another nationality who had long periods of residence in the U.S. and was an influence on American culture. The signed entries, written by scholars, begin with a brief summary of the person's chronology and important accomplishments. This is followed by a narrative of the subject's life. . . . In many cases, a black-and-white photograph accompanies the narrative, which concludes with an assessment of the subject's overall contribution and a brief bibliography listing a few key sources. . . . Recommended for all high-school, public, and academic libraries wanting complete SEAL coverage or libraries wanting to supplement their collection of 1960s resources with a purely biographical approach." Booklist

Includes bibliographical references

Shipp, Steve
Latin American and Caribbean artists of the modern era; a biographical dictionary of more than 12,700 persons. McFarland & Co 2002 864p il $115   **920.003**
1. Reference books 2. Latin American art 3. Artists -- Dictionaries
ISBN 0-7864-1057-4

LC 2002-13828

"All entries include expected information such as birth date and place and artist's medium, and longer entries also feature biographical sketches, including education and influ-

ences, as well as lists of collections, exhibits, and titles. . . . A good starting point for further research." Libr J

Includes bibliographical references

St. James guide to Hispanic artists; profiles of Latino and Latin American artists. editor, Thomas Riggs. St. James Press 2002 xx, 682p il $195   **920.003**
1. Hispanic American art 2. Artists -- United States
ISBN 1-55862-470-8

LC 2001-41935

This "guide profiles some 375 of the most prominent Hispanic artists of the past century. The entries include basic biographical information, critical commentary, and lists of exhibitions, publications, and collections holding their works." Libr J

Includes bibliographical references

Wakeman, John
World authors, 1950-1970; a companion volume to Twentieth century authors. edited by John Wakeman; editorial consultant: Stanley J. Kunitz. Wilson, H.W. 1975 1594p il (Authors series) $160 **920.003**
1. Reference books 2. Authors -- Dictionaries 3. Literature -- Bio-bibliography
ISBN 0-8242-0419-0

This volume includes 959 "authors who came into prominence between 1950 and 1970. . . . Authors were chosen for literary importance or outstanding popularity." Wilson Libr Bull

World authors, 1970-1975; editor, John Wakeman; editorial consultant, Stanley J. Kunitz. Wilson, H.W. 1980 894p il (Authors series) $140 **920.003**
1. Reference books 2. Authors -- Dictionaries 3. Literature -- Bio-bibliography
ISBN 0-8242-0641-X

LC 79-21874

This volume provides biographical or autobiographical sketches for 348 of the most influential and popular men and women of letters who have come into prominence between 1970 and 1975

Waldrup, Carole Chandler
The **vice** presidents; biographies of the 45 men who have held the second highest office in the United States. McFarland & Co. 1996 271p il hardcover o.p. pa $39.95   **920.003**
1. Vice-presidents -- United States
ISBN 0-7864-0179-6; 978-0-7864-2611-9 pa; 0-7864-2611-X pa

LC 96-30538

"Well-written with clear, precise language and vocabulary, this informative book will be useful in either the reference section or with the collective biographies." Book Rep

Includes bibliographical references

Ware, Susan
Notable American women; a biographical dictionary completing the twentieth century. Su-

san Ware, editor; Stacy Braukman, assistant editor. Belknap Press 2004 xxx, 729p $45   **920.003**
1. Reference books 2. Women -- United States -- Biography 3. United States -- Biography -- Dictionaries
ISBN 0-674-01488-X
LC 2004-48859
This volume includes "stars of the golden ages of radio, film, dance, and television; scientists and scholars; politicians and entrepreneurs; authors and aviators; civil rights activists and religious leaders; Native American craftspeople and world-renowned artists. Women from a broad spectrum of ethnic, class, political, religious, and sexual identities are all acknowledged." Publisher's note
Includes bibliographical references

Who was who in America; with world notables. Marquis Who's Who 1942 23v set $999.95 **920.003**
1. Reference books 2. United States -- Biography -- Dictionaries
ISBN 978-0-8379-0282-1
"Includes sketches removed from 'Who's who in America' because of death of the biographee; date of death and, often, interment location is added." Guide to Ref Books. 11th edition

★ **Who's** who 2008; an annual biographical dictionary. 160th ed.; A. & C. Black 2007 2574p $325   **920.003**
1. Reference books 2. Great Britain -- Biography -- Dictionaries
ISBN 978-0-7136-8555-8; 0-7136-8555-7
Annual. First published 1849
"The pioneer work of the who's who type and still one of the most important. Until 1897, it was the handbook of titled and official classes and included lists of names rather than biographical sketches. . . . It is principally British, but a few prominent names of other nationalities are included. Biographies are reliable and fairly detailed; they give main facts, addresses, often telephone numbers and in case of authors, lists of works." Guide to Ref Books. 11th edition

Who's who among African Americans; 21st ed.; Gale Res. 2008 1477p $275   **920.003**
1. Reference books 2. African Americans -- Biography -- Dictionaries
ISBN 978-1-4144-0020-4; 1-4144-0020-9
First published 1976 by Educational Communications with title: Who's who among black Americans. Biennial schedule after 5th edition
"Short entries focusing on career achievements and positions. Indexes list entries by place of birth and profession." N Y Public Libr Book of How & Where to Look It Up

Who's who in America, 2008; 62nd ed.; Marquis Who's Who 2007 2v set $710.10   **920.003**
1. Reference books 2. United States -- Biography -- Dictionaries
ISBN 978-0-8379-7011-0; 0-8379-7011-3
Annual. First published 1899
"The standard dictionary of contemporary biography, containing concise biographical data, prepared according to established practices, with addresses and, in the case of au-

thors, lists of works. . . . Each edition is thoroughly revised, new biographies added, and others dropped. For names of persons dropped because of death, see 'Who was who in America'." Guide to Ref Books. 11th edition

★ **Who's** who in American art, 2008; 28th ed.; Marquis Who's Who 2007 1550p $267.30 **920.003**
1. Reference books 2. Artists -- United States -- Dictionaries
ISBN 978-0-8379-6307-5; 0-8379-6307-9
Companion volume to American art directory
Biennial. First published 1936 by American Federation of Arts as part of American art annual
"Profiles representatives of all segments of the art world including artists, administrators, and librarians. Entries give vital statistics, professional education and training, commissions and exhibitions, and membership in art societies. Includes geographic and professional classification indexes and cumulative necrology." N Y Public Libr Book of How & Where to Look It Up

Who's who in British history; beginnings to 1901. general editor, Geoffrey Treasure; authors and contributors, Ian Dawson {et al.} Fitzroy Dearborn Pubs. 1998 2v maps set $325   **920.003**
1. Reference books 2. Great Britain -- Biography -- Dictionaries
ISBN 1-884964-90-7
"The length of entries varies from many pages (Henry VIII) to a column for most persons. . . . The choice of entries (ending with 1901) reflects the traditional emphasis of history teaching, with heavy representation of statemen, royalty, military persons, diplomats, major writers, and leading ladies of the stage and aristocracy." Choice
Includes bibliographical references

★ **Who's** who in finance and business 2008-2009; 36th ed; Marquis Who's Who 2007 1,100 $349   **920.003**
1. Reference books 2. Business -- Biography -- Dictionaries
ISBN 978-0-8379-0356-9
Biennial. First published 1936 with title: Who's who in commerce and industry. Continues Who's who in finance and industry
"Gives international coverage of businessmen. Includes index of firms with references to personnel for whom sketches are included." Guide to Ref Books. 11th edition

★ **Who's** who of American women 2007; 26th ed; Marquis Who's Who 2006 1,700 $305 **920.003**
1. Reference books 2. Women -- United States -- Biography 3. United States -- Biography -- Dictionaries
ISBN 0-8379-0434-X
Biennial. First published for 1958/1959
"This title provides information on women who are successful in a variety of professions, including business, government, education, art and culture, and those who have received prestigious honors or have been selected for honorary institutions. The biographical data are provided by the women themselves so the quality varies. In general it includes name, occupation, birth date, education, career his-

tory, publications, professional activities, awards, and home and office addresses. This has long been a standard source in many public and academic libraries." Am Ref Books Annu, 2003

Women in world history; a biographical encyclopedia. Anne Commire, editor, Deborah Klezmer, associate editor. Gale Res. 1999 17v set $1,495 **920.003**
1. Reference books 2. Women -- Biography 3. Women -- History -- Encyclopedias
ISBN 0-7876-3736-X

LC 99-24692
ALA RUSA Dartmouth Medal (2001)
"The editors researched wives, daughters, mothers, and other women who were not documented in traditional, male-oriented sources, especially history books. . . . Some entries are only a sentence or two because of lack of information, but the majority include most or all of the following: dates, if known, or time of flourishing; an identifying summary of life and achievements; a personal profile with vital statistics and names of family members; events in the life of the biographee; vitae listing such things as works for authors or winning records for athletes; a quotation by or about the individual; and bibliographical references." Booklist
Includes bibliographical references

World explorers and discoverers; editor, Richard E. Bohlander; consultants, John L. Allen {et al.} Macmillan 1991 531p il maps $110 **920.003**
1. Reference books 2. Explorers -- Dictionaries
ISBN 978-0-02-897445-3; 0-02-897445-X

LC 91-23156
"Over 300 explorers and discoverers are featured in this attractive compilation that covers exploration from ancient times to the present and includes such notable moderns as Jacques Cousteau and Edmund Hillary." Am Libr

920.009 Ethnic and national groups

Great lives from history; editors, Carmen Tafolla and Martha P. Cotera. Salem Press 2012 3 v., xxvi, 1058 p.p ill. (set) $395 **920.009**
1. Latinos (U.S.) 2. Hispanic Americans -- Biography -- Encyclopedias
ISBN 9781587658112; 9781587658129; 9781587658136; 1587658100; 9781587658105

LC 2011043168
The authors "[Carmen] Tafolla, an award-winning author of Chicana literature for children and adults, . . . and librarian and activist [Martha P.] Cotera, . . . provide brief biographical essays covering 518 figures from Latino history." Among those profiled are actor Desi Arnaz, football player Tony Romo, and actress Rita Hayworth. (Library Journal)
Includes bibliographical references and indexes

Hernández, Daisy
A **cup** of water under my bed; a memoir. by Daisy Hernández. Beacon Press 2014 200 p. (hardback : alkaline paper) $24.95 **920.009**
1. Family 2. Women journalists 3. Women -- Social

conditions 4. Cuban Americans -- Biography 5. Colombian Americans -- Biography 6. Women -- New Jersey -- Biography 7. Identity (Psychology) -- United States 8. United States -- Social conditions -- 1980- 9. Bisexual women -- United States -- Biography 10. Young women -- Family relationships -- United States 11. Women journalists -- New York (State) -- New York -- Biography
ISBN 9780807014486; 0807014486

LC 2014000820
In this memoir author "Daisy Hernández chronicles what the women in her Cuban-Colombian family taught her about love, money, and race. In prose that is both memoir and commentary, Daisy reflects on reporting for the New York Times as the paper is rocked by the biggest plagiarism scandal in its history and plunged into debates about the role of race in the newsroom." (Publisher's note)
"She maintains a lively pace by flashing back-and-forth between childhood and adulthood, personal and professional lives, with an emphasis on her ascent from New York Times intern to regular columnist at Ms. An accessible, honest look at the often heart-wrenching effects of intergenerational tension on family ties." Booklist

McCullough, David G., 1933-
★ The **greater** journey; [by] David McCullough. Simon & Schuster 2011 558p. ill. (some col.), maps $37.50; ebook $19.99 **920.009**
1. Artists 2. Paris (France) -- History 3. Intellectuals -- United States 4. Paris (France) -- Intellectual life 5. Authors, American 6. Americans -- France 7. Biography, Collective 8. Paris (France) -- Intellectual life -- 19th century 9. Americans -- France -- Paris -- History -- 19th century
ISBN 978-1-4165-7176-6; 1-4165-7176-0; 978-1-4165-7689-1 ebook; 9781416571766; 9781416576891; 1416576894

LC 2010053001
In this book, "award-winning historian [David] McCullough . . . [tells the story of] a cluster of aspiring young people such as portraitist George Healy and lawyer Charles Sumner, eager to expand their horizons [in Paris] in the 1830s. . . . [The book] include[s] numerous other visitors over an entire eventful century. . . . [N]ovelist James Fenimore Cooper, widowed schoolteacher Emma Hart Willard and young medical student Oliver Wendell Holmes Sr. all knew their education was not complete without a stint in the medieval capital. For many of these American rubes, exposure to the fine arts, old-world architecture, fashion, fine dining, museums and teaching hospitals proved transformative, and the knowledge they gained would define their professional lives back in America." (Kirkus)
An "account of young Americans, driven by wanderlust, setting out in search of greener Parisian pastures. Well-known figures such as James Fenimore Cooper, Oliver Wendell Holmes Sr., and Mary Cassat, and long-forgotten entities like Elizabeth Blackwell and William Wells Brown, all walked along the Avenue des Champs-Élysées, went to the Musée du Louvre, ate wonderful meals, and became inspired. Their life-changing adventures played a vital role in transforming the course of US history." Christ Sci Monit
Includes bibliographical references (p. 519-537) and index.

920.073 Collective biography—United States

Isay, Dave

Callings; A Celebration of Lives of Purpose and Passion. Dave Isay. Penguin Group USA 2016 288 p. illustrations $26 **920.073**

1. Vocational guidance 2. Meaning (Philosophy) 3. Creation (Literary, artistic, etc.)

ISBN 1594205183; 9781594205187

This book, by Dave Isay, "presents unforgettable stories from people doing what they love. Some found their paths at a very young age, others later in life; some overcame great odds or upturned their lives in order to pursue what matters to them. Many of their stories have never been broadcast or published by StoryCorps until now." (Publisher's note)

"These wonderful stories reveal that work becomes meaningful to those who choose—or are in some cases chosen by—the calling that motivates, energizes, and inspires them." Pub Wkly

920.71 Men

Gates, Henry Louis

Thirteen ways of looking at a black man. Random House 1997 xxvii, 226p hardcover o.p. pa $12 **920.71**

1. Actors 2. Authors 3. Dancers 4. Singers 5. Generals 6. Novelists 7. Dramatists 8. Choreographers 9. Football players 10. Essayists 11. Memoirists 12. Screenwriters 13. Sportscasters 14. Literary critics 15. Music historians 16. Social activists 17. Short story writers 18. Young adult authors 19. Black Muslim leaders 20. Secretaries of state 21. African Americans -- Biography

ISBN 0-679-77666-4 pa

LC 96-33138

"Mr. Gates's strong suit is finding the common man in uncommon figures, without losing sight of the ways in which race, class and personal experience have shaped each life." N Y Times Book Rev

920.72 Women

Cohen, Lisa

All we know; three lives. Lisa Cohen. Farrar, Straus and Giroux 2012 429 p. ill. (alk. paper) $30.00 **920.72**

1. Women -- Biography 2. Biography -- 20th century 3. Women intellectuals -- Biography 4. Socialites -- United States -- Biography 5. Women fashion designers -- England -- Biography 6. Modernism (Aesthetics) -- History -- 20th century 7. Women authors, American -- 19th century -- Biography

ISBN 0374176493; 9780374176495

LC 2011041055

This collective biography examines the lives of "Esther Murphy (1897-1962) . . . Mercedes de Acosta (1893-1968) . . . and feminist Madge Garland (1898-1990). . . .They knew each other well from social circles, and none of them had

simple lives. [Lisa] Cohen . . . delineates the . . . biographical matters of ancestry, parents, schooling, marriages, affairs, friendships, breakups, work, and death. . . . [A] three-part inquiry into the meaning of failure, style, and sexual identity." (Publishers Weekly)

Includes bibliographical references (p. [359]-406) and index

Nimura, Janice P.

Daughters of the Samurai; A Journey from East to West and Back. by Janice P. Nimura. W W Norton & Co Inc 2015 352 p. illustrations, map, portraits $26.95 **920.72**

1. Japanese 2. Japanese American women 3. Japan -- Foreign relations -- United States 4. United States -- Foreign relations -- Japan

ISBN 0393077993; 9780393077995

LC 2014046933

This book, by Janice P. Nimura, focuses on "five young girls [who] were sent by the Japanese government to the United States. Their mission: learn Western ways and return to help nurture a new generation of enlightened men to lead Japan. Raised in traditional samurai households during the turmoil of civil war, three of these unusual ambassadors—Sutematsu Yamakawa, Shige Nagai, and Ume Tsuda—grew up as typical American schoolgirls." (Publisher's note)

Schatz, Kate

Rad women worldwide; Artists and Athletes, Pirates and Punks, and Other Revolutionaries Who Shaped History. by Kate Schatz; illustrated by Miriam Klein Stahl. Ten Speed Press 2016 112 p. illustrations (ebook) $47.97; (hardback) $15.99 **920.72**

1. Women -- History 2. Women -- Biography 3. Women -- History -- Juvenile literature 4. Women -- Biography -- Juvenile literature

ISBN 9780399578878; 9780399578861

LC 2016012179

This book by Kate Schatz, illustrated by Miriam Klein Stahl, offers "tales of perseverance and radical success by pairing well researched . . . biographies with . . . cut-paper portraits. From 430 BCE to 2016, . . . the book features an array of diverse figures, including Hatshepsut (. . . who ruled Egypt peacefully for two decades) and Malala Yousafzi (the youngest person to win the Nobel Peace Prize) to Poly Styrene (legendary teenage punk and lead singer of X-Ray Spex)." (Publisher's note)

"Readers of either gender could well find a role model in the India-born U.S. astronaut Kalpana Chawla, or in Wangari Maathai, whose Green Belt Movement in Africa resulted in the planting of more than 30 million environment-reviving trees." Booklist

Includes bibliographical references and index

Ware, Susan

Letter to the world; seven women who shaped the American century. Norton 1998 xxiv, 344p il $25.95 **920.72**

1. Actors 2. Dancers 3. Diplomats 4. Journalists 5. Choreographers 6. Anthropologists 7. Golfers 8. Curators 9. Hurdlers 10. Columnists 11. High jumpers 12. Humanitarians 13. Opera singers 14.

Dance teachers 15. Javelin throwers 16. Olympic athletes 17. Social activists 18. Women -- Biography 19. Writers on science 20. Spouses of presidents 21. United Nations officials
ISBN 0-393-04652-4

LC 97-45923

The author "considers the lives of seven women who had an exceptional impact on 20th-century American culture and society's perception of the role of women: Eleanor Roosevelt, Dorothy Thompson, Margaret Mead, Katharine Hepburn, Babe Didrikson Zaharias, Martha Graham, and Marian Anderson. In addition to focusing on outstanding achievements in their chosen fields, Ware looks at their often unconventional private lives." Libr J

Includes bibliographical references

929 Genealogy, names, insignia

Baxter, Angus

In search of your European roots; a complete guide to tracing your ancestors in every country in Europe. 3rd ed; Genealogical 2001 315p pa $18.95 **929**
1. Genealogy
ISBN 0-8063-1657-8

LC 00-136383

First published 1985

This work covers the various types of genealogical records available in approximately 30 European countries. Archival resources from the national to local level are described. Also included are telephone numbers, e-mail addresses, fax numbers, and URL's for various European archives and organizations

Includes bibliographical references (p. {303}-312) and index

Bentley, Elizabeth Petty

Directory of family associations; {by} Elizabeth Petty Bentley, & Deborah Ann Carl. 4th ed; Genealogical 2001 320p $34.95 **929**
1. Genealogy
ISBN 0-8063-1679-9

LC 2001-131456

First published 1991

Contains information on approximately 6,000 family name associations in the United States; lists addresses, phone numbers, contact persons, and publications (if any)

★ The **genealogist's** address book; state and local resources: with special resources including ethnic and religious organizations. 6th ed.; Genealogical Pub. Co. 2009 799p $69.95 **929**
1. Genealogy
ISBN 978-0-8063-1796-0

First published 1991. Periodically revised

This is a source for "fax, phone, web addresses, and contact names for genealogical, historical, and religious societies across the United States. Bentley . . . judiciously divides contact information into three subject segments. The first organizes genealogical and historical associations alphabetically, initially by state, then county, and finally by society

name. Essential for genealogists and regional historians." Libr J

Croom, Emily Anne

The **genealogist's** companion and sourcebook; 2nd ed; Betterway Bks. 2003 454p il map pa $19.99 **929**
1. Genealogy
ISBN 1-55870-651-8

LC 2003-50017

First published 1994

This how-to genealogy handbook seeks to explore "collections and libraries within the U.S. and the records that may be found within them. . . . In addition to covering government records, cemetery records, newspapers, city directories, and other sources, there are chapters of African American and Native American genealogy. . . . Because the volume is easy reading and instructive at the same time, it will be a very popular choice for public libraries." Booklist {review of 1994 edition}

Includes bibliographical references

Franklin, John Hope

★ **In** search of the promised land; a Black family and the Old South. [by] John Hope Franklin, Loren Schweninger. Oxford University Press 2005 286p il map (New narratives in American history) $23; pa $13.95 **929**
1. Slavery -- United States 2. United States -- Race relations 3. African Americans -- Southern States
ISBN 0-19-516087-8; 0-19-516088-6 pa

LC 2004-61666

The authors trace "the history of the Thomas-Rapier family during the antebellum and Civil War eras. Starting with matriarch Sally Thomas, born a slave in 1787, the book enables readers to distinguish the various complex modes within which slavery operated. The resulting family history also traces the evolution of race relations in diverse locations from New Orleans to New York City, Canada, Minnesota, and the Caribbean." Libr J

Includes bibliographical references

Greenwood, Val D.

The **researcher's** guide to American genealogy; 3rd ed; Genealogical 2000 662p il $29.95 **929**
1. Genealogy 2. Archives -- United States
ISBN 0-8063-1621-7

LC 99-73349

First published 1973

"This classic textbook for the more experienced researcher gives detailed answers to questions about primary records, including vital, census, probate, land, court (including adoption), church, military, cemetery, and wills. Completely updated, it remains the outstanding text and reference book in American genealogy and the benchmark against which others must be judged." Libr J {review of 1990 edition}

Includes bibliographical references

Kemp, Thomas Jay

International vital records handbook; 5th ed.; Genealogical Publishing Co. 2009 587p pa $49.95   **929**

1. Registers of births, etc.
ISBN 978-0-8063-1793-9

LC 2008-940022

First published 1988 with title: Vital records handbook

"The book is divided into these three major segments. The first offers approved-form facsimiles for the request of U.S. state-issued documents. The second segment covers request forms issued in U.S. Territories. The third details various procedures and forms necessary to attain official documents in foreign countries. . . . A crucial, time-saving resource." Libr J

Includes bibliographical references

Virtual roots 2.0; a guide to genealogy and local history on the World Wide Web. rev and updated; Scholarly Resources 2003 311p $75; pa $29.95 **929**

1. Genealogy 2. World Wide Web
ISBN 0-8420-2922-2; 0-8420-2923-0 pa

LC 2002-154366

First published 1997

The more than 1,000 "Web sites in this directory are arranged into four primary categories—general subjects, U.S., international, and family associations—each of which is further subdivided by topic, state, country, or family name. Web site entries include organization name, address, telephone number(s), Internet and e-mail addresses, and, where appropriate, other Web links that open even more doorways." Booklist {review of 1997 edition}

Includes bibliographical references

929.1 Genealogy

McCarthy, Andrew

Journeys home; inspiring stories, plus tips and strategies to find your family history. Andrew McCarthy, Joyce Maynard, Pico Iyer, Diane Johnson & the National Geographic travel team; foreword by Dr. Spencer Wells, National Geographic explorer-in-residence. National Geographic 2015 288 p. color illustrations (hardcover : alkaline paper) $26 **929.1**

1. Genealogy 2. Voyages and travels 3. Genealogy -- Anecdotes 4. Voyages and travels -- Anecdotes 5. Celebrities -- Travel -- Anecdotes 6. United States -- Genealogy -- Anecdotes 7. United States -- Genealogy -- Handbooks, manuals, etc 8. Celebrities -- United States -- Genealogy -- Anecdotes
ISBN 1426213816; 9781426213816

LC 2014033593

This book, by Andrew McCarthy, Joyce Maynard, Pico Iyer, Diane Johnson and the National Geographic travel team, "combines intriguing tales of discovery with tips on how to begin your own explorations. Actor and award-winning travel writer Andrew McCarthy's featured story recounts his recent quest to uncover his family's Irish history, while twenty-five other prominent writers tell their own heartfelt stories of connection." (Publisher's note)

"This poignant and information-filled travelog and genealogy primer is ideal for public libraries." LJ

Includes bibliographical references and index

929.2 Family histories

Teege, Jennifer

My grandfather would have shot me; a Black woman discovers her family's Nazi past. Jennifer Teege, Nikola Sellmair. The Experiment 2015 240 p. illustrations (cloth) $24.95 **929.2**

1. Grandfathers 2. War criminals 3. National socialists 4. Racially mixed people 5. Nazis -- Family relationships 6. Płaszów (Concentration camp) 7. Racially mixed people -- Germany -- Biography 8. Concentration camp commandants -- Family relationships 9. Grandchildren of war criminals -- Germany -- Biography
ISBN 1615192530; 9781615192533

LC 2014046242

This book, by Jennifer Teege, with Nikola Sellmair, is the "memoir of a German-Nigerian woman who learns that her grandfather was the brutal Nazi commandant depicted in Schindler's List, Amon Goeth." (Publisher's note)

"Originally published in German as Amon: mein Grossvater hätte mich erschossen, Teege's account is an important addition to narratives written by descendants of war criminals. A gripping read, highly recommended for anyone interested in history, memoirs, and biography." LJ

Includes bibliographical references

Well, François

Family trees; a history of genealogy in America. François Weil. Harvard University Press 2013 320 p. (hardcover) $27.95 **929.2**

1. Genealogy 2. United States -- Social conditions 3. National characteristics, American 4. Genealogy -- United States -- History 5. Genealogy -- Social aspects -- United States
ISBN 0674045831; 9780674045835

LC 2012044769

This book is a survey of genealogy in America, which has become easier with the advent of the Internet. "The author enumerates four growth stages in the endeavor," looking at colonial America, the late 18th-century, after the Civil War and modern day. François Weil "explains how the proliferation of genealogy-focused Web sites and DNA testing has transformed the pursuit into a lucrative commercial venture." (Publishers Weekly)

Includes bibliographical references and index

929.4 Personal names

Ciuraru, Carmela

Nom de plume; a (secret) history of pseudonyms. Harper 2011 xxiv, 343p $24.99 **929.4**

1. Authors 2. Pseudonyms
ISBN 978-0-06-173526-4

LC 2010-53603

The author "tells the stories of some of literature's most famous pen names by weaving in details about these secretive, often eccentric writers' lives and works to examine their decision to use pen names. From Lewis Carroll (born Charles Dodgson) to Mark Twain (Samuel Clemens) and Victoria Lucas (Sylvia Plath), one chapter is devoted to each with so much detail that the authors under discussion seem to become characters in Ciuraru's book. . . . For anyone who creates — writers, artists and performers — the book will enthrall. It's as much a meditation on the creative process as it is a tell-all about their names and the intrigue, branding or mind games that created them." Associated Press

Includes bibliographical references

Delahunty, Andrew

Oxford dictionary of nicknames. Oxford University Press 2003 229p $29.95; pa $24 **929.4**

1. Nicknames

ISBN 0-19-860539-0; 0-19-860948-5 pa

LC 2004-273526

"This volume is a treasure trove of popular linguistic creativity. From the Hanging Judge to Hanoi Jane, and from Queen Dick to the Queen of Hearts, it makes for delightful bathroom browsing with just a dab of history and culture." Publ Wkly

★ **Dictionary** of American family names; Patrick Hanks, editor. Oxford Univ. Press 2003 3v set $295 **929.4**

1. Personal names -- United States

ISBN 0-19-508137-4

LC 2003-3844

"This set will be useful for genealogists, historians, and others curious about their family roots." SLJ

Includes bibliographical references

Latham, Edward

A **dictionary** of names, nicknames, and surnames of persons, places, and things. Omnigraphics 1990 334p $48 **929.4**

1. Nicknames 2. Reference books 3. Names -- Dictionaries 4. Personal names -- Dictionaries

ISBN 1-55888-901-9

LC 89-26513

A reissue of the title first published 1904 by Dutton

Compiled as a supplement to the "ordinary dictionaries of biography, geography, mythology, etc. {wherein} a person or place is often alluded to by means of a surname or nickname without any clue being given to the reader, who does not happen to be aware of the actual name of the person or place." Preface

Shane, Neala

Inspired baby names from around the world; 6,000 favorite worldwide names and the meanings behind them. Neala Shane. New World Library 2015 712 p. (paperback : alkaline paper) $21.95 **929.4**

1. Personal names 2. Dictionaries

ISBN 1608683206; 9781608683208

LC 2014042449

This book of baby names, by Neala Shane, "includes 6,000-plus names from all corners of the globe, and each entry illuminates the name's distinctive spiritual, historical, and cultural background. . . . Pronunciation guide, origin,

alternate spellings, and meaning are enhanced by the affirmation carefully chosen for each name. Lists of names by meaning, names by ethnicity, and most popular names by decade provide easy reference." (Publisher's note)

"While readers can browse this book, it's intended for those putting extensive time and investigation into naming their child. Names can sometimes be tough to live up to. But from Aaron (Hebrew) to Zuri (Swahili), there will be plenty of conversation, controversy, and debate inspired by these pages." LJ

929.9 Forms of insignia and identification

Leepson, Marc

Flag: an American biography. Thomas Dunne Books/St. Martin's Press 2005 334p il $24.95; pa $14.95 **929.9**

1. Flags -- United States

ISBN 978-0-312-32308-0; 0-312-32308-5; 978-0-312-32309-7 pa; 0-312-32309-3 pa

LC 2004-65920

"From reverence to kitsch, Americans' attitudes to their flag and its mythology have changed over the years, and Leepson does a creditable job of recounting those changes." Publ Wkly

Includes bibliographical references

Minahan, James

The **complete** guide to national symbols and emblems. Greenwood Press 2010 2v il set $180 **929.9**

1. Reference books 2. Signs and symbols 3. National emblems -- Encyclopedias 4. National characteristics -- Encyclopedias

ISBN 978-0-313-34496-1; 978-0-313-34497-8 ebook

LC 2009-36963

"This set is an impressive compilation of material that should be quite useful for anyone looking for current information about flags, anthems, athletic teams, cuisines, and such. The 200-plus entries cover independent nations of the world and some dependent states and territories that seek greater visibility, such as Wallonia (an autonomous region within Belgium) and Puerto Rico. Volume 1 covers Asia and Oceania, Central and South America, and Europe. Volume 2 covers the Middle East and North Africa, North America and the Caribbean, and sub-Saharan Africa. National flags and coats of arms are shown in color." Booklist

Includes bibliographical references

Shearer, Benjamin F.

State names, seals, flags, and symbols; a historical guide. [by] Benjamin F. Shearer and Barbara S. Shearer. 3rd ed, rev and expanded; Greenwood Press 2001 495p il $73.95 **929.9**

1. Reference books 2. Seals (Numismatics) 3. Flags -- United States 4. Geographic names -- United States

ISBN 0-313-31534-5

LC 2001-23525

First published 1987

"Chapters on mottoes, flowers, trees, birds, songs, holidays, and license plates are just a sampling of what is covered, and the format is such that the concisely written material can be found as expeditiously as possible. Even though the book is touted predominantly as a reference tool, the information provided makes fascinating and enlightening reading." Libr J [review of 1994 edition]

Includes bibliographical references

Testi, Arnaldo

Capture the flag; the Stars and Stripes in American history. translated by Noor Giovanni Mazhar. New York University Press 2010 165p il $22.95 **929.9**

1. Patriotism 2. American national characteristics 3. Flags -- United States

ISBN 978-0-8147-83221; 0-8147-8322-8

LC 2009-39278

Original Italian edition, 2003

"From our July 4th celebrations to the iconic images from 9/11, the American flag is an all-pervasive, definitive symbol of American national identity. . . . [Testi] provides readers with an engaging and fresh perspective that can only be provided by an outsider standing above the fray. Whether discussing the evolution of flag etiquette or its relationship to the U.S. Constitution, Testi deftly explores the shifting cultural meanings of the American symbol, from 1776 through the growth of the American empire to the contentious debates occurring today." Libr J

Includes bibliographical references

Znamierowski, Alfred, 1940-

The **World** Encyclopedia of Flags; The definitive guide to international, flags, banners, standards and ensigns, with over 1400 illustration. by Alfred Znamierowski. Lorenz Books 2013 256 p. $16.99 **929.9**

1. Flags

ISBN 0754826295; 9780754826293

This book, by Alred Znamierowski, presents "a directory of flags and a fascinating history of their development and usage, featuring over 600 flags including military signs, royal standards, civic flags, ensigns and national flags, expertly illustrated throughout." (Publisher's note)

930 History of ancient world (to ca. 499)

Beard, Mary, 1955-

Confronting the classics; traditions, adventures, and innovations. Mary Beard. Liveright Publishing Corporation, a Division of W. W. Norton & Company 2013 320 p. (hardcover) $28.95 **930**

1. Classical education 2. Classical civilization 3. Classical antiquities 4. Civilization, Classical

ISBN 0871407167; 9780871407160

LC 2013016133

"This collection comprises a decade's worth of [Mary] Beard's . . . book reviews, mostly from the 'Times Literary Supplement' and the 'New York Review of Books,' plus one lecture not previously published. . . . The work follows a chronological arrangement, with the first section on ancient Greece, the next on early Rome, the third on Imperial Rome, and so forth, with later pieces focusing on the

classicists themselves across the subsequent centuries." (Library Journal)

Includes bibliographical references and index

The **Cambridge** ancient history. Cambridge Univ. Press 1970 il maps set $3500 **930**

1. Ancient history

ISBN 978-0-521-85073-5

Original 12 volume set published 1923-1939 with 5 volumes of plates

"An excellent reference history. Each chapter has been written by a specialist, with full bibliographies at the end of each volume." Guide to Ref Books. 11th edition

Cantor, Norman F.

Antiquity: the civilization of the ancient world. HarperCollins Pubs. 2003 240p map $24.95; pa $13.95 **930**

1. Ancient civilization

ISBN 0-06-017409-9; 0-06-093098-5 pa

LC 2003-42317

"Cantor's work provides the beginning classicist with an enticing yet sturdy foundation for further exploration." Booklist

Includes bibliographical references

★ **Encyclopedia** of the ancient world; editor, Thomas J. Sienkewicz. Salem Press 2002 3v il maps set $341 **930**

1. Reference books 2. Ancient civilization -- Encyclopedias

ISBN 0-89356-038-3

LC 2001-49896

This reference work encompasses "not only Greece and Rome but also 'the civilizations, cultures, traditions, monuments and artifacts, significant wars and battles, and important personages of the rest of the world: Europe (outside Greece and Rome), Africa, the Americas, Asia, and Oceania.' The time span is from prehistory to approximately 700 C.E." Booklist

Includes bibliographical references

Frammolino, Ralph

Chasing Aphrodite; the hunt for looted antiquities at the world's richest museum. [by] Jason Felch and Ralph Frammolino. Houghton Mifflin Harcourt 2011 375p il $28.00 **930**

1. Cultural property 2. Classical antiquities 3. J. Paul Getty Museum 4. Archaeological thefts 5. Classical antiquities -- Italy 6. Cultural property -- Repatriation -- Italy 7. Classical antiquities -- Destruction and pillage

ISBN 0151015015; 9780151015016

LC 2010-25835

In 1976 "oil billionaire J. Paul Getty left his estate to the museum that bears his name, which was suddenly the wealthiest collecting institution in the world—one whose problem was how to spend rather than raise money. The founder's narrow interests had determined the museum's collecting areas, one of which was Greek and Roman art. The stage was set for trouble, and the trouble is described in fascinating detail in 'Chasing Aphrodite,' an account of the Getty's travails in collection-building by Los Angeles Times reporters Jason Felch and Ralph Frammolino. In 2005, long-time Getty curator Marion True would be indicted by authorities in Rome for traffic in illicit antiquities; not long after, in a related controversy, she was forced to resign. The reporters covered these events, as well as the museum's agreements to repatriate works acquired before and during Ms. True's tenure. They were given access by unidentified sources to the museum's archives, and in this book they document a museum administration often motivated by ambition but eventually also by stirrings of conscience." Wall Street J

Includes bibliographical references and index

Great events from history, The ancient world, prehistory-476 C.E. editor, Mark W. Chavalas; consulting editors, Mark S. Aldenderfer ... [et al.] Salem Press 2004 2v il map set $160 **930**
1. Ancient history 2. Reference books
ISBN 1-58765-155-6; 978-1-58765-155-7
LC 2004-1360

Companion volume to Great lives from history, The ancient world, prehistory-476 C.E.

Some essays previously published in Great events from history (1972-1980), Chronology of European history, 15,000 B.C. to 1997 (1997), and Great events from history, North American series (1997)

"Articles are arranged chronologically, beginning around 25,000 B.C.E. with the San Peoples, who created the first discernible art in Africa, and ends on September 4, 476 C.E. with the fall of Rome, when the last Roman emperor, Romulus Augustulus, was deposed. Articles cover the entire world, with special attention paid to non-European areas. . . . All articles maintain the same structure and give the locale of the event, its category, a summary of the event, its significance, an annotated list of further readings, and cross references to related events." Ref & User Services Quarterly

Includes bibliographical references

Kapuscinski, Ryszard, 1932-2007
Travels with Herodotus; translated from the Polish by Klara Glowczewska. Alfred A. Knopf 2007 275p $25 **930**
1. Historians 2. Voyages and travels 3. Authors 4. Biographers 5. Journalists 6. Nonfiction writers
ISBN 1-400-04338-5; 9781400043385
LC 2006-39565

Original Polish edition, 2004

Kapuscinski describes his travels "to India, to Afghanistan, to China, to Cambodia, to Rangoon." (Publisher's note)

"A work of art: so eloquent, so simple, that you find yourself marveling at its prose, its gentle observation and the rhythm of the words. And you find yourself applauding such good translation as well." Washington Post Book World

Kemp, Barry
The **city** of Akhenaten and Nefertiti; Amarna and its people. Barry Kemp. Thames & Hudson 2012 320 p. (hardcover) $45 **930**
1. Egypt -- History 2. Egypt -- Antiquities 3. Tell el-Amarna (Egypt)
ISBN 0500051739; 9780500051733
LC 2011945993

This book by Barry Kemp describes the history of "the ancient site of Tell el-Amarna in Middle Egypt, [which] was the capital city of the heretic pharaoh Akhenaten and his chief consort, Nefertiti. Occupied for just sixteen or so years in the fourteenth century BC, the city lay largely abandoned and forgotten until excavations over the last hundred years brought it back into prominence." (Publisher's note)

930.1   Archaeology

Beneath the seven seas; adventures with the Intitute of Nautical Archaeology. edited by George F. Bass. Thames & Hudson 2005 256p il maps $39.95 **930.1**
1. Archeology 2. Shipwrecks 3. Underwater exploration
ISBN 978-0-500-05136-8; 0-500-05136-4
LC 2005-900862

This book features "accounts by many distinguished archaeologists associated with the INA [Institute of Nautical Archaeology]. They tell of the discovery, excavation, and preservation of more than 40 shipwrecks—and one sunken city—the world over, from ancient times through the Byzantine, medieval, and Renaissance eras and on through World War II. . . . This book will appeal to general readers and specialists alike in nautical archaeology." Libr J

Includes bibliographical references

Ceram, C. W.
Gods, graves, and scholars; the story of archaeology. translated from the German by E. B. Garside and Sophie Wilkins. 2nd rev and substantially enl ed; Knopf 1967 441p il maps hardcover o.p. pa $11.16 **930.1**
1. Mayas 2. Aztecs 3. Archeology 4. Hieroglyphics 5. Babel, Tower of 6. Cuneiform inscriptions 7. Rosetta stone inscription 8. Kings 9. Crete (Greece) 10. Egypt -- Antiquities
ISBN 0-394-74319-9 pa

Original German edition, 1949; first English language edition, 1951

"The story of Champollion and the reading of the Rosetta Stone, the decipherment of the inscriptions on the monument of Darius the Great, Leonard Woolley's famous excavations at Ur, and John Lloyd Stephens' discovery of the ruins of a great Mayan city are ... told in this book." Doors to More Mature Read

Includes bibliographical references

Childs, Craig Leland
Finders keepers; a tale of archaeological plunder and obsession. Little, Brown and Co. 2010 274p $24.99 **930.1**
1. Archeologists -- Ethics
ISBN 978-0-316-06642-6; 0-316-06642-7
LC 2009-51921

"Childs treks the canyon-incised Colorado Plateau in search of pre-Columbian artifacts. Their legal regulation collides with collectors' obsessions to possess them. Childs, though, does not remove what he finds, an ethic that vies with other precepts for the proper preservation of antiquities.

For every stand he takes on archaeological morality in this narrative mix of his backcountry experiences and conversations with collectors, curators, dealers, and an occasional looter, Childs engages their justifications for taking custody of ancient objects. . . . Alternating romantic and practical moods, Childs hunts virtue as much as baskets in this engaging discourse." Booklist

Includes bibliographical references

Hunt, Patrick
Ten discoveries that rewrote history. Plume 2007 226p pa $27.95 **930.1**
1. Antiquities 2. Ancient civilization 3. Archeology -- History
ISBN 978-0-452-28877-5; 0-452-28877-0
LC 2007-19808
The author "has produced a wonderful volume of of archaeological history. In doing so, he has provided a seldom seen look at some of the most important scientific developments in the field." Sci Books Films

Includes bibliographical references

Johnson, Marilyn
Lives in ruins; archaeologists and the seductive lure of human rubble. Marilyn Johnson. Harper 2014 288 p. $25.99 **930.1**
1. Archeology 2. Archeologists 3. Archaeology -- Anecdotes 4. Archaeologists -- Anecdotes
ISBN 0062127187; 9780062127181
LC 2014028450
In this book the author, Marilyn Johnson, "turns her . . . eye and . . . wit to the real-life avatars of Indiana Jones-- the archaeologists who sort through the muck and mire of swamps, ancient landfills, volcanic islands, and other dirty places to reclaim history for us all. . . . [She] digs and drinks alongside archaeologists, chases them through the Mediterranean, the Caribbean, and even Machu Picchu, and excavates their lives." (Publisher's note)

"Without glitz, the author has created a very enjoyable work that will be appreciated by experts in the field and casual readers alike. Well suited to anyone contemplating archaeology as a career, those curious about what the profession is like, lovers of history and science, and readers who enjoy and are grateful for the lure of prehistory and discovery as a mental process." LJ

Includes bibliographical references

MacGregor, Neil, 1946-
A history of the world in 100 objects; Neil MacGregor. Viking 2011 xxvi, 707 p. p col. ill., maps $45 **930.1**
1. Antiques 2. Art objects 3. World history 4. Material culture 5. Ceremonial objects 6. Archaeology, Medieval 7. Classical antiquities 8. Antiquities, Prehistoric
ISBN 0670022705; 1846144132; 9780670022700; 9781846144134
LC 2011021769
The book by Neil MacGregor is the result of "a joint project between the [British M]useum and the British Broadcasting Corporation's Radio Four. . . . In this project, . . . one hundred objects from the museum's enormous holdings [were be chosen]. . . . The book . . . is . . . a compilation of

the one hundred objects, arranged more or less chronologically, . . . each with essay and commentary as edited for final broadcast format." (New York Review of Books)

Includes bibliographical references (p. 671-678) and index

The **Oxford** Companion to Archaeology; Edited by Neil Asher Silberman. 2nd edition Oxford University Press 2012 3 vol. illustrations $595 **930.1**
1. Archeology
ISBN 0199735786; 9780199735785
LC 2011051893
"Much has changed in the field [of archaeology] since 1996. Recent developments in methods and analytical techniques (e.g., laser-based mapping and survey systems, new applications of the scanning electron microscope) have revolutionized the ways excavations are performed. Cultural tourism, cultural resource management, heritage, and conservation have been redefined as areas within archaeology, and have been newly emphasized by scholars and administrators. Major site discoveries have expanded our understanding of prehistory and human developments through time. The second edition explores each of these advances in the field, adding approximately 150 entries." (Publisher's note)

932 Egypt to 640

Brier, Bob
The **murder** of Tutankhamen; a true story. Berkley Books 2005 xx, 264p il pa $14 **932**
1. Kings 2. Egypt -- History
ISBN 0-425-20690-4; 978-0-425-20690-4
LC 2005-41085
First published 1998 by Putnam
"Brier obviously knows his subject and is impassioned by it. Readers who enjoy history or true-crime stories will be intrigued by this work." SLJ

Includes bibliographical references

Bunson, Margaret R.
Encyclopedia of ancient Egypt; Margaret R. Bunson. 3rd edition Facts On File 2012 xxviii, 516 p.p ill., maps (alk. paper) $95 **932**
1. Egypt -- History 2. Egypt -- Antiquities -- Encyclopedias 3. Egypt -- Civilization -- Encyclopedias 4. Egypt -- Antiquities -- Dictionaries 5. Egypt -- Civilization -- To 332 B.C. -- Dictionaries
ISBN 0816082162; 9780816082162
LC 2011026433
"Entries are detailed and concise; some have bibliographies, and many summarize why a subject is notable, with references to related entries. The volume explores every aspect of Egyptian culture, from warfare to burial rites. Interesting entries include the ones on Akhenaten, the heretical pharaoh who introduced monotheism; his famous wife Nefertiti; and son Tutankhamun. Alexander the Great's conquest of Egypt and its historical impact are covered extensively in a detailed entry. Deities are discussed for many of the historical periods, and the information concerning Hatshepsut, the female pharaoh, is detailed and enlighten-

ing. This volume features a list of illustrations and maps, brief introduction, historical/geographical overview, chronology, and glossary." (Choice)

"This is a useful one-stop, ready-reference resource for general readers interested in ancient Egyptian civilization." LJ

Includes bibliographical references and index

David, A. Rosalie

Handbook to life in ancient Egypt; [by] Rosalie David. rev ed; Facts on File 2003 417p il map (Facts on File library of world history) $50   **932**
1. Egypt -- Civilization
ISBN 0-8160-5034-1

LC 2002-35229

First published 1998

This covers such topics as the geography of Ancient Egypt, society and government, religion, funerary beliefs and customs, architecture, trade and transport, the army and navy, economy and industry, and everyday life.

Includes bibliographical references

Dreyfus, Renee

Hatshepsut: from queen to Pharaoh; edited by Catharine H. Roehrig with Renée Dreyfus and Cathleen A. Keller. Yale University Press 2005 339p il map $65   **932**
1. Queens 2. Egypt -- History 3. Egypt -- Civilization
ISBN 0-300-11139-8

LC 2005-20286

The editors "offer a magnificent portrait of this remarkable woman and all aspects of Egyptian life in the 18th Dynasty, from religion and politics to art and jewelry." Publ Wkly

Includes bibliographical references

Fletcher, Joann

The **Story** of Egypt; The Civilization that Shaped the World. by Joann Fletcher. Hachette Books 2016 496 p. color illustrations, maps $29.95   **932**
1. Egypt -- History
ISBN 1444785184; 1681771349; 9781444785180; 9781681771342

In this book, "Professor Joann Fletcher pulls together the complete story of Egypt—charting the rise and fall of the ancient Egyptians while putting their whole world into a context to which we can all relate. Fletcher uncovers some . . . revelations: new evidence shows that women became pharaohs on at least ten occasions; that the ancient Egyptians built the first Suez Canal and then circumnavigated Africa." (Publisher's note)

"The authoritative author imparts her vast knowledge in an orderly chronology and lively, intimate history. A perfect choice for budding Egyptologists." Kirkus

Includes bibliographical references (pages 381-460) and index.

Hawass, Zahi A.

Hidden treasures of ancient Egypt; unearthing the masterpieces of Egyptian history. [by] Zahi Hawass; photographs by Kenneth Garrett. National Geographic Society 2004 256p il $35   **932**
1. Egyptian art 2. Egypt -- Antiquities 3. Excavations (Archeology) -- Egypt
ISBN 0-7922-6319-7

LC 2004-44845

The author "narrates the past 150 years of excavation, from the colonial period—when Westerners overwhelmed the ranks of those recovering the nation's treasures—through Egypt's independence and the present era of international cooperation. . . . This breathtaking glimpse at the country's archeological wealth should excite curious and adventurous minds worldwide." Publ Wkly

★ **Tutankhamun** and the golden age of the pharaohs; [by] Zahi Hawass; photographs by Kenneth Garrett. National Geographic Books 2005 285p il map $35   **932**
1. Kings 2. Egypt -- Antiquities
ISBN 0-7922-3873-7

LC 2005-41678

This companion to an exhibition displaying about 130 items found in the tombs of Tutankhamun and other kings from the same dynasty "describes the physical and symbolic attributes of each object and explains its purpose in the afterlife. . . . An arrestingly visual album destined for high demand." Booklist

Includes bibliographical references

Mertz, Barbara

Temples, tombs, & hieroglyphs; a popular history of ancient Egypt. 2nd ed., 1st William Morrow ed.; William Morrow 2007 xxvi, 324p il map $26.95   **932**
1. Queens 2. Hieroglyphics 3. Egyptian language 4. Kings 5. Syria 6. Egypt -- Antiquities 7. Egypt -- Civilization 8. Thebes (Egypt: Extinct city)
ISBN 978-0-06-125276-1; 0-06-125276-X

LC 2007-29118

First published 1964 by Coward-McCann

This is an "introduction to the history of ancient Egypt and Egyptology. . . . Mertz gives special attention to such topics as the kingship (yes) of Queen Hatshepsut, the exploits of Thutmose III, and the Amarna Period with its intriguing players Akhenaten, Nefertiti, and Tutankhamen. Presenting both pros and cons of current theories, Mertz also explains in simple language archaeological techniques such as carbon 14 dating and historical chronology. . . . [This is] an excellent introduction for patrons interested in the land of the pharaohs." Libr J

The **Oxford** encyclopedia of ancient Egypt; Donald B. Redford, editor in chief. Oxford Univ. Press 2001 3v set $450   **932**
1. Reference books 2. Egypt -- Antiquities -- Encyclopedias 3. Egypt -- Civilization -- Encyclopedias
ISBN 0-19-510234-7

LC 99-54801

ALA RUSA Dartmouth Medal (2002)

This reference work covers "archaeology, biography, history, language, social history, and more. . . . [It features] essays from more than 250 contributors from various countries and scholarly pursuits, all with solid academic credentials. . . . One is not likely to encounter another work of this magnitude on a subject of such universal interest for some time." Booklist

Includes bibliographical references

Romer, John

A **history** of ancient Egypt; from the first farmers to the Great Pyramid. John Romer. Thomas Dunne Books 2013 512 p. (hardcover) $29.99   **932**

1. Archeology 2. Egypt -- History 3. Egypt -- History -- To 332 B.C

ISBN 1250030110; 9781250030115

LC 2013012485

This book, "the first of John Romer's promised two-volume history of ancient Egypt, . . .takes us from the earliest farming communities in northeast Africa, to the building of the Great Pyramid of King Khufu. . . . The evidence he looks at goes well beyond the written sources . . . to archaeological evidence . . . which allows him to explore pre-unification Egypt in some detail." (History Today)

Includes bibliographical references and index

Verner, Miroslav

The **pyramids**; the mystery, culture, and science of Egypt's great monuments. translated from the German by Steven Rendall. Grove Press 2001 495p il map hardcover o.p. pa $17.50   **932**

1. Pyramids 2. Egypt -- Antiquities

ISBN 0-8021-3935-3 pa

LC 2001-35084

In this study, the author "focuses on research of the last decade and excavations over the past 20 years. Verner divides his book into chapters according to pharaonic dynasty, spotlighting individual pharaohs' pyramids. He not only explains the layout of each pyramid but also presents various theories on how each pyramid was built and tells stories about the people that were buried there." Booklist

Includes bibliographical references

Wilkinson, Toby

★ The **rise** and fall of ancient Egypt; [by] Toby Wilkinson. Random House 2011 611p il map $35   **932**

1. Egypt -- History 2. Egypt -- History -- 332-30 B.C. 3. Egypt -- History -- To 332 B.C.

ISBN 978-0-553-80553-6; 0-553-80553-3

LC 2009-47322

The author "offers a revisionist view of the ugly life hidden by the splendors and dazzling treasures of pharaonic Egypt. He shows in rich detail that it was a brutal society where life was cheap, royal power absolute and established through fear and coercion. . . . This is a penetrating and authoritative overview of a violent ancient civilization often revered by contemporary scholars and enthusiasts." Publ Wkly

Includes bibliographical references

933   Palestine to 70

Burleigh, Nina

Unholy business; a true tale of faith, greed, and forgery in the holy land. Smithsonian Books 2008 271p $27.50   **933**

1. Forgery 2. Engineers 3. Entrepreneurs 4. Antiquarians 5. Israel -- Antiquities

ISBN 978-0-06-145845-3

LC 2008-23425

"In 2002, the James Ossuary, an ancient limestone box for bones with an inscription on it that said 'James, son of Joseph, brother of Jesus' was publicized as the first real physical evidence of Jesus Christ's existence. The plot thickened when the ossuary went on tour, creating lots of publicity, a book by advocate Hershel Shanks, and a Discovery Channel documentary. Then the ossuary's owner, Oded Golan, and his antique-dealer associates were charged with forgery. . . . Whether or not readers believe the ossuary is authentic, they will thoroughly enjoy this book." Libr J

Goodman, Martin

Rome and Jerusalem; the clash of ancient civilizations. Alfred A. Knopf 2007 598p il map $35 **933**

1. Jews -- Rome 2. Jews -- History

ISBN 978-0-375-41185-4; 0-375-41185-2

LC 2007-5267

"For scholars of Roman and Jewish history as well as well-informed general readers, this work provides a definitive account." Booklist

Includes bibliographical references

Korb, Scott

Life in year one; what the world was like in first-century Palestine. Riverhead Books 2010 241p $25.95   **933**

1. Palestine 2. Jews -- History 3. Bible -- History

ISBN 978-1-59448-899-3

LC 2010-146

The author "calls his retrospective 'a lively romp through the land of Palestine,' circa 5 B.C.E.–70 C.E., but the picture he draws from archeology, ancient historical accounts, and religious texts is anything but lighthearted. . . . Korb's vivid, breezy prose makes accessible a mountain of scholarship that illuminates the past." Publ Wkly

Includes bibliographical references

935   Mesopotamia to 637 and Iranian Plateau to 637

Kriwaczek, Paul

Babylon; Mesopotamia and the birth of civilization. Paul Kriwaczek. Thomas Dunne Books/St. Martin's Press 2012 310 p.   **935**

1. Tigris River 2. Euphrates River 3. Iraq -- History 4. Ancient civilization 5. Babylon (Extinct city) 6. Iraq -- History -- To 634 7. Iraq -- Civilization -- To 634 8. Iraq -- Politics and government 9. Babylon (Extinct city) -- History 10. Babylon (Extinct city) -- Civilization 11. Babylon (Extinct city) -- Politics and

government

ISBN 9781250000071; 9781429941068

LC 2012003104

This book is an "overview of the rich, ancient civilizations that flourished in the land between the two rivers. . . . The ancient simmering conflict of the Fertile Crescent boils down to the question: "Should the Tigris-Euphrates Valley be mastered from the west or the east"? . . . The need to organize systems of irrigation in Eridu . . . spawned an "urban revolution," with the invention of cities and all that came with them: division of labor, social classes, engineering, the arts, education, numbers and law, to mention a few. . . . The author keeps close to biblical readings for comparative accounts of the Flood and the succession of kings of the city-states to the founder of the first true empire, Sargon." (Kirkus)

Includes bibliographical references and index

936 Europe north and west of Italian Peninsula to ca. 499

★ **Ancient** Europe 8000 B.C.-A.D. 1000; encyclopedia of the Barbarian world. Peter Bogucki & Pam J. Crabtree, editors-in-chief. Thomson/Gale 2004 2v il, maps set $280   **936**
1. Ancient history 2. Reference books 3. Europe -- History -- Encyclopedias
ISBN 0-684-80668-1

LC 2003-15251

"Any public and academic library that has a clientele interested in European archeology or the featured historical period covered will find this a valuable purchase." Booklist
Includes bibliographical references

Cunliffe, Barry
The **ancient** Celts. Penguin Books 1999 324p il map pa $21.95   **936**
1. Celts
ISBN 0-14-025422-6
First published 1997 by Oxford Univ. Press
This is a "survey of the origins of the Celts and their expansion during the Iron Age through their largely successful subjection by the Romans. . . . [Cunliffe] has written a readable and informative book with many attractive illustrations." Libr J
Includes bibliographical references

Higgins, Charlotte
Under another sky; journeys in Roman Britain. Charlotte Higgins. The Overlook Press 2015 282 p. illustrations, maps (hardback) $27.95   **936**
1. Rome -- Antiquities 2. Great Britain -- Antiquities 3. Great Britain -- History -- 0-1066 4. Monuments -- Great Britain 5. Landscapes -- Great Britain 6. Great Britain -- History, Local 7. Romans -- Great Britain -- History 8. Great Britain -- Antiquities, Roman 9. Cultural landscapes -- Great Britain
ISBN 1468310895; 9781468310894

LC 2015011873

In this book, by Charlotte Higgins, shortlisted for the Samuel Johnson Prize, the author "sets out to explore the ancient monuments of Roman Britain. She explores the land that was once Rome's northernmost territory and how it has changed since the years after the empire fell. Under Another Sky invites us to see the British landscape, and British history, . . . as indelibly marked by how the Romans first imagined and wrote, these strange and exotic islands." (Publisher's note)

"A thoroughly researched, elegantly written history." Kirkus

Includes bibliographical references and index

936.2 England to 410 and Wales to 410

Hill, Rosemary
Stonehenge. Harvard University Press 2008 242p il map (Wonders of the world) $19.95   **936.2**
1. Stonehenge (England) 2. Megalithic monuments -- Great Britain
ISBN 9780674031326; 0674031326

LC 2008-12024

Hill's "book is a treasure: stylish, thoughtful, miraculously condensed, and as full of knowledge as a megalith is full of megalith." Sunday Times (London)

Includes bibliographical references (p. 211-222)

Pearson, Mike Parker
Stonehenge; a new understanding: solving the mysteries of the greatest stone age monument. by Mike Parker Pearson. The Experiment 2013 432 p. (hardcover) $27.50   **936.2**
1. Stonehenge (England) 2. Excavations (Archeology) 3. England -- Antiquities 4. Megalithic monuments -- England 5. Stonehenge (England) -- History 6. Stonehenge World Heritage Site (England)
ISBN 1615190791; 9781615190799

LC 2012047688

This book, by Mike Parker Pearson, "changes the way we think about [Stonehenge] correcting previously erroneous dating, filling gaps in our knowledge about its builders and how they lived, clarifying the monument's significance both celestially and as a burial ground, and contextualizing Stonehenge . . . within the broader landscape of the Neolithic Age." (Publisher's note)

"Renowned archaeologist Pearson . . . presents the findings of the most ambitious and scientifically informed investigation of Stonehenge thus far. . . . Filled with maps, drawings, photographs and diagrams, the book details the group's findings in a well-organized, absorbing manner." Kirkus

Includes bibliographical references and index

937 Italian Peninsula to 476 and adjacent territories to 476

Allan, Tony
Life, myth, and art in Ancient Rome. J. Paul Getty Museum 2005 144p il pa $19.95   **937**
1. Roman art 2. Roman mythology 3. Rome -- Antiquities 4. Rome -- Civilization
ISBN 0-89236-821-7

LC 2004-114326

This is an "illustrated guide to the cultural and political heritage of ancient Rome, including the enduring legacy of its art and architecture, the engineering innovations of its vast system of roads and aqueducts, the . . . myths of its gods and goddesses, and the power of its emperors and legions." Publisher's note

Includes bibliographical references

Beard, Mary

The **fires** of Vesuvius; Pompeii lost and found. Belknap Press of Harvard University Press 2008 360p il map $26.95; pa $17.95 **937**

1. Pompeii (Extinct city)

ISBN 978-0-674-02976-7; 0-674-02976-3; 978-0-674-04586-6 pa; 0-674-04586-6 pa

LC 2008-27513

"The eruption of Mt. Vesuvius in 79 A.D. preserved a uniquely rich sample of Roman life. Buried among the ruins of Pompeii are frescoes, graffiti ('Atimetus got me pregnant'), campaign ads, and housewares; the victims themselves left hollows in the lava that, when cast in plaster, yield details as fine as the imprint of one man's eyebrows. In this lively survey, Beard, a classicist at Cambridge, tempers erudition with a skepticism toward interpretive overreach." New Yorker

Includes bibliographical references

SPQR; a history of ancient Rome. Mary Beard. Liveright Publishing Corp. 2015 608 p. ill. (some col.), maps (hardcover) $35 **937**

1. Rome -- History 2. Ancient civilization 3. Rome -- History -- Kings, 753-510 B.C 4. Rome -- History -- Republic, 510-30 B.C 5. Rome -- History -- Empire, 30 B.C.-476 A.D

ISBN 0871404230; 9780871404237

LC 2015036060

National Book Critics Circle Award Finalist: Nonfiction (2015)

Author Mary Beard presents this book "exploring how the Romans themselves challenged the idea of imperial rule, how they responded to terrorism and revolution, and how they invented a new idea of citizenship and nation, while also keeping her eye open for those overlooked in traditional histories: women, slaves and ex-slaves, conspirators, and losers. Beard separates fact from fiction, myth and propaganda from historical record." (Publisher's note)

"Since the author is a well-known popularizer of classical studies, it is no surprise that this is a humorous and accessible work, but it is also extremely rigorous in its questioning of standard conclusions and methods. . . . At all points, her approaches are easy to follow." LJ

Includes bibliographical references and index

Berry, Joanne

The **complete** Pompeii. Thames & Hudson 2007 256p il map $40 **937**

1. Pompeii (Extinct city)

ISBN 978-0-500-05150-4; 0-500-05150-X

LC 2007-922095

This book "covers the origins and evolution of the city, the daily life of its residents, the geography of the region, and the eruption of Mt. Vesuvius, as well as a history of the excavation of the site. Easy to read and with full color pictures of the excavation, along with maps, time lines, diagrams, and vivid art reproductions, this book gives a broad and comprehensive introduction to the Pompeian world. . . . High school libraries should be advised that there is a section on eroticism that contains visually and verbally explicit sexual material." Libr J

Includes bibliographical references

Bunson, Matthew

Encyclopedia of ancient Rome; Matthew Bunson. 3rd ed. Facts On File 2012 xxxvii, 788 p.p ill., maps (acid-free paper) $95.00 **937**

1. Rome -- Antiquities 2. Rome -- Civilization 3. Rome -- History -- Encyclopedias 4. Rome -- History -- Empire, 30 B.C.-476 A.D. -- Encyclopedias

ISBN 0816082170; 9780816082179

LC 2011038366

This encyclopedia, by Matthew Bunson, "provides . . . coverage of the people, places, events, and ideas of ancient Rome. Each entry . . . reflect[s] recent advances in archaeology, historical and literary criticism, and social analysis. In addition, the scope . . . include[s] the entire history of ancient Rome, from the first founding of the city . . . to the final collapse of Roman power in the fifth century CE." (Publisher's note)

"A superb source of detailed, engaging information on the ever fascinating and often perplexing ancient Roman civilization, Bunson's work is a handy reference for classics students and enthusiasts alike." LJ

Includes bibliographical references (p. 757-760) and index

The **Cambridge** illustrated history of the Roman world; edited by Greg Woolf. Cambridge University Press 2003 384p il map (Cambridge illustrated history) $45 **937**

1. Rome -- History

ISBN 0-521-82775-2

LC 2004-298480

This book explores such topics as "religion, Rome's relationship with Greece, warfare and Empire, and science and culture." Publisher's note

Includes bibliographical references

Everitt, Anthony

The **rise** of Rome; the making of the world's greatest empire. Anthony Everitt. 1st ed. Random House 2012 xxxii, 478 p., [8] p. of platesp col. ill., maps (ebook) $85.00; (hardcover : alk. paper) $30.00 **937**

1. Rome -- History 2. Rome -- Politics and government 3. Rome -- History -- Empire, 284-476 4. Rome -- History -- Empire, 30 B.C.-284 A.D

ISBN 1400066638; 9780679645160; 9781400066636; 0679645160

LC 2011048318

This book by Anthony Everitt examines the history of "Rome and its . . . ascent from an obscure agrarian backwater. . . . He chronicles the clash between patricians and plebeians that defined the politics of the Republic. He shows how Rome's . . . strategy of offering citizenship to her defeated subjects was instrumental in expanding the reach of her burgeoning empire. And he outlines the corrosion of constitutional norms that accompanied Rome's . . . expansion." (Publisher's note)

Includes bibliographical references (p. [423]-426) and index.

Fowler, Brenda

Iceman; uncovering the life and times of a prehistoric man found in an alpine glacier. University of Chicago Press ed; University of Chicago Press 2001 315p il pa $15   937
    1. Mummies 2. Prehistoric peoples 3. Italy -- Antiquities
    ISBN 0-226-25823-8
                                        LC 2001-27805
First published 2000 by Random House
"In September 1991, hikers in the Alps discovered a well-preserved frozen corpse; nearby lay a stone ax and swatches of leather and fur. The man turned out to have died in the early Bronze Age, making him an incalculable treasure for students of early human beings. Fowler . . . offers a brisk and easy-to-follow narrative, first of the great discovery, then of the personal and political struggles for control of the frozen body." Publ Wkly
    Includes bibliographical references

Freisenbruch, Annelise

Caesars' wives; sex, power, and politics in the Roman Empire. Free Press 2010 xxvi, 337p il $28; ebook $14.99   937
    1. Empresses 2. Women -- Rome 3. Rome -- History
    ISBN 978-1-4165-8303-5; 1-4165-8303-3; 978-1-4165-8357-8 ebook; 1-4165-8357-2 ebook
                                        LC 2010-19368
"Providing well-chosen, scintillating details—e.g., enemies being boiled alive, familial bonds savagely snapped in an instant—alongside careful historical analysis, the author breathes new life into these overlooked subjects. . . . A captivating look at imperial Rome's roots in the making of the modern stateswoman " Kirkus
    Includes bibliographical references

Gibbon, Edward

★ The **decline** and fall of the Roman empire; Edward Gibbon; edited, abridged, and with a critical introduction by Hans-Friedrich Mueller; introduction by Daniel J. Boorstin; illustrations by Giovanni Battista Piranesi. Modern Library paperback ed.; Modern Library 2003 xxxvii, 1258p il map pa $15.95   937
    1. Rome -- History 2. Byzantine Empire
    ISBN 0-375-75811-9
                                        LC 2002-32585
First published 1776-1788 in the United Kingdom with title: The history of the decline and fall of the Roman Empire
"In this substantial history of the Roman Empire, Gibbon bridges the abyss between the ancient and the modern world. It is the one historical work of the eighteenth century that is still accepted as authoritative. It covers thirteen centuries of

history, during which time paganism was breaking down and Christianity was taking its place." Reader's Adviser
    Includes bibliographical references

Goldsworthy, Adrian

Pax romana; War, Peace and Conquest in the Roman World. Adrian Goldsworthy. Yale University Press 2016 528 p. illustrations, maps (alk. paper) $32.50   937
    1. Rome 2. Peace
    ISBN 9780300178821
                                        LC 2016941493
This book, by Adrian Goldsworthy, is a "comprehensive history of the Roman Peace. . . . Goldsworthy turns his attention to the Pax Romana, the famous peace and prosperity brought by the Roman Empire at its height in the first and second centuries AD. Yet the Romans were conquerors, imperialists who took by force a vast empire stretching from the Euphrates to the Atlantic coast." (Publisher's note)
"An engrossing account of how the Roman Empire grew and operated." Kirkus
    Includes bibliographical references and index.

O'Connell, Robert L.

The **ghosts** of Cannae; Hannibal and the darkest hour of the Roman republic. Random House 2010 310p map $27   937
    1. Generals 2. Punic Wars, 264 B.C.-146 B.C. 3. Rome -- History 4. Punic Wars, 264-146 B.C.
    ISBN 978-1-4000-6702-2; 1-4000-6702-2
                                        LC 2009-40006
"The distinctive edge of The Ghosts of Cannae is Robert L. O'Connell's consistently professional instinct for the behavior of men and units on the battlefield. He is able to put himself and his reader on the ground at Cannae, gagging in the heat of a southern Italian midsummer, assailed by an overload from every one of the five senses." N Y Times Book Rev
    Includes bibliographical references

The **Oxford** history of the Roman world; edited by John Boardman, Jasper Griffin, Oswyn Murray. Oxford Univ. Press 1991 518p il maps hardcover o.p. pa $17.95   937
    1. Rome -- History
    ISBN 0-19-280203-8
                                        LC 91-11763
This "work tells the story of the rise of Rome from its origins as a cluster of villages to the foundation of the Roman Empire by Augustus, to its consolidation in the first two centuries CE. It also discusses aspects of the later Empire and its influence on Western civilization." Publisher's note
    Includes bibliographical references

Pellegrino, Charles R.

★ **Ghosts** of Vesuvius; a new look at the last days of Pompeii, how the towers fell, and other strange connections. [by] Charles Pellegrino. 1st ed; W. Morrow 2004 489p il map $25.95; pa $15.95   937
    1. Pompeii (Extinct city) 2. Excavations (Archeology)

-- Italy

ISBN 0-380-97310-3; 0-06-075100-2 pa

LC 2003-71055

"In August A.D. 79, Mt. Vesuvius erupted and famously buried the city of Pompeii and, less famously, the city of Herculaneum. From this node of history, Pellegrino goes off on a . . . search for the connections and ruptures that have shaped not only human civilization but the very course of life on Earth and the universe at large. . . . This is a book to be savored, reread and passed along to future generations." Publ Wkly

Includes bibliographical references

Strauss, Barry

The **death** of Caesar; the story of history's most famous assassination. Barry Strauss. Simon & Schuster 2015 352 p. 8 plates; illustrations $27 **937**

1. Assassination

ISBN 1451668791; 9781451668797

LC 2014032045

This book, by Barry Strauss, presents the "dramatic story of one of history's most famous events--the death of Julius Caesar. . . . [William] Shakespeare shows Caesar's assassination to be an amateur and idealistic affair. The real killing, however, was a carefully planned paramilitary operation, a generals' plot, put together by Caesar's disaffected officers and designed with precision." (Publisher's note)

"The author explains how Caesar's funeral was even more dramatic than Shakespeare's version—especially Mark Antony's eulogy. Once again, Strauss takes us deep into the psyche of ancient history in an exciting, twisted tale that is sure to please." Kirkus

Includes bibliographical references and index

938   Greece to 323

★ **Ancient** Greece; edited by Thomas J. Sienkewicz. Salem Press 2007 3v il map (Magill's choice) set $207   **938**

1. Reference books 2. Greece -- History -- Encyclopedias

ISBN 1-58765-281-1; 978-1-58765-281-3

LC 2006-16525

Some of the essays in this work appeared in various other Salem Press sets

This is a "comprehensive examination of Greek civilization and its impact on Western history, 'from its earliest archaeological remains until the Battle of Actium in 31 B.C.E,' . . . [The essays included] cover art, daily life and customs, government, literature, medicine and science, war, the role of women, and mythology. Biographical entries profile statesmen, artists, writers, scientists, and philosophers, and relevant entries probe battles, philosophical movements, and types of literature." SLJ

Includes bibliographical references

Burckhardt, Jacob

The **Greeks** and Greek civilization; translated by Sheila Stern; edited with an introduction by Oswyn

Murray. St. Martin's Press 1998 449p hardcover o.p. pa $16.95   **938**

1. Greece -- Civilization

ISBN 0-312-24447-9 pa

LC 98-30107

Translation of selected lectures on ancient Greece delivered by the German cultural historian in the 1870s

"These lectures provide not only a rich overview of Burckhardt's learning but a precious glimpse into the intellectual world of the late nineteenth century. . . . Here his topics range from the importance of the 'agon' in forging individualism to the pessimism and violence that underlay much of Greek culture." New Yorker

Includes bibliographical references

★ The **Cambridge** dictionary of classical civilization; edited by Graham Shipley . . . [et al.] Cambridge University Press 2006 xliv, 966p il map $180   **938**

1. Reference books 2. Classical civilization -- Dictionaries

ISBN 0-521-48313-1; 978-0-521-48313-1

LC 2006-299203

The "entries and more than 500 illustrations focus on social, economic, and cultural aspects of these civilizations from the mid-eighth century BCE to the end of the fifth century." Booklist

Includes bibliographical references

Cartledge, Paul

Ancient Greece; a history in eleven cities. Oxford University Press 2009 261p il map $19.95 **938**

1. Greece -- Civilization 2. Greece -- History -- 0-323

ISBN 978-0-19-923338-0

LC 2009-26999

"Aiming for a general audience, Cartledge achieves a fast-paced, highly readable romp through ancient Greece. An excellent choice for anyone seeking an introduction to the topic; for all its readability, this book doesn't skimp on the research." Libr J

Includes bibliographical references

Great moments in Greek archaeology; academic coordinator, Panos Valavanis; translated by David Hardy; foreword by Angelos Delivorrias; essays by George F. Bass . . . [et al.] The J. Paul Getty Museum 2007 379p il $75   **938**

1. Greece -- Antiquities 2. Excavations (Archeology) -- Greece

ISBN 978-0-89236-910-2; 0-89236-910-8

LC 2007-16609

"This magnificently illustrated book with essays by leading scholars—frequently the excavators themselves—tells the story of Greek archaeological discoveries, capturing the excitement and rendering details accessible to a wide audience." Libr J

Includes bibliographical references

Green, Peter

The **Hellenistic** age; a history. Modern Library 2007 xxxiii, 199p map (Modern Library chronicles) hardcover o.p. pa $14   **938**
1. Hellenism 2. Greece -- History 3. Mediterranean region -- History
ISBN 978-0-679-64279-4; 0-679-64279-X; 978-0-8129-6740-1 pa; 0-8129-6740-2 pa
LC 2006-46657

Tis study "traces the unfolding of Hellenistic civilization in a linear fashion, while at the same time drawing connections between successive alterations in the political, economic and social landscape of the Hellenistic East and the appearance of new cultural and intellectual perspectives. . . . [The book] provides an interesting and well-written overview of a historical period that Green aptly describes as covering 'some of the most crucial and transformational history of the ancient world. . . . The changes are lasting and fundamental.' If only for this, students of world history are in Green's debt." Philadelphia Inquirer

Includes bibliographical references

Herodotus, ca. 484 B.C.-425 B.C.

The **Histories**; Herodotus; translated by Tom Holland; introduction and notes by Paul Cartledge. Viking Adult 2014 880 p. maps (hbk.) $40   **938**
1. Ancient history 2. Greece -- History -- 0-323 3. History, Ancient 4. Greece -- History -- To 146 B.C
ISBN 0670024899; 9780670024896
LC 2012474647

This book by Herodotus, translated by Tom Holland, "is the earliest surviving work of nonfiction and a thrilling narrative account of (among other things) the war between the Persian Empire and the Greek city-states in the fifth century BC." This edition includes "an introduction and notes by Professor Paul Cartledge, a translator's preface, an index of significant persons and places, maps, and a supplementary index." (Publisher's note)

"This ancient Greek historian could easily be called the father of humor. . . he irreverently describes events, players and their countless harebrained schemes." Kirkus

Includes bibliographical references (pages 745-746) and indexes

★ The **landmark** Herodotus; the Histories: a new translation. a new translation by Andrea L. Purvis with maps, annotations, appendices, and encyclopedic index; edited by Robert B. Strassler; with an introduction by Rosalind Thomas. Pantheon Books 2007 lxiv, 953p $45   **938**
1. History, Ancient 2. Greece -- History 3. Greece -- History -- To 146 B.C.
ISBN 978-0-375-42109-9; 0-375-42109-2; 0375421092; 9780375421099
LC 2007024149

This is a new translation of Herodotus' Histories. Indexes.

"A major theme of the Histories is the way in which time can effect surprising changes in the fortunes and reputations of empires, cities, and men; all the more appropriate, then, that Herodotus' reputation has once again been riding very high. In the academy, his technique, once derided as haphazard, has earned newfound respect, while his popular-

ity among ordinary readers will likely get a boost from the publication of perhaps the most densely annotated, richly illustrated, and user-friendly edition of his Histories ever to appear: 'The Landmark Herodotus,' edited by Robert B. Strassler and bristling with appendices, by a phalanx of experts, on everything from the design of Athenian warships to ancient units of liquid measure." New Yorker

Includes bibliographical references

Higgins, Charlotte

It's all Greek to me: from Homer to the Hippocratic Oath, how ancient Greece has shaped our world. Harper 2010 229p il map $16.99   **938**
1. Greece -- Civilization
ISBN 978-0-06-180400-7; 0-06-180400-2
LC 2010-06737

First published 2008 in the United Kingdom

"The book has plenty of useful aspects, perhaps most notably in the rich back matter, comprising an alphabet, map, timeline, key to important Greek gods and notables and a sampling of Greek sayings and words (and root words) that still inhabit our language (tantalizing, Draconian). Anyone reading The Iliad or any other of the Greek classic texts for the first time would do well to keep the section bookmarked. Higgins covers Homer, the playwrights, the historians, the nascent scientists and the philosophers, and she gives special attention to the warriors, wars and other aspects of the ancient world that continue to make us uncomfortable—e.g., homosexuality, women's rights, slavery. Periodically, she pauses to offer mini-disquisitions on topics as varied as the plots of The Iliad and The Odyssey, the architecture of the Parthenon and the uneven verisimilitude of the 2007 film 300." Kirkus

Includes bibliographical references

Kagan, Donald

The **Peloponnesian** War. Viking 2003 xxvii, 511p il map $29.95; pa $15   **938**
1. Greece -- History -- 431-404 B.C., Peloponnesian War
ISBN 0-670-03211-5; 0-14-200437-5 pa
LC 2002-193377

This is a study of "the conflict between Athens and Sparta in the fifth century B.C.E. . . . {Kagan's} primary source is, of course, Thucydides' epic history, but {he} draws on Aristotle, Xenophon, and others to provide an objective, nuanced perspective on the military drama. And it's quite a drama: the clash of democracy and oligarchy, the testing of great leaders, the innovative military tactics, and the unprecedented human cost." Booklist

Includes bibliographical references

Thucydides; the reinvention of history. Viking 2009 257p map $26.95   **938**
1. Historians 2. Historiography 3. Greece -- Historiography 4. Greece -- Intellectual life -- To 146 B.C. 5. Greece -- History -- 431-404 B.C., Peloponnesian War 6. Greece -- History -- Peloponnesian War, 431-404 B.C.
ISBN 0670921296; 9780670021291
LC 2009-08368

Kagan argues that "The Peloponnesian War differs significantly from other accounts offered by Thucydides' contemporaries and stands as the first modern work of political history." (Publisher's note) Index.

"Kagan's utter mastery is on display in this vigorous, elegantly written, provocative book." PopMatters

Includes bibliographical references

★ The **Landmark** Xenophon's Hellenika; a new translation. translation by John Marincola; with maps, annotations, appendices, and encyclopedic index edited by Robert B. Strassler; with an introduction by David Thomas. Pantheon Books 2009 lxxxii, 579p il map $40 **938**

1. Greece -- History -- To 146 B.C. 2. Greece -- History -- 431-404 B.C., Peloponnesian War 3. Greece -- History -- Peloponnesian War, 431-404 B.C.

ISBN 9780375422553

LC 2009-20970

"The Hellenika is often messy: Athens and Sparta are the primary players, but Corinth and Thebes constantly jump into the fray, and Persia, Sparta's sometime ally, is always lurking at the periphery. All this can be confusing, and one of the more impressive things about the Landmark edition is how much it tries—and succeeds—in making the texts of ancient Greece accessible to contemporary audiences. The extensive footnotes are both informative and readable. . . . Side notes, meanwhile, offer a running plot summary, in case the casual reader neglects to follow, say, the hostilities between Agesilaos and Phleious. The maps generously sprinkled across these pages are uniformly clear, showing both battle maneuvers and shifting geopolitical alliances. And the appendix is a veritable treasure trove of secondary material." New Criterion

Includes bibliographical references and index

Lane Fox, Robin

The **classical** world; an epic history from Homer to Hadrian. Basic Books 2006 656p il map $35 **938**

1. Classical civilization 2. Rome -- Civilization 3. Greece -- Civilization

ISBN 978-0-465-02496-4; 0-465-02496-3

LC 2006-20247

First published 2005 in the United Kingdom

A "portrait of Greek and Roman culture over a period of roughly 900 years. Although he utilizes a broadly chronological approach, Fox goes well beyond the usual, dreary narrative of battles, dynastic changes, and political conflicts that often characterize surveys of the period. Instead, Fox focuses on the gradual development and transformation of various cultural aspects of Greek and Roman societies, and he discusses in often fascinating detail topics that are normally given short shrift in general histories." Booklist

The **Oxford** classical dictionary; general editors, Simon Hornblower and Antony Spawforth; assistant editor, Esther Eidinow. 4th ed; Oxford University Press 2012 lv, 1592 p **938**

1. Classical dictionaries 2. Classical civilization -- Dictionaries

ISBN 0199545561; 9780199545568

LC 2012009579

First published 1949 under the editorship of M. Cary and others

This reference book "offers nearly 1600 pages of entries that detail important topics of the Classical world from agriculture to war, social history to science, biography to religion. . . .Two focus areas are new to this edition: anthropology and reception, an area of study that examines how a Classical idea or concept affected various societies during different periods of history, depending on the context of the people reading the narrative, viewing the art . . . etc." (Library Journal)

"A scholarly dictionary, with signed articles, covering biography, literature, mythology, philosophy, religion, science, geography, etc. Most of the articles are brief, but there are some longer survey articles, e.g. Rome, music, scholarship, etc." Guide to Ref Books. 11th edition

Includes bibliographical references

Thucydides

The **landmark** Thucydides; a comprehensive guide to the Peloponnesian War. edited by Robert B. Strassler; introduction by Victor Davis Hanson. A newly revised edition of the Richard Crawley translation with maps, annotations, appendices, and e **938**

Free Press 1996 xxxiii,713 $45; pa $25

1. Greece -- History -- 431-404 B.C., Peloponnesian War

ISBN 978-1-416-59087-3; 0-684-82790-5

LC 96-24555

"Strassler, an unaffiliated scholar of classical studies, has remedied many of the flaws of Richard Crawley's 1874 translation of The Peloponnesian War. He has added descriptive paragraph-by-paragraph synopses, topic headers on every page, numerous maps keyed to the adjoining text, explanatory footnotes, an extensive index, an excellent introduction by Victor Davis Hanson . . . . and 11 appendixes (by various scholars) on politics, warfare, and society in the Greece of the fifth century B.C.E." Libr J

938.03 Persian Wars, 500-479 B.C.

Karnazes, Dean

The **legend** of Marathon; Reliving the Ancient Battle and Epic Run That Inspired the World's Greatest Footrace. by Dean Karnazes. St. Martin's Press 2016 304 p. $25.99 **938.03**

1. Marathon running 2. Democracy -- History 3. Sparta (Extinct city) 4. Marathon, Battle of, 490 B.C.

ISBN 1609614747; 9781609614744

This book, by Dean Karnazes, "is the story of the 153-mile run from Athens to Sparta that inspired the marathon and saved democracy. . . . In 490 BCE, Pheidippides ran for 36 hours straight from Athens to Sparta to seek help in defending Athens from a Persian invasion in the Battle of Marathon. In doing so, he saved the development of Western civilization and inspired the birth of the marathon as we know it." (Publisher's note)

"This is a remarkable and inspiring memoir that will have casual and serious runners cheering." Pub Wkly

939 Other parts of ancient world

★ **Civilizations** of the Ancient Near East; Jack M. Sasson, editor in chief; John Baines, Gary Beckman, Karen S. Rubinson, associate editors. Hendrickson Publishers 2000 4v in 2 il map set $169.95 **939**
1. Middle East -- Civilization
ISBN 1-56563-607-4

LC 00-63144

First published 1995 by Scribner

This "work concentrates on the Near East, broadly defined to include a region from Northeast Africa to India, Pakistan, and Burma, with principal focus on the core areas of Egypt, Syro-Palestine, Mesopotamia, and Anatolia. The time span ranges from the third millennium B.C.E., when writing was invented, to 330 B.C.E., when Alexander triumphed over the Persian Empire. The 189 contributors from five continents and 16 countries include some of the world's finest scholars." Libr J [review of 1995 edition]

Includes bibliographical references

Wood, Michael
In search of the Trojan War. University of Calif. Press 1998 288p il pa $19.95 **939**
1. Bronze Age 2. Trojan War 3. Troy (Extinct city) 4. Turkey -- Antiquities
ISBN 0-520-21599-0

LC 98-4958

First published 1985 by Facts on File

"This is a first-rate book. . . . The book makes a readable and clear approach to some of the knottiest problems of Bronze Age archaeology." Choice [review of 1985 edition]

Includes bibliographical references

940 History of Europe

Beyond Rosie; a documentary History of Women and World War II. edited by Julia Brock, Jennifer W. Dickey, Richard J. W. Harker. University of Arkansas Press 2015 245 p. (pbk. : alk. paper) $22.95 **940**
1. World War, 1939-1945 -- Women 2. World War, 1939-1945 -- United States
ISBN 9781557286697; 9781557286703; 9781610755573

LC 2014949011

This book, edited by Julia Brock, Jennifer W. Dickey, Richard Harker, and Catherine Lewis, "offers readers an opportunity to see the numerous contributions [women] made to the fight against the Axis powers and how American women's roles changed during the war. The primary documents (newspapers, propaganda posters, cartoons, excerpts from oral histories and memoirs, speeches, photographs, and editorials) collected here represent cultural, political, economic, and social perspectives on the diverse roles women played during World War II." (Publisher's note)

"The editors indicate that their intent in assembling this collection was to interest high-school history students and readers of wartime history, as well as students in universities supporting research in women's studies, history, and social-science disciplines. Summing Up: Recommended. All academic audiences; general readers." Choice

940.1 Europe--Early history to 1453

English, Edward D.
Encyclopedia of the medieval world. Facts on File 2004 2v il map (Facts on File library of world history) set $150 **940.1**
1. Reference books 2. Middle Ages -- Encyclopedias
ISBN 0-8160-4690-5

LC 2003-27825

This encyclopedia "covers the time period from the late antique world to about 1500 C.E and includes events, people, institutions, and culture in western and eastern Europe, Scandinavia, North Africa, Byzantium, and the Near East. The 2,000 entries discuss significant people, art, politics, literature, religion, economics, law, science, and warfare in an A-Z format." Booklist

Includes bibliographical references

Freeman, Charles
The **closing** of the Western mind; the rise of faith and the fall of reason. Knopf 2003 xxiii, 432p il map $32.50; pa $16.95 **940.1**
1. Hellenism 2. Western civilization 3. Europe -- Intellectual life 4. Europe -- History -- 476-1492 5. Church history -- 30-600, Early church
ISBN 1-400-04085-X; 1-400-03380-2 pa

LC 2002-44821

"This is one of the best books to date on the development of Christianity. . . . Beautifully written and impressively annotated, this is an indispensable read for anyone interested in the roots of Christianity and its implications for our modern worldview." Choice

Includes bibliographical references

Gies, Frances
Life in a medieval village; [by] Frances and Joseph Gies. Harper & Row 1990 257p il maps hardcover o.p. pa $14.95 **940.1**
1. Middle Ages 2. Medieval civilization
ISBN 0-06-016215-5; 0-06-092046-7 pa

LC 89-33759

"Elton, England, is the focal point of the authors' efforts to portray the everyday life and social structure of the High Middle Ages. After giving a brief summary of Elton's origins and development in the Roman and Anglo-Saxon periods, the book examines just how the residents lived and worked within the feudal structure at the beginning of the fourteenth century." Booklist

Includes bibliographical references

Gies, Joseph
Life in a medieval city; [by] Joseph and Frances Gies. HarperPerennial 1981 274p il map pa $13.95 **940.1**
1. Middle Ages 2. Medieval civilization
ISBN 0-06-090880-7

First published 1969 by Crowell

"A portrait of a medieval city [Troyes], a flourishing settlement of a type not known in Europe before the Middle Ages." Cincinnati Public Libr

Includes bibliographical references

Herlihy, David

The **black** death and the transformation of the west; edited and with an introduction by Samuel K. Cohn, Jr. Harvard Univ. Press 1997 117p hardcover o.p. pa $12 **940.1**

1. Plague 2. Renaissance 3. Medieval civilization 4. Europe -- History -- 476-1492

ISBN 0-674-07613-3 pa

LC 96-54637

These "essays redefine the historical study of the Black Death. . . . Herlihy's contention is that we can learn from this 'devastating natural disaster': for example, parallels can be drawn to today's pandemic of AIDS, especially in the resultant bigotries that both engendered. Cohn introduces the lectures, admirably setting the scene. This book, which opens a new chapter on the history and implications of the plague, is essential for all readers of medieval history." Libr J

Includes bibliographical references

Knights; in history and in legend. chief consultant Constance Brittain Bouchard. Firefly Books 2009 304p il map $40 **940.1**

1. Knights and knighthood 2. Military art and science -- History

ISBN 978-1-55407-480-8

The history of knights, from their everyday lives to their clothing, training, heraldry and orders, as well as their role in literature and film, and the decline of traditional knighthood.

"Aimed at history and art history lovers, this work would be excellent reading for medieval history enthusiasts and should be welcomed as a library reference resource." Libr J

Includes bibliographical references

The **New** Cambridge medieval history; edited by Paul Fouracre . . . [et al.] Cambridge Univ. Press 2005 7v in 8 il maps set $1600 **940.1**

1. Middle Ages 2. Medieval civilization

ISBN 978-0-521-85360-6; 0-521-85360-5

This set replaces the Cambridge medieval history, published 1929-1967

"An excellent reference history, written by specialists, with full bibliographies at the end of each volume." Guide to Ref Books. 11th edition [entry for Cambridge medieval history]

Pye, Michael

The **Edge** of the World; a cultural history of the North Sea and the transformation of Europe. by Michael Pye. W W Norton & Co Inc 2015 360 p. 8 plates; color ills., maps (hardcover) $27.95 **940.1**

1. North Sea 2. Europe -- History -- 476-1492

ISBN 1605986992; 9781605986999

This book, by Michael Pye, offers a history of Medieval cultural history "ranging from the terror of the Vikings to the golden age of cities. . . . Saints and spies, pirates and philosophers, artists and intellectuals: they all criss-crossed the grey North Sea in the so-called 'dark ages.' . . . Now the critically acclaimed Michael Pye reveals the cultural transformation sparked by those men and women." (Publisher's note)

"This said, for beginners desirous of a well-written and eclectic glimpse of the medieval period, this is a good book. Those more advanced in their studies will find the thesis and generalizations a bit overdone. Summing Up: Recommended. General readers/public libraries only." Choice

Reston, James

The **last** apocalypse; Europe at the year 1000 A.D. Doubleday 1998 299p il map hardcover o.p. pa $14.95 **940.1**

1. Europe -- History -- 476-1492

ISBN 0-385-48336-8 pa

LC 97-18812

"Reston's seemingly encyclopedic knowledge of the tenth century, combined with his disarming interpretations of the period's events, makes for fascinating reading." Booklist

Includes bibliographical references

Wickham, Chris

★ The **inheritance** of Rome; a history of Europe from 400 to 1000. Viking 2009 650p il map (The Penguin history of Europe) $35 **940.1**

1. Middle Ages 2. Medieval civilization 3. Rome -- Civilization

ISBN 978-0-670-02098-0

LC 2009-15169

"Wickham's achievement contributes richly to our picture of this often narrowly understood period." Publ Wkly

Includes bibliographical references

940.2 Europe--1453-

Adkin, Mark

The **Trafalgar** companion; a guide to history's most famous sea battle and the life of Admiral Lord Nelson. Aurum Press 2005 560p il map $75 **940.2**

1. Admirals 2. Trafalgar (Spain), Battle of, 1805

ISBN 1-84513-018-9

"Beginning with a prologue that describes the wounding and death of Vice-Admiral Horatio Nelson, the book introduces readers to the history of the campaign from 1802 to 1805 and to . . . information about the men and ships of the Royal Navy, in alternate chapters. . . . It will long stand as the definitive one-volume study of Great Britain's foremost naval hero and his times." Choice

Includes bibliographical references

Barbero, Alessandro

The **Battle**; a new history of Waterloo. Walker & Company 2005 340p il map $28; pa $16 **940.2**

1. Waterloo, Battle of, 1815

ISBN 0-8027-1453-6; 978-0-8027-1453-4; 0-8027-1500-1 pa; 978-0-8027-1500-5 pa

Original Italian edition, 2003

The author's "narrative flows smoothly, making readers feel part of the battle's events. The chapters are short—never more than a few pages—and they pull the reader along with the action." Choice

Includes bibliographical references (p. 318-324)

Barzun, Jacques

From dawn to decadence; 500 years of Western cultural life, 1500 to the present. HarperCollins Pubs. 2000 877p hardcover o.p. pa $20   **940.2**
1. Western civilization 2. Europe -- Civilization 3. Europe -- Intellectual life
ISBN 0-06-092883-2 pa

LC 99-16194

"Encyclopedic without being discontinuous, the book hardly seems as long, as carefully constructed or as densely packed as it is. Though the ideas it explains are often complicated, the explanations it offers are limpidly clear, sparkling with biographical anecdote and counter-canonical observations." N Y Times Book Rev

Includes bibliographical references

Blanning, T. C. W.

★ The pursuit of glory; Europe, 1648-1815. [by] Tim Blanning. Viking 2007 xxvii, 707p il map (The Penguin history of Europe) $39.95   **940.2**
1. Europe -- Civilization 2. Europe -- History -- 1492-1789 3. Europe -- History -- 1789-1815
ISBN 978-0-670-06320-8; 0-670-06320-7

LC 2006-37324

The author "thoroughly covers the politics and endless wars of the period. . . . 'The Pursuit of Glory' is history writing at its glorious best." N Y Times (Late N Y Ed)

Includes bibliographical references

Blom, Philipp, 1970-

The vertigo years; Europe 1900-1914. Basic Books 2008 466p il $29.95   **940.2**
1. Europe -- History -- 1871-1918 2. Europe -- History -- 20th century 3. Europe -- Civilization -- 20th century
ISBN 0-465-01116-0; 978-0-465-01116-2

LC 2008-935053

Blom examines the period between 1900 and the outbreak of the First World War, as cities grew, "education changed the outlook of millions; mass-produced items transformed daily life; industrial laborers demanded a share of political power; and women sought to change their place in society." (Publisher's note) Bibliography. Index.

"Blom's engrossing history begins with an invitation: 'Imagine yourself looking at the years 1900 to 1914 without the long shadows of the future darkening their historical present.' His imaginative recreation of this period argues that speed—both literal and figurative—came to typify and, ultimately, define modern life. This was the age that gave rise not only to Futurism and Vorticism but also to car racing and the electric chair. Precipitate change also ushered in an age of uncertainty and attraction to the seeming stability of the past. The book's strength is also its charm—a multifaceted, panoramic approach animated by vivacious narration of individual stories." New Yorker

Includes bibliographical references

Coote, Stephen

Napoleon and the Hundred Days. DaCapo Press 2005 308p il $27.50   **940.2**
1. Emperors 2. France -- History -- 1799-1815
ISBN 0-306-81408-0

LC 2004-65505

First published 2004 in the United Kingdom

This history "of the 100 days between Napoleon's escape from Elba and his capitulation after Waterloo uses the period as a lens through which to examine his character in general. . . . This accessible work is reminiscent of the finest classical Roman histories and biographies." Publ Wkly

Includes bibliographical references

Cornwell, Bernard, 1944-

Waterloo; The History of Four Days, Three Armies, and Three Battles. Bernard Cornwell. HarperCollins 2015 352 p. illustrations, maps, portraits $35   **940.2**
1. Waterloo, Battle of, 1815
ISBN 0062312057; 9780062312051

LC 2015487235

"In his first work of nonfiction, [author] Bernard Cornwell combines his storytelling skills with a meticulously researched history to give a . . . chronicle of every dramatic moment, from Napoleon's daring escape from Elba to the smoke and gore of the three battlefields and their aftermath." (Publisher's note)

Corrigan, Gordon

Waterloo; A New History. Gordon Corrigan. W W Norton & Co Inc 2014 341 p. 16 plates; color ills; map $28.95   **940.2**
1. Waterloo, Battle of, 1815
ISBN 1605986526; 9781605986524

LC 2014407633

This book, by historian Gordon Corrigan, focuses on the Battle of Waterloo. "Fought on Sunday, June 18th, 1815, by some 220,000 men over rain-sodden ground in what is now Belgium, [it] brought an end to twenty-three years of almost continual war between imperial France and her enemies. A decisive defeat for Napoleon and a hard-won victory for the Allied armies of the Duke of Wellington and the Prussians, led by the stalwart Marshal Blucher, it brought about the French emperor's final exile." (Publisher's note)

"Those interested in military history, particularly that of England or France, will love the detail in this volume. Corrigan keeps things exciting by blending his own brand of wit with historical fact." LJ

Includes bibliographical references (pages 327-329) and index

Crane, David, 1942-

Went the day well? witnessing Waterloo. by David Crane. Alfred A. Knopf 2015 384 p. 24 plates; illustrations; maps (hardback) $30   **940.2**
1. War and civilization 2. Waterloo, Battle of, 1815 3. England -- History, Military -- 19th century -- Sources 4. England -- Social conditions -- 19th century -- Sources 5. War and society -- England -- History -- 19th century -- Sources 6. Waterloo, Battle of, Waterloo, Belgium, 1815 -- Personal narratives, British 7. Waterloo, Battle of, Waterloo, Belgium, 1815 -- Social aspects -- England -- Sources
ISBN 0307594920; 9780307594921

LC 2014044143

This book, by by David Crane, offers an "hour-by-hour chronicle that starts the day before the battle [of Waterloo]

that reset the course of world history and continues to its aftermath. Switching perspectives between Britain and Belgium, prison and palace, poet and pauper, lover and betrothed, husband and wife, David Crane paints a picture of Britain as it was that summer when everything changed." (Publisher's note)

"History buffs will relish both of these works. Readers should also consider Brendan Simms's The Longest Afternoon." LJ

Includes bibliographical references and index

Esdaile, Charles J.

Napoleon's wars; an international history, 1803-1815. [by] Charles Esdaile. Viking 2008 621p il map $35   940.2

1. Emperors 2. Europe -- History -- 1789-1815 3. France -- History -- 1799-1815

ISBN 978-0-670-02030-0; 0-670-02030-3

First published 2007 in the United Kingdom

"Recapturing the flux of international diplomacy and Napoléon's congenital rejection of compromise, Esdaile persuasively places the diplomatic foundation to popular military histories about the Napoleonic wars." Booklist

Includes bibliographical references (p. 567-602)

Europe 1789 to 1914: encyclopedia of the age of industry and empire. Merriman and Jay Winter, editors in chief. Charles Scribner's Sons 2006 5v il map (Scribner library of modern Europe) set $595   940.2

1. Reference books 2. Europe -- Civilization -- Encyclopedias 3. Europe -- History -- 1789-1900 -- Encyclopedias 4. Europe -- History -- 1871-1918 -- Encyclopedias

ISBN 0-684-31359-6; 978-0-684-31359-7

LC 2006-7335

This encyclopedia covers "the time period between the onset of the French Revolution to the outbreak of World War I." Publisher's note

Includes bibliographical references

Gies, Joseph

Life in a medieval castle; [by] Joseph and Frances Gies. Harper & Row 1979 272p il pa $14.95 940.2

1. Castles 2. Feudalism 3. Middle Ages 4. Knights and knighthood 5. Hunting -- Great Britain

ISBN 0-06-090674-X

LC 79-103901

First published 1974 by Crowell

Using Chepstow Castle on the Welsh border as a model, the authors provide "descriptions of the medieval world where the castle was household, feudal center, and military target, and by concentrating on Anglo-Norman examples illustrate what existence was like as the dark ages began to brighten." Booklist

Includes glossary and bibliographical references

Grayling, A. C.

★ The **Age** of Genius; The Seventeenth Century and the Birth of the Modern Mind. by A. C. Grayling.

St. Martin's Press 2016 368 p. illustrations, map, portraits $30   940.2

1. Europe -- Intellectual life 2. Europe -- History -- 17th century

ISBN 1620403447; 9781620403440

This book, by A. C. Grayling, "explores . . . the story of the 17th century in Europe. . . . Grayling vividly reconstructs this unprecedented era and breathes new life into the major figures of the seventeenth century intelligentsia who span literature, music, science, art, and philosophy--Shakespeare, Monteverdi, Galileo, Rembrandt, Locke, Newton, Descartes, Vermeer, Hobbes, Milton, and Cervantes, among many more." (Publisher's note)

"Grayling does a fantastic job of proving his assertion that the 17th century saw a dramatic shift in Western thought. Readers with an interest in the history of philosophy and scientific discovery will enjoy this highly engaging book." LJ

Greenblatt, Stephen

★ The **swerve**; [by] Stephen Greenblatt. W.W. Norton 2011 356p il $26.95   940.2

1. Poets 2. Renaissance 3. Philosophers 4. Modern civilization 5. Civilization, Modern 6. Science, Renaissance 7. Philosophy, Renaissance

ISBN 0393064476; 9780393064476

LC 2011019765

National Book Award: Nonfiction (2011)

Pulitzer Prize: General Nonfiction (2012)

The book presents a history of the "ancient Roman philosophical epic, On the Nature of Things, by Lucretius - a beautiful poem of the most dangerous ideas: that the universe functioned without the aid of gods, that religious fear was damaging to human life, and that matter was made up of very small particles in eternal motion, colliding and swerving in new directions." According to the author, "the copying and translation of this ancient book—the greatest discovery of the greatest book-hunter of his age—fueled the Renaissance, inspiring artists such as Botticelli and thinkers such as Giordano Bruno; shaped the thought of Galileo and Freud, Darwin and Einstein; and had a revolutionary influence on writers such as Montaigne and Shakespeare and even Thomas Jefferson." (Publisher's note)

"A fascinating, intelligent look at what may well be the most historically resonant book-hunt of all time." Booklist

Includes bibliographical references (p. [309]-335) and index.

Hobsbawm, E. J.

The **age** of revolution 1789-1848. Vintage Books 1996 356p il map pa $15.95   940.2

1. Industries -- History 2. Europe -- History -- 1789-1900

ISBN 978-0-679-77253-8; 0-679-77253-7

First published 1962 by World Pub. Co.

"This book traces the transformation of the world between 1789 and 1848 insofar as it was due to what is here called the 'dual revolution'—the French Revolution of 1789 and the contemporaneous (British) Industrial Revolution." Preface

Includes bibliographical references

King, David

Vienna, 1814; how the conquerors of Napoleon made love, war, and peace at the Congress of Vienna. Harmony Books 2008 434p il $27.50   **940.2**
1. Congress of Vienna (1814-1815) 2. Europe -- History -- 1789-1815 3. Europe -- Politics and government
ISBN 978-0-307-33716-0; 0-307-33716-2

LC 2007-24680

"The conquerors of Napoleon were in a festive mood when they met in Vienna in the fall of 1814 to decide the fate of Europe. . . . [The author] does a superb job of evoking the bedazzling social scene that served as the backdrop to the Congress of Vienna. His characterizations of such luminaries as Czar Alexander, Metternich, Talleyrand, and Castlereagh are lucid and thoroughly grounded in primary sources. . . . This is a worthy contribution to the study of a critical historical event long neglected by historians." Libr J
Includes bibliographical references

Lieven, D. C. B.

Russia against Napoleon; the true story of the campaigns of War and Peace. [by] Dominic Lieven. Viking 2010 617p il map $35.95   **940.2**
1. Emperors 2. Russia -- History 3. Europe -- History -- 1789-1815 4. Napoleonic Wars, 1800-1815 -- Campaigns -- Russia
ISBN 978-0-670-02157-4

LC 2009-42564

First published 2009 in the United Kingdom

"Lieven's book is lucid, engaging and reflects his deep love for Russia. This is a fascinating, exhaustively researched work, an elegant handling of a welter of confusing sources and a vital account of Russia from 1807 to 1814 that is unlikely to be bettered." Hist Today
Includes bibliographical references

Manchester, William

A **world** lit only by fire; the medieval mind and the Renaissance: portrait of an age. Little, Brown 1992 318p il maps hardcover o.p. pa $15.95 **940.2**
1. Explorers 2. Renaissance
ISBN 0-316-54556-2 pa

LC 91-39928

The author covers "the tumultuous span from the Dark Ages to the dawn of the Renaissance. He delineates an age when invisible spirits infested the air, when tolerance was seen as treachery and 'a mafia of profane popes desecrated Christianity.' Besides re-creating the arduous lives of ordinary people, . . . {Manchester} peoples his tapestry with such figures as Leonardo, Machiavelli, Lucrezia Borgia, Erasmus, Luther, Henry VIII and Anne Boleyn." Publ Wkly
Includes bibliographical references

Mostert, Noel

The **line** upon a wind; the great war at sea, 1793-1815. W.W. Norton & Co. 2008 xxv, 774p il map $35   **940.2**
1. Naval history 2. Seafaring life 3. Europe -- History -- 1789-1900 4. France -- History -- 1799-1815
ISBN 978-0-393-06653-1; 0-393-06653-3

LC 2007-39313

First published 2007 in the United Kingdom

"This is a vast, fast-moving chronicle that ranges across great distances while examining a host of characters, both well known and relatively obscure. Mostert does justifiably place great emphasis on Admiral Nelson and the critical battle at Trafalgar. He also offers useful and interesting descriptions of less-prominent aspects of the wars, including conflicts with the Barbary pirates and the British struggles against the rise of American naval power. This is an outstanding survey of a prolonged struggle that helped shape world history." Booklist
Includes bibliographical references (p. 748-752)

O'Brien, Michael

Mrs. Adams in winter; a journey in the last days of Napoleon. Farrar, Straus and Giroux 2010 364p il map $27   **940.2**
1. Presidents 2. Senators 3. Members of Congress 4. Secretaries of state 5. Spouses of presidents 6. Europe -- History -- 1789-1815 7. Europe -- Description and travel
ISBN 978-0-374-21581-1; 0-374-21581-2

LC 2009-25437

The author "pursues Louisa Adams's 40-day trek through a Europe in the process of transformation. The Mrs. Adams in question is not to be confused with Abigail Adams, the Colonial matriarch and wife of the second president. Rather, Louisa Catherine Adams was her London-born daughter-in-law, the wife to Abigail's son John Quincy Adams. . . . O'Brien's narrative is richly contextual, encompassing not only the great personalities of the age, whom Mrs. Adams met, but penetrating the secrets of a complicated marriage. A wide-sweeping historical survey and original intellectual journey." Kirkus
Includes bibliographical references

O'Keeffe, Paul

Waterloo; The Aftermath. by Paul O'Keeffe. Penguin Group USA 2014 400 p. $37.50   **940.2**
1. Waterloo, Battle of, 1815
ISBN 1468311301; 9781468311303

LC 2015010800

This book moves "from the horrors of the battlefield [at Waterloo] to the drawing rooms of London and Paris, from Napoleon's retreat and surrender to British triumph and celebration. . . . [Author] Paul O'Keeffe employs a multiplicity of contemporary sources and viewpoints to create a reading experience that brings the sights, sounds and smells of the battlefield, of conquest and defeat, of celebration and riot, into focus as never before." (Publisher's note)

Pagden, Anthony

The **Enlightenment;** and why it still matters. Anthony Pagden. 1st ed. Random House 2013 xx, 501 p.p ill. (ebook) $85.00; (hardcover) $30.00 **940.2**
1. Enlightenment
ISBN 1400060680; 9780679645313; 9781400060689

LC 2012043848

This book, by Anthony Pagden, "takes a fresh look at the revolutionary intellectual movement that laid the foundation for the modern world. Liberty and equality. Human rights. Freedom of thought and expression. Belief in reason and progress. The value of scientific inquiry. These are just some of the ideas that were conceived and developed during the Enlightenment, and which changed forever the intellectual landscape of the Western world." (Publisher's note)

Includes bibliographical references (pages 417-480) and index

Pocock, Tom

The **terror** before Trafalgar; Nelson, Napoleon and the secret war. Naval Institute Press 2005 255p il map pa $16.95 **940.2**

1. Admirals 2. Emperors 3. Europe -- History -- 1789-1815

ISBN 978-1-5911-4681-0; 1-5911-4681-X

LC 2004-58185

First published 2003 by Norton

The author "retells the story of the four years in which the French confidently prepared to invade Britain, overrun its army, take out its armaments and replace the government with something easier to control. . . . Pocock's little book . . . gives a chilling insight into ineffectual undercover operations and groundbreaking weaponry: rockets, torpedos, submarines, airships and the construction of an undersea tunnel, all so far ahead of their time that none turned out in the end to be much use in practical terms to either side." N Y Times Book Rev

Includes bibliographical references

Renaissance Society of America

Encyclopedia of the Renaissance; Paul F. Grendler, editor in chief. Scribner 1999 6v set $750 **940.2**

1. Reference books 2. Renaissance -- Encyclopedias

ISBN 0-684-80514-6

LC 99-48290

ALA RUSA Dartmouth Medal (2000)

This set covers "aspects of the Renaissance from the origins of humanism in Italy (ca. 1350) through 1750. . . . The encyclopedia's strength lies in its scholarship and in the comprehensiveness and diversity of its scope." Booklist

Reston, James

Defenders of the faith; Charles V, Suleyman the Magnificent, and the battle for Europe, 1520-1536. Penguin Press 2009 xxi, 407p il map $29.95 **940.2**

1. Emperors 2. Holy Roman Empire 3. Sultans 4. Turkey -- History -- Ottoman Empire, 1288-1918

ISBN 978-1-59420-225-4

LC 2008-54655

"Fast-paced and engaging, this is excellent reading for popular audiences." Libr J

Includes bibliographical references

Roberts, Andrew

Waterloo: June 18, 1815; the battle for modern Europe. HarperCollins 2005 143p il maps (Making history) $21.95; pa $12.95 **940.2**

1. Waterloo, Battle of, 1815

ISBN 0-06-008866-4; 0-06-076215-2 pa

LC 2005-282517

This is a study of the defeat of Napoleon's army at the Battle of Waterloo in June, 1815.

The author "instills an appreciation for Waterloo as a horrific experience saturated with alternative possible outcomes. A must for the military shelf." Booklist

Includes bibliographical references (p. 135-136)

Simms, Brendan

The **longest** afternoon; the 400 men who decided the Battle of Waterloo. Basic Books 2015 186 p. maps $24.99 **940.2**

1. Waterloo, Battle of, 1815

ISBN 0465064825; 9780465064823

LC 2015451024

This book on the Battle of Waterloo by Brendan Simms presents an "account of the bloody, heroic defense of La Haye Sainte, a farmhouse that Napoleon had to capture to reach the Duke of Wellington's army. The massive stone building survives intact; not so its defenders, a battle-tested unit of the British army." (Kirkus Reviews)

"This thoroughly engrossing account will thrill all history lovers." LJ

Talty, Stephan

The **illustrious** dead; the terrifying story of how typhus killed Napoleon's greatest army. Crown Publishers 2009 315p map $27 **940.2**

1. Typhus 2. Emperors 3. Europe -- History -- 1789-1815 4. France -- History -- 1799-1815

ISBN 978-0-307-39404-0

LC 2008-50646

"Talty delivers a breezy, popular account of a gruesome campaign, emphasizing the equally gruesome epidemic that accompanied it." Publ Wkly

Includes bibliographical references

Wells, C. M.

Sailing from Byzantium; how a lost empire shaped the world. Colin Wells. Delacorte Press 2006 xxx, 335p map $22 **940.2**

1. Byzantine Empire

ISBN 0-553-80381-6

LC 2006-42665

The author "considers how Byzantium, the Eastern, Greek-language Roman Empire of the Middle Ages, influenced three successor civilizations Western Europe, Islam, and the eastern Slavic world of the Balkans and Russia. . . . This history is a needed reminder of the debt that three of our major civilizations owe to Byzantium." Libr J

Includes bibliographical references

Wilson, Ellen Judy

★ **Encyclopedia** of the Enlightenment; Peter Hanns Reill, consulting editor; Ellen Judy Wilson, principal author. rev ed; Facts on File 2004 670p $75 **940.2**

1. Reference books 2. Europe -- Intellectual life 3. Philosophy -- Encyclopedias 4. Enlightenment -- Encyclopedias

ISBN 0-8160-5335-9

LC 2003-22973

First published 1996

This reference provides a "review of the important ideas, people, and events that shaped the world during the Enlightenment. [It] covers the major changes in science, education, philosophy, art and architecture, and politics which took place during the 17th and 18th centuries and led to the birth of the modern era. . . . The biographical entries cover such notables as Robespierre, Schiller, Fielding, Kant, and Voltaire. . . . Larger public, school, and academic libraries looking for a comprehensive overview of the subject for the student or interested reader will find this a valuable and accessible resource." Libr J

Includes bibliographical references

Wilson, Peter H.
The **Thirty** Years War; Europe's tragedy. Belknap Press of Harvard University Press 2009 xxii, 996p il map $35   **940.2**
1. Thirty Years' War, 1618-1648
ISBN 978-0-674-03634-5

LC 2009-11266
This "is a history of prodigious erudition that manages to corral the byzantine complexity of the Thirty Years War into a coherent narrative." Wall Street J

Includes bibliographical references

Zamoyski, Adam
Rites of peace; the fall of Napoleon and the Congress of Vienna. HarperColins 2007 634p il map $29.95   **940.2**
1. Congress of Vienna (1814-1815) 2. Europe -- History -- 1789-1815
ISBN 0-06-077518-1; 978-0-06-077518-6

This "book is old-fashioned, impressively detailed diplomatic history." Economist

Includes bibliographical references

940.3   World War I, 1914-1918

Audoin-Rouzeau, Stephane
14-18, understanding the Great War; {by} Stéphane Audoin-Rouzeau and Annette Becker; translated from the French by Catherine Temerson. Hill & Wang 2002 280p $24; pa $14   **940.3**
1. World War, 1914-1918
ISBN 0-8090-4642-3; 0-8090-4643-1 pa
LC 2002-111422
Original French edition, 2000
"The authors take an anthropological approach to the cataclysm that engulfed Europe in 1914 and examine three significant aspects of the war: violence, crusade, and mourning. . . . Supported by contemporary documentation, this unique work will become a classic study." Libr J

Includes bibliographical references

Burg, David F.
Almanac of World War I; [by] David F. Burg and L. Edward Purcell; introduction by William Manchester. University Press of Ky. 1998 320p il maps hardcover o.p. pa $22   **940.3**
1. World War, 1914-1918
ISBN 0-8131-2072-1; 0-8131-9087-8 pa;

9780813190877

LC 98-26625
"The bulk of the text is arranged chronologically by year and date, listing almost daily occurrences from 1914 through 1918. . . . The work is international in scope, covering political and military happenings from around the world. . . . There is really nothing comparable to this volume." Booklist

Includes bibliographical references

Carter, Miranda
George, Nicholas, and Wilhelm; three royal cousins and the road to World War I. Alfred A. Knopf 2010 498p il map $30   **940.3**
1. Emperors 2. Kings 3. Biography, Individual 4. World War, 1914-1918 -- Causes 5. Europe -- Politics and government -- 1871-1918
ISBN 978-1-4000-4363-7; 1-4000-4363-8

LC 2009-37690
First published 2009 in the United Kingdom with title: The three emperors

In the years before World War I, the great European powers were ruled by three first cousins: King George V, Kaiser Wilhelm II, and Tsar Nicholas II. Carter uses the cousins' correspondence and a host of historical sources to tell their tragicomic stories.

The author "writes with lusty humour at times, has a fresh clarifying intelligence when unravelling knotty problems of ancien régime life and a sharp eye for telling details about people's gestures, temper, appearance and attitudes. . . . This is traditional narrative history with a 21st-century zing—a real corker of a book." Hist Today

Includes bibliographical references

Clark, Christopher
The **sleepwalkers**; how Europe went to war in 1914. Christopher Clark. Harper 2013 697 p. $29.99   **940.3**
1. Europe -- History -- 1871-1918 2. World War, 1914-1918 -- Causes 3. World War, 1914-1918 -- Diplomatic history 4. Europe -- Politics and government -- 1871-1918
ISBN 006114665X; 9780061146657

LC 2012038473
In this book on the origins of World War I, author Christopher Clark "posits a bad brew of diplomatic contingencies and individual agency as the cause. . . . Clark . . . begins by describing the interactions of Serbia and Austria-Hungary, which sparked the conflict. He presents the former as a 'raw and fragile democracy' whose 'turbulent' politics challenged a neighboring empire held together by habit. Indeed, the instability across Europe further polarized alliance networks." (Publishers Weekly)

Includes bibliographical references and index

The **Encyclopedia** of World War I; a political, social, and military history. ABC-CLIO 2005 5v il map set $485   **940.3**
1. Reference books 2. World War, 1914-1918 -- Encyclopedias
ISBN 1-85109-420-2

LC 2005-22937

This set opens with "four essays discussing the origins, outbreak, overview, and legacy of the war. They are followed by alphabetical entries on virtually every aspect of the conflict, including battles, people, military equipment and strategies, and social and political changes associated with it." SLJ

Includes bibliographical references

Englund, Peter

★ The **beauty** and the sorrow; an intimate history of the First World War. translated by Peter Graves. Alfred A. Knopf 2011 540p il $35   **940.3**

1. World War, 1914-1918 -- Personal narratives
ISBN 978-0-307-59386-3; 0-307-59386-X
    LC 2011-20828

Original Swedish edition, 2009

This work "threads together the wartime experiences of 20 more or less unremarkable men and women, on both sides of the war, from schoolgirls and botanists to mountain climbers, doctors, ambulance drivers and clerks. A few of these people will become heroes. A few will become prisoners of war, or lose limbs, go mad or die. . . . Mr. Englund's book is a deviation from standard history books. It is a corrective too to the notion that World War I was only about the dire trench warfare on the Western Front. . . . [It] expertly pans across other theaters of war: the Alps, the Balkans, the Eastern Front, Mesopotamia, East Africa." N Y Times Book Rev

Includes bibliographical references

Gilbert, Martin

The **First** World War; a complete history. Holt & Co. 1994 xxiv, 615p il maps hardcover o.p. pa $25   **940.3**

1. World War, 1914-1918
ISBN 0-8050-1540-X; 0-8050-7617-4 pa
    LC 94-27268

"What Mr. Gilbert seeks to do, and frequently succeeds in doing, is to humanize, indeed to personalize, World War I. His effort and accomplishment make this a rewarding and significant book." N Y Times Book Rev

Includes bibliographical references

Grant, R. G.

World War I; The Definitive Visual History : from Sarajevo to Versailles. R. G. Grant. Dk Pub. 2014 360 p. ill. (some color), color maps $40 **940.3**

1. Weapons -- History 2. World War, 1914-1918
ISBN 1465419381; 9781465419385
    LC 2013387827

"Written by historian R. G. Grant, and created by DK's award-winning editorial and design team, World War I charts the . . . war. . . . Using illustrated timelines, detailed maps, and personal accounts, readers will see the oft-studied war in a new light. Key episodes are set clearly in the wider context of the conflict, in-depth profiles look at the key generals and political leaders, and full-color photo galleries showcase . . . weapons, inventions, and new technologies." (Publisher's note)

"This is a broad, moving, informative account of the war that's perfect for both the young, budding historian and the well-versed WWI reader." Pub Wkly

Hastings, Max

Catastrophe 1914; Europe goes to war. by Max Hastings. Alfred A. Knopf 2013 672 p. (hardback) $35   **940.3**

1. Europe -- History -- 1871-1918 2. World War, 1914-1918 -- Causes 3. Europe -- History -- July Crisis, 1914
ISBN 0307597059; 9780307597052; 9780307743831
    LC 2013027865

Author Max Hastings "traces the path to [World War I] making clear why Germany and Austria-Hungary were primarily to blame, and describes the gripping first clashes in the West, where the French army marched into action. Hastings gives us frank assessments of generals and political leaders. He argues passionately against the contention that the war was not worth the cost, maintaining that Germany's defeat was vital to the freedom of Europe." (Publisher's note)

Readers accustomed to Hastings' vivid battle descriptions, incisive anecdotes from all participants, and shrewd, often unsettling opinions will not be disappointed. Among the plethora of brilliant accounts of this period, this is one of the best." (Kirkus)

Includes bibliographical references (pages 595-603) and index

Hochschild, Adam

To end all wars; a story of loyalty and rebellion, 1914-1918. Houghton Mifflin Harcourt 2011 xx, 448p map $28; ebook $28   **940.3**

1. Pacifism 2. Soldiers -- Great Britain 3. World War, 1914-1918 -- Great Britain 4. World War, 1914-1918 -- Social aspects 5. World War, 1914-1918 -- Psychological aspects 6. World War, 1914-1918 -- Conscientious objectors
ISBN 978-0-618-75828-9; 0-618-75828-3; 978-0-54754-921-7 ebook; 0-54754-921-0 ebook
    LC 2010-25836

"An ambitious narrative that presents a teeming worldview through intimate, human portraits." Kirkus

Includes bibliographical references=

Hughes-Wilson, John

The **First** World War in 100 objects; by John Hughes-Wilson. Firefly Books Ltd 2014 448 p. color illustrations; maps $39.95   **940.3**

1. World War, 1914-1918
ISBN 1770854134; 9781770854130

This book, by John Hughes-Wilson, "draws on the most interesting 100 items that describe the causes, progress and outcome of the First World War. From weapons that created carnage to affectionate letters home, these 100 objects are as extraordinary in their diversity and storytelling power as they are devastating in their poignancy. This is the stuff of war at its most horrible." (Publisher's note)

"The text packs in an impressive amount of detail, making it seem fussy at times, but the explanations of facts and events are always clear. Altogether, this is a stunning read that is exciting in its depth, scope and personal feel. After seeing and reading about objects touched, used, cherished and hated by those who experienced the war, it will be impossible not to gain a greater understanding and appreciation of the struggle that 'truly... still shapes the world in which we live.'" Pub Wkly

MacMillan, Margaret

Paris 1919; six months that changed the world. Random House 2002 560p $35; pa $16.95 **940.3**
1. Governors 2. Presidents 3. College presidents 4. Treaty of Versailles 5. Nobel laureates for peace 6. World War, 1914-1918 -- Peace 7. Germany -- History -- 1918-1933 8. Paris Peace Conference (1919-1920)
ISBN 0-375-50826-0; 0-375-76052-0 pa
LC 2002-23707
First published 2001 in the United Kingdom with title: Peacemakers

The author examines the Paris Peace Conference of 1919. Economist John Maynard Keynes blamed "the failure of the conference on the vindictiveness of the French in general and of Clemenceau in particular. Margaret MacMillan . . . argues that the conference has been blamed for many disasters that were, in fact, determined either by events that took place before it began or by later troubles." (Economist) Index.

"MacMillan's lucid prose brings her participants to colorful and quotable life, and the grand sweep of her narrative encompasses all the continents the peacemakers vainly carved up." Publ Wkly

Includes bibliographical references

McMeekin, Sean

★ The **Berlin**-Baghdad express; the Ottoman Empire and Germany's bid for world power. The Belknap Press of Harvard University Press 2010 460p il map **940.3**
1. Jihad 2. Railroads 3. Geopolitics 4. World War, 1914-1918 5. Germany -- Foreign relations -- Turkey 6. Turkey -- Foreign relations -- Germany
ISBN 0-0674-05739-2; 978-0-674-05739-5
LC 2010019199
"Germany saw the ambitious Berlin-to-Baghdad railway as a powerful tool to win World War I. But the doomed project wasn't completed until 1940. The railway debacle provides a colorful backdrop for historian McMeekin's look at the Great War from the German-Turk perspective; as a cast of ruthless characters illustrate Germany's attempt to topple what was then the largest Middle East power: the British Empire." N Y Post

Includes bibliographical references

★ **July** 1914; countdown to war. Sean McMeekin. Basic Books, a member of the Perseus Books Group 2013 xviii, 461 p.p ill. (hardcover) $29.99 **940.3**
1. Austria -- History 2. World War, 1914-1918 -- Causes 3. Europe -- History -- July Crisis, 1914
ISBN 0465031455; 9780465031450
LC 2012049777
This book is a "political history of the weeks between the assassination of Austria's Archduke Franz Ferdinand and the beginning of World War I. . . . Relying on extensive research in numerous archives, as well as diaries and correspondence from key national leaders, [Sean] McMeekin

examines the intricacies of Austrian politics and diplomacy." (Publishers Weekly)

Includes bibliographical references and index.

Slotkin, Richard, 1942-

Lost battalions; the Great War and the crisis of American nationality. Richard Slotkin. H. Holt 2005 639p il maps **940.3**
1. African American soldiers 2. Minorities -- United States 3. United States -- Ethnic relations 4. African American soldiers -- History 5. World War, 1914-1918 -- United States 6. World War, 1914-1918 -- Regimental histories 7. United States -- Army -- Infantry Regiment, 369th 8. World War, 1914-1918 -- Participation, African American 9. World War, 1914-1918 -- Regimental histories -- United States 10. United States -- Army -- Infantry Division, 77th -- Joint Assault Signal Company, 292nd
ISBN 0-8050-4124-9
LC 2005-46312
Slotkin "follows the Negro soldiers of the 369th and the Jewish, Italian, and other immigrants of the 77th into conflict." (Publisher's note) Index.

This is a "history of the African-American 369th Infantry, known as the 'Harlem Hellfighters,' and the 77th Division, dubbed the 'Melting Pot' for its ranks of Italians, Jews and other eastern Europeans. . . . Slotkin smoothly telescopes from the trenches to the political and social implications for decades to come in this insightful, valuable account." Publ Wkly

Stone, Norman

★ **World** War One. Basic Books 2009 226p il map $25 **940.3**
1. World War, 1914-1918
ISBN 978-0-465-01368-5; 0-465-01368-6
First published 2007 in the United Kingdom
The author presents a narrative history of the First World War.

"Stone is as unconventional as he is brilliant, and this provocative interpretation of the Great War combines impressive command of the literature with a telling eye for relevant facts and a sensitive ear for telling epigrams." Publ Wkly

Includes bibliographical references

Strachan, Hew

The **First** World War. Viking 2004 364p il maps hardcover o.p. pa $16 **940.3**
1. World War, 1914-1918
ISBN 0-14-303518-5 pa; 0-670-03295-6
LC 2003-62191
This book examines "the causes, the major campaigns, and the consequences of the First World War." (Publisher's note) Index.

"Readers already familiar with the sequence of events in strict order will benefit most. But all readers will eventually be gripped, and even the most seasoned ones will praise the insights and the original choice of illustrations." Publ Wkly

Includes bibliographical references

Tooze, Adam

★ The **deluge**; the Great War and the remaking of global order, 1916-1931. Adam Tooze. Viking Adult 2014 672 p. illustrations, maps (hardback) $40 **940.3**

1. World politics 2. Economic conditions 3. World War, 1914-1918 -- Influence 4. Balance of power 5. World politics -- 1919-1932 6. International relations -- History -- 20th century

ISBN 0670024929; 9780670024926

LC 2014005314

Los Angeles Times Book Prize: History (2014)

This book, by Adam Tooze, is an "analysis of the First World War and its anguished aftermath. . . . [The author] revisits this seismic moment in history, challenging the existing narrative of the war, its peace, and its aftereffects. From the day the United States enters the war in 1917 to the precipice of global financial ruin, Tooze delineates the world remade by American economic and military power." (Publisher's note)

"Tooze's grand economic history is stimulating, persuasive, and surprisingly accessible." Pub Wkly

Includes bibliographical references and index

Tuchman, Barbara Wertheim

★ The **guns** of August; [by] Barbara W. Tuchman; [with a new foreword by Robert K. Massie] 1st Ballantine Books ed; Ballantine 1994 xxiv, 511p il, maps pa $14 **940.3**

1. World War, 1914-1918

ISBN 0-345-38623-X

LC 93-90461

First published 1962 by Macmillan

A history of the negotiations that preceded World War I and the course of the war's first month.

Includes bibliographical references

The **Zimmermann** telegram. Ballantine Books 1985 244p il pa $14 **940.3**

1. World War, 1914-1918 -- Causes

ISBN 0-345-32425-0

LC 84-91737

First published 1958 by Macmillan

The author discusses the German plan to induce Mexico to attack the U.S. during World War I.

Includes bibliographical references

The **United** States in the First World War; an encyclopedia. editor, Anne Cipriano Venzon; consulting editor, Paul L. Miles. Garland 1995 xx, 830p maps (Garland reference library of the humanities) $155; pa $45 **940.3**

1. Reference books 2. World War, 1914-1918 -- Encyclopedias

ISBN 0-8240-7055-0; 0-8153-3353-6 pa

LC 95-1782

"Biography, economics, civil rights, women's issues, foreign relations, battles, armaments, and conferences are among the topics included. Arrangement is alphabetical, and most articles are brief—between one column and a page. .

. . Most articles include brief bibliographies. There are six maps, but no other illustrations." Libr J

Woodward, David R.

World War I almanac. Facts On File 2009 554p il map (Almanacs of American wars) $95 **940.3**

1. Almanacs 2. Reference books 3. World War, 1914-1918

ISBN 978-0-8160-7134-0; 978-1-4381-1896-3 ebook

LC 2008-41575

This book "would be a welcome addition to public, school, and academic libraries where a student needs to find basic information quickly." Booklist

Includes glossary and bibliographical references

940.4 Military history of World War I

Anderson, Scott, 1959-

Lawrence in Arabia; war, deceit, imperial folly and the making of the modern Middle East. Scott Anderson. Doubleday 2013 592 p. $28.95 **940.4**

1. Middle East -- History 2. Great Britain. Army -- Biography 3. Middle East -- History -- 1914-1923 4. Soldiers -- Great Britain -- Biography 5. World War, 1914-1918 -- Campaigns -- Turkey 6. World War, 1914-1918 -- Campaigns -- Middle East

ISBN 038553292X; 9780385532921

LC 2012049719

In this biography of Lawrence of Arabia, Scott Anderson "reasons that 'Lawrence was both eyewitness to and participant in some of the most pivotal events leading to the creation of the modern Middle East . . . a corner of the earth where even the simplest assertion is dissected and parsed and argued over.' Too many biographers of Lawrence, he suggests, have let political biases and academic hobbyhorses overshadow their work." (Publishers Weekly)

Includes bibliographical references

Davenport, Matthew J.

First over there; the attack on Cantigny, America's first battle of World War I. Matthew J. Davenport. Thomas Dunne Books/St. Martin's Press 2015 384 p. illustrations, maps (hardcover) $28.99 **940.4**

1. World War, 1914-1918 -- United States 2. World War, 1914-1918 -- Campaigns -- France 3. Cantigny, Battle of, Cantigny, France, 1918 4. United States. Army. Infantry Division, 1st

ISBN 1250056446; 9781250056443

LC 2015012154

This book, by Matthew J. Davenport, tells the "true story of America's first modern military battle, its first military victory during World War One, and its first steps onto the world stage. At first light on Tuesday, May 28th, 1918, waves of American riflemen from the U.S. Army's 1st Division climbed from their trenches, charged across the shell-scarred French dirt of no-man's-land, and captured the hilltop village of Cantigny from the grip of the German Army." (Publisher's note)

"From the "creeping barrage" of artillery to the eventual American victory, the reader will hear every explosion, feel each bullet whiz past, and sometimes cry at the loss of a comrade. This is a brilliant work for every library." LJ

Includes bibliographical references and index

Downing, Taylor

Secret Warriors; The Spies, Scientists and Code Breakers of World War I. Taylor Downing. W W Norton & Co Inc 2015 464 p. 16 plates; illustrations $28.95   **940.4**

1. Espionage 2. World War, 1914-1918

ISBN 1605986941; 9781605986944

Author Taylor Downing presents this "account of World War I that uncovers how wartime code-breaking, aeronautics, and scientific research that laid the foundation for much of the innovations of the twentieth century. [It] provides an invaluable and fresh history of the World War I, profiling a number of the key incidents and figures which lead to great leaps forward for the twentieth century." (Publisher's note)

"This volume should be of interest to most readers, especially those interested in military history." LJ

Dyer, Geoff

The **missing** of the Somme; Geoff Dyer. Vintage Books 2011 176p.   **940.4**

1. Memory 2. Veterans 3. World War, 1914-1918

ISBN 9780307742971; 9780307743237

LC 2002327412

This book offers an "exploration of the meaning and formal remembrance of British participation in World War I. . . . [Author Geoff] Dyer argues that our perceptions of the WWI are shaped by impressions of the war presented through the literature and public statuary (and, to a lesser degree, photography) produced within 15 years of the Armistice. The dominant theme of these cultural works is . . . sacrifice as a virtue in itself and its formal remembrance, and he believes this was evident even in works produced at the very beginning of the war. . . . Dyer intertwines the story of his travels with two friends to visit monuments and military cemeteries of the Western Front with . . . observations on statuary by Charles Sargeant Jagger, the poetry of Wilfred Owen and the literary criticism of Paul Fussell, among others." (Kirkus)

Eisenhower, John S. D.

Yanks: the epic story of the American Army in World War I; {by} John S. D. Eisenhower with Joanne Thompson Eisenhower. Free Press 2001 353p il maps hardcover o.p. pa $16   **940.4**

1. United States -- Army 2. World War, 1914-1918 -- Campaigns

ISBN 0-684-86304-9; 0-7432-2385-3 pa

LC 2001-23124

"This is an important work that should help alter the historical picture of the American role in the conflict." Booklist

Includes bibliographical references

Farwell, Byron

Over there; the United States in the Great War, 1917-1918. Norton 1999 336p $27.95; pa $15.95   **940.4**

1. World War, 1914-1918 -- United States

ISBN 0-393-04698-2; 0-393-32028-6 pa

LC 98-35705

This history of American intervention in World War I focuses primarily on the military aspects of the war but also discusses its social and economic impact

"This title does provide good coverage on the intervention in Russia and the role of women in the war, notably the 'Hello Girls.' " Libr J

Includes bibliographical references

Harries, Meirion

The **last** days of innocence; America at war, 1917-1918. {by} Meirion and Susie Harries. Random House 1997 573p il hardcover o.p. pa $16   **940.4**

1. World War, 1914-1918 -- United States

ISBN 0-679-74376-6 pa

LC 96-21756

"This is an excellent study of US participation in WWI. The research is in far greater depth than the usual 'popular history,' the analysis is sharp and informative, and the writing is clear and a pleasure to read. The authors strike an even balance between necessity for condensation and the accuracy that comes from detailed treatment." Choice

Includes bibliographical references

Hart, Peter

The **Somme**; the darkest hour on the Western Front. Pegasus Books 2008 589p il map $35; pa $17.95   **940.4**

1. World War, 1914-1918 -- Campaigns -- France

ISBN 978-1-60598-016-4; 1-60598-016-1; 978-1-60598-081-2 pa; 1-60598-081-1 pa

First published 2005 in the United Kingdom

This is an "account of the Somme offensive. . . . [The author evokes] the horrors of combat on the western front, skillfully blending these personal accounts with strategic considerations of a battle that slaughtered nearly a million French, German, and British soldiers. . . . Military history at its best." Libr J

Includes bibliographical references

Herwig, Holger H.

The **Marne**, 1914; the opening of World War I and the battle that changed the world. Random House 2009 391p il map $28   **940.4**

1. World War, 1914-1918 -- Campaigns -- France

ISBN 9781400066711; 1-4000-6671-9

LC 2009-5687

This fine history of World War I's opening battle argues persuasively that it was decisive in setting the pattern for the war, a pattern that made World War II inevitable. . . . Herwig's research has been exhaustive, including of archives long since thought destroyed that help him fill in a great many details about the German side. . . . As fine an addition to scholarly World War I literature as has been seen in some time. Booklist

Includes bibliographical references

Hynes, Samuel

The **unsubstantial** air; American fliers in the First World War. Samuel Hynes. Farrar, Straus & Giroux 2014 336 p. illustrations (cloth : alkaline paper) $26   **940.4**

1. Air pilots 2. World War, 1914-1918 -- Aerial

operations 3. Fighter pilots -- United States -- Biography 4. World War, 1914-1918 -- Aerial operations, American 5. World War, 1914-1918 -- Personal narratives, American 6. Fighter pilots -- United States -- History -- 20th century

ISBN 0374278008; 9780374278007

LC 2014008673

This book, by Samuel Hynes, is the "story of the Americans who fought and died in the aerial battles of World War I. Much more than a traditional military history, it is an account of the excitement of becoming a pilot and flying in combat over the Western Front, told through the words and voices of the aviators themselves." (Publisher's note)

"The reader quickly becomes aware of the acute danger pilots faced—the narratives Haynes utilizes to tell the story often end abruptly with a terse account of a death due to a training accident, mechanical failure, or combat. It is a must read for anyone interested in aviation history, military history, and the American experience in the Great War." Pub Wkly

Includes bibliographical references and index

Larson, Erik

★ **Dead** wake; the last voyage of the Lusitania. by Erik Larson. Crown Publishers 2015 464 p. maps (hardcover) $28 **940.4**
1. Lusitania (Steamship) 2. World War, 1914-1918 -- Naval operations

ISBN 0307408868; 9780307408860; 9780307408877

LC 2014034182

This book by Erik Larson describes the history and events surrounding the sinking of the British passenger vessel Lusitania during World War I. "For months, German U-boats had brought terror to the North Atlantic. But the Lusitania . . . and her captain . . . placed tremendous faith in the gentlemanly strictures of warfare that for a century had kept civilian ships safe from attack. Germany, however, was determined to change the rules of the game." (Publisher's note)

"Reader engrossment is tightly sustained as we move back and forth between the Lusitania on its return from New York City to its home port of Liverpool under a black cloud of warnings that the imperial German government considered the waters around Britain to be a war zone, and the rapacious German submarine U-20, stalking the seas for prey like a lion on the Serengeti. Factual and personal to a high degree, the narrative reads like a grade-A thriller." Booklist

Includes bibliographical references and index

Lawrence, T. E.

Seven pillars of wisdom; a triumph. Doubleday 1935 672p il maps hardcover o.p. pa $19.95 **940.4**
1. Arabs 2. Bedouins 3. Wahhabis 4. World War, 1914-1918 -- Middle East

ISBN 0-385-41895-7 pa

"Not only a history of the Arab revolt during the {First} World War, but a commentary on the national characteristics, and political policies of Arabs, Turks and British." Cleveland Public Libr

Lussu, Emilio, 1890-1975

A **soldier** on the southern front; the classic Italian memoir of World War I. Emilio Lussu. Rizzoli Ex Libris 2014 278 p. (alk. paper) $26.95 **940.4**
1. Autobiographies 2. World War, 1914-1918 -- Campaigns -- Italy 3. World War, 1914-1918 -- Personal narratives

ISBN 0847842789; 9780847842780

LC 2013943440

Written by Emilio Lussu, translated by Gregory Conti, this memoir is "a rediscovered Italian masterpiece chronicling the author's experience as an infantryman, newly translated and reissued to commemorate the centennial of World War I. . . . A classic in Italy but virtually unknown in the English-speaking world, it reveals . . . the almost farcical side of the war as seen by a Sardinian officer fighting the Austrian army on the Asiago plateau in northeastern Italy." (Publisher's note)

A "compelling read that enters the mind of a man at the front, exposed daily to terrible scenes and decisions that change who he is." LJ

Massie, Robert K.

Castles of steel; Britain, Germany, and the winning of the Great War at sea. Random House 2003 865p il map pa $17.95; $35 **940.4**
1. Germany -- Kriegsmarine 2. Great Britain -- Royal Navy 3. World War, 1914-1918 -- Naval operations 4. World War, 1914-1918 -- Naval operations, German 5. World War, 1914-1918 -- Naval operations, British

ISBN 0-345-40878-0 pa; 0-679-45671-6

LC 2003-41373

Focusing on Britain's Grand Fleet and Germany's High Seas Fleet, Massie examines the role of sea power in determining the outcome of the First World War. Index.

The author "makes a coherent if long narrative out of a sequence of events familiar to students of naval history but probably not to many other potential readers." Publ Wkly

Millman, Chad

The **detonators**; the secret plot to destroy America and an epic hunt for justice. Little, Brown 2006 330p il map $24.99 **940.4**
1. Sabotage 2. World War, 1914-1918 -- United States

ISBN 978-0-316-73496-7; 0-316-73496-9

LC 2005-24401

"With its obvious contemporary resonance, Millman's able account of an earlier foreign attack on America should draw the espionage audience and more." Booklist

Includes bibliographical references

Mosier, John

The **myth** of the Great War; a new military history of World War I. HarperCollins Pubs. 2001 381p il hardcover o.p. pa $14.95 **940.4**
1. World War, 1914-1918 -- Campaigns

ISBN 0-06-019676-9; 0-06-008433-2 pa

LC 00-46103

"After dissecting the major campaigns on the western front, Mosier concludes that Germany's ultimate defeat was the direct result of the influx of American soldiers into France in 1917 and 1918. . . . This is revisionist history that

convincingly smashes the myths that Allied governments, leaders, and propagandists worked so hard to promulgate. Mosier's masterful account is a welcome addition." Booklist
Includes bibliographical references

Neiberg, Michael
★ **Fighting** the Great War; a global history. [by] Michael S. Neiberg. Harvard University Press 2005 xx, 395p il map $27.95   **940.4**
1. World War, 1914-1918
ISBN 0-674-01696-3

LC 2004-54330
"Readers interested in a general overview of WW I can do no better than Neiberg's excellent account." Choice
Includes bibliographical references

Ousby, Ian
The **road** to Verdun; World War I's most momentous battle and the folly of nationalism. Doubleday 2002 393p il maps $30; pa $16   **940.4**
1. World War, 1914-1918 -- Campaigns
ISBN 0-385-50393-8; 0-385-72173-0 pa

LC 2002-19475
This is a study of the Battle of Verdun which "killed 700,000 French and German soldiers, 10% of all those killed in the war. Yet a sense of glory was maintained, however inappropriately, amid the gore: the road leading to the battlefield was called the Sacred Way, and the French General Neville gained immortality by his brave statement, 'They {the Germans} shall not pass.'" Publ Wkly

Paice, Edward
World War I: the African Front. Pegasus 2008 xxxix, 488p il map $35   **940.4**
1. World War, 1914-1918 -- Campaigns -- East Africa
ISBN 978-1-933648-90-3
"An authoritative summing-up of a grim, complex and little-known part of World War I." Kirkus
Includes bibliographical references

Philpott, William
Three armies on the Somme; the first battle of the twentieth century. [by] William Philpott. Alfred A. Knopf 2010 631p il map $35; ebook $35 **940.4**
1. Germany -- Heer 2. France -- Armée 3. Great Britain -- Army 4. World War, 1914-1918 -- Campaigns -- France
ISBN 978-0-307-26585-2; 978-0-307-59372-6 ebook
LC 2010-4070
First published 2009 in the United Kingdom with title: Bloody victory
"The Battle of the Somme is branded in British memory as the exemplar of WWI: a months-long cataclysm that, at the cost of monumental casualties, repelled the Germans from a few square miles of shell-blasted French countryside. This account by a descendant of an artillerist in the battle has two aims: to narrate the battle from its initial strategic concept to its sputtering-out in late 1916 and to refute historical and popular opinion about the battle. . . . Comprehensive research and convention-bucking argument qualify Philpott for the WWI shelf." Booklist
Includes bibliographical references

Preston, Diana
A **higher** form of killing; six weeks in spring 1915 that changed the nature of warfare forever. Diana Preston. Bloomsbury 2015 352 p. 16 plates; ills.; maps; ports (hardback) $28   **940.4**
1. Strategy 2. World War, 1914-1918 3. Lusitania (Steamship) 4. World War, 1914-1918 -- Chemical warfare 5. Ypres, 2nd Battle of, Ieper, Belgium, 1915 6. War (Philosophy) -- History -- 20th century 7. Just war doctrine -- History -- 20th century 8. Airships -- Germany -- History -- 20th century 9. World War, 1914-1918 -- Naval operations -- Submarine 10. Bombing, Aerial -- England -- London -- History -- 20th century 11. Weapons of mass destruction -- Germany -- History -- 20th century 12. Germany -- Armed Forces -- Weapons systems -- History -- 20th century
ISBN 1620402122; 9781620402122

LC 2014019999
This book by Diana Preston "places the creation of poison gas, the torpedo, and the zeppelin into the context of warfare and the human toll exacted. . . . She explains the scorched-earth policy of Germany under Kaiser Wilhelm II, which mandated a complete triumph for the Fatherland at all cost during the infamous six-week period in 1915 where this trio of deadly weapons was introduced to untold suffering for soldiers and civilians alike." (Publishers Weekly)
"In what is often difficult but necessary reading, Preston provides haunting descriptions of the effects of poison gas. A harrowing—and, in this era of drones, absolutely pertinent—look at the rapacious reaches of man's murderous imagination." Kirkus
Includes bibliographical references and index

Sacco, Joe
The **Great** War; July 1, 1916 : the first day of the Battle of the Somme : an illustrated panorama. Joe Sacco. W.W. Norton & Co. Inc. 2013 54 p. chiefly ill. $35   **940.4**
1. World War, 1914-1918 2. Great Britain -- Military history 3. World War, 1939-1945 -- Campaigns -- France 4. Somme, 1st Battle of the, France, 1916 5. Somme, 1st Battle of the, France, 1916 -- Comic books, strips, etc
ISBN 0393088804; 9780393088809

LC 2013010710
This art book by Joe Sacco presents "a single continuous panorama, eight inches tall and twenty-four feet long," which "illustrates, in minutely detailed black-and-white drawings, events just before and during a summer day when the British army suffered morethan fifty-seven thousand dead and wounded, its greatest single-day loss. . . . An accompanying booklet" presents a "brief account of the day by Adam Hoschchild." (Bookforum)

Scott, R. Neil
★ **Many** were held by the sea; the tragic sinking of HMS Otranto. R. Neil Scott. Rowman & Littlefield 2012 249 p. (cloth : alk. paper) $35.00 **940.4**
1. Shipwrecks 2. World War, 1914-1918 -- Naval operations 3. Kashmir (Troopship) 4. Otranto (Troopship) 5. Shipwrecks -- Scotland -- Islay 6. World War, 1914-1918 -- Naval operations, British 7.

World War, 1914-1918 -- Casualties -- Great Britain 8.
Transports -- Great Britain -- History -- 20th century 9.
World War, 1914-1918 -- Transportation -- Great Britain
10. Marine accidents -- Great Britain -- History -- 20th
century
ISBN 1442213426; 9781442213425; 9781442213449
LC 2012003033

This book by R. Neil Scott tells the story of a 1918 disaster in which the "HMS Kashmir rammed HMS Otranto off
Islay, Scotland. . . . On board were 372 British officers and
sailors and 701 American soldiers. . . . The Kashmir managed to back away and follow the harsh wartime order . .
. to continue on her prescribed course rather than stop and
take on survivors. Thus it was that . . . the severely damaged
Otranto was left dead in the water with more than a thousand
souls aboard." (Publisher's note)

Includes bibliographical references and index

Sebag-Montefiore, Hugh

Somme; into the breach. Hugh Sebag-Montefiore. The Belknap Press of Harvard University Press
2016 xlviii, 607 p.p illustrations, maps (hardcover)
$35; (ebook) $43.95   **940.4**
1. Somme, 1st Battle of the, France, 1916 2. World
War, 1914-1918 -- Campaigns -- France 3. World War,
1914-1918 -- France -- Personal narratives 4. World
War, 1914-1918 -- Campaigns -- France -- Somme
ISBN 9780674545199; 0674545192; 9780674970038
LC 2016025276

This book on the Battle of the Somme during World War
I by Hugh Sebag-Montefiore presents eyewitness accounts
that "relive scenes of extraordinary courage and sacrifice, as
soldiers ordered 'over the top' ventured into No Man's Land
and enemy trenches, where they met a hail of machine-gun
fire, thickets of barbed wire, and exploding shells." (Publisher's note)

"A beautifully crafted, blow-by-blow account with deep
insight into the lives of these diverse young men." Kirkus

Includes bibliographical references (pages [581]-586)
and index

Thompson, Mark

The **white** war; life and death on the Italian
front, 1915-1919. Basic Books 2009 454p il map
$30   **940.4**
1. World War, 1914-1918 -- Campaigns -- Italy
ISBN 978-0-465-01329-6; 0-465-01329-5
First published 2008 in the United Kingdom

"Penetrating study of one of the forgotten fronts of the
Great War. . . . A much-needed addition to the literature of
World War I." Kirkus

Includes bibliographical references

Wawro, Geoffrey

A **mad** catastrophe; the outbreak of World War
I and the collapse of the Habsburg Empire. Geoffrey Wawro. Basic Books 2014 472 p. illustrations,
maps (hardback) $29.99   **940.4**
1. Austria -- History 2. Hungary -- History 3. World
War, 1914-1918 4. World War, 1914-1918 -- Causes 5.
Austria -- History -- Franz Joseph I, 1848-1916 6. World
War, 1914-1918 -- Campaigns -- Balkan Peninsula 7.

World War, 1914-1918 -- Campaigns -- Galicia (Poland
and Ukraine)
ISBN 0465028357; 9780465028351
LC 2013039393

"The Austro-Hungarian army that marched east and
south to confront the Russians and Serbs in the opening
campaigns of World War I had a glorious past but a pitiful present. . . . As prizewinning historian Geoffrey Wawro explains in 'A Mad Catastrophe,' the doomed Austrian
conscripts were an unfortunate microcosm of the Austro-Hungarian Empire itself--both equally ripe for destruction."
(Publisher's note)

"Wawro's authoritative account is a damning analysis of
an empire and a people unready for war." Pub Wkly

Includes bibliographical references and index

Weber, Thomas

Hitler's first war; Adolf Hitler, the men of the
List Regiment, and the First World War. Oxford University Press 2010 450p il $34.95   **940.4**
1. Heads of state 2. Nazi leaders 3. Soldiers -- Germany
4. World War, 1914-1918 5. Biography, Individual 6.
World War, 1914-1918 -- Germany 7. World War, 1914-1918 -- Campaigns 8. Germany -- Heer -- Bayerisches
Reserve-Infanterie-Regiment 16
ISBN 0199233209; 9780199233205

"Hitler claimed that his years as a soldier in the First
World War were the most formative years of his life. However, for the six decades since his death in the ruins of
Berlin, Hitler's time as a soldier on the Western Front has
remained a blank spot. . . . [Weber's book] looks at what
really happened to Private Hitler and the men of the Bavarian List Regiment of which he was a member." (Publisher's
note) Index.

"A triumph of original research in a very stony field. The
conclusion that might be drawn is that Hitler was far more of
the opportunist than is generally supposed. He made things
up as he went along, including his own past." Wall Street J

Includes bibliographical references

Yockelson, Mitchell A., 1962-

Forty-seven days; how Pershing's warriors came
of age to defeat the German Army in World War I.
Mitchell Yockelson. New American Library 2016
400 p. illustrations (hardcover) $28   **940.4**
1. United States -- Military history 2. World War, 1914-1918 -- United States 3. United States. Army. American
Expeditionary Forces 4. World War, 1914-1918 --
Campaigns -- Western Front
ISBN 9780451466952
LC 2015039121

This book, by Mitchell Yockelson, offers "the gripping
account of the U.S. First Army's . . . triumph over the Germans in America's bloodiest battle of the First World War—
the Battle of the Meuse-Argonne. . . . Historian Mitchell
Yockelson tells how General John J. 'Black Jack' Pershing's
exemplary leadership led to the unlikeliest of victories."
(Publisher's note)

"An accessible, elucidating study by a knowledgeable
expert." Kirkus

Includes bibliographical references (pages 339-379)
and index.

940.436 Allied offensives of September 25-November 11, 1918

Walker, William T.

Betrayal at Little Gibraltar; a German fortress, a treacherous American general, and the battle to end World War I. William T. Walker. Scribner 2016 464 p. $28 **940.436**

1. World War, 1914-1918 2. Military art and science 3. Argonne, Battle of the, France, 1918 4. World War, 1914-1918 -- Campaigns -- Meuse River Valley 5. Montfaucon (Meuse, France) -- History, Military -- 20th century 6. United States. Army. Infantry Division, 79th -- History -- World War, 1914-1918

ISBN 9781501117893; 9781501117916; 1501117890

LC 2015044665

This book, by William Walker, "tells vivid human stories of the soldiers who fought to capture the giant fortress [Montfaucon] and push the American advance. Using unpublished first-person accounts—and featuring photographs, documents, and maps that place you in the action—Walker describes the horrors of World War I combat, the sacrifices of the doughboys, and the determined efforts of two participants to pierce the cover-up and to solve the mystery of Montfaucon." (Publisher's note)

"He creates a convincing argument for a postwar cover-up of Bullard's actions. A military history for all libraries" LJ

Includes bibliographical references and index

940.44 Air operations

Hamilton-Paterson, James

Marked for death; The First War in the Air. James Hamilton-Paterson. Head of Zeus 2015 356 p. illustrations (some color) (hbk.) $27.95 **940.44**

1. World War, 1914-1918 -- Aerial operations 2. World War, 1914-1918 -- Casualties

ISBN 9781681771588; 1681771586; 1784970395; 9781784970390

LC 2014495526

This book, by James Hamilton-Paterson, is an "account of aerial combat during World War I, revealing the terrible risks taken by the men who fought and died in the world's first war in the air. . . . [It] debunks popular myth to explore the brutal truths of wartime aviation: of flimsy planes and unprotected pilots; of burning nineteen-year-olds falling screaming to their deaths; of pilots blinded by the entrails of their observers." (Publisher's note)

"Best of all, the author—who has a solid body of fiction to his credit—is a consummate storyteller; not only does the book tell a fascinating story, it is nearly impossible to put down." Kirkus

Includes bibliographical references (pages 331-334) and index

940.5 Europe--1918-

Jarausch, Konrad H.

Out of ashes; a new history of Europe in the twentieth century. Konrad H. Jarausch. Princeton University Press 2015 880 p. illustrations, maps (hardback : acid-free paper) $39.50 **940.5**

1. Europe -- History -- 20th century 2. Europe -- Social conditions -- 20th century 3. Europe -- Politics and government -- 20th century 4. Social change -- Europe -- History -- 20th century

ISBN 0691152799; 9780691152790

LC 2014031328

This book, by Konrad H. Jarausch, offers a "history of twentieth-century Europe. . . [It] tells the story of an era of unparalleled violence and barbarity yet also of humanity, prosperity, and promise. . . . [It also] explores the paradox of the European encounter with modernity in the twentieth century, shedding new light on why it led to cataclysm, inhumanity, and self-destruction, but also social justice, democracy, and peace." (Publisher's note)

"The work isn't designed to be encyclopedic, yet it should be on the shelf of everyone seeking a panoramic, narrative guide to history's most violent century. This comprehensive history of 20th-century Europe is bound to become the standard work on its subject: a bold, major achievement." Pub Wkly

Includes bibliographical references and index

Kershaw, Ian

To Hell and Back; Europe 1914-1949. Ian Kershaw. Penguin Group USA 2015 592 p. illustrations, maps $35 **940.5**

1. World War, 1914-1918 2. World War, 1939-1945 3. Europe -- History -- 1918-1945

ISBN 0670024589; 9780670024582

LC 2015040523

This book, by Ian Kershaw, part of the "Penguin History of Europe" series, offers an "analysis of the pivotal years of World War I and World War II. The European catastrophe, the long continuous period from 1914 to 1949, was unprecedented in human history. . . . This new volume . . . offers comprehensive coverage of this tumultuous era." (Publisher's note)

"Kershaw concludes with a somewhat less successful appraisal of the vastly altered geopolitical landscape following WWII, the social and economic disruptions, the physical ruin of the continent, and the responses to the devastation offered by the Christian churches, leading intellectuals, and popular entertainments. An ambitious, dense , sometimes-difficult treatment of a vast topic." Kirkus

Mak, Geert

★ **In** Europe; travels through the twentieth century. translated from the Dutch by Sam Garrett. Pantheon 2007 876p map $35 **940.5**

1. Europe -- Description and travel 2. Europe -- History -- 20th century

ISBN 0-375-42495-4; 978-0-375-42495-3

LC 2007-9260

Original Dutch edition, 2004

This book recounts the author's travels through Europe and examines the history of European countries, particularly focusing on the the the effects of the Treaty of Rome.

"Mak's brilliant compendium is difficult to define—is it a history book, a travelogue, a memoir?—but stands out as a remarkable, insightful, exhilarating exposition on that peculiar continent across the Atlantic." Publ Wkly

Sachar, Howard Morley

Dreamland; Europeans and Jews in the aftermath of the Great War. {by} Howard M. Sachar. Knopf 2002 385p map hardcover o.p. pa $15   **940.5**
1. Jews -- Europe 2. Europe -- History -- 1918-1945
ISBN 0-375-70829-4 pa

LC 2001-38471

An overview of Jewish life in Europe during the three decades before the Holocaust

"This scholarly analysis provides a completely original slant on the much-studied interwar period." Booklist

Includes bibliographical references

Talty, Stephan

Agent Garbo; the brilliant, eccentric secret agent who tricked Hitler and saved D-Day. Stephan Talty. Houghton Mifflin Harcourt 2012 301 p.   **940.5**
1. Spies 2. Normandy (France), Attack on, 1944 3. World War, 1939-1945 -- Secret service 4. Spies -- Great Britain -- Biography 5. World War, 1939-1945 -- Secret service -- Great Britain
ISBN 0547614810; 9780547614816

LC 2012005470

This book by Stephan Talty tells the story of "Juan Pujol, the Spanish hotel manager who, in January 1941, waltzed into the British Embassy in Madrid and announced that he wanted to help the Allied war effort. . . . Turned down by the British, Pujol came up with a stunningly audacious plan: he would approach the Germans, offer his services as a spy, gather intelligence, and then go back to the British, operating as a double agent. And here's the thing: it worked." (Booklist)

Includes bibliographical references (pages [281]-283) and index

940.53   World War II, 1939-1945

Ackerman, Diane, 1948-

★ The **zookeeper's** wife. W.W. Norton 2007 368p il $24.95   **940.53**
1. Zoos 2. Jews -- Poland 3. Holocaust, 1933-1945 4. World War, 1939-1945 -- Jews -- Rescue
ISBN 978-0-393-06172-7; 0-393-06172-8

LC 2007-12635

This is an account of how the director of the Warsaw Zoo and his wife, Jan and Antonina Zabinski, respectively, saved 300 Jews during World War II.

"An exemplary work of scholarship and an 'ecstasy of imagining,' Ackerman's affecting telling of the heroic Zabinskis' dramatic story illuminates the profound connection between humankind and nature, and celebrates life's beauty, mystery, and tenacity." Booklist

Includes bibliographical references

Arrington, Leonard J.

Japanese Americans, from relocation to redress; edited by Roger Daniels, Sandra C. Taylor, Harry H.L. Kitano; contributions by Leonard J. Arrington {et al.} rev & updated ed; University of Wash. Press 1991 xxi, 242p il pa $25   **940.53**
1. World War, 1939-1945 -- Reparations 2. Japanese Americans -- Evacuation and relocation, 1942-1945
ISBN 0-295-97117-7

LC 91-2892

First published 1986 by University of Utah Press

A collection of essays on Japanese Americans focusing on their wartime relocation and their efforts to seek reparations.

Includes bibliographical references

Barr, Niall

Eisenhower's Armies; The American-british Alliance During World War II. Niall Barr. W W Norton & Co Inc 2015 544 p. 16 plates; illustrations; maps $35   **940.53**
1. World War, 1939-1945 2. United States -- Foreign relations -- Great Britain
ISBN 1605988162; 9781605988160

This book by Niall Bar "is the story of two very different armies learning to live, work, and fight together even in the face of serious strategic disagreements. The book is also a very human story about the efforts of many individuals . . . who worked and argued together to defeat Hitler's Germany. In highlighting the cooperation, tensions, and disagreements inherent in this military alliance, this work shows that Allied victory was far from pre-ordained and proves that the business of making this alliance work was vital for eventual success." (Publisher's note)

"This dramatic work isn't just for military historians or World War II scholars. It is also highly recommended for students of World War II and of the Atlantic Alliance of the mid-20th century and is a great read for anyone interested in leadership, decision making, international relations and diplomacy, and 20th-century history." LJ

Barrett, Duncan

GI brides; the wartime girls who crossed the Atlantic for love. Duncan Barrett & Nuala Calvi. William Morrow Paperbacks 2014 592 p. 16 plates; illustrations (paperback) $14.99   **940.53**
1. Military spouses 2. World War, 1939-1945 3. British -- United States 4. British Americans -- Biography 5. War brides -- Great Britain -- Biography 6. Women immigrants -- United States -- Biography 7. World War, 1939-1945 -- Women -- Great Britain
ISBN 0062328050; 9780062328052

LC 2014010526

Authors Duncan Barrett and Nuala Calvi present the " tale of romance and resilience--the true story of four British women who crossed the Atlantic for love, coming to America at the end of World War II to make a new life with the American servicemen they married." (Publisher's note)

"Alternating among the women, the authors bring to light the joys and sorrows of each woman, but readers may find it easier to read each story in its entirety before switching to another one. Entertaining stories about four women who embraced life with American soldiers after the end of World War II." Kirkus

Includes bibliographical references and index

Berenbaum, Michael

The **world** must know; the history of the Holocaust as told in the United States Holocaust Memorial Museum. Arnold Kramer, editor of photographs. 2nd ed; United States Holocaust Memorial Museum 2006 xxi, 250p il pa $29.95   **940.53**

1. Holocaust, 1933-1945 2. United States Holocaust Memorial Museum

ISBN 0-8018-8358-X

First published 1993 by Little, Brown

"Visually evocative and unsettling, the book, supplemented with a useful bibliography, is an excellent choice for those with little acquaintance of the subject or those needing a concise synopsis." Libr J [review of 1993 edition]

Includes bibliographical references

Berthon, Simon

Warlords; an extraordinary recreation of World War II through the eyes and minds of Hitler, Roosevelt, Churchill, and Stalin. [by] Simon Berthon and Joanna Potts. Da Capo Press 2006 358p il $24.95   **940.53**

1. Governors 2. Statesmen 3. Historians 4. Presidents 5. Heads of state 6. Prime ministers 7. People with disabilities 8. Memoirists 9. Nazi leaders 10. Philatelists 11. Cabinet members 12. Communist leaders 13. Political leaders 14. Members of Parliament 15. Nobel laureates for literature 16. World War, 1939-1945 -- Diplomatic history

ISBN 0-306-81467-6

LC 2005-432583

First published 2005 in the United Kingdom

This book focuses "on the day-to-day actions of Hitler, Stalin, Churchill, and Roosevelt as they grapple with the war's events and plot strategy. . . . For anyone interested in how these four leaders engaged in the war, here is a great place to start." Libr J

Includes bibliographical references

Beschloss, Michael R.

★ The **conquerors**: Roosevelt, Truman, and the destruction of Hitler's Germany, 1941-1945; {by} Michael Beschloss. Simon & Schuster 2002 377p il maps $26.95; pa $15   **940.53**

1. Governors 2. Presidents 3. Vice-presidents 4. People with disabilities 5. Reconstruction (1939-1951) 6. Senators 7. Philatelists 8. World War, 1939-1945 -- Germany 9. Germany -- Foreign relations -- United States 10. United States -- Foreign relations -- Germany

ISBN 0-684-81027-1; 0-7432-4454-0 pa

LC 2002-30331

"As German forces were driven back in 1943-45, American leaders were anxious that in 20 years, just as it had done after its defeat in 1918, a vengeful Germany would start another world war. To prevent this, two schools of thought flowed through DC's salons of power: punishment or rehabilitation. . . . Beschloss covers the meeting-by-meeting, memo-by-memo political battle between the two approaches.

. . . Beschloss' comprehensive research and narration into every nuance opens a significant perspective on bureaucratic politics' effect on the Germany that eventually formed in the early cold war." Booklist

Includes bibliographical references

Bowman, Constance

Slacks and calluses; our summer in a bomber factory. Constance Bowman; illustrated by Clara Marie Allen; introduction by Sandra M. Gilbert. Smithsonian Institution Press 1999 xiv, 181p illustrations   **940.53**

1. World War, 1939-1945 -- Women 2. World War, 1939-1945 -- United States

ISBN 1-560-98368-X; 9781560983682; 1-560-98387-6

LC 99031365

This book, by Constance Bowman and illustrated by Clara Marie Allen, describes how "in 1943 two spirited young teachers decided to do their part for the war effort by spending their summer vacation working the swing shift on a B-24 production line at a San Diego bomber plant. Entering a male-dominated realm . . . , they learned to use tools that they had never seen before, live with aluminum shavings in their hair, and get along with . . . coworkers from all walks of life." (Publisher's note)

Buruma, Ian

Year zero; 1945 and the aftermath of war. Ian Buruma. Penguin Press 2013 384 p. $29.95 **940.53**

1. World history -- 1945- 2. World politics -- 1945- 3. World War, 1939-1945 -- Influence 4. History, Modern -- 1945-1989 5. World War, 1939-1945 -- Peace

ISBN 1594204365; 9781594204364

LC 2013007702

This book by Ian Buruma "explores the nascent social and political forces that later influenced the Cold War and post-colonial movements. . . . Starting with a world ruined by war, Buruma moves . . . from describing the elation of victory and the desire for revenge to the Allies' attempts to reform societies by eliminating all traces of militarism or fascism and establishing a European welfare state, as destroyed cities are rebuilt and fallen nations reimagined." (Publishers Weekly)

Buruma... offers a vivid portrayal of the first steps toward normalcy in human affairs amid the ruins of Europe and Asia. (Kirkus)

Includes bibliographical references and index

Carley, Michael Jabara

1939; the alliance that never was and the coming of World War II. Dee, I.R. 1999 xxv, 321p maps $28.95   **940.53**

1. World War, 1939-1945 -- Causes 2. World War, 1939-1945 -- Diplomatic history

ISBN 1-56663-252-8

LC 99-24873

The author "provides a detailed and fascinating perspective on one of the major causes of World War II." Libr J

Includes bibliographical references (p. {299}-308) and index

Cesarani, David, 1956-2015

Final Solution; The Fate of the Jews 1933-1949. by David Cesarani. St. Martin's Press 2016 960 p. illustrations, maps (hbk) $40 **940.53**

1. Holocaust, 1939-1945
ISBN 9781250000835; 1250000831

LC 2016033310

This book, by David Cesarani, "is a magisterial work of history that chronicles the fate of Europe's Jews. Based on decades of scholarship, documentation newly available from the opening of Soviet archives, declassification of western intelligence service records, as well as diaries and reports written in the camps, Cesarani provides a sweeping reappraisal challenging accepted explanations for the anti-Jewish politics of Nazi Germany and the inevitability of the Final Solution." (Publisher's note)

"Cesarani's overwhelming evidence of brutality makes this book unbearably painful to read and makes his analysis hard to accept. Even before an official plan, Hitler's anti-Semitic rants inspired his army and his nation. A highly learned but problematic examination of Nazi decision-making." Kirkus

Includes bibliographic references and index.

Churchill, Winston

Closing the ring. Houghton Mifflin 1951 749p maps (Second World War) hardcover o.p. pa $18 **940.53**

1. World War, 1939-1945 2. World War, 1939-1945 -- Great Britain
ISBN 0-395-41059-2 pa

"'Closing the Ring' sets forth the year of conflict from June 1943 to June 1944. Aided by the command of the oceans, the mastery of the U-boats, and our ever growing superiority in the air, the Western Allies were able to conquer Sicily and invade Italy, with the result that Mussolini was overthrown and the Italian nation came over to our side." Preface

The **gathering** storm. Houghton Mifflin 1948 784p maps (Second World War) hardcover o.p. pa $19 **940.53**

1. World War, 1939-1945 2. World War, 1939-1945 -- Great Britain
ISBN 0-395-41055-X pa

The first volume of Churchill's monumental history of the Second World War describes the days between the false peace and Hitler's near-victory just before Dunkirk

The **grand** alliance. Houghton Mifflin 1950 903p maps (Second World War) hardcover o.p. pa $18 **940.53**

1. World War, 1939-1945 2. World War, 1939-1945 -- Great Britain
ISBN 0-395-41057-6 pa

This volume begins with the German drive in the East, covers the War in Africa and describes the entrance into the war of Russia and, after Pearl Harbor, the United States

The **hinge** of fate. Houghton Mifflin 1950 1000p maps (Second World War) hardcover o.p. pa $18 **940.53**

1. World War, 1939-1945 2. World War, 1939-1945 -- Great Britain
ISBN 0-395-41058-4 pa

Describing events leading to the invasion of Sicily, warfare in Africa, the discouragingly slow job of reconquest in Europe, meetings with Roosevelt, and efforts at collaboration with Stalin, this volume covers the period from January 1942 to May 1943

Their finest hour. Houghton Mifflin 1949 751p maps (Second World War) hardcover o.p. pa $19 **940.53**

1. World War, 1939-1945 2. World War, 1939-1945 -- Great Britain
ISBN 0-395-41056-8 pa

This volume starts with the problems confronting Churchill as he assumed the office of Prime Minister in 1940 and continues with accounts of the Battle of Britain, the Battle of France and Dunkirk

Triumph and tragedy. Houghton Mifflin 1953 800p maps (Second World War) hardcover o.p. pa $18 **940.53**

1. World War, 1939-1945 2. World War, 1939-1945 -- Great Britain
ISBN 0-395-41060-6 pa

The concluding volume of Churchill's history of World War II begins with D-Day and covers campaigns leading to the defeat of Germany and Japan

Clendinnen, Inga

Reading the Holocaust. Cambridge Univ. Press 1999 227p il map $69; pa $19.99 **940.53**

1. Holocaust, 1933-1945 -- Historiography
ISBN 0-521-64174-8; 0-521-01269-4 pa

LC 98-53636

In this reexamination of the Holocaust Clendinnen "first considers the problematic nature of eyewitness accounts, then turns to an unflinching inquiry into the Nazi mentality and finally takes on the tough question of artistic representation. . . . This slim, powerful book forces a reader to reexamine almost all the assumptions we've accepted since the Holocaust occurred." N Y Times Book Rev

Includes bibliographical references

Cohen, Rich

The **avengers**. Knopf 2000 261p il hardcover o.p. pa $13 **940.53**

1. Poets 2. Authors 3. Underground leaders 4. Holocaust, 1933-1945 5. World War, 1939-1945 -- Underground movements
ISBN 0-375-70529-5 pa

LC 00-21062

Cohen chronicles the resistance efforts of a small group of European Jews during the Second World War. Attention is focused primarily on the activities of three individuals: Rozka Korczak, Vitka Kempner, and Abba Kovner.

"Cohen is a skilled writer. His language is spare and muscular, his descriptions evocative, his technique suspenseful." N Y Times Book Rev

Collingham, Lizzie

The **taste** of war; World War II and the battle for food. Lizzie Collingham. Penguin Press 2012 xv, 634 p.p il map $36   **940.53**
1. Strategy 2. World War, 1939-1945 -- Food supply 3. Starvation -- History -- 20th century 4. Food habits -- History -- 20th century 5. Food supply -- History -- 20th century 6. Food security -- History -- 20th century 7. War and society -- History -- 20th century 8. Nutrition policy -- History -- 20th century
ISBN 1594203296; 9781594203299
LC 2011043783

This book examines "the fundamental role that food played in the planning, conduct, and course of the Second World War." Author Lizzie Collingham "explicates how Italy's plans for colonizing Ethiopia and further infiltrating Libya, Japan's expansion into Manchuria and China, and Germany's drive into Russia and the Ukraine were in essence 'battle[s] for Food.'" (Atlantic Monthly)

Includes bibliographical references (p. 581-620) and index

Colors of confinement; rare Kodachrome photographs of Japanese American incarceration in World War II. edited by Eric L. Muller; with photographs by Bill Manbo. Univ. of North Carolina Pr. in ass. w/the Ctr. for Documentary Studies at Duke Univ. 2012 122 p. ill. (some col.) (Documentary arts and culture) (cloth : alk. paper) $35   **940.53**
1. World War, 1939-1945 -- Pictorial works 2. World War, 1939-1945 -- Prisoners and prisons, American 3. Japanese Americans -- Evacuation and relocation, 1942-1945 4. Heart Mountain Relocation Center (Wyo.) -- Pictorial works 5. World War, 1939-1945 -- Concentration camps -- Wyoming -- Pictorial works 6. Japanese Americans -- Evacuation and relocation, 1942-1945 -- Pictorial works
ISBN 0807835730; 9780807835739
LC 2011052817

This book, edited by Eric L. Muller, as part of the "Documentary Arts and Culture" series, with photographs by Bill Manbo, presents images of the Japanese American internments of World War II. "In 1942, Bill Manbo . . . and his family were forced . . . into the Japanese American internment camp at Heart Mountain in Wyoming. While there, Manbo documented . . . his family's struggle to maintain a normal life under the harsh conditions of racial imprisonment." (Publisher's note)

Includes bibliographical references and index

Cooke, Alistair

American home front, 1941-1942. Atlantic Monthly 2006 xx, 327p il $24   **940.53**
1. United States -- Social conditions 2. World War, 1939-1945 -- United States 3. United States --

Description and travel 4. United States -- Social life and customs
ISBN 978-0-87113-939-9; 0-87113-939-1
LC 2005-58860

"Crisscrossing the American continent from east to west and north to south, stopping in diners and bus stations and newly humming industrial plants, Mr. Cooke brings to life an America stepping into the unknown, committing its muscle and blood to an enterprise that most citizens could barely articulate, in places most of them had never heard of." N Y Times (Late N Y Ed)

Costigliola, Frank

Roosevelt's lost alliances; how personal politics helped start the Cold War. Frank Costigliola. Princeton University Press 2012 533 p. $35.00 **940.53**
1. World politics -- 1945-1991 2. Cold war 3. Governors 4. Statesmen 5. Historians 6. Memoirists 7. Presidents 8. Philatelists 9. Heads of state 10. Cabinet members 11. Prime ministers 12. Communist leaders 13. Political leaders 14. Members of Parliament 15. Nobel laureates for literature 16. United States -- Foreign relations 17. World War, 1939-1945 -- Diplomatic history 18. Soviet Union -- Foreign relations -- United States 19. United States -- Foreign relations -- Soviet Union 20. Great Britain -- Foreign relations -- United States 21. United States -- Foreign relations -- Great Britain
ISBN 069112129X; 9780691121291
LC 2011025271

Author Frank Costigliola "describes the functional alliance among the big three--Roosevelt, Churchill, and Stalin--during World War II and how, after Roosevelt's death, it was undermined. . . . Churchill is presented as an unchanging warrior and colonialist, whereas Stalin is portrayed" as "a 'realist' who, despite his brutality, sought secure borders, internal order, modernization, and respect. . . . FDR is pictured as being in reasonable health at Yalta and not bamboozled by Stalin." (Library Journal)

Includes bibliographical references.

Daniels, Roger

Prisoners without trial; Japanese Americans in World War II. Rev. ed.; Hill and Wang 2004 162p il (Critical issue series) pa $12   **940.53**
1. World War, 1939-1945 -- United States 2. Japanese Americans -- Evacuation and relocation, 1942-1945
ISBN 0-8090-7896-1
LC 2004-47328

First published 1993

An account of "the relocation of Japanese Americans during World War II, an injustice prompted not by military necessity but by political and racial motivations. The purpose of this volume is to tell the story in light of the redress legislation enacted in 1988." Libr J [review of 1993 edition]

Includes bibliographical references

Dawidowicz, Lucy S.

The **war** against the Jews, 1933-1945; 10th anniversary ed; Bantam Books 1986 xxxx, 466p il pa $19	**940.53**

1. Jews -- Europe 2. Holocaust, 1933-1945

ISBN 978-0-553-34532-2; 0-553-34532-X

LC 85-48051

A reissue with new introduction and supplementary bibliography of the title first published 1975 by Holt, Rinehart & Winston

"One of the best histories of the mass murder of Jews in World War II. Argues for the centrality of anti-Semitism in Hitler's program." Reader's Adviser

Includes bibliographical references

Dobbs, Michael

Six months in 1945; FDR, Stalin, Churchill, Truman, and the birth of the modern world. by Michael Dobbs. 1st ed. Alfred A. Knopf 2012 418 p. (hardcover) $28.95	**940.53**

1. Cold war 2. World War, 1939-1945 -- Peace 3. World War, 1939-1945 -- Diplomatic history 4. World politics -- 1945-1955 5. Cold War -- Diplomatic history 6. Soviet Union -- Foreign relations -- United States 7. United States -- Foreign relations -- Soviet Union

ISBN 030727165X; 9780307271655

LC 2012021747

This book, by Michael Dobbs, provides an "account of the pivotal six-month period spanning the end of World War II, the dawn of the nuclear age, and the beginning of the Cold War. When Roosevelt, Stalin, and Churchill met in Yalta in February 1945, . . . victory was imminent. The Big Three wanted to draft a blueprint for a lasting peace--but instead set the stage for a forty-four-year division of Europe into Soviet and western spheres of influence." (Publisher's note)

Includes bibliographical references and index

Dower, John W., 1938-

★ **Ways** of forgetting, ways of remembering; Japan in the modern world. John W. Dower. New Press 2012 336 p. (hardcover : alk. paper) $26.95 **940.53**

1. Propaganda 2. American essays 3. Japan -- History 4. Japan -- History -- 1945- 5. World War, 1939-1945 -- Japan 6. World War, 1939-1945 -- Influence 7. Japan -- Social conditions -- 1945 8. Japan -- Politics and government -- 1945 9. Japan -- History -- 1945- -- Historiography 10. World War, 1939-1945 -- Japan -- Historiography 11. World War, 1939-1945 -- Social aspects -- Japan 12. Social change -- Japan -- History -- 20th century 13. Collective memory -- Japan -- History -- 20th century

ISBN 1595586180; 9781595586186

LC 2011033861

This book "brings together a number of [John W. Dower's] essays written between 1993 and 2007. . . . Most deal with Japan since WWII, although Dower . . . invokes much earlier history." Particular focus is given to "national hypocrisy and the misuses of history and memory, American as well as Japanese. His topics include Japanese racism along with the enthusiasm with which Japan went to war. . . . Essays on Hiroshima round out the volume." (Publishers Weekly)

Includes bibliographical references and index

Dwork, Deborah

★ **Holocaust**: a history; {by} Deborah Dwork, Robert Jan Van Pelt. Norton 2002 xx, 444p il $27.95; pa $15.95	**940.53**

1. Jews -- Germany 2. Holocaust, 1933-1945 3. Germany -- Politics and government -- 1933-1945

ISBN 0-393-05188-9; 0-393-32524-5 pa

LC 2002-23565

"The authors examine such issues as the historic relationship between Jews, gentiles, and Germans; World War I and its consequences; National Socialism in the Weimar Republic; the Third Reich and its anti-Semitic measures; worldwide refugee policies that became a disaster for the Jews; and Jewish and gentile life under German occupation. They also examine the efforts by Allied nations to help the Jews. . . . This is a monumental work of impeccable scholarship." Booklist

Includes bibliographical references

Edsel, Robert M.

The **monuments** men; Allied heros, Nazi thieves, and the greatest treasure hunt in history. Robert M. Edsel with Bret Witter. Center Street 2009 p. cm.	**940.53**

1. Art thefts 2. World War, 1939-1945 3. Europe -- History

ISBN 9781599951492

LC 2009012255

Includes bibliographical references.

Eisner, Peter

The **Pope's** Last Crusade; How an American Jesuit Helped Pope Pius XI's Campaign to Stop Hitler. HarperCollins 2013 352 p. $27.99	**940.53**

1. Holocaust, 1939-1945 2. Catholic Church -- Relations -- Judaism

ISBN 0062049143; 9780062049148

This book by Peter Eisner offers an account of the "efforts by the Vatican to counter the Nazis before WWII. . . . According to Eisner, the Vatican's track record [regarding the Holocaust] might have been different if Pius XI had lived to deliver a speech in 1939 condemning the German regime" that was "based on the thinking of the Rev. John LaFarge, an American . . . whom Pius XI had commissioned to write a papal encyclical on" church action against racism. (Publishers Weekly)

Encyclopedia of Jewish life before and during the Holocaust; edited by Shmuel Spector and Geoffrey Wigoder. New York Univ. Press 2001 3v il maps set $99	**940.53**

1. Reference books 2. Jews -- Europe 3. Holocaust, 1933-1945 -- Encyclopedias

ISBN 0-8147-9356-8

"Each entry provides vital information on the town's Jewish inhabitants on the eve of German occupation, gives the dates of Jewish roundups and mass executions and estimates how many Jews from that community survived the war." Publ Wkly

★ **Encyclopedia** of World War II; a political, social and military history. Spencer C. Tucker, editor, Priscilla Mary Roberts, editor volume 5. ABC-CLIO 2004 5v il map set $485 **940.53**
1. Reference books 2. World War, 1939-1945 -- Encyclopedias
ISBN 1-576-07999-6

LC 2004-23745

"The 1,465 alphabetically arranged articles provide an international perspective on people; key battles, campaigns, and events; military equipment and strategy; countries; and other relevant topics. . . . Country entries not only cover the main Allied and Axis powers but also such countries as Afghanistan, Brazil, Estonia, Iraq, Mexico, New Zealand, and Somalia as well as world regions. . . . An excellent resource for high-school, public, and academic libraries." Booklist
Includes bibliographical references

Evans, Richard J.
★ The **Third** Reich at war. Penguin Press 2009 926p il map $40 **940.53**
1. Germany -- History -- 1933-1945 2. World War, 1939-1945 -- Germany
ISBN 978-1-59420-206-3

LC 2008-44765

First published 2008 in the United Kingdom
This is a "very readable, well-paced account that is fully familiar with the huge amount of specialist scholarship in this field but never gets bogged down by excessive detail." Hist Today
Includes bibliographical references

Faber, David
Munich, 1938; appeasement and World War II. Simon & Schuster 2009 520p il $30 **940.53**
1. World War, 1939-1945 -- Causes 2. Munich Four-Power Agreement (1938) 3. World War, 1939-1945 -- Diplomatic history 4. Europe -- Politics and government -- 1918-1945
ISBN 978-1-4391-3233-3

LC 2008-44896

"The 1938 Munich Conference has been referred to as the Great Betrayal, virtually guaranteeing the start of war in Europe the following year. In return for Hitler's empty promises of peace, the British and French governments acquiesced to his demand to annex the Sudetenland, a largely German-speaking region of Czechoslovakia. The appeasement emboldened Hitler and led directly to the German-Soviet nonaggression pact and their joint invasion of Poland. Faber's account of the preparation for and actual unfolding of the conference is comprehensive, engrossing, and depressing, like viewing a slow-motion train wreck. . . . He does a masterful job of recounting the political maneuvers and infighting within both the British and German camps." Booklist
Includes bibliographical references

Friedlander, Saul
Nazi Germany and the Jews. vl HarperCollins Pubs. 1997 436p vl hardcover o.p. pa $19.95 **940.53**
1. Jews -- Germany 2. Holocaust, 1933-1945 3. Jews

-- Persecutions 4. Germany -- History -- 1933-1945
ISBN 0-06-019042-6; 0-06-092878-6 pa

LC 96-21915

"Not the least impressive aspect of Friedländer's book is the skill with which he juxtaposes different levels of reality within an overall chronological frame, moving from high-level Nazi debates on Jewish policy to the routine brutalities of the SA and SS, and from the perceptions of the average German citizen to those of the victims." N Y Rev Books
Includes bibliographical references

The **years** of extermination; Nazi Germany and the Jews, 1939-1945. HarperCollins Publishers 2007 xxvi, 870p $39.95 **940.53**
1. Jews -- Germany 2. Holocaust, 1933-1945 3. Jews -- Persecutions 4. Germany -- History -- 1933-1945
ISBN 0-06-019043-4; 978-0-06-019043-9

LC 2006-48982

The second part of a two-part series starting with Nazi Germany and the Jews: vl: The years of persecution, 1933-1939 (1997)
"This is a masterful synthesis that draws on a lifetime of learning and research." Publ Wkly
Includes bibliographic references

Friedman, Anita
Rywka's Diary; The Writings of a Jewish Girl from the Lodz Ghetto. Anita Friedman. HarperCollins 2015 288 p. 8 plates; color ills., map (hardcover) $35 **940.53**
1. Jewish children in the Holocaust 2. Holocaust, 1939-1945 -- Personal narratives
ISBN 9780062389688; 0062389688

This book, by Anita Friedman, "is the diary of a girl named Rywka Lipszyc who detailed the brutal conditions that Jews in the Lodz ghetto, the second largest in Poland, endured under the Nazis: poverty, hunger and malnutrition, religious oppression, and, in Rywka's case, the death of her parents and siblings. Handwritten in a school notebook between October 1943 and April 1944, the diary ends literally in mid-sentence. What became of Rywka is a mystery." (Publisher's note)
"An incredible addition to Holocaust literature. The historical essays are informative and absorbing to a general audience." LJ

Gilbert, Martin
Kristallnacht; prelude to destruction. Harper-Collins Publishers 2006 314p il map (Making history) hardcover o.p. pa $14.99 **940.53**
1. Jews -- Persecutions 2. Germany -- History -- 1933-1945
ISBN 0-06-057083-0; 978-0-06-057083-5; 0-06-112135-5 pa; 978-0-06-112135-7 pa

LC 2005-58169

This is "an account of the Night of Broken Glass, which was unleashed against the Jewish communities across Germany on November 10, 1938. . . . A powerful account of the helplessness of the Jews." Booklist

Includes bibliographical references

The **Routledge** atlas of the Holocaust; 4th ed.; Routledge 2009 286p map $120; pa $30.95 **940.53**
1. Atlases 2. Reference books 3. Holocaust, 1933-1945 -- Maps
ISBN 978-0-415-48481-7; 0-415-48481-2; 978-0-415-48486-2 pa; 0-415-48486-3 pa

LC 2008-43844

First published 1982 in the United Kingdom with title: The Dent atlas of the Holocaust

The author uses "maps, text, and photographs to document Hitler's attempt to destroy Europe's Jews. . . . Commentary offers statistical information, historical background, and something about the people of the area. Archival photographs bring the events to life. . . . This small but effective work demonstrates the magnitude of the Nazi terror by bringing it down to a personal level." Am Ref Books Annu, 2003 [review of 2002 edition]

Includes bibliographical references

The **Second** World War; a complete history. Holt & Co. 1989 846p il maps hardcover o.p. pa $25 **940.53**
1. World War, 1939-1945
ISBN 0-8050-1788-7 pa

LC 89-11129

The author begins this study "with the invasion of Poland. Gilbert's flowing narrative is spiced with anecdotal details culled from diaries, memoirs and official documents. He is especially skillful at interweaving summaries of military strategy with vignettes of civilian suffering—the genocide of the Jews is never far from view." Newsweek

Includes bibliographical references

Goldhagen, Daniel Jonah

Hitler's willing executioners; ordinary Germans and the Holocaust. [by] Daniel Jonah Goldhagen. Knopf 1996 622p il maps hardcover o.p. pa $16 **940.53**
1. Antisemitism 2. National socialism 3. Holocaust, 1933-1945 4. Germany -- History -- 1933-1945
ISBN 0-679-44695-8; 0-679-77268-5 pa

LC 95-38591

The author "endeavors to show that the common apologia for the Germans—that Hitler 'brainwashed' them—is nonsense and that most Germans gave their active assent to genocide. An ordinary German commander, for example, might feel himself bound by a strict code of conduct yet not be at all averse to murdering Jews. The book ends with a detailed notes section and an appendix that explains the correct methodology for studying the Nazi period." Libr J

Goldsmith, Martin

The **inextinguishable** symphony; a true story of music and love in Nazi Germany. Wiley 2000 346p il hardcover o.p. pa $15.95 **940.53**
1. Drummers 2. Jews -- Germany 3. Holocaust, 1933-

1945
ISBN 0-471-35097-4; 0-471-07864-6 pa

LC 00-25955

Goldsmith's "weaving together of cultural and personal history constitutes a gripping tale of persecution, intrigue, and love and an insider's—or two insiders'—view of a dark time." Booklist

Includes bibliographical references

Goodman, Simon, 1948-

The **Orpheus** Clock; the search for my family's art treasures stolen by the Nazis. Simon Goodman. Scribner 2015 368 p. 8 pages of color plates; ills. (hardback) $28 **940.53**
1. Art thefts 2. Jews -- Germany 3. World War, 1939-1945 -- Reparations 4. Art thefts -- Investigation 5. Jewish bankers -- Germany -- Biography 6. Holocaust, Jewish (1939-1945) -- Germany 7. Art thefts -- Germany -- History -- 20th century
ISBN 1451697635; 9781451697636; 9781451697643

LC 2015017171

This book, by Simon Goodman, presents the "true story of one man's single-minded quest to reclaim what the Nazis stole from his family, their beloved art collection, and to restore their legacy. Simon Goodman's grandparents . . . , the Gutmanns, as they were known then, . . . amassed a magnificent, world-class art collection. . . . But the Nazi regime snatched from them everything they had worked to build." (Publisher's note)

Groom, Winston

★ **1942**; the year that tried men's souls. Atlantic Monthly Press 2005 459p il maps $27.50 **940.53**
1. World War, 1939-1945
ISBN 0-8711-3889-1

LC 2004-62779

In this military history of one year during World War II, the author "delivers the traditional worshipful portrait of General MacArthur while admitting he made several key blunders that doomed the Philippines in the year's early months. . . . He adds that brains and luck win more battles than courage, providing a perfect illustration in Midway, fought in June 1942. . . . Groom has written a page-turner; readers needing an introduction will love it." Publ Wkly

Includes bibliographical references

Guttenplan, D. D.

The **Holocaust** on trial. Norton 2001 328p il hardcover o.p. pa $15.95 **940.53**
1. Trials 2. Historians 3. College teachers 4. Holocaust, 1933-1945 -- Historiography
ISBN 0-393-32292-0 pa

LC 2001-30370

The author chronicles the "libel trial in Britain brought by historian David Irving. Irving, widely viewed as an apologist for Hitler, sued American scholar Deborah Lipstadt, whose Denying the Holocaust (1993) had labeled Irving as a right-wing extremist. . . . Interspersing essayistic diversions, the author presents a thoughtful work as well as a courtroom thriller." Booklist

Includes bibliographical references

Hackett, David A.

The **Buchenwald** report; translated, edited, and with an introduction by David A. Hackett; foreword by Frederick A. Praeger. Westview Press 1995 397p map hardcover o.p. pa $29   **940.53**

1. Buchenwald (Germany: Concentration camp) 2. Holocaust, 1933-1945 -- Personal narratives

ISBN 0-8133-1777-0; 0-8133-3363-6 pa

LC 94-39714

"This seminal document, published here in its entirety for the first time, is a report compiled for the Allied Army from interviews with the inmates of the Buchenwald concentration camp, located near Weimar, Germany in April 1945, shortly after the camp's liberation. . . . It is immediate, direct, and, as the product of the testimony of many people, more inclusive and wide-ranging than any single individual's personal testament. A classic of Holocaust literature that should be in any library that covers European history." Libr J

Includes bibliographical references

Hamilton, Nigel, 1944-

Commander in chief; FDR's battle with Churchill, 1943. Nigel Hamilton. Houghton Mifflin Harcourt 2016 496 p. illustrations, maps (hardcover) $30   **940.53**

1. World War, 1939-1945 2. Command of troops -- Case studies 3. World War, 1939-1945 -- Campaigns 4. World War, 1939-1945 -- United States 5. World War, 1939-1945 -- Diplomatic history 6. Great Britain -- Foreign relations -- United States 7. United States -- Foreign relations -- Great Britain

ISBN 0544279115; 9780544279117

LC 2015037253

This book, by Nigel Hamilton, presents a "look at Franklin Roosevelt's role in the Allied strategy midway through World War II, with an emphasis on his relations with Winston Churchill. Hamilton shows Roosevelt's clear vision of how to win the war and how to create a postwar society that would prevent such wars from recurring." (Kirkus Reviews)

"This is an outstanding contribution to understanding the wartime alliance and Roosevelt's role in it." Booklist

Includes bibliographical references and index

Helm, Sarah

Ravensbruck; life and death in Hitler's concentration camp for women. Sarah Helm. Nan A. Talese/Doubleday 2014 656 p. 16 plates; illustrations; maps (hardback) $37.50   **940.53**

1. Concentration camps 2. Holocaust, 1939-1945 3. World War, 1939-1945 -- Women 4. Ravensbrück (Concentration camp) 5. Women prisoners -- Germany -- Ravensbrück 6. World War, 1939-1945 -- Prisoners and prisons, German 7. Women concentration camp inmates -- Germany -- Ravensbrück

ISBN 038552059X; 9780385520591

LC 2014014974

This book by Sarah Helm focuses on "Ravensbrück, a concentration camp designed specifically for women by Heinrich Himmler, prime architect of the Holocaust. Using testimony unearthed since the end of the Cold War and interviews with survivors who have never talked before, . . . Helm has ventured into the heart of the camp, demonstrating

for the reader in riveting detail how easily and quickly the unthinkable horror evolved." (Publisher's note)

Henderson, Bruce B., 1946-

Rescue at Los Banos; the most daring prison camp raid of World War II. Bruce Henderson. William Morrow 2015 366 p. illustrations (hardcover) $27.99   **940.53**

1. World War, 1939-1945 -- Philippines 2. World War, 1939-1945 -- Aerial operations 3. World War, 1939-1945 -- Prisoners and prisons 4. Los Baños Internment Camp 5. World War, 1939-1945 -- Campaigns -- Philippines 6. World War, 1939-1945 -- Prisoners and prisons, Japanese 7. World War, 1939-1945 -- Aerial operations, American -- Philippines 8. World War, 1939-1945 -- Amphibious operations, American -- Philippines

ISBN 006232506X; 9780062325068; 9780062325075; 9780062370020

LC 2015007141

This book by Bruce Henderson tells the "true story of one of the greatest military rescues of all time, the 1945 World War II prison camp raid at Los Baños in the Philippines. Combining personal interviews, diaries, correspondence, memoirs, and archival research, [Henderson] tells the story of a remarkable group of prisoners . . . and of the young American soldiers and Filipino guerrillas who risked their lives to save them." (Publisher's note)

"This narrative of one event depicting the horrors of war and its resolution should broaden the perspective of general readers of 20th-century military history. Although a monument, a ceremony, and a joint U.S. congressional resolution honored this liberation on its 60th anniversary, the event was underpublicized at the time since Joe Rosenthal's iconic photograph of the raising of the American flag on Iwo Jima taken the same day received more media coverage." LJ

Includes bibliographical references and index

Herman, Arthur

Freedom's forge; how American business produced victory in World War II. Arthur Herman. Random House 2012 xiv, 413 p.p   **940.53**

1. Economic policy -- United States 2. Industrial mobilization -- United States 3. Manufacturing industries -- United States 4. United States -- Economic conditions -- 1933-1945 5. World War, 1939-1945 -- Economic aspects -- United States 6. United States -- Economic policy -- 1933-1945 7. Industrial management -- United States -- History -- 20th century 8. Industrial mobilization -- United States -- History -- 20th century 9. Manufacturing industries -- Military aspects -- United States -- History -- 20th century

ISBN 1400069645; 9780679604631; 9781400069644

LC 2011040661

In this book, "the author argues . . . against the conventional wisdom that America's rearmament [during World War II] took place under the guidance of a competent federal government. . . . The production of the flood of war materiel that drowned the Axis was achieved by the voluntary cooperation of businesses driven as much by the profit motive as by patriotism, solving problems through their own

ingenuity rather than waiting for government directives."
(Kirkus Reviews)

Includes bibliographical references (p. [387-399)
and index

Hoffman, Eva

    After such knowledge; memory, history and the
legacy of the Holocaust. Public Affairs 2004 301p
$25; pa $14   **940.53**
    1. Holocaust, 1933-1945
    ISBN 1-586-48046-4; 0-586-48304-8 pa
                        LC 2003-66443
    The author "focuses on the consciousness and experi-
ence of the Holocaust's second generation—the children of
survivors. . . . The book considers such diverse concepts as
how the 'trauma' of the Holocaust is constructed, the role of
emigration and national identity in shaping the second generation's narratives of their lives. . . . Hoffman writes with a
subdued but vibrant passion." Publ Wkly

    Includes bibliographical references

Horwitz, Gordon J.

    Ghettostadt; Lodz and the making of a Nazi city.
The Belknap Press of Harvard University Press 2008
395p il map   **940.53**
    1. Holocaust, 1933-1945 2. Jews -- Persecutions 3.
ódz (Poland) 4. ódz (Poland) -- Ethnic relations 5.
Holocaust, Jewish (1939-1945) -- Poland -- ódz 6. Jews
-- Persecutions -- Poland -- ódz -- History
    ISBN 0-674-02799-X; 978-0-674-02799-2
                        LC 2007-50934
    The author discusses how the Nazis transformed Lodz,
whose population was more than one-third Jewish, into a
new German city called Litzmannstadt. Index.

    "The Nazis' use of bureaucracy to achieve their geno-
cidal aims comes through clearly in this historical tour de
force. The Nazis attempted to 're-engineer' the Polish city
of Lodz, home to more than 230,000 Jews (one-third of the
city's population) before the war, into a model—and Juden-
frei—German city embodying health and beauty they called
Litzmannstadt. This required forcing the Jews into a ghetto
with the help of Jewish leaders, especially the . . . report-
edly lascivious industrialist Chaim Rumkowski. . . . With a
graceful style rare in academic history, Horwitz . . . marshals
a host of primary sources to highlight the gradual destruction
of the ghetto." Publ Wkly

    Includes bibliographical references

Jones, Michael

    After Hitler; the last ten days of World War II in
Europe. Michael Jones. NAL Caliber 2015 400 p. 16
plates; illustrations; maps (hardback) $27.95 **940.53**
    1. World War, 1939-1945 -- Peace 2. World War,
1939-1945 -- Europe -- End 3. World War, 1939-1945
-- Diplomatic history
    ISBN 0451477014; 9780451477019
                        LC 2015018149
    "After Hitler shines a light on ten fascinating days after
that infamous suicide that changed the course of the twentieth century. Combining exhaustive research with masterfully paced storytelling, Michael Jones recounts the Führer's
frantic last stand; the devious maneuverings of his hand-

picked successor, Karl Dönitz; the grudging respect Joseph
Stalin had for Churchill and FDR, as well as his distrust of
Harry Truman; the bold negotiating by General Dwight D.
Eisenhower that hastened Germany's surrender but drew the
ire of the Kremlin; the journalist who almost scuttled the
cease-fire; and the thousands of ordinary British, American,
and Russian soldiers caught in the swells of history, from the
Red Army's march on Berlin to the liberation of the Nazis'
remaining concentration camps. Through it all, Jones traces
the shifting loyalties between East and West that sowed the
seeds of the Cold War and nearly unraveled the Grand Alliance." From the Publisher

    "Unlike connoisseurs of military history, casual read-
ers may not be concerned with martial unit designations
and some of the gritty details of battle formation, but the
exploits of the men and women they represented are engrossing, sometimes even heartbreaking. A skillful historian
demonstrates how courage and hope characterized the last
act of the great campaign to bring peace to Europe 70 years
ago." Kirkus

Joukowsky, Artemis

    Defying the Nazis; The Sharps' War. Artemis
Joukowsky, foreword by Ken Burns. Beacon Press
2016 255 p. illustrations (hardcover : alk. paper)
$25.95; (ebook) $15.99   **940.53**
    1. Holocaust, 1939-1945 2. Righteous Gentiles in the
Holocaust 3. World War, 1939-1945 -- Jews -- Rescue
4. Holocaust, Jewish (1939-1945) 5. Righteous Gentiles
in the Holocaust -- Massachusetts -- Wellesley Hills
    ISBN 080707182X; 9780807071823; 9780807071830
                        LC 2016007704
    This book by Artemis Joukowsky, with foreword by
Ken Burns, tells the story of the Reverend Waitstill Sharp,
a young Unitarian minister, and his wife, Martha, "whose
faith and commitment to social justice inspired them to
undertake dangerous rescue and relief missions across war-
torn Europe, saving the lives of countless refugees, political
dissidents, and Jews on the eve of World War II." (Publisher's note)

    "A harrowing and ultimately inspirational tribute to a
brave couple." Booklist

    Includes bibliographical references (pages 235-244)
and index.

Karski, Jan, 1914-2000

    ★ **Story** of a secret state; my report to the
world. Jan Karski; foreword by Madeleine Albright.
Georgetown University Press 2013 464 p. (hbk. :
alk. paper) $26.95   **940.53**
    1. World War, 1939-1945 -- Poland 2. World War,
1939-1945 -- Personal narratives 3. Poland -- History
-- Occupation, 1939-1945 4. World War, 1939-1945 --
Personal narratives, Polish
    ISBN 1589019830; 9781589019836
                        LC 2012037549
    This book, by Jan Karski, is a memoir of a diplomat who
served during "World War II and the Holocaust. With elements of a spy thriller, documenting his experiences in the
Polish Underground, and as one of the first accounts of the
systematic slaughter of the Jews by the German Nazis, this
volume is a remarkable testimony of one man's courage and

a nation's struggle for resistance against overwhelming oppression." (Publisher's note)

Includes bibliographical references and index

Kershaw, Alex

Avenue of spies; a true story of terror, espionage, and one American family's heroic resistance in Nazi-occupied Paris. by Alex Kershaw. Crown 2015 304 p. 8 plates; ills; maps; ports. (hardback) $28 **940.53**
1. Spies 2. Americans -- France 3. Physicians -- Biography 4. Paris (France) -- History 5. World War, 1914-1918 -- France 6. Spies -- France -- Paris -- Biography 7. World War, 1939-1945 -- France -- Paris 8. Americans -- France -- Paris -- Biography 9. Physicians -- France -- Paris -- Biography 10. France -- History -- German occupation, 1940-1945 11. Paris (France) -- History, Military -- 20th century 12. World War, 1939-1945 -- Underground movements -- France -- Paris
ISBN 0804140030; 9780804140034

LC 2015016861

This book, by Alex Kershaw, is the "true story of an American doctor in Paris. . . . Avenue Foch, one of the most exclusive residential streets in Nazi-occupied France, was Paris's hotbed of daring spies, murderous secret police, amoral informers, and Vichy collaborators. So when American physician Sumner Jackson, who lived with his wife and young son Phillip at Number 11, found himself drawn into the Liberation network of the French resistance, he knew the stakes were impossibly high." (Publisher's note)

"Kershaw tells their story in an intense, moving account that also serves to vividly describe the life of ordinary Parisians under the occupation." Booklist

Kinney, David

The devil's diary; Alfred Rosenberg and the stolen secrets of the Third Reich. Robert K. Wittman and David Kinney. Harper 2016 528 p. illustrations (hardcover : alkaline paper) $35 **940.53**
1. National socialism 2. National socialists 3. Holocaust, 1939-1945 4. Nazis -- Diaries 5. National socialism -- Philosophy 6. Holocaust, Jewish (1939-1945) -- Philosophy 7. Germany -- Foreign relations -- Soviet Union 8. Soviet Union -- Foreign relations -- Germany 9. United States. Federal Bureau of Investigation -- Officials and employees -- Biography
ISBN 9780062319012; 9780062319029

LC 2015036609

This book, by Robert K. Wittman and David Kinney, "investigates the disappearance of a private diary penned by one of Adolf Hitler's top aides—Alfred Rosenberg, his 'chief philosopher'—and mines its long-hidden pages to deliver a fresh, eye-opening account of the Nazi rise to power and the genesis of the Holocaust." (Publisher's note)

"Wittman and Kinney's chronicle of the efforts historians took to gain access to the diary feels like it's pulled from a movie, especially when they add in Rosenberg's story. This is an outstanding piece of journalism." Pub Wkly

Includes bibliographical references (pages [447]-494) and index.

Klein, Maury

A call to arms; mobilizing America for World War II. by Maury Klein. 1st U.S. ed. Bloomsbury 2013 912 p. (hardcover) $40.00 **940.53**
1. Military weapons 2. World War, 1939-1945 3. United States -- Armed forces 4. United States -- Economic policy -- 1933-1945 5. World War, 1939-1945 -- Economic aspects -- United States 6. Industrial mobilization -- United States -- History -- 20th century 7. United States -- Armed Forces -- Mobilization -- History -- 20th century
ISBN 1596916079; 9781596916074

LC 2012039497

This book, written by Maury Klein, examines U.S. efforts to "create, outfit, transport, and supply huge armies, navies, and air forces" for World War II. It looks at how American productivity, "American industry, and American workers, won World War II [and how it] [n]ot only . . . determine[d] the outcome of the war, but it transformed the American economy and society." (Publisher's note)

Includes bibliographical references and index.

Koker, David

At the edge of the abyss; a concentration camp diary, 1943-1944. David Koker; edited by Robert Jan van Pelt; translated from the Dutch by Michiel Horn and John Irons. Northwestern University Press 2012 xii, 396 p.p **940.53**
1. Diaries 2. Jews -- Biography 3. World War, 1939-1945 -- Prisoners and prisons 4. Vught (Concentration camp) 5. Prisoners of war -- Netherlands -- Biography 6. World War, 1939-1945 -- Personal narratives, Dutch
ISBN 0810126362; 9780810126367

LC 2011026584

The book presents the diary of David Koker from 1943-1944. "During his time in the Vught concentration camp, the 21-year-old David recorded on an almost daily basis his observations, thoughts, and feelings. He mercilessly probed the abyss that opened around him and, at times, within himself. David's diary covers almost a year, both charting his daily life in Vught as it developed over time and tracing his spiritual evolution as a writer. Until early February 1944, David was able to smuggle some 73,000 words from the camp to his best friend Karel van het Reve, a non-Jew." (Publisher's note)

Includes bibliographical references

Kruk, Herman

The last days of the Jerusalem of Lithuania; chronicles from the Vilna ghetto and the camps, 1939-1944. edited and introduced by Benjamin Harshav; translated by Barbara Harshav. Yivo Inst. for Jewish Res. 2002 732p il maps $45 **940.53**
1. Jews -- Lithuania 2. Holocaust, 1933-1945 3. World War, 1939-1945 -- Underground movements
ISBN 0-300-04494-1

LC 2002-16736

This a collection of Kruk's journals and other writings from the Jewish ghetto of Vilna and a labor camp in Estonia This "is a major addition to Holocaust literature and Jewish history. In 1961 a Yiddish edition of the Vilna diaries was published. This larger new edition has been painstakingly assembled from those diaries and other documents and writings by Kruk that were widely scattered and only found since the 1961 edition; Harshav has also added a wealth of new footnotes." Publ Wkly

Includes bibliographical references

Langer, Lawrence L.

Admitting the Holocaust; collected essays. Oxford Univ. Press 1995 202p hardcover o.p. pa $14.95 **940.53**

1. Poets 2. Authors 3. Novelists 4. Dramatists 5. Holocaust, 1939-1945, in literature 6. Essayists 7. Short story writers 8. Holocaust, 1933-1945 9. Nobel laureates for literature 10. Holocaust, 1933-1945, in literature

ISBN 0-19-510648-2 pa

LC 94-13368

"A horribly bleak, undeniably important book." Booklist

Includes bibliographical references

Art from the ashes; a Holocaust anthology. edited by Lawrence L. Langer. Oxford Univ. Press 1995 689p il hardcover o.p. pa $47.95; $76.95 **940.53**

1. Holocaust, 1939-1945, in literature 2. Holocaust, 1933-1945, in literature 3. Holocaust, 1933-1945 -- Personal narratives

ISBN 0-19-507732-6 pa; 9780195077322

LC 94-11446

A "remarkable volume, perfectly suited for anyone studying the Holocaust. . . . Compared with [the] firsthand accounts, fiction could be, one would think, only a pallid version of reality. Yet the fiction Mr. Langer collects . . . highlights the reality of the Holocaust with stunning intensity." N Y Times Book Rev

Levi, Primo

★ **Survival** in Auschwitz; the Nazi assault on humanity. translated from the Italian by Stuart Woolf; including "A conversation with Primo Levi" by Philip Roth. Touchstone 1997 187p hardcover o.p. pa $16.00 **940.53**

1. Auschwitz (Poland: Concentration camp) 2. Holocaust, 1933-1945 -- Personal narratives 3. World War, 1939-1945 -- Personal narratives

ISBN 0-02-029192-2; 9780684826806 pa

LC 86-13656

Originally published 1958 in Italy; first United States editon published 1959 by Orion Press with title: If this is a man

This volume tells of the Italian Jewish chemist's ten months as a concentration camp inmate

Lewy, Guenter

★ The **Nazi** persecution of the gypsies. Oxford Univ. Press 2000 306p il hardcover o.p. pa $24.95 **940.53**

1. Gypsies 2. National socialism 3. World War, 1939-1945 -- Atrocities

ISBN 0-19-512556-8; 0-19-514240-3 pa

LC 98-52545

The author "begins with a brief history of the maltreatment of Gypsies all over Europe, from the fifteenth century

onward; then, by dint of exhaustive research, Lewy documents the horrors of their expulsions, detentions, deportations, and deaths during the systematic madness of the Holocaust." Booklist

Includes bibliographical references

Lifton, Robert Jay

The **Nazi** doctors; medical killing and the psychology of genocide. Basic Bks. 1986 561p hardcover o.p. pa $23 **940.53**

1. Physicians 2. War criminals 3. Concentration camps 4. Murderers 5. Nazi leaders 6. Holocaust, 1933-1945 7. World War, 1939-1945 -- Atrocities

ISBN 0-465-04905-2 pa

LC 85-73874

"How could German physicians trained as scientist-healers carry out Nazi orders for mass killings? . . . Lifton, an American Jewish physician, seeks answers through interviews with surviving doctors, family members, and victims and by painstakingly gleaning Holocaust archives." Sci Books Films

Includes bibliographical references

Lipstadt, Deborah E.

Denying the Holocaust; the growing assault on truth and memory. with a new preface by the author. Plume 1994 278p pa $16 **940.53**

1. Antisemitism 2. Holocaust, 1933-1945 -- Historiography

ISBN 0-452-27274-2; 978-0-452-27274-3

LC 93-45586

First published 1993 by Free Press

"Lipstadt has written a disturbing book that deserves a wide readership." Libr J

Includes bibliographical references

★ **History** on trial; my day in court with David Irving. Ecco 2005 xxi, 346p il $25.95; pa $14.95 **940.53**

1. Trials 2. Historians 3. Holocaust, 1933-1945 -- Historiography

ISBN 0-06-059376-8; 0-06-059377-6 pa

LC 2004-57533

"No one who cares about historical truth, freedom of speech or the Holocaust will avoid a sense of triumph from Gray's decision—or a sense of dismay that British libel laws allowed such intimidation by Irving of a historian and a publisher in the first place." Publ Wkly

Includes bibliographical references

Lukacs, John, 1924-

Five days in London, May 1940. Yale Univ. Press 1999 236p $19.95; pa $11.95 **940.53**

1. Diplomats 2. Statesmen 3. Historians 4. Prime ministers 5. Memoirists 6. Cabinet members 7. Government officials 8. Members of Parliament 9. Colonial administrators 10. Nobel laureates for literature 11. World War, 1939-1945 -- Great Britain 12. World war, 1939-1945 -- Great Britain 13. Great Britain -- Politics and government 14. World War, 1939-1945 -- Diplomatic history 15. Great Britain -- Politics and government -- 1936-1945 16. Great Britain

-- Politics and government -- 20th century
ISBN 0-300-08030-1; 0-300-08466-8 pa

LC 99-27583

Lukacs discusses Prime Minister Winston Churchill's war policy during the five days between May 24 and May 28, 1940. "In that period, Belgium surrendered; and it became clear that France must shortly do the same. . . . Churchill also had to face a political threat within his own inner War Cabinet, from Lord Halifax. . . . Defiance of Hitler in those final days of May 1940 looked rash to Halifax. He wanted to discover what terms Hitler was prepared to offer, . . . and hinted that he might resign if Churchill refused to consider all options." (Natl Rev) Index.

This work focuses on the "chaotic few days during which, according to the author, Hitler came closest to winning the war. . . . Lukacs concentrates on the struggle within the British War Cabinet, which pitted the Prime Minister, Winston Churchill, against the Foreign Secretary, Lord Halifax, a Tory idol and a friend of the King. The point of contention was Halifax's belief that England should attempt to negotiate a general European settlement with Hitler. Churchill's stubborn refusal won out. The author's equally stubborn digging uncovered a stunning amount of defeatism and intrigue against Churchill by contemporary statesmen." New Yorker

Includes bibliographical references

Maitland, Leslie

Crossing the borders of time; a true story of war, exile, and love reclaimed. Leslie Maitland. Other Press 2012 494 p. **940.53**
1. Love stories 2. Jews -- France 3. Jewish refugees -- Biography 4. World War, 1939-1945 -- Jews 5. Immigrants -- United States -- Biography 6. First loves -- France -- Biography 7. Jewish refugees -- United States -- Biography 8. World War, 1939-1945 -- Jews -- France -- Biography 9. World War, 1939-1945 -- Refugees -- France -- Biography
ISBN 1590514963; 9781590514962

LC 2011047110

This book focuses on "love lost in Alsace during World War II, rediscovered 50 years later in New Jersey. . . . [Author Leslie] Maitland's mother Janine, along with her German-speaking parents, sister and brother, originally fled in 1938 from Freiburg,. . . . The family then landed in Lyon, where Janine . . . reignited a friendship with a dashing Catholic law student, Roland Arcieri. After falling in love during their brief time together, Janine was yanked away again with her family." (Kirkus Reviews)

Includes bibliographical references (p. 489-492)

Mazower, Mark

Hitler's empire; how the Nazis ruled Europe. Penguin Press 2008 xl, 725p il map **940.53**
1. National socialism 2. Europe -- History -- 1918-1945 3. Germany -- History -- 1918-1945 4. Germany -- History -- 1933-1945 5. World War, 1939-1945 -- Germany
ISBN 1-594-20188-9; 978-1-594-20188-2

LC 2008-26997

This is an account of how the Nazis designed, maintained, and ultimately lost their European empire. (Publisher's note) Index.

The author's compelling analysis of the contradictions underpinning the Nazis' dream of Lebensraum impressively demonstrates that the Nazis were destined to lose World War II. But he soberly reminds us that, inefficient as the Nazis may have been at running an empire, they were brutally effective at suppressing resistance to it. New Leader

Includes bibliographical references

Mazzeo, Tilar J.

★ Irena's children; the extraordinary story of the woman who saved 2,500 children from the Warsaw ghetto. Tilar J. Mazzeo. Gallery Books 2016 336 p. (hardcover : alk. paper) $26 **940.53**
1. World War, 1939-1945 -- Jews -- Rescue 2. Holocaust, Jewish (1939-1945) -- Poland 3. World War, 1939-1945 -- Jews -- Rescue -- Poland 4. Righteous Gentiles in the Holocaust -- Poland -- Biography
ISBN 1476778507; 9781476778501; 9781476778518

LC 2015051244

This book, by Tilar J. Mazzeo, gives the "account of . . . the 'female Oskar Schindler' who took staggering risks to save 2,500 children from death and deportation in Nazi-occupied Poland during World War II. In 1942, one young social worker, Irena Sendler, was granted access to the Warsaw ghetto as a public health specialist. While there, she reached out to the trapped Jewish families, going from door to door and asking the parents to trust her with their young children." (Publisher's note)

"Mazzeo chronicles a ray of hope in desperate times in this compelling biography of a brave woman who refused to give up." Kirkus

Includes bibliographical references and index.

McDougall, Christopher

Natural Born Heroes; How a Daring Band of Misfits Mastered the Lost Secrets of Strength and Endurance. Christopher McDougall. Knopf 2015 368 p. map $26.95 **940.53**
1. Crete (Greece) 2. Heroes and heroines 3. World War, 1939-1945 -- Greece
ISBN 0307594963; 9780307594969

LC 2014047459

In this book Christopher McDougall explains how he "finds his next great adventure on the razor-sharp mountains of Crete, where a band of Resistance fighters in World War II plotted the daring abduction of a German general from the heart of the Nazi occupation. McDougall makes his way to the island to find the answer and retrace their steps, experiencing firsthand the extreme physical challenges the Resistance fighters and their local allies faced." (Publisher's note)

"As long as McDougall sticks to their exploits, this narrative is riveting. Unfortunately, his ruminations upon the nature of heroism and his efforts to link these men to ancient and modern heroes ring false. Still, at its best, this is a well-done recounting of a truly heroic episode of WWII." Booklist

Moorhouse, Roger

The Devils' Alliance; Hitler's Pact With Stalin, 1939-1941. by Roger Moorhouse. Basic Books 2014 432 p. 16 plates; illustrations; maps $29.99 **940.53**
1. World War, 1939-1945 -- Treaties 2. Soviet Union

-- Foreign relations -- Germany
ISBN 0465030750; 9780465030750

LC 2012278241

This book, by Roger Moorhouse, "explores the causes and implications of the Nazi-Soviet Pact, a . . . covenant whose creation and dissolution were crucial turning points in World War II. Forged by the German foreign minister, Joachim von Ribbentrop, and his Soviet counterpart, Vyacheslav Molotov, the nonaggression treaty briefly united the two powers in a brutally efficient collaboration. Together, the Germans and Soviets quickly conquered and divided central and eastern Europe." (Publisher's note)

"Moorhouse's accessible prose and clear explication make this a great story for history readers, and his extensive research and documentation help create a critical text for academics focusing on World War II, German history, and Soviet history." LJ

Mortimer, Gavin

The **longest** night; the bombing of London on May 10, 1941. Berkley Caliber 2005 356p il $24.95   **940.53**
1. World War, 1939-1945 -- Great Britain 2. World War, 1939-1945 -- Aerial operations
ISBN 0-425-20557-6

LC 2005-45281

"This account is given special power and poignancy by using the recollections of surviving men and women who endured that terrible night. An outstanding addition to World War II collections." Booklist

Nagorski, Andrew

The **Nazi** hunters; Andrew Nagorski. Simon & Schuster 2016 416 p. illustrations (hardcover) $30   **940.53**
1. War criminals 2. Holocaust, 1939-1945 3. Fugitives from justice 4. World War, 1939-1945 -- Atrocities 5. Nuremberg Trial of Major German War Criminals, 1945-1946 6. Nazi hunters -- History 7. Holocaust, Jewish (1939-1945) 8. War criminals -- Germany -- History 9. Fugitives from justice -- Germany -- History
ISBN 9781476771861; 9781476771878

LC 2015027334

This book, by Andrew Nagorski, "reveals the experiences of the young American prosecutors in the Nuremberg and Dachau trials, Benjamin Ferencz and William Denson; the Polish investigating judge Jan Sehn, who handled the case of Auschwitz commandant Rudolf Höss; Germany's judge and prosecutor Fritz Bauer; . . . the Mossad agent Rafi Eitan, who was in charge of the Israeli team that nabbed Eichmann; and Eli Rosenbaum, who rose to head the US Justice Department's Office of Special Investigations." (Publisher's note)

"A detailed look at the grim work of tracking Nazis over the decades since World War II." Kirkus

Includes bibliographical references and index

Neiberg, Michael

Potsdam; the end of World War II and the remaking of Europe. Michael Neiber. Basic Books 2015 336 p. illustrations (hardcover : alk. paper) $29.99   **940.53**
1. World War, 1939-1945 -- Treaties 2. World War,

1939-1945 -- Armistices 3. World War, 1939-1945 -- Peace
ISBN 0465075258; 9780465075256

LC 2015007545

In this book author "Michael Neiberg brings the turbulent Potsdam conference to life, vividly capturing the delegates' personalities: Truman, trying to escape from the shadow of Franklin Roosevelt; Churchill, bombastic and seemingly out of touch; Stalin, cunning and meticulous. The delegates arrived at Potsdam determined to learn from the mistakes their predecessors made. But, riven by tensions and dramatic debates over how to end the most recent war, they only dimly understood that their discussions of peace were giving birth to a new global conflict." (Publisher's note)

"A must-have account for everyone from students of world history at the undergraduate and graduate levels to knowledgeable recreational readers." LJ

Includes bibliographical references and index

The **New** York Times complete World War II, 1939-1945; the coverage from the battlefields to the home front. edited by Richard Overy. Black Dog & Leventhal Pub 2013 611 p. $40   **940.53**
1. World War, 1939-1945 2. Newspapers -- United States
ISBN 1579129447; 9781579129446

This book, edited by Richard Overy, features "hundreds of . . . articles from the archives of the 'Times'—including firsthand accounts of major events and little-known anecdotes. . . . The book covers the biggest battles of the war, from the Battle of the Bulge to the Battle of Iwo Jima, as well as moving stories from the home front and profiles of noted leaders and heroes such as Winston Churchill and George Patton." (Publisher's note)

"This is a book to lose yourself in, to witness the war transmuted into print for the masses of readers living through it and anxious to follow its twists and turns." LJ

Olson, Lynne

Those angry days; Roosevelt, Lindbergh, and America's fight over World War II, 1939-1941. by Lynne Olson. Random House Inc. 2013 576 p. (hardcover) $30.00; (ebook) $85.00   **940.53**
1. World War, 1939-1945 -- United States 2. United States -- Military policy 3. World War, 1939-1945 -- Diplomatic history 4. United States -- Foreign relations -- 1933-1945 5. United States -- Politics and government -- 1933-1945 6. Isolationism -- United States -- History -- 20th century 7. Intervention (International law) -- History -- 20th century 8. Political culture -- United States -- History -- 20th century
ISBN 9781400069743; 1400069742; 9780679604716

LC 2012025381

This book, by Lynne Olson, offers an "account of the debate over American intervention in World War II. . . . At the center of this controversy stood the two most famous men in America: President Franklin D. Roosevelt, who championed the interventionist cause, and aviator Charles Lindbergh, who as unofficial leader and spokesman for America's isolationists emerged as the president's most formidable adversary." (Publisher's note)

Includes bibliographical references (p. [509]-518)

and index.

Orbach, Danny

The **plots** against Hitler; Danny Orbach. Houghton Mifflin Harcourt 2016 432 p. (hardcover) $28 **940.53**

1. Heads of state 2. World War, 1939-1945 -- Underground movements 3. Germany -- Politics and government -- 1933-1945 4. Heads of state -- Germany -- Biography 5. Assassins -- Germany -- History -- 20th century 6. Anti-Nazi movement -- Germany -- History -- 20th century 7. Opposition (Political science) -- Germany -- History -- 20th century

ISBN 9780544714434

LC 2015043037

This book, by Danny Orbach, is an "account of the anti-Nazi underground in Germany and its numerous efforts to assassinate Adolf Hitler. In 1933, Adolf Hitler became Chancellor of Germany. A year later, all parties but the Nazis had been outlawed. . . . Yet over the next few years, an unlikely clutch of conspirators emerged—soldiers, schoolteachers, politicians, diplomats, theologians, even a carpenter—who would try repeatedly to end the Fuhrer's genocidal reign." (Publisher's note)

"Likely to become the definitive general history of the subject and the starting place for all future research, Orbach's work is a fascinating story of courage and an excellent study of the struggle of individuals to act morally and honorably." Pub Wkly

Includes bibliographical references and index

Overy, Richard

Why the Allies won; {by} Richard Overy. W W Norton & Co Inc 1996 416 p. il maps hardcover o.p. (pbk.) $19.95 **940.53**

1. Strategy 2. World War, 1939-1945

ISBN 039331619X; 978-0393316193

LC 95-52444

This is an analysis of the reasons for the Allied victory over the Axis powers in 1945. "Professor Overy has chosen to divide his book into two . . . distinct parts. In the first part he gives summary accounts of the four military arenas which he considered decisive: the war at sea; the Eastern Front in 1942-3; the strategic air offensive; and the invasion of France in 1944. In the second part, he turns to the underlying political, social and industrial factors." (Times Lit Suppl) Bibliography. Index.

"Eschewing the belief that the Allies won solely because of their prodigious production of weapons and equipment, Mr. Overy points out that in the early stages of the war, before the Allies were fully mobilized, the Axis countries held the production advantage, yet failed to achieve victory because Germany's management of supply logistics was far inferior to that of the Allies—frequently as a result of Hitler's wrongheaded interference. . . . Assiduously researched and concisely written, this is a highly perceptive study." N Y Times Book Rev

Includes bibliographical references

Pick, Hella

Simon Wiesenthal; a life in search of justice. Northeastern Univ. Press 1996 349p il $35 **940.53**

1. Authors 2. Architects 3. Holocaust survivors 4. Essayists 5. Memoirists 6. Nazi hunters 7. Jewish leaders

ISBN 1-55553-273-X

LC 96-11808

This biography "has interesting things to say about forgiveness, including an extraordinary hallucinogenic encounter with a dying SS officer, and conveys a broadly sympathetic picture of a man capable of distinguishing between individuals and their political rhetoric." Times Lit Suppl

Includes bibliographical references

Pivnik, Sam

Survivor; Auschwitz, the Death March and My Fight for Freedom. Sam Pivnik. St. Martin's Press 2013 320 p. (hardcover) $26.99 **940.53**

1. Holocaust, 1939-1945

ISBN 125002952X; 9781250029522

This book, by Sam Pivnik, presents a memoir of a Jewish Holocaust survivor. "On fourteen occasions he should have been killed, but luck, his physical strength, and his determination not to die all played a part in Sam Pivnik living to tell his . . . story. In 1939, . . . Pivnik's life changed forever when the Nazis invaded Poland. He survived the two ghettoes . . . , six months [in] Auschwitz . . . , [and] the brutal Fürstengrube mining camp." (Publisher's note)

Plokhy, S. M.

Yalta; the price of peace. [by] S.M. Plokhy. Viking 2010 xxviii, 451p il map **940.53**

1. Yalta Conference (1945) 2. World politics -- 1945-1991 3. World War, 1939-1945 -- Peace 4. World War, 1939-1945 -- Diplomatic history

ISBN 978-0-670-02141-3

LC 2009-26833

Plokhy "has produced a colorful and gripping portrait of the three aging leaders at their historic encounter." Wall Street J

Includes bibliographical references

Raghavan, Srinath

India's war; World War ll and the making of modern South Asia. Srinath Raghavan. Basic Books 2016 592 p. illustrations (hardcover) $35 **940.53**

1. India -- History -- 20th century 2. World War, 1939-1945 -- Campaigns -- South Asia

ISBN 9780465030224

LC 2016933273

This book, by Srinath Raghavan, discusses the experience of World War II in India. The author "paints a compelling picture of battles abroad and of life on the home front, arguing that the war is crucial to explaining how and why colonial rule ended in South Asia. World War II forever altered the country's social landscape, overturning many Indians' settled assumptions and opening up new opportunities for the nation's most disadvantaged people." (Publisher's note)

"This book will be appreciated by scholars and general readers alike who wish to discover more answers to India's role in World War II." LJ

Includes bibliographical references and index.

Rees, Laurence

Auschwitz: a new history; Laurence Rees. Public Affairs 2005 xxii, 327p il $30; pa $16   **940.53**

1. Holocaust, 1933-1945 2. Auschwitz (Poland: Concentration camp)

ISBN 1-586-48303-X; 1-586-48357-9 pa

LC 2004-43196

For this history of the concentration camp, the author "interviewed 100 former Nazi perpetrators and survivors from the camp and drew on hundreds of interviews conducted for his previous research on the Third Reich, many with former members of the Nazi Party. . . . This is a significant contribution to our understanding of the intricacies of Nazi racial and ethnic policy that resulted in this ultimate abomination." Booklist

Includes bibliographical references

Reeves, Richard

Infamy; the shocking story of the Japanese American internment in World War II. Richard Reeves. Henry Holt & Co. 2015 368 p. 16 plates; illustrations; maps (hardcover) $32   **940.53**

1. World War, 1939-1945 2. Japanese -- United States 3. Concentration camps -- United States 4. World War, 1939-1945 -- Japanese Americans 5. Japanese Americans -- Evacuation and relocation, 1942-1945

ISBN 0805094083; 9780805094084

LC 2014033329

In this book author "Richard Reeves provides an authoritative account of the internment of more than 120,000 Japanese-Americans and Japanese aliens during World War II. Reeves has interviewed survivors, read numerous private letters and memoirs, and combed through archives to deliver a sweeping narrative of this atrocity." (Publisher's note)

Reeves mixes intimate narratives with historical documents to give an authoritative account of one of the darkest periods in American history." LJ

Includes bibliographical references and index

Reporting World War II. Library of Am. 1995 2v ea $35   **940.53**

1. World War, 1939-1945 2. Reporters and reporting

ISBN 1-883011-04-3 v1; 1-883011-05-1 v2

LC 94-45463

This "collection of some 200 entries by nearly 90 writers, drawn from newspapers, magazine articles, broadcast transcripts and book excerpts, recalls WW II campaigns and battles in all theaters but pays attention to the home front as well. It begins with an excerpt from William L. Shirer's Berlin Diary and ends with one from John Hersey's Hiroshima. . . . This is a treasure trove of war reporting, featuring writing of the highest order." Publ Wkly

Reynolds, David

In command of history; Churchill fighting and writing the Second World War. by David Reynolds. Random House 2005 xxiv, 631p il $35   **940.53**

1. Statesmen 2. Historians 3. Prime ministers 4. Memoirists 5. Cabinet members 6. Members of Parliament 7. Nobel laureates for literature 8. World War, 1939-1945 -- Historiography

ISBN 0-679-45743-7

LC 2004-51087

"Packed with detail and vivid characterizations . . . [this book is] a different take on one of the few men capable of both making history and writing it." Publ Wkly

Includes bibliographical references

Richmond Mouillot, Miranda

A **fifty**-year silence; love, war, and a ruined house in France. Miranda Richmond Mouillot. Crown Publishers 2015 288 p. illustrations, maps $26 **940.53**

1. Divorce 2. Grandparents 3. World War, 1939-1945 -- Refugees 4. Grandparents -- Biography 5. Jews -- France -- Biography 6. Divorced people -- Biography 7. World War, 1939-1945 -- France 8. Holocaust survivors -- Biography 9. Jews -- United States -- Biography 10. Holocaust, Jewish (1939-1945) -- France

ISBN 0804140642; 9780804140645

LC 2014015315

This book is an "account of [author] Miranda Richmond Mouillot's journey to find out what happened between her grandmother, a physician, and her grandfather, an interpreter at the Nuremberg Trials, who refused to utter his wife's name aloud after she left him. To discover the roots of their embittered and entrenched silence, Miranda abandons her plans for the future and moves to their stone house, now a crumbling ruin; immerses herself in letters, archival materials, and secondary sources." (Publisher's note)

"The corrosive effects of the Holocaust—upon those directly involved and generations thereafter—are illustrated vividly in this candid saga of familial love and misunderstanding." LJ

Rosenfeld, Oskar

In the beginning was the ghetto; 890 days in Lodz. edited and with an introduction by Hanno Loewy; translated from the German by Brigitte M. Goldstein. Northwestern Univ. Press 2002 xxxviii, 313p $40   **940.53**

1. Łódz (Poland) 2. Jews -- Poland 3. Holocaust, 1933-1945 -- Personal narratives

ISBN 0-8101-1488-7

LC 2001-6691

Original German edition, 1994

These entries from Rosenfeld's diary "contain vivid descriptions of daily life in the ghetto, including details about deportations, forced labor, hunger, diseases, cold, terror, and the struggle to maintain human dignity. . . . This book is one of the most important and lasting works documenting the horrors of the Holocaust." Booklist

Includes bibliographical references

Rosenzveig, Charles H.

The **World** reacts to the Holocaust; David S. Wyman, editor; Charles H. Rosenzveig, project director. Johns Hopkins Univ. Press 1996 xxiii, 981p $80   **940.53**

    1. Holocaust, 1933-1945
    ISBN 0-8018-4969-1

                       LC 96-15395

This is a "country-by-country chronicle of the impact of the Holocaust on world history. Covering 22 countries and the United Nations, the volume carefully traces the contentions and controversies involved in coming to terms with the events leading up to the Holocaust, from prewar attitudes and perceptions to the political, economic, and cultural legacies in the 1990s." Univ Press Books for Public and Second Sch Libr

    Includes bibliographical references

Russell, Jan Jarboe, 1951-

The **Train** to Crystal City; FDR's Secret Prisoner Exchange Program and America's Only Family Internment Camp During World War II. Jan Jarboe Russell. Simon & Schuster 2015 416 p. 8 plates; illustrations; map $30   **940.53**

    1. Crystal City (Tex.) -- History   2. Concentration camps -- United States   3. World War, 1939-1945 -- United States
    ISBN 1451693664; 9781451693669

                       LC 2014030862

This book, by Jan Jarboe Russell, tells the history of "a secret FDR-approved American internment camp in Texas during World War II, where thousands of families . . . were incarcerated. . . . Focusing her story on two American-born teenage girls who were interned, [the] author . . . uncovers the details of their years spent in the camp." (Publisher's note)

"Based in part on interviews with camp survivors, Russell documents in chilling detail a shocking story of national betrayal." Kirkus

Sakamoto, Pamela Rotner, 1962-

Midnight in broad daylight; a Japanese American family caught between two worlds. Pamela Rotner Sakamoto. Harper 2016 464 p. 8 plates; portraits (hardback) $29.99   **940.53**

    1. World War, 1939-1945 -- Japan   2. Japanese Americans -- Evacuation and relocation, 1942-1945   3. Soldiers -- Japan -- Biography   4. Japan -- Relations -- United States   5. United States -- Relations -- Japan   6. Translators -- United States -- Biography   7. World War, 1939-1945 -- Japanese Americans   8. World War, 1939-1945 -- Japan -- Hiroshima-shi   9. Japanese American families -- Washington -- Seattle
    ISBN 9780062351937

                       LC 2015017943

This book, by Pamela Rotner Sakamoto, "alternating between the American and Japanese perspectives, . . . captures the uncertainty and intensity of those charged with the fighting [of World War II] as well as the deteriorating home front of Hiroshima . . . and provides a fresh look at the dropping of the first atomic bomb. . . . It is . . . a scathing examination of racism and xenophobia [and] an homage to the tremen-

dous Japanese American contribution to the American war effort." (Publisher's note)

"A beautifully rendered work wrought with enormous care and sense of compassionate dignity." Kirkus

    Includes bibliographical references and index

Scheyer, Moriz

Asylum; A Survivor's Flight from Nazi-Occupied Vienna Through Wartime France. Moriz Scheyer; P. N. Singer (translator, Epilogue) Little, Brown and Co. 2016 320 p. ill., maps, portraits $28   **940.53**

    1. Asylum   2. Journalists   3. Holocaust survivors   4. World War, 1939-1945
    ISBN 9780316272889

                       LC 2016932793

This memoir by Austrian Jewish writer Moriz Scheyer, translated and with an epilogue by P. N. Singer, provides an account of Scheyer's "flight, persecution, and clandestine life in wartime France. As arts editor for one of Vienna's principal newspapers, Scheyer knew many of the city's foremost artists, and was an important literary journalist. With the advent of the Nazis he was forced from both job and home. In 1943, . . . Scheyer began drafting what was to become this book." (Publisher's note)

"A well-written book full of desperate hope, intense fear, and a demand for vigilance against the mentality of hate." Kirkus

    Includes bibliographical references (pages 304-305).

Shephard, Ben

The **long** road home; the aftermath of the Second World War. Alfred A. Knopf 2011 489p map $35; ebook $35   **940.53**

    1. World War, 1939-1945 -- Refugees   2. World War, 1939-1945 -- Forced repatriation   3. United Nations Relief and Rehabilitation Administration
    ISBN 978-1-4000-4068-1; 978-1-4000-4068-1 ebook

                       LC 2010-23894

First published 2010 in the United Kingdom

The book examines the experience of "roughly eleven million foreigners stranded in Germany [after World War II], often in ghastly conditions, after surviving years of hard labor and imprisonment in labor camps, concentration camps, death camps, and POW camps. . . . The Allied armies, chiefly the Americans, Soviets, and British, were faced with the kind of catastrophe left in the wake of most wars, but the scale in 1945 was unprecedented. . . . Shephard describes . . . the . . . confrontation of well-fed people from a relatively secure world with human beings who had indeed been reduced to a state that seemed lower than animals." (New York Review of Books)

"Ben Shephard's account of this demanding and important subject is a triumph. He has unearthed new and moving testimony by former DPs and has burrowed into official and personal papers without ever letting his deep scholarship get in the way of the riveting story he has to tell." Hist Today

    Includes bibliographical references

Smith, Lyn

Remembering, voices of the holocaust; a new history in the words of the men and women who sur-

vived. [foreword by Laurence Rees] Carroll & Graf 2006 351p il map $27 **940.53**
1. Holocaust, 1933-1945 -- Personal narratives
ISBN 0-7867-1640-1

LC 2006-284769

First published 2005 in the United Kingdom

The author, "who has recorded the experiences of survivors for London's Imperial War Museum, weaves together more than 100 accounts to construct a narrative of Nazi persecutions from the first anti-Semitic measures in 1933 through the liberation of the concentration camps. . . . This is an extraordinary work of scholarship and a reminder of the power of individual stories, which can bring home the horrors of WWII more forcefully than abstract numbers." Publ Wkly

Includes bibliographical references

Snyder, Timothy D., 1969-
Black Earth; The Holocaust As History and Warning. Timothy Snyder. Random House Inc. 2015 480 p. maps $30 **940.53**
1. Atrocities 2. Holocaust, 1939-1945 3. World War, 1939-1945
ISBN 1101903457; 9781101903452

LC 2015016818

This book, by Timothy Snyder, exploring the legacy of the Jewish Holocaust, "presents a new explanation of the great atrocity of the twentieth century, and reveals the risks that we face in the twenty-first. Based on new sources from eastern Europe and forgotten testimonies from Jewish survivors, . . . [it] recounts the mass murder of the Jews as an event that is still close to us, more comprehensible than we would like to think, and thus all the more terrifying." (Publisher's note)

"Snyder brings two fresh elements to his dizzying, harrowing tale. The first is his extraordinarily wide and deep research into the remarkable stories, many unknown, of individual Holocaust survivors, the subject of the last half of his book. The second element, likely to be controversial, is his argument, asserted and reasserted, that, at its roots, the Holocaust was made possible by the failure of national states." Pub Wkly

Includes bibliographical references and index

Spiegelman, Art
★ **Maus**; a survivor's tale. Art Spiegelman. 25th anniversary ed. Pantheon Bks. 1996 295 p. 2v in 1 ill., maps (some col.) $35 **940.53**
1. Graphic novels 2. Biographical graphic novels 3. Holocaust, 1933-1945 -- Graphic novels
ISBN 0-679-40641-7

LC 96-32796

A combined edition of Maus I : My father bleeds history (1986) and Maus II : And here my troubles began (1991)

Awards: 1992 Pulitzer Prize Special Award; Eisner Award for Best Graphic Album: Reprint for Maus II; Harvey Award for Best Graphic Album of Previously Published Work (for Maus II); 1993 Los Angeles Times Book Prize for Fiction (for Maus II)

"An undisputed classic and award-winning title (including a Pulitzer Prize in 1992) in which renowned cartoonist Spiegelman depicts his father's experiences as a World War

II Nazi concentration camp survivor. The memoir is also a chronicle of Spiegelman's relationship with his father as we witness their visits and disagreements. The black-and-white drawings are straightforward, but with an interesting twist: all of the Jews are depicted as mice and the Nazis as cats." LJ

★ **MetaMaus**. Pantheon Books 2011 299p il $35 **940.53**
1. Authors 2. Cartoonists 3. Graphic novels 4. Autobiographical graphic novels 5. Nonfiction writers 6. Cartoonists -- Graphic novels 7. Holocaust survivors -- Graphic novels 8. Holocaust, 1933-1945 -- Graphic novels
ISBN 978-0-375-42394-9

LC 2010052045

The New York cartoonist traces the creative process that went into drawing his Pulitzer Prizewinning classic, revealing the sources of his inspiration and describing his parents' emotional struggles as Holocaust survivors after the end of World War II.

"Informative about everything you may or may not have thought to ask about Maus and the Spiegelmans, this exhaustive purgative has been well organized and packaged and succeeds in being grimly entertaining, indeed almost addictive." Libr J

Stargardt, Nicholas
Witnesses of war; children's lives under the Nazis. Distributed by Random House 2006 493p il map $30; pa $16.95 **940.53**
1. World War, 1939-1945 -- Children
ISBN 1-4000-4088-4; 978-1-4000-4088-9; 1-4000-3379-9 pa; 978-1-4000-3379-9 pa

LC 2005-50409

First published 2005 in the United Kingdom

This is "a sharp and taut account of misery." Publ Wkly

Includes bibliographical references

Takaki, Ronald T.
Double victory; a multicultural history of America in World War II. [by] Ronald Takaki. Little, Brown 2000 282p il hardcover o.p. pa $19.99 **940.53**
1. United States -- Race relations 2. World War, 1939-1945 -- United States
ISBN 0-316-83155-7; 0-316-83156-5 pa

LC 99-40374

"Takaki discusses the experiences of African Americans, Indians, Chicanos, Asian Americans from several nations, German and Italian Americans, and Jewish Americans. . . . Despite Jim Crow, internment camps, neglected slums, barrios, reservations, and rejection of Jewish refugees, the nation's not-quite-Americans fought bravely in World War II." Booklist

Includes bibliographical references

Tate, Tim
Hitler's forgotten children; a true story of the Lebensborn program and one woman's search for her real identity. Ingrid von Oelhafen and Tim Tate; with Dr. Dorothee Schmitz-Koster. Berkley Caliber 2016 288 p. illustrations, plates (hardback) $28 **940.53**
1. World War, 1939-1945 -- Children 2. Lebensborn

e.V. (Germany) 3. World War, 1939-1945 -- Children -- Biography 4. Eugenics -- Germany -- History -- 20th century 5. World War, 1939-1945 -- Personal narratives, Yugoslav
ISBN 9780425283325

LC 2015034223

This book, by Ingrid von Oelhafen and Tim Tate, with Dorothee Schmitz-Koster, describes how "in the summer of 1942, parents across Nazi-occupied Yugoslavia were required to submit their children to medical checks designed to assess racial purity. One such child, Erika Matko, was . . . taken to Germany and placed with politically vetted foster parents, Erika was renamed Ingrid von Oelhafen. Many years later, Ingrid began to uncover the truth of her identity." (Publisher's note)

"This riveting, raw, and heart-wrenching story of misplaced identity and one woman's quest to find peace and hope in the darkest of times will intrigue a variety of readers interested in a mix of history nestled among personal memoir." LJ

Includes bibliographical references (page 275).

United States Holocaust Memorial Museum

The **Holocaust** and history; the known, the unknown, the disputed, and the reexamined. edited by Michael Berenbaum and Abraham J. Peck. Indiana Univ. Press 1998 836p $58.71; pa $35   **940.53**
  1. Holocaust, 1933-1945
  ISBN 0-253-33374-1; 0-253-21529-3 pa

LC 97-40030

"Papers collected here originated at a 1993 conference organized by the US Holocaust Memorial Museum's Research Institute. . . . The 50 contributors treat the subject from every conceivable angle: the role of antisemitism and racism; the politics of 'racial hygiene'; Nazi leadership and bureaucracy; the complicity of 'ordinary' people; the experiences of Gypsies, homosexuals, and blacks; the concentration camps; the Holocaust as reflected in international relations; the response of Jews, rescuers, and survivors. Recognizing the passionately controversial nature of the field, the editors have opted for variety over unanimity." Choice

Wachsmann, Nikolaus

Kl; A History of the Nazi Concentration Camps. Nikolaus Wachsmann. Farrar, Straus & Giroux 2015 880 p. 32 plates; illustrations; maps $40   **940.53**
  1. Holocaust, Jewish (1939-1945) 2. World War, 1939-1945 -- Concentration camps 3. World War, 1939-1945 -- Atrocities -- Germany 4. Concentration camps -- History -- 20th century 5. World War, 1939-1945 -- Prisoners and prisons, German
  ISBN 0374118256; 9780374118259

LC 2014031269

Author Nicholas Wachsumann "presents startling revelations, based on many years of archival research, about the functioning and scope of the [Nazi concentration] camp system. Examining, close up, life and death inside the camps, and adopting a wider lens to show how the camp system was shaped by changing political, legal, social, economic, and military forces, Wachsmann produces a unified picture of the Nazi regime." (Publisher's note)

"A comprehensive, encyclopedic work that should be included in the collections of libraries, schools and other institutions." Kirkus

Includes bibliographical references (pages 779-826) and index

Weinberg, Gerhard L.

★ A **world** at arms; a global history of World War II. 2nd ed; Cambridge University Press 2005 xxix, 1178p map $65; pa $25.99   **940.53**
  1. World War, 1939-1945
  ISBN 0-521-85316-8; 978-0-521-85316-3; 0-521-61826-6 pa; 978-0-521-61826-7 pa

LC 2005-41954

First published 1994

"Weinberg's unrivaled command of archival sources combine with a smooth writing style to produce a definitive one-volume history of World War II." Libr J [review of 1994 edition]

Includes bibliographical references

Weissova, Helga, 1929-

Helga's diary; a young girl's account of life in a concentration camp. Helga Weiss; translated by Neil Bermel; Introduction by Francine Prose. 1st American ed. W.W. Norton & Co Inc. 2013 256 p. (hardcover) $24.95   **940.53**
  1. Concentration camps 2. Terezin (Czechoslovakia: Concentration camp) 3. Holocaust, Jewish (1939-1945) 4. Jewish children in the Holocaust 5. Jews -- Czech Republic -- Prague 6. Theresienstadt (Concentration camp) 7. Prague (Czech Republic) -- Biography
  ISBN 0393077977; 9780393077971

LC 2013003775

Helga Weiss "begins her diary as a frightened eight-year-old in a bomb shelter . . . . The scene sets the tone of fear and confusion that will dominate her life for the next several years, the bulk of which she spends in the Jewish ghetto, Terezin. Her writings describe both the torturous physical circumstances of daily life, as well as the psychological toll wrought by ceaseless anxiety, degradation, and survivor's guilt." (Publishers Weekly)

Includes bibliographical references.

Weller, George

Weller's war; a legendary foreign correspondent's saga of World War II on five continents. edited by Anthony Weller. Crown Publishers 2009 644p il map $30   **940.53**
  1. World War, 1939-1945 -- Campaigns 2. World War, 1939-1945 -- Personal narratives
  ISBN 978-0-307-40655-2; 0-307-40655-5

The author "wrote for the Chicago Daily News for 35 years, achieving fame for his widely ranging dispatches from the many fronts of World War II. He was captured by the Gestapo in Greece, escaped from Java on a boat strafed by Japanese fighters, marched with Belgian colonial troops fighting Italian colonial troops in Ethiopia, and slogged through swamps with Americans and Australians locked in grim struggles in New Guinea. Weller's war reporting won him the Pulitzer Prize in 1943. Here, his son assembles many of his dispatches, which add tremendously to our understanding of the war at ground level, the people's war." Libr J

West Point History of World War II; The United States Military Academy; Editors: Clifford J. Rogers, Ty Seidule, and Steve R. Waddell. Simon & Schuster 2015 432 p. illustrations; color maps (hardcover) $55 **940.53**
1. World War, 1939-1945 2. United States Military Academy
ISBN 1476782733; 9781476782737
LC 2015031711

This book, published by the United States Military Academy, edited by Clifford J. Rogers, Ty Seidule, and Steve R. Waddell, offers "an outstanding new military history of the first half of World War II, featuring a rich array of images, . . . graphics, . . . maps, and expert analysis commissioned by the United States Military Academy to teach the art of war to West Point cadets." (Publisher's note)

"An astonishing, important book that will inform and entertain all readers, this is an essential purchase. Fans of military history, strategy, warfare, and human conflict will reap the benefits of this work." LJ

Winik, Jay
1944; FDR and the year that changed history. Jay Winik. Simon & Schuster 2015 512 p. illustrations (hardcover) $35 **940.53**
1. World War, 1939-1945 2. Holocaust, Jewish (1939-1945) 3. World War, 1939-1945 -- United States 4. Political leadership -- United States -- History -- 20th century
ISBN 1439114080; 9781439114087; 9781501125362
LC 2015013912

This book by "author Jay Winik brings to life in gripping detail the year 1944, which determined the outcome of World War II and put more pressure than any other on an ailing yet determined President Roosevelt. [It] is the first book to tell these events with such moral clarity and unprecedented sweep, and a moving appreciation of the extraordinary struggles of the era's outsized figures." (Publisher's note)

"An accomplished popular historian unpacks the last full year of World War II and the excruciatingly difficult decisions facing Franklin Roosevelt. . . . A complex history rendered with great color and sympathy." Kirkus
Includes bibliographical references and index

A **woman** in Berlin; eight weeks in the conquered city: a diary. by Anonymous; translated by Philip Boehm. Metropolitan Books/Henry Holt 2005 261p $23 **940.53**
1. Berlin, Battle of, 1945 2. World War, 1939-1945 -- Women 3. World War, 1939-1945 -- Personal narratives
ISBN 0-8050-7540-2
LC 2005-41984

Original German edition, 2003; Expurgated edition translated by James Stern published 1954 by Harcourt, Brace
This "is one of the most important documents to emerge from World War II." N Y Times Book Rev

World War II; Douglas Brinkley, general editor; edited and with chapter introductions by David Ru-

bel. Times Books 2003 2v il (New York Times living history) $30 ea **940.53**
1. World War, 1939-1945
ISBN 0-8050-7246-2 v1; 0-8050-7247-0 v2
LC 2003-59658

Yellin, Emily
Our mothers' war; American women at home and at the Front during World War II. Free Press 2004 447p il hardcover o.p. pa $14 **940.53**
1. World War, 1939-1945 -- Women
ISBN 0-7432-4514-8; 0-7432-4516-4 pa
LC 2004-40496

"Yellin reveals all of the responsibilities held by women, including helping to manufacture aircraft, ships, and other munitions; and, in the process, outproducing all of America's allies and enemies, by far. Readers see war brides who worked hard to maintain the morale of their husbands while surviving long separation, fear, and shortages of virtually everything necessary to support a family. . . . [This book] is an important book because the role played by women in World War II has been regularly ignored." SLJ
Includes bibliographical references

Zuccotti, Susan
Père Marie-Benoît and Jewish rescue; how a French priest together with Jewish friends saved thousands during the Holocaust. Susan Zuccotti. Indiana University Press 2013 280 p. (cloth : alkaline paper) $35 **940.53**
1. World War, 1939-1945 -- Jews -- Rescue 2. Marseille (France) -- Biography 3. Priests -- France -- Marseille -- Biography 4. Capuchins -- France -- Marseille -- Biography 5. Marseille (France) -- History -- 20th century 6. Holocaust, Jewish (1939-1945) -- France -- Marseille 7. Jews -- France -- Marseille -- History -- 20th century 8. World War, 1939-1945 -- Jews -- Rescue -- France -- Marseille 9. Righteous Gentiles in the Holocaust -- France -- Marseille -- Biography
ISBN 0253008530; 9780253008534
LC 2012047187

In this book, Susan Zuccotti offers an account "of the life of Capuchin priest Père Marie-Benoît and his successful efforts to save thousands of Jews." Her "approach begins before Marie-Benoît's birth in 1895, with a review of the geography and history of the region in France where he was born. She then moves on to profile the courageous priest in the trenches of the First World War, . . . and afterward during his high-level religious studies in Rome after the war." (Publishers Weekly)
Includes bibliographical references and index

Under his very windows; the Vatican and the Holocaust in Italy. Yale Univ. Press 2000 408p il $29.95; pa $16.95 **940.53**
1. Popes 2. Jews -- Italy 3. Holocaust, 1933-1945 4. Catholic Church -- Relations -- Judaism
ISBN 0-300-08487-0; 0-300-09310-1 pa
LC 00-43307

Zuccotti's "aim is to show that whatever help was given to the Jews by the Catholic Church during the war resulted almost entirely from spontaneous acts by courageous individuals—priests, monks and nuns, and occasionally prel-ates—and not from any interventions by the Vatican. . . . Zuccotti makes her case strongly. . . . This is a serious and well-researched book." N Y Times Book Rev

Includes bibliographical references (p.) and index

940.531   Social, political, economic history of the Holocaust

Goldberg, Rita
Motherland;   growing up with the holocaust. Rita Goldberg. Halban 2014 xvi, 340 p.p illustra-tions $27.95   **940.531**
  1. Holocaust survivors 2. Jews -- Netherlands 3. Holocaust, 1939-1945 4. World War, 1939-1945 -- Jewish resistance 5. Holocaust, Jewish (1939-1945) 6. World War, 1939-1945 -- Participation, Jewish 7. World War, 1939-1945 -- Underground movements 8. Holocaust survivors -- Netherlands -- Biography 9. Jews -- Netherlands -- 20th century -- Biography 10. Jews -- Netherlands -- Social conditions -- 20th century
  ISBN 1620970732; 1905559623; 9781620970737; 9781905559626
                                 LC 2013496141
  This book, by Rita Goldberg, is a "deeply moving sec-ond-generation Holocaust memoir. . . . Proud of her mother and yet struggling to forge an identity in the shadow of such heroic accomplishments (in a family setting that included close relationships with the iconic Frank family), Goldberg reveals a little-explored aspect of Holocaust survival: the often-wrenching family and interpersonal struggles of the children and grandchildren whose own lives are haunted by historic tragedy." (Publisher's note)
  "Of course, the family story, and especially the Frank connection, will draw readers (she knew Otto very well, right up to his postwar visits to the U.S.), who will be open to discussion of the big issues of perpetrators, victims, and, especially, bystanders, then and now." Booklist
  Includes bibliographical references

Holden, Wendy
Born Survivors; Three Young Mothers and Their Extraordinary Story of Courage, Defiance, and Hope. Wendy Holden. HarperCollins 2015 400 p. map, illustrations $26.99   **940.531**
  1. Mothers 2. Survival skills 3. Concentration camps
  ISBN 0062370251; 9780062370259
  This book by Wendy Holden "celebrates three moth-ers who defied death to give their children life. The Nazis murdered their husbands but concentration camp prisoners Priska, Rachel, and Anka would not let evil take their un-born children too." (Publisher's note) Holden draws on "in-terviews, letters, historical records, and personal visits to the sites where this story unfolded." (Kirkus Reviews)
  "An engrossing, intense, and highly descriptive narrative chronicling the ghastly conditions three pregnant women suffered through at the hands of the Nazis." Kirkus

Simon, Marie Jalowicz
Underground in Berlin; A Young Woman's Ex-traordinary Tale of Survival in the Heart of Nazi Ger-

many. Marie Jalowicz Simon; translated by Anthea Bell. Little, Brown & Co. 2015 384 p. illustrations, map $28   **940.531**
  1. Jews -- Germany 2. Berlin (Germany) 3. Holocaust, 1939-1945
  ISBN 0316382094; 9780316382090
                                 LC 2015935821
  This memoir tells how "in 1941, [author] Marie Jalowicz Simon, a nineteen-year-old Berliner, made an extraordinary decision. All around her, Jews were being rounded up for deportation, forced labor, and extermination. Marie took off her yellow star, turned her back on the Jewish community, and vanished into the city. In the years that followed, Ma-rie lived under an assumed identity, forced to accept shelter wherever she found it." (Publisher's note)

940.54   Military history of World War II

Alperovitz, Gar
The **decision** to use the atomic bomb and the ar-chitecture of an American myth; {by} Gar Alpero-vitz with the assistance of Sanho Tree {et al.} Knopf 1995 843p hardcover o.p. pa $18   **940.54**
  1. United States -- Foreign relations 2. World War, 1939-1945 -- United States 3. Hiroshima (Japan) -- Bombardment, 1945
  ISBN 0-679-76285-X pa
                                 LC 95-8778
  "Alperovitz is the dean of revisionist scholars who argue that the nuclear bombing of Japan was unnecessary and that America bears a hefty responsibility for the cold war. . . . His main and probably most controversial contention is that certain documents pertaining to the decision were doctored, some by none other than Truman himself. Further, Alpero-vitz sees James Byrnes, Truman's Mephistophelian secre-tary of state, as a furtive player who nixed such alternative plans as modifying the unconditional-surrender demand and encouraging a Russian declaration of war." Booklist
  Includes bibliographical references

Ambrose, Stephen E.
  ★ **Band** of brothers; E Company, 506th Regi-ment, 101st Airborne from Normandy to Hitler's Ea-gle's Nest. [by] Stephen Ambrose. Simon & Schus-ter 2001 333p il maps $25; pa $16   **940.54**
  1. World War, 1939-1945 -- Europe 2. United States -- Army -- Parachute Infantry Regiment, 506th -- Company E
  ISBN 0-7432-1638-5; 0-7432-2454-X pa
                                 LC 2001-20134
  A reissue of the title first published 1992
  "Moving, poignant, and uplifting, this book is high-ly recommended for medium and large World War II collections." Booklist
  Includes bibliographical references

  Citizen soldiers; the U.S. Army from the Nor-mandy beaches to the Bulge to the surrender of Ger-

many, June 7, 1944-May 7, 1945. Simon & Schuster 1997 512p il maps hardcover o.p. pa $17 **940.54**
1. World War, 1939-1945 -- Campaigns -- France
ISBN 0-684-84801-5 pa

LC 97-23876

This continuation of D-Day focuses on the front-line experiences of American soldiers who fought in northwestern Europe in the war's last years

"These events have all been well documented, but in Ambrose's capable hands, the bloody and dramatic battles fought in northwest Europe in 1944-45 come alive as never before." N Y Times Book Rev

Includes bibliographical references

D-Day, June 6, 1944; the climactic battle of World War II. Simon & Schuster 1994 655p il maps $30; pa $17 **940.54**
1. Normandy (France), Attack on, 1944 2. World War, 1939-1945 -- Campaigns -- France
ISBN 0-671-88403-4; 0-684-80137-X pa

LC 93-40353

This is an account of the Allied invasion of Normandy in 1944. The author argues "that the invasion represented a triumph of the old United States Army, whose officers had transformed millions of civilians into a cohesive, highly trained and motivated mass army that, backed by a united nation, won with relative ease." (Christ Sci Monit) Index.

"Mr. Ambrose wonderfully illuminates the mind of the very young soldier of any nation anywhere who has never been in fighting before." N Y Times Book Rev

Includes bibliographical references

The **victors**; Eisenhower and his boys, the men of World War II. Simon & Schuster 1998 396p hardcover o.p. pa $16 **940.54**
1. Generals 2. Presidents 3. College presidents 4. United States -- Army 5. World War, 1939-1945 -- Campaigns
ISBN 0-684-85629-8 pa

LC 98-37808

"The author is a master of letting his subjects tell the story, of standing back and allowing the large lessons to unfold. The result is history with lasting impact." SLJ

Includes bibliographical references

The **wild** blue; the men and boys who flew the B-24s over Germany 1944-45. Simon & Schuster 2001 299p il $26; pa $16 **940.54**
1. Air pilots 2. B-24 bomber 3. Senators 4. Members of Congress 5. Government officials 6. Presidential candidates 7. World War, 1939-1945 -- Aerial operations
ISBN 0-7432-0339-9; 0-7432-2309-8 pa

LC 2001-20563

Ambrose presents profiles of American pilots who flew B-24 bombers focusing on the Dakota Queen piloted by future senator and presidential candidate George McGovern

"Ambrose's narrative flows smoothly, even as he manages to cover each man's story." Libr J

Includes bibliographical references

Atkinson, Rick, 1952-
★ An **army** at dawn; the war in North Africa, 1942-1943. Holt & Co. 2002 681p il maps (The liberation trilogy) $30; pa $16 **940.54**
1. Africa, North -- History, Military 2. World War, 1939-1945 -- North Africa 3. World War, 1939-1945 -- Campaigns -- North Africa 4. World War, 1939-1945 -- Campaigns -- Africa, North
ISBN 0-8050-6288-2; 0-8050-7448-1 pa

LC 2002-24130

This is the first volume of a projected World War II trilogy.

This "volume covers the conception of Operation Torch through the German surrender in Tunisia in May 1943. . . . An exemplary work that feeds anticipation of the succeeding volumes." Booklist

Includes bibliographical references

Followed by The day of battle (2007)

★ The **day** of battle; the war in Sicily and Italy, 1943-1944. H. Holt 2007 791p il map (The liberation trilogy) $35; pa $17 **940.54**
1. World War, 1939-1945 -- Campaigns -- Italy
ISBN 978-0-8050-6289-2; 0-805-06289-0; 978-0-8050-8861-8 pa; 0-8050-8861-X pa

LC 2007-7653

"The second volume of . . . [the author's] 'Liberation' trilogy, which began with the Pulitzer Prizewinning An Army at Dawn: The War in North Africa, 1942–1943, this is probably the most eagerly awaited World War II book of the year. Atkinson's clear prose, perceptive analysis, and grasp of the personalities and nuances of the campaigns make his book an essential purchase." Libr J

Includes bibliographical references

The **guns** at last light; the war in Western Europe, 1944-1945. Rick Atkinson. Henry Holt and Co. 2013 877 p. ill. (The liberation trilogy) $40 **940.54**
1. Generals 2. Soldiers 3. World War, 1939-1945 4. World War, 1939-1945 -- Campaigns -- Western Front
ISBN 0805062904; 9780805062908

LC 2012034312

This book concludes Rick Atkinson's series about World War II. "Peopling the pages [of the book] are German, British, French, Canadian, and (primarily) American generals and common soldiers. Excerpts from the letters of dead soldiers on both sides, as well as from the diaries of captain generals, fill out the story." (Publishers Weekly)

"[L]ively, occasionally lyric prose brings the vast theater of battle, from the beaches of Normandy deep into Germany, brilliantly alive." Pub Wkly

Includes bibliographical references (pages 813-841) and index

Ballard, Robert D.
Return to Midway; {by} Robert D. Ballard and Rick Archbold; principal photography by David Doubilet. . . . National Geographic Soc. 1999 191p il maps $40 **940.54**
1. Shipwrecks 2. Midway, Battle of, 1942 3. World

War, 1939-1945 -- Naval operations
ISBN 0-7922-7500-4

LC 99-10831

In this narrative, Ballard "intersperses chapters on the Battle of Midway with a fascinating account of his search for the U.S.S. Yorktown, which was sunk by a Japanese destroyer on June 7, 1942. Period photographs from the battle are combined with those of the Yorktown as she rests today, and paintings by marine artist Ken Marschall add detail to complete the record. The lively narrative is punctuated with two Japanese and two American oral history accounts of the battle." Libr J

Includes bibliographical references

Bascomb, Neal

The **winter** fortress; the epic mission to sabotage Hitler's superbomb. Neal Bascomb. Houghton Mifflin Harcourt 2016 400 p. ill., portraits, maps (hardcover) $28   **940.54**
   1. Atomic bomb 2. World War, 1939-1945 3. Atomic bomb -- Germany -- History 4. Sabotage -- Norway -- History -- 20th century 5. World War, 1939-1945 -- Germany -- Technology 6. World War, 1939-1945 -- Commando operations -- Norway 7. World War, 1939-1945 -- Underground movements -- Norway
   ISBN 0544368053; 9780544368057

LC 2015042716

In this book, by Neal Bascomb, "It's 1942 and the Nazis are racing to be the first to build a weapon unlike any known before. They have the physicists, they have the uranium, and now all their plans depend on amassing a single ingredient: heavy water, which is produced in Norway's Vemork. . . . For the Allies, the plant must be destroyed. But how would they reach the castle fortress set on a precipitous gorge in one of the coldest, most inhospitable places on Earth?" (Publisher's note)

"Parts of the book read like an adventure novel, others like straightforward history, but the combination will appeal to readers of both WWII fiction and nonfiction." Booklist

Includes bibliographical references and index

Beevor, Antony, 1946-

Ardennes 1944; The Battle of the Bulge. by Antony Beevor. Penguin Group USA 2015 480 p. illustrations, maps $35   **940.54**
   1. Ardennes (France), Battle of the, 1944-1945 2. World War, 1914-1918 -- Campaigns -- France
   ISBN 0670025313; 9780670025312

LC 2015490442

In this book, historian Antony Beevor "reconstructs the Battle of the Bulge. . . . On December 16, 1944, Hitler launched his 'last gamble' in the snow-covered forests and gorges of the Ardennes in Belgium. . . . The allies, taken by surprise, found themselves fighting two panzer armies. Belgian civilians abandoned their homes. . . . Panic spread even to Paris. While some American soldiers, overwhelmed by the German onslaught, fled or surrendered, others held on heroically." (Publisher's note)

"Beevor skewers the pretensions and weaknesses of generals and details atrocities and mistreatment of both civilians and surrendering enemies by both sides. The author takes for granted more knowledge of the battle, the terrain, and the

German language than general readers may possess, and he occasionally repeats information attentive readers will recall from previous mentions. But these are small quibbles. On the whole, this is a treasure of memorable portraits, striking details, fascinating revelations, and broad insights—likely to be the definitive account of the battle for years to come. Essential reading for anyone interested in World War II." Kirkus

D-day; the Battle for Normandy. Viking 2009 591p il map $32.95   **940.54**
   1. Normandy (France), Attack on, 1944
   ISBN 978-0-670-02119-2

LC 2009-23574

This "is a vibrant work of history that honors the sacrifice of tens of thousands of men and women." Time

Includes bibliographical references

The **fall** of Berlin 1945. Viking 2002 xxxvii, 489p il maps $29.95; pa $16   **940.54**
   1. Berlin, Battle of, 1945 2. World War, 1939-1945 -- Germany
   ISBN 0-670-03041-4; 0-14-200280-1 pa

LC 2002-510674

The author "relies on material from American, German, British, French, and Swedish archives and documents from former Soviet files, making the book an invaluable and meticulous account." Booklist

Includes bibliographical references (p. 466-475) and index

The **Second** World War; Antony Beevor. Little, Brown & Co 2012 xii, 863 p.p   **940.54**
   1. Military history 2. World War, 1939-1945 3. Europe -- History -- 1918-1945
   ISBN 0316023744; 9780316023740

LC 2012007028

In this book on World War II Anthony Beevor describes how "the war was set in motion by a single person--Adolf Hitler--and its extension reflected specific decisions by specific people, and its course changed lives across the globe in ways impossible to predict. . . . And from heads of state to front-line riflemen, from field marshals to teenaged girls, Beevor's protagonists exercise choice in the context of 'the greatest man-made disaster in history.'" (Publishers Weekly)

Includes bibliographical references and index.

Blair, Clay

Hitler's U-boat war; the hunted, 1942-1945. Random House 1998 xxviii, 909p 2v il map hardcover o.p. pa $19.95   **940.54**
   1. World War, 1939-1945 -- Atlantic Ocean 2. World War, 1939-1945 -- Naval operations -- Submarine
   ISBN 0-6794-5742-9

LC 96-2275

This is a history of the German submarine campaign against Allied forces during the Second World War

This is "the most thorough study of the U-Boat campaign available; it includes a massive amount of detailed statistics." Libr J {review of volume 1}

Includes bibliographical references

Blum, Howard

The **Last** Goodnight; A World War II Story of
Espionage, Adventure, and Betrayal. Howard Blum.
Harper Collins Publishers 2016 528 p. illustrations
(hardcover) $28.99   **940.54**
1. Women spies 2. World War, 1939-1945 -- Secret
service 3. Women spies -- United States -- Biography
4. World War, 1939-1945 -- Secret service -- United
States 5. Espionage, American -- Europe -- History --
20th century
ISBN 9780062307675; 9780062307798;
9780062307804
                                        LC 2015019329

This book, by Howard Blum, offers a "biography of
Betty Pack, the dazzling American debutante who became
an Allied spy during WWII and was hailed by OSS chief
General 'Wild Bill' Donovan as 'the greatest unsung heroine
of the war.' . . . Beneath Betty's cool, professional determination, Blum reveals a troubled woman conflicted by the
very traits that made her successful." (Publisher's note)
"Occasionally breathless and torrid in description, this is
a well-documented work that certainly never bores." Kirkus
Includes bibliographical references

Bradley, James

Flags of our fathers; [by] James Bradley with
Ron Powers. Bantam Bks. 2000 376p $24.95; pa
$14   **940.54**
1. Iwo Jima, Battle of, 1945 2. Photojournalists 3.
United States -- Marine Corps
ISBN 0-553-11133-7; 0-553-38415-5 pa
                                        LC 00-25803

This is the "story of the most famous photograph to
come out of World War II, the flag-raising on Mount Suribachi during the Battle of Iwo Jima in February 1945. Bradley
is the son of one of the six men immortalized in that remarkable photo, and his gripping narrative, vivid descriptions,
and heartfelt style make this a powerful story of courage,
humility, and tragedy." Libr J
Includes bibliographical references

Breitman, Richard

Official secrets; what the Nazis planned, what
the British and Americans knew. Hill & Wang 1998
325p hardcover o.p. pa $22   **940.54**
1. Holocaust, 1933-1945 2. World War, 1939-1945 --
Atrocities 3. Germany -- Politics and government --
1933-1945
ISBN 0-8090-3819-6; 0-8090-0184-5 pa
                                        LC 98-7997

This "is a remarkable study, concise yet carefully nuanced." N Y Times Book Rev
Includes bibliographical references

Brokaw, Tom

An **album** of memories; personal histories from
the greatest generation. Random House 2001 314p
il maps $29.95; pa $14.95   **940.54**
1. United States -- History -- 1933-1945 2. World War,
1939-1945 -- Personal narratives
ISBN 0-375-50581-4; 0-375-76041-5 pa
                                        LC 2001-273436

This volume "gathers letters written to Brokaw by Americans who lived through the Depression and World War II
and, in some cases, letters written by their children. Brokaw
provides a brief introduction and a time line for each chapter; these cover the Depression, the war in Europe and in the
Pacific, and the wartime 'home front,' closing with 'Reflections.' The book is lavishly illustrated with reproductions of
photographs, drawings, documents, and other memorabilia
of the era." Booklist

Burgin, R. V.

Islands of the damned; a Marine at war in the
Pacific. [by] R.V. Burgin with William Marvel. New
American Library 2010 296p il $24.95   **940.54**
1. World War, 1939-1945 -- Pacific Ocean 2. World
War, 1939-1945 -- Personal narratives
ISBN 978-0-451-22990-8
                                        LC 2009-40454

"As this well-written, excellently detailed personal narrative makes clear, some Marines who fought alongside him
did not make it home alive. They and thousands more died
amid war's confusing and unspeakable horrors. Sometimes
they were killed by the enemy, sometimes by friendly fire,
sometimes by accidents, and sometimes by shocking, split-
second decisions where one life was sacrificed to save others. . . . Time is thinning the ranks of America's Pacific War
veterans. But Islands of the Damned is a taut, engrossing,
haunting book that will help keep their accomplishments and
enormous sacrifices alive." Dallas Morning News

Burleigh, Michael

Moral combat; good and evil in World War II.
Harper 2011 xxi, 650p il map $29.95   **940.54**
1. World War, 1939-1945 -- Ethical aspects
ISBN 978-0-06-058097-1; 0-06-058097-6
First published 2010 in the United Kingdom
"No-one with an interest in the Second World War
should be without this book; and indeed nor should any-
one who cares about how our world has come about."
Daily Telegraph
Includes bibliographical references

Clark, Lloyd

Blitzkrieg; Myth, Reality, and Hitler's Lightning
War: France 1940. Lloyd Clark. Atlantic Monthly
Press 2016 480 p. illustrations, maps $27 **940.54**
1. Military history 2. Strategy -- History 3. World War,
1939-1945 4. Dunkerque (France), Battle of, 1940 5.
Ardennes (France), Battle of the, 1944-1945
ISBN 0802125131; 9780802125132
This book by Lloyd Clark delivers a new history of Germany's 1940 invasion of France. "Germans launched a military offensive in France . . . that married superb intelligence,
the latest military thinking, and new technology to achieve
. . . what their fathers had failed to achieve in . . . the First
World War. It was a . . . victory, altering the balance of power
in Europe in one stroke, and convinced the entire world that
the Nazi war machine was unstoppable." (Publisher's note)
"A solid, well-documented military history, Clark's newest work will appeal to anyone interested in World War II
and early operations on the western front." LJ
Includes bibliographical references (pages 420-439)

and index.

Conant, Jennet

A **covert** affair; Julia Child and Paul Child in the OSS. Simon & Schuster 2011 395p il $28 **940.54**
1. Cooks 2. Artists 3. Diplomats 4. Intelligence service 5. Anticommunist movements 6. Television personalities 7. Senators 8. Cookbook writers 9. Spouses of prominent persons 10. World War, 1939-1945 -- Secret service 11. United States -- Office of Strategic Services 12. United States -- Politics and government -- 1945-1953 13. World War, 1939-1945 -- Secret service -- United States 14. Anti-communist movements -- United States -- History -- 20th century
ISBN 978-1-4391-6352-8; 978-1-4391-6850-9 ebook
LC 2011-02875
This is an "account of Julia and Paul Child's experiences as members of the Office of Strategic Services (OSS) in the Far East during World War II." (Publisher's note) Index.
"Paul and Julia Child are merely supporting players in this book about the Office of Strategic Services in World War II and the McCarthy witch hunts that followed. Despite this blatant marketing ploy, the book is a well-researched and well-written account of this period in American history." Seattle Times
Includes bibliographical references

The **irregulars**; Roald Dahl and the British spy ring in wartime Washington. Simon & Schuster 2008 xx, 393p il $27.95 **940.54**
1. Authors 2. Children's authors 3. Short story writers 4. Intelligence service -- Great Britain 5. World War, 1939-1945 -- Secret service
ISBN 978-0-7432-9458-4; 0-7432-9458-0
LC 2008-12483
Conant tells the story of young writer Roald Dahl who is assigned by His Majesty's Government to Washington, D.C. as a diplomat to gather intelligence about America's isolationist circles. In the course of his "spying," he meets or works closely with David Ogilvy, Ian Fleming, and the great spymaster William Stephenson (aka Intrepid).
"Entertaining social history that also reveals a little-known aspect of an important literary figure's life." Kirkus
Includes bibliographical references

Costello, John

The **Pacific** War. Quill 1982 742p il $21.95 **940.54**
1. World War, 1939-1945 -- Pacific Ocean
ISBN 0-688-01620-0; 978-0-688-01620-3
LC 82-15054
First published 1981 by Rawson, Wade
A "history of World War II as it was played out in the Pacific theater. . . . Emphasizing the role played by Allied intelligence sources during the early period of the war, Costello analyzes the actual battles from Pearl Harbor to the atomic bombing of Japan." Booklist
Includes bibliographical references

Curtis, Brian

Fields of Battle; Pearl Harbor, the Rose Bowl, and the Boys Who Went to War. by Brian Curtis. St. Martin's Press 2016 320 p. $29.99 **940.54**
1. Football players 2. College football -- History 3. World War, 1939-1945 -- United States
ISBN 1250059585; 9781250059581
LC 2016020829
This book by Brian Curtis recalls how, "in the wake of the bombing of Pearl Harbor, the 1942 Rose Bowl was moved from Pasadena to Duke University out of fear of further Japanese attacks on the West Coast. Shortly after this unforgettable game, many of the players and coaches left their respective colleges, entered the military, and went on to serve around the world in famous battlegrounds, . . . where fate and destiny would bring them back together." (Publisher's note)
"A fine sports book with a stirring extra dimension." Kirkus
Includes bibliographical references and index.

Daws, Gavan

Prisoners of the Japanese; POWs of World War II in the Pacific. Morrow 1994 462p il map hardcover o.p. pa $19.95 **940.54**
1. Prisoners of war 2. World War, 1939-1945 -- Pacific Ocean 3. World War, 1939-1945 -- Prisoners and prisons
ISBN 0-688-11812-7; 0-688-14370-9 pa
LC 93-49363
"Daws offers a well-written thoroughly researched account of these POWs. . . . An exceptionally worthwhile addition to the literature on the war in the Pacific." Booklist
Includes bibliographical references

Dimbleby, Jonathan

The **Battle** of the Atlantic; how the allies won the war. Jonathan Dimbleby. Oxford University Press 2016 560 p. illustrations, maps $34.95 **940.54**
1. World War, 1939-1945 -- Campaigns 2. World War, 1939-1945 -- Naval operations 3. World War, 1939-1945 -- Campaigns -- Atlantic Ocean 4. World War, 1939-1945 -- Naval operations -- Submarine
ISBN 9780190495855
LC 2015032726
This book, by Jonathan Dimbleby, focuses on the "Battle of the Atlantic and the men who fought it. . . . Had Germany succeeded in cutting off the supply of American ships, England might not have held out. Yet had Churchill siphoned reinforcements to the naval effort earlier, thousands of lives might have been preserved. The battle consisted of not one but hundreds of battles, ranging from hours to days in duration, and forcing both sides into constant innovation." (Publisher's note)
"The history of the battle for the Atlantic is well documented, but Dimbleby's work, with its emphasis on the strategic importance of the battle, is an excellent addition to the story, and expert historians as well as general readers can enjoy this effort." Pub Wkly
Includes bibliographical references and index

Doyle, William

PT 109; an American epic of war, survival, and the destiny of John F. Kennedy. William Doyle. William Morrow 2015 352 p. 8 plates; illustrations; maps (hardcover) $27.99 **940.54**

1. World War, 1939-1945 -- Naval operations 2. PT-109 (Torpedo boat) 3. World War, 1939-1945 -- Naval operations, American 4. World War, 1939-1945 -- Campaigns -- Solomon Islands

ISBN 9780062346582; 9780062346599

LC 2015021575

This book, by William Doyle, tells "the extraordinary World War II story of shipwreck and survival that paved John F. Kennedy's path to power. . . . Author William Doyle has crafted a thrilling and definitive account of the sinking of PT 109 and its shipwrecked crew's heroics. . . . The story's second act . . . explores in new detail how this extraordinary episode shaped Kennedy's character and fate, proving instrumental to achieving his presidential ambitions." (Publisher's note)

"Dramatic and revealing. Readers unfamiliar with the Joe Kennedy back story will be startled to learn of his puppet master-like role in orchestrating JFK's rise to the presidency." Kirkus

Includes bibliographical references and index

Duffy, James P., 1941-

War at the end of the world; Douglas MacArthur and the forgotten fight for New Guinea, 1942-1945. James P. Duffy. NAL Caliber 2016 448 p. illustrations, maps $28 **940.54**

1. World War, 1939-1945 -- Campaigns -- New Guinea

ISBN 9780451418302

LC 2015019828

This book, by James P. Duffy, is an "account of an epic, yet nearly forgotten, battle of World War II—General Douglas MacArthur's four-year assault on the Pacific War's most hostile battleground: the mountainous, jungle-cloaked island of New Guinea." (Publisher's note)

"Duffy's portrait of the South Pacific is an entertaining and well-researched war history that will satisfy intrigued novices and devoted students alike." Kirkus

Includes bibliographical references and index

Dunnigan, James F.

The Pacific War encyclopedia; {by} James F. Dunnigan and Albert A. Nofi. Facts on File 1998 2v il maps set $137.50 **940.54**

1. Reference books 2. World War, 1939-1945 -- Encyclopedias

ISBN 0-8160-3439-7

LC 97-15634

This work "is lively as well as informative, and . . . will be attractive to military buffs while still useful to more serious researchers." Libr J

Felton, Mark

Zero Night; the untold story of World War Two's greatest escape. Mark Felton. Thomas Dunne Books/ St. Martin's Press 2015 320 p. illustrations, maps (hardcover) $25.99 **940.54**

1. Escapes 2. World War, 1939-1945 -- Prisoners and prisons 3. Oflag VI B (Concentration camp) 4. World War, 1939-1945 -- Germany -- Warburg 5. World War, 1939-1945 -- Prisoners and prisons, German 6. Prisoners of war -- Germany -- Warburg -- History -- 20th century 7. Prisoner-of-war escapes -- Germany -- Warburg -- History -- 20th century

ISBN 9781250073747

LC 2015017591

This book, by Mark Felton, describes how "on August 30, 1942 - 'Zero Night' - 40 Allied officers staged . . . [a] mass escape. . . . Months of meticulous planning and secret training hung in the balance during three minutes of mayhem as the officers boldly stormed the huge double fences at Oflag Prison. . . . The highly coordinated effort succeeded and set 36 men free into the German countryside." (Publisher's note)

"The author grippingly tracks the evaders' trek to freedom, an event that would warrant a book in itself. Even the epilogue will bring a smile. In this exciting book, Felton has captivatingly captured the bravery of the prisoners." Kirkus

Includes bibliographical references and index

Frank, Richard B.

★ Downfall; the end of the Imperial Japanese Empire. Penguin 2001 484p il map pa $18 **940.54**

1. Japan -- History -- 1868-1945 2. World War, 1939-1945 -- Japan 3. World War, 1939-1945 -- Aerial operations

ISBN 0-14-100146-1

First published 1999 by Random House

"Weaving together the strands of military and diplomatic events, Frank contends that absent the bombings of Hiroshima and Nagasaki the war would have continued for at least several more months, at a cost in Japanese and Allied civilian and combatant lives far in excess of the admittedly awful toll that the atomic bombs exacted. A powerful work of history." Libr J

Includes bibliographical references

Geroux, William

The Mathews Men; Seven Brothers and the War Against Hitler's U-boats. by William Geroux. Penguin Group USA 2016 400 p. ill., maps, portraits $28 **940.54**

1. Virginia -- History 2. Merchant marine -- United States 3. World War, 1939-1945 -- United States

ISBN 0525428151; 9780525428152

This book, by William Geroux, focuses on "One of the last unheralded heroic stories of World War II: the U-boat assault off the American coast against the men of the U.S. Merchant Marine who were supplying the European war, and one community's monumental contribution to that effort. Mathews County, Virginia, is a remote outpost on the Chesapeake Bay with little to offer except unspoiled scenery—but it sent an unusually large concentration of sea captains to fight in World War II." (Publisher's note)

"Geroux presents an unflinching, inspiring, and long-delayed tribute to the sacrifice of these men." Booklist

Includes bibliographical references (pages 371-375)

and index.

Giangreco, D. M.

Hell to pay; Operation Downfall and the invasion of Japan, 1945-47. Naval Institute Press 2009 xxiii, 362p il map $36.95   **940.54**

  1. World War, 1939-1945 -- Campaigns -- Japan

ISBN 978-1-59114-316-1

LC 2009-27766

"Illustrative of just how much the war with Japan was a close-run thing, this is essential reading." Libr J

Includes bibliographical references

Glass, Charles

The **deserters**; a hidden history of World War II. Charles Glass. The Penguin Press 2013 400 p. (hardcover) $27.95   **940.54**

  1. Military desertion   2. World War, 1939-1945   3. Military policy -- United States   4. Combat -- Psychological aspects   5. World War, 1939-1945 -- Desertions   6. Military deserters -- History -- 20th century   7. World War, 1939-1945 -- Psychological aspects   8. Desertion, Military -- History -- 20th century

ISBN 1594204284; 9781101617816; 9781594204289

LC 2012046881

This book follows three World War II soldiers court-martialed for desertion. "Tracking in detail the wartime biographies of three privates in the infantry—Tennessee farm boy Alfred Whitehead, Brooklyner Steve Weiss and Britisher John Bain—the author constructs a frame for his much broader . . . discussion of military personnel policy." (Kirkus Reviews)

Includes bibliographical references and index

The **good** war; an oral history of World War Two. [edited by] Studs Terkel. New Press 1997 589p pa $16.95   **940.54**

  1. World War, 1939-1945 -- Personal narratives

ISBN 1-56584-343-6

LC 2003-389322

First published 1984 by Pantheon Bks.

In a series of interviews Terkel depicts how WWII affected the lives of average Americans.

Grayling, A. C.

Among the dead cities; the history and moral legacy of the WWII bombing of civilians in Germany and Japan. Walker & Co. 2006 361p il maps $25.95   **940.54**

  1. World War, 1939-1945 -- Ethical aspects   2. World War, 1939-1945 -- Aerial operations

ISBN 0-8027-1471-4

LC 2005-58597

"Was it wrong for the Allies to bomb German and Japanese civilians in World War II? In this book, . . . [the author] attends to one of the twentieth-century's largest unexploded moral conundrums. . . . Grayling's book builds careful, generous cases for and against the bombing, admitting as evidence both the experience of the bombed as well as the bombers." Booklist

Includes bibliographical references

Groom, Winston

The **generals**; Patton, MacArthur, Marshall, and the winning of World War II. by Winston Groom. National Geographic 2015 496 p. maps; 16 plates (hardcover : alk. paper) $30   **940.54**

  1. Generals   2. World War, 1939-1945 -- United States   3. Generals -- United States -- Biography   4. World War, 1939-1945 -- United States -- Biography

ISBN 9781426215490

LC 2015021562

This book, by Winston Groom, "tells the intertwined and uniquely American tales of George Patton, Douglas MacArthur, and George Marshall - from the World War I battle that shaped them to their greatest victory: leading the allies to victory in World War II. These three remarkable men-of-arms who rose from the gruesome hell of the First World War to become the finest generals of their generation during World War II redefined America's ideas of military leadership." (Publisher's note)

"There is much material on the battle tactics of both World Wars, which should appeal to military buffs, while general readers will welcome a review of the facts about these men conveyed through felicitous prose." LJ

Includes bibliographical references and index

Ham, Paul

Hiroshima Nagasaki; the real story of the atomic bombings and their aftermath. Paul Ham. Doubleday 2012 ix, 629 p.p ill. (some color), maps (hbk.) $35   **940.54**

  1. Atomic bomb -- History   2. Nagasaki (Japan) -- Bombardment, 1945   3. Hiroshima (Japan) -- Bombardment, 1945   4. Atomic bomb victims -- Japan   5. World War, 1939-1945 -- Japan -- Nagasaki-shi   6. World War, 1939-1945 -- Japan -- Hiroshima-shi   7. Atomic bomb -- Government policy -- United States -- History -- 20th century   8. Nagasaki-shi (Japan) -- History -- Bombardment, 1945 -- Moral and ethical aspects   9. Hiroshima-shi (Japan) -- History -- Bombardment, 1945 -- Moral and ethical aspects

ISBN 1250047110; 9781448126279; 1448126274; 9781250047113

LC 2012515240

"In this harrowing history of the Hiroshima and Nagasaki bombings, Paul Ham argues against the use of nuclear weapons, drawing on extensive research and hundreds of interviews to prove that the bombings had little impact on the eventual outcome of the Pacific War. More than 100,000 people were killed instantly by the atomic bombs. . . . Many hundreds of thousands more succumbed to their horrific injuries later, or slowly perished of radiation-related sickness." (Publisher's note)

"A valuable contribution to the literature of World War II that asks its readers to rethink much of what they've been taught about America's just cause." Kirkus

Includes bibliographical references and index

Hamilton, Nigel, 1944-

The **mantle** of command; FDR at war, 1941-1942. Nigel Hamilton. Houghton Mifflin Har-

court 2014 528 p. illustrations, maps (hardcover)
$30   **940.54**
1. Strategy 2. World War, 1939-1945 -- United States
3. World War, 1939-1945 -- Campaigns 4. Command
of troops -- United States -- Case studies 5. World War,
1939-1945 -- United States -- Biography 6. United
States -- Foreign relations -- Great Britain
ISBN 0547775245; 9780544227842; 9780547775241
LC 2013045586

"Based on years of archival research and interviews with
the last surviving aides and Roosevelt family members, Nigel Hamilton offers a definitive account of FDR's masterful-
-and underappreciated--command of the Allied war effort.
Hamilton takes readers inside FDR's White House Oval
Study--his personal command center--and into the meetings
where he battled with Churchill about strategy and tactics
and overrode the near mutinies of his own generals and secretary of war." (Publisher's note)

"Though it's a weighty tome, and is based extensively
on Roosevelt's own notes, Hamilton keeps a brisk pace
throughout to produce what will likely be seen as a definitive volume on this aspect of Roosevelt's career." Pub Wkly
Includes bibliographical references and index

Harding, Stephen

Last to die; a defeated empire, a forgotten mission, and the last American killed in World War
II. Stephen Harding. Da Capo Press 2015 vii,
253 p.p 16 plates; maps (hardcover : alk. paper)
$26.99   **940.54**
1. World War, 1939-1945 -- Aerial operations -- Japan 2.
Pottstown (Pa.) -- Biography 3. World War, 1939-1945
-- Aerial operations, American 4. World War, 1939-
1945 -- Campaigns -- Japan -- Tokyo 5. World War,
1939-1945 -- Reconnaissance operations, American
6. United States. Army Air Forces -- Aerial gunners --
Biography 7. United States. Army Air Forces. Photo
Reconnaissance Squadron, 20th -- Biography
ISBN 0306823381; 9780306823381
LC 2015003486

This book, by Stephen Harding, describes the events
surrounding the final U.S. combat death of World War II.
"Based on official American and Japanese histories, personal memoirs, and the author's exclusive interviews with many
of the story's key participants, . . . [this book] is a . . . tale of
air combat, bravery, cowardice, hubris, and determination,
all set during the turbulent and confusing final days of World
War II." (Publisher's note)

"Harding treats the youth with admiration and affection
that elicit compassion without becoming cloying or melodramatic. This is a superb look at the life and death of one
young man among millions of others who loved, were loved
by others, and died too soon." Booklist

Includes bibliographical references (pages 213-221)
and index

Hastings, Max

Armageddon: the battle for Germany, 1944-45.
A.A. Knopf 2004 584p il maps $30   **940.54**
1. World War, 1939-1945
ISBN 0-375-41433-9
LC 2004-46468

The author "tells the grim tale of the final collapse of
the Third Reich. It does so from the viewpoints of the upper
millstone (the Western Allies), the lower millstone (the Russians) and the grain being ground in between (the Germans).
The research includes previously untapped Russian archives
(particularly in the accounts of Soviet veterans) and leads
to a gripping and horrifying story that serious students of
military history will find almost impossible to put down."
Publ Wkly

Includes bibliographical references

Inferno; by Max Hastings. Alfred A. Knopf
2011 xx, 729 p.p [48] p. of plates ill maps   **940.54**
1. Military history 2. World War, 1939-1945 3.
Military art and science -- History
ISBN 9780307273598
LC 2011013890

'This book "offers an account of the [Second World]
war that concentrates on the lived experience of the men and
women who took part in it. On almost every page there is
. . . material from interviews, diaries, letters, memoirs and
personal documents of many kinds. . . . This is at its core
very much a military history, despite the space devoted to
the experiences of civilians. . . . [Author Max] Hastings argues that the navies of the United Kingdom and the United
States were their best fighting forces; he thinks the armies
of the two Allied powers were mostly no match for the ruthless fighting prowess of the Germans and Japanese, whose
willingness to sacrifice themselves contrasted with the care
taken by Allied generals to minimize casualties among their
own men. Red Army troops behaved in a manner not unlike
that of the Germans, their reckless disregard for their own
safety driven on by the knowledge that the Soviet secret police would shoot them if they hesitated." (N Y Times)

Includes bibliographical references and index.

Retribution; the battle for Japan, 1944-45. Alfred A. Knopf 2008 615p il map $35   **940.54**
1. World War, 1939-1945 -- Japan
ISBN 978-0-307-26351-3; 0-307-26351-7
LC 2007-34202

First published 2007 in the United Kingdom with title:
Nemesis

This chronicle of the final year of the Pacific war discusses such topics as the events leading to Allied victory,
Japan's war against China, and the decision to bomb Hiroshima and Nagasaki.

"Encompassing the British, Chinese, and Soviet roles
in vanquishing Japan, Hastings is both comprehensive and
finely acute in this masterful interpretive narrative." Booklist

Includes bibliographical references

The **secret** war; Spies, Ciphers, and Guerrillas,
1939-1945. by Max Hastings. HarperCollins 2016
640 p. illustrations $35   **940.54**
1. Spies 2. Espionage 3. Intelligence service 4. World
War, 1939-1945 -- Military intelligence
ISBN 006225927X; 9780062259271

This book, by Max Hastings, "is a sweeping examination of one of the most important yet underexplored aspects
of World War II—intelligence—showing how espionage
successes and failures by the United States, Britain, Russia,

Germany, and Japan influenced the course of the war and its final outcome." (Publisher's note)

"This wide-ranging account is filled with compelling characters, some admirable, others morally dubious. Hastings also illustrates that even great intelligence coups can be wasted by politicians who fail to properly utilize the information." Booklist

Includes bibliographical references (pages 579-585) and index.

Haynes, Fred
The **lions** of Iwo Jima; [by] Fred Haynes and James A. Warren. Henry Holt 2008 272p il map $26; pa $17 **940.54**
1. Iwo Jima, Battle of, 1945 2. World War, 1939-1945 -- Personal narratives 3. United States -- Marine Corps -- Marines, 28th
ISBN 978-0-8050-8325-5; 0-8050-8325-1; 978-0-8050-9017-8 pa; 0-8050-9017-7 pa
LC 2007-42245
"The account focuses on the experience of Combat Team 28, a unit of 4,500 marines; their best-known accomplishment was the raising of the flag atop Mount Suribachi. However, that event, immortalized by the classic photograph, occurred only four days into the monthlong battle. Ahead lay a cauldron of merciless slaughter, with marines inching forward against Japanese troops entrenched in a series of interlocking caves and tunnels. The authors capture the horror of their advance as close-range combat in confined areas became the norm. This is a disturbing, sometimes sickening chronicle, but the harsh face of war in the Pacific theater has rarely been portrayed so effectively." Booklist
Includes bibliographical references

Hellbeck, Jochen
Stalingrad; the city that defeated the Third Reich. Jochen Hellbeck. PublicAffairs 2015 500 p. illustrations (hardcover) $29.99 **940.54**
1. Stalingrad, Battle of, 1942-1943 2. World War, 1939-1945 -- Soviet Union 3. Stalingrad, Battle of, Volgograd, Russia, 1942-1943 4. Stalingrad, Battle of, Volgograd, Russia, 1942-1943 -- Personal narratives, German 5. Stalingrad, Battle of, Volgograd, Russia, 1942-1943 -- Personal narratives, Russian
ISBN 1610394968; 9781610394963
LC 2015002880
Author Jochen Hellbeck presents "a definitive new portrait of the most fateful battle of World War II. The turning point of World War II came at Stalingrad. During the battle and shortly after its conclusion, scores of Red Army commanders and soldiers, party officials and workers spoke with a team of historians who visited from Moscow to record their conversations. The tapestry of their voices provides groundbreaking insights into the thoughts and feelings of Soviet citizens during wartime." (Publisher's note)
Includes bibliographical references and index

Hersey, John
Hiroshima; a new edition with a final chapter written forty years after the explosion. Knopf 1985 196p il $26; pa $6.50 **940.54**
1. Atomic bomb 2. World War, 1939-1945 -- Japan 3.

Hiroshima (Japan) -- Bombardment, 1945
ISBN 0-394-54844-2; 0-679-72103-7 pa
LC 85-40346
First published 1946
An account of the aftermath of the first atomic bomb as reflected in the lives of six survivors

Hervieux, Linda
Forgotten; the untold story of D-Day's Black heroes, at home and at war. Linda Hervieux. HarperCollins 2015 368 p. 16 plates; ills; portraits $27.99 **940.54**
1. African American soldiers 2. Normandy (France), Attack on, 1944 3. World War, 1939-1945 -- Campaigns -- France 4. African American soldiers -- Biography 5. World War, 1939-1945 -- Balloons -- United States 6. World War, 1939-1945 -- Campaigns -- France -- Normandy 7. World War, 1939-1945 -- Participation, African American 8. World War, 1939-1945 -- Regimental histories -- United States 9. United States. Army. Anti-Aricraft Barrage Balloon Battalion, 320th -- History
ISBN 9780062313799
LC 2015017941
This book, by Linda Hervieux, "pays tribute to the valor of an all-black battalion whose crucial contributions at D-Day have gone unrecognized. . . . [T]he 320th Barrage Balloon Battalion . . . landed on the beaches of France. Their orders were to man a curtain of armed balloons meant to deter enemy aircraft. One member . . . would be nominated for the Medal of Honor, an award he would never receive. The nation's highest decoration was not given to black soldiers in World War II. (Publisher's note)
"Recommended for aviation buffs, chroniclers of World War II, and anyone who wants a nondense military read." LJ
Includes bibliographical references and index

Hicks, George
The **comfort** women; Japan's brutal regime of enforced prostitution in the Second World War. Norton 1995 303p il maps hardcover o.p. pa $14.95 **940.54**
1. Comfort women 2. Sino-Japanese Conflict, 1937-1945 3. World War, 1939-1945 -- Women 4. World War, 1939-1945 -- Atrocities
ISBN 0-393-03807-6; 0-393-31694-7 pa
LC 95-2162
The author begins his "report with a historical survey of wartime sexual exploitation of women, then narrows the focus to the 'comfort women' system developed by the Japanese. The copious testimony of victims is shockingly graphic. . . . This significant addition to 'the poor record of mankind to womankind, especially in war,' properly approaches the subject as a human-rights issue tied to the rise of feminism in Asia." Publ Wkly
Includes bibliographical references

Hillenbrand, Laura, 1967-
Unbroken. Random House 2010 473p il map $27; ebook $27 **940.54**
1. Veterans 2. Prisoners of war 3. Evangelists 4. Olympic athletes 5. Air force officers 6. Runners

(Athletes) 7. Biography, Individual 8. World War, 1939-1945 -- Aerial operations 9. World War, 1939-1945 -- Prisoners and prisons

ISBN 978-1-4000-6416-8; 1-4000-6416-3; 978-0-679-60375-7 ebook; 0-679-60375-1 ebook

LC 2010017517

This is an account of Army Air Force bomber Louis Zamperini's plane crash in 1943 and his abuse as a Japanese prisoner of war.

"Hillenbrand's triumph is that in telling Louie's story . . . she tells the stories of thousands whose suffering has been mostly forgotten. She restores to our collective memory this tale of heroism, cruelty, life, death, joy, suffering, remorselessness, and redemption." Publ Wkly

Includes bibliographical references

Holland, James

Battle of Britain; five months that changed history, May-October 1940. St. Martin's Press 2011 677p il map $40; ebook $19.99   **940.54**

1. Britain, Battle of, 1940

ISBN 978-0-312-67500-4; 978-1-4299-1941-8 ebook

LC 2010-40646

First published 2010 in the United Kingdom

"This massive volume is informative, enthralling, and moving—often all three at once. It effectively combines narrative and analysis to tell the story of the confrontation between the Luftwaffe and RAF Fighter Command from May through October 1940." Booklist

Includes bibliographical references

The **rise** of Germany 1939-1941; The Rise of Germany, 1939-1941. James Holland. Atlantic Monthly Press 2015 512 p. illustrations (some color) $30   **940.54**

1. World War, 1939-1945 -- Germany

ISBN 080212397X; 9780802123978

This book, by James Holland, presents a reappraisal of traditional World War II historiography. "It is commonly held that at the outset of war, Germany had the best army in the world and Britain barely managed to hold out against it until the Americans declared war. . . . But the picture looked much different in 1939. . . . Hitler was bluffing when he called for the wholesale destruction of Poland, but his bet that Western Europe wouldn't get involved turned out to be fatally wrong." (Publisher's note)

"Holland skillfully integrates the broad political, diplomatic, economic, and military narrative with stories of individuals, civilians, and soldiers from all the belligerents." LJ

Hornfischer, James D.

Ship of ghosts; the story of the USS Houston, FDR's legendary lost cruiser, and the epic saga of her survivors. Bantam Books 2006 530p il map $26   **940.54**

1. Houston (Cruiser) 2. World War, 1939-1945 -- Naval operations

ISBN 0-553-80390-5; 978-0-553-80390-7

LC 2006-47530

This book "recounts the exploits of the Houston, mainstay of the skimpy Allied fleet opposing the Japanese onslaught in the war's early days, until her sinking in a des-

perate battle with overwhelming Japanese forces in the Java Sea in 1942. . . . The narrative then shifts gears to follow the Houston's several hundred survivors through Japanese POW camps in Southeast Asia, focusing on the labor camps on the Burma-Thailand railway (glamorized in the movie Bridge on the River Kwai). . . . [This is] a gripping, well-told memorial to Greatest Generation martyrdom." Publ Wkly

Includes bibliographical references

Hotta, Eri

Japan 1941; countdown to infamy. by Eri Hotta. Alfred A. Knopf 2013 352 p. (hardcover) $27.95   **940.54**

1. World War, 1939-1945 -- Japan 2. Japan -- Politics and government 3. Pearl Harbor (Oahu, Hawaii), Attack on, 1941 4. War -- Decision making 5. Pearl Harbor (Hawaii), Attack on, 1941 6. Japan -- Politics and government -- 1926-1945 7. Japan -- Military policy -- History -- 20th century 8. Military planning -- Japan -- History -- 20th century

ISBN 0307594017; 9780307594013

LC 2013014781

In this book, author Eri Hotta presents his attempt "to examine the lead up to the attack on Pearl Harbor from a Japanese perspective [and] portrays the dilemma faced by the Japanese government and military in 1941. She indicts American policy makers for their failure to understand Japan's views [and] condemns U.S. demands that Japan withdraw from China." (Booklist)

Includes bibliographical references and index

Iwo Jima; World War II veterans remember the greatest battle of the Pacific. [edited by] Larry Smith. W.W. Norton 2008 xxiv, 345p il map $26.95; pa $17.95   **940.54**

1. Iwo Jima, Battle of, 1945 2. World War, 1939-1945 -- Personal narratives

ISBN 978-0-393-06234-2; 0-393-06234-1; 978-0-393-33491-3 pa; 0-393-33491-0 pa

LC 2008-1301

This is "a superb collection of 22 oral histories from Iwo Jima veterans, including two Medal of Honor winners, a Navajo 'Code-Talker,' the last surviving flag raiser from the first flag raising on Mount Suribachi, a war correspondent, and an African American marine who served in an ammo company." Libr J

Jacobsen, Annie

Operation Paperclip; the secret intelligence program to bring Nazi scientists to America. Annie Jacobsen. Little Brown & Co 2014 544 p. illustrations (hardcover) $30   **940.54**

1. Cold war 2. German scientists 3. National socialists 4. Scientists -- Germany -- History 5. Scientists -- United States -- History

ISBN 031622104X; 9780316221047

LC 2013028255

This book by Annie Jacobsen describes how "in the chaos following World War II, the U.S. government faced many difficult decisions, including what to do with the Third Reich's scientific minds. These were the brains behind the Nazis' once-indomitable war machine. So began Operation

Paperclip, a decades-long, covert project to bring Hitler's scientists and their families to the United States." (Publisher's note)

"Built upon archival records, court transcripts, declassified documents, and interviews, Jacobsen's impressive book plumbs the dark depths of this postwar recruiting and shows the historical truths behind the space race and postwar U.S. dominance." LJ

Includes bibliographical references and index

Jones, Michael K.

The **retreat**; Hitler's first defeat. [by] Michael Jones. Thomas Dunne Books/St. Martin's Press 2010 xxi, 328p il map $27.99   **940.54**
1. World War, 1939-1945 -- Campaigns -- Soviet Union
ISBN 978-0-312-62819-2
LC 2010-34784
First published 2009 in the United Kingdom
"Fluently written with good sourcing, this book covers both sides of a vast conflict that dwarfed any other in Western Europe." Libr J
Includes bibliographical references

Kaplan, Alice Yaeger

The **interpreter**; [by] Alice Kaplan. University of Chicago Press 2007 240p il map pa $15 **940.54**
1. Authors 2. Veterans 3. Novelists 4. Trials (Homicide) 5. African American soldiers 6. Army officers 7. World War, 1939-1945 -- African Americans
ISBN 978-0-226-42425-5; 0-226-42425-1
LC 2006-35822
First published 2005 by Free Press
This is an "account of the trials of two American soldiers accused of murdering French citizens in the waning days of World War II. One of the accused soldiers, a black man named James Hendricks, was sentenced to death, while the other, George Whittington, a white who had been proclaimed a war hero, was acquitted. French political novelist Louis Guilloux served as an interpreter at these trials, and Kaplan draws from Guilloux's diaries as well as from a novel he based upon the trials. . . . Inventive, moving, and beautifully written, this is a major contribution to investigative history." Libr J
Includes bibliographical references

Karnad, Raghu

Farthest field; an Indian story of the Second World War. Raghu Karnad. W W Norton & Co Inc. 2015 320 p. maps (hardcover) $25.95   **940.54**
1. War and civilization 2. World War, 1939-1945 3. Social change -- India 4. India -- History -- 1765-1947, British occupation 5. World War, 1939-1945 -- India 6. Soldiers -- India -- Biography 7. World War, 1939-1945 -- India -- Madras 8. World War, 1939-1945 -- India -- Calicut 9. Social change -- India -- History -- 20th century 10. War and society -- India -- History -- 20th century 11. Great Britain. Army. British Indian Army -- Biography 12. Great Britain. Army. British Indian Army -- History -- World War, 1939-1945
ISBN 0393248097; 9780393248098
LC 2015018733

This book, by journalist Raghu Karnad, "narrates the lost epic of India's [role in World War II], in which the largest volunteer army in history fought for the British Empire, even as its countrymen fought to be free of it. It carries us from Madras to Peshawar, Egypt to Burma—unfolding the saga of a young family amazed by their swiftly changing world and swept up in its violence." (Publisher's note)

"An appealing, if necessarily fictionalized in places, portrait of three officers who did their best fighting a war widely opposed by many countrymen and that provided little benefit to the nation and was quickly forgotten after Indian independence in 1947." Kirkus

Includes bibliographical references and index

Katz, Robert

The **battle** for Rome; the Germans, the allies, the partisans and the Pope, September 1943-June 1944. Simon & Schuster 2003 418p il map $28; pa $16   **940.54**
1. World War, 1939-1945 -- Italy
ISBN 0-7432-1642-3; 0-7432-5808-8 pa
LC 2003-45677
"This narrative history describes the Eternal City at a key time of struggle—the dark year of German occupation between the overthrow of Mussolini in 1943 and liberation by the Allies in 1944. Four parties wrestle for Rome: the ruthless yet wary German occupiers, the Holy See in self-preservation mode, a gutsy band of patriotic students with homemade explosives, and the U.S. Fifth Army under Mark Clark. . . . This is challenging research presented fluidly, and Katz's fascination with a key moment for a fascinating city shines through." Booklist
Includes bibliographical references

Kennedy, Paul M., 1945-

Engineers of victory; the problem solvers who turned the tide in the Second World War. Paul Kennedy. Random House 2013 464 p. (alk. paper) $30   **940.54**
1. World War, 1939-1945 2. World War, 1939-1945 -- Campaigns 3. Germany -- Armed Forces -- Organization 4. World War, 1939-1945 -- Naval operations 5. World War, 1939-1945 -- Aerial operations 6. Bombing, Aerial -- History -- 20th century 7. Amphibious warfare -- History -- 20th century 8. World War, 1939-1945 -- Amphibious operations 9. World War, 1939-1945 -- Campaigns -- Pacific Area 10. Germany -- Armed Forces -- History -- World War, 1939-1945 11. Naval convoys -- Atlantic Ocean -- History -- 20th century
ISBN 1400067618; 9781400067619; 9781588368980
LC 2012024284
This book by Paul Kennedy "provides a new and unique look at how World War II was won." The book is a "nuts-and-bolts account of the strategic factors that led to Allied victory. Kennedy reveals how the leaders' grand strategy was carried out by the ordinary soldiers, scientists, engineers, and businessmen responsible for realizing their commanders' visions of success." (Publisher's note)
Includes bibliographical references and index

Kershaw, Alex

Escape from the deep; the epic story of a legendary submarine and her courageous crew. Da Capo Press 2008 270p il map $26; pa $15.95   **940.54**
1. Tang (Ship) 2. World War, 1939-1945 -- Pacific Ocean 3. World War, 1939-1945 -- Naval operations 4. World War, 1939-1945 -- Prisoners and prisons
ISBN 978-0-306-81519-5; 0-306-81519-2; 978-0-306-81790-8 pa; 0-306-81790-X pa

LC 2008-298762

Details the history of the U.S. Navy submarine Tang in the Pacific theater of World War II, the explosion that led to its sinking, the ordeal of its surviving crew members and their capture by the Japanese, followed by months of brutal captivity.

The author "has researched exhaustively, including interviewing the last two living survivors, and written compactly the portrait of nine Americans who rose to heroism and of a ship that well deserved its status . . . as a legend in the naval history of World War II." Booklist

Includes bibliographical references

Keuning-Tichelaar, An

Passing on the comfort; the war, the quilts, and the women who made a difference. [by] An Keuning-Tichelaar and Lynn Kaplanian-Buller. Good Books 2005 186p il pa $14.95   **940.54**
1. Quilts 2. World War, 1939-1945 -- Personal narratives
ISBN 1-561484-82-2

LC 2005-01932

This is the "narrative of a Dutch resistance operation during WWII conducted by Keuning-Tichelaar and her husband, Herman, a Mennonite minister. With the support of their townspeople, the two young newlyweds sheltered and saved the lives of Jewish adults and children, and others in danger from the Nazis. As part of a relief effort, quilts were created by women in North American Mennonite circles and sent to the Netherlands. Beautifully illustrated with 19 color photographs of the quilts, this book describes in an understated voice the harrowing events and the daily acts of courage that Keuning-Tichelaar undertook. When, decades later, coauthor Kaplanian-Buller, a U.S. citizen living in Amsterdam, found the old quilts, she persuaded An to share her story." Publ Wkly

Includes bibliographical references

Korda, Michael

With wings like eagles; a history of the Battle of Britain. Harper 2009 322p il map $25.95   **940.54**
1. Britain, Battle of, 1940 2. Great Britain -- Royal Air Force 3. World War, 1939-1945 -- Aerial operations
ISBN 978-0-06-112535-5; 0-06-112535-0

LC 2008-09293

This "is a skillful, absorbing, often moving contribution to the popular understanding of one of the few episodes in history to live on untarnished and undiminished in the collective memory and to deserve the description 'heroic.'" Washington Post

Includes bibliographical references (p. 303-305)

Leckie, Robert, 1920-

Okinawa; the last battle of World War II. Viking 1995 220p il hardcover o.p. pa $13.95   **940.54**
1. World War, 1939-1945 -- Campaigns -- Okinawa Island
ISBN 0-670-84716-X; 0-14-017389-7 pa

LC 94-39145

In this history of the Battle of Okinawa "Leckie supplies an accessible historical overview of a perplexing war tactic, the kamikaze attack." Booklist

Lee, Bruce

Marching orders; the untold story of World War II. Da Capo Press 2001 608p map pa $24 **940.54**
1. Cryptography 2. World War, 1939-1945 -- Japan 3. World War, 1939-1945 -- Secret service
ISBN 978-0-306-81036-7; 0-306-81036-0
First published 1995 by Crown

"Many of the mysteries that have eluded historians since the end of the war are much clarified. . . . This is the most significant publication about World War II since the recent series of books on the Ultra revelations and should be purchased by all libraries." Libr J

Includes bibliographical references

Letts, Elizabeth

The **perfect** horse; The Daring U.S. Mission to Rescue the Priceless Stallions Kidnapped by the Nazis. Elizabeth Letts. Ballantine Books 2016 400 p. illustrations, map (hardcover : alk. paper) $28 **940.54**
1. Horses 2. World War, 1939-1945 -- Austria 3. Arabian horse -- Poland -- History -- 20th century 4. Lipizzaner horse -- Austria -- History -- 20th century 5. Spanische Reitschule (Vienna, Austria) -- History -- 20th century 6. United States. Army. Cavalry Regiment, Mechanized, 2nd -- History 7. World War, 1939-1945 -- Confiscations and contributions -- Germany 8. World War, 1939-1945 -- Confiscations and contributions -- United States 9. World War, 1939-1945 -- Commando operations -- Czech Republic -- Hostouň
ISBN 0345544803; 9780345544803

LC 2016010501

This book, by Elizabeth Letts, tells the "story of the heroic rescue of priceless horses in the closing days of World War II. . . . A small troop of . . . American soldiers captures a German spy and makes an astonishing find—his briefcase is empty but for photos of beautiful white horses that have been stolen and kept on a secret farm behind enemy lines. Hitler has stockpiled the world's finest purebreds in order to breed the perfect military machine—an equine master race." (Publisher's note)

"The author's elegant narrative conveys how the love for these amazing creatures transcends national animosities." Kirkus

Includes bibliographical references and index

Lewis, Damien

The **Dog** Who Could Fly; The Incredible True Story of a WWII Airman and the Four-legged Hero

Who Flew at His Side. Damien Lewis. Pocket Books 2014 304 p. illustrations $26 **940.54**
1. Dogs 2. World War, 1939-1945 -- Aerial operations
ISBN 1476739145; 9781476739144

LC 2014015567
This book by Damien Lewis "is the true account of a German shepherd who was adopted by the Royal Air Force during World War II, joined in flight missions, and survived everything from crash-landings to parachute bailouts--ultimately saving the life of his owner and dearest friend. . . . Airman Robert Bozdech stumbled across the tiny German shepherd--whom he named Ant--after being shot down on a daring mission over enemy lines." (Publisher's note)

A "heartwarming and well-paced man-and-his-dog story. . . . Lewis has captured the spirit of the era and told the story using Bozdech's manuscript as source material without making it maudlin or sentimental." Pub Wkly

Includes bibliographical references

Liebling, A. J.
World War II writings. Library of America 2008 1089p map (The library of America) $40 **940.54**
1. World War, 1939-1945 -- Campaigns 2. World War, 1939-1945 -- Personal narratives
ISBN 978-1-59853-018-6

LC 2007-938791
"The war brought out the best in [Liebling]. Here he . . . relied on straightforward observation, delivered in a style less mannered than Hemingway's, less sentimental than Ernie Pyle's, less excitable than Michael Herr's. It's the kind of writing that looks easy, except that very few war correspondents have ever done it so well." N Y Times Book Rev

Includes bibliographical references

Lifton, Robert Jay
Hiroshima in America; a half century of denial. [by] Robert Jay Lifton & Greg Mitchell; with a new afterword by the authors. Avon Books 1996 427p il pa $18.95 **940.54**
1. Atomic bomb 2. Hiroshima (Japan) -- Bombardment, 1945
ISBN 978-0-380-72764-3; 0-380-72764-1

First published 1995 by Putnam with title: Hiroshima in America: fifty years of denial

Lifton and Mitchell examine "the reaction of the American people to the bombing of Hiroshima in 1945 and its domestic aftermath. The authors examine what they perceive to be a conspiracy by the government to mislead and suppress information about the actual bombing, Truman's decision to drop the bomb, and the birth and mismanagement of the beginning of the nuclear age." Libr J

Includes bibliographical references

Lineberry, Cate
The secret rescue; Cate Lineberry. Little, Brown and Co. 2013 320 p. $27 **940.54**
1. Nurses 2. World War, 1939-1945 3. Special forces (Military science) -- United States
ISBN 0316220221; 9780316220224

LC 2013934814
This book looks at the Medical Air Evacuation Transport Squadron during World War II. Cate Lineberry "looks in par-ticular at the 807th MAETS, consisting of 25 female nurses, 24 medics and other enlisted men from all over the country. They were assembled at Bowman Field in Louisville, Ky., for training before being shipped off in mid-August 1943." When they were forced down over enemy territory, there "ensued many weeks of near-comical confusion" before a rescue took place. (Kirkus Reviews)

Lukacs, John D.
Escape from Davao; the forgotten story of the most daring prison break of the Pacific war. Simon & Schuster 2010 xiii, 433p il $27.99 **940.54**
1. Davao City (Philippines) 2. Soldiers -- United States 3. World War, 1939-1945 -- Philippines 4. World War, 1939-1945 -- Prisoners and prisons 5. World War, 1939-1945 -- Underground movements
ISBN 978-0-7432-6278-1; 0-7432-6278-6

LC 2010-03238
The author "is a gifted stylist and storyteller. He doesn't flinch at the grim or the gruesome. . . . At bottom, 'Escape From Davao' is a morality tale, not unlike the war movies of the 1940s and '50s, about pluck, luck, courage, comradeship, Yankee humor, ingenuity, and religious faith." Pittsburgh Post-Gazette

Includes bibliographical references

Lulushi, Albert
Donovan's Devils; OSS commandos behind enemy lines : Europe, World War II. Albert Lulushi. Arcade Pubishing 2016 398 p. illustrations, maps (hardcover : alk. paper) $25.99 **940.54**
1. World War, 1939-1945 -- Commando operations 2. World War, 1939-1945 -- Secret service -- United States 3. World War, 1939-1945 -- Commando operations -- Europe 4. United States. Office of Strategic Services -- History
ISBN 9781628725674

LC 2015037691
This book, by Albert Lulushi, presents a history of "the OSS—Office of Strategic Services—created under the command of William Donovan . . . [and] its cloak-and-dagger operations during World War II . . . as the precursor of the CIA. . . . [This book] provides the most comprehensive account to date of the Operational Group activities, including a detailed narrative of the ill-fated Ginny mission, which resulted in the one of the OSS's gravest losses of the war." (Publisher's note)

"A proficient, well-wrought work that emphasizes the actual fighting men, their deeds, and their fates." Kirkus

Includes bibliographical references and index

Macintyre, Ben, 1963-
Double cross; the true story of the D-day spies. Ben Macintyre. Crown 2012 399 p. ill., maps **940.54**
1. Spies 2. World War, 1939-1945 3. Normandy (France), Attack on, 1944 4. Spies -- Europe -- Biography 5. World War, 1939-1945 -- Deception 6. World War, 1939-1945 -- Secret service 7. World War, 1939-1945 -- Military intelligence 8. Espionage -- Europe -- History -- 20th century 9. Deception (Military science) -- History -- 20th century 10. World War, 1939-

1945 -- Campaigns -- France -- Normandy
ISBN 9780307888754; 9780307888761

LC 2012003089

This book looks at the "deceit operation [that] was aimed at convincing the Nazis that Calais and Norway, not Normandy, were the targets of the 150,000-strong [D-Day] invasion force. The deception involved every branch of Allied wartime intelligence - the Bletchley Park code-breakers, MI5, MI6, SOE, Scientific Intelligence, the FBI and the French Resistance. But at its heart was the 'Double Cross System', a team of double agents controlled by the secret Twenty Committee." The squad comprised 'a bisexual Peruvian playgirl, a tiny Polish fighter pilot, a Serbian seducer, a wildly imaginative Spaniard with a diploma in chicken farming, and a hysterical Frenchwoman whose obsessive love for her pet dog very nearly wrecked the entire deception,' as well as a "sixth spy." (Publisher's note)

Includes bibliographical references (p. [383]-386) and index.

Operation Mincemeat; how a dead man and a bizarre plan fooled the Nazis and assured an allied victory. Harmony Books 2010 400p il $25.99 **940.54**
1. Lawyers 2. Intelligence service agents 3. World War, 1939-1945 -- Secret service
ISBN 978-0-307-45327-3; 0-307-45327-8

LC 2009-47562

A "true WWII tale that reads like something by Ian Fleming. In fact, two of Fleming's fellow British intelligence officers hatched the title operation. They dressed a corpse in uniform and arranged for it to wash up on a Nazi-friendly stretch of the Spanish coast bearing a suitcase with false war plans. Against all odds, Operation Mincemeat succeeded — and helped convince the Germans that the Allies planned to invade Sardinia and Greece in 1943 instead of their real target, Sicily. Relying on a cache of once-classified documents, Macintyre provides the fullest account yet of this curious episode and enlivens his yarn with quirky details." Entertainment Wkly

Includes bibliographical references

Rogue Heroes; The History of the SAS, Britain's Secret Special Forces Unit That Sabotaged the Nazis and Changed the Nature of War. by Ben Macintyre. Random House Inc 2016 352 p. illustrations, maps (ebook) $65; $28 **940.54**
1. Special forces (Military science) 2. World War, 1939-1945 -- Great Britain
ISBN 9781101904176; 110190416X; 9781101904169

This book, by Ben Macintyre, shares the "untold story of WWII's greatest secret fighting force. . . Britain's Special Air Service—or SAS—was the brainchild of David Stirling. . . . Where most of his colleagues looked at a battlefield map of World War II's African theater and saw a protracted struggle with Rommel's desert forces, Stirling saw an opportunity: given a small number of elite, well-trained men, he could parachute behind enemy lines and sabotage their airplanes and war material." (Publisher's note)

"He demonstrates that even in a global war, a few uniquely talented, imaginative, and bold individuals of relatively junior rank can have a major impact. Macintyre delivers a solid history and an enjoyable read that will appeal to those interested in military history as well as readers who enjoy real-life tales of adventure." Pub Wkly

Includes bibliographical references (pages 363-364) and index.

Manchester, William

Goodbye, darkness; a memoir of the Pacific War. Little, Brown 1980 401p il hardcover o.p. pa $16.95 **940.54**
1. World War, 1939-1945 -- Pacific Ocean 2. World War, 1939-1945 -- Personal narratives
ISBN 0-316-50111-5 pa

LC 80-17310

This memoir arises from a 1978 trip the author made "to Pacific battlefields, seeking to exorcise three decades of nightmares dating to wartime days as a Marine Corps sergeant. . . . First tracing his family background, youth, enlistment, training, and embarkation from San Diego, Manchester unravels a memoir featuring historical reconstruction, disjointed flash-forwards, shocking vignettes, {and} redoubtable vocabulary." Choice

McKay, Sinclair

The **secret** lives of codebreakers; the men and women who cracked the Enigma code at Bletchley Park. Sinclair McKay. Penguin Group 2012 vi, 338 p.p (paperback) $16.00 **940.54**
1. Cryptography 2. World War, 1939-1945 -- Great Britain 3. World War, 1939-1945 -- Military intelligence 4. World War, 1939-1945 -- Cryptography 5. Bletchley Park (Milton Keynes, England) -- History 6. Great Britain. Government Communications Headquarters -- History 7. World War, 1939-1945 -- Electronic intelligence -- Great Britain
ISBN 0452298717; 9780452298712

LC 2012018408

This book by Sinclair McKay looks at the staff of "the Government Code & Cypher School, where [during World War II] British experts deciphered German communications, including those encrypted by the Enigma coding machine. . . . McKay presents a sociological history of the scientists, engineers, and other academics . . . thrown together at Bletchley Park with debutantes and ordinary workers, all with a common goal." (Library Journal)

Includes bibliographical references and index.

Merridale, Catherine

★ **Ivan's** war; life and death in the Red Army, 1939-1945. Metropolitan Books 2006 426p il map $30 **940.54**
1. Soviet Union -- Red Army 2. World War, 1939-1945 -- Soviet Union
ISBN 0-8050-7455-4

LC 2005-50457

The author discusses the life of the ordinary Russian soldier during World War II.

Merridale "succeeds admirably in fashioning a compelling portrait, helped immensely by her talent as a writer." Foreign Affairs

Includes bibliographical references

Miller, Nathan

War at sea; a naval history of World War II. Oxford University Press 1996 592p il map pa $29.95 **940.54**

1. World War, 1939-1945 -- Naval operations
ISBN 0-19-511038-2

LC 96-31787

First published 1995 by Scribner

"Miller's research—primarily on the Royal Navy—and a reading of hundreds of pertinent monographs has enabled him to fashion a briskly paced narrative that will both inform and entertain." Choice

Includes bibliographical references

Moses, Sam

At all costs; how a crippled ship and two American merchant mariners turned the tide of World War II. Random House 2006 335p il $25.95 **940.54**

1. World War, 1939-1945 -- Naval operations 2. World War, 1939-1945 -- Mediterranean Sea
ISBN 1-4000-6318-3

LC 2006-40425

"The remarkable heroism that won the day, as well as Moses' thorough retelling, makes this an exciting, imperative read for anyone interested in WWII." Publ Wkly

Includes bibliographical references

Moynahan, Brian

Leningrad; Siege and Symphony : The Story of the Great City Terrorized by Stalin, Starved by Hitler, Immortalized by Shostakovich. Brian Moynahan. Atlantic Monthly Press 2014 496 p. 16 plates; illustrations; maps $30 **940.54**

1. Symphony 2. World War, 1939-1945 -- Soviet Union
ISBN 0802123163; 9780802123169

In this book author Brian Moynahan "sets the composition of Shostakovich's most famous work against the tragic canvas of the siege itself and the years of repression and terror that preceded it. In vivid . . . detail he tells the story of the cruelties heaped by the twin monsters of the twentieth century on a city of exquisite beauty and fine minds, and of its no less remarkable survival." (Publisher's note)

"Moynahan's rapturous commentary on the music at times amounts to puffery. Nonetheless an admirable tribute to the human spirit and artistic integrity. Highly recommended for all readers interested in the era and the wellsprings of artistic creation." LJ

Murphy, Brian, 1959-

81 days below zero; the incredible survival story of a World War II pilot in Alaska's frozen wilderness. Brian Murphy. Da Capo Press 2015 264 p. 8 plates; illustrations (hardback) $24.99 **940.54**

1. Survival skills 2. Wilderness survival 3. Survival after airplane accidents, shipwrecks, etc. 4. Wilderness survival -- Alaska 5. World War, 1939-1945 -- Alaska 6. Airplane crash survival -- Alaska 7. B-24 (Bomber) -- Accidents -- Alaska 8. Aeronautics, Military -- Accidents -- Alaska 9. Air pilots, Military -- United States -- Biography 10. World War, 1939-1945 -- Aerial

operations, American
ISBN 0306823284; 9780306823282; 9780306823299

LC 2015003484

This book by Brian Murphy tells how "shortly before Christmas in 1943, five Army aviators left Alaska's Ladd Field on a test flight. Only one ever returned: Leon Crane, a city kid from Philadelphia with little more than a parachute on his back when he bailed from his B-24 Liberator before it crashed into the Arctic. Alone in subzero temperatures, Crane managed to stay alive in the dead of the Yukon winter for nearly twelve weeks and, amazingly, walked out of the ordeal intact." (Publisher's note)

Includes bibliographical references and index

Neiberg, Michael

The **blood** of free men; the liberation of Paris, 1944. Michael Neiberg. Basic Books, A Member of the Perseus Books Group 2012 309 p. (hardcover : alk. paper) $28.99 **940.54**

1. World War, 1939-1945 -- France -- Paris 2. World War, 1939-1945 -- Campaigns -- France -- Paris
ISBN 0465023991; 9780465023998

LC 2012016282

This book by Michael Neiber focuses on Paris, France during World War II. "As the Allies struggled inland from Normandy in August of 1944, the fate of Paris hung in the balance. Other jewels of Europe . . . were, or would soon be, reduced to rubble during attempts to liberate them. But Paris endured, thanks to a fractious cast of characters, from Resistance cells to Free French operatives to an unlikely assortment of diplomats, Allied generals, and governmental officials." (Publisher's note)

Includes bibliographical references and index.

Neitzel, Sönke, 1968-

Soldaten; On Fighting, Killing, and Dying: The Secret WWII Transcripts of German POWs. Sönke Neitzel and Harald Welzer; translated from the German by Jefferson Chase. Alfred A. Knopf 2012 x, 437 p.p $30.50 **940.54**

1. World War, 1939-1945 -- Prisoners and prisons, German 2. Eavesdropping -- Great Britain 3. World War, 1939-1945 -- Anecdotes 4. Soldiers -- Germany -- Attitudes -- Sources 5. Prisoners of war -- Germany -- Attitudes -- Sources 6. World War, 1939-1945 -- Prisoners and prisons, British 7. Prisoners of war -- Great Britain -- Attitudes -- Sources 8. Germany -- Armed Forces -- History -- 20th century -- Sources 9. World War, 1939-1945 -- Military intelligence -- Great Britain
ISBN 0307958124; 9780307958129

LC 2012005744

This book, by Sönke Neitzel and Harald Welzer, "closely examines. . . recorded interrogations of German POWs. . . and the casual, pitiless brutality omnipresent in them, from a historical and psychological perspective. What factors led to the degradation of the soldiers' sense of awareness and morality? How much did their social environments affect their interpretation of the war and their actions during combat? . . . [An] unflinching narrative of wartime experience emerges." (Publisher's note)

Includes bibliographical references (p. [397]-412)

Nelson, Craig

The **first** heroes; the extraordinary story of the Doolittle Raid--America's first World War II victory. Viking 2002 430p il $27.95; pa $15   **940.54**
1. Generals 2. Air force officers 3. World War, 1939-1945 -- Japan 4. United States -- Army Air Forces 5. World War, 1939-1945 -- Aerial operations
ISBN 0-670-03087-2; 0-14-200341-7 pa
LC 2002-28092
"The most interesting part of the book is the harrowing story of survival as crew members are forced to ditch their planes on the Asian mainland. This is a thrilling real-life saga that both informs and inspires." Booklist
Includes bibliographical references

Pearl Harbor; from infamy to greatness. Craig Nelson. Scribner, an imprint of Simon & Schuster 2016 800 p. (hardcover) $32   **940.54**
1. United States -- Military history 2. Pearl Harbor (Oahu, Hawaii), Attack on, 1941 3. Pearl Harbor (Hawaii), Attack on, 1941
ISBN 9781451660494
LC 2016018490
This book, by Craig Nelson, is a "definitive account of the event that changed twentieth-century America—Pearl Harbor. . . . Beginning in 1914, . . . Craig Nelson maps the road to war, beginning with Franklin D. Roosevelt, then the Assistant Secretary of the Navy . . . , [and] traces Japan's leaders as they lurch into ultranationalist fascism, which culminates in their insanely daring yet militarily brilliant scheme to terrify America with one of the boldest attacks ever waged." (Publisher's note)
"Nelson's well written history of Pearl Harbor will be enjoyed by the general reader and appropriately highlights the battle's historical significance." Pub Wkly
Includes bibliographical references

Norman, Elizabeth M.

★ **Tears** in the darkness; the story of the Bataan Death March and its aftermath. [by] Michael Norman and Elizabeth M. Norman. Farrar, Straus, and Giroux 2009 463p il $30   **940.54**
1. Prisoners of war 2. World War, 1939-1945 -- Atrocities 3. World War, 1939-1945 -- Prisoners and prisons 4. World War, 1939-1945 -- Campaigns -- Philippines 5. Prisoners of war -- Philippines -- Bataan (Province) 6. World War, 1939-1945 -- Prisoners and prisons, Japanese
ISBN 0-374-27260-3; 978-0-374-27260-9
LC 2008-47163
"For the first four months of 1942, U.S., Filipino, and Japanese soldiers fought what was America's first major land battle of World War II, the battle for the tiny Philippine peninsula of Bataan. It ended with the surrender of 76,000 Filipinos and Americans, the single largest defeat in American military history. The defeat, though, was only the beginning, as Michael and Elizabeth M. Norman [argue in this] . . . book. From then until the Japanese surrendered in August 1945, the prisoners of war suffered an ordeal of unparalleled cruelty and savagery: forty-one months of captivity, starvation rations, dehydration, hard labor, deadly disease, and torture." (Publisher's note) Index.

This book "is authoritative history. Ten years in the making, it is based on hundreds of interviews with American, Filipino and Japanese combatants. But it is also a narrative achievement. The book seamlessly blends a wide-angle view with the stories of many individual participants." N Y Times (Late N Y Ed)
Includes bibliographical references

Olson, Lynne

Citizens of London; the Americans who stood with Britain in its darkest, finest hour. Random House 2010 471p il $28   **940.54**
1. Diplomats 2. Governors 3. Radio reporters 4. Government officials 5. Television reporters 6. Television news anchors 7. World War, 1939-1945 -- Diplomatic history 8. Great Britain -- Foreign relations -- United States 9. United States -- Foreign relations -- Great Britain
ISBN 978-1-4000-6758-9
The story of how the United States forged its wartime alliance with Britain, told from the perspective of three key American players in London: Edward R. Murrow, Averell Harriman, and John Gilbert Winant.
A nuanced history that captures the intensity of life in a period when victory was not a foregone conclusion. Kirkus
Includes bibliographical references

The **Pacific** War; from Pearl Harbor to Hiroshima. editor, Daniel Marston. Pbk. ed.; Osprey Pub. 2010 272p il map pa $19.95   **940.54**
1. World War, 1939-1945 -- Campaigns -- Pacific Ocean
ISBN 978-1-84908-382-9
LC 2010-292672
First published 2005 with title: The Pacific war companion
"These essays on the Pacific theater of WW II, written by a group of international scholars representing Australia, Great Britain, Japan, and the US, cover the wellknown events at Pearl Harbor, the Coral Sea, and Midway; MacArthur's push to the Philippines; Nimitz's island campaign in the central Pacific; Okinawa; and the dropping of the atomic bomb on Hiroshima and Nagasaki. . . . A chronology, detailed maps, and photographs greatly enhance this excellent volume on the Pacific phase of WW II." Choice
Includes bibliographical references

Patton, George S.

War as I knew it; by George S. Patton, Jr.; annotated by Paul D. Harkins. Houghton Mifflin 1947 425p il maps hardcover o.p. pa $18   **940.54**
1. World War, 1939-1945 -- Campaigns
ISBN 0-395-73529-7 pa
An account of the General's WWII European campaigns from the fight for Sicily to the conquest of Germany based on a series of "open letters" written to his wife

Peffer, Randall

Where divers dare; the hunt for the last U-boat. Randall Peffer. Berkley Calibre 2016 320 p. illustrations (hardback) $28   **940.54**
1. Shipwrecks 2. Submarines 3. Marine salvage 4. World War, 1939-1945 -- Campaigns 5. U-550

(Submarine) 6. Shipwrecks -- North Atlantic Ocean 7. Salvage -- United States -- History 8. Divers -- United States -- Biography 9. Deep diving -- United States -- History 10. Underwater archaeology -- North Atlantic Ocean 11. Shipwrecks -- Massachusetts -- Nantucket Island 12. World War, 1939-1945 -- Naval operations, German 13. World War, 1939-1945 -- Naval operations -- Submarine 14. World War, 1939-1945 -- Campaigns -- North Atlantic Ocean

ISBN 9780425276365

LC 2015028313

This book, by Randall Peffer, is the "true account of the search for German U-boat U-550. . . . In 2012, a team found it—the last undiscovered U-boat in dive-able waters off the Eastern Seaboard of the United States, more than three hundred feet below the surface. This is the story of their twenty-year quest to find this 'Holy Grail' of deep-sea diving and their tenacious efforts to dive on this treacherous wreck." (Publisher's note)

"Peffer conveys the tension, fear, and exhilaration of deep wreck diving in this uncomfortable true story of bravery, compassion, and death that characterized the violent last hours of U-550." Pub Wkly

Pellegrino, Charles

To hell and back; the last train from Hiroshima. Charles Pellegrino. Rowman & Littlefield 2015 432 p. illustrations, map (Asia/Pacific/perspectives) (cloth : alk. paper) $29.95 **940.54**

1. Atomic bomb 2. Atomic bomb victims 3. Hiroshima (Japan) -- Bombardment, 1945 4. Forensic archaeology -- Japan -- Hiroshima-shi 5. World War, 1939-1945 -- Japan -- Hiroshima-shi 6. Atomic bomb victims -- Japan -- Hiroshima-shi -- Biography 7. Atomic bomb -- Social aspects -- Japan -- Hiroshima-shi -- History -- 20th century

ISBN 1442250585; 9781442250581

LC 2015014341

This book, by Charles Pellegrino, part of the "Asia/Pacific/Perspectives" series, "drawing on the voices of atomic bomb survivors and the new science of forensic archaeology, . . . describes the events and the aftermath of two days in August when nuclear devices, detonated over Japan, changed life on Earth forever. . . . At the narrative's core are eyewitness accounts of those who experienced the atomic explosions firsthand--the Japanese civilians on the ground." (Publisher's note)

"This is horrifying, painful, and necessary reading." Kirkus

Includes bibliographical references and index

Pleshakov, Konstantin

★ Stalin's folly; the tragic first ten days of World War II on the Eastern Front. [by] Constantine Pleshakov. Houghton Mifflin 2005 326p il map $26 **940.54**

1. Heads of state 2. Communist leaders 3. Political leaders 4. World War, 1939-1945 -- Europe

ISBN 0-618-36701-2

LC 2004-65133

This is an account of the German invasion of the Soviet Union in 1941.

This book "belongs in every World War II collection." Libr J

Includes bibliographical references

Prados, John

Storm over Leyte; The Philippine Invasion and the Destruction of the Japanese Navy. John Prados. New American Library 2016 400 p. illustrations, map $28 **940.54**

1. World War, 1939-1945 -- Campaigns -- Philippines 2. Leyte Gulf, Battle of, Philippines, 1944 3. Leyte Island (Philippines) -- History, Military 4. World War, 1939-1945 -- Campaigns -- Philippines -- Leyte Island

ISBN 9780451473615

LC 2015047067

This book, by John Prados, presents the "story of the Battle of Leyte Gulf in World War II. . . . As Allied ships prepared for the invasion of the Philippine island of Leyte, every available warship, submarine and airplane was placed on alert while Japanese admiral Kurita Takeo stalked Admiral William F. Halsey's unwitting American armada." (Publisher's note)

"The work is exceedingly balanced and provides detailed portraits of the personalities of the Japanese commanders, their understanding of events, and their decision-making processes." Pub Wkly

Includes bibliographical references and index.

Prange, Gordon William

At dawn we slept; the untold story of Pearl Harbor. {by} Gordon W. Prange in collaboration with Donald M. Goldstein and Katherine V. Dillon. Viking 1991 889p il hardcover o.p. **940.54**

1. Pearl Harbor (Oahu, Hawaii), Attack on, 1941

LC 91-50176

First published 1981 by McGraw-Hill

The author "offers a comprehensive account of Japanese preparations for the attack, the origins and extent of American unpreparedness, and the aftermath of the attack on both sides." Booklist

Includes bibliographical references

Read, Anthony

The fall of Berlin; [by] Anthony Read and David Fisher. Da Capo Press 1995 513p il map pa $18.50 **940.54**

1. Berlin, Battle of, 1945 2. Germany -- History -- 1933-1945 3. World War, 1939-1945 -- Germany

ISBN 0-306-80619-3; 978-0-306-80619-3

LC 94-47998

First published 1992 in the United Kingdom

A description of "the bombing of Berlin by the British and Americans and how the Russian Army fought its way toward and through Berlin in 1945. The authors intend no startling new interpretations or profound analysis. Instead, they offer vignettes, often based on diaries, to describe life in Berlin late in the war. They also retell the story of fanatical Nazi leaders and of the Wehrmacht's desperate efforts to defend the city. The result is a highly readable and, at the same time, sophisticated and reliable narrative history." Libr J

Includes bibliographical references

Roberts, Andrew, 1963-

Masters and commanders; how four titans won the war in the West, 1941-1945. HarperCollins 2009 xl, 673p il map $35   **940.54**

1. Generals 2. Governors 3. Statesmen 4. Historians 5. Presidents 6. Prime ministers 7. People with disabilities 8. Marshals 9. Memoirists 10. Philatelists 11. Cabinet members 12. Secretaries of state 13. Members of Parliament 14. Secretaries of defense 15. Nobel laureates for peace 16. Great Britain -- War Cabinet 17. Nobel laureates for literature 18. World War, 1939-1945 -- Campaigns 19. Strategy -- History -- 20th century 20. World War, 1939-1945 -- Military intelligence 21. World War, 1939-1945 -- Personal narratives, British 22. World War, 1939-1945 -- Personal narratives, American

ISBN 0-06-122857-5; 978-0-06-122857-5

First published 2008 in the United Kingdom with subtitle: how Roosevelt, Churchill, Marshall and Alanbrooke won the war in the West

Roberts contends that various events "of the Second World War turned on the personalities and relationships between two political masters—Winston Churchill and Franklin D. Roosevelt—and the military commanders of their armed forces—the Chief of the Imperial General Staff, General Sir Alan Brooke, and the US Army Chief of Staff, General George C. Marshall. In reconstructing the debates between these four principals and . . . [other] senior Allied figures, Roberts draws upon the private papers of . . . contemporaries and on verbatim accounts of Churchill's War Cabinet meetings." (Publisher's note)

Roberts reinforces his reputation for high-quality military history with this comprehensive synthesis of primary sources about the fundamental strategic decisions of WWII." Booklist

The **storm** of war; a new history of the Second World War. HarperCollins 2011 lvi, 712p il map $29.99   **940.54**

1. World War, 1939-1945

ISBN 978-0-06-122859-9; 0-06-122859-1

First published 2009 in the United Kingdom

"In general, histories of the Second World War in the English language can be divided sharply into those written by Americans, which downplay the British role in the war, and those written by British historians, which downplay the role of the Americans (and also give less space and attention to the Pacific theater than the European theater). Roberts has managed to write a book that both strives and succeeds in giving more or less equal time to both, and also manages to include enough about events in China and the war on the Eastern Front to give the reader a well-balanced and excitingly written account of the whole war. . . . His scholarship is superb, and the 'packaging' of the book, with very good illustrations and ample first-class maps, makes it a real pleasure to read." Daily Beast

Includes bibliographical references

Roberts, Geoffrey

Stalin's general; the life of Georgy Zhukov. Geoffrey Roberts. Random House 2012 375 p. (alk. paper) $30   **940.54**

1. Biography 2. National socialism 3. Soviet Union -- History -- 1939-1945 4. World War, 1939-1945 -- Soviet Union 5. Marshals -- Soviet Union -- Biography

ISBN 1400066921; 9780679645177; 9781400066926

LC 2011040663

Author Geoffrey Roberts presents a "biography of the ruthless Red Army general who defeated the Nazis and then spent decades alternately disgraced and rehabilitated in Soviet Russia. . . . As [Georgy] Zhukov, a rising cavalry commander in the rapidly modernizing Red Army, managed to escape being a victim of the army purges of 1937-38 and was then appointed on his first important mission for Stalin: to 'conduct a purge' of the Japanese from the Mongolian-Manchurian border in 1939." (Kirkus Reviews)

Includes bibliographical references and index.

Rooney, Andrew A.

My war; [by] Andy Rooney. PublicAffairs 2000 333p il $20; pa $14   **940.54**

1. Authors 2. Humorists 3. Journalists 4. World War, 1939-1945 -- Personal narratives

ISBN 1-58648-010-3; 1-58648-159-2 pa

LC 00-59228

First published 1995 by Random House

The author "relates how he became a notable combat journalist in WW II, a war he calls 'the ultimate experience for anyone in it.' For the Army newspaper Stars and Stripes, he covered the air war over Germany, the D-Day invasion of Normandy and the Allied drive into Germany. Rooney's simple, ruminative style . . . grips the reader as he describes famous events of the war." Publ Wkly

Scott, James M., 1964-

Target Tokyo; Jimmy Doolittle and the raid that avenged Pearl Harbor. James M. Scott. W W Norton & Co Inc 2015 xv, 648 p.p ill. (hbk.) $35 **940.54**

1. World War, 1939-1945 -- Aerial operations -- Japan 2. Tokyo (Japan) -- History -- Bombardment, 1942 3. World War, 1939-1945 -- Aerial operations, American

ISBN 9780393089622; 0393089622

LC 2014043257

Pulitzer Prize Finalist: History (2016)

This book, by James M. Scott, describes the events of the U.S. Doolittle Raid on Japan in the aftermath of the Pearl Harbor bombing. "On April 18, 1942, sixteen U.S. Army bombers under the command of daredevil pilot Jimmy Doolittle lifted off from the deck of the USS Hornet on a one-way mission to pummel the enemy's factories, refineries, and dockyards and then escape to Free China." (Publisher's note)

"This popular history will appeal to fans of Laura Hillebrand's Unbroken and is comparable to other histories of the Tokyo Raid including Craig Nelson's The First Heroes and Carroll V. Glines's The Doolittle Raid." LJ

Includes bibliographical references (pages 613-622) and index.

Scott-Clark, Cathy

The **Amber** Room; the fate of the world's greatest lost treasure. [by] Catherine Scott-Clark & Adrian Levy. Walker & Co. 2004 386p il $26 **940.54**
1. Art thefts 2. World War, 1939-1945 -- Destruction and pillage
ISBN 0-8027-1424-2

LC 2004-49625

The authors "tell an exciting, intense, and surprising story. It is filled with episodes of cold-war intrigue, cynicism, amoral betrayal, and bureaucratic stalling that degenerates into absurdity." Booklist

Includes bibliographical references

Sebag-Montefiore, Hugh

Enigma: the battle for the code. Wiley 2000 422p il hardcover o.p. pa $16.95 **940.54**
1. Cryptography 2. World War, 1939-1945 -- Secret service
ISBN 0-471-40738-0; 0-471-49035-0 pa

LC 00-43920

This is the story of the German Enigma code.

"Describing the breaking of the German naval code during World War II, is both engrossing and exciting. Much of the information presented here is based on recently declassified documents." Booklist

Includes bibliographical references

Sheftall, Mordecai G.

Blossoms in the wind; the human legacy of the Kamikaze. [by] M.G. Sheftall. NAL Caliber 2005 480p il $24.95 **940.54**
1. Kamikaze airplanes 2. World War, 1939-1945 -- Aerial operations
ISBN 0-451-21487-0

LC 2004-27356

This account of the "design, training, and execution [of Japanese suicide missions] includes interviews with the families of dead pilots and, harder to reach, pilots who survived the missions." Booklist

Includes bibliographical references

Sides, Hampton

Ghost soldiers; the forgotten epic story of World War II's most dramatic mission. Doubleday 2001 342p il maps $24.95 **940.54**
1. World War, 1939-1945 -- Prisoners and prisons 2. United States -- Army -- Ranger Battalion, 6th 3. World War, 1939-1945 -- Campaigns -- Philippines
ISBN 0-385-49564-1

LC 2001-17337

"The author's excellent grasp of human emotions and bravery makes this a compelling book hard to put down." Publ Wkly

Smyth, Denis

Deathly deception; the real story of Operation Mincemeat. Oxford University Press 2010 xx, 367p il **940.54**
1. Lawyers 2. Intelligence service agents 3. World War, 1939-1945 -- Secret service
ISBN 978-0-19-923398-4

LC 2010-923437

"When the Allies decided to invade Sicily in summer 1943, they floated the body of a British military officer ashore in German-friendly Spain with the hope that the documents he carried would influence the Germans to believe that the Greek islands or Sardinia would be the Allies' actual target—and the ruse appeared to work. . . . [This is an] administrative history of both sides."

"This superlative and almost unexpurgated account of Operation Mincemeat will enthrall serious students of WWII." Booklist

Includes bibliographical references

Snyder, Timothy D., 1969-

Bloodlands; Europe between Hitler and Stalin. Basic Books 2010 524p map $29.95 **940.54**
1. Genocide 2. Massacres 3. Heads of state 4. Nazi leaders 5. Eastern Europe 6. Communist leaders 7. Political leaders 8. Genocide -- Europe 9. Holocaust, 1933-1945 10. Soviet Union -- History 11. Holocaust, Jewish (1939-1945) 12. Germany -- History -- 1933-1945 13. World War, 1939-1945 -- Atrocities 14. Soviet Union -- History -- 1917-1936 15. Eastern Europe -- History -- 1918-1945
ISBN 9780465002399; 0465002390

LC 2010-16816

The book "tr[ies] to explain mass violence in parts of Eastern Europe in the twentieth century. . . . Snyder deals with territories that were ruled for some time by both Nazi Germany and the USSR from 1930 to 1953. He covers most of today's Poland and Ukraine (the focus of his interest), Belarus, the three Baltic countries, and the most western strip of Russia. . . . Snyder gives a[n] . . . account of political history. . . . [He] places . . . emphasis on the exploitation of the countryside and enforced hunger, which claimed half of the fourteen million victims in the 'bloodlands.' Economically speaking, he emphasizes the extraction of resources by imperialists as the cause of mass starvation." (American Historical Review)

"Mr. Snyder's book is revisionist history of the best kind: in spare, closely argued prose, with meticulous use of statistics, he makes the reader rethink some of the best-known episodes in Europe's modern history." Economist

Includes bibliographical references

Spector, Ronald

Eagle against the sun; the American war with Japan. {by} Ronald H. Spector. Free Press 1985 589p il hardcover o.p. pa $18 **940.54**
1. World War, 1939-1945 -- Japan 2. World War, 1939-1945 -- United States 3. World War, 1939-1945 -- Campaigns -- Pacific Ocean
ISBN 0-394-74101-3 pa

LC 84-47888

While "policy, strategy and military operations are emphasized . . . Mr. Spector makes a real attempt to give readers some idea of what the war was like for the men and women who fought it. It is here that the book is at its best." N Y Times Book Rev

Includes bibliographical references

Takaki, Ronald T.

Hiroshima; why America dropped the atomic bomb. [by] Ronald Takaki. Little, Brown 1995 193p il $28; pa $14.95   **940.54**
  1. Atomic bomb 2. World War, 1939-1945 -- United States 3. Hiroshima (Japan) -- Bombardment, 1945
  ISBN 0-316-83122-0; 0-316-83124-7 pa
                                        LC 95-13546
This study of the bombings of Hiroshima and Nagasaki focuses on the psychological motivations of the American decision-makers, especially Harry Truman.

"Right or wrong, the study is a provocative addition to the unresolved debate over the dropping of the atomic bombs." Publ Wkly

Includes bibliographical references

Thomas, Evan

★ **Sea** of thunder; four commanders and the last great naval campaign, 1941-1945. Simon & Schuster 2006 415p il map $27   **940.54**
  1. World War, 1939-1945 -- Naval operations 2. World War, 1939-1945 -- Campaigns -- Pacific Ocean
  ISBN 978-0-7432-5221-8; 0-7432-5221-7
                                        LC 2006-47511
This is an "account of the Battle of Leyte Gulf, October 1944, one of history's largest naval battles, where Admiral William 'Bull' Halsey, the commander of the U.S. Third Fleet, and his commander, Ernest Evans, met the forces of Japanese admirals Takeo Kurita and Matome Ugaki. . . . Thomas paints compelling portraits of these men, offering insight into their characters and actions throughout the war in the Pacific." Libr J

Includes bibliographical references

Toll, Ian W.

The **conquering** tide; war in the Pacific Islands, 1942-1944. Ian W. Toll. W. W. Norton & Company 2015 672 p. 32 plates; illustrations; maps (hardcover) $35   **940.54**
  1. World War, 1939-1945 -- Naval operations 2. World War, 1939-1945 -- Campaigns -- Pacific Ocean
  ISBN 0393080641; 9780393080643
                                        LC 2015009591
This book, by Ian W. Toll, "encompasses the heart of the Pacific War--the period between mid-1942 and mid-1944--when parallel Allied counteroffensives north and south of the equator washed over Japan's far-flung island empire like a 'conquering tide,' concluding with Japan's irreversible strategic defeat in the Marianas." (Publisher's note)

"Toll successfully captures the drama and excitement of the Pacific War. Readers of military history will anticipate the final volume in this excellent history that should be a part of every library's collection on World War II." LJ

Pacific crucible; war at sea in the Pacific, 1941-1942. Ian W. Toll. W.W. Norton 2011 xxxvi, 597p il map $35   **940.54**
  1. United States -- Naval history 2. World War, 1939-1945 -- Naval operations 3. Pearl Harbor (Oahu, Hawaii), Attack on, 1941 4. World War, 1939-1945 --

Campaigns -- Pacific Ocean
  ISBN 978-0-393-06813-9; 0-393-06813-7
                                        LC 2011028907
In this book, "[p]rize-winning freelance naval historian [Ian W.] Toll . . . chronicles one of the U.S. Navy's finest performances of WWII in this . . . narrative of the months following the . . . attacks on Pearl Harbor. Eyewitness accounts and . . . research in American and Japanese print and archival sources" form the book's basis. (Publishers Weekly)

"The author makes vast quantities of technological and tactical concepts intelligible to all but the rankest beginner—for whom this book is not remotely suitable. A particular gift of the author is intelligent character portraits: Yamamoto, MacArthur, Halsey, and Nimitz (clearly one of the author's favorites). Add to all these other attributes a thorough scholarly apparatus, and it is difficult to think of a recent book on this subject that is of such consistently outstanding value." Booklist

Includes bibliographical references and index.

Weale, Adrian

Army of evil; a history of the SS. Adrian Weale. NAL Caliber 2012 xiii, 459 p.p $28.95   **940.54**
  1. Waffen-SS 2. World War, 1939-1945 -- Germany 3. World War, 1939-1945 -- Regimental histories 4. National Socialism 5. Waffen-SS -- History 6. Germany -- Politics and government -- 1933-1945 7. World War, 1939-1945 -- Regimental histories -- Germany 8. Nationalsozialistische Deutsche Arbeiter-Partei. Schutzstaffel
  ISBN 0451237919; 9780451237910
                                        LC 2012014170
This book by Adrian Weale presents a "look at the formation of the Schutzstaffeln (aka the SS), from [Adolf] Hitler's early private bodyguards to Heinrich Himmler's elite extermination squads. Weale . . . plots the evolution of the SS as the embodiment and implementation of the Nazi racist ideology. . . . Weale delineates the consolidation of Himmler's power, including the implementation of the concentration camp system . . . as the SS soldiers evolved into instruments of genocide." (Kirkus Reviews)

Includes bibliographical references (p. 433-440) and index

World War II; the definitive visual history : from Blitzkrieg to the atom bomb. senior editor, Alison Sturgeon. DK Publishing 2015 372 p. illustrations, color maps (hardcover) $40   **940.54**
  1. World War, 1939-1945
  ISBN 9781465436023; 1465436022
                                        LC 2015288118
This book, edited Alison Sturgeon and the Dorling Kindersley company, part of the Smithsonian Visual History series, "is a comprehensive, authoritative, yet accessible guide to the people, politics, events, and lasting effects of World War II. . . . [It] presents a complete overview of the war, including the rise of [Adolf] Hitler and the Nazi party, fascism, Pearl Harbor, Hiroshima, and the D-Day landings." (Publisher's note)

"This is a good quick-reference source for information on not just what happened in this great conflict but also on the causes and consequences of it as well. Additionally, it is attractively packaged and provides solid competition to similar Internet resources. The organization and layout are simple, clear, and intuitive. Recommended for all types of libraries." Booklist

Wukovits, John F., 1944-

Hell from the heavens; the epic story of the USS Laffey and World War II's greatest kamikaze attack. John F. Wukovits. Da Capo Press, a member of the Perseus Books Group 2015 336 p. 16 plates; illustrations (hardcover) $25.99   **940.54**

1. World War, 1939-1945 -- Naval operations 2. World War, 1939-1945 -- Aerial operations -- Japan 3. Laffey (Ship) 4. Kamikaze pilots -- Japan 5. Japan. Kaigun. Kamikaze Tokubetsu Kōgekitai 6. World War, 1939-1945 -- Campaigns -- Pacific Area 7. World War, 1939-1945 -- Naval operations, American 8. World War, 1939-1945 -- Aerial operations, Japanese

ISBN 0306823241; 9780306823244

LC 2014042127

This book, by John F. Wukovits, presents the story of "the largest single-ship kamikaze attack of World War II. On April 16, 1945, the crewmen of the USS Laffey were battle hardened and prepared. They had engaged in combat off the Normandy coast in June 1944. . . . But nothing could have prepared the crew for this moment--an eighty-minute ordeal in which the single small ship was targeted by no fewer than twenty-two Japanese suicide aircraft." (Publisher's note)

"For WWII buffs, surely, but also for general readers looking to understand the damage inflicted and the terror in s pired by the Japanese suicide squadrons." Kirkus

Includes bibliographical references and index

Zuckoff, Mitchell

Frozen in Time; An Epic Story of Survival and a Modern Quest for Lost Heroes of World War II. Mitchell Zuckoff. HarperCollins 2013 384 p. (hardcover) $28.99   **940.54**

1. Rescue work 2. Arctic regions

ISBN 0062133438; 9780062133434

This book, by Mitchell Zuckoff, tells of how "on November 5, 1942, a US cargo plane slammed into the Greenland Ice Cap." Several subsequent rescue attempts themselves crashed. This book "tells the story of these crashes and the fate of the survivors, bringing vividly to life their battle to endure 148 days of the brutal Arctic winter, until an expedition headed by famed Arctic explorer Bernt Balchen brought them to safety." (Publisher's note)

"Zuckoff's...complex narrative involves the fates of three downed missions to Greenland in late 1942, juxtaposed with the events of the modern-day search effort, led by an exploration company in August 2012 and joined by the author. As a result of the many competing strands and characters, some confusion in the details ensues--though maps and a cast of characters are included to help orient readers... An exhaustively layered but exciting account involving characters of enormous courage and stamina." Kirkus

Lost in Shangri-la. HarperCollins 2011 xii, 384p.p ill. $26.99   **940.54**

1. Primitive societies 2. Survival after airplane accidents, shipwrecks, etc. 3. New Guinea 4. Aircraft accidents -- New Guinea 5. Primitive societies -- New

Guinea 6. World War, 1939-1945 -- Missing in action 7. World War, 1939-1945 -- Aerial operations, American 8. World War, 1939-1945 -- Search and rescue operations

ISBN 978-0-06-198834-9; 0-06-198834-0

LC 201034508

L.L. Winship/PEN New England Award: Nonfiction (2012)

This book describes "how three World War II sightseers survived a crash in remote New Guinea." (N Y Times Book Rev) Bibliography. Index.

"On May 13, 1945, an American transport plane carrying 24 servicemen and women crashed into a mountain in the tropical jungles of Dutch New Guinea (now Papua), leaving three survivors. Learning about the event while researching another subject, the author recognized the ingredients of a terrific tale: a beautiful young WAC, a hidden valley reminiscent of the Shangri-La in James Hilton's Lost Horizon, primitive tribal people and a daring air rescue. In this well-crafted book, Zuckoff turns the long-forgotten episode into an unusually exciting narrative. Drawing on the young WAC survivor Margaret Hastings' diary as well as journals and interviews, the author hones in on life at the U.S. military base in Hollandia, on the northern coast of uncharted New Guinea; a soldier's chance discovery a year earlier of Baliem Valley, a verdant area about 150 miles into the interior, with its hundreds of native villages surrounded by gardens; and the doomed flight of officers and enlisted personnel out on a joy ride to view this much-talked-about land of Stone Age people from the air." Kirkus

Includes bibliographical references and index.

940.55   Europe--1945-1999

Judt, Tony

Postwar; a history of Europe since 1945. Penguin Press 2005 878p il maps $39.95   **940.55**

1. Europe -- History -- 1945-

ISBN 1-59420-065-3

LC 2005-52126

"This is the best history we have of Europe in the postwar period and not likely to be surpassed for many years." Publ Wkly

Includes bibliographical references

Lowe, Keith

Savage continent; Europe in the aftermath of World War II. St. Martin's Press 2012 460 p. $30.00   **940.55**

1. Europe -- History -- 1945- 2. Reconstruction (1939-1951) 3. World War, 1939-1945 -- Occupied territories

ISBN 1250000203; 9781250000200

LC 2011279703

Includes bibliographical references and index.

This book offers an "account of the violent and vengeful aftermath of the Second World War in Europe. . . . The aftermath was in part a product of inherited political tensions and ideological conflicts from before 1939 but chiefly a consequence of the massive destruction, displacement and criminality unleashed by Hitler's invasion of Poland and, perhaps more important, the Anglo-French decision to resist it." (New Statesman)

Mazower, Mark

Dark continent: Europe's twentieth century. Knopf 1999 487p il maps hardcover o.p. pa
$16   **940.55**

1. Europe -- History -- 20th century
ISBN 0-679-75704-X pa

LC 98-15886

The author's "relative unconcern with international and
great-power politics probably accounts for a rather intra-Eu-
ropean perspective . . . just as it contributes to some exaggera-
tion of the points of comparison and convergence in East and
West European economic history. . . . But these are minor defects, the price to be paid for a confident and unconventional
work of historical interpretation." N Y Times Book Rev

Includes bibliographical references

941   British Isles

Burns, William E.

A brief history of Great Britain. Facts On File
2010 xxiv, 296p il map (Brief history) $49.50; pa
$19.95   **941**

1. Great Britain -- History
ISBN 978-0-8160-7728-1; 978-0-8160-8124-0 pa

LC 2009-8217

This book "narrates the history of Great Britain from the
earliest times to the 21st century, covering the entire island—
England, Wales, and Scotland—as well as associated archipelagos such as the Channel Islands, the Orkneys, and Ireland as
they have influenced British history. The central story of this
volume is the development of the British kingdom, including
its rise and decline on the world stage." Publisher's note

Includes bibliographical references

Farquhar, Michael

Behind the palace doors; five centuries of sex,
adventure, vice, treachery, and folly from royal Britain. Random House Trade Paperbacks 2011 307p
pa $15; ebook $11.99   **941**

1. Great Britain -- Kings and rulers
ISBN 978-0-8129-7904-6 pa; 978-0-679-60453-2
ebook

LC 2010-21116

The author "probes 500 years of monarchical mishaps
and misdeeds, screaming headlines and gleeful attacks by
cartoonists. He uncloaks secrets, schemes, scandals, blood-
soaked sheets, public humiliations, intrigues, and adultery.
Illustrated with lineage charts and chronologically organized, chapters cover the houses of Tudor, Stuart, Hanover,
Saxe-Coburg-Gotha, and Windsor. . . . [His] style is a breezy
pleasure throughout." Publ Wkly

Includes bibliographical references

Fraser, Rebecca

★ The story of Britain; from the Romans to the
present: a narrative history. Norton 2005 829p il
map $35   **941**

1. Great Britain -- History
ISBN 0-393-06010-1

LC 2004-26049

First published 2003 in the United Kingdom with title: A
people's history of Britain

The author's "narrative advances with the emphasis on
the roles of a litany of historical icons, from Queen Boudica
to Margaret Thatcher. For those readers who are primarily
interested in the 'who, what, when, where, why' of British
history, this is a valuable general study." Booklist

Includes bibliographical references

Guy, John

The Children of Henry VIII. Oxford University
Press 2013 272 p. (hardcover) $27.95   **941**

1. Great Britain -- History -- 1485-1603, Tudors
ISBN 0192840908; 9780192840905

This book by John Guy looks at "the heirs of Henry VIII.
. . . Rather than attempt the massive undertaking of covering in depth the histories of Edward, Mary, and Elizabeth,
Guy has chosen to give the most salient details regarding
the monarchs . . . present[ing] an overall picture of their
lives and upbringings under Henry's rule and during their
later reigns. His particular focus is on how their relationships with each other--and . . . their father--affected them."
(Library Journal)

Hunt, Tristram, 1974-

Cities of empire; the British colonies and the
creation of the urban world. Tristram Hunt. Metropolitan Books 2014 544 p. illustrations, maps (hardback) $35   **941**

1. Colonies 2. City and town life 3. Great Britain
-- Colonies 4. Cities and towns -- Case studies 5.
Metropolitan areas -- Case studies 6. Imperialism --
History -- Case studies 7. Great Britain -- Colonies --
History -- Case studies
ISBN 0805093087; 9780805093087

LC 2014030024

Author Tristram Hunt presents a "history of the most enduring colonial creation, the city, explored through ten portraits of powerful urban centers the British Empire left in its
wake. He traces the collaboration of cultures and traditions
that produced these influential urban centers, the work of an
army of administrators, officers, entrepreneurs, slaves, and
renegades." (Publisher's note)

"A book to be enjoyed by an array of readers, including historians of various stripes, particularly those who have
traveled to any of the book's cities." LJ

Includes bibliographical references and index

Lacey, Robert

Great tales from English history; the truth about
King Arthur, Lady Godiva, Richard the Lionheart,
and more. Little, Brown and Co. 2004 254p maps
$22.95   **941**

1. Great Britain -- History
ISBN 0-316-10910-X

LC 2003-115660

First published 2003 in the United Kingdom

"This volume begins in 7150 BC with the life and death of Cheddar Man and ends in 1381 with Wat Tyler and the Peasants' Revolt." Publisher's note

Includes bibliographical references

Great tales from English history [2] Joan of Arc, the princes in the Tower, Bloody Mary, Oliver Cromwell, Sir Isaac Newton, and more. Little, Brown and Co. 2005 271p il map $23.95   **941**
1. Great Britain -- History
ISBN 0-316-10924-X

         LC 2004-63351
First published 2004 in the United Kingdom

The author's "second volume on English history opens in 1348, the year of the Black Plague, which wiped out half of England's five million people, and proceeds through the astonishing scientific discoveries of Sir Isaac Newton in 1687. . . . Lacey's animated prose, energetic storytelling and spirited approach to British history bring the past to life." Publ Wkly

Includes bibliographical references

★ **Great** tales from English history [3] Captain Cook, Samuel Johnson, Queen Victoria, Charles Darwin, Edward the Abdicator, and more. Little, Brown and Co. 2006 305p $23.99   **941**
1. Great Britain -- History
ISBN 978-0-316-11459-2; 0-316-11459-6

         LC 2006-931723
"The third volume in Lacey's series of edifying and entertaining stories from English history abounds in fascinating profiles. Industrial and agricultural pioneers such as Jethro Tull, James Hargreaves and Isambard Kingdom Brunel abide alongside human rights protestors such as Thomas Clarkson, who founded the British antislavery movement; feminist philosopher Mary Wollstonecraft; and journalist Annie Besant, who initiated a successful 1888 match girls' strike." Publ Wkly

Includes bibliographical references

The **Oxford** history of Britain; edited by Kenneth O. Morgan. Rev ed, New ed; Oxford University Press 2010 821p map pa $18.95   **941**
1. Great Britain -- History
ISBN 978-0-19-957925-9; 0-19-957925-3

         LC 2010279308
Text based on The Oxford illustrated history of Britain, published 1984. This version first published 2001

This "volume tells the story of Britain and its people over two thousand years, from the coming of the Roman legions to the present day." Publisher's note

Includes bibliographical references

Schama, Simon
A **history** of Britain. Hyperion 2000 3v ea $40   **941**
1. Great Britain -- History
ISBN 0-7868-6675-6 v1; 0-7868-6752-3 v2; 0-7868-6899-6 v3

         LC 00-61442
Schama "writes wonderfully, in an easygoing yet elegant manner, with an eye for the telling aesthetic detail, and

throughout brimming with intelligence and passion." N Y Times Book Rev

Includes bibliographical references

941.06   House of Stuart and Commonwealth periods, 1603-1714

Ackroyd, Peter, 1949-
Rebellion; the history of England from James I to the Glorious Revolution. Peter Ackroyd. Thomas Dunne Books, an imprint of St. Martin's Press 2014 512 p. illustrations (some color) (hardcover) $29.99   **941.06**
1. Great Britain -- History -- 1603-1714, Stuarts 2. Great Britain -- History -- Stuarts, 1603-1714
ISBN 1250003636; 9781250003638

         LC 2014026045
This book, by Peter Ackroyd, presents the "history of England, beginning the progress south of the Scottish king, James VI, who on the death of Elizabeth I became the first Stuart king of England, and ending with the deposition and flight into exile of his grandson, James II. . . . In addition to its account of England's royalty, [it] also gives us a very real sense of the lives of ordinary English men and women" (Publisher's note)

"Although general readers in the U.S. may find some of the names and places unfamiliar, this masterful work of popular history will remind them that the ideas that launched our own revolution were forged during this seminal period of English history." Booklist

Long, James
The **plot** against Pepys; [by] James Long & Ben Long. Overlook Press 2008 322p il $27.95 **941.06**
1. Trials 2. Diarists 3. Military officials 4. Government officials 5. Members of Parliament 6. Great Britain -- History -- 1603-1714, Stuarts
ISBN 978-1-59020-069-8; 1-59020-069-1
First published 2007 in the United Kingdom

"The book is packed with marvellous asides that add colour to an already kaleidoscopic cavalcade of crass credulousness, court drama and crookery. . . . I couldn't put it down, and there aren't many books on the seventeenth century you can say that about." Hist Today

Includes bibliographical references

Pepys, Samuel
★ The **diary** of Samuel Pepys; edited and with a preface by Richard Le Gallienne; introduction by Robert Louis Stevenson. Modern Lib. 2001 xxxv, 310p $22; pa $15.95   **941.06**
1. Diarists 2. Military officials 3. Government officials 4. Members of Parliament
ISBN 0-679-64221-8; 0-8129-7071-3 pa

         LC 00-54817
An abridged edition of Pepys' eleven-volume diary, originally written between 1660 and 1669.

Tomalin, Claire

Samuel Pepys; the unequalled self. Knopf 2002 xxiii, 470p il $30; pa $16.95   **941.06**
1. Diarists 2. Military officials 3. Government officials 4. Members of Parliament 5. Great Britain -- Social life and customs 6. Great Britain -- History -- 1603-1714, Stuarts
ISBN 0-375-41143-7; 0-375-72553-9 pa
LC 2002-75701

"Tomalin mines the diary, and she also expands upon the characters and events, great and small, that affected Pepys' life and livelihood to bring the man and his milieu to life— pungently as well as vibrantly." Booklist
Includes bibliographical references

941.066: Reign of Charles II, 1660-1685 (Restoration)

Jordan, Don

The **king's** revenge; Charles II and the Greatest Manhunt in British History. Don Jordan and Michael Walsh. Little, Brown & Co. 2012 383 p. illustrations $27.95   **941.066**
1. Great Britain -- History 2. Regicides -- England -- History -- 17th century 3. Great Britain -- History -- Charles II, 1660-1685 4. Great Britain -- History -- Puritan Revolution, 1642-1660
ISBN 1408703270; 1681771683; 9781408703274; 9781681771687
LC 2012545486

In this book, by Don Jordan and Michael Walsh, "when Charles I was executed, his son Charles II made it his role to seek out retribution, producing the biggest manhunt Britain had ever seen, one that would span Europe and America and would last for thirty years. . . . Many of the most senior figures in England were hanged, drawn and quartered; imprisoned for life; or consigned to a self-imposed exile, in constant fear of the assassin's bullet." (Publisher's note)

"Crafted like a spy novel as Charles II set about to find the living regicides, this work will intrigue readers with the breadth and ruthlessness of the king's search." LJ
Includes bibliographical references (p. [357]-360) and index

941.07   Period of House of Hanover, 1714-1837

Brewer, John

The **pleasures** of the imagination; English culture in the eighteenth century. University of Chicago Press 2000 721p il pa $20   **941.07**
1. Great Britain -- Civilization 2. Great Britain -- Intellectual life 3. Great Britain -- Social life and customs
ISBN 0-226-07419-6; 978-0-226-07419-1
LC 99-57059

First published 1997 by Farrar, Straus and Giroux
"A remarkable feat of scholarship, this volume will quickly establish itself as an indispensable reference." Booklist
Includes bibliographical references

Foreman, Amanda

Georgiana, Duchess of Devonshire. Random House 2000 454p hardcover o.p. pa $15.95 **941.07**
1. Socialites 2. Spouses of prominent persons 3. Nobility -- Great Britain -- Biography 4. Women politicians -- Great Britain -- Biography 5. Great Britain -- Politics and government -- 1789-1820 6. Great Britain -- Social life and customs -- 18th century 7. Great Britain -- History -- George III, 1760-1820 -- Biography
ISBN 0-375-75383-4 pa
LC 99-23580

Georgiana "was the society leader of her day. Daughter of the fabulously wealthy Earl Spencer (and ancestor of the late princess of Wales) and married to the even more wealthy duke of Devonshire, Georgiana was watched, adored, and imitated. But she evolved herself into more than just a fashionable hostess; she got involved in Whig politics, to an extent unprecedented for women. . . . The tenor of the subject's time and place—in this instance, aristocratic Britain in the late 1700s and early 1800s—is both colorfully and meaningfully realized." Booklist
Includes bibliographical references

McLynn, Frank

1759: the year Britain became master of the world. Atlantic Monthly Press 2004 422p il map $26   **941.07**
1. Seven Years' War, 1756-1763 2. Great Britain -- Colonies 3. Great Britain -- Foreign relations
ISBN 0-87113-881-6
LC 2004-57397

First published 2004 in the United Kingdom
1759 "was the fourth [year] in the Seven Years War, a struggle between France and England for global dominance that was fought worldwide. McLynn focuses on the deadly conflict, contrasting the two nations' differing wartime policies and showing how the combination of Britain's maritime prowess and sheer good luck helped it emerge triumphant, albeit by a narrow margin. . . . Splendidly narrated, with balanced insights into the Native American aspect of the French and Indian Wars, McLynn's book will enthrall all lovers of history told well." Publ Wkly
Includes bibliographical references

941.08   Period of Victoria and House of Windsor, 1837-

McKillop, A. B.

The **spinster** & the prophet; H.G. Wells, Florence Deeks, and the case of the plagiarized text. Four Walls Eight Windows 2002 477p il $26.95 **941.08**
1. Authors 2. Novelists 3. Historians 4. Plagiarism 5. Historiography 6. Feminists 7. Writers on science 8. Writers on politics 9. Science fiction writers
ISBN 1-56858-236-6
LC 2002-71292

"When, in 1920, Florence Deeks finally received her rejected manuscript—a feminist history of the world—from Macmillan after eight months, she couldn't understand why it appeared in such bad condition. . . . Later that year, when she read H.G. Wells's new book, The Outline of History, published by Macmillan, she felt a chill. There were so many similarities to her own work: shared themes, organization, word choice, even the same mistakes. Florence made a dramatic decision—she would sue Wells and his publisher for plagiarism. . . . The author handles the dual story line brilliantly, weaving together two opposing characters into one altogether gripping tale of literary theft." Publ Wkly

Includes bibliographical references

Vallone, Lynne

    Becoming Victoria. Yale Univ. Press 2001 256p il $26.95   **941.08**

    1. Queens 2. Great Britain -- History -- 19th century

    ISBN 0-300-08950-3

                     LC 00-68561

  "Analyzing Victoria's girlhood diaries, drawings and fiction, as well as records of her education and scores of accounts of her childhood, Valone . . . constructs a revisionist account of the princess's youthful persona but also traces the process by which Victoria was molded into the 'right' kind of adult: capable of assuming the throne and also a clear embodiment of all that was womanly and pure. . . . Well-researched, and with sophisticated cultural criticism, this sound scholarship will engage the interest of academics and nonacademics alike." Publ Wkly

  Includes bibliographical references

941.081   British Isles--Reign of Victoria, 1837-1901

Encyclopedia of the Victorian era; James Eli Adams, editor in chief; Tom Pendergast, Sara Pendergast, editors. Grolier Academic Reference 2004 4v il map set $499   **941.081**

    1. Great Britain -- Civilization 2. Great Britain -- History -- 19th century

    ISBN 0-7172-5860-2

                   LC 2003-57101

  "Entries ranging in length from a few paragraphs to several pages are written by experts, treat topics from William Acton to zoological gardens, and seek to encompass the important issues, people, and events of the Victorian era. . . . While predictable figures such as Queen Victoria and Benjamin Disraeli appear, so too do social history topics such as the sporting life, penny dreadfuls, and cholera." Choice

  Includes bibliographical references

Murphy, Paul Thomas

  Shooting Victoria; madness, mayhem, and the rebirth of the British monarchy. Paul Thomas Murphy. Pegasus Books 2012 669 p. $35.00   **941.081**

    1. Victoria, Queen of Great Britain, 1819-1901 -- Assassination attempts

    ISBN 9781605983547; 1605983543

  This book on various attempts to assassinate Queen Victoria of England "recounts . . . how these deluded subjects managed to channel their mental instability or optimistic naïveté into assassination attempts with barely functioning pistols or stout canes. . . . [Paul Thomas] Murphy . . . weaves their life stories in with the reactions of Victoria and Albert

and other notables as the government struggled to define a policy for punishing assassins." (Publishers Weekly)

Summerscale, Kate

  Mrs. Robinson's disgrace; the private diary of a Victorian lady. Kate Summerscale. Bloomsbury 2012 xvi, 303 p.p geneal. tables $26.00   **941.081**

    1. Diaries 2. Divorce 3. Great Britain -- History -- Victoria, 1837-1901

    ISBN 1608199134; 9781608199136

                 LC 2012451243

  This book considers the experience of Victorian woman "Isabella Robinson [who] defended herself in the newly created English divorce court over a mislaid diary filled with passionate erotic entries, philosophical musings, and complaints against her husband. . . . In two sections, the book first describes Isabella's flowery, coy memories of [her lover] . . . the second part focuses on her trial on an adultery charge and the scrambling of her male friends to preserve their reputations." (Publishers Weekly)

  Includes bibliographical references and index

Wilson, A. N.

  The **Victorians**. Norton 2003 724p il $35; pa $17.95   **941.081**

    1. Great Britain -- Civilization 2. Great Britain -- History -- 19th century

    ISBN 0-393-04974-4; 0-393-32543-1 pa

                 LC 2002-33809

  First published 2002 in the United Kingdom

  "Even to fastidious readers, Wilson's failings are minor, and the colorful tapestry he presents of a smoky world peopled with the likes of Carlyle, Mill, Marx, Ruskin, and Darwin can hardly fail to enthrall. Both professional scholars and laypeople will love to relax with this book, although some knowledge of the age is a must." Choice

  Includes bibliographical references

941.084   Great Britain -- 1936-1945

Cadbury, Deborah

  Princes at war; the bitter battle inside Britain's royal family in the darkest days of wwii. Deborah Cadbury. PublicAffairs 2014 384 p. 16 plates; illustrations (hardcover) $28.99   **941.084**

    1. Great Britain -- Kings and rulers 2. Great Britain -- History -- 20th century

    ISBN 1610394038; 9781610394031; 9781610394048

                 LC 2014957933

  This book, by Deborah Cadbury, explores how "In 1936, the British monarchy faced the greatest threats to its survival in the modern era--the crisis of abdication and the menace of Nazism. The fate of the country rested in the hands of George V's sorely unequipped sons. . . . [The book portrays] these four very different men . . . , one of whom had to save the monarchy . . . as the old order was overturned." (Publisher's note)

  "Bias aside, this is an engaging, well-told history of England and its royals during its most fragile period; conveying wartime tensions, worldwide scandals, and familial devotions and rivalries with equal vividness." LJ

Clarke, Peter

Mr. Churchill's profession; the statesman as author and the book that defined the 'special relationship' Peter Clarke. 1st US ed. Bloomsbury Press 2012 xix, 347 p.p ill. (alk. paper) $30.00 **941.084**
  1. Politicians' writings 2. Prime ministers -- Great Britain 3. Great Britain -- History -- 20th century 4. Prime ministers -- Great Britain -- Biography
  ISBN 1608193721; 9781608193721
  LC 2011044274

This book "traces the making of the . . . work that occupied [Winston] Churchill for a quarter century, his four-volume 'History of the English-Speaking Peoples.' Churchill signed the contract for 'History' in 1932, at a time when his political career seemed over. His . . . return to power when the Nazis swept across Europe meant the book went uncompleted until the 1950s. But long before he took office, the . . . project was shaping his worldview, his speeches, and his leadership." (Publisher's note)

Includes bibliographical references (p.318 -331) and index

Maier, Thomas

When lions roar; the Churchills and the Kennedys. Thomas Maier. Crown Publishers 2014 784 p. 16 plates; illustrations $30 **941.084**
  1. Kennedy family 2. Great Britain -- Relations -- United States 3. United States -- Relations -- Great Britain 4. Great Britain -- Politics and government -- 20th century 5. United States -- Politics and government -- 20th century
  ISBN 0307956792; 9780307956798; 9780307956811
  LC 2014007201

This book, by Thomas Maier, provides "the first comprehensive history of the deeply entwined personal and public lives of the Churchills and the Kennedys and what their 'special relationship' meant for Great Britain and the United States. . . . Thomas Maier tells this dynastic saga . . . providing . . . insight into the Churchill and Kennedy families and the profound forces of duty, loyalty, courage and ambition that shaped them." (Publisher's note)

"An excellent work for all history collections, especially those devoted to 20th-century political history." LJ

Includes bibliographical references and index
Churchills and the Kennedys

Morton, Andrew

17 carnations; the royals, the nazis and the biggest cover-up in history. Andrew Morton. Grand Central Publishing 2015 384 p. illustrations (hardcover) $28 **941.084**
  1. Conspiracies -- Great Britain -- History -- 20th century
  ISBN 9781455527090; 9781455527113; 9781478959151; 9781619695887
  LC 2014957815

This book, by Andrew Morton, "tells the story of the feckless Edward VIII, later Duke of Windsor, his American wife, Wallis Simpson, the bizarre wartime Nazi plot to make him a puppet king after the invasion of Britain, and the attempted cover-up by Churchill, General Eisenhower, and King George VI of the duke's relations with Hitler." (Publisher's note)

Includes bibliographical references (pages [329]-362) and index.

941.085 Great Britain -- 1945-1999

Andersen, Christopher

Game of crowns; Elizabeth, Camilla, Kate, and the throne. Christopher Andersen. Gallery Books 2016 352 p. color illustrations $28 **941.085**
  1. Queens 2. Princesses 3. Great Britain -- Kings and rulers
  ISBN 9781476743950; 9781476743974
  LC 2015050619

This book, by Christopher Anderson, takes a "look into the relationships and rivalries of Queen Elizabeth, Camilla Parker Bowles, and Kate Middleton. Andersen reveals what transpires within the royal family away from the public's prying eyes; how the women actually feel about each other; how they differ as lovers, wives, and mothers; and how they are reshaping the landscape of the monarchy." (Publisher's note)

"With gaspworthy and laugh-out-loud moments revealing scandalous and sympathetic details of the royal family, Andersen humanizes this privileged yet embattled group." Kirkus

Includes bibliographical references (pages 315-319) and index.

Junor, Penny

The Firm: the troubled life of the House of Windsor. Thomas Dunne Books 2005 xxi, 442p il $25.95 **941.085**
  1. Queens 2. Kings 3. Great Britain -- Kings and rulers
  ISBN 0-312-35274-3
  LC 2005-45528

"Readers of this interesting and occasionally jaw-dropping look at the world's most famous dysfunctional family will find plenty to engage them." Libr J

Includes bibliographical references

Kynaston, David

Austerity Britain; 1945-51. Walker & Co. 2008 692p il (Tales of a new Jerusalem) $45 **941.085**
  1. Great Britain -- Social conditions 2. Great Britain -- History -- 1945-1952 3. Great Britain -- Politics and government -- 20th century
  ISBN 978-0-8027-1693-4; 0-8027-1693-8
  First published 2007 in the United Kingdom

"Drawing on a remarkable array of diaries, letters, memoirs, and surveys, Kynaston assembles a polyphonic history of a pivotal time." New Yorker

Includes bibliographic references

Family Britain, 1951-1957. Walker & Co 2010 776p il $47.50 **941.085**
  1. Great Britain -- History -- 1952- 2. Great Britain -- Social conditions 3. Great Britain -- Politics and government -- 20th century
  ISBN 978-0-8027-1797-9

"Picking up where the much-lauded Austerity Britain, 1945-1951 (2008) left off, Kynaston's latest presents a panoramic view of a transformative period. . . . Leading us on an immersive tour of headlines and correspondence, diaries and sociological studies, Kynaston narrates moments and motifs both great and small, among them the Festival of Britain, Council housing, the queen's coronation, pub culture, Kingsley Amis, smog, labor strikes, skiffle, the 'colour bar,' grammar schools, football, the Suez Crisis, young Mick Jagger, and the BBC." Booklist

Includes bibliographical references

941.1   Scotland

Herman, Arthur
How the Scots invented the modern world; the true story of how western Europe's poorest nation created our world & everything in it. Crown 2001 392p $25.95; pa $14.95   **941.1**
1. Scottish national characteristics 2. Scotland -- Civilization
ISBN 0-609-60635-2; 0-609-80999-7 pa
LC 2001-28951
"This is a worthwhile book for the general reader." Publ Wkly
Includes bibliographical references (p. 362-376) and index

Nicolson, Adam
Sea room: an island life in the Hebrides. North Point Press 2002 391p il maps $27; pa $14 **941.1**
1. Hebrides (Scotland) -- Social life and customs
ISBN 0-86547-636-5; 0-86547-667-5 pa
LC 2002-19816
First published 2001 in the United Kingdom
"Magnificent and poetic, this is a literary and ecological masterpiece." Booklist
Includes bibliographical references

941.3   Southeastern Scotland

Stewart, Rory
The **Marches**; A Borderland Journey Between England and Scotland. by Rory Stewart. Houghton Mifflin Harcourt 2016 304 p. $26   **941.3**
1. England 2. Scotland 3. Boundaries
ISBN 0544108884; 9780544108882
This book, by Rory Stewart, is "an exploration of the Marches—the borderland between England and Scotland—and the people, history, and conflicts that have shaped it. . . . Following the lines of Neolithic standing stones, wading through floods and ruined fields, he walks Hadrian's Wall with soldiers who have fought in Afghanistan and visits the Buddhist monks who outnumber Christian monks in the Scottish countryside today." (Publisher's note)

941.5   Ireland

★ **Encyclopedia** of Irish history and culture; James S. Donnelly Jr., editor in chief; Karl S. Bottigheimer . . . [et al.], associate editors. Macmillan Reference USA 2004 2v il map set $270 **941.5**
1. Reference books 2. Ireland -- Encyclopedias
ISBN 0-02-865902-3
LC 2004-5353
"The A-Z entries are preceded by a chronology and followed by a selection of almost 150 primary documents ranging from the Confession of St. Patrick (c. 450) to the Belfast/Good Friday Agreement (1998). . . . Providing the latest in scholarship, entries are well written and cover the gamut of historical, social, and cultural topics." Booklist
Includes bibliographical references

Ferriter, Diarmaid
The **transformation** of Ireland. Overlook Press 2005 884p $37.50   **941.5**
1. Ireland -- History
ISBN 1-58567-681-0
LC 2005-49849
First published 2004 in the United Kingdom
"This book isn't a political history of 20th-century Ireland; it's more a chronicle of the social reaction to the events that shaped that century. . . . [The author] has written an informative, funny, at times derisive book that takes a fresh approach to 20th-century Ireland." Publ Wkly
Includes bibliographical references

Kelly, John
The **graves** are walking; the great famine and the saga of the Irish people. John Kelly. Henry Holt and Co. 2012 397 p.   **941.5**
1. Famines -- Ireland 2. Ireland -- History 3. Ireland -- Immigration and emigration 4. Ireland -- History -- Famine, 1845-1852 5. Famines -- Ireland -- History -- 19th century 6. Irish -- Migrations -- History -- 19th century 7. Ireland -- Emigration and immigration -- History -- 19th century
ISBN 080509184X; 9780805091847
LC 2012011493
This book, by John Kelly, offers an "account of . . . the Great Irish Potato Famine. . . . It started in 1845, . . . [a] perfect storm of bacterial infection, political greed, and religious intolerance. . . . But even more extraordinary . . . were its political underpinnings, and [the author] . . . provides . . . analysis on the role that Britain's nation-building policies played in exacerbating the devastation by attempting to use the famine to reshape Irish society and character." (Publisher's note)
Includes bibliographical references and index

Nic Dhiarmada, Bríona
The **1916** Irish Rebellion; Bríona Nic Dhiarmada; foreword by Mary McAleese. University of Notre Dame Press 2016 ix, 205 p.p illustrations, map (hardcover : alk. paper) $45   **941.5**
1. Irish Americans 2. Ireland -- History -- 20th century 3. Irish question 4. Ireland -- History -- Easter Rising,

1916
ISBN 0268036144; 9780268036140
LC 2015042508

In this book, "scholar Bríona Nic Dhiarmada has seized the occasion of the centenary of the Irish Rising to reassess this event and its historical significance. Her book explores the crucial role of Irish Americans in both the lead-up to and the aftermath of the events in Dublin and places the Irish Rising in its European and global context, as an expression of the anti-colonialism that found its full voice in the wake of the First World War." (Publisher's note)

"Rich in fascinating historical photographs and informative and poignant documents that capture each phase of the struggle and its inevitable and tragic outcome, this striking volume tells the complex tale of a singular chapter in the long war against colonialism in plain and ringing language." Booklist

Includes bibliographical references and index

State, Paul F.
A **brief** history of Ireland. Facts On File 2009 xxiv, 408p il map (Brief history) $49.50; pa $19.95   **941.5**
1. Ireland -- History
ISBN 978-0-8160-7516-4; 0-8160-7516-6; 978-0-8160-7517-1 pa; 0-8160-7517-4 pa
LC 2008-29243

The author "opens this vibrant reference with an introduction to Ireland's landscape, people, economics, natural resources, and current government. Following this essay-style overview are 11 chronologically organized chapters. Each is devoted to a significant historical watershed, tracing events from Ireland's prehistory to its contemporary prosperity. Appendixes provide at-a-glance portraits of Northern Ireland and the Irish Republic, including a list of presidents, prime ministers, and a time line of notable dates." Libr J

Includes bibliographical references

Walsh, Maurice
Bitter freedom; Ireland in a Revolutionary World, 1918-1923. Maurice Walsh. Liveright Publishing Corp., a division of W.W. Norton & Company 2016 544 p. (hardcover) $35   **941.5**
1. Revolutions 2. World politics 3. World War, 1914-1918 -- Influence 4. Ireland -- History -- 20th century 5. World politics -- 1919-1932 6. Ireland -- History -- 1910-1921 7. World War, 1914-1918 -- Ireland 8. Revolutions -- History -- 20th century 9. World War, 1914-1918 -- Political aspects 10. Ireland -- Politics and government -- 1910-1921 11. Ireland -- History -- War of Independence, 1919-1921 12. Ireland -- History -- War of Independence, 1919-1921 -- Social aspects
ISBN 1631491954; 9781631491955
LC 2016002970

This book, by Maurice Walsh, "places revolutionary Ireland within the panorama of nationalist movements born out of World War I. Beginning with the Easter Rising of 1916, [it] follows through from the War of Independence to the end of the post-partition civil war in 1924." (Publisher's note)

"An excellent history, but more importantly, a sharply written portrait of a people and their long struggle to survive." Kirkus

Includes bibliographical references and index

941.501   Early history to 1086

Cahill, Thomas
How the Irish saved civilization; the untold story of Ireland's heroic role from the fall of Rome to the rise of medieval Europe. {by} Thomas Cahill. Talese 1995 246p il maps $27.50; pa $12.95   **941.501**
1. Medieval civilization 2. Learning and scholarship 3. Ireland -- Civilization
ISBN 0-385-41848-5; 0-385-41849-3 pa
LC 94-28130

"Highly literate and affectionate, if somewhat rambling and indulgent. . . . As a freewheeling, witty popular history of Irish Christianity in the Dark Ages, this will amuse and enlighten." Libr J

Includes bibliographical references

941.505   Period under House of Tudor, 1485-1603

Ekin, Des
The **Last** Armada; Queen Elizabeth, Juan Del Águila, and the 100-day Invasion of England. by Des Ekin. W W Norton & Co Inc 2016 420 p. 8 plates; illustrations; maps $27.95   **941.505**
1. Naval battles 2. Spain -- History 3. Great Britain -- History
ISBN 1605989444; 9781605989440

This book, by Des Ekin, is the "story of the last great naval battle between England and Spain. . . . General Juan del Águila has been sprung from a prison cell to command the last great Spanish armada. His mission: to seize a bridgehead in Queen Elizabeth's England and hold it. Facing him is Charles Blount, a brilliant English strategist. . . . Meanwhile, Irish insurgent Hugh O'Neill knows that this is his final chance to drive the English out of Ireland." (Publisher's note)

"The author explains the terrain, battles, siege construction, and weaponry well enough to please any military historian, but the real prizes here are the author's discussions of the effect of the battle on Spain as its empire died and England's colonies grew, the end of Spain's religious wars, the shift of power in England, and the cataclysm as Gaelic Ireland declined and died. A fantastic book that finally assigns Kinsale its rightful place in history." Kirkus

941.6   Northern Ireland; Donegal, Monaghan, Cavan counties of Republic of Ireland

Campbell, Julieann
Setting the truth free; the inside story of the Bloody Sunday Justice Campaign. Julieann Camp-

bell. Liberties Press 2012 219 p. ill. (some col.) (pbk.) $24.95 **941.6**

1. Civil rights demonstrations 2. Northern Ireland -- History 3. Bloody Sunday, Derry, Northern Ireland, 1972 4. Bloody Sunday Justice Campaign 5. Londonderry (Northern Ireland) -- History -- 20th century 6. Massacres -- Northern Ireland -- Londonderry -- History -- 20th century

ISBN 1907593373; 9781907593376

LC 2012379691

In this book about the "1972 Bloody Sunday massacre during a peaceful civil rights march in Derry, Northern Ireland ... . [Julieann] Campbell, an Irish journalist . . . niece of the first person slain on that tragic day . . . [and] the press officer for the campaign to find justice for those killed and wounded, not only tells the tale of her murdered 17-year-old uncle, Jackie Duddy, but also details the planning of the march, the . . . slaughter by the British troops, and the traumatic remembrances of the survivors. . . . A need to seek justice, as Campbell writes, motivated the Irish community to protest and pressure the British government to launch a real inquiry into the shootings." (Publishers Weekly)

Coogan, Tim Pat

The **troubles**; Ireland's ordeal, 1966-1996, and the search for peace. Palgrave 2002 589p il map pa $22.95 **941.6**

1. Northern Ireland

ISBN 978-0-312-29418-2; 0-312-29418-2

First published 1995 in the United Kingdom

In this political history the author "examines all parties to the struggle. . . . He reconstructs the past 30 years, from the 1969 marching and riots to the H-Block protests, the MacBride Principles, the Anglo-Irish agreement, and the recent paramilitary cease-fire. Coogan traces the current peace process, stalled by Great Britain's insistence that the IRA hand in its weapons, to the 1979 visit of Pope John Paul II." Libr J

Includes bibliographical references

942 England and Wales

Ackroyd, Peter

London: the biography. Talese 2001 xxvi, 801p il $45; pa $18.95 **942**

1. London (England) -- History

ISBN 0-385-49770-9; 0-385-49771-7 pa

LC 2001-27153

First published 2000 in the United Kingdom

"A sweeping, highly readable account of London's colorful and complicated history." Libr J

Includes bibliographical references

Thames; the biography. Nan A. Talese/Doubleday 2008 481p il map $40 **942**

1. Thames River (England) 2. London (England) -- History

ISBN 978-0-385-52623-4; 0-385-52623-7

LC 2008-02864

First published 2007 in the United Kingdom

"Eschewing standard organization, Ackroyd jumps from today's posh London banks to Roger Bacon's observatory at Grandpont to Dickens's 'deathlike and mysterious' waterway. We learn about the riverbank's many species of willow (white, weeping, crack, cane osier), and about the Retribution and the Belliqueux, eighteenth-century prison boats that each held hundreds of men. . . . A survey of the many ways in which the river can kill notes that most Thames suicides remain 'anonymous and unlamented.' Not every tidbit will appeal to every reader, but the book demands to be read as it was written, according to one's fancy." New Yorker

Includes bibliographical references

Cartwright, Justin

Oxford revisited. Bloomsbury 2009 223p pa $18 **942**

1. Oxford (England) 2. University of Oxford

ISBN 978-1-59691-093-5; 1-59691-093-3

First published 2008 in the United Kingdom with title: This secret garden

"A South African-born novelist who graduated from Oxford University in the 1960s, Cartwright returns to the medieval campus nearly four decades later on a combination nostalgic tour and journalistic inquiry. Seeking to define the university's greatness, Cartwright offers erudite meditations on everything from the solidity of its buildings . . . to the fiercely individualistic lives of its students. . . . He offers sharply observed homages to the thinkers and writers—Isaiah Berlin, J. R. R. Tolkien, Charles Dodgson—who shaped Oxford's discourse, and maps out the university's peculiar mix of silly rituals and sublime intellectual life. In addition, the book retraces Cartwright's own journey from callow teenager to confident young scholar-athlete." N Y Times Book Rev

Gott, Richard

Britain's empire; resistance, repression and revolt. Richard Gott. Verso Books 2011 vii, 568 p.p $34.95 **942**

1. Imperialism 2. Resistance to government 3. Great Britain -- Colonies 4. Imperialism -- History 5. Great Britain -- Civilization 6. Commonwealth countries -- History 7. Great Britain -- Colonies -- History 8. Government, Resistance to -- Commonwealth countries -- History 9. Government, Resistance to -- Great Britain -- Colonies -- History

ISBN 1844677389; 9781844677382

LC 2011456112

This book, by Richard Gott, offers a "history of the foundation of the British empire, . . . punctur[ing] the still widely held belief that the British Empire was a . . . civilizing enterprise of great benefit to its subject peoples. Instead, [it] reveals a history of systemic repression . . . and . . . military dictatorship. . . . [But w]herever Britain tried to plant its flag, there was resistance. From Ireland to India, from the American colonies to Australia." (Publisher's note)

Includes bibliographical references and index.

Hollis, Leo

London rising; the men who made modern London. Walker & Co. 2008 390p il map $27.99 **942**

1. Authors 2. Architects 3. Economists 4. Physicians

5. Physicists 6. Philosophers 7. Diarists 8. Essayists 9. Biographers 10. College teachers 11. Members of Parliament 12. London (England) -- History 13. Political and social philosophers 14. St. Paul's Cathedral (London, England)
ISBN 978-0-8027-1632-3; 0-8027-1632-6

LC 2008-000179

"London in the mid-17th century remained a medieval city. The civil war, a plague that claimed 100,000 lives and the Great Fire of 1666 would have been sufficient to send it back to the Dark Ages. Instead, London was transformed into a modern metropolis. . . . Hollis controls the narrative by focusing on the five figures who best represent the spirit of the age. John Locke, the philosopher, outlined a daring theory of universal natural rights; social observer John Evelyn grappled with the specific meaning of Englishness; real estate developer and speculator Nicholas Barbon rebuilt the center of London (with designs by the scientific polymath Robert Hooke); and lastly, Christopher Wren, who created St. Paul's Cathedral, eternal symbol of the glittering city." Publ Wkly

Includes bibliographical references

Livingstone, Natalie

The **mistresses** of Cliveden; three centuries of scandal, power, and intrigue in an English stately home. Natalie Livingstone. Ballantine Books 2016 512 p. illustrations (hardback) $32   **942**
1. Nobility 2. Women -- England 3. Country homes -- England 4. Cliveden (England) -- History 5. Women -- England -- Biography 6. Cliveden (England) -- Biography 7. Nobility -- England -- Biography 8. Rich people -- England -- Biography
ISBN 9780553392074

LC 2015049927

In this book, by Natalie Livingstone, "five miles from Windsor Castle, home of the royal family, sits the Cliveden estate. . . . Throughout its storied history, Cliveden has been a setting for misbehavior, intrigue, and passion—from its salacious, deadly beginnings in the seventeenth century to the 1960s Profumo Affair, the sex scandal that toppled the British government." (Publisher's note)

"In her debut book, Livingstone ably avoids tabloidlike gossip to profile five remarkable women, and she provides a helpful cast of characters at the beginning of the story. Readers who enjoy English history will be happy to have this in their libraries." Kirkus

Includes bibliographical references and index

Nicolson, Juliet

The **perfect** summer; England 1911, just before the storm. Grove Press 2007 290p il $25; pa $15   **942**
1. Great Britain -- Social conditions 2. Great Britain -- History -- 20th century 3. Great Britain -- Social life and customs
ISBN 0-8021-1846-1; 978-0-8021-1846-2; 0-8021-4367-9 pa; 978-0-8021-4367-9 pa

LC 2006-48854

First published 2006 in the United Kingdom

"With her sparkling social history about Edwardian society on the brink of World War I, Nicolson has created the perfect beach reading for Anglophiles." Christ Sci Monit

Includes bibliographical references

Tombs, Robert

The **English** and their history; Robert Tombs. Knopf 2014 x, 1012 p.p 32 plates; illustrations; maps $45   **942**
1. Great Britain -- History 2. Great Britain -- Civilization 3. English
ISBN 1101874767; 1846140188; 9781101874769; 9781846140181

LC 2014486349

This book by Robert Tombs is an "account of the people who have a claim to be the oldest nation in the world. The English first came into existence as an idea, before they had a common ruler and before the country they lived in even had a name. They have lasted as a recognizable entity ever since, and their defining national institutions can be traced back to the earliest years of their history." (Publisher's note)

"All readers will benefit from a history that reveals the "connections and disconnections," the "continuities and discontinuities" that make the English who they think they are. Summing Up: Essential. All levels/libraries." Choice

Includes bibliographical references and index

942.01 England--Early history to 1066

King Arthur in legend and history; edited by Richard White; foreword by Allan Massie. Routledge 1998 xxv, 570p il maps hardcover o.p. pa $34.95   **942.01**
1. Kings 2. Great Britain -- History -- 0-1066
ISBN 0-415-92063-9 pa

LC 97-47726

First published 1997 in the United Kingdom

"This book is a compilation of source material excerpted primarily from longer works. . . . The documents themselves are arranged in roughly chronological and geographical order, ranging from Gildas (c. 548) to The Buik of the Chronicles of Scotland (1535). The anthology presents both historical and literary works and draws from French and German as well as English sources." Libr J

Includes bibliographical references

942.02 England--Norman period, 1066-1154

Morris, Marc

★ The **Norman** Conquest; The Battle of Hastings and the Fall of Anglo-saxon England. by Marc Morris. W W Norton & Co Inc 2013 464 p. $32   **942.02**
1. Hastings (East Sussex, England), Battle of, 1066 2. Great Britain -- History -- 1066-1154, Norman period
ISBN 1605984515; 9781605984513

This book by Marc Morris "explains why the Norman Conquest was the most significant cultural and military episode in English history. It explain[s] why England was at once so powerful and yet so vulnerable to William the Conqueror's attack; why the Normans, in some respects less sophisticated, possessed the military cutting edge; how William's hopes of a united Anglo-Norman realm unraveled, dashed by English rebellions, Viking invasions, and the insatiable demands of his fellow conquerors." (Publisher's note)

942.03   England--Period of House of Plantagenet, 1154-1399

Jones, Dan

★ The **Plantagenets**; the warrior kings and queens who made England. Dan Jones. Viking 2013 xxv, 534 p.p (hardcover) $36   **942.03**
1. Great Britain -- Kings and rulers 2. Great Britain -- History -- 1154-1399, Plantagenets 3. Great Britain -- Kings and rulers -- Biography 4. Great Britain -- History -- Plantagenets, 1154-1399 5. Great Britain -- Politics and government -- 1154-1399
ISBN 0670026654; 9780670026654
LC 2012039998
First published in Great Britain in 2012.

This book, by Dan Jones, examines how "the first Plantagenet king inherited a blood-soaked kingdom from the Normans and transformed it into an empire stretched at its peak from Scotland to Jerusalem. . . . We meet . . . Eleanor of Aquitaine, . . . her son, Richard the Lionheart, . . . and King John, a tyrant who was forced to sign Magna Carta. . . . This is the era of chivalry, . . . the Black Death, the founding of Parliament, . . . and the Hundred Year's War." (Publisher's note)

"The great battles against the Scots and French and the subjugation of the Welsh make for thrilling reading but so do the equally enthralling struggles over succession, the Magna Carta, and the Provisions of Oxford...Written with prose that keeps the reader captivated throughout accounts of the span of centuries and the not-always-glorious trials of kingship, this book is at all times approachable, academic, and entertaining." Booklist

Includes bibliographical references and index

Seward, Desmond

The **Demon's** Brood; A History of the Plantagenet Dynasty. by Desmond Seward. W W Norton & Co Inc 2014 400 p. 16 plates; ills; portraits (hardback) $28.95   **942.03**
1. Great Britain -- History -- 1154-1399, Plantagenets
ISBN 1605986186; 9781605986180; 9781605988696

This book, by Desmond Seward, offers a "history of the most dominant royal dynasty in English history, from Richard the Lionheart and Edward the Black Prince to Henry IV and Richard III. The Plantagenets reigned over England longer than any other family--from Henry II to Richard III. . . . Based on major contemporary sources and recent research, acclaimed historian Desmond Seward provides the first readable overview of the whole extraordinary dynasty, in one volume." (Publisher's note)

"Seward is a good author to turn to for ease in reading history; his writing style is quick, vibrant and delightfully pithy in its simplicity of phrase." Kirkus

942.04   England--Period of Houses of Lancaster and York, 1399-1485

Gristwood, Sarah

Blood sisters; the women behind the Wars of the Roses. Sarah Gristwood. Basic Books, A Member of the Perseus Books Group 2013 432 p. (hard cover : alk. paper) $29.99   **942.04**
1. Courts and courtiers 2. Queens -- Great Britain 3. Great Britain -- History -- 1455-1485, Wars of the Roses 4. Great Britain -- History -- Henry VII, 1485-1509 5. Great Britain -- History -- Wars of the Roses, 1455-1485
ISBN 0465018319; 9780465018314
LC 2012044813

This book, by historian Sarah Gristwood, examines the female dynamics behind the War of the Roses. "While the events of this turbulent time are usually described in terms of the male leads who fought and died seeking the throne, a handful of powerful women would prove just as decisive as their kinfolks' clashing armies. . . . Gristwood traces the rise and rule of the seven most critical women in the wars." (Publisher's note)

Includes bibliographical references and index

Jones, Dan

The **Wars** of the Roses; the fall of the Plantagenets and the rise of the Tudors. Dan Jones. Viking 2014 416 p. ills., maps, genealogical tab. $36 **942.04**
1. Great Britain -- History -- 1455-1485, Wars of the Roses 2. Great Britain -- History -- Wars of the Roses, 1455-1485 3. Great Britain -- History -- Lancaster and York, 1399-1485
ISBN 0670026670; 9780670026678
LC 2014010099

This book, by Dan Jones, describes how "the crown of England changed hands five times over the course of the fifteenth century, as two branches of the Plantagenet dynasty fought to the death for the right to rule. . . . [The volume chronicles] how the longest-reigning British royal family tore itself apart until it was finally replaced by the Tudors." (Publisher's note)

"This excellent and fairly accessible contribution to the history of the Wars of the Roses serves as a helpful corrective to previous mythologized versions. It is highly recommended for studies of British royal history and for readers of popular narrative nonfiction." LJ

Includes bibliographical references and index

Jones, Michael K.

Bosworth 1485; The Battle That Transformed England: the Rise of the Tudor Dynasty. Michael K. Jones. W W Norton & Co Inc. 2015 256 p. 16 plates; illustrations $27.95   **942.04**
1. Great Britain -- History -- 1455-1485, Wars of the Roses
ISBN 1605988596; 9781605988597

This book, by Michael K. Jones, offers an "authoritative reinterpretation of the Battle of Bosworth Field, where the Wars of the Roses ended and the Tudor dynasty began. . . . With startling detail of Henry Tudor's reliance on French mercenaries, plus a new account of the battle itself, the author turns Shakespeare on its head, painting an entirely fresh picture of the dramatic life and death of Richard III, England's most infamous monarch." (Publisher's note)

"Jones recounts the actual battle in easily understood terms for laymen and offers unusual insights into the role of foreign fighters. This is a well-done reexamination of the conflict that truly altered the course of history." Booklist

Weir, Alison

The **Wars** of the Roses. Ballantine Bks. 1995 462p il hardcover o.p. pa $15.95   **942.04**

1. Great Britain -- History -- 1455-1485, War of the Roses

ISBN 0-345-39117-9; 0-345-40433-5 pa

"No history collection should do without this perfectly focused and beautifully unfolded account." Booklist

942.05   England--Period of House of Tudor, 1485-1603

Ackroyd, Peter, 1949-

Tudors; The History of England from Henry VIII to Elizabeth I. by Peter Ackroyd. Thomas Dunne Books 2013 512 p. (History of England) $29.99   **942.05**

1. England 2. Great Britain -- History -- 1485-1603, Tudors 3. Great Britain -- History -- Tudors, 1485-1603

ISBN 1250003628; 9781250003621

LC 2013024573

This book, the "second title in [Peter Ackroyd's] projected six-volume history of England," focuses on "the 16th-century religious reformation that began, as a dynastic matter, with Henry VIII's divorce from Katherine of Aragon in 1533. . . . The Reformation in England was marked by upheaval and bloodshed, as the Tudors imposed religious changes upon an initially reluctant populace." (Publishers Weekly)

Includes bibliographical references (pages 473-481) and index

Fletcher, Catherine

The **divorce** of Henry VIII; the untold story from inside the Vatican. Catherine Fletcher. Palgrave Macmillan 2012 xviv, 266 p.p ill., map (hardcover) $28   **942.05**

1. Great Britain -- Foreign relations 2. Catholic Church -- Foreign relations 3. Reformation -- England 4. Catholic Church -- Foreign relations -- Great Britain 5. Great Britain -- Foreign relations -- Catholic Church 6. Great Britain -- Politics and government -- 1509-1547 7. Church and state -- Great Britain -- History -- 16th century

ISBN 0230341519; 9780230341517

LC 2011050335

This book, by historian Catherine Fletcher, explores the history and politics of the formation of the Church of England from Vatican archive sources. "In 1533 . . . Henry VIII decided to divorce his wife of twenty years. . . . But getting his freedom involved a terrific web of intrigue. . . . Henry's man in Rome was a wily Italian diplomat named Gregorio Casali who drew no limits on skullduggery including kid-

napping, bribery and theft to make his king a free man." (Publisher's note)

Includes bibliographical references and index

Goodman, Ruth

How to be a Tudor; a dawn-to-dusk guide to Tudor life. Ruth Goodman. Liveright Publishing Corporation 2016 336 p. illustrations (some color) (hardcover) $29.95   **942.05**

1. Great Britain -- Social life and customs 2. Great Britain -- History -- 1485-1603, Tudors 3. Great Britain -- History -- Tudors, 1485-1603 4. Great Britain -- Social conditions -- 16th century 5. Great Britain -- Social life and customs -- 16th century

ISBN 9781631491399

LC 2015038420

This book, by Ruth Goodman, is "an erudite romp through the intimate details of life in Tudor England. . . . Drawing on her own adventures living in re-created Tudor conditions, Goodman serves as our intrepid guide to sixteenth-century living. Proceeding from daybreak to bedtime, this . . . work celebrates the ordinary lives of those who labored through the era." (Publisher's note)

"Throughout, Goodman's palpable enthusiasm and clear appreciation for the resourcefulness of the era's people make these men and women entirely relatable and yet full of surprises." Pub Wkly

Includes bibliographical references and index

Lipscomb, Suzannah

★ A **Journey** Through Tudor England; Hampton Court Palace and the Tower of London to Stratford-upon-avon and Thornbury Castle. by Suzannah Libscomb. 1st ed. W W Norton & Co Inc 2013 336 p. (hardcover) $26.95   **942.05**

1. Great Britain -- Description and travel 2. Great Britain -- History -- 1485-1603, Tudors

ISBN 1605984604; 9781605984605

This is "a guidebook that introduces readers to the history of the [Tudor] period through 50 of 'the best and most interesting' buildings associated with Tudor royalty. Each chapter tells the story of how a specific building served as the physical backdrop to the lives of those who inhabited it or to a particularly important visit from a famous personage." (Publishers Weekly)

Meyer, G. J.

The **Tudors**; the complete story of England's most notorious dynasty. Delacorte Press 2010 xxvi, 612p il map $30   **942.05**

1. Queens 2. Kings 3. Great Britain -- Kings and rulers 4. Great Britain -- History -- 1485-1603, Tudors

ISBN 978-0-385-34076-2

LC 2009-40032

"History buffs will savor Meyer's cheeky, nuanced, and authoritative perspective on an entire dynasty, and his study brims with enriching background discussions, ranging from class structure and the medieval Catholic Church to the Tudor connection to Spanish royalty." Publ Wkly

Includes bibliographical references

Mortimer, Ian

The **time** traveler's guide to Elizabethan England; Ian Mortimer. Viking 2013 416 p. (hardcover) $27.95 **942.05**

1. Great Britain -- Social conditions -- History 2. Great Britain -- History -- 1558-1603, Elizabeth 3. England -- Social conditions -- 16th century 4. Great Britain -- History -- Elizabeth, 1558-1603 5. England -- Social life and customs -- 16th century

ISBN 0670026077; 9780670026074

LC 2013001566

In this book, British historian Ian Mortimer offers an "account of life during Queen Elizabeth's 1558-1603 reign. The average Elizabethan paid little attention to politics but a great deal to domestic technology. Thus, bricks and clear glass became cheaper." Topic include the advent of chimneys, Elizabethan professionals, bathing habits, and personal hygiene. (Kirkus Reviews)

Includes bibliographical references and index

Ronald, Susan

Heretic queen; Queen Elizabeth I and the wars of religion. Susan Ronald. St. Martin's Press 2012 350 p. (hardcover) $27.99 **942.05**

1. Religious tolerance 2. War -- Religious aspects 3. Great Britain -- History -- 1485-1603, Tudors 4. Reformation -- England 5. England -- Church history -- 16th century 6. Great Britain -- History -- Elizabeth, 1558-1603

ISBN 0312645384; 9780312645380; 9781250015211

LC 2012010248

In this "companion volume to 'Pirate Queen,' [Susan] Ronald's 2007 study of . . . England's Elizabeth I , the author sets the Elizabethan age within the context of the Catholic-Protestant wars of religion" of "the latter half of the 16th century. Elizabeth had witnessed the religious divisions that marked the reigns of" Henry VIII, Edward VI, and Mary I, "so upon her ascension to the throne in 1558 she was eager to grant a measure of religious tolerance to her subjects." (Publishers Weekly)

Includes bibliographical references and index

Starkey, David

Six wives: the queens of Henry VIII. HarperCollins Pubs. 2003 xxvii, 852p il hardcover o.p. pa $16.95 **942.05**

1. Queens 2. Great Britain -- History -- 1485-1603, Tudors

ISBN 0-694-01043-X; 0-06-000550-5 pa

"Solidly researched and delightfully told, this is highly recommended." Libr J

Includes bibliographical references

Weir, Alison

Henry VIII; the king and his court. Ballantine Bks. 2001 632p il $28; pa $16.95 **942.05**

1. Kings 2. Great Britain -- History -- 1485-1603, Tudors

ISBN 0-345-43659-8; 0-345-43708-X pa

LC 2001-116042

In this biography of the Tudor king, the author "examines the minutiae of his daily life and gives prominence to the background players of his court. . . . At times, the weighty detail and numerous characters will make the work inaccessible; however, as a scholarly study it is a significant achievement." Libr J

Includes bibliographical references

The **life** of Elizabeth I. Ballantine Bks. 1998 532p il hardcover o.p. pa $15.95 **942.05**

1. Queens 2. Great Britain -- History -- 1485-1603, Tudors

ISBN 0-345-42550-2 pa

LC 98-34917

"Weir brings a fine sense of selection and considerable zest to her portrait of the self-styled Virgin Queen." Publ Wkly

Includes bibliographical references

The **six** wives of Henry VIII. Grove Weidenfeld 1992 643p il hardcover o.p. pa $15 **942.05**

1. Kings 2. Great Britain -- History -- 1485-1603, Tudors

ISBN 0-8021-3683-4 pa

LC 91-29522

First published 1991 in the United Kingdom

This is a collective biography of the wives of the Tudor king of England

"Wonderfully detailed, extensively researched. . . . The narrative is free flowing, humorous, informative, and readable." SLJ

Includes bibliographical references

942.055   Reign of Elizabeth I, 1558-1603

MacGregor, Neil, 1946-

Shakespeare's restless world; A Portrait of an Era in Twenty Objects. Neil MacGregor. Allen Lane 2012 xvi, 320 p.p ill. (some color), color maps $36 **942.055**

1. Great Britain -- Social conditions -- History 2. England -- Social conditions -- 16th century 3. England -- Social conditions -- 17th century

ISBN 0670026344; 9780670026340

LC 2013376339

This book, by Neil MacGregor, "brings the world of Shakespeare and the Tudor era of Elizabeth I into focus. . . . MacGregor and his team at the British Museum, working together in a landmark collaboration with the Royal Shakespeare Company and the BBC, bring us twenty objects that capture the essence of Shakespeare's universe. . . . This was . . . [a] time when discoveries in science and technology altered the parameters of the known world." (Publisher's note)

"Beautifully illustrated, MacGregor's history offers a vibrant portrait of Shakespeare's dramatic, perilous and exhilarating world." Kirkus

Includes bibliographical references and index

942.06   England--House of Stuart and Commonwealth periods to present, 1603-

Fraser, Antonia

Faith and treason; the story of the Gunpowder Plot. Doubleday 1996 xxxv, 347p il hardcover o.p. pa $16   **942.06**
   1. Gunpowder plot, 1605 2. Conspirators 3. Revolutionaries 4. Great Britain -- History -- 1603-1714, Stuarts
   ISBN 0-385-47190-4 pa

                      LC 96-21709
"A small group of Roman Catholics planned to blow up Parliament on its opening day in 1605, when the Protestant King James and his older son would be present, and to proclaim the nine-year-old princess Elizabeth queen, raise her as a Catholic, and so restore Catholicism as the state religion. . . . The Gunpowder Plot was both cruel and crackpot, but Fraser does a wonderful job of conveying to the modern reader just why a few Catholics felt that it was justified and also was likely to succeed." New Yorker
   Includes bibliographical references

942.1   London (England)

Flanders, Judith

The **Victorian** city; everyday life in Dickens' London. Judith Flanders. Thomas Dunne Books 2014 xxiii, 520 p.p 16 plates; illustrations; maps (hardback) $27.99   **942.1**
   1. London (England) -- History 2. London (England) -- In literature 3. London (England) -- Intellectual life -- 19th century 4. London (England) -- Social life and customs -- 19th century
   ISBN 1250040213; 9781250040213

                  LC 2014007566
Los Angeles Times Book Prize Finalist: History (2014)
This book, by Judith Flanders, offers a "portrait of everyday life on the streets of [Victorian] London. . . . From the moment Charles Dickens . . . arrived in the city in 1822, he obsessively walked its streets. . . . Now, with him, Judith Flanders leads us through the markets, transport systems, sewers, . . . chop-houses and entertainment emporia of Dickens' London, to reveal the Victorian capital in all its variety, vibrancy, and squalor." (Publisher's note)
"This is a superb portrait of an exciting, thriving, and dangerous city." Booklist
   Includes bibliographical references (pages 479-499) and index

Jones, Nigel

Tower; an epic history of the Tower of London. Nigel Jones. St. Martin's Press 2012 464 p. (hardcover) $35.00   **942.1**
   1. Great Britain -- History 2. London (England) -- History 3. Prisons -- England -- London -- History 4. Tower of London (London, England) -- History 5. Fortification -- England -- London -- History 6. London (England) -- Buildings, structures, etc
   ISBN 0312622961; 9780312622961; 9781250018144
                  LC 2012028273

The book presents a history of the Tower of London in which the author "seeks to conjure the many characters that have lived, been imprisoned and perished within its walls. His concern is not so much with the building itself: he pays only fleeting attention to its architectural development. Instead, he is interested in the 'great actors in the dramas of English history' who trod its passages." These include "Henry VII . . . Simon de Montfort . . . Elizabeth I . . . [and] Sir Walter Raleigh". (TLS)
   Includes bibliographical references and index

942.9   Wales

Morris, Jan

A **writer's** house in Wales. National Geographic Soc. 2002 143p (National Geographic directions) $25   **942.9**
   1. Wales
   ISBN 0-7922-6523-8

                  LC 2001-44731
The author "reflects on her home in Wales, its beautiful setting and the nature of being Welsh. . . . This slim and charming volume offers a crisp account of the turbulent history of the Welsh and their battle to maintain their language and culture in the shadow of their more powerful neighbor." Publ Wkly

942.901   Historical periods

Charles-Edwards, T. M.

Wales and the Britons, 350-1064; by T.M. Charles-Edwards. Oxford University Press 2013 xx, 795 p.p (The history of Wales) $185   **942.901**
   1. Wales -- History 2. Great Britain -- History -- 0-1066 3. Wales -- History -- To 1063
   ISBN 0198217315; 9780198217312

                  LC 2012376060
This book, by T.M. Charles-Edwards, "provides a detailed history of Wales in the period in which it was created out of the remnants of Roman Britain. It thus begins in the fourth century, with accelerating attacks from external forces, and ends shortly before the Norman Conquest of England. The narrative history is interwoven with chapters on the principal sources, the social history of Wales, the Church, the early history of the Welsh language, and its early literature, both in Welsh and in Latin." (Publisher's note)
   Includes bibliographical references (p. [680]-739) and index

943 Germany and neighboring central European countries

Coy, Jason Philip

A **brief** history of Germany; [by] Jason P. Coy. Facts on File 2011 288p il map (Brief history) $49.50; pa $19.95   **943**

1. Germany -- History
ISBN 978-0-8160-8142-4; 978-0-8160-8329-9 pa
LC 2010-23139

This book provides an "account of the events, people, and special customs and traditions that have shaped Germany from ancient times to the present." Publisher's note
Includes bibliographical references

Fulbrook, Mary

★ A **concise** history of Germany; 2nd ed; Cambridge University Press 2004 277p il, maps (Cambridge concise histories) hardcover o.p. pa $22 **943**

1. Princes 2. Statesmen 3. Heads of state 4. Prime ministers 5. National socialism 6. Nazi leaders 7. Germany -- History
ISBN 0-521-83320-5; 0-521-54071-2 pa
LC 2004-271599

First published 1990 in the United Kingdom
This history of Germany "spans the early Middle Ages to the present day. . . . Mary Fulbrook explores the interrelationships between social, political and cultural factors in the light of the latest scholarly controversies." Publ Wkly
Includes bibliographical references

Gay, Peter

My German question; growing up in Nazi Berlin. Yale Univ. Press 1998 208p il $40; pa $11.95 **943**

1. Historians 2. National socialism 3. Jews -- Germany 4. College teachers 5. Nonfiction writers 6. Jews -- Persecutions 7. Germany -- Politics and government -- 1933-1945
ISBN 0-300-07670-3; 0-300-08070-0 pa
LC 98-26686

"A searching, sensitive portrait of Gay's youth, as crystalline as memory can be made." Booklist

Gay, Ruth

The **Jews** of Germany; a historical portrait. with an introduction by Peter Gay. Yale Univ. Press 1992 297p il maps hardcover o.p. pa $35   **943**

1. Jews -- Germany
ISBN 0-300-05155-7; 0-300-06052-1 pa
LC 91-30235

This is a history of Germany's Jews from the first century to the Holocaust.
"Illustrated sumptuously with paintings, photographs and excerpts from letters and historical documents, . . . this affirming history survives the sad end of the centuries-old German Jewish way of life." N Y Times Book Rev

Gorra, Michael Edward

The **bells** in their silence; travels through Germany. {by} Michael Gorra. Princeton University Press 2004 211p $24.95   **943**

1. Germany -- Description and travel
ISBN 0-691-11765-9

Gorra's "account of his travels through Germany is shaped—perhaps even haunted—by figures from the past: historical, literary, personal. A captivating, unique work of synthesis." Booklist
Includes bibliographical references

Harding, Thomas

The **House** by the Lake; One House, Five Families, and a Hundred Years of German History. Thomas Harding. St. Martin's Press 2016 464 p. ill., maps, genealogical table (hardcover) $28   **943**

1. Houses 2. Germany
ISBN 1250065062; 9781250065063
LC 2015044339

"In the summer of 1993, [author] Thomas Harding traveled to Germany with his grandmother to visit a small house by a lake on the outskirts of Berlin. . . . Slowly he began to piece together the lives of the five families who had lived there: a wealthy landowner, a prosperous Jewish family, a renowned composer, a widow and her children, a Stasi informant. All had made the house their home, and all but one had been forced out." (Publisher's note)
"This personal saga centered on a family home will appeal to enthusiasts of German history, especially post-World War II division and reunification." LJ
Includes bibliographical references (pages 361-414) and index.

MacDonogh, Giles

Frederick the Great; a life in deed and letters. St. Martin's Press 2000 436p il hardcover o.p. pa $16.95   **943**

1. Kings
ISBN 0-312-27266-9 pa
LC 00-24799

First published 1999 in the United Kingdom
"Both general readers and those with a strong background in European history will find great value in this outstanding biography." Booklist
Includes bibliographical references

MacGregor, Neil, 1946-

Germany; memories of a nation. Neil MacGregor. Alfred A. Knopf 2015 656 p. color illustrations; maps (hardback) $40   **943**

1. Germany -- History 2. Germany -- Civilization
ISBN 1101875666; 9781101875667
LC 2014048396

In this book, Neil MacGregor presents a history of Germany in objects. The author "argues that, uniquely for any European country, no coherent, overarching narrative of Germany's history can be constructed, for in Germany both geography and history have always been unstable. . . . German history may be inherently fragmented, but it contains a large number of widely shared memories, awarenesses, and experiences; examining some of these is the purpose of this book." (Publisher's note)

"Most importantly, the author finds post-World War II Germany hyperattuned to the need for memorials to victims of terror and oppression—e.g., via the work of painter and printmaker Käthe Kollwitz. A comprehensive record jam-packed with visuals." Kirkus

Includes bibliographical references and index

Moorhouse, Roger

Berlin at war. Basic Books 2010 432p il $29.95   **943**

1. Berlin (Germany) -- History 2. World War, 1939-1945 -- Germany

ISBN 978-0-465-00533-8

LC 2010-907169

"Election results in the fading days of the Weimar Republic indicate that Berliners were not particularly sympathetic to Hitler or his movement. Yet Berlin endured horrible physical destruction, deprivation, and death. This included intense Allied bombings by day and night, and a siege and eventual ravaging by the Russian army. . . . [Moorhouse] begins with an almost idyllic scene as huge crowds in Berlin witness the celebration of Hitler's birthday in April 1939; at the time, of course, Germany seemed to have achieved its foreign-policy goals without firing a shot. As the fortunes of Germany and Berlin deteriorate, Moorhouse uses the testimonies of a variety of Berliners to describe some memorable scenes and struggles.This is a hard, unrelenting saga of the effects of total warfare on citizens just hoping to survive." Booklist

Includes bibliographical references

Watson, Peter, 1943-

The **German** genius; Europe's third renaissance, the second scientific revolution, and the twentieth century. Harper 2010 964p il $35   **943**

1. Germany -- Civilization 2. Germany -- Intellectual life

ISBN 0060760222; 9780060760229

LC 2010-06738

This is a "cultural history of German ideas and influence, from 1750 to the present day." (Publisher's note) Index.

This is "a panoramic review of German cultural and intellectual development from 1750 to the present. Examining the contributions of literally hundreds of German thinkers and doers and mapping the conceptual connections between them, the author demonstrates the breadth, volume, and influence of German output in philosophy, science, industry, art, literature, and all forms of scholarly activity. But Watson's true focus is the cultural crucible, forged in the eighteenth and nineteenth centuries and informed by notions of Bildung and inwardness, that gave rise to such accomplishments but also set the stage for the evil actions of the Third Reich. To some extent an effort to untether our understanding of German history from the conflicts of the twentieth century, this study is also a reminder that our modern Western worldview has deep German roots." Booklist

Includes bibliographical references

943.08   Germany since 1866

Craig, Gordon Alexander

Germany, 1866-1945; by Gordon A. Craig. Oxford Univ. Press 1978 825p (Oxford history of modern Europe) hardcover o.p. pa $41.95   **943.08**

1. Germany -- History

ISBN 0-19-502724-8 pa

LC 78-58471

"An impressive . . . survey of modern German history, this book is an indispensable reference." New Statesman (1913)

Includes bibliographical references

Evans, Richard J.

★ The **coming** of the Third Reich; a history. Penguin Press 2004 622p il map hardcover o.p. pa $18   **943.08**

1. National socialism 2. Germany -- History -- 1866-1918 3. Germany -- History -- 1918-1933

ISBN 1-594-20004-1; 0-14-303469-3 pa

LC 2003-63205

First published 2003 in the United Kingdom

"This is a first-rate narrative history that informs and educates and may inspire readers to delve even deeper into the subject." Booklist

Includes bibliographical references

Stern, Fritz Richard

Five Germanys I have known; [by] Fritz Stern. Farrar, Straus & Giroux 2006 546p il map $30   **943.08**

1. Germany -- History

ISBN 978-0-374-15540-7; 0-374-15540-2

LC 2006-60

In this "memoir, Stern looks back over the 'five Germanys' his generation has seen—the Weimar Republic, Nazi tyranny, the post-1945 Federal Republic, the Soviet-controlled German Democratic Republic and, lastly, the reunited Germany of the present—and explains how he came to reconcile himself with his birth country (which his Jewish family fled in 1938) as it has come to terms with its new place in today's more cohesive and peaceful Europe. . . . The book's intriguing structure makes it a wonderful combination of history, memoir, analysis and even poetry." Publ Wkly

943.085   Period of Weimar Republic, 1918-1933

Haffner, Sebastian

Defying Hitler; a memoir. translated from the German by Oliver Pretzel. Farrar, Straus & Giroux 2002 309p il $24; pa $14   **943.085**

1. Germany -- History -- 1918-1933

ISBN 0-374-16157-7; 0-312-42113-3 pa

LC 2002-17058

"In August 1938 a young German lawyer and journalist with the . . . name of Raimund Pretzel arrived in England. . . . Pretzel, a non-Jew, was fleeing to join and marry a Jewish woman pregnant with their first child. . . . Choosing a new name—Sebastian Haffner—to keep the Nazis from retaliating against his relatives, he went on to a . . . career as a journalist and historian in England, where he died in 1999. Afterward, while perusing his father's papers, Oliver Pretzel . . . found a . . . typescript in German. It was Haffner's unfinished memoir about his early years, begun in 1939, that sought through autobiography to understand how Hitler came to power." New Leader

943.086 Germany--Period of Third Reich, 1933-1945

Album of the damned; snapshots from the Third Reich. Academy Chicago Publishers 2008 408p il $50 **943.086**
    1. Germany -- History -- 1933-1945 2. World War, 1939-1945 -- Pictorial works
    ISBN 978-0-89733-576-8; 0-89733-576-7

"Photographed almost exclusively by amateurs — both soldiers and civilians — the pictures in Album of the Damned center on the daily life within the Third Reich, both at home and on the battlefield. . . . Garson assembled the exclusively black-and-white photos from private collections around the world, including many captured by the Soviets that only became available after the fall of the Soviet Union. . . . Critics might maintain that by focusing on showing how Nazis were 'human,' attention is diverted from their crimes against humanity. But it's impossible to thumb through the book on any page and not see the ghosts of the six million floating around every photo. A narrative that snakes through the book provides an overview of the time period and background on what's taking place in the photos." Jerusalem Post

Aycoberry, Pierre
    The **social** history of the Third Reich; 1933-1945. translated from the French by Janet Lloyd. New Press 2000 380p $30; pa $15.95 **943.086**
    1. National socialism 2. Germany -- Social conditions 3. Germany -- Politics and government -- 1933-1945
    ISBN 1-56584-549-8; 1-56584-635-4 pa
        LC 99-14059

"In examining the actions of individuals and social groups, {the author} illustrates that German citizens' response to the Nazi regime varied wildly. Some resisted bravely; others saw an opportunity for advancement. Most people sought merely to survive. In fact, what is extremely unsettling is how so many could maintain a semblance of normalcy in their lives. Aycoberry does not attempt to answer the unanswerable questions posed by the Nazi era, but his disturbing, brutally honest, and scrupulously fair work may be a landmark in the field." Booklist
    Includes bibliographical references

Bascomb, Neal
    Hunting Eichmann; how a band of survivors and a young spy agency chased down the world's most notorious Nazi. Houghton Mifflin Harcourt 2009 390p il map $26 **943.086**
    1. War criminals 2. Nazi leaders 3. Secret service

-- Israel
    ISBN 978-0-618-85867-5; 0-618-85867-9
        LC 2008-35757

The author recounts the pursuit, capture, and abduction of Nazi war criminal Adolf Eichmann. "Bascomb spread a wide net in researching the 15-year hunt, and he fills his book with previously unknown or neglected details, utilizing the remembrances of former Mossad agents, German and American intelligence operatives, and Argentine Nazi sympathizers who tried to find Eichmann after his seizure. . . . This is an outstanding account of a sustained and worthy manhunt." Booklist
    Includes bibliographical references

Burleigh, Michael
    The **Third** Reich; a new history. Hill & Wang 2000 xxv, 965p il maps hardcover o.p. pa $18 **943.086**
    1. Germany -- History -- 1933-1945
    ISBN 0-8090-9326-X pa
        LC 00-31838

"This brilliant and unique view of a great tyranny is an important addition to our understanding of the first half of the twentieth century." Booklist
    Includes bibliographical references

Evans, Richard J.
    ★ The **Third** Reich in power, 1933-1939. Penguin Press 2005 941p il map hardcover o.p. pa $20 **943.086**
    1. National socialism 2. Germany -- History -- 1933-1945
    ISBN 1-594-20074-2; 0-14-303790-0 pa
        LC 2005-52128

This "is a major achievement. No other recent synthetic history has quite the range and narrative power of Evans's work." Publ Wkly
    Includes bibliographical references

Fischer, Klaus P.
    Nazi Germany; a new history. Continuum 1995 734p il hardcover o.p. pa $32.95 **943.086**
    1. Heads of state 2. National socialism 3. Nazi leaders 4. Germany -- History -- 1933-1945
    ISBN 0-8264-0906-7 pa
        LC 94-41796

"An indispensable, compellingly readable political, military and social history of the Third Reich." Publ Wkly
    Includes bibliographical references

Fleming, Gerald
    Hitler and the final solution; with an introduction by Saul Friedlander. University of Calif. Press 1984 xxxvi, 219p il hardcover o.p. pa $18.95 **943.086**
    1. Heads of state 2. Nazi leaders 3. Holocaust, 1933-1945
    ISBN 0-520-06022-9 pa
        LC 83-24352

Original German edition, 1982

This work attempts to prove "that the Final Solution was deliberately designed and personally willed and ordered by Hitler. Fleming reveals the elaborate precautions taken not only to disguise the nature of the operation but also to ensure that it could not be connected with Hitler." Publisher's note

Includes bibliographical references

Fritzsche, Peter

Life and death in the Third Reich. Belknap Press of Harvard University Press 2008 368p   **943.086**
1. National socialism 2. Holocaust, 1933-1945 3. Germany -- Ethnic relations 4. Collective memory -- Germany 5. Holocaust, Jewish (1939-1945) 6. Germany -- History -- 1933-1945 7. Holocaust, Jewish (1939-1945) -- Germany

ISBN 0-674-02793-0; 0-674-03465-1 pa; 978-0-674-02793-0; 978-0-674-03465-5 pa

LC 2007-40552

This is a sequel to the author's Germans into Nazis (1998). In this study, Fritzsche seeks to explain the success of the ideology of Nazism. He argues that "its basic appeal lay in the Volksgemeinschaft—a 'people's community' that appealed to Germans to be part of a great project to redress the wrongs of the Versailles treaty, make the country strong and vital, and rid the body politic of unhealthy elements. The goal was to create a new national and racial self-conscious-ness among Germans. For Germany to live, others—espe-cially Jews—had to die. . . . Fritzsche examines the efforts of Germans to adjust to new racial identities, to believe in the necessity of war, to accept the dynamic of uncondi-tional destruction—in short, to become Nazis." (Publisher's note) Index.

"This book combines a compelling historical narrative with a thought-provoking analysis and will be of much inter-est to scholars in the field as well as a more general reader-ship." Times Higher Ed

Includes bibliographical references

Johnson, Eric A.

What we knew; terror, mass murder and every-day life in Nazi Germany: an oral history. [by] Eric A. Johnson and Karl-Heinz Reuband. Basic Books 2005 xxiii, 434p $27.50   **943.086**
1. Holocaust, 1933-1945 2. Germany -- History -- 1933-1945

ISBN 0-465-08571-7

"The authors posit that 'far from living in a state of con-stant fear and discontent, most Germans led happy and even normal lives in Nazi Germany.' They believe that the Holo-caust could not have been possible without the complicity of the majority of the German population. . . . This scholarly work is a major contribution to the understanding of life in Nazi Germany and a compelling narrative that is certain to be the standard work on the subject." Booklist

Includes bibliographical references

Kershaw, Ian

Hitler, 1936-1945: nemesis. Norton 2000 832p hardcover o.p. pa $25   **943.086**
1. Dictators 2. Heads of state 3. National socialism 4. Nazi leaders 5. Germany -- Politics and government -- 1933-1945

ISBN 0-393-04994-9; 0-393-32252-1 pa

"The second volume of Kershaw's biography of Hitler covers the period from the Anschluss with Austria to 1945. .

. . By 1938, Hitler's word was the equivalent of written law. After 1936, Hitler also came to believe his own propaganda. . . . Without any reasonable restraint, he led Germany inexo-rably to destruction. . . . Kershaw's two volumes will prob-ably be the standard source for many years." Libr J

Klemperer, Victor

★ I will bear witness; a diary of the Nazi years, 1933-1941. translated by Martin Chalmers. Random House 1998 556p hardcover o.p. pa $15.95 **943.086**
1. Holocaust survivors 2. Diarists 3. Germany -- History -- 1933-1945

ISBN 0-375-75378-8 pa

LC 98-15429

"Never has the isolation of living in a world that wishes one's people dead been rendered with greater pathos. Every act of cruelty as well as every gesture of kindness is scrupu-lously recorded." Nation

Nelson, Anne

Red Orchestra; the story of the Berlin under-ground and the circle of friends who resisted Hitler. Random House 2009 388p il $27   **943.086**
1. National socialism 2. Rote Kapelle (Resistance group) 3. World War, 1939-1945 -- Underground movements

ISBN 978-1-4000-6000-9; 1-4000-6000-1

LC 2008-23465

The author "documents the wartime journey of Greta Kuckhoff, a young German, and her valiant colleagues who formed a potent resistance to the Hitler regime in its glory days. . . . Nelson's riveting book speaks proudly of Greta . . . and all of the nearly three million Germans who resisted Hitler's iron will, and gives the reader a somber view of hell from the inside." Publ Wkly

Includes bibliographical references

Ortner, Helmut

The lone assassin; the epic true story of the man who almost killed Hitler. Helmut Ortner; translated by Ross Benjamin. Skyhorse Pub. 2012 183 p. (hardcover : alk. paper) $24.95   **943.086**
1. World War, 1939-1945 -- Underground movements 2. Germany -- History -- 1933-1945 3. Anti-Nazi movement -- Germany -- Biography

ISBN 1616083832; 9781616083830

LC 2011049214

"In this book . . . author [Helmut] Ortner . . . lays out the story of Georg Elser, the carpenter who attempted to as-sassinate [Adolf] Hitler in 1939, courtesy of a bomb in the Munich Beer Hall. . . . Ortner examines Elser's life as well as covering the conditions that led to Hitler's rise to power, including the 1923 failed coup that made the Munich Beer Hall so symbolic to the Nazi regime." (Publishers Weekly)

Parssinen, Terry M.

The Oster conspiracy of 1938; the unknown story of the military plot to kill Hitler and avert World War II. {by} Terry Parssinen. HarperCollins Pubs. 2003 xxii, 232p il map $27.95; pa $13.95 **943.086**
1. Generals 2. Heads of state 3. Nazi leaders 4.

Underground leaders 5. Germany -- Politics and government -- 1933-1945
ISBN 0-06-019587-8; 0-06-095525-2 pa
LC 2002-68896

"A fascinating, blow-by-blow account of a seemingly feasible but failed attempt to prevent World War II. . . . Even knowing the outcome, readers feel suspense and hope as events unfold; alternate history buffs and history students alike will gain new insight into the past and into human character from this tragic story." SLJ

Includes bibliographical references

Rosenbaum, Ron

Explaining Hitler; the search for the origins of his evil. HarperPerennial 1999 444p pa $16 **943.086**
1. Heads of state 2. National socialism 3. Nazi leaders
4. Germany -- Politics and government -- 1933-1945
ISBN 0-06-095339-X; 978-0-06-095339-3
LC 99-25965

First published 1998 by Random House

This book examines interpretations of Hitler made by his contemporaries and by historians.

"In this brilliantly skeptical inventory of the world's Hitler-thinking, Rosenbaum analyzes not only the multiple Hitler theories but also the agendas and fantasies that the theorizers bring to their subject." Time

Includes bibliographical references

Shirer, William L.

The rise and fall of the Third Reich; a history of Nazi Germany. with a new afterword by the author. Simon & Schuster 1990 1249p hardcover o.p. pa $25 **943.086**
1. Heads of state 2. Nazi leaders 3. Germany -- History -- 1933-1945 4. World War, 1939-1945 -- Germany
ISBN 0-671-72868-7 pa
LC 90-221762

First published 1960

This is a comprehensive, documented history of Germany from the beginning of the Nazi party in 1918 to the World War II defeat of Germany in 1945. Here is a detailed account of the events, and the leading figures of the Nazi era, especially Adolf Hitler

Includes bibliographical references

Speer, Albert

Inside the Third Reich; memoirs. translated from the German by Richard and Clara Winston; introduction by Eugene Davidson. Simon & Schuster 1997 596p il pa $18 **943.086**
1. Heads of state 2. Nazi leaders 3. Germany -- History -- 1933-1945 4. World War, 1939-1945 -- Germany
ISBN 0-684-82949-5; 978-0-684-82949-4
Original German edition, 1969

The author, Hitler's "architect and later his armaments minister, was in the dictator's inner circle for almost 12 years. . . . After the war Speer used the enforced leisure of his 20 prison years as a war criminal to plan and write these memoirs." Libr J

Includes bibliographical references

Stargardt, Nicholas

The German War; A Nation Under Arms. Nicholas Stargardt. Basic Books, a member of the Perseus Books Group 2015 720 p. 24 plates; illustrations; maps $35 **943.086**
1. World War, 1939-1945 2. Germany -- History -- 1933-1945
ISBN 0465018998; 9780465018994
LC 2015945013

This book, by Nicholas Stargardt, "draws on an extraordinary range of primary source materials--personal diaries, court records, and military correspondence--to answer [why Germany continued World War II for 3 years after its strategic defeat.] . . . He offers an unprecedented portrait of wartime Germany, bringing the hopes and expectations of the German people--from infantrymen and tank commanders on the Eastern front to civilians on the home front--to vivid life." (Publisher's note)

"A well-researched, unsettling social history of war that will prove deeply thought-provoking—even worrying—for readers who wonder what they might have done under the same circumstances." Kirkus

Tubach, Frederic C.

German voices; memories of life during Hitler's Third Reich. [by] Frederic C. Tubach with Sally Patterson Tubach. University of California Press 2011 273p il $26.95 **943.086**
1. National socialism 2. Germany -- History -- 1933-1945 3. World War, 1939-1945 -- Germany 4. Germany -- Social life and customs
ISBN 978-0-520-26964-4; 0-520-26964-0
LC 2010-51218

"Tubach approaches his mission with a nice, unobtrusive blend of sympathetic warmth and scholarly detachment. . . . The best recommendation I can make—and it is a warm one—is that readers go into German Voices prepared to treat it as one facet of a larger investigation into the phenomenon that was the Third Reich—as a uniquely accessible, honest and frequently thought-provoking window enabling some valuable ground-level insight into the much larger evil behavior that prevailed—until it imploded." PopMatters

Includes bibliographical references

Turner, Henry Ashby

Hitler's thirty days to power; January 1933. {by} Henry Ashby Turner, Jr. Addison-Wesley 1996 255p il hardcover o.p. pa $16 **943.086**
1. Heads of state 2. National socialism 3. Nazi leaders
4. Germany -- Politics and government -- 1918-1933
ISBN 0-201-32800-3 pa
LC 96-20012

The author explores "the fateful 30 days before Hitler became chancellor of Germany in January 1933. Although many of the facts are known, this study reveals that the Nazi dictator did not come to power as the result of 'impersonal forces.' The slender, analytical volume indicates that rather, at a time of mortal peril for Germany—and the world—intrigue was the order of the day in Berlin. . . . Students of German history and extremist movements should enjoy this fast-paced narrative." Publ Wkly

Includes bibliographical references

943.087 Germany--1945-1990

Bessel, Richard

Germany 1945; from war to peace. HarperCollins 2009 522p il map $28.99 **943.087**
1. Reconstruction (1939-1951) 2. World War, 1939-1945 -- Peace 3. Germany -- History -- 1945-1990 4. World War, 1939-1945 -- Germany
ISBN 978-0-06-054036-4; 0-06-054036-2

This is an account of the German home front during the last months of the war. Bessel also writes about the country's path to economic recovery in the second half of 1945.

The author "does an excellent job of evoking the blasted landscape of a conquered Germany—the homelessness and the hunger, the rubble and the mass rape." New Yorker

Includes bibliographical references

Darnton, Robert

Berlin journal, 1989-1990. Norton 1991 352p il hardcover o.p. pa $12.95 **943.087**
1. Berlin (Germany) 2. Germany (East) -- Politics and government
ISBN 0-393-31018-3 pa

LC 90-19745

"Darnton spent parts of 1989 and 1990 in Germany, witnessing the end of that country's division into East and West as the Berlin Wall fell. . . . {He} focuses more on events and aftereffects in East Germany as experienced by ordinary citizens, rather than trying to write a definitive study. Darnton talks with workers, bureaucrats, and government officials and describes what was happening and what the people understood about these momentous events." Booklist

Reeves, Richard

Daring young men; the heroism and triumph of the Berlin Airlift, June 1948-May 1949. Simon & Schuster 2010 316p il map $28 **943.087**
1. Air pilots 2. Air pilots -- Biography 3. Air pilots, Military -- History 4. Berlin (Germany) -- History -- Blockade, 1948-1949
ISBN 978-1-4165-4119-6; 1-4165-4119-5

LC 2009-15333

"'The American people will not allow the German people to starve,' Colonel Frank Howley, one of the top American commanders in Berlin, said in June, 1948, after the Soviets cut off all supply routes except an air corridor to the Western sectors of the city. But when the blockade began, as Reeves notes in his appealing account, almost no one believed that food and fuel for an urban population of more than two million could be delivered by air, and many American officials thought the question was how Berlin could be abandoned with the least embarrassment. Ten and a half months and a quarter-million American and British flights later—an unmatched act of politico-logistical bravado—the Soviets abandoned their blockade." New Yorker

Includes bibliographical references

Sarotte, Mary Elise

The **collapse**; the accidental opening of the Berlin Wall. Mary Elise Sarotte. Basic Books 2014 320 p. illustrations, maps (hardback) $27.99 **943.087**
1. Berlin Wall (1961-1989) 2. Berlin (Germany) --

History 3. Germany (East) -- Politics and government 4. Berlin Wall, Berlin, Germany,1961-1989 5. Berlin (Germany) -- History -- 1945-1990 6. Germany (East) -- Politics and government -- 1989-1990
ISBN 0465064949; 9780465064946

LC 2014026435

In this book on the factors contributing to the fall of the Berlin Wall, "historian Mary Elise Sarotte reveals how a perfect storm of decisions made by daring underground revolutionaries, disgruntled Stasi officers, and dictatorial party bosses sparked an unexpected series of events culminating in the chaotic fall of the Wall." (Publisher's note)

"Amply researched and emotive, this work shares the full narrative of events leading to the fall of the Berlin Wall in a way that both academics and lay readers will appreciate. Those already familiar with the subjects and time frames involved will definitely benefit from the author's extensive research and emphasis on personal narratives." LJ

Includes bibliographical references and index
Accidental opening of the Berlin Wall

Taylor, Frederick

Exorcising Hitler; the occupation and denazification of Germany. [by] Frederick Taylor. Bloomsbury Press 2011 xxxvii, 438p il $30 **943.087**
1. Nazi leaders 2. Denazification 3. Heads of state 4. Germany -- History -- 1945-1955 5. Germany -- History -- 1945-1990 6. Reconstruction (1939-1951) -- Germany 7. Germany -- Politics and government -- 1945-1990
ISBN 1-59691-536-6; 978-1-59691-536-7

LC 2010-46282

This is a "history of the birth of democracy in the ruins of Hitler's Germany." (Publisher's note)

It "chronicles the bitter endgame of war, the murderous Nazi resistance, the vast displacement of people in Central and Eastern Europe, and the nascent cold war struggle between Soviet and Western occupiers." (New York Times Book Review)

Includes bibliographical references

943.155 Berlin (Germany)

Mitchell, Greg

The **tunnels**; Escapes Under the Berlin Wall and the Historic Films the JFK White House Tried to Kill. Greg Mitchell. Crown Publishing 2016 400 p. illustrations, maps (ebook) $65; (hardback) $28 **943.155**
1. Escapes 2. Cold war 3. Refugees 4. Political activists 5. Berlin Wall (1961-1989) 6. Escapes -- Germany (East) -- History 7. Berlin Wall, Berlin, Germany, 1961-1989 8. Refugees -- Germany (East) -- Biography 9. National Broadcasting Company -- History 10. Columbia Broadcasting System, inc. -- History 11. Political activists -- Germany (West) -- Biography 12. Escapes -- Germany -- Berlin -- History -- 20th century 13. Tunnels -- Germany -- Berlin -- History -- 20th century 14. Documentary films -- Censorship -- United States -- History -- 20th century
ISBN 9781101903865; 9781101903858;

9781101903872

LC 2016013452

This book, by Greg Mitchell, is a "Cold War narrative of superpower showdowns, media suppression, and two escape tunnels beneath the Berlin Wall. In the summer of 1962, . . . a group of young West Germans risked prison, Stasi torture, and even death to liberate friends, lovers, and strangers in East Berlin by digging tunnels under the Wall. Then two U.S. television networks heard about the secret projects and raced to be first to document them from the inside." (Publisher's note)

"Mitchell's tense, fascinating account reveals how the U.S. undermined a freedom struggle for the sake of diplomacy." Pub Wkly

Includes bibliographical references and index.

943.703 Czech Republic and Slovakia -- 1918-1992

McNamara, Kevin J.

Dreams of a great small nation; the mutinous army that threatened a revolution, destroyed an empire, founded a republic, and remade the map of Europe. Kevin J. McNamara. PublicAffairs 2016 416 p. maps (hardcover) $28.99   **943.703**
 1. Slovenia 2. Revolutions 3. Czechoslovakia
ISBN 9781610394840; 9781610394857

LC 2016930908

This book, by Kevin J. McNamara, tells how "in 1917, two empires that had dominated much of Europe and Asia teetered on the edge of the abyss, exhausted by the ruinous cost in blood and treasure of the First World War. As Imperial Russia and Habsburg-ruled Austria-Hungary began to succumb, a small group of Czech and Slovak combat veterans stranded in Siberia saw an opportunity to realize their long-held dream of independence." (Publisher's note)

"McNamara's work presents a vital first entry that opens the doors on this integral part of World War I history and the shaping of the Soviet-influenced Eastern European political and social fabric." LJ

Includes bibliographical references (pages 331-379) and index.

943.71 Czech Republic

Albright, Madeleine Korbel

Prague winter; a personal story of remembrance and war, 1937-1948. Madeleine Albright with Bill Woodward. HarperCollins 2012 x, 467 p.p $29.99   **943.71**
 1. Czechoslovakia -- History -- 1918-1968 2. World War, 1939-1945 -- Personal narratives 3. Prague (Czech Republic) -- Biography 4. Czechoslovakia -- History -- 1938-1945 5. World War, 1939-1945 -- Czechoslovakia 6. World War, 1939-1945 -- Czech Republic -- Prague 7. Prague (Czech Republic) -- History -- 20th century 8. Jewish families -- Czech Republic -- Prague -- Biography
ISBN 0062030310; 9780062030313

LC 2011049416

This book by Madeleine Albright chronicles her personal "experiences, and those of her family . . . [during] the years of 1937 to 1948. . . . The book takes readers from the Bohemian capital . . . to the bomb shelters of London, from the desolate prison ghetto of Terezin to the highest councils of European and American government. Albright reflects on her discovery of her family's Jewish heritage many decades after the war, [and] on her Czech homeland's tangled history." (Publisher's note)

Includes bibliographical references and index.

Demetz, Peter

Prague in black and gold; scenes from the life of a European city. Hill & Wang 1997 411p maps hardcover o.p. pa $15   **943.71**
 1. Prague (Czech Republic) -- History
ISBN 0-8090-1609-5 pa

LC 96-52216

The author presents an "account of the city's history and culture by focusing on epic events as well as heroes, villains and martyrs throughout the millennia of its existence. . . . A highly literate panorama of a focal point of European culture." Publ Wkly

Includes bibliographical references

943.8 Poland

The **Chronicle** of the Lodz ghetto, 1941-1944; edited by Lucjan Dobroszycki; translated by Richard Lourie {et al.} Yale Univ. Press 1984 lxviii, 551p il hardcover o.p. pa $37   **943.8**
 1. Jews -- Poland 2. Holocaust, 1933-1945 3. Lodz (Poland) -- Social conditions
ISBN 0-300-03924-7 pa

LC 84-3614

"The record is made more profoundly melancholic by the restrained archivist style employed by the chroniclers." New Statesman (1913)

943.9 Hungary

Michener, James A.

The **bridge** at Andau. Fawcett Crest 1983 277p pa $6.99   **943.9**
 1. Hungarian refugees 2. Hungary -- History -- 1956, Revolution
ISBN 978-0-449-21050-5; 0-449-21050-2
First published 1957 by Random House

"The heroism, horror and tragedy of the 1956 Hungarian revolt is revealed through interviews with many refugees who crossed the bridge at Andau to freedom." Cleveland Public Libr

944 France and Monaco

Baldwin, Rosecrans, 1977-

Paris, I love you but you're bringing me down; Rosecrans Baldwin. Farrar, Straus and Giroux 2012 286 p. **944**

1. Autobiographies 2. Americans -- France 3. Paris (France) -- Description and travel 4. Paris (France) -- Biography 5. Couples -- France -- Paris -- Biography 6. Americans -- France -- Paris -- Biography 7. Paris (France) -- Social life and customs

ISBN 0374146683; 9780374146689

LC 2011045886

This expatriate memoir by Rosecrans Baldwin presents an account of his time living in Paris, France. "Baldwin discovered some very French things about office life in Paris: You have to eat lunch, because the company docks a portion of your pay and returns it to you as meal coupons. . . . It's virtually impossible to get fired. . . . The author also discovered that French banks seem never to have heard of credit cards, and although he and wife qualified as legal residents for health-insurance coverage, the cards permitting them to actually use the insurance didn't arrive until a month before they left. Nonetheless, despite tight finances and loud construction work around their apartment, Baldwin fell in love just like everyone else." (Kirkus)

Buckley, Veronica

The **secret** wife of Louis XIV; Francoise d'Aubigne, Madame de Maintenon. Farrar, Straus and Giroux 2009 498p il map $35 **944**

1. Kings 2. Royal favorites 3. France -- History -- 1589-1789, Bourbons

ISBN 978-0-374-15830-9; 0-374-15830-4

LC 2008-16210

This is "a lively, sympathetic portrayal of the woman who, against all odds, succeeded in taming the royal tomcat." N Y Times Book Rev

Includes bibliographical references

Downie, David

A **passion** for Paris; romanticism and romance in the City of Light. David Downie. St. Martin's Press 2015 320 p. illustrations (hardback) $26.99 **944**

1. Romanticism 2. Paris (France)

ISBN 1250043158; 9781250043153

LC 2015007261

This memoir, by David Downie, is the author's "irreverent quest to uncover why Paris is the world's most romantic city--and has been for over 150 years. . . . Weaving together his own with the lives and loves of Victor Hugo, Georges Sand, Charles Baudelaire, Balzac, Nadar and other great Romantics, Downie delights in the city's secular romantic pilgrimage sites." (Publisher's note)

"The author's encyclopedic knowledge of the city and its artists grants him a mystical gift of access: Doors left ajar and carriage gates left open foster his search for the city's magical story. Anyone who loves Paris will adore this joyful book. Readers visiting the city are advised to take it with them to discover countless new experiences." Kirkus

Fiennes, Ranulph, 1944-

Agincourt; The Fight for France. Ranulph Fiennes. Pegasus 2015 336 p. plts; ills; mps; chrt; g tabls $26.95 **944**

1. War 2. France -- History -- 1589-1789, Bourbons

ISBN 1605989150; 9781605989150

Author Ranulph Fiennes "account of the Battle of Agincourt gives a unique perspective on one of the most significant battles in English history. With fascinating detail on the battle plans, weaponry, and human drama of Agincourt, this is a gripping evocation of a historical event integral to English identity. Six hundred years after the Battle of Agincourt, Sir Ranulph Fiennes casts new light on this epic event that has resonated throughout British and French history." (Publisher's note)

"Despite its shortcomings, Fiennes's strong narrative style pulls readers along quickly, leaving plenty of time to tackle another more authoritative book on Agincourt such as Juliet Barker's Agincourt: Henry V and the Battle That Made England." Library Journal

Fraser, Antonia

Marie Antoinette; the journey. Talese 2001 xxii, 512p il $35; pa $16.95 **944**

1. Queens 2. France -- History -- 1589-1789, Bourbons

ISBN 0-385-48948-X; 0-385-48949-8 pa

LC 2001-23493

"A well-researched biography that may cause one to rethink the role in which history has cast Marie Antoinette." Libr J

Includes bibliographical references

Goldstone, Nancy

The **rival** queens; Catherine De' Medici, her daughter Marguerite De Valois, and the betrayal that ignited a kingdom. Nancy Goldstone. Little, Brown & Co. 2015 448 p. 8 plates; color ills., maps $30 **944**

1. France -- History -- 1328-1589, House of Valois

ISBN 0316409650; 9780316409650

LC 2014955135

This book by Nancy Goldstone is the "true story of mother-and-daughter queens Catherine de' Medici and Marguerite de Valois, whose wildly divergent personalities and turbulent relationship changed the shape of their tempestuous and dangerous century. Treacherous court politics, poisonings, inter-national espionage, and adultery form the background to a story that includes such celebrated figures as Elizabeth I, Mary, Queen of Scots, and Nostradamus." (Publisher's note)

"This highly accessible account is recommended for general but serious readers interested in European history and royal biography." LJ

Gordon, Mary

★ **Joan** of Arc. Viking 2000 xxv, 180p (Penguin lives series) $19.95 **944**

1. Saints 2. Christian saints 3. France -- History -- 1328-1589, House of Valois

ISBN 0-670-88537-1

LC 99-55678

"This biography rehearses the well-known highlights in Joan's short life: the voices she heard who charged her with the mission to save France, her participation in the Battle of Orléans and the coronation of King Charles VII; her trial by an ecclesiastical court, where she was charged with witchcraft, heresy and idolatry.... The strength of this 'biographical meditation' lies in the penultimate chapter, in which Gordon investigates the numerous re-creations of Joan on stage and screen." Publ Wkly

Includes bibliographical references

Green, David

The **Hundred** Years War; a people's history. David Green. Yale University Press 2014 360 p. 16 plates; illustrations; maps (cl : alk. paper) $40 **944**
1. Hundred Years' War, 1339-1453 2. France -- History -- 1328-1589, House of Valois 3. Great Britain -- History -- 1066-1485, Medieval period 4. France -- History, Military -- 1328-1589 5. France -- Foreign relations -- Great Britain 6. Great Britain -- Foreign relations -- France 7. Great Britain -- History, Military -- 1066-1485

ISBN 0300134517; 9780300134513
LC 2014014233

This book, by David Green, profiles "the Hundred Years War (1337-1453) [which] dominated life in England and France for well over a century. . . . [The author] focuses on the ways the war affected different groups, among them knights, clerics, women, peasants, soldiers, peacemakers, and kings. He also explores how the long war altered governance in England and France and reshaped peoples' perceptions of themselves and of their national character." (Publisher's note)

"This impressive survey ought to be included in any collection on the Middle Ages or the history of England and France. Summing Up: Highly recommended. All levels/libraries." Choice

100 Years War

Horne, Alistair

★ La belle France; a short history. Knopf 2005 485p il map $30 **944**
1. France -- History

ISBN 1-4000-4140-6
LC 2004-42329

First published 2004 in the United Kingdom with title: Friend or foe: an Anglo-Saxon history of France

"This compelling narrative belongs in any public library needing an excellent, current one-volume history of France." Booklist

Includes bibliographical references

Seven ages of Paris. Knopf 2002 448p $35; pa $16 **944**
1. Paris (France)

ISBN 0-679-45481-0; 1-4000-3446-9 pa
LC 2002-29653

The author traces "the history of Paris through seven periods, beginning in the 12th century and ending with the death of Charles de Gaulle in 1969. . . . Each section includes fascinating insights into the social and cultural life of the age, fashions in clothing, architectural developments, leading personalities, and lifestyles of rich and poor alike.

With the verve of a master storyteller, Horne captures Parisians' 'zest for living.'" Libr J

Includes bibliographical references

Jones, Colin

Paris; biography of a city. Colin Jones. Viking 2005 xxv, 566p il map $29.95 **944**
1. Paris (France)

ISBN 0-670-03393-6
LC 2004-53608

First published 2004 in the United Kingdom

"Moving from prehistoric tribal habitation through Roman times, medieval uncertainty and splendor, early modern religious wars, Enlightenment, revolution, and two world wars, Jones examines how rulers, economy, religion and violence have shaped the city. . . . Anyone who loves Paris will find connections and revelations here, a Paris of the mind that resonates through the centuries." Publ Wkly

Includes bibliographical references

Jonnes, Jill

Eiffel's tower; and the World's Fair where Buffalo Bill beguiled Paris, the artists quarreled, and Thomas Edison became a count. Viking 2009 354p il map $27.95 **944**
1. Structural engineers 2. Eiffel Tower (Paris, France) 3. Exposition Universelle de 1889 (Paris, France)

ISBN 978-0-670-02060-7; 0-670-02060-5
LC 2008-49839

"Not long after Gustave Eiffel, an engineer and builder of railway bridges, won the contract to build a centerpiece attraction for the 1889 World's Fair, he faced a barrage of criticism of its design as well as financial, architectural, mechanical, and political obstacles to its construction. Jonnes . . . captures the verve and personality of the Belle Epoque as Paris struggled to show the world its glory. . . . [She also] details the iconic figures who added to the allure of the fair—James McNeill Whistler, Paul Gauguin, Thomas Edison, Annie Oakley, and Buffalo Bill—and the excitement and ambitions of the era." Booklist

Includes bibliographical references

Kaplan, Alice

Dreaming in French; the Paris years of Jacqueline Bouvier Kennedy, Susan Sontag, and Angela Davis. Alice Kaplan. University of Chicago Press 2012 x, 289 p.p **944**
1. Paris (France) -- History 2. Foreign students -- France 3. Women -- United States -- Biography 4. Women -- United States -- Intellectual life 5. Students, Foreign -- France -- Paris -- Biography 6. United States -- Civilization -- French influences

ISBN 0226424383; 9780226424385
LC 2011026598

This book by Alice Kaplan offers a biographical account of the "transformative Parisian experiences of three strikingly different young women: Jacqueline Bouvier Kennedy, Susan Sontag, and Angela Davis. . . . In her comparisons of the three women's experiences, . . . she argues . . . about the impact of Paris on the rest of their lives: Bouvier's, aesthetic; Sontag's, intellectual; and Davis's, political." (Choice: Current Reviews for Academic Libraries)

Includes bibliographical references and index

Karnow, Stanley

Paris in the fifties; illustrations by Annette Karnow. Times Bks. 1997 352p il hardcover o.p. pa $14　　　**944**

1. French national characteristics 2. France -- Politics and government 3. Paris (France) -- Social life and customs

ISBN 0-8129-3137-8 pa

LC 97-18521

"Not content with simply ensconcing himself in the Time bureau offices, . . . Karnow created a personal life for himself and took in all that Paris and the provinces had to offer. And now he offers this succulent book, which Francophiles will devour." Booklist

Lever, Evelyne

Madame de Pompadour; translated from the French by Catherine Temerson. Farrar, Straus & Giroux 2002 310p il $26; pa $16.95　　　**944**

1. Royal favorites 2. France -- History -- 1589-1789, Bourbons

ISBN 0-374-11308-4; 0-312-31050-1 pa

LC 2002-22811

Original French edition, 2000

"Lever has crafted a detailed and fascinating portrait of the woman who pretty well ran France from 1745 to 1764." Publ Wkly

Includes bibliographical references

Moorehead, Caroline

Village of Secrets; Defying the Nazis in Vichy France. by Caroline Moorehead. HarperCollins 2014 384 p. illustrations, maps $27.99　　　**944**

1. World War, 1939-1945 -- France 2. World War, 1939-1945 -- Underground movements

ISBN 0062202472; 9780062202475

LC 2014497785

This book, by Caroline Moorehead, tells the "story of a French village that helped save thousands hunted by the Gestapo during World War II. . . . Le Chambon-sur-Lignon is a small village . . . high in the mountains of the Ardèche. . . . During the Second World War, the inhabitants of this tiny mountain village and its parishes saved thousands wanted by the Gestapo: resisters, freemasons, communists, OSS and SOE agents, and Jews." (Publisher's note)

"Moorehead not only recounts the heroics but also the everyday ordinariness of those involved, busting the embellished mythology while emphasizing the essential humanity of the entire operation." Booklist

Paris was ours; thirty-two writers reflect on the City of Light. edited by Penelope Rowlands. Algonquin Books of Chapel Hill 2011 279p pa $15.95　　　**944**

1. Paris (France) -- Description and travel

ISBN 978-1-56512-953-5; 1-56512-953-9

LC 2010-30560

In this anthology "Penelope Rowlands culled 32 essays, stories and poems, some original, some previously published, from writers who include professors, single mothers, gay men, a homeless woman, a wealthy Iranian and a poor young Cuban. The collection takes some of the shine off Paris but not the allure — not unlike the pull of a troubled but passionate lover who could never be more than a fling. . . . Ultimately, the writers fall in love with Paris, a city that embraces sorrow, depression, snarkiness, human frailty and living in the moment no matter the menial task that entails. In dismantling the dream of Paris, they reveal an infinitely more complex city and people." Minneapolis Star Tribune

Riding, Alan

And the show went on; cultural life in Nazi-occcupied Paris. Alfred A. Knopf 2010 399p il map $28.95　　　**944**

1. Popular culture -- France 2. World War, 1939-1945 -- France 3. France -- Social life and customs 4. Paris (France) -- Intellectual life 5. France -- History -- 1940-1945, German occupation

ISBN 978-0-307-26897-6; 0-307-26897-7

LC 2010-16841

"This engrossing work, rich in detail, should appeal to French historians and serious readers interested in 20th-century cultural history." Libr J

Includes bibliographical references

Robb, Graham

Parisians; an adventure history of Paris. W.W. Norton & Co. 2010 475p il map $28.95　　　**944**

1. Paris (France) -- History

ISBN 978-0-393-06724-8; 0-393-06724-6

LC 2009-54279

Part history, part travelog, part Ripley's Believe It or Not!, this creative historical geography takes us on a tour of Paris via a series of chronologically arranged vignettes stretching from the eve of the Revolution of 1789 to the present. . . . The book records a series of moments and meetings when characters both obscure and famous interacted with key landmarks like the Palais Royal, Notre Dame, or Place de la Concorde. Robb . . . recreates the drama and turmoil of key events like the bloody horrors of the Commune, De Gaulle's triumphant 1944 entry into Paris, or the tumultuous student demonstrations of May 1968. Libr J

Includes bibliographical references

Sante, Luc

The **other** Paris; Luc Sante. Farrar, Straus & Giroux 2015 320 p. illustrations, map (hardback) $27　　　**944**

1. Poverty 2. Paris (France) 3. France -- Social conditions 4. Poor -- France -- Paris -- History 5. Paris (France) -- Social conditions 6. Criminals -- France -- Paris -- History 7. Paris (France) -- Description and travel 8. Working class -- France -- Paris -- History 9. City and town life -- France -- Paris -- History 10. Paris (France) -- Social life and customs -- 19th century 11. Paris (France) -- Social life and customs -- 20th century 12. Eccentrics and eccentricities -- France -- Paris --

History
ISBN 0374299323; 9780374299323; 9781429944588
LC 2015004988

In this book on Paris, France, author "Luc Sante gives us a panoramic view of that second metropolis, which has nearly vanished but whose traces are in the bricks and stones of the contemporary city, in the culture of France itself, and, by extension, throughout the world.Drawing on testimony from a great range of witnesses-from Balzac and Hugo to assorted boulevardiers, rabble-rousers, and tramps-Sante . . . takes the reader on a whirlwind tour." (Publisher's note)

"A fascinating stroll through a vanished, wild past. Recommended for general readers." LJ

Includes bibliographical references and index

Tuchman, Barbara Wertheim

A **distant** mirror; the calamitous 14th century. {by} Barbara W. Tuchman. Knopf 1978 xx, 677p il maps hardcover o.p. pa $17.95   **944**
1. Plague 2. Crusades 3. Medieval civilization 4. Women -- Europe 5. World history -- 14th century 6. Church history -- 600-1500, Middle Ages 7. France -- History -- 1328-1589, House of Valois 8. Great Britain -- History -- 1154-1399, Plantagenets
ISBN 0-345-34957-1 pa

LC 78-5985

The author traces the history of the fourteenth century by following the career of a "feudal lord, Enguerrand de Coucy VII, the seigneur of some 150 towns and villages in Picardy. He was born in 1340, and he died in captivity in 1397, having been made a prisoner by the Turks." Time

Includes bibliographical references

Williams, Charles

The **last** great Frenchman; a life of General de Gaulle. Wiley 1995 544p il $30; pa $19.95 **944**
1. Generals 2. Statesmen 3. Presidents 4. Prime ministers
ISBN 0-471-11711-0; 0-471-18071-8 pa

LC 94-42881

The author offers "appraisals of de Gaulle's career as soldier, politician and head of state. Williams contrasts the infuriatingly obstinate public figure with the private man, emotional and affectionate in the bosom of his family. Especially interesting is the account of de Gaulle's tender relationship with his retarded daughter. . . . The author also sheds light on de Gaulle's determined anti-Americanism during his final years." Publ Wkly

Includes bibliographical references

Yalom, Marilyn

How the French invented love; nine hundred years of passion and romance. HarperCollins 2012 416 p. $15.99   **944**
1. Cultural critique 2. French literature 3. Love in literature
ISBN 0062048317; 9780062048318

This book offers author Marilyn Yalom's literary investigation into "how the French manage their romances, marriages, affairs, and obsession with love and sex." She "argues that it's not only gender-specific traits and roles that are socially constructed, but love, too. For example, 'Les liaisons dangereuses' . . . is still on the list of required reading in French high schools." (Publishers Weekly)

944.04   France since 1789

Burke, Edmund

★ **Reflections** on the Revolution in France; edited by J.C.D. Clark. Stanford Univ. Press 2001 446p $65; pa $29.95   **944.04**
1. France -- History -- 1789-1799, Revolution
ISBN 0-8047-3923-4; 978-0-8047-3923-8; 0-8047-4205-7 pa; 0-8047-4205-4 pa

LC 00-63732

First published 1790

"A treatise by Edmund Burke, written in the form of a letter to a Frenchman. It attacks the leaders and principles of the French Revolution for their violence and excesses, and urges reform, rather than rebellion, as a means of correcting social and political abuses." Benet's Reader's Ency. 4th edition

Includes bibliographical references

Lefebvre, Georges

The **French** Revolution. Columbia Univ. Press 1962 2v hardcover o.p. v1 pa $32; v2 pa $32 **944.04**
1. France -- History -- 1789-1799, Revolution
ISBN 0-231-08598-2 v1 pa; 0-231-08599-0 v2 pa

Original French edition, 1930; this translation is based on 1957 reprintings

An account of the political, military, social, economic and intellectual aspects of the French Revolution.

Includes bibliographical references

McPhee, Peter

★ **Liberty** or death; the French Revolution, 1789-1799. Peter McPhee. Yale University Press 2016 488 p. (cloth : alk. paper) $35   **944.04**
1. France -- History -- 1789-1799, Revolution 2. France -- History -- Revolution, 1789-1799
ISBN 9780300189933

LC 2015040677

This book, by Peter McPhee, discusses "the French Revolution [which] has fascinated, perplexed, and inspired for more than two centuries. It was a seismic event that radically transformed France and launched shock waves across the world. In this . . . new history, Peter McPhee draws on a lifetime's study of eighteenth-century France and Europe to create an entirely fresh account of the world's first great modern revolution—its origins, drama, complexity, and significance." (Publisher's note)

"McPhee (emeritus, history, Univ. of Melbourne; Robespierre: A Life) has written on many aspects of the French Revolution but never more beneficially than in this articulate and perceptive volume. McPhee's revolution is truly national in scope; Paris interacting with the hinterlands rather than a case of Paris playing the dog and the rest of France the tail. The author also makes solid use of primary source materials from outside France. . . . Numerous histories of the French Revolution exist; while many are good, none is so current on the literature and lucidly presented as this. Scholars and history lovers will rejoice." LJ

Reiss, Tom, 1964-

★ The **Black** Count; glory, revolution, betrayal, and the real Count of Monte Cristo. Tom Reiss; [maps by David Lindroth Inc.] Crown Trade 2012 ix, 414 p.p maps (hardcover) $27   **944.04**
1. Generals -- France -- Biography 2. France. Armée -- Biography 3. France -- History, Military -- 1789-1815
ISBN 030738246X; 9780307382467; 9780307952950

LC 2012017633

Pulitzer Prize: Biography (2013)

This book by Tom Reiss, which won the Pulitzer Prize for biography presents the story of "General Alex Dumas, . . . the son of a black slave--who rose higher in the white world than any man of his race. . . . Born in Saint-Domingue (now Haiti), Alex Dumas was briefly sold into bondage but made his way to Paris where he was schooled as a sword-fighting member of the French aristocracy. Enlisting as a private, he rose to command armies at the height of the Revolution." (Publisher's note)

Includes bibliographical references (p. [341]-403) and index

944.05   Period of First Empire, 1804-1815

Johnson, Paul

★ **Napoleon.** Viking 2002 190p (Penguin lives series) hardcover o.p. pa $13   **944.05**
1. Emperors 2. France -- Kings and rulers
ISBN 0-670-03078-3; 0-14-303745-5 pa

LC 2001-45605

Johnson "presents a concise appraisal of Napoleon's career and a precise understanding of his enigmatic character. The author views Napoleon, not as an 'idea man' whose ideology was the ladder by which he propelled himself to heights of power, but as an opportunist who took advantage of a series of events and situations he could manipulate into achieving supreme control." Booklist

Includes bibliographical references

Schom, Alan

One hundred days; Napoleon's road to Waterloo. Oxford University Press 1993 398p pa $45 **944.05**
1. Emperors 2. Waterloo, Battle of, 1815
ISBN 978-0-19-508177-0; 0-19-508177-3

LC 93-11787

First published 1992 by Atheneum

This is an account of "Napoleon's escape from Elba in February 1815 and his return . . . to France. Rallying the nation behind him, he mustered his army and marched off to meet Wellington at Waterloo. . . . This is a first-class reconstruction of Napoleon's final campaign." Publ Wkly

Includes bibliographical references

944.081   Period of Third Republic, 1870-1945

Bredin, Jean-Denis

The **affair**; the case of Alfred Dreyfus. translated from the French by Jeffrey Mehlman. Braziller 1986 628p il hardcover o.p. pa $19.95   **944.081**
1. Antisemitism 2. Trials 3. Army officers 4. France -- Politics and government -- 1815-1914
ISBN 0-8076-1175-1 pa

LC 85-22374

Original French edition, 1983

In his examination of the case, the author seeks to "set the affair within the . . . currents of French history and the rising tide of anti-Semitism." (Choice) Bibliography. Index. Originally published in France in 1983.

"That Bredin manages to be both passionate and exact is his first outstanding virtue. He is admirably free of the baroque conspiracy theories that sprout so luxuriantly on both sides of this case." N Y Rev Books

Includes bibliographical references

Brown, Frederick

For the soul of France; culture wars in the age of Dreyfus. Alfred A. Knopf 2010 304p il $28.95   **944.081**
1. French national characteristics 2. Nationalism -- France 3. France -- History -- 1815-1914
ISBN 978-0-307-26631-6; 0-307-26631-1

LC 2009-30912

"Brown recounts the history of France, following its 1789 revolution, as an ongoing contest between the champions and foes of the Enlightenment. . . . The humiliating defeat of the Franco-Prussian War of 1870-71 was followed by the economic crash of 1882 and the Panama Company bribery scandal of 1893, both of which were reputedly executed by Jewish masters. . . . In 1894, an opportunity for revenge presented itself in the person of Alfred Dreyfus, a 34-year-old Jewish army officer. Accused of espionage on the flimsiest of evidence—fabrications, and forgeries—Dreyfus was twice tried and convicted. Dreyfus was eventually freed in 1906, one year after a law requiring the separation of church and state had passed. Secularism seemed to hold sway. But, as Brown demonstrates in his brilliant study, religious fervor and bellicose patriotism combined in World War I to shift the balance yet again." Boston Globe

Includes bibliographical references

Derfler, Leslie

★ The **Dreyfus** affair. Greenwood Press 2002 xxii, 167p il (Greenwood guides to historic events, 1500-1900) $44.95   **944.081**
1. Antisemitism 2. Army officers 3. France -- Politics and government -- 1815-1914
ISBN 0-313-31791-7

LC 2001-38365

"Following a chronology is a 'Historical Overview' containing several chapters of background and analysis. These chapters provide context for what is commonly known as the Dreyfus affair, discuss how anti-Semitism and socialism played into and were affected by the affair, and summarize how the affair has been viewed through history. The next section is an A-Z collection of biographies of almost 20 key individuals. . . . Primary documents comprise the next chapter and most documents are accompanied by short explanations. . . . This guide is useful for researchers who need more information than they can find in an encyclopedia." Booklist

Includes bibliographical references

Read, Piers Paul, 1941-

The **Dreyfus** affair; the scandal that tore France in two. Piers Paul Read. Bloomsbury Press 2012 408 p. **944.081**

1. Treason 2. Scandals 3. Antisemitism 4. France -- History -- 1815-1914 5. France -- Intellectual life -- 19th century 6. Scandals -- France -- History -- 19th century 7. France -- History -- Third Republic, 1870-1940 8. France -- Politics and government -- 1870-1940 9. Trials (Treason) -- Political aspects -- France 10. Antisemitism -- France -- History -- 19th century 11. Religion and politics -- France -- History -- 19th century ISBN 1608194329; 9781608194322

LC 2011034456

This historical work by Piers Paul Read reviews the Dreyfus Affair. "Captain Alfred Dreyfus was a rising star in the French artillery command. . . . However, Dreyfus had enemies as a result of his ambition. . . . On the basis of flimsy evidence, Dreyfus was placed under arrest for the crime of high treason. Not long afterward, he was sentenced to spend the rest of his life on the legendary, lethal Devil's Island. The saga of Dreyfus's many trials . . . the fight to free him, and the intrigues on both sides, is a . . . story rife with heroes and villains. . . . The anti-Semitism and deceit on display in the Dreyfus case was an ominous prelude to the Holocaust and the long, bloody twentieth century to come." (Publisher's note)

Includes bibliographical references and index.

944.083 Period of Fifth Republic, 1958-

Mayle, Peter

Encore Provence; new adventures in the south of France. Knopf 1999 226p **944.083**

1. Authors 2. Humorists 3. Provence (France) 4. Children's authors 5. Nonfiction writers 6. Provence (France) -- Social life and customs ISBN 0679441247; 0679762698

LC 99-62335

Mayle, the author of A Year in Provence (1990) and Toujours Provence (1991), discusses his experiences after "he and his wife returned to Provence after an absence of four years." (Booklist)

Mayle's "book is all about the renewal of his acquaintance with the land he so loves. Essays range widely over Provençal life. . . . His observations and commentaries are laced with humor but encompass true respect and admiration for his adopted homeland." Booklist

A **year** in Provence; illustrations by Judith Clancy. Knopf 1990 207p il $19.95 **944.083**

1. Provence (France) -- Social life and customs ISBN 0394572300

LC 89-38475

First published 1989 in the United Kingdom

"Peter Mayle recently emigrated to the South of France, where he has bought and modernized a house close to the village of Ménerbes in the Lubéron. A Year in Provence is his account of a settler's experiences, beginning with his arrival in January and ending with a party for the builders to celebrate the house's completion the following Christmas." (Times Lit Suppl)

White, Edmund

The **flaneur**; a stroll through the paradoxes of Paris. Bloomsbury Pub. 2001 211p maps $16.95 **944.083**

1. Paris (France) -- Description and travel ISBN 1-58234-135-4

LC 00-46812

"White is richly informed, and his evocative writing should appeal to both armchair travelers and visitors to Paris." Libr J

944.084 France -- 2000-

Chirac, Jacques, 1932-

My life in politics; Jacques Chirac; edited by Catherine Spencer. Palgrave Macmillan 2012 352 p. **944.084**

1. France -- Politics and government 2. Presidents -- France -- Biography 3. France -- Politics and government -- 1958-
ISBN 0230340881; 9780230340886

LC 2012018097

This book by "[t]wo-time president of France, mayor of Paris, and international politician" Jacques Chirac "covers the full scope of Chirac's political career of more than 50 years. . . . As mayor of Paris, Chirac was famed for his success in beautifying the City of Lights and keeping it whole during the heady days of the 1968 riots. As president in the 1990s and early 2000s, Chirac took controversial steps to privatize the economy and plan the European Union." (Publisher's note)

944.36 France -- Paris

Anselmo, Lisa

My (part-time) Paris life; How Running Away Brought Me Home. Lisa Anselmo. Thomas Dunne Books/St. Martin's Press 2016 256 p. (hardcover) $25.99; (ebook) $66 **944.36**

1. Self-realization 2. Mother-daughter relationship 3. Paris (France) -- Description and travel 4. Paris (France) -- Biography 5. Self-actualization (Psychology) 6. Mothers -- United States -- Death 7. Women -- France -- Paris -- Biography 8. Mothers and daughters -- United States 9. Americans -- France -- Paris -- Biography 10. Paris (France) -- Desctription and travel 11. Paris (France) -- Social life and customs ISBN 9781250067470; 9781466875821

LC 2016007864

This memoir by Lisa Anselmo, "is for anyone who's ever felt lost or hopeless, but still dreams of something more.

... [It] explores one woman's search for peace and meaning, and how the ups and downs of expat life in Paris taught her to let go of fear, find self-worth, and create real, lasting happiness in the City of Light." (Publisher's note)

"In the end, this is a sweet and inspiring account of one woman's taxing yet rewarding search for peace, happiness, and contentment in the City of Light." Pub Wkly

Brassaï, 1899-1984

Brassai; Paris by Night. by Brassai. Random House Inc. 2012 96 p. illustrations $45   **944.36**
1. Night 2. Photography 3. Paris (France)
ISBN 2080200992; 9782080200990

In this book, by Brassaï, "he sensed that photography was the tool that would allow him to document his vision of a dying society. Fascinated by the night, which he found disconcerting, enigmatic, and suggestive, Brassaï photographed its every aspect, from police to prostitutes to the homeless to socialites, all in a dreamlike and mysterious manner." (Publisher's note)

Carhart, Thad

Finding Fontainebleau; an American boy in France. Thad Carhart. Viking 2016 304 p. map (hardback) $27   **944.36**
1. Americans -- France 2. France -- Description and travel 3. Fontainebleau (France) -- Biography 4. Boys -- France -- Fontainebleau -- Biography 5. Americans -- France -- Fontainebleau -- Biography 6. Fontainebleau (France) -- Buildings, structures, etc 7. Château de Fontainebleau (Fontainebleau, France) 8. Fontainebleau (France) -- Social life and customs -- 20th century
ISBN 9780525428800; 0525428801
LC 2016008395

This book, by Thad Carhart, is a "memoir of a childhood in 1950s Fontainebleau. Each trip to Fontainebleau introduces him to entirely new aspects of the château's history, enriching his memories and leading him to Patrick Ponsot, the head of the château's restoration, who becomes Carhart's guide to the hidden Fontainebleau." (Publisher's note)

"Carhart's meandering, warmly evocative anecdotes register both the quirkiness of France's traditions and the civilizing, humanizing influence they exert." Pub Wkly

945   Italy, San Marino, Vatican City, Malta

Berendt, John

The city of falling angels; a Venice story. Penguin Press 2005 414p $25.95; pa $15   **945**
1. Venice (Italy) -- Social life and customs
ISBN 1-59420-058-0; 1-59420-061-0 pa
LC 2005-47661

The author describes some of his encounters with contemporary Venetians. The starting point for his travels was the investigation of the fire which destroyed La Fenice opera house in 1996.

Berendt "delivers an urbane, beautifully fashioned book with much exotic charm. . . . [The author] makes erudite, inquisitive, nicely skeptical company as he leads the reader through the shadows of what was heretofore better known as a tourist attraction." N Y Times (Late N Y Ed)

Bosworth, R. J. B.

Mussolini's Italy; life under the dictatorship, 1915-1945. Penguin 2006 xxvi, 692p il map $35   **945**
1. Heads of state 2. Fascism -- Italy 3. Italy -- History -- 1914-1945
ISBN 1-59420-078-5
LC 2005-52127

First published 2005 in the United Kingdom
Bosworth "combines prodigious research with a clear writing style that will appeal to all readers interested in the Italy of Il Duce." Libr J
Includes bibliographical references

Capponi, Niccolo

The Day the Renaissance Was Saved; The Battle of Anghiari and Da Vinci's Lost Masterpiece. Niccolo Capponi; translated by Andre Naffis-Sahely. Random House Inc 2015 240 p. 16 plates; illustrations $26.95   **945**
1. Renaissance 2. Painting -- 15th and 16th centuries
ISBN 1612194605; 9781612194608
LC 2015955589

In this book author "Niccolò Capponi--a direct descendent of Niccolò Machiavelli, as well as of a Florentine general who was a key strategist of the campaign at Anghiari--weaves the story of da Vinci's lost masterpiece through the narrative of the history-changing battle, and offers context on the development of humanist thought and the political intrigues of fifteenth-century Italy." (Publisher's note)

"A significant survey of an important battle and its outcomes as retold by an expert of Italian Renaissance military and political history, this book will be of interest mostly to scholars, graduate students, and some general readers of the subject. For both large public and academic libraries." LJ

Clark, Robert

Dark water; flood and redemption in the city of masterpieces. Doubleday 2008 354p il $26   **945**
1. Floods 2. Florence (Italy)
ISBN 978-0-7679-2648-5; 0-7679-2648-X
LC 2008-1695

This is an account of the Florence flood of 1966.
The author "tells an enthralling true story in a way that makes it read like a novel." Economist
Includes bibliographical references

Crowley, Roger

★ City of fortune; how Venice ruled the seas. Roger Crowley. Random House 2011 xxix, 432 p.p (alk. paper) $32.00   **945**
1. Venice (Italy) 2. Italy -- History 3. Medieval civilization 4. Venice (Italy) -- Commerce -- History 5. Venice (Italy) -- History -- 697-1508 6. Merchants -- Italy -- Venice -- History 7. Mediterranean Region -- Commerce -- History 8. Venice (Italy) -- Economic conditions -- To 1797
ISBN 1400068207; 9780679644262; 9781400068203
LC 2011005529

Author Roger Crowley "narrate[s] the rise and apogee of the empire acquired by Venice [Italy] between 1000 and 1500 . . . [It discusses] . . . the collective nature of the medieval Venetian state, its organisation and its awe-inspiring effectiveness [and] . . . draws the substantive difference between Venice and Genoa in their centuries-long struggle for commercial and economic dominance." (History Today)

Includes bibliographical references (p. [407]-415) and index

Frieda, Leonie

The **Deadly** Sisterhood; A Story of Women, Power, and Intrigue in the Italian Renaissance, 1427-1527. Leonie Frieda. HarperCollins 2013 xi, 403 p.p (hardcover) $32.50 **945**
1. Renaissance 2. Women -- Biography 3. Italy -- History -- 0-1559
ISBN 0061563080; 9780061563089

This book, by Leonie Frieda, provides a biography of "eight women whose lives . . . encompass the spectacle, opportunity, and depravity of Italy's Renaissance. Lucrezia Turnabuoni, Clarice Orsini, Beatrice d'Este, Isabella d'Este, Caterina Sforza, Giulia Farnese, Isabella d'Aragona, and Lucrezia Borgia shared the riches of their birthright: wealth, political influence, and friendship, but none were not exempt from personal tragedies, exile, and poverty." (Publisher's note)

Hazzard, Shirley

The **ancient** shore; dispatches from Naples. [by] Shirley Hazzard and Francis Steegmuller. University of Chicago Press 2008 129p il $18; pa $13 **945**
1. Italy -- Description and travel
ISBN 978-0-2263-2201-8; 0-2263-2201-7; 978-0-226-32202-5 pa; 0-226-32202-5 pa
LC 2008-15420

"Much larger than all its parts, this book does full justice to a place, and a time, where 'nothing was pristine, except the light.'" Bookforum

Hibbert, Christopher

The **Borgias** and their enemies; 1431-1519. Harcourt, Inc. 2008 328p $26 **945**
1. Kings 2. Italy -- History
ISBN 978-0-15-101033-2; 0-15-101033-1
LC 2008-03076

"Lucrezia Borgia, on hearing that her father, Pope Alexander VI, was choosing her third husband, noted that her first two had been 'very unlucky.' Luck had little to do with it, as Hibbert shows in this vivid chronicle of the notoriously corrupt Renaissance family. One husband was killed on the orders of her brother Cesare, whose ruthlessness made him the model for Machiavelli's 'The Prince'; the other was discarded after ceasing to be politically useful to the Pope. Hibbert ably traces the web of alliances through which the Spanish-born Alexander hoped to secure his hold on Italy and his family's place in power." New Yorker

Includes bibliographical references

Hughes, Robert

Rome; a cultural, visual, and personal history. Alfred A. Knopf 2011 498p il $35 **945**
1. Rome -- History
ISBN 978-0-307-26844-0; 0-307-26844-6
LC 2011-14600

The author "gives us a guided tour through the city in its many incarnations, excavating the geologic layers of its cultural past and creating an indelible portrait of a city in love with spectacle and power . . . The reader need not agree with Mr. Hughes's acerbic assessments or even be interested in Rome as a destination on the map to relish this volume, so captivating is his narrative. Although his book is a biography of Rome, it is also an acutely written historical essay informed by his wide-ranging knowledge of art, architecture and classical literature, and a thought-provoking meditation on how gifted artists (like Bernini and Michelangelo) and powerful politicians and church leaders (like Augustus, Mussolini and Pope Sixtus V) can reshape the map and mood of a city." n Y times Book Rev

Includes bibliographical references

Keahey, John

Seeking Sicily; a cultural journey through myth and reality in the heart of the Mediterranean. Thomas Dunne Books/St. Martin's Press 2011 312p il $27.99; ebook $14.99 **945**
1. Sicily (Italy) -- Description and travel 2. Sicily (Italy) -- Social life and customs
ISBN 978-0-312-59705-4; 978-1-4299-9067-7 ebook
LC 2011026786

The author "takes a meandering and inspiring tour through the history, culture, and landscape of Sicily, an island that has been a crossroads for the various peoples of the Mediterranean for millennia. . . . Keahey's thoroughly researched book will inspire any traveler to look past the Sicily of the traditional tourist's guide and appreciate its diverse, layered, and sometimes dark history." Libr J

Includes bibliographical references

Lee, Alexander

The **ugly** Renaissance; Alexander Lee. Doubleday 2013 448 p. 16 plts; ills; gen. tabl; map $30 **945**
1. Renaissance 2. Italy -- History -- 0-1559 3. Art -- 15th and 16th centuries 4. Renaissance -- Italy 5. Italy -- Civilization -- 1268-1559 6. Italy -- Social life and customs -- To 1500 7. Degeneration -- Social aspects -- Italy -- History -- To 1500
ISBN 0385536593; 9780385536592
LC 2013015480

This book, by Alexander Lee, offers "a . . . counterintuitive portrait of the sordid, hidden world behind the dazzling artwork of Michelangelo, Leonardo da Vinci, Botticelli, and more. . . . Renaissance scholar Alexander Lee illuminates the dark and titillating contradictions that were hidden beneath the surface of the period's best-known artworks." (Publisher's note)

"This highly inviting history should appeal widely to both scholars and casual readers." LJ

Includes bibliographical references and index

Leon, Donna

My Venice and Other Essays; by Donna Leon. Pgw 2013 240 p. $26 **945**
1. Venice (Italy)
ISBN 0802120369; 9780802120366

This book, by Donna Leon, presents "over fifty . . . essays that range from battles over garbage in the canals to the troubles with rehabbing Venetian real estate. She shares episodes from her life in Venice, explores her love of opera, and recounts tales from in and around her country house in the mountains. With pointed observations and humor, she also explores her family history and former life in New Jersey, and the idea of the Italian man." (Publisher's note)

Madden, Thomas F.

Venice; a new history. Thomas F. Madden. Viking 2012 xi, 446 p.p (hbk. : alk. paper) $35   **945**
    1. Venice (Italy) -- History
    ISBN 0670025429; 9780670025428
                    LC 2012005304

This book on the history of Venice by Thomas Madden "trac[es] an arc from the city's humble origins as a lagoon refuge to its apex as a vast maritime empire and Renaissance epicenter to its rebirth as a modern tourist hub. Madden explores all aspects of Venice's . . . achievements . . . its role as an economic powerhouse and birthplace of capitalism, its popularization of opera, the stunning architecture of its watery environs, and more." (Publisher's note)

Includes bibliographical references and index.

Mayes, Frances

Under the Tuscan sun; at home in Italy. Chronicle Bks. 1996 280p $22.95   **945**
    1. Italian cooking 2. Tuscany (Italy) -- Social life and customs
    ISBN 0-8118-0842-4
                    LC 96-15137

"Casual and conversational, {Ms. Mayes's} chapters are filled with craftsmen and cooks, with exploratory jaunts into the countryside—but what they all boil down to is an intense celebration of what she calls 'the voluptuousness of Italian life.' Occasionally, this leads to the sort of gushy observations you might expect from a besotted lover. But more often it produces an appealing and very vivid snapshot imagery." N Y Times Book Rev

Parks, Tim

Italian ways; on and off the rails from Milan to Palermo. Tim Parks. W W Norton & Co Inc 2013 288 p. (hardcover) $25.95   **945**
    1. Railroad travel -- Italy 2. Italy -- Description and travel 3. Italy -- Social life and customs
    ISBN 0393239322; 9780393239324
                    LC 2013011386

In this book, author Tim Parks "pokes affectionate fun at his fellow train travelers and surveys a rapidly changing Italian landscape. . . . Here, he chronicles his adventures on the nation's rails. . . . Train travel in Italy is the ultimate leveler, Parks finds, and it provides a microcosm of what is transpiring in the society as a whole since globalization has taken root. His observations mingle travelogue, history and memoir, spanning the years from 2005 to the present." (Kirkus Reviews)

Strathern, Paul, 1940-

Death in Florence; the Medici, Savonarola and the battle for the soul of the Renaissance city. Paul Strathern. W W Norton & Co Inc 2015 464 p. 8 plates; color ills., maps $29.95   **945**
    1. Martyrs 2. Renaissance 3. Florence (Italy) 4. Monks 5. Political leaders 6. Patrons of the arts 7. Writers on religion 8. Florence (Italy) -- History -- 1421-1737
    ISBN 160598826X; 9781605988269

In this book on Florence, Italy author "Paul Strathern reveals the paradoxes, self-doubts, and political compromises that made the battle for the soul of the Renaissance city one of the . . . important moments in Western history. By the end of the fifteenth century . . . the ruling Medici embodied the progressive humanist spirit. In the form of Savonarola, an unprepossessing provincial monk, Lorenzo [de Medici] found his nemesis. The battle between these two men would be a fight to the death, a series of sensational events." (Publisher's note)

"Strathern brings his two opponents to life by including a great deal about their physicality (Lorenzo was plagued by gout and arthritis; Savonarola had a plain face but eyes that burned with intensity). The juxtaposition of Lorenzo's and Savonarola's lives and approaches to life adds to the sense of a 'cat and mouse game' throughout this riveting narrative history." Booklist

Taylor, Benjamin

Naples declared; a walk around the bay. Benjamin Taylor. G.P. Putnam's Sons 2012 240 p.   **945**
    1. Local history 2. Naples (Italy) 3. City and town life 4. Naples (Italy) -- History 5. Naples, Bay of (Italy) -- History 6. City and town life -- Italy -- Naples 7. Naples (Italy) -- Description and travel 8. Naples (Italy) -- Social life and customs 9. Naples, Bay of (Italy) -- Description and travel
    ISBN 0399159177; 9780399159176
                    LC 2011049450

This book by Benjamin Taylor provides a description of Naples, Italy with "discussions of history, philosophy, religion, art, culture, literature, [and] customs. The book meanders between past and present, wanders in stream-of-thought fashion through the Naples streets, delves . . . into the city's stories, lives, and lore, and drops in for conversations with locals . . ." (Library Journal)

"[including] present-day encounters with a fervently communist doctor, with a chain-smoking student of Faulkner, and with novelist Shirley Hazzard." (Kirkus)

Includes bibliographical references and index

945.091   Reign of Victor Emmanuel III, 1900-1946

Bosworth, R. J. B.

Mussolini. Oxford Univ. Press 2002 584p il hardcover o.p. pa $14.95   **945.091**
    1. Heads of state 2. Fascism -- Italy 3. Italy -- Politics and government
    ISBN 0-340-73144-3; 0-340-80988-4 pa
                    LC 2002-283267

This is "the definitive study of the Italian dictator and belongs in every public and academic library with a strong European history collection." Libr J

Includes bibliographical references

Corner, Paul

The **Fascist** Party and popular opinion in Mussolini's Italy; by Paul Corner. Oxford University Press 2012 302 p. (hbk.) $125   **945.091**

1. Public opinion 2. Fascism -- Italy 3. Fascism -- Italy -- History 4. Fascism -- Italy -- Public opinion 5. Partito nazionale fascista (Italy) 6. Public opinion -- Italy -- History -- 20th century

ISBN 0198730691; 9780198730699

LC 2012462711

Focusing on fascism in Italy, author Paul Corner "argues that 'real existing Fascism', as lived by a large part of the population, was in fact an increasingly negative experience and reflected few of those colourful and attractive features of fascist propaganda which have induced more favourable interpretations of the regime. Distinguishing clearly between the fascist project and its realisation, Corner examines the ways in which the fascist party asserted itself at the local level." (Publisher's note)

945.093   Italy -- 2000-

Hooper, John

The **Italians**; John Hooper. Penguin Group USA 2015 336 p. illustrations $28.95   **945.093**

1. Italians 2. Italy -- Civilization

ISBN 0525428070; 9780525428077

LC 2014038474

This book, by John Hooper, "a vivid and surprising portrait of the Italian people. . . . Digging deep into their history, culture, and religion, Hooper offers keys to understanding everything from their bewildering politics to their love of life and beauty. Looking at the facts that lie behind the stereotypes, he sheds new light on many aspects of Italian life." (Publisher's note)

"'Few countries,' writes the author, 'are as comprehensively associated with happiness as Italy. Just the mention of its name brings to mind sunny days, blue skies, glittering seas; delicious, comforting food; good-looking, well-dressed people; undulating hills topped with cypress trees; museums crammed with much of the best of Western art.' What's not to love? A thoroughly researched, well-written, ageless narrative of a fascinating people." Kirkus

945.51   Florence

Strathern, Paul, 1940-

The **Medici**; Power, Money, and Ambition in the Italian Renaissance. by Paul Strathern. W W Norton & Co Inc 2016 464 p. $28.95   **945.51**

1. Renaissance 2. Medici, House of 3. Florence (Italy) -- History

ISBN 1605989665; 9781605989662

In this book, author Paul Strathern "explores the . . . rise and fall of the Medici family in Florence, as well as the

Italian Renaissance which they did so much to sponsor and encourage. Strathern also follows the lives of many of the great Renaissance artists with whom the Medici had dealings, including Leonardo, Michelangelo and Donatello; as well as scientists like Galileo and Pico della Mirandola." (Publisher's note)

"A fantastically comprehensive history covering the breadth of the great learning, art, politics, and religion of the period." Kirkus

Includes bibliographical references (pages 413-417) and index.

945.731   Italy -- Naples

Wilson, Katherine

Only in Naples; lessons in food and famiglia from my Italian mother-in-law. Katherine Wilson. Random House Inc 2016 304 p. (hardback : acid-free paper) $27   **945.731**

1. Naples (Italy) 2. Cooking -- Italy -- Naples 3. Families -- Italy -- Naples 4. Naples (Italy) -- Biography 5. Americans -- Italy -- Naples -- Biography 6. Naples (Italy) -- Social life and customs 7. Mothers-in-law -- Italy -- Naples -- Biography 8. Daughters-in-law -- Family relationships -- Italy -- Naples

ISBN 9780812998160

LC 2015016098

This memoir, by Katherine Wilson, "follows American-born Katherine Wilson on her adventures abroad. Thanks to a surprising romance—and a spirited woman who teaches her to laugh, to seize joy, and to love—a three-month rite of passage in Naples turns into a permanent embrace of this boisterous city on the Mediterranean." (Publisher's note)

"Each experience, each delicious meal is insightfully described as the reader follows Wilson's path toward carnale, becoming confident and comfortable in one's own skin." Booklist

945.8   Sicily and adjacent islands

Norwich, John Julius

Sicily; John Julius Norwich. Random House 2015 400 p. 16 plates; color ills; map (hardback : acid-free paper) $32   **945.8**

1. Sicily (Italy) 2. Italy -- History 3. Sicily (Italy) -- History 4. Sicily (Italy) -- Civilization 5. Sicily (Italy) -- History, Military 6. Sicily (Italy) -- Kings and rulers -- History

ISBN 0812995171; 9780812995176

LC 2015007371

Author "John Julius Norwich's engrossing narrative is the first to knit together all of the colorful strands of Sicilian history into a single comprehensive study. Here is a vivid, erudite, page-turning chronicle of an island and the remarkable kings, queens, and tyrants who fought to rule it." (Publisher's note)

"This excellent, informative source on natural features, art and architecture, and regional lifestyles is not to be missed by armchair travelers, history lovers, and fans of Norwich's previous works." LJ

Includes bibliographical references and index

946 Spain, Andorra, Gibraltar, Portugal

Goodwin, Robert

Spain; The Center of the World 1519-1682. by Robert Goodwin. St. Martin's Press 2015 608 p. 16 plates; ills.; maps; ports. $40 **946**

1. Spain -- History

ISBN 1620403609; 9781620403600

LC 2014415759

This book, by Robert Goodwin, focuses on the "Golden Age of the Spanish Empire. . . . From scholars and playwrights, to poets and soldiers, Goodwin is in complete command of the history of this tumultuous and exciting period. But the superstars alone will not tell the whole tale--Goodwin delves deep to find previously unrecorded sources and accounts of how Spain's Golden Age would unfold, and ultimately, unravel." (Publisher's note)

"Anyone wanting a better idea of the feel of this phase of Spanish history will be well served by this title. Accompanying maps and a genealogical chart are helpful." LJ

Kamen, Henry

Philip of Spain. Yale Univ. Press 1997 384p il maps hardcover o.p. pa $18.95 **946**

1. Kings 2. Spain -- History

ISBN 0-300-07081-0; 0-300-07800-5 pa

LC 96-52421

"Kamen's prose is lucid, succinct, and thorough. . . . In humanizing a man too often viewed as a cardboard tyrant, Kamen has made a valuable contribution to European historiography." Booklist

Includes bibliographical references

Kurlansky, Mark

The **Basque** history of the world. Penguin 2001 387p il map pa $15 **946**

1. Basque Provinces (France and Spain)

ISBN 978-0-14-029851-2; 0-14-029851-7

First published 1999 by Walker & Co.

"This book traces the history of the Basques from their mysterious origins to their politically fraught existence in this century. . . . Kurlansky shows how Basques, famed for their geographic and linguistic isolation, have played significant roles in world history-as mercenaries in ancient Greece, whalers in the Middle Ages, explorers in the Americas, and even cautious supporters of modern European integration." New Yorker

Lowney, Chris

A **vanished** world; medieval Spain's golden age of enlightenment. Free Press 2005 320p il map $26 **946**

1. Spain -- Civilization

ISBN 0-7432-4359-5

LC 2004-56362

This is a history of Spain between the Muslim conquest in 711 and the driving of Muslims from Iberia in 1492, during which the author argues there was a tentative peace between Christians, Muslims, and Jews.

The author "successfully brings the story of medieval Spain to a wider audience and draws out of this rich history important lessons for the post-9/11 world." Christ Sci Monit

Includes bibliographical references

Tremlett, Giles

Ghosts of Spain; travels through Spain and its secret past. Walker 2007 386p $26.95 **946**

1. Spain -- Description and travel 2. Spain -- Social life and customs

ISBN 0-8027-1574-5; 978-0-8027-1574-6

First published 2006 in the United Kingdom

An "examination of the Franco years and their legacy make a somber backdrop for an otherwise cheery tale. Having summoned the ghosts, [the author] moves along to offer a guided tour of modern Spain, making stops at the usual journalistic destinations. The educational system, politics, health care, child rearing and the national character are dealt with in well-organized chapters that move the reader briskly along. . . . A highly informative, well-written introduction to post-Franco Spain." N Y Times (Late N Y Ed)

946.081 Period of Second Republic, 1931-1939

Hochschild, Adam

Spain in our hearts; Americans in the Spanish Civil War, 1936/1939. Adam Hochschild. Houghton Mifflin Harcourt 2016 464 p. illustrations, maps (hardcover) $30 **946.081**

1. Americans -- Spain 2. Spain -- History -- 1936-1939, Civil War

ISBN 9780547973180; 9780547974538

LC 2015037244

This book, by Adam Hochschild, offers "a sweeping history of the Spanish Civil War, told through a dozen [American expatriate] characters, including Ernest Hemingway and George Orwell: a tale of idealism, heartbreaking suffering, and a noble cause that failed. . . . It was in many ways the opening battle of World War II, and we still have much to learn from it." (Publisher's note)

"Hochschild ably explores subtle shades of the conflict that contemporary authors and participants did not want to consider." Kirkus

Includes bibliographical references and index

Lewis, Norman

The **tomb** in Seville; crossing Spain on the brink of civil war. introduction by Julian Evans. Carroll & Graf 2005 150p $20; pa $14.95 **946.081**

1. Spain -- Description and travel

ISBN 0-7867-1439-5; 0-7867-1687-8 pa

First published 2003 in the United Kingdom

"Reading the author's account of his travels in a country on the brink of war is almost as satisfying as being there." Booklist

Rhodes, Richard

Hell and Good Company; The Spanish Civil War and the World It Made. Richard Rhodes. Simon &

Schuster 2015 384 p. 16 plates; illustrations; maps $30 **946.081**
    1. War stories 2. Spain -- History -- 1936-1939, Civil War
ISBN 1451696213; 9781451696219

This book by Richard Rhodes looks at the "story of the Spanish Civil War through the eyes of the reporters, writers, artists, doctors, and nurses who witnessed it. He takes us into battlefields and bomb shelters, into the studios of artists, into the crowded wards of war hospitals, and into the hearts and minds of a rich cast of characters to show how the ideological, aesthetic, and technological developments that emerged in Spain changed the world forever." (Publisher's note)

"Despite the inclusion of a superb bibliography, the author's interpretation seems stuck in 1936. Other recent histories offer a more complicated and, in many instances, a more nuanced understanding of events and the actions of key personalities and groups. Summing Up: Recommended. General and undergraduate libraries." Choice

946.083 Reign of Juan Carlos I, 1975-

Stewart, Chris
    Driving over lemons; an optimist in Andalucia. Pantheon Bks. 2000 248p il maps hardcover o.p. pa $13.95 **946.083**
    1. Spain -- Description
ISBN 978-0-375-41028-4; 978-0-375-70915-9 pa; 0-375-70915-0 pa

                        LC 99-56675

"The ability to write hilarious travelogues featuring excruciating scenes of discomfort may well be a {British} national characteristic. It's certainly possessed by Chris Stewart." N Y Times Book Rev

947 Russia and neighboring east European countries

Applebaum, Anne
    ★ **Iron** curtain; the crushing of Eastern Europe, 1945-1956. Anne Applebaum. Doubleday 2012 xxxvi, 566 p.p (hardcover) $35.00 **947**
    1. Communism -- Russia 2. Soviet Union -- Social conditions 3. Communist countries -- Social conditions 4. Europe, Eastern -- Relations -- Soviet Union 5. Soviet Union -- Relations -- Europe, Eastern 6. Communist countries -- Politics and government 7. Europe, Eastern -- Social conditions -- 20th century 8. Communism -- Europe, Eastern -- History -- 20th century 9. Europe, Eastern -- Politics and government -- 1945-1989 10. Political culture -- Europe, Eastern -- History -- 20th century 11. Political persecution -- Europe, Eastern -- History -- 20th century 12. Communism -- Social aspects -- Europe, Eastern -- History -- 20th century
ISBN 9780385515696; 0385515693

                        LC 2012022086

In this book, "journalist Anne Applebaum delivers a . . . history of how Communism took over Eastern Europe after World War II." She "describes how the Communist regimes of Eastern Europe were created and what daily life was like

once they were complete. She draws on newly opened East European archives, interviews, and personal accounts translated for the first time to portray . . . the dilemmas faced by millions of individuals." (Publisher's note)
    Includes bibliographical references and index.

Drakulic, Slavenka
    Cafe Europa; life after communism. Penguin Books 1999 213p pa $14 **947**
    1. Eastern Europe -- Social conditions 2. Eastern Europe -- Politics and government
ISBN 978-0-14-027772-2; 0-14-027772-2

    First published 1996 in the United Kingdom; first United States edition published 1997 by Norton

    The author of these pieces is "at once critical of a culture that remains bleakly conformist in the aftermath of Communist rule and empathetic for its having known nothing else. With consistent equanimity, she examines the frustrating plight of the novice Balkan democracies. On a more quotidian level, too, she finds that much is wanting, measured against Western standards of richesse, congeniality, and even taxi service. Owing largely to Drakulic's knack for drawing humor from an abundance of anecdotes—whether about a toothpaste monopoly or the bureaucratic cartwheels required to purchase a vacuum cleaner—these essays read like stories." New Yorker

Erickson, Carolly
    Great Catherine. St. Martin's Griffin 1995 392p pa $18.95 **947**
    1. Empresses 2. Russia -- History 3. Russia -- Kings and rulers
ISBN 0-312-13503-3

                        LC 95-22619

    First published 1994 by Crown
    "Erickson's fluid, captivating portrait of Catherine the Great reads like a first-rate historical novel." Booklist

Figes, Orlando, 1959-
    The **Crimean** War; a history. Metropolitan Books 2010 576p il map $35; e-book $16.99 **947**
    1. Crimean War, 1853-1856
ISBN 978-0-8050-7460-4; 0-8050-7460-0; 978-1-4299-9724-9 e-book; 1-4299-9724-9 e-book

                        LC 2010-23152

    Published in the United Kingdom with title: Crimea
    This "is a complex tale, told vividly by Mr Figes. Perhaps it should serve as a healthy cold shower for any modern civilisational warrior who sets out to present the course of history as a simple tug-of-war between Christianity and Islam." Economist
    Includes bibliographical references

Hosking, Geoffrey A.
    ★ **Russia** and the Russians; a history. {by} Geoffrey Hosking. Belknap Press 2001 718p il map $35; pa $18.95 **947**
    1. Russia -- History 2. Soviet Union -- History
ISBN 0-674-00473-6; 0-674-01114-7 pa

                        LC 00-65085

"This is a high-quality overview, suitable for all libraries." Booklist

Russia: people and empire, 1552-1917; {by} Geoffrey Hosking. Harvard Univ. Press 1997 548p maps $33; pa $15.16　　　　**947**

1. Russian national characteristics 2. Russia -- History
ISBN 0-674-78118-X; 0-674-78119-8 pa

LC 97-5069

The author explores the question "of how and why the Russians never developed a sense of nation. He argues that the Russian monarchy and aristocracy were always more interested in building an expansive empire than in promoting the belief in nationhood, something understood by the powerless peasantry. The expensive and inefficient bureaucracy that emerged over the centuries weighed against any possibility of community, and in the end this tottering edifice was unable to withstand the cataclysm of World War I. Hosking has brought a powerful intellect and great erudition to this work." Libr J

Includes bibliographical references

King, David

Red star over Russia; a visual history of the Soviet Union from the revolution to the death of Stalin: posters, photographs and graphics from the David King collection. Abrams 2009 345p il $50　　**947**

1. Russian art 2. Soviet Union -- History -- Pictorial works
ISBN 978-0-8109-8279-6; 0-8109-8279-X

In this survey "the graphics used to promote the workers' paradise deserve admiration. But the rest of this extraordinarily illustrated book provides witness to the corrosive effects of ham-handed propaganda, and to the role of state-sanctioned imagery in demeaning and subjugating the arts. Red Star Over Russia is a mammoth collection of rare Soviet applied art and photographs . . . organized not into individual chapters, but into pages and spreads devoted to a range of themes addressed in graphic and photographic materials, including 'Political Abstraction,' 'Urban Proletariat' and 'Workers of the World, Unite.' Prominent artists like El Lissitzky and Gustav Klutsis are featured." N Y Times Book Rev

Kotkin, Stephen

Uncivil society; 1989 and the implosion of the communist establishment. with a contribution by Jan T. Gross. Modern Library 2009 197p il map (Modern Library chronicles) $24　　　　**947**

1. Soviet Union -- Social conditions 2. Eastern Europe -- Social conditions 3. Soviet Union -- Politics and government 4. Eastern Europe -- Politics and government
ISBN 978-0-679-64276-3; 0-679-64276-5

LC 2009-12903

"Combining scholarship with sparkling prose, the authors recount a thoroughly satisfying historical struggle in which the good guys won." Publ Wkly

Includes bibliographical references

Massie, Robert K., 1929-

Catherine the Great; portrait of a woman. Robert K. Massie. Random House 2011 xiii, 625p ill. (some col.), maps　　　　**947**

1. Biography 2. Empresses 3. Russia -- Kings and rulers
ISBN 9780679456728; 9781588360441

LC 2011015279

Presents a reconstruction of the eighteenth-century empress's life that covers her efforts to engage Russia in the cultural life of Europe, her creation of the Hermitage, and her numerous scandal-free romantic affairs.

"Massie delivers a fascinating account of dog-eat-dog politics in 18th-century Europe and the larger-than-life Russian empress who gave as good as she got." Kirkus

Includes bibliographical references

Massie, Suzanne

Land of the firebird; the beauty of old Russia. Hearttree 1980 493p il pa $32　　　　**947**

1. Russian art 2. Russia -- Civilization
ISBN 978-0-9644184-1-7; 0-9644184-1-X

First published 1980 by Simon & Schuster

The author's intent "is to give 'a sense of the whole, now-vanished culture of old Russia . . . to describe that beauty which the Russians once knew how to create, what they loved, and admired and how they once lived and rejoiced.'" N Y Times Book Rev

Includes bibliographical references

Pleshakov, Konstantin

There is no freedom without bread! 1989 and the civil war that brought down communism. [by] Constantine Pleshakov. Farrar, Straus, and Giroux 2009 289p $26　　　　**947**

1. Communism 2. Berlin Wall (1961-1989) 3. Poland -- Politics and government 4. Soviet Union -- Politics and government 5. Eastern Europe -- Politics and government
ISBN 978-0-374-28902-7; 0-374-28902-6

LC 2009-10185

The author's "explanation of the 1989 collapse respects the complexity of Eastern Europe, yet his account is both clear and beautifully lyrical. His greatest strength lies in not being burdened by doctrine; he finds worth in communists and in Reagan. . . . Pleshakov writes history with a human face." Washington Post Book World

Includes bibliographical references

Polonsky, Rachel

Molotov's magic lantern; travels in Russian history. Farrar, Straus and Giroux 2011 390p map $27; ebook $14.99　　　　**947**

1. Diplomats 2. Authors, Russian 3. Communism and literature 4. Cabinet members 5. Communist leaders 6. Soviet Union -- Intellectual life 7. Moscow (Russia) -- Description and travel 8. Russia (Federation) -- Description and travel
ISBN 978-0-374-21197-4; 978-1-4299-7490-5 ebook

LC 2010-23037

Polonsky "has produced a spectacular and enjoyable display of intellectual fireworks for the general reader. . . . Her finely drawn literary travelogues on Taganrog, Murmansk, Vologda, Irkutsk and other places depict squalor, pomp, misery, exhilaration, heroism and brutishness, each cameo framed in its historical, cultural and physical context. . . . She has a knack for putting herself into other people's shoes with empathy and skill. . . . The author has grit, charm and style—and a gift for traveller's tales." Economist

Riasanovsky, Nicholas V.

A **history** of Russia; 8th ed; Oxford University Press 2011 various paging il map pa $64.95 **947**
1. Russia -- History 2. Soviet Union -- History
ISBN 978-0-19-534197-3
LC 2010-23174
First published 1963
This narrative history includes discussions of economics, social organization, religion, and culture.
Includes bibliographical references

Sebestyen, Victor

Revolution 1989; the fall of the Soviet empire. Pantheon Books 2009 xxi, 451p il $30 **947**
1. Soviet Union -- Politics and government 2. Eastern Europe -- Politics and government
ISBN 978-0-375-42532-5; 0-375-42532-2
LC 2009-23045
"Numerous books have come out that attempt to synthesize the compelling story of the fall of communism, but Revolution 1989 comes closest to being the essential volume. Sebestyen's elegant narrative lays out in crisp episodes what was happening in Russia, Bulgaria, East Germany, Hungary, Czechoslovakia, and Afghanistan throughout the tumultuous 1980s. His portrait of Gorbachev is particularly sharp—and asks us to reconsider the Soviet leader's surprising role 20 years ago. As a refugee from Hungary in 1956, Sebestyen brings a personal touch to these historic moments." Daily Beast
Includes bibliographical references

Volkov, Solomon

St. Petersburg; a cultural history. translated by Antonina W. Bouis. Free Press 1995 598p il hardcover o.p. pa $26.50 **947**
1. Poets 2. Authors 3. Dancers 4. Composers 5. Dramatists 6. Choreographers 7. Essayists 8. Nobel laureates for literature 9. Saint Petersburg (Russia) -- History
ISBN 0-684-83296-8 pa
LC 95-24116
Four of Volkov's "six very long chapters revolve around figures representative of certain periods or trends in the evolution of the St. Petersburg myth: Akhmatova, Balanchine, Shostakovich and Brodsky. Aspects of these central biographical and cultural portraits lead him . . . into countless mini-biographies of related figures." N Y Times Book Rev

Warnes, David

Chronicle of the Russian tsars; the reign-by-reign record of the rulers of imperial Russia. Thames & Hudson 1999 224p il $34.95 **947**
1. Russia -- History 2. Russia -- Kings and rulers
ISBN 0-500-05093-7
LC 98-61289
The introduction provides a "historical overview of how Tsarism came into being. The succeeding chapters are divided by major political events and social upheaval. . . . The reign of each tsar is analyzed within this framework, highlighting major events, but also giving abundant personal details such as marriages, children, etc." SLJ
Includes bibliographical references (p. 218-219) and index

947.08   Russia since 1855

Kurth, Peter

Tsar: the lost world of Nicholas and Alexandra; photographs by Peter Christopher. Little, Brown 1995 229p il hardcover o.p. pa $29.95 **947.08**
1. Emperors 2. Empresses 3. Russia -- History
ISBN 0-316-50787-3; 0-316-55788-9 pa
LC 95-12820
In text and photographs, this volume examines the lives of Tsar Nicholas II, the Empress Alexandra, and the Russian Imperial family.
"A large format and a profusion of illustrations ostensibly mark it a picture book; instead it is a remarkably comprehensive overview of the reign of the last czar and his consort. . . . Kurth sensitively documents the imperial family's suffering as prisoners of the Bolsheviks and their eventual execution." Booklist
Includes bibliographical references

Massie, Robert K., 1929-

The **Romanovs;** the final chapter. Random House 1995 308p il hardcover o.p. pa $14.95 **947.08**
1. Emperors 2. Empresses 3. Forensic anthropology 4. Impostors 5. Royal pretenders 6. Russia -- Kings and rulers
ISBN 0-394-58048-6; 0-345-40640-0 pa
LC 95-4718
This book "is divided into three major parts. The first segment—by far the most fascinating and original—focuses on the complex scientific process used in identifying the Romanovs' remains. . . . The second part concerns the various impostors who have claimed to be members of the Russian imperial family. . . . [The] third segment [is] a report on those Romanov émigrés—close relatives of the Czar's—who survived the Bolsheviks' persecution." N Y Times Book Rev
Includes bibliographical references

Pipes, Richard

The **Russian** Revolution. Knopf 1990 xxiv, 944p il maps hardcover o.p. pa $25 **947.08**
1. Russia -- History
ISBN 0-679-73660-3 pa
LC 89-35129

This is a "massive, wonderfully vivid, gripping chronicle. . . . No other book so brilliantly clarifies the inner dynamics of the Russian Revolution." Publ Wkly

Includes bibliographical references

947.084   Russia (Soviet Union)--1917-1991

Amis, Martin

Koba the dread; laughter and the twenty million. Hyperion 2002 306p il $24.95   **947.084**
1. Heads of state 2. Communist leaders 3. Political leaders 4. Soviet Union -- Politics and government
ISBN 0-7868-6876-7

"Amis create{s} a compelling narrative, summarizing vast amounts of information and presenting it in a lucid, accessible form." New York Times

Brent, Jonathan

Stalin's last crime; the plot against the Jewish doctors, 1948-1953. {by} Jonathan Brent and Vladimir P. Naumov. HarperCollins 2003 399p $26.95; pa $14.95   **947.084**
1. Heads of state 2. Communist leaders 3. Political leaders 4. Jews -- Persecutions
ISBN 0-06-019524-X; 0-06-093310-0 pa
LC 2002-191930

"This book points out suspicious inconsistencies in official accounts of Stalin's death and fingers chief of secret police Beria as a likely assassin. . . . Brent and Naumov link Stalin's famously anti-Semitic 'Doctors' Plot,' in which Jewish doctors were unjustly accused of conspiring to murder important politicians, to the ridiculous 'plan of the internal blow,' another alleged conspiracy of officials supposedly aiding an American plan to nuke the Kremlin itself. The authors argue that these Stalin-engineered plots were to be used by the paranoid dictator as justification for nuclear war. Tales of Stalin's paranoia are nothing new, but rarely are his subtle, yet relentless, machinations laid out in such intricate detail." Booklist

Includes bibliographical references

Competing voices from the Russian Revolution; edited by Michael C. Hickey. Greenwood 2011 xiii, 599p ill. (alk. paper) $65.00   **947.084**
1. History -- Sources 2. World War, 1914-1918 3. Russia -- History -- 1917-1921, Revolution 4. Social conflict -- Soviet Union -- History -- Sources 5. Soviet Union -- History -- Revolution, 1917-1921 -- Sources 6. Soviet Union -- Politics and government -- 1917-1936 -- Sources 7. Soviet Union -- History -- Revolution, 1917-1921 -- Personal narratives 8. Soviet Union -- History -- Revolution, 1917-1921 -- Social aspects -- Sources
ISBN 9780313385230; 0313385238; 9780313385247; 0313385246
LC 2010039676

This book "presents documents that underscore the . . . public discussion about key events and issues during the 1917 Russian Revolution, one of the pivotal events in modern history. . . . [T]he documents . . . clarify the issues while revealing the broad range of ways in which Russians understood the events unfolding around them. Focusing on

public rhetoric and debate in Russia from the outbreak of World War I in 1914 through the dissolution of the Constituent Assembly in January 1918, the documents present the views not only of key political figures, but also of ordinary men and women—mothers, soldiers, factory workers, peasants, students, businesspeople, and educated professionals." (Publisher's note)

Includes bibliographical references (p. 583-588) and index.

Figes, Orlando

A **people's** tragedy; the Russian Revolution, 1891-1924. Viking 1997 xx, 923p hardcover o.p. pa $25   **947.084**
1. Soviet Union -- History -- 1917-1921, Revolution
ISBN 0-14-024364-X pa
LC 96-36761

First published 1996 in the United Kingdom

The author has "produced an engagingly written and well-researched book that will leave few readers with any doubts that the Bolsheviks, and especially their leader, Lenin, were ruthless killers, willing to sacrifice millions of lives for the sake of power and their own personal ambitions." N Y Times Book Rev

Includes bibliographical references

★ The **whisperers**; private life in Stalin's Russia. Metropolitan Books 2007 xxxviii, 739p il map $35   **947.084**
1. Communism -- Soviet Union 2. Soviet Union -- Social conditions
ISBN 978-0-8050-7461-1; 0-8050-7461-9
LC 2007-24223

"This is a humbling monument to the evil and endurance of Russia's Soviet past and, implicitly, a guide to its present." Economist

Includes bibliographical references

Gellately, Robert

Stalin's curse; battling for communism in war and Cold War. by Robert Gellately. Knopf 2013 496 p. $32.50   **947.084**
1. Communism -- Russia 2. Communism -- Europe -- History -- 20th century 3. Soviet Union -- Politics and government -- 1936-1953
ISBN 0307269159; 9780307269157
LC 2012028768

Author Robert Gellately presents an "account based on newly released Russian documentation that reveals Joseph Stalin's true motives--and the extent of his enduring commitment to expanding the Soviet empire--during the years in which he seemingly collaborated with Franklin D. Roosevelt, Winston Churchill, and the capitalist West." (Publisher's note)

Includes bibliographical references and index

Hochschild, Adam

The **unquiet** ghost; Russians remember Stalin. Houghton Mifflin 2003 304p il map pa $14.95   **947.084**
1. Heads of state 2. Communist leaders 3. Political

leaders 4. Soviet Union -- History
ISBN 978-0-618-25747-8; 0-618-25747-0
First published 1994 by Viking
In this look at Stalin's legacy the author "visits the ruins of the old prison camps of Kazakhstan and Kolyma, digs through the K.G.B. archives and spends a night at Stalin's seaside retreat. Most important, he interviews camp survivors, camp guards and the children of both. The questions he asks are of universal significance. . . . By asking these questions while traveling through today's Russia, Mr. Hochschild effectively places Stalinism in a modern context." N Y Times Book Rev
Includes bibliographical references

Medvedev, Roy Aleksandrovich, 1925-
★ **Let** history judge; the origins and consequences of Stalinism. {by} Roy Medvedev. rev and expanded ed; Columbia Univ. Press 1989 xxi, 903p $104; pa $35 **947.084**
1. Heads of state 2. Communist leaders 3. Political leaders 4. Political crimes and offenses 5. Soviet Union -- Politics and government 6. Soviet Union -- Politics and government -- 1925-1953
ISBN 0-231-06350-4; 0-231-06351-2 pa
LC 89-758
Original Russian edition copyrighted 1967; first United States edition published 1972 by Knopf
The first two parts of this book examine Stalin's rise in the Communist Party, and his assumption of power and reliance on repression. The last two sections consider the nature and causes of Stalinism as well as the effects of Stalin's dictatorship. Glossary. Index. For the first edition see BRD 1972.
"Never have Stalin's crimes against humanity been more forcefully or more thoroughly documented than in . . . {this book, which} distills firsthand testimonies of the mass arrests, torture, imprisonment and executions that befell millions of innocent Soviet citizens." Publ Wkly
Includes bibliographical references

Pipes, Richard
A **concise** history of the Russian Revolution. Knopf 1995 431p il maps hardcover o.p. pa $16 **947.084**
1. Russia -- History
ISBN 0-679-74544-0 pa
LC 95-3127
A one volume condensation of the author's The Russian Revolution and Russia under the Bolshevik regime
"Forcefully showing why the 70-year-old Communist experiment failed {Pipes} provides the nonacademic reader with accurate historical events in a highly readable format." Libr J
Includes bibliographical references

Russia under the Bolshevik regime. Vintage Books 1995 587p il map pa $21 **947.084**
1. Heads of state 2. Revolutionaries 3. Communist leaders 4. Political leaders 5. Soviet Union -- History
ISBN 978-0-679-76184-6; 0-679-76184-5
First published 1994 by Knopf

"In this sequel to The Russian Revolution Pipes persuasively argues that Lenin's one-party dictatorship, through its terrorizing, suppression of the press, censorship and monopolistic control of cultural organizations, set the stage for Stalin's genocidal totalitarianism. . . . Pipes shows how both Hitler and Mussolini drew on Lenin's tyrannical methods, and he perceptively analyzes the mindset of Western fellow-travelers who wove fantasies of the U.S.S.R. as an egalitarian Eden while rationalizing its evils." Publ Wkly
Includes bibliographical references

Reed, John
Ten days that shook the world. Penguin Books 2007 368p (Penguin classics) pa $12 **947.084**
1. Soviet Union -- History -- 1917-1921. Revolution
ISBN 978-0-14-144212-9; 0-14-144212-3
First published 1919 by International Pubs.
"A reportorial, firsthand, and sympathetic account of the November Revolution in Russia (1917). . . . After prefatory explanation of political groups and other organizations, and of the background of the uprising, the work tells with graphic detail of the fall of the provisional government, the revolution and counterrevolution, the solidifying of power, and the resultant congress." Oxford Companion to Am Lit. 5th edition

Service, Robert
Lenin--a biography. Harvard Univ. Press 2000 xxv, 561p il maps $38.95; pa $19.95 **947.084**
1. Heads of state 2. Revolutionaries 3. Communist leaders 4. Political leaders
ISBN 0-674-00330-6; 0-674-00828-6 pa
LC 00-21394
This biography focuses "on Lenin the man. It draws on a wealth of new material to provide a subtle and complex portrait. . . . In particular, Service's account adds much to our knowledge of Lenin's early years and his final years as a man cut down by a series of strokes. . . . It is lucidly written, sharply observed, full of good sense, packed with vivid anecdote and, above all, succeeds—where so many have failed—in creating a Lenin who is believably human." Hist Today
Includes bibliographical references

Volkogonov, Dmitrii Antonovich
Lenin; a new biography. {by} Dmitri Volkogonov; translated and edited by Harold Shukman. Free Press 1994 xxxix, 529p il $30 **947.084**
1. Heads of state 2. Revolutionaries 3. Communist leaders 4. Political leaders
ISBN 0-02-933435-7
LC 94-31752
A condensed English version of the two-volume Russian edition published in 1994
"The author draws heavily on newly declassified KGB archives that he oversees as special assistant to President Boris Yeltsin. . . . Volkogonov's narrative is indispensable for understanding the Bolshevik coup, their crushing of the democratic opposition and the tragic aftermath." Publ Wkly
Includes bibliographical references

947.085   Russia (Soviet Union)--1953-1991

Carlson, Peter

K blows top; a Cold War comic interlude starring Nikita Khrushchev, America's most unlikely tourist. PublicAffairs 2009 327p il $26.95   **947.085**
1. Cold war 2. Heads of state 3. Communist leaders 4. Political leaders 5. Soviet Union -- Foreign relations -- United States 6. United States -- Foreign relations -- Soviet Union
ISBN 9781586484972; 1-58648-497-4
LC 2008-39090
Recounts Khrushchev's 1959 trip across America against the backdrop of the Cold War and a capitalist America living under the shadow of the hydrogen bomb.

"Drawing on contemporary news reports, modern interviews, and memoirs written by some of the participants, [this is] . . . a story about a poorly educated but extraordinarily powerful man who became, for a brief time, a pop-culture icon. . . . A fine example of popular history at its most engaging—anecdotal but informative and written with great feeling for the comedic side of current events." Booklist

Includes bibliographical references

Gorbachev, Mikhail

On my country and the world; {by} Gorbachev. Columbia Univ. Press 1999 300p $50; pa $17.95   **947.085**
1. World politics -- 1965- 2. Soviet Union -- Politics and government 3. Russia (Federation) -- Politics and government
ISBN 0-231-11514-8; 0-231-11515-6 pa
LC 99-31273
The former Soviet leader presents an analysis of his country's Communist past and an account of his role in government in the 1980s. Gorbachev also includes ideas for political change

Gorbachev is "fresh and candid in its initial section on the pluses and minuses of the Revolution of 1917." Nation

Remnick, David

★ **Lenin's** tomb; Russia and the fall of Communism. Random House 1993 576p hardcover o.p. pa $15.95   **947.085**
1. Soviet Union -- Politics and government
ISBN 0-679-75125-4 pa
LC 92-56841
"This book is a record of almost four years beginning in 1988 when David Remnick, a Washington Post reporter, was assigned to Moscow. . . . He argues convincingly that what did in the old Soviet leadership, right down through Mikhail Gorbachev, was its unending assault not only on people but on memory. By making a secret of history, it made its people increasingly distracted, and desperate, until they overthrew it." N Y Times Book Rev

Satter, David

Age of delirium; the decline and fall of the Soviet Union. Yale University Press 2001 424p pa $30   **947.085**
1. Soviet Union -- History
ISBN 0-300-08705-5; 978-0-300-08705-5

First published 1996 by Knopf
The author "appraises the Russians by writing about the travails of average people in the last decade of Soviet rule. Objects of the Communist ideology's enforced unanimity, his subjects include dissidents sent to psychiatric wards, persecuted religious people, a TASS journalist learning how to write the party line, and miners exploited by the workers' state. . . . An insightful from-the-ground-up view of typical Russians whom the top-down politicians are now courting." Booklist

Stokes, Gale

The **walls** came tumbling down; the collapse of communism in Eastern Europe. Oxford Univ. Press 1993 319p hardcover o.p. pa $31.95   **947.085**
1. Communism 2. Eastern Europe -- Politics and government
ISBN 0-19-506644-8; 0-19-506645-6 pa
LC 92-44862
This book "can be recommended as a coherent, well-written history that defines its time frame well, provides sound coverage, makes prudent judgments, and wears its analysis lightly. . . . Stokes's overview traces the ebb and flow of personalities and events in a manner that is both accessible to lay readers and informative to scholars." Libr J

947.086   Commonwealth of Independent States, 1991-

Aleksievich, Svetlana, 1948-

★ **Secondhand** time; Svetlana Alexievich; translated by Bela Shayevich. Random House 2016 496 p. (hardback : acid-free paper) $30   **947.086**
1. Russia 2. Oral history 3. Soviet Union -- Social conditions 4. Soviet Union -- Biography 5. Oral history -- Soviet Union 6. Russia (Federation) -- Biography 7. Oral history -- Russia (Federation) 8. Post-communism -- Russia (Federation) 9. Russia (Federation) -- Social conditions -- 1991-
ISBN 9780399588808
LC 2016005925
This book, by Svetlana Alexievich, translated by Bela Shayevich, "chronicles the demise of communism. Everyday Russian citizens recount the past thirty years, showing us what life was like during the fall of the Soviet Union and what it's like to live in the new Russia left in its wake. Through interviews spanning 1991 to 2012, Alexievich takes us behind the propaganda and contrived media accounts, giving us a panoramic portrait of contemporary Russia and Russians." (Publisher's note)

"Journalist Alexievich (Voices from Chernobyl), who won the 2015 Nobel Prize in Literature, captures the heartache, excitement, and harsh realities of life at the end of the Soviet era and the birth of modern Russia. A collection of oral histories linked by topic, theme, and the author's own musings, this impassioned and critical study, originally published in Russian in 2013, documents the immense changes the Russian people underwent in the 1990s and 2000s. . . . A must for historians, lay readers, and anyone who enjoys well-curated personal narratives. All readers will appreciate the revelations about Russia's turbulent transition and present cultural and political status." LJ

Baker, Peter

Kremlin rising; Vladimir Putin's Russia and the end of revolution. [by] Peter Baker and Susan Glasser. Scribner 2005 453p il $27.50   **947.086**
1. Russia (Federation) -- Politics and government
ISBN 0-743-26431-2
LC 2005-44157
The authors chronicle the transformation of contemporary Russia under President Vladimir Putin.

"Well written, well reported and well organized, the book consists of freestanding chapters that touch on the most important events and trends in contemporary Russia, from the war in Chechnya to the spread of AIDS and the dire state of the Russian judicial system." N Y Times (Late N Y Ed)

Includes bibliographical references

Brent, Jonathan

Inside the Stalin archives; discovering the new Russia. Atlas & Company 2008 335p il $26 **947.086**
1. Heads of state 2. Communist leaders 3. Political leaders 4. Russia (Federation) 5. Archives -- Soviet Union
ISBN 978-0-9777-4333-9; 0-9777-4333-0

This work, which draws upon the author's fifteen years of unprecedented access to high-level Soviet Archives, "reveals as much about the grim realities of post-Soviet life and bureaucracy as it does about the archives themselves. Equipped with little Russian and few contacts, but with an almost palpable sense of decency and honest intentions that illuminate his book, Brent explains for the general reader as well as for specialists how he went about his work in the new Russia." N Y Times Book Rev

Dawisha, Karen

Putin's kleptocracy; who owns Russia? Karen Dawisha. Simon & Schuster 2014 vii, 445 p.p illustrations $30   **947.086**
1. Russia -- History -- 1991- 2. Racketeering -- Russia (Federation) 3. Political corruption -- Russia (Federation) 4. Russia (Federation) -- Politics and government -- 1991-
ISBN 1476795193; 9781476795195
LC 2014948969
Author Rachel Dawisha's book is "the result of years of research into the KGB and the various Russian crime syndicates. [It] describes and exposes the origins of [Vladimir] Putin's kleptocratic regime. She presents extensive new evidence about the Putin circle's use of public positions for personal gain even before Putin became president in 2000." (Publisher's note)

"A rich and exhaustive account of Putin and his regime that supports a forecast of its 'hard authoritarian' drift and dependence on 'European public goods' for survival." LJ

Includes bibliographical references and index

Lieven, Anatol

Chechnya; tombstone of Russian power. with photographs by Heidi Bradner. Yale Univ. Press 1998 436p il $55; pa $28   **947.086**
1. Chechnya (Russia)
ISBN 0-300-07398-4; 0-300-07881-1 pa
LC 98-84479
"The book is a great, ostentatiously erudite festival of ideas, sometimes brilliant, sometimes dubious, but never less than interesting." N Y Times Book Rev

Meier, Andrew

Black earth; a journey through Russia after the fall. Norton 2003 511p il map $28.95; pa $15.95   **947.086**
1. Russia (Federation)
ISBN 0-393-05178-1; 0-393-32641-1 pa
LC 2003-6562
"After talking to scores of people—from survivors of the Aldy massacre to a harrowed Russian lieutenant colonel who runs the body-collection point closest to the Chechen battleground—Meier paints in this heartbreaking book a devastating picture of contemporary life in a country where, as one man put it, people have 'lived like the lowest dogs for more than eighty years.'" Publ Wkly

Includes bibliographical references

Ostrovsky, Arkady

The **Invention** of Russia; From Gorbachev's Freedom to Putin's War. by Arkady Ostrovsky. Penguin Group USA 2016 384 p. $30   **947.086**
1. Cold war 2. World politics -- 1945-1991 3. Russia -- Politics and government 4. Russia -- History -- 1917-1991, Soviet Union
ISBN 0399564160; 9780399564161
This book, by Arkady Ostrovsky, "reaches back to the darkest days of the cold war to tell the story of the fight for the soul of a nation. With the deep insight only possible of a native son, Ostrovsky introduces us to the propagandists, oligarchs, and fixers who have set Russia's course since the collapse of the Soviet Union, inventing a new and more ominous identity for a country where ideas are all too often wielded like a cudgel." (Publisher's note)

"A troubling and superbly documented book that will make readers wonder what comes next for Russia and its propagandists." Booklist

Includes bibliographical references (pages [351]-355) and index.

Politkovskaya, Anna

A **Russian** diary; a journalist's final account of life, corruption, and death in Putin's Russia. translated by Arch Tait; foreword by Scott Simon. Random House 2007 369p map $25.95   **947.086**
1. Presidents 2. Prime ministers 3. Russia (Federation) -- Politics and government
ISBN 1-4000-6682-4; 978-1-4000-6682-7
LC 2007-296943
These are the journals kept by the Russian journalist who was killed in Moscow in 2006.

This is a "brilliant . . . portrayal of Russian life during the middle years of Putin's rule." New York Rev Books

Remnick, David

Resurrection; the struggle for a new Russia. Random House 1997 398p hardcover o.p. pa $15   **947.086**

1. Russia (Federation) -- Politics and government
ISBN 0-375-75023-1 pa

LC 96-47360

In this companion volume to Lenin's tomb, "Remnick concentrates on the post-Soviet scene and its prospects. . . . Chaotic uncertainty, massive corruption, and crime are notoriously present, yet the possibility of a different, better life also beckons. . . . This is an interesting, highly informative portrait of a country struggling toward a fateful future." Libr J

Includes bibliographical references

Richards, Susan

Lost and found in Russia; lives in a post-Soviet landscape. Other Press 2010 544p pa $15.95; ebook $15.95   **947.086**

1. Russia (Federation) -- Description and travel 2. Russia (Federation) -- Social life and customs
ISBN 978-1-59051-348-4 pa; 978-1-59051-369-9 ebook

First published 2010 in the United Kingdom

"During many trips from 1992 to 1998, Richards . . . traveled to visit friends in Russia, particularly in the southwestern towns of Saratov and Marx. . . . She fashions the narrative around the friends she met and lived with closely. Vera, follower of the Vissarion cult, was an inhabitant of Saratov, once called the Athens of the Volga, now a forsaken place closed to foreigners because of its military industry (presently defunct). In Marx, once the nexus of the Russian Germans, Richards stayed with Anna, a tensely coiled journalist—a pravednik, or 'truth bearer'—who had been punished for her honest writing; the volatile couple Natasha and Igor, lured to the dead-end town by Gorbachev's promise of a German homeland, now mostly unemployed and alcoholic; and the couple Misha and Tatiana, marooned in Marx after their engineering training, who became thriving entrepreneurs and part of the rising Russian middle class. . . . Other trips took her through Siberia and the Crimea to view the residues of Russian Orthodoxy, the Old Believers and folksy spiritualism. A patiently crafted glimpse 'through a crack in the wardrobe' of the devastation wrought on Russian society during the turbulent post-Communist '90s." Kirkus

Treisman, Daniel

The **return**; Russia's journey from Gorbachev to Medvedev. Free Press 2011 523p il $30; ebook $14.99   **947.086**

1. Russia (Federation) -- Politics and government
ISBN 978-1-4165-6071-5; 1-4165-6071-8; 978-1-4516-0574-7 ebook; 1-4516-0574-9 ebook; 1416560718; 1451605749 ebook; 978141656071-5; 9781451605747 ebook

LC 2010011520

"The politics and economics of post-Communist Russia occupy this survey of the past two decades. Treisman . . . works commentary about Russia's successive leaders—Gorbachev, Yeltsin, Putin, and Medvedev—into the problems they confronted. . . . Encompassing foreign policy and Rus-

sian public opinion, Treisman's knowledgeable presentation is a reliable current-affairs source for Russia's economic revival and reassertion in international affairs." Booklist

947.43   Ural Mountains (Russia)

Garrels, Anne

Putin country; a journey into the real Russia. Anne Garrels. Farrar, Straus & Giroux 2015 240 p. (hardback) $26   **947.43**

1. Russia -- Description and travel 2. Cheliabinsk (Russia) -- Biography 3. Cheliabinsk (Russia) -- Social conditions 4. Cheliabinsk (Russia) -- Description and travel 5. Cheliabinsk (Russia) -- Social life and customs 6. Interviews -- Russia (Federation) -- Cheliabinsk 7. Subculture -- Russia (Federation) -- Cheliabinsk 8. Political culture -- Russia (Federation) -- Cheliabinsk
ISBN 9780374247720

LC 2015034644

In this book, the NPR correspondent Anne Garrels "began visiting a crumbling military-industrial center called Chelyabinsk that lies 1,000 miles east of Moscow. Here she profiles economic chaos, political corruption, and surging xenophobia, bursting cosmopolitanism and sudden wealth for rising professionals and Mafiosi. . . . All to clarify what the fall of communism has meant for the population at large. And she explains why so many Russians love Vladimir Putin." (Library Journal)

"This book will be of interest to general readers seeking to learn more about the country that exists beyond Moscow and St. Petersburg, as well as those wanting to gain better insight into its interior political and social conditions." LJ

947.5   Caucasus

Baiev, Khassan

The **Oath**; a surgeon under fire. [by] Khassan Baiev; with Ruth and Nicholas Daniloff. Walker & Co. 2003 376p il $26   **947.5**

1. Chechnya (Russia)
ISBN 0-8027-1404-8

LC 2003-52502

The author "is modest, which only adds to his heroism. But more than that, he has humanized the Chechens, whom others have portrayed as terrorists. Russian president Vladimir Putin has tried to equate Russia's fight against the Chechens with the U.S. battle against al-Qaida. Those who read this stirring memoir will be hard-pressed to see the situation so simply." Publ Wkly

Seierstad, Asne

The **angel** of Grozny; orphans of a forgotten war. translated by Nadia Christensen. Basic Books 2008 340p $25.95   **947.5**

1. Chechnya (Russia) -- History -- 1994- (Civil War)
ISBN 978-0-465-01122-3; 0-465-01122-5

LC 2008-925222

In the early hours of New Year's 1994, Russian troops invaded the Republic of Chechnya, plunging the country into a prolonged and bloody conflict that continues to this day. A foreign correspondent in Moscow at the time, "Asne Seierstad traveled regularly to Chechnya to report on the war, describing its affects on those trying to live their daily lives amidst violence.

"Seierstad's searing, evocative recounting brings Chechnya to life, especially the unimaginable suffering and strength of the Chechen people. Powerful, painful, and raw, . . . [this] is essential reading." Booklist

947.7   Ukraine

King, Charles
Odessa; genius and death in a city of dreams. W.W. Norton & Co. 2011 336p il map $27.95 **947.7**
1. Jews -- Ukraine 2. Odessa (Ukraine) 3. Odessa (Ukraine) -- History 4. Jews -- Ukraine -- Odessa -- History 5. Odessa (Ukraine) -- Politics and government
ISBN 9780393070842; 0-393-07084-0
LC 2010-38000
This is a "finely written and evocative portrait of the city. . . . [Its] detail, coupled with a fine feel for the sweep of history . . . makes this book a worthy tribute to one of Europe's greatest and least-known cities." Economist
Includes bibliographical references

Kurtz, Glenn
Three minutes in Poland; discovering a lost world in a 1938 family film. Glenn Kurtz. Farrar, Straus & Giroux 2014 432 p. illustrations, maps (hardback) $30 **947.7**
1. Community life 2. Jews -- Poland 3. Holocaust, 1939-1945 4. Poland -- History -- 1918-1945 5. Nasielsk (Poland) -- Biography 6. Holocaust survivors -- Biography 7. Jews -- PolandHistory -- 20th century 8. Holocaust, Jewish (1939-1945) -- Poland 9. Nasielsk (Poland) -- History -- 20th century 10. Community life -- Poland -- Nasielsk -- History -- 20th century
ISBN 0374276773; 9780374276775
LC 2014008516
In this book, author "Glenn Kurtz stumbles upon an old family film in his parents' closet in Florida. . . . The film, shot long ago by his grandfather on a sightseeing trip to Europe, includes shaky footage of Paris and the Swiss Alps. . . . Astonishingly, David Kurtz also captured on color 16mm film the only known moving images of the thriving, predominantly Jewish town of Nasielsk, Poland, shortly before the community's destruction." (Publisher's note)

"Engrossing detective work and chance encounters--one casual online viewer recognized a 13-year-old boy in the film as her still-living grandfather--allowed Kurtz to assemble a vibrant portrait of Jewish Nasielsk, its homely shops, proud synagogue, quarreling Hasidim and Zionists, impish kids, and, not least, of its harrowing war-time dissolution. He also explores the resurrection of the community's history, as survivors find images of loved ones lost for generations and forge new bonds." Pub Wkly

947.98   Estonia

Theroux, Alexander
Estonia: a ramble through the periphery. Fantagraphics Books 2011 351p il $29.99 **947.98**
1. Estonia -- Description and travel
ISBN 978-1-60699-465-8; 1-60699-465-4
Theroux "follows his wife, Sarah, to [Estonia] in 2008, where she paints on her Fulbright grant scenes of its stolid towns. Brother of the equally waspish travel writer Paul, Alexander Theroux, meanwhile, skulks, fulminates, studies, and walks wherever he can, soaking up the frigid atmosphere of its people. . . . He deploys bombast, overkill, and ridicule to pepper his perennial pop-up targets of greed, lassitude, and stupidity. He includes here his caustic if characteristic habit of lists, ruminations, and rants. For all his predilection for careful observation of how people look, sound, and move, he inflates, if maybe in sly self-deprecation, the impact others have on him—rather than vice versa. . . . Full of endnotes, translating many phrases he quotes in their original languages, and graced by a few of the couple's photos and Sarahs plein air oil paintings, this provides a suitably quirky introduction to Theroux as an essayist and critic." PopMatters

948   Scandinavia

Booth, Michael
The **Almost** Nearly Perfect People. Jonathan Cape 2014 416 p. map $26 **948**
1. Scandinavia -- Civilization 2. Scandinavia -- Social conditions 3. Scandinavia -- Social life and customs
ISBN 0224089625; 9780224089623; 9781250061966; 1250061962
In this book, Michael Booth "covers the countries that invariably dominate the top ten lists of best/healthiest/most egalitarian places to live: Denmark, Finland, Iceland, Norway, and Sweden. Beginning with his adopted home of Denmark, Booth sets out to address whether the quality of life in Nordic countries is really so high. . . . He . . . discovers . . . some chinks in the utopian armor: isolationism, persistent racism . . . and growing fissures in a classless society." (Publishers Weekly)

"Thanks to Booth's good-natured description of his adventures—and his honest admiration—we may head for Scandinavia after all (bringing some elf-off spray, just in case)." Booklist

Ferguson, Robert
The **Vikings**; a history. Viking 2009 450p il map **948**
1. Vikings 2. Europe -- History -- 476-1492
ISBN 978-0-670-02079-9
LC 2009-26818
"Ferguson's scholarly study requires close attention, but the intellectual rewards are plentiful. Provides a significant deepening of our knowledge of the Vikings." Kirkus
Includes bibliographical references

The **Oxford** illustrated history of the Vikings; edited
by Peter Sawyer. Oxford Univ. Press 1997 298p
il maps hardcover o.p. pa $27.50   **948**
1. Vikings
ISBN 0-19-820526-0; 0-19-285434-8 pa

LC 97-16649

This illustrated collection of articles includes discussion of the Vikings' impact on England, Iceland, Greenland,
Russia, and the Frankish and Danish Empires; Viking ships
and ship-building; Viking religion; and the ways in which
Vikings have been portrayed throughout history. Significant
archaeological finds are featured.
Includes bibliographical references

Roesdahl, Else

The **Vikings**; translated by Susan M. Margeson
and Kirsten Williams. 2nd ed; Penguin Books 1998
324p il map pa $17   **948**
1. Vikings
ISBN 0-14-025282-7; 978-0-14-025282-8
Original Danish edition, 1987
A survey of Viking civilization from c.750-c.1050.
"About one-third of the book deals with Viking expansion into Russia, Normandy, the British Isles, Iceland,
Greenland, etc. . . . Most of the book surveys the geography,
people, society, religion, art, etc., of the Vikings' Scandinavian homelands." Libr J
Includes bibliographical references

948.97   Finland

Beach, Hugh

A **year** in Lapland; guest of the reindeer herders.
with a new afterword by the author. University of
Washington Press 2001 242p il map pa $25 **948.97**
1. Sami (European people) 2. Lapland
ISBN 0-295-98037-0; 978-0-295-98037-9

LC 00-47936

First published 1993 by Smithsonian Institution Press
The author "tells of his first year among the Saami reindeer herders of Swedish Lapland. His narrative interweaves
adventure, descriptions of the harsh beauty of the landscape,
supernatural tales and ancient myths. Beach also explores
topics of change in the lives of the herders brought on by
laws requiring village groups to move and by adaptations to
new items such as rubber boots, seaplanes, and appliances."
Libr J

Edwards, Robert

The **Winter** War; Russia's invasion of Finland,
1939-1940. Pegasus Books 2008 319p il map
$27.95   **948.97**
1. Russo-Finnish War, 1939-1940 2. World War, 1939-
1945 -- Finland
ISBN 978-1-933648-50-7
First published 2006 in the United Kingdom
"A brisk, efficient account of one of the most overlooked episodes of World War II. . . . Highly readable and
informative." Kirkus
Includes bibliographical references

949.12   Iceland

Johanneson, Gudni Thorlacius

The **history** of Iceland; Guðni Thorlacius Jóhan-
nesson. Greenwood 2013 xv, 172 p.p (The Greenwood Histories of the Modern Nations) (hardcopy :
acid-free paper) $58   **949.12**
1. Iceland -- History
ISBN 0313376204; 9780313376207

LC 2012031759

This book divides the "history of Iceland into seven sections chronicling events and conditions in the country from
874 through mid-2012. . . . The author enlivens his coverage with . . . stories, such as one of an early chronicler who
marveled that the midnight sun was so bright that lice could
easily be picked out of clothing." (Booklist)
Includes bibliographical references (pages 157-160)
and index

949.2   Netherlands

Schama, Simon

The **embarrassment** of riches; an interpretation
of Dutch culture in the Golden Age. Knopf 1987
698p il maps hardcover o.p. pa $23   **949.2**
1. Netherlands -- Civilization
ISBN 0-679-78124-2 pa

LC 86-45418

"Delving into customs, beliefs, popular art and quirks
of behavior, Schama has fashioned a tour de force, a profound, unconventional and rewarding portrait of a people."
Publ Wkly
Includes bibliographical references

Shorto, Russell

Amsterdam; a history of the world's most lib-
eral city. Russell Shorto. Doubleday 2013 368 p.
$28.95   **949.2**
1. Liberalism 2. Netherlands -- History 3. Amsterdam
(Netherlands) -- History 4. Liberalism -- Netherlands
-- Amsterdam -- History
ISBN 0385534574; 9780385534574

LC 2013003544

Author Russell Shorto's book presents a history of the
city of Amsterdam. "Weaving in his own experiences of
his adopted home, Shorto provides" a "story of Amsterdam
from the building of its first canals in the 1300s, through its
brutal struggle for independence, its golden age as a vast
empire, to its complex present in which its cherished ideals
of liberalism are under siege." (Publisher's note)
Includes bibliographical references

949.5 Greece

Brownworth, Lars

Lost to the West; the forgotten Byzantine Empire that rescued Western civilization. Crown Publishers 2009 329p map $26; pa $15 **949.5**

1. Byzantine Empire

ISBN 978-0-307-40795-5; 978-0-307-40796-2 pa

"Brownworth delivers just enough of the big picture for interested readers to pursue specific events in greater detail. An energetic look at a still-misunderstood period in late antiquity." Kirkus

Includes bibliographical references

Mazower, Mark

Salonica, city of ghosts; Christians, Muslims, and Jews, 1430-1950. Knopf 2005 490p il maps $35 **949.5**

1. Thessalonike (Greece)

ISBN 0-375-41298-0

LC 2004-57690

First published 2004 in the United Kingdom

This is a history of the Greek city.

The author's "graceful, evocative prose, his deft attention to details and his empathetic presentation of all sides of the story add up to a magnificent tale of this unique city." Publ Wkly

Includes bibliographical references

Norwich, John Julius

Byzantium: the apogee. Knopf 1991 xxiv, 389p il map $49.95 **949.5**

1. Byzantine Empire

ISBN 0-394-53779-3

LC 91-53119

This is the second volume of a three-volume narrative history of the Byzantine Empire. "Beginning with Charlemagne's coronation in 800 A.D. and the resulting split in the Christian world, Norwich traces the return of iconoclasm, political intrigues, military campaigns, atrocities, and alliances, ending with the fateful battle at Nanzikert from which the Empire never recovered. . . . [The author] deftly brings to life the frozen icons of the history books." Libr J

Includes bibliographical references

Byzantium: the decline and fall. Knopf 1995 xxxvii, 488p il maps $49.95 **949.5**

1. Byzantine Empire

ISBN 0-679-41650-1

This final volume of the author's three volume narrative history chronicles the last four centuries of the Byzantine Empire.

Includes bibliographical references

Byzantium: the early centuries. Knopf 1989 407p il $49.95 **949.5**

1. Byzantine Empire

ISBN 0-394-53778-5

LC 88-45508

First published 1988 in the United Kingdom

This is the first of a three-volume narrative history of the Byzantine Empire. It traces Byzantium's history "from the birth of Constantine c.274 to the coronation of Charlemagne on Christmas Day 800." Libr J

Includes bibliographical references

949.6 Balkan Peninsula

Pamuk, Orhan

Istanbul; memories and the city. translated from the Turkish by Maureen Freely. Knopf 2005 384p il $26.95 **949.6**

1. Istanbul (Turkey)

ISBN 1-400-04095-7

LC 2004-61537

Original Turkish edition, 2003

The novelist writes about his life as a resident of Istanbul. "The author mingles 'personal memoir with cultural history', and a fascinating read it is too for anyone who has even the slightest acquaintance with this fabled bridge between east and west." Economist

949.7 Serbia, Croatia, Slovenia, Bosnia and Hercegovina, Montenegro, Macedonia

Di Giovanni, Janine

Madness visible; a memoir of war. Knopf 2003 285p map hardcover o.p. pa $14 **949.7**

1. Kosovo (Serbia)

ISBN 0-375-41073-2; 978-0-375-72455-8 pa; 0-375-72455-9 pa

LC 2002-44820

This "narrative of the 1999 war in Kosovo, NATO's campaign against Serbia, and the ouster of Milosevic offers an unbiased view of the enormous suffering of Yugoslav Albanians and Serbs following the genocidal rage of the Belgrade regime against the Kosovo Liberation Army's (KLA) drive for an independent Kosovo. . . . This exciting work is highly recommended for all libraries." Libr J

Includes bibliographical references

Rieff, David

Slaughterhouse; Bosnia and the failure of the West. Simon & Schuster 1995 240p hardcover o.p. pa $18.95 **949.7**

1. Yugoslav War, 1991-1995 2. Bosnia and Hercegovina

ISBN 0-684-81903-1 pa

LC 94-40148

This account of the war in the former Yugoslavia grew out of Rieff's travels in the region from 1992 through 1994

"Slaughterhouse is perhaps the most powerful, passionate, and penetrating dissection of a Westerner of the ongoing Bosnian tragedy." Booklist

Rohde, David

Endgame; the betrayal and fall of Srebrenica, Europe's worst massacre since World War II. Westview Press 1998 450p il pa $20 **949.7**

1. Yugoslav War, 1991-1995 2. Srebrenica (Bosnia and

Hercegovina)
ISBN 0-8133-3533-7; 978-0-8133-3533-9

LC 98-26127

First published 1997 by Farrar, Straus & Giroux

"Rohde argues that the fall of Srebrenica could have been prevented, but he is ultimately unable to explain the 'collective failure' of the United States, the United Nations, and NATO in stopping the massacre. His investigation is carefully documented by over 300 footnotes. This is an important and revealing book." Libr J

Includes bibliographical references

West, Richard

Tito; and the rise and fall of Yugoslavia. Carroll & Graf Pubs. 1995 436p il hardcover o.p. pa $15.95　　　　**949.7**

1. Heads of state 2. Communist leaders 3. Political leaders 4. Yugoslavia -- Politics and government
ISBN 0-7867-0332-6 pa

LC 95-10404

First published 1994 in the United Kingdom

This biography "describes Tito's rise to power, his creation of the Partisan Army during the Axis occupation, his consolidation of southern Slavs after the war and establishment of a Communist Yugoslavia, the break with Stalin in 1948, Tito's subsequent rivalry with the Soviet bloc and his leadership of nonaligned states. . . . The book also clarifies the present three-way conflict among Serbs, Croats and Muslims." Publ Wkly

Includes bibliographical references

949.702　Yugoslavia, 1918-1991

Maass, Peter

Love thy neighbor; a story of war. Knopf 1996 305p hardcover o.p. pa $14　　　　**949.702**

1. Yugoslav War, 1991-1995 2. Bosnia and Hercegovina
ISBN 0-679-76389-9 pa

LC 95-39250

This book on the Yugoslav conflict is based on Maass's experiences as the Washington Post's reporter in Bosnia

"Maass was only in Bosnia for about a year, from 1992 to 1993, but he saw a great deal. And he displays extraordinary sensitivity to the ambiguities of his position." Nation

Includes bibliographical references

949.703　Period as sovereign nations, 1991-

Clark, Wesley K.

★ **Waging** modern war; Bosnia, Kosovo, and the future of combat. PublicAffairs 2001 xxxi, 479p il map hardcover o.p. pa $18　　　　**949.703**

1. Yugoslav War, 1991-1995 2. Kosovo (Serbia) -- History
ISBN 1-58648-139-8 pa

LC 01-19717

This is an account of the former Supreme Allied Commander's experiences during the Kosovo crises. "Clark tells a story of frustration with NATO allies, who had to approve each operation and target selection, and with U.S. policy-

makers as he tried to formulate a strategy that would achieve his military goals." Libr J

949.71　Serbia

McAllester, Matthew

Beyond the Mountains of the Damned; the war inside Kosovo. New York Univ. Press 2002 227p il $30; pa $17.95　　　　**949.71**

1. Kosovo (Serbia) -- History
ISBN 0-8147-5660-3; 0-8147-5661-1 pa

LC 2001-4370

"McAllester's spare, understated prose . . . is potent, as is his exploration of the human side of geopolitics and war." Publ Wkly

Includes bibliographical references

949.8　Romania

Kaplan, Robert D., 1952-

In Europe's shadow; two cold wars and a thirty-year journey through Romania and beyond. Robert D. Kaplan. Random House Inc 2015 336 p. 16 plates; illustrations; maps (hardcover) $28　　　**949.8**

1. Geopolitics 2. Romania -- Civilization 3. Europe -- History -- 20th century 4. Romania -- History -- 1989- 5. Romania -- History -- 1944-1989 6. Romania -- Description and travel
ISBN 9780812996814

LC 2015012726

This book, by Robert D. Kaplan, "illuminates the fusion of the Latin West and the Greek East that created Romania, the country that gave rise to . . . [Adolf] Hitler's chief foreign accomplice during World War II, and the country that was home to the most brutal strain of Communism. . . . Kaplan finds himself in dialogue with the great thinkers of the past, and with the Romanians of today, the philosophers, priests, and politicians—those who struggle to keep the flame of humanism alive in the era of a resurgent Russia." (Publisher's note)

"Despite the lack of a clear focus and the somewhat incoherent organization, this is a well-written, intriguing, and informative book." Pub Wkly

Includes bibliographical references and index

950　History of Asia

Fallows, James M.

Looking at the sun; {by} James Fallows. Pantheon Bks. 1994 517p hardcover o.p. pa $15　**950**

1. East Asia
ISBN 0-679-76162-4 pa

LC 93-38367

"A fascinating, fresh, and potentially controversial contemplation of the global market." Booklist

"In a timely, even prophetic, portrait of Asia's rise and the magnitude of its challenge to the West, Fallows demolishes the myth that Japan is a capitalist country built on the

Western model. He demonstrates instead how Japan's economic system treats business as an instrument of national interest while casting aside the traditional Western values of individual enterprise and human rights." (Publisher's note)

Mishra, Pankaj

From the ruins of empire; the intellectuals who remade Asia. Pankaj Mishra. Farrar, Straus and Giroux 2012 368 p. ill. (alk. paper) $27.00; (pbk.) $18.00 **950**

1. Intellectuals
ISBN 9780374249595; 0374249598; 1250037719; 9781250037718

LC 2012940483

"Originally published in 2012 by Allen Lane, an imprint of Penguin Books, Great Britain as From the ruins of empire : the revolt against the West and the remaking of Asia"--Title page verso.

This book "looks at how, between about 1870 and 1940, 'some of the most intelligent and sensitive people in the East responded to the encroachments of the West (both physical and intellectual) on their societies.' In particular, he focuses on Jamal al-Din al-Afghani and Liang Qichao, intellectuals and political activists." (Publishers Weekly)

Includes bibliographical references (pages 311-340) and index.

Weatherford, Jack

Genghis Khan and the Quest for God; How the World's Greatest Conqueror Gave Us Religious Freedom. by Jack Weatherford. Penguin Group USA 2016 304 p. $28 **950**

ISBN 0735221154; 9780735221154

This biography, by Jack Weatherford, "reveals how Genghis [Khan] harnessed the power of religion to rule the largest empire the world has ever known. . . . He created the world's greatest trading network, . . . but he knew that if his empire was going to last, he would need something stronger and more binding than trade. He needed religion. And so, unlike the Christian, Taoist and Muslim conquerors who came before him, he gave his subjects freedom of religion." (Publisher's note)

"This sound examination of Khan, his methods of rule, and his views on religious tolerance presents a valid and welcome addition to scholarship on the subject." LJ

951 China and adjacent areas

Berkshire encyclopedia of China; modern and historic views of the world's newest and oldest global power. Berkshire Pub. Group 2009 5v il map set $675 **951**

1. Reference books 2. China -- Civilization -- Encyclopedias 3. China -- Social life and customs -- Encyclopedias
ISBN 978-0-9770159-4-8; 0-9770159-4-7

LC 2009-7589

"Arranged alphabetically, the nearly 1000 articles cover an . . . array of subjects as they relate to China. Among those explored are the country's history (both ancient and mod-

ern), politicians, architecture, food, international relations, and medicine." Libr J

Includes bibliographical references

The **Cambridge** history of China; general editors, Denis Twitchett and John K. Fairbank. Cambridge Univ. Press 1978 12v v1 $205; v3 $205; v6 $178; v7 $205; v8 $178; v9 $178; v10 $195; v11 $205; v12 $205; v13 $205; v14 $180; v15 $195 **951**

1. China -- History
ISBN 0-521-24327-0 v1; 0-521-21446-7 v3; 0-521-24331-9 v6; 0-521-24332-7 v7; 0-521-24333-5 v8; 0-521-24334-3 v9; 0-521-21447-5 v10; 0-521-22029-7 v11; 0-521-23541-3 v12; 0-521-24338-6 v13; 0-521-24336-X v14; 0-521-24337-8 v15

LC 76-29852

"An important series for scholars, this is also a valuable reference tool for general collections." Libr J

Includes bibliographical references

Chetham, Deirdre

Before the deluge; the vanishing world of the Yangtze's Three Gorges. Palgrave 2002 xxiii, 296p il map hardcover o.p. pa $17.95 **951**

1. Yangtze River valley (China) 2. China -- Social life and customs
ISBN 1-4039-6428-9 pa

LC 2002-16939

The author "paints a pulsating picture of the great river, the countryside, the people and their occupations, the amazingly fluid political philosophies and the sheer endurance of all parties, past and present, involved with the overwhelming project." Publ Wkly

Includes bibliographical references

Clunas, Craig

Ming; 50 Years That Changed China. by Craig Clunas, Jessica Harrison-Hall. University of Washington Press 2014 304 p. color illustrations, color map (hardcover) $60 **951**

1. China -- History
ISBN 0295994509; 9780714124841; 9780295994505

This book, by Craig Clunas and Jessica Harrison-Hall, "by focusing on the significant years of the early Ming dynasty and through the themes of court people and their lives, extraordinary developments in culture, the military, religion, diplomacy and trade, . . . brings the wider history of this fascinating period to colorful life." (Publisher's note)

"For anyone interested in Chinese art and history." LJ

Dalai Lama, XIV, 1935-

My appeal to the world; in quest of truth and justice on behalf of the Tibetan people, 1961-2010.... Presented by Sofia Stril-Rever. Tibet House U.S. 2015 400 p. (hardback : alk. paper) $29.95 **951**

1. Peace 2. Tibet (China) 3. Tibetans -- Social conditions 4. Tibet Autonomous Region (China) -- History 5. Peace-building -- China -- Tibet Autonomous Region 6. Tibet Autonomous Region (China) -- Politics

and goverment
ISBN 0967011566; 9780967011561

LC 2014034290

In this book, "[a]ll of the Dalai Lama's March 10th speeches, at their most poignant and eloquent, are collected, . . . introduced and historically contextualized by Sofia Stril-Rever, an author and scholar of Tibetan history and culture and Buddhist spirituality who has long served as his French translator." (Publisher's note)

"Those who wish to learn more about the late 20th-century history of Sino-Tibetan relations will find this a respectable resource, but it should be noted that this set of writings does not offer Chinese perspectives on the thorny issue." Pub Wkly

Includes bibliographical references and index

My Tibet; text by His Holiness the fourteenth Dalai Lama of Tibet; photographs and introduction by Galen Rowell. University of Calif. Press 1990 162p il hardcover o.p. pa $34.95 **951**
1. Buddhism 2. Tibet (China) -- Pictorial works
ISBN 0-520-08948-0 pa

LC 90-10868

This is "a volume of photographs taken in recent years by Galen Rowell, with a text drawn from interviews with the Dalai Lama or essays written previously by him." N Y Times Book Rev

DeWoskin, Rachel
Foreign babes in Beijing; behind the scenes of a new China. W. W. Norton 2005 332p $24.95; pa $13.95 **951**
1. China -- Social life and customs
ISBN 0-393-05902-2; 0-393-32859-7 pa

LC 2005-939

The author recounts her experiences living in China in the 1990s, where she had a starring role in the soap opera "Foreign Babes in Beijing."

"Ms DeWoskin's portrait of the complexities of urban China is not uncritical. But her book is written with enormous warmth for its people. And it is all the better for avoiding neat conclusions." Economist

Dong, Stella
Shanghai, 1842-1949; the rise and fall of a decadent city. Morrow 2000 318p il hardcover o.p. pa $15 **951**
1. Shanghai (China)
ISBN 0-06-093481-6 pa

LC 99-41902

An "account of a city legendary for decadence, violence, and greedy imperialism. Dong meticulously details the European commercial interests that deliberately promoted opium trafficking and exploited the land and people of Shanghai with every conceivable vice for nearly 100 years." Booklist

Fairbank, John King
★ **China**; a new history. [by] John King Fairbank and Merle Goldman. 2nd enl. ed.; Belknap

Press of Harvard University Press 2006 560p il map pa $24 **951**
1. China -- History
ISBN 0-674-01828-1; 978-0-674-01828-0

LC 2005-53695

First published 1992

Fairbank covers the history of China from paleolithic cultures of 400,000 B.C. up to 1989. Goldman adds a chapter on events in the post-Mao period and an epilogue on China at the beginning of the 21st century.

Includes bibliographical references

The **great** Chinese revolution: 1800-1985. Harper & Row 1986 396p maps hardcover o.p. pa $16 **951**
1. China -- History
ISBN 0-06-039057-3; 0-06-039076-X pa

LC 86-665

"The book is never pedantic, but gathers together a lifetime of scholarship plus a true gift for presentation of complex issues and a fine eye for telling illustration." Libr J

Includes bibliographical references

Hessler, Peter
★ **Oracle** bones; a journey between China's past and present. HarperCollins 2006 491p il $26.95; pa $15.99 **951**
1. China -- Civilization 2. China -- Description and travel
ISBN 0-06-082658-4; 0-06-082659-2 pa

LC 2005-52607

The author "has a marvelous sense of the intonations and gestures that give life to the moment; he knows when to join in the action and when simply to wait for things to happen. Today's China could have been made for him." N Y Times Book Rev

Includes bibliographical references

Meyer, Michael J.
The **last** days of old Beijing; life in the vanishing backstreets of a city transformed. [by] Michael Meyer. Walker & Company 2008 355p il map $25.99; pa $16 **951**
1. Beijing (China)
ISBN 978-0-8027-1652-1; 0-8027-1652-0; 978-0-8027-1750-4 pa; 0-8027-1750-4 pa

LC 2008-15546

This is a "revealing portrait of urban change, and the consequences of China's unquenchable thirst for modernization." Kirkus

Includes bibliographical references

Palmer, James
Heaven cracks, earth shakes; James Palmer. Basic Books, a member of the Perseus Books Group 2012 ix, 273p.p ill. **951**
1. Earthquakes 2. China -- History -- 1949-1976
ISBN 9780465014781; 9780465023493

LC 2011934180

In this book, "Beijing-based author [James] Palmer . . . lays out the devastation wrought by 10 years of the Cultural

Revolution, and how over the space of a few months the Chinese people managed to rebound and move forward. The year was scarred irrevocably by three events: the death in January of the people's beloved prime minister Zhou Enlai; the earthquake in Tangshan, which had been predicted several days before yet warnings ignored, flattening the coal-mining town in the space of 23 seconds and killing more than 650,000 people; and Mao's death in September, which set off a power struggle between the Gang of Four, led by Mao's widow, Jiang Qing, and the supporters of Deng Xiaoping." (Kirkus)

Includes bibliographical references (p. 261-264) and index.

Platt, Stephen R.

Autumn in the Heavenly Kingdom; China, the West, and the epic story of the Taiping Civil War. by Stephen R. Platt. Alfred A. Knopf 2012 468 p. **951**
1. Manchus 2. China -- Foreign relations 3. Europeans -- China -- History 4. Christian missionaries -- History 5. China -- History -- 1850-1864, Taiping Rebellion 6. Ethnic conflict -- China 7. Americans -- China -- History -- 19th century
ISBN 9780307271730

LC 2011035137

The book is author Stephen R. Platt's account of "[t]he cataclysmic Taiping rebellion. . . . In 1837 a peasant named Hong Xiuquan announced that he was Jesus' younger brother, sent to rid China of 'devils' including its weak, corrupt, ethnically foreign Manchu rulers. His charisma attracted a vast following that by the 1850s had conquered a large area, the Taiping Heavenly Kingdom, with a capital at Nanjing." (Publishers Weekly)

Includes bibliographical references

Preston, Diana

The **Boxer** Rebellion; the dramatic story of China's war on foreigners that shook the world in the summer of 1900. Walker & Co. 2000 xxvii, 436p il maps $28 **951**
1. China -- History
ISBN 0-8027-1361-0

LC 00-39243

"Preston's account, compiled from the many letters, diaries, and memoirs by European survivors of the siege, captures an odd strain of mordant humor." N Y Times Book Rev
Includes bibliographical references

Schell, Orville

★ **Wealth** and power; Orville Schell & John Delury. Random House Inc 2013 496 p. $30 **951**
1. China -- Social conditions 2. China -- Politics and government 3. China -- History -- 20th century -- Biography 4. China -- History -- 21st century -- Biography 5. China -- Politics and government -- 20th century 6. China -- Politics and government -- 21st century
ISBN 0679643478; 9780679643470

LC 2013002596

In this book, the authors "track the intellectual and political pursuit of fuqiang, or wealth and power, by Chinese thinkers and leaders in response to the humiliations heaped upon their country by Western powers, beginning with the Opium Wars of the mid-19th century. The work comprises chronologically ordered minibiographies, . . . with long sections devoted to Mao Zedong and Deng Xiaoping." (Publishers Weekly)

Includes bibliographical references and index

Spence, Jonathan D.

The **Chan's** great continent; China in Western minds. Norton 1998 279p hardcover o.p. pa $14.95 **951**
1. China -- Civilization
ISBN 0-393-31989-X pa

LC 98-10823

"Spence's book will appeal not only to those interested in history and literature, but to anyone looking for a perspective on contemporary discourse about China." Publ Wkly
Includes bibliographical references

God's Chinese son; the Taiping Heavenly Kingdom of Hong Xiuquan. Norton 1996 400p il maps hardcover o.p. pa $15.95 **951**
1. Revolutionaries 2. Religious leaders 3. China -- History -- 1850-1864, Taiping Rebellion
ISBN 0-393-31556-8 pa

LC 95-17245

"In 1836, twenty-two-year-old Hong Xiuquan failed the civil-service examinations in Canton and came across some Christian tracts. When he later fell sick and had visions, he became convinced that he was the Christian God's second son, destined to rule a 'heavenly kingdom' on earth. Many were attracted to Hong's egalitarian policies—despite his enforced separation of the sexes—and his sect prospered. But its attempts to overthrow the Qing dynasty resulted in unprecedented bloodshed: twenty million people died before the uprising was defeated, in 1864. Spence's present-tense narrative is riveting." New Yorker
Includes bibliographical references

The **search** for modern China. Norton 1990 xxv, 876p il maps hardcover o.p. pa $27.70 **951**
1. China -- History
ISBN 0-393-30780-8 pa

LC 89-9241

Spence's "own sense of China's past is so vivid, his understanding so sure and his writer's skill so powerful that the reader apprehends distant events as if they were contemporary." New Statesman (1913)
Includes bibliographical references

Treason by the book; {by} Jonathan Spence. Viking 2001 300p map $24.95; pa $14 **951**
1. China -- History 2. China -- Politics and government
ISBN 0-670-89292-0; 0-14-200041-8 pa

LC 00-43805

"Spence's story of emperor, officials, and conspirators is both rousingly unlikely and highly informative." Libr J

Tsering Shakya

The **dragon** in the land of snows; a history of modern Tibet since 1947. Columbia Univ. Press 1999 574p il $32.50   **951**

1. Tibet (China)

ISBN 0-231-11814-7

LC 99-14020

"Drawing on Tibetan, Chinese, British, Indian and American sources, Shakya weaves an authoritative and easily readable narrative. 'The Dragon in the Land of Snows' is likely to be the definitive history of modern Tibet for a generation or more." N Y Times Book Rev

Includes bibliographical references

951.04   China--Period of Republic, 1912-1949

Chang, Iris

★ The **rape** of Nanking; the forgotten holocaust of World War II. Penguin 1998 290p il pa $16   **951.04**

1. Sino-Japanese Conflict, 1937-1945 2. Nanjing (Jiangsu Province, China) massacre, 1937

ISBN 0-14-027744-7; 978-0-14-027744-9

LC 97-24137

First published 1997 by Basic Books

"Chang's book is a memorial to the victims of Nanking, a damning indictment of Japanese political historiography, a valuable addition to Pacific war literature, and a literary model of how to speak about the unspeakable." Booklist

Includes bibliographical references

Sun Shuyun

The **Long** March; the true history of Communist China's founding myth. Doubleday 2007 270p il map $26   **951.04**

1. Heads of state 2. Communist leaders 3. Political leaders 4. China -- History -- 1912-1949

ISBN 978-0-385-52024-9; 0-385-52024-7

First published 2006 in the United Kingdom

"In 1934, surrounded by Chiang Kai-shek's forces in the south, Mao's Red Army marched more than eight thousand miles to a new base, in the northwest. The march, completed by only a fifth of the original army, was a defeat in all ways but one: it returned Mao from the political wilderness to power. Mao transformed the march into the founding myth of modern China and, in doing so, created a new narrative around victories that never happened. Shuyun, a Chinese-born BBC documentary producer, retraces the route and interviews the few remaining survivors, in an account that shows the human cost of Mao's revisionism." New Yorker

951.05   China--Period of People's Republic, 1949-

August, Oliver

Inside the red mansion; on the trail of China's most wanted man. Houghton Mifflin Company 2007 268p map $26   **951.05**

1. Smugglers 2. Commercial agents 3. China --

Description and travel

ISBN 978-0-618-71498-8; 0-618-71498-7

LC 2006-26930

"In 1999, China's Public Enemy No. 1 was 'Fatty' Lai Changxing, an illiterate rice farmer turned real-estate and shipping mogul who fled the country, accused of heading a multibillion-dollar smuggling ring. This account . . . casts Lai's rise and fall as a cautionary tale of boomtown China. The author tours the remains of Lai's empire—a film studio built as a replica of the Forbidden City; a posh brothel where he bribed Party officials with the company of 'Miss Temporarys'—but he reserves his most vivid prose for the 'fakers and fortune seekers, oddballs and outlaws' he meets along the way." New Yorker

Becker, Jasper

The **Chinese**. Oxford University Press 2002 493p il map pa $21.95   **951.05**

1. China -- Social conditions 2. China -- Economic conditions

ISBN 0-19-514940-8

First published 2000 by Free Press

This "is a captivating and enlightening read for anyone interested in Asian or cultural studies." Booklist [review of 2000 edition]

Includes bibliographical references

Chang, Jung

Wild swans; three daughters of China. Simon & Schuster 1991 524p il hardcover o.p. pa $15 **951.05**

1. Women -- China 2. China -- History

ISBN 0-7432-4698-5 pa

LC 91-20696

The author "tells the harrowing life stories of her maternal grandmother, her mother, and herself. Their tales span a period of radical change in China that has touched every aspect of life." Booklist

Chen, Da

Sounds of the river; a memoir. HarperCollins Pubs. 2002 307p hardcover o.p. pa $12.95 **951.05**

1. Lawyers 2. Linguists 3. Calligraphers 4. China -- History -- 1949-

ISBN 0-06-095872-3 pa

LC 2001-39215

"Da Chen once again describes his past with fondness and buoyancy." N Y Times Book Rev

Dikötter, Frank

Mao's great famine; the history of China's most devastating catastrophe, 1958-1962. Walker & Co. 2010 420p il map $30   **951.05**

1. Food supply 2. Heads of state 3. Famines -- China 4. Communist leaders 5. Political leaders 6. Food supply -- China 7. Economic policy -- China 8. China -- Economic policy -- 1949-1976

ISBN 978-0-8027-7768-3; 0-8027-7768-6

LC 2010-13141

This book on the 1958-1962 famine in China "focuses on describing and conveying to the reader the stark effects of the famine at the local level. . . . [T]he first two . . . parts retrace major events of the Great Leap Forward disaster and famine. . . stressing the crucial role of the Lushan Conference." Other chapters depict "survival strategies, repressive violence . . . the various ways in which people died, and the places where most deaths occurred." (China Perspectives)

The author parses this study of the Great Leap Forward into three "components: Mao Zedong's bloody-minded resolve to implement the accelerated collectivization of the countryside, and the stifling of all opposition; the effects of these devastating policies on agriculture, industry, trade, housing and nature; and the catastrophic human toll (at least 45 million people died unnecessarily between 1958 and 1962')." Kirkus

Includes bibliographical references and index

Fallows, James M.

Postcards from Tomorrow Square; reports from China. [by] James Fallows. Vintage Books 2009 262p pa $14.95 **951.05**
1. China -- History -- 1976-
ISBN 978-0-307-45624-3; 0-307-45624-2

LC 2008-28083

"In this series of articles, Fallows reports on interesting trends and personalities in China—ambitious entrepreneurs and the rise in popularity of reality shows on state-run television. Despite the Western view of a powerful, single-minded China, Fallows presents a portrait of a huge and complex nation with such a vast range of ages and regional, geographic, and cultural differences that it defies simple definition." Booklist

Leibovitz, Liel

Fortunate sons; the 120 Chinese boys who came to America, went to school, and revolutionized an ancient civilization. [by] Liel Leibovitz & Matthew Miller. W.W. Norton 2011 319p il $26.95 **951.05**
1. Educators 2. China -- History 3. Education -- China 4. China -- History -- 1861-1912 5. China -- Politics and government 6. China -- History -- Reform movement, 1898 7. Chinese students -- United States -- History 8. China -- Politics and government -- 19th century
ISBN 0-393-07004-2; 978-0-393-07004-0

LC 2010-37724

The book "begins with Yung Wing, who came to America in the late 1840s. The first Chinese student admitted to Yale, he returned to his homeland in 1854. . . . Under his tutelage, 120 Chinese boys crossed the Pacific in the 1870s, intent on learning Western skills that might help their country modernize." (N Y Times Book Rev) Index.

"A curious, little-known episode of Sino-American history vividly told." Kirkus

Includes bibliographical references

Levine, Steven I.

Deng Xiaoping; A Revolutionary Life. by Alexander V. Pantsov, with Steven I. Levine. Oxford University Press 2015 648 p. illustrations, maps $34.95 **951.05**
ISBN 019939203X; 9780199392032

LC 2014042299

This biography on Chinese Communist leader Deng Xiaoping, by Alexander V. Pantsov and Steven Levine, "does what no other biography has done: based on newly discovered documents, it covers his entire life, from his childhood and student years to the post-Tiananmen era. Thanks to unprecedented access to Russian archives containing massive files on the Chinese Communist Party, the authors present a wealth of new material on Deng dating back to the 1920s." (Publisher's note)

"Aiming for and largely achieving a balanced perspective, Pantsov and Levine give Deng credit for his accomplishments but do not shy away from his crimes. The result is a nuanced portrait of a genuine reformer who nevertheless kept his foot firmly on the brakes; a man of the people with an authoritarian bent; and, in the end, a man more similar to Mao than he was different." Booklist

★ **Mao**; the real story. Alexander V. Pantsov with Steven I. Levine. 1st Simon & Schuster hardcover Simon & Schuster 2012 xix, 755 p.p $35 **951.05**
1. Communism -- China 2. China -- Politics and government 3. Heads of state -- China -- Biography 4. China -- Politics and government -- 1949-1976
ISBN 1451654472; 9781451654479; 9781451654493

LC 2011053113

This book offers a biography of Communist leader Mao Zedong. It relates "how Mao, who joined the Communist Party in 1920, fought his way . . . to its leadership in the 1930s. . . . Taking power in 1949, Mao established a Stalinist autocracy featuring purges, massive social upheaval, and disastrous economic policies. . . . [Alexander V.] Pantsov reveals that Mao took pains to remain a faithful follower until Stalin's 1952 death." (Publishers Weekly)

Includes bibliographical references and index

Lord, Bette Bao

Legacies: a Chinese mosaic. Knopf 1990 245p hardcover o.p. pa $19 **951.05**
1. China -- Politics and government 2. China -- Social life and customs
ISBN 0-449-90620-5 pa

LC 89-43452

The author lived in China from 1985 to 1989. Her book is based on interviews with Chinese people, including an actress, a teacher, a veteran of the Long March, an artist, a journalist, a peasant, an entrepreneur and a Communist Party cadre, who recount their experiences of persecution during the Cultural Revolution. The author also describes her own experiences and her family history

"A vivid and startling mosaic of the political struggles that foreshadowed the Tiananmen Square uprising." Time

Ma Jian

Red dust; a path through China. translated from the Chinese by Flora Drew. Pantheon Bks. 2001 324p maps hardcover o.p. pa $14 **951.05**
1. China -- Description and travel
ISBN 0-385-72023-8 pa

LC 2001-21575

"Faced with imprisonment, Jian fled to the Chinese countryside, eventually making his way to Tibet. His journey is presented as a combination travelogue and a narrative of sheer poetry and spirituality." Booklist

Pan, Philip P.

★ **Out** of Mao's shadow; the struggle for the soul of a new China. Simon & Schuster 2008 349p il map $28; pa $16 **951.05**

1. China -- History -- 1949- 2. China -- Social conditions

ISBN 978-1-4165-3705-2; 1-4165-3705-8; 978-1-4165-3706-9 pa; 1-4165-3706-6 pa

LC 2008-11550

This is "one of the most revealing books about China since it opened up to the outside world in the 1970s." N Y Rev Books

Includes bibliographical references

Pomfret, John

Chinese lessons; five classmates and the story of the new China. H. Holt 2006 315p il map $26 **951.05**

1. China

ISBN 978-0-8050-7615-8; 0-8050-7615-8

LC 2006-41211

This "is a highly personal, honest, funny and well-informed account of China's hyperactive effort to forget its past and reinvent its future." N Y Times Book Rev

Salzman, Mark

Iron & silk. Random House 1987 211p hardcover o.p. pa $12.95 **951.05**

1. Martial arts 2. China -- Description and travel

ISBN 0-394-55156-7; 0-394-75511-1 pa

LC 86-11846

The author tells of his two years teaching English to medical students in China's Hunan Province following his graduation from Yale University in 1982.

This book is "not so much a treatise on modern Chinese mores as a series of telling vignettes. . . . [The author] describes his encounter with Pan Qingfu, the country's foremost master of wushu, the traditional Chinese martial art." Time

Schoppa, R. Keith

The **Columbia** guide to modern Chinese history. Columbia Univ. Press 2000 356p il map (Columbia guides to Asian history) $49 **951.05**

1. China -- History

ISBN 0-231-11276-9

LC 99-53420

This narrative overview of Chinese history focuses on five areas: domestic politics, society, the economy, culture, and relations with the outside world. Contains approximately 500 annotated entries for further research in English as well as electronic resources and films. A chronology, excerpts from primary documents, and numerous graphs and tables are appended

Includes bibliographical references

Short, Philip

Mao; a life. Holt & Co. 2000 782p il maps hardcover o.p. pa $20 **951.05**

1. Heads of state 2. Communist leaders 3. Political

leaders 4. China -- Politics and government

ISBN 0-8050-6638-1 pa

LC 99-41839

This biography "takes Mao from his 1893 birth in the village of Shaoshan to school in Changsha, where he trained to be a teacher, and then into revolutionary activity, the long fight with Chiang Kai-shek, and leadership of the most populous nation on Earth." Booklist

Includes bibliographical references

Spence, Jonathan D.

Mao Zedong; {by} Jonathan Spence. Viking 1999 188p map (Penguin lives series) $19.95 **951.05**

1. Heads of state 2. Communist leaders 3. Political leaders 4. China -- Politics and government

ISBN 0-670-88669-6

LC 99-27739

"This specialist's book for nonspecialists concisely recounts the life of the Communist leader who revolutionized China. Ideas travel fast: Mao, a peasant son born in 1893, was able to read Darwin and Marx in translation and add Western ideas to his heritage of classical Chinese thought, and Spence helps us understand why he eventually embraced Communism. What is less clear is why a gifted, high-minded youth became a ruthless, crackpot tyrant." New Yorker

Includes bibliographical references

Vogel, Ezra F.

Deng Xiaoping and the transformation of China; Ezra F. Vogel. Belknap Press of Harvard University Press 2011 xxiv, 876p ill. **951.05**

1. Communism -- China 2. China -- Economic conditions 3. China -- Politics and government 4. Biography, Individual

ISBN 978-0-674-05544-5; 0-674-05544-6; 9780674062832

LC 2011006925

Lionel Gelber Prize (Canada) (2012)

This book, a 2012 Lionel Gelber Prize winner, offers a biography of Chinese politician Deng Xiaoping. "Deng was the pragmatic yet disciplined driving force behind China's radical transformation in the late twentieth century. He confronted the damage wrought by the Cultural Revolution, dissolved Mao's cult of personality, and loosened the economic and social policies that had stunted China's growth. Obsessed with modernization and technology, Deng opened trade relations with the West, which lifted hundreds of millions of his countrymen out of poverty. Yet at the same time he answered to his authoritarian roots, most notably when he ordered the crackdown in June 1989 at Tiananmen Square. . . . In the fifty years of his tumultuous rise to power, he endured accusations, purges, and even exile before becoming China's preeminent leader from 1978 to 1989 and again in 1992. When he reached the top, Deng saw an opportunity to creatively destroy much of the economic system he had helped build for five decades as a loyal follower of Mao—and he did not hesitate." (Publisher's note)

Includes bibliographical references and index

951.056   China -- 1960-1969

Dikötter, Frank

The **Cultural** Revolution; A People's History, 1962-1976. by Frank Dikötter. St. Martin's Press 2016 432 p. map $32   **951.056**
   1. China -- History -- 1949-1976
   ISBN 1632864215; 9781632864215
   This book on the Chinese Cultural Revolution, by Frank Dikötter, "draws for the first time on hundreds of previously classified party documents, from secret police reports to unexpurgated versions of leadership speeches. . . . Dikötter uses this wealth of material to undermine the picture of complete conformity that is often supposed to have characterized the last years of the Mao era." (Publisher's note)
   "Dikotter tells a harrowing tale of unbelievable suffering. A potent combination of precise history and moving examples, plus a useful chronology of events." Kirkus
   Includes bibliographical references and index.

951.06   China -- 2000-

Osnos, Evan

★ **Age** of ambition; chasing fortune, truth, and faith in the new China. Evan Osnos. 1st edition Farrar Straus & Giroux 2014 416 p. map (hardback) $27   **951.06**
   1. China -- Social conditions 2. China -- Politics and government 3. China -- Civilization 4. Individualism -- China 5. Social change -- China 6. Authoritarianism -- China 7. Economic development -- China
   ISBN 0374280746; 9780374280741
                                            LC 2013041338
   Pulitzer Prize Finalist: General Nonfiction (2015)
   Author "Evan Osnos was on the ground in China for years, witness to profound political, economic, and cultural upheaval. In 'Age of Ambition,' he describes the greatest collision taking place in that country: the clash between the rise of the individual and the Communist Party's struggle to retain control." (Publisher's note)
   "Osnos combines scintillating reportage with an eye for telling ironies that illuminate broader trends; without downplaying the uniqueness of Chinese society, he makes its tensions feel achingly familiar for Western readers." Pub Wkly
   Includes bibliographical references index

Schmitz, Rob

Street of Eternal Happiness; big city dreams along a Shanghai road. Rob Schmitz. Crown Publishers 2016 336 p. maps (hardback) $28 **951.132**
   1. Shanghai (China) 2. City and town life -- China -- Shanghai 3. Streets -- China -- Shanghai 4. Shanghai (China) -- Biography 5. Neighborhoods -- China -- Shanghai 6. Shanghai (China) -- Economic conditions 7. Americans -- China -- Shanghai -- Biography 8. Shanghai (China) -- Social life and customs
   ISBN 9780553418088
                                            LC 2015041162
   This book, by Rob Schmitz, offers a "portrait of individuals who hope, struggle, and grow along a single street cutting through the heart of China's most exhilarating metropolis: . . . Modern Shanghai: a global city in the midst of a renaissance, where dreamers arrive each day to partake in a mad torrent of capital, ideas, and opportunity." (Publisher's note)
   "Probing human-interest stories that mine the heart of today's China." Kirkus
   Includes bibliographical references (pages 316-322) and index.

951.249   Taiwan (Formosa) and adjacent islands

Copper, John F.

Taiwan; nation-state or province? John F. Copper. Westview Press 2013 xiii, 259 p.p ill., maps (pbk. : alk. paper) $36   **951.249**
   1. Taiwan 2. Taiwan -- International status
   ISBN 0813346924; 9780813346922; 9780813346939
                                            LC 2012031338
   This book, by John Copper, focuses on Taiwan. The "country's culture, history, and geography are explored in detail, allowing readers a chance to see how people live. . . . Sidebars highlight especially interesting people, places, and events [and] recipes give readers the opportunity to experience foreign cuisine first-hand." (Publisher's note)
   "[A] comprehensive yet concise introduction to Taiwan." Choice
   Includes bibliographical references (p. 237-246) and index

951.9   Korea

Brady, James

The **coldest** war; a memoir of Korea. St. Martin's Griffin 2000 248p il map pa $15.95   **951.9**
   1. Korean War, 1950-1953 -- Personal narratives
   ISBN 978-0-312-26511-3; 0-312-26511-5
   First published 1990 by Orion Bks.
   "From November 1951 to July 1952, the author was a marine lieutenant who frequently found himself called upon to fight and kill Chinese and North Korean soldiers on the battlefields of Korea. His memoir of that experience is a well-crafted piece told in a voice that skillfully mixes the sardonic insight of an older man looking back on a highly extraordinary episode of his past with the naivete of the young warrior he once was." Booklist

Breen, Michael

The **Koreans**; who they are, what they want, where their future lies. St. Martin's Press 1999 276p hardcover o.p. pa $14.95   **951.9**
   1. Korean national characteristics 2. Korea -- History
   ISBN 0-312-32609-2 pa
                                            LC 99-45599
   First published 1998 in the United Kingdom
   In this survey of Korea's culture, the author "probes such diverse topics as the status of civil liberties, generational social strains within families, and the massive corruption that permeates Korean society. He writes with a snappy, readable style." Booklist
   Includes bibliographical references

Cumings, Bruce

★ **Korea's** place in the sun; a modern history. Updated ed; W. W. Norton 2005 542p il map pa $16.95　　　**951.9**

1. Korea -- History

ISBN 0-393-32702-7; 0-393-31681-5

LC 2006-276040

First published 1997

This history of Korea from 1860 focuses primarily on the post-1945 period

"Mr. Cumings has pored over the historical documents and he argues intelligently. His book is important precisely because he marshals considerable evidence to challenge conventional understanding." N Y Times Book Rev

Includes bibliographical references

The **Korean** War; a history. Modern Library 2010 288p il map (Modern Library chronicles)　　　**951.9**

1. Korean War, 1950-1953　2. Korean War, 1950-1953 -- United States

ISBN 0-679-64357-5; 978-0-679-64357-9

LC 2010005629

This is a "revisionist history of America's intervention in Korea." (N Y Times (Late N Y Ed)) Index.

A "revisionist history of America's intervention in Korea. Beneath its bland title, Mr. Cumings's book is a squirm-inducing assault on America's moral behavior during the Korean War, a conflict that he says is misremembered when it is remembered at all. It's a book that puts the reflexive anti-Americanism of North Korea's leaders into sympathetic historical context. . . . [Cumings] mows down a host of myths about the war in his short new book, which is a distillation of his own scholarship and that of many other historians." N Y Times (Late N Y Ed)

Includes bibliographical references

Halberstam, David

★ The **coldest** winter; America and the Korean War. Hyperion 2007 719p map $35　　　**951.9**

1. Korean War, 1950-1953

ISBN 1-401-30052-9; 978-1-401-30052-4

LC 2007-1635

"Alive with the voices of the men who fought, Halberstam's telling is a virtuoso work of history." Publ Wkly

Includes bibliographical references

Oberdorfer, Don

The **two** Koreas; a contemporary history. New ed; Basic Bks. 2001 521p il map pa $21　　　**951.9**

1. Korea -- History

ISBN 0-465-05162-6

LC 2001-43486

First published 1997 by Addison-Wesley

This is a study of North and South Korean politics and an analysis of U.S. policy from the 1970s to the present

Includes bibliographical references

Peterson, Mark

A **brief** history of Korea; [by] Mark Peterson with Phillip Margulies. Facts On File 2010 328p il map (Brief history) $49.50　　　**951.9**

1. Korea -- History

ISBN 978-0-8160-5085-7

LC 2009-18889

This book "covers the history of Korea from the origins of the Korean people in prehistoric times to the economic and political situation in North and South Korea today." Publisher's note

Includes bibliographical references

951.904　Korea 1945-1999

Hickey, Michael

The **Korean** War; the West confronts communism. Overlook Press 2000 397p il maps $35　　　**951.904**

1. Korean War, 1950-1953　2. United Nations -- Armed Forces -- Korea

ISBN 1-58567-035-9

LC 00-27692

First published 1999 in the United Kingdom

An "analysis of both the military and political factors that caused the war and the conduct on all sides. . . . The author does not mince words when criticizing General MacArthur and other UN commanders. Using declassified documents as well as regimental and personal diaries, he wades through political intrigue and military disasters and triumphs to give us a memorable account." Libr J

Includes bibliographical references

Hutton, Robin

Sgt. Reckless; America's war horse. Robin Hutton. Regnery Publishing 2014 346 p. illustrations (alk. paper) $27.99　　　**951.904**

1. Horses　2. Animals -- War use　3. Korean War, 1950-1953 -- Biography　4. Korean War, 1950-1953 -- Campaigns　5. Korean War, 1950-1953 -- Artillery operations　6. United States. Marine Corps -- History -- 20th century　7. War horses -- Korea (South) -- History -- 20th century　8. War horses -- United States -- History -- 20th century　9. United States. Marine Corps. Marine Regiment, 5th -- Biography

ISBN 1621572633; 9781621572633

LC 2014019750

This book, by Robin Hutton, tells the story of "a Mongolian mare who was bred to be a racehorse . . . purchased . . . and renamed . . . Reckless, for the Recoilless Rifles Platoon, Anti-Tank Division, of the 5th Marines she'd be joining. . . . This . . . equine became an American hero. Reckless was awarded two Purple Hearts for her valor and was officially promoted to staff sergeant twice, a distinction never bestowed upon an animal before or since." (Publisher's note)

"Hutton's passion and admiration for her subject (she also heads an effort to create a monument to Reckless) shines through in this sparkling and engaging portrait of a most remarkable and courageous animal." Pub Wkly

Includes bibliographical references and index

Sergeant Reckless, America's war horse

Makos, Adam

Devotion; An Epic Story of Heroism, Friendship, and Sacrifice. by Adam Makos. Random House Inc. 2015 464 p. 16 plates; illustrations; maps $28 **951.904**

ISBN 0804176582; 9780804176583

LC 2015023955

This book, by Adam Makos, "tells the inspirational story of the U.S. Navy's most famous aviator duo, Lieutenant Tom Hudner and Ensign Jesse Brown, and the Marines they fought to defend. A white New Englander from the country-club scene, Tom passed up Harvard to fly fighters for his country. An African American sharecropper's son from Mississippi, Jesse became the navy's first black carrier pilot, defending a nation that wouldn't even serve him in a bar." (Publisher's note)

Weintraub, Stanley, 1929-

A **Christmas** far from home; an epic tale of courage and survival during the Korean War. Stanley Weintraub. Da Capo Press, a member of the Perseus Books Group Press 2014 304 p. illustrations; maps (hardcover) $26.99 **951.904**

1. Christmas 2. United States. Army 3. Korean War, 1950-1953 4. Soldiers -- United States 5. Courage -- Korea (North) -- History -- 20th century 6. Escapes -- Korea (North) -- History -- 20th century 7. Marines -- United States -- History -- 20th century 8. Soldiers -- United States -- History -- 20th century 9. Survival -- Korea (North) -- History -- 20th century 10. Christmas -- Korea (North) -- History -- 20th century 11. United States. Army. Corps, 10th -- History -- 20th century 12. Korean War, 1950-1953 -- Regimental histories -- United States 13. Korean War, 1950-1953 -- Campaigns -- Korea (North) -- Changjin Reservoir

ISBN 0306822326; 9780306822322

LC 2014011944

In this book, by Stanley Weintraub, "five months into the Korean War, General Douglas MacArthur flew to American positions in the north and grandly announced an end-the-war-by-Christmas offensive. . . . Marching north in plunging temperatures, General Edward Almond's X Corps, which included a Marine division under the able leadership of General Oliver Smith, encountered little resistance. But thousands of Chinese . . . were lying in wait and would soon trap tens of thousands of US troops." (Publisher's note)

"The tragic tale of how the arrogance of a general led to disastrous consequences for the American troops in North Korea in 1950... Weintraub expertly delineates the unraveling disaster for the entrapped, frozen, dispirited troops on the ground." Kirkus

Includes bibliographical references and index

951.93 North Korea (People's Democratic Republic of Korea)

Demick, Barbara

Nothing to envy; ordinary lives in North Korea. Spiegel & Grau 2009 314p il map **951.93**

1. Koreans 2. Korea (North) 3. Korea (North) -- Social

conditions 4. Korea (North) -- Economic conditions

ISBN 0-385-52390-4; 978-0-385-52390-5

LC 2009-22420

This book "follows the lives of six ordinary North Koreans, including a female doctor, a pair of star-crossed lovers, a factory worker and an orphan." (N Y Times (Late N Y Ed))

"A fascinating and deeply personal look at the lives of six defectors from the repressive totalitarian regime of the Republic of North Korea, in which Demick . . . draws out details of daily life that would not otherwise be known to Western eyes because of the near-complete media censorship north of the arbitrary border drawn after Japan's surrender ending WWII." Publ Wkly

Includes bibliographical references

Hassig, Ralph C.

The **hidden** people of North Korea; everyday life in the hermit kingdom. [by] Ralph Hassig and Kongdan Oh. Rowman & Littlefield Publishers 2009 300p il $39.95 **951.93**

1. Heads of state 2. Korea (North) 3. Communist leaders 4. Korea (North) -- Social conditions 5. Political culture -- Korea (North) 6. Korea (North) -- Economic conditions 7. Korea (North) -- Politics and government

ISBN 978-0-7425-6718-4; 0-7425-6718-4

LC 2009-29786

The authors "gather behind-the-curtain research to expose day-to-day life, and the powers that control it, in North Korea, a developed nation where meat is a luxury and the Internet doesn't exist for anyone but the dictator. . . . The uninformed will find much that's fascinating and shocking: a nation of castes and concentration camps, replete with a politics of fear that rivals the worst Orwell could imagine." Publ Wkly

Includes bibliographical references

Lankov, Andrei

The **real** North Korea; life and politics in the failed Stalinist utopia. Andrei Lankov. Oxford University Press 2013 304 p. (hardcover) $27.95 **951.93**

1. Korea (North) -- Social conditions 2. Korea (North) -- Politics and government 3. Korea (North) -- Foreign relations 4. Korea (North) -- Politics and government -- 1994-

ISBN 0199964297; 9780199964291

LC 2012046992

This first half of this book by Andrei Lankov "provides an overview of North Korea's past history, and discusses how it has changed in the years since the famine of the 1990s. The second half predicts that the North Korean regime will ultimately collapse, then discusses likely outcomes of this event." (Library Journal)

Includes bibliographical references and index

952   Japan

Jansen, Marius B.

★ The **making** of modern Japan. Belknap Press
2000 871p il maps $35; pa $18.95   **952**
1. Japan -- History
ISBN 0-674-00334-9; 0-674-00991-6 pa
LC 00-41352

"Jansen has produced what is sure to become the standard narrative history of modern Japan. . . . In every way
this is a remarkable book . . . and no reference collection on
Japan can pretend to be complete without it." Choice

Includes bibliographical references

McClain, James L.

Japan, a modern history. Norton 2001 632p il
maps $35; pa $31.25   **952**
1. Japan -- History
ISBN 0-393-04156-5; 0-393-97720-X pa
LC 2001-34545

"This is a well-written, well-researched, and easily readable survey of the modern history of a fascinating and important nation." Booklist

Includes bibliographical references

Mockett, Marie Mutsuki

Where the Dead Pause, and the Japanese Say
Goodbye; A Journey. by Marie Mutsuki Mockett. W
W Norton & Co Inc 2015 336 p. $26.95   **952**
1. Grief 2. Sendai Earthquake, Japan, 2011 3.
Fukushima Nuclear Accident, Fukushima, Japan, 2011
ISBN 0393063011; 9780393063011
LC 2014032438

In this memoir, "Marie Mutsuki Mockett's family owns
a Buddhist temple 25 miles from the Fukushima Daiichi
nuclear power plant. In March 2011, after the earthquake
and tsunami, radiation levels prohibited the burial of her
Japanese grandfather's bones. As Japan mourned thousands
of people lost in the disaster, Mockett also grieved for her
American father, who had died unexpectedly. Seeking consolation, Mockett is guided by a colorful cast of Zen priests
and ordinary Japanese." (Publisher's note)

"Mockett's involving and revelatory chronicle of Japanese spirituality in a time of crisis greatly enriches our perceptions of both a unique culture and the human longing for
connection with the dead." Booklist

Perez, Louis G.

The **history** of Japan; 2nd ed.; Greenwood Press
2009 266p map (Greenwood histories of the modern
nations) $49.95   **952**
1. Reference books 2. Japan -- History
ISBN 978-0-313-36442-6
LC 2008-52242

First published 1998

This history covers prehistoric and early feudal Japan to
the 21st Century. Cultural aspects examined include theater
and cinema, marriage customs, and youth culture as well as
the women's movement and political scandals.

"With its essential chronology, term glossary, and premier list, the volume serves as both engaging read and
quick-reference." Libr J

Includes bibliographical references

952.03   Japan--1868-1945

Buruma, Ian

Inventing Japan, 1853-1964. Modern Lib. 2003
194p hardcover o.p. pa $12.95   **952.03**
1. Japan -- History
ISBN 0-679-64085-1; 0-8129-7286-4 pa
LC 2002-26346

"Buruma traces the remarkable metamorphosis that
transformed an isolated island shogunate into an expansive
military empire and then into a pacified and prosperous democracy. . . . An excellent introductory study." Booklist

Includes bibliographical references

Gordon, Andrew

The **modern** history of Japan. Oxford University
Press 2003 384p il $35; pa $29.95   **952.03**
1. Japan -- History
ISBN 0-19-511060-9; 0-19-511061-7 pa
LC 2002-70916

The author examines "Japan's political, economic, social, and cultural inventions of its modernity in evolving
international contexts, incorporating inside viewpoints and
debates. Beyond identifying the national stages (feudalism,
militarism, democracy), the author innovatively emphasizes
how labor unions, cultural figures, and groups in society
(especially women) have been affected over time and have
responded." Libr J

Includes bibliographical references and index

Keene, Donald

Emperor of Japan; Meiji and His world, 1852-
1912. Columbia Univ. Press 2002 922p il $82.50;
pa $27.95   **952.03**
1. Emperors 2. Japan -- History -- 1868-1945
ISBN 0-231-12340-X; 0-231-12341-8 pa
LC 2001-28826

This is a "biography-cum-history of Emperor Meiji and
his times. . . . Meiji's reign saw Japan become fully industrialized under a brand new constitution, and with new economic and educational systems adopted. Despite the book's
massive scale, Keene's graceful writing holds the reader's
interest throughout." Booklist

Includes bibliographical references

Pleshakov, Konstantin

The **Tsar's** last armada; the epic journey to the
Battle of Tsushima. {by} Constantine Pleshakov.
Basic Bks. 2002 xx, 396p il maps hardcover o.p.
pa $17.50   **952.03**
1. Russo-Japanese War, 1904-1905
ISBN 0-465-05792-6 pa
LC 2001-52532

This is an account of events leading to the Russo-Japanese War and the defeat of the Russian fleet in the Tsushima
Straits in 1905

"A compulsively readable account told from the Russian viewpoint." Booklist

Includes bibliographical references

Seagrave, Sterling

The **Yamato** dynasty; the secret history of Japan's Imperial family. Broadway Bks. 2000 394p il hardcover o.p. pa $23   **952.03**
1. Emperors 2. Japan -- Kings and rulers 3. Japan -- Politics and government

ISBN 0-7679-0497-4 pa

LC 99-49888

This "history of Japan from the mid-19th century to the present weaves together an iconoclastic historical narrative with a mostly caustic view of Japan's imperial family. The Seagraves depict modern Japan as a country consistently dominated by a closed financial oligarchy in league with politicians, bureaucrats, the imperial family, and underworld bosses." Libr J

Includes bibliographical references

952.04   Japan 1945-1999

Dower, John W.

Embracing defeat; Japan in the wake of World War II. by John Dower. Norton 1999 676p il $29.95; pa $17.95   **952.04**
1. Japan -- History -- 1945-1952, Allied occupation

ISBN 0-393-04686-9; 0-393-32027-8 pa

LC 98-22133

"Dower demonstrates an impressive mastery of voluminous sources, both American and Japanese, and he deftly situates the political story within a rich cultural context." Publ Wkly

Includes bibliographical references

953   Arabian Peninsula and adjacent areas

Filiu, Jean-Pierre

Gaza; A History. Jean-Pierre Filiu; translated by John King. Oxford University Press 2014 384 p. maps $29.95   **953**
1. Gaza Strip 2. Gaza -- History 3. Arab-Israeli conflict 4. Gaza Strip -- History 5. Land settlement -- Gaza 6. Gaza Strip -- Social conditions 7. Gaza Strip -- Economic conditions 8. Gaza Strip -- Politics and government 9. Social conflict -- Gaza Strip -- History

ISBN 0190201894; 9780190201890

LC 2013497342

This book, by Jean-Pierre Filiu, presents the history of Gaza. "Wedged between the Negev and Sinai deserts on one side and the Mediterranean Sea on the other, Gaza was contested by the Pharaohs, Persians, Greeks, Romans, Byzantines, Arabs, Fatimids, Mamluks, Crusaders, and Ottomans. Then in 1948, 200,000 people sought refuge in Gaza. . . . It is here that Palestinian nationalism grew and sprouted into a dream of statehood, a journey much filled with strife." (Publisher's note)

"While the chronological account leaves out some significant discussions, such as everyday politics in Gaza,

as in Asef Bayat's Life as Politics: How Ordinary People Change the Middle East (CH, Aug'10, 47-7167), Filiu is at his best when he engages with various sources in uncovering histories mostly ignored or even unknown to many. A must read for students and scholars of the modern Middle East, and anyone who wants to understand Palestinian history. Summing Up: Essential. All public and academic libraries." Choice

Includes bibliographical references (pages 375-379) and indexes

Krane, Jim

City of gold; Dubai and the dream of capitalism. St. Martin's Press 2009 356p il map $27.99   **953**
1. Dubai (United Arab Emirates)

ISBN 9780312535742

LC 2009-13188

The author "traces the historical roots and economic and political changes of 'a small Arab village that grew into a big city' and profiles the members of the ruling royal family—Sheikh Rashid, Sheikh Zayed, and Sheikh Mohammed—whose vision brought Dubai to where it is today. . . . This landmark work is recommended to those interested in the history, politics, and economics of the Middle East; an excellent choice for anyone who wishes to learn more about Dubai." Libr J

Includes bibliographical references

953.305   Yemen -- 1918-

Kasinof, Laura

Don't be afraid of the bullets; an accidental war correspondent in Yemen. Laura Kasinof. Arcade Publishing 2014 304 p. map (hardcover) $24.95   **953.305**
1. Yemen 2. Protest movements 3. Arab Spring, 2010- 4. War correspondents 5. Americans -- Yemen (Republic) -- Biography 6. anā (Yemen) -- Biography 7. Yemen (Republic) -- History -- 1990- -- Biography 8. War correspondents -- Yemen (Republic) -- Biography 9. Foreign correspondents -- Yemen (Republic) -- Biography 10. Yemen (Republic) -- Politics and government -- 21st century 11. anā (Yemen) -- Description and travel 12. Protest movements -- Yemen (Republic) -- History -- 21st century 13. anā (Yemen) -- Social conditions -- 21st century

ISBN 1628724455; 9781628724455

LC 2014019103

This memoir tells the story of freelance journalist Laura Kasinof. "When she first moved to [Yemen] in 2009, she was the only American reporter based in the country. . . . When antigovernment protests broke out in [2011], . . . she contacted the 'New York Times' to see if she could cover the rapidly unfolding events for the newspaper. Laura never planned to be a war correspondent, but found herself in the middle of brutal government attacks on peaceful protesters." (Publisher's note)

"By the book's end, she is sharper, savvier and a confirmed Yemenophile. Even if the reader doesn't fully grasp the appeal Yemen holds for Kasinof, her passion for the country still makes for a compelling tale."

953.8   Saudi Arabia

House, Karen Elliott

On Saudi Arabia; its people, past, religion, fault lines--and future. Karen Elliott House. 1st ed. Alfred A. Knopf 2012 x, 308 p.p ill., map (hardcover) $28.95   **953.8**
1. Saudi Arabia -- History 2. Saudi Arabia -- Politics and government 3. Saudi Arabia -- Religion 4. Saudi Arabia -- Civilization 5. Saudi Arabia -- Social life and customs
ISBN 0307272168; 9780307272164

LC 2012018977

This book, by Pulitzer Prize-winning reporter Karen Elliott House, "explores all facets of life in . . . [Saudi Arabia]: its tribal past, its complicated present, its precarious future. Through observation, anecdote, extensive interviews, and analysis Karen Elliot House navigates the maze in which Saudi citizens find themselves trapped and reveals the mysterious nation that is the world's largest exporter of oil, critical to global stability, and a source of Islamic terrorists." (Publisher's note)

Includes bibliographical references (p. 281-289)

Lacey, Robert

Inside the Kingdom; kings, clerics, modernists, terrorists, and the struggle for Saudi Arabia. Viking 2009 404p il map $27.95   **953.8**
1. Saudi Arabia -- Social conditions
ISBN 978-0-670-02118-5; 0-670-02118-0

LC 2009-08367

Sequel to The kingdom (1982)

The author's "eye for sweeping trends and the telling detail combined with the depth, breadth and evenhandedness of his research makes for an indispensable guide." Publ Wkly

Includes bibliographical references

Wynbrandt, James

A brief history of Saudi Arabia; foreword by Fawaz A. Gerges. 2nd ed; Facts On File 2010 364p il map (Brief history) $49.50; pa $19.95   **953.8**
1. Saudi Arabia -- History
ISBN 978-0-8160-7876-9; 978-0-8160-8250-6 pa

LC 2010-5466

First published 2004

This history of Saudi Arabia covers "pre-Islamic Arabia; Bedouin society and culture; the birth and spread of Islam; the development of and philosophy behind Wahhabism; the origins of House Saud; Saudi Arabia's role in the Middle East; Saudi Arabia's relationship to the United States; the battle between conservative and progressive elements in the monarchy today; [and] the reign of King Abdullah." Publisher's note

Includes glossary and bibliographical references

954   India and neighboring south Asian countries

Dalrymple, William

White Mughals; love and betrayal in the eighteenth-century India. Viking 2003 xlvii, 459p il map $34.95; pa $16   **954**
1. British -- India
ISBN 0-670-03184-4; 0-14-200412-X pa

LC 2002-191082

James Kirkpatrick was the Resident of the East India Company in Hyderabad. This book documents his marriage to Khair-un-Nissa, a Mughal aristocrat

This "book, ambitious in scope and rich in detail, demonstrates that a century before Kipling's 'never the twain'— and two centuries before neocons and radical Islamists trumpeted the clash of civilizations—the story of the Westerner in Muslim India was one not of conquest but of appreciation, adaptation, and seduction." New Yorker

Includes bibliographical references

Hardy, Justine

In the valley of mist; Kashmir: one family in a changing world. Free Press 2009 209p il map $25   **954**
1. Jammu and Kashmir (India)
ISBN 978-1-4391-0289-3; 1-4391-0289-9

LC 2008-55093

The author "channels the story of Kashmir's dark transformation from an idyllic place . . . of beauty and freedom to a realm of chaos and bloodshed through the lives of one family, the Dars. . . . Hardy's intimate and dramatic chronicle clarifies and humanizes Kashmir's torments, which are of grave global consequence." Booklist

Lapierre, Dominique

The City of Joy. Warner Books 1991 528p il pa $7.99   **954**
1. Calcutta (India) -- Social conditions
ISBN 0-446-35556-9

Original French edition, 1985

An account of life in the most squalid of Calcutta's slums, Anand Nagar (The City of Joy). The author focuses on the lives of a rickshaw driver, a Polish Catholic priest, an American doctor and an Assamese nurse.

McLeod, John

The history of India. Greenwood Press 2002 xx, 223p (Greenwood histories of the modern nations) $39.95   **954**
1. Mogul Empire 2. India -- History -- 1526-1765
ISBN 0-313-31459-4

LC 2002-276829

The author presents "in broad outlines some of the major events and episodes that make up India's history. . . . This is a useful compilation of important facts relating to Indian history. Its strength lies primarily in the last six chapters in which brief narratives of the struggle for independence and post-independence India down to the close of the twentieth century are nicely presented. All in all, this is a book that

all libraries should have." Recomm Ref Books for Small &
Medium-sized Libr & Media Cent, 2003
Includes bibliographical references

Mehta, Suketu
★ **Maximum** city; Bombay lost and found. Alfred A. Knopf 2004 542p $27.95 **954**
1. Bombay (India)
ISBN 0-375-40372-8
LC 2004-48969
The author "explores various aspects of Bombay life,
from setting up residence to exploring the hugely successful domestic film industry; from detailing Bombay's sex
industry to profiling the reasons behind India's own 'September 11,' the 1993 riots and bombings that exposed a
vast enmity between extremist Hindus and Muslims. . . .
Mehta delivers a fresh and unblinking look at contemporary
Bombay." Booklist

Miller, Sam
Delhi; adventures in a megacity. St. Martin's
Press 2010 291p il map $25.99 **954**
1. India -- Social life and customs 2. Delhi (India) --
Description and travel
ISBN 978-0-312-61237-5
LC 2010-13043
First published 2009 in the United Kingdom
The author "presents a highly entertaining and witty account of a walking tour of Delhi. He describes 12 walks that
begin in the center of the city and proceed outward to the satellite towns at the outskirts. Miller's portrayal of the changing landscape and street life is engrossing." Libr J

Rashid, Ahmed
Descent into chaos; the US and the failure of
nation building in Pakistan, Afghanistan, and Central
Asia. Viking 2008 lviii, 484p il map $27.95; pa
$18 **954**
1. Pakistan -- Politics and government 2. Afghanistan
-- Politics and government 3. Central Asia -- Foreign
relations -- United States 4. United States -- Foreign
relations -- Central Asia
ISBN 978-0-670-01970-0; 0-670-01970-4; 978-0-14-
311557-1 pa; 0-14-311557-X pa
LC 2008-02949
This is a "lucid, insightful, and highly readable tome on
the existent and emergent threats in Central Asia." Choice
Includes bibliographical references

Roy, Arundhati
Walking with the comrades. Penguin Books
2011 220p il map pa $15 **954**
1. Terrorism 2. Atrocities 3. Guerrillas 4. Social
conflict 5. India -- Politics and government
ISBN 978-0-14-312059-9
LC 2011039307
The author "exposes the violent contradictions of India's
economic miracle in this blistering critique of the Indian
government's campaign against the Maoist insurgents in the
country's central tribal lands encompassing several states.
Roy, who recounts time spent on the move with a cadre
of rebels, argues forcefully that Operation Green Hunt—

launched by the state under the rubric of the threat of terrorism—is an all-out war to remove indigenous communities
from lands already promised to corporations eager to exploit
their extremely valuable resources. . . . Informed, impassioned, at times strident, and fleet and fascinating when describing life on the ground among the rebels, Roy's prose
will both rouse and ruffle." Publ Wkly
Includes bibliographical references

Sen, Amartya Kumar
The **argumentative** Indian; writings on Indian
history, culture, and identity. [by] Amartya Sen. Farrar, Straus and Giroux 2006 xx, 409p il **954**
1. India -- Civilization
ISBN 0-374-10583-9
LC 2005-49460
"Sen's lucid reasoning and thoroughgoing humanism . .
. ensure a lively and commanding defense of diversity and
dialogue." Publ Wkly
Includes bibliographical references

Walsh, Judith E.
A **brief** history of India; 2nd ed.; Facts On File,
Inc. 2010 414p il map (Brief history) $49.50; pa
$19.95 **954**
1. India -- History
ISBN 978-0-8160-8143-1; 978-0-8160-8362-6 pa
LC 2010-26316
First published 2006
"The Brief History series introduces readers to the dramatic events, notable people, and special customs and traditions that have shaped many of the world's countries. Each
engaging volume covers a specific country and offers a concise history of the struggles and triumphs of the peoples and
cultures that have called that country home." (Publisher's
note)
"The book surveys India's history in about 300 pages,
with a number of pictures and short in-depth sidebars on
items such as "Rajput Clans" and "Dowry Deaths," Walsh
(SUNY, Old Westbury) begins with India's geography and
concludes with a section on contemporary India. . . . The
book is most suitable for those wanting a very quick, basic
introduction to India's history and culture." Choice
Includes bibliographical references

Wolpert, Stanley A.
A **new** history of India; 7th ed; Oxford University Press 2004 530p il map $63.95; pa $43 **954**
1. Mogul Empire
ISBN 0-19-516677-9; 0-19-516678-7 pa
LC 2003-53589
First published 1977. Periodically revised
A comprehensive survey of Indian history from its early
beginnings to the present. Includes discussion of the assassination of Rajiv Gandhi; violence in Kashmir, Punjab, and
Assam; and the effects of rural development
Includes bibliographical references

954.03   India--Period of British rule, 1785-1947

Chadha, Yogesh

Gandhi; a life. Wiley 1998 546p il hardcover o.p. pa $19.95   **954.03**

1. Authors 2. Journalists 3. Essayists 4. Pacifists 5. Memoirists 6. Political leaders 7. Writers on politics 8. India -- Politics and government

ISBN 0-471-35062-1 pa

LC 97-37406

First published 1997 in the United Kingdom with title: Rediscovering Gandhi

"Chadha reexamines Gandhi's life with an eye to restoring its complications and contradictions, noting that 'to suppress his weaknesses would be to undermine his strengths.' And he succeeds in his mission, presenting the great leader not as a holy man but as a humanist and politician." Booklist

Includes bibliographical references

Wolpert, Stanley A.

★ Gandhi's passion; the life and legacy of Mahatma Gandhi. [by] Stanley Wolpert. Oxford Univ. Press 2001 308p il hardcover o.p. pa $17.95 **954.03**

1. Authors 2. Journalists 3. Essayists 4. Pacifists 5. Memoirists 6. Political leaders 7. Writers on politics 8. India -- Politics and government

ISBN 0-19-513060-X; 0-19-515634-X pa

LC 00-45298

"From his pampered childhood to his ascetic final years, the text follows the Mahatma ('Great Soul') on a paradoxical pilgrimage in which the deliberate acceptance of suffering endowed him with the power he needed to challenge the leading politicians of Europe, Africa, and Asia." Booklist

Includes bibliographical references

954.04   India -- 1947-1971

French, Patrick

India; a portrait. Alfred A. Knopf 2011 398p il $30   **954.04**

1. India -- History -- 1947-

ISBN 978-0-307-27243-0; 0-307-27243-5

LC 2011-03921

This work "combines deep research about the country's history with a series of vignettes culled from French's street-level reporting. Taken together, his reading of seminal texts and his interviews with politicians, pimps, businessmen, laborers, farmers, scholars and people from all levels of India's caste system result in a fittingly vigorous and colorful book about what it means to live in India six decades after the nation freed itself from British rule." San Francisco Chron

Includes bibliographical references

Guha, Ramachandra

India after Gandhi; the history of the world's largest democracy. Ecco 2007 893p il map $34.95   **954.04**

1. India -- History -- 1947-

ISBN 978-0-06-019881-7; 0-06-019881-8

LC 2006-52180

This book documents India's transformation from a colonial state to independence.

The author "builds his story by making us witnesses of events as they occur, drawing on contemporary accounts. His voluminous account may seem daunting, but it is crucial for the understanding of modern India. . . . Guha is patient in his approach, gentle in his criticism, exasperated by what he does not like, and eclectic in drawing on evidence that supports his argument." New Statesman

Includes bibliographical references

Tharoor, Shashi

India; from midnight to the millennium. Arcade Pub. 1997 392p map hardcover o.p. pa $15.95   **954.04**

1. India -- History

ISBN 1-55970-384-9; 978-1-55970-803-6 pa; 1-55970-803-4 pa

LC 97-8376

"Each telling anecdote illuminates some aspect of Indian culture, from politics to religion, creating a mosaic that reflects India's endless variations on the theme of life." Booklist

Nehru: the invention of India. Arcade Pub 2003 282p $24.95; pa $13.95   **954.04**

1. Prime ministers 2. Nonfiction writers 3. Prime ministers -- India

ISBN 1-559-70697-X; 1-559-70737-2 pa

LC 2003-58274

The author touches "on key points in Nehru's life: his English education, the importance of guidance he received from his father and Gandhi, his prison years during the drive for independence, and his administration of the new Indian republic. He neatly pulls together the essence of Nehru's beliefs in democratic institution building, pan-Indian secularism, Socialist democratic economy, and the foreign policy of nonalignment. . . . If readers could choose only one narrative about Nehru, this would suffice." Libr J

Includes bibliographical references

954.05   India -- 1971-

Deb, Siddhartha

The **beautiful** and the damned; Siddhartha Deb. Faber and Faber, Inc. 2011 253p.   **954.05**

1. Journalism 2. Globalization 3. Cultural critique 4. India -- Social conditions 5. India -- Civilization -- 21st century 6. India -- Social conditions -- 21st century 7. India -- Economic conditions -- 21st century 8. India -- Politics and government -- 21st century

ISBN 9780865478732; 0865478627; 9780865478626

LC 2011024408

This book "examines India's many contradictions through various individual . . . perspectives. . . . [Author Siddhartha] Deb introduces the reader to an unforgettable group of Indians, including a Gatsby-like mogul in Delhi whose hobby is producing big-budget gangster films that no one sees; a wiry, dusty farmer named Gopeti whose village is plagued by suicides and was the epicenter of a riot; and a sad-eyed waitress named Esther who has set aside her dual degrees in biochemistry and botany to serve Coca-Cola to arms dealers at an upscale hotel called Shangri La." (Publisher's note)

Giridharadas, Anand

India calling; an intimate portrait of a nation's remaking. Times Books/Henry Holt and Co. 2011 273p $25; ebook $11.99 **954.05**

1. Journalists 2. India -- Civilization 3. Social change -- India 4. India -- Social conditions 5. India -- Civilization -- 1947- 6. India -- Description and travel 7. India -- Social life and customs 8. India -- Social conditions -- 1947- 9. National characteristics, East Indian

ISBN 0-8050-9177-7; 1-4299-5062-5 ebook; 978-0-8050-9177-9; 978-1-4299-5062-6 pa

LC 2010-18447

The author, who is "an American, traces his parents' journey from India." (N Y Times Book Rev) Index.

This "is a fine book, elegant, self-aware and unafraid of contradictions and complexity. Giridharadas captures fundamental changes in the nature of family and class relationships and the very idea of what it means to be an Indian." N Y Times Book Rev

Mishra, Pankaj

★ Temptations of the West; how to be modern in India, Pakistan, Tibet, and beyond. Farrar, Straus & Giroux 2006 323p $25 **954.05**

1. South Asia -- Description and travel

ISBN 0-374-17321-4; 978-0-374-17321-0

LC 2006-11987

"It is impossible in a short form to do justice to the density and complexity of . . . . [the author's] arguments, to his comprehensive illustrations, to his scathing demolition of the comfort zones of both East and West, and to the intrepid and endlessly questioning spirit which lies behind his book." N Y Rev Books

954.9 Other jurisdictions

Napoli, Lisa

Radio Shangri-La; what I learned in the happiest kingdom on earth. Crown Publishers 2010 xx, 277p $25 **954.9**

1. Bhutan -- Description and travel

ISBN 978-0-307-45302-0; 978-0-307-45304-4 ebook

LC 2009-49176

"The author provides a readable account of her life-changing decision to leave the comforts of her cosmopolitan Los Angeles life and serve as a volunteer at Kuzoo FM 90, a radio station for young people in the remote Himalayan kingdom of Bhutan. Disillusioned with her love life and fed up with her job as a public-radio commentator, Napoli took a chance on a mysterious stranger's offer of unpaid work in a country where '[b]eing, not having' and '[h]appiness above wealth' were the prevailing national philosophies. . . . The author's authentic voice and light, pleasant cultural insights make for a refreshingly uplifting book." Kirkus

Includes bibliographical references

954.91 Pakistan

Gull, Imtiaz

The **most** dangerous place; Pakistan's lawless frontier. Viking 2010 xxx, 282p map **954.91**

1. Terrorism 2. Taliban 3. Al Qaeda (Organization)

ISBN 0-670-02225-X; 978-0-670-02225-0

LC 2010-01898

First published 2009 in India with title: The al Qaeda connection

Gul "tracks the Taliban and al-Qaeda insurgents into the mountainous tribal regions to investigate the tangle of perilous allegiances. The destabilized Afghanistan-Pakistan border region is constantly in the news as the Obama administration attempts to flush out the militants using the area as a base to train soldiers and launch terrorist attacks. In a dense, timely study, the author investigates the complicated makeup of these groups. . . . Informational rather than didactic, Gul's insider take will serve as an excellent resource."

Inskeep, Steve

Instant city; life and death in Karachi. Penguin Press 2011 284p il map $27.95 **954.91**

1. Karachi (Pakistan) -- Social conditions 2. Karachi (Pakistan) -- Description and travel

ISBN 978-1-59420-315-2; 1-59420-315-6

LC 2011020673

Analyzes the growing metropolis of Karachi, Pakistan, including the importance of regional stability to American security interests, the terrorist bombing of a Shia religious procession, and the challenging religious, ethnic, and political divides.

"This is an intimate book about a megacity, and Inskeep succeeds by keeping his ambitions modest. By trying to understand the horrific event of one particular day, he keeps his narrative well paced and full of small surprises. The book sparkles when Inskeep takes an unexpected turn and follows a stranger, or when he tracks down a new trend to illuminate a new facet of the city." Publ Wkly

Includes bibliographical references

Lieven, Anatol

Pakistan; a hard country. PublicAffairs 2011 558p il $35 **954.91**

1. Pakistan -- History 2. Pakistan -- Social conditions 3. Pakistan -- Politics and government 4. Pakistan -- Politics and government -- 1988-

ISBN 978-1-61039-021-7; 1-61039-021-0

LC 2011-921821

"Lieven breaks down his study by specific region; considers the structures of justice, religion, the military and politics in turn; and, finally, in a skillful, insightful synthesis, addresses the history of and issues concerning the Taliban, both Pakistani and Afghani. A well-reasoned, welcome resource for Western 'experts' and lay readers alike." Kirkus

Schmidle, Nicholas

To live or to perish forever; two tumultuous years in Pakistan. Henry Holt and Co. 2009 254p il map $25 **954.91**

1. Pakistan -- Description and travel 2. Pakistan --

Politics and government
ISBN 978-0-8050-8938-7; 0-8050-8938-1

LC 2008-48373

"Schmidle offers a gripping, grim account of his two years as a journalism fellow in Pakistan, where his travels took him into the most isolated and unfriendly provinces, and into the thick of interests and beliefs that impede that nation's peace and progress. . . . Schmidle has, with this effort, established himself as a fresh, eloquent and informed contributor to the ongoing dialogue regarding Pakistan, terrorism and the strategic importance of engaging Central Asia in efforts toward peace and stability." Publ Wkly

954.93   Sri Lanka

Deraniyagala, Sonali

Wave; Sonali Deraniyagala. Alfred A. Knopf 2013 240 p. (hardcover) $24   954.93
1. Grief 2. Indian Ocean earthquake and tsunami, 2004 3. Bereavement 4. Parents -- Death 5. Children -- Death 6. Widows -- Biography 7. Indian Ocean Tsunami, 2004 8. Disaster victims -- Sri Lanka -- Biography
ISBN 0307962695; 9780307962690

LC 2012040980

This book offers author Sonali Deraniyagala's experience coping with the loss of her parents, husband, and two young sons, who perished in the "Indian Ocean tsunami that broke loose on December 26, 2004" and "killed something like 230,000 people." This is "an account of her coping with her grief while also celebrating the memories of those she loved. . . . She ranges over her childhood in Colombo, meeting her English husband at Cambridge, and the birth of her children." (Library Journal)

955   Iran

Follett, Ken

On wings of eagles. New American Library 1984 415p il pa $7.99   955
1. Iran hostage crisis, 1979-1981
ISBN 0-451-16353-2; 978-0-451-16353-0
First published 1983 by Morrow

The author "recounts the efforts of successful Texas industrialist Ross Perot to rescue from a Teheran jail two senior corporate executives arrested during the anti-American and revolutionary period in Iran in 1979." Libr J

Housden, Roger

Saved by beauty; an American romantic in Iran. Broadway Books 2011 290p map $24; ebook $11.99   955
1. Iran -- Description and travel 2. Iran -- Social life and customs
ISBN 978-0-307-58773-2; 978-0-307-58775-6 ebook
LC 2011003323

The author "documents his travels to Iran in late 2008 and early 2009. The narrative flows seamlessly as the author visits Tehran, paradise gardens in Shiraz, the Pasargadae archaeological site where Cyrus the Great is buried,

Persepolis, the Jewish quarter in Yazd, Esfaha-n, Sanandaj, Mashhad, Neysha-bur, Tu-s, Kermanshah, Ahvaz, and Turkey's Bursa and Konya, as well as surrounding settlements, plains, deserts, and mountainous areas. . . . Poetry lovers and adventurers alike will appreciate this work." Libr J

Mackey, Sandra

The **Iranians**; Persia, Islam, and the soul of a nation. W. Scott Harrop, research assistant. Dutton 1996 xxii, 426p maps hardcover o.p. pa $15.95 955
1. Iran -- Politics and government
ISBN 04-522-7563-6 pa

LC 95-44135

The author presents "information on Iranian civilization from Cyrus the Great to the present. Throughout this turbulent history of invasions and conquerors, the Persian soul, with its foundations in the Zoroastrian concept of justice overlaid with Shia Islam, has steadfastly endured. Since many Westerners had little familiarity with Iran until the overthrow of the Shah in 1979, this very readable book provides a perspective on what led up to those events, what is happening in Iran today, and how the current situation is likely to affect the future of Iran and its relationship with the West." Libr J

Peterson, Scott

Let the swords encircle me; Iran--a journey behind the headlines. Simon & Schuster 2010 732p il $32; ebook $16.99   955
1. Iran -- History -- 1979- 2. Iran -- Social conditions 3. Iran -- Politics and government 4. Iran -- Foreign relations -- United States 5. United States -- Foreign relations -- Iran
ISBN 978-1-4165-9728-5; 978-1-4165-9739-1 ebook
LC 2010-17761

"Reading 'Let the Swords Encircle Me' is like taking a seminar on modern Iran with a patient guide who knows and loves both Iran and the US, and wants only for them to reconcile. The book's deep understanding of the nuances and many shades of Iran are valuable." Christ Sci Monit

Includes bibliographical references

Wright, Robert A.

Our man in Tehran; the true story behind the secret mission to save six Americans during the Iran Hostage Crisis and the foreign ambassador who worked with the CIA to bring them home. [by] Robert Wright. Other Press ed.; Other Press 2011 xxvi, 406p il $25.95; ebook $25.95   955
1. Escapes 2. Diplomats 3. Iran hostage crisis, 1979-1981 4. Iran -- Foreign relations -- United States 5. United States -- Foreign relations -- Iran
ISBN 978-1-59051-413-9; 978-1-59051-414-6 ebook
LC 2010-20376

First published 2010 in Canada

"Much of Iran's relationship with the West—and their mutual antipathy—stems from the muddled events of a single day: November 4, 1979, when Iranian militants overran the U.S. embassy in Tehran, launching a 444-daylong hostage drama. What's often forgotten is that six Americans evaded their would-be captors and were protected and eventually extracted from Iran by Canadian diplomats. In this fascinating account of spycraft and compassion, Wright . . . puts newly unclassified documents to excellent use in recounting how Canadian ambassador Ken Taylor hid the Americans who had slipped out a side door and gathered intelligence for the U.S. government." Publ Wkly

Includes bibliographical references

955.05   Iran--1906-2005

Abrahamian, Ervand

The **coup**; 1953, the CIA, and the roots of modern U.S.-Iranian relations. Ervand Abrahamian. The New Press 2013 277 p. (hardcover) $26.95 **955.05**
1. Iran -- History -- 1941-1979 2. United States. Central Intelligence Agency 3. Great Britain -- Foreign relations -- Iran 4. Iran -- Foreign relations -- Great Britain 5. Iran -- Foreign relations -- United States 6. Iran -- History -- Coup d'état, 1953 7. United States -- Foreign relations -- Iran 8. Iran -- Politics and government -- 1941-1979 9. United States. Central Intelligence Agency -- History -- 20th century 10. Petroleum industry and trade -- Political aspects -- Iran -- History -- 20th century 11. Petroleum industry and trade -- Political aspects -- United States -- History -- 20th century
ISBN 1595588264; 9781595588265

LC 2012031402

This book, by Ervand Abrahamian, profiles how "in August 1953, the U.S. Central Intelligence Agency orchestrated the swift overthrow of Iran's democratically elected leader and installed Muhammad Reza Shah Pahlavi in his place. Over the next twenty-six years, the United States backed the unpopular, authoritarian shah. . . . The blowback was almost inevitable, as this new and revealing history of the coup and its consequences shows." (Publisher's note)

Includes bibliographical references and index

Baglio, Matt

Argo; how the CIA and Hollywood pulled off the most audacious rescue in history. Antonio J. Mendez and Matt Baglio. Viking 2012 viii, 310 p.p $26.95   **955.05**
1. Iran -- History 2. United States -- History 3. United States -- Foreign relations -- Iran 4. Iran Hostage Crisis, 1979-1981 5. Canada -- Foreign relations -- Iran 6. Iran -- Foreign relations -- Canada 7. United States. Central Intelligence Agency 8. Diplomats -- United States -- History -- 20th century
ISBN 0670026220; 9780670026227

LC 2012014991

In this book, Antonio J. Mendez tells the story of "November 4, 1979, [when] Iranian militants stormed the American embassy in Tehran and captured dozens of American hostages. . . . Disguising himself as a Hollywood producer, and supported by [under]cover CIA operatives . . . Mendez traveled to Tehran under the guise of scouting locations for a fake science fiction film called 'Argo.' While pretending to find the perfect film backdrops, Mendez and a colleague succeeded in contacting the escapees, and smuggling them out of Iran." (Publisher's note)

Includes bibliographical references and index.

Buchan, James

Days of God; the revolution in Iran and its consequences. James Buchan. Simon & Schuster 2013 432 p. illustrations, maps (hardcover) $27.99 **955.05**
1. Islam and politics 2. Iran -- History -- 1979- 3. Iran -- Politics and government -- 20th century 4. Iran -- History -- 1979-1997 5. Iran -- History -- Revolution, 1979 6. Iran -- History -- Revolution, 1979 -- Causes 7. Iran -- History -- Revolution, 1979 -- Influence 8. Political violence -- Iran -- History -- 20th century
ISBN 1416597778; 9781416597773

LC 2013008890

This book by James Buchan examines how "the Iranian Revolution of 1979 was a turning-point in modern history. The destruction of the Iranian monarchy not only upset the political order in the Middle East and brought on a quarter-century of warfare, but introduced a new way to look at history. In 'Days of God' James Buchan lives each moment of the revolution through the eyes of ordinary people." (Publisher's note)

Includes bibliographical references and index

Cooper, Andrew Scott

The **fall** of heaven; the Pahlavis and the final days of imperial Iran. Andrew Scott Cooper. Henry Holt & Co. 2016 624 p. (hardback) $35   **955.05**
1. Iran -- History 2. Iran -- History -- Mohammad Reza Pahlavi, 1941-1979
ISBN 9780805098976; 9780805098983

LC 2015046095

This book, by Andrew Scott Cooper, is an "account of the rise and fall of Iran's glamorous Pahlavi dynasty, written with the cooperation of the late Shah's widow, Empress Farah, Iranian revolutionaries and US officials from the Carter administration." (Publisher's note)

"A thorough new appraisal of an enigmatic ruler who died believing his people still loved him." Kirkus

Includes bibliographical references and index

Secor, Laura

Children of Paradise; The Struggle for the Soul of Iran. Laura Secor. Penguin Group USA 2016 528 p. map (hardcover) $30   **955.05**
1. Iran -- History -- 1979- 2. Iran -- Politics and government
ISBN 9781594487101; 1594487103

This book, by Laura Secor, presents a history of Iran from 1979 to the present. "Inside Iran, a breathtaking drama has unfolded since then, as religious thinkers, political operatives, poets, journalists, and activists have imagined and reimagined what Iran should be. They have drawn as deeply on the traditions of the West as of the East and have acted upon their beliefs with urgency and passion, frequently staking their lives for them." (Publisher's note)

"Secor's clear writing offers a firm grounding in the last 40 years of Iranian political thought and the many actions it has inspired in a complicated and fascinating country." Pub Wkly

Includes bibliographical references (pages [470]-494) and index.

956 Middle East (Near East)

Armenian Golgotha; translated by Peter Balakian
with Aris Sevag. Alfred A. Knopf 2009 509p il
map $35 **956**
1. Genocide 2. Armenian massacres, 1915-1923 3.
Priests 4. Genocide -- Turkey 5. Biography, Individual
6. Armenian massacres, 1915-1923 -- Personal
narratives
ISBN 0-307-26288-X; 978-0-307-26288-2

LC 2008-39957

This is a first-person account of the Armenian massacre.
Chronology. Glossary. Bibliography. Index.

"On the night of April 24, 1915, Grigoris Balakian, an
Armenian priest, and more than two hundred other Armenian politicians and intellectuals were arrested in Constantinople. Soon, Armenians across Turkey were massacred
or forced to join a death march to the desert of Der Zor.
Balakian walked among the displaced for months before he
fled, disguising himself variously as a German engineer, a
soldier, and a worker in the vineyards; he began this book
while in hiding. (It was published in Armenian in 1922 and
in 1959; the translator is Balakian's great-nephew.) Both a
memoir and an attempt at a history of the genocide, it assumes considerable familiarity with Ottoman politics, but
remains fascinating firsthand testimony to a monumental
crime." New Yorker

Includes bibliographical references

Barr, James

A **line** in the sand. W. W. Norton & Co. 2012
xii, 450 p. ill. 12 p. of plates **956**
1. Diplomats 2. Middle East 3. World War, 1914-
1918 4. Sykes-Picot Agreement 5. France -- Foreign
relations -- Great Britain 6. Great Britain -- Foreign
relations -- France 7. Middle East -- Foreign relations --
20th century 8. Middle East -- Politics and government
-- 1914-1945
ISBN 1-84737-453-0 Simon & Schuster; 978-1-
84737-453-0 Simon & Schuster; 9780393070651
W.W. Norton & Co. 2012; 0393070654 W.W. Norton
& Co., 2012

LC 2011038037

"In 1916, in the middle of the First World War, two men
secretly agreed to divide the Middle East between them. Sir
Mark Sykes was a visionary politician; François Georges-
Picot a diplomat with a grudge. The deal they struck, which
was designed to relieve tensions that threatened to engulf the
Entente Cordiale, drew a line in the sand from the Mediterranean to the Persian frontier. Territory north of that stark
line would go to France; land south of it, to Britain. . . . Their
pact survived the war to form the basis for the postwar division of the region into five new countries Britain and France
would rule. The creation of Britain's mandates of Palestine,
Transjordan and Iraq, and France's in Lebanon and Syria,
made the two powers uneasy neighbours for the following
thirty years. . . . [This book] tells the story of the . . . era
when Britain and France ruled the Middle East. It [aims to]
explain . . . how the old antagonism between these two powers inflamed the . . . modern rivalry between the Arabs and
the Jews, and ultimately led to war between the British and

the French in 1941 and between the Arabs and the Jews in
1948." (Publisher's note)

Includes bibliographical references and index.

Congressional Quarterly, Inc.

★ The **Middle** East; 11th ed; CQ Press 2007
xix, 663p il map $70; pa $46.95 **956**
1. Middle East -- Politics and government
ISBN 978-0-87289-368-9; 0-87289-368-5; 978-0-
87289-369-6 pa; 0-87289-369-3 pa

LC 2007-19956

First published 1974. Periodically revised

Covers topics such as oil, Islam, the Arab-Israeli conflict, the Persian Gulf, and the arms trade in the Middle
East. Also presents profiles of Middle Eastern nations and
twentieth-century leaders and includes documents such as
UN resolutions and peace treaties

Includes bibliographical references

Finkel, Caroline

★ **Osman's** dream; the story of the Ottoman
Empire, 1300-1923. Basic Books 2006 660p il
map **956**
1. Turkey -- History 2. Turkey -- History -- Ottoman
Empire, 1288-1918
ISBN 0465023967; 9780465023967

First published 2005 in the United Kingdom

This is a history "of the Ottoman Empire from its origins
in the thirteenth century through its destruction on the battlefields of World War I." (Publisher's note)

This is a history "of the Ottoman Empire from its origins
in the thirteenth century through its destruction on the battlefields of World War I." Publisher's note

Includes bibliographical references

Friedman, Thomas L.

From Beirut to Jerusalem. Farrar, Straus & Gir-
oux 1989 541p il maps $32 **956**
1. Jewish-Arab relations 2. Lebanon -- History 3.
Israel -- Politics and government 4. Middle East --
Politics and government
ISBN 0-374-15895-9

LC 92-148666

First published 1989

The author presents an account of the political situation
in the Middle East as he witnessed it in his years as a reporter
in Lebanon and Jerusalem

"When recounting his frequently harrowing experiences in that troubled region, Friedman can be absolutely
riveting; similarly, his historical insights, his explanation of
the root causes of the Arab-Israeli conflict, and his impressions of people and places in the Holy Land never fail to
fascinate." Booklist

Herzog, Chaim

The **Arab**-Israeli wars; war and peace in the
Middle East from the 1948 War of Independence
to the present. updated by Shlomo Gazit; introduction by Isaac Herzog and Michael Herzog. 2nd ed,

rev and updated; Vintage Books 2005 476p il pa
$16.95 **956**
 1. Jewish-Arab relations
 ISBN 1-4000-7963-2

LC 2005-280207

First published 1982 by Random House
This book traces "the Arab-Israeli wars and military conflicts from the 1948 War of Independence through the 1973 Yom Kippur War." Libr J
Includes bibliographic references

Lewis, Bernard
 The **Middle** East; a brief history of the last 2,000 years. Scribner 1995 433p il hardcover o.p. pa
$16 **956**
 1. Middle East -- History
 ISBN 0-684-80712-2; 0-684-83280-1 pa

LC 96-4384

"Lewis has chosen to accentuate the social, economic, and cultural changes that have occurred over 20 centuries. He ranges from seemingly trivial concerns (changes in dress and manners in an Arab coffeehouse) to earth-shaking events (the Mongol conquest of Mesopotamia) in painting a rich, varied, and fascinating portrait of a region that is steeped in traditionalism while often forced by geography and politics to accept change." Booklist
Includes bibliographical references

 Notes on a century; reflections of a Middle East historian. Bernard Lewis; with Buntzie Ellis Churchill. Viking 2012 388 p. **956**
 1. Autobiographies 2. International relations 3. Middle East -- Politics and government 4. Middle East -- Historiography 5. Middle East -- History -- 20th century 6. Middle East -- History -- 21st century 7. Middle East specialists -- Great Britain -- Biography
 ISBN 0670023531; 9780670023530

LC 2011049267

This memoir by political consultant and historian Bernard Lewis provides the author's personal reflections on his international career and his views on the major themes of world politics spanning "World War II, up through the Arab Spring. . . . Lewis . . . was the first to warn of a coming 'clash of civilizations,' a term he coined in 1957, and has led [a] life, as much a political actor as a scholar of the Middle East." (Publisher's note)
Includes bibliographical references and index.

Meyer, Karl E.
 Kingmakers; the invention of the modern Middle East. [by] Karl E. Meyer and Shareen Blair Brysac. Norton 2008 507p il map $27.95 **956**
 1. Middle East -- History
 ISBN 978-0-393-06199-4; 0-393-06199-X

LC 2008-07378

The authors "have written a timely and engrossing study of the men and women who were instrumental in giving birth to some of the nations, institutions, and chronic problems of the area." Booklist
Includes bibliographical references

Morris, Benny
 Righteous victims; a history of the Zionist-Arab conflict, 1881-1998. Knopf 1999 751p hardcover o.p. pa $18 **956**
 1. Israel-Arab conflicts 2. Jewish-Arab relations
 ISBN 0-679-74475-4 pa

LC 98-42774

Morris traces the history of Arab-Israeli conflicts and examines major events and their aftereffects
"The author displays a remarkable grasp of the history of the Zionist-Arab conflict and an analytical style that is devoid of the polemics that have characterized so many books on this subject." Libr J
Includes bibliographical references

Wallach, Janet
 Desert queen; the extraordinary life of Gertrude Bell: adventurer, adviser to kings, ally of Lawrence of Arabia. Talese 1996 xxv, 419p hardcover o.p. pa $15.95 **956**
 1. Explorers 2. Travelers 3. Archeologists 4. Archaeologists 5. Women -- Travel
 ISBN 0-385-47408-3; 978-1-4000-9619-0 pa; 1-4000-9619-7 pa

LC 95-44868

"High-spirited, outspoken, and self-reliant, . . . {Bell} was the first woman to earn a degree in history at Oxford, a skilled mountain climber and equestrienne, and an avid and fearless traveler who found her spiritual home in the deserts of Iraq and Arabia. . . . Fluent in Arabic and on good terms with powerful men, Bell became an invaluable asset to British intelligence and was drafted as a spy during World War I. . . . Wallach . . . brings the resolute Bell and her complex world vividly to life." Booklist
Includes bibliographical references

956.04   Middle East--1945-1980

MacFarquhar, Neil
 The **media** relations department of Hizbollah wishes you a happy birthday; unexpected encounters in the changing Middle East. PublicAffairs 2009 387p il map $26.95; pa $15.95 **956.04**
 1. Middle East -- Description and travel 2. Middle East -- Politics and government
 ISBN 978-1-58648-635-8; 978-1-58648-811-6 pa

LC 2009-2004

The author "offers something fresh and unexpected for readers steeped in a decade of news reports about suicide bombers, absolutist imams and tyrannical despots. . . . [This book] is MacFarquhar's effort to write a funny (yet penetrating) account about real Arabs—and a few Persians—struggling against long odds to bring their societies into the modern age. . . . For those who care about the Middle East and want to start listening to weak but growing voices calling for reform and modernization on local rather than Western terms, MacFarquhar's account is a fine place to begin." N Y Times Book Rev
Includes bibliographical references

Oren, Michael

Six days of war; June 1967 and the making of the modern Middle East. {by} Michael B. Oren. Oxford Univ. Press 2002 446p il $30   **956.04**

1. Israel-Arab War, 1967
ISBN 0-19-515174-7

LC 2001-58823

This is a history of the June 1967 Arab-Israeli War

"What makes this book important is the breadth and depth of the research. Oren draws on archives, newly declassified documents, memoirs and interviews from Israel, America, Britain and what was then the Soviet Union." N Y Times Book Rev

Includes bibliographical references

Sacco, Joe

Footnotes in Gaza. Metropolitan Books 2009 418p il $29.95   **956.04**

1. Graphic novels 2. Massacres -- Graphic novels 3. Israel-Arab conflicts -- Graphic novels
ISBN 978-0-8050-7347-8; 0-8050-7347-7

LC 2009-28433

"Cartoonist and journalist Joe Sacco is the world's foremost creator of 'comics journalism'—a contemporary field he basically invented. . . . [This] book, whose 'footnotes' refer both to facts and metaphorically to history's forgotten people, is about two massacres of Palestinians in the Gaza Strip in November 1956. . . . Very little has been written about either event. Sacco conducted extensive research of U.N. documents and other materials, and additionally set out to interview as many eyewitnesses as he could track down. This is really the heart of this moving, precisely drawn work." Time Out N Y

Includes bibliographical references

Shlaim, Avi

The **iron** wall; Israel and the Arab world since 1948. Norton 1999 704p il hardcover o.p. pa $17.95   **956.04**

1. Israel-Arab conflicts 2. Jewish-Arab relations 3. Israel -- Foreign relations
ISBN 0-393-32112-6 pa

LC 99-23121

"A thorough analysis of Israel's relationships with the West as well as its neighbors from a controversial but thoughtful point of view." Booklist

Includes bibliographical references

Wright, Lawrence, 1947-

★ **Thirteen** Days in September; Carter, Begin, and Sadat at Camp David. Lawrence Wright. First edition Alfred A. Knopf 2014 368 p. illustrations, maps $27.95   **956.04**

1. Egypt -- History 2. Arab countries -- Foreign relations -- Israel 3. Camp David Agreements (1978) 4. Israel-Arab War, 1973 -- Peace 5. United States -- Foreign relations -- 1977-1981
ISBN 0385352034; 9780385352031

LC 2013497329

Carnegie Medal Shortlist: Nonfiction (2015)
Los Angeles Times Book Prize Finalist: History (2014)

This book by Lawrence Wright is a "day-by-day account of the 1978 Camp David conference, when President Jimmy Carter persuaded Israeli prime minister Menachem Begin and Egyptian president Anwar Sadat to sign the first peace treaty in the modern Middle East, one which endures to this day. . . . Wright draws vivid portraits of other fiery personalities who were present at Camp David--including Moshe Dayan, Osama el-Baz, and Zbigniew Brzezinski." (Publisher's note)

"The author alternates among each day's events, biographical sketches of the central and supporting players, and insightful sociopolitical essays on the three leaders and their countries as he explains the process that led to a Nobel Peace Prize for Sadat and Begin and laid the foundation for the subsequent Oslo Accords." LJ

Includes bibliographical references and index

956.05   Middle East -- 1980-

Engel, Richard, 1973-

And then all hell broke loose; two decades in the Middle East. by Richard Engel. Simon & Schuster 2016 400 p. 8 plates; illustrations, maps (hardback) $27   **956.05**

1. Journalists 2. Middle East -- History 3. Middle East -- History -- 21st century 4. Foreign correspondents -- United States -- Biography 5. Middle East -- Politics and government -- 21st century
ISBN 9781451635119; 9781451635126; 9781451635133

LC 2015030898

This book, by journalist Richard Engel, is the "story of the Middle East revolutions, the Arab Spring, war, and terrorism. . . . Engel has been under fire, blown out of hotel beds, taken hostage. He has watched Mubarak and Morsi in Egypt arrested and condemned, reported from Jerusalem, been through the Lebanese war, covered the whole shooting match in Iraq, interviewed Libyan rebels who toppled Gaddafi, [and] reported from Syria as Al-Qaeda stepped in." (Publisher's note)

"Clear, candid, and concise, Engel's overview of the ongoing battleground should be required reading for anyone desiring a thorough and informed portrait of what the past has created and what the future holds for the Middle East and the world at large." Booklist

Includes bibliographical references and index

Hider, James

The **spiders** of Allah; travels of an unbeliever on the frontline of holy war. St. Martin's Griffin 2009 323p pa $14.95   **956.05**

1. Religion and politics 2. Religious fundamentalism 3. Terrorism -- Religious aspects 4. Middle East -- Description and travel 5. Middle East -- Politics and government
ISBN 978-0-312-56585-5; 0-312-56585-2

LC 2009-7378

"A British journalist's firsthand account of fanaticism and bloodshed in the Middle East. . . . [The author] loosely examines the ways in which radical Islam and fundamentalist Christianity have continually warped and damaged an already difficult situation. . . . The author's dense, vivid descriptions, frequently steeped in irony and humor, make for a slow but powerful read." Kirkus

Miller, Aaron David

The **much** too promised land; America's elusive search for Arab-Israeli peace. Bantam Books 2008 407p $26; pa $16 **956.05**

1. Israel-Arab conflicts 2. Middle East -- Foreign relations -- United States 3. United States -- Foreign relations -- Middle East

ISBN 978-0-553-80490-4; 0-553-80490-1; 978-0-553-38414-7 pa; 0-553-38414-7 pa

LC 2007-38982

The author presents advice on Mideast policy after having been a participant in diplomatic efforts made by the administrations of Presidents Carter, Clinton, and George W. Bush.

This is "an indispensable guide to the recent history of American peacemaking efforts in the defining conflict of the Middle East." Bookforum

Includes bibliographical references

Pope, Hugh

Dining with al-Qaeda; three decades exploring the many worlds of the Middle East. Thomas Dunne Books/St. Martin's Press 2010 332p il map $26.99 **956.05**

1. Middle East -- Description and travel 2. Middle East -- Politics and government

ISBN 978-0-312-38313-8

Pope's "criticisms of the invasion and of Israel may grate some readers, but those interested in the interpersonal rather than the international will enjoy Pope's bold curiosity in meeting people all over the Middle East." Booklist

Said, Edward W.

The **end** of the peace process; Oslo and after. Pantheon Bks. 2000 345p $27.50; pa $14 **956.05**

1. Israel-Arab conflicts 2. Jewish-Arab relations

ISBN 0-375-40930-0; 0-375-72574-1 pa

LC 99-44765

The author provides "analysis of the pitfalls of the Oslo agreement. Most of the essays in this collection have appeared in Cairo's al-Ahram Weekly and al-Hayat, London's Arabic-language daily. Each essay is Said's reflection on a dimension of the Palestinian predicament.... He is as critical of the corruption, incompetence, and authoritarianism of the Palestinian Authority as he is of American and Israeli postures." Libr J

Shavit, Ari, 1957-

My promised land; Ari Shavit. Spiegel & Grau 2013 464 p. **956.05**

1. Zionism 2. Israel -- History 3. Israel-Arab conflicts 4. Israel -- Politics and government 5. Arab-Israeli conflict

ISBN 9780385521703; 9780812984644

LC 2012046122

In this book, "Israeli journalist [Ari] Shavit . . . presents a history of and meditation on Zionism's successes and failures. . . .He traces the rise and demise of the kibbutzim, the 1948 displacement of Palestinians, the shock of 1967's

Six-Day War victory, and the near defeat in the 1973 Yom Kippur War." He asks, "Can Israel fully integrate its Arab citizens, do justice to the Palestinians, and assure security in the face of looming military and demographic threats? " (Library Journal)

Stack, Megan

Every man in this village is a liar; an education in war. [by] Megan K. Stack. Doubleday 2010 257p $26.95 **956.05**

1. War and civilization 2. War on terrorism 3. Middle East -- Description and travel

ISBN 978-0-385-52716-3; 0-385-52716-0

LC 2009-34473

"As a 25-year-old correspondent for the Los Angeles Times, Stack covered Afghanistan in the days immediately following 9/11, then traveled to other outposts in the war on terror, from Iraq to Iran, Libya, and Lebanon. In a disquieting series of essays, Stack now takes readers deep into the carnage where she was exposed to the insanity, innocence, and inhumanity of wars with no beginning, middle, or end. Her soaring imagery sears itself into the brain, in acute and accurate tales that should never be forgotten by the wider world, and yet always are." Booklist

Weiss, Michael

Isis; inside the army of terror. Michael Weiss, Hassan Hassan. Regan Arts 2015 270 p. map $14; (hbk) $28.95 **956.05**

1. Iraq 2. Syria 3. Terrorism

ISBN 1682450201; 1941393578; 9781941393574; 9781682450291; 9781682450208

LC 2015930621

This book, by Michael Weiss and Hassan Hassan, presents a "look inside the world's most dangerous terrorist group . . . the Islamic State of Iraq and Syria (ISIS). . . . [The authors] explain how these violent extremists evolved from a nearly defeated Iraqi insurgent group into a jihadi army of international volunteers who behead Western hostages in slickly produced videos and have conquered territory equal to the size of Great Britain." (Publisher's note)

Includes bibliographical references (pages 367-402) and index.

Wright, Robin

Dreams and shadows; the future of the Middle East. Penguin Press 2008 464p map $26.95 **956.05**

1. Middle East -- Politics and government

ISBN 1-59420-111-0; 978-1-59420-111-0

LC 2007-46267

"Absorbing accounts of brave activists are interwoven with relevant context and history in clear, vivid language. These elements make the book an engaging read, and a useful one for people who want to better understand this important part of the world." Christ Sci Monit

Includes bibliographical reference

956.054 Middle East -- 2000-

Bacevich, Andrew J., 1947-

America's war for the greater Middle East; a military history. Andrew J. Bacevich. Random House Inc 2016 480 p. maps (hardcover) $30 **956.054**
1. Middle East -- History 2. United States -- Military history 3. Middle East -- Foreign relations -- United States 4. United States -- Foreign relations -- Middle East 5. United States -- History, Military -- 20th century 6. United States -- History, Military -- 21st century
ISBN 9780553393941; 9780553393934

LC 2015038868

This book, by Andrew J. Bacevich, "provides a searing reassessment of U.S. military policy in the Middle East over the past four decades. During the 1980s, Bacevich argues, a great transition occurred. As the Cold War wound down, the United States initiated a new conflict—a War for the Greater Middle East. Bacevich weaves a compelling narrative out of episodes as varied as the Beirut bombing of 1983, the Mogadishu firefight of 1993, the invasion of Iraq in 2003, and the rise of ISIS." (Publisher's note)

Includes bibliographical references and index

956.1 Turkey

Goodwin, Jason

Lords of the horizons; a history of the Ottoman Empire. Holt & Co. 1999 351p il map hardcover o.p. pa $15 **956.1**
1. Turkey -- History -- Ottoman Empire, 1288-1918
ISBN 0-312-42066-8 pa

LC 98-41601

"A history of distinctive originality, Goodwin's account imbibes deeply of traveler's impressions and seeks to see and describe, rather than explain and judge. A valuable synthesis." Booklist

Includes bibliographical references

Kinzer, Stephen

Crescent and star; Turkey between two worlds. Farrar, Straus & Giroux 2001 252p hardcover o.p. pa $14 **956.1**
1. Turkey -- Politics and government
ISBN 0-374-52866-7 pa

LC 2001-23298

The author "gives a concise introduction to Turkey: Kemal Atatürk's post-WWI establishment of the modern secular Turkish state; the odd makeup of contemporary society, in which the military enforces Atatürk's reforms. In stylized but substantive prose, he devotes chapters to the problems he sees plaguing Turkish society: Islamic fundamentalism, frictions regarding the large Kurdish minority and the lack of democratic freedoms." Publ Wkly

Mango, Andrew

The **Turks** today; Andrew Mango. 1st ed; Overlook Press 2004 292p map $29.95; pa $17.95 **956.1**
1. Turkey -- History
ISBN 1-585-67615-2; 1-585-67756-6 pa

LC 2004-58339

"This fascinating and timely survey is both a political history and a cultural examination of a diverse, dynamic society." Booklist

Includes bibliographical references

Ureneck, Lou

The **Great** Fire; One American's Mission to Rescue Victims of the 20th Century's First Genocide. HarperCollins 2015 496 p. 16 plates; ills.; maps; ports. $28.99 **956.1**
1. Genocide 2. Armenian massacres, 1915-1923
ISBN 0062259881; 9780062259882

This book by Lou Ureneck tells the story of Asa Jennings "a Methodist Minister and [Halsey Powell] a principled American naval officer who helped rescue more than 250,000 refugees during the genocide of Armenian and Greek Christians." (Publisher's note)

"This account is written with fans of popular narrative history in mind. Despite the muddled material, many will find this a worthwhile read. Students of this dark part of history, however, will most appreciate Ureneck's research." LJ

956.6 Eastern Turkey

Akcam, Taner

A **shameful** act; the Armenian genocide and the question of Turkish responsibility. translated by Paul Bessemer. Metropolitan Books 2006 483p map $30 **956.6**
1. Genocide 2. Armenian massacres, 1915-1923
ISBN 0-8050-7932-7; 978-0-8050-7932-6

LC 2005-58401

Original Turkish edition, 1999

"This groundbreaking and lucid account by a prominent Turkish scholar speaks forcefully to all." Publ Wkly

Includes bibliographical references

Balakian, Peter

★ The **burning** Tigris; the Armenian genocide and America's response. HarperCollins 2003 xx, 475p il $26.95; pa $14.95 **956.6**
1. Genocide 2. Armenian massacres, 1915-1923
ISBN 0-06-019840-0; 0-06-055870-9 pa

LC 2003-44986

"The book's real power derives from the eyewitness accounts of the genocide itself. The sheer volume of outsiders' testimony that Balakian compiles, and the horrifying similarity of their observations of men, women and children beaten, tortured, burned to death in churches or sent out into the desert to starve, is an overwhelmingly convincing retort to genocide deniers." N Y Times Book Rev

Includes bibliographical references

Suny, Ronald Grigor

They Can Live in the Desert but Nowhere Else; A History of the Armenian Genocide. by Ronald Grigor Suny. Princeton University Press 2015 520 p. illustrations, maps $35   **956.6**
1. Armenian massacres, 1915-1923
ISBN 0691147302; 9780691147307

LC 2014041347

In this book on the Armenian genocide, historian Ronald Grigor Suny "cuts through nationalist myths, propaganda, and denial to provide an unmatched account of when, how, and why the atrocities of 1915-16 were committed. . . . Drawing on archival documents and eyewitness accounts, this is an unforgettable chronicle of a cataclysm that set a tragic pattern for a century of genocide and crimes against humanity." (Publisher's note)

"Suny weaves this complex story into a nuanced, meticulously researched, and compellingly argued book. Summing Up: Highly recommended. Advanced undergraduate and graduate collections." Choice

956.7 Iraq

Allawi, Ali A.

The **occupation** of Iraq; winning the war, losing the peace. Yale University Press 2007 xxiv, 518p il map $28   **956.7**
1. Iraq War, 2003-2011 2. Iraq War, 2003- 3. Iraq -- Politics and government
ISBN 978-0-300-11015-9; 0-300-11015-4

LC 2006-39445

This "scholarly yet immensely readable exposition of Iraqi society and politics will likely become the standard reference on post-9/11 Iraq." Publ Wkly

Includes bibliographical references

Atkinson, Rick

Crusade; the untold story of the Persian Gulf War. Houghton Mifflin 1993 575p il maps hardcover o.p. pa $17   **956.7**
1. Persian Gulf War, 1991
ISBN 0-395-71083-9 pa

LC 93-14388

The author provides an "account of the actions and utterances of those who directed and fought in the Persian Gulf War. He also provides a thorough analysis of diplomatic and political aspects of the conflict. Rich in pertinent details, the powerful narrative leaps nimbly from Washington to Riyadh, from Baghdad to Kuwait City, and to various battle sites across the sands. Expectedly, the book's dominant personality is General H. Norman Schwarzkopf." Publ Wkly

Includes bibliographical references

In the company of soldiers; a chronicle of combat. H. Holt 2004 319p il maps $25; pa $14 **956.7**
1. Iraq War, 2003-2011 2. Iraq War, 2003- 3. United States -- Army -- Airborne Division, 101st
ISBN 0-8050-7561-5; 0-8050-7773-1 pa

LC 2003-67607

This is an eyewitness account of the war in Iraq. "In the spring of 2003, the author accompanied combat units to Iraq. He spent two months embedded with the 101st Airborne Division's headquarters staff, sharing their daily experiences from initial deployment out of Fort Campbell, KY, to overseas staging areas in Kuwait, and ultimately bearing witness to the unit's march on Baghdad. His view of the war was from a vantage point that permitted scrutiny of strategy, planning, and decision making at the senior command level." SLJ

Filkins, Dexter

★ The **forever** war. Alfred A. Knopf 2008 368p il $25   **956.7**
1. Iraq War, 2003-2011 2. Journalists 3. Iraq War, 2003- 4. War on Terrorism, 2001- 5. Iraq War, 2003- -- Personal narratives 6. Afghanistan -- Politics and government -- 2001-
ISBN 0-307-26639-7; 978-0-307-26639-2

LC 2008-11761

Filkins, a "New York Times correspondent, furnishes a firsthand account of the battle against Islamic fundamentalism, from the rise of the Taliban in the 1990s, to the terrorist attacks of 9/11, to the modern-day wars in Afghanistan and Iraq." (Publisher's note)

This is "wonderfully written and carefully researched [book]. . . . Filkins's gripping account gives readers a clear, though disturbing, view of what's happening on the ground in Iraq. And he has put himself in the middle of this madness to deliver a stunning and illuminating story." Christ Sci Monit

Includes bibliographical references

Finkel, David

The **good** soldiers. Sarah Crichton Books 2009 287p il $26   **956.7**
1. Iraq War, 2003-2011 2. Iraq War, 2003- 3. United States -- Army 4. Counterinsurgency -- Iraq 5. Soldiers -- United States 6. Iraq War, 2003- -- Campaigns 7. Soldiers -- United States -- Biography
ISBN 0-374-16573-4; 978-0-374-16573-4

LC 2009-19391

This is an account of the Iraq "war as experienced on the ground . . . by members of an Army battalion sent to Baghdad during the surge in 2007." (N Y Times (Late N Y Ed))

"Finkel's keen firsthand reportage, its grit and impact only heightened by the literary polish of his prose, gives us one of the best accounts yet of the American experience in Iraq." Publ Wkly

Frederick, Jim

Black hearts; one platoon's descent into madness in Iraq's triangle of death. Harmony Books 2010 439p il map $26   **956.7**
1. War crimes 2. Iraq War, 2003- -- Atrocities 3. United States -- Army -- Airborne Division, 101st
ISBN 978-0-307-45075-3; 0-307-45075-9

LC 2009-35537

"Frederick recounts the events leading up to and following the rape and murder of 14-year-old Iraqi Abeer al-Janabi and the subsequent murder of her family—parents Qassim and Fakhriah and six-year-old sister Hadeel—committed by members of one U.S. Army deployment in Iraq's 'Triangle of Death.'" Publ Wkly

Includes bibliographical references

Gordon, Michael R.

The **generals'** war; the inside story of the conflict in the Gulf. by Michael R. Gordon and Bernard E. Trainor. Little, Brown 1994 551p il map hardcover o.p. pa $18.95   **956.7**

1. Persian Gulf War, 1991
ISBN 0-316-32100-1 pa

LC 94-27144

"This cogent analysis provides several disturbing answers worthy of our attention." Libr J

Includes bibliographical references

Gordon, Michael R., 1951-

The **endgame**; the inside story of the struggle for Iraq, from George W. Bush to Barack Obama. Michael R. Gordon and Bernard E. Trainor. Pantheon Books 2012 xix, 779 p.p $35   **956.7**

1. Iraq War, 2003-2011 2. Iraq -- Politics and government 3. Iraq -- Foreign relations -- United States 4. United States -- Foreign relations -- Iraq 5. Insurgency -- Iraq 6. Iraq -- Ethnic relations 7. Iraq -- Relations -- United States 8. United States -- Relations -- Iraq 9. Iraq -- Politics and government -- 21st century 10. United States -- Armed Forces -- Iraq -- History 11. Iraq War, 2003-2011 -- Political aspects -- United States
ISBN 0307377229; 9780307377227

LC 2012024746

This book by Michael R. Gordon and Bernard E. Trainor presents a "chronicle of the Iraq War, emphasizing military maneuvers and Iraqi participation at all levels." It offers a "record of the nine years of conflict between the 'inside-out' versus 'outside-in' strategies of the U.S. government in dealing with Iraqi intransigence and conversion to democracy. . . . The authors take great pains to delineate the makeup of the Iraqi government in the prickly transition to sovereignty." (Kirkus Reviews)

Includes bibliographical references and index.

Gourevitch, Philip

Standard operating procedure; [by] Philip Gourevitch and Errol Morris. Penguin Press 2008 286p il $25.95   **956.7**

1. Prisoners of war 2. Iraq War, 2003-2011 3. Iraq War, 2003- 4. Abu Ghraib (Baghdad, Iraq: Prison)
ISBN 978-1-59420-132-5

LC 2008-10215

"This deft piece of reportage will stir readers' anger, at both the actions and the consequences. . . . A thorough, terrifying account of an American-made 'bedlam.'" Publ Wkly

Haass, Richard

War of necessity: war of choice; a memoir of two Iraq wars. by Richard N. Haass. Simon & Schuster 2009 336 p. $27   **956.7**

1. Iraq War, 2003- -- Causes 2. Persian Gulf War, 1991 -- Causes 3. United States -- Military policy 4. Iraq War, 2003- -- Political aspects 5. Persian Gulf War,

1991 -- Political aspects 6. Middle East -- Foreign relations -- United States 7. United States -- Foreign relations -- Middle East
ISBN 978-1-4165-4902-4; 1-4165-4902-1; 1416549021; 9781416549024

LC 2009004495

"A unique perspective on how war policy was formed by two very different presidents." Kirkus

Includes bibliographical references and index

Hoffmann, Andrea C.

The **girl** who escaped ISIS; this is my story. Farida Khalaf, Andrea C. Hoffmann. Atria Books 2016 240 p. map (hardback) $24   **956.7**

1. Refugees 2. Terrorism 3. IS (Organization) 4. Iraq -- Refugees 5. Yezidi women -- Iraq -- Biography
ISBN 1501131710; 9781501131714; 9781501152337

LC 2016022449

In this memoir, by Farida Khalaf with Andrea C. Hoffmann, translated from the German by Jamie Bulloch, the author "describes her world as it was [under the Islamic State.] . . . Held in a slave market in Syria and sold into the homes of several ISIS soldiers, she stubbornly attempts resistance at every turn. Farida is ultimately brought to an ISIS training camp in the middle of the desert, where she plots an against-all-odds escape for herself and five other girls." (Publisher's note)

Kennedy, Hugh

When Baghdad ruled the Muslim world; the rise and fall of Islam's greatest dynasty. Da Capo Press 2005 xxv, 326p il map hardcover o.p. pa $18.95   **956.7**

1. Islamic civilization 2. Baghdad (Iraq)
ISBN 0-306-81435-8; 978-0-306-81435-8; 0-306-81480-3 pa; 978-0-306-81480-8 pa

LC 2006-295518

First published 2004 in the United Kingdom with title: The Court of the Caliphs

The author "has written an informative and sobering lesson for those who idolize the past." Choice

Includes bibliographical references

Mansoor, Peter R.

Baghdad at sunrise; a Brigade Commander's war in Iraq. foreword by Donald Kagan and Frederick Kagan. Yale University Press 2008 xxvii, 376p il map (Yale library of military history) $28   **956.7**

1. Iraq War, 2003- -- Personal narratives
ISBN 978-0-300-14069-9; 0-300-14069-X

LC 2008-07366

"This is a unique contribution to the burgeoning literature on the Iraq war. . . . The critique is balanced, perceptive and merciless." Publ Wkly

Includes bibliographical references

Mills, Dan

Sniper one; on scope and under siege with a sniper team in Iraq. St. Martin's Press 2008 xxvi, 349p il map $26.95 **956.7**

1. Iraq War, 2003- -- Personal narratives

ISBN 978-0-312-53126-3; 0-312-53126-5

LC 2008-20438

First published 2007 in the United Kingdom

"When a battalion of the Prince of Wales' Royal Regiment landed in Iraq in 2004, Mills commanded the 18 men of the sniper platoon. His gripping combat narrative covers how the platoon did more than its share of the fighting during the months when the Iraqis virtually besieged the battalion." Booklist

Murray, Williamson

The **Iraq** war; a military history. by Williamson Murray and Robert H. Scales, Jr. Belknap Press of Harvard University Press 2003 312p il map $29.95; pa $20 **956.7**

1. Iraq War, 2003-2011 2. Iraq War, 2003- 3. United States -- Armed forces

ISBN 0-674-01280-1; 0-674-01968-7 pa

This is a military history of the 2003 American-led war against Iraq

"Williamson Murray and Robert Scales, both American military academics, have produced a superlative record of the invasion—part history, part critique and part doctrinal template for the future. Technical and operational aspects are explained clearly without losing the depth required to make this a serious study." Economist

Includes bibliographical references

Packer, George

The **assassins'** gate; America in Iraq. Farrar, Straus & Giroux 2005 467p hardcover o.p. pa $15 **956.7**

1. Iraq War, 2003-2011 2. Iraq War, 2003- 3. Iraq -- Politics and government 4. United States -- Politics and government -- 2001-

ISBN 0-374-29963-3; 0-374-53055-6 pa

LC 2005-11521

This "book rests on three main pillars: analysis of the intellectual origins of the Iraq war, summary of the political argument that preceded and then led to it, and firsthand description of the consequences on the ground. . . . The Iraq debate has long needed someone who is both tough-minded enough, and sufficiently sensitive, to register all its complexities. In George Packer's work, this need is answered." Publ Wkly

Includes bibliographical references

Polk, William Roe

★ **Understanding** Iraq; the whole sweep of Iraqi history, from Genghis Khan's Mongols to the Ottoman Turks to the British mandate to the American occupation. [by] William R. Polk. HarperCollins 2005 221p map $22.95; pa $13.95 **956.7**

1. Iraq -- History

ISBN 0-06-076468-6; 0-06-076469-4 pa

LC 2005-281319

The author presents an account of the history of Iraq, from the Dark Ages to the American occupation that began in 2003.

This is "a sober and informed account of Iraq's history, culminating in a compelling critique of the U.S. intervention there." Foreign Affairs

Includes bibliographical references

Raddatz, Martha

The **long** road home; a story of war and family. Putnam 2007 310p il map hardcover o.p. pa $15 **956.7**

1. Soldiers -- United States 2. United States -- Army -- Cavalry, 1st 3. Iraq War, 2003- -- Personal narratives

ISBN 0-399-15382-9; 978-0-399-15382-2; 0-425-21934-8 pa; 978-0-425-21934-8 pa

LC 2006-37332

This "account has grit and high drama. . . . Sometimes the level of detail is astonishing." N Y Times (Late N Y Ed)

Ricks, Thomas E.

Fiasco: the American military adventure in Iraq. Penguin Press 2006 482p il map hardcover o.p. pa $16 **956.7**

1. Iraq War, 2003-2011 2. Iraq War, 2003 3. Iraq War, 2003-

ISBN 0-14-303891-5 pa; 1-59420-103-X; 978-0-14-303891-7 pa; 978-1-59420-103-5

LC 2006-45357

This book is "not a political rant nor is it shrill. But in its low-key, extraordinarily well-sourced, highly-detailed portrait of the run-up to and conduct of the war it is devastating." Christ Sci Monit

Includes bibliographical references

Robertson, John

Iraq; A Short History. John Robertson. Oneworld Publications 2015 336 p. 8 plates; illustrations; maps $35 **956.7**

1. Iraq -- History 2. Iraq War, 2003-2011 3. Iraq -- Civilization

ISBN 1851685863; 9781851685868

In this book author "John Robertson canvases the entirety of Iraq's rich history, from the seminal advances of its Neolithic inhabitants to the aftermath of the American-led invasion and Iraq today. Grounded in extensive research, this balanced account of a country and its people explores the greatness and grandeur of Iraq's achievements, the brutality and magnificence of its ancient empires, [and] its contributions to the emergence of the world's enduring monotheistic faiths." (Publisher's note)

"Few books in English cover Iraq's entire history in such a holistic manner. This highly readable and informative book will be a valuable tool in teaching and research for informed general readers and Middle East specialists." LJ

Seierstad, Asne

A **hundred** and one days; a Baghdad journal. translated by Ingrid Christophersen. Basic Books 2005 321p il maps hardcover o.p. pa $14 **956.7**

1. Iraq War, 2003- -- Personal narratives

ISBN 0-465-07600-9; 0-465-07601-7 pa

First published 2005 in the United Kingdom

The author "writes about her stay as a reporter for Scandinavian, Dutch, and German media in Baghdad in the days before the war in Iraq through the fall of Baghdad. . . . Seierstad puts a human face to and provides insight into the mosaic of the people of Iraq, the Bath party supporters, the dissidents, and the average person caught in the nightmare of the Saddam regime and the horrors of war." SLJ

Shadid, Anthony

Night draws near; Iraq's people in the shadow of America's war. Picador 2006 507p map pa $15   **956.7**

1. Iraq War, 2003-2011 2. Iraq War, 2003-
ISBN 978-0-312-42603-3; 0-312-42603-8

First published 2005 by Holt & Co.

"Evenhanded and keenly observed, containing just enough (and no more) of the author to suggest a decent man worthy of our trust, . . . [this book] is written for the inexpert but has fresh material for scholars." Economist

Includes bibliographical references

Sheeler, Jim

Final salute; a story of unfinished lives. Penguin Press 2008 280p il $25.95   **956.7**

1. Death 2. Bereavement 3. Iraq War, 2003-2011 4. Iraq War, 2003- 5. Military personnel -- United States
ISBN 978-1-59420-165-3; 1-59420-165-X

LC 2007-44130

This is a "tribute to the soldiers who have died in Iraq and their devastated families. The author spent two years shadowing Maj. Steve Beck, a marine in charge of casualty notification, as he delivered the news of battlefield death to families. Sheeler puts readers in Beck's shoes as he walks up to houses, delivers the knock on the door so dreaded by military families and tries to comfort distraught spouses and parents. . . . Sheeler's book is a devastating account of the sacrifices military families make and should be required reading for all Americans." Publ Wkly

Sky, Emma

The **Unraveling**; High Hopes and Missed Opportunities in Iraq. Emma Sky. PublicAffairs 2015 400 p. illustrations, maps, portraits (hardcover) $28.99   **956.7**

1. Iraq War, 2003-2011 2. Postwar reconstruction
ISBN 161039593X; 9781610395939

LC 2015932207

This book, by Emma Sky, "provides unique insights into the US military as well as the complexities, diversity, and evolution of Iraqi society. [The memoir] . . . is an intimate insider's portrait of how and why the Iraq adventure failed and contains a unique analysis of the course of the war." (Publisher's note)

"At once informative and emotional, this book will find a wide audience of adult readers, especially those interested in global politics and current events." LJ

Stewart, Rory

★ The **prince** of the marshes; and other occupational hazards of a year in Iraq. Harcourt, Inc. 2006 396p il $25   **956.7**

1. Diplomats 2. Nonfiction writers 3. Iraq -- Social conditions 4. Iraq -- Description and travel 5. Iraq -- Politics and government
ISBN 0-15-101235-0; 978-0-15-101235-0

LC 2006-06905

"In August 2003, at the age of thirty, Rory Stewart took a taxi from Jordan to Baghdad. A Farsi-speaking British diplomat who had recently completed an epic walk from Turkey to Bangladesh, he was soon appointed deputy governor of Amarah and then Nasiriyah, provinces in the remote, impoverished marsh regions of southern Iraq. He spent the next eleven months negotiating hostage releases, holding elections, and splicing together some semblance of an infrastructure for a population of millions. . . . The Prince of the Marshes tells the story of Stewart's year." (Publisher's note) Chronology.

"In 2003, Stewart, a former British diplomat, joined the Coalition Provisional Authority in Iraq and was posted to the southern province of Maysan, where he found himself the de-facto governor of a restive populace whose allegiances were split among fifty-four political parties, twenty major tribes, and numerous militias. Stewart's account of his attempts to placate the various local figures who continually threaten to kill each other, or him, is both shrewd and self-deprecating." New Yorker

Tripp, Charles

A **history** of Iraq; 3rd ed.; Cambridge University Press 2007 xxiii, 357p il map $70; pa $24.99 **956.7**

1. Iraq -- History
ISBN 978-0-521-87823-4; 978-0-521-70247-8 pa

LC 2007-282451

First published 2000

This book traces the political history of Iraq from the Ottoman Empire to the fall of Saddam Hussein and the American occupation.

Includes bibliographical references

Woodward, Bob

★ **Plan** of attack. Simon & Schuster 2004 467p il map hardcover o.p. pa $14   **956.7**

1. Iraq War, 2003-2011 2. Iraq War, 2003- 3. United States -- Politics and government -- 2001-
ISBN 0-7432-5547-X; 0-7432-5548-8 pa

LC 2004-351204

The author "delivers an engrossing blow-by-blow of the run-up to war in Iraq. . . . With this book, Woodward . . . has delivered his most important and impressive work in years. Ultimately, this first-class work of contemporary history will be remembered for shedding needed light on the Iraq War." Publ Wkly

Wright, Evan

Generation kill; Devil Dogs, Iceman, Captain America, and the new face of American war. G.P.

Putnam's Sons 2004 354p il maps hardcover o.p.
pa $15 **956.7**
1. Iraq War, 2003- -- Personal narratives
ISBN 0-399-15193-1; 0-425-20040-X pa
LC 2004-44682

The author discusses his experiences when embedded with the First Marine Division in Iraq. This book is based on a series of articles that originally appeared in Rolling Stone.

This "account is a personality-driven, readable and insightful look at the Iraq War's first month from the Marine grunt's point of view." Publ Wkly

956.704 Iraq--1920-

Bolger, Daniel P.

Why We Lost; A General's Inside Account of the Iraq and Afghanistan Wars. Daniel Bolger. Houghton Mifflin Harcourt 2014 400 p. 16 plates; illustrations; maps $28 **956.704**
1. Afghan War, 2001- 2. Iraq War, 2003-2011 3. United States -- Military history 4. Military personnel -- United States 5. Leadership -- United States 6. Afghan War, 2001- -- Campaigns 7. Iraq War, 2003-2011 -- Campaigns 8. Strategic culture -- United States 9. Afghan War, 2001- -- Personal narratives, American 10. Iraq War, 2003-2011 -- Personal narratives, American 11. War on Terrorism, 2001-2009 -- Personal narratives, American 12. Civil-military relations -- United States -- History -- 21st century
ISBN 0544370481; 9780544370487
LC 2014026908

This book, by Daniel Bolger, is an "insider account of the U.S. wars in Iraq and Afghanistan, and how it all went wrong. Over a thirty-five-year career, . . . Bolger rose through the army infantry to become a three-star general, commanding in both theaters of the U.S. campaigns in Iraq and Afghanistan. . . . Now, as a witness to all levels of military command, Bolger offers a unique assessment of these wars, from 9/11 to the final withdrawal from the region." (Publisher's note)

"Bolger does a fine job of delineating the technical aspects of military workings (while making good fun of the euphemistic names of the various operations labeled by the 'guys in the Pentagon basement') and candidly describes America's efforts after a decade of attrition as 'global containment of Islamic threats.' With vigorous, no-nonsense prose and an impressive clarity of vision, this general does not mince blame in this chronicle o f failure." Kirkus

Includes bibliographical references (pages 438-485) and index

General's inside account of the Iraq and Afghanistan Wars

Castner, Brian

The **long** walk; a story of war and the life that follows. Brian Castner. Doubleday 2012 222 p. **956.704**
1. Autobiographies 2. Ordnance disposal units 3. Post-traumatic stress disorder 4. Iraq War, 2003-2011 -- Personal narratives 5. Ordnance disposal units -- Iraq 6. Ordnance disposal units -- United States 7. United States. Air Force -- Officers -- Biography 8. Iraq War,

2003-2011 -- Personal narratives, American 9. Iraq War, 2003-2011 -- Veterans -- United States -- Biography
ISBN 0385536208; 9780385536202
LC 2011052419

This memoir by Brian Castner describes his life during and after the Iraq War. "[A]s the commander of an Explosive Ordnance Disposal unit in Iraq . . . [d]ays and nights he and his team . . . would . . . engage in . . . disarming the deadly improvised explosive devices that had been discovered. . . . When Castner returned home to his wife and family, he began a struggle with . . . an unshakable feeling of fear and confusion and survivor's guilt that he terms The Crazy." (Publisher's note)

Includes bibliographical references and index.

Chandrasekaran, Rajiv

Imperial life in the emerald city; inside Iraq's green zone. Rajiv Chandrasekaran. Alfred A. Knopf 2006 x, 320p maps (alk. paper) $25.95 **956.704**
1. Iraq 2. Iraq War, 2003-2011 3. Political corruption 4. United States -- Politics and government 5. Iraq War, 2003- 6. Iraq -- Coalition Provisional Authority 7. United States -- Politics and government -- 2001- 8. United States -- Politics and government -- 2001-2009
ISBN 1400044871; 9781400044870
LC 2006041014

BBC Samuel Johnson Prize for Non-Fiction (2007)

This book discusses "the Green Zone in Baghdad, headquarters for the American occupation in Iraq, . . . [and provides a] portrait of the Green Zone and the Coalition Provisional Authority (which ran Iraq's government from April 2003 to June 2004) that becomes a metaphor for the [U.S.] administration's larger failings in Iraq. An insular, often blinkered approach to decision making; a reluctance to listen to experts; Pollyannaish expectations leading to inadequate allocations of resources and staff; a willful ignorance of Iraqi culture and history; and an obliviousness to realities on the ground: all are on unfortunate display in the Emerald City." (New York Times)

"This is a clearly written, blessedly undidactic book. It should be read by anyone who wants to understand how things went so badly wrong in Iraq." N Y Times Book Rev

Includes bibliographical references (p. [303]-306) and index.

Edmonds, Bill Russell

God Is Not Here; A Soldier's Struggle With Torture, Trauma, and the Moral Injuries of War. Bill Russell Edmonds. W.W. Norton & Co. Inc. 2015 312 p. illustrations $27.95 **956.704**
1. War -- Ethical aspects 2. Iraq War, 2003-2011 -- Personal narratives
ISBN 1605987743; 9781605987743

In this book, by Lieutenant Colonel Bill Russell Edmonds, "the focus is on a young man struggling to learn what is right when fighting wrong. [The author] . . . provides a disturbing and thought-provoking account of the morally ambiguous choices faced when living with and fighting within a foreign religion and culture, as well as the resulting psychological and spiritual impacts on a soldier." (Publisher's note)

"Edmonds doesn't reach the depth attained in recent books by Ben Fountain, Phil Klay, or Michael Pitre, but he does provide a useful adjunct to the work on PTSD done by Jonathan Shay and other writers and analysts. War is hell, and hell is other people. In this serviceable account, Edmonds assures us that both adage s are true." Kirkus

Fair, Eric

Consequence; A Memoir. Eric Fair. Henry Holt & Co. 2016 256 p. (hardcover) $26   956.704

1. Ethics 2. Iraq War, 2003-2011 3. Torture -- Iraq 4. Linguists -- Iraq -- Biography 5. Military interrogation -- Iraq 6. Iraq War, 2003-2011 -- Atrocities 7. Military interrogation -- United States 8. Government contractors -- United States -- Biography 9. Iraq War, 2003-2011 -- Personal narratives, American 10. Iraq War, 2003-2011 -- Prisoners and prisons, American 11. Heart -- Transplantation -- Patients -- United States -- Biography
ISBN 9781627795135; 9781627795142

LC 2015031396

In this memoir, author Eric Fair "questions everything--his faith, his morality, his country--as he recounts his experience as an interrogator in Iraq. It is a story of a man who chases his own demons from Egypt, where he served as an Army translator, to a detention center in Iraq, to seminary at Princeton, and eventually, to a heart transplant ward at the University of Pennsylvania." (Publisher's note)

"A startling debut from a haunted individual who wishes he had left Iraq earlier 'with my soul intact.' " Kirkus

Hornfischer, James D.

Service; a Navy SEAL at war. Marcus Luttrell; with James D. Hornfischer. Little, Brown and Co. 2012 xv, 364 p.p (hardcover) $27.99   956.704

1. War 2. Soldiers -- United States 3. Voluntary military service 4. Afghan War, 2001- -- Campaigns 5. Iraq War, 2003-2011 -- Campaigns 6. Afghan War, 2001- -- Personal narratives, American 7. United States. Navy. SEALs -- Officers -- Biography 8. Iraq War, 2003-2011 -- Personal narratives, American
ISBN 0316185361; 9780316185363

LC 2012904468

Author Marcus "Luttrell chronicles his missions preserving democracy for America . . . During their time in Iraq, his SEAL combat brothers killed perceived enemies, suffered countless wounds, and died at a rapid pace, making the narrative occasionally difficult to follow. In some chapters, battle tactics predominate, and the sentences are quick and graphic . . . Luttrell explains why some men answer the call of war no matter the risk to themselves or their loved ones. The author seeks to explain the honor of military service to . . . readers who have never experienced it." (Kirkus)

Includes bibliographical references.

Swofford, Anthony

Jarhead: a Marine's chronicle of the Gulf War and other battles. Scribner 2003 260p hardcover o.p. pa $15   956.704

1. United States -- Marine Corps 2. Persian Gulf War, 1991 -- Personal narratives
ISBN 0-7432-3535-5; 0-7432-8721-5 pa

LC 2002-30866

This book offers "an unflinching portrayal of the loneliness and brutality of modern warfare and sophisticated analyses of—and visceral reactions to—its politics." Publ Wkly

Thorpe, Helen

Soldier girls; the battles of three women at home and at war. Helen Thorpe. Scribner 2014 416 p. (hardcover : alk. paper) $28   956.704

1. Afghan War, 2001- 2. Iraq War, 2003-2011 3. United States. Army 4. Women in the military 5. United States -- National Guard 6. Women -- Indiana -- Biography 7. Afghan War, 2001- -- Campaigns 8. Iraq War, 2003-2011 -- Campaigns 9. Indiana. National Guard -- Biography 10. United States. Army -- Women -- Biography 11. Single mothers -- United States -- Biography 12. Women soldiers -- United States -- Biography 13. Women veterans -- United States -- Biography 14. Afghan War, 2001- -- Women -- United States -- Biography 15. Iraq War, 2003-2011 -- Women -- United States -- Biography
ISBN 1451668104; 9781451668100; 9781451668117

LC 2014000658

This book, by Helen Thorpe, is an "account of three women deployed to Afghanistan and Iraq, and how their military service affected their friendship, their personal lives, and their families. . . . These women, who are quite different in every way, become friends, and we watch their interaction and also what happens when they are separated. . . . We see them work extremely hard, deal with the attentions of men on base and in war zones, and struggle to stay connected to their families back home." (Publisher's note)

"Thorpe fills this gripping tale with the women's own words, texts, and letters (from friends and their children, as well), and the story is engrossing and heartbreaking at once. Thorpe notes in the acknowledgments that the women's full-bore contributions to the book were not just to enlighten readers but also to let other war veterans know that they are not alone in their struggle to put their lives back together after a deployment." Booklist

Battles of three women at home and at war

956.91 Syria

Di Giovanni, Janine

The Morning They Came For Us; Dispatches from Syria. Janine di Giovanni. W W Norton & Co Inc 2016 320 p. maps $25.95   956.91

1. Jihad 2. Syria 3. War correspondents
ISBN 0871407132; 9780871407139

LC 2016007537

In this book, journalist Janine di Giovanni "gives us a tour de force of war reportage [in Syria], all told through the perspective of ordinary people—among them a doctor, a nun, a musician, and a student. What emerges is an extraordinary picture of the devastating human consequences of armed conflict, one that charts an apocalyptic but at times the tender story of life in a jihadist war zone." (Publisher's note)

"Di Giovanni presents a devastating picture of the horrors of civil war and the disintegration of Syrian society. Her vivid depictions of suffering may be overwhelming for some readers." LJ

Includes bibliographical references (pages [173]-176) and index.

Erlich, Reese

Inside Syria; the backstory of their civil war and what the world can expect. Reese Erlich; foreword by Noam Chomsky. Prometheus Books 2014 287 p. 8 plates; illustrations; maps (hardback) $25   **956.91**

1. War 2. Syria -- Politics and government 3. Syria -- History -- Civil War, 2011- 4. Syria -- Politics and government -- 2000- 5. Protest movements -- Syria -- History -- 21st century 6. Political violence -- Syria -- History -- 21st century

ISBN 1616149485; 9781616149482

LC 2014015840

In this book author "Reese Erlich unravels the complex dynamics underlying the Syrian civil war. Through vivid, on-the-ground accounts and interviews with both rebel leaders and Syrian President Bashar al-Assad, Erlich gives the reader a better understanding of this momentous power struggle and why it matters." (Publisher's note)

"A timely, immediate description and explanation of social and political disintegration at huge human cost in war-torn Syria." LJ

Includes bibliographical references and index

Warrick, Joby, 1960-

Black flags; the rise of ISIS. Joby Warrick. Doubleday 2015 368 p. 8 plates (hardback) $28.95   **956.91**

1. Islamic fundamentalism 2. Terrorism -- Middle East 3. IS (Organization) 4. Terrorism -- Iraq 5. Terrorism -- Religious aspects -- Islam 6. Middle East -- Politics and government -- 21st century

ISBN 0385538219; 9780385538213

LC 2015020949

Pulitzer Prize: General Nonfiction (2016)

This book, by Joby Warrick, "traces how the strain of militant Islam behind ISIS first arose in a remote Jordanian prison and spread with the unwitting aid of two American presidents. . . . Drawing on unique high-level access to CIA and Jordanian sources, Warrick weaves gripping, moment-by-moment operational details with the perspectives of diplomats and spies, generals and heads of state, many of whom foresaw a menace worse than al Qaeda and tried desperately to stop it." (Publisher's note)

"The author focuses on dramatic flashpoints and the roles of key players, creating an exciting tale with a rueful tone, emphasizing how the Iraq invasion's folly bir t hed ISIS and created many missed opportunities to stop al-Zarqawi quickly. Warrick stops short of offering policy solutions, but he provides a valuable, readable introduction to a pressing international security threat." Kirkus

956.92   Lebanon

Friedman, Matti

Pumpkinflowers; a soldier's story of a forgotten war. Matti Friedman. Algonquin Books of Chapel Hill 2016 256 p. map (hardcover) $25.95   **956.92**

1. Lebanon -- History -- Civil War, 1975-1990 2. Lebanon -- History -- Civil War, 1975-1990 -- Personal narratives, Israeli

ISBN 1616204583; 9781616204587

LC 2015031466

This book, by Matti Friedman, describes the author's experiences serving in the Israeli military during the Lebanese civil war. "Part memoir, part reportage, part history, . . . [it] captures the birth of today's chaotic Middle East and the rise of a twenty-first-century type of war in which there is never a clear victor and media images can be as important as the battle itself." (Publisher's note)

"A haunting yet wry tale of young people at war, cursed by political forces beyond their control, that can stand alongside the best narrative nonfiction coming out of Afghanistan and Iraq." Kirkus

Includes bibliographical references.

956.94   Palestine; Israel

Armstrong, Karen

Jerusalem; one city, three faiths. Knopf 1996 xxi, 471p il maps hardcover o.p. pa $17.95   **956.94**

1. Jerusalem -- History

ISBN 0-679-43596-4; 0-345-39168-3 pa

LC 96-75888

Armstrong's "overarching theme, that Jerusalem has been central to the experience and 'sacred geography' of Jews, Muslims and Christians and thus has led to deadly struggles for dominance, is a familiar one, yet she brings to her sweeping, profusely illustrated narrative a grasp of sociopolitical conditions seldom found in other books." Publ Wkly

Bregman, Ahron

A **history** of Israel. Palgrave Macmillan 2002 xx, 320p map (Palgrave essential histories) $70; pa $21.95   **956.94**

1. Israel -- History

ISBN 0-333-67631-9; 0-333-67632-7 pa

LC 2002-72304

"Bregman takes into account all the major issues involving Israel's history." Booklist

Includes bibliographical references and index

Carroll, James, 1943-

Jerusalem, Jerusalem; how the ancient city ignited our modern world. Houghton Mifflin Harcourt 2011 418p $20   **956.94**

1. Jerusalem

ISBN 978-0-547-19561-2; 0-547-19561-3

LC 2010-43034

"Carroll examines the enigma that is Jerusalem—the holiest and most blood-soaked spot on earth. . . . While various religions flourished all over the ancient world, it was in Jerusalem that God emerged. Not just a god, but God, one who recognizes how both the need for violence and the hatred of violence reside within the human spirit. These conflicting impulses are the subthemes that propel Carroll's story across the ages, through Jerusalem's wreckages and rebirths, as the three Abrahamic religions claim the city as its own. Carroll's writing is so compelling, so beautifully constructed, that, ironically, the book can be a very slow read. There is something on almost every page that makes the reader want to stop and contemplate." Booklist

Includes bibliographical references

Cohen, Rich

Israel is real. Farrar, Straus, and Giroux 2009 383p map $27; pa $16   **956.94**
1. Jews -- History 2. Israel -- Description and travel
ISBN 978-0-374-17778-2; 0-374-17778-3; 978-0-312-42976-8 pa; 0-312-42976-2 pa
LC 2008-49223

The author explains "the history of a people and its religion from the time Zealots revolted against their Roman occupiers to the rise of the Zionists, who helped build the current republic. . . . A must-read for those who want to understand the context of the modern Jewish state." Kirkus

Includes bibliographical references

Collins, Larry

O Jerusalem! {by} Larry Collins and Dominique Lapierre. Simon & Schuster 1972 637p il maps hardcover o.p. pa $17   **956.94**
1. Israel-Arab War, 1948-1949 2. Jerusalem -- History -- 1948, Siege
ISBN 0-671-66241-4 pa

This is an account of the struggle for the city of Jerusalem during the Israel-Arab War of 1948

Includes bibliographical references

Ephron, Dan

Killing a king; the assassination of Yitzhak Rabin and the remaking of Israel. Dan Ephron. W W Norton & Co Inc 2015 304 p. 8 plates; color illustrations (hardcover) $27.95   **956.94**
1. Assassination 2. Israel -- History 3. Israel -- Politics and government -- 1993-
ISBN 0393242099; 9780393242096
LC 2015025695

Los Angeles Times Book Prize: History (2015)

In this book author Dan Ephron "relates the parallel stories of [Israeli Prime Minister Yitzhak] Rabin and his stalker, Yigal Amir, over the two years leading up to the assassination, as one of them planned political deals he hoped would lead to peace, and the other plotted murder. Through the prism of the assassination, much about Israel today comes into focus, from the paralysis in peacemaking to the fraught relationship between current Prime Minister Benjamin Netanyahu and President Barack Obama." (Publisher's note)

"Fascinating characterizations of real people and intrigue make this book appealing to readers of both fiction and nonfiction thrillers and anyone interested in the history of Israel." LJ

Includes bibliographical references and index

Gilbert, Martin

Jerusalem in the twentieth century. Wiley 1996 412p il maps $30; pa $16.95   **956.94**
1. Jerusalem 2. Palestine -- History
ISBN 0-471-16308-2; 0-471-28328-2 pa
LC 96-18458

"Gilbert's history is heavily Zionist. . . . Nonetheless, despite his tilt, Gilbert is well worth reading. He has an unrivalled ability to tell a story through the eyes of (some of) those taking part and his book is good popular history." London Rev Books

Includes bibliographical references

Gorenberg, Gershom

The **accidental** empire; Israel and the birth of the settlements, 1967-1977. Times Books 2006 454p il map $30   **956.94**
1. West Bank 2. Gaza Strip 3. Israel -- Politics and government
ISBN 0-8050-7564-X; 978-0-8050-7564-9
LC 2005-52988

This is an account of the settler movement in Israel, beginning with the aftermath of the 1967 war.

This is "an absorbing narrative with extensive references to archives, private papers, oral histories, books and articles." Nation

Includes bibliographical references

Hoffman, Adina

Till we have built Jerusalem; architects of a new city. Adina Hoffman. Farrar, Straus & Giroux 2016 368 p. illustrations (hardback) $28   **956.94**
1. Jerusalem 2. Architects 3. Architecture 4. Jerusalem -- Buildings 5. Architects -- Jerusalem -- Biography 6. Jerusalem -- History -- 20th century
ISBN 9780374289102; 9780374709785
LC 2015034650

This book, by Adina Hoffman, is a "journey into the very different lives of three architects who helped shape modern Jerusalem. The book unfolds as an excavation and opens with the arrival in 1930s Jerusalem of the celebrated Berlin architect Erich Mendelsohn. . . . Next we meet Austen St. Barbe Harrison, Palestine's chief government architect from 1922-1937. . . . And in the riveting . . . section, Hoffman herself sets out through the battered streets of today's Jerusalem." (Publisher's note)

"This is a well-done survey of the period and of a city that continues to attract and sadden both visitors and residents." Booklist

Hoffman, Bruce

Anonymous soldiers; the struggle for Israel, 1918-1947. Bruce Hoffman. Alfred A. Knopf, a division of Random House LLC 2015 640 p. 24 plates; illustrations $35   **956.94**
1. Zionism 2. Counterinsurgency 3. Israel -- History 4. Palestine -- History 5. World War, 1939-1945 6. Israel-Arab conflicts 7. Palestine -- History -- 1917-1948 8. World War, 1939-1945 -- Palestine 9. Zionism -- Palestine -- History -- 20th century 10. Palestine -- Politics and government -- 1917-1948 11.

Counterinsurgency -- Palestine -- History -- 20th century
ISBN 0307594718; 9780307594716

LC 2014018177

This book, by Bruce Hoffman, is "based on newly available documents, of the battles between Jews, Arabs, and the British that led to the creation of Israel. . . . Hoffman . . . shines new light on the bombing of the King David Hotel, the assassination of Lord Moyne in Cairo, the leadership of Menachem Begin, the life and death of Abraham Stern, and much else. Above all, Hoffman shows exactly how the underdog 'anonymous soldiers' of Irgun and Lehi defeated the British." (Publisher's note)

"A must-read for anyone interested in the origins of the State of Israel." LJ

Laqueur, Walter

A **history** of Zionism; with a new preface by the author. Schocken Bks. 1989 xxii, 639p il hardcover o.p. pa $16.95 **956.94**
1. Zionism
ISBN 0-8052-1149-7 pa

LC 88-38221

A reissue with new introduction of the title first published 1972 by Holt, Rinehart & Winston

The author examines the history of Zionism over the past three centuries from its European roots to the establishment of the state of Israel

Includes bibliographical references

LeBor, Adam

City of oranges; an intimate history of Arabs and Jews in Jaffa. W.W. Norton 2007 xxxviii, 424p il map pa $14.95 **956.94**
1. Israel-Arab conflicts
ISBN 0-393-32984-4; 978-0-393-32984-1

LC 2007-2389

First published 2006 in the United Kingdom

LeBor presents interviews with Arab and Jewish families in Jaffa, Israel.

"Those looking for a well-rounded and truly human insight into the conflict will enjoy this account." Publ Wkly

Includes bibliographical references

Miller, Jennifer

★ **Inheriting** the Holy Land; an American's search for hope in the Middle East. Ballantine Books 2005 xxxiii, 261p map $24.95; pa $14.95 **956.94**
1. Israel-Arab conflicts
ISBN 0-345-46924-0; 978-0-345-46924-3; 0-345-46925-9 pa; 978-0-345-46925-0 pa

LC 2004-66349

The author "is the daughter of one of the chief American negotiators in the Israeli-Palestinian conflict and a longtime participant in the Seeds of Peace program, bringing together Israeli and Palestinian children. Using the many contacts that she has made, from the highest leaders to the children on the street, Miller explores . . . the many different viewpoints and preconceptions of the people involved in the conflict, not excluding her own. . . . This is a superb book on a crucial issue of our time." SLJ

Includes bibliographical references

Mitchell, George J. (George John), 1933-

A **Path** to Peace; A Brief History of Israeli-Palestinian Negotiations and a Way Forward in the Middle East. George J. Mitchell; Alon Sachar. Simon & Schuster 2016 192 p. $26 **956.94**
1. Diplomacy 2. Palestine 3. Israel-Arab conflicts 4. Israel -- Foreign relations -- Arab countries
ISBN 1501153919; 9781501153914

LC 2016027278

This book by former US Special Envoy for Middle East Peace George J. Mitchell and Alon Sachar offers an "insider account of how the Israelis and the Palestinians have progressed (and regressed) in their negotiations through the years and outlines the specific concessions each side must make to finally achieve lasting peace." (Publisher's note)

"Mitchell's careful statements may simply seem inconclusive to the more casual reader, but this is only a testament to the level of nuance in this scrupulous book." Pub Wkly

Includes bibliographical references and index.

Montefiore, Sebag

Jerusalem; the biography. [by] Simon Sebag Montefiore. Knopf 2011 638p il map $35 **956.94**
1. Jerusalem -- History
ISBN 978-0-307-26651-4; 0-307-26651-6

"An epic history of the holy city at the heart of Judaism, Christianity and Islam is presented through the lives of its creators and conquerors from King David and Jesus to the Maccabees and Sir Moses Montefiore, in a chronicle that draws on new archival materials, current scholarship and family records. By the award-winning author of Stalin." (Publisher's note)

"If, as some have maintained, the word Jerusalem means "city of peace," it is a grand historical irony. For, as this beautifully written, absorbing, but often grim account shows, there are few stones of the city that have not been stained with the blood of its inhabitants during the past 3,000 years. Acclaimed historian and biographer Montefiore views Jerusalem as a living, breathing organism bearing the genetic imprint of many conquerors, including Jews, Greeks, Arabs, crusading Franks, Turks, and the British. . . . While sometimes painful to read, this is an essential book for those who wish to understand a city that remains a nexus of world affairs." Booklist

O'Malley, Padraig

The **two**-state delusion; Israel and Palestine: a tale of two narratives. Padraig O'Malley. Viking 2015 432 p. maps $30 **956.94**
1. Israel-Arab conflicts 2. Israel -- Politics and government 3. Jews -- Identity 4. Arab-Israeli conflict -- Causes 5. Israel -- History -- 21st century 6. Palestinian Arabs -- Ethnic identity 7. Arab-Israeli conflict -- 1993- -- Peace 8. Arab-Israeli conflict -- Political aspects 9. Palestinian Arabs -- History -- 21st century 10. Israel -- Politics and government -- 21st century 11. Palestinian Arabs -- Politics and government -- 21st century
ISBN 0670025054; 9780670025053

LC 2014038545

In this book author Padraig O'Malley "argues that a two-state solution is no longer a viable path to create lasting peace in Israel and Palestine. O'Malley concludes that even if such an agreement could be reached, it would be nearly impossible to implement given the staggering costs, Palestine's political disunity and the viability of its economy, rapidly changing demographics, Israel's continuing political shift to the right, global warming's effect on the water supply, and more." (Publisher's note)

"If O'Malley's out-of-the-box advice lacks a comprehensive one-state solution, it could galvanize readers to engage in the discussion in new and more creative ways." Booklist

Includes bibliographical references and index

Palestine Speaks; Voices from the West Bank and Gaza. edited by Cate Malek and Mateo Hoke. McSweeney's 2014 320 p. illustrations, map $16   **956.94**
1. Palestine 2. Military occupation
ISBN 1940450241; 9781940450247
                                        LC 2015452323

In this "oral history collection" edited by Cate Malek and Mateo Hoke, "men and women from Palestine--including a fisherman, a settlement administrator, and a marathon runner--describe in their own words how their lives have been shaped by the historic crisis. The occupation of the West Bank and Gaza has been one of the world's most widely reported yet least understood human rights crises for over four decades." (Publisher's note)

"An absolute must for anyone interested in the Arab-Israeli conflict or with an interest in human rights. This book, similar to the other titles in the series, is an excellent way of developing a deeper understanding of people living the encounters about which we read in the papers and watch on the news." LJ

Sachar, Howard Morley
A **history** of Israel; from the rise of Zionism to our time. [by] Howard M. Sachar. 3rd ed, rev and updated; Knopf 2007 xxii, 1270p map pa $39.95   **956.94**
1. Zionism 2. Israel -- History
ISBN 978-0-375-71132-9; 0-375-71132-5
                                        LC 2006-101970

First published in two volumes 1976-1987

This is a history of the state of Israel. "When first published in 1976, this truly monumental history was hailed as a definitive work. . . . As extraordinarily stimulating as the first edition." Booklist

Includes bibliographical references

Shipler, David K.
Arab and Jew; wounded spirits in a promised land. rev ed; Penguin Bks. 2002 xxxix, 565p maps pa $17   **956.94**
1. Palestinian Arabs 2. Israel-Arab conflicts 3. Jewish-Arab relations 4. Israel -- Social conditions
ISBN 0-14-200229-1
                                        LC 2001-54862

First published 1986 by Times Bks.

The author examines the stereotypes that Arabs and Jews have of one another and "the origins of the prejudices that have been intensified by war, terrorism, and nationalism. . . . Shipler examines the process of indoctrination that begins in schools; he discusses the far-ranging effects of socioeco-

nomic differences, historical conflicts between Islam and Judaism, attitudes about the Holocaust, and much more." Publisher's note

Includes bibliographical references

Tolan, Sandy
The **lemon** tree; an Arab, a Jew, and the heart of the Middle East. Bloomsbury Pub. 2006 362p $24.95   **956.94**
1. Israel-Arab conflicts
ISBN 1-58234-343-8; 978-1-58234-343-3
                                        LC 2005-30360

The author "captures the Arab-Israeli struggle in this story of a house and the two families, first Palestinian then Jewish, who successively lived in it. . . . This wonderful human story vividly depicts the depths of attachment to contested ground." Libr J

956.940   Israel -- 1948-

Bar-On, Mordechai
Moshe Dayan; Israel's controversial hero. Mordechai Bar-On. 1st ed. Yale University Press 2012 xii, 247 p.p photograph (alk. paper) $25   **956.940**
1. Soldiers -- Israel 2. Israel -- Politics and government 3. Generals -- Israel -- Biography 4. Statesmen -- Israel -- Biography 5. Arab-Israeli conflict -- Biography
ISBN 0300149417; 9780300149418
                                        LC 2012000595

"In this . . . biography [of Israeli leader Moshe Dayan], Mordechai Bar-On . . . offers a . . . view of Dayan's private life, public career, and political controversies, set against an . . . analysis of Israel's political environment from pre-Mandate Palestine through the early 1980s. . . . Drawing on . . . Israeli archives, accounts by Dayan and members of his circle, and firsthand experiences, Bar-On reveals Dayan as a man unwavering in his devotion to Zionism and . . . Israel." (Publisher's note)

Includes bibliographical references (p. 219-236) and index

Cohen, Richard
Israel; Is It Good for the Jews? Richard Cohen. Simon & Schuster 2014 288 p. (hardback) $26   **956.940**
1. Israel 2. Jews -- History 3. Israel -- History
ISBN 1416575685; 9781416575689; 9781416575696
                                        LC 2014021062

National Jewish Book Awards Finalist: Modern Jewish Thought and Experience (2014)

This book, by Richard M. Cohen, "is part reportage, part memoir--an intimate journey through the history of Europe's Jews, culminating in the establishment of Israel. A veteran, syndicated columnist for 'The Washington Post,' . . . [the author] began this journey as a skeptic, wondering in a national column whether the creation of a Jewish State was 'a mistake.'" (Publisher's note)

"A thoughtful study recommended for both general and academic readers of history." LJ

Horovitz, David Phillip

A **little** too close to God; the thrills and panic of a life in Israel. {by} David Horovitz. Knopf 2000 311p $27.50 **956.940**

1. Israeli national characteristics 2. Israel -- Social conditions 3. Israel -- Politics and government

ISBN 0-375-40381-7

The author, editor of the Jerusalem Report, argues "that in recent years the conservative Netanyahu government and the continued influence of extreme Orthodox Jews have done little except complicate daily life in Israel and prevent serious peace negotiations from taking place. He presents a highly informative history and current-events narrative in a manner that makes it personal and relevant to Jews and non-Jews alike." Libr J

La Guardia, Anton

War without end; Israelis, Palestinians, and the struggle for a promised land. St. Martin's Griffin 2003 xxii, 436p il map pa $16.95 **956.940**

1. Zionism 2. Palestinian Arabs 3. Israel-Arab conflicts 4. Israeli national characteristics

ISBN 0-312-31633-X

LC 2003-41288

First published 2001 in the United Kingdom with title: Holy Land, unholy war: Israelis and Palestinians

"This is fundamentally an examination of two wounded peoples, neither of whom seems capable of surmounting national myths and past hatreds to forge a new future. La Guardia is evenhanded in his criticism of both Israeli and Palestinian leaders, but he does not spare ordinary people. . . . This is an absorbing but heartbreaking examination of a seemingly endless tragedy that continues to unfold before our eyes." Booklist [review of 2002 edition]

Includes bibliographical references

Lozowick, Yaacov

Right to exist; a moral defense of Israel's wars. Doubleday 2003 326p map $26; pa $15 **956.940**

1. Israel-Arab conflicts

ISBN 0-385-50905-7; 1-4000-3243-1 pa

LC 2003-48477

The author "asserts that Israel is now, as before, struggling against opponents whose goal is the eventual destruction of the Jewish state. In examining the entire history of the Zionist enterprise, he illustrates both the moral justification of that enterprise and of the wars Israelis have been compelled to fight to preserve their independence. . . . {This} is an eloquent and necessary justification of Israel's right to defend itself." Booklist

Rubin, Barry

Israel; an introduction. Barry Rubin. Yale University Press 2012 ix, 340 p.p (paperback : alk. paper) $30.00 **956.940**

1. Israel

ISBN 0300162308; 9780300162301

LC 2011028927

This book presents a "survey of the many . . . . facets of Israeli history, society, government, economics and culture . . . Such issues include existential insecurity, ongoing Palestinian conflict, fluid borders, diverse immigrant population,

living with daily terrorist violence and the sense of being 'misunderstood by outside observers.' . . . [Barry Rubin] reminds readers that Jews even in exile acted as a 'national people, arguably the first such in history,' and thus the establishment of Israel was 'the continuation of a long historical process,' not merely the result of the Holocaust." (Kirkus)

Includes bibliographical references and index

Shilon, Avi

Menachem Begin; a life. Avi Shilon; translated from the Hebrew by Danielle Zilberberg and Yoram Sharett. Yale University Press 2012 545 p. (clothbound : alk. paper) $40 **956.940**

1. Prime ministers -- Israel 2. Israel -- Politics and government 3. Prime ministers -- Israel -- Biography 4. Revisionist Zionists -- Israel -- Biography 5. Israel -- Politics and government -- 20th century

ISBN 0300162359; 9780300162356

LC 2012012189

Author Avi Shilon discusses Menachem Begin. "The book presents a detailed new portrait of Israel's founding leader. Among the many topics Avi Shilon holds up to new light are Begin's antagonistic relationship with David Ben-Gurion, his controversial role in the 1982 Lebanon War, his unique leadership style, the changes in his ideology over the years, and the mystery behind the total silence he maintained at the end of his career." (Publisher's note)

Includes bibliographical references and index

956.95 Jordan and West Bank

Ehrenreich, Ben

The **Way** to the Spring; Life and Death in Palestine. by Ben Ehrenreich. Penguin Group USA 2016 448 p. illustrations, maps $28 **956.95**

1. Palestine 2. West Bank 3. Journalists 4. Palestinian Arabs

ISBN 1594205906; 9781594205903

LC 2016016951

This book, by journalist Ben Ehrenreich, is an "immersion into the everyday struggles of Palestinian life. . . . Ruled by the Israeli military, set upon and harassed constantly by Israeli settlers who admit unapologetically to wanting to drive them from the land, forced to negotiate an ever more elaborate and more suffocating series of fences, checkpoints, and barriers that have sundered home from field, home from home, this is a population whose living conditions are unique." (Publisher's note)

"Ehrenreich's journal conveys how the Israeli-Palestinian conflict truly plays out at ground level, where "normal" might include the sounds of screaming, being arrested and questioned for hours, or simply being shot at." Booklist

Includes bibliographical references (pages 371-411) and index.

Grossman, David

The **yellow** wind; translated from the Hebrew by Haim Watzman; {with a new afterword by the author} Picador 2002 222p map pa $13 **956.95**

1. Palestinian Arabs 2. Jewish-Arab relations 3. West

Bank
ISBN 0-312-42098-6

LC 2002-67325

Original Hebrew edition, 1987; this translation first published 1988

"Grossman was assigned to report for a weekly newspaper on life for both occupied and occupier on the West Bank during the 20th anniversary of its conquest. With an eye and ear for revealing detail, he argues that the Jews are now doing to Palestinians what has been done to them through the ages." Libr J

957 Siberia (Asiatic Russia)

Frazier, Ian
Travels in Siberia. Farrar, Straus and Giroux 2010 529p il map $30 **957**
1. Siberia (Russia) -- Description and travel
ISBN 978-0-374-27872-4; 0-374-27872-4

LC 2010-05784

"Frazier records several visits [to Siberia]: a summer's trip via cantankerous automobile across the entire region, in the company of a couple of local companions; a winter's journey by train and car, during which the car sometimes used frozen waterways for roads; and a return visit to see the effects of the emerging Russian energy industry. . . . The contrasts are stark—one day, he walked through the ruins of a remote, frozen Soviet-era prison camp and later saw a ballet in St. Petersburg—and the writing is consistently rich. A dense, challenging, dazzling work that will leave readers exhausted but yearning for more." Kirkus

Includes bibliographical references

Thubron, Colin
In Siberia. HarperCollins Pubs. 2000 287p hardcover o.p. pa $14 **957**
1. Siberia (Russia) -- Description and travel
ISBN 0-06-095373-X pa

LC 99-41346

"Thubron elegantly encompasses both awe-inspiring landscapes and their dark histories as well as immersing himself in local eccentricities." Times Lit Suppl

957.7 Birobidzhan (Russia) -- History

Gessen, Masha
Where the Jews aren't; The Sad and Absurd Story of Birobidzhan, Russia's Jewish Autonomous Region. Masha Gessen. Nextbook/Schocken 2016 192 p. map (hardback) $25 **957.7**
1. Jews -- Russia 2. Russia -- History 3. Birobidzhan (Russia) -- History 4. Jews -- Russia (Federation) -- Birobidzhan 5. Evreĭskaia avtonomnaia oblast (Russia) -- History
ISBN 9780805242461

LC 2015049370

This book, by Masha Gessen, tells the "story of the Jews in twentieth-century Russia . . . . In 1929, the Soviet Union declared the area of Birobidzhan a homeland for Jews. It was championed by a group of intellectuals who envisioned

a place of post-oppression Jewish culture. . . . After the Second World War, the newly named 'Jewish Autonomous Region' received an influx of Jews dispossessed from what had once been the Pale, most of whom had lost families in the Holocaust." (Publisher's note)

"Gessen ably tells one of the 20th century's most chilling stories of struggle, perseverance, and despair." Pub Wkly

Includes bibliographical references (pages [151]-163) and index.

958 Central Asia

Hanks, Reuel R.
★ Central Asia; a global studies handbook. ABC-CLIO 2005 xvii, 467p il map (Global studies) $55 **958**
1. Central Asia
ISBN 1-85109-656-6

LC 2005-14716

"The superb text makes accessible, whether for reports or general reading, former Silk Road lands that may play increasingly important roles—think of oil-rich Kazakhstan—in the world's economy." SLJ

Includes bibliographical references

958.1 Afghanistan

Ansary, Mir Tamim
West of Kabul, East of New York; an Afghan American story. Farrar, Straus & Giroux 2002 292p hardcover o.p. pa $13 **958.1**
1. Islamic civilization 2. Afghanistan -- Social conditions
ISBN 0-374-28757-0; 0-312-42151-6 pa

The author, an Afghan American, reflects on his dual heritage. In light of the events of September 11, he focuses particular attention on the relationship between Islam and the West.

"While Ansary's political insights can be detached or perhaps purposefully aloof his descriptions of having lived in and identified alternately with the West and the Islamic world are utterly compelling." Publ Wkly

Badkhen, Anna, 1976-
★ The world is a carpet; four seasons in an Afghan village. Anna Badkhen. Riverhead Hardcover 2013 288 p. (hardback) $26.95 **958.1**
1. Nomads 2. Afghanistan 3. Carpets -- Afghanistan 4. Weaving -- Afghanistan 5. Women weavers -- Afghanistan 6. Rugs, Oriental -- Afghanistan 7. Afghanistan -- Social life and customs 8. Women -- Afghanistan -- Social conditions -- 21st century
ISBN 1594488320; 9781594488320

LC 2013003827

This book relates the year author Anna Badkhen spent in a "Balkh village in northern Afghanistan that could not be found on the map, where the illiterate Turkoman women fashioned the most exquisite rugs in the world." She chronicles "the hard lives of the inhabitant survivors," who deal with opium addiction, poverty, and colonizers. (Kirkus Reviews)

Coll, Steve

Ghost wars; the secret history of the CIA, Afghanistan, and bin Laden, from the Soviet invasion to September 10, 2001. Penguin Press 2004 695p maps $29.95; pa $16 **958.1**

1. Terrorists 2. Afghanistan 3. United States -- Central Intelligence Agency

ISBN 1-594-20007-6; 0-14-303466-9 pa

LC 2003-58593

The author "has given us what is certainly the finest historical narrative so far on the origins of Al Qaeda in the post-Soviet rubble of Afghanistan." N Y Times Book Rev

Includes bibliographical references

Dalrymple, William

Return of a king; the battle for Afghanistan, 1839-42. William Dalrymple. 1st ed. Alfred A. Knopf 2013 xxix, 515 p.p ill. (some col.), maps (hardcover) $30 **958.1**

1. Afghan War, 2001- 2. Afghanistan -- History -- British Intervention, 1838-1842 3. Afghanistan -- History, Military -- 19th century 4. British -- Afghanistan -- History -- 19th century

ISBN 0307958280; 9780307958280

LC 2012040998

This book, by William Dalrymple, "gives us the . . . account yet of the spectacular first battle for Afghanistan: the British invasion of the remote kingdom in 1839. . . . Dalrymple takes us beyond the bare outline of this infamous battle, and . . . illuminates the uncanny similarities between the West's first disastrous entanglement with Afghanistan and the situation today." (Publisher's note)

Includes bibliographical references (pages 493-497) and index.

Elliot, Jason

An unexpected light; travels in Afghanistan. St. Martin's Press 2001 473p map hardcover o.p. pa $18 **958.1**

1. Afghanistan -- Description and travel

ISBN 0-312-28846-8 pa

LC 2001-50036

This "is an account of Elliot's two visits to Afghanistan. The first occurred when he joined the mujaheddin circa 1979 and was smuggled into Soviet-occupied Afghanistan; the second happened nearly ten years later, when he returned to the still war-torn land. The skirmishes that Elliot painstakingly describes here took place between the Taliban and the government of Gen. Ahmad Shah Massoud in Kabul. . . . Elliot traveled widely in the hinterland, visiting Faizabad in the north and Herat in the west. The result is some of the finest travel writing in recent years." Libr J

Ewans, Martin

Afghanistan; a short history of its people and politics. HarperCollins Pubs. 2002 244p il maps hardcover o.p. pa $13.95 **958.1**

1. Afghanistan -- History

ISBN 0-06-050508-7 pa

LC 2002-17342

"This is a fascinating story and the best book-length examination of Afghanistan's history we're likely to have for some time." Booklist

Includes bibliographical references

Feifer, Gregory

The great gamble; the Soviet war in Afghanistan. Harper 2009 326p il map $27.99 **958.1**

1. Afghanistan -- History -- Soviet occupation, 1979-1989

ISBN 978-0-06-114318-2; 0-06-114318-9

LC 2008-22594

This is a history of the Soviet Union's 1979-1989 war in Afghanistan. "Taking advantage of his skills, experience, and contacts . . . as a foreign correspondent, Feifer's narrative relies greatly on the experiences of those involved on all sides of the conflict—from Soviet political and military insiders to various participants in the mujahideen resistance and even former CIA operatives—but he leans most heavily on the poignant stories of Soviet veterans. Fortunately for the reader, Feifer's research also includes a prudent mix of combat analyses, contemporary reports, and historical studies that inform a balanced treatment of his complex subject." Open Letters

Includes bibliographical references

Guibert, Emmanuel

★ The photographer; [by] Emmanuel Guibert, Didier Lefèvre and Frédéric Lemercier; translated by Alexis Siegel. First Second 2009 267p il map pa $29.95 **958.1**

1. Graphic novels 2. Photojournalism -- Graphic novels 3. Médecins Sans Frontières (Organization) -- Graphic novels 4. Afghanistan -- History -- Soviet occupation, 1979-1989 -- Graphic novels

ISBN 978-1-59643-375-5; 1-59643-375-2

"Originally published as three volumes in France from 2003 to 2006, this graphic novel follows photojournalist Didier Lefèvre during his three months in Pakistan and Afghanistan in 1986 as he documented the medical missions of Doctors without Borders. . . . The graphic novel combines traditional comic art with some of the four thousand photographs Lefevre shot while in Afghanistan. . . . Many images will stay with readers as both horrifying and glorious. The Afghan children being treated for burns, bullet wounds, and shrapnel are page by page next to the beauty of the Afghan mountainous landscapes. . . . [This book] has a powerful message and images of a part of the world that should be discussed more often." Voice Youth Advocates

Junger, Sebastian

War. Twelve 2010 287p map $26.99 **958.1**

1. Afghan War, 2001- -- Personal narratives 2. United

States -- Army -- Airborne Brigade, 173rd
ISBN 978-0-446-55624-8

LC 2009-49493

"The war in Afghanistan contains brutal trauma but also transcendent purpose in this riveting combat narrative. Junger spent 14 months in 2007-2008 intermittently embedded with a platoon of the 173rd Airborne brigade in Afghanistan's Korengal Valley, one of the bloodiest corners of the conflict. . . . Junger experiences everything they do—nerve-racking patrols, terrifying roadside bombings and ambushes, stultifying weeks in camp when they long for a firefight to relieve the tedium. . . . The result is an unforgettable portrait of men under fire." Publ Wkly

Includes bibliographical references

Rashid, Ahmed

Taliban; militant Islam, oil and fundamentalism in Central Asia. 2nd ed; Yale University Press 2010 319p map pa $17.95   **958.1**
1. Islam and politics 2. Islamic fundamentalism 3. Taliban 4. Afghanistan -- Politics and government
ISBN 978-0-300-16368-1; 0-300-16368-1

LC 2009-938249

First published 2000

The author explains "the Taliban's rise to power, its impact on Afghanistan and the region, its role in oil and gas company decisions, and the effects of changing American attitudes toward the Taliban. He also describes the new face of Islamic fundamentalism and explains why Afghanistan has become the world center for international terrorism." Publisher's note

Includes bibliographical references

Romesha, Clinton L., 1981-

★ **Red** platoon; a true story of American valor. Clinton Romesha. Penguin Group USA 2016 400 p. illustrations (hardcover) $28   **958.1**
1. Battles 2. Afghan War, 2001- -- Personal narratives 3. Taliban 4. Kamdesh, Battle of, Afghanistan, 2009
ISBN 9780525955054; 0525955054

This book is "the only comprehensive, firsthand account of the fourteen hour firefight at the Battle of Keating [in the Afghan War] by Medal of Honor recipient Clinton Romesha. . . . On October 3, 2009, after years of constant smaller attacks, the Taliban finally decided to throw everything they had at Keating. The ensuing 14-hour battle—and eventual victory—cost 8 men their lives." (Publisher's note)

"This firsthand account by former U.S. Army staff sergeant Romesha, who earned the Medal of Honor for his actions during this battle, expertly disentangles the complicated threads of the effort, accounting for the actions (and deaths) of every participant, including the massive air support, medical care, and command decisions related to the action. . . . A clear and expertly crafted account of an iconic fight during the Afghan War, this work is sure to be popular with readers of military history." LJ

Schroen, Gary C.

First in; an insider's account of how the CIA spearheaded the war on terror in Afghanistan. Pre-

sidio Press/Ballantine Books 2005 $25.95; pa $14.95   **958.1**
1. Afghanistan 2. United States -- Central Intelligence Agency
ISBN 0-89141-872-5; 0-89141-875-X pa

LC 2005-43171

The author describes his experiences after he "was tapped to lead the effort to establish contact with the Northern Alliance in the days following 9/11; the 35-year CIA veteran commanded the first American team on the ground in Afghanistan. . . . Schroen delivers what he advertises: a powerful account that takes the reader inside war councils and 19th-century- style cavalry charges in the months just after 9/11." Publ Wkly

Seierstad, Asne

The **bookseller** of Kabul; translated by Ingrid Christophersen. Little, Brown 2003 287p $19.95; pa $12.95   **958.1**
1. Afghanistan 2. Women -- Afghanistan
ISBN 0-316-73450-0; 0-316-15941-7 pa

LC 2003-54643

The author "entered Kabul with Northern Alliance soldiers after they ousted the Taliban. She took the rare opportunity to live with and write a book about the extended family of Sultan Khan, bookseller and entrepreneur. The result, organized around events in the lives of individual members of Khan's large clan . . . provides appropriate information about recent Afghani history, a glimpse from the inside at an Islamic family, and an understanding of the harshness and difficulty of the daily grind in Afghanistan—both under the Taliban and after the U.S. antiterrorist campaign." Booklist

Shah, Saira

The **storyteller's** daughter. Knopf 2003 253p $24; pa $13.95   **958.1**
1. Afghanistan
ISBN 0-375-41531-9; 1-4000-3147-8 pa

LC 2004-295126

The author "weaves oral traditions with history to describe life as an Afghani raised in the West but with solid roots in the East. . . . We learn about Shah's documentary work in Afghanistan, the power of myth through which Afghanistan's tradition is born, the brave work of peoples and organizations such as the Revolutionary Association of the Women of Afghanistan (RAWA), and the West's (and even East's) misconceptions regarding Muslim teachings. . . This rare personal and historic account of the region is a great addition to public and academic libraries." Libr J

Wahab, Shaista

★ A **brief** history of Afghanistan; [by] Shaista Wahab and Barry Youngerman. 2nd ed; Facts on File 2010 354p il map (Brief history) $49.50; pa $19.95   **958.1**
1. Afghanistan -- History
ISBN 978-0-8160-8218-6; 978-0-8160-8219-3 pa; 978-1-4381-0819-3 ebook

LC 2010-19656

First published 2006

This history of Afghanistan "examines this country's isolation and how it found itself involved in 30 years of war and anarchy. . . . [It] explores the culture and politics of the Pashtun tribes whose homeland extends across much of Afghanistan and northern Pakistan, as well as the Taliban insurgency and the relationship between local leaders and the central government in Kabul." Publisher's note

Includes bibliographical references

West, Bing

The **wrong** war; grit, strategy, and the way out of Afghanistan. [by] Bing West. Random House 2011 307p il map $28 **958.1**

1. Afghan War, 2001-

ISBN 978-1-4000-6873-9; 1-4000-6873-8

LC 2010043107

West argues that "the central premise of counterinsurgency doctrine holds that if the Americans sacrifice on behalf of the Afghan government, then the Afghan people will risk their lives for that same government in return. They will fight the Taliban. . . . This isn't happening. . . . [The author contends that] the Afghans are waiting to see who prevails, but prevailing is impossible without their help." (N Y Times Book Rev) Bibliography. Index.

This is "a crushing and seemingly irrefutable critique of the American plan in Afghanistan. It should be read by anyone who wants to understand why the war there is so hard." N Y Times Book Rev

Includes bibliographical references

Zoya

Zoya's story; an Afghan woman's struggle for freedom. {by} Zoya with John Follain and Rita Cristofari. HarperCollins Pubs. 2002 239p $24.95; pa $12.95 **958.1**

1. Afghanistan 2. Women -- Afghanistan

ISBN 0-06-009782-5; 0-06-009783-3 pa

"After both her parents were killed by the Mujahideen, Zoya took up her mother's work in the Revolutionary Association of the Women of Afghanistan and, with her grandmother, journeyed to Pakistan, where she could receive an education. A few years later, Zoya returned to Afghanistan, where she witnessed public executions but also saw heartening displays of courage. A stirring memoir by an uncompromisingly brave woman." Booklist

958.104 Afghanistan--1919-

Bruning, John R.

Level zero heroes; the story of U.S. Marine Special Operations in Bala Murghab, Afghanistan. Michael Golembesky with John R. Bruning. St. Martin's Press 2014 320 p. 16 plates; illustrations; maps (hardcover) $26.99 **958.104**

1. Afghan War, 2001- 2. Special forces (Military science) -- United States 3. Taliban 4. Close air support -- History -- 21st century 5. Afghan War, 2001- -- Personal narratives, American 6. Bādghīs (Afghanistan) -- History, Military 7. Afghan War, 2001- -- Campaigns -- Afghanistan -- Bādghīs 8. United States. Marine Corps -- Non-commissioned officers -- Biography 9. Murgab River Region (Afghanistan and Turkmenistan)

-- History, Military 10. United States. Marine Special Operations Command. Marine Special Operations Team 8222 -- Biography

ISBN 1250030404; 9781250030405

LC 2014016597

Author "Michael Golembesky follows the members of U.S. Marine Special Operations Team 8222 on their assignment to . . . Taliban stronghold known as Bala Murghab as they conduct special operations. [It] brings to life the mission of these selected few that fought side-by-side in Afghanistan, in a narrative as action-packed and emotional as anything to emerge from the Special Operations community contribution to the Afghan War." (Publisher's note)

"Readers who enjoy first-person accounts of battles laced with nonstop action will have a tough time putting this one down." LJ

Includes bibliographical references

Story of U.S. Marine Special Operations in Bala Murghab, Afghanistan

Castner, Brian

All the ways we kill and die; an elegy for a fallen comrade and the hunt for his killer, Brian Castner. Arcade Pub. 2016 356 p. (hardcover : alk. paper) $25.99 **958.104**

1. Explosives 2. Afghan War, 2001- 3. Military personnel -- United States 4. Afghan War, 2001- -- Campaigns 5. Ordnance disposal units -- Afghanistan 6. United States. Air Force -- Officers -- Biography 7. Afghan War, 2001- -- Personal narratives, American 8. Improvised explosive devices -- Detection -- Afghanistan

ISBN 1628726547; 9781628726541

LC 2015040029

In this memoir, author "Brian Castner, an Iraq War vet, learns that his friend and [explosive ordnance disposal] brother Matt has been killed by an IED in Afghanistan, he . . . begins a personal investigation. Is the bomb maker who killed Matt the same man American forces have been hunting since Iraq, known as the Engineer? Castner takes us inside the manhunt for this elusive figure, meeting maimed survivors, interviewing the forensics teams who gather post-blast evidence, [and] the wonks who collect intelligence." (Publisher's note)

"Castner's writing is evocative and engaging, completely absorbing from beginning to end. A must-read for military buffs and a should-read for anyone who has given even a cursory thought to the U.S. efforts in Afghanistan and Iraq." Kirkus

Includes bibliographical references

Elegy for a fallen comrade and the hunt for his killer

Gall, Carlotta

The **wrong** enemy; America in Afghanistan, 2001/2014. Carlotta Gall. Houghton Mifflin Harcourt 2014 352 p. illustrations $28 **958.104**

1. Taliban 2. Afghan War, 2001- 3. Qaida (Organization) 4. Pakistan -- Politics and government 5. Pakistan. Inter Services Intelligence 6. Afghanistan -- Politics and government 7. Pakistan -- Foreign relations -- United States 8. United States -- Foreign relations -- Pakistan 9. Afghanistan -- Foreign relations -- United States 10.

United States -- Foreign relations -- Afghanistan
ISBN 0544046692; 9780544046696

LC 2013044257

"Carlotta Gall has reported from Afghanistan and Pakistan for almost the entire duration of the American invasion and occupation, beginning shortly after 9/11. She knows just how much this war has cost the Afghan people, and how much damage can be traced to Pakistan and its duplicitous government and intelligence forces. Now that American troops are withdrawing, it is time to tell the full history of how we have been fighting the wrong enemy, in the wrong country." Publisher's Note

"The author offers a compelling account of the attack on bin Laden's compound, the repercussions of which are still being felt. Gall admirably never loses sight of the human element in this tragedy." Kirkus

Includes bibliographical references and index

Ghouri, Nadene

The **lightless** sky; a twelve-year-old refugee's harrowing escape from Afghanistan and his extraordinary journey across half the world. Gulwali Passarlay with Nadene Ghouri. HarperOne 2016 368 p. color illustrations, maps (hardback) $25.99   **958.104**
1. Taliban 2. Afghan War, 2001- 3. Political refugees 4. Political refugees -- Afghanistan -- Biography
ISBN 9780062443878

LC 2015042841

In this memoir, Gulwali Passarlay "was caught between the Taliban who wanted to recruit him, and the Americans who wanted to use him. To protect her son, Gulwali's mother sent him away. The search for safety would lead the twelve-year-old across eight countries. . . . Eventually granted asylum in England, Gulwali was sent to a good school, learned English, won a place at a top university, and was chosen to help carry the Olympic Torch in the 2012 London Games." (Publisher's note)

"A vivid, timely story of survival. If spies live in boredom punctuated by flashes of terrifying action, then refugees on the run live in constant high anxiety punctuated by flashes of horror and panic." Kirkus

Gopal, Anand, 1980-

No good men among the living; America, the Taliban, and the war through Afghan eyes. Anand Gopal. Metropolitan Books 2014 320 p. map (hardback) $27   **958.104**
1. Taliban 2. Afghan War, 2001- 3. Peace-building -- Afghanistan 4. Counterinsurgency -- Afghanistan 5. Internal security -- Afghanistan 6. United States -- Military policy 7. Afghan War, 2001 -- Personal narratives, Afghani
ISBN 0805091793; 9780805091793

LC 2014001384

Pulitzer Prize Finalist: General Nonfiction (2015)

In this book, "Anand Gopal traces in vivid detail the lives of three Afghans caught in America's war on terror. He follows a Taliban commander, who rises from scrawny teenager to leading insurgent; a US-backed warlord, who uses the American military to gain personal wealth and power; and a village housewife trapped between the two sides, who discovers the devastating cost of neutrality." (Publisher's note)

"Policymakers and informed readers will benefit immensely from this illuminating book." LJ

Grenier, Robert L.

88 days to Kandahar; a CIA diary. Robert L. Grenier. Simon & Schuster 2014 448 p. 16 plates; illustrations; maps (hardcover) $28   **958.104**
1. Taliban 2. Afghan War, 2001- 3. Intelligence service -- United States 4. United States. Central Intelligence Agency 5. Afghan War, 2001- -- Campaigns 6. Afghan War, 2001- -- Secret service 7. Pakistan -- Relations -- United States 8. United States -- Relations -- Pakistan 9. Afghan War, 2001- -- Personal narratives, American 10. Intelligence officers -- United States -- Biography 11. Afghanistan -- Politics and government -- 21st century 12. United States. Central Intelligence Agency -- Biography
ISBN 1476712077; 9781476712079; 9781476712086

LC 2014036555

This book focuses on the "First American-Afghan War, a CIA war, [that] was approved by President George W. Bush and directed by the author, Robert Grenier, the CIA station chief in Islamabad. Forging separate alliances with warlords, Taliban dissidents, and Pakistani Intelligence, Grenier launched the 'southern campaign,' orchestrating the final defeat of the Taliban and Hamid Karzai's rise to power in eighty-eight chaotic days." (Publisher's note)

"This eye-opening account of how things really "work" in the Middle East and in modern war will appeal to general readers and those interested in political science, war memoirs, contemporary battle accounts, American history, Middle Eastern politics, and books about spies/covert operations. Highly Recommended." LJ

Eighty eight days to Kandahar, a CIA diary

Maurer, Kevin

No easy day; the autobiography of a Navy SEAL : the firsthand account of the mission that killed Osama Bin Laden. Mark Owen; with Kevin Maurer. Dutton 2012 xiii, 316 p.p $26.95   **958.104**
1. Afghan War, 2001- -- Personal narratives 2. Special forces (Military science) -- United States 3. Qaida (Organization) 4. United States. Navy. SEALs -- Biography 5. United States. Navy -- Commando troops -- Biography
ISBN 0525953728; 9780525953722

LC 2012371921

This book, by Mark Owen with Kevin Mauer, offers a "first-person account of the planning and execution of the Bin Laden raid from a Navy Seal" who was present on the mission. The book follows "Owen and the other handpicked members of the twenty-four-man team as they train[ed] for the biggest mission of their lives." It provides a "narrative of the assault, beginning with the helicopter crash . . . straight through to the radio call confirming Bin Laden's death." (Publisher's note)

Includes bibliographical references.

Nordland, Rod

The **Lovers**; Afghanistan's Romeo and Juliet, the True Story of How They Defied Their Families and

Escaped an Honor Killing. HarperCollins 2016 384
p. chiefly col. ill., map $26.99   **958.104**
    1. Love 2. Honor 3. Islamic law 4. Women --
Afghanistan
    ISBN 0062378821; 9780062378828

    This book, by Rod Nordland, tells the "story of a young
couple. . . . Zakia and Ali were from different tribes, but they
grew up on neighboring farms in the hinterlands of Afghanistan. By the time they were young teenagers, [they] had
fallen in love. Defying their families, sectarian differences,
cultural conventions, and Afghan civil and Islamic law, they
ran away together only to live under constant threat from
Zakia's large and vengeful family, who have vowed to kill
her." (Publisher's note)

    "Nordland offers a stark, eye-opening look at the deplor-
able state of women's rights in Afghanistan through the travails of a brave, determined young couple." Booklist

    Includes bibliographical references and index.

Omar, Qais Akbar

    ★ A **fort** of nine towers; an Afghan family story.
by Qais Akbar Omar. 1st ed. Farrar, Straus and Giroux 2013 396 p. maps (hardcover) $27.00 **958.104**
    1. Family 2. Afghanistan -- Social conditions 3.
Afghanistan -- Biography 4. Afghanistan -- Social
conditions -- 20th century
    ISBN 0374157642; 9780374157647

LC 2012034566

    In this book, author Qais Akbar Omar presents a com-
ing-of-age memoir about his experiences in Afghanistan
during the Afghan Civil War. "With rockets falling around
them, Omar's family fled, leaving behind everything they
owned to take shelter in an old fort. As the violence escalated, Omar's father decided he must take his children out
of the country to safety. Omar recounts terrifyingly narrow
escapes and absurdist adventures, as well as moments of intense joy and beauty." (Publisher's note)

Partlow, Joshua

    A **kingdom** of their own; The Family Karzai
and the Afghan Disaster. Joshua Partlow. Alfred
A. Knopf 2016 432 p. illustrations (hardback)
$30   **958.104**
    1. Afghan War, 2001- 2. Afghanistan -- Politics and
government 3. United States -- Foreign relations
-- Afghanistan 4. Afghanistan -- Foreign relations --
United States
    ISBN 9780307962645

LC 2016007281

    This book by Joshua Partlow focuses on the failed rela-
tionship between the powerful Karzai family and the United
States. "The United States went to Afghanistan on a simple
mission: avenge the September 11 attacks and drive the
Taliban from power. . . . [In] the ensuing fight for power
and money, . . . President Hamid Karzai and his brothers
began the war as symbols of a new Afghanistan: . . . the antithesis of the brutish and backward Taliban regime." (Publisher's note)

    "American military and political arrogance butts up
against deep-rooted cultural customs and family networks

throughout this excellent account of a vastly difficult topic."
Pub Wkly

    Includes bibliographical references (pages [391]-402)
and index.

Slahi, Mohamedou Ould, 1970-

    Guantanamo diary; Mohamedou Ould Slahi;
edited by Larry Siems. Little, Brown & Co. 2015
400 p. $29   **958.104**
    1. Torture 2. Prisoners 3. Guantanamo Bay Detention
Camp 4. War on Terrorism, 2001-2009 -- Biography 5.
Prisoners of war -- United States -- Diaries 6. Political
prisoners -- United States -- Diaries 7. Guantánamo Bay
Detention Camp -- Biography 8. Mauritanians -- Cuba
-- Guantánamo Bay Naval Base -- Diaries 9. Political
prisoners -- Cuba -- Guantánamo Bay Naval Base --
Diaries
    ISBN 0316328685; 9780316328685

LC 2014023763

    This memoir, edited by Larry Siems, tells how "since
2002, [author] Mohamedou Slahi has been imprisoned at the
detention camp at Guantánamo Bay, Cuba. In all these years,
the United States has never charged him with a crime. . . .
Three years into his captivity Slahi began a diary. . . . His
diary is not merely a vivid record of a miscarriage of justice,
but a deeply personal memoir--terrifying, darkly humorous,
and surprisingly gracious." (Publisher's note)

    "Slahi may or may not be a reliable narrator; readers are
called on to suspend disbelief. By his account, of course,
he is not guilty. His memoir is essential reading for anyone
concerned with human rights and the rule of law."

Smith, Graeme

    The **Dogs** Are Eating Them Now; Our War in
Afghanistan. by Graeme Smith. Knopf Canada 2013
320 p. illustrations, maps $26   **958.104**
    1. Journalists 2. Afghan War, 2001-
    ISBN 0307397807; 1619024799; 9780307397805;
9781619024793

LC 2014034083

    This book, by foreign correspondent Graeme Smith, "is
a highly personal narrative of our war in Afghanistan. . . .
Smith was not simply embedded with the military: he operated independently and at great personal risk to report from
inside the war, and the heroes of his story are the translators,
guides, and ordinary citizens who helped him find the truth.
They revealed sad, absurd, touching stories that provide the
key to understanding why the mission failed to deliver peace
and democracy." (Publisher's note)

    "Recommended for readers of battlefield accounts and
those seeking a better understanding of the Afghani people.
For another excellent journalistic account, see Edward Gira-
det's Killing the Cranes." LJ

959   Southeast Asia

Somers Heidhues, Mary F.

Southeast Asia: a concise history. Thames & Hudson 2000 192p il maps hardcover o.p. pa $18.95   **959**

1. Southeast Asia -- History
ISBN 0-500-28303-6 pa

LC 99-66014

This "history ranges from Southeast Asia's prehistoric times to the most recent political developments in Indonesia. Heidhues . . . divides her study into seven well-balanced chapters, touching on the political history, economics, society, and culture of Burma, Thailand, Cambodia, Vietnam, Malaysia, Singapore, Brunei, Indonesia, and the Philippines." Libr J

959.1   Myanmar

Aung San Suu Kyi

Freedom from fear, and other writings; edited with an introduction by Michael Aris; foreword to the first edition by Vaclav Havel, foreword to the second edition by Archbishop Desmond Tutu. rev ed; Penguin Bks. 1995 xxxi, 374p il pa $14.95   **959.1**

1. Myanmar -- Politics and government
ISBN 0-14-025317-3

LC 96-902734

First published 1991

This is a collection of essays, letters, speeches, and other writings by the Burmese opposition leader, Winner of the 1991 Nobel Peace Prize

"Mrs. Aung San Suu Kyi's excellent book offers inspiration to many other peoples in the region as much as it reflects Myanmar's own desire for change." N Y Times Book Rev {review of 1991 edition}

Includes bibliographical references

Larkin, Emma

Everything is broken; a tale of catastrophe in Burma. Penguin Press 2010 271p map $25.95 **959.1**

1. Cyclones 2. Disaster relief 3. Myanmar
ISBN 978-1-59420-257-5; 1-59420-257-5

LC 2010-04029

"Larkin is such a facile observer and writer, she tempts comparisons to Orwell, and certainly ranks with Ryszard Kapuscinski as a lyric writer of reportage." Cleveland Plain Dealer

Thant Myint-U

The river of lost footsteps; histories of Burma. Farrar, Straus & Giroux 2006 361p il map $25; pa $15   **959.1**

1. Myanmar
ISBN 978-0-374-16342-6; 0-374-16342-1; 978-0-374-53116-4 pa; 0-374-53116-1 pa

LC 2006-09199

"This readable, reflective history will support revived interest in Burma." Booklist

Includes bibliographical references

Where China meets India; Burma and the new crossroads of Asia. Farrar, Straus and Giroux 2011 361p map $27   **959.1**

1. Myanmar -- Description and travel 2. China -- Foreign relations -- Myanmar 3. India -- Foreign relations -- Myanmar 4. Myanmar -- Foreign relations -- China 5. Myanmar -- Foreign relations -- India
ISBN 978-0-374-29907-1; 0-374-29907-2

LC 2011024406

In the book, "Thant Myint-U advances the . . . argument for changing Western policy [regarding Burma]: isolation is useless because Burma is . . . becoming a bridge between two rising global giants. Writing of his travels through the borderlands of China, India and Burma, Thant Myint-U hopes to demonstrate how this region of Asia, home to more than 600 million people, is integrating, and how Burma will be at the center of it." (Nation)

Focusing "on his home country of Burma, and the area encompassed by a diameter of 1,000 miles drawn from the city of Mandalay on the edge of the Shan Plateau, Thant suggests that this corner of the world (with a population of 600 million) is destined to become a bridge between Bengal, Bangladesh, India's North Eastern Provinces, and China's Yunnan province." Publ Wkly

Includes bibliographical references

959.3   Thailand

Krauss, Erich

Wave of destruction; the stories of four families and history's deadliest tsunami. Rodale 2006 244p il map $24.95   **959.3**

1. Tsunamis 2. Survival after airplane accidents, shipwrecks, etc. 3. Thailand
ISBN 1-59486-378-4

LC 2005-24531

The author provides an "account of four families in a Thai village devastated by the tsunami of December 26, 2004. . . . Passionately told, this tragic story portrays the full human cost of natural devastation." Publ Wkly

Wyatt, David K.

★ Thailand: a short history; 2nd ed; Yale Univ. Press 2003 352p il maps pa $20   **959.3**

1. Thailand -- History
ISBN 0-3000-8475-7

First published 1984

This volume provides a general history of Thailand beginning with the migrations of the Tai peoples from southern China, examining the social and economic changes to the present

Includes bibliographical references

959.6 Cambodia

Brinkley, Joel, 1952-2014

Cambodia's curse; the modern history of a troubled land. PublicAffairs 2011 386p il $27.99 **959.6**

1. Heads of state 2. Communist leaders 3. Political leaders 4. Democracy -- Cambodia 5. Cambodia -- History -- 1979- 6. Cambodia -- Social conditions 7. Cambodia -- Politics and government 8. Cambodia -- Politics and government -- 1979-

ISBN 978-1-58648-787-4; 1-58648-787-6

LC 2010-44806

"Brinkley cuts a clear narrative path through the bewildering, cynical politics and violent social life of one of the worlds most brutalized and hard-up countries." Foreign Affairs

Includes bibliographical references

Kiernan, Ben

The **Pol** Pot regime; race, power, and genocide in Cambodia under the Khmer Rouge, 1975-79. 2nd ed; Yale Univ. Press 2002 xxiii, 477p il map (Yale Nota bene) pa $19.95 **959.6**

1. Atrocities 2. Communism -- Cambodia 3. Cambodia -- Politics and government

ISBN 0-300-09649-6

LC 2002-100979

First published 1996

This is an account of "the Cambodian catastrophe; the significant internal resistance to the Khmer Rouge; and the racialist and totalitarian attitudes by which Pol Pot's regime justified the death, by starvation and disease as well as torture and murder, of some 1.5 million of their 8 million countrymen." Booklist {review of 1996 edition}

Includes bibliographical references

Ung, Loung

First they killed my father; a daughter of Cambodia remembers. HarperCollins Pubs. 2000 240p il hardcover o.p. pa $13.95 **959.6**

1. Cambodia -- History -- 1975-

ISBN 0-06-019332-8; 0-06-085626-2 pa

LC 99-34707

The author's father was a "high-ranking government official in Phnom Penh. She was only five when the Khmer Rouge stormed the city and her family was forced to flee. They sought refuge in various camps, hiding their wealth and education, always on the move and ever fearful of being betrayed. After 20 months, Ung's father was taken away, never to be seen again. Her story of starvation, forced labor, beatings, attempted rape, separations, and the deaths of her family members is one of horror and brutality." SLJ

959.604 Cambodia -- 1949-

Bizot, Francois

The **gate**; translated from the French by Euan Cameron; with a preface by John Le Carré. Knopf 2003 275p $24; pa $14 **959.604**

1. Atrocities 2. Communism -- Cambodia 3. Cambodia

-- History -- 1970-1975, Civil War

ISBN 0-375-41293-X; 0-375-72723-X pa

LC 2002-69428

Original French edition, 2000

Bizot's "tale of his experiences, both in the camp and as translator at the gate of the French embassy, leaves readers with haunting images of the doomed." Booklist

Him, Chanrithy, 1965-

When broken glass floats; growing up under the Khmer Rouge. Norton 2000 330p il map hardcover o.p. pa $13.95 **959.604**

1. Refugees 2. Memoirists 3. Interpreters 4. Cambodia -- History 5. Political refugees -- Cambodia 6. Political atrocities -- Cambodia 7. Political refugees -- United States 8. Cambodia -- Politics and government -- 1975-1979

ISBN 0-393-32210-6 pa

LC 99-58417

This is an account of the author's experiences as a child in Cambodia under the Khmer Rouge. Him "watched {her} father hauled away to be killed, saw {her} mother and several siblings die by execution, starvation and disease. After the Khmer Rouge's downfall, {she} eventually escaped to Thailand and then to the United States." (N Y Times Book Rev)

Him "was 10 in 1975 when the Khmer Rouge overtook her country in what she calls the time of broken glass. Feeling a survivor's responsibility to do so, Him vividly recalls the brutality of the camps, the strict social control, and alienation from family that the Khmer Rouge enforced." Booklist

959.7 Vietnam

Blehm, Eric

Legend; A Harrowing Story from the Vietnam War of One Green Beret's Heroic Mission to Rescue a Special Forces Team Caught Behind Enemy Lines. Eric Blehm. Random House Inc. 2015 288 p. 16 plates; ills.; maps; ports. $27 **959.7**

1. Rescue work 2. Vietnam War, 1961-1975 3. Special forces (Military science) -- United States

ISBN 0804139512; 9780804139519

LC 2015451022

In this book, Eric Blehm looks at the Vietnam War through "a single mission that occurred on May 2, 1968. A twelve-man Special Forces team had been covertly inserted into a small clearing in the jungles of neutral Cambodia. Soon they found themselves surrounded by hundreds of NVA, under attack. When Special Forces Staff Sergeant Roy Benavidez heard the distress call, he jumped aboard the next helicopter bound for the combat zone." (Publisher's note)

"Overall, the narrative seems a good magazine article pulled into book length, with some slipshod moments (e.g., one doesn't get a master's degree in Shakespeare) and too many draggy stretches. In the hands of a Junger or Krakauer, this story might have taken more memorable form . Still, Vietnam War completists will be interested." Kirkus

Goscha, Christopher

Vietnam; Christopher Goscha. Basic Books 2016 592 p. illustrations, maps $35   **959.7**
1. Vietnam -- History 2. Vietnam -- Colonization
ISBN 9780465094363

LC 2016017630

In this book, author Christopher Goscha "tells the full history of Vietnam, from antiquity to the present day. Generations of emperors, rebels, priests, and colonizers left complicated legacies in this remarkable country. Periods of Chinese, French, and Japanese rule reshaped and modernized Vietnam, but so too did the colonial enterprises of the Vietnamese themselves as they extended their influence southward from the Red River Delta." (Publisher's note)

"A vigorous, eye-opening account of a country of great importance to the world, past and future." Kirkus

Includes bibliographical references and index

959.704   Vietnam--1945-

Anderson, David L.

★ The **Columbia** guide to the Vietnam War. Columbia Univ. Press 2002 308p maps (Columbia guides to American history and cultures) $47; pa $22.50   **959.704**
1. Vietnam War, 1961-1975
ISBN 0-231-11492-3; 0-231-11493-1 pa

LC 2002-20143

"Anderson's guide successfully compresses the copiously documented, labyrinthine history of the Vietnamese conflict into a single economical volume. In five parts, the guide's narrative and encyclopedia sections provide a fascinating survey of the war, while the remaining elements of the work link modern researchers to a host of richly documented resources. . . . The guide will become an important resource for those seeking a historical overview as well as direction for further research. Strongly recommended." Choice

Includes bibliographical references

Appy, Christian G.

American Reckoning; The Vietnam War and Our National Identity. Christian G. Appy. Penguin Group USA 2015 416 p. $28.95   **959.704**
1. Vietnam War, 1961-1975 2. National characteristics
3. United States -- Politics and government
ISBN 0670025399; 9780670025398

LC 2014038477

In this book on the Vietnam War, Christian G. Appy argues "that the way the war was fought and its outcome put an indelible dent in the idea of American exceptionalism. The war, he argues, 'shattered the central tenet of American national identity--the broad faith that the United States is a unique force for good in the world.'" (Publishers Weekly)

"Appy paints with a broad brush and may interpret our national security needs too narrowly. Still, his assertion that our current policies could guarantee constant warfare deserves to be seriously considered." Booklist

Caputo, Philip

★ A **rumor** of war; with a twentieth anniversary postscript by the author. Henry Holt and Co. 1996 xxi, 356p pa $15   **959.704**
1. Vietnam War, 1961-1975 -- Personal narratives
ISBN 0-8050-4695-X

LC 96-19314

First published 1977 by Holt, Rinehart & Winston

These are "the combat recollections of a very young Marine officer in Vietnam in 1965-1966. Caputo later became a newspaperman. . . . He remembers himself as a patriotic youngster, eager to prove his manhood, and then . . . he takes us through his step-by-step discovery that war and manhood and their interrelation are more complicated than he had dreamed." New Yorker

Duiker, William J.

Ho Chi Minh; by William Duiker. Hyperion 2000 695p il maps $35; pa $16.95   **959.704**
1. Heads of state 2. Communist leaders 3. Political leaders
ISBN 0-7868-6387-0; 0-7868-8701-X pa

LC 00-26757

In this biography the author "examines Ho's life primarily in the context of his political activity in Paris, Moscow, southern China, and Vietnam, occasionally spiced with anecdotes of Ho's highly secretive personal life. . . . Duiker handles the complicated political and diplomatic issues with ease, and his narrative, though it sometimes strays from Ho's life to fill in the bigger picture, never bogs down." Booklist

Includes bibliographical references

Ellsberg, Daniel

Secrets: a memoir of Vietnam and the Pentagon papers. Viking 2002 498p il $29.95; pa $16   **959.704**
1. Vietnam War, 1961-1975 2. Pentagon Papers
ISBN 0-670-03030-9; 0-14-200342-5 pa

LC 2002-16874

Ellsberg recalls how he leaked "the Pentagon Papers, which documented U.S. foreign-policy failures and deceit in Vietnam from 1945 to 1968. . . . Ellsberg's autobiographical account provides insight into the disturbing abuses of presidential power that plagued the Vietnam/Watergate era." Libr J

Includes bibliographical references

FitzGerald, Frances

Fire in the lake; the Vietnamese and the Americans in Vietnam. Little, Brown 1972 491p maps hardcover o.p. pa $16.95   **959.704**
1. Vietnam War, 1961-1975 2. Vietnam -- Politics and government
ISBN 0-316-15919-0 pa

This book looks at the effects American intervention had on the Vietnamese social and intellectual landscape.

Includes bibliographical references

Glasser, Ronald J.

365 days. Braziller 1971 292p hardcover o.p. pa $14.95 **959.704**

1. Vietnam War, 1961-1975 -- Medical care 2. Vietnam War, 1961-1975 -- Personal narratives

ISBN 0-8076-1527-7 pa

The author, a military doctor who was stationed in Japan, recounts his experiences treating wounded American military personnel during the Vietnam War

Goldstein, Donald M.

The **Vietnam** War: the story and photographs; by Donald M. Goldstein, Katherine V. Dillon, and J. Michael Wenger. Brassey's 1997 179p il maps hardcover o.p. pa $19.95 **959.704**

1. Vietnam War, 1961-1975

ISBN 1-57488-210-4 pa

LC 97-11574

This history of the Vietnam War "proceeds both chronologically and thematically, beginning with the French colonial era and the Indochina War, then covering successive stages of the U.S. involvement. The text is sufficiently detailed, clear, and balanced to serve as a narrative introduction to the subject, but the real strength lies in the photographs. They cover the subject with admirable thoroughness. . . . They do not include too many chestnuts, and they adequately cover the Vietnamese, the navy, and other subjects relatively neglected in the literature thus far." Booklist

Includes bibliographical references

Hampton, Dan

The **hunter** killers; the extraordinary story of the first Wild Weasels, the band of maverick aviators who flew the most dangerous missions of the Vietnam War. Dan Hampton. William Morrow 2015 416 p. 16 plates; illustrations; maps (hardcover) $27.99 **959.704**

1. Air pilots 2. Electronic warfare 3. Vietnam War, 1961-1975 -- Aerial operations 4. Vietnam War, 1961-1975 -- Campaigns 5. Vietnam War, 1961-1975 -- Political aspects 6. Vietnam War, 1961-1975 -- Aerial operations, American 7. Electronic warfare aircraft -- United States -- History -- 20th century

ISBN 006237513X; 9780062375124; 9780062375131; 9780062392947

LC 2015007013

This book, by Dan Hampton, tells the story of how, "at the height of the Cold War, America's most elite aviators bravely volunteered for a covert program aimed at eliminating an impossible new threat. . . . Vietnam, 1965: . . . a USAF F-4 Phantom jet was suddenly blown from the sky by a mysterious and lethal weapon--a Soviet SA-2 surface-to-air missile (SAM). . . . the Pentagon ordered a top secret program called Wild Weasel I to counter the SAM problem." (Publisher's note)

"Hampton uses a lot of military terminology, some of which might be difficult for the lay reader to understand, but his overall writing style is excellent; in particular, his vivid, fast-paced combat narratives. His latest work will appeal to military history fans or anyone looking for an absorbing read." LJ

Includes bibliographical references and index

Extraordinary story of the first Wild Weasels, the band of maverick aviators who flew the most dangerous missions of the Vietnam War

Hendrickson, Paul

The **living** and the dead; Robert McNamara and five lives of a lost war. Knopf 1996 427p il hardcover o.p. pa $15 **959.704**

1. Vietnam War, 1961-1975 2. Bankers 3. Secretaries of defense 4. International organization officials

ISBN 0-679-7811-X pa

LC 96-7445

"Exhaustively researched, probing, important contribution to the annals of American history." Publ Wkly

Includes bibliographical references

Inside the Pentagon papers; edited by John Prados and Margaret Pratt Porter. University Press of Kansas 2004 248p (Modern war studies) $29.95 **959.704**

1. Vietnam War, 1961-1975 2. Pentagon Papers

ISBN 0-7006-1325-0

LC 2004-1961

The editors "reexamine the secret government papers that blew the whistle on the Vietnam War, led to the federal attempts to restrain the press and ultimately resulted in President Richard Nixon's resignation. . . . Volumes about these issues abound, but Prados and Porter offer a concise look at those pivotal events and their long-term effects." Publ Wkly

Includes bibliographical references

Kaiser, David E.

American tragedy; Kennedy, Johnson, and the origins of the Vietnam War. {by} David Kaiser. Harvard Univ. Press 2000 566p il $36; pa $18.95 **959.704**

1. Presidents 2. Vice-presidents 3. Vietnam War, 1961-1975 4. Senators 5. Members of Congress 6. United States -- Politics and government -- 1961-1974

ISBN 0-674-00225-3; 0-674-00672-0 pa

LC 99-52925

"The first-rate research is complemented by an intriguing model of intergenerational policy-making." Libr J

Includes bibliographical references and index

Karnow, Stanley

Vietnam; a history. 2nd rev & updated ed; Penguin Bks. 1997 768p il maps pa $17.95 **959.704**

1. Vietnam War, 1961-1975 2. Vietnam -- History

ISBN 0-14-026547-3

First published 1983

A summation "of over two centuries of conflict in Indochina. Chronicling a tragic history, Karnow presents a balanced and sympathetic view of Vietnamese aspirations and the mishaps that led to American involvement in a 'war nobody won.'" Voice Youth Advocates [review of 1983 edition]

Includes bibliographical references

Kissinger, Henry

Ending the Vietnam War; a history of America's involvement in and extrication from the Vietnam War. Touchstone 2002 640p map pa $18   **959.704**

1. Vietnam War, 1961-1975

ISBN 0-7432-1532-X

LC 2002-17996

"Readers interested in the Vietnam period but unfamiliar with Kissinger's previous books will find this new volume worthwhile. . . . Kissinger's account of America's venture in Vietnam and his role in that shipwreck is factually accurate, eminently informed and masterfully crafted." Publ Wkly

Includes bibliographical references

Langguth, A. J.

Our Vietnam; the war, 1954-1975. Simon & Schuster 2000 766p il maps hardcover o.p. pa $20   **959.704**

1. Vietnam War, 1961-1975 2. Vietnam -- Politics and government

ISBN 0-7432-1231-2 pa

LC 00-57384

This book "is unique in its perspective of the major players on both sides." Booklist

Includes bibliographical references

Lind, Michael

Vietnam, the necessary war; a reinterpretation of America's most disastrous military conflict. Free Press 1999 314p $25; pa $14   **959.704**

1. Vietnam War, 1961-1975 2. United States -- Foreign relations

ISBN 0-684-84254-8; 0-684-87027-4 pa

LC 99-28449

"Lind's arguments, if not always persuasive, are always provocative." Publ Wkly

Includes bibliographical references and index

Logevall, Fredrik, 1963-

★ Embers of War; The Fall of an Empire and the Making of America's Vietnam. Fredrik Logevall. Random House 2012 xxii, 839 p.p ill.   **959.704**

1. France -- Colonies 2. Vietnam War, 1961-1975 3. Indochinese War, 1946-1954 4. United States -- Foreign relations -- Vietnam 5. United States -- Politics and government -- 1961-1974

ISBN 0375504427; 9780375504426

LC 2011034971

Pulitzer Prize: History (2013)

This book examines "the [Vietnam] war's roots in the U.S. reaction to the French colonial experience." Discussing "the global changes wrought by WWII, the beginning of the cold war, and America's new role as the pre-eminent power in Asian and world affairs . . . [Fredrik] Logevall makes" the "case that America's Vietnam involvement replicated the French experience: the U.S. was fighting against an anticolonialist revolution and giving the Democratic Republic of Vietnam legitimacy." (Publishers Weekly)

Includes bibliographical references and index.

Mann, Robert

A grand delusion; America's descent into Vietnam. Basic Bks. 2000 821p il $35; pa $22 **959.704**

1. Vietnam War, 1961-1975 2. Vietnam -- Politics and government 3. United States -- Politics and government -- 20th century

ISBN 0-465-04369-0; 0-465-04370-4 pa

LC 00-49824

This account of the United States involvement in the Vietnam War focuses on the political causes and "collision of personalities throughout the White House, Congress, and elsewhere during that era. Mann's history concentrates on seven American leaders in the halls of power rather than on the battlefield." Libr J

Includes bibliographical references and index

Maraniss, David

They marched into sunlight; war and peace in Vietnam and America, October, 1967. Simon & Schuster 2003 592p il map hardcover o.p. pa $16   **959.704**

1. Vietnam War, 1961-1975

ISBN 0-7432-1780-2; 0-7432-6104-6 pa

LC 2003-52885

This is a "narrative by a reporter who juxtaposes a ghastly little battle in Vietnam with an antiwar and anti-Dow demonstration at the University of Wisconsin, Madison, on the same day; it captures moral ambiguity everywhere, without stereotyping or condescension." N Y Times Book Rev

Includes bibliographical references

McNamara, Robert S.

In retrospect; the tragedy and lessons of Vietnam. Vintage Bks. 1996 518p il map pa $16.95 **959.704**

1. Vietnam War, 1961-1975

ISBN 0-679-76749-5; 978-0-679-76749-7

First published 1995 by Times Books

"Former defense secretary McNamara seeks 'to put Vietnam in context' and counter 'the cynicism and even contempt with which so many people view our political institutions and leaders.' . . . He identifies 'eleven major causes for our disaster in Vietnam' and six points when the U.S. could legitimately have withdrawn. Certainly not the last word on this still-controversial subject but an essential acquisition for most libraries." Booklist

Includes bibliographical references

Miller, Edward

Misalliance; Ngo Dinh Diem, the United States, and the fate of South Vietnam. Edward Miller. Harvard University Press 2013 419 p. (hardcover : alk. paper) $39.95   **959.704**

1. Vietnam -- Foreign relations -- United States 2. Vietnam (Republic) -- Politics and government 3. United States -- Foreign relations -- Vietnam (Republic) 4. Vietnam (Republic) -- Foreign relations -- United States

ISBN 0674072987; 9780674072985

LC 2012035332

This book is a "reassessment of former South Vietnamese leader Ngo Dinh Diem and his relationship with the US. . . . Miller takes a . . . transnational approach by utilizing

Vietnamese and foreign language sources and presenting an analysis that is much more Vietnamese centered. . . . The author argues that it was, in fact, the politics of nation building that shaped the evolution and ultimate collapse of the US alliance with Diem." (Choice)

Includes bibliographical references and index

Moore, Harold G.

We are soldiers still; a journey back to the battlefields of Vietnam. [by] Harold G. Moore and Joseph L. Galloway. Harper 2008 248p il $24.95; pa $14.99 **959.704**

1. Vietnam -- Description and travel 2. Vietnam War, 1961-1975 -- Personal narratives

ISBN 978-0-06-114776-0; 0-06-114776-1; 978-0-06-114777-7 pa; 0-06-114777-X pa

LC 2008-11034

Sequel to We were soldiers once and young (1992)

"A worthy and wise successor to one of the best books ever about combat in Vietnam." Kirkus

We were soldiers once--and young; Ia Drang: the battle that changed the war in Vietnam. [by] Harold G. Moore and Joseph L. Galloway. Random House 1992 412p il maps $26.95; pa $7.50 **959.704**

1. Vietnam War, 1961-1975 -- Personal narratives

ISBN 0-679-41158-5; 0-345-47264-0 pa

LC 92-53642

"On Nov. 14, 1965, the 1st Battalion of the 7th Cavalry, commanded by Col. Moore and accompanied by UPI reporter Galloway, helicoptered into Vietnam's remote Ia Drang Valley and found itself surrounded by a numerically superior force of North Vietnamese regulars. Moore and Galloway here offer a detailed account, based on interviews with participants and on their own recollections, of what happened during the four-day battle." Publ Wkly

Includes bibliographical references

Followed by We are soldiers still (2008)

Morgan, Ted

Valley of death; the tragedy at Dien Bien Phu that led America into the Vietnam War. Random House 2010 722p il map $35 **959.704**

1. Indochinese War, 1946-1954 2. Dien Bien Phu, Battle of, 1954 3. United States -- Foreign relations -- Vietnam 4. Vietnam -- Foreign relations -- United States

ISBN 978-1-4000-6664-3

LC 2009-19714

"This absorbing account of the prelude, battle, and aftermath that ended the 'first Viet Nam War' is a sad tale of misconception, missed opportunities, and massive blunders by French and even American military and civilian officials. . . . This is a superb chronicle of a sad and avoidable conflict that led to an even more destructive one." Booklist

Includes bibliographical references

Napoli, Philip F.

Bringing it all back home; oral histories of New York's Vietnam veterans. by Philip F. Napoli. 1st

ed. Hill and Wang 2012 254 p., [8] p. of platesp ill. (hardcover) $27 **959.704**

1. Oral history 2. Vietnam War, 1961-1975 -- Veterans 3. New York (N.Y.) -- Biography 4. Vietnam War, 1961-1975 -- New York (State) -- New York 5. Vietnam War, 1961-1975 -- Personal narratives, American 6. Vietnam War, 1961-1975 -- Veterans -- New York (State) -- New York -- Interviews

ISBN 0809073188; 9780809073184

LC 2012034731

For this book, Philip F. Napoli "spent six years conducting extensive interviews with more than 200 Vietnam vets who either grew up in New York City or who currently live there. The result of those 600 hours of recordings is a readable chronicle that uses the personal histories of the soldiers (in the interviewees' transcribed words) to tell the human story of the American war in Vietnam." (Publishers Weekly)

Includes bibliographical references.

Nguyen, Viet Thanh, 1971-

Nothing ever dies; Vietnam and the memory of war. Viet Thanh Nguyen. Harvard University Press 2016 356 p. illustrations $27.95 **959.704**

1. Vietnam War, 1961-1975 2. Art and war 3. War and society 4. Identity (Psychology) in art 5. Memory -- Sociological aspects 6. Vietnam War, 1961-1975 -- Social aspects 7. Vietnam War, 1961-1975 -- Art and the war

ISBN 9780674660342

LC 2015037444

National Book Award Finalist: Nonfiction (2016)

This book, by Viet Thanh Nguyen, "brings a comprehensive vision of the [Vietnam] war into sharp focus. At stake are ethical questions about how the war should be remembered by participants that include not only Americans and Vietnamese but also Laotians, Cambodians, South Koreans, and Southeast Asian Americans." (Publisher's note)

"Essentially a critical study, Nguyen's work is a powerful reflection on how we choose to remember and forget." Kirkus

Includes bibliographical references and index

Sallah, Michael

Tiger Force; a true story of men and war. [by] Michael Sallah and Mitch Weiss. Little, Brown 2006 403p il map $25.95 **959.704**

1. Vietnam War, 1961-1975 2. United States -- Army -- Infantry Regiment, 327th -- Battalion, 1st

ISBN 0-316-15997-2; 978-0-316-15997-5

LC 2005-20921

"In 1967, the Tiger Force platoon of the 101st Airborne went on a seven-month-long rampage through South Vietnam's central highlands that left dead more than 325 civilians, mostly children, women, and old men. . . . [This] is a searing narrative, difficult to read yet difficult to put down, about Tiger Force's descent into a leaderless and ruthless unit, in which, as one of the ex-soldiers puts it to the authors, the objective was to 'kill anything that moves.'" Libr J

Includes bibliographical references

Sheehan, Neil

A **bright** shining lie: John Paul Vann and America in Vietnam. Random House 1988 861p il hardcover o.p. pa $18   **959.704**

1. Vietnam War, 1961-1975 2. Army officers
ISBN 0-679-72414-1 pa

LC 87-43330

The author "tells the story of the war through the focus of John Paul Vann, an army officer who faced down South Vietnamese politicians and American generals to expose the corruption that undermined our efforts and later was President Nixon's civilian adviser in Vietnam until he was killed in a helicopter crash in 1972. It is a dramatic device that lets Mr. Sheehan bring the very palpable feel of the war to us with passionate power." N Y Times Book Rev

Includes bibliographical references

Shultz, Richard H.

The **secret** war against Hanoi; Kennedy and Johnson's use of spies, saboteurs, and covert warriors in North Vietnam. {by} Richard H. Shultz, Jr. HarperCollins Pubs. 1999 408p il hardcover o.p. pa $15   **959.704**

1. Subversive activities 2. Vietnam War, 1961-1975 -- Secret service 3. United States -- Politics and government -- 1961-1974 4. United States -- Military Assistance Command, Vietnam -- Studies and Observations Group
ISBN 0-06-093253-8 pa

LC 99-44524

"Organized in a military entity euphemistically named the Studies and Observation Group (SOG), the covert war, it was hoped, would annoy Hanoi enough to force it to scale back its war in the south. . . . Schultz was given access to SOG archives and veterans and has produced a professional volume on how SOG originated and operated over its eight-year existence." Booklist

Includes bibliographical references

Tucker, Spencer C.

The **encyclopedia** of the Vietnam War; a political, social, and military history. Spencer C. Tucker, editor. 2nd ed.; ABC-CLIO 2011 4v il map set $395   **959.704**

1. Reference books 2. Vietnam War, 1961-1975 -- Encyclopedias
ISBN 978-1-85109-960-3; 978-1-85109-961-0 ebook

LC 2011007604

First published 1998

"Written to provide multidimensional perspectives into the conflict, . . . [this encyclopedia] covers not only the American experience in Vietnam, but also the entire scope of Vietnamese history, including the French experience and the Indochina War, as well as the origins of the conflict, how the United States became involved, and the extensive aftermath of this prolonged war." Publisher's note

Includes bibliographical references

Ulander, Perry A.

Walking point; from the ashes of the Vietnam War. Perry A. Ulander. North Atlantic Books 2016 252 p. (trade pbk.) $18.95   **959.704**

1. United States. Army 2. Vietnam War, 1961-1975 3. Soldiers -- United States 4. Soldiers -- Drug use -- Vietnam 5. Soldiers -- United States -- Biography 6. Vietnam War, 1961-1975 -- Vietnam -- Central Highlands 7. Vietnam War, 1961-1975 -- Personal narratives, American 8. United States. Army. Airborne Brigade, 173rd. Bravo Company 9. United States. Army -- Military life -- History -- 20th century
ISBN 9781623170127

LC 2015022372

In this memoir, author "Perry A. Ulander chronicles . . . the bewildering predicament he confronted and the fellowship and guidance that transformed him during the year he served as an American GI in the jungles of Vietnam. Conveying . . . . the harrowing experiences that shatter his core beliefs, Ulander also captures the camaraderie and humor of his platoon." (Publisher's note)

"Ulander's fine memoir should take a place among the best works in the Vietnam War autobiographical canon." Pub Wkly

The **Vietnam** War; editor, Mark Lawrence; introduction by David K. Shipler. Fitzroy Dearborn Pubs. 2001 2v il maps (New York Times 20th century in review) set $150   **959.704**

1. Vietnam War, 1961-1975
ISBN 1-57958-368-7

LC 2002-726953

"A must-have for all libraries." Recomm Ref Books for Small & Medium-sized Libr & Media Cent, 2003

Wolf, Marvin J.

Abandoned in hell; the fight for Vietnam's Fire Base Kate. Captain William Albracht (Ret.) and Captain Marvin J. Wolf (Ret.) NAL Caliber 2015 384 p. 16 plates; illustrations (hardback) $27.95   **959.704**

1. Vietnam War, 1961-1975 -- Personal narratives 2. Courage -- Case studies 3. Fire Base Kate (Vietnam) 4. Command of troops -- Case studies 5. Heroes -- United States -- Biography 6. Soldiers -- United States -- Biography 7. Vietnam War, 1961-1975 -- Personal narratives, American 8. United States. Army. Special Forces -- Officers -- Biography 9. Escapes -- Vietnam -- Central Highlands -- History -- 20th century
ISBN 0451468082; 9780451468086

LC 2014028501

This memoir, by William Albracht and Marvin J. Wolf, describes how "in October 1969, ... the youngest Green Beret captain in Vietnam took command of a remote hilltop outpost called Fire Base Kate, held by only 27 American soldiers and 150 Montagnard militiamen. He found their defenses woefully unprepared. At dawn the next morning, three North Vietnamese Army regiments . . . crossed the Cambodian border and attacked." (Publisher's note)

"This fast-paced narrative encapsulates Vietnam War themes, significantly the bravery of grunts and company grade officers and their loyalty to one another, and also bureaucratic mistakes with tragic consequences made by inexperienced officers and government officials too far removed from front-line action. Ultimately, Firebase Kate, as Albracht says, was built in a vulnerable location and its men were "written off" when they could no longer defend it. Readers of such excellent battlefield works as Harold Moore and Joseph Galloway's We Were Soldiers Once And Young will delve into this one." LJ

959.8 Indonesia and East Timor

Taylor, Jean Gelman
★ **Indonesia**: peoples and histories. Yale University Press 2003 420p il maps hardcover o.p. pa $24 **959.8**
1. Indonesia
ISBN 0-300-09709-3; 0-300-10518-5 pa
LC 2002-152348

This is "an account of Indonesia from the earliest migrations and settlements in the archipelago to the collapse of yet another government just a few years ago. While basically historical in design, this is no ordinary history. The book is one great historical essay . . . that allows the historian's search for the past to wander into social, religious, artistic, and anthropological byways." Choice
Includes bibliographical references

959.9 Philippines

Jones, Gregg
Honor in the dust; Theodore Roosevelt, war in the Philippines, and the rise and fall of America's imperial dream. Gregg Jones. New American Library 2012 xvi, 430 p.p (hbk.) $26.95 **959.9**
1. Philippenes -- History -- Philippine American War, 1899-1902 2. Philippines -- Annexation to the United States 3. Philippines -- History -- Philippine American War, 1899-1902 -- Atrocities 4. Philippines -- History -- Philippine American War, 1899-1902 -- Campaigns -- Philippines -- Samar 5. Philippines -- History -- Philippine American War, 1899-1902 -- Political aspects -- United States
ISBN 0451229045; 9780451229045
LC 2011033386

This book by Gregg Jones is the story of how "an up-and-coming Theodore Roosevelt set out to transform the U.S. into a major world power. The Spanish-American War would forever change America's standing in global affairs, and drive the young nation into its own imperial showdown in the Philippines. . . . [Jones] captures an era brimming with American optimism and confidence as the nation expanded its influence abroad." (Publisher's note)
Includes bibliographical references (p. 382-420) and index

Karnow, Stanley, 1925-2013
In our image; America's empire in the Philippines. Random House 1989 494p il maps hardcover o.p. pa $27 **959.9**
1. Philippines -- History 2. Philippines -- Foreign relations -- United States 3. United States -- Foreign relations -- Philippines
ISBN 0-345-32816-7 pa
LC 88-42676

This is an account of Philippine history from Magellan to Corazon Aquino. It focuses on the role of the United States in Philippine affairs from the annexation of the country following the Spanish-American war to the present. Chronology. Annotated chapter bibliographies. Index.
The author's "treatment of the indecisiveness of President McKinley over the issue of empire and of the egotistical General MacArthur make the work a definite purchase for libraries. . . . Those who love swashbuckling history will enjoy this work." Libr J
Includes bibliographical references

960 History of Africa

Lefkowitz, Mary R.
Not out of Africa; how Afrocentrism became an excuse to teach myth as history. [by] Mary Lefkowitz. Basic Bks. 1996 222p il map hardcover o.p. pa $19 **960**
1. Africa -- Historiography 2. History -- Study and teaching
ISBN 0-465-09837-1; 0-465-09838-X pa
LC 95-49109

"The book is a case study in historical methods, the value and limits of scholarship, and the preciousness of hard-bitten reason and objectivity. The book is also lucid and accessible." Christ Sci Monit
Includes bibliographical references

Meredith, Martin
Born in Africa; by Martin Meredith. 1st ed.; PublicAffairs 2011 xxiv, 230p ill. **960**
1. Africa 2. Anthropology 3. Human origins
ISBN 9781586486631 pa; 9781610391054
LC 2010043985

This book presents an "account of human evolution and the fiercely competitive anthropologists who are unearthing our ancestors' remains and arguing over what they mean. . . . [It] describ[es] the nuts-and-bolts of field research, the meaning of the often headline-producing findings and the ever-changing variety of species who split off from the common ancestors of chimpanzees and hominids." (Kirkus) "Scientists . . . have firmly established Africa as the birthplace not only of humankind but of modern humans. They have revealed how early technology, language ability, and artistic endeavour all originated in Africa; and they have shown how small groups of Africans spread out from Africa in an exodus sixty thousand years ago to populate the rest of the world." (Publisher's note)
Includes bibliographical references (p. 199-218) and index.

The **fortunes** of Africa; a history of the continent over fifty centuries. Martin Meredith. PublicAffairs

2014 784 p. 16 plates; illustrations; maps (hardcover) $35   **960**

1. Africa -- History
ISBN 1610394593; 9781610394598; 9781610394604
LC 2014939816

This book, by Martin Meredith, "follows the fortunes of Africa over a period of 5,000 years. With compelling narrative, he traces the rise and fall of ancient kingdoms and empires; the spread of Christianity and Islam; the enduring quest for gold and other riches; the exploits of explorers and missionaries; and the impact of European colonization. He examines, too, the fate of modern African states and concludes with a glimpse of their future." (Publisher's note)

"A gripping tale of insatiable greed—personal and collective." Booklist

Pakenham, Thomas

The **scramble** for Africa; the White man's conquest of the dark continent from 1876 to 1912. Avon 1992 xxv, 738p il map pa $22.95   **960**

1. Africa -- History
ISBN 0-380-71999-1
First published 1991 by Random House

This book is an account of the colonization and conquest of Africa by five European nations—Great Britain, France, Belgium, Germany, and Italy.

This is a "sweeping narrative, refreshingly old fashioned in its appreciation of the fact that imperialism did have some virtues, which offers as good an introduction to the 'scramble' as has ever been written." Libr J

Includes bibliographical references

Soyinka, Wole, 1934-

Of Africa; Wole Soyinka. Yale University Press 2012 199 p. (cloth : alk. paper) $24   **960**

1. Africa -- History 2. Africa -- Civilization
ISBN 0300140460; 9780300140460
LC 2012013544

In this book 1986 Nobel Laureate Wole Soyinka "argues that the abuse of Africa and Africans (i.e., the slave trade) belongs in company with the Holocaust and Hiroshima in the museum of human inhumanity. . . . He offers anecdotal accounts of non-Western medical achievements and paeans to a more accepting, less intrusive, nonviolent set of spiritual beliefs encompassed by the Yoruba deity Orisa." (Kirkus Reviews)

961.204 Libya -- 1952-2011

Chorin, Ethan

Exit the colonel; the hidden history of the Libyan revolution. Ethan Chorin. PublicAffairs 2012 viii, 374 p.p map (hardcover) $29.99; (ebook) $29.99   **961.204**

1. Libya -- History -- Civil War, 2011-
ISBN 1610391713; 9781610391719; 9781610391726 pdf
LC 2012021266

This book, by, Ethan Chorin, "goes . . . beyond recent reporting on the Arab Spring to link the Libyan uprising to a flawed reform process, egregious human rights abuses, re-

gional disparities, and inconsistent stories spun by Libya and the West to justify the Gaddafi regime's 'rehabilitation.' . . . . [The book] is based upon extensive interviews with senior US, EU, and Libyan officials, and with rebels and loyalists." (Publisher's note)

Includes bibliographical references (p. 347-354) and index

962   Egypt, Sudan, South Sudan

Jeal, Tim

Explorers of the Nile; the triumph and tragedy of a great Victorian adventure. Yale 2011 510p il map $32.50   **962**

1. Explorers 2. East Africa -- History 3. Central Africa -- History 4. Nile River -- Exploration
ISBN 978-0-300-14935-7
LC 2011933872

In this book on Victorian "efforts to find the source of the [Nile River]," the author focuses on a "quintet of great Victorian explorers," namely David Livingstone, Henry Morton Stanley, John Hanning Speke, Richard Burton, and Samuel Baker. "He recreates the mosquito-infested journeys and reveals the complex personal relationships, as Livingtone's early ventures to Lake Nyasa give way to the rivalry between Burton and Speke, who ventured north to Lakes Tanganyika, Victoria and Albert." Details on "the geopolitical consequences of finding the source of the Nile" are also presented. (History Today)

"Jeal's judicious account is a must-read for anyone hoping to understand the internal dynamics of modern state-building in central Africa." Booklist

Includes bibliographical references

Morrison, Dan

The **black** Nile; one man's amazing journey through peace and war on the world's longest river. Viking 2010 307p il map $26.95   **962**

1. Canoes and canoeing 2. War and civilization 3. Nile River -- Social conditions 4. Nile River -- Description and travel
ISBN 978-0-670-02198-7
LC 2010-4709

A foreign correspondent traces the four-thousand-mile plank-board boat journey he took with an inexperienced childhood friend along the Nile River from Lake Victoria to the Mediterranean Sea.

"Morrison's account transcends the travel genre to provide authentic and timely information on a complicated part of the world." Libr J

Stothard, Peter

Alexandria; The Last Nights of Cleopatra. Penguin Group USA 2013 400 p. $26.95   **962**

1. Alexandria (Egypt) 2. Egypt -- Description and travel
ISBN 1468303708; 9781468303704

In this book, "when Peter Stothard, editor of the 'Times Literary Supplement,' finds himself stranded in Alexandria in the winter of 2010 after his flight to South Africa has been cancelled, he sets out to explore a nation on the brink of revolution. Guided by two native Egyptians, Stothard traces his own life-long interest in the history of Cleopatra, and his repeated failure to write the book about her that he had always wanted to." (Publisher's note)

Strathern, Paul

Napoleon in Egypt; Bantam hardcover ed; Bantam Books 2008 480p il map $30 **962**
1. Emperors 2. Egypt -- History -- 1798-1801, French occupation
ISBN 978-0-553-80678-6; 0-553-80678-5
LC 2008-28135
First published 2007 in the United Kingdom
"Strathern's skillful use of memoir and other primary sources brings to life one of the most fascinating campaigns in military history." Libr J
Includes bibliographical references (p. 429-460)

962.05   Egypt since 1922

Cambanis, Thanassis

Once upon a revolution; an Egyptian story. Thanassis Cambanis. Free Press 2015 274 p. (hardcover) $26 **962.05**
1. Revolutionaries 2. Egypt -- History 3. Arab Spring, 2010- 4. Political activists 5. Social change -- Arab countries 6. Civic leaders -- Egypt -- Biography 7. Egypt -- History -- Protests, 2011- 8. Revolutionaries -- Egypt -- Biography 9. Egypt -- History -- 1981- -- Biography 10. Political activists -- Egypt -- Biography 11. Social change -- Egypt -- History -- 21st century
ISBN 1451658990; 9781451658996; 9781451659009
LC 2014022751
This book, on the 2011 Egyptian revolution by Thanassis Cambanis, "follows two leaders of the uprising from the beginnings of their political involvement to the military coup that overthrew Mohamed Morsi. Basem, an unassuming architect, becomes one of the few liberal members of parliament, while Moaz, a Muslim Brother, grows increasingly disenchanted with political Islam." (Publishers Weekly)
"Cambanis is master of the compelling detail: for example, in relating that Kamel was born in 1937, he notes that this was the year King Farouk I was crowned, a king who ate oysters by the hundred in his palace while his people endured WWII bombings. Wonderfully readable and insightful." Booklist
Includes bibliographical references and index

Khalil, Ashraf

Liberation Square; Ashraf Khalil. St. Martin's Press 2012 x, 324p.p **962.05**
1. Revolutions 2. Political corruption 3. Egypt -- History -- 1970- 4. Egypt -- History -- Protests, 2011 5. Egypt -- Politics and government -- 21st century
ISBN 9781250006691; 9781429962445
LC 2011038194
This book covers "the rise and fall of Hosni Mubarak's dictatorship. . . . The . . . combination of judicial corruption and police brutality began to awake significant opposition, and the tipping point was the brutal beating death of Khalid Saieed in Alexandria on June 6, 2010. . . . [Author Ashraf]

Khalil's discussion of the role of the Internet and social media . . . [shows] how large numbers of people were organized to achieve specific objectives--for example, converging on Cairo's squares and other public areas. The author . . . examines how the opposition to Egypt's paramilitary police gained strength, and how American diplomacy contributed to the cause. Khalil closes with the battle for Tahrir Square and the overthrow of the dictatorship." (Kirkus)

Steavenson, Wendell, 1970-

Circling the Square; Stories from the Egyptian Revolution. by Wendell Steavenson. HarperCollins 2015 384 p. illustrations $26.99 **962.05**
1. Arab Spring, 2010- 2. Egypt -- History -- 1970- 3. Egypt -- Politics and government
ISBN 0062375253; 9780062375254
In this book, author Wendell Steavenson "recounts the events of the Egyptian Revolution-- from Mubarak's fall to Morsi's. Here is the panoply of Tahrir Square, a pointillist portrait of a people enacting and reacting to change and hope. . . . Steavenson takes us to the heart of the Revolution and paints indelible portraits of ordinary Egyptians grappling with hope and change amid violence and bloodshed." (Publisher's note)
"A moving, empathetic portrayal of a central movement of our time: the brave Egyptian people's attempt to end repression without the tools or the leaders to succeed." LJ

962.4   Sudan and South Sudan

Deng, Benson

They poured fire on us from the sky; the true story of three lost boys from Sudan. [by] Benson Deng, Alephonsion Deng, Benjamin Ajak; with Judy Bernstein. Public Affairs 2005 xxiii, 311p map hardcover o.p. pa $13.95 **962.4**
1. Refugees 2. Sudan
ISBN 1-58648-269-6; 1-58648-388-9 pa
LC 2005-42566
"This collection is moving in its depictions of unbelievable courage." Publ Wkly

963   Ethiopia and Eritrea

Shah, Tahir

In search of King Solomon's mines. Little, Brown 2003 240p il map $24.95; pa $13.95 **963**
1. Ethiopia -- Description and travel
ISBN 1-55970-641-4; 1-55970-724-0 pa
First published in 2002 in the United Kingdom
This is an account of the author's search for "the mysterious mines of Ophir, where King Solomon, the Bible's wisest king, was supposed to have buried a fortune in gold. . . . According to his reckoning, the mines should be in modern-day Ethiopia, so he set out on an adventure of a lifetime with a shifty bookseller named (no kidding) Ali Baba. Along the way, readers are treated to his accounts of everything from the California gold rush to a sadistic Sultan." Libr J
Includes bibliographical references

964   Morocco, Ceuta, Melilla, Western Sahara, Canary Islands

Shah, Tahir

The **Caliph's** house; Tahir Shah. Bantam Books 2006 349p il $22   **964**

1. Morocco -- Description and travel
ISBN 0-553-80399-9

LC 2005-53656

"Shah's picture of Moroccan society, its deeply held Islamic faith, its primitive superstition, and its raucous economy makes for endlessly fascinating reading." Booklist

965   Algeria

Camus, Albert, 1913-1960

Algerian chronicles; Albert Camus; translated by Arthur Goldhammer; with an introduction by Alice Kaplan. Harvard University Press 2013 240 p. (hardcover) $21.95   **965**

1. Algeria -- History 2. French-Algerian War, 1954-1962 3. Algeria -- History -- Revolution, 1954-1962 4. Algeria -- Social conditions -- 20th century 5. Algeria -- Politics and government -- 20th century
ISBN 0674072588; 9780674072589

LC 2012036100

This book is "the first English translation of [Albert Camus'] 'Chroniques Algériennes' (1958)." It includes his "reportage of the 1939 famine in Kabylia" as well as other observations "fixed historically in the French-Algerian war." Camus' struggles "with the concept and conflicts of colonialism" are shared. (Publishers Weekly)

Includes bibliographical references and index.

Evans, Martin

Algeria; France's undeclared war. Martin Evans. Oxford University Press 2012 xxi, 457 p.p (hardcover) $35.00   **965**

1. Torture 2. Nationalism 3. War and civilization 4. Algeria -- Foreign relations 5. France -- Colonies -- Africa 6. France -- Foreign relations -- 1945- 7. Algeria -- Foreign relations -- France 8. France -- Foreign relations -- Algeria 9. Algeria -- History -- Revolution, 1954-1962 10. Algeria -- History -- Revolution, 1954-1962 -- Causes
ISBN 0192803506; 9780192803504

LC 2012371069

Author "Martin Evans argues that it was the Socialist led Republican Front, in power from January 1956 until May 1957, which was the defining moment in the [Algerian revolutionary] war [of 1954-1962 . . . [and] underlines the conflict of values between the Republican Front and Algerian nationalism, explaining how this clash produced patterns of thought and action, such as the institutionalization of torture and the raising of pro-French Muslim militias, which tragically polarized choices and framed all subsequent stages of the conflict." (Publisher's note)

Includes bibliographical references (p. [415]-429) and index

Morgan, Ted

My battle of Algiers; by Ted Morgan. Collins/Smithsonian 2006 284p maps $24.95   **965**

1. Algeria -- History -- 1954-1962, Revolution
ISBN 0-06-085224-0

LC 2005-52160

The author "recalls his service as a young officer in France's bitter war in Algeria. . . . Anyone interested in the origins of modern terrorist tactics will benefit from his recollections." Publ Wkly

966.62   Liberia

Dwyer, Johnny

American warlord; the true story of a father and son. Johnny Dwyer. Alfred A. Knopf 2015 368 p. 8 plates; illustrations, maps $27.95   **966.62**

1. Americans -- Africa 2. Soldiers -- Liberia 3. Political violence -- Liberia 4. Liberia -- Politics and government -- 1980- 5. Liberia -- History -- Civil War, 1989-1996 -- Atrocities 6. Liberia -- History -- Civil War, 1999-2003 -- Atrocities
ISBN 0307273482; 9780307273482

LC 2014025451

This book by Johnny Dwyer is the story of "Chucky Taylor . . . the American son of the infamous African dictator Charles Taylor. Raised by his mother in the Florida suburbs, at the age of 17 he followed his father to Liberia, where he ended up leading a murderous militia. Chucky is now in a federal penitentiary, the only American ever convicted of torture." (Publisher's note)

"Dwyer deftly captures both the larger implications of Taylor's reign and the human-scaled horror of his son's descent: "Chucky's story had been improbable and at times surreal, but its brutality was real." A dark triumph—a meticulous geopolitic a l narrative and gripping tale of an American son lost to evil." Kirkus

966.68   Côte d'Ivoire (Ivory Coast)

Erdman, Sarah

Nine hills to Nambonkaha; two years in the heart of an African village. Holt & Co. 2003 322p $23; pa $14   **966.68**

1. Ivory Coast 2. Peace Corps (U.S.)
ISBN 0-8050-7381-7; 0-312-42312-8 pa

LC 2003-44955

"This is an engrossing, well-told tale certain to appeal to armchair travelers and to anyone—especially women—considering international volunteer work." Publ Wkly

966.705   Ghana -- 1957-

Mahama, John Dramani, 1958-

My first coup d'etat and other true stories from the lost decades of Africa; John Dramani Mahama. Bloomsbury 2012 318 p. $25.00   **966.705**

1. Revolutions 2. Ghana -- History 3. Ghana

-- Biography 4. Ghana -- History -- 1957- 5. Vice-presidents -- Ghana -- Biography 6. Ghana -- History -- Coup d'état, 1966
ISBN 1608198596; 9781608198597

LC 2011053052

In "this memoir, [vice president of Ghana John Dramani] Mahama, the son of a member of parliament, recounts how [African] affairs of state became real in his young mind on the day in 1966 when no one came to collect him from boarding school—the government had been overthrown, his father arrested, and his house confiscated. . . . Mahama unspools Ghana's recent history via . . . personal anecdotes." (Publishers Weekly)

966.905 Nigeria -- 1960-

Maier, Karl
This house has fallen; midnight in Nigeria. PublicAffairs 2000 xxxvii, 327p hardcover o.p. pa $18 **966.905**
1. Nigeria -- Politics and government
ISBN 0-8133-4045-4 pa

LC 00-28199

The author "explores the promise and paradox of Nigeria. {He} . . . recounts the history of this nation cobbled together from British colonial interests in its formative years and dominated by international oil interests in more recent years." Booklist
Includes bibliographical references

967.5 Democratic Republic of the Congo, Rwanda, Burundi

Hochschild, Adam
★ King Leopold's ghost; a story of greed, terror, and heroism in Colonial Africa. Houghton Mifflin 1998 366p il map hardcover o.p. pa $15 **967.5**
1. Atrocities 2. Belgium -- Colonies 3. Congo (Republic) -- History
ISBN 0-395-75924-2; 0-618-00190-5 pa

LC 98-16813

"Hochschild's impressively researched history records the roles of the famous and obscure, missionaries, journalists, opportunists, politicians, and royalty in this long-forgotten drama." Booklist
Includes bibliographical references

967.51 Democratic Republic of the Congo

Stearns, Jason K.
Dancing in the glory of monsters; the collapse of the Congo and the great war of Africa. PublicAffairs 2011 380p $28.99 **967.51**
1. Genocide 2. Massacres 3. Congo (Republic) 4. Massacres -- Congo (Democratic Republic) 5. Congo (Democratic Republic) -- History -- 1997- 6. Political

violence -- Congo (Democratic Republic)
ISBN 978-1-58648-929-8; 1-58648-929-1

LC 2010-43075

This book does not tell "the story of the Rwanda genocide in 1994, in which 800,000 people—almost all civilians—were massacred by their ethnic rivals in the space of a hundred days. That great atrocity is now relatively well known. Instead, this book tells of the war that broke out in the same region two years later, and that was in many ways its consequence. . . . As the Rwandan invaders penetrated into the eastern Congo, atrocities broke out. The Rwandans murdered the Hutus who had not fled. . . . Robert Mugabe of Zimbabwe and Eduardo Dos Santos of Angola pulled their troops out of the war, warning Kabila to negotiate for peace. . . . As well as 'big men' actors, [Jason K.] Stearns questioned many survivors of battle and massacre." (New York Review of Books)

A "look at the war that began in Congo in 1996 and that eventually involved nine countries and 20 different rebel movements, resulting in the deaths of more than five million people. In sheer brutality, this mostly unremarked upon cataclysm ranks with the two world wars, the Great Leap Forward and the Cambodia genocide. . . . Mr. Stearns has spoken to everyone—villagers, child soldiers, Mobutu's commanders, Kabila's ministers, Rwandan intelligence officers. In these conversations he found gold, bringing clarity—and humanity—to a place that usually seems inexplicable and barbaric. "Dancing in the Glory of Monsters" is riveting and certain to become essential reading for anyone looking to understand Central Africa." Wall Street J

Sundaram, Anjan
Stringer; a reporter's journey in the Congo. Anjan Sundaram. Doubleday 2014 265 p. $25.95 **967.51**
1. Journalism 2. Congo (Democratic Republic) 3. Congo (Democratic Republic) -- Description and travel 4. Congo (Democratic Republic) -- Social conditions -- 21st century
ISBN 0385537751; 9780345806321; 9780385537759; 9780385537766

LC 2013000980

Author Anjan "Sundaram exchanged mathematics for journalism, starting out as a stringer in dangerous Congo with little in the way of experience or contacts. This memoir sees him struggling to learn his craft while battling malaria, isolation, financial woes, and the tendency of editors to send in name reporters when a big story breaks. In addition, Sundaram offers an intensely rendered account of the immeasurable sadness of Congo through the tumultuous 2006 elections. " (Library Journal)

"The author skillfully captures the smallest details of life in a destitute land, blending the sordid history of Congo with his battle to forge a career in a troubled and forsaken country." Pub Wkly

967.571 Rwanda

Gourevitch, Philip
We wish to inform you that tomorrow we will be killed with our families; stories from Rwanda. Far-

rar, Straus & Giroux 1998 355p hardcover o.p. pa
$15   967.571
  1. Genocide 2. Rwanda -- Politics and government
  ISBN 0-374-28697-3; 0-312-24335-9 pa
                                            LC 98-22132
  This work is "readable and moving, Gourevitch is an
impassioned and thoughtful observer. But this is not a work
that gives much pleasure or comfort. Nor are its arguments
fool-proof, its evidence complete, or its documentation
thorough. . . . Still Gourevitch does struggle to come close
to a great mystery of evil, and he makes us attend to great
crimes." Commonweal

Hatzfeld, Jean
  The **antelope's** strategy; living in Rwanda after
the genocide. a report by Jean Hatzfeld; translated
from the French by Linda Coverdale. Farrar, Straus
and Giroux 2009 242p map $25   967.571
  1. Genocide 2. Hutu (African people) 3. Tutsi (African
people) 4. Rwanda
  ISBN 978-0-374-27103-9; 0-374-27103-8
                                            LC 2008-52489
  Original French edition, 2007
  This "is a book that illustrates vividly the thorny realities
that accompany survival and appeasement." Washington Post

  Machete season; the killers in Rwanda speak: a
report. translated from the French by Linda Coverdale; preface by Susan Sontag. Farrar, Straus and
Giroux 2005 253p il maps hardcover o.p. pa
$14   967.571
  1. Genocide 2. Hutu (African people) 3. Tutsi (African
people) 4. Rwanda
  ISBN 0-374-28082-7; 0-312-42503-1 pa
                                            LC 2004-61600
  Original French edition, 2003
  "Steering clear of politics, this important book succeeds
in offering the reader some grasp of how such unspeakable
acts unfolded." Publ Wkly

967.6 Uganda and Kenya

Beard, Peter H. (Peter Hill), 1938-
  The **end** of the game; the last word from paradise. [by] Peter Beard; [foreword by Paul Theroux]
Taschen 2008 280p il $39.99   967.6
  1. Hunting 2. East Africa -- Description and travel
  ISBN 3-83650-530-4; 978-3-83650-530-7
  First published 1965 by Viking; updated 1977 and published by Doubleday
  "This landmark book, with a chilling (and acerbic) new
introduction by travel writer and novelist Paul Theroux, contains photographs many of them shocking that reveal the
sad situation of African wildlife, and most particularly the
elephant. Beard mourns the end of a continent from a diverse
and interdependent ecosystem to a land suffocated by cement, wire, walls and ditches (not to mention war)." Stuart
News (Stuart, Florida)

Chretien, Jean-Pierre
  ★ The **great** lakes of Africa; two thousand years
of history. translated by Scott Straus. Zone Books
2003 504p map $36   967.6
  1. Rwanda 2. Uganda 3. Burundi 4. East Africa
  ISBN 1-89095-134-X
                                            LC 2002-191001
  "This is an impressive and important book surveying 2,000 years of history. . . . The preeminence accorded
Rwanda and Burundi . . . leads to the book's most significant
contribution: to demonstrate that the region's recent interrelated conflicts claiming over four million lives are not based
on ancient, unchanging 'ethnic' cleavages, most notably between Tutsi and Hutu." Choice
  Includes bibliographical references

Rice, Andrew
  The **teeth** may smile but the heart does not forget;
murder and memory in Uganda. Metropolitan Books/
Henry Holt and Co. 2009 363p il map $26   967.6
  1. Generals 2. Atrocities 3. Presidents 4. Uganda 5.
Murderers 6. Murder victims 7. Government officials
8. Children of prominent persons
  ISBN 978-0-8050-7965-4; 0-8050-7965-3
                                            LC 2008-41984
  "At the core of the book is an unsolved disappearance:
Eliphaz Laki, a local leader with ties to the anti-Amin oppo-
sition, vanished in the early days of the Amin regime. When
his son, Duncan, uncovered a clue to his father's disappear-
ance 30 years later, the investigation eventually implicated
Amin's second-in-command, Maj. Gen. Yusuf Gowon. With
Amin living out his years safely in Saudi Arabia, the trial of
Gowon forced Uganda to confront its brutal past. Treating
the Lakis' story as a microcosm of Uganda's own, the author
weaves together the family's search for truth and justice with
Uganda's history." Publ Wkly

967.61 Uganda

David, Saul
  Operation Thunderbolt; Flight 139 and the Raid
on Entebbe Airport, the Most Audacious Hostage
Rescue Mission in History. Saul David. Little Brown
& Co. 2015 464 p. 16 unnumbered pages of plates
(hardcover) $30   967.61
  1. Hostages 2. Special forces (Military science) -- Israel
  ISBN 9780316245418; 0316245410
                                            LC 2015946917
  This book, by Saul David, offers a "definitive account of
one of the greatest Special Forces missions ever. . . . On June
27, 1976, an Air France flight from Tel Aviv to Paris was hijacked by a group of . . . terrorists. . . . The plane was forced
to divert to Entebbe, in Uganda. . . . Days later, Israeli commandos disguised as Ugandan soldiers assaulted the airport
terminal, killed all the terrorists, and rescued all the hostages
but three who were killed in the crossfire." (Publisher's note)
  "A definitive history of the Entebbe operation, likely
to be popular among readers of military and terrorism
works." LJ

967.62 Kenya

Anderson, David M.

Histories of the hanged; the dirty war in Kenya and the end of the empire. [by] David Anderson. Norton 2005 406p il map $25.95; pa $15.95 **967.62**
1. Kenya 2. Mau Mau 3. Great Britain -- Colonies -- Africa

ISBN 0-393-05986-3; 0-393-32754-X pa

LC 2004-24804

This "history of the last days of the British Empire in Kenya focuses on the colonial judicial system, which sent over 1,000 native Kenyans to the gallows between 1952 and 1959, during the state of emergency triggered by the Mau Mau insurrection. . . . This is vital reading for any student of British colonial and African history." Publ Wkly

Includes bibliographical references

Dinesen, Isak

★ Out of Africa and Shadows on the grass. Vintage Bks. 1989 462p pa $13.95 **967.62**
1. Kenya

ISBN 0-679-72475-3

LC 89-40144

Out of Africa is a recording of the author's life on a Kenya coffee plantation. Shadows on the grass consists of four short essays which present the author's recollections of her servants in Africa

967.73 Somalia

Bowden, Mark

Black Hawk down; a story of modern war. Atlantic Monthly Press 1999 386p il maps $25; pa $13.95 **967.73**
1. Somalia 2. United States -- Army -- Task Force Ranger

ISBN 0-87113-738-0; 0-14-028850-3 pa

LC 98-46688

The author describes "both sides of the October 1993 raid into the heart of Mogadishu, Somalia, a raid that quickly became the most intensive close combat Americans have engaged in since the Vietnam War. But Bowden's gripping narrative of the fighting is only a framework for an examination of the internal dynamics of America's elite forces and a critique of the philosophy of sending such high-tech units into combat with minimal support." Publ Wkly

Fergusson, James

The world's most dangerous place; inside the outlaw state of Somalia. James Fergusson. Da Capo Press 2013 432 p. (hardcover) $27.50 **967.73**
1. Violence 2. Somalia -- Social conditions

ISBN 0306821176; 9780306821172

LC 2013933566

This book "investigates the civil war, foreign interventions and mass starvation of Somalia. . . . The vast majority of Somalians is illiterate, desperately poor and so committed to genetic ties within their particular geographic clan that pulling together as a nation seems hopeless. Many of the peacekeeping soldiers are from Uganda, ironic given that nation's recent bouts of sectarian violence." (Kirkus)

Rawlence, Ben

City of thorns; nine lives in the world's largest refugee camp. by Ben Rawlence. Picador 2016 352 p. (hardcover) $26 **967.73**
1. Refugees 2. Somali-Ethiopian Conflict, 1979- 3. Refugees -- Kenya 4. Refugees -- Somalia 5. Refugee camps -- Kenya

ISBN 1250067634; 9781250067630

LC 2015029505

In this book, by Ben Rawlence, "deep within the inhospitable desert of northern Kenya where only thorn bushes grow, Dadaab [refugee camp] is a city like no other. Its buildings are made from mud, sticks or plastic, its entire economy is grey, and its citizens survive on rations and luck. . . . Rawlence interweaves the stories of nine individuals to show what life is like in the camp and to sketch the wider political forces that keep the refugees trapped there." (Publisher's note)

968.04 Republic of South Africa 1814-1910

Meredith, Martin

Diamonds, gold, and war; the British, the Boers, and the making of South Africa. PublicAffairs 2007 570p il map $35 **968.04**
1. South African War, 1899-1902 2. South Africa -- History 3. Great Britain -- Colonies -- Africa

ISBN 978-1-58648-473-6; 1-58648-473-7

LC 2007-34540

A history of the tumultuous period leading up to the 1910 founding of the modern state of South Africa explores how the discovery of vast diamond and gold deposits led to a fierce struggle between the British and the Boers for control of the region.

"Meredith thoroughly involves us in this gripping history. Highly recommended for all libraries." Libr J

Includes bibliographical references (p. 540-550)

Millard, Candice

★ Hero of the empire; the Boer war, a daring escape, and the making of Winston Churchill. Candice Millard. Doubleday 2016 416 p. (hardcover) $30 **968.04**
1. South African War, 1899-1902 2. South African War, 1899-1902 -- Participation, British 3. South African War, 1899-1902 -- Prisoners and prisons, British

ISBN 0385535732; 9780385535731

LC 2015049806

In this book, author Candice Millard presents a "narrative of Winston Churchill's extraordinary and little-known exploits during the Boer War. just two weeks after his arrival, the soldiers he was accompanying on an armored train were ambushed, and Churchill was taken prisoner. Remarkably, he pulled off a daring escape--but then had to traverse hundreds of miles of enemy territory, alone, with nothing but a crumpled wad of cash, four slabs of chocolate, and his wits to guide him." (Publisher's note)

"Here the author documents the equally risky adventures of Winston Churchill (1874-1965) during the Second Boer War, in which Churchill and his fellow soldiers were captured upon arriving in South Africa. Churchill managed an escape, eventually returning to South Africa to free the men with whom he was imprisoned. . . . Enjoyable for all readers, especially fans of Churchill, military and world history, narrative nonfiction, and survival stories." LJ

968.06 South Africa--Period as Republic, 1961-

Carlin, John

Playing the enemy; Nelson Mandela and the game that made a nation. Penguin 2008 274p il $24.95 **968.06**

1. Presidents 2. Rugby football 3. Political prisoners 4. Rugby 5. Political leaders 6. Human rights activists 7. Nobel laureates for peace

ISBN 978-1-59420-174-5; 1-59420-174-9

LC 2008-298721

"Deftly sketched characters make up both an audience for the big game and a gallery of South Africa, through which Carlin will recount the absorbing story of a country emerging from its cruelly absurd racist experiment." N Y Times Book Rev

Includes bibliographical references

Duke, Lynne

Mandela, Mobutu, and me; a newswoman's African journey. Doubleday 2003 294p $24 **968.06**

1. Generals 2. Presidents 3. Political prisoners 4. Political leaders 5. Human rights activists 6. Nobel laureates for peace 7. South Africa -- Politics and government

ISBN 0-385-50398-9

LC 2002-73365

The author covers "some of the bloodier postcolonial wars of southern Africa as well as one of the most constructive struggles: the shaping of a postapartheid government. Her interviews with Mandela and Mobutu 'bookend' . . . conversations with common folk: township women struggling for clean water, AIDS nurses battling superstitious villagers and even a quiet old Zulu man impressed to meet his 'first foreign black folk.' A consummate journalist, Duke gives readers concise but thorough background briefings on a country's relevant history before cutting to the chase: who's taken control now, why, and what that means for the balance of power. . . . She deftly combines solid information and personal perspective to produce a powerful, readable chronicle." Publ Wkly

Mandela, Nelson

Mandela; an illustrated autobiography. Little, Brown 1996 208p il map $29.95 **968.06**

1. Presidents 2. Political prisoners 3. Political leaders 4. Human rights activists 5. Nobel laureates for peace 6. South Africa -- Race relations 7. South Africa -- Politics and government

ISBN 0-316-55038-8

LC 96-77497

"The photos, from a variety of archives and journalistic sources, ably illustrate Mandela and, even more so, the South Africa around him." Libr J

Tutu, Desmond

No future without forgiveness; [by] Desmond Mpilo Tutu. Doubleday 1999 287p hardcover o.p. pa $15.95 **968.06**

1. South Africa -- Race relations 2. South Africa -- Commission for Truth and Reconciliation

ISBN 0-385-49690-7 pa

LC 99-34451

The author reflects on his role "as chairman of the Truth and Reconciliation Commission. Tutu speaks frankly of . . . the struggle that preceded it and of the betrayals and jubilations of this unique commission. The TRC's work was unprecedented not only in its emphasis on restorative over retributive justice but in the spirituality that permeated its work, the bulk of which constituted hearings from the 'victims' and 'perpetrators' of apartheid." Publ Wkly

Includes bibliographical references

The **rainbow** people of God; the making of a peaceful revolution. edited by John Allen. Doubleday 1994 xxii, 281p il hardcover o.p. pa $15.95 **968.06**

1. Sermons 2. South Africa -- Race relations

ISBN 0-385-48374-0 pa

LC 94-16011

This collection of Tutu's "speeches, letters, and sermons—from the time of the 1976 Soweto Uprising, through the long years of repression and defiance, up to the triumph of the democratic election—serves as an immediate contemporary history of South Africa. Tutu's media secretary, John Allen, provides a general historical introduction and a connecting narrative that places the individuals pieces in dramatic context." Booklist

Includes bibliographical references

Waldmeir, Patti

Anatomy of a miracle; the end of apartheid and the birth of the new South Africa. Rutgers University Press 1998 289p pa $22.95 **968.06**

1. South Africa -- Race relations 2. South Africa -- Politics and government

ISBN 0-8135-2582-9; 978-0-8135-2582-2

LC 98-15628

First published 1997 by W.W. Norton

Waldmeir traces the political and personal struggles that ultimately contributed to the dismantling of apartheid in South Africa

"Although Mandela attributes greatness to de Klerk for his courage, it is Mandela's own character that dominates this history. . . . Engrossing in its sweep, this account also describes the obstacles facing the regime." Publ Wkly

Includes bibliographical references

968.91   Zimbabwe

Lamb, Christina

House of stone; the true story of a family divided in war-torn Zimbabwe. Lawrence Hill Books 2007 290p il map   **968.91**
1. Farmers 2. Nannies 3. Zimbabwe -- Race relations
ISBN 978-1-55652-735-7; 1-55652-735-7

LC 2007-19814

"Through the parallel accounts of two people in Zimbabwe, one a poor black maid, one a rich white farmer, . . . Lamb tells the compelling story of a country ravaged first by colonial settlers and now by brutal civil war. . . . The anguished personal detail, true to the changing viewpoints, makes for a gripping read." Booklist

Rogers, Douglas

The **last** resort; a memoir of Zimbabwe. Harmony Books 2009 309p map $24.99   **968.91**
1. Resorts 2. Zimbabwe
ISBN 978-0-307-40797-9; 0-307-40797-7

"A nuanced, funny, and heartbreaking story of one community's experience of survival in Mugabe's Zimbabwe." New Yorker

970   History of North America

Morgan, Ted

Wilderness at dawn; the settling of the North American continent. Simon & Schuster 1993 541p il maps hardcover o.p. pa $20   **970**
1. North America -- History 2. Canada -- History -- 0-1763 (New France) 3. United States -- History -- 1600-1775, Colonial period
ISBN 0-671-88237-6 pa

LC 93-2628

Morgan "tells a good story, emphasizing the ordinary people who did the actual settlement. . . . A useful survey of the colonial frontier." Libr J
Includes bibliographical references

970.004   North American native peoples

American Indians; consulting editor, Harvey Markowitz. Salem Press 1995 3v il maps (Ready reference) set $331   **970.004**
1. Reference books 2. Native Americans -- Encyclopedias 3. Native Americans -- Mexico -- Encyclopedias
ISBN 0-89356-757-4

LC 94-47633

"This set contains 1,129 articles ranging in length from 200 to 3,000 words. The entries cover a wide range of persons, tribes, organizations, cultural and historical events, and contemporary issues of U.S., Canadian, and some Mesoamerican Indian groups. Individual entries appear for 275 North American tribes. Entries are arranged alphabetically and are illustrated with 250 black-and-white photographs, maps, charts, tables, and drawings." Booklist

Bragdon, Kathleen J.

The **Columbia** guide to American Indians of the Northeast. Columbia Univ. Press 2001 292p il maps (Columbia guides to American Indian history and culture) $53.50; pa $25.50   **970.004**
1. Native Americans
ISBN 0-231-11452-4; 0-231-11453-2 pa

LC 2001-47341

This handbook "includes not only a broad overview of the history of Native Americans in the Northeast but also a partially annotated listing of materials for further research including published primary sources, oral traditions, films, and Internet sites." Libr J
Includes bibliographical references

Brown, Dee Alexander

★ **Bury** my heart at Wounded Knee; an Indian history of the American West. [by] Dee Brown. Thirtieth anniversary ed; Holt & Co. 2001 487p il hardcover o.p. pa $16   **970.004**
1. Generals 2. Civil engineers 3. Government officials 4. West (U.S.) -- History 5. Native Americans -- Wars 6. Native Americans -- West (U.S.)
ISBN 0-8050-6634-9; 0-8050-6669-1 pa

LC 00-40958

First published 1970
This is an account of the experience of the American Indian during the white man's expansion westward.
Includes bibliographical references

Bruchac, Joseph

Our stories remember; American Indian history, culture, & values through storytelling. Fulcrum 2003 192p map pa $16.95   **970.004**
1. Storytelling 2. Native Americans -- History
ISBN 1-555-91129-3

LC 2002-151236

"This important volume includes a wealth of traditional stories and solid information." SLJ
Includes bibliographical references

Deloria, Vine

Custer died for your sins; an Indian manifesto. by Vine Deloria, Jr. University of Oklahoma Press 1988 278p pa $19.95   **970.004**
1. Native Americans
ISBN 0-8061-2129-7

LC 87-40561

First published 1969 by Macmillan
The author examines how anthropologists, missionaries, and government agencies have mistreated American Indians.

Documents of American Indian diplomacy; treaties, agreements, and conventions, 1775-1979. {compiled by} Vine Deloria, Jr., and Raymond J. DeMallie; with a foreword by Daniel K. Inouye. University of Okla. Press 1999 2v (Legal history of North America) set $125   **970.004**
1. Treaties 2. Native Americans -- Government relations
ISBN 0-8061-3118-7

LC 98-45365

This is a collection of hundreds of treaties and agreements made by American Indian nations with the Continental Congress, England, Spain, and other foreign countries, the Confederacy, the Republic of Texas, railroad companies, other Indian nations, and the U.S. government, with chapter introductions which put them in historical and political context

"A must for all libraries." Libr J

Includes bibliographical references

Dunbar-Ortiz, Roxanne

An **indigenous** peoples' history of the United States; Roxanne Dunbar-Ortiz. Beacon Press 2014 296 p. (ReVisioning American history) (hardcover : alk. paper) $27.95   **970.004**
   1. United States -- Race relations 2. Native Americans -- United States 3. United States -- History -- 1600-1775, Colonial period 4. United States -- Colonization 5. United States -- Politics and government
   ISBN 080700040X; 9780807000403
                      LC 2013050262

This book, by Roxanne Dunbar-Ortiz, "offers a history of the United States told from the perspective of Indigenous peoples and reveals how Native Americans, for centuries, actively resisted expansion of the US empire. . . . [It] challenges the founding myth of the United States and shows how policy against the Indigenous peoples was colonialist and designed to seize the territories of the original inhabitants, displacing or eliminating them." (Publisher's note)

"His belief in the separation of church and state is obvious (he states in the introduction that he was raised a Jew but is now an atheist); his legal arguments are solid, and he is not contemptuous of religion. However, some readers are bound to be put off by his cavalier and sometimes sarcastic tone, although others will appreciate its humor. Should find many general readers." LJ

Includes bibliographical references and index

Encyclopedia of Native American wars and warfare; general editors, William B. Kessel, Robert Wooster. Facts on File 2005 398p il map $75; pa $21.95   **970.004**
   1. Reference books 2. Native Americans -- Wars -- Encyclopedias
   ISBN 0-8160-3337-4; 0-8160-6430-X pa
                      LC 00-56200

"This encyclopedia offers readers a wide range of information about Native American history in North America after 1492." Choice

Includes bibliographical references

Fenton, William Nelson

The **Great** Law and the Longhouse; a political history of the Iroquois Confederacy. {by} Willam N. Fenton. University of Okla. Press 1998 xxii, 786p il map (Civilization of the American Indian series) $75   **970.004**
   1. Iroquois Indians -- History
   ISBN 0-8061-3003-2
                      LC 97-19842

"If a library has only one book about the Iroquois . . . it should be this title." Libr J

Includes bibliographical references

Fowler, Loretta

The **Columbia** guide to American Indians of the Great Plains. Columbia Univ. Press 2003 283p il maps (Columbia guides to American Indian history and culture) $53.50; pa $26.50   **970.004**
   1. Native Americans -- Great Plains
   ISBN 0-231-11700-0; 0-231-11701-9 pa
                      LC 2002-73708

"This work is divided into four parts: a general survey of the history and cultures of the native peoples of the region; alphabetically arranged entries focusing on individuals, places, and events; a chronology; and a listing of resources for further research that includes published primary sources, oral traditions, films, and Internet sites. . . . Highly recommended." Libr J

Includes bibliographical references

Harmon, Alexandra

Indians in the making; ethnic relations and Indian identities around Puget Sound. University of Calif. Press 1998 393p il maps (American crossroads) hardcover o.p. pa $21.95   **970.004**
   1. Washington (State) -- History 2. Native Americans -- Northwest Coast of North America
   ISBN 0-520-22685-2 pa
                      LC 98-17665

The author "examines how both the federal government and the native peoples of western Washington were constantly redefining Indian identity to their advantage over a 150-year period. Harmon's examination of the native fishing rights controversy of the 1960s and 1970s is particularly useful." Libr J

Includes bibliographical references

Hendricks, Steve

The **unquiet** grave; the FBI and the struggle for the soul of Indian country. Thunder's Mouth Press 2006 490p il map $27.95   **970.004**
   1. Educators 2. Dissenters 3. Indian leaders 4. Social activists 5. American Indian Movement 6. Native Americans -- Government relations 7. United States -- Federal Bureau of Investigation
   ISBN 1-56025-735-0; 978-1-56025-735-6

The author tells "the story of the American Indian Movement (AIM) to reclaim civil and treaty rights. . . . Bracketed by the 1976 murder of AIM activist Anna Mae Aquash and the 2004 trial related to it, Hendricks's swift narrative is riddled with judicial travesties, coverups, vigilantism, COINTELPRO-style tactics, mounting paranoia and lawlessness on both sides, as activists and ordinary American Indians confront the devastating neglect and outright hostility of government authorities." Publ Wkly

Includes bibliographical references

Iverson, Peter

We are still here; American Indians in the twentieth century. Davidson, H. 1998 255p il (American history series) pa $14.95   **970.004**
    1. Native Americans
ISBN 0-88295-940-9
                        LC 97-38321
    The author "begins at Wounded Knee and tells the stories of Indian communities throughout the United States, including not only political leaders and activists, but also professionals, artists, soldiers and athletes." Publisher's note
    Includes bibliographical references

Johansen, Bruce E.

The **Native** peoples of North America; a history. Praeger 2005 2v il set $99.95   **970.004**
    1. Native Americans -- History
ISBN 0-275-98159-2
                      LC 2004-28732
    This is a history of "cultures indigenous to North America from their earliest origins to the present. . . . Encompassing not only traditional historical records but also oral histories and biographical sketches, these two volumes will undoubtedly become an integral part of Native American history, an increasingly popular field." Booklist
    Includes bibliographical references

Johnson, Michael G.

Encyclopedia of native tribes of North America; Michael Johnson; illustrator, Richard Hook. Compendium 2007 320 p. color illustrations; maps $49.95   **970.004**
    1. Native Americans -- North America 2. Native Americans -- Encyclopedias
ISBN 1770854614; 190557374X; 9781770854611; 9781905573745
                      LC 2008360036
    First published 1993 in the United Kingdom with title: The native tribes of North America
    This book, by Michael Johnson, illustrated by Richard Hook, "offers the most up-to-date and essential facts on the identity, kinships, locations, populations and cultural characteristics of some 400 separately identifiable peoples native to the North American continent, both living and extinct, from the Canadian Arctic to the Rio Grande." (Publisher's note)
    "The maps, photographs, and beautiful illustrations by Hook, combined with concise, accurate entries, make this volume a good purchase, especially for libraries that lack the 2007 edition. Summing Up: Recommended. Lower-division undergraduates and above; general readers." Choice

Josephy, Alvin M.

America in 1492; the world of the Indian peoples before the arrival of Columbus. edited and with an introduction by Alvin Josephy, Jr.; developed by Frederick E. Hoxie. Knopf 1992 477p il maps hardcover o.p. pa $20   **970.004**
    1. America -- Antiquities 2. America -- Exploration 3. Native Americans -- History 4. Native Americans

-- Antiquities
ISBN 0-394-56438-3; 0-679-74337-5 pa
                      LC 90-26222
    These essays depict "the diverse lives of the approximately 75 million people living in the Americas around the turn of the fifteenth century. Geography guides the first section. . . . Another section focuses on languages, spiritual beliefs and customs, art, and 'systems of knowledge.'" Booklist
    Includes bibliographical references

The **Nez** Perce Indians and the opening of the Northwest; {by} Alvin M. Josephy, Jr. Houghton Mifflin 1997 xx, 705p il map pa $19   **970.004**
    1. Nez Percé Indians 2. Pacific Northwest
ISBN 0-395-85011-8
                      LC 96-54278
    First published 1965 by Yale University Press
    This history of the Nez Perce tribe traces its contact with white settlers from Lewis and Clark to Chief Joseph and war in 1877
    Includes bibliographical references

Josephy, Alvin M., 1915-2005

The **longest** trail; writings on American Indian history, culture, and politics. by Alvin M. Josephy, Jr.; edited by Marc Jaffe and Rich Wandschneider. Vintage Books, A Division of Penguin Random House LLC 2015 544 p. (paperback) $16.95   **970.004**
    1. Native Americans -- History 2. Native Americans -- Politics and government 3. Native Americans -- Social life and customs
ISBN 9780345806918
                      LC 2015010197
    This book, by Alvin M. Josephy, Jr., edited by Marc Jaffe and Rich Wandschneider, reviews "five hundred years of Indian history in North America from first settlements in the East to the long trek of the Nez Perce Indians in the Northwest. The essays deal with the origins of still unresolved troubles with treaties and territories to fishing and land rights, and who should own archeological finds, as well as the ideologies that underpin our Indian policy." (Publisher's note)
    "Essential for anyone interested in contemporary Native American history and culture and should be read alongside Josephy's autobiography A Walk Toward Oregon: A Memoir." LJ

McLoughlin, William Gerald

After the Trail of Tears; the Cherokees' struggle for sovereignty, 1839-1880. {by} William G. McLoughlin. University of N.C. Press 1993 439p maps hardcover o.p. pa $21.95   **970.004**
    1. Cherokee Indians 2. Indian chiefs
ISBN 0-8078-4433-0 pa
                      LC 93-18532
    The author "recounts the tragedy that continued to afflict the Cherokee Nation after their forced removal from their traditional home to Oklahoma during the 1820s and 1830s. In Oklahoma the Cherokee Nation set out to reconstruct their society, reestablishing their newspaper, which published in the Cherokee language, and governing themselves

according to a constitution modeled on that of the United States. . . . McLoughlin vividly depicts the conflicts between 'full-bloods,' who sought to live by more traditional ways, and Cherokees of mixed ancestry who favored assimilation into the dominant culture." Publ Wkly

Includes bibliographical references

McReynolds, Edwin C.

The **Seminoles**. University of Okla. Press 1957 397p il maps (Civilization of the American Indian series) hardcover o.p. pa $21.95   **970.004**

1. Seminole Indians

ISBN 0-8061-1255-7 pa

"This is almost strictly a military and political history, in great detail, spiced with a few incidents which reveal the courageous character of the Seminoles, and stressing their relations with the Creeks." Libr J

Includes bibliographical references

Milton, Giles

Big Chief Elizabeth; the adventures and fate of the First English Colonists in America. Farrar, Straus & Giroux 2000 358p il maps hardcover o.p. pa $14   **970.004**

1. Queens 2. Native Americans 3. Virginia -- History 4. America -- Exploration 5. Great Britain -- Colonies -- America

ISBN 0-312-42018-8 pa

LC 00-31522

"Nearly 500 years ago, a small group of white men landed on the shores of North America and named it Virginia (for the Virgin Queen [Elizabeth]). Their purpose was to capture some natives and bring them to England to learn their language and everything else they could about the country they wished to colonize. . . . [Milton] chronicles the century-long battle to establish a permanent settlement in Virginia." Christ Sci Monit

Includes bibliographical references

Native America in the twentieth century; an encyclopedia. edited by Mary B. Davis; assistant editors, Joan Berman, Mary E. Graham, Lisa A. Mitten. Garland 1994 xxxvii, 787p il maps (Garland reference library of social science) hardcover o.p. pa $50   **970.004**

1. Reference books   2. Native Americans -- Encyclopedias

ISBN 0-8153-2583-5 pa

LC 94-768

This volume offers "tribal-specific information on the art, daily life, economic development, and religion of 20th-century American Indians and Alaskan Natives and the government policy that affects them." Libr J

★ **Native** American testimony; a chronicle of Indian-white relations from prophecy to the present, 1492-2000. edited by Peter Nabokov; with a foreword by Vine Deloria, Jr. Rev and updated ed; Penguin Bks. 1999 xxiii, 506p il maps pa $16.95   **970.004**

1. Native Americans -- History -- Sources 2. Native

Americans -- Government relations

ISBN 0-14-028159-2

First published 1978 by Crowell with subtitle: An anthology of Indian and white relations, first encounter to dispossession

"A collection of primary-source material, grouped by key issues that arose during 500 years of Indian and white encounters in North America. Nabokov uses traditional narratives, old government transcripts, reservation newspapers, and firsthand interviews to highlight this chronological volume. Photographs appear throughout." SLJ {review of 1991 edition}

Includes bibliographical references

Osborn, William M.

The **wild** frontier; atrocities during the American-Indian War from Jamestown Colony to Wounded Knee. Random House 2000 363p hardcover o.p. pa $19   **970.004**

1. Frontier and pioneer life 2. Native Americans -- Wars 3. Native Americans -- Government relations

ISBN 0-375-75856-9 pa

LC 00-27171

"Characterizing the years between 1622 and 1890 as the era of the American-Indian War, Osborn provides a balanced analysis of the vicious atrocities committed by white settlers and Native Americans during the prolonged period of westward expansion. . . . Laden with stark, unsparing descriptions . . . the detailed narrative retains an admirable objectivity." Booklist

Includes bibliographical references

Perdue, Theda

The **Columbia** guide to American Indians of the Southeast; [by] Theda Perdue and Michael D. Green. Columbia Univ. Press 2001 325p il maps (Columbia guides to American Indian history and culture) $53.50; pa $27.50   **970.004**

1. Native Americans -- Southern States

ISBN 0-231-11570-9; 0-231-11571-7 pa

LC 2001-35338

"The first half of the text focuses on the history and culture of the region's native groups. This includes not only the Mississippian Moundbuilder cultures that arose between 800 and 1000 C.E. but also well-known native groups such as the Cherokee and Creeks. . . . Immediately following the survey are alphabetically arranged entries focusing on individuals, places, and events. The final two sections are a chronology and a listing of resources for further research, which include published primary sources, oral traditions, films, and Internet sites. . . . An essential purchase for all libraries collecting books about Native Americans." Libr J

Includes bibliographical references

Philip, Neil

The **great** circle; a history of the First Nations. foreword by Dennis Hastings. Clarion Books 2006 153p il map $25   **970.004**

1. Native Americans

ISBN 978-0-618-15941-3; 0-618-15941-X

LC 2005032743

"Philip takes on a huge challenge here: to present a unified narrative that explains the complex and confrontational relationships between Native Americans and white settlers. . . . He pulls it off, however, thanks to solid research, an engaging writing style, and a talent for making individual stories serve the whole. . . . Top marks, too, for the volume's photographs and historical renderings, which so intensely illustrate the pages." Booklist

Includes bibliographical references

Pritzker, Barry

A **Native** American encyclopedia; history, culture, and peoples. [by] Barry M. Pritzker. Oxford Univ. Press 2000 591p il hardcover o.p. pa $29.95   **970.004**

1. Reference books 2. Native Americans -- Encyclopedias

ISBN 0-19-513897-X; 0-19-513877-5 pa

LC 99-53677

First published 1998 by ABC-CLIO as a two-volume set with title: Native Americans

"Organized geographically, each section begins with an introduction to the area and its original inhabitants. Tribal entries follow, with some smaller related groups discussed together. Each article includes sections on location, population, language, history, religion, government, customs, dwellings, diet, key technology, trade, notable arts, transportation, dress, and war/weapons. A contemporary section follows, with information on government/reservations, economy, legal status, and daily life." Libr J [review of 1998 edition]

Includes bibliographical references

Rajtar, Steve

Indian war sites; a guidebook to battlefields, monuments, and memorials, state by state with Canada and Mexico. McFarland & Co. 1999 330p $39.95   **970.004**

1. Native Americans -- Wars

ISBN 0-7864-0710-7

LC 99-25893

This is a "reference to hundreds of conflicts, both major and minor, between American Indians and Europeans. Divided alphabetically by state and then chronologically within each, entries include name and date, a nonspecific location (e.g., Spring River), a brief description, and bibliographic sources. If the battle was a part of a larger war Rajtar also gives the name of the war; and if there is a monument, he tells its location and briefly describes what's there." Libr J

Includes bibliographical references

Richter, Daniel K.

Facing east from Indian country; a Native history of early America. Harvard Univ. Press 2001 317p il maps $27.50; pa $15.95   **970.004**

1. Native Americans

ISBN 0-674-00638-0; 0-674-01117-1 pa

LC 2001-24997

The author "recasts early American history from the Native American point of view and in doing so illuminates as much about the Europeans as about the original Americans. . . . Exploring the varying complexities of different native people's relationships with England, France and Spain, he argues that the Native Americans were safer during the colonial era than after the Revolution. . . . Gracefully written and argued, Richter's compelling research and provocative claims make this an important addition to the literature for general readers of both Native American and U.S. studies." Publ Wkly

Includes bibliographical references and index

Robbins, Catherine C.

All Indians do not live in teepees (or casinos) University of Nebraska Press 2011 385p il map $26.95   **970.004**

1. Native Americans -- Social life and customs

ISBN 978-0-8032-3973-9; 0-8032-3973-4

LC 2011011320

"A solid, insightful overview of the way American Indians live now." Kirkus

Includes bibliographical references

Roberts, David

Once they moved like the wind; Cochise, Geronimo, and the Apache wars. Simon & Schuster 1993 368p il hardcover o.p. pa $22   **970.004**

1. Apache Indians 2. Indian chiefs 3. Native Americans -- Wars

ISBN 0-671-70221-1; 0-671-88556-1 pa

LC 93-7112

"The book is history at its most engrossing." Publ Wkly

Includes bibliographical references

Treuer, Anton

Atlas of Indian nations; by Anton Treuer. National Geographic Books 2013 319 p. ills.; maps; photos (color) (hardcover : alk. paper) $40 **970.004**

1. Native Americans -- North America 2. Native Americans -- History

ISBN 1426211600; 9781426211607; 9781426212567

LC 2013036634

This book, by Anton Treuer, "is a comprehensive resource for those interested in Native American history and culture. Told through maps, photos, art, and archival cartography, this is the story of American Indians. . . . Organized by region, this encyclopedic reference details Indian tribes in these areas: beliefs, sustenance, shelter, alliances and animosities, key historical events, and more." (Publisher's note)

"'The land made the first people of North America,' insists Ojibwe scholar Treuer (Everything You Wanted to Know About Indians but Were Afraid to Ask), and in this gorgeously illustrated volume employs the atlas format to demonstrate this reality. Chock full of historical and contemporary maps, photographs, and paintings, this smart hybrid of art book and textbook is irresistible to leaf through because of the eye-catching images on every page. But Treuer's clear, accessible text is the complementary gem." Pub Wkly

Includes bibliographical references and index

Waldman, Carl

Atlas of the North American Indian; 3rd ed; Facts on File 2009 450p il map (Facts on file library of American history) $85; pa $24.95　　**970.004**

1. Atlases 2. Reference books 3. Native Americans

ISBN 978-0-8160-6858-6; 0-8160-6858-5; 978-0-8160-6859-3 pa; 0-8160-6859-3 pa

LC 2008-40736

First published 1985

"This is a very well-designed book, a bargain for any library." Voice Youth Advocates [review of 2000 edition]

Includes glossary and bibliographical references

Encyclopedia of Native American tribes; 3rd rev ed; Facts on File 2006 xxiv, 360p il map (Facts on File library of American history) $75; pa $21.95　　**970.004**

1. Reference books 2. Native Americans -- Encyclopedias

ISBN 978-0-8160-6273-7; 0-8160-6273-0; 978-0-8160-6274-4 pa; 0-8160-6274-9 pa

LC 2006-12529

First published 1988

"This well-written and easily accessible encyclopedia of a good starting point for research on Native American tribes." Libr Media Connect

Includes bibliographical references

Weatherford, J. McIver

Native roots; how the Indians enriched America. [by] Jack Weatherford. Fawcett 1992 310p il map pa $13.95　　**970.004**

1. Native Americans

ISBN 978-0-449-90713-9; 0-449-90713-9

First published 1991 by Crown

"A valuable corrective to the sentimentality with which we regard the first U.S. settlers and developers." Booklist

Includes bibliographical references

Wilson, James

The **earth** shall weep; the history of Native Americans. Atlantic Monthly Press 1999 xxix, 466p maps hardcover o.p. pa $16　　**970.004**

1. Native Americans

ISBN 0-8021-3680-X pa

LC 99-13098

"Employing elegiac prose and steady narrative momentum, Wilson has written a richly informative history that places Native Americans 'at the center of the historical stage.'" Publ Wkly

Includes bibliographical references

Woodard, Colin

American nations; a history of the eleven rival regional cultures of North America. Viking 2011 371p map $30　　**970.004**

1. Multiculturalism 2. Regionalism -- North America 3. North America -- Race relations

ISBN 978-0-670-02296-0

LC 2011015196

The author's "take on American history identifies the original cultural settlements that became the United States, and proceeds with the thesis that these regional and cultural divisions are responsible for clashes stretching back to Revolutionary times. The 11 nations don't follow state or even country territory lines, but rather the paths taken by the earliest settlers of these areas; while later immigrants added to the mix, they didn't change the fundamental culture. . . . The book's compelling explanations and apt descriptions will fascinate anyone with an interest in politics, regional culture, or history." Publ Wkly

Includes bibliographical references

970.01　North America--Early history to 1599

Adovasio, J. M.

The **first** Americans; in pursuit of archaeology's greatest mystery. {by} J.M. Adovasio with Jake Page. Random House 2002 328p il maps hardcover o.p. pa $14.95　　**970.01**

1. America -- Antiquities 2. Native Americans -- Origin

ISBN 0-375-75704-X pa

LC 2002-69766

"Readers get a lively, close-up view of how archaeologists study America's original discoverers." Booklist

Includes bibliographical references

Archaeology of prehistoric native America; an encyclopedia. editor, Guy Gibbon; associate editors, Kenneth M. Ames [et al.] Garland 1998 lxxvii, 941p il map (Garland reference library of the humanites) $205　　**970.01**

1. Reference books 2. North America -- Antiquities -- Encyclopedias 3. Native Americans -- Antiquities -- Encyclopedias

ISBN 0-8153-0725-X

LC 98-11443

This encyclopedia includes alphabetically arranged entries covering North American prehistory and archaeology.

"This superb reference source . . . has no equal in its coverage of Native American cultures in North America prior to European contact." Libr J

Includes bibliographical references

Dillehay, Tom D.

★ The **settlement** of the Americas; a new prehistory. {by} Thomas D. Dillehay. Basic Bks. 2000 xxi, 371p il hardcover o.p. pa $22　　**970.01**

1. America -- Antiquities 2. America -- Exploration

ISBN 0-465-07669-6 pa

LC 00-27572

This "is a seminal work in the field that is accessible to lay readers." Libr J

Includes bibliographical references

Horwitz, Tony

★ A **voyage** long and strange; rediscovering the new world. Henry Holt and Co. 2008 445p il map $27.50 **970.01**

1. Explorers 2. America -- Exploration
ISBN 978-0-8050-7603-5; 0-8050-7603-4

LC 2007-45883

"Realizing that his knowledge of American history between Columbus's discovery and Plymouth Rock over 100 years later was sketchy at best, . . . [the author] sets out to educate himself with his own explorations. He intertwines his experiences retracing the early conquistadors, adventurers, and entrepreneurs through such regions as Newfoundland, the Dominican Republic, and the American South, Southwest, and New England with thoroughly researched accounts of the territories themselves, the natives who were historically affected, and the motives of the explorers. . . . This readable and vastly entertaining history travelog is highly recommended for public libraries." Libr J

Includes bibliographical references

Mann, Charles C.

1491; new revelations of the Americas before Columbus. Knopf 2005 465p il maps **970.01**

1. America -- Antiquities 2. Native Americans -- History
ISBN 1-4000-3205-9 pa; 1-4000-4006-X

LC 2005-42178

This is a portrait "of the Americas before the arrival of the Europeans in 1492." (Publisher's note) Index.

"Mann navigates adroitly through the controversies. He approaches each in the best scientific tradition, carefully sifting the evidence, never jumping to hasty conclusions, giving everyone a fair hearing—the experts and the amateurs; the accounts of the Indians and their conquerors. And rarely is he less than enthralling." N Y Times Book Rev

Includes bibliographical references

National Museum of Natural History (U.S.)

Vikings: the North Atlantic saga; edited by William W. Fitzhugh and Elisabeth I. Ward. Smithsonian Institution Press 2000 432p il maps hardcover o.p. pa $34.95 **970.01**

1. Vikings 2. America -- Exploration
ISBN 1-56098-970-X; 1-56098-995-5 pa

LC 99-57983

This book is "well designed, heavily illustrated and almost encyclopedic in scope and detail." Publ Wkly

Includes bibliographical references

Schneider, Paul

Brutal journey: the epic story of the first crossing of North America. Holt 2006 366p il maps $26 **970.01**

1. Explorers 2. America -- Exploration
ISBN 978-0-8050-6835-1; 0-8050-6835-X

LC 2005-50246

"Equally able in his dramatizations of the privations and brutalities suffusing this extraordinary tale, Schneider scores big with fans of historical (mis)adventure." Booklist

Includes bibliographical references

Schobinger, Juan

★ The **ancient** Americans; a reference guide to the art, culture, and history of pre-Columbian North and South America. translation, Carys Evans-Corrales; consultant, Susan Kart. Sharpe, M.E. 2000 2v il maps set $159 **970.01**

1. Native American art 2. Rock drawings, paintings, and engravings 3. America -- Antiquities 4. Native Americans -- Antiquities
ISBN 0-7656-8034-3

LC 00-56280

Original Spanish language edition, 1997

This reference "surveys the entire Western Hemisphere prior to the arrival of Europeans in the Americas. This copiously illustrated work is especially notable for its numerous full-color plates of Native American rock art." Libr J

Includes bibliographical references

970.3 Specific native peoples

Nabokov, Peter

How the World Moves; The Odyssey of an American Indian Family. Peter Nabokov. Penguin Group USA 2015 560 p. illustrations $32.95 **970.3**

1. Immigrants 2. Pueblo Indians
ISBN 0670024880; 9780670024889

In this book author Peter Nabokov "narrates the . . . story of [Edward Proctor] Hunt's life within a multicultural and historical context. Chronicling Pueblo Indian life and Anglo/Indian relations over the last century and a half, he explores how this entrepreneurial family capitalized on the nation's passion for Indian culture. Nabokov dramatizes how the Hunts, like immigrants throughout history, faced anguishing decisions over staying put or striking out for economic independence." (Publisher's note)

"The pull of the Pueblo was always powerful, and the familial ties and love of ceremony and song were sufficient to bring them back often. The lure of the Land of Enchantment is irresistible, as Nabokov draws us into the simple, cooperative life of the Pueblo Indians and their magnificent territory. A great choice for lovers of the Southwest." Kirkus

971 Canada

Black, Conrad, 1944-

Rise to greatness; the history of Canada from Vikings to the present. Conrad Black. McClelland & Stewart 2014 1106 p. 24 plates; ills.; portraits (hardcover : alk. paper) $50 **971**

1. Canada -- History
ISBN 1468309943; 9780771013546; 9780771013553

LC 2014944153

This book, by Conrad Black, "Spanning 874 to 2014, . . . challenges our perception of our history and Canada's role in the world. From Champlain to Carleton, Baldwin and Lafontaine, to MacDonald, Laurier, and King, Canada's role in peace and war, to Quebec's quest for autonomy, [author Conrad] Black takes on sweeping themes and vividly recounts the story of Canada's development from colony to dominion to country." (Publisher's note)

Gray, Charlotte

Gold diggers; striking it rich in the Klondike. Counterpoint 2010 413p il map $29.95 **971**

1. Gold mines and mining 2. Klondike River valley (Yukon) -- Gold discoveries 3. Frontier and pioneer life -- Klondike River valley (Yukon)

ISBN 978-1-58243-611-1

LC 2010-17805

This is "an enchanting recitation of lives—and deaths—in the Klondike during the gold rush over 100 years ago. Combining a keen eye for detail and firsthand histories of contemporary witnesses, Gray sets forth the lives of six 'stampeders,' including Jack London (who almost died in the wild before writing so wonderfully of those who did), Mountie Sam Steele, business wiz Belinda Mulrooney, highborn journalist Flora Shaw, devoted Jesuit priest William Judge, and, most of all, Bill Haskell, a simple soul who left America with a dream of exploration and riches." Libr J

Includes bibliographical references

MacDonald, Laura M.

Curse of the Narrows. Walker & Co. 2005 355p il maps $26 **971**

1. Explosions 2. Halifax (N.S.)

ISBN 0-8027-1458-7

LC 2005-44255

This "book captures in vivid detail the history of this catastrophe." Booklist

Includes bibliographical references

Mowat, Farley

High latitudes; an Arctic journey. foreword by Margaret Atwood. Steerforth Press 2003 300p map pa $15.95 **971**

1. Arctic regions 2. Natural history -- Canada

ISBN 1-58642-061-5

LC 2002-151151

First published 2002 in Canada

"In 1966, Mowat's publisher, Jack McClelland, sent Mowat into northern Canada to research an illustrated volume on the region. This book is the tale of that journey. Hopscotching by creaky plane from one isolated settlement to another, Mowat witnesses the devastation being wrought on the native peoples by encroaching white men, lured by a mirage of the north's supposedly limitless minerals and the raw beauty of the land and its people. A cavalcade of vivid, fiction-worthy characters fills these pages. . . . Voiced with a passionate sense of justice, this work is stirring reading from the bard of the Canadian north." Publ Wkly

Riendeau, Roger E.

★ A brief history of Canada; [by] Roger Riendeau. 2nd ed; Facts on File 2007 444p il map (Brief history) $45 **971**

1. Canada -- History

ISBN 978-0-8160-6335-2

LC 2006-47130

First published 2000

This is a history of Canada "beginning with the exploration of the Northern American frontier and continuing through the rise and fall of the French and British empires to the foundations of Canadian nationhood and the present day." Publisher's note

Includes bibliographical references

971.01 Early history to 1763

Macleod, D. Peter

Northern Armageddon; the Battle of the Plains of Abraham and the making of the American Revolution. Peter MacLeod. Alfred A. Knopf 2016 448 p. (hardcover : alk. paper) $35 **971.01**

1. Seven Years' War, 1756-1763 2. Canada -- History -- 1755-1763 3. Canada -- History -- To 1763 (New France) 4. Québec Campaign, Québec, 1759 5. Plains of Abraham, Battle of the, Québec, 1759

ISBN 0307269892; 9780307269898

LC 2015015893

In this book author Peter MacLeod "using original research--diaries, journals, letters, and firsthand accounts--and bringing to bear all of his extensive knowledge and grasp of warfare and colonial North American history, tells the epic story on a human scale. He writes of the British at Quebec through the eyes of a master's mate on one of the ships embroiled in the battle. And from the French perspective, as the British bombarded Quebec, of four residents of the city—a priest, a clerk, a nun, and a notary—caught in the crossfire." (Publisher's note)

"This is a superbly researched and written account of a seminal episode in world history." Booklist

Includes bibliographical references

972 Mexico, Central America, West Indies, Bermuda

Coe, Michael D.

The Maya; Michael D. Coe. 7th ed fully rev and expanded; Thames and Hudson 2005 272p il map (Ancient peoples and places) pa $22.50 **972**

1. Mayas

ISBN 978-0-500-28505-3; 0-500-28505-5

First published 1966 by Praeger

An illustrated survey of the Maya civilization, focusing on the achievements of the Classic Period, A.D. 300-900

Includes bibliographical references

Crutchfield, James A.

Revolt at Taos; The New Mexican and Indian Insurrection of 1847. James A. Crutchfield. Westholme Pub Llc 2015 400 p. illustrations, maps (hardcover) $29.95 **972**

1. Insurgency 2. Taos (N.M.) -- History

ISBN 1594162239; 9781594162237

LC 2015451017

This book, by James A. Crutchfield, describes the events surrounding the New Mexican/Indian revolt of Taos in 1847 and its aftermath. "On the morning of January 19, 1847,

Charles Bent, the newly appointed governor of the American-claimed territory of New Mexico, was savagely killed at his home in Don Fernando de Taos, a small, remote town located north of Santa Fe." (Publisher's note)

"This broad treatment of the Taos Revolt is a sincere attempt to view events and consequences from the perspectives of all peoples involved. Recommended for the examination of civil rights during the forced Americanization of established residents of New Mexico territory." LJ

Diaz del Castillo, Bernal

The **discovery** and conquest of Mexico, 1517-1521; translated by A.P. Maudslay. Da Capo Press 2003 478p il map pa $24 **972**
1. Mexico -- History
ISBN 0-306-81319-X; 978-0-306-81319-1
First published 1956 by Farrar, Straus & Giroux
"The memoirs of an old man, who began to write of his experiences half a century after they occurred and completed his account at the age of 84, they are not free from minor inaccuracies, but they are the most reliable narrative that exists." Chicago Sunday Trib

Foster, Lynn V.

★ A **brief** history of Mexico; 4th ed; Facts On File 2009 324p il map (Brief history) $49.50; pa $19.95 **972**
1. Mexico -- History
ISBN 978-0-8160-7405-1; 978-0-8160-7406-8 pa
LC 2009-18298
First published 1997
An overview of Mexican history covering pre-Columbian civilizations and contemporary indigenous cultures. Language, art, religion, politics and economics are discussed. A chronology and bibliography are included.
Includes bibliographical references

Henderson, Timothy J.

The **Mexican** Wars for Independence. Hill and Wang 2009 xxiii, 246p il map $27.50 **972**
1. Mexico -- History
ISBN 978-0-8090-9509-4; 0-8090-9509-2
LC 2008-48141
"A solid overview of a decidedly difficult time and place, and a lucid introduction for those unfamiliar with Mexican history." Kirkus
Includes bibliographical references

Kirkwood, Burton

The **history** of Mexico; 2nd ed.; Greenwood Press/ABC-CLIO 2010 258p il map (Greenwood histories of the modern nations) $49.95 **972**
1. Mexico -- History
ISBN 978-0-313-36601-7; 0-313-36601-2
LC 2009036964
First published 2000
A historical survey of Mexico and its people from the arrival of the first humans in the Western Hemisphere to the first decade of the 21st century. Topics range from Mexico's cultural past to more current issues such as the war on drugs and the North American Free Trade Agreement.
Includes bibliographical references

Meyer, Michael C.

★ The **course** of Mexican history; [by] Michael C. Meyer, William L. Sherman, Susan M. Deeds. 8th ed.; Oxford University Press 2007 688p il map hardcover o.p. pa $64.95 **972**
1. Mexico -- History
ISBN 0-19-517835-1; 978-0-19-517835-7; 0-19-517836-X pa; 978-0-19-517836-4 pa
LC 2006-51741
A chronologically arranged survey of the political, economic, social, and cultural history of Mexico, ranging from the pre-Columbian period to the present.
Includes bibliographical references

The **Oxford** history of Mexico; edited by Michael C. Meyer and William H. Beezley. Oxford Univ. Press 2000 709p il maps $45 **972**
1. Mexico -- History
ISBN 0-19-511228-8
LC 99-56044
The editors "have compiled 20 previously unpublished essays by experts who explore Mexico from precolonial times to the present. . . . Examining the country with new and different approaches, the contributors challenge traditional historical concepts on a variety of issues." Libr J
Includes bibliographical references

Prescott, William Hickling

History of the conquest of Mexico. Modern Lib. 1998 xxvi, 1005p hardcover o.p. pa $17.95 **972**
1. Aztecs 2. Explorers 3. Mexico -- History 4. Colonial administrators
ISBN 0-375-75803-8 pa
LC 98-10173
First published 1843 in three volumes
This is a history of the subjugation of the Aztec people by Hernan Cortez and his soldiers between 1519 and 1522.

Smith, Michael Ernest

The **Aztecs**; [by] Michael E. Smith. 2nd ed; Blackwell 2003 367p il maps (Peoples of America) hardcover o.p. pa $29.95 **972**
1. Aztecs 2. Mexico -- Antiquities
ISBN 0-631-23015-7; 0-631-23016-5 pa
LC 2001-6950
First published 1996
The author "summarizes the results of archaeological research conducted largely in the past 30 years into the everyday lives of ordinary people in the villages, hamlets, and farmsteads from many regions of central Mexico. His method permits a fresh view of such topics as agricultural methods, population size, market system, relations between city-states and the empire, and even human sacrifice. Smith carries his social account of these people through transformation under Spanish rule and their legacy in modern Mexico." Libr J [review of 1996 edition]
Includes bibliographical references

Townsend, Richard F.

The **Aztecs**; 3rd ed; Thames & Hudson 2009 256p il map (Ancient peoples and places) pa $24.95   **972**
1. Aztecs
ISBN 978-0-500-28791-0
LC 2008-908216
First published 1992
"Examines the history of these accomplished people through a review of the monuments and artifacts they left behind; exploring how their water-control projects worked, the purposes of their ceremonial centers, and the way they built their incredible ancient structures that still stand today." Publisher's note
Includes bibliographical references

972.08   Mexico since 1867

Fuentes, Carlos

A **new** time for Mexico; translated from the Spanish by Marina Gutman Castañeda and the author. University of Calif. Press 1997 226p pa $16.95   **972.08**
1. Mexico -- Politics and government
ISBN 0-520-21183-9
LC 97-8427
First published 1996 by Farrar, Straus, & Giroux
In these essays "Fuentes calls on Mexican president Ernesto Zedillo to take definitive steps toward a full democracy—electoral reform; equal access of candidates to the media; independent, aggressive labor unions; and, above all, true separation between the ruling party and the government. . . . Offering lapidary, lyrical meditations on Mexico as a land of continual metamorphosis, Fuentes nostalgically reminisces about his home in Veracruz, whose port his father defended against a Yankee invasion in 1914." Publ Wkly

Katz, Friedrich

The **life** and times of Pancho Villa. Stanford Univ. Press 1998 985p hardcover o.p. pa $30.95 **972.08**
1. Outlaws 2. Revolutionaries 3. Mexico -- History
ISBN 0-8047-3046-6 pa
LC 97-47271
The author "traces Pancho Villa's rise from relatively obscure outlaw to national leader of the Mexican Revolution (1910-20) and his subsequent decline to guerrilla leader. . . .{This} is likely to be the definitive account of Villa for years to come." Libr J
Includes bibliographical references

Lewis, Oscar

★ The **children** of Sanchez; autobiography of a Mexican family. Random House 1961 xxxi, 499p hardcover o.p. pa $17   **972.08**
1. Family 2. Poor -- Mexico City (Mexico) 3. Mexico City (Mexico) -- Social conditions
ISBN 0-394-70280-8 pa
"Oscar Lewis has made something brilliant and of singular significance, a work of such unique concentration and sympathy." N Y Times Book Rev

Womack, John

Zapata and the Mexican Revolution. Knopf 1969 435p il hardcover o.p. pa $17   **972.08**
1. Revolutionaries 2. Mexico -- History
ISBN 0-394-70853-9 pa
The author reconstructs the "history of the agrarian revolution in southern Mexico from the late Diaz period to about 1920. The work is well written {and} carefully conceived." Choice

972.8   Other parts of Middle America

Perez-Brignoli, Hector

A **brief** history of Central America; translated by Ricardo B. Sawrey A. and Susana Stettri de Sawrey. University of Calif. Press 1989 223p maps hardcover o.p. pa $18.97   **972.8**
1. Central America -- History
ISBN 0-520-06832-7 pa
LC 89-31889
This book presents the economic, political and cultural history of Guatemala, Honduras, El Salvador, Nicaragua and Costa Rica, the five national states of Central America
"For interested laypersons, this is an excellent introduction with an accurate sense of the region." Libr J
Includes bibliographical references

972.81   Guatemala

Carlsen, William

Jungle of Stone; The True Story of Two Men, Their Extraordinary Journey, and the Discovery of the Lost Civilization of the Maya. by William Carlsen (Author) HarperCollins 2016 496 p. ill. (some color), maps $28.99   **972.81**
1. Explorers 2. Ancient civilization 3. Mayas -- Antiquities 4. Central America -- Civilization
ISBN 0062407392; 9780062407399
In this book, by William Carlsen, "In 1839 rumors of . . . stone ruins buried within the unmapped jungles of Central America reached two of the world's most intrepid travelers. . . . [John Lloyd] Stephens and [Frederick] Catherwood . . . documented the remains of an astonishing civilization that had flourished in the Americas. . . . [They] were the first to grasp the significance of the Maya remains." (Publisher's note)
"A captivating history of two men who dramatically changed their contemporaries' view of the past." Kirkus
Includes bibliographical references (pages [467]-515) and index.

Coe, Michael D.

Royal cities of the ancient Maya; Michael D. Coe; photographs by Barry Brukoff. Vendome Press 2012 224 p. $50   **972.81**
1. Mayas -- History 2. Cities and towns -- HIstory 3. Maya architecture 4. Mayas -- Antiquities 5. Central

America -- Antiquities
ISBN 0865652848; 9780865652842

LC 2011051139

This book presents the "history of Mayan civilization as seen through the development and decline of its many impressive city-states." It offers "glimpses, through dated stone monuments, into the hereditary lines of dynastic kings who ruled Mayan city-states and frequently did battle with each other." (Library Journal)

Includes bibliographical references

Encyclopedia of the ancient Maya; edited by Walter R. T. Witschey. Rowman & Littlefield 2015 574 p. (cloth : alk. paper) $95   **972.81**
1. Mayas 2. Mayas -- Encyclopedias
ISBN 9780759122840

LC 2015032712

This book, edited by Walter R. T. Witschey, "offers an A-to-Z overview of the ancient Maya culture from its inception around 3000 BC to the Spanish Conquest after AD 1600. Over two hundred entries written by more than sixty researchers explore subjects ranging from food, clothing, and shelter to the sophisticated calendar and now-deciphered Maya writing system." (Publisher's note)

"The work would be a valuable resource for undergraduate students of archaeology, anthropology, history, Latino studies, and art history." Booklist

Includes bibliographical references and index

Goldman, Francisco
The **art** of political murder; who killed the Bishop? Grove Press 2007 396p il map $25   **972.81**
1. Bishops 2. Trials (Homicide) 3. Murder victims 4. Human rights activists 5. Guatemala -- Politics and government
ISBN 978-0-8021-1828-8; 0-8021-1828-3

This book "is a tour de force, not just for . . . [the author's] reportorial tenacity . . . but because his novelist's eye and his deep understanding of Guatemalan society take you places no other reporter could." Nation

Includes bibliographical references

972.87   Panama

McCullough, David G.
★ The **path** between the seas; the creation of the Panama Canal, 1870-1914. [by] David McCullough. Simon & Schuster 1977 698p il maps hardcover o.p. pa $18   **972.87**
1. Diplomats 2. Governors 3. Physicians 4. Presidents 5. Panama Canal 6. Vice-presidents 7. Army officers 8. Public health officials 9. Nobel laureates for peace
ISBN 0-671-24409-4

LC 76-57967

"Not only is this a well-told story of the building of the Panama Canal but it also supplies welcome background for the . . . debate on the canal's role in inter-American relations." Booklist

Includes bibliographical references

972.9   West Indies (Antilles) and Bermuda

Gibson, Carrie
Empire's Crossroads; A History of the Caribbean from Columbus to the Present Day. Carrie Gibson. Atlantic Monthly Press 2014 448 p. color illustrations; maps $28   **972.9**
1. World history 2. Caribbean Region
ISBN 0802126146; 9780802126146

LC 2015430678

In this book author "Carrie Gibson traces the story of [the Caribbean] from the northern rim of South America up to Cuba, and from discovery through colonialism to today, offering a . . . panoramic view of this complex region and its rich, important history. Gibson wields . . . detail to combat the myths that have romanticized this region as one of uniform white sand beaches where the palm trees always sway." (Publisher's note)

"Alongside her stark descriptions of the slave economies, Gibson recounts geopolitical events that have periodically wracked the Caribbean Sea, from wars galore in the 1700s to the Cold War, as well as the supplanting of European suzerainty by American influence, expressed today more by cruise ship than by gunboat. Sympathetically attuned to the hard actualities of life in ostensibly paradisaical tropics, Gibson delivers a fine, faceted history for general-interest readers." Booklist

Kincaid, Jamaica, 1946-
A **small** place. Farrar, Straus & Giroux 1988 81p hardcover o.p. pa $11   **972.9**
1. Antigua and Barbuda 2. Antigua (Antigua and Barbuda)
ISBN 0-374-52707-5 pa

LC 88-376

The author of Annie John (BRD 1986) addresses foreign visitors to her country, the island of Antigua. In this essay, she discusses the poverty and political corruption of the island, which she views as a legacy of British colonialism and also as a result of an economy controlled by tourism.

Von Tunzelmann, Alex
Red heat; conspiracy, murder, and the Cold War in the Caribbean. Henry Holt 2011 449p il $30; ebook $14.99   **972.9**
1. Generals 2. Physicians 3. Presidents 4. Revolutionaries 5. Haiti -- History 6. Communist leaders 7. Political leaders 8. Cuba -- History -- 1959- 9. Caribbean region -- History 10. Dominican Republic -- History 11. Haiti -- History -- 1934-1986 12. Caribbean region -- History -- 1945- 13. Dominican Republic -- History -- 1930-1961 14. Caribbean region -- Foreign relations -- United States 15. United States -- Foreign relations -- Caribbean region
ISBN 978-0-8050-9067-3; 978-1-4299-6673-3 ebook

LC 2010-37585

"Three dictators, circa 1960—Castro in Cuba, François Duvalier in Haiti, and Rafael Trujillo in the Dominican Republic—are the principals in von Tunzelmann's political history. Recounting alarms that trio set off in Washington, she ponders how well the Eisenhower and Kennedy administrations understood situations on the islands of Cuba and

Hispaniola. Not very realistically, runs the tenor of von Tunzelmann's narrative. . . . Punctuated by accounts of such major incidents as the Bay of Pigs, the assassination of Trujillo, the Cuban missile crisis, and LBJ's 1965 intervention in the Dominican Republic, von Tunzelmann's diligent work will widen the eyes of cold war buffs." Booklist

Includes bibliographical references

972.91   Cuba

Cooke, Julia

The **other** side of paradise; life in the new Cuba. Julia Cooke. Seal Press 2014 248 p. (paperback) $17   **972.91**
1. Havana (Cuba) 2. Cuba -- Social life and customs 3. Havana (Cuba) -- Biography 4. Cuba -- History -- 1990- -- Biography 5. Cuba -- Politics and government -- 1990- 6. Young adults -- Cuba -- Havana -- Biography 7. Havana (Cuba) -- Social conditions -- 21st century 8. Havana (Cuba) -- Social life and customs -- 21st century 9. Social change -- Cuba -- Havana -- History -- 21st century
ISBN 1580055311; 9781580055314
LC 2013044413

This book by Julia Cook describes how "[t]his last generation of Cubans raised under Fidel Castro animate life in a waning era of political stagnation as the rest of the world beckons: waiting out storms at rummy hurricane parties and attending raucous drag cabarets, planning ascendant music careers and black-market business ventures, trying to reconcile the undefined future with the urgent today." (Publisher's note)

"An absorbing and educational read about contemporary Cuba, the love of its people for their country, and their hope for opportunity." LJ

Includes bibliographical references

Gimbel, Wendy

Havana dreams; a story of Cuba. Knopf 1998 234p il hardcover o.p. pa $13   **972.91**
1. Defectors 2. Presidents 3. Mistresses 4. Socialites 5. Cuba -- History 6. Communist leaders 7. Children of prominent persons
ISBN 0-679-75070-3 pa
LC 98-14571

Gimbel "succeeds in showing the complexity of family relationships resulting from the Cuban revolution, which extends into two countries." Libr J

Includes bibliographical references

Guevara March, Aleida, 1960-

Remembering Che; my life with Che Guevara. Aleida March; [translated by Pilar Aguilera] Ocean Press 2012 viii, 168 p.p ill.   **972.91**
1. Cuba -- History -- 1958-1959, Revolution 2. Cuba -- History -- 1990- 3. Cuba -- History -- 1959-1990 4. Revolutionaries -- Latin America -- Biography 5. Revolutionaries' spouses -- Latin America -- Biography
ISBN 0987077937; 9780987077936; 9780987077998
LC 2011943980

Author Aleida March "evokes the memories of her partner, Ernesto Che Guevara. She describes their great romance and life together from the days when they first met as fellow guerrillas in Cuba's revolutionary war up to the tragic moment when she learned of Che's assassination in Bolivia less than a decade later. . . . She also describes her efforts to raise her four children as ordinary children despite their father's legendary status in Cuba and abroad." (Publisher's note)

Includes bibliographical references

Guillermoprieto, Alma

Dancing with Cuba; a memoir of the revolution. translated from the Spanish by Esther Allen. Pantheon 2004 290p $25; pa $13   **972.91**
1. Cuba -- Description and travel
ISBN 0-375-42093-2; 0-375-72581-4 pa
LC 2003-44200

"Guillermoprieto vividly and purposefully recounts her acute discomfort with the strained and ludicrous rhetoric of the revolution, her sorrow over Castro's catastrophic failures, her astonishment at the great valor of Cuba's people, and her gradual recognition of her true calling as a journalist." Booklist

Martinez-Fernandez, Luis

Encyclopedia of Cuba; people, history, culture. edited by Luis Martinez-Fernández [et al.] Greenwood Press 2003 2v il maps set $174.95   **972.91**
1. Reference books 2. Cuba -- Encyclopedias
ISBN 1-57356-334-X
LC 2002-70030

"The editors intend this work to be a non-politicized look at Cuban people, politics, history, and culture. Chapters cover topics such as history, government, and popular culture. Within each chapter, entries are in alphabetical order. An excellent introduction to a colorful and important nation." Booklist

Includes bibliographical references

Perez, Louis A.

Cuba; between reform and revolution. Oxford University Press 2006 442p il map (Latin American histories) $77.95; pa $34.95   **972.91**
1. Cuba -- History
ISBN 0-19-517911-0; 978-0-19-517911-8; 0-19-517912-9 pa; 978-0-19-517912-5 pa
LC 2004-65477

First published 1988

"A narrative history that emphasizes the antecedents of the Cuban revolution and concludes with an analysis of Fidel Castro's successes and failures." N Y Public Libr Book of How & Where to Look It Up [entry for 1988 edition]

Includes bibliographical references

Rasenberger, Jim

The **brilliant** disaster; JFK, Castro, and America's doomed invasion of Cuba's Bay of Pigs. Scribner 2011 460p il   **972.91**
1. Presidents 2. Senators 3. Communist leaders 4. Members of Congress 5. Cuba -- History -- 1961, Invasion 6. Cuba -- Foreign relations -- United States

7. United States -- Foreign relations -- Cuba
ISBN 978-1-4165-9650-9

LC 2011-4178

"On Apr., 17, 1961, a CIA-trained brigade of 1,400 Cuban exiles, mostly students and former soldiers, made an unsuccessful amphibious assault on the Bay of Pigs, in southern Cuba, hoping to spur a popular revolt and overthrow the Castro regime. Fifty years later, Rasenberger . . . succeeds admirably in offering a nuanced view of the entire botched operation, from its planning in two U.S. administrations to the Cuban armed forces' quick defeat of the exiles, whose attack lacked air cover and the element of surprise." Kirkus
Includes bibliographical references

Suchlicki, Jaime
Cuba; from Columbus to Castro and beyond.
{by} Jaime Suchlicki. 5th ed; Brassey's 2002 285p
pa $24.95 **972.91**
1. Cuba -- History
ISBN 1-57488-436-0

LC 2002-3953

First published 1997
A summary of Cuba's development, with emphasis on the twentieth century and the factors that led to the Cuban revolution
Includes bibliographical references

Symmes, Patrick
The **boys** from Dolores; Fidel Castro's schoolmates from revolution to exile. Pantheon Books 2007 352p $26.95 **972.91**
1. Presidents 2. Communist leaders 3. Colegio de Dolores (Cuba) 4. Cuba -- Description and travel
ISBN 978-0-375-42283-6; 0-375-42283-8

LC 2006-30323

"The author writes of Castro's schoolmates from Dolores, the private Jesuit academy in Santiago de Cuba on the island's eastern end, and he visits several of them. . . . Among the Dolores students were Castro's brothers Raul and Ramon and a future star in North American television, Desi Arnaz. But it is Cuban intellectuals like Lundy Aguilar to whom Symmes turns for insights into Cuba before and after Castro's revolution. The result is a remarkable account of the country and its people." Libr J

972.94 Haiti

Dubois, Laurent
Haiti; the aftershocks of history. Laurent Dubois.
1st ed.; Henry Holt and Co. 2012 p. cm. $32 **972.94**
1. Haiti -- History
ISBN 978-0-8050-9335-3

LC 2011020162

"Building on his landmark synthesis of revolutionary Haiti. . . , Dubois summarizes colonial slave society and the liberation era, then thoroughly covers poorly understood 19th-century developments. Ongoing tensions between ruling elites and rural citizens characterized this period. Elites hoped to restore the plantation regime's coercive labor relations; peasants sought title to land for subsistence farming and local market production. Dubois persuasively argues that the resulting stalemate defines much of Haiti's history, shaping political as well as agricultural life." (Choice Reviews)
Includes bibliographical references

Laferriee, Dany
The **World** Is Moving Around Me; A Memoir of the Haiti Earthquake. Dany Laferrière; translated by David Homel. Arsenal Pulp Press 2013 192 p. $15.95 **972.94**
1. Natural disasters 2. Haiti Earthquake, Haiti, 2010
ISBN 1551524988; 9781551524986

LC 2012517880

This book by Dany Laferriere "is an eyewitness account of the [January 12, 2010 earth]quake and its aftermath. In a series of vignettes, Laferrière reveals the shock, rage, and grief experienced by those around him, the acts of heroism he witnessed, and his own sense of survivor guilt. This book is not only the chronicle of a natural disaster; it is also a personal meditation about the responsibility and power of the written word." (Publisher's note)

973 United States

Alvarez, Alex
Native America and the question of genocide; Alex Alvarez. Rowman & Littlefield Publishers, Inc. 2014 222 p. (Studies in genocide: religion, history, and human rights) (cloth : alk. paper) $40 **973**
1. Genocide 2. Native Americans -- United States 3. United States -- Social policy 4. United States -- Race relations 5. United States -- Politics and government
ISBN 1442225815; 9781442225817; 9781442225824

LC 2013048466

"Did Native Americans suffer genocide? This controversial question lies at the heart of 'Native America and the Question of Genocide.' After reviewing the various meanings of the word genocide, author Alex Alvarez examines a range of well-known examples . . . to determine where genocide occurred and where it did not. The book explores the destructive beliefs of the European settlers, and then looks at topics including disease, war, and education through the lens of genocide." (Publisher's note)
"In his sensitive treatment of this difficult issue, Alvarez strikes a balance between scholarly pragmatism and a humanist's empathy for the victims of this immense tragedy." Booklist
Includes bibliographical references and index

Americans at war; society, culture, and the homefront. John P. Resch, Editor in Chief. Macmillan Reference USA 2005 4v il set $395 **973**
1. War and civilization 2. United States -- Civilization 3. United States -- Military history
ISBN 0-02-865806-X

LC 2004-17314

This book "delivers well-written articles and would make an excellent addition to high-school, academic, and public libraries." Booklist
Includes bibliographical references

Appleby, Joyce Oldham

Inheriting the revolution; the first generation of Americans. {by} Joyce Appleby. Belknap Press 2000 322p il hardcover o.p. pa $16   973

    1. United States -- Social conditions 2. United States -- History -- 1783-1865

    ISBN 0-674-00236-9; 0-674-00663-1 pa

                     LC 99-49787

"This book provides a splendid introduction to the period for students and general readers." Libr J

Includes bibliographical references

Ashby, Ruth

The **great** american documents; Volume 1, 1620-1830. Ruth Ashby; illustrated by Ernie Colón; editorial consultant Russell Motter. Hill and Wang 2014 160 p. col. ill. (hardcover) $40   973

    1. United States -- History -- Sources 2. United States -- Politics and government -- Sources

    ISBN 0809094606; 9780809094608

                   LC 2013956401

Written by Ruth Ashby and illustrated by Ernie Colón, "'The Great American Documents: Volume 1' introduces as series narrator none other than Uncle Sam, who walks us through twenty essential documents. Each document gets a chapter, in which Uncle Sam explains its key passages, its origins, how it came to be written, and its impact. This graphic primer is an indispensable resource for students and anyone else who wants the facts of American history close at hand." (Publisher's note)

"Colon uses well-designed, full-color panel layouts to eloquently blend charts and other informative graphics with straightforward images of events, clothing, and customs as well as clear, concise metaphors, all with an eye toward promoting a solid understanding of the basic facts and their impact." Booklist

Includes bibliographical references

Berger, Joseph

The **pious** ones; the world of Hasidim and their battles with America. Joseph Berger. Harper Perennial 2014 384 p. (paperback) $15.99   973

    1. Ethnic relations 2. Jews -- New York (N.Y.) 3. Hasidim -- Social conditions 4. New York (N.Y.) -- Ethnic relations 5. Hasidim -- New York (State) -- New York -- Social conditions 6. Jews -- New York (State) -- New York -- Social life and customs

    ISBN 0062123343; 9780062123343; 9780062123350

                   LC 2014011724

In this book, "journalist Joseph Berger takes us inside the notoriously insular world of the Hasidim to explore their origins, beliefs, and struggles--and the social and political implications of their expanding presence in America. . . . Berger traces their origins in eighteenth-century Eastern Europe, illuminating their dynamics and core beliefs that remain so enigmatic to outsiders." (Publisher's note)

"Through Berger's solid research and approachable writing, readers will gain a clear, well-rounded understanding of who the Hasidim are, where they came from and where they are going as a people." Kirkus

Boorstin, Daniel J.

The **Americans**: The colonial experience. Random House 1958 434p hardcover o.p. pa $15 973

    1. Puritans 2. Americanisms 3. Society of Friends 4. American national characteristics 5. Georgia -- History 6. Law -- United States 7. United States -- Civilization 8. United States -- Intellectual life 9. Colleges and universities -- United States 10. United States -- History -- 1600-1775, Colonial period

    ISBN 0-394-70513-0 pa

The first volume of the author's trilogy entitled: The Americans

"This study of colonial America attempts to show that it was not merely an offshoot of the mother country, but a new civilization. . . . The author centers his highly informative work on colonial education, the special qualities of American speech, and the growth of a distinct culture." Booklist

Includes bibliographical references

The **Americans**: The democratic experience. Random House 1973 717p hardcover o.p. pa $19   973

    1. Advertising 2. American art 3. Americanisms 4. Higher education 5. Automobile industry 6. United States -- Civilization 7. Cities and towns -- United States 8. United States -- Social conditions 9. United States -- Economic conditions

    ISBN 0-394-71011-8 pa

Concluding volume of the author's trilogy which began with The Americans: The colonial experience and continued with The Americans: The national experience

This volume is concerned with the democratization of the national character over the past hundred years and the growth of technology

Includes bibliographical references

The **Americans**: The national experience. Random House 1965 517p hardcover o.p. pa $16 973

    1. Americanisms 2. Federal government 3. Heroes and heroines 4. American national characteristics 5. America -- Exploration 6. African Americans -- Religion 7. United States -- Civilization 8. United States -- Intellectual life 9. Constitutional history -- United States 10. Colleges and universities -- United States

    ISBN 0-394-70358-8 pa

This is the second volume of the author's trilogy

A cultural interpretation of American history, this book traces "the roots of contemporary American life to the years between the Revolution and the Civil War." Booklist

Includes bibliographical references

Hidden history; selected and edited by Daniel J. Boorstin and Ruth F. Boorstin. Vintage Books 1989 332p pa $15   973

    1. United States -- Civilization

    ISBN 978-0-679-72223-6; 0-679-72223-8

First published 1987 by Harper & Row

"A collection of essays and abridgments from [Boorstin's] books that investigates certain overlooked or disregarded corners of history. . . . History engagingly written, deeply felt, widely appealing." Booklist

Bracks, Lean'tin

African American almanac; 400 years of triumph, courage and excellence. Lean'tin Bracks. Visible Ink Press 2012 xiii, 543 p.p ill. (pbk.) $22.95   **973**

1. Almanacs 2. African Americans -- History 3. African Americans -- Encyclopedias 4. African Americans -- Biography -- Encyclopedias 5. African Americans -- Biography 6. African Americans -- Intellectual life 7. African Americans -- Social life and customs
ISBN 1578593239; 9781578593231

LC 2011038636

This reference book by Lean'tin Bracks "chronicles the African American experience from the arrival of the first Africans to North America in the early 1600s to the present day," including an almanac of topics such as Civil Rights, politics, and music, as well as biographies of various notable African Americans. "Bracks also gives context to less documented areas of African American history." (Booklist)

"This mostly excellent overview of African American contributions to the United States will be a welcome addition to school, public, and community college libraries." LJ

Includes bibliographical references (p. 469-477) and index

Burke, Kevin M.

And Still I Rise; Black America Since MLK. Henry L. Gates, Kevin M. Burke. HarperCollins 2015 336 p. illustrations (chiefly color) (ebook) $32.99; (hardcover) $35   **973**

1. United States -- Race relations 2. African Americans -- Social conditions 3. African Americans -- History -- Chronology
ISBN 9780062427014; 0062427008; 9780062427007

This book by Henry L. Gates and Kevin M. Burke explores "the last half-century of the African American experience. More than fifty years after the passage of the Civil Rights Act and the birth of Black Power, the United States has both a black president and black CEOs running Fortune 500 companies—and a large black underclass beset by persistent poverty, inadequate education, and an epidemic of incarceration. . . . [Gates] raises . . . vital questions about this dichotomy." (Publisher's note)

"This is an amazing collection of images of achievement on the long road to equality in the U.S." Booklist

Includes bibliographical references (pages 287-307) and index.

Churchill, Winston S.

The great republic; a history of America. edited by Winston S. Churchill. Random House 1999 454p hardcover o.p. pa $15.95   **973**

1. United States -- History
ISBN 0-375-50320-X; 978-0-375-75440-1 pa; 0-375-75440-7 pa

LC 99-28511

"The first half of the volume offers an old-fashioned narrative history of America's political development, from the age of exploration to the 1880s. The second half reprints articles that Churchill penned for English publications on such themes as Prohibition, the muckracking of Upton Sinclair, and the death of Franklin Delano Roosevelt." Libr J

Includes bibliographical references

Commager, Henry Steele

The American mind; an interpretation of American thought and character since the 1880's. Yale Univ. Press 1950 476p hardcover o.p. pa $14.95   **973**

1. Authors 2. Lawyers 3. Economics 4. Sociology 5. Economists 6. Journalism 7. Pragmatism 8. Philosophers 9. Psychologists 10. Law teachers 11. Sociologists 12. Social critics 13. College teachers 14. Authors, American 15. Nonfiction writers 16. Writers on science 17. Law -- United States 18. Supreme Court justices 19. United States -- Religion 20. United States -- Civilization 21. National characteristics, American 22. United States -- Intellectual life 23. United States -- Economic conditions 24. United States -- Politics and government
ISBN 0-300-00046-4 pa

Cornelison, Pam

★ The great American history fact-finder; the who, what, where, when, and why of American history. [by] Pam Cornelison and Ted Yanak. 2nd ed, updated and expanded; Houghton Mifflin 2004 608p il, maps pa $14.95   **973**

1. Reference books 2. United States -- History -- Dictionaries
ISBN 0-618-43941-2

LC 2004-47480

First published 1993 with authors' names in reverse order

This book provides "information about significant persons as well as political, legal, sporting, and cultural events in American history. Entries are alphabetically arranged, and related entries cross-referenced. . . . Besides an index, there are suggested readings and information on the states, presidents, vice presidents, population, Supreme Court, Articles of Confederation, Declaration of Independence, and US Constitution (with signers and nonsigners). This is a good quick reference." Choice

Curtis, Nancy C.

Black heritage sites; an African American odyssey and finder's guide. American Lib. Assn. 1996 677p il $75   **973**

1. Historic sites 2. African Americans -- History
ISBN 0-8389-0643-5

LC 95-5788

This "guide locates significant places in African-American history and supplies . . . recent addresses, phone numbers, and visitors' information. . . . Organized by region, a historical essay introduces each section, presenting the culture and history in that area." Publisher's note

Daily life through American history in primary documents; Randall M. Miller, general editor. Greenwood 2012 1099 p.   **973**

1. Archives -- United States 2. United States -- History -- Chronology 3. United States -- Social life and customs
ISBN 161069032X; 1610690338; 9781610690324; 9781610690331

LC 2011040023

In this history book, "four volumes are organized chronologically and then thematically and present the 'many small things that made up Americans' daily life.' Volumes are 'The

Colonial Period through the American Revolution,' 'The American Revolution to the Civil War,' 'The Civil War to World War I,' and 'World War I to the Present.' Each volume begins with a time line of selected events and a lengthy historical-overview essay describing significant themes, events, and concerns of the period. This is followed by about 100 primary documents that illustrate daily life." (Booklist)

Includes bibliographical references and index

★ **Encyclopedia** of American historical documents; edited by Susan Rosenfeld. Facts on File 2004 3v (Facts on File library of American history) set $300 **973**
1. United States -- History -- Sources
ISBN 0-8160-4995-5

LC 2003-51610

"Each section begins with an overview of the period and each document is introduced with commentary on when and why it was created and its significance, then and now. Entries include material 'with resonance for the 21st century' that represents turning points in U.S. history, and documents of a controversial nature. Students can read Supreme Court justices' opinions, presidential announcements and inaugural addresses, excerpts from noteworthy books that influenced American thought and action, and speeches of women and people of color. . . . Students and teachers will welcome this mammoth resource." SLJ

Includes bibliographical references

Encyclopedia of American history; Gary B. Nash, general editor. Rev. ed.; Facts on File 2010 11v il map (Facts on File library of American history) set $1,150 **973**
1. Reference books 2. United States -- History -- Encyclopedias
ISBN 978-0-8160-7136-4

LC 2008-35422

First published 2003

This encyclopedia provides a "presentation of the political, social, economic, and cultural events that have shaped the land and the nation." Publisher's note

Includes bibliographical references

Encyclopedia of rural America; the land and people. Gary A. Goreham, editor. 2nd ed; Grey House Pub. 2008 2v il map set $250 **973**
1. Reference books 2. United States -- Geography -- Encyclopedias 3. Country life -- United States -- Encyclopedias 4. United States -- Rural conditions -- Encyclopedias
ISBN 978-1-59237-115-0; 1-59237-115-9

First published 1997 by ABC-CLIO

"This encyclopedia covers a broad range of topics, such as agriculture, the arts, economics, the environment, health, humanities, and political and social science. The . . . alphabetically arranged entries, from addiction to worker's compensation, are listed in the front of each volume for handy reference." Booklist [review of 1997 edition]

Includes bibliographical references

Encyclopedia of the new American nation; the emergence of the United States, 1754-1829. Paul

Finkelman, editor in chief. Thomson Gale 2005 3v il map set $395 **973**
1. Reference books 2. United States -- History -- 1783-1865 -- Encyclopedias 3. United States -- History -- 1775-1783, Revolution -- Encyclopedias 4. United States -- History -- 1600-1775, Colonial period -- Encyclopedias
ISBN 0-684-31346-4

LC 2005-17783

The editor and contributors "have produced a wonderful reference source." Ref & User Services Quarterly

Includes bibliographical references

Encyclopedia of U.S. political history. CQ Press 2009 7v il map set $1200 **973**
1. Reference books 2. Political science -- Encyclopedias 3. United States -- Politics and government -- Encyclopedias
ISBN 978-0-87289-320-7

LC 2010-2253

"An impressive work remarkable for its breath and scope, this encyclopedia covers U.S. political history chronologically from the year 1500 to the present day. . . . Written in a vivid and accessible yet scholarly manner, this wonderful synthesis of history and political science will greatly benefit students, lovers of political history, and academics alike." Libr J

Includes bibliographical references

Encyclopedia of women and American politics; edited by Lynne E. Ford. Facts On File 2008 xx, 636 p.p (hc : alk. paper) $85 **973**
1. Feminism -- History 2. Women political activists 3. Women -- Political activity 4. Women in politics -- United States -- Encyclopedias 5. Women legislators -- United States -- Encyclopedias 6. United States -- Politics and government -- Encyclopedias
ISBN 0816054916; 9780816054916

LC 2007004331

Author Lynne E. Ford discusses "the role of women throughout America's political history. . . . [The book] contains more than 500 entries covering the people, events, and terms involved in the history of women and politics. . . . [The] encyclopedia also provides a biography for every woman who has served in the U.S. House of Representatives, the Senate, and the Supreme Court. Broad topics, such as sexual harassment, are cross-referenced with key events and people who are relevant to the topic." (Publisher's note)

Includes bibliographical references and index.

Eyewitness to America; 500 years of America in the words of those who saw it happen. edited by David Colbert. Pantheon Bks. 1997 xxx, 599p hardcover o.p. pa $16.95 **973**
1. United States -- History -- Sources
ISBN 0-679-44224-3; 0-679-76724-X pa

LC 96-24150

This volume contains a "panorama of first-person accounts of moments in the country's story that stretch from an October 10, 1492, diary entry by one of Columbus's crewmen to a 1994 e-mail message from Bill Gates. The nearly 300 entries tend to be short, preceded by informative introductions. The result is a feeling for history that is both immediate and dramatic." Publ Wkly

Includes bibliographical references

Glass, Brent D.

50 great American places; essential historic sites across the U.S. Brent D. Glass. Simon & Schuster 2016 320 p. illustrations $16 **973**

1. Historic sites 2. United States -- Description and travel 3. Historic sites -- United States -- Guidebooks

ISBN 1451682034; 9781451682038

LC 2015031714

This book, by Brent D. Glass, is a "guide to fifty of the most important cultural and historic sites in the United States. From Massachusetts to Florida to Washington to California, [it] takes you on a journey through our nation's history. Sharing the inside stories of sites as old as Mesa Verde (Colorado) and Cahokia (Illinois) and as recent as Silicon Valley (California) and the Mall of America (Minnesota), each essay provides the historical context." (Publisher's note)

"This book will whet the appetite of history buffs interested in possible destinations, or anybody who would like to learn American history through the places where it happened." Library Journal

Includes bibliographical references and index

Hofstadter, Richard

The **American** political tradition, and the men who made it; with a foreword by Christopher Lasch. 25th anniversary ed; Knopf 1973 xxxiii, 378p hardcover o.p. pa $14 **973**

1. Authors 2. Lawyers 3. Generals 4. Governors 5. Statesmen 6. Architects 7. Presidents 8. Abolitionists 9. Philanthropists 10. Vice-presidents 11. People with disabilities 12. Orators 13. Essayists 14. Handicapped 15. Philatelists 16. Political leaders 17. State legislators 18. College presidents 19. Secretaries of war 20. Members of Congress 21. Secretaries of state 22. Presidential candidates 23. Secretaries of commerce 24. Nobel laureates for peace 25. United States -- Politics and government

ISBN 0-679-72315-3 pa

First published 1948

This volume contains twelve essays, ten of which analyze the political careers of Lincoln, Jefferson, Jackson, Calhoun, Wendell Phillips, Bryan, Theodore Roosevelt, Wilson, Hoover and Franklin D. Roosevelt.

Includes bibliographical references

Kendall, Joshua C.

First dads; parenting and politics from George Washington to Barack Obama. Joshua Kendall. Grand Central Publishing 2016 400 p. illustrations (hardcover) $27 **973**

1. Presidents -- United States -- Children 2. Presidents -- United States -- Biography 3. Presidents -- United States -- History 4. Children of presidents -- United States -- History 5. Children of presidents -- United States -- Biography 6. Presidents -- Family relationships

-- United States -- History

ISBN 9781455551958

LC 2015050559

This book, by Joshua Kendall, explores how "every [U.S.] president has had some experience as a parent. . . . Each president's parenting style reveals much about his beliefs as well as his psychological make-up. . . . Based on research in archives around the country, Kendall shows presidential character in action." (Publisher's note)

"Kendall's research puts all the presidents and their parenting practices in perspective, giving readers great insight into these men and their children. Rich in detail, this informative book gives new understanding to our nation's leaders and their offspring." Kirkus

Includes bibliographical references and index

Lee, Erika

The **making** of Asian America; a history. by Erika Lee. Simon & Schuster 2015 416 p. illustrations, map (hardback) $29.95 **973**

1. Asian Americans -- History 2. Asians -- United States -- History 3. Racism -- United States -- History 4. United States -- Race relations -- History 5. United States -- Ethnic relations -- History 6. South Asia -- Emigration and immigration -- History 7. United States -- Emigration and immigration -- History

ISBN 9781476739403; 9781476739410

LC 2015010372

This book, by Erika Lee, "shows how generations of Asian immigrants and their American-born descendants have made and remade Asian American life in the United States: sailors who came on the first trans-Pacific ships in the 1500s; indentured 'coolies' who worked alongside African slaves in the Caribbean; and Chinese, Japanese, Filipino, Korean, and South Asian immigrants who were recruited to work in the United States only to face massive racial discrimination." (Publisher's note)

"An impressive work that details how this diverse population has both swayed and been affected by the United States." LJ

Lepore, Jill

★ The **mansion** of happiness; a history of life and death. Jill Lepore. 1st ed. Alfred A. Knopf 2012 xxxiii, 282 p.p $27.95 **973**

1. Life 2. Death 3. Popular culture 4. United States -- Intellectual life 5. United States -- Social conditions 6. United States -- Social life and customs 7. Popular culture -- United States -- History 8. Politics and culture -- United States -- History 9. Life -- Social aspects -- United States -- History 10. Death -- Social aspects -- United States -- History 11. Happiness -- Social aspects -- United States -- History 12. Life (Biology) -- Social aspects -- United States -- History 13. Life cycle, Human -- Social aspects -- United States -- History

ISBN 0307592995; 9780307592996

LC 2011050566

In this book Jill Lepore examines "the history of American ideas about life and death. . . . Lepore starts . . . with the story of a seventeenth-century Englishman who had the idea that all life begins with an egg and ends it with an American who, in the 1970s, began freezing the dead. . . . Investigating the surprising origins of the stuff of everyday life . . . Lepore argues that the age of discovery, Darwin, and the Space Age turned ideas about life on earth topsy-turvy." (Publisher's note)

Includes bibliographical references and index.

The **story** of America; essays on origins. Jill Lepore. Princeton University Press 2012 viii, 416 p.p (acid-free paper) $27.95   **973**
1. United States -- History 2. Democracy -- United States -- History 3. United States -- Politics and government 4. United States -- History -- Sources 5. United States -- Politics and government -- Sources
ISBN 069115399X; 9780691153995

LC 2012016854

In this book, "Jill Lepore investigates American origin stories . . . to show how American democracy is bound up with the history of print. . . . Part civics primer, part cultural history, 'The Story of America' excavates the origins of everything from the paper ballot and the Constitution to the I.O.U. and the dictionary. . . . From past to present, Lepore argues, Americans have wrestled with the idea of democracy by telling stories." (Publisher's note)

Includes bibliographical references and index.

Loewen, James W.

Lies across America; what our historic sites get wrong. Simon & Schuster 2007 464p pa $16   **973**
1. Monuments 2. Historic sites
ISBN 978-0-7432-9629-8; 0-7432-9629-X
First published 1999 by New Press

"The book consists of 95 brief commentaries on specific sites from Alaska to Florida to Maine, sandwiched between essays that offer advice on how to interpret what you read or are told at historic sites." N Y Times Book Rev [review of 1999 edition]

Marcus, Greil

The **shape** of things to come; prophecy and the American voice. Farrar, Straus & Giroux 2006 320p $25   **973**
1. American national characteristics 2. Nationalism -- United States 3. United States -- Civilization
ISBN 978-0-374-10438-2; 0-374-10438-7

LC 2005-33139

Marcus "posits that the United States of America is a cultural construction, grounded in the Declaration of Independence and the Constitution. Without those bedrocks, Marcus believes, the nation would be 'little more than a collection of buildings and people who have no special reason to speak to each other, and nothing to say.' Marcus builds his own erudite vision upon John Winthrop's 1630 speech 'A Modell of Christian Charity,' Abraham Lincoln's second inaugural address in 1865, Martin Luther King Jr.'s 1963 exhortation from the steps of the Lincoln Memorial in Washington, the later novels of Philip Roth, the films of David Lynch and the music of David Thomas with his band Pere Ubu. More than most books, Marcus's latest tour de force is quite likely to divide readers into two camps: those who find it brilliant and those who find it baffling." Publ Wkly

Morison, Samuel Eliot

The **growth** of the American Republic; {by} Samuel Eliot Morison, Henry Steele Commager, and William E. Leuchtenburg. 7th ed; Oxford Univ. Press 1980 2v il maps ea $59.95   **973**
1. United States -- History
ISBN 0-19-502593-8 v1; 0-19-502594-6 v2

LC 79-52432

First published 1930 in a single volume

A history of the United States that deals with military, political, economic, social, literary and spiritual aspects of the nation's development

"A good general history, well-written." Sheehy. Guide to Ref Books. 10th edition

Olson, James Stuart

Encyclopedia of the industrial revolution in America; {by} James S. Olson; technical editor: Robert L. Shadle. Greenwood Press 2002 xxv, 313p il $69.95   **973**
1. Reference books 2. Industrial revolution -- Encyclopedias
ISBN 0-313-30830-6

LC 00-52129

"A well-organized and comprehensive ready reference." Voice Youth Advocates

Includes bibliographical references

Prothero, Stephen

The **American** Bible; how our words unite, divide, and define a nation. Stephen Prothero. 1st ed. HarperOne 2012 vii, 533 p.p (hardback) $29.99 **973**
1. American national characteristics 2. United States -- Politics and government 3. American literature -- History and criticism 4. Group identity in literature 5. United States -- Civilization 6. National characteristics, American 7. Language and culture -- United States 8. Nationalism and literature -- United States 9. National characteristics, American, in literature 10. Literature and society -- United States -- History 11. Rhetoric -- Political aspects -- United States -- History 12. Speeches, addresses, etc., American -- History and criticism
ISBN 0062123432; 9780062123435

LC 2012005054

In this book, Stephen Prothero has "assembl[ed] a version of the American canon: 'Not the books I revere but those that Americans themselves have made sacred.' His scripture comprises a set of essays, speeches and fiction that, in his judgment, have largely influenced the United States' self-image. By recovering their teachings, he believes, we can heal the divisiveness and self-interest that ail our politics." (Washington Post)

Includes bibliographical references (p. 491-510) and index.

Puleo, Stephen

American treasures; The Secret Efforts to Save the Declaration of Independence, the Constitution and the Gettysburg Address. Stephen Puleo. St.

Martin's Press 2016 432 p. illustrations (hardback) $28.99 **973**
  1. Historic preservation 2. United States. Constitution 3. Democracy -- United States -- History 4. United States. Declaration of independence 5. United States -- History -- Sources 6. Hiding places -- United States -- History 7. United States. Declaration of Independence 8. United States -- Politics and government -- Sources 9. Historic preservation -- Political aspects -- United States -- History 10. Manuscripts -- Collection and preservation -- United States -- History 11. United States -- Antiquities -- Collection and preservation -- History
  ISBN 9781250065742
  LC 2016003702
This book, by Stephen Puleo, focuses on how "FDR set about hiding the country's valuables: . . . the Declaration of Independence, the Constitution, the Gettysburg Address, and more, guarded by a battery of agents and bound for safekeeping in the nation's most impenetrable hiding place." (Publisher's note)
  "This unique, easily digestible, well-researched saga is ideal for general readers." Booklist
  Includes bibliographical references and index

Reynolds, David, 1952-
  America, empire of liberty; a new history of the United States. Basic Books 2009 563p map **973**
  1. United States -- History
  ISBN 9780465015009
  LC 2009-17831
This is "a one-volume history of the United States, from the mound-builders of the 11th century to the challenges facing President Barack Obama. . . . Mr. Reynold's book provides an entertaining and fair-minded introduction to American history." Economist
  Includes bibliographical references

Schlesinger, Arthur M. (Arthur Meier), 1917-2007
  The **cycles** of American history; {by} Arthur M. Schlesinger, Jr. Houghton Mifflin 1986 498p hardcover o.p. pa $16 **973**
  1. United States -- History 2. United States -- Foreign relations 3. United States -- Politics and government
  ISBN 0-395-95793-1 pa
  LC 86-7706
"For this volume, Schlesinger has revised and updated papers, reviews, and essays that have appeared in various forms over the past quarter-century. . . . Each of the 14 essays that make up the book offers a fresh, demanding, and lively argument about important issues in American intellectual, political, or diplomatic history." Choice
  Includes bibliographical references

Shenkman, Richard
  Legends, lies & cherished myths of American history. HarperPerennial 1989 213p il pa $13 **973**
  1. Legends -- United States 2. United States -- History
  ISBN 978-0-06-097261-5; 0-06-097261-0
  First published 1988 by Morrow
  The author "debunks a host of popular myths associated with U.S. history. From the Founding Fathers to the Reagan

presidency, heretofore undisputed facts are exposed as fiction. Misquotes, misinterpretations, and downright fabrications are all duly recorded in an amusing and illuminating fashion. An irresistible browsing item." Booklist
  Includes bibliographical references

Stark, Peter
  The **last** empty places; a past and present journey through the blank spots on the American map. Ballantine Books 2010 325p il map $26 **973**
  1. Wilderness areas 2. United States -- Local history 3. United States -- Description and travel
  ISBN 978-0-345-49537-2; 0-345-49537-3
  LC 2010-09942
Stark writes "about exploring Maine's northern woods and the St. John River, the forests and glens of western Pennsylvania, the vast empty deserts of southeast Oregon and the High Desert of New Mexico, deep within the Gila Wilderness. Often he takes his family with him, and we get to read about the trials and tribulations of tents, backpacks, river crossings, switchbacks, towering cliffs and shadowy canyons. At the same time he intersperses his journeys with historical tales and horrors. . . . Stark keeps his writing sharp and clear and, wonderfully, does not slip into celebration of some mystical state of oneness with nature." Providence J
  Includes bibliographical references

State by state; a panoramic portrait of America. edited by Matt Weiland & Sean Wilsey. Ecco 2008 xxxi, 572p il map $29.95 **973**
  1. United States
  ISBN 978-0-06-147090-5; 0-06-147090-2
  LC 2008-300642
"Taking as their inspiration the state guides published by the Federal Writers' Project during and shortly after the Great Depression, Weiland and Wilsey assembled 50 of America's finest writers and asked them to contribute essays on the same general theme: why my state is special—or not. The result is a funny, moving, rousing collection, greater than the sum of its excellent parts, a convention of literary super-delegates, each one boisterously nominating his or her piece of the Republic." N Y Times Book Rev

Steinbeck, John
  Travels with Charley; in search of America. Viking 1962 246p hardcover o.p. pa $14 **973**
  1. United States -- Civilization 2. United States -- Description and travel
  ISBN 0-670-72508-0; 0-14-200070-1 pa
  The Nobel laureate recounts his impressions and observations of America gathered during a trip through forty states in the company of his French poodle Charley

Virga, Vincent
  Eyes of the nation; a visual history of the United States. by Vincent Virga and curators of the Library of Congress; historical commentary by Alan Brinkley. Knopf 1997 399p il $75 **973**
  1. United States -- History -- Pictorial works
  ISBN 0-679-44330-4
  LC 97-36603

This visual history "showcases more than 500 illustrations, manuscripts, engravings, prints, movie stills and other artifacts stretching back to the 15th century. The accompanying text by the historian Alan Brinkley rolls through the high and low points of the nation's history, but it is the captions that sparkle the brightest, adding context while offering surprising information." N Y Times Book Rev

Vowell, Sarah

Assassination vacation. Simon & Schuster 2005 258p il hardcover o.p. pa $14 **973**
1. United States -- Local history 2. United States -- Description and travel 3. Presidents -- United States -- Assassination
ISBN 0-7432-6003-1; 0-7432-6004-X pa
LC 2004-59134

"[Vowell] has done her homework, providing lucid descriptions of the murders and agile summations of the scholarly assessments of each era." America

Walker, Jesse

The **United** States of paranoia; a conspiracy theory. Jesse Walker. Harper 2013 448 p. $25.99 **973**
1. Paranoia 2. Conspiracies 3. United States -- Civilization 4. National characteristics, American 5. Political culture -- United States 6. Conspiracy theories -- United States 7. United States -- Politics and government 8. Paranoia -- Social aspects -- United States 9. Paranoia -- Political aspects -- United States
ISBN 0062135554; 9780062135551
LC 2013011426

In this book, Jesse Walker offers an analysis of conspiracy theories in the U.S., dividing them into five types: "those dealing with the perceived enemy within (e.g., militia and hate groups); the enemy outside (e.g., al-Qaeda); the enemy above (e.g., the Illuminati); and the enemy below (e.g., the Occupy movement). The fifth category relates to theories of a so-called benevolent conspiracy, which assume that someone or something is working for the betterment of humanity." (Publishers Weekly)

Wills, Garry

A **necessary** evil; a history of American distrust of government. Simon & Schuster 1999 365p hardcover o.p. pa $15 **973**
1. Resistance to government 2. United States -- Politics and government
ISBN 0-684-87026-6 pa
LC 99-35879

This "analysis of the distorted mythology that has grown up around government in the U.S. takes on hot-button issues from the Second Amendment and term limits to the idea that the Founders sought to create an inefficient government. Provocative and enlightening." Booklist

Includes bibliographical references

Zimmermann, Warren

First great triumph; how five Americans made their country a world power. Farrar, Straus & Giroux 2002 562p il $30; pa $15 **973**
1. Poets 2. Lawyers 3. Admirals 4. Diplomats 5. Governors 6. Statesmen 7. Historians 8. Presidents 9.

Vice-presidents 10. Spanish-American War, 1898 11. Senators 12. Biographers 13. Secretaries of war 14. Secretaries of state 15. Nobel laureates for peace 16. United States -- History -- 1898-1919
ISBN 0-374-17939-5; 0-374-52893-4 pa
LC 2002-25015

The author credits five men "for the vision, determination and political skill that first gave the United States its global ambition. His book is a history of the American rise to power and a collective biography of [his] five heroes: Theodore Roosevelt, the assistant secretary of the Navy and later president; Alfred T. Mahan, the naval strategist; Senator Henry Cabot Lodge of Massachusetts; Secretary of State John Hay; and the first American colonial administrator, Elihu Root." N Y Times (Late N Y Ed)

Includes bibliographical references

Zinn, Howard, 1922-2010

★ A **people's** history of the United States; 1492-present. Howard Zinn. HarperCollins 2003 729 p. **973**
1. United States -- History
ISBN 0060528427
LC 2002032895

"According to this classic of revisionist American history, narratives of national unity and progress are a smoke screen disguising the ceaseless conflict between elites and the masses whom they oppress and exploit. Historian [Howard] Zinn sides with the latter group in chronicling Indians' struggle against Europeans, blacks' struggle against racism, women's struggle against patriarchy, and workers' struggle against capitalists." (Publishers Weekly)

Includes bibliographical references (p. [689]-708) and index

973.09   Presidents--United States

Carlson, Brady

Dead presidents; an American adventure into the strange deaths and surprising afterlives of our nation's leaders. Brady Carlson. W W Norton & Co Inc 2016 336 p. illustrations (hardcover) $26.95 **973.09**
1. Monuments -- United States 2. Presidents -- United States -- Death and burial 3. Presidents -- United States -- Death 4. Presidents -- United States -- Biography
ISBN 9780393243932
LC 2015032329

This book, by Brady Carlson, offers an "exploration into the death stories of our nation's greatest leaders—and the wild ways we choose to remember and memorialize them. . . . With an engaging mix of history and contemporary reporting, Carlson recounts the surprising origin stories of the Washington Monument, Mount Rushmore, Grant's Tomb, and JFK's Eternal Flame." (Publisher's note)

"A brisk, lighthearted travelogue with an exuberant guide." Kirkus

Includes bibliographical references and index

Chronology of the U.S. presidency; Mathew Manweller, editor. ABC-CLIO 2012 4 v. xxii, 1556 p.p (hbk. : acid-free paper) $399.00 **973.09**
1. Cabinet officers 2. United States -- History 3. Presidents -- United States 4. Presidents -- United States -- Biography 5. Presidents -- United States -- History -- Chronology 6. United States -- Politics and government -- Chronology
ISBN 1598846450; 9781598846454; 9781598846461
LC 2011053314

This book looks at the 44 U.S. presidents. "Entries begin with a portrait of the president and contain a biographical sketch of both the man himself and the First Family, information on each member of the cabinet, a chronology of significant term events, and primary-source materials." (Library Journal)
Includes bibliographical references and index.

Freedman, Eric

Presidents and Black America; a documentary history. Stephen A. Jones, Eric Freedman. CQ Press 2011 xxxiv, 546 p.p (cloth : alk. paper) $145 **973.09**
1. African Americans 2. Presidents -- Attitudes 3. Presidents -- United States 4. African Americans -- Political activity 5. United States -- Race relations -- History 6. African Americans -- Attitudes -- History -- Sources 7. Presidents -- United States -- Racial attitudes -- Sources 8. Presidents -- Relations with African Americans -- History -- Sources
ISBN 1608710084; 9781608710089
LC 2011032618

This reference book "features a mixture of primary source material with introductory essays outlining each president's views on blacks in America. . . . The work is arranged in chronological order, with each chapter covering a president. . . . Chapters open with an introductory essay. . . . One can clearly see how the successive Republican presidencies of Harding, Coolidge, and Hoover turned American blacks . . . to the Democratic party of Franklin Roosevelt." (Booklist)
Includes bibliographical references and index.

★ The **presidency** A to Z; Gerhard Peters, editor; John T. Woolley, editor. 5th ed. CQ Press 2012 xix, 715 p.p ill. (hardcover) $125 **973.09**
1. Presidents -- United States -- Biography 2. Presidents -- United States -- Encyclopedias
ISBN 1608719081; 9781608719082
LC 2012023290

This book, by Gerhard Peters, presents a dictionary of the U.S. presidency. The book is a "tool for understanding the presidency, both historically and today and for appraising how it and the executive branch have responded to the challenges facing the nation. It provides readers with quick information and in-depth background on the presidency through a comprehensive encyclopedia of over 300 easy-to-read entries." (Publisher's note)
"At over 700 pages and also available online, this core title. . . provid[es] a comprehensive encyclopedic treatment of the U.S. presidency. . . . A recommended purchase for all

libraries and a required one for those with earlier editions, which it supplants." LJ
Includes bibliographical references (p. 684-690) and index.

Greenberg, David

Republic of spin; an inside history of the American presidency. David Greenberg. W.W. Norton & Co. 2016 560 p. 16 plates; illustrations (hardcover) $35 **973.099**
1. Presidents -- United States 2. United States -- Politics and government 3. Critics -- United States -- Biography 4. Presidents -- United States -- History 5. Presidents -- United States -- Biography 6. Spin doctors -- United States -- Biography 7. Political consultants -- United States -- Biography 8. Communication in politics -- United States -- History 9. Presidents -- United States -- Public opinion -- History 10. Public relations and politics -- United States -- History 11. Public opinion -- Political aspects -- United States -- History
ISBN 0393067068; 9780393067064
LC 2015031998

In this book author David Greenberg "recounts the rise of the White House spin machine, from Teddy Roosevelt to Barack Obama. His sweeping, startling narrative takes us behind the scenes to see how the tools and techniques of image making and message craft work. Greenberg also examines the profound debates Americans have waged over the effect of spin on our politics. Does spin help our leaders manipulate the citizenry? Or does it allow them to engage us more fully in the democratic project?" (Publisher's note)
"This revealing account of politics as image in U.S. presidential culture should be read by any student of the American presidency and American politics." LJ
Includes bibliographical references and index

973.2 United States--Colonial period, 1607-1775

Anderson, Fred

The **crucible** of war; the Seven Years' War and the fate of empire in British North America, 1754-1766. with illustrations from the William L. Clements Library. Knopf 2000 862p il hardcover o.p. pa $21 **973.2**
1. Seven Years' War, 1756-1763 2. United States -- History -- 1600-1775, Colonial period
ISBN 0-375-70636-4 pa
LC 99-18512

The author "demonstrates that the conflict was more than just a peripheral squabble that anticipated the American Revolution. Not only did the war decisively alter relations among the French, the English and the Native American allies of the two powers, who for decades had played the English and French off one another to their own advantage, but just as critical, argues Anderson, the war also changed the character of British imperialism, with the mother country trying to reshape the terms of empire and the colonists' place in it." Publ Wkly

The **dominion** of war; empire and liberty in North America, 1500-2000. [by] Fred Anderson and

Andrew Cayton. Viking 2005 520p il maps $27.95; pa $16   **973.2**

1. United States -- Military history 2. United States -- Territorial expansion

ISBN 0-670-03370-7; 0-14-303651-3 pa

The authors provide an "account of the U.S. rise to global preeminence over five centuries. Central to their thesis is the assertion that military conflict has been essential in determining the cultural and political evolution of North America. . . . Anderson and Cayton have provided a well-written and important reinterpretation of our past." Booklist

Includes bibliographical references

Bailyn, Bernard

★ The **barbarous** years; the peopling of British North America : the conflict of civilizations, 1600-1675. Bernard Bailyn. Alfred A. Knopf 2012 614 p. $35   **973.2**

1. Colonization 2. Immigration and emigration 3. Great Britain -- Colonies -- America 4. United States -- History -- 1600-1775, Colonial period 5. Canada -- History -- To 1763 (New France) 6. North America -- Civilization -- 17th century 7. Immigrants -- North America -- History -- 17th century 8. United States -- History -- Colonial period, ca. 1600-1775 9. Great Britain -- Colonies -- America -- History -- 17th century

ISBN 0394515706; 9780394515700

LC 2012034223

This book, by Bernard Bailyn, presents an account of the 17th century colonial migrations to North America. "They moved . . . from different social backgrounds and cultures . . . and circumstances. . . . They came hoping to re-create if not to improve these diverse lifeways in a remote . . . environment. But their stories are mostly of confusion, failure, violence, and the loss of civility as they sought to normalize abnormal situations and recapture lost worlds." (Publisher's note)

Includes bibliographical references and index.

The **peopling** of British North America; an introduction. Knopf 1986 177p hardcover o.p. pa $12   **973.2**

1. United States -- History -- 1600-1775, Colonial period

ISBN 0-394-75779-3 pa

LC 85-82144

In this introductory volume of a projected multivolume work, the author "gives first airing to his overall argument on settling patterns in history. Though designed to introduce the subsequent volumes, this superbly articulate study is understandable on its own." Booklist

Includes bibliographical references

Demos, John

The **unredeemed** captive; a family story from early America. Knopf 1994 315p maps hardcover o.p. pa $14   **973.2**

1. Clergy 2. Mohawk Indians 3. Native Americans -- Captivities 4. Massachusetts -- History -- 1600-1775, Colonial period

ISBN 0-679-75961-1 pa

LC 93-23907

This "is a lively introduction to an authentically multicultural colonial North America." N Y Times Book Rev

Fowler, William M.

Empires at war; the French & Indian War and the struggle for North America, 1754-1763. [by] William M. Fowler, Jr. Walker & Company 2005 xxv, 332p il maps $27; pa $15   **973.2**

1. United States -- History -- 1755-1763, French and Indian War

ISBN 0-8027-1411-0; 0-8027-7737-6 pa

LC 2004-43064

In this history of the French and Indian War, the author "glances occasionally at the European and Caribbean theaters of this 'first world war,' but concentrates on the North American operations that determined Britain's victory over France in the struggle for imperial supremacy. . . . The result is a judicious, well-paced and engaging introduction to a turning point in American and world history." Publ Wkly

Includes bibliographical references

Goetzmann, William H.

Beyond the Revolution; a history of American thought from Paine to pragmatism. Basic Books 2009 456p $35   **973.2**

1. American philosophy 2. United States -- Intellectual life

ISBN 978-0-465-00495-9; 0-465-00495-4

LC 2008-25590

"It's conventional to spin American history as a story of unfolding freedom, a quest to perfect our founding ideals, but Beyond the Revolution introduces something of a countervailing narrative. The country was as free and limitless as it would ever want to be right after the founding, Mr. Goetzmann contends, and the task since then has been to find a workable frame to harness that freedom. . . . [This book argues that] the entire frenzy of American enterprise from the founding to the present can be understood as an effort to invent, peddle, connive or discern, a model for how to choose and what to value in country where anything is possible." N Y Observer

Includes bibliographical references (p. 403-436)

Hawke, David Freeman

Everyday life in early America. Harper & Row 1988 195p il (Everyday life in America) hardcover o.p. pa $13   **973.2**

1. United States -- Social life and customs 2. United States -- History -- 1600-1775, Colonial period

ISBN 0-06-091251-0 pa

LC 87-17667

The author "provides enlightening and colorful descriptions of early Colonial Americans and debunks many widely held assumptions about 17th century settlers." Publ Wkly

Includes bibliographical references

Lepore, Jill

The **name** of war; King Philip's War and the origins of American identity. Knopf 1998 xxviii, 337p il maps hardcover o.p. pa $15   **973.2**

1. King Philip's War, 1675-1676 2. Native Americans

-- Wars 3. Great Britain -- Colonies -- America
ISBN 0-375-70262-8 pa

LC 97-2820

"This is a powerful book that doesn't shy away from depicting the sheer horror of what must be termed a race war." Booklist

Includes bibliographical references

Philbrick, Nathaniel

★ **Mayflower**; a story of courage, community, and war. Viking 2006 461p il $29.95; pa $16 **973.2**
1. Pilgrims (New England colonists) 2. Massachusetts -- History -- 1600-1775, Colonial period
ISBN 0-670-03760-5; 978-0-670-03760-5; 978-0-14-311197-9 pa; 0-14-311197-3 pa

LC 2005-58470

The author "has written a judicious, fascinating work of revisionist history. 'Mayflower' is a surprise-filled account of what are supposed to be some of the best-known events in this country's past but are instead an occasion for collective amnesia." N Y Times (Late N Y Ed)

Includes bibliographical references

Schultz, Eric B.

King Philip's War; the history and legacy of America's forgotten conflict. {by} Eric B. Schultz, Michael J. Tougias. Countryman Press 1999 416p il maps hardcover o.p. pa $18.95 **973.2**
1. King Philip's War, 1675-1676 2. Native Americans -- Government relations 3. New England -- History -- 1600-1775, Colonial period
ISBN 0-88150-483-1 pa

LC 99-23481

The first part of this volume provides a "chronological retelling of the war. The second part, organized geographically and the heart of the volume, takes readers through New England to various sites associated with the conflict. . . . The third part offers three contemporary narratives reflecting the significance of the war on the people of the era. Useful maps assist the reader throughout." Libr J

Includes bibliographical references

973.3 United States--Periods of Revolution and Confederation, 1775-1789

Allen, Danielle

Our Declaration; A Reading of the Declaration of Independence in Defense of Equality. Danielle Allen. W W Norton & Co Inc 2014 288 p. illustrations $27.95 **973.3**
1. Freedom 2. United States. Declaration of independence 3. Equality -- United States 4. United States. Declaration of Independence -- Criticism, Textual
ISBN 087140690X; 9780871406903

LC 2014009825

"Troubled by the fact that so few Americans actually know what it says, Danielle Allen . . . set out to explore the arguments of the Declaration, reading it with both adult night students and University of Chicago undergraduates. Keenly aware that the Declaration is riddled with contradictions--liberating some while subjugating slaves and Native

Americans--Allen and her students nonetheless came to see that the Declaration makes a coherent and riveting argument about equality." (Publisher's note)

"As if conducting a friendly conversation, sentence by sentence, [Allen] takes readers through all the text's words, and she proves a patient, informed and friendly guide." Kirkus

Includes bibliographical references and index

The **American** Revolution: writings from the War of Independence. Library of Am. 2001 878p $40 **973.3**
1. United States -- History -- 1775-1783, Revolution
ISBN 1-88301-191-4

LC 00-45373

"This work will serve as a marvelous research tool for specialists, but general readers with an interest in American history will also find fascinating gems." Booklist

Includes bibliographical references

Beck, Derek W.

Igniting the American Revolution; 1773-1775. Derek W. Beck. Sourcebooks, Inc. 2015 480 p. (hardcover : alk. paper) $26.99 **973.3**
1. United States -- History -- Revolution, 1775-1783 -- Causes
ISBN 1492613959; 9781492613954

LC 2015016941

Includes bibliographical references and index

The **war** before independence, 1775-1776; Derek W. Beck. Sourcebooks Inc 2016 480 p. illustrations, maps (hardcover) $26.99 **973.3**
1. United States -- History -- 1775-1783, Revolution
2. United States -- History -- Revolution, 1775-1783 -- Campaigns
ISBN 9781492633099

LC 2015049006

This book, by Derek W. Beck, "transports readers into the violent years of 1775 and 1776, with the infamous Battle of Bunker Hill--a turning point in the Revolution--and the snowy, wind-swept march to the frozen ground at the Battle of Quebec, ending with the exciting conclusion of the Boston Campaign. Meticulous research and new material . . . throws open the doors . . . to . . . little-known triumphs and tribulations of America's greatest military leaders." (Publisher's note)

"Beck writes exceptionally vividly, and as such, even readers slow to respond to battleground to-and-fro will be fully engaged." Booklist

Includes bibliographical references and index

Becker, Carl

The **Declaration** of Independence; a study in the history of political ideas. Knopf 1942 286p hardcover o.p. pa $11 **973.3**
1. Architects 2. Presidents 3. Vice-presidents 4. Essayists 5. United States -- Declaration of Independence 6. United States -- Politics and government -- 1775-1783, Revolution
ISBN 0-394-70060-0 pa

A reprint, with a new preface, of a book first published 1922 by Harcourt Brace & Co.

"A study of the Declaration, the philosophy that lay behind it, the history of its several drafts, an estimate of its literary quality." Wis Libr Bull

Includes bibliographical references

Beeman, Richard R.

Our lives, our fortunes and our sacred honor; the forging of American independence, 1774-1776. Richard R. Beeman. Basic Books, A Member of the Perseus Books Group 2013 528 p. (hardcover) $29.99   973.3

1. United States -- History 2. United States -- Politics and government 3. United States. Continental Congress, 1774 4. Statesmen -- United States -- Biography 5. Revolutionaries -- United States -- Biography 6. United States. Continental Congress -- History 7. United States -- History -- Revolution, 1775-1783 8. United States -- Politics and government -- To 1775 9. United States -- Politics and government -- 1775-1783 10. United States -- History -- Revolution, 1775-1783 -- Biography
ISBN 046502629X; 9780465026296; 9780465037827
LC 2013001875

This book by Richard B. Beeman "examines the . . . period between the meeting of the Continental Congress on September 5, 1774 and the . . . decision for independence in July of 1776. Beeman brings to life a cast of characters, including the . . . passionate John Adams, Adams much-misunderstood foil John Dickinson, the fiery political activist Samuel Adams, and the relative political neophyte Thomas Jefferson, and . . . reveals their path from subjects of England to citizens of a new nation." (Publisher's note)

Includes bibliographical references and index

Blumrosen, Alfred W.

Slave nation; how slavery united the colonies & sparked the American Revolution. [by] Alfred W. Blumrosen and Ruth G. Blumrosen; introduction by Eleanor Holmes Norton. Sourcebooks 2005 336p il map $24.95   973.3

1. Slavery -- United States 2. African Americans -- History 3. United States -- History -- 1775-1783, Revolution -- Causes
ISBN 1-4022-0400-0
LC 2004-27271

The authors "use the Somerset case of 1772, which freed all slaves in Britain, to illustrate how the price of freedom from English rule ensured continued bondage for slaves in the American South. The Blumrosens argue that Southerners feared that the ruling might be extended to the entire empire and therefore joined the move to win independence from Britain. . . . This well-researched book is sure to be controversial." Libr J

Includes bibliographical references

Bobrick, Benson

Angel in the whirlwind; the triumph of the American Revolution. Penguin Bks. 1998 553p map pa $18   973.3

1. United States -- History -- 1775-1783, Revolution
ISBN 0-14-027500-2; 978-0-14-027500-1
LC 97-11320

First published 1997 by Simon & Schuster

"Many of the stories are familiar—Paul Revere's ride, Arnold's descent into infamy—but the book's strength lies in its many lesser-known details on the battlefield and beyond. . . . Though the format demands only brief treatment of complicated issues, what emerges is a highly impressive show of exhaustive research and engaging storytelling." Publ Wkly

Includes bibliographical references

Borneman, Walter R., 1952-

American spring; Lexington, Concord, and the road to revolution. Walter R. Borneman. Little Brown & Co 2014 480 p. illustrations, maps, portraits (hardcover) $30   973.3

1. United States -- History -- 1775-1783, Revolution
ISBN 0316221023; 9780316221016; 9780316221023
LC 2014932742

Includes bibliographical references and index

This book, by Walter R. Borneman, "look[s] at the American Revolution's first months. . . . [It] follows a fledgling nation from Paul Revere's little-known ride of December 1774 and the first shots fired on Lexington Green through the catastrophic Battle of Bunker Hill, culminating with a Virginian named George Washington taking command of colonial forces on July 3, 1775." (Publisher's note)

"Taking advantage of massive documentation, Borneman delivers a gripping, almost moment-by-moment account of the nasty exchanges and bloody retreat of British troops followed by hundreds and then thousands of militia who camped around Boston and laid siege." Kirkus

Breen, T. H.

American insurgents, American patriots; the revolution of the people. Hill and Wang 2010 337p $27   973.3

1. United States -- History -- 1775-1783, Revolution 2. United States -- Militia -- History -- Revolution, 1775-1783 3. United States -- History -- Revolution, 1775-1783 -- Social aspects 4. United States -- History -- Revolution, 1775-1783 -- Committees of safety
ISBN 978-0-8090-7588-1; 0-8090-7588-1
LC 2009-42496

Breen "uses correspondence, diaries, outtakes from clergy sermons and newspaper reports to build a mosaic representation of the popular mood, and the escalating willingness to take up arms. . . . [The] book shows an energetic and necessarily untidy process of invention on the part of a people, and captures well its improvisatory nature." Chicago Trib

Includes bibliographical references and index

Bunker, Nick

★ An **empire** on the edge; how Britain came to fight America. Nick Bunker. 1st edition Alfred A. Knopf 2014 448 p. illustrations, map hbk $30 **973.3**

1. Boston Tea Party, 1773 2. Great Britain -- Foreign relations -- United States 3. United States -- Foreign relations -- Great Britain 4. United States -- History -- 1600-1775, Colonial period 5. United States -- History -- 1775-1783, Revolution -- Causes

ISBN 030759484X; 9780307594846

LC 2014001032

Pulitzer Prize Finalist: History (2015)

This book, by Nick Bunker, "tells the story of the last three years of mutual embitterment that preceded the outbreak of America's war for independence in 1775. . . . At the heart of the book lies the Boston Tea Party, an event that arose from fundamental flaws in the way the British managed their affairs. . . . By the late summer of 1774, when the rebels in New England began to arm themselves, the descent into war had become irreversible." (Publisher's note)

"Bunker's book argues that, for the British, America was 'a continent she did not comprehend and could not hope to rule.' The author is particularly attuned to economic context and concerned with how events unfolded in practice, rather than what was said in theory." LJ

Includes bibliographical references and index

Cohen, I. Bernard

Science and the founding fathers; science in the political thought of Jefferson, Franklin, Adams and Madison. Norton 1995 368p il hardcover o.p. pa $15.95 **973.3**

1. Authors 2. Diplomats 3. Inventors 4. Statesmen 5. Architects 6. Presidents 7. Scientists 8. Vice-presidents 9. Political science 10. Senators 11. Essayists 12. Writers on science 13. Members of Congress 14. Secretaries of state 15. Science -- United States -- History

ISBN 0-393-31510-X pa

LC 94-26731

The author "analyzes how Thomas Jefferson, Benjamin Franklin, John Adams, and James Madison incorporated their scientific beliefs and knowledge into their political lives. Cohen examines each man's scientific education and then searches for examples of how that knowledge was expressed in their published works. He looks closely at phrases from the Declaration of Independence and the Constitution and shows that they have a Newtonian basis." Libr J

Dunn, Susan

Sister revolutions; French lightning, American light. Faber & Faber 1999 258p il hardcover o.p. pa $14 **973.3**

1. France -- History -- 1789-1799, Revolution 2. United States -- History -- 1775-1783, Revolution

ISBN 0-571-19989-5 pa

LC 99-18178

"The American Revolution, according to Dunn, was more peaceful and practical, in part because its leaders were both intellectuals and men of political experience. The French Revolution, on the other hand, veered into extravagant abstractions because its leaders were intellectuals with

litttle or no previous political experience. This book is clearly written and should appeal particularly to undergraduate students and members of the general public." Choice

Includes bibliographical references

DuVal, Kathleen

★ **Independence** Lost; Lives on the Edge of the American Revolution. Kathleen DuVal. Random House Inc. 2015 464 p. illustrations, maps $28 **973.3**

1. United States -- History -- 1775-1783, Revolution 2. West Florida -- History, Military -- 18th century 3. Gulf Coast (U.S.) -- History, Military -- 18th century 4. United States -- History -- Revolution, 1775-1783 -- Biography 5. United States -- History -- Revolution, 1775-1783 -- Social aspects 6. Autonomy -- Social aspects -- Gulf Coast (U.S.) -- History -- 18th century

ISBN 1400068959; 9781400068951

LC 2014042511

"Focusing on the frontier struggle in the Gulf of Mexico region, DuVal . . . illustrates how multipronged the American Revolution was. It involved three empires (Britain, France, and Spain), several major Native American peoples, and both free and enslaved Africans. DuVal personalizes the conflict by tracing the fates of eight individuals: two tribal leaders, a loyalist couple, a merchant couple backing the colonists, a transplanted pro-colonist Acadian, and a slave who served as a cattle driver and later as a courier for the Spanish." (Publishers Weekly)

"By describing these lives and how the revolution affected them, DuVal accurately theorizes that independence was lost by many, and that the idea of 'empire' was often a place of security and affluence." LJ

Includes bibliographical references and index

Egerton, Douglas R.

Death or liberty; African Americans and revolutionary America. Oxford University Press 2009 342p il map $29.95 **973.3**

1. Slavery -- United States 2. African Americans -- History 3. United States -- History -- 1775-1783, Revolution

ISBN 978-0-19-530669-9; 0-19-530669-4

LC 2008-27862

The author "traverses the rise and the debatable inevitability of slavery in the United States between the end of the Seven Years' War (1763) and Jefferson's election (1800), arguing that the 'division of the Republic into free wage labor sections and proslavery regions did not have to happen that way.'" Publ Wkly

Includes bibliographical references and index

Ellis, Joseph J.

American creation; triumphs and tragedies at the founding of the republic. A. A. Knopf 2007 283p **973.3**

1. United States -- History -- 1783-1809 2. United States -- History -- 1775-1783, Revolution 3. United States -- Politics and government -- 1783-1809 4. United States -- Politics and government -- 1775-1783,

Revolution

ISBN 978-0-307-26369-8; 0-307-26369-X

LC 2007-5273

The author "selects 'certain propitious moments' from the American Revolution and early republic, dramatizes them, and analyzes their crucial ramifications for America's future. . . . A history bound for phenomenal popularity." Booklist

Includes bibliographical references

The **Quartet**; Orchestrating the Second American Revolution, 1783-1789. Joseph J. Ellis. Knopf 2015 320 p. $27.95   **973.3**

1. Founding Fathers of the United States 2. United States -- Politics and government -- 1783-1809 3. Constitutional history -- United States 4. Statesmen -- United States -- Biography 5. Politicians -- United States -- Biography 6. United States -- Politics and government -- 1783-1789 7. Federal government -- United States -- History -- 18th century 8. Confederation of states -- United States -- History -- 18th century

ISBN 0385353405; 9780385353403

LC 2014034503

In this book, author Joseph J. Ellis presents "the story of this second American founding and of the men most responsible--George Washington, Alexander Hamilton, John Jay, and James Madison. These men, with the help of Robert Morris and Gouverneur Morris, shaped the contours of American history by diagnosing the systemic dysfunctions created by the Articles of Confederation." (Publisher's note)

"Ellis's approach employs deft characterizations and insights into these politicians and philosophers. . . . With his usual skill, Ellis brings alive what otherwise might seem dry constitutional debates, with apt quotations and bright style." Pub Wkly

Includes bibliographical references and index

★ **Revolutionary** summer; the birth of American independence. by Joseph J. Ellis. 1st ed. Alfred A. Knopf 2013 xiii, 219 p., 8 unnumbered pages of platesp col. ill., map (hardcover) $26.95   **973.3**

1. Founding Fathers of the United States 2. United States -- History -- 1775-1783, Revolution 3. United States -- History -- Revolution, 1775-1783

ISBN 0307701220; 9780307701220

LC 2012026140

This book, by Pulitzer-winning historian Joseph Ellis, discusses "the summer months of 1776 . . . in the story of our country's founding. . . . The Continental Congress and the Continental Army were forced to make decisions on the run, improvising as history congealed around them. . . . Ellis . . . examines the most influential figures in this propitious moment . . . [and] weaves together the political and military experiences as two sides of a single story." (Publisher's note)

Includes bibliographical references (pages 189-208) and index.

Ferling, John

Whirlwind; the American Revolution and the war that won it. John Ferling. Bloomsbury 2015 432 p. 16 plates; illustrations; maps (alk. paper) $30   **973.3**

1. United States -- History -- 1775-1783, Revolution

2. United States -- History -- Revolution, 1775-1783 -- Campaigns

ISBN 162040172X; 9781620401729

LC 2014033315

This book, by John Ferling, "is a fast-paced and scrupulously told one-volume history of [the American Revolution]. Balancing social and political concerns of the period and perspectives of the average American revolutionary with a careful examination of the war itself, Ferling has crafted . . . a book about the causes of the American Revolution, the war that won it, and the meaning of the Revolution overall." (Publisher's note)

"Ferling has created another accessible yet scholarly work on the American Revolution. While its primary appeal is to history buffs, academics looking for an introductory survey history should also find this work useful." LJ

Includes bibliographical references and index

Fischer, David Hackett

Paul Revere's ride. Oxford Univ. Press 1994 445p il maps $37.50; pa $19.95   **973.3**

1. Concord (Mass.), Battle of, 1775 2. Lexington (Mass.), Battle of, 1775 3. Artisans 4. Metalworkers 5. Revolutionaries

ISBN 0-19-508847-6; 0-19-509831-5 pa

LC 93-25739

"Fischer's solid study of Paul Revere and his infamous ride debunks the myths surrounding the event, reconstructing the circumstances leading to the Battle of Lexington and Concord. Fischer's extensive use of primary sources affords an intimate glimpse of the participants' thoughts and feelings." Booklist

Includes bibliographical references

Washington's crossing. Oxford University Press 2004 564p il maps (Pivotal moments in American history) $35; pa $16.95   **973.3**

1. Generals 2. Presidents 3. United States -- History -- 1775-1783, Revolution -- Campaigns

ISBN 0-19-517034-2; 0-19-518159-X pa

LC 2003-19858

The author describes how "Washington, his officers, and their men turn the early military defeats of Long Island and New York City into victory at Trenton and Princeton. The opening chapter is devoted to the painting Washington Crossing the Delaware. Then the author discusses the British, Hessian, and American military units that were involved in these campaigns and gives background on their officers. This is Fischer's strong suit: he tells stories and gives details that bring history alive. . . . In the hands of such a thorough researcher and talented writer, this is powerful stuff." SLJ

Includes bibliographical references

Fleming, Thomas J.

Washington's secret war; the hidden history of Valley Forge. [by] Thomas Fleming. Smithsonian Books/Collins 2005 384p il map $27.95; pa $14.95   **973.3**

1. Generals 2. Presidents 3. United States -- Continental Army 4. United States -- History -- 1775-

1783, Revolution -- Campaigns

ISBN 0-06-082962-1; 0-06-087293-4 pa

LC 2005-52157

"Fleming has provided an original and provocative reinterpretation of a critical period in the struggle for independence." Booklist

Includes bibliographical references

Fowler, William M.

American crisis; George Washington and the dangerous two years after Yorktown, 1781-1783. Walker & Co. 2011 340p il map $28 **973.3**

1. Generals 2. Presidents 3. United States -- History -- 1775-1783, Revolution

ISBN 978-0-8027-1706-1; 0-8027-1706-3

The author "artfully records the dangerous situation in the United States during the time between Cornwallis's surrender at Yorktown in 1781 and the evacuation of British troops from New York two years later. Drawing from a wealth of letters, he describes General Washington's skill as a leader, his humble and respectful character, and his noble motives in fighting to keep the army organized and disciplined. . . . This well-documented and highly readable account will engage and enrich scholars and general readers alike." Libr J

Includes bibliographical references

Gould, Eliga H.

Among the powers of the earth; the American Revolution and the making of a new world empire. Eliga H. Gould. Harvard University Press 2012 301 p., [22] p. of platesp ill., maps (alk. paper) $45 **973.3**

1. Imperialism 2. United States -- Foreign relations 3. United States -- History -- 1775-1783, Revolution 4. United States -- Territorial expansion 5. United States -- Foreign relations -- 1775-1783 6. United States -- Foreign relations -- 1783-1815 7. United States -- International status -- History 8. United States -- History -- Revolution, 1775-1783 -- Influence

ISBN 0674046080; 9780674046085

LC 2011035333

"In this reappraisal of the American Revolution . . . Gould argues that the nation's founding was far from a straightforward bid for liberty and independence. Even as Americans strove to be free from . . . imperialism, they sought the recognition of Europe's imperial powers -- and the authority to become colonizers in their own right and rule a New World empire." (Publisher's note)

Includes bibliographical references and index

Hibbert, Christopher

Redcoats and rebels; the American Revolution through British eyes. Norton 1990 xx, 375p il maps hardcover o.p. pa $18.95 **973.3**

1. United States -- History -- 1775-1783, Revolution

ISBN 0-393-02895-X; 0-393-32293-9 pa

LC 90-31753

"Mr. Hibbert has an eye for the telling anecdote and the graphic quotation, and his bibliography indicates that he has consulted a wealth of manuscript material as well as research published during the last 30 years that illuminates what lay behind the British defeat." N Y Times Book Rev

Hogeland, William

Declaration; the nine tumultuous weeks when America became independent, May 1-July 4, 1776. Simon & Schuster 2010 273p il $26; ebook $12.99 **973.3**

1. United States -- Continental Congress 2. United States -- Declaration of Independence 3. United States -- History -- 1775-1783, Revolution -- Causes 4. United States -- Politics and government -- 1775-1783, Revolution

ISBN 978-1-4165-8409-4; 1-4165-8409-9; 978-1-4165-8425-4 ebook

LC 2010-3239

The author "forges a compelling narrative from the dozens of intricate political imbroglios that culminated with the signing of the Declaration of Independence. By casting a light on the daily interests of colonial Americans, particularly those whose homes and businesses patterned the spaces of bustling 18th-century Philadelphia, the author animates the discontents of the soon-to-be independent citizenry. With charming detail, the narrative brings together the diverse political players working during the nine weeks prior to the signing of the Declaration. These included rural militias, landed aristocrats, city merchants and immigrants, all of whom found a voice in Philadelphia." Kirkus

Includes bibliographical references

Jasanoff, Maya

Liberty's exiles; Maya Jasanoff. Alfred A. Knopf 2011 xvi, 460p.p col. ill., maps $30 **973.3**

1. Refugees 2. American Loyalists 3. American loyalists 4. Great Britain -- Colonies 5. United States -- History -- 1775-1783, Revolution 6. United States -- History -- Revolution, 1775-1783

ISBN 978-1-4000-4168-8; 1-4000-4168-6; 978-0-307-59530-0 e-book

LC 201023514

National Book Critics Circle Award: General Nonfiction (2011)

This book offers a "global history of the [American] loyalist exodus to Canada, the Caribbean, Sierra Leone, India, and beyond. . . . [Loyalists discussed include] Elizabeth Johnston, a young mother from Georgia, who led her growing family to Britain, Jamaica, and Canada, questing for a home; black loyalists . . . and Mohawk Indian leader Joseph Brant, who tried to find autonomy for his people in Ontario." (Publisher's note)

The author "examines the effects of the American Revolution on those whose loyalty to the Crown compelled them to flee the new United States." Kirkus

Includes bibliographical references and index.

Ketchum, Richard M.

Saratoga; turning point of America's Revolutionary War. Holt & Co. 1997 545p il maps hardcover o.p. pa $18 **973.3**

1. Saratoga Campaign, 1777

ISBN 0-8050-6123-1 pa

LC 97-2773

A "narrative account of the Saratoga campaign of 1777. . . . Ketchum provides the full political context within which the fighting took place while penning dozens of colorful portraits of the principal characters. The author also succeeds in his goal of telling the story from the perspective of the participants, illustrating what the American Revolution in upstate New York meant for soldiers and civilians alike." Libr J

Includes bibliographical references

Lockhart, Paul Douglas

The **whites** of their eyes; Bunker Hill, the first American Army, and the emergence of George Washington. Harper 2011 414p il map $27.99   **973.3**

1. Generals 2. Presidents 3. Bunker Hill (Boston, Mass.), Battle of, 1775 4. United States -- Continental Army 5. United States -- Military history 6. United States -- History -- 1775-1783, Revolution

ISBN 978-0-06-195886-1; 0-06-195886-7

LC 2010-43033

"Lockhart's shrewd, well-judged interpretation corrects myths about the battle and the men who fought it while doing full justice to their achievement in creating an army—and a nation—out of chaos." Publ Wkly

Includes bibliographical references

Maier, Pauline

American scripture; making the Declaration of Independence. Knopf 1997 xxi, 304p hardcover o.p. pa $14   **973.3**

1. United States -- Declaration of Independence 2. United States -- Politics and government -- 1775-1783, Revolution

ISBN 0-679-77908-6 pa

LC 97-2769

"In the spring of 1776, with a British invasion fleet on its way, the Second Continental Congress appointed a committee to compose a statement explaining America's decision to seek independence. Thomas Jefferson was the principal drafter of the statement, but Maier makes it clear that his task was to express the sentiments of the Congress, not his personal views, and she shows that when the congressmen edited his draft they improved it greatly (rather than 'mangling' it, as Jefferson ever after maintained). The Declaration of Independence is, she argues, a profoundly collective document, both in its origins and in our still-evolving interpretation of its self-evident truths." New Yorker

McCullough, David G., 1933-

1776; [by] David McCullough. Simon & Schuster 2005 386p il map $32   **973.3**

1. United States -- History -- 1775-1783, Revolution

ISBN 0-7432-2671-2

LC 2005-42505

"This is a narrative tour de force, exhibiting all the hallmarks the author is known for: fascinating subject matter, expert research and detailed, graceful prose." Publ Wkly

Includes bibliographical references

Middlekauff, Robert

★ The **glorious** cause; the American Revolution, 1763-1789. Rev. and expanded ed.; Oxford

University Press 2004 736p il map (Oxford history of the United States) $37.50   **973.3**

1. United States -- History -- 1775-1783, Revolution

ISBN 0-19-516247-1

LC 2004-16295

First published 1982

"This is narrative history at its best, written in a conversational and engaging style." Libr J

Includes bibliographical references

Morgan, Edmund Sears

The **birth** of the Republic, 1763-89; 3rd ed; University of Chicago Press 1992 206p (Chicago history of American civilization) hardcover o.p. pa $13   **973.3**

1. United States -- History -- 1783-1809 2. United States -- History -- 1775-1783, Revolution

ISBN 0-226-53756-0; 0-226-53757-9 pa

LC 92-8871

First published 1956

A brief study of the American revolutionary period from 1763 to 1789.

Includes bibliographical references

Nelson, James L.

With fire & sword; the battle of Bunker Hill and the beginning of the American Revolution. Thomas Dunne Books 2011 364p il map $27.99; ebook $14.99   **973.3**

1. Bunker Hill (Boston, Mass.), Battle of, 1775 2. United States -- History -- 1775-1783, Revolution -- Causes

ISBN 978-0-312-57644-8; 978-1-4299-6807-2 ebook

LC 2010-40653

"This rousing history rescues Bunker Hill from its folkloric shroud and presents it as one of the revolution's more significant and dramatic battles. . . . Nelson's gripping portrait of the battle caps a lively chronicle of the early days of the rebellion in Massachusetts and of the revolutionaries' scramble to establish a government and organize an army as they edged uneasily toward independence." Publ Wkly

Includes bibliographical references

O'Donnell, Patrick K.

Washington's Immortals; The Untold Story of an Elite Regiment Who Changed the Course of the Revolution. by Patrick K. O'Donnell. Atlantic Monthly Press 2016 336 p. ill. (some color), maps $28   **973.3**

1. United States -- History -- 1775-1783, Revolution

ISBN 0802124593; 9780802124593

This book, by Patrick K. O'Donnell, focuses on the U.S. revolutionary war "regiment, famously known as the 'Immortal 400.' . . . O'Donnell pieces together the stories of these brave men--their friendships, loves, defeats, and triumphs. He explores their arms and tactics, their struggles with hostile loyalists and shortages of clothing and food, their development into an elite unit, and their dogged opponents, including British General Lord Cornwallis." (Publisher's note)

"Using primary sources from both sides of the Atlantic, O'Donnell effectively traces the story of Maryland's immortals, describing the battles authentically along with the precariousness of the American cause." LJ

Includes bibliographical references (pages 387-442) and index.

Parkinson, Robert G.

The **common** cause; Creating Race and Nation in the American Revolution. by Robert G. Parkinson. Univ. of North Carolina Pr. for the Omohundro Inst. of Early Am. History & Culture 2016 768 p. illustrations, map (cloth : alk. paper) $45   **973.3**
1. Racism -- History 2. United States -- Race relations -- History 3. United States -- History -- 1775-1783, Revolution 4. Racism -- United States -- History -- 18th century 5. United States -- History -- Revolution, 1775-1783 -- Propaganda 6. United States -- History -- Revolution, 1775-1783 -- Social aspects
ISBN 9781469626635
LC 2016000574

In this book, author Robert G. Parkinson "argues that to unify the patriot side, political and communications leaders linked British tyranny to colonial prejudices, stereotypes, and fears about insurrectionary slaves and violent Indians. Manipulating newspaper networks, Washington, Jefferson, Adams, Franklin, and their fellow agitators broadcast stories of British agents inciting African Americans and Indians to take up arms against the American rebellion." (Publisher's note)

Includes bibliographical references and index.

Paul, Joel R.

Unlikely allies; how a merchant, a playwright, and a spy saved the American Revolution. [by] Joel Richard Paul. Riverhead Books 2009 405p il $25.95   **973.3**
1. Spies 2. Authors 3. Diplomats 4. Dramatists 5. Cross-dressers 6. Saratoga Campaign, 1777 7. Transvestites 8. Secret service -- United States 9. United States -- History -- 1775-1783, Revolution
ISBN 978-1-59448-883-2; 1-59448-883-5
LC 2009-34986

"A rip-roaring account of the American Revolution, told from a fresh, and undeniably offbeat, perspective." Booklist
Includes bibliographical references (p. 384-396)

Philbrick, Nathaniel

Bunker Hill; A City, a Siege, a Revolution. Nathaniel Philbrick. Viking Adult 2013 400 p. (hardcover) $32.95   **973.3**
1. Boston (Mass.) -- History 2. Bunker Hill (Boston, Mass.), Battle of, 1775 3. United States -- History -- 1775-1783, Revolution 4. Bunker Hill, Battle of, Boston, Mass., 1775 5. Boston (Mass.) -- History -- Revolution, 1775-1783
ISBN 0670025445; 9780670025442
LC 2013001534

This book, by Nathaniel Philbrick, profiles the history of the Battle of Bunker Hill. "After the Boston Tea Party, British and American soldiers and Massachusetts residents have warily maneuvered around each other until April 19, [1775]

when violence finally erupts. . . . In June, . . . skirmishes give way to outright war in the Battle of Bunker Hill. It would be the bloodiest battle of the Revolution to come, and the point of no return for the rebellious colonists." (Publisher's note)

Includes bibliographical references and index

★ **Valiant** Ambition; George Washington, Benedict Arnold, and the Fate of the American Revolution. by Nathaniel Philbrick. Penguin Group USA 2016 448 p. ill., maps, portraits $30   **973.3**
1. United States -- History -- 1775-1783, Revolution
ISBN 0525426787; 9780525426783

This book, by Nathaniel Philbrick, is an "account of the middle years of the American Revolution, and the tragic relationship between George Washington and Benedict Arnold. . . . As a country wary of tyrants suddenly must figure out how it should be led, Washington's unmatched ability to rise above the petty politics of his time enables him to win the war that really matters." (Publisher's note)

"Philbrick weaves exciting accounts of Arnold's impulsive battlefield exploits with the activities of self-interested military and civil associates into the demythified story of the circumstances of a tragic betrayal." LJ

Includes bibliographical references (pages 329-403) and index.

Phillips, Kevin, 1940-

1775; a good year for revolution. Kevin Phillips. Viking 2012 656 p. $36   **973.3**
1. Great Britain -- History 2. United States -- History -- 1775-1783, Revolution 3. United States -- Foreign relations -- Great Britain 4. United States. Continental Congress 5. Concord, Battle of, Concord, Mass., 1775 6. Fort Ticonderoga (N.Y.) -- Capture, 1775 7. Lexington, Battle of, Lexington, Mass., 1775 8. Boston (Mass.) -- History -- Siege, 1775-1776 9. United States -- History -- Revolution, 1775-1783 10. United States -- Politics and government -- 1775-1783
ISBN 0670025127; 9780670025121
LC 2012001786

Author Kevin Phillips looks at "the myth that 1776 was the watershed year of the American Revolution. He suggests that the great events and confrontations of 1775--Congress's belligerent economic ultimatums to Britain . . . and the new provincial congresses and hundreds of local committees that quickly reconstituted local authority in Patriot hands--achieved a sweeping Patriot control of territory and local government that Britain was never able to overcome." (Publisher's note)

Includes bibliographical references and index.

Rakove, Jack

Revolutionaries; a new history of the invention of America. [by] Jack Rakove. Houghton Mifflin Harcourt 2010 487p $30   **973.3**
1. Statesmen -- United States 2. United States -- Intellectual life 3. United States -- History -- 1775-1783, Revolution 4. United States -- History -- Revolution, 1775-1783 5. United States -- Intellectual life -- 18th century 6. United States -- Politics and government -- 1775-1783 7. Revolutionaries -- United States -- History -- 18th century 8. United States -- Politics and

government -- 1775-1783, Revolution
ISBN 978-0-618-26746-0

LC 2009-47557

The author "reflects on how a group of lawyers and planters came to wage the American Revolution. Instead of focusing on the battlefield, the author examines what might be called a revolution of the mind—that is, how the early Founding Fathers' ideas developed and took hold. . . . An ambitious, intelligent exploration into the intellectual underpinnings of the Revolution." Kirkus

Includes bibliographical references

Raphael, Ray

★ A **people's** history of the American Revolution; how common people shaped the fight for independence. 1st Perennial ed; Perennial 2002 506p pa $13.95 **973.3**

1. United States -- History -- 1775-1783, Revolution
ISBN 0-06-000440-1

LC 2002-16992

First published 2001 by New Press

"Moving from broad overviews to stories of small groups or individuals, Raphael's study is impressive in both its sweep and its attention to the particular." Publ Wkly

Includes bibliographical references

The **spirit** of 74; how the American Revolution began. Ray Raphael and Marie Raphael. The New Press 2015 288 p. (hardcover : alk. paper) $26.95 **973.3**

1. United States -- Politics and government 2. United States -- History -- 1775-1783, Revolution 3. Massachusetts -- History -- Revolution, 1775-1783 4. United States -- History -- Revolution, 1775-1783 -- Causes

ISBN 9781620971260; 1620971267

LC 2015008420

This book by Ray Raphael and Marie Raphael "fills in this gap in our nation's founding narrative, showing how in these mislaid months, step by step, real people made a revolution. A 'Spirit of '74' initiated the American Revolution, much as the better-known 'Spirit of '76' sparked independence." (Publisher's note)

The Raphaels expertly contextualize how the outbreak of a shooting war at Lexington and Concord marked a crucial 'turning point' in, rather than the beginning of, the American Revolution." Pub Wkly

Includes bibliographical references and index

Taylor, Alan

American Revolutions; A Continental History, 1750-1804. Alan Taylor. W W Norton & Co Inc 2016 736 p. $37.5 **973.3**

1. United States -- History -- 1775-1783, Revolution 2. United States -- History -- 1600-1775, Colonial period
ISBN 0393082814; 9780393082814

Author Alan Taylor, "gives us a different creation story in this magisterial history of the nation's founding. Taylor's Revolution builds like a ground fire overspreading Britain's mainland colonies, fueled by local conditions, destructive, hard to quell. Taylor skillfully draws France, Spain, and native powers into a comprehensive narrative of the war that

delivers the major battles, generals, and common soldiers with insight and power." (Publisher's note)

"A clear, authoritative, well-organized look at the messy Colonial march toward revolution and self-rule." Kirkus

Tuchman, Barbara Wertheim

The **first** salute; [by] Barbara W. Tuchman. Knopf 1988 347p il maps hardcover o.p. pa $16.95 **973.3**

1. United States -- History -- 1775-1783, Revolution
ISBN 0-394-55333-0; 0-345-33667-4 pa

LC 88-45216

"The book is a tightly woven narrative, ingeniously structured. It is not a blow-by-blow account of the conflict; familiarity with issues and events is assumed. Instead, Tuchman takes a specific incident and through it elucidates the course and outcome of the war." Christ Sci Monit

Includes bibliographical references

Unger, Harlow Giles

American tempest; how the Boston Tea Party sparked a revolution. [by] Harlow Giles Unger. Da Capo Press 2011 288p il map $26 **973.3**

1. Boston Tea Party, 1773 2. United States -- History -- 1775-1783, Revolution -- Causes
ISBN 978-0-306-81962-9; 0-306-819627

LC 2010-47734

"As Unger makes clear, the true impact of the Boston Tea Party came from Britain's ill-advised overreaction to the symbolic act of vandalism. It was exactly the response [Sam] Adams had dreamed of, with an enraged British government closing the port of Boston, sending more troops, imposing martial law, and requiring permits for any large Boston meetings. These 'Coercive Acts,' along with Adams's constant drumbeat of anti-British propaganda, helped unify the colonies around the idea of independence. Unger ends the book with British soldiers marching out to Lexington and Concord hoping to arrest Adams and Hancock (who, tipped off by Paul Revere, had fled). The rest, as they say, is history, and Unger has brought it brilliantly to life." Boston Globe

Includes bibliographical references

Vowell, Sarah, 1969-

Lafayette in the Somewhat United States; by Sarah Vowell. Penguin Group USA 2015 288 p. illustrations $27.95 **973.3**

1. United States -- History -- 1775-1783, Revolution
ISBN 1594631743; 9781594631740

LC 2015024639

This book, by Sarah Vowell, is an "account of George Washington's trusted officer and friend, that swashbuckling teenage French aristocrat the Marquis de Lafayette. Chronicling General Lafayette's years in Washington's army, Vowell reflects on the ideals of the American Revolution versus the reality of the Revolutionary War." (Publisher's note)

"In this crash course on the fledgling nation's teenaged French general, undoubtedly the only American Revolution narrative to offhandedly drop a Ferris Bueller reference, Vowell . . . retains her familiar casual tone and displays her crow-like ability to find the shiny, nearly forgotten historical details." Pub Wkly

Weintraub, Stanley

Iron tears; America's battle for freedom, Britain's quagmire, 1775-1783. Free Press 2005 375p il maps $28 **973.3**

1. United States -- History -- 1775-1783, Revolution
ISBN 0-7432-2687-9

LC 2004-56363

The author "examines the possibility that the British lost the war because of protest and lack of support at home. . . . The British failure to win a war against ill-trained but determined guerrilla forces in often unpredictable circumstances and weather appears now as an eerie harbinger of modern conflicts such as the Vietnam War. Weintraub's fast-paced narrative and impeccable historical research provide a stimulating challenge to conventional histories of the Revolutionary War that focus exclusively on the heroism of American forces." Publ Wkly

Includes bibliographical references

Wood, Gordon S.

The **radicalism** of the American Revolution. Knopf 1992 447p hardcover o.p. pa $16 **973.3**

1. United States -- Social life and customs 2. United States -- History -- 1775-1783, Revolution 3. United States -- Politics and government -- 1775-1783, Revolution
ISBN 0-679-73688-3 pa

LC 91-19719

"Under the broad categories of monarchy, republicanism, and democracy, Wood explains how the US was transformed from a society that took for granted a nonworking elite and a dependent servile underclass to one in which the free-standing individualist, who worked for a living, became the norm. . . . {A} readable book based on hundreds of primary and secondary sources." Choice

Includes bibliographical references

973.385   American secret service and spies

Nagy, John A.

George Washington's secret spy war; The Making of America's First Spymaster. John A. Nagy. St. Martin's Press 2016 384 p. illustrations (ebook) $60; (hardcover) $27.99 **973.385**

1. Spies -- United States 2. American espionage -- History 3. United States -- History -- 1775-1783, Revolution 4. Spies -- United States -- Biography 5. Espionage -- United States -- History -- 18th century 6. United States -- History -- Revolution, 1775-1783 -- Secret service
ISBN 9781250096821; 9781250096814

LC 2016021588

This book by John A. Nagy tells "how George Washington took a disorderly, ill-equipped rabble and defeated the best trained and best equipped army of its day in the Revolutionary War. . . . Using George Washington's diary as the primary source, Nagy tells the story of Washington's experiences during the French and Indian War and his first steps in the field of espionage." (Publisher's note)

"Nagy's fast-paced chronicle reveals a little-known side of America's Revolutionary War hero." Pub Wkly

Includes bibliographical references and index

973.4   United States--Constitutional period, 1789-1809

Brookhiser, Richard

America's first dynasty; the Adamses, 1735-1918. Free Press 2002 244p il $25; pa $14 **973.4**

1. Authors 2. Diplomats 3. Novelists 4. Historians 5. Presidents 6. Vice-presidents 7. Senators 8. Essayists 9. Political leaders 10. Members of Congress 11. Secretaries of state
ISBN 0-684-86881-4; 0-684-86864-4 pa

LC 2001-51276

An "account of the lives of John, John Quincy, Charles Francis and Henry, four generations of men often brilliant but often shortsighted as well: two presidents, one diplomat and, finally, a historian who felt he had failed the ancestors." N Y Times Book Rev

Includes bibliographical references

Burstein, Andrew

Madison and Jefferson; [by] Andrew Burstein and Nancy Isenberg. Random House 2010 809p il map $35; e-book $35 **973.4**

1. Architects 2. Presidents 3. Vice-presidents 4. Essayists 5. Members of Congress 6. Secretaries of state 7. Presidents -- United States 8. United States -- Politics and government -- 1783-1865 9. United States -- Politics and government -- 1775-1783, Revolution
ISBN 978-1-4000-6728-2; 978-0-679-60410-5 e-book

LC 2010-5884

This "dual biography promotes Madison from junior partner to full-fledged colleague of the 'more magnetic' Jefferson. According to the authors, Madison's popular image peaked in 1789 as 'father of the Constitution.' But Burstein . . . and Isenberg . . . see him as a canny, effective politician for four decades, from the Continental Congress through his two terms as America's fourth president. . . . An important, thoughtful, and gracefully written political history from the viewpoint of the young nation's two most intellectual founding fathers." Publ Wkly

Includes bibliographical references and index

Cerami, Charles A.

Jefferson's great gamble; the remarkable story of Jefferson, Napoleon and the men behind the Louisiana Purchase. Sourcebooks 2003 309p il $22.95; pa $14.95 **973.4**

1. Emperors 2. Architects 3. Presidents 4. Vice-presidents 5. Louisiana Purchase 6. Essayists
ISBN 1-57071-945-4; 1-40220-240-7 pa

LC 2002-153440

"Anyone wanting to read the story of a momentous turning point in American history, a story of diplomatic maneuvering and international politics, will be hard-pressed to find a better version than this." Publ Wkly

Includes bibliographical references

Ellis, Joseph J.

Founding brothers; the revolutionary generation. Knopf 2000 288p $26.95; pa $14   **973.4**
1. United States -- Biography 2. Presidents -- United States 3. United States -- History -- 1783-1809 4. United States -- Politics and government -- 1783-1809
ISBN 0-375-40544-5; 0-375-70524-4 pa
LC 99-59304
"Ellis' essays are angled, fascinating, and perfect for general-interest readers." Booklist
Includes bibliographical references

Gordon-Reed, Annette

Thomas Jefferson and Sally Hemings; an American controversy. University Press of Va. 1997 xx, 288p hardcover o.p. pa $14.95   **973.4**
1. Slaves 2. Architects 3. Presidents 4. Vice-presidents 5. Essayists 6. Mistresses
ISBN 0-8139-1833-2 pa
LC 96-34550
"Hemings, a slave who was one-quarter African, was also a half sister of Jefferson's deceased wife, and she lived at Monticello for many years. In this understated, brilliant study an African-American law professor examines the allegation that Jefferson was the father of Hemings' children." New Yorker
Includes bibliographical references

Hamilton, Alexander

Writings. Library of Am. 2001 1108p $40 **973.4**
1. United States -- Politics and government -- 1783-1809 2. United States -- Politics and government -- 1775-1783, Revolution
ISBN 1-931082-04-9
LC 2001-23043
"The text consists of more than 170 letters, speeches, essays, reports, and memoranda written between 1769 and 1804, including all of Hamilton's material presented in The Federalist. This additionally sports several conflicting eyewitness accounts of Hamilton's lethal duel with Aaron Burr." Libr J
Includes bibliographical references

Hogeland, William

★ The **Whiskey** Rebellion; George Washington, Alexander Hamilton, and the frontier rebels who challenged America's newfound sovereignty. Scribner 2006 302p map $26.95; pa $16   **973.4**
1. Whiskey Rebellion, Pa., 1794
ISBN 978-0-7432-5490-8; 0-7432-5490-2; 978-0-7432-5491-5 pa; 0-7432-5491-0 pa
LC 2005-56340
"Soon after Americans ousted inequitable British taxation, Secretary of Finance Alexander Hamilton, hatched a plan to put the new nation on steady financial footing by imposing the first American excise tax, on whiskey makers. The tax favored large distillers over small farmers with stills in the mountains of Pennsylvania, Maryland and Virginia, and the farmers fomented their own new revolution— a challenge to the sovereignty of the new government and the power of the wealthy eastern seaboard. In a fast-paced, blow-by-blow account of this 'primal national drama,' jour-

nalist Hogeland energetically chronicles the skirmishes that made the Whiskey Rebellion from 1791 to 1795 a symbol of the conflict between republican ideals and capitalist values." Publ Wkly
Includes bibliographical references

Kranish, Michael

Flight from Monticello; Thomas Jefferson at war. Michael Kranish. Oxford University Press 2010 xii, 388 p.p   **973.4**
1. Statesmen 2. Architects 3. Presidents 4. Vice-presidents 5. Governors -- Virginia -- Biography 6. Presidents -- United States -- Biography 7. Virginia -- History -- Revolution, 1775-1783 8. Virginia -- Politics and government -- 1775-1783 9. United States -- Politics and government -- 1783-1809
ISBN 0195374622; 9780195374629 (acid-free paper)
LC 2009018156
This is an account of Jefferson's life during the period when he served as governor of Virginia. He became governor "in 1779 and had to face repeated invasions of his state by British forces." (Newsweek) Index.
"Crisply written and well documented, this book is popular history at its best and will appeal to a wide readership. Highly recommended." Libr J
Includes bibliographical references (p. [371]-373)

Kukla, Jon

A **wilderness** so immense; the Louisiana Purchase and the destiny of America. Knopf 2003 430p il map $30; pa $16   **973.4**
1. Louisiana Purchase
ISBN 0-375-40812-6; 0-375-70761-1 pa
LC 2002-27395
"This judicious, aptly illustrated work will gratify all its readers. Rarely does a work of history combine grace of writing with such broad authority." Publ Wkly
Includes bibliographical references

The **Louisiana** Purchase; a historical and geographical encyclopedia. Junius P. Rodriguez, editor. ABC-CLIO 2002 xxxv, 513p il maps $95 **973.4**
1. Louisiana Purchase 2. United States -- History -- 1783-1809
ISBN 1-57607-188-X
LC 2002-3228
"The reasons for as well as the immediate and historical repercussions of the purchase are explored in nearly 300 articles written by 85 distinguished scholars. Coverage includes native peoples, noteworthy personalities, and geographical areas associated with a land acquisition that nearly doubled the size of our nation. An extensive bibliography, 49 pertinent documents, a chronology, and an index round out this excellent volume." Libr J
Includes bibliographical references

Miller, John Chester

The **Federalist** era, 1789-1801; by John C. Miller. Waveland Press 1998 304p il pa $16.95 **973.4**
1. Statesmen 2. Architects 3. Presidents 4. Vice-presidents 5. Essayists 6. Federal Party (U.S.) 7. Secretaries of the treasury 8. United States -- History

-- 1783-1809
ISBN 978-1-57766-031-6; 1-57766-031-5
First published 1960 by Harper & Row
A chronicle of the administrations of George Washington and John Adams, concentrating on the politics and diplomacy.
Includes bibliographical references

Purcell, Sarah J.
The **early** national period; [by] Sarah Purcell. Facts on File 2004 420p il map (Eyewitness history) $75   **973.4**
1. United States -- History -- 1783-1865
ISBN 0-8160-4769-3
LC 2003-14969
"A serious history student will find this book invaluable." Libr Media Connect
Includes bibliographical references

Sedgwick, John
War of two; Alexander Hamilton, Aaron Burr, and the duel that stunned the nation. John Sedgwick. Berkley Books 2015 480 p. color illustrations (hardcover : alk. paper) $27.95   **973.4**
1. United States -- Politics and government -- 1783-1809 2. Burr-Hamilton Duel, Weehawken, N.J., 1804 3. United States -- Politics and government -- 1801-1809
ISBN 9781592408528
LC 2015014275
This book, by John Sedgwick, is an "investigation into the rivalry between Alexander Hamilton and Aaron Burr, whose infamous duel left the Founding Father dead and turned a sitting Vice President into a fugitive. . . . A series of letters between Burr and Hamilton suggest the duel was fought over an unflattering comment made at a dinner party. But another letter . . . provides critical insight into his true motivation. It was addressed to former Speaker of the House Theodore Sedgwick." (Publisher's note)
"A fine rendition of a storied episode in American history." Booklist
Includes bibliographical references and index

Staloff, Darren
Hamilton, Adams, Jefferson; the politics of enlightenment and the American founding. Hill & Wang 2005 419p $30   **973.4**
1. Statesmen 2. Architects 3. Presidents 4. Enlightenment 5. Vice-presidents 6. Essayists 7. Secretaries of the treasury
ISBN 0-8090-7784-1; 978-0-8090-7784-7
LC 2005-40433
"Staloff has created a work that is a must-read for any serious scholar of US history." Choice
Includes bibliographical references

Stewart, David O.
American emperor; Aaron Burr's challenge to Jefferson's America. Simon & Schuster 2011 xx, 410p il map $30; ebook $14.99   **973.4**
1. Architects 2. Presidents 3. Vice-presidents 4. Essayists 5. Presidents -- United States -- Election -- 1800 6. United States -- Politics and government --

1783-1809
ISBN 978-1-4391-5718-3; 978-1-4391-6032-9 ebook
LC 2011002647
Traces the career of the third U.S. vice president and would-be secession leader, discussing his acrimonious relationship with Thomas Jefferson; his ambitious vision of expansion; and his historical, self-defended trial for treason.
"A persuasive, engaging examination of the post-political career of a shadowy and much-maligned figure from the era of the Founders." Kirkus
Includes bibliographical references

Vidal, Gore
Inventing a nation: Washington, Adams, Jefferson. Yale University Press 2003 224p $22; pa $14   **973.4**
1. Generals 2. Architects 3. Presidents 4. Vice-presidents 5. Essayists
ISBN 0-300-10171-6; 0-300-10592-4 pa
LC 2003-015612
Vidal offers "characteristically brilliant and acerbic reflections on power and personality. . . . This entertaining and enlightening reappraisal of the Founders is a must for buffs of American civilization and its discontents." Booklist

Washington, George, 1732-1799
★ **Writings.** Library of Am. 1997 xxiii, 1149p $40   **973.4**
1. Virginia -- History 2. United States -- Politics and government -- 1783-1809 3. United States -- Politics and government -- 1775-1783, Revolution
ISBN 1-883011-23-X
LC 96-9665
This "selection of Washington's letters, speeches, diary entries, maxims and military orders reveals a writer of surprising versatility and a statesman consciously involved with the forging of our national character." Publ Wkly

Wiencek, Henry
★ An **imperfect** god; George Washington, his slaves, and the creation of America. Farrar, Straus and Giroux 2003 404p il map $26; pa $15 **973.4**
1. Generals 2. Presidents 3. Presidents -- United States
ISBN 0-374-17526-8; 0-374-52951-5 pa
LC 2003-6984
"This work of stylish scholarship and genealogical investigation makes Washington an even greater and more human figure than he has seemed before." Publ Wkly
Includes bibliographical references

★ **Master** of the mountain; Thomas Jefferson and his slaves. Henry Wiencek. Farrar, Straus and Giroux 2012 352 p. ill. maps, geneal. tables (alk. paper) $28.00   **973.4**
1. Slavery -- United States 2. United States -- History -- 1775-1865 3. Monticello (Va.) -- History 4. Slaves -- Virginia -- Albemarle County -- History 5. Plantation life -- Virginia -- Albemarle County -- History
ISBN 0374299560; 9780374299569
LC 2011052231
In this book, Henry Wiencek "explores the economic calculus behind [Thomas] Jefferson's gradual cooling to-

ward emancipation and eventual acceptance of human capital as a great 'investment opportunity.' Wiencek argues . . . that Jefferson not only failed to follow the advice and example of his peers . . . and embrace emancipation but was in fact a 'pioneer in the monetizing of slaves' and went to great lengths to impose 'his own reality' on his 'little familial empire.'" (Library Journal)

"Wiencek's insightful and engaging account is recommended to both the illustrious Virginian's detractors and to his devotees." LJ

Includes bibliographical references (p.305-315) and index.

Wood, Gordon S., 1933-

★ **Empire** of liberty; a history of the early Republic, 1789-1815. Oxford University Press 2009 778p il map (Oxford history of the United States) $35 **973.4**

1. United States--Civilization 2. National characteristics, American 3. United States -- Civilization -- 1783-1865 4. United States -- Politics and government -- 1783-1809 5. United States -- Politics and government -- 1783-1865

ISBN 978-0-19-503914-6

LC 2009-10762

"Skillfully traversing seminal topics such as slavery, westward expansion, social leveling, diplomacy, evangelicalism, the arts and sciences, and the transformation of the American legal system, Wood's authoritative and compelling narrative presents a picture of early Americans engaged in pursuit of cultural, social, and economic self-discovery. . . . [This is] a brilliant, definitive, and thought-provoking historical synthesis; sure to become indispensable to any study of the era." Libr J

Includes bibliographical references

Yaeger, Don

George Washington's secret six; the spy ring that saved the American Revolution. Brian Kilmeade and Don Yaeger. Sentinel 2013 256 p. illustrations, map $27.95 **973.4**

1. American espionage 2. United States -- History -- 1775-1783, Revolution 3. Spies -- United States -- History -- 18th century 4. Spies -- New York (State) -- History -- 18th century 5. United States -- History -- Revolution, 1775-1783 -- Secret service 6. New York (State) -- History -- Revolution, 1775-1783 -- Secret service

ISBN 159523103X; 9781595231031

LC 2013032285

This book by Brian Kilmeade and Don Yaeger examines the American Revolution and General George Washington's "little-known, top-secret group called the Culper Spy Ring. Kilmeade and . . . Yaeger have painted compelling portraits of George Washington's secret six [including]: Robert Townsend, the reserved Quaker merchant . . . Austin Roe, the tavern keeper . . . [and] Agent 355, a woman whose identity remains unknown." (Publisher's note)

"While Kilmeade and Yaeger don't provide deep analysis, the narrative should please enthusiastic fans of the upheaval surrounding the founding of the United States. In a slim, quick-moving book, the authors bring attention to a group that exerted an enormous influence over events during the Revolutionary War." Kirkus

Includes bibliographical references and index

Zacks, Richard

The **pirate** coast; Thomas Jefferson, the first marines, and the secret mission of 1805. Hyperion 2005 432p il map $25.95; pa $15.95 **973.4**

1. Diplomats 2. Architects 3. Presidents 4. Vice-presidents 5. Essayists 6. Army officers 7. United States -- History -- 1801-1805, Tripolitan War

ISBN 1-401-30003-0; 1-401-30849-X pa

LC 2004-60635

"This is the book that Captain Eaton has long deserved." Publ Wkly

Includes bibliographical references

973.5   United States--1809-1845

Cook, Jane Hampton

American phoenix; John Quincy and Louisa Adams, the War of 1812, and the exile that saved American independence. Jane Hampton Cook. Thomas Nelson 2013 x, 502 p.p ill. (some col.) (hardcover) $26.99 **973.5**

1. Diplomats -- United States -- Biography 2. Presidents -- United States -- Biography 3. Russia -- Foreign relations -- United States 4. United States -- Foreign relations -- Russia 5. United States -- History -- War of 1812 -- Peace 6. Presidents' spouses -- United States -- Biography 7. United States -- History -- War of 1812 -- Biography 8. United States -- History -- War of 1812 -- Diplomatic history

ISBN 1595555412; 9781595555410

LC 2012039898

This is a "dual biography of John Quincy and Louisa Adams during the former's service as United States envoy to Russia (1809-1814) and throughout his negotiations with Britain that produced the Treaty of Ghent and ended the War of 1812." Jane Hampton Cook "draws heavily from diaries and voluminous correspondences to render the couple's daily and inner struggles." (Publishers Weekly)

Includes bibliographical references and index

Daughan, George C.

1812: the Navy's war; George C. Daughan. Basic Books 2011 xxix, 491p il map $32.50 **973.5**

1. War of 1812 2. United States -- Navy -- History

ISBN 978-0-465-02046-1; 978-0-465-02808-5 ebook

LC 2011020923

This book provides an account of "the U.S. Navy's surprising performance in the war that finally reconciled the British to America's independence. . . . If the U.S. Navy . . . didn't win the War of 1812, it probably kept the nation from losing. The . . . exploits of outstanding officers like Isaac Hull, David Porter, Stephen Decatur and Oliver Hazard Perry earned new respect for America's fleet; victories by the Essex, the Hornet and the Constitution . . . set off national celebrations. Daughan supplies . . . the big picture-the dismal struggles of both armies, Napoleon's off-stage machinations that determined so much of the war's progress, the outcome of domestic political squabbles upon which the navy's survival depended . . , but he focuses on the personalities, ships and battles that prevented the British from suffocating the infant nation's maritime ambitions." (Kirkus)

"Daughan narrates the story of the War of 1812, focusing on the tiny, 20-ship U.S. Navy. In doing so, from the poorly conducted chase of HMS Belvidera by Commodore John Rogers in June 1812 to the capture of HMS Penguin by USS Hornet in March 1815, Daughan also traces the development of the U.S. Navy." Libr J

Includes bibliographical references

Groom, Winston

Patriotic fire; Andrew Jackson and Jean Laffite at the Battle of New Orleans. Alfred A. Knopf 2006 xxiv, 292p il map $26 **973.5**

1. Pirates 2. Generals 3. Presidents 4. New Orleans (La.), Battle of, 1815

ISBN 1-4000-4436-7; 978-1-4000-4436-8

LC 2005-51001

"This is a beautifully written and exciting work of popular history." Booklist

Includes bibliographical references

Hahn, Steven

A **Nation** Without Borders; The United States and Its World in an Age of Civil Wars, 1830-1910. Steven Hahn; edited by Eric Foner. Penguin Group USA 2016 608 p. $35 **973.5**

1. Capitalism 2. Mexican War, 1846-1848 3. United States -- History -- 19th century 4. United States -- History -- 1861-1865, Civil War

ISBN 0670024686; 9780670024681

LC 2016018053

This book by Pulitzer Prize-winning historian Steven Hahn "takes on the conventional histories of the nineteenth century and offers a perspective that promises to be as enduring as it is controversial. It begins and ends in Mexico and, throughout, is internationalist in orientation. . . . It places the Civil War in the context of many domestic rebellions against state authority. . . . It reconfigures the history of capitalism." (Publisher's note)

"Given Hahn's unimpeachable body of knowledge, readers can be confident that they're getting the most current understanding of the history of the U.S." Pub Wkly

Howe, Daniel Walker, 1937-

★ **What** hath God wrought; the transformation of America, 1815-1848. Oxford University Press 2007 904p il map (Oxford history of the United States) $35 **973.5**

1. Social change -- United States 2. United States -- History -- 1815-1861 3. United States -- Foreign relations -- 1815-1861 4. United States -- Politics and government -- 1815-1861

ISBN 978-0-19-507894-7; 0-19-507894-2

LC 2007-12370

The author "narrates a crucial period in U.S. history— a time of territorial growth, religious revival, booming industrialization, a recalibrating of American democracy and the rise of nationalist sentiment. . . . Supported by engaging prose, Howe's achievement will surely be seen as one of the most outstanding syntheses of U.S. history published this decade." Publ Wkly

Includes bibliographical references

Inskeep, Steve

Jacksonland; President Andrew Jackson, Cherokee Chief John Ross, and a Great American Land Grab. by Steve Inskeep. Penguin Group USA 2015 448 p. 8 plates; ills.; maps; ports. $29.95 **973.5**

1. Cherokee Indians 2. Land settlement -- United States

ISBN 1594205566; 9781594205569

LC 2015300789

This book, by Steve Inskeep, "is the thrilling narrative history of two men-- President Andrew Jackson and Cherokee chief John Ross-- who led their respective nations at a crossroads of American history. Five decades after the Revolutionary War, the United States approached a constitutional crisis. At its center stood two former military comrades locked in a struggle that tested the boundaries of our fledgling democracy." (Publisher's note)

"This superb book is highly recommended for readers interested in Native American studies or Southern history. For more on Catherine Beecher and her movement, see Alisse Portnoy's Their Right To Speak: Women's Activism in the Indian and Slave Debates." LJ

Langguth, A. J., 1933-2014

Driven West; Andrew Jackson and the Trail of Tears to the Civil War. Simon & Schuster 2010 466p il map $30; ebook $14.99 **973.5**

1. Generals 2. Presidents 3. Trail of Tears, 1838-1839 4. Native Americans -- Relocation 5. United States -- History -- 1815-1861

ISBN 978-1-4165-4859-1; 1-4165-4859-9; 978-1-4391-9327-3 ebook; 1-4391-9327-4 ebook

LC 2010-20455

Langguth argues "that the passage of the Indian Removal Act of 1830, Jackson's breaking of Indian treaties and his support of the Southern states, especially Georgia, in resisting a Supreme Court ruling in favor of the Cherokees were 'salvos . . . fired in the nation's first civil war.'" (N Y Times Book Rev) Bibliography. Index.

"A disturbing reconsideration of a key period of history and a powerful indictment of its main actors." Kirkus

Includes bibliographical references

Lincoln, Abraham, 1809-1865

★ **Speeches** and writings, 1832-1858; speeches, letters, and miscellaneous writings: the Lincoln Douglas debates. Library of Am. 1989 898p $35 **973.5**

1. Lincoln-Douglas debates, 1858 2. United States -- Politics and government -- 1815-1861

ISBN 0-940450-43-7

LC 88-82723

Based on the "eight volumes of 'The Collected Works of Abraham Lincoln,' edited by Roy P. Basler, Marion Dolores Pratt and Lloyd A. Dunlap, the present . . . [volume contains] all seven of the Lincoln-Douglas debates, as well as the . . . speeches, before and after the debates, that attacked the repeal of the Missouri Compromise of 1820 and 'squatter sovereignty' in the territories." N Y Times Book Rev

Includes bibliographical references

Miller, William Lee

Arguing about slavery; the great battle in the United States Congress. Knopf 1996 577p hardcover o.p. pa $17   **973.5**

1. Presidents 2. Senators 3. Members of Congress 4. Secretaries of state 5. Slavery -- United States 6. United States -- Congress 7. United States -- Politics and government -- 1815-1861

ISBN 0-679-76844-0 pa

LC 95-35075

"Miller lays out the arcane workings of the proceedings with admirable detail, clarity, and verve." Christ Sci Monit

Includes bibliographical references

Oates, Stephen B.

The **approaching** fury; voices of the storm, 1820-1861. Buz Wyeth, editor. HarperCollins Pubs. 1997 495p hardcover o.p. pa $15   **973.5**

1. United States -- History -- 1815-1861 2. United States -- History -- 1861-1865, Civil War -- Causes

ISBN 0-06-092885-9 pa

LC 96-31965

Companion volume to The whirlwind of war

"Taken on its own terms, this book powerfully re-creates some of the momentous events that produced the catastrophe of 1861. Mr. Oates succeeds in bringing his characters alive and in creating highly dramatic scenes for them to act out." N Y Times Book Rev

Includes bibliographical references

Reynolds, David S.

Waking giant; America in the age of Jackson. Harper 2008 466p il $29.95   **973.5**

1. Generals 2. Presidents 3. United States -- History -- 1815-1861

ISBN 978-0-06-082656-7

LC 2007-51751

This is "a terrific introduction of succinct length to . . . a time when the foundations of much of modern America were laid." N Y Times (Late N Y Ed)

Includes bibliographical references

Smith, Gene Allen

The **slaves'** gamble; choosing sides in the War of 1812. Gene Allen Smith. Palgrave Macmillan 2013 272 p. $27   **973.5**

1. War of 1812 2. Slavery -- United States

ISBN 0230342086; 9780230342088

LC 2012045726

This book by Gene Allen Smith explains that "in the [19th] century's first two decades, the [United States] waged war against Britain, Spain, and various Indian tribes. Slaves played a role in the military operations, and the different sides viewed them as a potential source of manpower. While surprising numbers did assist the Americans, the wars created opportunities for slaves to find freedom among the Redcoats, the Spaniards, or the Indians." (Publisher's note)

Includes bibliographical references and index.

Taylor, Alan

The **civil** war of 1812; American citizens, British subjects, Irish rebels, & Indian allies. Alfred A. Knopf 2010 620p il map $35; e-book $35   **973.5**

1. War of 1812 2. Ontario -- History -- War of 1812 3. United States -- History -- War of 1812 4. Northern boundary of the United States -- History

ISBN 978-1-4000-4265-4; 1-4000-4265-8; 978-0-307-59459-4 e-book

LC 2010-12783

In this book, Alan "Taylor examines themes pertinent to the period and the war [of 1812], blending narrative with analysis. He sees this upheaval, and the earlier American Revolution, as part of an anglophone civil war that defined America, Canada, and the British Empire in the nineteenth century. It was a peculiar type of civil war, to be certain, as it involved more than one state and more than one culture. . . . Many Canadians were in fact displaced American loyalists who hoped to undo the revolution. . . . Taylor draws on the conceptual frameworks created in the burgeoning field of borderlands history to construct his study. He uses this approach to situate the character of the war along the American-Canadian border, which he sees as central to the entire conflict." (American Historical Review)

"Instead of a traditional narrative of the war from its beginnings in June 1812 to its end in early 1815, [this] book is structured topically. . . . Such a neat and methodical organization helps Taylor bring the confused and chaotic events of the war under control. It also allows him to present an enormous amount of material—on persons, events, and stories—without overwhelming the reader. And the amount of material is enormous." N Y Rev Books

Includes bibliographical references

Tocqueville, Alexis de

Democracy in America; with an introduction by Alan Ryan. Knopf 1994 lxxii, 434, xi, 394p (Everyman's library) $27   **973.5**

1. Democracy 2. American national characteristics 3. United States -- Social conditions 4. United States -- Politics and government

ISBN 978-0-679-43134-3; 0-679-43134-9

LC 94-1752

First part originally published in France, 1835; the second in 1840

Based partly on the French author's observations of American political and social conditions during a visit in 1831-1832. "It remains the best philosophical discussion of Democracy illustrated by the experience of the United States, up to the time when it was written, which can be found in any language." Pratt Alcove

Includes bibliographical references

Vogel, Steve

Through the perilous fight; six weeks that saved the nation. Steve Vogel. Random House Inc 2013 560 p. (acid-free paper) $30   **973.5**

1. War of 1812 2. Baltimore, Battle of, Baltimore, Md., 1814 3. Maryland -- History -- War of 1812 -- Campaigns 4. United States -- History -- War of 1812 -- Campaigns 5. Washington (D.C.) -- History -- Capture

by the British, 1814
ISBN 1400069130; 9780679603474; 9781400069132
LC 2012039797

This book is a "chronicle of the critical closing months of the War of 1812—specifically, the British attacks on Washington and Baltimore." Steve Vogel "begins in the summer of 1814 with the British planning their attack. They were eager for payback after the American invasion of Canada two years earlier. Vogel focuses on Rear Adm. George Cockburn—a figure he revisits throughout—who was especially intent on capturing and torching Washington." (Kirkus Reviews)

Includes bibliographical references and index

Wilentz, Sean

The **rise** of American democracy; Jefferson to Lincoln. Norton 2005 xxiii, 1044p il $35   **973.5**
1. Democracy 2. Democracy -- United States 3. United States -- Politics and government -- 1783-1865
ISBN 0-393-05820-4
LC 2004-29466

Wilentz traces the evolution of democratic principles in the United States from the American Revolution to the Civil War. Index.

This "is a magnificent chronicle, the life of an idea that, although it is mentioned nowhere in the Constitution, nevertheless slowly elbowed its way into the heart of American life. . . . Wilentz shows what [the] fight has cost, and why it's worth it." Newsweek

Includes bibliographical references

973.6   United States--1845-1861

Bordewich, Fergus M.

America's great debate; Henry Clay, Stephen A. Douglas, and the compromise that preserved the Union. Fergus M. Bordewich. Simon & Schuster 2012 x, 480 p.p   **973.6**
1. Debates and debating 2. Slavery -- United States -- History 3. United States -- History -- 1861-1865, Civil War 4. United States -- Politics and government -- 1861-1865 5. Compromise of 1850 6. Slavery -- United States -- History -- 19th century 7. United States -- Politics and government -- 1815-1861 8. United States -- History -- Civil War, 1861-1865 -- Causes
ISBN 1439124604; 9781439124604; 9781439141687
LC 2011029547

In this book, "Historian [Fergus M.] Bordewich . . . recounts the amazing story of the cliffhanging compromise hammered out in both houses of Congress in 1850 that pitted the rival pro- and antislavery factions against each other and saved the country, temporarily, from dissolution. . . . Bordewich portrays a colorful cast of characters--Democrats, Whigs, Free Soilers and abolitionists--whose passionate rhetoric attained lyrical heights and brought the debate about America's very identity to the forefront. Chief architect Henry Clay . . . warned his colleagues of the dire consequences of disunion. . . . Warring factions . . . threatened to defeat the omnibus bill, until the rhetorical arm-wringing

by . . . Stephen A. Douglas squeezed a compromise and the necessary passage." (Kirkus)

Includes bibliographical references (p. [403]-463) and index

Guelzo, Allen C.

Lincoln and Douglas; the debates that defined America. Simon & Schuster 2008 xxvii, 383p il map $26   **973.6**
1. Lawyers 2. Presidents 3. Lincoln-Douglas debates, 1858 4. Senators 5. Political leaders 6. State legislators 7. Members of Congress 8. Presidential candidates 9. United States -- Politics and government -- 1815-1861
ISBN 978-0-7432-7320-6; 0-7432-7320-6
LC 2007-44254

"This Lincoln-Douglas rendition will engage every interest in Civil War and black history." Booklist

Includes bibliographical references

Wineapple, Brenda

Ecstatic nation; confidence, crisis, and compromise, 1848-1877. Brenda Wineapple. Harper 2013 736 p. $35   **973.6**
1. United States -- History 2. Slavery -- United States -- History 3. United States -- History -- 1849-1877 4. Reconstruction (U.S. history, 1865-1877) 5. United States -- History -- Civil War, 1861-1865 6. Slavery -- United States -- History -- 19th century 7. United States -- History -- Civil War, 1861-1865 -- Causes 8. Antislavery movements -- United States -- History -- 19th century 9. United States -- Territorial expansion -- History -- 19th century
ISBN 0061234575; 9780061234576
LC 2012051538

Author Brenda Wineapple's book focuses on the history of the U.S. and discusses people "such as P. T. Barnum, Walt Whitman, George Armstrong Custer, Horace Greeley, and Jefferson Davis." The book discusses "slavery through the devastations of the Civil War and its aftermath. It explores the terrible complexities of Reconstruction and the fledgling hope that women would share equally in a new definition of American citizenship, and it traces the lust for land and the lure of its beauty from a frenzied rush to riches to the displacement of Indians." (Publisher's note)

Includes bibliographical references and index

973.7   Administration of Abraham Lincoln, 1861-1865

Abbott, Karen

Liar, Temptress, Soldier, Spy; Four Women Undercover in the Civil War. by Karen Abbott. HarperCollins Publishers 2014 368 p. illustrations, map $27.99   **973.7**
1. American espionage 2. Women -- United States -- History 3. United States -- History -- 1861-1865, Civil War
ISBN 0062092898; 9780062092892
LC 2014013602

In this book, author Karen Abbott "illuminates . . . little known aspects of the Civil War: the stories of four courageous women--a socialite, a farmgirl, an abolitionist, and a widow--who were spies. . . . Using a wealth of primary source material and interviews with the spies' descendants, Abbott seamlessly weaves the adventures of these four heroines throughout the tumultuous years of the war." (Publisher's note)

"Remarkable, brave lives rendered in a fluidly readable, even romantic history lesson." Kirkus

Includes bibliographical references and index

Ash, Stephen V.

Firebrand of liberty; the story of two Black regiments that changed the course of the Civil War. W.W. Norton & Co. 2008 282p il map $25.95   **973.7**
1. African American soldiers 2. United States -- Army -- South Carolina Volunteers, 1st 3. United States -- History -- 1861-1865, Civil War -- Campaigns 4. United States -- Army -- South Carolina Volunteers, 2nd (1863-1864)

ISBN 978-0-393-06586-2; 0-393-06586-3
LC 2008-2503

"The titular firebrand in this revealing history is not an individual but a curious and ambitious project: the establishment, in March 1863, of a permanent Union outpost in Florida to serve as a haven for fugitive slaves and to 'help ignite the destruction of Southern slavery from within.' In readable prose and relying exclusively on primary sources, historian Ash . . . tells the little-known but crucial story of how 900 newly freed slaves, under the leadership of white abolitionist officers, captured Jacksonville." Publ Wkly

Includes bibliographical references (p. [256]-265) and index.

Berg, Scott W.

★ **38** nooses; Lincoln, Little Crow, and the beginning of the frontier's end. Scott W. Berg. Pantheon Books 2012 384 p. $27.95   **973.7**
1. Native Americans -- Wars 2. United States -- History -- 1775-1865 3. Native Americans -- Government relations -- History 4. Dakota Indians -- Relocation 5. Dakota Indians -- Wars, 1862-1865 6. Dakota Indians -- Government relations -- History -- 19th century 7. Executions and executioners -- United States -- History -- 19th century

ISBN 0307377245; 9780307377241
LC 2012002807

Author Scott W. Berg discusses "events within the larger context of the Civil War, the history of the Dakota people, and the subsequent United States-Indian wars. . . . In August 1862, after decades of broken treaties, increasing hardship, and relentless encroachment on their lands, a group of Dakota warriors convened a council at the tepee of their leader, Little Crow. . . . So began six weeks of intense conflict along the Minnesota frontier as the Dakotas clashed with settlers and federal troops, all the while searching for allies in their struggle." (Publisher's note)

Includes bibliographical references and index.

Blanton, DeAnne

They fought like demons; women soldiers in the American Civil War. {by} DeAnne Blanton and Lau-

ren M. Cook. Louisiana State Univ. Press 2002 277p il (Conflicting worlds) $29.95   **973.7**
1. Women soldiers 2. United States -- History -- 1861-1865, Civil War

ISBN 0-8071-2806-6
LC 2002-4441

"The authors reconstruct the reasons why women entered the armed forces: many were simply patriotic, while others followed their husbands or lovers and yet others yearned to break free from the constraints that Victorian society had laid on them as women. Blanton and Cook detail women soldiers in combat, on the march, in camp and in the hospital, where many were discovered after getting sick. Some even wound up in grim prisons kept by both sides, while a few hid pregnancies and were only discovered after giving birth. . . . Solid research by the authors, including a look at the careers of a few women soldiers after the war, makes this a compelling book that belongs in every Civil War library." Publ Wkly

Includes bibliographical references

Blight, David W.

American oracle. Belknap Press of Harvard University Press 2011 314p $27.95   **973.7**
1. Poets 2. Authors 3. Novelists 4. Dramatists 5. Historians 6. Journalists 7. Essayists 8. Screenwriters 9. Poets laureate 10. Literary critics 11. Magazine editors 12. Short story writers 13. Writers on politics 14. Young adult authors 15. United States -- History -- 1861-1865, Civil War -- Historiography

ISBN 978-0-674-04855-3
LC 2011006653

This book by David W. Blight "examines how we handled the centennial [of the U.S. Civil War,] which occurred at the infancy of the civil rights movement, and the persistent questioning about all the elements that were at the heart of the nation-rending civil conflict." It focuses on "the works of four writers -- Robert Penn Warren, southern-born novelist; Bruce Catton, historian and journalist; Edmund Wilson, literary critic; and James Baldwin, northern-born essayist and race critic." (Booklist)

This "book is a set of critical reflections on the racial attitudes and historical views of four great American writers—James Baldwin, Bruce Catton, Robert Penn Warren, and Edmund Wilson (and in an epilogue, Ralph Ellison)— around the time of the Civil War centennial 50 years ago." Publ Wkly

Includes bibliographical references

Boatner, Mark Mayo

The **Civil** War dictionary; by Mark Mayo Boatner III; maps and diagrams by Allen C. Northrop and Lowell I. Miller. 1st Vintage Civil War Library ed.; Vintage Civil War Library 1991 974p il map pa $24   **973.7**
1. Reference books 2. United States -- History -- 1861-1865, Civil War -- Encyclopedias

ISBN 0-679-73392-2; 978-0-679-73392-8
LC 91-50013

First published 1959 by McKay

"With more than 4,000 entries . . . this dictionary remains the most comprehensive and consistently accurate reference tool on the American Civil War. In addition to the biographical sketches there are entries relating to campaigns and battles, naval engagements, weapons, issues and incidents, military terms and definitions, politics, literature, and statistics." Choice

Includes bibliographical references

Bordewich, Fergus M.

★ **Bound** for Canaan; the epic story of the underground railroad, America's first integrated civil rights movement. Fergus M. Bordewich. Amistad 2005 540p il map $27.95; pa $14.95   **973.7**

1. Underground railroad 2. Slavery -- United States

ISBN 0-06-052430-8; 0-06-052431-6 pa
                                        LC 2004-52082

"The men and women of this remarkable account will remain with readers for a long time to come." Publ Wkly

Includes bibliographical references

Boritt, G. S.

The **Gettysburg** gospel; the Lincoln speech that nobody knows. Simon & Schuster 2006 415p il $28   **973.7**

1. Lawyers 2. Presidents 3. State legislators 4. Members of Congress

ISBN 978-0-7432-8820-0; 0-7432-8820-3
                                        LC 2006-50578

"The author sets the speech in its contemporary context and, most interestingly, demonstrates that it was not only minimally noticed by Lincoln's peers and the press at the time but was virtually forgotten to history until the 20th century. He addresses many of the myths surrounding the address, such as that Lincoln wrote it in haste on the train to Gettysburg. In fact, it went through a number of careful revisions. He includes images of the known copies of the handwritten address, broadsides and programs relating to the dedication ceremony at Gettysburg, selections of photos from the era, and a line-byline analysis of the various drafts of the address. Boritt's narrative style will appeal to lay readers . . . , while his extensive research and insightful conclusions will appeal to scholars." Libr J

Brewster, Todd

Lincoln's Gamble; The Tumultuous Six Months That Gave America the Emancipation Proclamation and Changed the Course of the Civil War. Todd Brewster. Simon & Schuster Scribner 2014 368 p. illustrations $27   **973.7**

1. Emancipation Proclamation 2. United States -- History -- 1861-1865, Civil War 3. Slaves -- Emancipation -- United States 4. United States -- Politics and government -- 1861-1865 5. United States. President (1861-1865 : Lincoln). Emancipation Proclamation

ISBN 1451693869; 9781451693867
                                        LC 2013497336

Author Todd Brewster offers an "account of the most critical six months in Abraham Lincoln's presidency, when he penned the Emancipation Proclamation and changed the course of the Civil War. Brewster focuses on these critical six months to ask: was it through will or by accident, in-

tention or coincidence, personal achievement or historical determinism that he freed the slaves?" (Publisher's note)

"Featuring vignettes of figures who met Lincoln during his formulation of the proclamation, Brewster's work illuminates Lincoln's lines of thought during this turning point in American history." Booklist

Includes bibliographical references (pages 321-335) and index

Catton, Bruce, 1899-1978

A **stillness** at Appomattox. Doubleday 1953 438p maps hardcover o.p. pa $14.95   **973.7**

1. Appomattox Campaign, 1865 2. United States -- History -- 1861-1865, Civil War -- Campaigns

ISBN 0-385-04451-8 pa

Concluding volume of trilogy which began with Mr. Lincoln's army (1951) and Glory road (1952). This final volume of the author's study of the Army of the Potomac covers the period from early 1864 to April, 1865

The author's "approach is judicious, his interpretation unbiased and his coverage comprehensive." N Y Times Book Rev

Includes bibliographical references

The **Causes** of the Civil War; edited by Kenneth M. Stampp. 3rd rev ed; Simon & Schuster 1991 255p pa $14   **973.7**

1. Nationalism 2. State rights 3. Slavery -- United States 4. Southern States -- Economic conditions 5. United States -- History -- 1861-1865, Civil War -- Causes 6. United States -- History -- 1861-1865, Civil War -- Sources

ISBN 0-671-75155-7
                                        LC 91-36819

First published 1959 by Prentice-Hall

This book integrates the conclusions of various post-war historians with the thoughts of contemporary commentators like Jefferson Davis, Horace Greeley, and Lincoln. Political, cultural and economic aspects are emphasized

Includes bibliographical references

Center for the National Archives Experience

Discovering the Civil War; by the National Archives Experience's "Discovering the Civil War" Exhibition Team with a message from David S. Ferriero, Archivist of the United States; foreword by Ken Burns. D. Giles Ltd. 2010 208p il map $44.95 **973.7**

1. United States -- History -- 1861-1865, Civil War

ISBN 978-1-904832-91-1
                                        LC 2010-27924

"Created to accompany the major National Archives Civil War exhibit that mined our national trove of photographs, manuscripts, maps, ephemera, realia, and more, this book is spectacular in its presentation of the wide array of seemingly mundane but surprisingly revealing sources from both the well known and the obscure. . . . The intelligent framing of issues (e.g., government controls, technological and scientific innovation) for each chapter will invite readers to consider many questions about war and society, war making, and the economy of war." Libr J

Includes bibliographical references

★ The **Civil** War; the first year told by those who lived it. edited by Brooks D. Simpson, Stephen W. Sears, Aaron Sheehan-Dean. Library of America 2011 xxv, 814p map $37.50   **973.7**
1. United States -- History -- 1861-1865, Civil War -- Sources
ISBN 978-1-59853-088-9; 1-59853-088-7
LC 2010-931718

"Drawing on diaries, letters, speeches, newspaper reports and editorials, memoirs, songs, poems, and other sources, the editors bring together a rich variety of voices relating or remembering the crisis of the Union from Lincoln's election in 1860 through the first year of war. . . . Readable and riveting, this 'you are there' collection makes real the sense of urgency that gripped Americans as the nation came apart and as the war began, 175 years ago. An excellent primer on why the Civil War mattered to those living it." Libr J

Includes bibliographical references

The **Civil** War: a visual history; [produced in association with the Smithsonian Institution] DK Publishing 2011 360p il map $40   **973.7**
1. United States -- History -- 1861-1865, Civil War -- Pictorial works
ISBN 978-0-7566-7185-3

"Drawing on Smithsonian Institution collections, this fact-filled and richly illustrated history brings the war fully to life, along with time lines, sidebars on particular issues, chapter introductions, lengthy captions, and detailed maps. The emphasis throughout is on the military. Multiple examples of weapons, supplies, uniforms, camp life necessities, transport, and battle scenes dominate and show the variety, complexity, and prolixity of making war. Espionage, the home front, and politics get a nod, but this book is for those wanting to smell the sulfur and hear the thunder of guns." Libr J

Colaiaco, James A.
Frederick Douglass and the Fourth of July. Palgrave Macmillan 2006 247p hardcover o.p. pa $16.95   **973.7**
1. Slaves 2. Authors 3. Abolitionists 4. Memoirists 5. Slavery -- United States
ISBN 1-4039-7033-5; 1-4039-8072-1 pa
LC 2005-51520

"Colaiaco's careful study recaptures Douglass' reputation as one of America's greatest orators." Booklist

Includes bibliographical references

Craughwell, Thomas J.
Stealing Lincoln's body. Belknap Press of Harvard University Press 2007 250p il $24.95   **973.7**
1. Lawyers 2. Presidents 3. Grave robbing 4. Counterfeits and counterfeiting 5. State legislators 6. Members of Congress
ISBN 978-0-674-02458-8; 0-674-02458-3
LC 2006-50842

"Summoning the raw spirit of crime novels and horror stories, as well as the forensic detail of a coroner's inquest, Thomas J. Craughwell has turned the eerie final chapter of

the Lincoln story into a guilty pleasure." Washington Post Book World

Includes bibliographical references

Daniel, Larry J.
Shiloh; the battle that changed the Civil War. Simon & Schuster 1997 430p il map hardcover o.p. pa $14   **973.7**
1. Shiloh (Tenn.), Battle of, 1862
ISBN 0-684-83857-5 pa
LC 96-51539

The author "has crafted a superbly researched volume that will appeal to both the beginning Civil War reader as well as those already familiar with the course of fighting in the wooded terrain bordering the Tennessee River." Publ Wkly

Includes bibliographical references

Davis, Burke
Sherman's march. Random House 1980 335p il maps hardcover o.p. pa $14   **973.7**
1. Generals 2. Bentonville (N.C.), Battle of, 1865 3. Memoirists 4. Secretaries of war 5. United States -- History -- 1861-1865, Civil War -- Campaigns
ISBN 0-394-75763-7 pa
LC 79-5550

The author "reconstructs Sherman's infamous, but vastly consequential march through Georgia and the Carolinas, which sent the Confederacy into its death throes. Basing his narrative on eyewitness accounts, Davis brings the event down to a personal level." Booklist

Includes bibliographical references

To Appomattox; nine April days, 1865. Burford Books 2002 433p map pa $18.95   **973.7**
1. Appomattox Campaign, 1865 2. United States -- History -- 1861-1865, Civil War
ISBN 1-580-80097-1; 978-1-580-80097-6
LC 2001-56744

First published 1959 by Rinehart

"The story of the last nine days of the Civil War from the march on Richmond to the surrender at Appomattox. Quotations from diaries, letters, newspapers and military reports create a sense of immediacy as the reader follows each day's events in the city, in the Confederate camp, and with the Union Army." Publ Wkly

Includes bibliographical references

Davis, William C.
Battle at Bull Run; a history of the first major campaign of the Civil War. Louisiana State University Press 1981 298p il map pa $19.95   **973.7**
1. Bull Run, 1st Battle of, 1861
ISBN 978-0-8071-0867-3; 0-8071-0867-7

First published 1977 by Doubleday

In this account of the war's first major engagement Davis' "sketches of the commanders, which will particularly delight Civil War enthusiasts, delve into the officer's backgrounds and unusual characteristics and include critical appraisals of their leadership capabilities. In addition,

Davis includes fascinating human interest stories about the troops." Libr J

Includes bibliographical references

An **honorable** defeat; the last days of the Confederate government. Harcourt 2001 496p il maps $30; pa $16   **973.7**

1. Generals 2. Statesmen 3. Vice-presidents 4. Senators 5. Political leaders 6. Secretaries of war 7. Presidential candidates 8. Confederate States of America

ISBN 0-15-100564-8; 0-15-600748-7 pa

LC 00-46143

Davis "knows his two principal players well, and a marvelous supporting cast of politicians and soldiers helps him to fashion a story rich in pathos and humor." N Y Times Book Rev

Includes bibliographical references

Detzer, David

Allegiance; Fort Sumter, Charleston, and the beginning of the Civil War. Harcourt 2001 367p $27   **973.7**

1. Charleston (S.C.) -- History 2. Fort Sumter (Charleston, S.C.) 3. United States -- History -- 1861-1865, Civil War -- Causes

ISBN 0-15-100641-5

LC 00-50570

"The central figure in this drama is Maj. Robert Anderson, commander of the Union garrison in Charleston Harbor. . . . Detzer's writing style brings the reader into close contact with soldiers, civilians and politicians as they struggle to solve the fate of Anderson and his men." Publ Wkly

Includes bibliographical references

Doyle, Don H.

The **Cause** of All Nations; An International History of the American Civil War. by Don H. Doyle. Basic Books 2014 400 p. illustrations $29.99 **973.7**

1. War -- Public opinion 2. United States -- History -- 1861-1865, Civil War

ISBN 0465029671; 9780465029679

LC 2014024140

In this book, "historian Don H. Doyle explains that the Civil War was viewed abroad as part of a much larger struggle for democracy that spanned the Atlantic Ocean, and had begun with the American and French Revolutions. While battles raged, . . . a parallel contest took place abroad, both in the marbled courts of power and in the public square. Foreign observers held widely divergent views on the war--from radicals such as Karl Marx and Giuseppe Garibaldi, . . . to aristocratic monarchists." (Publisher's note)

Egerton, Douglas R.

Year of meteors; Stephen Douglas, Abraham Lincoln, and the election that brought on the Civil War. Bloomsbury Press 2010 399p il $29   **973.7**

1. Presidents -- United States -- Election -- 1860 2. United States -- Politics and government -- 1815-1861 3. United States -- Politics and government -- 1857-1861 4. United States -- History -- 1861-1865, Civil War -- Causes 5. United States -- History -- Civil War,

1861-1865 -- Causes

ISBN 978-1-59691-619-7

LC 2010-4965

In this book on the causes of the U.S. Civil War, Douglas R. Egerton "asserts that the reason strains evolved into full-scale hostilities was the result of actions by a relatively few men. Egerton views the election of [Abraham] Lincoln, which seemed inconceivable at the beginning of 1860, as the trigger for secession. He suggests that to some extent the election was the result of what amounted to a conspiracy on the part of Southern radicals." (Booklist)

The author "examines the importance of race in the presidential election of 1860, when a relatively unknown candidate came from behind to be elected to the nation's highest office. Following the fortunes of Democrat Stephen Douglas, Republican Abraham Lincoln, and a host of others significant to the election, Egerton highlights the central role played by race in the dynamics of political party, sectionalism, and politics generally in the election after which the nation was plunged into Civil War. . . . Heavily documented, relying on substantial primary and manuscript sources, this book sheds new light on an often researched topic. All those with an interest in the importance of race in the nation's history will want to acquire this highly readable work." Libr J

Includes bibliographical references and index.

Eicher, David J.

The **longest** night; a military history of the Civil War. foreword by James M. McPherson; maps by Lee Vande Visse. Simon & Schuster 2001 990p maps $40; pa $22   **973.7**

1. United States -- History -- 1861-1865, Civil War -- Campaigns

ISBN 0-684-84944-5; 0-684-84945-3 pa

LC 2001-34153

An account of battles and military strategies in the Civil War

"Civil War buffs and military history scholars will find Eicher's superb analyses and original insights into oft-neglected theaters of operations extremely valuable. An important work that will be an essential component of Civil War collections." Booklist

Includes bibliographical references

★ **Encyclopedia** of the American Civil War; a political, social, and military history. David S. Heidler and Jeanne T. Heidler, editors; foreword by James W. McPherson; David J. Coles, associate editor; Gary W. Gallagher, James M. McPherson, Mark E. Neely, Jr., editorial board. ABC-CLIO 2000 5v il maps set $425   **973.7**

1. Reference books 2. United States -- History -- 1861-1865, Civil War -- Encyclopedias

ISBN 1-57607-066-2

LC 00-11195

ALA RUSA Dartmouth Medal honorable mention (2001)

"The editors have compiled a comprehensive source that provides a first-stop reference on broad areas or specific topics on the Civil War. The contemporary photographs and lithographs bring the human element into the encyclopedia, a type of reference known more for facts and figures than emotions. The primary-source-documents volume brings obscure resources together, which will further illumine the period for students."—"Outstanding Reference Sources." American Libraries, May 2001

Includes bibliographical references

Faust, Drew Gilpin

Mothers of invention; women of the slaveholding South in the American Civil War. University of N.C. Press 1996 326p il $37.50; pa $19.95 **973.7**
1. Women -- Southern States 2. United States -- History -- 1861-1865, Civil War -- Women
ISBN 0-8078-2255-8; 0-8078-5573-1 pa

LC 95-8896

Based on journals, letters and memoirs, this is an "analysis of the impact of secession, invasion and conquest on Southern white women. Antebellum images based on helplessness and dependence were challenged as women assumed an increasing range of social and economic responsibilities. . . . Faust's provocative analysis of a complex subject merits a place in all collections of U.S. history." Publ Wkly

Includes bibliographical references

Faust, Drew Gilpin, 1947-

This republic of suffering; death and the American Civil War. Alfred A. Knopf 2008 346p il $27.95 **973.7**
1. Death 2. Burial -- History 3. Death -- Social aspects -- United States 4. United States -- History -- 1861-1865, Civil War 5. United States -- History -- Civil War, 1861-1865 -- Influence 6. United States -- History -- Civil War, 1861-1865 -- Social aspects
ISBN 0-375-40404-X; 978-0-375-40404-7

LC 2007-14658

The author "surveys the many ways the Civil War generation coped with the trauma: the concept of the Good Death—conscious, composed and at peace with God; the rise of the embalming industry; the sad attempts of the bereaved to get confirmation of a soldier's death, sometimes years after war's end; the swelling national movement to recover soldiers' remains and give them decent burials; the intellectual quest to find meaning—or its absence—in the war's carnage. . . . The result is an insightful, often moving portrait of a people torn by grief." Publ Wkly

Includes bibliographical references

Foner, Eric

The **fiery** trial; Abraham Lincoln and American slavery. W.W. Norton 2010 426p il map $29.95 **973.7**
1. Lawyers 2. Presidents 3. State legislators 4. Members of Congress 5. Biography, Individual 6. Slavery -- United States 7. Slaves -- Emancipation -- United States
ISBN 978-0-393-06618-0; 0-393-06618-5

LC 2010-23425

The author "explores the evolution—from frontier lawyer to Great Emancipator—of Lincoln's thought about and response to slavery. The book . . . showcases Foner's engaging style and insight, while keeping a tight focus on Lincoln in his own historical context. [This work] explains how a man who was more skilled politician than reformer came

to issue one of the most sweeping, consequential edicts in American history." Am Scholar

Includes bibliographical references

★ **Gateway** to Freedom; The Hidden History of the Underground Railroad. Eric Foner. W W Norton & Co Inc 2015 320 p. ill, maps, port hbk $26.95 **973.7**
1. Fugitive slaves 2. Underground railroad 3. Slavery -- United States
ISBN 0393244075; 9780393244076

LC 2014036993

Author Eric Foner examines "the dramatic story of fugitive slaves and the antislavery activists who defied the law to help them reach freedom. [He] elevates the underground railroad from folklore to sweeping history. The story is inspiring--full of memorable characters making their first appearance on the historical stage--and significant--the controversy over fugitive slaves inflamed the sectional crisis of the 1850s." (Publisher's note)

"The author eschews the common approach of documenting the phenomenon from the South, instead centering his monograph on New York City. Through individuals such as abolitionist Sydney Howard Gay and minister Charles Ray, he demonstrates that ferrying escaped slaves from the city's waterfront to other locales throughout the North was fraught with extreme danger." LJ

Includes bibliographical references and index

Foote, Shelby

The **Civil** War; a narrative. Random House 1958 3v maps set $165; pa $75 **973.7**
1. United States -- History -- 1861-1865, Civil War
ISBN 0-394-49517-9; 0-394

"In objectivity, in range, in mastery of detail, in beauty of language and feeling for the people involved, this work surpasses anything else on the subject." New Repub

Includes bibliographical references

The **Civil** War, a narrative; by Shelby Foote. Vintage Books 1986 (pbk. : v. 1) : $15.95; $50.00 **973.7**
1. United States -- History -- 1861-1865, Civil War 2. United States -- History -- Civil War, 1861-1865
ISBN 0394746236 (per vol.); 0394749138 (set); 9780394746210; 9780394746227; 9780394746234

LC 86040135

This book, by Shelby Foote, presents a reprint of a multivolume narrative history of the U.S. Civil War written between 1958 and 1974. In it the author covers the political and social forces, the battles, and the major figures of the conflict from its beginning at the siege of Fort Sumpter to the final battle of Appomattox.

Includes bibliographies and indexes

Stars in their courses; the Gettysburg campaign, June-July 1863. Shelby Foote. Modern Library 1994 viii, 290 p.p maps $23 **973.7**
1. Gettysburg (Pa.), Battle of, 1863 2. Gettysburg Campaign, 1863
ISBN 0679601120; 9780679601128

LC 94196068

This book, by Shelby Foote, "brilliantly re-creates the three-day conflict [at Gettysburg]: it is a masterly treatment of a key great battle and the events that preceded it - not as legend has it but as it really was, before it became distorted by controversy and overblown by remembered glory." (Publisher's note)

Ford, Lacy K.

Deliver us from evil; the slavery question in the old South. Oxford University Press 2009 673p $34.95   **973.7**

1. Slavery -- United States 2. Southern States -- History 3. Southern States -- Race relations 4. Slavery -- United States -- History

ISBN 0-19-511809-X; 978-0-19-511809-4

LC 2008-47533

This book focuses "on the period from the drafting of the federal consitution in 1787 through the age of Jackson. . . . [Ford] examines the political, intellectual, economic , and social thought of leading white southerners." (N Y Times Book Rev) Index.

This book provides "an intricate, textured argument about the intellectual, social, and political interests shaping 'the slavery question,' as well as a reminder that Southern white commitment to a hardened proslavery position was not preordained or one-dimensional. Essential for all students of this subject." Libr J

Includes bibliographical references

Foreman, Amanda

A **world** on fire; Britain's crucial role in the American Civil War. Random House 2011 958p il map $35   **973.7**

1. United States -- History -- 1861-1865, Civil War 2. Great Britain -- Foreign relations -- United States 3. United States -- Foreign relations -- Great Britain 4. United States -- History -- Civil War, 1861-1865 -- Participation, British 5. United States -- History -- Civil War, 1861-1865 -- Foreign public opinion, British

ISBN 0-375-50494-X; 978-0-375-50494-5

First published 2010 in the United Kingdom

Amanda Foreman tells the "story of the American Civil War and the major role played by Britain and its citizens in that struggle. . . . Between 1861 and 1865, thousands of British citizens volunteered for service on both sides of the Civil War. From the first cannon blasts on Fort Sumter to Lee's surrender at Appomattox, they served as officers and infantrymen, sailors and nurses, blockade runners and spies." (Publisher's note)

"Ranging from the drawing rooms of Washington and London to the battlefields of Gettysburg and Antietam, to the high seas, and to Confederate and Union home fronts, Foreman has written a diplomatic, military, and social kaleidoscope of the Civil War. She superbly conveys the horror, pathos, and chaos of battle, the political and moral ambiguities, and the devotion of those who fought. She has also restored an international dimension missing from many histories. The fall of Fort Sumter in April 1861 set off a furious diplomatic contest between North and South for the favors of Great Britain, then the world's superpower. Britain had a tangle of economic interests in the United States; it was bound to the South by cotton, which kept the British tex-

tile industry spinning, and British investors held millions in stocks and securities." Boston Globe

Fredrickson, George M.

Big enough to be inconsistent; Abraham Lincoln confronts slavery and race. Harvard University Press 2008 156p (The W.E.B. Du Bois lectures) $19.95   **973.7**

1. Lawyers 2. Presidents 3. State legislators 4. Members of Congress 5. Slavery -- United States 6. African Americans -- Civil rights

ISBN 978-0-674-02774-9; 0-674-02774-4

LC 2007-34018

The author "wades into a controversial arena: was Lincoln a heroic emancipator or a racist who didn't care about slaves at all? Stating that in between 'pathological' racism and egalitarianism lies a spectrum of possibilities, Fredrickson says that Lincoln is not easily classified. . . . This brief book will be widely discussed by historians and will provide nonacademic readers a lucid introduction to some of the most heated debates about the 16th president." Publ Wkly

Includes bibliographical references

Fredriksen, John C.

Civil War almanac. Facts on File, Inc. 2007 858p il map (Almanacs of American wars) $85   **973.7**

1. United States -- History -- 1861-1865, Civil War

ISBN 0-8160-6459-8; 978-0-8160-6459-5

LC 2006-29985

First published 1983 under the editorship of John Stewart Bowman

This book contains a "day-by-day chronology of the events and people of this monumental war, along with an A-to-Z dictionary offering biographical information on leading military and political figures involved in the conflict." Publisher's note

Includes bibliographical references

Furgurson, Ernest B.

Chancellorsville, 1863; the souls of the brave. Knopf 1992 405p il maps hardcover o.p. pa $16   **973.7**

1. Chancellorsville (Va.), Battle of, 1863

ISBN 0-679-72831-7 pa

LC 91-47059

"Mr. Furgurson has written what should become the standard account of the battle. He is especially good at discussing both larger tactical issues and the experiences of ordinary soldiers. He is also evenhanded." N Y Times Book Rev

Includes bibliographical references

Gallagher, Gary W.

The **Confederate** War. Harvard Univ. Press 1997 218p il hardcover o.p.   **973.7**

1. Confederate States of America 2. United States -- History -- 1861-1865, Civil War

LC 97-2495

This book "is the best thing that has happened to Confederate historiography in many years. Gallagher has a more thorough command of the sources for Confederate history than any other historian I have read and he brings that mastery to bear in a concise, hard-hitting book." NY Rev Books

Includes bibliographical references

The **union** war. Harvard University Press 2011 215p il $27.95   **973.7**
1. United States -- History -- 1861-1865, Civil War 2. United States -- History -- Civil War, 1861-1865 3. United States -- Politics and government -- 1861-1865 4. Popular culture -- United States -- History -- 19th century

ISBN 978-0-674-04562-0; 0-674-04562-9

LC 2010-51977

In this book, "Gary Gallagher argues . . . that Northerners, ranging from President Lincoln all the way down to the conscripts in the Army of the Potomac, didn't fight the Civil War to free the slaves or to topple white supremacy in the South. Instead, they fought for the Union, an admittedly diffuse concept, Gallagher admits, but nevertheless their central animating principle." (Times Literary Supplement)

"Gallagher offers not so much a history of wartime patriotism as a series of meditations on the meaning of the Union to Northerners, the role of slavery in the conflict and how historians have interpreted (and in his view misinterpreted) these matters." N Y Times Book Rev

Includes bibliographical references

Gienapp, William E.

Abraham Lincoln and Civil War America; a biography. Oxford Univ. Press 2001 239p il maps hardcover o.p. pa $24.95   **973.7**
1. Lawyers 2. Presidents 3. State legislators 4. Members of Congress 5. Presidents -- United States 6. United States -- History -- 1861-1865, Civil War

ISBN 0-19-515099-6; 0-19-515100-3 pa

LC 2001-50056

This biography focuses on the American president's leadership during the Civil War.

"In spite of the book's size, its discriminating history of Lincoln's life is surprisingly rich, and the narrative of his presidency and the unfolding of the war is crisp and coherent." Bookmarks

Includes bibliographical references

Goldfield, David R.

★ **America** aflame; how the Civil War created a nation. [by] David Goldfield. Bloomsbury Press 2011 632p il $35   **973.7**
1. United States -- History -- 1861-1865, Civil War -- Causes 2. United States -- History -- Civil War, 1861-1865 -- Causes 3. United States -- History -- Civil War, 1861-1865 -- Campaigns 4. United States -- History -- Civil War, 1861-1865 -- Influence 5. United States -- History -- Civil War, 1861-1865 -- Social aspects 6. United States -- History -- 1861-1865, Civil War -- Religious aspects

ISBN 978-1-59691-702-6; 1-59691-702-4

LC 2010-25241

"A provocatively written, scrupulously researched, and well-framed consideration of evangelical religion's ques-

tionable role in the antebellum, Civil War, and Reconstruction periods of our history." Libr J

Includes bibliographical references

Goodheart, Adam

★ **1861**; the Civil War awakening. 1st ed.; Alfred A. Knopf 2011 481p il $28.95   **973.7**
1. United States -- Intellectual life 2. United States -- Politics and government -- 1861-1865 3. United States -- History -- 1861-1865, Civil War -- Causes

ISBN 978-1-4000-4015-5; 1-4000-4015-9

LC 2010-51326

"Goodheart leads us on a journey through the frenzied, frightening months between Abraham Lincoln's election to the presidency in 1860 — followed with breakneck speed by the secession of the Confederate States and the outbreak of war — and July 4, 1861, when President Lincoln delivered his first message to Congress, laying out the case not only for the necessity of war, but for a more democratic vision of the United States. The election of Lincoln and the secession crisis is, of course, familiar terrain. But Goodheart's version is at once more panoramic and more intimate than most standard accounts, and more inspiring. This is fundamentally a history of hearts and minds, rather than of legislative bills and battles." N Y Times Book Rev

Gopnik, Adam

Angels and ages; a short book about Darwin, Lincoln, and modern life. Alfred A. Knopf 2009 211p $24.95   **973.7**
1. Lawyers 2. Presidents 3. Naturalists 4. Modern civilization 5. Travel writers 6. State legislators 7. Writers on science 8. Members of Congress

ISBN 978-0-307-27078-8; 0-307-27078-5

LC 2008-36224

"The book is worth reading . . . for the author's unquestioned skill as a craftsman and the light he sheds on what has become, for many, settled history." Bookmarks

Groom, Winston

Shiloh, 1862; the first great and terrible battle of the civil war. Winston Groom. National Geographic Books 2012 446 p.   **973.7**
1. Shiloh (Tenn.), Battle of, 1862 2. Tennessee -- History -- 1861-1865, Civil War 3. United States -- History -- 1861-1865, Civil War -- Campaigns 4. Shiloh, Battle of, Tenn., 1862

ISBN 9781426208744

LC 2012372339

This book "presents Shiloh, fought on April 6-7 in western Tennessee, as a turning point in the [U.S. Civil War]." (Kirkus) "[Winston] Groom . . . compels the reader to appreciate the enormous toll to both sides owing to advanced arms, outmoded battle tactics, and poor generalship. Although Groom lays responsibility on both sides, he especially blames General [Ulysses] Grant and General [William] Sherman . . . for failure to fortify positions, properly reconnoiter, read the signs of enemy advances, and have a battle plan in case of attack. . . . Groom sees Shiloh as a learning experience for Grant, who finally understood that no single battle, no matter how costly or geographically significant, could end the rebellion: the Union could be restored only through the total conquest of the South." (Libr J)

Includes bibliographical references (p. 409-419) and index

Vicksburg, 1863. Alfred A. Knopf 2009 482p il $30   973.7

1. Vicksburg (Miss.) -- Siege, 1863 2. United States -- History -- 1861-1865, Civil War -- Campaigns

ISBN 978-0-307-26425-1

LC 2008-45984

"Rarely has the story of such a lengthy and complicated campaign been told with such clarity and grace." Washington Post

Includes bibliographical references

Guelzo, Allen C.

Gettysburg; the last invasion. by Allen C. Guelzo. 1st ed. Alfred A. Knopf 2013 xix, 632 p., 16 unnumbered pages of platesp ill., maps (hardcover) $35   973.7

1. Gettysburg (Pa.), Battle of, 1863 2. United States -- History -- 1861-1865, Civil War

ISBN 0307594084; 9780307594082

LC 2012047013

The book offers an account of the battle of Gettysburg. Though "the battle site was not inevitable, the actual battle was . . . . The Union had reason to be concerned, but, as [Allen C.] Guelzo documents, their foe was scattered and divided, with rivalries and miscommunication . . . keeping James Longstreet from attacking, J.E.B. Stuart from arriving on the battlefield in time, and the much-disliked George Pickett from enjoying a better fate than being cannon fodder." (Kirkus Reviews)

Includes bibliographical references (pages 483-599) and index.

Harper, Judith E.

Women during the Civil War; an encyclopedia. Routledge 2003 472p il map $170; pa $59.95 973.7

1. Reference books 2. United States -- History -- 1861-1865, Civil War -- Women -- Encyclopedias

ISBN 0-415-93723-X; 0-415-95574-2 pa

LC 2003-7181

"The 128 entries range in length from 400 to 4000 words, and include biographies of women from all regions of the U.S. Well-known figures such as Harriet Tubman, Clara Barton, Louisa May Alcott, and Mary Todd Lincoln are represented but so too are African-American sculptor Edmonia Lewis, poet Lucy Larcom, and Emma LeConte. . . As well as biographies, there are superb thematic entries on women living in the West, prostitutes, industrial workers, family life, and invasion and occupation. . . . This encyclopedia is a welcomed addition to reference collections." SLJ

Includes bibliographical references

Hearts touched by fire; the best of battles and leaders of the Civil War. edited with an introduction by Harold Holzer; with contributions by James M. McPherson ... [et al.] Modern Library 2011 xxiii, 1230p il map $38   973.7

1. United States -- History -- 1861-1865, Civil War --

Personal narratives

ISBN 978-0-679-64364-7

An anthology of excerpts from the four-volume classic "Battles and Leaders of the Civil War" features firsthand recollections by the Civil War's commanders and subordinates on both sides, with commentary by such leading scholars as James McPherson and Joan Waugh.

Hodes, Martha

Mourning Lincoln; Martha Hodes. Yale University Press 2015 408 p. illustrations $30   973.7

1. Bereavement 2. Public opinion

ISBN 030019580X; 9780300195804

LC 2014952310

In this "exploration of diaries, letters, and other personal writings penned during the spring and summer of 1865, Martha Hodes, one of our finest historians, captures the full range of reactions to the president's death--far more diverse than public expressions would suggest. She tells a story of shock, glee, sorrow, anger, blame, and fear." (Publisher's note)

Holzer, Harold

The **Civil** War in 50 objects; Harold Holzer and the New-York Historical Society; with an introduction by Eric Foner. Viking 2013 416 p. (hardcover) $36   973.7

1. United States -- Antiquities 2. United States -- History -- 1861-1865, Civil War 3. New-York Historical Society 4. United States -- History -- Civil War, 1861-1865 -- Museums 5. United States -- History -- Civil War, 1861-1865 -- Anecdotes 6. United States -- History -- Civil War, 1861-1865 -- Antiquities 7. United States -- History -- Civil War, 1861-1865 -- Collectibles

ISBN 067001463X; 9780670014637

LC 2013001532

This book, by Harold Holzer, explores the U.S. Civil War through a set of preserved objects "from a soldier's diary with the pencil still attached to John Brown's pike, the Emancipation Proclamation, a Confederate Palmetto flag, and the leaves from Abraham Lincoln's bier. . . . Lincoln scholar Harold Holzer sheds new light on the war by examining fifty objects from the New-York Historical Society's acclaimed collection." (Publisher's note)

Includes bibliographical references and index

A **just** and generous nation; Abraham Lincoln and the fight for American opportunity. Harold Holzer and Norton Garfinkle. Basic Books, a member of the Perseus Books Group 2015 320 p. illustrations (hardcover) $27.99   973.7

1. Equality 2. Economic development 3. United States -- History -- 1861-1865, Civil War 4. United States -- Politics and government -- 1861-1865 5. United States -- History -- Civil War, 1861-1865 -- Causes 6. Social mobility -- United States -- History -- 19th century 7. Economic development -- United States -- History -- 19th century 8. United States -- History -- Civil War, 1861-1865 -- Social aspects 9. United States -- History -- Civil War, 1861-1865 -- Economic aspects 10. Equality -- Economic aspects -- United States -- History

-- 19th century
ISBN 0465028306; 9780465028306

LC 2015022842

In this book on Abraham Lincoln, authors Harold Holzer and Norton Garfinkle "present a groundbreaking new account of the beliefs that inspired our sixteenth president to go to war when the Southern states seceded from the Union. Rather than a commitment to eradicating slavery or a defense of the Union, they argue, Lincoln's guiding principle was the defense of equal economic opportunity." (Publisher's note)

"This review of Lincoln's thoughts and actions and examination of subsequent administrations' willingness to promote and secure the American Dream will generate much-needed debate on the history, efficacy, and morality of government's role and responsibility in shaping an economy of fairness and growth. The future of America depends on that question." LJ

Includes bibliographical references and index

Lincoln and the power of the press; the war for public opinion. Harold Holzer. Simon & Schuster 2014 768 p. illustrations (hardcover) $37.50 **973.7**
1. Press 2. Presidents -- United States -- Press relations 3. United States -- Politics and government -- 1861-1865 4. Press and politics -- United States -- History -- 19th century 5. United States -- History -- Civil War, 1861-1865 -- Journalists 6. United States -- History -- Civil War, 1861-1865 -- Press coverage
ISBN 1439192715; 9781439192719; 9781439192726

LC 2014021392

This book by Harold Holzer describes how, "From his earliest days, [U.S. President Abraham] Lincoln devoured newspapers. As he started out in politics he wrote editorials and letters to argue his case. He spoke to the public directly through the press. He even bought a German-language newspaper to appeal to that growing electorate in his state. Lincoln alternately pampered, battled, and manipulated the three most powerful publishers of the day." (Publisher's note)

Includes bibliographical references (pages 665-697) and index

Horwitz, Tony
Confederates in the attic; dispatches from the unfinished Civil War. Pantheon Bks. 1998 406p map hardcover o.p. pa $14.95 **973.7**
1. United States -- History -- 1861-1865, Civil War
ISBN 0-679-75833-X pa

LC 97-26759

This "is the work of a skilled journalist looking at how—and why—the War Between the States continues to live in so many issues still with us." Libr J

Howard, David
Lost rights; the misadventures of a stolen American relic. Houghton Mifflin Harcourt 2009 344p $26 **973.7**
1. Theft 2. Manuscripts 3. United States -- Constitution -- 1st-10th amendments
ISBN 978-0-618-82607-0; 0-618-82607-6

LC 2009-18046

"The tale pulsates with dynamic personalities greatly affected by their connection to one of the rarest, most influential and valuable documents in American history. Howard has produced a marvelously compelling read." Publ Wkly

Includes bibliographical references

Hyslop, Stephen G.
Atlas of the Civil War; a comprehensive guide to the tactics and terrain of battle. edited by Neil Kagan; narrative by Stephen G. Hyslop; introduction by Harris J. Andrews. National Geographic Society 2009 255p il map $40 **973.7**
1. Reference books 2. Historical atlases 3. United States -- History -- 1861-1865, Civil War -- Maps
ISBN 978-1-4262-0347-3

LC 2008-35066

"Arranged chronologically, this atlas combines period photographs and illustrations, rare period maps and modern cartography, with just enough narrative to explain the two-page spread devoted to each subject (the majority being about particular battles or campaigns). . . . The text also features numerous sidebars throughout, offering micro-timelines, biographies, and images showing the human side of the war. All of these special features make this large-format atlas a superior choice for Civil War buffs as well as those new to the subject." Libr J

Jordan, Brian Matthew, 1986-
Marching Home; Union Veterans and Their Unending Civil War. Brian Matthew Jordan. W W Norton & Co Inc 2015 384 p. illustrations $28.95 **973.7**
1. Veterans 2. United States -- History -- 1861-1865, Civil War
ISBN 0871407817; 9780871407818

LC 2014032544

Pulitzer Prize Finalist: History (2016)

In this book, U.S. "Civil War historian Brian Matthew Jordan" looks at Union veterans, who, "tending rotting wounds, battling alcoholism, campaigning for paltry pensions . . . tragically realized that they stood as unwelcome reminders to a new America. Mining previously untapped archives, Jordan uncovers anguished letters and diaries, essays by amputees, and gruesome medical reports, all deeply revealing of the American psyche." (Publisher's note)

Katz, Harry L.
Civil War sketch book; drawings from the battlefront. Harry L. Katz and Vincent Virga; with a preface by Alan Brinkley. W.W. Norton & Co Inc. 2012 xxv, 251 p.p. col. ill. (hardcover) $50 **973.7**
1. United States -- History -- 1861-1865, Civil War -- Pictorial works 2. United States -- History -- 1861-1865, Civil War -- Personal narratives 3. Drawing, American -- 19th century 4. United States -- History -- Civil War, 1861-1865 -- Art and the war 5. United States -- History -- Civil War, 1861-1865 -- Pictorial works
ISBN 0393072207; 9780393072204

LC 2011044004

In this book, Harry L. Katz and Vincent Virga "look at the illustrators—including Winslow Homer and Thomas Nast—who covered the war for popular newspapers of the time . . . by traveling with the troops and sketching among the dead and wounded as well as bullets, fire, and the general chaos of the battlefield. . . . The book's text, which follows the chronology of the war, includes selections from the artists' letters, logbooks, diaries, and other firsthand accounts." (Library Journal)

Includes bibliographical references and index

Keegan, John

The **American** Civil War; a military history. Alfred A. Knopf 2009 396p il map $35   **973.7**

1. Military geography -- United States 2. United States -- History -- 1861-1865, Civil War -- Campaigns

ISBN 978-0-307-26343-8; 0-307-26343-6

LC 2009-19469

The author "provides the single best one-volume assessment of the military character and conduct of America's ordeal by fire." Libr J

Includes bibliographical references

Klein, Maury

Days of defiance; Sumter, secession, and the coming of the Civil War. Knopf 1997 496p il hardcover o.p. pa $16   **973.7**

1. United States -- History -- 1861-1865, Civil War

ISBN 0-679-76882-3 pa

LC 96-39156

"With a novelist's skill, Klein has crafted an engrossing portrait of the nation's descent into chaos and war." Publ Wkly

Includes bibliographical references

Krauthamer, Barbara

Envisioning emancipation; Black Americans and the end of slavery. Deborah Willis and Barbara Krauthamer. Temple University Press 2013 223 p. ill. (cloth : alk. paper) $35   **973.7**

1. Slaves -- Emancipation 2. Slavery -- United States 3. African Americans -- Portraits 4. Documentary photography -- United States 5. Historiography and photography -- United States 6. African Americans -- History -- 1863-1877 -- Pictorial works 7. United States -- History -- Civil War, 1861-1865 -- African Americans -- Pictorial works

ISBN 1439909857; 9781439909850

LC 2012032600

This book is a collection "of nearly 150 photographs reaching from the mid-19th to the early 20th century" that are meant to help readers "contemplate not only the history of slavery and emancipation but also our continued ties to that history and its legacies." Subjects include the "escaped slave Dolly pictured on a reward notice, a group gathered for a 1916 slave reunion, Emancipation Day celebrations, fugitives fording a river, chimney sweeps, family groups, and penal slavery crews." (Publishers Weekly)

Includes bibliographical references and index

Leaders of the American Civil War; a biographical and historiographical dictionary. edited by Charles F. Ritter and Jon L. Wakelyn. Greenwood Press 1998 xxxiv, 465p $85   **973.7**

1. Reference books 2. United States -- History -- 1861-

1865, Civil War -- Biography -- Dictionaries

ISBN 0-313-29560-3

LC 98-12156

This dictionary "includes 47 articles on outstanding military and civilian Union and Confederate leaders as well as entries for other significant figures, including Frederick Douglass, Clara Barton, Dorothea Dix, and even Walt Whitman." Libr J

Includes bibliographical references

Leonard, Elizabeth D.

All the daring of the soldier; women of the Civil War armies. Norton 1999 368p il hardcover o.p. pa $22.95   **973.7**

1. Women soldiers 2. United States -- Army 3. Confederate States of America -- Army 4. United States -- History -- 1861-1865, Civil War

ISBN 978-0-393-04712-7; 0-393-04712-1; 978-0-393-33547-7 pa; 0-393-33547-X pa

LC 98-52304

The author presents "stories of dozens of women who served in both the Union and Confederacy during the Civil War. Some were spies, but many more adopted men's names, dressed in men's clothes and lived and fought and died alongside mostly unsuspecting men." Publ Wkly

Includes bibliographical references

Levine, Bruce

The **fall** of the house of Dixie; how the Civil War remade the American South. Bruce Levine. Random House 2013 xix, 439 p., [16] p. of platesp ill., map $30   **973.7**

1. Confederate States of America -- History 2. United States -- History -- 1861-1865, Civil War 3. Confederate States of America 4. Confederate States of America -- Social conditions 5. Confederate States of America -- Economic conditions 6. United States -- History -- Civil War, 1861-1865 -- Social aspects 7. United States -- History -- Civil War, 1861-1865 -- Economic aspects 8. Elite (Social sciences) -- Southern States -- History -- 19th century 9. Slavery -- Social aspects -- Southern States -- History -- 19th century 10. Slavery -- Economic aspects -- Southern States -- History -- 19th century

ISBN 1400067030; 9780679645351; 9781400067039

LC 2011048310

In this book Bruce Levine tells the "story of how [the American Civil War] upended the economic, political, and social life of the old South, utterly destroying the Confederacy and the society it represented and defended. Told through the words of the people who lived it, 'The Fall of the House of Dixie' illuminates the way a war undertaken to preserve the status quo became a second American Revolution whose impact on the country was as strong and lasting as that of our first." (Publishing note)

Includes bibliographical references (p. [377]-415) and index.

Lincoln, Abraham, 1809-1865

★ **Speeches** and writings, 1859-1865; speeches, letters, and miscellaneous writings, presidential

messages and proclamations. Library of Am. 1989 xxxiii, 787p $35   973.7
1. United States -- Politics and government -- 1861-1865
ISBN 0-940450-63-1

LC 89-45349

This volume is based upon The Collected Works of Abraham Lincoln. It includes public statements, business letters, "poems, personal letters, telegrams to generals in the field, and other [writings]." Libr J
Includes bibliographical references

Manning, Chandra
Troubled refuge; Struggling for Freedom in the Civil War. Chandra Manning. Alfred A. Knopf 2016 416 p. illustrations, maps $30   973.7
1. Slaves -- Emancipation -- United States 2. United States -- History -- 1861-1865, Civil War 3. United States -- History -- Civil War, 1861-1865 -- Social aspects 4. United States -- History -- Civil War, 1861-1865 -- African Americans
ISBN 9780307271204

LC 2015039724

This book, by Chandra Manning, is "a vivid portrait of the Union army's escaped-slave refugee camps and how they shaped the course of emancipation and citizenship in the United States. . . . Drawing on records of the Union and Confederate armies, the letters and diaries of soldiers, transcribed testimonies of former slaves, and more, . . . Manning allows us to accompany the black men, women, and children who sought out the Union army in hopes of achieving autonomy." (Publisher's note)
"An essential contribution to the history of the Civil War and its aftermath." Booklist
Includes bibliographical references

Marten, James
Civil War America; voices from the home front. ABC-CLIO 2003 346p il $85   973.7
1. United States -- History -- 1861-1865, Civil War -- Personal narratives
ISBN 1-576-07237-1

LC 2002-154377

"Marten offers a view of the war through the eyes of diverse noncombatants. Four parts of this five-part work each deal with Southerners, Northerners, children, and African Americans . . . Part five, 'Aftermaths,' includes descriptions of the postwar lives of veterans, orphans, and ex-slaves, and concludes with a chapter on the Civil War stories by Ambrose Bierce. Readers will find Marten's overarching theme of change—both immediate and long-range—revelatory and instructional." SLJ
Includes bibliographical references

Masur, Louis P.
The **Civil** War: a concise history. Oxford University Press 2011 118p il $18.95   973.7
1. United States -- History -- 1861-1865, Civil War
ISBN 978-0-19-974048-2

LC 2010-19460

The author provides "a concise but compelling narrative of the Civil War era, packing in the critical information to track the trajectory of secession, war, emancipation, and

Reconstruction. He focuses on the political and the military, with Lincoln, Jefferson Davis, and the generals especially getting their due." Libr J
Includes bibliographical references

McPherson, James M.
Abraham Lincoln and the second American Revolution. Oxford Univ. Press 1991 173p hardcover o.p. pa $16.95   973.7
1. Lawyers 2. Presidents 3. State legislators 4. Members of Congress 5. United States -- History -- 1861-1865, Civil War
ISBN 0-19-507606-0 pa

LC 90-6885

The author "examines Lincoln's role in the transformation wrought by the Civil War—the liberation of four million slaves, the overthrow of the social and political order of the South." Publ Wkly
Includes bibliographical references

Drawn with the sword; reflections on the American Civil War. Oxford Univ. Press 1996 258p $45; pa $18.95   973.7
1. Authors 2. Lawyers 3. Generals 4. Novelists 5. Statesmen 6. Presidents 7. Abolitionists 8. Vice-presidents 9. Orators 10. State legislators 11. Children's authors 12. Nonfiction writers 13. Secretaries of war 14. Members of Congress 15. Short story writers 16. Secretaries of state 17. Glory (Motion picture) 18. Emancipation Proclamation (1863) 19. United States -- History -- 1861-1865, Civil War
ISBN 0-19-509679-7; 0-19-511796-4 pa

LC 95-38107

"These pieces provide a lively reminder that the best scholarship is also often a pleasure to read." N Y Times Book Rev

For cause and comrades; why men fought in the Civil War. Oxford Univ. Press 1997 237p $25; pa $15.95   973.7
1. Soldiers -- United States 2. United States -- History -- 1861-1865, Civil War
ISBN 0-19-509023-3; 0-19-512499-5 pa

LC 96-24760

"Volumes have been written on the causes of the Civil War, but less has been written on what caused soldiers to risk their lives on the battlefield. McPherson . . . fills the gap. After studying thousands of letters and diaries, he discusses what really led soldiers to enlist, what kept them in the army, and what led them to the front lines." Libr J
Includes bibliographical references

Hallowed ground; a walk at Gettysburg. Crown Publishers 2003 144p map (Crown Journeys series) $16   973.7
1. Gettysburg (Pa.), Battle of, 1863
ISBN 0-609-61023-6

LC 2002-35154

"If it were only a pointer to the physical ground and commemorative markers, this guide would be ordinary, but McPherson so articulately injects reminders—as of a free black farmer who fled the approaching battle lest Confederates enslave him—of what the Civil War was about as to display the crystalline style that has made him one of our finest Civil War historians." Booklist

★ **This** mighty scourge; perspectives on the Civil War. Oxford University Press 2007 260p $28 **973.7**
1. Lawyers 2. Presidents 3. State legislators 4. Members of Congress 5. United States -- History -- 1861-1865, Civil War
ISBN 0-19-531366-6

LC 2006-35523

These essays "stand as a remarkably elegant and clarifying narrative exploration of the most basic questions concerning the Civil War, issues over which scholars and activists still contend. . . 'This Mighty Scourge,' in fact, is an exemplary exercise in the contribution a great historian and eloquent writer can make to a people's understanding of themselves." Los Angeles Times

McPherson, James M., 1936-
Battle cry of freedom; the Civil War era. Oxford Univ. Press 1988 904p il maps (Oxford history of the United States) $47.50; pa $18.95 **973.7**
1. United States -- History -- 1861-1865, Civil War
ISBN 0-19-503863-0; 0-19-516895-X pa

LC 87-11045

This narrative covers events "from the Mexican War through Appomattox. . . . {There are} political and economic discussions . . . . {as well as} descriptions of military campaigns and personalities." (Libr J) Bibliography. Index.
This volume "is comprehensive yet succinct, scholarly without being pedantic, eloquent but unrhetorical. It is compellingly readable." N Y Times Book Rev
Includes bibliographical references

The **war** that forged a nation; why the Civil War still matters. James M. McPherson. Oxford University Press 2015 232 p. (hardback) $27.95 **973.7**
1. United States -- History -- 1861-1865, Civil War 2. Social change -- United States -- History 3. War and society -- United States -- History 4. National characteristics, American -- History 5. United States -- History -- Civil War, 1861-1865 -- Influence 6. United States -- History -- Civil War, 1861-1865 -- Social aspects 7. United States -- History -- Civil War, 1861-1865 -- Psychological aspects
ISBN 0199375771; 9780199375776

LC 2014018008

In this book "historian James M. McPherson considers why the Civil War remains so deeply embedded in our national psyche and identity. The drama and tragedy of the war, from its scope and size--an estimated death toll of 750,000, far more than the rest of the country's wars combined--to the nearly mythical individuals involved--Abraham Lincoln, Robert E. Lee, Stonewall Jackson--help explain why the Civil War remains a topic of interest." (Publisher's note)
"In a discussion of Lincoln and slavery, the author agrees with Eric Foner that the president was anti-slavery (deeming it a violation of natural rights) but not an abolitionist (he expected slavery would eventually die out). These authoritative essays, most of which appeared previously in

various formats, will appeal mainly to serious students and specialists." Kirkus
Includes bibliographical references and index

The **New** York Times disunion; A History of the Civil War. edited by Edward L. Widmer, with Clay Risen and George Kalogerakis. Oxford University Press 2016 392 p. illustrations $34.95 **973.7**
1. United States -- History -- 1861-1865, Civil War 2. United States -- History -- Civil War, 1861-1865
ISBN 9780190621834

LC 2016015114

This book, edited by Edward L. Widmer, presents "a series [of New York Times articles] marking the long string of anniversaries around the Civil War. . . . Moving chronologically and thematically across all four years of hostilities, this comprehensive and engrossing work examines secession, slavery, battles, and domestic and global politics." (Publisher's note)
(Noted academics, scholars, editors, and historians contribute to a collection of fresh, provocative essays on the Civil War." (Kirkus)
Includes bibliographical references and index

Oakes, James
Freedom national; the destruction of slavery in the United States, 1861-1865. James Oakes. W. W. Norton & Co. 2013 608 p. (hardcover) $29.95 **973.7**
1. Slavery -- United States 2. Slaves -- Emancipation -- United States 3. United States -- History -- 1861-1865, Civil War 4. Slavery -- United States -- History 5. United States -- History -- Civil War, 1861-1865 6. Antislavery movements -- United States -- History 7. United States. President (1861-1865 : Lincoln). Emancipation Proclamation
ISBN 0393065316; 9780393065312

LC 2012035601

This book by James Oakes "shows how deftly [Abraham] Lincoln and congressional Republicans pursued anti-slavery throughout the [American Civil] war, pragmatic in policy but steadfast on principle. . . . As the devastating war continued with slavery still entrenched, Republicans embraced a more aggressive military emancipation, triggered by the Emancipation Proclamation. Finally it took a constitutional amendment on abolition to achieve the Union's primary goal in the war." (Publisher's note)
Includes bibliographical references and index

Paludan, Phillip S.
The **presidency** of Abraham Lincoln; {by} Phillip Shaw Paludan. University Press of Kan. 1994 xx, 384p (American presidency series) $29.95; pa $15.95 **973.7**
1. Lawyers 2. Presidents 3. State legislators 4. Members of Congress 5. United States -- Politics and government -- 1861-1865
ISBN 0-7006-0671-8; 0-7006-0745-5 pa

LC 93-46830

The author "traces the year-by-year chronology of a Presidency engaged with recruiting, placating, appeasing and coercing the various and competing factions of the war years, and sees in Lincoln 'a commitment to the political-constitutional system that would itself move the nation toward its highest ambitions.' . . . Equally interesting is Mr. Paludan's depiction of how the war transformed the national Government, not only establishing the foundations for the Gilded Age but more subtly strengthening and enriching the role of government." NY Times Book Rev

Includes bibliographical references

Perry, James M.

Touched with fire; five presidents and the Civil War battles that made them. PublicAffairs 2003 335p il map $26; pa $16 **973.7**
1. Generals 2. Governors 3. Presidents 4. Senators 5. Members of Congress 6. Presidents -- United States 7. United States -- History -- 1861-1865, Civil War
ISBN 1-586-48114-2; 1-586-48290-4 pa
LC 2003-46625

"All chief executives during the Gilded Age volunteered for the Union in the Civil War (excluding Grover Cleveland, who paid for a substitute). Perry here recounts their war records with an eye to the subsequent electoral advertising of their bravery and patriotism. . . . Perry, a wry storyteller, delivers the regimental-level detail that buffs crave while dusting events with the skepticism that presidential electoral campaigning invites." Booklist

Includes bibliographical references

Rable, George C.

God's almost chosen peoples; a religious history of the American Civil War. University of North Carolina Press 2010 586p il (Littlefield history of the Civil War era) $35 **973.7**
1. United States -- History -- 1861-1865, Civil War -- Religious aspects
ISBN 978-0-8078-3426-8; 0-8078-3426-2
LC 2010-23646

"Rable draws upon newspapers, sermons, diaries, letters, and journals to show that many people on both sides of the conflict turned to faith to help explain the war's causes, course, and consequences. Rable demonstrates that both Northerners and Southerners tried to make sense of the brutal war by thumbing through their Bibles, listening to their preachers, and interpreting battles as a fulfillment of a divine plan. . . . Because of its thorough research and its chronicle of the lives of ordinary people, Rable's engrossing study of the role of religion in the Civil War will stand as the definitive religious history of America's most divisive conflict." Publ Wkly

Includes bibliographical references and index

Roper, Robert

Now the drum of war; Walt Whitman and his brothers in the Civil War. Walker & Co. 2008 421p il $28 **973.7**
1. Poets 2. Authors 3. Essayists 4. Army officers 5. United States -- History -- 1861-1865, Civil War
ISBN 978-0-8027-1553-1; 0-8027-1553-2

This is a "history of the Civil War by means of a family portrait, presenting the war through the eyes and words of the Whitman family. . . . The book provides a simultaneous historical perspective on the war and on an exceptional family, giving general readers and students a vivid depiction of

both and a deeper understanding of one of America's greatest poets." Libr J

Includes bibliographical references and index

Sarna, Jonathan D.

Lincoln and the Jews; a history. by Jonathan Sarna and Benjamin Shapell. Thomas Dunne Books 2015 288 p. color illustrations; map (hardcover) $40 **973.7**
1. Jews -- United States 2. Jews -- United States -- History -- 19th century 3. United States -- History -- Civil War, 1861-1865 -- Jews
ISBN 1250059534; 9781250059536
LC 2014033453

In this book, authors "Jonathan D. Sarna and collector Benjamin Shapell reveal how Lincoln's remarkable relationship with American Jews impacted both his path to the presidency and his policy decisions as president. The volume uncovers a new and previously unknown feature of Abraham Lincoln's life, one that broadened him, and, as a result, broadened America." (Publishers' note)

"The authors provide extensive discussion of Lincoln's efforts to restrain anti-Semitic attitudes in the army, most notably General Ulysses Grant's infamous expulsion order, and extensive prejudice by General Benjamin Butler. This attractive volume featuring a plethora of primary documents highlights the political contributions of numerous Jews to Lincoln's decisions both small and momentous." Choice

Includes bibliographical references and index

Sears, Stephen W.

★ **Chancellorsville**. Houghton Mifflin 1996 593p hardcover o.p. pa $17 **973.7**
1. Generals 2. Chancellorsville (Va.), Battle of, 1863
ISBN 0-395-87744-X pa
LC 96-31220

In this history of the campaign that ended in Chancellorsville, the author argues that "a chain of errors, assumptions, and communications failures combined with the genuine brilliance and good luck of the Confederates to lead to a stinging if indecisive Union defeat." Booklist

Includes bibliographical references

★ **Gettysburg**. Houghton Mifflin 2003 623p il map $30; pa $17 **973.7**
1. Gettysburg (Pa.), Battle of, 1863
ISBN 0-395-86761-4; 0-618-48538-4 pa
LC 2002-191259

This is an "assessment of the battle of Gettysburg and the events leading up to it. . . . Sears examines several turning points during the battle's buildup and three-day duration. The resulting insights add to the excellent and dramatic narrative flow. . . . For all Civil War collections and academic libraries." Libr J

Includes bibliographical references

★ **Landscape** turned red; the Battle of Antietam. Houghton Mifflin 2003 431p il pa $17 **973.7**
1. Antietam (Md.), Battle of, 1862
ISBN 978-0-618-34419-2; 0-618-34419-5
First published 1983 by Ticknor & Fields

This "account of the Battle of Antietam, the bloodiest day of the Civil War, is wide-ranging, detailed, and copiously documented. Stephen Sears . . . describes the tension-filled days preceding September 17, 1862, especially the political climate of Union pessimism and Confederate optimism. . . . The battle itself is then exhaustively recounted." Booklist

★ To the gates of Richmond; the peninsula campaign. Mariner 2001 468p il map pa $17 **973.7**
1. Peninsular Campaign, 1862
ISBN 978-0-618-12713-9; 0-618-12713-5
First published 1992 by Ticknor & Fields
"The campaign on the peninsula between the James and York rivers in Virginia in the spring of 1862 was McClellan's major strategic effort and the first major Union offensive in the East. . . . Sears does an outstanding job in making intelligible an extremely complex campaign." Booklist
Includes bibliographical references

Sinha, Manisha
The **Slave's** cause; a history of abolition. Manisha Sinha. Yale University Press 2016 784 p. illustrations (alk. paper) $37.50 **973.7**
1. Abolitionists 2. Slaves -- Emancipation 3. Slavery -- United States
ISBN 9780300181371
LC 2015948091
"Drawing on extensive archival research, including newly discovered letters and pamphlets, [author Manisha] Sinha documents the influence of the Haitian Revolution and the centrality of slave resistance in shaping the ideology and tactics of abolition. This book is a comprehensive new history of the abolition movement in a transnational context." (Publisher's note)
"Sinha's book is a tour de force that surpasses all previous works in scope, scale, and scholarship." LJ
Includes bibliographic references and index.

Slotkin, Richard, 1942-
Long Road to Antietam; how the Civil War became a revolution. Richard Slotkin. Liveright Publishing Corporation 2012 512 p. (hardcover) $32.95 **973.7**
1. Emancipation Proclamation 2. United States -- History -- 1861-1865, Civil War 3. Antietam, Battle of, Md., 1862 4. United States. President (1861-1865 : Lincoln). Emancipation Proclamation
ISBN 0871404117; 9780871404114
LC 2012007795
This book looks at the germination of the U.S. Civil War which "became a revolution in summer 1862, when Lincoln acknowledged that peaceful compromise was at that point impossible and thoroughly committed himself to war. First up in this new strategy: the Emancipation Proclamation. As Lincoln clashed with ambitious general George McClellan, the country started on the bloody road to Antietam." (Library Journal)
Includes bibliographical references and index

No quarter; the Battle of the Crater, 1864. Random House 2009 411p il map $28 **973.7**
1. Petersburg (Va.) -- History -- Siege, 1864-1865 2.

United States -- History -- 1861-1865, Civil War -- Campaigns
ISBN 978-1-4000-6675-9; 1-4000-6675-1
LC 2008-36260
"By 1864, the North and South had settled into a positional war around Richmond and Petersburg, VA, with trenches, cannon, disease, and delay. Gen. Grant decided to try a mine, digging under a portion of the fortifications and cramming the tunnel with explosives. It was the largest explosion ever seen at the time—and led to a crushing Union defeat, with 4500 dead. There have been lots of books about the Crater, but the eminent Slotkin does a respectable job. Civil War history enthusiasts will want this." Libr J
Includes bibliographical references

Snodgrass, Mary Ellen
★ The **Underground** Railroad; an encyclopedia of people, places, and operations. Sharpe Reference 2007 2v il map set $199 **973.7**
1. Reference books 2. Underground railroad -- Encyclopedias 3. Slavery -- United States -- Encyclopedias
ISBN 978-0-7656-8093-8
LC 2007-9199
The author "has compiled an important and extensively researched encyclopedia of the Underground Railroad. Beginning with a concise, informative general introduction, this ambitious two-volume set neatly identifies the key people, places, documents, organizations, and publications of the Underground Railroad movement, along with significant actions, events, and ideas underlying it in the US and Canada. Offering photographs, bookplates, sketches, and handbills, the set is visually attractive." Choice
Includes bibliographical references

Stout, Harry S.
Upon the altar of the nation : a moral history of the American Civil War. Viking 2006 552p il $29.95 **973.7**
1. United States -- History -- 1861-1865, Civil War
ISBN 0-670-03470-3
LC 2005-42420
"Impeccably sourced and highly engaging, the book will surely be controversial—the best histories often are." Booklist
Includes bibliographical references

Swanson, Mark
Atlas of the Civil War, month by month; major battles and troop movements. maps by Mark Swanson, with Jacqueline D. Langley. University of Georgia Press 2004 141p il map $39.95 **973.7**
1. Reference books 2. Historical atlases 3. United States -- History -- 1861-1865, Civil War -- Maps
ISBN 0-8203-2658-5
LC 2004-12264
This Civil War atlas depicts "multiple aspects of the war's action in a month-by-month sequence from April 1861 to June 1865. . . . An absolute must for Civil War studies." Univ Press Books for Public and Second Sch Libr, 2006
Includes bibliographical references

Tobin, Jacqueline

Hidden in plain view; the secret story of quilts and the underground railroad. [by] Jacqueline L. Tobin and Raymond G. Dobard. Doubleday 1999 208p il map hardcover o.p. pa $14 **973.7**

1. Quilts 2. Ciphers 3. Underground railroad

ISBN 0-385-49137-9; 0-385-49767-9 pa

LC 98-49804

This is "a needed and valuable contribution to the literature of African American culture." Libr J

Includes bibliographical references

Trudeau, Noah Andre

Like men of war; black troops in the Civil War, 1862-1865. Little, Brown 1998 xxii, 548p il maps hardcover o.p. pa $18 **973.7**

1. African American soldiers 2. United States -- History -- 1861-1865, Civil War

ISBN 0-316-85325-9; 0-316-85344-5 pa

LC 97-15380

A "study of the battlefield experiences of black Union regiments. Some 60 maps help the reader make sense of famous engagements (Fort Wagner and the Crater) and notorious incidents (Fort Pillow) in which black soldiers fought, as well as scores of lesser-known clashes. Rich archival research is integrated into a lively narrative that places the raising and deployment of black regiments in broader contexts. This book will become a basic source of information on the subject." Libr J

Includes bibliographical references

Walters, Kerry

The **Underground** Railroad; a reference guide. Kerry Walters. ABC-CLIO 2012 x, 223 p.p ill. (hardcover : acid-free paper) $58.00; (ebook) $58.00 **973.7**

1. Abolitionists 2. Slavery -- United States -- History 3. Underground railroad -- Encyclopedias 4. Underground railroad 5. Fugitive slaves -- United States -- History 6. Abolitionists -- United States -- History -- 19th century 7. Antislavery movements -- United States -- History -- 19th century

ISBN 1598846477; 9781598846478; 9781598846485

LC 2011041517

"This book, part of the Guides to Historic Events in America series, brings into perspective what the Underground Railroad did and how it operated. This guide begins with a chronology from 1690 to 1870, followed by an introduction that attempts to separate the legends from the reality of the times. Subsequent chapters cover the major aspects of slavery and the Underground Railroad." (Booklist)

Includes bibliographical references and index.

Ward, Andrew

★ The **slaves'** war; the Civil War in the words of former slaves. Houghton Mifflin Co. 2008 386p il $28 **973.7**

1. Slavery -- United States 2. Freedmen -- United States 3. Slaves -- Southern States -- Biography 4. United States -- History -- Civil War, 1861-1865 -- Social aspects 5. United States -- History -- Civil War,

1861-1865 -- African Americans 6. United States -- History -- 1861-1865, Civil War -- Personal narratives 7. United States -- History -- Civil War, 1861-1865 -- Personal narratives

ISBN 0-618-63400-2; 978-0-618-63400-2

LC 2008-1532

Collected from "interviews, diaries, letters, and memoirs, here is the Civil War as seen from not only battlefields, capitals, and camps, but also slave quarters, kitchens, roadsides, farms, towns, and swamps." (Publisher's note) Index.

The author "has provided a . . . narrative that gives voice to the experiences and attitudes of slaves who endured the conflict. Ward utilizes testimonials, diaries, and letters, and organizes them in chronological order from the months before the commencement of hostilities to the aftermath of the surrender at Appomattox. . . . This is a work that will interest both scholars and general readers." Booklist

Includes bibliographical references

Ward, Geoffrey C.

The **Civil** War; an illustrated history. {by} Geoffrey C. Ward with Ken Burns and Ric Burns. Knopf 1990 425p il maps $75; pa $29.95 **973.7**

1. United States -- History -- 1861-1865, Civil War

ISBN 0-394-56285-2; 0-679-74277-8 pa

LC 89-43475

"A companion to a nine-part Public Broadcasting System documentary, this superbly designed book easily stands on its own." N Y Times Book Rev

Includes bibliographical references

Wert, Jeffry D.

Mosby's Rangers. Simon & Schuster 1990 384p il hardcover o.p. pa $14 **973.7**

1. United States -- History -- 1861-1865, Civil War 2. Confederate States of America -- Army -- Virginia Cavalry Battalion, 43rd

ISBN 0-671-74745-2 pa

LC 90-37917

"Well-researched, objectively written, this is a first-class history." Publ Wkly

Includes bibliographical references

The **West** Point History of the Civil War; by The United States Military Academy with Colonel Ty Seidule and Clifford Rogers. Simon & Schuster 2014 352 p. color illustrations, maps (hardcover) $55 **973.7**

1. Military art and science 2. United States Military Academy 3. United States -- History -- 1861-1865, Civil War

ISBN 9781476782621; 1476782628

This book, published by United States Military Academy, with Colonel Ty Seidule and Clifford Rogers, offers a "definitive military history of the Civil War, featuring the same exclusive images, tactical maps, and expert analysis commissioned by The United States Military Academy to teach the history of the art of war to West Point cadets." (Publisher's note)

Wiley, Bell Irvin

The **life** of Billy Yank; the common soldier of the Union. with a foreword by James I. Robertson, Jr. Updated ed.; Louisiana State University Press 2008 454p il pa $21.95   **973.7**
1. United States -- Army -- Military life 2. United States -- History -- 1861-1865, Civil War
ISBN 978-0-8071-3375-0; 0-8071-3375-2
LC 2008-24243
First published 1952 by Bobbs-Merrill
"The soldiers' own writings—their letters and diaries—are . . . used as chief source for a picture of the response of the Union men to the call to arms, their training, army life, reactions to Southerners they encountered, opinions of Negroes, and comments on their Reb counterparts." Booklist
Includes bibliographical references

The **life** of Johnny Reb; the common soldier of the Confederacy. Updated ed.; Louisiana State University Press 2008 444p il pa $21.95   **973.7**
1. United States -- History -- 1861-1865, Civil War 2. Confederate States of America -- Army -- Military life
ISBN 978-0-8071-3325-5
LC 2007-33859
First published 1943 by Bobbs-Merrill
"Composite biography of the ordinary soldier of the Confederacy—his behavior in camp and under fire, his food, clothing, weapons, religion, amusements, attitude toward women, and so on. Taken mostly from firsthand accounts in letters, diaries, and records." New Yorker
Includes bibliographical references

Williams, David

★ **Bitterly** divided; the South's inner Civil War. David Williams. New Press 2008 310p ill., ports. (hbk.) o.p.; (pbk.) $14; (hbk.) o.p.   **973.7**
1. Social conflict 2. Southern States -- History 3. Secession -- Southern States 4. Confederate States of America 5. United States -- History -- 1861-1865, Civil War 6. Social conflict -- Southern States -- History -- 19th century
ISBN 1-59558-108-1; 978-1595584755; 9781595581082
LC 2007045285
In this book, author and "historian David Williams lays bare the myth of a united confederacy, revealing that the South was in fact fighting two civil wars--an external one that we know so much about and an internal one about which there is scant literature and virtually no public awareness. . . . [The book] shows that from the Confederacy's very beginnings white Southerners were as likely to have opposed secession as supported it, and they undermined the Confederate war effort at nearly every turn. In just one of many telling examples in . . . narrative history, Williams shows that when planters grew too much cotton and tobacco and exempted themselves from the draft, plain folk called the conflict a 'rich man's war' and rioted. Many formed armed anti-Confederate bands. Southern blacks, in what W.E.B. DuBois called 'a general strike against the Confederacy,' resisted in increasingly overt ways, escaped by the thousands, and forced a change in the war's direction that led to emancipation." (Publisher's note)

"Williams marshals abundant evidence to demonstrate that the Confederacy also lost an internal civil war during 1861-65. . . . This firm repudiation of the myth of the solid Confederate South is absolutely essential Civil War reading." Booklist
Includes bibliographical references (p. [275]-291) and index

Wills, Garry

Lincoln at Gettysburg; the words that remade America. Simon & Schuster 1992 317p hardcover o.p. pa $14   **973.7**
1. Lawyers 2. Presidents 3. State legislators 4. Members of Congress
ISBN 0-671-86742-3 pa
LC 92-3546
This is a "tour de force that will cause much discussion and argument." Libr J
Includes bibliographical references

Woodworth, Steven E.

Atlas of the Civil War; by Steven Woodworth and Kenneth J. Winkle; foreword by James M. McPherson. Oxford University Press 2004 400p il map $75   **973.7**
1. Reference books 2. Historical atlases 3. United States -- History -- 1861-1865, Civil War -- Maps
ISBN 0-19-522131-1
LC 2004-53112
"Richly illustrated, this publication will be wanted by all types of libraries. . . . The text entries are useful, while the maps and illustrations are both informative and eye-catching." Choice

973.775   Administration of Abraham Lincoln, 1861-1865 -- Medical services

Toler, Pamela D.

Heroines of Mercy Street; the real nurses of the Civil War. Pamela D. Toler. Little, Brown & Co. 2016 287 p. illustrations $27   **973.775**
1. Nurses 2. United States -- History -- 1861-1865, Civil War
ISBN 0316392073; 9780316392075
LC 2015953905
This book, by Pamela D. Toler, " tells the true stories of the nurses at Mansion House, the Alexandria, Virginia, mansion turned war-time hospital and setting for the new PBS drama 'Mercy Street.' Among the Union soldiers, doctors, wounded men from both sides, freed slaves, politicians, speculators, and spies who passed through the hospital in the crossroads of the Civil War, were nurses who gave their time freely and willingly to save lives and aid the wounded." (Publisher's note)
"Accessible and well researched, Toler's book coincides with the recent PBS series Mercy Street and successfully illustrates the beginnings of nursing as a designated field of medical practice." LJ
Includes bibliographical references (pages 263-274) and index.

973.8   United States--Reconstruction period, 1865-1901

Algeo, Matthew

The **president** is a sick man; wherein the supposedly virtuous Grover Cleveland survives a secret surgery at sea and vilifies the courageous newspaperman who dared expose the truth. Chicago Review Press 2011 255p il $24.95   **973.8**
1. Mayors 2. Governors 3. Journalism 4. Presidents 5. Journalists 6. District attorneys 7. United States -- Politics and government -- 1865-1898
ISBN 978-1-56976-350-6; 1-56976-350-X
LC 2010-44639

"Incredibly, shortly after his second term began in 1893, Cleveland boarded a friend's yacht and sailed into the Long Island Sound where surgeons, in a makeshift operating theater, cut away cancerous tissue in his mouth and part of his jawbone. . . . Cancer was virtually taboo in Cleveland's day. He didn't want to lose public confidence or become a spectacle like former President Grant, who had died from cancer. Also, Cleveland was in a contentious political struggle over whether the U.S. should return to the gold standard to back its money (his position), or continue with a policy that also accepted silver, the view of his vice president, Adlai Stevenson. Cleveland feared that should he become incapacitated, Stevenson would assume power and sway the country's financial direction. The yacht's crew and surgeons kept mum, except for a dentist serving as anesthetist, who told a fellow doctor. Word found its way to Philadelphia Press reporter E.J. Edwards, who confirmed enough of the tale to print it. Cleveland's circle squatted on the scoop and undermined the reporter's reputation. . . . Only decades later would one of the surgeons tell all in an article, and make amends to Edwards for the harm done to him." Milwaukee J Sentinel

Includes bibliographical references

Connell, Evan S.

★ **Son** of the Morning Star. North Point Press 1984 441p il hardcover o.p. pa $18   **973.8**
1. Generals 2. Little Bighorn, Battle of the, 1876 3. Army officers
ISBN 0-86547-160-6; 0-86547-510-5 pa
LC 84-60681

This book is "impressive in its massive presentation of information, and in the conclusions it draws about the probable events that led to the fracas on the banks of the Little Bighorn. But its strength lies in the way the author has shaped his material." N Y Times Book Rev

Includes bibliographical references

Diner, Steven J.

A **very** different age; Americans of the progressive era. Hill & Wang 1997 320p hardcover o.p. pa $14   **973.8**
1. Progressivism (United States politics) 2. United States -- History -- 20th century
ISBN 0-8090-1611-7 pa
LC 97-3801

The author examines the "social, economic, political, and other changes experienced by Americans during the first two decades of the 20th century. . . . The writing is succinct

and fluid. . . . This rewarding social history is an excellent book for both experienced historians and novices." Libr J

Includes bibliographical references

Donovan, James

A **terrible** glory; Custer and the Little Bighorn-- the last great battle of the American West. [by] James Donovan. Little, Brown and Co. 2008 528p il map pa $16.99; $26.99   **973.8**
1. Generals 2. Little Bighorn, Battle of the, 1876 3. Army officers 4. Western States -- History, Military 5. Native Americans -- Government relations 6. Little Bighorn, Battle of the, Mont., 1876
ISBN 0-316-06747-4 pa; 0-316-15578-0; 978-0-316-06747-8 pa; 978-0-316-15578-6
LC 2007-26156

The author "collects the multiple threads that led to the 1876 massacre at Little Big Horn. . . . Exhaustive research, lively prose and fresh interpretation make for a valuable addition to literature on this otherwise well-trodden historical event." Publ Wkly

Includes bibliographical references (p. [487]-511) and index

Foner, Eric

Forever free; the story of emancipation and Reconstruction. illustrations edited and with commentary by Joshua Brown. Knopf 2005 xxx, 268p il $27.50; pa $15   **973.8**
1. Reconstruction (1865-1876) 2. Slavery -- United States 3. United States -- Politics and government -- 1865-1898
ISBN 0-375-40259-4; 978-0-375-40259-3; 0-375-70274-1 pa; 978-0-375-70274-7 pa
LC 2005-40706

This "is an invaluable and timely book about a subject central to U.S. history and still of obvious significance today—slavery, the Civil War, emancipation, Reconstruction, and both the immediate aftermath and longer-term consequences of those things." Rev Am Hist

Includes bibliographical references

★ **Reconstruction**; America's unfinished revolution, 1863-1877. HarperCollins Pubs. 1988 xxvii, 690p il maps hardcover o.p. pa $23.95   **973.8**
1. Reconstruction (1865-1876) 2. United States -- History -- 1865-1898
ISBN 0-06-093716-5 pa
LC 87-45615

"Incorporating much eyewitness material, this book emphasizes the centrality of the Black experience. The book also examines the themes of race and class, the remodeling of Southern society, and the national context. A complete, modern, scholarly text." N Y Public Libr Book of How & Where to Look It Up

Includes bibliographical references

Franklin, John Hope

Reconstruction after the Civil War; John Hope Franklin; with a new foreword by Eric Foner. 3rd

edition University of Chicago Press 2013 279 p. $20 **973.8**
1. Reconstruction (1865-1876) 2. United States -- History -- 1865-1898
ISBN 9780226923376; 0226923371

LC 2012010482

This is an "account of American life in a time of great challenge, unfamiliar problems, and uncertain leadership. Discusses the Radicals' effort to secure racial justice in the South, the fact that corruption existed not only in the South, and that some worthwhile measures emerged from 'carpetbag' legislatures." Guide to Read in Am Hist {review of 1961 edition}

Grant, Ulysses S. (Ulysses Simpson), 1822-1885

Memoirs and selected letters; personal memoirs of U.S. Grant, selected letters, 1839-1865. Library of Am. 1990 2v in 1 il maps $35 **973.8**
1. Generals 2. Presidents 3. United States -- History -- 1861-1865, Civil War
ISBN 0-940450-58-5

LC 90-60013

This volume includes Grant's personal memoirs, first published in 1885 and 175 letters written between 1839 and 1865
Includes bibliographical references

Grumet, Bridget Hall

Reconstruction era: primary sources; Lawrence W. Baker, project editor. UXL 2004 xxv, 228p il (Reconstruction Era reference library) $60 **973.8**
1. Reconstruction (1865-1876)
ISBN 0-7876-9219-0

LC 2004-17309

This book "contains 19 complete or partial documents, such as the Fourteenth Amendment of the U.S. Constitution and Rutherford B. Hayes' inaugural address. Each document is accompanied by an introduction, keys to reading the document, a discussion of subsequent events related to the document, and other material." Booklist
Includes bibliographical references

Howes, Kelly King

Reconstruction era: almanac; Lawrence W. Baker, project editor. UXL 2004 xxxvii, 228p il map (Reconstruction Era reference library) $60 **973.8**
1. Reconstruction (1865-1876)
ISBN 0-7876-9217-4

LC 2004-17301

This book "covers the political and social aspects of Reconstruction, including carpetbaggers and scalawags, amnesty for white Southerners, 'Black Codes,' the impeachment of President Johnson, the rise of the Ku Klux Klan, attempts to restore the old order in the South and much more." Publisher's note
Includes bibliographical references

Langguth, A. J., 1933-2014

After Lincoln; how the north won the Civil War and lost the peace. A. J. Langguth. Simon & Schuster 2014 464 p. illustrations (hardcover) $28 **973.8**
1. Reconstruction (1865-1876) 2. United States -- Politics and government -- 1865-1898 3. Reconstruction (U.S. history, 1865-1877) 4. United States -- Politics and government -- 1865-1877
ISBN 1451617321; 9781451617320; 9781451617337

LC 2013051340

This book, by A. J. Langguth, "tells the story of the Reconstruction, which set back black Americans and isolated the South for a century. . . . President Andrew Johnson, a former slave owner from Tennessee, was challenged by Northern Congressmen, Radical Republicans led by Thaddeus Stephens and Charles Sumner, who wanted to punish the defeated South. . . . By the 1868 election, united Republicans nominated Ulysses Grant, Lincoln's winning Union general." (Publisher's note)

"The power of the Ku Klux Klan to strike fear was very real, no matter how foreign it seems today. This is a cogent, well-researched, well-told history of that important period. Langguth shows rather than explains, and the result is a rich history of an understudied period of American history." Kirkus
Includes bibliographical references and index

Lears, T. J. Jackson

Rebirth of a nation; the making of modern America, 1877-1920. [by] Jackson Lears. HarperCollins 2009 418p il $27.99 **973.8**
1. United States -- History -- 1865-1898 2. United States -- History -- 1898-1919
ISBN 978-0-06-074749-7; 0-06-074749-8

"A fascinating cultural history. . . . [This] is a major work by a leading historian at the top of his game—at once engaging and tightly argued. Like the best histories, it is also a book that speaks to our own time." N Y Times Book Rev

McFarland, Philip

Mark Twain and the Colonel; Samuel L. Clemens, Theodore Roosevelt, and the arrival of a new century. Philip McFarland. Rowman & Littlefield Publishers, Inc. 2012 499 p. (cloth : alk. paper) $28.00 **973.8**
1. Biography 2. United States -- Civilization -- 1865-1918
ISBN 1442212268; 9781442212268; 9781442212282

LC 2011051861

In this book, "[Philip] McFarland . . . presents [satirist Mark Twain and U.S. President Theodore Roosevelt] as dynamic foils, indicative of the social and political growing pains of the country. Differences in background and beliefs abounded: Roosevelt was an expansionist; Twain was a staunch anti-imperialist. McFarland doesn't shy away from the complex notions each man had of the other." (Publishers Weekly)
Includes bibliographical references and index.

Millard, Candice

The **destiny** of the republic; Candice Millard. Doubleday 2011 x, 319 p., [16] p. of platesp ill. **973.8**

1. United States -- History -- 1865-1898 2. Presidents -- United States -- Assassination 3. Presidents -- United States -- Biography 4. Medicine -- United States -- History -- 19th century 5. United States -- Politics and government -- 1881-1885 6. Political culture -- United States -- History -- 19th century 7. Power (Social sciences) -- United States -- History -- 19th century 8. Presidents -- Medical care -- United States -- History -- 19th century 9. Medical instruments and apparatus -- United States -- History -- 19th century

ISBN 9780307939654; 0385535007; 9780385526265; 9780385535007

LC 2011001549

This book explores U.S. history during the presidency and assassination of U.S. president James Garfield. "As [the author] . . . builds to the president's fatal encounter with his assassin, she details the intra-party struggle among Republicans that led to Garfield's surprise 1880 nomination. . . . During the nearly three excruciating months Garfield lay dying, Alexander Graham Bell . . . scrambled to perfect his induction balance (a metal detector) in time to locate the lead bullet lodged in the stricken president's back. Meanwhile, Garfield's medical team persistently failed to observe British surgeon Joseph Lister's methods of antisepsis--the American medical establishment rejected the idea of invisible germs as ridiculous--a neglect that almost surely killed the president." (Kirkus)

Includes bibliographical references (p. 313-323) and index

Miller, Scott

The **President** and the assassin; McKinley, terror, and empire at the dawn of the American century. Random House 2011 422p il **973.8**

1. Governors 2. Presidents 3. Anarchism and anarchists 4. Murderers 5. Anarchists 6. Members of Congress 7. Anarchism -- United States -- History 8. United States -- Social conditions -- 1865-1918 9. United States -- Politics and government -- 1865-1898 10. United States -- Politics and government -- 1897-1901 11. United States -- Politics and government -- 1898-1919 12. United States -- Territorial expansion -- History -- 19th century

ISBN 1-4000-6752-9; 978-1-4000-6752-7

LC 2010-38857

"Miller examines the social, economic and political forces that underlay the transformation of the U.S. after the Civil War from a feeble newcomer in world affairs to the global power we know today in a way that keeps you learning and turning pages at the same time. Rewarding as it is to be able to grasp at last such late 19th-century mysteries as the monetary debates that have befuddled college students ever since, what makes the book compelling is neither the narrative nor the explanations but the sense of familiarity that pervades it all. Indeed, so many of the circumstances and events of the earlier time have parallels in our own that the experience of reading it is practically eerie." Oregonian

Includes bibliographical references (p. [385]-403) and index

Philbrick, Nathaniel

★ The **last** stand; Custer, Sitting Bull, and the Battle of the Little Bighorn. Viking 2010 466p il map $30 **973.8**

1. Generals 2. Dakota Indians 3. Little Bighorn, Battle of the, 1876 4. Army officers 5. Indian chiefs 6. Dakota Indians -- Wars, 1876 7. Little Bighorn, Battle of the, Mont., 1876

ISBN 978-0-670-02172-7

LC 2009-47209

The author "writes a lively narrative that brushes away the cobwebs of mythology to reveal the context and realities of Custer's unexpected 1876 defeat at the hands of his Indian enemies under Sitting Bull, and the character of each leader. Judicious in his assessments of events and intentions, Philbrick offers a rounded history of one of the worst defeats in American military history, a story enhanced by his minute examination of the battle's terrain and interviews with descendants in both camps." Publ Wkly

Includes bibliographical references

Rauchway, Eric

Murdering McKinley; the making of Theodore Roosevelt's America. Hill & Wang 2003 250p il $25; pa $14 **973.8**

1. Governors 2. Presidents 3. Vice-presidents 4. Murderers 5. Anarchists 6. Members of Congress 7. Nobel laureates for peace 8. United States -- Politics and government -- 1898-1919

ISBN 0-8090-7170-3; 0-8090-1638-9 pa

LC 2003-40666

The author "uses a search for the motive of President William McKinley's assassin as a means to comment on the Progressive Era and show how Theodore Roosevelt manipulated the emotions of rage and despair after the tragic event to give it meaning, thereby advancing his own political vision. . . . Novel in its conception and well written, the book is appropriate for public as well as academic libraries." Choice

Includes bibliographical references

Sandoz, Mari

★ The **Battle** of the Little Bighorn. Lippincott 1966 191p maps (Great battles of history series) hardcover o.p. pa $12.95 **973.8**

1. Generals 2. Little Bighorn, Battle of the, 1876 3. Army officers

ISBN 0-397-00410-9; 0-8032-9100-0 pa

"An account of the United States Army expedition against the Sioux Nation with emphasis on the political motives and ambitions of General Custer." Publ Wkly

Includes bibliographical references

Schlereth, Thomas J.

Victorian America; transformations in everyday life, 1876-1915. HarperCollins Pubs. 1991 363p (Everyday life in America) hardcover o.p. pa $15 **973.8**

1. United States -- Social life and customs

ISBN 0-06-092160-9 pa

LC 89-46555

The author surveys the objects, events, experiences, products and tastes that comprised what he terms America's

Victorian culture (1876-1915) and shows how its values shaped modern life.

"What a wonderful book. . . . Schlereth is no wry compiler of trivia. His analysis of social context reveals truly profound, intangible transformations in how and where Americans spent their time during four pivotal decades." Booklist

Includes bibliographical references

Thomas, Evan

The **war** lovers; Roosevelt, Lodge, Hearst, and the rush to empire, 1898. Little, Brown and Co. 2010 471p il $29.99 **973.8**

1. Governors 2. Presidents 3. Vice-presidents 4. Spanish-American War, 1898 5. Senators 6. Biographers 7. Newspaper editors 8. Political leaders 9. Members of Congress 10. Newspaper executives 11. Speakers of the House 12. Nobel laureates for peace 13. Spanish-American War, 1898 -- Causes 14. United States -- Territorial expansion 15. United States -- Politics and government -- 1897-1901 16. United States -- Politics and government -- 1898-1919 17. Business and politics -- United States -- History -- 19th century

ISBN 0-316-00409-X; 978-0-316-00409-1

LC 2009-43616

This book focuses on the "Spanish American War and [on the involvement of] Roosevelt, Lodge, Hearst, McKinley, William James, and Thomas Reed." (Publisher's note) Index.

The author's multifaceted portraits lend the book a sweeping, almost cinematic quality. A lively, well-rounded look at politics and personalities in late-19th-century America. Kirkus

Includes bibliographical references

Tuccille, Jerome

The **roughest** riders; the untold story of the Black soldiers in the Spanish-American War. Jerome Tuccille. Chicago Review Press 2015 304 p. illustrations, maps (cloth) $26.95 **973.8**

1. African American soldiers 2. Spanish-American War, 1898 3. United States -- Military history 4. Spanish-American War, 1898 -- Campaigns 5. African American soldiers -- History -- 19th century 6. Spanish-American War, 1898 -- Participation, African American

ISBN 1613730462; 9781613730461

LC 2015001414

This book, by Jerome Tuccille, "is the inspiring story of the first African American soldiers to serve during the post-slavery era, first in the West and later in Cuba, when full equality, legally at least, was still a distant dream. They fought heroically and courageously, making [Teddy] Roosevelt's campaign [in the Spanish-American War] a great success that added to the future president's legend as a great man of words and action." (Publisher's note)

"Tuccille's excellent descriptions give readers a graphic feel for the vicissitudes of jungle warfare and the grim racial and social realities that these men endured." Pub Wkly

Includes bibliographical references and index

Welch, James

Killing Custer; the Battle of the Little Bighorn and the fate of the Plains Indians. by James Welch

with Paul Stekler. Norton 1994 320p il hardcover o.p. pa $14.95 **973.8**

1. Little Bighorn, Battle of the, 1876 2. Native Americans -- Wars

ISBN 0-393-32939-9 pa

LC 94-5617

"Welch produced this history of the Indian wars of the northern plains as a by-product of his work scripting a television documentary on the Battle of the Little Bighorn. In addition to military history, it contains long sections describing the life of the Plains Indians, accounts of contemporary Indian radical groups, and Welch's reactions while visiting the various historic sites in the area." Libr J

Includes bibliographical references

West, Elliott

The **last** Indian war; the Nez Perce story. Oxford University Press 2009 397p il map (Pivotal moments in American history) **973.8**

1. Indian chiefs 2. Nez Percé War, 1877 3. Big Hole, Battle of the, 1877 4. Nez Percé Indians -- Wars, 1877 5. Nez Percé Indians -- History -- 19th century

ISBN 9780195136753

LC 2008051382

This is an account of the 1877 war between the Nez Perce Indians and the United States government. Chronology. Index.

The author "uses the story of the Nez Percé War of 1877 and its origins and aftermath to illuminate the era of expansion and consolidation between 1845 and 1877 that forged the American identity, a period he calls the 'Greater Reconstruction.' . . . This well-written book is an excellent place to start in understanding the Nez Percé War and is highly recommended for all libraries." Libr J

Includes bibliographical references (p. 325-328) and index.

973.9   United States--1901-

Boorstin, Daniel J. (Daniel Joseph), 1914-2004

The **image**; a guide to pseudo-events in America. Daniel J. Boorstin. Vintage Books, a division of Random House, Inc. 2012 x, 321 p.p (pbk.) $16 **973.9**

1. Fame 2. Popular culture -- United States 3. National characteristics, American 4. United States -- Civilization -- 1945- 5. Popular culture -- United States -- History -- 20th century

ISBN 0679741801; 9780679741800

LC 2012464128

This book, by Daniel J. Boorstin, "first published in 1962, . . . introduced the notion of 'pseudo-events'--events such as press conferences and presidential debates, which are manufactured solely in order to be reported--and the contemporary definition of celebrity. . . . Since then Daniel J. Boorstin's prophetic vision of an America inundated by its own illusions has become an essential resource for any reader who wants to distinguish the manifold deceptions of our culture." (Publisher's note)

Cooke, Alistair

Letter from America, 1946-2004. Knopf 2004 xx, 503p il $35 **973.9**

1. United States -- Social life and customs 2. United States -- Politics and government -- 20th century

ISBN 1-4000-4402-2

LC 2004-304550

"Arranged into chapters by decades, these commentaries reveal not only Cooke's mastery of clear prose but also the range of American topics that caught his interest, from politics to culture. . . . A book for appreciators of American culture in the second half of the previous century as well as those who relish the essay in either oral or written form." Booklist

Galbraith, John Kenneth

Name-dropping; from F.D.R. on. Houghton Mifflin 1999 194p $26; pa $14 **973.9**

1. Politicians -- United States -- Anecdotes 2. United States -- Politics and government -- 20th century

ISBN 0-395-82288-2; 0-618-15453-1 pa

LC 99-20070

The author "reminisces about important figures with whom he has been involved in his long and distinguished life in the public arena. Among the brief portraits are those of Franklin and Eleanor Roosevelt, Harry Truman, JFK, LBJ, Nehru, and others. More than the self-effacing title indicates, this book offers important insights into the people and times on which its author reflects. Galbraith writes with a wit, style, and elegance few can match." Libr J

Gilmore, Glenda Elizabeth

These United States; a nation in the making, 1890 to the present. by Glenda Elizabeth Gilmore, Thomas J. Sugrue. W W Norton & Co Inc 2015 672 p. 16 plates (hardcover) $39.95 **973.9**

1. United States -- History 2. United States -- Politics and government

ISBN 0393239527; 9780393239522

LC 2015019091

This book, by Glenda Elizabeth Gilmore and Thomas J. Sugrue, offers a "history of the making and unmaking of American democracy and global power [during the long 20th century.] . . . The history begins and ends in periods of concentrated wealth, with immigration roiling politics and racial divisions flaring. Its arc over those hundred-plus years raises key questions: how far has our democracy come?" (Publisher's note)

"Sure to be enjoyed by those who appreciate Howard Zinn's A People's History of the United States." LJ

Menand, Louis

The Metaphysical Club. Farrar, Straus & Giroux 2001 546p il $30; pa $15 **973.9**

1. Educators 2. Metaphysics 3. Philosophers 4. Psychologists 5. Logicians 6. Writers on science 7. Supreme Court justices 8. United States -- Intellectual life

ISBN 0-374-19963-9; 0-374-52849-7 pa

LC 00-66279

"Menand brings rare common sense and graceful, witty prose to his richly nuanced reading of American intellectual history." N Y Times Book Rev

Includes bibliographical references

Morgan, Ted

Reds: McCarthyism in twentieth-century America. Random House 2003 685p $35; pa $16.95 **973.9**

1. Anticommunist movements 2. Senators 3. Communism -- United States 4. United States -- Politics and government -- 20th century

ISBN 0-679-44399-1; 0-812-97302-X pa

LC 2003-46509

"Senator Joseph McCarthy's demagogic career is just part of this sweeping account of anti-Communist purges and Communist espionage." N Y Times Book Rev

Includes bibliographical references

St. James encyclopedia of popular culture; editors, Tom Pendergast and Sara Pendergast; with an introduction by Jim Cullen. St. James Press 1999 5v il set $695 **973.9**

1. Reference books 2. United States -- Civilization -- Encyclopedias 3. Popular culture -- United States -- Encyclopedias

ISBN 1-55862-400-7

LC 99-46540

This is an "overview of popular culture in twentieth-century America with a particular emphasis on the second half of the century. In more than 2,700 entries, the nearly 450 contributors attempt to cover the major personalities, productions, products, events, and developments from film, music, print culture, social life, sports, television and radio, art, and performances (which include theater, dance, stand-up comedy, and other live performances). . . . The entries seldom sink to trivialization. They are generally thoughtful and well written, providing information and insight. . . . The editors have done a masterful job of providing something for nearly everyone." Am Ref Books Annu, 2001

Includes bibliographical references

Tintori, Karen

Trapped: the 1909 Cherry Mine disaster. Simon & Schuster 2002 273p il $25; pa $14 **973.9**

1. Coal mines and mining -- Accidents

ISBN 0-7434-2194-9; 0-7434-2195-7 pa

LC 2002-104596

"On November 13, 1909, a fire trapped 480 coal miners . . . 400 feet below ground in a mine at Cherry, Illinois. Only 221 escaped. . . . Tintori describes the life-and-death struggle of the miners below ground and the terror of the women and children gathered at the mine's entrance. . . . Tintori's graphic account of this tragedy is a sad but gripping story." Booklist

973.91   United States--1901-1953

Allen, Frederick Lewis

Only yesterday; an informal history of the 1920's. Wiley 1997 285p (Wiley investment classics) $21.95   **973.91**
1. United States -- Social conditions 2. United States -- History -- 1919-1933 3. United States -- Economic conditions -- 1919-1933
ISBN 0-471-18952-9

LC 97-19930

A reissue of the title first published 1931 by Harper and Brothers

"An account of the years from the spring of 1919 to . . . {1931}. It is a kaleidoscopic picture of American politics, society, manners, morals, and economic conditions." Booklist

Includes bibliographical references

Beam, Alex

A great idea at the time; the rise, fall, and curious afterlife of the Great Books. PublicAffairs 2008 245p il $24.95   **973.91**
1. Books and reading 2. United States -- Intellectual life 3. Great books of the Western world (Franklin Center, Pa.)
ISBN 978-1-58648-487-3; 1-58648-487-7

LC 2008-33115

This is a "look at the marketing phenomenon and cultural-icon status of the Great Books of Western Civilization, a 54-volume collection compiled by university-affiliated academics. . . . Beam's book will have readers looking at volumes in the series from a whole new perspective owing to its witty handling of popular culture." Libr J

Includes bibliographical references (p. 223-228) and index

Burns, Eric

1920; The Year That Made the Decade Roar. Eric Burns. W W Norton & Co Inc 2015 400 p. $27.95   **973.91**
1. Nineteen twenties 2. United States -- History -- 20th century
ISBN 1605987727; 9781605987729

"Eric Burns investigates the year of 1920, which was not only a crucial twelve-month period of its own, but one that foretold the future, foreshadowing the rest of the 20th century and the early years of the 21st, whether it was Sacco and Vanzetti or the stock market crash that brought this era to a close." (Publisher's note)

"Burns makes it possible to recognize the century to come in this intimate study of a single year, and the result is downright fascinating." Pub Wkly

Includes bibliographical references (pages 313-321) and index

Burns, James MacGregor

The three Roosevelts; patrician leaders who transformed America. by James MacGregor Burns & Susan Dunn. Atlantic Monthly Press 2001 678p il $37.50; pa $18   **973.91**
1. Diplomats 2. Governors 3. Presidents 4. Vice-presidents 5. People with disabilities 6. Columnists 7.

Philatelists 8. Humanitarians 9. Social activists 10. Spouses of presidents 11. United Nations officials 12. Nobel laureates for peace 13. United States -- Politics and government -- 20th century
ISBN 0-87113-780-1; 0-8021-3872-1 pa

LC 00-60896

Burns and Dunn "succeed in approaching their subjects with grace, respect and insight. In the end, they do great justice to three remarkable lives." Publ Wkly

Includes bibliographical references

Davis, Deborah

Guest of honor; Booker T. Washington, Theodore Roosevelt, and the White House dinner that shocked a nation. by Deborah Davis. Atria Books 2012 x, 308 p.p   **973.91**
1. Presidents -- United States -- Biography 2. United States -- Race relations -- History 3. United States -- Politics and government -- 1898-1919 4. United States -- Social conditions -- 1865-1918 5. United States -- Politics and government -- 1901-1909 6. United States -- Race relations -- History -- 20th century
ISBN 1439169810; 9781439169810; 9781439169827; 9781439169834

LC 2012009045

This book is a "portrayal of the . . . oppressive racial attitudes prevalent at the turn of the twentieth century. As [Deborah] Davis indicates, even many so-called Progressives adhered to pseudoscientific doctrines of social Darwinism and Anglo-Saxon racial superiority Given that context, the unprecedented dinner invitation extended by President Teddy Roosevelt to preeminent black educator Booker T. Washington assumed great importance. Davis first expends considerable effort in drawing parallels between the two men . . . showing both as intense strivers. . . . When she gets to the meeting itself and the reactions to it, she . . . provid[es a] . . . snapshot of the prejudices and schisms in American society a century ago." (Booklist)

Includes bibliographical references (p.[285]-295) and index

Dickstein, Morris

Dancing in the dark; a cultural history of the Great Depression. W. W. Norton 2009 598p il $29.95   **973.91**
1. Great Depression, 1929-1939 2. Popular culture -- United States 3. United States -- History -- 1919-1933 4. United States -- History -- 1933-1945 5. United States -- Social life and customs
ISBN 978-0-393-07225-9

LC 2009-17389

A cultural history of the 1930s explores the anxiety, despair, and optimism of the period while evaluating such factors as the Dust Bowl migrations, "screwball comedy," and swing band music to evaluate how period culture provided a dynamic lift to the country's morale.

"Whether discussing Citizen Kane or Porgy and Bess, the poetry of Langston Hughes, William Carlos Williams or Robert Frost, Faulkner's unique achievement and odd relation to the period, the films of Cary Grant or the elegance and energy of Art Deco, Dickstein always has something smart and lively to say. His scintillating commentary illumi-

nates an important dimension of a decade too often considered only in political or economic terms. It's hard to imagine
a more astute, more graceful guide to a remarkably creative
period." Kirkus

Includes bibliographical references

Egan, Timothy

★ The **big** burn; Teddy Roosevelt and the fire
that saved America. Houghton Mifflin Harcourt
2009 324p il map $27   **973.91**

1. Governors 2. Presidents 3. Forest fires 4. Vice-
presidents 5. Conservationists 6. Forest conservation
7. Nature conservation 8. Foresters 9. Nobel laureates
for peace 10. United States -- Forest Service 11. Forest
conservation -- United States 12. Forest fires -- United
States -- History 13. National parks and reserves --
United States 14. Forest conservation -- United States
-- History 15. Nature conservation -- United States --
History 16. National parks and reserves -- United States
-- History

ISBN 978-0-618-96841-1; 0-618-96841-5

LC 2009-21881

"This is history that is well researched, vividly set into
the context of the early twentieth century, and written with
such skill in character development and pacing that readers
will be lost in a vivid reimagining of those surreal days in
1910 when an ecological event unfolded with the spectacle
of a modern summer blockbuster." Orion

Includes bibliographical references (p. [287]-305)
and index.

Fraser, Steve, 1945-

The **age** of acquiescence; the life and death of
American resistance to organized wealth and power.
Steve Fraser. Little, Brown & Co. 2015 480 p.
(hardback) $28   **973.91**

1. Income 2. Power (Social sciences) 3. United States
-- Social conditions 4. Acquiescence (Psychology) --
History 5. Social conflict -- United States -- History
6. Protest movements -- United States -- History 7.
Social psychology -- United States -- History 8. Income
distribution -- United States -- History 9. United States
-- Politics and government -- 1945- 10. Elite (Social
sciences) -- United States -- History 11. Power (Social
sciences) -- United States -- History

ISBN 0316185434; 9780316185431

LC 2014020466

This book by Steve Fraser "examines the rise of American capitalism, the visionary attempts to protect the democratic commonwealth, and the great surrender to today's
delusional fables of freedom and the politics of fear. Mass
movements envisioned a new world supplanting dog-eat-
dog capitalism. But over the last half-century that political
will and cultural imagination have vanished. Why? [Fraser]
seeks to solve that mystery." (Publisher's note)

"Though the implications for both present and future are
bleak, few books feature such an ambitious premise or cover
as much historical ground over such a complex era as skillfully as does Fraser's. Summing Up: Highly recommended.
All levels/libraries."

Gardner, Mark Lee

Rough Riders; Theodore Roosevelt, his cowboy
regiment, and the immortal charge up San Juan Hill.
Mark Lee Gardner. William Morrow 2016 352 p.
illustrations (hardcover) $26.99   **973.91**

1. Spanish-American War, 1898 -- Regimental histories
2. San Juan Hill, Battle of, Cuba, 1898 3. United States.
Army. Volunteer Cavalry, 1st 4. Spanish-American
War, 1898 -- Campaigns -- Cuba

ISBN 9780062312082; 9780062312099;
9780062466433

LC 2015046230

This narrative history book, by Mark Lee Gardner,
profiles Theodore Roosevelt and his Rough Riders cavalry
regiment. "In February 1898, Congress authorized President
McKinley to recruit a volunteer army to drive the Spaniards
from Cuba. From this army emerged the legendary 'Rough
Riders,' a mounted regiment drawn from America's western
territories and led by the indomitable Theodore Roosevelt."
(Publisher's note)

"Gardner provides some terrifying, exhilarating stories
of the battle, including the valiant charge up San Juan Hill
through enemy gunfire. Throughout, Gardner celebrates
Roosevelt, who as a postwar commander-in-chief never for-
got the lesson of war and the heroic sacrifices of the fighters." Pub Wkly

Goodwin, Doris Kearns, 1943-

★ The **Bully** Pulpit; Theodore Roosevelt, William Howard Taft, and the Golden Age of Journalism.
Doris Kearns Goodwin. Simon & Schuster 2013
848 p. illustrations $40   **973.91**

1. Journalism -- United States -- History 2. United
States -- Politics and government -- 1901-1909 3.
United States -- Politics and government -- 1909-1913
4. Republican Party (U.S. : 1854-) -- History -- 20th
century 5. Press and politics -- United States -- History
-- 20th century 6. Progressivism (United States politics)
-- History -- 20th century

ISBN 141654786X; 9781416547860

LC 2013032709

Andrew Carnegie Medal for Excellence in Nonfiction
(2014)

This book, by Doris Kearns Goodwin, examines "the
friendship of two very different Presidents, [Theodore]
Roosevelt and William Howard Taft. . . . Though the book
is primarily concerned with the intervening private lives
of two politicians, a prominent second narrative emerges
as Goodwin links both presidents' fortunes to the rise of
'muckraking' journalism, specifically the magazine 'Mc-
Clure's' and its influence over political and social discussion." (Publishers Weekly)

"By shining a light on a little-discussed President and
a much-discussed one, Goodwin manages to make history
very much alive and relevant." Pub Wkly

Includes bibliographical references (pages 753-867)
and index

Hagedorn, Ann

Savage peace; hope and fear in America, 1919.
Simon & Schuster 2007 543p il $30   **973.91**

1. United States -- Race relations 2. United States --

History -- 1919-1933
ISBN 978-0-7432-4371-1; 0-7432-4371-4
LC 2006-51258

Hagedorn "weaves numerous threads of history together to provide a clear vision of American society at the dawn of the modern age. This is not the dull history of academia: Her writing is concise, colorful and compelling." PopMatters

Includes bibliographical references (p. [499]-510) and index.

Hofstadter, Richard

The **age** of reform from Bryan to F.D.R. Knopf 1955 328, xxp hardcover o.p. pa $12.95 **973.91**
1. United States -- Politics and government -- 20th century
ISBN 0-394-70095-3 pa

This analysis of the reform movements in American politics from 1890-1940 reviews: The agrarian uprising that found its expression in the Populist movement of the 1890's; The Progressive movement from about 1900-1914; The New Deal of the 1930's. Emphasis is placed upon the ideas of the leading political reformers.

Includes bibliographical references

Kennedy, David M.

★ **Freedom** from fear; the American people in depression and war, 1929-1945. Oxford Univ. Press 1999 936p il maps (Oxford history of the United States) $39.95; pa $22.50 **973.91**
1. United States -- History -- 1919-1933 2. United States -- History -- 1933-1945
ISBN 0-19-503834-7; 0-19-514403-1 pa
LC 98-49580

This narrative history of the United States spans the period from the Great Depression to the end of the Second World War

"Rarely does a work of historical synthesis combine such trenchant analysis and elegant writing. For its scope, its insight and its purring narrative engine, Kennedy's book will stand for years to come as the definitive account of the critical decades of the American century." Publ Wkly

Includes bibliographical references

Lunde, Darrin

The **naturalist**; Theodore Roosevelt, a lifetime of exploration, and the triumph of American natural history. Darrin Lunde. Crown 2016 352 p. illustrations, map (hardback) $28 **973.91**
1. Presidents -- United States -- Biography 2. Nature conservation -- United States -- History 3. Nature conservation -- United States 4. Natural history museums -- United States 5. Naturalists -- United States -- Biography 6. Conservationists -- United States -- Biography
ISBN 9780307464309
LC 2015036683

This book, by Darrin Lunde, is a "captivating new account of how Theodore Roosevelt's lifelong passion for the natural world set the stage for America's wildlife conservation movement and determined his legacy as a founding father of today's museum naturalism." (Publisher's note)

"Colloquially and anecdotally written, sometimes graphically detailing the pursuit and skinning of game, this book is accessible to the lay reader and authenticated for the historian." LJ

Includes bibliographical references and index.

Millard, Candice

The **river** of doubt; Theodore Roosevelt's darkest journey. Doubleday 2005 416p il map $26 **973.91**
1. Governors 2. Presidents 3. Vice-presidents 4. Amazon River valley 5. Nobel laureates for peace 6. Roosevelt-Rondon Scientific Expedition (1913-1914)
ISBN 0-385-50796-8
LC 2005-46541

This is an account of the Amazon expedition Theodore Roosevelt undertook in 1912, with his son Kermit and the Brazilian explorer Col. Candido Rondon.

The author "turns this incredible story into one that easily matches an Indiana Jones screen adventure." Libr J

Includes bibliographical references

Miller, Nathan

New world coming; the 1920s and the making of modern America. Da Capo Press 2004 433p pa $19.95 **973.91**
1. Authors 2. Novelists 3. Screenwriters 4. Short story writers 5. United States -- History -- 1919-1933
ISBN 978-0-306-81379-5; 0-306-81379-3
LC 2004-56140

First published 2003 by Scribner

The author "illuminates the United States as it existed under presidents Harding, Coolidge and Hoover, using the life of F. Scott Fitzgerald, with all its peaks and valleys during the 1920s, as the backbone of his narrative. . . . In addition to events in the arts and sciences, Miller details bitter labor struggles, the rise of the reconstituted Ku Klux Klan and Prohibition. . . . This volume comprises an excellent chronicle of that turbulent, troubled and tempestuous decade called 'the roaring '20s.'" Publ Wkly

Includes bibliographical references

Moore, Lucy

Anything goes; a biography of the roaring twenties. Overlook Press 2010 352p il $25.95 **973.91**
1. United States -- History -- 1919-1933
ISBN 978-1-59020-313-2
LC 2009-46437

First published 2008 in the United Kingdom

"Rather than presenting her material as an extended survey of the period, Moore focuses on a single Jazz Age trope per chapter, resulting in easily digestible takes on prohibition and the high-spirited criminal culture it engendered; the explosion in popularity of jazz music; the evolution of the flapper; the emergence of Hollywood as creator of a national cultural consciousness; the financial scandals of the Harding presidency; the Sacco/Vanzetti and Scopes trials; the resurgence of the Ku Klux Klan; the Algonquin round table and the founding of the New Yorker; Charles Lindbergh's historic trans-Atlantic flight; the spectacular boxing career of Jack Dempsey; and the financial devastation of the Wall Street crash that ended the party and ushered in the Great

Depression. . . . Snappy, vivid account of America's most glittering decade." Kirkus

Includes bibliographical references

Pietrusza, David

1920: the year of the six presidents. Carroll & Graf 2007 533p il $28.95   **973.91**

1. Presidents -- United States -- Election -- 1920

ISBN 978-0-78671-622-7; 0-7867-1622-3

"Six men—a sitting president, former president, and four eventual presidents—competed in the 1920 presidential election. . . . [The author] contends that this election marked the birth of modern American politics. . . . The many issues and forces that swirled during that time, from the fear of Communists and Socialists and the terrorism they allegedly perpetrated to technological advances and Prohibition, make for a fascinating and compelling tale of an often-overlooked election in our history." Libr J

Includes bibliographical references

Schlesinger, Arthur M. (Arthur Meier), 1917-2007

The **crisis** of the old order, 1919-1933; [by] Arthur M. Schlesinger, Jr. Houghton Mifflin 2003 557p (Age of Roosevelt) pa $17   **973.91**

1. Governors 2. Presidents 3. People with disabilities 4. Philatelists 5. United States -- History -- 1919-1933

ISBN 0-618-34085-8

LC 2003-47884

First published 1957

This is the first of three volumes which interpret the political, economic, social, and intellectual life of the United States during the time when Franklin D. Roosevelt was in office. This volume covers the years preceding his first term

Includes bibliographical references

Followed by The coming of the New Deal, and The politics of upheaval

Shlaes, Amity

The **forgotten** man; a new history of the Great Depression. Amity Shlaes. HarperCollins 2007 464 p.   **973.91**

1. New Deal, 1933-1939 2. Great Depression, 1929-1939 3. Depressions -- 1929 -- United States 4. Presidents --United States -- Policies 5. Economic stabilization -- United States -- History -- 20th century

ISBN 0066211700; 9780066211701

"Reminding readers that the reputedly do-nothing Hoover pulled hard on the fiscal levers (raising tariffs, increasing government spending), Shlaes nevertheless emphasizes that his enthusiasm for intervention paled against the ebullient FDR's glee in experimentation. She focuses closely on the influence of his fabled Brain Trust, her narrative shifting among Raymond Moley, Rexford Tugwell, and other prominent New Dealers. Businesses that litigated their resistance to New Deal regulations attract Shlaes' attention, as do individuals who coped with the despair of the 1930s through self-help, such as Alcoholics Anonymous cofounder Bill Wilson. The book culminates in the rise of Wendell Willkie, and Shlaes' accent on personalities is an appealing avenue into her skeptical critique of the New Deal." Booklist

Includes bibliographical references

Smith, Hedrick

Who stole the American dream? Hedrick Smith. Random House 2012 xxxi, 557 p.p   **973.91**

1. American dream 2. Middle class -- United States 3. United States -- Politics and government 4. Public interest -- United States 5. Divided government -- United States 6. Income distribution -- United States 7. Polarization (Social sciences) -- United States 8. United States -- Politics and government -- 1989- 9. Middle class -- Political activity -- United States 10. Middle class -- United States -- Economic conditions 11. United States -- Politics and government -- 1945-1989 12. Political culture -- United States -- History -- 20th century 13. Political culture -- United States -- History -- 21st century

ISBN 1400069661; 9780679604648; 9781400069668

LC 2012005865

This book, by Pulitzer Prize winner Hedrick Smith, offers an "account of how, over the past four decades, the American Dream has been dismantled. . . . Smith reveals how pivotal laws and policies were altered while the public wasn't looking, how Congress often ignores public opinion, why moderate politicians got shoved to the sidelines, and how Wall Street often wins politically by hiring over 1,400 former government officials as lobbyists." (Publisher's note)

Includes bibliographical references (p. [527]-538) and index

Starobin, Paul

After America; narratives for the next global age. Viking 2009 358p $26.95   **973.91**

1. International relations 2. United States -- Civilization 3. United States -- Foreign relations

ISBN 978-0-670-02094-2

LC 2008-46685

This "is a narrative of extraordinary range and contemporary relevance." Publ Wkly

Includes bibliographical references

Terkel, Studs, 1912-2008

★ **Hard** times; an oral history of the great depression. Norton 2000 462p pa $14.95   **973.91**

1. Great Depression, 1929-1939 2. United States -- Social conditions 3. United States -- Economic conditions -- 1919-1933 4. United States -- Economic conditions -- 1933-1945

ISBN 1-56584-656-7

LC 2003-389318

A reissue of the title first published 1970 by Pantheon Bks.

"Persons of all ages, occupations, and classes scattered across the U.S. remember what they experienced or were told about the economic crisis of the 1930's. The result is a social document of immense interest." Booklist

973.917   Administration of Franklin Delano Roosevelt, 1933-1945

The **40s**; the story of a decade. The New Yorker; edited by Henry Finder with Giles Harvey; introduction by David Remnick. Random House

Inc 2014 720 p. illustrations (acid-free paper) $30 **973.917**

1. Nineteen forties 2. New York (N.Y.) -- Intellectual life 3. United States -- In literature 4. New Yorker (New York, N.Y. : 1925) 5. United States -- History -- 1933-1945 6. United States -- History -- 1945-1953 7. United States -- Social customs -- 1945- 8. United States -- Social customs -- 1933-1945 9. United States -- Social life and customs -- 20th century

ISBN 0679644792; 9780679644798; 9780679644804

LC 2013047082

"The 1940s were when 'The New Yorker' came of age. A magazine that was best known for its humor and wry social observation would extend itself, offering the first in-depth reporting from Hiroshima and introducing American readers to the fiction of Vladimir Nabokov and the poetry of Elizabeth Bishop. In this . . . book, . . . contributions from the . . . writers who graced [the magazine's] pages throughout the decade are placed in history by the magazine's current writers." (Publisher's note)

"Readers are certain to enjoy the beautiful writing, clever thinking and insightful thoughts across a vast range of topics." Kirkus

Cook, Blanche Wiesen

Eleanor Roosevelt. v1 Penguin Bks. 1993 587p v1 il pa $18 **973.917**

1. Diplomats 2. Columnists 3. Humanitarians 4. Social activists 5. Spouses of presidents 6. United Nations officials 7. Presidents' spouses -- United States

ISBN 0-14-009460-1

LC 87040632

First published 1992

This first volume of a two-volume biography of Eleanor Roosevelt "spans the years from Eleanor's birth to her husband Franklin Delano's inauguration." Publisher's note

Includes bibliographical references

Fullilove, Michael

Rendezvous with destiny; how Franklin D. Roosevelt and five extraordinary men took America into the war and into the world. Michael Fullilove. The Penguin Press 2013 480 p. (hardcover) $29.95 **973.917**

1. World War, 1939-1945 -- United States 2. World War, 1939-1945 -- Diplomatic history 3. United States -- Foreign relations -- 1933-1945

ISBN 1594204357; 9781594204357

LC 2012047003

This book by Michael Fullilove looks at the lead-up to the U.S. entry in to World War II. President Franklin D. Roosevelt "had to jump some big hurdles: he had to convince his fellow Americans of the necessity of getting involved, and he had to support Britain's efforts to keep Hitler from overwhelming the U.K.'s skies and shores. In 1940, Roosevelt enlisted five capable men to cross the Atlantic to visit, negotiate, observe the war-weary British, and assess how the U.S. could help." (Publishers Weekly)

Includes bibliographical references and index

Golay, Michael

★ **America** 1933; the Great Depression, Lorena Hickok, Eleanor Roosevelt, and the shaping of the New Deal. by Michael Golay. Free Press 2013 336 p. $26.99 **973.917**

1. Great Depression, 1929-1939 2. United States -- History -- 1919-1933 3. Depressions -- 1929 -- United States 4. United States -- History -- 1933-1945 5. United States -- Social conditions -- 1918-1945 6. United States -- Economic conditions -- 1918-1945 7. Investigative reporting -- United States -- History -- 20th century

ISBN 143919601X; 9781439196014

LC 2012041139

In this book, author Michael Golay "writes of the 1933-34 cross-country trip undertaken by Lorena Hickok to evaluate and report to the new Federal Emergency Relief Administration (FERA) on how the Great Depression was impacting ordinary families. . . . She had been an Associated Press reporter; her friendship with Eleanor Roosevelt (ER) helped her to create FERA reports that captured President Roosevelt's attention. Golay focuses here on the grinding poverty that Hickok witnessed." (Library Journal)

Includes bibliographical references and index

Jordan, Jonathan W.

American warlords; how Roosevelt's high command led America to victory in World War II. Jonathan W. Jordan. NAL Caliber 2015 624 p. illustrations $28.95 **973.917**

1. Generals 2. World War, 1939-1945 -- Campaigns 3. World War, 1939-1942 -- United States 4. Generals -- United States -- Biography 5. Presidents -- United States -- Biography 6. Command of troops -- History -- 20th century 7. United States -- Politics and government -- 1933-1945

ISBN 0451414578; 9780451414571

LC 2014036427

This book by Jonathan W. Jordan "explores the relationship between Franklin D. Roosevelt and his top military advisers, extending the analysis to the Asian and South Pacific dimension of World War II. Focusing on the leadership tension of the era, the author proves how Roosevelt was often pitted against his Secretary of War Henry Stimson, Army Chief of Staff George C. Marshall, and Chief of Naval Operations Ernest J. King." (Library Journal)

"Jordan's wonderful new insight into the leaders shows how lucky we were regarding Stimson's prescient warnings about nuclear war, Marshall's long-suffering, self-effacing loyalty, and King's rough-and-ready fighting abilities. In addition to World War II buffs, other readers will enjoy the intrigue, back-stabbing, action, and diplomacy in this well-written book." Kirkus

Includes bibliographical references and index

Katznelson, Ira

Fear itself; the New Deal and the origins of our time. Ira Katznelson. Liveright Publishing Corporation 2013 512 p. (hardcover) $29.95 **973.917**

1. New Deal, 1933-1939 2. United States -- Economic conditions -- 1919-1933 3. World politics, 1933-1945 4. United States -- Politics and government -- 1933-

1945 5. Political culture -- United States -- History -- 20th century
ISBN 0871404508; 9780871404503
LC 2012041794
Author Ira Katznelson looks at the New Deal in this book. "Rather than seeing [Franklin D. Roosevelt]'s brainchild as simply a great experiment in economic recovery and the enlargement of government responsibility, Katznelson emphasizes three often neglected aspects of that extraordinary era"--fear, pressure from Nazi and Soviet regimes, and the "southern cage." (Publishers Weekly)
Includes bibliographical references and index

Leuchtenburg, William Edward

Franklin D. Roosevelt and the New Deal, 1932-1940; {by} William E. Leuchtenburg. Harper & Row 1963 393p il (New American nation series) hardcover o.p. pa $16   **973.917**
1. Governors 2. Presidents 3. New Deal, 1933-1939 4. People with disabilities 5. Philatelists 6. United States -- History -- 1933-1945
ISBN 0-06-133025-6 pa
This treatment of Roosevelt's first two terms in office emphasizes the economic crisis and New Deal reforms. The author shows how social forces influenced government action: the San Francisco strike in 1934, the careers of Huey Long and Father Coughlin, the sharecroppers' revolt, and unemployment
This book "is comprehensive, logically organized, and written with clarity and detachment." Am Hist Rev
Includes bibliographical references

Moe, Richard

Roosevelt's second act; the election of 1940 and the politics of war. Richard Moe. Oxford University Press 2013 392 p. $29.95   **973.917**
1. World War, 1939-1945 -- United States 2. Presidents -- Term of office -- United States 3. Presidents -- United States -- Election -- 1940 4. United States -- Foreign relations -- 1933-1945 5. United States -- Politics and government -- 1933-1945
ISBN 0199981914; 9780199981915
LC 2013004529
This book by Richard Moe looks at the "the lead-up to the U.S. election of 1940 and war in Europe. . . . Moe aims to get inside FDR's head and delineate the president's decision-making process step by step. From 'shifting gears' from trying to jump-start the crippled economy in his first term to focusing on German aggression and bolstering England in his second, Roosevelt never let himself be pinned down." (Kirkus Reviews)
Includes bibliographical references and index

Schlesinger, Arthur M. (Arthur Meier), 1917-2007

The coming of the New Deal, 1933-1935; {by} Arthur M. Schlesinger, Jr. Houghton Mifflin 2003 669p (Age of Roosevelt) pa $17   **973.917**
1. Governors 2. Presidents 3. New Deal, 1933-1939 4. People with disabilities 5. Philatelists 6. United States -- History -- 1933-1945
ISBN 0-618-34086-6
LC 2003-47859

First published 1959
"This second volume of 'The Age of Roosevelt' continues the work begun with 'The Crisis of the Old Order, 1919-1933'. . . . The dramatic story of how representative democracy began the battle to conquer economic collapse is followed through the first two years of the New Deal." Libr J
Includes bibliographical references
Followed by The politics of upheaval

The **politics** of upheaval, 1935-1936; {by} Arthur M. Schlesinger, Jr. Houghton Mifflin 2003 749p (Age of Roosevelt) pa $17   **973.917**
1. Governors 2. Presidents 3. New Deal, 1933-1939 4. People with disabilities 5. Philatelists 6. United States -- History -- 1933-1945
ISBN 0-618-34087-4
LC 2003-47889
First published 1960
This third volume of The age of Roosevelt "concentrates on the turbulent concluding years of Franklin D. Roosevelt's first term." Publisher's note
Includes bibliographical references

Simon, James F.

FDR and Chief Justice Hughes; the president, the Supreme Court, and the epic battle over the New Deal. James F. Simon. Simon & Schuster 2012 461 p. ill. $28   **973.917**
1. New Deal, 1933-1939 2. Presidents -- United States 3. United States -- Foreign relations 4. United States. Supreme Court -- Biography 5. United States -- Politics and government -- 1933-1945 6. Executive power -- United States -- History -- 20th century 7. Political questions and judicial power -- United States -- History -- 20th century
ISBN 9781416573289; 9781416573296; 9781416578895
LC 2011028825
Author James F. Simon focuses on "the struggle between FDR and Chief Justice Charles Evans Hughes that decided the fate of the New Deal. . . . In 1936, FDR was reelected by a landslide and the exasperated president proposed legislation to relieve, he said, the overburdened and elderly justices of their heavy workload. He proposed the appointment of an additional justice for each sitting member over seventy years old. . . . The proposal would have permitted the president to stack the Court with justices favorable to the New." (Publisher's note)
Includes bibliographical references and index.

Wortman, Marc

1941: Fighting the Shadow War; A Divided America in a World at War. Marc Wortman. Atlantic Monthly Press 2016 416 p. illustrations, map $27   **973.917**
1. World War, 1939-1945 -- United States 2. United States -- Politics and government -- 1933-1945
ISBN 0802125115; 9780802125118
This book, by Marc Wortman, "explores the little-known history of America's clandestine involvement in World War II before the attack on Pearl Harbor. Wortman tells the story through the eyes of the powerful as well as

ordinary citizens. Their stories weave throughout the intricate tapestry of events that unfold during the crucial year of 1941." (Publisher's note)

"The author displays a nice sense of the dramatic scene and a solid ear for telling quotes, and ample documentation gives readers the opportunity to look further into the history." Kirkus

973.918   Administration of Harry S Truman, 1945-1953

Brands, H. W.

★ The **General** Vs. the President; MacArthur and Truman at the Brink of Nuclear War. by H.W. Brands. Random House Inc 2016 448 p. illustrations, maps (ebook) $65; $30   **973.918**
1. Nuclear weapons -- United States -- History 2. United States -- Politics and government -- 1945-
ISBN 9780385540582; 0385540574; 9780385540575
LC 2016021412

This book, by H.W. Brands, presents the "story of how President Harry Truman and General Douglas MacArthur squared off to decide America's future in the aftermath of World War II. . . . In the nuclear era, when the Soviets, too, had the bomb, the specter of a catastrophic third World War lurked menacingly close on the horizon." (Publisher's note)

"An exciting, well-written comparison study of two American leaders at loggerheads during the Korean War crisis." Kirkus

Includes bibliographical references and index.

Weisbrode, Kenneth

The **Year** of Indecision, 1946; A Tour Through the Crucible of Harry Truman's America. by Kenneth Weisbrode. Penguin Group USA 2016 320 p. $28   **973.918**
1. Nineteen forties 2. United States -- History -- 20th century
ISBN 0670016845; 9780670016846

This book, by Kenneth Weisbrode, is an "account of America at the pivot point of the postwar era, Harry Truman's first full year in office. . . . Relations broke down with the Soviet Union, and nearly did with the British. The United States suffered shortages and strikes of a magnitude it had not seen in years. In November 1946, the Democrats lost both houses of Congress. The tension between fear and optimism expressed itself too in popular culture." (Publisher's note)

"A solid, fact-filled study, especially relevant for those who thought life was better then." Kirkus

Includes bibliographical references (pages [267]-285) and index.

973.92   United States--1953-2001

The **50s**; the story of a decade. The New Yorker; edited by Henry Finder; introduction by David Remnick. Random House 2015 784 p. illustrations (hardcover) $35   **973.92**
1. Nineteen fifties 2. United States -- Civilization -- 1945-
ISBN 9780679644811; 0679644814
LC 2015030067

In this book, edited by Henry Finder, articles from "The New Yorker" magazine from the 1950s are presented to chronicle the era. "In this . . . volume, classic works of reportage, criticism, and fiction are complemented by new contributions from the magazine's present all-star lineup of writers, including Jonathan Franzen, Malcolm Gladwell, and Jill Lepore." (Publisher's note)

Includes bibliographical references

American empire, 1945-2000; the rise of a global power, the democratic revolution at home. Joshua Freeman. Viking 2012 512 p.   **973.92**
1. United States -- History -- 1945- 2. United States -- Foreign relations 3. United States -- Politics and government -- 1945- 4. United States -- Economic conditions -- 20th century 5. United States -- Foreign relations -- 1989- 6. United States -- Economic conditions -- 1945- 7. United States -- Foreign relations -- 1945-1989 8. United States -- Politics and government -- 1989- 9. United States -- Politics and government -- 1945-1989
ISBN 0670023787; 9780670023783
LC 2011049263

In this book, author Joshua B. Freeman examines a postwar dominant America . . . . Covering the glory years of 1945-2000, Freeman . . . turns his critical eye on America's turbulent internal affairs, delving into Truman's contested Fair Deal reforms, the McCarthy communist witch-hunts, Eisenhower's cautious civil rights record, LBJ's ambitious Great Society programs, Nixon's Watergate disgrace, the return of 'corporate capitalism' and Reagan conservatism. Freeman deals with the Clinton administration's economic policies . . . followed by the Republican victory in 2000. Though at its peak, America's power exceeded that of the Roman and British empires in cultural, economic, military, and political terms, the nation's postwar dreams were never completely fulfilled, says Freeman." (Publishers Weekly)

Includes bibliographical references and index

Bloom, Allan David

The **closing** of the American mind. Simon & Schuster 1987 392p hardcover o.p. pa $14 **973.92**
1. Higher education 2. United States -- Intellectual life
ISBN 0-671-65715-1 pa
LC 86-24768

This is the author's assessment of liberal arts education today. "In essence, he argues that over the last 25 years the academy has all but abandoned the intellectual and moral principles that have traditionally informed and given substance to liberal education, becoming prey to the enthusiasms—increasingly politicized—of the moment." N Y Times Book Rev

Duffy, Michael

★ The **presidents** club; inside the world's most exclusive fraternity. Nancy Gibbs and Michael Duffy. Simon & Schuster 2012 vii, 641 p.p   **973.92**
1. Interpersonal relations 2. Presidents -- United States 3. United States -- Politics and government -- 1945- 4. Presidents -- United States -- History 5. Ex-presidents -- United States -- History
ISBN 1439127700; 9781439127704
LC 2011042047

This book "chart[s] the zigzag arc of relationships among the men who have occupied the White House since the mid 20th century. . . . [T]he authors present numerous instances of presidents warming to their predecessors. . . . Sometimes mutual admiration was already in place (Truman and Eisenhower--though it later disintegrated); sometimes, antipathy (Clinton and Bush II). But almost always the sitting presidents found in their predecessors some solace, willing ears and sound advice." (Kirkus)
Includes bibliographical references.

Frum, David

How we got here; the 70's: the decade that brought you modern life (for better or worse) Basic Bks. 2000 xxiv, 418p il hardcover o.p. pa $18.95   **973.92**
1. United States -- Civilization -- 1970-
ISBN 0-465-01496-5 pa

The author "aims 'to describe—and to judge' the transformation of American values during the '70s. Surveying politics, legal cases and opinion polls as well as popular culture, he links what he sees as America's loss of faith in government, the rise of 'sourness and cynicism' and the culture of licentiousness and divorce, among other social changes, to events in that decade." Publ Wkly
Includes bibliographical references

Gregory, Ross

Cold War America, 1946 to 1990; Richard Balkin, general editor. Facts on File 2003 670p il map (Almanacs of American life) $105   **973.92**
1. Cold war 2. United States -- History -- 1945- 3. United States -- Social conditions
ISBN 0-8160-3868-6
LC 2001-51136

"This is a treasure trove of statistical information documenting the enormous changes in American life from 1945 to 1990. . . . Found herein are data on everything from the population by sex . . . region, and race, business formations and failures, bull and bear markets, and operations of the postal service to the federal debt, high school seniors and drugs, executions by gender and race, and recipients of National Book Awards and Pulitzer Prizes. . . . Enhancing the work's appeal are photographs throughout the text and an exhaustive index." Am Ref Books Annu, 2003
Includes bibliographical references

Halberstam, David

The **fifties**. Villard Bks. 1993 800p il hardcover o.p. pa $17.95   **973.92**
1. Popular culture -- United States 2. United States -- Social life and customs 3. United States -- Politics and government -- 20th century
ISBN 0-449-90933-6 pa
LC 92-56815

This is a social history of the United States during the 1950s

The author's "sources are secondary and derivative, but his instinct for the revealing anecdote, his ear for the memorable quote, and his awesome powers of organization add up to a variegated overview that moves seamlessly between the serious shenanigans of Chief Justice Earl Warren and the frivolous ones of . . . Grace Metalious." Natl Rev
Includes bibliographical references

Hayden, Tom

The **long** sixties; from 1960 to Barack Obama. Paradigm Publishers 2009 272p $26.95   **973.92**
1. Lawyers 2. Presidents 3. Social change 4. Social movements 5. Senators 6. State legislators 7. Nobel laureates for peace 8. United States -- Social conditions 9. United States -- History -- 1961-1974
ISBN 978-1-59451-739-6; 1-59451-739-8

"With elements of a new Rules for Radicals and knowing takes on such old New Left moments as The Port Huron Statement, Hayden's book could be a worthy foundational document." Kirkus
Includes bibliographical references

King, Martin Luther, Jr., 1929-1968

The **trumpet** of conscience; [by] Martin Luther King, Jr. Beacon Press 2010 80p (King legacy series) $22; pa $12   **973.92**
1. United States -- Social conditions
ISBN 978-0-8070-0071-7; 0-8070-0071-X; 978-0-8070-0170-7 pa; 0-8070-0170-8 pa
LC 2010007881

First published 1968 by Harper & Row
"In November and December 1967, Dr. Martin Luther King, Jr., delivered five lectures for the renowned Massey Lecture Series of the Canadian Broadcasting Corporation. The collection was immediately released as a book under the title Conscience for Change, but after King's assassination in 1968, it was republished as The Trumpet of Conscience. The collection . . . is his final testament on racism, poverty, and war. Each oration in this volume encompasses a distinct theme, . . . addressing issues of equality, conscience and war, the mobilization of young people, and nonviolence." Publisher's note

Kirkpatrick, Rob

1969; the year everything changed. Skyhorse Pub. 2009 302p $24.95   **973.92**
1. United States -- Social conditions 2. United States -- History -- 1961-1974 3. United States -- Civilization -- 1945- 4. United States -- Social life and customs
ISBN 978-1-60239-366-0
LC 2008-43073

The author "asserts that 1969 was the birth of modern America and sets out to relate how this incredible year reflected deep underlying changes in American culture. The book is divided into four parts that roughly outline the year, including 'sexual revolutions of springtime' and 'the apocalyptic standoffs at year's end.' A riveting look at a pivotal year." Booklist

Includes bibliographical references

Klosterman, Chuck

Eating the dinosaur. Scribner 2009 245p $25 **973.92**

1. Sports 2. Consumption (Economics) 3. Popular culture -- United States 4. United States -- Civilization -- 1970-

ISBN 978-1-4165-4420-3; 1-4165-4420-8

LC 2009-18719

"Klosterman delivers his findings like earth-shattering epiphanies, letting the layers of subtle humor and irony fill in any gaps in logic. The result is a collection as much about the author and his way of thinking as it is about his topics. In both cases, the author is unique. Funny, irreverent and fascinating-Klosterman at his best." Kirkus

Kort, Michael

The **Columbia** guide to the Cold War. Columbia Univ. Press 1998 366p (Columbia guides to American history and cultures) $60; pa $19.50 **973.92**

1. Cold war 2. United States -- History -- 1945- 3. United States -- Foreign relations

ISBN 0-231-10772-2; 0-231-10773-0 pa

LC 98-7154

The author begins "with a narrative survey of the Cold War which explains some of the historiographical debates that have occupied historians for more than 50 years. Following this section is a mini-encyclopedia consisting of one- or two-page essays on a wide range of Cold War topics. The book concludes with a concise chronology and a comprehensive bibliography of books, films, novels, journal articles, and archival sources. Finally . . . Kort points out some of the relevant current websites and CD-ROM products." Libr J

Kuralt, Charles

Charles Kuralt's America. Anchor Books 1996 279p il pa $14.95 **973.92**

1. United States -- Description and travel 2. United States -- Social life and customs

ISBN 0-385-48510-7; 978-0-385-48510-4

LC 96-18992

First published 1995 by Putnam

"Kuralt is not in search of crises or epiphanies; he values nature and good food, neighborliness and craftsmanship, quaintness and quirkiness. Though no literary match for American chroniclers like Calvin Trillin, the effable Kuralt does, in un-fancy style, convey his enthusiasm and his engagement." Publ Wkly

On the road with Charles Kuralt. Fawcett 1986 363p il pa $19 **973.92**

1. United States -- Description and travel 2. United States -- Social life and customs

ISBN 0-449-00740-5; 978-0-449-00740-2

First published 1985 by Putnam

"As a CBS reporter specializing in 'soft' news, Kuralt has been roaming around the U.S. since 1967 in search of 'just plain folks.' Some 100 of the television interviews that resulted from that search have been transcribed for this collection. Loosely organized by themes emphasizing the individuality, altruism, and humor that characterize small town and rural Americans, the interviews and anecdotes are consistently entertaining." Booklist

Marling, Karal Ann

As seen on TV; the visual culture of everyday life in the 1950s. Harvard Univ. Press 1994 328p il map $27.50; pa $20.50 **973.92**

1. Television broadcasting 2. Popular culture -- United States 3. United States -- Social life and customs

ISBN 0-674-04882-2; 0-674-04883-0 pa

LC 94-2814

"A nostalgic, informative and sometimes funny view of 1950's American culture." Publ Wkly

Includes bibliographical references

Morrow, Lance

Second drafts of history; essays. Lance Morrow. Basic Books 2006 323p $26.95 **973.92**

1. United States -- Social conditions 2. United States -- Politics and government -- 1989-

ISBN 0-4650-4750-5

LC 2005-17092

"Loosely arranged by subject, these essays cover the gamut of human experience, seen through Morrow's practiced yet unjaundiced point of view. Whether offering a fact-laden piece on the AIDS epidemic or a personal meditation on the Jonesboro, Ark., school shootings, Morrow manages—without becoming sentimental—to evoke the spirit of a collective America. . . . Since Morrow is a weekly columnist, the news of the day is often the primary subject." Publ Wkly

Patterson, James T.

Grand expectations; the United States, 1945-1974. James T. Patterson. Oxford Univ. Press 1996 xviii, 829p ill., maps (pbk.) $27.95; o.p. **973.92**

1. United States -- History -- 1945- 2. United States -- Economic conditions 3. United States -- Politics and government -- 1945-

ISBN 9780195117974; 019507680X

LC 9513878

Bancroft Prize (1996)

In this book, author "James T. Patterson['s] . . . work . . . weaves [together] the major political, cultural, and economic events of . . . America from 1945 through Watergate. . . . [The book explores events from] the bloody campaigns in Korea and . . . McCarthyism to the assassinations of the Kennedys and Martin Luther King, to the Vietnam War, Watergate, and Nixon's resignation. Patterson . . . portray[s] the . . . [economic] growth after World War II . . . as well as the resultant buoyancy of spirit reflected in everything from streamlined toasters, to big, flashy cars, to the soaring, butterfly roof of TWA's airline terminal in New York. . . . [A]n important thread running through the book is a . . . depiction of the civil rights movement--from the electrifying Brown v. Board of Education decision, to the violent confrontations in Little Rock, Birmingham, and Selma, to the landmark civil rights acts of 1964 and 1965." (Publisher's note)

Includes bibliographical references (p. 791-802)

and index.

Restless giant; the United States from Watergate to Bush v. Gore. James T. Patterson. Oxford University Press 2005 xii, 448p ill., maps $45   **973.92**
1. United States -- History -- 1945- 2. United States -- Politics and government -- 1945- 3. United States -- History -- 1969-
ISBN 019512216X; 9780195122169
LC 2005016711

This book provides an "assessment of the twenty-seven years between the resignation of Richard Nixon and the election of George W. Bush in a . . . narrative that . . . weaves together social, cultural, political, economic, and international developments. . . . [Author James T.] Patterson describes how America began facing bewildering developments in places such as Panama, Somalia, Bosnia, and Iraq, and discovered that it was far from easy to direct the outcome of global events, and at times even harder for political parties to reach a consensus over what attempts should be made. At the same time, domestic issues such as the persistence of racial tensions, high divorce rates, alarm over crime, and urban decay led many in the media to portray the era as one of decline." (Publisher's note)

Includes bibliographical references and index.

Pietrusza, David

1960: LBJ vs. JFK vs. Nixon; the epic campaign that forged three presidencies. Union Square Press 2008 xx, 523p il $24.95   **973.92**
1. Presidents 2. Vice-presidents 3. Senators 4. Nonfiction writers 5. Members of Congress 6. Presidents -- United States -- Election -- 1960
ISBN 978-1-402-76114-0
LC 2009-291219

"The 1960 presidential campaign season was dominated by the personalities of three men, each of whom became president. . . . Pietrusza chronicles their roles and character in a stirring, hard-edged political saga." Booklist

Includes bibliographical references

Postwar America; an encyclopedia of social, political, cultural, and economic history. James Ciment, editor. M.E. Sharpe 2006 4v il set $399   **973.92**
1. Reference books 2. United States -- Civilization -- Encyclopedias
ISBN 0-7656-8067-X; 978-0-7656-8067-9
LC 2004-13120

"A-Z entries address specific persons, groups, concepts, events, geographical locations, organizations, and cultural and technological phenomena. Sidebars highlight primary source materials, items of special interest, statistical data, and other information; and Cultural Landmark entries chronologically detail the music, literature, arts, and cultural history of the era. Bibliographies covering literature from the postwar era and about the era are also included, as well as illustrations and specialized indexes." Publisher's note

Includes bibliographical references

Schultz, Kevin M.

Buckley and Mailer; the difficult friendship that shaped the Sixties. Kevin M. Schultz. W. W. Norton & Company, Inc. 2015 400 p. 8 plates; illustrations (hardcover) $28.95   **973.92**
1. Nineteen sixties 2. United States -- History -- 1961-1969 3. United States -- Civilization -- 1945- 4. Journalists -- United States -- Biography 5. Authors, American -- 20th century -- Biography 6. United States -- Social conditions -- 1960-1980
ISBN 0393088715; 9780393088717
LC 2015001553

This book, by Kevin M. Schultz, offers a "chronicle of the 1960s through the surprisingly close and incredibly contentious friendship of its two most colorful characters. William F. Buckley, Jr., and Norman Mailer . . . lived remarkably parallel lives. Both became best-selling authors in their twenties . . . both started hugely influential papers . . . both ran for mayor of New York City; . . . and both became the figurehead of their respective social movements." (Publisher's note)

"By contextualizing the friendship, this volume, in addition to its considerable virtues as quasi-biography, is also a provocative and thorough, if not quite comprehensive (it's pretty much all East Coast, and there's no music), social and political history of the sixties, among the very best we have had." Booklist

Includes bibliographical references and index

Shelley, Fred M.

★ **Atlas** of American politics, 1960-2000; [by] Fred M. Shelley [et al.] CQ Press 2002 242p maps $156.25   **973.92**
1. United States -- Politics and government -- Maps
ISBN 1-56802-665-X
LC 2001-18267

This work "examines U.S. government and politics at the congressional district, state, and national levels from a combined historical, geographical, and political perspective. More than 200 maps from a variety of government and private sources show the relationship between the nation's geography and its political life. . . . This book provides a unique look at U.S. politics during the last 40 years and will be useful to students and researchers from the high-school level up." Booklist

Includes bibliographical references

Sirota, David

Back to our future; how the 1980s explains the world we live in now--our culture, our politics, our everything. Ballantine Books 2011 276p $25; ebook $12.99   **973.92**
1. Popular culture -- United States 2. United States -- Social conditions 3. United States -- Civilization -- 1970-
ISBN 978-0-345-51878-1; 0-345-51878-0; 978-0-345-51880-4 ebook
LC 2010-41627

"The scope of the author's period knowledge is indisputable, and he parlays his experience as a Democratic strategist into politically charged discussions about the anti-governmental preaching on The A-Team, Ronald Reagan's questionable approach to Vietnam veterans and the bulletproof vigor of movies like Rambo, Red Dawn and Top Gun. . . . A sharp, dizzying history lesson that packs a punch." Kirkus

Includes bibliographical references.

Thomas, Evan

★ **Ike's** bluff; president Eisenhower's secret battle to save the world. Evan Thomas. Little, Brown and Co. 2012 496 p. $29.99 **973.92**

1. Generals 2. Presidents -- United States 3. Cold war -- Diplomatic history 4. United States -- Foreign relations -- 1953-1961 5. National security -- United States -- History -- 20th century 6. Nuclear warfare -- Government policy -- United States -- History -- 20th century 7. Nuclear weapons -- Government policy -- United States -- History -- 20th century

ISBN 0316091049; 9780316091046; 9780316224161

LC 2012019640

In this book about U.S. President Dwight Eisenhower, Evan Thomas makes a "case for the way that Eisenhower, the World War II Allied forces' supreme commander and one of the greatest shoo-ins in American electoral history, brought his military instincts form the battlefield to the White House . . . Eisenhower's combination of courage, petulance and cunning are hard qualities to reconcile." (New York Times)

Includes bibliographical references and index.

Von Tunzelmann, Alex

Blood and Sand; Suez, Hungary, and Eisenhower's Campaign for Peace. by Alex von Tunzelmann. HarperCollins 2016 560 p. illustrations, maps $32.50 **973.92**

1. Cold war 2. World politics 3. Hungary -- History -- 1956, Revolution

ISBN 006224924X; 9780062249241

This book by Alex von Tunzelmann "tells the story of both the Suez Crisis and the Hungarian Revolution of 1956—a tale of conspiracy and revolutions, spies and terrorists, kidnappings and assassination plots, the fall of the British Empire and the rise of American hegemony under the heroic leadership of President Dwight D. Eisenhower—which shaped the Middle East and Europe we know today." (Publisher's note)

"This is an outstanding reexamination of these sad, history-altering events." Booklist

Includes bibliographical references (pages 503-509) and index.

Wheen, Francis

Strange days indeed; the golden age of paranoia. Public Affairs 2010 344p $26.95 **973.92**

1. Paranoia 2. Presidents 3. Prime ministers 4. Vice-presidents 5. Senators 6. Nonfiction writers 7. Members of Congress 8. Members of Parliament 9. World politics -- 1945-1991

ISBN 978-1-58648-845-1; 1-58648-845-7

LC 2009-941854

First published 2009 in the United Kingdom

"A hugely entertaining book that makes you laugh, think, and look over your shoulder—sometimes all at the same time." Booklist

Includes bibliographical references

Woodward, Bob

Shadow; five presidents and the legacy of Watergate. Simon & Schuster 1999 592p il hardcover o.p. pa $16 **973.92**

1. Actors 2. Diplomats 3. Governors 4. Presidents 5. Vice-presidents 6. Watergate Affair, 1972-1974 7. Senators 8. Nonfiction writers 9. Members of Congress 10. Parents of presidents 11. United Nations officials 12. Nobel laureates for peace 13. Presidents -- United States 14. United States -- Politics and government -- 1989- 15. United States -- Politics and government -- 1974-1989

ISBN 0-684-85263-2 pa

LC 99-37045

Woodward examines the long-term effect of the Watergate Affair on the presidencies of Gerald Ford, Jimmy Carter, Ronald Reagan, George Bush, and Bill Clinton

The author is an "effective investigative journalist. These skills are on full display in Shadow. . . . {The book} is most interesting as a reconstruction of the many scandals that have troubled the Clinton Administration." Nation

Includes bibliographical references

973.921 Administration of Dwight David Eisenhower, 1953-1961

Branch, Taylor

★ **Parting** the waters: America in the King years, 1954-63. Simon & Schuster 1988 1064p il hardcover o.p. pa $22 **973.921**

1. Clergy 2. Nonfiction writers 3. Civil rights activists 4. Nobel laureates for peace 5. African Americans -- Civil rights 6. United States -- History -- 1953-1961

ISBN 0-671-46097-8; 0-671-68742-5 pa

LC 88-24033

This history of the American civil rights movement from 1954 to 1963 focuses on the life of Dr. Martin Luther King.

The author "has searched out the hidden reality and often tragic human drama of the King years. On his best pages, the past, miraculously, seems to spring back to life. King himself appears human, all too human. Yet when the reader is done, his remarkable virtues and ordinary vices seem of a piece, the component parts of a coherent, towering personality." Newsweek

Includes bibliographical references

Frank, Jeffrey

Ike and dick; portrait of a strange political marriage. Jeffrey Frank. Simon & Schuster 2013 448 p. (hardcover) $30 **973.921**

1. Presidents -- United States -- Biography 2. Nixon, Richard M. (Richard Milhous), 1913-1994 3. United States -- Politics and government -- 1945-1989

ISBN 1416587012; 9781416587019; 9781416588207

LC 2012015138

Author Jeffrey Frank's book on the "1952 presidential election focuses on Republican vice presidential candidate" Richard Nixon. "Easily winning the Republican presidential nomination, Eisenhower left the choice of a running mate to advisers, who picked Nixon: a first-term senator, he was much younger, politically astute, and possessing suitably fierce anticommunist credentials." (Publishers Weekly)

Includes bibliographical references and index

Gellman, Irwin F.

The **President** and the Apprentice; Eisenhower and Nixon, 1952-1961. Yale University Press 2015 816 p. 16 plates; illustrations $40   **973.921**
1. Nixon, Richard M. (Richard Milhous), 1913-1994
ISBN 0300181051; 9780300181050
LC 2015935011

This book by Irwin F. Gellman "reveals a different [Dwight] Eisenhower, and a different [Richard] Nixon. Ike trusted and relied on Nixon, sending him on many sensitive overseas missions. Based on twenty years of research in numerous archives, many previously untouched, this book offers a fresh and surprising account of the Eisenhower presidency." (Publisher's note)

"Although he doesn't discount Nixon's character flaws, Gellman asserts that Eisenhower respected Nixon and valued his views on a variety of issues. This is hardly the final word on their relationship, but Gellman has certainly made a worthy effort at reappraisal." Booklist

Johnson, Haynes Bonner

The **age** of anxiety; McCarthyism to terrorism. [by] Haynes Johnson. Harcourt 2005 609p il $26   **973.921**
1. Anticommunist movements 2. Senators 3. War on terrorism
ISBN 0-15-101062-5; 978-0-15-101062-2
LC 2005-13117

The author "offers an engrossing account of the career of red-baiting demagogue Joseph McCarthy and a chilling description of his legacy for today." Publ Wkly

Includes bibliographical references

Smith, Jean Edward

Eisenhower; in war and peace. by Jean Edward Smith. Random House 2012 950 p. (hbk : alk. paper) $40.00   **973.921**
1. Biography 2. Presidents -- United States -- Biography 3. Generals 4. Presidents 5. College presidents 6. Presidents -- United States 7. United States. Army -- Biography 8. United States -- Politics and government -- 1953-1961
ISBN 9781400066933; 140006693X; 9780679644293
LC 2011008605

This book presents a biography of former U.S. President Dwight D. Eisenhower. Jean Edward Smith "provides . . . insight into Ike's . . . apprenticeship under Douglas MacArthur in Washington and the Philippines. Then the whole panorama of World War II unfolds, with Eisenhower's . . . generalship forging the Allied path to victory. . . . Domestically, Eisenhower reduced defense spending, balanced the budget, constructed the interstate highway system, and pro-

vided social security coverage for millions who were self-employed." (Publisher's note)

Includes bibliographical references

Wicker, Tom

Dwight D. Eisenhower. Times Bks. 2002 158p (American presidents series) $20   **973.921**
1. Generals 2. Presidents 3. College presidents 4. Presidents -- United States 5. United States -- Politics and government -- 1953-1961
ISBN 0-8050-6907-0
LC 2002-20397

This work "captures the key events of the Eisenhower presidency in a way that is highly accessible and intellectually compelling." Libr J

Includes bibliographical references

973.922   Administration of John Fitzgerald Kennedy, 1961-1963

Branch, Taylor, 1947-

★ **Pillar** of fire; America in the King years, 1963-65. Simon & Schuster 1998 746p il hardcover o.p.   **973.922**
1. Clergy 2. Nonfiction writers 3. Civil rights activists 4. Nobel laureates for peace 5. African Americans -- Civil rights 6. United States -- History -- 1961-1969 7. United States -- History -- 1961-1974 8. Afro-Americans -- Civil rights -- History -- 20th century
ISBN 0-684-84809-0 pa
LC 97-46076

"Branch began telling the story of the civil rights movement in his . . . Parting the Waters: America in the King Years, 1954-63. Here he picks up where he left off, narrating the history of the years 1963-65, when the movement won . . . the Civil Rights Act of 1964 and the Voting Rights Act of 1965." (Commonweal) Bibliography. Index.

"Branch's research is impeccable and his knowledge of his material solid. . . . The book is significant for marshaling so much information, particularly the profiles of all the many individuals involved in the race issues of that time." Booklist

Includes bibliographical references

Bugliosi, Vincent

Reclaiming history; the assassination of President John F. Kennedy. W.W. Norton & Co. 2007 xlv, 1612p il $49.95   **973.922**
1. Presidents 2. Conspiracies 3. Senators 4. Murderers 5. Members of Congress
ISBN 978-0-393-04525-3; 0-393-04525-0
LC 2007-01545

The author argues that Lee Harvey Oswald was the lone assassin of John F. Kennedy.

"Destined to be the most significant challenge (save the Warren Report) to conspiracy theories, Bugliosi's study will provoke controversy and debate." Booklist

Includes bibliographical references

Cohen, Andrew

Two days in June; John F. Kennedy and the 48 hours that changed history. Andrew Cohen. McClelland & Stewart 2014 416 p. (hardcover : alk. paper) $29.95 **973.922**

ISBN 0771023871; 9780771023873; 9780771023880

LC 2014944155

This book, by Andrew Cohen, focuses on how "on two consecutive days in June 1963, in two lyrical speeches, John F. Kennedy . . . [addressed] the two greatest issues of his time: nuclear arms and civil rights. . . . His speech on June 10 leads to the Limited Nuclear Test Ban Treaty of 1963; his speech on June 11 to the Civil Rights Act of 1964." (Publisher's note)

"This book is a page-turner. Undoubtedly, Kennedy supporters will love it. More important, it serves as a first-rate introduction to why the president made such a significant impression on the nation and the world despite his brief tenure." LJ

Coleman, David G.

The **fourteenth** day; JFK and the aftermath of the Cuban Missile Crisis. David G. Coleman. 1st ed. W.W. Norton & Co. 2012 192 p. (hardcover) $25.95 **973.922**

1. Cuban Missile Crisis, 1962 2. United States -- History -- 1961-1974 3. United States -- Foreign relations -- Soviet Union 4. Cuban Missile Crisis, 1962 -- Influence 5. United States -- Foreign relations -- 1961-1963 6. Soviet Union -- Foreign relations -- United States 7. United States -- Politics and government -- 1961-1963

ISBN 0393084418; 9780393084412

LC 2012025397

In this book on the aftermath of the 1962 Cuban Missile Crisis, "[David G.] Coleman . . . reveals that the possibility of a U.S.-USSR war did not end . . . when . . . [John F.] Kennedy lifted the naval blockade. The author draws on Kennedy's 260 hours of secret White House tapes and presidential and foreign relations records to offer a narrative covering from October 29, 1962, through February 1963, when tensions subsided and relations between the two superpowers began to improve." (Library Journal)

Includes bibliographical references and index.

Dobbs, Michael

★ **One** minute to midnight; Kennedy, Khrushchev, and Castro on the brink of nuclear war. Alfred A. Knopf 2008 426p $28.95 **973.922**

1. Cuban Missile Crisis, 1962

ISBN 978-1-4000-4358-3; 1-4000-4358-1

LC 2007-52250

The author discusses the Cuban Missile Crisis of 1962.

This book "is filled with . . . insights that will change the views of experts and help inform a new generation of readers." N Y Times Book Rev

Includes bibliographical references

Freedman, Lawrence

Kennedy's wars; Berlin, Cuba, Laos, and Vietnam. Oxford Univ. Press 2000 xx, 528p il hardcover o.p. pa $18.95 **973.922**

1. Presidents 2. Vietnam War, 1961-1975 3. Cuban Missile Crisis, 1962 4. Senators 5. Members of Congress 6. Berlin Wall (1961-1989) 7. Military policy

-- United States 8. United States -- Foreign relations

ISBN 0-19-513453-2; 0-19-515243-3 pa

LC 99-87898

"Lawrence's book is an excellent treatment of U.S. foreign policy during this dynamic era and an insightful portrait of John F. Kennedy as a leader." Libr J

Includes bibliographical references

Fursenko, A. V.

One hell of a gamble; Khrushchev, Castro, and Kennedy, 1958-1964. {by} Aleksandr Fursenko and Timothy Naftali. Norton 1997 420p il hardcover o.p. pa $15.95 **973.922**

1. Cuban Missile Crisis, 1962 2. Soviet Union -- Foreign relations -- United States 3. United States -- Foreign relations -- Soviet Union

ISBN 0-393-31790-0 pa

LC 97-1022

For this diplomatic history of the Cuban Missile Crisis, the authors were granted "permission to review Krushchev's papers; they were also able to draw on archival material from other official Soviet sources." N Y Times Book Rev

Includes bibliographical references

Gitlin, Todd

The **sixties**; years of hope, days of rage. Bantam Bks. 1987 513p hardcover o.p. pa $19.95 **973.922**

1. Students -- Political activity 2. United States -- Social conditions 3. United States -- History -- 1961-1974

ISBN 0-553-37212-2 pa

LC 87-47575

"Though ex-SDS leader Gitlin occasionally falls prey to the self-indulgence that snares most sixties' commentators, his analysis of the decade's politics is thought-provoking and clearheaded. Rather than singing the familiar hymn of praise to youthful idealism, Gitlin carefully dissects why the activist spirit developed when it did and what its legacy has been." Am Libr

Includes bibliographical references

Halberstam, David

The **best** and the brightest; foreword by John McCain. Modern Library ed; Modern Lib. 2001 xxviii, 780p $24.95; pa $16.95 **973.922**

1. Authors 2. Generals 3. Diplomats 4. Educators 5. Statesmen 6. Presidents 7. Vice-presidents 8. Bankers 9. Senators 10. Army officers 11. College teachers 12. Nonfiction writers 13. Members of Congress 14. Foundation officials 15. Government officials 16. Political scientists 17. Secretaries of state 18. Presidential advisers 19. Secretaries of defense 20. Nobel laureates for peace 21. International organization officials 22. United States -- Foreign relations -- Vietnam 23. Vietnam -- Foreign relations -- United States 24. United States -- Politics and government -- 1961-1974

ISBN 0-679-64099-1; 0-449-90870-4 pa

LC 2001-31261

A reissue of the title first published 1972

"The author describes analytically rather than narratively, how the Kennedy-Johnson intellectual (McNamara, Bundy, Rusk, Ball, Taylor, et al.) men praised as 'the best and the brightest' men of this century, became the architects of the disastrous American policy of Indochina." Libr J

Includes bibliographical references

Hill, Clint

Five days in November; Clint Hill and Lisa Mc-Cubbin. Gallery Books 2013 256 p. (hardback) $30   **973.922**
1. Kennedy, John F. (John Fitzgerald), 1917-1963 -- Assassination 2. United States. Secret Service -- Officials and employees -- Biography

ISBN 1476731497; 9781476731490; 9781476731506

LC 2013019272

Author Clint Hill presents a book of photographs pertaining to the day that President John F. Kennedy was assassinated. Through the pictures, "we witness three-year-old John Kennedy Jr.'s pleas to come to Texas with his parents and the rapturous crowds of mixed ages and races that greeted the Kennedys at every stop in Texas. We stand beside a shaken Lyndon Johnson as he is hurriedly sworn in as the new president. We experience the first lady's steely courage when she insists on walking through the streets of Washington, D.C., in her husband's funeral procession." (Publisher's note)

Mrs. Kennedy and me; Clint Hill; with Lisa Mc-Cubbin. Gallery Books 2012 viii, 343 p.p **973.922**
1. Bodyguards -- Biography 2. Secret service -- United States 3. Presidents' spouses -- United States 4. Presidents -- United States -- Assassination 5. Presidents' spouses -- Protection -- United States 6. United States. Secret Service -- Officials and employees -- Biography

ISBN 1451648448; 9781451648447; 9781451648461

LC 2011051017

This book is a "memoir of guarding First Lady Jacqueline Kennedy through the young and sparkling years of the Kennedy presidency and the dark days following the assassination. Secret Service Special Agent [Clint] Hill . . . first met a young and pregnant soon-to-be First Lady in November 1960. For the next four years Hill would seldom leave her side. Theirs would be an odd relationship of always-proper formality combined with deep intimacy crafted through close proximity and mutual trust and respect. . . .When the bullet ripped into the president's brain with Hill not five feet away, he remained with her, through the public and private mourning. . . . Soon after, both would go on with their lives, but Hill would . . . never stop feeling he could have done more to save the president." (Kirkus)

Kaiser, David E.

The road to Dallas; the assassination of John F. Kennedy. [by] David Kaiser. Belknap Press of Harvard University Press 2008 509p il map $35 **973.922**
1. Presidents 2. Senators 3. Members of Congress

ISBN 978-0-674-02766-4; 0-674-02766-3

LC 2007-27305

"This is a deeply disturbing look at a national tragedy, and Kaiser's sober tone and reasoned analysis may well convince some in the Oswald-was-alone-nut camp." Publ Wkly

Includes bibliographical references

Kennedy, Caroline, 1957-

Jacqueline Kennedy; foreword by Caroline Kennedy; introduction and annotations by Michael Beschloss. Hyperion 2011 xxxii, 368 p.p 8 sound discs   **973.922**
1. Interviews 2. Presidents' spouses -- United States 3. United States -- History -- 1953-1961 4. Presidents -- United States -- Biography 5. Presidents' spouses -- United States -- Interviews 6. United States -- Politics and government -- 1961-1963

ISBN 9781401324254; 1401324258

LC 2012372265

This book, accompanied by a set of 8 compact discs (CDs), presents "seven historic interviews" by U.S. First Lady Jacqueline Kennedy "about her life with John F. Kennedy" (JFK). Recorded in 1964, "shortly after President . . . Kennedy's assassination," the interviews discuss JFK's political career and his views on various subjects, "including his thoughts and feelings about his brothers Robert and Ted, and his take on world leaders past and present." (Publisher's note) Other topics include JFK's reading habits, U.S. relations with Cuba, and Kennedy's relationship with her husband.

Includes bibliographical references and index.

Kennedy, Robert F., 1925-1968

Make gentle the life of this world; the vision of Robert F. Kennedy. edited and with an introduction by Maxwell Taylor Kennedy. Broadway Books 1999 188p il pa $15   **973.922**
1. Quotations

ISBN 0-7679-0371-4

LC 98-55988

First published 1998 by Harcourt Brace & Co.

This is a collection of quotations by Robert F. Kennedy and the authors who inspired him

"Chapters are arranged by issues that were most important to Kennedy and remain timely today—the responsibilities of citizens to their government, the tragedy of poverty in the midst of plenty, the importance of dissent in a democratic society, and work as the solution for the welfare crises. The book's haunting photos convey Kennedy's spirit as successfully as the words." Libr J

Includes bibliographical references

Thirteen days; a memoir of the Cuban missile crisis. with introductions by Robert S. McNamara and Harold Macmillan. Norton 1969 224p il hardcover o.p. pa $12.95   **973.922**
1. Cuban Missile Crisis, 1962 2. Soviet Union -- Foreign relations -- United States 3. United States -- Foreign relations -- Soviet Union 4. United States -- Politics and government -- 1961-1974

ISBN 0-393-31834-6 pa

A behind-the-scenes account of the Cuban Missile Crisis of 1962. Includes reproductions of pertinent documents and speeches by both President Kennedy and Nikita Khrushchev.

Leaming, Barbara

Mrs. Kennedy; the missing history of the Kennedy years. Free Press 2001 406p il $25; pa $14 **973.922**

1. Editors 2. Socialites 3. Spouses of presidents

ISBN 0-684-86209-3; 0-7432-2749-2 pa

LC 2001-40442

"Asserting that Jacqueline Kennedy's role in shaping her husband's presidency has been under-examined, Leaming . . . offers a corrective in this intimate look at a very private woman. Initially inclined to keep herself as much in the background as possible, says Leaming, Jacqueline Kennedy became an increasingly visible and vocal first lady as she realized how effective she could be as an image maker. It's in this capacity that Leaming convincingly depicts her as being instrumental in shaping the course of her husband's administration." Publ Wkly

Includes bibliographical references

Matthews, Chris

Kennedy & Nixon; the rivalry that shaped postwar America. {by} Christopher Matthews. Simon & Schuster 1996 377p il hardcover o.p. pa $14 **973.922**

1. Presidents 2. Vice-presidents 3. Senators 4. Nonfiction writers 5. Members of Congress 6. United States -- Politics and government -- 20th century

ISBN 0-684-83246-1 pa

LC 96-15677

This exploration of the rift between Kennedy and Nixon "shows how these two anti-New Dealers, anti-Communists, and freshmen members of Congress in 1946 became enemies as their political careers advanced." Libr J

Includes bibliographical references

Minutaglio, Bill

Dallas 1963; Bill Minutaglio, Steven L. Davis. Twelve 2013 336 p. (hardcover) $28 **973.922**

1. Conspiracies 2. Kennedy, John F. (John Fitzgerald), 1917-1963 -- Assassination

ISBN 9781455522095; 9781455522118; 9781619692794

LC 2013939303

Author Bill Minutaglio's book focuses on the assassination of President John F. Kennedy. "Beginning with the campaign for Kennedy's election and set against a nation in transition, Bill Minutaglio and Steven L. Davis ingeniously explore the swirling forces that led numerous friends and aides to warn the president against stopping in Dallas on his fateful trip to Texas." (Publisher's note)

Includes bibliographical references (pages 341-362) and index

Neff, James

Vendetta; Bobby Kennedy Versus Jimmy Hoffa. by James Neff. Little, Brown & Co. 2015 384 p. illustrations $28 **973.922**

1. United States -- Politics and government -- 20th century

ISBN 0316738344; 9780316738347

LC 2015939408

In this book, author James Neff "brings to life the . . . clash of two American titans: Robert Kennedy and his nemesis Jimmy Hoffa. . . . Kennedy's battle with Hoffa burst into the public consciousness with the 1957 Senate Rackets Committee hearings and intensified when his brother named him attorney general in 1961. RFK put together a . . . squad within the Justice Department, devoted to destroying [him]. But Hoffa, with nearly unlimited Teamster funds, was not about to roll over." (Publisher's note)

"This enthralling account, based mostly on archival research, will appeal to Kennedy followers, true crime fans, and students and scholars of modern American history." LJ

Posner, Gerald L.

Case closed; Lee Harvey Oswald and the assassination of JFK. [by] Gerald Posner. Anchor Books 2003 608p il pa $17.95 **973.922**

1. Presidents 2. Senators 3. Murderers 4. Members of Congress

ISBN 1-400-03462-0; 978-1-400-03462-8

LC 2003-283539

First published 1993

In this book Posner argues that Lee Harvey Oswald was solely responsible for the assassination of President Kennedy and that none of the theories alleging conspiracy is valid.

"One of the strongest and most important features of the book, indeed, is Posner's painstaking dissection of each and every one of the competing conspiracy theories. None of them stands up under scrutiny." Natl Rev

Includes bibliographical references

Reeves, Richard

President Kennedy; profile of power. Simon & Schuster 1993 798p il hardcover o.p. pa $22 **973.922**

1. Presidents 2. Senators 3. Members of Congress 4. Biography, Individual 5. Presidents -- United States 6. United States -- Politics and government -- 1961-1974

ISBN 0-671-89289-4 pa

LC 93-24805

This is an account "of John F. Kennedy's three years as president, with an emphasis on leadership techniques." (Choice)

"Reeves doesn't try to soft-pedal the distasteful, but his account of the Kennedy presidency is resolutely matter of fact and not an indictment." Time

Includes bibliographical references

Shenon, Philip

A cruel and shocking act; The secret history of the Kennedy assassination. Philip Shenon. Henry Holt & Co. 2013 625 p. 32 plates; illustrations; maps (hardback) $32 **973.922**

1. United States -- History -- 20th century 2. Kennedy, John F. (John Fitzgerald), 1917-1963 -- Assassination 3. United States. Warren Commission

ISBN 0805094202; 9780805094206

LC 2013031968

This book, by Philip Shenon, is an "account of the Kennedy assassination. . . . Shenon shows how the commission's ten-month investigation was doomed to fail because the man leading it-- Chief Justice Earl Warren-- was more committed to protecting the Kennedy family than getting to the full truth about what happened on that tragic day." (Publisher's note)

"But the combination of destroyed records, unpursued investigative leads, and lies by senior government officials--"most especially at the CIA"--will leave most reasonable readers unsettled as to whether the truth has yet been discovered. Maps and photos." Pub Wkly.

Includes bibliographical references (pages 593-598) and index

Stoll, Ira

JFK, conservative; Ira Stoll. Houghton Mifflin Harcourt 2013 288 p. $27   **973.922**
1. Conservatism -- United States -- History 2. United States -- Politics and government -- 1961-1974 3. United States -- Politics and government -- 1961-1963 4. Conservatism -- United States -- History -- 20th century
ISBN 0547585985; 9780547585987

LC 2013001595

It was the author's intent to demonstrate that "John F. Kennedy's priorities as president . . . were not to promote large government and federally funded social programs but to seek tax reductions, maintain a strong department of defense, fight communism, and reduce federal spending. . . . [Ira] Stoll posits that Ronald Reagan is the true inheritor of the Kennedy legacy because . . . he advocated the same priorities as JFK and made similar fiery, anticommunist speeches." (Library Journal).

Includes bibliographical references and index

Swanson, James L.

End of Days; The Assassination of John F. Kennedy. James L. Swanson. HarperCollins 2013 416 p. illustrations, map $29.99   **973.922**
1. Kennedy, John F. (John Fitzgerald), 1917-1963 -- Assassination
ISBN 0062083481; 9780062083487

LC 2013498445

This book, by James L. Swanson, on the assassination of U.S. President John F. Kennedy "follows the event hour-by-hour, from the moment Lee Harvey Oswald conceived of the crime three days before its execution, to his own murder two days later at a Dallas Police precinct at the hands of Jack Ruby, a two-bit nightclub owner." (Publisher's note)

"Drawing on the decades of technological advances that have deepened the knowledge of the assassination, the author presents the stunning unfolding of the event in punchy, poignant vignettes, following one character after another to the inexorable conclusion." Kirkus

Includes bibliography and index

973.923   Administration of Lyndon Baines Johnson, 1963-1969

Branch, Taylor, 1947-

★ At Canaan's edge; America in the King years, 1965-68. Simon & Schuster 2006 1039p il hardcover o.p.   **973.923**
1. Clergy 2. Nonfiction writers 3. Civil rights activists

4. Civil rights movements 5. Nobel laureates for peace 6. African Americans -- Civil rights 7. United States -- History -- 1961-1969 8. United States -- History -- 1961-1974 9. African Americans -- Civil rights -- History -- 20th century 10. Civil rights movements -- United States -- History -- 20th century
ISBN 0-684-85712-X; 0-684-85713-8 pa

LC 2005-40177

This is "the third and final volume of Taylor Branch's . . . history of the life and times of King." (N Y Times (Late N Y Ed)) Index.

In this history that follows the life of Martin Luther King "from the protest at Selma and the 1966 Meredith March through King's expanding political concern for the poor to his 1968 assassination in Memphis, Tenn., Branch gives us not only the civil rights leader's life but also the rapidly changing pulse of American culture and politics. . . . This magisterial book is a fitting tribute to a magisterial man." Publ Wkly

Includes bibliographical references

Busby, Horace W.

The **thirty-**first of March; an intimate portrait of Lyndon Johnson's final days in office. [by] Horace Busby; with a preface by Scott Busby and an introduction by Hugh Sidey. Farrar, Straus and Giroux 2005 250p il $24; pa $14   **973.923**
1. Presidents 2. Vice-presidents 3. Senators 4. Members of Congress 5. United States -- Politics and government -- 1961-1974
ISBN 0-374-27574-2; 0-374-53021-1 pa

This book "covers the 20 years during which Busby served as a trusted advisor and speechwriter for Johnson. This previously unpublished manuscript was discovered by Busby's son after his father's death in 2000. . . . This is an engrossing and important contribution to our understanding of a compelling political personality." Booklist

The **Columbia** guide to America in the 1960s; David Farber and Beth Bailey, editors. Columbia Univ. Press 2001 508p il map (Columbia guides to American history and cultures) $60; pa $25   **973.923**
1. United States -- Social conditions 2. United States -- History -- 1961-1974
ISBN 0-231-11372-2; 0-231-11373-0 pa

LC 00-65577

This reference work includes "a dictionary, an extensive annotated bibliography, a chronology of the era, and statistical information [and] two extraordinary bonuses: a section 'Debating the Sixties,' which includes ten essays by prominent historians . . . and an excellent 77-page history of the 1960s. This book is a fine addition to any library's collection." Choice

Includes bibliographical references

Patterson, James T.

The **eve** of destruction; how 1965 transformed America. James T. Patterson. Basic Books 2012 344 p. (hardcover : alk. paper) $28.99   **973.923**
1. Vietnam War, 1961-1975 2. United States -- History -- 1961-1974 3. Civil rights -- United States -- History

4. United States -- Politics and government -- 1961-1974
5. United States -- History -- 1961-1969 6. Vietnam War, 1961-1975 -- United States 7. United States -- Social conditions -- 1960-1980 8. United States -- Politics and government -- 1963-1969
ISBN 0465013589; 9780465013586; 9780465033485
LC 2012033786

In this book, James T. Patterson "asserts that 1965 was 'a pivotal year in American life.' He sets the stage with a picture of 'buoyant and confident' white America in late 1964, before addressing the 'shifts of mood . . . politics, culture, and foreign policies' that many found unsettling and divisive. . . . The bulk of his attention is turned toward the civil rights movement . . . the Great Society programs of President Johnson and the escalation of the Vietnam War." (Publishers Weekly)

Risen, Clay
A **nation** on fire; America in the wake of the King assassination. John Wiley & Sons 2009 292p il $25.95   **973.923**
1. Riots 2. Clergy 3. Nonfiction writers 4. Civil rights activists 5. Nobel laureates for peace 6. United States -- Race relations 7. African Americans -- Social conditions
ISBN 978-0-470-17710-5
LC 2008-26789

The author "has crafted a crucial addition to civil rights history, sure to absorb anyone interested in the times, the movement or MLK Jr." Publ Wkly
Includes bibliographical references

Taking charge; the Johnson White House tapes, 1963-1964. edited and with commentary by Michael R. Beschloss. Simon & Schuster 1997 591p il hardcover o.p. pa $16   **973.923**
1. Presidents 2. Vice-presidents 3. Senators 4. Members of Congress 5. United States -- Politics and government -- 1961-1974
ISBN 0-684-84792-2 pa
LC 97-26749

This book is a "selection of conversations taped by Lyndon B. Johnson during the first nine months of his Presidency—beginning on the day of the Kennedy assassination and continuing through the close of the Democratic National Convention in 1964. . . . There are no stunning revelations and no recorded moments of epochal importance. But 'Taking Charge' is a riveting book nevertheless. This is partly because it has been superbly edited and annotated by the historian Michael R. Beschloss, who has made everything—even the most arcane references—accessible to ordinary readers." N Y Times Book Rev

The **Times** were a changin' the sixties reader. edited by Irwin Unger and Debi Unger. Three Rivers Press (NY) 1998 355p hardcover o.p. pa $16   **973.923**
1. United States -- History -- 1961-1974
ISBN 0-609-80337-9 pa
LC 97-39844

"The broad range of viewpoints and the easy access to such an array of primary sources make the book a powerful adjunct for study of the sixties, as well as an interesting book for browsing." Book Rep

Witcover, Jules
The **year** the dream died; revisiting 1968 in America. Warner Bks. 1997 544p $25; pa $16   **973.923**
1. United States -- History -- 1961-1974
ISBN 0-446-51849-2; 0-446-67471-0 pa
LC 96-42017

Political columnist Witcover reviews "the tumultuous year in which the nation came 'unglued.' Nixon and Agnew vie for the villain's role, although neither would have been significant, contends the author, had LBJ not eroded his Kennedy legacy by escalating American involvement in Vietnam. . . . This backward look is enriched by the 20/20 hindsight of surviving participants, some still prominent in public life." Publ Wkly

Woods, Randall B.
Prisoners of hope; Lyndon B. Johnson, the Great Society, and the limits of liberalism. Randall B. Woods. Basic Books 2016 480 p. illustrations (hardback) $32   **973.923**
1. Social policy -- United States 2. United States -- Economic policy -- 1961-1971 3. United States -- Social policy -- 20th century 4. United States -- Politics and government -- 1963-1969 5. Liberalism -- United States -- History -- 20th century 6. Social legislation -- United States -- History -- 20th century 7. Economic assistance, Domestic -- United States -- History -- 20th century
ISBN 9780465050963
LC 2015040042

This book, by Randall B. Woods, "presents the first comprehensive history of the Great Society [policies of U.S. President Lyndon B. Johnson], exploring both the breathtaking possibilities of visionary politics, as well as its limits. . . . A cautionary tale about the unintended consequences of even well-intentioned policy, . . . [the book] offers a nuanced portrait of America's most ambitious--and controversial--domestic policy agenda since the New Deal." (Publisher's note)

"A sympathetic but also gimlet-eyed scholar's look at a towering physical and political presence who learned, to his sorrow, that good intentions were insufficient." Kirkus
Includes bibliographical references and index

973.924 Administration of Richard Milhous Nixon, 1969-1974

Abuse of power; the new Nixon tapes. edited with an introduction and commentary by Stanley I. Kutler. Free Press 1997 xxiii, 675p hardcover o.p. pa $30.95   **973.924**
1. Presidents 2. Vice-presidents 3. Watergate Affair, 1972-1974 4. Senators 5. Nonfiction writers 6. Members of Congress 7. United States -- Politics and government -- 1961-1974
ISBN 0-684-85187-3 pa
LC 97-32096

"This is an edited collection of transcripts of President Nixon's Watergate-related conversations made available under a 1974 Congressional directive covering tapes related to 'abuse of governmental power.' More than 90 percent of the volume covers the year after the June 1972 break-in and focuses on Watergate." Choice

Bernstein, Carl

All the president's men; {by} Carl Bernstein, Bob Woodward. Simon & Schuster 1999 349p il hardcover o.p. pa $14   **973.924**
1. Watergate Affair, 1972-1974 2. Washington post
ISBN 0-684-86355-3; 0-671-89441-2 pa
LC 98-54773
A reissue of the title first published 1974
The two Washington Post reporters whose investigative journalism first revealed the Watergate scandal tell the way it happened from the first suspicions, through the trail of false leads, lies, secrecy, and high-level pressure, to the final moments when they were able to put the pieces of the puzzle together and write the series that won the Post a Pulitzer Prize

Dean, John W. (John Wesley), 1938-

The **Nixon** Defense; What He Knew and When He Knew It. John W. Dean. Viking 2014 416 p. $35   **973.924**
1. Watergate Affair, 1972-1974 2. Nixon, Richard M. (Richard Milhous), 1913-1994
ISBN 0670025364; 9780670025367
LC 2014020821
In this book, author and former White House Counsel John W. Dean "connects the dots between what we've come to believe about Watergate and what actually happened. . . . [He] draws on his own transcripts of almost a thousand conversations, a wealth of Nixon's secretly recorded information, and more than 150,000 pages of documents in the National Archives and the Nixon Library to provide the definitive answer to the question: What did President Nixon know and when did he know it?" (Publisher's note)
"[O]ne of the best and fullest accounts of the Watergate cover-up, one that conveys in Nixon's own voice the casual criminality of his troubled presidency." Pub Wkly
Includes bibliographical references (pages 661-719) and index

Emery, Fred

Watergate; the corruption of American politics and the fall of Richard Nixon. Touchstone 1994 xvi, 559p il pa $25.95   **973.924**
1. Presidents 2. Vice-presidents 3. Watergate Affair, 1972-1974 4. Senators 5. Nonfiction writers 6. Members of Congress
ISBN 0-684-81323-8
LC 95-12511
First published 1994 by Times Bks.
"In addition to an introductory section on the cast of characters involved, Emery provides a detailed examination of the Committee To Reelect the President (CRP) and its dirty tricks: wiretapping, money laundering campaigns, and the infamous burglary of Democratic National Committee headquarters. Unlike much of the psychopersonal material that has come out on Nixon, Emery's book focuses

on the tough political problems, documenting the need for impeachment and ultimately endorsing it. Riveting reading that is based on an unprecedented combing of the primary sources." Libr J
Includes bibliographical references

Feldstein, Mark

Poisoning the press; Richard Nixon, Jack Anderson, and the rise of Washington's scandal culture. [by] Mark Feldstein. Farrar, Straus and Giroux 2010 461p il $30; ebook $14.99   **973.924**
1. Press -- Government policy 2. Political culture -- Washington (D.C.) 3. Presidents -- United States -- Press relations 4. United States -- Politics and government -- 1961-1974 5. United States -- Politics and government -- 1969-1974 6. Political culture -- United States -- History -- 20th century 7. Press and politics -- United States -- History -- 20th century
ISBN 978-0-374-23530-7; 978-1-4299-7897-2 ebook
LC 2010-10272
"This fast-moving narrative will fascinate readers of recent American political and journalism history." Libr J
Includes bibliographical references

Glasser, Joshua M.

The **eighteen**-day running mate; McGovern, Eagleton, and a campaign in crisis. Joshua M. Glasser. Yale University Press 2012 381 p. ill. (hardcover) $26   **973.924**
1. United States -- Politics and government -- 1961-1974 2. Presidents -- United States -- Election -- 1972 3. United States -- Politics and government -- 1969-1974
ISBN 0300176295; 9780300176292
LC 2012002582
This book, by Joshua M. Glasser, examines the brief 1972 U.S. vice-presidential campaign of Thomas Eagleton with Democratic nominee George McGovern. "Within days of Eagleton's nomination, a pair of anonymous phone calls brought to light his history of hospitalizations . . . and past treatment with electroshock therapy. The revelation rattled the campaign and placed McGovern's organization under intense public and media scrutiny." (Publisher's note)
Includes bibliographical references and index

Hughes, Ken

Chasing shadows; the Nixon tapes, the Chennault affair, and the origins of Watergate. Ken Hughes. University of Virginia Press 2014 x, 228 p.p (cloth ; acid-free paper) $24.95   **973.924**
1. Watergate Affair, 1972-1974 2. Nixon, Richard M. (Richard Milhous), 1913-1994 3. Audiotapes 4. United States -- Politics and government -- 1961-1963 5. United States -- Politics and government -- 1963-1969 6. United States -- Politics and government -- 1969-1974
ISBN 0813936632; 9780813936635
LC 2014013429
This book, by by Ken Hughes, explores the larger picture surrounding the Watergate Scandal of the Richard Nixon administration. The author "unearth[s] a pattern of actions by Nixon . . . that begins during the 1968 campaign, when Nixon, concerned about the impact on his presidential bid of the Paris peace talks with the Vietnamese, secretly un-

dermined the negotiations through a Republican fundraiser named Anna Chennault." (Publisher's note)

"Through its foremost practitioners in Johnson and Nixon, Hughes reveals the realities of see American politics as a blood sport." Pub Wkly

Includes bibliographical references and index

Killen, Andreas

1973 nervous breakdown; Watergate, Warhol, and the birth of post-sixties America. Bloomsbury 2006 312p $24.95 **973.924**

1. United States -- Civilization -- 1970-
ISBN 1-59691-059-3; 978-1-59691-059-1

LC 2005-23661

This "is a high-definition snapshot, both nostalgic and perceptive, of a transitional time." Libr J

Includes bibliographical references

Kissinger, Henry

Years of renewal. Simon & Schuster 1999 1151p il maps hardcover o.p. pa $24 **973.924**

1. College teachers 2. Nonfiction writers 3. Writers on politics 4. Secretaries of state 5. Presidential advisers 6. Nobel laureates for peace 7. United States -- Foreign relations 8. International relations specialists
ISBN 0-684-85572-0 pa

LC 98-41038

"Statecraft defies simple solutions, and one of the merits of Kissinger's memoir—especially this somber and reflective third volume—is that he so rarely provides them." N Y Times Book Rev

Includes bibliographical references

The **Nixon** tapes; 1973. edited and annotated by Douglas Brinkley and Luke A. Nichter. Houghton Mifflin Harcourt 2015 848 p. 8 plates; color illustrations (hardcover) $35 **973.924**

1. Sound recordings 2. Presidents -- United States -- Archives 3. Nixon, Richard M. (Richard Milhous), 1913-1994 4. Audiotapes 5. United States -- Foreign relations -- 1969-1974 -- Sources 6. United States -- Politics and government -- 1969-1974 -- Sources
ISBN 0544610539; 9780544610538

LC 2015028189

In this book, authors Douglas Brinkley and Luke A. Nichter "conclude their project of publishing highlights from Richard Nixon's infamous tapes. . . . This volume finds Nixon often exulting publicly thanks to the emerging success of his rapprochement and trip to China, the winding down of the Vietnam War, and growing détente with the Soviet Union. Some of the most affecting conversations on these tapes take place between Nixon and Soviet Premier Leonid Brezhnev." (Kirkus Reviews)

"General readers might prefer earlier transcription efforts, such as Watergate principal John Dean's 2014 The Nixon Defense, since the excerpts in that book are shorter and more context is given. Even so, these longer excerpts resemble an oddly fascinating reality show, and historians will like that Brinkley and Nichter worked with the most complete body of recordings and used audio equipment of the highest quality to ensure transcription accuracy." LJ

Olson, Keith W.

Watergate; the presidential scandal that shook America. University Press of Kansas 2003 220p il $35; pa $15.95 **973.924**

1. Watergate Affair, 1972-1974
ISBN 0-7006-1250-5; 0-7006-1251-3 pa

LC 2002-38058

The author describes "the White House-approved break-in at Democratic National Committee headquarters in Washington's Watergate complex and its aftermath—most importantly, the dramatic proceedings of the Senate Watergate Committee. . . . {This} book provides an excellent, compact narrative of a crucial moment in the history of the American presidency." Publ Wkly

Includes bibliographical references

Packer, George

★ The **unwinding**; an inner history of the new America. George Packer. Farrar Straus & Giroux 2013 448 p. (hardcover) $27 **973.924**

1. Economics -- History 2. United States -- Economic conditions 3. Crises -- United States 4. United States -- Biography 5. Social problems -- United States 6. United States -- History -- 1969- 7. Celebrities -- United States -- Biography 8. Politicians -- United States -- Biography 9. United States -- Social conditions -- 1980- 10. United States -- Politics and government -- 1989-
ISBN 0374102414; 9780374102418

LC 2013004431

In this book, George Packer "charts the erosion of the social compact that kept the country stable and middle class. Readers experience three decades of change via the personal histories of an Ohio factory worker, a Washington political operative, a North Carolinian small businessman, and an Internet billionaire. Their lives follow the ups and downs of a changing country, where manufacturing jobs vanish, businesses thrive and fail, and political fortunes crest and recede." (Publishers Weekly)

Includes bibliographical references (pages 431-434)

Perlstein, Rick

The **Invisible** Bridge; The Fall of Nixon and the Rise of Reagan. by Rick Perlstein. Simon & Schuster 2014 800 p. illustrations (some color) $37.50 **973.924**

1. Conservatism -- United States 2. United States -- History -- 20th century 3. Nixon, Richard M. (Richard Milhous), 1913-1994
ISBN 1476782415; 9781476782416

LC 2014381509

This book, by Rick Perlstein, is a "portrait of America on the verge of a nervous breakdown in the tumultuous political and economic times of the 1970s. In January of 1973 Richard Nixon announced the end of the Vietnam War and prepared for a triumphant second term--until televised Watergate hearings revealed his White House as little better than a mafia den." Ronald Reagan was "inventing the new conservative political culture we know now." (Publisher's note)

"Although the book only goes up to Reagan's loss of the 1976 Republican nomination to President Gerald Ford, the scope of the work never feels limited. . . . A compelling, astute chronicle of the politics and culture of late-20th-century America." Kirkus

★ **Nixonland**; the rise of a president and the fracturing of America. Scribner 2008 881p il **973.924**
1. Presidents 2. Vice-presidents 3. Senators 4. Nonfiction writers 5. Members of Congress 6. Presidents -- United States 7. United States -- Politics and government -- 1961-1974 8. United States -- Politics and government -- 1969-1974 9. United States -- Politics and government -- 1974-1977
ISBN 0743243021; 074324303X; 9780743243025; 9780743243032 pa
                                        LC 20080273706
This book focuses on U.S. President Richard Nixon, from the "tumultuous years of 1965, on the eve of the Watts Riot, through Nixon's landslide victory in 1972. [Rick] Perlstein has twin objectives. First, he develops a . . . narrative about how Richard Nixon . . . came to epitomize and personify the values of the 'silent majority.' Second, Nixon's ability to exploit voters' anxieties about race, poverty, law and order, and patriotism has produced bitter partisan divisions." (Choice: Current Reviews for Academic Libraries)
This "is an exceptionally broad and thorough social, cultural and political history of eight tumultuous years. . . . It sings with outstanding storytelling and insight." Washington Monthly
Includes bibliographical references

Reeves, Richard
President Nixon; alone in the White House. Simon & Schuster 2001 702p il $35; pa $16 **973.924**
1. Presidents 2. Vice-presidents 3. Senators 4. Nonfiction writers 5. Members of Congress 6. Presidents -- United States 7. United States -- Politics and government -- 1961-1974
ISBN 0-684-80231-7; 0-7432-2719-0 pa
                                        LC 2001-34417
This narrative "is chronological, from Nixon's inauguration in January 1969 to April 1973, when he realized that he had lost control over the Watergate scandals. . . . In between are Vietnam and crime in the streets, affirmative action and the end of the gold standard, Chile and the antiballistic missile treaty, the opening to China and, of course, Watergate. A fascinating study of the brilliant, profoundly flawed man elected to lead the nation through a troubled time." Booklist
Includes bibliographical references

Reston, James
The **conviction** of Richard Nixon; the untold story of the Frost/Nixon interviews. Harmony Books 2007 207p $22   **973.924**
1. Presidents 2. Vice-presidents 3. Watergate Affair, 1972-1974 4. Senators 5. Talk show hosts 6. Nonfiction writers 7. Members of Congress 8. Television producers 9. Presidents -- United States
ISBN 978-0-307-39420-0; 0-307-39420-4
                                        LC 2007-1238
"In 1977, three years after his resignation, Richard Nixon returned to the public eye in a series of interviews with British television journalist David Frost, for which Nixon received $1 million. Figuring his political and lawyerly

skills were more than a match for Frost's interrogation, Nixon instead found himself doing exactly what his successor, Gerald Ford, had tried to prevent with a presidential pardon: publicly admitting that he had broken the law. Reston Jr. was one of the aides Frost hired to help him plan his line of attack; this book, written at the time of the interviews, is being published for the first time now. . . . Reston's passion for finding the chinks in Nixon's armor makes for fascinating reading." Publ Wkly

Weiner, Tim
One man against the world; the tragedy of Richard Nixon. Tim Weiner. Henry Holt & Co. 2015 384 p. illustration (hardcover) $30   **973.924**
1. Presidents -- United States 2. Nixon, Richard M. (Richard Milhous), 1913-1994 3. Presidents -- United States -- Biography 4. United States -- Politics and government -- 1969-1974
ISBN 1627790837; 9781627790833
                                        LC 2015012381
In this book, author Tim Weiner argues that "President Richard Nixon's (1913-94) most tragic flaw was his idea that the presidency was above the law; a delusion that drove him to the "gutter politics" that led to the Watergate scandal in 1972 and his inevitable resignation in 1974." The book draws on "archival documents that were not declassified until the 21st century . . . notably about bombings in Southeast Asia and a near-nuclear confrontation with the former Soviet Union." (Library Journal)
"Those seeking to understand America in the second half of the twentieth century and, distressingly, beyond would do well to begin here. The tragedy was not Nixon's alone, but his role in it has never been portrayed more vividly." Booklist
Includes bibliographical references (pages [325]-356) and index.

Woodward, Bob
The **final** days; {by} Bob Woodward, Carl Bernstein. Simon & Schuster 1976 476p il hardcover o.p. pa $16   **973.924**
1. Presidents 2. Vice-presidents 3. Watergate Affair, 1972-1974 4. Senators 5. Nonfiction writers 6. Members of Congress 7. United States -- Politics and government -- 1961-1974
ISBN 0-7432-7406-7 pa
The title refers to the final days of the Nixon Presidency. The authors have "constructed a two-part narrative, the first half covering the period from April 30, 1973—the day John Dean was fired as White House counsel—until late July 1974, and the second half covering the last two weeks in detail." N Y Times Book Rev

Zinn, Howard, 1922-2010
The **historic** unfulfilled promise; Howard Zinn; introduction by Mathew Rothschild. City Lights Books 2012 250 p. $16.95   **973.924**
1. Military policy -- United States 2. United States -- Economic conditions 3. United States -- Politics and government 4. World politics -- 20th century 5. United States -- History -- 1969- 6. United States -- Foreign relations -- 1989- 7. United States -- Foreign relations -- 1981-1989 8. United States -- Politics and government

-- 1989- 9. United States -- Politics and government
-- 1981-1989
ISBN 087286555X; 9780872865556

LC 2012007955

This book by Howard Zinn collects "the dozens of articles he penned for 'The Progressive' magazine from 1980 to 2009," Topics include "the Barack Obama White House, the sorry state of US government and politics, the tragic futility of US military actions in Afghanistan and Iraq, or the plight of working people in an economy rigged to benefit the rich and powerful." (Publisher's note)

Includes index.

973.925   Administration of Gerald Rudolph Ford, 1974-1977

Schulman, Bruce J.

The **seventies**; the great shift in American culture, society, and politics. Da Capo 2002 334p pa $17.95   **973.925**

1. United States -- Civilization -- 1970-
ISBN 0-306-81126-X; 978-0-306-81126-5

First published 2001 by Free Press

"This is an important contribution to modern American social history and the literature of popular culture." Publ Wkly

Includes bibliographical references

973.927   Administration of Ronald Reagan, 1981-1989

Brokaw, Tom

The **time** of our lives; past, present, promise. Random House 2011 xxii, 291p il $26; ebook $12.99   **973.927**

1. Social problems 2. American national characteristics 3. United States -- Social conditions 4. United States -- Politics and government -- 1989-
ISBN 978-1-4000-6458-8; 978-0-679-64392-0 ebook

LC 2011022825

"At this troubled point in the nation's history, . . . Brokaw offers a perspective from his own life and career. Drawing on interviews and observations, he ponders how the U.S. has come to a point where the country is suffering from eroding confidence, a financial crisis, declining education, and fears about China's progress. . . . Through the prism of his family and career, Brokaw looks back on the Great Depression, the civil rights era, the Cold War, and more recent history and looks forward to the future for his grandchildren and the nation. With commonsense values, he appeals to Americans to recommit to family and community, increase civic engagement, and make sacrifices in an effort to ensure some security for generations to come. An engaging recollection of the achievements of the past, the realities of the present, and the promise of the future." Booklist

D'Souza, Dinesh

Ronald Reagan; how an ordinary man became an extraordinary leader. Free Press 1997 292p hardcover o.p. pa $13   **973.927**

1. Actors 2. Governors 3. Presidents 4. Presidents -- United States 5. United States -- Politics and government -- 1974-1989
ISBN 0-684-84823-6 pa

LC 97-31396

The author's "provocative argument for Reagan's greatness opens a necessary and complicated debate." Commentary

Includes bibliographical references

FitzGerald, Frances

Way out there in the blue; Reagan, Star Wars, and the end of the Cold War. Simon & Schuster 2000 592p hardcover o.p. pa $17   **973.927**

1. Actors 2. Cold war 3. Governors 4. Presidents 5. Strategic Defense Initiative 6. United States -- Politics and government -- 1974-1989
ISBN 0-7432-0023-3 pa

LC 99-59913

Fitzgerald offers a history of U.S. missile-defense programs over the last two decades, focusing particular attention on the Strategic Defense Initiative (SDI) supported by President Reagan

"Explaining the Star Wars saga, Fitzgerald delivers all the information that any nonexpert could absorb." Booklist

Includes bibliographical references

The **Iran-Contra** scandal; the declassified history. edited by Peter Kornbluh and Malcolm Byrne. New Press 1993 xxxiii, 412p hardcover o.p. pa $24.95   **973.927**

1. Iran-Contra Affair, 1985-1990
ISBN 1-56584-047-X pa

LC 92-53732

This volume contains "one hundred documents concerning the Iran-Contra Scandal, covering the period from Reagan's original presidential finding of Dec. 1, 1981 to Bush's grant of executive clemency of Dec. 24, 1992. With a helpful chronology of key events and a glossary of major participants, the volume sets forth with contextual introductions the documents, the paper trail of this major controversy in contemporary American politics." Libr J

Includes bibliographical references

Johnson, Haynes Bonner

Sleepwalking through history; America in the Reagan years. {by} Haynes Johnson. Norton 1991 524p il hardcover o.p. pa $15.95   **973.927**

1. Actors 2. Governors 3. Presidents 4. United States -- History -- 1974-1989 5. United States -- Politics and government -- 1974-1989
ISBN 0-393-32434-6 pa

LC 90-38623

This is a study of American politics, history, and culture during the 1980s

The author "concentrates on major events like the Iran-contra affair and the Wall street scene, and briefly touches on other domestic scandals. . . . Not the definitive history of the 1980s, but recommended as an important book by an important author." Libr J

Includes bibliographical references

Mann, James

The **rebellion** of Ronald Reagan; a history of the end of the Cold War. [by] James Mann. Viking 2009 396p il   **973.927**

1. Actors 2. Cold war 3. Governors 4. Presidents 5. Cold War 6. Cabinet members 7. Communist leaders 8. Nobel laureates for peace 9. Soviet Union -- Foreign relations -- United States 10. United States -- Foreign relations -- Soviet Union 11. Political leadership -- United States -- History -- 20th century

ISBN 0670020540; 9780670020546

LC 2008029029

Ronald Reagan did not win the Cold War, nor was he just historically lucky, as two contrasting viewpoints would sometimes have it. Instead, . . . [the author writes,] after a career of hard line anticommunism Reagan proved more flexible and visionary than many other leaders of American foreign policy and more opportunistic and insightful into the motives of Mikhail Gorbachev when the Soviet leader signaled change in the USSR's own conventional hard-line position. . . . Mann bases his argument upon impressive original research, including interviews with principals who range from George Shultz, to Colin Powell, to Helmut Kohl, to Nancy Reagan. Libr J

Includes bibliographical references

Ratnesar, Romesh

Tear down this wall; a city, a president, and the speech that ended the Cold War. Simon & Schuster 2009 229p $27   **973.927**

1. Actors 2. Cold war 3. Governors 4. Presidents 5. American speeches 6. Cabinet members 7. Communist leaders 8. Berlin Wall (1961-1989) 9. Nobel laureates for peace 10. Soviet Union -- Foreign relations -- United States 11. United States -- Foreign relations -- Soviet Union

ISBN 978-1-4165-5690-9

LC 2009-24213

Drawing on interviews with Reagan administration officials, journalists, historians, and eyewitnesses, the author focuses on Ronald Reagan's June 1987 speech at the Brandenburg Gate and his historic challenge to Mikhail Gorbachev to tear down the Berlin Wall.

"This book may be read with pleasure by many, from trained historians to curious general readers. Generally objective in its approach, it will yet lead readers to understand why Reagan is remembered fondly by many and why both he and Gorbachev were key figures in this significant element of 20th-century history." Libr J

Includes bibliographical references

Reagan, Ronald,1911-2004

Reagan, in his own hand; edited, with an introduction and commentary by Kiron K. Skinner, Annelise Anderson, Martin Anderson; with a foreword by George P. Schultz. Free Press 2001 xxvi, 549p il $30; pa $16   **973.927**

1. United States -- Politics and government -- 1989-

ISBN 0-7432-0123-X; 0-7432-1938-4 pa

LC 00-66304

"A collection of . . . manuscripts is presented here, just as Reagan wrote them, including his corrections and notes. With a few exceptions, they are very short radio commentaries delivered during the pre-presidential period (1975-1979), focusing mostly on foreign policy and the economy." Publ Wkly

Reeves, Richard

President Reagan: the triumph of imagination. Simon & Schuster 2005 571p il $30   **973.927**

1. Actors 2. Governors 3. Presidents 4. United States -- Politics and government -- 1974-1989

ISBN 0-7432-3022-1

LC 2005-54198

This is an examination of the Reagan presidency.

This book "is a compelling read, fast-paced and scrupulously fair. . . . Anybody who is interested in Reagan's extraordinary presidency needs to reckon with Reeves." N Y Times Book Rev

Includes bibliographical references

973.928   Administration of George Bush, 1989-1993

Schell, Jonathan

Writing in time; a political chronicle. Moyer Bell 1997 303p hardcover o.p. pa $14.95 **973.928**

1. United States -- Politics and government -- 1989-

ISBN 1-55921-295-0 pa

LC 96-8516

This volume "traces the 1992 Presidential campaign, the election and President Clinton's first term through Jonathan Schell's columns for Newsday. This chronicle is a distinctly partisan one: Schell's views of the White House and its wannabes are seen strictly from the left. But the author's eye for issues and motives is so sure that even those who detest his opinions will find 'Writing in Time' a lively refresher course on five years of American history." N Y Times Book Rev

Woodward, Bob

The **commanders**. Simon & Schuster 1991 398p il hardcover o.p. pa $16   **973.928**

1. Diplomats 2. Presidents 3. Vice-presidents 4. Persian Gulf War, 1991 5. Members of Congress 6. Parents of presidents 7. United Nations officials 8. United States -- Dept. of Defense 9. United States -- Foreign relations

ISBN 0-671-41367-8; 0-7432-3475-8 pa

LC 91-13037

This book discusses "top-level White House [and] Pentagon decisionmaking, first in the attack on Panama, and then in the 5½ months of diplomatic and especially military maneuvering that preceded the [1991] war with Iraq." Christ Sci Monit

973.929   Administration of Bill Clinton, 1993-2001

Chafe, William H.

Bill and Hillary; the politics of the personal. William H. Chafe. 1st ed. Farrar Strauss and Giroux 2012 x, 387 p.p (hardcover : alk. paper) $28.00   **973.929**
1. Married people 2. Presidents -- United States -- Biography 3. Presidents' spouses -- United States -- Biography 4. United States -- Politics and government -- 1993-2001
ISBN 0809094657; 9780809094653

LC 2011041302

This book offers a "portrait of how the dynamic between Bill and Hillary Clinton affected their achievements in public life. Both fiercely ambitious super-achievers from dysfunctional families, their personalities were complementary (he charming and brilliant, she disciplined and demanding)." They worked as a team, which "caused controversy when he was Arkansas governor and threatened disaster when he became president in 1992." (Publishers Weekly)

Includes bibliographical references and index.

Gormley, Ken

The **death** of American virtue; Clinton vs. Starr. Crown Publishers 2010 789p il $35   **973.929**
1. Judges 2. Lawyers 3. Governors 4. Presidents 5. Political ethics 6. Misconduct in office 7. Interns 8. Senators 9. Law teachers 10. Presidential aides 11. Government officials 12. Secretaries of state 13. Spouses of presidents 14. Presidential candidates 15. Clothing industry executives 16. Whitewater Inquiry, 1993-2000 17. Special prosecutors -- United States 18. Misconduct in office -- United States 19. Governmental investigations -- United States
ISBN 0-307-40944-9; 978-0-307-4094-4

The author presents an analysis of the events leading up to the impeachment trial of President William Jefferson Clinton, from Ken Starr's initial Whitewater investigation through the Paula Jones sexual harassment suit to the Monica Lewinsky affair. . . . [The book includes material from interviews with] Bill Clinton, Ken Starr, Monica Lewinsky, Paula Jones, [and] Susan McDougal. (Publisher's note) Index.

For those wishing to understand exactly what happened during this confusing, dismal time, Gormley's informed reporting and evenhanded analysis is the place to start. The entire nightmare vividly recalled. Kirkus

Includes bibliographical references

McDougal, Susan

The **woman** who wouldn't talk; {by} Susan McDougal with Pat Harris; introduction by Helen Thomas. Carroll & Graf Pubs. 2003 384p il $25; pa $14   **973.929**
1. Governors 2. Prisoners 3. Presidents 4. Real estate developers 5. Spouses of prominent persons
ISBN 0-7867-1128-0; 0-7867-1302-X pa

LC 2002-192705

"In the 1996 Whitewater investigation, McDougal was indicted for fraud over a $300,000 loan, claiming that only her ex-husband, Jim McDougal, knew the money's intended purpose. Kenneth Starr, head of the Office of the Independent Counsel investigating Whitewater, offered her leniency if she would implicate President Clinton and Hillary Clinton. McDougal refused to testify, she writes, because she didn't want her statements about the Clintons' innocence twisted into perjury by the Starr Commission. She spent the next 21 months in prison on a charge of civil contempt. McDougal has written an engaging, sometimes gossipy, insightful biography, notable for its accounts of her different trials and more so for the depiction of life in women's prisons." Libr J

Reich, Robert B.

Locked in the cabinet. Knopf 1997 338p hardcover o.p. pa $15   **973.929**
1. United States -- Dept. of Labor 2. United States -- Politics and government -- 1989-
ISBN 0-375-70061-7 pa

LC 97-71921

The author writes about his tenure as Secretary of Labor in the first Clinton administration

"Reich has an acid pen, and he is by turns witty, churlish, and plain vulgar. . . . The specificity of detail in this book adds up not only to an absorbing accounting of failed service in the Cabinet but also to a powerful indictment of the Clinton Presidency." New Leader

Stephanopoulos, George

All too human; a political education. Little, Brown 1999 456p $32; pa $14.95   **973.929**
1. Governors 2. Presidents 3. Presidents -- United States 4. United States -- Politics and government -- 1989-
ISBN 0-316-92919-0; 0-316-93016-4 pa

LC 99-13817

This is a political memoir by a former senior advisor to President Clinton

"A fascinating if controversial insiders account of life inside the Clinton pressure cooker administration during its early years." Libr J

Includes bibliographical references

Toobin, Jeffrey R.

A **vast** conspiracy; the real story of the sex scandal that nearly brought down a president. 1st Touchstone ed.; Simon & Schuster 2000 422p pa $20   **973.929**
1. Governors 2. Presidents 3. United States -- Politics and government -- 1989-
ISBN 0-7432-0413-1; 978-0-7432-0413-2

LC 00-59524

First published 1999 by Random House

"It was the most extraordinary public saga of our time, and Jeffrey Toobin gives us a definitive history of the ordeal that very nearly brought down a president. Here is the whole story of the Clinton sex scandals -- from its beginnings in a Little Rock hotel to its climax on the floor of the United States Senate with only the second vote on presidential removal in American history. Rich with Shakespearean characters and dramatic secrets, fueled with the high octane of a sensational legal thriller, and tinged by misguided, outlandish behavior that was played out at the very highest levels, Toobin's A Vast Conspiracy brings a dignity and integrity to this story that it has never before received. " (Publisher's note)

"Even for those who disagree with [Toobin's] assessment, the book is still hugely entertaining. There are plenty of scandal pellets to be found scattered throughout the analysis." Christ Sci Monit

Includes bibliographical references

973.93 United States--2001-

Caputo, Philip

The **longest** road; overland in search of America from Key West to the Arctic Ocean. by Philip Caputo. Henry Holt and Company 2013 352 p. $28 **973.93**
1. Travel writing 2. United States -- Social conditions 3. United States -- Biography 4. National characteristics, American 5. United States -- Description and travel 6. United States -- Social conditions -- 21st century 7. United States -- Social life and customs -- 21st century
ISBN 0805094466; 9780805094466

LC 2012050451

In this book author Philip Caputo takes a "journey across America, Airstream in tow, and asks everyday Americans what unites and divides a country as endlessly diverse as it is large. What he found is a story [designed to] entertain and inspire readers as much as it informs them about the state of today's United States, the glue that holds us all together, and the conflicts that could cause us to pull apart." (Publisher's note)

Schama, Simon

The **American** future; a history. Ecco 2009 400p il $29.99 **973.93**
1. American national characteristics 2. United States -- History 3. United States -- Civilization
ISBN 978-0-06-053923-8; 0-06-053923-2

LC 2009-358875

First published 2008 in the United Kingdom

Schama "has begun wandering through the literature of the American past to snap up unconsidered trifles. The result is a book of mixed genre-history, memoir and journalism-and none the worse for that. In four successive chapters, Schama considers the American relationship to war, religion, immigration and prosperity. Within each, he moves between historical narratives and vignettes from the contemporary scene, usually involving his own presence. So the book's architecture is crisp, even as its rationale is mysterious." Times Lit Suppl

Shorris, Earl

The **politics** of heaven; America in fearful times. Norton 2007 371p $25.95 **973.93**
1. Conservatism 2. Christian fundamentalism 3. Christianity and politics 4. United States -- Politics and government -- 2001-
ISBN 978-0-393-05963-2; 0-393-05963-4

LC 2007-12726

The author "offers a historical perspective on religion in the U.S., from Calvinist doctrine marrying religion and capitalism to the conservative modern-day gospels as preached by Billy Graham and Jerry Falwell. Drawing on research

and interviews with political figures and advisors, academics, and theologians, Shorris examines the confluence of history, philosophy, experiences, and 'elemental feelings' that have gained enough momentum to become a movement of the fearful . . . Shorris eloquently offers a penetrating and unsettling look at American fear birthed by the horrors of the atom bomb and nurtured by 9/11 that promises to have an enduring impact on global and domestic policy for generations to come.." Booklist

973.931 Administration of George W. Bush, 2001-2009

Bernstein, Richard

Out of the blue; the story of September 11, 2001, from Jihad to Ground Zero. {by} Richard Bernstein and the staff of the New York Times. Times Bks. 2002 287p il hardcover o.p. pa $15 **973.931**
1. Terrorism 2. September 11 terrorist attacks, 2001
ISBN 0-8050-7240-3; 0-8050-7410-4 pa

LC 2002-20396

This account of the September 11, 2001 terrorist attacks focuses "on the personal—the victims, the perpetrators and heroes whose lives became tangled in catastrophe. . . . It uses these stories as a jumping-off point for a comprehensive look at the terror attacks—the reactions of New Yorkers, the nation and the world; the criticism of U.S. government agencies; the lingering effects of the tragedy. While some of this information has been published elsewhere, it has not been gathered so comprehensively—nor has it been written so well." Publ Wkly

Bruni, Frank

Ambling into history: the unlikely odyssey of George W. Bush. HarperCollins Pubs. 2002 278p hardcover o.p. pa $12.95 **973.931**
1. Governors 2. Presidents 3. Baseball executives 4. Children of presidents 5. Energy industry executives 6. Presidents -- United States
ISBN 0-06-093782-3 pa

The author, who covered Bush's 2000 presidential campaign for the New York Times, focuses on Bush's personality and mannerisms as well as his basic interactions with family, friends, and the public.

"Given [Bruni's] familiarity with Bush, one would expect his book to contain revealing insights, and this superb, incisive, and surprising account does not disappoint." Booklist

Includes bibliographical references

Eichenwald, Kurt

500 days; secrets and lies in the terror wars. by Kurt Eichenwald. 1st Touchstone hardcover ed. Touchstone 2012 xxiii, 611 p.p (hardcover) $30.00; (paperback) $18.00 **973.931**
1. International relations 2. Terrorism -- Prevention 3. September 11 terrorist attacks, 2001 4. War on Terrorism, 2001-2009 5. World politics -- 21st century 6. September 11 Terrorist Attacks, 2001
ISBN 1451669380; 9781451669381; 9781451674132;

9781451669398

LC 2012001214

This book offers an "episodic reconstruction of the fallout from 9/11 in the highest spheres of terrorist strategy. Former 'New York Times' reporter [Kurt] Eichenwald . . . chronicles the entire post-9/11 year-and-a-half spectacular, demonstrating literally how the anti-terrorist hysteria in the United States, and the hatred of America and general global paranoia, forged the 'trauma that haunts the world to this day.'" (Kirkus Reviews)

Includes bibliographical references (p. [525]-576) and index.

Farmer, John J.

The **ground** truth; the untold story of America under attack on 9/11. [by] John Farmer. Riverhead Books 2009 388p $26.95   **973.931**

1. Terrorism 2. September 11 terrorist attacks, 2001
ISBN 978-1-59448-894-8; 1-59448-894-0

LC 2009-23297

The author "presents a dismaying catalogue of incompetence and dissembling before and after the attack on the World Trade Center and the Pentagon. The author makes excellent use of declassified primary-source documents from 9/11—including transcriptions of frantic last-minute phone calls of air-traffic controllers—to demonstrate how a massively funded national-security system, a relic of the Cold War, failed to counter a small band of terrorists. . . . An important systematic brief on how an elaborately constructed national-defense system was penetrated, and why lessons of that day for disaster response remain dimly understood." Kirkus

Includes bibliographical references

Franks, Tommy

American soldier; [by] Tommy Franks, with Malcolm McConnell. Regan Bks. 2004 590p il map $27.95; pa $16.95   **973.931**

1. Generals
ISBN 0-06-073158-3; 0-06-077954-3 pa

LC 2004-558617

"The real value of 'American Soldier' . . . is not what it says about the war on terror, but what it reveals about Tommy Franks. . . . The chapter on Vietnam, where Franks spent a year in brutal combat as a field artillery officer, is a cleareyed, mordant memoir." N Y Times Book Rev

Hersh, Seymour M.

★ **Chain** of command; the road from 9/11 to Abu Ghraib. HarperCollins 2004 394p map $25.95; pa $14.95   **973.931**

1. Iraq War, 2003-2011 2. September 11 terrorist attacks, 2001 3. Iraq War, 2003- 4. War on terrorism 5. Abu Ghraib (Baghdad, Iraq: Prison)
ISBN 0-06-019591-6; 0-06-095537-6 pa

"This sobering book is the closest anyone without a security clearance will get to operatives in the inner sanctums of America's intelligence, military, political and diplomatic worlds." Publ Wkly

Kaplan, Robert D.

Imperial grunts; the American military on the ground. Random House 2005 421p maps $27.95   **973.931**

1. Soldiers -- United States 2. Military policy -- United States
ISBN 1-4000-6132-6

LC 2004-61466

Kaplan's "on-the-ground reportage makes for riveting reading." N Y Times (Late N Y Ed)

Includes bibliographical references

Kessler, Ronald

The **CIA** at war; inside the secret campaign against terror. St. Martin's Press 2003 362p il $27.95; pa $15.95   **973.931**

1. War on terrorism 2. United States -- Central Intelligence Agency
ISBN 0-312-31932-0; 0-312-31933-9 pa

LC 2003-58487

The author "takes us from the formation of the CIA as an outgrowth of World War II OSS intelligence activities, when most agents were East Coast Ivy League elites focused on cold war scrimmages, through the current war on terror, where the enemy is often unknown and the agency elite are somewhat more diverse. Through numerous interviews with both agents and operatives, Kessler brings to life a world generally described only in fiction." Booklist

Includes bibliographical references

Mayer, Jane

The **dark** side; the inside story of how the war on terror turned into a war on American ideals. Doubleday 2008 392p il $27.50   **973.931**

1. September 11 terrorist attacks, 2001 2. War on terrorism 3. United States -- Politics and government -- 2001-
ISBN 978-0-385-52639-5; 0-385-52639-3

LC 2008-299452

This is an account of how the Bush administration has fought the war on terror.

This is a "brilliantly researched and deeply unsettling book." N Y Times Book Rev

Includes bibliographical references (p. 361-369)

Miller, John

The **cell**: inside the 9/11 plot and why the FBI and CIA failed to stop it; {by} John Miller and Michael Stone, with Chris Mitchell. Hyperion 2002 336p $24.95; pa $13.95   **973.931**

1. Terrorism 2. September 11 terrorist attacks, 2001 3. Intelligence service -- United States 4. United States -- Central Intelligence Agency 5. United States -- Federal Bureau of Investigation
ISBN 0-7868-6900-3; 0-7868-8782-6 pa

LC 2002-27322

The authors analyze the circumstances inside and outside the United States that culminated in the September 11 terrorist attack. Included is an account of Miller's face-to-face meeting with Osama bin Laden in Afghanistan in 1998. This is a "frightening and important book." Publ Wkly

National Commission on Terrorist Attacks Upon the United States

★ The **9** /11 Commission report; final report of the National Commission on Terrorist Attacks Upon the United States. Norton 2004 567p il $19.95; pa $10   **973.931**

> 1. Terrorism 2. September 11 terrorist attacks, 2001 3. War on terrorism 4. Qaida (Organization) 5. National security -- United States
> ISBN 0-393-06041-1; 0-393-32671-3 pa
> > LC 2004-57564

This work aims to describe how the terrorist attacks of September 11, 2001 occurred and to provide recommendations for the prevention of future attacks.

This book "reads like a Shakespearean drama. . . . This multi-author document produces an absolutely compelling narrative intelligence, one with clarity, a sense of shared mission and an overriding desire to do something about the situation." Publ Wkly

Includes bibliographical references

Noonan, Peggy

A **heart,** a cross & a flag; America today. Free Press 2003 270p (Wall Street journal book) hardcover o.p. pa $19.95   **973.931**

> 1. American national characteristics 2. September 11 terrorist attacks, 2001 3. War on terrorism 4. United States -- Politics and government -- 2001-
> ISBN 0-7432-5005-2; 978-0-7432-5048-1; 0-7432-5048-6
> > LC 2003-48336

"Noonan's essays are thoughtful, introspective, and deeply patriotic. Although she is devastated by the horror of 9/11, her spirits are lifted by the heroism and kindness she sees in her fellow New Yorkers, from the firemen who bravely raced into the doomed towers to the people who turned out to cheer on the rescue workers and firemen who toiled in the wreckage." Booklist

Ramo, Joshua Cooper

The **age** of the unthinkable; why the new world disorder constantly surprises us and what we can do about it. Little, Brown and Company 2009 279p $25.99   **973.931**

> 1. World politics -- 1991- 2. Military policy -- United States 3. United States -- Foreign relations
> ISBN 978-0-316-11808-8; 0-316-11808-7
> > LC 2009-00854

This is "a fascinating look at various aspects of today's complicated world and how interconnecting systems often come to bear in unexpected ways." Libr J

Includes bibliographical references

Smith, Jean Edward

Bush; Jean Edward Smith. Simon & Schuster 2016 768 p. $35   **973.931**

> 1. Presidents -- United States 2. United States -- Politics and government -- 2001-2009
> ISBN 1476741190; 9781476741192
> > LC 2015034690

This book, by Jean Edward Smith "demonstrates that it was not Dick Cheney, Donald Rumsfeld, or Condoleezza Rice, but President [George W.] Bush himself who took personal control of foreign policy. Bush drew on his deep religious conviction that important foreign-policy decisions were simply a matter of good versus evil. Domestically, he overreacted to 9/11 and endangered Americans' civil liberties." (Publisher's note)

"This is a superb recap and critical analysis of Bush's controversial administration." Pub Wkly

Includes bibliographical references and index

Soufan, Ali H.

★ The **black** banners; the inside story of 9/11 and the war against Al-Qaeda. [by] Ali H. Soufan; with Daniel Freedman. W.W. Norton & Co. 2011 xxvi, 572p il map $26.95   **973.931**

> 1. Terrorism 2. September 11 terrorist attacks, 2001 3. War on terrorism 4. Al Qaeda (Organization) 5. War on Terrorism, 2001- 6. Terrorism -- United States -- Prevention
> ISBN 978-0-393-07942-5; 0-393-07942-2
> > LC 2011026938

A former FBI special agent offers an insider's account of how the September 11th attacks could have been prevented, as well as his role in the war on terror.

"The best and most original book published in the West on al-Qaeda, this is highly recommended." Libr J

Includes bibliographical references

Spiegelman, Art

In the shadow of no towers. Pantheon Books 2004 il $19.95   **973.931**

> 1. Graphic novels 2. September 11 terrorist attacks, 2001 -- Graphic novels
> ISBN 0-375-42307-9
> > LC 2004-43870

The author "provides a hair-raising and wry account of his family's frantic efforts to locate one another on September 11 as well as a morbidly funny survey of his trademark sense of existential doom. . . . This is a powerful and quirky work of visual storytelling by a master comics artist." Publ Wkly

Suskind, Ron

The **one** percent doctrine; deep inside America's pursuit of its enemies since 9/11. Simon & Schuster 2006 367p $27   **973.931**

> 1. Terrorism 2. War on terrorism 3. United States -- Politics and government -- 2001-
> ISBN 0-7432-7109-2; 978-0-7432-7109-7
> > LC 2006-279373

"Relying on . . . access to former and current government officials, this book [seeks to] . . . reveal for the first time how the U.S. government—from President Bush on down—is frantically improvising to fight a new kind of war." Publisher's note

The **torture** papers; the road to Abu Ghraib. edited by Karen J. Greenberg, Joshua L. Dratel; intro-

duction by Anthony Lewis. Cambridge University Press 2005 xxxiv, 1249p il $30 **973.931**
1. Iraq War, 2003-2011 2. Iraq War, 2003- 3. Abu Ghraib (Baghdad, Iraq: Prison)
ISBN 0-521-85324-9
"A gripping and alarming read about the use of government power." Choice
Includes bibliographical references

Woodward, Bob
State of denial. Simon & Schuster 2006 560p il hardcover o.p. pa $16 **973.931**
1. Governors 2. Presidents 3. Iraq War, 2003-2011 4. Iraq War, 2003- 5. Baseball executives 6. Children of presidents 7. Energy industry executives
ISBN 0-7432-7223-4; 978-0-7432-7223-0; 0-7432-7224-2 pa; 978-0-7432-7224-7 pa
LC 2006-285190
This is a critique of the Bush administration's handling of the war in Iraq.
"If journalism is the first page of history, then Woodward's opus will be required reading for any would-be historians of the time." Publ Wkly
Includes bibliographical references

Wright, Lawrence, 1947-
★ The **looming** tower; Al Qaeda and the road to 9/11. Knopf 2006 469p map $27.95 **973.931**
1. Terrorism 2. September 11 terrorist attacks, 2001 3. Al Qaeda (Organization) 4. Intelligence service -- United States 5. Terrorism -- Government policy -- United States
ISBN 0-375-41486-X; 9780375414862
LC 2006-41032
This is a "narrative history of the events leading to 9/11." (Publisher's note)
The author "goes back—way back—to 1948 to dissect the personal influences and political radicalization that would lead to al Qaeda's attack on America." Libr J
Includes bibliographical references

973.932 Administration of Barack Obama, 2009-

Balz, Daniel J.
The **battle** for America, 2008; the story of an extraordinary election. [by] Dan Balz and Haynes Johnson. Viking Press 2009 415p $29.95 **973.932**
1. Presidents -- United States -- Election -- 2008 2. United States -- Politics and government -- 2001-
ISBN 978-0-670-02111-6; 0-670-02111-3
LC 2009-17129
This is an account of the 2008 American presidential campaign and election.
"Although we all know how things turned out, the authors know how to work a cliffhanger, and, as they effectively demonstrate, things could have turned out differently at any number of turns. Essential for watchers of politics and a model for similar electoral analyses in the future." Kirkus
Includes bibliographical references

Berry, Mary Frances
Power in words; the stories behind Barack Obama's speeches, from the state house to the White House. [by] Mary Frances Berry, Josh Gottheimer; foreword by Ted Sorensen. Beacon Press 2010 xxxiii, 267p $24.95 **973.932**
1. American speeches 2. Presidents -- United States -- Election -- 2008 3. United States -- Politics and government -- 2001-
ISBN 978-0-8070-0104-2
LC 2010004085
Collection of 18 of Obama's most memorable speeches between 2002 and 2008, each introduced by Berry and Gottheimer with political analysis, historical context, and commentary from the speechwriters.
"A book to savor and return to for subsequent readings." Kirkus
Includes bibliographical references

Johnston, David Cay
The **making** of Donald Trump; David Cay Johnston. Melville House 2016 xvi, 263 p.p (hardcover) $24.99 **973.932**
1. Businessmen -- Biograpy 2. Businessmen -- United States -- Biography 3. Celebrities -- United States -- Biography 4. Real estate developers -- United States -- Biography 5. Presidential candidates -- United States -- Biography 6. Television personalities -- United States -- Biography 7. Political campaigns -- United States -- History -- 21st century
ISBN 1612196322; 9781612196329
LC 2016947664
This book, by David Cay Johnston, is the "culmination of nearly 30 years of reporting on Donald Trump. . . . Covering the long arc of Trump's career, Johnston tells the full story of how a boy from a quiet section of Queens, NY would become an entirely new, and complex, breed of public figure. Trump is a man of great media savvy, entrepreneurial spirit, and political clout. Yet his career has been plagued by legal troubles and mounting controversy." (Publisher's note)
"By exposing what he argues is Trump's strategic flouting of the law, as well as his belief in revenge as a 'guiding principle' and his strategy of 'sowing doubt and threatening litigation,' Johnston hopes that his book will prompt readers to carefully 'evaluate the prospect of a Trump presidency.' " Booklist
Includes bibliographic references (pages 215-258) and index

Kantor, Jodi
The **Obamas**; Jodi Kantor. Little, Brown and Co. 2012 viii, 359 p.p $16 **973.932**
1. Presidents -- United States -- Family 2. White House (Washington, D.C.) 3. Presidents -- United States -- Biography
ISBN 0316098760; 9780316098755; 9780316098762
LC 2011940240
This book profiles the marriage of U.S. President Barack Obama and his wife Michelle. Author Jodi Kantor, "a 'New York Times' Washington correspondent, offers a prolonged peek behind the curtain at the evolving role of the Obama

marriage as a driver of White House East and West Wing sensibility." (AudioFile)

Includes bibliographical references (p. 343-347) and index

Sunstein, Cass R. (Cass Robert), 1954-

Simpler; The Future of Government. Cass R. Sunstein. Simon & Schuster 2013 240 p. $26 **973.932**
1. Economics 2. Political science 3. United States -- Economic policy -- 2009- 4. United States -- Politics and government -- 2009-
ISBN 1476726590; 9781476726595

LC 2012048234

This book, written by Cass R. Sunstein, discusses simpler government. "Behavioral economics has influenced business and politics. Sunstein [shows] why Americans are better off as a result, and what the future has in store. Backed by historic executive orders ensuring transparency and accountability, simpler government can be found in new initiatives that save money and time, improve health, and lengthen lives." (Publisher's note)

Includes bibliographical references and index

Taibbi, Matt

Griftopia; bubble machines, vampire squids, and the long con that is breaking America. Spiegel & Grau 2010 252p $26 **973.932**
1. Despotism 2. Political corruption 3. Global Financial Crisis, 2008-2009 4. United States -- Politics and government -- 2001-
ISBN 978-0-385-52995-2; 978-0-385-52997-6 ebook

LC 2010-15067

This is a study of the causes and consequences of the 2008 financial crisis.

"Taibbi's glib prose is punctuated with just enough irreverence and wit to allow him to appeal to more casual readers while providing sufficient detail to satisfy those looking for a serious discussion of the high-level manipulation of the economy. Recommended for anyone interested in understanding the economy and how it got that way." Libr J

974 Specific states of United States

Macdonald, Cameron

The **endangered** species road trip; a summer's worth of dingy motels, poison oak, ravenous insects, and the rarest species in North America. by Cameron MacDonald. Pgw 2013 216 p. $17.95 **974**
1. Travel 2. Rare animals
ISBN 155365935X; 9781553659358

In this book, author Cameron MacDonald discusses his "road trip of a lifetime to observe North America's rarest species. MacDonald offers fascinating details about the natural history of the endangered species he seeks, as well as threats like overpopulation, commercial fishing, and climate change that are driving them towards extinction." (Publisher's note)

"Documenting the ongoing simplification of North America's ecologies could be grim work . . . but MacDonald's comedic sense and his engaging style are addictive and the resulting tale is intensely charming." Pub Wkly

Vowell, Sarah

The **wordy** shipmates. Riverhead Books 2008 254p map $25.95 **974**
1. Puritans 2. Pilgrims (New England colonists) 3. New England -- History -- 1600-1775, Colonial period
ISBN 978-1-59448-999-0; 1-59448-999-8

LC 2008-30491

"Focusing on the Puritans who settled in 1692 in the Massachusetts Bay Colony, Vowell laments their image as 'boring killjoys' when in fact they were 'fascinating killjoys.' A book dense with detail, insight, and humor." Booklist

974.4 Massachusetts

Bradford, William

Of Plymouth Plantation, 1620-1647; the complete text, with notes and an introduction by Samuel Eliot Morison. Knopf 1952 xliii, 448p maps $25 **974.4**
1. Pilgrims (New England colonists) 2. Massachusetts -- History -- 1600-1775, Colonial period
ISBN 0-394-43895-7

Written between 1630 and 1650; first published 1856 with title: History of Plymouth Plantation

"The opening book sketches the origin of the Separatist movement, the flight from England to Holland, the settlement at Leiden, the plans for the settlement in New England, and the Mayflower voyage. The second book, which includes the major part of the history, is in the form of annals from 1620 to 1646, and describes every aspect of the life of the Pilgrims. Besides being a primary historical source, the work has artistic value because of its dignified, sonorous style, deriving from the Geneva Bible." Oxford Companion to Am Lit. 5th edition

Bremer, Francis J.

John Winthrop; America's forgotten founding father. Oxford University Press 2003 478p il hardcover o.p. pa $21.95 **974.4**
1. Clergy 2. Government officials 3. Colonial administrators
ISBN 0-19-514913-0; 978-0-19-517981-1 pa; 0-19-517981-1 pa

LC 2002-38143

"Bremer's definitive biography gracefully portrays Winthrop as a man of his time, whose influence in the new colony grew out of his own struggles to establish his identity before he left England." Publ Wkly

Includes bibliographical references

Bunker, Nick

★ **Making** haste from Babylon; the Mayflower Pilgrims and their world: a new history. Alfred A. Knopf 2010 489p il map $30 **974.4**
1. Pilgrims (New England colonists) 2. Mayflower (Ship) 3. Pilgrims (New Plymouth Colony) 4. Massachusetts -- History -- New Plymouth, 1620-1691 5. Massachusetts -- History -- 1600-1775, Colonial

period

ISBN 978-0-307-26682-8; 0-307-26682-6

LC 2009038520

This is an "account of the Mayflower project and the first decade of the Plymouth Colony." (Publisher's note)

"Never before has such a comprehensive and thoroughly researched study of the subject appeared. . . . [This book] scoops up every relevant character and links all to the basic tale of indomitable courage, religious faith, commercial ambition, international rivalry, and domestic politics. The results are stunning. Certain to be the dominating work on the Pilgrims for decades." Publ Wkly

Includes bibliographical references

East, Elyssa

Dogtown; death and enchantment in a New England ghost town. Free Press 2009 291p map $26   **974.4**

1. Dogtown (Mass.)

ISBN 978-1-4165-8704-0; 1-4165-8704-7

LC 2009-17197

"A true-crime story, an art appreciation course and an American history lesson stitched together, and it succeeds as all three. . . . Plaudits to East for exploring the relationship of the land to artists, as well as to the people who live upon it, in this case for generations." N Y Times Book Rev

Kidder, Tracy

Home town. Washington Square Press 2000 432p pa $14.95   **974.4**

1. City and town life 2. Northampton (Mass.)

ISBN 978-0-671-78521-5; 0-671-78521-4

First published 1999 by Random House

This "acutely observed, crisply written, and utterly absorbing documentary proves that there is nothing on this spinning earth more amazing and full of grace than everyday life." Booklist

Includes bibliographical references

Manegold, Catherine

Ten Hills Farm; the forgotten history of slavery in the North. [by] C.S. Manegold. Princeton University Press 2010 317p il map $29.95   **974.4**

1. Slaves -- Massachusetts 2. Massachusetts -- History 3. Slavery -- Massachusetts 4. Slavery -- United States 5. Slave trade -- Massachusetts

ISBN 978-0-691-13152-8; 0-691-13152-X

LC 2009030875

This book tells the story "of five generations of slave owners in colonial New England. Settled in 1630, . . . Ten Hills Farm, a six-hundred-acre estate just north of Boston, passed from the Winthrops to the Ushers, to the Royalls—all . . . dynasties tied to the Native American and Atlantic slave trades." (Publisher's note) Index.

"Full of rich historical detail, this is a story that needed to be told." Kirkus

Includes bibliographical references

Masur, Louis P.

The **soiling** of Old Glory; the story of a photograph that shocked America. Bloomsbury Press 2008 224p il $24.95   **974.4**

1. Demonstrations 2. Photojournalism 3. Busing (School integration) 4. Boston (Mass.) -- Race relations

ISBN 978-1-59691-364-6; 1-59691-364-9

LC 2007-31215

"On April 5, 1976, an antibusing rally in Boston grew violent when African American lawyer Ted Landsmark was attacked by some of the protesters. News photographer Stanley Forman captured the ruckus on film; one photo gained international attention and is the subject of this . . . study by Masur. . . . Masur writes descriptively about the photo while creating an ethnographic history of 1970s Boston, with diversions into the political and cultural uses of the American flag and the history of photojournalism in the United States. He also describes the aftermath of the photo's front-page publication. . . . A compelling story; highly recommended for all high school, public, and academic libraries." Libr J

Includes bibliographical references

974.5   Rhode Island

Barry, John M.

Roger Williams and the creation of the American soul; church, state, and the birth of liberty. John M. Barry. Viking 2012 464 p.   **974.5**

1. Puritans 2. Religion and politics -- United States 3. United States -- History -- 1600-1775, Colonial period 4. United States -- History -- 17th century 5. United States -- Civilization -- 17th century

ISBN 0670023051; 9780670023059

LC 2011032995

This book by John M. Barry offers a "look at how Roger Williams shaped the nature of religion, political power, and individual rights in America. . . . Americans have [always] wrestled with . . . two concepts that define the nature of the nation: the proper relation between church and state and between a free individual and the state. These debates began with the extraordinary thought and struggles of Roger Williams. . . . This is a story . . . set against Puritan America and the English Civil War. Williams's interactions with King James, Francis Bacon, Oliver Cromwell, and his mentor Edward Coke set his course, but his fundamental ideas came to fruition in America, as Williams, though a Puritan, collided with John Winthrop's vision of his 'City upon a Hill.'" (Publisher's note)

Includes bibliographical references (p. 427-438) and index

974.7   New York

★ **After** the fall; edited by Mary Marshall Clark ... [et al.] New Press 2011 xxiii, 263 p.p $26.95 **974.7**

1. September 11 terrorist attacks, 2001 -- Personal narratives

ISBN 978-1-59558-647-6; 9781595586476

LC 2011012833

This book was produced by "Columbia University's Oral History Research Office, headed by [the book's editor,] Mary Marshall Clark, [who] went to work immediately after September 11, 2001, and has now issued a selection from its hundreds of interviews with those most directly involved— first responders, victims' families, residents of lower Manhattan. . . . The interviews make clear the distance between those who will go on distressfully reliving their experience forever and those of us who were merely bystanders." (Columbia Journalism Review)

"The Columbia Center for Oral History (CCOH) is committed to building 'repositories of living memory,' and after 9/11 began to gather narratives from a variety of New York survivors and witnesses, eventually collecting over 600 histories. The skilled interviewers . . . are trained in oral history methods and richly summon forth from interviewees the repercussions of the attack on individuals, families, and communities. Those interviewed reflect a variety of perspectives, including both professional and unskilled workers, in the Twin Towers, neighbors, first responders, and many of New York's immigrant groups, including Muslims." Libr J

Anasi, Robert

The **last** bohemia; scenes from the life of Williamsburg, Brooklyn. Robert Anasi. Farrar, Straus and Giroux 2012 240 p. (alk. paper) $15.00 **974.7**
1. Brooklyn (New York, N.Y.) 2. New York (N.Y.) -- Social conditions 3. New York (N.Y.) -- Description and travel 4. New York (N.Y.) -- Social life and customs 5. Bohemianism -- New York (State) -- New York 6. Social change -- New York (State) -- New York 7. City and town life -- New York (State) -- New York 8. Williamsburg (New York, N.Y.) -- Social conditions 9. Williamsburg (New York, N.Y.) -- Description and travel 10. Williamsburg (New York, N.Y.) -- Social life and customs

ISBN 0374533318; 9780374533311
LC 2011051267

This memoir about Brooklyn, New York focuses on the "eternal clash between authenticity, art, and real estate development." Author "[Robert] Anasi witnessed Williamsburg's progress in the 1990s and 2000s from crime-ridden working-class neighborhood overshadowed by crumbling factories . . . to edgy arts scene and hipster mecca to end-stage self-parody as an unaffordably upscale 'Bohemian theme park.'" (Publishers Weekly)

Burns, Cherie

The **great** hurricane-1938. Atlantic Monthly Press 2005 240p il $24 **974.7**
1. Hurricanes 2. Northeastern States
ISBN 0-8711-3893-X
LC 2005-41211

The author discusses the hurricane of September 1938, which affected the northeastern United States from Long Island to Providence, Rhode Island.

The author "has dug up old newspaper accounts and local histories to reconstruct the terror and destruction that accompanied the 1938 hurricane. Those who suffered the most, of course, did not survive to tell their tales. Nearly 700 people died, and about 63,000 were left homeless. . . . Survivor's stories, however, give ample feeling for the power of the rain, tide, and wind." Nat Hist

Burrows, Edwin G.

Gotham; a history of New York City to 1898. {by} Edwin G. Burrows and Mike Wallace. Oxford Univ. Press 1998 xxiv, 1383p il maps hardcover o.p. pa $29.95 **974.7**
1. New York (N.Y.) -- History
ISBN 0-19-514049-4 pa
LC 97-39308

This history "begins with the Indian settlements and the subsequent seizure of the city by the Dutch in 1626 and continues up to the consolidation of the five boroughs in 1898. The authors . . . cover an extraordinary range of topics, including religion, race, gender and class, architecture, society and the arts, noted personalities, sports and the special customs immigrants brought with them." America

Includes bibliographical references

Calhoun, Ada

St. Marks Is Dead; The Many Lives of America's Hippest Street. by Ada Calhoun. W.W. Norton & Co. Inc. 2015 400 p. illustrations, map (ebook) $50; $27.95 **974.7**
1. Counter culture 2. Manhattan (New York, N.Y.)
ISBN 9780393249798; 039324038X; 9780393240382
LC 2015028040

This book, by Ada Calhoun, is a "narrative history of three hallowed Manhattan blocks . . . St. Marks Place. . . . Calhoun profiles iconic characters from W. H. Auden to Abbie Hoffman, from Keith Haring to the Beastie Boys, among many others. She argues that St. Marks has variously been an elite address, an immigrants' haven, a mafia warzone, a hippie paradise, and a backdrop to the film Kids—but it has always been a place that outsiders call home." (Publisher's note)

"As Calhoun traces the neighborhood's evolution from wealthy and respectable to gritty and poverty-stricken and back again, she shows how one street can become a microcosm of America's political and cultural history." Pub Wkly

Includes bibliographical references (pages 341-397) and index.

Clancy, Tara

The **Clancys** of Queens; A Memoir. Tara Clancy. Crown Publishers 2016 256 p. (hardcover) $27 **974.7**
1. Working class 2. Women -- United States 3. Queens (New York, N.Y.) 4. New York (N.Y.) -- Social life and customs 5. Queens (New York, N.Y.) -- Social life and customs
ISBN 9781101903117
LC 2016003555

This memoir, by Tara Clancy, "is not merely an authentic coming-of-age tale or a rowdy barstool biography. Chock-full of characters who escape the popular imaginings of this city, it offers a bold portrait of real people, people whose stories are largely absent from our shelves. Most crucially, it captures—in inimitable prose—the rarely-heard voices of New York's working-class women." (Publisher's note)

" The varied settings of her childhood, like the nautical-themed bar with regulars, including English Billy and a tall, mustachioed man known as Daisy, are full-fledged characters in themselves. As Clancy whirls with feverish tomboy energy from one escapade to the next, she gives a fantastically vivid view into her many worlds." Booklist

Cliff, Nigel

The **Shakespeare** riots; revenge, drama, and death in nineteenth-century America. Random House 2007 312p il $26.95 **974.7**

1. Poets 2. Actors 3. Authors 4. Dramatists 5. Riots -- New York (N.Y.) 6. Astor Place (New York, N.Y.) 7. New York (N.Y.) -- Social life and customs

ISBN 9780345486943; 0-345-48694-3

LC 2006-49139

"Cliff argues persuasively that 'the Astor Place riot,' as it came to be known, marked a turning point in America's search for a national identity. . . . [This] is an intriguing, thought-provoking book." Washington Post Book World

Includes bibliographical references

Dwyer, Jim

102 minutes; the untold story of the fight to survive inside the Twin Towers. [by] Jim Dwyer and Kevin Flynn. Times Books 2005 322p il $26; pa $15 **974.7**

1. September 11 terrorist attacks, 2001 2. World Trade Center terrorist attack, 2001

ISBN 0-8050-7682-4; 0-8050-8032-5 pa

LC 2004-55321

Dwyer and Flynn have "given us a fitting tribute to the people caught up in one of the great dramas of our time. And for people still haunted by the events of that day, reading '102 Minutes' provides a cathartic release." N Y Times Book Rev

Friend, David

Watching the world change; the stories behind the images of 9/11. Farrar, Straus and Giroux 2006 435p il $30 **974.7**

1. Documentary photography 2. World Trade Center (New York, N.Y.) 3. September 11 terrorist attacks, 2001 -- Pictorial works

ISBN 978-0-374-29933-0; 0-374-29933-1

LC 2005-36158

In this "analysis of how images of 9/11 and the 'war on terror' have altered our understanding of power, world politics, religion and identity, . . . [the author] successfully merges reportage and analysis as he interprets the images of falling towers, panic in Manhattan streets and prisoners at Abu Ghraib that have been burned into our brains." Publ Wkly

Includes bibliographical references

Gage, Beverly

The **day** Wall Street exploded; a story of America in its first age of terror. Oxford University Press 2009 400p il **974.7**

1. Bombings 2. Terrorism 3. Wall Street (New York, N.Y.) 4. Terrorism -- New York (N.Y.) 5. Terrorism -- United States -- History

ISBN 0-19-514824-X; 978-0-19-514824-4

LC 2008022074

This is an account of the "1920 terrorist attack on Wall Street—why it happened [and] how it shaped American politics." (Publisher's note) Index.

"Gage has performed a real service, both in presenting such a complicated case in such a fair and balanced way and in reminding readers how large a space terrorism once occupied on the political landscape." San Francisco Chron

Includes bibliographical references

Gill, Jonathan

Harlem; the four hundred year history from Dutch village to capital of black America. Grove Press 2011 520p il map $29.95 **974.7**

1. New York (N.Y.) -- Harlem

ISBN 978-0-8021-1910-0

"Comprehensive and compassionate—an essential text of American history and culture." Kirkus

Includes bibliographical references

Goodman, Matthew

The **Sun** and the moon; the remarkable true account of hoaxers, showmen, dueling journalists, and lunar man-bats in nineteenth-century New York. Basic Books 2008 350p il $26; pa $15 **974.7**

1. Fraud 2. Journalism 3. Moon 4. New York sun (Newspaper: 1833-1950)

ISBN 978-0-465-00257-3; 0-465-00257-9; 978-0-465-01900-7 pa; 0-465-01900-5 pa

LC 2008-23617

"These incredible events occurred during a great democratization of media, with affordable news for all and the seeds of pop culture beginning to take root. To read The Sun and the Moon is to enter a world of aeronauts, automaton chess players, and glorious lunar temples. It is the old New York of P.T. Barnum brought into incredible focus and Goodman's research couldn't be more comprehensive." PopMatters

Includes bibliographical references

Griswold, Mac

★ The **Manor**; Three Centuries at a Slave Plantation on Long Island. Mac Griswold. Farrar Straus & Giroux 2013 304 p. $28 **974.7**

1. Plantations 2. Slavery -- United States 3. Long Island (N.Y.) -- History 4. Long Island (N.Y.) -- Biography 5. Shelter Island (N.Y.) -- History 6. Sylvester Manor Plantation Site (N.Y.) 7. Slavery -- New York (State) -- Long Island -- History 8. Plantations -- New York (State) -- Long Island -- History 9. Excavations (Archaeology) -- New York (State) -- Long Island 10. Plantation life -- New York (State) -- Long Island -- History 11. Plantation owners -- New York (State) -- Long Island -- Biography

ISBN 0374266298; 9780374266295

LC 2013005463

This book is Mac Griswold's exploration of a 1652 plantation house on Long Island. She uncovers the histories of "those who lived in it or passed through its grounds: Native Americans, generation after generation of Sylvesters (the original owners), and—most surprisingly, considering that the Sylvesters were Quakers—the family's slaves." (Publishers Weekly)

Includes bibliographical references and index

In the Catskills; a century of Jewish experience in the mountains. Phil Brown, editor. Columbia

University Press 2002 xvi, 415 p.p illustrations $60 **974.7**

1. Jews -- United States 2. Catskill Mountains (N.Y.) 3. Catskill Mountains Region (N.Y.)/Social life and customs 4. Jews/Recreation/New York (State)/Catskill Mountains region 5. Catskill Mountains Region (N.Y.) -- Social life and customs 6. Jews/New York (State)/ Catskill Mountains Region/Social life and customs ISBN 0231123604; 9780231123600

LC 2001042319

"Through fiction, memoir, music, and art, this book offers a glimpse of the Catskills experience over a century and assesses its continuing impact on American culture. The book features contributions from such writers as Isaac Bashevis Singer and Vivian Gornick; and original contributions from historians, sociologists, and scholars of American and Judaic studies." Publisher's Note

"This is a great look at the history of Catskill culture for readers new to the material, but those looking for more depth will be disappointed." Pub Wkly

Includes bibliographical references (p. 393-412)

It happened in the Catskills; an oral history in the words of busboys, bellhops, guests, proprietors, comedians, agents, and others who lived it. Myrna Katz Frommer and Harvey Frommer. Excelsior Editions/ State University of New York Press 2009 245 p. il $24.95 **974.7**

1. Jews -- History 2. Catskill Mountains (N.Y.) ISBN 1438427484; 9781438427485

LC 2004054619

Originally published 1991 by Harcourt

Khan, Yasmin Sabina

Enlightening the world; the creation of the Statue of Liberty. Cornell University Press 2010 231p il $24.95 **974.7**

1. Artists 2. Sculptors 3. National monuments 4. Statue of Liberty (New York, N.Y.) 5. France -- Foreign relations -- United States 6. United States -- Foreign relations -- France ISBN 978-0-8014-4851-5; 0-8014-4851-4

LC 2009035711

This is "a lucid account connecting France's widespread grief over Abraham Lincoln's 1865 assassination with that country's own struggles to establish a lasting democracy. Khan shows how Édouard-René Lefebvre de Laboulaye, a legal scholar and celebrant of French-American friendship, led others to design and construct what was officially called Liberty Enlightening the World. . . . An important book for general audiences." Publ Wkly

Includes bibliographical references

Langewiesche, William

American ground, unbuilding the World Trade Center. North Point Press 2002 205p $22; pa $13 **974.7**

1. September 11 terrorist attacks, 2001 2. World Trade Center (New York, N.Y.) ISBN 0-86547-582-2; 0-86547-675-6 pa

LC 2002-75153

First published as a three part series of articles in Atlantic Monthly

"This is a genuinely monumental story, told without melodrama, an intimate depiction of ordinary Americans reacting to grand-scale tragedy at their best—and sometimes their worst." Publ Wkly

Lepore, Jill

New York burning; liberty, slavery, and conspiracy in an eighteenth-century Manhattan. Alfred A. Knopf 2005 323p il maps $26.95 **974.7**

1. Slavery -- United States 2. New York (N.Y.) -- History ISBN 1-4000-4029-9

LC 2004-57625

"In this first-rate social history, Lepore not only adroitly examines the case's travesty, questioning whether such a conspiracy ever existed, but also draws a splendid portrait of the struggles, prejudices and triumphs of a very young New York City in which fully 'one in five inhabitants was enslaved.'" Publ Wkly

Includes bibliographical references

MacColl, Gail

To marry an English Lord; by Gail MacColl and Carol McD. Wallace. Workman Pub. 1989 x, 403 p.p ill. (pbk.) $15.95; o.p. **974.7**

1. Marriage 2. Nobility 3. Great Britain -- History 4. Women -- Social conditions 5. Women -- United States -- History 6. England -- Social life and customs ISBN 9780761171959; 0894809393

LC 85040529

This book traces how "[f]rom the Gilded Age until 1914, more than 100 American heiresses invaded Britannia and swapped dollars for titles--just like Cora Crawley, Countess of Grantham, the first of the Downton Abbey characters Julian Fellowes was inspired to create [for the television program] after reading 'To Marry An English Lord.' Filled with . . . personalities, . . . anecdotes, grand houses, and . . . period details--plus photographs, illustrations, quotes, and the finer points of Victorian and Edwardian etiquette--'To Marry An English Lord' is [a] social history." (Publisher's note)

Martin, Wednesday

Primates of Park Avenue; a memoir. Wednesday Martin, Ph.D. Simon & Schuster 2015 256 p. (hardcover) $26 **974.7**

1. Mothers 2. Upper class 3. New York (N.Y.) 4. Primates -- Behavior 5. New York (N.Y.) -- Biography 6. Primates -- Behavior -- Miscellanea 7. New York (N.Y.) -- Social life and customs 8. Upper East Side (New York, N.Y.) -- Biography 9. Mothers -- New York (State) -- New York -- Biography 10. Interpersonal relations -- New York (State) -- New York 11. Upper East Side (New York, N.Y.) -- Social life and customs 12. Mothers -- New York (State) -- New York -- Social life and customs ISBN 1476762627; 9781476762623; 9781476762715

LC 2014041481

In this memoir, "Wednesday Martin decodes the primate social behaviors of Upper East Side mothers. . . . After marrying a man from the Upper East Side and moving to the neighborhood, ... Martin struggled to fit in. Drawing on her background in anthropology and primatology, she tried looking at her new world through that lens, and suddenly things fell into place. . . . . [S]he analyzed tribal migration patterns; display rituals; physical adornment, mutilation, and mating practices." (Publisher's note)

"This anthropological journey into the wilds of New York City's most exclusive zip code could have easily devolved into condescension, but instead it proves that mothers everywhere want the same thing: health and happiness for their progeny." LJ

Includes bibliographical references

McCourt, Malachy

A **monk** swimming. Hyperion 1998 290p $23.95; pa $14   **974.7**
1. Actors
ISBN 0-7868-6398-6; 0-7868-8414-2 pa
      LC 97-46720
"The memoir, which covers ground through 1963, will have readers smiling and laughing constantly." Publ Wkly

Singing my him song. HarperCollins Pubs. 2000 242p hardcover o.p. pa $14   **974.7**
1. Actors
ISBN 0-06-095548-1 pa
      LC 00-59774
In this sequel to A monk swimming, "McCourt tells us the rest of his story; how he got from there to here, how he went from living the headlong and heedless life of a world-class drunk to becoming a sober, loving father and grandfather, still happily married after thirty-five years." Publisher's note

Miller, Donald L.

★ **Supreme** city; How Jazz Age Manhattan gave birth to modern America. Donald L. Miller. Simon & Schuster 2014 784 p. illustrations, map $37.50   **974.7**
1. Manhattan (New York, N.Y.) 2. New York (N.Y.) -- History 3. New York (N.Y.) -- History -- 20th century 4. New York (N.Y.) -- Politics and government -- 1898-1951 5. New York (N.Y.) -- Social life and customs -- 20th century
ISBN 1416550194; 9781416550198
      LC 2013020154
This book, by Donald L. Miller, "is the story of Manhattan's growth and transformation in the 1920s and the brilliant people behind it. . . . As mass communication emerged, the city moved from downtown to midtown through a series of engineering triumphs--Grand Central Terminal . . . . the Holland Tunnel, and the modern skyscraper. In less than ten years Manhattan became the social, cultural, and commercial hub of the country. The 1920s was the Age of Jazz and the Age of Ambition." (Publisher's note)

"Conveying the panoramic sweep of the era with wit, illuminating details, humor, and style, Miller illustrates how Midtown Manhattan became the nation's communications, entertainment, and commercial epicenter." Pub Wkly

Includes bibliographical references and index

Reid, David

The **brazen** age; New York City and the American empire : politics, art, and bohemia. David Reid. Pantheon Books 2015 528 p. illustrations (hbk. : alk. paper) $30   **974.7**
1. New York (N.Y.) -- History 2. Bohemianism -- New York (N.Y.) 3. Greenwich Village (New York, N.Y.) -- History 4. New York (N.Y.) -- Civilization 5. New York (N.Y.) -- History -- 1898-1951 6. New York (N.Y.) -- Intellectual life -- 20th century 7. Bohemianism -- New York (State) -- New York -- History -- 20th century 8. Greenwich Village (New York, N.Y.) -- Intellectual life -- 20th century
ISBN 9780394572376
      LC 2015024900
This book, by David Reid, presents a "look at the extraordinarily rich culture and turbulent politics of New York City between the years 1945 and 1950. . . . [It] opens with Franklin Delano Roosevelt's campaign tour through the city's boroughs in 1944. . . . But the political tone would be set by the next president, and Reid looks closely at Thomas Dewey, Henry Wallace, and Harry Truman." (Publisher's note)

"Reid delivers his opinion in a score of unrelated but brilliant chapters on iconic New York individuals (Berenice Abbott, Weegee), groups (returning soldiers, homosexuals), politics (the 1948 elections, leftist magazines), and bohemia (Greenwich village again and again). A historical tour de force." Kirkus

Includes bibliographical references and index

Rips, Nicolaia

Trying to float; Coming of Age in the Chelsea Hotel. Nicolaia Rips. Scribner 2016 272 p. illustrations (hardcover) $25   **974.7**
1. Teenage girls 2. New York (N.Y.) 3. Eccentrics and eccentricities 4. Bohemianism -- New York (N.Y.) 5. Hotels and motels -- United States 6. Chelsea Hotel -- Biography 7. New York (N.Y.) -- Biography 8. New York (N.Y.) -- Social life and customs 9. Bohemianism -- New York (State) -- New York 10. Coming of age -- New York (State) -- New York 11. Girls -- New York (State) -- New York -- Biography 12. Teenage girls -- New York (State) -- New York -- Biography 13. Eccentrics and eccentricities -- New York (State) -- New York
ISBN 9781501132988
      LC 2016014365
In this memoir, "meet the family Rips: father Michael, a lawyer turned writer with a penchant for fine tailoring; mother Sheila, a former model and renowned artist who matches her welding outfits with couture; and daughter Nicolaia, a precocious high school junior at work on a record of her peculiar seventeen years. Nicolaia is a perpetual outsider. . . . But at the Chelsea, Nicolaia need not look far to find her tribe." (Publisher's note)

"This heartfelt memoir balances pathos and humor, proving that Rips, still only a senior in high school, is a promising writer who is wise beyond her years." Pub Wkly

Schneider, Paul

The **Adirondacks**; a history of America's first wilderness. Holt & Co. 1997 368p il maps hardcover o.p. pa $16   **974.7**
   1. Adirondack Mountains (N.Y.) -- History
   ISBN 0-8050-5990-3 pa

                   LC 96-39844

The author presents a "history of New York State's Adirondack region. He relates here the life and lore of these scenic mountains and lakes (Whiteface, Mt. Marcy, Fulton Chain Lakes) from the region's earliest inhabitants (Haudenosaunce/Iroquois) through the advent of Henry Hudson (1609), the Revolutionary War, abolitionists (John Brown), 19th-century homesteaders, Hudson River School artists, tuberculosis patients to Melville Dewey's Lake Placid Club, the Adirondack Mountain Club, and the present environmental conservation efforts." Libr J

Smith, Dennis

A **decade** of hope; stories of grief and endurance from 9/11 families and friends. [by] Dennis Smith with Deirdre Smith. Viking 2011 364p $26.95 **974.7**
   1. September 11 terrorist attacks, 2001 -- Personal narratives
   ISBN 978-0-670-02293-9

               LC 2011023325

The author, "a former firefighter, collects 25 moving personal narratives in this significant addition to the literature of September 11. Featuring notable figures such as NYPD Commissioner Ray Kelly and Congressman Peter King alongside rescue workers and victims' family members and loved ones, Smith's interviewees offer their experiences of that tragic day, illustrating how the pain and losses are still acutely felt. . . . With restraint and pathos, Smith's book provides powerful tribute and testimony." Publ Wkly

Stanton, Brandon

Humans of New York; Brandon Stanton. St. Martin's Press 2013 304 p. color illustrations (hardback) $29.99   **974.7**
   1. Photography 2. Street life 3. New York (N.Y.) 4. Photography, Artistic 5. New York (N.Y.) -- Pictorial works 6. Street photography -- New York (State) -- New York 7. City and town life -- New York (State) -- New York -- Hisotry -- 21st century -- Pictorial works
   ISBN 9781250038814; 9781250038821; 1250038820

              LC 2013027586

This book, by photographer Brandon Stanton, is "inspired by the blog [of the same name]. With four hundred color photos, including exclusive portraits and all-new stories, 'Humans of New York' is a stunning collection of images that showcases the outsized personalities of New York." (Publisher's note)

"There's the Yugoslavian janitor who studied for 12 years to earn his classics degree; Banana George, the world's oldest barefoot water-skier who's now in a wheelchair; Muslims in prayer; and shots of adorable kids, crazy fashionistas, and young lovers, all paired with a comment from Stanton or from the subjects themselves. There's no judgment, just

observation and in many cases reverence, making for an inspiring reading and visual experience." Pub Wkly

Humans of New York: stories; Brandon Stanton. St. Martin's Press 2015 432 p. chiefly color illustrations (hardcover) $29.99   **974.7**
   1. New York (N.Y.) 2. Portrait photography 3. New York (N.Y.) -- Biography 4. Interviews -- New York (State) -- New York 5. New York (N.Y.) -- Biography -- Pictorial works 6. Street photography -- New York (State) -- New York 7. New York (N.Y.) -- Social life and customs -- Pictorial works 8. City and town life -- New York (State) -- New York -- Pictorial works
   ISBN 9781250058904; 9781466886964; 1250058902

              LC 2015025568

  Alex Award (2016)

"In the summer of 2010, photographer Brandon Stanton began an ambitious project--to single-handedly create a photographic census of New York City. The photos he took and the accompanying interviews became the blog Humans of New York. Ever since Brandon began interviewing people on the streets of New York, the dialogue he's had with them has increasingly become as in-depth, intriguing and moving as the photos themselves." (Publisher's note)

"Photographer and author Stanton returns with a companion volume to Humans of New York (2013), this one with similarly affecting photographs of New Yorkers but also with some tales from his subjects' mouths. . . . A wondrous mix of races, ages, genders, and social classes, and on virtually every page is a surprise." Kirkus

Strausbaugh, John

The **Village**; 400 Years of Beats and Bohemians, Radicals and Rogues, a History of Greenwich Village. HarperCollins 2013 640 p. (hardcover) $29.99   **974.7**
   1. Bohemianism -- New York (N.Y.) 2. Greenwich Village (New York, N.Y.) -- History 3. Greenwich Village (New York (N.Y.) -- Social life and customs
   ISBN 0062078194; 9780062078193

In this book, author John Strausbaugh "traces the history of [Greenwich Village, New York City] . . . from its early settlement in the 1600s to the present day. He examines its role in the arts within the context of broader issues and periods such as Prohibition, World War II, McCarthyism, organized crime, and gay liberation. Among the writers, artists, and musicians discussed are Amy Lowell, Maxwell Bodenheim, Norman Mailer, Allen Ginsberg . . . and Edward Albee." (Library Journal)

Taylor, Alan

The **divided** ground; Indians, settlers and the northern borderland of the American Revolution. Alfred A. Knopf 2006 542p il maps $35; pa $16.95   **974.7**
   1. Iroquois Indians -- History 2. New York (State) -- History 3. United States -- History -- 1775-1783, Revolution
   ISBN 0-679-45471-3; 1-4000-7707-9 pa

              LC 2005-43582

"Taylor's exquisite writing and thorough research in both Canadian and US archives and manuscript collections make this a major work." Choice

Includes bibliographical references

Von Drehle, Dave

★ **Triangle**: the fire that changed America. Atlantic Monthly Press 2003 340p il hardcover o.p. pa $14   **974.7**

1. Fires 2. Factories 3. Clothing industry 4. New York (N.Y.) 5. Triangle Shirtwaist Company, Inc.

ISBN 0-87113-874-3; 0-8021-4151-X pa

LC 2003-41835

"Von Drehle's engrossing account, which emphasizes the humanity of the victims and the theme of social justice, brings on of the pivotal and most shocking episodes of American labor history to life." Publ Wkly

Includes bibliographical references

Ward, Geoffrey C.

A **disposition** to be rich; how a small-town pastor's son ruined an American president, brought on a Wall Street crash, and made himself the best-hated man in the United States. by Geoffrey C. Ward. Alfred A. Knopf 2012 418 p.   **974.7**

1. Financial crises 2. Capitalists and financiers 3. United States -- Biography 4. Swindlers and swindling -- United States -- History 5. New York (N.Y.) -- Biography 6. Rochester (N.Y.) -- Biography 7. Children of clergy -- New York (State) -- Biography 8. Swindlers and swindling -- United States -- Biography 9. Capitalists and financiers -- United States -- Biography 10. Financial crises -- United States -- History -- 19th century 11. Ponzi schemes -- New York (State) -- New York -- History -- 19th century

ISBN 0679445307; 9780679445302

LC 2011035140

This book by Geoffrey C. Ward looks at "American financial swindler . . . Ferdinand Ward. . . . The secret of his success was the classic pyramid scheme, which entailed paying off earlier investors with proceeds from newer ones. . . . In 1884, it all came crashing down . . . ruining countless individuals . . . and arguably contributing to the Panic of 1884. Ward went to prison but never acknowledged responsibility." (Library Journal)

Includes bibliographical references

974.71 New York (N.Y.)

Anbinder, Tyler

★ **City** of Dreams; Tyler Anbinder. Houghton Mifflin Harcourt 2016 768 p. illustrations, maps (ebook) $35; (hardcover) $35   **974.71**

1. Immigrants -- New York (State) -- New York -- History 2. New York (N.Y.) -- Emigration and immigration -- History

ISBN 9780544103856; 9780544104655; 054410465X

This book about immigrants features "memorable characters both beloved and unfamiliar, whose lives unfold in rich detail. . . . [Author] Tyler Anbinder's story is one of innovators and artists, revolutionaries and rioters, staggering

deprivation and soaring triumphs, all playing out against the powerful backdrop of New York City, at once ever-changing and profoundly, permanently itself." (Publisher's note)

"An endlessly fascinating kaleidoscope of American history. A fantastic historical resource" Kirkus

Includes bibliographical references (pages 579-700) and index.

Gopnik, Adam

Through the children's gate; a home in New York. Alfred A. Knopf 2006 318p $25   **974.71**

1. New York (N.Y.) -- Description and travel 2. New York (N.Y.) -- Social life and customs. 3. Home -- Social aspects -- New York (State) -- New York.

ISBN 1-4000-4181-3; 978-1-4000-4181-7

LC 2006-45260

"Gopnik writes about returning to New York after five years in Paris." (N Y Times Book Rev)

"You don't have to be a New Yorker or even necessarily an enthusiast of the city to be alternately amused, touched, and charmed by Gopnik's well-crafted pieces." Christ Sci Monit

974.73 New York - Hudson River Valley

Daughan, George C.

Revolution on the Hudson; New York City and the Hudson River Valley in the American War of Independence. George C. Daughan. W W Norton & Co Inc 2016 432 p. ill., maps, portraits (hardcover) $28.95   **974.73**

1. Hudson River (N.Y. and N.J.) -- History 2. United States -- History -- 1775-1783, Revolution

ISBN 9780393245721; 0393245721

LC 2016007017

This book, by George C. Daughan, tells "the untold story of the fight for the Hudson River Valley, control of which, both the Americans and the British firmly believed, would determine the outcome of the Revolutionary War. . . . It unpacks intricate military maneuvers on land and sea, introduces the personalities presiding over each side's strategy, and reinterprets the vagaries of colonial politics." (Publisher's note)

"A stimulating look at the American Revolution by a diligent historian and talented writer." Kirkus

Includes bibliographical references (pages [355]-395) and index.

974.8 Pennsylvania

Pennsylvania: a history of the Commonwealth; edited by Randall M. Miller and William Pencak. Pennsylvania State Univ. Press 2002 xxxi, 654p il maps $49.95; pa $29.95   **974.8**

1. Pennsylvania -- History

ISBN 0-271-02213-2; 0-271-02214-0 pa

LC 2002-5457

"More than half of this book is an unusual and inspired hybrid of history and nine other disciplines from geography to literature. . . . . The editors profess to discover the sources of Pennsylvania's greatness and significance but also expose its faults and declining significance in the 20th century. They succeed at both." Choice

975   Southeastern United States (South Atlantic states)

Blount, Roy
Long time leaving; dispatches from up South. [by] Roy Blount, Jr. Knopf 2007 383p $25   **975**
1. Southern States -- Humor 2. Southern States -- Civilization
ISBN 978-0-307-26618-7; 0-307-26618-4
LC 2007-6799
"This delightful collection is not only fun and funny but insightful as well." Libr J

Bragg, Rick
Ava's man. Knopf 2001 259p $25; pa $13 **975**
1. Carpenters 2. Factory workers
ISBN 0-375-41062-7; 0-375-72444-3 pa
LC 2001-32677
In this account of his maternal grandfather's life as a roofer and bootlegger in Appalachia, the author "creates a soulful, poignant portrait of working-class Southern life." Publ Wkly

Cash, Wilbur Joseph
The mind of the South; with a new introduction by Bertram Wyatt-Brown. Vintage Bks. 1991 xliv, 444p pa $16   **975**
1. Southern States -- Civilization
ISBN 0-679-73647-6
LC 91-50042
First published 1941 by Knopf
A psychological, cultural, and social history of the old South

Lemann, Nicholas
Redemption: the last battle of the Civil War. Farrar, Straus and Giroux 2006 257p $24   **975**
1. African Americans -- Segregation 2. Southern States -- Race relations
ISBN 978-0-374-24855-0; 0-374-24855-9
LC 2006-91
This book "offers a vigorous, necessary reminder of how racist reaction bred an American terrorism that suppressed black political activity and crushed Reconstruction in the South." N Y Times Book Rev
Includes bibliographical references

Southern living 50 years; a celebration of people, places, and culture. Sid Evans and the editors of Southern Living Magazine. Oxmoor House 2015 320 p. color illustrations (hardcover) $40   **975**
1. Southern cooking 2. Southern States -- Description and travel
ISBN 9780848744144; 0848744144
LC 2015942383

This book, by Sid Evans and the editors of the "Southern Living" magazine, celebrates the magazine's 50-year anniversary by profiling the Southern States. "Filled with evocative images, fascinating stories, revealing explorations, and time-honored recipes, [This book] . . . is about how Southerners live, what they value, how they cook, how they welcome people into their homes." (Publisher's note)

Theroux, Paul, 1941-
Deep South; four seasons on back roads. Paul Theroux. Houghton Mifflin Harcourt 2015 464 p. 16 unnumbered pages of plates (hardcover : alkaline paper) $29.95   **975**
1. Southern States 2. United States -- Description and travel 3. Seasons -- Southern States 4. Southern States -- Biography 5. Scenic byways -- Southern States 6. Southern States -- Social conditions 7. Southern States -- Description and travel 8. Southern States -- Social life and customs
ISBN 0544323521; 9780544323520
LC 2015006631
In this book author Paul Theroux "explores a piece of America—the Deep South. He finds there a paradoxical place, full of incomparable music, unparalleled cuisine, and yet also some of the nation's worst schools, housing, and unemployment rates. It's these parts of the South, so often ignored, that have caught Theroux's keen traveler's eye." (Publisher's note)
"Theroux's books always appear on the best-seller list, and his latest may prove to be his most popular book yet." Booklist
Includes bibliographical references and index

975.3   District of Columbia (Washington)

Bordewich, Fergus M.
Washington: the making of the American capital. Amistad 2008 367p map $27.95; pa $15.99 **975.3**
1. Washington (D.C.)
ISBN 978-0-06-084238-3; 0-06-084238-5; 978-0-06-084239-0 pa; 0-06-084239-3 pa
LC 2007-52053
The author explains "how the city's site was chosen and how political scheming, personal conflicts, and greed almost doomed the project of designing and constructing a capital city from scratch. Two themes are woven throughout his narrative: the important but often overlooked role played by slaves and former freed slaves and the constant North-South debate at the root of the bitter dispute over the capital's locale. . . . Bordewich introduces readers to the key players: George Washington, Thomas Jefferson, African American surveyor Benjamin Banneker, intractable and ill-fated architect and city planner Maj. Pierre Charles L'Enfant, the city's triumvirate of commissioners, and a host of pernicious financial speculators." Libr J
Includes bibliographical references

Brower, Kate Andersen

The **residence**; inside the private world of the White House. Kate Andersen Brower. Harper 2015 320 p. 16 plates; color illustrations $27.99 **975.3**
1. Presidents -- United States 2. White House (Washington, D.C.) 3. Presidents -- United States -- Biography -- Anecdotes 4. Washington (D.C.) -- Social life and customs -- Anecdotes 5. Presidents' spouses -- United States -- Biography -- Anecdotes 6. Presidents -- Family relationships -- United States -- Anecdotes 7. Children of presidents -- United States -- Biography -- Anecdotes 8. White House (Washington, D.C.) -- History -- 20th century -- Anecdotes 9. Household employees -- Washington (D.C.) -- Social life and customs -- Anecdotes
ISBN 0062305190; 9780062305190
LC 2014040404
This book by Kate Brower Anderson "reveals daily life in the White House as it is really lived through the voices of the maids, butlers, cooks, florists, doormen, engineers, and others who tend to the needs of the President and First Family. She reveals the intimacy between the First Family and the people who serve them, as well as tension that has shaken the staff over the decades." (Publisher's note)

"Fans of Downton Abbey will find this look into the secret world of the White House fascinating. History buffs who would like to learn more about the personal lives of the presidents and their families will definitely enjoy all the intriguing vignettes." LJ

Gordon, John S., 1944-

Washington's monument; and the fascinating history of the obelisk. John Steele Gordon. Blooms-bury USA 2016 224 p. illustrations (hardback) $27 **975.3**
1. Monuments 2. Washington Monument (Washington, D.C.) 3. Washington (D.C.) -- Buildings, structures, etc 4. Washington Monument (Washington, D.C.) -- History
ISBN 1620406500; 9781620406502
LC 2015036462
This book, by John Steele Gordon, examines the history of the Washington Monument. "The story behind its construction is a largely untold and intriguing piece of American history, which acclaimed historian John Steele Gordon relates with verve, connecting it to the colorful saga of the ancient obelisks of Egypt. Nobody knows how many obelisks were crafted in ancient Egypt, or even exactly how they were created. Their stories illuminate that of the Washington Monument." (Publisher's note)

"Filled with fascinating facts and interesting anecdotes, this is a book that will delight history and architecture buffs and enrich both past and planned visits to Washington, D.C., and its sights." Booklist

Includes bibliographical references (pages 215-216) and index.

Gugliotta, Guy

Freedom's cap; Guy Gugliotta. Hill and Wang 2012 viii, 486 p.p **975.3**
1. Capitols 2. Historic buildings -- United States 3. United States -- History -- 1815-1861 4. United States -- History -- 1849-1877 5. Washington (D.C.)

-- Buildings, structures, etc. 6. United States Capitol (Washington, D.C.) -- History
ISBN 9780809046812
LC 2011025750
This book takes place in "Washington [in the] 1850s. . . . [Author Guy Gugliotta provides an] account of the transformation of the U. S. Capitol from a[n] . . . inadequate . . . structure into today's massive marble symbol of democracy. . . . The author begins in the mid-1850s with the issue of Thomas Crawford's statue, 'Freedom,' now perched atop the Capitol dome. The . . . contest that Gugliotta outlines was between Army engineer Montgomery C. Meigs and architect Thomas Ustick Walter, both of whom would, at times, have control of the project. Both had ferocious work ethics, as well as enormous egos. . . . Gugliotta . . . includ[es] stories about marble quarries and ironworks; John Brown (whom he labels a terrorist); Presidents Fillmore, Pierce, Buchanan and Lincoln; and the many artisans and artists, principally Constantino Brumidi." (Kirkus)

Includes bibliographical references and index

Herken, Gregg

The **Georgetown** set; the establishment elite who waged--and won--the Cold War. by Gregg Herken. Alfred A. Knopf 2014 512 p. illustrations, map $30 **975.3**
1. Cold war 2. Washington (D.C.) -- Biography 3. Cold War 4. Georgetown (Washington, D.C.) -- Biography 5. Washington (D.C.) -- History -- 20th century 6. Georgetown (Washington, D.C.) -- History -- 20th century 7. Upper class -- Washington (D.C.) -- History -- 20th century 8. Washington (D.C.) -- Social life and customs -- 20th century 9. Political culture -- Washington (D.C.) -- History -- 20th century
ISBN 0307271188; 9780307271181
LC 2013047033
This book, by Gregg Herken, offers a "behind-the-scenes history of postwar Washington--a . . . portrait of the close-knit group of journalists, spies, and government officials who waged the Cold War over cocktails and dinner. . . . The Georgetown set included Phil and Kay Graham, . . . Joe and Stewart Alsop, . . . Frank Wisner, . . . and a host of other diplomats . . . and scholars responsible for crafting America's response to the Soviet Union from Truman to Reagan." (Publisher's note)

"Dense and scholarly with over 1,100 endnotes, this work will delight committed lay readers and scholars interested in political and diplomatic history, biography, and old-fashioned high society scandal." LJ

Includes bibliographical references and index

Katharine Graham's Washington; {compiled by} Katharine Graham. Knopf 2002 813p il $30; pa $16.95 **975.3**
1. Washington (D.C.)
ISBN 0-375-41471-1; 1-4000-3059-5 pa
LC 2002-111640
"The late newspaper publisher's posthumous legacy is a delightful and insightful anthology of writings on the city that formed so much of her personality and her professional life. She draws from her personal collection of writings by a range of writers, many of them personal friends." Booklist

Lusane, Clarence

The **Black** history of the White House. City Lights Books 2011 575p il (Open Media series)   **975.3**

1. Slavery -- United States 2. White House (Washington, D.C.) 3. United States -- Race relations 4. Presidents -- United States -- Staff 5. African Americans -- Washington (D.C.)

ISBN 978-0-8728-6532-7

LC 2010-36925

The author "offers a comprehensive and well-documented account of African Americans who have graced the White House as builders, slaves, servants, entertainers, policy professionals, and finally as the nation's First Family. . . . This is an important work of historical scholarship, bringing together chronicles of the African Americans who have played major roles in the annals of the presidential mansion." Libr J

Includes bibliographical references

Monkman, Betty C.

★ The **White** House; its historic furnishings and first families. principal photography by Bruce White. Abbeville Press 2000 320p il $65   **975.3**

1. White House (Washington, D.C.)

ISBN 0-7892-0624-2

LC 00-27085

"Monkman, the White House curator, documents the furnishings and decorative objects as well as the metamorphoses of White House interiors. The impact of the presidents and first ladies is particularly intriguing." Libr J

Includes bibliographical references

Snow, Peter

When Britain burned the White House; the 1814 invasion of Washington. Peter Snow. Thomas Dunne Books/St. Martin's Press 2014 320 p. 8 plates; illustrations; maps (hardcover : alk. paper) $25.99 **975.3**

1. War of 1812 2. United States -- Foreign relations -- Great Britain 3. Maryland -- History -- War of 1812 -- Campaigns 4. United States -- History -- War of 1812 -- Campaigns 5. Washington (D.C.) -- History -- Capture by the British, 1814

ISBN 1250048281; 9781250048288

LC 2014010743

In this book on the War of 1812, author "Peter Snow recounts the fast-changing fortunes of that summer's extraordinary confrontations. Drawing from a wealth of material, including eyewitness accounts, Snow describes the colorful personalities on both sides of those spectacular events: including the beleaguered President James Madison and First Lady Dolley, American heroes such as Joshua Barney and Sam Smith, and flawed military leaders like Army Chief William Winder." (Publisher's note)

"Although the author ultimately tells a riveting true story, he offers little new about the campaign, which is disappointing. Summing Up: Recommended. Public libraries/general collections." Choice

Includes bibliographical references and index

975.5   Virginia

Firstbrook, Peter

A **Man** Most Driven; Captain John Smith, Pocahontas and the Founding of America. Peter Firstbrook. Oneworld Publications 2014 352 p. illustrations $30   **975.5**

1. America -- Exploration

ISBN 1851689508; 9781851689507

In this biography of explorer John Smith, author "Peter Firstbrook traces the adventurer's astonishing exploits across three continents, testing Smith's claimed biography against the historical and geographical reality on the ground. [It] delivers an enlightening dissection of this mythology-making man and the founding of America." (Publisher's note)

"Firstbrook gives Smith the benefit of the doubt in his account of being saved from the Powhatans' chopping block by chief Wahunsenacawh's favorite daughter, Pocahontas—as befits an intrepid leader who was fiercely committed to the New World effort and instrumental in its survival over the first two murderous winters. Exciting historical tales with romantic overtones." Kirkus

Fox, James

Five sisters; the Langhornes of Virginia. Simon & Schuster 2000 496p il $30; pa $16   **975.5**

1. Members of Parliament 2. Spouses of prominent persons

ISBN 0-684-80812-9; 0-7432-0042-X pa

LC 99-41815

First published 1998 in the United Kingdom with title: The Langhorne sisters

"Irene Langhorne, the last great Southern belle, moved North in 1895, when she married Charles Dana Gibson, creator of the Gibson girl. In her wake, three younger sisters (her elder, Lizzie, was already married) burst onto the glittering society stage. Nancy, the most famous, married Waldorf Astor and threw herself into English political activism; Phyllis, the author's grandmother, was more introverted; Nora, with 'a heart like a hotel,' repeatedly led the family to the brink of scandal. Fox brings intimacy to these semipublic personalities, elevating a century's gossip and legend into absorbing history." New Yorker

Includes bibliographical references

Furgurson, Ernest B.

Ashes of glory; Richmond at war. Knopf 1996 419p il maps hardcover o.p. pa $16   **975.5**

1. Richmond (Va.) -- History 2. United States -- History -- 1861-1865, Civil War -- Campaigns

ISBN 0-679-74660-9 pa

LC 95-49591

The author "tells the story of a city that between 1861 and 1865 epitomized the experience of the Civil War as a revolutionary one. Capital of a state that had long opposed secession, Richmond now became the symbol of Southern independence. It also remained a center of clandestine Unionism that hosted a struggle between espionage networks matching anything seen in Cold War Berlin." Publ Wkly

Includes bibliographical references

Horn, James P. P.

A **land** as God made it; Jamestown and the birth of America. [by] James Horn. Basic Books 2005 337p il maps $26 **975.5**

1. Jamestown (Va.) -- History

ISBN 0-465-03094-7

LC 2005-13054

"Possessing Jamestown's inherent drama, this is a solid rendition of the saga." Booklist

Includes bibliographical references

Poole, Robert M.

Section 60; Arlington National Cemetery : where war comes home. Robert M. Poole. Bloomsbury 2014 256 p. illustrations, map (alk. paper) $27 **975.5**

1. Afghan War, 2001- 2. Iraq War, 2003-2011 3. Arlington National Cemetery (Va.) 4. Memorial Day 5. Families of military personnel -- United States 6. Afghan War, 2001- -- Casualties -- United States 7. Iraq War, 2003-2011 -- Casualties -- United States 8. Arlington National Cemetery (Arlington, Va.) -- History -- 21st century

ISBN 1620402939; 9781620402931

LC 2014017528

Author Robert M. Poole's book on Arlington National Cemetary presents a "biography of a five-acre plot where many of those killed in Iraq and Afghanistan have been laid to rest alongside service members from earlier wars. Poole recounts stories of courage and sacrifice by fallen heroes, and explores the ways in which soldiers' comrades, friends, and families honor and remember those lost to war-carrying on with life in the aftermath of wartime tragedy." (Publisher's note)

"Nonfiction enthusiasts will appreciate this work; it will especially satisfy those with an interest in the human condition. It is a book that will linger in the reader's mind." LJ

Includes bibliographical references and index

Section 60, Arlington National Cemetery

Arlington National Cemetery, where war comes home

Price, David

★ **Love** and hate in Jamestown; John Smith, Pocahontas, and the heart of a new nation. {by} David A. Price. Knopf 2003 305p maps $25.95; pa $14.95 **975.5**

1. Princesses 2. Colonists 3. Indian leaders 4. Travel writers 5. Jamestown (Va.) -- History

ISBN 0-375-41541-6; 1-4000-3172-9 pa

LC 2002-43437

"For those general readers who wish to move beyond the myths and obtain a better understanding of them and the early years of the colony, this book will be an enjoyable and valuable tool." Booklist

Includes bibliographical references

Taylor, Alan

★ The **internal** enemy; slavery and war in Virginia, 1772-1832. Alan Taylor. W.W. Norton & Co. Inc. 2013 624 p. (hardcover) $35 **975.5**

1. Virginia -- History 2. Slavery -- United States --

History 3. United States -- History -- 1783-1815 4. Virginia -- History -- War of 1812 5. Slaves -- Virginia -- Tidewater (Region) -- History 6. Slavery -- Virginia -- Tidewater (Region) -- History 7. Plantation life -- Virginia -- Tidewater (Region) -- History 8. United States -- History -- War of 1812 -- Naval operations, British 9. United States -- History -- War of 1812 -- Participation, African American

ISBN 0393073718; 9780393073713

LC 2013009643

Pulitzer Prize: History (2014)

Author Alan Taylor "illustrates that a great factor in the liberation of thousands of slaves was the policy and intervention of the British government and military. Taylor concentrates on the six decades between the American Revolution and the slave revolt of Nat Turner, and he focuses on the Chesapeake region of Virginia. The area is dotted with numerous rivers flowing to the bay, and here hundreds of slaves paddled out to British warships, especially during the War of 1812." (Booklist)

"Exemplary work of history by Pulitzer and Bancroft winner Taylor (History/Univ. of Virginia; Colonial America: A Very Short Introduction, 2012, etc.), who continues his deep-searching studies of American society on either side of the Revolution. The world the slaves made was one of fear and loathing—on the part of the masters, that is, who indeed waited in a 'cocoon of dread' for the day when their 'internal enemy' would finally pounce. That day first came with a series of events that form the heart of the book: namely, the arrival of the War of 1812 in Virginia...One of the ironies of the war, which would eventually produce just the uprising of the internal enemy the Virginians dreaded, was that, so inept was the federal response, it advanced the cause of states' rights, which would lead to the broader Civil War two decades after Nat Turner's revolt. Full of implication, an expertly woven narrative that forces a new look at 'the peculiar institution' in a particular time and place." (Kirkus)

Includes bibliographical references and index

975.6   North Carolina

Horn, James

A **kingdom** strange; the brief and tragic history of the lost colony of Roanoke. [by] James Horn. Basic Books 2010 296p il map $26 **975.6**

1. Roanoke Island (N.C.) -- History

ISBN 978-0-465-00485-0

LC 2010-563

"The author creates an engaging, you-are-there feel to the narrative, with rich descriptions of European politics, colonists' daily struggles and the vagaries of relations between Native American tribes. . . . A satisfying recounting of some of the earliest American history." Kirkus

Includes bibliographical references

975.7   South Carolina

Ball, Edward

Slaves in the family. Ballantine Books 1999 505p il map pa $17.95   **975.7**

1. Plantation life 2. Slaveholders 3. South Carolina 4. Plantation owners 5. Slavery -- United States 6. United States -- Race relations

ISBN 978-0-345-43105-9; 0-345-43105-7

First published 1998 by Farrar, Straus & Giroux

"For nearly a hundred and seventy years before the Civil War, members of the Ball family owned a string of plantations worked by slaves along South Carolina's Cooper River. After the war, the author's ancestors lost or sold their land and scattered to make new lives, but he wondered what happened to the slaves. This book, a brilliant blend of archival research and oral history, tells what he found." New Yorker

Includes bibliographical references

975.8   Georgia

Berendt, John

Midnight in the garden of good and evil; a story of Savannah. Random House 1994 388p $25; pa $14   **975.8**

1. Savannah (Ga.)

ISBN 0-679-42922-0; 0-679-75152-1 pa

LC 93-3955

"Berendt has fashioned a Baedeker to Savannah that, while it flirts with condescension, is always contagiously affectionate. Few cities have been introduced more seductively." Newsweek

★ Foxfire 40th anniversary book; faith, family, and the land. edited by Angie Cheek, Lacy Hunter Nix, and Foxfire students. Anchor Books 2006 xxxix, 512p il pa $17.95   **975.8**

1. Handicraft 2. Country life -- Georgia 3. Appalachian region -- Social life and customs

ISBN 0-307-27551-5; 978-0-307-27551-6

LC 2006-45311

"Drawing on the magazine's published talks by local high school students with elderly rural inhabitants, the books have explored the crafts, cooking, music, gardening and stories that have been passed down through the generations. The focus in this anniversary volume is on devotion to religion, family and the land. Collecting pieces from 40 years' worth of the magazine, the book inevitably covers topics covered in previous Foxfire collections, including snake handling, childhood toys and recipes. But the spoken words remain captivating, eloquent if plainspoken." Publ Wkly

Jones, Jacqueline

Saving Savannah; the city and the Civil War. Alfred A. Knopf 2008 510p il map $30   **975.8**

1. Savannah (Ga.) 2. United States -- History -- 1861-1865, Civil War

ISBN 978-1-4000-4293-7; 1-4000-4293-3

LC 2008-11508

"Synthesizing the perspectives of the mercantile elite, the aristocratic upper crust and the downtrodden, . . . [the author has] fashioned a compelling social and political history." Washington Post Book World

Includes bibliographical references

Pressly, Paul M.

★ On the rim of the Caribbean; colonial Georgia and the British Atlantic world. Paul M. Pressly. University of Georgia Press 2013 xii, 354 p.p (hardcover : alk. paper) $69.95   **975.8**

1. Georgia -- History 2. International trade 3. United States -- History -- 1600-1775, Colonial period 4. Georgia -- Economic conditions -- 18th century 5. Plantations -- Georgia -- History -- 18th century 6. Georgia -- History -- Colonial period, ca. 1600-1775 7. Georgia -- Commerce -- West Indies, British -- History -- 18th century 8. West Indies, British -- Commerce -- Georgia -- History -- 18th century

ISBN 0820335673; 0820345032; 9780820335674; 9780820345031

LC 2012033964

In this book, "Paul M. Pressly interprets Georgia's place in the Atlantic world in light of recent work in transnational and economic history." He "examines the ways in which Georgia came to share many of the characteristics of the sugar islands, how Savannah developed as a 'Caribbean' town, the dynamics of an emerging slave market, and the role of merchant-planters as leaders in forging a highly adaptive economic culture open to innovation." (Publisher's note)

"This richly documented, analytically complex, and well-written book is a major contribution to the study of Colonial Georgia and the 18th-century Atlantic world." Choice

Includes bibliographical references (p. [301]-335) and index

Sherrod, Shirley

The courage to hope; how I stood up to the right wing media, the Obama administration, and the forces of fear. Shirley Sherrod; with Catherine Whitney. 1st Atria Books hardcover ed. Atria Books 2012 240 p., [8] p. of plates p col. ill. (hardcover : alk. paper) $24.99; (trade paper : alk. paper) $15.00   **975.8**

1. Rural development 2. Sherrod, Shirley, 1948- 3. United States -- Race relations 4. Rural poor -- Georgia 5. Georgia -- Rural conditions 6. Rural development -- Georgia 7. Farmers -- Georgia -- Economic conditions 8. Mass media -- Objectivity -- United States 9. African American farmers -- Georgia -- Economic conditions 10. United States. Dept. of Agriculture -- Officials and employees -- Biography

ISBN 1451650949; 9781451650945; 9781451651010; 9781451651027

LC 2011050718

In this memoir, "[Shirley] Sherrod sets the record straight on her forced resignation from the Department of Agriculture in 2010. The author . . . was director for the USDA's Rural Development in Georgia when conservative political blogger Andrew Breitbart attacked her for allegedly reverse racist comments she made at an NAACP event. The threat of exposure on national TV was enough to send the USDA running for cover, and she was dismissed. Sherrod decided she had to fight back." (Kirkus Reviews)

Includes bibliographical references and index.

975.9   Florida

Allman, T. D.

Finding Florida. Pgw 2013 528 p. (hardcover) $27.50   **975.9**

1. Florida -- History 2. Political corruption

ISBN 0802120768; 9780802120762

This book by T. D. Allman offers a history of Florida that "spans half a millennium, from the myth of Ponce de León's Fountain of Youth to the 2012 shooting of 17-year-old Trayvon Martin, and it is a . . . cavalcade of would-be 'conquistadors,' epically corrupt and racist politicians, and oligarch-wannabes. Allman argues that these individuals' ideas about Florida were wildly wrong." (Booklist)

Gaines, Steven S.

Fool's paradise; players, poseurs, and the culture of excess in South Beach. Crown Publishers 2009 274p il $25.95   **975.9**

1. South Beach (Miami Beach, Fla.) -- Social life and customs

ISBN 978-0-307-34627-8; 0-307-34627-7

LC 2008-36067

This is a "terrific social history buffet. . . . [Gaines is] a gifted storyteller. He fills the book with telling anecdotes and bons mots, but the narrative never gets off track. It would be easy to focus on the drug-and-sleaze aspect of South Beach. But Gaines lets a little bit go a long way. He could fill the book with stupid celebrity tricks. But again, less is more. This book succeeds not because of star power but because of story power. The centerpiece of the book is a war of dueling architects and builders fighting to build the iconic Fontainebleau hotel and then to destroy it out of spite." St. Petersburg Times

Includes bibliographical references

Grunwald, Michael

The **swamp**; the Everglades, Florida, and the politics of paradise. Simon & Schuster 2005 450p il map hardcover o.p. pa $15   **975.9**

1. Everglades (Fla.)

ISBN 0-7432-5105-9; 978-0-7432-5105-1; 978-0-7432-5107-5 pa; 0-618-12749-6 pa

LC 2005-56329

This is a "chronicle of the history of the Everglades. . . . [This] is a riveting tale of ambition versus ecological reality, politics versus science, and, on the upside, our gradual awakening to the true nature of nature." Booklist

Includes bibliographical references

976.1   Alabama

Agee, James, 1909-1955

★ **Cotton** Tenants; Three Families. Random House Inc 2013 224 p. $24.95   **976.1**

1. Farm family -- Alabama -- History -- 20th century
2. Farm tenancy -- Alabama -- History -- 20th century

ISBN 1612192122; 9781612192123

This book, written during the Great Depression, was "commissioned by Fortune magazine' as a 'report on working conditions of poor white farmers in the deep south.' The report itself was never published. . . . It follows the lives of three impoverished tenant farmers--Floyd Burroughs, Bud Fields, and Frank Tingle--and their families". Topics include "diet, shelter, and labor". (Publishers Weekly)

Let us now praise famous men; [by] James Agee, Walker Evans; with an introduction to the new edition by John Hersey. Houghton Mifflin 2000 il $30; pa $18   **976.1**

1. Farm tenancy 2. Alabama -- Social conditions

ISBN 978-0-395-95771-4; 0-395-95771-0; 978-0-618-12749-8 pa; 0-618-12749-6 pa

First published 1941

This work documents "the ways of life of three Alabama tenant-farming families. . . . It is a unique and complex book, deeply honest and compassionate, and remarkable for its extraordinary descriptive, lyric, and meditative prose." Benet's Reader's Ency of Am Lit

McWhorter, Diane

Carry me home; Birmingham, Alabama: the climactic battle of the civil rights revolution. Simon & Schuster 2001 701p il hardcover o.p. pa $17 **976.1**

1. African Americans -- Civil rights 2. Birmingham (Ala.) -- Race relations

ISBN 0-684-80747-5; 0-7432-1772-1 pa

LC 00-53827

McWhorter presents an account of the struggle for civil rights in Birmingham, Ala., both from a personal and societal perspective

"A daughter of Birmingham's privileged elite, Mc-Whorter weaves a personal narrative through this startling account of the history, events, and major players on both sides of the civil rights battle in that city." Booklist

Includes bibliographical references

976.2   Mississippi

Welty, Eudora

One time, one place; Mississippi in the Depression : a snapshot album. rev ed; University Press of Miss. 1996 115p il $35   **976.2**

1. Mississippi -- Pictorial works

ISBN 0-87805-866-4

LC 95-46057

First published 1971 by Random House

This is a "collection of photographs of Mississippians that Welty took in the 1930s, when she worked for the Works Progress Administration (WPA). This Silver Anniversary Edition contains a great foreword by William Maxwell that absolutely nails the importance of the book for many readers." Booklist

976.3 Louisiana

Baum, Dan

Nine lives; death and life in New Orleans. Spiegel & Grau 2009 335p $26   **976.3**

1. New Orleans (La.) -- Social life and customs
ISBN 978-0-385-52319-6; 0-385-52319-X

LC 2008-31483

"Baum's in-depth reporting (he was on scene during Katrina, even turning himself in at the Convention Center to chronicle the out-of-sight outrages) is evident on every page." Booklist

Includes bibliographical references

Brinkley, Douglas

The great deluge; Hurricane Katrina, New Orleans, and the Mississippi Gulf Coast. Morrow 2006 716p il hardcover o.p. pa $17.95   **976.3**

1. Disaster relief 2. Hurricane Katrina, 2005
ISBN 0-06-112423-0; 0-06-114849-0 pa

LC 2006-43338

This is an account of Hurricane Katrina, which ravaged the Gulf Coast in late summer 2005.

The author "captures the human toll of Katrina as graphically as the most vivid newspaper and television accounts did, and by pulling together a huge, choral portrait of what happened during that first week of havoc and distress (from Saturday, Aug. 27, through Saturday, Sept. 3), he gives the reader a richly detailed timeline of disaster—a timeline in which the sheer cumulative power of details impresses upon us, again, just how abysmally inept relief efforts were on every level, from FEMA to the Red Cross to the New Orleans police department, from the federal government to state and local authorities." N Y Times (Late N Y Ed)

Dyson, Michael Eric

Come hell or high water; Hurricane Katrina and the color of disaster. Basic Civitas 2006 258p $23; pa $14.95   **976.3**

1. Disaster relief 2. Hurricane Katrina, 2005 3. African Americans -- Social conditions
ISBN 978-0-465-01761-4; 0-465-01761-4; 978-0-465-01772-0 pa; 0-465-01772-X pa

LC 2007-310210

This book on Hurrican Katrina "not only chronicles what happened when, it also argues that the nation's failure to offer timely aid to Katrina's victims indicates deeper problems in race and class relations. . . . [The author's] contention that Katrina exposed a dominant culture pervaded not only by 'active malice' toward poor blacks but also by a long history of 'passive indifference' to their problems is both powerful and unsettling." Publ Wkly

Includes bibliographical references

Horne, Jed

★ Breach of faith; Hurricane Katrina and the near death of a great American city. Random House 2006 412p map hardcover o.p. pa $16   **976.3**

1. Disaster relief 2. Hurricane Katrina, 2005 3. New Orleans (La.) -- Description and travel
ISBN 978-1-4000-6552-3; 1-4000-6552-6; 978-0-

8129-7650-2 pa; 0-8129-7650-9 pa

LC 2006-46468

This book does "an admirable job of detailing the design flaws that left New Orleans underwater." New Repub

Includes bibliographical references

Krist, Gary

Empire of sin; a story of sex, jazz, murder, and the battle for modern New Orleans. Gary Krist. Crown 2014 432 p. illustrations (hardback) $26   **976.3**

1. Prostitution 2. Crime -- United States 3. New Orleans (La.) -- History 4. New Orleans (La.) -- History -- 20th century 5. New Orleans (La.) -- Social conditions -- 20th century 6. Storyville (New Orleans, La.) -- History -- 20th century 7. Crime -- Louisiana -- New Orleans -- History -- 20th century 8. Murder -- Louisiana -- New Orleans -- History -- 20th century 9. Corruption -- Louisiana -- New Orleans -- History -- 20th century 10. Sex customs -- Louisiana -- New Orleans -- History -- 20th century 11. Storyville (New Orleans, La.) -- Social conditions -- 20th century 12. Jazz -- Social aspects -- Louisiana -- New Orleans -- History -- 20th century
ISBN 0770437060; 9780770437060; 9780770437084

LC 2014003191

This book, by Gary Krist, "re-creates the remarkable story of New Orleans' thirty-years war against itself, pitting the city's elite 'better half' against its powerful and long-entrenched underworld of vice, perversity, and crime. This early-20th-century battle centers on one man: Tom Anderson, the undisputed czar of the city's Storyville vice district, who fights desperately to keep his empire intact as it faces onslaughts from all sides." (Publisher's note)

"Krist's lively book is only marred by an overlong section devoted to a series of axe murders that plagued the city. A wild, well-told tale." Kirkus

Includes bibliographical references (pages 333-344) and index

Lane, Charles

The day freedom died; the Colfax massacre, the Supreme Court, and the betrayal of Reconstruction. Henry Holt and Co. 2008 326p il map $27   **976.3**

1. Massacres 2. Trials (Homicide) 3. Reconstruction (1865-1876) 4. Louisiana -- Race relations 5. African Americans -- History 6. United States -- Supreme Court
ISBN 978-0-8050-8342-2; 0-8050-8342-1

LC 2007-37514

"The Colfax Massacre . . . took place on an Easter Sunday afternoon in 1873. Within four hours, at least eighty black American men had been brutally murdered by white vigilantes in Colfax, La. Journalist Lane's groundbreaking and persuasive work illustrates this 'pivotal event in the political and constitutional history of post-Civil War America' and its social, political and judicial aftermath. . . . Students of American and African-American history will find it particularly valuable; fans of American history will find it a moving and instructive drama." Publ Wkly

Includes bibliographical references

Neufeld, Josh

A.D. New Orleans after the deluge. Pantheon Books 2009 193p il $24.95 **976.3**

1. Graphic novels 2. New Orleans (La.) -- Graphic novels 3. Hurricane Katrina, 2005 -- Graphic novels
ISBN 978-0-307-37814-9; 0-307-37814-4

LC 2008-55687

"Graphic artist Neufeld paints an emotive portrait of New Orleans during and after Hurricane Katrina, as seen through the eyes of seven of the city's citizens. The opening panels coalesce into a long cinematic pan, a thrumming set-up for the disaster. The half-page and quarter-page panels—satellite views of weather patterns and close inspections of neighborhoods—are crisp, and the two-page spreads are softly focused. . . . Neufeld's words and images are commensurable and rhythmic, and the vernacular is sharp. Bristling with attitude and pungent with social awareness." Kirkus

Rasmussen, Daniel

American uprising; the untold story of America's largest slave revolt. Harper 2011 276p map **976.3**

1. Slavery -- United States 2. New Orleans (La.) -- History 3. African Americans -- Louisiana 4. New Orleans (La.) -- Race relations 5. Slavery -- Louisiana -- New Orleans 6. African Americans -- Louisiana -- New Orleans 7. Slave insurrections -- Louisiana -- New Orleans
ISBN 0061995215; 0062084356; 9780061995217; 9780062084354

LC 2010017855

This is a history of the 1811 slave rebellion in New Orleans. Bibliography. Index.

This is an "account of a large-scale, three-day slave revolt on the sugar plantations near New Orleans during the 1811 Carnival (Mardi Gras) season. The author argues that the slave-rebels, who had learned warfare tactics in their native Africa, were inspired by the successful Haitian revolution. . . . This is a welcome addition to popular history and an engaging read for anyone interested in this important chapter in the tragic story of American slavery." Libr J

Includes bibliographical references

Rivlin, Gary

Katrina; After the Flood. Gary Rivlin. Simon & Schuster 2015 480 p. maps $27 **976.3**

1. New Orleans (La.) 2. Hurricane Katrina, 2005
ISBN 1451692226; 9781451692228

LC 2015431412

In this book, "ten years after Hurricane Katrina made landfall in southeast Louisiana--on August 29, 2005--journalist Gary Rivlin traces the storm's immediate damage, the city of New Orleans's efforts to rebuild itself, and the storm's lasting affects not just on the city's geography and infrastructure--but on the psychic, racial, and social fabric of one of this nation's great cities." (Publisher's note)

"Rivlin captures the snark, the bellyaching, and the outright denial of those in charge—and many aimed to be in charge (while many dodged responsibility as well). A fascinating lesson in urban planning in the face of calamity and financial shenanigans about what has been deemed 'the most expensive disaster in history.'" Booklist

Van Heerden, Ivor Ll.

The **storm**; what went wrong and why during Hurricane Katrina. [by] Ivor van Heerden and Mike Bryan. Viking 2006 308p il map hardcover o.p. pa $15 **976.3**

1. Disaster relief 2. Hurricane Katrina, 2005
ISBN 0-670-03781-8; 0-14-311213-9 pa

LC 2006-44727

This book focuses on public mismanagement relating to Hurricane Katrina.

"This serious, scientific explanation of what exactly happened in the hours—and years—leading up to Hurricane Katrina's devestation of New Orleans brings a fresh perspective to a tragedy that has generated remarkably similar news accounts over the past eight months." Publ Wkly

Includes bibliographical references

★ **Voices** rising; stories from the Katrina Narrative Project. edited by Rebeca Antoine; [afterword by Fredrick Barton] UNO Press 2008 244p pa $12.95 **976.3**

1. Hurricane Katrina, 2005 -- Personal narratives
ISBN 978-0-9728143-6-2; 0-9728143-6-1

In this "collection of personal narratives, readers come face-to-face with the stark reality wrought by Hurricane Katrina and the failure of the federal levees. . . . Every aspect of the post-Katrina New Orleans experience is present here, from areas as divergent as the I10 overpass, the French Quarter, and shelters across the South. The rescuers and rescued have equal voices and share memories poignant and startling. . . . Miles away from academic analysis, this is American social history from the ground up and staggering in its significance." Booklist

976.4 Texas

Davis, William C.

Three roads to the Alamo; the lives and fortunes of David Crockett, James Bowie and William Barret Travis. HarperCollins Pubs. 1998 791p il hardcover o.p. pa $20 **976.4**

1. Lawyers 2. Soldiers 3. Pioneers 4. Army officers 5. Texas -- History 6. Members of Congress 7. Alamo (San Antonio, Tex.)
ISBN 0-06-093094-2 pa

LC 97-43815

This "is a readable, stimulating, and exceptionally well-researched narrative history." Libr J

Includes bibliographical references

Donovan, James

The **blood** of heroes; the 13-day struggle for the Alamo-- and the sacrifice that forged a nation. James Donovan. 1st ed. Little, Brown and Co. 2012 x, 500 p.p ill., maps $29.99 **976.4**

1. Texas -- History 2. Alamo (San Antonio, Tex.) -- History 3. Alamo (San Antonio, Tex.) -- Siege, 1836
ISBN 0316053740; 9780316053747

LC 2011050067

This book chronicles "the Battle of the Alamo" which the author characterizes as "the signal event of the Texas struggle for independence.... [James] Donovan's ... story focuses on the 13-day standoff, but he also supplies ... context, helping us to understand the history of the breakaway province and notable characters in the revolution like [Sam] Houston, Stephen Austin, Ben Milam and James C. Neill." (Kirkus Reviews)

Includes bibliographical references (p. [467]-488) and index.

Roker, Al, 1954-

The **storm** of the century; tragedy, heroism, survival, and the epic true story of America's deadliest natural disaster : the great Gulf hurricane of 1900. Al Roker. William Morrow 2015 320 p. 8 plates; ills., maps (hardcover) $27.99   **976.4**

1. Storms 2. Natural disasters -- United States 3. Galveston (Tex.) -- History -- 20th century 4. Hurricanes -- Texas -- Galveston -- History -- 20th century

ISBN 0062364650; 9780062364654; 9780062364661

LC 2015007009

In this book, author Al Roker "brings to life the Great Gulf Hurricane of 1900, the deadliest natural disaster in American history. Exploring the impact of the disaster on a rising nation's confidence--the pain and trauma of the loss and the determination of the response--Al Roker illuminates both the energy and the limitations of the American Century, and of nature itself." (Publisher's note)

"Roker's account will interest readers who previously knew nothing about the Galveston hurricane. However, Isaac's Storm is not out of date and deserves its place as the recommended version." Kirkus

Includes bibliographical references

Valby, Karen

Welcome to Utopia; notes from a small town. Spiegel & Grau 2010 238p il $25   **976.4**

1. City and town life 2. Utopia (Tex.)

ISBN 978-0-385-52286-1; 0-385-52286-X

LC 2009-37970

"Entertainment Weekly magazine sent intrepid reporter Karen Valby into the great flyover zone in 2006 in search of a 'small town somewhere in America without popular culture.' She found Utopia, a town of a few hundred souls 90 miles west of the nation's seventh-largest city, San Antonio. Utopia is not exactly off the grid, and one suspects that its name appealed to Valby more than its isolation. Her book . . . is a pleasant moment-in-time postcard of a typical U.S. town." Minneapolis Star Tribune

Includes bibliographical references

976.6 Oklahoma

Hirsch, James S.

Riot and remembrance; the Tulsa race war and its legacy. Houghton Mifflin 2002 358p il $25; pa $14   **976.6**

1. Riots 2. Tulsa (Okla.) -- Race relations 3. African

Americans -- Tulsa (Okla.)

ISBN 0-618-10813-0; 0-618-34076-9 pa

LC 2001-51615

"Hirsch unearths an important episode in U.S. history with verve, intelligence and compassion." Publ Wkly

Includes bibliographical references

976.8 Tennessee

Kiernan, Denise

The **girls** of atomic city; the secret history of the women who built WWII's most powerful weapon. by Denise Kiernan. Simon & Schuster 2013 400 p. $26   **976.8**

1. Atomic bomb 2. Women -- Tennessee -- Oak Ridge -- History 3. World War, 1939-1945 -- Tennessee -- Oak Ridge 4. Oak Ridge (Tenn.) -- History -- 20th century

ISBN 1451617526; 9781451617528

LC 2012045467

This book by Denise Kiernan tells the "story of the young women of Oak ridge, Tennessee, who unwittingly played a crucial role in . . . enriching uranium for the atomic bomb. . . . Few could piece together the true nature of their work until the bomb 'Little Boy' was dropped over Hiroshima, Japan, and the secret was out. Kiernan traces the astonishing story of these unsung WWII workers through interviews with dozens of surviving women and other Oak Ridge residents." (Publisher's note)

Includes bibliographical references

Lauterbach, Preston

Beale Street Dynasty; Sex, Song, and the Struggle for the Soul of Memphis. Preston Lauterbach. W W Norton & Co Inc 2015 368 p. 8 plates; ills.; maps $26.95   **976.8**

1. Race relations 2. Political corruption 3. Memphis (Tenn.) -- History

ISBN 0393082571; 9780393082579

LC 2014039928

Author Preston Lauterbach presents this "history of Beale Street . . . and the battle for the soul of Memphis. Following the Civil War, Beale Street in Memphis, Tennessee, thrived as a cauldron of sex and song, violence and passion. But out of this turmoil emerged a center of black progress, optimism, and cultural ferment. Lauterbach tells this . . . story through the multigenerational saga of a family whose ambition, race pride, and moral complexity indelibly shaped the city." (Publisher's note)

"While sex and song (as promised in the book's subtitle) are present at times, this account is really about politics and power in a major Southern city. Recommended for all readers interested in Memphis or in African American history." LJ

977 North central United States

Barry, John M.

Rising tide; the great Mississippi flood of 1927 and how it changed America. Simon & Schuster 1997 524p il maps hardcover o.p. pa $16 **977**
1. Generals 2. Bridge engineers 3. Military engineers 4. Floods -- Mississippi River 5. Mississippi River valley -- History
ISBN 0-684-84002-2 pa

LC 96-40077

This is the "story of human defeat by a savage, unpredictable river. . . . The flood of 1927, three times greater than the flood of 1993, was an unprecedented disaster that spurred a political innovation. Congress's agreement to rebuild the Mississippi's shattered flood-control system marked the federal government's first assumption of full financial responsibility for a regional calamity. Much of the book recounts how the greed of New Orleans bankers and Delta planters increased the sufferings of the rural poor. . . . Barry's book is a virtuoso piece of exposition." New Yorker
Includes bibliographical references

Boissoneault, Lorraine

The Last Voyageurs; Retracing La Salle's Journey Across America: Sixteen Teenagers on an Adventure of a Lifetime. by Lorraine Boissoneault. W W Norton & Co Inc 2016 368 p. color illustrations, map $27.95 **977**
1. Teachers 2. Mississippi River 3. Voyages and travels
ISBN 1605989762; 9781605989761

In this book, by Lorraine Boissoneault, "Reid Lewis never wanted to be an ordinary French teacher. With the approach of the American Bicentennial, he decided to . . . [recreate] the voyage of René Robert Cavelier, Sieur de La Salle, the first European to travel from Montreal to the end of the Mississippi River. Lewis' crew of modern voyageurs was comprised of 16 high school students and 6 teachers." (Publisher's note)

"All the elements of an exciting adventure story are here. Boissoneault describes interesting, complicated people facing life-threatening perils, and in alternating Lewis's story with that of La Salle's journey, she makes fascinating historical comparisons." Pub Wkly

Dennis, Jerry

The living Great Lakes; searching for the heart of the inland seas. Thomas Dunne Bks. 2003 296p il maps hardcover o.p. pa $14.95 **977**
1. Great Lakes
ISBN 0-312-25193-9; 0-312-33103-7 pa

LC 2002-32500

The author offers a "description of being a crew member on the schooner Malabar on a six-week trip through the waters of Lakes Huron, Ontario, Michigan, Erie and Superior. . . . Dennis weaves anecdotes from his childhood, such as a family-fishing trip on Lake Michigan, together with informed commentary on the natural history of the lakes and the people who live there." Publ Wkly
Includes bibliographical references

Eckert, Allan W.

A sorrow in our heart: the life of Tecumseh. Bantam Bks. 1992 862p maps hardcover o.p. pa $7.99 **977**
1. Shawnee Indians 2. Indian chiefs
ISBN 0-553-56174-X pa

LC 91-31858

This is a "narrative biography of Tecumseh, the remarkable Shawnee warrior and statesman who succeeded in organizing a group of disparate tribes into a cohesive confederacy of nations. . . . Eckert places his subject firmly within his proper social and historical context by providing a tremendous amount of meticulously researched and authenticated background information, including illuminating details of tribal life and Shawnee culture." Booklist
Includes bibliographical references

Laskin, David

The children's blizzard; . HarperCollins 2004 307p map $24.95; pa $13.95 **977**
1. Blizzards
ISBN 0-06-052075-2; 0-06-052076-0 pa

LC 2005-295018

"An adroit, sensitive drama and a skillful addition to a popular genre." Booklist
Includes bibliographical references

977.1 Ohio

Gup, Ted

A secret gift; how one man's kindness--and a trove of letters--revealed the hidden history of the Great Depression. Penguin Press 2010 365p il $25.95 **977.1**
1. Charity 2. Businesspeople 3. Philanthropists 4. Great Depression, 1929-1939 5. Canton (Ohio)
ISBN 978-1-59420-270-4; 1-59420-270-2

LC 2010-17302

"As Gup interweaves the sagas of recipient families with the life of their anonymous benefactor, 'A Secret Gift' never fails to entertain, inform and sometimes astound." Cleveland Plain Dealer
Includes bibliographical references

Ryan, Terry

The prize winner of Defiance, Ohio; how my mother raised 10 kids on 25 words or less. foreword by Suze Orman. Simon & Schuster 2001 351p il $24; pa $13 **977.1**
1. Homemakers 2. Prizewinners 3. Defiance (Ohio) -- Biography 4. Prize contests in advertising
ISBN 0-7432-1122-7; 0-7432-1123-5 pa

LC 2001-18379

"Although Terry Ryan's father, Kelly Ryan, drank away most of his weekly machinist's paycheck, her mother responded by finding a use for her skill with words {by entering and winning contests}." (Women's Rev Books)

The author recounts the life of her mother, "a small-town Ohio housewife in the nineteen-fifties who lived on the brink of dire poverty, thanks to a brood of ten kids and an ineffectual drunk of a husband. Since Evelyn couldn't work outside her home, she worked inside it, penning hundreds of product jingles and entering them in the national contests that drove the advertising industry of the day." New Yorker

977.3   Illinois

Abbott, Karen

Sin in the Second City; madams, ministers, playboys, and the battle for America's soul. Random House 2007 xxiv, 356p il $25.95   977.3
1. Prostitution 2. Madams 3. Everleigh Club (Chicago, Ill.) 4. Prostitution -- Illinois -- Chicago 5. Chicago (Ill.) -- Social life and customs
ISBN 1-4000-6530-5; 978-1-4000-6530-1

LC 2006-51878

This book by Karen Abbott examines "the history of the Everleigh Club that operated on Chicago's Near South Side from 1900 to 1911. At this renowned high-class brothel, enterprising sisters Ada and Minna Everleigh challenged the stereotype of the victimized immature woman by hiring only willing adults whose comportment, education, meals, and health they closely monitored." (Library Journal)

"Lavish in her details, nicely detached in her point of view, [and with] scrupulous concern for historical accuracy, Ms. Abbott has written an immensely readable book. Sin in the Second City offers much in the way of reflection for those interested in the unending puzzle that goes by the name of human nature." Wall Street Journal

Includes bibliographical references

Cohen, Adam

American pharaoh: Mayor Richard J. Daley: his battle for Chicago and the nation; {by} Adam Cohen and Elizabeth Taylor. Little, Brown 2000 614p map hardcover o.p. pa $16.95   977.3
1. Mayors 2. Political party leaders 3. Chicago (Ill.) -- Politics and government
ISBN 0-316-83489-0 pa

LC 99-42157

"Penetrating, nonsensationalistic and exhaustive, this is an impressive and important biography." Publ Wkly

Includes bibliographical references

Dyja, Thomas

The third coast; when Chicago built the American dream. Thomas Dyja. The Penguin Press 2013 xxxiv, 544 p.p ill. (hardcover) $29.95   977.3
1. Chicago (Ill.) -- History -- 20th century 2. Chicago (Ill.) -- Social conditions -- 20th century 3. Chicago (Ill.) -- Relations -- United States 4. Chicago (Ill.) -- Intellectual life -- 20th century
ISBN 1594204322; 9781594204326

LC 2012039710

This book, by Thomas Dyja, explores the industrial and cultural history of Chicago, Illinois in the mid-20th century. "Much of what defined the nation as it grew into a superpower was produced in Chicago. . . . Yet even as Chicago led the way in creating mass-market culture, its artists pushed back in their own distinct voices. . . . Thomas Dyja re-creates the story of the city in its postwar prime and explains its profound impact on modern America." (Publisher's note)

"A readable, richly detailed history of America's second city." Kirkus

Includes bibliographical references and index

Miller, Donald L.

City of the century; the epic of Chicago and the making of America. {by} Donald Miller. Simon & Schuster 1996 704p il maps hardcover o.p. pa $18   977.3
1. Chicago (Ill.) -- History
ISBN 0-684-83138-4 pa

LC 96-4018

In this account of Chicago's history in the nineteenth century "Miller tells of Chicago's historical and literary figures, reform leaders, architects, industrialists, and entrepreneurs." Libr J

977.4   Michigan

LeDuff, Charlie

Detroit; an American autopsy. Charlie LeDuff. Penguin Press 2013 xvi, 286 p.p ill. (hardcover) $27.95   977.4
1. Detroit (Mich.) -- History 2. Detroit (Mich.) -- Economic conditions 3. Detroit (Mich.) -- Social conditions 4. Detroit (Mich.) -- Politics and government 5. Journalists -- Michigan -- Detroit -- Biography
ISBN 1594205345; 9781594205347

LC 2012030924

In this book, Charlie LeDuff profiles Detroit, Michigan. "Having led us on the way up, Detroit now seems to be leading us on the way down. Once the richest city in America, Detroit is now the nation's poorest. Once the vanguard of America's machine age . . . , Detroit is now America's capital for unemployment, illiteracy, dropouts, and foreclosures. . . . LeDuff sets out to uncover what destroyed his city." (Publisher's note)

Maraniss, David

Once in a great city; a Detroit story. David Maraniss. Simon & Schuster 2015 512 p. 16 plates; illustrations; maps (hardcover) $32.50   977.4
1. Detroit (Mich.) -- Economic conditions
ISBN 9781476748382; 1476748381

LC 2015017134

This book, by David Maraniss, "highlights the class and race frictions that demarcated and defined the city [of Detroit in the mid-20th century] and gives readers a glimpse of the colorful life of mobsters and moguls, entertainers and entrepreneurs. Among the famous Detroiters he highlights are Henry Ford II, Lee Iacocca, Berry Gordy Jr., George Romney, and the Reverend C. L. Franklin. Maraniss captures Detroit just as it is both thriving and dying." (Booklist)

"Although overstuffed with facts (for example, that Cavanagh 'kept four extra suits, thirteen striped ties,' and abundant shirts in his office for a quick change), and sometimes breaching the city's boundaries to become a history of the whole country, Maraniss' brawny narrative evokes a city still 'vibrantly alive' and striving for a renaissance. An illuminating history of a golden era in a city desperately seeking to reclaim the glory." Kirkus

Martelle, Scott

Detroit; a biography. Scott Martelle. Chicago Review Press 2012 xvi, 288 p.p **977.4**

1. Detroit (Mich.) -- History 2. Detroit (Mich.) -- Population 3. Detroit (Mich.) -- Economic conditions 4. African Americans -- Detroit (Mich.) -- History 5. African Americans -- Michigan -- Detroit -- History
ISBN 156976526X; 9781569765265

LC 2011041173

This book on Detroit, Michigan "recounts the rise and downfall of a once-great city, from its origins as a French military outpost to protect fur traders and tame local Indian tribes, to the industrial giant, known colloquially as Motown, and now when its "economy seized up like an engine run dry." Founded by a French naval officer named Cadillac, the city became a vibrant river town with the Erie Canal's opening, exporting both to the east and westward to Chicago. The 1855 opening of Lake Superior later expanded its postbellum shipping capacity and brought heavy industry. . . . But a series of downturns ravaged the city: the 1973 OPEC oil embargo helped destroy the city's auto-industry dominance, and drug-dealing gangs caused a murder rate that far out-stripped New York's." (Publishers Wkly)

Includes bibliographical references (p. 261-280) and index

McDonnell, Michael A.

Masters of Empire; Great Lakes Indians and the Making of America. Michael McDonnell. Farrar, Straus & Giroux 2015 402 p. illustrations, maps $35 **977.4**

1. Great Lakes region 2. Native Americans -- United States
ISBN 0809029537; 9780809029532

LC 2015022331

This book, by Michael A. McDonnell, "reveals the pivotal role played by the native peoples of the Great Lakes in the history of North America. Though less well known than the Iroquois or Sioux, the Anishinaabeg, who lived across Lakes Michigan and Huron, were equally influential. Masters of Empire charts the story of one group, the Odawa, who settled at the straits between those two lakes." (Publisher's note)

"McDonnell's scholarly yet compelling history will be a valuable addition to American history and Native American collections." Booklist

Includes bibliographical references and index.

977.7 Iowa

Blair, Joe

By the Iowa Sea; a memoir. Joe Blair. Scribner 2012 280 p. **977.7**

1. Adultery 2. Midlife crisis 3. Marriage problems 4. Middle aged men -- Biography 5. Iowa -- Biography
ISBN 1451636059; 9781451636055

LC 2011038073

This memoir describes "[o]ne man's midlife crisis surrounding love, marriage and parenthood. As a child, [Joe] Blair imagined his adulthood including motorcycles and the freedom to come and go as he pleased. Years later, he

was tied down with a heating-and-air-conditioning repair job, a wife, four children (one of them severely autistic), a mortgage and no motorcycle. . . . The author's need for a change became more urgent. Excessive drinking and sexual fantasies of his wife with another man were not enough, and Blair, desperate for an escape route, turned to another woman, finding passion and excitement in her arms. Internal confusion over his infidelity collided with the outer reality of his wife's anger, and the resulting changes surprised even the author." (Kirkus)

Includes bibliographical references and index

978 Western United States

Brown, Dee Alexander

The **American** West; photos edited by Martin F. Schmitt. Scribner 1994 461p il maps hardcover o.p. pa $17 **978**

1. Rodeos 2. Cowhands 3. Kiowa Indians 4. Apache Indians 5. Dakota Indians 6. Cheyenne Indians 7. Little Bighorn, Battle of the, 1876 8. Outlaws 9. Indian chiefs 10. Nez Percé Indians 11. West (U.S.) -- History 12. Frontier and pioneer life -- West (U.S.)
ISBN 0-684-80441-7 pa

LC 94-37444

"This narrative history of westward expansion paints a vivid portrait of the settlers, pioneers, entrepreneurs, and Native Americans of the old West. Useful as collateral research material and for recreational reading." Booklist

Includes bibliographical references

Buck, Rinker

The **Oregon** Trail; an American journey. Rinker Buck. Simon & Schuster 2015 464 p. illustrations, maps (hardcover) $28 **978**

1. Oregon Trail 2. Frontier and pioneer life -- West (U.S.) 3. Oregon National Historic Trail
ISBN 1451659164; 9781451659160; 9781451659177

LC 2015001159

This book, by Rinker Buck, presents an "account of traveling the length of the Oregon Trail the old-fashioned way. . . . Spanning two thousand miles and traversing six states from Missouri to the Pacific coast, the Oregon Trail is the route that made America. In the fifteen years before the Civil War, . . . it united the coasts, doubled the size of the country, and laid the groundwork for the railroads. Today, amazingly, the trail is all but forgotten." (Publisher's note)

"Recommended for folk interested in the Oregon Trail, pioneer history, or mules." LJ

Calloway, Colin G.

One vast winter count; the Native American West before Lewis and Clark. University of Nebraska Press 2003 631p il (History of the American West) $39.95 **978**

1. West (U.S.) -- History 2. Native Americans -- West (U.S.)
ISBN 0-8032-1530-4

LC 2003-44757

"Calloway concentrates on the Indian experience from the Appalachians to the Pacific, in a time frame from prehistory to the 18th century. The scope is staggering, but Calloway masters it, demonstrating a remarkable command of a broad spectrum of historical, ethnographic and archeological sources including printed material and oral traditions." Publ Wkly

Includes bibliographical references

Carter, Robert A.

Buffalo Bill Cody; the man behind the legend. Wiley 2000 496p il hardcover o.p. pa $18.95 **978**

1. Entertainers 2. Scouts 3. Hunters 4. Circus executives 5. Circus performers 6. Frontier and pioneer life -- West (U.S.)

ISBN 0-471-31996-1; 0-471-07780-1 pa

LC 00-20368

This is "a stolid sifting of facts from fiction." Booklist

Includes bibliographical references

Dary, David

★ The **Oregon** Trail; an American saga. Knopf 2004 414p il map $35 **978**

1. Oregon Trail 2. Frontier and pioneer life -- West (U.S.)

ISBN 0-375-41399-5

LC 2004-46512

The author "looks at the men and women who trekked the trouble-strewn paths to the nation's northwest coast. . . . Dary opens with 18th-century maritime explorers and carries us into the late 19th century, when the trail west from Independence, Mo., had ceded its importance to the railroads. . . . His closing chapter on the Oregon Trail's rebirth as a tourist draw in the 20th century is a real contribution to modern western lore. It's hard to imagine a more informative introduction to the westering itch along the Oregon Trail and to those who responded to it." Publ Wkly

Includes bibliographical references

Egan, Timothy

The **worst** hard time; the untold story of those who survived the great American dust bowl. Timothy Egan. Houghton Mifflin Co. 2006 340p ill., map $28; $28 **978**

1. Dust storms 2. Great Depression, 1929-1939 3. United States -- History -- 20th century 4. Great Plains -- History 5. Great Plains -- Social conditions -- 20th century

ISBN 061834697X; 9780618346974

LC 2005-08057

National Book Awards: Nonfiction (2006), Oklahoma Book Awards: Nonfiction Category (2006), Western Heritage Award: Outstanding Nonfiction (2007)

This book presents an "account of how America's . . . plains turned to dust, and how the ferocious plains winds stirred up an endless series of 'black blizzards' . . . in what became known as the Dust Bowl. But the plague was manmade, as Egan shows: the plains weren't suited to farming, and plowing up the grass to plant wheat, along with a confluence of economic disaster—the Depression—and natural disaster—eight years of drought—resulted in an ecological and human catastrophe. . . . [The author] grounds his tale in portraits of the people who settled the plains: hardy Americans and immigrants desperate for a piece of land to call

their own and lured by the lies of promoters who said the ground was arable." (Publishers Weekly)

"With characters who seem to have sprung from a novel by Sinclair Lewis or Steinbeck, and Egan's powerful writing, this account will long remain in readers' minds." Publ Wkly

Includes bibliographical references (p. 315-327) and index

Faulkner, Steven

Bitterroot; Echoes of Beauty & Loss. by Steven Faulkner. Midpoint Trade Books Inc 2016 384 p. illustrations, map $24.95 **978**

1. Pacific Northwest 2. Lewis and Clark Expedition (1804-1806)

ISBN 0825307929; 9780825307928

In this book, "using the letters of the 19th-century explorer Pierre Jean De Smet, Steven Faulkner and his eighteen-year-old son, Alex, follow De Smet across the High Plains to the fur trappers' rendezvous on the Green River, then on to the Lewis and Clark Trail. . . . By road, foot, mountain bike, and canoe, Steven and Alex experience the vast landscape and try to capture an understanding of the Wild Northwest." (Publisher's note)

"Faulkner's verbs vivify, his quotes enlarge his experience, and his poetic descriptions exploit all five senses colorfully; still, keener editing would have pared the backwoods baroque." Pub Wkly

Hyde, Anne F.

Empires, nations, and families; a history of the North American West, 1800-1860. Anne F. Hyde. University of Nebraska Press 2011 xv, 628 p.p **978**

1. Frontier and pioneer life -- West (U.S.) 2. Families -- West (U.S.) -- History -- 19th century 3. West (U.S.) -- Commerce -- History -- 19th century 4. Fur trade -- Social aspects -- West (U.S.) -- History -- 19th century

ISBN 0803224052; 9780803224056

LC 2011000174

Bancroft Prize (2012)

Pulitzer Prize Nominee (2012)

Includes bibliographical references and index.

McLynn, Frank

Wagons west; the epic story of America's overland trails. Grove Press 2002 509p il maps $32.50; pa $16.50 **978**

1. Overland journeys to the Pacific 2. Frontier and pioneer life -- West (U.S.)

ISBN 0-8021-1731-7; 0-8021-4063-7 pa

LC 2002-33859

This "account of the westward migration covers the years 1840-49, spanning the time between the eclipse of the mountain men and the beginning of the gold rush. . . . Relying on original diaries and memoirs, McLynn eloquently illustrates how diverse groups of people, including midwestern farmers, Native Americans, Mormons, and missionaries, played their parts in transforming the West while being transformed by it. This work will be a valuable addition to western history collections." Booklist

Includes bibliographical references

Raban, Jonathan, 1942-

Bad land; an American romance. Pantheon Bks. 1996 324p hardcover o.p. **978**

1. West (U.S.) -- History 2. West (U.S.) -- Description 3. Frontier and pioneer life -- West (U.S.)

ISBN 0-679-75906-9 pa

LC 96-13432

This "book about Montana examines the present remains and historical origins of the last great wave of American western settlement, the migration of homesteaders to eastern Montana in the first decade of this century." (London Rev Books)

Raban "turns Montana into a profound symbol for America's sense of displacement; for its tragic romance with rootlessness, its search for identity under that big blue sky." New Statesman (1913)

Schmidt, Thomas

The **Lewis** & Clark Trail; foreword by Stephen E. Ambrose. Bicentennial ed completely rev; National Geographic Soc. 2002 192p il maps pa $16 **978**

1. Lewis and Clark Expedition (1804-1806) 2. West (U.S.) -- Description and travel

ISBN 0-7922-6471-1

LC 2001-7003

First published 1998

Color photographs and maps provide a guide to the Lewis and Clark National Historic Trail

Sides, Hampton

Blood and thunder; an epic of the American West. Doubleday 2006 460p il $26.95 **978**

1. Navajo Indians 2. Scouts 3. Pioneers 4. West (U.S.) -- History 5. United States -- Territorial expansion 6. Frontier and pioneer life -- West (U.S.)

ISBN 978-0-385-50777-6; 0-385-50777-1

LC 2006-16579

This book "will surely capture readers, and it ought to. It's a riveting account of a vast swath of history with which few Americans are familiar." New Yorker

Includes bibliographical references

Slatta, Richard W.

The **cowboy** encyclopedia. Norton 1996 474p il pa $17 **978**

1. Reference books 2. Cowhands -- Encyclopedias

ISBN 0-393-31473-1

LC 94-19824

First published 1994 by ABC-CLIO

"Focusing on the cowboy experience in North and South America, The Cowboy Encyclopedia provides history, definitions, and commentary in an A-to-Z arrangement with major topics such as saddles and cowboy films receiving longer topical entries. Excellent cross-references and an extensive index provide easy access to all aspects of a topic. Appendixes cover cowboy films and videotape sources, museums, periodicals, and western cultural happenings." Am Libr

Slaughter, Thomas P.

Exploring Lewis and Clark; reflections on men and wilderness. Knopf 2003 231p il maps $24; pa $14 **978**

1. Slaves 2. Explorers 3. Lewis and Clark Expedition (1804-1806) 4. Interpreters 5. Guides (Persons) 6. Territorial governors 7. West (U.S.) -- Exploration

ISBN 0-375-40078-8; 0-375-70071-4 pa

LC 2002-69376

"It may be easy to dismiss as a nitpicking revisionist potshot at our beloved heroes, but as the expedition's bicentennial approaches, this book's perspective will help keep our understanding well nuanced and grounded in fact." Booklist

Includes bibliographical references

Stark, Peter

Astoria; John Jacob Astor and Thomas Jefferson's lost Pacific empire : a story of wealth, ambition, and survival. by Peter Stark. HarperCollins Publishers 2014 366 p. ill. (some col.), maps, port $27.99 **978**

1. Scientific expeditions 2. United States -- Exploring expeditions

ISBN 0062218298; 9780062218292

The launch -- The journey -- Pacific Empire and war -- Fate of the Astorians

This book, by Peter Stark, relates how "in 1810, entrepreneur John Jacob Astor proposed to Thomas Jefferson that Astor start a trading colony in what is now Oregon. . . . [Peter] Stark . . . chronicles Astor's mad dash to establish a fur-trading company, Astoria, which would capture the territory's wealth and allow Jefferson to inaugurate his vision of a democracy from sea to shining sea." (Publishers Weekly)

"A fast-paced, riveting account of exploration and settlement, suffering and survival, treachery and death." Kirkus

Includes bibliographical references and index

Ward, Geoffrey C.

The **West**; an illustrated history. narrative by Geoffrey C. Ward; based on a documentary film script by Geoffrey C. Ward and Dayton Duncan; with a preface by Stephen Ives and Ken Burns; and contributions by Dayton Duncan {et al.} Little, Brown 1996 445p il hardcover o.p. pa $24.95 **978**

1. West (U.S.) -- History

ISBN 0-316-73589-2 pa

LC 96-4323

"The book's eight chapters, each written by a different historian, are arranged according to the corresponding PBS series. Beginning with Western America in the 1500s, the work presents all aspects of Western culture from the reality to the myth, moving chronologically from the Spanish exploration of the West, Native Americans, Hispanic Westerners, women in the West, and the Gold Rush, and ending with Buffalo Bill's Wild West Show. If one is looking for an in-depth, comprehensive history of the westward movement, this is not it, but as an introduction, this work is an enjoyable and interesting place to start." Libr J

978.1   Kansas

Frank, Thomas
What's the matter with Kansas? how conservatives won the heart of America. Metropolitan Books 2004 306p map $24; pa $14   **978.1**
1. Conservatism 2. Kansas
ISBN 0-8050-7339-6; 0-8050-7774-X pa
LC 2004-44824
This is "a brilliant book, one of the best so far this decade on American politics." Nation
Includes bibliographical references

Stratton, Joanna L.
Pioneer women; voices from the Kansas frontier. introduction by Arthur M. Schlesinger, Jr. Simon & Schuster 1981 319p il hardcover o.p. $15   **978.1**
1. Women -- Kansas 2. Kansas -- History 3. Frontier and pioneer life -- Kansas
ISBN 0-671-44748-3 pa
LC 80-15960
"A unique book based on the memoirs of nearly 800 pioneer women who lived in Kansas between 1854 and 1890. . . . The book presents personal and detailed accounts of life inside homes, the schools, and the social organizations of early Kansas." Choice
Includes bibliographical references

978.3   South Dakota

Mort, Terry
Thieves' Road; The Black Hills Betrayal and Custer's Path to Little Bighorn. Terry Mort. Random House Inc 2015 340 p. 8 plates; illustrations; maps $25   **978.3**
1. Native Americans -- Wars
ISBN 1616149604; 9781616149604
LC 2014035457
This book, by Terry Mort, describes how "in the summer of 1874, Brevet Major General George Armstrong Custer led an expedition of some 1,000 troops and more than one hundred wagons into the Black Hills of South Dakota. This . . . work of narrative history tells the little-known story of this exploratory mission and reveals how it set the stage for the climactic Battle of the Little Bighorn two years later." (Publisher's note)
"This highly readable and insightful work is recommended as an essential backstory to Custer's subsequent downfall at the aforementioned battle." LJ

978.7   Wyoming

Black, George
Empire of shadows; the epic story of Yellowstone. George Black. St. Martin's Press 2012 548 p   **978.7**
1. West (U.S.) -- Exploration 2. Yellowstone National Park -- History 3. United States -- History -- 19th century 4. Native Americans -- West (U.S.) -- History 5.

Yellowstone National Park -- Discovery and exploration
ISBN 9780312383190; 9781429989749
LC 2011041351
This book is an "account of the discovery and imaginative creation of Yellowstone National Park is told through the lives of the park's colorful and often tragically egotistic explorers and promoters. . . . Waging an irreverent battle against now traditional fakelore, [George] Black particularly emphasizes Native American presence in the region of geysers, hot springs, and the headwaters of the Yellowstone River and the role of Lt. Gustavus Doane's military exploration, which opened the wonderland to international attention." (Libr J) "Divided into five sections and beginning with the familiar expedition of Lewis and Clark, the book spans nearly the entire 19th century. . . . As the book continues, the government enters with paleontologists, entomologists, botanists, and mineralogists, among others." (Kirkus)
Includes bibliographical references

Meyer, Judith L.
The **spirit** of Yellowstone; the cultural evolution of a national park. photographs by Vance Howard. Roberts Rinehart 2003 145p il pa $19.95   **978.7**
1. Human influence on nature 2. Yellowstone National Park
ISBN 1-570-98395-X
LC 2002-156320
First published 1996 by Rowman & Littlefield
The author "pays tribute to the park and all its glories, covering the park's history, its prime landmarks, and its prominence in art. The photographs are truly striking and not the typical landscape fare. Howard plays with light and texture to capture images that will amaze even those already familiar with the park's unprecedented beauty." Libr J
Includes bibliographical references

978.8   Colorado

Enss, Chris
Mochi's war; the tragedy of Sand Creek. Chris Enss and Howard Kazanjian. TwoDot, an imprint of Rowman & Littlefield Publishers 2015 184 p. illustrations (pbk.) $16.95   **978.8**
1. Cheyenne Indians 2. Prisoners of war 3. Sand Creek, Battle of, 1864 4. Cheyenne Indians -- Biography 5. Cheyenne Indians -- Wars, 1864 6. Native Americans -- Relocation 7. Sand Creek Massacre, Colo., 1864 8. Sand Creek Massacre National Historic Site (Colo.) 9. Prisoners of war -- Florida -- Castillo de San Marcos National Monument (Saint Augustine) -- Biography
ISBN 9780762760770; 076276077X
LC 2015005372
This book, by Chris Enss and Howard Kazanjian, focuses on "the brutal and unprovoked massacre of a sleeping village of Cheyenne and Arapaho peoples at Sand Creek (present-day Colorado) by troops of the Colorado Volunteers in November 1864. This still controversial military engagement sets the background in which Mochi, a Cheyenne woman, lost her entire family and barely survived herself, by killing a soldier and then fleeing her camp." (Library Journal)

"Highly recommended for adult readers of Western and Native American history, this biographical account provides a counterpoint to the many works that have mythologized such women as Pocahontas and Sacajawea." LJ

Includes bibliographical references and index

978.9   New Mexico

Childs, Craig Leland

House of rain; tracking a vanished civilization across the American Southwest. [by] Craig Childs. Little, Brown and Co. 2006 496p il map $24.99   **978.9**

1. Pueblo Indians 2. Southwestern States -- Antiquities 3. Chaco Culture National Historical Park (N.M.)

ISBN 978-0-316-60817-6; 0-316-60817-3

LC 2006-19112

"Beginning at the monumental cultural center of Chaco Canyon, where the Anasazi flourished, Childs's quest to understand their apparent disappearance leads him to the numerous great houses of New Mexico, such as Pueblo Bonito, to the Four Corners area of northeastern Arizona, southern Colorado and Utah, and beyond to northern Mexico. In these places, he identifies features that had not appeared prior to the apparent abandonment of Chaco (thus implying that the Anasazi migrated to these areas). Childs vividly weaves his personal narrative, imbued with a deep respect for the geography and cultural landscape, with scientific research and numerous interactions with foremost scholars." Libr J

979   Great Basin and Pacific Slope region of United States

Durham, Michael S.

Desert between the mountains; Mormons, miners, padres, mountain men, and the opening of the Great Basin, 1772-1869. University of Oklahoma Press 1999 336p il map pa $19.95   **979**

1. Mormons 2. Great Basin 3. Frontier and pioneer life -- West (U.S.)

ISBN 0-8061-3186-1; 978-0-8061-3186-3

LC 99-23572

First published 1997 by Holt & Co.

This is a history of the settlement of the Great Basin area in what is now Utah and Nevada.

"This is well-written history at its most easygoing." Publ Wkly

Includes bibliographical references

Groom, Winston

Kearny's march; the epic journey that created the American southwest, 1846-1847. Alfred A. Knopf 2011 310p il map $27.95; ebook $13.99   **979**

1. Generals 2. West (U.S.) -- History

ISBN 978-0-307-27096-2; 978-0-307-70141-1 ebook

LC 2011013889

"Groom brings to life the events of 1846–47 that transformed northern Mexico into the American Southwest during the Mexican War. He highlights General Stephen Ke-

arny's Army of the West and the taking of New Mexico and California, Captain John Charles Fremont's expedition to California and his administrative battle with Kearny, the Mormon Battalion attached to Kearny's army, Colonel Alexander Doniphan's capture of Chihuahua, and the civilian emigration horror of the Reed-Donner overland wagon train disaster. Groom's narrative of national political scheming and the constant threat of British involvement in the Mexican War creates an intriguing international drama." Libr J

Includes bibliographical references

Hutton, Paul Andrew

The **Apache** wars; the hunt for Geronimo, the Apache Kid, and the captive boy who started the longest war in American history. by Paul Andrew Hutton. Crown Publishing 2016 528 p. illustrations, map (hardcover) $30   **979**

1. Apache Indians -- Wars

ISBN 9780770435813; 9780770435837

LC 2015050712

This book, by Paul Andrew Hutton, is a "historical account of the manhunt for Geronimo and the 25-year Apache struggle for their homeland. They called him Mickey Free. His kidnapping started the longest war in American history, and both sides--the Apaches and the white invaders—blamed him for it. A mixed-blood warrior who moved uneasily between the worlds of the Apaches and the American soldiers, he was never trusted by either but desperately needed by both." (Publisher's note)

"What happened to Felix Ward is less important to the larger historical picture than how the situation with the Apaches was resolved, but Hutton provides an unexpected twist that keeps the story fresh until the end." Pub Wkly

Includes bibliographical references and index

979.1   Arizona

Dolnick, Edward

Down the great unknown; John Wesley Powell's 1869 journey of discovery and tragedy through the Grand Canyon. HarperCollins Pubs. 2001 367p il maps $27.50; pa $13.95   **979.1**

1. Explorers 2. Geologists 3. Large print books 4. Grand Canyon (Ariz.) 5. Colorado River (Colo.-Mexico) 6. Explorers -- United States -- Biography 7. Grand Canyon (Ariz.) -- Description and travel 8. Grand Canyon (Ariz.) -- Discovery and exploration 9. Colorado River (Colo.-Mexico) -- Discovery and exploration

ISBN 006019619X; 0060955864

LC 2001-24819

This is an account of Major John Wesley Powell's survey of the Grand Canyon. "Powell (one-armed since Shiloh) and nine men, six of them Civil War veterans, set out on May 24, 1869, at Green River Station on the Union Pacific Railroad in what was then Wyoming Territory. . . . One day before they reached the end of the canyon, three deserted, thinking that a rapids they could see ahead was certain death. These three climbed the walls of the canyon and were never seen again. The survivors came out into the flat country at the mouth of the Virgin River, ninety-nine days after they had set out." (Harpers)

"Dolnick, a science journalist who has rafted down the Grand, turns in a most estimable rendition of that storied expedition. It skillfully integrates the notes and journals of expedition members with technical insight about the perils of roiling whitewater." Booklist

Includes bibliographical references

Pasternak, Judy

Yellow dirt; an American story of a poisoned land and a people betrayed. Free Press 2010 317p il map $26; ebook $12.99 **979.1**

1. Navajo Indians 2. Uranium mines and mining
ISBN 1416594825; 1439100462; 9781416594826; 9781439100462

LC 2010-5546

"In the 1940s, when the U.S. government was embarking on developing atomic weapons, it discovered huge uranium deposits in Navajo territory covering parts of Utah, New Mexico, and Arizona. . . . The Navajo themselves saw little of the huge profits from uranium but as workers and land dwellers would suffer radiation exposure four times that of the Japanese targeted by the A-bomb. . . . Pasternak follows four generations of Navajo families, from the patriarch who warned against violating the land to those tempted by the prospects of jobs and money. . . . A stunning look at a shameful chapter in American history with long-lasting implications for all Americans concerned with environmental justice." Booklist

Includes bibliographical references

979.2 Utah

Walker, Ronald W.

★ **Massacre** at Mountain Meadows; an American tragedy. by Ronald W. Walker, Richard E. Turley, Jr., [and] Glen M. Leonard. Oxford University Press 2008 430p il map $29.95 **979.2**

1. Mountain Meadows Massacre, 1857
ISBN 978-0-19-516034-5

LC 2008-14451

The authors tell the story of "the titular 1857 tragedy in which 157 emigrants traveling to California were killed by local Mormons. With its understated prose, an essential purchase." Libr J

Includes bibliographical references

979.3 Nevada

D'Agata, John

About a mountain. W. W. Norton 2010 236p $23.95 **979.3**

1. Yucca Mountain Repository (Nev.) 2. Las Vegas metropolitan area (Nev.) -- Social life and customs
ISBN 978-0-393-06818-4; 0-393-06818-8

LC 2009-39295

D'Agata "uses the federal government's highly controversial (and recently rejected) proposal to entomb the U.S.'s nuclear waste located in Yucca Mountain, near Las Vegas, as

his way into a spiraling and subtle examination of the modern city, suicide, linguistics, Edvard Munch's The Scream, ecological and psychic degradation, and the gulf between information and knowledge. Acting as a counterpoint to Yucca is the story of a teenager named Levi who leapt to his death off Las Vegas' Stratosphere Motel. . . . A sublime reading experience, aesthetically rewarding and marked by moral courage and humility." Publ Wkly

Denton, Sally

The **money** and the power; the making of Las Vegas and its hold on America, 1947-2000. by Sally Denton and Roger Morris. Knopf 2001 479p hardcover o.p. pa $15 **979.3**

1. Gambling 2. Organized crime 3. Political corruption 4. Las Vegas (Nev.)
ISBN 0-375-70126-5 pa

LC 00-62011

"The idea of Las Vegas as the epitome of crass American pop culture has become at least a surface truism in most circles. But Denton and Morris . . . go much deeper than the surface in this sobering account of the famous Nevada resort town." Booklist

Includes bibliographical references

979.4 California

Brands, H. W.

The **Age** of Gold; The California Gold Rush & the New American Dream. by H.W. Brands. Anchor Books 2003 549 p. 16 plates; illustrations; maps $19.95 **979.4**

1. California -- History 2. California -- Gold discoveries 3. United States -- Civilization -- 1783-1865 4. United States -- Social conditions -- To 1865 5. California -- Gold discoveries -- Social aspects
ISBN 0385720882; 9780385720885

LC 200223776

This book, by H.W. Brands, focuses on the "gold rush of 1848. . . . For most of the hundreds of thousands who flocked to California, though, life in the mines of the Sierras was hard and rarely paid off. Yet the hopeful kept coming not only from the East but from around the world, with profound implications for California and the rest of the country." (Publishers Weekly)

"Combining this wealth of ideas with vivid biographies of actors great and small in the expansionist drama, Brands has produced a work that stands far above the tide of mostly forgettable titles that accompanied the 150th anniversary of the Gold Rush three years ago. A lucid, literate survey of events that transformed the nation, for better and worse." Kirkus

Didion, Joan

Where I was from. Knopf 2003 226p $23; pa $13.95 **979.4**

1. American national characteristics 2. California -- History 3. California -- Social conditions
ISBN 0-679-43332-5; 0-679-75286-2 pa

LC 2002-43325

This "is a complex and challenging memoir, difficult to enter into but just as difficult to put down. . . . Those who have long admired the clarity and precision of her prose will not be disappointed with this partly autobiographical, partly historical, but fully engrossing account." Libr J

Lee, Helie

In the absence of sun; a Korean American woman's promise to reunite three lost generations of her family. Harmony Bks. 2002 342p il maps hardcover o.p. pa $18.95   **979.4**
1. Korean Americans 2. Korea (North)
ISBN 0-449-91171-3 pa

LC 2002-1680

"Lee's Still Life with Rice (1996) was a novelized account of her grandmother's life and escape from what would become North Korea. As she now recounts her and her father's struggles to get other people out of the North, she continues to wrestle with her own Korean heritage—in particular, the paternalistic and patronizing attitudes toward women." Booklist

Menuez, Doug

Fearless genius; the digital revolution in Silicon Valley, 1985-2000. by Doug Menuez; foreword by Elliott Erwitt; introduction by Kurt Andersen. Atria Books 2014 192 p. illustrations (hardcover : alk. paper) $39.99   **979.4**
1. Microelectronics 2. High technology industry 3. Computer industry -- United States 4. Santa Clara Valley (Santa Clara County, Calif.) 5. Santa Clara Valley (Santa Clara County, Calif.) -- Pictorial works 6. Documentary photography -- California -- Santa Clara Valley (Santa Clara County) 7. High technology -- California -- Santa Clara Valley (Santa Clara County) -- History 8. Microelectronics industry -- California -- Santa Clara Valley (Santa Clara County) -- History
ISBN 1476752699; 9781476752693

LC 2013045228

This book, by Doug Menuez, is a "chronicle of the Silicon Valley technology boom, capturing key moments in the careers of Steve Jobs and more than seventy other leading innovators . . . [including] John Warnock at Adobe, John Sculley at Apple, Bill Gates at Microsoft, John Doerr at Kleiner Perkins, Bill Joy at Sun Microsystems, Gordon Moore and Andy Grove at Intel, Marc Andreessen at Netscape." (Publisher's note)

"Menuez even makes the innovators' solitude--sequestered behind drawn blinds for days or cordoned off from the rest of the pack in lonely cubicles--surprisingly compelling. The accompanying text is both complementary and instructive." Kirkus

Includes bibliographical references and index

Muir, John

The **Yosemite**; the original John Muir text. illustrated with photographs by Galen Rowell; each photograph accompanied by an excerpt from the works of John Muir and an annotation by Galen Rowell; intro-

duction by the photographer. Sierra Club Bks. 1989 218p il hardcover o.p. pa $14.95   **979.4**
1. Yosemite National Park (Calif.)
ISBN 0-87156-782-2 pa

LC 88-34919

New photographs complement Muir's classic 1912 natural history of the national park
Includes bibliographical references

Randall, David K.

The **King** and Queen of Malibu; The True Story of the Battle for Paradise. by David K. Randall. W W Norton & Co Inc 2016 256 p. illustrations $26.95   **979.4**
1. California -- History 2. United States -- History
ISBN 0393240991; 9780393240993

LC 2015038696

This book, by David K. Randall, "traces the path of one family as the country around them swept off the last vestiges of the Civil War and moved into what we would recognize as the modern age. The story of Malibu ranges from the halls of Harvard to the Old West in New Mexico to the beginnings of San Francisco's counter culture amid the Gilded Age, and culminates in the glamour of early Hollywood." (Publisher's note)

"An engaging story about wealth, entitlement, property rights, change, loss, and pain." Kirkus

Includes bibliographical references.

Stein, Jean

West of Eden; an American place. Jean Stein. Random House Inc 2016 352 p. illustrations (hardback) $30   **979.4**
1. Oral history 2. Hollywood (Calif.) 3. Los Angeles (Calif.) 4. Los Angeles (Calif.) -- History 5. Beverly Hills (Calif.) -- History 6. Los Angeles (Calif.) -- Biography 7. Beverly Hills (Calif.) -- Biography 8. Los Angeles (Calif.) -- Social conditions 9. Oral history -- California -- Los Angeles 10. Hollywood (Los Angeles, Calif.) -- History 11. Hollywood (Los Angeles, Calif.) -- Biography 12. Los Angeles (Calif.) -- Social life and customs
ISBN 9780812998405

LC 2015022411

This book, by Jean Stein, presents the "aspirations of five larger-than-life individuals and their families. . . . At the center of each family is a dreamer who finds fortune and strife in Southern California: Edward Doheny, the . . . oil tycoon; . . . Jack Warner, the son of Polish-Jewish immigrants; . . . Jane Garland, the troubled daughter of an aspiring actress; . . . Jennifer Jones, an actress. . . . Finally, Stein chronicles . . . her own father, Jules Stein, an eye doctor." (Publisher's note)

"Stein's exhaustive research and brand-new interviews make this an invaluable resource for any student of pop culture, or indeed of 20th-century American history." Pub Wkly

Williams, Mary

The **lost** daughter; Mary Williams. Blue Rider Press, A member of Penguin Group (USA) Inc 2013 320 p. $26.95   **979.4**
1. Abandoned children 2. Oakland (Calif.) -- Biography

3. Black Panther Party -- History 4. Adoptees -- California -- Biography 5. Mothers and daughters -- California -- Biography 6. Oakland (Calif.) -- Social conditions -- 20th century 7. African Americans -- California -- Oakland -- Biography 8. African Americans -- California -- Oakland -- Social conditions -- 20th century

ISBN 0399160868; 9780399160868

LC 2013001245

This book is a memoir by Mary Williams. Her "father was a [Black] Panther who served time in prison, her mother eventually succumbed to drinking and withdrew from family life, and her sister died a violent death. Traumatized by poverty and neglect at 16, Williams took the opportunity to flee to Santa Monica to live with Jane Fonda. . . . What followed was an extraordinary life of wealth and privilege." She discusses her achievements and her attempts to reconcile with her biological family. (Booklist)

Winchester, Simon

A **crack** in the edge of the world; America and the great California earthquake of 1906. HarperCollins 2005 462p il maps $27.95 **979.4**

1. Earthquakes -- California 2. San Francisco (Calif.) -- History 3. San Francisco (Calif.) -- Earthquake, 1906 4. Earthquakes -- California -- San Francisco -- History -- 20th century

ISBN 0-06-057199-3

LC 2005-46009

"Winchester writes about the earthquake and fire that destroyed San Francisco almost 100 years ago." (N Y Times Book Rev)

"In this brawny page-turner, . . . [the author] has crafted a magnificent testament to the power of planet Earth and the efforts of humankind to understand her." Publ Wkly

Includes bibliographical references

979.7 Washington

Kluger, Richard

The **bitter** waters of Medicine Creek; a tragic clash between white and native America. Alfred A. Knopf 2011 330p il map $28.95 **979.7**

1. Generals 2. Indian chiefs 3. Territorial governors 4. Territorial legislators 5. Puget Sound region (Wash.) 6. Nisqualli Indians -- History 7. Puget Sound (Wash.) -- History 8. Native Americans -- Washington (State) 9. Nisqualli Indians -- Government relations

ISBN 978-0-307-26889-1; 0-307-26889-6

LC 2010-34249

"When Isaac Stevens, territorial governor of Washington, implemented plans to move the Nisquallies from their ancestral lands to reservations in 1853, Chief Leschi turned from 'good Indian' to incendiary. Implacably opposed to removal to a place 'where the sting of an insect killed like the stroke of a spear, and the streams were foul and muddy,' he organized armed resistance to the whites in Washington. Gov. Stevens' resolve to punish him became an obsession. . . . [Kluger] recounts the confrontation between the two men. Meticulously researched, elegantly written and sophisticated, the book uses this all but forgotten episode in American

history to give a human face to the injustices visited on Indians in treaty-making, on the battlefield and, surprisingly, in the courtroom." Minneapolis Star Tribune

Krist, Gary

The **white** cascade; the Great Northern Railway disaster and America's deadliest avalanche. Henry Holt and Company 2007 315p il map $26 **979.7**

1. Avalanches 2. Railroad accidents

ISBN 978-0-8050-7705-6; 0-8050-7705-7

LC 2006-49047

"This is a tale in which snow falls, a mountain looms, and most of the protagonists simply sit. The outcome is predetermined. Mr. Krist does wonders with this unpromising material, however. Adopting a restrained, documentary tone, he slowly builds a picture of massing natural forces and helpless humanity, brought closer and closer to catastrophe with each tick of the clock. The pacing is expertly judged, and the potentially confusing narrative threads, involving multiple actors in scattered locations, are tied together neatly." N Y Times (Late N Y Ed)

Includes bibliographical references

Sone, Monica

Nisei daughter; Monica Sone; introduction to the 2014 edition by Marie Rose Wong; introduction to the 1979 edition by S. Frank Miyamoto; preface to the 1979 edition by the author. University of Washington Press 2014 238 p. (paperback : alkaline paper) $18.95 **979.7**

1. World War, 1939-1945 -- United States 2. Japanese Americans -- Evacuation and relocation, 1942-1945 3. Seattle (Wash.) -- Biography 4. Puyallup Assembly Center (Puyallup, Wash.) 5. Japanese Americans -- Washington (State) -- Seattle -- Biography

ISBN 9780295993553

LC 2013036826

In this memoir, author Monica Sone "tells what it was like to grow up Japanese American on Seattle's waterfront in the 1930s and to be subjected to 'relocation' during World War II. Along with over one hundred thousand other persons of Japanese ancestry—most of whom were U.S. citizens—Sone and her family were uprooted from their home and imprisoned in a camp." (Publisher's note)

979.8 Alaska

Borneman, Walter R.

★ **Alaska**: saga of a bold land. HarperCollins Pubs. 2003 608p il maps $34.95; pa $16.95 **979.8**

1. Alaska -- History

ISBN 0-06-050306-8; 0-06-050307-6 pa

LC 2002-27271

"Separated into nine chronologically based chapters, the text explores a recurring theme in Alaska's development: conflict among disparate groups over how the land would be used for personal enrichment. . . . Engaging chapters detail the important events and those who helped shape Alaska's history. . . . This expansive, comprehensive history is recommended for all libraries." Libr J

Includes bibliographical references

Heacox, Kim

Rhythm of the wild; a life inspired by Alaska's Denali National Park. Kim Heacox. Lyons Press 2015 304 p. (hardcover : alkaline paper) $25.95 **979.8**

1. National parks and reserves -- Alaska 2. Denali National Park and Preserve (Alaska) -- History 3. Natural history -- Alaska -- Denali National Park and Preserve 4. Denali National Park and Preserve (Alaska) -- Description and travel 5. Denali National Park and Preserve (Alaska) -- Environmental conditions 6. Nature conservation -- Alaska -- Denali National Park and Preserve (Alaska) 7. Landscape protection -- Alaska -- Denali National Park and Preserve (Alaska)

ISBN 1493003895; 9781493003891

LC 2014048442

This book, by Kim Heacox, is "an Alaska memoir focused on Denali National Park. . . . an Alaska memoir focused on Denali National Park. . . . We hitchhike with Kim through Idaho, camp on the Colorado Plateau, and fly off the sand cliffs of Hangman Creek with a little terrier named Super Max, the Wonder Dog." (Publisher's note)

"The park's wildlife—moose, eagles, red fox, sandhill cranes, grizzly bears, porcupines and wolves—share the stage with human actors in Heacox's chronicle. Topnotch environmental writing to shelve alongside George Perkins Marsh, Aldo Leopold, Robert Marshall and Barry Lopez." Kirkus

Includes bibliographical references and index

Jenkins, Peter

Looking for Alaska. St. Martin's Press 2002 434p il $25.95; pa $14.95 **979.8**

1. Alaska -- Description and travel 2. Alaska -- Social life and customs

ISBN 0-312-26178-0; 0-312-30289-4 pa

LC 2001-48871

This book "sparkles with adventure, quirky characters, unbelievable hardships, and indescribable beauty." Libr J

McPhee, John A.

Coming into the country; {by} John McPhee. Farrar, Straus & Giroux 1977 438p maps hardcover o.p. pa $15 **979.8**

1. Alaska -- Description and travel

ISBN 0-374-52287-1 pa

LC 77-12249

This book "is actually three lengthy bulletins about Alaska. . . . The first describes a canoe trip that McPhee and four companions took. . . . Second, McPhee tells of a helicopter ride with a committee looking for a site on which to build a new state capital. The last and longest section covers some wintry months spent in Eagle, a tiny settlement on the Yukon River." Time

Raban, Jonathan, 1942-

Passage to Juneau; a sea and its meanings. Pantheon Bks. 1999 435p $26.50; pa $15 **979.8**

1. Native Americans -- Art 2. Native Americans -- Folklore 3. Alaska -- Description and travel 4. Romanticism -- History -- 18th century 5. Inside Passage -- Description and travel 6. Northwest, Pacific -- Description and travel 7. Northwest Coast of North America -- Description 8. Northwest Coast of North America -- Description and travel

ISBN 0-679-44262-6; 0-679-77614-1 pa

LC 99-28777

"Sailing from Seattle to Alaska, {Raban} aims to replicate the 1792 explorations of English Capt. George Vancouver. . . . Then, suddenly, in the middle of his trip, Raban's father dies. . . . In the last half of the book, Raban finishes out his itinerary while reckoning with his father's memory." (Newsweek)

"Long fascinated by the Inside Passage (the protected waterway that runs from Washington State up to Alaska), Raban casts off in his 35'ketch from his home port in Seattle to follow in the wake of generations of salmon fishermen. He draws a rather dark portrait of the region as he fills out its history, through the cranky journals of Captain Vancouver and others, and meditates on the beautiful but threatening and lonesome landscape, with its struggling communities, submerged mountains, tricky waters, and names like Deception Pass and Desolation Sound." Libr J

980 History of South America

Brown, Matthew

From Frontiers to Football; An Alternative History of Latin America Since 1800. by Matthew Brown. University of Chicago Press 2014 224 p. illustrations, map $30 **980**

1. Latin America -- History

ISBN 1780233531; 9781780233536

In this book, author Matthew Brown "provides a much-needed historical analysis to rebut misconceptions about Latin America's past while giving readers the tools with which to understand the region's complex present. . . . Brown restores a cultural history to the continent, giving as much attention to pop singer Shakira and retired footballer Pelé as he does to coffee producers, copper miners, government policies, and covert imperialism." (Publisher's note)

"Brown highlights cultural figures such as footballer Pelé, novelist and Nobel Peace Prize-winner Rigoberto Menchú, cyclist Lucho Herrera, and musical superstar Shakira alongside political figures such as Chilean dictator Augusto Pinochet, Brazilian President Luiz Inácio Lula da Silva, and Venezuelan President Hugo Chavez. This book is an excellent starting point for readers looking for an introduction to Latin American history." Pub Wkly

Casey, Michael

Che's afterlife; the legacy of an image. Vintage Books 2009 388p il pa $15.95 **980**

1. Physicians 2. Photographers 3. Revolutionaries

ISBN 978-0-307-27930-9; 0-307-27930-8

LC 2008-32186

Casey "has written a book that is not only a cultural history of an image, but also a sociopolitical study of the mechanisms of fame. It is a book about how ideas travel and mutate in this age of globalization, how concepts of political ideology have increasingly come to be trumped by notions of commerce and cool and chic, and how the historical Che

Guevara gave way, postmortem, to a host of other Ches." N Y Times (Late N Y Ed)

Includes bibliographical references.

Chasteen, John Charles

Born in blood and fire; a concise history of Latin America. 2nd ed; W.W. Norton 2006 372p il map pa $43.25 **980**

1. Latin America -- History

ISBN 978-0-393-92769-6; 0-393-92769-5

LC 2005-48248

First published 2000

"Chasteen focuses on major political, social and economic topics and trends that helped shape Latin America, including liberalism, the caste system, the mixing of races, nationalism and the Western notion of 'Progress'; he also examines the role that Europe and the United States played in the development of these phenomena. Also refreshing is Chasteen's examination of the periods he covers from the perspective of women." Publ Wkly [review of 2000 edition]

Includes bibliographical references

Thomas, Hugh

Rivers of gold; the rise of the Spanish Empire, from Columbus to Magellan. Random House 2003 xxi, 696p il map $35 **980**

1. Spain -- Colonies 2. America -- Exploration

ISBN 0-375-50204-1

LC 2003-69316

"Engagingly presented, this book clearly shows the author's passion for his subject." Booklist

Includes bibliographical references

Williamson, Edwin

The **Penguin** history of Latin America; Edwin Williamson. Penguin Books 2010 705p ill., maps pa $20 **980**

1. Latin America -- History

ISBN 9780141034751

LC 2005-412242

"The book is organized topically, rather than by country, and the author wisely selected regional examples of his major themes, rather than attempting a detailed analysis of each country. The work ends with an unusual exploration of literature and culture in relation to identity and modernization, followed by a helpful bibliographic essay." Libr J

Includes bibliographical references

981 Brazil

Meade, Teresa

A **brief** history of Brazil; [by] Teresa A. Meade. 2nd ed; Facts On File 2009 280p il (Brief history) $49.50; pa $19.95 **981**

1. Brazil -- History

ISBN 978-0-8160-7788-5; 0-8160-7788-6; 978-0-8160-7789-2 pap; 0-8160-7789-4 pap; 978-1-4381-2736-1 ebook

LC 2009-33853

First published 2003

An account of Brazil's political, economic, and cultural landscape.

Includes bibliographical references

Reel, Monte

The **last** of the tribe; the epic quest to save a lone man in the Amazon. Scribner 2010 273p il map $26 **981**

1. Native Americans -- Brazil 2. Guapore River valley (Brazil and Bolivia)

ISBN 978-1-4165-9474-1; 1-4165-9474-4

LC 2009-37974

"In the opening scene of Monte Reel's 'The Last of the Tribe,' Brazilian government workers approach the deep jungle hideout of an Amazonian Indian they suspect to be the last living member of his tribe. The Indian sits in his hut, cornered, an arrow drawn on his bow, and waits. After two hours, the standoff ends. The government workers leave; the Indian disappears into the jungle. Again. 'The Last of the Tribe' is the story of the 20-year pursuit of that solitary Indian by aid workers who want to contact and protect him, and by loggers and miners who want him dead or moved before he gives the government a reason to protect more land from resource extraction. . . . Reel's tale is expertly told: perfectly timed, thoroughly researched and descriptively written." San Francisco Chron

Includes bibliographical references

Skidmore, Thomas E.

Brazil; five centuries of change. Oxford Univ. Press 1999 254p maps hardcover o.p. pa $28.95 **981**

1. Brazil

ISBN 0-19-505810-0 pa

LC 98-23122

Skidmore explores the country's "history, its political and economic development, and social and racial relationships. . . . This is a well-researched look at a fascinating country." Booklist

Includes bibliographical references

Whitaker, Robert

The **mapmaker's** wife; a true tale of love, murder, and survival in the Amazon. Basic Books 2004 352p il maps $25 **981**

1. Travelers 2. Scientific expeditions 3. Amazon River valley

ISBN 0-7382-0808-6; 978-0-7382-0808-4

LC 2003-26902

"The harrowing journey of Isabel Godin across the Andes and down the Amazon to rejoin her husband after a 20-year separation is only a small part of the extended history of the Charles-Marie de la Condamine expedition, which in turn is set within its context of the history of Enlightenment science, 18th-century mapping methods, the debate over the shape of the earth, and the sorry history of the Spanish and Portuguese conquest of South America." Sci Books Films

Includes bibliographical references

981.53 Brazil--Rio de Janeiro

Barbassa, Juliana

Dancing With the Devil in the City of God; Rio de Janeiro and the Olympic Dream. Juliana Barbassa. Simon & Schuster 2015 336 p. color illustrations, map (ebook) $16.99; (hardback : alkaline paper) $27   **981.53**

1. Social problems -- Brazil -- Rio de Janeiro 2. City and town life -- Brazil -- Rio de Janeiro 3. Rio de Janeiro (Brazil) -- Economic conditions 4. Economic development -- Brazil -- Rio de Janeiro

ISBN 9781476756271; 1476756252; 9781476756257

LC 2014042530

In this book by Juliana Barbassa, "Rio has always aspired to the pantheon of global capitals, and under the spotlight of the 2014 World Cup and the 2016 Olympic Games it seems that its moment has come. But in order to prepare itself for the world stage, Rio must vanquish the entrenched problems that Barbassa recalls from her childhood. Turning this beautiful but deeply flawed place into a pristine showcase of the best that Brazil has to offer." (Publisher's note)

"Her interviews with police, prostitutes, drug dealers, ecologists, businesspeople, academics, movers and shakers, and the moved and shaken offer a fascinating look at the people who live in and aspire to change one of the world's most impressive cities." Booklist

Includes bibliographical references and index.

982 Argentina

Brown, Jonathan C.

A **brief** history of Argentina; 2nd ed; Facts On File 2010 354p il map (Brief history) $49.50; pa $19.95   **982**

1. Argentina -- History

ISBN 978-0-8160-7796-0; 978-0-8160-8361-9 pa; 978-1-4381-3111-5 ebook

LC 2010004887

First published 2002

This book covers "Argentina's diverse geography and its varied natural resources; the origins of the deep-seated practices of discrimination, which continue today; the effects of neoliberalism on Argentina's large working class and urban poor, culminating in the caserola movement, the piqueteros movement, and the birth of the cartoneros; the impact a changing global economy has had within Argentina's borders; [and] the rich culture of Argentina, which has created five Nobel laureates, vibrant cities that draw millions of tourists annually, and sports teams that have won multiple world championships." Publisher's note

Includes bibliographical references

Parrado, Nando

★ **Miracle** in the Andes; 72 days on the mountain and my long trek home. [by] Nando Parrado with Vince Rause. Crown Publishers 2006 291p il map hardcover o.p. pa $13.95   **982**

1. Survival after airplane accidents, shipwrecks, etc. 2.

Andes

ISBN 1-4000-9767-3; 978-1-4000-9767-8; 1-4000-9769-X pa; 978-1-4000-9769-2 pa

LC 2005-21629

"In October 1972, a plane carrying an Uruguayan rugby team crashed in the Andes. Not immediately rescued, the survivors turned to cannibalism to survive and after 72 days were saved. Rugby team member Parrado has written a beautiful story of friendship, tragedy and perseverance." Publ Wkly

985 Peru

Adams, Mark

Turn right at Machu Picchu. Dutton 2011 333p il map $26.95   **985**

1. Explorers 2. Governors 3. Historians 4. Senators 5. Machu Picchu (Peru) 6. Peru -- Antiquities

ISBN 978-0-525-95224-4; 0-525-95224-1

LC 2011-10211

Traces the author's recreation of Hiram Bingham III's discovery of the ancient citadel, Machu Picchu, in the Andes Mountains of Peru, describing his struggles with rudimentary survival tools and his experiences at the sides of local guides.

"While some readers may prefer a more straightforward version of Bingham's exploits . . . , those favoring a quirkier retelling will relish Mr. Adams's wry, revealing romp through the Andes." Wall Street J

Bingham, Hiram

★ **Lost** city of the Incas; the story of Machu Picchu and its builders, with an introduction by Hugh Thomson; photographs by Hugh Thomson. Sterling 2002 274p il hardcover o.p. pa $12.95   **985**

1. Incas 2. Machu Picchu (Peru) 3. Peru -- Antiquities

ISBN 0-2976-0759-6; 1-84212-585-0 pa

LC 2002-483039

A reissue of the title first published 1948 by Duell

"In 1911 Bingham, an American explorer, found the Inca city of Machu Picchu, which had been lost for 300 years. In this volume he tells of its origin, how it came to be lost and how it was finally discovered." Libr J

Includes bibliographical references

Hunefeldt, Christine

A **brief** history of Peru; 2nd ed; Facts On File 2010 xx, 332p il map (Brief history) $49.50   **985**

1. Peru -- History

ISBN 978-0-8160-8144-8; 978-1-4381-0828-5 ebook

LC 2010-20748

First published 2004

This is a history of Peru ranging "from its ancient peoples and the Inca Empire through . . . recent political, social, and economic developments." Publisher's note

Includes bibliographical references

Moseley, Michael Edward

★ The **Incas** and their ancestors; the archaeology of Peru. rev ed; Thames & Hudson 2001 288p il maps $27.50   **985**

1. Incas 2. Peru -- Antiquities
ISBN 0-500-28277-3

LC 00-108866
First published 1992

This account of Andean prehistory and archaeology takes us from the first settlement of 10,000 years ago to the Spanish conquest

"Clearly presented, with a generous ration of maps and illustrations, {the volume} is thoughtful and welcome." Times Lit Suppl {review of 1992 edition}

Includes bibliographical references

Thomson, Hugh

The **white** rock; an exploration of the Inca heartland. Overlook Press 2003 316p il map $27.95; pa $16.95   **985**

1. Incas
ISBN 1-585-67355-2; 1-585-67503-2 pa

LC 2002-34606
First published 2001 in the United Kingdom

"So entertaining and appealing is Thomson's story of his exploration of the Inca empire that readers will wish they could take off and follow in his footsteps. . . . Thomson's wit, eye for detail and reverence for humanity set him apart from the average travel-adventure writer—he is as good a companion as a traveler could hope for." Publ Wkly

Includes bibliographical references

990 History of Australasia, Pacific Ocean islands, Atlantic Ocean islands, Arctic islands, Antarctica, extraterrestrial worlds

Michener, James A.

Return to paradise. Random House 1951 437p hardcover o.p. pa $7.99   **990**

1. Islands of the Pacific
ISBN 0-449-20650-5 pa

"Alternate chapters describe each island followed by a short story set against the region described." Ont Libr Rev

Treister, Kenneth

Easter Island's silent sentinels; the sculpture and architecture of Rapa Nui. Kenneth Treister, Patricia Vargas Casanova, and Claudio Cristino; foreword by Daniel Libeskind; maps and illustrations by Roberto Izaurieta and Kenneth Treister. University of New Mexico Press 2013 xv, 144 p.p color illustrations (cloth : alk. paper) $45   **990**

1. Sculpture 2. Architecture 3. Easter Island
ISBN 0826352642; 9780826352644

LC 2013013728
Written by Kenneth Treister, Patricia Vargas Casanova, and Claudio Cristino, "this richly illustrated book of the history, culture, and art of Easter Island is the first to examine in detail the island's vernacular architecture, often overshadowed by its giant stone statues. It shows the conjecturally re-

constructed prehistoric pole houses . . . and the Easter Island Statue Project's inventory of the colossal moai sculptures." (Publisher's note)

Includes bibliographical references (pages 123-132) and index

994   Australia

Clarke, F. G.

The **history** of Australia. Greenwood Press 2002 236p (Greenwood histories of the modern nations) $45   **994**

1. Australia -- History
ISBN 0-313-31498-5

LC 2001-54704
This volume "begins with a timeline of historical events. The first chapter is a very short overview of Australia (geography, climate, culture, and so on). The rest of the text is a chronological study in short, concise chapters beginning 60,000 years ago with Aboriginal Australia and ending with 2001 and beyond. Each chapter is broken down into smaller sections, with headings, covering such essential topics as colonization, war, government, and politics. The work ends with smaller sections for notable people, notes, a bibliographic essay, and an index." Recomm Ref Books for Small & Medium-sized Libr & Media Cent, 2003

Includes bibliographical references (p. {225}-227) and index

Clendinnen, Inga

Dancing with strangers; Europeans and Australians at first contact. Inga Clendinnen. Cambridge University Press 2005 324p il map $60; pa $21.99   **994**

1. Aboriginal Australians 2. Australian national characteristics 3. Australia -- Race relations 4. Great Britain -- Colonies -- Australia
ISBN 0-5218-5137-8; 0-5216-1681-6 pa

LC 2005-11523
First published 2003 in Australia

"In January 1788, the First Fleet arrived in New South Wales, Australia and a thousand British men and women encountered the people who would be their new neighbors. . . . [This book] tells the story of what happened between the first British settlers of Australia and these Aborigines." Publisher's note

Includes bibliographical references

Hughes, Robert

The **fatal** shore. Knopf 1987 688p il maps hardcover o.p. pa $18   **994**

1. Penal colonies 2. Australia -- History
ISBN 0-394-75366-6 pa

LC 86-45272
"This epic account chronicles the history of Australia during the 80 years (1788-1868) of England's convict transportation system, when some 160,000 convicts reached 'the fatal shore.' Interweaving his own lucid narrative with untapped original sources—including the diaries and letters of the prisoners themselves—Hughes shows the evolution of

the system and of the fledgling nation that emerged from the brutal penal colony." Libr J

Includes bibliographical references

Keneally, Thomas

A **commonwealth** of thieves; the improbable birth of Australia. Nan A. Talese/Doubleday 2006 385p map hardcover o.p. pa $15.95 **994**

1. Admirals 2. Penal colonies 3. Australia -- History 4. Colonial administrators 5. Frontier and pioneer life -- Australia

ISBN 0-385-51459-X; 978-0-385-51459-0; 1-4000-7956-X pa; 978-1-4000-7956-8 pa

LC 2006-44470

First published 2005 in Australia

This "book offers an engaging treatment of a subject which over the years has provoked a long and sometimes heated debate." Times Lit Suppl

Includes bibliographical references

995 New Guinea and neighboring countries of Melanesia

Hoffman, Carl

★ A **Savage** Harvest; A Tale of Cannibals, Colonialism, and Michael Rockefeller's Tragic Quest for Primitive Art. by Carl Hoffman. HarperCollins 2014 304 p. illustrations $26.99 **995**

1. New Guinea 2. Cannibalism 3. Missing persons

ISBN 0062116150; 9780062116154

This book, by Carl Hoffman, focuses on "the mysterious disappearance of Michael Rockefeller in New Guinea in 1961. . . . Soon after his disappearance, rumors surfaced that he'd been killed and ceremonially eaten by the local Asmat--a native tribe of warriors whose complex culture was built around sacred, reciprocal violence, head hunting, and ritual cannibalism. The Dutch government and the Rockefeller family denied the story, and Michael's death was officially ruled a drowning." (Publisher's note)

"[An] unforgettable story of a soothing and politically expedient cover-up and a brutal and tragic collision of cultures." Booklist

Includes bibliographical references (pages 310-312) and index.

995.3 Papua New Guinea

Flannery, Tim F.

Throwim way leg; tree-kangaroos, possums, and penis gourds--on the track of unknown mammals in wildest New Guinea. [by] Tim Flannery. Atlantic Monthly Press 1998 326p il map hardcover o.p. pa $14 **995.3**

1. Ethnology -- New Guinea 2. New Guinea -- Description

ISBN 0-8021-3665-6 pa

LC 98-38435

This "is more than an account of [the author's] fieldwork. It is an enthralling introduction to the mountain people of New Guinea." N Y Times Book Rev

996 Polynesia and other Pacific Ocean islands

Alexander, Caroline

The **Bounty**: the true story of the mutiny on the Bounty. Viking 2003 491p il hardcover o.p. pa $17 **996**

1. Admirals 2. Explorers 3. Oceania 4. Mutineers 5. Bounty (Ship) 6. Naval officers 7. Government officials 8. Colonial administrators

ISBN 978-0-670-03133-7; 0-670-03133-X; 978-0-14-200469-2 pa; 0-14-200469-3 pa

LC 2003-50158

"A rollicking sea adventure told with enormous confidence and style." Booklist

Includes bibliographical references

Severin, Timothy

In search of Robinson Crusoe. Basic Bks. 2002 333p il hardcover o.p. pa $16.95 **996**

1. Authors 2. Sailors 3. Novelists 4. Historians 5. Survival after airplane accidents, shipwrecks, etc. 6. Essayists 7. Pamphleteers 8. Writers on politics

ISBN 0-465-07699-8 pa

LC 2002-71661

The author examines "the fictional Crusoe alongside the historic realities of colonization and human ingenuity. . . . Readers learn about the history of marooning among plunderers, blockade navies and other piratical sailors, as well as the ethnography of the so-called 'Moskito Man' (aka Man Friday) and all the ways to provide for oneself on a deserted island. . . . The work is energetic and Severin is an ideal guide to the world behind the word. This will surely appeal to the lovers of maritime history." Publ Wkly

996.9 Hawaii and neighboring north central Pacific Ocean islands

Haley, James L.

Captive paradise; the United States and Hawai'i. James L. Haley. St. Martin's Press 2014 448 p. illustrations (hardcover : alk. paper) $29.99 **996.9**

1. Hawaii -- History 2. United States -- History 3. Hawaii -- Annexation to the United States

ISBN 0312600658; 9780312600655

LC 2014026108

This book "focuses on Hawaii's annexation by the United States. Weaving a vast web of culture clashes amid the military and ideological conquests that turned native Hawaiians into 'strangers in their own land,' [James L.] Haley delivers his narrative through big personalities: royalty, missionaries, and conquerors of various backgrounds." (Publishers Weekly)

"Haley underscores how remarkable it was that the islands were able to withstand coercion by French, British and

American forces for as long as they did. A pertinent work of keen understanding of the complex Hawaiian story." Kirkus

Includes bibliographical references and index

Moore, Susanna, 1948-

Paradise of the Pacific; approaching Hawaii. Susanna Moore. Farrar, Straus & Giroux 2015 320 p. illustrations, map (hardback) $26   **996.9**

1. Hawaii -- History 2. Folklore -- Hawaii 3. Hawaii -- Description and travel 4. Legends -- Hawaii 5. Hawaii -- History -- 18th century 6. Hawaii -- Social conditions -- 18th century 7. Hawaii -- Social life and customs -- 18th century 8. Acculturation -- Hawaii -- History -- 18th century 9. Social change -- Hawaii -- History -- 18th century 10. Culture conflict -- Hawaii -- History -- 18th century 11. Hawaii -- Emigration and immigration -- History -- 18th century

ISBN 0374298777; 9780374298777

LC 2015002967

NBA Longlist

Author Susanna Moore "pieces together the elusive, dramatic story of late-eighteenth-century Hawaii—its kings and queens, gods and goddesses, missionaries, migrants, and explorers—a not-so-distant time of abrupt transition, in which an isolated pagan world of human sacrifice and strict taboo, without a currency or a written language, was confronted with the equally ritualized world of capitalism, Western education, and Christian values." (Publisher's note)

"Moore's background in storytelling radiates throughout this work, creating a quick- paced and well-crafted narrative. Highly recommended for the armchair historian and those intrigued by Hawaiian history, maritime exploration, and the history of Christian missionaries. For readers with a continued fascination in the development of the Hawaiian Islands, perusing Julia Flynn Siler's Lost Kingdom might also prove a rewarding endeavor." LJ

Includes bibliographical references and index

Vowell, Sarah, 1969-

Unfamiliar fishes. Riverhead Books 2011 238p il map $25.95   **996.9**

1. Hawaii -- History 2. United States -- Territorial expansion 3. Hawaii -- Annexation to the United States

ISBN 978-1-59448-787-3

LC 2010-47943

"While Vowell's take on Hawaii's Americanization is abbreviated, it's never bereft of substance—her repartee manages to be filling, her insights astute and comprehensive." N Y Times Book Rev

Includes bibliographical references

998   Arctic islands and Antarctica

Alexander, Caroline

The **Endurance**; Shackleton's legendary Antarctic expedition. Knopf 1998 211p il $29.95   **998**

1. Explorers 2. Endurance (Ship) 3. Antarctica -- Exploration 4. Imperial Trans-Antarctic Expedition (1914-1917)

ISBN 0-375-40403-1

In 1914, Sir Ernest Shackleton "sailed to Antarctica with 27 men in hopes of being the first human to transverse the continent. But his ship, the Endurance, was trapped, then crushed, by ice in the Weddell Sea, propelling the party into a nightmare of cold and near starvation. Alexander, relying extensively on journals by crew members, some never published, as well as on myriad other sources, delivers a spellbinding story of human courage. . . . What makes this book especially exciting, however, are the 170 previously unpublished photos by the expedition's photographer, Frank Hurley." Publ Wkly

Ehrlich, Gretel

This cold heaven; seven seasons in Greenland. Pantheon Bks. 2001 377p il maps hardcover o.p. pa $14   **998**

1. Inuit 2. Greenland

ISBN 0-679-44200-6; 0-679-75852-6 pa

LC 00-69277

"Ehrlich began traveling to Greenland during her recovery from a nearly fatal lightning strike, and her keen, often poetic responses to the beauty of the frigid landscape and the warmth of Inuit families, combined with a profound immersion in Greenland history, infuse her captivating account with both drama and reflection." Booklist

Includes bibliographical references

Emmerson, Charles

The **future** history of the Arctic. PublicAffairs 2010 405p il map   **998**

1. Geopolitics 2. Arctic regions

ISBN 978-1-58648-636-5

LC 2009-35094

"It's easy to romanticise the Arctic, and over the years plenty of authors have. Oddly though, given the region's increasing geopolitical significance, it's rare to find books that treat it as something other than a chilly adventure playground or an excuse for reams of purple prose. Thank goodness, then, for Charles Emmerson. In this book he looks at how the frozen north has played a key role in world affairs in the past and how it could prove more important in the years to come." Scotsman

Includes bibliographical references

The **ends** of the earth; an anthology of the finest writing on the Arctic and the Antarctic. Bloomsbury 2007 2v in 1 map $29.95   **998**

1. Antarctica 2. Polar regions 3. Arctic regions

ISBN 1-59691-443-2; 978-1-59691-443-8

The editors "present an anthology of writings about the Arctic and Antarctic, which is actually two books in one. Halfway through, readers can turn the book upside down for writings about the opposite end of the earth. . . . Included are primary-source accounts by early explorers such as Ernest Shackleton, John Franklin, and Kund Rasmussen, nature writings by Barry Lopez and Gretel Ehrlich, excerpts from novels by Jules Verne, Jack London, and H.P. Lovecraft, and essays by journalists and scientists. Each excerpt is just long enough to whet the reader's appetite. Great reading for the armchair adventurer." Libr J

Griffiths, Tom

Slicing the silence; voyaging to Antarctica. Harvard University Press 2007 399p map $29.95 **998**

1. Antarctica -- Description and travel

ISBN 978-0-674-02633-9; 0-674-02633-0

LC 2007-06549

Simultaneously published in Australia

"Believing that to understand the experiences of explorers and the history of Antarctica one must experience its mighty winds, cold, danger, and silence, the author, in 2002, joined a ship delivering scientists and supplies to Casey Station. This book is part diary of that voyage and part history of that most southerly land. . . . This enjoyable and highly readable book would be an excellent addition to any natural history, polar history, or adventure travel collection." Libr J

Includes bibliographical references

Kavenna, Joanna

The **ice** museum; in search of the lost land of Thule. Viking 2006 294p il map $24.95; pa $15 **998**

1. Arctic regions -- Exploration

ISBN 0-670-03473-8; 0-14-303846-X pa

First published 2005 in the United Kingdom

The author "chronicles her personal journey into the myth and reality of the legendary Arctic land of Thule. . . . [This book] transcends all genre description, and holds its own as a journey into a world that somehow vibrantly exists on paper and nowhere else." Booklist

McGonigal, David

Antarctica; secrets of the southern continent. chief consultant, David McGonigal. Firefly Books 2008 400p il map $59.95 **998**

1. Antarctica

ISBN 978-1-55407-398-6; 1-55407-398-7

This "book covers all aspects of the continent, including ecology, geography, wildlife, and exploration. . . . Sumptuously illustrated with photos, maps, and paintings, this will be the go-to reference on Antarctica for years to come. A truly superb production." Booklist

Riffenburgh, Beau

Shackleton's forgotten expedition; the voyage of the Nimrod. by Beau Riffenburgh. Bloomsbury, Distributed to the trade by Holtzbrinck Publishers 2004 xxiv, 358p il map $25.95; pa $15.95 **998**

1. Explorers 2. Antarctica -- Exploration

ISBN 1-58234-488-4; 1-58234-611-9 pa

LC 2004-11999

The author recounts Shackleton's "voyage to the Antarctic from 1907 to 1909, during which he led a small group of men to within 97 miles of the South Pole. . . . For those who thrilled to the Endurance saga, Riffenburgh offers an equally gripping adventure, which laid the foundations of Shackleton's capacity for brilliant leadership under pressure." Publ Wkly

Includes bibliographical references

Smith, Roff

Life on the ice; no one goes to Antarctica alone. National Geographic 2005 208p pa $16 **998**

1. Antarctica -- Description and travel

ISBN 0-7922-9345-2

LC 2005-298454

First published 2002 in Australia

"Smith is the most exceptional of travel writers: his portraits of people are deeply sympathetic, while his language is at once lyrical and knowledgeable. Not to be missed." Booklist

Streever, Bill

Cold; adventures in the world's frozen places. Little, Brown and Co. 2009 292p $24.99; pa $14.99 **998**

1. Cold 2. Arctic regions -- Description and travel

ISBN 978-0-316-04291-8; 0-316-04291-9; 978-0-316-04292-5 pa; 0-316-04292-7 pa

LC 2008-45350

Strever "delivers a poetic, anecdotal narrative complete with polar expeditions, Ice Age mysteries, igloos, permafrost and hailstorms. . . . This is a wonderful collection of one man's first-rate observations and commentary about the history and importance of cold to the earth and its occupants." Publ Wkly

Includes bibliographical references

Turney, Chris

1912; the year the world discovered Antarctica. Pgw 2012 358 p. $27 **998**

1. Explorers 2. Antarctica -- Exploration

ISBN 1582437890; 9781582437897

This book by Chris Turney presents "an in-depth look at a year in which five different expeditions set out to explore Antarctica. . . . The continent would see no fewer than five different national exploration teams during that year, and geologist Turney . . . examines each expedition in turn, after outlining some of the earliest attempts at exploring Antarctica, including Ernest Shackleton's 1907-1909 expedition." (Kirkus Reviews)

Includes bibliographical references and index.

AUTHOR, TITLE, AND SUBJECT INDEX

This index to the books in the Classified Collection includes author, title, and subject entries; added entries for publishers' series, illustrators, joint authors, and editors of works entered under title; and name and subject cross-references; all arranged in one alphabet.

The number or symbol in bold face type at the end of each entry refers to the Dewey Decimal Classification or to the Fiction (Fic) or Story Collection (S C), or Easy Books (E) section where the main entry for the book will be found. Works classed in 92 will be found under the headings for the biographies' subject.

The **$100** startup. Guillebeau, C. **658.1**

$2.00 a Day. Shaefer, H. L. **339.4**

$40 million slaves. Rhoden, W. C. **796**

1-2-3 magic. Phelan, T. W. **649**

10 Granny Squares 30 Blankets. Hubert, M. **746.43**

10 Mississippi. Healey, S. **811**

10% happier. Harris, D. **158.1**

10% human. Collen, A. **612.3**

The **100** best business books of all time. Covert, J. **016.6**

100 Best Jewish Recipes. Rose, E. **641.5**

100 days of real food. Leake, L. **613.2**

100 essential modern poems. **821**

100 essential things you didn't know you didn't know. Barrow, J. D. **510**

100 flowers and how they got their names. Wells, D. **582.13**

100 great poems of the twentieth century. **821**

100 most important science ideas. Henderson, M. **500**

100 most popular nonfiction authors. Drew, B. A. **920.003**

100 notes on violence. Carr, J. **811**

100 suns, 1945-1962. Light, M. **355.8**

100 YEARS' WAR *See* Hundred Years' War, 1339-1453

1001 Movies You Must See Before You Die. **791.43**

101 careers in healthcare management. **362.106**

101 classic cookbooks. **641**

101 essential tips [series]
Mills, D. Aquarium fish **639.34**

101 great, ready-to-use book lists for teens. Keane, N. J. **028.5**

101 magic tricks. Miles, B. **793.8**

101 outstanding graphic novels. **741.5**

101 quantum questions. Ford, K. W. **530.1**

101 Saturday morning projects. **643**

101 top tips from professional manga artists. **741.5**

102 minutes. Dwyer, J. **974.7**

1080 recipes. Ortega, S. **641.5**

112 Mercer Street. Feldman, B. **920**

13 bankers. Johnson, S. **332.1**

13 things that don't make sense. Brooks, M. **500**

13.8. Gribbin, J. **523.1**

14-18, understanding the Great War. Audoin-Rouzeau, S. **940.3**

1491. Mann, C. C. **970.01**

1493. Mann, C. C. **909**

15 stars. Weintraub, S. **920**

15 things you should give up to be happy. Saviuc, L. D. **152.4**

The **150** best American recipes. **641.5**

150+ screen-free activities for kids. Citro, A. **796.5**

The **15:17** to Paris. Sadler, A. **363.325**

17 carnations. Morton, A. **941.084**

1759: the year Britain became master of the world. McLynn, F. **941.07**

1775. Phillips, K. **973.3**

1776. McCullough, D. G. **973.3**

180 more. **811**

1812: the Navy's war. Daughan, G. C. **973.5**

1861. Goodheart, A. **973.7**

1912. Turney, C. **998**

1913. Emmerson, C. **909.82**

1916. Jeffery, K. **909.82**

The **1916** Irish Rebellion. Nic Dhiarmada, B. **941.5**

1920. Burns, E. **973.91**

1920: the year of the six presidents. Pietrusza, D. **973.91**

1920S *See* Nineteen twenties

1939. Carley, M. J. **940.53**

1940S *See* Nineteen forties

1941 : Fighting the Shadow War. Wortman, M. **973.917**

1942. Groom, W. **940.53**

1944. Winik, J. **940.53**

1946. Sebestyen, V. **909.82**

1950S *See* Nineteen fifties

1960: LBJ vs. JFK vs. Nixon. Pietrusza, D. **973.92**

1960S *See* Nineteen sixties

1966. Savage, J. **781.66**

1968. Kurlansky, M. **909.82**

1969. Kirkpatrick, R. **973.92**

1970S *See* Nineteen seventies

1973 nervous breakdown. Killen, A. **973.924**

1980S *See* Nineteen eighties

The **1990s.** Schwartz, R. A. **909.82**

2 weeks to a younger brain. Small, G. **616.8**

2,100 Asanas. Lacerda, D.   **613.7**

The **2-step** low-FODMAP eating plan. Shepherd, S.   **641.5**

2009 poet's market.   **808.1**

2010: the best women's stage monologues and scenes.   **808.82**

2015 getting financial aid.   **378.3**

2015 songwriter's market.   **338.4**

The **20th** Century in Poetry.   **808.81**

21. Santiago, W.   **92**

21 short plays. Wilson, L.   **812**

The **21st** century economy. Epping, R. C.   **330.9**

The **21st-century** black librarian in America.   **020**

3-D PRINTING *See* Three-dimensional printing

30 lessons for living. Pillemer, K. A.   **305.26**

300 tips for painting & decorating. Jenkins, A.   **698**

301 smart answers to tough business etiquette questions. Oliver, V.   **395**

32 yolks. Chambers, V.   **92**

33 revolutions per minute. Lynskey, D.   **782.42**

The **36-hour** day. Mace, N. L.   **618.97**

The **36-Hour** Day. Mace, N. L.   **616.8**

365 days. Glasser, R. J.   **959.704**

The **37th** parallel. Mezrich, B.   **001.942**

38 nooses. Berg, S. W.   **973.7**

3d printing for dummies. Horne, R.   **621.9**

The **4** disciplines of execution. Covey, S.   **658.4**

4 plays. Inge, W.   **812**

The **40s.**   **973.917**

41. Bush, G. W.   **92**

438 days. Franklin, J.   **910.916**

The **50** best sights in astronomy and how to see them. Schaaf, F.   **520**

50 great American places. Glass, B. D.   **973**

The **50** most extreme places in our solar system. Baker, D.   **523.2**

500 crochet stitches. Knight, E.   **746.43**

500 days. Eichenwald, K.   **973.931**

The **50s.**   **973**

52 loaves. Alexander, W.   **641.8**

52 McGs. Thomas, R. M.   **920**

The **52** new foods challenge. Lee, J. T.   **641.5**

56. Kennedy, K.   **92**

The **60s.**   **909.826**

660 curries. Iyer, R.   **641.5**

7 Greeks.   **881**

The **7** habits of highly effective people. Covey, S. R.   **158**

7 things your teenager won't tell you. Lippincott, J. M.   **649**

75 years of Marvel Comics.   **741.5**

75 years of the Oscar. Osborne, R. A.   **791.43**

750 knitting stitches. Knight, E.   **746.432**

8 keys to end bullying. Whitson, S.   **302.34**

8 keys to mental health series
   Whitson, S. 8 keys to end bullying   **302.34**

8 keys to raising the quirky child. Bowers, M.   **649**

81 days below zero. Murphy, B.   **940.54**

88 days to Kandahar. Grenier, R. L.   **958.104**

The **8th** habit. Covey, S. R.   **158**

The **9/11** Commission report. National Commission on Terrorist Attacks Upon the United States **973.931**

The **9/11** report. Jacobson, S.   **741.5**

@stickyjesus. Heim, T.   **248.4**

@WAR. Harris, S.   **355.3**

[Sic] Cody, J.   **362.196**

[The nest] home design handbook. Roney, C.

A

A is for American. Lepore, J.   **306.44**

A to Z of African Americans [series]
   Bader, P. African-American writers   **920.003**

A to Z of chemists. Oakes, E. H.   **920.003**

A to Z of crochet.   **746.434**

A to Z of earth scientists. Gates, A. E.   **920.003**

A to Z of Latino Americans [series]
   Friedman, I. C. Latino athletes   **920.003**
   Martinez Wood, J. Latino writers and journalists   **920.003**
   Newton, D. E. Latinos in science, math, and professions   **920.003**
   Otfinoski, S. Latinos in the arts   **920.003**

The **A** to Z of plant names. Coombes, A. J.   **635**

A to Z of women in world history. Kuhlman, E. A.   **920.003**

A-z of Ribbon Embroidery.   **746.44**

Ā'ishah, 7th cent.
About
   Hazleton, L. After the prophet   **297**

A-Z of Whitework.   **746.44**

A. Lincoln. White, R. C.   **92**

A. Poulin Jr. new poets of America series
   Harrington, J. N. Even the hollow my body made is gone   **811**

A.D. Neufeld, J.   **976.3**

Aaron, Hank, 1934-
About
   Bryant, H. The last hero   **92**

Aaronovitch, David
   Voodoo histories   **909.08**

Aaronson, Naomi
   Pilates for breast cancer survivors   **616.99**

The **AARP** Retirement Survival Guide. Jason, J.   **332.024**

The **abacus** and the cross. Brown, N. M.   **92**

Abad Faciolince, Héctor Joaquín
About
   Abad, H. Oblivion   **868**

Abad Gómez, Héctor
About
   Abad, H. Oblivion   **868**

ABANDONED CHILDREN

Williams, M. The lost daughter **979.4**

ABANDONED CHILDREN
See also Child welfare; Children

Abandoned in hell. Wolf, M. J. **959.704**

ABANDONED TOWNS *See* Extinct cities; Ghost towns

Abani, Adesina
(jt. auth) Falk, B. Teaching matters **370.9**

Abbate, Carolyn
A history of opera **782.1**

Abbey, Cherie D.
(ed) Holidays, festivals, and celebrations of the world dictionary **394.26**

Abbotson, Susan C. W.
Critical companion to Arthur Miller **812**

Abbott, Alysia
About
Abbott, A. Fairyland **813**

Abbott, Christmas
The Badass Body Diet **613.2**

Abbott, Jack Henry, 1944-2002
In the belly of the beast **365**

Abbott, Karen
American rose **92**
Liar, Temptress, Soldier, Spy **973.7**
Sin in the Second City **977.3**

ABBREVIATIONS
See also Writing

ABCS *See* Alphabet

Abdelkareem, Moaz
About
Cambanis, T. Once upon a revolution **962.05**

Abdi, Hawa
Keeping hope alive **92**

ABDOMINAL EXERCISES
See also Exercise

ABDUCTION *See* Kidnapping

Abdul Rauf, Feisal, 1948-
Moving the mountain **297.09**

Abdul-Jabbar, Kareem, 1947-
Black profiles in courage **920**
About
Abdul-Jabbar, K. On the shoulders of giants **92**

Abdullahi, Asad
About
Steinberg, J. A man of good hope **92**

Abegg, Martin G.
The Dead Sea scrolls **296.1**

Abel, Jessica
Drawing words & writing pictures **741.5**
Mastering comics **741.5**

Abel, Niels Henrik, 1802-1829
About
Bell, E. T. Men of mathematics **920**
Livio, M. The equation that couldn't be solved **512**

Abel, Paul

(jt. auth) North, C. How to Read the Solar System **523.2**

Abigail Adams. Holton, W. **92**

ABILITY
Ericsson, A. Peak **153.9**
Shenk, D. The genius in all of us **155.2**

ABILITY -- TESTING
Gould, S. J. The mismeasure of man **153.9**

ABILITY -- TESTING
See also Educational tests and measurements; Intelligence tests; Psychological tests

ABILITY GROUPING IN EDUCATION
See also Education; Educational psychology; Grading and marking (Education)

ABNORMAL CHILDREN *See* Children with disabilities; Exceptional children

ABNORMAL PSYCHOLOGY
Ronson, J. The psychopath test **616.85**
Smoller, J. The other side of normal **591.5**

ABNORMAL PSYCHOLOGY
See also Mind and body; Nervous system

ABOLITION OF CAPITAL PUNISHMENT *See* Capital punishment

ABOLITION OF SLAVERY *See* Abolitionists; Slavery; Slaves -- Emancipation

ABOLITIONISTS
Abdul-Jabbar, K. Black profiles in courage **920**
Benfey, C. E. G. A summer of hummingbirds **920**
Berkin, C. Civil War wives **920**
Carretta, V. Equiano, the African **92**
Clinton, C. Harriet Tubman: the road to freedom **92**
Colaiaco, J. A. Frederick Douglass and the Fourth of July **973.7**
Douglass, F. Autobiographies **92**
Douglass, F. My bondage and my freedom **92**
Douglass, F. Narrative of the life of Frederick Douglass, an American slave **92**
Failure is impossible **92**
Hague, W. J. William Wilberforce **92**
Hedrick, J. D. Harriet Beecher Stowe **92**
Hofstadter, R. The American political tradition, and the men who made it **973**
Horwitz, T. Midnight rising **92**
Humez, J. M. Harriet Tubman **92**
Kantrowitz, S. More than freedom **323.1**
Larson, K. C. Bound for the promised land **92**
McPherson, J. M. Drawn with the sword **973.7**
Painter, N. I. Sojourner Truth **305.5**
Reynolds, D. S. Mightier than the sword **813**
Reynolds, D. S. John Brown, abolitionist **92**
Sinha, M. The Slave's cause **973.711**
Slaughter, T. P. The beautiful soul of John Woolman, apostle of abolition **92**
Tobin, J. From Midnight to Dawn **322**
Walters, K. The Underground Railroad **973.7**
Wilson, E. Patriotic gore **810**

ABOLITIONISTS -- BIOGRAPHY
Stauffer, J. Picturing Frederick Douglass   92
ABOLITIONISTS -- UNITED STATES -- BIOGRAPHY
Douglass, F. My bondage and my freedom   92
Stauffer, J. Picturing Frederick Douglass   92
ABOLITIONISTS -- UNITED STATES -- HISTORY -- 19TH CENTURY
Walters, K. The Underground Railroad   **973.7**
Abominable science! Prothero, D. R.   **001.944**
Abood, Maureen
Rose water and orange blossoms
ABORIGINAL AUSTRALIAN ART
   See also Art
ABORIGINAL AUSTRALIANS
Clendinnen, I. Dancing with strangers   **994**
ABORIGINAL AUSTRALIANS
   See also Australians; Indigenous peoples
ABORIGINES *See* Indigenous peoples
ABORIGINES, AUSTRALIAN *See* Aboriginal Australians
ABORTION
Moreno, J. D. The body politic   **303.48**
Pollitt, K. Pro   **363.46**
Press, E. Absolute convictions   **363.46**
Reagan, L. J. When abortion was a crime   **363.46**
ABORTION -- ENCYCLOPEDIAS
Palmer, L. J. Encyclopedia of abortion in the United States   **363.46**
ABORTION -- ETHICAL ASPECTS
   See also Ethics
ABORTION -- LAW AND LEGISLATION
Hull, N. E. H. Roe v. Wade   **344**
ABORTION -- LAW AND LEGISLATION
   See also Law; Legislation
ABORTION -- RELIGIOUS ASPECTS -- CHRISTIANITY
Joyce, K. The child catchers   **362.734**
ABORTION PROVIDERS
Press, E. Absolute convictions   **363.46**
ABORTION, INDUCED -- PERSONAL NARRATIVES
Ilse, S. The prenatal bombshell   **618.3**
Abousteit, Nora
BurdaStyle sewing vintage modern   **646.4**
About a mountain. D'Agata, J.   **979.3**
About Alice. Trillin, C.   **92**
About behaviorism. Skinner, B. F.   **150.19**
About now. Kyger, J.   **811**
About time. Frank, A.   **523.1**
Above the line. MacLaine, S.   **92**
Above the river. Wright, J. A.   **811**
Abraham Lincoln. McPherson, J. M.   **92**
Abraham Lincoln. Keneally, T.   **92**
Abraham Lincoln. Burlingame, M.   **92**
Abraham Lincoln and Civil War America. Gienapp,
W. E.   **973.7**
Abraham Lincoln and the second American Revolution. McPherson, J. M.   **973.7**
Abraham Lincoln: The prairie years and The war years. Sandburg, C.   **92**
Abraham, Ken, 1951-
   (jt. auth) Aldrin, B. No dream is too high   **92**
Abrahamian, Ervand
The coup   **955.05**
Abram, Norm
Measure twice, cut once   **684**
Abrams studio [series]
Micklewright, K. Drawing: mastering the language of visual expression   **741.2**
Abrams, Douglas
   (jt. auth) Gottman, J. The man's guide to women   **155.3**
Abrams, Douglas Carlton
   (ed) The book of forgiving   **179**
   (ed) Made for goodness   **170**
Abrams, J., 1886-1953
           About
Healy, T. The great dissent   **342.73**
Abrams, John
Companies we keep   **338.7**
Abrams, Jonathan
Boys among men   **796.323**
Abrams, M. H. (Meyer Howard), 1912-2015
The fourth dimension of a poem   **808.1**
A glossary of literary terms   **803**
   (ed) The Norton anthology of English literature **820**
Abrams, Rachel Carlton
   (jt. auth) Gottman, J. The man's guide to women   **155.3**
Abramson, Albert
The History of Television 1880 to 1941   **621.388**
The history of television, 1942 to 2000   **621.388**
ABRASIVES
   See also Ceramics
The **Abridged** History of Rainfall. Hopler, J. **811.6**
ABRIDGMENTS
   See also Literature
Abroad at home.   **917.3**
ABSENTEE FATHERS
   See also Absentee parents; Fathers
ABSENTEE PARENTS
   See also Parents
ABSENTEEISM (LABOR)
   See also Hours of labor; Personnel management
Absolute convictions. Press, E.   **363.46**
Absolute zero and the conquest of cold. Shachtman, T.   **536**
Absolutely American. Lipsky, D.   **355**
ABSTRACT ART
   See also Art

ABSTRACT EXPRESSIONISM
Albers, P. Joan Mitchell **92**
Livingston, J. The paintings of Joan Mitchell **759.13**
Solomon, D. Jackson Pollock **92**
ABU GHRAIB (BAGHDAD, IRAQ: PRISON)
Gourevitch, P. Standard operating procedure **956.7**
Hersh, S. M. Chain of command **973.931**
The torture papers **973.931**
Abu-Jaber, Diana.
About
Abu-Jaber, D. Life Without a Recipe **92**
Abundance. Kotler, S. **303.48**
Aburedwan, Ramzi
About
Tolan, S. Children of the stone **780**
ABUSE OF ANIMALS *See* Animal welfare
ABUSE OF CHILDREN *See* Child abuse
Abuse of power. Theoharis, A. G. **363.325**
Abuse of power. **973.924**
ABUSE OF SUBSTANCES *See* Substance abuse
ABUSED CHILDREN *See* Child abuse
ABUSED CHILDREN -- UNITED STATES -- BIOGRAPHY
Grande, R. The distance between us **92**
ABUSED PERSONS
Ali, N. I am Nujood, age 10 and divorced **92**
Latus, J. If I am missing or dead **92**
ABUSED WIVES *See* Abused women; Wife abuse
ABUSED WOMEN
Crompton, V. Saving beauty from the beast **362.88**
Latus, J. If I am missing or dead **92**
ABUSED WOMEN
See also Victims of crimes; Women
ABUSED WOMEN -- MASSACHUSETTS -- BOSTON -- SOCIAL CONDITIONS
Sered, S. S. Can't catch a break **362.83**
ABUSIVE MEN -- ALASKA -- MCCARTHY -- BIOGRAPHY
Pilgrim's wilderness **92**
ABUSIVE PERSONS
Woo, I. The great divorce **92**
ABYSSAL ZONE
Hoyt, E. Creatures of the deep **591.7**
AC\DC (MUSICAL GROUP)
Englehart, M. AC/DC **920**
ACADEMIC ACHIEVEMENT
Duckworth, A. Grit **158.1**
Kennedy-Moore, E. Smart parenting for smart kids **649**
ACADEMIC ACHIEVEMENT
See also Success
ACADEMIC ACHIEVEMENT -- UNITED STATES
Bain, K. What the best college students do **378.1**
ACADEMIC DEGREES

See also Colleges and universities
ACADEMIC DISSERTATIONS *See* Dissertations
ACADEMIC FAILURE *See* Academic achievement
ACADEMIC FREEDOM
See also Intellectual freedom; Toleration
ACADEMIC LIBRARIES
Butler, P. M. Joint libraries **027**
ACADEMIC LIBRARIES
See also Libraries
ACADEMIC WRITING -- HANDBOOKS, MANUALS, ETC
A manual for writers of research papers, theses, and dissertations **808.06**
ACADEMY AWARDS (MOTION PICTURES)
Harris, M. Pictures at a revolution **791.43**
Osborne, R. A. 75 years of the Oscar **791.43**
ACADEMY AWARDS (MOTION PICTURES)
See also Motion pictures
ACADEMY OF NATURAL SCIENCES OF PHILADELPHIA -- HISTORY
A glorious enterprise **508**
Accepted. Patterson, P. **92**
Access to Asia. Alexander, L. **395.5**
ACCESS TO HEALTH CARE
Brawley, O. W. How we do harm **362.109**
Gruber, J. Health care reform **362.1**
Hoffman, B. Health care for some **362.1**
Topol, E. The creative destruction of medicine **610.28**
ACCESS TO HEALTH CARE
See also Medical care
ACCESSIBILITY OF HEALTH SERVICES *See* Access to health care
The **accessible** home. Pierce, D. **728.087**
Accessing the classics. Rosow, L. V. **011.6**
The **accidental** empire. Gorenberg, G. **956.94**
Accidental genius. Fine, M. **791**
The **accidental** guerrilla. Kilcullen, D. **355.4**
Accidental saints. Bolz-Weber, N. **284.1**
ACCIDENTS -- PREVENTION
Halsted, D. D. Disaster planning **025.8**
ACCLIMATIZATION *See* Adaptation (Biology); Environmental influence on humans
The **accordion** family. Newman, K. S. **306.874**
ACCORDIONISTS
Wolfe, C. K. The life and legend of Leadbelly **92**
ACCOUNTABILITY *See* Liability (Law); Responsibility
ACCOUNTING
See also Business; Business education; Business mathematics
ACCOUNTING -- HANDBOOKS, MANUALS, ETC
Shim, J. K. Accounting handbook **657**
Accounting handbook. Shim, J. K. **657**

ACCOUNTS, COLLECTING OF *See* Collecting of accounts

ACCULTURATION
Frankopan, P. The Silk Roads   **909**
Gibbon, P. Tribe   **305.8**
Handlin, O. The uprooted   **325**

ACCULTURATION
   See also Anthropology; Civilization; Culture; Ethnology

ACCULTURATION -- HAWAII -- HISTORY -- 18TH CENTURY
Moore, S. Paradise of the Pacific   **996.9**

ACCULTURATION -- HISTORY
Frankopan, P. The Silk Roads   **909**

Acedia & me. Norris, K.   **92**

Acemoglu, Daron
Why nations fail   **330**

Acharya, Viral V.
Guaranteed to fail   **332.7**

Achebe, Chinua, 1930-2013
The education of a British-protected child   **92**
There was a country   **823**
Achebe, C. Home and exile   **823**

Acheson. Chace, J.   **92**

Acheson, Dean, 1893-1971
     About
Chace, J. Acheson   **92**
Halberstam, D. The best and the brightest **973.922**

Acheson, Hugh
The broad fork   **641.597**
A New Turn in the South   **641.59**

The **Achievement** Habit. Roth, B.   **158.1**

ACHIEVEMENT MOTIVATION
   See also Educational psychology; Motivation (Psychology); Performance

ACHIEVEMENT TESTS
   See also Academic achievement; Educational tests and measurements

ACHIEVEMENT, ACADEMIC *See* Academic achievement

Achor, Shawn
Before happiness   **158**

ACID (DRUG) *See* LSD (Drug)

ACID RAIN
   See also Rain; Water pollution
Acid test. Shroder, T.   **615.7**

ACIDS
   See also Chemicals; Chemistry

Acitelli, Tom
The audacity of hops   **641.2**

Ackerman, Diane, 1948-
Deep play   **155.6**
A natural history of love   **152.4**
A natural history of the senses   **152.1**
Origami bridges   **811**
The rarest of the rare   **578.68**

A slender thread   **362.28**
The zookeeper's wife   **940.53**

Ackerman, Jennifer
Ah-choo!   **616.2**
The Genius of Birds   **598**

Ackerman-Leist, Philip
Rebuilding the foodshed   **338.1**

Ackmann, Martha
The Mercury 13: the untold story of thirteen American women and the dream of space flight **629.45**

Ackroyd's brief lives [series]
Ackroyd, P. Charlie Chaplin   **92**
Ackroyd, P. Chaucer   **92**
Ackroyd, P. Poe   **92**

Ackroyd, Peter, 1949-
Charlie Chaplin   **92**
Chaucer   **92**
The death of King Arthur   **398.2**
London: the biography   **942**
Poe   **92**
Rebellion   **941.06**
Thames   **942**
Tudors   **942.05**

ACNE
   See also Skin -- Diseases

Acocella, Joan Ross
Twenty-eight artists and two saints   **920**

Acosta, Mercedes de, 1893-1968
     About
Cohen, L. All we know   **920.72**

Acosta-Belen, Edna
The Norton anthology of Latino literature   **810**

ACOUSTICS *See* Architectural acoustics; Hearing; Music -- Acoustics and physics; Sound

ACQUAINTANCE RAPE *See* Date rape

ACQUIESCENCE (PSYCHOLOGY) -- HISTORY
Fraser, S. The age of acquiescence   **973.91**

ACQUIRED IMMUNE DEFICIENCY SYNDROME *See* AIDS (Disease)

ACQUIRED IMMUNODEFICIENCY SYNDROME -- EPIDEMIOLOGY -- AFRICA
Halperin, D. Tinderbox   **614.5**

ACQUISITIONS (LIBRARIES)
Rethinking collection development and management   **025.2**

ACQUISITIONS (LIBRARIES) *See* Libraries -- Acquisitions

ACQUISITIONS, CORPORATE *See* Corporate mergers and acquisitions

Acquista, Angelo
The Mediterranean Family Table   **641.59**

ACROBATS -- BIOGRAPHY
Wall, D. The ordinary acrobat   **796.47**

ACROBATS AND ACROBATICS
Wall, D. The ordinary acrobat   **796.47**

ACROBATS AND ACROBATICS
See also Circus

ACRONYMS -- DICTIONARIES
Acronyms, initialisms, & abbreviations diction-
ary **421**
Acronyms, initialisms, & abbreviations diction-
ary. **421**
Across the land and the water. **831**

ACRYLIC PAINTING
Kloosterboer, L. Painting in acrylics **751.426**

ACRYLIC PAINTING
See also Painting
Act of Congress. Kaiser, R. G. **346.73**
An **act** of state. Pepper, W. F. **364.1**

ACT UP (ORGANIZATION)
Schiavi, M. Celluloid activist **92**

ACTING
2010: the best women's stage monologues and
scenes **808.82**
Adler, S. Stella Adler: the art of acting **792**
The Best Men's Stage Monologues 2016 **792**
The best stage scenes of 2007 **808.82**
Chekhov, M. To the actor **792**
Hagen, U. Respect for acting **792**
Mamet, D. True and false **792**
Moore, S. The Stanislavski system **792**
Stanislavsky, K. An actor's work **792**
Stanislavsky, K. Creating a role **792**
The Ultimate audition book **808.82**

ACTING
See also Drama; Public speaking
Active liberty. Breyer, S. G. **342**

ACTIVITIES CURRICULUM *See* Creative activities

ACTIVITY SCHOOLS *See* Education -- Experi-
mental methods
An **actor** and his time. Gielgud, J. **92**
An **actor's** work. Stanislavsky, K. **792**

ACTORS
Abbott, K. American rose **92**
Andrews, J. Home **92**
Angelou, M. Letter to my daughter **92**
Angelou, M. I know why the caged bird sings **92**
Angelou, M. A song flung up to heaven **818**
Apatow, J. Sick in the head **792.7**
Arkin, A. An improvised life **92**
Bacall, L. By myself and then some **92**
Bach, S. Leni: the life and work of Leni Riefens-
tahl **92**
Balbirer, N. Take your shirt off and cry **92**
Ball, L. Love, Lucy **92**
Belafonte, H. My song **92**
Berg, A. S. Kate remembered **92**
Biskind, P. Star **92**
Black women writers (1950-1980) **810**
Bogle, D. Heat wave **92**

Buckley, W. F. The Reagan I knew **92**
Buford, K. Burt Lancaster **92**
Callow, S. Orson Welles **92**
Carroll, D. The legs are the last to go **92**
Clarke, G. Get happy: the life of Judy Garland **92**
Cliff, N. The Shakespeare riots **974.4**
Curtis, J. Spencer Tracy **92**
D'Souza, D. Ronald Reagan **973.927**
Dyson, M. E. Holler if you hear me: searching for
Tupac Shakur **92**
Eliot, M. American titan **92**
The essential Chaplin **92**
Fey, T. Bossypants **92**
Fine, M. Accidental genius **791**
Fisher, C. Wishful drinking **92**
FitzGerald, F. Way out there in the blue **973.927**
Flinn, C. Brass diva **92**
Foote, H. Beginnings **812**
Fox, M. J. Always looking up **92**
Fox, M. J. Lucky man **92**
Friedwald, W. Sinatra! the song is you **92**
Gary Cooper **92**
Gates, H. L. Thirteen ways of looking at a black
man **920.71**
Gavin, J. Stormy weather **92**
Gehring, W. D. James Dean: rebel with a cause **92**
George-Warren, H. Public cowboy no. 1 **92**
Giddins, G. Bing Crosby: a pocketful of dreams:
the early years, 1903-1940 **92**
Gielgud, J. An actor and his time **92**
Gillespie, M. A. Maya Angelou **92**
Goudsouzian, A. Sidney Poitier **92**
Guralnick, P. Careless love: the unmaking of Elvis
Presley **92**
Hepburn, K. Me **92**
Hoskyns, B. Lowside of the road **92**
Ice-T Ice **92**
Jackson, C. Hattie: the life of Hattie McDaniel **92**
Jaffrey, M. Climbing the mango trees **92**
Jobrani, M. I'm not a terrorist, but I've played one
on tv **92**
Johnson, H. B. Sleepwalking through histo-
ry **973.927**
Kaplan, J. Frank **92**
Kashner, S. Furious love **92**
Kaufman, D. Doris Day **92**
Leider, E. W. Myrna Loy **92**
Levy, S. Paul Newman **92**
Lewis, J. Dean & me **92**
Life stories **920**
Mann, J. The rebellion of Ronald Reagan **973.927**
Mann, W. J. Kate: the woman who was Hepburn **92**
Martin, S. Born standing up **92**
Mason, B. A. Elvis Presley **92**
McCabe, J. Cagney **92**
McCourt, M. A monk swimming **974.7**

McCourt, M. Singing my him song   974.7

Meade, M. Buster Keaton   92

Min, A. Red Azalea   92

Mooney, P. Black is the new white   92

Moore, M. T. Growing up again   92

Moore, S. The Stanislavski system   792

Palin, M. Halfway to Hollywood   92

Pierpont, C. R. Passionate minds   810

Playwrights at work   812

Plummer, C. In spite of myself   92

Poitier, S. The measure of a man   92

Quirk, L. J. Bob Hope: the road well-traveled   92

Ratnesar, R. Tear down this wall   973.927

Reagan, R. Reagan   92

Reagan, R. My father at 100   92

Reeve, C. Still me   92

Reeves, R. President Reagan: the triumph of imagination   973.927

Rhodes, R. Hedy's folly   92

Ripken, C. The only way I know   92

Robeson, P. Here I stand   92

Robeson, P. The undiscovered Paul Robeson   92

Santopietro, T. Sinatra in Hollywood   92

Shearer, S. M. Beautiful   92

Singer, M. Character studies   920

Spoto, D. Notorious   92

Swanson, J. L. Manhunt   364.152

Taraborrelli, J. R. The secret life of Marilyn Monroe   92

Thomson, D. Bette Davis   92

Thomson, D. Humphrey Bogart   92

Thomson, D. Ingrid Bergman   92

Thursby, J. S. Critical companion to Maya Angelou   818

Trimborn, J. Leni Riefenstahl   92

Victor, A. The Elvis encyclopedia   781.66

Walker, A. Audrey   92

Wallach, E. The good, the bad, and me   92

Ware, S. Letter to the world   920.72

Wasson, S. Fifth Avenue, 5 AM   791.43

Watts, J. Hattie McDaniel   92

Waxman, S. Rebels on the backlot   920

Whitfield, E. Pickford   92

Woodward, B. Shadow   973.92

Wranovics, J. Chaplin and Agee   92

ACTORS

See also Entertainers

ACTORS -- DICTIONARIES

Monush, B. Screen world presents the encyclopedia of Hollywood film actors   920.003

Otfinoski, S. Latinos in the arts   920.003

ACTORS -- GREAT BRITAIN -- BIOGRAPHY

Cleese, J. So, anyway...   92

ACTORS -- UNITED STATES

Ackroyd, P. Charlie Chaplin   92

ACTORS -- UNITED STATES

See also Actors

ACTORS -- UNITED STATES -- BIOGRAPHY

Alford, T. Fortune's Fool   92

Eyman, S. John Wayne: the life and legend   92

Goessel, T. The first king of Hollywood   92

McGilligan, P. Young Orson   92

ACTORS -- UNTED STATES -- BIOGRAPHY

Kaling, M. Why not me?   92

ACTORS AND ACTRESSES *See* Actors

**ACTORS, BLACK -- UNITED STATES -- BIOG-
RAPHY**

Smith, J. E. Becoming Belafonte   92

ACTRESSES

Bergen, C. A fine romance   92

Kaling, M. Is everyone hanging out without me?
  (and other concerns)   818

Kaling, M. Why not me?   92

MacLaine, S. Above the line   92

Mulgrew, K. Born With Teeth   791.45

Reynolds, D. Make 'em Laugh   92

ACTRESSES

See also Actors

ACTRESSES -- BIOGRAPHY

Day, F. You're Never Weird on the Internet (Almost)

Huston, A. Watch me   92

Poole, W. S. Vampira   92

**ACTRESSES -- KOREA (SOUTH) -- BIOGRA-
PHY**

Fischer, P. A Kim Jong-Il production   791.43

**ACTRESSES -- UNITED STATES -- ANEC-
DOTES**

Douglas, I. I blame Dennis Hopper   792.02

**ACTRESSES -- UNITED STATES -- BIOGRA-
PHY**

Alden, G. Elvis and Ginger   92

Douglas, I. I blame Dennis Hopper   792.02

Poole, W. S. Vampira   92

Riley, K. The Astaires   92

Acts of faith. Patel, E.   92

ACTUAL INNOCENCE

Bozella, D. Stand Tall   365.6

ACUPRESSURE

See also Alternative medicine; Massage

ACUPUNCTURE

See also Alternative medicine

Acurio, Gastón

Peru   641.598

Aczel, Amir D., 1950-2015

The artist and the mathematician   500

Finding zero   513.5

God's equation   523.1

Present at the creation   539.7

The riddle of the compass   912

Ad Hoc at home. Keller, T.   641.5

Ad infinitum. Ostler, N.   470

Ada Blackjack. Niven, J.   92

Ada's algorithm. Essinger, J. **92**

ADAGES *See* Proverbs

Adair, Virginia Hamilton

Ants on the melon **811**

Beliefs and blasphemies **811**

Adam's curse. Sykes, B. **599.93**

Adam, David

The man who couldn't stop **616.85**

Adam, Helen

A Helen Adam reader **811**

Adam, John A.

A mathematical nature walk **510**

Adam, Philip

Jack London, photographer **92**

Adamchak, Raoul W.

Tomorrow's table **664**

Adamec, Christine

When your adult child breaks your heart **616.89**

Adams family

About

Brookhiser, R. America's first dynasty **973.4**

Adams, Abigail, 1744-1818

About

Adams, J. My dearest friend **92**

Holton, W. Abigail Adams **92**

Adams, Ansel, 1902-1984

Ansel Adams in Yosemite Valley

Szarkowski, J. Ansel Adams at 100 **770**

Alinder, M. S. Ansel Adams **92**

Adams, Charles Francis, 1807-1886

About

Brookhiser, R. America's first dynasty **973.4**

Adams, Henry, 1838-1918

About

Adams, H. The education of Henry Adams **92**

Brookhiser, R. America's first dynasty **973.4**

Kazin, A. An American procession **810**

Tom and Jack **92**

Adams, James Eli

(ed) Encyclopedia of the Victorian era **941.081**

Adams, Jocelyn Delk

Grandbaby cakes **641.86**

Adams, John

About

Adams, J. Hallelujah junction **92**

McCullough, D. G. John Adams **92**

My dearest friend **92**

Adams, John Quincy, 1767-1848

About

Brookhiser, R. America's first dynasty **973.4**

Cohen, I. B. Science and the founding fathers **973.3**

Cook, J. H. American phoenix **973.5**

Giles Unger, H. John Quincy Adams **92**

Kaplan, F. John Quincy Adams **92**

Kennedy, J. F. Profiles in courage **920**

Miller, W. L. Arguing about slavery **973.5**

Nagel, P. C. John Quincy Adams **92**

O'Brien, M. Mrs. Adams in winter **940.2**

Remini, R. V. John Quincy Adams **92**

Traub, J. John Quincy Adams **92**

Thomas, L. Louisa **92**

Adams, John, 1735-1826

About

Adams, J. My dearest friend **92**

Brookhiser, R. America's first dynasty **973.4**

Ellis, J. J. Founding brothers **973.4**

Grant, J. John Adams **92**

Holton, W. Abigail Adams **92**

Larson, E. J. A magnificent catastrophe **324**

McCullough, D. G. John Adams **92**

Staloff, D. Hamilton, Adams, Jefferson **973.4**

Vidal, G. Inventing a nation: Washington, Adams, Jefferson **973.4**

Adams, Laurie

Italian Renaissance art **709.02**

Adams, Liza

Needle felting **746**

Adams, Louisa Catherine, 1775-1852

About

Cook, J. H. American phoenix **973.5**

O'Brien, M. Mrs. Adams in winter **940.2**

Thomas, L. Louisa **92**

Adams, Mark, 1967-

Meet Me in Atlantis **398.23**

Turn right at Machu Picchu **985**

Adams, Maureen B.

Shaggy muses **920**

Adams, Rachel, 1968-

About

Adams, R. Raising Henry **92**

Adamson, Joy

Born free **599.75**

Adamson, Lynda G.

Notable women in American history **016**

Notable women in world history **016**

Adamson, Robert

The goldfinches of Baghdad **821**

ADAPTABILITY (PSYCHOLOGY) *See* Adjustment (Psychology)

ADAPTATION (BIOLOGY)

Barrington, R. Life **578.4**

Francis, R. C. Epigenetics **572.8**

Toffler, A. Future shock **303.4**

Zuk, M. Riddled with life **616.07**

ADAPTATION (BIOLOGY)

See also Biology; Ecology; Genetics; Variation (Biology)

ADAPTATION (PSYCHOLOGY) *See* Adjustment (Psychology)

Adarme, Adrianna

The year of cozy **641.3**

Adcock, Fleur

Poems 1960-2000 **821**

ADD (CHILD BEHAVIOR DISORDER) *See* Attention deficit disorder

Addams, Jane, 1860-1935

Twenty years at Hull-House **361.7**

      About

Knight, L. W. Jane Addams **92**

Addario, Lynsey

      About

Addario, L. It's What I Do **92**

ADDICTION -- POETRY

Huntington, C. Heavenly bodies **811**

Addiction by design. Schüll, N. D. **362.2**

ADDICTION TO ALCOHOL *See* Alcoholism

ADDICTION TO DRUGS *See* Drug abuse

ADDICTION TO GAMBLING *See* Compulsive gambling

ADDICTION TO NICOTINE *See* Tobacco habit

ADDICTION TO TOBACCO *See* Tobacco habit

ADDICTIVE BEHAVIOR *See* Compulsive behavior

ADDICTS *See* Drug addicts

ADDICTS -- REHABILITATION

Fletcher, A. M. Inside rehab **362.29**

ADDITIVES, FOOD *See* Food additives

Addonizio, Kim

The poet's companion **808.1**

ADDRESSES *See* Lectures and lecturing; Speeches

Adelson-Goldstein, Jayme

The Oxford picture dictionary **423**

Aderkas, P. von

Turner, N. J. The North American guide to common poisonous plants and mushrooms **581.6**

ADHD does not exist. Saul, R. **618.92**

ADHD nation. Schwarz, A. **618.92**

ADHESIVES

      See also Materials

Adichie, Chimamanda Ngozi, 1977-

We Should All Be Feminists **305.42**

ADIRONDACK MOUNTAINS (N.Y.) -- HISTORY

Schneider, P. The Adirondacks **974.7**

The **Adirondacks**. Schneider, P. **974.7**

ADJUSTMENT (PSYCHOLOGY)

Brizendine, J. Stunned by grief **248**

Gonzales, L. Surviving survival **155.9**

Kingma, D. R. The ten things to do when your life falls apart **155.9**

Seligman, M. E. P. Learned optimism **155.2**

Thomas, A. What Comes Next and How to Like It **92**

Tuck, S. Getting from me to we **155.4**

ADJUSTMENT (PSYCHOLOGY)

      See also Psychology

ADJUSTMENT (PSYCHOLOGY) IN CHILDREN

Tuck, S. Getting from me to we **155.4**

ADJUSTMENT, SOCIAL *See* Social adjustment

Adkin, Mark

The Trafalgar companion **940.2**

Adler, Margot

Drawing down the moon **133.4**

Adler, Mortimer J.

Aristotle for everybody **185**

How to think about the great ideas **080**

Adler, Moshe

Economics for the rest of us **330**

Adler, Robert E.

Medical firsts **610**

Adler, Stella

Stella Adler on America's master playwrights **812**

Stella Adler: the art of acting **792**

Adler, Stephen J.

Grunwald, L. Women's letters **305.4**

Adler, William M.

The man who never died **92**

ADMINISTRATION *See* Civil service; Management; Public administration

ADMINISTRATION OF CRIMINAL JUSTICE

Benforado, A. Unfair **364.3**

Bogira, S. Courtroom 302 **345**

Burns, S. The Central Park Five **364.1**

Encyclopedia of crime and punishment **346**

Feige, D. Indefensible **345**

Morris, E. A wilderness of error **364.152**

Oshinsky, D. M. Worse than slavery **365**

Stevenson, B. Just Mercy **353.4**

Stuntz, W. J. The collapse of American criminal justice **364.4**

ADMINISTRATION OF CRIMINAL JUSTICE

      See also Administration of justice; Criminal law

ADMINISTRATION OF CRIMINAL JUSTICE -- UNITED STATES

The divide **303.3**

Garrett, B. L. Too big to jail **345.73**

Smith, C. S. The injustice system **345.73**

ADMINISTRATION OF JUSTICE

Legal systems of the world **340**

ADMINISTRATION OF JUSTICE

      See also Law

ADMINISTRATION OF JUSTICE -- UNITED STATES

Bernstein, N. Burning down the house **365**

ADMINISTRATIVE ABILITY *See* Executive ability

ADMINISTRATIVE AGENCIES

Kettl, D. F. The next government of the United States **351**

ADMINISTRATIVE AGENCIES -- LAW AND LEGISLATION *See* Administrative agencies

ADMINISTRATIVE AGENCIES -- UNITED

STATES -- REORGANIZATION
Gates, R. M. A passion for leadership **92**
ADMINISTRATIVE LAW
See also Law
Admiral of the ocean sea: a life of Christopher Columbus. Morison, S. E. **92**
The **admirals.** Borneman, W. R. **920**
ADMIRALS
Adkin, M. The Trafalgar companion **940.2**
Alexander, C. The Bounty: the true story of the mutiny on the Bounty **996**
Beyer, K. W. Grace Hopper and the invention of the information age **92**
Hibbert, C. Nelson **92**
Keneally, T. A commonwealth of thieves **994**
Pocock, T. The terror before Trafalgar **940.2**
Spencer, C. E. M. S. Prince Rupert **92**
Sugden, J. Nelson: a dream of glory, 1758-1797 **92**
Woodward, B. The commanders **973.928**
Zimmermann, W. First great triumph **973**
ADMIRALS
See also Military personnel; Navies
ADMIRALS -- UNITED STATES -- BIOGRAPHY
Berman, L. Zumwalt **92**
Borneman, W. R. The admirals **920**
Thomas, E. John Paul Jones **92**
ADMISSIONS APPLICATIONS *See* College applications
ADMISSIONS ESSAYS *See* College applications
Admitting the Holocaust. Langer, L. L. **940.53**
Adnan's Story. Chaudry, R. **364.152**
ADOLESCENCE
Auster, P. Report from the interior **92**
Bazelon, E. Sticks and stones **302.34**
Columbia University/Health Service The Go ask Alice book of answers **613**
Damour, L. Untangled **305.235**
Flanagan, C. Girl land **305.235**
Hine, T. The rise and fall of the American teenager **305.235**
Mead, M. Coming of age in Samoa **306**
ADOLESCENCE -- PSYCHOLOGY *See* Adolescent psychology
ADOLESCENT
Gnaulati, E. Back to normal **618.92**
Adolescent literacy in the academic disciplines. **428**
ADOLESCENT MOTHERS *See* Teenage mothers
ADOLESCENT PROSTITUTION *See* Juvenile prostitution
ADOLESCENT PSYCHIATRY
See also Psychiatry
ADOLESCENT PSYCHOLOGY
Barkley, R. A. Taking Charge of ADHD **618.92**
Gnaulati, E. Back to normal **618.92**
Jackson, L. Freaks, geeks and asperger syndrome **618.92**
Jensen, F. E. The teenage brain **612.6**
Lippincott, J. M. 7 things your teenager won't tell you **649**
Siegel, D. J. Brainstorm **155.5**
Wiseman, R. Masterminds and wingmen **649**
ADOLESCENT PSYCHOLOGY
See also Psychology
ADOLESCENTS *See* Teenagers
Adonis to Zorro. **422**
ADOPTED CHILDREN
Sweeney, J. If it's not one thing, it's your mother **362.734**
Winterson, J. Why be happy when you could be normal? **823**
ADOPTED CHILDREN
See also Adoptees; Children
ADOPTED CHILDREN -- AUSTRALIA -- TASMANIA -- BIOGRAPHY
Brierley, S. A long way home **92**
ADOPTED CHILDREN -- CALIFORNIA
Sweeney, J. If it's not one thing, it's your mother **362.734**
ADOPTEES -- CALIFORNIA -- BIOGRAPHY
Williams, M. The lost daughter **979.4**
ADOPTEES -- UNITED STATES -- IDENTIFICATION -- CASE STUDIES
Marshall, S. Reunited **362.82**
Adopting older children. Groza, V. **362.7**
ADOPTION
Caughman, S. You can adopt **362.7**
Fessler, A. The girls who went away **362.82**
Gammage, J. China ghosts **362.7**
Groza, V. Adopting older children **362.7**
Joyce, K. The child catchers **362.734**
Marshall, S. Reunited **362.82**
Rosswood, E. Journey to Same-sex Parenthood **306.874**
Seek, A. God and Jetfire **92**
ADOPTION
See also Parent-child relationship
ADOPTION -- RELIGIOUS ASPECTS -- CHRISTIANITY
Joyce, K. The child catchers **362.734**
Adovasio, J. M.
The first Americans **970.01**
ADULT CHILD ABUSE VICTIMS
Calcaterra, R. Girl Unbroken **306**
ADULT CHILD ABUSE VICTIMS
See also Victims of crimes
ADULT CHILD SEXUAL ABUSE VICTIMS
Bass, E. The courage to heal **616.85**
ADULT CHILD SEXUAL ABUSE VICTIMS
See also Adult child abuse victims
ADULT CHILDREN -- FAMILY RELATIONSHIPS

Newman, K. S. The accordion family   **306.874**

ADULT CHILDREN -- PSYCHOLOGY
Budd, K. The voluntourist   **361.7**

ADULT CHILDREN LIVING WITH PARENTS
Newman, K. S. The accordion family   **306.874**

ADULT CHILDREN OF AGING PARENTS -- FAMILY RELATIONSHIPS
Butler, K. Knocking on Heaven's Door   **616.02**

ADULT CHILDREN OF AGING PARENTS -- UNITED STATES -- BIOGRAPHY
Hodgman, G. Bettyville   **306.874**

ADULT EDUCATION
Rose, M. Back to school   **374**

ADULT EDUCATION
See also Education; Higher education; Secondary education; University extension

ADULTERY
Barash, D. P. The myth of monogamy   **306.7**
Blair, J. By the Iowa Sea   **977.7**

ADULTHOOD
Jackson, L. Sex, drugs and Asperger's syndrome (ASD)   **618.92**
Kaling, M. Why not me?   **92**
Ray, B. E. Not quite adults   **306.8**
Sheehy, G. New passages   **305.24**

ADULTHOOD -- HUMOR
Kaling, M. Why not me?   **92**

ADVANCE DIRECTIVES (MEDICAL CARE)
Volandes, A. E. The conversation   **616.02**
Advanced bushcraft. Canterbury, D.   **613.69**
Advanced chain maille jewelry workshop. Karon, K.   **745.594**
Advancing the story. Wenger, D. H.   **070.1**

ADVENT
See also Church year; Religious holidays

ADVENTURE AND ADVENTURERS
Cordingly, D. Women sailors and sailors' women   **910.4**
Lawrence, S. River house   **92**
Points unknown   **910**

ADVENTURE AND ADVENTURERS -- CHINA -- SHANHAI -- BIOGRAPHY
Grescoe, T. Shanghai grand   **951.132**

ADVENTURE AND ADVENTURERS -- FICTION *See* Adventure fiction

ADVENTURE AND ADVENTURERS -- UNITED STATES -- BIOGRAPHY
Groom, W. The aviators   **920**

ADVENTURE FICTION
Kurson, R. Pirate hunters   **910.91**

ADVENTURE FICTION
See also Fiction

ADVENTURE FILMS
See also Motion pictures

ADVENTURE GRAPHIC NOVELS
See also Graphic novels

The **adventure** of English. Bragg, M.   **420**

ADVENTURE STORIES *See* Adventure fiction

ADVENTURE TELEVISION PROGRAMS
See also Television programs

ADVENTURE TRAVEL
Foer, J. Atlas Obscura   **910.41**

ADVENTURE TRAVEL
See also Travel; Voyages and travels

ADVENTURERS
Morris-Suzuki, T. To the Diamond Mountains   **915**
Adventures among ants. Moffett, M. W.   **595.7**
Adventures in chicken. Flores, E. K.   **641.665**
Adventures in human being. Francis, G.   **612**
Adventures in the screen trade. Goldman, W.   **791.43**
The **adventures** of Amos 'n' Andy. Ely, M. P.   **791.44**
The **adventures** of Grandmaster Flash. Grandmaster Flash   **92**

ADVERTISING
Boorstin, D. J. The Americans: The democratic experience   **973**
Jantsch, J. The referral engine   **658.8**
Miles, J. YouTube marketing power   **658.8**
Turow, J. The daily you   **659.1**

ADVERTISING
See also Business; Retail trade

ADVERTISING -- LIBRARIES
Imhoff, K. R. Library contests   **021.7**

ADVERTISING AND CHILDREN
Linn, S. The case for make believe   **155.4**

ADVERTISING AND CHILDREN
See also Advertising; Children

ADVERTISING ART *See* Commercial art

ADVERTISING COPY
See also Advertising; Authorship

ADVERTISING LAYOUT AND TYPOGRAPHY
See also Advertising; Printing; Typography

ADVICE COLUMNISTS
Dickinson, A. The mighty queens of Freeville   **92**
Life stories   **920**

ADVICE COLUMNS
See also Counseling; Newspapers -- Sections, columns, etc.

ADVOCACY (POLITICAL SCIENCE)
See also Political science
The **Aeneid.** Virgil   **873**

AERIAL PHOTOGRAPHY
Haas, R. B. Through the eyes of the Vikings   **779**
Malin, G. Beaches   **779.37**

AERIAL PHOTOGRAPHY
See also Photography

AERIAL PROPELLERS
See also Airplanes

AERIAL ROCKETS *See* Rockets (Aeronautics)

AERIALISTS -- UNITED STATES -- BIOGRAPHY
Jensen, D. Queen of the air   **791.3**

AEROBICS
See also Exercise

AERODYNAMICS
See also Air; Dynamics; Pneumatics

AERONAUTICAL ENGINEERS
Clary, D. A. Rocket man   **92**
Hargittai, I. The Martians of science   **920**

AERONAUTICAL INSTRUMENTS
See also Scientific apparatus and instruments

AERONAUTICAL SPORTS
Higgins, M. Bird dream   **797.5**

AERONAUTICAL SPORTS
See also Aeronautics; Sports

AERONAUTICS
Alexander, D. E. Why don't jumbo jets flap their wings?   **629.13**
McCullough, D. The Wright brothers   **92**
Ryan, C. Sonic wind   **92**

AERONAUTICS
See also Engineering; Locomotion

AERONAUTICS -- ACCIDENTS *See* Aircraft accidents

AERONAUTICS -- CHINA
Fallows, J. China airborne   **387.7**

AERONAUTICS -- COMPETITIONS
Jackson, J. Atlantic fever   **629.130**

AERONAUTICS -- FLIGHTS
Botting, D. Dr. Eckener's dream machine   **629.133**
Lindbergh, C. The spirit of St. Louis   **629.13**

AERONAUTICS -- FLIGHTS
See also Voyages and travels

AERONAUTICS -- HISTORY
Goldstone, L. Birdmen   **629.13**
Jackson, J. Atlantic fever   **629.130**

AERONAUTICS -- PILOTING *See* Airplanes -- Piloting

AERONAUTICS -- POPULAR WORKS
Vanhoenacker, M. Skyfaring   **629.132**

AERONAUTICS -- SAFETY MEASURES
McGee, W. J. Attention all passengers   **387.7**

AERONAUTICS -- SAFETY MEASURES -- RESEARCH -- UNITED STATES -- HISTORY -- 20TH CENTURY
Ryan, C. Sonic wind   **92**

AERONAUTICS -- UNITED STATES -- BIOGRAPHY
McCullough, D. The Wright brothers   **92**

AERONAUTICS -- UNITED STATES -- HISTORY
Kessner, T. The flight of the century   **92**
Pyne, S. J. Voyager   **919**

AERONAUTICS -- UNITED STATES -- HISTORY -- 20TH CENTURY
Groom, W. The aviators   **920**
McCullough, D. The Wright brothers   **92**

AERONAUTICS AND CIVILIZATION
See also Aeronautics; Civilization

AERONAUTICS IN AGRICULTURE
See also Aeronautics; Agriculture; Spraying and dusting

AERONAUTICS, COMMERCIAL -- CHINA
Fallows, J. China airborne   **387.7**

AERONAUTICS, MILITARY -- ACCIDENTS -- ALASKA
Murphy, B. 81 days below zero   **940.54**

AEROSPACE ENGINEERING
Whittle, R. Predator   **623.74**

AEROSPACE ENGINEERING
See also Aeronautics; Astronautics; Engineering

AEROSPACE ENGINEERS
Biddle, W. Dark side of the moon   **92**
Clary, D. A. Rocket man   **92**
Hickam, H. H. Rocket boys   **629.1**
Neufeld, M. J. Von Braun   **92**

AEROSPACE INDUSTRIES -- CALIFORNIA, SOUTHERN -- HISTORY
Whittle, R. Predator   **623.74**

AEROTHERMODYNAMICS
See also Astronautics; High speed aeronautics; Supersonic aerodynamics; Thermodynamics

Aeschylus. Aeschylus   **882**

Aeschylus
Aeschylus   **882**
The Oresteia   **882**

AESTHETICS
Donoghue, D. Speaking of beauty   **801**
Eco, U. History of beauty   **111**
Kaufman, S. L. The art of grace   **302.1**
Keene, D. The pleasures of Japanese literature   **895.6**
On ugliness   **111**
Whitefield-Madrano, A. Face value   **111.85**
Williams, T. T. Finding beauty in a broken world   **814**

AESTHETICS
See also Philosophy

The **affair.** Bredin   **944.081**

Affairs of honor. Freeman, J. B.   **306.2**

AFFECTION *See* Friendship; Love

AFFECTIVE DISORDERS
See also Abnormal psychology

AFFECTIVE DISORDERS -- TREATMENT
Greenberger, D. Mind over mood   **616.89**

AFFIRMATIONS
Osteen, J. The power of I am   **248.4**

AFFIRMATIONS
See also Self-help techniques

AFFIRMATIVE ACTION PROGRAMS
Katznelson, I. When affirmative action was white   **323.1**

AFFIRMATIVE ACTION PROGRAMS
   See also Discrimination in employment; Personnel management
AFFLICTION *See* Joy and sorrow; Suffering
AFFLUENT PEOPLE *See* Rich
AFFORDABLE HOUSING *See* Housing
AFGHAN LITERATURE
  I am the beggar of the world   **891**
AFGHAN WAR, 2001-
  Addario, L. It's What I Do   **92**
  Bannerman, S. Homefront 911   **362.86**
  Dalrymple, W. Return of a king   **958.1**
  Ghouri, N. The lightless sky   **958.104**
  Khan, M. R. My Guantanamo diary   **909.83**
  Lemmon, G. T. Ashley's war   **92**
  Luttrell, M. Lone survivor   **92**
  Partlow, J. A kingdom of their own   **958.104**
  Poole, R. M. Section 60   **975.5**
  Rodriguez, D. Rise   **92**
  Smith, G. The Dogs Are Eating Them Now   **958.104**
  West, B. The wrong war   **958.1**
AFGHAN WAR, 2001- -- CAMPAIGNS
  Bolger, D. P. Why We Lost   **956.704**
  Castner, B. All the ways we kill and die   **958.104**
  Grenier, R. L. 88 days to Kandahar   **958.104**
  Hornfischer, J. D. Service   **956.704**
  Luttrell, M. Lone survivor   **92**
  Thorpe, H. Soldier girls   **956.704**
AFGHAN WAR, 2001- -- CAMPAIGNS -- AFGHANISTAN -- BĀDGHĪS
  Bruning, J. R. Level zero heroes   **958.104**
AFGHAN WAR, 2001- -- CASUALTIES -- UNITED STATES
  Poole, R. M. Section 60   **975.5**
AFGHAN WAR, 2001- -- ENCYCLOPEDIAS
  The encyclopedia of Middle East wars   **355**
AFGHAN WAR, 2001- -- PERSONAL NARRATIVES
  Maurer, K. No easy day   **958.104**
  Romesha, C. L. Red platoon   **958.1**
  Sites, K. The things they cannot say   **355**
AFGHAN WAR, 2001- -- PERSONAL NARRATIVES, AMERICAN
  Bolger, D. P. Why We Lost   **956.704**
  Bruning, J. R. Level zero heroes   **958.104**
  Castner, B. All the ways we kill and die   **958.104**
  Grenier, R. L. 88 days to Kandahar   **958.104**
  Hornfischer, J. D. Service   **956.704**
  Luttrell, M. Lone survivor   **92**
  Rodriguez, D. Rise   **92**
AFGHAN WAR, 2001- -- SECRET SERVICE
  Grenier, R. L. 88 days to Kandahar   **958.104**
AFGHAN WAR, 2001- -- VETERANS -- UNITED STATES
  Bannerman, S. Homefront 911   **362.86**
AFGHAN WAR, 2001- -- WOMEN -- UNITED

STATES -- BIOGRAPHY
  Thorpe, H. Soldier girls   **956.704**
Afghanistan. Evans, M.   **958.1**
AFGHANISTAN
  Badkhen, A. The world is a carpet   **958.1**
AFGHANISTAN -- BIOGRAPHY
  Omar, Q. A. A fort of nine towers   **958.104**
AFGHANISTAN -- DESCRIPTION AND TRAVEL
  Elliot, J. An unexpected light   **958.1**
  Jubber, N. Drinking arak off an ayatollah's beard   **915**
AFGHANISTAN -- FOREIGN RELATIONS -- UNITED STATES
  Gall, C. The wrong enemy   **958.104**
  Partlow, J. A kingdom of their own   **958.104**
AFGHANISTAN -- HISTORY
  Coll, S. Ghost wars   **958.1**
  Ewans, M. Afghanistan   **958.1**
  Wahab, S. A brief history of Afghanistan   **958.1**
AFGHANISTAN -- HISTORY -- BRITISH INTERVENTION, 1838-1842
  Dalrymple, W. Return of a king   **958.1**
AFGHANISTAN -- HISTORY -- SOVIET OCCUPATION, 1979-1989
  Coll, S. Ghost wars   **958.1**
  Feifer, G. The great gamble   **958.1**
AFGHANISTAN -- HISTORY -- SOVIET OCCUPATION, 1979-1989 -- GRAPHIC NOVELS
  Guibert, E. The photographer   **958.1**
AFGHANISTAN -- POLITICS AND GOVERNMENT -- 2001-
  Filkins, D. The forever war   **956.7**
  Rashid, A. Descent into chaos   **954**
  Rashid, A. Taliban   **958.1**
AFGHANISTAN -- POLITICS AND GOVERNMENT -- 21ST CENTURY
  Grenier, R. L. 88 days to Kandahar   **958.104**
AFGHANISTAN -- SOCIAL CONDITIONS
  Nordberg, J. The underground girls of Kabul **305.42**
  Omar, Q. A. A fort of nine towers   **958.104**
AFGHANISTAN -- SOCIAL CONDITIONS -- 20TH CENTURY
  Omar, Q. A. A fort of nine towers   **958.104**
AFGHANISTAN -- SOCIAL LIFE AND CUSTOMS
  Badkhen, A. The world is a carpet   **958.1**
AFGHANS (COVERLETS)
  Chachula, R. Unexpected afghans   **746.43**
Afremow, Jim
  The champion's mind   **796.01**
AFRICA
  Badkhen, A. Walking With Abel   **305.896**
  Meredith, M. Born in Africa   **960**
AFRICA -- CIVILIZATION
  Soyinka, W. Of Africa   **960**

AFRICA -- CIVILIZATION
See also Civilization

AFRICA -- DESCRIPTION
Matthiessen, P. African silences   **916**

AFRICA -- DESCRIPTION AND TRAVEL
Perry, A. The Rift   **320.9**

AFRICA -- ENCYCLOPEDIAS
Africana: the encyclopedia of the African and African American experience   **909**

AFRICA -- HISTORIOGRAPHY
Lefkowitz, M. R. Not out of Africa   **960**

AFRICA -- HISTORY
Meredith, M. The fortunes of Africa   **960**
Soyinka, W. Of Africa   **960**

AFRICA -- POLITICS AND GOVERNMENT
Burgis, T. The looting machine   **338.2**

AFRICA -- SOCIAL CONDITIONS
Burgis, T. The looting machine   **338.2**
Gevisser, M. Lost and Found in Johannesburg, a memoir   **92**
Perry, A. The Rift   **320.9**
Varty, B. Cathedral of the wild   **639.9**

AFRICA, NORTH -- HISTORY, MILITARY
Atkinson, R. An army at dawn   **940.54**

AFRICAN AMERICAN ABOLITIONISTS -- BIOGRAPHY
Douglass, F. My bondage and my freedom   **92**
Stauffer, J. Picturing Frederick Douglass   **92**

AFRICAN AMERICAN ABOLITIONISTS -- HISTORY
Berlin, I. The long emancipation   **326.8**

AFRICAN AMERICAN ACTORS
Bogle, D. Bright boulevards, bold dreams   **791.43**
Carroll, D. The legs are the last to go   **92**
Lane, S. F. Black Broadway   **792**

AFRICAN AMERICAN ACTORS
See also Actors; Black actors

AFRICAN AMERICAN ACTORS AND ACTRESSES *See* African American actors

The **African** American almanac.   **305.8**
African American almanac. Bracks, L.   **973**

AFRICAN AMERICAN ANTHROPOLOGISTS -- BIOGRAPHY
Ransby, B. Eslanda   **92**

AFRICAN AMERICAN ART
Farrington, L. E. Creating their own image   **709**
Murray, A. The blue devils of Nada   **780.89**
Patton, S. F. African-American art   **704.03**

AFRICAN AMERICAN ART
See also Art; Black art

AFRICAN AMERICAN ASTRONAUTS
Hardesty, V. Black wings   **920**
Paul, R. We could not fail   **920**

AFRICAN AMERICAN ASTRONAUTS -- BIOGRAPHY
Gubert, B. K. Distinguished African Americans in aviation and space science   **629.13**
Paul, R. We could not fail   **920**

AFRICAN AMERICAN ATHLETES
Assael, S. The murder of Sonny Liston   **796.83**
Balf, T. Major   **92**
Biddle, D. R. Tasting freedom   **92**
Bryant, H. The last hero   **92**
Donovan, B. Hard driving: the Wendell Scott story   **92**
Hogan, L. D. Shades of glory   **796.357**
Joyner-Kersee, J. A kind of grace   **796.42**
Levy, A. H. Floyd Patterson   **92**
Remnick, D. King of the world: Muhammad Ali and the rise of an American hero   **92**
Rhoden, W. C. $40 million slaves   **796**
Roberts, R. Joe Louis   **92**
Robinson, J. I never had it made   **92**
Ross, C. K. Mavericks, money, and men   **796.332**
Ruck, R. Raceball   **796.357**
Runstedtler, T. Jack Johnson, rebel sojourner   **796.83**
Schaap, J. Triumph   **92**
Tye, L. Satchel   **92**
White, B. Uppity   **92**

AFRICAN AMERICAN ATHLETES
See also Athletes; Black athletes

AFRICAN AMERICAN AUTHORS
Angelou, M. Letter to my daughter   **92**
Angelou, M. I know why the caged bird sings   **92**
Boyd, V. Wrapped in rainbows   **92**
Gillespie, M. A. Maya Angelou   **92**
Hooks, B. Belonging   **92**
Hughes, L. I wonder as I wander   **818**
Hurston, Z. N. Dust tracks on a road   **92**
Marshall, P. Triangular road   **92**
Norrell, R. J. Alex Haley and the books that changed a nation   **92**
Rampersad, A. The life of Langston Hughes Volume I: 1902-1941   **92**
Rampersad, A. The life of Langston Hughes Volume II: 1941-1967   **818**
Wright, R. Black boy   **92**
Zora Neale Hurston: a life in letters   **92**

AFRICAN AMERICAN AUTHORS
See also American authors; Black authors

AFRICAN AMERICAN AUTHORS -- BIOGRAPHY
Gifford, J. Street poison   **813**

AFRICAN AMERICAN AUTHORS -- DICTIONARIES
Bader, P. African-American writers   **920.003**

AFRICAN AMERICAN BASEBALL PLAYERS
Kashatus, W. C. Jackie and Campy   **92**
Lazenby, R. Michael Jordan   **92**
Maraniss, A. Strong inside   **92**
McGregor, R. K. A Calculus of Color   **796.357**

AFRICAN AMERICAN BASEBALL PLAYERS

See also Baseball players

AFRICAN AMERICAN BASEBALL PLAYERS -- BIOGRAPHY

Kashatus, W. C. Jackie and Campy 92

AFRICAN AMERICAN BOXERS -- BIOGRAPHY

Assael, S. The murder of Sonny Liston 796.83

Gildea, W. The longest fight 796.83

Runstedtler, T. Jack Johnson, rebel sojourner 796.83

Stratton, W. K. Floyd Patterson 92

AFRICAN AMERICAN BUSINESS PEOPLE

See African American businesspeople

AFRICAN AMERICAN BUSINESSPEOPLE

White, S. Prince of darkness 92

AFRICAN AMERICAN BUSINESSPEOPLE

See also Black businesspeople; Businesspeople

AFRICAN AMERICAN CAPITALISTS AND FINANCIERS -- BIOGRAPHY

White, S. Prince of darkness 92

AFRICAN AMERICAN CHILDREN

See also Black children; Children

AFRICAN AMERICAN CHILDREN -- EDUCATION

Tough, P. Whatever it takes 362.7

AFRICAN AMERICAN CIVIL RIGHTS WORKERS

Lewis, J. March 92

Sugrue, T. J. Sweet land of liberty 323

AFRICAN AMERICAN CIVIL RIGHTS WORKERS -- BIOGRAPHY

Dyson, M. E. I may not get there with you: the true Martin Luther King, Jr 323

Lewis, A. B. The shadows of youth 323.1

Smith, J. E. Becoming Belafonte 92

AFRICAN AMERICAN COLLEGE GRADUATES

Hobbs, J. The short and tragic life of Robert Peace 92

AFRICAN AMERICAN COOKING

Afro-vegan 641.59

Miller, A. Soul food 641.59

Soul food love 641.59

Terry, B. Vegan Soul kitchen 641.5

AFRICAN AMERICAN COOKING -- HISTORY

Miller, A. Soul food 641.59

AFRICAN AMERICAN COOKS -- UNITED STATES -- BIOGRAPHY

Chambers, V. Yes, chef 92

African American cultural theory and heritage [series]

Inaba, M. Willie Dixon 92

AFRICAN AMERICAN DANCERS

Jones, B. T. Story/Time 814

AFRICAN AMERICAN DANCERS

See also African Americans; Dancers

AFRICAN AMERICAN DANCERS -- BIOGRAPHY

Copeland, M. Life in motion 92

AFRICAN AMERICAN EDUCATORS

Biddle, D. R. Tasting freedom 92

Davis, D. Guest of honor 973.91

Harlan, L. R. Booker T. Washington: the making of a black leader, 1856-1901 92

Harlan, L. R. Booker T. Washington: the wizard of Tuskegee, 1901-1915 92

McCluskey, A. T. A forgotten sisterhood 370.922

Norrell, R. J. Up from history 92

Smock, R. W. Booker T. Washington 92

Uncle Tom or new Negro 370

Washington, B. T. Up from slavery 92

AFRICAN AMERICAN EDUCATORS

See also African Americans; Educators

AFRICAN AMERICAN EDUCATORS -- SOUTHERN STATES -- BIOGRAPHY

McCluskey, A. T. A forgotten sisterhood 370.922

AFRICAN AMERICAN ELDERLY

See also Elderly

AFRICAN AMERICAN ENGINEERS -- BIOGRAPHY

Paul, R. We could not fail 920

AFRICAN AMERICAN ENTERTAINERS -- BIOGRAPHY

Common One day it'll all make sense 92

AFRICAN AMERICAN FAMILIES

Haley, A. Roots 920

Swarns, R. L. American tapestry 92

AFRICAN AMERICAN FAMILIES -- HISTORY

Williams, H. A. Help me to find my people 306.3

AFRICAN AMERICAN FARMERS -- GEORGIA -- ECONOMIC CONDITIONS

Sherrod, S. The courage to hope 975.8

AFRICAN AMERICAN FEMINISTS -- BIOGRAPHY

Bell-Scott, P. The firebrand and the First Lady 92

AFRICAN AMERICAN FOOTBALL PLAYERS

Ross, C. K. Mavericks, money, and men 796.332

AFRICAN AMERICAN GENERALS -- BIOGRAPHY

Koltz, T. It worked for me 92

AFRICAN AMERICAN GIRLS -- ILLINOIS -- CHICAGO REGION -- SOCIAL CONDITIONS -- 20TH CENTURY

Jefferson, M. Negroland 92

AFRICAN AMERICAN JOURNALISTS -- BIOGRAPHY

Norrell, R. J. Alex Haley and the books that changed a nation 92

AFRICAN AMERICAN LAWYERS -- BIOGRAPHY

Slevin, P. Michelle Obama **92**

AFRICAN AMERICAN LEGISLATORS

Dray, P. Capitol men **920**

Lewis, J. March **92**

AFRICAN AMERICAN LIBRARIANS

The 21st-century black librarian in America **020**

AFRICAN AMERICAN LIBRARIANS

    See also Black librarians; Librarians

African American literature. **810.9**

AFRICAN AMERICAN LITERATURE *See*
    American literature -- African American authors

African American lives. **920**

AFRICAN AMERICAN MEN -- BIOGRAPHY

Gates, H. L. Thirteen ways of looking at a black
man **920.71**

Moore, W. The work **92**

AFRICAN AMERICAN MEN -- MISSISSIPPI

Ward, J. Men We Reaped **92**

**AFRICAN AMERICAN MODELS -- BIOGRA-
PHY**

Cleveland, P. Walking with the muses **92**

AFRICAN AMERICAN MUSIC

Baraka, I. A. The LeRoi Jones/Amiri Baraka reader **818**

Lomax, A. The land where the blues began **781.643**

Ware, C. P. Slave songs of the United States **781.62**

AFRICAN AMERICAN MUSIC

    See also Black music; Music

AFRICAN AMERICAN MUSICIANS

Basie, C. Good morning blues: the autobiography
of Count Basie **92**

Cohodas, N. Princess Noire **92**

Coleman, R. Blue Monday **92**

Cook, R. It's about that time **92**

Davis, M. Miles, the autobiography **92**

Dyson, M. E. Holler if you hear me: searching for
Tupac Shakur **92**

Feather, L. From Satchmo to Miles **920**

Govenar, A. B. Lightnin' Hopkins **92**

Ice-T Ice **92**

Inaba, M. Willie Dixon **92**

Kelley, R. D. G. Thelonious Monk **92**

King, B. B. Blues all around me **781.643**

Lowe, J. Digging for dirt **92**

Murray, A. The blue devils of Nada **780.89**

Ratliff, B. Coltrane **92**

Scott-Heron, G. The last holiday **920**

Wald, E. Escaping the delta **92**

White, C. The life and times of Little Richard **92**

Wolfe, C. K. The life and legend of Leadbelly **92**

AFRICAN AMERICAN MUSICIANS

    See also Black musicians; Musicians

The **African** American national biography. **920.003**

**AFRICAN AMERICAN NEIGHBORHOODS --
DRAMA**

Wilson, A. Two trains running **812**

AFRICAN AMERICAN NEWSPAPERS

Michaeli, E. The defender **071**

AFRICAN AMERICAN PHOTOGRAPHERS

Willis, D. Reflections in Black **770.92**

AFRICAN AMERICAN PILOTS

Gubert, B. K. Distinguished African Americans in
aviation and space science **629.13**

Hardesty, V. Black wings **920**

AFRICAN AMERICAN POETRY *See* American
poetry -- African American authors

African American religious leaders. Haskins, J. **920**

AFRICAN AMERICAN SINGERS

Belafonte, H. My song **92**

Bogle, D. Heat wave **92**

Brown, J. James Brown, the godfather of soul **92**

Carroll, D. The legs are the last to go **92**

Cohodas, N. Princess Noire **92**

Epstein, D. M. Nat King Cole **92**

Gavin, J. Stormy weather **92**

Holiday, B. Lady sings the blues **92**

Keiler, A. Marian Anderson **92**

Sullivan, J. The hardest working man **92**

AFRICAN AMERICAN SINGERS

    See also African Americans; Singers

**AFRICAN AMERICAN SINGERS -- BIOGRA-
PHY**

Ritz, D. Respect **92**

AFRICAN AMERICAN SOLDIERS

Ash, S. V. Firebrand of liberty **973.7**

Kaplan, A. Y. The interpreter **940.54**

Sutherland, J. African Americans at war **355**

Trudeau, N. A. Like men of war **973.7**

Tuccille, J. The roughest riders **973.8**

**AFRICAN AMERICAN SOLDIERS -- BIOGRA-
PHY**

Buckley, G. L. American patriots **355**

Hervieux, L. Forgotten **940.54**

AFRICAN AMERICAN SOLDIERS -- HISTORY

Ash, S. V. Firebrand of liberty **973.7**

Slotkin, R. Lost battalions **940.3**

Slotkin, R. No quarter **973.7**

**AFRICAN AMERICAN SOLDIERS -- HISTORY
-- 19TH CENTURY**

Ash, S. V. Firebrand of liberty **973.7**

Tuccille, J. The roughest riders **973.8**

AFRICAN AMERICAN SONGS *See* African
American music

**AFRICAN AMERICAN TELEVISION JOUR-
NALISTS -- UNITED STATES -- ANEC-
DOTES**

Roberts, D. Been there, done that **92**

AFRICAN AMERICAN THEATER

Lane, S. F. Black Broadway **792**

**AFRICAN AMERICAN UNIVERSITIES AND
COLLEGES**

Williams, J. I'll find a way or make one **378**

AFRICAN AMERICAN WOMEN

Clinton, C. Harriet Tubman: the road to freedom **92**

Dove, R. On the bus with Rosa Parks **811**

Farrington, L. E. Creating their own image **709**

Gavin, J. Stormy weather **92**

Hill, A. Reimagining equality **305.8**

Humez, J. M. Harriet Tubman **92**

Lee Shetterly, M. Hidden Figures **510.92**

Longing to tell **306.7**

Smith, P. Shoulda been Jimi Savannah **811**

Walker-Hill, H. From spirituals to symphonies **780**

AFRICAN AMERICAN WOMEN

See also Black women; Women

**AFRICAN AMERICAN WOMEN -- BIOGRA-
PHY**

Cleveland, P. Walking with the muses **92**

**AFRICAN AMERICAN WOMEN -- CIVIL
RIGHTS -- HISTORY -- 20TH CENTURY**

McGuire, D. L. At the dark end of the street **323.1**

**AFRICAN AMERICAN WOMEN -- DICTION-
ARIES**

Black women in America **920.003**

Notable black American women, book I **920.003**

Notable black American women, Book III **920.003**

**AFRICAN AMERICAN WOMEN -- HEALTH
AND HYGIENE**

Essence total makeover **646.7**

**AFRICAN AMERICAN WOMEN -- ILLINOIS
-- CHICAGO -- BIOGRAPHY**

Jefferson, M. Negroland **92**

**AFRICAN AMERICAN WOMEN -- MASSA-
CHUSETTS -- CAMBRIDGE -- BIOGRAPHY**

Nathans, S. To free a family **306.3**

**AFRICAN AMERICAN WOMEN -- VIOLENCE
AGAINST**

McGuire, D. L. At the dark end of the street **323.1**

**AFRICAN AMERICAN WOMEN AUTHORS --
BIOGRAPHY**

Smith, T. K. Ordinary light **92**

Ward, J. Men We Reaped **92**

**AFRICAN AMERICAN WOMEN CIVIL
RIGHTS WORKERS -- ALABAMA -- MONT-
GOMERY -- BIOGRAPHY**

Brinkley, D. Rosa Parks **92**

Theoharis, J. The rebellious life of Mrs. Rosa
Parks **92**

**AFRICAN AMERICAN WOMEN CIVIL
RIGHTS WORKERS -- BIOGRAPHY**

Bell-Scott, P. The firebrand and the First Lady **92**

McCluskey, A. T. A forgotten sisterhood **370.922**

**AFRICAN AMERICAN WOMEN LAWYERS --
BIOGRAPHY**

Slevin, P. Michelle Obama **92**

AFRICAN AMERICAN YOUTH

See also Youth

AFRICAN AMERICANS

The African American almanac **305.8**

Africana: the encyclopedia of the African and African American experience **909**

Du Bois, W. E. B. The souls of Black folk **305.8**

The Fire This Time **305.896**

Gates, H. L. The African-American century **305**

Gates, H. L. In search of our roots **305.8**

Hurston, Z. N. Novels and stories **813**

Jefferson, M. Negroland **92**

Jones, J. A dreadful deceit **305.8**

The Oxford W. E. B. Du Bois reader **305.896**

Presidents and Black America **973.09**

Robeson, P. The undiscovered Paul Robeson **92**

AFRICAN AMERICANS

See also Blacks

**AFRICAN AMERICANS -- ATTITUDES -- HIS-
TORY -- SOURCES**

Presidents and Black America **973.09**

AFRICAN AMERICANS -- BIOGRAPHY

Buckley, G. L. The Black Calhouns **92**

Haley, A. Roots **920**

Jacoby, K. The strange career of William Ellis **92**

Macy, B. Truevine **791.3**

Moore, W. The work **92**

Smith, J. Blood brothers **92**

White, S. Prince of darkness **92**

**AFRICAN AMERICANS -- BIOGRAPHY --
DICTIONARIES**

The African American national biography **920.003**

Notable black American men, book I **920.003**

Notable black American men, book II **920.003**

Notable black American scientists **509**

Who's who among African Americans **920.003**

**AFRICAN AMERICANS -- BIOGRAPHY -- EN-
CYCLOPEDIAS**

Bracks, L. African American almanac **973**

**AFRICAN AMERICANS -- CALIFORNIA --
OAKLAND -- BIOGRAPHY**

Williams, M. The lost daughter **979.4**

AFRICAN AMERICANS -- CHICAGO (ILL.)

Common One day it'll all make sense **92**

Michaeli, E. The defender **071**

Writers of the Black Chicago renaissance **810.9**

AFRICAN AMERICANS -- CIVIL RIGHTS

Kantrowitz, S. More than freedom **323.1**

Morris, J. M. Eye on the Struggle **92**

Rieder, J. Gospel of freedom **323.1**

Sokol, J. All eyes are upon us **323.1**

Stratton, W. K. Floyd Patterson **92**

AFRICAN AMERICANS -- CIVIL RIGHTS

See also Blacks -- Civil rights; Civil rights

**AFRICAN AMERICANS -- CIVIL RIGHTS --
ALABAMA -- BIRMINGHAM**

Rieder, J. Gospel of freedom **323.1**

**AFRICAN AMERICANS -- CIVIL RIGHTS --
ALABAMA -- MONTGOMERY -- HISTORY**

-- 20TH CENTURY

Brinkley, D. Rosa Parks **92**

Theoharis, J. The rebellious life of Mrs. Rosa Parks **92**

AFRICAN AMERICANS -- CIVIL RIGHTS -- GRAPHIC NOVELS

Lewis, J. R. March **92**

Lewis, J. March **92**

AFRICAN AMERICANS -- CIVIL RIGHTS -- HISTORY -- 19TH CENTURY

Blackmon, D. A. Slavery by another name **305.8**

Douglass, F. Frederick Douglass: selected speeches and writings **326**

AFRICAN AMERICANS -- CIVIL RIGHTS -- HISTORY -- 20TH CENTURY

Blackmon, D. A. Slavery by another name **305.8**

Boyle, K. Arc of justice **345**

Branch, T. At Canaan's edge **973.923**

Dyson, M. E. I may not get there with you: the true Martin Luther King, Jr **323**

Joseph, P. E. Waiting 'til the midnight hour **323.1**

Katznelson, I. When affirmative action was white **323.1**

King, M. L. The autobiography of Martin Luther King, Jr **323**

Lewis, A. B. The shadows of youth **323.1**

Sugrue, T. J. Sweet land of liberty **323**

Sullivan, P. Lift every voice **323.1**

AFRICAN AMERICANS -- CIVIL RIGHTS -- HISTORY -- 20TH CENTURY -- PICTORIAL WORKS

Kelley, K. Let Freedom Ring **323.1**

AFRICAN AMERICANS -- CIVIL RIGHTS -- MASSACHUSETTS -- BOSTON REGION -- HISTORY -- 19TH CENTURY

Kantrowitz, S. More than freedom **323.1**

AFRICAN AMERICANS -- CIVIL RIGHTS -- NORTHEASTERN STATES -- HISTORY -- 20TH CENTURY

Sokol, J. All eyes are upon us **323.1**

AFRICAN AMERICANS -- CIVIL RIGHTS -- PENNSYLVANIA -- PHILADELPHIA

Biddle, D. R. Tasting freedom **92**

AFRICAN AMERICANS -- CIVIL RIGHTS -- POETRY

Wright, C. D. One with others **811**

AFRICAN AMERICANS -- CIVIL RIGHTS -- SOUTHERN STATES -- HISTORY

McCluskey, A. T. A forgotten sisterhood **370.922**

Remembering Jim Crow **305.896**

AFRICAN AMERICANS -- CIVIL RIGHTS -- SOUTHERN STATES -- HISTORY -- 20TH CENTURY

Arsenault, R. Freedom riders **323**

Sokol, J. There goes my everything **305.8**

AFRICAN AMERICANS -- CRIMES AGAINST

-- MISSISSIPPI

Anderson, D. S. Emmett Till **364.1**

AFRICAN AMERICANS -- DETROIT (MICH.) -- HISTORY

Martelle, S. Detroit **977.4**

AFRICAN AMERICANS -- DRAMA

Wilson, A. Two trains running **812**

AFRICAN AMERICANS -- ECONOMIC CONDITIONS

Katznelson, I. When affirmative action was white **323.1**

Robinson, E. Disintegration **305.8**

AFRICAN AMERICANS -- ECONOMIC CONDITIONS

See also Blacks -- Economic conditions; Economic conditions

AFRICAN AMERICANS -- EDUCATION

McWhorter, J. H. Losing the race **305.8**

Williams, J. I'll find a way or make one **378**

AFRICAN AMERICANS -- EDUCATION

See also Blacks -- Education; Education

AFRICAN AMERICANS -- EDUCATION (HIGHER) HISTORY

Wilder, C. S. Ebony and Ivy **379.26**

AFRICAN AMERICANS -- EDUCATION -- HISTORY

McCluskey, A. T. A forgotten sisterhood **370.922**

AFRICAN AMERICANS -- ENCYCLOPEDIAS

Bracks, L. African American almanac **973**

AFRICAN AMERICANS -- FICTION

Hurston, Z. N. Novels and stories **813**

AFRICAN AMERICANS -- FOLKLORE

See also Blacks -- Folklore; Folklore

AFRICAN AMERICANS -- FOLKLORE -- ENCYCLOPEDIAS

Prahlad, A. The Greenwood encyclopedia of African American folklore **398**

AFRICAN AMERICANS -- HARLEM (NEW YORK, N.Y.)

Brown, C. Manchild in the promised land **92**

AFRICAN AMERICANS -- HEALTH AND HYGIENE

Tweedy, D. Black Man in a White Coat **92**

AFRICAN AMERICANS -- HISTORY

Anderson, D. S. Emmett Till **364.1**

Austen, J. Darkest America **791**

Black Firsts: 4,000 Ground-breaking and Pioneering Historical Events **920**

Bracks, L. African American almanac **973**

AFRICAN AMERICANS -- HISTORY -- 1863-1877 -- PICTORIAL WORKS

Krauthamer, B. Envisioning emancipation **973.7**

AFRICAN AMERICANS -- HISTORY -- CHRONOLOGY

Burke, K. M. And Still I Rise **973**

AFRICAN AMERICANS -- HISTORY -- ENCY-

CLOPEDIAS

Black firsts   **920**

AFRICAN AMERICANS -- HISTORY -- SOURCES

Freedom on my mind   **305.8**

Remembering slavery   **326**

AFRICAN AMERICANS -- HOUSING

Hill, A. Reimagining equality   **305.8**

AFRICAN AMERICANS -- HOUSING

   See also Blacks -- Housing; Housing

AFRICAN AMERICANS -- ILLINOIS -- CHICAGO -- BIOGRAPHY

Gifford, J. Street poison   **813**

Street poison   **813**

AFRICAN AMERICANS -- ILLINOIS -- CHICAGO -- NEWSPAPERS

Michaeli, E. The defender   **071**

AFRICAN AMERICANS -- ILLINOIS -- CHICAGO -- SOCIAL LIFE AND CUSTOMS -- 20TH CENTURY

Jefferson, M. Negroland   **92**

AFRICAN AMERICANS -- INTELLECTUAL LIFE

Bracks, L. African American almanac   **973**

Ellison, R. The collected essays of Ralph Ellison   **814**

Gates, H. L. The African-American century   **305**

Gates, H. L. The future of the race   **305.896**

Marshall, P. Triangular road   **92**

AFRICAN AMERICANS -- INTELLECTUAL LIFE

   See also Blacks -- Intellectual life; Intellectual life

AFRICAN AMERICANS -- INTELLECTUAL LIFE -- BIBLIOGRAPHY

African American literature   **810.9**

AFRICAN AMERICANS -- LOUISIANA

Rasmussen, D. American uprising   **976.3**

AFRICAN AMERICANS -- MICHIGAN -- DETROIT

Boyle, K. Arc of justice   **345**

AFRICAN AMERICANS -- MICHIGAN -- DETROIT -- HISTORY

Martelle, S. Detroit   **977.4**

AFRICAN AMERICANS -- MIGRATIONS -- HISTORY

Berlin, I. The making of African America   **305.8**

AFRICAN AMERICANS -- MIGRATIONS -- HISTORY -- 20TH CENTURY

Wilkerson, I. The warmth of other suns   **307**

AFRICAN AMERICANS -- MISSISSIPPI

Evers, M. W. The autobiography of Medgar Evers: a hero's life and legacy revealed through his writings, letters, and speeches   **92**

Ferris, W. Give my poor heart ease   **781.643**

Hendrickson, P. Sons of Mississippi   **305.8**

Lomax, A. The land where the blues began   **781.643**

Trethewey, N. D. Beyond Katrina   **818**

AFRICAN AMERICANS -- NEW YORK (STATE) -- NEW YORK -- INTELLECTUAL LIFE

Bernard, E. Carl Van Vechten and the Harlem Renaissance   **92**

AFRICAN AMERICANS -- PICTORIAL WORKS

The Scurlock Studio and Black Washington   **779**

AFRICAN AMERICANS -- POETRY

Clifton, L. The collected poems of Lucille Clifton 1965-2010   **811**

AFRICAN AMERICANS -- POLITICAL ACTIVITY

Presidents and Black America   **973.09**

Writers of the Black Chicago renaissance   **810.9**

AFRICAN AMERICANS -- POLITICS AND GOVERNMENT

Dyson, M. E. The Black presidency   **305.8**

AFRICAN AMERICANS -- PORTRAITS

Krauthamer, B. Envisioning emancipation   **973.7**

AFRICAN AMERICANS -- RACE IDENTITY

Ellison, R. The collected essays of Ralph Ellison   **814**

Family affair   **305.8**

Jefferson, M. Negroland   **92**

Robinson, E. Disintegration   **305.8**

Sandweiss, M. A. Passing strange   **92**

Smith, T. K. Ordinary light   **92**

AFRICAN AMERICANS -- RACE IDENTITY

   See also Blacks -- Race identity; Race awareness

AFRICAN AMERICANS -- RACE IDENTITY -- HISTORY

Jones, J. A dreadful deceit   **305.8**

AFRICAN AMERICANS -- RELIGION

Blum, E. J. The color of Christ   **232**

AFRICAN AMERICANS -- RELIGION

   See also Blacks -- Religion; Religion

AFRICAN AMERICANS -- RELIGION -- ENCYCLOPEDIAS

The Encyclopedia of African and African-American religions   **299.6**

AFRICAN AMERICANS -- REPARATIONS

Berry, M. F. My face is black is true   **92**

AFRICAN AMERICANS -- SEGREGATION

Arsenault, R. Freedom riders   **323**

Lemann, N. Redemption: the last battle of the Civil War   **975**

Loewen, J. W. Sundown towns   **363.5**

Packard, J. M. American nightmare   **305.8**

Remembering Jim Crow   **305.896**

Woodward, C. V. The strange career of Jim Crow   **305.8**

AFRICAN AMERICANS -- SEGREGATION

   See also Blacks -- Segregation; Segregation

**AFRICAN AMERICANS -- SEGREGATION --
NORTHEASTERN STATES -- HISTORY**
Sokol, J. All eyes are upon us   323.1
**AFRICAN AMERICANS -- SEGREGATION --
SOUTHERN STATES**
Arsenault, R. Freedom riders   323
**AFRICAN AMERICANS -- SEGREGATION --
SOUTHERN STATES -- HISTORY**
McCluskey, A. T. A forgotten sisterhood   370.922
Packard, J. M. American nightmare   305.8
Remembering Jim Crow   305.896
**AFRICAN AMERICANS -- SOCIAL CONDI-
TIONS**
Burke, K. M. And Still I Rise   973
Coates Between the World and Me   305.8
Hobbs, J. The short and tragic life of Robert
Peace   92
**AFRICAN AMERICANS -- SOCIAL CONDI-
TIONS**
See also Blacks -- Social conditions; Social
conditions
**AFRICAN AMERICANS -- SOCIAL CONDI-
TIONS -- 19TH CENTURY**
White, S. Prince of darkness   92
**AFRICAN AMERICANS -- SOCIAL LIFE AND
CUSTOMS**
Bracks, L. African American almanac   973
Prahlad, A. The Greenwood encyclopedia of Afri-
can American folklore   398
**AFRICAN AMERICANS -- SOCIAL LIFE AND
CUSTOMS**
See also Blacks -- Social life and customs;
Manners and customs
**AFRICAN AMERICANS -- SOCIAL LIFE AND
CUSTOMS -- ENCYCLOPEDIAS**
Prahlad, A. The Greenwood encyclopedia of Afri-
can American folklore   398
**AFRICAN AMERICANS -- SOUTH CAROLINA
-- CHARLESTON -- SOCIAL CONDITIONS**
Kelly, J. America's longest siege   305.896
AFRICAN AMERICANS -- SOUTHERN STATES
Dray, P. At the hands of persons unknown   364.1
Franklin, J. H. In search of the promised land 929
Griffin, J. H. Black like me   305.8
Remembering Jim Crow   305.896
Wiencek, H. The Hairstons   920
**AFRICAN AMERICANS -- SOUTHERN
STATES -- SOCIAL CONDITIONS**
McCluskey, A. T. A forgotten sisterhood   370.922
AFRICAN AMERICANS -- SUFFRAGE
Dudden, F. E. Fighting chance   324.6
Watson, B. Freedom summer   323.1
AFRICAN AMERICANS -- SUFFRAGE
See also African Americans -- Civil rights;
Blacks -- Suffrage; Suffrage
AFRICAN AMERICANS -- TEXAS -- POLITICS

AND GOVERNMENT
Jacoby, K. The strange career of William Ellis   92
AFRICAN AMERICANS -- TULSA (OKLA.)
Hirsch, J. S. Riot and remembrance   976.6
**AFRICAN AMERICANS -- WASHINGTON
(D.C.)**
Lusane, C. The Black history of the White
House   975.3
AFRICAN AMERICANS AND LIBRARIES
The 21st-century black librarian in America   020
African Americans at war. Sutherland, J.   355
AFRICAN AMERICANS IN ART
Willis, D. Reflections in Black   770.92
AFRICAN AMERICANS IN LITERATURE
African American literature   810.9
Bader, P. African-American writers   920.003
Bernard, E. Carl Van Vechten and the Harlem Re-
naissance   92
Ellison, R. The collected essays of Ralph Elli-
son   814
**AFRICAN AMERICANS IN LITERATURE --
BIBLIOGRAPHY**
African American literature   810.9
**AFRICAN AMERICANS IN MOTION PIC-
TURES**
Bogle, D. Bright boulevards, bold dreams 791.43
**AFRICAN AMERICANS IN MOTION PIC-
TURES**
See also Blacks in motion pictures; Minorities
in motion pictures; Motion pictures
AFRICAN AMERICANS IN TELEVISION *See*
African Americans on television
**AFRICAN AMERICANS IN TELEVISION
BROADCASTING**
Ely, M. P. The adventures of Amos 'n' Andy 791.44
**AFRICAN AMERICANS IN TELEVISION
BROADCASTING**
See also Television broadcasting
**AFRICAN AMERICANS IN THE MOTION PIC-
TURE INDUSTRY**
See also Blacks in the motion picture industry;
Minorities in the motion picture industry; Mo-
tion picture industry
**AFRICAN AMERICANS IN THE PERFORM-
ING ARTS -- NEW YORK (STATE) -- NEW
YORK -- HISTORY -- 20TH CENTURY**
Lane, S. F. Black Broadway   792
**AFRICAN AMERICANS IN THE TELEVISION
INDUSTRY** *See* African Americans in television
broadcasting
AFRICAN ART
Visona, M. B. A history of art in Africa   709
AFRICAN ART
See also Art
AFRICAN CIVILIZATION *See* Africa -- Civili-
zation

AFRICAN COOKING
Samuelsson, M. The soul of a new cuisine **641.5**

AFRICAN DIASPORA -- ENCYCLOPEDIAS
Africana: the encyclopedia of the African and African American experience **909**

AFRICAN ELEPHANT -- EFFECT OF POACHING ON
Orenstein, R. Ivory, horn and blood **333.95**

AFRICAN LITERATURE
See also Literature

AFRICAN LITERATURE -- HISTORY AND CRITICISM
Achebe, C. The education of a British-protected child **92**

AFRICAN METHODIST EPISCOPAL CHURCH
Newman, R. S. Freedom's prophet **92**

AFRICAN MUSIC
See also Music

AFRICAN MYTHOLOGY
See also Mythology

AFRICAN NATIONAL CONGRESS
Smith, D. J. Young Mandela **92**

AFRICAN NATIONAL CONGRESS -- BIOGRAPHY
Jones, B. Mandela **92**

AFRICAN POETRY -- COLLECTIONS
The Penguin book of modern African poetry **896**
African queen. Holmes, R. **92**

AFRICAN REFUGEES
Steinberg, J. A man of good hope **92**
African silences. Matthiessen, P. **916**

AFRICAN SONGS
See also Songs

African-American art. Patton, S. F. **704.03**
The African-American century. Gates, H. L. **305**
African-American poetry of the nineteenth century. **811**

AFRICAN-AMERICAN STUDENTS FEDERATION
Shachtman, T. Airlift to America **378.1**
African-American writers. Bader, P. **920.003**
Africana: the encyclopedia of the African and African American experience. **909**

AFRICANS -- UNITED STATES
Fuller, A. Leaving Before the Rains Come **305.409**

AFRO-AMERICANS See African Americans

AFRO-AMERICANS -- CIVIL RIGHTS -- HISTORY -- 20TH CENTURY
Branch, T. Pillar of fire **973.922**
Afro-vegan. **641.59**

Aftel, Mandy
Fragrant **612.8**
After. Hirshfield, J. **811**
After all. Matthews, W. **811**
After America. Starobin, P. **973.91**
After broadcast news. Carpini, M. X. D. **071**

After Camelot. Taraborrelli, J. R. **920**

AFTER DINNER SPEECHES
See also Speeches
After Dolly. Wilmut, I. **176**
After Hitler. Jones, M. **940.53**
After Lincoln. Langguth, A. J. **973.8**
After such knowledge. Hoffman, E. **940.53**
After the Dance. Ritz, D. **782.42**
After the fall. **974.7**
After the music stopped. Blinder, A. S. **330.973**
After the prophet. Hazleton, L. **297**
After the Trail of Tears. McLoughlin, W. G. **970.004**
After you hear it's cancer. Leifer, J. **616.99**

AFTERLIFE See Future life
Aftermath. Cusk, R. **823**

AFTERNOON TEAS
See also Cooking
Aftershock. Reich, R. B. **330.9**
Against security. Molotch, H. **363.325**
Against the tide. Dean, C. **333.91**

Agassi, Andre, 1970-
About
Agassi, A. Open **92**

Agassiz, Louis, 1807-1873
About
Irmscher, C. Louis Agassiz **92**

Agatston, Patricia W.
(jt. auth) Kowalski, R. M. Cyberbullying **302.34**

AGE -- PHYSIOLOGICAL EFFECT See Aging

AGE AND EMPLOYMENT
See also Age; Employment

AGE DISCRIMINATION
See also Discrimination
The age of acquiescence. Fraser, S. **973.91**
Age of ambition. Osnos, E. **951.06**
The age of anxiety. Johnson, H. B. **973.921**
The age of Bowie. Morley, P. **92**
Age of delirium. Satter, D. **947.085**
The Age of Edison. Freeberg, E. **303.48**
The age of empathy. **152.4**
The age of entanglement. Gilder, L. **530.1**
The Age of Genius. Grayling, A. C. **940.2**
The Age of Gold. Brands, H. W. **979.4**
Age of greed. Madrick, J. G. **330.9**
The age of insight. Kandel, E. R. **154.2**
The age of movies. Kael, P. **791.43**
The age of radiance. Nelson, C. **539.7**
The age of reform from Bryan to F.D.R. Hofstadter, R. **973.91**
The age of revolution 1789-1848. Hobsbawm, E. J. **940.2**

Age of Roosevelt [series]
Schlesinger, A. M. The coming of the New Deal, 1933-1935 **973.917**
Schlesinger, A. M. The crisis of the old order, 1919-1933 **973.91**

Schlesinger, A. M. The politics of upheaval, 1935-1936 **973.917**

The **age** of sustainable development. Sachs, J. **338.9**

The **age** of the unthinkable. Ramo, J. C. **973.931**

The **age** of turbulence. Greenspan, A. **92**

The **age** of wonder. Holmes, R. **509**

AGED See Elderly

AGED -- UNITED STATES

Jacoby, S. Never say die **305.26**

AGED MEN See Elderly men

AGED PARENTS See Aging parents

Agee, James, 1909-1955

Cotton Tenants **976.1**

Let us now praise famous men **976.1**

About

Wranovics, J. Chaplin and Agee **92**

AGEING See Aging

AGENT (PHILOSOPHY)

Black, J. Other pasts, different presents, alternative futures **900**

Agent Garbo. Talty, S. **940.5**

Agent Zigzag. Macintyre, B. **92**

The **ages** of Gaia. Lovelock, J. **570.1**

AGGREGATES See Set theory

AGGRESSIVE BEHAVIOR See Aggressiveness (Psychology)

AGGRESSIVENESS (PSYCHOLOGY)

Simmons, R. Odd girl out **305.23**

AGGRESSIVENESS (PSYCHOLOGY)

See also Human behavior; Psychology

AGGRESSIVENESS IN CHILDREN

Simmons, R. Odd girl out **305.23**

Whitson, S. 8 keys to end bullying **302.34**

The **agile** gene. Ridley, M. **155.7**

Agincourt. Fiennes, R. **944**

AGING

Athill, D. Somewhere towards the end **92**

Carter, J. The virtues of aging **305.26**

Crystal, B. Still foolin' 'em **92**

Ephron, N. I feel bad about my neck **814**

Esmonde-White, M. Aging backwards **613.2**

Goldman, B. Brain fitness **153.1**

Greer, G. The change **618.1**

Haycock, D. B. Mortal coil **571.8**

Jacoby, S. Never say die **305.26**

Kinsley, M. Old age **814.54**

Lachs, M. Treat me, not my age **612.6**

Lawrence-Lightfoot, S. The third chapter **305.26**

Northrup, C. Goddesses never age **613**

Pillemer, K. A. 30 lessons for living **305.26**

Sheehy, G. New passages **305.24**

Vaillant, G. E. Triumphs of experience **305.31**

Weil, A. Healthy aging **612.6**

AGING

See also Age; Elderly; Gerontology; Longevity; Middle age; Old age

AGING -- PHYSIOLOGICAL ASPECTS

Sagan, D. Cracking the aging code **612.67**

AGING -- PHYSIOLOGY

Gawande, A. Being mortal **362.17**

AGING -- PREVENTION

Esmonde-White, M. Aging backwards **613.2**

Goldman, B. Brain fitness **153.1**

AGING -- PSYCHOLOGICAL ASPECTS

Guiliano, M. French women don't get facelifts **613**

AGING -- PSYCHOLOGICAL ASPECTS -- UNITED STATES -- LONGITUDINAL STUDIES

Vaillant, G. E. Triumphs of experience **305.31**

AGING -- RELIGIOUS ASPECTS

Chittister, J. The gift of years **200**

AGING -- SOCIAL ASPECTS -- UNITED STATES -- LONGITUDINAL STUDIES

Vaillant, G. E. Triumphs of experience **305.31**

AGING -- UNITED STATES

Kinsley, M. Old age **814.54**

Aging backwards. Esmonde-White, M. **613.2**

AGING PARENTS

Block, S. When Your Parent Moves in **306.874**

Chast, R. Can't We Talk About Something More Pleasant? **741.5**

Delehanty, H. Caring for your parents **362.6**

Hogan, P. R. Stages of senior care **362.6**

Pipher, M. B. Another country **306.874**

AGING PARENTS

See also Elderly; Parents

AGING PERSONS See Elderly

Agnew, Connie L.

Twins! **649**

Agnostic. Hazleton, L. **211**

AGNOSTICISM

Hazleton, L. Agnostic **211**

AGNOSTICISM

See also Free thought; Religion

AGORAPHOBIA

Shawn, A. Wish I could be there **92**

AGORAPHOBIA

See also Phobias

AGRARIAN QUESTION See Agriculture -- Economic aspects; Agriculture -- Government policy; Land tenure

AGREEMENTS See Contracts; Covenants

AGRIBUSINESS EXECUTIVES

Rathbone, J. P. The sugar king of Havana **92**

Agricola cookbook. Tomlinson, S. **641.564**

Agricola, Gnaeus Julius, 40-93

About

Tacitus, C. Complete works of Tacitus **878**

AGRICULTURAL INNOVATIONS

Fukuoka, M. Sowing seeds in the desert **631.6**

AGRICULTURAL INNOVATIONS

See also Technological innovations

AGRICULTURAL LABORERS
Shaw, R. Beyond the fields **331.8**

AGRICULTURAL LABORERS
See also Labor

AGRICULTURAL MACHINERY
Tractor **629.225**

AGRICULTURAL MACHINERY
See also Machinery; Tools

AGRICULTURAL PESTS
Gardiner, M. M. Good garden bugs **635**

AGRICULTURAL POLICY *See* Agriculture --
Government policy

AGRICULTURAL PROCESSING
Reese, J. Make the bread, buy the butter **641.3**

AGRICULTURAL PRODUCTS *See* Farm produce

AGRICULTURAL TOOLS *See* Agricultural machinery

AGRICULTURE
Barber, D. The third plate **641.3**
Bittman, M. Food matters **613.2**
Markham, B. L. Mini farming **635**
Standage, T. An edible history of humanity **394.1**

AGRICULTURE
See also Life sciences

AGRICULTURE -- ECONOMIC ASPECTS
See also Economics

**AGRICULTURE -- ENVIRONMENTAL AS-
PECTS**
Fukuoka, M. Sowing seeds in the desert **631.6**

AGRICULTURE -- GOVERNMENT POLICY
Ackerman-Leist, P. Rebuilding the foodshed **338.1**

AGRICULTURE -- GOVERNMENT POLICY
See also Industrial policy

AGRICULTURE -- HISTORY
Mann, C. C. 1493 **909**

AGRICULTURE -- UNITED STATES
Fine, D. Hemp bound **633.5**
McMillan, T. The American way of eating **338.4**

AGRICULTURE AND ENERGY
Animal, vegetable, miracle **641**

AGRICULTURE AND STATE *See* Agriculture --
Government policy

**AGRICULTURE AND STATE -- UNITED
STATES**
Bittman, M. A bone to pick **338.1**

AGRONOMY *See* Agriculture

Ah-choo! Ackerman, J. **616.2**

Ahamed, Liaquat
Lords of finance **332.1**

Ahead of the curve. Kenny, B. **796.357**

Ahern, Daniel
(jt. auth) Ahern, S. J. Gluten-Free Girl American
classics reinvented **641.597**
(jt. auth) Ahern, S. J. Gluten-free girl every
day **641.5**

Ahern, Shauna James
Gluten-Free Girl American classics reinvent-
ed **641.597**
Gluten-free girl every day **641.5**

Ahlstrom, Sydney E.
A religious history of the American people **200**

Ahuja, Nita
Johns Hopkins patients' guide to colon and rectal
cancer **616.99**

AI (ARTIFICIAL INTELLIGENCE) *See* Artificial intelligence

Ai, Weiwei
About
Ai weiwei **709.5**
Martin, B. Hanging man **709**

AID TO DEPENDENT CHILDREN *See* Child
welfare

AID TO DEVELOPING AREAS *See* Foreign aid;
Technical assistance

Aidells, Bruce
The complete meat cookbook **641.6**

AIDS (DISEASE)
Duberman, M. B. Hold tight gently **920**
Garrett, L. The coming plague **614.4**
Halperin, D. Tinderbox **614.5**
Monette, P. Borrowed time **362.1**
Shilts, R. And the band played on **362.1**
Steinberg, J. Sizwe's test **362.1**
Stratton, S. E. The encyclopedia of HIV and
AIDS **362.196**

AIDS (DISEASE)
See also Communicable diseases; Diseases

AIDS (DISEASE) -- POETRY
Powell, D. A. Repast **811**

AIDS (DISEASE) -- PREVENTION
Pisani, E. The wisdom of whores **614.5**

**AIDS (DISEASE) -- SOCIAL ASPECTS -- NIGE-
RIA**
Iweala, U. Our kind of people **362.196**

AIDS (DISEASE) -- TREATMENT
See also Therapeutics

AIDS ACTIVISTS
Becker, S. I had brain surgery, what's your excuse? **92**

AIDS VACCINES
Jacobs, C. D. Jonas Salk **92**
Jonas Salk **92**

Aiken, Joan
The way to write for children **808.06**

Aiken, Mary
The cyber effect **155.9**

Aikman, Becky
About
Aikman, B. Saturday night widows **306.88**

Aim true. Budig, K. **613.7**

Ainslie's complete guide to thoroughbred racing.

Ainslie, T.   **798.401**
Ainslie, Ricardo C.
The fight to save Juárez   **363.45**
Ainslie, Tom
Ainslie's complete guide to thoroughbred racing   **798.401**
Air. Logan, W. B.   **551.5**
AIR
See also Meteorology
AIR
Logan, W. B. Air   **551.5**
AIR -- MICROBIOLOGY
See also Microbiology
AIR -- SOCIAL ASPECTS
Logan, W. B. Air   **551.5**
Air apparent. Monmonier, M. S.   **551.63**
AIR CARRIERS *See* Airlines
AIR CRASHES *See* Aircraft accidents
AIR FORCE OFFICERS
Carney, J. T. No room for error   **356**
Geary, R. The Lindbergh child   **364.1**
Hillenbrand, L. Unbroken   **940.54**
Kessner, T. The flight of the century   **92**
Lindbergh, C. The spirit of St. Louis   **629.13**
Lindbergh, R. Under a wing   **92**
Nelson, C. The first heroes   **940.54**
Sheehan, N. A fiery peace in a cold war   **92**
Woodward, B. The commanders   **973.928**
Worden, A. Falling to Earth   **92**
AIR GUITAR
See also Guitars
AIR LINES *See* Airlines
AIR PILOTS
Ambrose, S. E. The wild blue   **940.54**
Butler, S. East to the dawn   **629.13**
Geary, R. The Lindbergh child   **364.1**
Hampton, D. The hunter killers   **959.704**
Haynsworth, L. Amelia Earhart's daughters **629.13**
Hynes, S. The unsubstantial air   **940.4**
Kessner, T. The flight of the century   **92**
Lindbergh, C. The spirit of St. Louis   **629.13**
Lindbergh, R. Under a wing   **92**
Mondor, C. C. The map of my dead pilots   **387.7**
Reeves, R. Daring young men   **943.087**
Trzebinski, E. The lives of Beryl Markham **629.13**
Winters, K. C. Amelia Earhart   **92**
AIR PILOTS
See also Aeronautics
AIR PILOTS -- BIOGRAPHY
Barbree, J. Neil Armstrong   **92**
Groom, W. The aviators   **920**
Jackson, J. Atlantic fever   **629.130**
AIR PILOTS -- UNITED STATES -- BIOGRAPHY
Groom, W. The aviators   **920**
Lindbergh, C. The spirit of St. Louis   **629.13**

AIR PILOTS, MILITARY -- HISTORY
Reeves, R. Daring young men   **943.087**
AIR PILOTS, MILITARY -- UNITED STATES -- BIOGRAPHY
Groom, W. The aviators   **920**
Murphy, B. 81 days below zero   **940.54**
AIR PIRACY *See* Hijacking of airplanes
Air plants.   **628.5**
AIR POLLUTION
Jacobs, C. Smogtown   **363.7**
Logan, W. B. Air   **551.5**
AIR POLLUTION
See also Environmental health; Pollution
AIR TRAVEL
McGee, W. J. Attention all passengers   **387.7**
AIR TRAVEL
See also Transportation; Travel; Voyages and travels
AIR-SHIPS *See* Airships
AIRCRAFT *See* Airplanes; Airships; Balloons; Gliders (Aeronautics); Helicopters
AIRCRAFT ACCIDENTS
Gonzales, L. Flight 232   **363.12**
Mondor, C. C. The map of my dead pilots   **387.7**
Ollestad, N. Crazy for the storm   **92**
Sabbag, R. Down around midnight   **92**
AIRCRAFT ACCIDENTS -- NEW GUINEA
Zuckoff, M. Lost in Shangri-la   **940.54**
AIRCRAFT INDUSTRY EXECUTIVES
Botting, D. Dr. Eckener's dream machine   **629.133**
Wright, O. How we invented the airplane   **92**
Airlift to America. Shachtman, T.   **378.1**
AIRLINE EXECUTIVES
Singer, M. Character studies   **920**
Slater, R. No such thing as over-exposure   **92**
AIRLINES -- HIJACKING *See* Hijacking of airplanes
AIRLINES -- UNITED STATES
McGee, W. J.   **387.7**
AIRPLANE ACCIDENTS *See* Aircraft accidents
AIRPLANE CRASH SURVIVAL -- ALASKA
Murphy, B. 81 days below zero   **940.54**
AIRPLANE CRASHES *See* Aircraft accidents
AIRPLANE HIJACKING *See* Hijacking of airplanes
AIRPLANE PILOTS *See* Air pilots
AIRPLANE RACING
See also Aeronautical sports; Racing
AIRPLANES
Alexander, D. E. Why don't jumbo jets flap their wings?   **629.13**
Wright, O. How we invented the airplane   **92**
AIRPLANES
See also Aeronautics
AIRSHIPS
Botting, D. Dr. Eckener's dream machine   **629.133**

AIRSHIPS
   See also Aeronautics
AIRSHIPS -- GERMANY -- HISTORY -- 20TH CENTURY
   Preston, D. A higher form of killing   **940.4**
AIRWAYS *See* Aeronautics
Aitken, Gillon R.
   Naipaul, V. S. Between father and son   **823**
Aitkenhead, Decca
      About
   Aitkenhead, D. All at sea   **92**
Ajak, Benjamin
   Deng, B. They poured fire on us from the sky **962.4**
Akcam, Taner
   A shameful act   **956.6**
Akhenaton, King of Egypt, fl. ca. 1388-1358 B.C.
      About
   Mertz, B. Temples, tombs, & hieroglyphs   **932**
Akhmatova, Anna Andreevna, 1889-1966
   The complete poems of Anna Akhmatova **891.71**
   Selections./English. Poems   **891.7**
      About
   Feinstein, E. Anna of all the Russias   **92**
   Volkov, S. St. Petersburg   **947**
Akiyama, Lance
   Rubber band engineer   **745**
Akkam, Alia
   (jt. auth) Tanguay, P. The Tippling bros.   **641.87**
Akst, Daniel
   We have met the enemy   **153.8**
Al Jundi, Sami, 1962-
      About
   Al Jundi, S. The hour of sunlight   **92**
Al-Khairi, Bashir
      About
   Tolan, S. The lemon tree   **956.94**
Al-Khalili, Jim
   The house of wisdom   **509**
   (jt. auth) McFadden, J. Life on the Edge   **572**
Al-Maria, Sophia
      About
   Al-Maria, S. The Girl Who Fell to Earth   **92**
Āl Saʻūd, House of
      About
   House, K. E. On Saudi Arabia   **953.8**
Al-Shaykh, Hanan
   Hikayati sharhun yatul./English The locust and the bird   **92**
ALA fundamentals series
   Giesecke, J. Fundamentals of library supervision   **023**
ALA glossary of library and information science. **020**
ALA reader's advisory series
   Wyatt, N. The readers' advisory guide to nonfiction   **025.5**
ALABAMA -- BIOGRAPHY

   Mills, M. The Mockingbird Next Door   **92**
ALABAMA -- RACE RELATIONS
   Greenhaw, W. Fighting the devil in Dixie   **323.1**
ALABAMA -- SOCIAL CONDITIONS
   Agee, J. Let us now praise famous men   **976.1**
ALABAMA CRIMSON TIDE (FOOTBALL TEAM)
   St. John, W.   Rammer jammer yellow hammer   **796.332**
Alabaster, Carol
   Developing an outstanding core collection   **025.2**
ALAMO (SAN ANTONIO, TEX.)
   Davis, W. C. Three roads to the Alamo   **976.4**
ALAMO (SAN ANTONIO, TEX.) -- SIEGE, 1836
   Donovan, J. The blood of heroes   **976.4**
Alan Lomax. Szwed, J. F.   **92**
Alan's war. Guibert, E.   **741.5**
Alanbrooke, Alan Francis Brooke, Viscount, 1883-1963
      About
   Roberts, A. Masters and commanders   **940.54**
ALASKA
   Dixon, K. The Tutka Bay Lodge cookbook **641.59**
   Heacox, K. John Muir and the ice that started a fire   **92**
   Mondor, C. C. The map of my dead pilots **387.7**
   Pilgrim's wilderness   **92**
   Tape, K. D. The changing arctic landscape **551.69**
ALASKA -- BIOGRAPHY
   Krakauer, J. Into the wild   **917**
ALASKA -- CLIMATE
   Tape, K. D. The changing arctic landscape **551.69**
ALASKA -- DESCRIPTION
   Krakauer, J. Into the wild   **917**
ALASKA -- ENVIRONMENTAL CONDITIONS
   Wohlforth, C. The fate of nature   **304.2**
ALASKA -- HISTORY
   Borneman, W. R. Alaska: saga of a bold land **979.8**
   Hensley, W. L. Fifty miles from tomorrow   **92**
ALASKA -- SOCIAL LIFE AND CUSTOMS
   Jenkins, P. Looking for Alaska   **979.8**
ALASKA HIGHWAY (ALASKA AND CANADA)
   See also Roads
Alaska: saga of a bold land. Borneman, W. R. **979.8**
Albee, Edward, 1928-
   Who's afraid of Virginia Woolf?   **812**
      About
   Gussow, M. Edward Albee   **92**
   Playwrights at work   **812**
Albers, Anni, 1899-1994
      About
   Weber, N. F. The Bauhaus group   **920**
Albers, Josef, 1888-1976
      About
   Weber, N. F. The Bauhaus group   **920**
Albers, Patricia

Joan Mitchell   **92**

Albert Camus. Todd, O.   **848**

Albert Moore. Asleson, R.   **759.2**

Albert Speer. Sereny, G.   **92**

Albertine, Viv, 1954-

About

Albertine, V. Clothes, Clothes, Clothes. Music, Music, Music. Boys, Boys, Boys   **92**

Albitz, Becky

(ed) Rethinking collection development and management   **025.2**

Albom, Mitch, 1958-

Tuesdays with Morrie   **378.1**

Albracht, William

About

Wolf, M. J. Abandoned in hell   **959.704**

Albrecht, Donald

The Work of Charles and Ray Eames   **745.4**

Albright, Madeleine Korbel, 1937-

About

Woodward, B. Prague winter   **943.71**

An **album** of memories. Brokaw, T.   **940.54**

Album of the damned.   **943.086**

ALCHEMISTS

Webster, C. Paracelsus   **92**

ALCHEMY

See also Chemistry; Occultism

ALCOHOL

See also Chemicals

ALCOHOL -- HISTORY

Bitters   **641.8**

Rogers, A. Proof   **663**

ALCOHOLIC BEVERAGES

Bar Book   **641.87**

Bitters   **641.8**

Conigliaro, T. The cocktail lab   **641.87**

Risen, C. American Whiskey, Bourbon & Rye   **641.2**

Stewart, A. The drunken botanist   **581.6**

ALCOHOLIC BEVERAGES

See also Alcohol; Beverages

ALCOHOLIC BEVERAGES -- UNITED STATES

Mitenbuler, R. Bourbon empire   **663**

ALCOHOLICS

Bingham, E. Irrepressible   **306.76**

Karr, M. Lit   **92**

Schaap, R. Drinking with men   **92**

ALCOHOLICS -- REHABILITATION

Steinberg, N. Drunkard   **92**

ALCOHOLICS -- UNITED STATES

Laing, O. The Trip to Echo Spring   **810.9**

ALCOHOLISM

Bailey, B. The Splendid Things We Planned   **92**

Bowman, D. Bottled   **362.292**

Breslin, E. Drinking with Miss Dutchie   **92**

Dorris, M. The broken cord   **362.292**

Glaser, G. Her best-kept secret   **362.292**

Johnston, A. D. Drink   **362.292**

Laing, O. The Trip to Echo Spring   **810.9**

McWilliam, C. What to look for in winter   **92**

ALCOHOLISM

See also Social problems

ALCOHOLISM IN LITERATURE

Laing, O. The Trip to Echo Spring   **810.9**

Alcott, Amos Bronson, 1799-1888

About

Matteson, J. Eden's outcasts   **92**

Alcott, Louisa May, 1832-1888

The sketches of Louisa May Alcott   **818**

About

Matteson, J. Eden's outcasts   **92**

Reisen, H. Louisa May Alcott   **92**

Alden, Ginger

About

Alden, G. Elvis and Ginger   **92**

Aldenderfer, Mark S.

(ed) Great events from history, The ancient world, prehistory-476 C.E.   **930**

Alder, Ken

The measure of all things   **526**

Alderfer, Jonathan

(ed) National Geographic complete birds of North America   **598**

National Geographic birding essentials   **598**

Aldersey-Williams, Hugh, 1959-

Periodic tales   **546**

The tide   **551.464**

Aldrich, Nelson W.

(ed) George, being George   **92**

Aldrin, Buzz, 1930-

Mission to mars   **629.44**

About

Aldrin, B. No dream is too high   **92**

Aleixandre, Vicente

A longing for the light   **861**

Aleksievich, Svetlana, 1948-

Secondhand time   **947.086**

Aletti, Vince

(ed) Thompson, M. Michael Thompson: Portraits   **779**

Alex Haley and the books that changed a nation. Norrell, R. J.   **92**

Alexander Hamilton. Chernow, R.   **92**

Alexander, Amir

Infinitesimal   **511**

Alexander, Caroline

The Bounty: the true story of the mutiny on the Bounty   **996**

The Endurance   **998**

The war that killed Achilles   **883**

Alexander, David E.

Why don't jumbo jets flap their wings?   **629.13**

Alexander, Elizabeth, 1962-

Alexander, E.   Crave radiance   811
(ed)   Brooks, G.   The essential Gwendolyn
   Brooks   811
About
Alexander, E.   The light of the world   92
Alexander, Larry
Biggest brother   92
Alexander, Liz
Access to Asia   395.5
Alexander, William
52 loaves   641.8
Alexandra, Empress, consort of Nicholas II, Emperor of Russia, 1872-1918
About
Kurth, P.   Tsar: the lost world of Nicholas and Alexandra   947.08
Massie, R. K.   Nicholas and Alexandra   92
Alexandria. Stothard, P.   962
ALEXANDRIA (EGYPT)
Stothard, P.   Alexandria   962
Alexie, Sherman
Face   811
Alexis De Tocqueville. Epstein, J.   92
Alford, Jeffrey
Beyond the Great Wall   641.5
Flatbreads and flavors   641.8
Hot, sour, salty, sweet   641.59
Alford, Terry
Fortune's Fool   92
Alfred E. Smith, the happy warrior. Finan, C. M. 92
Alfred Kazin's journals. Cook, R. M.   92
Alfred Stieglitz: the key set. Stieglitz, A. 770
Algar, Ayla Esen
Classical Turkish cooking   641.59
ALGEBRA
See also Mathematical analysis; Mathematics
Algeo, Matthew
The president is a sick man   973.8
Alger, Kajsa
Susan Feniger's street food   641.59
Algeria. Evans, M.   965
ALGERIA -- BIOGRAPHY
Macey, D.   Frantz Fanon   92
ALGERIA -- HISTORY -- 1954-1962, REVOLUTION
Morgan, T.   My battle of Algiers   965
ALGERIA -- HISTORY -- REVOLUTION, 1954-1962
Camus, A.   Algerian chronicles   965
Algerian chronicles. Camus, A.   965
ALGORITHMS
Domingos, P.   The master algorithm   003
Michael, T. S.   How to guard an art gallery and other discrete mathematical adventures 511
Ali, Khaliah
About

Ali, K.   Fighting weight   92
Ali, Muhammad, 1942-2016
About
Kindred, D.   Sound and fury   796
Kram, M.   The ghosts of Manila   796.83
Remnick, D.   King of the world: Muhammad Ali and the rise of an American hero   92
Shanahan, T.   Runnng with the champ   796.830
Smith, J.   Blood brothers   92
Ali, Naheed
Understanding celiac disease   616.3
Understanding lung cancer   616.99
(jt. auth) Lewis, M.   Understanding pain   616
Ali, Nujood
About
Ali, N.   I am Nujood, age 10 and divorced   92
Ali, Taha Muhammad
About
Hoffman, A.   My happiness bears no relation to happiness   92
Ali, Wajahat
(ed) All-American   297.092
Alice. Cordery, S. A.   92
Alice Neel. Hoban, P.   92
Alice Starmore's book of Fair Isle knitting. Starmore, A.   746.43
Alice Walker.   813
Alice Walker's The color purple.   813
ALIEN LABOR
Bacon, D.   Illegal people   331.6
ALIEN LABOR
See also Labor
ALIEN PESTS *See* Nonindigenous pests
ALIENATION (SOCIAL PSYCHOLOGY)
James, J.   The glamour of strangeness   700.19
ALIENATION (SOCIAL PSYCHOLOGY)
See also Social psychology
ALIENS -- CHINA -- SHANHAI -- BIOGRAPHY
Grescoe, T.   Shanghai grand   951.132
ALIENS FROM OUTER SPACE *See* Extraterrestrial beings
ALIENS, ILLEGAL *See* Unauthorized immigrants
ALIMENTARY CANAL -- POPULAR WORKS
Roach, M.   Gulp   612.3
ALIMONY
See also Divorce
Alinder, Mary Street
Ansel Adams   92
Group f.64   770.92
Alink, Merissa
Little house living   640
Alison Glass Appliqué. Glass, A.   746
Alison, Jane
About
Alison, J.   The sisters antipodes   92
Alive. Read, P. P.   910.4

Alix G. Mautner memorial lectures [series]
Feynman, R. P. QED   **539.7**
All about braising.   **641.7**
All about Eve.   **770**
All about roasting.   **641.7**
All American. Crawford, B.   **92**
All at sea. Aitkenhead, D.   **92**
All creatures great and small. Herriot, J.   **92**
All eyes are upon us. Sokol, J.   **323.1**
All Fishermen Are Liars. Gierach, J.   **799.12**
All for love. Dryden, J.   **822**
All governments lie. MacPherson, M.   **92**
ALL HALLOWS' EVE *See* Halloween
All in. Levs, J.   **306.3**
All in. Elton, C.   **658.3**
All in the dances: a brief life of George Balanchine.
Teachout, T.   **92**
All Indians do not live in teepees (or casinos) Robbins, C. C.   **970.004**
All is change. Sutin, L.   **294.3**
All Joy and No Fun. Senior, J.   **306.874**
All music guide to classical music.   **016**
The **all** new ball book of canning and preserving.   **641.42**
All new square foot gardening. Bartholomew, M.   **635**
All of it singing. Gregg, L.   **811**
All of us. Carver, R.   **811**
All points patchwork. Gilleland, D.   **746.46**
All rivers run to the sea. Wiesel, E.   **813**
All strangers are kin. O'Neill, Z.   **910.917**
All the best, George Bush. Bush, G.   **92**
All the daring of the soldier. Leonard, E. D.   **973.7**
All the devils are here. McLean, B.   **330.9**
All the laws but one. Rehnquist, W. H.   **342**
All the poems of Muriel Spark. Spark, M.   **821**
All the president's men. Bernstein, C.   **973.924**
All the presidents' gardens. McDowell, M.   **635.09**
All the Shah's men. Kinzer, S.   **327**
All the Songs. Margotin, P.   **781.66**
All the stops. Whitney, C. R.   **786.5**
All the time in the world. Jenkins, J. K.   **390**
All the truth is out. Bai, M.   **328.73**
All the ways we kill and die. Castner, B.   **958.104**
All the whiskey in heaven. Bernstein, C.   **811**
All the Wild That Remains. Gessner, D.   **363.7**
All These Things That I've Done. Cohen, M.   **781.66**
All things Austen. Olsen, K.   **823**
All Tomorrow's Parties. Spillman, R.   **070.4**
All too human. Stephanopoulos, G.   **973.929**
All under heaven. Phillips, C.   **641.5**
All we know. Cohen, L.   **920.72**
All work, no pay. Berger, L.   **650.14**
All-American.   **297.092**
Allaby, Michael
The gardener's guide to weather and climate   **635**

(jt. auth) Park, C. A dictionary of environment and conservation   **333.7**
Allaby, Michael
The encyclopedia of Earth   **910**
Allan Pinkerton. Mackay, J. A.   **363.28**
Allan, Tony
Life, myth, and art in Ancient Rome   **937**
Allawi, Ali A.
The occupation of Iraq   **956.7**
ALLEGED CRIMINALS
Heard, A. The eyes of Willie McGee   **364.66**
Allegiance. Detzer, D.   **973.7**
ALLEGORIES
     See also Fiction
ALLEGORY
     See also Arts; Fiction
Allen, Arthur
The fantastic laboratory of Dr. Weigl   **614.5**
Vaccine   **614.4**
Allen, Danielle
Our Declaration   **973.3**
Allen, Frederick Lewis
Only yesterday   **973.91**
Allen, John L., 1965-
The Catholic church   **282**
Tutu, D. The rainbow people of God   **968.06**
Allen, R.
(ed) Bulletproof feathers   **570.1**
Allen, Richard, 1760-1831
           About
Newman, R. S. Freedom's prophet   **92**
Allen, William Francis
Ware, C. P. Slave songs of the United States   **781.62**
Allen, Woody, 1935-
           About
Allen, W. Woody Allen on Woody Allen   **791.43**
Allende family
           About
Allende, I. Paula   **92**
Allende, Isabel
My invented country   **863**
Paula   **92**
The sum of our days   **92**
ALLERGY
Sears, W. The allergy book   **618.92**
ALLERGY
     See also Immunity
The **allergy** book. Sears, W.   **618.92**
ALLERGY, FOOD *See* Food allergy
Alley, Richard B., 1957-
Earth   **621**
Allgor, Catherine
A perfect union   **92**
Allied Forces/Supreme Headquarters/Psychological Warfare Division/Intelligence Team
Hackett, D. A. The Buchenwald report   **940.53**

Alligator candy. Kushner, D.   **362.88**

ALLIGATORS

  See also Reptiles

Allilueva, Svetlana, 1926-2011

     About

  Sullivan, R. Stalin's daughter   **92**

Allin, Craig W.

  (ed) Encyclopedia of global resources   **333.7**

Allison, Courtney

  (jt. auth) Peacock, J. The soup club cookbook   **641.81**

Allison, Graham T.

  Nuclear terrorism   **363.32**

Allison, Jay

  (ed) This I believe   **170**

  (ed) This I believe II   **170**

Allitt, Patrick

  The conservatives   **320.5**

Allman, T. D.

  Finding Florida   **975.9**

ALLOCATION OF TIME *See* Time management

ALLOSAURUS

  See also Dinosaurs

ALLUSIONS

  Adonis to Zorro   **422**

  Ayto, J. Brewer's dictionary of modern phrase & fable   **803**

  Manser, M. H. The Facts on File dictionary of allusions   **422**

  McMahon, S. Brewer's dictionary of Irish phrase & fable   **427**

  Oxford dictionary of phrase and fable   **803**

  Rockwood, C. Brewer's dictionary of phrase & fable   **803**

Allyn, Pam

  What to read when   **028.5**

The **almanac** of American politics 2012. Barone, M.   **328**

Almanac of Famous People.   **920**

Almanac of World War I. Burg, D. F.   **940.3**

ALMANACS

  Barone, M. The almanac of American politics 2012   **328**

  Bracks, L. African American almanac   **973**

  The CIA World Factbook   **028**

  Our Sunday Visitor Catholic almanac   **282**

  Woodward, D. R. World War I almanac   **940.3**

  The World Almanac and Book of Facts 2015   **030**

Almanacs of American life [series]

  Gregory, R. Cold War America, 1946 to 1990   **973.92**

Almanacs of American wars [series]

  Fredriksen, J. C. Civil War almanac   **973.7**

  Woodward, D. R. World War I almanac   **940.3**

Almereyda, Michael

  (ed) Night wraps the sky   **92**

Almond, Gabriel Abraham

  Strong religion   **200.9**

Almond, Steve

     About

  Almond, S. Candyfreak: a journey through the chocolate underbelly of America   **338.4**

  Almond, S. Rock and roll will save your life **781.66**

Almost everyone's guide to science. Gribbin, J. R.   **500**

The **Almost** Nearly Perfect People. Booth, M. **948**

Almost president. Farris, S.   **920**

Alone on the ice. Roberts, D.   **919**

Alone together. Turkle, S.   **303.4**

Alone! alone!: lives of some outsider women. Dinnage, R.   **920**

Alperovitz, Gar

  The decision to use the atomic bomb and the architecture of an American myth   **940.54**

Alpert, Abby, 1961-

  Read on-- graphic novels   **016**

ALPHABET

  Rosen, M. Alphabetical   **421**

Alphabetical. Rosen, M.   **421**

ALPHABETS

  See also Alphabet; Sign painting

Alphabetter juice, or, The joy of text. Blount, R.   **818**

Als, Hilton, 1960-

  White Girls   **814**

Alschuler, Lise N.

  (jt. auth) Gazella, K. A. The definitive guide to thriving after cancer   **616.99**

Alson, Peter

  Atlas, T. Atlas   **92**

ALTAMONT FESTIVAL

  Russell, E. A. Let it bleed   **781.66**

An **altar** in the world. Taylor, B. B.   **92**

Alter, David

  Staying sharp   **612.8**

Alter, Jonathan

  The promise   **92**

Alter, Linda Lee

     About

  The female gaze   **704**

ALTERNATIVE FUEL VEHICLES

  Sperling, D. Two billion cars   **388.3**

ALTERNATIVE GRAINS

  Ancient grains for modern meals   **641.59**

  Robertson, C. Tartine Book No. 3   **641.81**

ALTERNATIVE HISTORIES

  Black, J. Other pasts, different presents, alternative futures   **900**

ALTERNATIVE HISTORIES

  See also Fantasy fiction

ALTERNATIVE LIFESTYLES

  Rawles, J. W. Tools for survival   **613.6**

ALTERNATIVE LIFESTYLES
See also Lifestyles

ALTERNATIVE MEDICINE
Backes, M. Cannabis Pharmacy **615.7**
Borins, M. A doctor's guide to alternative medicine **615.5**
Bowling, A. C. Optimal health with multiple sclerosis **616.8**
Marchant, J. Cure **616.89**
Murray, M. T. The encyclopedia of natural medicine **615.5**
Weil, A. Eight weeks to optimum health **613**

ALTERNATIVE MEDICINE
See also Medicine

ALTERNATIVE MEDICINE -- ENCYCLOPEDIAS
The Gale encyclopedia of alternative medicine **615.5**

ALTERNATIVE MEDICINE -- POPULAR WORKS
Romm, A. J. The natural pregnancy book **618.2**

ALTERNATIVE MEDICINE PRACTITIONERS
Lattin, D. The Harvard Psychedelic Club **920**

ALTERNATIVE PRESS
Ostertag, B. People's movements, people's press **071**

ALTERNATIVE PRESS
See also Press

ALTERNATIVE ROCK MUSIC
See also Rock music

ALTITUDE, INFLUENCE OF *See* Environmental influence on humans

Altman, Ellen
Hernon, P. Assessing service quality **025.5**
Altman, Howard
In this house **811**
Altman, Nancy J.
The battle for Social Security **368.4**
Altman, Robert, 1925-2006
About
Zuckoff, M. Robert Altman **92**
Altmann, Tanya Remer
What to feed your baby **649.3**
(ed) Caring for your baby and young child **618.92**

ALTRUISM
Doty, J. R. Into the Magic Shop **92**
Keltner, D. Born to be good **155.2**
ALTRUISM
See also Conduct of life

ALTRUISTIC BEHAVIOR *See* Altruism

ALTRUISTS *See* Philanthropists

Altshuler, Alyssa
(jt. auth) Ladd, D. L. The Medical Library Association guide to finding out about diabetes **016**

ALUMINUM -- RECYCLING
See also Recycling

Alvarenga, Salvador, approximately 1977
About
Franklin, J. 438 days **910.916**
Alvarez, Alex
Native America and the question of genocide **973**
Alvarez, Julia, 1950-
The woman I kept to myself **811**
About
Alvarez, J. A wedding in Haiti **818**
Alvarez, Walter
A Most Improbable Journey **508**
T. rex and the Crater of Doom **551.7**
Always hungry? Ludwig, D. **613.2**
Always looking. **700**
Always looking up. Fox, M. J. **92**
Alworth, Jeff
The beer bible **641.2**
The **Alzheimer's** advisor. James, V. E. **344**
ALZHEIMER'S DISEASE
See also Brain -- Diseases
ALZHEIMER'S DISEASE -- BIOGRAPHY
Kozol, J. The theft of memory **92**
ALZHEIMER'S DISEASE -- DIET THERAPY
Estep, P. The mindspan diet **616.8**
ALZHEIMER'S DISEASE -- PREVENTION
Kosik, K. S. Outsmarting alzheimer's **616.8**
Alzheimer's early stages. Kuhn, D. **616.8**
Amar, Akhil Reed
America's constitution **342**
Amarcord, Marcella remembers. Hazan, M. **92**
Amaro. **641.874**
AMATEUR FILMS
See also Motion pictures
AMATEUR RADIO STATIONS
Silver, H. W. Ham radio for dummies **621.384**
AMATEUR THEATER
See also Amusements; Theater
The **amateurs.** Halberstam, D. **797.1**
Amato, Paula
(ed) Pregnancy day by day **618.2**
(ed) The pregnancy encyclopedia **618.2**
Amazing grace. Kozol, J. **362.7**
The **amazing** story of quantum mechanics. Kakalios, J. **530.1**
AMAZON RIVER VALLEY
Stafford, E. Walking the Amazon **918.1**
AMAZON RIVER VALLEY -- LANGUAGES
Everett, D. L. Don't sleep, there are snakes **305.8**
Amazons to fighter pilots. **355**
AMBASSADORS
See also Diplomats
AMBASSADORS -- UNITED STATES -- BIOGRAPHY
Gaddis, J. L. George F. Kennan **327**
Nasaw, D. The patriarch **92**
AMBER

Poinar, G. O. The quest for life in amber 560

The **Amber** Room. Scott-Clark, C. 940.54

AMBERGRIS

Aftel, M. Fragrant 612.8

AMBITION

See also Social psychology

Ambition and desire. Williams, K. 92

Ambling into history: the unlikely odyssey of George W. Bush. Bruni, F. 973.931

Ambrose Bierce. Morris, R. 92

Ambrose, Stephen E., 1936-2002

Ambrose, S. E. D-Day, June 6, 1944 940.54

Ambrose, S. E. Undaunted courage 917

Band of brothers 940.54

Citizen soldiers 940.54

Eisenhower 92

Nothing like it in the world 385

The victors 940.54

The wild blue 940.54

Amelia Earhart. Winters, K. C. 92

Amelia Earhart's daughters. Haynsworth, L. 629.13

Amelia, Princess, daughter of George III, King of Great Britain, 1783-1810

About

Fraser, F. Princesses 920

AMERICA -- ANTIQUITIES

Adovasio, J. M. The first Americans 970.01

Dillehay, T. D. The settlement of the Americas 970.01

Josephy, A. M. America in 1492 970.004

Mann, C. C. 1491 970.01

Schobinger, J. The ancient Americans 970.01

AMERICA -- ANTIQUITIES

See also Antiquities

AMERICA -- CIVILIZATION

Watson, P. The great divide 909

AMERICA -- CIVILIZATION

See also Civilization

AMERICA -- DESCRIPTION

Theroux, P. The old Patagonian express 918

AMERICA -- DISCOVERY AND EXPLORATION

Fernandez-Armesto, F. Amerigo 92

Horwitz, T. A voyage long and strange 970.01

Mann, C. C. 1493 909

AMERICA -- DISCOVERY AND EXPLORATION *See* America -- Exploration

AMERICA -- EXPLORATION

Firstbrook, P. A Man Most Driven 975.5

AMERICA -- MAPS

Lester, T. The fourth part of the world 912

America 1933. Golay, M. 973.917

America aflame. Goldfield, D. R. 973.7

America and the pill. May, E. T. 363.9

America in 1492. Josephy, A. M. 970.004

America the philosophical. Romano, C. 191

America the possible. Speth, J. G. 338.9

America's Bank. Lowenstein, R. 332.1

America's constitution. Amar, A. R. 342

America's first dynasty. Brookhiser, R. 973.4

America's first families. Anthony, C. S. 920

America's great debate. Bordewich, F. M. 973.6

America's great hiking trails. Berger, K. 796.51

America's library. Conaway, J. 027.5

America's longest siege. Kelly, J. 305.896

America's musical life. Crawford, R. 780.9

America's obsessives. Kendall, J. 609.2

America's other Audubon. Kiser, J. M. 598

America's pastor. Wacker, G. 92

America's Test Kitchen (Company)

(ed) The America's test kitchen do-it-yourself cookbook 641.597

(comp) The America's Test Kitchen healthy family cookbook 641.5

(comp) The America's Test Kitchen new family cookbook 641.5

(comp) The complete vegetarian cookbook 641.5

(comp) Cook it in cast iron 641.7

(comp) Cook's Country eats local 641.597

(comp) The cook's illustrated meat book 641.6

(comp) Foolproof preserving 641.4

(comp) The make-ahead cook 641.5

(comp) Master of the grill 641.578

(comp) Naturally sweet 641.86

(ed) The science of good cooking 641.3

AMERICA'S TEST KITCHEN (TELEVISION PROGRAM)

The America's test kitchen family baking book 641.8

The **America's** test kitchen do-it-yourself cookbook. 641.597

The **America's** test kitchen family baking book. 641.8

The **America's** Test Kitchen healthy family cookbook. 641.5

The **America's** Test Kitchen new family cookbook. 641.5

America's vice presidents. Witcover, J. 352.23

America's war for the greater Middle East. Bacevich, A. J. 956.054

America's women. Collins, G. 305.4

America, a cultural history [series]

Fischer, D. H. Liberty and freedom 323.44

America, empire of liberty. Reynolds, D. 973

America--farm to table. 641.597

American Academy of Pediatrics

Caring for your school-age child 649

AMERICAN ACTORS *See* Actors -- United States

AMERICAN ACTORS AND ACTRESSES *See* Actors -- United States

American apocalypse. Sutton, M. A. 277.3

AMERICAN ARCHITECTURE

Wiencek, H. National Geographic guide to America's great houses **728.8**

AMERICAN ARCHITECTURE *See* Architecture

-- United States

American art. Craven, W. **709**

AMERICAN ART

Boorstin, D. J. The Americans: The democratic experience **973**

Craven, W. American art **709**

FitzGerald, M. C. Picasso and American art **709**

Gerdts, W. H. American impressionism **759.13**

Harvey, E. J. The Civil War and American art **709**

Haskell, B. The American century **709**

Hassrick, P. H. Art of the American West **709**

Hughes, R. American visions **709**

AMERICAN ART

See also Art

AMERICAN ART -- ENCYCLOPEDIAS

The Grove encyclopedia of American art **709**

AMERICAN ARTISTS *See* Artists -- United States

American Association of Retired Persons

Delehanty, H. Caring for your parents **362.6**

Jason, J. The AARP Retirement Survival Guide **332.024**

AMERICAN AUTHORS

Begley, A. Updike **92**

Bram, C. Eminent outlaws **810.9**

Daugherty, T. The Last Love Song **92**

Melton, G. D. Love warrior **92**

Miles, B. Call Me Burroughs **92**

Mills, M. The Mockingbird Next Door **92**

The moment **818**

Parini, J. Empire of self **92**

Robbins, T. Tibetan Peach Pie **92**

Suitable accommodations **92**

AMERICAN AUTHORS

See also Authors

AMERICAN AUTHORS -- BIOGRAPHY

As consciousness is harnessed to flesh **818**

Beller, T. J.D. Salinger **92**

Johnson, J. The voice is all **818**

Labor, E. Jack London **92**

Leader, Z. The Life of Saul Bellow **92**

Niven, P. Thornton Wilder **809**

Weiner, J. Hungry heart **92**

White, E. The Tastemaker **92**

AMERICAN AUTHORS -- CORRESPONDENCE

Burroughs, W. S. Rub out the words **813**

AMERICAN BALLADS

See also American poetry

American ballads and folk songs. **781.62**

American Bar Association

The American Bar Association legal guide for small business **346**

AMERICAN BAR ASSOCIATION

Tamanaha, B. Z. Failing law schools **340**

The **American** Bar Association legal guide for small business. American Bar Association **346**

American bee. Maguire, J. **372.6**

The **American** Bible. Prothero, S. **973**

American biographies [series]

Oakes, E. H. American writers **920.003**

American Bird Conservancy

Lebbin, D. J. The American Bird Conservancy guide to bird conservation **333.95**

The **American** Bird Conservancy guide to bird conservation. Lebbin, D. J. **333.95**

AMERICAN BISON *See* Bison

American Bloomsbury. Cheever, S. **810**

American book trade directory. **070.5**

American buffalo. Rinella, S. **599.64**

American cake. Byrn, A. **641.86**

American Cancer Society complete guide to family caregiving. **649.8**

American Canoe Association

Canoeing **797.1**

Kayaking **797.1**

An **American** Cardinal. Boyle, C. **92**

American catch. Greenberg, P. **333.95**

The **American** century. Haskell, B. **709**

American century series

Hughes, L. I wonder as I wander **818**

AMERICAN CHARACTERISTICS *See* American national characteristics

American chica. Arana, M. **92**

An **American** childhood. Dillard, A. **92**

American Civil Liberties Union

The rights of women **346.01**

The **American** Civil War. Keegan, J. **973.7**

AMERICAN CIVIL WAR *See* United States -- History -- 1861-1865, Civil War

AMERICAN CIVILIZATION *See* America -- Civilization

American College of Sports Medicine

Complete guide to fitness & health **613.7**

AMERICAN COLONIAL STYLE IN ARCHITECTURE

See also Architecture

AMERICAN COLONIES *See* United States -- History -- 1600-1775, Colonial period

AMERICAN COLONIZATION SOCIETY

Davis, D. B. The problem of slavery in the age of emancipation **306.3**

AMERICAN COMPOSERS *See* Composers -- United States

AMERICAN COOKING

101 classic cookbooks **641**

Acheson, H. The broad fork **641.597**

Acheson, H. A New Turn in the South **641.59**

Ahern, S. J. Gluten-Free Girl American classics reinvented **641.597**

America--farm to table **641.597**

The America's test kitchen do-it-yourself cookbook **641.597**

The America's Test Kitchen healthy family cookbook **641.5**

The America's Test Kitchen new family cookbook **641.5**

Beard on food **641.5**

The Beetlebung Farm cookbook **641**

Besh, J. My family table **641.59**

Brennan, K. Keepers **641.5**

Brock, S. Heritage **641.59**

Bryson, F. Blue ribbon baking from a redneck kitchen **641.597**

Charlie Palmer's American fare **641.59**

Cooking my way back home **641.5**

Cook's Country eats local **641.597**

Currence, J. Pickles, pigs & whiskey **641.59**

Disbrowe, P. Down south **641.59**

Dixon, K. The Tutka Bay Lodge cookbook **641.59**

Dupree, N. Mastering the art of Southern cooking **641.59**

Erickson, R. A boat, a whale, and a walrus **641.597**

Flinn, K. Burnt toast makes you sing good **641.597**

Food in the Civil War era **641.597**

Foose, M. H. A southerly course **641.59**

Gartland, A. Heartlandia **641.597**

Hamilton, G. Prune **641.3**

Home **641.5**

Humm, D. I love New York **641.59**

Jamison, B. The border cookbook **641.59**

Kostow, C. A new Napa cuisine **641.59**

Lee, M. The Lee Bros. Charleston kitchen **641.59**

Mario Batali Big American cookbook **641.597**

McMillan, T. The American way of eating **338.4**

Miller, A. Soul food **641.59**

Moore, C. Little Flower baking **641.815**

Moore, R. This is Camino **641.5**

Moulton, S. Sara Moulton's Home Cooking 101 **641.5**

My perfect pantry **641.5**

Phillips, M. The Chelsea Market cookbook **641.59**

Red Rooster Cookbook **641.5**

Ridge, B. The Beekman 1802 heirloom dessert cookbook **641.5**

Rodgers, R. The essential James Beard cookbook **641.597**

Rollins, K. A taste of cowboy **641.597**

Sewall, J. The New England kitchen **641.597**

The Silver Palate cookbook **641.5**

Thompson-Anderson, T. Texas on the Table **641.597**

Victuals **641.5**

AMERICAN COOKING

    See also Cooking

AMERICAN COOKING -- HISTORY

Coe, A. A square meal **641.5**

American Council of Learned Societies

Garraty, J. A. American national biography **920.003**

American creation. Ellis, J. J. **973.3**

American crescent. Qazwini, H. **92**

American crisis. Fowler, W. M. **973.3**

American crossroads [series]

Harmon, A. Indians in the making **970.004**

American crucifixion. Beam, A. **289.3**

American dance. Fuhrer, M. **792.8**

American Diabetes Association

(comp) Ask the experts **616.4**

American Diabetes Association complete guide to diabetes **616.4**

American Diabetes Association complete guide to diabetes. American Diabetes Association **616.4**

AMERICAN DIARIES

    See also American literature; Diaries

American Dietetic Association complete food and nutrition guide. Duyff, R. L. **613.2**

AMERICAN DIPLOMATIC AND CONSULAR SERVICE

Neu, C. E. Colonel House **92**

AMERICAN DRAMA

Critical survey of drama **809**

AMERICAN DRAMA

    See also American literature; Drama

AMERICAN DRAMA -- 20TH CENTURY

Gurney, A. R. Love letters and two other plays: The golden age and What I did last summer **812**

AMERICAN DRAMA -- 20TH CENTURY -- HISTORY AND CRITICISM

Adler, S. Stella Adler on America's master playwrights **812**

Playwrights at work **812**

AMERICAN DRAMA -- AFRICAN AMERICAN AUTHORS -- HISTORY AND CRITICISM

Lane, S. F. Black Broadway **792**

AMERICAN DRAMA -- DICTIONARIES

Critical survey of drama **809**

AMERICAN DRAMATISTS

Adler, S. Stella Adler on America's master playwrights **812**

Dowling, R. M. Eugene O'Neill **92**

Lahr, J. Tennessee Williams **92**

AMERICAN DRAMATISTS

    See also American authors; Dramatists

AMERICAN DRAWING

    See also Drawing

AMERICAN DREAM

Mettler, S. Degrees of inequality **378.73**

Quinones, S. Dreamland **362.29**

Roberts, J. A. Shiny objects **339.4**

Smith, H. Who stole the American dream? **973.91**

Swift, E. Auto Biography **629.222**

American dreamer. Hilfiger, T. **92**

American drive. Cox, H. H. **338**

American earth. **333.72**

American Eden. Graham, W. **712**

American electricians' handbook. **621.3**

American emperor. Stewart, D. O. **973.4**

The American empire project [series]

McCoy, A. W. A question of torture **323.4**

American empire, 1945-2000. **973.92**

AMERICAN ENGRAVING

See also Engraving

AMERICAN ESPIONAGE

Abbott, K. Liar, Temptress, Soldier, Spy **973.7**

Laird, T. Into Tibet **327.12**

Lichtblau, E. The Nazis next door **324.1**

Yaeger, D. George Washington's secret six **973.4**

AMERICAN ESPIONAGE

See also Espionage

AMERICAN ESPIONAGE -- HISTORY

Nagy, J. A. George Washington's secret spy war **973.385**

AMERICAN ESSAYS

Abrams, M. H. The fourth dimension of a poem **808.1**

As consciousness is harnessed to flesh **818**

Baker, N. The way the world works **814**

The best American essays 2012 **808**

The Best American essays 2013 **814**

The best American essays 2014 **814**

Dower, J. W. Ways of forgetting, ways of remembering **940.53**

Flanagan, C. Girl land **305.235**

Franzen, J. Farther away **814**

Hitchens, C. Arguably **814**

Hustvedt, S. Living, thinking, looking **814**

Kaling, M. Is everyone hanging out without me? (and other concerns) **818**

Moody, R. On celestial music **780.9**

Morris, E. This living hand **814**

Rankine, C. Citizen **811**

Robinson, M. When I was a child I read books **814**

Sedaris, D. Let's explore diabetes with owls **814**

Solnit, R. The Faraway Nearby **814**

Tevis, J. The world is on fire **814**

This explains everything **500**

AMERICAN ESSAYS

See also American literature; Essays

American experience [series]

Reef, C. Working in America **305**

AMERICAN EXPLORING EXPEDITIONS *See* United States -- Exploring expeditions

AMERICAN FICTION

The Facts on File companion to the American novel **813**

Helbig, A. Dictionary of American young adult fiction, 1997-2001 **028.5**

Herald, D. T. Genreflecting **016**

AMERICAN FICTION

See also American literature; Fiction

AMERICAN FICTION -- 20TH CENTURY -- BIBLIOGRAPHY

Vnuk, R. Women's fiction **016**

AMERICAN FICTION -- BIO-BIBLIOGRAPHY

The Columbia companion to the twentieth-century American short story **813**

Contemporary Jewish-American novelists **813**

The Facts on File companion to the American novel **813**

AMERICAN FICTION -- ENCYCLOPEDIAS

The Facts on File companion to the American novel **813**

AMERICAN FICTION -- HISTORY AND CRITICISM

The Columbia companion to the twentieth-century American short story **813**

The Facts on File companion to the American novel **813**

AMERICAN FICTION -- JEWISH AUTHORS

Contemporary Jewish-American novelists **813**

AMERICAN FICTION -- STORIES, PLOTS, ETC

Herald, D. T. Genreflecting **016**

AMERICAN FICTION -- WOMEN AUTHORS

Vnuk, R. Read on-- women's fiction **016**

Vnuk, R. Women's fiction **016**

AMERICAN FILMS *See* Motion pictures -- United States

AMERICAN FOLK ART

Encyclopedia of American folk art **745**

AMERICAN FOLK ART

See also American art; Folk art

AMERICAN FOLK DRAMA

See also American drama; Folk drama

AMERICAN FOLK MUSIC *See* Folk music -- United States

AMERICAN FOLK SONGS *See* Folk songs -- United States

American food in history [series]

Food in the Civil War era **641.597**

American food writing. **641.5**

AMERICAN FOOTBALL LEAGUE -- HISTORY

Ross, C. K. Mavericks, money, and men **796.332**

AMERICAN FOREIGN AID

See also Foreign aid

American foreign relations since 1600. **016**

AMERICAN FURNITURE

Macy, B. Factory man **338.7**

AMERICAN FURNITURE

See also Furniture

The American future. Schama, S. **973.93**

American girls. Sales, N. J. **004.67**

American Gothic. Biel, S. **759.13**

AMERICAN GOVERNMENT *See* United States

-- Politics and government

American ground, unbuilding the World Trade Center. Langewiesche, W. **974.7**

American grown. Obama, M. **635**

American Heart Association

New American Heart Association cookbook The new American Heart Association cookbook **641.5**

American Heiress. Toobin, J. **322.4**

The American Heritage dictionary of idioms. Ammer, C. **423.13**

The American Heritage dictionary of the English language. **423**

The American Heritage guide to contemporary usage and style. Houghton Mifflin Co. **423**

American heroes. Morgan, E. S. **920**

American heroines. Hutchison, K. B. **920**

AMERICAN HISTORY See America -- History; United States -- History

American history series

Iverson, P. We are still here **970.004**

American home front, 1941-1942. Cooke, A. **940.53**

American honor killings. McConnell, D. **364.15**

American Horticultural Society encyclopedia of plants & flowers. **635.9**

AMERICAN HOSTAGES

See also Hostages

American huckster. Thompson, T. **796.334**

American hymns old and new. Christ-Janer, A. **782.27**

AMERICAN ILLUSTRATORS See Illustrators -- United States

American impressionism. Gerdts, W. H. **759.13**

AMERICAN INDIAN MOVEMENT

Hendricks, S. The unquiet grave **970.004**

American Indians. **970.004**

AMERICAN INDIANS See Native Americans

American Institute for Cancer Research

The new American plate cookbook **641.5**

American Institute of Parliamentarians

(comp) American Institute of Parliamentarians standard code of parliamentary procedure **060.4**

American insurgents, American patriots. Breen, T. H. **973.3**

AMERICAN INTERNATIONAL GROUP, INC.

Boyd, R. Fatal risk **368**

American inventors, entrepreneurs & business visionaries. Carey, C. W. **920**

American Islam. Barrett, P. M. **920**

American Judaism. Sarna, J. D. **296**

American Kennel Club

(comp) The American Kennel Club's meet the breeds **636.7**

(comp) The new complete dog book **636.7**

The complete dog book **636.7**

Burch, M. R. Citizen canine **636.7**

The American Kennel Club's meet the breeds. **636.7**

American law in the 20th century. Friedman, L. M. **349**

The American Leonardo. Brewer, J. **759**

AMERICAN LETTERS

Letters of the century **816**

Vonnegut, K. Kurt Vonnegut **813**

AMERICAN LETTERS

See also American literature; Letters

AMERICAN LETTERS -- AFRICAN AMERICAN AUTHORS

Letters from Black America **305.8**

AMERICAN LIBRARY ASSOCIATION PUBLICATIONS

Saricks, J. G. The readers' advisory guide to genre fiction **025.5**

American Library Association. Office for Intellectual Freedom

(comp) Intellectual Freedom Manual **025.2**

American lightning. Blum, H. **364.152**

American lion. Meacham, J. **92**

AMERICAN LITERATURE

The Cambridge guide to literature in English **820**

Facts on File, I. Encyclopedia of American literature **810**

Magill's survey of American literature **810**

Youn, M. Blackacre **811.6**

AMERICAN LITERATURE

See also Literature

AMERICAN LITERATURE (SPANISH)

Latino literature **016**

AMERICAN LITERATURE (SPANISH)

See also American literature

AMERICAN LITERATURE -- 20TH CENTURY

Bohemians, bootleggers, flappers, and swells **810.8**

The Portable sixties reader **810**

AMERICAN LITERATURE -- 20TH CENTURY -- HISTORY AND CRITICISM

Elie, P. The life you save may be your own **810**

Laing, O. The Trip to Echo Spring **810.9**

Morgan, B. The typewriter is holy **810**

Pierpont, C. R. Passionate minds **810**

Writers of the Black Chicago renaissance **810.9**

AMERICAN LITERATURE -- 21ST CENTURY

The moment **818**

AMERICAN LITERATURE -- AFRICAN AMERICAN AUTHORS

African American literature **810.9**

Writers of the Black Chicago renaissance **810.9**

AMERICAN LITERATURE -- AFRICAN AMERICAN AUTHORS -- BIBLIOGRAPHY

African American literature **810.9**

AMERICAN LITERATURE -- AFRICAN AMERICAN AUTHORS -- BIO-BIBLIOGRAPHY

Bader, P. African-American writers **920.003**

Encyclopedia of African-American writing **810**

AMERICAN LITERATURE -- AFRICAN AMERICAN AUTHORS -- COLLECTIONS

Crossing the danger water 810
The Norton anthology of African American literature 810
The Portable Harlem Renaissance reader 810

AMERICAN LITERATURE -- AFRICAN AMERICAN AUTHORS -- HISTORY AND CRITICISM

Bader, P. African-American writers 920.003
Black literature criticism 809
Hooks, B. Remembered rapture 808
Writers of the Black Chicago renaissance 810.9

AMERICAN LITERATURE -- AFRICAN AMERICAN AUTHORS -- HISTORY AND CRITICISM -- HANDBOOKS, MANUALS, ETC

African American literature 810.9

AMERICAN LITERATURE -- AFRO-AMERICAN AUTHORS See American literature -- African American authors

AMERICAN LITERATURE -- BIO-BIBLIOGRAPHY

The Cambridge handbook of American literature 810
Elie, P. The life you save may be your own 810
Hart, J. D. The Oxford companion to American literature 810
Oakes, E. H. American writers 920.003
The Oxford companion to English literature 820

AMERICAN LITERATURE -- BLACK AUTHORS See American literature -- African American authors

AMERICAN LITERATURE -- COLLECTIONS

Baseball: a literary anthology 810
The Chronology of American literature 810
Crossing the danger water 810
I thought my father was God and other true tales from the National Story Project 810
Jewish American literature 810
Modern American memoirs 810
The Norton book of modern war 808.8
The Oxford book of women's writing in the United States 810
The Portable beat reader 810
The Portable sixties reader 810
Pushcart Prize XXXVI: best of the small presses 2012 810

AMERICAN LITERATURE -- DICTIONARIES

The Cambridge guide to literature in English 820
The Cambridge handbook of American literature 810
Hart, J. D. The Oxford companion to American literature 810
Oakes, E. H. American writers 920.003
The Oxford companion to English literature 820

AMERICAN LITERATURE -- ENCYCLOPEDIAS

Facts on File, I. Encyclopedia of American literature 810
The Oxford encyclopedia of American literature 810

AMERICAN LITERATURE -- HISPANIC AMERICAN AUTHORS

Latino and Latina writers 810
Latino literature 016
The Norton anthology of Latino literature 810
Salem Press Inc. Notable Latino writers 810

AMERICAN LITERATURE -- HISPANIC AMERICAN AUTHORS -- BIO-BIBLIOGRAPHY

Martinez Wood, J. Latino writers and journalists 920.003

AMERICAN LITERATURE -- HISTORY AND CRITICISM

Begley, A. Updike 92
Laing, O. The Trip to Echo Spring 810.9
Levy, A. Huck Finn's America 813
Michaels, J. R. Passing by the dragon 813
Philbrick, N. Why read Moby-Dick? 813
Prothero, S. The American Bible 973

AMERICAN LITERATURE -- ILLINOIS -- CHICAGO -- HISTORY AND CRITICISM

Writers of the Black Chicago renaissance 810.9

AMERICAN LITERATURE -- JEWISH AUTHORS

Jewish American literature 810

AMERICAN LITERATURE -- LATIN AMERICAN AUTHORS See American literature -- Latino authors

AMERICAN LITERATURE -- LATINO AUTHORS

Latino literature 016

AMERICAN LITERATURE -- MEXICAN AMERICAN AUTHORS

See also American literature -- Latino authors

AMERICAN LITERATURE -- NEW ENGLAND

Stuart, S. P. Perfectly miserable 92

AMERICAN LITERATURE -- SOUTHERN STATES -- COLLECTIONS

The Oxford book of the American South 810

AMERICAN LITERATURE -- SOUTHERN STATES -- ENCYCLOPEDIAS

The Companion to southern literature 810

AMERICAN LITERATURE -- WEST (U.S.) -- COLLECTIONS

The Portable Western reader 810

AMERICAN LITERATURE -- WOMEN AUTHORS

Black women writers (1950-1980) 810
The Oxford book of women's writing in the United States 810

Showalter, E. A jury of her peers **810**

AMERICAN LITERATURE -- WOMEN AUTHORS -- BIO-BIBLIOGRAPHY
Showalter, E. A jury of her peers **810**

AMERICAN LITERATURE -- WOMEN AUTHORS -- COLLECTIONS
The Oxford book of women's writing in the United States **810**

AMERICAN LITERATURE -- WOMEN AUTHORS -- HISTORY AND CRITICISM
Hooks, B. Remembered rapture **808**
Pierpont, C. R. Passionate minds **810**
Showalter, E. A jury of her peers **810**
American lives [series]
Borich, B. J. Body geographic **818**

AMERICAN LOYALISTS
See also United States -- History -- 1775-1783, Revolution

AMERICAN LOYALISTS
Jasanoff, M. Liberty's exiles **973.3**

AMERICAN LOYALISTS -- BIOGRAPHY
Kamensky, J. A revolution in color **759.13**

American Lung Association
Goldfarb, T. L. American Lung Association 7 steps to a smoke-free life **616.86**
American Lung Association 7 steps to a smoke-free life. Goldfarb, T. L. **616.86**
The **American** meadow garden. Greenlee, J. **635.9**
American military leaders. Fredriksen, J. C. **355**
The **American** mind. Commager, H. S. **973**
American mirror. Solomon, D. **92**
The American moment [series]
Zieger, R. H. American workers, American unions **331.8**

AMERICAN MOTION PICTURES *See* Motion pictures -- United States

American Museum of Natural History
Alexander, C. The Endurance **998**
Animal life **591.5**

AMERICAN MUSIC
See also Music

AMERICAN MUSIC -- HISTORY AND CRITICISM
Crawford, R. America's musical life **780.9**

AMERICAN MUSICIANS *See* Musicians -- United States

American national biography. Garraty, J. A. **920.003**

AMERICAN NATIONAL CHARACTERISTICS
Boorstin, D. J. The Americans: The colonial experience **973**
Boorstin, D. J. The Americans: The national experience **973**
Brokaw, T. The time of our lives **973.927**
Didion, J. Where I was from **979.4**
Fischer, D. H. Liberty and freedom **323.44**
Marcus, G. The shape of things to come **973**

Noonan, P. A heart, a cross & a flag **973.931**
Parini, J. Promised land **810**
Prothero, S. The American Bible **973**
Schama, S. The American future **973.93**
Terkel, S. My American century **920**
Testi, A. Capture the flag **929.9**
Tocqueville, A. d. Democracy in America **973.5**
White, R. Railroaded **385**
Wulf, A. Founding gardeners **712**

AMERICAN NATIONAL CHARACTERISTICS
See also National characteristics
American nations. Woodard, C. **970.004**
American nerd. Nugent, B. **305.9**
American newspaper comics. Holtz, A. **741.5**
AMERICAN NEWSPAPERS *See* Newspapers -- United States
American nightmare. Packard, J. M. **305.8**

AMERICAN NOVELISTS
Lennon, J. M. Norman Mailer **92**

AMERICAN NOVELISTS
See also American authors; Novelists
The **American** opera singer. Davis, P. G. **920**
American oracle. Blight, D. W. **973.7**

AMERICAN ORATIONS *See* American speeches

AMERICAN PAINTING
Marin, C. Chicano visions **709**
Wilton, A. American sublime **759.13**

AMERICAN PAINTING
See also Painting
American passage. Cannato, V. J. **325**
American patriots. Buckley, G. L. **355**

AMERICAN PERIODICALS *See* Periodicals -- United States
American pharaoh: Mayor Richard J. Daley: his battle for Chicago and the nation. Cohen, A. **977.3**
American Pharoah. Drape, J. **798.4**
American philosophy. Kaag, J. **191**

AMERICAN PHILOSOPHY
See also Philosophy

AMERICAN PHILOSOPHY
Goetzmann, W. H. Beyond the Revolution **973.2**
Kaag, J. American philosophy **191**
Rand, A. The voice of reason; essays in objectivist thought **191**
Romano, C. America the philosophical **191**
American phoenix. Cook, J. H. **973.5**
American photographs. Evans, W. **779**

AMERICAN POETRY
180 more **811**
The best American poetry **811**
Best of the Best American Poetry **811**
The Best poems of the English language **821**
Brock-Broido, L. Stay, Illusion **811**
Dove, R. Collected poems **811**
Glück, L. Faithful and virtuous night **811**
Good poems **811**

The Making of a poem **821**
The Oxford book of American poetry **811**
Poems to read **808.81**
Postmodern American poetry **811**
Raab, L. Mistaking each other for ghosts **811**
Weise, J. The book of goodbyes **813**
Youn, M. Blackacre **811.6**
Young, K. Blue laws **811.54**
Zapruder, M. Come on all you ghosts **811**

AMERICAN POETRY
    See also American literature; Poetry

AMERICAN POETRY -- 20TH CENTURY
The Penguin anthology of twentieth-century American poetry **811**

AMERICAN POETRY -- 21ST CENTURY
Angles of ascent **811**
Jones, S. Prelude to bruise **811**
Poetry 180 **811**
Postmodern American poetry **811**

AMERICAN POETRY -- AFRICAN AMERICAN AUTHORS
Angles of ascent **811**
Moten, F. The Feel Trio **811**

AMERICAN POETRY -- AFRICAN AMERICAN AUTHORS -- COLLECTIONS
African-American poetry of the nineteenth century **811**
Every shut eye ain't asleep **811**
The Oxford anthology of African-American poetry **811**
The Vintage book of African American poetry **811**

AMERICAN POETRY -- AFRO-AMERICAN AUTHORS *See* American poetry -- African American authors

AMERICAN POETRY -- BIO-BIBLIOGRAPHY
Contemporary poets **821**
Encyclopedia of American poetry, the twentieth century **811**

AMERICAN POETRY -- BLACK AUTHORS
See American poetry -- African American authors

AMERICAN POETRY -- COLLECTIONS
Barnett, C. The game of boxes **811**
Doty, M. Deep lane **811**
Gerstler, A. Scattered at sea **811**
Hayes, T. How to be drawn **811**
Hicok, B. Elegy owed **811**
Hirshfield, J. The beauty **811**
Padgett, R. Collected Poems **811**
Pardlo, G. Digest **811**
The Penguin anthology of twentieth-century American poetry **811**
Perillo, L. On the spectrum of possible deaths **811**
Shapiro, A. Reel to reel **811**
Stanford, F. What about this **811.54**

AMERICAN POETRY -- HISTORY AND CRITICISM

The Columbia history of American poetry **811**
Gioia, D. Disappearing ink **811**
Jarrell, R. No other book **809**
Logan, W. Our savage art **811**
MacGowan, C. J. Twentieth-century American poetry **811**
Paglia, C. Break, blow, burn **809.1**
Pinsky, R. Democracy, culture, and the voice of poetry **811**
Schmidt, M. Lives of the poets **821**
Vendler, H. H. Coming of age as a poet **820**

AMERICAN POETRY -- NATIVE AMERICAN AUTHORS
Harper's anthology of 20th century Native American poetry **811**

AMERICAN POETRY -- WOMEN AUTHORS
Oliver, M. A thousand mornings **811**

AMERICAN POETRY -- WOMEN AUTHORS -- COLLECTIONS
Cronk, L. Having been an accomplice **811**
Gerstler, A. Scattered at sea **811**
Perillo, L. On the spectrum of possible deaths **811**
American poetry, the twentieth century. **811**
American poetry: the seventeenth and eighteenth centuries. **811**

AMERICAN POETS
Dove, R. Collected poems **811**
Hammer, L. James Merrill **92**

AMERICAN POETS
    See also American authors; Poets
American poets continuum series
Clifton, L. Mercy **811**
Nye, N. S. You & yours: poems **811**
Simpson, L. A. M. The owner of the house **811**
Snodgrass, W. D. Not for specialists **811**
The **American** political tradition, and the men who made it. Hofstadter, R. **973**

AMERICAN POLITICIANS *See* Politicians -- United States

AMERICAN POLITICS *See* United States -- Politics and government

AMERICAN POTTERY
    See also Pottery
American presidency series
Paludan, P. S. The presidency of Abraham Lincoln **973.7**
American presidents series
Brands, H. W. Woodrow Wilson **92**
Bunting, J. Ulysses S. Grant **92**
Calhoun, C. W. Benjamin Harrison **92**
Dallek, R. Harry S. Truman **92**
Finkelman, P. Millard Fillmore **92**
Gordon-Reed, A. Andrew Johnson **92**
Graff, H. F. Grover Cleveland **92**
May, G. John Tyler **92**
Parmet, H. S. George Bush **92**

Peters, C. Lyndon B. Johnson   92
Phillips, K. P. William McKinley   92
Remini, R. V. John Quincy Adams   92
Wicker, T. Dwight D. Eisenhower   973.921
Widmer, E. L. Martin Van Buren   92
Wilentz, S. Andrew Jackson   92
Wills, G. James Madison   92
An **American** procession. Kazin, A.   810
American Prometheus. Bird, K.   92

AMERICAN PROPAGANDA
   See also Propaganda

AMERICAN PROSE LITERATURE
   Wilson, R. V. Farther traveler   818

AMERICAN PROSE LITERATURE
   See also American literature
American queen. Oller, J.   92
American radical. Guttenplan, D. D.   92
American Reckoning. Appy, C. G.   959.704
American reference books annual 2016.   011
American religious poems.   811
American renaissance. Matthiessen, F. O.   810

AMERICAN REVOLUTION *See* United States --
   History -- 1775-1783, Revolution

AMERICAN REVOLUTION BICENTENNIAL,
   1776-1976 -- COLLECTIBLES
   See also Collectors and collecting
The **American** Revolution: writings from the War of
   Independence.   973.3
American Revolutions. Taylor, A.   973.3
An **American** River. Mary, B.
American rose. Abbott, K.   92
American saint. Barthel, J.   92

AMERICAN SATIRE
   See also American literature; Satire
American Savage. Savage, D.   306.76
American scoundrel: the life of the notorious Civil
   War General Dan Sickles. Keneally, T.   92
American scripture. Maier, P.   973.3

AMERICAN SCULPTURE
   See also Sculpture
The **American** Senate. Baker, R. A.   328.73
American sermons.   252

AMERICAN SERMONS
   See also American literature; Sermons

AMERICAN SHORT STORIES
   Let me tell you   818

AMERICAN SHORT STORIES
   See also Short stories
American Sign Language. Sternberg, M. L. A.   419
The **American** Sign Language handshape diction-
   ary. Tennant, R. A.   419
American smooth. Dove, R.   811
American soldier. Franks, T.   973.931
American soldiers. Kindsvatter, P. S.   355
The **American** songbag. Sandburg, C.   781.62

AMERICAN SONGS

Porter, C. Selected lyrics   **782.42**

AMERICAN SONGS
   See also Songs
American speeches.   **815**

AMERICAN SPEECHES
   American speeches   **815**
   Berry, M. F. Power in words   **973.932**
   Fellow citizens   **352.23**
   Ratnesar, R. Tear down this wall   **973.927**
   State of the union   **352.23**

AMERICAN SPEECHES
   See also American literature; Speeches
American sphinx: the character of Thomas Jeffer-
   son. Ellis, J. J.   **92**
American spring. Borneman, W. R.   **973.3**
American statesmen.   **920.003**
American sublime. Wilton, A.   **759.13**
American tapestry. Swarns, R. L.   **92**

AMERICAN TEENAGERS *See* Teenagers --
   United States
American tempest. Unger, H. G.   **973.3**
American titan. Eliot, M.   **92**
American tragedy. Kaiser, D. E.   **959.704**

AMERICAN TRAVELERS
   See also Travelers
American treasures. Puleo, S.   **973**
American Ulysses. White, R. C.   **92**
American uprising. Rasmussen, D.   **976.3**
American Veda. Goldberg, P.   **294.5**
American visions. Hughes, R.   **709**
American war poetry.   **811**
American warlord. Dwyer, J.   **966.62**
American warlords. Jordan, J. W.   **973.917**
American wasteland. Bloom, J.   **363.7**
The **American** way of death revisited. Mitford,
   J.   **338.4**
The **American** way of eating. McMillan, T.   **338.4**
The **American** West. Brown, D. A.   **978**
American Whiskey, Bourbon & Rye. Risen,
   C.   **641.2**
American widow. Torres, A.   **741.5**

AMERICAN WIT AND HUMOR
   Blount, R. Alphabetter juice, or, The joy of text **818**
   Brunetti, I. An anthology of graphic fiction, car-
   toons & true stories, vol. 2   **741.5**
   Brunetti, I. An Anthology of graphic fiction, car-
   toons, and true stories   **741.5**
   Carlin, G. Napalm & silly putty   **817**
   Crystal, B. Still foolin' 'em   **92**
   Fey, T. Bossypants   **92**
   Humbug   **741.5**
   Kaling, M. Is everyone hanging out without me?
   (and other concerns)   **818**
   Meyerowitz, R. Drunk stoned brilliant dead   **051**
   Mirth of a nation   **817**
   The Oxford book of humorous prose   **827**

Trillin, C. Quite enough of Calvin Trillin **817**
Twain, M. Mark Twain's library of humor **817**
AMERICAN WIT AND HUMOR
   See also American literature; Wit and humor
American wits. **811**
American women scientists. Reynolds, M. D. **509**
The **American** woodland garden. Darke, R. **635.9**
American workers, American unions. Zieger, R. H. **331.8**
American writers. Oakes, E. H. **920.003**
American writers. **920.003**
AMERICAN YOUTH *See* Youth -- United States
American-made. Taylor, N. **331.1**
AMERICAN-SPANISH WAR, 1898 *See* Spanish-American War, 1898
AMERICANA
   See also Collectors and collecting; Popular culture -- United States; United States -- Civilization; United States -- History
AMERICANISMS
Bailey, R. W. Speaking American **427**
Boorstin, D. J. The Americans: The colonial experience **973**
Boorstin, D. J. The Americans: The democratic experience **973**
Boorstin, D. J. The Americans: The national experience **973**
Bryson, B. Made in America **420**
Davidson, M. Right, wrong, and risky **423**
Do you speak American ?(Television program) Do you speak American? **427**
Lepore, J. A is for American **306.44**
Little, B. &. C. I. Bartlett's Roget's thesaurus **423**
Spears, R. A. McGraw-Hill's dictionary of American slang and colloquial expressions **427**
AMERICANISMS -- DICTIONARIES
Garner, B. A. Garner's modern American usage **423**
New Oxford American dictionary **423**
AMERICANISMS -- ENCYCLOPEDIAS
Home ground **917**
AMERICANIZATION
   See also Socialization
Americanos. Monterrey, M. **305.8**
The **Americans.** Frank, R. **779.997**
AMERICANS -- AFRICA
Dwyer, J. American warlord **966.62**
AMERICANS -- AUSTRALIA -- SYDNEY (N.S.W.) -- BIOGRAPHY
Corrigan, K. Glitter and Glue **92**
AMERICANS -- CHINA -- HISTORY -- 19TH CENTURY
Platt, S. R. Autumn in the Heavenly Kingdom **951**
AMERICANS -- CHINA -- SHANGHAI -- BIOGRAPHY
Schmitz, R. Street of Eternal Happiness **951.132**

AMERICANS -- CHINA -- SHANGHAI -- BIOGRAPHY
Grescoe, T. Shanghai grand **951.132**
AMERICANS -- ENGLAND -- BIOGRAPHY
Byrne, P. Kick **92**
AMERICANS -- ENGLAND -- LONDON -- BIOGRAPHY
Leaming, B. Kick Kennedy **92**
AMERICANS -- FOREIGN COUNTRIES
Sadler, A. The 15:17 to Paris **363.325**
AMERICANS -- FRANCE
Baldwin, R. Paris, I love you but you're bringing me down **944**
James, E. Paris in love **92**
Kershaw, A. Avenue of spies **940.53**
AMERICANS -- FRANCE -- FONTAINEBLEAU -- BIOGRAPHY
Carhart, T. Finding Fontainebleau **944.36**
AMERICANS -- FRANCE -- PARIS -- BIOGRAPHY
Anselmo, L. My (part-time) Paris life **944.361**
Baldwin, R. Paris, I love you but you're bringing me down **944**
James, E. Paris in love **92**
Kershaw, A. Avenue of spies **940.53**
AMERICANS -- FRANCE -- PARIS -- HISTORY -- 19TH CENTURY
McCullough, D. G. The greater journey **920.009**
AMERICANS -- ITALY -- NAPLES -- BIOGRAPHY
Wilson, K. Only in Naples **945.731**
AMERICANS -- SPAIN
Hochschild, A. Spain in our hearts **946.081**
AMERICANS -- YEMEN (REPUBLIC) -- BIOGRAPHY
Kasinof, L. Don't be afraid of the bullets **953.305**
Americans at war. **973**
Americans' favorite poems. **808.81**
The **Americans:** The colonial experience. Boorstin, D. J. **973**
The **Americans:** The democratic experience. Boorstin, D. J. **973**
The **Americans:** The national experience. Boorstin, D. J. **973**
The Americas [series]
Timerman, J. Prisoner without a name, cell without a number **92**
Americi, Hugo
(ed) Tea **641.3**
Amerigo. Fernandez-Armesto, F. **92**
Améry, Jean
            About
Sebald, W. G. On the natural history of destruction **833**
Ames, Kenneth M.
(ed) Archaeology of prehistoric native Ameri-

ca **970.01**

Ames, Louise Bates
Your eight-year-old **649**
Your five-year-old **649**
Your four-year-old **649**
Your one-year-old **649**
Your seven-year-old **649**
Your six-year-old **649**
Your two-year-old **649**
Ilg, F. L. Your three-year-old **649**

Ames, Robert, 1934-1983
About
Bird, K. The Good Spy **92**

Amichai, Yehuda
Open closed open **892.4**
Poems of Jerusalem; and, Love poems **892**
The selected poetry of Yehuda Amichai **892**

Amidon, Stephen
Something like the gods **306.4**
The sublime engine **612.1**

Amidon, Thomas W.
Amidon, S. The sublime engine **612.1**

Amin, Idi, 1925-2003
About
Rice, A. The teeth may smile but the heart does not forget **967.6**

Amini, Fari
Lewis, T. A general theory of love **152.4**

Amis, Kingsley, 1922-1995
Bradford, R. Lucky him: the life of Kingsley Amis **92**
Leader, Z. The life of Kingsley Amis **92**

Amis, Martin
Koba the dread **947.084**
About
Amis, M. Experience **92**

AMISH
Hostetler, J. A. Amish society **289.7**
Kraybill, D. B. Amish grace **364.152**
Kraybill, D. B. Concise encyclopedia of Amish, Brethren, Hutterites, and Mennonites **289.7**
Kraybill, D. B. On the backroad to heaven **289.7**
Kraybill, D. B. The riddle of Amish culture **289.7**
Mackall, J. Plain secrets **289.7**
Shachtman, T. Rumspringa **305.23**

AMISH
See also Christian sects; Mennonites
Amish society. Hostetler, J. A. **289.7**

AMISTAD (SCHOONER)
Rediker, M. The Amistad rebellion **326**

AMISTAD (SCHOONER) -- POETRY
Young, K. Ardency **811**
The Amistad rebellion. Rediker, M. **326**

Ammann, Karl
Elephant reflections **599.67**

Ammer, Christine.

The American Heritage dictionary of idioms. **423.13**

AMMUNITION
See also Explosives; Ordnance; Projectiles

AMNESIA
Crais, C. History lessons **92**

AMNESIA
See also Memory

AMNESIA, ANTEROGRADE
Dittrich, L. Patient H.M. **616.85**

AMNESTY
See also Administration of criminal justice; Executive power
Among African apes. **599.8**
Among stone giants. Van Tilburg, J. **92**
Among the dead cities. Grayling, A. C. **940.54**
Among the heroes. Longman, J. **364.1**
Among the powers of the earth. Gould, E. H. **973.3**

Amore, Anthony M.
The art of the con **702.8**

AMOS 'N' ANDY (RADIO PROGRAM)
Ely, M. P. The adventures of Amos 'n' Andy **791.44**

AMOS 'N' ANDY (TELEVISION PROGRAM)
Ely, M. P. The adventures of Amos 'n' Andy **791.44**

AMPHIBIANS
Attenborough, D. Life in cold blood **597.9**
Conant, R. A field guide to reptiles & amphibians **597.9**
Firefly Encyclopedia of Reptiles and Amphibians **597.9**
A guide to amphibians and reptiles **597.9**
Mattison, C. What reptile? **639.3**
Stebbins, R. C. A field guide to Western reptiles and amphibians **597.9**

AMPHIBIANS
See also Animals

AMPHIBIOUS WARFARE -- HISTORY -- 20TH CENTURY
Kennedy, P. M. Engineers of victory **940.54**

AMPLIFIERS (ELECTRONICS)
See also Electronics

AMPUTEES
Cleland, M. Heart of a patriot **92**

AMPUTEES
See also People with disabilities

AMPUTEES -- REHABILITATION
Witter, B. Stronger **92**
The AMS weather book. Williams, J. **551.5**

Amster, Linda
(ed) The New York Times Jewish cookbook **641.5**
(ed) The New York Times Passover cookbook **641.5**
Amsterdam. Shorto, R. **949.2**

AMSTERDAM (NETHERLANDS)
Gies, M. Anne Frank remembered **92**

AMSTERDAM (NETHERLANDS) -- BIOGRA-PHY
Anne Frank **92**

AMSTERDAM (NETHERLANDS) -- HISTORY
Shorto, R. Amsterdam **949.2**
Amundsen, Darrel W.
(ed) The History of science and religion in the western tradition **201**
Amundsen, Roald
About
Larson, E. J. An empire of ice **919**
Amundsen, Roald, 1872-1928
About
Bown, S. R. The last Viking **92**
AMUSEMENT PARKS
Kirby, D. Death at SeaWorld **599.53**
AMUSEMENTS
Denmead, K. Geek dad **790**
Amusing ourselves to death. Postman, N. **302.23**
Amy Butler's style stitches. Butler, A. **646.4**
An Deming
Yang Lihui Handbook of Chinese mythology **299.5**
The **Analects.** Confucius **181**
ANALOGY
Hofstadter, D. Surfaces and essences **169**
Pollack, J. Shortcut **808**
Anand, Anita
Sophia **92**
Ananthaswamy, Anil
The edge of physics **530**
ANARCHISM AND ANARCHISTS
Avrich, K. Sasha and Emma **335**
Butterworth, A. The world that never was **335**
Merriman, J. M. The dynamite club **363.32**
Miller, S. The President and the assassin **973.8**
Strang, D. A. Worse than the devil **345**
Tuchman, B. W. The proud tower **909.82**
Watson, B. Sacco and Vanzetti **345**
ANARCHISM AND ANARCHISTS
See also Freedom; Political crimes and offenses; Political science
ANARCHISM AND ANARCHISTS -- GRAPHIC NOVELS
Rudahl, S. A dangerous woman **335**
ANARCHISTS
Rauchway, E. Murdering McKinley **973.8**
Rudahl, S. A dangerous woman **335**
Watson, B. Sacco and Vanzetti **345**
Anasi, Robert, 1966-
About
Anasi, R. The last bohemia **974.7**
ANATOMY
Gray's anatomy **611**
Wilkinson, M. Restless creatures **591.47**
ANATOMY
See also Biology; Medicine
Anatomy 360 degrees. Roebuck, J.
Anatomy of a business plan. Pinson, L. **658.4**
The **anatomy** of a calling. Rankin, L. **92**

Anatomy of a miracle. Waldmeir, P. **968.06**
Anatomy of an epidemic. Whitaker, R. **616.89**
The **anatomy** of fascism. Paxton, R. O. **321.9**
The **anatomy** of hope. Groopman, J. E. **616**
The **anatomy** of influence. Bloom, H. **801**
Anatomy of Love. Fisher, H. **302.3**
The **anatomy** of violence. Raine, A. **616.85**
ANATOMY, ARTISTIC
Hart, C. Human anatomy made amazingly easy **743.4**
Loomis, A. Figure drawing for all it's worth **743.4**
Winslow, V. L. Classic human anatomy **743.49**
ANATOMY, ARTISTIC See Artistic anatomy
Anbinder, Tyler
City of Dreams **974.71**
Ancell, R. Manning
The biographical dictionary of World War II generals and flag officers **920.003**
ANCESTOR WORSHIP
See also Religion
The **ancestor's** tale. Dawkins, R. **576.8**
ANCESTRY See Genealogy; Heredity
ANCHOR & HOPE (RESTAURANT)
Cooking my way back home **641.5**
Anchor Bible reference library [series]
Brown, R. E. An introduction to the New Testament **225**
Meier, J. P. A marginal Jew **232.9**
The **ancient** Americans. Schobinger, J. **970.01**
ANCIENT ARCHITECTURE
See also Archeology; Architecture
ANCIENT ART
See also Art
The **ancient** Celts. Cunliffe, B. **936**
ANCIENT CIVILIZATION
Beard, M. SPQR **937**
Cantor, N. F. Antiquity: the civilization of the ancient world **930**
Carlsen, W. Jungle of Stone **972.81**
Hancock, G. Underworld: the mysterious origins of civilization **551.7**
Hunt, P. Ten discoveries that rewrote history **930.1**
Kriwaczek, P. Babylon **935**
The Oxford history of the biblical world **220.9**
Teresi, D. Lost discoveries **509**
ANCIENT CIVILIZATION
See also Ancient history; Civilization
ANCIENT CIVILIZATION -- ENCYCLOPEDIAS
Encyclopedia of the ancient world **930**
Ancient Europe 8000 B.C.-A.D. 1000. **936**
ANCIENT GEOGRAPHY
See also Ancient history; Historical geography
Ancient grains for modern meals. **641.59**
Ancient Greece. **938**

Ancient Greece. Cartledge, P.   938

ANCIENT GREECE See Greece -- History -- 0-323

Ancient Greek athletics. Miller, S. G.   796

ANCIENT HISTORY

Ancient Europe 8000 B.C.-A.D. 1000   936

The Cambridge ancient history   930

Great events from history, The ancient world, prehistory-476 C.E.   930

Great lives from history, The ancient world, prehistory-476 C.E   920.003

Herodotus, c. 4. B. B. C. The Histories   938

Weinberg, S. To explain the world   509

ANCIENT HISTORY

See also World history

The **ancient** Olympics. Spivey, N. J.   796.48

Ancient peoples and places [series]

Coe, M. D. The Maya   972

Townsend, R. F. The Aztecs   972

ANCIENT PHILOSOPHY

Freely, J. The flame of Miletus   509

Lucretius Carus, T. On the nature of things: De rerum natura   187

Shields, C. J. Aristotle   185

ANCIENT PHILOSOPHY

See also Philosophy

The **ancient** shore. Hazzard, S.   945

--And a time to die. Kaufman, S. R.   362.1

--and never let her go. Rule, A.   364.1

And so it goes: Kurt Vonnegut: a life. Shields, C. J.   92

And Still I Rise. Burke, K. M.   973

And the band played on. Shilts, R.   362.1

And the sea is never full. Wiesel, E.   813

And the show went on. Riding, A.   944

And then all hell broke loose. Engel, R.   956.05

And they all sang. Terkel, S.   780.9

Andalibian, Rahimeh

About

Andalibian, R. The rose hotel   92

Andelman, Bob

Will Eisner: A Spirited Life   741.5

Andersch, Alfred, 1914-1980

About

Sebald, W. G. On the natural history of destruction   833

Andersen, Christopher

Game of crowns   941.085

(jt. auth) Anderson, C. The good son   92

Andersen, Hans Christian, 1805-1875

About

Andersen, J. Hans Christian Andersen: a new life   92

Wullschlager, J. Hans Christian Andersen   839.8

Andersen, Jens

Hans Christian Andersen: a new life   92

Anderson, Anna, d. 1984

About

Massie, R. K. The Romanovs   947.08

Anderson, Annelise Graebner

(ed) Reagan, in his own hand   973.927

(ed) Reagan, R. Reagan   92

Anderson, Chris

The numbers game   796.334

Anderson, Christopher

The good son   92

Anderson, Clayton C., 1959-

About

Anderson, C. The ordinary spaceman   92

Anderson, Daniel

(ed) Nemerov, H. The selected poems of Howard Nemerov   811

Anderson, David L.

The Columbia guide to the Vietnam War   959.704

Anderson, David M.

Histories of the hanged   967.62

Anderson, Devery S.

Emmett Till   364.1

Anderson, Edward F.

The cactus family   583

Anderson, Fred

The crucible of war   973.2

The dominion of war   973.2

Anderson, Herbert

The divine art of dying   202

Anderson, Jack, 1922-2005

About

Feldstein, M. Poisoning the press   973.924

Anderson, Jean

The food of Portugal   641.5

Anderson, Jon Lee

Che Guevara   92

Anderson, Julie

The art of medicine   610

Anderson, Lars

Carlisle vs. Army   796.332

The Mannings   796.332

Anderson, Marian, 1897-1993

About

Keiler, A. Marian Anderson   92

Ware, S. Letter to the world   920.72

Anderson, Mark

The day the world discovered the sun

Anderson, Marlow

(ed) Sherlock Holmes in Babylon   510

Anderson, Martin

(ed) Reagan, in his own hand   973.927

(ed) Reagan, R. Reagan   92

Anderson, Pam

How to cook without a book   641.5

Perfect one-dish dinners   641.8

Perfect recipes for having people over   641.5

Anderson, Paul Thomas
> **About**
> Waxman, S. Rebels on the backlot **920**

Anderson, Sarah
> The spinner's book of yarn designs **746.14**

Anderson, Scott, 1959-
> Lawrence in Arabia **940.4**

Anderson, Sean
> Historical dictionary of terrorism **363.32**

Anderson, Sulome
> The Hostage's Daughter **92**

Anderson, Susan B.
> Susan B. Anderson's kids' knitting workshop **746.43**

Anderson, Teoti
> The ultimate guide to dog training **636.7**

Anderson, Terry A., 1949-
> **About**
> Anderson, S. The Hostage's Daughter **92**

Anderson, Thomas Charles, 1858-1931
> **About**
> Krist, G. Empire of sin **976.3**

Anderson, Tim, 1972-
> **About**
> Anderson, T. Sweet Tooth **92**

Anderson, William T.
> Laura Ingalls Wilder country **92**

ANDES
> Parrado, N. Miracle in the Andes **982**
> Read, P. P. Alive **910.4**

Andoe, Joe
> **About**
> Andoe, J. Jubilee city **92**

Andrée, Salomon August, 1854-1897
> **About**
> Wilkinson, A. The ice balloon **910.91**

André, Christophe
> Looking at Mindfulness **158.1**

Andrea Palladio. Boucher, B. **720.9**

Andrea, Alfred J.
> Encyclopedia of the crusades **909.07**

Andres, Jose
> Tapas **641.8**

Andrew Carnegie. Nasaw, D. **92**
Andrew Carnegie. Wall, J. F. **92**
Andrew Jackson. Wilentz, S. **92**
Andrew Jackson. Remini, R. V. **92**
Andrew Jackson. Brands, H. W. **92**
Andrew Johnson. Gordon-Reed, A. **92**
Andrew Wyeth. Wyeth, A. **92**

Andrew, Christopher M.
> Defend the realm **327.12**

Andrews, Anthony
> (ed) Black's veterinary dictionary **636.089**

Andrews, Colman
> Country cooking of Ireland **641.5**

Andrews, James R.

(jt. auth) Yaeger, D. Any given Monday **617.1**

Andrews, Julie
> **About**
> Andrews, J. Home **92**

Andrews, William L.
> (ed) Washington, B. T. Up from slavery **92**

ANDROGYNY
> *See also* Gender role; Sex differences (Psychology)

ANDROIDS
> *See also* Robots

ANDROIDS -- POPULAR WORKS
> Dufty, D. F. How to build an android **629.8**

Andrzejewski, Jerzy, 1910-1983
> Milosz, C. Legends of modernity **891.8**
> **About**
> Milosz, C. To begin where I am **891.8**

Andy Grove. Tedlow, R. S. **92**

Andy Warhol was a hoarder. Kalb, C. **616.89**

ANECDOTES
> The New Oxford book of literary anecdotes **828**
> A reader's book of days **809**

Ang, Tom
> Digital photographer's handbook **775**
> Digital photography masterclass **775**
> Photography **770.9**

Angel in the whirlwind. Bobrick, B. **973.3**

The **angel** of Grozny. Seierstad, A. **947.5**

Angel on my shoulder. Cole, N. **92**

Angel, Katherine
> **About**
> Angel, K. Unmastered **828**

Angela's ashes. McCourt, F. **92**

Angell, Roger, 1920-
> **About**
> Angell, R. This old man **92**

Angelo, Bonnie
> First families **920**

Angelou, Maya, 1928-2014
> The complete collected poems of Maya Angelou **811**
> I shall not be moved **811**
> Wouldn't take nothing for my journey now **814**
> **About**
> Angelou, M. Letter to my daughter **92**
> Angelou, M. Mom & me & mom **818**
> Angelou, M. I know why the caged bird sings **92**
> Angelou, M. A song flung up to heaven **818**
> Black women writers (1950-1980) **810**
> Gillespie, M. A. Maya Angelou **92**
> Mom & me & mom **818**
> Thursby, J. S. Critical companion to Maya Angelou **818**

Angels. Bussagli, M. **704.9**

ANGELS
> *See also* Heaven; Spirits

ANGELS
Bussagli, M. Angels   **704.9**
Angels and ages. Gopnik, A.   **973.7**
Angels in America. Kushner, T.   **812**
Anger. Tavris, C.   **152.4**
ANGER
Lerner, H. G. The dance of anger   **152.4**
Tavris, C. Anger   **152.4**
ANGER
    See also Emotions
Angier, Bradford
Field guide to edible wild plants   **581.6**
Angier, Carole
The double bond: Primo Levi, a biography   **92**
Angier, Natalie
Woman   **612.6**
ANGINA PECTORIS
    See also Heart diseases
Angle of yaw. Lerner, B.   **811**
Angles of ascent.   **811**
ANGLING *See* Fishing
ANGLO-AMERICAN CATALOGUING RULES
Oliver, C. Introducing RDA   **025.3**
ANGLO-SAXONS
    See also Great Britain -- History -- 0-1066;
    Teutonic peoples
ANGOLA -- DESCRIPTION AND TRAVEL
Theroux, P. Last train to Zona Verde   **916**
Angry wind. Tayler, J.   **916**
Angwin, Julia
Dragnet nation   **323.44**
Stealing MySpace   **338.7**
ANHEUSER-BUSCH, INC.
MacIntosh, J. Dethroning the king   **338.8**
ANHEUSER-BUSCH, INC. -- HISTORY
Knoedelseder, W. Bitter brew   **338.7**
ANIMAL ABUSE *See* Animal welfare
ANIMAL ATTACKS
Kirby, D. Death at SeaWorld   **599.53**
ANIMAL BABIES
    See also Animals
ANIMAL BEHAVIOR
The age of empathy   **152.4**
Animal life   **591.5**
Bagemihl, B. Biological exuberance   **591.56**
Balcombe, J. The exultant ark   **591.5**
Balcombe, J. Second nature   **591.5**
Balcombe, J. What a Fish Knows   **597.15**
Barrington, R. Life   **578.4**
Bekoff, M. Wild justice   **591.5**
Berger, J. The better to eat you with   **591.5**
Boysen, S. T. The smartest animals on the planet   **591.5**
Braitman, L. Animal madness   **591.5**
Encyclopedia of animal behavior   **591.5**
Foster, C. Being a Beast   **591.5**

Grandin, T. Animals in translation   **591.5**
Grandin, T. Animals make us human   **636**
Griffin, D. R. Animal minds   **591.5**
Hart, B. L. Your ideal cat   **636.8**
Heinrich, B. Life everlasting   **591.7**
Heinrich, B. Summer world   **591.7**
Masson, J. M. When elephants weep   **591.5**
McCarthy, S. Becoming a tiger   **591.5**
Miller, P. The smart swarm   **156**
Morell, V. Animal wise   **591.5**
Peterson, D. The moral lives of animals   **156**
Safina, C. Beyond words   **591.56**
The secret language of animals   **591.5**
ANIMAL BEHAVIOR
    See also Animals; Zoology
ANIMAL CAMOUFLAGE *See* Camouflage (Biology)
ANIMAL COMMUNICATION
Fouts, R. Next of kin   **156**
Friend, T. Animal talk   **591.59**
Halloran, A. R. The song of the ape   **599.885**
Heinrich, B. Life everlasting   **591.7**
Link, T. Talking with dogs and cats   **636.088**
ANIMAL COMMUNICATION
    See also Animal behavior
ANIMAL COURTSHIP
    See also Animal behavior; Sexual behavior in animals
ANIMAL DEALERS
Smith, J. E. Stolen world   **364.1**
ANIMAL DEFENSES
Eisner, T. Secret weapons   **595.7**
Emlen, D. J. Animal weapons   **591.47**
ANIMAL DEFENSES
    See also Animal behavior
ANIMAL DRAWING *See* Animal painting and illustration
ANIMAL ECOLOGY
Berger, J. The better to eat you with   **591.5**
Heinrich, B. Life everlasting   **591.7**
Animal evolution. Nielsen, C.   **591.3**
ANIMAL EXPERIMENTATION
Greek, C. R. Sacred cows and golden geese   **179**
Preston, R. The hot zone   **614.5**
ANIMAL EXPERIMENTATION
    See also Research
ANIMAL EXPERIMENTATION -- MORAL AND ETHICAL ASPECTS
Greek, C. R. Sacred cows and golden geese   **179**
Westoll, A. The chimps of Fauna Sanctuary   **636.9**
ANIMAL EXPLOITATION *See* Animal welfare
Animal eye. Rekdal, P.   **811**
Animal factory. Kirby, D.   **363.7**
ANIMAL FLIGHT
Alexander, D. E. Why don't jumbo jets flap their wings?   **629.13**

ANIMAL FLIGHT
> *See also* Animal locomotion; Flight

ANIMAL FOOD *See* Animals -- Food; Food of animal origin

ANIMAL HOUSING
Johnson, S. How to build chicken coops   **636.5**

ANIMAL HOUSING
> *See also* Animals

ANIMAL HUSBANDRY *See* Livestock industry

ANIMAL INDUSTRY *See* Livestock industry

ANIMAL INTELLIGENCE
Ackerman, J. The Genius of Birds   **598**
Balcombe, J. Second nature   **591.5**
Bekoff, M. Wild justice   **591.5**
Boysen, S. T. The smartest animals on the planet   **591.5**
Bradshaw, J. Dog sense   **636.7**
Bradshaw, J. Cat sense   **636.8**
Masson, J. M. When elephants weep   **591.5**
McCarthy, S. Becoming a tiger   **591.5**
Montgomery, S. The soul of an octopus   **594**
Peterson, D. The moral lives of animals   **156**
Safina, C. Beyond words   **591.56**
Waal, F. B. M. d. Are We Smart Enough to Know How Smart Animals Are?   **591.5**

ANIMAL INTELLIGENCE
> *See also* Animals

Animal investigators. Neme, L. A.   **363.2**

ANIMAL KINGDOM *See* Zoology

ANIMAL LANGUAGE *See* Animal communication; Animal sounds

Animal life.   **591.5**

ANIMAL LIFE CYCLES
Heinrich, B. Life everlasting   **591.7**

ANIMAL LOCOMOTION
Wilkinson, M. Restless creatures   **591.47**

ANIMAL LOCOMOTION
> *See also* Animals; Locomotion

ANIMAL LORE *See* Animals -- Folklore; Animals in literature; Mythical animals; Natural history

Animal madness. Braitman, L.   **591.5**
Animal minds. Griffin, D. R.   **591.5**

ANIMAL PAINTING AND ILLUSTRATION
Hand, D. Draw Horses in 15 Minutes   **743.6**
Kiser, J. M. America's other Audubon   **598**

ANIMAL PAINTING AND ILLUSTRATION
> *See also* Painting

ANIMAL PARASITES *See* Parasites

ANIMAL PHOTOGRAPHY *See* Photography of animals

ANIMAL PHYSIOLOGY *See* Zoology

ANIMAL PICTURES *See* Animals -- Pictorial works

ANIMAL PSYCHOLOGY
Griffin, D. R. Animal minds   **591.5**

ANIMAL PSYCHOLOGY *See* Animal intelligence; Comparative psychology

ANIMAL REPRODUCTION
> *See also* Animals; Reproduction

ANIMAL RESCUE
The art of raising a puppy   **636.7**
Bradley, C. Last chain on Billie   **639.97**
Katz, J. Saving Simon   **636.1**
Williams, T. M. The odyssey of KP2   **599.79**
Zheutlin, P. Rescue road   **636.7**

ANIMAL RESCUE
> *See also* Animal welfare

ANIMAL RESCUE -- ANECDOTES
Miracle dogs   **636.7**

ANIMAL RIGHTS
Goodall, J. The ten trusts   **333.95**
Hargrove, J. Beneath the surface   **599.53**
The lives of animals   **179**
Wise, S. M. Drawing the line   **179**

ANIMAL RIGHTS MOVEMENT
Beers, D. L. For the prevention of cruelty   **179**
Kuipers, D. Operation Bite Back   **92**
Shevelow, K. For the love of animals   **179**

ANIMAL RIGHTS MOVEMENT
> *See also* Social movements

ANIMAL SOUNDS
Halloran, A. R. The song of the ape   **599.885**

ANIMAL SOUNDS
> *See also* Animal behavior

Animal talk. Friend, T.   **591.59**

ANIMAL TRACKS
Elbroch, M. Mammal tracks & sign   **599**
Elbroch, M. The Peterson field guide to animal tracks   **599**

Animal weapons. Emlen, D. J.   **591.47**

ANIMAL WEAPONS
Emlen, D. J. Animal weapons   **591.47**

ANIMAL WELFARE
Baur, G. Farm Sanctuary   **179**
Danforth, A. Butchering poultry, rabbit, lamb, goat, and pork   **664**
Do unto animals   **590**
Faruqi, S. Project Animal Farm   **338.1**
Foer, J. S. Eating animals   **641.3**
Goodall, J. The ten trusts   **333.95**
The lives of animals   **179**
Masson, J. M. When elephants weep   **591.5**

ANIMAL WELFARE -- MORAL AND ETHICAL ASPECTS
Pierce, J. Run, Spot, run   **636.08**

ANIMAL WELFARE -- UNITED STATES
Beers, D. L. For the prevention of cruelty   **179**
Bradley, C. Last chain on Billie   **639.97**

ANIMAL WELFARE MOVEMENT *See* Animal rights movement

Animal wise. Morell, V.   **591.5**
Animal, vegetable, miracle.   **641**

ANIMALS
Heinrich, B. Summer world   **591.7**
Wildlife of the world   **591**
ANIMALS -- ANATOMY
   See also Anatomy; Zoology
ANIMALS -- ANTARCTICA
Matthiessen, P. End of the earth   **508**
ANIMALS -- BEHAVIOR *See* Animal behavior
ANIMALS -- CAMOUFLAGE *See* Camouflage (Biology)
ANIMALS -- COLOR
   See also Color
ANIMALS -- DISEASES
Quammen, D. Spillover   **614.4**
ANIMALS -- DISEASES
   See also Diseases
ANIMALS -- ENCYCLOPEDIAS
The cat encyclopedia   **636.8**
ANIMALS -- HABITATIONS
Do unto animals   **590**
ANIMALS -- HOUSING *See* Animal housing
ANIMALS -- LANGUAGE *See* Animal communication
ANIMALS -- LONGEVITY
Kerasote, T. Pukka's Promise   **636.7**
ANIMALS -- MIGRATION
Wilcove, D. S. No way home   **591.56**
ANIMALS -- MIGRATION
   See also Animal behavior
ANIMALS -- MISTREATMENT *See* Animal welfare
ANIMALS -- MOVEMENTS *See* Animal locomotion
ANIMALS -- NORTH AMERICA
Ernst, C. H. Venomous reptiles of the United States, Canada, and northern Mexico   **597.9**
Flores, D. Coyote America   **599.77**
ANIMALS -- PHOTOGRAPHY *See* Photography of animals
ANIMALS -- PICTORIAL WORKS
Friedman, E. W. The Dogist   **779**
Giraffe reflections   **599.638**
Wildlife of the world   **591**
ANIMALS -- POLAR REGIONS -- PICTORIAL WORKS
Seaman, C. Melting away   **910.91**
ANIMALS -- PROTECTION *See* Animal welfare
ANIMALS -- PSYCHOLOGICAL ASPECTS
Heinrich, B. Life everlasting   **591.7**
ANIMALS -- RELIGIOUS ASPECTS
Wintz, J. Will I see my dog in heaven?   **231.7**
ANIMALS -- WAR USE
Hutton, R. Sgt. Reckless   **951.904**
ANIMALS AS CARRIERS OF DISEASE
Quammen, D. Spillover   **614.4**
ANIMALS AS FOOD *See* Food of animal origin

ANIMALS IN ART
Hayakawa, H. Kirigami menagerie   **736**
ANIMALS IN MOTION PICTURES
   See also Motion pictures
ANIMALS IN POLICE WORK
   See also Police; Working animals
Animals in translation. Grandin, T.   **591.5**
Animals make us human. Grandin, T.   **636**
ANIMALS' RIGHTS *See* Animal rights
ANIMALS, EDIBLE *See* Food of animal origin
ANIMALS, EXTINCT *See* Extinct animals
ANIMALS, FOSSIL
Taylor, P. D. A history of life in 100 fossils   **560**
ANIMALS, MYTHICAL
Prothero, D. R. Abominable science!   **001.944**
ANIMALS, MYTHICAL -- HISTORY
Kaplan, M. Medusa's gaze and vampire's bite   **001.944**
ANIMATED CARTOONS *See* Animated films; Animated television programs
ANIMATED FILMS
Cavalier, S. The world history of animation   **791.43**
Harryhausen, R. The art of Ray Harryhausen **778.5**
Suskind, R. Life, animated   **618.92**
ANIMATED FILMS
   See also Cartoons and caricatures; Motion pictures
ANIMATED FILMS -- HISTORY AND CRITICISM
Cavalier, S. The world history of animation **791.43**
ANIMATED FILMS -- UNITED STATES -- HISTORY AND CRITICISM
Ghez, D. They drew as they pleased   **741.58**
ANIMATED TELEVISION PROGRAMS
Cavalier, S. The world history of animation **791.43**
ANIMATED TELEVISION PROGRAMS
   See also Television programs
ANIMATION (CINEMATOGRAPHY)
Cavalier, S. The world history of animation **791.43**
Williams, R. The animator's survival kit   **778.53**
ANIMATION (CINEMATOGRAPHY)
   See also Cinematography
The **animator's** survival kit. Williams, R.   **778.53**
ANIMATORS
Cavalier, S. The world history of animation **791.43**
ANIMATORS -- UNITED STATES -- BIOGRAPHY
Gabler, N. Walt Disney   **92**
ANIME
Brenner, R. E. Understanding manga and anime   **025.2**
ANIME
   See also Animated films; Animated television programs
ANIMISM
   See also Religion

Anna and the King of Siam. Landon, M. **92**
Anna in the tropics. Cruz, N. **812**
Anna of all the Russias. Feinstein, E. **92**
The **annals** of unsolved crime. Epstein, E. J. **364.152**
Annan, Kofi A. (Kofi Atta)
            About
Annan, K. A. Interventions **341.23**
The **Annapolis** Book of Seamanship. Rousmaniere,
    J. **623.88**
Anne Boleyn, Queen, consort of Henry VIII, King
    of England, 1507-1536
            About
Fraser, A. The wives of Henry VIII **920**
Starkey, D. Six wives: the queens of Henry
    VIII **942.05**
Weir, A. The lady in the tower **92**
Anne Frank. **92**
Anne Frank. Prose, F. **839.3**
Anne Frank. Jacobson, S. **92**
Anne Frank House
Jacobson, S. Anne Frank **92**
Anne Frank remembered. Gies, M. **92**
Anne Morrow Lindbergh. Hertog, S. **92**
Anne Morrow Lindbergh. Winters, K. C. **92**
Anne of Cleves, Queen, consort of Henry VIII,
    King of England, 1515-1557
            About
Fraser, A. The wives of Henry VIII **920**
Starkey, D. Six wives: the queens of Henry
    VIII **942.05**
Anne Sexton. Middlebrook, D. W. **811**
Anne, Queen of Great Britain, 1665-1714
            About
Somerset, A. Queen Anne **92**
Anne, Queen, consort of Richard III, King of Eng-
    land, 1456-1485
            About
Gristwood, S. Blood sisters **942.04**
The **Annie** Dillard reader. Dillard, A. **818**
Annie Leibovitz at work. Leibovitz, A. **779**
Annie Oakley. Kasper, S. **92**
Annie's ghosts. Luxenberg, S. **92**
Annigoni, Tony
            About
McCumber, D. Playing off the rail **794.7**
Annis, Barbara
Work with me **306.3**
ANNIVERSARIES
    See also Manners and customs
The **annotated** and illustrated double helix. **572.8**
The **annotated** U.S. Constitution and Declaration of
    Independence. **342**
Annoying. Palca, J. **612.8**
ANNUALS See Almanacs; Calendars; Periodicals;
    School yearbooks; Yearbooks
ANNUALS (PLANTS)

Ellis, B. W. Taylor's guide to annuals **635.9**
ANNUALS (PLANTS)
    See also Cultivated plants; Flower gardening;
    Flowers
ANNUITIES
    See also Investments; Retirement income
ANONYMOUS (GROUP)
Olson, P. We are Anonymous **005.8**
Anonymous soldiers. Hoffman, B. **956.94**
ANONYMS See Pseudonyms
ANOREXIA NERVOSA
Hornbacher, M. Wasted: a memoir of anorexia and
    bulimia **616.85**
ANOREXIA NERVOSA
    See also Eating disorders
Another bullshit night in Suck City. Flynn, N. **92**
Another country. Pipher, M. B. **306.874**
Another day at the front. Reed, I. **305.8**
Ansary, Mir Tamim
West of Kabul, East of New York **958.1**
Ansel Adams. Alinder, M. S. **92**
Ansel Adams at 100. Szarkowski, J. **770**
Ansel, Dominique
Dominique Ansel **641.86**
Anselmo, Lisa
            About
Anselmo, L. My (part-time) Paris life **944.361**
Anstett, Patricia
Breast cancer surgery and reconstruction **618.1**
Answering teens' tough questions. Eagle, M. **027.62**
ANTARCTIC EXPEDITIONS See Antarctica --
    Exploration
ANTARCTIC REGIONS/DISCOVERY AND EX-
    PLORATION
Larson, E. J. An empire of ice **919**
Antarctica. McGonigal, D. **998**
ANTARCTICA
    See also Earth; Polar regions
ANTARCTICA
The ends of the earth **998**
McGonigal, D. Antarctica **998**
ANTARCTICA -- DESCRIPTION AND TRAVEL
Griffiths, T. Slicing the silence **998**
Montaigne, F. Fraser's penguins **577.2**
Roberts, D. Alone on the ice **919**
Smith, R. Life on the ice **998**
Solomon, S. The coldest March **919**
ANTARCTICA -- EXPLORATION
Anthony, J. C. Hoosh **394.1**
Larson, E. J. An empire of ice **919**
Roberts, D. Alone on the ice **919**
Smith, M. Shackleton **92**
Turney, C. 1912 **998**
ANTARCTICA -- EXPLORATION
    See also Exploration; Scientific expeditions
ANTARCTICA -- HISTORY -- ANECDOTES

Anthony, J. C. Hoosh   **394.1**

ANTARCTICA -- SOCIAL LIFE AND CUS-TOMS

Anthony, J. C. Hoosh   **394.1**

The **antelope's** strategy. Hatzfeld, J.   **967.571**

Anterooms. Wilbur, R.   **811**

Anthes, Emily

Frankenstein's cat   **616.02**

ANTHOLOGIES

Ephron, N. The Most of Nora Ephron   **814**

ANTHOLOGIES

See also Books

An **Anthology** of Chinese literature.   **895.1**

An **anthology** of graphic fiction, cartoons & true stories, vol. 2. Brunetti, I.   **741.5**

An **Anthology** of graphic fiction, cartoons, and true stories. Brunetti, I.   **741.5**

Anthology of modern Chinese poetry.   **895.1**

An **anthology** of modern Irish poetry.   **821**

Anthology of modern Palestinian literature.   **892.7**

Anthony Blunt: his lives. Carter, M.   **92**

Anthony, Carl Sferrazza

America's first families   **920**

Nellie Taft   **92**

Anthony, Jason C.

Hoosh   **394.1**

Anthony, Lawrence, 1950-2012

The elephant whisperer   **599.67**

Anthony, Michael, 1968-

V Is for Vegetables   **641.6**

Anthony, Susan B., 1820-1906

        About

Failure is impossible   **92**

An **anthropologist** on Mars. Sacks, O. W.   **616.8**

ANTHROPOLOGISTS

Li, C. N. The bitter sea   **92**

Maples, W. R. Dead men do tell tales   **614**

Mead, M. Blackberry winter   **92**

Ware, S. Letter to the world   **920.72**

ANTHROPOLOGY

Kaplan, M. Medusa's gaze and vampire's bite   **001.944**

Leakey, R. E. Origins reconsidered   **599.93**

Levi-Strauss, C. The savage mind   **155.8**

Meredith, M. Born in Africa   **960**

ANTHROPOLOGY

See also Social sciences

ANTHROPOMETRY

Fabian, A. The skull collectors   **599.9**

ANTHROPOMETRY

See also Anthropology; Ethnology; Human beings

ANTI-ABORTION MOVEMENT *See* Pro-life movement

ANTI-APARTHEID MOVEMENT

Smith, D. J. Young Mandela   **92**

ANTI-APARTHEID MOVEMENT

See also Civil rights; Social movements; South Africa -- Race relations

ANTI-COMMUNIST MOVEMENTS -- UNITED STATES -- HISTORY -- 20TH CENTURY

Conant, J. A covert affair   **940.54**

Lichtblau, E. The Nazis next door   **324.1**

Thompson, N. The hawk and the dove   **92**

ANTI-FASCIST MOVEMENTS *See* World War, 1939-1945 -- Underground movements

ANTI-ISLAM PREJUDICE *See* Islamophobia

Anti-Judaism. Nirenberg, D.   **305.892**

ANTI-MUSLIM PREJUDICE *See* Islamophobia

ANTI-NAZI MOVEMENT *See* World War, 1939-1945 -- Underground movements

ANTI-NAZI MOVEMENT -- GERMANY -- BIOGRAPHY

The lone assassin   **943.086**

ANTI-NAZI MOVEMENT -- GERMANY -- HISTORY -- 20TH CENTURY

Orbach, D. The plots against Hitler   **940.53**

ANTI-NAZI MOVEMENT -- POLAND

Allen, A. The fantastic laboratory of Dr. Weigl   **614.5**

ANTI-TERRORISM *See* Terrorism -- Prevention

ANTI-WAR POETRY *See* War poetry

ANTI-WAR STORIES *See* War stories

ANTIABORTION MOVEMENT *See* Pro-life movement

ANTIBIOTICS

Blaser, M. J. Missing microbes   **615.7**

ANTIBIOTICS

See also Drug therapy

ANTIBUSING *See* Busing (School integration)

ANTICOMMUNIST MOVEMENTS

Conant, J. A covert affair   **940.54**

Johnson, H. B. The age of anxiety   **973.921**

Morgan, T. Reds: McCarthyism in twentieth-century America   **973.9**

ANTICOMMUNIST MOVEMENTS

See also Communism

ANTICORROSIVE PAINT *See* Corrosion and anticorrosives

ANTIDEPRESSANTS

Kramer, P. D. Ordinarily well   **615.7**

ANTIDEPRESSANTS

See also Psychotropic drugs

ANTIDEPRESSANTS -- EFFECTIVENESS

Kramer, P. D. Ordinarily well   **615.7**

ANTIDEPRESSANTS -- HISTORY

Kramer, P. D. Ordinarily well   **615.7**

ANTIETAM (MD.), BATTLE OF, 1862

Sears, S. W. Landscape turned red   **973.7**

Slotkin, R. Long Road to Antietam   **973.7**

ANTIETAM (MD.), BATTLE OF, 1862

See also Battles; United States -- History --

1861-1865, Civil War -- Campaigns

ANTIGUA (ANTIGUA AND BARBUDA)
Kincaid, J. A small place   **972.9**

ANTIGUA AND BARBUDA
Kincaid, J. A small place   **972.9**

ANTIMALARIALS -- HISTORY -- UNITED STATES
Masterson, K. M. The malaria project   **616.9**

Antine, Stacey, 1968-
Appetite for life   **641.5**

ANTINUCLEAR MOVEMENT
   See also Arms control; Nuclear weapons; Social movements

ANTIQUARIAN BOOKS *See* Rare books

ANTIQUARIANS
Burleigh, N. Unholy business   **933**

ANTIQUE AND CLASSIC CARS
Swift, E. Auto Biography   **629.222**

ANTIQUE AND CLASSIC CARS
   See also Automobiles

ANTIQUE AND CLASSIC CARS -- EXHIBITIONS
Gross, K. Dream cars   **629.222**

ANTIQUE AND VINTAGE MOTORCYCLES
   See also Motorcycles

ANTIQUE AUTOMOBILES *See* Antique and classic cars

ANTIQUE CARS *See* Antique and classic cars

ANTIQUES
MacGregor, N. A history of the world in 100 objects   **930.1**
Miller, J. Miller's antiques handbook & price guide   **745.1**
Stanton, M. Killer stuff and tons of money   **381**

ANTIQUES
   See also Antiquities; Collectors and collecting; Decoration and ornament; Decorative arts

ANTIQUITIES
Brown, N. M. Ivory Vikings   **736**
Hunt, P. Ten discoveries that rewrote history   **930.1**
Levine, L. I. Visual Judaism in late antiquity   **704.9**

ANTIQUITIES -- COLLECTION AND PRESERVATION
Atwood, R. Stealing history   **364.1**

ANTIQUITIES -- COLLECTION AND PRESERVATION
   See also Collectors and collecting

ANTIQUITIES, PREHISTORIC
MacGregor, N. A history of the world in 100 objects   **930.1**

ANTIQUITY OF MAN *See* Human origins

Antiquity: the civilization of the ancient world.
Cantor, N. F.   **930**

ANTISEMITISM
Arendt, H. Origins of totalitarianism   **321.9**

Baldwin, N. Henry Ford and the Jews   **305**
Bredin The affair   **944.081**
Chesler, P. The new anti-semitism   **305.8**
Derfler, L. The Dreyfus affair   **944.081**
Goldhagen, D. Hitler's willing executioners   **940.53**
Kamen, H. The Spanish Inquisition   **272**
Kertzer, D. I. The Popes against the Jews   **261.2**
Lipstadt, D. E. Denying the Holocaust   **940.53**
Those who forget the past   **305.8**
Wasserstein, B. On the eve   **305.892**
Watts, S. The people's tycoon   **92**
The World reacts to the Holocaust   **940.53**

ANTISEMITISM
   See also Prejudices

ANTISEMITISM -- EUROPE -- HISTORY
Nirenberg, D. Anti-Judaism   **305.892**

ANTISEMITISM -- FRANCE -- HISTORY -- 19TH CENTURY
Read, P. P. The Dreyfus affair   **944.081**

ANTISEMITISM -- HISTORY -- 20TH CENTURY
Goldhagen, D. J. The Devil That Never Dies   **305.892**

ANTISEPTICS
   See also Therapeutics

ANTISLAVERY *See* Abolitionists; Slavery; Slaves -- Emancipation

ANTISLAVERY MOVEMENTS
Davis, D. B. The problem of slavery in the age of emancipation   **306.3**

ANTISLAVERY MOVEMENTS -- UNITED STATES
Colaiaco, J. A. Frederick Douglass and the Fourth of July   **973.7**
Rediker, M. The Amistad rebellion   **326**

ANTISLAVERY MOVEMENTS -- UNITED STATES -- HISTORY
Berlin, I. The long emancipation   **326.8**
Oakes, J. Freedom national   **973.7**

ANTISLAVERY MOVEMENTS -- UNITED STATES -- HISTORY -- 19TH CENTURY
Clinton, C. Harriet Tubman: the road to freedom   **92**
Douglass, F. Frederick Douglass: selected speeches and writings   **326**
Douglass, F. My bondage and my freedom   **92**
Walters, K. The Underground Railroad   **973.7**
Wineapple, B. Ecstatic nation   **973.6**

ANTITRUST LAW
   See also Commercial law

ANTIVIVISECTION MOVEMENT *See* Animal rights movement

ANTIWAR MOVEMENTS *See* Peace movements

Antoine, Rebeca
(ed) Voices rising   **976.3**

Anton Chekhov's life and thought. Chekhov, A. P.   **92**

Antonia, Mother
About
Jordan, M. The prison angel 92
Antoniou, Antonis
(ed) A Map of the World 912
Antonius, Marcus, ca. 83-30 B.C.
About
Goldsworthy, A. K. Antony and Cleopatra 92
Antony and Cleopatra. Goldsworthy, A. K. 92
The **ants**. Holldobler, B. 595.79
ANTS
Holldobler, B. The ants 595.79
Holldobler, B. Journey to the ants 595.79
Holldobler, B. The leafcutter ants 595.7
Keller, L. The lives of ants 595.7
Moffett, M. W. Adventures among ants 595.7
ANTS
See also Insects
ANTS -- BEHAVIOR
Moffett, M. W. Adventures among ants 595.7
ANTS -- ECOLOGY
Moffett, M. W. Adventures among ants 595.7
Ants on the melon. Adair, V. H. 811
Antunes, Antonio Lobo
The fat man and infinity 869
ANXIETIES *See* Anxiety
ANXIETY
Chansky, T. E. Freeing your child from anxiety 618.92
Clark, T. Nerve 152.4
Enayati, A. Seeking serenity 155.9
Smith, D. Monkey mind 616.85
Tillich, P. The courage to be 179
ANXIETY
See also Emotions; Neuroses; Stress (Psychology)
ANXIETY -- TREATMENT
Trainor, K. Calming your anxious child 618.92
ANXIETY IN CHILDREN
Chansky, T. E. Freeing your child from anxiety 618.92
ANXIETY IN CHILDREN -- POPULAR WORKS
Trainor, K. Calming your anxious child 618.92
The **anxiety** toolkit. Boyes, A. 616.85
ANXIOUSNESS *See* Anxiety
Any given Monday. Yaeger, D. 617.1
Anything goes. Moore, L. 973.91
Anything goes. Mordden, E. 782.1
Anzovin, Steven
(ed) Famous first facts, international edition 031.02
APACHE INDIANS
Brown, D. A. The American West 978
APACHE INDIANS -- HISTORY
Roberts, D. Once they moved like the wind 970.004
Utley, R. M. Geronimo 92
APACHE INDIANS -- WARS

Hutton, P. A. The Apache wars 979
Utley, R. M. Geronimo 92
The **Apache** wars. Hutton, P. A. 979
Apana, Chang, 1871-1933
About
Yunte Huang Charlie Chan 92
APARTHEID
Smith, D. J. Young Mandela 92
APARTHEID
See also Segregation; South Africa -- Race relations
APARTHEID -- SOUTH AFRICA
Mandela, N. Conversations with myself 92
APARTMENT HOUSES
See also Buildings; Domestic architecture; Houses; Housing
APARTMENTS
Smith, M. The nesting place 248.4
APATHY
Norris, K. Acedia & me 92
Apatow, Judd, 1967-
Sick in the head 792.7
APES
Among African apes 599.8
Bearzi, M. Beautiful minds 599.8
Morris, D. Planet ape 599.8
Stanford, C. B. Planet without apes 599.88
Waal, F. d. Bonobo 599.88
World atlas of great apes and their conservation 599.8
APES
See also Primates
Apess, William, 1798-1839
About
Gura, P. F. The life of William Apess, Pequot 92
APHASIA
See also Brain -- Diseases; Language disorders; Speech disorders
APHRODITE (GREEK DEITY)
See also Gods and goddesses
APICULTURE *See* Beekeeping
Apocalypses. Weber, E. 200
APOCALYPTIC FICTION
Kallio, J. Read on ... speculative fiction for teens 016
APOCALYPTIC FICTION
See also Fiction
APOCALYPTIC FILMS
See also Motion pictures
Apocalyptic planet. Childs, C. 550
The **Apocrypha.** Bible/O.T./Apocrypha 229
APOLLO (GREEK DEITY)
See also Gods and goddesses
APOLLO PROJECT
Mailer, N. Of a fire on the moon 629.45
Nelson, C. Rocket men 629.45

Pyle, R. Destination moon **629.45**
Smith, A. Moondust **920**
Worden, A. Falling to Earth **92**
APOLLO PROJECT
 See also Life support systems (Space envi-
ronment); Orbital rendezvous (Space flight);
Space flight to the moon
Apollo's angels. Homans, J. **792.8**
Apollo's fire. Sims, M. **529**
Apollonius
 The voyage of Argo: the Argonautica **881**
APOLOGETICS
 Armstrong, K. The case for God **211**
 De civitate Dei./English Concerning the city of
 God against the pagans **239**
 John Paul Crossing the threshold of hope **282**
 Keller, T. J. The reason for God **239**
APOLOGETICS
 See also Theology
APOSTLES
 Borg, M. J. The first Paul **227**
 Gubar, S. Judas **92**
 Kung, H. Great Christian thinkers **230**
 Murphy-O'Connor, J. Paul **225.9**
 Ruden, S. Paul among the people **225.9**
APOSTLES
 See also Christian saints; Church history --
 30-600, Early church
Apostol, Tom M., 1923-2016
 New Horizons in Geometry **516**
APOSTOLIC CHURCH *See* Church history -- 30-
 600, Early church
APPALACHIA *See* Appalachian Region
APPALACHIAN MOUNTAINS REGION *See*
 Appalachian Region
APPALACHIAN REGION
 See also United States
APPALACHIAN REGION
 Animal, vegetable, miracle **641**
 Smith, L. Dimestore **92**
APPALACHIAN REGION -- DESCRIPTION
 AND TRAVEL
 Bryson, B. A walk in the woods **917**
APPALACHIAN REGION -- SOCIAL LIFE AND
 CUSTOMS
 Foxfire 40th anniversary book **975.8**
APPALACHIAN REGION, SOUTHERN -- EN-
 VIRONMENTAL CONDITIONS
 House, S. Something's rising **338.2**
APPALACHIAN REGION, SOUTHERN --
 GUIDEBOOKS
 Spira, T. P. Waterfalls and wildflowers in the South-
 ern Appalachians **796.51**
APPALACHIAN REGION, SOUTHERN -- SO-
 CIAL LIFE AND CUSTOMS
 Victuals **641.5**

APPARATUS, ELECTRONIC *See* Electronic ap-
 paratus and appliances
APPARATUS, SCIENTIFIC *See* Scientific appa-
 ratus and instruments
APPARITIONS
 See also Parapsychology; Spirits
APPEARANCE (PHILOSOPHY)
 Whitefield-Madrano, A. Face value **111.85**
APPEARANCE, PERSONAL *See* Personal ap-
 pearance
Appelfeld, Aron
   About
 Langer, L. L. Admitting the Holocaust **940.53**
APPERCEPTION
 See also Educational psychology; Psychology
APPETITE -- PSYCHOLOGICAL ASPECTS
 Christensen, K. Blue plate special **92**
Appetite for life. Fitch, N. R. **92**
Appetite for life. Antine, S. **641.5**
An **appetite** for poetry. Kermode, F. **801**
Appetite for self-destruction. Knopper, S. **384**
An **Appetite** for Wonder. Dawkins, R. **92**
Appetites. Bourdain, A. **641**
APPETIZERS
 Andres, J. Tapas **641.8**
 Fine cooking appetizers **641.8**
APPETIZERS
 See also Cooking
Appiah, Anthony
 (ed) Africana: the encyclopedia of the African and
 African American experience **909**
Appignanesi, Lisa
 Trials of passion **364.152**
APPLE *See* Apples
APPLE COMPUTER, INC
 Lashinsky, A. Inside Apple **338.7**
APPLE COMPUTER, INC. -- HISTORY
 Isaacson, W. Steve Jobs **92**
APPLE COMPUTER, INC. -- MANAGEMENT
 Tetzeli, R. Becoming Steve Jobs **92**
The **apple** trees at Olema. Hass, R. **811**
Applebaum, Anne
 Gulag **365**
 Iron curtain **947**
Applebaum, Wilbur
 (ed) Encyclopedia of the scientific revolution **509**
Appleby, Joyce Oldham
 Inheriting the revolution **973**
 Appleby, J. The relentless revolution **330.1**
Appleby, R. Scott
 Almond, G. A. Strong religion **200.9**
Applegate, Debby
 The most famous man in America **92**
APPLES
 Apples of uncommon character **634**
 Means, H. B. Johnny Appleseed **92**

Pollan, M. The botany of desire **306.4**

Wood, S. M. Apples to cider **663**

APPLES

See also Fruit

APPLES -- VARIETIES

Apples of uncommon character **634**

Apples and oranges. Brenner, M. **92**

Apples of uncommon character. **634**

Apples to cider. Wood, S. M. **663**

Appleseed, Johnny, 1774-1845

About

Means, H. B. Johnny Appleseed **92**

APPLIANCES, ELECTRONIC See Electronic apparatus and appliances

APPLICATIONS FOR COLLEGE See College applications

APPLICATIONS FOR POSITIONS

Knock 'em dead cover letters **650.14**

APPLICATIONS FOR POSITIONS

See also Job hunting; Personnel management

APPLIED PSYCHOLOGY

Beattie, M. Beyond codependency **616.86**

Bloomfield, H. H. Making peace with your past **158**

Carnegie, D. How to win friends and influence people **158**

Csikszentmihalyi, M. Flow: the psychology of optimal experience **155.2**

Kessel, B. It's not about the money **332.024**

Klauser, H. A. Write it down, make it happen **158**

May, R. Freedom and destiny **158**

Michels, B. The tools **158**

Mischel, W. The marshmallow test **155.2**

Mlodinow, L. Subliminal **154.2**

Peale, N. V. The power of positive living **248**

Peck, M. S. Further along the road less traveled **158**

Peck, M. S. The road less traveled **158**

Peck, M. S. The road less traveled and beyond **158**

Robbins, T. Unlimited power **158**

APPLIED PSYCHOLOGY

See also Psychology

APPLIED SCIENCE See Technology

APPLIQUÉ

See also Needlework

APPOMATTOX CAMPAIGN, 1865

Catton, B. A stillness at Appomattox **973.7**

Davis, B. To Appomattox **973.7**

APPOMATTOX CAMPAIGN, 1865

See also United States -- History -- 1861-1865, Civil War -- Campaigns

APPRAISAL OF BOOKS See Book reviewing; Books and reading; Criticism; Literature -- History and criticism

APPRECIATION OF ART See Art appreciation

APPRECIATION OF MUSIC See Music appreciation

The **apprentice:** my life in the kitchen. Pepin, J. **641.5**

APPRENTICES

See also Labor; Technical education

APPRENTICESHIP NOVELS See Bildungsromans

The **approaching** fury. Oates, S. B. **973.5**

APPROXIMATE COMPUTATION

Mahajan, S. Street-fighting mathematics **510**

Appy, Christian G.

American Reckoning **959.704**

APRIL FOOLS' DAY

See also Holidays

APTITUDE See Ability

Aptowicz, Cristin O'Keefe

Dr. Mütter's Marvels **92**

AQUACULTURE

See also Agriculture; Marine resources

AQUARIAN AGE MOVEMENT See New Age movement

Aquarium fish. Mills, D. **639.34**

AQUARIUMS

Bailey, M. The Ultimate Encyclopedia of Aquarium Fish & Fish Care **639.34**

Mills, D. Aquarium fish **639.34**

AQUARIUMS

See also Freshwater biology; Natural history

Aquash, Anna Mae, 1945-1976

About

Hendricks, S. The unquiet grave **970.004**

AQUATIC ANIMAL WELFARE

Hargrove, J. Beneath the surface **599.53**

Kirby, D. Death at SeaWorld **599.53**

AQUATIC ANIMALS

See also Animals

AQUATIC EXERCISES

See also Exercise

AQUATIC GARDENS See Water gardens

AQUATIC PLANTS See Freshwater plants; Marine plants

AQUATIC SPORTS -- SAFETY MEASURES See Water safety

AQUEDUCTS

See also Civil engineering; Hydraulic structures; Water supply

Aqui, 1962-

About

Lamb, C. House of stone **968.91**

Aquino, Lucia

Leonardo Da Vinci **92**

ARAB AMERICAN YOUTH

Bayoumi, M. How does it feel to be a problem? **305.8**

ARAB AMERICANS

Al-Maria, S. The Girl Who Fell to Earth **92**

Halaby, L. My name on his tongue **811**

Shadid, A. House of stone **306**

ARAB AMERICANS -- SOCIAL CONDITIONS

Bayoumi, M. How does it feel to be a problem? **305.8**

Eggers, D. Zeitoun **92**

Malek, A. A country called Amreeka **305.8**

Arab and Jew. Shipler, D. K. **956.94**

ARAB CIVILIZATION

Hourani, A. H. A history of the Arab peoples **909**

Rogan, E. The Arabs **909**

ARAB COUNTRIES

Fargues, P. The atlas of the Arab world **909**

Lamb, D. The Arabs **909**

ARAB COUNTRIES

    See also Islamic countries; Middle East

ARAB COUNTRIES -- DESCRIPTION AND TRAVEL

O'Neill, Z. All strangers are kin **910.917**

ARAB COUNTRIES -- FOREIGN RELATIONS -- ISRAEL

Wright, L. Thirteen Days in September **956.04**

ARAB COUNTRIES -- HISTORY

Hourani, A. H. A history of the Arab peoples **909**

Rogan, E. The Arabs **909**

ARAB COUNTRIES -- HISTORY -- ARAB SPRING, 2010- *See* Arab Spring, 2010-

ARAB COUNTRIES -- INTELLECTUAL LIFE

Al-Khalili, J. The house of wisdom **509**

ARAB COUNTRIES -- KINGS AND RULERS

Owen, R. The rise and fall of Arab presidents for life **352.23**

ARAB COUNTRIES -- MAPS

Fargues, P. The atlas of the Arab world **909**

The new atlas of the Arab world **912**

ARAB COUNTRIES -- POLITICS AND GOVERNMENT

Cole, J. The New Arabs **909**

Culbertson, S. The fires of spring **909**

ARAB COUNTRIES -- POLITICS AND GOVERNMENT

    See also Politics

ARAB COUNTRIES -- POLITICS AND GOVERNMENT -- 1945-

Owen, R. The rise and fall of Arab presidents for life **352.23**

ARAB COUNTRIES -- POLITICS AND GOVERNMENT -- 21ST CENTURY

Culbertson, S. The fires of spring **909**

Worth, R. F. A rage for order **909**

The **Arab** of the Future. Sattouf, R. **92**

The **Arab** of the Future 2. Sattouf, R. **92**

ARAB REFUGEES

    See also Refugees

ARAB SPRING, 2010-

Cambanis, T. Once upon a revolution **962.05**

Cole, J. The New Arabs **909**

Culbertson, S. The fires of spring **909**

Kasinof, L. Don't be afraid of the bullets **953.305**

Steavenson, W. Circling the Square **962.05**

Worth, R. F. A rage for order **909**

ARAB-ISRAEL CONFLICTS *See* Israel-Arab conflicts

ARAB-ISRAEL RELATIONS *See* Arab countries -- Foreign relations -- Israel; Israel -- Foreign relations -- Arab countries

ARAB-ISRAEL WAR, 1948-1949 *See* Israel-Arab War, 1948-1949

ARAB-ISRAEL WAR, 1967 *See* Israel-Arab War, 1967

ARAB-ISRAELI CONFLICT

Chesler, P. The new anti-semitism **305.8**

Filiu Gaza **953**

La Guardia, A. War without end **956.940**

Landau, D. Arik **92**

Lozowick, Y. Right to exist **956.940**

Morris, B. Righteous victims **956**

Shavit, A. My promised land **956.05**

Shipler, D. K. Arab and Jew **956.94**

Shlaim, A. The iron wall **956.04**

Tolan, S. The lemon tree **956.94**

ARAB-ISRAELI CONFLICT -- 1973-1993

Grossman, D. The yellow wind **956.95**

Halevi, Y. K. Like dreamers **356**

ARAB-ISRAELI CONFLICT -- 1993- -- PEACE

Morris, B. Righteous victims **956**

O'Malley, P. The two-state delusion **956.94**

Said, E. W. The end of the peace process **956.05**

ARAB-ISRAELI CONFLICT -- BIOGRAPHY

Bar-On, M. Moshe Dayan **956.940**

ARAB-ISRAELI RELATIONS *See* Arab countries -- Foreign relations -- Israel; Israel -- Foreign relations -- Arab countries

The **Arab-Israeli** wars. Herzog, C. **956**

ARAB-JEWISH RELATIONS *See* Jewish-Arab relations

Arabesque: a taste of Morocco, Turkey, and Lebanon. Roden, C. **641.5**

ARABIAN HORSE -- POLAND -- HISTORY -- 20TH CENTURY

Letts, E. The perfect horse **940.54**

ARABIC CIVILIZATION

    See also Civilization

ARABIC LANGUAGE

O'Neill, Z. All strangers are kin **910.917**

ARABIC LANGUAGE

    See also Language and languages

ARABIC LITERATURE

Tales of the Marvellous and News of the Strange **892.7**

ARABIC LITERATURE

    See also Literature

ARABIC LITERATURE -- COLLECTIONS

Anthology of modern Palestinian literature **892.7**

Night and horses and the desert **892.7**

ARABIC POETRY -- COLLECTIONS
 Music of a distant drum **808.81**
 The Poetry of Arab women **892.7**
The **Arabs.** Rogan, E. **909**
The **Arabs.** Lamb, D. **909**
ARABS
 Braude, J. The honored dead **364.152**
 Lawrence, T. E. Seven pillars of wisdom **940.4**
 Sattouf, R. The Arab of the Future **92**
ARABS -- PALESTINE *See* Palestinian Arabs
ARACHNIDA
 Beccaloni, J. Arachnids **595.4**
 Eisner, T. Secret weapons **595.7**
Arachnids. Beccaloni, J. **595.4**
ARACHNIDS
 See also Animals
Arafat, Yasir, 1929-2004
     About
 Remnick, D. Reporting **814**
Arana, Marie
 Bolivar **92**
     About
 Arana, M. American chica **92**
Arbesman, Samuel
 The half-life of facts **501**
ARBITRATION AND AWARD
 See also Commercial law; Courts
ARBORICULTURE *See* Forests and forestry;
 Fruit culture; Trees
Arbus, Diane, 1923-1971
     About
 Arbus, D. Diane Arbus **779.2**
 Lubow, A. Diane Arbus **92**
ARC LIGHT *See* Electric lighting
Arc of justice. Boyle, K. **345**
Arcadia. Stoppard, T. **822**
ARCHAEOLOGICAL THEFTS
 Atwood, R. Stealing history **364.1**
 Frammolino, R. Chasing Aphrodite **930**
ARCHAEOLOGISTS
 Brown, M. T.E. Lawrence **92**
 Howell, G. Gertrude Bell **92**
 Korda, M. Hero **92**
 Ryan, D. P. Beneath the sands of Egypt **92**
 Van Tilburg, J. Among stone giants **92**
 Wallach, J. Desert queen **956**
ARCHAEOLOGISTS -- GREAT BRITAIN -- BI-
 OGRAPHY
 Sattin, A. The Young T. E. Lawrence **92**
ARCHAEOLOGY -- ANECDOTES
 Johnson, M. Lives in ruins **930.1**
Archaeology of prehistoric native America. **970.01**
ARCHAEOLOGY, MEDIEVAL
 MacGregor, N. A history of the world in 100 ob-
 jects **930.1**

ARCHAEOPTERYX
 See also Dinosaurs
ARCHBISHOPS *See* Bishops
Archbold, Rick
 Ballard, R. D. Return to Midway **940.54**
ARCHEOLOGICAL SPECIMENS *See* Antiqui-
 ties
ARCHEOLOGISTS
 Howell, G. Gertrude Bell **92**
 Johnson, M. Lives in ruins **930.1**
 Ryan, D. P. Beneath the sands of Egypt **92**
 Wallach, J. Desert queen **956**
ARCHEOLOGISTS
 See also Historians
ARCHEOLOGISTS -- ETHICS
 Childs, C. L. Finders keepers **930.1**
ARCHEOLOGY
 Beneath the seven seas **930.1**
 Ceram, C. W. Gods, graves, and scholars **930.1**
 Johnson, M. Lives in ruins **930.1**
 The Oxford Companion to Archaeology **930.1**
 Romer, J. A history of ancient Egypt **932**
ARCHEOLOGY
 See also History
ARCHEOLOGY -- HISTORY
 Hunt, P. Ten discoveries that rewrote history **930.1**
Archeophonics. Gizzi, P. **811.54**
Archer, J. Clark
 Lavin, S. J. Atlas of the great plains **912**
ARCHERY
 See also Martial arts; Shooting
Archibald MacLeish: reflections. **92**
Archimedes, ca. 287-212 B.C.
     About
 Bell, E. T. Men of mathematics **920**
 Hirshfeld, A. Eureka man **92**
The **architect** of genocide. Breitman, R. **92**
ARCHITECTS
 Albrecht, D. The Work of Charles and Ray
 Eames **745.4**
 Boucher, B. Andrea Palladio **720.9**
 Burstein, A. Madison and Jefferson **973.4**
 Cohen, I. B. Science and the founding fathers **973.3**
 Ellis, J. J. American sphinx: the character of Thom-
 as Jefferson **92**
 Fest, J. C. Speer: the final verdict **92**
 Hoffman, A. Till we have built Jerusalem **956.94**
 Hofstadter, R. The American political tradition, and
 the men who made it **973**
 Hollis, L. London rising **942**
 Huxtable, A. L. Frank Lloyd Wright **92**
 Isenberg, B. Conversations with Frank Gehry **92**
 King, R. Brunelleschi's dome **726**
 King, R. Michelangelo & the Pope's ceiling **759**
 Kranish, M. Flight from Monticello **973.4**
 Larson, E. J. A magnificent catastrophe **324**

Lepore, J. A is for American **306.44**

Malone, J. W. It doesn't take a rocket scientist **920**

Miller, J. C. The Federalist era, 1789-1801 **973.4**

Mormando, F. Bernini **92**

Pick, H. Simon Wiesenthal **940.53**

Rybczynski, W. The perfect house: a journey with the Renaissance architect Andrea Palladio **720.9**

Secrest, M. Frank Lloyd Wright **92**

Segev, T. Simon Wiesenthal **92**

Sereny, G. Albert Speer **92**

Simon, J. F. What kind of nation **342**

Stewart, D. O. American emperor **973.4**

Storrer, W. A. The Frank Lloyd Wright companion **720.9**

Unger, H. G. The last founding father **92**

Weber, N. F. The Bauhaus group **920**

Wills, G. 'Negro president' **326**

Zacks, R. The pirate coast **973.4**

ARCHITECTS

   See also Artists

ARCHITECTS -- JERUSALEM -- BIOGRAPHY

Hoffman, A. Till we have built Jerusalem **956.94**

ARCHITECTS -- UNITED STATES -- BIOGRAPHY

Goldberger, P. Building art **92**

Secrest, M. Frank Lloyd Wright **92**

ARCHITECTURAL ACOUSTICS

   See also Sound

ARCHITECTURAL DECORATION AND ORNAMENT

   See also Architecture; Decoration and ornament

ARCHITECTURAL DESIGN

Eck, J. The distinctive home **728**

Rybczynski, W. The look of architecture **721**

Wansink, B. Slim by design **613.2**

ARCHITECTURAL DESIGN

   See also Architecture; Design

ARCHITECTURAL DRAWING

   See also Drawing

ARCHITECTURAL ENGINEERING *See* Building; Structural analysis (Engineering); Structural engineering

ARCHITECTURAL HISTORIANS

Wilson, A. N. Betjeman **92**

ARCHITECTURAL METALWORK

   See also Metalwork

ARCHITECTURAL PERSPECTIVE *See* Perspective

Architecture. **720.9**

ARCHITECTURE

Architecture **720.9**

Easter Island's silent sentinels **990**

Hoffman, A. Till we have built Jerusalem **956.94**

Hollis, E. The secret lives of buildings **720.9**

Howard, H. Architecture's odd couple **720.973**

Inside the not so big house **728.37**

Palladio, A. The four books on architecture **720**

Rybczynski, W. The look of architecture **721**

The Seventy wonders of the modern world **720.9**

ARCHITECTURE

   See also Art

ARCHITECTURE -- 15TH AND 16TH CENTURIES

Rybczynski, W. The perfect house: a journey with the Renaissance architect Andrea Palladio **720.9**

ARCHITECTURE -- 20TH CENTURY

Curtis, W. J. R. Modern architecture since 1900 **724**

Gropius, W. The new architecture and the Bauhaus **724**

Huxtable, A. L. On architecture **724**

Wolfe, T. From Bauhaus to our house **720.9**

ARCHITECTURE -- COMPOSITION, PROPORTION, ETC.

   See also Composition (Art)

ARCHITECTURE -- DETAILS

The elements of style **728**

Inside the not so big house **728.37**

ARCHITECTURE -- GREAT BRITAIN

The elements of style **728**

ARCHITECTURE -- HISTORY

Jarzombek, M. A global history of architecture **720.9**

Watkin, D. A history of Western architecture **720**

ARCHITECTURE -- PHILOSOPHY

Davies, C. Thinking about architecture **720**

ARCHITECTURE -- THEMES, MOTIVES

Architecture **720.9**

ARCHITECTURE -- UNITED STATES

Creating a new old house **728**

The elements of style **728**

Goldberger, P. Building art **92**

McAlester, V. S. A field guide to American houses **728**

Rybczynski, W. Mysteries of the mall **720**

ARCHITECTURE -- UNITED STATES -- HISTORY -- 20TH CENTURY

Howard, H. Architecture's odd couple **720.973**

ARCHITECTURE AND PEOPLE WITH DISABILITIES

Pierce, D. The accessible home **728.087**

ARCHITECTURE AND PEOPLE WITH DISABILITIES

   See also People with disabilities

Architecture's odd couple. Howard, H. **720.973**

ARCHITECTURE, AMERICAN *See* Architecture -- United States

ARCHITECTURE, DOMESTIC *See* Domestic architecture

ARCHITECTURE, DOMESTIC -- GREAT BRITAIN

The elements of style **728**

ARCHITECTURE, DOMESTIC -- MAINE

The house with sixteen handmade doors   728

ARCHITECTURE, DOMESTIC -- UNITED STATES

The best homes from This old house   643

Creating a new old house   728

The elements of style   728

Susanka, S. Creating the not so big house   728

ARCHITECTURE, DOMESTIC -- UNITED STATES -- GUIDEBOOKS

McAlester, V. S. A field guide to American houses   728

ARCHITECTURE, MODERN See Modernism in architecture

ARCHIVE OF FOLK CULTURE (U.S.)

Wade, S. The beautiful music all around us   781.62

ARCHIVES

Williams, H. A. Help me to find my people   306.3

ARCHIVES

See also Bibliography; Documentation; History -- Sources; Information services

ARCHIVES -- SOVIET UNION

Brent, J. Inside the Stalin archives   947.086

ARCHIVES -- UNITED STATES

Daily life through American history in primary documents   973

ARCHIVISTS

Persico, J. E. Franklin and Lucy   920

ARCHIVISTS -- PROFESSIONAL ETHICS

Defending professionalism   020

ARCTIC EXPEDITIONS See Arctic regions -- Exploration

Arctic labyrinth. Williams, G.   910.4

ARCTIC REGIONS

Braverman, B. Welcome to the Goddamn Ice Cube   974.81

Tape, K. D. The changing arctic landscape   551.69

Zuckoff, M. Frozen in Time   940.54

ARCTIC REGIONS See Canadian Arctic

See also Earth; Polar regions

ARCTIC REGIONS -- DESCRIPTION AND TRAVEL

Fredston, J. A. Rowing to latitude   797.1

Streever, B. Cold   998

Wheeler, S. The magnetic north   910.4

ARCTIC REGIONS -- DISCOVERY AND EXPLORATION

Cookman, S. Ice blink   919

Fleming, F. Ninety degrees North   919

Kavenna, J. The ice museum   998

McGoogan, K. Race to the Polar Sea   92

Niven, J. Ada Blackjack   92

Wilkinson, A. The ice balloon   910.91

ARCTIC REGIONS -- DISCOVERY AND EXPLORATION -- NORWEIGIAN

Bown, S. R. The last Viking   92

ARCTIC REGIONS -- EXPLORATION

Sides, H. In the kingdom of ice   910.4

Wilkinson, A. The ice balloon   910.91

ARCTIC REGIONS -- EXPLORATION

See also Exploration; Scientific expeditions

ARCTIC REGIONS -- PICTORIAL WORKS

Haas, R. B. Through the eyes of the Vikings   779

ARCTIC SUNRISE (SHIP)

Stewart, B. Don't trust, don't fear, don't beg   363.738

Arctic wings.   598

Arden, Lynie

The work-at-home sourcebook   338.7

Ardency. Young, K.   811

ARDENNES (FRANCE), BATTLE OF THE, 1944-1945

Beevor, A. Ardennes 1944   940.54

Clark, L. Blitzkrieg   940.54

ARDENNES (FRANCE), BATTLE OF THE, 1944-1945

See also Battles; World War, 1939-1945 -- Campaigns

Ardennes 1944. Beevor, A.   940.54

Ardent spirits. Price, R.   92

Ardor. Calasso, R.   294.5

Are we hardwired? Clark, W. R.   155.7

Are We Smart Enough to Know How Smart Animals Are? Waal, F. B. M. d.   591.5

Are you my mother? Bechdel, A.   741.5

Are you somebody. O'Faolain, N.   070

Area 51. Jacobsen, A.   358.4

AREA 51 (NEV.)

Jacobsen, A. Area 51   358.4

AREA STUDIES

See also Education

ARENA THEATER

See also Theater

Arendt, Hannah

Origins of totalitarianism   321.9

About

Pierpont, C. R. Passionate minds   810

Arfons, Art, 1926-

About

Hawley, S. J. Speed duel   796.72

ARGENTINA -- HISTORY

Bascomb, N. Hunting Eichmann   943.086

Brown, J. C. A brief history of Argentina   982

ARGENTINE COOKING

Mallmann, F. Seven fires   641.5

Argentini, Paul

Boland, R. Musicals!   792.6

Argo. Baglio, M.   955.05

ARGONAUTS (GREEK MYTHOLOGY)

Apollonius The voyage of Argo: the Argonautica   881

ARGONNE, BATTLE OF THE, FRANCE, 1918

Walker, W. T. Betrayal at Little Gibraltar **940.436**

Arguably. Hitchens, C. **814**

Arguing about slavery. Miller, W. L. **973.5**

ARGUMENTATION *See* Debates and debating; Logic

The **argumentative** Indian. Sen, A. K. **954**

ARID REGIONS

    See also Earth

ARID REGIONS -- DESCRIPTION AND TRAVEL

    Streever, B. Heat **551.41**

Ariel. Plath, S. **811**

Ariely, Dan

    (ed) The best American science and nature writing 2012 **810.8**

Ariely, Dan

    The honest truth about dishonesty **177**

Ariet, María del Carmen

    (ed) Diary of a combatant **92**

Arik. Landau, D. **92**

Ariosto, Lodovico

    Orlando Furioso/The frenzy of Orlando, part 1 **851**

    Orlando Furioso/The frenzy of Orlando, part 2 **851**

Aris, Michael

    Aung San Suu Kyi Freedom from fear, and other writings **959.1**

ARISTOCRACY

    Jefferson, M. Negroland **92**

ARISTOCRACY

    See also Political science; Upper class

ARISTOCRACY (SOCIAL CLASS) -- GREAT BRITAIN -- BIOGRAPHY

    Byrne, P. Kick **92**

    Leaming, B. Kick Kennedy **92**

ARISTOCRACY (SOCIAL CLASS) -- RUSSIA -- HISTORY -- 20TH CENTURY

    Smith, D. Former people **305.5**

Aristophanes

    The complete plays **882**

Aristotle. Shields, C. J. **185**

Aristotle for everybody. Adler, M. J. **185**

Aristotle's children. Rubenstein, R. E. **189**

Aristotle, 384-322 B.C.

    About

    Adler, M. J. Aristotle for everybody **185**

    The basic works of Aristotle **888**

    Durant, W. J. The story of philosophy **109**

    The lagoon **570.1**

    Nicomachean ethics **170**

    Politics **320**

    The Renaissance philosophy of man **189**

    Rubenstein, R. E. Aristotle's children **189**

    Russell, B. A history of Western philosophy **109**

    Shields, C. J. Aristotle **185**

ARITHMETIC

    See also Mathematics; Set theory

ARITHMETIC -- ESTIMATION *See* Approximate computation

ARITHMETIC -- FOUNDATIONS

    Thaller, B. Numbers **513.5**

ARIZONA JUSTICE PROJECT

    Siegel, B. Manifest injustice **364.152**

ARKANSAS -- RACE RELATIONS

    Margolick, D. Elizabeth and Hazel **92**

Arkin, Alan, 1934-

    About

    Arkin, A. An improvised life **92**

Arkison, Cheryl

    Sunday morning quilts **746.46**

ARLINGTON NATIONAL CEMETERY (VA.)

    Poole, R. M. Section 60 **975.5**

The **Arm.** Passan, J. **796.357**

Arm knitting. Bassetti, A. **746.43**

Armageddon: the battle for Germany, 1944-45. Hastings, M. **940.54**

ARMAMENTS *See* Military readiness; Military weapons

Armantrout, Rae

    Versed **811**

The **armchair** James Beard. Beard, J. **641.5**

ARMED FORCES

    See also Military art and science

ARMED FORCES -- WOMEN *See* Women in the military

ARMENIA -- RELATIONS -- TURKEY

    Toumani, M. There was and there was not **327**

Armenian Golgotha. **956**

ARMENIAN MASSACRES SURVIVORS -- BIOGRAPHY

    MacKeen, D. A. The hundred-year walk **92**

ARMENIAN MASSACRES, 1915-1923

    Akcam, T. A shameful act **956.6**

    Armenian Golgotha **956**

    Balakian, P. The burning Tigris **956.6**

    Suny, R. G. They Can Live in the Desert but Nowhere Else **956.6**

    Ureneck, L. The Great Fire **956.1**

ARMIES

    See also Armed forces; Military personnel

ARMIES -- MEDICAL CARE

    See also Medical care; Military medicine

Armitage's garden perennials. Garden perennials **635.9**

Armitage's native plants for North American gardens. Armitage, A. M. **635.9**

Armitage's vines and climbers. Armitage, A. M. **635.9**

Armitage, Allan M.

    Armitage's native plants for North American gardens **635.9**

    Armitage's vines and climbers **635.9**

    Garden perennials Armitage's garden perennials   635.9

ARMOR
> See also Art metalwork; Costume; Military art and science

ARMS AND ARMOR See Armor; Weapons

Arms and the man. Shaw, B.   822

ARMS CONTROL

Hodge, N. A nuclear family vacation   623.4

Langewiesche, W. The atomic bazaar   355

Wilson, W. Five myths about nuclear weapons   355.02

ARMS CONTROL
> See also International relations; International security; War

ARMS PROLIFERATION See Arms race

ARMS RACE

Gordin, M. D. Red cloud at dawn   355

Rhodes, R. Arsenals of folly   355

ARMS RACE
> See also Arms control; International security

ARMS TRANSFERS
> See also International trade

Armstrong, Frank

The retirement challenge--will you sink or swim?   332.024

Armstrong, Helen Joseph

Patternmaking for fashion design   646.4

Armstrong, Jennifer Keishin

Sexy feminism   305.42

Armstrong, John

Love, life, Goethe   92

Armstrong, Karen, 1944-

Armstrong, K. Twelve steps to a compassionate life   177

The battle for God   200.9

Buddha   294.3

The case for God   211

Fields of Blood   201

The great transformation   200.9

A history of God   200

Islam   297

Jerusalem   956.94

Muhammad   297

A short history of myth   398.2

Twelve steps to a compassionate life   177

Visions of God   248.2

About

Armstrong, K. The spiral staircase   92

Armstrong, Lance

About

Louis Armstrong, in his own words   92

Strickland, B. Tour de Lance   92

Armstrong, Louis, 1900-1971

About

Armstrong, L. Louis Armstrong, in his own words   92

Brothers, T. Louis Armstrong, master of modernism   92

Feather, L. From Satchmo to Miles   920

Murray, A. The blue devils of Nada   780.89

Teachout, T. Pops   92

Armstrong, Nancy

Friedman, V. M. Field guide to stains   648

Armstrong, Neil, 1930-2012

About

Barbree, J. Neil Armstrong   92

Armstrong, Richard B.

Rough Guides (Firm) The Rough Guide to film   791.43

ARMY See Armies; Military art and science

An army at dawn. Atkinson, R.   940.54

ARMY BASES See Military bases

ARMY DESERTION See Military desertion

ARMY LIFE See Soldiers

Army of evil. Weale, A.   940.54

ARMY OFFICERS

Alexander, L. Biggest brother   92

Bredin The affair   944.081

Brighton, T. Patton, Montgomery, Rommel   920

Connell, E. S. Son of the Morning Star   973.8

Davis, W. C. Three roads to the Alamo   976.4

Derfler, L. The Dreyfus affair   944.081

Donovan, J. A terrible glory   973.8

Falkner, D. Great time coming: the life of Jackie Robinson, from baseball to Birmingham   92

Halberstam, D. The best and the brightest   973.922

Hanson, V. D. The soul of battle   355

Hirshson, S. P. General Patton: a soldier's life   92

Kaplan, A. Y. The interpreter   940.54

Kennedy, J. F. Profiles in courage   920

Mansoor, P. R. Baghdad at sunrise   956.7

McCullough, D. G. The path between the seas   972.87

Millard, C. The river of doubt   973.91

Moore, W. The other Wes Moore   92

Philbrick, N. The last stand   973.8

Robinson, J. I never had it made   92

Roper, R. Now the drum of war   973.7

Sandoz, M. The Battle of the Little Bighorn   973.8

Schama, C. Wild romance   92

Sheehan, N. A bright shining lie: John Paul Vann and America in Vietnam   959.704

Showalter, D. E. Patton and Rommel   92

Sielski, M. Fading echoes   92

Tuchman, B. W. The proud tower   909.82

Tygiel, J. Baseball's great experiment   796.357

Wert, J. D. Custer   92

Wilson, E. Patriotic gore   810

Witter, B. Until Tuesday   362.4

Zacks, R. The pirate coast   973.4

ARMY POSTS See Military bases

Arnason, H. Harvard

History of modern art   **709.04**

Arnauld, Antoine, 1612-1694
>About

Nadler, S. M. The best of all possible worlds   190

Arnell, Charles

Bennett, J. The complete snowboarder   **796.9**

Arney, Kat

Herding Hemingway's Cats   **572.8**

Arney, Tommy
>About

Swift, E. Auto Biography   **629.222**

Arnold, Dave

Liquid intelligence   **641.87**

Arnold, James R.

(ed) Cold War   **909.82**

Jungle of snakes   355

Arnold, Jeremy

The essentials   **791.43**

AROMATHERAPY

Keville, K. The aromatherapy garden   **635.9**

AROMATHERAPY
>See also Therapeutics

The **aromatherapy** garden. Keville, K.   **635.9**

AROMATIC PLANTS
>See also Plants

AROMATIC PLANTS -- THERAPEUTIC USE

Keville, K. The aromatherapy garden   **635.9**

Aron, Wendy
>About

Aron, W. Hide & seek   92

Aronica, Lou

Creative schools   **371.2**

Aronson, Jane

Carried in Our Hearts   **362.734**

Aronson, Joseph

The encyclopedia of furniture   **749.03**

Aronson, Ronald

(ed) Sartre, J. P. Truth and existence   121

(ed) We Have Only This Life to Live   848

Arora, Pankaj

To the cloud   **004.67**

Around America. Cronkite, W.   917

Around my French table. Greenspan, D.   641.5

Around the corner crochet borders. Eckman, E.   **746.43**

Around the World in 50 Years. Podell, A.   910.4

Arousal, the secret logic of sexual fantasies. Bader, M. J.   **306.7**

Arrested. Denham, W.   **362.82**

Arrieta, Marie-Clarie

(jt. auth) Finlay, B. B. Let Them Eat Dirt   616.9

Arrington, Leonard J.

Japanese Americans, from relocation to redress   **940.53**

Arrival city. Saunders, D.   **307.24**

Arrival of the fittest. Wagner, A.   **572.8**

The **ARRL** handbook for radio communications.   **621.384**

ARROWSIC (ME.) -- BUILDINGS, STRUCTURES, ETC

The house with sixteen handmade doors   **728**

Arsenals of folly. Rhodes, R.   355

Arsenault, Raymond

Freedom riders   323

ARSENIC

Hempel, S. The inheritor's powder   **364.152**

Art. Cumming, R.   **700**

ART

The Art Book   **709**

Bailey, G. A. Art in time   709

Bonair-Agard, R. Bury my clothes   **811**

Parkinson, R. B. A little gay history   **306.76**

Szostak, P. The art of Star Wars   **791.43**

ART
>See also Arts

ART -- 15TH AND 16TH CENTURIES

Kline, F. R. Leonardo's holy child   **741.945**

Lee, A. The ugly Renaissance   945

ART -- 19TH CENTURY

Craske, M. Art in Europe, 1700-1830   **709.03**

ART -- 20TH CENTURY

Barnes, J. Keeping an eye open   **709.04**

Gompertz, W. What Are You Looking at?   **709**

Gooch, B. Smash Cut   **92**

Stein, J. E. Eye of the sixties   92

ART -- 21ST CENTURY

Gompertz, W. What Are You Looking at?   **709**

Perry, G. Playing to the gallery   **709.05**

ART -- ANALYSIS, INTERPRETATION, APPRECIATION See Art -- Study and teaching; Art appreciation; Art criticism

ART -- ATTRIBUTION

Cumming, L. The Vanishing Velazquez   **759.6**

ART -- COLLECTIONS See Art collections

ART -- COLLECTORS AND COLLECTING

Brysac, S. B. The China collectors   **709.5**

Prose, F. Peggy Guggenheim   **92**

ART -- DICTIONARIES

Encyclopedia of artists   **709**

Frazier, N. The Penguin concise dictionary of art history   **703**

ART -- ECONOMIC ASPECTS

Congdon, L. Art, Inc.   **702**

ART -- EXHIBITIONS

The female gaze   **704**

Galitz, K. C. The Metropolitan Museum of Art   **700**

ART -- EXHIBITIONS
>See also Exhibitions

ART -- EXPERTISING

Brewer, J. The American Leonardo   **759**

Kline, F. R. Leonardo's holy child   **741.945**

ART -- FORGERIES

Amore, A. M. The art of the con   **702.8**

ART -- FORGERIES
   See also Counterfeits and counterfeiting; Forgery

ART -- HISTORY
Bailey, G. A. Art in time   **709**
Barnes, J. Keeping an eye open   **709.04**
Cumming, R. Art   **700**
Ebert-Schifferer, S. Caravaggio   **92**
Florence   **759.5**
King, R. Leonardo and the Last supper   **759**
Lester, T. Da Vinci's ghost   **741.092**

ART -- HISTORY
   See also History

ART -- HISTORY -- MAPS
Atlas of world art   **709**

ART -- MARKETING
Thornton, S. Seven days in the art world   **709.05**

ART -- MUSEUMS *See* Art museums

ART -- PENNSYLVANIA -- PHILADELPHIA -- EXHIBITIONS
The female gaze   **704**

ART -- POETRY
Hayes, T. How to be drawn   **811**
Hong, C. P. Engine empire   **811**

ART -- PRIVATE COLLECTIONS -- MASSACHUSETTS -- CAMBRIDGE -- EXHIBITIONS
In harmony   **704**

ART -- PRIVATE COLLECTIONS -- OKLAHOMA -- NORMAN -- CATALOGS
The James T. Bialac Native American Art Collection   **704.03**

ART -- PRIVATE COLLECTIONS -- WASHINGTON (STATE) -- TACOMA -- CATALOGS
Hassrick, P. H. Art of the American West   **709**

ART -- PSYCHOLOGICAL ASPECTS
Kandel, E. R. The age of insight   **154.2**

ART -- PSYCHOLOGY
Always looking   **700**

ART -- STUDY AND TEACHING
Painting the great masters   **751.45**

ART -- VOCATIONAL GUIDANCE
Congdon, L. Art, Inc.   **702**
Art and madness. Roiphe, A. R.   **92**

ART AND MUSIC
The art of music   **708**
The visual blues   **704.03**

ART AND MYTHOLOGY
   See also Art; Mythology

ART AND MYTHOLOGY -- DICTIONARIES
Impelluso, L. Gods and heroes in art   **700**
The art and politics of science. Varmus, H.   **92**

ART AND RELIGION
Bussagli, M. Angels   **704.9**

ART AND RELIGION
   See also Art; Religion
Art and social justice education.   **372.5**

ART AND SOCIETY
Rich, A. A human eye   **814**

ART AND SOCIETY
   See also Art

ART AND SOCIETY -- UNITED STATES -- HISTORY -- 20TH CENTURY
Stein, J. E. Eye of the sixties   **92**

ART AND SOCIOLOGY *See* Art and society
The art and soul of baking. Mushet, C.   **641.8**

ART AND WAR
Nguyen, V. T. Nothing ever dies   **959.704**

ART APPRECIATION
André, C. Looking at Mindfulness   **158.1**
Beckett, W. Sister Wendy's American collection   **709**
Hoving, T. Art for dummies   **709**
King, R. Art: over 2,500 works from cave to contemporary   **709**
Kundera, M. Encounter   **809**
Salle, D. How to see   **709.04**
White, M. Travels in Vermeer   **92**

ART APPRECIATION
   See also Aesthetics; Art criticism
The Art Book.   **709**

ART CATALOGS
   See also Art

Art classics [series]
Aquino, L. Leonardo Da Vinci   **92**

ART COLLECTIONS
Harvey, E. J. The Civil War and American art   **709**
In harmony   **704**
The James T. Bialac Native American Art Collection   **704.03**

ART COLLECTORS
Brandon, R. Ugly beauty   **646.7**
Brewer, J. The American Leonardo   **759**
Cannadine, D. Mellon   **92**
De Waal, E. The hare with amber eyes   **920**
Gill, A. Art lover   **92**
McPhee, J. A. The ransom of Russian art   **709**
Walsh, J. The J. Paul Getty Museum and its collections   **708.1**

ART CRITICISM
Always looking   **700**
As consciousness is harnessed to flesh   **818**
Lester, T. Da Vinci's ghost   **741.092**
Perry, G. Playing to the gallery   **709.05**

ART CRITICISM
   See also Criticism

ART CRITICS
Richardson, J. The sorcerer's apprentice   **92**

ART DECO
Art deco 1910-1939   **709.04**

ART DECO

See also Art -- 20th century

Art deco 1910-1939.   **709.04**

ART EDUCATION *See* Art -- Study and teaching

Art for dummies. Hoving, T.   **709**

ART FORGERIES *See* Art -- Forgeries

Art from the ashes. Langer, L. L.   **940.53**

ART GALLERIES *See* Art museums; Commercial
art galleries

ART HISTORIANS

Bard, E. Lunch in Paris   **92**

Carter, M. Anthony Blunt: his lives   **92**

Grant, G. M. At the elbows of my elders **920**

Humbert, A. Resistance   **92**

Richardson, J. The sorcerer's apprentice **92**

ART IN ADVERTISING *See* Commercial art

ART IN EDUCATION -- SOCIAL ASPECTS

Art and social justice education   **372.5**

Art in Europe, 1700-1830. Craske, M.   **709.03**

Art in the modern era. Dempsey, A.   **709.04**

Art in time. Nadel, D.   **741.5**

Art in time. Bailey, G. A.   **709**

Art lover. Gill, A.   **92**

ART METALWORK

See also Decorative arts; Metalwork

ART MOVEMENTS

Bailey, G. A. Art in time   **709**

ART MUSEUM CURATORS

Obrist Ways of curating   **707.5**

ART MUSEUMS

Galitz, K. C. The Metropolitan Museum of Art **700**

ART MUSEUMS

See also Museums

ART MUSIC *See* Music

ART OBJECTS

MacGregor, N. A history of the world in 100 objects   **930.1**

Von Habsburg, G. Faberge revealed   **739.2**

ART OBJECTS

See also Antiques; Art; Decoration and ornament; Decorative arts

ART OBJECTS, RUSSIAN -- CATALOGS

Von Habsburg, G. Faberge revealed   **739.2**

The art of ancient Egypt. Robins, G.   **709.3**

The art of choosing. Iyengar, S.   **153.8**

The art of comic book writing. Kneece, M. **741.5**

The art of conversation. Blyth, C.   **395**

The art of creative pruning. Hobson, J. **715**

The art of dressing curves. Moses, S. **746.92**

The art of eating. Fisher, M. F. K.   **641**

The art of electronics. Horowitz, P.   **621.381**

The art of fermentation. Katz, S. E.   **664**

The art of fiction. Gardner, J.   **808.3**

The art of French pastry. Shulman, M. R. **641.86**

The art of grace. Kaufman, S. L.   **302.1**

The art of hand reading. Reid, L.   **133.6**

The art of Harvey Kurtzman. Kitchen, D. **741.5**

The art of immersion. Rose, F.   **306.4**

The art of loving. Fromm, E.   **152.4**

The art of making money. Kersten, J.   **92**

The art of medicine. Anderson, J.   **610**

The art of metal clay. Haab, S.   **739.27**

The art of movement. Browar, K.   **792**

The art of music.   **708**

The Art of natural building.   **690**

The art of negotiation. Wheeler, M.   **658.4**

The art of Neil Gaiman. Campbell, H.   **92**

The art of people. Kerpen, D.   **650.1**

The art of political murder. Goldman, F. **972.81**

The Art of preserving. Field, R.   **641.4**

The art of raising a puppy.   **636.7**

The art of Ray Harryhausen. Harryhausen, R. **778.5**

The art of rivalry. Smee, S.   **700.92**

The art of Robert Frost. Kendall, T.   **811**

The Art of Seamanship. Naranjo, R.   **623.8**

The art of simple food. Streiff, F.   **641.5**

The art of Star Wars. Szostak, P.   **791.43**

The Art of Stillness.   **302.23**

The art of teaching. Parini, J.   **371.1**

Art of the American West. Hassrick, P. H. **709**

The art of the con. Amore, A. M.   **702.8**

The Art of the Map. Reinhartz, D.   **526**

The Art of the personal essay.   **808.84**

Art of the pie. McDermott, K.   **641.86**

The art of the start 2.0.   **658.1**

The art of thinking clearly. Dobelli, R. **153.4**

The Art of tinkering. Wilkinson, K.   **500**

The art of waiting. Boggs, B.   **618.178**

ART PATRONAGE

See also Art and society

ART POTTERY

Burnett, J. B. Graphic clay   **738.1**

ART POTTERY

See also Pottery

ART ROBBERIES *See* Art thefts

ART SCHOOLS *See* Art -- Study and teaching

ART TEACHERS

Small, D. Stitches   **741.5**

Thomas Eakins   **759.13**

Weber, N. F. The Bauhaus group   **920**

ART THEFTS

Amore, A. M. The art of the con   **702.8**

Atwood, R. Stealing history   **364.1**

Dolnick, E. The rescue artist   **364.1**

Edsel, R. M. The monuments men   **940.53**

Goodman, S. The Orpheus Clock   **940.53**

Muller, M. Lost lives, lost art   **709**

Petropoulos, J. The Faustian bargain   **709**

Scott-Clark, C. The Amber Room   **940.54**

Scotti, R. A. Vanished smile   **759**

Wittman, R. Priceless   **364.1**

ART THEFTS

See also Theft

ART THEFTS -- INVESTIGATION
Goodman, S. The Orpheus Clock   **940.53**
ART THERAPY
    See also Therapeutics
ART, AFRICAN
Visona, M. B. A history of art in Africa   **709**
ART, AMERICAN *See* American art
ART, AMERICAN -- 19TH CENTURY -- THEMES, MOTIVES -- EXHIBITIONS
Harvey, E. J. The Civil War and American art   **709**
ART, AMERICAN -- WEST (U.S.) -- CATALOGS
Hassrick, P. H. Art of the American West   **709**
ART, BUDDHIST *See* Buddhist art
ART, CHINESE -- APPRECIATION -- UNITED STATES
Brysac, S. B. The China collectors   **709.5**
ART, EGYPTIAN
Robins, G. The art of ancient Egypt   **709.3**
ART, GREEK *See* Greek art
Art, Inc. Congdon, L.   **702**
ART, IRANIAN -- EXHIBITIONS
In harmony   **704**
ART, ISLAMIC *See* Islamic art
ART, ITALIAN
Adams, L. Italian Renaissance art   **709.02**
ART, ITALIAN -- EXHIBITIONS
The Renaissance portrait   **704.9**
ART, LATIN AMERICAN
Barnitz, J. Twentieth-century art of Latin America   **709**
ART, MODERN
Gill, A. Art lover   **92**
ART, MODERN -- 20TH CENTURY
Barnes, J. Keeping an eye open   **709.04**
Salle, D. How to see   **709.04**
Tomkins, C. Lives of the artists   **920**
ART, MODERN -- 20TH CENTURY *See* Art -- 20th century
ART, MODERN -- 20TH CENTURY -- EXHIBITIONS
The female gaze   **704**
ART, MODERN -- 20TH CENTURY -- LATIN AMERICA
Barnitz, J. Twentieth-century art of Latin America   **709**
ART, MODERN -- 20TH CENTURY -- PUBLIC OPINION
Perry, G. Playing to the gallery   **709.05**
ART, MODERN -- 21ST CENTURY
Salle, D. How to see   **709.04**
ART, MODERN -- 21ST CENTURY *See* Art -- 21st century
ART, MODERN -- 21ST CENTURY -- EXHIBITIONS
The female gaze   **704**
ART, POLISH -- 20TH CENTURY

Rynecki, E. Chasing portraits   **700.92**
ART, RENAISSANCE *See* Art -- 15th and 16th centuries
ART, ROMAN *See* Roman art
Art: a new history. Johnson, P.   **709**
Art: over 2,500 works from cave to contemporary. King, R.   **709**
Artemis, Nadine, 1971-
    Holistic dental care   **617.6**
The **artful** parent. Van't Hul, J.   **745.5**
The **artful** year. Van't Hul, J.   **745.594**
Artfully embroidered. Shimoda, N.   **746.44**
ARTHRITIS
    See also Diseases
ARTHROPODA -- CONSERVATION
Fortey, R. Horseshoe crabs and velvet worms   **595**
Arthur Conan Doyle. Doyle, A. C.   **92**
ARTHUR M. SACKLER MUSEUM -- EXHIBITIONS
In harmony   **704**
Arthur Miller. Bigsby, C.   **92**
Arthur Miller. Gottfried, M.   **92**
Arthur, King
         About
Ackroyd, P. The death of King Arthur   **398.2**
King Arthur in legend and history   **942.01**
Malory, T. Le morte Darthur, or, The hoole book of Kyng Arthur and of his noble knyghtes of the Rounde Table   **398.2**
ARTHURIAN ROMANCES
Sir Gawain and the Green Knight   **398.2**
ARTHURIAN ROMANCES
    See also Romances
ARTICULATION (EDUCATION)
    See also Education -- Curricula; Schools -- Administration
The **artificial** ape. Taylor, T.   **599.93**
ARTIFICIAL FLIES
Gathercole, P. The fly-tying bible   **688.7**
The history of fly fishing in fifty flies   **799.124**
Rosenbauer, T. The Orvis guide to the essential American flies   **799.1**
ARTIFICIAL FLIES
    See also Fishing -- Equipment and supplies; Fly casting
ARTIFICIAL FLOWERS
Cetti, L. The exquisite book of paper flowers   **745.594**
ARTIFICIAL FLOWERS
    See also Decoration and ornament
ARTIFICIAL FOODS
    See also Food; Synthetic products
ARTIFICIAL HEART
    See also Artificial organs; Heart
ARTIFICIAL INSEMINATION
    See also Reproduction

ARTIFICIAL INTELLIGENCE
Baker, S. Final Jeopardy   **006.3**
Christian, B. The most human human   **128**
Dufty, D. F. How to build an android   **629.8**
Kurzweil, R. How to create a mind   **612.8**
Zarkadakis, G. In Our Own Image   **006.3**

ARTIFICIAL INTELLIGENCE
See also Computer science

ARTIFICIAL LANGUAGES
Okrent, A. In the land of invented languages   **499**

ARTIFICIAL LIFE
Venter, J. C. Life at the Speed of Light   **303.48**

ARTIFICIAL ORGANS
See also Surgery

ARTILLERY
See also Military art and science
Artisan Preserving. Macdonald, E.   **641.4**

ARTISANS
Faber, T. Faberge's eggs   **739.2**
Fischer, D. H. Paul Revere's ride   **973.3**
Lepore, J. A is for American   **306.44**
The **artist** and the mathematician. Aczel, A. D. **500**
The **artist** as critic. Wilde, O.   **824**
The **artist** blacksmith. Parkinson, P.   **682**
An **artist** in treason. Linklater, A.   **92**
The **artist's** compass. Moore, R. S.   **791.023**
The **artist's** complete guide to figure drawing. Ryder, A.   **743.4**
The **artist's** library.   **021.2**
Artist's painting techniques.   **751.4**
The **artist,** the philosopher, and the warrior. Strathern, P.   **920**

ARTISTIC ANATOMY
Hart, C. Human anatomy made amazingly easy   **743.4**

ARTISTIC ANATOMY
See also Anatomy; Art; Drawing; Nude in art

ARTISTIC PHOTOGRAPHY
Roden, S. . . . i listen to the wind that obliterates my traces   **781.64**
Thompson, M. Michael Thompson: Portraits **779**

ARTISTIC PHOTOGRAPHY
See also Art; Photography

ARTISTS
Acocella, J. R. Twenty-eight artists and two saints   **920**
Adams, H. Tom and Jack   **92**
Albers, P. Joan Mitchell   **92**
Andoe, J. Jubilee city   **92**
The Art Book   **709**
The art of music   **708**
Asleson, R. Albert Moore   **759.2**
Bailey, A. Velazquez: surrendering at Breda **759**
Baillio, J. Claude Monet, 1840-1926   **759**
Bechdel, A. Fun home   **741.5**
Benfey, C. E. G. A summer of hummingbirds **920**

Bentley, G. E. The stranger from paradise: a biography of William Blake   **821**
Biel, S. American Gothic   **759.13**
Bilal, W. Shoot an Iraqi   **92**
Blackburn, J. Old man Goya   **92**
Brainard, J. The Nancy book   **759**
Brewer, J. The American Leonardo   **759**
Brombert, B. A. Edouard Manet   **92**
Carter, A. A. The Red Rose girls   **759.13**
Cikovsky, N. Winslow Homer   **759.13**
Cockburn, H. Henry's demons   **92**
Conant, J. A covert affair   **940.54**
Congdon, L. Art, Inc.   **702**
Crabapple, M. Drawing Blood   **92**
Dippie, B. W. The Frederic Remington Art Museum collection   **709**
Dolnick, E. The rescue artist   **364.1**
Drohojowska-Philp, H. Full bloom   **92**
Edouard Vuillard   **759**
Elderfield, J. De Kooning: a retrospective **759.13**
Ellis, R. Tuna   **333.95**
Ellison, R. The collected essays of Ralph Ellison   **814**
Ellison, R. Going to the territory   **818**
Evans, R. T. Grant Wood   **92**
Faber, T. Faberge's eggs   **739.2**
Feiffer, J. Backing into forward   **92**
Finch, C. Chuck Close   **92**
FitzGerald, M. C. Picasso and American art **709**
Fraser, K. Ornament and silence   **809**
Frey, J. Toulouse-Lautrec   **92**
Gioia, D. Can poetry matter?   **809.1**
Graham-Dixon, A. Caravaggio   **92**
Hennessey, M. H. Norman Rockwell   **759.13**
Henri Matisse   **709.2**
Hoban, P. Alice Neel   **92**
Hudson, M. Titian   **92**
Hughes, R. Goya   **760**
James, C. Cultural amnesia   **920**
James, J. The glamour of strangeness   **700.19**
Kambalu, S. The jive talker   **92**
Khan, Y. S. Enlightening the world   **974.7**
King, R. Brunelleschi's dome   **726**
King, R. The judgment of Paris   **759**
King, R. Michelangelo & the Pope's ceiling **759**
Kirshenblatt, M. They called me Mayer July **92**
Leal, B. The ultimate Picasso   **759**
Lear, L. J. Beatrix Potter   **92**
Lepore, J. A is for American   **306.44**
Levin, G. Lee Krasner   **92**
Liedtke, W. A. Vermeer and the Delft school **759.9**
Livingston, J. The paintings of Joan Mitchell   **759.13**
Lottman, H. R. Man Ray's Montparnasse **709**
Lozano Frida Kahlo   **759.9**
Mailer, N. C. A ticket to the circus   **92**

Malcolm, J. Forty-one false starts 808.02
Mathews, N. M. Mary Cassatt 759.13
Matthiessen, F. O. American renaissance 810
McCullough, D. G. The greater journey 920.009
Michaelis, D. N.C. Wyeth 92
Min, A. Red Azalea 92
Morgan, J. Dr. Seuss & Mr. Geisel 92
Morris-Suzuki, T. To the Diamond Mountains 915
Murray, A. The blue devils of Nada 780.89
Nathan, D. Sybil exposed 616.85
Norman, P. John Lennon 92
Penrose, R. Picasso: his life and work 709
Peppiatt, M. Francis Bacon in Your Blood 759.2
Prideaux, S. Edvard Munch 92
Rhodes, R. John James Audubon 92
Robinson, R. Georgia O'Keeffe: a life 709
Ross, C. The world of Edward Gorey 700.92
Rothkopf, S. Jeff Koons 709.2
Sassoon, D. Becoming Mona Lisa 759
Satrapi, M. The complete Persepolis 741.5
Schama, S. Rembrandt's eyes 92
Scherman, T. Pop 92
Scotti, R. A. Vanished smile 759
Sebald, W. G. On the natural history of destruction 833
Small, D. Stitches 741.5
Solomon, D. Jackson Pollock 92
Spurling, H. Matisse the master 92
Spurling, H. The unknown Matisse 92
Stanton, T. Road to Cooperstown 92
Steinberg, S. Steinberg at the New Yorker 741.5
Strathern, P. The artist, the philosopher, and the warrior 920
Swan, A. De Kooning: an American master 92
Tate, M. J. Critical companion to F. Scott Fitzgerald 813
Thomas Eakins 759.13
Thomson, B. Van Gogh paintings 759.9
Tomkins, C. Duchamp 709
Tran, G. B. Vietnamerica 741.5
Uglow, J. S. Nature's engraver 92
Vaill, A. Everybody was so young 759.13
Weidensaul, S. Return to wild America 578
Wyeth, A. Andrew Wyeth 92
ARTISTS -- BIOGRAPHY
Andelman, B. Will Eisner: A Spirited Life 741.5
Danchev, A. Cézanne 759.4
Maurice Sendak 741.6
Unger, M. J. Michelangelo 92
ARTISTS -- BIOGRAPHY -- ENCYCLOPEDIAS
Biographical encyclopedia of artists 920.003
ARTISTS -- DICTIONARIES
Encyclopedia of artists 709
Otfinoski, S. Latinos in the arts 920.003
Shipp, S. Latin American and Caribbean artists of the modern era 920.003

ARTISTS -- GREAT BRITAIN -- BIOGRAPHY
Sykes, C. S. David Hockney 92
ARTISTS -- HUNGARY -- BIOGRAPHY
The burning of the world 92
ARTISTS -- PSYCHOLOGY
Acocella, J. R. Twenty-eight artists and two saints 920
James, J. The glamour of strangeness 700.19
Smee, S. The art of rivalry 700.92
ARTISTS -- RUSSIA
Romanov riches 891.7
ARTISTS -- UNITED STATES
Felisbret, E. Graffiti New York 751.7
Staiti, P. Of Arms and Artists 759.13
ARTISTS -- UNITED STATES -- BIOGRAPHY
Kamensky, J. A revolution in color 759.13
ARTISTS -- UNITED STATES -- DICTIONARIES
Who's who in American art, 2008 920.003
ARTISTS AS CARTOGRAPHERS
A Map of the World 912
ARTISTS' BOOKS
Rivers, C. Little book of book making 686
ARTISTS' MATERIALS
See also Materials
ARTISTS' MODELS
Bocquet Kiki de Montparnasse 759.4
ARTISTS' MODELS
See also Art
ARTISTS' MODELS -- ITALY -- FLORENCE -- BIOGRAPHY
Hales, D. Mona Lisa 759.5
ARTISTS, AMERICAN *See* Artists -- United States
ARTISTS, BRITISH
Peacock, M. The paper garden 92
Sykes, C. S. David Hockney 92
ARTISTS, CHINESE
Ai weiwei 709.5
ARTISTS, FRENCH
Brombert, B. A. Edouard Manet 92
Frey, J. Toulouse-Lautrec 92
Hudson, M. Titian 92
Roe, S. The private lives of the impressionists 759
Tomkins, C. Duchamp 709
ARTISTS, GERMAN
Weber, N. F. The Bauhaus group 920
ARTISTS, ITALIAN
Aquino, L. Leonardo Da Vinci 92
Bramly, S. Leonardo 709
Klein, S. Leonardo's legacy 709
Langdon, H. Caravaggio 709
Mormando, F. Bernini 92
Nuland, S. B. Leonardo da Vinci 709
Prose, F. Caravaggio 92
Robb, P. M: the man who became Caravaggio 759

Secrest, M. Modigliani 92
Unger, M. J. Michelangelo 92
White, M. Leonardo 92
ARTISTS, MEXICAN
Herrera, H. Frida: a biography of Frida Kahlo 709
Kahlo, F. The diary of Frida Kahlo 92
Marnham, P. Dreaming with his eyes open 92
ARTISTS, RUSSIAN
Wullschlager, J. Chagall 92
ARTISTS, SPANISH
Bailey, A. Velazquez: surrendering at Breda 759
ARTS
Boorstin, D. J. The creators 909
Hyde, L. Common as air 346.04
Spillman, R. All Tomorrow's Parties 070.4
ARTS
See also Humanities
Arts & crafts furniture projects. Paolini, G. 684.1
ARTS -- BIBLIOGRAPHY
Perrault, A. H. Information resources in the humanities and the arts 016
ARTS -- BIOGRAPHY
Andelman, B. Will Eisner: A Spirited Life 741.5
ARTS -- GOVERNMENT POLICY
See also Social policy
ARTS -- HISTORY
Arts and humanities through the eras 700
ARTS -- LIBRARY RESOURCES
The artist's library 021.2
ARTS -- PHILOSOPHY
Eco, U. History of beauty 111
On ugliness 111
ARTS -- STUDY AND TEACHING
The muses go to school 700
ARTS -- UNITED STATES
Haskell, B. The American century 709
ARTS AND CRAFTS *See* Handicraft
ARTS AND CRAFTS MOVEMENT
Lindsay, V. Sewing to sell 646.2
Miller, J. Miller's arts & crafts 745.4
Paolini, G. Arts & crafts furniture projects 684.1
Van't Hul, J. The artful year 745.594
ARTS AND CRAFTS MOVEMENT
See also Art; Decoration and ornament; Decorative arts; Industrial arts
Arts and humanities through the eras. 700
ARTS IN THE CHURCH *See* Art and religion
Arts of the possible. Rich, A. 811
ARTS, GRAPHIC *See* Graphic arts
ARTS, RUSSIAN
Romanov riches 891.7
As always, Julia. 92
As big as the West. Milner, C. A. 92
As China goes, so goes the world. Gerth, K. 339.4
As consciousness is harnessed to flesh. 818
As if. Saler, M. 823

As of this writing. James, C. 824
As seen on TV. Marling, K. A. 973.92
As Texas goes. Collins, G. 320.6
As we speak. Meyers, P. 808.5
ASBESTOS
See also Minerals
Asbridge, Thomas
The crusades 909.07
The Greatest Knight 92
The **ascent** of money. Ferguson, N. 330
The **ascent** of the A-word. Nunberg, G. 427
ASCETICISM
See also Ethics; Religious life
Ascher, Steven
The filmmaker's handbook 777
ASD, the complete autism spectrum disorder health & diet guide. Smith, R. G. 616.85
Ash, Avner
Elliptic tales 515
Ash, Jennifer
Brott, A. A. The expectant father 649
Ash, John
(jt. auth) Fraioli, J. O. Culinary birds 641.6
Ash, Stephen V.
Firebrand of liberty 973.7
ASHANTI (AFRICAN PEOPLE)
See also Africans; Indigenous peoples
Ashbery, John
Collected poems 1956-1987 811
Notes from the air 811
Planisphere 811
Selected poems 811
Where shall I wander 811
A worldly country 811
Ashby, Ruth
The great american documents 973
Ashcroft, Frances
The spark of life 612
Ashe, Arthur
About
McPhee, J. Levels of the game 796.34
Ashes of glory. Furgurson, E. B. 975.5
ASHKENAZIM -- SOCIAL LIFE AND CUS-TOMS
Wex, M. Rhapsody in schmaltz 641.5
Ashley's war. Lemmon, G. T. 92
Ashley, Dwayne
Williams, J. I'll find a way or make one 378
Ashley, James Mitchell, 1824-1896
About
Richards, L. L. Who freed the slaves? 342.73
Ashton, Dianne
Hanukkah in America 296.4
Ashton, Nigel
King Hussein of Jordan 92
ASIA -- CIVILIZATION

See also Civilization; East and West

ASIA -- DESCRIPTION AND TRAVEL

Houton, J. A geek in Thailand   **915.9**

ASIA -- DESCRIPTION AND TRAVEL -- EARLY WORKS TO 1800

Bergreen, L. Marco Polo   **92**

Polo, M. The travels of Marco Polo   **915**

ASIA -- POLITICS AND GOVERNMENT

See also Politics

Asia/Pacific/perspectives [series]

Pellegrino, C. To hell and back   **940.54**

ASIAN AMERICANS -- HISTORY

Lee, E. The making of Asian America   **973**

ASIAN ARCHITECTURE

See also Architecture

ASIAN ART

See also Art

ASIAN COOKING

Alger, K. Susan Feniger's street food   **641.59**

Asian dumplings   **641.59**

Bowl   **641.81**

Chang, D. Momofuku   **641.5**

Duguid, N. Burma   **641.59**

Hair, J. The steamy kitchen cookbook   **641.5**

Henry, D. A Change of Appetite   **641.5**

Jaffrey, M. At home with Madhur Jaffrey   **641.5**

Meehan, P. Lucky Peach 101 easy Asian recipes   **641.595**

Trang, C. Essentials of Asian cuisine   **641.5**

Tsai, M. Blue Ginger   **641.5**

Wong, L. A. Dumplings All Day Wong   **641.59**

Asian dumplings   **641.59**

ASIAN MYTHOLOGY

Yang Lihui Handbook of Chinese mythology **299.5**

ASIAN STUDIES SPECIALISTS

Grant, R. Crazy river   **916**

Lovell, M. S. A rage to live: a biography of Richard and Isabel Burton   **92**

Salzman, M. True notebooks   **371.9**

ASIANS -- UNITED STATES -- HISTORY

Lee, E. The making of Asian America   **973**

ASIATIC ELEPHANT -- EFFECT OF POACHING ON

Orenstein, R. Ivory, horn and blood   **333.95**

Asimov, Isaac, 1920-1992

About

Gunn, J. E. Isaac Asimov   **813**

Ask the experts.   **616.4**

Aslan, Reza

No god but God   **297**

Asleep. Crosby, M. C.   **362.1**

Asleson, Robyn

Albert Moore   **759.2**

Asma, Stephen T.

On monsters   **398.2**

Asmal, Kader

(ed) In his own words   **92**

Asperger Syndrome. Bashe, P. R.   **618.92**

ASPERGER'S SYNDROME

Bashe, P. R. Asperger Syndrome   **618.92**

Dawson, G. A parent's guide to high-functioning autism spectrum disorder   **618.92**

Jackson, L. Freaks, geeks and asperger syndrome   **618.92**

Robison, J. E. Look me in the eye   **92**

Robison, J. E. Switched on   **616.85**

Rodriguez, A. M. Autism spectrum disorders   **616.85**

Saperstein, J. A. Getting a life with Asperger's **92**

Tammet, D. Born on a blue day   **92**

ASPERGER'S SYNDROME

See also Autism

ASPERGER'S SYNDROME -- PATIENTS -- FAMILY RELATIONSHIPS

Jackson, L. Freaks, geeks and asperger syndrome   **618.92**

Jackson, L. Sex, drugs and Asperger's syndrome (ASD)   **618.92**

ASPERGER'S SYNDROME -- PATIENTS -- UNITED STATES -- BIOGRAPHY

Robison, J. E. Switched on   **616.85**

Saperstein, J. A. Getting a life with Asperger's **92**

ASPERGER'S SYNDROME -- POPULAR WORKS

Dawson, G. A parent's guide to high-functioning autism spectrum disorder   **618.92**

Rodriguez, A. M. Autism spectrum disorders   **616.85**

Assael, Shaun

The murder of Sonny Liston   **796.83**

ASSASSINATION

Ephron, D. Killing a king   **956.94**

Hakkakiyan, R. Assassins of the Turquoise Palace   **364.152**

Sides, H. Hellhound on his trail   **364.152**

Strauss, B. The death of Caesar   **937**

ASSASSINATION

See also Crime; Homicide; Political crimes and offenses

ASSASSINATION ATTEMPTS

Murphy, P. T. Shooting Victoria   **941.081**

ASSASSINATION -- HISTORY

Epstein, E. J. The annals of unsolved crime **364.152**

Assassination vacation. Vowell, S.   **973**

ASSASSINS -- GERMANY -- HISTORY -- 20TH CENTURY

Orbach, D. The plots against Hitler   **940.53**

Assassins of the Turquoise Palace. Hakkakiyan, R.   **364.152**

The **assassins'** gate. Packer, G.   **956.7**

ASSAULT, SEXUAL *See* Rape

ASSERTIVENESS (PSYCHOLOGY)

See also Aggressiveness (Psychology); Psychology

Assessing service quality. Hernon, P. **025.5**

The **assist.** Swidey, N. **796.323**

ASSISTED SUICIDE

Humphry, D. Final exit **179.7**

Yount, L. Right to die and euthanasia **179.7**

ASSISTED SUICIDE

See also Suicide

ASSISTED SUICIDE -- LAW AND LEGISLATION -- UNITED STATES

Ball, H. At liberty to die **344**

ASSOCIATIONS

Encyclopedia of Associations **060.4**

ASSOCIATIONS, INSTITUTIONS, ETC. *See* Associations

ASSOCIATIONS, INTERNATIONAL *See* International agencies

Astaire, Adele

About

Riley, K. The Astaires **92**

Astaire, Fred

About

Riley, K. The Astaires **92**

The **Astaires.** Riley, K. **92**

ASTEROIDS

Randall, L. Dark Matter and the Dinosaurs **523.1**

ASTEROIDS

See also Astronomy; Solar system

ASTHMA

Brazelton, T. B. To listen to a child **155.4**

ASTHMA

See also Allergy; Lungs -- Diseases

ASTOR PLACE (NEW YORK, N.Y.)

Cliff, N. The Shakespeare riots **974.4**

Astor, Nancy Witcher Langhorne Astor, Viscountess, 1879-1964

About

Livingstone, N. The mistresses of Cliveden **942.009**

Fox, J. Five sisters **975.5**

Astoria. Stark, P. **978**

ASTRAL PROJECTION

See also Parapsychology

Astrobiology. Catling, D. C. **576.8**

ASTROBIOLOGY *See* Life on other planets; Space biology

ASTROGEOLOGY

See also Geology

ASTROLOGY

Goodman, L. Linda Goodman's star signs **130**

Goodman, L. Linda Goodman's sun signs **133.5**

Lewis, J. R. The astrology book **133.5**

Miller, S. Planets and possibilities **133.5**

Snodgrass, M. E. Signs of the zodiac **133.5**

ASTROLOGY

See also Astronomy; Divination; Occultism

ASTROLOGY -- ENCYCLOPEDIAS

Lewis, J. R. The astrology book **133.5**

The **astrology** book. Lewis, J. R. **133.5**

The **Astronaut** Wives Club. Koppel, L. **629.45**

An **astronaut's** guide to life on earth. Hadfield, C. **92**

ASTRONAUTICS

Milestones of space **629.4**

Wohlforth, C. Beyond Earth **629.455**

ASTRONAUTICS

See also Aeronautics

ASTRONAUTICS -- COMMUNICATION SYSTEMS

See also Interstellar communication; Telecommunication

ASTRONAUTICS -- POPULAR WORKS

Clegg, B. Final Frontier **629.4**

ASTRONAUTICS -- UNITED STATES

Bell, J. The interstellar age **919**

Dean, M. L. Leaving orbit **629.4**

Space chronicles **629.4**

ASTRONAUTICS -- UNITED STATES -- EQUIPMENT AND SUPPLIES -- PICTORIAL WORKS

Milestones of space **629.4**

ASTRONAUTICS -- UNITED STATES -- FORECASTING -- POPULAR WORKS

Piantadosi, C. A. Mankind beyond Earth **629.45**

ASTRONAUTICS -- UNITED STATES -- HISTORY

Koppel, L. The Astronaut Wives Club **629.45**

Nelson, C. Rocket men **629.45**

Pyne, S. J. Voyager **919**

Sheehan, N. A fiery peace in a cold war **92**

ASTRONAUTICS AND CIVILIZATION

See also Aeronautics and civilization; Astronautics; Civilization

ASTRONAUTICS AND STATE -- UNITED STATES

Space chronicles **629.4**

ASTRONAUTS

Gubert, B. K. Distinguished African Americans in aviation and space science **629.13**

Hadfield, C. An astronaut's guide to life on earth **92**

Wolfe, T. The right stuff **629.45**

Worden, A. Falling to Earth **92**

ASTRONAUTS

See also Air pilots; Space flight

ASTRONAUTS -- NUTRITION

See also Nutrition

ASTRONAUTS -- UNITED STATES

Mailer, N. Of a fire on the moon **629.45**

Pyle, R. Destination moon **629.45**

Smith, A. Moondust **920**

ASTRONAUTS -- UNITED STATES -- BIOGRAPHY

Aldrin, B. No dream is too high 92
Anderson, C. The ordinary spaceman 92
Barbree, J. Neil Armstrong 92
Massimino, M. Spaceman 92
Sherr, L. Sally Ride 92

ASTRONAUTS' SPOUSES -- BIOGRAPHY
Koppel, L. The Astronaut Wives Club 629.45

ASTRONOMERS
Alder, K. The measure of all things 526
Bartusiak, M. The day we found the universe 520
Bell, E. T. Men of mathematics 920
Brown, M. How I killed Pluto and why it had it coming 523.4
Ferris, T. Seeing in the dark 520
Heilbron, J. L. Galileo 92
Hirshfeld, A. c. Starlight Detectives 523.1
Hofstadter, D. The Earth moves 509
Johnson, G. Miss Leavitt's stars 92
Malone, J. W. It doesn't take a rocket scientist 920
Miller, A. I. Empire of the stars 520
Nicastro, N. Circumference 526
Poundstone, W. Carl Sagan 92
Repcheck, J. Copernicus' secret 92
Snyder, L. J. The philosophical breakfast club 509
Sobel, D. Galileo's daughter 92
Sobel, D. A more perfect heaven 520
Vollmann, W. T. Uncentering the Earth 92

ASTRONOMERS
See also Scientists

ASTRONOMERS -- HISTORY -- 18TH CEN-TURY
Anderson, M. The day the world discovered the sun

ASTRONOMICAL INSTRUMENTS
See also Scientific apparatus and instruments; Space optics

ASTRONOMICAL PHOTOGRAPHY
Astronomy photographer of the year 520

ASTRONOMICAL PHOTOGRAPHY
See also Astronomical instruments; Photography

ASTRONOMICAL PHOTOGRAPHY -- COM-PETITIONS
Astronomy photographer of the year 520

ASTRONOMICAL PHYSICS See Astrophysics

ASTRONOMY
Benson, M. Cosmigraphics 523.1
Chown, M. Solar system 523.2
Consolmagno, G. Turn left at Orion 520
Dickinson, T. The backyard astronomer's guide 522
Dickinson, T. NightWatch: a practical guide to viewing the universe 520
Ferris, T. Seeing in the dark 520
Geach, J. Galaxy 523.1
Hirshfeld, A. c. Starlight Detectives 523.1
Hofstadter, D. The Earth moves 509
North, C. How to Read the Solar System 523.2

Raymo, C. An intimate look at the night sky 520
Ridpath, I. The monthly sky guide 523.8
Ridpath, I. Stars and planets 520
Sagan, C. Broca's brain 500
Sagan, C. Cosmos 520
Schaaf, F. The 50 best sights in astronomy and how to see them 520
Scharf, C. The Copernicus complex 523.1
Schilling, G. Deep Space 520
Schneider, H. Backyard guide to the night sky 520
Sims, M. Apollo's fire 529
Sobel, D. A more perfect heaven 520
Universe 523.1
White, V. The Total Skywatcher's Manual 523.8
Wulf, A. Chasing Venus 523.9

ASTRONOMY
See also Physical sciences; Science; Universe

ASTRONOMY -- ATLASES See Stars -- Atlases

ASTRONOMY -- HISTORY
Bauer, S. W. The story of Western science 509

ASTRONOMY -- HISTORY -- 18TH CENTURY
Anderson, M. The day the world discovered the sun
Wulf, A. Chasing Venus 523.9

ASTRONOMY -- HISTORY -- 20TH CENTURY
Bartusiak, M. The day we found the universe 520
Sobel, D. The glass universe 522.197

ASTRONOMY -- MATHEMATICS
See also Mathematics

ASTRONOMY -- PICTORIAL WORKS
Astronomy photographer of the year 520

ASTRONOMY -- POPULAR WORKS
Scagell, R. Complete Guide to Stargazing 520
Trotta, R. The edge of the sky 520

ASTRONOMY -- RELIGIOUS ASPECTS -- CHRISTIANITY
Hofstadter, D. The Earth moves 509
Astronomy photographer of the year. 520

ASTROPHYSICISTS
Miller, A. I. Empire of the stars 520
Poundstone, W. Carl Sagan 92

ASTROPHYSICS
Goodstein, D. L. Feynman's lost lecture 521
Hawking, S. W. The nature of space and time 530.1
The universe 523.1

ASTROPHYSICS
See also Astronomy; Physics

Astyk, Sharon
A nation of farmers 338.1

Asylum. Scheyer, M. 940.53

ASYLUM
See also International law

ASYLUM
Scheyer, M. Asylum 940.53
Asylum denied. Kenney, D. N. 92

ASYLUM, RIGHT OF See Asylum
At all costs. Moses, S. 940.54

At Canaan's edge. Branch, T. **973.923**
At dawn we slept. Prange, G. W. **940.54**
At day's close. Ekirch, A. R. **306.4**
At home. Bryson, B. **643**
At home in the garden. Kristal, M. **635.09**
At home in the whole food kitchen. Chaplin, A. **641.3**
At home with Madhur Jaffrey. Jaffrey, M. **641.5**
At liberty to die. Ball, H. **344**
AT RISK STUDENTS
Fenn, L. Carry on **920**
AT RISK STUDENTS
    See also Students
At the dark end of the street. McGuire, D. L. **323.1**
At the edge of the abyss. **940.53**
At the elbows of my elders. Grant, G. M. **920**
At the Existentialist Cafe. Bakewell, S. **142**
At the fights. **796.8**
At the hands of persons unknown. Dray, P. **364.1**
At the same time. Sontag, S. **814**
AT&T (FIRM)
Lapsley, P. Exploding the Phone **384**
AT-HOME EMPLOYMENT *See* Home-based business
Atanasoff, John V.
                About
Smiley, J. The man who invented the computer **92**
ATHEISM
Dawkins, R. An Appetite for Wonder **92**
Dawkins, R. The God delusion **200**
De Botton, A. Religion for atheists **200**
Gay, P. A Godless Jew **150.19**
Hitchens, C. God is not great **200**
ATHEISM
    See also Religion; Secularism; Theology
ATHEISM -- HISTORY
Minois, G. The atheist's Bible **200**
The **atheist's** Bible. Minois, G. **200**
ATHEISTS
De Botton, A. Religion for atheists **200**
ATHENA (GREEK DEITY)
    See also Gods and goddesses
ATHENS (GREECE) -- DRAMA.
Aristophanes The complete plays **882**
ATHENS (GREECE) -- FICTION
Democracy **741.5**
ATHENS (GREECE) -- HISTORY
Hughes, B. The hemlock cup **92**
Athens, Lonnie H.
                About
Rhodes, R. Why they kill **364.3**
Athill, Diana
                About
Athill, D. Somewhere towards the end **92**
ATHLETES
Amidon, S. Something like the gods **306.4**

Buford, K. Native American son **92**
ATHLETIC STATES
Caesar, E. Two hours **796.42**
Connolly, K. M. Double take **92**
Crawford, B. All American **92**
Epstein, D. The sports gene **613.7**
Nocera, J. Indentured **796.04**
Strickland, B. Tour de Lance **92**
ATHLETES -- ATTITUDES
Rotella, B. How champions think in sports and in life **796.01**
ATHLETES -- DICTIONARIES
Friedman, I. C. Latino athletes **920.003**
ATHLETES -- HISTORY
Amidon, S. Something like the gods **306.4**
ATHLETES -- NUTRITION
Lim, A. The feed zone cookbook **641.5**
Lim, A. Feed zone portables **641.5**
ATHLETES -- TRAINING
McClusky, M. Faster, higher, stronger **613.7**
ATHLETES -- WOUNDS AND INJURIES
Starrett, K. Ready to run **613.7**
Yaeger, D. Any given Monday **617.1**
ATHLETES WITH DISABILITIES
Connolly, K. M. Double take **92**
ATHLETIC COACHING *See* Coaching (Athletics)
ATHLETIC MEDICINE *See* Sports medicine
ATHLETICS
Miller, S. G. Ancient Greek athletics **796**
Atik, Chiara
Modern Dating **646.7**
Atkins, Peter William, 1940-
Reactions **541**
Atkins, Vera, 1908-2000
                About
Helm, S. A life in secrets **92**
Atkinson, Rick, 1952-
An army at dawn **940.54**
Crusade **956.7**
The day of battle **940.54**
In the company of soldiers **956.7**
The guns at last light **940.54**
Atkinson, Sam
(ed) Complete cat care
ATLANTA (GA.) -- RACE RELATIONS
Burns, R. Burial for a King **92**
Atlantic. Winchester, S. **551.46**
ATLANTIC COAST (NORTH AMERICA)
Gimlette, J. Theatre of fish **917**
ATLANTIC COAST CONFERENCE
Feinstein, J. A march to madness **796.323**
Atlantic fever. Jackson, J. **629.130**
ATLANTIC OCEAN
Rackley, A. Salt, sweat, tears **92**
ATLANTIC OCEAN
    See also Ocean

The **Atlantic** slave trade. Postma, J.   **306.3**

ATLANTIC STATES
>   *See also* United States

ATLANTIS (LEGENDARY PLACE)
>   Adams, M.   Meet Me in Atlantis   **398.23**

Atlas. Atlas, T.   **92**

ATLAS (MISSILE)
>   *See also* Ballistic missiles; Intercontinental ballistic missiles

Atlas A-Z.   **912**

Atlas Obscura. Foer, J.   **910.41**

Atlas of American politics, 1960-2000. Shelley, F. M.   **973.92**

The **atlas** of bird migration.   **598**

The **atlas** of birds. Unwin, M.   **598**

The **atlas** of cities.   **912**

The **atlas** of climate change. Dow, K.   **551.6**

Atlas of exploration.   **911**

The **atlas** of global conservation. Hoekstra, J. M.   **333.95**

Atlas of Indian nations. Treuer, A.   **970.004**

The **atlas** of new librarianship. Lankes, R. D.   **020**

The **atlas** of the Arab world. Fargues, P.   **909**

Atlas of the Civil War.   **973.7**

Atlas of the Civil War. Woodworth, S. E.   **973.7**

Atlas of the Civil War, month by month. Swanson, M.   **973.7**

Atlas of the great plains. Lavin, S. J.   **912**

Atlas of the North American Indian. Waldman, C.   **970.004**

Atlas of the transatlantic slave trade. Eltis, D.   **381**

Atlas of the World.   **912**

Atlas of world art.   **709**

Atlas of Yellowstone.   **912.09**

Atlas, James
>   Bellow   **813**

Atlas, Nava
>   Plant power   **641.5**

Atlas, Scott W.
>   In excellent health   **362.109**

Atlas, Teddy
>   ### About
>   Atlas, T. Atlas   **92**
>   Remnick, D. Reporting   **814**

ATLASES
>   *See also* Geography; Maps

ATLASES, ASTRONOMICAL *See* Stars -- Atlases

ATMOSPHERE
>   Logan, W. B. Air   **551.5**
>   Roston, E. The carbon age   **577**

ATMOSPHERE
>   *See also* Air; Earth

ATMOSPHERE -- POLLUTION *See* Air pollution

ATMOSPHERIC GREENHOUSE EFFECT *See* Global warming

The **atom** and the apple. Balibar, S.   **530**

The **atomic** bazaar. Langewiesche, W.   **355**

ATOMIC BOMB
>   Baggott, J. E. The first war of physics   **355.8**
>   Bascomb, N. The winter fortress   **940.54**
>   Feynman   **92**
>   Hersey, J. Hiroshima   **940.54**
>   Kiernan, D. The girls of atomic city   **976.8**
>   Lifton, R. J. Hiroshima in America   **940.54**
>   Pellegrino, C. To hell and back   **940.54**
>   Preston, D. Before the fallout   **355.8**
>   Takaki, R. T. Hiroshima   **940.54**

ATOMIC BOMB
>   *See also* Bombs; Nuclear weapons

ATOMIC BOMB -- GERMANY -- HISTORY
>   Bascomb, N. The winter fortress   **940.54**
>   Sheinkin, S. Bomb   **623.4**

ATOMIC BOMB -- GERMANY -- HISTORY -- 20TH CENTURY
>   Cassidy, D. C. Beyond uncertainty   **92**

ATOMIC BOMB -- HISTORY
>   Ham, P. Hiroshima Nagasaki   **940.54**
>   Monk, R. Robert Oppenheimer   **92**

ATOMIC BOMB -- SOCIAL ASPECTS -- JAPAN -- HIROSHIMA-SHI -- HISTORY -- 20TH CENTURY
>   Pellegrino, C. To hell and back   **940.54**

ATOMS
>   Challoner, J. The Elements   **546**
>   Feynman, R. P. Six easy pieces   **530**

Atoms Under the Floorboards. Woodford, C.   **502**

ATONEMENT -- CHRISTIANITY
>   *See also* Christianity; Sacrifice; Salvation

ATONEMENT -- JUDAISM
>   *See also* Judaism

ATROCITIES
>   Bizot, F. The gate   **959.604**
>   Hochschild, A. King Leopold's ghost   **967.5**
>   Kiernan, B. The Pol Pot regime   **959.6**
>   Rice, A. The teeth may smile but the heart does not forget   **967.6**
>   Roy, A. Walking with the comrades   **954**
>   Snyder, T. D. Black Earth   **940.53**
>   Sontag, S. Regarding the pain of others   **303.6**

ATROCITIES
>   *See also* Crime; Cruelty

ATTACHMENT BEHAVIOR
>   *See also* Developmental psychology

ATTEMPTED SUICIDE *See* Suicide

Attenborough, David
>   Life in cold blood   **597.9**
>   Life in the undergrowth   **592**
>   The life of birds   **598**

ATTENTION
>   Csikszentmihalyi, M. Flow: the psychology of optimal experience   **155.2**

Goleman, D. Focus   **153.7**
Newport, C. Deep work   **650.1**
Parr, B. Captivology   **153.7**

ATTENTION
  See also Apperception; Educational psychology; Memory; Psychology; Thought and thinking

Attention all passengers. McGee, W. J.   **387.7**

ATTENTION DEFICIT DISORDER
  See also Abnormal psychology

ATTENTION-DEFICIT DISORDERED ADULTS -- LIFE SKILLS GUIDES
Matlen, T. The queen of distraction   **616.85**

ATTENTION-DEFICIT HYPERACTIVITY DISORDER
Barkley, R. A. Taking Charge of ADHD   **618.92**
Saul, R. ADHD does not exist   **618.92**

ATTENTION-DEFICIT HYPERACTIVITY DISORDER -- UNITED STATES
Schwarz, A. ADHD nation   **618.92**

ATTENTION-DEFICIT-DISORDERED ADULTS -- BIOGRAPHY
Denevi, T. Hyper   **92**

Atterberry, Tara E.
  (ed) Encyclopedia of Associations   **060.4**

ATTICA PRISON
Thompson, H. A. Blood in the water   **365**

Attila, King of the Huns, d. 453
    About
Kelly, C. The end of empire   **92**

ATTITUDE (PSYCHOLOGY)
Viscott, D. S. Emotional resilience   **158**

ATTITUDE (PSYCHOLOGY)
  See also Emotions; Psychology

ATTITUDES *See* Attitude (Psychology)

ATTORNEYS *See* Lawyers

ATTORNEYS GENERAL
Clarke, T. The last campaign   **92**
Feldman, N. Scorpions   **920**
Goodwin, D. K. Team of rivals   **92**
Mahoney, R. D. Sons and brothers: the days of Jack and Bobby Kennedy   **92**
Schlesinger, A. M. Robert Kennedy and his times   **92**
Thomas, E. Robert Kennedy   **92**

Attracting beneficial bugs to your garden. Walliser, J.   **628.9**

Attridge, Harold W.
  (ed) The HarperCollins encyclopedia of Catholicism   **282**

Attucks, Crispus, d. 1770
    About
Abdul-Jabbar, K. Black profiles in courage   **920**

Attwater, Donald
The Penguin dictionary of saints   **920.003**
  (ed) Butler's Lives of the saints   **920.003**

Attwell, David
J. M. Coetzee and the Life of Writing   **823**

Atwan, Robert
  (ed) The best American essays 2012   **808**
  (ed) The best American essays 2014   **814**
  (ed) The best American essays 2010   **814**
  (ed) The Best American essays of the century   **814**

Atwood, Craig D.
Handbook of denominations in the United States   **280**

Atwood, Lisa
  (jt. auth) Field, R. The Art of preserving   **641.4**

Atwood, Margaret, 1939-
In other worlds   **809**
Payback   **332.7**
Writing with intent   **814**

Atwood, Rebecca
Living with pattern   **701.85**

Atwood, Roger
Stealing history   **364.1**

Auburn, David
Proof   **812**

Auchincloss, Louis
  (ed) Poems./Selections Selected poems   **811**

AUCTION BRIDGE *See* Bridge (Game)

The **audacity** of hops. Acitelli, T.   **641.2**

Auday, Bryan C.
  (ed) Magill's medical guide   **610**

Auden, W. H. (Wystan Hugh), 1907-1973
    About
Brodsky, J. Less than one   **809.1**
Heaney, S. Finders keepers   **821**
Jarrell, R. No other book   **809**

Audi, Robert
  (ed) The Cambridge dictionary of philosophy   **103**

Audibert-Boulloche, Christiane
    About
Kaiser, C. The cost of courage   **92**

AUDIENCES
  See also Communication; Social psychology

AUDIO CASSETTES *See* Sound recordings

AUDIOBOOKS
Grover, S. Listening to learn   **372.4**

AUDIOBOOKS
  See also Sound recordings

AUDIOBOOKS -- CATALOGS
Saricks, J. G. Read on--audiobooks   **011**

AUDIOTAPES
Hughes, K. Chasing shadows   **973.924**
The Nixon tapes   **973.924**

AUDIOTAPES *See* Sound recordings

AUDIOVISUAL EDUCATION
  See also Education

AUDIOVISUAL MATERIALS CENTERS *See* Instructional materials centers

Audition. Walters, B.   **92**

AUDITORIUMS
See also Buildings; Centers for the performing arts

Audoin-Rouzeau, Stephane
14-18, understanding the Great War   **940.3**

Audrey. Walker, A.   **92**

Audubon birdhouse book. Wolfson, E.   **728**

The **Audubon** Society field guide to North American butterflies. Pyle, R. M.   **595.7**

The **Audubon** Society field guide to North American fossils. Thompson, I.   **560**

The **Audubon** Society field guide to North American insects and spiders. Milne, L. J.   **595.7**

The **Audubon** Society field guide to North American rocks and minerals. Chesterman, C. W.   **549**

The **Audubon** Society field guide to North American trees. Little, E. L.   **582.16**

The **Audubon** Society field guide to North American weather. Ludlum, D. M.   **551.6**

Audubon, John James, 1785-1851
About
Rhodes, R. John James Audubon   **92**

August, Oliver
Inside the red mansion   **951.05**

AUGUSTA NATIONAL GOLF CLUB
Sampson, C. Masters   **796.352**

Augusta Sophia, Princess, daughter of George III, King of Great Britain, 1768-1840
About
Fraser, F. Princesses   **920**

Augusta, Princess of Wales, 1719-1772
About
Livingstone, N. The mistresses of Cliveden **942.009**

Augustine, Saint, Bishop of Hippo
Confessions   **242**
De civitate Dei./English Concerning the city of God against the pagans   **239**
About
Kung, H. Great Christian thinkers   **230**
Russell, B. A history of Western philosophy   **109**
Wills, G. Saint Augustine   **270.2**

Augustus. Everitt, A.   **92**

Augustus. Goldsworthy, A.   **92**

Augustus, Emperor of Rome, 63 B.C.-14 A.D
About
Goldsworthy, A. Augustus   **92**
Everitt, A. Augustus   **92**
The twelve Caesars   **878**

Auletta, Ken
Googled   **338.7**
Media man   **92**

AUM SHINRIKYO
Murakami, H. Underground   **364.1**

Aung San Suu Kyi
Freedom from fear, and other writings   **959.1**
About

Wintle, J. Perfect hostage   **92**

AUNTS
See also Family

Auricchio, Laura
The marquis   **92**

AURORAS
See also Geophysics; Meteorology

AUSCHWITZ (POLAND: CONCENTRATION CAMP)
Levi, P. Survival in Auschwitz   **940.53**
Moorehead, C. A train in winter   **940.53**
Rees, L. Auschwitz: a new history   **940.53**

AUSCHWITZ (POLAND: CONCENTRATION CAMP)
See also Concentration camps

Auschwitz: a new history. Rees, L.   **940.53**

Ausenda, Fabio
(ed) Green volunteers   **333.72**

Aust, Stefan
Baader-Meinhof   **363.32**

Austen, Jake
Darkest America   **791**

Austen, Jane, 1775-1817
About
Baker, W. Critical companion to Jane Austen   **823**
Bloom, H. The Western canon   **809**
The Cambridge companion to Jane Austen   **823**
Harman, C. Jane's fame   **92**
Lee, H. Virginia Woolf's nose   **820**
Nabokov, V. V. Lectures on literature   **808.3**
Nokes, D. Jane Austen   **823**
Olsen, K. All things Austen   **823**
Shields, C. Jane Austen   **823**
Tomalin, C. Jane Austen   **823**
A truth universally acknowledged   **823**

Auster, Paul, 1947-
(ed) I thought my father was God and other true tales from the National Story Project   **810**
(ed) The Random House book of twentieth-century French poetry   **841**
About
Auster, P. Report from the interior   **92**

Austerity Britain. Kynaston, D.   **941.085**

Austin, Paul, 1955-
About
Austin, P. Beautiful eyes   **92**

AUSTRALIA -- DESCRIPTION
Chatwin, B. The songlines   **919**

AUSTRALIA -- DESCRIPTION AND TRAVEL
Bryson, B. In a sunburned country   **919**
Flannery, T. F. Chasing kangaroos   **599.2**

AUSTRALIA -- HISTORY
Clarke, F. G. The history of Australia   **994**
Hughes, R. The fatal shore   **994**
Keneally, T. A commonwealth of thieves   **994**

AUSTRALIA -- RACE RELATIONS

Clendinnen, I. Dancing with strangers **994**

AUSTRIA -- HISTORY
McMeekin, S. July 1914 **940.3**
Wawro, G. A mad catastrophe **940.4**
Authentic Mexican. Bayless, R. **641.597**
AUTHOR AND PUBLISHER *See* Authors and publishers
AUTHORITARIANISM *See* Fascism; Totalitarianism
AUTHORITARIANISM -- ARAB COUNTRIES
Owen, R. The rise and fall of Arab presidents for life **352.23**
AUTHORITARIANISM -- CHINA
Osnos, E. Age of ambition **951.06**
AUTHORITARIANISM -- SOCIAL ASPECTS -- RUSSIA (FEDERATION)
Pomerantsev, P. Nothing is true and everything is possible **306**
AUTHORITIES (PERSONS) *See* Specialists
AUTHORITY
See also Political science
AUTHORS -- BIOGRAPHY
Andelman, B. Will Eisner: A Spirited Life **741.5**
Collins, P. Edgar Allan Poe **92**
McGrath, A. E. C. S. Lewis **92**
AUTHORS -- CORRESPONDENCE
Cather, W. The selected letters of Willa Cather **813**
Meanwhile there are letters **92**
Vonnegut, K. Kurt Vonnegut **813**
AUTHORS -- CORRESPONDENCE
See also Letters
AUTHORS -- DICTIONARIES
Colby, V. World authors, 1975-1980 **920.003**
Colby, V. World authors, 1980-1985 **809**
Colby, V. World authors, 1985-1990 **809**
Drew, B. A. 100 most popular nonfiction authors **920.003**
Rich, M. World authors, 2000-2005 **920.003**
Thompson, C. World authors, 1990-1995 **809**
Thompson, C. World authors, 1995-2000 **809**
Wakeman, J. World authors, 1950-1970 **920.003**
Wakeman, J. World authors, 1970-1975 **920.003**
AUTHORS -- FAMILY LIFE
Oates, J. C. The Lost Landscape **92**
Russo, R. Elsewhere **92**
When I first held you **306.874**
AUTHORS -- HOMES AND HAUNTS *See* Literary landmarks
AUTHORS -- INTERVIEWS
See also Interviews
AUTHORS -- UNITED STATES -- BIOGRAPHY
McGilligan, P. Young Orson **92**
AUTHORS AND PUBLISHERS
Getting it published **070.5**
Herman, J. Jeff Herman's guide to book publishers, editors, & literary agents **070.5**

MFA vs NYC **808.02**
AUTHORS AND PUBLISHERS
See also Authorship; Contracts; Publishers and publishing
AUTHORS AND PUBLISHERS -- DIRECTORIES
Guide to literary agents **070.5**
AUTHORS AND PUBLISHERS -- UNITED STATES
MFA vs NYC **808.02**
AUTHORS AND PUBLISHERS -- UNITED STATES -- HISTORY -- 20TH CENTURY
Turner, F. Renegade **813**
AUTHORS AND READERS
Bloom, H. The anatomy of influence **801**
Authors series
Colby, V. World authors, 1975-1980 **920.003**
Colby, V. World authors, 1980-1985 **809**
Colby, V. World authors, 1985-1990 **809**
Rich, M. World authors, 2000-2005 **920.003**
Thompson, C. World authors, 1990-1995 **809**
Thompson, C. World authors, 1995-2000 **809**
Wakeman, J. World authors, 1950-1970 **920.003**
Wakeman, J. World authors, 1970-1975 **920.003**
AUTHORS' SPOUSES -- GREAT BRITAIN -- BIOGRAPHY
Santamaria, A. Joy **92**
AUTHORS, ALGERIAN -- 20TH CENTURY -- BIOGRAPHY
Carroll, S. B. Brave genius **920**
AUTHORS, AMERICAN *See* American authors
AUTHORS, AMERICAN -- 20TH CENTURY
Bram, C. Eminent outlaws **810.9**
The Columbia companion to the twentieth-century American short story **813**
Kerouac, J. Selected letters, 1957-1969 **813**
Kiernan, F. Seeing Mary plain: a life of Mary McCarthy **818**
Laing, O. The Trip to Echo Spring **810.9**
AUTHORS, AMERICAN -- 20TH CENTURY -- BIOGRAPHY
Angelou, M. Mom & me & mom **818**
Angelou, M. A song flung up to heaven **818**
Auster, P. Report from the interior **92**
Begley, A. Updike **92**
Beller, T. J.D. Salinger **92**
Borich, B. J. Body geographic **818**
Dearborn, M. V. Mailer **813**
Drew, B. A. 100 most popular nonfiction authors **920.003**
Elie, P. The life you save may be your own **810**
Hertog, S. Anne Morrow Lindbergh **92**
Hogan, L. The woman who watches over the world **818**
Johnson, J. The voice is all **818**
King, S. On writing **813**

Kingston, M. H. The woman warrior **92**
Labor, E. Jack London **92**
Lardner, R. I'd hate myself in the morning **813**
Lennon, J. M. Norman Mailer **92**
Mayes, F. Under magnolia **92**
Mills, M. The Mockingbird Next Door **92**
Nabokov, V. V. Speak, memory **813**
Norrell, R. J. Alex Haley and the books that changed a nation **92**
Parini, J. Empire of self **92**
Paterson, K. Stories of my life **92**
Pierpont, C. R. Passionate minds **810**
The play that changed my life **812**
Rowley, H. Richard Wright **813**
Savigneau, J. Carson McCullers **813**
Schultz, K. M. Buckley and Mailer **973.92**
Society for the Study of the Short Story A Reader's companion to the short story in English **809**
Stuart, S. P. Perfectly miserable **92**
Trillin, C. Quite enough of Calvin Trillin **817**
Watts, S. Self-help Messiah **92**
Weiner, J. Hungry heart **92**
White, E. The Tastemaker **92**
Wideman, J. E. Hoop roots **813**

AUTHORS, AMERICAN -- 20TH CENTURY -- BIOGRAPHY.
Pitzer, A. The Secret History of Vladimir Nabokov **891.73**

AUTHORS, AMERICAN -- 20TH CENTURY -- CORRESPONDENCE
Burroughs, W. S. Rub out the words **813**
Meanwhile there are letters **92**
Suitable accommodations **92**

AUTHORS, AMERICAN -- 20TH CENTURY -- DIARIES
As consciousness is harnessed to flesh **818**

AUTHORS, AMERICAN -- 21ST CENTURY -- BIOGRAPHY
Becker, D. L. Many subtle channels **840.9**
Christensen, K. Blue plate special **92**
The moment **818**
Rosenfelt, D. Dogtripping **636.7**
Smith Rakoff, J. My Salinger year **92**
Strayed, C. Wild **92**
Stuart, S. P. Perfectly miserable **92**

AUTHORS, AMERICAN -- ANECDOTES
The New Oxford book of literary anecdotes **828**

AUTHORS, AMERICAN -- BIOGRAPHY
Bailey, B. The Splendid Things We Planned **92**
The Cambridge guide to literature in English **820**
Estreich, G. The Shape of the Eye **618.92**
Harrison, K. The kiss **813**
Hitchens, C. Mortality **304.6**
James, E. Paris in love **92**
Kinsley, M. Old age **814.54**

AUTHORS, AMERICAN -- DICTIONARIES

American writers **920.003**
Oakes, E. H. American writers **920.003**

AUTHORS, AUSTRIAN
Joseph Roth **92**

AUTHORS, AUSTRIAN -- 20TH CENTURY -- BIOGRAPHY
Kafka, the years of insight **833**
Prochnik, G. The Impossible Exile **92**

AUTHORS, CANADIAN
Mowat, F. Born naked **92**

AUTHORS, CANADIAN See Canadian authors

AUTHORS, CATALAN -- 20TH CENTURY -- BIOGRAPHY
The Gray Notebook **849**

AUTHORS, CHILEAN
Allende, I. My invented country **863**
Allende, I. Paula **92**
Allende, I. The sum of our days **92**

AUTHORS, COLOMBIAN
Martin, G. Gabriel Garcia Marquez **92**

AUTHORS, COLOMBIAN -- 20TH CENTURY -- BIOGRAPHY
Abad, H. Oblivion **868**
Garcia Marquez, G. Living to tell the tale **92**

AUTHORS, CONGOLESE (BRAZZAVILLE) -- BIOGRAPHY
Mabanckou, A. The lights of Pointe-Noire **848**

AUTHORS, DANISH
Andersen, J. Hans Christian Andersen: a new life **92**
Wullschlager, J. Hans Christian Andersen **839.8**

AUTHORS, ENGLISH
Barnes, J. Nothing to be frightened of **92**
Bond, J. Who the hell is Pansy O'Hara? **920**
Briggs, J. Virginia Woolf: an inner life **92**
Fraser, A. Must you go? **92**
Gaskell, E. C. The life of Charlotte Bronte **92**
Gordon, L. Charlotte Bronte **92**
Harman, C. Jane's fame **92**
Hastings, S. The secret lives of Somerset Maugham **92**
Hughes, K. George Eliot **823**
Lee, H. Virginia Woolf **823**
Meyers, J. Samuel Johnson **92**
Moffat, W. A great unrecorded history **92**
The New Oxford book of literary anecdotes **828**
Nokes, D. Jane Austen **823**
Roiphe, K. Uncommon arrangements **920**
Scammell, M. Koestler **92**
Seymour, M. Mary Shelley **92**
Shields, C. Jane Austen **823**
Slater, M. Charles Dickens **92**
Smiley, J. Charles Dickens **823**
Sturrock, D. Storyteller **92**
Tomalin, C. Jane Austen **823**
Under the sun **92**

Waugh, A. Fathers and sons 920
Wilson, F. The ballad of Dorothy Wordsworth 92
Woolf, V. A moment's liberty: the shorter diary 92
Woolf, V. Moments of being 823
AUTHORS, ENGLISH *See* English authors
AUTHORS, ENGLISH -- 18TH CENTURY
Moore, W. How to create the perfect wife 823
AUTHORS, ENGLISH -- 20TH CENTURY -- BIOGRAPHY
Cusk, R. Aftermath 823
Huxley, E. The flame trees of Thika 828
McGrath, A. E. C. S. Lewis 92
Meyers, J. Orwell 828
Pierpont, C. R. Passionate minds 810
Roiphe, K. Uncommon arrangements 920
Seth, V. Two lives 92
Shakespeare, N. Bruce Chatwin 823
Society for the Study of the Short Story A Reader's companion to the short story in English 809
Thompson, L. The six 92
Weldon, F. Auto da Fay 823
Winterson, J. Why be happy when you could be normal? 823
AUTHORS, ENGLISH -- ANECDOTES
The New Oxford book of literary anecdotes 828
AUTHORS, FRENCH
Bakewell, S. How to live, or, A life of Montaigne in one question and twenty attempts at an answer 92
Sartre, J. P. The words 92
Todd, O. Albert Camus 848
AUTHORS, FRENCH -- 20TH CENTURY -- BIOGRAPHY
Carroll, S. B. Brave genius 920
Kaplan, A. The collaborator: the trial & execution of Robert Brasillach 848
AUTHORS, GERMAN
Across the land and the water 831
AUTHORS, INDIC -- GREAT BRITAIN -- BIOGRAPHY
Rushdie, S. Joseph Anton 92
AUTHORS, INDIC -- HOMES AND HAUNTS -- ENGLAND -- LONDON
Seth, V. Two lives 92
AUTHORS, IRISH
Bowker, G. James Joyce 823
Damrosch, L. Jonathan Swift 92
AUTHORS, ITALIAN
The Oxford companion to Italian literature 850
Tuck, L. Woman of Rome: a life of Elsa Morante 92
AUTHORS, ITALIAN -- BIOGRAPHY
Unger, M. J. Machiavelli 92
AUTHORS, JAPANESE
Modern Japanese writers 895.6
AUTHORS, KENYAN -- 20TH CENTURY -- BIOGRAPHY

Ngugi wa Thiong'o In the house of the interpreter 823
AUTHORS, NIGERIAN -- 20TH CENTURY -- BIOGRAPHY
Achebe, C. The education of a British-protected child 92
Achebe, C. There was a country 823
Achebe, C. Home and exile 823
AUTHORS, POLISH -- 20TH CENTURY -- CORRESPONDENCE.
Milosz, C. Legends of modernity 891.8
AUTHORS, RUSSIAN
Bartlett, R. Tolstoy 891.7
Boyd, B. Vladimir Nabokov: the American years 813
Boyd, B. Vladimir Nabokov: the Russian years 813
Frank, J. Dostoevsky 92
Nabokov, V. V. Speak, memory 813
Polonsky, R. Molotov's magic lantern 947
Popoff, A. The wives 891.7
Romanov riches 891.7
AUTHORS, RUSSIAN -- 20TH CENTURY -- BIOGRAPHY
Finn, P. The Zhivago affair 891.73
Nabokov, V. V. Speak, memory 813
AUTHORS, RUSSIAN -- 20TH CENTURY -- BIOGRAPHY.
Pitzer, A. The Secret History of Vladimir Nabokov 891.73
AUTHORS, SCOTTISH
Doyle, A. C. Arthur Conan Doyle 92
Stannard, M. Muriel Spark 92
AUTHORS, SCOTTISH -- 18TH CENTURY -- BIOGRAPHY
Boswell's enlightenment 828
Martin, P. A life of James Boswell 828
Zaretsky, R. Boswell's enlightenment 92
AUTHORS, SOUTH AFRICAN
Mda, Z. Sometimes there is a void 828
AUTHORS, SOUTH AFRICAN -- 20TH CENTURY -- BIOGRAPHY
Gevisser, M. Lost and Found in Johannesburg, a memoir 92
Mda, Z. Sometimes there is a void 828
AUTHORS, SPANISH
The Gray Notebook 849
AUTHORS, SWEDISH -- 19TH CENTURY -- BIOGRAPHY
Prideaux, S. Strindberg 839.7
AUTHORSHIP
Aiken, J. The way to write for children 808.06
Ballard, J. G. Miracles of life 823
Becker, D. L. Many subtle channels 840.9
Bond, J. Who the hell is Pansy O'Hara? 920
Boyd, B. On the origin of stories 809
Burn this book 814

Butler, R. O. From where you dream **808.3**

Chabon, M. Maps and legends **814**

The Chicago manual of style **808**

Dirda, M. Browsings **028**

Eco, U. Confessions of a young novelist **808.3**

Gardner, J. On becoming a novelist **808.3**

Gutkind, L. You can't make this stuff up **808**

Hiney, T. Raymond Chandler **813**

Hooks, B. Remembered rapture **808**

Hustvedt, S. Living, thinking, looking **814**

King, S. On writing **813**

Knight, R. M. Journalistic writing **070**

Koch, S. The modern library writer's workshop **808.3**

Lamott, A. Bird by bird **808**

LaRocque, P. The book on writing **808**

Malcolm, J. Forty-one false starts **808.02**

MFA vs NYC **808.02**

Morrell, J. P. Thanks, but this isn't for us **808.3**

Morris, E. This living hand **814**

Naipaul, V. S. Reading & writing **92**

Pinker, S. The sense of style **808**

Pinsky, R. Singing School **808.1**

The play that changed my life **812**

Popoff, A. The wives **891.7**

Rabiner, S. Thinking like your editor **808**

A reader's book of days **809**

Seuling, B. How to write a children's book and get it published **808.06**

Smiley, J. Thirteen ways of looking at the novel **813**

Stein, S. Stein on writing **808**

The Writer's digest guide to good writing **808**

AUTHORSHIP

See also Literature

AUTHORSHIP -- DATA PROCESSING -- HANDBOOKS, MANUALS, ETC.

Walker, J. R. The Columbia guide to online style **808**

AUTHORSHIP -- GRAPHIC NOVELS

Barry, L. What it is **741.5**

AUTHORSHIP -- HANDBOOKS, MANUALS, ETC.

Bingham, H. The writers' and artists' yearbook guide to how to write **808.3**

AUTHORSHIP -- PSYCHOLOGICAL ASPECTS

Laing, O. The Trip to Echo Spring **810.9**

AUTHORSHIP -- STYLE MANUALS

The Chicago manual of style **808**

Garvey, M. Stylized **808**

AUTHORSHIP -- VOCATIONAL GUIDANCE

MFA vs NYC **808.02**

AUTISM

Barnett, K. The spark **618.92**

Bashe, P. R. Asperger Syndrome **618.92**

Dawson, G. A parent's guide to high-functioning autism spectrum disorder **618.92**

Donvan, J. In a different key **616.85**

Grandin, T. The autistic brain **616.85**

Grandin, T. Animals in translation **591.5**

Grinker, R. R. Unstrange minds **616.85**

Harris, S. L. Essential first steps for parents of children with autism **618.92**

Harris, S. L. Siblings of Children With Autism **618.92**

Jackson, L. Freaks, geeks and asperger syndrome **618.92**

Lintala, J. The un-prescription for Autism **616.85**

Prizant, B. M. Uniquely human **618.92**

The reason I jump **92**

Rodriguez, A. M. Autism spectrum disorders **616.85**

Smith, R. G. ASD, the complete autism spectrum disorder health & diet guide **616.85**

Stephens, K. The Prodigy's Cousin **155.45**

Suskind, R. Life, animated **618.92**

Tammet, D. Born on a blue day **92**

AUTISM -- POPULAR WORKS

Rodriguez, A. M. Autism spectrum disorders **616.85**

AUTISM -- RESEARCH

Grandin, T. The autistic brain **616.85**

AUTISM -- TREATMENT

Robison, J. E. Switched on **616.85**

Autism Adulthood. Senator, S. **616.85**

AUTISM IN CHILDREN

Lazebnik, C. Overcoming Autism **618.92**

Prizant, B. M. Uniquely human **618.92**

AUTISM IN CHILDREN -- CASE STUDIES

Barnett, K. The spark **618.92**

AUTISM IN CHILDREN -- POPULAR WORKS

Rodriguez, A. M. Autism spectrum disorders **616.85**

Autism spectrum disorders. Rodriguez, A. M. **616.85**

AUTISM SPECTRUM DISORDERS

Donvan, J. In a different key **616.85**

Grandin, T. The autistic brain **616.85**

Lintala, J. The un-prescription for Autism **616.85**

The **autistic** brain. Grandin, T. **616.85**

AUTISTIC CHILDREN

Bowers, M. 8 keys to raising the quirky child **649**

Dawson, G. A parent's guide to high-functioning autism spectrum disorder **618.92**

Harris, S. L. Siblings of Children With Autism **618.92**

Lazebnik, C. Overcoming Autism **618.92**

Lintala, J. The un-prescription for Autism **616.85**

Mutch, M. Know the night **92**

The reason I jump **92**

Rodriguez, A. M. Autism spectrum disorders **616.85**

Smith, R. G. ASD, the complete autism spectrum

disorder health & diet guide **616.85**

Stephens, K. The Prodigy's Cousin **155.45**

AUTISTIC CHILDREN

See also Autistic people; Children with mental disabilities

AUTISTIC CHILDREN -- FAMILY RELATIONSHIPS

Harris, S. L. Siblings of Children With Autism **618.92**

AUTISTIC CHILDREN -- REHABILITATION

Barnett, K. The spark **618.92**

AUTISTIC PEOPLE

Senator, S. Autism Adulthood **616.85**

AUTISTIC PEOPLE

See also People with mental disabilities

AUTISTIC PEOPLE -- JAPAN -- BIOGRAPHY

The reason I jump **92**

AUTISTIC PEOPLE -- LIFE SKILLS GUIDES

Jackson, L. Sex, drugs and Asperger's syndrome (ASD) **618.92**

AUTISTIC PEOPLE -- MENTAL HEALTH

Grandin, T. The autistic brain **616.85**

AUTISTIC PEOPLE -- PSYCHOLOGY

The reason I jump **92**

AUTISTIC SPECTRUM DISORDERS *See* Autism

AUTISTIC YOUTH

Jackson, L. Freaks, geeks and asperger syndrome **618.92**

AUTISTIC YOUTH -- LIFE SKILLS GUIDES

Jackson, L. Sex, drugs and Asperger's syndrome (ASD) **618.92**

Auto Biography. Swift, E. **629.222**

Auto da Fay. Weldon, F. **823**

AUTOBIOGRAPHICAL COMIC BOOKS, STRIPS, ETC.

Lewis, J. March **92**

AUTOBIOGRAPHICAL GRAPHIC NOVELS

B., D. Epileptic **741.5**

Bechdel, A. Are you my mother? **741.5**

Bechdel, A. Fun home **741.5**

Georges, N. J. Calling Dr. Laura **92**

My friend Dahmer **741.5**

Satrapi, M. The complete Persepolis **741.5**

Small, D. Stitches **741.5**

Spiegelman, A. MetaMaus **940.53**

Torres, A. American widow **741.5**

AUTOBIOGRAPHICAL GRAPHIC NOVELS

See also Graphic novels

AUTOBIOGRAPHICAL MEMORY

Bloomfield, H. H. Making peace with your past **158**

Crais, C. History lessons **92**

Autobiographies. Douglass, F. **92**

AUTOBIOGRAPHIES

See also Biography

Autobiography. Mill, J. S. **92**

An **autobiography.** Gandhi, M. **92**

AUTOBIOGRAPHY

See also Biography as a literary form

AUTOBIOGRAPHY

Baroni, B. Fat kid got fit **362.196**

Conway, J. K. When memory speaks **808**

Encyclopedia of women's autobiography **920.003**

Ishida, S. Sewing happiness **646.2**

The Norton book of American autobiography **920**

Roche, R. Read on-- biography **016**

Yagoda, B. Memoir **809**

AUTOBIOGRAPHY -- AUTHORSHIP

Kephart, B. Handling the truth **808.06**

AUTOBIOGRAPHY -- BIBLIOGRAPHY

Roche, R. Read on-- biography **016**

AUTOBIOGRAPHY -- HISTORY AND CRITICISM *See* Autobiography

AUTOBIOGRAPHY -- TECHNIQUE *See* Autobiography

AUTOBIOGRAPHY AS A LITERARY FORM *See* Autobiography

Autobiography of a recovering skinhead. Meeink, F. **92**

The **autobiography** of Alice B. Toklas. Stein, G. **92**

The **autobiography** of Benjamin Franklin. Franklin, B. **92**

The **autobiography** of Lincoln Steffens. Steffens, L. **92**

The **autobiography** of Malcolm X. Malcolm X **92**

Autobiography of Mark Twain. **818**

Autobiography of Mark Twain. **92**

Autobiography of Mark Twain. **92**

The **autobiography** of Martin Luther King, Jr. King, M. L. **323**

The **autobiography** of Medgar Evers: a hero's life and legacy revealed through his writings, letters, and speeches. Evers, M. W. **92**

Autobiography of red. Carson, A. **811**

Autobiography, Poor Richard, and later writings. Franklin, B. **818**

AUTOGRAPHED EDITIONS

See also Autographs; Editions

AUTOGRAPHS

Tingey, J. The Englishman who posted himself and other curious objects **92**

AUTOGRAPHS

See also Biography; Writing

AUTOIMMUNE DISEASES

Cahalan, S. Brain on fire **616.8**

Myers, A. The autoimmune solution **616.97**

AUTOIMMUNE DISEASES

See also Diseases

AUTOIMMUNE DISEASES -- TREATMENT

Blum, S. Your immune system recovery plan **616.97**

The **autoimmune** solution. Myers, A. **616.97**

AUTOMATION OF LIBRARY PROCESSES --

HANDBOOKS, MANUALS, ETC.
Cohn, J. M. The complete library technology planner **025**
AUTOMATONS *See* Robots
Automats, taxi dances, and vaudeville. Freeland, D.
AUTOMOBILE DESIGN *See* Automobiles -- Design and construction
AUTOMOBILE DRIVER EDUCATION
   See also Education
AUTOMOBILE DRIVERS
   Vanderbilt, T. Traffic **629.28**
AUTOMOBILE DRIVING *See* Automobile drivers
AUTOMOBILE EXECUTIVES
   Baldwin, N. Henry Ford and the Jews **305**
   Brinkley, D. Wheels for the world **338.7**
   Grandin, G. Fordlandia **307.7**
   Lutz, B. Car guys vs. bean counters **338.7**
   Watts, S. The people's tycoon **92**
AUTOMOBILE INDUSTRY
   Baldwin, N. Henry Ford and the Jews **305**
   Boorstin, D. J. The Americans: The democratic experience **973**
   Brinkley, D. Wheels for the world **338.7**
   Cox, H. H. American drive **338**
   Goldstone, L. Drive! **338.4**
   Lutz, B. Car guys vs. bean counters **338.7**
   Michelli, J. A. Driven to delight **658**
   Sperling, D. Two billion cars **388.3**
   Vlasic, B. Once upon a car **338.4**
AUTOMOBILE INDUSTRY
   See also Industries
AUTOMOBILE INDUSTRY AND TRADE -- CUSTOMER SERVICES -- GERMANY
   Michelli, J. A. Driven to delight **658**
AUTOMOBILE INDUSTRY AND TRADE -- UNITED STATES -- FINANCE
   Lutz, B. Car guys vs. bean counters **338.7**
AUTOMOBILE INSURANCE
   See also Insurance
AUTOMOBILE PARTS
   See also Automobiles
AUTOMOBILE RACING
   Baime, A. J. Go like hell **796.72**
   Donovan, B. Hard driving: the Wendell Scott story **92**
   Hawley, S. J. Speed duel **796.72**
   Levy, S. Paul Newman **92**
AUTOMOBILE REPAIRS *See* Automobiles -- Maintenance and repair
AUTOMOBILE TOURING *See* Automobile travel
AUTOMOBILE TRAVEL
   The open road **770**
   Podell, A. Around the World in 50 Years **910.4**
AUTOMOBILE TRAVEL
   See also Transportation; Travel; Voyages and travels

AUTOMOBILE TRAVEL -- GUIDEBOOKS
   See also Maps
AUTOMOBILE TRAVEL -- UNITED STATES -- HISTORY -- 20TH CENTURY
   Davis, D. The trip **700.92**
AUTOMOBILES
   The Beaulieu encyclopedia of the automobile **629.222**
AUTOMOBILES
   See also Highway transportation; Motor vehicles; Vehicles
AUTOMOBILES -- DRAWINGS -- EXHIBITIONS
   Gross, K. Dream cars **629.222**
AUTOMOBILES -- DRIVING *See* Automobile drivers
AUTOMOBILES -- ENCYCLOPEDIAS
   The Beaulieu encyclopedia of the automobile **629.222**
AUTOMOBILES -- FUEL CONSUMPTION
   Sperling, D. Two billion cars **388.3**
AUTOMOBILES -- FUEL CONSUMPTION
   See also Energy consumption; Fuel
AUTOMOBILES -- HISTORY
   Car **629.222**
   Parissien, S. The life of the automobile **629.222**
AUTOMOBILES -- LAW AND LEGISLATION
   See also Law; Legislation
AUTOMOBILES -- SOCIAL ASPECTS
   Ladd, B. Autophobia **303.4**
AUTOMOBILES -- SOCIAL ASPECTS -- UNITED STATES -- HISTORY
   Ingrassia, P. Engines of change **629.222**
AUTONOMY (PSYCHOLOGY)
   Nielsen, K. E. A disability history of the United States **362.4**
AUTONOMY (PSYCHOLOGY)
   See also Psychology
AUTONOMY -- SOCIAL ASPECTS -- GULF COAST (U.S.) -- HISTORY -- 18TH CENTURY
   DuVal, K. Independence Lost **973.3**
Autophobia. Ladd, B. **303.4**
Autry, Gene, 1907-1998
             About
   George-Warren, H. Public cowboy no. 1 **92**
AUTUMN
   See also Seasons
Autumn in the Heavenly Kingdom. Platt, S. R. **951**
Ava's man. Bragg, R. **975**
AVAILABILITY OF HEALTH SERVICES *See* Access to health care
AVALANCHES
   Fredston, J. A. Snowstruck **551.3**
   Krist, G. The white cascade **979.7**

Avallone, Eugene A.
(ed) Marks' standard handbook for mechanical engineers **621**
AVANT-GARDE (AESTHETICS)
Weber, N. F. The Bauhaus group **920**
AVANT-GARDE (AESTHETICS)
See also Aesthetics; Modernism (Aesthetics)
AVARICE
See also Sin
The **avengers.** Cohen, R. **940.53**
Avenue of spies. Kershaw, A. **940.53**
AVERAGE
See also Arithmetic; Probabilities; Statistics
Averno. Gluck, L. **811**
Aversa, Elizabeth S.
(jt. auth) Perrault, A. H. Information resources in the humanities and the arts **016**
Avery, Christine
(ed) Rethinking collection development and management **025.2**
Avery, Kevin
Everything is an afterthought **92**
AVIATION *See* Aeronautics
AVIATION ACCIDENTS *See* Aircraft accidents
AVIATION MEDICINE
See also Medicine
The **aviators.** Groom, W. **920**
AVIATORS *See* Air pilots
Avineri, Shlomo
Herzl's vision **320.54**
Avitabile, Alphonse
(jt. auth) Sammataro, D. The beekeeper's handbook **638.1**
AVOCATIONS *See* Hobbies
Avoid boring people. Watson, J. D. **92**
Avonmore, William Charles Yelverton, Viscount, 1824-1883
About
Schama, C. Wild romance **92**
Avrich, Karen
Sasha and Emma **335**
Avrich, Paul
(jt. auth) Avrich, K. Sasha and Emma **335**
Axelrod, Alan
The encyclopedia of the American armed forces **355**
Whiskey tango foxtrot **427**
Axelrod, David, 1955-
Believer **92**
Axelrod, Howard, 1973-
About
Axelrod, H. The point of vanishing **92**
Axelrod, Matt
Your guide to the Jewish holidays **296.4**
AXIOLOGY *See* Values
Ayala, Francisco Jose, 1934-

Darwin's gift to science and religion **576.8**
Aycoberry, Pierre
The social history of the Third Reich **943.086**
Ayers, Edward L.
(ed) The Oxford book of the American South **810**
Ayers, Nathaniel Anthony
About
Lopez, S. The soloist **92**
Aykroyd, Peter
A history of ghosts **133.1**
Ayn Rand and the world she made. Heller, A. C. **92**
Ayres, Alex
(ed) Twain, M. The wit and wisdom of Mark Twain **818**
Ayres, Chris
Osbourne, O. I am Ozzy **92**
Ayto, John
Brewer's dictionary of modern phrase & fable **803**
The Oxford dictionary of slang **427**
(ed) Oxford dictionary of English idioms **423**
AYURVEDA
Fondin, M. S. The wheel of healing with ayurveda **615.5**
Azam Zanganeh, Lila
My sister, guard your veil; my brother guard, your eyes **305**
Azri, Stephanie
(jt. auth) Ilse, S. The prenatal bombshell **618.3**
The **Aztecs.** Townsend, R. F. **972**
AZTECS
Ceram, C. W. Gods, graves, and scholars **930.1**
Prescott, W. H. History of the conquest of Mexico **972**
Smith, M. E. The Aztecs **972**
Townsend, R. F. The Aztecs **972**
The **Aztecs.** Smith, M. E. **972**
Azzarelli, Kim K.
(jt. auth) Verveer, M. Fast forward **650.1**

B

B+ grades, A+ college application. Jager-Hyman, J. **378.1**
B-24 (BOMBER) -- ACCIDENTS -- ALASKA
Murphy, B. 81 days below zero **940.54**
B-24 BOMBER
Ambrose, S. E. The wild blue **940.54**
B., David. B., D.Epileptic **741.5**
B.F. Skinner. Bjork, D. W. **92**
B.T.C. OLD-FASHIONED GROCERY
Grimes, D. The B.T.C. old-fashioned grocery cookbook **641.59**
The **B.T.C.** old-fashioned grocery cookbook. Grimes, D. **641.59**
BĀDGHĪS (AFGHANISTAN) -- HISTORY, MILITARY
Bruning, J. R. Level zero heroes **958.104**

Baader-Meinhof. Aust, S.   363.32

Baartman, Saartjie

     About

   Crais, C. C.   Sara Baartman and the Hottentot Venus   92

   Holmes, R.   African queen   92

Babb, Sam, 1891-1937

     About

   Reeder, L.   Dust bowl girls   796.323

Babbage, Charles, 1791-1871

     About

   Essinger, J.   Ada's algorithm   92

   Snyder, L. J.   The philosophical breakfast club   509

Babe. Creamer, R. W.   92

BABEL, TOWER OF

   Ceram, C. W.   Gods, graves, and scholars   930.1

BABIES See Infants

BABOONS

   Sapolsky, R. M.   A primate's memoir   599.8

BABOONS

     See also Apes

Baby Birds. Zickefoose, J.   598

The **baby** book. Cross, C.   649.122

The **baby** book. Sears, W.   649

BABY BOOM GENERATION

     See also Population

BABY BOOM GENERATION -- UNITED STATES

   Kinsley, M.   Old age   814.54

BABY CARE See Infants -- Care

Baby catcher. Vincent, P.   618.2

BABY CLOTHES See Infants' clothing

BABY FOODS

   White, D. A.   First bites   641.3

BABY NAMES See Personal names

Babylon. Kriwaczek, P.   935

BABYLON (EXTINCT CITY)

   Kriwaczek, P.   Babylon   935

The **Babylonian** theorem. Rudman, P. S.   510

BABYSITTING

     See also Child care; Infants -- Care

Baca, Jimmy Santiago

   Spring poems along the Rio Grande   811

Bacall, Lauren, 1924-2014

     About

   Bacall, L.   By myself and then some   92

Bacci, Ingrid

   Effortless pain relief   616

Bacevich, Andrew J., 1947-

   America's war for the greater Middle East   956.054

   Washington rules   355

Bach. Gardiner, J. E.   92

Bach family

     About

   Schonberg, H. C.   The great pianists   920

Bach, Johann Sebastian, 1685-1750

     About

   Gardiner, J. E.   Bach   92

   Geck, M.   Johann Sebastian Bach   92

   Siblin, E.   The cello suites   787.3

   Wolff, C.   Johann Sebastian Bach   92

Bach, Maria, 1896-1978

     About

   Porter, C. H.   Five lives in music   780.92

Bach, Steven

   Leni: the life and work of Leni Riefenstahl   92

BACK -- DISEASES -- TREATMENT

   Deyo, R. A.   Watch your back!   617.5

The **back** chamber. Hall, D.   811

Back from the dead. Walton, B.   92

Back in the Day Bakery, made with love. Day, C.   641.81

The **back** in the swing cookbook. Fertig, J.   641.5

BACK PACKING See Backpacking

Back to normal. Gnaulati, E.   618.92

Back to our future. Sirota, D.   973.92

Back to school. Rose, M.   374

Back yard series

   Muller, K.   The potter's studio handbook   738.1

BACKACHE -- TREATMENT

   Deyo, R. A.   Watch your back!   617.5

Backes, Michael

   Cannabis Pharmacy   615.7

Backfire: Carly Fiorina's high-stakes battle for the soul of Hewlett-Packard. Burrows, P.   338.7

Backing into forward. Feiffer, J.   92

BACKPACK CYCLING See Bicycle touring

BACKPACKING

   Baggett, J.   The lost girls   910.4

BACKPACKING

     See also Camping; Hiking

Backstabbing for beginners. Soussan, M.   363.8

The **backyard** astronomer's guide. Dickinson, T.   522

The **backyard** beekeeper. Flottum, K.   638.1

Backyard Building. Stiles, D.   690

Backyard guide to the night sky. Schneider, H.   520

The **backyard** homestead.   641

BACON'S REBELLION, 1676

     See also United States -- History -- 1600-1775, Colonial period

Bacon, David

   Illegal people   331.6

Bacon, Francis, 1561-1626

     About

   Durant, W. J.   The story of philosophy   109

Bacon, Francis, 1909-1992

     About

   Smee, S.   The art of rivalry   700.92

BACTERIA

   Blaser, M. J.   Missing microbes   615.7

   Tetro, J.   The Germ Files   579.3

Zimmer, C. Microcosm **579.3**

BACTERIA

See also Microorganisms; Parasites

BACTERIAL WARFARE See Biological warfare

BACTERIOLOGY

See also Microbiology

BAD BEHAVIOR

See also Human behavior

Bad Feminist. Gay, R. **814**

Bad girls go everywhere: the life of Helen Gurley Brown. Scanlon, J. **92**

Bad land. Raban, J. **978**

Bad paper. Halpern, J. **332.7**

Bad Pharma. Goldacre, B. **615.107**

Bad science. Goldacre, B. **500**

The **bad-ass** librarians of Timbuktu. Hammer, J. **025.8**

The **Badass** Body Diet. Abbott, C. **613.2**

Bader, Christopher D.

Paranormal America **133.8**

Bader, Michael J.

Arousal, the secret logic of sexual fantasies **306.7**

Bader, Philip

African-American writers **920.003**

BADGERS

See also Mammals

Badkhen, Anna, 1976-

Walking With Abel **305.896**

About

Badkhen, A. The world is a carpet **958.1**

Baer, Max, 1909-1959

About

Schaap, J. Cinderella Man **92**

Báez, Fernando

A universal history of the destruction of books **900**

Bageant, Joe

Deer hunting with Jesus **305.5**

Bagemihl, Bruce

Biological exuberance **591.56**

Bagg, Mary

(ed) Berkshire encyclopedia of China **951**

Baggett, Jennifer

About

Baggett, J. The lost girls **910.4**

Baggott, J. E.

The first war of physics **355.8**

Baggott, J. The quantum story **530.1**

Baggott, Jim

The quantum story **530.1**

BAGHDAD (IRAQ)

Kennedy, H. When Baghdad ruled the Muslim world **956.7**

BAGHDAD (IRAQ) -- SOCIAL LIFE AND CUS-TOMS

Ciezadlo, A. Day of honey **92**

Baghdad at sunrise. Mansoor, P. R. **956.7**

Baghdad without a map, and other misadventures in Arabia. Horwitz, T. **915**

Baglio, Matt

Argo **955.05**

BAGS

See also Containers

BAHAI FAITH

See also Religions

Bahn, Paul G.

Lister, A. Mammoths **569**

Bai, Matt

All the truth is out **328.73**

Baiev, Khassan

About

Baiev, K. The Oath **947.5**

Baigrie, Brian S.

(ed) History of modern science and mathematics **500**

Bailey, Anthony

Velazquez: surrendering at Breda **759**

Bailey, Beth L.

(ed) The Columbia guide to America in the 1960s **973.923**

Bailey, Blake, 1963-

Cheever **92**

About

Bailey, B. The Splendid Things We Planned **92**

Bailey, Elisabeth Tova

About

Bailey, E. T. The sound of a wild snail eating **92**

Bailey, Elizabeth

Safe kids, smart parents **613.6**

Bailey, Gauvin Alexander

Art in time **709**

Bailey, Mary

The Ultimate Encyclopedia of Aquarium Fish & Fish Care **639.34**

Bailey, Rebecca

(jt. auth) Bailey, E. Safe kids, smart parents **613.6**

Easy to love, difficult to discipline **155**

Bailey, Richard W.

Speaking American **427**

Baillet, Christine

(jt. auth) Bruno, I. Reinventing Ikea **684.1**

Baillio, Joseph

Claude Monet, 1840-1926 **759**

Bailyn, Bernard

The barbarous years **973.2**

The peopling of British North America **973.2**

Sometimes an art, never a science, always a craft **907.2**

Baime, A. J.

Go like hell **796.72**

Bain, David Haward

Empire express **385**

Bain, Ken

What the best college students do   **378.1**

Bainbridge, David A.
Gardening with less water   **635.9**

Bainton, Roland Herbert
Here I stand: a life of Martin Luther   **92**

Baiocchi, Regina A. Harris, 1956-
About
Walker-Hill, H. From spirituals to symphonies **780**

Bair, Deirdre
Saul Steinberg   **741.092**
Simone de Beauvoir   **848**

Baird, Julia
Victoria   **92**

Bais, Sander
In praise of science   **500**

Bajac, Quentin
Photography at MOMA   **770**

BAKED PRODUCTS
Baker, L. Fat witch bake sale   **641.81**
Daykin, R. Butter baked goods   **641.81**
Matheson, C. Flour   **641.8**
Ovenly   **641.81**

Baker, David
The 50 most extreme places in our solar system   **523.2**

Baker, Deborah
The convert   **92**

Baker, Ella, 1903-1986
About
Cornel West on Black prophetic fire   **92**

Baker, Houston A.
(ed) Douglass, F. Narrative of the life of Frederick Douglass, an American slave   **92**

Baker, James W.
Thanksgiving   **394.26**

Baker, Jean H.
Margaret Sanger   **92**
Mary Todd Lincoln   **92**

Baker, Jennifer S., 1953-
The readers' advisory guide to historical fiction **026**

Baker, Joanne
Henderson, M. 100 most important science ideas   **500**

Baker, John F.
The Washingtons of Wessyngton Plantation   **920**

Baker, Joseph O.
(jt. auth) Bader, C. D. Paranormal America **133.8**

Baker, Josephine, 1906-1975
About
Mackrell, J. Flappers   **920**

Baker, Josh
(ed) 75 years of Marvel Comics   **741.5**

Baker, Lawrence W.
(ed) Grumet, B. H. Reconstruction era: primary sources   **973.8**
(ed) Howes, K. K. Reconstruction era: almanac   **973.8**
(ed) Matuz, R. Reconstruction era: biographies **920**

Baker, Lucy
Fat witch bake sale   **641.81**

Baker, Nicholson, 1957-
Double fold   **025.2**
The way the world works   **814**
The World on Sunday   **071**

Baker, Peter
Kremlin rising   **947.086**

Baker, Richard A.
The American Senate   **328.73**

Baker, Russell, 1925-
About
Baker, R. Growing up   **92**

Baker, Stephen
Final Jeopardy   **006.3**
The numerati   **303.4**

Baker, Stewart A.
Skating on stilts   **363.32**

Baker, William
Critical companion to Jane Austen   **823**
The facts on file companion to Shakespeare **822.3**

BAKERS
Bullock-Prado, G. Confections of a closet master baker   **92**

Bakewell, Sarah
At the Existentialist Cafe   **142**
How to live, or, A life of Montaigne in one question and twenty attempts at an answer   **92**

BakeWise. Corriher, S.   **641.8**

Baking. Peterson, J.   **641.8**

BAKING
See also Cooking

BAKING
Adams, J. D. Grandbaby cakes   **641.86**
The America's test kitchen family baking book   **641.8**
Baker, L. Fat witch bake sale   **641.81**
Baking illustrated   **641.8**
Beranbaum, R. L. The baking Bible   **641.81**
Berry, M. Baking with Mary Berry   **641.865**
The Best Casserole cookbook ever   **641.8**
Bittman, M. How to Bake Everything   **641.86**
Black, S. One dough, ten breads   **641.81**
Blakeslee, R. L. Your time to bake   **641.8**
Bouchon Bakery   **641.59**
Boyle, T. Flavorful   **641.86**
Breakfast at Huckleberry   **641.5**
Bullock-Prado, G. Confections of a closet master baker   **92**
Chang, J. Baking with less sugar   **641.5**
Child, J. Baking with Julia   **641.7**
Corriher, S. BakeWise   **641.8**
Cunningham, M. The Fannie Farmer baking book   **641.7**

Daley, R. In the sweet kitchen **641.8**
Day, C. Back in the Day Bakery, made with love **641.81**
Daykin, R. Butter baked goods **641.81**
DeMasco, K. The craft of baking **641.8**
Dodge, A. J. The everyday baker **641.815**
Flavor flours **641.3**
Food52 baking **641.81**
Forkish, K. Flour water salt yeast **641.81**
Goldman, D. Duff Bakes **641.81**
Greenspan, D. Baking chez moi **641.86**
Haedrich, K. Pie: 300 tried-and-true recipes for delicious homemade pie **641.8**
Heatter, M. Maida Heatter's cakes **641.8**
Heatter, M. Maida Heatter's cookies **641.8**
Holiday cookies **641.86**
Kaminsky, P. Bien Cuit **641.815**
Lawson, N. How to be a domestic goddess **641.815**
Matheson, C. Flour **641.8**
McDermott, K. Art of the pie **641.86**
Moore, C. Little Flower baking **641.815**
Moore, K. Delicious dump cakes **641.86**
Mushet, C. The art and soul of baking **641.8**
Naturally sweet **641.86**
Ovenly **641.81**
Patent, G. Baking in America **641.8**
Peterson, J. Baking **641.8**
Ptak, C. The Violet Bakery cookbook **641.86**
Robertson, C. Tartine Book No. 3 **641.81**
Robicelli, A. Robicelli's **641.86**
Sarabeth's good morning cookbook **641.5**
Shulman, M. R. The art of French pastry **641.86**
Tosi, C. Momofuku Milk Bar **641.8**
Tye, D. Baking as biography **92**
Wright, C. Mix + Match Cakes **641.86**

BAKING -- MASSACHUSETTS -- BOSTON
Matheson, C. Flour **641.8**

Baking as biography. Tye, D. **92**
The baking Bible. Beranbaum, R. L. **641.81**
Baking chez moi. Greenspan, D. **641.86**
Baking illustrated. **641.8**
Baking in America. Patent, G. **641.8**
Baking with Julia. Child, J. **641.7**
Baking with less sugar. Chang, J. **641.5**
Baking with Mary Berry. Berry, M. **641.865**
Balaban, Naomi E.
The handy anatomy answer book **611**
(ed) The handy science answer book **500**
Balakian, Peter
The burning Tigris **956.6**

BALANCE OF NATURE See Ecology
BALANCE OF PAYMENTS
See also International economic relations
BALANCE OF POWER
Kennedy, P. M. The rise and fall of the great powers **909.08**

BALANCE OF POWER
See also International relations
BALANCE OF POWER -- FORECASTING
Brzezinski, Z. Strategic vision **327.1**
BALANCE OF TRADE
See also International trade
A balanced life. Smith, T. **362.1**
Balanchine, George, 1904-1983
About
Gottlieb, R. A. George Balanchine: the ballet maker **92**
Teachout, T. All in the dances: a brief life of George Balanchine **92**
Volkov, S. St. Petersburg **947**
Balay, Robert
(ed) Guide to reference books **011**
Balbirer, Nancy
About
Balbirer, N. Take your shirt off and cry **92**
Balch, Thomas J.
(jt. auth) Robert, H. M. Robert's rules of order newly revised **060.4**
(jt. auth) Robert, H. M. Robert's rules of order, newly revised, in brief **060.4**
Balcombe, Jonathan
The exultant ark **591.5**
Second nature **591.5**
What a Fish Knows **597.15**
Balcon, Jill
(ed) The complete poems of C. Day Lewis **821**
Bald Is Better With Earrings. Hutton, A. **616.99**
Baldrige, Letitia
Letitia Baldrige's new manners for new times **395**
Baldwin, Debra Lee
Succulents simplified **635.9**
Baldwin, James, 1924-1987
Collected essays **814**
About
Blight, D. W. American oracle **973.7**
Gates, H. L. Thirteen ways of looking at a black man **920.71**
Baldwin, Lewis V.
(ed) Thou, dear God **242**
Baldwin, Louisa, 1845-1925
About
Flanders, J. A circle of sisters **920**
Baldwin, Neil
Henry Ford and the Jews **305**
Baldwin, Peter
The copyright wars **346**
Baldwin, Rosecrans, 1977-
About
Baldwin, R. Paris, I love you but you're bringing me down **944**
Balf, Todd
Major **92**

Balibar, Sebastien
The atom and the apple   530
Balick, Michael J.
Rodale's 21st-century herbal   635
Ball family
      About
Ball, E. Slaves in the family   975.7
BALL GAMES
    See also Games
Ball, Edward
Slaves in the family   975.7
The sweet hell inside   920
Ball, George W.
      About
Galbraith, J. K. Name-dropping   973.9
Ball, Howard, 1937-
At liberty to die   344
Ball, Lucille, 1911-1989
      About
Ball, L. Love, Lucy   92
Ball, Philip, 1962-
Invisible   535
Nature's patterns   500.2
Patterns in nature   500.2
Balla, Nicolaus
Bar Tartine   641.59
The **ballad** of Dorothy Wordsworth. Wilson, F.   92
BALLADS
American ballads and folk songs   781.62
Our singing country   781.62
BALLADS
    See also Literature; Poetry; Songs
Ballance, Laura Jane
Cook, J. Our noise   338
Ballard, J. G., 1930-2009
      About
Ballard, J. G. Miracles of life   823
Ballard, Robert D.
The eternal darkness   551.46
Return to Midway   940.54
BALLET
Copeland, M. Life in motion   92
Craine, D. The Oxford dictionary of dance   792.8
Gottlieb, R. A. George Balanchine: the ballet maker   92
Homans, J. Apollo's angels   792.8
Minden, E. G. The ballet companion   792.8
Reynolds, N. No fixed points   792.8
Teachout, T. All in the dances: a brief life of George Balanchine   92
BALLET
    See also Dance; Drama; Performing arts; Theater
The **ballet** companion. Minden, E. G.   792.8
BALLET DANCERS
Diaghilev   92

Kavanagh, J. Nureyev   92
Life stories   920
Marshall, L. Every step you take   92
Minden, E. G. The ballet companion   792.8
Tallchief, M. Maria Tallchief   92
BALLET DANCERS
    See also Dancers
BALLETS (MUSIC)
    See also Dance music
BALLISTIC MISSILES
Sheehan, N. A fiery peace in a cold war   92
BALLISTIC MISSILES
    See also Guided missiles; Nuclear weapons; Rockets (Aeronautics)
BALLOON ASCENSIONS -- ARCTIC REGIONS
Wilkinson, A. The ice balloon   910.91
BALLOONING -- HISTORY
Holmes, R. Falling upwards   387.7
BALLOONS
    See also Aeronautics
BALLOONS, DIRIGIBLE *See* Airships
BALLROOM DANCING
    See also Dance
Ballyhoo, buckeroo, and spuds. Quinion, M.   422
Balsamo, John
Balsamo, W. Young Al Capone   92
Balsamo, William
Young Al Capone   92
BALTIMORE (MD.)
Watkins, D. The Cook Up   364.1
BALTIMORE (MD.) -- BIOGRAPHY
Moore, W. The work   92
BALTIMORE ORIOLES (BASEBALL TEAM)
Ripken, C. The only way I know   92
BALTIMORE RAVENS (FOOTBALL TEAM)
Feinstein, J. Next man up   796.332
BALTIMORE, BATTLE OF, BALTIMORE, MD., 1814
Vogel, S. Through the perilous fight   973.5
Balz, Daniel J.
The battle for America, 2008   973.932
Balzac. Robb, G.   92
Balzac, Honoré de, 1799-1850
      About
Robb, G. Balzac   92
Bambara, Toni Cade
      About
Black women writers (1950-1980)   810
Bambaradeniya, Channa N. B.
The illustrated atlas of wildlife   591.9
BAMBOO
    See also Wood
Bambrick, Yvonne
The urban cycling survival guide   796.6
Bamford, James
The shadow factory   327.12

Banai, Noit
(jt. auth) Bailey, G. A. Art in time **709**
BANANA REPUBLIC TRAVEL AND SAFARI COMPANY
Ziegler, M. Wild company **381**
BANANA TRADE -- LOUISIANA -- NEW ORLEANS -- HISTORY
Cohen, R. The fish that ate the whale **338.7**
BAND LEADERS
Armstrong, L. Louis Armstrong, in his own words **92**
Basie, C. Good morning blues: the autobiography of Count Basie **92**
Cook, R. It's about that time **92**
Dance, S. The world of Count Basie **920**
Davis, M. Miles, the autobiography **92**
Ellison, R. Going to the territory **818**
Feather, L. From Satchmo to Miles **920**
Lees, G. You can't steal a gift **781.65**
Murray, A. The blue devils of Nada **780.89**
Nolan, T. Three chords for beauty's sake: the life of Artie Shaw **92**
Band of brothers. Ambrose, S. E. **940.54**
The **band** that played on. Turner, S. **910.4**
BANDAGES
See also First aid
BANDITS *See* Thieves
BANDMASTERS *See* Conductors (Music)
BANDS (MUSIC)
Cohen, R. The Sun and the Moon and the Rolling Stones **782.42**
Fogerty, J. Fortunate son **92**
Bane, Theresa
Encyclopedia of vampire mythology **398**
Banerjee, Abhijit V.
Poor economics **339.4**
Banfield, Kelsey
The family calendar cookbook **641.5**
Bang, Mary Jo
The bride of E **811**
Elegy **811**
BANGLADESH
Bass, G. J. The Blood telegram **327.73**
BANGLADESH -- HISTORY -- REVOLUTION, 1971 -- ATROCITIES
Bass, G. J. The Blood telegram **327.73**
BANJO PLAYERS
Stanley, R. Man of constant sorrow **92**
BANJOS
Seeger, P. How to play the 5-string banjo **787.8**
BANK CAPITAL -- LAW AND LEGISLATION
Friedman, J. Engineering the financial crisis **330.9**
BANK FAILURES
Bartiromo, M. The weekend that changed Wall Street **330.9**
Farrell, G. Crash of the titans **332.1**

Johnson, S. 13 bankers **332.1**
Kelly, K. Street fighters **332.6**
BANK FAILURES
See also Bankruptcy; Banks and banking; Business failures
BANK FAILURES -- UNITED STATES -- HISTORY
Grind, K. The lost bank **332.3**
BANK OF AMERICA NA
Farrell, G. Crash of the titans **332.1**
BANK ROBBERIES
See also Theft
Banker to the world. Rhodes, W. R. **92**
BANKERS
Ahamed, L. Lords of finance **332.1**
Chernow, R. The Warburgs **920**
De Waal, E. The hare with amber eyes **920**
Ferguson, N. High financier **92**
Greenspan, A. The age of turbulence **92**
Halberstam, D. The best and the brightest **973.922**
Hendrickson, P. The living and the dead **959.704**
Hibbert, C. The House of Medici **920**
Millman, C. The detonators **940.4**
Overtveldt, J. v. Bernanke's test **332.1**
Parks, T. Medici money **332.1**
Rhodes, W. R. Banker to the world **92**
Rockefeller, D. Memoirs **332.1**
Strouse, J. Morgan **92**
Weintraub, S. Charlotte and Lionel **92**
Woodward, B. Maestro: Greenspan's Fed and the American boom **331.1**
Bankhead, Tallulah, 1902-1968
About
Mackrell, J. Flappers **920**
BANKING *See* Banks and banking
BANKRUPTCY
Elias, S. Chapter 13 bankruptcy **346**
Elias, S. How to file for Chapter 7 bankruptcy **346.07**
BANKRUPTCY
See also Business failures; Commercial law; Debtor and creditor; Finance
BANKS AND BANKING
Cassidy, J. How markets fail **381**
Cohan, W. D. Money and power **332.6**
Cox, H. H. American drive **338**
Ferguson, N. High financier **92**
King, M. A. The End of Alchemy **330.122**
McGee, S. Chasing Goldman Sachs **332.6**
Parks, T. Medici money **332.1**
Rhodes, W. R. Banker to the world **92**
Wessel, D. In Fed we trust **332.1**
BANKS AND BANKING
See also Business; Capital; Commerce; Finance
BANKS AND BANKING -- CORRUPT PRAC-

TICES

Lefevre, J. Straight to Hell   **332.1**

BANKS AND BANKING -- DATA PROCESSING
  See also Data processing

BANKS AND BANKING -- UNITED STATES
  Friedman, J. Engineering the financial crisis 330.9
  Grind, K. The lost bank   332.3
  Lane, C. A Nation Wholly Free   336.3
  Lowenstein, R. America's Bank   332.1

BANKS AND BANKING -- VATICAN CITY
  Posner, G. God's Bankers   **364.16**

BANKS AND BANKING -- WASHINGTON (STATE) -- SEATTLE -- HISTORY
  Grind, K. The lost bank   332.3

BANKS AND BANKING, COOPERATIVE *See*
  Cooperative banks

BANKS AND BANKING, INTERNATIONAL
  Rhodes, W. R. Banker to the world   **92**

Bankston, Carl L.
  (ed) Great lives from history: Notorious lives   **920.003**

BANNED BOOKS *See* Books -- Censorship
Banned in the U.S.A. Foerstel, H. N.   **025.2**

Bannerman, Stacy
  Homefront 911   **362.86**

BANNERS *See* Flags
BANQUETS *See* Dining; Dinners
Banyas, Stephanie
  Brunch @ Bobby's   **641.5**

Bao Pu
  (tr) Prisoner of the state   **92**

Baptist, Edward E.
  The half has never been told   **306.3**

BAR *See* Lawyers
Bar Book.   **641.87**

BAR MITZVAH
    See also Judaism -- Customs and practices
Bar Tartine. Balla, N.   **641.59**

BAR TARTINE (SAN FRANCISCO, CALIF.)
  Balla, N. Bar Tartine   **641.59**

Bar-Itzhak, Haya
  (ed) Encyclopedia of Jewish folklore and traditions   **398.2**

Bar-On, Mordechai
  Moshe Dayan   **956.940**

Bara, Brett
  (ed) Crochet at home   **746.43**

Barack Obama. Maraniss, D.   **92**

Baraka, Imamu Amiri
  Dutchman, and The slave   **812**
  The LeRoi Jones/Amiri Baraka reader   **818**

Baranczak, Stanislaw
  Monologue of a dog   **891.8**
  Szymborska, W. Poems, new and collected, 1957-1997   **891.8**

Barash, David P.

Homo mysterious   **303.4**
The myth of monogamy   **306.7**

Baratay, Eric
  Zoo: a history of zoological gardens in the West   **590.73**

BARBADOS -- HISTORY
  Stuart, A. Sugar in the Blood   **338.1**
Barbarian Days. Finnegan, W.   **92**
The **barbarous** years. Bailyn, B.   **973.2**
The **Barbary** plague. Chase, M.   **362.1**

Barbash, Tom
  Lutnick, H. On top of the world   **332.6**

Barbassa, Juliana
  Dancing With the Devil in the City of God   **981.53**

BARBECUE COOKING
  Batali, M. Italian grill   **641.5**
  Blonder, G. Meathead   **641.7**
  Byres, T. Smoke   **641.6**
  Carroll, J. Feeding the fire   **641.7**
  Carruthers, J. Eat street   **641.76**
  Cramby, J. Tex-Mex from Scratch   **641.59**
  The essential New York times grilling cookbook   **641.5**
  The grilling book   **641.5**
  Jamison, C. A. The big book of outdoor cooking and entertaining   **641.5**
  Kaminsky, P. Charred & scruffed   **641.7**
  Kaminsky, P. Mallmann on fire   **641.598**
  Lang, A. P. Serious barbecue   **641.5**
  Mackay, J. Franklin barbecue   **641.7**
  Mallmann, F. Seven fires   **641.5**
  Master of the grill   **641.578**
  Neely, P. Down home with the Neelys   **641.5**
  The one true barbecue   **641.5**
  Raichlen, S. The barbecue! bible   **641.5**
  Raichlen, S. Project smoke   **641.6**

BARBECUE COOKING
    See also Outdoor cooking
The **barbecue!** bible. Raichlen, S.   **641.5**

BARBECUING -- SOUTHERN STATES -- HISTORY
  The one true barbecue   **641.5**

Barber, Dan
  The third plate   **641.3**

BARBERING *See* Hair
Barbero, Alessandro
  The Battle   **940.2**

BARBERSHOP (MUSIC)
    See also Songs
Barbie. Capella, M.   **688.722**

BARBIE DOLLS
  Capella, M. Barbie   **688.722**
Barbon, Nicholas, d. 1698
                  About
  Hollis, L. London rising   **942**
Barbour, Ian G.

When science meets religion **261.5**

Barbree, Jay
Neil Armstrong **92**
The **bard.** Crawford, R. **92**

Bard, Elizabeth
About
Bard, E. Lunch in Paris **92**

Bardwell, Sandra
Sewing Basics **746**

Bare bones young adult services. Vaillancourt, R. J. **027.62**

Barefield, Eddie, 1909-1991
About
Dance, S. The world of Count Basie **920**

Barefoot Contessa (East Hampton, N.Y.: Store)
Garten, I. Barefoot Contessa family style **641.5**
Garten, I. Barefoot Contessa, how easy is that? **641.5**
Garten, I. Barefoot in Paris **641**
Make it ahead **641.5**

Barefoot Contessa at home. Garten, I. **641**
Barefoot Contessa family style. Garten, I. **641.5**
Barefoot Contessa, how easy is that? Garten, I. **641.5**
Barefoot in Paris. Garten, I. **641**

Baret, Jeanne, 1740-1807
About
Ridley, G. The discovery of Jeanne Baret **92**

BARGAINING *See* Negotiation

Barilla, James
My Backyard Jungle **577.5**

Barker, Margaret A., 1952-
(jt. auth) Wolfson, E. Audubon birdhouse book **728**

Barker, Teresa
Deak, J. Girls will be girls **649**
(jt. auth) Steiner-Adair, C. The Big Disconnect **303.48**

Barkley, Russell A.
Taking charge of ADHD **618.92**

Barks, Coleman
Rumi: the big red book **891**

Barlett, Donald L.
The betrayal of the American dream **330.973**

Barlow, Julie
Nadeau The story of French **440**
The story of Spanish **460**

Barnavi, Eli
(ed) A Historical atlas of the Jewish people **909**

Barnes, Emm
(jt. auth) Anderson, J. The art of medicine **610**

Barnes, Jane, 1942-
About
Barnes, J. Falling in love with Joseph Smith **92**

Barnes, Julian, 1946-
Keeping an eye open **709.04**
Levels of life **823**

About
Barnes, J. Nothing to be frightened of **92**

Barnett, Catherine
The game of boxes **811**

Barnett, Cynthia
Rain **551.57**

Barnett, Jacob, 1998-
About
Barnett, K. The spark **618.92**

Barnett, Kristine
The spark **618.92**

Barney Ross. Century, D. **92**

Barnham, Keith
The Burning Answer **333.79**

Barnitz, Jacqueline
Twentieth-century art of Latin America **709**

Barnosky, Anthony D.
Dodging extinction **576.8**

Barnouw, David
The diary of Anne Frank: the critical edition **92**

Barnstone, Willis
(ed) The Gnostic Bible **299**

Barnum, P. T. (Phineas Taylor), 1810-1891
About
Saxon, A. H. P. T. Barnum: the legend and the man **338.7**

Barone, Michael
The almanac of American politics 2012 **328**

Baroni, Bill
About
Baroni, B. Fat kid got fit **362.196**

BAROQUE ARCHITECTURE
See also Architecture

BAROQUE ART
See also Art

Barr, James
A line in the sand **956**

Barr, Luke
Provence, 1970 **641.59**

Barr, Nevada
About
Barr, N. Seeking enlightenment--hat by hat **92**

Barr, Niall
Eisenhower's Armies **940.53**

Barr, Patricia
(jt. auth) Wallace, D. Ultimate Star wars

Barr, Roseanne
About
Life stories **920**

Barr, Stephen M.
Modern physics and ancient faith **201**

Barra, Allen
Inventing Wyatt Earp **92**
Yogi Berra **92**

Barratt, David
(ed) Manser, M. H. Critical companion to the Bi-

ble   220.6

Barrenechea, Teresa
The Basque table   641.59

Barrett, Duncan
GI brides   940.53

Barrett, Faith
(ed) Words for the hour   811

Barrett, Justin L.
Born believers   200.1

Barrett, Paul
Dinosaurs   567.9

Barrett, Paul M.
American Islam   920
Law of the jungle   344

Barrett, William
Irrational man   142

BARRIER FREE DESIGN *See* Architecture and
people with disabilities

Barringer, Bruce
Launching a Business   658.1

Barringer, T. J.
Wilton, A. American sublime   759.13

Barrington, Rupert
Life   578.4

BARRISTERS *See* Lawyers

Barron's Educational Series Inc.
(comp) Profiles of American colleges 2015 **378.73**

BARROOMS *See* Bars

Barrow, Cathy
Mrs. Wheelbarrow's practical pantry   641.4

Barrow, John D.
100 essential things you didn't know you didn't
know   510
The book of nothing   111
The constants of nature   530.8
The infinite book   111

Barrow, Mark V.
Nature's ghosts   333.95

Barry, Dan
Bottom of the 33rd   796.357

Barry, Dave, 1947-
You can date boys when you're forty   306.85

Barry, John M.
The great influenza   614.5
Rising tide   977
Roger Williams and the creation of the American
soul   974.5

Barry, Lynda
What it is   741.5

Barry, Marion, 1936-2014
               About
Halberstam, D. The children   323.1

BARS
The Dead Rabbit drinks manual   641.87
Fauchald, N. Death & Co   641.87
Fraioli, J. O. The Canon Cocktail Book   641

Schaap, R. Drinking with men   92
Simonson, R. A proper drink   641.87
Sultan, T. Sunny's nights   641.87

**BARS -- CALIFORNIA -- SAN FRANCISCO --
HISTORY**
Drinking the devil's acre   641.87

Barsanti, Chris
The science fiction movie guide   016

BARTENDING
Arnold, D. Liquid intelligence   641.87
Bar Book   641.87
Conigliaro, T. The cocktail lab   641.87
Fauchald, N. Death & Co   641.87
Hellmich, M. Ultimate bar book   641.8

**BARTENDING -- NEW YORK (STATE) -- NEW
YORK**
Sultan, T. Sunny's nights   641.87

BARTER
        See also Commerce; Economics; Money;
        Subsistence economy; Underground economy

Barth, Karl, 1787-1853
               About
Kung, H. Great Christian thinkers   230

Barthel, Joan
American saint   92

Barthelme, Donald
               About
Daugherty, T. Hiding man   92

Bartholdi, Frédéric Auguste, 1834-1904
               About
Khan, Y. S. Enlightening the world   974.7

Bartholomew, Mel, 1931-2016
All new square foot gardening   635
Square foot gardening high-value veggies   635

Bartiromo, Maria
The weekend that changed Wall Street   330.9

Bartle, Lisa R.
Burgess, M. Reference guide to science fiction,
fantasy, and horror   016

Bartlett's familiar quotations. O'Brien, G.   808.88
Bartlett's Roget's thesaurus. Little, B. &. C. I.   423

Bartlett, Jamie
The Dark Net   302.23

Bartlett, Rosamund
Tolstoy   891.7

Bartlett, Wendy K.
Floating collections   025.2

Bartusiak, Marcia
Black hole   523.8
The day we found the universe   520

Baryshnikov, Mikhail, 1948-
               About
Life stories   920

Barzun, Jacques
From dawn to decadence   940.2

Basbanes, Nicholas A.

Every book its reader 028
On paper 676
Patience & fortitude 002
Bascomb, Neal
Hunting Eichmann 943.086
The new cool 629.8
The winter fortress 940.54
BASEBALL
Barry, D. Bottom of the 33rd 796.357
Baseball: a literary anthology 810
Geist, B. Little League confidential 796.357
Goodwin, D. K. Wait till next year 796.357
Hample, Z. Watching baseball smarter 796.357
Hogan, L. D. Shades of glory 796.357
Kurkjian, T. I'm fascinated by sacrifice flies 796.357
Kurlansky, M. The Eastern stars 796.357
Lewis, M. Moneyball 796.357
Miller, S. The Only Rule Is It Has to Work 796.357
Molina, B. Molina 92
Posnanski, J. The soul of baseball 796.357
Ripken, C. Play baseball the Ripken way 796.357
Ruck, R. Raceball 796.357
Smith, R. Red Smith on baseball 796.357
Thorn, J. Baseball in the Garden of Eden 796.357
Tygiel, J. Baseball's great experiment 796.357
BASEBALL
See also Ball games; Sports
BASEBALL -- BIOGRAPHY
Barra, A. Yogi Berra 92
Biddle, D. R. Tasting freedom 92
Breslin, J. Branch Rickey 92
Bryant, H. The last hero 92
Clavin, T. Roger Maris 92
Creamer, R. W. Babe 92
D'Antonio, M. Forever blue 92
Darling, R. The complete game 92
Fox, W. P. Satchel Paige's America 92
Halberstam, D. The teammates 796
Hirsch, J. S. Willie Mays 92
Kennedy, K. 56 92
Leavy, J. The last boy 92
Maraniss, D. Clemente 92
Ripken, C. The only way I know 92
Ritter, L. S. The glory of their times 920
Robinson, J. I never had it made 92
Robinson, R. Iron horse: Lou Gehrig in his time 92
Stanton, T. Road to Cooperstown 92
Torre, J. The Yankee years 92
Tye, L. Satchel 92
White, B. Uppity 92
BASEBALL -- COACHING
Kettmann, S. Baseball maverick 92
Pennington, B. Billy Martin 92
BASEBALL -- COLLECTORS AND COLLECT-ING.
Wong, S. Smithsonian baseball 796

BASEBALL -- ECONOMIC ASPECTS -- UNIT-ED STATES
Sawchik, T. Big data baseball 796.357
BASEBALL -- GRAPHIC NOVELS
Santiago, W. 21 92
BASEBALL -- HISTORY
Kenny, B. Ahead of the curve 796.357
McGregor, R. K. A Calculus of Color 796.357
BASEBALL -- IOWA -- CLARINDA
Tackett, M. The Baseball Whisperer 796.357
BASEBALL -- PICTORIAL WORKS
Leifer, N. Neil Leifer: Ballet in the dirt 796.357
BASEBALL -- PSYCHOLOGICAL ASPECTS
Svrluga, B. The grind 796.357
BASEBALL -- PUERTO RICO
Molina, B. Molina 92
BASEBALL -- RECORDS
Barry, D. Bottom of the 33rd 796.357
BASEBALL -- UNITED STATES
Bradlee, B. C. The kid 92
BASEBALL -- UNITED STATES -- HISTORY
Russo, F. The Cooperstown chronicles 92
Smith, R. Red Smith on baseball 796.357
Thorn, J. Baseball in the Garden of Eden 796.357
BASEBALL -- UNITED STATES -- MISCELLA-NEA
Kenny, B. Ahead of the curve 796.357
Kurkjian, T. I'm fascinated by sacrifice flies 796.357
BASEBALL CARDS
Jamieson, D. Mint condition 796.357
BASEBALL CLUBS *See* Baseball teams
BASEBALL EXECUTIVES
Auletta, K. Media man 92
Breslin, J. Branch Rickey 92
Bruni, F. Ambling into history: the unlikely odyssey of George W. Bush 973.931
D'Antonio, M. Forever blue 92
Farmer, J. J. The ground truth 973.931
George-Warren, H. Public cowboy no. 1 92
Hersh, S. M. Chain of command 973.931
Lewis, M. Moneyball 796.357
Schlesinger, A. M. War and the American presidency 327.1
White, B. Uppity 92
Woodward, B. Plan of attack 956.7
Woodward, B. State of denial 973.931
Baseball in the Garden of Eden. Thorn, J. 796.357
BASEBALL MANAGERS
Barra, A. Yogi Berra 92
Bissinger, H. G. Three nights in August 796.357
Breslin, J. Branch Rickey 92
Creamer, R. W. Stengel 796.357
Dierker, L. This ain't brain surgery 796
Gay, T. M. Tris Speaker 92
Halberstam, D. The teammates 796
Linn, E. Hitter: the life and turmoils of Ted Wil-

liams 92
Posnanski, J. The soul of baseball 796.357
Torre, J. The Yankee years 92

BASEBALL MANAGERS -- NEW YORK (STATE) -- NEW YORK -- BIOGRAPHY
Billy Martin 92
Pennington, B. Billy Martin 92
Baseball maverick. Kettmann, S. 92

BASEBALL PITCHERS
Passan, J. The Arm 796.357
Rivera, M. The closer 92

BASEBALL PLAYERS
Barra, A. Yogi Berra 92
Bissinger, H. G. Three nights in August 796.357
Bryant, H. The last hero 92
Clavin, T. Roger Maris 92
Cramer, R. B. Joe DiMaggio 796.357
Creamer, R. W. Babe 92
Creamer, R. W. Stengel 796.357
Darling, R. The complete game 92
Dykstra, L. House of nails 796.357
Falkner, D. Great time coming: the life of Jackie Robinson, from baseball to Birmingham 92
Feinstein, J. Where nobody knows your name 796.357
Fox, W. P. Satchel Paige's America 92
Gay, T. M. Tris Speaker 92
Halberstam, D. The teammates 796
Hirsch, J. S. Willie Mays 92
Kennedy, K. 56 92
Knight, M. The best team money can buy 796.357
Leavy, J. The last boy 92
Life stories 920
Linn, E. Hitter: the life and turmoils of Ted Williams 92
Maraniss, D. Clemente 92
Posnanski, J. The soul of baseball 796.357
Ripken, C. The only way I know 92
Robinson, J. I never had it made 92
Robinson, R. Iron horse: Lou Gehrig in his time 92
Stump, A. Cobb 796.357
Torre, J. The Yankee years 92
Tye, L. Satchel 92
Tygiel, J. Baseball's great experiment 796.357
White, B. Uppity 92
Wilson, D. Pudge 92

BASEBALL PLAYERS
See also Athletes

BASEBALL PLAYERS -- BIOGRAPHY
Kennedy, K. Pete Rose 92
Leerhsen, C. Ty Cobb 92
Russo, F. The Cooperstown chronicles 92

BASEBALL PLAYERS -- GRAPHIC NOVELS
Santiago, W. 21 92

BASEBALL PLAYERS -- NEW YORK (STATE) -- NEW YORK -- BIOGRAPHY

Billy Martin 92
Pennington, B. Billy Martin 92

BASEBALL PLAYERS -- UNITED STATES -- BIOGRAPHY
Bradlee, B. C. The kid 92
Dierker, L. This ain't brain surgery 796
Kashatus, W. C. Jackie and Campy 92
Leavy, J. Sandy Koufax 796.357
Leerhsen, C. Ty Cobb 92
Russo, F. The Cooperstown chronicles 92
The **Baseball** Whisperer. Tackett, M. 796.357
Baseball's great experiment. Tygiel, J. 796.357
Baseball: a literary anthology. 810

BASEL ACCORD (1988)
Friedman, J. Engineering the financial crisis 330.9

BASEL II (2004)
Friedman, J. Engineering the financial crisis 330.9

BASEMENTS
Black & Decker Corp. The complete guide to finishing basements 643
The complete guide to finishing basements 643
German, R. Remodeling a basement 643

BASEMENTS -- REMODELING -- AMATEURS' MANUALS
The complete guide to finishing basements 643

BASES (CHEMISTRY)
See also Chemistry
Bashe, Patricia Romanowski, 1949-
Asperger Syndrome 618.92
Bashe, Philip
McFarlane, R. The complete bedside companion 649.8

BASHFULNESS *See* Shyness
BASHFULNESS IN CHILDREN
Fonseca, C. Raising the shy child 649
The **basic** beliefs of Judaism. Epstein, L. J. 296.3
Basic book repair methods. Schechter, A. A. 025.7
The **basic** business library. 016
Basic economics. Sowell, T. 330

BASIC EDUCATION
See also Education
Basic fishing. Bourne, W. 799.1
Basic ideas [series]
Devlin, K. J. The unfinished game 519.2
BASIC LIFE SKILLS *See* Life skills
A **basic** music library. 016

BASIC NEEDS
Corning, P. The fair society 303.3
BASIC RIGHTS *See* Civil rights; Human rights
The **basic** works of Aristotle. Aristotle 888
Basic writings. Heidegger, M. 193
The **basic** writings of C. G. Jung. Jung, C. G. 150.19
Basic writings of Kant. Kant, I. 193
Basic writings of Nietzsche. Nietzsche, F. W. 193
The **basic** writings of Sigmund Freud. 150.19
Basie, Count, 1904-1984

About

Basie, C. Good morning blues: the autobiography
  of Count Basie   92

Dance, S. The world of Count Basie   920

Feather, L. From Satchmo to Miles   920

Murray, A. The blue devils of Nada   780.89

BASKET MAKING

  See also Weaving

BASKETBALL

Blais, M. In these girls, hope is a muscle   796.323

Colton, L. Counting coup   796.323

Davis, S. When March went mad   796.323

Dohrmann, G. Play their hearts out   796.323

Feinstein, J. Last dance   796.323

Feinstein, J. A march to madness   796.323

FreeDarko presents the macrophenomenal pro basketball almanac   796.323

Merlino, D. The hustle   796.323

Reynolds, B. Hope   796.323

Simmons, B. The book of basketball   796.323

Swidey, N. The assist   796.323

Wideman, J. E. Hoop roots   813

BASKETBALL

  See also Ball games; Sports

BASKETBALL -- BIOGRAPHY

Knight, B. Knight: my story   92

Lazenby, R. Jerry West   92

BASKETBALL -- ECONOMIC ASPECTS --
UNITED STATES

Glockner, A. Chasing perfection   796.323

BASKETBALL -- HISTORY

Fury, S. Rise & fire   796.323

McCallum, J. Dream team   796.323

BASKETBALL COACHES -- OKLAHOMA --
BIOGRAPHY

Reeder, L. Dust bowl girls   796.323

BASKETBALL COACHES -- UNITED STATES
-- BIOGRAPHY

Davis, S. Wooden   92

Feinstein, J. The legends club   796.323

BASKETBALL DRAFT

Abrams, J. Boys among men   796.323

BASKETBALL PLAYERS

Abdul-Jabbar, K. On the shoulders of giants   92

Dohrmann, G. Play their hearts out   796.323

Joyner-Kersee, J. A kind of grace   796.42

Kriegel, M. Pistol   92

Lazenby, R. Jerry West   92

BASKETBALL PLAYERS -- UNITED STATES
-- BIOGRAPHY

Lazenby, R. Michael Jordan   92

McCallum, J. Dream team   796.323

Walton, B. Back from the dead   92

Williams, J. Life is not an accident   92

BASKETBALL TEAMS

  See also Basketball; Sports teams

BASKETS

  See also Containers

The **Basque** book.   641.5

BASQUE COOKING

Barrenechea, T. The Basque table   641.59

The Basque book   641.5

Hirigoyen, G. Pintxos   641.8

The **Basque** history of the world. Kurlansky, M.   946

The **Basque** table. Barrenechea, T.   641.59

BASS (FISH)

Greenberg, P. Four fish   333.95

Bass, Diana Butler

Grounded   231

Bass, Ellen

The courage to heal   616.85

Bass, Gary Jonathan, 1969-

The Blood telegram   327.73

Freedom's battle   341.5

Bass, George Fletcher

(ed) Beneath the seven seas   930.1

About

Bass, R. Why I came West   92

Bass, William M.

Death's acre   614

Bassetti, Amanda

Arm knitting   746.43

BASSISTS

Lees, G. You can't steal a gift   781.65

Bastards of Utopia. Razsa, M.   303.48

Bastianich, Joseph

Healthy pasta   641.82

Bastianich, Lidia

Lidia cooks from the heart of Italy   641.5

Lidia's Italian-American kitchen   641.59

Lidia's commonsense Italian cooking   641.59

Lidia's family table   641.5

Lidia's favorite recipes   641.594

Lidia's mastering the art of Italian cuisine   641.594

BASTOGNE, BATTLE OF *See* Ardennes (France),
  Battle of the, 1944-1945

Baszile, Jennifer, 1969-

About

Baszile, J. The Black girl next door   92

BAT MITZVAH

  See also Judaism -- Customs and practices

Batali, Mario, 1960-

Italian grill   641.5

About

Buford, B. Heat   641.5

America--farm to table   641.597

Mario Batali Big American cookbook   641.597

Bate, Jonathan

John Clare: a biography   92

Soul of the age   822.3

Bates, Edward, 1793-1869

About

Goodwin, D. K.   Team of rivals   **92**

BATHROOMS

See also Rooms

BATHS

See also Cleanliness; Hygiene; Physical therapy

Bathurst, Bella

The wreckers   **910.4**

BATIK

See also Dyes and dyeing

Batker, David K.

De Graaf, J.   What's the economy for, anyway?   **330.9**

BATMAN (FICTIONAL CHARACTER)

O'Neil, D.   Batman unauthorized   **741.5**

Batman unauthorized. O'Neil, D.   **741.5**

BATS

See also Mammals

BATTERED WIVES *See* Abused women

BATTERED WOMEN *See* Abused women

BATTERIES, ELECTRIC *See* Electric batteries; Storage batteries

Battilana, Jessica

(jt. auth) Fernald, A.   Home cooked   **641.5**

(jt. auth) Phan, C.   Vietnamese home cooking   **641.59**

Battista, Maggie

Food gift love   **642**

The **Battle**. Barbero, A.   **940.2**

Battle at Bull Run. Davis, W. C.   **973.7**

Battle at sea. Grant, R. G.   **359**

BATTLE CASUALTIES -- HISTORY

Stephenson, M.   The last full measure   **305.9**

Battle cries and lullabies. De Pauw, L. G.   **355**

Battle cry of freedom. McPherson, J. M.   **973.7**

The **battle** for America, 2008. Balz, D. J.   **973.932**

The **battle** for God. Armstrong, K.   **200.9**

The **battle** for Rome. Katz, R.   **940.54**

The **battle** for Social Security. Altman, N. J.   **368.4**

Battle hymn of the tiger mother. Chua, A.   **306.874**

The **battle** of Bretton Woods. Steil, B.   **339.5**

Battle of Britain. Holland, J.   **940.54**

The **Battle** of the Atlantic. Dimbleby, J.   **940.54**

BATTLE OF THE BULGE *See* Ardennes (France), Battle of the, 1944-1945

The **Battle** of the Little Bighorn. Sandoz, M.   **973.8**

The **Battle** of Versailles. Givhan, R.   **746.9**

BATTLEFIELDS

See also Battles

BATTLES

Hanson, V. D.   Carnage and culture   **904**

Keegan, J.   Fields of battle   **355.009**

Romesha, C. L.   Red platoon   **958.1**

BATTLES

See also Military art and science; Military history; War

Batuman, Elif

The possessed   **891.7**

Batykefer, Erinn

(ed) The artist's library   **021.2**

Baudelaire, Charles

Les fleurs du mal   **841**

Poems   **841**

Bauer, Jeni Britton

Jeni's splendid ice creams at home   **641.8**

Bauer, Juli

(jt. auth) Bryant, G.   The paleo kitchen   **641.5**

Bauer, Susan Wise

The story of Western science   **509**

Baughman, Judith

(ed) Fitzgerald, F. S.   A life in letters   **813**

BAUHAUS

Gropius, W.   The new architecture and the Bauhaus   **724**

Weber, N. F.   The Bauhaus group   **920**

BAUHAUS -- INFLUENCE

Wolfe, T.   From Bauhaus to our house   **720.9**

The **Bauhaus** group. Weber, N. F.   **920**

Baum, Dan

Gun guys   **683.4**

Nine lives   **976.3**

Bauman, Jeff

About

Witter, B.   Stronger   **92**

Baumann, Thea

It's all easy   **641.5**

Baumeister, Theodore

(ed) Marks' standard handbook for mechanical engineers   **621**

Baumgarten, Linda

Four centuries of quilts   **746.46**

Baur, Gene

Farm Sanctuary   **179**

Bausch, Paul

Dornfest, R.   Google hacks   **025.04**

BAVARIA (GERMANY) -- DESCRIPTION AND TRAVEL

DK Eyewitness Munich & the Bavarian Alps   **914.336**

Bawer, Bruce

Surrender   **297**

The victims' revolution   **320**

Baxter, Angus

In search of your European roots   **929**

Baxter, John, 1939-

The most beautiful walk in the world   **914**

The perfect meal   **641.59**

About

Baxter, J.   Five nights in Paris   **914.4**

BAY VIEW (MILWAUKEE, WIS.) -- HISTORY -- 20TH CENTURY

Strang, D. A. Worse than the devil   345
**BAYESIAN STATISTICAL DECISION THEO-
RY**
Silver, N. The signal and the noise   **519.5**
Bayless, Deann Groen
Bayless, R. Mexico: one plate at a time **641.597**
Bayless, R. Fiesta at Rick's   **641.5**
Bayless, R. Rick Bayless's Mexican kitchen **641.59**
Bayless, Rick, 1953-
Authentic Mexican   **641.597**
Fiesta at Rick's   **641.5**
Mexican everyday   **641.597**
Mexico: one plate at a time   **641.597**
More Mexican everyday   **641.597**
Rick Bayless's Mexican kitchen   **641.59**
Bayley, John, 1925-2015
                About
Bayley, J. Elegy for Iris   823
Bayoumi, Moustafa
How does it feel to be a problem?   **305.8**
Bazelon, Emily, 1971-
Sticks and stones   **302.34**
Bazin, Nancy Topping
(ed) Conversations with Nadine Gordimer 823
BCIS (BRAIN-COMPUTER INTERFACES) *See*
Brain-computer interfaces
Beach, Hugh
A year in Lapland   **948.97**
Beach, Sylvia
                About
The letters of Sylvia Beach   92
Beacham's encyclopedia of popular fiction. 809
Beaches. Malin, G.   **779.37**
BEACHES
Dean, C. Against the tide   **333.91**
Malin, G. Beaches   **779.37**
Van der Meer, A. Coastal living beach house hap-
py   747
BEACHES
    See also Seashore
Beachy, Robert
Gay Berlin   **306.76**
Bead metamorphosis. Kan, L.   **745.594**
The **beader's** color palette. Deeb, M. **745.594**
BEADS
Geary, T. F. The illustrated bead bible **745.594**
Michaels, C. F. Teach yourself visually jewelry
making & beading   **745.59**
BEADS
    See also Decoration and ornament
Beadweaving master class [series]
DeCoster, M. Marcia DeCoster's beaded opu-
lence   **739.27**
BEADWORK
DeCoster, M. Marcia DeCoster's beaded opu-
lence   **739.27**

Deeb, M. The beader's color palette   **745.594**
Geary, T. F. The illustrated bead bible **745.594**
Kan, L. Bead metamorphosis   **745.594**
Katz, A. Seed bead chic   **745.594**
Michaels, C. F. Teach yourself visually jewelry
making & beading   **745.59**
BEADWORK
    See also Handicraft
BEADWORK -- PATTERNS
Katz, A. Seed bead chic   **745.594**
Wiseman, J. Jill Wiseman's beautiful beaded
ropes   **745.594**
BEAGLE EXPEDITION (1831-1836)
Darwin, C. The Beagle letters   **576.8**
Darwin, C. The voyage of the Beagle   **508**
The **Beagle** letters. Darwin, C.   **576.8**
Beah, Ishmael
                About
Beah, I. A long way gone   92
Beaks, bones, and bird songs. Lederer, R. J. **598**
Beale Street Dynasty. Lauterbach, P. **976.8**
Beall, Julianne
(ed) Dewey decimal classification and relative in-
dex   **025.4**
Beam, Alex
American crucifixion   **289.3**
A great idea at the time   **973.91**
Beam, Cris
To the end of June   **362.73**
Beane, Billy, 1962-
                About
Lewis, M. Moneyball   **796.357**
**BEANIE BABIES (TRADEMARK) -- COLLEC-
TORS AND COLLECTING -- HISTORY**
Bissonnette, Z. The great Beanie Baby bub-
ble   **338.7**
BEAR, STEARNS & CO. INC.
Kelly, K. Street fighters   **332.6**
Beard on bread. Beard, J.   **641.8**
Beard on food.   **641.5**
Beard, Amanda
                About
Beard, A. In the water they can't see you cry **797.2**
Beard, James, 1903-1985
The armchair James Beard   **641.5**
Beard on bread   **641.8**
Beard on food   **641.5**
The fireside cook book   **641.5**
James Beard's American cookery   **641.5**
(jt. auth) Rodgers, R. The essential James Beard
cookbook   **641.597**
                About
Barr, L. Provence, 1970   **641.59**
Beard, Jocelyn
(ed) The Ultimate audition book   **808.82**
Beard, Mary, 1955-

Confronting the classics   **930**

The fires of Vesuvius   **937**

SPQR   **937**

Beard, Peter H. (Peter Hill), 1938-

The end of the game   **967.6**

Bearden, Romare, 1914-1988

About

Ellison, R. The collected essays of Ralph Ellison   **814**

Ellison, R. Going to the territory   **818**

Murray, A. The blue devils of Nada   **780.89**

BEARINGS (MACHINERY)

See also Machinery

Bearman, Peter

(ed) After the fall   **974.7**

BEARS

See also Mammals

Bearzi, Maddalena

Beautiful minds   **599.8**

Beasley, Sandra

About

Beasley, S. Don't kill the birthday girl   **92**

BEASTS *See* Animals

The **Beat** generation.   **810**

BEAT GENERATION

The Beat generation   **810**

Beat poets   **811**

Kerouac, J. Selected letters, 1957-1969   **813**

Miles, B. Call Me Burroughs   **92**

Morgan, B. I celebrate myself   **92**

Morgan, B. The typewriter is holy   **810**

Sandison, D. Neal Cassady   **92**

Spontaneous mind   **811**

BEAT GENERATION

See also American literature; Bohemianism

BEAT GENERATION -- BIOGRAPHY

Johnson, J. The voice is all   **818**

BEAT GENERATION -- CORRESPONDENCE

Burroughs, W. S. Rub out the words   **813**

Beat poets.   **811**

BEATBOXING

See also Popular music; Vocal music

BEATLES

Margotin, P. All the Songs   **781.66**

Starr, R. Photograph   **782.4**

Thomson, G. George Harrison   **92**

BEATLES

See also Bands (Music)

The **Beatles** anthology.   **782.421**

The **Beatles:** the biography. Spitz, B.   **920**

BEATNIKS *See* Beat generation

Beatrix Potter. Lear, L. J.   **92**

BEATS *See* Beat generation

Beattie, Melody

Beyond codependency   **616.86**

Codependent no more   **616.86**

Beattie, Owen

(jt. auth) Geiger, J. Frozen in time   **919**

Beatty, Michael A.

County name origins of the United States   **917**

Beatty, Scott

The DC Comics encyclopedia   **741.5**

Beatty, Warren, 1937-

About

Biskind, P. Star   **92**

Beaty, H. Wayne

(ed) Standard Handbook for Electrical Engineers   **621.3**

Beaufort, Margaret, Countess of Richmond and Derby, 1443-1509

About

Gristwood, S. Blood sisters   **942.04**

The **Beaulieu** encyclopedia of the automobile.   **629.222**

Beaumarchais. Lever, M.   **92**

Beaumarchais, Pierre Augustin Caron de, 1732-1799

About

Lever, M. Beaumarchais   **92**

Paul, J. R. Unlikely allies   **973.3**

Beaumont, Stephen

The world atlas of beer   **641.2**

BEAUTIFICATION OF LANDSCAPE *See* Landscape protection

Beautiful. Shearer, S. M.   **92**

Beautiful & pointless. Orr, D.   **809.1**

The **beautiful** and the damned. Deb, S.   **954.05**

Beautiful bracelets by hand. Gedeon, J.   **745.594**

The **beautiful** cigar girl. Stashower, D.   **364.152**

Beautiful eyes. Austin, P.   **92**

A **beautiful** mess happy handmade home. Chapman, E.   **747**

Beautiful minds. Bearzi, M.   **599.8**

The **beautiful** music all around us. Wade, S.   **781.62**

The **beautiful** soul of John Woolman, apostle of abolition. Slaughter, T. P.   **92**

Beautiful thing. Faleiro, S.   **792.7**

The **beauty.** Hirshfield, J.   **811**

BEAUTY *See* Aesthetics

The **beauty** and the sorrow. Englund, P.   **940.3**

BEAUTY CONTEST WINNERS

Schiller, L. Perfect murder, perfect town   **364.15**

BEAUTY CONTESTS

See also Contests

The **beauty** myth. Wolf, N.   **305.4**

The **beauty** of the husband. Carson, A.   **811**

BEAUTY SHOPS

Rodriguez, D. Kabul Beauty School   **305.4**

BEAUTY SHOPS

See also Business enterprises

BEAUTY, PERSONAL

Berg, R. Beauty: the new basics   **646.7**

DuPriest, L. Natural beauty   **646.7**
Essence total makeover   **646.7**
Halbreich, B. I'll drink to that   **92**
Thomas, M. The French beauty solution   **646.7**
Volk, P. Shocked   **92**
BEAUTY, PERSONAL *See* Personal appearance;
  Personal grooming
BEAUTY, PERSONAL -- SOCIAL ASPECTS
  Whitefield-Madrano, A. Face value   **111.85**
Beauty: the new basics. Berg, R.   **646.7**
Beauvoir, Simone de, 1908-1986
  The second sex   **305.4**

About

  Bair, D. Simone de Beauvoir   **848**
Beavan, Colin
  No impact man   **333.72**
BEAVERS
    See also Furbearing animals; Mammals
Because I said so.   **306.8**
Beccaloni, Jan
  Arachnids   **595.4**
Bechdel, Alison, 1960-

About

  Bechdel, A. Are you my mother?   **741.5**
  Bechdel, A. Fun home   **741.5**
Beck, Astrid B.
  (ed) Eerdmans dictionary of the Bible   **220.3**
Beck, Derek W.
  The war before independence, 1775-1776   **973.3**
Beck, Simone
  Child, J. Mastering the art of French cooking **641.5**
Beck, Warren A.
  Historical atlas of the American West   **911**
Becker, Annette
  Audoin-Rouzeau, S. 14-18, understanding the
    Great War   **940.3**
Becker, Carl
  The Declaration of Independence   **973.3**
Becker, Daniel Levin
  Many subtle channels   **840.9**
Becker, Elizabeth
  Overbooked   **338.4**
Becker, Ethan
  Rombauer, I. v. S. Joy of cooking   **641.5**
Becker, Holly
  Decorate   **747**
Becker, Jasper
  The Chinese   **951.05**
Becker, Jo
  Forcing the spring   **346.73**
Becker, Josh, 1958-
  The more of less   **241.68**
Becker, Marion Rombauer
  Rombauer, I. v. S. Joy of cooking   **641.5**
Becker, Suzy

About

Becker, S. I had brain surgery, what's your ex-
  cuse?   **92**
Becker-Phelps, Leslie
  Love   **646.7**
Beckert, Sven
  Empire of cotton   **338.4**
Beckett, Samuel, 1906-1989
  Collected poems in English and French   **841**
  Dramatic works   **842**

About

  Bloom, H. The Western canon   **809**
  Gordon, L. G. The world of Samuel Beckett, 1906-
    1946   **848**
  Playwrights at work   **812**
  Samuel Beckett's Waiting for Godot   **842**
Beckett, Wendy
  Sister Wendy's American collection   **709**
Becoming a graphic & digital designer. Heller,
  S.   **741.6**
Becoming a supple leopard. Cordoza, G.   **613.7**
Becoming a tiger. McCarthy, S.   **591.5**
Becoming Belafonte. Smith, J. E.   **92**
Becoming Dr. Q. Quiñones-Hinojosa, A.   **92**
Becoming Elektra. Houghton, M.   **781.64**
Becoming Jewish. Reuben, S. C.   **296.7**
Becoming Justice Blackmun. Greenhouse, L.   **92**
Becoming King. Jackson, T.   **92**
Becoming Madison. Signer, M.   **92**
Becoming Mona Lisa. Sassoon, D.   **759**
Becoming Nicole. Nutt, A. E.   **306.76**
Becoming Queen Victoria. Williams, K.   **92**
Becoming Ray Bradbury. Eller, J. R.   **92**
Becoming Steve Jobs. Tetzeli, R.   **92**
Becoming vegan. Davis, B.   **613.2**
Becoming Victoria. Vallone, L.   **941.08**
Becoming Wise. Tippett, K.   **158.1**
BED AND BREAKFAST ACCOMMODATIONS
    See also Hotels and motels
A **bed** for the night. Rieff, D.   **361.2**
Beddall, Catherine
  The magic of gingerbread   **641.86**
Bede, Pam Nisevich
  The Runner's world big book of marathon and half-
    marathon training   **796.425**
Bednar, Nancy
  The encyclopedia of sewing machine tech-
    niques   **646.2**
Bedor, Deborah
  Getting in by standing out   **371**
BEDOUINS
  Lawrence, T. E. Seven pillars of wisdom   **940.4**
BEDOUINS
    See also Arabs
BEDSPREADS
    See also Interior design
BEDTIME

See also Night; Sleep

The **bee** book.   595.799

BEE CULTURE *See* Beekeeping

BEE HIVES *See* Beehives

BEE HOUSES *See* Beehives

The **bee-friendly** garden. Frey, K. 595.799

Beecher, Henry Ward, 1813-1887
About
Applegate, D. The most famous man in America 92

BEEF
    See also Meat

BEEF CATTLE
Lewis, C. The illustrated guide to cows   636.2

BEEHIVES
Flottum, K. The backyard beekeeper   638.1

BEEHIVES
    See also Animal housing

The **beekeeper's** handbook. Sammataro, D. 638.1

The **beekeeper's** lament. Nordhaus, H.   638

BEEKEEPING
The bee book   595.799

Ellis, H. Sweetness & light   595.7

Flottum, K. The backyard beekeeper   638.1

Jacobsen, R. Fruitless fall   638

McKibben, B. Oil and Honey   363.7

Nordhaus, H. The beekeeper's lament   638

Sammataro, D. The beekeeper's handbook 638.1

BEEKEEPING
    See also Agriculture

BEEKEEPING -- HANDBOOKS, MANUALS, ETC
Sammataro, D. The beekeeper's handbook 638.1

The **Beekman** 1802 heirloom dessert cookbook. Ridge, B.   641.5

Beeman, Richard
Plain, honest men   342

Beeman, Richard R.
Our lives, our fortunes and our sacred honor 973.3

Been there, done that. Roberts, D.   92

BEER
Alworth, J. The beer bible   641.2

Beaumont, S. The world atlas of beer   641.2

Beer bites   641.5

Huckelbridge, D. The United States of beer 641.23

BEER
    See also Alcoholic beverages

BEER -- UNITED STATES
Acitelli, T. The audacity of hops   641.2

The **beer** bible. Alworth, J.   641.2

Beer bites.   641.5

BEER INDUSTRY -- UNITED STATES -- HISTORY
Knoedelseder, W. Bitter brew   338.7

BEER MAKING *See* Brewing

Beers, Diane L.
For the prevention of cruelty   179

BEES
Ellis, H. Sweetness & light   595.7

Frey, K. The bee-friendly garden 595.799

Hubbell, S. A book of bees   638

Jacobsen, R. Fruitless fall   638

Nordhaus, H. The beekeeper's lament   638

Seeley, T. D. Honeybee democracy 595.799

BEES
    See also Insects

BEES -- HOUSING *See* Beehives

Beethoven. Suchet, J.   92

Beethoven. Swafford, J.   92

Beethoven, Ludwig van, 1770-1827
About
Lockwood, L. Beethoven: the music and the life   780

Morris, E. Beethoven: the universal composer 92

Rosen, C. The classical style   780.9

Sachs, H. The Ninth   785

Schonberg, H. C. The great pianists   920

Suchet, J. Beethoven   92

Swafford, J. Beethoven   92

Beethoven: the music and the life. Lockwood, L.   780

Beethoven: the universal composer. Morris, E. 92

The **Beetlebung** Farm cookbook.   641

BEETLES
Evans, A. V. An inordinate fondness for beetles   595.7

BEETLES
    See also Insects

Beetz, Kirk H.
(ed) Beacham's encyclopedia of popular fiction 809

Beevor, Antony, 1946-
Ardennes 1944   940.54

D-day   940.54

The fall of Berlin 1945   940.54

The Second World War   940.54

Beezley, William H.
(ed) The Oxford history of Mexico   972

Before amen. Lucado, M.   248.3

Before happiness. Achor, S.   158

Before the dawn. Wade, N.   599.93

Before the deluge. Chetham, D.   951

Before the fallout. Preston, D.   355.8

Before the lights go out. Koerth-Baker, M. 333.79

Before they pass away.   305.8

Before Victoria. Denlinger, E. C.   920

Before you buy! Corbett, M.   643

The **beggar's** opera. Gay, J.   822

BEGGING
    See also Poor

Begin again. Silverman, K.   92

Begin, Menachem, 1913-1992
About
Menachem Begin   956.940

Wright, L. Thirteen Days in September **956.04**

A **beginner's** guide to 3D printing. Rigsby, M. **621.9**

The **Beginner's** photography guide. Gatcum, C. **770**

The **beginning** of infinity. Deutsch, D. **501**

The **beginning** of wisdom. Kass, L. **222**

Beginnings. Foote, H. **812**

Begley, Adam
Updike **92**

BEHAVIOR *See* Animal behavior; Human behavior

BEHAVIOR -- PERSONAL NARRATIVES
Montross, C. Falling into the fire **92**

BEHAVIOR DISORDERS IN CHILDREN -- PREVENTION
Dunckley, V. L. Reset your child's brain **004.67**

BEHAVIOR EVOLUTION
Maestripieri, D. Games primates play **155.7**

BEHAVIOR GENETICS
Clark, W. R. Are we hardwired? **155.7**
Kean, S. The violinist's thumb **572.8**
Smoller, J. The other side of normal **591.5**
Weiner, J. Time, love, memory **591.5**

BEHAVIOR GENETICS
See also Genetics; Psychology

BEHAVIOR IN ORGANIZATIONS *See* Organizational behavior

BEHAVIOR MODIFICATION
Goldsmith, M. Triggers **155.2**

BEHAVIOR MODIFICATION
See also Applied psychology; Human behavior; Psychology of learning

BEHAVIOR OF CHILDREN *See* Child psychology; Children -- Conduct of life; Etiquette for children and teenagers

BEHAVIOR OF TEENAGERS *See* Adolescent psychology; Etiquette for children and teenagers; Teenagers -- Conduct of life

BEHAVIOR PROBLEMS (CHILDREN) *See* Emotionally disturbed children

BEHAVIOR, HELPING *See* Helping behavior

BEHAVIORAL ASSESSMENT
Rudder, C. Dataclysm **155.2**

BEHAVIORISM
Skinner, B. F. About behaviorism **150.19**

BEHAVIORISM
See also Human behavior; Psychology; Psychophysiology

BEHAVIORISTIC PSYCHOLOGY *See* Behaviorism

Behind my eyes. Lee **811**

Behind the beautiful forevers. Boo, K. **305.5**

Behind the Berkshire Hathaway curtain. Chan, R. W. **658.4**

Behind the Mask. Dennison, M. **92**

Behind the palace doors. Farquhar, M. **941**

Behind the screen. Mann, W. J. **791.43**

Behnke, Robert J.
Trout and salmon of North America **597**

The **beholder's** eye. **814**

Behr, Edward
The Food and Wine of France **641.5**

Beier, Ulli
(ed) The Penguin book of modern African poetry **896**

BEIJING (CHINA)
Meyer, M. J. The last days of old Beijing **951**

Beilock, Sian
Choke **153.9**
How the body knows its mind **153.7**

Beinfeld, Solon
(ed) Comprehensive Yiddish-English Dictionary **439**

BEING *See* Ontology

Being a Beast. Foster, C. **591.5**
Being and nothingness. Sartre, J. P. **142**
Being and time. Heidegger, M. **111**
Being Jewish. Goldman, A. L. **296.4**
Being mortal. Gawande, A. **362.17**
Being Nixon. Thomas, E. **92**
Being wrong. Schulz, K. **153**

Beisner, Robert L.
(ed) American foreign relations since 1600 **016**

Bekoff, Marc
Wild justice **591.5**
(ed) Encyclopedia of animal behavior **591.5**
Goodall, J. The ten trusts **333.95**

Belafonte, Harry, 1927-
About
Belafonte, H. My song **92**
Gates, H. L. Thirteen ways of looking at a black man **920.71**
Smith, J. E. Becoming Belafonte **92**

Belfiore, Michael
The department of mad scientists **355**

BELGIUM -- COLONIES
Hochschild, A. King Leopold's ghost **967.5**

BELIEF AND DOUBT
Barrett, J. L. Born believers **200.1**
Hecht, J. M. Doubt: a history **121**
Nasr, A. A. My Isl@m **297.09**
Shermer, M. The believing brain **153.4**
Shermer, M. Why people believe weird things **001.9**
This I believe **170**
This I believe II **170**

BELIEF AND DOUBT
See also Philosophy; Theory of knowledge

BELIEF AND DOUBT -- POETRY
Pankey, E. Trace **811**

Belief beyond boundaries. **209**
Beliefs and blasphemies. Adair, V. H. **811**
Believer. Axelrod, D. **92**
Believer, beware. **200.9**

The **believing** brain. Shermer, M.   **153.4**

Believing is seeing. Morris, E.   **770.9**

BELL TELEPHONE LABORATORIES

Gertner, J. The idea factory   **384**

Bell, Alexander Graham, 1847-1922

About

Gray, C. Reluctant genius   **92**

Lepore, J. A is for American   **306.44**

Millard, C. The destiny of the republic   **973.8**

Shulman, S. The telephone gambit   **621.3**

Bell, Anne Olivier

(ed) Woolf, V. A moment's liberty: the shorter diary   **92**

Bell, Dana

(comp) Smithsonian atlas of world aviation **629.13**

Bell, Eric Temple

Men of mathematics   **920**

Bell, Gertrude Margaret Lowthian, 1868-1926

About

Howell, G. Gertrude Bell   **92**

Wallach, J. Desert queen   **956**

Bell, Ian

Once upon a time   **92**

Bell, Jim, 1965-

The interstellar age   **919**

The space book   **523.1**

Bell, Julian

Van Gogh   **92**

Bell, Laura, 1954-

About

Bell, L. Claiming ground   **92**

Bell, Madison Smartt

Toussaint Louverture   **92**

Bell, Suzanne

Encyclopedia of forensic science   **363.2**

Librarian's guide to online searching   **025.04**

Bell-Scott, Patricia

The firebrand and the First Lady   **92**

Bellamy, Andrea

Small-space vegetable gardens   **635**

Bellamy, Charles L.

Evans, A. V. An inordinate fondness for beetles   **595.7**

Bellamy, Richard

About

Stein, J. E. Eye of the sixties   **92**

Belle. Byrne, P.   **92**

Belle, Dido Elizabeth, 1761-1804

About

Byrne, P. Belle   **92**

Bellec, Francois

Unknown lands   **910.4**

Beller, Thomas

J.D. Salinger   **92**

BELLES LETTRES *See* Literature

BELLEVUE HOSPITAL

Manheimer, E. Twelve patients   **362.11**

Belliveau, Denis

In the footsteps of Marco Polo   **915**

Bellos, Alex

Here's looking at Euclid   **513**

Bellow. Atlas, J.   **813**

Bellow, Saul, 1915-2005

About

Atlas, J. Bellow   **813**

Bellow, S. Saul Bellow   **92**

Langer, L. L. Admitting the Holocaust   **940.53**

Leader, Z. The Life of Saul Bellow   **92**

BELLS

See also Musical instruments

The **bells** in their silence. Gorra, M. E.   **943**

BELLY DANCING

Soffee, A. T. Snake hips   **793.3**

BELLY DANCING

See also Dance

Belonging. Davis, D.   **821**

Belonging. Hooks, B.   **92**

Beloof, Douglas E.

Victims' rights   **345.73**

Belozerskaya, Marina

The Medici giraffe   **636**

BELTS AND BELTING

See also Machinery

Belva Lockwood. Norgren, J.   **92**

Belzoni. Noël Hume, I.   **92**

Belzoni, Giovanni Battista, 1778-1823

About

Noël Hume, I. Belzoni   **92**

Ben Jelloun, Tahar

Islam explained   **297**

Ben-Barak, Idan

The invisible kingdom   **579**

Benanav, Michael

Men of salt   **916**

Bend, not break. Ping Fu   **92**

Bender, Michele

(jt. auth) Blum, S. Your immune system recovery plan   **616.97**

(jt. auth) Massey, L. Curly girl   **646.7**

Bender, Richard W.

Bountiful bonsai   **635.9**

Bender, Steve

The New Southern Living Garden Book   **635.9**

Bendersky, Jorge

DIY dog grooming, from puppy cuts to best in show   **636.7**

Beneath blossom rain. Grange, K.   **915**

Beneath the sands of Egypt. Ryan, D. P.   **92**

Beneath the seven seas.   **930.1**

Beneath the surface. Hargrove, J.   **599.53**

Benedict XVI, Pope, 1927-

Jesus of Nazareth. part two   **232.9**

Pope Francis among the wolves 282
Benedict, Jeff
Little pink house 343
QB 92
The System 796.332
Benedict, Saint, Abbot of Monte Cassino
About
Butcher, C. A. Man of blessing 271
BENEFICIAL INSECTS
Gardiner, M. M. Good garden bugs 635
Walliser, J. Attracting beneficial bugs to your garden 628.9
BENEFICIAL INSECTS
See also Economic zoology; Insects
Benet's reader's encyclopedia. 803
Benfey, Christopher E. G.
A summer of hummingbirds 920
Benforado, Adam
Unfair 364.3
Benford, Gregory
Popular mechanics magazine. The wonderful future that never was 609
Benga, Ota
About
Newkirk, P. Spectacle 92
BENGALI LANGUAGE
See also Indian languages; Language and languages
Benjamin Britten. Powell, N. 92
Benjamin Franklin. Isaacson, W. 92
Benjamin Franklin's numbers. Pasles, P. C. 510
Benjamin Harrison. Calhoun, C. W. 92
Benjamin, Arthur
The Magic of Math 510
Benjamin, Kate
(jt. auth) Galaxy, J. Catification 636
Bennett, Alan
The history boys 822
Bennett, Alexander C.
Kendo 796.86
Bennett, Denise Beaubien
(ed) Guide to reference in medicine and health 025.06
Bennett, James Gordon, 1841-1918
About
Sides, H. In the kingdom of ice 910.4
Bennett, Jeff
The complete snowboarder 796.9
Benson, Herbert
The relaxation response 155.9
Benson, Kathleen
Haskins, J. African American religious leaders 920
Benson, Michael
Cosmigraphics 523.1
Far out 778.3
Bentley, Elizabeth Petty

Directory of family associations 929
The genealogist's address book 929
Bentley, Eric
The life of the drama 809
Bentley, G. E.
The stranger from paradise: a biography of William Blake 821
Benton, Charlotte
(ed) Art deco 1910-1939 709.04
Benton, Maya
(ed) Roman vishniac rediscovered 779.092
Benton, Thomas Hart, 1782-1858
About
Kennedy, J. F. Profiles in courage 920
Benton, Thomas Hart, 1889-1975
About
Adams, H. Tom and Jack 92
Benton, Tim
(ed) Art deco 1910-1939 709.04
BENTONVILLE (N.C.), BATTLE OF, 1865
Davis, B. Sherman's march 973.7
Benyus, Janine M., 1958-
The secret language of animals 591.5
Benzer, Seymour, 1921-2007
About
Weiner, J. Time, love, memory 591.5
BEQUESTS See Gifts; Inheritance and succession; Wills
Beranbaum, Rose Levy
The baking Bible 641.81
The cake bible 641.8
Berard, G. Lynn
Science and technology resources 025.5
Berberova, Nina
About
Fraser, K. Ornament and silence 809
Bercovitch, Sacvan
(ed) The Cambridge history of American literature 810
Berdik, Chris
Mind over mind 153.4
BEREAVEMENT
Aitkenhead, D. All at sea 92
Alexander, E. The light of the world 92
Barnes, J. Levels of life 823
The Book of eulogies 808.8
Brizendine, J. Stunned by grief 248
Brock-Broido, L. Stay, Illusion 811
Doka, K. J. Grief is a journey 155.9
Dresser, N. Saying goodbye to someone you love 155.9
Edelman, H. Motherless daughters 155.9
Edelman, H. Motherless mothers 155.9
Emswiler, M. A. Guiding your child through grief 155.9
Gilbert, S. M. Death's door 155.9

Hodes, M. Mourning Lincoln   **973.7**
Jamison, K. R. Nothing was the same   **92**
Levy, N. To begin again   **296.7**
McCracken, E. An exact replica of a figment of my imagination   **92**
Oates, J. C. A widow's story   **92**
O'Rourke, M. The long goodbye   **92**
Rasmussen, M. Black aperture   **811**
Remembrances and celebrations   **808.8**
Roiphe, A. R. Epilogue   **92**
Rosenblatt, R. Making toast   **92**
Sheeler, J. Final salute   **956.7**
Sife, W. The loss of a pet   **155.9**
Strayed, C. Wild   **92**

BEREAVEMENT
   See also Emotions

BEREAVEMENT -- PERSONAL NARRATIVES
Ilse, S. The prenatal bombshell   **618.3**

BEREAVEMENT -- PSYCHOLOGICAL ASPECTS
Levy, A. The orphaned adult   **152.4**
Smith, C. B. The rules of inheritance   **616.99**

Berebitsky, Julie
Sex and the office   **331.4**

Berenbaum, Michael
(ed) Encyclopaedia Judaica   **296**
(ed) The Holocaust and history   **940.53**
The world must know   **940.53**

Berendt, John
The city of falling angels   **945**
Midnight in the garden of good and evil   **975.8**

Berg, A. Scott
Kate remembered   **92**
Wilson   **92**

Berg, Rona
Beauty: the new basics   **646.7**

Berg, Ryan, 1974-
      About
Berg, R. No house to call my home   **362.786**

Berg, Scott W.
38 nooses   **973.7**

Bergen, Candice, 1946-
      About
Bergen, C. A fine romance   **92**

Bergen, Peter L.
The longest war   **909.83**
Manhunt   **363.325**

BERGEN-BELSEN (GERMANY: CONCENTRATION CAMP)
   See also Concentration camps

Berger, James
(ed) Keller, H. The story of my life   **92**

Berger, Joel
The better to eat you with   **591.5**

Berger, Jonah
Invisible Influence   **302.13**

Berger, Joseph
The pious ones   **973**

Berger, Karen
America's great hiking trails   **796.51**

Berger, Lauren
All work, no pay   **650.14**

Berger, Lisa
Goldman, B. Brain fitness   **153.1**

Berger, William
Puccini without excuses   **92**
Verdi with a vengeance   **782.1**

Berger, Zackary
Talking to your doctor   **610.69**

Bergman, Ingrid, 1915-1982
      About
Spoto, D. Notorious   **92**
Thomson, D. Ingrid Bergman   **92**

Bergner, Daniel
The other side of desire   **306.7**
What Do Women Want?   **305**

Bergreen, Laurence
Capone   **364.1**
Marco Polo   **92**
Over the edge of the world   **910.4**

Bergson, Henri, 1859-1941
      About
Durant, W. J. The story of philosophy   **109**
Russell, B. A history of Western philosophy   **109**

Berkeley, George, 1685-1753
      About
Russell, B. A history of Western philosophy   **109**

Berkin, Carol
A brilliant solution   **342**
Civil War wives   **920**

Berkman, Alexander, 1870-1936
      About
Avrich, K. Sasha and Emma   **335**

Berkowitz, Eric
The boundaries of desire   **306.7**

Berkshire encyclopedia of China.   **951**

BERKSHIRE HATHAWAY INC.
Chan, R. W. Behind the Berkshire Hathaway curtain   **658.4**

Berkson, Bill
Portrait and dream   **811**

BERLIN (GERMANY)
Spillman, R. All Tomorrow's Parties   **070.4**
Underground in Berlin   **940.531**

BERLIN (GERMANY) -- HISTORY -- BLOCKADE, 1948-1949
Reeves, R. Daring young men   **943.087**
Berlin at war. Moorhouse, R.   **943**
Berlin journal, 1989-1990. Darnton, R.   **943.087**

BERLIN WALL (1961-1989)
Freedman, L. Kennedy's wars   **973.922**
Mitchell, G. The tunnels   **943.155**

Pleshakov, K. There is no freedom without bread! **947**

Berlin, Adele
(ed) The Oxford dictionary of the Jewish religion **296**

BERLIN, BATTLE OF, 1945
Beevor, A. The fall of Berlin 1945 **940.54**
Read, A. The fall of Berlin **940.54**
A woman in Berlin **940.53**

Berlin, Edward A.
King of ragtime: Scott Joplin and his era **92**

Berlin, Ira
Generations of captivity **326**
The long emancipation **326.8**
The making of African America **305.8**
(ed) Remembering slavery **326**

The **Berlin-Baghdad** express. McMeekin, S. **940.3**

Berlinerblau, Jacques
How to be secular **211**

Berlinski, David
The king of infinite space **516.2**

Berlitz Korean compact dictionary. **495.7**

Berlo, Janet Catherine
Native North American art **709.01**

Berman, Ari
Give us the ballot **324.6**

Berman, Dorothy Matthews
Matthews, J. L. Social security, Medicare & government pensions **344**

Berman, Larry
Zumwalt **92**

BERMUDA PETREL
Gehrman, E. Rare birds **598**

BERMUDA TRIANGLE
See also Atlantic Ocean

Bernadac, Marie-Laure
Leal, B. The ultimate Picasso **759**

Bernan Press (Company)
(comp) Social security handbook **368.4**

Bernanke's test. Overtveldt, J. v. **332.1**

Bernanke, Ben
About
The Courage to Act **92**
Overtveldt, J. v. Bernanke's test **332.1**
Wessel, D. In Fed we trust **332.1**

Bernard Shaw. Peters, S. **822**

Bernard, Emily
Carl Van Vechten and the Harlem Renaissance **92**

Bernard, Juliet
(ed) Knitting masterclass **746.432**

Bernard, Pierre, 1875-1955
About
Love, R. The Great Oom **92**

Bernard, Wendy
Up, down, all-around stitch dictionary **746.43**

Berners-Lee, Mike
How bad are bananas? **363.7**

Bernie. Rall, T. **92**

Bernier, Celeste-Marie
(jt. auth) Stauffer, J. Picturing Frederick Douglass **92**

Bernini. Mormando, F. **92**

Bernini, Gian Lorenzo, 1598-1680
About
Mormando, F. Bernini **92**

Bernoulli family
About
Bell, E. T. Men of mathematics **920**

Bernstein, Aaron
(ed) Sustaining life **333.95**

Bernstein, Burton
Leonard Bernstein **92**

Bernstein, Carl
All the president's men **973.924**
A woman in charge **92**
Woodward, B. The final days **973.924**

Bernstein, Charles, 1950-
Bernstein, C. All the whiskey in heaven **811**
(ed) Zukofsky, L. Selected poems **811**

Bernstein, Jeremy
Oppenheimer **92**
Plutonium **546**

Bernstein, Judy
Deng, B. They poured fire on us from the sky **962.4**

Bernstein, Leonard, 1918-1990
About
Bernstein, B. Leonard Bernstein **92**

Bernstein, Nell
Burning down the house **365**

Bernstein, Nina
The lost children of Wilder **362.73**

Bernstein, Peter L.
Wedding of the waters **386**

Bernstein, Richard
Out of the blue **973.931**

Bernstein, Richard B.
Thomas Jefferson **92**

Bernstein, Richard, 1944-
China 1945 **327.73**

Bernstein, William
The four pillars of investing **332.6**
The investor's manifesto **332.6**

Berra, Yogi, 1925-
About
Barra, A. Yogi Berra **92**

BERRIES
Bowling, B. L. Homegrown berries **634**

BERRIES
See also Fruit; Fruit culture

Berrigan, Anselm
(ed) Poems/Selections The collected poems of Ted Berrigan **811**

Berrigan, Edmund
(ed) Poems/Selections The collected poems of Ted
  Berrigan **811**
Berrigan, Sandy
About
Berrigan, T. Dear Sandy, hello **92**
Berrigan, Ted, 1934-1983
Dear Sandy, hello **92**
Poems/Selections The collected poems of Ted Ber-
  rigan **811**
Berry, Joanne
The complete Pompeii **937**
Berry, Mary
Baking with Mary Berry **641.865**
Berry, Mary Frances
My face is black is true **92**
Power in words **973.932**
Berry, Wendell, 1934-
Bringing it to the table **630**
Collected poems, 1957-1982 **811**
Given **811**
Imagination in place **814**
New collected poems **811**
A timbered choir **811**
Berryman, John
Collected poems, 1937-1971 **811**
The dream songs **811**
Bertholf, Robert J.
(ed) Duncan, R. E. Selected poems **811**
Bertholle, Louisette
Child, J. Mastering the art of French cooking **641.5**
Berthon, Simon
Warlords **940.53**
Beschloss, Michael R., 1955-
The conquerors: Roosevelt, Truman, and the de-
  struction of Hitler's Germany, 1941-1945 **940.53**
Jacqueline Kennedy **973.922**
(ed) Taking charge **973.923**
Besh, John
Cooking from the heart **641.5**
My family table **641.59**
My New Orleans **641.59**
Bessel, Richard
Germany 1945 **943.087**
The best American essays 2010. **814**
The best American essays 2012. **808**
The Best American essays 2013. **814**
The best American essays 2014. **814**
The Best American essays of the century. **814**
The best American poetry. **811**
The best American science and nature writing
  2012. **810.8**
The best American science and nature writing
  2014. **810.8**
The best American series
The best American essays 2010 **814**

The Best American short plays. **812**
The Best American Sports Writing 2014. **814**
The Best American sports writing of the century. **796**
The best American travel writing 2012. **808**
The best and the brightest. Halberstam, D. **973.922**
BEST BOOKS
Alabaster, C. Developing an outstanding core col-
  lection **025.2**
Alpert, A. Read on-- graphic novels **016**
Baker, J. S. The readers' advisory guide to histori-
  cal fiction **026**
Basbanes, N. A. Every book its reader **028**
Covert, J. The 100 best business books of all
  time **016.6**
Dirda, M. Book by book **028**
Ellington, E. A year of reading **011**
Frolund, T. Read on...history **016**
Helbig, A. Dictionary of American young adult fic-
  tion, 1997-2001 **028.5**
Hooper, B. Read on....historical fiction **016**
Horror: another 100 best books **823**
Moyer, J. E. The readers' advisory handbook **025.5**
Pearl, N. Book lust **011**
Pearl, N. More book lust **025**
Pearl, N. Now read this **016**
Pearl, N. Now read this II **016**
Pearl, N. Now read this III **016**
Quillen, C. L. Read on... romance **016**
Required reading **301**
Rosow, L. V. Accessing the classics **011.6**
Saricks, J. G. The readers' advisory guide to genre
  fiction **025.5**
Saricks, J. G. Readers' advisory service in the pub-
  lic library **025.5**
Wyatt, N. The readers' advisory guide to nonfic-
  tion **025.5**
BEST BOOKS
See also Books
The best business writing 2013. **330.9**
The Best Casserole cookbook ever. **641.8**
The best chicken recipes. Cook's illustrated (Peri-
  odical) **641.6**
Best food writing 2014. **641.3**
The best homemade kids' lunches on the planet.
  Fuentes, L. **641.5**
The best homemade kids' snacks on the planet.
  Fuentes, L. **641.5**
The best homes from This old house. **643**
The best International recipe. Cook's illustrated
  (Periodical) **641.5**
The Best Men's Stage Monologues 2016. **792**
The best of all possible worlds. Nadler, S. M. **190**
The best of it. Ryan, K. **811**
Best of the Best American Poetry. **811**
The best one-dish suppers. **641.8**
The best plays of 2006-2007. **808.82**

Best plays theater yearbook [series]

The best plays of 2006-2007   **808.82**

The **Best** poems of the English language.   **821**

The **best** quick breads. Hensperger, B.   **641.8**

The **best** recipe.   **641.5**

BEST SELLERS (BOOKS)

    See also Books and reading

Best skillet recipes. Cook's illustrated (Periodical)   **641.7**

The **best** stage scenes of 2007.   **808.82**

The **best** team money can buy. Knight, M. **796.357**

The **Best** Women's Stage Monologues 2016.   **792**

The **best** year of their lives. Morrow, L.   **920**

Best, Joel

Stat-spotting   **301**

BEST-BOOK LISTS *See* Best books

Best-Boss, Angie

Your child's teeth   **617.6**

BESTIARIES

    See also Books

Bestor, Leslie Ann

Cast on, bind off   **746.43**

Betjeman. Wilson, A. N.   **92**

Betjeman, John Sir, 1906-1984

    About

Wilson, A. N. Betjeman   **92**

Betrayal.   **282**

BETRAYAL

Macintyre, B. A Spy Among Friends   **327.12**

Betrayal at Little Gibraltar. Walker, W. T. **940.436**

The **betrayal** of the American dream. Barlett, D. L.   **330.973**

Betrayal of trust. Garrett, L.   **362.1**

The **betrayal** of work. Shulman, B.   **331.2**

BETROTHAL

    See also Courtship; Marriage

Betsy Ross and the making of America. Miller, M. R.   **92**

Bette Davis. Thomson, D.   **92**

Bettelheim, Bruno

Freud and man's soul   **150.19**

Bettencourt, Megan Feldman

Triumph of the heart   **155.9**

Better. Gawande, A.   **616**

The **better** angels of our nature. Pinker, S.   **301**

The **better** bag maker. Mallalieu, N.   **646.4**

Better for all the world. Bruinius, H.   **363.9**

Better Homes & Gardens (Company)

(comp) Do it yourself kitchens   **643**

(comp) New decorating book   **747**

Better homes and gardens new cook book. Better homes and gardens   **641.5**

Better Homes and Gardens New Cook Book.   **641.5**

Better than before. Rubin, G.   **158.1**

The **better** to eat you with. Berger, J.   **591.5**

BetterPhoto basics. Miotke, J.   **771**

BETTING *See* Gambling

Betting the farm on a drought. McGraw, S. **363.738**

Betty Crocker cookbook.   **641.5**

Betty Crocker cookie book. Crocker, B.   **641.8**

Betty Crocker's cooking basics.   **641.5**

Betty Shabazz: a remarkable story of survival and faith before and after Malcolm X. Rickford, R. J. **92**

Bettyville. Hodgman, G.   **306.874**

Between earth and sky. Nadkarni, N.   **582.16**

Between father and son. Naipaul, V. S.   **823**

Between the Dark and the Daylight. Chittister, J. **128**

Between the World and Me. Coates   **305.8**

Between you & me. Norris, M.   **428**

Betzina, Sandra

Power sewing step-by-step   **646.4**

Bevan, A. W. R.

Meteorites: a journey through space and time **523.5**

Bevel, James Luther, 1936-2008

    About

Halberstam, D. The children   **323.1**

BEVERAGE INDUSTRY

    See also Food industry

BEVERAGE INDUSTRY EXECUTIVES

MacIntosh, J. Dethroning the king   **338.8**

BEVERAGES

Helwig, J. Smoothie-licious   **641.87**

The Oxford encyclopedia of food and drink in America   **641.3**

BEVERAGES

    See also Diet; Food

BEVERAGES -- HISTORY

Standage, T. A history of the world in 6 glasses   **394.1**

Beverley, James A.

(ed) Melton, J. G. Melton's encyclopedia of American religions   **200.9**

BEVERLY HILLS (CALIF.) -- BIOGRAPHY

Stein, J. West of Eden   **979.4**

Bevill, Amanda

World spice at home   **641.6**

Bewes, Diccon

Slow Train to Switzerland   **914.94**

Bewick, Thomas, 1753-1828

    About

Uglow, J. S. Nature's engraver   **92**

Bewilderment. Ferry, D.   **811**

Beyer, Jinny

The quilter's album of patchwork patterns **746.46**

Beyer, Kurt W.

Grace Hopper and the invention of the information age   **92**

Beyond belief. Pagels, E. H.   **229**

Beyond codependency. Beattie, M.   **616.86**

Beyond Earth. Wohlforth, C.   **629.455**

Beyond glory. Margolick, D.   **796.8**

Beyond innocence. Goodall, J.   **92**

Beyond intelligence. Foster, J. **649**

Beyond Katrina. Trethewey, N. D. **818**

Beyond Rosie. **940**

Beyond silence. Hoffman, D. **811**

Beyond the asterisk. **378.1**

Beyond the blue horizon. Fagan, B. **910.4**

Beyond the fields. Shaw, R. **331.8**

Beyond the god particle. Lederman, L. **539.7**

Beyond the Great Wall. Alford, J. **641.5**

Beyond the Mountains of the Damned. McAllester, M. **949.71**

Beyond the Revolution. Goetzmann, W. H. **973.2**

Beyond the square crochet motifs. Eckman, E. **746.434**

Beyond tolerance. Niebuhr, G. **201**

Beyond uncertainty. Cassidy, D. C. **92**

Beyond words. Safina, C. **591.56**

Bezanson, Randall P.
How free can the press be? **342**

Bhagavad Gita. Mahabharata/Bhagavadgita **294.5**

The **Bhagavad** Gita. Davis, R. H. **294.5**

BHAGAVADGĪTĀ -- HISTORY
Davis, R. H. The Bhagavad Gita **294.5**

Bhattacharya, Shaoni
(jt. auth) Cross, C. The baby book **649.122**
Watch my baby grow **649.122**

BHUTAN -- DESCRIPTION AND TRAVEL
Grange, K. Beneath blossom rain **915**
Napoli, L. Radio Shangri-La **954.9**

Bhutto, Benazir
          About
Bhutto, B. Reconciliation **92**

Bi. Eisner, S. **306.76**

BI-RACIAL PEOPLE See Racially mixed people

Bialac, James T.
          About
The James T. Bialac Native American Art Collection **704.03**

Biale, David
(ed) Cultures of the Jews **909**

Bianchi, Luciana
(jt. auth) Castanho, T. Brazilian Food **641.598**

BIAS (PSYCHOLOGY) See Prejudices

BIAS ATTACKS See Hate crimes

BIAS CRIMES See Hate crimes

Biba's Italy. Caggiano, B. **641.59**

Bible
The Oxford study Bible **220.5**

BIBLE (AS SUBJECT) -- ANTIQUITIES
Currie, R. The letter and the scroll **220.9**

BIBLE (AS SUBJECT) -- DICTIONARIES
Eerdmans dictionary of the Bible **220.3**
The Oxford companion to the Bible **220.3**

BIBLE -- BIOGRAPHY
Tischler, N. M. Men and women of the Bible **220.9**

BIBLE -- COMMENTARIES

Bowker, J. The complete Bible handbook **220.6**

Manser, M. H. Critical companion to the Bible **220.6**

BIBLE -- CONCORDANCES
Cruden, A. Cruden's Complete concordance **220.5**
Strong, J. The strongest Strong's exhaustive concordance of the Bible **220.5**

BIBLE -- CRITICISM
Manser, M. H. Critical companion to the Bible **220.6**
Murphy, C. The Word according to Eve **220.8**
Wray, T. J. What the Bible really tells us **220.6**

BIBLE -- DICTIONARIES
The HarperCollins Bible dictionary **220.3**
Zondervan illustrated Bible dictionary **220.3**

BIBLE -- GEOGRAPHY
Curtis, A. Oxford Bible atlas **220.9**

BIBLE -- HISTORY
Ferrell, L. A. The Bible and the people **220.5**
Korb, S. Life in year one **933**

BIBLE -- HISTORY OF BIBLICAL EVENTS
The Cambridge companion to the Bible **220.9**

BIBLE -- HISTORY OF BIBLICAL EVENTS
The Oxford history of the biblical world **220.9**

BIBLE -- MEDITATIONS
Carter, J. Sources of strength **248.4**

BIBLE -- N.T. -- CRITICISM
Brown, R. E. An introduction to the New Testament **225**

BIBLE -- N.T. -- EPISTLES OF PAUL -- CRITICISM
Borg, M. J. The first Paul **227**
Ruden, S. Paul among the people **225.9**

BIBLE -- N.T. -- GOSPELS -- CRITICISM
Benedict XVI, P. Jesus of Nazareth. part two **232.9**
Bonhoeffer, D. The cost of discipleship **226**
Gordon, M. Reading Jesus **232**
Pagels, E. H. The origin of Satan **235**

BIBLE -- O.T. -- BIOGRAPHY -- DICTIONARIES
Mandel, D. Who's who in the Jewish Bible **920.003**

BIBLE -- O.T. -- CRITICISM
Kugel, J. L. How to read the Bible **221**
Telushkin, J. Biblical literacy **221**

BIBLE -- O.T. -- GENESIS -- CRITICISM
Kass, L. The beginning of wisdom **222**
Kushner, H. S. How good do we have to be? **296.7**
Moyers, B. Genesis: a living conversation **222**

BIBLE -- O.T. -- HISTORY OF BIBLICAL EVENTS
Cahill, T. The gifts of the Jews **909**

BIBLE -- O.T. -- INTRODUCTIONS
The Jewish Bible **221**
Bible/O.T./Pentateuch The five books of Moses **222**

BIBLE -- O.T. -- PENTATEUCH -- GEOGRA-

PHY

Feiler, B. S. Walking the Bible   **915**

BIBLE AND SCIENCE

See also Religion and science; Science

The **Bible** and the people. Ferrell, L. A.   **220.5**

BIBLE AS LITERATURE

Manser, M. H.   Critical companion to the Bible   **220.6**

BIBLE. MATTHEW -- CRITICISM, INTERPRETATION, ETC

Spong, J. S. Biblical literalism   **226.2**

BIBLE. N.T. -- CHRONOLOGY

Borg, M. J. Evolution of the Word   **225**

BIBLE. O.T. JOB -- COMMENTARIES

Kushner, H. S. The book of Job   **223**

BIBLE. OLD TESTAMENT -- CRITICISM, INTERPRETATION, ETC

Kirsch, A. The people and the books   **809.889**

BIBLE. PENTATEUCH -- COMMENTARIES

Bible/O.T./Pentateuch   The five books of Moses   **222**

Bible/N.T./Gospels

The three Gospels   **226.3**

Bible/O.T.

Tanakh   **221**

Bible/O.T./Genesis

Bible/O.T./Pentateuch   The five books of Moses   **222**

The **Bible**: Authorized King James Version.   **220.5**

BIBLICAL COSMOLOGY

See also Cosmology

Biblical literacy. Telushkin, J.   **221**

Biblical literalism. Spong, J. S.   **226.2**

BIBLIOGRAPHIC CONTROL -- HISTORY

Wright, A. Cataloging the world   **020.9**

BIBLIOGRAPHIC INSTRUCTION

See also Library services

BIBLIOGRAPHICAL CITATIONS

Walker, J. R.   The Columbia guide to online style   **808**

BIBLIOGRAPHY -- BEST BOOKS *See* Best books

BIBLIOGRAPHY -- RARE BOOKS *See* Rare books

BIBLIOMANIA *See* Book collecting

BIBLIOPHILY *See* Book collecting

BICYCLE CAMPING *See* Bicycle touring

BICYCLE COMMUTING

Bike Snob The enlightened cyclist   **796.6**

Bicycle design. Lessing   **629.2**

Bicycle diaries. Byrne, D.   **796.6**

BICYCLE RACING

Balf, T. Major   **92**

Hamilton, T. The Secret Race   **796.62**

Moore, T. Gironimo!   **796.6**

BICYCLE RACING

See also Cycling; Racing

BICYCLE TOURING

Byrne, D. Bicycle diaries   **796.6**

Moore, T. Gironimo!   **796.6**

BICYCLE TOURING

See also Camping; Cycling; Travel

Bicycles. Giovanni, N.   **811**

BICYCLES

Petersen, G. Just ride   **796.6**

BICYCLES -- DESIGN AND CONSTRUCTION -- HISTORY

Hallett, R. Bike deconstructed   **629.227**

Lessing Bicycle design   **629.2**

BICYCLES -- MAINTENANCE AND REPAIR

Henderson, B. The Haynes bicycle book   **629.28**

Zinn & the art of road bike maintenance   **629.227**

BICYCLING *See* Cycling

Bidart, Frank

Watching the spring festival   **811**

(ed) Lowell, R. Collected poems   **811**

Bidart, Frank, 1939-

Metaphysical dog   **811**

Star dust   **811**

Biddle, Daniel R.

Tasting freedom   **92**

Biddle, Wayne

Dark side of the moon   **92**

A field guide to germs   **616**

Biedermann, Hans

Dictionary of symbolism   **302.2**

Biel, Steven

American Gothic   **759.13**

Bien Cuit. Kaminsky, P.   **641.815**

Bierce, Ambrose, 1842-1914?

About

Drabelle, D. The great American railroad war **385**

Morris, R. Ambrose Bierce   **92**

Wilson, E. Patriotic gore   **810**

Biever, John A.

The wandering mind   **612.8**

BIG BANG THEORY

Clark, S. The Unknown Universe   **523.1**

Frank, A. About time   **523.1**

Halpern, P. Edge of the universe   **523.1**

Kaku, M. Parallel worlds   **523.1**

Rees, M. J. Just six numbers   **523.1**

Singh, S. Big bang: the origins of the universe **523.1**

BIG BANG THEORY

See also Cosmology

Big bang: the origins of the universe. Singh, S. **523.1**

The **Big** Book of a Miniature House. Frisoni   **745**

The **big** book of cross-stitch designs. Reader's Digest Association   **746.44**

The **big** book of outdoor cooking and entertaining. Jamison, C. A.   **641.5**

The **big** book of preserving the harvest. Costenbader, C. W.   **641.4**

The **big** book of symptoms.   **618.92**

BIG BOOKS

     See also Children's literature; Reading materials

The **big** burn. Egan, T.   **973.91**

BIG BUSINESS

     Power, Inc.   **322**

BIG BUSINESS -- UNITED STATES

     Coll, S. Private empire   **338.7**

Big Chief Elizabeth. Milton, G.   **970.004**

Big data. Cukier, K.   **306.46**

BIG DATA -- POLITICAL ASPECTS -- UNITED STATES

     O'Neil, C. Weapons of math destruction   **005.7**

BIG DATA -- SOCIAL ASPECTS -- UNITED STATES

     O'Neil, C. Weapons of math destruction   **005.7**

Big data baseball. Sawchik, T.   **796.357**

The **Big** Disconnect. Steiner-Adair, C.   **303.48**

Big enough to be inconsistent. Fredrickson, G. M.   **973.7**

BIG GAME HUNTING

     The complete guide to hunting, butchering, and cooking big game   **799.2**

BIG GAME HUNTING

     See also Hunting

Big girls don't cry. Traister, R.   **324**

A **big** history. Brown, C. S.   **909**

BIG HOLE, BATTLE OF THE, 1877

     West, E. The last Indian war   **973.8**

Big ideas simply explained [series]

     The politics book   **320.01**

Big ideas/small books [series]

     Orbach, S. Bodies   **362.1**

Big magic. Gilbert, E.   **153.3**

The **big** miss. Haney, H.   **796.352**

Big money. Vogel, K. P.   **324.7**

The **big** necessity. George, R.   **363.7**

The **big** payback. Charnas, D.   **781.64**

The **Big** Picture. Carroll, S.   **577**

The **big** policeman. Conway, J. N.   **92**

The **big** rich. Burrough, B.   **338.2**

The **big** screen. Thomson, D.   **791.43**

The **big** short. Lewis, M.   **330.9**

The **big** sort. Bishop, B.   **305.8**

The **big** switch. Carr, N. G.   **303.4**

The **big** thirst. Fishman, C.   **333.91**

The **big** truck that went by. Katz, J. M.   **363.34**

The **big-ass** book of home decor. Montano, M.   **645**

Big-box swindle. Mitchell, S.   **381**

Big-time sports in American universities. Clotfelter, C. T.   **796**

Biggers, Jeff

     Reckoning at Eagle Creek   **333.73**

Biggest brother. Alexander, L.   **92**

Bigon, Mario

     The Morrow guide to knots   **623.88**

BIGOTRY *See* Prejudices; Toleration

BIGOTRY-MOTIVATED CRIMES *See* Hate crimes

Bigsby, Christopher

     Arthur Miller   **92**

Bike deconstructed. Hallett, R.   **629.227**

Bike Snob

     The enlightened cyclist   **796.6**

The **bikeriders.** Lyon, D.   **796.7**

BIKES *See* Bicycles

BIKING *See* Cycling

Biklé, Anne

     (jt. auth) Montgomery, D. R. The hidden half of nature   **579**

Bilal, Wafaa, 1966-

     About

     Bilal, W. Shoot an Iraqi   **92**

Bilderback, Leslie

     No-churn ice cream   **641.86**

BILDUNGSROMANS

     Lamarche, U. Unabrow   **92**

     Mayes, F. Under magnolia   **92**

BILDUNGSROMANS

     See also Fiction

BILINGUAL BOOKS

     See also Books; Editions

BILINGUALISM

     See also Language and languages

Bill and Hillary. Chafe, W. H.   **973.929**

BILL COLLECTING *See* Collecting of accounts

Bill Mauldin. DePastino, T.   **92**

The **Bill** McKibben reader. McKibben, B.   **333.72**

The **bill** of the century. Risen, C.   **342.73**

BILLIARDS

     Byrne, R. Byrne's new standard book of pool and billiards   **794.7**

Billing, Kelly

     (jt. auth) Helm, B. The water gardener's bible   **635.9**

Billings, J. Todd

     About

     Billings, J. T. Rejoicing in lament   **248.8**

Billings, Lee

     Five billion years of solitude   **576.8**

The **Billion** Dollar Spy. Hoffman, D. E.   **327.12**

Billion-Dollar Ball. Gaul, G. M.   **796.332**

The **billionaire's** vinegar. Wallace, B.   **641.2**

Billions and billions. Sagan, C.   **500**

BILLS OF CREDIT *See* Credit; Negotiable instruments

BILLS OF FARE *See* Menus

Billy Martin. Pennington, B.   **92**

Billy Martin.   **92**

Billy the Kid. Wallis, M.   **92**

Billy, the Kid
>> **About**
>> Brown, D. A. The American West **978**
>> Gardner, M. L. To hell on a fast horse **92**
>> Wallis, M. Billy the Kid **92**

Bilton, Nick
>> Hatching Twitter **006.7**

Bin Laden family
>> **About**
>> Coll, S. The Bin Ladens **920**

Bin Laden, Osama, 1957-2011
>> **About**
>> Bergen, P. L. Manhunt **363.325**
>> Hersh, S. The killing of Osama Bin Laden **327.73**
>> Maurer, K. No easy day **958.104**

The **Bin** Ladens. Coll, S. **920**

BINARY SYSTEM (MATHEMATICS)
>> *See also* Mathematics; Numbers

BINDING OF BOOKS *See* Bookbinding

Binelli, Mark
>> Detroit City is the place to be **307.1**

Bing Crosby: a pocketful of dreams: the early years, 1903-1940. Giddins, G. **92**

BINGE EATING BEHAVIOR *See* Bulimia

BINGE-PURGE BEHAVIOR *See* Bulimia

Bingham family
>> **About**
>> Bingham, E. Irrepressible **306.76**

Bingham, Emily
>> Irrepressible **306.76**

Bingham, Henrietta Worth, 1901-1968
The writers' and artists' yearbook guide to how to write **808.3**
>> **About**
>> Bingham, E. Irrepressible **306.76**

Bingham, Hiram, 1875-1956
>> Lost city of the Incas **985**
>> **About**
>> Adams, M. Turn right at Machu Picchu **985**
>> Heaney, C. Cradle of gold **92**

Binns, Brigit Legere
>> Psilakis, M. How to roast a lamb **641.5**

Binyon, T. J.
>> Pushkin: a biography **92**

BIO-INVASIONS *See* Biological invasions

BIOCHEMISTRY
>> Wilcox, C. Venomous **572**

BIOCHEMISTRY
>> *See also* Biology; Chemistry; Medicine

BIOCHEMISTS
>> Gunn, J. E. Isaac Asimov **813**
>> Ridley, M. Francis Crick **92**
>> Winchester, S. The man who loved China **92**

BIOCONVERSION *See* Biomass energy

BIODIVERSITY
>> A window on eternity **333.95**

BIODIVERSITY
>> *See also* Biology

BIODIVERSITY -- ENCYCLOPEDIAS
>> Rice, S. A. Encyclopedia of biodiversity **578.7**

BIODIVERSITY -- MOZAMBIQUE -- PARQUE NACIONAL DA GORONGOSA
>> A window on eternity **333.95**

BIODIVERSITY -- SOUTH AFRICA
>> Girling, R. The Hunt for the Golden Mole **591.68**

BIODIVERSITY CONSERVATION
>> Fraser, C. Rewilding the world **333.95**

BIODIVERSITY CONSERVATION
>> *See also* Conservation of natural resources

BIODYNAMIC AGRICULTURE
>> Citizen farmers **635**
>> Biodynamic gardening. **635**

BIOELECTRICITY *See* Electrophysiology

BIOENGINEERING
>> *See also* Biology; Engineering

BIOETHICS
>> *See also* Ethics

BIOFEEDBACK TRAINING
>> *See also* Feedback (Psychology); Mind and body; Psychology of learning; Psychotherapy

BIOFUELS *See* Biomass energy

BIOGENESIS -- POPULAR WORKS
>> Rutherford, A. Creation **576.8**

BIOGEOGRAPHY
Bambaradeniya, C. N. B. The illustrated atlas of wildlife **591.9**
World atlas of great apes and their conservation **599.8**

BIOGEOGRAPHY
>> *See also* Ecology; Geography

BIOGRAPHERS
>> Bair, D. Simone de Beauvoir **848**
>> Bloom, H. The anatomy of influence **801**
>> Brookhiser, R. Right time, right place **92**
>> Existentialism from Dostoevsky to Sartre **142**
>> Farrell, S. E. Critical companion to Kurt Vonnegut **813**
>> Fraser, K. Ornament and silence **809**
>> Goodwin, D. K. Wait till next year **796.357**
>> Hollis, L. London rising **942**
>> Jarrell, R. No other book **809**
>> Ker, I. G. K. Chesterton **828**
>> King, D. Patrick O'Brian **823**
>> Maraniss, D. Into the story **92**
>> Martin, P. A life of James Boswell **828**
>> Morgan, T. My battle of Algiers **965**
>> Oates, J. C. A widow's story **92**
>> Parini, J. The art of teaching **371.1**
>> Reiss, T. The Orientalist **92**
>> Richardson, J. The sorcerer's apprentice **92**
>> Schlesinger, A. M. Journals: 1952-2000 **92**
>> Schlesinger, A. M. A life in the twentieth centu-

ry   92
Shields, C. J. And so it goes: Kurt Vonnegut: a life   92
Simon, J. F. What kind of nation   342
Sisman, A. Boswell's presumptuous task   828
Smith, J. E. John Marshall   347
Spurling, H. Pearl Buck in China   92
Stannard, M. Muriel Spark   92
Starr, W. W. Whisky, kilts, and the Loch Ness Monster   914
Steffens, L. The autobiography of Lincoln Steffens   92
Sutherland, J. Stephen Spender   92
Thomas, E. The war lovers   973.8
Thomson, D. Try to tell the story   92
Thurman, J. Secrets of the flesh: a life of Colette   92
Travels with Herodotus   930
Ulrich, L. Well-behaved women seldom make history   305.4
Von Mehren, J. Minerva and the muse: a life of Margaret Fuller   92
White, E. City boy   92
White, E. The flaneur   944.083
White, E. My lives   813
Zimmermann, W. First great triumph   973

BIOGRAPHERS -- UNITED STATES -- BIOGRAPHY
Bailey, B. The Splendid Things We Planned   92
The **biographical** dictionary of World War II generals and flag officers. Ancell, R. M.   920.003
Biographical encyclopedia of artists.   920.003
The **biographical** encyclopedia of jazz. Feather, L.   781.65

BIOGRAPHICAL FICTION
    See also Fiction
BIOGRAPHICAL FILMS
    See also Motion pictures
BIOGRAPHICAL GRAPHIC NOVELS
Geary, R. J. Edgar Hoover   363.2
Guibert, E. Alan's war   741.5
I see the promised land   92
Jacobson, S. Anne Frank   92
Kleist, R. Johnny Cash   92
Rall, T. Bernie   92
Rudahl, S. A dangerous woman   335
Spiegelman, A. Maus   940.53
Van Sciver, N. The Hypo   92
BIOGRAPHICAL GRAPHIC NOVELS
    See also Graphic novels
A **biographical** guide to the great jazz and pop singers. Friedwald, W.   920.003
BIOGRAPHICAL TELEVISION PROGRAMS
    See also Television programs
Biography. Hamilton, N.   907
BIOGRAPHY
    See also History

BIOGRAPHY
Abad, H. Oblivion   868
Bartlett, R. Tolstoy   891.7
Booknotes (Television program) Booknotes: life stories   920
Brinkley, A. John F. Kennedy   92
Burt, D. S. The biography book   016
Caro, R. A. The passage of power   92
Cee-Lo Everybody's brother   782.421
Cohen, R. The fish that ate the whale   338.7
Cusk, R. Aftermath   823
Holroyd, M. A book of secrets   306.874
Johnson, P. Darwin   576.8
Kephart, B. Handling the truth   808.06
Kidder, T. Good prose   808.02
Massie, R. K. Catherine the Great   947
McFarland, P. Mark Twain and the Colonel   973.8
Miller, J. Examined lives   190
Reisner, R. Read on-- life stories   016
Roberts, G. Stalin's general   940.54
Russo, R. Elsewhere   92
Scott, R. J. Freedom papers   305.896
Smith, J. E. Eisenhower   973.921
Taylor, S. Commander   92
Telushkin, J. Rebbe   92
Thomas Becket   92
Turner, J. G. Brigham Young, pioneer prophet   289.3
BIOGRAPHY -- 20TH CENTURY
Cohen, L. All we know   920.72
Life stories   920
The Scribner encyclopedia of American lives, The 1960s   920.003
Thomas, R. M. 52 McGs   920
Ware, S. Letter to the world   920.72
BIOGRAPHY -- AUTHORSHIP
Morris, E. This living hand   814
BIOGRAPHY -- BIBLIOGRAPHY
Roche, R. Read on-- biography   016
BIOGRAPHY -- DICTIONARIES
Great lives from history, The 17th century, 1601-1700   920.003
Great lives from history, The 19th century, 1801-1900   920.003
Great lives from history, The ancient world, prehistory-476 C.E   920.003
Great lives from history, the Middle Ages, 477-1453   920.003
Great lives from history, the Renaissance & early modern era, 1454-1600   920.003
Great lives from history: Notorious lives   920.003
Great lives from history: the 20th century, 1901-2000   920.003
Powell, J. Great lives from history, The 18th century, 1701-1800   920.003
BIOGRAPHY -- DICTIONARIES

See also Encyclopedias and dictionaries

BIOGRAPHY -- HISTORY AND CRITICISM
See Biography as a literary form

BIOGRAPHY -- INDEXES
Havlice, P. P. Index to artistic biography **920.003**

BIOGRAPHY -- INDIVIDUAL
Ker, I. G. K. Chesterton **828**

BIOGRAPHY -- TECHNIQUE *See* Biography as a literary form

BIOGRAPHY AS A LITERARY FORM
Conway, J. K. When memory speaks **808**
Hamilton, N. Biography **907**
Helfand, J. Scrapbooks: an American history **745.54**
Lee, H. Virginia Woolf's nose **820**
Piercy, M. So you want to write **808.3**

BIOGRAPHY AS A LITERARY FORM
See also Authorship; Literature
The **biography** book. Burt, D. S. **016**

BIOGRAPHY, COLLECTIVE
Adams, M. B. Shaggy muses **920**
Ahamed, L. Lords of finance **332.1**
Ancell, R. M. The biographical dictionary of World War II generals and flag officers **920.003**
Barrett, P. M. American Islam **920**
Baum, D. Nine lives **976.3**
Burrough, B. The big rich **338.2**
Cheever, S. American Bloomsbury **810**
Darling, D. J. Gravity's arc **530**
Davis, P. G. The American opera singer **920**
Dinnage, R. Alone! alone!: lives of some outsider women **920**
Feldman, B. 112 Mercer Street **920**
Feldman, N. Scorpions **920**
Fraser, F. Princesses **920**
Fraser, K. Ornament and silence **809**
Friedwald, W. A biographical guide to the great jazz and pop singers **920.003**
Gates, H. L. Thirteen ways of looking at a black man **920.71**
Gray, C. Gold diggers **971**
Grunwald, L. Women's letters **305.4**
Hargittai, I. The Martians of science **920**
Hart, J. D. The Oxford companion to American literature **810**
The Harvard biographical dictionary of music **780**
Hastings, M. Warriors **355**
Holroyd, M. A book of secrets **306.874**
Marton, K. The great escape **920**
Marton, K. Hidden power **920**
McCullough, D. G. The greater journey **920.009**
Miller, J. Examined lives **190**
Montefiore, S. Jerusalem **956.94**
Morgan, E. S. American heroes **920**
The Norton/Grove dictionary of women composers **780.92**

Raddatz, M. The long road home **956.7**
Roiphe, K. Uncommon arrangements **920**
Schiff, K. G. Lighting the way **920**
Singer, M. Character studies **920**
Smith, A. Moondust **920**
This I believe II **170**
Tinniswood, A. The Verneys **920**
Tomkins, C. Lives of the artists **920**
Waldrup, C. C. The vice presidents **920.003**
Waxman, S. Rebels on the backlot **920**
Weber, N. F. The Bauhaus group **920**
Weir, A. The six wives of Henry VIII **942.05**
World explorers and discoverers **920.003**
Xinran China witness **920**

BIOLOGICAL ANTHROPOLOGY *See* Physical anthropology

BIOLOGICAL CHEMISTRY *See* Biochemistry

BIOLOGICAL CLOCKS *See* Biological rhythms

BIOLOGICAL DIVERSIFICATION *See* Biodiversity

BIOLOGICAL DIVERSITY
Earle, S. A. The world is blue **551.46**
Margulis, L. What is life? **570.1**
Sustaining life **333.95**
Wilson, E. O. The diversity of life **333.95**
Wilson, E. O. In search of nature *j* **113**

BIOLOGICAL DIVERSITY *See* Biodiversity

BIOLOGICAL DIVERSITY CONSERVATION *See* Biodiversity conservation

Biological exuberance. Bagemihl, B. **591.56**

BIOLOGICAL INVASIONS
Burdick, A. Out of Eden **577**
Hamilton, G. Super species **578.6**
Perez, L. Snake in the grass **597.96**

BIOLOGICAL PSYCHIATRY
Smoller, J. The other side of normal **591.5**

BIOLOGICAL RHYTHMS
Foster, R. G. Rhythms of life **571.7**

BIOLOGICAL TERRORISM *See* Bioterrorism

BIOLOGICAL WARFARE
Engelberg, S. Germs **358**
Guillemin, J. Biological weapons **358**
Lockwood, J. A. Six-legged soldiers **358**
Preston, R. The demon in the freezer **616.9**
Weapons of mass destruction **358**

BIOLOGICAL WARFARE
See also Military art and science; Tactics
Biological weapons. Guillemin, J. **358**

BIOLOGISTS
Barrow, M. V. Nature's ghosts **333.95**
Berger, J. The better to eat you with **591.5**
DeStefano, S. Coyote at the kitchen door **578.7**
Maathai, W. Unbowed **92**
Maddox, B. Rosalind Franklin: the dark lady of DNA **92**
McCalman, I. Darwin's armada **576.8**

Offit, P. A. Vaccinated **92**

Owens, M. Secrets of the savanna **599**

Streever, B. Cold **998**

BIOLOGISTS

    See also Naturalists; Scientists

BIOLOGISTS -- UNITED STATES -- BIOGRA-PHY

Jahren, H. Lab girl **92**

BIOLOGISTS -- UNITED STATES -- CORRE-SPONDENCE

Wilson, E. O. Letters to a Young Scientist **570**

BIOLOGY

Ashcroft, F. The spark of life **612**

Collen, A. 10% human **612.3**

Gerald, M. C. The Biology Book **570.9**

Mesler, B. A Brief History of Creation **576.8**

Souder, W. On a farther shore **92**

Tattersall, I. Masters of the planet **599.93**

BIOLOGY

    See also Life sciences; Science

BIOLOGY -- CLASSIFICATION

Yoon, C. K. Naming nature **570.1**

BIOLOGY -- DICTIONARIES

A dictionary of biology **570**

BIOLOGY -- ECOLOGY *See* Ecology

BIOLOGY -- ENCYCLOPEDIAS

Rice, S. A. Encyclopedia of biodiversity **578.7**

BIOLOGY -- HISTORY

The lagoon **570.1**

Stott, R. Darwin's ghosts **576.8**

BIOLOGY -- PERIODICITY *See* Biological rhythms

BIOLOGY -- PHILOSOPHY

Lovelock, J. The ages of Gaia **570.1**

Margulis, L. What is life? **570.1**

Thomas, L. The lives of a cell **570.1**

Venter, J. C. Life at the Speed of Light **303.48**

Watson, L. Dark nature **111**

BIOLOGY -- RELIGIOUS ASPECTS -- CHRISTIANITY

Wathey, J. C. The illusion of God's presence **204**

BIOLOGY -- SIMULATION METHODS

Long, J. Darwin's devices **629.8**

BIOLOGY -- SOCIAL ASPECTS *See* Sociobiology

The **Biology** Book. Gerald, M. C. **570.9**

BIOMASS ENERGY

Koerth-Baker, M. Before the lights go out **333.79**

BIOMASS ENERGY

    See also Energy resources; Fuel

BIOMATHEMATICS

    See also Biology; Mathematics

BIOMECHANICS *See* Ergonomics; Human locomotion

BIOMEDICAL TECHNOLOGY

Topol, E. The creative destruction of medi-cine **610.28**

BIOMIMICRY

Harman, J. The shark's paintbrush **600**

BIONICS

Bulletproof feathers **570.1**

BIOPHYSICISTS

Weiner, J. Time, love, memory **591.5**

BIOPHYSICISTS -- UNITED STATES -- BIOG-RAPHY

Ryan, C. Sonic wind **92**

BIOPHYSICS

    See also Biology; Physics

BIORHYTHMS *See* Biological rhythms

BIOSCIENCES *See* Life sciences

BIOSPHERE

Lovelock, J. The ages of Gaia **570.1**

BIOSPHERE

    See also Life (Biology)

BIOTECHNOLOGY

Anthes, E. Frankenstein's cat **616.02**

Kurpinski, K. How to defeat your own clone **660.6**

BIOTECHNOLOGY

    See also Chemical engineering; Microbiology

BIOTERRORISM

Guillemin, J. Biological weapons **358**

Willman, D. The mirage man **363.325**

BIOTERRORISM

    See also Terrorism

BIOTIC COMMUNITIES

Burdick, A. Out of Eden **577**

Wills, C. Green Equilibrium **577**

The **biplane** houses. Murray, L. A. **821**

BIPOLAR DISORDER *See* Manic-depressive illness

Birch, Dinah

(ed) The Oxford companion to English litera-ture **820**

Birch, Helen (Artist)

Freehand **741.2**

The **bird.** Tudge, C. **598**

Bird. National Audubon Society **598**

BIRD ATTRACTING -- UNITED STATES

Wolfson, E. Audubon birdhouse book **728**

Bird by bird. Lamott, A. **808**

Bird cloud. Proulx, A. **92**

Bird dream. Higgins, M. **797.5**

The **bird** feeder book. Stokes, D. W. **598**

BIRD HOUSES *See* Birdhouses

A **Bird** in the Hand. Henry, D. **641.665**

Bird sense. Birkhead, T. **598**

BIRD SONG *See* Birdsongs

BIRD WATCHERS

Cokinos, C. The fallen sky **523.5**

Gentile, O. Life list **92**

BIRD WATCHERS -- ANECDOTES

Hayward, N. Lost among the birds **598.072**

Welcome to subirdia   598

BIRD WATCHING

Alderfer, J. National Geographic birding essentials   598

Dunne, P. Pete Dunne on bird watching   598

Gentile, O. Life list   92

Hayward, N. Lost among the birds   598.072

Karlson, K. T. Birding by Impression   598

Leahy, C. W. The birdwatcher's companion to North American birdlife   598

Sibley, D. Sibley's birding basics   598

Stokes, D. W. The bird feeder book   598

Weidensaul, S. Of a feather   598

Welcome to subirdia   598

What the robin knows   598.8

Zickefoose, J. The bluebird effect   598

BIRD WATCHING

    See also Natural history

BIRD WATCHING -- ANECDOTES

Hayward, N. Lost among the birds   598.072

Strycker, N. The thing with feathers   598

BIRD WATCHING -- WASHINGTON (STATE) -- SEATTLE

Welcome to subirdia   598

Bird, Kai, 1951-

American Prometheus   92

The Good Spy   92

BIRDBANDING

    See also Wildlife conservation

BIRDHOUSES

Wolfson, E. Audubon birdhouse book   728

BIRDHOUSES

    See also Animal housing

BIRDING *See* Bird watching

Birding by Impression. Karlson, K. T.   598

BirdLife International

National Audubon Society Bird   598

Birdmen. Goldstone, L.   629.13

Birdology. Montgomery, S.   598

BIRDS

Ackerman, J. The Genius of Birds   598

Arctic wings   598

Attenborough, D. The life of birds   598

Birkhead, T. Ten thousand birds   598

Elphick, J. The World of Birds   598

Hanson, T. Feathers   598

Kiser, J. M. America's other Audubon   598

Montgomery, S. Birdology   598

National Audubon Society Bird   598

The Princeton encyclopedia of birds   598

Sibley, D. Sibley's birding basics   598

Tudge, C. The bird   598

Unwin, M. The atlas of birds   598

Welcome to subirdia   598

Zickefoose, J. Baby Birds   598

BIRDS

    See also Animals

BIRDS -- ANATOMY

Masear, T. Fastest Things on Wings   598

BIRDS -- ANATOMY

    See also Anatomy

BIRDS -- BEHAVIOR

Birkhead, T. Bird sense   598

Lederer, R. J. Beaks, bones, and bird songs   598

Strycker, N. The thing with feathers   598

Zickefoose, J. The bluebird effect   598

BIRDS -- BEHAVIOR

    See also Animal behavior

BIRDS -- COLOR

    See also Color

BIRDS -- CONSERVATION

The world's rarest birds   598

BIRDS -- CONSERVATION -- CALIFORNIA

Raffin, M. The birds of Pandemonium   639.97

BIRDS -- COUNTING -- ANECDOTES

Hayward, N. Lost among the birds   598.072

BIRDS -- EGGS

    See also Eggs

BIRDS -- EGGS AND NESTS *See* Birds -- Eggs; Birds -- Nests

BIRDS -- ENCYCLOPEDIAS

The Princeton encyclopedia of birds   598

BIRDS -- EVOLUTION

Lederer, R. J. Beaks, bones, and bird songs   598

BIRDS -- FLIGHT

    See also Animal flight

BIRDS -- HABITAT

Welcome to subirdia   598

BIRDS -- HABITS AND BEHAVIOR *See* Birds -- Behavior

BIRDS -- IDENTIFICATION

Karlson, K. T. Birding by Impression   598

BIRDS -- MIGRATION

The atlas of bird migration   598

Weidensaul, S. Living on the wind   598

BIRDS -- NESTS

Davies, N. Cuckoo   598.7

BIRDS -- NORTH AMERICA -- PICTORIAL WORKS

Kiser, J. M. America's other Audubon   598

BIRDS -- PHYSIOLOGY

Birkhead, T. Bird sense   598

BIRDS -- PROTECTION

Raffin, M. The birds of Pandemonium   639.97

BIRDS -- PROTECTION

    See also Wildlife conservation

BIRDS -- PSYCHOLOGY

Ackerman, J. The Genius of Birds   598

Birkhead, T. Bird sense   598

BIRDS -- SONG *See* Birdsongs

BIRDS -- UNITED STATES

Lebbin, D. J. The American Bird Conservancy

guide to bird conservation **333.95**

Sibley, D. The Sibley field guide to birds of Western North America **598**

Zickefoose, J. The bluebird effect **598**

BIRDS -- WASHINGTON (STATE) -- SEATTLE -- IDENTIFICATION

Welcome to subirdia **598**

BIRDS IN ART

Kiser, J. M. America's other Audubon **598**

The **birds** of Pandemonium. Raffin, M. **639.97**

BIRDS OF PREY

See also Birds; Predatory animals

BIRDS' NESTS *See* Birds -- Nests

Birdseye. Kurlansky, M. **338.7**

Birdseye, Clarence, 1886-1956

About

Kurlansky, M. Birdseye **338.7**

BIRDSONGS

Kroodsma, D. E. The singing life of birds **598**

What the robin knows **598.8**

BIRDSONGS

See also Animal sounds

The **birdwatcher's** companion to North American birdlife. Leahy, C. W. **598**

Birkhead, Tim

Bird sense **598**

The Most Perfect Thing **598**

Ten thousand birds **598**

BIRMINGHAM (ALA.) -- RACE RELATIONS

Rieder, J. Gospel of freedom **323.1**

BIROBIDZHAN (RUSSIA) -- HISTORY

Gessen, M. Where the Jews aren't **957.7**

Biron, Rebecca E.

Elena Garro and Mexico's modern dreams **868**

BIRTH *See* Childbirth

BIRTH ATTENDANTS *See* Midwives

BIRTH CONTROL

Baker, J. H. Margaret Sanger **92**

Weschler, T. Taking charge of your fertility **613.9**

BIRTH CONTROL

See also Population; Sexual hygiene

BIRTH CONTROL -- ETHICAL ASPECTS

See also Ethics

BIRTH CUSTOMS *See* Childbirth

BIRTH DEFECTS

See also Medical genetics; Pathology

The **Birth** of a Nation. Lehr, D. **305.8**

BIRTH OF A NATION (MOTION PICTURE)

Lehr, D. The Birth of a Nation **305.8**

Birth of a theorem. **92**

The **birth** of an opera. Rose, M. **782.1**

The **birth** of pleasure. Gilligan, C. **152.4**

The **birth** of Satan. Wray, T. J. **235**

The **birth** of the pill. Eig, J. **618.1**

The **birth** of the Republic, 1763-89. Morgan, E. S. **973.3**

BIRTH ORDER

See also Children; Family

The **Birth** Partner. Simkin, P. **618.2**

BIRTH RATE

See also Vital statistics

BIRTH RECORDS *See* Registers of births, etc.

BIRTH WEIGHT, LOW -- COMPLICATIONS

Linden, D. W. Preemies **618.92**

Birth without violence. **618.4**

BIRTHDAY BOOKS

See also Birthdays; Calendars

BIRTHDAYS

Nowlan, R. A. Born this day **808.88**

BIRTHDAYS

See also Anniversaries; Days

BIRTHPARENTS

See also Parents

BIRTHPARENTS -- INDIA -- IDENTIFICATION

Brierley, S. A long way home **92**

BIRTHPARENTS -- UNITED STATES -- IDENTIFICATION -- CASE STUDIES

Marshall, S. Reunited **362.82**

BIRTHS, REGISTERS OF *See* Registers of births, etc.

BISEXUAL PEOPLE

See also LGBT people

BISEXUAL STUDENTS -- UNITED STATES

Cahill, S. LGBT youth in America's schools **371.82**

BISEXUAL WOMEN -- UNITED STATES -- BIOGRAPHY

Bingham, E. Irrepressible **306.76**

Hernández, D. A cup of water under my bed **920.009**

BISEXUALITY

Bingham, E. Irrepressible **306.76**

Eisner, S. Bi **306.76**

BISEXUALITY

See also Sex

Bishara, Rawia

Olives, lemons & za'atar **641.59**

Bishop, Bill

The big sort **305.8**

Bishop, Elizabeth, 1911-1979

Edgar Allan Poe & the juke-box **811**

Poems, prose, and letters **818**

About

Heaney, S. Finders keepers **821**

BISHOPS

Burstein, A. Madison and Jefferson **973.4**

Goldman, F. The art of political murder **972.81**

Kung, H. Great Christian thinkers **230**

Newman, R. S. Freedom's prophet **92**

Russell, B. A history of Western philosophy **109**

Wills, G. Saint Augustine **270.2**

BISHOPS

See also Clergy

Biskind, Peter

Easy riders, raging bulls   **791.43**
(ed) My Lunches With Orson   **791.43**
Star   **92**
Biskupic, Joan
Sandra Day O'Connor   **92**
Bismarck. Steinberg, J.   **92**
Bismarck, Otto, Furst von, 1815-1898
About
Fulbrook, M. A concise history of Germany   **943**
Kissinger, H. Diplomacy   **327.2**
Steinberg, J. Bismarck   **92**
BISON
Rinella, S. American buffalo   **599.64**
BISON
See also Mammals
Biss, Eula, 1977-
Notes from no man's land   **305.8**
On immunity   **616.07**
Bissell, Tom
Extra lives   **794.8**
Bissinger, H. G.
Friday night lights   **796.332**
Three nights in August   **796.357**
Bissonnette, Matt, 1976-
(jt. auth) Maurer, K. No easy day   **958.104**
Bissonnette, Zac
The great Beanie Baby bubble   **338.7**
Biswas, Chandrima
(ed) The pregnancy encyclopedia   **618.2**
Bitter.   **664**
Bitter brew. Knoedelseder, W.   **338.7**
Bitter freedom. Walsh, M.   **941.508**
The **bitter** sea. Li, C. N.   **92**
The **bitter** waters of Medicine Creek. Kluger, R.   **979.7**
Bitterly divided. Williams, D.   **973.7**
BITTERNESS (TASTE)
Amaro   **641.874**
Bitter   **664**
Bitterroot. Faulkner, S.   **978**
Bitters.   **641.8**
BITTERS
Amaro   **641.874**
Bitters   **641.8**
Bittle, Scott
(jt. auth) Johnson, J. Where did the jobs go-- and how do we get them back?   **331.1**
Bittman, Mark, 1950-
A bone to pick   **338.1**
Food matters   **613.2**
The food matters cookbook   **641.3**
How to Bake Everything   **641.86**
How to cook everything   **641.5**
How to Cook Everything Fast   **641.5**
How to cook everything vegetarian   **641.5**
Mark Bittman's Kitchen express   **641.5**

Mark Bittman's kitchen matrix   **641.5**
The VB6 cookbook   **641.5**
Bix, Herbert P.
Hirohito and the making of modern Japan   **92**
Bizet. MacDonald, H.   **92**
Bizet, Georges, 1838-1875
About
MacDonald, H. Bizet   **92**
Bizot, Francois
The gate   **959.604**
Bjork, Daniel W.
B.F. Skinner   **92**
Bjornerud, Marcia
Reading the rocks   **551.7**
Black & Decker Corp.
(comp) The complete guide to finishing basements   **643**
(comp) The complete guide to plumbing   **696**
(comp) The complete guide to roofing & siding   **695**
The complete guide to finishing basements   **643**
The complete guide to patios & walkways   **690**
The complete guide to plumbing   **696**
The complete guide to roofing, siding & trim   **695**
The complete photo guide to home improvement   **643**
The complete photo guide to home repair   **643**
The **black** 100. Salley, C.   **920**
BLACK ACTORS
See also Actors
BLACK AMERICANS *See* African Americans
Black aperture. Rasmussen, M.   **811**
The **black** banners. Soufan, A. H.   **973.931**
Black boy. Wright, R.   **92**
Black Broadway. Lane, S. F.   **792**
BLACK BUSINESSPEOPLE
See also Businesspeople
The **Black** Calhouns. Buckley, G. L.   **92**
BLACK CHILDREN
See also Children
The **Black** Count.   **944.04**
BLACK DEATH *See* Plague
The **black** death and the transformation of the west. Herlihy, D.   **940.1**
BLACK DIASPORA *See* African diaspora
Black earth. Meier, A.   **947.086**
Black Earth. Snyder, T. D.   **940.53**
Black Elk speaks. Black Elk   **92**
Black Elk, 1863-1950
About
Black Elk Black Elk speaks   **92**
Steltenkamp, M. F. Black Elk, holy man of the Oglala   **92**
Black Elk, holy man of the Oglala. Steltenkamp, M. F.   **92**
Black firsts.   **920**
Black Firsts: 4,000 Ground-breaking and Pioneering

Historical Events. **920**

Black flags. Warrick, J. **956.91**

The **Black** girl next door. Baszile, J. **92**

Black Hawk down. Bowden, M. **967.73**

BLACK HAWK WAR, 1832

    See also Native Americans -- Wars; United
States -- History -- 1815-1861

Black hearts. Frederick, J. **956.7**

Black heritage sites. Curtis, N. C. **973**

The **Black** history of the White House. Lusane,
C. **975.3**

Black hole. Bartusiak, M. **523.8**

The **black** hole war. Susskind, L. **530.1**

BLACK HOLES (ASTRONOMY)

  Bartusiak, M. Black hole **523.8**

  Hawking, S. My brief history **92**

  Miller, A. I. Empire of the stars **520**

  Rovelli, C. Seven Brief Lessons on Physics **530**

  Scharf, C. Gravity's engines **523.8**

  Susskind, L. The black hole war **530.1**

  Tyson, N. d. Death by black hole **523.8**

BLACK HOLES (ASTRONOMY)

    See also Astronomy; Astrophysics; Stars

Black holes and baby universes and other essays.
Hawking, S. **523.1**

BLACK HUMOR (LITERATURE)

    See also Fiction; Literature; Wit and humor

Black is the new white. Mooney, P. **92**

Black Kettle, Cheyenne Chief, 1803?-1868

     About

  Brown, D. A. The American West **978**

BLACK LIBRARIANS

    See also Librarians

Black like me. Griffin, J. H. **305.8**

BLACK LITERATURE (AMERICAN) *See*
American literature -- African American authors

Black literature criticism. **809**

Black maestro. Drape, J. **92**

BLACK MAGIC (WITCHCRAFT) *See* Magic;
Witchcraft

Black Man in a White Coat. Tweedy, D. **92**

BLACK MARKET

  Voigt, E. The dragon behind the glass **597.176**

BLACK MUSIC

    See also Music

BLACK MUSICIANS

  Smith, J. E. Becoming Belafonte **92**

BLACK MUSICIANS

    See also Musicians

BLACK MUSLIM LEADERS

  Carson, C. Malcolm X: the FBI file **92**

  Evanzz, K. The messenger: the rise and fall of Elijah Muhammad **297.8**

  Gardell, M. In the name of Elijah Muhammad **297**

  Gates, H. L. Thirteen ways of looking at a black
man **920.71**

Levinsohn, F. H. Looking for Farrakhan **297.8**

Malcolm X The autobiography of Malcolm X **92**

Marable, M. Malcolm X **92**

Perry, B. Malcolm **92**

BLACK MUSLIMS

  Gardell, M. In the name of Elijah Muhammad **297**

  Levinsohn, F. H. Looking for Farrakhan **297.8**

  Malcolm X The autobiography of Malcolm X **92**

  Marable, M. Malcolm X **92**

BLACK MUSLIMS

    See also African Americans -- Religion; Black
nationalism; Muslims -- United States

BLACK MUSLIMS -- BIOGRAPHY

  Evanzz, K. The messenger: the rise and fall of Elijah Muhammad **297.8**

  Smith, J. Blood brothers **92**

BLACK NATIONALISM

    See also African Americans -- Political activi-
ty; African Americans -- Race identity; Blacks
-- Political activity; Blacks -- Race identity

Black nature. **808**

The **black** Nile. Morrison, D. **962**

BLACK PANTHER PARTY -- HISTORY

  Williams, M. The lost daughter **979.4**

BLACK POETRY (AMERICAN) *See* American
poetry -- African American authors

Black postcards. Wareham, D. **92**

BLACK POWER

  Joseph, P. E. Waiting 'til the midnight hour **323.1**

BLACK POWER

    See also African Americans -- Political activ-
ity; Blacks -- Political activity

The **Black** presidency. Dyson, M. E. **305.8**

Black profiles in courage. Abdul-Jabbar, K. **920**

BLACK SABBATH (MUSICAL GROUP)

  Osbourne, O. I am Ozzy **92**

BLACK SEA REGION -- HISTORY

  Mayor, A. The Poison King **92**

Black stars [series]

  Haskins, J. African American religious leaders **920**

The **black** swan. Taleb, N. N. **003**

Black trials. Weiner, M. S. **342**

Black wings. Hardesty, V. **920**

BLACK WOMEN

  Lewis, R. C. Voyage of the Sable Venus and other
poems **811**

BLACK WOMEN

    See also Women

Black women in America. **920.003**

Black women writers (1950-1980) **810**

Black's law dictionary. **340**

Black's veterinary dictionary. **636.089**

Black, Brian C.

  (ed) Climate change **363.738**

Black, Conrad M.

  Richard M. Nixon **92**

Rise to greatness **971**
Black, George
Empire of shadows **978.7**
Black, Hugo LaFayette, 1886-1971
About
Feldman, N. Scorpions **920**
Black, Jeremy
Other pasts, different presents, alternative futures **900**
Black, Sarah
One dough, ten breads **641.81**
Black, Scott Hoffman
Gardening for butterflies **638**
Blackacre. Youn, M. **811.6**
BLACKBERRY (SMARTPHONE)
McNish, J. Losing the signal **338.4**
Blackberry winter. Mead, M. **92**
Blackburn, Julia
Old man Goya **92**
Blackburn, Lucie, d. 1895
About
Smardz Frost, K. I've got a home in glory land **92**
Blackburn, Paul
The collected poems of Paul Blackburn **811**
Blackburn, Simon, 1944-
The Oxford dictionary of philosophy **103**
Think: a compelling introduction to philosophy **100**
Truth **121**
Blackburn, Thornton, 1813 or 14-1890
About
Smardz Frost, K. I've got a home in glory land **92**
BLACKFACE ENTERTAINERS -- UNITED STATES -- HISTORY
Austen, J. Darkest America **791**
Blackjack, Ada, 1898-1983
About
Niven, J. Ada Blackjack **92**
Blackman, Lucie Jane, 1978-2000
About
Parry, R. L. People who eat darkness **364.152**
Blackmon, Douglas A.
Slavery by another name **305.8**
Blackmun, Harry A.
About
Greenhouse, L. Becoming Justice Blackmun **92**
BLACKS
Raboteau, E. Searching for Zion **305.896**
BLACKS -- ATLANTIC OCEAN REGION -- SOCIAL CONDITIONS
Scott, R. J. Freedom papers **305.896**
BLACKS -- BIOGRAPHY
See also Biography
BLACKS -- CIVIL RIGHTS
See also Blacks -- Political activity; Civil rights
BLACKS -- ECONOMIC CONDITIONS

See also Economic conditions
BLACKS -- FOLKLORE
See also Folklore
BLACKS -- RACE IDENTITY
See also Race awareness
BLACKS -- RELIGION
The Encyclopedia of African and African-American religions **299.6**
BLACKS -- RELIGION
See also Religion
BLACKS -- SEGREGATION
Green, K. Something Must Be Done About Prince Edward County **379.26**
BLACKS IN LITERATURE
Black literature criticism **809**
BLACKS IN MOTION PICTURES
Bogle, D. Bright boulevards, bold dreams **791.43**
The **blacks:** a clown show. Genet, J. **842**
BLACKSMITHING
Parkinson, P. The artist blacksmith **682**
Blackwell critical biographies [series]
Brown, T. The life of W.B. Yeats **821**
Blackwell guides to literature [series]
MacGowan, C. J. Twentieth-century American poetry **811**
Blackwell, Andrew
Visit sunny Chernobyl **363.73**
Blackwell, Lewis, 1958-
Blackwell, L. The life and love of dogs **636.7**
Blagojevich, Rod R., 1956-
About
Brackett, E. Pay to play **92**
Blainey, Geoffrey
Sea of dangers **92**
Blair, Barb
Furniture Makeovers **684.1**
Furniture makes the room **684.1**
Blair, Clay
Hitler's U-boat war **940.54**
Blair, Gabrielle Stanley
Design mom **747**
Blair, Joe, 1962-
About
Blair, J. By the Iowa Sea **977.7**
Blair, Louise
Worrall-Thompson, A. The essential diabetes cookbook **641.5**
Blair, Tony
About
Blair, T. A journey **92**
Remnick, D. Reporting **814**
Blais, Madeleine
In these girls, hope is a muscle **796.323**
Blake, Jenny
Life after college **646.7**
Blake, William, 1757-1827

The complete poetry and prose of William Blake **821**

About

Bentley, G. E. The stranger from paradise: a biography of William Blake **821**

Blakeney, Justina
The new Bohemians **747**

Blakeslee, Robert L.
Your time to bake **641.8**

Blakeslee, Sandra
Wallerstein, J. S. The unexpected legacy of divorce **306.89**

Blanchard, Zechariah
Saltwater Fish and Reef Tanks **639**

Blanco, Richard, 1968-
The Prince of Los Cocuyos **92**

Bland, Jeffrey S.
The disease delusion **615.5**

The **blank** slate. Pinker, S. **155.2**

Blank spots on the map. Paglen, T. **355.3**

BLANK VERSE
See also Poetry

Blank, Hanne
Straight **306.76**

Blanning, T. C. W.
The pursuit of glory **940.2**
The triumph of music **780.9**

Blanning, Tim
Frederick the Great **92**

Blanton, DeAnne
They fought like demons **973.7**

Blaser, Martin J.
Missing microbes **615.7**

Blashford-Snell, Victoria
(ed) The illustrated kitchen bible **641.5**

BLASPHEMY (ISLAM) -- HISTORY -- 20TH CENTURY
Rushdie, S. Joseph Anton **92**

Blass, Steve, 1942-
About
Life stories **920**

Blatner, David
Spectrums **539.2**

Blauvelt, Robert P.
(jt. auth) Gates, A. E. Encyclopedia of pollution **363.7**

Blazer, Chuck, 1945-
About
Thompson, T. American huckster **796.334**

BLEACHING
See also Cleaning; Industrial chemistry; Textile industry

Bleeding Orange. Boeheim, J. **92**

Blehm, Eric
Legend **959.7**

Bleicher, Isaac

(jt. auth) Greenstein, E. A Jewish baker's pastry secrets **641.86**

Bleiler, Richard
Reference and research guide to mystery and detective fiction **016**
(ed) Supernatural fiction writers **809**

BLENDED LEARNING -- UNITED STATES
Vander Ark, T. Getting smart **371.33**

BLETCHLEY PARK (MILTON KEYNES, ENGLAND) -- HISTORY
McKay, S. The secret lives of codebreakers **940.54**

Bligh, William, 1754-1817
About
Alexander, C. The Bounty: the true story of the mutiny on the Bounty **996**

Blight, David W.
American oracle **973.7**
A slave no more **326**

BLIMPS *See* Airships

BLIND
Bloom, H. The Western canon **809**
Campbell, G. John Milton **92**
Feather, L. From Satchmo to Miles **920**
Gibson, W. The miracle worker **812**
Gray, M. Hand me my travelin' shoes **92**
Hawkes, D. John Milton **92**
Herrmann, D. Helen Keller **92**
Keller, H. Helen Keller: selected writings **92**
Keller, H. The story of my life **92**
Kermode, F. An appetite for poetry **801**
Kurson, R. Crashing through **92**
McWilliam, C. What to look for in winter **92**
Roberts, J. A sense of the world **92**
Vendler, H. H. Coming of age as a poet **820**

BLIND
See also People with physical disabilities

BLIND -- BOOKS AND READING
See also Books and reading

BLIND -- EDUCATION
See also Education

Blind descent. Tabor, J. M. **796.52**

Blind eye. Stewart, J. B. **364.1**

The **blind** side. Lewis, M. **92**

Blinder, Alan S.
After the music stopped **330.973**

BLINDNESS
See also Vision disorders

Blink: the power of thinking without thinking. Gladwell, M. **153.4**

Blitzkrieg. Clark, L. **940.54**

BLIZZARDS
Laskin, D. The children's blizzard **977**
Tougias, M. Ten hours until dawn **363.34**

BLIZZARDS
See also Storms

Bloch-Bauer, Adele, 1881-1925

About

O'Connor The lady in gold   **759.36**

Block city. Kearney, K.   **794**

BLOCK PRINTING *See* Color prints; Linoleum block printing; Textile printing; Wood engraving; Woodcuts

Block, Geoffrey Holden

(ed) The Richard Rodgers reader   **782.1**

Block, Shira

When Your Parent Moves in   **306.874**

Blockbusters. Elberse, A.   **384**

Blockley, D. I.

Bridges   **624.2**

BLOGGERS

Bageant, J. Deer hunting with Jesus   **305.5**

Beavan, C. No impact man   **333.72**

Eteraz, A. Children of dust   **92**

A homemade life   **92**

Lobdell, W. Losing my religion   **92**

Blom, Philipp, 1970-

The vertigo years   **940.2**

Blomquist, Jeff

Goldberg, D. A user's guide to the universe   **530**

Blonder, Greg

Meathead   **641.7**

BLOOD

Englert, R. Blood secrets   **363.2**

BLOOD

See also Physiology

BLOOD -- DISEASES

See also Diseases

Blood and politics. Zeskind, L.   **305.8**

Blood and Sand. Von Tunzelmann, A.   **973.92**

Blood and thunder. Sides, H.   **978**

Blood at the root. Phillips, P.   **305.8**

Blood brothers. Smith, J.   **92**

Blood brothers. Weisskopf, M.   **92**

BLOOD GROUPS

See also Blood

Blood in the cage. Wertheim, L. J.   **92**

Blood in the water. Thompson, H. A.   **365**

Blood knot and other plays. Fugard, A.   **822**

Blood lyrics. Ford, K.   **811**

The **blood** of free men. Neiberg, M.   **940.54**

The **blood** of heroes. Donovan, J.   **976.4**

Blood of the tiger. Mills, J. A.   **639.97**

BLOOD PRESSURE

See also Blood

Blood secrets. Englert, R.   **363.2**

Blood sisters. Gristwood, S.   **942.04**

The **Blood** telegram. Bass, G. J.   **327.73**

Blood will out. Kirn, W.   **364.152**

Blood, bones & butter. Hamilton, G.   **92**

Blood, iron, & gold. Wolmar, C.   **385**

BLOODBORNE INFECTIONS -- PREVENTION

Goldfarb, T. L. The patient survival guide

Bloodlands. Snyder, T. D.   **940.54**

Bloody murder. Symons, J.   **809**

BLOODY SUNDAY JUSTICE CAMPAIGN

Campbell, J. Setting the truth free   **941.6**

The **bloody** white baron. Palmer, J.   **92**

Bloom, Allan David

The closing of the American mind   **973.92**

Bloom, Harold, 1930-

(ed) Alice Walker   **813**

(ed) Alice Walker's The color purple   **813**

(ed) American religious poems   **811**

(ed) The Best poems of the English language   **821**

Bloom, H. The anatomy of influence   **801**

Genius   **153.9**

Hamlet: poem unlimited   **822.3**

Shakespeare: the invention of the human   **822.3**

The Western canon   **809**

(ed) Geoffrey Chaucer's The Canterbury tales   **821**

(ed) J.D. Salinger   **813**

(ed) John Steinbeck   **813**

(ed) Samuel Beckett's Waiting for Godot   **842**

(ed) Selected poems   **811**

(ed) Till I end my song   **808.81**

(ed) William Faulkner   **813**

(ed) Zora Neale Hurston   **813**

About

Bloom, H. The anatomy of influence   **801**

Bloom, Howard

The God problem   **500**

The Lucifer principle   **128**

Bloom, Jonathan

American wasteland   **363.7**

Bloom, Ken

Broadway musicals   **792.6**

Bloom, Leora

Theo Chocolate   **641.6**

Bloom, Paul

How pleasure works   **152.4**

Bloomfield, April

A Girl and Her Greens   **641.65**

Bloomfield, Harold H.

Making peace with your past   **158**

The **Bloomsbury** Guide to Christian Spirituality.   **270**

Bloomston, Carrie

The little spark   **153.3**

Blossoms in the wind. Sheftall, M. G.   **940.54**

Blott, Maggie

(ed) Pregnancy day by day   **618.2**

Blouin, Jacques

Peynaud, E. The taste of wine   **641.2**

Blount, RoyJr., 1941-

Alphabetter juice, or, The joy of text   **818**

Long time leaving   **975**

Robert E. Lee   **92**

Save room for pie   **641.3**

Twain, M. Mark Twain's library of humor **817**

BLOWING THE WHISTLE *See* Whistle blowing

Blowout in the Gulf. Freudenburg, W. R. **363.7**

BLOWOUTS, OIL WELL *See* Oil wells -- Blowouts

BLUE COLLAR WORKERS *See* Labor; Working class

The **blue** devils of Nada. Murray, A. **780.89**

Blue Ginger. Tsai, M. **641.5**

Blue highways. Heat Moon, W. L. **917**

Blue hour. Forche, C. **811**

Blue laws. Young, K. **811.54**

Blue like jazz. Miller, D. **92**

Blue Monday. Coleman, R. **92**

Blue plate special. Christensen, K. **92**

Blue ribbon baking from a redneck kitchen. Bryson,
F. **641.597**

The **blue** sweater. Novogratz, J. **339.4**

The **Blue** Zones solution. Buettner, D. **613.2**

The **bluebird** effect. Zickefoose, J. **598**

BLUEGRASS MUSIC

Stanley, R. Man of constant sorrow **92**

BLUEGRASS MUSIC

See also Music

BLUEGRASS MUSICIANS

Stanley, R. Man of constant sorrow **92**

Blues. Giovanni, N. **811**

Blues all around me. King, B. B. **781.643**

Blues all day long. Goins, W. E. **92**

BLUES MUSIC

Baraka, I. A. The LeRoi Jones/Amiri Baraka reader **818**

Ferris, W. Give my poor heart ease **781.643**

Gioia, T. Delta blues **781.643**

Govenar, A. B. Lightnin' Hopkins **92**

Govenar, A. B. Texas blues **781.64**

Gray, M. Hand me my travelin' shoes **92**

King, B. B. Blues all around me **781.643**

Lomax, A. The land where the blues began **781.643**

Murray, A. The blue devils of Nada **780.89**

Nothing but the blues **781.643**

Robertson, D. W.C. Handy **92**

Wald, E. Escaping the delta **92**

Wolfe, C. K. The life and legend of Leadbelly **92**

BLUES MUSIC

See also African American music; Folk music
-- United States; Popular music

BLUES MUSIC -- HISTORY AND CRITICISM

Inaba, M. Willie Dixon **92**

Murray, A. The blue devils of Nada **780.89**

Nothing but the blues **781.643**

BLUES MUSIC -- POETRY

Blues poems **811**

BLUES MUSICIANS

Feather, L. From Satchmo to Miles **920**

Goins, W. E. Blues all day long **92**

Govenar, A. B. Lightnin' Hopkins **92**

Gray, M. Hand me my travelin' shoes **92**

Holiday, B. Lady sings the blues **92**

Hoskyns, B. Lowside of the road **92**

Inaba, M. Willie Dixon **92**

James, E. Rage to survive **92**

King, B. B. Blues all around me **781.643**

Robertson, D. W.C. Handy **92**

Wald, E. Escaping the delta **92**

Blues poems. **811**

BLUES POETRY

See also American poetry -- African American
authors

BLUES SONGS *See* Blues music

Bluestein, Jane

The perfection deception **155.2**

Bluhm, Lisa

Creative soldered jewelry & accessories **745.594**

Blum, Andrew

Tubes **384.3**

Blum, Deborah

(ed) The best American science and nature writing
2014 **810.8**

Ghost hunters **133.9**

The poisoner's handbook **614**

Blum, Edward J.

The color of Christ **232**

Blum, Howard

American lightning **364.152**

The Last Goodnight **940.54**

Blum, Susan

Your immune system recovery plan **616.97**

Blume, Lesley M. M.

Everybody behaves badly **813**

Blumenreich, Megan

(jt. auth) Falk, B. Teaching matters **370.9**

Blumenthal, David

The heart of power **362.1**

Blumenthal, Eileen

Puppetry **791.5**

Blumenthal, Sidney, 1948-

A self-made man **92**

Blumrosen, Alfred W.

Slave nation **973.3**

Blumrosen, Ruth Gerber

Blumrosen, A. W. Slave nation **973.3**

Blunt, Anthony, 1907-1983

About

Carter, M. Anthony Blunt: his lives **92**

Blunt, Judy

Breaking clean **92**

Blunt, Judy, 1954-

About

Blunt, J. Breaking clean **92**

Blunt, Wilfrid

Linnaeus, the compleat naturalist **92**

Blur. Kovach, B.   **070**

Bly, Robert
Eating the honey of words   **811**
Iron John   **305.31**
The night Abraham called to the stars   **811**
(tr) Jacobsen, R. The roads have come to an end now   **839.8**

About
Gioia, D. Can poetry matter?   **809.1**

Blyth, Catherine
The art of conversation   **395**

BOARD BOOKS FOR CHILDREN
    See also Picture books for children

BOARD GAMES
Botermans, J. The book of games   **794**

BOARD GAMES
    See also Games

BOARD OF GOVERNORS OF THE FEDERAL RESERVE SYSTEM
Woodward, B. Maestro: Greenspan's Fed and the American boom   **331.1**

BOARDING HOUSES *See* Hotels and motels

BOARDING SCHOOLS -- DRAMA.
Bennett, A. The history boys   **822**

Boardman, John
Greek art   **709.3**
(ed) The Oxford history of the Roman world   **937**

BOAT RACERS
Auletta, K. Media man   **92**

BOAT RACING
    See also Boats and boating; Racing
A **boat,** a whale, and a walrus. Erickson, R. **641.597**

BOATING *See* Boats and boating

Boatner, Mark Mayo
The Civil War dictionary   **973.7**

BOATS AND BOATING
Chapman piloting & seamanship   **623.88**
Stone, N. On the water   **917**

Bob Dylan. Margotin, P.   **782.42**
Bob Dylan. Brown, D.   **92**
The **Bob** Dylan encyclopedia. Gray, M.   **782.42**
Bob Hope: the road well-traveled. Quirk, L. J.   **92**

Bobbitt, Philip
Terror and consent   **363.32**

Bobby Fischer teaches chess. Fischer, B.   **794.1**
Bobby Kennedy. Tye, L.   **92**

Bobick, James E.
(jt. auth) Berard, G. L. Science and technology resources   **025.5**
Balaban, N. E. The handy anatomy answer book   **611**
(ed) The handy science answer book   **500**

Bobrick, Benson
Angel in the whirlwind   **973.3**

Bochner, Harry
(ed) Comprehensive Yiddish-English Diction-

ary   **439**

Bock, Laszlo
Work rules!   **658.4**

Bocquet, José-Louis
Kiki de Montparnasse   **759.4**

Bodanis, David
E   **530.1**
Electric universe   **537**

Boden, Edward
(ed) Black's veterinary dictionary   **636.089**

Bodies. Orbach, S.   **362.1**

BODY *See* Human body

BODY AND MIND *See* Mind and body

BODY CARE *See* Hygiene

Body geographic. Borich, B. J.   **818**

The **body** hunters. Shah, S.   **362.1**

BODY IMAGE
Brown, H. Body of truth   **613.2**
Durham, M. G. The Lolita effect   **302.23**
Orbach, S. Bodies   **362.1**
Shinner, P. You feel so mortal   **814**

BODY IMAGE
    See also Human body; Mind and body; Personality; Self-perception

BODY IMAGE IN WOMEN
Whitefield-Madrano, A. Face value   **111.85**
Body intelligence. Cardillo, J.   **158.1**
The **body** keeps the score. Van der Kolk, B. A.   **616.85**

BODY LANGUAGE
Dimitrius Reading people   **155.2**
Pease, A. The definitive book of body language   **153.6**

BODY LANGUAGE
    See also Nonverbal communication

Body of truth. Brown, H.   **613.2**

BODY PIERCING
    See also Personal appearance
The **body** politic. Moreno, J. D.   **303.48**

BODY SURFING *See* Surfing

BODY TEMPERATURE
    See also Diagnosis; Physiology

BODY WEIGHT
Brown, H. Body of truth   **613.2**

BODY WEIGHT
    See also Human body; Weight

BODYBUILDING
    See also Exercise; Physical fitness

BODYGUARDS -- BIOGRAPHY
Hill, C. Mrs. Kennedy and me   **973.922**

Boeckh, J. Anthony
The great reflation   **332.6**

Boeheim, Jim, 1944-
Bleeding Orange   **92**

Boehm, Arthur
Tsai, M. Blue Ginger   **641.5**

Boesch, Christophe
(ed) Among African apes 599.8

Bogard, Paul
The end of night 551.56

Bogard, Travis
(ed) O'Neil, E. Complete plays 812

Bogart, Humphrey, 1899-1957
About
Thomson, D. Humphrey Bogart 92

Boggs, Belle
The art of waiting 618.178

Boggs, Jacey
Spin art 746.12

Bogira, Steve
Courtroom 302 345

Bogle, Donald
Bright boulevards, bold dreams 791.43
Heat wave 92

Bogle, John C., 1929-
The clash of the cultures 332.6

Bogucki, Peter I.
(ed) Ancient Europe 8000 B.C.-A.D. 1000 936

Bogus, Carl T.
Buckley 92

BOHEMIANISM
The Portable beat reader 810

BOHEMIANISM
See also Counter culture; Manners and customs

BOHEMIANISM -- NEW YORK (N.Y.)
Invisible City 779
Martin, J. Rebel Souls 92
Strausbaugh, J. The Village 974.7

BOHEMIANISM -- NEW YORK (STATE) -- NEW YORK
Anasi, R. The last bohemia 974.7
Rips, N. Trying to float 974.7

BOHEMIANISM -- NEW YORK (STATE) -- NEW YORK -- HISTORY -- 20TH CENTURY
Reid, D. The brazen age 974.7

Bohemians, bootleggers, flappers, and swells. 810.8

Bohlander, Richard E.
(ed) World explorers and discoverers 920.003

Bohnet, Iris
What works 331.4

Bohr, Niels Henrik David, 1885-1962
About
Bolles, E. B. Einstein defiant 530.1

Boissoneault, Lorraine
The Last Voyageurs 977

Bolan, Kimberly
Technology made simple 025

Boland, Eavan
New collected poems 821
(ed) The Making of a poem 821
A woman without a country 821

Boland, Robert
Musicals! 792.6

The **bold** dry garden. 635.9

A **bold** fresh piece of humanity. O'Reilly, B. 92

Bolger, Daniel P.
Why We Lost 956.704

Bolick, Kate
About
Bolick, K. Spinster 92

Bolivar. Arana, M. 92

Bolivar, Simon, 1783-1830
About
Arana, M. Bolivar 92

Bolkovac, Kathryn
About
Bolkovac, K. The whistleblower 92

Bollas, Christopher
When the Sun Bursts 616.89

Boller, Paul F.
Presidential wives 920
They never said it 808.88

Bolles, Edmund Blair
Einstein defiant 530.1

Bolles, Richard Nelson
What color is your parachute? 2017 650.1

Bollingen series
Plato The collected dialogues of Plato, including the letters 888

Bollinger, Don
Hardwood floors 690

Bolman, Lee G.
How great leaders think 658.4

BOLSHEVISM See Communism

Bolsta, Hyla Shifra
The illuminated Kaddish 296.4

Bolt, Robert
A man for all seasons 822

Boltzmann's tomb. Green, B. 509

Bolz-Weber, Nadia
Accidental saints 284.1

Bomb. Sheinkin, S. 623.4

BOMB ATTACKS See Bombings

The **bomb** in the basement. Karpin, M. I. 355

BOMBAY (INDIA)
Boo, K. Behind the beautiful forevers 305.5
Faleiro, S. Beautiful thing 792.7

Bomber County. Swift, D. 821

BOMBERS
See also Airplanes; Military airplanes

BOMBING, AERIAL -- ENGLAND -- LONDON -- HISTORY -- 20TH CENTURY
Preston, D. A higher form of killing 940.4

BOMBING, AERIAL -- HISTORY -- 20TH CENTURY
Kennedy, P. M. Engineers of victory 940.54

BOMBINGS

Blum, H. American lightning   **364.152**

Gage, B. The day Wall Street exploded   **974.7**

Merriman, J. M. The dynamite club   **363.32**

BOMBINGS

     See also Offenses against public safety; Political crimes and offenses; Terrorism

BOMBS

     See also Ammunition; Explosives; Ordnance; Projectiles

The **Bon** appetit cookbook. Fairchild, B.   **641.5**

The **Bon** appetit fast easy fresh cookbook. Fairchild, B.   **641.5**

Bonair-Agard, Roger

   Bury my clothes   **811**

Bonaparte. Gueniffey, P.   **92**

Bonaparte, Paolina, 1780-1825

     About

   Fraser, F. Pauline Bonaparte   **92**

Bond's Top 100 Franchises, 2015.   **381**

Bond, Jenny

   Who the hell is Pansy O'Hara?   **920**

Bond, Robert E.

   (ed) Bond's Top 100 Franchises, 2015   **381**

Bondar, Carin

   Wild Sex   **591.562**

Bondil, Nathalie

   (ed) Cuba: art and history, from 1868 to today   **709**

BONDS

     See also Finance; Investments; Negotiable instruments; Securities; Stock exchanges

Bonds, Margaret, 1913-1972

     About

   Walker-Hill, H. From spirituals to symphonies **780**

BONE MARROW -- TRANSPLANTATION

   Whitehouse, B. The match   **92**

A **bone** to pick. Bittman, M.   **338.1**

Bone wars. Rea, T.   **560**

BONES -- DISEASES

     See also Diseases

Bonewitz, Ronald

   Rocks and minerals   **549**

Bonhoeffer. Metaxas, E.   **92**

Bonhoeffer, Dietrich, 1906-1945

   The cost of discipleship   **226**

     About

   Marsh, C. Strange glory   **92**

   Metaxas, E. Bonhoeffer   **92**

Bonifonte, Philip

   T'ai chi for seniors   **613.7**

Bonk. Roach, M.   **612.6**

Bonney, Grace

   Design*Sponge at home   **747**

Bonnie, 1910-1934

     About

   Guinn, J. Go down together   **364.1**

Bonobo. Waal, F. d.   **599.88**

BONSAI

   Bender, R. W. Bountiful bonsai   **635.9**

Boo, Katherine

   Behind the beautiful forevers   **305.5**

The **Book.** Houston, K.   **002.09**

BOOK BURNING

   Bosmajian, H. A. Burning books   **098**

BOOK BUYING (LIBRARIES) *See* Libraries -- Acquisitions

Book by book. Dirda, M.   **028**

BOOK CLUBS (DISCUSSION GROUPS)

   Hollands, N. Fellowship in a ring   **809**

BOOK COLLECTING

   American book trade directory   **070.5**

   Basbanes, N. A. Patience & fortitude   **002**

   Lansky, A. Outwitting history   **002.07**

   Mays, A. E. The millionaire and the bard   **822.33**

   Rasmussen, E. The Shakespeare thefts   **822.3**

BOOK COLLECTING

     See also Book selection; Collectors and collecting

BOOK COLLECTORS

   Lansky, A. Outwitting history   **002.07**

   Singer, M. Character studies   **920**

   Strouse, J. Morgan   **92**

BOOK DESIGN

   Rivers, C. Little book of book making   **686**

BOOK DESIGN

     See also Book industry

BOOK DESIGNERS

   Rivers, C. Little book of book making   **686**

BOOK DISCUSSION GROUPS *See* Book clubs (Discussion groups)

BOOK EDITORS -- UNITED STATES -- BIOGRAPHY

   The tender hour of twilight   **070.5**

BOOK ILLUSTRATION *See* Illustration of books

The **book** in the Renaissance. Pettegree, A.   **070.5**

BOOK INDUSTRY

   American book trade directory   **070.5**

   Lee, M. Bookmaking: editing, design, production   **686**

   Pettegree, A. The book in the Renaissance   **070.5**

BOOK INDUSTRY

     See also Industries

BOOK LENDING *See* Library circulation

BOOK LISTS *See* Best books

Book lust. Pearl, N.   **011**

Book of ages. Lepore, J.   **92**

The **book** of basketball. Simmons, B.   **796.323**

A **book** of bees. Hubbell, S.   **638**

Book of blues. Kerouac, J.   **811**

The **book** of calamities. Trachtenberg, P.   **128**

The **Book** of common prayer and administration of the sacraments and other rites and ceremonies of the church. Episcopal Church/Book of common prayer **264**

The **book** of decorating. **747**

The **Book** of eulogies. **808.8**

The **book** of forgiving. **179**

The **book** of games. Botermans, J. **794**

The **book** of Genesis. Crumb, R. **741.5**

The **book** of goodbyes. Weise, J. **813**

The **book** of home how-to. **643**

The **book** of home how-to. **643**

Book of honor. Gup, T. **327.12**

The **Book** of Isaias. Connolly, D. **305.235**

The **book** of Jewish food. Roden, C. **641.5**

The **book** of Job. Kushner, H. S. **223**

The **book** of Klezmer. Strom, Y. **781.62**

The **book** of love. McConnachie, J. **306.7**

The **book** of love. Rosenblatt, R. **152.4**

A **Book** of love poetry. **808.81**

A **Book** of lumininous things. Milosz, C. **808.81**

Book of Majors. **378**

The **Book** of Matt. Jimenez, S. **364.1**

A **book** of Mediterranean food. David, E. **641.5**

The **book** of miracles. Woodward, K. L. **231.7**

The **Book** of Mormon. Book of Mormon **289.3**

Book of Mormon

The Book of Mormon **289.3**

Givens, T. By the hand of Mormon **289.3**

The **Book** of Mormon. Gutjahr, P. C. **289.3**

BOOK OF MORMON -- CRITICISM

Hardy, G. Understanding the Book of Mormon **289.3**

The **book** of my lives. Hemon, A. **814**

The **book** of New Israeli food. Gur, J. **641.5**

The **book** of nothing. Barrow, J. D. **111**

The **book** of numbers. Conway, J. H. **512.7**

A **book** of saints for Catholic moms. Hendey, L. M. **248.8**

A **book** of secrets. Holroyd, M. **306.874**

The **book** of shells. Harasewych, M. G. **594**

Book of sketches, 1952-53. Kerouac, J. **811**

The **Book** of Spice. O'Connell, J. **641.3**

The **book** of the states. **352.13**

The **book** of trees. Lima, M. **001.2**

The **book** of U.S. government jobs. Damp, D. V. **331.1**

The **Book** of war. **355**

The **book** of William. Collins, P. **822.3**

The **book** on the bookshelf. Petroski, H. **022**

The **book** on writing. LaRocque, P. **808**

BOOK RARITIES See Rare books

Book repair. Lavender, K. **025.7**

BOOK REVIEWING

See also Books and reading; Criticism

BOOK SELECTION

Keane, N. J. 101 great, ready-to-use book lists for teens **028.5**

Ramsdell, K. Romance fiction **016**

Reference Sources for Small and Medium-Sized Libraries **011**

Roche, R. Read on-- biography **016**

What Do I Read Next? **020**

BOOK SELECTION

See also Libraries -- Acquisitions; Libraries -- Collection development

BOOK SELECTION -- UNITED STATES

Foerstel, H. N. Banned in the U.S.A **025.2**

BOOK TALKS

Schall, L. Teen talkback with interactive book-talks! **021.7**

BOOK TALKS

See also Book reviews; Libraries -- Public relations; Public speaking

BOOK TRADE *See* Book industry; Booksellers and bookselling; Publishers and publishing

Bookbinding. Cambras, J. **686.3**

BOOKBINDING

See also Book industry; Books

BOOKBINDING

Cambras, J. Bookbinding **686.3**

Diehn, G. Real life journals: designing & using handmade books **686.3**

Ekrem, E. Bound **686.3**

Golden, A. Making handmade books **686.3**

LaPlantz, S. Cover to cover **686.3**

Petroski, H. The book on the bookshelf **022**

Rivers, C. Little book of book making **686**

BOOKBINDING -- REPAIRING -- HAND-BOOKS, MANUALS, ETC

Lavender, K. Book repair **025.7**

Booker T. Washington. Smock, R. W. **92**

Booker T. Washington: the making of a black leader, 1856-1901. Harlan, L. R. **92**

Booker T. Washington: the wizard of Tuskegee, 1901-1915. Harlan, L. R. **92**

Booker, Cory

About

Russakoff, D. The prize **371.2**

BOOKKEEPING

See also Business; Business education; Business mathematics

BOOKMAKING (BETTING) *See* Gambling

Bookmaking: editing, design, production. Lee, M. **686**

Booknotes (Television program)

Booknotes: life stories **920**

Booknotes: life stories. Booknotes (Television program) **920**

Books. McMurtry, L. **92**

BOOKS

Golden, A. Making handmade books **686.3**

Lee, M. Bookmaking: editing, design, production **686**

Novel living **002.075**

Petroski, H. The book on the bookshelf 022

BOOKS -- APPRAISAL *See* Book reviewing; Books and reading; Criticism; Literature -- History and criticism

BOOKS -- CENSORSHIP
Finn, P. The Zhivago affair 891.73
Scales, P. R. Books under fire 016

BOOKS -- CENSORSHIP
See also Censorship

BOOKS -- COLLECTORS AND COLLECTING
See Book collecting

BOOKS -- CONSERVATION AND RESTORATION
Schechter, A. A. Basic book repair methods 025.7

BOOKS -- CONSERVATION AND RESTORATION -- HANDBOOKS, MANUALS, ETC
Lavender, K. Book repair 025.7

BOOKS -- DESIGN *See* Book design

BOOKS -- EUROPE -- HISTORY -- 1400-1600
Pettegree, A. The book in the Renaissance 070.5

BOOKS -- EXHIBITIONS
See also Exhibitions

BOOKS -- LARGE PRINT *See* Large print books

BOOKS -- PRESERVATION *See* Library resources -- Conservation and restoration

BOOKS -- PRICES
See also Booksellers and bookselling; Prices

BOOKS -- SELECTION *See* Book selection
Books and islands in Ojibwe country. Erdrich, L. 92

BOOKS AND READING
Baker, N. The way the world works 814
Basbanes, N. A. Every book its reader 028
Basbanes, N. A. Patience & fortitude 002
Beam, A. A great idea at the time 973.91
Brottman, M. The Maximum Security Book Club 365.66
Clark, C. A. Read on...sports 016
Cords, S. S. The real story 025.5
Dirda, M. Book by book 028
Dirda, M. Browsings 028
Ellington, E. A year of reading 011
Fiore, C. D. Fiore's summer library reading program handbook 027.62
Herald, D. T. Genreflecting 016
Hirshfield, J. Ten windows 808.1
Hollands, N. Fellowship in a ring 809
James, C. Latest readings 828
John, L. Z. Running book discussion groups 374
Keane, N. J. 101 great, ready-to-use book lists for teens 028.5
Manguel, A. A reader on reading 818
Mendelsund, P. What we see when we read 028
Nafisi, A. Reading Lolita in Tehran 92
Nafisi, A. The Republic of Imagination 819
Naipaul, V. S. Reading & writing 92
Pearl, N. Book lust 011

Pearl, N. More book lust 025
Prose, F. Reading like a writer 808
Ross, C. S. The pleasures of reading 028
Saler, M. As if 823
Schwalbe, W. The end of your life book club 616.99
Smiley, J. Thirteen ways of looking at the novel 813
Szymborska, W. Nonrequired reading 028.1
Walton, J. What Makes This Book So Great 813
What Do I Read Next? 020

BOOKS AND READING
See also Communication; Education; Reading

BOOKS AND READING -- BEST BOOKS *See* Best books

BOOKS AND READING -- HISTORY
Houston, K. The Book 002.09

BOOKS AND READING -- PSYCHOLOGICAL ASPECTS
Mutch, M. Know the night 92

BOOKS AND READING -- UNITED STATES
Parini, J. Promised land 810
Walton, J. What Makes This Book So Great 813

BOOKS AND READING FOR CHILDREN *See* Children -- Books and reading

BOOKS AND READING.
Ross, C. S. Reading matters 028

BOOKS FOR CHILDREN *See* Children's literature

BOOKS FOR SIGHT SAVING *See* Large print books

BOOKS FOR TEENAGERS *See* Young adult literature

Books in action [series]
The artist's library 021.2

BOOKS IN MACHINE-READABLE FORM *See* Electronic books

BOOKS OF HOURS
See also Books

BOOKS ON CASSETTE *See* Audiobooks
BOOKS ON TAPE *See* Audiobooks
Books that changed the world [series]
Browne, J. Darwin's Origin of species 576.8
Manguel, A. Homer's The Iliad and The Odyssey 883
Books under fire. Scales, P. R. 016
The **bookseller** of Kabul. Seierstad, A. 958.1
BOOKSELLERS
The letters of Sylvia Beach 92
BOOKSELLERS AND BOOKSELLING
Buzbee, L. The yellow-lighted bookshop 002
Cumming, L. The Vanishing Velazquez 759.6
The letters of Sylvia Beach 92
McMurtry, L. Books 92
BOOKSELLERS AND BOOKSELLING
See also Book industry

BOOKSELLERS AND BOOKSELLING -- ENG-LAND -- READING

Cumming, L. The Vanishing Velazquez   **759.6**

BOOKSELLERS AND BOOKSELLING -- FRANCE -- PARIS

The letters of Sylvia Beach   **92**

BOOKSELLERS' CATALOGS

See also Booksellers and bookselling

BOOKTALKING *See* Book talks

BOOKTALKS *See* Book talks

Boole, George, 1815-1864

About

Bell, E. T. Men of mathematics   **920**

BOOLEAN ALGEBRA

See also Group theory; Set theory; Symbolic logic

Boom, Bust, Boom. Carter, B.   **622**

Boomhower, Daniel F., 1976-

(ed) A basic music library   **016**

Boone. Morgan, R.   **92**

Boone, Daniel, 1734-1820

About

Faragher, J. M. Daniel Boone   **92**

Morgan, R. Boone   **92**

Boorstin, Daniel J.

The Americans: The colonial experience   **973**

The Americans: The democratic experience   **973**

The Americans: The national experience   **973**

The creators   **909**

Hidden history   **973**

The image   **973.9**

Boorstin, Ruth Frankel

(ed) Boorstin, D. J. Hidden history   **973**

Boot, Max

War made new   **355**

Booth, John Wilkes, 1838-1865

About

Alford, T. Fortune's Fool   **92**

Swanson, J. L. Manhunt   **364.152**

Booth, Michael

The Almost Nearly Perfect People   **948**

Booth, Philip

Selves   **811**

Booth, Wayne C., 1921-2005

(ed) A manual for writers of research papers, theses, and dissertations   **808.06**

BOOTLEGGERS

Balsamo, W. Young Al Capone   **92**

Bergreen, L. Capone   **364.1**

Eig, J. Get Capone   **92**

BOOTS *See* Shoes

Bootstrapper. Link, M.   **92**

Borba, Michele

Unselfie   **649.7**

The **border** cookbook. Jamison, B.   **641.59**

BORDER LIFE *See* Frontier and pioneer life

Border patrol nation. Miller, T.   **363.28**

BORDER PATROLS

Carr, M. Fortress Europe   **363.28**

Miller, T. Border patrol nation   **363.28**

BORDER PATROLS

See also Police

BORDERLANDS -- EUROPE

Carr, M. Fortress Europe   **363.28**

Borderless economics. Guest, R.   **303.48**

BORDERS (GEOGRAPHY) *See* Boundaries

BORDERS, ORNAMENTAL (DECORATIVE ARTS)

Eckman, E. Around the corner crochet borders   **746.43**

Bordewich, Fergus M.

America's great debate   **973.6**

Bound for Canaan   **973.7**

The First Congress   **327.73**

Washington: the making of the American capital   **975.3**

Borg, Marcus J., 1942-2015

Evolution of the Word   **225**

The first Paul   **227**

Borges, a life. Williamson, E.   **92**

Borges, Jorge Luis, 1899-1986

Selected non-fictions   **864**

Selected poems   **861**

This craft of verse   **809.1**

About

Bloom, H. The Western canon   **809**

Williamson, E. Borges, a life   **92**

Borgia family

About

Hibbert, C. The Borgias and their enemies   **945**

Borgia, Cesare, 1476?-1507

About

Strathern, P. The artist, the philosopher, and the warrior   **920**

Borgia, Lucrezia, 1480-1519

About

Bradford, S. Lucrezia Borgia   **92**

The **Borgias** and their enemies. Hibbert, C.   **945**

Borich, Barrie Jean, 1959-

About

Borich, B. J. Body geographic   **818**

BORING *See* Drilling and boring (Earth and rocks); Drilling and boring (Metal, wood, etc.)

Borins, Mel

A doctor's guide to alternative medicine   **615.5**

Boritt, G. S.

The Gettysburg gospel   **973.7**

Borman, Tracy

Thomas Cromwell   **92**

Born believers. Barrett, J. L.   **200.1**

Born digital. Palfrey, J.   **302.23**

Born free. Adamson, J.   **599.75**

The **born** frees. Burge, K.   305.242

Born in Africa. Meredith, M.   960

Born in blood and fire. Chasteen, J. C.   980

Born naked. Mowat, F.   92

Born on a blue day. Tammet, D.   92

Born round. Bruni, F.   92

Born standing up. Martin, S.   92

Born Survivors. Holden, W.   940.531

Born this day. Nowlan, R. A.   808.88

Born to be good. Keltner, D.   155.2

Born to be king. Mayer, C.   92

Born to Be Wild. Garlick, H.   796.083

Born to run. McDougall, C.   796.42

Born With Teeth. Mulgrew, K.   791.45

Born, Max, 1882-1970

    About

  Greenspan, N. T. The end of the certain world   92

Borneman, Walter R., 1952-

  The admirals   920

  Alaska: saga of a bold land   979.8

  American spring   973.3

  Macarthur at war   92

  Polk   92

Borrowed time. Monette, P.   362.1

BORROWING *See* Loans

Borsics, Angelin

  Styled   747

Bortolotti, Dan

  Hope in hell   610

  Wild blue   599.5

Borukhova, Mazoltuv

    About

  Malcolm, J. Iphigenia in Forest Hills   345

Borzutzky, Daniel

  The performance of becoming human   811.6

Bosco-Ruggiero, Stephanie

  (jt. auth) Groza, V. Adopting older children   362.7

Bosmajian, Haig A.

  Burning books   098

Bosman, Ellen

  Gay, lesbian, bisexual, and transgendered literature   016

BOSNIA AND HERCEGOVINA

  Shapiro, S. The Bosnia list   92

BOSNIA AND HERCEGOVINA -- ETHNIC RELATIONS -- HISTORY -- 20TH CENTURY

  Shapiro, S. The Bosnia list   92

The **Bosnia** list. Shapiro, S.   92

BOSNIAN AMERICANS -- BIOGRAPHY

  Shapiro, S. The Bosnia list   92

Boss Cupid. Gunn, T.   821

Boss Life. Downs, P.   92

BOSS RULE *See* Political corruption

BOSSA NOVA (MUSIC)

  See also Dance music; Popular music

BOSSINESS

    See also Personality

Bossypants. Fey, T.   92

BOSTON (MASS.)

  Sered, S. S. Can't catch a break   362.83

BOSTON (MASS.) -- BIOGRAPHY

  Lepore, J. Book of ages   92

BOSTON (MASS.) -- HISTORY

  Philbrick, N. Bunker Hill   973.3

  Phillips, K. 1775   973.3

BOSTON (MASS.) -- RACE RELATIONS

  Lehr, D. The fence   364.1

  Lukas, J. A. Common ground   305.8

  Masur, L. P. The soiling of Old Glory   974.4

BOSTON MARATHON BOMBING, BOSTON, MASS., 2013

  Russell, J. Long mile home   363.325

  Witter, B. Stronger   92

BOSTON RED SOX (BASEBALL TEAM)

  Halberstam, D. Summer of '49   796.357

  Halberstam, D. The teammates   796

  Linn, E. Hitter: the life and turmoils of Ted Williams   92

  Stout, G. Fenway 1912   796.357

BOSTON REGION (MASS.) -- RACE RELATIONS -- HISTORY -- 19TH CENTURY

  Kantrowitz, S. More than freedom   323.1

BOSTON TEA PARTY, 1773

  Bunker, N. An empire on the edge   973.3

  Unger, H. G. American tempest   973.3

BOSTON TEA PARTY, 1773

    See also United States -- History -- 1775-1783, Revolution

Boston Women's Health Book Collective

  Our bodies, ourselves   613

Boston, Sarah

  Lucky Dog   636.089

Bostridge, Ian

  Schubert's winter journey   782.4

Bostridge, Mark

  Florence Nightingale   92

Bostrom, Nick, 1973-

  Superintelligence   006.3

Boswell's enlightenment. Zaretsky, R.   92

Boswell's enlightenment.   828

Boswell's presumptuous task. Sisman, A.   828

Boswell, James, 1740-1795

  The journal of a tour to the Hebrides with Samuel Johnson   914

  The life of Samuel Johnson   92

    About

  Boswell's enlightenment   828

  Martin, P. A life of James Boswell   828

  Sisman, A. Boswell's presumptuous task   828

  Starr, W. W. Whisky, kilts, and the Loch Ness Monster   914

  Zaretsky, R. Boswell's enlightenment   92

Bosworth 1485. Jones, M. K.   942.04
Bosworth, R. J. B.
  Mussolini   945.091
  Mussolini's Italy   945
BOTANICAL CHEMISTRY
  See also Chemistry
BOTANICAL GARDENS
  See also Gardens; Parks
**BOTANICAL GARDENS -- ENGLAND -- HIS-
  TORY -- 19TH CENTURY**
  Holway, T. The flower of empire   727
BOTANICAL ILLUSTRATION
  Flora illustrata   016
BOTANICAL ILLUSTRATION
  See also Art; Illustration of books
**BOTANICAL SPECIMENS -- COLLECTION
  AND PRESERVATION** *See* Plants -- Collec-
  tion and preservation
BOTANISTS
  Blunt, W. Linnaeus, the compleat naturalist 92
  Fraser, K. Ornament and silence   809
  Lowman, M. Life in the treetops   577.34
  McCalman, I. Darwin's armada   576.8
  Preston, R. The wild trees   577.3
  Pringle, P. The murder of Nikolai Vavilov   92
  Ridley, G. The discovery of Jeanne Baret   92
BOTANISTS
  See also Naturalists
**BOTANISTS -- UNITED STATES -- ANEC-
  DOTES**
  Kassinger, R. A Garden of Marvels   580
BOTANY
  Fortey, R. Horseshoe crabs and velvet worms 595
  Kassinger, R. A Garden of Marvels   580
BOTANY
  See also Biology; Science
BOTANY -- ENCYCLOPEDIAS
  Magill's encyclopedia of science   580
**BOTANY -- GREAT BRITAIN -- DICTIONAR-
  IES**
  Coombes, A. J. The A to Z of plant names   635
BOTANY -- HISTORY
  Holway, T. The flower of empire   727
  Mabey, R. The cabaret of plants   580
BOTANY -- NOMENCLATURE
  Coombes, A. J. The A to Z of plant names   635
**BOTANY -- NORTH AMERICA -- DICTIONAR-
  IES**
  Coombes, A. J. The A to Z of plant names   635
BOTANY -- PATHOLOGY *See* Plant diseases
BOTANY -- PHILOSOPHY
  Marder, M. The philosopher's plant   580
The **botany** of desire. Pollan, M.   306.4
BOTANY, ECONOMIC *See* Economic botany
BOTANY, MEDICAL *See* Medical botany
Botermans, Jack

  The book of games   794
Botting, Douglas
  Dr. Eckener's dream machine   629.133
BOTTLE FEEDING
  Porto, A. The pediatrician's guide to feeding babies
    and toddlers   618.92
Bottled. Bowman, D.   362.292
Bottled lightning. Fletcher, S.   621.31
Bottom of the 33rd. Barry, D.   796.357
Bottomfeeder. Grescoe, T.   641.6
Bottura, Massimo
  Never Trust a Skinny Italian Chef   641.594
Bouchard, Constance Brittain
  (ed) Knights   940.1
Boucher, Bruce
  Andrea Palladio   720.9
Bouchon Bakery.   641.59
BOUCHON BAKERY
  Bouchon Bakery   641.59
Boudreau, Jamie
  (jt. auth) Fraioli, J. O. The Canon Cocktail
    Book   641
Boukreev, Anatoli
  The climb   796.522
BOULDER (COLO.) -- POLICE DEPT.
  Schiller, L. Perfect murder, perfect town   364.15
BOULDER DAM (ARIZ. AND NEV.) *See* Hoover
  Dam (Ariz. and Nev.)
Boulloche, André
                       About
  Kaiser, C. The cost of courage   92
Bound. Ekrem, E.   686.3
Bound for Canaan. Bordewich, F. M.   973.7
Bound for the promised land. Larson, K. C. 92
BOUNDARIES
  Stewart, R. The Marches   941.3
BOUNDARIES
  See also Geography; International law; Inter-
    national relations
The **boundaries** of desire. Berkowitz, E. 306.7
Boundless. Winter, K.   910.9
Bountiful bonsai. Bender, R. W.   635.9
BOUNTY (SHIP)
  Alexander, C. The Bounty: the true story of the mu-
    tiny on the Bounty   996
The **Bounty:** the true story of the mutiny on the
  Bounty. Alexander, C.   996
Bourbaki, Nicolas
                       About
  Aczel, A. D. The artist and the mathematician 500
Bourbon empire. Mitenbuler, R.   663
BOURBON WHISKEY -- UNITED STATES
  Mitenbuler, R. Bourbon empire   663
Bourdain, Anthony, 1956-
  Appetites   641
  A cook's tour   641

About
Bourdain, A. Kitchen confidential 92
Bourdain, A. Medium raw 92
BOURGEOISIE *See* Middle class
Bouricius, Ann
The romance readers' advisory 016
Bourne, Joyce
The Oxford Dictionary of Music 780.3
Bourne, Wade
Basic fishing 799.1
Boustani, Rafic
Fargues, P. The atlas of the Arab world 909
Boutique bags. Kim, S. 646.4
BOUTIQUE BREWERIES *See* Microbreweries
Bouton, Katherine, 1947-
About
Bouton, K. Shouting won't help 617.8
BOW AND ARROW
See also Weapons
Bowden, Charles
Murder city 364.152
Bowden, Ken
Nicklaus, J. Jack Nicklaus 796.352
Bowden, Mark
Black Hawk down 967.73
**BOWED STRINGED INSTRUMENTS -- CON-
STRUCTION**
Pagliaro, M. The musical instrument desk refer-
ence 784.192
Bowen, Zackery, d. 2006
About
Brown, E. Shake the devil off 364.152
Bowers, Edgar
Collected poems 811
Bowers, Kathryn
Zoobiquity 636.089
Bowers, Mark
8 keys to raising the quirky child 649
BOWHUNTING
See also Hunting
Bowie on Bowie. 92
Bowie, David
About
Bowie on Bowie 92
Morley, P. The age of Bowie 92
Bowie, Jim, 1796-1836
About
Davis, W. C. Three roads to the Alamo 976.4
Bowien, Danny, 1982-
(jt. auth) Ying, C. The Mission Chinese Food
Cookbook 641.595
Bowker, Gordon, 1934-
James Joyce 823
Bowker, John
The complete Bible handbook 220.6
World religions 200

(ed) The Cambridge illustrated history of reli-
gions 200.9
Bowl. 641.81
Bowles, Chester, 1901-1986
About
Galbraith, J. K. Name-dropping 973.9
Bowles, Hamish
Jacqueline Kennedy 92
Vogue and the Metropolitan Museum of Art Cos-
tume Institute 391
BOWLING
Manzione, G. Pin Action 794.6
Bowling, Allen C.
Optimal health with multiple sclerosis 616.8
Bowling, Barbara L.
Homegrown berries 634
Bowman, Carl F.
Kraybill, D. B. On the backroad to heaven 289.7
Bowman, Constance
Slacks and calluses 940.53
Bowman, Dana
Bottled 362.292
Bown, Stephen R.
The last Viking 92
Merchant kings 338.8
Bowser, Mary Elizabeth, approximately 1840-
About
Abbott, K. Liar, Temptress, Soldier, Spy 973.7
The **Boxer** Rebellion. Preston, D. 951
BOXERS (PERSONS)
Century, D. Barney Ross 92
Haygood, W. Sweet thunder 92
Kahn, R. A flame of pure fire: Jack Dempsey and
the roaring '20s 92
Kimball, G. Four kings 920
Kindred, D. Sound and fury 796
Kram, M. The ghosts of Manila 796.83
Levy, A. H. Floyd Patterson 92
Life stories 920
Margolick, D. Beyond glory 796.8
Remnick, D. King of the world: Muhammad Ali
and the rise of an American hero 92
Remnick, D. Reporting 814
Schaap, J. Cinderella Man 92
Ward, G. C. Unforgivable blackness 92
**BOXERS (SPORTS) -- UNITED STATES -- BI-
OGRAPHY**
Assael, S. The murder of Sonny Liston 796.83
Gildea, W. The longest fight 796.83
Kram, M. The ghosts of Manila 796.83
Runstedtler, T. Jack Johnson, rebel sojourn-
er 796.83
Shanahan, T. Runnng with the champ 796.830
Stratton, W. K. Floyd Patterson 92
BOXES
See also Containers

BOXES -- COLLECTORS AND COLLECTING
   See also Collectors and collecting

BOXING
   At the fights   796.8
   Butler   The domino diaries   796.83
   Hauser, T.   Boxing is--   796.8
   Kram, M.   The ghosts of Manila   796.83
   Liebling, A. J.   The sweet science   796.83
   Margolick, D.   Beyond glory   796.8

BOXING
   See also Athletics;   Self-defense

BOXING -- CUBA -- ANECDOTES
   Butler   The domino diaries   796.83

BOXING -- HISTORY
   Margolick, D.   Beyond glory   796.8
   Roberts, R.   Joe Louis   92

BOXING -- UNITED STATES -- HISTORY
   Runstedtler, T.   Jack Johnson, rebel sojourner   796.83

Boxing is-- Hauser, T.   796.8

The **boy** who harnessed the wind. Kamkwamba, W.   92

Boyatzis, Richard
   (jt. auth) Goleman, D.   Primal Leadership   658.4

Boyce, Charles
   Critical companion to William Shakespeare   822.3

BOYCOTTS
   See also Commerce;   Consumers;   Passive resistance

Boyd, Belle, 1844-1900
       About
   Abbott, K.   Liar, Temptress, Soldier, Spy   973.7

Boyd, Brian
   On the origin of stories   809
   Vladimir Nabokov: the American years   813
   Vladimir Nabokov: the Russian years   813

Boyd, Danah
   It's complicated   004.67

Boyd, Gerald
       About
   Boyd, G. M.   My Times in black and white   92

Boyd, Herb
   We shall overcome   323.1

Boyd, John
   Zimbardo, P. G.   The time paradox   153.7

Boyd, Roddy
   Fatal risk   368

Boyd, Valerie
   Wrapped in rainbows   92

Boyer, Carl B.
   A history of mathematics   510

Boyes, Alice
   The anxiety toolkit   616.85

Boylan, Jennifer Finney, 1958-
       About
   Boylan, J. F.   I'm looking through you   92

Boyle. Hunter, M.   92

Boyle, Christina
   An American Cardinal   92

Boyle, Gregory J.
   Tattoos on the heart   277

Boyle, Kevin
   Arc of justice   345

Boyle, Robert, 1627-1691
       About
   Hunter, M.   Boyle   92

Boyle, Tish
   The cake book   641.8
   Flavorful   641.86

Boynton, Robert S.
   (ed) The New new journalism   071

Boynton, Victoria
   (ed)   Encyclopedia of women's autobiography   920.003

BOYS
   See also Children

BOYS -- EDUCATION
   See also Education

BOYS -- EMPLOYMENT *See* Youth -- Employment

BOYS -- FRANCE -- FONTAINEBLEAU -- BIOGRAPHY
   Carhart, T.   Finding Fontainebleau   944.36

BOYS -- PSYCHOLOGY
   Wiseman, R.   Masterminds and wingmen   649

Boys among men. Abrams, J.   796.323

The **boys** from Dolores. Symmes, P.   972.91

The **Boys** in the Boat. Brown, D. J.   797.12

Boys in the trees. Simon, C.   92

Boysen, Sarah Till
   The smartest animals on the planet   591.5

Bozella, Dewey, 1959-
   Stand Tall   365.6

Braafladt, Keith
   Technology and literacy   027.62

Braasch, Gary
   Earth under fire   363.7

BRACELETS
   Gedeon, J.   Beautiful bracelets by hand   745.594

BRACHIOSAURUS
   See also Dinosaurs

Bracken, Peg
   The I hate to cook book   641.5

Brackett, Charles, 1892-1969
       About
   It's the pictures that got small   92

Brackett, Elizabeth
   Pay to play   92

Brackett, Virginia
   (ed) The Facts on File companion to the British novel   823

Bracks, Lean'tin

African American almanac 973

Brad and Michele Moore roots music series
Bradley, A. House of hits **781.64**
The **Bradbury** chronicles. Weller, S. 92
Bradbury speaks. Bradbury, R. **814**
Bradbury, Dominic
The iconic interior 747
Bradbury, Ray, 1920-2010
Bradbury speaks **814**
About
Eller, J. R. Becoming Ray Bradbury 92
Weller, S. The Bradbury chronicles 92
Braddock, James J., 1906-1974
About
Schaap, J. Cinderella Man 92
Bradford, John P.
Bosman, E. Gay, lesbian, bisexual, and transgendered literature 016
Bradford, Richard
Lucky him: the life of Kingsley Amis 92
Bradford, Sarah
Lucrezia Borgia 92
Bradford, Stacey L.
The Wall Street Journal: financial guidebook for new parents **332.024**
Bradford, William
Of Plymouth Plantation, 1620-1647 **974.4**
Bradlee, Benjamin C., 1921-2014
The kid 92
Bradley, Adam
Common One day it'll all make sense 92
Bradley, Andy
House of hits **781.64**
Bradley, Barbara
Drawing people **743.4**
Bradley, Carol
Last chain on Billie **639.97**
Bradley, Fern Marshall
(ed) Rodale's ultimate encyclopedia of organic gardening 635
Saving vegetable seeds 635
Bradley, James
Flags of our fathers **940.54**
Bradley, Lloyd
This is reggae music **781.646**
Bradshaw, John, 1950-
Cat sense **636.8**
Dog sense **636.7**
The trainable cat **636.8**
Bradstreet, Anne, 1612?-1672
About
Gordon, C. Mistress Bradstreet 92
Brady vs Manning. Myers, G. 92
Brady, Frank
Endgame 92
Brady, James

The coldest war **951.9**
Brady, Mathew B., approximately 1823-1896
About
Panzer, M. Mathew Brady and the image of history **770.92**
Wilson, R. Mathew Brady **770.92**
Brady, Patricia
Martha Washington 92
Brady, Tom, 1977-
About
Myers, G. Brady vs Manning 92
Bragdon, Kathleen J.
The Columbia guide to American Indians of the Northeast **970.004**
Bragg, Melvyn
The adventure of English 420
Bragg, Rick
Ava's man **975**
About
Bragg, R. The prince of Frogtown 92
BRAHMANISM
See also Religions
Brahms, Johannes, 1833-1897
About
Swafford, J. Johannes Brahms 92
BRAIDS (HAIRSTYLING)
See also Hair
BRAILLE
See also Writing
BRAILLE BOOKS
See also Books
The **brain.** Eagleman, D. **612.82**
The **brain.** DeSalle, R. **612.8**
BRAIN
See also Head; Nervous system
BRAIN
Buonomano, D. Brain bugs **612.8**
Carter, R. The human brain book **612.82**
DeSalle, R. The brain **612.8**
Doidge, N. The brain that changes itself **612.8**
Eagleman, D. The brain **612.82**
Eagleman, D. Incognito **153**
Eliot, L. What's going on in there? **612.8**
Gazzaniga, M. S. Human **612.8**
Gazzaniga, M. S. Tales from Both Sides of the Brain 92
Hood, B. The self illusion **155.2**
Kozol, J. The theft of memory 92
Kurzweil, R. How to create a mind **612.8**
Medina, J. Brain rules **153**
Pinker, S. How the mind works **153**
Ramachandran, V. S. The tell-tale brain **616.8**
Ros, H. Neurocomic **612.82**
Sagan, C. The dragons of Eden **153**
Schacter, D. L. Searching for memory **153.1**
Small, G. 2 weeks to a younger brain **616.8**

Zimmer, C. Soul made flesh   **612.8**

BRAIN -- CARE AND HYGIENE
Alter, D. Staying sharp   **612.8**

BRAIN -- CONCUSSION
Esty, M. L. Conquering Concussion   **617.4**
Fainaru, S. League of Denial   **617.1**
Laskas, J. M. Concussion   **617.5**
Stoler, D. R. Coping with concussion and mild traumatic brain injury   **617.4**

BRAIN -- DISEASES
Cahalan, S. Brain on fire   **616.8**
Kean, S. The tale of the dueling neurosurgeons   **617.4**
Ropper, A. H. Reaching down the rabbit hole **616.8**

BRAIN -- DISEASES
See also Diseases

BRAIN -- DISEASES -- ANECDOTES
Ropper, A. H. Reaching down the rabbit hole **616.8**

BRAIN -- EVOLUTION
DeSalle, R. The brain   **612.8**

BRAIN -- GROWTH
Jensen, F. E. The teenage brain   **612.6**

BRAIN -- HEMORRHAGE -- PATIENTS
Taylor, J. B. My stroke of insight   **362.19**

BRAIN -- LOCALIZATION OF FUNCTIONS
Kurzweil, R. How to create a mind   **612.8**

BRAIN -- MATHEMATICAL MODELS
Kaku, M. The future of the mind   **612.8**

BRAIN -- PHYSIOLOGY
Carter, R. The human brain book   **612.82**
Doidge, N. The brain's way of healing   **612.8**
Gonzales, L. Surviving survival   **155.9**

BRAIN -- PHYSIOLOGY -- POPULAR WORKS
Kean, S. The tale of the dueling neurosurgeons   **617.4**

BRAIN -- POPULAR WORKS
Burnett, D. Idiot brain   **612.8**

BRAIN -- SURGERY
Marsh, H. Do No Harm   **92**

BRAIN -- TUMORS
Coutts, M. The Iceberg   **92**

BRAIN -- WOUNDS AND INJURIES
Esty, M. L. Conquering Concussion   **617.4**
Krug, L. Louise   **617.4**
Padgett, J. Struck by genius   **155.9**
Stoler, D. R. Coping with concussion and mild traumatic brain injury   **617.4**

BRAIN -- WOUNDS AND INJURIES
See also Brain -- Concussion
Brain bugs. Buonomano, D.   **612.8**

BRAIN DAMAGED CHILDREN
See also Children with disabilities; Exceptional children

BRAIN DEATH
Ball, H. At liberty to die   **344**
Teresi, D. The undead   **610**

BRAIN DEATH
See also Death

BRAIN DISEASES -- POPULAR WORKS
Kean, S. The tale of the dueling neurosurgeons   **617.4**
Brain fitness. Goldman, B.   **153.1**
Brain on fire. Cahalan, S.   **616.8**
Brain rules. Medina, J.   **153**
Brain rules for baby. Medina, J.   **649**
Brain storms. Palfreman, J.   **616.8**
The brain that changes itself. Doidge, N.   **612.8**
The brain's way of healing. Doidge, N.   **612.8**
Brain, Marshall
The engineering book   **620.009**

BRAIN-COMPUTER INTERFACES
Kaku, M. The future of the mind   **612.8**
Brainard, Joe, 1942-1994
About
Brainard, J. The Nancy book   **759**
Brainstorm. Siegel, D. J.   **155.5**
Braintrust. Churchland, P. S.   **612.8**
Brainwashed. Lilienfeld, S. O.   **612.8**

BRAINWASHING
Huxley, A. Brave new world revisited   **303.3**

BRAINWASHING
See also Behavior modification; Mental suggestion; Psychological warfare; Psychology of learning

BRAISING (COOKING)
All about braising   **641.7**
Ruhlman's how to braise   **641.7**
Braitman, Laurel
Animal madness   **591.5**
Bram, Christopher
Eminent outlaws   **810.9**
Bramly, Serge
Leonardo   **709**
Branch Rickey. Breslin, J.   **92**
BRANCH STORES *See* Chain stores
Branch, Taylor, 1947-
At Canaan's edge   **973.923**
The Clinton tapes   **92**
Parting the waters: America in the King years, 1954-63   **973.921**
Pillar of fire   **973.922**
Brancheau, Dawn, 1969-2010
About
Kirby, D. Death at SeaWorld   **599.53**

BRAND NAME PRODUCTS
Lindström, M. Small Data   **658.8**
Watkins, A. Hello, my name is awesome   **658.8**

BRAND NAME PRODUCTS
See also Commercial products; Manufactures

BRAND NAME PRODUCTS -- COMPOSITION -- TABLES
Netzer, C. T. The complete book of food

counts   613.2

Brand, Cristo
About
Jones, B. Mandela   92

Brand, Phyllis, 1880-1937
About
Fox, J. Five sisters   975.5

BRANDED MERCHANDISE *See* Brand name products

BRANDEIS UNIVERSITY -- FACULTY -- BIOGRAPHY
Albom, M. Tuesdays with Morrie   378.1

Brandeis, Louis Dembitz, 1856-1941
About
Urofsky, M. I. Louis D. Brandeis   92

BRANDING (MARKETING)
Lindström, M. Small Data   658.8
Watkins, A. Hello, my name is awesome   658.8

Brando, Marlon, 1924-2004
About
Life stories   920

Brandon, Ruth
Surreal lives   709.04
Ugly beauty   646.7

Brandow, Todd
Edward Steichen   779

Brands, H. W.
The Age of Gold   979.4
Andrew Jackson   92
The General Vs. the President   973.918
The man who saved the union   355.009
Reagan   92
Traitor to his class   92
Woodrow Wilson   92

Brandt, Anthony
The man who ate his boots   910.4

Brannan, Karen
The Family Tree   364.134

Branson, Richard
Reach for the skies   629.1

Brasillach, Robert, 1909-1945
About
Kaplan, A. The collaborator: the trial & execution of Robert Brasillach   848

Brass diva. Flinn, C.   92

Brassaï. Brassaï   944.361

Brassaï, 1899-1984
Brassaï   944.361

BRASSES
    See also Art metalwork; Brass; Inscriptions; Sculpture; Tombs

Brathwaite, Edward Kamau
Elegguas   811

Braude, Joseph
The honored dead   364.152

Braukman, Stacy Lorraine

Ware, S. Notable American women   920.003

Braun, Eva
About
Gortemaker, H. B. Eva Braun   92

Brave genius. Carroll, S. B.   920

Brave new words.   809.3

Brave new world revisited. Huxley, A.   303.3

Braverman, Blair
Welcome to the Goddamn Ice Cube   974.81

BRAVERY *See* Courage

Brawley, Otis Webb
How we do harm   362.109

Bray, Adam
(jt. auth) Wallace, D. Ultimate Star wars

Bray, Hiawatha
You are here   910.285

Bray, Ilona M.
Nolo's essential guide to buying your first home 643
(jt. auth) Lewis, L. N. How to Get a Green Card 342
U.S. Immigration Made Easy   342

Bray, Willie Reginald, 1879-1939
About
Tingey, J. The Englishman who posted himself and other curious objects   92

Brazelton, T. Berry
The irreducible needs of children   155.4
To listen to a child   155.4
Touchpoints birth to 3   649

The **brazen** age. Reid, D.   974.7

Brazil. Skidmore, T. E.   981

Brazil.   918.1

BRAZIL
Skidmore, T. E. Brazil   981

BRAZIL -- DESCRIPTION AND TRAVEL
Brazil   918.1
Rigby, C. Fodor's Rio de Janeiro & Sao Paulo   918.15

BRAZIL -- HISTORY
Meade, T. A brief history of Brazil   981
Skidmore, T. E. Brazil   981

BRAZILIAN COOKING
Castanho, T. Brazilian Food   641.598

Brazilian Food. Castanho, T.   641.598

BRAZILIAN LITERATURE
    See also Latin American literature; Literature

BRČKO (BOSNIA AND HERCEGOVINA) -- BIOGRAPHY
Shapiro, S. The Bosnia list   92

BRCA GENES
Stark, L. Pandora's DNA   616.99

Breach of faith. Horne, J.   976.3

BREAD
Alexander, W. 52 loaves   641.8
Alford, J. Flatbreads and flavors   641.8
Beard, J. Beard on bread   641.8
Black, S. One dough, ten breads   641.81

Della Fattoria bread **641.81**

Dodge, A. J. The everyday baker **641.815**

Forkish, K. Flour water salt yeast **641.81**

Fromartz, S. In search of the perfect loaf **641.81**

Hensperger, B. The best quick breads **641.8**

Kaminsky, P. Bien Cuit **641.815**

Ovenly **641.81**

Robertson, C. Tartine bread **641.8**

Rodriguez, J. W. The Hot Bread Kitchen cookbook **641.59**

BREAD

See also Baking; Cooking; Food

The **bread** of angels. Saldana, S. **92**

BREAK DANCING

See also Dance

Break on through: the life and death of Jim Morrison. Riordan, J. **92**

Break, blow, burn. Paglia, C. **809.1**

BREAKERS *See* Ocean waves

Breakfast at Huckleberry. **641.5**

Breakfast at Sally's. LeMieux, R. **92**

BREAKFAST AT TIFFANY'S (MOTION PICTURE)

Wasson, S. Fifth Avenue, 5 AM **791.43**

BREAKFASTS

Sarabeth's good morning cookbook **641.5**

BREAKFASTS

See also Cooking; Menus

Breaking clean. Blunt, J. **92**

Breaking free, starting over. Dalpiaz, C. M. **362.82**

Breaking night. Murray, L. **92**

Breaking the Chains of Gravity. Teitel, A. S. **629.4**

Breaking through bias. Kramer, A. S. **650.101**

Breaking through concrete. Hanson, D. **630**

BREAKING UP (INTERPERSONAL RELATIONS)

Waxman, J. How to break up with anyone **158.2**

Wright, J. It Ended Badly **302**

Breakout nations. Sharma, R. **330.91**

BREAKTHROUGHS, SCIENTIFIC *See* Discoveries in science

BREAST

Love, S. M. Dr. Susan Love's Breast Book **618.1**

Williams, F. Breasts **612.6**

BREAST -- CANCER *See* Breast cancer

BREAST CANCER

Aaronson, N. Pilates for breast cancer survivors **616.99**

Anstett, P. Breast cancer surgery and reconstruction **618.1**

Corrigan, K. The middle place **92**

Fertig, J. The back in the swing cookbook **641.5**

Jacobs, H. The Silver Lining **616.99**

Love, S. M. Dr. Susan Love's Breast Book **618.1**

Lunden, J. Had I Known **791.450**

Port, E. The new generation breast cancer

book **616.99**

Prijatel, P. Surviving triple negative breast cancer **616.99**

Queller, J. Pretty is what changes **92**

Sikka, M. A breast cancer alphabet **616.99**

Silver, M. Breast cancer husband **616.99**

Stark, L. Pandora's DNA **616.99**

Williams, F. Breasts **612.6**

BREAST CANCER

See also Cancer; Women -- Diseases

BREAST CANCER -- DIAGNOSIS

Port, E. The new generation breast cancer book **616.99**

BREAST -- CANCER -- DIET THERAPY -- RECIPES

Fertig, J. The back in the swing cookbook **641.5**

BREAST CANCER -- GRAPHIC NOVELS

Hayden, J. The Story of My Tits **741.5**

BREAST CANCER -- TREATMENT

Hutton, A. Bald Is Better With Earrings **616.99**

Port, E. The new generation breast cancer book **616.99**

Prijatel, P. Surviving triple negative breast cancer **616.99**

A **breast** cancer alphabet. Sikka, M. **616.99**

Breast cancer husband. Silver, M. **616.99**

Breast cancer surgery and reconstruction. Anstett, P. **618.1**

BREAST NEOPLASMS -- REHABILITATION -- POPULAR WORKS

Aaronson, N. Pilates for breast cancer survivors **616.99**

BREASTFEEDING

The womanly art of breastfeeding **649**

BREASTFEEDING

See also Infants -- Nutrition

BREASTFEEDING -- POPULAR WORKS

Huggins, K. The nursing mother's companion **649**

BREASTFEEDING -- SAFETY MEASURES

Pitman, T. Sweet sleep **649**

Breasts. Williams, F. **612.6**

Breath. Levine, P. **811**

The **breath** of a wok. Richardson, A. **641.59**

BREATHING EXERCISES -- POPULAR WORKS

Aaronson, N. Pilates for breast cancer survivors **616.99**

Breathturn into timestead. Celan, P. **635.9**

Brecht and company. Fuegi, J. **92**

Brecht, Bertolt, 1898-1956

About

Fuegi, J. Brecht and company **92**

Breckinridge, John Cabell, 1821-1875

About

Davis, W. C. An honorable defeat **973.7**

Bredeson, Michelle

(ed) BurdaStyle modern sewing **646.4**

Bredin, Jean-Denis

The affair **944.081**

BREEDING

See also Reproduction

BREEDING BEHAVIOR *See* Sexual behavior in animals

Breedlove, Craig, 1938-

About

Hawley, S. J. Speed duel **796.72**

Breen, Bill

Brick by brick **338.7**

Breen, Michael

The Koreans **951.9**

Breen, Nancy

(ed) 2009 poet's market **808.1**

Breen, T. H.

American insurgents, American patriots **973.3**

George Washington's journey **92**

Bregman, Ahron

Cursed victory

A history of Israel **956.94**

Brehm, Matthew

Drawing perspective **742**

Breitman, Richard

The architect of genocide **92**

Official secrets **940.54**

Bremer, Francis J.

John Winthrop **974.4**

Brendon, Piers

The decline and fall of the British Empire, 1781-1997 **909**

Brennan, Gerald

(ed) All music guide to classical music **016**

Brennan, Jason

Libertarianism **320.51**

Brennan, Kathy

Keepers **641.5**

Brenner, Carl

About

Brenner, M. Apples and oranges **92**

Brenner, Frederic

Diaspora: homelands in exile **909**

Brenner, Joel Glenn

The emperors of chocolate **338.7**

Brenner, Marie

About

Brenner, M. Apples and oranges **92**

Brenner, Robin E.

Understanding manga and anime **025.2**

Brent, Jonathan

Inside the Stalin archives **947.086**

Stalin's last crime **947.084**

Brentano, Margaret

Baker, N. The World on Sunday **071**

Breslin, Ed

About

Breslin, E. Drinking with Miss Dutchie **92**

Breslin, Jimmy

Branch Rickey **92**

I want to thank my brain for remembering me **92**

The short sweet dream of Eduardo Gutierrez **331.6**

Breslow, Lester

(ed) Encyclopedia of public health **362.1**

Bressett, Kenneth E.

Yeoman, R. S. A guide book of United States coins **737.4**

Brewer's dictionary of Irish phrase & fable. McMahon, S. **427**

Brewer's dictionary of modern phrase & fable. Ayto, J. **803**

Brewer's dictionary of phrase & fable. Rockwood, C. **803**

Brewer, John

The American Leonardo **759**

The pleasures of the imagination **941.07**

Brewer, Robert Lee

Writer's Market **808**

Brewer, Stephen C.

The Canyon Ranch guide to men's health **613**

BREWERIES

See also Factories

BREWING

Acitelli, T. The audacity of hops **641.2**

Beaumont, S. The world atlas of beer **641.2**

Huckelbridge, D. The United States of beer **641.23**

Proulx, A. Cider **641.2**

Watman, M. Chasing the white dog **363.4**

Wood, S. M. Apples to cider **663**

BREWING INDUSTRY -- UNITED STATES -- HISTORY

Knoedelseder, W. Bitter brew **338.7**

Brewster, Todd

Lincoln's Gamble **973.7**

Breyer, Stephen G., 1938-

Active liberty **342**

Making our democracy work **347**

Brian, Denis

The Curies **92**

Brick by brick. Breen, B. **338.7**

Brick, Michael

Saving the school **373.22**

Brickell, Christopher

(ed) American Horticultural Society encyclopedia of plants & flowers **635.9**

(jt. auth) Joyce, D. Pruning & training

BRICKLAYING

See also Building

BRICKS

See also Building materials

BRIDAL CUSTOMS *See* Marriage customs and rites

The **bride** of E. Bang, M. J. — 811
The **bridge.** Remnick, D. — 92
BRIDGE (GAME)
    Lerner, B. The bridge ladies — 92
BRIDGE (GAME)
    See also Card games
The **bridge** at Andau. Michener, J. A. — 943.9
The **bridge** at the end of the world. Speth, J. G. — 333.7
BRIDGE ENGINEERS
    Barry, J. M. Rising tide — 977
The **bridge** ladies. Lerner, B. — 92
Bridges. Blockley, D. I. — 624.2
BRIDGES
    See also Civil engineering; Transportation
BRIDGES
    Blockley, D. I. Bridges — 624.2
    McGinty, B. Lincoln's Greatest Case — 346
Bried, Erin
    How to sew a button — 640
Brief Candle in the Dark. Dawkins, R. — 570
A **brief** guide to Islam. Grieve, P. — 297
Brief history [series]
    Brown, J. C. A brief history of Argentina — 982
    Burns, W. E. A brief history of Great Britain — 941
    Coy, J. P. A brief history of Germany — 943
    Foster, L. V. A brief history of Mexico — 972
    Hunefeldt, C. A brief history of Peru — 985
    Meade, T. A brief history of Brazil — 981
    Peterson, M. A brief history of Korea — 951.9
    Riendeau, R. E. A brief history of Canada — 971
    State, P. F. A brief history of Ireland — 941.5
    Wahab, S. A brief history of Afghanistan — 958.1
    Walsh, J. E. A brief history of India — 954
    Wynbrandt, J. A brief history of Saudi Arabia — 953.8
A **brief** history of Afghanistan. Wahab, S. — 958.1
A **brief** history of Argentina. Brown, J. C. — 982
A **brief** history of Brazil. Meade, T. — 981
A **brief** history of Canada. Riendeau, R. E. — 971
A **brief** history of Central America. Perez-Brignoli, H. — 972.8
A **Brief** History of Creation. Mesler, B. — 576.8
A **brief** history of Germany. Coy, J. P. — 943
A **brief** history of Great Britain. Burns, W. E. — 941
A **brief** history of India. Walsh, J. E. — 954
A **brief** history of Ireland. State, P. F. — 941.5
A **brief** history of Korea. Peterson, M. — 951.9
A **brief** history of Mexico. Foster, L. V. — 972
A **brief** history of Peru. Hunefeldt, C. — 985
A **brief** history of Saudi Arabia. Wynbrandt, J. — 953.8
A **brief** history of thought. Ferry, L. — 100
A **brief** history of time. Hawking, S. — 523.1
A **briefer** history of time. Hawking, S. — 523.1
Brier, Bob
    The murder of Tutankhamen — 932
Brierley, Saroo
    About

Brierley, S. A long way home — 92
BRIGANDS *See* Thieves
Briggs, Julia
    Virginia Woolf: an inner life — 92
Brigham Young, pioneer prophet. Turner, J. G. — 289.3
Bright boulevards, bold dreams. Bogle, D. — 791.43
Bright brave phenomena. Nadelberg, A. — 811
BRIGHT CHILDREN *See* Gifted children
Bright dead things. Limon, A. — 811
A **bright** shining lie: John Paul Vann and America in Vietnam. Sheehan, N. — 959.704
Bright, Deb
    The truth doesn't have to hurt — 158.2
Bright-sided. Ehrenreich, B. — 155.2
Brightman, Carol
    Sweet chaos — 920
Brighton Beach memoirs. Simon, N. — 812
Brighton, Terry
    Patton, Montgomery, Rommel — 920
Brill, A. A.
    (ed) The basic writings of Sigmund Freud — 150.19
Brill, David
    Johanson, D. C. From Lucy to language — 599.93
Brill, Steven
    Class — warfare
Brilliant. Brox, J. — 621.32
A **brilliant** darkness. Magueijo, J. — 92
The **brilliant** disaster. Rasenberger, J. — 972.91
A **brilliant** solution. Berkin, C. — 342
Brin, Sergey
    About
    Auletta, K. Googled — 338.7
Brinckle, Gordon, 1915-2007
    About
    Messick, K. The projectionist — 92
Bring me her heart. Getty, S. — 811
Bringing Adam home. Matthews, J. — 364.1
Bringing it all back home. Napoli, P. F. — 959.704
Bringing it to the table. Berry, W. — 630
Brinkley, Alan
    John F. Kennedy — 92
    The publisher — 92
    Virga, V. Eyes of the nation — 973
Brinkley, Douglas
    Cronkite — 92
    Rightful heritage — 92
    (ed) The Nixon tapes — 973.924
    The great deluge — 976.3
    The quiet world — 333.72
    Rosa Parks — 92
    Wheels for the world — 338.7
    The wilderness warrior — 92
    (ed) The Reagan diaries — 92
    (ed) World War II — 940.53
Brinkley, Joel, 1952-2014
    Cambodia's curse — 959.6

Brinkley, John Richard, 1885-1942
    About
  Brock, P. Charlatan   **92**
Brinkley-Rogers, Paul
  Please Enjoy Your Happiness   **070.92**
Briscione, James
  The great cook   **641.5**
The **brisket** book. Pierson, S.   **641.3**
Bristow, Barbara A., 1957-
  (ed) Sears List of Subject Headings   **025.4**
Bristow, M. J.
  (ed) National anthems of the world   **782.42**
Britain's empire. Gott, R.   **942**
BRITAIN, BATTLE OF, 1940
  Holland, J. Battle of Britain   **940.54**
  Korda, M. With wings like eagles   **940.54**
BRITAIN, BATTLE OF, 1940
  See also Battles; World War, 1939-1945 --
    Campaigns
**BRITISH -- AFGHANISTAN -- HISTORY --
19TH CENTURY**
  Dalrymple, W. Return of a king   **958.1**
BRITISH -- INDIA
  Dalrymple, W. White Mughals   **954**
BRITISH -- UNITED STATES
  Barrett, D. GI brides   **940.53**
**BRITISH ANTARCTIC ("TERRA NOVA") EX-
PEDITION (1910-1913)**
  Preston, D. A first rate tragedy   **919**
  Solomon, S. The coldest March   **919**
BRITISH ART
  Sykes, C. S. David Hockney   **92**
BRITISH COOKING
  David, E. Summer cooking   **641.5**
  Fearnley-Whittingstall, H. River Cottage every
    day   **641.5**
BRITISH EMPIRE *See* Great Britain -- Colonies
BRITISH PETROLEUM CO. PLC
  Freudenburg, W. R. Blowout in the Gulf   **363.7**
BRITISH PETROLEUM COMPANY
  Magner, M. Poisoned legacy   **338.7**
British women poets of the Romantic era.   **821**
BRITONS -- FICTION.
  Ackroyd, P. The death of King Arthur   **398.2**
Britten, Benjamin, 1913-1976
    About
  Powell, N. Benjamin Britten   **92**
Britton, Sarah
  My new roots   **641.3**
Brizendine, Judy
  Stunned by grief   **248**
The **broad** fork. Acheson, H.   **641.597**
Broad, William
  Engelberg, S. Germs   **358**
  The science of yoga   **613.7**
BROADBAND INTERNET

  See also Internet; Internet access
Broadcast hysteria. Schwartz, A. B.   **791.44**
BROADCAST JOURNALISM
  Carpini, M. X. D. After broadcast news   **071**
  Walters, B. Audition   **92**
  Wenger, D. H. Advancing the story   **070.1**
BROADCAST JOURNALISM
  See also Broadcasting; Journalism; Press
**BROADCAST JOURNALISM -- GRAPHIC
NOVELS**
  Gladstone, B. The influencing machine   **302.23**
**BROADCAST JOURNALISM -- POLITICAL
ASPECTS -- UNITED STATES**
  Carpini, M. X. D. After broadcast news   **071**
BROADCASTERS
  Brock, P. Charlatan   **92**
BROADCASTING
  Walton, B. Back from the dead   **92**
BROADCASTING
  See also Telecommunication
BROADCASTING EXECUTIVES
  Auletta, K. Media man   **92**
  Baggett, J. The lost girls   **910.4**
  George-Warren, H. Public cowboy no. 1   **92**
  Wolff, M. The man who owns the news   **92**
Broadwater, Jeff
  George Mason, forgotten founder   **92**
  James Madison   **92**
Broadway. Maslon, L.   **792.6**
BROADWAY (NEW YORK, N.Y.) -- HISTORY
  Lane, S. F. Black Broadway   **792**
Broadway musicals. Bloom, K.   **792.6**
Broca's brain. Sagan, C.   **500**
Brock, James P.
  Kaufman field guide to butterflies of North Ameri-
    ca   **595.7**
Brock, Julia
  (ed) Beyond Rosie   **940**
Brock, Pope
  Charlatan   **92**
Brock, Sean
  Heritage   **641.59**
Brock-Broido, Lucie
  Stay, Illusion   **811**
Brockett, Oscar G.
  History of the theatre   **792.09**
Brockman, John
  (ed) This explains everything   **500**
  (ed) The universe   **523.1**
  (ed) This will change everything   **501**
Brodsky, Joseph, 1940-1996
  Collected poems in English, 1972-1999   **891.7**
  Less than one   **809.1**
    About
  Volkov, S. St. Petersburg   **947**
Brody, Jane E.

Jane Brody's guide to the great beyond   **616.02**

Broers, Michael

Napoleon   **92**

Brogaard, Berit

The superhuman mind   **153.9**

Brognart, Gilbert

About

Milosz, C. To begin where I am   **891.8**

BROILING

Kaminsky, P. Mallmann on fire   **641.598**

Brokaw, Tom

An album of memories   **940.54**

A long way from home   **070**

The time of our lives   **973.927**

About

Brokaw, T. A Lucky Life Interrupted   **92**

Broke, USA. Rivlin, G.   **339.4**

The **broken** cord. Dorris, M.   **362.292**

The **broken** tower: a life of Hart Crane. Mariani, P. L.   **811**

The **broken** word. Foulds, A.   **821**

Broken: my story of addiction and redemption. Moyers, W. C.   **92**

Broker, trader, lawyer, spy. Javers, E.   **364.1**

BROKERS (STOCKS) See Stockbrokers

Brombert, Beth Archer

Edouard Manet   **92**

BRONCHIAL ASTHMA See Asthma

Bronfman, Edgar M., 1929-2013

Why be Jewish?   **296**

Bronk, William

Selected poems   **811**

Bronner, Simon J.

(ed) Encyclopedia of American folklife   **398**

Bronowski, Jacob

Science and human values   **500**

Bronski, Michael

A queer history of the United States   **306.76**

Brontë, Charlotte, 1816-1855

About

Gaskell, E. C. The life of Charlotte Bronte   **92**

Gordon, L. Charlotte Bronte   **92**

Brontë, Emily, 1818-1848

The complete poems of Emily Jane Bronte   **821**

About

Adams, M. B. Shaggy muses   **920**

BRONX (NEW YORK, N.Y.) -- SOCIAL CONDITIONS

Kozol, J. Ordinary resurrections   **305.23**

LeBlanc, A. N. Random family   **305.5**

BRONZE AGE

Wood, M. In search of the Trojan War   **939**

BRONZE AGE

See also Civilization

BRONZES

See also Archeology; Art; Art metalwork; Decoration and ornament; Metalwork; Sculpture

Brook, Peter

The empty space   **792**

About

Brookhiser, R. Right time, right place   **92**

Brookhiser, Richard

America's first dynasty   **973.4**

Founders' son   **92**

Founding father: rediscovering George Washington   **92**

Right time, right place   **92**

What would the Founders do?   **320**

BROOKLYN (NEW YORK, N.Y.)

Anasi, R. The last bohemia   **974.7**

Jones, C. The Brooklyn bartender   **641.874**

BROOKLYN (NEW YORK, N.Y.) -- ETHNIC RELATIONS

Bayoumi, M. How does it feel to be a problem?   **305.8**

BROOKLYN (NEW YORK, N.Y.) -- GUIDEBOOKS

Freudenheim, E. The Brooklyn experience   **917.47**

BROOKLYN (NEW YORK, N.Y.) -- SOCIAL LIFE AND CUSTOMS

Sultan, T. Sunny's nights   **641.87**

The **Brooklyn** bartender. Jones, C.   **641.874**

BROOKLYN DODGERS (BASEBALL TEAM)

Breslin, J. Branch Rickey   **92**

D'Antonio, M. Forever blue   **92**

Goodwin, D. K. Wait till next year   **796.357**

The **Brooklyn** experience. Freudenheim, E.   **917.47**

Brookover, Sophie

Pop goes the library   **021.2**

Brooks, Christopher Antonio

(ed) The African American almanac   **305.8**

Brooks, David, 1961-

(ed) The best American essays 2012   **808**

The Road to Character   **170**

The social animal   **305.5**

Brooks, Gwendolyn

The essential Gwendolyn Brooks   **811**

In Montgomery, and other poems   **811**

About

Black women writers (1950-1980)   **810**

Brooks, Joanna

(jt. auth) Cooper, A. Saving Alex   **92**

Brooks, Michael

13 things that don't make sense   **500**

Brooks, Robert B.

Raising resilient children   **649**

Broom, Dave

The World Atlas of Whisky   **641.2**

Brosens, Koenraad

European tapestries in the Art Institute of Chicago   **746.3**

Broth.   **641.813**

The **brother** gardeners. Wulf, A.   **635**

Brother, I'm dying. Danticat, E.   **92**

BROTHERHOOD OF ETERNAL LOVE

  Schou, N. Orange sunshine   **363.45**

BROTHERS

  Gigante, D. The Keats brothers   **920**

  Kushner, D. Alligator candy   **362.88**

  Louvin, C. Satan is real   **920**

  Macy, B. Truevine   **791.3**

  Von Ziegesar, P. The looking glass brother   **92**

BROTHERS

  See also Men; Siblings

BROTHERS AND SISTERS *See* Siblings

Brothers, Thomas

  Armstrong, L. Louis Armstrong, in his own words   **92**

  Louis Armstrong, master of modernism   **92**

Brotherton, Rob

  Suspicious Minds   **153.4**

Brott, Armin A.

  The expectant father   **649**

Brottman, Mikita

  The Maximum Security Book Club   **365.66**

Brotton, Jerry

  Great maps   **912.09**

Brougher, Kerry

  (ed) Ai weiwei   **709.5**

Brousse, Amy Elizabeth Thorpe, 1910-1963

         About

  Blum, H. The Last Goodnight   **940.54**

Broven, John

  Record makers and breakers   **781.64**

Browar, Ken

  The art of movement   **792**

Brower, Kate Andersen

  First women   **973.099**

  The residence   **975.3**

Brower, Sam

  Prophet's prey   **306.8**

Brown, Alton, 1962-

  Everydaycook   **641.5**

Brown, Amanda

  Spruce   **747**

Brown, Amy

  Let's start the music   **027.62**

Brown, Archie

  The rise and fall of communism   **320.5**

Brown, Brandon P.

  (ed) Magill's medical guide   **610**

Brown, Brene

  Rising strong   **158**

Brown, Brian Arthur

  (ed) Three Testaments   **208**

Brown, Carolyn

         About

Brown, C. Chance and circumstance   **92**

Brown, Carrie

  The new Christmas tree   **745.594**

Brown, Christia Spears

  Parenting beyond pink and blue   **649**

Brown, Claude, 1937-2002

         About

  Brown, C. Manchild in the promised land   **92**

Brown, Cynthia Stokes

  A big history   **909**

Brown, Daniel

  The indifferent stars above   **92**

  Under a flaming sky   **634.9**

Brown, Daniel James

  The Boys in the Boat   **797.12**

Brown, David Alan

  Leonardo da Vinci   **759**

Brown, David Blayney

  (ed)   J.m.w.   turner

Brown, Dee Alexander

  The American West   **978**

  Bury my heart at Wounded Knee   **970.004**

Brown, Donald

  Bob Dylan   **92**

Brown, Ethan

  Shake the devil off   **364.152**

Brown, Frederick

  Flaubert   **92**

  For the soul of France   **944.081**

Brown, Harriet

  Body of truth   **613.2**

Brown, Helen Gurley

         About

  Hauser, B. Enter Helen   **92**

  Hirshey, G. Not pretty enough   **92**

  Scanlon, J. Bad girls go everywhere: the life of Helen Gurley Brown   **92**

Brown, James, 1933-2006

         About

  Brown, J. James Brown, the godfather of soul   **92**

  Brown, J. The Los Angeles diaries   **92**

  McBride, J. Kill 'em and leave   **92**

  Smith, R. J. The one   **92**

  Sullivan, J. The hardest working man   **92**

Brown, Jeff

  The Runner's Brain   **796.42**

Brown, John, 1800-1859

         About

  Horwitz, T. Midnight rising   **92**

  Reynolds, D. S. John Brown, abolitionist   **92**

Brown, Jonathan C.

  A brief history of Argentina   **982**

Brown, Judith M.

  Nehru: a political life   **92**

Brown, Kate

  Plutopia   **363.17**

Brown, Laura
How to write anything   **808**
Brown, Leanne
Good and cheap   **641.5**
Brown, Lesley
(ed) Shorter Oxford English dictionary on histori-
cal principles   **423**
Brown, Malcolm
T.E. Lawrence   **92**
Brown, Marianne Gluszak
Tennant, R. A. The American Sign Language hand-
shape dictionary   **419**
Brown, Matthew
From Frontiers to Football   **980**
Brown, Michael E.
         About
Brown, M. How I killed Pluto and why it had it
coming   **523.4**
Brown, Mick
Tearing down the wall of sound   **92**
Brown, Mike
How I killed Pluto and why it had it coming   **523.4**
Brown, Nancy Marie
The abacus and the cross   **92**
Ivory Vikings   **736**
Brown, Pete, 1968-
Shakespeare's Pub   **647.9**
Brown, Peter
Through the eye of a needle   **270.2**
Brown, Phil
(ed) In the Catskills   **974.7**
Brown, Raymond Edward
An introduction to the New Testament   **225**
Brown, Samuel Morris
In heaven as it is on earth   **236**
Brown, Stephen
Glitterville's handmade Christmas   **745.594**
Glitterville's handmade Halloween   **745.594**
Brown, Stephen C.
(ed) Arctic wings   **598**
Brown, Terence
The life of W.B. Yeats   **821**
Brown, Theresa
The shift   **616.02**
Brown, Tina
The Diana chronicles   **92**
Browne, David
Fire and rain   **781.66**
Browne, John
The Glass Closet   **331.5**
Brownfield, Christopher J.
         About
Brownfield, C. J. My nuclear family   **92**
Browning, Elizabeth Barrett, 1806-1861
Sonnets from the Portuguese   **821**
         About

Adams, M. B. Shaggy muses   **920**
Browning, Michael
Maples, W. R. Dead men do tell tales   **614**
Browning, Robert
Robert Browning   **821**
Robert Browning's poetry   **821**
Brownmiller, Susan
In our time   **305.42**
Brownson, JeanMarie
Bayless, R. Mexico: one plate at a time   **641.597**
Bayless, R. Rick Bayless's Mexican kitchen **641.59**
Brownstein, Carrie, 1974-
Hunger Makes Me a Modern Girl   **92**
         About
Brownstein, C. Hunger Makes Me a Modern
Girl   **92**
Brownworth, Lars
Lost to the West   **949.5**
Browsings. Dirda, M.   **028**
Brox, Jane
Brilliant   **621.32**
Broyard, Anatole
         About
Gates, H. L. Thirteen ways of looking at a black
man   **920.71**
Life stories   **920**
Bruccoli, Matthew Joseph
(ed) Fitzgerald, F. S. A life in letters   **813**
Bruce. Carlin, P. A.   **92**
Bruce Chatwin. Shakespeare, N.   **823**
Bruchac, Joseph
Our stories remember   **970.004**
Bruck, Connie
When Hollywood had a king   **338.7**
Bruinius, Harry
Better for all the world   **363.9**
Brunch @ Bobby's.   **641.5**
BRUNCHES
Brunch @ Bobby's   **641.5**
Sarabeth's good morning cookbook   **641.5**
Brunelleschi's dome. King, R.   **726**
Brunelleschi, Filippo, 1377-1446
         About
King, R. Brunelleschi's dome   **726**
Brunetti, Ivan
An anthology of graphic fiction, cartoons & true
stories, vol. 2   **741.5**
An Anthology of graphic fiction, cartoons, and true
stories   **741.5**
Cartooning   **741.5**
Bruni, Frank
Ambling into history: the unlikely odyssey of
George W. Bush   **973.931**
Where You Go Is Not Who You'll Be   **378.161**
         About
Bruni, F. Born round   **92**

Bruning, John R.
Level zero heroes   **958.104**

Bruno, Isabelle
Reinventing Ikea   **684.1**

Bruns, Catharina
(jt. auth) Pester, S. Supercraft   **745.5**

Bruns, Roger
(ed) Congress investigates   **328**

Brunvand, Jan Harold
The vanishing hitchhiker   **398.2**

Brutal imagination. Eady, C.   **811**

Brutal journey: the epic story of the first crossing of
North America. Schneider, P.   **970.01**

Bryan, Mike
Ripken, C. The only way I know   **92**
Van Heerden, I. L. The storm   **976.3**

Bryan, Patricia L.
Midnight assassin   **364.152**

Bryan, William Jennings, 1860-1925
About
Hofstadter, R. The American political tradition, and
the men who made it   **973**
Kazin, M. A godly hero   **92**

Bryant, Charity
About
Cleves, R. H. Charity and Sylvia   **306.84**

Bryant, Geoff
(ed) The plant finder   **635.9**

Bryant, George
The paleo kitchen   **641.5**

Bryant, Howard
The last hero   **92**

Bryant-Davis, Thelma
(ed) Surviving sexual violence   **362.88**

Bryant-Waugh, Rachel
(jt. auth) Lask, B. Eating disorders   **616.85**

Brysac, Shareen Blair
The China collectors   **709.5**
Meyer, K. E. Kingmakers   **956**

Bryson, Bill
Bryson, B. A short history of nearly everything **500**
At home   **643**
I'm a stranger here myself   **818**
In a sunburned country   **919**
Made in America   **420**
Notes from a small island   **914**
Shakespeare   **822.3**
A walk in the woods   **917**
(ed) Seeing further   **506**
About
Bryson, B. The life and times of the thunderbolt
kid   **92**
Bryson, B. The road to Little Dribbling   **914**

Bryson, Francine
Blue ribbon baking from a redneck kitchen **641.597**

Bryson, Lew
Tasting whiskey   **663**

Bryson, Lucy
(jt. auth) Rigby, C. Fodor's Rio de Janeiro & Sao
Paulo   **918.15**

Bryson, Tina Payne
(jt. auth) Siegel, D. J. No-drama discipline   **649**
(jt. auth) Siegel, D. J. The whole-brain child   **649**

Brzezinski, Mika, 1967-
Obsessed   **362.196**

Brzezinski, Zbigniew, 1928-
Strategic vision   **327.1**

BUBBLES
    See also Air; Gases

Buber, Martin, 1878-1965
I and thou   **181**
About
Friedman, M. S. Encounter on the narrow ridge: a
life of Martin Buber   **92**

BUBONIC PLAGUE *See* Plague

BUCCANEERS *See* Pirates

Buchan, James
Days of God   **955.05**

Buchanan, Edna
About
Life stories   **920**

Buchanan, Mark
Nexus: small worlds and the groundbreaking science of networks   **530**

Buchanan, Rita
Taylor's master guide to landscaping   **712**

Buchberg, Karl
(ed) Henri Matisse   **709.2**

**BUCHENWALD (GERMANY: CONCENTRA-
TION CAMP)**
Hackett, D. A. The Buchenwald report   **940.53**

**BUCHENWALD (GERMANY: CONCENTRA-
TION CAMP)**
    See also Concentration camps
The **Buchenwald** report. Hackett, D. A.   **940.53**

Bucher, Julia A.
(ed) American Cancer Society complete guide to
family caregiving   **649.8**

BUCK V. BELL
Lombardo, P. A. Three generations, no imbeciles   **344**

Buck, Carrie, 1906-1983
About
Lombardo, P. A. Three generations, no imbe-
ciles   **344**

Buck, Pearl S. (Pearl Sydenstricker), 1892-1973
About
Spurling, H. Pearl Buck in China   **92**

Buck, Rinker
The Oregon Trail   **978**

Buck, Rinker, 1950-
About

Buck, R. The Oregon Trail 978
The Oregon Trail 978
Buckell studies in Latin American literature and theory [series]
Biron, R. E. Elena Garro and Mexico's modern dreams 868
Buckland, Gail
Evans, H. They made America 920
Who shot rock & roll 781.66
Who shot sports 779.97
Buckley. Bogus, C. T. 92
Buckley and Mailer. Schultz, K. M. 973.92
Buckley, Bruce
Weather: a visual guide 551.5
Buckley, Bryan
About
Sielski, M. Fading echoes 92
Buckley, Christopher Taylor, 1952-
About
Buckley, C. T. Losing Mum and Pup 92
Buckley, Gail Lumet, 1937-
American patriots 355
About
Buckley, G. L. The Black Calhouns 92
Buckley, Pat
About
Buckley, C. T. Losing Mum and Pup 92
Buckley, Veronica
The secret wife of Louis XIV 944
Bogus, C. T. Buckley 92
Buckley, William F., 1925-2008
About
Brookhiser, R. Right time, right place 92
Buckley, C. T. Losing Mum and Pup 92
Buckley, W. F. Miles gone by 92
Buckley, W. F. Nearer, my God 282
The Reagan I knew 92
Schultz, K. M. Buckley and Mailer 973.92
Bucknam, Robert
(jt. auth) Ezzo, G. On becoming baby wise 649
Bud, Robert
(ed) Instruments of science 502.8
Budbill, David
Happy life 811
Budd, Ann
The knitter's handy book of patterns 746.43
Knitter's handy book of top-down sweaters 746.432
New directions in sock knitting 746.432
Sock knitting master class 746.432
Budd, Ken
About
Budd, K. The voluntourist 361.7
Buddha. Armstrong, K. 294.3
The **Buddha** walks into a bar. Rinzler, L. 294.3
BUDDHISM
Bstan-'dzin-rgya-mtsho, D. L. X. Freedom in exile 92
Bstan-'dzin-rgya-mtsho, D. L. X. My Tibet 951
Bstan-'dzin-rgya-mtsho, D. L. X. Violence and compassion 294.3
Chödrön, P. How to meditate 294.3
Eastern religions 200.9
Emet, J. Finding the blue sky 294.3
Greenblat, M. R. A. Dharma Delight 294.3
Harris, D. 10% happier 158.1
How to be compassionate 294.3
Keown, D. A dictionary of Buddhism 294.3
Kerouac, J. Some of the dharma 294.3
Mullin, G. H. The second Dalai Lama 92
Nichtern, E. The road home 294.3
Rinzler, L. The Buddha walks into a bar 294.3
Sogyal The Tibetan book of living and dying 294.3
Sutin, L. All is change 294.3
Thondup, T. Enlightened journey 294.3
Thurman, R. A. F. Why the Dalai Lama matters 294.3
BUDDHISM
See also Religions
BUDDHISM -- DICTIONARIES
Olson, C. Historical dictionary of Buddhism 294.3
BUDDHISM -- PRAYERS
See also Prayers
BUDDHIST ART
Suzuki, D. T. Manual of Zen Buddhism 294.3
BUDDHIST ART
See also Art
BUDDHIST LEADERS
Armstrong, K. Buddha 294.3
Bstan-'dzin-rgya-mtsho, D. L. X. Freedom in exile 92
Iyer, P. The open road 92
Johnson, T. Tragedy in crimson 294.3
Thurman, R. A. F. Why the Dalai Lama matters 294.3
Budge, Don, 1915-2000
About
Fisher, M. A terrible splendor 796.342
BUDGET
See also Public finance
BUDGET -- UNITED STATES
Kramer, M. A people's guide to the federal budget 352.4
BUDGET DEFICIT -- UNITED STATES
Johnson, S. White House burning 336.3
BUDGETS, HOUSEHOLD *See* Household budgets
BUDGETS, PERSONAL *See* Personal finance
Budig, Kathryn
Aim true 613.7
Buell, Hal
Moments 070.4
Buelow, Beth L.

The Introvert Entrepreneur   **658.11**

Buettner, Dan

The Blue Zones solution   **613.2**

Buffalo Bill Cody. Carter, R. A.   **978**

Buffalo Bill's America. Warren, L. S.   **92**

Buffalo Bill, 1846-1917

About

Carter, R. A. Buffalo Bill Cody   **978**

Warren, L. S. Buffalo Bill's America   **92**

BUFFALO, AMERICAN *See* Bison

Buffering. Hart, H.   **792.702**

Buffett, Mary

Warren Buffett and the art of stock arbitrage   **332.6**

Buffett, Warren E.

About

Buffett, M. Warren Buffett and the art of stock arbitrage   **332.6**

Chan, R. W. Behind the Berkshire Hathaway curtain   **658.4**

Schroeder, A. D. The snowball: Warren Buffett and the business of life   **92**

Buford, Bill

Heat   **641.5**

Buford, Kate

Burt Lancaster   **92**

Native American son   **92**

Bugliosi, Vincent

Helter skelter   **364.1**

Reclaiming history   **973.922**

Buhle, Paul

Kitchen, D. The art of Harvey Kurtzman   **741.5**

(ed) Rudahl, S. A dangerous woman   **335**

(ed) Students for a Democratic Society   **378.1**

Buhrke, Thomas

(ed) Renewable energy   **333**

BUILDING

The Art of natural building   **690**

Eck, J. The distinctive home   **728**

Kidder, T. House   **690**

Stiles, D. Backyard Building   **690**

BUILDING AND LOAN ASSOCIATIONS *See* Savings and loan associations

Building and managing e-book collections.   **025.2**

Building art. Goldberger, P.   **92**

BUILDING DESIGN *See* Architecture

BUILDING FAILURES

Levy, M. Why buildings fall down   **690**

BUILDING FAILURES

See also Structural failures

BUILDING MATERIALS

The Art of natural building   **690**

BUILDING MATERIALS

See also Materials

BUILDING NESTS *See* Nest building

Building the Getty. Meier, R.   **708**

BUILDING, WOODEN -- AMATEURS' MANU-

ALS

The complete outdoor builder   **690**

BUILDINGS

Hollis, E. The secret lives of buildings   **720.9**

BUILDINGS -- EARTHQUAKE EFFECTS

See also Earthquakes

BUILT-IN FURNITURE

See also Furniture

Buisseret, David

(ed) The Oxford companion to world exploration   **910.3**

Buk-Swienty, Tom

The other half   **92**

Buker, Derek M.

The science-fiction and fantasy readers' advisory   **025.5**

Bukowski, Charles

The pleasures of the damned   **811**

Bulb. Pavord, A.   **635.9**

BULBS

Pavord, A. Bulb   **635.9**

BULBS

See also Flower gardening; Plants

Bulbs in the basement, geraniums on the windowsill. McGowan, A.   **635.9**

Bulfinch's mythology. Bulfinch, T.   **398.2**

Bulfinch, Thomas

Bulfinch's mythology   **398.2**

BULGE, BATTLE OF THE *See* Ardennes (France), Battle of the, 1944-1945

Bulger, Whitey, 1929-

About

Cullen, K. Whitey Bulger   **364.1**

Bulik, Cynthia M.

Midlife eating disorders   **616.85**

BULIMIA

Forrest, E. Your voice in my head   **362.196**

Hornbacher, M. Wasted: a memoir of anorexia and bulimia   **616.85**

BULIMIA

See also Eating disorders

BULL RIDING

Peter, J. Fried twinkies, buckle bunnies & bull riders   **791.8**

BULL RUN, 1ST BATTLE OF, 1861

Davis, W. C. Battle at Bull Run   **973.7**

Bull!: a history of the boom, 1982-1999. Mahar, M.   **332.6**

Bull, Jane

Get set, sew   **646.2**

Bull, John L.

The National Audubon Society field guide to North American birds, Eastern region   **598**

Bullard, Robert Lee, 1861-1947

About

Walker, W. T. Betrayal at Little Gibraltar   **940.436**

Bullard, Sara
  Teaching tolerance   **649**
Bullard, Thomas E.
  The myth and mystery of UFOs   **001.9**
Bulletproof feathers.   **570.1**
BULLFIGHTS
  Hemingway, E. The dangerous summer   **791.8**
  Hemingway, E. Death in the afternoon   **791.8**
BULLFIGHTS
  See also Sports
BULLIES
  Bazelon, E. Sticks and stones   **302.34**
  Bully   **371.5**
  Cahill, S. LGBT youth in America's schools **371.82**
  Kurzweil, A. Whipping Boy   **92**
  Strauss, S. L. Sexual harassment and bullying   **302.34**
  Whitson, S. 8 keys to end bullying   **302.34**
BULLIES
  See also Aggressiveness (Psychology)
Bulliet, Richard W.
  (ed) The Columbia history of the 20th century   **909.82**
BULLION *See* Precious metals
Bullock-Prado, Gesine, 1970-
      About
  Bullock-Prado, G. Confections of a closet master baker   **92**
Bully.   **371.5**
The **Bully** Pulpit. Goodwin, D. K.   **973.91**
BULLYING
  Bazelon, E. Sticks and stones   **302.34**
  Bully   **371.5**
  Kowalski, R. M. Cyberbullying   **302.34**
  Strauss, S. L. Sexual harassment and bullying   **302.34**
Bülow, Hans von, 1830-1894
      About
  Schonberg, H. C. The great pianists   **920**
BUMBLEBEES
  The bee book   **595.799**
Bunch, Robert, 1820-
      About
  Dickey, C. Our Man in Charleston   **92**
Bundrum, Charlie, d. 1958
      About
  Bragg, R. Ava's man   **975**
Bundy, McGeorge, 1919-1996
      About
  Halberstam, D. The best and the brightest **973.922**
Bundy, Ted
      About
  Rule, A. The stranger beside me   **92**
Bungalow style. Crochet, T.   **747**
Bunker Hill. Philbrick, N.   **973.3**
BUNKER HILL (BOSTON, MASS.), BATTLE

OF, 1775
  Lockhart, P. D. The whites of their eyes   **973.3**
  Nelson, J. L. With fire & sword   **973.3**
  Philbrick, N. Bunker Hill   **973.3**
BUNKER HILL (BOSTON, MASS.), BATTLE OF, 1775
    See also Battles; United States -- History -- 1775-1783, Revolution -- Campaigns
Bunker, Nick
  An empire on the edge   **973.3**
  Making haste from Babylon   **974.4**
Bunny Williams' on garden style.
Bunson, Margaret R.
  Encyclopedia of ancient Egypt   **932**
Bunson, Matthew
  Encyclopedia of ancient Rome   **937**
Bunting, Basil
  Complete poems   **821**
Bunting, Josiah
  Ulysses S. Grant   **92**
BUNYAN, PAUL (LEGENDARY CHARACTER)
    See also Folklore -- United States
Bunyan, Paul (Legendary character)
      About
  Hustvedt, S. Living, thinking, looking   **814**
Buonomano, Dean
  Brain bugs   **612.8**
Burana, Lily
      About
  Burana, L. I love a man in uniform   **92**
Buratovich, Michael A.
  (ed) Magill's medical guide   **610**
Burbank, Luther, 1849-1926
      About
  Smith, J. S. The garden of invention   **92**
Burch, Mary R.
  Citizen canine   **636.7**
Burcher, Nick
  Paid, owned, earned   **658.8**
Burckhardt, Jacob
  The Greeks and Greek civilization   **938**
BurdaStyle modern sewing.   **646.4**
BurdaStyle sewing vintage modern. Abousteit, N.   **646.4**
Burdick, Alan
  Out of Eden   **577**
Bureau of Labor Statistics
  Occupational outlook handbook   **331.7**
BUREAUCRACY
    See also Political science; Public administration
Burfoot, Amby
  (jt. auth) Bede, P. N. The Runner's world big book of marathon and half-marathon training **796.425**
  Runner's world complete book of running **796.42**
Burg, David F.

Almanac of World War I **940.3**

Burge, Kimberly
The born frees **305.242**

Burger, Jeff
(ed) Leonard Cohen on Leonard Cohen **92**

Burgers. **641.66**

Burgess, Michael
Reference guide to science fiction, fantasy, and horror **016**

Burgin, Angus
The great persuasion **330.12**

Burgin, R. V., 1922-
About
Burgin, R. V. Islands of the damned **940.54**

Burgin, Robert
(ed) Cords, S. S. The real story **025.5**
Going places **910.4**

Burgis, Tom
The looting machine **338.2**

BURGLARS See Thieves

**BURGLARY INVESTIGATION -- ENGLAND --
LONDON -- CASE STUDIES**
Crosby, M. C. The great pearl heist **364.16**

BURGLARY PROTECTION
See also Crime prevention

Burhans, Dirk E.
Crunch! **338.4**

BURIAL
Kammen, M. G. Digging up the dead **393**

BURIAL
See also Archeology; Public health

BURIAL -- HISTORY
Faust, D. G. This republic of suffering **973.7**
The **burial** at Thebes. Heaney, S. **822**

BURIAL CUSTOMS See Burial
Burial for a King. Burns, R. **92**
BURIAL STATISTICS See Mortality; Registers of births, etc.; Vital statistics
The **buried** book. Damrosch, D. **809**
BURIED CITIES See Extinct cities
Buried in the sky. Zuckerman, P. **796.522**

BURIED TREASURE
See also Archeology; Underwater exploration

BURIED TREASURE -- FICTION
Kurson, R. Pirate hunters **910.91**

Burk, Kathleen
Old world, new world **327**

Burke, Carolyn
Lee Miller **92**
No regrets **92**

Burke, Dennis
Law man **92**

Burke, Edmund, 1729-1797
Reflections on the Revolution in France **944.04**
About
Norman, J. Edmund Burke **92**

Burke, John (John J.)
Neal-Schuman library technology companion **025**

Burke, Kevin M.
And Still I Rise **973**

Burke, Larry
Ripken, C. Play baseball the Ripken way **796.357**

Burke, Monte
Saban **796.332**

Burke, Timothy M.
The Paradiso files **364.152**

Burkett, Richard
Nelson, G. C. Ceramics: a potter's handbook **738.1**

Burkhardt, Frederick
(ed) Darwin, C. The Beagle letters **576.8**

Burkholder, J. Peter
(ed) Norton Anthology of Western Music **780**
(jt. auth) Palisca, C. V. A history of Western music **780.9**

Burleigh, Michael
Moral combat **940.54**
The Third Reich **943.086**

Burleigh, Nina
Unholy business **933**

BURLESQUE (LITERATURE)
See also Comedy; Parody; Satire

BURLESQUE (THEATER)
See also Theater

Burlingame, Michael
Abraham Lincoln **92**
Burma. Duguid, N. **641.59**

BURMA See Myanmar

BURMA -- SOCIAL LIFE AND CUSTOMS
Duguid, N. Burma **641.59**

Burman, Leonard, 1953-
Taxes in America **336.2**

BURN OUT (PSYCHOLOGY)
See also Job satisfaction; Job stress; Mental health; Motivation (Psychology); Occupational health and safety; Stress (Psychology)
Burn this book. **814**

Burne-Jones, Georgiana, Lady, 1840-1920
About
Flanders, J. A circle of sisters **920**

Burnett, Bill
(jt. auth) Evans, D. Designing your life **650.1**

Burnett, Carol, 1933-
In such good company **791.45**

Burnett, Dean
Idiot brain **612.8**

Burnett, Jason Bige
Graphic clay **738.1**
The **Burning** Answer. Barnham, K. **333.79**
Burning books. Bosmajian, H. A. **098**
Burning down the house. Bernstein, N. **365**
The **burning** of the world. **92**
The **burning** Tigris. Balakian, P. **956.6**

Burns. Burns, R.   **821**

Burns, Cherie
The great hurricane-1938   **974.7**

Burns, Cortney
(jt. auth) Balla, N. Bar Tartine   **641.59**

Burns, David D.
Feeling good   **158**

Burns, Deborah
(ed) Storey's horse-lover's encyclopedia   **636.1**

Burns, Elizabeth
Brookover, S. Pop goes the library   **021.2**

Burns, Eric
1920   **973.91**
The Golden Lad   **92**
Infamous scribblers   **071**

Burns, James MacGregor
The three Roosevelts   **973.91**

Burns, Ken, 1953-
Duncan, D. Lewis & Clark   **917**
The Roosevelts   **920**
Ward, G. C. The Civil War   **973.7**
Ward, G. C. Jazz   **781.65**

Burns, Mike, 1865?-1934
About
Burns, M. The only one living to tell   **305.897**

Burns, Rebecca
Burial for a King   **92**

Burns, Ric
Ward, G. C. The Civil War   **973.7**

Burns, Robert
Burns   **821**

Burns, Robert, 1759-1796
About
Crawford, R. The bard   **92**
Heaney, S. Finders keepers   **821**

Burns, Sarah
The Central Park Five   **364.1**

Burns, Thomas S.
A history of the Ostrogoths   **909.07**

Burns, Tom
Our Necessary Shadow   **616.89**

Burns, William E.
A brief history of Great Britain   **941**

Burnshaw, Stanley
The collected poems and selected prose   **811**

Burnt toast makes you sing good. Flinn, K. **641.597**

Burr, Aaron, 1756-1836
About
Ellis, J. J. Founding brothers   **973.4**
Larson, E. J. A magnificent catastrophe   **324**
Sedgwick, J. War of two   **973.4**
Stewart, D. O. American emperor   **973.4**

Burr, Brooks M.
Page, L. M. Peterson field guide to freshwater fishes of North America north of Mexico   **597**

Burr, Ty

Gods like us   **306.4**

BURR-HAMILTON DUEL, WEEHAWKEN, N.J., 1804
Sedgwick, J. War of two   **973.4**

Burrell, Brian David
(jt. auth) Ropper, A. H. Reaching down the rabbit hole   **616.8**

Burrough, Bryan
The big rich   **338.2**
Days of Rage   **303.48**

Burroughs, Augusten
About
Burroughs, A. Lust and Wonder   **92**
Burroughs, A. Running with scissors   **813**

Burroughs, William S., 1914-1997
Burroughs, W. S. Rub out the words   **813**
About
Miles, B. Call Me Burroughs   **92**

Burroway, Janet, 1936-
(ed) Butler, R. O. From where you dream   **808.3**
(ed) A story larger than my own   **810.9**

Burrows, Edwin G.
Gotham   **974.7**

Burrows, John
(ed) The complete classical music guide   **780**

Burrows, Larry
Vietnam   **770.92**

Burrows, Peter
Backfire: Carly Fiorina's high-stakes battle for the soul of Hewlett-Packard   **338.7**

Burstein, Andrew
Madison and Jefferson   **973.4**

Burt Lancaster. Buford, K.   **92**

Burt, Daniel S.
The biography book   **016**
(ed) The Chronology of American literature   **810**

Burt, John
(ed) The collected poems of Robert Penn Warren   **811**

Burt, Stephen
Close calls with nonsense   **809.1**

Burt, William
Marshes   **578.7**

Burton, Isabel, Lady, 1831-1896
About
Lovell, M. S. A rage to live: a biography of Richard and Isabel Burton   **92**

Burton, Richard Francis Sir, 1821-1890
About
Grant, R. Crazy river   **916**
Lovell, M. S. A rage to live: a biography of Richard and Isabel Burton   **92**

Burton, Richard, 1925-1984
About
Kashner, S. Furious love   **92**

Burton, Virgil L.

(ed) Encyclopedia of Business Information Sources 330

Buruma, Ian
Inventing Japan, 1853-1964   **952.03**
Murder in Amsterdam   **364.152**
Year zero   **940.53**

BURUNDI
Chretien The great lakes of Africa   **967.6**
Kidder, T. Strength in what remains   **92**

Bury my clothes. Bonair-Agard, R.   **811**

Bury my heart at Wounded Knee. Brown, D. A.   **970.004**

Bury the chains. Hochschild, A.   **326**

BURYING GROUNDS See Burial; Cemeteries

Busbee, Jay
Earnhardt Nation   **796.72**

Busby, Horace W.
The thirty-first of March   **973.923**

Busch family
About
Knoedelseder, W. Bitter brew   **338.7**
MacIntosh, J. Dethroning the king   **338.8**

Busch, Akiko
The incidental steward   **363.7**

Busch, Benjamin
About
Busch, B. Dust to dust   **92**

Busch, Robert
The wolf almanac   **599.77**

Buschendorf, Christa
(ed) Cornel West on Black prophetic fire   **92**

BUSES
See also Automobiles; Highway transportation; Local transit; Motor vehicles

Bush. Smith, J. E.   **973.931**

BUSH SURVIVAL See Wilderness survival

Bush, George W.
All the best, George Bush   **92**
About
Bruni, F. Ambling into history: the unlikely odyssey of George W. Bush   **973.931**
Bush, G. W. Decision points   **92**
Schlesinger, A. M. War and the American presidency   **327.1**
Woodward, B. State of denial   **973.931**
41   **92**
Duffy, M. The presidents club   **973.92**
About
Haass, R. War of necessity: war of choice   **956.7**
Smith, J. E. Bush   **973.931**

Bush, George W. (George Walker), 1946-
About
Bush, G. W. 41   **92**
Bush, G. All the best, George Bush   **92**
Haass, R. War of necessity: war of choice   **956.7**
Parmet, H. S. George Bush   **92**

Woodward, B. The commanders   **973.928**
Woodward, B. Shadow   **973.92**

Bush, Lawrence
Rosten, L. The new joys of Yiddish   **422**

Bushcraft 101. Canterbury, D.   **613.6**

The **Bushcraft** field guide to trapping, gathering, and cooking in the wild. Canterbury, D.   **641.691**

Bushman, Barbara Ann
(ed) Complete guide to fitness & health   **613.7**

Bushman, Richard L.
Joseph Smith   **92**
Joseph Smith and the beginnings of Mormonism   **289.3**
Mormonism   **289.3**

Bushmiller, Ernie, 1905-1982
About
Brainard, J. The Nancy book   **759**

BUSINESS
Chan, R. W. Behind the Berkshire Hathaway curtain   **658.4**

BUSINESS
See also Commerce; Economics

BUSINESS -- BIBLIOGRAPHY
The basic business library   **016**
Covert, J. The 100 best business books of all time   **016.6**
Guide to Reference in Business and Economics **016**

BUSINESS -- BIOGRAPHY -- DICTIONARIES
Who's who in finance and business 2008-2009   **920.003**

BUSINESS -- CORRUPT PRACTICES
Lewis, M. Flash boys   **332.6**

BUSINESS -- DATABASES -- HANDBOOKS, MANUALS, ETC
Ernsthausen, D. G. Strauss's handbook of business information   **016**

BUSINESS -- DICTIONARIES
Cheng & Tsui English-Chinese lexicon of business terms with pinyin   **495.1**

BUSINESS -- ENCYCLOPEDIAS
Encyclopedia of Business Information Sources **330**

BUSINESS -- INFORMATION SERVICES
The basic business library   **016**

BUSINESS -- SOCIAL RESPONSIBILITY See Social responsibility of business

BUSINESS ADMINISTRATION See Management

BUSINESS AND GOVERNMENT See Economic policy

BUSINESS AND POLITICS
Cohen, R. The fish that ate the whale   **338.7**
Friedman, T. L. The Lexus and the olive tree   **337**
Power, Inc.   **322**

BUSINESS AND POLITICS
See also Politics

BUSINESS AND POLITICS -- UNITED STATES

Reich, R. B. Saving capitalism   330.973

**BUSINESS AND POLITICS -- UNITED STATES
-- HISTORY -- 19TH CENTURY**
Thomas, E. The war lovers   973.8

BUSINESS BUDGETS
   See also Business

BUSINESS COMMUNICATION
Alexander, L. Access to Asia   395.5
Annis, B. Work with me   306.3
Goulston, M. Just listen   650.1
Kramer, A. S. Breaking through bias   650.101
Meyers, P. As we speak   808.5
Morrison, T. Kiss, bow, or shake hands 395
Port, M. Steal the show   658.4

BUSINESS CYCLES
Boeckh, J. A. The great reflation   332.6
Mahar, M. Bull!: a history of the boom, 1982-
   1999   332.6
Reinhart, C. M. This time is different 338.5

BUSINESS CYCLES
   See also Cycles; Economic conditions

BUSINESS DEPRESSION, 1929-1939 *See* Great
   Depression, 1929-1939

BUSINESS DEPRESSIONS *See* Depressions

BUSINESS EDUCATION
   See also Education

BUSINESS ENTERPRISES
Micklethwait, J. The company   338.7
Nalebuff, B. Mission in a bottle   338.7
Pakroo, P. The small business start-up kit 346
Spector, R. The mom & pop store   381
Taylor, W. Practically radical   658.4

**BUSINESS ENTERPRISES -- CORRUPT PRAC-
TICES**
The best business writing 2013   330.9

**BUSINESS ENTERPRISES -- DATA PROCESS-
ING**
Arora, P. To the cloud   004.67

BUSINESS ENTERPRISES -- PLANNING *See*
   Business planning

BUSINESS ENTERTAINING
RoAne, S. How to work a room   650.1

BUSINESS ENTERTAINING
   See also Entertaining; Public relations

BUSINESS ETHICS
Abrams, J. Companies we keep   338.7
Callahan, D. The cheating culture   174
Covey, S. M. R. Smart trust   174
Gentile, M. C. Giving voice to values   174
Sandel, M. J. What money can't buy   330.1

BUSINESS ETHICS
   See also Ethics; Professional ethics

BUSINESS ETIQUETTE
Morrison, T. Kiss, bow, or shake hands 395
Oliver, V. 301 smart answers to tough business eti-
   quette questions   395

Post, P. Emily Post's The etiquette advantage in
   business   395
RoAne, S. How to work a room   650.1

BUSINESS ETIQUETTE
   See also Etiquette

BUSINESS ETIQUETTE -- ASIA
Alexander, L. Access to Asia   395.5

BUSINESS FAILURES
Acharya, V. V. Guaranteed to fail   332.7
Dwyer, J. More awesome than money   384.3

BUSINESS FAILURES
   See also Business

BUSINESS INTELLIGENCE
Javers, E. Broker, trader, lawyer, spy 364.1

BUSINESS LAW *See* Commercial law

BUSINESS MANAGERS
McCourt, A. A long stone's throw   92

BUSINESS NETWORKS
Guest, R. Borderless economics   303.48
Ryckman, P. Stiletto network   331.4

The **business** of baby. Margulis, J.   649

BUSINESS ORGANIZATIONS *See* Business enterprises

BUSINESS PEOPLE *See* Businesspeople

BUSINESS PLANNING
Arora, P. To the cloud   004.67
How to write a business plan   658.15
Lashinsky, A. Inside Apple   338.7
Pinson, L. Anatomy of a business plan   658.4
The power of habit   158.1
Sarillo, N. A slice of the pie   658.02
Wheeler, M. The art of negotiation   658.4

BUSINESS PLANNING
   See also Planning

BUSINESS PRESENTATIONS
Duarte, N. Resonate   658.452
Gallo, C. Talk like TED   658.4
Port, M. Steal the show   658.4

BUSINESS RECESSIONS *See* Recessions

BUSINESS WRITING
The best business writing 2013   330.9

BUSINESS WRITING
   See also Authorship

BUSINESSES *See* Business enterprises

BUSINESSMEN
Cohen, R. The fish that ate the whale   338.7
Dykstra, L. House of nails   796.357
Kurlansky, M. Birdseye   338.7
Mezrich, B. Once Upon a Time in Russia 330
Rathbone, J. P. The sugar king of Havana 92
Renehan, E. J. Commodore   92
Stiles, T. J. The first tycoon   92
Walton, S. Sam Walton, made in America 92
Wolff, M. The man who owns the news   92

BUSINESSMEN
   See also Businesspeople

BUSINESSMEN -- UNITED STATES -- BIOGRAPHY

Johnston, D. C. The making of Donald Trump **973.932**
Kurlansky, M. Birdseye **338.7**
Lewis, M. D. The new new thing **338.4**

BUSINESSPEOPLE

Browne, J. The Glass Closet **331.5**
Carey, C. W. American inventors, entrepreneurs & business visionaries **920**
Encyclopedia of Business Information Sources **330**
Gup, T. A secret gift **977.1**
Keefe, P. R. The snakehead **364.1**
Parrado, N. Miracle in the Andes **982**
Stone, B. Things a little bird told me **006.7**
Strouse, J. Morgan **92**

BUSINESSPEOPLE

See also Business

BUSINESSPEOPLE -- UNITED STATES -- BIOGRAPHY

Bilton, N. Hatching Twitter **006.7**
Isaacson, W. Steve Jobs **92**
Knight, P. H. Shoe dog **92**
Nasaw, D. The patriarch **92**
Tetzeli, R. Becoming Steve Jobs **92**
Zuckerman, G. The frackers **338.2**

BUSINESSPEOPLE -- UNITED STATES -- CONDUCT OF LIFE

Jacobs, B. Life is good **650.1**

BUSINESSWOMEN

Davidds, Y. Your own terms **658.4**
Huston, T. How women decide **155.333**
Lemmon, G. T. The dressmaker of Khair Khana **92**
Levinson, D. J. The seasons of a woman's life **155.6**
Pepper, C. The seven pearls of financial wisdom **332.024**
Pimsleur, J. Million Dollar Women **658.4**
Verveer, M. Fast forward **650.1**

BUSINESSWOMEN

See also Businesspeople; Women

BUSINESSWOMEN -- ENCYCLOPEDIAS

Krismann, C. Encyclopedia of American women in business **920.003**

BUSINESSWOMEN -- UNITED STATES -- BIOGRAPHY

Ping Fu Bend, not break **92**

BUSING (SCHOOL INTEGRATION)

Lukas, J. A. Common ground **305.8**
Masur, L. P. The soiling of Old Glory **974.4**

BUSING (SCHOOL INTEGRATION)

See also School children -- Transportation; School integration

Buskin, Richard
Diller, P. Like a lampshade in a whorehouse **92**
Busoni, Ferruccio, 1866-1924
About

Schonberg, H. C. The great pianists **920**
Bussagli, Marco
Angels **704.9**
Buster Keaton. Meade, M. **92**
But I could never go. **641.5**
But What If We're Wrong? Klosterman, C. **909.83**
Butcher, Carmen Acevedo
Man of blessing **271**
Butcher, Tim
Chasing the Devil **916**
Butchering poultry, rabbit, lamb, goat, and pork. Danforth, A. **664**
Butler's Lives of the saints. **920.003**
Butler, Alban
Butler's Lives of the saints **920.003**
Butler, Amy
Amy Butler's style stitches **646.4**
Butler, Brin-Jonathan
About
Butler The domino diaries **796.83**
Butler, Chris (Private investigator)
About
Crooks, P. The setup **363.28**
Butler, Colin
The practical Shakespeare **822.3**
Butler, Katy
Knocking on Heaven's Door **616.02**
Butler, Patricia M.
Joint libraries **027**
Butler, Rebecca P.
Copyright for teachers & librarians in the 21st century **346**
Butler, Robert Olen
From where you dream **808.3**
Butler, Rosa Johnson
Gillespie, M. A. Maya Angelou **92**
Butler, Susan
East to the dawn **629.13**
Butler, Tom
(ed) Overdevelopment, Overpopulation, Overshoot **363.9**
Buttala, Lee Alan
(ed) The seed garden
BUTTER
See also Dairy products
Butter baked goods. Daykin, R. **641.81**
Butterflies. **595.78**
BUTTERFLIES
Black, S. H. Gardening for butterflies **638**
Brock, J. P. Kaufman field guide to butterflies of North America **595.7**
Butterflies **595.78**
Leach, W. Butterfly people **595.78**
Pyle, R. M. The Audubon Society field guide to North American butterflies **595.7**
Stokes, D. W. The butterfly book **595.7**

BUTTERFLIES

　　See also Insects

The **butterfly** book. Stokes, D. W.　　**595.7**

BUTTERFLY GARDENING

　Black, S. H.　Gardening for butterflies　　**638**

Butterfly people. Leach, W.　　**595.78**

Butterick, George F.

　(ed) Olson, C.　The Maximus poems　　**811**

Butterworth, Alex

　The world that never was　　**335**

Buttiglione, Rocco

　Karol Wojtyla　　**282**

BUTTONS

　　See also Clothing and dress

Buy-in. Kotter, J. P.　　**650.1**

BUYERS' GUIDES *See* Consumer education; Shopping

BUYOUTS, CORPORATE *See* Corporate mergers and acquisitions

Buzbee, Lewis, 1957-

　　About

　Buzbee, L.　The yellow-lighted bookshop　　**002**

A **Buzz** in the Meadow. Goulson, D.　　**638**

Buzzed. Kuhn, C.　　**615.7**

By hook or by crook. Crystal, D.　　**427**

By myself and then some. Bacall, L.　　**92**

By the hand of Mormon. Givens, T.　　**289.3**

By the Iowa Sea. Blair, J.　　**977.7**

By the sword. Cohen, R.　　**796.8**

Byatt, A. S. (Antonia Susan), 1936-

　Peacock & vine　　**700.92**

Bynum, W. F.

　(ed) Oxford dictionary of scientific quotations **500**

BYRD ANTARCTIC EXPEDITION

　　See also Antarctica -- Exploration

Byrd, Rudolph P.

　(ed) Johnson, J. W.　The essential writings of James Weldon Johnson　　**818**

Byres, Tim

　Smoke　　**641.6**

Byrn, Anne

　American cake　　**641.86**

Byrne's new standard book of pool and billiards. Byrne, R.　　**794.7**

Byrne, David

　　About

　Byrne, D.　Bicycle diaries　　**796.6**

　How Music Works　　**781.1**

Byrne, Eugene

　Darwin　　**576.8**

Byrne, Malcolm

　(ed) The Iran-Contra scandal　　**973.927**

Byrne, Paula

　Belle　　**92**

　Kick　　**92**

Byrne, Robert

Byrne's new standard book of pool and billiards　　**794.7**

Byrnes, Thomas, 1842-1910

　　About

　Conway, J. N.　The big policeman　　**92**

Byron, George Gordon Byron, 6th Baron, 1788-1824

　Selected poetry of Lord Byron　　**821**

　　About

　Eisler, B.　Byron--child of passion, fool of fame **92**

Byron--child of passion, fool of fame. Eisler, B. **92**

Bystrolětov, D. A., 1901-1975

　　About

　Draitser, E.　Stalin's Romeo spy　　**92**

BYZANTINE ARCHITECTURE

　　See also Ancient architecture; Architecture; Medieval architecture

BYZANTINE ART

　　See also Ancient art; Art; Medieval art

BYZANTINE EMPIRE

　Brownworth, L.　Lost to the West　　**949.5**

　Gibbon, E.　The decline and fall of the Roman empire　　**937**

　Norwich, J. J.　Byzantium: the apogee　　**949.5**

　Norwich, J. J.　Byzantium: the decline and fall **949.5**

　Norwich, J. J.　Byzantium: the early centuries **949.5**

　Wells, C. M.　Sailing from Byzantium　　**940.2**

Byzantium: the apogee. Norwich, J. J.　**949.5**

Byzantium: the decline and fall. Norwich, J. J. **949.5**

Byzantium: the early centuries. Norwich, J. J. **949.5**

C

C & B crafts [series]

　Crowfoot, J.　Ultimate crochet bible　　**746.43**

C & T Asian dictionary series

　Cheng & Tsui English-Chinese lexicon of business terms with pinyin　　**495.1**

C. Eric Lincoln series on the black experience [series]

　Gardell, M.　In the name of Elijah Muhammad **297**

C. S. Lewis. McGrath, A. E.　　**92**

C.S. Lewis. Wilson, A. N.　　**823**

CABALA

　　See also Hebrew literature; Jewish literature; Judaism; Mysticism; Occultism

The **cabaret** of plants. Mabey, R.　　**580**

CABINET OFFICERS

　Chronology of the U.S. presidency　　**973.09**

　Downey, K.　The woman behind the New Deal **92**

CABINET OFFICERS -- UNITED STATES -- BIOGRAPHY

　Gates, R. M.　A passion for leadership　　**92**

　Kissinger, H.　Years of renewal　　**973.924**

　Marvel, W.　Lincoln's autocrat　　**92**

　Rice, C.　No higher honor　　**327.73**

　Stahr, W.　Seward　　**92**

Unger, I. George Marshall   92

CABINETMAKERS -- UNITED STATES
Downs, P. Boss Life   92

CABINETWORK
    See also Carpentry

CABINS *See* Log cabins and houses

CABLE KNITTING
Durant, J. Cable left, cable right   **746.432**
Cable left, cable right. Durant, J.   **746.432**

CABLE TELEVISION -- UNITED STATES -- HISTORY
Martin, B. Difficult men   **791.450**

Cable, George Washington, 1844-1925
            About
Wilson, E. Patriotic gore   **810**

CABLES
    See also Power transmission; Rope

CABLES, SUBMARINE *See* Submarine cables

CACTUS
Anderson, E. F. The cactus family   **583**
Hewitt, T. The complete book of cacti & succulents   **635.9**

CACTUS
    See also Desert plants
The **cactus** family. Anderson, E. F.   **583**

CAD *See* Computer-aided design

CAD SOFTWARE *See* Computer-aided design software

CAD--CAM SYSTEMS
Rigsby, M. A beginner's guide to 3D printing **621.9**

CAD\CAM SOFTWARE *See* Computer-aided design software

CADAVERS *See* Dead

Cadbury, Deborah
Princes at war   **941.084**

Caddel, Richard
(ed) Bunting, B. Complete poems   **821**

Cadillac Man
            About
Cadillac Man Land of the lost souls   92
Caesar. Goldsworthy, A. K.   92
Caesar, Caius, 20 B.C.-4 A.D.
            About
The twelve Caesars   **878**
Caesar, Ed
Two hours   **796.42**
Caesar, Julius, 100-44 B.C.
The Gallic War   **878**
Strauss, B. The death of Caesar   **937**
            About
Goldsworthy, A. K. Caesar   **92**
Caesars' wives. Freisenbruch, A.   **937**
Cafe Europa. Drakulic, S.   **947**
Cafe Society. Josephson, B.   **792.7**
CAFÉ SOCIETY (NEW YORK, N.Y.: NIGHT-CLUB)

Josephson, B. Cafe Society   **792.7**

CAFES *See* Coffeehouses; Restaurants

CAGE BIRDS
    See also Birds

Cage, John
            About
Brown, C. Chance and circumstance   **92**
Larson, K. Where the heart beats   **700.1**
Silverman, K. Begin again   **92**

Caggiano, Biba
Biba's Italy   **641.59**

Cagney. McCabe, J.   **92**

Cagney, James, 1899-1986
            About
McCabe, J. Cagney   **92**

Cahalan, Susannah
            About
Cahalan, S. Brain on fire   **616.8**

Cahill, Sean
LGBT youth in America's schools   **371.82**

Cahill, Thomas
The gifts of the Jews   **909**
How the Irish saved civilization   **941.501**
Sailing the wine-dark sea   **909**

Cahn, Naomi
(jt. auth) Carbone, J. Marriage markets   **306.85**

CAI *See* Computer-assisted instruction

Caillebotte, Gustave, 1848-1894
            About
Shackelford, G. T. M. Gustave Caillebotte   **759.4**

Cain, Susan
Quiet   **155.2**

Cairns, Huntington
(ed) Plato The collected dialogues of Plato, including the letters   **888**

Cairns, Scott
The end of suffering   **231**

CAIRO GENIZAH
Cole, P. Sacred trash   **296.09**

CAJUN MUSIC
    See also Music

CAKE
Adams, J. D. Grandbaby cakes   **641.86**
Beranbaum, R. L. The cake bible   **641.8**
Boyle, T. The cake book   **641.8**
DeMasco, K. The craft of baking   **641.8**
Desaulniers, M. Death by chocolate cakes   **641.8**
Goldman, D. Duff Bakes   **641.81**
Heatter, M. Maida Heatter's cakes
A la mode   **641.865**
Moore, K. Delicious dump cakes   **641.86**
Vintage cakes   **641.86**
Wright, C. Mix + Match Cakes   **641.86**

CAKE
    See also Baking; Confectionery; Cooking; Desserts

CAKE -- UNITED STATES -- HISTORY
Byrn, A. American cake   **641.86**
The **cake** bible. Beranbaum, R. L.   **641.8**
The **cake** book. Boyle, T.   **641.8**
CAKE DECORATING
Blakeslee, R. L. Your time to bake   **641.8**
Boyle, T. The cake book   **641.8**
Byrn, A. American cake   **641.86**
Calamar, Gary
Record store days   **780.2**
Calaprice, Alice
(ed) Einstein, A. The ultimate quotable Einstein   **530**
(jt. auth) Schulmann, R. An Einstein encyclopedia   **530.092**
Calasso, Roberto
Ardor   **294.5**
Calcaterra, Regina
Girl Unbroken   **306**
      About
Calcaterra, R. Etched in Sand   **92**
CALCULUS
Alexander, A. Infinitesimal   **511**
Apostol, T. M. New Horizons in Geometry   **516**
Ouellette, J. The calculus diaries   **515**
CALCULUS
      See also Mathematical analysis; Mathematics
The **calculus** diaries. Ouellette, J.   **515**
A **Calculus** of Color. McGregor, R. K.   **796.357**
CALCUTTA (INDIA) -- SOCIAL CONDITIONS
Lapierre, D. The City of Joy   **954**
CALDECOTT MEDAL
      See also Children's literature; Illustration of books; Literary prizes
Caldecott, Julian Oliver
(ed) World atlas of great apes and their conservation   **599.8**
Calderazzo, John
Rising fire: volcanoes and our inner lives   **551.2**
Calderon de la Barca, Pedro
Life's a dream   **862**
Calderwood, Norma Jean
      About
In harmony   **704**
Caldwell, Erskine, 1903-1987
      About
Ellison, R. The collected essays of Ralph Ellison   **814**
Caldwell, Gail, 1951-
      About
Caldwell, G. Let's take the long way home   **92**
Caldwell, G. New life, no instructions   **92**
Caldwell, Gianaclis
Mastering artisan cheesemaking   **637**
CALENDARS
      See also Time

Calhoun, Ada
St. Marks Is Dead   **974.7**
Calhoun, Charles W.
Benjamin Harrison   **92**
Calhoun, Craig J.
Dictionary of the social sciences   **300**
Calhoun, John C. (John Caldwell), 1782-1850
      About
Hofstadter, R. The American political tradition, and the men who made it   **973**
McPherson, J. M. Drawn with the sword   **973.7**
CALIFORNIA
Moore, R. This is Camino   **641.5**
Moulle, J. P. French roots   **641.594**
CALIFORNIA -- BIOGRAPHY
Kingston, M. H. The woman warrior   **92**
CALIFORNIA -- CHURCH HISTORY -- 20TH CENTURY
Dochuk, D. From Bible belt to sunbelt   **277**
CALIFORNIA -- HISTORY
Brands, H. W. The Age of Gold   **979.4**
Dvorak, J. Earthquake Storms   **551.22**
Randall, D. K. The King and Queen of Malibu   **979.4**
Stillman, D. Desert reckoning   **363.2**
CALIFORNIA -- PICTORIAL WORKS
Watkins, C. E. Carleton Watkins: the complete mammoth photographs   **778.9**
CALIFORNIA -- POLITICS AND GOVERNMENT -- 1951-
Rosenfeld, S. Subversives   **378.1**
CALIFORNIA -- SOCIAL CONDITIONS
Didion, J. Where I was from   **979.4**
CALIFORNIA GOLD RUSH *See* California -- Gold discoveries
California legacy book [series]
Steffens, L. The autobiography of Lincoln Steffens   **92**
California studies in food and culture [series]
Nabhan, G. P. Cumin, camels, and caravans   **382**
Nesheim, M. Why calories count   **613.2**
Pasta, a. d. p. t. Encyclopedia of pasta   **641.8**
CALIFORNIA. PROPOSITION 8 (2008)
Becker, J. Forcing the spring   **346.73**
Yoshino, K. Speak now   **346.73**
California/Milbank books on health and the public [series]
Foege, W. H. House on fire   **614.5**
Caligula & three other plays. Camus, A.   **842**
Caligula, Emperor of Rome, 12-41
      About
The twelve Caesars   **878**
The **Caliph's** house. Shah, T.   **964**
CALIPHS
Hazleton, L. After the prophet   **297**
Calishain, Tara

Dornfest, R. Google hacks **025.04**

CALISTHENICS *See* Gymnastics; Physical education

Call Me Burroughs. Miles, B. **92**

The **call** of the mall. Underhill, P. **306**

The **call** of trains. Shaughnessy, J. **779**

A **call** to arms. Klein, M. **940.53**

A **call** to mercy. **234.5**

Callahan, Daniel

Taming the beloved beast **338.4**

Callahan, David

The cheating culture **174**

Callahan, Gail

Hand dyeing yarn and fleece **746.6**

Callahan, John F.

(ed) Ellison, R. The collected essays of Ralph Ellison **814**

Callahan, Tom

In search of Tiger **92**

Called again. Davis, J.P. **92**

Called out of darkness. Rice, A. **92**

Callen, Michael, 1955-1993

About

Duberman, M. B. Hold tight gently **920**

CALLIGRAPHERS

Chen, D. Colors of the mountain **92**

Chen, D. Sounds of the river **951.05**

CALLIGRAPHY

Godfrey-Nicholls, G. Mastering calligraphy **745.6**

Modern calligraphy **745.6**

Shepherd, M. Learn calligraphy **745.6**

CALLIGRAPHY

See also Decorative arts; Handwriting; Writing

Calling Dr. Laura. Georges, N. J. **92**

Callings. Isay, D. **920.073**

Callow, Philip

Chekhov, the hidden ground **891.7**

From noon to starry night: a life of Walt Whitman **811**

Calloway, Colin G.

One vast winter count **978**

Calloway, Stephen

(ed) The elements of style **728**

Calming your anxious child. Trainor, K. **618.92**

CALORIC CONTENT OF FOODS *See* Food -- Caloric content

CALORIES (FOOD) *See* Food -- Caloric content

Calvi, Nuala

(jt. auth) Barrett, D. GI brides **940.53**

CALVINISM

See also Reformation

Calvino, Italo

Why read the classics? **809**

About

Becker, D. L. Many subtle channels **840.9**

Calvino, I. Collection of Sand **854**

CALYPSO (MUSIC)

See also Folk music

Camarata, Stephen M.

Late-talking children **618.92**

Cambanis, Thanassis

Once upon a revolution **962.05**

CAMBODIA

DK Eyewitness Travel Cambodia & Laos **915.9**

CAMBODIA -- HISTORY -- 1970-1975, CIVIL WAR

Bizot, F. The gate **959.604**

CAMBODIA -- HISTORY -- 1975-

Ung, L. First they killed my father **959.6**

Ung, L. Lucky child **92**

CAMBODIA -- POLITICS AND GOVERNMENT

Brinkley, J. Cambodia's curse **959.6**

Kiernan, B. The Pol Pot regime **959.6**

CAMBODIA -- POLITICS AND GOVERNMENT -- 1975-1979

Him, C. When broken glass floats **959.604**

Cambodia's curse. Brinkley, J. **959.6**

Cambras, Josep

Bookbinding **686.3**

CAMBRIDGE (MASS.) -- BIOGRAPHY

Nathans, S. To free a family **306.3**

The **Cambridge** ancient history. **930**

The **Cambridge biography D.H. Lawrence, 1885-1930** [series]

Worthen, J. D.H. Lawrence, the early years, 1885-1912 **92**

The **Cambridge** companion to Jane Austen. **823**

The **Cambridge** companion to Native American literature. **897**

The **Cambridge** companion to Newton. **530**

The **Cambridge** companion to the Bible. **220.9**

Cambridge companions to literature [series]

The Cambridge companion to Jane Austen **823**

Cambridge concise histories [series]

Fulbrook, M. A concise history of Germany **943**

The **Cambridge** dictionary of classical civilization. **938**

The **Cambridge** dictionary of philosophy. **103**

The **Cambridge** dictionary of scientists. Millar, D. **920.003**

The **Cambridge** dictionary of statistics. Everitt, B. **519.5**

The **Cambridge** encyclopedia of language. Crystal, D. **400**

The **Cambridge** encyclopedia of the English language. Crystal, D. **420**

The **Cambridge** grammar of the English language. Huddleston, R. D. **425**

The **Cambridge** guide to children's books in English. **028.5**

The **Cambridge** guide to English usage. Peters,

P. **428**

The **Cambridge** guide to literature in English. **820**

The **Cambridge** guide to the solar system. Lang, K. R. **523.2**

The **Cambridge** guide to women's writing in English. **820**

The **Cambridge** handbook of American literature. **810**

Cambridge historical studies in American law and society [series]

Rabban, D. M. Free speech in its forgotten years **342**

The **Cambridge** history of American literature. **810**

The **Cambridge** history of China. **951**

The **Cambridge** history of Judaism. **296**

The **Cambridge** history of Judaism. **296**

The **Cambridge** history of Judaism. **296.09**

The **Cambridge** history of Latin American literature. Gonzalez Echevarria, R. **860**

The **Cambridge** history of Russian literature. **891.7**

The **Cambridge** history of Spanish literature. **860**

Cambridge illustrated history [series]

The Cambridge illustrated history of religions **200.9**

The Cambridge illustrated history of the Islamic world **909**

The Cambridge illustrated history of the Roman world **937**

The **Cambridge** illustrated history of medicine. **610**

The **Cambridge** illustrated history of religions. **200.9**

The **Cambridge** illustrated history of the Islamic world. **909**

The **Cambridge** illustrated history of the Roman world. **937**

The **Cambridge** introduction to modern British fiction, 1950-2000. Head, D. **823**

The **Cambridge** star atlas. Tirion, W. **523.8**

Cambridge texts in the history of political thought [series]

Plato The republic **888**

The **Cambridge** world history of food. **641.3**

CAMDEN (N.J.)

Hedges, C. Days of destruction, days of revolt **305.5**

CAMELS

See also Desert animals; Mammals

CAMERAS

See also Photography; Photography -- Equipment and supplies

Cameron, Angus

The L.L. Bean game and fish cookbook **641.6**

Cameron, Julia B., 1948-

It's never too late to begin again **155.67**

Cameron, Steve

(ed) Hockey Hall of Fame Book of Players **796.962**

Camfield, Gregg

(ed) The Oxford companion to Mark Twain **818**

Camilla, Duchess of Cornwall, 1947-

About

Andersen, C. Game of crowns **941.085**

CAMINO (RESTAURANT)

Moore, R. This is Camino **641.5**

Camoes, Luis de

Selected sonnets **869**

CAMOUFLAGE (BIOLOGY)

Forbes, P. Dazzled and deceived **578.4**

CAMOUFLAGE (BIOLOGY)

See also Animal defenses

CAMOUFLAGE (MILITARY SCIENCE)

See also Military art and science; Naval art and science

CAMP COOKING *See* Outdoor cooking

CAMP DAVID AGREEMENTS (1978)

Wright, L. Thirteen Days in September **956.04**

CAMP SONGS

See also Songs

CAMPAIGN FUNDS -- UNITED STATES

Vogel, K. P. Big money **324.7**

CAMPAIGN LITERATURE

See also Literature; Politics

Campaigning for president in America, 1788-2016. Roberts, R. N. **324.709**

CAMPAIGNS, POLITICAL *See* Politics

CAMPAIGNS, PRESIDENTIAL -- UNITED STATES *See* Presidents -- United States -- Election

Campanella, Roy, 1921-1993

About

Kashatus, W. C. Jackie and Campy **92**

Campany, David

(ed) The open road **770**

Campbell, Gordon

John Milton **92**

Campbell, Greg

Selby, S. A. Flawless **364.1**

Campbell, Hayley

The art of Neil Gaiman **92**

Campbell, James T.

Middle passages **916**

Campbell, Jeremy

The liar's tale **177**

Campbell, Jonathan

The venomous reptiles of the Western Hemisphere **597.96**

Campbell, Joseph

Creative mythology **201**

Occidental mythology **201**

Oriental mythology **201**

The power of myth **201**

Primitive mythology **201**

Campbell, Julieann

Setting the truth free **941.6**

Campbell, Stu

How to mulch **635**

Campbell, W. Joseph

Getting it wrong **071**

Campbell, William, 1730?-1778

About

Harris, J. W. The hanging of Thomas Jeremiah **92**

Campbell-Kelly, Martin

From airline reservations to Sonic the Hedgehog **005**

CAMPING

Canterbury, D. Bushcraft 101 **613.6**

White, D. Under the stars **796.54**

CAMPING

See also Outdoor recreation

CAMPING -- HANDBOOKS, MANUALS, ETC

Canterbury, D. Advanced bushcraft **613.69**

Canterbury, D. Bushcraft 101 **613.6**

Canterbury, D. The Bushcraft field guide to trapping, gathering, and cooking in the wild **641.691**

CAMPING -- UNITED STATES

White, D. Under the stars **796.54**

Campion, Caroline

(jt. auth) Brennan, K. Keepers **641.5**

Campo, Juan Eduardo

Encyclopedia of Islam **297**

Camus, Albert, 1913-1960

Algerian chronicles **965**

Caligula & three other plays **842**

The myth of Sisyphus, and other essays **844**

The rebel **303.6**

Resistance, rebellion, and death **844**

About

Carroll, S. B. Brave genius **920**

Todd, O. Albert Camus **848**

Can I tell you about eating disorders? **616.85**

Can poetry matter? Gioia, D. **809.1**

Can you get hooked on lip balm? Romanowski, P. **646.7**

Can't buy me love. Gould, J. **920**

Can't catch a break. Sered, S. S. **362.83**

Can't stop, won't stop. Chang, J. **781.64**

Can't We Talk About Something More Pleasant? Chast, R. **741.5**

Canada. **917.104**

CANADA -- DESCRIPTION *See* Canada -- Description and travel

CANADA -- DESCRIPTION AND TRAVEL

Canada **917.104**

CANADA -- FOREIGN RELATIONS -- IRAN

Baglio, M. Argo **955.05**

CANADA -- HISTORY

Black, C. Rise to greatness **971**

CANADA -- HISTORY -- 0-1763 (NEW FRANCE)

Morgan, T. Wilderness at dawn **970**

CANADA -- HISTORY -- 1755-1763

Macleod, D. P. Northern Armageddon **971.01**

CANADA -- HISTORY -- 1812-1815, WAR OF 1812 *See* War of 1812

CANADA -- HISTORY -- TO 1763 (NEW FRANCE)

Bailyn, B. The barbarous years **973.2**

Macleod, D. P. Northern Armageddon **971.01**

CANADA -- SOCIAL LIFE AND CUSTOMS

Tye, D. Baking as biography **92**

Canada, Geoffrey

Fist, stick, knife, gun **305.23**

About

Tough, P. Whatever it takes **362.7**

CANADIAN ARCTIC EXPEDITION (1913-1918)

See also Arctic regions -- Exploration; Canada -- Exploring expeditions

CANADIAN AUTHORS

Mowat, F. Born naked **92**

CANADIANS

O'Brady, T. Seven spoons **641.597**

Canal house cooks every day. Hirsheimer, C. **641.5**

CANALS

See also Civil engineering; Hydraulic structures; Transportation; Waterways

CANAPÉS *See* Appetizers

CANARIES

See also Birds; Cage birds

CANASTA (GAME)

See also Card games

CANCER

Brenner, M. Apples and oranges **92**

DeVita-Raeburn, E. The death of cancer **92**

Kaplan, L. Help Your Dog Fight Cancer **636.7**

Leaf, C. The truth in small doses **616.99**

Mukherjee, S. The emperor of all maladies **616.99**

Ross, T. A cancer in the family **616.99**

Skloot, R. The immortal life of Henrietta Lacks **92**

CANCER

See also Diseases; Tumors

CANCER -- CHEMOTHERAPY

Geiger, C. The Cancer Survivors' Club **362.196**

Hitchens, C. Mortality **304.6**

CANCER -- CHEMOTHERAPY

See also Drug therapy

CANCER -- DIET THERAPY

See also Diet therapy

CANCER -- ENVIRONMENTAL ASPECTS

Williams, F. Breasts **612.6**

CANCER -- EXERCISE THERAPY

Will my cancer come back? **616.99**

CANCER -- GENETIC ASPECTS

Stark, L. Pandora's DNA **616.99**

CANCER -- GENETIC ASPECTS

See also Medical genetics

CANCER -- GRAPHIC NOVELS

Small, D. Stitches **741.5**

CANCER -- HISTORY

DeVita-Raeburn, E. The death of cancer **92**

Mukherjee, S. The emperor of all maladies **616.99**

CANCER -- NURSING

Brown, T. The shift **616.02**

CANCER -- NURSING

See also Nursing

CANCER -- PALLIATIVE TREATMENT

American Cancer Society complete guide to family caregiving **649.8**

CANCER -- PATIENTS *See* Cancer patients

CANCER -- PREVENTION

Gazella, K. A. The definitive guide to thriving after cancer **616.99**

CANCER -- PSYCHOLOGICAL ASPECTS

Fullbright, C. D. How to help your friend with cancer **616.99**

Gubar, S. Memoir of a debulked woman **616.99**

Will my cancer come back? **616.99**

CANCER -- RELIGIOUS ASPECTS -- CHRISTIANITY

Billings, J. T. Rejoicing in lament **248.8**

CANCER -- SURGERY

See also Surgery

CANCER -- TOMS RIVER REGION

Fagin, D. Toms River **363.72**

A **cancer** in the family. Ross, T. **616.99**

CANCER PATIENTS

Aaronson, N. Pilates for breast cancer survivors **616.99**

Ali, N. Understanding lung cancer **616.99**

American Cancer Society complete guide to family caregiving **649.8**

Boston, S. Lucky Dog **636.089**

Brokaw, T. A Lucky Life Interrupted **92**

Cody, J. [Sic] **362.196**

Dent, J. Courage beyond the game **796.332**

Fullbright, C. D. How to help your friend with cancer **616.99**

Gazella, K. A. The definitive guide to thriving after cancer **616.99**

Geiger, C. The Cancer Survivors' Club **362.196**

Hitchens, C. Mortality **304.6**

Hutton, A. Bald Is Better With Earrings **616.99**

Jacobs, H. The Silver Lining **616.99**

Leifer, J. After you hear it's cancer **616.99**

Lunden, J. Had I Known **791.450**

Manheimer, E. Twelve patients **362.11**

Prijatel, P. Surviving triple negative breast cancer **616.99**

Rufus, R. Die young with me **92**

Sikka, M. A breast cancer alphabet **616.99**

Von Furstenberg, D. The woman I wanted to be **92**

Will my cancer come back? **616.99**

CANCER PATIENTS

See also Patients

CANCER PATIENTS -- BIOGRAPHY

James, E. Paris in love **92**

Rufus, R. Die young with me **92**

CANCER PATIENTS -- FAMILY RELATIONSHIPS

Marshall, D. Home is burning **92**

CANCER PATIENTS -- FAMILY RELATIONSHIPS -- UNITED STATES

Schwalbe, W. The end of your life book club **616.99**

CANCER PATIENTS -- HOME CARE

American Cancer Society complete guide to family caregiving **649.8**

CANCER PATIENTS -- RELIGIOUS LIFE

Billings, J. T. Rejoicing in lament **248.8**

CANCER PATIENTS -- UNITED STATES -- BIOGRAPHY

Hitchens, C. Mortality **304.6**

Marshall, D. Home is burning **92**

Schwalbe, W. The end of your life book club **616.99**

Von Furstenberg, D. The woman I wanted to be **92**

CANCER PATIENTS' CHILDREN *See* Children of cancer patients

The **Cancer** Survivors' Club. Geiger, C. **362.196**

The **cancer-fighting** kitchen. Katz, R. **641.5**

The **candidate.** Popkin, S. L. **324.9**

CANDIES *See* Candy

CANDLE 79 (RESTAURANT)

Vegan holiday cooking from Candle Cafe **641.5**

CANDLE CAFE

Vegan holiday cooking from Candle Cafe **641.5**

Candlemaker's companion. Oppenheimer, B. **745.59**

CANDLES

Oppenheimer, B. Candlemaker's companion **745.59**

CANDLES

See also Lighting

CANDY

Almond, S. Candyfreak: a journey through the chocolate underbelly of America **338.4**

DeMasco, K. The craft of baking **641.8**

Candyfreak: a journey through the chocolate underbelly of America. Almond, S. **338.4**

Canellos, Peter S.

English, B. Last lion **92**

Canfield, Jack

The success principles **158**

CANNABIS *See* Marijuana

The **Cannabis** Encyclopedia. Cervantes, J. **633.79**

Cannabis Pharmacy. Backes, M. **615.7**

Cannadine, David

Mellon **92**

The undivided past **128**

Cannan, Edwin

(ed) Smith, A. The wealth of nations **330.1**

Cannato, Vincent J.

American passage **325**

CANNED GOODS *See* Canning and preserving

Cannibal. Sinclair, S.   **811.6**

CANNIBALISM

  Hoffman, C. A Savage Harvest   **995**

CANNIBALISM

    See also Ethnology; Human behavior

CANNING AND PRESERVING

  The all new ball book of canning and preserving   **641.42**

  Barrow, C. Mrs. Wheelbarrow's practical pantry   **641.4**

  Better Homes and Gardens New Cook Book **641.5**

  Canning for a New Generation   **641**

  Complete book of home preserving   **641.4**

  Costenbader, C. W. The big book of preserving the harvest   **641.4**

  Field, R. The Art of preserving   **641.4**

  Foolproof preserving   **641.4**

  Katz, S. E. The art of fermentation   **664**

  Macdonald, E. Artisan Preserving   **641.4**

  Mackenzie, J. The complete book of pickling **641.4**

  West, K. Saving the season   **641.4**

CANNING AND PRESERVING

    See also Cooking; Food -- Preservation; Industrial chemistry

Canning for a New Generation.   **641**

CANNON *See* Ordnance

Cannon, Byron

  (ed) Great events from history, The Middle Ages, 477-1453   **909.07**

Cannon, John

  The kings & queens of Britain   **920**

Canoeing.   **797.1**

CANOES AND CANOEING

  Canoeing   **797.1**

  Fredston, J. A. Rowing to latitude   **797.1**

  Kayaking   **797.1**

  Morrison, D. The black Nile   **962**

CANOES AND CANOEING

    See also Boats and boating; Water sports

CANON (LITERATURE)

  Beam, A. A great idea at the time   **973.91**

  Calvino, I. Why read the classics?   **809**

  Mendelsohn, D. Waiting for the barbarians   **801**

The **Canon** Cocktail Book. Fraioli, J. O.   **641**

CANONIZATION

    See also Christian saints; Rites and ceremonies

CANTATAS

    See also Choral music; Vocal music

Canterbury, Dave

  Advanced bushcraft   **613.69**

  Bushcraft 101   **613.6**

  The Bushcraft field guide to trapping, gathering, and cooking in the wild   **641.691**

CANTIGNY, BATTLE OF, CANTIGNY,

FRANCE, 1918

  Davenport, M. J. First over there   **940.4**

CANTON (OHIO)

  Gup, T. A secret gift   **977.1**

CANTOR FITZGERALD LP

  Lutnick, H. On top of the world   **332.6**

Cantor, Georg, 1845-1918

      About

  Bell, E. T. Men of mathematics   **920**

Cantor, Norman F.

  Antiquity: the civilization of the ancient world **930**

  In the wake of the plague   **614.5**

The **cantos** of Ezra Pound. Pound, E.   **811**

CANVAS EMBROIDERY

  Christensen, J. I. The needlepoint book   **746.44**

CANVAS EMBROIDERY *See* Needlepoint

The **Canyon** Ranch guide to men's health. Brewer, S. C.   **613**

Capa, Robert, 1913-1954

      About

  Marton, K. The great escape   **920**

Capacity. McMichael, J.   **811**

Capano, Thomas J., 1949-

      About

  Rule, A. --and never let her go   **364.1**

Cape Cod. Thoreau, H. D.   **917**

CAPE COD (MASS.) -- DESCRIPTION AND TRAVEL

  Thoreau, H. D. Cape Cod   **917**

Capek, Josef

  Capek, K. R.U.R. and The insect play   **891.8**

Capek, Karel

  R.U.R. and The insect play   **891.8**

Capella, Massimiliano

  Barbie   **688.722**

Capers, Valerie

      About

  Walker-Hill, H. From spirituals to symphonies **780**

Caperton, Hugh

      About

  Leamer, L. The price of justice   **346.730**

Capinera, John L.

  Field guide to grasshoppers, crickets, and katydids of the United States   **595.7**

CAPITAL

  Marx, K. Capital: an abridged edition   **330.1**

CAPITAL

    See also Economics; Finance

CAPITAL AND LABOR *See* Industrial relations

Capital dames. Roberts, C.   **793.7**

CAPITAL GAINS

  Bogle, J. C. The clash of the cultures   **332.6**

Capital in the twenty-first century.   **332**

CAPITAL MARKET

    See also Finance; Financial institutions; Loans; Securities

Capital of the world. Mires, C.   **341.23**
CAPITAL PUNISHMENT
   Heard, A. The eyes of Willie McGee   **364.66**
   Prejean, H. The death of innocents   **364.66**
   Turow, S. Ultimate punishment   **345**
CAPITAL PUNISHMENT
   See also Criminal law; Punishment
CAPITAL PUNISHMENT -- UNITED STATES
   Smith, C. S. The injustice system   **345.73**
Capital: an abridged edition. Marx, K.   **330.1**
CAPITALISM
   Appleby, J. The relentless revolution   **330.1**
   Baptist, E. E. The half has never been told   **306.3**
   Davies, W. The happiness industry   **304**
   Hahn, S. A Nation Without Borders   **973.5**
   Heilbroner, R. L. The worldly philosophers   **330.1**
   Klein, N. This changes everything   **363.738**
   Lehmann, C. The money cult   **261.8**
   McChesney, R. W. Digital disconnect   **302.23**
   McMillan, J. Reinventing the bazaar   **330.12**
   Reich, R. B. Saving capitalism   **330.973**
   Sandel, M. J. What money can't buy   **330.1**
   Soto, H. d. The mystery of capital   **330.12**
   Speth, J. G. The bridge at the end of the world   **333.7**
   Zizek, S. First as tragedy, then as farce   **337**
CAPITALISM
   See also Economics; Labor; Profit
CAPITALISM -- ETHICAL ASPECTS
   Mackey, J. Conscious capitalism   **174**
CAPITALISM -- HISTORY
   Appleby, J. The relentless revolution   **330.1**
   Beckert, S. Empire of cotton   **338.4**
   McMillan, J. Reinventing the bazaar   **330.12**
CAPITALISM -- POLITICAL ASPECTS
   Power, Inc.   **322**
CAPITALISM -- SOCIAL ASPECTS
   Davies, W. The happiness industry   **304**
   Friedman, T. L. The Lexus and the olive tree   **337**
CAPITALISM -- UNITED STATES
   Reich, R. B. Saving capitalism   **330.973**
CAPITALISM -- UNITED STATES -- HISTORY
   Lehmann, C. The money cult   **261.8**
CAPITALISTS AND FINANCIERS
   Ahamed, L. Lords of finance   **332.1**
   Hagstrom, R. G. The Warren Buffett Way   **332.6**
   Madrick, J. G. Age of greed   **330.9**
   Partnoy, F. The match king   **92**
   Schroeder, A. D. The snowball: Warren Buffett and the business of life   **92**
   Shiller, R. J. Irrational exuberance   **332.63**
   Ward, G. C. A disposition to be rich   **974.7**
CAPITALISTS AND FINANCIERS
   See also Businesspeople
CAPITALISTS AND FINANCIERS -- ILLINOIS -- CHICAGO -- BIOGRAPHY
   Jobb, D. Empire of deception   **92**

CAPITALISTS AND FINANCIERS -- UNITED STATES -- BIOGRAPHY
   Strouse, J. Morgan   **92**
   Ward, G. C. A disposition to be rich   **974.7**
CAPITALIZATION (FINANCE) *See* Corporations -- Finance; Securities; Valuation
CAPITALS (CITIES)
   See also Cities and towns
Capitol men. Dray, P.   **920**
CAPITOLS
   Gugliotta, G. Freedom's cap   **975.3**
Capone. Bergreen, L.   **364.1**
Capone, Al, 1899-1947
      About
   Balsamo, W. Young Al Capone   **92**
   Bergreen, L. Capone   **364.1**
   Eig, J. Get Capone   **92**
Caponigro, Dara
   (ed) The book of decorating   **747**
Capote, Truman, 1924-1984
   In cold blood   **364.1**
   Long, R. E. Truman Capote, enfant terrible   **92**
   Music for chameleons   **818**
   Plimpton, G. Truman Capote   **813**
   Portraits and observations   **814**
   Too brief a treat   **92**
Capponi, Niccolo
   The Day the Renaissance Was Saved   **945**
The captain asks for a show of hands. Flynn, N.   **811**
Captain James Cook. Hough, R. A.   **92**
CAPTIVE ELEPHANTS -- UNITED STATES -- ANECDOTES
   Bradley, C. Last chain on Billie   **639.97**
CAPTIVE MARINE MAMMALS
   Kirby, D. Death at SeaWorld   **599.53**
Captive paradise. Haley, J. L.   **996.9**
CAPTIVE REPTILES -- BREEDING
   Mattison, C. What reptile?   **639.3**
CAPTIVITY NARRATIVES
   See also Autobiography
Captivology. Parr, B.   **153.7**
Capture the flag. Testi, A.   **929.9**
CAPUCHINS -- FRANCE -- MARSEILLE -- BIOGRAPHY
   Zuccotti, S. Père Marie-Benoît and Jewish rescue   **940.53**
Caputo, Philip
   A rumor of war   **959.704**
      About
   Caputo, P. The longest road   **973.93**
Car.   **629.222**
CAR DESIGN *See* Automobiles -- Design and construction
CAR DRIVERS *See* Automobile drivers
Car guys vs. bean counters. Lutz, B.   **338.7**
Caravaggio. Ebert-Schifferer, S.   **92**

Caravaggio. Graham-Dixon, A. **92**

Caravaggio. Prose, F. **92**

Caravaggio. Langdon, H. **709**

Caravaggio, Michelangelo Merisi da, 1573-1610
About
Ebert-Schifferer, S. Caravaggio **92**

Graham-Dixon, A. Caravaggio **92**

Langdon, H. Caravaggio **709**

Prose, F. Caravaggio **92**

Robb, P. M: the man who became Caravaggio **759**

CARBOHYDRATES
> See also Biochemistry; Nutrition

CARBOLIC ACID
> See also Acids; Chemicals

CARBON
Berners-Lee, M. How bad are bananas? **363.7**

Roston, E. The carbon age **577**

CARBON
> See also Chemical elements

CARBON 14 DATING See Radiocarbon dating

The **carbon** age. Roston, E. **577**

The **carbon** crunch. Helm, D. **333.79**

CARBON DIOXIDE GREENHOUSE EFFECT
> See Global warming

Carbone, June
Marriage markets **306.85**

CARCINOMA See Cancer

CARD GAMES
Gibson, W. B. Hoyle's modern encyclopedia of card games **795.4**

Ho, O. The Ultimate Book of Family Card Games **795.4**

Hoyle, E. Hoyle's rules of games **795.4**

CARD GAMES
> See also Games

CARD GAMES -- JUVENILE LITERATURE
Ho, O. The Ultimate Book of Family Card Games **795.4**

CARD TRICKS
> See also Card games; Magic tricks; Tricks

The **Cardamom** Trail. Makan, C. **641.5**

Carde, Ring T.
Encyclopedia of insects **595.7**

Cardenal, Ernesto
Pluriverse **861**

CARDIAC DISEASES See Heart diseases

CARDIAC RESUSCITATION
Casarett, D. Shocked **616.02**

CARDIAC RESUSCITATION
> See also Emergency medicine

Cardillo, Joseph
Body intelligence **158.1**

CARDINALS
Boyle, C. An American Cardinal **92**

CARDINALS -- UNITED STATES -- BIOGRAPHY

Boyle, C. An American Cardinal **92**

CARDIOVASCULAR SYSTEM
> See also Anatomy; Physiology

CARDIOVASCULAR SYSTEM -- DISEASES -- BIBLIOGRAPHY
De Richemond, J. The Medical Library Association guide to finding out about heart disease **016**

Cardozo, Christopher
Edward S. Curtis **770**

CARDS, GREETING See Greeting cards

Carducci, Tad
(jt. auth) Tanguay, P. The Tippling bros. **641.87**

Carduff, Christopher
(ed) Always looking **700**

(ed) Higher gossip **818**

CARE GIVERS See Caregivers

CARE OF CHILDREN See Child care

CARE OF THE DYING See Terminal care

CARE OF THE SICK -- PSYCHOLOGICAL ASPECTS
Pogrebin, L. C. How to be a friend to a friend who's sick **610**

CAREER CHANGES
Harris, C. A. Strategize to win **650.1**

Kreamer, A. Risk/reward **650.1**

CAREER CHANGES
> See also Age and employment; Vocational guidance

CAREER CHOICE -- UNITED STATES
101 careers in healthcare management **362.106**

The **career** code. Power, K. **650.1**

CAREER COUNSELING See Vocational guidance

CAREER DEVELOPMENT
Harris, C. A. Strategize to win **650.1**

Kay, A. This is how to get your next job **650.14**

Kreamer, A. Risk/reward **650.1**

Licht, A. Leave Your Mark **650.1**

Smith, L. R. No fears, no excuses **650.1**

CAREER DEVELOPMENT See Personnel management; Vocational guidance

CAREER GUIDANCE See Vocational guidance

The **career** playbook. Citrin, J. M. **650.14**

CAREERS See Occupations; Professions; Vocational guidance

CAREGIVERS
Ali, N. Understanding lung cancer **616.99**

Carter, R. Helping yourself help others **649.8**

Gillies, A. Keeper **616.8**

James, V. E. The Alzheimer's advisor **344**

Kessler, L. Dancing with Rose **362.1**

Kuhn, D. Alzheimer's early stages **616.8**

McFarlane, R. The complete bedside companion **649.8**

Pogrebin, L. C. How to be a friend to a friend who's sick **610**

Silver, M. Breast cancer husband **616.99**
Twelve breaths a minute **616**
CAREGIVERS
See also Volunteer work
CAREGIVERS -- HANDBOOKS, MANUALS, ETC.
American Cancer Society complete guide to family caregiving **649.8**
What if it's not Alzheimer's? **616.8**
CAREGIVERS -- POPULAR WORKS
Ali, N. Understanding lung cancer **616.99**
CAREGIVERS -- UNITED STATES -- BIOGRAPHY
Hodgman, G. Bettyville **306.874**
Careless love: the unmaking of Elvis Presley. Guralnick, P. **92**
Carey, Benedict
How we learn **153.1**
Carey, Charles W.
American inventors, entrepreneurs & business visionaries **920**
Carey, Sarah
Stewart, M. Martha Stewart's cooking school **641.5**
Cargas, Harry J.
Wiesenthal, S. The sunflower **179.7**
Carhart, Thaddeus
About
Carhart, T. Finding Fontainebleau **944.36**
CARIBBEAN AREA *See* Caribbean Region
CARIBBEAN ART -- ENCYCLOPEDIAS
Encyclopedia of Latin American & Caribbean art **709**
CARIBBEAN COOKING
Afro-vegan **641.59**
Goldberg, D. Cuba! **641.5**
New World kitchen **641.59**
CARIBBEAN REGION
Gibson, C. Empire's Crossroads **972.9**
CARIBBEAN REGION -- FOREIGN RELATIONS -- UNITED STATES
Von Tunzelmann, A. Red heat **972.9**
Caring for your baby and young child. **618.92**
Caring for your parents. Delehanty, H. **362.6**
Caring for your school-age child. **649**
Carl Sagan. Poundstone, W. **92**
Carl Van Vechten and the Harlem Renaissance. Bernard, E. **92**
Carl, Deborah Ann
Bentley, E. P. Directory of family associations **929**
Carleton Watkins: the complete mammoth photographs. Watkins, C. E. **778.9**
Carley, Michael Jabara
1939 **940.53**
A **Carlin** Home Companion. Carlin, K. **92**
Carlin, George
Napalm & silly putty **817**

Carlin, John
Playing the enemy **968.06**
(ed) Masters of American comics **741.5**
Carlin, Kelly, 1963-
About
Carlin, K. A Carlin Home Companion **92**
Carlin, Peter Ames
Bruce **92**
Carlisle vs. Army. Anderson, L. **796.332**
Carlo, Philip
Gaspipe **92**
Carlos, Prince of Asturias, 1545-1568
About
Schiller, F. Don Carlos and Mary Stuart **832**
Carlsen, William
Jungle of Stone **972.81**
Carlson, Brady
Dead presidents **973.09**
Carlson, Julie
Remodelista **747**
Carlson, Laurie M.
A fever in Salem **133.4**
Carlson, Peter
K blows top **947.085**
Carlson, W. Bernard
Tesla **92**
Carluccio, Antonio
Pasta **641.82**
Carlyle, Thomas
Sartor resartus **824**
Carmellini, Andrew
Hyman, G. Urban Italian **641.5**
Carnage and culture. Hanson, V. D. **904**
Carnegie. Krass, P. **338.7**
Carnegie, Andrew, 1835-1919
About
Krass, P. Carnegie **338.7**
Nasaw, D. Andrew Carnegie **92**
Rea, T. Bone wars **560**
Wall, J. F. Andrew Carnegie **92**
Carnegie, Dale
How to win friends and influence people **158**
Watts, S. Self-help Messiah **92**
Carnes, Mark C.
Garraty, J. A. American national biography **920.003**
Carney, John T.
No room for error **356**
Carney, Scott
The red market **364.1**
CARNIVAL
See also Festivals
CARNIVALS
See also Amusements; Festivals
CARNIVOROUS ANIMALS
See also Animals
CARNIVOROUS PLANTS

See also Plants

Caro, Ina

Paris to the past   **914**

Caro, Robert A., 1935-

The passage of power   **92**

The path to power   **92**

The power broker: Robert Moses and the fall of New York   **92**

CAROL BURNETT SHOW (TELEVISION PROGRAM : 1967-1978)

Burnett, C. In such good company   **791.45**

Caroli, Betty Boyd

First ladies   **920**

Lady Bird and Lyndon   **92**

CAROLS

See also Christmas music; Church music; Folk songs; Hymns; Songs; Vocal music

CARPAL TUNNEL SYNDROME

Gambaro, J. The truth about carpal tunnel syndrome   **616.85**

Carpenter, Bogdana

(ed) Milosz, C. To begin where I am   **891.8**

Carpenter, Dale

Flagrant conduct   **342.73**

CARPENTERS

Bragg, R. Ava's man   **975**

CARPENTRY

Abram, N. Measure twice, cut once   **684**

CARPENTRY

See also Building

CARPENTRY -- HANDBOOKS, MANUALS, ETC

Kelsey, J. Woodworking   **684**

CARPETBAG RULE *See* Reconstruction (1865-1876)

CARPETS *See* Rugs and carpets

CARPETS -- AFGHANISTAN

Badkhen, A. The world is a carpet   **958.1**

Carpini, Michael X. Delli

After broadcast news   **071**

Carr, Caleb

The lessons of terror   **303.6**

Carr, David

About

Carr, D. The night of the gun   **92**

Carr, Jonathan

The Wagner clan   **920**

Carr, Julie

100 notes on violence   **811**

Carr, Matthew, 1953-2011

Fortress Europe   **363.28**

Carr, Nicholas G., 1959-

The big switch   **303.4**

The shallows   **612.8**

Utopia is creepy   **303.483**

Carr, Tina

(jt. auth) Peacock, J. The soup club cookbook   **641.81**

Carreño, Carolynn

Meat   **641.6**

Mozza at home   **641.5**

Carretta, Vincent

Equiano, the African   **92**

Carried in Our Hearts. Aronson, J.   **362.734**

Carriere, Jean-Claude

Bstan-'dzin-rgya-mtsho, D. L. X. Violence and compassion   **294.3**

Carrillo Arronte, Margarita

Mexico   **641.59**

Carroll, Diahann

About

Carroll, D. The legs are the last to go   **92**

Carroll, James, 1943-

House of war   **355**

About

Carroll, J. Practicing Catholic   **92**

Jerusalem, Jerusalem   **956.94**

Carroll, Joe

Feeding the fire   **641.7**

Carroll, Lewis, 1832-1898

About

Cohen, M. N. Lewis Carroll   **92**

Carroll, Rebecca

(ed) Uncle Tom or new Negro   **370**

Carroll, Sean

The Big Picture   **577**

The particle at the end of the Universe   **539.7**

Carroll, Sean B.

Brave genius   **920**

Endless forms most beautiful   **571.8**

The making of the fittest   **572.8**

Remarkable creatures   **508**

The Serengeti Rules   **570**

Carroll, Sean M.

From eternity to here   **530.1**

Carruth, Hayden

Toward the distant islands   **811**

Carruthers, Gerard

(ed) Burns, R. Burns   **821**

Carruthers, John

Eat street   **641.76**

Carry me home. McWhorter, D.   **976.1**

Carry on. Fenn, L.   **920**

CARS (AUTOMOBILES) *See* Automobiles

Carsick. Waters, J.   **92**

Carson McCullers. Savigneau, J.   **813**

Carson, Anne, 1950-

Autobiography of red   **811**

The beauty of the husband   **811**

Carson, A. Nox   **811**

Men in the off hours   **811**

Nox   **811**

Red doc> 811
(tr) Sappho If not, winter 884
Carson, Clayborne
Malcolm X: the FBI file 92
(ed) The Eyes on the prize civil rights reader 323.1
(ed) King, M. L. The autobiography of Martin Luther King, Jr 323
Carson, Johnny, 1925-2005
About
Life stories 920
Carson, Kit, 1809-1868
About
Sides, H. Blood and thunder 978
Carson, Rachel, 1907-1964
The edge of the sea 577.7
The sea around us 551.46
Silent spring 363.7
Under the sea wind 578.7
About
Lytle, M. H. The gentle subversive 92
Souder, W. On a farther shore 92
Carson, Susannah
(ed) Living with Shakespeare 822.3
(ed) A truth universally acknowledged 823
CARTER FAMILY (MUSICAL GROUP)
Zwonitzer, M. Will you miss me when I'm gone? 781.642
Carter, A. P., 1891-1960
About
Zwonitzer, M. Will you miss me when I'm gone? 781.642
Carter, Alice A.
The Red Rose girls 759.13
Carter, Bill
Boom, Bust, Boom 622
Carter, David
(ed) Spontaneous mind 811
Stonewall 306.76
Carter, Graydon
(ed) Bohemians, bootleggers, flappers, and swells 810.8
Vanity Fair, the portraits 779
Carter, Gregg Lee
(ed) Guns in American society 363.33
Carter, James
About
Wertheim, M. Physics on the fringe 530.1
Carter, Jimmy, 1924-
Sources of strength 248.4
The virtues of aging 305.26
About
Carter, J. A full life 92
Carter, J. White House diary 92
Carter, J. Everything to gain 92
Carter, J. An hour before daylight 92
Carter, J. Keeping faith: memoirs of a president 92

Carter, J. Sharing good times 92
Woodward, B. Shadow 973.92
Wright, L. Thirteen Days in September 956.04
Carter, Maybelle, 1909-1978
About
Zwonitzer, M. Will you miss me when I'm gone? 781.642
Carter, Miranda
Anthony Blunt: his lives 92
George, Nicholas, and Wilhelm 940.3
Carter, Rita
The human brain book 612.82
Carter, Robert A.
Buffalo Bill Cody 978
Carter, Robert, 1728-1804
About
Levy, A. The first emancipator 92
Carter, Rosalynn
Carter, J. Everything to gain 92
Helping yourself help others 649.8
Carter, Sara, 1898-1979
About
Zwonitzer, M. Will you miss me when I'm gone? 781.642
Carter, Thomas L.
Evans, G. E. Introduction to library public services 025.5
Carter, Toni M.
(ed) ALA glossary of library and information science 020
Carter, William C.
Marcel Proust 843
CARTHAGE (EXTINCT CITY)
See also Extinct cities
Cartier-Bresson, Henri,
About
Cartier-Bresson, H. The Decisive Moment 770
Cartier-Bresson, Henri, 1908-2004
The Decisive Moment 770
Cartledge, Paul
Ancient Greece 938
Democracy 321.8
CARTOGRAPHERS
Lester, T. The fourth part of the world 912
CARTOGRAPHERS -- UNITED STATES -- BIOGRAPHY
Felt, H. Soundings 526
Cartographies of time. Grafton, A. 902
CARTOGRAPHY
A Map of the World 912
CARTOGRAPHY *See* Map drawing; Maps
CARTOGRAPHY -- HISTORY
Brotton, J. Great maps 912.09
Lester, T. The fourth part of the world 912
Cartooning. Brunetti, I. 741.5
CARTOONING

Goldstein, N. Jackie Ormes   741.5
Holtz, A. American newspaper comics   741.5
CARTOONING
    See also Cartoons and caricatures; Wit and
humor
Cartooning for the beginner. Hart, C.   741.5
CARTOONISTS
  Abel, J. Mastering comics   741.5
  Bechdel, A. Fun home   741.5
  Becker, S. I had brain surgery, what's your ex-
    cuse?   92
  Brainard, J. The Nancy book   759
  DePastino, T. Bill Mauldin   92
  Feiffer, J. Backing into forward   92
  Ghez, D. They drew as they pleased   741.58
  Goldstein, N. Jackie Ormes   741.5
  Jones, G. Men of tomorrow   741.5
  Kitchen, D. The art of Harvey Kurtzman 741.5
  Leopold, D. The Hirschfeld century   741.5
  Masters of American comics   741.5
  Michaelis, D. Schulz and Peanuts   92
  Satrapi, M. The complete Persepolis   741.5
  Schumacher, M. Will Eisner   92
  Spiegelman, A. MetaMaus   940.53
  Steinberg, S. Steinberg at the New Yorker 741.5
CARTOONISTS -- BIOGRAPHY
  Bechdel, A. Are you my mother?   741.5
CARTOONISTS -- GRAPHIC NOVELS
  Spiegelman, A. MetaMaus   940.53
**CARTOONISTS -- UNITED STATES -- BIOG-
RAPHY**
  Andelman, B. Will Eisner: A Spirited Life 741.5
  Jones, G. Men of tomorrow   741.5
  Mankoff, B. How about never--is never good for
    you?   92
  Ricca, B. Super boys   92
CARTOONS AND CARICATURES
  The complete cartoons of the New Yorker 741.5
  Diffee, M. Hand drawn jokes for smart attractive
    people   741.5
  Hart, C. Cartooning for the beginner   741.5
  Hirschfeld, A. Hirschfeld on line   741.5
  Holtz, A. American newspaper comics   741.5
  Kitchen, D. The art of Harvey Kurtzman 741.5
  Mankoff, B. How about never--is never good for
    you?   92
  McCloud, S. Reinventing comics   741.5
  Steinberg, S. Steinberg at the New Yorker 741.5
CARTOONS, ANIMATED *See* Animated films
CARTOONS, TELEVISION *See* Animated televi-
sion programs
Cartwright, Justin
  Oxford revisited   942
Carver, Raymond
  All of us   811
  A new path to the waterfall   811

              About
  Sklenicka, C. Raymond Carver   92
Carville, James
  It's the middle class, stupid!   320.51
CARVING (MEAT, ETC.)
  Guggiana, M. Primal cuts   641.6
CARVING (MEAT, ETC.)
    See also Dining; Entertaining; Meat
Carwardine, Richard
  Lincoln: a life of purpose and power   92
Casals, Pablo, 1876-1973
              About
  Siblin, E. The cello suites   787.3
Casanova, Patricia Vargas
  Easter Island's silent sentinels   990
Casarett, David
  Shocked   616.02
Cascadia. Hillman, B.   811
Case closed. Posner, G. L.   973.922
The **case** for books. Darnton, R.   002
The **case** for God. Armstrong, K.   211
The **Case** for Grace. Strobel, L.   234
The **case** for make believe. Linn, S.   155.4
A **case** for the existence of God. Overman, D. L. 212
The **cases** that haunt us. Douglas, J. E. 364.1
Casey, Michael
  Che's afterlife   980
Casey, Susan
  Voices in the Ocean   599.53
  The wave   551.46
Cash, Jean W.
  Flannery O'Connor: a life   92
Cash, Johnny
              About
  Hilburn, R. Johnny Cash   92
  Kleist, R. Johnny Cash   92
  Streissguth, M. Johnny Cash   92
Cash, Rosanne
  Composed   92
              About
  Cash, R. Composed   92
Cash, Wilbur Joseph
  The mind of the South   975
CASINOS -- NEVADA -- LAS VEGAS
  Schüll, N. D. Addiction by design   362.2
Casnocha, Ben
  My start-up life   338.7
Cass, Ronald A.
  (jt. auth) Hylton, K. N. Laws of creation 346.04
Cassady, Neal
              About
  Sandison, D. Neal Cassady   92
Cassatt, Mary, 1844-1926
              About
  Mathews, N. M. Mary Cassatt   759.13
Cassavetes, John

About

Fine, M. Accidental genius **791**

CASSEROLE COOKING

The Best Casserole cookbook ever **641.8**

CASSETTE BOOKS *See* Audiobooks

CASSETTE TAPES, AUDIO *See* Sound recordings

Cassidy, Butch, b. 1866

About

Hatch, T. The Last Outlaws **364.15**

Cassidy, David C., 1945-

Beyond uncertainty **92**

Cassidy, Gerald

About

Kaiser, R. G. So damn much money **328**

Cassidy, John

How markets fail **381**

Cassirer, Ernst

(ed) The Renaissance philosophy of man **189**

Casso, Gaspipe, 1942-

About

Carlo, P. Gaspipe **92**

Cast on, bind off. Bestor, L. A. **746.43**

Castaneda, Carlos

The teachings of Don Juan **299.7**

Castanho, Thiago

Brazilian Food **641.598**

CASTAWAYS *See* Survival after airplane accidents, shipwrecks, etc.

CASTAWAYS IN LITERATURE

Frank, K. Crusoe **823**

CASTE

Jadhav, N. Untouchables **305.5**

CASTE

See also Manners and customs

Castelli, Leo, 1907-1999

About

Cohen-Solal, A. Leo & his circle **92**

Castle, Alison

(ed) McCartney, L. Life in photographs **779**

Castle, David

(ed) Genetically modified foods **363.1**

Castle, Sheri

The Southern Living community cookbook

CASTLES

Gies, J. Life in a medieval castle **940.2**

CASTLES

See also Buildings

Castles of steel. Massie, R. K. **940.4**

Castner, Brian

About

Castner, B. All the ways we kill and die **958.104**

Castner, B. The long walk **956.704**

Castor, Helen

Joan of Arc **92**

She-wolves **920**

Castro, Fidel, 1926-2016

About

Castro, F. Fidel Castro: my life **92**

Coltman, L. The real Fidel Castro **92**

Cooke, J. The other side of paradise **972.91**

Gimbel, W. Havana dreams **972.91**

Rasenberger, J. The brilliant disaster **972.91**

Symmes, P. The boys from Dolores **972.91**

Szulc, T. Fidel **92**

Von Tunzelmann, A. Red heat **972.9**

Castro, M. Regina

(ed) Mayo Clinic, the essential diabetes book **616.4**

Castro, Raúl, 1931-

About

Von Tunzelmann, A. Red heat **972.9**

CASUALTY INSURANCE

See also Insurance

CAT BREEDS

The complete cat breed book **636.8**

Hart, B. L. Your ideal cat **636.8**

The **cat** encyclopedia. **636.8**

CAT OWNERS

Bradshaw, J. Cat sense **636.8**

Cat sense. Bradshaw, J. **636.8**

The **cat** whisperer. Nagelschneider, M. **636.8**

CATACOMBS

See also Burial; Cemeteries; Christian antiquities; Tombs

Catalog of Unabashed Gratitude. Gay, R. **811.6**

CATALOGING

Maxwell, R. L. Maxwell's handbook for RDA, resource description & access **025.3**

Mitchell, A. M. Cataloging and organizing digital resources **025.3**

Oliver, C. Introducing RDA **025.3**

Sears List of Subject Headings **025.4**

CATALOGING

See also Bibliographic control; Documentation; Library science; Library technical processes

CATALOGING -- STANDARDS

Oliver, C. Introducing RDA **025.3**

Cataloging and organizing digital resources. Mitchell, A. M. **025.3**

CATALOGING OF MUSIC

See also Cataloging

Cataloging the world. Wright, A. **020.9**

CATALOGUING *See* Cataloging

CATAMARANS

See also Boats and boating

Catastrophe 1914. Hastings, M. **940.3**

CATASTROPHES *See* Disasters

CATASTROPHES (GEOLOGY)

Alvarez, W. T. rex and the Crater of Doom **551.7**

Dauber, P. M. The three big bangs **523.1**

CATASTROPHES (GEOLOGY)

See also Geology

CATCHERS (BASEBALL) -- UNITED STATES -- BIOGRAPHY

Wilson, D. Pudge   **92**

Catching fire. Wrangham, R. W.   **641.3**

Catching the Sky. O'Brien, K.   **796.94**

Cate, Martin

Smuggler's Cove   **647.95**

Cate, Rebecca

(jt. auth) Cate, M. Smuggler's Cove   **647.95**

Category 5. Zebrowski, E.   **363.34**

CATERING

See also Cooking; Food service

CATERPILLARS

See also Butterflies; Moths

Catharine Howard, Queen, consort of Henry VIII, King of England, d. 1542

About

Fraser, A. The wives of Henry VIII   **920**

Starkey, D. Six wives: the queens of Henry VIII   **942.05**

Catharine Parr, Queen, consort of Henry VIII, King of England, 1512-1548

About

Fraser, A. The wives of Henry VIII   **920**

Porter, L. Katherine the queen   **92**

Starkey, D. Six wives: the queens of Henry VIII   **942.05**

CATHAY HOTEL (SHANGHAI, CHINA) -- HISTORY

Grescoe, T. Shanghai grand   **951.132**

CATHEDRAL HIGH SCHOOL (SPRINGFIELD, MASS.)

Blais, M. In these girls, hope is a muscle   **796.323**

Cathedral of the wild. Varty, B.   **639.9**

CATHEDRALS

See also Church buildings

Cathedrals of science. Coffey, P.   **540**

Cather, Willa, 1873-1947

Stories, poems, and other writings   **818**

About

Cather, W. The selected letters of Willa Cather **813**

Lee, H. Willa Cather   **92**

Woodress, J. L. Willa Cather   **92**

Catherine II, the Great, Empress of Russia, 1729-1796

About

Catherine The memoirs of Catherine the Great **92**

Erickson, C. Great Catherine   **947**

Jaques, S. The Empress of Art   **92**

Massie, R. K. Catherine the Great   **947**

Rounding, V. Catherine the Great   **92**

Catherine the Great. Massie, R. K.   **947**

Catherine the Great. Rounding, V.   **92**

Catherine, Duchess of Cambridge, 1982-

About

Andersen, C. Game of crowns   **941.085**

Catherine, of Aragon, Queen, consort of Henry VIII, King of England, 1485-1536

About

Fraser, A. The wives of Henry VIII   **920**

CATHOLIC CHARISMATIC MOVEMENT

See also Catholic Church; Episcopal Church

The **Catholic** church. Allen, J. L.   **282**

CATHOLIC CHURCH

See also Christian sects; Christianity

CATHOLIC CHURCH

Betrayal   **282**

Buttiglione, R. Karol Wojtyla   **282**

Carroll, J. Practicing Catholic   **92**

Francis, P. The church of mercy   **282**

John Paul Crossing the threshold of hope   **282**

Magill, R. J. Sincerity   **179**

Martin, J. The Jesuit guide to almost everything   **248.4**

New Catholic encyclopedia   **282**

Pope Francis among the wolves   **282**

Rice, A. Called out of darkness   **92**

Russell, B. A history of Western philosophy   **109**

Vallely, P. Pope Francis   **92**

Wills, G. The Future of the Catholic Church With Pope Francis   **282**

Woodward, K. L. Making saints   **235**

CATHOLIC CHURCH -- CLERGY -- BIOGRAPHY

Shriver, M. Pilgrimage   **282.092**

CATHOLIC CHURCH -- CLERGY -- SEXUAL BEHAVIOR

D'Antonio, M. Mortal Sins   **261.8**

CATHOLIC CHURCH -- DIRECTORIES

Our Sunday Visitor Catholic almanac   **282**

CATHOLIC CHURCH -- DOCTRINES

A call to mercy   **234.5**

CATHOLIC CHURCH -- DOCTRINES -- HISTORY -- 17TH CENTURY

Hofstadter, D. The Earth moves   **509**

CATHOLIC CHURCH -- ENCYCLOPEDIAS

The HarperCollins encyclopedia of Catholicism   **282**

New Catholic encyclopedia   **282**

CATHOLIC CHURCH -- FINANCE

Posner, G. God's Bankers   **364.16**

CATHOLIC CHURCH -- FOREIGN RELATIONS

Fletcher, C. The divorce of Henry VIII   **942.05**

CATHOLIC CHURCH -- HISTORY

Allen, J. L. The Catholic church   **282**

CATHOLIC CHURCH -- HISTORY -- 21ST CENTURY

Pope Francis among the wolves   **282**

Posner, G. God's Bankers   **364.16**

CATHOLIC CHURCH -- IRELAND

O'Faolain, N. A radiant life   **824**

CATHOLIC CHURCH -- LITURGY

Lucatero, H. The living Mass   **264**

Norris, K. The cloister walk   **255**

CATHOLIC CHURCH -- LITURGY

See also Liturgies; Rites and ceremonies

CATHOLIC CHURCH -- MISSIONS

Fisher, J. T. On the Irish waterfront   **331.7**

CATHOLIC CHURCH -- PRAYERS AND DE-VOTIONS

Hendey, L. M. A book of saints for Catholic moms   **248.8**

CATHOLIC CHURCH -- RELATIONS (DIPLO-MATIC) *See* Catholic Church -- Foreign relations

CATHOLIC CHURCH -- RELATIONS -- JUDA-ISM

Eisner, P. The Pope's Last Crusade   **940.53**

CATHOLIC CHURCH -- UNITED STATES

Carroll, J. Practicing Catholic   **92**

D'Antonio, M. Mortal Sins   **261.8**

CATHOLIC CHURCH -- UNITED STATES -- BI-OGRAPHY

Rodríguez, R. Darling   **92**

CATHOLICS

Hendey, L. M. A book of saints for Catholic moms   **248.8**

CATHOLICS -- ENGLAND -- BIOGRAPHY

Leaming, B. Kick Kennedy   **92**

Catification. Galaxy, J.   **636**

Catlin, George, 1796-1872

    About

Eisler, B. The Red Man's Bones   **92**

Catling, David C.

Astrobiology   **576.8**

Catlos, Brian A.

Infidel kings and unholy warriors   **909.07**

CATS

Bradshaw, J. Cat sense   **636.8**

Bradshaw, J. The trainable cat   **636.8**

The complete cat breed book   **636.8**

Cooper, G. Homer's odyssey   **636.8**

Cox, T. Close encounters of the furred kind   **636.8**

Galaxy, J. Catification   **636**

Halligan, K. Doc Halligan's What every pet owner should know   **636**

Hart, B. L. Your ideal cat   **636.8**

Herriot, J. James Herriot's cat stories   **636.8**

Link, T. Talking with dogs and cats   **636.088**

Myron, V. Dewey   **636.8**

Wild cats of the world   **599.75**

CATS

See also Domestic animals; Mammals

CATS -- BEHAVIOR

Bradshaw, J. Cat sense   **636.8**

Bradshaw, J. The trainable cat   **636.8**

Hart, B. L. Your ideal cat   **636.8**

Nagelschneider, M. The cat whisperer   **636.8**

CATS -- CARE

Complete cat care

CATS -- ENCYCLOPEDIAS

The cat encyclopedia   **636.8**

CATS -- ENGLAND -- NORFOLK -- ANEC-DOTES

Cox, T. Close encounters of the furred kind   **636.8**

CATS -- EQUIPMENT AND SUPPLIES

Galaxy, J. Catification   **636**

CATSKILL MOUNTAINS (N.Y.)

In the Catskills   **974.7**

It happened in the Catskills   **974.7**

CATTLE

See also Domestic animals; Mammals

CATTLE -- VACCINATION

See also Vaccination

Catto, Octavius V., 1839-1871

    About

Biddle, D. R. Tasting freedom   **92**

Catton, Bruce, 1899-1978

A stillness at Appomattox   **973.7**

    About

Blight, D. W. American oracle   **973.7**

Cauchy, Augustin Louis, Baron, 1789-1857

    About

Bell, E. T. Men of mathematics   **920**

Caughman, Susan

You can adopt   **362.7**

Caught up in crime. Niebuhr, G. W.   **016**

CAUSALITY *See* Causation

CAUSATION

Gladwell, M. The tipping point   **302**

CAUSATION

See also Metaphysics; Philosophy

CAUSE AND EFFECT *See* Causation

The **Cause** of All Nations. Doyle, D. H.   **973.7**

CAUSES OF DISEASES *See* Diseases -- Causes

The **Causes** of the Civil War.   **973.7**

Cavafy, Constantine P., 1863-1933

Collected poems   **889**

The unfinished poems   **889**

    About

Brodsky, J. Less than one   **809.1**

Cavalier, Stephen

The world history of animation   **791.43**

Cavalryman of the lost cause. Wert, J. D.   **92**

Cavanagh, Clare

(tr) Eternal enemies   **891.8**

(tr) Map   **891.8**

(tr) Monologue of a dog   **891.8**

(tr) Szymborska, W. Nonrequired reading   **028.1**

Szymborska, W. Poems, new and collected, 1957-1997   **891.8**

(tr) Unseen hand   **891.8**

(tr) Zagajewski, A. Without end   **891.8**

CAVE DRAWINGS AND PAINTINGS
   See also Rock drawings, paintings, and engravings

CAVE DWELLERS
   See also Prehistoric peoples

CAVE ECOLOGY
   See also Ecology

CAVES
Tabor, J. M. Blind descent   **796.52**

Cawley, A. C.
   (ed) Everyman, and medieval miracle plays   **822**

Cayce, Edgar, 1877-1945
         About
Kirkpatrick, S. Edgar Cayce   **92**

Cayley, Arthur, 1821-1895
         About
Bell, E. T. Men of mathematics   **920**

Cayton, Andrew R. L.
Anderson, F. The dominion of war   **973.2**

CBC Massey lectures [series]
Atwood, M. Payback   **332.7**

CBS INC.
Diehl, D. Rather outspoken   **92**

CD-ROMS
Borges, J. L. This craft of verse   **809.1**
The Oxford English dictionary   **423**

Cézanne, Paul, 1839-1906
         About
Danchev, A. Cézanne   **759.4**

Cee-Lo (Musician)
         About
Cee-Lo Everybody's brother   **782.421**

Celan, Paul, 1920-1970
Breathturn into timestead   **635.9**
Poems of Paul Celan   **831**

CELEBRITIES
Carter, G. Vanity Fair, the portraits   **779**
An Innocent Abroad   **910.4**
Kalb, C. Andy Warhol was a hoarder   **616.89**
Kipnis, L. How to become a scandal   **306.7**
Leibovitz, A. Annie Leibovitz at work   **779**
The muses go to school   **700**
Strauss, N. Everyone loves you when you're dead   **920**

CELEBRITIES -- APPALACHIAN REGION, SOUTHERN -- INTERVIEWS
House, S. Something's rising   **338.2**

CELEBRITIES -- BIOGRAPHY
Cooper, A. The rainbow comes and goes   **92**
Dennison, M. Behind the Mask   **92**
Lovejoy, B. Rest in pieces   **306.9**

CELEBRITIES -- ENCYCLOPEDIAS
Almanac of Famous People   **920**

CELEBRITIES -- PSYCHOLOGY -- BIOGRAPHY

Kalb, C. Andy Warhol was a hoarder   **616.89**

CELEBRITIES -- TRAVEL -- ANECDOTES
McCarthy, A. Journeys home   **929.1**

CELEBRITIES -- UNITED STATES -- BIOGRAPHY
Cooper, A. The rainbow comes and goes   **92**
Johnston, D. C. The making of Donald Trump   **973.932**
Leaming, B. Jacqueline Bouvier Kennedy Onassis   **92**
Packer, G. The unwinding   **973.924**

CELEBRITIES -- UNITED STATES -- GENEALOGY -- ANECDOTES
McCarthy, A. Journeys home   **929.1**

CELEBRITY *See* Fame

CELERY
   See also Vegetables

CELIAC DISEASE
Ali, N. Understanding celiac disease   **616.3**

CELIBACY
   See also Clergy; Religious life

The **cell**: inside the 9/11 plot and why the FBI and CIA failed to stop it. Miller, J.   **973.931**

CELLARS *See* Basements

CELLISTS
Siblin, E. The cello suites   **787.3**
The **cello** suites. Siblin, E.   **787.3**

CELLS
   See also Biology; Physiology; Reproduction

CELLS, ELECTRIC *See* Electric batteries

CELLULAR TELEPHONES
   See also Telephone

Celluloid activist. Schiavi, M.   **92**

CELTS
Cunliffe, B. The ancient Celts   **936**

CELTS
   See also France -- History -- 0-1328; Great Britain -- History -- 0-1066

CEMENT
   See also Adhesives; Building materials; Ceramics; Masonry; Plaster and plastering

CEMETERIES
   See also Burial; Public health; Sanitation

CENSORSHIP
Báez, F. A universal history of the destruction of books   **900**
Burn this book   **814**
Intellectual Freedom Manual   **025.2**
Pinnell-Stephens, J. Protecting intellectual freedom in your public library   **025.2**
Simon, J. The new censorship   **363.31**

CENSORSHIP
   See also Intellectual freedom

CENSORSHIP -- HISTORY -- 21ST CENTURY
Simon, J. The new censorship   **363.31**

CENSORSHIP -- UNITED STATES

Foerstel, H. N. Banned in the U.S.A   **025.2**

CENSORSHIP -- UNITED STATES -- HISTORY -- 20TH CENTURY

Turner, F. Renegade   **813**

CENSUS

   See also Population; Statistics; Vital statistics

CENSUS OF MARINE LIFE (PROJECT)

Crist, D. T. World ocean census   **578.7**

Centamore, Adam

Tasting wine & cheese

CENTENARIANS

Bach, S. Leni: the life and work of Leni Riefenstahl   **92**

Davis, J. E. An Everglades providence   **92**

Delany, S. Having our say   **92**

Gorn, E. J. Mother Jones   **331.88**

Kennan, G. F. Sketches from a life   **92**

Nelson, J. C. The remains of Company D   **920**

Summerscale, K. The suspicions of Mr. Whicher   **364.152**

Thompson, N. The hawk and the dove   **92**

Tucker, T. The great starvation experiment   **174.2**

Center books in Anabaptist studies [series]

Kraybill, D. B. On the backroad to heaven   **289.7**

Kraybill, D. B. The riddle of Amish culture   **289.7**

The **center** cannot hold. Saks, E. R.   **92**

Center for the National Archives Experience

Discovering the Civil War   **973.7**

CENTERS FOR THE PERFORMING ARTS

   See also Performing arts

CENTERS FOR THE PERFORMING ARTS -- NEW YORK (STATE) -- NEW YORK

Levy, R. They told me not to take that job   **792.09**

CENTRAL AFRICA

   See also Africa

CENTRAL AFRICA -- HISTORY

Jeal, T. Explorers of the Nile   **962**

CENTRAL AMERICA

   See also North America

CENTRAL AMERICA -- ANTIQUITIES

Coe, M. D. The Maya   **972**

Royal cities of the ancient Maya   **972.81**

CENTRAL AMERICA -- CIVILIZATION

Carlsen, W. Jungle of Stone   **972.81**

CENTRAL AMERICA -- DESCRIPTION AND TRAVEL

Hely, S. The wonder trail   **917.28**

CENTRAL AMERICA -- HISTORY

Perez-Brignoli, H. A brief history of Central America   **972.8**

Central Asia. Hanks, R. R.   **958**

CENTRAL ASIA

Hanks, R. R. Central Asia   **958**

CENTRAL ASIA -- DESCRIPTION AND TRAVEL

MacLean, R. Magic bus   **915**

CENTRAL ASIA -- FOREIGN RELATIONS -- UNITED STATES

Rashid, A. Descent into chaos   **954**

CENTRAL EUROPE -- HISTORICAL GEOGRAPHY -- MAPS

Magocsi, P. R. Historical atlas of Central Europe   **911**

CENTRAL HIGH SCHOOL (LITTLE ROCK, ARK.)

Margolick, D. Elizabeth and Hazel   **92**

CENTRAL PACIFIC RAILROAD

Ambrose, S. E. Nothing like it in the world   **385**

Bain, D. H. Empire express   **385**

CENTRAL PACIFIC RAILROAD COMPANY -- HISTORY

Drabelle, D. The great American railroad war   **385**

The **Central** Park Five. Burns, S.   **364.1**

CENTRAL PLANNING *See* Economic policy

CENTRE DE DOCUMENTATION ET DE RECHERCHES 'AHMED BABA.'

Hammer, J. The bad-ass librarians of Timbuktu   **025.8**

Centre National d'Art et de Culture Georges Pompidou

Dickerman, L. Dada   **709.04**

A **century** of recorded music. Day, T.   **780.26**

Century, Douglas

Barney Ross   **92**

Ice-T Ice   **92**

Making a difference   **303.3**

Cepo, Julie

(jt. auth) Steinhart, A. H. Crohn's & colitis diet guide   **616.3**

Ceram, C. W.

Gods, graves, and scholars   **930.1**

Cerami, Charles A.

Jefferson's great gamble   **973.4**

CERAMIC INDUSTRY

   See also Industries

CERAMIC MATERIALS *See* Ceramics

CERAMICS

Burnett, J. B. Graphic clay   **738.1**

De Waal, E. The white road   **738.209**

Nelson, G. C. Ceramics: a potter's handbook   **738.1**

Taylor, B. Glaze   **738.1**

CERAMICS

   See also Industrial chemistry; Materials

Ceramics: a potter's handbook. Nelson, G. C.   **738.1**

CEREBRAL DOMINANCE

Edwards, B. Drawing on the Right Side of the Brain   **741.2**

CEREBRAL PALSY

The fall   **92**

CEREBRAL PALSY

   See also Brain -- Diseases

CEREMONIAL OBJECTS

MacGregor, N. A history of the world in 100 objects **930.1**

CEREMONIES See Etiquette; Manners and customs; Rites and ceremonies

Cermele, Joe
The total fishing manual **799.1**

CERN
Aczel, A. D. Present at the creation **539.7**

Certain trumpets. Wills, G. **303.3**

CERTAINTY
See also Logic; Theory of knowledge

Cervantes Saavedra, Miguel de, 1547-1616
Man of La Mancha **812**
About
Bloom, H. The Western canon **809**

Cervantes, Jorge
The Cannabis Encyclopedia **633.79**

Cerveny, Randall S.
Weather's greatest mysteries solved! **304.2**

Césaire, Aimé
About
Baraka, I. A. The LeRoi Jones/Amiri Baraka reader **818**

Cesarani, David, 1956-2015
Final Solution **940.53**

Cetti, Livia
The exquisite book of paper flowers **745.594**

Cézanne. Danchev, A. **759.4**

Ch'oe, Ŭn-hŭi, 1930-
About
Fischer, P. A Kim Jong-Il production **791.43**

CHÂTEAU DE FONTAINEBLEAU (FONTAINEBLEAU, FRANCE)
Carhart, T. Finding Fontainebleau **944.36**

CHÂTEAU DE VERSAILLES (VERSAILLES, FRANCE)
Givhan, R. The Battle of Versailles **746.9**

CHABAD-LUBAVITCH
Telushkin, J. Rebbe **92**

Chabon, Michael
Maps and legends **814**
About
Chabon, M. Manhood for amateurs **92**

Chabris, Christopher
The invisible gorilla **153.7**

Chace, James
Acheson **92**

Chachula, Robyn, 1978-
Unexpected afghans **746.43**

CHACO CULTURE NATIONAL HISTORICAL PARK (N.M.)
Childs, C. L. House of rain **978.9**

Chadha, Yogesh
Gandhi **954.03**

Chadwick, Douglas H.
The company we keep **333.95**

Chadwick, Fergus
The bee book **595.799**

Chadwick, Henry
(ed) Augustine Confessions **242**

Chafe, William H.
Bill and Hillary **973.929**
(ed) Remembering Jim Crow **305.896**

Chagall. Wullschlager, J. **92**

Chagall, Marc, 1887-1985
About
Wullschlager, J. Chagall **92**

The chain. Genoways, T. **338.7**

Chain of command. Hersh, S. M. **973.931**

CHAIN STORES
Mitchell, S. Big-box swindle **381**

CHAIN STORES
See also Retail trade; Stores

CHAINS (JEWELRY)
Karon, K. Advanced chain maille jewelry workshop **745.594**

CHAIR CANING
See also Handicraft

CHAIRS
See also Furniture

CHAIRS -- HISTORY
Rybczynski, W. Now I sit me down **749.32**

CHAKRAS
Dale, C. Llewellyn's complete book of chakras **131**

CHAKRAS
See also Yoga

CHAKRAS -- MISCELLANEA
Judith, A. Eastern body, Western mind **150.19**

Chaline, Eric
Fifty minerals that changed the course of history **549**

CHALK TALKS
See also Public speaking

Chalk, Peter
(ed) Encyclopedia of terrorism **363.32**

The challenge of library management. Mosley, P. A. **025.1**

CHALLENGED BOOKS -- UNITED STATES -- BIBLIOGRAPHY
Scales, P. R. Books under fire **016**

Challenger, Melanie
(ed) Stolen voices **920**

Challoner, Jack
The Elements **546**

Chalmers, David Mark
Hooded Americanism: the history of the Ku Klux Klan **322.4**

Chaloner, William, d. 1699
About
Levenson, T. Newton and the counterfeiter **92**

CHAMBER MUSIC
See also Instrumental music; Music

Chambers, Veronica
32 yolks   **92**
Yes, chef   **92**
Chambers, Whittaker
        About
Chambers, W. Witness   **92**
The **chameleon** couch. Komunyakaa, Y.   **811**
Chametzky, Jules
(ed) Jewish American literature   **810**
CHAMPAGNE (WINE)
Tardi, A. Champagne, uncorked   **641.2**
Champagne, uncorked. Tardi, A.   **641.2**
The **champion's** mind. Afremow, J.   **796.01**
Champlain's dream. Fischer, D. H.   **92**
Champlain, Samuel de, 1567-1635
        About
Fischer, D. H. Champlain's dream   **92**
Champollion, Jean-François, 1790-1832
        About
Robinson, A. Cracking the Egyptian code   **493**
The **Chan's** great continent. Spence, J. D.   **951**
CHAN, CHARLIE (FICTIONAL CHARACTER)
Yunte Huang Charlie Chan   **92**
Chan, Ronald W.
Behind the Berkshire Hathaway curtain   **658.4**
Chan, Simon
(ed) Zondervan dictionary of Christian spirituality   **248**
CHANCE
Dolnick, B. Luck   **130**
Howe, F. Second childhood   **811**
Mazur, J. Fluke   **519.2**
Mlodinow, L. The Drunkard's walk   **519.2**
Chance and circumstance. Brown, C.   **92**
Chancellorsville. Sears, S. W.   **973.7**
CHANCELLORSVILLE (VA.), BATTLE OF, 1863
Furgurson, E. B. Chancellorsville, 1863   **973.7**
Sears, S. W. Chancellorsville   **973.7**
Chancellorsville, 1863. Furgurson, E. B.   **973.7**
Chandler, Charlotte
It's only a movie   **92**
Chandler, Raymond, 1888-1959
        About
Hiney, T. Raymond Chandler   **813**
Chandrasekaran, Rajiv
Imperial life in the emerald city   **956.704**
Chandrasekhar, Subrahmanyan, 1910-1995
        About
Miller, A. I. Empire of the stars   **520**
CHANEL (FIRM)
Mazzeo, T. J. The secret of Chanel No. 5   **338.7**
Chanel, Coco, 1883-1971
        About
Garelick, R. K. Mademoiselle   **92**
Mazzeo, T. J. The secret of Chanel No. 5   **338.7**

Vaughan, H. Sleeping with the enemy   **92**
Chang, Andrew C.
(comp) Cheng & Tsui English-Chinese lexicon of business terms with pinyin   **495.1**
Chang, David
Momofuku   **641.5**
Chang, Ha-Joon
Economics   **330**
Chang, Iris
The rape of Nanking   **951.04**
Chang, Jeff
Can't stop, won't stop   **781.64**
Chang, Joanne
Baking with less sugar   **641.5**
(jt. auth) Matheson, C. Flour   **641.8**
Chang, Jung
Mao: the unknown story   **92**
Wild swans   **951.05**
Chang, Leslie T.
Factory girls   **331.4**
Chang, Tina
(ed) Language for a new century   **808.81**
The **change.** Greer, G.   **618.1**
CHANGE
   See also Metaphysics
CHANGE (PSYCHOLOGY)
Achor, S. Before happiness   **158**
Bright, D. The truth doesn't have to hurt   **158.2**
Heath, C. Switch   **303.4**
McGraw, P. C. Life strategies   **158**
Michels, B. The tools   **158**
The power of habit   **158.1**
Rubin, G. Better than before   **158.1**
Weber, R. J. The created self   **155.2**
CHANGE (PSYCHOLOGY)
   See also Psychology
CHANGE (PSYCHOLOGY) -- CASE STUDIES
Clarke, T. JFK's last hundred days   **92**
A **Change** of Appetite. Henry, D.   **641.5**
The **changing** arctic landscape. Tape, K. D.   **551.69**
CHANGING CAREERS *See* Career changes
The **changing** light at Sandover. Merrill, J.   **811**
Changing lives. Tunstall, T.   **780.7**
Changing my mind. Smith, Z.   **824**
Chansky, Tamar E.
Freeing your child from anxiety   **618.92**
Chanson de Roland
The song of Roland   **841**
CHANUKAH *See* Hanukkah
CHAOS (SCIENCE)
Ball, P. Nature's patterns   **500.2**
Harford, T. Messy   **153.35**
CHAOS (SCIENCE)
   See also Dynamics; Science; System theory
Chaos Monkeys. Martinez, A. G.   **338.4**
CHAOTIC BEHAVIOR IN SYSTEMS *See* Chaos

(Science)

CHAPBOOKS

See also Books; Folklore; Literature; Pamphlets; Periodicals; Wit and humor

Chapin, Kari
The handmade marketplace **745.5**

CHAPLAINS
See also Clergy

Chaplin and Agee. Wranovics, J. **92**

Chaplin, Amy
At home in the whole food kitchen **641.3**

Chaplin, Charlie, 1889-1977
About
Ackroyd, P. Charlie Chaplin **92**
The essential Chaplin **92**
Wranovics, J. Chaplin and Agee **92**

Chaplin, Joyce E.
Round about the earth **910.4**

Chapman piloting & seamanship. **623.88**

Chapman, Adam
(jt. auth) Barrington, R. Life **578.4**

Chapman, Bob
Everybody matters **658.4**

Chapman, C. C.
Handley, A. Content rules **658.8**

Chapman, Eddie, 1914-1997
About
Macintyre, B. Agent Zigzag **92**

Chapman, Emma
A beautiful mess happy handmade home **747**

Chapman, Eunice, 1778-1863
About
Woo, I. The great divorce **92**

Chapman, Gary D.
Love as a way of life **241**

Chapman, James, 1763-1852
About
Woo, I. The great divorce **92**

Chapman, Richard
The new complete guitarist **787.87**

Chapman, Robert L.
(ed) Roget's international thesaurus **423**

Chappell, Jon
Guitar All-in-one for Dummies **787.87**

Chapter 13 bankruptcy. Elias, S. **346**

CHARACTER
Brooks, D. B. The Road to Character **170**
Brooks, D. The social animal **305.5**

CHARACTER
See also Ethics; Personality

CHARACTER -- POLITICAL ASPECTS -- UNITED STATES -- HISTORY -- 20TH CENTURY
Bai, M. All the truth is out **328.73**

Character studies. Singer, M. **920**

CHARACTERS *See* Characters and characteristics

in literature

CHARACTERS AND CHARACTERISTICS IN LITERATURE
Bloom, H. Shakespeare: the invention of the human **822.3**
Cyclopedia of literary characters **803**
Ellis, S. How to Be a Heroine **809.3**
Swain, D. V. Creating characters **808.3**

CHARACTERS AND CHARACTERISTICS IN LITERATURE
See also Literature

CHARACTERS AND CHARACTERISTICS ON TELEVISION
Martin, B. Difficult men **791.450**

CHARADES
See also Amateur theater; Amusements; Literary recreations; Riddles

Charbonneau, Diane
(ed) Chihuly **748.2**

CHARCOAL
See also Fuel

CHARCOAL DRAWING
See also Drawing

Charcuteria. **641.594**

Charcuterie and French pork cookery. Grigson, J. **641.6**

Chariot. Cotterell, A. **357**

CHARITIES
Zunz, O. Philanthropy in America **361.7**

CHARITY
Gup, T. A secret gift **977.1**

CHARITY
See also Ethics; Virtue

Charity and Sylvia. Cleves, R. H. **306.84**

Charlatan. Brock, P. **92**

Charlemagne. Wilson, D. A. **92**

Charlemagne, Emperor, 742-814
About
Bulfinch, T. Bulfinch's mythology **398.2**
Wilson, D. A. Charlemagne **92**

Charles Darwin. Browne, J. **92**

Charles Darwin's On the Origin of Species. Keller, M. **576.8**

Charles Dickens. Smiley, J. **823**
Charles Dickens. Slater, M. **92**
Charles Dickens. Tomalin, C. **92**

Charles Eliot Norton lectures [series]
Borges, J. L. This craft of verse **809.1**

Charles Fort. Steinmeyer, J. **92**

Charles II, King of England, 1630-1685
About
Jordan, D. The king's revenge **941.062**
About
Uglow, J. S. A gambling man **92**

Charles Ives. Swafford, J. **92**

Charles Kuralt's America. Kuralt, C. **973.92**

Charles V, Holy Roman Emperor, 1500-1558
About
Reston, J. Defenders of the faith   **940.2**
Charles, John A.
The mystery readers' advisory   **025.2**
Charles, Prince of Wales, 1948-
About
Mayer, C. Born to be king   **92**
Charles, Ray
About
Feather, L. From Satchmo to Miles   **920**
Charles-Edwards, T. M.
Wales and the Britons, 350-1064   **942.901**
CHARLESTON (S.C.) -- HISTORY
Detzer, D. Allegiance   **973.7**
CHARLESTON (S.C.) -- HISTORY -- 1775-1865
Kelly, J. America's longest siege   **305.896**
CHARLESTOWN HIGH SCHOOL (BOSTON, MASS.)
Swidey, N. The assist   **796.323**
Charlie Chan. Yunte Huang   **92**
Charlie Chaplin. Ackroyd, P.   **92**
Charlie Palmer's American fare.   **641.59**
Charlotte and Lionel. Weintraub, S.   **92**
Charlotte Augusta, Princess of Great Britain, 1796-1817
About
Williams, K. Becoming Queen Victoria   **92**
Charlotte Bronte. Gordon, L.   **92**
Charlotte Moss. Moss, C.   **747**
Charlotte, Queen, Consort of Frederick I, King of Württemberg, 1766-1828
About
Fraser, F. Princesses   **920**
CHARMS
See also Folklore; Superstition
Charnas, Dan
The big payback   **781.64**
Charred & scruffed. Kaminsky, P.   **641.7**
CHARTERS
See also History -- Sources
Charters, Ann
(ed) Kerouac, J. Selected letters, 1940-1956   **92**
(ed) Kerouac, J. Selected letters, 1957-1969   **813**
(ed) The Portable beat reader   **810**
(ed) The Portable sixties reader   **810**
Chartier, Roger
(ed) Aries, P. A History of private life   **909**
CHARTOGRAPHY *See* Maps
CHARTS *See* Charts, diagrams, etc.
CHARTS, DIAGRAMS, ETC.
Lima, M. The book of trees   **001.2**
CHASE MANHATTAN BANK, N.A.
Rockefeller, D. Memoirs   **332.1**
Chase, Marilyn
The Barbary plague   **362.1**

Chase, Salmon P. (Salmon Portland), 1808-1873
About
Goodwin, D. K. Team of rivals   **92**
Oller, J. American queen   **92**
CHASIDISM *See* Hasidism
Chasing Aphrodite. Frammolino, R.   **930**
Chasing Gideon. Houppert, K.   **345.73**
Chasing Goldman Sachs. McGee, S.   **332.6**
Chasing Icarus. Mortimer, G.   **629.13**
Chasing kangaroos. Flannery, T. F.   **599.2**
Chasing perfection. Glockner, A.   **796.323**
Chasing portraits. Rynecki, E.   **700.92**
Chasing science at sea. Prager, E. J.   **551.46**
Chasing shadows. Hughes, K.   **973.924**
Chasing the Devil. Butcher, T.   **916**
Chasing the white dog. Watman, M.   **363.4**
Chasing Utopia. Giovanni, N.   **811**
Chasing Venus. Wulf, A.   **523.9**
Chast, Roz
Can't We Talk About Something More Pleasant?   **741.5**
Chasteen, John Charles
Born in blood and fire   **980**
CHASTITY
See also Sexual ethics; Virtue
CHATEAUX *See* Castles
Chatterjee, Pria
The dirty little secrets of getting into a top college   **378.161**
Chatterton, John
About
Kurson, R. Pirate hunters   **910.91**
Chattman, Lauren
Maangchi's real Korean cooking   **641.595**
Chatwin, Bruce
In Patagonia   **918**
The songlines   **919**
About
Shakespeare, N. Bruce Chatwin   **823**
Under the sun   **92**
Chatwin, Elizabeth
(ed) Under the sun   **92**
Chaucer. Ackroyd, P.   **92**
Chaucer, 1340-1400. West, R.   **821**
Chaucer, Geoffrey, d. 1400
The complete poetry and prose of Geoffrey Chaucer   **821**
About
Ackroyd, P. Chaucer   **92**
Bloom, H. The Western canon   **809**
Geoffrey Chaucer's The Canterbury tales   **821**
The Oxford companion to Chaucer   **821**
Rossignol, R. Critical companion to Chaucer   **821**
West, R. Chaucer, 1340-1400   **821**
Chaudry, Rabia
Adnan's Story   **364.152**

Chavalas, Mark W.
(ed) Great events from history, The ancient world, prehistory-476 C.E. **930**

Chaves, Mark
Ordaining women **262**

Chavez, Cesar, 1927-1993
About
Pawel, M. The Crusades of Cesar Chavez **92**
Shaw, R. Beyond the fields **331.8**

Chayes, Sarah
Thieves of state **364.1**

Che Guevara. Anderson, J. L. **92**

Che's afterlife. Casey, M. **980**

The **cheapskate** next door. Yeager, J. **332.024**

CHEATING (EDUCATION)
See also Honesty
The **cheating** culture. Callahan, D. **174**

CHEATING IN SPORTS *See* Sports -- Corrupt practices

Chechnya. Lieven, A. **947.086**

CHECHNYA (RUSSIA)
Baiev, K. The Oath **947.5**
Lieven, A. Chechnya **947.086**

CHECHNYA (RUSSIA) -- HISTORY -- 1994-(CIVIL WAR)
Seierstad, A. The angel of Grozny **947.5**

CHECKERS
See also Board games
The **checklist** manifesto. Gawande, A. **610.28**

Checkoway, Julie
The three-year swim club **797.2**

Cheek, Angie
(ed) Foxfire 40th anniversary book **975.8**

CHEERLEADERS *See* Cheerleading

CHEERLEADING
Laskas, J. M. Hidden America **305.5**

CHEERS AND CHEERLEADING *See* Cheerleading

CHEESE
Centamore, A. Tasting wine & cheese
Darlington, T. Dibruno Bros. House of Cheese **641.3**
World cheese book **641.3**

CHEESE
See also Dairy products

CHEESE -- MICROBIOLOGY
See also Microbiology

CHEESE MAKING *See* Cheesemaking

CHEESECAKE (COOKING)
See also Cake

CHEESEMAKING
Caldwell, G. Mastering artisan cheesemaking **637**
Lucero, C. One-hour cheese **637**

Cheetham, Kathleen
Singer perfect plus **646.2**

Cheever. Bailey, B. **92**

Cheever, John, 1912-1982

About
Bailey, B. Cheever **92**

Cheever, Susan
American Bloomsbury **810**
Drinking in America **394.1**

Chekhov. Chekhov, A. P. **891.7**

Chekhov, Anton Pavlovich, 1860-1904
Chekhov **891.7**
The complete plays **891.7**
The portable Chekhov **891.7**
About
Callow, P. Chekhov, the hidden ground **891.7**
Chekhov, A. P. Anton Chekhov's life and thought **92**
Malcolm, J. Reading Chekhov **891.7**
Nabokov, V. V. Lectures on Russian literature **891.7**

Chekhov, Michael
To the actor **792**

Chekhov, the hidden ground. Callow, P. **891.7**

CHELIABINSK (RUSSIA) -- BIOGRAPHY
Garrels, A. Putin country **947.43**

CHELSEA HOTEL -- BIOGRAPHY
Rips, N. Trying to float **974.7**

CHELSEA MARKET (NEW YORK, N.Y.)
Phillips, M. The Chelsea Market cookbook **641.59**
The **Chelsea** Market cookbook. Phillips, M. **641.59**

CHEMICAL APPARATUS
See also Scientific apparatus and instruments

CHEMICAL DEPENDENCY *See* Substance abuse

CHEMICAL ELEMENTS
Aldersey-Williams, H. Periodic tales **546**
Challoner, J. The Elements **546**
The elements **546**
Gray, T. Molecules **541**
Kean, S. The disappearing spoon **546**

CHEMICAL ELEMENTS
See also Chemistry

CHEMICAL ELEMENTS -- PICTORIAL WORKS
The elements **546**

CHEMICAL REACTIONS
Atkins, P. W. Reactions **541**

CHEMICAL REACTIONS
See also Chemistry

CHEMICAL SPILLS
Lerner, S. Sacrifice zones **363.738**

CHEMICAL WARFARE
Tucker, J. B. War of nerves **358**
Weapons of mass destruction **358**

CHEMICALS
Winter, R. A consumer's dictionary of cosmetic ingredients **668**

CHEMICALS -- TOXICOLOGY *See* Toxicology

CHEMISTRY
Cobb, C. The joy of chemistry **540**
Kamozawa, A. Ideas in food **641.5**
Lange's handbook of chemistry **540**

CHEMISTRY
See also Physical sciences; Science
CHEMISTRY -- DICTIONARIES
A dictionary of chemistry **540**
CHEMISTRY -- DICTIONARIES
See also Encyclopedias and dictionaries
CHEMISTRY -- HISTORY
Cobb, C. Creations of fire **540**
Coffey, P. Cathedrals of science **540**
Greenberg, A. From alchemy to chemistry in picture and story **540**
CHEMISTRY -- TABLES
CRC Handbook of Chemistry and Physics **540**
Lange's handbook of chemistry **540**
CHEMISTS
Angier, C. The double bond: Primo Levi, a biography **92**
Brandon, R. Ugly beauty **646.7**
Brian, D. The Curies **92**
Coffey, P. Cathedrals of science **540**
Dry, S. Curie **92**
Ewing, H. P. The lost world of James Smithson **92**
Garfield, S. Mauve **667**
Gordin, M. D. A well-ordered thing: Dmitrii Mendeleev and the shadow of the periodic table **92**
Hamblyn, R. The invention of clouds **551.57**
Hirshfeld, A. The electric life of Michael Faraday **92**
Hunter, M. Boyle **92**
Johnson, S. The invention of air **92**
Levi, P. The periodic table **92**
Maddox, B. Rosalind Franklin: the dark lady of DNA **92**
Malone, J. W. It doesn't take a rocket scientist **920**
Oakes, E. H. A to Z of chemists **920.003**
Pauling, L. C. Linus Pauling in his own words **081**
Stern, J. Denial **92**
CHEMISTS
See also Scientists
CHEMISTS -- ENGLAND -- BIOGRAPHY
Garfield, S. Mauve **667**
CHEMISTS -- FRANCE
Dry, S. Curie **92**
CHEMISTS -- POLAND
Dry, S. Curie **92**
CHEMOTHERAPY See Cancer -- Chemotherapy; Drug therapy
Chen, Da, 1962-
About
Chen, D. Colors of the mountain **92**
Chen, D. Sounds of the river **951.05**
Chen, Pauline W.
About
Chen, P. W. Final exam **92**
Cheney, Lynne V., 1941-
James Madison **92**

Cheng & Tsui English-Chinese lexicon of business terms with pinyin. **495.1**
Cheng, Chui-ping
About
Keefe, P. R. The snakehead **364.1**
Cheng, Eugenia
How to bake pi **510.1**
Cheng, Linsun
(ed) Berkshire encyclopedia of China **951**
Cheng, Nien, 1915-2009
About
Cheng, N. Life and death in Shanghai **92**
Chennault, Anna
About
Hughes, K. Chasing shadows **973.924**
Chenoweth, Juneal M.
American reference books annual 2016 **011**
Cherniavsky, Mark
The cookbook library **641.509**
Chernow, Ron
Alexander Hamilton **92**
Titan: the life of John D. Rockefeller, Sr. **92**
The Warburgs **920**
Washington **92**
CHEROKEE INDIANS
Inskeep, S. Jacksonland **973.5**
Mankiller, W. Mankiller: a chief and her people **92**
McLoughlin, W. G. After the Trail of Tears **970.004**
Chertavian, Gerald.
A Year Up **331.25**
Chesler, Phyllis
The new anti-semitism **305.8**
CHESS
Brady, F. Endgame **92**
Brown, N. M. Ivory Vikings **736**
Fischer, B. Bobby Fischer teaches chess **794.1**
Hallman, J. C. The chess artist **794.1**
U.S. Chess Federation's official rules of chess **794.1**
CHESS
See also Board games
The chess artist. Hallman, J. C. **794.1**
Chester Himes. Sallis, J. **813**
Chesterman, Charles W.
The Audubon Society field guide to North American rocks and minerals **549**
Chesterton, G. K., (Gilbert Keith), 1874-1936
About
Ker, I. G. K. Chesterton **828**
CHESTS
See also Furniture
Chetham, Deirdre
Before the deluge **951**
Chevannes, Barry
Rastafari: roots and ideology **299.6**
CHEVRON CORPORATION -- TRIALS, LITIGATION, ETC

Barrett, P. M. Law of the jungle **344**

Chewy gooey crispy crunchy melt-in-your-mouth cookies. Medrich, A. **641.8**

CHEYENNE INDIANS

Brown, D. A. The American West **978**

Enss, C. Mochi's war **978.8**

Chezar, Ariella

The flower workshop **745.92**

Chiang, Kai-shek, 1887-1975
About
Bernstein, R. China 1945 **327.73**

Taylor, J. The generalissimo **92**

Tuchman, B. W. Stilwell and the American experience in China, 1911-45 **327**

Chiang, Mei-ling, 1898-2003
About
Li, L. T. Madame Chiang Kai-Shek **92**

Pakula, H. The last empress **92**

Chiang, Renee

(tr) Prisoner of the state **92**

CHIAPAS (MEXICO) -- BIOGRAPHY

Franklin, J. 438 days **910.916**

CHICAGO (ILL.)

Borich, B. J. Body geographic **818**

CHICAGO (ILL.) -- ANTIQUITIES

See also Antiquities

CHICAGO (ILL.) -- BIOGRAPHY

Eire, C. M. N. Waiting for snow in Havana **92**

Jobb, D. Empire of deception **92**

CHICAGO (ILL.) -- ECONOMIC CONDITIONS -- 20TH CENTURY

Jobb, D. Empire of deception **92**

CHICAGO (ILL.) -- HISTORY

Michaeli, E. The defender **071**

CHICAGO (ILL.) -- INTELLECTUAL LIFE -- 20TH CENTURY

Dyja, T. The third coast **977.3**

Writers of the Black Chicago renaissance **810.9**

CHICAGO (ILL.) -- MAPS

See also Maps

CHICAGO (ILL.) -- POETRY

Smith, P. Shoulda been Jimi Savannah **811**

CHICAGO (ILL.) -- POLITICS AND GOVERN-MENT

Cohen, A. American pharaoh: Mayor Richard J. Daley: his battle for Chicago and the nation **977.3**

CHICAGO (ILL.) -- RACE RELATIONS -- HISTORY -- 20TH CENTURY -- ANECDOTES

Jefferson, M. Negroland **92**

CHICAGO (ILL.) -- SOCIAL CONDITIONS

Addams, J. Twenty years at Hull-House **361.7**

Knight, L. W. Jane Addams **92**

CHICAGO (ILL.) -- SOCIAL CONDITIONS

See also Social conditions

CHICAGO (ILL.) -- SOCIAL LIFE AND CUSTOMS

Abbott, K. Sin in the Second City **977.3**

CHICAGO DEFENDER -- HISTORY

Michaeli, E. The defender **071**

Chicago guides to writing, editing, and publishing [series]

A manual for writers of research papers, theses, and dissertations **808.06**

Turabian, K. L. Student's guide to writing college papers **808**

Chicago history of American civilization [series]

Morgan, E. S. The birth of the Republic, 1763-89 **973.3**

The **Chicago** manual of style. **808**

CHICAGO REGION (ILL.) -- BIOGRAPHY

Jefferson, M. Negroland **92**

CHICANERY See Deception

Chicano visions. Marin, C. **709**

CHICANOS See Mexican Americans

CHICKENPOX

See also Diseases; Viruses

CHICKENS

Johnson, S. How to build chicken coops **636.5**

Lawler, A. Why did the chicken cross the world? **636.5**

Rude, E. Tastes Like Chicken **636.5**

CHICKENS

See also Poultry

CHICKENS -- HISTORY

Lawler, A. Why did the chicken cross the world? **636.5**

CHICKENS -- HOUSING

Johnson, S. How to build chicken coops **636.5**

Chicoine, Brian

The guide to good health for teens & adults with Down syndrome **618.92**

Chidester, David

(ed) In his own words **92**

Chideya, Farai

The episodic career **650.1**

CHIEF JUSTICES See Judges

The **chief**: the life of William Randolph Hearst. Nasaw, D. **070.5**

Chihuly. **748.2**

CHILD ABUSE

Calcaterra, R. Etched in Sand **92**

Hayden, T. L. Twilight children **618.92**

Zacharias, K. S. A silence of mockingbirds **364.152**

CHILD ABUSE

See also Child welfare; Domestic violence; Parent-child relationship

CHILD ARTISTS

Van't Hul, J. The artful parent **745.5**

CHILD ARTISTS

See also Artists; Gifted children

CHILD AUTHORS

See also Authors; Gifted children

CHILD BEHAVIOR *See* Child psychology; Children -- Conduct of life; Etiquette for children and teenagers

CHILD BENEFACTORS
Joyner-Kersee, J. A kind of grace   **796.42**

CHILD BIRTH *See* Childbirth

CHILD CARE
Caring for your baby and young child   **618.92**
Caring for your school-age child   **649**
Leach, P. Child care today   **362.7**
Leach, P. Your baby & child   **649**
Spock, B. Dr. Spock's baby and child care   **649**
Spock, B. Dr. Spock's the first two years   **649**
Spock, B. Dr. Spock's the school years   **649**

CHILD CARE SERVICES
Gold, T. Secrets of the nanny whisperer   **649**

CHILD CARE SERVICES
See also Public welfare; Social work

CHILD CARE SERVICES -- UNITED STATES
Gold, T. Secrets of the nanny whisperer   **649**
Child care today. Leach, P.   **362.7**
The child catchers. Joyce, K.   **362.734**

CHILD CUSTODY
Woo, I. The great divorce   **92**

CHILD CUSTODY
See also Divorce mediation; Parent-child relationship

CHILD DEVELOPMENT
Brazelton, T. B. The irreducible needs of children   **155.4**
Brazelton, T. B. To listen to a child   **155.4**
Brazelton, T. B. Touchpoints birth to 3   **649**
Camarata, S. M. Late-talking children   **618.92**
Caring for your school-age child   **649**
Clinton, H. R. It takes a village   **305.23**
Egan, A. Is it a big problem or a little problem?   **649**
Eliot, L. Pink brain, blue brain   **612.6**
Gopnik, A. The gardener and the carpenter   **155.4**
Gopnik, A. The scientist in the crib   **155.4**
Kagan, J. The human spark   **155**
Karr-Morse, R. Scared sick   **155.9**
Konner, M. The evolution of childhood   **305.23**
Leach, P. Your baby & child   **649**
Leach, P. Your Baby and Child From Birth to Age Five   **618.92**
Levine, M. D. A mind at a time   **370.15**
Mayes, L. C. The Yale Child Study Center guide to understanding your child   **649**
Miller, L. The Spiritual Child   **649**
Prosek, J. Raising Can-Do Kids   **649.7**
Siegel, D. J. The whole-brain child   **649**
Spock, B. Dr. Spock's the first two years   **649**
Spock, B. Dr. Spock's the school years   **649**
Suskind, D. Thirty Million Words   **612.8**
Tough, P. Helping Children Succeed   **372.1**
Tuck, S. Getting from me to we   **155.4**

Watch my baby grow   **649.122**
Willingham, E. The informed parent   **649.1**

CHILD DEVELOPMENT
See also Children

CHILD DEVELOPMENT -- UNITED STATES
Clinton, H. R. It takes a village   **305.23**
A child is born. Nilsson, L.   **612.6**

CHILD LABOR
Levine, M. J. Children for hire   **331.3**

CHILD LABOR
See also Age and employment; Child welfare; Labor; Social problems

CHILD MARRIAGE
Ali, N. I am Nujood, age 10 and divorced   **92**

CHILD MOLESTING *See* Child sexual abuse

CHILD NEGLECT *See* Child abuse

CHILD PLACING *See* Adoption; Foster home care

CHILD PROSTITUTION *See* Juvenile prostitution

CHILD PSYCHIATRY
See also Psychiatry

CHILD PSYCHOLOGY
Barkley, R. A. Taking Charge of ADHD   **618.92**
Barrett, J. L. Born believers   **200.1**
Brazelton, T. B. The irreducible needs of children   **155.4**
Brazelton, T. B. To listen to a child   **155.4**
Brazelton, T. B. Touchpoints birth to 3   **649**
Chansky, T. E. Freeing your child from anxiety   **618.92**
Dunckley, V. L. Reset your child's brain   **004.67**
Egan, A. Is it a big problem or a little problem?   **649**
Foss, B. The dyslexia empowerment plan   **618.92**
Gnaulati, E. Back to normal   **618.92**
Gopnik, A. The gardener and the carpenter   **155.4**
Karr-Morse, R. Scared sick   **155.9**
Kubler-Ross, E. On children and death   **155.9**
Louv, R. Last child in the woods   **155.4**
Medina, J. Brain rules for baby   **649**
Piaget, J. The moral judgment of the child   **155.4**
Sears, W. Parenting the fussy baby and high-need child   **649**
Stephens, K. The Prodigy's Cousin   **155.45**
White, B. L. The new first three years of life   **155.4**
Young-Eisendrath, P. The self-esteem trap   **155.2**

CHILD PSYCHOLOGY
See also Psychology

CHILD RAISING *See* Child rearing

CHILD REARING
Ames, L. B. Your eight-year-old   **649**
Ames, L. B. Your five-year-old   **649**
Ames, L. B. Your four-year-old   **649**
Ames, L. B. Your one-year-old   **649**
Ames, L. B. Your seven-year-old   **649**
Ames, L. B. Your six-year-old   **649**

Ames, L. B. Your two-year-old **649**

Bailey, R. A. Easy to love, difficult to discipline **155**

Barkley, R. A. Taking charge of ADHD **618.92**

Borba, M. Unselfie **649.7**

Bowers, M. 8 keys to raising the quirky child **649**

Brazelton, T. B. The irreducible needs of children **155.4**

Brazelton, T. B. Touchpoints birth to 3 **649**

Brooks, R. B. Raising resilient children **649**

Caring for your school-age child **649**

Chua, A. Battle hymn of the tiger mother **306.874**

Cross, C. The baby book **649.122**

Deak, J. Girls will be girls **649**

DeSouza, L. Eat, Play, Sleep **649.122**

Economides, A. The moneysmart family system **332.024**

Edelman, M. W. The measure of our success **170**

Edgerton, C. Papadaddy's book for new fathers **649**

Elman, N. M. The unwritten rules of friendship **649**

Emswiler, M. A. Guiding your child through grief **155.9**

Fonseca, C. Raising the shy child **649**

Furedi, F. Paranoid parenting **649**

Greene, R. W. Raising human beings **306.874**

The happy sleeper **649**

Hurley, K. The happy kid handbook **649**

Ilg, F. L. Your three-year-old **649**

Karp, H. The happiest baby on the block **649**

Kazdin, A. E. The Everyday Parenting Toolkit **649**

Kennedy-Moore, E. Smart parenting for smart kids **649**

Lazebnik, C. Overcoming Autism **618.92**

Leach, P. The essential first year **649**

Mayes, L. C. The Yale Child Study Center guide to understanding your child **649**

Murkoff, H. E. What to expect the first year **649**

Murkoff, H. E. What to expect the second year **649**

Murkoff, H. What to Expect the First Year **649**

Phelan, T. W. 1-2-3 magic **649**

Porto, A. The pediatrician's guide to feeding babies and toddlers **618.92**

Richey, M. A. The impulsive, disorganized child **649**

Sampson, S. D. How to raise a wild child **508**

Siegel, D. J. No-drama discipline **649**

Siegel, D. J. The whole-brain child **649**

Spock, B. Dr. Spock's baby and child care **649**

Spock, B. Dr. Spock's the first two years **649**

Spock, B. Dr. Spock's the school years **649**

Suskind, D. Thirty Million Words **612.8**

Tough, P. Helping Children Succeed **372.1**

Willingham, E. The informed parent **649.1**

CHILD REARING

    See also Child care; Child-adult relationship; Parent-child relationship

CHILD REARING -- RELIGIOUS ASPECTS --

JUDAISM

Ingall, M. Mamaleh knows best **649.1**

CHILD REARING -- UNITED STATES

Lahey, J. The gift of failure **649**

Mintz, S. Huck's raft **305.23**

CHILD REARING -- UNITED STATES -- HANDBOOKS, MANUALS, ETC

Scott, J. Raising children in the military **355.1**

CHILD SEX ABUSE *See* Child sexual abuse

CHILD SEXUAL ABUSE

Bass, E. The courage to heal **616.85**

Betrayal **282**

Rabinowitz, D. No crueler tyrannies **345**

CHILD SEXUAL ABUSE

    See also Child abuse; Incest; Sex crimes

CHILD SEXUAL ABUSE BY CLERGY

D'Antonio, M. Mortal Sins **261.8**

CHILD SNATCHING BY PARENTS *See* Parental kidnapping

CHILD SOLDIERS

    See also Children; Soldiers

CHILD STUDY *See* Child development; Child psychology

CHILD SUPPORT

    See also Child welfare; Desertion and nonsupport; Divorce mediation

CHILD WELFARE

Bernstein, N. The lost children of Wilder **362.73**

Clinton, H. R. It takes a village **305.23**

CHILD WELFARE

    See also Charities; Public welfare; Social work

CHILD WELFARE -- UNITED STATES

Clinton, H. R. It takes a village **305.23**

Kozol, J. Fire in the ashes **362.7**

A **child's** Christmas in Wales. Thomas, D. **828**

Child, Julia, 1912-2004

Child, J. The way to cook **641.5**

Baking with Julia **641.7**

From Julia Child's kitchen **641.5**

Julia and Jacques cooking at home **641.59**

Mastering the art of French cooking **641.5**

My life in France **92**

About

As always, Julia **92**

Barr, L. Provence, 1970 **641.59**

Child, J. My life in France **92**

Conant, J. A covert affair **940.54**

Fitch, N. R. Appetite for life **92**

Prud'homme, A. The French chef in America **641.509**

Spitz, B. Dearie **92**

Child, Paul

About

Conant, J. A covert affair **940.54**

CHILD-ADULT RELATIONSHIP

See also Children

CHILDBIRTH

Birth without violence **618.4**

Epstein, R. H. Get me out **618.2**

Mayo Clinic guide to a healthy pregnancy **618.2**

The mommy docs' ultimate guide to pregnancy and birth **618.2**

Murkoff, H. What to expect when you're expecting **618.2**

Nilsson, L. A child is born **612.6**

Pregnancy day by day **618.2**

Simkin, P. The Birth Partner **618.2**

CHILDBIRTH -- POPULAR WORKS

The pregnancy encyclopedia **618.2**

CHILDBIRTH -- PSYCHOLOGICAL ASPECTS

The kind mama **618.1**

CHILDLESSNESS

Maybe baby **306.8**

CHILDLESSNESS

See also Children; Family size

The **children**. Halberstam, D. **323.1**

CHILDREN

See also Age; Family

CHILDREN

Abdul-Jabbar, K. Black profiles in courage **920**

Ali, N. I am Nujood, age 10 and divorced **92**

Anne Frank **92**

Bailey, E. Safe kids, smart parents **613.6**

Barnouw, D. The diary of Anne Frank: the critical edition **92**

Bullard, S. Teaching tolerance **649**

Canada, G. Fist, stick, knife, gun **305.23**

Christakis, E. The Importance of Being Little **372.21**

Frank, A. The diary of a young girl: the definitive edition **92**

Jacobson, S. Anne Frank **92**

Jones, G. Killing monsters **302.23**

Konner, M. The evolution of childhood **305.23**

Kozol, J. Ordinary resurrections **305.23**

Kubler-Ross, E. On children and death **155.9**

Matthews, J. Bringing Adam home **364.1**

Ozick, C. Quarrel & quandary **814**

Prose, F. Anne Frank **839.3**

Schiller, L. Perfect murder, perfect town **364.15**

Summerscale, K. The suspicions of Mr. Whicher **364.152**

Toffler, A. Future shock **303.4**

CHILDREN -- ABUSE *See* Child abuse

CHILDREN -- ADOPTION *See* Adoption

CHILDREN -- ANTHROPOMETRY

Konner, M. The evolution of childhood **305.23**

CHILDREN -- BOOKS AND READING

Newman, N. Raising passionate readers **649.58**

CHILDREN -- BOOKS AND READING

See also Books and reading

CHILDREN -- BOOKS AND READING -- UNITED STATES

Scales, P. R. Books under fire **016**

CHILDREN -- CARE *See* Child care

CHILDREN -- CHARITIES, PROTECTION, ETC. *See* Child welfare

CHILDREN -- CHINA

Xinran Message from an unknown Chinese mother **305.4**

CHILDREN -- CIVIL RIGHTS

See also Civil rights

CHILDREN -- CLOTHING *See* Children's clothing

CHILDREN -- CONDUCT OF LIFE

Dunckley, V. L. Reset your child's brain **004.67**

Phelan, T. W. 1-2-3 magic **649**

CHILDREN -- CONDUCT OF LIFE

See also Conduct of life

CHILDREN -- CRIMES AGAINST -- PREVENTION

Bailey, E. Safe kids, smart parents **613.6**

CHILDREN -- CUSTODY *See* Child custody

CHILDREN -- DEATH

Deraniyagala, S. Wave **954.93**

CHILDREN -- DEATH

See also Death

CHILDREN -- DENTAL CARE

Best-Boss, A. Your child's teeth **617.6**

CHILDREN -- FINANCE, PERSONAL

Economides, A. The moneysmart family system **332.024**

CHILDREN -- FOOD *See* Children -- Nutrition

CHILDREN -- GROWTH

See also Child development

CHILDREN -- HEALTH AND HYGIENE

The big book of symptoms **618.92**

Finlay, B. B. Let Them Eat Dirt **616.9**

Sears, R. W. The vaccine book **614.4**

Smith, R. G. ASD, the complete autism spectrum disorder health & diet guide **616.85**

Thurow, R. The first 1,000 days **618.92**

CHILDREN -- HEALTH AND HYGIENE

See also Health; Hygiene

CHILDREN -- HOSPITAL CARE

Keene, N. Your Child in the Hospital **362.1**

CHILDREN -- HYGIENE *See* Children -- Health and hygiene

CHILDREN -- INSTITUTIONAL CARE

See also Child welfare; Institutional care

CHILDREN -- LANGUAGE

Camarata, S. M. Late-talking children **618.92**

CHILDREN -- LANGUAGE

See also Language and languages

CHILDREN -- LIFE SKILLS GUIDES

Dawson, P. Smart but scattered **649**

CHILDREN -- MANAGEMENT *See* Child rearing

CHILDREN -- MEDICAL CARE
Keene, N. Your Child in the Hospital　　**362.1**

CHILDREN -- MOLESTING *See* Child sexual abuse

CHILDREN -- NUTRITION
Antine, S. Appetite for life　　**641.5**
Shetreat-Klein, M. The Dirt Cure　　**618.92**

CHILDREN -- NUTRITION
See also Children -- Health and hygiene; Nutrition

CHILDREN -- PHYSICAL FITNESS
See also Children -- Health and hygiene; Physical fitness

CHILDREN -- PLACING OUT *See* Adoption; Foster home care

CHILDREN -- PROTECTION
Bailey, E. Safe kids, smart parents　　**613.6**

CHILDREN -- PSYCHOLOGY *See* Child psychology

CHILDREN -- RELIGIOUS LIFE
Barrett, J. L. Born believers　　**200.1**

CHILDREN -- SLEEP
The happy sleeper　　**649**

CHILDREN -- SOCIALIZATION *See* Socialization

CHILDREN -- SURGERY
See also Surgery

CHILDREN -- TRAINING *See* Child rearing

CHILDREN -- TRAVEL
Maraniss, D. Barack Obama　　**92**

CHILDREN -- UNITED STATES
Tough, P. How children succeed　　**372.21**

CHILDREN -- UNITED STATES -- SOCIAL CONDITIONS
Kozol, J. Fire in the ashes　　**362.7**

CHILDREN AND ADVERTISING *See* Advertising and children

CHILDREN AND DEATH
See also Death

CHILDREN AND THE INTERNET *See* Internet and children

CHILDREN AND WAR
Beah, I. A long way gone　　**92**
Stolen voices　　**920**

CHILDREN AND WAR
See also Children; War
Children for hire. Levine, M. J.　　**331.3**

CHILDREN OF ALCOHOLICS
See also Children

CHILDREN OF ANTHROPOLOGISTS -- BIOGRAPHY
Kushner, D. Alligator candy　　**362.88**

CHILDREN OF CANCER PATIENTS
Marshall, D. Home is burning　　**92**

CHILDREN OF CANCER PATIENTS
See also Cancer patients

CHILDREN OF CANCER PATIENTS -- UNITED STATES -- BIOGRAPHY
Smith, C. B. The rules of inheritance　　**616.99**

CHILDREN OF CLERGY -- NEW YORK (STATE) -- BIOGRAPHY
Ward, G. C. A disposition to be rich　　**974.7**
Children of crisis. Coles, R.　　**305.23**

CHILDREN OF DIVORCED PARENTS
Wallerstein, J. S. The unexpected legacy of divorce　　**306.89**

CHILDREN OF DIVORCED PARENTS
See also Children; Divorce; Parent-child relationship

CHILDREN OF DRUG ADDICTS
Murray, L. Breaking night　　**92**

CHILDREN OF DRUG ADDICTS
See also Children; Drug addicts

CHILDREN OF DRUG ADDICTS -- MASSACHUSETTS -- BIOGRAPHY
Ruta, D. With or without you　　**362.29**
Children of dust. Eteraz, A.　　**92**

CHILDREN OF GAY PARENTS
Abbott, A. Fairyland　　**813**
Garner, A. Families like mine　　**306.8**

CHILDREN OF GAY PARENTS
See also Children

CHILDREN OF HEADS OF STATE -- SOVIET UNION -- BIOGRAPHY
Sullivan, R. Stalin's daughter　　**92**
The **Children** of Henry VIII. Guy, J.　　**941**

CHILDREN OF ILLEGAL ALIENS -- EDUCATION -- LAW AND LEGISLATION -- UNITED STATES
Truax, E. Dreamers　　**325**

CHILDREN OF IMMIGRANTS
Shteyngart, G. Little failure　　**92**

CHILDREN OF IMMIGRANTS
See also Children; Immigration and emigration

CHILDREN OF IMMIGRANTS -- EDUCATION
Connolly, D. The Book of Isaias　　**305.235**

CHILDREN OF MINORITIES -- EDUCATION -- UNITED STATES -- CASE STUDIES
Falk, B. Teaching matters　　**370.9**

CHILDREN OF NARCOTIC ADDICTS *See* Children of drug addicts
Children of Paradise. Secor, L.　　**955.05**

CHILDREN OF PRESIDENTS
Bruni, F. Ambling into history: the unlikely odyssey of George W. Bush　　**973.931**
Bush, G. W. Decision points　　**92**
Cordery, S. A. Alice　　**92**
Farmer, J. J. The ground truth　　**973.931**
Hersh, S. M. Chain of command　　**973.931**
Korda, M. Ulysses S. Grant: the unlikely hero　　**92**

Millard, C. The river of doubt   **973.91**

Schlesinger, A. M. War and the American presidency   **327.1**

Woodward, B. Plan of attack   **956.7**

Woodward, B. State of denial   **973.931**

CHILDREN OF PRESIDENTS -- UNITED STATES -- BIOGRAPHY

Anderson, C. The good son   **92**

Kendall, J. C. First dads   **973**

CHILDREN OF PRESIDENTS -- UNITED STATES -- BIOGRAPHY -- ANECDOTES

Brower, K. A. The residence   **975.3**

CHILDREN OF PRESIDENTS -- UNITED STATES -- HISTORY

Kendall, J. C. First dads   **973**

CHILDREN OF PROMINENT PERSONS

Ali, K. Fighting weight   **92**

Gimbel, W. Havana dreams   **972.91**

Lindbergh, R. Under a wing   **92**

Rice, A. The teeth may smile but the heart does not forget   **967.6**

Sobel, D. Galileo's daughter   **92**

The **children** of Sanchez. Lewis, O.   **972.08**

CHILDREN OF SEXUAL MINORITY PARENTS -- BOOKS AND READING -- UNITED STATES

Naidoo, J. C. Rainbow family collections   **028.1**

CHILDREN OF SINGLE PARENTS

See also Children; Single parents

Children of the stone. Tolan, S.   **780**

CHILDREN OF WORKING PARENTS

See also Children; Parent-child relationship

CHILDREN WITH AUTISM *See* Autistic children

CHILDREN WITH DISABILITIES

Adams, R. Raising Henry   **92**

Siegel, L. M. The complete IEP guide   **371.9**

CHILDREN WITH DISABILITIES

See also Children; Exceptional children; People with disabilities

CHILDREN WITH DISABILITIES -- BIOGRAPHY

Estreich, G. The Shape of the Eye   **618.92**

CHILDREN WITH DISABILITIES -- FAMILY RELATIONSHIPS

Palmer, S. Just one of the kids   **649**

CHILDREN WITH DISABILITIES -- UNITED STATES -- PSYCHOLOGY

Solomon, A. Far from the tree   **362.4**

CHILDREN WITH MENTAL DISABILITIES

Richey, M. A. The impulsive, disorganized child   **649**

CHILDREN WITH MENTAL DISABILITIES

See also Child psychiatry; Children with disabilities; People with mental disabilities

CHILDREN WITH MENTAL DISABILITIES --

EDUCATION

See also Education; Special education

CHILDREN WITH MENTAL DISABILITIES -- UNITED STATES -- BIOGRAPHY

Austin, P. Beautiful eyes   **92**

CHILDREN WITH PHYSICAL DISABILITIES

Palmer, S. Just one of the kids   **649**

CHILDREN WITH PHYSICAL DISABILITIES

See also Children with disabilities; People with physical disabilities

CHILDREN WITH SOCIAL DISABILITIES

Coles, R. Children of crisis   **305.23**

Kozol, J. Amazing grace   **362.7**

Kozol, J. Savage inequalities   **371.9**

CHILDREN WITH SOCIAL DISABILITIES

See also Children with disabilities; People with social disabilities

CHILDREN'S ALLOWANCES

See also Child rearing; Money; Personal finance

CHILDREN'S ART

See also Art

CHILDREN'S AUTHORS

Allende, I. My invented country   **863**

Allende, I. Paula   **92**

Allende, I. The sum of our days   **92**

Andersen, J. Hans Christian Andersen: a new life   **92**

Anderson, W. T. Laura Ingalls Wilder country   **92**

Andrews, J. Home   **92**

Angelou, M. Letter to my daughter   **92**

Angelou, M. I know why the caged bird sings   **92**

Angelou, M. A song flung up to heaven   **818**

Benfey, C. E. G. A summer of hummingbirds   **920**

Black women writers (1950-1980)   **810**

Cohen, M. N. Lewis Carroll   **92**

Conant, J. The irregulars   **940.54**

Danticat, E. Brother, I'm dying   **92**

Danticat, E. Create dangerously   **92**

Downing, D. C. Into the region of awe   **248.2**

Elledge, S. E. B. White   **92**

Eller, J. R. Becoming Ray Bradbury   **92**

Ellis, R. Tuna   **333.95**

Erdrich, L. Books and islands in Ojibwe country **92**

Feiffer, J. Backing into forward   **92**

Ford, P. F. Companion to Narnia   **823**

Garvey, M. Stylized   **808**

Gillespie, M. A. Maya Angelou   **92**

Gilmour, D. The long recessional: the imperial life of Rudyard Kipling   **92**

Gunn, J. E. Isaac Asimov   **813**

Hedrick, J. D. Harriet Beecher Stowe   **92**

Hooks, B. Belonging   **92**

Hooks, B. Wounds of passion   **92**

Jarrell, R. No other book   **809**

King, J. Farley: the life of Farley Mowat   **92**

Lear, L. J. Beatrix Potter **92**
Life stories **920**
Lindbergh, R. Under a wing **92**
Lively, P. A house unlocked **92**
Mayle, P. Encore Provence **944.083**
McPherson, J. M. Drawn with the sword **973.7**
Miller, L. The magician's book **823**
Morgan, J. Dr. Seuss & Mr. Geisel **92**
Mowat, F. Born naked **92**
Oates, J. C. A widow's story **92**
Oates, J. C. The journal of Joyce Carol Oates: 1973-1982 **92**
Parker, D. M. Ogden Nash **92**
Paulsen, G. Winterdance **798.8**
Rehak, M. Girl sleuth **813**
Reynolds, D. S. Mightier than the sword **813**
Ricketts, H. Rudyard Kipling **92**
Ross, C. The world of Edward Gorey **700.92**
Sanders, S. R. A private history of awe **92**
Seth, V. Two lives **92**
Singer, I. B. More stories from my father's court **839**
Small, D. Stitches **741.5**
Sturrock, D. Storyteller **92**
Tan, A. The opposite of fate **814**
Thursby, J. S. Critical companion to Maya Angelou **818**
Uhlberg, M. Hands of my father **92**
Weller, S. The Bradbury chronicles **92**
White, E. B. Letters of E.B. White **92**
Wilson, A. N. C.S. Lewis **823**
Wilson, E. Patriotic gore **810**
Wullschlager, J. Hans Christian Andersen **839.8**
The **children's** blizzard. Laskin, D. **977**
CHILDREN'S BOOKS *See* Children's literature
CHILDREN'S CLOTHING
Wilkes, L. Sew classic clothes for girls
Yaker, R. Little one-yard wonders **646.2**
CHILDREN'S LIBRARIES
Fiore, C. D. Fiore's summer library reading program handbook **027.62**
CHILDREN'S LIBRARIES
See also Libraries
CHILDREN'S LIBRARIES -- ACTIVITY PROGRAMS
Braafladt, K. Technology and literacy **027.62**
Brown, A. Let's start the music **027.62**
Del Negro, J. M. Folktales aloud **027.62**
Ghoting, S. N. STEP into storytime **027.62**
CHILDREN'S LIBRARIES -- ACTIVITY PROGRAMS -- UNITED STATES
Ghoting, S. N. STEP into storytime **027.62**
CHILDREN'S LIBRARIES -- COLLECTION DEVELOPMENT -- UNITED STATES
Naidoo, J. C. Rainbow family collections **028.1**
CHILDREN'S LIBRARIES -- SERVICES TO

MINORITIES -- UNITED STATES
Naidoo, J. C. Rainbow family collections **028.1**
CHILDREN'S LITERATURE
The Cambridge guide to children's books in English **028.5**
CHILDREN'S LITERATURE
See also Literature
CHILDREN'S LITERATURE -- CENSORSHIP -- UNITED STATES
Scales, P. R. Books under fire **016**
CHILDREN'S LITERATURE -- ENCYCLOPEDIAS
The Cambridge guide to children's books in English **028.5**
CHILDREN'S LITERATURE -- HISTORY AND CRITICISM
Miller, L. The magician's book **823**
CHILDREN'S LITERATURE -- TECHNIQUE
Aiken, J. The way to write for children **808.06**
Seuling, B. How to write a children's book and get it published **808.06**
Shulevitz, U. Writing with pictures **808.06**
CHILDREN'S PARAPHERNALIA
Yaker, R. Little one-yard wonders **646.2**
CHILDREN'S PARTIES
See also Amusements; Entertaining; Parties
Children's Picturebooks. Salisbury, M. **741**
CHILDREN'S RIGHTS ADVOCATES
Edelman, M. W. Lanterns **92**
CHILDREN'S SONGS
See also Children's poetry; School songbooks; Songs
CHILDREN'S STORIES
See also Children's literature; Fiction
CHILDREN'S STORIES -- AUTHORSHIP
Paterson, K. Stories of my life **92**
Children's writer's & illustrator's market. **808**
Childress, Alice, 1916 or 20-1994
About
Black women writers (1950-1980) **810**
Childs, Craig
Apocalyptic planet **550**
Finders keepers **930.1**
House of rain **978.9**
CHILE
Tobar, H. Deep down dark **363.11**
Chiles, James R.
The god machine **629.133**
Chilled. Jackson, T. **621.56**
Chilton, Bruce
(ed) The Cambridge companion to the Bible **220.9**
CHIMNEYS
See also Architecture -- Details; Buildings
CHIMPANZEES
Fouts, R. Next of kin **156**
Goodall, J. In the shadow of man **599.8**

Goodall, J. Through a window **599.8**
Halloran, A. R. The song of the ape **599.885**
CHIMPANZEES
    See also Apes
CHIMPANZEES -- BEHAVIOR
Waal, F. d. Bonobo **599.88**
Waal, F. d. Our inner ape **156**
Westoll, A. The chimps of Fauna Sanctuary **636.9**
CHIMPS *See* Chimpanzees
The **chimps** of Fauna Sanctuary. Westoll, A. **636.9**
China. Fairbank, J. K. **951**
CHINA
 Pomfret, J. Chinese lessons **951.05**
Spence, J. D. The Chan's great continent **951**
CHINA (REPUBLIC) *See* Taiwan
CHINA -- BIOGRAPHY
Chen, D. Sounds of the river **951.05**
Xinran China witness **920**
CHINA -- CHURCH HISTORY -- 20TH CENTURY
God is red **275.1**
CHINA -- CHURCH HISTORY -- 21ST CENTURY
God is red **275.1**
CHINA -- CIVILIZATION
Hessler, P. Oracle bones **951**
Osnos, E. Age of ambition **951.06**
Spence, J. D. The Chan's great continent **951**
CHINA -- CIVILIZATION -- ENCYCLOPEDIAS
Berkshire encyclopedia of China **951**
CHINA -- COMMERCE -- UNITED STATES
Dolin, E. J. When America first met China **382**
CHINA -- DESCRIPTION AND TRAVEL
Alford, J. Beyond the Great Wall **641.5**
August, O. Inside the red mansion **951.05**
Bergreen, L. Marco Polo **92**
Fallows, J. M. Postcards from Tomorrow Square **951.05**
Gargan, E. A. A river's tale **915**
Hessler, P. Country driving **303.4**
Hessler, P. Oracle bones **951**
Ma Jian Red dust **951.05**
Morris-Suzuki, T. To the Diamond Mountains **915**
Rose, D. A. Larry's kidney **915**
Rose, S. For all the tea in China **382**
Salzman, M. Iron & silk **951.05**
Sun Shuyun The Long March **951.04**
Theroux, P. Riding the iron rooster **915**
CHINA -- ECONOMIC CONDITIONS
Vogel, E. F. Deng Xiaoping and the transformation of China **951.05**
CHINA -- ECONOMIC CONDITIONS -- 1970-
Nolan, P. Is China buying the world? **332.67**
CHINA -- ECONOMIC CONDITIONS -- 2000-
Fallows, J. China airborne **387.7**
CHINA -- EMIGRATION AND IMMIGRATION

Keefe, P. R. The snakehead **364.1**
CHINA -- FOREIGN ECONOMIC RELATIONS
Dolin, E. J. When America first met China **382**
CHINA -- FOREIGN RELATIONS
Platt, S. R. Autumn in the Heavenly Kingdom **951**
CHINA -- FOREIGN RELATIONS -- HISTORY
Westad, O. A. Restless empire **327**
CHINA -- FOREIGN RELATIONS -- MYANMAR
Thant Myint-U Where China meets India **959.1**
CHINA -- FOREIGN RELATIONS -- UNITED STATES
Bernstein, R. China 1945 **327.73**
CHINA -- HISTORY
Dolin, E. J. When America first met China **382**
Ming **951**
CHINA -- HISTORY -- 1850-1864, TAIPING REBELLION
Platt, S. R. Autumn in the Heavenly Kingdom **951**
CHINA -- HISTORY -- 1861-1912
Jung Chang Empress Dowager Cixi **92**
Leibovitz, L. Fortunate sons **951.05**
CHINA -- HISTORY -- 1912-1949
Bernstein, R. China 1945 **327.73**
CHINA -- HISTORY -- 1949-
Chen, D. Colors of the mountain **92**
Chen, D. Sounds of the river **951.05**
Cheng, N. Life and death in Shanghai **92**
Li, C. N. The bitter sea **92**
Min, A. Red Azalea **92**
Pan, P. P. Out of Mao's shadow **951.05**
CHINA -- HISTORY -- 1949-1976
Dikötter, F. The Cultural Revolution **951.056**
Min, A. The Cooked Seed **92**
Palmer, J. Heaven cracks, earth shakes **951**
CHINA -- HISTORY -- 1976-
Fallows, J. China airborne **387.7**
CHINA -- HISTORY -- 19TH CENTURY
Jung Chang Empress Dowager Cixi **92**
CHINA -- HISTORY -- CULTURAL REVOLUTION, 1966-1976 -- PERSONAL NARRATIVES
Chen, D. Sounds of the river **951.05**
Ping Fu Bend, not break **92**
Xinran China witness **920**
CHINA -- HISTORY -- REFORM MOVEMENT, 1898
Leibovitz, L. Fortunate sons **951.05**
CHINA -- HISTORY -- REPUBLIC, 1912-1949
Bernstein, R. China 1945 **327.73**
Pakula, H. The last empress **92**
CHINA -- HISTORY -- TIANANMEN SQUARE INCIDENT, 1989
Prisoner of the state **92**
CHINA -- HISTORY -- TIANANMEN SQUARE INCIDENT, 1989 -- POETRY

Liu, X.   June fourth elegies **811**

CHINA -- POLITICS AND GOVERNMENT
Levine, S. I. Mao **951.05**
Osnos, E. Age of ambition **951.06**
Schell, O. Wealth and power **951**
Vogel, E. F. Deng Xiaoping and the transformation of China **951.05**

CHINA -- POLITICS AND GOVERNMENT -- 1976-2002
Prisoner of the state **92**

CHINA -- POLITICS AND GOVERNMENT -- 2002-
Martin, B. Hanging man **709**

CHINA -- POLITICS AND GOVERNMENT -- 20TH CENTURY
Chang, J. Mao: the unknown story **92**
Schell, O. Wealth and power **951**

CHINA -- SOCIAL CONDITIONS
Osnos, E. Age of ambition **951.06**
Schell, O. Wealth and power **951**

CHINA -- SOCIAL CONDITIONS -- 2000-
Martin, B. Hanging man **709**
Pan, P. P. Out of Mao's shadow **951.05**
Pomfret, J. Chinese lessons **951.05**

CHINA -- SOCIAL LIFE AND CUSTOMS
Phoenix claws and jade trees **641.595**

CHINA -- SOCIAL LIFE AND CUSTOMS -- EN-CYCLOPEDIAS
Berkshire encyclopedia of China **951**
China 1945. Bernstein, R. **327.73**
China airborne. Fallows, J. **387.7**
The **China** collectors. Brysac, S. B. **709.5**
China ghosts. Gammage, J. **362.7**
China men. Kingston, M. H. **920**

CHINA PAINTING
See also Decoration and ornament; Painting; Porcelain
China witness. Xinran **920**
Chinaberry sidewalks. Crowell, R. **92**

CHINATOWN (NEW YORK, NY) -- HISTORY -- 20TH CENTURY
Seligman, S. D. Tong wars **364.106**
The **Chinese.** Becker, J. **951.05**

CHINESE -- UNITED STATES -- BIOGRAPHY
Min, A. The Cooked Seed **92**

CHINESE AMERICAN CRIMINALS -- NEW YORK (STATE) -- NEW YORK--HISTORY--20TH CENTURY
Seligman, S. D. Tong wars **364.106**

CHINESE AMERICAN FAMILIES
Chua, A. Battle hymn of the tiger mother **306.874**

CHINESE AMERICAN WOMEN -- BIOGRA-PHY
Ping Fu Bend, not break **92**

CHINESE AMERICANS -- BIOGRAPHY
Kingston, M. H. China men **920**

Shen, A. J. A tiger's heart **92**

CHINESE AMERICANS -- CALIFORNIA -- BI-OGRAPHY
Kingston, M. H. The woman warrior **92**
Mah, A. Y. Falling leaves **305.48**
Chinese art. Tregear, M. **709**

CHINESE ART
Brysac, S. B. The China collectors **709.5**
Hearn, M. K. Splendors of Imperial China **709**
Tregear, M. Chinese art **709**

CHINESE CANADIANS
See also Canadians; Immigrants -- Canada

CHINESE COOKING
Alford, J. Beyond the Great Wall **641.5**
Dunlop, F. Every grain of rice **641.59**
Dunlop, F. Land of fish and rice **641.5**
Li, L. Daughter of heaven **92**
Mastering the art of Chinese cooking **641.59**
Phillips, C. All under heaven **641.5**
Phoenix claws and jade trees **641.595**
Ying, C. The Mission Chinese Food Cook-book **641.595**

CHINESE COOKING
See also Cooking

CHINESE ETHICS
Confucius The Analects **181**

CHINESE LANGUAGE
See also Language and languages

CHINESE LANGUAGE -- DICTIONARIES
Cheng & Tsui English-Chinese lexicon of business terms with pinyin **495.1**
Chinese lessons. Pomfret, J. **951.05**

CHINESE LITERATURE
See also Literature

CHINESE LITERATURE -- COLLECTIONS
An Anthology of Chinese literature **895.1**

CHINESE LITERATURE -- HISTORY AND CRITICISM
The Columbia history of Chinese literature **895.1**

CHINESE PHILOSOPHY
Confucius The Analects **181**

CHINESE POETRY
See also Chinese literature; Poetry

CHINESE POETRY -- COLLECTIONS
Liu, X. June fourth elegies **811**

CHINESE STUDENTS -- UNITED STATES -- HISTORY
Leibovitz, L. Fortunate sons **951.05**
Ching, Francis D. K.
(jt. auth) Jarzombek, M. A global history of archi-tecture **720.9**

CHIPMUNKS
See also Mammals; Squirrels
Chirac, Jacques, 1932-
                    About
Chirac, J. My life in politics **944.084**

CHIROPRACTIC

See also Alternative medicine; Massage

Chitnis, Christine

Little bites   641.5

Chittister, Joan

Between the Dark and the Daylight   128

Following the path   248.4

The gift of years   200

Chittum, Ryan

(ed) The best business writing 2013   330.9

Chitty, A. B.

Murolo, P. From the folks who brought you the weekend   331

CHIVALRY

Bulfinch, T. Bulfinch's mythology   398.2

CHIVALRY

See also Manners and customs

CHIVALRY -- ROMANCES See Romances

Chivian, Eric

(ed) Sustaining life   333.95

CHOCOLATE

Almond, S. Candyfreak: a journey through the chocolate underbelly of America   338.4

Brenner, J. G. The emperors of chocolate   338.7

Guittard Chocolate cookbook   641.6

Rosenblum, M. Chocolate: a bittersweet saga of dark and light   641.3

Theo Chocolate   641.6

CHOCOLATE

See also Food

CHOCOLATE DESSERTS

Higgins, K. Chocolate-covered Katie   641.6

Theo Chocolate   641.6

Chocolate-covered Katie. Higgins, K.   641.6

Chocolate: a bittersweet saga of dark and light. Rosenblum, M.   641.3

Chödrön, Pema

How to meditate   294.3

CHOICE (PSYCHOLOGY)

Glasser, W. Choice theory   150

Iyengar, S. The art of choosing   153.8

McKeown, G. Essentialism   153.8

Vanderbilt, T. You may also like   153.8

CHOICE (PSYCHOLOGY)

See also Psychology

CHOICE OF BOOKS See Best books; Book selection; Books and reading

CHOICE OF COLLEGE See College choice

CHOICE OF PROFESSION, OCCUPATION, VOCATION, ETC. See Vocational guidance

CHOICE OF SCHOOL See School choice

Choice theory. Glasser, W.   150

CHOICE, FREEDOM OF See Free will and determinism

Choke. Beilock, S. L.   153.9

CHOLERA

Johnson, S. The ghost map   614.5

CHOOSE-YOUR-OWN STORY PLOTS See Plot-your-own stories

Choosing hope. Fisher, R. G.   371.7

Choosing raw. Hamshaw, G.   641.3

Chopin's funeral. Eisler, B.   92

Chopin, Frédéric, 1810-1849

About

Eisler, B. Chopin's funeral   92

Schonberg, H. C. The great pianists   920

Chopra, Deepak, 1946-

(jt. auth) Tanzi, R. E. Super genes   613

Choral masterworks. Steinberg, M.   782.5

CHORAL MUSIC

Steinberg, M. Choral masterworks   782.5

CHORAL SPEAKING

See also Drama; Recitations

CHOREOGRAPHERS

Brown, C. Chance and circumstance   92

Gates, H. L. Thirteen ways of looking at a black man   920.71

Gottlieb, R. A. George Balanchine: the ballet maker   92

Hischak, T. The Oxford companion to the American musical   792.6

Jones, B. T. Story/Time   814

Life stories   920

Streb, E. Streb   92

Teachout, T. All in the dances: a brief life of George Balanchine   92

Vaill, A. Somewhere   92

Volkov, S. St. Petersburg   947

Ware, S. Letter to the world   920.72

Wasson, S. Fosse   92

CHOREOGRAPHERS -- UNITED STATES -- BIOGRAPHY

Wasson, S. Fosse   92

Chorin, Ethan

Exit the colonel   961.204

Chosen by a horse. Richards, S.   636.1

Chowdhury, Bernie

The last dive   363.14

Chown, Marcus

Solar system   523.2

Chretien, Jean-Pierre

The great lakes of Africa   967.6

Christ-Janer, Albert

American hymns old and new   782.27

Christakis, Erika

The Importance of Being Little   372.21

Christensen, Jo Ippolito

The needlepoint book   746.44

Christensen, Kate, 1962-

How to cook a moose   641.597

About

Christensen, K. Blue plate special   92

Christensen, Michael J.
(jt. auth) Nouwen, H. Discernment   248.4
Christgau, Robert
About
Christgau, R. Going Into the City   92
CHRISTIAN BIOGRAPHY
Hamilton, D. For the Glory   92
CHRISTIAN BIOGRAPHY
See also Biography; Religious biography
CHRISTIAN BIOGRAPHY -- UNITED STATES
Lamott, A. Small victories   248
Miller, D. Blue like jazz   92
Zierman, A. When we were on fire   92
CHRISTIAN CIVILIZATION
See also Christianity; Civilization
CHRISTIAN COALITION (ORGANIZATION)
Martin, W. C. With God on our side   261.8
CHRISTIAN CONSERVATISM -- UNITED STATES
Christian reconstruction   230
CHRISTIAN CONVERTS FROM JUDAISM -- UNITED STATES -- BIOGRAPHY
Santamaria, A. Joy   92
CHRISTIAN DOCTRINAL THEOLOGY *See* Christianity -- Doctrines
CHRISTIAN DOCTRINE *See* Christianity -- Doctrines
CHRISTIAN ETHICS
Kim, J. Under the same sky   92
Nouwen, H. Discernment   248.4
Price, R. A serious way of wondering   241
CHRISTIAN ETHICS
See also Ethics
CHRISTIAN ETHICS -- CHINA
Kim, J. Under the same sky   92
CHRISTIAN FICTION
Michaels, J. R. Passing by the dragon   813
CHRISTIAN FICTION
See also Fiction; Religious fiction
CHRISTIAN FICTION, AMERICAN -- CRITICISM AND INTERPRETATION
Michaels, J. R. Passing by the dragon   813
CHRISTIAN FUNDAMENTALISM
Armstrong, K. The battle for God   200.9
Brower, S. Prophet's prey   306.8
Martin, W. C. With God on our side   261.8
Shorris, E. The politics of heaven   973.93
CHRISTIAN FUNDAMENTALISM
See also Christianity -- Doctrines; Religious fundamentalism
CHRISTIAN GAYS -- UNITED STATES
Chu, J. Does Jesus Really Love Me?   261.8
CHRISTIAN HERESIES
Magill, R. J. Sincerity   179
CHRISTIAN HERESIES
See also Doctrinal theology; Heresy

CHRISTIAN HOLIDAYS
See also Church year; Religious holidays
CHRISTIAN LIFE
Armstrong, K. The case for God   211
Boyle, G. J. Tattoos on the heart   277
Carter, J. Sources of strength   248.4
Davis, W. Enough   241
Evans, R. H. Searching for Sunday   248
Girzone, J. F. Never alone   248.4
Girzone, J. F. A portrait of Jesus   232.9
Heim, T. @stickyjesus   248.4
John Paul Crossing the threshold of hope   282
Lewis, C. S. Letters to Malcolm: chiefly on prayer   248
Lewis, C. S. The Screwtape letters   248
Lucado, M. Before amen   248.3
Made for goodness   170
Martin, J. The Jesuit guide to almost everything   248.4
Mathewes-Green, F. Welcome to the Orthodox Church   281.9
Meyer, J. Seize the day   248.4
Miller, D. Blue like jazz   92
Nouwen, H. Discernment   248.4
Riess, J. Flunking sainthood   248.4
Winner, L. F. Wearing God   231.7
Zierman, A. When we were on fire   92
CHRISTIAN LIFE
See also Religious life
CHRISTIAN LIFE -- MEDITATIONS
Heim, T. @stickyjesus   248.4
CHRISTIAN LIFE -- SERMONS
See also Sermons
CHRISTIAN LITERATURE
McGrath, A. E. C. S. Lewis   92
CHRISTIAN MARTYRS -- ENGLAND -- BIOGRAPHY
Thomas Becket   92
CHRISTIAN MISSIONARIES
Spink, K. Mother Teresa   92
CHRISTIAN MISSIONARIES -- HISTORY
Platt, S. R. Autumn in the Heavenly Kingdom   951
CHRISTIAN MISSIONS
See also Christianity; Church history; Church work
CHRISTIAN MORAL THEOLOGY *See* Christian ethics
CHRISTIAN NAMES *See* Personal names
CHRISTIAN PHILOSOPHY
Lewis, C. S. Mere Christianity   230
Teilhard de Chardin, P. The divine milieu   230
CHRISTIAN PHILOSOPHY
See also Philosophy
CHRISTIAN PILGRIMS AND PILGRIMAGES -- ISRAEL
Rodríguez, R. Darling   92

CHRISTIAN POETRY, ENGLISH -- EARLY MODERN, 1500-1700.
Herbert, G. Herbert: poems   821
Christian reconstruction.   230
CHRISTIAN SAINTS
Gordon, M. Joan of Arc   944
Hendey, L. M. A book of saints for Catholic moms   248.8
Martin, J. My life with the saints   920
Pernoud, R. Joan of Arc: her story   92
Thomas Becket   92
Woodward, K. L. Making saints   235
CHRISTIAN SAINTS
See also Saints
CHRISTIAN SAINTS -- BIOGRAPHY
Barthel, J. American saint   92
CHRISTIAN SAINTS -- BIOGRAPHY -- HISTORY AND CRITICISM
McCarthy, D. M. Sharing God's Good Company   235
CHRISTIAN SAINTS -- DICTIONARIES
Attwater, D. The Penguin dictionary of saints   920.003
Butler's Lives of the saints   920.003
Farmer, D. H. The Oxford dictionary of saints   920.003
Guiley, R. E. The encyclopedia of saints   282
CHRISTIAN SAINTS -- ENGLAND -- BIOGRAPHY
Thomas Becket   92
CHRISTIAN SAINTS -- PRAYERS AND DEVOTIONS
Hendey, L. M. A book of saints for Catholic moms   248.8
CHRISTIAN SAINTS -- UNITED STATES -- BIOGRAPHY
Barthel, J. American saint   92
CHRISTIAN SCIENCE
Eddy, M. B. Science and health, with key to the Scriptures   289.5
Schoepflin, R. B. Christian Science on trial   289.5
Christian Science on trial. Schoepflin, R. B.   289.5
CHRISTIAN SECTS
See also Christianity; Church history; Sects
CHRISTIAN SOCIOLOGY
Buttiglione, R. Karol Wojtyla   282
Chaves, M. Ordaining women   262
CHRISTIAN SOCIOLOGY
See also Religion and sociology; Sociology
CHRISTIAN SYMBOLISM
See also Symbolism
CHRISTIAN UNION
See also Christian sects; Church
CHRISTIAN WOMEN -- RELIGIOUS LIFE
Winner, L. F. Wearing God   231.7
CHRISTIAN WOMEN SAINTS -- FRANCE --

BIOGRAPHY
Castor, H. Joan of Arc   92
Gordon, M. Joan of Arc   944
Christian, Brian
The most human human   128
Christian, Fletcher, 1764-1793
About
Alexander, C. The Bounty: the true story of the mutiny on the Bounty   996
Christian, Nicole
(ed) Reference guide to Russian literature   891.7
CHRISTIAN-OWNED BUSINESS ENTERPRISES
See also Business enterprises
Christianity. MacCulloch, D.   270
CHRISTIANITY
See also Religions
CHRISTIANITY
Armstrong, K. A history of God   200
Bolz-Weber, N. Accidental saints   284.1
Chu, J. Does Jesus Really Love Me?   261.8
Edman, E. M. Queer virtue   230
Ferry, L. A brief history of thought   100
Francis, P. Walking with Jesus   282
Gordon-Reed, A. Most Blessed of the Patriarchs   92
Jenkins, P. The new faces of Christianity   270
Moore, R. Onward   230
Pagels, E. H. Beyond belief   229
Tickle, P. The great emergence   270
Voices of early Christianity   270.1
CHRISTIANITY -- 21ST CENTURY
Bass, D. B. Grounded   231
CHRISTIANITY -- APOLOGETIC WORKS
See also Apologetics
CHRISTIANITY -- BIOGRAPHY See Christian biography
CHRISTIANITY -- CHINA
God is red   275.1
CHRISTIANITY -- DICTIONARIES
Zondervan dictionary of Christian spirituality   248
CHRISTIANITY -- DOCTRINES
Billings, J. T. Rejoicing in lament   248.8
CHRISTIANITY -- DOCTRINES
See also Doctrinal theology
CHRISTIANITY -- ECONOMIC ASPECTS -- UNITED STATES -- HISTORY
Lehmann, C. The money cult   261.8
CHRISTIANITY -- ENCYCLOPEDIAS
The Bloomsbury Guide to Christian Spirituality   270
CHRISTIANITY -- SPIRITUAL LIFE
Bass, D. B. Grounded   231
Lamott, A. Small victories   248
CHRISTIANITY -- UNITED STATES
Berlinerblau, J. How to be secular   211
Wacker, G. America's pastor   92

Yancey, P. Vanishing grace   277

CHRISTIANITY -- UNITED STATES -- HISTORY
Lehmann, C. The money cult   **261.8**

CHRISTIANITY AND OTHER RELIGIONS
Asbridge, T. The crusades   **909.07**
Crowley, R. Empires of the sea   **359**
Griswold, E. The tenth parallel   **297**
Karabell, Z. Peace be upon you   **201**
Saldana, S. The bread of angels   **92**
Three Testaments   **208**

CHRISTIANITY AND OTHER RELIGIONS
See also Religions

CHRISTIANITY AND OTHER RELIGIONS -- ISLAM
Crowley, R. Empires of the sea   **359**
Griswold, E. The tenth parallel   **297**
Saldana, S. The bread of angels   **92**

CHRISTIANITY AND OTHER RELIGIONS -- ISLAM -- HISTORY -- TO 1500
Cobb, P. M. The race for paradise   **909.07**

CHRISTIANITY AND POLITICS
Kimball, C. When religion becomes lethal   **201**
Martin, W. C. With God on our side   **261.8**
Shorris, E. The politics of heaven   **973.93**
Thomas Becket   **92**

CHRISTIANITY AND POLITICS
See also Church and state; Religion and politics

CHRISTIANITY AND POLITICS -- EVANGELICALISM
Dochuk, D. From Bible belt to sunbelt   **277**

CHRISTIANITY AND POLITICS -- UNITED STATES
Kruse, K. M. One nation under God   **322**

CHRISTIANITY AND SCIENCE
See also Christianity; Religion and science

CHRISTIANS
Cliff, N. Holy war   **909**
Zierman, A. When we were on fire   **92**

CHRISTIANS -- BIOGRAPHY *See* Christian biography

CHRISTIANS -- PERSECUTIONS
See also Church history; Persecution

Christiansen, Keith
(ed) The Renaissance portrait   **704.9**

Christie, Agatha
The mousetrap and other plays   **822**

Christie, Chris
About
Russakoff, D. The prize   **371.2**

Christina Rossetti. Rossetti, C. G.   **821**

Christine, de Pisan, ca. 1364-ca. 1431
About
Ulrich, L. Well-behaved women seldom make history   **305.4**

Christmas. Forbes, B. D.   **394.26**

CHRISTMAS
Brown, S. Glitterville's handmade christmas   **745.594**
Forbes, B. D. Christmas   **394.26**
Weintraub, S. A Christmas far from home **951.904**

CHRISTMAS
See also Christian holidays; Holidays

CHRISTMAS -- KOREA (NORTH) -- HISTORY -- 20TH CENTURY
Weintraub, S. A Christmas far from home **951.904**

CHRISTMAS -- POETRY
Christmas poems   **821**

CHRISTMAS -- WALES
Thomas, D. A child's Christmas in Wales   **828**

A **Christmas** far from home. Weintraub, S. **951.904**

CHRISTMAS MUSIC
See also Music

Christmas poems.   **821**

CHRISTMAS TREES
Brown, C. The new Christmas tree   **745.594**

CHRISTMAS TREES
See also Christmas decorations; Trees

Christopher Marlowe. Honan, P.   **92**

Christopher, Thomas
Essential perennials   **635.9**
Garden revolution   **577**

CHROMOSOME ABNORMALITIES
See also Chromosomes; Variation (Biology)

CHROMOSOMES
Sykes, B. Adam's curse   **599.93**
Sykes, B. DNA USA   **559.9**
Wapner, J. The Philadelphia chromosome   **616.99**

CHROMOSOMES
See also Genetics; Heredity

CHRONIC DISEASES
Bland, J. S. The disease delusion   **615.5**
Horowitz, R. I. Why can't I get better?   **616.9**
Snyder, R. d. 1. What you must know about dialysis   **617.4**
Steinhart, A. H. Crohn's & colitis diet guide **616.3**

CHRONIC DISEASES
See also Diseases

CHRONIC FATIGUE SYNDROME
Murphree, R. H. Treating and beating fibromyalgia and chronic fatigue syndrome   **616**

CHRONIC FATIGUE SYNDROME
See also Diseases

CHRONIC PAIN
Bacci, I. Effortless pain relief   **616**
Kaplan, G. Total recovery   **616**
Parks, T. Teach us to sit still   **616**

CHRONIC PAIN
See also Chronic diseases; Pain

CHRONIC PAIN -- COMPLICATIONS
Kaplan, G. Total recovery   **616**

CHRONICLE HISTORY (DRAMA) *See* Historical drama

The **chronicle** of jazz. Cooke, M.   **781.65**

The **Chronicle** of the Lodz ghetto, 1941-1944. **943.8**

Chronicle of the popes. Maxwell-Stuart, P. G. **282**

Chronicle of the Russian tsars. Warnes, D.   **947**

CHRONICLE PLAYS *See* Historical drama

Chronicles. Dylan, B.   **92**

Chronicles of old los angeles. Roman, J.

CHRONOLOGY

    See also Astronomy; History; Time

The **Chronology** of American literature.   **810**

Chronology of the U.S. presidency.   **973.09**

CHRONOLOGY, HISTORICAL *See* Historical chronology

CHRONOMETERS *See* Clocks and watches

CHRYSLER CORP.

    Vlasic, B. Once upon a car   **338.4**

Chu, Jeff, 1977-

        About

    Chu, J. Does Jesus Really Love Me? **261.8**

Chua, Amy, 1962-

        About

    Chua, A. Battle hymn of the tiger mother **306.874**

Chua-Eoan, Howard

    (jt. auth) Hargrove, J. Beneath the surface **599.53**

Chuck Close. Finch, C.   **92**

Chudnovsky, D. (David), 1947-

        About

    Life stories   **920**

Chudnovsky, G. (Gregory), 1952-

        About

    Life stories   **920**

Chura, David

    I don't wish nobody to have a life like mine **371.9**

CHURCH

    McKnight, S. Kingdom conspiracy   **231.7**

    Pattison, J. Slow church   **253**

CHURCH AND STATE

    Greenawalt, K.   Does God belong in public
        schools?   **379**

    Wexler, J. Holy hullabaloos   **342**

CHURCH AND STATE

    See also Church; State, The

**CHURCH AND STATE -- GREAT BRITAIN --
    HISTORY -- 16TH CENTURY**

    Fletcher, C. The divorce of Henry VIII   **942.05**

CHURCH AND STATE -- ITALY -- HISTORY

    Kertzer, D. I. The Pope and Mussolini   **322**

CHURCH AND STATE -- UNITED STATES

    Kruse, K. M. One nation under God   **322**

CHURCH BUILDINGS

    King, R. Brunelleschi's dome   **726**

CHURCH BUILDINGS

    See also Buildings

CHURCH DENOMINATIONS *See* Christian
sects; Sects

CHURCH ENTERTAINMENTS

    See also Amusements; Church work

CHURCH FESTIVALS *See* Religious holidays

CHURCH FINANCE

    Posner, G. God's Bankers   **364.16**

CHURCH FINANCE

    See also Finance

CHURCH FURNITURE

    See also Furniture

CHURCH HISTORY

    Kung, H. Great Christian thinkers   **230**

    MacCulloch, D. Christianity   **270**

    Stark, R. For the glory of God   **201**

CHURCH HISTORY

    See also History

**CHURCH HISTORY -- 600-1500, MIDDLE
    AGES**

    Asbridge, T. The crusades   **909.07**

    Phillips, J. Holy warriors   **909.07**

    Tuchman, B. W. A distant mirror   **944**

**CHURCH HISTORY -- 600-1500, MIDDLE
    AGES**

    See also Middle Ages

**CHURCH HISTORY -- PRIMITIVE AND EAR-
    LY CHURCH, CA. 30-600**

    Brown, P. Through the eye of a needle   **270.2**

    Gubar, S. Judas   **92**

**CHURCH HISTORY -- PRIMITIVE AND EAR-
    LY CHURCH, CA. 30-600 -- SOURCES**

    Voices of early Christianity   **270.1**

**CHURCH OF JESUS CHRIST OF LATTER-
    DAY SAINTS**

    Book of Mormon The Book of Mormon   **289.3**

    Brower, S. Prophet's prey   **306.8**

    Bushman, R. L. Joseph Smith and the beginnings
        of Mormonism   **289.3**

    Bushman, R. L. Mormonism   **289.3**

**CHURCH OF JESUS CHRIST OF LATTER-
    DAY SAINTS -- HISTORY**

    Beam, A. American crucifixion   **289.3**

    Brown, S. M. In heaven as it is on earth **236**

    Gutjahr, P. C. The Book of Mormon   **289.3**

**CHURCH OF JESUS CHRIST OF LATTER-DAY
    SAINTS -- PRESIDENTS -- BIOGRAPHY**

    Turner, J. G. Brigham Young, pioneer proph-
        et   **289.3**

The **church** of mercy. Francis, P.   **282**

CHURCH POLITY

    See also Church

CHURCH RENEWAL

    See also Church

CHURCH WORK

    Boyle, G. J. Tattoos on the heart   **277**

    McKnight, S. Kingdom conspiracy   **231.7**

CHURCH WORK

See also Church

CHURCH WORK WITH THE SICK

See also Church work; Sick

CHURCH WORK WITH THE TERMINALLY ILL

Egan, K. On living   **170.44**

CHURCH WORK WITH YOUTH

See also Church work; Youth

CHURCH YEAR

See also Calendars; Religious holidays; Worship

CHURCHES *See* Church buildings; Religious institutions

Churchill. Johnson, P.   **92**

Churchill family

About

Maier, T. When lions roar   **941.084**

Churchill's empire. Toye, R.   **92**

Churchill, Caryl

Mad forest   **822**

Churchill, Winston, 1874-1965

Closing the ring   **940.53**

The gathering storm   **940.53**

The grand alliance   **940.53**

The great republic   **973**

The hinge of fate   **940.53**

Their finest hour   **940.53**

Triumph and tragedy   **940.53**

About

Clarke, P. Mr. Churchill's profession   **941.084**

Dobbs, M. Six months in 1945   **940.53**

Hamilton, N. Commander in chief   **940.53**

Lukacs, J. Five days in London, May 1940 **940.53**

Maier, T. When lions roar   **941.084**

Manchester, W. The last lion, Winston Spencer Churchill   **92**

Millard, C. Hero of the empire   **968.04**

Churchill, Winston, S.

(ed) Churchill, W. The great republic   **973**

Churchland, Patricia S.

Braintrust   **612.8**

The **CIA** at war. Kessler, R.   **973.931**

The **CIA** World Factbook.   **028**

Cialdini, Robert B.

Influence: the psychology of persuasion   **153.8**

Cianciotto, Jason

(jt. auth) Cahill, S. LGBT youth in America's schools   **371.82**

Ciardi, John

The collected poems of John Ciardi   **811**

Cicero. Everitt, A.   **92**

Cicero, Marcus Tullius, 106-43 B.C.

On the good life   **878**

Political speeches   **875**

The republic; and, The laws   **320.1**

About

Everitt, A. Cicero   **92**

Cid

The poem of the Cid   **861**

Cider. Proulx, A.   **641.2**

CIDER

Proulx, A. Cider   **641.2**

Ciezadlo, Annia

About

Ciezadlo, A. Day of honey   **92**

Cifelli, Edward M.

(ed) Ciardi, J. The collected poems of John Ciardi   **811**

CIGARETTES

Proctor, R. N. Golden holocaust   **362.29**

Cikovsky, Nicolai

Winslow Homer   **759.13**

Ciment, James

(ed) Encyclopedia of conflicts since World War II   **909.82**

(ed) Postwar America   **973.92**

CINCO DE MAYO (HOLIDAY)

See also Holidays

Cinderella ate my daughter. Orenstein, P.   **305.23**

Cinderella Man. Schaap, J.   **92**

CINEMA *See* Motion pictures

CINEMAS *See* Motion picture theaters

CINEMATOGRAPHY

Ascher, S. The filmmaker's handbook   **777**

Harryhausen, R. The art of Ray Harryhausen **778.5**

Thomson, D. How to watch a movie   **791.43**

CINEMATOGRAPHY

See also Photography

CINEMATOGRAPHY -- HANDBOOKS, MANUALS, ETC

Ascher, S. The filmmaker's handbook   **777**

CINNAMON

Aftel, M. Fragrant   **612.8**

Cinque, 1811?-1879

About

Abdul-Jabbar, K. Black profiles in courage   **920**

CIPHER AND TELEGRAPH CODES

See also Ciphers; Telegraph

CIPHERS

Fox, M. The Riddle of the Labyrinth   **487**

Tobin, J. Hidden in plain view   **973.7**

CIPHERS

See also Signs and symbols

CIRCLE

See also Geometry; Shape

A **circle** of sisters. Flanders, J.   **920**

Circling faith.   **200.8**

Circling the Square. Steavenson, W.   **962.05**

Circular knitting workshop.   **746.43**

CIRCULATION OF LIBRARY MATERIALS

See Library circulation

Circumcision. Gollaher, D.   **392**

CIRCUMCISION
Gollaher, D. Circumcision   392
Circumference. Nicastro, N.   526
CIRCUMNAVIGATION *See* Voyages around the world
CIRCUS
Bradley, C. Last chain on Billie   639.97
Daly, M. Topsy   791.3
Jensen, D. Queen of the air   791.3
Macy, B. Truevine   791.3
CIRCUS
    See also Amusements
CIRCUS -- HISTORY
Wall, D. The ordinary acrobat   796.47
CIRCUS ANIMALS -- UNITED STATES -- AN-ECDOTES
Bradley, C. Last chain on Billie   639.97
CIRCUS EXECUTIVES
Carter, R. A. Buffalo Bill Cody   978
Saxon, A. H. P. T. Barnum: the legend and the man   338.7
Warren, L. S. Buffalo Bill's America   92
Ciribassi, John
(ed) Decoding Your Dog   636.7
CITIES AND TOWNS
The atlas of cities   912
Green, H. The company town   307.7
Mumford, L. The culture of cities   307.7
Winkless, L. Science and the City   307.76
CITIES AND TOWNS
    See also Sociology
CITIES AND TOWNS -- CASE STUDIES
Hunt, T. Cities of empire   941
CITIES AND TOWNS -- CIVIC IMPROVE-MENT
Wilson, D. S. The neighborhood project   307.7
CITIES AND TOWNS -- GROWTH
Saunders, D. Arrival city   307.24
CITIES AND TOWNS -- GROWTH
    See also Internal migration; Population
CITIES AND TOWNS -- HISTORY
Royal cities of the ancient Maya   972.81
Smith, P. D. City   307.76
CITIES AND TOWNS -- HISTORY
Mumford, L. The city in history   307.7
Smith, P. D. City   307.76
CITIES AND TOWNS -- MICHIGAN -- DE-TROIT
Binelli, M. Detroit City is the place to be   307.1
CITIES AND TOWNS -- PLANNING *See* City planning
CITIES AND TOWNS -- UNITED STATES
Rybczynski, W. Mysteries of the mall   720
The who, what, and where of America   317.3
CITIES AND TOWNS -- UNITED STATES -- STATISTICS

The who, what, and where of America   317.3
CITIES AND TOWNS, MOVEMENT TO *See* Cities and towns -- Growth; Urbanization
Cities of empire. Hunt, T.   941
Citizen. Rankine, C.   811
Citizen canine. Burch, M. R.   636.7
Citizen Coke. Elmore, B. J.   338.7
Citizen farmers.   635
Citizen Moore. Rapoport, R.   92
Citizen Sherman. Fellman, M.   92
Citizen soldier. Donald, A. D.   92
Citizen soldiers. Ambrose, S. E.   940.54
Citizens of London. Olson, L.   940.54
CITIZENS UNITED -- TRIALS, LITIGATION, ETC
Vogel, K. P. Big money   324.7
CITIZENSHIP
    See also Constitutional law; Political ethics; Political science
Citrin, James M.
The career playbook   650.14
Citro, Asia
150+ screen-free activities for kids   796.5
Citron, Danielle Keats
Hate crimes in cyberspace   364.15
CITRUS FRUITS
    See also Fruit
City. Smith, P. D.   307.76
CITY AND TOWN LIFE
Bambrick, Y. The urban cycling survival guide   796.6
Hunt, T. Cities of empire   941
Kidder, T. Home town   974.4
Mumford, L. The city in history   307.7
Taylor, B. Naples declared   945
Valby, K. Welcome to Utopia   976.4
CITY AND TOWN LIFE
    See also Cities and towns; Urban sociology
CITY AND TOWN LIFE -- BRAZIL -- RIO DE JANEIRO
Barbassa, J. Dancing With the Devil in the City of God   981.53
CITY AND TOWN LIFE -- CALIFORNIA -- SAN FRANCISCO -- HISTORY -- 20TH CENTU-RY
Talbot, D. Season of the witch   306
CITY AND TOWN LIFE -- CHINA -- SHANG-HAI
Schmitz, R. Street of Eternal Happiness   951.132
CITY AND TOWN LIFE -- FRANCE -- PARIS -- HISTORY
Sante, L. The other Paris   944
CITY AND TOWN LIFE -- HISTORY
Smith, P. D. City   307.76
CITY AND TOWN LIFE -- ITALY -- NAPLES
Taylor, B. Naples declared   945

CITY AND TOWN LIFE -- NEW YORK (STATE) -- NEW YORK

Anasi, R. The last bohemia   **974.7**

CITY AND TOWN LIFE -- NEW YORK (STATE) -- NEW YORK -- HISOTRY -- 21ST CENTURY -- PICTORIAL WORKS

Stanton, B. Humans of New York   **974.7**

City boy. White, E.   **92**

The **city** in history. Mumford, L.   **307.7**

CITY LIFE *See* City and town life

CITY LIFE -- HISTORY

Smith, P. D. City   **307.76**

City lights open media [series]

Miller, T. Border patrol nation   **363.28**

City lights pocket poets anthology.   **808.81**

City lights/sister spit [series]

McBee, T. P. Man alive   **92**

The **city** of Akhenaten and Nefertiti. Kemp, B. **930**

City of Dreams. Anbinder, T.   **974.71**

The **city** of falling angels. Berendt, J.   **945**

City of fortune. Crowley, R.   **945**

City of gold. Krane, J.   **953**

The **City** of Joy. Lapierre, D.   **954**

City of oranges. LeBor, A.   **956.94**

City of the century. Miller, D. L.   **977.3**

City of thorns. Rawlence, B.   **967.73**

CITY PLANNERS -- CANADA -- BIOGRAPHY

Kanigel, R. Eyes on the street   **92**

CITY PLANNING

Duany, A. Suburban nation   **307.76**

Kanigel, R. Eyes on the street   **92**

Mumford, L. The culture of cities   **307.7**

CITY PLANNING

See also Cities and towns -- Civic improvement; Planning

CITY PLANNING -- MICHIGAN -- DETROIT

Binelli, M. Detroit City is the place to be   **307.1**

CITY PLANNING -- ROME

McGregor, J. H. Rome from the ground up   **711**

City room. Gelb, A.   **92**

CITY SCHOOLS *See* Urban schools

CITY TRAFFIC

Vanderbilt, T. Traffic   **629.28**

CIUDAD JUAREZ (MEXICO)

Ainslie, R. C. The fight to save Juárez   **363.45**

Ciuraru, Carmela

(ed) Beat poets   **811**

Nom de plume   **929.4**

CIVIC LEADERS -- EGYPT -- BIOGRAPHY

Cambanis, T. Once upon a revolution   **962.05**

CIVICS *See* Citizenship; Political science

CIVIL DEFENSE

See also Military art and science

CIVIL DISOBEDIENCE

See also Resistance to government

CIVIL DISOBEDIENCE -- ALABAMA -- BIR-

MINGHAM -- HISTORY -- 20TH CENTURY

Rieder, J. Gospel of freedom   **323.1**

CIVIL DISORDERS *See* Riots

CIVIL ENGINEERING

See also Engineering

CIVIL ENGINEERS

Brown, D. A. Bury my heart at Wounded Knee   **970.004**

Hiltzik, M. A. Colossus   **627**

Winchester, S. The map that changed the world **526**

CIVIL GOVERNMENT *See* Political science

CIVIL LIBERTY *See* Freedom

CIVIL PROCEDURE

See also Courts

CIVIL RIGHTS

Brands, H. W. The man who saved the union **355.009**

Dershowitz, A. M. Rights from wrongs   **323**

Dickey, C. Securing the city   **363.32**

Ford, R. T. Rights gone wrong   **342**

Hickman, J. Murder at Camp Delta   **355.1**

Hirshman, L. Victory   **306.76**

Kenney, D. N. Asylum denied   **92**

King, G. Devil in the grove   **305.896**

Marshall, T. Thurgood Marshall   **347**

Mersky, R. M. Landmark Supreme Court cases   **347.73**

Rehnquist, W. H. All the laws but one   **342**

Shipler, D. K. The rights of the people   **323**

CIVIL RIGHTS

See also Constitutional law; Human rights; Political science

CIVIL RIGHTS (INTERNATIONAL LAW) *See* Human rights

CIVIL RIGHTS -- CONSTITUTIONAL HISTORY

Arsenault, R. Freedom riders   **323**

Colaiaco, J. A. Frederick Douglass and the Fourth of July   **973.7**

CIVIL RIGHTS -- HISTORY -- SOUTHERN STATES -- 20TH CENTURY

Maraniss, A. Strong inside   **92**

CIVIL RIGHTS -- UNITED STATES

Lewis, J. March   **92**

Purdum, T. S. An idea whose time has come **342.73**

CIVIL RIGHTS -- UNITED STATES -- HISTORY

Kluger, R. Indelible ink   **686.209**

Patterson, J. T. The eve of destruction   **973.923**

CIVIL RIGHTS -- UNITED STATES -- HISTORY -- 20TH CENTURY

Purdum, T. S. An idea whose time has come **342.73**

Sullivan, P. Lift every voice   **323.1**

CIVIL RIGHTS ACTIVISTS

Abdul-Jabbar, K. Black profiles in courage   **920**

Baraka, I. A. The LeRoi Jones/Amiri Baraka reader   **818**

Branch, T. At Canaan's edge   **973.923**

Branch, T. Pillar of fire **973.922**

Branch, T. Parting the waters: America in the King years, 1954-63 **973.921**

Brinkley, D. Rosa Parks **92**

Burns, R. Burial for a King **92**

Carson, C. Malcolm X: the FBI file **92**

Cleaver, E. Target zero **323**

Dyson, M. E. I may not get there with you: the true Martin Luther King, Jr **323**

Ellison, R. The collected essays of Ralph Ellison **814**

Evanzz, K. The messenger: the rise and fall of Elijah Muhammad **297.8**

Evers, M. W. The autobiography of Medgar Evers: a hero's life and legacy revealed through his writings, letters, and speeches **92**

Gardell, M. In the name of Elijah Muhammad **297**

Gates, H. L. The future of the race **305.896**

Giddings, P. Ida: a sword among lions **92**

Halberstam, D. The children **323.1**

Harlan, L. R. Booker T. Washington: the making of a black leader, 1856-1901 **92**

Harlan, L. R. Booker T. Washington: the wizard of Tuskegee, 1901-1915 **92**

I see the promised land **92**

Jackson, T. Becoming King **92**

Joseph, P. E. Waiting 'til the midnight hour **323.1**

King, M. L. The autobiography of Martin Luther King, Jr **323**

Kotz, N. Judgment days **323**

Lewis, D. L. W.E.B. Du Bois **92**

Malcolm X The autobiography of Malcolm X **92**

Marable, M. Malcolm X **92**

Marshall, T. Thurgood Marshall **347**

Norrell, R. J. Up from history **92**

Pepper, W. F. An act of state **364.1**

Perry, B. Malcolm **92**

Rickford, R. J. Betty Shabazz: a remarkable story of survival and faith before and after Malcolm X **92**

Risen, C. A nation on fire **973.923**

Robeson, P. Here I stand **92**

Robeson, P. The undiscovered Paul Robeson **92**

Rowan, C. T. Dream makers, dream breakers **92**

Sides, H. Hellhound on his trail **364.152**

Smock, R. W. Booker T. Washington **92**

Uncle Tom or new Negro **370**

Washington, B. T. Up from slavery **92**

Williams, J. Thurgood Marshall **92**

Wilson, E. Patriotic gore **810**

Young, A. An easy burden **92**

Zellner, R. The wrong side of Murder Creek **92**

CIVIL RIGHTS ACTIVISTS -- SOUTHERN STATES -- HISTORY

Arsenault, R. Freedom riders **323**

Civil rights and the struggle for Black equality in

the twentieth century [series]

Jackson, T. Becoming King **92**

CIVIL RIGHTS DEMONSTRATIONS

Campbell, J. Setting the truth free **941.6**

Euchner, C. Nobody turn me around **323.1**

Zellner, R. The wrong side of Murder Creek **92**

CIVIL RIGHTS DEMONSTRATIONS

See also Demonstrations

CIVIL RIGHTS DEMONSTRATIONS -- UNITED STATES -- PICTORIAL WORKS

Kelley, K. Let Freedom Ring **323.1**

CIVIL RIGHTS MOVEMENTS

Branch, T. At Canaan's edge **973.923**

Joseph, P. E. Waiting 'til the midnight hour **323.1**

Lewis, J. March **92**

CIVIL RIGHTS MOVEMENTS -- ALABAMA -- BIRMINGHAM -- HISTORY -- 20TH CENTURY

McWhorter, D. Carry me home **976.1**

Rieder, J. Gospel of freedom **323.1**

CIVIL RIGHTS MOVEMENTS -- NORTHEASTERN STATES

Sugrue, T. J. Sweet land of liberty **323**

CIVIL RIGHTS MOVEMENTS -- PENNSYLVANIA -- PHILADELPHIA

Biddle, D. R. Tasting freedom **92**

CIVIL RIGHTS MOVEMENTS -- SOUTHERN STATES

Arsenault, R. Freedom riders **323**

CIVIL RIGHTS MOVEMENTS -- SOUTHERN STATES -- HISTORY

McCluskey, A. T. A forgotten sisterhood **370.922**

CIVIL RIGHTS MOVEMENTS -- SOUTHERN STATES -- HISTORY -- 20TH CENTURY

McGuire, D. L. At the dark end of the street **323.1**

Sokol, J. There goes my everything **305.8**

CIVIL RIGHTS MOVEMENTS -- UNITED STATES -- HISTORY -- 20TH CENTURY

Branch, T. At Canaan's edge **973.923**

Dyson, M. E. I may not get there with you: the true Martin Luther King, Jr **323**

Lewis, A. B. The shadows of youth **323.1**

Sugrue, T. J. Sweet land of liberty **323**

CIVIL RIGHTS WORKERS -- ALABAMA -- MONTGOMERY -- BIOGRAPHY

Brinkley, D. Rosa Parks **92**

Theoharis, J. The rebellious life of Mrs. Rosa Parks **92**

CIVIL SERVICE

Gates, R. M. A passion for leadership **92**

CIVIL SERVICE

See also Administrative law; Political science; Public administration

CIVIL SERVICE -- UNITED STATES

Damp, D. V. The book of U.S. government jobs **331.1**

CIVIL UNIONS
    See also Rites and ceremonies
The Civil War.   **973.7**
The Civil War. Ward, G. C.   **973.7**
The Civil War. Foote, S.   **973.7**
CIVIL WAR -- HISTORY -- 17TH CENTURY
  Parker, G. Global crisis   **909**
CIVIL WAR -- UNITED STATES *See* United
    States -- History -- 1861-1865, Civil War
Civil War almanac. Fredriksen, J. C.   **973.7**
Civil War America. Marten, J.   **973.7**
Civil War America [series]
  Marvel, W. Lincoln's autocrat   **92**
The Civil War and American art. Harvey, E. J.   **709**
The Civil War dictionary. Boatner, M. M.   **973.7**
The Civil War in 50 objects. Holzer, H.   **973.7**
The civil war of 1812. Taylor, A.   **973.5**
Civil War sketch book. Katz, H. L.   **973.7**
Civil War wives. Berkin, C.   **920**
The Civil War, a narrative. Foote, S.   **973.7**
The Civil War: a concise history. Masur, L. P.   **973.7**
The Civil War: a visual history.   **973.7**
**CIVIL-MILITARY RELATIONS -- UNITED
    STATES**
  Bannerman, S. Homefront 911   **362.86**
**CIVIL-MILITARY RELATIONS -- UNITED
    STATES -- HISTORY -- 21ST CENTURY**
  Bolger, D. P. Why We Lost   **956.704**
The civility solution. Forni, P. M.   **395**
CIVILIZATION
  Boorstin, D. J. The creators   **909**
  Costa, R. D. The watchman's rattle   **501**
  Malone, M. S. The guardian of all things   **153.1**
  The revolt of the masses   **901**
  Smith, P. D. City   **307.76**
CIVILIZATION -- HISTORY
  History   **909**
  Lawler, A. Why did the chicken cross the
    world?   **636.5**
  McNeill, W. H. Plagues and peoples   **614.4**
  Watson, P. Ideas   **909**
CIVILIZATION -- HISTORY -- SOURCES
  Daily life through world history in primary docu-
    ments   **909**
CIVILIZATION -- HUMOR
  Trillin, C. Quite enough of Calvin Trillin   **817**
CIVILIZATION AND COMPUTERS *See* Com-
    puters and civilization
Civilization of the American Indian series
  Fenton, W. N. The Great Law and the Long-
    house   **970.004**
  McReynolds, E. C. The Seminoles   **970.004**
CIVILIZATION, ANCIENT *See* Ancient civiliza-
    tion
CIVILIZATION, CLASSICAL *See* Classical civi-
    lization

CIVILIZATION, GREEK *See* Greece -- Civiliza-
    tion
CIVILIZATION, MEDIEVAL *See* Medieval civi-
    lization
CIVILIZATION, MODERN
  Ridley, M. The evolution of everything   **303.48**
CIVILIZATION, MODERN *See* Modern civiliza-
    tion
**CIVILIZATION, MODERN -- 21ST CENTURY
    -- PICTORIAL WORKS**
  Reuters   **909.83**
CIVILIZATION, WESTERN *See* Western civili-
    zation
CIVILIZATION, WESTERN -- HISTORY
  Henry, J. A short history of scientific thought   **501**
**CIVILIZATION, WESTERN -- JEWISH INFLU-
    ENCES**
  Nirenberg, D. Anti-Judaism   **305.892**
Civilizations of the Ancient Near East.   **939**
Cixi, Empress dowager of China, 1835-1908
      About
  Jung Chang Empress Dowager Cixi   **92**
Claerbaut, A. Alyce
  (ed) Strayhorn   **781.650**
Claflin, Kyri
  (jt. auth) Cherniavsky, M. The cookbook li-
    brary   **641.509**
Claiming ground. Bell, L.   **92**
CLAIRVOYANCE
    See also Extrasensory perception; Occultism
CLAIRVOYANTS *See* Psychics
Clancy family
      About
  Clancy, T. The Clancys of Queens   **974.7**
Clancy, Tara, 1980-
      About
  Clancy, T. The Clancys of Queens   **974.7**
The Clancys of Queens. Clancy, T.   **974.7**
CLANS
    See also Family
Clapp, Henry, 1814-1875
      About
  Martin, J. Rebel Souls   **811**
Clapton. Clapton, E.   **92**
Clapton, Eric
      About
  Clapton, E. Clapton   **92**
  Schumacher, M. Crossroads   **92**
CLARA WARD SINGERS
  Ward-Royster, W. How I got over   **920**
Clara's war. Kramer, C.   **92**
Clare, John, 1793-1864
      About
  Bate, J. John Clare: a biography   **92**
  Heaney, S. Finders keepers   **821**
Clarence Darrow. Farrell, J. A.   **92**

CLARINETISTS

Dance, S. The world of Count Basie   920

Nolan, T. Three chords for beauty's sake: the life of Artie Shaw   92

Clark, Candace

Charles, J. A. The mystery readers' advisory **025.2**

Clark, Christopher

The sleepwalkers   **940.3**

Clark, Craig A.

Read on...sports   **016**

Clark, David

Buffett, M. Warren Buffett and the art of stock arbitrage   **332.6**

Clark, David Scott

The Oxford companion to American law   **349**

Clark, Ella Elizabeth

Sacagawea of the Lewis and Clark expedition   **92**

Clark, Huguette, 1906-2011

About

Dedman, B. Empty mansions   **92**

Clark, J. C. D.

(ed) Burke, E. Reflections on the Revolution in France   **944.04**

Clark, James H., 1944-

About

Lewis, M. D. The new new thing   **338.4**

Clark, Jim

About

Lewis, M. D. The new new thing   **338.4**

Clark, Lloyd

Blitzkrieg   **940.54**

Clark, Lynn Schofield

The parent app   **302.23**

Clark, Mary Marshall

(ed) After the fall   **974.7**

Clark, Melissa

Cook this now   **641.5**

Franny's   **641.594**

In the kitchen with a good appetite   **641.5**

Clark, Robert

Dark water   **945**

Clark, Stuart

The Unknown Universe   **523.1**

Clark, Taylor

Nerve   **152.4**

Starbucked   **338**

Clark, Thomas

(ed) The Writer's digest guide to good writing **808**

Clark, Tom

Light & shade   **811**

Clark, Wesley K.

Waging modern war   **949.703**

Clark, William Andrews, 1839-1925

About

Dedman, B. Empty mansions   **92**

Clark, William R.

Are we hardwired?   **155.7**

Clark, William S.

A field guide to hawks of North America   **598**

Clark, William, 1770-1838

About

Ambrose, S. E. Undaunted courage   **917**

Slaughter, T. P. Exploring Lewis and Clark   **978**

Clarke, Arthur C., 1917-2008

About

Malone, J. W. It doesn't take a rocket scientist **920**

Clarke, F. G.

The history of Australia   **994**

Clarke, Gerald

(ed) Capote, T. Too brief a treat   **92**

Get happy: the life of Judy Garland   **92**

Clarke, Peter

Mr. Churchill's profession   **941.084**

Clarke, Thurston

JFK's last hundred days   **92**

The last campaign   **92**

Clary, David A.

Rocket man   **92**

The **clash** of civilizations and the remaking of world order. Huntington, S. P.   **909.82**

The **clash** of the cultures. Bogle, J. C.   **332.6**

Class warfare. Brill, S.

CLASSES (MATHEMATICS) *See* Set theory

CLASSIC AUTOMOBILES *See* Antique and classic cars

CLASSIC CARS *See* Antique and classic cars

Classic home desserts.   **641.8**

Classic human anatomy. Winslow, V. L.   **743.49**

The **classic** of changes. I ching   **299.5**

Classic writings on poetry.   **809.1**

CLASSICAL ANTIQUITIES

Frammolino, R. Chasing Aphrodite   **930**

CLASSICAL CIVILIZATION

Beard, M. Confronting the classics   **930**

Cahill, T. Sailing the wine-dark sea   **909**

Freeman, C. Egypt, Greece, and Rome   **909**

Lane Fox, R. The classical world   **938**

CLASSICAL CIVILIZATION

See also Ancient civilization

CLASSICAL DICTIONARIES

Grant, M. A guide to the ancient world   **913**

The Oxford classical dictionary   **938**

CLASSICAL DICTIONARIES

See also Ancient history; Encyclopedias and dictionaries

CLASSICAL DRAMA

Thorburn, J. E. The Facts on File companion to classical drama   **880**

CLASSICAL DRAMA

See also Classical literature; Drama

CLASSICAL EDUCATION

Beard, M. Confronting the classics   **930**

CLASSICAL EDUCATION
See also Education

CLASSICAL LANGUAGES *See* Greek language;
Latin language

Classical literature. Jenkyns, R.   **880**

CLASSICAL LITERATURE
Mendelsohn, D. Waiting for the barbarians   **801**

CLASSICAL LITERATURE
See also Literature

CLASSICAL LITERATURE -- DICTIONARIES
The Oxford companion to classical literature   **880**

CLASSICAL MUSIC *See* Music

Classical music in America. Horowitz, J.   **781.6**

CLASSICAL MUSICIANS
Eisler, B. Chopin's funeral   **92**
Ellison, R. The collected essays of Ralph Ellison   **814**
Schonberg, H. C. The great pianists   **920**

CLASSICAL MYTHOLOGY
Graves, R. The Greek myths   **292**

CLASSICAL MYTHOLOGY
See also Mythology

CLASSICAL MYTHOLOGY -- DICTIONARIES
Impelluso, L. Gods and heroes in art   **700**
The Oxford dictionary of classical myth and religion   **292**

The **classical** style. Rosen, C.   **780.9**
Classical Turkish cooking. Algar, A. E.   **641.59**
The **classical** world. Lane Fox, R.   **938**

CLASSICISM
See also Aesthetics; Literature

CLASSICISM IN ARCHITECTURE
See also Architecture; Classicism

CLASSICISTS
Mendelsohn, D. The lost   **92**

Classico e moderno. Friedman, A.   **641.59**

Classics of naval literature [series]
Morison, S. E. John Paul Jones   **92**

CLASSIFICATION -- BOOKS
Wright, A. Cataloging the world   **020.9**

CLASSIFICATION, DEWEY DECIMAL *See*
Dewey Decimal Classification

CLASSROOM MANAGEMENT
Whitson, S. 8 keys to end bullying   **302.34**

CLASSROOM MANAGEMENT
See also School discipline; Teaching

Claude Monet, 1840-1926. Baillio, J.   **759**
Claudius, Emperor of Rome, 10 B.C.-54
About
The twelve Caesars   **878**

Clausen, Ruth Rogers
(jt. auth) Christopher, T. Essential perennials **635.9**

Clausen, Tammy Hennigh
Spratford, B. S. The horror readers' advisory **025.5**

Clausewitz, Carl von
On war   **355**

Clavin, Thomas
Roger Maris   **92**

Clavin, Tom
The DiMaggios   **796.357**
(jt. auth) Drury, B. The heart of everything that is   **92**

Clawson, Dan
(ed) Required reading   **301**

CLAY
Pavelka, L. The complete book of polymer clay   **738.1**

CLAY
See also Ceramics; Soils

CLAY MODELING *See* Modeling

CLAY POT COOKING
Wolfert, P. Mediterranean clay pot cooking **641.59**

Clay, Catrine
King, Kaiser, Tsar   **920**

Clay, Henry, 1777-1852
About
Bordewich, F. M. America's great debate   **973.6**
Heidler, D. S. Henry Clay   **92**

Clayman, Charles B.
(ed) The Human body   **612**

Clayton, Buck, 1911-1991
About
Dance, S. The world of Count Basie   **920**

Cleage, Pearl
About
Cleage, P. Things I Should Have Told My Daughter   **92**

Clean Tech Nation. Pernick, R.   **333.794**

CLEANING
Friedman, V. M. Field guide to stains   **648**

CLEANING
See also Sanitation

CLEANING COMPOUNDS
See also Cleaning

CLEANLINESS
See also Hygiene; Sanitation

A **clearing** in the distance: Frederick Law Olmsted and America in the nineteenth century. Rybczynski, W.   **712**

Cleaver, Eldridge, 1935-1998
About
Cleaver, E. Target zero   **323**

Cleaver, Kathleen
(ed) Cleaver, E. Target zero   **323**

Cleaves, H. James
(jt. auth) Mesler, B. A Brief History of Creation   **576.8**

Cleese, John
About
Cleese, J. So, anyway...   **92**

Clegg, Bill
About

Ninety days **362.29**

Clegg, Brian
Extra Sensory **133.8**
Final Frontier **629.4**

Cleland, Max, 1942-
About
Cleland, M. Heart of a patriot **92**

CLEMENCY
 See also Administration of criminal justice;
 Executive power
Clemente. Maraniss, D. **92**

Clemente, Roberto, 1934-1972
About
Maraniss, D. Clemente **92**
Santiago, W. 21 **92**

Clementi, Muzio, 1752-1832
About
Schonberg, H. C. The great pianists **920**
Clementine. Purnell, S. **92**

CLEMSON TIGERS (FOOTBALL TEAM)
Rodriguez, D. Rise **92**

Clendinnen, Inga
Dancing with strangers **994**
Reading the Holocaust **940.53**
Cleopatra. Schiff, S. **92**
Cleopatra the great. Fletcher, J. **92**

Cleopatra, Queen of Egypt, d. 30 B.C.
About
Dryden, J. All for love **822**
Fletcher, J. Cleopatra the great **92**
Goldsworthy, A. K. Antony and Cleopatra **92**
Schiff, S. Cleopatra **92**

CLERGY
Applegate, D. The most famous man in America **92**
Ash, S. V. Firebrand of liberty **973.7**
Baraka, I. A. The LeRoi Jones/Amiri Baraka reader **818**
Branch, T. At Canaan's edge **973.923**
Branch, T. Pillar of fire **973.922**
Branch, T. Parting the waters: America in the King years, 1954-63 **973.921**
Bremer, F. J. John Winthrop **974.4**
Burns, R. Burial for a King **92**
DeGategno, P. J. Critical companion to Jonathan Swift **828**
Demos, J. The unredeemed captive **973.2**
Dyson, M. E. I may not get there with you: the true Martin Luther King, Jr **323**
Gaustad, E. S. Roger Williams **92**
Graham, B. Just as I am **92**
Halberstam, D. The children **323.1**
I see the promised land **92**
Jackson, T. Becoming King **92**
Johnson, S. The invention of air **92**
King, M. L. The autobiography of Martin Luther King, Jr **323**

Kotz, N. Judgment days **323**
Malone, J. W. It doesn't take a rocket scientist **920**
Marsden, G. M. Jonathan Edwards **92**
Marsh, C. Strange glory **92**
Metaxas, E. Bonhoeffer **92**
Pepper, W. F. An act of state **364.1**
Risen, C. A nation on fire **973.923**
Sides, H. Hellhound on his trail **364.152**
Slaughter, T. P. The beautiful soul of John Woolman, apostle of abolition **92**
Snyder, L. J. The philosophical breakfast club **509**
Taylor, B. B. An altar in the world **92**
Wilson, E. Patriotic gore **810**
Young, A. An easy burden **92**

CLEVELAND CLINIC FOUNDATION
Cosgrove, T. The Cleveland Clinic way **362.11**
The **Cleveland** Clinic way. Cosgrove, T. **362.11**

Cleveland, Grover, 1837-1908
About
Algeo, M. The president is a sick man **973.8**
Graff, H. F. Grover Cleveland **92**

Cleveland, Pat
About
Cleveland, P. Walking with the muses **92**

Cleves, Rachel Hope
Charity and Sylvia **306.84**

CLIFF DWELLERS AND CLIFF DWELLINGS
 See also Archeology; Native Americans --
 Southwestern States

Cliff, Nigel
Holy war **909**
The Shakespeare riots **974.4**

Clifford, Denis
Make your own living trust **346.05**
Plan your estate **346.05**

Clifton, Lucille, 1936-2010
The collected poems of Lucille Clifton 1965-2010 **811**
Mercy **811**
About
Black women writers (1950-1980) **810**

CLIMACTERIC, FEMALE *See* Menopause
CLIMATE
Allaby, M. The gardener's guide to weather and climate **635**
Cerveny, R. S. Weather's greatest mysteries solved! **304.2**
Dow, K. The atlas of climate change **551.6**
Fagan, B. M. The long summer: how climate changed civilization **551.6**
Flannery, T. F. The weather makers **363.7**
Kolbert, E. Field notes from a catastrophe **363.7**
Linden, E. The winds of change **551.6**
Williams, J. The AMS weather book **551.5**
Wohlforth, C. The whale and the supercomputer **305.897**

CLIMATE
 See also Earth sciences
CLIMATE -- ENVIRONMENTAL ASPECTS
 Braasch, G. Earth under fire   **363.7**
 Cullen, H. The weather of the future   **551.63**
 DeBuys, W. E. A great aridness   **551.6**
 Dumanoski, D. The end of the long summer **551.6**
 Friedman, T. L. Hot, flat, and crowded   **363.7**
 Goodell, J. How to cool the planet   **551.6**
 Hansen, J. E. Storms of my grandchildren   **363.7**
 Hertsgaard, M. Hot   **304.2**
 Lynas, M. Six degrees   **551.6**
 McKibben, B. Eaarth   **253**
 Montaigne, F. Fraser's penguins   **577.2**
 Pearce, F. With speed and violence   **551.6**
 Pooley, E. The climate war   **363.7**
 Smith, L. C. The world in 2050   **304.2**
CLIMATE -- RESEARCH
 Stager, C. Deep future   **363.7**
Climate Central Inc.
 (comp) Global weirdness   **577.2**
Climate change.   **363.738**
CLIMATE CHANGE
 See also Climate
CLIMATE CHANGE
 Druse, K. The new shade garden
 The global warming reader   **363.738**
 Gore, A. The future   **303.4**
 Kelly, W. J. The People's Republic of Chemi-
 cals   **363.739**
 Klein, N. This changes everything   **363.738**
 Koerth-Baker, M. Before the lights go out **333.79**
 McGuire, B. Waking the giant   **551.5**
 O'Connor, M. R. Resurrection Science   **591.68**
 Roberts, C. The ocean of life   **551.46**
 Sobel, A. Storm surge   **551.55**
CLIMATE CHANGE -- HISTORY -- 17TH CEN-
 TURY
 Parker, G. Global crisis   **909**
CLIMATE CHANGE -- PUBLIC OPINION
 Marshall, G. Don't Even Think About It   **551.6**
The **climate** war. Pooley, E.   **363.7**
CLIMATIC CHANGES
 Flannery, T. F. The weather makers   **363.7**
 Fleming, J. R. Fixing the sky   **551.6**
 Hertsgaard, M. Hot   **304.2**
 Linden, E. The winds of change   **551.6**
 McKibben, B. Eaarth   **253**
 Pearce, F. With speed and violence   **551.6**
 Walker, G. The hot topic   **363.7**
 Wohlforth, C. The whale and the supercomput-
 er   **305.897**
CLIMATIC CHANGES -- ALASKA
 Heacox, K. John Muir and the ice that started a
 fire   **92**
CLIMATIC CHANGES -- ECONOMIC AS-

PECTS
 Guzman, A. T. Overheated   **363.738**
 Klein, N. This changes everything   **363.738**
CLIMATIC CHANGES -- ENCYCLOPEDIAS
 Encyclopedia of global warming & climate
 change   **363.738**
 Fry, J. L. The encyclopedia of weather and climate
 change   **551.6**
CLIMATIC CHANGES -- ENVIRONMENTAL
 ASPECTS
 Goodell, J. How to cool the planet   **551.6**
 McGuire, B. Waking the giant   **551.5**
 McKibben, B. Oil and Honey   **363.7**
CLIMATIC CHANGES -- ENVIRONMEN-
 TAL ASPECTS -- ALASKA -- PICTORIAL
 WORKS
 Tape, K. D. The changing arctic landscape **551.69**
CLIMATIC CHANGES -- ENVIRONMENTAL
 ASPECTS -- POLAR REGIONS -- PICTO-
 RIAL WORKS
 Seaman, C. Melting away   **910.91**
CLIMATIC CHANGES -- FORECASTING
 Cullen, H. The weather of the future   **551.63**
 Global weirdness   **577.2**
CLIMATIC CHANGES -- HISTORY -- ENCY-
 CLOPEDIAS
 Climate change   **363.738**
CLIMATIC CHANGES -- MATHEMATHICAL
 MODELS
 Global weirdness   **577.2**
CLIMATIC CHANGES -- PREVENTION
 Helm, D. The carbon crunch   **333.79**
CLIMATIC CHANGES -- RESEARCH -- ENCY-
 CLOPEDIAS
 Climate change   **363.738**
CLIMATIC CHANGES -- SOCIAL ASPECTS --
 HISTORY -- 17TH CENTURY
 Parker, G. Global crisis   **909**
CLIMATIC CHANGES -- UNITED STATES --
 POPULAR WORKS
 McGraw, S. Betting the farm on a drought **363.738**
CLIMATIC CHANGES IN LITERATURE
 Ghosh, A. The great derangement   **809**
CLIMATOLOGY *See* Climate
The **climb.** Boukreev, A.   **796.522**
CLIMBING PLANTS
 Armitage, A. M. Armitage's vines and climb-
 ers   **635.9**
 Ellis, B. W. Covering ground   **635.9**
 Michener, D. Taylor's guide to ground covers **635.9**
CLIMBING PLANTS
 See also Gardening; Plants
Climbing the mango trees. Jaffrey, M.   **92**
Clineff, Kindra
 Martin, T. The new terrarium   **635.9**
CLINICAL CHEMISTRY

See also Biochemistry; Diagnosis

CLINICAL COMPETENCE
Wachter, R. The digital doctor   **610.28**

CLINICAL DRUG TRIALS *See* Drugs -- Testing

CLINICAL GENETICS *See* Medical genetics

CLINICAL MEDICINE
Wachter, R. The digital doctor   **610.28**

CLINICAL RECORDS *See* Medical records

Clinical trials. Speid, L.   **615.5**

CLINICAL TRIALS --MORAL AND ETHICAL ASPECTS
Goldacre, B. Bad Pharma   **615.107**

CLINICAL TRIALS OF DRUGS *See* Drugs -- Testing

CLINICS *See* Health facilities; Medical practice

The **Clinton** tapes. Branch, T.   **92**

Clinton, Bill, 1946-
         About
Branch, T. The Clinton tapes   **92**
Chafe, W. H. Bill and Hillary   **973.929**
Clinton, B. My life   **92**
Gormley, K. The death of American virtue **973.929**
McDougal, S. The woman who wouldn't talk   **973.929**
Stephanopoulos, G. All too human   **973.929**
Toobin, J. R. A vast conspiracy   **973.929**
Woodward, B. Shadow   **973.92**

Clinton, Catherine
Harriet Tubman: the road to freedom   **92**
Mrs. Lincoln   **92**

Clinton, Hillary Rodham, 1947-
Clinton, H. R. It takes a village   **305.23**
Living history   **92**
         About
Bernstein, C. A woman in charge   **92**
Chafe, W. H. Bill and Hillary   **973.929**
Clinton, H. R. Hard choices   **92**
Gormley, K. The death of American virtue **973.929**
Traister, R. Big girls don't cry   **324**

CLIP ART
See also Graphic arts

CLIVEDEN (ENGLAND) -- BIOGRAPHY
Livingstone, N. The mistresses of Cliveden **942.009**

CLIVEDEN (ENGLAND) -- HISTORY
Livingstone, N. The mistresses of Cliveden **942.009**

CLOCK AND WATCH MAKERS
Sobel, D. Longitude   **526**

CLOCKS AND WATCHES
Marchant, J. Decoding the heavens   **681.1**

CLOCKS AND WATCHES
See also Time

The **clockwork** universe. Dolnick, E.   **509**

CLOG DANCING
See also Dance

The **cloister** walk. Norris, K.   **255**

CLONES AND CLONING *See* Cloning

CLONING
Kurpinski, K. How to defeat your own clone **660.6**
Wilmut, I. After Dolly   **176**

CLONING
See also Genetic engineering

CLONING -- ETHICAL ASPECTS
See also Ethics

CLOSE AIR SUPPORT -- HISTORY -- 21ST CENTURY
Bruning, J. R. Level zero heroes   **958.104**

Close calls with nonsense. Burt, S.   **809.1**

Close encounters of the furred kind. Cox, T.   **636.8**

Close, Chuck, 1940-
         About
Finch, C. Chuck Close   **92**

Close, F. E.
The infinity puzzle   **530.1**
Nothing   **530**

Close, Glenn, 1947-
         About
Earley, P. Resilience   **616.89**

Close, Jessie, 1953-
         About
Earley, P. Resilience   **616.89**

CLOSED CAPTION TELEVISION
See also Deaf; Television

CLOSED CAPTION VIDEO RECORDINGS
See also Deaf; Video recordings

The **closer.** Rivera, M.   **92**

The **closing** of the American mind. Bloom, A. D.   **973.92**

The **closing** of the Western mind. Freeman, C. **940.1**

Closing the ring. Churchill, W.   **940.53**

Clotfelter, Charles T.
Big-time sports in American universities   **796**

CLOTH *See* Fabrics

CLOTHES *See* Clothing and dress

Clothes, Clothes, Clothes. Music, Music, Music. Boys, Boys, Boys. Albertine, V.   **92**

CLOTHIERS *See* Clothing industry

CLOTHING AND DRESS
Halbreich, B. I'll drink to that   **92**
Herzog, A. Knit wear love   **746.432**
Murphy, M. Woven to wear   **746.1**
One-yard wonders   **646.2**
Stanley, S. H. DIY wardrobe makeovers   **646**
White, B. Sewing green   **646.4**

CLOTHING AND DRESS
See also Manners and customs

CLOTHING AND DRESS -- ALTERATION -- PICTORIAL WORKS
Veblen, S. The complete photo guide to perfect fitting   **646.4**

CLOTHING AND DRESS -- HISTORY
Stevenson, N. J. Fashion   **391.009**

CLOTHING AND DRESS -- REMAKING

Stanley, S. H. DIY wardrobe makeovers   **646**

CLOTHING AND DRESS MEASUREMENTS
Herzog, A. Knit to flatter   **746.43**

CLOTHING INDUSTRY
Gross, M. Focus   **770.92**
Snyder, R. L. Fugitive denim   **382**
Von Drehle, D. Triangle: the fire that changed America   **974.7**
Ziegler, M. Wild company   **381**

CLOTHING INDUSTRY
See also Industries

CLOTHING INDUSTRY EXECUTIVES
Crowe, L. G. The towering world of Jimmy Choo   **391**
Gormley, K. The death of American virtue **973.929**

CLOTHING TRADE *See* Clothing industry

CLOTHING TRADE -- UNITED STATES
Jacobs, B. Life is good   **650.1**
Ziegler, M. Wild company   **381**

CLOUD COMPUTING
Arora, P. To the cloud   **004.67**
The **cloud** corporation. Donnelly, T.   **811**

CLOUD SEEDING *See* Weather control
Cloud, Abigail
Sylph   **811**

CLOUDS
Hamblyn, R. The invention of clouds   **551.57**

CLOUDS
See also Atmosphere; Meteorology
Clouds of Glory. Korda, M.   **92**
Clough, Arthur Hugh
(ed) Plutarch: the lives of the noble Grecians and Romans   **920**
Cloutier, Mark
(ed) National electrical code handbook 2014 **621.3**
Clover, Charles
The end of the line   **333**

CLOWNS
See also Circus; Entertainers

CLUBS
See also Associations
Clunas, Craig
(ed) Ming   **951**
Clyde, 1909-1934

About
Guinn, J. Go down together   **364.1**

CO-DEPENDENCE *See* Codependency
CO-DEPENDENCY *See* Codependency
Co-Mix. Spiegelman, A.   **741.5**
CO-OPS *See* Cooperative societies
COACH DRIVERS
Smardz Frost, K. I've got a home in glory land **92**
Coache, Christopher D.
(ed) National electrical code handbook 2014 **621.3**
COACHING *See* Coaching (Athletics); Horsemanship

COACHING (ATHLETICS)
Boeheim, J. Bleeding Orange   **92**
COACHING (ATHLETICS)
See also Athletics; Physical education; Sports

COAL
See also Fuel
COAL MINERS
See also Miners
COAL MINES AND MINING
Biggers, J. Reckoning at Eagle Creek   **333.73**
Galuszka, P. A. Thunder on the Mountain **363.11**
House, S. Something's rising   **338.2**
Laskas, J. M. Hidden America   **305.5**

COAL MINES AND MINING
See also Coal; Mines and mineral resources

COAL MINES AND MINING -- ACCIDENTS
Tintori, K. Trapped: the 1909 Cherry Mine disaster   **973.9**

COAL MINES AND MINING -- APPALACHIAN REGION
Galuszka, P. A. Thunder on the Mountain **363.11**

COAL OIL *See* Petroleum
COAL TAR PRODUCTS
See also Petroleum

COAL TRADE -- APPALACHIAN REGION
Galuszka, P. A. Thunder on the Mountain **363.11**

COAL TRADE -- CORRUPT PRACTICES -- WEST VIRGINIA
Leamer, L. The price of justice   **346.730**

COAST CHANGES
Pilkey, O. H. The rising sea   **363.34**

COAST ECOLOGY *See* Coastal ecology
COASTAL ECOLOGY
Safina, C. The view from Lazy Point   **508**

COASTAL ECOLOGY
See also Ecology

COASTAL LANDFORMS *See* Coasts
Coastal living beach house happy. Van der Meer, A.   **747**

COASTAL ZONE ECOLOGY *See* Coastal ecology

COASTAL ZONE MANAGEMENT
See also Coasts; Regional planning

COASTS
Dean, C. Against the tide   **333.91**
Pilkey, O. H. The rising sea   **363.34**
The **coat** route. Noonan, M. L.   **338.4**
Coates, Ta-Nehisi, 1975-
The beautiful struggle
Between the World and Me   **305.8**
Cobain, Kurt, 1967-1994

About
Cross, C. R. Heavier than heaven: a biography of Kurt Cobain   **92**
Cross, C. R. Here we are now   **92**
Cobb. Stump, A.   **796.357**

Cobb, Cathy
Creations of fire **540**
The joy of chemistry **540**
Cobb, Geraldyn M., 1931-
About
Haynsworth, L. Amelia Earhart's daughters **629.13**
Cobb, Matthew
Life's Greatest Secret **572.8**
Cobb, Paul M.
The race for paradise **909.07**
Cobb, Ty, 1886-1961
About
Leerhsen, C. Ty Cobb **92**
Stump, A. Cobb **796.357**
COBBLERS (COOKING)
Moore, K. Delicious dump cakes **641.86**
COBOL (COMPUTER PROGRAM LANGUAGE)
Beyer, K. W. Grace Hopper and the invention of the information age **92**
Coburn, Broughton
Everest: mountain without mercy **796.522**
Jamling Tenzing Norgay Touching my father's soul **796.522**
COCA-COLA COMPANY
Elmore, B. J. Citizen Coke **338.7**
Cocaine. Streatfeild, D. **362.29**
COCAINE
Feiling, T. Cocaine nation **362.29**
Streatfeild, D. Cocaine **362.29**
COCAINE
See also Narcotics
COCAINE BABIES See Children of drug addicts
Cocaine nation. Feiling, T. **362.29**
Cochise, Apache Chief, d. 1874
About
Brown, D. A. The American West **978**
Brown, D. A. Bury my heart at Wounded Knee **970.004**
Roberts, D. Once they moved like the wind **970.004**
Cochran, Jacqueline, 1910?-1980
About
Haynsworth, L. Amelia Earhart's daughters **629.13**
Cochrane, Kira
(ed) Journalistas **808.8**
Cocina de la familia. Tausend, M. **641.5**
Cockburn, Andrew
Kill Chain **623.7**
Cockburn, George, Sir, 1772-1853
About
Vogel, S. Through the perilous fight **973.5**
Cockburn, Henry, 1982-
About
Cockburn, H. Henry's demons **92**
Cockburn, Patrick
(jt. auth) Cockburn, H. Henry's demons **92**

COCKROACHES
See also Insects
The **cocktail** lab. Conigliaro, T. **641.87**
COCKTAILS
Amaro **641.874**
Arnold, D. Liquid intelligence **641.87**
Bar Book **641.87**
Bitters **641.8**
Cate, M. Smuggler's Cove **647.95**
The craft cocktail party **641.87**
The Dead Rabbit drinks manual **641.87**
Del Mar Sacasa, M. Summer cocktails **641.87**
Drinking the devil's acre **641.87**
Fauchald, N. Death & Co **641.87**
Fraioli, J. O. The Canon Cocktail Book **641**
Hellmich, M. Ultimate bar book **641.8**
Humm, D. The NoMad cookbook **641.597**
Jones, C. The Brooklyn bartender **641.874**
Mix shake stir **641.8**
Tanguay, P. The Tippling bros. **641.87**
COCKTAILS -- HISTORY
Simonson, R. A proper drink **641.87**
COCOA
See also Beverages
COCOONS See Butterflies; Caterpillars; Moths; Silkworms
Cod. Kurlansky, M. **333.95**
CODE NAMES
See also Abbreviations; Names
CODEPENDENCY
Beattie, M. Codependent no more **616.86**
Codependent no more. Beattie, M. **616.86**
CODES See Ciphers
CODFISH
Greenberg, P. Four fish **333.95**
Kurlansky, M. Cod **333.95**
Codina, Carles
The complete book of jewelry making **739.27**
Codrescu, Andrei
New Orleans, mon amour **814**
Cody, Joshua
[Sic] **362.196**
Coe, Andrew
A square meal **641.5**
Coe, Michael D.
The Maya **972**
Royal cities of the ancient Maya **972.81**
COEDUCATION
See also Education
COELACANTH
Weinberg, S. A fish caught in time **597.3**
Coenraads, Robert Raymond
Rocks and fossils **552**
Coetzee, J. M.
The lives of animals **179**
COFFEE

See also Beverages

COFFEE -- HISTORY

Standage, T. A history of the world in 6 glasses **394.1**

COFFEE BARS *See* Coffeehouses

COFFEE HOUSES *See* Coffeehouses

COFFEE INDUSTRY

Clark, T. Starbucked **338**

Hoffmann, J. The world atlas of coffee **641.3**

Schultz, H. Onward **647.9**

COFFEEHOUSES

See also Coffee industry; Restaurants

Coffey, Patrick

Cathedrals of science **540**

Coffey, Wayne

When nobody was watching **796.334**

Coffin, Charles M.

(ed) Donne, J. The complete poetry and selected prose of John Donne **821**

Cogeval, Guy

(ed) Edouard Vuillard **759**

Cogito ergo sum: the life of Rene Descartes. Watson, R. A. **92**

COGNITION

DeSalle, R. The brain **612.8**

Dobelli, R. The art of thinking clearly **153.4**

Edelman, S. The happiness of pursuit **153**

Gopnik, A. The scientist in the crib **155.4**

Greenfield, S. Mind change **155.9**

Hood, B. The self illusion **155.2**

Newport, C. Deep work **650.1**

COGNITION *See* Theory of knowledge

COGNITION -- PHYSIOLOGICAL ASPECTS

Kounios, J. The Eureka factor **612.8**

COGNITION DISORDERS

Sacks, O. The mind's eye **616.85**

COGNITION IN ADOLESCENCE

Siegel, D. J. Brainstorm **155.5**

COGNITION IN ANIMALS

Griffin, D. R. Animal minds **591.5**

Morell, V. Animal wise **591.5**

COGNITIVE NEUROSCIENCE

Gazzaniga, M. S. Human **612.8**

Kaku, M. The future of the mind **612.8**

Lieberman, M. D. Social **302**

Shermer, M. The believing brain **153.4**

COGNITIVE PSYCHOLOGY

Lewis, M. The Undoing Project **153**

Lieberman, M. D. Social **302**

Rosenbaum, D. A. It's a jungle in there **153**

COGNITIVE SCIENCE

Bostrom, N. Superintelligence **006.3**

COGNITIVE STYLES

Kounios, J. The Eureka factor **612.8**

COGNITIVE STYLES

See also Intellect; Theory of knowledge

COGNITIVE STYLES IN CHILDREN

See also Child psychology

COGNITIVE STYLES IN CHILDREN -- UNITED STATES

Tough, P. How children succeed **372.21**

Cognitive surplus. Shirky, C. **303.4**

COGNITIVE THERAPY

Greenberger, D. Mind over mood **616.89**

Lewis, M. The Undoing Project **153**

Wax, R. Sane new world **158.1**

COGNITIVE THERAPY

See also Psychotherapy

COGNITIVE THERAPY -- POPULAR WORKS

Greenberger, D. Mind over mood **616.89**

Cohan, William D.

Money and power **332.6**

The price of silence **364.15**

Cohen, Adam

American pharaoh: Mayor Richard J. Daley: his battle for Chicago and the nation **977.3**

Imbeciles **344**

Cohen, Andrew

Two days in June **973.922**

Cohen, Carl

Copi, I. M. Introduction to logic **160**

Cohen, Donald J.

Mayes, L. C. The Yale Child Study Center guide to understanding your child **649**

Cohen, Eliot A.

Conquered into liberty **355**

Cohen, I. Bernard

(ed) The Cambridge companion to Newton **530**

Science and the founding fathers **973.3**

Cohen, J. M.

(ed) The Penguin book of Spanish verse **861**

Cohen, Lawrence J.

Playful parenting **649**

Cohen, Leonard, 1934-2016

About

Leonard Cohen on Leonard Cohen **92**

Simmons, S. I'm your man **92**

Cohen, Lisa

All we know **920.72**

Cohen, Lizabeth

A consumer's republic **339.4**

Cohen, Mitchell

All These Things That I've Done **781.66**

Cohen, Morton Norton

Lewis Carroll **92**

Cohen, Rich

The avengers **940.53**

The fish that ate the whale **338.7**

Israel is real **956.94**

The Sun and the Moon and the Rolling Stones **782.42**

Sweet and low **920**

Cohen, Richard M

By the sword 796.8

About

Cohen, R. Israel 956.940

Cohen, Saul Bernard
(ed) The Columbia gazetteer of North America 917
(ed) The Columbia gazetteer of the world 910.3

Cohen, Scott W.
Eat, sleep, poop 618.92

Cohen-Solal, Annie
Leo & his circle 92
Mark Rothko 759.13

Cohn, John M.
The complete library technology planner 025

Cohn, Lawrence
(ed) Nothing but the blues 781.643

Cohn, Roy, 1927-1986

About

Kushner, T. Angels in America 812

Cohn, Samuel K.
Herlihy, D. The black death and the transformation of the west 940.1

Cohodas, Nadine
Princess Noire 92

COIFFURE *See* Hair

Coile, D. Caroline
Encyclopedia of dog breeds 636.7

COINAGE
See also Money

COINAGE OF WORDS *See* New words

COINCIDENCE
Mazur, J. Fluke 519.2

COINCIDENCE THEORY (MATHEMATICS)
Mazur, J. Fluke 519.2

COINS
Krause, C. L. Standard catalog of world coins 737.4
Yeoman, R. S. A guide book of United States coins 737.4
Yeoman, R. S. Handbook of United States coins 737.4

COINS
See also Money

Cokinos, Christopher
The fallen sky 523.5

Colaiaco, James A.
Frederick Douglass and the Fourth of July 973.7

Colbert, David
(ed) Eyewitness to America 973

Colby, Vineta
World authors, 1975-1980 920.003
World authors, 1980-1985 809
World authors, 1985-1990 809

Colby, William Egan, 1920-1996

About

Woods, R. B. Shadow warrior 92

Cold. Streever, B. 998

COLD

Streever, B. Cold 998

COLD (DISEASE)
Ackerman, J. Ah-choo! 616.2

COLD (DISEASE)
See also Communicable diseases; Diseases

COLD -- THERAPEUTIC USE
See also Therapeutics

COLD CASES (CRIMINAL INVESTIGATION)
Epstein, E. J. The annals of unsolved crime 364.152
Halber, D. The skeleton crew 363.25
Nelson, M. The red parts 362.88
Presley, J. The Phantom Killer 364.152

COLD CASES (CRIMINAL INVESTIGATION) -- CALIFORNIA -- LOS ANGELES -- CASE STUDIES
Mann, W. J. Tinseltown 364.152

COLD STORAGE
See also Food -- Preservation

Cold War. 909.82
The **Cold** War. Hillstrom, K. 909.82

COLD WAR
Carlson, P. K blows top 947.085
Dallek, R. The lost peace 909.82
Dobbs, M. Six months in 1945 940.53
Finn, P. The Zhivago affair 891.73
FitzGerald, F. Way out there in the blue 973.927
Foner, E. The story of American freedom 323.44
Gaddis, J. L. George F. Kennan 327
Gates, R. M. From the shadows 327
Gregory, R. Cold War America, 1946 to 1990 973.92
Haynes, J. E. Spies 327.12
Herken, G. The Georgetown set 975.3
Hillstrom, K. The Cold War 909.82
Hoffman, D. E. The Billion Dollar Spy 327.12
Jacobsen, A. Operation Paperclip 940.54
Johnson, I. A mosque in Munich 297
Kissinger, H. Diplomacy 327.2
Kort, M. The Columbia guide to the Cold War 973.92
Lichtblau, E. The Nazis next door 324.1
Mann, J. The rebellion of Ronald Reagan 973.927
Mitchell, G. The tunnels 943.155
Ostrovsky, A. The Invention of Russia 947.086
Ratnesar, R. Tear down this wall 973.927
Rhodes, R. Arsenals of folly 355
Sheehan, N. A fiery peace in a cold war 92
Service, R. The End of the Cold War, 1985-1991 909.82
Sheehan, N. A fiery peace in a cold war 92
Theoharis, A. G. Abuse of power 363.325
Thompson, N. The hawk and the dove 92
Von Tunzelmann, A. Blood and Sand 973.92
Wheen, F. Strange days indeed 973.92

COLD WAR
See also World politics -- 1945-1991

COLD WAR -- DIPLOMATIC HISTORY
Dobbs, M. Six months in 1945 **940.53**
Gaddis, J. L. George F. Kennan **327**
Service, R. The End of the Cold War, 1985-1991 **909.82**
COLD WAR -- DIPLOMATIC HISTORY
Thomas, E. Ike's bluff **973.92**
COLD WAR -- ENCYCLOPEDIAS
Cold War **909.82**
Cold War America, 1946 to 1990. Gregory, R. **973.92**
The **coldest** March. Solomon, S. **919**
The **coldest** war. Brady, J. **951.9**
The **coldest** winter. Halberstam, D. **951.9**
Cole Porter. McBrien, W. **92**
Cole, Henri
Middle earth **811**
Cole, Juan
The New Arabs **909**
Cole, K. C.
The hole in the universe **530.01**
Something incredibly wonderful happens **92**
Cole, Nat King, 1919?-1965
About
Epstein, D. M. Nat King Cole **92**
Lees, G. You can't steal a gift **781.65**
Cole, Natalie
About
Cole, N. Angel on my shoulder **92**
Cole, Peter
Sacred trash **296.09**
Cole, Tyson
Uchi: the cookbook **641.6**
COLEGIO DE DOLORES (CUBA)
Symmes, P. The boys from Dolores **972.91**
Coleman, David G.
The fourteenth day **73.922**
Coleman, Eliot
Winter harvest handbook **635**
Coleman, Patrick
(ed) The art of music **708**
Coleman, Rick
Blue Monday **92**
Coleridge, Samuel Taylor
The complete poems **821**
Coles, David J.
(ed) Encyclopedia of the American Civil War **973.7**
Coles, Robert
Children of crisis **305.23**
Handing one another along **820**
Lives of moral leadership **170**
The spiritual life of children **204**
Colet, Louise, 1810-1876
About
Fraser, K. Ornament and silence **809**
The **Colette** sewing handbook. Mitnick, S. **646.4**
Colette, 1873-1954

About
Thurman, J. Secrets of the flesh: a life of Colette **92**
Coley, Byron
Moore, T. No wave **781.66**
Colgrove, Debbie
Teach yourself visually sewing **646.2**
Colicchio, Tom
'wichcraft **641.8**
Colin, Chris
(jt. auth) Moore, R. This is Camino **641.5**
Coll, Steve
The Bin Ladens **920**
Ghost wars **958.1**
Coll, Steve, 1958-
Private empire **338.7**
The **collaboration**. Urwand, B. **791.43**
COLLABORATIONISTS
Kaplan, A. The collaborator: the trial & execution of Robert Brasillach **848**
The **collaborator**: the trial & execution of Robert Brasillach. Kaplan, A. **848**
COLLABORATORS (TRAITORS) See Collaborationists
COLLAGE
Peacock, M. The paper garden **92**
COLLAGE
See also Art; Handicraft
The **collapse**. Sarotte, M. E. **943.087**
The **collapse** of American criminal justice. Stuntz, W. J. **364.4**
COLLAPSE OF STRUCTURES See Structural failures
Collapse: how societies choose to fail or succeed. Diamond, J. M. **304.2**
The **collected** dialogues of Plato, including the letters. Plato **888**
Collected early poems, 1950-1970. Rich, A. **811**
Collected essays. Baldwin, J. **814**
Collected essays and poems. Thoreau, H. D. **818**
The **collected** essays of Ralph Ellison. Ellison, R. **814**
Collected later poems. Hecht, A. **811**
The **Collected** Letters of Thomas Hardy. **823**
COLLECTED PAPERS (ANTHOLOGIES) See Anthologies
Collected plays. Foote, H. **812**
Collected plays. Norman, M. **812**
Collected plays & writings on theater. Wilder, T. **812**
The **collected** plays of Neil Simon. Simon, N. **812**
Collected plays, 1944-1961. Miller, A. **812**
Collected poems. Smith, S. **821**
The **collected** poems. Plath, S. **811**
Collected poems. Kenyon, J. **811**
Collected poems. Lowell, R. **811**
Collected poems. Hayden, R. E. **811**
Collected poems. Dove, R. **811**

Collected poems. Auden, W. H.   **821**

Collected poems. Williams, C. K.   **811**

The **collected** poems. Kunitz, S.   **811**

Collected poems. Constantine, D.   **821**

Collected poems. Larkin, P.   **821**

Collected poems. Strand, M.   **811**

Collected Poems. Padgett, R.   **811**

Collected poems. Millay, E. S. V.   **811**

Collected poems. Bowers, E.   **811**

Collected poems. Gilbert, J.   **811**

Collected poems. Larkin, P.   **821**

Collected poems. Hughes, T.   **821**

Collected poems. Auden, W. H.   **811**

Collected poems. Davie, D.   **821**

Collected poems. Cavafy, C. P.   **889**

Collected poems. Justice, D. R.   **811**

Collected poems. Gunn, T.   **821**

Collected poems. Schuyler, J.   **811**

Collected poems. Garcia Lorca, F.   **861**

Collected poems & translations. Emerson, R. W. **811**

Collected poems 1956-1987. Ashbery, J.   **811**

Collected poems and other verse. Mallarme, S. **841**

The **collected** poems and selected prose. Burnshaw, S.   **811**

Collected poems in English and French. Beckett, S.   **841**

Collected poems in English, 1972-1999. Brodsky, J.   **891.7**

The **collected** poems of A. E. Housman. Housman, A. E.   **821**

The **collected** poems of Audre Lorde. Lorde, A. **811**

The **collected** poems of Barbara Guest. Guest, B.   **811**

The **collected** poems of Eugenio Montale 1925-1977.   **851**

The **collected** poems of Frank O'Hara. O'Hara, F.   **811**

The **collected** poems of James Laughlin. Laughlin, J.   **811**

The **collected** poems of James Merrill. Merrill, J.   **811**

The **collected** poems of John Ciardi. Ciardi, J. **811**

The **collected** poems of Kathleen Raine. Raine, K.   **821**

The **collected** poems of Kenneth Koch. Koch, K.   **811**

The **collected** poems of Lucille Clifton 1965-2010. Clifton, L.   **811**

The **collected** poems of Octavio Paz, 1957-1987. Paz, O.   **861**

The **collected** poems of Odysseus Elytis. Elytes, O.   **889**

The **collected** poems of Paul Blackburn. Blackburn, P.   **811**

The **collected** poems of Robert Creeley. Creeley, R.   **811**

The **collected** poems of Robert Penn Warren.   **811**

The **collected** poems of Ted Berrigan. Poems/Selections   **811**

The **collected** poems of Theodore Roethke. Roethke, T.   **811**

The **collected** poems of W.B. Yeats. Yeats, W. B.   **821**

The **collected** poems of William Carlos Williams. Williams, W. C.   **811**

Collected poems, 1909-1962. Eliot, T. S.   **811**

Collected poems, 1912-1944.   **811**

Collected poems, 1917-1982. MacLeish, A.   **811**

Collected poems, 1920-1954. Montale, E.   **851**

Collected poems, 1937-1971. Berryman, J.   **811**

Collected poems, 1943-2004. Wilbur, R.   **811**

Collected poems, 1947-1997. Ginsberg, A.   **811**

Collected poems, 1953-1993. Updike, J.   **811**

The **collected** poems, 1956-1998. Herbert, Z. **891.8**

Collected poems, 1957-1982. Berry, W.   **811**

Collected poems, prose, & plays. Frost, R.   **811**

Collected poetry and prose. Stevens, W.   **811**

The **collected** poetry of Nikki Giovanni, 1968-1998. Giovanni, N.   **811**

Collected works. Niedecker, L.   **811**

COLLECTED WORKS *See* Anthologies; Literature -- Collections; Storytelling -- Collections

Collected works [series]

   Wilson, L. The Talley trilogy   **812**

The **collected** works. Gibran, K.   **818**

COLLECTIBLE CARD GAMES

   See also Card games

COLLECTIBLES

   See also Collectors and collecting

COLLECTING *See* Collectors and collecting

COLLECTING OF ACCOUNTS

   Halpern, J. Bad paper   **332.7**

COLLECTING OF ACCOUNTS

   See also Commercial law; Credit; Debt; Debtor and creditor

COLLECTION AGENCIES

   Halpern, J. Bad paper   **332.7**

COLLECTION DEVELOPMENT (LIBRARIES)

   Evans, G. E. Collection management basics **025.2**

   Johnson, P. Fundamentals of Collection Development and Management   **025.2**

   Rethinking collection development and management   **025.2**

COLLECTION DEVELOPMENT (LIBRARIES)

   See Libraries -- Collection development

COLLECTION DEVELOPMENT (LIBRARIES) -- UNITED STATES -- POLICY STATEMENTS

   Vnuk, R. The weeding handbook   **025.2**

COLLECTION DEVELOPMENT -- ADMINISTRATION

   Johnson, P. Fundamentals of Collection Development and Management **025.2**

COLLECTION DEVELOPMENT -- HAND-BOOKS, MANUALS, ETC.

Disher, W. Crash Course in Collection Development **025.2**

COLLECTION MANAGEMENT (LIBRARIES)

Rethinking collection development and management **025.2**

COLLECTION MANAGEMENT (LIBRARIES) -- UNITED STATES -- CASE STUDIES

Singer, C. A. Fundamentals of Managing Reference Collections **025.2**

Collection management basics. Evans, G. E. **025.2**

COLLECTIVE MEMORY

Crais, C. History lessons **92**

COLLECTIVE MEMORY

See also Memory; Social psychology

COLLECTIVE MEMORY -- GERMANY

Fritzsche, P. Life and death in the Third Reich **943.086**

COLLECTIVE MEMORY -- JAPAN -- HISTORY -- 20TH CENTURY

Dower, J. W. Ways of forgetting, ways of remembering **940.53**

COLLECTIVE MEMORY -- POLITICAL ASPECTS -- UNITED STATES

Sehat, D. The Jefferson rule **306.2**

COLLECTIVE SECURITY *See* International security

COLLECTIVE SETTLEMENTS

See also Communism; Cooperation; Socialism

COLLECTIVISM

See also Economics; Political science

COLLECTORS

Singer, M. Character studies **920**

Tingey, J. The Englishman who posted himself and other curious objects **92**

COLLECTORS AND COLLECTING

Frost, R. O. Stuff **616.85**

Jamieson, D. Mint condition **796.357**

Jasanoff, M. Edge of empire **909.08**

COLLECTORS AND COLLECTING

See also Art; Hobbies

COLLECTORS AND COLLECTING -- UNITED STATES -- BIOGRAPHY

Dedman, B. Empty mansions **92**

COLLECTS *See* Prayers

College. Delbanco, A. **378.73**

College (un)bound. Selingo, J. J. **378**

COLLEGE ADMINISTRATORS

Rice, C. Extraordinary, ordinary people **92**

Roosevelt, C. Too close to the sun **92**

COLLEGE ADMISSIONS ESSAYS *See* College applications

COLLEGE AND SCHOOL DRAMA

Sokolove, M. Drama high **92**

COLLEGE AND SCHOOL DRAMA

See also Amateur theater; Drama; Student activities

COLLEGE AND SCHOOL JOURNALISM

See also Journalism; Student activities

COLLEGE AND UNIVERSITY LIBRARIES *See* Academic libraries

COLLEGE APPLICATIONS

Bedor, D. Getting in by standing out **371**

Bruni, F. Where You Go Is Not Who You'll Be **378.161**

Chatterjee, P. The dirty little secrets of getting into a top college **378.161**

Fiske, E. B. Fiske Guide to Getting Into The Right College **378.1**

Jager-Hyman, J. B+ grades, A+ college application **378.1**

Steinberg, J. The gatekeepers **378.1**

COLLEGE ATHLETES -- UNITED STATES -- ECONOMIC CONDITIONS

Nocera, J. Indentured **796.04**

COLLEGE ATHLETICS *See* College sports

COLLEGE BASKETBALL

Boeheim, J. Bleeding Orange **92**

Davis, S. Wooden **92**

Feinstein, J. The legends club **796.323**

COLLEGE CHOICE

Bruni, F. Where You Go Is Not Who You'll Be **378.161**

Chatterjee, P. The dirty little secrets of getting into a top college **378.161**

Fiske, E. B. Fiske guide to colleges **378**

Fiske, E. B. Fiske Guide to Getting Into The Right College **378.1**

Morgan, G. Undecided **371.4**

Peterson's four-year colleges 2015 **378.73**

Peterson's two-year colleges 2015 **378.73**

Profiles of American colleges 2015 **378.73**

COLLEGE CHOICE

See also Colleges and universities; School choice

COLLEGE COSTS

Dreifus, C. Higher education? **378**

Getting financial aid **378.3**

Mettler, S. Degrees of inequality **378.73**

COLLEGE COSTS

See also Colleges and universities -- Finance

COLLEGE DEANS

Green, B. Boltzmann's tomb **509**

COLLEGE DRAMA *See* College and school drama

College Entrance Examination Board (comp) 2015 getting financial aid **378.3**

COLLEGE ENTRANCE REQUIREMENTS *See* Colleges and universities -- Entrance requirements

COLLEGE FOOTBALL

Benedict, J. The System   **796.332**
Dent, J. Courage beyond the game   **796.332**
Gaul, G. M. Billion-Dollar Ball   **796.332**
Rodriguez, D. Rise   **92**

COLLEGE FOOTBALL -- HISTORY
Curtis, B. Fields of Battle   **940.54**
Roberts, D. Tribal   **796.332**

COLLEGE FOOTBALL COACHES
Benedict, J. The System   **796.332**
Burke, M. Saban   **796.332**

COLLEGE GRADUATES
        See also Professions

COLLEGE GRADUATES -- EMPLOYMENT
Blake, J. Life after college   **646.7**
Sandberg, S. Lean in   **658.4**

**COLLEGE GRADUATES -- VOCATIONAL
    GUIDANCE**
Selingo, J. J. There Is Life After College **650.14**

COLLEGE LIBRARIES *See* Academic libraries
COLLEGE LIFE *See* College students
COLLEGE MAJORS
        See also Academic degrees; Colleges and uni-
        versities -- Curricula
COLLEGE PRESIDENTS
Ambrose, S. E. Eisenhower   **92**
Ambrose, S. E. The victors   **940.54**
Anderson, L. Carlisle vs. Army   **796.332**
Blount, R. Robert E. Lee   **92**
Brands, H. W. Woodrow Wilson   **92**
Burstein, A. Madison and Jefferson   **973.4**
Conway, J. K. True north   **92**
Cooper, J. M. The warrior and the priest: Woodrow
    Wilson and Theodore Roosevelt   **92**
Cooper, J. M. Woodrow Wilson   **92**
David, A. Once upon a country   **92**
Fellman, M. The making of Robert E. Lee   **92**
Freeman, D. S. Lee   **92**
Gregorian, V. The road to home   **92**
Hofstadter, R. The American political tradition, and
    the men who made it   **973**
Kissinger, H. Diplomacy   **327.2**
MacMillan, M. Paris 1919   **940.3**
Marsden, G. M. Jonathan Edwards   **92**
Smith, J. E. Eisenhower   **973.921**
Thomas, E. M. Robert E. Lee   **92**
Tuchman, B. W. Practicing history   **907**
Weintraub, S. 15 stars   **920**
Wicker, T. Dwight D. Eisenhower   **973.921**

COLLEGE SPORTS
Clotfelter, C. T. Big-time sports in American uni-
    versities   **796**
Cohan, W. D. The price of silence   **364.15**
Feinstein, J. The legends club   **796.323**
Lewis, M. The blind side   **92**
Nocera, J. Indentured   **796.04**
Roberts, D. Tribal   **796.332**

COLLEGE SPORTS
        See also Sports; Student activities
**COLLEGE SPORTS -- ECONOMIC ASPECTS
    -- UNITED STATES**
Nocera, J. Indentured   **796.04**

COLLEGE SPORTS -- UNITED STATES
Benedict, J. The System   **796.332**
Clotfelter, C. T. Big-time sports in American uni-
    versities   **796**
Lewis, M. The blind side   **92**

**COLLEGE SPORTS -- UNITED STATES -- HIS-
    TORY**
Roberts, D. Tribal   **796.332**

COLLEGE STUDENTS
Bain, K. What the best college students do **378.1**
Crossman, A. Getting the best out of college **378.1**
Rose, M. Back to school   **374**
Shachtman, T. Airlift to America   **378.1**

COLLEGE STUDENTS
        See also Students

**COLLEGE STUDENTS -- POLITICAL ACTIV-
    ITY -- CALIFORNIA -- BERKELEY -- HIS-
    TORY**
Rosenfeld, S. Subversives   **378.1**

**COLLEGE STUDENTS -- POLITICAL ACTIV-
    ITY -- GRAPHIC NOVELS**
Students for a Democratic Society   **378.1**

COLLEGE STUDENTS -- SEXUAL BEHAVIOR
Freitas, D. The end of sex   **176**

COLLEGE STUDENTS -- SEXUAL BEHAVIOR
        See also Sex

COLLEGE STUDENTS -- UNITED STATES
Bain, K. What the best college students do **378.1**
Selingo, J. J. College (un)bound   **378**

COLLEGE STUDENTS, FOREIGN *See* Foreign
students

COLLEGE TEACHERS
Albom, M. Tuesdays with Morrie   **378.1**
Alice Walker   **813**
Alice Walker's The color purple   **813**
Baszile, J. The Black girl next door   **92**
Bayley, J. Elegy for Iris   **823**
Bell, E. T. Men of mathematics   **920**
Berger, J. The better to eat you with   **591.5**
Bernstein, J. Oppenheimer   **92**
Bird, K. American Prometheus   **92**
Black women writers (1950-1980)   **810**
Bloom, H. The anatomy of influence   **801**
Boyd, B.   Vladimir Nabokov: the American
    years   **813**
Boyd, B. Vladimir Nabokov: the Russian years **813**
Brodsky, J. Less than one   **809.1**
Brown, M. How I killed Pluto and why it had it
    coming   **523.4**
Buruma, I. Murder in Amsterdam   **364.152**
Chua, A. Battle hymn of the tiger mother   **306.874**

Coffey, P. Cathedrals of science **540**

Cokinos, C. The fallen sky **523.5**

Cole, K. C. Something incredibly wonderful happens **92**

Commager, H. S. The American mind **973**

Conway, J. K. True north **92**

Dallek, R. Nixon and Kissinger **92**

Dennett, D. C. Darwin's dangerous idea **146**

DeStefano, S. Coyote at the kitchen door **578.7**

Downey, K. The woman behind the New Deal **92**

Eco, U. Confessions of a young novelist **808.3**

Eire, C. M. N. Learning to die in Miami **92**

Eire, C. M. N. Waiting for snow in Havana **92**

Everett, D. L. Don't sleep, there are snakes **305.8**

Ferguson, N. The ascent of money **330**

Fraser, K. Ornament and silence **809**

Garvey, M. Stylized **808**

Gates, H. L. Colored people **92**

Gay, P. My German question **943**

Gillespie, C. Critical companion to Alice Walker **813**

Gillespie, C. Critical companion to Toni Morrison **813**

Gioia, D. Can poetry matter? **809.1**

Green, B. Boltzmann's tomb **509**

Greenfield, R. Timothy Leary **92**

Guttenplan, D. D. The Holocaust on trial **940.53**

Halberstam, D. The best and the brightest **973.922**

Halberstam, D. The children **323.1**

Hargittai, I. The Martians of science **920**

Hartman, S. V. Lose your mother **323**

Heaney, S. Finders keepers **821**

Heinrich, B. Summer world **591.7**

Hofstadter, D. R. I am a strange loop **153**

Hollis, L. London rising **942**

Hooks, B. Belonging **92**

Hooks, B. Wounds of passion **92**

Hough, S. E. Richter's scale **92**

Jamison, K. R. Nothing was the same **92**

Jarrell, R. No other book **809**

Judt, T. Thinking the twentieth century **320.092**

Kandel, E. R. In search of memory **153**

Karr, M. Lit **92**

Kissinger, H. Years of renewal **973.924**

Kubler-Ross, E. The wheel of life **150**

Lattin, D. The Harvard Psychedelic Club **920**

Li, C. N. The bitter sea **92**

Life stories **920**

Lytle, M. H. The gentle subversive **92**

Mackall, J. Plain secrets **289.7**

Maples, W. R. Dead men do tell tales **614**

Marton, K. The great escape **920**

McPhee, J. A. The ransom of Russian art **709**

Mendelsohn, D. The lost **92**

Milosz, C. To begin where I am **891.8**

Murphy, T. W. Life in rewind **92**

Nabokov, V. V. Speak, memory **813**

Nafisi, A. Reading Lolita in Tehran **92**

Nafisi, A. Things I've been silent about **92**

Olson, R. Don't be such a scientist **501**

Orbinski, J. An imperfect offering **610**

Parini, J. The art of teaching **371.1**

Pauling, L. C. Linus Pauling in his own words **081**

Pierpont, C. R. Passionate minds **810**

Poetry in person **809.1**

Preston, R. The wild trees **577.3**

Price, R. Ardent spirits **92**

Raymo, C. Walking zero **526**

Rhodes, R. Why they kill **364.3**

Rice, C. Extraordinary, ordinary people **92**

Richards, S. Chosen by a horse **636.1**

Roberts, S. King of infinite space **92**

Rubin, L. D. My father's people **920**

Ryan, D. P. Beneath the sands of Egypt **92**

Sabar, A. My father's paradise **305.8**

Samet, E. D. Soldier's heart **810**

Sanders, S. R. A private history of awe **92**

Schultz, P. My dyslexia **92**

Singh, S. Fermat's enigma **512**

Spring, J. Secret historian **92**

Stern, F. R. Five Germanys I have known **943.08**

Stern, J. Denial **92**

Susskind, L. The black hole war **530.1**

Tedlow, R. S. Andy Grove **92**

Tucker, T. The great starvation experiment **174.2**

Unferth, D. O. Revolution **920**

Varmus, H. The art and politics of science **92**

Wainaina, B. One day I will write about this place **823**

Walker, A. The same river twice **813**

Watson, J. D. Avoid boring people **92**

Watson, J. D. Genes, girls, and Gamow **92**

Weiner, J. Time, love, memory **591.5**

Wideman, J. E. Hoop roots **813**

Wills, G. Outside looking in **92**

Wolff, T. This boy's life: a memoir **92**

Zellner, R. The wrong side of Murder Creek **92**

COLLEGE TEACHERS *See* Colleges and universities -- Faculty; Educators; Teachers

COLLEGE TEACHERS -- UNITED STATES

Dreifus, C. Higher education? **378**

COLLEGES AND UNIVERSITIES

Delbanco, A. College **378.73**

Peterson's four-year colleges 2015 **378.73**

Profiles of American colleges 2015 **378.73**

COLLEGES AND UNIVERSITIES

See also Education; Higher education; Professional education; Schools

COLLEGES AND UNIVERSITIES -- APPLICATIONS *See* College applications

COLLEGES AND UNIVERSITIES -- BUILDINGS

See also Buildings

**COLLEGES AND UNIVERSITIES -- CURRI-
CULA**
Book of Majors 378

**COLLEGES AND UNIVERSITIES -- EN-
TRANCE REQUIREMENTS**
Bedor, D. Getting in by standing out 371

COLLEGES AND UNIVERSITIES -- FACULTY
Dreifus, C. Higher education? 378
Goldstein, W. For the love of physics 92

COLLEGES AND UNIVERSITIES -- FACULTY
See also Teachers

COLLEGES AND UNIVERSITIES -- FINANCE
Gaul, G. M. Billion-Dollar Ball 796.332
Selingo, J. J. College (un)bound 378

COLLEGES AND UNIVERSITIES -- FINANCE
See also Finance

**COLLEGES AND UNIVERSITIES -- SELEC-
TION** *See* College choice

**COLLEGES AND UNIVERSITIES -- STU-
DENTS** *See* College students

**COLLEGES AND UNIVERSITIES -- UNITED
STATES**
Book of Majors 378
Crossman, A. Getting the best out of college 378.1
Fiske, E. B. Fiske guide to colleges 378
Fiske, E. B. Fiske Guide to Getting Into The Right
College 378.1

Collen, Alanna
10% human 612.3

Colletti, Maria
Terrariums 635.9

COLLIES
See also Dogs

Collinge, Alan
The student loan scam 378.3

Collingham, E. M. (Elizabeth M.)
Curry 394.1
Collingham, L. The taste of war 940.53

Collingham, Lizzie
The taste of war 940.53

Collins, Billy
(ed) 180 more 811
Nine horses 811
Sailing alone around the room 811
The trouble with poetry and other poems 811
(ed) Poetry 180 811

Collins, Francis S.
The language of life 616

Collins, Gail
America's women 305.4
As Texas goes 320.6
When everything changed 305.4
William Henry Harrison 92

Collins, James C.
Good to great 658

Collins, Joseph T.
Conant, R. A field guide to reptiles & amphibians 597.9

Collins, Larry
O Jerusalem! 956.94

Collins, Lauren
When in French 92

Collins, Paul
The book of William 822.3
Duel With the Devil 364.152
Edgar Allan Poe 92
The murder of the century 364.152
The trouble with Tom: the strange afterlife and
times of Thomas Paine 92

Collision Low Crossers. Dawidoff, N. 796.3

COLLISIONS, RAILROAD *See* Railroad accidents

Colman, Andrew M.
A dictionary of psychology 150

Colmez, Coralie
Math on trial 345

Colomb, Gregory G.
(ed) A manual for writers of research papers, theses, and dissertations 808.06

**COLOMBIA -- POLITICS AND GOVERNMENT
-- 1974-**
Abad, H. Oblivion 868

COLOMBIAN AMERICANS -- BIOGRAPHY
Hernández, D. A cup of water under my bed 920.009

**COLON (ANATOMY) -- CANCER -- POPULAR
WORKS**
Ahuja, N. Johns Hopkins patients' guide to colon
and rectal cancer 616.99

Colon, Ernie
Jacobson, S. The 9/11 report 741.5
Jacobson, S. Anne Frank 92

Colonel House. Neu, C. E. 92
Colonel Roosevelt. Morris, E. 92

COLONIAL ADMINISTRATORS
Alexander, C. The Bounty: the true story of the mu-
tiny on the Bounty 996
Bremer, F. J. John Winthrop 974.4
Harris, J. W. The hanging of Thomas Jeremiah 92
Keneally, T. A commonwealth of thieves 994
Lukacs, J. Five days in London, May 1940 940.53
Meredith, M. Diamonds, gold, and war 968.04
Prescott, W. H. History of the conquest of Mexi-
co 972
Schneider, P. Brutal journey: the epic story of the
first crossing of North America 970.01
Tacitus, C. Complete works of Tacitus 878

COLONIAL HISTORY (U.S.) *See* United States
-- History -- 1600-1775, Colonial period

COLONIAL LEADERS
Broadwater, J. George Mason, forgotten founder 92

Gaustad, E. S. Roger Williams **92**
Harris, J. W. The hanging of Thomas Jeremiah **92**
LaPlante, E. Salem witch judge **92**
COLONIAL WILLIAMSBURG FOUNDATION
-- CATALOGS
Baumgarten, L. Four centuries of quilts **746.46**
COLONIALISM See Colonies; Imperialism
COLONIALISM -- AFRICA
Halperin, D. Tinderbox **614.5**
COLONIES
Hunt, T. Cities of empire **941**
Pagden, A. Peoples and empires **909**
COLONIES
See also Imperialism
COLONIES, SPACE See Space colonies
COLONISTS
Abdul-Jabbar, K. Black profiles in courage **920**
Gordon, C. Mistress Bradstreet **92**
Price, D. Love and hate in Jamestown **975.5**
COLONIZATION
Bailyn, B. The barbarous years **973.2**
Kwarteng, K. Ghosts of empire **909**
COLONIZATION
See also Imperialism; Land settlement
The **Colony**. Tayman, J. **614.5**
COLOR
Deeb, M. The beader's color palette **745.594**
Eckstut, A. The Secret Language of Color **535.6**
COLOR
See also Aesthetics; Chemistry; Light; Optics; Painting; Photometry
COLOR -- PSYCHOLOGICAL ASPECTS
See also Color sense; Psychology
COLOR BLINDNESS
Sacks, O. W. The island of the colorblind **617.7**
COLOR BLINDNESS
See also Color sense; Vision disorders
Color concrete garden projects. **721**
COLOR IN INTERIOR DECORATION
Atwood, R. Living with pattern **701.85**
The **color** of Christ. Blum, E. J. **232**
COLOR OF FOOD
Vibrant food **641.5**
The **color** of water. McBride, J. **92**
COLOR PHOTOGRAPHY
See also Photography
COLOR PRINTING
See also Printing
COLOR PURPLE (MOTION PICTURE)
Walker, A. The same river twice **813**
Color recipes for painted furniture and more. Sloan, A.
COLOR SENSE
See also Psychophysiology; Senses and sensation; Vision
COLORADO RIVER (COLO.-MEXICO)
Dolnick, E. Down the great unknown **979.1**

COLORADO RIVER -- HOOVER DAM See
Hoover Dam (Ariz. and Nev.)
Colored people. Gates, H. L. **92**
COLORING BOOKS
See also Picture books for children
Colors of confinement. **940.53**
Colors of the mountain. Chen, D. **92**
Colors passing through us. Piercy, M. **811**
The **colossal** book of short puzzles and problems. Gardner, M. **793.8**
Colossus. Hiltzik, M. A. **627**
COLOUR See Color
Colquhoun, Kate
Did she kill him? **364.152**
Coltman, Leycester
The real Fidel Castro **92**
Colton, Larry
Counting coup **796.323**
Coltrane. Ratliff, B. **92**
Coltrane, John, 1926-1967
About
Kahn, A. The house that Trane built **781.65**
Ratliff, B. Coltrane **92**
COLUMBIA (SPACECRAFT)
White, R. Into the Black **629.44**
The **Columbia** anthology of British poetry. **821**
The **Columbia** book of Chinese poetry. **895.1**
COLUMBIA BROADCASTING SYSTEM, INC.
-- HISTORY
Mitchell, G. The tunnels **943.155**
The **Columbia** companion to the twentieth-century American short story. **813**
Columbia contemporary American religion series
Hamm, T. D. The Quakers in America **289.6**
Smith, J. I. Islam in America **297.092**
The **Columbia** documentary history of American women since 1941. Sigerman, H. **305.4**
The **Columbia** gazetteer of North America. **917**
The **Columbia** gazetteer of the world. **910.3**
The **Columbia** Granger's dictionary of poetry quotations. **808.81**
The **Columbia** Granger's index to poetry in anthologies. **808.81**
The **Columbia** Granger's Index to poetry in collected and selected works. **808.81**
The **Columbia** guide to America in the 1960s. **973.923**
The **Columbia** guide to American Indians of the Great Plains. Fowler, L. **970.004**
The **Columbia** guide to American Indians of the Northeast. Bragdon, K. J. **970.004**
The **Columbia** guide to American Indians of the Southeast. Perdue, T. **970.004**
The **Columbia** guide to modern Chinese history. Schoppa, R. K. **951.05**
The **Columbia** guide to online style. Walker, J.

R.   **808**

The **Columbia** guide to the Cold War. Kort, M.   **973.92**

The **Columbia** guide to the Vietnam War. Anderson, D. L.   **959.704**

Columbia guides to American history and cultures [series]

Anderson, D. L. The Columbia guide to the Vietnam War   **959.704**

The Columbia guide to America in the 1960s   **973.923**

Kort, M. The Columbia guide to the Cold War   **973.92**

Columbia guides to American Indian history and culture [series]

Bragdon, K. J. The Columbia guide to American Indians of the Northeast   **970.004**

Fowler, L. The Columbia guide to American Indians of the Great Plains   **970.004**

Perdue, T. The Columbia guide to American Indians of the Southeast   **970.004**

Columbia guides to Asian history [series]

Schoppa, R. K. The Columbia guide to modern Chinese history   **951.05**

The **Columbia** history of American poetry.   **811**

The **Columbia** history of Chinese literature. **895.1**

The **Columbia** history of the 20th century. **909.82**

The **Columbia** history of the British novel.   **823**

The **Columbia** history of Western philosophy.   **190**

Columbia Journalism Review books [series]

The best business writing 2013   **330.9**

Columbia journalism review books [series]

Simon, J. The new censorship   **363.31**

Columbia literary history of the United States. **810**

COLUMBIA RIVER

Harden, B. A river lost   **333.91**

Columbia studies in international and global history [series]

Fleming, J. R. Fixing the sky   **551.6**

Columbia University/Health Service

The Go ask Alice book of answers   **613**

Columbine. Cullen, D.   **364.152**

COLUMBINE HIGH SCHOOL (LITTLETON, COLO.)

Klebold, S. A mother's reckoning   **373**

COLUMBUS DAY

See also Holidays

Columbus, Christopher

About

Mann, C. C. 1493   **909**

Morison, S. E. Admiral of the ocean sea: a life of Christopher Columbus   **92**

COLUMNISTS *See* Journalists

Colvile, Robert

The Great Acceleration   **303.483**

Colwin, Laurie

Home cooking   **641.5**

More home cooking   **642**

COMANCHE INDIANS -- HISTORY

Gwynne, S. C. Empire of the summer moon   **92**

COMANCHE INDIANS -- WARS

Gwynne, S. C. Empire of the summer moon   **92**

COMBAT -- PSYCHOLOGICAL ASPECTS

Glass, C. The deserters   **940.54**

COMBAT PHOTOGRAPHY *See* War photography

Combs, Rebecca Ann

Kumihimo : basics & beyond   **745.594**

COMBUSTION

See also Chemistry

COMCATE (FIRM)

Casnocha, B. My start-up life   **338.7**

Come as you are. Nagoski, E.   **613.9**

Come hell or high water. Dyson, M. E.   **976.3**

Come on all you ghosts. Zapruder, M.   **811**

The **Comedians.** Nesteroff, K.   **792.7**

COMEDIANS

Diller, P. Like a lampshade in a whorehouse   **92**

Fey, T. Bossypants   **92**

Kanfer, S. Groucho: the life and times of Julius Henry Marx   **92**

Lewis, J. Dean & me   **92**

Life stories   **920**

Louvish, S. Monkey business   **920**

Martin, S. Born standing up   **92**

Mooney, P. Black is the new white   **92**

Nesteroff, K. The Comedians   **792.7**

Palin, M. Halfway to Hollywood   **92**

Quirk, L. J. Bob Hope: the road well-traveled   **92**

Short, M. I must say   **92**

COMEDIANS

See also Actors; Entertainers

COMEDIANS -- BIOGRAPHY

Ackroyd, P. Charlie Chaplin   **92**

Cleese, J. So, anyway...   **92**

Henry, D. Furious cool   **92**

COMEDIANS -- FAMILY RELATIONSHIPS

Carlin, K. A Carlin Home Companion   **92**

COMEDIANS -- UNITED STATES -- BIOGRAPHY

Ackroyd, P. Charlie Chaplin   **92**

Crystal, B. Still foolin' 'em   **92**

Henry, D. Furious cool   **92**

Jobrani, M. I'm not a terrorist, but I've played one on tv   **92**

Zoglin, R. Hope   **92**

COMEDIANS -- UNITED STATES -- INTERVIEWS

Apatow, J. Sick in the head   **792.7**

COMEDIES

See also Drama; Wit and humor

COMEDY

Nesteroff, K. The Comedians   792.7

COMEDY
   See also Drama; Wit and humor

COMEDY FILMS
Nesteroff, K. The Comedians   792.7

COMEDY FILMS
   See also Comedies; Motion pictures

COMEDY RADIO PROGRAMS
Nesteroff, K. The Comedians   792.7

COMEDY TELEVISION PROGRAMS
Burnett, C. In such good company   791.45
Lear, N. Even This I Get to Experience   92
Nesteroff, K. The Comedians   792.7
Shales, T. Live from New York   791.45

COMEDY TELEVISION PROGRAMS
   See also Comedies; Television programs

Comet. Sagan, C.   523.6

COMETS
Sagan, C. Comet   523.6

COMETS
   See also Astronomy; Solar system

COMFORT FOOD
Adarme, A. The year of cozy   641.3
Lawson, N. Simply Nigella   641.5

Comfort me with apples. Reichl, R.   92

The **comfort** women. Hicks, G.   940.54

COMFORT WOMEN
Hicks, G. The comfort women   940.54

Comfort, Alex, 1920-2000
The joy of sex   613.9

COMIC BOOK NOVELS *See* Graphic novels

COMIC BOOK WRITERS
Bechdel, A. Fun home   741.5
Schumacher, M. Will Eisner   92

COMIC BOOKS, STRIPS, ETC.
Abel, J. Drawing words & writing pictures   741.5
Brunetti, I. An anthology of graphic fiction, cartoons & true stories, vol. 2   741.5
Brunetti, I. An Anthology of graphic fiction, cartoons, and true stories   741.5
Crumb, R. The book of Genesis   741.5
Gladstone, B. The influencing machine   302.23
Hajdu, D. The ten-cent plague   741.5
Humbug   741.5
Jones, G. Men of tomorrow   741.5
Kitchen, D. The art of Harvey Kurtzman   741.5
Masters of American comics   741.5
McCloud, S. Reinventing comics   741.5
Morrison, G. Supergods   741.5
My friend Dahmer   741.5
Nadel, D. Art in time   741.5
Small, D. Stitches   741.5
Spiegelman, A. Co-Mix   741.5
Spiegelman, A. In the shadow of no towers 973.931
Understanding comics   741.5
Watterson, B. The complete Calvin and

Hobbes   741.5
Wednesday comics   741.5

COMIC BOOKS, STRIPS, ETC.
   See also Wit and humor

COMIC BOOKS, STRIPS, ETC. -- AUTHORSHIP
Kneece, M. The art of comic book writing   741.5

COMIC BOOKS, STRIPS, ETC. -- ENCYCLOPEDIAS
Beatty, S. The DC Comics encyclopedia   741.5

COMIC BOOKS, STRIPS, ETC. -- HISTORY
Howe, S. Marvel Comics   741.5

COMIC BOOKS, STRIPS, ETC. -- HISTORY AND CRITICISM
Graphic novels beyond the basics   025.2
O'Neil, D. Batman unauthorized   741.5

COMIC BOOKS, STRIPS, ETC. -- TECHNIQUE
Abel, J. Mastering comics   741.5

COMIC BOOKS, STRIPS, ETC. -- UNITED STATES
Morrison, G. Supergods   741.5

COMIC BOOKS, STRIPS, ETC. -- UNITED STATES -- HISTORY AND CRITICISM
Holtz, A. American newspaper comics   741.5
Howe, S. Marvel Comics   741.5
Ricca, B. Super boys   92

Comics and sequential art. Eisner, W.   741.5

Coming apart. Murray, C.   305.8

Coming clean. Miller, K. R.   92

Coming into the country. McPhee, J. A.   979.8

COMING OF AGE -- FRANCE -- PARIS
Chambers, V. 32 yolks   92

COMING OF AGE -- NEW YORK (STATE) -- NEW YORK
Rips, N. Trying to float   974.7

COMING OF AGE -- UNITED STATES
Lamarche, U. Unabrow   92
Smith, T. K. Ordinary light   92

Coming of age as a poet. Vendler, H. H.   820

Coming of age in Samoa. Mead, M.   306

COMING OF AGE STORIES *See* Bildungsromans

The **coming** of the New Deal, 1933-1935. Schlesinger, A. M.   973.917

The **coming** of the Third Reich. Evans, R. J. 943.08

Coming out to play. Marcus, E.   92

The **coming** plague. Garrett, L.   614.4

COMMA
Norris, M. Between you & me   428

Commager, Henry Steele
The American mind   973
Morison, S. E. The growth of the American Republic   973

Command and control. Schlosser, E.   363.17

COMMAND OF TROOPS
Korda, M. Clouds of Glory   92

Ricks, T. E. The generals 355.009
COMMAND OF TROOPS -- CASE STUDIES
Hamilton, N. Commander in chief 940.53
Wolf, M. J. Abandoned in hell 959.704
COMMAND OF TROOPS -- HISTORY -- 20TH CENTURY
Jordan, J. W. American warlords 973.917
COMMAND OF TROOPS -- HISTORY -- 20TH CENTURY -- CASE STUDIES
Ricks, T. E. The generals 355.009
COMMAND OF TROOPS -- UNITED STATES -- CASE STUDIES
Hamilton, N. The mantle of command 940.54
Commander. Taylor, S. 92
Commander in chief. Hamilton, N. 940.53
The **commanders.** Woodward, B. 973.928
COMMANDO TROOPS
Couch, D. Sua sponte 356
COMMEDIA DELL'ARTE
See also Acting; Comedy; Farces
COMMENCEMENTS
McCullough, D. J. You Are Not Special 170
Very good lives 158
COMMENCEMENTS
See also Colleges and universities; High schools; School assembly programs
COMMERCE
See also Economics; Finance
COMMERCE -- HISTORY
Mann, C. C. 1493 909
Micklethwait, J. The company 338.7
COMMERCE -- LAW AND LEGISLATION *See* Commercial law
COMMERCIAL AERONAUTICS
See also Freight; Transportation
COMMERCIAL AERONAUTICS -- CHINA
Fallows, J. China airborne 387.7
COMMERCIAL AGENTS
August, O. Inside the red mansion 951.05
COMMERCIAL ART
Heller, S. Becoming a graphic & digital designer 741.6
COMMERCIAL ART
See also Advertising; Art; Drawing; Visual communication
COMMERCIAL ART -- HISTORY
Eskilson, S. J. Graphic design 740
COMMERCIAL ART GALLERIES
See also Business enterprises
COMMERCIAL BUILDINGS
See also Buildings
COMMERCIAL CATALOGS
See also Advertising
COMMERCIAL CRIMES -- ILLINOIS -- CHICAGO -- HISTORY -- 20TH CENTURY
Jobb, D. Empire of deception 92

COMMERCIAL EMPLOYEES *See* Office workers
COMMERCIAL FISHING
Clover, C. The end of the line 333
Ellis, R. Tuna 333.95
Greenberg, P. Four fish 333.95
Hilborn, R. Overfishing 338.3
Jacobsen, R. The living shore 639.9
Kurlansky, M. Cod 333.95
Kurlansky, M. The last fish tale 639.2
Roberts, C. The unnatural history of the sea 909
COMMERCIAL FISHING
See also Industries
COMMERCIAL FISHING -- UNITED STATES
Greenberg, P. American catch 333.95
COMMERCIAL GEOGRAPHY
See also Commerce; Geography
COMMERCIAL LAW
Pakroo, P. The small business start-up kit 346
COMMERICAL ART -- HISTORY
Eskilson, S. J. Graphic design 740
Commerson, Philibert, 1727-1773
About
Ridley, G. The discovery of Jeanne Baret 92
Commire, Anne
(ed) Women in world history 920.003
COMMITMENT (PSYCHOLOGY)
See also Choice (Psychology)
Commodore. Renehan, E. J. 92
Common
One day it'll all make sense 92
Common (Musician)
About
Common One day it'll all make sense 92
Common as air. Hyde, L. 346.04
The **common** cause. Parkinson, R. G. 973.31
COMMON COLD *See* Cold (Disease)
Common ground. Lukas, J. A. 305.8
COMMON LAW
See also Law
The **common** man. Manning, M. 811
COMMON SENSE
Watts, D. J. Everything is obvious 153.4
The **common** thread. Sulston, J. 572.8
COMMONWEALTH COUNTRIES
Ferguson, N. Empire: the rise and demise of the British world order and the lessons for global power 909
COMMONWEALTH COUNTRIES -- HISTORY
Brendon, P. The decline and fall of the British Empire, 1781-1997 909
Gott, R. Britain's empire 942
Commonwealth Fund Book Program
Lovelock, J. The ages of Gaia 570.1
A **commonwealth** of thieves. Keneally, T. 994
COMMONWEALTH, THE *See* Political science;

Republics; State, The

COMMUNAL LIVING

See also Cooperation

COMMUNICABLE DISEASES

Encyclopedia of plague and pestilence **614.4**

Garrett, L. The coming plague **614.4**

Goldfarb, T. L. The patient survival guide

Oldstone, M. B. A. Viruses, plagues, and history **614.4**

COMMUNICABLE DISEASES

See also Diseases; Public health

COMMUNICABLE DISEASES -- HISTORY

Halperin, D. Tinderbox **614.5**

Murphy, M. Rabid **614.5**

COMMUNICABLE DISEASES -- PREVENTION

Allen, A. Vaccine **614.4**

Goldfarb, T. L. The patient survival guide

COMMUNICATION

Berger, Z. Talking to your doctor **610.69**

Duarte, N. Resonate **658.452**

Everett, D. L. Language **400**

How to Talk So Kids Will Listen and Listen So Kids Will Talk **649.1**

Kerpen, D. The art of people **650.1**

McGowan, B. Pitch Perfect **658.452**

McMillan, R. Crucial conversations **153.6**

O'Connor, R. Friends, followers, and the future **302.3**

Olson, R. Don't be such a scientist **501**

Poe, M. Learning to communicate in science and engineering **501**

Port, M. Steal the show **658.4**

Stone, D. Difficult conversations **158**

Suskind, R. Life, animated **618.92**

Tannen, D. I only say this because I love you **306.87**

COMMUNICATION

See also Sociology

COMMUNICATION -- GRAPHIC METHODS

Rendgen, S. Understanding the world **741.6**

COMMUNICATION AMONG ANIMALS *See* Animal communication

Communication and society [series]

McLuhan, M. The global village **302.2**

COMMUNICATION ARTS *See* Language arts

COMMUNICATION DISORDERS (MEDICINE)

See Communicative disorders

COMMUNICATION IN LEARNING AND SCHOLARSHIP -- HISTORY

Lima, M. The book of trees **001.2**

COMMUNICATION IN MANAGEMENT

Meyers, P. As we speak **808.5**

COMMUNICATION IN MANAGEMENT -- SEX DIFFERENCES

Kramer, A. S. Breaking through bias **650.101**

COMMUNICATION IN MARRIAGE

See also Marriage

COMMUNICATION IN MEDICINE

Berger, Z. Talking to your doctor **610.69**

COMMUNICATION IN ORGANIZATIONS

Annis, B. Work with me **306.3**

COMMUNICATION IN ORGANIZATIONS -- SEX DIFFERENCES

Kramer, A. S. Breaking through bias **650.101**

COMMUNICATION IN POLITICS -- UNITED STATES -- HISTORY

Greenberg, D. Republic of spin **973.099**

COMMUNICATION IN SCIENCE

Olson, R. Don't be such a scientist **501**

COMMUNICATIVE DISORDERS

Sacks, O. The mind's eye **616.85**

COMMUNICATIVE DISORDERS

See also Nervous system -- Diseases

COMMUNISM

Brown, A. The rise and fall of communism **320.5**

Marx, K. The Communist manifesto **335.4**

Pipes, R. Communism: a history **335.4**

Pleshakov, K. There is no freedom without bread! **947**

Priestland, D. The red flag **335.4**

Smith, D. Former people **305.5**

Stokes, G. The walls came tumbling down **947.085**

Wheen, F. Karl Marx **335.4**

Zizek, S. First as tragedy, then as farce **337**

COMMUNISM

See also Collectivism; Political science; Totalitarianism

COMMUNISM -- CAMBODIA

Bizot, F. The gate **959.604**

Kiernan, B. The Pol Pot regime **959.6**

COMMUNISM -- CHINA

God is red **275.1**

Levine, S. I. Mao **951.05**

Vogel, E. F. Deng Xiaoping and the transformation of China **951.05**

COMMUNISM -- RUSSIA

Applebaum, A. Iron curtain **947**

Gellately, R. Stalin's curse **947.084**

COMMUNISM -- SOVIET UNION

Figes, O. The whisperers **947.084**

Pleshakov, K. There is no freedom without bread! **947**

Service, R. Trotsky **92**

COMMUNISM -- SOVIET UNION *See* Communism -- Russia

COMMUNISM -- UNITED STATES

Chambers, W. Witness **92**

Haynes, J. E. Venona **327.12**

Morgan, T. Reds: McCarthyism in twentieth-century America **973.9**

COMMUNISM AND LITERATURE

Nabokov, V. V. Lectures on Russian literature **891.7**

Polonsky, R. Molotov's magic lantern   **947**

COMMUNISM AND LITERATURE
See also Communism; Literature

COMMUNISM AND RELIGION
See also Communism; Religion

Communism: a history. Pipes, R.   **335.4**

COMMUNIST COUNTRIES -- POLITICS AND GOVERNMENT
Applebaum, A. Iron curtain   **947**

COMMUNIST COUNTRIES -- SOCIAL CONDITIONS
Applebaum, A. Iron curtain   **947**

COMMUNIST LEADERS
Amis, M. Koba the dread   **947.084**
Berthon, S. Warlords   **940.53**
Brent, J. Inside the Stalin archives   **947.086**
Brent, J. Stalin's last crime   **947.084**
Brinkley, J. Cambodia's curse   **959.6**
Carlson, P. K blows top   **947.085**
Castro, F. Fidel Castro: my life   **92**
Chang, J. Mao: the unknown story   **92**
Coltman, L. The real Fidel Castro   **92**
Conquest, R. Stalin   **92**
Costigliola, F. Roosevelt's lost alliances   **940.53**
Dikötter, F. Mao's great famine   **951.05**
Dobbs, M. One minute to midnight   **973.922**
Duiker, W. J. Ho Chi Minh   **959.704**
Gimbel, W. Havana dreams   **972.91**
Gordin, M. D. Red cloud at dawn   **355**
Hassig, R. C. The hidden people of North Korea   **951.93**
Hochschild, A. The unquiet ghost   **947.084**
Kissinger, H. Diplomacy   **327.2**
Mann, J. The rebellion of Ronald Reagan   **973.927**
Medvedev, R. A. Let history judge   **947.084**
Montefiore, S. Stalin: the court of the red tsar   **92**
Montefiore, S. Young Stalin   **92**
Nikita Khrushchev   **92**
Pipes, R. Russia under the Bolshevik regime   **947.084**
Pleshakov, K. Stalin's folly   **940.54**
Polonsky, R. Molotov's magic lantern   **947**
Pomper, P. Lenin's brother   **92**
Pringle, P. The murder of Nikolai Vavilov   **92**
Prisoner of the state   **92**
Radzinsky, E. Stalin   **92**
Rasenberger, J. The brilliant disaster   **972.91**
Ratnesar, R. Tear down this wall   **973.927**
Service, R. Trotsky   **92**
Service, R. Lenin--a biography   **947.084**
Service, R. Stalin   **92**
Short, P. Mao   **951.05**
Snyder, T. D. Bloodlands   **940.54**
Spence, J. D. Mao Zedong   **951.05**
Sun Shuyun The Long March   **951.04**
Symmes, P. The boys from Dolores   **972.91**

Szulc, T. Fidel   **92**
Taubman, W. Khrushchev   **92**
Tolstaia, T. Pushkin's children   **891.7**
Volkogonov, D. A. Lenin   **947.084**
Von Tunzelmann, A. Red heat   **972.9**
West, R. Tito   **949.7**
The **Communist** manifesto. Marx, K.   **335.4**

COMMUNIST PARTY (CHINA)
McGregor, R. The Party   **324.2**
Sun Shuyun The Long March   **951.04**

COMMUNIST PARTY (U.S.)
Haynes, J. E. Venona   **327.12**

COMMUNISTS -- GERMANY -- BIOGRAPHY
Sperber, J. Karl Marx   **92**

COMMUNITIES -- RELIGIOUS ASPECTS -- CHRISTIANITY
Pattison, J. Slow church   **253**

COMMUNITY DEVELOPMENT
Cortese, A. Locavesting   **332.6**
Overdevelopment, Overpopulation, Overshoot   **363.9**

COMMUNITY DEVELOPMENT
See also Domestic economic assistance; Social change; Urban renewal

COMMUNITY DEVELOPMENT, URBAN -- UNITED STATES
Duany, A. Suburban nation   **307.76**

COMMUNITY GARDENS
Joy, L. Start a community food garden   **635**
Smith, J. N. Growing a garden city   **635**

COMMUNITY GARDENS
See also Gardens

COMMUNITY GARDENS -- UNITED STATES
Hanson, D. Breaking through concrete   **630**

COMMUNITY HEALTH SERVICES
See also Community services; Public health

COMMUNITY HISTORY *See* Local history
COMMUNITY IDENTITY *See* Group identity
COMMUNITY LIFE
Kurtz, G. Three minutes in Poland   **947.7**

COMMUNITY LIFE
See also Associations

COMMUNITY LIFE -- POLAND -- NASIELSK -- HISTORY -- 20TH CENTURY
Kurtz, G. Three minutes in Poland   **947.7**

COMMUNITY ORGANIZATION
See also Community life; Social work

A community resilience guide [series]
Ackerman-Leist, P. Rebuilding the foodshed **338.1**

COMMUNITY SERVICES
See also Social work

COMMUNITY-SUPPORTED AGRICULTURE
See also Agriculture; Food cooperatives

COMMUTING
See also Transportation

COMPACT CARS

See also Automobiles

COMPACT DISC READ-ONLY MEMORY *See* CD-ROMs

COMPACT DISCS
See also Optical storage devices; Sound recordings

Compagno, Leonard J. V.
Sharks of the world **597**

COMPANIES *See* Business enterprises; Corporations; Partnership

Companies we keep. Abrams, J. **338.7**

Companion to Asian studies [series]
Keene, D. The pleasures of Japanese literature **895.6**

Companion to Narnia. Ford, P. F. **823**

The **Companion** to southern literature. **810**

The **company.** Micklethwait, J. **338.7**

COMPANY SYMBOLS *See* Trademarks

The **company** town. Green, H. **307.7**

COMPANY TOWNS -- UNITED STATES -- HISTORY
Green, H. The company town **307.7**

The **company** we keep. Chadwick, D. H. **333.95**

COMPAQ COMPUTER CORPORATION
Burrows, P. Backfire: Carly Fiorina's high-stakes battle for the soul of Hewlett-Packard **338.7**

COMPARATIVE ANATOMY
See also Anatomy; Zoology

COMPARATIVE CIVILIZATION
Morris, I. Why the West rules--for now **909**

COMPARATIVE EDUCATION
Ripley, A. The smartest kids in the world **370.9**

COMPARATIVE GOVERNMENT
Fukuyama, F. Political Order and Political Decay **320.1**
Fukuyama, F. The origins of political order **320**

COMPARATIVE PHYSIOLOGY
See also Physiology

COMPARATIVE PSYCHOLOGY
Bearzi, M. Beautiful minds **599.8**
Bowers, K. Zoobiquity **636.089**
Braitman, L. Animal madness **591.5**
Masson, J. M. When elephants weep **591.5**
Safina, C. Beyond words **591.56**
Suddendorf, T. The gap **156**
Waal, F. d. Our inner ape **156**

COMPARATIVE PSYCHOLOGY
See also Zoology

COMPARATIVE RELIGION *See* Christianity and other religions; Religions

COMPARISON OF CULTURES *See* Cross-cultural studies

COMPASS
Aczel, A. D. The riddle of the compass **912**

COMPASS
See also Magnetism; Navigation

Compass Rose. Sze, A. **811**

COMPASSION
Armstrong, K. Twelve steps to a compassionate life **177**
Doty, J. R. Into the Magic Shop **92**
How to be compassionate **294.3**
Katz, J. Saving Simon **636.1**

COMPASSION
See also Emotions

COMPENSATION *See* Pensions; Salaries, wages, etc.; Workers' compensation

COMPETENCE *See* Performance

Competing voices from the Russian Revolution. **947.084**

COMPETITION
See also Business; Business ethics; Commerce

COMPETITION (PSYCHOLOGY)
Rosenbaum, D. A. It's a jungle in there **153**

COMPETITION (PSYCHOLOGY)
See also Interpersonal relations; Motivation (Psychology); Psychology

COMPETITION, INTERNATIONAL
Newman, K. S. The accordion family **306.874**

COMPLEMENTARY THERAPIES -- ENCYCLOPEDIAS -- ENGLISH
The Gale encyclopedia of alternative medicine **615.5**

The **complete** bedside companion. McFarlane, R. **649.8**

The **complete** Bible handbook. Bowker, J. **220.6**

The **complete** book of cacti & succulents. Hewitt, T. **635.9**

The **complete** book of food counts. Netzer, C. T. **613.2**

Complete book of home preserving. **641.4**

The **complete** book of jewelry making. Codina, C. **739.27**

The **Complete** book of pasta and noodles. **641.8**

The **complete** book of pickling. Mackenzie, J. **641.4**

The **complete** book of polymer clay. Pavelka, L. **738.1**

The **complete** Calvin and Hobbes. Watterson, B. **741.5**

The **complete** cartoons of the New Yorker. **741.5**

The **complete** cat breed book. **636.8**

Complete cat care.

The **complete** classical music guide. **780**

The **complete** collected poems of Maya Angelou. Angelou, M. **811**

The **complete** compost gardening guide. Pleasant, B. **631.8**

The **complete** dictionary of real estate terms explained simply. Haden, J. **333.3**

Complete do-it-yourself manual. Reader's Digest Association, I. **643**

Complete do-it-yourself manual. **643**

The **complete** dog book. American Kennel Club **636.7**

The **complete** game. Darling, R. **92**

The **complete** gods and goddesses of ancient Egypt. Wilkinson, R. H. **299**

Complete Greek tragedies [series]

  Aeschylus Aeschylus **882**

  Euripides Euripides **882**

  Euripides Euripides [2] **882**

  Sophocles Sophocles **882**

The **complete** guide to acquisitions management. Lewis, L. K. **025.2**

The **complete** guide to finishing basements. **643**

The **complete** guide to finishing basements. Black & Decker Corp. **643**

Complete guide to fitness & health. **613.7**

The **complete** guide to hunting, butchering, and cooking big game. **799.2**

The **Complete** Guide to Hunting, Butchering, and Cooking Wild Game. **799.2**

The **complete** guide to national symbols and emblems. Minahan, J. **929.9**

The **complete** guide to patios & walkways. Black & Decker Corp. **690**

The **complete** guide to plumbing. Black & Decker Corp. **696**

The **complete** guide to plumbing. **696**

Complete Guide to Prescription & Nonprescription Drugs. Griffith, H. W. **615**

The **complete** guide to roofing & siding. **695**

The **complete** guide to roofing, siding & trim. Black & Decker Corp. **695**

Complete Guide to Stargazing. Scagell, R. **520**

The **complete** guide to upholstery. Dobson, C. **684.1**

The **complete** guide to wiring. **621.319**

The **complete** houseplant survival manual. Pleasant, B. **635.9**

The **complete** IEP guide. Siegel, L. M. **371.9**

The **complete** jewelry making course. McGrath, J. **739.27**

The **complete** lesbian & gay parenting guide. Lev, A. I. **649**

The **complete** library technology planner. Cohn, J. M. **025**

The **complete** major prose plays. Ibsen, H. **839.8**

The **complete** meat cookbook. Aidells, B. **641.6**

The **complete** odes of Pindar. Pindar **884**

The **complete** oil painter. Gorst, B. **751.45**

The **complete** operas of Mozart. Osborne, C. **792.5**

The **complete** operas of Puccini. Osborne, C. **792.5**

The **complete** operas of Richard Wagner. Osborne, C. **792.5**

The **complete** outdoor builder. **690**

The **complete** Persepolis. Satrapi, M. **741.5**

The **Complete** Photo Guide to Cardmaking. Watanabe, J. **745.594**

The **complete** photo guide to crochet. Hubert, M. **746.43**

The **complete** photo guide to framing & displaying artwork. Kistler, V. C. **749**

The **complete** photo guide to home improvement. Black & Decker Corp. **643**

The **complete** photo guide to home repair. Black & Decker Corp. **643**

The **complete** photo guide to perfect fitting. Veblen, S. **646.4**

The **complete** photo guide to sewing. Creative Publishing International, I. **646.2**

The **complete** photo guide to window treatments. **646.2**

The **complete** plays. Plays **822**

The **complete** plays. Synge, J. M. **822**

The **complete** plays. Chekhov, A. P. **891.7**

The **complete** plays. Aristophanes **882**

The **complete** plays. Plays **822**

Complete plays. O'Neil, E. **812**

Complete poems. Poe, E. A. **811**

Complete poems. Bunting, B. **821**

The **complete** poems. Jonson, B. **821**

The **complete** poems. Coleridge, S. T. **821**

The **complete** poems. Jarrell, R. **811**

The **complete** poems. Lawrence, D. H. **821**

Complete poems. Johnson, J. W. **811**

The **complete** poems. **811**

The **complete** poems. Sexton, A. **811**

The **complete** poems and plays, 1909-1950. Eliot, T. S. **811**

Complete poems and selected letters. Crane, H. **811**

The **complete** poems of Anna Akhmatova. Akhmatova, A. A. **891.71**

The **complete** poems of C. Day-Lewis. **821**

The **complete** poems of Carl Sandburg. Sandburg, C. **811**

The **complete** poems of Emily Jane Bronte. Bronte, E. **821**

The **complete** poems of John Keats. Keats, J. **821**

The **complete** poems of Kenneth Rexroth. Rexroth, K. **811**

Complete poems, 1904-1962. Cummings, E. E. **811**

Complete poetry and collected prose. Whitman, W. **811**

The **complete** poetry and prose of Geoffrey Chaucer. Chaucer, G. **821**

The **complete** poetry and prose of William Blake. Blake, W. **821**

The **complete** poetry and selected prose of John Donne. Donne, J. **821**

Complete poetry: translations & selected prose. **821**

The **complete** Pompeii. Berry, J. **937**

Complete Roman drama in translation [series]

  Terence Terence, the comedies **872**

The **complete** sailing manual. Sleight, S. **797.124**

The **complete** serger handbook. James, C. **646.2**

The **complete** snowboarder. Bennett, J. **796.9**

The **complete** vegetarian cookbook. **641.5**

Complete verse. Kipling, R. **821**

The **complete** verse and other nonsense. Lear, E. **821**

Complete works. Pinter, H. **822**

The **complete** works. Shakespeare, W. **822.3**

Complete works of Tacitus. Tacitus, C. **878**

Complexity. Mitchell, M. **501**

COMPLEXITY (PHILOSOPHY)

    Costa, R. D. The watchman's rattle **501**

    Mitchell, M. Complexity **501**

Complications: a young surgeon's notes on an imperfect science. Gawande, A. **617**

Composed. Cash, R. **92**

COMPOSERS

    Adams, J. Hallelujah junction **92**

    Berger, W. Puccini without excuses **92**

    Berger, W. Verdi with a vengeance **782.1**

    Berlin, E. A. King of ragtime: Scott Joplin and his era **92**

    Bernstein, B. Leonard Bernstein **92**

    Brown, C. Chance and circumstance **92**

    Carr, J. The Wagner clan **920**

    Einstein, A. Mozart **92**

    Eisler, B. Chopin's funeral **92**

    Ellison, R. Going to the territory **818**

    Emerson, K. Doo-dah!: Stephen Foster and the rise of American popular culture **92**

    Feather, L. From Satchmo to Miles **920**

    Geck, M. Johann Sebastian Bach **92**

    Gilbert, S. E. The music of Gershwin **780**

    Gutman, R. W. Mozart **92**

    Hafner, K. A romance on three legs **92**

    Haydn **92**

    Hischak, T. The Oxford companion to the American musical **792.6**

    Hyland, W. G. George Gershwin **92**

    Jones, Q. Q: the autobiography of Quincy Jones **92**

    Joseph, C. M. Stravinsky inside out **92**

    Lebrecht, N. Why Mahler? **92**

    Lehman, D. A fine romance **782.42**

    Leiber, J. Hound dog **92**

    Leonard Cohen on Leonard Cohen **92**

    Lockwood, L. Beethoven: the music and the life **780**

    MacDonald, H. Bizet **92**

    McBrien, W. Cole Porter **92**

    Mercer-Taylor, P. J. The life of Mendelssohn **92**

    Morris, E. Beethoven: the universal composer **92**

    Murray, A. The blue devils of Nada **780.89**

    Nice, D. Prokofiev: from Russia to the West, 1891-1935 **92**

    Osborne, C. The complete operas of Mozart **792.5**

    Osborne, C. The complete operas of Puccini **792.5**

    Osborne, C. The complete operas of Richard Wagner **792.5**

    Pollack, H. George Gershwin **92**

    The Richard Rodgers reader **782.1**

    Robertson, D. W.C. Handy **92**

    Rose, M. The birth of an opera **782.1**

    Rosen, C. The classical style **780.9**

    Sachs, H. The Ninth **785**

    Schebera, J. Kurt Weill **92**

    Schonberg, H. C. The great pianists **920**

    Schonberg, H. C. The lives of the great composers **780**

    Servadio, G. Rossini **92**

    Shaffer, P. Peter Shaffer's Amadeus **822**

    Shawn, A. Wish I could be there **92**

    Siblin, E. The cello suites **787.3**

    Silverman, K. Begin again **92**

    Solomon, M. Mozart **92**

    Sondheim, S. Finishing the hat **92**

    Steinberg, M. The symphony **784.2**

    Strouse, C. Put on a happy face **92**

    Swafford, J. Charles Ives **92**

    Swafford, J. Johannes Brahms **92**

    Tuchman, B. W. The proud tower **909.82**

    Volkov, S. St. Petersburg **947**

    Walker-Hill, H. From spirituals to symphonies **780**

    Walsh, S. Stravinsky: a creative spring **92**

    Walsh, S. Stravinsky: the second exile **92**

    Wills, G. Verdi's Shakespeare **822.3**

    Wolff, C. Johann Sebastian Bach **92**

    Zappa, F. The real Frank Zappa book **92**

COMPOSERS

    See also Musicians

COMPOSERS -- BIOGRAPHY

    Gardiner, J. E. Bach **92**

    Glass, P. Words Without Music **92**

    Harris, E. T. George Frideric Handel **92**

    Powell, N. Benjamin Britten **92**

    Strayhorn **781.650**

    Suchet, J. Beethoven **92**

    Swafford, J. Beethoven **92**

COMPOSERS -- CANADA -- INTERVIEWS

    Leonard Cohen on Leonard Cohen **92**

COMPOSERS -- ENGLAND -- BIOGRAPHY

    Powell, N. Benjamin Britten **92**

COMPOSERS -- FRANCE -- BIOGRAPHY

    MacDonald, H. Bizet **92**

COMPOSERS -- GERMANY -- BIOGRAPHY

    Gardiner, J. E. Bach **92**

    Geck, M. Robert Schumann **92**

    Suchet, J. Beethoven **92**

    Swafford, J. Beethoven **92**

    Wolff, C. Johann Sebastian Bach **92**

COMPOSERS -- RUSSIA

    Romanov riches **891.7**

COMPOSERS -- UNITED STATES
Shawn, A. Leonard Bernstein 92
Sondheim, S. Look, I made a hat 782.1
COMPOSERS -- UNITED STATES -- BIOGRAPHY
McBrien, W. Cole Porter 92
Strayhorn 781.650
Walker-Hill, H. From spirituals to symphonies 780
COMPOSERS -- UNITED STATES -- BIOGRAPHY -- PICTORIAL WORKS
Strayhorn 781.650
Composers of the twentieth century [series]
Gilbert, S. E. The music of Gershwin 780
COMPOSERS, AMERICAN See Composers -- United States
COMPOSERS, GERMAN
Gardiner, J. E. Bach 92
Suchet, J. Beethoven 92
Swafford, J. Beethoven 92
COMPOSITION (ART)
Freehand 741.2
Peterson, B. Learning to see creatively 770.1
COMPOSITION (ART)
See also Art
COMPOSITION (MUSIC)
Margotin, P. Bob Dylan 782.42
COMPOSITION (MUSIC)
See also Music; Music -- Theory
COMPOSITION (RHETORIC) See Rhetoric
COMPOST
Pleasant, B. The complete compost gardening guide 631.8
COMPOST
See also Fertilizers; Soils
Comprehensive Yiddish-English Dictionary. 439
COMPROMISE OF 1850
Bordewich, F. M. America's great debate 973.6
COMPULSION (PSYCHOLOGY) See Compulsive behavior
COMPULSIVE BEHAVIOR
Bergner, D. The other side of desire 306.7
Kendall, J. America's obsessives 609.2
COMPULSIVE BEHAVIOR
See also Abnormal psychology; Human behavior
COMPULSIVE GAMBLING
Schüll, N. D. Addiction by design 362.2
COMPULSIVE GAMBLING
See also Compulsive behavior; Gambling
COMPULSIVE HOARDING
Frost, R. O. Stuff 616.85
Miller, K. R. Coming clean 92
COMPULSORY EDUCATION
See also Education -- Government policy
COMPULSORY MILITARY SERVICE See Draft
COMPUTABLE FUNCTIONS

Dyson, G. Turing's cathedral 004
COMPUTATION, APPROXIMATE See Approximate computation
COMPUTER AIDED DESIGN See Computer-aided design
COMPUTER ALGORITHMS
Fortnow, L. The golden ticket 511.3
COMPUTER ANIMATION
See also Animation (Cinematography)
COMPUTER ART
See also Art; Computer graphics
COMPUTER ASSISTED INSTRUCTION See Computer-assisted instruction
COMPUTER AWARENESS See Computer literacy
COMPUTER CRIMES
Moore, A. Cyber self-defense 613.6
Vamosi, R. When gadgets betray us 004
COMPUTER CRIMES
See also Crime
COMPUTER CRIMES -- PREVENTION -- GOVERNMENT POLICY
Harris, S. @WAR 355.3
COMPUTER CRIMES -- UNITED STATES
Krebs, B. Spam nation 364.16
Mitnick, K. D. Ghost in the wires 364.16
COMPUTER DRAFTING See Computer graphics
COMPUTER DRAWING See Computer graphics
COMPUTER ENGINEERS -- UNITED STATES -- BIOGRAPHY
Isaacson, W. Steve Jobs 92
Tetzeli, R. Becoming Steve Jobs 92
COMPUTER FONTS
See also Type and type-founding
COMPUTER FRAUD See Computer crimes
COMPUTER GAMES
Kearney, K. Block city 794
McGonigal, J. Reality is broken 306.4
COMPUTER GAMES
See also Computer software; Games
COMPUTER GRAPHICS
Heller, S. Becoming a graphic & digital designer 741.6
COMPUTER GRAPHICS
See also Data processing
COMPUTER HACKERS
Mitnick, K. D. Ghost in the wires 364.16
Olson, P. We are Anonymous 005.8
COMPUTER HACKERS
See also Computer crimes; Criminals
COMPUTER INDUSTRY
See also Industries
COMPUTER INDUSTRY -- CALIFORNIA -- SANTA CLARA COUNTY -- HISTORY
Maxfield, K. Starting up Silicon Valley 338.7
COMPUTER INDUSTRY -- UNITED STATES

Menuez, D. Fearless genius **979.4**

COMPUTER INDUSTRY -- UNITED STATES -- MANAGEMENT

Lashinsky, A. Inside Apple **338.7**

COMPUTER INDUSTRY EXECUTIVES

Burrows, P. Backfire: Carly Fiorina's high-stakes battle for the soul of Hewlett-Packard **338.7**

Norris, R. S. Racing for the bomb: General Leslie R. Groves, the Manhattan Project's indispensable man **92**

Schiller, L. Perfect murder, perfect town **364.15**

COMPUTER LITERACY

Heim, T. @stickyjesus **248.4**

COMPUTER LITERACY

See also Computers and civilization; Literacy

COMPUTER LITERACY -- STUDY AND TEACHING

Braafladt, K. Technology and literacy **027.62**

COMPUTER MUSIC

See also Music

COMPUTER NETWORK RESOURCES *See* Internet resources

COMPUTER NETWORK RESOURCES -- EVALUATION

Seife, C. Virtual unreality **025.04**

COMPUTER NETWORKS

Blum, A. Tubes **384.3**

COMPUTER NETWORKS

See also Data transmission systems; Telecommunication

COMPUTER PERIPHERALS

See also Computers

COMPUTER PROGRAMMING

Beyer, K. W. Grace Hopper and the invention of the information age **92**

COMPUTER PROGRAMMING

See also Computer science; Data processing

COMPUTER SCIENCE

Michael, T. S. How to guard an art gallery and other discrete mathematical adventures **511**

COMPUTER SCIENCE

See also Science

COMPUTER SCIENCE -- DICTIONARIES

See also Encyclopedias and dictionaries

COMPUTER SCIENCE -- HISTORY

Dyson, G. Turing's cathedral **004**

Isaacson, W. The innovators **004**

COMPUTER SCIENCE -- MISCELLANEA

Pogue, D. Pogue's basics **004**

COMPUTER SCIENTISTS

Auletta, K. Googled **338.7**

Beyer, K. W. Grace Hopper and the invention of the information age **92**

Hofstadter, D. R. I am a strange loop **153**

Isaacson, W. The innovators **004**

Remnick, D. Reporting **814**

Smiley, J. The man who invented the computer **92**

COMPUTER SECURITY

Moore, A. Cyber self-defense **613.6**

Vamosi, R. When gadgets betray us **004**

COMPUTER SECURITY

See also Computers

COMPUTER SECURITY -- UNITED STATES

Mitnick, K. D. Ghost in the wires **364.16**

COMPUTER SEX

See also Sex

COMPUTER SIMULATION

See also Mathematical models

COMPUTER SOFTWARE EXECUTIVES

Lewis, M. D. The new new thing **338.4**

COMPUTER SOFTWARE INDUSTRY

Campbell-Kelly, M. From airline reservations to Sonic the Hedgehog **005**

COMPUTER SOFTWARE INDUSTRY

See also Industries

COMPUTER SOFTWARE INDUSTRY -- UNITED STATES

Casnocha, B. My start-up life **338.7**

COMPUTER VIRUSES

See also Computer crimes; Computer software

COMPUTER-AIDED DESIGN

Rigsby, M. A beginner's guide to 3D printing **621.9**

COMPUTER-AIDED DESIGN

See also Computer graphics; Design

COMPUTER-ASSISTED INSTRUCTION

Vander Ark, T. Getting smart **371.33**

COMPUTER-ASSISTED INSTRUCTION -- UNITED STATES

Vander Ark, T. Getting smart **371.33**

COMPUTERS

Johnson, G. A shortcut through time **004.1**

COMPUTERS -- HEALTH ASPECTS

Vamosi, R. When gadgets betray us **004**

COMPUTERS -- HISTORY

Dyson, G. Turing's cathedral **004**

Essinger, J. Ada's algorithm **92**

Isaacson, W. The innovators **004**

COMPUTERS -- POETRY

Hong, C. P. Engine empire **811**

COMPUTERS AND CHILDREN

Kowalski, R. M. Cyberbullying **302.34**

COMPUTERS AND CHILDREN

See also Children; Computers

COMPUTERS AND CIVILIZATION

Carr, N. G. The big switch **303.4**

Markoff, J. What the dormouse said-- **004**

McGonigal, J. Reality is broken **306.4**

COMPUTERS AND CIVILIZATION

See also Civilization; Computers; Technology and civilization

COMPUTERS AND PEOPLE WITH DISABILI-

TIES
See also Computers; People with disabilities
A Comstock book [series]
The monarch butterfly **595.7**
Comstock books in herpetology [series]
Campbell, J. The venomous reptiles of the Western
Hemisphere **597.96**
Comte-Sponville, Andre
A small treatise on the great virtues **170**
CON ARTISTS See Swindlers and swindling
CON GAME See Swindlers and swindling
Conant, Douglas R.
Touchpoints **658.4**
Conant, Jennet
A covert affair **940.54**
The irregulars **940.54**
Conant, Roger
A field guide to reptiles & amphibians **597.9**
Conaway, James
America's library **027.5**
Conaway, Wayne A.
Morrison, T. Kiss, bow, or shake hands **395**
Concannon, Amy
(ed) J.m.w. turner
CONCENTRATION See Attention
**CONCENTRATION CAMP COMMANDANTS
-- FAMILY RELATIONSHIPS**
My grandfather would have shot me **929.2**
CONCENTRATION CAMPS
Applebaum, A. Gulag **365**
Helga's diary **940.53**
Helm, S. Ravensbruck **940.53**
Holden, W. Born Survivors **940.531**
Kizny, T. Gulag **365**
Lifton, R. J. The Nazi doctors **940.53**
CONCENTRATION CAMPS
See also Military camps; Political crimes and
offenses
**CONCENTRATION CAMPS -- HISTORY --
20TH CENTURY**
Wachsmann, N. Kl **940.53**
**CONCENTRATION CAMPS -- UNITED
STATES**
Reeves, R. Infamy **940.53**
Russell, J. J. The Train to Crystal City **940.53**
CONCEPT LEARNING
See also Concepts; Psychology of learning
The **concept** of anxiety. **233**
CONCEPTION -- PREVENTION See Birth con-
trol
CONCEPTS
See also Perception
Concerning E.M. Forster. Kermode, F. **823**
Concerning the city of God against the pagans. De
civitate Dei./English **239**
CONCERTS

See also Amusements; Music
The **Concise** American Heritage Spanish dictionary.
Houghton Mifflin Co. **463**
Concise encyclopedia of Amish, Brethren, Hutter-
ites, and Mennonites. Kraybill, D. B. **289.7**
Concise encyclopedia of Latin American litera-
ture. **860**
The **concise** guide to hip-hop music. Edwards,
P. **782.42**
A **concise** history of Germany. Fulbrook, M. **943**
Concise history of science & invention. **509**
A **concise** history of the Russian Revolution. Pipes,
R. **947.084**
Concise Oxford American thesaurus. **423**
CONCORD (MASS.), BATTLE OF, 1775
Fischer, D. H. Paul Revere's ride **973.3**
Phillips, K. 1775 **973.3**
CONCORD (MASS.), BATTLE OF, 1775
See also Battles; United States -- History --
1775-1783, Revolution -- Campaigns
CONCRETE
See also Building materials; Foundations;
Masonry; Plaster and plastering
CONCRETE BUILDING See Concrete construc-
tion
CONCRETE CONSTRUCTION
Color concrete garden projects **721**
Concussion. Laskas, J. M. **617.5**
CONCUSSION, BRAIN See Brain -- Concussion
CONDEMNATION OF LAND See Eminent do-
main
CONDENSERS (STEAM)
See also Steam engines
CONDIMENTS
Foolproof preserving **641.4**
CONDUCT OF LIFE
Aldrin, B. No dream is too high **92**
Armstrong, K. Twelve steps to a compassionate
life **177**
The Art of Stillness **302.23**
Coles, R. Lives of moral leadership **170**
Covey, S. R. The 7 habits of highly effective peo-
ple **158**
Covey, S. R. First things first **158**
Davis, W. Enough **241**
De Botton, A. Religion for atheists **200**
Egan, K. On living **170.44**
Engel, B. The nice girl syndrome **155.6**
Gilbert, E. Big magic **153.3**
Gottlieb, D. Learning from the heart **170**
Johnson, C. The information diet **303.48**
Kipnis, L. How to become a scandal **306.7**
Kirsch, M. The girl's guide to absolutely every-
thing **646.7**
Kubler-Ross, E. Life lessons **170**
Lamarche, U. Unabrow **92**

Made for goodness **170**

Manson, M. The subtle art of not giving a fu*k **158.1**

Miller, J. Examined lives **190**

Palmer, A. A life well played **92**

Pillemer, K. A. 30 lessons for living **305.26**

Rankin, L. The anatomy of a calling **92**

Reader's Digest Association Everyday greatness **170**

Rushkoff, D. Present Shock **303.48**

Saviuc, L. D. 15 things you should give up to be happy **152.4**

Soukup, R. Unstuffed **646.7**

Sull, D. Simple Rules **650.1**

This I believe **170**

This I believe II **170**

Walsh, P. Lighten up **332.024**

Wann, D. The new normal **306**

Westheimer, R. K. The Doctor Is in

CONDUCT OF LIFE

  See also Ethics; Human behavior; Life skills

CONDUCT OF LIFE -- HUMOR

Kaling, M. Why not me? **92**

CONDUCT OF LIFE -- PHILOSOPHY

Aldrin, B. No dream is too high **92**

CONDUCTING

  See also Music

Conducting the reference interview. Nilsen, K. **025.5**

CONDUCTORS (MUSIC)

Bernstein, B. Leonard Bernstein **92**

Jones, Q. Q: the autobiography of Quincy Jones **92**

Lebrecht, N. Why Mahler? **92**

Osborne, R. Herbert von Karajan **92**

Schonberg, H. C. The great pianists **920**

Tunstall, T. Changing lives **780.7**

CONDUCTORS (MUSIC)

  See also Musicians; Orchestra

Cone, Steve

Singer upholstery basics plus **684.1**

Conefrey, Mick

The Ghosts of K2 **796.522**

CONEY ISLAND (NEW YORK, N.Y.)

Handwerker, L. Famous Nathan **92**

CONFECTIONERY

  See also Cooking

Confections of a closet master baker. Bullock-Prado, G. **92**

CONFEDERACIES *See* Federal government

CONFEDERATE STATES OF AMERICA

Williams, D. Bitterly divided **973.7**

CONFEDERATE STATES OF AMERICA

  See also United States -- History --1861-1865, Civil War

CONFEDERATE STATES OF AMERICA -- ARMY

Blount, R. Robert E. Lee **92**

Leonard, E. D. All the daring of the soldier **973.7**

McPherson, J. M. For cause and comrades **973.7**

Robertson, J. I. Stonewall Jackson **92**

Wert, J. D. Cavalryman of the lost cause **92**

CONFEDERATE STATES OF AMERICA -- ARMY -- MILITARY LIFE

Wiley, B. I. The life of Johnny Reb **973.7**

CONFEDERATE STATES OF AMERICA -- BIOGRAPHY

Cooper, W. J. Jefferson Davis, American **92**

Warner, E. J. Generals in gray **920**

CONFEDERATE STATES OF AMERICA -- ECONOMIC CONDITIONS

Levine, B. The fall of the house of Dixie **973.7**

CONFEDERATE STATES OF AMERICA -- FOREIGN RELATIONS -- GREAT BRITAIN

Dickey, C. Our Man in Charleston **92**

CONFEDERATE STATES OF AMERICA -- HISTORY

Gwynne, S. C. Rebel Yell **92**

Levine, B. The fall of the house of Dixie **973.7**

Robertson, J. I. Stonewall Jackson **92**

CONFEDERATE STATES OF AMERICA -- SOCIAL CONDITIONS

Levine, B. The fall of the house of Dixie **973.7**

Williams, D. Bitterly divided **973.7**

CONFEDERATE STATES OF AMERICA. ARMY -- BIOGRAPHY

Davis, W. C. Crucible of commmand **920**

The **Confederate** War. Gallagher, G. W. **973.7**

Confederates in the attic. Horwitz, T. **973.7**

CONFEDERATION OF AMERICAN COLONIES *See* United States -- History -- 1783-1815

CONFEDERATION OF STATES -- UNITED STATES -- HISTORY -- 18TH CENTURY

Ellis, J. J. The Quartet **973.3**

Confessions. Augustine **242**

Confessions. Rousseau **92**

Confessions of a street addict. Cramer, J. J. **332.6**

Confessions of a young novelist. Eco, U. **808.3**

The **confessions** of an English opium-eater and other writings. De Quincey, T. **824**

CONFIDENCE

Gilbert, E. Big magic **153.3**

The **Confidence** Game. Konnikova, M. **364.163**

CONFIDENCE GAME *See* Swindlers and swindling

CONFLICT MANAGEMENT

Powell, J. Terrorists at the table **363.325**

Waxman, J. How to break up with anyone **158.2**

CONFLICT MANAGEMENT

  See also Management; Negotiation; Problem solving; Social conflict

CONFLICT OF CULTURES *See* Culture conflict

CONFLICT OF GENERATIONS

See also Child-adult relationship; Interpersonal relations; Parent-child relationship; Social conflict

CONFLICT OF INTERESTS
   See also Political ethics
CONFLICT OF INTERESTS -- UNITED STATES
   Elliott, C. White coat, black hat   **174.2**
CONFLICT RESOLUTION *See* Conflict management
CONFLICT, SOCIAL *See* Social conflict
Conflicting worlds [series]
   Blanton, D. They fought like demons   **973.7**
CONFORMITY
   Robbins, A. The geeks shall inherit the Earth
CONFORMITY
   See also Attitude (Psychology); Freedom
Confronting the classics. Beard, M.   **930**
CONFUCIANISM
   Eastern religions   **200.9**
CONFUCIANISM
   See also Religions
Confucius
   The Analects   **181**
Congdon, Lisa
   Art, Inc.   **702**
CONGENITAL DISEASES *See* Medical genetics
CONGLOMERATE CORPORATIONS
   See also Corporations
CONGO (DEMOCRATIC REPUBLIC)
   Sundaram, A. Stringer   **967.51**
CONGO (DEMOCRATIC REPUBLIC) -- DESCRIPTION AND TRAVEL
   Sundaram, A. Stringer   **967.51**
CONGO (DEMOCRATIC REPUBLIC) -- HISTORY -- 1997-
   Stearns, J. K. Dancing in the glory of monsters   **967.51**
CONGO (DEMOCRATIC REPUBLIC) -- SOCIAL CONDITIONS -- 21ST CENTURY
   Sundaram, A. Stringer   **967.51**
CONGO (REPUBLIC)
   Mabanckou, A. The lights of Pointe-Noire   **848**
CONGO (REPUBLIC) -- HISTORY
   Hochschild, A. King Leopold's ghost   **967.5**
CONGREGATIONALISM
   Marsden, G. M. Jonathan Edwards   **92**
CONGREGATIONS *See* Religious institutions
Congress A to Z. Congressional Quarterly, I.   **328**
Congress investigates.   **328**
CONGRESS OF RACIAL EQUALITY
   Arsenault, R. Freedom riders   **323**
CONGRESS OF VIENNA (1814-1815)
   King, D. Vienna, 1814   **940.2**
   Zamoyski, A. Rites of peace   **940.2**
Congressional Quarterly, Inc.
   Congress A to Z   **328**

The Middle East   **956**
Presidential elections 1789-2008   **324.6**
Conigliaro, Tony, 1971-
   The cocktail lab   **641.87**
Conis, Elena
   Vaccine nation   **614.4**
CONJURING *See* Magic tricks
Conley, Cort
   (ed) Modern American memoirs   **810**
Connect-the-shapes crochet motifs. Eckman, E.   **746.43**
CONNECTICUT
   Kristal, M. At home in the garden   **635.09**
Connecting the dots. Kumin, M.   **811**
Connell, Evan S.
   Son of the Morning Star   **973.8**
Conner, Bobbi
   Unplugged play   **790.1**
Conner, Claire, 1945-
         About
   Conner, C. Wrapped in the flag   **322.4**
Conniff, Richard
   House of Lost Worlds   **069**
Connolly, Daniel
   The Book of Isaias   **305.235**
Connolly, Kevin Michael, 1985-
         About
   Connolly, K. M. Double take   **92**
Connolly, William G.
   Siegal, A. The New York times manual of style and usage   **808**
Connor, James A.
   Pascal's wager   **92**
Connors, Joanna
   I Will Find You   **364.15**
Connors, Philip
         About
   Connors, P. Fire season   **634.9**
Conoley, Gillian
   Peace   **811**
Conover, Ted
   The routes of man   **388.1**
Conquered into liberty. Cohen, E. A.   **355**
Conquering Concussion. Esty, M. L.   **617.4**
The **conquering** tide. Toll, I. W.   **940.54**
Conquerors. Crowley, R.   **909**
The **conquerors:** Roosevelt, Truman, and the destruction of Hitler's Germany, 1941-1945. Beschloss, M. R.   **940.53**
Conquest of Everest. Lewis-Jones, H.   **796.522**
Conquest, Robert
   Stalin   **92**
Conrad, Ariane
   Jones, V. The green-collar economy   **363.7**
Conrad, Clyde Lee
         About

Herrington, S. A. Traitors among us   **327.12**

Conrad, Joseph, 1857-1924
About
Said, E. W. Reflections on exile and other essays   **814**

Conradi, Peter
Iris Murdoch   **823**

Conroy, John
Unspeakable acts, ordinary people   **323.4**

Conroy, Pat
About
Conroy, P. My losing season   **796.323**

CONSCIENCE
   See also Christian ethics; Duty; Ethics

CONSCIENTIOUS OBJECTORS
   See also Freedom of conscience; War -- Religious aspects

Conscious and verbal. Murray, L. A.   **821**
Conscious capitalism. Mackey, J.   **174**

CONSCIOUSNESS
Damasio, A. R. The feeling of what happens   **153**
Gazzaniga, M. S. Human   **612.8**
Hofstadter, D. R. I am a strange loop   **153**
Kurzweil, R. How to create a mind   **612.8**
May, R. The courage to create   **153.3**

CONSCIOUSNESS
   See also Apperception; Mind and body; Perception; Psychology

CONSCIOUSNESS -- POPULAR WORKS
Burnett, D. Idiot brain   **612.8**

CONSCIOUSNESS EXPANDING DRUGS *See*
Hallucinogens

CONSCRIPTION, MILITARY *See* Draft

CONSENSUS (SOCIAL SCIENCES)
Surowiecki, J. The wisdom of crowds   **303.3**
Consequence. Fair, E.   **956.704**

CONSERVATION OF NATURAL RESOURCES
Brinkley, D. The wilderness warrior   **92**
Grescoe, T. Bottomfeeder   **641.6**
Hoekstra, J. M. The atlas of global conservation   **333.95**
Koslow, J. A. The silent deep   **578.7**
Montgomery, D. R. The hidden half of nature   **579**
Park, C. A dictionary of environment and conservation   **333.7**
Wohlforth, C. The fate of nature   **304.2**

CONSERVATION OF NATURAL RESOURCES
   See also Environmental protection; Natural resources

CONSERVATION OF NATURAL RESOURCES -- ALASKA
Wohlforth, C. The fate of nature   **304.2**

CONSERVATION OF NATURAL RESOURCES -- DICTIONARIES
Park, C. A dictionary of environment and conservation   **333.7**

CONSERVATION OF NATURAL RESOURCES -- UNITED STATES -- HISTORY -- 20TH CENTURY
Brinkley, D. The wilderness warrior   **92**

CONSERVATIONISTS
Bass, R. Why I came West   **92**
Beavan, C. No impact man   **333.72**
Bell, L. Claiming ground   **92**
Davis, J. E. An Everglades providence   **92**
Egan, T. The big burn   **973.91**
Furmansky, D. Z. Rosalie Edge, hawk of mercy   **92**
Humes, E. Eco Barons   **363.7**
Lytle, M. H. The gentle subversive   **92**
Maathai, W. Unbowed   **92**
Miller, C. Gifford Pinchot and the making of modern environmentalism   **333.7**
Owens, M. Secrets of the savanna   **599**
Pooley, E. The climate war   **363.7**
Remnick, D. Reporting   **814**
Safina, C. The view from Lazy Point   **508**
Wilson, D. An unreasonable woman   **92**
Zelnick, B. Gore: a political life   **92**

CONSERVATIONISTS -- UNITED STATES -- BIOGRAPHY
Lunde, D. The naturalist   **973.91**

CONSERVATISM
Allitt, P. The conservatives   **320.5**
Brookhiser, R. Right time, right place   **92**
Conner, C. Wrapped in the flag   **322.4**
Dochuk, D. From Bible belt to sunbelt   **277**
Foner, E. The story of American freedom   **323.44**
Frank, T. What's the matter with Kansas?   **978.1**
Martin, W. C. With God on our side   **261.8**
Shorris, E. The politics of heaven   **973.93**

CONSERVATISM
   See also Political science; Social sciences

CONSERVATISM -- RELIGIOUS ASPECTS -- CHRISTIANITY
Christian reconstruction   **230**

CONSERVATISM -- RELIGIOUS ASPECTS -- CHRISTIANITY -- HISTORY -- 20TH CENTURY
Dochuk, D. From Bible belt to sunbelt   **277**

CONSERVATISM -- UNITED STATES
Hochschild, A. R. Strangers in their own land   **320.52**
Perlstein, R. The Invisible Bridge   **973.924**

CONSERVATISM -- UNITED STATES -- HISTORY
Bogus, C. T. Buckley   **92**
Goldwag, A. The new hate   **306.2**
Stoll, I. JFK, conservative   **973.922**

CONSERVATISM -- UNITED STATES -- HISTORY -- 20TH CENTURY
Kruse, K. M. One nation under God   **322**
Stoll, I. JFK, conservative   **973.922**

The **conservatives**. Allitt, P.   **320.5**

Consider the eel. Schweid, R.   **597**

Consider the fork.   **643**

Consider the lobster. Wallace, D. F.   **814**

Considine, Glenn D.

    (ed) Van Nostrand's scientific encyclopedia   **503**

Consilience. Wilson, E. O.   **121**

CONSOLATION

    See also Emotions; Human behavior

Console wars. Harris, B. J.   **338.7**

**CONSOLIDATION AND MERGER OF CORPO-
RATIONS** *See* Corporate mergers and acquisitions

Consolmagno, Guy

    Turn left at Orion   **520**

CONSORTIA, LIBRARY *See* Library cooperation

CONSPIRACIES

    Aaronovitch, D. Voodoo histories   **909.08**

    Brotherton, R. Suspicious Minds   **153.4**

    Bugliosi, V. Reclaiming history   **973.922**

    Goldwag, A. The new hate   **306.2**

    Mezrich, B. The 37th parallel   **001.942**

    Minutaglio, B. Dallas 1963   **973.922**

    Pepper, W. F. An act of state   **364.1**

    Ronson, J. Them: adventures with extremists **322.4**

    Walker, J. The United States of paranoia   **973**

CONSPIRACIES

    See also Crime; Political crimes and offenses

**CONSPIRACIES -- GREAT BRITAIN -- HIS-
TORY -- 20TH CENTURY**

    Morton, A. 17 carnations   **941.084**

**CONSPIRACY THEORIES -- POLITICAL AS-
PECTS -- UNITED STATES**

    Goldwag, A. The new hate   **306.2**

CONSPIRACY THEORIES -- UNITED STATES

    Walker, J. The United States of paranoia   **973**

CONSPIRATORS

    Fraser, A. Faith and treason   **942.06**

The **constant** fire. Frank, A.   **201**

Constantine, David

    Collected poems   **821**

    (ed & tr) Kleist, H. v. Selected writings   **838**

The **constants** of nature. Barrow, J. D.   **530.8**

CONSTELLATIONS

    Consolmagno, G. Turn left at Orion   **520**

CONSTELLATIONS

    See also Sky

The **Constitution**. Paulsen, M. S.   **342.73**

The **Constitution** of the United States of America.   **342**

CONSTITUTIONAL AMENDMENTS

    See also Constitutional law; Constitutions

The **Constitutional** Convention. Madison, J.   **342**

The **Constitutional** Convention of 1787. Vile, J. R.   **342**

CONSTITUTIONAL CONVENTIONS -- UNIT-

ED STATES

    Raphael, R. Mr. president   **352.23**

CONSTITUTIONAL HISTORY

    Broadwater, J. George Mason, forgotten founder   **92**

    Burns, E. Infamous scribblers   **071**

    Lombardo, P. A. Three generations, no imbeciles   **344**

    Paulsen, M. S. The Constitution   **342.73**

    Rabban, D. M. Free speech in its forgotten years   **342**

    Rehnquist, W. H. All the laws but one   **342**

    Simon, J. F. What kind of nation   **342**

CONSTITUTIONAL HISTORY

    See also History

**CONSTITUTIONAL HISTORY -- UNITED
STATES -- 18TH CENTURY**

    Raphael, R. Constitutional myths   **342.73**

**CONSTITUTIONAL HISTORY -- UNITED
STATES -- ENCYCLOPEDIAS**

    Maddex, R. L. The U.S. Constitution A to Z   **342**

    Vile, J. R. The Constitutional Convention of 1787   **342**

    Vile, J. R. Encyclopedia of constitutional amendments, proposed amendments, and amending issues, 1789-2010   **342**

**CONSTITUTIONAL HISTORY -- UNITED
STATES -- GRAPHIC NOVELS**

    Hennessey, J. The United States Constitution   **342**

CONSTITUTIONAL LAW

    The Oxford guide to United States Supreme Court decisions   **342**

CONSTITUTIONAL LAW -- UNITED STATES

    The Constitution of the United States of America   **342**

    Mandery, E. J. A wild justice   **345.73**

    Paulsen, M. S. The Constitution   **342.73**

    Shipler, D. K. Freedom of speech   **323.44**

    Tribe, L. H. Uncertain justice   **342.73**

**CONSTITUTIONAL LAW -- UNITED STATES
-- ENCYCLOPEDIAS**

    Maddex, R. L. The U.S. Constitution A to Z   **342**

    Schultz, D. A. Encyclopedia of the United States Constitution   **342**

    Vile, J. R. The Constitutional Convention of 1787   **342**

    Vile, J. R. Encyclopedia of constitutional amendments, proposed amendments, and amending issues, 1789-2010   **342**

Constitutional myths. Raphael, R.   **342.73**

CONSTRUCTION INDUSTRY EXECUTIVES

    Singer, M. Character studies   **920**

    Slater, R. No such thing as over-exposure   **92**

CONSTRUCTION OF ROADS *See* Roads

CONSTRUCTION WORKERS

    Breslin, J. The short sweet dream of Eduardo Gutierrez **331.6**

CONSUMER BEHAVIOR
Kolko, J. Well-designed **658.5**
Lindström, M. Small Data **658.8**
Miller, G. F. Spent **339.4**
CONSUMER BEHAVIOR See Consumers
CONSUMER CREDIT
Halpern, J. Bad paper **332.7**
Leonard, R. Credit repair **332.7**
McNaughton, D. The essential credit repair handbook **332.024**
CONSUMER CREDIT
See also Banks and banking; Credit; Personal finance
CONSUMER DEMAND See Consumption (Economics)
CONSUMER EDUCATION
Levine, J. Not buying it **640.73**
CONSUMER EDUCATION
See also Education; Home economics
CONSUMER EDUCATION -- POPULAR WORKS
Olmsted, L. Real food/fake food **641.3**
CONSUMER GOODS
See also Commercial products; Manufactures
CONSUMER ORGANIZATIONS See Cooperative societies
CONSUMER PRICE INDEXES
See also Cost and standard of living; Prices
CONSUMER PROFILING
Turow, J. The daily you **659.1**
CONSUMER PROTECTION
See also Industrial policy
CONSUMER SPENDING See Consumption (Economics)
A **consumer's** dictionary of cosmetic ingredients. Winter, R. **668**
A **consumer's** dictionary of food additives. Winter, R. **664**
A **consumer's** republic. Cohen, L. **339.4**
CONSUMERISM See Consumer protection; Consumption (Economics)
CONSUMERS
Becker, J. The more of less **241.68**
Cohen, L. A consumer's republic **339.4**
De Grazia, V. Irresistible empire **306**
Gerth, K. As China goes, so goes the world **339.4**
Goleman, D. Ecological intelligence **333.7**
Lindström, M. Small Data **658.8**
Miller, G. F. Spent **339.4**
Roberts, J. A. Shiny objects **339.4**
Underhill, P. The call of the mall **306**
Underhill, P. Why we buy **658.8**
Vanderbilt, T. You may also like **153.8**
CONSUMERS' COOPERATIVE SOCIETIES
See Cooperative societies

CONSUMERS' GUIDES See Consumer education
CONSUMERS' PREFERENCES
Vanderbilt, T. You may also like **153.8**
CONSUMPTION (ECONOMICS)
Akst, D. We have met the enemy **153.8**
Cohen, L. A consumer's republic **339.4**
De Grazia, V. Irresistible empire **306**
Gerth, K. As China goes, so goes the world **339.4**
Humes, E. Garbology **628.4**
Klosterman, C. Eating the dinosaur **973.92**
Leonard, A. The story of stuff **306.4**
Miller, G. F. Spent **339.4**
Underhill, P. The call of the mall **306**
Waldfogel, J. Scroogenomics **339.4**
CONSUMPTION (ECONOMICS)
See also Economics
CONSUMPTION (ECONOMICS) -- RELIGIOUS ASPECTS -- CHRISTIANITY
Becker, J. The more of less **241.68**
CONSUMPTION (ECONOMICS) -- UNITED STATES
Roberts, J. A. Shiny objects **339.4**
CONSUMPTION OF ALCOHOLIC BEVERAGES See Drinking of alcoholic beverages
CONSUMPTION OF ENERGY See Energy consumption
CONTACT PRINTING -- UNITED STATES
Longworth, K. Hollywood frame by frame **791.43**
Contact! Morris, J. **910.4**
CONTAGION (SOCIAL PSYCHOLOGY)
Gladwell, M. The tipping point **302**
CONTAGION AND CONTAGIOUS DISEASES
See Communicable diseases
CONTAGIOUS DISEASES See Communicable diseases
CONTAINER GARDENING
Smith, E. C. The vegetable gardener's container bible **635**
The unexpected houseplant **635.9**
CONTAINER GARDENING
See also Gardening
CONTAINERS
Kealing, B. Tupperware, unsealed **338.7**
CONTAMINATED FOOD See Food contamination
CONTAMINATION OF ENVIRONMENT See Pollution
Contemporary black biography, v68. **920**
Contemporary issues series
Genetically modified foods **363.1**
Contemporary Jewish-American novelists. **813**
Contemporary playwrights series
Norman, M. Collected plays **812**
Contemporary poets. **821**
The **contemporary** Torah. **222**
Contemporary women artists. **920.003**

Contemporary world fiction. Dilevko, J.   016

Contemporary world issues. Science, technology, and medicine [series]
   Newton, D. E. World energy crisis   333.79

Contemporary writers series
   Contemporary poets   821

Content rules. Handley, A.   658.8

CONTENTMENT -- RELIGIOUS ASPECTS -- CHRISTIANITY
   Davis, W. Enough   241

Contested Will. Shapiro, J.   822.3

CONTESTS
   Imhoff, K. R. Library contests   021.7

Continental divide. Isserman, M.   796.52

CONTINENTAL DRIFT
   See also Continents; Geology

CONTINENTAL SHELF
   See also Geology

CONTINENTS
   See also Earth

CONTINGENCY (PHILOSOPHY)
   Black, J. Other pasts, different presents, alternative futures   900

CONTINUING EDUCATION
   See also Education

The **Continuum** encyclopedia of British literature.   810

CONTRABAND TRADE *See* Smuggling

CONTRACEPTION *See* Birth control

CONTRACT BRIDGE *See* Bridge (Game)

CONTRACT LABOR
   Jordan, D. White cargo   326

CONTRACT LABOR
   See also Labor

CONTRACTING FOR SERVICES *See* Outsourcing

CONTRACTING OUT *See* Outsourcing

CONTRACTIONS *See* Abbreviations; Ciphers

CONTRACTORS
   Eggers, D. Zeitoun   92

Contracts. Stim, R.   346

CONTRACTS
   See also Commerce; Commercial law

CONTRACTS
   Stim, R. Contracts   346

Contrarian investment strategies. Dreman, D.   332.601

Contreras, Bret
   Strong curves   613.7

CONTROL (PSYCHOLOGY)
   Fontes, L. A. Invisible chains   158.2
   Maestripieri, D. Games primates play   155.7
   Viorst, J. Imperfect control   158.1

CONTROL OF GUNS *See* Gun control

The **control** of nature. McPhee, J.   304.2

Controversial New Religions.   200.9

CONVENIENCE COOKING *See* Quick and easy cooking

CONVENIENCE FOODS
   Schlosser, E. Fast food nation   394.1
   Spurlock, M. Don't eat this book   614.5

CONVENIENCE FOODS
   See also Food

CONVENIENCE STORES
   Howe, B. R. My Korean deli   92

Convergences [series]
   Said, E. W. Reflections on exile and other essays   814

The **conversation.** Volandes, A. E.   616.02

CONVERSATION
   See also Communication; Language and languages

CONVERSATION
   Blyth, C. The art of conversation   395
   Roffman, D. Talk to me first   613.907
   Tannen, D. You just don't understand   302.2
   Turkle, S. Reclaiming Conversation   302.23

Conversations at the American Film Institute with the great moviemakers.   791.43

Conversations with Frank Gehry. Isenberg, B.   92

Conversations with myself. Mandela, N.   92

Conversations with Nadine Gordimer.   823

CONVERSION
   James, W. The varieties of religious experience   210
   Reuben, S. C. Becoming Jewish   296.7

CONVERSION
   See also Evangelistic work; Salvation; Spiritual life

CONVERSION -- MORMON CHURCH
   Barnes, J. Falling in love with Joseph Smith   92

CONVERSION OF WASTE PRODUCTS *See* Recycling

The **convert.** Baker, D.   92

CONVERTS
   Baker, D. The convert   92
   Woo, I. The great divorce   92

CONVERTS
   See also Conversion

CONVERTS TO CATHOLICISM
   See also Catholics; Converts

CONVERTS TO JUDAISM
   Reuben, S. C. Becoming Jewish   296.7

CONVEYING MACHINERY
   See also Machinery; Materials handling

CONVICT LABOR
   Applebaum, A. Gulag   365
   Kizny, T. Gulag   365

CONVICT LABOR
   See also Forced labor; Prisoners

The **conviction** of Richard Nixon. Reston, J.   973.924

CONVICTS *See* Criminals; Prisoners

Conway, Ed

The Summit **339.5**

Conway, Erik M.
Merchants of doubt **174**

Conway, J. North
The big policeman **92**

Conway, Jill K., 1934-
When memory speaks **808**

About
Conway, J.K. True north **92**

Conway, John Horton
The book of numbers **512.7**

Coogan, Michael David
(ed) Eastern religions **200.9**
(ed) The Oxford companion to the Bible **220.3**
(ed) The Oxford history of the biblical world **220.9**

Coogan, Tim Pat
The troubles **941.6**

Cook. Thomas, N. **910**

Cook it in cast iron. **641.7**

Cook Korean! Ha, R. **641.595**

Cook this now. Clark, M. **641.5**

The **Cook** Up. Watkins, D. **364.1**

Cook with Jamie. Oliver, J. **641.5**

Cook's Country eats local. **641.597**

Cook's illustrated (Periodical)
The best chicken recipes **641.6**
The best International recipe **641.5**
Best skillet recipes **641.7**
The new best recipe **641.5**

The **cook's** illustrated meat book. **641.6**

A **cook's** tour. Bourdain, A. **641**

Cook, Blanche Wiesen
Eleanor Roosevelt **973.917**

Cook, Edward M.
Abegg, M. G. The Dead Sea scrolls **296.1**

Cook, James, 1728-1779
About
Blainey, G. Sea of dangers **92**
Hough, R. A. Captain James Cook **92**
Thomas, N. Cook **910**

Cook, Jane Hampton
American phoenix **973.5**

Cook, John
Our noise **338**

Cook, Kevin
Tommy's honor **92**

Cook, Lauren M.
Blanton, D. They fought like demons **973.7**

Cook, Richard
Cook, R. M. Alfred Kazin's journals **92**
It's about that time **92**
The Penguin guide to jazz recordings **781.65**

Cook, Richard M., 1941-
Alfred Kazin's journals **92**

Cook, Sarah
Customer care excellence **658.8**

Cook, Steven
Zahav **641.59**
The **cookbook** library. Cherniavsky, M. **641.509**

COOKBOOK WRITERS
As always, Julia **92**
Bittman, M. Food matters **613.2**
Buford, B. Heat **641.5**
Child, J. My life in France **92**
Conant, J. A covert affair **940.54**
Fisher, M. F. K. A stew or a story **641**
Fitch, N. R. Appetite for life **92**
Hazan, M. Amarcord, Marcella remembers **92**
Jaffrey, M. Climbing the mango trees **92**
Pepin, J. The apprentice: my life in the kitchen **641.5**

COOKBOOKS
101 classic cookbooks **641**
Abood, M. Rose water and orange blossoms **641.59**
Acheson, H. A New Turn in the South **641.59**
Ahern, S. J. Gluten-Free Girl American classics reinvented **641.597**
Ahern, S. J. Gluten-free girl every day **641.5**
Alford, J. Flatbreads and flavors **641.8**
Alford, J. Hot, sour, salty, sweet **641.59**
All about braising **641.7**
Amaro **641.874**
The America's test kitchen do-it-yourself cookbook **641.597**
The America's Test Kitchen healthy family cookbook **641.5**
The America's Test Kitchen new family cookbook **641.5**
Ancient grains for modern meals **641.59**
Ansel, D. Dominique Ansel **641.86**
Antine, S. Appetite for life **641.5**
Balla, N. Bar Tartine **641.59**
Banfield, K. The family calendar cookbook **641.5**
Bastianich, J. Healthy pasta **641.82**
Bastianich, L. M. Lidia's commonsense Italian cooking **641.59**
Bastianich, L. M. Lidia's family table **641.5**
Bastianich, L. M. Lidia's favorite recipes **641.594**
Battista, M. Food gift love **642**
Beard on food **641.5**
Beranbaum, R. L. The baking Bible **641.81**
Berry, M. Baking with Mary Berry **641.865**
Besh, J. Cooking from the heart **641.5**
Besh, J. My New Orleans **641.59**
The Best Casserole cookbook ever **641.8**
The best recipe **641.5**
Better Homes and Gardens New Cook Book **641.5**
Betty Crocker cookbook **641.5**
Bevill, A. World spice at home **641.6**
Bilderback, L. No-churn ice cream **641.86**
Bishara, R. Olives, lemons & za'atar **641.59**
Bittman, M. How to Bake Everything **641.86**

Bittman, M. How to Cook Everything Fast **641.5**

Bittman, M. Mark Bittman's kitchen matrix **641.5**

Blakeslee, R. L. Your time to bake **641.8**

Blonder, G. Meathead **641.7**

Bouchon Bakery **641.59**

Bourdain, A. Appetites **641**

Boyle, T. The cake book **641.8**

Boyle, T. Flavorful **641.86**

Breakfast at Huckleberry **641.5**

Brennan, K. Keepers **641.5**

Briscione, J. The great cook **641.5**

Brock, S. Heritage **641.59**

Brown, A. Everydaycook **641.5**

Bryant, G. The paleo kitchen **641.5**

Bryson, F. Blue ribbon baking from a redneck kitchen **641.597**

Burgers **641.66**

But I could never go **641.5**

Byres, T. Smoke **641.6**

Byrn, A. American cake **641.86**

Carrillo Arronte, M. Mexico **641.59**

Carroll, J. Feeding the fire **641.7**

Castanho, T. Brazilian Food **641.598**

Chaplin, A. At home in the whole food kitchen **641.3**

Clark, M. Franny's **641.594**

Classic home desserts **641.8**

Colwin, L. Home cooking **641.5**

Colwin, L. More home cooking **642**

Cook, S. Zahav **641.59**

Cooking my way back home **641.5**

The cook's illustrated meat book **641.6**

The country cooking of France **641.59**

Couscous and other good food from Morocco **641.59**

Cowin, D. Food & Wine Annual Cookbook 2015 **641**

Currence, J. Pickles, pigs & whiskey **641.59**

Davies, K. Q. What Katie Ate **641.5**

Day, C. Back in the Day Bakery, made with love **641.81**

Del Mar Sacasa, M. Summer cocktails **641.87**

Duguid, N. Burma **641.59**

Dunlop, F. Every grain of rice **641.59**

Dunlop, F. Land of fish and rice **641.5**

Dupree, N. Mastering the art of Southern cooking **641.59**

Erway, C. The food of Taiwan **641.595**

The essential New York times grilling cookbook **641.5**

Falk, D. The hungry fan's game day cookbook **641.5**

Farrow, J. Gingerbread Houses, Animals and Decorations **641.865**

Fearnley-Whittingstall, H. River Cottage Veg **641.5**

Fertig, J. The back in the swing cookbook **641.5**

Fine cooking appetizers **641.8**

Flores, E. K. Adventures in chicken **641.665**

The food of Morocco **641.59**

Foose, M. H. A southerly course **641.59**

Forkish, K. Flour water salt yeast **641.81**

Fraioli, J. O. Culinary birds **641.6**

Fuentes, L. The best homemade kids' lunches on the planet **641.5**

Garten, I. Cooking for Jeffrey **641.5**

Ghayour, S. Persiana **641.595**

Gluten-free & vegan pie **641.3**

Gluten-free wish list **641.5**

Goldberg, D. Cuba! **641.5**

Gran cocina latina **641.597**

The Great Big Pressure Cooker Book **641.5**

Greeley, A. Nong's Thai kitchen **641.595**

Green, A. Making artisan pasta **641.82**

The grilling book **641.5**

Grimes, D. The B.T.C. old-fashioned grocery cookbook **641.59**

Guggiana, M. Primal cuts **641.6**

Ha, R. Cook Korean! **641.595**

Harris, M. Magpie **641.86**

Hay, D. Life in Balance **641.563**

Hazan, M. Ingredienti **641.5**

The heart of the plate **641.5**

Heller, M. The everyday DASH diet cookbook **613.2**

Helou, A. Mediterranean street food **641.59**

Henry, D. A Change of Appetite **641.5**

Henry, D. Simple **641.5**

Hiroko Shimbo Hiroko's American kitchen **641.59**

Hirsheimer, C. Canal house cooks every day **641.5**

How to eataly **641.594**

Hoyer, D. Mayan cuisine **641.59**

It's all easy **641.5**

Iyer, R. Indian cooking unfolded **641.59**

Jaffrey, M. An invitation to Indian cooking **641.59**

Jamie Oliver's comfort food **641.5**

Jamie's Italy **641.59**

Jamison, B. The border cookbook **641.59**

Joachim, D. Cooking light global kitchen **641.59**

Jones, A. A modern way to eat **641.5**

Kaminsky, P. Mallmann on fire **641.598**

Kave, A. First prize pies **641.86**

Kijac, M. B. The South American table **641.59**

Koenig, L. Modern Jewish cooking **641.5**

Kord, T. A super upsetting cookbook about sandwiches **641.84**

Korean food made simple **641.595**

La Place, V. Verdura **641.6**

Lane, C. Dessert for Two **641.86**

Le, S. Easy Gourmet **641.5**

Leake, L. 100 days of real food **613.2**

Lee, M. The Lee Bros. Charleston kitchen **641.59**

Liddon, A. The oh she glows cookbook **641.5**

Lillien, L. Hungry girl clean & hungry   **641.302**
Lim, A. The feed zone cookbook   **641.5**
Lim, A. Feed zone portables   **641.5**
Little bites   **641.5**
The longevity kitchen   **612.6**
Madison, D. The new vegetarian cooking for everyone   **641.5**
Madison, D. Vegetarian suppers from Deborah Madison's kitchen   **641.5**
Make it ahead   **641.5**
The make-ahead cook   **641.5**
Mangini, C. The Vegetable Butcher   **641.65**
Marchetti, D. The glorious pasta of Italy   **641.82**
Marcus off duty   **641.5**
Massaad, B. A. Man'oushé   **641.5**
Mast Brothers Chocolate   **641.6**
Mastering pasta   **641.82**
Mastering the art of Chinese cooking   **641.59**
Matheson, C. Flour   **641.8**
McDermott, K. Art of the pie   **641.86**
The mom 100 cookbook   **641.5**
Moore, C. Little Flower baking   **641.815**
Moosewood Restaurant cooks at home   **641.5**
Morris, J. Superfood Kitchen   **641.5**
My perfect pantry   **641.5**
The naked cookbook   **641.302**
Natkin, M. Herbivoracious   **641.5**
New World kitchen   **641.59**
Nguyen, L. The food of Vietnam   **641.59**
Nolen, J. German cooking now   **641.594**
Olivier, M. Little Bento   **641.53**
Olney, R. Lulu's Provencal table   **641.59**
Olney, R. Simple French food   **641.59**
Oseland, J. Saveur   **641.5**
Ottolenghi   **641.5**
Ottolenghi, Y. Jerusalem   **641.5**
Ottolenghi, Y. Nopi   **641.5**
Ottolenghi, Y. Plenty more   **641.6**
Paleo takeout   **641.5**
Parachini, C. Roberta's   **641.82**
Pasta by hand   **641.82**
Patalsky, K. Healthy happy vegan kitchen   **641.5**
Patricia Wells at home in Provence   **641.59**
Pelaez, A. S. The Cuban table   **641.59**
Perelman, D. The smitten kitchen cookbook   **641.5**
The perfect scoop   **641.8**
Perlmutter, D. The grain brain cookbook   **641.563**
Peternell, C. Twelve Recipes   **641.5**
Peterson, J. Sauces   **641.81**
Phan, C. Vietnamese home cooking   **641.59**
Phillips, C. All under heaven   **641.5**
Phillips, M. The Chelsea Market cookbook   **641.59**
Pie school   **909**
Ramsay, G. Gordon Ramsay's fast food   **641.5**
Raw, vegan, not gross   **641.5**
Ray, R. Everyone is Italian on Sunday   **641.59**

Recipes   **641.5**
Reese, J. Make the bread, buy the butter   **641.3**
Rice, V. Recipes from many kitchens   **641.5**
Richardson, A. The breath of a wok   **641.59**
Rick Stein's complete seafood   **641.6**
Ripe   **641.6**
Robertson, C. Tartine   **641.8**
Robertson, C. Tartine Book No. 3   **641.81**
Roden, C. The book of Jewish food   **641.5**
Roden, N.   Ice   Pops!
Rodgers, R. The essential James Beard cookbook   **641.597**
Rodriguez, J. W. The Hot Bread Kitchen cookbook   **641.59**
Romero, T. H. Salad samurai   **641.83**
Ronnen, T. Crossroads   **641.59**
Rose, E. 100 Best Jewish Recipes   **641.5**
Rosenstrach, J. How to celebrate everything   **641.568**
Rossi, C. The Raging Skillet   **92**
Ruggiero, T. The truly healthy family cookbook   **641.5**
Ruhlman's twenty   **641.5**
Rule, C. S. Yogurt culture   **641.6**
Rustic Italian food   **641.59**
Saltsman, A. The Santa Monica Farmers' Market Cookbook   **641.5**
Sanfilippo, D. Practical paleo   **641.5**
Santibañez, R. Truly Mexican   **641.59**
The Scandinavian Kitchen   **641.59**
The science of good cooking   **641.3**
Seo, D. Naturally, delicious   **641.302**
Shulman, M. R. The simple art of vegetarian cooking   **641.5**
The Silver Palate cookbook   **641.5**
Simply ancient grains   **641.6**
Sodium girls limitless low-salt cookbook   **641.5**
Soul food love   **641.59**
Spices of life   **641.5**
The sprouted kitchen   **641.3**
Tanguay, P. The Tippling bros.   **641.87**
Tanis, D. One good dish   **641.82**
Tarlow, A. Dinner at the Long Table   **641.5**
Theo Chocolate   **641.6**
Thielen, A. The New Midwestern table   **641.59**
Thorisson, M. A kitchen in France   **641.594**
Two Moms in the Raw   **641.5**
Van Leeuwen Artisan Ice Cream   **641**
The VB6 cookbook   **641.5**
Vegan holiday cooking from Candle Cafe   **641.5**
Vegan, vegetarian, omnivore   **641.5**
The very best of recipes for health   **641.5**
Vintage cakes   **641.86**
Walter, C. Great cookies   **641.8**
Weight Watchers 50th anniversary cookbook   **641.5**
Well fed   **641.5**

West K-food **641.595**

Wolfert, P. Mediterranean clay pot cooking **641.59**

Wong, L. A. Dumplings All Day Wong **641.59**

Ying, C. The Mission Chinese Food Cookbook **641.595**

COOKBOOKS

See also Books

COOKBOOKS -- UNITED STATES -- HISTORY -- 19TH CENTURY

Food in the Civil War era **641.597**

Cooke, Alistair

American home front, 1941-1942 **940.53**

Letter from America, 1946-2004 **973.9**

Cooke, Jacob Ernest

(ed) The Federalist **342**

Cooke, John Byrne

On the road with Janis Joplin **92**

Cooke, Julia

The other side of paradise **972.91**

Cooke, Mervyn

The chronicle of jazz **781.65**

Cooke, Sam

About

Guralnick, P. Dream boogie **92**

Cooke, Tim

(ed) National Geographic concise history of world religions **200**

Cooked. Pollan, M. **641.5**

The **Cooked** Seed. Min, A. **92**

COOKERY *See* Cooking

COOKERY (PORK)

Grigson, J. Charcuterie and French pork cookery **641.6**

COOKERY -- SOUTH AMERICA

Kijac, M. B. The South American table **641.59**

COOKERY FOR THE SICK *See* Cooking for the sick

COOKERY, AMERICAN

Bastianich, L. Lidia's Italian-American kitchen **641.59**

Hesser, A. The essential New York Times cookbook **641.5**

Kamp, D. The United States of Arugula **641**

O'Neill, M. One big table **641.5**

The Oxford encyclopedia of food and drink in America **641.3**

Schlosser, E. Fast food nation **394.1**

COOKERY, AMERICAN *See* American cooking

COOKERY, FRENCH -- PROVENCAL STYLE

Olney, R. Lulu's Provencal table **641.59**

COOKERY, INTERNATIONAL

Jaffrey, M. Madhur Jaffrey's world vegetarian **641.5**

Rick Stein's complete seafood **641.6**

Robertson, R. Vegan planet **641.5**

COOKERY, LATIN AMERICAN

Kijac, M. B. The South American table **641.59**

COOKERY, MEDITERRANEAN

Helou, A. Mediterranean street food **641.59**

Shulman, M. R. Mediterranean harvest **641.5**

Wolfert, P. The slow Mediterranean kitchen **641.5**

COOKERY, MEXICAN

Bayless, R. Mexico: one plate at a time **641.597**

Kennedy, D. The essential cuisines of Mexico **641.59**

COOKERY, MIDDLE EASTERN

Roden, C. The new book of Middle Eastern food **641.59**

COOKERY, SOUTHEAST ASIAN

Alford, J. Hot, sour, salty, sweet **641.59**

COOKIES

Crocker, B. Betty Crocker cookie book **641.8**

DeMasco, K. The craft of baking **641.8**

Goldman, D. Duff Bakes **641.81**

The Gourmet cookie book **641.8**

Greenspan, D. Dorie's cookies **641.86**

Heatter, M. Maida Heatter's brand-new book of great cookies **641.8**

Heatter, M. Maida Heatter's cookies **641.8**

Holiday cookies **641.86**

Jaronsky, S. The cookies & cups cookbook **641.86**

Johnstone, C. F. Smart cookie **641.865**

Medrich, A. Chewy gooey crispy crunchy melt-in-your-mouth cookies **641.8**

Payard, F. Payard cookies **641.86**

Pillsbury Co. Pillsbury best cookies cookbook **641.8**

Walter, C. Great cookies **641.8**

Zabar, T. One sweet cookie **641.8**

COOKIES

See also Baking; Cooking

The **cookies** & cups cookbook. Jaronsky, S. **641.86**

Cooking. Peterson, J. **641.5**

COOKING

American food writing **641.5**

Beard, J. The armchair James Beard **641.5**

Betty Crocker's cooking basics **641.5**

Colwin, L. More home cooking **642**

Garten, I. Barefoot Contessa at home **641**

Garten, I. Barefoot Contessa family style **641.5**

A homemade life **92**

Lawson, N. How to Eat **641.5**

Oliver, J. Jamie's dinners **641**

Pepin, J. The apprentice: my life in the kitchen **641.5**

Pepin, J. Jacques Pepin celebrates **641.5**

Reichl, R. Comfort me with apples **92**

COOKING

See also Home economics

COOKING (BREAD)

Robertson, C. Tartine Book No. 3 **641.81**

COOKING (CEREALS)

Ancient grains for modern meals **641.59**
Simply ancient grains **641.6**
The sprouted kitchen **641.3**
COOKING (CHICKEN)
Davis, T. C. The hot chicken cookbook **641.7**
Flores, E. K. Adventures in chicken **641.665**
Henry, D. A Bird in the Hand **641.665**
Rude, E. Tastes Like Chicken **636.5**
COOKING (FRUIT)
Complete book of home preserving **641.4**
COOKING (GAME) -- TECHNIQUE
Canterbury, D. The Bushcraft field guide to trapping, gathering, and cooking in the wild **641.691**
COOKING (QUINOA)
Del Mar Sacasa, M. The quinoa [keen-wah] cookbook **641.3**
COOKING (SMOKED FOODS)
Raichlen, S. Project smoke **641.6**
COOKING (SPICES)
Bevill, A. World spice at home **641.6**
Duguid, N. Burma **641.59**
Hemphill, I. The spice & herb bible **641.3**
Sugar and spice **641.86**
COOKING (TEA)
Tea **641.3**
COOKING (VEGETABLES)
Atlas, N. Plant power **641.5**
Complete book of home preserving **641.4**
Dinki, N. Meat on the side **641.35**
Jacoby, K. Vedge **641.6**
Madison, D. Vegetable literacy **641.6**
Ottolenghi, Y. Plenty more **641.6**
Thug Kitchen **641.5**
COOKING (WILD FOODS) -- TECHNIQUE
Canterbury, D. The Bushcraft field guide to trapping, gathering, and cooking in the wild **641.691**
COOKING (YOGURT)
Rule, C. S. Yogurt culture **641.6**
COOKING -- ALASKA
Dixon, K. The Tutka Bay Lodge cookbook **641.59**
COOKING -- APPALACHIAN REGION, SOUTHERN
Victuals **641.5**
COOKING -- CALIFORNIA -- SAN FRANCISCO
Moore, R. This is Camino **641.5**
COOKING -- CHEESE
World cheese book **641.3**
COOKING -- CHOCOLATE
Higgins, K. Chocolate-covered Katie **641.6**
Mast Brothers Chocolate **641.6**
COOKING -- COMPETITIONS
Friedman, A. Knives at dawn **641.5**
COOKING -- CURRY
Iyer, R. 660 curries **641.5**
Ultimate curry bible Madhur Jaffrey's ultimate

curry bible **641.5**
COOKING -- EGGS
Ruhlman, M. Egg **641.675**
COOKING -- ENCYCLOPEDIAS
Larousse gastronomique **641.3**
COOKING -- FISH
Rick Stein's complete seafood **641.6**
Thompson, J. T. Fresh Fish **641.692**
COOKING -- FISH
See also Cooking -- Seafood
COOKING -- FRANCE -- MÉDOC
Thorisson, M. A kitchen in France **641.594**
COOKING -- FRANCE -- PARIS
The French kitchen cookbook **641.594**
COOKING -- FRANCE -- PROVENCE
The French kitchen cookbook **641.594**
COOKING -- FRUIT
Jacoby, K. Vedge **641.6**
Ripe **641.6**
COOKING -- GAME
Baxter, J. The perfect meal **641.59**
The Complete Guide to Hunting, Butchering, and Cooking Wild Game **799.2**
COOKING -- GRAINS
Ancient grains for modern meals **641.59**
Simply ancient grains **641.6**
COOKING -- GREECE -- IKARIA (MUNICIPALITY)
Kochilas, D. Ikaria **641.594**
COOKING -- HEALTH & HEALING -- HEART
Heller, M. The everyday DASH diet cookbook **613.2**
COOKING -- HERBS
Hemphill, I. The spice & herb bible **641.3**
Spices of life **641.5**
COOKING -- HISTORY
Cherniavsky, M. The cookbook library **641.509**
Consider the fork **643**
COOKING -- ITALY -- NAPLES
Wilson, K. Only in Naples **945.731**
COOKING -- LOUISIANA -- NEW ORLEANS
Besh, J. My New Orleans **641.59**
COOKING -- MASSACHUSETTS -- BOSTON
Matheson, C. Flour **641.8**
COOKING -- MEAT
Burgers **641.66**
Carreño, C. Meat **641.6**
Carruthers, J. Eat street **641.76**
Charcuteria **641.594**
The cook's illustrated meat book **641.6**
The everyday meat guide **641.36**
Guggiana, M. Primal cuts **641.6**
Stupak, A. Tacos **641.84**
COOKING -- MEAT
See also Meat
COOKING -- MEXICO -- YUCATÁN (STATE)

Hoyer, D. Mayan cuisine **641.59**

COOKING -- MUSHROOMS
Shroom **641.658**

COOKING -- NATURAL FOODS
Britton, S. My new roots **641.3**

Chaplin, A. At home in the whole food kitchen **641.3**

The family cooks **641.3**

Fong, H. Nom nom paleo **641.5**

Hamshaw, G. Choosing raw **641.3**

The heart of the plate **641.5**

Leake, L. 100 days of real food **613.2**

Lillien, L. Hungry girl clean & hungry **641.302**

Moosewood Restaurant cooks at home **641.5**

Moosewood restaurant favorites **641.5**

Morris, J. Superfood Kitchen **641.5**

The naked cookbook **641.302**

Patalsky, K. Healthy happy vegan kitchen **641.5**

Pouillon, N. My organic life **92**

Seo, D. Naturally, delicious **641.302**

The sprouted kitchen **641.3**

The sprouted kitchen bowl and spoon **641.3**

Two Moms in the Raw **641.5**

The very best of recipes for health **641.5**

COOKING -- NEW YORK (STATE) -- BROOKLYN
Clark, M. Franny's **641.594**

COOKING -- NEW YORK (STATE) -- NEW YORK
Humm, D. I love New York **641.59**

Red Rooster Cookbook **641.5**

COOKING -- PASTA PRODUCTS
Bastianich, J. Healthy pasta **641.82**

Carluccio, A. Pasta **641.82**

Green, A. Making artisan pasta **641.82**

Marchetti, D. The glorious pasta of Italy **641.82**

Pasta by hand **641.82**

Pasta modern **641.82**

Rustic Italian food **641.59**

COOKING -- PATAGONIA (ARGENTINA AND CHILE)
Kaminsky, P. Mallmann on fire **641.598**

COOKING -- PHILOSOPHY
Brennan, K. Keepers **641.5**

COOKING -- PORK
Grigson, J. Charcuterie and French pork cookery **641.6**

COOKING -- POULTRY
Fraioli, J. O. Culinary birds **641.6**

COOKING -- POULTRY
See also Poultry

COOKING -- RESEARCH
López-Alt, J. K. The food lab **664**

COOKING -- SEAFOOD
Pollinger, B. School of fish **641.6**

Rick Stein's complete seafood **641.6**

Seaver, B. Two if by sea **641.692**

Thompson, J. T. Fresh Fish **641.692**

COOKING -- SEAFOOD
See also Seafood

COOKING -- SOUTH CAROLINA -- CHARLESTON
Lee, M. The Lee Bros. Charleston kitchen **641.59**

COOKING -- SOUTHWESTERN STYLE
Jamison, B. The border cookbook **641.59**

COOKING -- STUDY AND TEACHING
Briscione, J. The great cook **641.5**

COOKING -- TECHNIQUE
López-Alt, J. K. The food lab **664**

COOKING -- TEXAS
Thompson-Anderson, T. Texas on the Table **641.597**

COOKING -- UNITED STATES
Ganeshram, R. Future Chefs **641.3**

COOKING -- VEGETABLES
Anthony, M. V Is for Vegetables **641.6**

Dinki, N. Meat on the side **641.35**

Donofrio, J. The Love and Lemons Cookbook **641.5**

Jacoby, K. Vedge **641.6**

Lang, R. The Southern vegetable book **641.65**

Malone, H. The Power of Pulses **635.65**

Mangini, C. The Vegetable Butcher **641.65**

Moosewood restaurant favorites **641.5**

Thug Kitchen **641.5**

Wilkinson, M. Mr. Wilkinson's vegetables **641.65**

COOKING -- VEGETABLES
See also Vegetables

COOKING -- YUCATAN PENINSULA
Sterling, D. Yucatán **641.59**

Cooking dirty. Sheehan, J. **92**

Cooking for Jeffrey. Garten, I. **641.5**

COOKING FOR LARGE NUMBERS *See* Quantity cooking

COOKING FOR ONE
See also Cooking

COOKING FOR THE SICK
Katz, R. The cancer-fighting kitchen **641.5**

COOKING FOR THE SICK
See also Cooking; Diet in disease; Nursing; Sick

COOKING FOR TWO
Lane, C. Dessert for Two **641.86**

COOKING FOR TWO
See also Cooking

Cooking from the heart. Besh, J. **641.5**

Cooking know-how. Weinstein, B. **641.5**

Cooking light global kitchen. Joachim, D. **641.59**

Cooking light mad delicious. Schroeder, K. **641.5**

Cooking my way back home. **641.5**

COOKING TEACHERS
Hazan, M. Amarcord, Marcella remembers **92**

Cooking with Italian grandmothers. Theroux, J. **641.5**

COOKING, AFRICAN
Afro-vegan **641.59**

COOKING, AMERICAN
Ahern, S. J. Gluten-Free Girl American classics reinvented **641.597**
America--farm to table **641.597**
The America's test kitchen do-it-yourself cookbook **641.597**
The America's Test Kitchen healthy family cookbook **641.5**
The America's Test Kitchen new family cookbook **641.5**
Besh, J. My family table **641.59**
Brennan, K. Keepers **641.5**
Charlie Palmer's American fare **641.59**
Cook's Country eats local **641.597**
Gartland, A. Heartlandia **641.597**
Gluten-Free Girl American classics reinvented **641.597**
Humm, D. I love New York **641.59**
Mario Batali Big American cookbook **641.597**
McMillan, T. The American way of eating **338.4**
Moore, C. Little Flower baking **641.815**
Phillips, M. The Chelsea Market cookbook **641.59**
Ridge, B. The Beekman 1802 heirloom dessert cookbook **641.5**
Rodgers, R. The essential James Beard cookbook **641.597**
Victuals **641.5**

COOKING, AMERICAN -- CALIFORNIA STYLE
Balla, N. Bar Tartine **641.59**
Cooking my way back home **641.5**
Kostow, C. A new Napa cuisine **641.59**
Moore, R. This is Camino **641.5**

COOKING, AMERICAN -- HISTORY -- 19TH CENTURY
Food in the Civil War era **641.597**

COOKING, AMERICAN -- HISTORY -- 20TH CENTURY
Barr, L. Provence, 1970 **641.59**

COOKING, AMERICAN -- LOUISIANA STYLE
Besh, J. My New Orleans **641.59**

COOKING, AMERICAN -- MIDWESTERN STYLE
Flinn, K. Burnt toast makes you sing good **641.597**
Thielen, A. The New Midwestern table **641.59**

COOKING, AMERICAN -- PACIFIC NORTHWEST STYLE
Dixon, K. The Tutka Bay Lodge cookbook **641.59**
Erickson, R. A boat, a whale, and a walrus **641.597**

COOKING, AMERICAN -- PHILOSOPHY
Barr, L. Provence, 1970 **641.59**

COOKING, AMERICAN -- SOUTHERN STYLE

Afro-vegan **641.59**
Bryson, F. Blue ribbon baking from a redneck kitchen **641.597**
Disbrowe, P. Down south **641.59**
Miller, A. Soul food **641.59**

COOKING, AMERICAN -- SOUTHWESTERN STYLE
Thompson-Anderson, T. Texas on the Table **641.597**

COOKING, AMERICAN -- WESTERN STYLE
Rollins, K. A taste of cowboy **641.597**

COOKING, ARGENTINE
Kaminsky, P. Mallmann on fire **641.598**

COOKING, ARMENIAN
Duguid, N. Taste of Persia **641.5**

COOKING, ASIAN
Asian dumplings **641.59**
Bowl **641.81**
Meehan, P. Lucky Peach 101 easy Asian recipes **641.595**

COOKING, AZERBAIJANI
Duguid, N. Taste of Persia **641.5**

COOKING, BASQUE
The Basque book **641.5**

COOKING, BURMESE
Duguid, N. Burma **641.59**

COOKING, CAJUN
Besh, J. My New Orleans **641.59**
Disbrowe, P. Down south **641.59**

COOKING, CANADIAN
O'Brady, T. Seven spoons **641.597**

COOKING, CARIBBEAN
Afro-vegan **641.59**
Gran cocina latina **641.597**
New World kitchen **641.59**

COOKING, CHOCOLATE
Guittard Chocolate cookbook **641.6**

COOKING, CREOLE
Besh, J. My New Orleans **641.59**

COOKING, EUROPEAN
Greenstein, E. A Jewish baker's pastry secrets **641.86**

COOKING, FRENCH
Chambers, V. 32 yolks **92**
Grigson, J. Charcuterie and French pork cookery **641.6**

COOKING, FRENCH -- PROVENCAL STYLE
Olney, R. Simple French food **641.59**

COOKING, GEORGIAN (SOUTH CAUCASIAN)
Duguid, N. Taste of Persia **641.5**

COOKING, ICELANDIC
Eddy, J. North **641.59**

COOKING, IRANIAN
Duguid, N. Taste of Persia **641.5**

COOKING, ITALIAN

Bastianich, J. Healthy pasta   **641.82**

Bastianich, L. M. Lidia's favorite recipes **641.594**

Bastianich, L. M. Lidia's mastering the art of Italian cuisine   **641.594**

Caggiano, B. Biba's Italy   **641.59**

Clark, M. Franny's   **641.594**

Friedman, A. Classico e moderno   **641.59**

Marchetti, D. The glorious pasta of Italy   **641.82**

Minchilli, E. Eating Rome   **641.594**

Mozza at home   **641.5**

Ray, R. Everyone is Italian on Sunday   **641.59**

Rustic Italian food   **641.59**

COOKING, KURDISH

Duguid, N. Taste of Persia   **641.5**

COOKING, MEDITERRANEAN

Ancient grains for modern meals   **641.59**

Ronnen, T. Crossroads   **641.59**

COOKING, MEXICAN

Gran cocina latina   **641.597**

COOKING, MIDDLE EASTERN

Ottolenghi, Y. Jerusalem   **641.5**

COOKING, RUSSIAN -- HISTORY -- 20TH CENTURY

Von Bremzen, A. Mastering the art of Soviet cooking   **641.59**

COOKING, SCANDINAVIAN

The Scandinavian Kitchen   **641.59**

COOKING, THAI

Greeley, A. Nong's Thai kitchen   **641.595**

Cookman, Scott

Ice blink   **919**

COOKS

As always, Julia   **92**

Barr, L. Provence, 1970   **641.59**

Bourdain, A. Kitchen confidential   **92**

Bourdain, A. Medium raw   **92**

Buford, B. Heat   **641.5**

Chambers, V. 32 yolks   **92**

Chambers, V. Yes, chef   **92**

Child, J. My life in France   **92**

Conant, J. A covert affair   **940.54**

Cowin, D. Mastering My Mistakes in the Kitchen   **641.5**

Fitch, N. R. Appetite for life   **92**

Friedman, A. One souffle at a time   **92**

Hamilton, G. Blood, bones & butter   **92**

Hazan, M. Amarcord, Marcella remembers   **92**

Moulle, J. P. French roots   **641.594**

Pepin, J. The apprentice: my life in the kitchen   **641.5**

Sheehan, J. Cooking dirty   **92**

Stabiner, K. Generation chef   **641.5**

COOKS -- BIOGRAPHY

Prud'homme, A. The French chef in America   **641.509**

Rossi, C. The Raging Skillet   **92**

COOKS -- FRANCE -- BIOGRAPHY

Spitz, B. Dearie   **92**

COOKS -- FRANCE -- PARIS -- BIOGRAPHY

Chambers, V. 32 yolks   **92**

COOKS -- SOUTHERN STATES -- BIOGRAPHY

The one true barbecue   **641.5**

COOKS -- UNITED STATES -- BIOGRAPHY

Chambers, V. Yes, chef   **92**

Martin, S. Life from scratch   **92**

Moulle, J. P. French roots   **641.594**

Pouillon, N. My organic life   **92**

Prud'homme, A. The French chef in America   **641.509**

Rossi, C. The Raging Skillet   **92**

Spitz, B. Dearie   **92**

COOKS -- UNITED STATES -- FAMILY RELATIONSHIPS

Martin, S. Life from scratch   **92**

COOKS -- UNTIED STATES -- BIOGRAPHY

Flinn, K. Burnt toast makes you sing good **641.597**

The **cool** factor. Linett, A.   **746.92**

Cool Springs Press (Company)

(comp) The book of home how-to   **643**

(comp) The complete guide to wiring   **621.319**

Cool, calm & collected. Kizer, C.   **811**

Cool, Michel

Francis, a new world pope   **92**

Cooler smarter. Shulman, S.   **363.7**

Coolidge. Shlaes, A.   **92**

Coolidge, Calvin, 1872-1933

About

Shlaes, A. Coolidge   **92**

COOLING APPLIANCES *See* Refrigeration

Coombes, Allen J.

The A to Z of plant names   **635**

Cooney, Kara, 1972-

The woman who would be king   **92**

Cooney, Seamus

(ed) Reznikoff, C. The poems of Charles Reznikoff   **811**

Coontz, Stephanie

A strange stirring   **305.42**

Cooper, Alex, 1994-

About

Cooper, A. Saving Alex   **92**

Cooper, Anderson, 1967-

About

Cooper, A. The rainbow comes and goes   **92**

Cooper, Andrew Scott

The fall of heaven   **955.05**

Cooper, Diana, 1892-1986

About

Mackrell, J. Flappers   **920**

Cooper, Douglas, 1911-1984

About

Richardson, J. The sorcerer's apprentice   **92**

Cooper, Gary, 1901-1961
About
Gary Cooper   **92**

Cooper, Gwen
Homer's odyssey   **636.8**

Cooper, Helene
About
Cooper, H. The house at Sugar Beach   **92**

Cooper, James Fenimore, 1789-1851
About
Franklin, W. James Fenimore Cooper   **92**

Cooper, John Milton
The warrior and the priest: Woodrow Wilson and
   Theodore Roosevelt   **92**
Woodrow Wilson   **92**

Cooper, William J.
Jefferson Davis, American   **92**

COOPERATION
Keltner, D. Born to be good   **155.2**

COOPERATION
   See also Associations; Commerce; Economics

COOPERATIVE AGRICULTURE
   See also Agriculture; Cooperation

COOPERATIVE BANKS
Friedman, J. Engineering the financial crisis **330.9**

COOPERATIVE BANKS
   See also Banks and banking; Cooperation;
   Cooperative societies; Personal loans

**COOPERATIVE COLLECTION DEVELOP-
MENT (LIBRARIES) -- UNITED STATES**
Bartlett, W. K. Floating collections   **025.2**

**COOPERATIVE ORGANIZATION ADMINIS-
TRATORS**
O'Shea, J. The deal from hell   **92**

COOPERATIVE SOCIETIES
Highfield, R. Supercooperators   **519.3**

COOPERATIVE SOCIETIES
   See also Cooperation; Corporations; Societies

COOPERATIVE STORES *See* Cooperative societies

COOPERATIVENESS
   See also Social psychology

COOPERATIVES *See* Cooperative societies
The **Cooperstown** chronicles. Russo, F.   **92**

Coote, Stephen
Napoleon and the Hundred Days   **940.2**

Cope, Alan Ingram, 1925-1999
About
Guibert, E. Alan's war   **741.5**

Copeland, B. Jack
Turing   **92**

Copeland, Edward
(ed) The Cambridge companion to Jane Austen **823**

Copeland, Lewis

(ed) The World's great speeches   **808.85**

Copeland, Misty, 1982
About
Copeland, M. Life in motion   **92**
The **Copernicus** complex. Scharf, C.   **523.1**
Copernicus' secret. Repcheck, J.   **92**

Copernicus, Nicolaus, 1473-1543
About
Repcheck, J. Copernicus' secret   **92**
Sobel, D. A more perfect heaven   **520**
Vollmann, W. T. Uncentering the Earth   **92**

Copestick, Joanna
(jt. auth) Becker, H. Decorate   **747**

Copi, Irving M.
Introduction to logic   **160**

COPING BEHAVIOR *See* Adjustment (Psychology)

COPING SKILLS *See* Life skills

Coping with concussion and mild traumatic brain
injury. Stoler, D. R.   **617.4**

Copley, John Singleton, 1738-1815
About
Kamensky, J. A revolution in color   **759.13**

COPPER
Carter, B. Boom, Bust, Boom   **622**

COPPER ENGRAVING *See* Engraving

COPPER MINES AND MINING
Carter, B. Boom, Bust, Boom   **622**
Tobar, H. Deep down dark   **363.11**

Copper, John F.
Taiwan   **951.249**

COPPERWORK
   See also Metalwork

Coppinger, Lorna
Coppinger, R. Dogs   **636.7**

Coppinger, Raymond
Dogs   **636.7**

COPY ART
   See also Art

COPYRIGHT
Butler, R. P. Copyright for teachers & librarians in
   the 21st century   **346**
Crews, K. D. Copyright law for librarians and edu-
   cators   **346.04**
Fishman, S. The copyright handbook   **346.04**
Fishman, S. The public domain   **346**
Hyde, L. Common as air   **346.04**
Hylton, K. N. Laws of creation   **346.04**
Lessig, L. The future of ideas   **004.67**
Lessig, L. Remix   **346**
Stim, R. Patent, copyright & trademark   **346**

**COPYRIGHT -- BROADCASTING RIGHTS --
UNITED STATES -- HISTORY**
Decherney, P. Hollywood's copyright wars **346.73**

COPYRIGHT -- EUROPE -- HISTORY
Baldwin, P. The copyright wars   **346**

COPYRIGHT -- MOTION PICTURES -- UNIT-ED STATES -- HISTORY

Decherney, P. Hollywood's copyright wars **346.73**

COPYRIGHT -- UNITED STATES

Crews, K. D. Copyright law for librarians and educators **346.04**

Gasaway, L. N. Copyright questions and answers for information professionals **346.73**

COPYRIGHT -- UNITED STATES -- HISTORY

Baldwin, P. The copyright wars **346**

Copyright for teachers & librarians in the 21st century. Butler, R. P. **346**

The copyright handbook. Fishman, S. **346.04**

Copyright law for librarians and educators. Crews, K. D. **346.04**

Copyright questions and answers for information professionals. Gasaway, L. N. **346.73**

The copyright wars. Baldwin, P. **346**

CORAL REEF ECOLOGY

See also Ecology

CORAL REEFS AND ISLANDS

See also Geology; Islands

CORALS

See also Marine animals

Corbeil, Jean-Claude

(ed) Merriam-Webster's visual dictionary **423**

Corbett, Holly C.

About

Baggett, J. The lost girls **910.4**

Corbett, Michael

Before you buy! **643**

Corbett, Sara

A house in the sky **92**

Corbett, William

The Whalen poem **811**

Corbin, Jennifer, d. 2004

About

Rule, A. Too late to say goodbye **364.152**

Cordery, Stacy A.

Alice **92**

Cordes, Kelly

The tower **796**

CORDIALS (LIQUOR) See Liquors

Cording, Robert

Walking with Ruskin **811**

Cordingly, David

Under the black flag **910.4**

Women sailors and sailors' women **910.4**

Cordon, Luis A.

Popular psychology **150**

Cordoza, Glen

Becoming a supple leopard **613.7**

Cords, Sarah Statz

The real story **025.5**

Pearl, N. Now read this III **016**

CORE CURRICULUM See Colleges and universi-ties -- Curricula; Education -- Curricula

Core samples from the world. **811**

Core technology competencies for librarians and library staff. **020**

Coren, Stanley

Why we love the dogs we do **636.7**

CORETTA SCOTT KING AWARD

See also Children's literature; Literary prizes

Corliss, Richard, 1944-2015

Mom in the movies **791.43**

Cornel West on Black prophetic fire. **92**

Cornelison, Pam

The great American history fact-finder **973**

Corner, Paul

The Fascist Party and popular opinion in Musso-lini's Italy **945.091**

Cornille, Didier

Skyscrapers **720**

Corning, Peter

The fair society **303.3**

Cornog, Martha

(ed) Graphic novels beyond the basics **025.2**

Corns, Thomas N.

Campbell, G. John Milton **92**

Cornthwaite, Julie

(jt. auth) Jones, M. Penguins **598.47**

Cornwell, Bernard, 1944-

Waterloo **940.2**

Cornwell, John

Hitler's pope: the secret history of Pius XII **92**

Cornwell, Neil

(ed) Reference guide to Russian literature **891.7**

Coronado, Rodney A., 1966-

About

Kuipers, D. Operation Bite Back **92**

Coronado, Shawna

Grow a living wall **635**

CORONARY DISEASES See Heart diseases

CORPORAL WORKS OF MERCY

A call to mercy **234.5**

CORPORATE ACCOUNTABILITY See Social responsibility of business

CORPORATE ACQUISITIONS See Corporate mergers and acquisitions

CORPORATE CULTURE

Alexander, L. Access to Asia **395.5**

Bock, L. Work rules! **658.4**

CORPORATE CULTURE

See also Corporations

CORPORATE CULTURE -- ASIA

Alexander, L. Access to Asia **395.5**

CORPORATE CULTURE -- CALIFORNIA -- SANTA CLARA COUNTY

Maxfield, K. Starting up Silicon Valley **338.7**

CORPORATE CULTURE -- UNITED STATES

Lashinsky, A. Inside Apple **338.7**

CORPORATE GOVERNANCE
Gramm, J. Dear chairman   **659.2**

CORPORATE GOVERNANCE -- LAW AND LEGISLATION -- UNITED STATES
Garrett, B. L. Too big to jail   **345.73**

CORPORATE GOVERNANCE -- UNITED STATES -- HISTORY
Gramm, J. Dear chairman   **659.2**

CORPORATE MERGERS AND ACQUISITIONS
Coll, S. Private empire   **338.7**
Farrell, G. Crash of the titans   **332.1**
MacIntosh, J. Dethroning the king   **338.8**

CORPORATE PLANNING See Business planning

CORPORATE POWER -- UNITED STATES
Coll, S. Private empire   **338.7**
Hayes, C. Twilight of the elites   **305.5**
Jenkins, M. Poison spring   **363.73**
Nader, R. Told you so   **303.3**

CORPORATE RESPONSIBILITY See Social responsibility of business

CORPORATE SYMBOLS See Trademarks

CORPORATE TAKEOVERS See Corporate mergers and acquisitions

CORPORATE TURNAROUNDS
Lutz, B. Car guys vs. bean counters   **338.7**

CORPORATION LAW
Garrett, B. L. Too big to jail   **345.73**

CORPORATION LAW
     See also Commercial law; Corporations; Law

CORPORATIONS
Denton, S. The Profiteers   **338.7**
Micklethwait, J. The company   **338.7**
Schultz, E. Retirement heist   **331.2**

CORPORATIONS
     See also Business enterprises

CORPORATIONS -- ACCOUNTING
     See also Accounting; Bookkeeping

CORPORATIONS -- CORRUPT PRACTICES -- UNITED STATES
Garrett, B. L. Too big to jail   **345.73**

CORPORATIONS -- ENVIRONMENTAL ASPECTS
Rigney, M. In pursuit of giants   **597**

CORPORATIONS -- FINANCE
     See also Finance

CORPORATIONS -- INVESTOR RELATIONS -- UNITED STATES -- HISTORY
Gramm, J. Dear chairman   **659.2**

CORPORATIONS -- MORAL AND ETHICAL ASPECTS
Mackey, J. Conscious capitalism   **174**

CORPORATIONS -- PLANNING See Business planning

CORPORATIONS -- POLITICAL ACTIVITY -- UNITED STATES -- HISTORY -- 20TH CEN-TURY
Kruse, K. M. One nation under God   **322**

CORPORATIONS -- SOCIAL RESPONSIBILITY See Social responsibility of business

CORPORATIONS, MULTINATIONAL See Multinational corporations

CORPORATIONS, NONPROFIT See Nonprofit organizations

CORPSES See Dead

CORPULENCE See Obesity

Correard, Marie-Helene
The Oxford-Hachette French dictionary   **443**

CORRECTIONAL INSTITUTIONS
     See also Punishment

CORRECTIONAL PERSONNEL -- SOUTH AFRICA -- BIOGRAPHY
Jones, B. Mandela   **92**

CORRECTIONS
     See also Administration of criminal justice

CORRESPONDENCE See Business letters; Letter writing; Letters

Corrigan, Gordon
Waterloo   **940.2**

Corrigan, Kelly
       About
Corrigan, K. Glitter and Glue   **92**
Corrigan, K. The middle place   **92**

Corriher, Shirley
BakeWise   **641.8**

CORROSION AND ANTI-CORROSIVES -- ANECDOTES
Waldman, J. Rust   **620.1**

CORRUPTION -- LOUISIANA -- NEW ORLEANS -- HISTORY -- 20TH CENTURY
Krist, G. Empire of sin   **976.3**

CORRUPTION -- RUSSIA (FEDERATION)
Pomerantsev, P. Nothing is true and everything is possible   **306**

CORRUPTION IN POLITICS See Political corruption

CORRUPTION IN SPORTS See Sports -- Corrupt practices

CORRUPTION, POLICE See Police corruption

CORSAIRS See Pirates

Corson, Richard
Stage makeup   **792**

Cortés, Hernán, 1485-1547
       About
Prescott, W. H. History of the conquest of Mexico   **972**

Cortese, Amy
Locavesting   **332.6**

Corwin, Lena
Lena Corwin's made by hand   **746.6**
Printing by hand   **745.5**

Cory, Steve

Ultimate guide: porches **690**

Cosby, Charlotte
(jt. auth) Studholme, J. Farrow & Ball How to
Decorate **747.94**

Cosell, Greg
The games that changed the game **796.332**

Cosell, Howard, 1918-1995
About
Kindred, D. Sound and fury **796**
Ribowsky, M. Howard Cosell **92**

Cosgrove, Alwyn
(jt. auth) Schuler, L. Strong **613.7**

Cosgrove, Toby
The Cleveland Clinic way **362.11**

COSMETIC SURGERY *See* Plastic surgery

COSMETICIANS
Brandon, R. Ugly beauty **646.7**

COSMETICS
Aftel, M. Fragrant **612.8**
DuPriest, L. Natural beauty **646.7**
Eldridge, L. Face paint **391.6**
Peiss, K. L. Hope in a jar **391.6**
Romanowski, P. Can you get hooked on lip
balm? **646.7**

COSMETICS
See also Personal grooming

COSMETICS -- DICTIONARIES
Winter, R. A consumer's dictionary of cosmetic ingredients **668**

COSMETICS INDUSTRY EXECUTIVES
Brandon, R. Ugly beauty **646.7**
Haynsworth, L. Amelia Earhart's daughters **629.13**
Mazzeo, T. J. The secret of Chanel No. 5 **338.7**
Vaughan, H. Sleeping with the enemy **92**

COSMIC RAYS
See also Nuclear physics; Radiation; Radioactivity; Space environment

Cosmigraphics. Benson, M. **523.1**

COSMOBIOLOGY *See* Space biology

COSMOCHRONOLOGY
Gribbin, J. 13.8 **523.1**

COSMOLOGY
Aczel, A. D. God's equation **523.1**
Alvarez, W. A Most Improbable Journey **508**
Ananthaswamy, A. The edge of physics **530**
Benson, M. Cosmigraphics **523.1**
Bloom, H. The God problem **500**
Clark, S. The Unknown Universe **523.1**
Close, F. E. Nothing **530**
Dauber, P. M. The three big bangs **523.1**
Frank, A. About time **523.1**
Frayn, M. The human touch **128**
Galfard, C. The Universe in Your Hand **523.1**
Gott, J. R. Welcome to the universe **523.1**
Greene, B. The hidden reality **530.1**
Greene, B. R. The elegant universe **539.7**

Greene, B. R. The fabric of the cosmos **523.1**
Gribbin, J. 13.8 **523.1**
Hawking, S. Black holes and baby universes and
other essays **523.1**
Hawking, S. A brief history of time **523.1**
Hawking, S. A briefer history of time **523.1**
Hawking, S. The grand design **530.1**
Hawking, S. My brief history **92**
Holt, J. Why does the world exist? **113**
Kaku, M. Parallel worlds **523.1**
Krauss, L. M. A universe from nothing **523.1**
Mitton, S. Heart of darkness **523.1**
Nothing **501**
Randall, L. Warped passages **530**
Rees, M. J. Just six numbers **523.1**
Scharf, C. Gravity's engines **523.8**
Singh, S. Big bang: the origins of the universe **523.1**
Smoot, G. Wrinkles in time **523.1**
The Stars **523.8**
Startalk **523.1**
Tegmark, M. Our mathematical universe **523.1**
Tyson, N. d. Death by black hole **523.8**
Tyson, N. d. Origins: fourteen billion years of cos-
mic evolution **523.1**
Weintraub, D. A. How old is the universe? **523.1**

COSMOLOGY
See also Universe

COSMOLOGY -- HISTORY
Bell, J. The space book **523.1**

COSMOLOGY -- MISCELLANEA
Bloom, H. The God problem **500**

COSMOLOGY -- POPULAR WORKS
Trotta, R. The edge of the sky **520**
Universe **523.1**

COSMONAUTS *See* Astronauts

COSMOPOLITANISM
Zuckerman, E. Rewire **302.23**

Cosmos. Sagan, C. **520**

COST ACCOUNTING
See also Accounting; Bookkeeping

COST AND STANDARD OF LIVING
Ridley, M. The rational optimist **339.2**
The value of a dollar **338.5**
The value of a dollar: colonial era to the Civil War,
1600-1865 **338.5**

COST AND STANDARD OF LIVING
See also Economics; Home economics; Quality of life; Social conditions; Wealth

Cost control for nonprofits in crisis. Smith, G.
S. **025.1**

COST EFFECTIVENESS
See also Economics

The cost of courage. Kaiser, C. **92**
The cost of discipleship. Bonhoeffer, D. **226**

COST OF LIVING *See* Cost and standard of living

COST OF MEDICAL CARE *See* Medical care --

Costs

Costa, Rebecca D.
The watchman's rattle **501**

Costello, Elaine
Random House Webster's American Sign Language
dictionary: unabridged **419**

Costello, Elvis, 1954-
About
Costello, E. Unfaithful Music & Disappearing
Ink **92**

Costello, John
The Pacific War **940.54**

Costello, Sara Ruffin
(ed) The book of decorating **747**

Costenbader, Carol W.
The big book of preserving the harvest **641.4**

Costigliola, Frank
Roosevelt's lost alliances **940.53**

COSTUME
See also Decorative arts; Ethnology; Manners and customs

COSTUME JEWELRY
Crowther, J. Make a statement **745.594**

Cote, Arthur E.
(ed) Fire protection handbook **628.9**

Cotera, Martha P.
(ed) Great lives from history **920.009**

Cott, Nancy F.
(ed) No small courage **305.4**

COTTAGE INDUSTRY *See* Home-based business

Cotterell, Arthur
Chariot **357**

COTTON
See also Economic botany; Fabrics; Fibers

COTTON MANUFACTURE
Beckert, S. Empire of cotton **338.4**
Johnson, W. River of dark dreams **305.8**

COTTON MANUFACTURE
See also Textile industry

Cotton Tenants. Agee, J. **976.1**

Couch, Dick
Sua sponte **356**
The warrior elite **359.9**

Couch, Julianne
Traveling the power line **333.793**

Coucy, Enguerrand de, 1340-1397
About
Tuchman, B. W. A distant mirror **944**

COUNCILS AND SYNODS
See also Christianity; Church history

COUNSELING
Crossman, A. Getting the best out of college **378.1**

COUNSELING
See also Applied psychology; Helping behavior; Personnel management

Counselor. Sorensen, T. C. **92**

Count on me. **177**

Countdown. Weisman, A. **304.2**

COUNTED THREAD EMBROIDERY
See also Embroidery

COUNTER CULTURE
Calhoun, A. St. Marks Is Dead **974.7**
Markoff, J. What the dormouse said-- **004**

COUNTER CULTURE
See also Lifestyles; Social conditions

COUNTER-REFORMATION
See also Christianity; Church history -- 1500-, Modern period

COUNTER-TERRORISM *See* Terrorism -- Prevention

COUNTERCULTURE *See* Counter culture

COUNTERCULTURE -- CALIFORNIA -- SAN FRANCISCO -- HISTORY -- 20TH CENTURY
Talbot, D. Season of the witch **306**

COUNTERCULTURE -- UNITED STATES
Kaiser, D. How the hippies saved physics **530.092**
Lattin, D. The Harvard Psychedelic Club **920**

COUNTERESPIONAGE *See* Intelligence service

COUNTERFACTUAL HISTORIES
See also Creative nonfiction; History

COUNTERFEITS AND COUNTERFEITING
Craughwell, T. J. Stealing Lincoln's body **973.7**
Kersten, J. The art of making money **92**
Levenson, T. Newton and the counterfeiter **92**

COUNTERFEITS AND COUNTERFEITING
See also Coinage; Crime; Forgery; Impostors and imposture; Money; Swindlers and swindling

COUNTERINSURGENCY
Arnold, J. R. Jungle of snakes **355**
Gentile, G. P. Wrong turn **355.02**
Hoffman, B. Anonymous soldiers **956.94**
Kilcullen, D. The accidental guerrilla **355.4**

COUNTERINSURGENCY
See also Guerrilla warfare; Insurgency

COUNTERINSURGENCY -- AFGHANISTAN
Gopal, A. No good men among the living **958.104**

COUNTERINSURGENCY -- AFGHANISTAN -- HISTORY -- 21ST CENTURY
Gentile, G. P. Wrong turn **355.02**

COUNTERINSURGENCY -- IRAQ
Finkel, D. The good soldiers **956.7**

COUNTERINSURGENCY -- PALESTINE -- HISTORY -- 20TH CENTURY
Hoffman, B. Anonymous soldiers **956.94**

COUNTERINTELLIGENCE *See* Intelligence service

Counterpoint. Piston, W. **781.2**

COUNTERPOINT
See also Composition (Music); Music -- Theory

COUNTERPOINT
Piston, W. Counterpoint **781.2**
Counties USA. 352.13
COUNTING
Thaller, B. Numbers **513.5**
Counting coup. Colton, L. **796.323**
COUNTRIES *See* Nations
COUNTRY AND WESTERN MUSIC *See* Country music
Country Bumpkin (Company)
(comp) A-z of Ribbon Embroidery **746.44**
A **country** called Amreeka. Malek, A. **305.8**
COUNTRY CAT DINNER HOUSE & BAR (PORTLAND, ORE.)
Gartland, A. Heartlandia **641.597**
The **country** cooking of France. **641.59**
Country cooking of Ireland. Andrews, C. **641.5**
Country driving. Hessler, P. **303.4**
Country Girl. O'Brien, E. **92**
COUNTRY HOMES -- ENGLAND
Livingstone, N. The mistresses of Cliveden **942.009**
COUNTRY LIFE
McDonnell, I. The Farmette cookbook **641.5**
Rebanks, J. The shepherd's life **92**
COUNTRY LIFE
See also Manners and customs
COUNTRY LIFE -- FRANCE
Thorisson, M. A kitchen in France **641.594**
COUNTRY LIFE -- GEORGIA
Foxfire 40th anniversary book **975.8**
COUNTRY LIFE -- IRELAND
McDonnell, I. The Farmette cookbook **641.5**
COUNTRY LIFE -- UNITED STATES -- ENCYCLOPEDIAS
Encyclopedia of rural America **973**
COUNTRY MUSIC
Cash, R. Composed **92**
Russell, T. Country music originals **781.642**
COUNTRY MUSIC
See also Folk music -- United States; Popular music
COUNTRY MUSIC -- ENCYCLOPEDIAS
The Encyclopedia of Country Music **781.64**
COUNTRY MUSIC -- HISTORY AND CRITICISM
Jennings, D. A. Sing me back home **781.642**
Mazor, B. Meeting Jimmie Rodgers **92**
COUNTRY MUSIC -- PICTORIAL WORKS
Kagarise, L. Pure country **781.642**
Country music originals. Russell, T. **781.642**
COUNTRY MUSICIANS
Cash, R. Composed **92**
Crowell, R. Chinaberry sidewalks **92**
The Encyclopedia of Country Music **781.64**
Escott, C. Hank Williams **92**
George-Warren, H. Public cowboy no. 1 **92**

Hemphill, P. Lovesick blues **92**
Kleist, R. Johnny Cash **92**
Kruth, J. To live's to fly **92**
Lynn, L. Still woman enough **92**
Mazor, B. Meeting Jimmie Rodgers **92**
McDonough, J. Tammy Wynette **92**
Patoski, J. N. Willie Nelson **92**
Russell, T. Country music originals **781.642**
Streissguth, M. Johnny Cash **92**
Zwonitzer, M. Will you miss me when I'm gone? **781.642**
COUNTRY MUSICIANS -- GRAPHIC NOVELS
Kleist, R. Johnny Cash **92**
A **country** of vast designs. Merry, R. W. **92**
COUNTRY SCHOOLS *See* Rural schools
COUNTY GOVERNMENT
Counties USA **352.13**
COUNTY LIBRARIES *See* Public libraries; Regional libraries
County name origins of the United States. Beatty, M. A. **917**
COUNTY OFFICERS *See* County government
COUNTY PLANNING *See* Regional planning
The **coup.** Abrahamian, E. **955.05**
Couper, Heather
The history of astronomy **520**
Coupland, Douglas
Marshall McLuhan **92**
COUPLES -- FRANCE -- PARIS -- BIOGRAPHY
Baldwin, R. Paris, I love you but you're bringing me down **944**
COUPONS (RETAIL TRADE)
Sennett, F. Groupon's biggest deal ever **381**
COUPONS (RETAIL TRADE)
See also Advertising
COUPS D'ÉTAT *See* Revolutions
COURAGE
Brown, B. Rising strong **158**
Kennedy, J. F. Profiles in courage **920**
May, R. The courage to create **153.3**
McCain, J. S. Why courage matters **179**
Tillich, P. The courage to be **179**
COURAGE
See also Virtue
COURAGE -- CASE STUDIES
Wolf, M. J. Abandoned in hell **959.704**
COURAGE -- KOREA (NORTH) -- HISTORY -- 20TH CENTURY
Weintraub, S. A Christmas far from home **951.904**
Courage beyond the game. Dent, J. **796.332**
The **Courage** to Act. Bernanke, B. **92**
The **courage** to be. Tillich, P. **179**
The **courage** to create. May, R. **153.3**
The **courage** to heal. Bass, E. **616.85**
The **courage** to hope. Sherrod, S. **975.8**
Courchesne, Rebecca

(jt. auth) Field, R. The Art of preserving **641.4**

COUREURS DE BOIS
    See also Fur trade; Fur trade -- Canada

The **course** of Mexican history. Meyer, M. C. **972**

COURSES OF STUDY *See* Education -- Curricula

COURT LIFE *See* Courts and courtiers

COURTESY
    Forni, P. M. The civility solution **395**

COURTESY
    See also Etiquette; Virtue

COURTIERS
    De Lisle, L. The sisters who would be queen **920**
    Massie, R. K. Nicholas and Alexandra **92**

COURTIERS *See* Courts and courtiers

COURTING *See* Courtship

Courtney, Nancy D.
    (ed) More technology for the rest of us **025**

Courtroom 302. Bogira, S. **345**

COURTS
    Bogira, S. Courtroom 302 **345**

COURTS
    See also Law

COURTS -- HISTORY
    O'Connor, S. D. Out of order **347.73**

COURTS AND COURTIERS
    Gristwood, S. Blood sisters **942.04**

COURTS OF LAST RESORT -- UNITED STATES -- HISTORY
    O'Connor, S. D. Out of order **347.73**

COURTSHIP
    Becker-Phelps, L. Love **646.7**

COURTSHIP
    See also Love

Courtwright, David T.
    Forces of habit **362.29**

Couscous and other good food from Morocco. **641.59**

COUSINS
    Peyser, M. Hissing cousins **92**

COUSINS
    See also Family

COUSINS -- UNITED STATES -- BIOGRAPHY
    Peyser, M. Hissing cousins **92**

Cousteau, Jacques Yves, 1910-1997
About
    Cousteau, J. Y. The human, the orchid, and the octopus **333.95**
    Matsen, B. Jacques Cousteau **92**

Coutts, Marion
    The Iceberg **92**

COUTURIERS *See* Fashion designers

Couvée, Petra
    (jt. auth) Finn, P. The Zhivago affair **891.73**

The **covenant** kitchen. Morgan, J. **641.5**

COVENANTS
    See also Contracts; Theology

COVENS *See* Witches

COVER LETTERS
    What color is your parachute? 2017 **650.1**
    Yate, M. Knock 'em dead cover letters **650.14**

COVER LETTERS
    See also Letters

Cover to cover. LaPlantz, S. **686.3**

Covering ground. Ellis, B. W. **635.9**

COVERLETS *See* Bedspreads; Quilts

A **covert** affair. Conant, J. **940.54**

Covert, Jack
    The 100 best business books of all time **016.6**

Covey, Sean
    The 4 disciplines of execution **658.4**

Covey, Stephen M. R.
    Smart trust **174**

Covey, Stephen R.
    The 7 habits of highly effective people **158**
    The 8th habit **158**
    First things first **158**
    Reader's Digest Association Everyday greatness **170**

Covington, Katie
    (jt. auth) Crowther, J. Make a statement **745.594**

Coward, Noel
    Three plays **822**

The **cowboy** encyclopedia. Slatta, R. W. **978**

COWBOYS
    George-Warren, H. Public cowboy no. 1 **92**

COWBOYS *See* Cowhands

COWBOYS -- WEST (U.S.) -- SOCIAL LIFE AND CUSTOMS
    Rollins, K. A taste of cowboy **641.597**

Cowboys full. McManus, J. **795.4**

Cowen, Tyler
    An economist gets lunch **394.1**

COWGIRLS *See* Cowhands

COWHANDS
    Brown, D. A. The American West **978**
    Rollins, K. A taste of cowboy **641.597**

COWHANDS
    See also Frontier and pioneer life; Ranch life

COWHANDS -- ENCYCLOPEDIAS
    Slatta, R. W. The cowboy encyclopedia **978**

Cowin, Dana
    Food & Wine Annual Cookbook 2015 **641**
    Mastering My Mistakes in the Kitchen **641.5**

Cox, Brian
    The quantum universe **530.12**

Cox, Hank H.
    American drive **338**

Cox, Jeff
    From vines to wines **634.8**

Cox, Lynne
About
    Cox, L. Swimming to Antarctica **92**

Cox, Madison

The Gardener's Garden **712**

Cox, Patsi Bale
Lynn, L. Still woman enough **92**

Cox, Rosamund Kidman
(ed) Wildlife Photographer of the Year **778.9**

Cox, Tom
Close encounters of the furred kind **636.8**

Coxeter, H. S. M. (Harold Scott Macdonald), 1907-2003
About
Roberts, S. King of infinite space **92**

Coy, Jason Philip
A brief history of Germany **943**

Coyle, Daniel
(jt. auth) Hamilton, T. The Secret Race **796.62**

Coyle, Marcia
The Roberts court **347.73**

Coyne, Jerry A.
Why evolution is true **576.8**

Coyote America. Flores, D. **599.77**

Coyote at the kitchen door. DeStefano, S. **578.7**

COYOTES
DeStefano, S. Coyote at the kitchen door **578.7**
Flores, D. Coyote America **599.77**

Cozzolino, Robert
(ed) The female gaze **704**

CPR (FIRST AID)
See also First aid

CQ's American government A to Z series
Congressional Quarterly, I. Congress A to Z **328**
Maddex, R. L. The U.S. Constitution A to Z **342**

Crabapple, Molly
The divide **303.3**
About
Crabapple, M. Drawing Blood **92**

Crabtree, Pam J.
(ed) Ancient Europe 8000 B.C.-A.D. 1000 **936**

CRACK (DRUG)
See also Cocaine

CRACK BABIES See Children of drug addicts

A **crack** in the edge of the world. Winchester, S. **979.4**

Cracking the aging code. Sagan, D. **612.67**

Cracking the Egyptian code. Robinson, A. **493**

Craddock, Ida C., 1857-1902
About
Schmidt, L. E. Heaven's bride **92**

Cradle of gold. Heaney, C. **92**

The **craft** cocktail party. **641.87**

The **craft** of baking. DeMasco, K. **641.8**

CRAFT SHOWS
See also Exhibitions; Festivals

CRAFTS (ARTS) See Arts and crafts movement;
Handicraft

Craig, Caroline
The little book of lunch **641.5**

Craig, Gordon Alexander
Germany, 1866-1945 **943.08**

Craig, Jennifer
Poe, M. Learning to communicate in science and
engineering **501**

Craig, William
Yankee come home **917.2**

Craine, Debra
The Oxford dictionary of dance **792.8**

Crais, Clifton C.
Sara Baartman and the Hottentot Venus **92**
About
Crais, C. History lessons **92**

Cramby, Jonas
Tex-Mex from Scratch **641.59**

Cramer, Alfred William
(ed) Musicians & composers of the 20th century **920.003**

Cramer, Deborah
Smithsonian ocean **578.7**

Cramer, James J.
Confessions of a street addict **332.6**

Cramer, Richard Ben
Joe DiMaggio **796.357**

Cramm, Gottfried, Freiherr von, 1909-1976
About
Fisher, M. A terrible splendor **796.342**

Cran, William
Do you speak American ?(Television program) Do
you speak American? **427**
McCrum, R. The story of English **420**

Crandall, Russell
Paleo takeout **641.5**

Crane, David, 1942-
Went the day well? **940.2**

Crane, Hart, 1899-1932
Complete poems and selected letters **811**
About
Mariani, P. L. The broken tower: a life of Hart
Crane **811**

Crane, Kathleen, 1951-
About
Crane, K. Sea legs **92**

Crane, Leon, 1919-2002
About
Murphy, B. 81 days below zero **940.54**

Crane, Stephen, 1871-1900
Prose and poetry **813**
About
Ellison, R. The collected essays of Ralph Elli-
son **814**
Kazin, A. An American procession **810**

CRANES (BIRDS)
Nigge, K. Whooping crane **598**

CRANIOLOGY -- HISTORY
Fabian, A. The skull collectors **599.9**

CRANKS *See* Eccentrics and eccentricities

Cranston, Maurice

Jean-Jacques: the early life and work of Jean-Jacques Rousseau, 1712-1754   **92**

The solitary self: Jean-Jacques Rousseau in exile and adversity   **92**

Crapol, Edward P.

John Tyler   **92**

Crash course [series]

Ford, C. Crash course in reference   **025.5**

Crash Course in Collection Development. Disher, W.   **025.2**

Crash course in library supervision. Tucker, D. C.   **023**

Crash course in readers' advisory. Orr, C.   **025.5**

Crash course in reference. Ford, C.   **025.5**

Crash course series

Tucker, D. C. Crash course in library supervision   **023**

Crash of the titans. Farrell, G.   **332.1**

CRASHES (FINANCE) *See* Financial crises

Crashing through. Kurson, R.   **92**

Craske, Matthew

Art in Europe, 1700-1830   **709.03**

Craske, Oliver

(ed) Punk rock   **781.66**

Craughwell, Thomas J.

Stealing Lincoln's body   **973.7**

Crave radiance. Alexander, E.   **811**

Craven, Wayne

American art   **709**

Crawford, Bill

All American   **92**

Crawford, Matthew B.

Shop class as soulcraft   **331**

The World Beyond Your Head   **155.2**

Crawford, Richard

America's musical life   **780.9**

Crawford, Robert, 1959-

The bard   **92**

Young Eliot   **92**

CRAYON DRAWING

See also Drawing

CRAZES *See* Fads

Crazy for the storm. Ollestad, N.   **92**

Crazy Horse. McMurtry, L.   **92**

Crazy Horse, Sioux Chief, ca. 1842-1877

About

McMurtry, L. Crazy Horse   **92**

Powers, T. The killing of Crazy Horse   **92**

Crazy river. Grant, R.   **916**

CRC Handbook of Chemistry and Physics.   **540**

Creamer, Robert W.

Babe   **92**

Stengel   **796.357**

Crease, Robert P.

The great equations   **509**

The quantum moment   **530.12**

Create dangerously. Danticat, E.   **92**

The **created** self. Weber, R. J.   **155.2**

Creating a new old house.   **728**

Creating a role. Stanislavsky, K.   **792**

Creating characters. Swain, D. V.   **808.3**

Creating the not so big house. Susanka, S.   **728**

Creating their own image. Farrington, L. E.   **709**

Creating your best life. Miller, C. A.   **158**

Creation. Rutherford, A.   **576.8**

CREATION

Mesler, B. A Brief History of Creation   **576.8**

CREATION (LITERARY, ARTISTIC, ETC.)

The artist's library   **021.2**

Bloomston, C. The little spark   **153.3**

Boorstin, D. J. The creators   **909**

Dillard, A. The writing life   **818**

Doctorow, E. L. Creationists: selected essays, 1993-2006   **814**

Gilbert, E. Big magic   **153.3**

Isay, D. Callings   **920.073**

Laing, O. The Trip to Echo Spring   **810.9**

Peacock, M. The paper garden   **92**

Sunset kitchen gypsy   **641.5**

CREATION (LITERARY, ARTISTIC, ETC.)

See also Genius; Imagination; Intellect; Inventions

CREATION -- STUDY AND TEACHING *See* Creationism; Evolution -- Study and teaching

CREATIONISM

Ayala, F. J. Darwin's gift to science and religion   **576.8**

Montgomery, D. R. The rocks don't lie   **551.48**

Young, C. C. Evolution and creationism   **576.8**

CREATIONISM

See also Christianity -- Doctrines

CREATIONISM -- POPULAR WORKS

Nye, B. Undeniable   **576.8**

Creationists: selected essays, 1993-2006. Doctorow, E. L.   **814**

Creations of fire. Cobb, C.   **540**

CREATIVE ABILITY

Aronica, L. Creative schools   **371.2**

The art of music   **708**

Bloomston, C. The little spark   **153.3**

Cameron, J. B. It's never too late to begin again   **155.67**

Csikszentmihalyi, M. Creativity   **153.3**

Harford, T. Messy   **153.35**

Kiyosaki, R. T. Why "A" Students Work for "C" Students and Why "B" Students Work for the Government   **332.024**

Kotter, J. P. Buy-in   **650.1**

May, R. The courage to create   **153.3**

Nugent, B. American nerd   **305.9**

CREATIVE ABILITY
See also Ability
CREATIVE ABILITY -- MISCELLANEA
Crispin, J. The creative tarot   133.3
**CREATIVE ABILITY -- PSYCHOLOGICAL AS-
PECTS**
Laing, O. The Trip to Echo Spring   810.9
**CREATIVE ABILITY -- STUDY AND TEACH-
ING -- UNITED STATES**
Aronica, L. Creative schools   371.2
**CREATIVE ABILITY -- UNITED STATES --
HISTORY -- 20TH CENTURY**
Gertner, J. The idea factory   384
CREATIVE ABILITY IN BUSINESS
Samit, J. Disrupt you!   650.1
CREATIVE ABILITY IN BUSINESS
See also Business; Creative ability
CREATIVE ABILITY IN OLD AGE
Peacock, M. The paper garden   92
CREATIVE ACTIVITIES
Citro, A. 150+ screen-free activities for kids 796.5
Doorley, R. Tinkerlab   600
Garlick, H. Born to Be Wild   796.083
CREATIVE ACTIVITIES
See also Amusements; Elementary education;
Kindergarten
CREATIVE ACTIVITIES AND SEAT WORK
Citro, A. 150+ screen-free activities for kids 796.5
Doorley, R. Tinkerlab   600
Frauenfelder, M. Maker dad   745.5
Van't Hul, J. The artful parent   745.5
The **creative** destruction of medicine. Topol,
E.   610.28
Creative Homeowner (Company)
(comp)   Ultimate   guide   to   plumbing
Creative lettering. Doh, J.   745.6
Creative mythology. Campbell, J.   201
CREATIVE NONFICTION
Boo, K. Behind the beautiful forevers   305.5
CREATIVE NONFICTION
See also Literature
CREATIVE NONFICTION -- AUTHORSHIP
D'Agata, J. The lifespan of a fact   808.02
Gutkind, L. You can't make this stuff up   808
Kidder, T. Good prose   808.02
CREATIVE NONFICTION -- TECHNIQUE
Gutkind, L. You can't make this stuff up   808
Creative Publishing International
The complete photo guide to window treat-
ments   646.2
(comp) First time sewing   646.2
Creative schools. Aronica, L.   371.2
The **creative** shrub garden. McIndoe, A.   635.9
Creative soldered jewelry & accessories. Bluhm,
L.   745.594
Creative stained glass. Stevenson, C.   748.5

The **creative** tarot. Crispin, J.   133.3
CREATIVE THINKING
Aronica, L. Creative schools   371.2
Csikszentmihalyi, M. Creativity   153.3
Grant, A. Originals   153.3
CREATIVE THINKING
See also Creative ability
Creative visualization. Gawain, S.   153.3
CREATIVE WRITING
Burge, K. The born frees   305.242
Gutkind, L. You can't make this stuff up   808
MFA vs NYC   808.02
Prose, F. Anne Frank   839.3
Prose, F. Reading like a writer   808
Salzman, M. True notebooks   371.9
Stein, S. How to grow a novel   808.3
The Writer's digest guide to good writing   808
CREATIVE WRITING
See also Authorship; Creation (Literary, artis-
tic, etc.); Language arts
**CREATIVE WRITING (HIGHER EDUCATION)
-- UNITED STATES**
MFA vs NYC   808.02
**CREATIVE WRITING (STUDY AND TEACH-
ING) -- SOUTH AFRICA**
Burge, K. The born frees   305.242
CREATIVE WRITING -- GRAPHIC NOVELS
Barry, L. What it is   741.5
Creativity. Csikszentmihalyi, M.   153.3
CREATIVITY *See* Creative ability
The **creators.** Boorstin, D. J.   909
CREATURE FILMS *See* Horror films
Creatures of a day. Gibbons, R.   811
Creatures of the deep. Hoyt, E.   591.7
CREDIBILITY *See* Truthfulness and falsehood
CREDIT
Leonard, R. Solve your money troubles   346
Credit repair. Leonard, R.   332.7
Creeley, Robert
The collected poems of Robert Creeley   811
Creevy, Bill
The pastel book   751.235
CREMATION
Doughty, C. Smoke gets in your eyes   92
Mitford, J. The American way of death revisit-
ed   338.4
CREMATION
See also Public health; Sanitation
**CREOLES -- ATLANTIC OCEAN REGION --
SOCIAL CONDITIONS**
Scott, R. J. Freedom papers   305.896
Crescent and star. Kinzer, S.   956.1
CRETE (GREECE)
McDougall, C. Natural Born Heroes   940.53
CREW (ROWING) *See* Rowing
CREWELWORK

See also Embroidery

Crews, Kenneth D.
Copyright law for librarians and educators **346.04**

Crick, Francis, 1916-2004
About
Ridley, M. Francis Crick **92**

Cricket radio. Himmelman, J. **595.7**

CRICKETS
Capinera, J. L. Field guide to grasshoppers, crickets, and katydids of the United States **595.7**
Himmelman, J. Cricket radio **595.7**

CRICKETS
See also Insects

Crilley, Mark
The realism challenge **751.4**

Crilly, A. J.
Henderson, M. 100 most important science ideas **500**

CRIME
Appignanesi, L. Trials of passion **364.152**
Great lives from history: Notorious lives **920.003**
James, B. Popular crime **364.1**
Kolker, R. Lost Girls **364.152**
Niebuhr, G. W. Caught up in crime **016**
Potter, M. Shadows in the vineyard **364.16**
Shaw, B. Major Barbara **822**

CRIME
See also Administration of criminal justice; Social problems

CRIME -- ENCYCLOPEDIAS
Encyclopedia of crime and punishment **346**
Nash, J. R. The great pictorial history of world crime **364**

CRIME -- FRANCE -- BURGUNDY -- CASE STUDIES
Potter, M. Shadows in the vineyard **364.16**

CRIME -- GERMANY -- NUREMBERG -- HISTORY
Harrington, J. F. The faithful executioner **364.66**

CRIME -- LOUISIANA -- NEW ORLEANS -- HISTORY -- 20TH CENTURY
Krist, G. Empire of sin **976.3**

CRIME -- MEXICO
Gibler, J. To die in Mexico **363.45**

CRIME -- NEW YORK (N.Y.)
Seligman, S. D. Tong wars **364.106**

CRIME -- NEW YORK (N.Y.) -- HISTORY -- 20TH CENTURY
Blum, D. The poisoner's handbook **614**

CRIME -- UNITED STATES
Connors, J. I Will Find You **364.15**
Krist, G. Empire of sin **976.3**
McConnell, D. American honor killings **364.15**

CRIME -- UNITED STATES -- HISTORY
James, B. Popular crime **364.1**

CRIME AND DRUGS *See* Drugs and crime

CRIME AND NARCOTICS *See* Drugs and crime

CRIME FILMS *See* Film noir; Gangster films; Mystery films

CRIME PREVENTION
Stuntz, W. J. The collapse of American criminal justice **364.4**

CRIME WRITING
Niebuhr, G. W. Caught up in crime **016**

The **Crimean** War. Figes, O. **947**

CRIMEAN WAR, 1853-1856
Figes, O. The Crimean War **947**

CRIMES *See* Crime

CRIMES AGAINST HUMANITY
See also Crime

CRIMES AGAINST PUBLIC SAFETY *See* Offenses against public safety

CRIMES OF HATE *See* Hate crimes

CRIMES OF PASSION -- CASE STUDIES
Appignanesi, L. Trials of passion **364.152**

CRIMES WITHOUT VICTIMS
See also Crime; Criminal law

CRIMES, POLITICAL *See* Political crimes and offenses

CRIMINAL BEHAVIOR *See* Criminal psychology

CRIMINAL INVESTIGATION
Crooks, P. The setup **363.28**
Englert, R. Blood secrets **363.2**
McCrery, N. Silent witnesses **363.25**
Niebuhr, G. W. Caught up in crime **016**
Stillman, D. Desert reckoning **363.2**
Wagner, E. J. The science of Sherlock Holmes **363.2**
Wittman, R. Priceless **364.1**

CRIMINAL INVESTIGATION
See also Law enforcement

CRIMINAL INVESTIGATION -- CALIFORNIA -- MOJAVE DESERT -- CASE STUDIES
Stillman, D. Desert reckoning **363.2**

CRIMINAL INVESTIGATION -- CASE STUDIES
McCrery, N. Silent witnesses **363.25**

CRIMINAL INVESTIGATION -- CORRUPT PRACTICES -- CALIFORNIA
Crooks, P. The setup **363.28**

CRIMINAL INVESTIGATION -- GREAT BRITAIN -- HISTORY
Crosby, M. C. The great pearl heist **364.16**

CRIMINAL INVESTIGATION -- UNITED STATES
Chaudry, R. Adnan's Story **364.152**
Halber, D. The skeleton crew **363.25**
Lance, P. Deal With the Devil **363.25**

CRIMINAL INVESTIGATION -- WASHINGTON METROPOLITAN AREA
Wilber, D. Q. A good month for murder **363.25**

CRIMINAL JUSTICE, ADMINISTRATION OF
See Administration of criminal justice

CRIMINAL JUSTICE, ADMINISTRATION OF
-- NEW YORK (N.Y.)
Burns, S. The Central Park Five   364.1
CRIMINAL JUSTICE, ADMINISTRATION OF
-- PSYCHOLOGICAL ASPECTS
Benforado, A. Unfair   364.3
CRIMINAL JUSTICE, ADMINISTRATION OF
-- UNITED STATES
Smith, C. S. The injustice system   345.73
Stuntz, W. J. The collapse of American criminal
justice   364.4
CRIMINAL LAW
See also Law
CRIMINAL LIABILITY OF JURISTIC PER-
SONS -- UNITED STATES
Garrett, B. L. Too big to jail   345.73
CRIMINAL PROCEDURE
See also Courts
CRIMINAL PROCEDURE -- GERMANY --
NUREMBERG -- HISTORY
Harrington, J. F. The faithful executioner   364.66
CRIMINAL PSYCHIATRY See Criminal psychol-
ogy
CRIMINAL PSYCHOLOGY
Benforado, A. Unfair   364.3
Douglas, J. E. The cases that haunt us 364.1
Paradis, C. The measure of madness   364.3
Rhodes, R. Why they kill   364.3
CRIMINAL PSYCHOLOGY
See also Psychology
CRIMINALISTICS See Forensic sciences
CRIMINALS
Balsamo, W. Young Al Capone   92
Carlo, P. Gaspipe   92
Chaudry, R. Adnan's Story   364.152
Eig, J. Get Capone   92
Great lives from history: Notorious lives 920.003
Guinn, J. Go down together   364.1
Kersten, J. The art of making money   92
Rhodes, R. Why they kill   364.3
Rule, A. The stranger beside me   92
CRIMINALS
See also Crime
CRIMINALS -- ALASKA -- MCCARTHY -- BI-
OGRAPHY
Pilgrim's wilderness   92
CRIMINALS -- FRANCE -- PARIS -- HISTORY
Sante, L. The other Paris   944
CRIMINALS -- IDENTIFICATION
See also Criminal investigation; Identification
CRIMINALS -- UNITED STATES -- BIOGRA-
PHY
Guinn, J. Manson   364.152
CRIMINOLOGISTS
Starr, D. The killer of little shepherds   364.152
CRIMINOLOGY See Crime

Crippen, Hawley Harvey, 1862-1910
About
Larson, E. Thunderstruck   364.152
CRIPPLED CHILDREN See Children with physi-
cal disabilities
CRIPPLED PEOPLE See People with physical
disabilities
CRISES -- UNITED STATES
Packer, G. The unwinding   973.924
CRISIS CENTERS
Ackerman, D. A slender thread   362.28
CRISIS CENTERS
See also Counseling; Social work
CRISIS COUNSELING See Hotlines (Telephone
counseling)
Crisis in employment. Jerrard, J.   025.5
The crisis of Islam. Lewis, B.   297
The crisis of the old order, 1919-1933. Schlesinger,
A. M.   973.91
Crispin, Jessa
The creative tarot   133.3
Crist, Darlene Trew
World ocean census   578.7
Crist, David
The twilight war   327
Crist, Steve
(ed) Edward weston   770
Cristino, Claudio
Easter Island's silent sentinels   990
Cristofari, Rita
Zoya Zoya's story   958.1
CRITICAL CARE NURSING -- PENNSYLVA-
NIA -- PERSONAL NARRATIVES
Brown, T. The shift   616.02
Critical companion to Alice Walker. Gillespie,
C.   813
Critical companion to Arthur Miller. Abbotson, S.
C. W.   812
Critical companion to Charles Dickens. Davis, P.
B.   823
Critical companion to Chaucer. Rossignol, R.   821
Critical companion to Dante. Ruud, J. 850
Critical companion to Edgar Allan Poe. Sova, D.
B.   818
Critical companion to Emily Dickinson. Leiter,
S.   811
Critical companion to Ernest Hemingway. Oliver,
C. M.   813
Critical companion to Eugene O'Neill. Dowling, R.
M.   812
Critical companion to F. Scott Fitzgerald. Tate, M.
J.   813
Critical companion to Flannery O'Connor. Kirk, C.
A.   813
Critical companion to George Orwell. Quinn, E. 828
Critical companion to Henry James. Haralson, E.

L. **813**

Critical companion to James Joyce. Fargnoli, A. N. **823**

Critical companion to Jane Austen. Baker, W. **823**

Critical companion to John Steinbeck. Schultz, J. D. **813**

Critical companion to Jonathan Swift. DeGategno, P. J. **828**

Critical companion to Kurt Vonnegut. Farrell, S. E. **813**

Critical companion to Maya Angelou. Thursby, J. S. **818**

Critical companion to Nathaniel Hawthorne. Wright, S. B. **813**

Critical companion to Philip Roth. Nadel, I. B. **813**

Critical companion to Ralph Waldo Emerson. Wayne, T. K. **818**

Critical companion to Robert Frost. Fagan, D. **811**

Critical companion to T.S. Eliot. Murphy, R. E. **811**

Critical companion to Tennessee Williams. Heintzelman, G. **812**

Critical companion to the Bible. Manser, M. H. **220.6**

Critical companion to Toni Morrison. Gillespie, C. **813**

Critical companion to Walt Whitman. Oliver, C. M. **811**

Critical companion to William Butler Yeats. Ross, D. A. **821**

Critical companion to William Faulkner. Fargnoli, A. N. **813**

Critical companion to William Shakespeare. Boyce, C. **822.3**

Critical companion to Zora Neale Hurston. Jones, S. L. **813**

Critical issue series
   Daniels, R. Prisoners without trial **940.53**
   Wallace, A. F. C. The long bitter trail **323.1**

Critical survey of drama. **809**

Critical survey of mystery and detective fiction. **809**

CRITICAL THINKING
   Levitin, D. J. A field guide to lies **153.4**
   Nisbett, R. E. Mindware **153.4**

CRITICAL THINKING
   See also Decision making; Logic; Problem solving; Reasoning; Thought and thinking

CRITICAL THINKING IN CHILDREN
   Bailey, E. Safe kids, smart parents **613.6**

CRITICISM
   Angell, R. This old man **92**
   Berry, W. Imagination in place **814**
   Bishop, E. Poems, prose, and letters **818**
   Capote, T. Portraits and observations **814**
   Crane, H. Complete poems and selected letters **811**
   Didion, J. We tell ourselves stories in order to live **814**

Doctorow, E. L. Creationists: selected essays, 1993-2006 **814**

Dyer, G. Otherwise known as the human condition **824**

Gioia, D. Can poetry matter? **809.1**

Kermode, F. An appetite for poetry **801**

Mendelsohn, D. Waiting for the barbarians **801**

Moretti, F. Distant reading **801**

Said, E. W. Reflections on exile and other essays **814**

Smith, Z. Changing my mind **824**

Sontag, S. At the same time **814**

Wallace, D. F. Consider the lobster **814**

Wilde, O. The artist as critic **824**

CRITICISM
   See also Aesthetics; Literature; Rhetoric

CRITICISM AND INTERPRETATION *See* Criticism

CRITICISM, FEMINIST *See* Feminist criticism

CRITICISM, INTERPRETATION, ETC. *See* Criticism

CRITICISM, PERSONAL
   Bright, D. The truth doesn't have to hurt **158.2**

CRITICS
   Gleiberman, O. Movie freak **791.43**
   Hopper, J. The first collection of criticism by a living female rock critic
   James, C. Latest readings **828**

CRITICS -- UNITED STATES -- BIOGRAPHY
   Caldwell, G. New life, no instructions **92**
   Greenberg, D. Republic of spin **973.099**

Critique of everyday life. Lefebvre, H. **301**

Critique of pure reason. Kant, I. **193**

CRO-MAGNONS
   See also Prehistoric peoples

CROATIA -- DESCRIPTION AND TRAVEL
   Wilson, J. Running away to home **305.8**

Croce, Benedetto, 1866-1952
        About
   Durant, W. J. The story of philosophy **109**

Crochet. Todhunter, T. **746.434**

The **crochet** answer book. Eckman, E. **746.43**

Crochet at home. **746.43**

Crochet one-skein wonders for babies. **746.434**

Crochet, Treena
   Bungalow style **747**

CROCHETING
   Chachula, R. Unexpected afghans **746.43**
   Crochet at home **746.43**
   Crochet one-skein wonders for babies **746.434**
   Crowfoot, J. Ultimate crochet bible **746.43**
   Eckman, E. Around the corner crochet borders **746.43**
   Eckman, E. Beyond the square crochet motifs **746.434**
   Eckman, E. Connect-the-shapes crochet mo-

tifs **746.43**

Eckman, E. The crochet answer book **746.43**

Gullberg, M. Tapestry crochet and more **746.434**

Hubert, M. 10 Granny Squares 30 Blankets **746.43**

Hubert, M. The complete photo guide to crochet **746.43**

Hubert, M. The granny square book **746.43**

Keim, C. Teach yourself visually crochet **746.43**

Loop-d-loop crochet **746.43**

Righetti, M. Crocheting in plain English **746.43**

Todhunter, T. Crochet **746.434**

CROCHETING

See also Needlework

CROCHETING -- HANDBOOKS, MANUALS, ETC

A to Z of crochet **746.434**

CROCHETING -- PATTERNS

Chachula, R. Unexpected afghans **746.43**

Crochet at home **746.43**

Crochet one-skein wonders for babies **746.434**

Eckman, E. Around the corner crochet borders **746.43**

Eckman, E. Beyond the square crochet motifs **746.434**

Eckman, E. Connect-the-shapes crochet motifs **746.43**

How to crochet **746.43**

Hubert, M. The granny square book **746.43**

Loop-d-loop crochet **746.43**

Omdahl, K. The finer edge **746.43**

CROCHETING -- TECHNIQUE

Knight, E. 500 crochet stitches **746.43**

A to Z of crochet **746.434**

Crocheting in plain English. Righetti, M. **746.43**

Crocker, Betty

Betty Crocker cookie book **641.8**

CROCKERY See Pottery

Crockett, Davy, 1786-1836

About

Davis, W. C. Three roads to the Alamo **976.4**

CROCODILES

See also Reptiles

Croddy, Eric

(ed) Weapons of mass destruction **358**

Croft, Terrell, 1880-1967

(ed) American electricians' handbook **621.3**

Crofton, Ian

Ayto, J. Brewer's dictionary of modern phrase & fable **803**

Crohn's & colitis diet guide. Steinhart, A. H. **616.3**

Croke, Vicki

The lady and the panda **599.78**

Crompton, Vicki

Saving beauty from the beast **362.88**

Cronk, Laura

Having been an accomplice **811**

Cronkite. Brinkley, D. **92**

Cronkite's war. Cronkite, W. **070.4**

Cronkite, Betsy, 1916-2005

About

Cronkite, W. Cronkite's war **070.4**

Cronkite, Walter, 1916-2009

Around America **917**

About

Brinkley, D. Cronkite **92**

Cronkite, W. Cronkite's war **070.4**

Cronkite, W. A reporter's life **070**

Cronkite's war **070.4**

Crook, David

The Wall Street Journal complete home owner's guidebook **643**

Crooks, Peter

The setup **363.28**

Croom, Emily Anne

The genealogist's companion and sourcebook **929**

CROP ROTATION

See also Agriculture

CROPS See Farm produce

CROPS AND CLIMATE

Allaby, M. The gardener's guide to weather and climate **635**

The gardener's guide to weather and climate **635**

Crosby, Bing, 1904-1977

About

Giddins, G. Bing Crosby: a pocketful of dreams: the early years, 1903-1940 **92**

Crosby, Guy

The science of good cooking **641.3**

Crosby, Molly Caldwell

Asleep **362.1**

The great pearl heist **364.16**

CROSBY, STILLS AND NASH (MUSICAL GROUP)

Browne, D. Fire and rain **781.66**

CROSS CULTURAL CONFLICT See Culture conflict

CROSS CULTURAL STUDIES See Cross-cultural studies

CROSS INFECTION -- PREVENTION

Goldfarb, T. L. The patient survival guide

Cross, Charles R.

Heavier than heaven: a biography of Kurt Cobain **92**

Here we are now **92**

Room full of mirrors **92**

Cross, Claire

The baby book **649.122**

Cross, Kim

What Stands in a Storm **363.34**

CROSS-CULTURAL PSYCHOLOGY See Ethnopsychology

CROSS-CULTURAL STUDIES

Alexander, L. Access to Asia **395.5**
Wroe, A. Orpheus **398.2**
CROSS-CULTURAL STUDIES
See also Culture; Social sciences
CROSS-DRESSERS
Paul, J. R. Unlikely allies **973.3**
CROSS-STITCH
Durant, J. Increase, decrease **746.43**
Improv handbook for modern quilters **746.46**
Reader's Digest Association The big book of
cross-stitch designs **746.44**
CROSS-STITCH
See also Embroidery
Crossan, John Dominic
Borg, M. J. The first Paul **227**
CROSSDRESSERS *See* Cross-dressers
Crossing the borders of time. Maitland, L. **940.53**
Crossing the danger water. **810**
Crossing the threshold of hope. John Paul **282**
Crossman, Anne
Getting the best out of college **378.1**
Crossroads. Schumacher, M. **92**
Crossroads. Ronnen, T. **641.59**
Crosstown traffic: Jimi Hendrix and the post-war
rock'n'roll revolution. Murray, C. S. **787.87**
CROSSWORD PUZZLES
See also Puzzles; Word games
Crouch, Stanley, 1945-
Kansas City lightning **92**
CROWDS
Surowiecki, J. The wisdom of crowds **303.3**
Crowe, David
Oskar Schindler **92**
Crowe, Francis Trenholm, 1882-1946
About
Hiltzik, M. A. Colossus **627**
Crowe, Lauren Goldstein
The towering world of Jimmy Choo **391**
Crowell, Rodney, 1950-
About
Crowell, R. Chinaberry sidewalks **92**
Crowfoot, Jane
Ultimate crochet bible **746.43**
Crowley, Bill
(ed) Defending professionalism **020**
Crowley, Roger
City of fortune **945**
Conquerors **909**
Empires of the sea **359**
Crown Journeys series
McPherson, J. M. Hallowed ground **973.7**
Crowther, Janet
Make a statement **745.594**
Crucial conversations. McMillan, R. **153.6**
Crucible of commmand. Davis, W. C. **920**
The **crucible** of war. Anderson, F. **973.2**

CRUDE OIL *See* Petroleum
Crude world. Maass, P. **338.2**
Cruden's Complete concordance. Cruden, A. **220.5**
Cruden, Alexander
Cruden's Complete concordance **220.5**
A **cruel** and shocking act. Shenon, P. **973.922**
CRUELTY
See also Ethics
CRUELTY TO ANIMALS *See* Animal welfare
CRUELTY TO CHILDREN *See* Child abuse
Cruikshank, Tiffany
Meditate your weight **613.25**
CRUISES *See* Ocean travel
Crumb, R.
The book of Genesis **741.5**
R. Crumb: the complete record cover collec-
tion **741.6**
Crump, R. W.
(ed) Rossetti, C. G. Christina Rossetti **821**
Crumpacker, Bunny
How to slice an onion **641.5**
Crunch! Burhans, D. E. **338.4**
Crusade. Atkinson, R. **956.7**
The **Crusades.** **909.07**
The **crusades.** Asbridge, T. **909.07**
CRUSADES
Asbridge, T. The crusades **909.07**
Cobb, P. M. The race for paradise **909.07**
The Crusades **909.07**
Haag, M. The Tragedy of the Templars **271**
The Oxford illustrated history of the Cru-
sades **909.07**
Phillips, J. Holy warriors **909.07**
Tuchman, B. W. A distant mirror **944**
CRUSADES -- ENCYCLOPEDIAS
Andrea, A. J. Encyclopedia of the crusades **909.07**
The Crusades **909.07**
CRUSADES -- INFLUENCE
Catlos, B. A. Infidel kings and unholy war-
riors **909.07**
The **Crusades** of Cesar Chavez. Pawel, M. **92**
CRUSHES
See also Friendship; Love
Crusoe. Frank, K. **823**
**CRUSOE, ROBINSON (FICTITIOUS CHARAC-
TER)**
Frank, K. Crusoe **823**
Crutchfield, James A.
Revolt at Taos **972**
Cruz, Nilo
Anna in the tropics **812**
CRYOBIOLOGY
See also Biology; Cold; Low temperatures
CRYONICS
See also Burial
CRYOSURGERY

See also Cold -- Therapeutic use; Surgery

CRYPTOGRAPHY

Lee, B. Marching orders **940.54**

McKay, S. The secret lives of codebreakers **940.54**

Sebag-Montefiore, H. Enigma: the battle for the code **940.54**

CRYPTOGRAPHY

See also Signs and symbols; Writing

CRYPTOZOOLOGY

Prothero, D. R. Abominable science! **001.944**

CRYSTAL CITY (TEX.) -- HISTORY

Russell, J. J. The Train to Crystal City **940.53**

CRYSTAL GAZING *See* Divination

CRYSTAL METH (DRUG)

See also Designer drugs; Methamphetamine

Crystal, Billy

About

Crystal, B. Still foolin' 'em **92**

Crystal, David

By hook or by crook **427**

The Cambridge encyclopedia of language **400**

The Cambridge encyclopedia of the English language **420**

A dictionary of language **410**

English as a global language **420**

How language works **401**

Spell It Out **421**

The stories of English **427**

The story of English in 100 words **422**

CRYSTALS

Harlow, G. E. Gems & Crystals **549**

Holden, A. Crystals and crystal growing **548**

Johnsen, O. Minerals of the world **549**

Crystals and crystal growing. Holden, A. **548**

Csikszentmihalyi, Mihaly

Creativity **153.3**

Flow: the psychology of optimal experience **155.2**

Cuba. Suchlicki, J. **972.91**

Cuba. Perez, L. A. **972.91**

CUBA

Baraka, I. A. The LeRoi Jones/Amiri Baraka reader **818**

Guillermoprieto, A. Dancing with Cuba **972.91**

CUBA -- DESCRIPTION AND TRAVEL

Guillermoprieto, A. Dancing with Cuba **972.91**

Symmes, P. The boys from Dolores **972.91**

CUBA -- ENCYCLOPEDIAS

Martinez-Fernandez, L. Encyclopedia of Cuba **972.91**

CUBA -- HISTORY

Gimbel, W. Havana dreams **972.91**

Perez, L. A. Cuba **972.91**

Rathbone, J. P. The sugar king of Havana **92**

Suchlicki, J. Cuba **972.91**

CUBA -- HISTORY -- 1958-1959, REVOLUTION

Diary of a combatant **92**

Remembering Che **972.91**

Weiss, M. The Yankee comandante **92**

CUBA -- HISTORY -- 1959-

Gimbel, W. Havana dreams **972.91**

Von Tunzelmann, A. Red heat **972.9**

CUBA -- HISTORY -- 1959-1990

Remembering Che **972.91**

CUBA -- HISTORY -- 1961, INVASION

Rasenberger, J. The brilliant disaster **972.91**

CUBA -- HISTORY -- 1990-

Remembering Che **972.91**

CUBA -- HISTORY -- 1990- -- BIOGRAPHY

Cooke, J. The other side of paradise **972.91**

CUBA -- HISTORY -- REVOLUTION, 1959 -- PARTICIPATION, AMERICAN

Weiss, M. The Yankee comandante **92**

CUBA -- POLITICS AND GOVERNMENT

Castro, F. Fidel Castro: my life **92**

Coltman, L. The real Fidel Castro **92**

Szulc, T. Fidel **92**

CUBA -- POLITICS AND GOVERNMENT -- 1990-

Cooke, J. The other side of paradise **972.91**

CUBA -- SOCIAL LIFE AND CUSTOMS

Butler The domino diaries **796.83**

Cooke, J. The other side of paradise **972.91**

Cuba! Goldberg, D. **641.5**

Cuba: art and history, from 1868 to today. **709**

CUBAN AMERICANS

Blanco, R. The Prince of Los Cocuyos **92**

Eire, C. M. N. Learning to die in Miami **92**

CUBAN AMERICANS -- BIOGRAPHY

Eire, C. M. N. Waiting for snow in Havana **92**

Hernández, D. A cup of water under my bed **920.009**

CUBAN ART

Cuba: art and history, from 1868 to today **709**

CUBAN COOKING

Goldberg, D. Cuba! **641.5**

Pelaez, A. S. The Cuban table **641.59**

CUBAN MISSILE CRISIS, 1962

Coleman, D. G. The fourteenth day **73.922**

Dobbs, M. One minute to midnight **973.922**

Freedman, L. Kennedy's wars **973.922**

Fursenko, A. V. One hell of a gamble **973.922**

Kennedy, R. F. Thirteen days **973.922**

CUBAN MISSILE CRISIS, 1962 -- INFLUENCE

Coleman, D. G. The fourteenth day **73.922**

The **Cuban** table. Pelaez, A. S. **641.59**

CUBIC EQUATIONS

Ash, A. Elliptic tales **515**

CUBIC EQUATIONS

See also Equations

CUBISM

See also Art

Cuckoo. Davies, N. **598.7**

CUCKOOS

Davies, N. Cuckoo   **598.7**

Cuddon, J. A.
The Penguin dictionary of literary terms and literary theory   **803**

Cuddy, Amy
Presence   **158.1**

Cukier, Kenneth
Big data   **306.46**

Culbertson, Shelly
The fires of spring   **909**

Culinary birds. Fraioli, J. O.   **641.6**

Culinary Institute of America
Vegetables   **641.6**

Culkin, Jennifer
        About
Culkin, J. A final arc of sky   **92**

Cullen, Bob
Golf is not a game of perfect   **796.352**

Cullen, Charles, 1960-
        About
Graeber, C. The good nurse   **364.152**

Cullen, Dave
Columbine   **364.152**

Cullen, Heidi
The weather of the future   **551.63**

Cullen, Kevin
Whitey Bulger   **364.1**

Cullin, Robert
Bolan, K. Technology made simple   **025**

Cullina, William
Native trees, shrubs & vines   **635.9**
Understanding perennials   **635.9**

Cullinan, Nicholas
(ed) Henri Matisse   **709.2**

Cullinane, Jan
The new retirement   **646.7**

Culp, David L.
The layered garden design lessons for year-round beauty from Brandywine Cottage   **635**

CULTIVATED PLANTS
Cullina, W. Native trees, shrubs & vines   **635.9**

CULTIVATED PLANTS
   See also Agriculture; Gardening; Plants

Cultivating garden style. Greayer, R.   **636.8**

CULTS
Belief beyond boundaries   **209**
The encyclopedia of cults, sects, and new religions   **200**
Wright, L. Going Clear   **299**

CULTS
   See also Religions

CULTS -- ALASKA -- MCCARTHY
Pilgrim's wilderness   **92**

Cultural amnesia. James, C.   **920**

CULTURAL ANTHROPOLOGY *See* Ethnology

CULTURAL CHANGE *See* Social change

CULTURAL CRITIQUE
Deb, S. The beautiful and the damned   **954.05**
Gill, A. A. To America with love   **917.3**
Yalom, M. How the French invented love   **944**

CULTURAL HERITAGE *See* Cultural property

A **cultural** history of physics.   **530**

CULTURAL LANDSCAPES -- GREAT BRITAIN
Higgins, C. Under another sky   **936**

CULTURAL PROGRAMS
Librarians as community partners   **021.2**

CULTURAL PROPERTY
Cole, P. Sacred trash   **296.09**
Frammolino, R. Chasing Aphrodite   **930**

CULTURAL PROPERTY -- PROTECTION
Hammer, J. The bad-ass librarians of Timbuktu   **025.8**

CULTURAL PROPERTY -- REPATRIATION -- ITALY
Frammolino, R. Chasing Aphrodite   **930**

CULTURAL RELATIONS
   See also Intellectual cooperation; International cooperation; International relations

CULTURAL RESOURCES MANAGEMENT *See* Cultural property -- Protection

The **Cultural** Revolution. Dikötter, F.   **951.056**

CULTURAL TOURISM
Becker, E. Overbooked   **338.4**

CULTURALLY DEPRIVED CHILDREN *See* Children with social disabilities

CULTURALLY HANDICAPPED CHILDREN *See* Children with social disabilities

CULTURE
Als, H. White Girls   **814**
Art and social justice education   **372.5**
Bloom, H. The Lucifer principle   **128**
Huxley, A. Brave new world revisited   **303.3**
Hyde, L. Common as air   **346.04**
Jenkins, J. K. All the time in the world   **390**
Moore, R. Onward   **230**
Pagel, M. Wired for culture   **303.4**
Wright, I. T. Darling Days   **92**

Culture and politics of health care work [series]
Deyo, R, A. Watch your back!   **617.5**

CULTURE CONFLICT
Al-Maria, S. The Girl Who Fell to Earth   **92**
Crabapple, M. Drawing Blood   **92**
Fadiman, A. The spirit catches you and you fall down   **306.4**
Frankopan, P. The Silk Roads   **909**

CULTURE CONFLICT
   See also Ethnic relations; Ethnopsychology; Race relations

CULTURE CONFLICT -- CALIFORNIA -- SAN FRANCISCO -- HISTORY -- 20TH CENTURY
Talbot, D. Season of the witch   **306**

CULTURE CONFLICT -- HAWAII -- HISTORY -- 18TH CENTURY
Moore, S.   Paradise of the Pacific   **996.9**
CULTURE CONFLICT -- HISTORY
Frankopan, P.   The Silk Roads   **909**
CULTURE CONFLICT -- UNITED STATES
Niose, D.   Nonbeliever nation   **211**
CULTURE CONTACT See Acculturation
The **culture** of cities. Mumford, L.   **307.7**
CULTURE SHOCK
Pipher, M.   The green boat   **303.4**
CULTURE SHOCK See Culture conflict
CULTURE, CORPORATE See Corporate culture
CultureAmerica [series]
Jellison, K.   It's our day   **392**
Cultures of the Jews.   **909**
Cultures of war. Dower, J. W.   **355**
CUMBERLAND PACKING CORPORATION
Cohen, R.   Sweet and low   **920**
Cumin, camels, and caravans. Nabhan, G. P.   **382**
Cumings, Bruce
Cumings, B.   The Korean War   **951.9**
Korea's place in the sun   **951.9**
The Korean War   **951.9**
Cumming, Laura
The Vanishing Velazquez   **759.6**
Cumming, Robert
Art   **700**
Cummings, E. E. (Edward Estlin), 1894-1962
Complete poems, 1904-1962   **811**
       About
Sawyer-Laucanno, C.   E.E. Cummings   **92**
Cunard, Nancy, 1896-1965
       About
Mackrell, J.   Flappers   **920**
CUNEIFORM INSCRIPTIONS
Ceram, C. W.   Gods, graves, and scholars   **930.1**
CUNEIFORM INSCRIPTIONS
   See also Inscriptions; Writing
Cunliffe, Barry
The ancient Celts   **936**
Cunningham, Jon
Waldman, C.   Encyclopedia of exploration   **910.3**
Cunningham, Marion
Cunningham, M.   The Fannie Farmer baking book   **641.7**
The Fannie Farmer cookbook   **641.5**
Cunningham, Merce
       About
Brown, C.   Chance and circumstance   **92**
A **cup** of water under my bed. Hernández, D. **920.009**
CUPCAKES
Robicelli, A.   Robicelli's   **641.86**
Cupcakes and cashmere at home. Schuman, E. **746.9**
CURATES See Clergy
CURATORS

James, J.   The snake charmer   **92**
Mead, M.   Blackberry winter   **92**
Novacek, M. J.   Time traveler   **92**
Ware, S.   Letter to the world   **920.72**
Cure. Marchant, J.   **616.89**
Cure unknown. Weintraub, P.   **616.9**
Cured. Holt, N.   **614.5**
Curie. Dry, S.   **92**
Curie, Eve, 1904-2007
       About
Emling, S.   Marie Curie and her daughters   **920**
Curie, Marie, 1867-1934
       About
Brian, D.   The Curies   **92**
Dry, S.   Curie   **92**
Emling, S.   Marie Curie and her daughters   **920**
Curie, Pierre, 1859-1906
       About
Brian, D.   The Curies   **92**
The **Curies.** Brian, D.   **92**
CURIOSITIES AND WONDERS
Bader, C. D.   Paranormal America   **133.8**
Foer, J.   Atlas Obscura   **910.41**
The Seventy wonders of the modern world   **720.9**
Steinmeyer, J.   Charles Fort   **92**
CURIOSITIES AND WONDERS -- CENTRAL AMERICA
Hely, S.   The wonder trail   **917.28**
CURIOSITIES AND WONDERS -- PERIODICALS
Guinness world records 2015   **031**
CURIOSITIES AND WONDERS -- SOUTH AMERICA
Hely, S.   The wonder trail   **917.28**
CURIOSITY
   See also Human behavior
Curious behavior. Provine, R. R.   **152.3**
The **Curious** Nature Guide. Leslie, C. W.   **508**
Curly girl. Massey, L.   **646.7**
Curly girl. Massey, L.   **646.7**
Currence, John
Pickles, pigs & whiskey   **641.59**
CURRENCY See Money
CURRENCY DEVALUATION See Monetary policy
Currency wars. Rickards, J.   **332.4**
Current Diagnosis and Treatment Surgery. Doherty, G. M.   **617**
Current medical diagnosis and treatment.   **610**
Current surgical diagnosis & treatment.   **617**
CURRICULA See Education -- Curricula
CURRICULUM MATERIALS CENTERS See Instructional materials centers
CURRICULUM PLANNING
   See also Education -- Curricula; Planning
Currie, Robin

The letter and the scroll **220.9**

Curry. Collingham, E. M. **394.1**

Curry, Constance
Zellner, R. The wrong side of Murder Creek **92**

Curry, Jennifer
Rich, M. World authors, 2000-2005 **920.003**

Curse of the Narrows. MacDonald, L. M. **971**

Cursed victory. Bregman, A.

The **curtain.** Kundera, M. **801**

Curtains. Jokinen, T. **393**

CURTAINS *See* Draperies

Curtan, Patricia
Streiff, F. The art of simple food **641.5**

Curtis, Adrian
Oxford Bible atlas **220.9**

Curtis, Brian
Fields of Battle **940.54**

Curtis, Edward E., 1970-
Muslims in America **305.8**

Curtis, Edward S., 1868-1952
About
Cardozo, C. Edward S. Curtis **770**
Egan, T. Short nights of the Shadow Catcher **770.92**
Gulbrandsen, D. Edward Sheriff Curtis **770**

Curtis, Garniss H.
Swisher, C. C. Java Man **599.93**

Curtis, Glade B.,1950-
Your pregnancy week by week **618.2**

Curtis, James
Spencer Tracy **92**

Curtis, Nancy C.
Black heritage sites **973**

Curtis, William J. R.
Modern architecture since 1900 **724**

Curtiss, Glenn Hammond, 1878-1930
About
Goldstone, L. Birdmen **629.13**

Curtiz, Michael, 1888-1962
About
Marton, K. The great escape **920**

The **cushion** in the road. Walker, A. **814**

Cushman, Clare
(ed) The Supreme Court justices **347.73**

Cushwa Center studies of Catholicism in Twentieth-century America [series]
Fisher, J. T. On the Irish waterfront **331.7**

Cusk, Rachel, 1967-
A life's work **306.874**
About
Cusk, R. Aftermath **823**

Custer. McMurtry, L. **92**

Custer. Wert, J. D. **92**

Custer died for your sins. Deloria, V. **970.004**

Custer's trials. Stiles, T. J. **92**

Custer, George A. (George Armstrong), 1839-1876
About

Connell, E. S. Son of the Morning Star **973.8**
Donovan, J. A terrible glory **973.8**
McMurtry, L. Custer **92**
Philbrick, N. The last stand **973.8**
Sandoz, M. The Battle of the Little Bighorn **973.8**
Stiles, T. J. Custer's trials **92**
Wert, J. D. Custer **92**

CUSTODY KIDNAPPING *See* Parental kidnapping

CUSTODY OF CHILDREN *See* Child custody

CUSTOM-MADE CLOTHING
Noonan, M. L. The coat route **338.4**

Customer care excellence. Cook, S. **658.8**

CUSTOMER RELATIONS
Cook, S. Customer care excellence **658.8**

CUSTOMER RELATIONS
See also Business; Public relations

CUSTOMER SERVICE *See* Customer services

CUSTOMER SERVICES
Cook, S. Customer care excellence **658.8**
Laughlin, S. The quality library **025.1**
Michelli, J. A. Driven to delight **658**

CUSTOMER SERVICES
See also Customer relations

CUSTOMER SERVICES -- TECHNOLOGICAL INNOVATIONS
Turow, J. The daily you **659.1**

CUSTOMS, SOCIAL *See* Manners and customs

Cut me loose. Vincent, L. **305.892**

Cut the Clutter. Ewer, C. T. **648.5**

Cutler, David
The savvy musician **780.2**

Cutler, Sam
You can't always get what you want **781.66**

Cutler, Thomas J.
Dutton's nautical navigation **623.89**

CYBER COMMERCE *See* Electronic commerce

The **cyber** effect. Aiken, M. **155.9**

Cyber self-defense. Moore, A. **613.6**

Cyberbullying. Kowalski, R. M. **302.34**

CYBERBULLYING
See also Bullies; Computer crimes

CYBERBULLYING
Kowalski, R. M. Cyberbullying **302.34**

CYBERBULLYING -- PREVENTION
Bully **371.5**

CYBERCOMMERCE *See* Electronic commerce

CYBERNETICS
See also Communication; Electronics; System theory

CYBERSPACE
See also Computer networks; Space and time

CYBERSPACE -- SECURITY MEASURES -- GOVERNMENT POLICY
Harris, S. @WAR **355.3**

CYBERSTALKING

Citron, D. K. Hate crimes in cyberspace **364.15**
**CYBERTERRORISM -- PREVENTION -- UNIT-
ED STATES -- HISTORY**
Kaplan, F. Dark territory **363.325**
The **cycles** of American history. Schlesinger, A.
M. **973**
CYCLING
Bambrick, Y. The urban cycling survival
guide **796.6**
Bike Snob The enlightened cyclist **796.6**
Henderson, B. The Haynes bicycle book **629.28**
Herlihy, D. V. The lost cyclist **92**
Petersen, G. Just ride **796.6**
CYCLING
See also Exercise; Outdoor recreation; Sports
CYCLING -- ENVIRONMENTAL ASPECTS
Byrne, D. Bicycle diaries **796.6**
CYCLING -- HANDBOOKS, MANUALS, ETC
Petersen, G. Just ride **796.6**
Weiss, E. The ultimate bicycle owner's manu-
al **796.6**
CYCLISTS
Balf, T. Major **92**
Herlihy, D. V. The lost cyclist **92**
Strickland, B. Tour de Lance **92**
CYCLONES
Larkin, E. Everything is broken **959.1**
CYCLONES
See also Meteorology; Storms; Winds
Cyclopedia of literary characters. **803**
Cyclopedia of literary places. **809**
CYCLOPEDIAS *See* Encyclopedias and dictionar-
ies
CYCLOPES (GREEK MYTHOLOGY)
Kaplan, M. Medusa's gaze and vampire's
bite **001.944**
CYCLOTRONS
See also Atoms; Nuclear physics; Transmuta-
tion (Chemistry)
Cylinder, Carly
The flower chef **745.92**
Cyndi Lauper. Lauper, C. **92**
Cyrano de Bergerac. Rostand, E. **842**
Cyrano de Bergerac, 1619-1655
About
Rostand, E. Cyrano de Bergerac **842**
CZECH AUTHORS
Zantovsky, M. Havel **943.704**
**CZECH REPUBLIC -- POLITICS AND GOV-
ERNMENT**
Havel, V. To the castle and back **92**
CZECHOSLOVAKIA
McNamara, K. J. Dreams of a great small na-
tion **943.703**
CZECHOSLOVAKIA -- HISTORY -- 1918-1968
Woodward, B. Prague winter **943.71**

**CZECHOSLOVAKIA -- POLITICS AND GOV-
ERNMENT**
Havel, V. To the castle and back **92**
Czolgosz, Leon F., 1873?-1901
About
Miller, S. The President and the assassin **973.8**
Rauchway, E. Murdering McKinley **973.8**

D

D DAY *See* Normandy (France), Attack on, 1944
D'Agata, John
About a mountain **979.3**
The lifespan of a fact **808.02**
D'Agnese, Joseph
The money book for freelancers, part-time, and the
self-employed **332.024**
D'Agostino, Ryan
(ed) The Eat Like a Man Guide to Feeding a
Crowd **641.5**
D'Alessandro, Emilio
About
D'Alessandro, E. Stanley Kubrick and me **791.43**
D'Annunzio, Gabriele, 1863-1938
About
Hughes-Hallett, L. Gabriele d'Annunzio **858**
D'Antonio, Michael
Forever blue **92**
Mortal Sins **261.8**
Spielman, A. Mosquito **595.77**
D'Este, Carlo
Warlord **92**
D'Souza, Dinesh
Ronald Reagan **973.927**
D-day. Beevor, A. **940.54**
D-Day, June 6, 1944. Ambrose, S. E. **940.54**
D.H. Lawrence. Worthen, J. **92**
D.H. Lawrence, the early years, 1885-1912. Worth-
en, J. **92**
Da Vinci's ghost. Lester, T. **741.092**
Daalder, Ivo H.
In the shadow of the Oval Office **355**
Dabney, Lewis M.
(ed) Wilson, E. Literary essays and reviews of the
1930s & 40s **814**
Dada. Dickerman, L. **709.04**
DADAISM
Dickerman, L. Dada **709.04**
Dahl, Linda
Loving Our Addicted Daughters Back to Life **362.29**
Dahl, Roald
About
Conant, J. The irregulars **940.54**
Sturrock, D. Storyteller **92**
Dahmer, Jeffrey
About
My friend Dahmer **741.5**

Daily life through American history in primary documents. **973**

Daily life through world history in primary documents. **909**

Daily painting. Marine, C. **751.4**

The **daily** you. Turow, J. **659.1**

DAIMLERCHRYSLER
Michelli, J. A. Driven to delight **658**

DAIRY CATTLE
Lewis, C. The illustrated guide to cows **636.2**

DAIRY PRODUCTS
English, A. Home dairy with Ashley English **637**
Hamilton, A. Got milked? **641.5**
Rule, C. S. Yogurt culture **641.6**

DAIRY-FREE COOKING
See also Cooking

DAIRYING
See also Agriculture; Livestock industry

DAKOTA INDIANS
Brown, D. A. The American West **978**
Philbrick, N. The last stand **973.8**
Yenne, B. Sitting Bull **92**

DAKOTA INDIANS -- GOVERNMENT RELATIONS -- HISTORY -- 19TH CENTURY
Berg, S. W. 38 nooses **973.7**

DAKOTA INDIANS -- WARS
Powers, T. The killing of Crazy Horse **92**

Daks, Nongkran
(jt. auth) Greeley, A. Nong's Thai kitchen **641.595**

Dalai Lama II, 1476-1542.
About
Mullin, G. H. The second Dalai Lama **92**

Dalai Lama XIV, 1935-
Freedom in exile **92**
How to be compassionate **294.3**
My appeal to the world **951**
My Tibet **951**
Violence and compassion **294.3**
About
Bstan-'dzin-rgya-mtsho, D. L. X. Freedom in exile **92**
Iyer, P. The open road **92**
Johnson, T. Tragedy in crimson **294.3**
Thurman, R. A. F. Why the Dalai Lama matters **294.3**

Dale, Cyndi
Llewellyn's complete book of chakras **131**

Dale, Steve
(ed) Decoding Your Dog **636.7**

Daley, Regan
In the sweet kitchen **641.8**

Daley, Richard J., 1902-1976
About
Cohen, A. American pharaoh: Mayor Richard J. Daley: his battle for Chicago and the nation **977.3**

Daley, Rosie

Weil, A. The healthy kitchen **641.5**

Dali, Keren
(jt. auth) Dilevko, J. Contemporary world fiction **016**

Dallas 1963. Minutaglio, B. **973.922**

DALLAS COWBOYS (FOOTBALL TEAM)
Ribowsky, M. The last cowboy **92**

Dallek, Robert
Harry S. Truman **92**
Let every nation know **92**
The lost peace **909.82**
Nixon and Kissinger **92**
An unfinished life: John F. Kennedy, 1917-1963 **92**

Dalpiaz, Christina M.
Breaking free, starting over **362.82**

Dalrymple, William
Nine lives **294**
Return of a king **958.1**
White Mughals **954**

Dalton, David
Scherman, T. Pop **92**

Dalton, Tony
Harryhausen, R. The art of Ray Harryhausen **778.5**

Daly, Michael
Topsy **791.3**

Dalzell, Tom
(ed) The new Partridge dictionary of slang and unconventional English **427**

DAMASCUS (SYRIA) -- DESCRIPTION AND TRAVEL
Saldana, S. The bread of angels **92**

Damasio, Antonio R.
The feeling of what happens **153**
Looking for Spinoza **152.4**

Damon-Moore, Laura
(ed) The artist's library **021.2**

Damour, Lisa
Untangled **305.235**

Damp, Dennis V.
The book of U.S. government jobs **331.1**

Damrosch, Barbara
The garden primer **635**

Damrosch, David
The buried book **809**

Damrosch, Leo
Jean-Jacques Rousseau **848**
Jonathan Swift **92**

DAMS
See also Civil engineering; Hydraulic structures; Water supply

Dana, Richard Henry
Two years before the mast **910.4**

DANCE
Browar, K. The art of movement **792**
Craine, D. The Oxford dictionary of dance **792.8**
Duncan, I. My life **92**

Reynolds, N. No fixed points   **792.8**
Streb, E. Streb   **92**
DANCE
   See also Amusements; Performing arts
DANCE -- DICTIONARIES
   Craine, D. The Oxford dictionary of dance   **792.8**
DANCE -- PICTORIAL WORKS
   Matter, J. Dancers among us   **770**
DANCE -- UNITED STATES
   Fuhrer, M. American dance   **792.8**
DANCE IN ART
   Matter, J. Dancers among us   **770**
The **dance** most of all. Gilbert, J.   **811**
DANCE MUSIC
   Matos, M. The underground is massive   **781.648**
DANCE MUSIC
   See also Music
The **dance** of anger. Lerner, H. G.   **152.4**
The **dance** of deception. Lerner, H. G.   **155.3**
The **dance** of intimacy. Lerner, H. G.   **155.6**
DANCE TEACHERS
   Tallchief, M. Maria Tallchief   **92**
   Ware, S. Letter to the world   **920.72**
Dance, Stanley
   The world of Count Basie   **920**
DANCERS
   Browar, K. The art of movement   **792**
   Brown, C. Chance and circumstance   **92**
   Faleiro, S. Beautiful thing   **792.7**
   Gates, H. L. Thirteen ways of looking at a black man   **920.71**
   Gottlieb, R. A. George Balanchine: the ballet maker   **92**
   Life stories   **920**
   Streb, E. Streb   **92**
   Teachout, T. All in the dances: a brief life of George Balanchine   **92**
   Vaill, A. Somewhere   **92**
   Volkov, S. St. Petersburg   **947**
   Ware, S. Letter to the world   **920.72**
DANCERS
   See also Entertainers
DANCERS -- PORTRAITS
   Matter, J. Dancers among us   **770**
DANCERS -- UNITED STATES -- BIOGRAPHY
   Riley, K. The Astaires   **92**
Dancers among us. Matter, J.   **770**
DANCES *See* Dance
DANCES (MUSIC) *See* Dance music
Danchev, Alex
   Cézanne   **759.4**
DANCING *See* Dance
Dancing in the dark. Dickstein, M.   **973.91**
Dancing in the glory of monsters. Stearns, J. K.   **967.51**
Dancing to the precipice: Lucie de la Tour du Pin and

the French Revolution. Moorehead, C.   **92**
Dancing with Cuba. Guillermoprieto, A.   **972.91**
Dancing with Rose. Kessler, L.   **362.1**
Dancing with strangers. Clendinnen, I.   **994**
Dancing With the Devil in the City of God. Barbassa, J.   **981.53**
Dando, Marc
   (jt. auth) Ebert, D. A. A pocket guide to sharks of the world   **597.3**
Dando, Marc
   Compagno, L. J. V. Sharks of the world   **597**
Danford, Natalie
   How to eataly   **641.594**
Danforth, Adam
   Butchering poultry, rabbit, lamb, goat, and pork **664**
DANGEROUS ANIMALS
   Quammen, D. Monster of God   **591.6**
DANGEROUS ANIMALS
   See also Animals
DANGEROUS ANIMALS -- FOLKLORE -- HISTORY
   Kaplan, M. Medusa's gaze and vampire's bite   **001.944**
Dangerous games. MacMillan, M.   **901**
The **dangerous** summer. Hemingway, E.   **791.8**
A **dangerous** woman. Rudahl, S.   **335**
Daniel Boone. Faragher, J. M.   **92**
Daniel Webster. Remini, R. V.   **328**
Daniel, Larry J.
   Shiloh   **973.7**
Danielle Walker's against all grain. Walker, D.   **641.563**
Daniels, Patricia
   The new solar system   **523.2**
Daniels, Roger
   Prisoners without trial   **940.53**
   (ed) Japanese Americans, from relocation to redress   **940.53**
Daniloff, Nicholas
   Baiev, K. The Oath   **947.5**
Daniloff, Ruth
   Baiev, K. The Oath   **947.5**
DANISH LANGUAGE
   See also Language and languages; Norwegian language; Scandinavian languages
DANISH LITERATURE
   See also Literature; Scandinavian literature
Danson, Edwin
   Weighing the world   **526**
Dante Alighieri, 1265-1321
   The divine comedy   **851**
   The Inferno   **851**
   Paradiso   **851**
   The portable Dante   **851**
   Purgatorio   **851**
       About

Bloom, H. The Western canon **809**
Ruud, J. Critical companion to Dante **850**
Danticat, Edwidge, 1969-
        About
Danticat, E. Brother, I'm dying **92**
Danticat, E. Create dangerously **92**
Danton, Georges Jacques, 1759-1794
        About
Lawday, D. The giant of the French Revolution **92**
Dare to repair. Sussman, J. **643**
Daring. Sheehy, G. **92**
Daring young men. Reeves, R. **943.087**
Darion, Joe
Cervantes Saavedra, M. d. Man of La Mancha **812**
DARK AGES *See* Middle Ages
Dark continent: Europe's twentieth century. Mazower, M. **940.55**
DARK ENERGY (ASTRONOMY)
Halpern, P. Edge of the universe **523.1**
DARK MATTER (ASTRONOMY)
Carroll, S. The particle at the end of the Universe **539.7**
Mitton, S. Heart of darkness **523.1**
DARK MATTER (ASTRONOMY)
    See also Matter
Dark Matter and the Dinosaurs. Randall, L. **523.1**
Dark money. Mayer, J. **320.52**
Dark nature. Watson, L. **111**
The **Dark** Net. Bartlett, J. **302.23**
DARK NIGHT OF THE SOUL *See* Mysticism
The **dark** side. Mayer, J. **973.931**
The **dark** side of genius. Spoto, D. **791.43**
Dark side of the moon. Biddle, W. **92**
Dark star safari. Theroux, P. **916**
Dark territory. Kaplan, F. **363.325**
Dark tide. Puleo, S. **363.1**
Dark water. Clark, R. **945**
Darke, Rick
The American woodland garden **635.9**
Darkest America. Austen, J. **791**
Darkness visible. Styron, W. **616.85**
DARKROOM TECHNIQUE IN PHOTOGRAPHY *See* Photography -- Processing
Darling. Rodríguez, R. **92**
Darling Days. Wright, I. T. **92**
Darling, David J.
Gravity's arc **530**
The universal book of mathematics **510**
Darling, Ron, 1960-
        About
Darling, R. The complete game **92**
Darlington, Tenaya
Dibruno Bros. House of Cheese **641.3**
Darms, Lisa
(ed) The riot grrrl collection **781.64**
Darnley, Henry Stewart, Lord, 1545-1567

        About
Weir, A. Mary, Queen of Scots, and the murder of Lord Darnley **92**
Darnton, Robert
Berlin journal, 1989-1990 **943.087**
The case for books **002**
Darrow, Clarence, 1857-1938
        About
Boyle, K. Arc of justice **345**
Farrell, J. A. Clarence Darrow **92**
Strang, D. A. Worse than the devil **345**
Darwin. Johnson, P. **576.8**
Darwin. Byrne, E. **576.8**
The **Darwin** reader. Darwin, C. **576.8**
Darwin's armada. McCalman, I. **576.8**
Darwin's dangerous idea. Dennett, D. C. **146**
Darwin's devices. Long, J. **629.8**
Darwin's ghost. Jones, S. **576.8**
Darwin's ghosts. Stott, R. **576.8**
Darwin's gift to science and religion. Ayala, F. J. **576.8**
Darwin's Origin of species. Browne, J. **576.8**
Darwin, Charles, 1809-1882
The Beagle letters **576.8**
The Darwin reader **576.8**
On the origin of species **576.8**
The origin of species by means of natural selection, or, The preservation of favored races in the struggle for life **576.8**
The voyage of the Beagle **508**
        About
Stott, R. Darwin's ghosts **576.8**
DARWINISM *See* Evolution
Darwish, Mahmud
If I were another **892.7**
Dary, David
The Oregon Trail **978**
Das Reboot. Honigstein, R. **796.334**
Dash, Mike
The first family **364.1**
Tulipomania **635.9**
DATA PROCESSING
Baker, S. The numerati **303.4**
Cukier, K. Big data **306.46**
DATA PROCESSING
    See also Computers; Information systems
DATA STORAGE AND RETRIEVAL SYSTEMS
    See Information systems
DATA TRANSMISSION SYSTEMS
    See also Telecommunication
DATABASE MANAGEMENT
Baker, S. Final Jeopardy **006.3**
DATABASE MANAGEMENT
    See also Computer science; Data processing; Information systems
DATABASE SEARCHING

Devine, J. Going beyond Google again   025.042

DATABASES
   See also Information resources

Dataclysm. Rudder, C.   155.2

DATE ETIQUETTE *See* Dating (Social customs)

DATE RAPE
   Krakauer, J. Missoula   362.883

DATE RAPE
   See also Dating (Social customs); Rape

DATES, HISTORICAL *See* Historical chronology

DATING (SOCIAL CUSTOMS)
   Atik, C. Modern Dating   646.7
   Becker-Phelps, L. Love   646.7
   Burroughs, A. Lust and Wonder   92
   Pincott, J. Do gentlemen really prefer blondes?   155.3

DATING (SOCIAL CUSTOMS)
   See also Courtship; Etiquette; Manners and customs

DATING, RADIOCARBON *See* Radiocarbon dating

Dauber, Nick
   (jt. auth) Shim, J. K. Accounting handbook   657

Dauber, Philip M.
   The three big bangs   523.1

Dauch, Richard E., 1942-2013
   (jt. auth) Cox, H. H. American drive   338

Daughan, George C.
   1812: the Navy's war   973.5
   Revolution on the Hudson   974.73

Daugherty, Tracy
   Hiding man   92
   Just one catch   92
   The Last Love Song   92

Daughter of heaven. Li, L.   92

DAUGHTERS
   Boland, E. A woman without a country   821

DAUGHTERS
   See also Family; Women

DAUGHTERS -- UNITED STATES -- BIOGRA-PHY
   Smith, C. B. The rules of inheritance   616.99

DAUGHTERS AND FATHERS *See* Father-daughter relationship

DAUGHTERS AND MOTHERS *See* Mother-daughter relationship

Daughters of the Samurai. Nimura, J. P.   920.72

DAUGHTERS-IN-LAW -- FAMILY RELATION-SHIPS -- ITALY -- NAPLES
   Wilson, K. Only in Naples   945.731

Daum, Meghan
   The unspeakable   814

DAVAO CITY (PHILIPPINES)
   Lukacs, J. D. Escape from Davao   940.54

Davenport, Basil
   (ed) The Portable Roman reader   870

Davenport, Matthew J.
   First over there   940.4

Davenport-Hines, R. P. T. (Richard Peter Treadwell), 1953-
   Universal Man   92

David and Goliath. Gladwell, M.   155.2

The **David** Foster Wallace Reader. Wallace, D. F.   813

David Hockney. Sykes, C. S., 1937-1975   92

David Hockney. Sykes, C. S., 1975-2012   92

David, A. Rosalie
   Handbook to life in ancient Egypt   932

David, Anthony
   Once upon a country   92

David, Elizabeth
   A book of Mediterranean food   641.5
   French provincial cooking   641.5
   Italian food   641.5
   Summer cooking   641.5

David, King of Israel
         About
   Pinsky, R. The life of David   92

David, Laurie
   The family cooks   641.3

David, Leonard
   (jt. auth) Aldrin, B. Mission to mars   629.44

David, Saul
   Operation Thunderbolt   967.61
   (ed) War: from ancient Egypt to Iraq   355

Davidds, Yasmin
   Your own terms   658.4

Davidman, Joy
         About
   Santamaria, A. Joy   92

Davidson, Alan, 1924-2003
   The Oxford companion to food   641

Davidson, Anthony H.
   Dolnick, B. Luck   130

Davidson, Cathy N.
   (ed) The Oxford book of women's writing in the United States   810

Davidson, Keay
   Smoot, G. Wrinkles in time   523.1

Davidson, Mark
   Right, wrong, and risky   423

Davidson, Michael
   (ed) Oppen, G. New collected poems   811

Davidson, Sara
   The December Project   296.7

Davie, Donald
   Collected poems   821

Davies, Brian
   The thought of Thomas Aquinas   189

Davies, Colin
   Thinking about architecture   720

Davies, Katie Quinn

What Katie Ate   **641.5**

Davies, Nick, 1953-
Cuckoo   **598.7**

Davies, P. C. W.
The eerie silence   **576.8**

Davies, Penelope J. E.
Janson, H. W. Janson's history of art   **709**

Davies, William
The happiness industry   **304**

DAVIS CUP
Fisher, M. A terrible splendor   **796.342**

Davis, Angela Y. (Angela Yvonne), 1944-
About
Kaplan, A. Dreaming in French   **944**

Davis, Bette, 1908-1989
About
Thomson, D. Bette Davis   **92**

Davis, Brenda
Becoming vegan   **613.2**

Davis, Burke
Sherman's march   **973.7**
To Appomattox   **973.7**

Davis, Dan M.
(jt. auth) Consolmagno, G. Turn left at Orion   **520**

Davis, David Brion, 1927-
The problem of slavery in the age of emancipation   **306.3**

Davis, Deborah
Guest of honor   **973.91**
The trip   **700.92**

Davis, Dick
Belonging   **821**

Davis, Eddie, 1922-1986
About
Dance, S. The world of Count Basie   **920**

Davis, Garth
(jt. auth) Jacobson, H. Proteinaholic   **613.2**

Davis, Jack E.
An Everglades providence   **92**

Davis, Jefferson, 1808-1889
About
Cooper, W. J. Jefferson Davis, American   **92**
Davis, W. C. An honorable defeat   **973.7**

Davis, Jennifer Pharr
About
Davis, J. P. Called again   **92**

Davis, John H.
Jacqueline Bouvier   **92**

Davis, Joshua
Spare parts   **629.8**

Davis, Kellie
(jt. auth) Contreras, B. Strong curves   **613.7**

Davis, Laura
Bass, E. The courage to heal   **616.85**

Davis, Lee Allyn
Man-made catastrophes   **904**

Davis, Lennard J.
Enabling acts   **342.73**

Davis, Mark W.
(jt. auth) Davis, M. Digital assassination   **005**

Davis, Mary B.
(ed) Native America in the twentieth century   **970.004**

Davis, Miles
About
Cook, R. It's about that time   **92**
Davis, M. Miles, the autobiography   **92**
Feather, L. From Satchmo to Miles   **920**

Davis, Paul B.
Critical companion to Charles Dickens   **823**

Davis, Peter G.
The American opera singer   **920**

Davis, Richard H.
The Bhagavad Gita   **294.5**

Davis, Seth
When March went mad   **796.323**
Wooden   **92**

Davis, Steven L., 1963-
(jt. auth) Minutaglio, B. Dallas 1963   **973.922**

Davis, Thomas J.
Plessy v. Ferguson   **342**

Davis, Timothy Charles
The hot chicken cookbook   **641.7**

Davis, Todd
Handy dad   **745.592**

Davis, Varina, 1826-1906
About
Berkin, C. Civil War wives   **920**

Davis, Wes
(ed) An anthology of modern Irish poetry   **821**

Davis, Will
Enough   **241**

Davis, William C.
Battle at Bull Run   **973.7**
Crucible of commmand   **920**
An honorable defeat   **973.7**
Three roads to the Alamo   **976.4**

Dawidoff, Nicholas
(ed) Baseball: a literary anthology   **810**
Collision Low Crossers   **796.3**

Dawidowicz, Lucy S.
The war against the Jews, 1933-1945   **940.53**

Dawisha, Karen
Putin's kleptocracy   **947.086**

Dawkins, Richard, 1941-
The ancestor's tale   **576.8**
Brief Candle in the Dark   **570**
Dawkins, R. The magic of reality   **501**
A devil's chaplain   **500**
The God delusion   **200**
The greatest show on Earth   **576.8**
The magic of reality   **501**

Pagel, M. Wired for culture   303.4
The selfish gene   576
Unweaving the rainbow   501
          About
Dawkins, R. An Appetite for Wonder   92
Daws, Gavan
Prisoners of the Japanese   940.54
Dawson, Alma
(ed) African American literature   810.9
Dawson, Geraldine
A parent's guide to high-functioning autism spec-
     trum disorder   618.92
Dawson, Ian
(ed) Who's who in British history   920.003
Dawson, Peg
Smart but scattered   649
DAY
          See also Chronology; Time
DAY CARE CENTERS
          See also Child care; Child welfare; Children
          -- Institutional care
DAY DREAMS *See* Fantasy
The day freedom died. Lane, C.   976.3
Day Lewis, C.
The complete poems of C. Day Lewis   821
The day of battle. Atkinson, R.   940.54
Day of honey. Ciezadlo, A.   92
DAY OF THE DEAD
          See also Holidays
The **Day** the Renaissance Was Saved. Capponi,
N.   945
The day the world discovered the sun. Anderson, M.
DAY TRADING (SECURITIES)
          See also Securities
The day Wall Street exploded. Gage, B.   974.7
The day we found the universe. Bartusiak, M. 520
Day, Alex
(jt. auth) Fauchald, N. Death & Co   641.87
Day, Cheryl
Back in the Day Bakery, made with love 641.81
Day, David
Jackson, A. Popular mechanics complete home
     how-to   643
Day, Doris, 1924-
          About
Kaufman, D. Doris Day   92
Day, Dorothy, 1897-1980
          About
Elie, P. The life you save may be your own 810
Day, Felicia
You're Never Weird on the Internet (Almost)
Day, Griffith
(jt. auth) Day, C. Back in the Day Bakery, made
     with love   641.81
Day, Thomas, 1748-1789
          About

Moore, W. How to create the perfect wife 823
Day, Timothy
A century of recorded music   780.26
Day, Trevor
Oceans   551.46
Dayan, Mosheh, 1931-1979
          About
Bar-On, M. Moshe Dayan   956.940
Daykin, Rosie
Butter baked goods   641.81
DAYS
Sims, M. Apollo's fire   529
Days of defiance. Klein, M.   973.7
Days of destruction, days of revolt. Hedges, C. 305.5
Days of God. Buchan, J.   955.05
Days of Rage. Burrough, B.   303.48
DAYS OF THE WEEK *See* Days
Days of wonder. Schulman, G.   811
Dazzled and deceived. Forbes, P.   578.4
The **DC** Comics encyclopedia. Beatty, S. 741.5
DC COMICS GROUP
Beatty, S. The DC Comics encyclopedia   741.5
The **DC** comics guide to writing comics. O'Neil,
D.   741.5
De Barros, Paul
Shall we play that one together?   92
De Botton, Alain, 1969-
The pleasures and sorrows of work   331
Religion for atheists   200
De civitate Dei./English
Concerning the city of God against the pagans 239
De Forest, John William, 1826-1906
          About
Wilson, E. Patriotic gore   810
De Give, Tassy
(jt. auth) Heibel, T. Rooted in design   635.9
De Graaf, John
What's the economy for, anyway?   330.9
De Grazia, Victoria
Irresistible empire   306
De Haven, Tom
Our hero   741.5
De Kooning, Willem, 1904-1997
          About
Elderfield, J. De Kooning: a retrospective 759.13
Smee, S. The art of rivalry   700.92
Swan, A. De Kooning: an American master   92
De Kooning: a retrospective. Elderfield, J. 759.13
De Kooning: an American master. Swan, A.   92
De Laszlo, Violet S.
(ed) Jung, C. G. The basic writings of C. G.
     Jung   150.19
De Laurentiis, Giada, 1970-
Happy cooking   641.5
De Lisle, Leanda
The sisters who would be queen   920

De Long, George W. (George Washington), 1844-1881

About

Sides, H. In the kingdom of ice   **910.4**

De Madariaga, Isabel

Ivan the Terrible   **92**

De Mille, Cecil B., 1881-1959

About

Eyman, S. Empire of dreams   **92**

De Pauw, Linda Grant

Battle cries and lullabies   **355**

De Quincey, Thomas

The confessions of an English opium-eater and other writings   **824**

De Reyna, Rudy

How to draw what you see   **741.2**

De Richemond, Jeanette

The Medical Library Association guide to finding out about heart disease   **016**

De Roy, Tui

(jt. auth) Jones, M. Penguins   **598.47**

De Sena, Joe, 1969-

(jt. auth) Durant, J. Spartan Fit   **613.7**

DE TRIBUS IMPOSTORIBUS

Minois, G. The atheist's Bible   **200**

De Villiers, Marq

The end   **363.34**

Sahara: a natural history   **508**

De Voto, Avis, 1904-1989

About

As always, Julia   **92**

De Vries, Alexandra

Frommer's Rio de Janeiro day By day   **918.15**

De Waal, Edmund

The hare with amber eyes   **920**

About

De Waal, E. The white road   **738.209**

De Young, Karen

Soldier: the life of Colin Powell   **92**

DEAD

Roach, M. Stiff   **611**

DEAD

See also Burial; Cremation; Death; Funeral rites and ceremonies; Obituaries

DEAD -- MISCELLANEA

Lovejoy, B. Rest in pieces   **306.9**

Dead men do tell tales. Maples, W. R.   **614**

Dead Mountain. Eichar, D.   **914.7**

Dead presidents. Carlson, B.   **973.09**

The Dead Rabbit drinks manual.   **641.87**

DEAD RABBIT GROCERY AND GROG (NEW YORK, N.Y.)

The Dead Rabbit drinks manual   **641.87**

The Dead Sea scrolls. Abegg, M. G.   **296.1**

Dead Sea scrolls

Abegg, M. G. The Dead Sea scrolls   **296.1**

The Encyclopedia of the Dead Sea scrolls   **296.1**

Golb, N. Who wrote the Dead Sea scrolls?   **296.1**

Schiffman, L. H. Reclaiming the Dead Sea scrolls   **296.1**

Dead wake. Larson, E.   **940.4**

Deadlines and disruption. Shepard, S. B.   **070.5**

Deadly choices. Offit, P. A.   **614.4**

Deadly monopolies. Washington, H. A.   **338.4**

The Deadly Sisterhood. Frieda, L.   **945**

DEAF

Bouton, K. Shouting won't help   **617.8**

Gibson, W. The miracle worker   **812**

Herrmann, D. Helen Keller   **92**

Keller, H. Helen Keller: selected writings   **92**

Keller, H. The story of my life   **92**

Sacks, O. W. Seeing voices   **362.4**

Uhlberg, M. Hands of my father   **92**

DEAF

See also Hearing impaired; People with physical disabilities

DEAF -- EDUCATION

Hauser, P. C. How deaf children learn   **371.91**

DEAF -- EDUCATION

See also Education

DEAF -- LEGAL STATUS, LAWS, ETC. -- UNITED STATES

Legal rights   **346.73**

DEAF -- MEANS OF COMMUNICATION

Hauser, P. C. How deaf children learn   **371.91**

DEAF -- MEANS OF COMMUNICATION

See also Communication

DEAF -- SIGN LANGUAGE *See* Sign language

DEAF CHILDREN

Hauser, P. C. How deaf children learn   **371.91**

DEAFNESS

Bouton, K. Shouting won't help   **617.8**

Deak, JoAnn

Girls will be girls   **649**

The deal from hell. O'Shea, J.   **92**

Deal With the Devil. Lance, P.   **363.25**

Deal, Terrence E.

(jt. auth) Bolman, L. G. How great leaders think   **658.4**

DEALERS, ART *See* Art dealers

Dean & me. Lewis, J.   **92**

Dean, Cornelia

Against the tide   **333.91**

Dean, Eddie

Kagarise, L. Pure country   **781.642**

Stanley, R. Man of constant sorrow   **92**

Dean, James, 1931-1955

About

Gehring, W. D. James Dean: rebel with a cause   **92**

Dean, John W. (John Wesley), 1938-

About

Dean, J. W. The Nixon Defense   **973.924**

Dean, Margaret Lazarus
Leaving orbit   **629.4**
Deane, Silas, 1737-1789
About
Paul, J. R. Unlikely allies   **973.3**
Dear chairman. Gramm, J.   **659.2**
Dear ghosts, Gallagher, T.   **811**
Dear Leader. Jang Jin-sung   **92**
Dear Prudence. Trinidad, D.   **811**
Dear Sandy, hello. Berrigan, T.   **92**
Dearborn, Mary V.
Mailer   **813**
Deardorff, David
What's wrong with my fruit garden?   **634**
What's wrong with my houseplant?   **635.9**
What's wrong with my vegetable garden?   **635**
Deardorff, David C.
What's wrong with my plant (and how do I fix
it?)   **635**
Dearie. Spitz, B.   **92**
DEATH
Anderson, H. The divine art of dying   **202**
Barnes, J. Nothing to be frightened of   **92**
Brody, J. E. Jane Brody's guide to the great be-
yond   **616.02**
Brown, S. M. In heaven as it is on earth   **236**
Butler, K. Knocking on Heaven's Door   **616.02**
Chen, P. W. Final exam   **92**
Davidson, S. The December Project   **296.7**
Dresser, N. Saying goodbye to someone you
love   **155.9**
Egan, K. On living   **170.44**
Emswiler, M. A. Guiding your child through
grief   **155.9**
Faust, D. G. This republic of suffering   **973.7**
Gilbert, S. M. Death's door   **155.9**
Giraldi, W. The Hero's Body   **92**
Haycock, D. B. Mortal coil   **571.8**
Heinrich, B. Life everlasting   **591.7**
The Inevitable   **814**
Kaufman, S. R. --And a time to die   **362.1**
Kiernan, S. P. Last rights   **179.7**
Kubler-Ross, E. Life lessons   **170**
Kubler-Ross, E. On children and death   **155.9**
Kubler-Ross, E. On death and dying   **155.9**
Lepore, J. The mansion of happiness   **973**
Levy, A. The orphaned adult   **152.4**
Mead, J. World of made and unmade   **811.54**
Moody, R. A. Life after life   **133.9**
Nuland, S. B. How we die   **616.07**
Peck, M. S. Denial of the soul   **179.7**
Phillips, P. Elegy for a broken machine   **811**
Roach, M. Spook   **133.9**
Schechter, H. The whole death catalog   **306.9**
Sheeler, J. Final salute   **956.7**
Sife, W. The loss of a pet   **155.9**

Simon, S. Unforgettable   **92**
Sogyal The Tibetan book of living and dying **294.3**
Spong, J. S. Eternal life   **236**
Teresi, D. The undead   **610**
Terkel, S. Will the circle be unbroken?   **128**
Twelve breaths a minute   **616**
Ward, J. Men We Reaped   **92**
DEATH
See also Biology; Eschatology; Life
Death & Co. Fauchald, N.   **641.87**
DEATH & CO. (BAR : NEW YORK, N.Y.)
Fauchald, N. Death & Co   **641.87**
DEATH -- AUTOBIOGRAPHY
Teresi, D. The undead   **610**
DEATH -- POETRY
Ferry, D. Bewilderment   **811**
Perillo, L. On the spectrum of possible deaths **811**
**DEATH -- PSYCHOLOGICAL ASPECTS --
CASE STUDIES**
Albom, M. Tuesdays with Morrie   **378.1**
DEATH -- QUOTATIONS
The Oxford book of death   **808.88**
DEATH -- RELIGIOUS ASPECTS
Anderson, H. The divine art of dying   **202**
**DEATH -- SOCIAL ASPECTS -- UNITED
STATES**
Faust, D. G. This republic of suffering   **973.7**
Kaufman, S. R. --And a time to die   **362.1**
**DEATH -- SOCIAL ASPECTS -- UNITED
STATES -- HISTORY**
Lepore, J. The mansion of happiness   **973**
The **death** and life of the great American school sys-
tem. Ravitch, D.   **379**
Death at SeaWorld. Kirby, D.   **599.53**
Death by black hole. Tyson, N. d.   **523.8**
Death by chocolate cakes. Desaulniers, M.   **641.8**
Death from the skies! Plait, P. C.   **520**
Death in Florence. Strathern, P.   **945**
Death in the afternoon. Hemingway, E.   **791.8**
Death in the city of light. King, D.
DEATH NOTICES *See* Obituaries
Death of a ventriloquist. Fay-LeBlanc, G.   **811**
The **death** of American virtue. Gormley, K. **973.929**
The **death** of Caesar. Strauss, B.   **937**
The **death** of cancer. DeVita-Raeburn, E.   **92**
The **death** of innocents. Prejean, H.   **364.66**
The **death** of King Arthur. Ackroyd, P.   **398.2**
Death or liberty. Egerton, D. R.   **973.3**
DEATH PENALTY *See* Capital punishment
DEATH RATE *See* Mortality; Vital statistics
**DEATH ROW INMATES -- UNITED STATES --
BIOGRAPHY**
Echols, D. Life after death   **364.66**
Death's acre. Bass, W. M.   **614**
Death's door. Gilbert, S. M.   **155.9**
Deathly deception. Smyth, D.   **940.54**

DEATHS, REGISTERS OF *See* Registers of births, etc.

Deb, Siddhartha
The beautiful and the damned **954.05**

DeBaggio, Francesco
Tucker, A. O. The encyclopedia of herbs **635**

DeBaggio, Thomas
Tucker, A. O. The encyclopedia of herbs **635**

The **Debate** on the Constitution. **342**

DEBATES AND DEBATING
Bordewich, F. M. America's great debate **973.6**

DEBATES AND DEBATING
See also Public speaking; Rhetoric

DeBenedetti, Christian
Beer bites **641.5**

DEBIT CARDS
See also Banks and banking

DEBT
Atwood, M. Payback **332.7**
Kobliner, B. Get a financial life **332.024**
McNaughton, D. The essential credit repair handbook **332.024**
Tamanaha, B. Z. Failing law schools **340**

DEBT
See also Finance

DEBT -- MORAL AND ETHICAL ASPECTS
Atwood, M. Payback **332.7**

DEBTOR AND CREDITOR
Leonard, R. Solve your money troubles **346**

DEBTOR AND CREDITOR
See also Commercial law

DeBuys, William
The last unicorn **591.68**

DeBuys, William Eno
A great aridness **551.6**

A **decade** of hope. Smith, D. **974.7**

Decade of the wolf. Smith, D. W. **599.77**

DECATHLETES
Anderson, L. Carlisle vs. Army **796.332**
Crawford, B. All American **92**

DECEASED *See* Dead

DECEIT *See* Deception; Fraud

December 8, 1980. Greenberg, K. E. **92**

The **December** Project. Davidson, S. **296.7**

DECEPTION
Ariely, D. The honest truth about dishonesty **177**
Konnikova, M. The Confidence Game **364.163**
Triandis, H. C. Fooling ourselves **155.2**

DECEPTION
See also Truthfulness and falsehood

DECEPTION (MILITARY SCIENCE) -- HISTORY -- 20TH CENTURY
Macintyre, B. Double cross **940.54**

DECEPTION -- PSYCHOLOGICAL ASPECTS
Trivers, R. The folly of fools **153.4**

DECEPTION -- SOCIAL ASPECTS

Trivers, R. The folly of fools **153.4**

DECEPTIVE ADVERTISING
See also Advertising; Business ethics

Decherney, Peter
Hollywood's copyright wars **346.73**

DECIMAL SYSTEM
See also Numbers

DECISION MAKING
Berger, J. Invisible Influence **302.13**
Dennett, D. C. Freedom evolves **153.8**
Dobelli, R. The art of thinking clearly **153.4**
Duhigg, C. Smarter faster better **158**
Gladwell, M. Blink: the power of thinking without thinking **153.4**
Groopman, J. E. Your medical mind **610**
Hall, S. S. Wisdom **179**
Iyengar, S. The art of choosing **153.8**
Kahneman, D. Thinking, fast and slow **153.4**
Kowitz, B. Sprint **658.4**
Lehrer, J. How we decide **153.8**
MacMillan, M. Dangerous games **901**
McKeown, G. Essentialism **153.8**
Meyer, J. Decision quality **658.4**
Michelson, L. D. The patient's playbook **610.69**
Miller, P. The smart swarm **156**
Mlodinow, L. Subliminal **154.2**
Mudd, P. The Head Game **153.4**
Partnoy, F. Wait **153.8**
Rhodes, W. R. Banker to the world **92**
Schulz, K. Being wrong **153**

DECISION MAKING -- PERSONAL NARRATIVES
Ilse, S. The prenatal bombshell **618.3**

DECISION MAKING -- PSYCHOLOGICAL ASPECTS
Huston, T. How women decide **155.333**

DECISION MAKING -- SEX DIFFERENCES
Huston, T. How women decide **155.333**

Decision points. Bush, G. W. **92**

Decision quality. Meyer, J. **658.4**

The **decision** to use the atomic bomb and the architecture of an American myth. Alperovitz, G. **940.54**

The **Decisive** Moment. Cartier-Bresson, H. **770**

DECKS (DOMESTIC ARCHITECTURE) *See* Patios

DECLAMATIONS *See* Monologues; Recitations

Declaration. Hogeland, W. **973.3**

The **Declaration** of Independence. Becker, C. **973.3**

The **decline** and fall of the British Empire, 1781-1997. Brendon, P. **909**

The **decline** and fall of the Roman empire. Gibbon, E. **937**

The **decline** of the West, volume one. Spengler, O. **901**

Decoding the heavens. Marchant, J. **681.1**

Decoding Your Dog. **636.7**

DECOLONIZATION -- HISTORY
Kwarteng, K. Ghosts of empire   **909**
Decorate. Becker, H.   **747**
DECORATION AND ORNAMENT
Becker, H. Decorate   **747**
Bonney, G. Design*Sponge at home   **747**
Doh, J. More creative lettering   **745.6**
Eckman, E. Around the corner crochet borders   **746.43**
Giramonti, L. B. Novel interiors   **747**
Logan, M. D. Mat, mount and frame it yourself **749**
Studholme, J. Farrow & Ball How to Decorate   **747.94**
DECORATION AND ORNAMENT
See also Art; Decorative arts
DECORATIVE ART *See* Decoration and ornament; Decorative arts
DECORATIVE ARTS
See also Arts
DECORATIVE ARTS -- ENCYCLOPEDIAS
The Greenwood encyclopedia of homes through American history   **728**
Decorative techniques [series]
Cambras, J. Bookbinding   **686.3**
DeCoster, Marcia
Marcia DeCoster's beaded opulence   **739.27**
DECOUPAGE
See also Decoration and ornament; Decorative arts; Paper crafts
DECOYS (HUNTING)
See also Hunting; Shooting
Dedekind, Richard, 1831-1916
             About
Bell, E. T. Men of mathematics   **920**
Dedman, Bill, 1960-
Empty mansions   **92**
DEDUCTION (LOGIC) *See* Logic
Deeb, Margie
The beader's color palette   **745.594**
Deeds, Susan M.
Meyer, M. C. The course of Mexican history   **972**
Deeks, Florence Amelia
             About
McKillop, A. B. The spinster & the prophet **941.08**
Deep. Nestor, J.   **797.2**
DEEP DIVING
Kurson, R. Pirate hunters   **910.91**
DEEP DIVING
See also Underwater exploration; Water sports
DEEP DIVING -- UNITED STATES -- HISTORY
Peffer, R. Where divers dare   **940.54**
Deep down dark. Tobar, H.   **363.11**
Deep future. Stager, C.   **363.7**
Deep lane. Doty, M.   **811**
Deep lane.   **811**
Deep play. Ackerman, D.   **155.6**

DEEP SEA DRILLING (PETROLEUM) *See* Offshore oil well drilling
DEEP SEA MINING *See* Ocean mining
Deep South.   **975**
Deep Space. Schilling, G.   **520**
Deep work. Newport, C.   **650.1**
DEEP-SEA PHOTOGRAPHY *See* Underwater photography
Deeply rooted. Hamilton, L. M.   **338.1**
DEER
See also Game and game birds; Mammals
Deer hunting with Jesus. Bageant, J.   **305.5**
Deeter, Kirk
The little red book of fly fishing   **799.124**
DEFECTIVE SPEECH *See* Speech disorders
DEFECTIVE VISION *See* Vision disorders
DEFECTORS
Gimbel, W. Havana dreams   **972.91**
Kenney, D. N. Asylum denied   **92**
DEFECTORS
See also Political refugees
DEFECTORS -- UNITED STATES -- BIOGRAPHY
Sullivan, R. Stalin's daughter   **92**
Defend the realm. Andrew, C. M.   **327.12**
The **defender.** Michaeli, E.   **071**
Defenders of the faith. Reston, J.   **940.2**
Defending professionalism.   **020**
DEFENSE INDUSTRY
See also Industries
DEFENSE MECHANISMS OF ANIMALS *See* Animal defenses
DEFENSE RESEARCH *See* Military research
DEFENSIVE (MILITARY SCIENCE)
Emlen, D. J. Animal weapons   **591.47**
DEFIANCE (OHIO) -- BIOGRAPHY
Ryan, T. The prize winner of Defiance, Ohio **977.1**
DEFICIENCIES *See* Scarcity
DEFICIT FINANCING
See also Public finance
DEFICIT FINANCING -- UNITED STATES
Johnson, S. White House burning   **336.3**
The **definitive** book of body language. Pease, A.   **153.6**
The **definitive** guide to thriving after cancer. Gazella, K. A.   **616.99**
DEFLATION (FINANCE)
See also Finance
Defoe, Daniel, 1661?-1731
             About
Frank, K. Crusoe   **823**
Severin, T. In search of Robinson Crusoe   **996**
Deford, Frank, 1938-
             About
Deford, F. Over time   **92**
DEFORESTATION

See also Forests and forestry

Defying Hitler. Haffner, S.   **943.085**

Defying the Nazis. Joukowsky, A.   **940.53**

DeGarmo, John

  The foster parenting manual   **306.874**

Degas. Hauptman, J.   **709**

Degas, Edgar, 1834-1917

          About

  Hauptman, J. Degas   **709**

  Smee, S. The art of rivalry   **700.92**

DeGategno, Paul J.

  Critical companion to Jonathan Swift   **828**

**DEGENERATION -- SOCIAL ASPECTS -- ITA-
LY -- HISTORY -- TO 1500**

  Lee, A. The ugly Renaissance   **945**

DeGeneres, Ellen, 1958-

  Home   **747**

Degraaf, Leonard

  Edison and the rise of innovation   **92**

Degrees of inequality. Mettler, S.   **378.73**

DEGREES OF LATITUDE AND LONGITUDE

  See Geodesy; Latitude; Longitude

Deheane, Stanislas

  Reading in the brain   **418**

DEISM

  See also Religion; Theology

DEITIES *See* Gods and goddesses

DeJean, Joan E.

  The essence of style   **391**

DEJECTION *See* Depression (Psychology)

Del Giocondo, Lisa, 1479-

          About

  Hales, D. Mona Lisa   **759.5**

Del Mar Sacasa, María

  The quinoa [keen-wah] cookbook   **641.3**

  Summer cocktails   **641.87**

Del Negro, Janice M.

  Folktales aloud   **027.62**

Delahunty, Andrew

  Oxford dictionary of nicknames   **929.4**

  (ed) Adonis to Zorro   **422**

  (ed) From bonbon to cha-cha   **422**

Delambre, J. B. J., 1749-1822

          About

  Alder, K. The measure of all things   **526**

Delancey. Wizenberg, M.   **647.95**

DELANCEY (PIZZARIA : SEATTLE, WASH.)

  Wizenberg, M. Delancey   **647.95**

DeLano, Sharon

  (ed) Leibovitz, A. Annie Leibovitz at work   **779**

Delany family

          About

  Delany, S. Having our say   **92**

Delany, Bessie

          About

  Delany, S. Having our say   **92**

Delany, Mary Granville Pendarves, 1700-1788

          About

  Peacock, M. The paper garden   **92**

Delany, Sadie

          About

  Delany, S. Having our say   **92**

Delbanco, Andrew

  College   **378.73**

  Melville   **92**

Delbruck, Max

          About

  Segrè, G. Ordinary geniuses   **572.8**

Delehanty, Hugh

  Caring for your parents   **362.6**

Delhi. Miller, S.   **954**

**DELHI (INDIA) -- DESCRIPTION AND TRAV-
EL**

  Miller, S. Delhi   **954**

Deliberate prose. Ginsberg, A.   **814**

Delicious dump cakes. Moore, K.   **641.86**

Delights & shadows. Kooser, T.   **811**

DeLillo, Don

          About

  Remnick, D. Reporting   **814**

DELINQUENCY, JUVENILE *See* Juvenile delinquency

DELINQUENTS *See* Criminals

Delisle, Guy

  Pyongyang: a journey in North Korea   **741.5**

Deliver us from evil. Ford, L. K.   **973.7**

Delivered. Gambito, S. V.   **811**

DELIVERY OF HEALTH CARE *See* Medical
care

DELIVERY OF HEALTH CARE -- TRENDS

  Topol, E. The creative destruction of medicine   **610.28**

**DELIVERY OF HEALTH CARE -- TRENDS --
UNITED STATES**

  Jauhar, S. Doctored   **92**

DELIVERY OF MEDICAL CARE *See* Medical
care

DELLA FATTORIA (BAKERY)

  Della Fattoria bread   **641.81**

Della Fattoria bread.   **641.81**

Delli Carpini, Michael X.

  (jt. auth) Carpini, M. X. D. After broadcast
news   **071**

Delmolino, Lara

  (jt. auth) Harris, S. L. Essential first steps for parents of children with autism   **618.92**

Deloria, Vine

  Custer died for your sins   **970.004**

  (comp) Documents of American Indian diplomacy   **970.004**

DELPHI (EXTINCT CITY)

  See also Extinct cities -- Greece; Greece --

Antiquities

Delta blues. Gioia, T.   **781.643**

The **deluge.** Tooze, A.   **940.3**

DeLuna, Carlos

About

Liebman, J. S. The wrong Carlos   **364.152**

Delury, John

(jt. auth) Schell, O. Wealth and power   **951**

DELUSIONS *See* Hallucinations and illusions

DeMallie, Raymond J.

(comp) Documents of American Indian diplomacy   **970.004**

DeMasco, Karen

The craft of baking   **641.8**

Demasio, Nunyo

(jt. auth) Parcells, B. Parcells   **796.332**

DEMENTIA

Kosik, K. S. Outsmarting Alzheimer's   **616.8**

Solnit, R. The Faraway Nearby   **814**

DEMENTIA

See also Brain -- Diseases

Demetz, Peter

Prague in black and gold   **943.71**

(ed) Lessing, G. E. Nathan the Wise, Minna von Barnhelm, and other plays and writings   **832**

Demick, Barbara

Nothing to envy   **951.93**

Democracy. Cartledge, P.   **321.8**

DEMOCRACY

See also Constitutional history; Constitutional law; Political science

DEMOCRACY

Democracy   **741.5**

Dobson, W. J. The dictator's learning curve   **321.8**

Dyson, M. E. Come hell or high water   **976.3**

Ferris, T. The science of liberty   **303.4**

Fukuyama, F. Political Order and Political Decay   **320.1**

Fukuyama, F. The origins of political order   **320**

McChesney, R. W. Digital disconnect   **302.23**

Morozov, E. The net delusion   **303.48**

Nafisi, A. The Republic of Imagination   **819**

Patel, R. The value of nothing   **330.1**

Schoen, D. E. The power of the vote   **324**

Seeley, T. D. Honeybee democracy   **595.799**

Tocqueville, A. d. Democracy in America   **973.5**

Toffler, A. Future shock   **303.4**

Wilentz, S. The rise of American democracy **973.5**

Democracy.   **741.5**

DEMOCRACY -- CAMBODIA

Brinkley, J. Cambodia's curse   **959.6**

DEMOCRACY -- ECONOMIC ASPECTS -- UNITED STATES

Reich, R. B. Saving capitalism   **330.973**

DEMOCRACY -- HISTORY

Cartledge, P. Democracy   **321.8**

Karnazes, D. The legend of Marathon   **938.03**

DEMOCRACY -- UNITED STATES

O'Neil, C. Weapons of math destruction   **005.7**

Speth, J. G. America the possible   **338.9**

DEMOCRACY -- UNITED STATES -- HISTORY

Han, L. C. Handbook to American democracy   **320.4**

Lepore, J. The story of America   **973**

Puleo, S. American treasures   **973**

Democracy and education. Dewey, J.   **370.1**

Democracy in America. Tocqueville, A. d.   **973.5**

Democracy, culture, and the voice of poetry. Pinsky, R.   **811**

DEMOCRATIC PARTY (U.S.)

Edwards, M. The parties versus the people   **320**

Kazin, M. A godly hero   **92**

Schoen, D. E. The power of the vote   **324**

DEMOCRATIC PARTY (U.S.)

See also Political parties

DEMOCRATIC PARTY (U.S.) -- HISTORY -- 20TH CENTURY

Lofgren, M. The party is over   **324.273**

DEMOCRATIC REPUBLIC OF THE CONGO

See Congo (Democratic Republic)

DEMOCRATIZATION

Dobson, W. J. The dictator's learning curve   **321.8**

DEMOGRAPHY *See* Population

Demon fish. Eilperin, J.   **597**

The **demon** in the freezer. Preston, R.   **616.9**

The **Demon's** Brood. Seward, D.   **942.03**

DEMONIAC POSSESSION

See also Demonology

DEMONOLOGY

See also Occultism

DEMONSTRATIONS

Masur, L. P. The soiling of Old Glory   **974.4**

DEMONSTRATIONS

See also Crowds; Public meetings

DEMONSTRATIONS FOR CIVIL RIGHTS *See* Civil rights demonstrations

Demos, John

The unredeemed captive   **973.2**

Dempsey, Amy

Art in the modern era   **709.04**

Dempsey, Jack, 1895-1983

About

Kahn, R. A flame of pure fire; Jack Dempsey and the roaring '20s   **92**

Dempsey, Rachel

(jt. auth) Williams, J. What works for women at work   **650.1**

Demystifying Islam. Zafar, H.   **297**

DENALI NATIONAL PARK AND PRESERVE (ALASKA) -- HISTORY

Heacox, K. Rhythm of the wild   **979.8**

DENATURED ALCOHOL

See also Alcohol

DENAZIFICATION

Taylor, F. Exorcising Hitler   **943.087**

Denevi, Timothy

About

Denevi, T. Hyper   **92**

Deng Xiaoping. Levine, S. I.   **951.05**

Deng Xiaoping and the transformation of China. Vogel, E. F.   **951.05**

Deng Xiaoping, 1904-1997

About

Vogel, E. F. Deng Xiaoping and the transformation of China   **951.05**

Deng, Alephonsion

Deng, B. They poured fire on us from the sky **962.4**

Deng, Benson

They poured fire on us from the sky   **962.4**

Denham, Wes

Arrested   **362.82**

Denial. Stern, J.   **92**

Denial of the soul. Peck, M. S.   **179.7**

Denlinger, Elizabeth Campbell

Before Victoria   **920**

Denmead, Ken

Geek dad   **790**

Dennett, Daniel Clement

Darwin's dangerous idea   **146**

Freedom evolves   **153.8**

Intuition Pumps and Other Tools for Thinking **121**

Dennis, Jerry

The living Great Lakes   **977**

Dennis-Bryan, Kim

(ed) The complete cat breed book   **636.8**

Dennison, Matthew

Behind the Mask   **92**

Denny, Glen

Valley walls   **796.52**

Denny, Walter B.

How to read Islamic carpets   **746.7**

DENOMINATIONS, RELIGIOUS *See* Sects

Dent, Jim

Courage beyond the game   **796.332**

DENTAL CARE

See also Medical care

DENTAL CARE -- POPULAR WORKS

Artemis, N. Holistic dental care   **617.6**

DENTISTRY

See also Medicine

DENTISTRY -- HISTORY

Wynbrandt, J. The excruciating history of dentistry   **617.6**

DENTISTRY -- POPULAR WORKS

Artemis, N. Holistic dental care   **617.6**

DENTISTS

Delany, S. Having our say   **92**

Malcolm, J. Iphigenia in Forest Hills   **345**

Seth, V. Two lives   **92**

Denton, Sally

The money and the power   **979.3**

The Profiteers   **338.7**

Denver, Rorke

About

Henican, E. Worth dying for   **359.984**

Denying the Holocaust. Lipstadt, D. E.   **940.53**

Denyse Schmidt.   **746.46**

Denyse Schmidt quilts.   **746.46**

DEOXYRIBONUCLEIC ACID *See* DNA

The **department** of mad scientists. Belfiore, M. **355**

DEPARTMENT STORES

Whitaker, J. Service and style   **381**

DEPARTMENT STORES

See also Business; Retail trade; Stores

DePastino, Todd

Bill Mauldin   **92**

DEPENDENCIES *See* Colonies

Deppe, Carol

The Tao of vegetable gardening   **635**

DEPRESSION (PSYCHOLOGY)

Aron, W. Hide & seek   **92**

Beard, A. In the water they can't see you cry **797.2**

Burns, D. D. Feeling good   **158**

Kaplan, G. Total recovery   **616**

Kramer, P. D. Ordinarily well   **615.7**

Max, D. T. c. Every love story is a ghost story **92**

Serani, D. Depression in later life   **618.97**

Solomon, A. The noonday demon   **616.85**

Styron, W. Darkness visible   **616.85**

Van Sciver, N. The Hypo   **92**

DEPRESSION (PSYCHOLOGY)

See also Abnormal psychology; Affective disorders; Neuroses

DEPRESSION (PSYCHOLOGY) -- POETRY

Pankey, E. Trace   **811**

Depression in later life. Serani, D.   **618.97**

DEPRESSION (PSYCHOLOGY) IN OLD AGE -- POPULAR WORKS

Serani, D. Depression in later life   **618.97**

DEPRESSION, MENTAL *See* Depression (Psychology)

DEPRESSIONS

Heilbroner, R. L. The worldly philosophers **330.1**

DEPRESSIONS

See also Business cycles

DEPRESSIVE PSYCHOSES *See* Depression (Psychology)

DEPROGRAMMING *See* Brainwashing

DERAILMENTS *See* Railroad accidents

Deraniyagala, Sonali

About

Deraniyagala, S. Wave   **954.93**

Derbyshire, John

Prime obsession   **512.7**

DEREGULATION
    See also Industrial policy
Derfler, Leslie
    The Dreyfus affair   **944.081**
DERIVATIVE SECURITIES
    See also Securities
Derks, Scott
    (ed) The value of a dollar   **338.5**
    (ed) The value of a dollar: colonial era to the Civil
    War, 1600-1865   **338.5**
DERMATITIS *See* Skin -- Diseases
DERMATOLOGY -- POPULAR WORKS
    Yosipovitch, G. Living with itch   **616.5**
Dershowitz, Alan M.
    Rights from wrongs   **323**
    Why terrorism works   **303.6**
DeSalle, Rob
    The brain   **612.8**
Desaulniers, Marcel
    Death by chocolate cakes   **641.8**
Descartes to Derrida. Sedgwick, P.   **190**
Descartes' loneliness. Grossman, A. R.   **811**
Descartes, René, 1596-1650
            About
    Bell, E. T. Men of mathematics   **920**
    Russell, B. A history of Western philosophy   **109**
    Watson, R. A. Cogito ergo sum: the life of Rene
    Descartes   **92**
DESCENT *See* Genealogy; Heredity
Descent into chaos. Rashid, A.   **954**
Descharnes, Robert, 1926-2014
    Salvador Dalí, 1904-1989   **759.6**
DESCRIPTIVE CATALOGING -- STANDARDS
    Oliver, C. Introducing RDA   **025.3**
**DESCRIPTIVE CATALOGING -- STANDARDS
-- HANDBOOKS, MANUALS, ETC**
    Maxwell, R. L. Maxwell's handbook for RDA, re-
    source description & access   **025.3**
DESCRIPTIVE GEOMETRY
    See also Geometrical drawing; Geometry
DESEGREGATED SCHOOLS *See* School inte-
gration
DESEGREGATION *See* Segregation
DESEGREGATION IN EDUCATION *See* School
integration
Desert America. Martínez, R.   **330.9**
DESERT ANIMALS
    See also Animals; Deserts
Desert between the mountains. Durham, M. S. **979**
DESERT ECOLOGY
    See also Ecology
DESERT PLANTS
    Duffield, M. R. Plants for dry climates   **635.9**
DESERT PLANTS
    See also Deserts; Plant ecology; Plants
Desert queen. Wallach, J.   **956**

Desert reckoning. Stillman, D.   **363.2**
DESERT RECLAMATION
    Fukuoka, M. Sowing seeds in the desert   **631.6**
**DESERT SURVIVAL -- SYRIA -- HISTORY --
20TH CENTURY**
    MacKeen, D. A. The hundred-year walk   **92**
The **deserters.** Glass, C.   **940.54**
DESERTIFICATION
    See also Climate; Deserts
DESERTIFICATION -- CONTROL
    Fukuoka, M. Sowing seeds in the desert   **631.6**
DESERTION *See* Desertion and nonsupport; Mili-
tary desertion
DESERTION AND NONSUPPORT
    See also Divorce; Domestic relations
DESERTION, MILITARY *See* Military desertion
**DESERTION, MILITARY -- HISTORY -- 20TH
CENTURY**
    Glass, C. The deserters   **940.54**
DESERTS
    See also Physical geography
Desharnais, Jasmin
    (ed) Tea   **641.3**
DESIGN
    See also Decoration and ornament
DESIGN
    Albrecht, D. The Work of Charles and Ray
    Eames   **745.4**
    Evans, D. Designing your life   **650.1**
    Kearney, K. Block city   **794**
    Kolko, J. Well-designed   **658.5**
    Petroski, H. To forgive design   **620**
    Petroski, H. Success through failure   **620**
    Rybczynski, W. The look of architecture   **721**
DESIGN -- SOCIAL ASPECTS
    Evans, D. Designing your life   **650.1**
Design mom. Blair, G. S.   **747**
DESIGN OF BOOKS *See* Book design
The **design** of everyday things. Norman, D. **745.2**
DESIGN PERCEPTION *See* Pattern perception
Design*Sponge at home. Bonney, G.   **747**
DESIGN, BOOK *See* Book design
DESIGNED GENETIC CHANGE *See* Genetic
engineering
DESIGNER DRUGS
    See also Drugs
DESIGNERS
    See also Artists
Designing and planting a woodland garden. Wiley,
K.   **635.9**
Designing With Light: An Introduction to Stage
Lighting. Gillette, J. M.   **792**
Designing your life. Evans, D.   **650.1**
DESIGNS, FLORAL *See* Flower arrangement
DESIRE
    Irvine, W. B. On desire   **128**

DESKTOP COMPUTERS *See* Personal computers

Desmond, Matthew, ca. 1970-
Evicted   **339.4**

DeSouza, Luiza
Eat, Play, Sleep   **649.122**

DESPOTISM
Taibbi, M. Griftopia   **973.932**

Dessert Divas. Manfield, C.   **641**

Dessert for Two. Lane, C.   **641.86**

DESSERTS
Blakeslee, R. L. Your time to bake   **641.8**
Boyle, T. Flavorful   **641.86**
Bryson, F. Blue ribbon baking from a redneck kitchen   **641.597**
Classic home desserts   **641.8**
DeMasco, K. The craft of baking   **641.8**
Dodge, A. J. The everyday baker   **641.815**
Food52 baking   **641.81**
Gerson, F. My sweet Mexico   **641.5**
Greenspan, D. Baking chez moi   **641.86**
Heatter, M. Maida Heatter's book of great desserts   **641.8**
Higgins, K. Chocolate-covered Katie   **641.6**
Jaronsky, S. The cookies & cups cookbook   **641.86**
Jordan, C. Sweetness   **641**
A la mode   **641.865**
Lane, C. Dessert for Two   **641.86**
Manfield, C. Dessert Divas   **641**
Mast Brothers Chocolate   **641.6**
Naturally sweet   **641.86**
The perfect scoop   **641.8**
Ptak, C. The Violet Bakery cookbook   **641.86**
Robertson, C. Tartine   **641.8**
Schreiber, C. Rustic fruit desserts   **641.8**
Tosi, C. Momofuku Milk Bar   **641.8**
Wright, C. Mix + Match Cakes   **641.86**

DESSERTS
See also Cooking

DeStefano, Stephen
Coyote at the kitchen door   **578.7**

Destination moon. Pyle, R.   **629.45**

Destiny. Jakes, T. D.   **248.4**

DESTINY *See* Fate and fatalism

Destiny and Power. Meacham, J.   **92**

The **destiny** of the republic. Millard, C.   **973.8**

DESTITUTION *See* Poverty

Destler, I. M.
Daalder, I. H. In the shadow of the Oval Office   **355**

DESTRUCTIVE INSECTS *See* Insect pests

DETECTIVE AND MYSTERY FILMS *See* Mystery films

DETECTIVE AND MYSTERY STORIES *See* Mystery fiction

DETECTIVE AND MYSTERY STORIES -- BIBLIOGRAPHY
Bleiler, R. Reference and research guide to mystery and detective fiction   **016**
Charles, J. A. The mystery readers' advisory   **025.2**
Niebuhr, G. W. Make mine a mystery II   **016**

DETECTIVE AND MYSTERY STORIES, ENGLISH -- HISTORY AND CRITICISM
James, P. D. Talking about detective fiction   **823**

DETECTIVE FICTION *See* Mystery fiction

DETECTIVE STORIES *See* Mystery fiction

DETECTIVES
Blum, H. American lightning   **364.152**
Conway, J. N. The big policeman   **92**
Leovy, J. Ghettoside   **364.152**
Summerscale, K. The suspicions of Mr. Whicher   **364.152**
Wilber, D. Q. A good month for murder   **363.25**
Yunte Huang Charlie Chan   **92**

DETECTIVES
See also Police

DETECTIVES -- FICTION
Flanders, J. The invention of murder   **364.152**

DETENTION OF UNLAWFUL COMBATANTS -- CUBA -- GUANTÁNAMO BAY NAVAL BASE
Hickman, J. Murder at Camp Delta   **355.1**

DETERGENT POLLUTION OF RIVERS, LAKES, ETC. *See* Water pollution

DETERMINISM AND INDETERMINISM *See* Free will and determinism

Dethroning the king. MacIntosh, J.   **338.8**

The **detonators.** Millman, C.   **940.4**

DETOXIFICATION (HEALTH)
Grigore, A. Skin cleanse   **613**
Smith, R. Toxin toxout   **613**

Detroit. Martelle, S.   **977.4**

Detroit. LeDuff, C.   **977.4**

DETROIT (MICH.)
Binelli, M. Detroit City is the place to be   **307.1**

DETROIT (MICH.) -- ECONOMIC CONDITIONS
LeDuff, C. Detroit   **977.4**
Maraniss, D. Once in a great city   **977.4**
Martelle, S. Detroit   **977.4**

DETROIT (MICH.) -- RACE RELATIONS
Boyle, K. Arc of justice   **345**

Detroit City is the place to be. Binelli, M.   **307.1**

Detz, Joan
How to write & give a speech   **808.5**

Detzer, David
Allegiance   **973.7**

Deuki Hong
Koreatown   **641.59**

DEUTERIUM OXIDE
See also Chemicals

Deutsch, Babette
Poetry handbook: a dictionary of terms   **808.1**

Deutsch, David

The beginning of infinity   501
Deutsch, Robin M.
Lippincott, J. M. 7 things your teenager won't tell
you   649
Deutscher, Guy
Through the language glass   410
DEVALUATION OF CURRENCY See Monetary
policy
Deveaux, Scott
Jazz   781.65
Developing an outstanding core collection. Alabaster, C.   025.2
Developing and managing electronic collections.
Johnson, P.   025.2
DEVELOPING COUNTRIES
Shah, S. The body hunters   362.1
DEVELOPING COUNTRIES
See also Economic conditions; Industrialization
**DEVELOPING COUNTRIES -- ECONOMIC
CONDITIONS**
Sharma, R. Breakout nations   330.91
**DEVELOPING COUNTRIES -- ECONOMIC
POLICY**
Acemoglu, D. Why nations fail   330
DEVELOPING COUNTRIES -- ENCYCLOPEDIAS
Encyclopedia of the developing world   909
DEVELOPING COUNTRIES -- SOCIAL POLICY
Acemoglu, D. Why nations fail   330
Developing library collections for today's young
adults. Pattee, A. S.   027.62
DEVELOPMENT See Embryology; Evolution;
Growth disorders; Modernization (Sociology)
DEVELOPMENT, ECONOMIC See Economic
development
DEVELOPMENTAL BIOLOGY
Carroll, S. B. The Serengeti Rules   570
Nielsen, C. Animal evolution   591.3
DEVELOPMENTAL DISABILITIES -- POPULAR WORKS
Rodriguez, A. M. Autism spectrum disorders   616.85
DEVELOPMENTAL NEUROBIOLOGY
Jensen, F. E. The teenage brain   612.6
DEVELOPMENTAL PSYCHOBIOLOGY
Jensen, F. E. The teenage brain   612.6
DEVELOPMENTAL PSYCHOLOGY
Eliot, L. What's going on in there?   612.8
Gopnik, A. The gardener and the carpenter   155.4
DEVELOPMENTAL PSYCHOLOGY
See also Psychology
**DEVELOPMENTALLY DISABLED CHILDREN
-- EDUCATION**
Camarata, S. M. Late-talking children   618.92

DEVIANCY See Deviant behavior
DEVIANT BEHAVIOR
Kipnis, L. How to become a scandal   306.7
DEVIANT BEHAVIOR
See also Human behavior
Devices and desires. Tone, A.   363.9
DEVIL
Pagels, E. H. The origin of Satan   235
Wray, T. J. The birth of Satan   235
Devil in the grove. King, G.   305.896
The **devil** in the shape of a woman. Karlsen, C.
F.   133.4
The **devil** in the white city. Larson, E.   364.15
The **Devil** That Never Dies. Goldhagen, D.
J.   305.892
The **Devil** within. Levack, B. P.   133.4
A **devil's** chaplain. Dawkins, R.   500
The **Devil's** Chessboard. Talbot, D.   92
The **devil's** diary. Kinney, D.   940.53
The **devil's** highway. Urrea, L. A.   325
The **Devils'** Alliance. Moorhouse, R.   940.53
Devine, Jane
Going beyond Google again   025.042
Devine, Lauren
(ed) Complete book of home preserving   641.4
DeVita, Vincent T., Jr., 1935-
About
DeVita-Raeburn, E. The death of cancer   92
DeVita-Raeburn, Elizabeth, 1966-
The death of cancer   92
Devlin, Keith J.
The unfinished game   519.2
Devlin, Naomi
River Cottage Gluten Free   641.5
**Devonshire, Deborah Vivien Freeman-Mitford
Cavendish, Duchess of, 1920-2014**
About
Thompson, L. The six   92
Devonshire, Georgiana Spencer Cavendish, Duchess of, 1757-1806
About
Foreman, A. Georgiana, Duchess of Devonshire   941.07
Devonshire, William Cavendish, Duke of, 1748-1811
About
Foreman, A. Georgiana, Duchess of Devonshire   941.07
Devotion. Makos, A.   951.904
DEVOTION See Prayer; Worship
DEVOTIONAL CALENDARS
See also Calendars; Devotional literature
DEVOTIONAL EXERCISES
Hendey, L. M. A book of saints for Catholic
moms   248.8
DEVOTIONAL LITERATURE

Lucado, M. Before amen **248.3**

DEVOTIONAL LITERATURE FOR CHILDREN
See also Devotional literature

DEVOTIONAL THEOLOGY See Devotional exercises; Prayer

DEVOTIONS See Devotional exercises

DeVoto, Mark
(ed) Harmony **781.2**

DeWalt, G. Weston
Boukreev, A. The climb **796.522**

Dewey. Myron, V. **636.8**

DEWEY DECIMAL CLASSIFICATION
Dewey decimal classification and relative index **025.4**
Dewey decimal classification and relative index. **025.4**

Dewey, John, 1859-1952
Democracy and education **370.1**
The school and society, and The child and the curriculum **372**
About
Durant, W. J. The story of philosophy **109**
Menand, L. The Metaphysical Club **973.9**

Dewey, Melvil
Dewey decimal classification and relative index **025.4**

Dewey, Thomas E. (Thomas Edmund), 1902-1971
About
Karabell, Z. The last campaign **324.9**

Dewitt, Dave
(jt. auth) Dewitt, D. Precious Cargo **306.3**

DeWitt, Sarah Hyman
(ed) Let me tell you **818**

DeWolf, Thomas Norman
Gather at the table **306.3**

DeWoskin, Rachel
Foreign babes in Beijing **951**

Deyo, Richard A.
Watch your back! **617.5**

Dharma Delight. Greenblat, M. R. A. **294.3**

Di Capua, Michael
(ed) Sendak, M. My brother's book **811**

Di Giovanni, Janine
Madness visible **949.7**
The Morning They Came For Us **956.91**

Di Maio, Vincent J. M., 1941-
About
Franscell, R. Morgue **616.07**

DIABETES
American Diabetes Association American Diabetes Association complete guide to diabetes **616.4**
Duyff, R. L. American Dietetic Association complete food and nutrition guide **613.2**
Flippin, R. The diabetes reset **616.4**
Hurley, D. Diabetes rising **362.1**
Mayo Clinic, the essential diabetes book **616.4**

Moore, M. T. Growing up again **92**

DIABETES
See also Diseases

DIABETES -- BIBLIOGRAPHY
Ladd, D. L. The Medical Library Association guide to finding out about diabetes **016**

DIABETES -- DIET THERAPY -- RECIPES
Heller, M. The everyday DASH diet cookbook **613.2**

DIABETES -- MISCELLANEA
Ask the experts **616.4**

DIABETES -- PREVENTION
Wright, H. The prediabetes diet plan **616.4**

DIABETES -- TREATMENT -- HANDBOOKS, MANUALS, ETC
Rubin, R. R. The Johns Hopkins guide to diabetes **616.4**
The **diabetes** reset. Flippin, R. **616.4**
Diabetes rising. Hurley, D. **362.1**
Diaghilev. **92**

Diaghilev, Serge, 1872-1929
About
Diaghilev **92**

DIAGNOSIS
The big book of symptoms **618.92**
Doherty, G. M. Current Diagnosis and Treatment Surgery **617**
Groopman, J. E. How doctors think **610**
Horowitz, R. I. Why can't I get better? **616.9**
Pagana, T. J. Mosby's diagnostic and laboratory test reference **616.07**
Sanders, L. Every patient tells a story **616.07**

DIAGNOSIS
See also Medicine

DIAGNOSTIC ERRORS
Gnaulati, E. Back to normal **618.92**

DIAGNOSTIC ERRORS -- UNITED STATES
Schwarz, A. ADHD nation **618.92**

DIAGNOSTIC ERRORS -- UNITED STATES -- CASE STUDIES
Cahalan, S. Brain on fire **616.8**

DIAGNOSTIC IMAGING
See also Pathology

Diagram Group
Lambert, D. The field guide to geology **551**

DIALECT LITERATURE
See also Literature

DIALECTICAL MATERIALISM
See also Communism; Socialism

DIALECTICS See Logic

DIALOGUE -- RELIGIOUS ASPECTS
Harris, S. Islam and the future of tolerance **297.2**

Diamandis, Peter, 1961-
(jt. auth) Kotler, S. Abundance **303.48**

Diamant, Anita
Pitching my tent **296.7**

The **diamond** dog. Wakoski, D. **811**

Diamond, Jared M.

Collapse: how societies choose to fail or succeed **304.2**

Guns, germs, and steel **303.4**

Diamond: a journey to the heart of an obsession. Hart, M. **553.8**

DIAMONDS

Hart, M. Diamond: a journey to the heart of an obsession **553.8**

Selby, S. A. Flawless **364.1**

Zoellner, T. The heartless stone **553.8**

DIAMONDS

See also Carbon; Precious stones

Diamonds, gold, and war. Meredith, M. **968.04**

The **Diana** chronicles. Brown, T. **92**

Diana, Princess of Wales, 1961-1997

About

Brown, T. The Diana chronicles **92**

Diane Arbus. Lubow, A. **92**

Diane Arbus. Arbus, D. **779.2**

Diano, Giada

(ed) Writing Across the Landscape **92**

Diaries. Orwell, G. **828**

DIARIES

At the edge of the abyss **940.53**

Diary of a combatant **92**

Diehn, G. Real life journals: designing & using handmade books **686.3**

The Gray Notebook **849**

Orwell, G. Diaries **828**

Summerscale, K. Mrs. Robinson's disgrace **941.081**

DIARIES

See also Literature

DIARISTS

Barnouw, D. The diary of Anne Frank: the critical edition **92**

Blight, D. W. A slave no more **326**

Frank, A. The diary of a young girl: the definitive edition **92**

Hertog, S. Anne Morrow Lindbergh **92**

Hollis, L. London rising **942**

Jacobson, S. Anne Frank **92**

Klemperer, V. I will bear witness **943.086**

LaPlante, E. Salem witch judge **92**

Lee, H. Virginia Woolf's nose **820**

Lindbergh, R. Under a wing **92**

Long, J. The plot against Pepys **941.06**

Ozick, C. Quarrel & quandary **814**

Pepys, S. The diary of Samuel Pepys **941.06**

Pierpont, C. R. Passionate minds **810**

Prose, F. Anne Frank **839.3**

Slaughter, T. P. The beautiful soul of John Woolman, apostle of abolition **92**

Tomalin, C. Samuel Pepys **941.06**

Wilson, F. The ballad of Dorothy Wordsworth **92**

Winters, K. C. Anne Morrow Lindbergh **92**

Diary of a combatant. **92**

The **diary** of a young girl: the definitive edition. Frank, A. **92**

The **diary** of Anne Frank. Goodrich, F. **812**

The **diary** of Anne Frank: the critical edition. Barnouw, D. **92**

The **diary** of Frida Kahlo. Kahlo, F. **92**

The **diary** of Samuel Pepys. Pepys, S. **941.06**

DIASPORA (PROJECT)

Dwyer, J. More awesome than money **384.3**

DIASPORA, AFRICAN *See* African diaspora

DIASPORA, JEWISH *See* Jewish diaspora

Diaspora: homelands in exile. Brenner, F. **909**

Diaz del Castillo, Bernal

The discovery and conquest of Mexico, 1517-1521 **972**

Diaz, Tom

The last gun **338.4**

Dibenedetto, David

(ed) The good dog **636.7**

Dibruno Bros. House of Cheese. Darlington, T. **641.3**

Dick, Philip K

About

Dufty, D. F. How to build an android **629.8**

The exegesis of Philip K. Dick **818**

Dickens, Charles, 1812-1870

About

Bloom, H. The Western canon **809**

Davis, P. B. Critical companion to Charles Dickens **823**

Flanders, J. The Victorian city **942.1**

Nabokov, V. V. Lectures on literature **808.3**

Slater, M. Charles Dickens **92**

Smiley, J. Charles Dickens **823**

Tomalin, C. Charles Dickens **92**

Dickerman, Leah

Dada **709.04**

Dickerman, Sara

The food lover's cleanse **641.5**

Dickey, Bronwen

Pit bull **636.755**

Dickey, Christopher

Our Man in Charleston **92**

Securing the city **363.32**

Dickey, Colin

Ghostland **133.1**

Dickey, Jennifer W.

(ed) Beyond Rosie **940**

Dickey, Lisa

Then comes marriage **346**

Dickinson, Amy

About

Dickinson, A. The mighty queens of Freeville **92**

Dickinson, Emily, 1830-1886

About

Adams, M. B. Shaggy muses   **920**
Benfey, C. E. G. A summer of hummingbirds **920**
Bloom, H. The Western canon   **809**
Gordon, L. Lives like loaded guns   **92**
Kazin, A. An American procession   **810**
Leiter, S. Critical companion to Emily Dickinson   **811**

Dickinson, Richard
Weeds of North America   **632**

Dickinson, Terence
The backyard astronomer's guide   **522**
NightWatch: a practical guide to viewing the universe   **520**

Dickman, Kyle
On the burning edge   **363.37**

Dickman, Michael
The end of the west   **811**

Dickson, Paul
(comp) Toasts   **808.88**

Dickstein, Morris
Dancing in the dark   **973.91**

The **dictator's** learning curve. Dobson, W. J. **321.8**

DICTATORS
Conquest, R. Stalin   **92**
Dobson, W. J. The dictator's learning curve **321.8**
Great lives from history: Notorious lives **920.003**
Hitler   **92**
Kershaw, I. Hitler, 1936-1945: nemesis **943.086**
Montefiore, S. Stalin: the court of the red tsar **92**
Montefiore, S. Young Stalin   **92**
Owen, R. The rise and fall of Arab presidents for life   **352.23**
Radzinsky, E. Stalin   **92**
Service, R. Stalin   **92**

DICTATORS
See also Heads of state; Totalitarianism

DICTATORS -- GERMANY -- BIOGRAPHY
Hitler   **92**

DICTATORS -- SOVIET UNION -- BIOGRAPHY
Kotkin, S. Stalin   **92**
Stalin   **92**

DICTATORSHIP
Dobson, W. J. The dictator's learning curve **321.8**

Dictionary of American family names. **929.4**
Dictionary of American young adult fiction, 1997-2001. Helbig, A.   **028.5**
A dictionary of biology.   **570**
A dictionary of Buddhism. Keown, D. **294.3**
A dictionary of chemistry.   **540**
Dictionary of confusable words.   **423**
A dictionary of environment and conservation. Park, C.   **333.7**
Dictionary of gods and goddesses. Jordan, M. **201**
The dictionary of imaginary places. Manguel, A.   **809**

A **dictionary** of language. Crystal, D. **410**
A **dictionary** of modern English usage. Fowler, H. W.   **428**
A **dictionary** of names, nicknames, and surnames of persons, places, and things. Latham, E. **929.4**
A **dictionary** of psychology. Colman, A. M. **150**
Dictionary of symbolism. Biedermann, H. **302.2**
Dictionary of the Middle Ages.   **909.07**
Dictionary of the social sciences. Calhoun, C. J. **300**
Dictionary of wars.   **355**
Did Adam and Eve have navels? Gardner, M. **500**
Did she kill him? Colquhoun, K. **364.152**

Didion, Joan
We tell ourselves stories in order to live **814**
Where I was from   **979.4**

About
Daugherty, T. The Last Love Song **92**
The year of magical thinking   **92**
Die young with me. Rufus, R.   **92**

Diedricksen, Derek
Microshelters   **690**

Diehl, Digby
Cole, N. Angel on my shoulder   **92**
Rather outspoken   **92**

Diehn, Gwen
Real life journals: designing & using handmade books   **686.3**

DIEN BIEN PHU, BATTLE OF, 1954
Morgan, T. Valley of death   **959.704**

Dierker, Larry, 1946-
About
Dierker, L. This ain't brain surgery **796**

DIES (METALWORKING)
See also Metalwork

DIESEL AUTOMOBILES
See also Automobiles

DIET
Abbott, C. The Badass Body Diet   **613.2**
Acquista, A. The Mediterranean Family Table   **641.59**
Anthony, M. V Is for Vegetables   **641.6**
Bittman, M. A bone to pick   **338.1**
Bittman, M. Food matters   **613.2**
Buettner, D. The Blue Zones solution **613.2**
Dickerman, S. The food lover's cleanse **641.5**
Flippin, R. The diabetes reset   **616.4**
Hay, D. Life in Balance   **641.563**
Mann, T. Secrets from the eating lab **613.2**
Mitchell, A. Eating in the middle   **641.3**
Nesheim, M. Why calories count   **613.2**
Steinhart, A. H. Crohn's & colitis diet guide **616.3**
Wansink, B. Slim by design   **613.2**
The whole30   **613.2**

DIET
See also Health; Hygiene

DIET -- THERAPEUTIC USE *See* Diet therapy

DIET -- UNITED STATES -- HISTORY -- 20TH CENTURY
Coe, A. A square meal   **641.5**
Diet for a hot planet. Lappé, A.   **641**
DIET IN DISEASE
Jacobson, H. Proteinaholic   **613.2**
DIET IN DISEASE
    See also Therapeutics
DIET IN DISEASE -- BIBLIOGRAPHY
De Richemond, J. The Medical Library Association guide to finding out about heart disease   **016**
DIET SUPPLEMENTS *See* Dietary supplements
DIET THERAPY
Gazella, K. A. The definitive guide to thriving after cancer   **616.99**
Low Dog, T. Healthy at home   **615.5**
Netzer, C. T. The complete book of food counts   **613.2**
Pascal, C. The whole foods allergy cookbook **641.5**
Shepherd, S. The 2-step low-FODMAP eating plan   **641.5**
DIET THERAPY
    See also Cooking for the sick; Diet in disease; Therapeutics
DIET THERAPY -- POPULAR WORKS
The whole30   **613.2**
DIETARY SUPPLEMENTS
Lee, J. The supplement handbook   **613.2**
Price, C. Vitamania   **612.3**
DIETARY SUPPLEMENTS
    See also Nutrition; Vitamins
DIETARY SUPPLEMENTS -- SOCIAL ASPECTS -- UNITED STATES
Price, C. Vitamania   **612.3**
Dietert, Rodney
The human superorganism   **613**
DIETETIC FOODS
    See also Diet; Food
DIETETICS *See* Diet
DIETING *See* Weight loss
Dietrich & Riefenstahl.   **791.43**
Dietrich, Marlene
        About
Dietrich & Riefenstahl   **791.43**
DIETS, REDUCING *See* Weight loss
Dietz, Maggie
(ed) Americans' favorite poems   **808.81**
(ed) Poems to read   **808.81**
Diffee, Matthew
Hand drawn jokes for smart attractive people **741.5**
Different hours. Dunn, S.   **811**
A **Different** Kind of Daughter. Holstein, K.   **92**
DIFFERENTIAL EQUATIONS
    See also Calculus
Difficult conversations. Stone, D.   **158**
Difficult men. Martin, B.   **791.450**

DIFFUSION OF INNOVATION
Topol, E. The creative destruction of medicine   **610.28**
DIFFUSION OF INNOVATIONS
Guest, R. Borderless economics   **303.48**
Ridley, M. The evolution of everything   **303.48**
Digest. Pardlo, G.   **811**
DIGESTION
    See also Physiology
DIGESTIVE ORGANS -- POPULAR WORKS
Roach, M. Gulp   **612.3**
DIGESTIVE SYSTEM
Shepherd, S. The 2-step low-FODMAP eating plan   **641.5**
Steinhart, A. H. Crohn's & colitis diet guide **616.3**
DIGESTIVE SYSTEM
    See also Anatomy
Digging for dirt. Lowe, J.   **92**
Digging up the dead. Kammen, M. G.   **393**
Digital assassination. Davis, M.   **005**
DIGITAL CAMERAS
Ang, T. Digital photographer's handbook   **775**
DIGITAL CINEMATOGRAPHY -- HANDBOOKS, MANUALS, ETC
Ascher, S. The filmmaker's handbook   **777**
Digital disconnect. McChesney, R. W.   **302.23**
DIGITAL DIVIDE
    See also Information society
The **digital** doctor. Wachter, R.   **610.28**
DIGITAL ELECTRONICS
    See also Electronics
DIGITAL LIBRARIES
Kovacs, D. K. The Kovacs guide to electronic library collection development   **025**
Managing Electronic Resources   **025.1**
Mitchell, A. M. Cataloging and organizing digital resources   **025.3**
White, A. C. E-metrics for library and information professionals   **025.2**
DIGITAL LIBRARIES
    See also Information systems; Libraries
DIGITAL LIBRARIES.
More technology for the rest of us   **025**
DIGITAL MEDIA
Burcher, N. Paid, owned, earned   **658.8**
Handley, A. Content rules   **658.8**
DIGITAL MEDIA
    See also Mass media
DIGITAL MEDIA -- SOCIAL ASPECTS
Lanier, J. You are not a gadget   **303.4**
DIGITAL MEDIA AND FAMILIES
Clark, L. S. The parent app   **302.23**
Digital photographer's handbook. Ang, T.   **775**
Digital photography. Horenstein, H.   **770**
DIGITAL PHOTOGRAPHY
Ang, T. Digital photographer's handbook   **775**

Ang, T. Digital photography masterclass **775**
Freeman, M. The photographer's mind **775**
Horenstein, H. Digital photography **770**
DIGITAL PHOTOGRAPHY
See also Digital electronics; Photography
Digital photography complete course. Hallett, T. **770**
Digital photography masterclass. Ang, T. **775**
DIGITAL PRESERVATION.
More technology for the rest of us **025**
DIGITAL REFERENCE SERVICES (LIBRAR-IES) *See* Electronic reference services (Libraries)
DIGITAL RIGHTS MANAGEMENT
See also Copyright; Data processing
DIGITAL VIDEO -- HANDBOOKS, MANUALS, ETC
Ascher, S. The filmmaker's handbook **777**
Dignen, Sheila
(ed) Adonis to Zorro **422**
Dikötter, Frank
The Cultural Revolution **951.056**
Mao's great famine **951.05**
Dilevko, Juris
Contemporary world fiction **016**
DILIGENCE
Duckworth, A. Grit **158.1**
Dillard, Annie, 1945-
The Annie Dillard reader **818**
Pilgrim at Tinker Creek **818**
(ed) Modern American memoirs **810**
About
Dillard, A. The writing life **818**
Dillard, A. An American childhood **92**
Dillehay, Tom D.
The settlement of the Americas **970.01**
Diller, Phyllis, 1917-
About
Diller, P. Like a lampshade in a whorehouse **92**
Dillon, Katherine V.
Goldstein, D. M. The Vietnam War: the story and photographs **959.704**
Prange, G. W. At dawn we slept **940.54**
Dillon, Pamela
(ed) Canoeing **797.1**
(ed) Kayaking **797.1**
Dillow, Gordon
White, B. Uppity **92**
Dilonardo, Paolo
(ed) Sontag, S. At the same time **814**
DiMaggio, Dina
(jt. auth) Porto, A. The pediatrician's guide to feeding babies and toddlers **618.92**
DiMaggio, Dom, 1917-2009
About
Halberstam, D. The teammates **796**
DiMaggio, Joe

About
Cramer, R. B. Joe DiMaggio **796.357**
Kennedy, K. 56 **92**
The **DiMaggios.** Clavin, T. **796.357**
DiMaio, Vincent
(jt. auth) Franscell, R. Morgue **616.07**
Dimarco, Damon
(jt. auth) Baroni, B. Fat kid got fit **362.196**
Dimbleby, Jonathan
The Battle of the Atlantic **940.54**
DIMENSION, FOURTH *See* Fourth dimension
Dimestore. Smith, L. **92**
Dimitrius, Jo-Ellan
Reading people **155.2**
Dimkovska, Lidija, 1971-
About
pH neutral history **891.8**
The **din** in the head. Ozick, C. **809**
Diner, Hasia R.
A time for gathering **305.8**
Diner, Steven J.
A very different age **973.8**
Dinerstein, Eric
The kingdom of rarities **596**
Dinesen, Isak, 1885-1962
Out of Africa and Shadows on the grass **967.62**
About
Thurman, J. Isak Dinesen **92**
DINING
Dinner Made Simple **641.555**
Kamp, D. The United States of Arugula **641**
Swift, S. The Splendid table's how to eat supper **641.5**
DINING
See also Food
Dining with al-Qaeda. Pope, H. **956.05**
Dinki, Nikki
Meat on the side **641.35**
Dinnage, Rosemary
Alone! alone!: lives of some outsider women **920**
Dinner. Rosenstrach, J. **642**
Dinner at the Long Table. Tarlow, A. **641.5**
Dinner Made Simple. **641.555**
Dinner solved! **641.5**
Dinner with Edward. Vincent, I. **158.1**
DINNERS
See also Cooking; Menus
DINNERS AND DINING
Bruni, F. Born round **92**
The make-ahead cook **641.5**
Michael Symon's 5 in 5 for every season **641.81**
Rosenstrach, J. Dinner **642**
Rosenstrach, J. How to celebrate everything **641.568**
Tarlow, A. Dinner at the Long Table **641.5**
DINNERS AND DINING *See* Dining; Dinners

DINNERS AND DINING -- HISTORY
Consider the fork   **643**
DINNERS AND DINING -- ITALY -- ROME
Minchilli, E. Eating Rome   **641.594**
DINNERS AND DINING -- NEW YORK (STATE) -- NEW YORK
Vincent, I. Dinner with Edward   **158.1**
DINNERS AND DINING -- TERMS AND PHRASES
Jurafsky, D. The language of food   **641.3**
Dinosaur odyssey. Sampson, S. D.   **567.9**
Dinosaurs.   **567.9**
Dinosaurs. Barrett, P.   **567.9**
DINOSAURS
Alvarez, W. T. rex and the Crater of Doom   **551.7**
Barrett, P. Dinosaurs   **567.9**
Dinosaurs   **567.9**
Dinosaurs the grand tour   **567.9**
Hone, D. The Tyrannosaur Chronicles   **567.91**
Horner, J. R. How to build a dinosaur   **567.9**
Larson, P. L. Rex appeal   **567.9**
Paul, G. S. The Princeton field guide to dinosaurs   **567.9**
Randall, L. Dark Matter and the Dinosaurs   **523.1**
Rea, T. Bone wars   **560**
Sampson, S. D. Dinosaur odyssey   **567.9**
DINOSAURS -- EGGS
See also Eggs
Dinosaurs the grand tour.   **567.9**
Dinwiddie, Robert, 1953-
The Stars   **523.8**
DIONYSUS (GREEK DEITY)
See also Gods and goddesses
DIPHTHERIA
See also Diseases
DIPLODOCUS
Rea, T. Bone wars   **560**
DIPLODOCUS
See also Dinosaurs
Diplomacy. Kissinger, H.   **327.2**
DIPLOMACY
Ferguson, N. Kissinger   **92**
Kissinger, H. Diplomacy   **327.2**
Mitchell, G. J. A Path to Peace   **956.94**
Reynolds, D. Summits   **909.82**
DIPLOMACY
See also International relations
DIPLOMATS
See also Diplomacy; International relations; Statesmen
DIPLOMATS -- GREAT BRITAIN -- BIOGRAPHY
Dickey, C. Our Man in Charleston   **92**
DIPLOMATS -- UNITED STATES -- BIOGRAPHY
Cook, J. H. American phoenix   **973.5**

DIPLOMATS -- UNITED STATES -- HISTORY -- 20TH CENTURY
Baglio, M. Argo   **955.05**
Dippie, Brian W.
The Frederic Remington Art Museum collection   **709**
Dirda, Michael
Book by book   **028**
Browsings   **028**
On Conan Doyle; or, The whole art of storytelling   **823**
DIRECT MARKETING
See also Mail-order business; Marketing
DIRECT SELLING
See also Marketing; Retail trade; Selling
DIRECT TAXATION *See* Taxation
Directed by desire. Jordan, J.   **811**
DIRECTION SENSE
Ellard, C. You are here   **153.7**
Directory of family associations. Bentley, E. P.   **929**
Directory of special libraries and information centers.   **026**
DIRECTORY, FRENCH, 1795-1799 *See* France -- History -- 1789-1799, Revolution
DIRIGIBLE BALLOONS *See* Airships
Dirix, Emmanuelle
Dressing the Decades   **391.009**
Dirr's encyclopedia of trees and shrubs. Dirr, M. A.   **635.9**
Dirr's Hardy trees and shrubs. Dirr, M.   **635.9**
Dirr's trees and shrubs for warm climates. Dirr, M.   **635.9**
Dirr, Michael A.
Dirr's encyclopedia of trees and shrubs   **635.9**
Dirr's Hardy trees and shrubs   **635.9**
Dirr's trees and shrubs for warm climates   **635.9**
Manual of woody landscape plants   **635.9**
The Reference Manual of Woody Plant Propagation   **631.5**
The **Dirt** Cure. Shetreat-Klein, M.   **618.92**
The **dirty** life. Kimball, K.   **92**
The **dirty** little secrets of getting into a top college. Chatterjee, P.   **378.161**
The **dirty** little secrets of getting your dream job. Raskin, D.   **650.14**
Dirty South. Westhoff, B.   **781.64**
Dirty wars. Scahill, J.   **355.02**
DiSabato-Aust, Tracy
The well-tended perennial garden   **635.9**
DISABILITIES
See also Diseases; Wounds and injuries
A **disability** history of the United States. Nielsen, K. E.   **362.4**
DISABILITY INSURANCE
See also Insurance
DISABILITY LAW *See* People with disabilities --

Legal status, laws, etc.

DISABLED *See* People with disabilities

DISADVANTAGED CHILDREN *See* Children with social disabilities

DISADVANTAGED STUDENTS *See* At risk students

Disappearing ink. Gioia, D.   **811**

The **disappearing** spoon. Kean, S.   **546**

DISAPPOINTMENT

    See also Emotions

DISARMAMENT

    Service, R.   The End of the Cold War, 1985-1991   **909.82**

DISARMAMENT *See* Arms control

DISASTER HOSPITALS -- LOUISIANA -- NEW ORLEANS -- CASE STUDIES

    Fink, S.   Five days at memorial   **362.11**

Disaster planning. Halsted, D. D.   **025.8**

DISASTER PREPAREDNESS *See* Disaster relief

DISASTER RELIEF

    Bortolotti, D.   Hope in hell   **610**

    Brinkley, D.   The great deluge   **976.3**

    De Villiers, M.   The end   **363.34**

    Dyson, M. E.   Come hell or high water   **976.3**

    Fink, S.   Five days at memorial   **362.11**

    Halsted, D. D.   Disaster planning   **025.8**

    Horne, J.   Breach of faith   **976.3**

    Larkin, E.   Everything is broken   **959.1**

    Miles, K.   Superstorm   **551.55**

    Ripley, A.   The unthinkable   **155.9**

    Van Heerden, I. L.   The storm   **976.3**

    Welky, D.   The thousand-year flood   **363.34**

DISASTER RELIEF

    See also Charities; Humanitarian intervention; Public welfare

Disaster response and planning for libraries. Kahn, M. B.   **025.8**

DISASTER RESPONSE AND RECOVERY

    Kahn, M. B.   Disaster response and planning for libraries   **025.8**

    Katz, J. M.   The big truck that went by   **363.34**

DISASTER VICTIMS -- JAPAN -- TŌHOKU REGION

    Ehrlich, G.   Facing the wave   **363.34**

DISASTER VICTIMS -- SRI LANKA -- BIOGRAPHY

    Deraniyagala, S.   Wave   **954.93**

DISASTERS

    Davis, L. A.   Man-made catastrophes   **904**

    Junger, S.   Fire   **909.82**

    Khan, A. S.   The next pandemic   **362.1**

    Ripley, A.   The unthinkable   **155.9**

    Solnit, R.   A paradise built in hell   **303.4**

DISASTERS -- HISTORY -- 17TH CENTURY

    Parker, G.   Global crisis   **909**

DISASTERS -- PSYCHOLOGICAL ASPECTS

    Gonzales, L.   Surviving survival   **155.9**

    Solnit, R.   A paradise built in hell   **303.4**

Disbrowe, Paula

    Down south   **641.59**

    Link, D.   Real Cajun   **641.5**

    Neely, P.   Down home with the Neelys   **641.5**

DISC JOCKEYS

    See also Musicians; Radio and music

DISC JOCKEYS (CLUB)

    Grandmaster Flash   The adventures of Grandmaster Flash   **92**

DISCARDING OF BOOKS, PERIODICALS, ETC. -- HANDBOOKS, MANUALS, ETC

    Vnuk, R.   The weeding handbook   **025.2**

Discernment. Nouwen, H.   **248.4**

DISCERNMENT (CHRISTIAN THEOLOGY)

    Nouwen, H.   Discernment   **248.4**

DISCIPLES, TWELVE *See* Apostles

DISCIPLINE *See* Punishment

DISCIPLINE OF CHILDREN

    Bailey, R. A.   Easy to love, difficult to discipline   **155**

    Phelan, T. W.   1-2-3 magic   **649**

DISCIPLINE OF CHILDREN *See* Child rearing; School discipline

DISCLOSURE OF INFORMATION

    See also Truthfulness and falsehood

DISCOGRAPHY *See* Sound recordings

The **discomfort** zone. Franzen, J.   **92**

Discontent and its civilizations. Hamid, M.   **814**

DISCOUNT STORES

    See also Retail trade; Stores

DISCOVERERS *See* Explorers

The **discoveries.** Lightman, A. P.   **509**

DISCOVERIES AND EXPLORATION *See* Exploration

DISCOVERIES IN GEOGRAPHY *See* Exploration

DISCOVERIES IN GEOGRAPHY -- HISTORY

    Bellec, F.   Unknown lands   **910.4**

    Lester, T.   The fourth part of the world   **912**

DISCOVERIES IN MEDICINE

    See also Discoveries in science; Medicine

DISCOVERIES IN SCIENCE

    Bartusiak, M.   Black hole   **523.8**

    Coffey, P.   Cathedrals of science   **540**

    Dyson, F. J.   Dreams of earth and sky   **500**

    Firestein, S.   Ignorance   **501**

    Green, B.   Boltzmann's tomb   **509**

    Morton, O.   Eating the sun   **572**

    Seeing further   **506**

DISCOVERIES IN SCIENCE

    See also Research; Science

DISCOVERIES IN SCIENCE -- ANECDOTES

    Brown, M.   How I killed Pluto and why it had it coming   **523.4**

DISCOVERIES, SCIENTIFIC *See* Discoveries in

science

Discovering America [series]

Smith, J. E. Becoming Belafonte **92**

Discovering the Civil War. Center for the National Archives Experience **973.7**

The **discovery** and conquest of Mexico, 1517-1521. Diaz del Castillo, B. **972**

The **discovery** of being. May, R. **150.19**

The **discovery** of global warming. Weart, S. R. **551.6**

The **discovery** of Jeanne Baret. Ridley, G. **92**

DISCRIMINATION

Benforado, A. Unfair **364.3**

Cahill, S. LGBT youth in America's schools **371.82**

Ford, R. T. Rights gone wrong **342**

DISCRIMINATION

See also Ethnic relations; Interpersonal relations; Prejudices; Race relations; Social problems; Social psychology

DISCRIMINATION AGAINST PEOPLE WITH DISABILITIES

See also Discrimination; People with disabilities

DISCRIMINATION AGAINST PEOPLE WITH DISABILITIES -- LAW AND LEGISLATION -- UNITED STATES

Davis, L. J. Enabling acts **342.73**

DISCRIMINATION IN CRIMINAL JUSTICE ADMINISTRATION -- FLORIDA -- GROVELAND

King, G. Devil in the grove **305.896**

DISCRIMINATION IN CRIMINAL JUSTICE ADMINISTRATION -- PSYCHOLOGICAL ASPECTS

Benforado, A. Unfair **364.3**

DISCRIMINATION IN EDUCATION

Perez, W. We are Americans **371.82**

DISCRIMINATION IN EDUCATION

See also Discrimination

DISCRIMINATION IN EMPLOYMENT

See also Discrimination

DISCRIMINATION IN EMPLOYMENT -- UNITED STATES -- HISTORY -- 20TH CENTURY

Paul, R. We could not fail **920**

DISCRIMINATION IN HIGHER EDUCATION -- UNITED STATES

Wilder, C. S. Ebony and Ivy **379.26**

DISCRIMINATION IN HOUSING

Loewen, J. W. Sundown towns **363.5**

Satter, B. Family properties **363.5**

DISCRIMINATION IN HOUSING

See also Discrimination; Housing

DISCRIMINATION IN PUBLIC ACCOMMODATIONS

See also Discrimination

DISCRIMINATION IN SPORTS -- UNITED

STATES

Kashatus, W. C. Jackie and Campy **92**

DISCRIMINATION IN SPORTS -- UNITED STATES -- HISTORY

Ross, C. K. Mavericks, money, and men **796.332**

DISCUSSION See Conversation; Debates and debating; Negotiation

DISCUSSION GROUPS

John, L. Z. Running book discussion groups **374**

DISCUSSION GROUPS

See also Conversation

DISEASE (PATHOLOGY) See Pathology

A **Disease** Called Childhood. Wedge, M. **618.92**

The **disease** delusion. Bland, J. S. **615.5**

DISEASE GERMS See Bacteria; Germ theory of disease

DISEASE MANAGEMENT

Khan, A. S. The next pandemic **362.1**

DISEASE MANAGEMENT

See also Medical care

DISEASE MODELS, ANIMAL

Bowers, K. Zoobiquity **636.089**

DISEASE OUTBREAKS

Khan, A. S. The next pandemic **362.1**

DISEASE OUTBREAKS -- HISTORY -- POPULAR WORKS

Quammen, D. Ebola **614.5**

DISEASES

The Cambridge world history of food **641.3**

Karr-Morse, R. Scared sick **155.9**

Moalem, S. Survival of the sickest **616**

Zuk, M. Riddled with life **616.07**

DISEASES -- CAUSES

Bland, J. S. The disease delusion **615.5**

DISEASES -- POETRY

Powell, D. A. Useless landscape **811**

DISEASES -- PREVENTION See Preventive medicine

DISEASES -- PSYCHOLOGICAL ASPECTS

Pogrebin, L. C. How to be a friend to a friend who's sick **610**

DISEASES -- TREATMENT See Therapeutics

DISEASES AND PESTS See Agricultural bacteriology; Agricultural pests; Fungi; Household pests; Insect pests; Parasites; Plant diseases

DISEASES IN LITERATURE

Murphy, M. Rabid **614.5**

DISEASES OF ANIMALS See Animals -- Diseases

DISEASES OF PLANTS See Plant diseases

DISEASES, CHRONIC See Chronic diseases

DISENGAGEMENT (MILITARY SCIENCE)

Rose, G. How wars end **355**

DISGUISE

See also Costume; Deception

Disher, Wayne

Crash Course in Collection Development   **025.2**

DISHES *See* Porcelain; Pottery; Tableware

DISHONESTY *See* Honesty

DiSilvestro, Roger L.
    Theodore Roosevelt in the Badlands   **92**

DISINFECTION AND DISINFECTANTS
     See also Hygiene; Pharmaceutical chemistry;
     Public health; Sanitation

Disintegration. Robinson, E.   **305.8**

Disney, Walt, 1901-1966
About
  Gabler, N. Walt Disney   **92**
  Ghez, D. They drew as they pleased   **741.58**
  Suskind, R. Life, animated   **618.92**

DISORDERS OF COMMUNICATION *See* Communicative disorders

The **dispensable** nation. Nasr, V.   **327.73**

DiSpirito, Rocco
  Now eat this!   **641.5**

DISPLACED PERSONS *See* Political refugees; Refugees

DISPOSAL OF REFUSE *See* Refuse and refuse disposal

A **disposition** to be rich. Ward, G. C.   **974.7**

DISPUTE SETTLEMENT *See* Conflict management

Disrupt you! Samit, J.   **650.1**

Disrupt yourself. Johnson, W.   **658.4**

DISRUPTIVE TECHNOLOGIES
  Johnson, W. Disrupt yourself   **658.4**

DISSECTION
  Roach, M. Stiff   **611**

Dissent. Young, R.   **303.48**

DISSENT
     See also Freedom of conscience; Freedom of
     religion

Dissent and the Supreme Court. Urofsky, M.
I.   **342.73**

DISSENTERS
  Abdul-Jabbar, K. Black profiles in courage   **920**
  Cleaver, E. Target zero   **323**
  Ellsberg, D. Secrets: a memoir of Vietnam and the
   Pentagon papers   **959.704**
  Havel, V. To the castle and back   **92**
  Hendricks, S. The unquiet grave   **970.004**
  Metaxas, E. Bonhoeffer   **92**
  Remnick, D. Reporting   **814**
  Schou, N. Orange sunshine   **363.45**
  Wintle, J. Perfect hostage   **92**

**DISSENTERS -- LEGAL STATUS, LAWS, ETC.
 -- UNITED STATES**
  Urofsky, M. I. Dissent and the Supreme
   Court   **342.73**

**DISSENTERS -- SOVIET UNION -- BIOGRA-
PHY**
  Finn, P. The Zhivago affair   **891.73**

DISSENTERS -- UNITED STATES -- HISTORY
  Wills, G. A necessary evil   **973**
  Young, R. Dissent   **303.48**

**DISSENTERS, ARTISTIC -- CHINA -- SOCIAL
 CONDITIONS -- 21ST CENTURY**
  Martin, B. Hanging man   **709**

DISSENTING OPINIONS -- UNITED STATES
  Urofsky, M. I. Dissent and the Supreme
   Court   **342.73**

DISSERTATIONS
  A manual for writers of research papers, theses, and
   dissertations   **808.06**
  Turabian, K. L. Student's guide to writing college
   papers   **808**

DISSERTATIONS
     See also Research

**DISSERTATIONS, -- HANDBOOKS, MANU-
ALS, ETC**
  A manual for writers of research papers, theses, and
   dissertations   **808.06**

DISSOCIATION (PSYCHOLOGY)
  Biever, J. A. The wandering mind   **612.8**

The **distance** between us. Grande, R.   **92**

DISTANCE EDUCATION
     See also Education

A **distant** mirror. Tuchman, B. W.   **944**

Distant reading. Moretti, F.   **801**

DISTILLATION
  Watman, M. Chasing the white dog   **363.4**

DISTILLATION
     See also Analytical chemistry; Industrial
     chemistry; Technology

The **distinctive** home. Eck, J.   **728**

Distinguished African Americans in aviation and
space science. Gubert, B. K.   **629.13**

Distinguished African Americans series
  Gubert, B. K. Distinguished African Americans in
   aviation and space science   **629.13**

DISTRACTED DRIVING
     See also Automobile drivers; Distraction
     (Psychology)

District and circle. Heaney, S.   **821**

DISTRICT ATTORNEYS
  Algeo, M. The president is a sick man   **973.8**
  Graff, H. F. Grover Cleveland   **92**
  Hull, N. E. H. Roe v. Wade   **344**
  Karabell, Z. The last campaign   **324.9**
  Rule, A. --and never let her go   **364.1**
  Siegel, F. F. The prince of the city   **92**

DISTRICT SCHOOLS *See* Rural schools

Dittrich, Luke
  Patient H.M.   **616.85**

DIVERS
  Cousteau, J. Y. The human, the orchid, and the oc-
   topus   **333.95**
  Matsen, B. Jacques Cousteau   **92**

DIVERS -- UNITED STATES -- BIOGRAPHY
Peffer, R. Where divers dare   **940.54**
Skolnick, A. One breath   **797.2**
DIVERSITY IN THE WORKPLACE
    See also Multiculturalism; Personnel management
DIVERSITY MOVEMENT *See* Multiculturalism
The **diversity** of life. Wilson, E. O.   **333.95**
DIVERSITY, BIOLOGICAL *See* Biodiversity
The **divide.**   **303.3**
DIVIDED ATTENTION *See* Distraction (Psychology)
DIVIDED GOVERNMENT -- UNITED STATES
Edwards, M. The parties versus the people   **320**
Smith, H. Who stole the American dream?   **973.91**
The **divided** ground. Taylor, A.   **974.7**
DIVIDENDS *See* Securities; Stocks
DIVINATION
I ching The classic of changes   **299.5**
DIVINATION
    See also Occultism
The **divine** art of dying. Anderson, H.   **202**
The **divine** comedy. Dante Alighieri   **851**
DIVINE HEALING *See* Spiritual healing
The **divine** milieu. Teilhard de Chardin, P.   **230**
Divine wind. Emanuel, K. A.   **551.55**
DIVING
    See also Swimming; Water sports
DIVISION OF POWERS *See* Separation of powers
DIVORCE
Moffett, K. Not your mother's divorce   **306.89**
Patchett, A. This Is the Story of a Happy Marriage   **92**
Richmond Mouillot, M. A fifty-year silence **940.53**
Summerscale, K. Mrs. Robinson's disgrace **941.081**
Wallerstein, J. S. The unexpected legacy of divorce   **306.89**
White, M. Travels in Vermeer   **92**
Woo, I. The great divorce   **92**
DIVORCE
    See also Family
Divorce & money. Woodhouse, V.   **346.01**
DIVORCE -- LAW AND LEGISLATION
Doskow, E. Nolo's essential guide to divorce **346.01**
Woodhouse, V. Divorce & money   **346.01**
DIVORCE -- PSYCHOLOGICAL ASPECTS
Cusk, R. Aftermath   **823**
Moffett, K. Not your mother's divorce   **306.89**
DIVORCE MEDIATION
    See also Divorce
The **divorce** of Henry VIII. Fletcher, C.   **942.05**
DIVORCED PEOPLE
Weldon, M. Escape Points   **362.196**
DIVORCED PEOPLE -- BIOGRAPHY
Richmond Mouillot, M. A fifty-year silence **940.53**
DIVORCED PEOPLE -- POETRY

Olds, S. Stag's leap   **811**
DIVORCED PERSONS *See* Divorced people
DIVORCED WOMEN
Link, M. Bootstrapper   **92**
Melton, G. D. Love warrior   **92**
DIVORCED WOMEN
    See also Divorced people; Single women
DIVORCED WOMEN -- BIOGRAPHY
Fuller, A. Leaving Before the Rains Come **305.409**
DIVORCED WOMEN -- UNITED STATES -- BIOGRAPHY
Melton, G. D. Love warrior   **92**
Dixie, Quinton Hosford
Williams, J. This far by faith   **200**
Dixon, Anne
The handweaver's pattern directory   **746.1**
Dixon, Kirsten
The Tutka Bay Lodge cookbook   **641.59**
Dixon, Mandy
(jt. auth) Dixon, K. The Tutka Bay Lodge cookbook   **641.59**
Dixon, Matt
The well-built triathlete   **796.42**
Dixon, Wheeler W., 1950-
A Short History of Film   **791.43**
Dixon, Willie
About
Inaba, M. Willie Dixon   **92**
DIY dog grooming, from puppy cuts to best in show. Bendersky, J.   **636.7**
DIY wardrobe makeovers. Stanley, S. H.   **646**
Django: the life and music of a Gypsy legend. Dregni, M.   **92**
DK Books (Company)
(comp) World War I   **940.3**
Dk Eyewitness Back Roads Spain.   **914.6**
Dk Eyewitness Munich & the Bavarian Alps. **914.336**
Dk Eyewitness Top 10 Rio De Janeiro.   **918.15**
DK Eyewitness Travel Cambodia & Laos.   **915.9**
DK Publishing (Company)
(comp) Atlas A-Z   **912**
(comp) The bee book   **595.799**
(comp) Biodynamic gardening   **635**
(comp) Brazil   **918.1**
(comp) The cat encyclopedia   **636.8**
(comp) Cross, C. The baby book   **649.122**
(comp) Dk Eyewitness Top 10 Rio De Janeiro   **918.15**
(comp) Firearms   **683.4**
(comp) The pregnancy encyclopedia   **618.2**
(comp) The tea book   **641.3**
(comp) Tractor   **629.225**
(comp) Wildlife of the world   **591**
(comp) World War II   **940.54**
DK Smithsonian nature guide [series]
Bonewitz, R. Rocks and minerals   **549**

DNA

The annotated and illustrated double helix   **572.8**

Carroll, S. B. The making of the fittest   **572.8**

Cobb, M. Life's Greatest Secret   **572.8**

Kean, S. The violinist's thumb   **572.8**

Kenneally, C. The invisible history of the human race   **616**

Maddox, B. Rosalind Franklin: the dark lady of DNA   **92**

DNA

    See also Cells; Heredity; Nucleic acids

DNA -- HISTORY

Kenneally, C. The invisible history of the human race   **616**

DNA FINGERPRINTING

Sykes, B. DNA USA   **559.9**

DNA USA. Sykes, B.   **559.9**

Do gentlemen really prefer blondes? Pincott, J. **155.3**

Do it for le$$! weddings. Vivaldo, D.   **395**

Do it yourself kitchens.   **643**

Do less, get more. Wasmund, S.   **650.1**

Do No Harm. Marsh, H.   **92**

Do unto animals.   **590**

Do you speak American ?(Television program)

Do you speak American?   **427**

Do you speak American? Do you speak American ?(Television program)   **427**

Do your om thing. Pacheco, R.   **181**

DO-IT-YOURSELF WORK

101 Saturday morning projects   **643**

Adarme, A. The year of cozy   **641.3**

New fix-it-yourself manual   **643**

DO-IT-YOURSELF WORK -- AMATEURS' MANUALS

The complete outdoor builder   **690**

Dobard, Raymond

Tobin, J. Hidden in plain view   **973.7**

Dobbs, Michael

One minute to midnight   **973.922**

Six months in 1945   **940.53**

Dobelli, Rolf

The art of thinking clearly   **153.4**

Dobroszycki, Lucjan

(ed) The Chronicle of the Lodz ghetto, 1941-1944   **943.8**

Dobson, Cherry

The complete guide to upholstery   **684.1**

Dobson, Michael

(ed) The Oxford companion to Shakespeare **822.3**

Dobson, William J.

The dictator's learning curve   **321.8**

Doc Halligan's What every pet owner should know. Halligan, K.   **636**

Dochuk, Darren

From Bible belt to sunbelt   **277**

The **Doctor** Is in. Westheimer, R. K.

A **doctor's** guide to alternative medicine. Borins, M.   **615.5**

The **doctor's** kidney diets. Kang, M. S.   **616.6**

DOCTOR-ASSISTED SUICIDE *See* Assisted suicide

DOCTORAL THESES *See* Dissertations

Doctored. Jauhar, S.   **92**

Doctorow, E. L.

Creationists: selected essays, 1993-2006   **814**

DOCTORS *See* Physicians

The **doctors'** plague. Nuland, S. B.   **92**

DOCTRINAL THEOLOGY

Davies, B. The thought of Thomas Aquinas   **189**

Holifield, E. B. Theology in America   **230**

Magill, R. J. Sincerity   **179**

Pelikan, J. J. Mary through the centuries   **232.91**

DOCTRINAL THEOLOGY

    See also Theology

Documentary arts and culture [series]

Colors of confinement   **940.53**

DOCUMENTARY FILMS

    See also Motion pictures

DOCUMENTARY FILMS -- CENSORSHIP -- UNITED STATES -- HISTORY -- 20TH CENTURY

Mitchell, G. The tunnels   **943.155**

DOCUMENTARY PHOTOGRAPHY

Frank, R. The Americans   **779.997**

Friend, D. Watching the world change   **974.7**

Light, M. 100 suns, 1945-1962   **355.8**

Lyon, D. Memories of myself   **779**

Magnum Photos, I. New York September 11   **770**

Morris, E. Believing is seeing   **770.9**

National Geographic Society (U.S.) Through the lens   **779**

National Geographic, the photographs   **778**

Sontag, S. Regarding the pain of others   **303.6**

Speaking Out   **306.76**

DOCUMENTARY PHOTOGRAPHY

    See also Photography

DOCUMENTARY PHOTOGRAPHY -- CALIFORNIA -- SANTA CLARA VALLEY (SANTA CLARA COUNTY)

Menuez, D. Fearless genius   **979.4**

DOCUMENTARY PHOTOGRAPHY -- UNITED STATES

Krauthamer, B. Envisioning emancipation   **973.7**

DOCUMENTARY TELEVISION PROGRAMS

    See also Television programs

DOCUMENTATION

Wright, A. Cataloging the world   **020.9**

DOCUMENTATION

    See also Information science

DOCUMENTS *See* Archives; Charters; Government publications

Documents of American Indian diplomacy. **970.004**

Dodge, Abigail Johnson
The everyday baker   **641.815**

Dodge, Norton T., 1927-
About
McPhee, J. A. The ransom of Russian art   **709**

Dodging extinction. Barnosky, A. D.   **576.8**

Dodson, James
Palmer, A. A golfer's life   **92**

Doerr, Bobby, 1918-
About
Halberstam, D. The teammates   **796**

Does God belong in public schools? Greenawalt, K.   **379**

Does Jesus Really Love Me? Chu, J.   **261.8**

Does this make my assets look fat? Hirshman, S. L.   **332.024**

DOG See Dogs

DOG ADOPTION
Rosenfelt, D. Dogtripping   **636.7**

DOG ADOPTION -- ANECDOTES
Miracle dogs   **636.7**

DOG BREEDING See Dogs -- Breeding

DOG BREEDS
The American Kennel Club's meet the breeds **636.7**
The new complete dog book   **636.7**

DOG CARE See Dogs -- Care

Dog days. Katz, J.   **636**

Dog Gone. Toutonghi, P.   **636.7**

The **Dog** Merchants. Kavin, K.   **636.7**

Dog owner's home veterinary handbook. Eldredge, D.   **636.7**

Dog owner's manual. Fogle, B.   **636.7**

DOG OWNERS -- ANECDOTES
Kerasote, T. Pukka's Promise   **636.7**

DOG PARKS
See also Dogs; Parks

DOG RESCUE
Zheutlin, P. Rescue road   **636.7**

Dog sense. Bradshaw, J.   **636.7**

DOG SHOWS
The American Kennel Club's meet the breeds **636.7**

DOG SHOWS
See also Dogs

DOG SLED RACING See Sled dog racing

DOG TRAINERS -- PSYCHOLOGY
Pierson, M. H. The secret history of kindness **636.7**

The **Dog** Who Could Fly. Lewis, D.   **940.54**

Dog years. Doty, M.   **92**

The **Dogist.** Friedman, E. W.   **779**

DOGMATIC THEOLOGY See Doctrinal theology

DOGMATICS See Doctrinal theology

Dogs. Coppinger, R.   **636.7**

DOGS
See also Domestic animals; Mammals

DOGS
Adams, M. B. Shaggy muses   **920**

American Kennel Club The complete dog book   **636.7**
Breslin, E. Drinking with Miss Dutchie   **92**
Coppinger, R. Dogs   **636.7**
Coren, S. Why we love the dogs we do   **636.7**
Doty, M. Dog years   **92**
Fogle, B. Dog owner's manual   **636.7**
Franklin, J. The wolf in the parlor   **636.7**
Friedman, E. W. The Dogist   **779**
The good dog   **636.7**
Halligan, K. Doc Halligan's What every pet owner should know   **636**
Herriot, J. James Herriot's dog stories   **636.7**
Herriot, J. James Herriot's favorite dog stories   **636.7**
Katz, J. The new work of dogs   **636.7**
Kerasote, T. Merle's door   **636.7**
Kerasote, T. Pukka's Promise   **636.7**
Lewis, D. The Dog Who Could Fly   **940.54**
Link, T. Talking with dogs and cats   **636.088**
McConnell, P. For the love of a dog   **636.7**
The new complete dog book   **636.7**
Rosenfelt, D. Dogtripping   **636.7**
Thomas, E. M. The social lives of dogs   **636.7**
Toutonghi, P. Dog Gone   **636.7**
Zheutlin, P. Rescue road   **636.7**

DOGS -- ANECDOTES
The good dog   **636.7**
Miracle dogs   **636.7**

DOGS -- BEHAVIOR
Anderson, T. The ultimate guide to dog training   **636.7**
Bradshaw, J. Dog sense   **636.7**
Decoding Your Dog   **636.7**
Stilwell, V. Train your dog positively   **636.7**
Thomas, E. M. The hidden life of dogs   **599.77**

DOGS -- BIOGRAPHY
Rosenfelt, D. Dogtripping   **636.7**

DOGS -- BREEDING
The American Kennel Club's meet the breeds **636.7**
Dickey, B. Pit bull   **636.755**
Kavin, K. The Dog Merchants   **636.7**

DOGS -- CARE
The art of raising a puppy   **636.7**
Bendersky, J. DIY dog grooming, from puppy cuts to best in show   **636.7**
Kaplan, L. Help Your Dog Fight Cancer   **636.7**
Miracle dogs   **636.7**

DOGS -- DISEASES
Eldredge, D. Dog owner's home veterinary handbook   **636.7**

DOGS -- ENCYCLOPEDIAS
Coile, D. C. Encyclopedia of dog breeds   **636.7**

DOGS -- EXHIBITIONS See Dog shows

DOGS -- GROOMING
Bendersky, J. DIY dog grooming, from puppy cuts

to best in show **636.7**

DOGS -- PICTORIAL WORKS

Blackwell, L. The life and love of dogs **636.7**

DOGS -- PSYCHOLOGY

Bradshaw, J. Dog sense **636.7**

Thomas, E. M. The hidden life of dogs **599.77**

DOGS -- PSYCHOLOGY

See also Animal intelligence; Comparative psychology; Psychology

DOGS -- STANDARDS -- UNITED STATES

The new complete dog book **636.7**

DOGS -- TRAINING

Anderson, T. The ultimate guide to dog training **636.7**

Decoding Your Dog **636.7**

Stilwell, V. Train your dog positively **636.7**

DOGS -- TRAINING -- PHILOSOPHY

Pierson, M. H. The secret history of kindness **636.7**

DOGS -- WAR USE

See also Animals -- War use

The **Dogs** Are Eating Them Now. Smith, G. **958.104**

Dogs that know when their owners are coming home. Sheldrake, R. **133.8**

Dogtown. East, E. **974.4**

DOGTOWN (MASS.)

East, E. Dogtown **974.4**

Dogtripping. Rosenfelt, D. **636.7**

Doh, Jenny

Creative lettering **745.6**

More creative lettering **745.6**

Signature styles **646.4**

Doherty, Gerard M.

(ed) Current surgical diagnosis & treatment **617**

Dohrmann, George

Play their hearts out **796.323**

Doidge, Norman

The brain that changes itself **612.8**

The brain's way of healing **612.8**

Dojny, Brooke

The New England cookbook **641.5**

Doka, Kenneth J.

Grief is a journey **155.9**

Dolan, Timothy Michael

About

Boyle, C. An American Cardinal **92**

Dolin, Eric Jay

Fur, fortune, and empire **381**

Leviathan **639.2**

When America first met China **382**

DOLL FURNITURE

Frisoni The Big Book of a Miniature House **745**

DOLL FURNITURE

See also Miniature objects; Toys

DOLLHOUSES

See also Miniature objects; Toys

Dolnick, Barrie

Luck **130**

Dolnick, Edward

The clockwork universe **509**

Down the great unknown **979.1**

The rescue artist **364.1**

Dolphin diaries. Herzing, D. L. **599.5**

DOLPHINS

Bearzi, M. Beautiful minds **599.8**

Casey, S. Voices in the Ocean **599.53**

Herzing, D. L. Dolphin diaries **599.5**

Montgomery, S. Journey of the pink dolphins **599.53**

DOLPHINS

See also Marine mammals

DOMAINE TEMPIER

Olney, R. Lulu's Provencal table **641.59**

DOMAINE TEMPIER VINEYARD

Olney, R. Lulu's Provencal table **641.59**

DOMESDAY BOOK

See also Great Britain -- History -- 1066-1154, Norman period

DOMESTIC ANIMAL DWELLINGS *See* Animal housing

DOMESTIC ANIMALS

Herriot, J. James Herriot's animal stories **636.089**

Katz, J. Dog days **636**

DOMESTIC ANIMALS

See also Animals

DOMESTIC ANIMALS -- DISEASES *See* Animals -- Diseases

DOMESTIC ANIMALS -- HISTORY

Francis, R. C. Domesticated **636**

DOMESTIC ANIMALS -- HOUSING *See* Animal housing

DOMESTIC ARCHITECTURE

The best homes from This old house **643**

Bradbury, D. The iconic interior **747**

Creating a new old house **728**

Crochet, T. Bungalow style **747**

The elements of style **728**

The house with sixteen handmade doors **728**

O'Keeffe, L. Heart and home

Susanka, S. Creating the not so big house **728**

Susanka, S. The not so big house **728**

Wiencek, H. National Geographic guide to America's great houses **728.8**

DOMESTIC ARCHITECTURE

See also Architecture

DOMESTIC ARCHITECTURE -- DESIGNS AND PLANS

Eck, J. The distinctive home **728**

Jordan, W. A. Universal design for the home **728**

Susanka, S. Not so big solutions for your home **728**

DOMESTIC ARCHITECTURE -- ENCYCLOPEDIAS

The Greenwood encyclopedia of homes through

American history   **728**

DOMESTIC ARCHITECTURE -- GUIDE-BOOKS
McAlester, V. S. A field guide to American houses   **728**

DOMESTIC ECONOMIC ASSISTANCE
See also Economic policy

DOMESTIC ECONOMIC ASSISTANCE -- DE-VELOPING COUNTRIES
Novogratz, J. The blue sweater   **339.4**

DOMESTIC RELATIONS -- UNITED STATES
Carbone, J. Marriage markets   **306.85**

DOMESTIC TERRORISM
See also Terrorism

DOMESTIC TERRORISM -- NORWAY
One of Us   **363.325**

DOMESTIC VIOLENCE
Dalpiaz, C. M. Breaking free, starting over **362.82**
Domestic violence sourcebook   **362.82**
Fontes, L. A. Invisible chains   **158.2**
Weiss, E. Family & friends' guide to domestic violence   **362.82**
Weiss, E. Surviving domestic violence   **362.82**

DOMESTIC VIOLENCE
See also Violence

Domestic violence sourcebook.   **362.82**
Domesticated. Francis, R. C.   **636**
DOMESTICATION *See* Domestic animals

DOMESTICS
Yellin, J. F. Harriet Jacobs: a life   **92**

DOMINANCE (PSYCHOLOGY)
Fontes, L. A. Invisible chains   **158.2**
Maestripieri, D. Games primates play   **155.7**

Domingos, Pedro
The master algorithm   **003**

DOMINICAN AMERICANS
Alvarez, J. A wedding in Haiti   **818**
Padilla Peralta Undocumented   **92**

The **dominion** of war. Anderson, F.   **973.2**

DOMINION THEOLOGY
Christian reconstruction   **230**

Dominique Ansel. Ansel, D.   **641.86**
Domino : your guide to a stylish home.   **747**
The **domino** diaries. Butler   **796.83**
Domino, Fats, 1928-
About
Coleman, R. Blue Monday   **92**
Domitian, Emperor of Rome, 51-96
About
The twelve Caesars   **878**
Don Carlos and Mary Stuart. Schiller, F.   **832**

DON'T ASK, DON'T TELL (MILITARY POLICY)
Nicholson, A. Fighting to serve   **355**
Don't be afraid of the bullets. Kasinof, L. **953.305**
Don't be such a scientist. Olson, R.   **501**

Don't eat this book. Spurlock, M.   **614.5**
Don't Even Think About It. Marshall, G.   **551.6**
Don't kill the birthday girl. Beasley, S.   **92**
Don't let's go to the dogs tonight. Fuller, A.   **92**
Don't make me think, revisited. Krug, S.   **006.7**
Don't sleep, there are snakes. Everett, D. L.   **305.8**
Don't trust, don't fear, don't beg. Stewart, B. **363.738**
Donald, Aida D.
Citizen soldier   **92**
Donald, David Herbert
Lincoln   **92**
Donaldson, Scott
(ed) Robinson, E. A. Poems   **821**
Donaldson-Pressman, Stephanie
(jt. auth) Jackson, R. The learning habit   **371.3**

DONATION OF ORGANS, TISSUES, ETC.
See also Gifts

DONATIONS *See* Gifts
Dong, Stella
Shanghai, 1842-1949   **951**
Doniger, Wendy
On Hinduism   **294.5**

DONKEYS -- NEW YORK (STATE) -- WEST HEBRON -- ANECDOTES
Katz, J. Saving Simon   **636.1**
Donnan, Kristin
Larson, P. L. Rex appeal   **567.9**
Donne, John
The complete poetry and selected prose of John Donne   **821**
Poems and prose   **821**
Donnelly, James S.
(ed) Encyclopedia of Irish history and culture **941.5**
Donnelly, Timothy
The cloud corporation   **811**

DONNER PARTY
Brown, D. The indifferent stars above   **92**
Donner, Thomas W.
(jt. auth) Rubin, R. R. The Johns Hopkins guide to diabetes   **616.4**
Donofrio, Jeanine
The Love and Lemons Cookbook   **641.5**
Donoghue, Denis
Speaking of beauty   **801**
Donoghue, Emma
Inseparable   **809**
Donohue, Nanette
(jt. auth) Vnuk, R. Women's fiction   **016**
Donovan's Devils. Lulushi, A.   **940.54**
Donovan, Brian
Hard driving: the Wendell Scott story   **92**
Donovan, James
The blood of heroes   **976.4**
A terrible glory   **973.8**
Donovan, William J. (William Joseph), 1883-1959
About

Fullilove, M. Rendezvous with destiny **973.917**

Lulushi, A. Donovan's Devils **940.54**

Donvan, John

In a different key **616.85**

Donziger, Steven R

About

Barrett, P. M. Law of the jungle **344**

Doo-dah!: Stephen Foster and the rise of American popular culture. Emerson, K. **92**

Doody, Kate

(jt. auth) Taylor, B. Glaze **738.1**

Doolittle, James Harold, 1896-1993

About

Groom, W. The aviators **920**

Nelson, C. The first heroes **940.54**

Scott, J. M. Target Tokyo **940.54**

Doomed to succeed. Ross, D. B. **327.73**

Door in the mountain. Valentine, J. **811**

Doorley, Rachelle

Tinkerlab **600**

DOORS

See also Architecture -- Details; Buildings

DOORS (MUSICAL GROUP)

Hopkins, J. No one here gets out alive **92**

Riordan, J. Break on through: the life and death of Jim Morrison **92**

Dorie's cookies. Greenspan, D. **641.86**

Doris Day. Kaufman, D. **92**

The **Dorito** effect. Schatzker, M. **641.3**

Dorland's illustrated medical dictionary. **610**

Dorling Kindersley Eyewitness Travel (Company)

(comp) DK Eyewitness Travel Cambodia & Laos **915.9**

(comp) Eyewitness Travel Malaysia & Singapore **915.9**

Dorling Kindersley Publishing Inc.

(comp) Artist's painting techniques **751.4**

(comp) Atlas A-Z **912**

(comp) Canada **917.104**

(comp) Design

(comp) Dk Eyewitness Back Roads Spain **914.6**

(comp) Dk Eyewitness Munich & the Bavarian Alps **914.336**

(comp) France **914.4**

(comp) The gardener's year **635**

(comp) Gem **553.8**

(comp) Germany **914.304**

(comp) Grow All You Can Eat in Three Square Feet **635**

(comp) Handmade interiors **646.2**

(comp) The history book **909**

(comp) History of the world in 1,000 objects **909**

(comp) Music **780.9**

(comp) The politics book **320.01**

(comp) Pruning plant by plant **635**

(comp) The Stars **523.8**

(comp) Style your perfect wedding **392.5**

(comp) Train **625.1**

(comp) Watch my baby grow **649.122**

Dorn, Chris

(jt. auth) Dorn, M. Staying alive **613.6**

Dorn, Edward

Way more West **811**

Dorn, Michael

Staying alive **613.6**

Dornenburg, Andrew

Page, K. The flavor bible **641.5**

Dornfest, Rael

Google hacks **025.04**

Doron, Mia Wechsler

(jt. auth) Linden, D. W. Preemies **618.92**

Dorothea Lange. Gordon, L. **92**

Dorothy Parker. Meade, M. **92**

Dorren, Gaston

Lingo **306.44**

Dorril, Stephen

MI6 **327.12**

Dorris, Michael

The broken cord **362.292**

Dos Passos, John

About

Kazin, A. An American procession **810**

Dosen, Stephanie

Woodland knits **746.43**

Doskow, Emily

(jt. auth) Hertz, F. A legal guide for lesbian and gay couples **346.01**

Nolo's essential guide to divorce **346.01**

Doss, Jason R.

Armstrong, F. The retirement challenge--will you sink or swim? **332.024**

Dostoevsky. Frank, J. **92**

Dostoyevsky, Fyodor, 1821-1881

About

Existentialism from Dostoevsky to Sartre **142**

Frank, J. Dostoevsky **92**

Nabokov, V. V. Lectures on Russian literature **891.7**

Ozick, C. Quarrel & quandary **814**

Doty, James R.

About

Doty, J. R. Into the Magic Shop **92**

Doty, Mark, 1953-

(ed) The best American poetry **811**

Deep lane **811**

Doty, M. Dog years **92**

Fire to fire **811**

The **double** bond: Primo Levi, a biography. Angier, C. **92**

DOUBLE CONSCIOUSNESS *See* Multiple personality

Double cross. Macintyre, B. **940.54**

Double Down. Halperin, M. **324.9**

Double fold. Baker, N. 025.2
Double take. Connolly, K. M. 92
Double victory. Takaki, R. T. 940.53
DOUBT See Belief and doubt
Doubt: a history. Hecht, J. M. 121
Doughten, Kevin
(ed) Pilgrim's wilderness 92
Doughty, Caitlin
About
Doughty, C. Smoke gets in your eyes 92
Douglas MacArthur. Herman, A. 92
Douglas, Auriel
Strumpf, M. The grammar bible 428
Douglas, Illeana, 1965-
About
Douglas, I. I blame Dennis Hopper 792.02
Douglas, J. D.
(ed) Zondervan illustrated Bible dictionary 220.3
Douglas, John E.
The cases that haunt us 364.1
Douglas, Marjory Stoneman
About
Davis, J. E. An Everglades providence 92
Douglas, Scott
Meb for mortals 796.42
Douglas, Stephen A. (Stephen Arnold), 1813-1861
About
Bordewich, F. M. America's great debate 973.6
Egerton, D. R. Year of meteors 973.7
Guelzo, A. C. Lincoln and Douglas 973.6
Douglas, William O. (William Orville), 1898-1980
About
Feldman, N. Scorpions 920
Douglass, Frederick, 1817?-1895
About
Abdul-Jabbar, K. Black profiles in courage 920
Colaiaco, J. A. Frederick Douglass and the Fourth of July 973.7
Cornel West on Black prophetic fire 92
Douglass, F. Autobiographies 92
Douglass, F. My bondage and my freedom 92
Douglass, F. Narrative of the life of Frederick Douglass, an American slave 92
Stauffer, J. Picturing Frederick Douglass 92
Dove, Rita
American smooth 811
On the bus with Rosa Parks 811
Selected poems 811
The Penguin anthology of twentieth-century American poetry 811
DOW JONES INDUSTRIAL AVERAGE
Shiller, R. J. Irrational exuberance 332.63
Dow, Kirstin, 1963-
The atlas of climate change 551.6
Dower, John W., 1938-
Cultures of war 355

Embracing defeat 952.04
Ways of forgetting, ways of remembering 940.53
Dowling, Robert M.
Critical companion to Eugene O'Neill 812
Eugene O'Neill 92
Down around midnight. Sabbag, R. 92
Down home with the Neelys. Neely, P. 641.5
Down size. Spiker, T. 92
Down south. Disbrowe, P. 641.59
DOWN SYNDROME
Adams, R. Raising Henry 92
Chicoine, B. The guide to good health for teens & adults with Down syndrome 618.92
DOWN SYNDROME -- BIOGRAPHY
Mutch, M. Know the night 92
DOWN SYNDROME -- PATIENTS -- BIOGRAPHY
Austin, P. Beautiful eyes 92
Estreich, G. The Shape of the Eye 618.92
Down the great unknown. Dolnick, E. 979.1
Down the up escalator. Garson, B. 339.2
DOWN'S SYNDROME See Down syndrome
Downer, Lesley
Women of the pleasure quarters 792.7
Downes, John
Finance and investment handbook 332.6
Downey, Kirstin
Isabella 92
The woman behind the New Deal 92
Downey, Scott
Bennett, J. The complete snowboarder 796.9
Downfall. Frank, R. B. 940.54
DOWNHILL SKIING -- UNITED STATES -- HISTORY
Vinton, N. The fall line 796.935
Downie, David
A passion for Paris 944
Downing, Brandon
Lake Antiquity 811
Downing, David C.
Into the region of awe 248.2
Downing, Taylor
Secret Warriors 940.4
Downing, Thomas E.
Dow, K. The atlas of climate change 551.6
Downs, Paul
Boss Life 92
Downs, Todd
Essential road bike maintenance handbook 629.28
DOWNSIZING OF ORGANIZATIONS
See also Organizational change
Downsizing the family home. Jameson, M. 346.04
Doyle, Arthur Conan Sir, 1859-1930
About
Dirda, M. On Conan Doyle; or, The whole art of storytelling 823

Doyle, A. C. Arthur Conan Doyle **92**
Jaher, D. The witch of Lime Street **92**
Doyle, Don H.
  The Cause of All Nations **973.7**
Doyle, William
  PT 109 **940.54**
Dr. Eckener's dream machine. Botting, D. **629.133**
Dr. Mütter's Marvels. Aptowicz, C. O. **92**
Dr. Patrick Walsh's guide to surviving prostate cancer. Walsh, P. C. **616.99**
Dr. Seuss & Mr. Geisel. Morgan, J. **92**
Dr. Spock on parenting. Spock, B. **649**
Dr. Spock's baby and child care. Spock, B. **649**
Dr. Spock's the first two years. Spock, B. **649**
Dr. Spock's the school years. Spock, B. **649**
Dr. Susan Love's Breast Book. Love, S. M. **618.1**
Drabeck, Bernard A.
  (ed) Archibald MacLeish: reflections **92**
Drabelle, Dennis
  The great American railroad war **385**
DRAFT
  Hicks, G. The comfort women **940.54**
A **draft** of light. Hollander, J. **811**
DRAFTERS
  Dippie, B. W. The Frederic Remington Art Museum collection **709**
  Schama, S. Rembrandt's eyes **92**
DRAG CULTURE
  See also Counter culture
Dragnet nation. Angwin, J. **323.44**
The **dragon** behind the glass. Voigt, E. **597.176**
The **dragon** in the land of snows. Tsering Shakya **951**
Dragonflies. Van Dokkum, P. **595.7**
DRAGONS
  See also Animals -- Folklore; Folklore; Monsters; Mythical animals
The **dragons** of Eden. Sagan, C. **153**
DRAINAGE
  See also Agricultural engineering; Civil engineering; Hydraulic engineering; Municipal engineering; Reclamation of land; Sanitary engineering
Draitser, Emil
  Stalin's Romeo spy **92**
Drake, Sylvia, 1784-1868
                About
  Cleves, R. H. Charity and Sylvia **306.84**
Drakulic, Slavenka
  Cafe Europa **947**
Drama. Lithgow, J. **92**
DRAMA
  See also Literature
DRAMA
  The best stage scenes of 2007 **808.82**
  Brook, P. The empty space **792**

DRAMA -- COLLECTIONS
  The Best American short plays **812**
  The best plays of 2006-2007 **808.82**
  Nine plays of the modern theater **808.82**
  The Ultimate audition book **808.82**
DRAMA -- DICTIONARIES
  Critical survey of drama **809**
DRAMA -- EXPLICATION
  Adler, S. Stella Adler on America's master playwrights **812**
DRAMA -- HISTORY AND CRITICISM
  Bentley, E. The life of the drama **809**
  Brockett, O. G. History of the theatre **792.09**
  Critical survey of drama **809**
  Masterplots II, drama series **809**
  The play that changed my life **812**
DRAMA -- INDEXES
  Montgomery, D. L. Ottemiller's index to plays in collections **016**
DRAMA -- STORIES, PLOTS, ETC.
  Masterplots II, drama series **809**
DRAMA -- TECHNIQUE
  Adler, S. Stella Adler on America's master playwrights **812**
DRAMA -- TECHNIQUE
  See also Authorship
Drama high. Sokolove, M. **92**
Dramatic works. Beckett, S. **842**
DRAMATISTS
  Abbotson, S. C. W. Critical companion to Arthur Miller **812**
  Allende, I. My invented country **863**
  Allende, I. Paula **92**
  Allende, I. The sum of our days **92**
  Andersen, J. Hans Christian Andersen: a new life **92**
  Angelou, M. Letter to my daughter **92**
  Angelou, M. I know why the caged bird sings **92**
  Angelou, M. A song flung up to heaven **818**
  Armstrong, J. Love, life, Goethe **92**
  Aron, W. Hide & seek **92**
  Atlas, J. Bellow **813**
  Bair, D. Simone de Beauvoir **848**
  Baraka, I. A. The LeRoi Jones/Amiri Baraka reader **818**
  Bartlett, R. Tolstoy **891.7**
  Bate, J. Soul of the age **822.3**
  Bellow, S. Saul Bellow **92**
  Bigsby, C. Arthur Miller **92**
  Black women writers (1950-1980) **810**
  Blight, D. W. American oracle **973.7**
  Bloom, H. Hamlet: poem unlimited **822.3**
  Bloom, H. Shakespeare: the invention of the human **822.3**
  Bloom, H. The Western canon **809**
  Boyce, C. Critical companion to William Shake-

speare 822.3
Boyd, V. Wrapped in rainbows 92
Brown, T. The life of W.B. Yeats 821
Bryson, B. Shakespeare 822.3
Butler, C. The practical Shakespeare 822.3
Callow, P. Chekhov, the hidden ground 891.7
Chekhov, A. P. Anton Chekhov's life and thought 92
Cliff, N. The Shakespeare riots 974.4
Collins, P. The book of William 822.3
Conversations with Nadine Gordimer 823
Danticat, E. Brother, I'm dying 92
Danticat, E. Create dangerously 92
Dowling, R. M. Critical companion to Eugene O'Neill 812
Eisler, B. Chopin's funeral 92
Eisler, B. Naked in the marketplace 92
Ellison, R. The collected essays of Ralph Ellison 814
Ellison, R. Going to the territory 818
Ellmann, R. James Joyce 92
Ellmann, R. Oscar Wilde 92
Existentialism from Dostoevsky to Sartre 142
Fargnoli, A. N. Critical companion to James Joyce 823
Feiffer, J. Backing into forward 92
Fisher, J. T. On the Irish waterfront 331.7
Folklore, memoirs, and other writings 398
Foote, H. Beginnings 812
Foster, R. F. W.B. Yeats: a life 821
Foster, R. F. W.B. Yeats: a life 821
Fraser, A. Must you go? 92
Fraser, K. Ornament and silence 809
Frye, N. Northrop Frye on Shakespeare 822.3
Fuegi, J. Brecht and company 92
Garber, M. Shakespeare after all 822.3
Garber, M. Shakespeare and modern culture 822.3
Gates, H. L. Thirteen ways of looking at a black man 920.71
Gibson, I. Federico Garcia Lorca: a life 92
Gillespie, C. Critical companion to Toni Morrison 813
Gillespie, M. A. Maya Angelou 92
Gioia, D. Can poetry matter? 809.1
Gordon, L. G. The world of Samuel Beckett, 1906-1946 848
Gordon, L. T.S. Eliot 92
Gottfried, M. Arthur Miller 92
Greenblatt, S. J. Will in the world 822.3
The Greenwood companion to Shakespeare 822.3
Hansberry, L. To be young, gifted, and Black 92
Harlan, E. George Sand 92
Hastings, S. The secret lives of Somerset Maugham 92
Havel, V. To the castle and back 92
Heaney, S. Finders keepers 821
Heilpern, J. John Osborne 92

Heintzelman, G. Critical companion to Tennessee Williams 812
Hellman, L. Pentimento 92
Heylin, C. So long as men can breathe 822.3
Hogan, L. The woman who watches over the world 818
Honan, P. Christopher Marlowe 92
Hooks, B. Belonging 92
Hooks, B. Wounds of passion 92
Hughes, L. I wonder as I wander 818
Hurston, Z. N. Dust tracks on a road 92
Jack, B. E. George Sand 843
Jones, S. L. Critical companion to Zora Neale Hurston 813
Kazin, A. An American procession 810
Keene, D. Five modern Japanese novelists 895.6
Kenji Yoshino A thousand times more fair 822.3
Kermode, F. An appetite for poetry 801
Kermode, F. Shakespeare's language 822.3
Kiberd, D. Ulysses and us 823
Lamb, C. Tales from Shakespeare 822.3
Langer, L. L. Admitting the Holocaust 940.53
Lessing, D. M. Under my skin 92
Lever, M. Beaumarchais 92
Leverich, L. Tom 92
Malcolm, J. Reading Chekhov 891.7
Marshall, P. Triangular road 92
Martin, S. Born standing up 92
Martinson, D. Lillian Hellman 92
McCrum, R. Wodehouse 92
Meade, M. Dorothy Parker 92
Middlebrook, D. W. Anne Sexton 811
Milford, N. Savage beauty: the life of Edna St. Vincent Millay 92
Milosz, C. To begin where I am 891.8
Morris, S. J. Rage for fame: the ascent of Clare Boothe Luce 92
Murphy, R. E. Critical companion to T.S. Eliot 811
Nabokov, V. V. Lectures on literature 808.3
Nabokov, V. V. Lectures on Russian literature 891.7
Nicholl, C. The reckoning 92
Night wraps the sky 92
Norwich, J. J. Shakespeare's kings 822.3
O'Brien, E. James Joyce 823
The Oxford companion to Shakespeare 822.3
Paul, J. R. Unlikely allies 973.3
Pearson, R. Voltaire almighty 92
Peters, S. Bernard Shaw 822
Pierpont, C. R. Passionate minds 810
Playwrights at work 812
Rampersad, A. The life of Langston Hughes Volume I: 1902-1941 92
Rampersad, A. The life of Langston Hughes Volume II: 1941-1967 818
Rao, C. In Hanuman's hands 92
Rasmussen, E. The Shakespeare thefts 822.3

Remnick, D. Reporting **814**

Rosenbaum, R. The Shakespeare wars **822.3**

Ross, D. A. Critical companion to William Butler Yeats **821**

Rowley, H. Richard Wright **813**

Rudnick, P. I shudder **92**

Salamon, J. Wendy and the lost boys

Samuel Beckett's Waiting for Godot **842**

Sartre, J. P. The words **92**

Savigneau, J. Carson McCullers **813**

Sebald, W. G. On the natural history of destruction **833**

Shakespeare, W. The complete works **822.3**

Shapiro, J. Contested Will **822.3**

Shapiro, J. A year in the life of William Shakespeare, 1599 **822.3**

Simon, N. The play goes on **812**

Simon, N. Rewrites **812**

Soyinka, W. You must set forth at dawn **92**

Spoto, D. The kindness of strangers: the life of Tennessee Williams **92**

Stoppard, T. Rosencrantz and Guildenstern are dead **822**

Strathern, P. The artist, the philosopher, and the warrior **920**

Thursby, J. S. Critical companion to Maya Angelou **818**

Todd, O. Albert Camus **848**

Unger, M. J. Machiavelli **92**

Vendler, H. H. Coming of age as a poet **820**

Vidal, G. Point to point navigation **92**

Viroli, M. Niccolo's smile: a biography of Machiavelli **92**

Volkov, S. St. Petersburg **947**

Wall, C. A. Women of the Harlem Renaissance **810**

Weldon, F. Auto da Fay **823**

Wells, S. W. Shakespeare: for all time **822.3**

Wills, G. Verdi's Shakespeare **822.3**

Worthen, J. D.H. Lawrence **92**

Worthen, J. D.H. Lawrence, the early years, 1885-1912 **92**

Wright, R. Black boy **92**

Wullschlager, J. Hans Christian Andersen **839.8**

Zora Neale Hurston **813**

Zora Neale Hurston: a life in letters **92**

DRAMATISTS

See also Authors; Drama

DRAMATISTS -- BIOGRAPHY

Lahr, J. Joy ride **792.02**

Prideaux, S. Strindberg **839.7**

DRAMATISTS, AMERICAN

Bigsby, C. Arthur Miller **92**

Gussow, M. Edward Albee **92**

Hansberry, L. To be young, gifted, and Black **92**

Hellman, L. Pentimento **92**

Leverich, L. Tom **92**

Martinson, D. Lillian Hellman **92**

The play that changed my life **812**

Rudnick, P. I shudder **92**

DRAMATISTS, AMERICAN See American dramatists

DRAMATISTS, AMERICAN -- 20TH CENTURY -- BIOGRAPHY

Dowling, R. M. Eugene O'Neill **92**

Foote, H. Beginnings **812**

Simon, N. The play goes on **812**

DRAMATISTS, AMERICAN -- BIOGRAPHY

Lahr, J. Joy ride **792.02**

DRAMATISTS, ENGLISH

Fraser, A. Must you go? **92**

Honan, P. Christopher Marlowe **92**

Nicholl, C. The reckoning **92**

Peters, S. Bernard Shaw **822**

DRAMATISTS, FRENCH

Lever, M. Beaumarchais **92**

Drape, Joe

American Pharoah **798.4**

Black maestro **92**

DRAPERIES

The complete photo guide to window treatments **646.2**

DRAPERIES

See also Interior design; Upholstery

DRAPERY See Draperies

DRAPERY IN ART

Bradley, B. Drawing people **743.4**

Dratel, Joshua L.

(ed) The torture papers **973.931**

Draw Horses in 15 Minutes. Hand, D. **743.6**

DRAWING

Abel, J. Mastering comics **741.5**

Bradley, B. Drawing people **743.4**

Brehm, M. Drawing perspective **742**

Crilley, M. The realism challenge **751.4**

Hand, D. Draw Horses in 15 Minutes **743.6**

Huston, S. Figure drawing for artists **743.4**

Norling, E. R. Perspective made easy **742**

Willenbrink, M. Drawing for the absolute beginner **741.2**

DRAWING

See also Art; Graphic arts

DRAWING -- TECHNIQUE

101 top tips from professional manga artists **741.5**

De Reyna, R. How to draw what you see **741.2**

Edwards, B. Drawing on the Right Side of the Brain **741.2**

Freehand **741.2**

Parks, C. S. Secrets to drawing realistic faces **743.42**

Drawing Blood. Crabapple, M. **92**

Drawing down the moon. Adler, M. **133.4**

Drawing for the absolute beginner. Willenbrink,

M.   **741.2**

Drawing on the Right Side of the Brain. Edwards, B.   **741.2**

Drawing people. Bradley, B.   **743.4**

Drawing perspective. Brehm, M.   **742**

Drawing the line. Wise, S. M.   **179**

Drawing words & writing pictures. Abel, J.   **741.5**

DRAWING, AMERICAN -- 19TH CENTURY

   Katz, H. L. Civil War sketch book   **973.7**

Drawing: mastering the language of visual expression. Micklewright, K.   **741.2**

DRAWINGS *See* Drawing

Drawn with the sword. McPherson, J. M.   **973.7**

DRAWN WORK

   See also Embroidery; Needlework

Dray, Philip

   At the hands of persons unknown   **364.1**

   Capitol men   **920**

   There is power in a union   **331.8**

A **dreadful** deceit. Jones, J.   **305.8**

Dream boogie. Guralnick, P.   **92**

Dream cars. Gross, K.   **629.222**

The **dream** encyclopedia. Lewis, J. R.   **154.6**

Dream home. Scott, D.   **643.12**

DREAM INTERPRETATION *See* Dreams

Dream makers, dream breakers. Rowan, C. T.   **92**

The **dream** manager. Kelly, M.   **658.3**

The **dream** of enlightenment. Gottlieb, A.   **190**

The **dream** of reason. Gottlieb, A.   **180**

The **dream** of the unified field. Graham, J.   **811**

The **dream** songs. Berryman, J.   **811**

Dream team. McCallum, J.   **796.323**

Dreamer of Dune. Herbert, B.   **813**

Dreamers. Truax, E.   **325**

DREAMING *See* Dreams

Dreaming in French. Kaplan, A.   **944**

Dreaming with his eyes open. Marnham, P.   **92**

Dreamland. Sachar, H. M.   **940.5**

Dreamland. Randall, D. K.   **612.8**

Dreamland. Quinones, S.   **362.29**

DREAMS

   The basic writings of Sigmund Freud   **150.19**

   Freud, S. Interpretation of dreams   **154.6**

   Jung, C. G. Man and his symbols   **150.19**

   Randall, D. K. Dreamland   **612.8**

DREAMS -- ENCYCLOPEDIAS

   Lewis, J. R. The dream encyclopedia   **154.6**

Dreams and shadows. Wright, R.   **956.05**

Dreams from my father. Obama, B.   **92**

Dreams of a great small nation. McNamara, K. J.   **943.703**

Dreams of earth and sky. Dyson, F. J.   **500**

Dreams to remember. Ribowsky, M.   **92**

Dreazen, Yochi

   The invisible front   **92**

DREDGING

   See also Civil engineering; Hydraulic engineering

Dreger, Alice

   Galileo's middle finger   **174.2**

Dregni, Michael

   Django: the life and music of a Gypsy legend   **92**

Dreifus, Claudia

   Higher education?   **378**

Dreiser, Theodore, 1871-1945

   About

   Kazin, A. An American procession   **810**

   A Theodore Dreiser encyclopedia   **813**

Dreman, David

   Contrarian investment strategies   **332.601**

DRESS *See* Clothing and dress

DRESS ACCESSORIES

   Doh, J. Signature styles   **646.4**

   Dosen, S. Woodland knits   **746.43**

DRESS ACCESSORIES *See* Fashion accessories

Dress your family in corduroy and denim. Sedaris, D.   **814**

Dresser, Norine

   Multicultural manners   **395**

   Saying goodbye to someone you love   **155.9**

Dressing the Decades. Dirix, E.   **391.009**

The **dressmaker** of Khair Khana. Lemmon, G. T.   **92**

DRESSMAKERS

   Lemmon, G. T. The dressmaker of Khair Khana   **92**

   Miller, M. R. Betsy Ross and the making of America   **92**

Dressmaking. Smith, A.   **646.4**

DRESSMAKING

   Betzina, S. Power sewing step-by-step   **646.4**

   Doh, J. Signature styles   **646.4**

   Hirsch, G. Gertie's ultimate dress book   **646.4**

   Lemmon, G. T. The dressmaker of Khair Khana   **92**

   Mitnick, S. The Colette sewing handbook   **646.4**

   New complete guide to sewing   **646.2**

   Smith, A. Dressmaking   **646.4**

   Veblen, S. The complete photo guide to perfect fitting   **646.4**

DRESSMAKING

   See also Clothing and dress; Clothing industry

DRESSMAKING -- PATTERN DESIGN -- PICTORIAL WORKS

   Veblen, S. The complete photo guide to perfect fitting   **646.4**

DRESSMAKING -- PATTERNS

   Abousteit, N. BurdaStyle sewing vintage modern   **646.4**

   BurdaStyle modern sewing   **646.4**

   Ito, M. Simply sewn   **646.4**

Drew, Bernard A.

   100 most popular nonfiction authors   **920.003**

DREW, NANCY (FICTITIOUS CHARACTER)
Rehak, M. Girl sleuth   **813**
The **Dreyfus** affair. Derfler, L.   **944.081**
The **Dreyfus** affair. Read, P. P.   **944.081**
Dreyfus, Alfred, 1859-1935
       About
Bredin The affair   **944.081**
Derfler, L. The Dreyfus affair   **944.081**
Read, P. P. The Dreyfus affair   **944.081**
Tuchman, B. W. The proud tower   **909.82**
Dreyfus, Renee
Hatshepsut: from queen to Pharaoh   **932**
DRIED FOODS
    See also Food
DRIED MILK
    See also Dried foods; Milk
Drift. Maddow, R.   **306.2**
DRILLING AND BORING (EARTH AND ROCKS)
    See also Hydraulic engineering; Mining engineering; Water supply engineering
DRILLING AND BORING (METAL, WOOD, ETC.)
Norwegian wood   **634.9**
DRILLING PLATFORMS
Freudenburg, W. R. Blowout in the Gulf   **363.7**
DRILLING PLATFORMS
    See also Ocean engineering; Offshore oil well drilling
Drink. Johnston, A. D.   **362.292**
Drinking arak off an ayatollah's beard. Jubber, N.   **915**
Drinking in America. Cheever, S.   **394.1**
DRINKING OF ALCOHOLIC BEVERAGES
Okrent, D. Last call   **363.4**
DRINKING OF ALCOHOLIC BEVERAGES -- HISTORY
Standage, T. A history of the world in 6 glasses   **394.1**
DRINKING OF ALCOHOLIC BEVERAGES -- UNITED STATES
Cheever, S. Drinking in America   **394.1**
DRINKING PROBLEM *See* Alcoholism; Drinking of alcoholic beverages
Drinking the devil's acre.   **641.87**
DRINKING WATER
Fagan, B. Elixir   **553.7**
DRINKING WATER
    See also Water; Water supply
DRINKING WATER -- CONTAMINATION -- HEALTH ASPECTS -- TOMS RIVER REGION
Fagin, D. Toms River   **363.72**
Drinking with men. Schaap, R.   **92**
Drinking with Miss Dutchie. Breslin, E.   **92**
DRINKS *See* Alcoholic beverages; Beverages; Liquors

Drive. Pink, D. H.   **153.1**
Drive! Goldstone, L.   **338.4**
Driven to abstraction. Waldrop, R.   **811**
Driven to delight. Michelli, J. A.   **658**
Driven to Distraction. Hallowell, E. M.   **616.85**
Driven West. Langguth, A. J.   **973.5**
DRIVERS, AUTOMOBILE *See* Automobile drivers
Driving hungry. Mosler, L.   **92**
Driving over lemons. Stewart, C.   **946.083**
Drohojowska-Philp, Hunter
Full bloom   **92**
DRONE AIRCRAFT
Cockburn, A. Kill Chain   **623.7**
Maurer, K. Hunter Killer   **92**
DRONE AIRCRAFT -- UNITED STATES -- DESIGN AND CONSTRUCTION
Whittle, R. Predator   **623.74**
DROPOUTS
    See also Students; Youth
DROUGHT-TOLERANT PLANTS
Penick, P. The water-saving garden   **635.9**
DROUGHTS
DeBuys, W. E. A great aridness   **551.6**
DROUGHTS
    See also Meteorology
DROWNING PREVENTION *See* Water safety
The **Drucker** lectures. Drucker, P. F.   **658**
Drucker, Peter F.
The Drucker lectures   **658**
DRUG ABUSE
Bailey, B. The Splendid Things We Planned   **92**
Beattie, M. Beyond codependency   **616.86**
Beattie, M. Codependent no more   **616.86**
Courtwright, D. T. Forces of habit   **362.29**
De Quincey, T. The confessions of an English opium-eater and other writings   **824**
Hamilton, T. The Secret Race   **796.62**
Kuhn, C. Buzzed   **615.7**
Peter, J. Hero of the underground   **92**
Quinones, S. Dreamland   **362.29**
Ritz, D. After the Dance   **782.42**
Streatfeild, D. Cocaine   **362.29**
DRUG ABUSE
    See also Social problems; Substance abuse
DRUG ABUSE -- PREVENTION -- HANDBOOKS, MANUALS, ETC
Larsen, L. Drug abuse sourcebook   **362.29**
DRUG ABUSE -- STUDY AND TEACHING *See* Drug education
DRUG ABUSE -- TREATMENT
Fletcher, A. M. Inside rehab   **362.29**
DRUG ABUSE -- TREATMENT
    See also Therapeutics
DRUG ABUSE -- TREATMENT -- HAND-

BOOKS, MANUALS, ETC
Larsen, L. Drug abuse sourcebook   362.29
DRUG ABUSE COUNSELING
Dahl, L. Loving Our Addicted Daughters Back to
  Life   362.29
DRUG ABUSE COUNSELING
  See also Counseling
DRUG ABUSE COUNSELORS
O'Dell, C. Miss O'Dell   92
DRUG ABUSE EDUCATION *See* Drug education
Drug abuse sourcebook. Larsen, L.   362.29
DRUG ADDICTION *See* Drug abuse
**DRUG ADDICTION -- TREATMENT -- HAND-
  BOOKS, MANUALS, ETC**
Larsen, L. Drug abuse sourcebook   362.29
DRUG ADDICTION -- UNITED STATES
Quinones, S. Dreamland   362.29
DRUG ADDICTION COUNSELING *See* Drug
  abuse counseling
DRUG ADDICTION EDUCATION *See* Drug
  education
DRUG ADDICTS
Carr, D. The night of the gun   92
Dahl, L. Loving Our Addicted Daughters Back to
  Life   362.29
Rao, C. In Hanuman's hands   92
Sacks, O. On the move   92
**DRUG ADDICTS -- MASSACHUSETTS -- BI-
  OGRAPHY**
Ruta, D. With or without you   362.29
DRUG ADDICTS -- REHABILITATION
Fletcher, A. M. Inside rehab   362.29
Ninety days   362.29
DRUG ADDICTS -- REHABILITATION
  See also Drug abuse counseling
**DRUG CONTROL -- MEXICO -- CIUDAD
  JUÁREZ**
Ainslie, R. C. The fight to save Juárez   363.45
DRUG COUNSELING *See* Drug abuse counseling
DRUG DEALERS
Hobbs, J. The short and tragic life of Robert
  Peace   92
DRUG DEALING *See* Drug traffic
DRUG EDUCATION
Hart, C. High Price   362.29
DRUG HABIT *See* Drug abuse
DRUG INDUSTRY
Elliott, C. White coat, black hat   174.2
Goldacre, B. Bad Pharma   615.107
Hilts, P. J. Protecting America's health   353.9
Petersen, M. Our daily meds   338.4
Shah, S. The body hunters   362.1
Stipp, D. The youth pill   612.6
Washington, H. A. Deadly monopolies   338.4
**DRUG INDUSTRY -- HISTORY -- UNITED
  STATES**

Tobbell, D. A. Pills, power, and policy   338.4
DRUG MISUSE *See* Drug abuse
DRUG PLANTS *See* Medical botany
DRUG PUSHERS *See* Drug traffic
DRUG RESISTANCE IN MICROORGANISMS
Blaser, M. J. Missing microbes   615.7
DRUG RESISTANCE IN MICROORGANISMS
  See also Microorganisms
DRUG THERAPY
Kramer, P. D. Ordinarily well   615.7
DRUG THERAPY
  See also Therapeutics
DRUG TRADE, ILLICIT *See* Drug traffic
DRUG TRAFFIC
Bowden, C. Murder city   364.152
Feiling, T. Cocaine nation   362.29
Garcia Marquez, G. News of a kidnapping   364.15
Gibler, J. To die in Mexico   363.45
Grillo, I. Gangster Warlords   364.106
Jimenez, S. The Book of Matt   364.1
Schou, N. Orange sunshine   363.45
Streatfeild, D. Cocaine   362.29
Watkins, D. The Cook Up   364.1
DRUG TRAFFIC
  See also Drugs and crime
DRUG TRAFFIC -- MEXICO
Ainslie, R. C. The fight to save Juárez   363.45
Quinones, S. Dreamland   362.29
Slater, D. Wolf Boys   364
DRUG USE *See* Drug abuse; Drugs
DRUG-FOOD INTERACTIONS
  See also Drug interactions; Metabolism; Nu-
  trition
DRUGS
Griffith, H. W. Complete Guide to Prescription &
  Nonprescription Drugs   615
Kuhn, C. Buzzed   615.7
Tobbell, D. A. Pills, power, and policy   338.4
DRUGS
  See also Pharmacy; Therapeutics
DRUGS -- ABUSE *See* Drug abuse
DRUGS -- ADULTERATION AND ANALYSIS
  See Pharmacology
DRUGS -- DICTIONARIES
O'Neil, M. J. The Merck index   615
DRUGS -- EFFECTIVENESS -- EVALUATION
Elliott, C. White coat, black hat   174.2
DRUGS -- MARKETING
Washington, H. A. Deadly monopolies   338.4
DRUGS -- MISUSE *See* Drug abuse
DRUGS -- PHYSIOLOGICAL EFFECT
  See also Pharmacology
DRUGS -- PSYCHOLOGICAL ASPECTS
  See also Applied psychology
**DRUGS -- RESEARCH -- UNITED STATES --
  HISTORY -- 20TH CENTURY**

Tobbell, D. A. Pills, power, and policy **338.4**

DRUGS -- TESTING

Goldacre, B. Bad Pharma **615.107**

DRUGS -- TESTING

    See also Consumer protection; Pharmacology

DRUGS AND CRIME

Martínez, R. Desert America **330.9**

DRUMMERS

The Beatles anthology **782.421**

Dance, S. The world of Count Basie **920**

Goldsmith, M. The inextinguishable symphony **940.53**

Spitz, B. The Beatles: the biography **920**

The **Drummond** Girls. Link, M. J. **92**

DRUMS

    See also Musical instruments; Percussion instruments

DRUNK DRIVING

    See also Crime; Drinking of alcoholic beverages

Drunk stoned brilliant dead. Meyerowitz, R. **051**

Drunkard. Steinberg, N. **92**

The **Drunkard's** walk. Mlodinow, L. **519.2**

DRUNKARDS See Alcoholics

The **drunken** botanist. Stewart, A. **581.6**

DRUNKENNESS See Alcoholism; Temperance

Drury, Bob

The heart of everything that is **92**

Druyan, Ann

Sagan, C. Comet **523.6**

DRY CLEANING

    See also Cleaning

DRY FARMING

    See also Agriculture

DRY GOODS See Fabrics

Dry, Sarah

Curie **92**

Dryden, John

All for love **822**

John Dryden **821**

(tr) Plutarch: the lives of the noble Grecians and Romans **920**

Drysdale, Rosemary

Entrelac **746.432**

DSK. Solomon, J. **306.77**

Du Bois, W. E. B. (William Edward Burghardt), 1868-1963

The souls of Black folk **305.8**

Writings **814**

The Oxford W. E. B. Du Bois reader **305.896**

    About

Cornel West on Black prophetic fire **92**

Gates, H. L. The future of the race **305.896**

Lewis, D. L. W.E.B. Du Bois **92**

Morris, A. D. The scholar denied **301**

DUAL-CAREER FAMILIES

Warner, J. Perfect madness **306.8**

Duany, Andrés, 1949-

Suburban nation **307.76**

Duarte, Nancy

Resonate **658.452**

DUBAI (UNITED ARAB EMIRATES)

Krane, J. City of gold **953**

Duberman, Martin

Hold tight gently **920**

Howard Zinn **92**

    About

Duberman, M. B. The Martin Duberman reader **306.76**

Dubin, Murray

(jt. auth) Biddle, D. R. Tasting freedom **92**

Dubner, Stephen J.

Dubner, S. J. Freakonomics **330**

Levitt, S. D. Superfreakonomics **330**

Dubofsky, Melvyn

Labor in America **331.8**

Dubois, Laurent

Haiti **972.94**

Dubus, Andre, 1959-

    About

Dubus, A. Townie **92**

Duchamp. Tomkins, C. **709**

Duchamp, Marcel, 1887-1968

    About

Tomkins, C. Duchamp **709**

DUCKS

    See also Birds; Poultry

Duckworth, Angela

Grit **158.1**

Duclos, Andrea

The plantiful table **641.5**

Dudamel, Gustavo

    About

Tunstall, T. Changing lives **780.7**

Dudden, Faye E.

Fighting chance **324.6**

Due considerations. Updike, J. **814**

DUE PROCESS OF LAW

    See also Administration of justice; Civil rights

Duel With the Devil. Collins, P. **364.152**

DUELING

    See also Manners and customs; Martial arts

Duff Bakes. Goldman, D. **641.81**

Duff Bakes.

Duffield, Mary Rose

Plants for dry climates **635.9**

Duffy, Eamon

Saints & sinners **282**

Duffy, James P., 1941-

War at the end of the world **940.54**

Duffy, Michael

The presidents club **973.92**

Duffy, Scott
Launch!   **658.1**

Duflo, Esther
(jt. auth) Banerjee, A. V. Poor economics   **339.4**

Dufty, David F.
How to build an android   **629.8**

Dufty, William
Holiday, B. Lady sings the blues   **92**

Dugan, Alan
Poems seven   **811**

Duguid, Naomi
Alford, J. Beyond the Great Wall   **641.5**
(jt. auth) Alford, J. Flatbreads and flavors   **641.8**
(jt. auth) Alford, J. Hot, sour, salty, sweet   **641.59**
Burma   **641.59**
Taste of Persia   **641.5**

Duhamel, Denise
Ka-ching!   **811**

Duhigg, Charles
Smarter faster better   **158**

Duiker, William J.
Ho Chi Minh   **959.704**

Duino elegies. Rilke, R. M.   **831**

Duke. Teachout, T.   **92**

DUKE UNIVERSITY
Cohan, W. D. The price of silence   **364.15**

DUKE UNIVERSITY -- BASKETBALL -- HISTORY
Feinstein, J. The legends club   **796.323**

Duke University/Center for Documentary Studies
Hirsch, E. How to read a poem   **808.1**

Duke, James A.
Peterson field guide to medicinal plants and herbs of eastern and central North America   **581.6**

Duke, Lynne
Mandela, Mobutu, and me   **968.06**

Dull Knife, Cheyenne Chief, d. 1883
       About
Brown, D. A. The American West   **978**

Dulles, Allen Welsh, 1893-1969
       About
Grose, P. Gentleman spy   **92**
Talbot, D. The Devil's Chessboard   **92**

Dulles, Foster Rhea
Dubofsky, M. Labor in America   **331.8**

Dumanoski, Dianne
The end of the long summer   **551.6**

Dumas, Alexandre, 1802-1870
       About
The Black Count   **944.04**

Dumas, Thomas Alexandre, 1762-1806
       About
The Black Count   **944.04**

DUMPLINGS
Asian dumplings   **641.59**
Wong, L. A. Dumplings All Day Wong   **641.59**

Dumplings All Day Wong. Wong, L. A.   **641.59**

DUMPS, TOXIC *See* Hazardous waste sites

Dunaway, David King
How can I keep from singing?   **92**

Dunbar, Robin
Human evolution   **155.7**

Dunbar-Ortiz, Roxanne
An indigenous peoples' history of the United States   **970.004**

Duncan, Dayton
Lewis & Clark   **917**
The national parks   **333.7**
Ward, G. C. The West   **978**

Duncan, Isadora, 1877-1927
       About
Duncan, I. My life   **92**
Life stories   **920**

Duncan, James
(ed) 2015 songwriter's market   **338.4**

Duncan, Robert Edward
Selected poems   **811**

Dunckley, Victoria L.
Reset your child's brain   **004.67**

Dungy, Camille T.
(ed) Black nature   **808**

Dunham, William
The mathematical universe   **510**

Dunjee, Roscoe, 1883-1965
       About
Ellison, R. The collected essays of Ralph Ellison   **814**

DUNKERQUE (FRANCE), BATTLE OF, 1940
Clark, L. Blitzkrieg   **940.54**

Dunlop, Fuchsia
Every grain of rice   **641.59**
Land of fish and rice   **641.5**

Dunn Chace, Teri
Seeing seeds   **581.4**

Dunn, Anna
(jt. auth) Tarlow, A. Dinner at the Long Table **641.5**

Dunn, Gwenavere W.
(ed) The who, what, and where of America   **317.3**

Dunn, Jancee
(jt. auth) Lauper, C. Cyndi Lauper   **92**

Dunn, Jon
Alderfer, J. National Geographic birding essentials   **598**

Dunn, Patricia A.
Grammar rants   **428**

Dunn, Rob
The wild life of our bodies   **579**

Dunn, Stephen
Different hours   **811**
Local visitations   **811**
Loosestrife   **811**
New & selected poems, 1974-1994   **811**

Dunn, Susan
Burns, J. M. The three Roosevelts   973.91
Sister revolutions   973.3
Dunnavant, Keith
Montana   92
Dunne, Jemima
(ed) Tractor   629.225
Dunne, John Gregory, 1932-2003
About
Didion, J. The year of magical thinking   92
Dunne, Pete, 1951-
Pete Dunne on bird watching   598
Dunne, P. Pete Dunne's essential field guide companion   598
Dunnigan, James F.
The Pacific War encyclopedia   940.54
Dunning, John B.
(ed) Sibley, D. The Sibley guide to bird life & behavior   598
DUPLICATE BRIDGE See Bridge (Game)
Dupree, Nathalie
Mastering the art of Southern cooking   641.59
DuPriest, Laura
Natural beauty   646.7
Dupuy, Jessica
Cole, T. Uchi: the cookbook   641.6
Duran, Roberto
About
Kimball, G. Four kings   920
Durand, Faith
The Kitchn cookbook   641.5
Durant, John
Spartan Fit   613.7
Durant, Judith
(ed) Crochet one-skein wonders for babies 746.434
Cable left, cable right   746.432
Increase, decrease   746.43
(ed) One-skein wonders for babies   746.43
Durant, William James
The story of philosophy   109
Durham, Eddie, 1906-1987
About
Dance, S. The world of Count Basie   920
Durham, M. Gigi
The Lolita effect   302.23
Durham, Michael S.
Desert between the mountains   979
Durham, Teva
Loop-d-loop crochet   746.43
Durieux, Arnaud
Englehart, M. AC/DC   920
Durkheim, Emile
Suicide, a study in sociology   179.7
Duron, Lori
Raising my rainbow   306.87
Durrenmatt, Friedrich

The visit   832
Dusoulier, Clotilde
The French market cookbook   641.5
DUST
See also Air pollution
Dust bowl girls. Reeder, L.   796.323
DUST STORMS
Egan, T. The worst hard time   978
DUST STORMS
See also Droughts; Erosion; Storms
Dust to dust. Busch, B.   92
Dust tracks on a road. Hurston, Z. N.   92
DUTCH PAINTING
Liedtke, W. A. Vermeer and the Delft school 759.9
Dutchman, and The slave. Baraka, I. A.   812
DUTIES See Tariff; Taxation
Dutrow, Barbara
Klein, C. Manual of mineral science   549
Dutton's nautical navigation. Cutler, T. J. 623.89
Dutton, Benjamin
Cutler, T. J. Dutton's nautical navigation 623.89
Dutton, Kevin
Split-second persuasion   153.8
DUTY
See also Ethics; Human behavior
Duty first. Ruggero, E.   355
DuVal, Kathleen
Independence Lost   973.3
Duvalier, Francois, 1907-1971
About
Von Tunzelmann, A. Red heat   972.9
Duveen, Joseph Duveen, Baron, 1869-1939
About
Brewer, J. The American Leonardo   759
Duyff, Roberta Larson
American Dietetic Association complete food and nutrition guide   613.2
Dvorak, John
Earthquake Storms   551.22
DWARF TREES
See also Trees
DWELLINGS See Domestic architecture; Houses; Housing
DWELLINGS -- BARRIER-FREE DESIGN
Pierce, D. The accessible home   728.087
DWELLINGS -- ELECTRIC EQUIPMENT -- AMATEURS' MANUALS
The complete guide to wiring   621.319
DWELLINGS -- FIRES AND FIRE PREVENTION -- UNITED STATES
Soles, C. The fire smart home handbook   643
DWELLINGS -- REMODELING
Carlson, J. Remodelista   747
Petersik, S. Lovable livable home   645
Scott, D. Dream home   643.12
DWELLINGS -- REMODELING -- AMATEURS'

MANUALS
101 Saturday morning projects **643**
The complete guide to plumbing **696**
**DWELLINGS -- UNITED STATES -- MAINTE-
NANCE AND REPAIR**
The best homes from This old house **643**
DWELLINGS IN ART
Van Doren, A. The house tells the story **728**
Dwight D. Eisenhower. Wicker, T. **973.921**
Dwork, Deborah
Holocaust: a history **940.53**
Dwyer, Jim
102 minutes **974.7**
More awesome than money **384.3**
Dwyer, Johnny
American warlord **966.62**
Dwyer, Timothy
(jt. auth) Peyser, M. Hissing cousins **92**
Dyce, Carol
(jt. auth) Cross, C. The baby book **649.122**
DYE INDUSTRY -- GREAT BRITAIN
Garfield, S. Mauve **667**
Dyer, Alan
Dickinson, T. The backyard astronomer's guide **522**
Dyer, Geoff
The missing of the Somme **940.4**
Otherwise known as the human condition **824**
Dyer, Wayne W.
The power of intention **158**
DYES AND DYEING
Callahan, G. Hand dyeing yarn and fleece **746.6**
Garfield, S. Mauve **667**
Greenfield, A. B. A perfect red **667**
DYES AND DYEING
See also Color; Pigments; Textile chemistry;
Textile industry
DYING CHILDREN *See* Terminally ill children
DYING PATIENTS *See* Terminally ill
Dyja, Thomas
The third coast **977.3**
Dykstra, Lenny, 1963-
House of nails **796.357**
Dylan Goes Electric! Wald, E. **781.66**
Dylan Thomas: a new life. Lycett, A. **92**
Dylan, Bob, 1941-
About
Bell, I. Once upon a time **92**
Brown, D. Bob Dylan **92**
Dylan, B. Chronicles **92**
Gray, M. The Bob Dylan encyclopedia **782.42**
DYNAMICS
See also Mathematics; Mechanics
DYNAMITE
See also Explosives
The **dynamite** club. Merriman, J. M. **363.32**
DYSFUNCTIONAL FAMILIES

Pilgrim's wilderness **92**
DYSLEXIA
Foss, B. The dyslexia empowerment plan **618.92**
Schultz, P. My dyslexia **92**
DYSLEXIA
See also Reading disability
The **dyslexia** empowerment plan. Foss, B. **618.92**
Dyson, Freeman J.
About
Schewe, P. F. Maverick Genius **92**
Dyson, Freeman J., 1923-
Dreams of earth and sky **500**
Dyson, George
Turing's cathedral **004**
Dyson, Michael Eric
The Black presidency **305.8**
Come hell or high water **976.3**
Holler if you hear me: searching for Tupac
Shakur **92**
I may not get there with you: the true Martin Luther
King, Jr **323**
DYSTOPIAN FICTION
Kallio, J. Read on ... speculative fiction for
teens **016**
DYSTOPIAN FICTION
See also Fantasy fiction; Science fiction
DYSTOPIAS
See also Political science
DYSTOPIAS -- FICTION *See* Dystopian fiction

E

E. Bodanis, D. **530.1**
E-MAIL
D'Agata, J. The lifespan of a fact **808.02**
E-MAIL
See also Data transmission systems; Telecom-
munication
**E-MAIL REFERENCE SERVICES (LIBRAR-
IES)** *See* Electronic reference services (Librar-
ies)
E-metrics for library and information professionals.
White, A. C. **025.2**
E. B. White. Elledge, S. **92
E.E. Cummings. Sawyer-Laucanno, C. **92**
Eaarth. McKibben, B. **253**
Eads, James Buchanan, 1820-1887
About
Barry, J. M. Rising tide **977**
Eady, Cornelius
Brutal imagination **811**
Eagle against the sun. Spector, R. **940.54**
Eagle, Ellen
Pastel painting atelier **741.235**
Eagle, MK
Answering teens' tough questions **027.62**
Eagleman, David

The brain   **612.82**
Incognito   **153**
EAGLES
    See also Birds; Birds of prey
Eagleton, Thomas F., 1929-2007
       About
Glasser, J. M. The eighteen-day running mate   **973.924**
Eakins, Thomas, 1844-1916
       About
Thomas Eakins   **759.13**
Eames, Charles
       About
Albrecht, D. The Work of Charles and Ray Eames   **745.4**
Eames, Ray
       About
Albrecht, D. The Work of Charles and Ray Eames   **745.4**
Earhart, Amelia, 1898-1937
       About
Butler, S. East to the dawn   **629.13**
Winters, K. C. Amelia Earhart   **92**
Earle, Sylvia A.
The world is blue   **551.46**
Earley, Mark W.
(ed) National electrical code handbook 2014 **621.3**
Earley, Pete
Resilience   **616.89**
EARLY CHILDHOOD EDUCATION
Ghoting, S. N. STEP into storytime   **027.62**
EARLY CHILDHOOD EDUCATION
    See also Education
EARLY CHILDHOOD EDUCATION -- UNITED STATES
Lahey, J. The gift of failure   **649**
Tough, P. How children succeed   **372.21**
EARLY CHRISTIAN LITERATURE
    See also Christian literature; Literature; Medieval literature
EARLY CHURCH HISTORY *See* Church history -- 30-600, Early church
The early national period. Purcell, S. J.   **973.4**
EARLY PRINTED BOOKS
    See also Books
Earnhardt Nation. Busbee, J.   **796.72**
Earp, Wyatt, 1848-1929
       About
Barra, A. Inventing Wyatt Earp   **92**
Tefertiller, C. Wyatt Earp   **92**
Earth. Alley, R. B.   **621**
Earth. Fortey, R. A.   **551.7**
Earth.   **550**
EARTH
    See also Planets; Solar system
EARTH

Earth. Siinger de Boer, J. Earthquakes in hum   **550**
EARTH -- AGE
Hazen, R. M. The story of Earth   **550**
EARTH -- CRUST
    See also Earth -- Internal structure
EARTH -- GRAVITY *See* Gravity
EARTH -- HISTORY -- POPULAR WORKS
Childs, C. Apocalyptic planet   **550**
EARTH -- INTERNAL STRUCTURE
Hazen, R. M. The story of Earth   **550**
Whitehouse, D. Into the Heart of Our World   **551**
EARTH -- MAPS
Oxford Atlas of the world   **912**
EARTH -- ORIGIN
Flannery, T. Here on Earth   **551**
Shubin, N. H. The universe within   **550**
The **earth** moved. Stewart, A.   **592**
The **Earth** moves. Hofstadter, D.   **509**
Earth ponds. Matson, T.   **627**
EARTH SCIENCES
Alvarez, W. A Most Improbable Journey   **508**
Flannery, T. Here on Earth   **551**
Gates, A. E. A to Z of earth scientists   **920.003**
Hazen, R. M. The story of Earth   **550**
Lamothe, M. The where, the why, and the how **502**
Rothman, J. Nature anatomy   **508**
Startalk   **523.1**
EARTH SCIENCES
    See also Physical sciences; Science
EARTH SCIENCES -- ENCYCLOPEDIAS
Allaby, M. The encyclopedia of Earth   **910**
EARTH SCIENCES -- HISTORY
Rudwick, M. J. S. Earth's deep history   **550**
EARTH SCIENCES -- STUDY AND TEACHING (MIDDLE SCHOOL) -- PICTORIAL WORKS
Rothman, J. Nature anatomy   **508**
The **earth** shall weep. Wilson, J.   **970.004**
EARTH SHELTERED HOUSES
    See also House construction; Houses; Underground architecture
Earth under fire. Braasch, G.   **363.7**
Earth's deep history. Rudwick, M. J. S.   **550**
EARTH, EFFECT OF MAN ON *See* Human influence on nature
EARTH-FRIENDLY TECHNOLOGY *See* Green technology
EARTHENWARE *See* Pottery
Earthly measures. Hirsch, E.   **811**
EARTHQUAKE RELIEF -- HAITI
Katz, J. M. The big truck that went by   **363.34**
EARTHQUAKE SEA WAVES *See* Tsunamis
Earthquake Storms. Dvorak, J.   **551.22**
EARTHQUAKES
Hough, S. E. Richter's scale   **92**
Palmer, J. Heaven cracks, earth shakes   **951**
Whitehouse, D. Into the Heart of Our World   **551**

Zeilinga de Boer, J. Earthquakes in human history **363.34**

EARTHQUAKES
>See also Earth; Geology; Natural disasters; Physical geography

EARTHQUAKES -- CALIFORNIA
Dvorak, J. Earthquake Storms **551.22**

EARTHQUAKES -- CALIFORNIA -- SAN FRANCISCO -- HISTORY -- 20TH CENTURY
Winchester, S. A crack in the edge of the world **979.4**

EARTHQUAKES -- ENCYCLOPEDIAS
Gates, A. E. Encyclopedia of earthquakes and volcanoes **551.2**

EARTHQUAKES -- PSYCHOLOGICAL ASPECTS
McClelland, M. Irritable hearts **92**

EARTHQUAKES -- UNITED STATES
Feldman, J. When the Mississippi ran backwards **551.2**

Earthquakes in human history. Zeilinga de Boer, J. **363.34**

EARTHWORKS (ARCHEOLOGY) See Excavations (Archeology)

EARTHWORKS (ART)
>See also Art

EARTHWORMS
Stewart, A. The earth moved **592**

Easson, Angus
(ed) Gaskell, E. C. The life of Charlotte Bronte **92**

EAST AFRICA
Chretien The great lakes of Africa **967.6**

EAST AFRICA
>See also Africa

EAST AFRICA -- DESCRIPTION AND TRAVEL
Beard, P. H. The end of the game **967.6**
Grant, R. Crazy river **916**

EAST AFRICA -- FOREIGN RELATIONS -- UNITED STATES
Shachtman, T. Airlift to America **378.1**

EAST AFRICA -- HISTORY
Jeal, T. Explorers of the Nile **962**

EAST AFRICA -- SOCIAL CONDITIONS
Grant, R. Crazy river **916**

EAST AND WEST
Ernst, C. W. Following Muhammad **297**
Fuller, G. E. A world without Islam **297**
Morris, I. Why the West rules--for now **909**

EAST AND WEST
>See also International relations

EAST AND WEST -- HISTORY
Frankopan, P. The Silk Roads **909**

EAST ASIA
Fallows, J. M. Looking at the sun **950**

EAST ASIA -- RELIGION

Eastern religions **200.9**

EAST ASIAN POETRY
Hong, C. P. Engine empire **811**

EAST INDIAN AMERICANS
Rao, C. In Hanuman's hands **92**

EAST INDIANS -- AUSTRALIA -- BIOGRAPHY
Brierley, S. A long way home **92**

EAST INDIANS -- ENGLAND -- LONDON
Seth, V. Two lives **92**

EAST INDIANS -- SOUTH AFRICA -- POLITICS AND GOVERNMENT
Guha, R. Gandhi before India **92**

East to the dawn. Butler, S. **629.13**

East West Street. Sands, P. **345**

East, Elyssa
Dogtown **974.4**

EASTER
>See also Christian holidays; Holy Week

EASTER ISLAND
Easter Island's silent sentinels **990**
Easter Island's silent sentinels. **990**
Eastern body, Western mind. Judith, A. **150.19**

EASTERN CHURCHES
>See also Christian sects; Christianity

EASTERN EUROPE
The fault line **914**
Hercules, O. Mamushka **641.594**

EASTERN EUROPE -- HISTORY -- 1918-1945
Snyder, T. D. Bloodlands **940.54**

EASTERN EUROPE -- POLITICS AND GOVERNMENT
Drakulic, S. Cafe Europa **947**
Kotkin, S. Uncivil society **947**
Pleshakov, K. There is no freedom without bread! **947**
Sebestyen, V. Revolution 1989 **947**
Stokes, G. The walls came tumbling down **947.085**

EASTERN EUROPE -- POLITICS AND GOVERNMENT -- 1945-1989
Applebaum, A. Iron curtain **947**

EASTERN EUROPE -- SOCIAL CONDITIONS
Drakulic, S. Cafe Europa **947**
Kotkin, S. Uncivil society **947**

EASTERN HEMISPHERE -- HISTORY
Watson, P. The great divide **909**
Eastern religions. **200.9**
The **Eastern** stars. Kurlansky, M. **796.357**

EASY AND QUICK COOKING See Quick and easy cooking

An **easy** burden. Young, A. **92**
Easy Gourmet. Le, S. **641.5**
Easy information sources for ESL, adult learners, & new readers. Riechel, R. **016**

EASY READING MATERIALS
>See also Children's literature; Reading materials

Easy riders, raging bulls. Biskind, P.   **791.43**

Easy to love, difficult to discipline. Bailey, R. A. **155**

Eat it up! Vinton, S. B.   **641.5**

The **Eat** Like a Man Guide to Feeding a Crowd. **641.5**

Eat Mexico. Tellez, L.   **641.597**

Eat Pray Love Made Me Do It.   **910.4**

Eat street. Carruthers, J.   **641.76**

Eat that frog! Tracy, B.   **640**

Eat, Play, Sleep. DeSouza, L.   **649.122**

Eat, pray, love. Gilbert, E.   **92**

Eat, sleep, poop. Cohen, S. W.   **618.92**

Eataly Srl

  (comp) How to eataly   **641.594**

Eathorne, Alison Malone

  (jt. auth) Malone, H. The Power of Pulses **635.65**

EATING *See* Dining; Gastronomy

Eating animals. Foer, J. S.   **641.3**

EATING CUSTOMS

  Altmann, T. R. What to feed your baby **649.3**

  Animal, vegetable, miracle   **641**

  Barber, D. The third plate   **641.3**

  Behr, E. The Food and Wine of France **641.5**

  Bittman, M. Food matters   **613.2**

  Collingham, E. M. Curry   **394.1**

  Consider the fork   **643**

  First bite   **641.01**

  The food of a younger land   **394.1**

  Jurafsky, D. The language of food   **641.3**

  Lappé, A. Diet for a hot planet   **641**

  Mayle, P. French lessons   **394.1**

  McWilliams, J. E. Just food   **394.1**

  Nestle, M. Why calories count   **613.2**

  Pollan, M. The omnivore's dilemma   **394.1**

  Pollan, M. In defense of food   **613**

  Rosenstrach, J. Dinner   **642**

  Rude, E. Tastes Like Chicken   **636.5**

  Standage, T. An edible history of humanity **394.1**

  Tye, D. Baking as biography   **92**

  Wrangham, R. W. Catching fire   **641.3**

EATING CUSTOMS

  See also Diet; Human behavior; Nutrition

EATING CUSTOMS -- UNITED STATES -- HISTORY

  Food in the Civil War era   **641.597**

Eating disorders. Lask, B.   **616.85**

EATING DISORDERS

  See also Abnormal psychology

EATING DISORDERS

  Brzezinski, M. Obsessed   **362.196**

  Bulik, C. M. Midlife eating disorders **616.85**

  Can I tell you about eating disorders? **616.85**

  Lock, J. Help your teenager beat an eating disorder   **616.85**

EATING DISORDERS IN ADOLESCENCE

  Lask, B. Eating disorders   **616.85**

  Lock, J. Help your teenager beat an eating disor-

der   **616.85**

EATING HABITS

  Brzezinski, M. Obsessed   **362.196**

  Consider the fork   **643**

  Fisher, M. F. K. The art of eating   **641**

  Fuentes, L. The best homemade kids' snacks on the
planet   **641.5**

  Mann, T. Secrets from the eating lab **613.2**

  Milk Bar Life   **641.86**

  Mitchell, A. Eating in the middle   **641.3**

  Wansink, B. Mindless eating   **616.85**

EATING HABITS -- ECONOMIC ASPECTS

  Cowen, T. An economist gets lunch   **394.1**

Eating in the middle. Mitchell, A.   **641.3**

Eating on the wild side. Robinson, J.   **306.4**

Eating Rome. Minchilli, E.   **641.594**

Eating the dinosaur. Klosterman, C.   **973.92**

Eating the honey of words. Bly, R.   **811**

Eating the sun. Morton, O.   **572**

Eatingwell (Company)

  (comp) Eatingwell Vegetables   **641.65**

Eatingwell Vegetables.   **641.65**

Eaton, Jan

  (jt. auth) Thomas, M. Mary Thomas's dictionary of
embroidery stitches   **746.44**

Eaton, Jonathan

  (ed) Chapman piloting & seamanship **623.88**

Eaton, William, 1764-1811

          About

  Zacks, R. The pirate coast   **973.4**

Eats, shoots & leaves. Truss, L.   **421**

The eaves of heaven. Pham, A. X.   **92**

EAVESDROPPING

  See also Criminal investigation; Right of privacy

EAVESDROPPING -- GREAT BRITAIN

  Soldaten   **940.54**

Ebadi, Shirin, 1947-

  Until We Are Free   **92**

          About

  Ebadi, S. Until We Are Free   **92**

Eberly, Merl

          About

  Tackett, M. The Baseball Whisperer **796.357**

Ebert, David A.

  A pocket guide to sharks of the world **597.3**

Ebert, Roger, 1942-2013

          About

  Ebert, R. Life itself   **92**

Ebert-Schifferer, Sybille

  Caravaggio   **92**

Ebola. Quammen, D.   **614.5**

EBOLA VIRUS

  Garrett, L. The coming plague   **614.4**

  Preston, R. The hot zone   **614.5**

  Quammen, D. Ebola   **614.5**

**EBOLA VIRUS -- PATHOGENICITY -- POPU-
LAR WORKS**
Quammen, D. Ebola **614.5**
Ebony and Ivy. Wilder, C. S. **379.26**
ECCENTRICS
The Mitfords **920**
Tingey, J. The Englishman who posted himself and
other curious objects **92**
**ECCENTRICS -- UNITED STATES -- BIOGRA-
PHY**
Dedman, B. Empty mansions **92**
ECCENTRICS AND ECCENTRICITIES
Rips, N. Trying to float **974.7**
Singer, M. Character studies **920**
ECCENTRICS AND ECCENTRICITIES
See also Curiosities and wonders; Personality
**ECCENTRICS AND ECCENTRICITIES --
FRANCE -- PARIS -- HISTORY**
Sante, L. The other Paris **944**
**ECCENTRICS AND ECCENTRICITIES -- NEW
YORK (STATE) -- NEW YORK**
Rips, N. Trying to float **974.7**
Echoes: the complete history of Pink Floyd. Povey,
G. **920**
Echols, Damien
About
Echols, D. Life after death **364.66**
Eck, Jeremiah
The distinctive home **728**
Eckener, Hugo, 1868-1954
About
Botting, D. Dr. Eckener's dream machine **629.133**
Eckert, Allan W.
A sorrow in our heart: the life of Tecumseh **977**
Eckford, Elizabeth, 1942-
About
Margolick, D. Elizabeth and Hazel **92**
Ecklund, Elaine Howard
Science vs. religion **215**
Eckman, Edie
(ed) Crochet one-skein wonders for babies **746.434**
Around the corner crochet borders **746.43**
Beyond the square crochet motifs **746.434**
Connect-the-shapes crochet motifs **746.43**
The crochet answer book **746.43**
Eckstut, Arielle
The Secret Language of Color **535.6**
Eckstut, Joann
(jt. auth) Eckstut, A. The Secret Language of Col-
or **535.6**
The **eclogues** of Virgil. Virgil **871**
Eco Barons. Humes, E. **363.7**
Eco, Umberto
History of beauty **111**
How to travel with a salmon & other essays **854**
(ed) On ugliness **111**

About
Eco, U. Confessions of a young novelist **808.3**
Ecological intelligence. Goleman, D. **333.7**
ECOLOGICAL MOVEMENT *See* Environmental
movement
ECOLOGICAL TOURISM *See* Ecotourism
ECOLOGISTS
Montaigne, F. Fraser's penguins **577.2**
ECOLOGY
Ball, P. Patterns in nature **500.2**
Burdick, A. Out of Eden **577**
Carroll, S. B. The Serengeti Rules **570**
Dinerstein, E. The kingdom of rarities **596**
Fraser, C. Rewilding the world **333.95**
Gore, A. An inconvenient truth **363.7**
Mooallem, J. Wild ones **333.95**
Novacek, M. J. Terra **576.8**
Wills, C. Green Equilibrium **577**
Wilson, E. O. The diversity of life **333.95**
A window on eternity **333.95**
ECOLOGY
See also Biology; Environment
ECOLOGY -- HISTORY
Mann, C. C. 1493 **909**
ECOLOGY -- JUVENILE LITERATURE
Leslie, C. W. The Curious Nature Guide **508**
ECOLOGY, HUMAN *See* Human ecology
ECOLOGY, SOCIAL *See* Human ecology
ECONOMIC AID *See* Foreign aid
ECONOMIC ASSISTANCE
Novogratz, J. The blue sweater **339.4**
ECONOMIC ASSISTANCE *See* Domestic eco-
nomic assistance; Foreign aid
**ECONOMIC ASSISTANCE -- DEVELOPING
COUNTRIES**
Banerjee, A. V. Poor economics **339.4**
**ECONOMIC ASSISTANCE, DOMESTIC --
UNITED STATES -- HISTORY -- 20TH CEN-
TURY**
Woods, R. B. Prisoners of hope **973.923**
ECONOMIC BIOLOGY *See* Economic botany;
Economic zoology
ECONOMIC BOTANY
Pollan, M. The botany of desire **306.4**
ECONOMIC BOTANY
See also Agriculture; Botany
ECONOMIC CONDITIONS
Acemoglu, D. Why nations fail **330**
Appleby, J. The relentless revolution **330.1**
Epping, R. C. The 21st century economy **330.9**
Kennedy, P. M. The rise and fall of the great pow-
ers **909.08**
Lanchester, J. I.O.U. **330.9**
Mann, C. C. 1493 **909**
Steil, B. The battle of Bretton Woods **339.5**
Tooze, A. The deluge **940.3**

ECONOMIC CONDITIONS
See also Business; Economics; Social conditions; Wealth

ECONOMIC CYCLES See Business cycles

ECONOMIC DEPRESSIONS See Depressions

ECONOMIC DEVELOPMENT
Brzezinski, Z. Strategic vision   **327.1**
De Graaf, J. What's the economy for, anyway?   **330.9**
Gilding, P. The great disruption   **304.2**
Harden, B. A river lost   **333.91**
Holzer, H. A just and generous nation   **973.7**
Pernick, R. Clean Tech Nation   **333.794**
Sharma, R. Breakout nations   **330.91**

ECONOMIC DEVELOPMENT
See also Economic policy; Economics

ECONOMIC DEVELOPMENT -- BRAZIL -- RIO DE JANEIRO
Barbassa, J. Dancing With the Devil in the City of God   **981.53**

ECONOMIC DEVELOPMENT -- CHINA
Osnos, E. Age of ambition   **951.06**

ECONOMIC DEVELOPMENT -- DEVELOPING COUNTRIES
Acemoglu, D. Why nations fail   **330**

ECONOMIC DEVELOPMENT -- ENVIRONMENTAL ASPECTS
Sachs, J. The age of sustainable development **338.9**

ECONOMIC DEVELOPMENT -- HISTORY
Capital in the twenty-first century   **332**

ECONOMIC DEVELOPMENT -- UNITED STATES -- HISTORY -- 19TH CENTURY
Holzer, H. A just and generous nation   **973.7**

ECONOMIC FORECASTING
Capital in the twenty-first century   **332**
Liveris, A. Make it in America   **330.9**
Sharma, R. Breakout nations   **330.91**

ECONOMIC FORECASTING
See also Business cycles; Economics; Forecasting

ECONOMIC GEOLOGY
See also Geology

ECONOMIC GROWTH See Economic development

ECONOMIC HISTORY
Appleby, J. The relentless revolution   **330.1**
Ferguson, N. The ascent of money   **330**
Kennedy, P. M. The rise and fall of the great powers   **909.08**
Lanchester, J. I.O.U.   **330.9**
Mann, C. C. 1493   **909**
McMillan, J. Reinventing the bazaar   **330.12**
Micklethwait, J. The company   **338.7**

ECONOMIC HISTORY See Economic conditions

ECONOMIC HISTORY -- 21ST CENTURY
Gore, A. The future   **303.4**

Rajan, R. G. Fault lines   **330.9**
Sharma, R. Breakout nations   **330.91**

ECONOMIC HISTORY -- ENCYCLOPEDIAS
The Oxford encyclopedia of economic history **330**

ECONOMIC HISTORY -- POLITICAL ASPECTS
Acemoglu, D. Why nations fail   **330**

ECONOMIC INDICATORS
See also Economics

ECONOMIC PLANNING See Economic policy

ECONOMIC POLICY
Patel, R. The value of nothing   **330.1**

ECONOMIC POLICY
See also Economics; Planning

ECONOMIC POLICY -- CHINA
Dikötter, F. Mao's great famine   **951.05**
McGregor, R. The Party   **324.2**

ECONOMIC POLICY -- TEXAS
Collins, G. As Texas goes   **320.6**

ECONOMIC POLICY -- UNITED STATES
Barlett, D. L. The betrayal of the American dream   **330.973**
The economists' voice 2.0   **330.9**
The great divergence   **339.2**
Haass, R. N. Foreign policy begins at home **327.73**
Herman, A. Freedom's forge   **940.53**
Krugman, P. R. End this depression now!   **330.9**
Pernick, R. Clean Tech Nation   **333.794**
Reich, R. B. Saving capitalism   **330.973**
Stone, J. M. Five easy theses   **330.973**
Vogel, K. P. Big money   **324.7**

ECONOMIC POLICY -- UNITED STATES -- HISTORY
Burgin, A. The great persuasion   **330.12**

ECONOMIC RECESSIONS See Recessions

ECONOMIC RELATIONS, FOREIGN See International economic relations

ECONOMIC STABILIZATION -- UNITED STATES -- HISTORY -- 20TH CENTURY
The forgotten man   **973.91**

ECONOMIC SUSTAINABILITY See Sustainable development

ECONOMIC ZOOLOGY
See also Zoology

Economics. Chang   **330**

ECONOMICS
Adler, M. Economics for the rest of us   **330**
Chang Economics   **330**
Commager, H. S. The American mind   **973**
Dubner, S. J. Freakonomics   **330**
The economics of inequality   **339.2**
Guest, R. Borderless economics   **303.48**
Heilbroner, R. L. The worldly philosophers **330.1**
Keynes, J. M. The general theory of employment, interest and money   **330.1**
King, M. A. The End of Alchemy   **330.122**

Lanchester, J. How to Speak Money 330.1
Levitt, S. D. Superfreakonomics 330
Marx, K. Capital: an abridged edition 330.1
Roth, A. E. Who gets what--and why 330.01
Shiller, R. J. Irrational exuberance 332.63
Smith, A. The wealth of nations 330.1
Smith, G. Standard deviations 519.5
Sowell, T. Basic economics 330
Speth, J. G. America the possible 338.9
Sunstein, C. R. Simpler 973.932
Taylor, T. The instant economist 330

ECONOMICS
    See also Social sciences

ECONOMICS -- BIBLIOGRAPHY
Guide to Reference in Business and Economics 016

ECONOMICS -- HISTORY
Packer, G. The unwinding 973.924
Power, Inc. 322

ECONOMICS -- PHILOSOPHY
Sandel, M. J. What money can't buy 330.1

ECONOMICS -- POLITICAL ASPECTS
Acemoglu, D. Why nations fail 330
Friedman, J. Engineering the financial crisis 330.9

ECONOMICS -- PSYCHOLOGICAL ASPECTS
Thaler, R. H. Misbehaving 330.01

ECONOMICS -- SOCIOLOGICAL ASPECTS
Dubner, S. J. Freakonomics 330
Levitt, S. D. Superfreakonomics 330

ECONOMICS -- TERMINOLOGY
Velshi, A. How to speak money 332.024

ECONOMICS -- UNITED STATES
The economists' voice 2.0 330.9

ECONOMICS AND CHRISTIANITY See Christianity and economics

Economics for the rest of us. Adler, M. 330
The economics of inequality. 339.2

Economides, Annette, 1961-
The moneysmart family system 332.024

Economides, Steve, 1958-
(jt. auth) Economides, A. The moneysmart family system 332.024

An economist gets lunch. Cowen, T. 394.1

ECONOMISTS
Commager, H. S. The American mind 973
Ellison, R. The collected essays of Ralph Ellison 814
Greenspan, A. The age of turbulence 92
Heilbroner, R. L. The worldly philosophers 330.1
Hollis, L. London rising 942
McPhee, J. A. The ransom of Russian art 709
Mill, J. S. Autobiography 92
Overtveldt, J. v. Bernanke's test 332.1
Snyder, L. J. The philosophical breakfast club 509
Wessel, D. In Fed we trust 332.1
Woodward, B. Maestro: Greenspan's Fed and the American boom 331.1

ECONOMISTS -- BIOGRAPHY
Davenport-Hines, R. P. T. Universal Man 92
The economists' voice 2.0. 330.9

Ecosystem [series]
Day, T. Oceans 551.46

ECOSYSTEM HEALTH
Wills, C. Green Equilibrium 577

ECOSYSTEM MANAGEMENT
Wills, C. Green Equilibrium 577

ECOSYSTEMS See Ecology

ECOTERRORISM
Potter, W. Green is the new red 320.5

ECOTERRORISM
    See also Environmental movement; Terrorism

ECOTOURISM
Blackwell, A. Visit sunny Chernobyl 363.73

ECSTASY (DRUG)
Shroder, T. Acid test 615.7

ECSTASY (DRUG) -- THERAPEUTIC USE
Shroder, T. Acid test 615.7

The ecstasy of influence. Lethem, J. 814

Ecstatic nation. Wineapple, B. 973.6

ECUMENICAL MOVEMENT
    See also Christian sects; Church

EDAPHOLOGY See Soil ecology

EDDAS
    See also Old Norse literature; Poetry; Scandinavian literature

Eddington, Arthur Stanley Sir, 1882-1944
    About
Miller, A. I. Empire of the stars 520

Eddy, Jody
North 641.59
(jt. auth) Goldberg, D. Cuba! 641.5

Eddy, Mary Baker
Science and health, with key to the Scriptures 289.5

Edelman, Hope
Motherless daughters 155.9
Motherless mothers 155.9

Edelman, Marian Wright, 1939-
The measure of our success 170
    About
Edelman, M. W. Lanterns 92

Edelman, Shimon
The happiness of pursuit 153

Edelson, Mat
Katz, R. The cancer-fighting kitchen 641.5
The longevity kitchen 612.6

Eden's outcasts. Matteson, J. 92

Edey, Maitland Armstrong
Johanson, D. C. Lucy: the beginnings of humankind 599.93

Edgar A. Poe. Silverman, K. 92
Edgar Allan Poe. Collins, P. 92
Edgar Allan Poe & the juke-box. Bishop, E. 811

EDGAR ALLAN POE AWARDS

See also Literary prizes; Mystery fiction

Edgar Cayce. Kirkpatrick, S. **92**

Edgar, Blake
Johanson, D. C. From Lucy to language **599.93**

Edge of empire. Jasanoff, M. **909.08**

The **edge** of physics. Ananthaswamy, A. **530**

The **edge** of the sea. Carson, R. **577.7**

The **edge** of the sky. Trotta, R. **520**

Edge of the universe. Halpern, P. **523.1**

The **Edge** of the World. Pye, M. **940.1**

Edge, Rosalie
About
Furmansky, D. Z. Rosalie Edge, hawk of mercy **92**

Edgerton, Clyde
Papadaddy's book for new fathers **649**

Edgson, Vicki
Broth **641.813**

An **edible** history of humanity. Standage, T. **394.1**

EDIBLE LANDSCAPING
Jabbour, N. Groundbreaking food gardens **635**

EDIBLE MUSHROOMS
Russell, S. The essential guide to cultivating mushrooms **635**

EDIBLE PLANTS
Angier, B. Field guide to edible wild plants **581.6**

The Cambridge world history of food **641.3**

Gibbons, E. Stalking the wild asparagus **581.6**

Jabbour, N. Groundbreaking food gardens **635**

Russell, S. The essential guide to cultivating mushrooms **635**

Stewart, A. The drunken botanist **581.6**

Van Wyk Food plants of the world **581.6**

EDIBLE PLANTS
See also Economic botany; Food; Plants

EDIFICES See Buildings

Edin, Kathryn, 1962-
(jt. auth) Shaefer, H. L. $2.00 a Day **339.4**

Edison. Israel, P. **92**

Edison and the rise of innovation. Degraaf, L. **92**

Edison, Harry, 1915-1999
About
Dance, S. The world of Count Basie **920**

Edison, Thomas A. (Thomas Alva), 1847-1931
About
Degraaf, L. Edison and the rise of innovation **92**

Freeberg, E. The Age of Edison **303.48**

Israel, P. Edison **92**

Edith Wharton. Lee, H. **92**

EDITING
See also Authorship; Publishers and publishing

EDITORS
Alice Walker **813**

Alice Walker's The color purple **813**

Arana, M. American chica **92**

As always, Julia **92**

Athill, D. Somewhere towards the end **92**

Black women writers (1950-1980) **810**

Bloom, H. The anatomy of influence **801**

Bowles, H. Jacqueline Kennedy **92**

Breslin, E. Drinking with Miss Dutchie **92**

Burana, L. I love a man in uniform **92**

Danticat, E. Brother, I'm dying **92**

Danticat, E. Create dangerously **92**

Davis, J. H. Jacqueline Bouvier **92**

Gates, H. L. The future of the race **305.896**

Gillespie, C. Critical companion to Alice Walker **813**

Gioia, D. Can poetry matter? **809.1**

Glendinning, V. Leonard Woolf **92**

Gordon, L. Lives like loaded guns **92**

Gordon, L. T.S. Eliot **92**

Heaney, S. Finders keepers **821**

Howe, B. R. My Korean deli **92**

Kazin, A. An American procession **810**

Kermode, F. An appetite for poetry **801**

Leaming, B. Mrs. Kennedy **973.922**

Lewis, D. L. W.E.B. Du Bois **92**

Manguel, A. A reader on reading **818**

Manguso, S. The two kinds of decay **362**

Milosz, C. To begin where I am **891.8**

Murphy, R. E. Critical companion to T.S. Eliot **811**

Proulx, A. Bird cloud **92**

Rao, C. In Hanuman's hands **92**

Vendler, H. H. Coming of age as a poet **820**

Walker, A. The same river twice **813**

Wall, C. A. Women of the Harlem Renaissance **810**

Winchester, S. The professor and the madman **423**

EDITORS -- UNITED STATES -- BIOGRAPHY
Hirshey, G. Not pretty enough **92**

Edlin, Aaron S.
(ed) The economists' voice 2.0 **330.9**

Edman, Elizabeth M., 1962-
Queer virtue **230**

Edmonds, Bill Russell
God Is Not Here **956.704**

Edmonds, David
Wittgenstein's poker **192**

Edmonds, Margot
Clark, E. E. Sacagawea of the Lewis and Clark expedition **92**

EDMONTOSAURUS
See also Dinosaurs

Edmund Burke. Norman, J. **92**

Edmundson, Mark, 1952-
About
Edmundson, M. Why football matters **92**

Edouard Manet. Brombert, B. A. **92**

Edouard Vuillard. **759**

Edsel, Robert M.
The monuments men **940.53**

Edson, Margaret

Wit   812

Edson, Russell
The rooster's wife   811

EDUCATION
Toffler, A. Future shock   303.4

EDUCATION
See also Civilization

EDUCATION -- AIMS AND OBJECTIVES
Kiyosaki, R. T. Why "A" Students Work for "C" Students and Why "B" Students Work for the Government   332.024
The muses go to school   700
Rhee, M. A. Radical   371.01

EDUCATION -- AUTOMATION *See* Computer-assisted instruction

EDUCATION -- CASE STUDIES
Falk, B. Teaching matters   370.9

EDUCATION -- CHINA
Leibovitz, L. Fortunate sons   951.05

EDUCATION -- CURRICULA
Art and social justice education   372.5

EDUCATION -- DATA PROCESSING *See* Computer-assisted instruction

EDUCATION -- DRAMA
Bennett, A. The history boys   822

EDUCATION -- EXPERIMENTAL METHODS
Vander Ark, T. Getting smart   371.33

EDUCATION -- FINANCE
See also Finance

EDUCATION -- FINLAND
Ripley, A. The smartest kids in the world   370.9

EDUCATION -- GOVERNMENT POLICY
Russakoff, D. The prize   371.2

EDUCATION -- GOVERNMENT POLICY
See also Social policy

EDUCATION -- INTEGRATION *See* School integration; Segregation in education

EDUCATION -- KOREA (SOUTH)
Ripley, A. The smartest kids in the world   370.9

EDUCATION -- PHILOSOPHY
Dewey, J. Democracy and education   370.1
Hirsch, E. D. The schools we need and why we don't have them   370.9

EDUCATION -- POLAND
Ripley, A. The smartest kids in the world   370.9

EDUCATION -- POLITICAL ASPECTS -- NEW JERSEY -- NEWARK
Russakoff, D. The prize   371.2

EDUCATION -- SEGREGATION *See* Segregation in education

EDUCATION -- SOCIAL ASPECTS -- UNITED STATES
Art and social justice education   372.5

EDUCATION -- STATISTICS
See also Statistics

EDUCATION -- UNITED STATES

Aronica, L. Creative schools   371.2
Gionfriddo, P. Losing Tim   92
Mettler, S. Degrees of inequality   378.73
Rhee, M. A. Radical   371.01
Ripley, A. The smartest kids in the world   370.9

EDUCATION -- UNITED STATES -- HISTORY
Wolff, D. How Lincoln learned to read   920

EDUCATION AND STATE *See* Education -- Government policy

EDUCATION AND STATE -- NEW JERSEY
Russakoff, D. The prize   371.2

EDUCATION FOR LIBRARIANSHIP *See* Library education

The **education** of a British-protected child. Achebe, C.   92

The **education** of a woman. Heilbrun, C. G.   92

EDUCATIONAL ACCOUNTABILITY -- UNITED STATES
Ravitch, D. The death and life of the great American school system   379

EDUCATIONAL ACHIEVEMENT *See* Academic achievement

EDUCATIONAL ADMINISTRATION *See* Schools -- Administration

EDUCATIONAL CHANGE
More Than a Score   371.26
Russakoff, D. The prize   371.2

EDUCATIONAL CHANGE
See also Education

EDUCATIONAL CHANGE -- NEW JERSEY -- NEWARK
Russakoff, D. The prize   371.2

EDUCATIONAL CHANGE -- UNITED STATES
Aronica, L. Creative schools   371.2
Mettler, S. Degrees of inequality   378.73
Rhee, M. A. Radical   371.01

EDUCATIONAL GAMES
McGonigal, J. Reality is broken   306.4

EDUCATIONAL PLANNING -- UNITED STATES
Selingo, J. J. College (un)bound   378

EDUCATIONAL POLICY *See* Education -- Government policy

EDUCATIONAL PSYCHOLOGY
Levine, M. D. A mind at a time   370.15

EDUCATIONAL PSYCHOLOGY
See also Psychology; Teaching

EDUCATIONAL REFORM *See* Educational change

EDUCATIONAL SOCIOLOGY
Hirsch, E. D. The schools we need and why we don't have them   370.9

EDUCATIONAL SOCIOLOGY
See also Sociology

EDUCATIONAL STANDARDS
See also Education

EDUCATIONAL TECHNOLOGY

Grover, S. Listening to learn **372.4**

EDUCATIONAL TECHNOLOGY

See also Education

Educational Testing Service

(comp) The official guide to the HiSET exam **373.126**

EDUCATIONAL TESTS AND MEASUREMENTS

More Than a Score **371.26**

Ravitch, D. The death and life of the great American school system **379**

EDUCATORS

Art and social justice education **372.5**

Ellison, R. The collected essays of Ralph Ellison **814**

Halberstam, D. The best and the brightest **973.922**

Halberstam, D. The children **323.1**

Harlan, L. R. Booker T. Washington: the making of a black leader, 1856-1901 **92**

Harlan, L. R. Booker T. Washington: the wizard of Tuskegee, 1901-1915 **92**

Hendricks, S. The unquiet grave **970.004**

Kozol, J. Letters to a young teacher **371.1**

Leibovitz, L. Fortunate sons **951.05**

Matteson, J. Eden's outcasts **92**

Menand, L. The Metaphysical Club **973.9**

Norrell, R. J. Up from history **92**

Singer, M. Character studies **920**

Smock, R. W. Booker T. Washington **92**

Taylor, A. The divided ground **974.7**

Torres, A. American widow **741.5**

Uncle Tom or new Negro **370**

Washington, B. T. Up from slavery **92**

Wilson, E. Patriotic gore **810**

EDUCATORS

See also Education

Edvard Munch. Prideaux, S. **92**

Edward Albee. Gussow, M. **92**

Edward I

About

Morris, M. A Great & Terrible King **92**

Edward III. Ormrod, W. M. **92**

Edward III, King of England, 1312-1377

About

Ormrod, W. M. Edward III **92**

Edward R. Murrow and the birth of broadcast journalism. Edwards, B. **92**

Edward S. Curtis. Cardozo, C. **770**

Edward Sheriff Curtis. Gulbrandsen, D. **770**

Edward Steichen. Brandow, T. **779**

Edward Steichen: the early years. Smith, J. **779**

Edward Teller, the real Dr Strangelove. Goodchild, P. **92**

Edward VII, King of Great Britain, 1841-1910

About

Carter, M. George, Nicholas, and Wilhelm **940.3**

Ridley, J. The heir apparent **92**

Edward weston. **770**

Edwards, Betty

Drawing on the Right Side of the Brain **741.2**

Edwards, Bob

Edward R. Murrow and the birth of broadcast journalism **92**

Edwards, Brent Hayes

(ed) Du Bois, W. E. B. The souls of Black folk **305.8**

Edwards, E. Jay, 1847-1924

About

Algeo, M. The president is a sick man **973.8**

Edwards, Jonathan, 1703-1758

About

Marsden, G. M. Jonathan Edwards **92**

Edwards, Laurie J.

(jt. auth) Moore, A. Cyber self-defense **613.6**

Edwards, Mickey

The parties versus the people **320**

Edwards, Paul

The concise guide to hip-hop music **782.42**

Edwards, Robert

The Winter War **948.97**

EELS

Schweid, R. Consider the eel **597**

Eerdmans dictionary of the Bible. **220.3**

The **eerie** silence. Davies, P. C. W. **576.8**

The **effective** manager. Horstman, M. **658**

Effort at speech. Meredith, W. **811**

Effortless healing. Mercola, J. M. **613.2**

Effortless pain relief. Bacci, I. **616**

Egan, Amy

Is it a big problem or a little problem? **649**

Egan, Kerry

On living **170.44**

Egan, Sean

(ed) Bowie on Bowie **92**

Egan, Timothy

The big burn **973.91**

The immortal Irishman **92**

Short nights of the Shadow Catcher **770.92**

The worst hard time **978**

Egerton, Douglas R.

Death or liberty **973.3**

Year of meteors **973.7**

Egg. Ruhlman, M. **641.675**

EGG DECORATION

See also Decoration and ornament; Handicraft

Egger-Sider, Francine

(jt. auth) Devine, J. Going beyond Google again **025.042**

Eggers, Dave, 1970-

Zeitoun **92**

EGGS

Birkhead, T. The Most Perfect Thing   598
EGGS
    See also Food
EGO
    Edelman, S. The happiness of pursuit   153
EGO (PSYCHOLOGY)
    See also Personality; Psychoanalysis; Psychology; Self
EGOISM
    Rand, A. The virtue of selfishness   171
EGYPT -- ANTIQUITIES
    Kemp, B. The city of Akhenaten and Nefertiti 930
EGYPT -- ANTIQUITIES -- ENCYCLOPEDIAS
    Bunson, M. R. Encyclopedia of ancient Egypt 932
EGYPT -- CIVILIZATION
    David, A. R. Handbook to life in ancient Egypt 932
    Hatshepsut: from queen to Pharaoh   932
    Mertz, B. Temples, tombs, & hieroglyphs   932
    Said, E. W. Reflections on exile and other essays   814
EGYPT -- DESCRIPTION AND TRAVEL
    Stothard, P. Alexandria   962
EGYPT -- HISTORY
    Bunson, M. R. Encyclopedia of ancient Egypt 932
    Cambanis, T. Once upon a revolution   962.05
    Fletcher, J. The Story of Egypt   932
    Kemp, B. The city of Akhenaten and Nefertiti 930
    Romer, J. A history of ancient Egypt   932
    Wright, L. Thirteen Days in September   956.04
EGYPT -- HISTORY -- 1798-1801, FRENCH OCCUPATION
    Strathern, P. Napoleon in Egypt   962
EGYPT -- HISTORY -- 1970-
    Khalil, A. Liberation Square   962.05
    Steavenson, W. Circling the Square   962.05
EGYPT -- HISTORY -- 1981- -- BIOGRAPHY
    Cambanis, T. Once upon a revolution   962.05
EGYPT -- HISTORY -- 332-30 B.C.
    Goldsworthy, A. K. Antony and Cleopatra   92
    Wilkinson, T. The rise and fall of ancient Egypt 932
EGYPT -- HISTORY -- EIGHTEENTH DYNASTY, CA. 1570-1320 B.C
    Cooney, K. The woman who would be king   92
EGYPT -- HISTORY -- PROTESTS, 2011
    Khalil, A. Liberation Square   962.05
EGYPT -- HISTORY -- TO 332 B.C
    Romer, J. A history of ancient Egypt   932
EGYPT -- RELIGION
    Wilkinson, R. H. The complete gods and goddesses
        of ancient Egypt   299
Egypt, Greece, and Rome. Freeman, C.   909
EGYPTIAN ART
    Hawass, Z. A. Hidden treasures of ancient
        Egypt   932
    Robins, G. The art of ancient Egypt   709.3
EGYPTIAN LANGUAGE

Mertz, B. Temples, tombs, & hieroglyphs   932
EGYPTIAN LANGUAGE -- WRITING, HIEROGLYPHIC
    Robinson, A. Cracking the Egyptian code   493
EGYPTIAN MYTHOLOGY
    Wilkinson, R. H. The complete gods and goddesses
        of ancient Egypt   299
EGYPTIAN MYTHOLOGY
    See also Mythology
EGYPTOLOGISTS -- BIOGRAPHY
    Noël Hume, I. Belzoni   92
EGYPTOLOGISTS -- FRANCE -- BIOGRAPHY
    Robinson, A. Cracking the Egyptian code   493
EGYPTOLOGY *See* Egypt -- Antiquities
Ehmann, Sven
    (ed) A Map of the World   912
Ehrenreich, Barbara
    Bright-sided   155.2
    Nickel and dimed   305.5
Ehrenreich, Ben
    The Way to the Spring   956.95
Ehrlich, Gretel
    Facing the wave   363.34
    This cold heaven   998
Eichar, Donnie
                    About
    Eichar, D. Dead Mountain   914.7
Eichenseer, Erika
    (ed) The turnip princess   398.209
Eichenwald, Kurt
    500 days   973.931
Eicher, David J.
    The longest night   973.7
Eichmann before Jerusalem.   92
The **Eichmann** trial. Lipstadt, D. E.   345
Eidinow, Esther
    (ed) The Oxford classical dictionary   938
Eidinow, John
    Edmonds, D. Wittgenstein's poker   192
EIFFEL TOWER (PARIS, FRANCE)
    Jonnes, J. Eiffel's tower   944
Eiffel's tower. Jonnes, J.   944
Eiffel, Alexandre Gustave, 1832-1923
                    About
    Jonnes, J. Eiffel's tower   944
Eig, Jonathan
    The birth of the pill   618.1
    Get Capone   92
Eight weeks to optimum health. Weil, A.   613
Eight world cups. Vecsey, G.   796.334
The **eighteen-day** running mate. Glasser, J.
M.   973.924
The **eighty-dollar** champion. Letts, E.   798.2
Eilperin, Juliet
    Demon fish   597
Einstein 1905. Rigden, J. S.   530.1

Einstein defiant. Bolles, E. B.   530.1
An **Einstein** encyclopedia. Schulmann, R. 530.092
Einstein on politics. Einstein, A.   92
Einstein's clocks and Poincare's maps. Galison, P.
L.   529
Einstein's dice and Schrödinger's cat. Halpern,
P.   530.13
Einstein's Masterwork. Gribbin, J.   530.11
Einstein's mistakes. Ohanian, H. C.   530
Einstein, Albert, 1879-1955
  Einstein on politics   92
  The evolution of physics   530
  The meaning of relativity   530.1
  A stubbornly persistent illusion   530.1
  The ultimate quotable Einstein   530
       About
  Aczel, A. D. God's equation   523.1
  Bodanis, D. E   530.1
  Bolles, E. B. Einstein defiant   530.1
  Einstein, A. Einstein on politics   92
  Feldman, B. 112 Mercer Street   920
  Galison, P. L. Einstein's clocks and Poincare's
    maps   529
  Halpern, P. Einstein's dice and Schrödinger's
    cat   530.13
  Isaacson, W. Einstein: his life and universe 92
  Levenson, T. The hunt for Vulcan   523.4
  Ohanian, H. C. Einstein's mistakes   530
  Rigden, J. S. Einstein 1905   530.1
  Sagan, C. Broca's brain   500
  Schulmann, R. An Einstein encyclopedia 530.092
Einstein, Alfred
  Mozart   92
Einstein: his life and universe. Isaacson, W.   92
Eire, Carlos M. N.
  A very brief history of eternity   236
       About
  Eire, C. M. N. Learning to die in Miami   92
  Eire, C. M. N. Waiting for snow in Havana 92
Eiseley, Loren C.
  The immense journey   576.8
Eisenberg, Arlene
  Murkoff, H. E. What to expect the first year 649
Eisenberg, John
  The great match race   798.4
Eisenberg, Ronald L.
  The JPS guide to Jewish traditions   296.4
Eisenhardt, Kathleen M.
  (jt. auth) Sull, D. Simple Rules   650.1
Eisenhower. Smith, J. E.   973.921
Eisenhower. Johnson, P.   92
Eisenhower. Ambrose, S. E.   92
Eisenhower's Armies. Barr, N.   940.53
Eisenhower, Dwight D. (Dwight David), 1890-1969
       About
  Ambrose, S. E. Eisenhower   92

  Ambrose, S. E. The victors   940.54
  Anderson, L. Carlisle vs. Army   796.332
  Frank, J. Ike and dick   973.921
  Johnson, P. Eisenhower   92
  Jordan, J. W. American warlords   973.917
  Smith, J. E. Eisenhower   973.921
  Thomas, E. Ike's bluff   973.92
  Weintraub, S. 15 stars   920
  Wicker, T. Dwight D. Eisenhower   973.921
Eisenhower, Joanne Thompson
  Eisenhower, J. S. D. Yanks: the epic story of the
    American Army in World War I   940.4
Eisenhower, John S. D.
  Yanks: the epic story of the American Army in
    World War I   940.4
Eisenstadt, Benjamin, 1906-1996
       About
  Cohen, R. Sweet and low   920
Eisler, Benita
  Byron--child of passion, fool of fame   92
  Chopin's funeral   92
  Naked in the marketplace   92
  The Red Man's Bones   92
Eisner, Maria
  Eisner, T. Secret weapons   595.7
Eisner, Peter
  The Pope's Last Crusade   940.53
Eisner, Shiri
  Bi   306.76
Eisner, Thomas
  For love of insects   595.7
  Secret weapons   595.7
Eisner, Will, 1917-2005
  Comics and sequential art   741.5
       About
  Schumacher, M. Will Eisner   92
Ekarius, Carol
  The field guide to fleece   677
Ekin, Des
  The Last Armada   941.505
Ekirch, A. Roger, 1950-
  At day's close   306.4
Ekrem, Erica
  Bound   686.3
Elaine de kooning. Fortune, B. B.   759.13
Elberse, Anita
  Blockbusters   384
Elbert, Samuel H.
  Pukui, M. K. Hawaiian dictionary   499
Elbroch, Mark
  Mammal tracks & sign   599
  The Peterson field guide to animal tracks 599
Elderfield, John
  De Kooning: a retrospective   759.13
ELDERLY
  Chittister, J. The gift of years   200

Jacoby, S. Never say die **305.26**
ELDERLY -- CARE
Delehanty, H. Caring for your parents **362.6**
Hogan, P. R. Stages of senior care **362.6**
ELDERLY -- HEALTH AND HYGIENE
Lachs, M. Treat me, not my age **612.6**
ELDERLY -- LAW AND LEGISLATION
Sember, B. M. Seniors' rights **346.01**
ELDERLY -- MEDICAL CARE
Gawande, A. Being mortal **362.17**
Volandes, A. E. The conversation **616.02**
ELDERLY -- MEDICAL CARE
See also Elderly -- Care; Medical care
ELDERLY -- PSYCHOLOGY
Serani, D. Depression in later life **618.97**
ELDERLY -- UNITED STATES
Lawrence-Lightfoot, S. The third chapter **305.26**
Pillemer, K. A. 30 lessons for living **305.26**
ELDERLY ABUSE
See also Domestic violence
ELDERLY MEN
Hall, D. Essays After Eighty **814**
Vaillant, G. E. Triumphs of experience **305.31**
ELDERLY MEN
See also Elderly
ELDERLY MEN -- EMPLOYMENT
Fideler, E. F. Men still at work **331.3**
ELDERLY WOMEN -- EMPLOYMENT
Fideler, E. F. Women still at work **331.4**
Eldredge, Debra
Dog owner's home veterinary handbook **636.7**
Eldredge, Niles
Extinction and Evolution **560**
Why we do it **155.3**
Eldridge, Lisa
Face paint **391.6**
Eleanor and Hick. Quinn, S. **92**
Eleanor of Aquitaine. Weir, A. **92**
Eleanor Roosevelt. Cook, B. W. **973.917**
Eleanor Roosevelt. Cook, B. W. **92**
**Eleanor, of Aquitaine, Queen, consort of Henry II,
  King of England, 1122?-1204**
About
Weir, A. Eleanor of Aquitaine **92**
ELECTION LAW
See also Constitutional law
ELECTIONEERING See Politics
ELECTIONS
See also Politics
ELECTRIC BATTERIES
Fletcher, S. Bottled lightning **621.31**
ELECTRIC CIRCUITS
See also Electric lines; Electricity
ELECTRIC CONDUCTORS
See also Electronics
ELECTRIC COOKING, SLOW

One pot **641.82**
ELECTRIC CURRENTS
See also Electricity
Electric Eden. Young, R. **781.62**
ELECTRIC ENGINEERING See Electrical engineering
**ELECTRIC ENGINEERING -- HANDBOOKS,
  MANUALS, ETC**
American electricians' handbook **621.3**
ELECTRIC GUITAR
See also Electronic musical instruments; Guitars
**ELECTRIC HOUSEHOLD APPLIANCES --
  MAINTENANCE AND REPAIR**
New fix-it-yourself manual **643**
The **electric** life of Michael Faraday. Hirshfeld, A. **92**
Electric light. Heaney, S. **821**
ELECTRIC LIGHT See Electric lighting; Photometry; Phototherapy
ELECTRIC LIGHTING
See also Lighting
**ELECTRIC LIGHTING -- UNITED STATES --
  HISTORY**
Freeberg, E. The Age of Edison **303.48**
ELECTRIC MACHINERY
See also Machinery
ELECTRIC MEASUREMENTS
See also Electric currents; Weights and measures
ELECTRIC POWER
Couch, J. Traveling the power line **333.793**
ELECTRIC POWER
See also Electricity; Energy resources; Power (Mechanics)
ELECTRIC POWER PRODUCTION -- MALAWI
Kamkwamba, W. The boy who harnessed the wind **92**
ELECTRIC PRODUCTS INDUSTRY
See also Industries
ELECTRIC RAILROADS
See also Railroads
ELECTRIC SIGNS
See also Advertising; Signs and signboards
Electric universe. Bodanis, D. **537**
ELECTRIC WAVES
See also Electricity; Waves
ELECTRIC WIRING
The complete guide to wiring **621.319**
Richter, H. P. Wiring simplified **621.319**
ELECTRIC WIRING, INTERIOR -- AMATEURS' MANUALS
The complete guide to wiring **621.319**
ELECTRICAL ENGINEERING
Platt, C. Make **621.381**

ELECTRICAL ENGINEERING

See also Engineering; Mechanical engineering

ELECTRICAL ENGINEERING -- HANDBOOKS, MANUALS, ETC.

American electricians' handbook   **621.3**

Horowitz, P. The art of electronics   **621.381**

National electrical code handbook 2014   **621.3**

Standard Handbook for Electrical Engineers **621.3**

ELECTRICAL ENGINEERS

Larson, E. Thunderstruck   **364.152**

ELECTRICAL ENGINEERS -- ITALY -- BIOGRAPHY

Raboy, M. Marconi   **92**

ELECTRICAL ENGINEERS -- UNITED STATES -- BIOGRAPHY

Carlson, W. B. Tesla   **92**

ELECTRICITY

Bodanis, D. Electric universe   **537**

Schultz, M. E. Grob's basic electronics   **621.381**

ELECTRICITY

See also Physics

ELECTRICITY -- HISTORY

Carlson, W. B. Tesla   **92**

ELECTRONIC APPARATUS AND APPLIANCES

Vamosi, R. When gadgets betray us   **004**

ELECTRONIC APPARATUS AND APPLIANCES

See also Electronics; Scientific apparatus and instruments

ELECTRONIC APPARATUS AND APPLIANCES -- MISCELLANEA

Pogue, D. Pogue's basics   **004**

ELECTRONIC BOOK READERS

See also Electronic apparatus and appliances; Reading -- Aids and devices

ELECTRONIC BOOKS

Baker, N. The way the world works   **814**

No shelf required   **025.17**

No shelf required 2   **070.5**

ELECTRONIC BOOKS

See also Books; Digital media

ELECTRONIC CIRCUIT DESIGN

Horowitz, P. The art of electronics   **621.381**

ELECTRONIC CIRCUITS

Horowitz, P. The art of electronics   **621.381**

ELECTRONIC CIRCUITS

See also Electric circuits; Electronics

ELECTRONIC COMMERCE

Angwin, J. Stealing MySpace   **338.7**

Siegel, D. Pull   **658.8**

ELECTRONIC GAMES -- COLLECTIONS

Gallaway, B. Game on!   **025.2**

ELECTRONIC GAMES INDUSTRY -- HISTORY

Harris, B. J. Console wars   **338.7**

ELECTRONIC INFORMATION RESOURCE LITERACY

Seife, C. Virtual unreality   **025.04**

ELECTRONIC INFORMATION RESOURCE SEARCHING

MacLeod, D. How to find out anything   **001.4**

ELECTRONIC INFORMATION RESOURCES

MacLeod, D. How to find out anything   **001.4**

ELECTRONIC INFORMATION RESOURCES -- MANAGEMENT

Johnson, P. Developing and managing electronic collections   **025.2**

Managing Electronic Resources   **025.1**

ELECTRONIC INFORMATION RESOURCES -- MARKETING

Laguardia, C. Marketing your library's electronic resources   **025.2**

ELECTRONIC INFORMATION RESOURCES -- SOCIAL ASPECTS

Cukier, K. Big data   **306.46**

ELECTRONIC MUSIC

Matos, M. The underground is massive **781.648**

ELECTRONIC MUSIC

See also Music

ELECTRONIC MUSICAL INSTRUMENTS

See also Musical instruments

ELECTRONIC PUBLISHING

No shelf required 2   **070.5**

ELECTRONIC PUBLISHING

See also Information services; Publishers and publishing

ELECTRONIC PUBLISHING AND LIBRARIES

See Libraries and electronic publishing

ELECTRONIC REFERENCE SERVICES (LIBRARIES)

Johnson, P. Developing and managing electronic collections   **025.2**

Managing Electronic Resources   **025.1**

Mulac, C. M. Fundamentals of reference   **025.5**

Nilsen, K. Conducting the reference interview   **025.5**

Singer, C. A. Fundamentals of Managing Reference Collections   **025.2**

ELECTRONIC REFERENCE SERVICES (LIBRARIES)

See also Reference services (Libraries)

ELECTRONIC SURVEILLANCE

Angwin, J. Dragnet nation   **323.44**

Bamford, J. The shadow factory   **327.12**

Theoharis, A. G. Abuse of power   **363.325**

ELECTRONIC TOYS

See also Electronic apparatus and appliances; Toys

ELECTRONIC WARFARE

Hampton, D. The hunter killers   **959.704**

ELECTRONICS
Fletcher, S. Bottled lightning   **621.31**
Platt, C. Make   **621.381**
Schultz, M. E. Grob's basic electronics   **621.381**
ELECTRONICS
    See also Engineering; Physics; Technology
ELECTRONICS -- HANDBOOKS, MANUALS, ETC.
Horowitz, P. The art of electronics   **621.381**
ELECTRONICS -- SOCIAL ASPECTS
Dunckley, V. L. Reset your child's brain   **004.67**
ELECTRONICS IN NAVIGATION -- HISTORY
Bray, H. You are here   **910.285**
ELECTRONICS INDUSTRY EXECUTIVES
Tedlow, R. S. Andy Grove   **92**
ELECTRONS
Feynman, R. P. QED   **539.7**
ELECTRONS
    See also Atoms; Particles (Nuclear physics)
ELECTROPHYSIOLOGY
Ashcroft, F. The spark of life   **612**
ELECTROPHYSIOLOGY
    See also Physiology
ELECTROPLATING
    See also Electrochemistry; Metalwork
ELECTROTHERAPEUTICS
    See also Massage; Physical therapy; Therapeutics
ELECTROTYPING
    See also Electrochemistry; Printing
The **elegant** universe. Greene, B. R.   **539.7**
Elegguas. Brathwaite, E. K.   **811**
ELEGIAC POETRY
    See also Poetry
Elegy. Bang, M. J.   **811**
Elegy for a broken machine. Phillips, P.   **811**
Elegy for Iris. Bayley, J.   **823**
Elegy owed. Hicok, B.   **811**
ELEKTRA RECORDS (FIRM)
Houghton, M. Becoming Elektra   **781.64**
ELEMENTARY EDUCATION
Dewey, J. The school and society, and The child and the curriculum   **372**
Hauser, P. C. How deaf children learn   **371.91**
ELEMENTARY SCHOOL LIBRARIES -- ACTIVITY PROGRAMS
Del Negro, J. M. Folktales aloud   **027.62**
The **Elements.** Challoner, J.   **546**
The **elements.**   **546**
The **elements** of journalism. Kovach, B.   **071**
The **elements** of pizza. Forkish, K.   **641.82**
The **elements** of story. Flaherty, F.   **808.5**
The **elements** of style. Strunk, W.   **808**
Elements of style. Gates, E.   **747**
The **elements** of style.   **728**
ELEMENTS, CHEMICAL *See* Chemical elements

Elena Garro and Mexico's modern dreams. Biron, R. E.   **868**
Elephant reflections. Ammann, K.   **599.67**
The **elephant** whisperer. Anthony, L.   **599.67**
ELEPHANTS
Ammann, K. Elephant reflections   **599.67**
Anthony, L. The elephant whisperer   **599.67**
Bradley, C. Last chain on Billie   **639.97**
Daly, M. Topsy   **791.3**
Orenstein, R. Ivory, horn and blood   **333.95**
Owens, D. The eye of the elephant   **333.95**
Owens, M. Secrets of the savanna   **599**
ELEPHANTS
    See also Mammals
ELEPHANTS -- PSYCHOLOGY
Safina, C. Beyond words   **591.56**
ELEPHANTS -- UNITED STATES -- ANECDOTES
Bradley, C. Last chain on Billie   **639.97**
Elia Kazan. Schickel, R.   **92**
Elias, Stephen
    Chapter 13 bankruptcy   **346**
    The foreclosure survival guide   **346**
    How to file for Chapter 7 bankruptcy   **346.07**
    Trademark   **346.04**
Eliav-Feldon, Miriam
    (ed) A Historical atlas of the Jewish people   **909**
Elie, Paul
    The life you save may be your own   **810**
Elijah Muhammad, 1897-1975
       About
    Evanzz, K. The messenger: the rise and fall of Elijah Muhammad   **297.8**
    Gardell, M. In the name of Elijah Muhammad   **297**
Eliot, George, 1819-1880
       About
    Bloom, H. The Western canon   **809**
    Hughes, K. George Eliot   **823**
Eliot, George, 1819-1880. Middlemarch
       About
    Mead, R. My life in Middlemarch   **823**
Eliot, Lise
    Pink brain, blue brain   **612.6**
    What's going on in there?   **612.8**
Eliot, Marc
    American titan   **92**
Eliot, T. S. (Thomas Stearns), 1888-1965
    Collected poems, 1909-1962   **811**
    The complete poems and plays, 1909-1950   **811**
    Inventions of the March Hare   **811**
       About
    Crawford, R. Young Eliot   **92**
    Gordon, L. T.S. Eliot   **92**
    Heaney, S. Finders keepers   **821**
    Kazin, A. An American procession   **810**
    Kermode, F. An appetite for poetry   **801**

Milosz, C. To begin where I am **891.8**

Murphy, R. E. Critical companion to T.S. Eliot **811**

Vendler, H. H. Coming of age as a poet **820**

ELITE (SOCIAL SCIENCES)

Brooks, D. The social animal **305.5**

Ferguson, C. Predator nation **330.973**

Freeland, C. Plutocrats **305.5**

ELITE (SOCIAL SCIENCES)

See also Leadership; Power (Social sciences);
Social classes; Social groups

**ELITE (SOCIAL SCIENCES) -- ILLINOIS --
CHICAGO REGION**

Jefferson, M. Negroland **92**

**ELITE (SOCIAL SCIENCES) -- SOUTHERN
STATES -- HISTORY -- 19TH CENTURY**

Levine, B. The fall of the house of Dixie **973.7**

**ELITE (SOCIAL SCIENCES) -- UNITED
STATES**

Hayes, C. Twilight of the elites **305.5**

**ELITE (SOCIAL SCIENCES) -- UNITED
STATES -- HISTORY**

Fraser, S. The age of acquiescence **973.91**

Elixir. Fagan, B. **553.7**

Elizabeth. Hilton, L. **92**

Elizabeth. Guy, J. **92**

Elizabeth and Hazel. Margolick, D. **92**

Elizabeth Cady Stanton. Ginzberg, L. D. **92**

Elizabeth I, Queen of England, 1533-1603

About

Castor, H. She-wolves **920**

Guy, J. Elizabeth **92**

Milton, G. Big Chief Elizabeth **970.004**

Norton, E. The Temptation of Elizabeth Tudor **92**

Ronald, S. Heretic queen **942.05**

Weir, A. The life of Elizabeth I **942.05**

Elizabeth II, Queen of Great Britain, 1926-

About

Andersen, C. Game of crowns **941.085**

Elizabeth, Princess of England, 1770-1840

About

Fraser, F. Princesses **920**

**Elizabeth, Queen, consort of Edward IV, King of
England, 1437?-1492**

About

Gristwood, S. Blood sisters **942.04**

**Elizabeth, Queen, consort of Henry VII, King of
England, 1465-1503**

About

Gristwood, S. Blood sisters **942.04**

Elkind, David

The power of play **155.4**

Ellard, Colin

You are here **153.7**

Elledge, Scott

E. B. White **92**

Ellenberg, Jordan, 1971-

How not to be wrong **510**

Eller, Jonathan R.

Becoming Ray Bradbury **92**

Ellington, Duke, 1899-1974

About

Ellison, R. Going to the territory **818**

Feather, L. From Satchmo to Miles **920**

Murray, A. The blue devils of Nada **780.89**

Teachout, T. Duke **92**

Ellington, Elisabeth

A year of reading **011**

Elliot, Jason

Mirrors of the unseen **915**

An unexpected light **958.1**

Elliott, Carl

White coat, black hat **174.2**

Elliott, Emory

(ed) Columbia literary history of the United
States **810**

ELLIPTIC CURVES

Ash, A. Elliptic tales **515**

ELLIPTIC FUNCTIONS

Ash, A. Elliptic tales **515**

Elliptic tales. Ash, A. **515**

Ellis Island and the peopling of America. Yans-
McLaughlin, V. **325**

ELLIS ISLAND IMMIGRATION STATION

Cannato, V. J. American passage **325**

Yans-McLaughlin, V. Ellis Island and the peopling
of America **325**

Ellis, Barbara W.

Covering ground **635.9**

Taylor's guide to annuals **635.9**

Taylor's guide to perennials **635.9**

(ed) Rodale's ultimate encyclopedia of organic gardening **635**

Ellis, Cassandra

Home sewn **646.21**

Ellis, Catherine

(ed) After the fall **974.7**

Ellis, Don, 1934-1978

About

Feather, L. From Satchmo to Miles **920**

Ellis, Hattie

Sweetness & light **595.7**

Ellis, Helen E.

(ed) Archibald MacLeish: reflections **92**

Ellis, Joseph J.

American creation **973.3**

American sphinx: the character of Thomas Jefferson **92**

Founding brothers **973.4**

His Excellency **92**

The Quartet **973.3**

Revolutionary summer **973.3**

Ellis, Richard

The empty ocean   577.7
On thin ice   599.78
Tuna   333.95
Ellis, Samantha
How to Be a Heroine   809.3
Ellis, Sarah
(jt. auth) Bradshaw, J. The trainable cat   636.8
Ellis, Sherry
(ed) Now write! screenwriting   808.2
Ellis, Thomas Sayers, 1963-
Skin, Inc.   811
Ellis, William Henry, 1864-1923
                    About
Jacoby, K. The strange career of William Ellis 92
Ellison, Ralph
The collected essays of Ralph Ellison   814
Going to the territory   818
                    About
Rampersad, A. Ralph Ellison   92
Ellmann, Richard
James Joyce   92
Oscar Wilde   92
(ed) The Norton anthology of modern and contem-
porary poetry   821
(ed) Wilde, O. The artist as critic   824
Ellsberg, Daniel, 1931-
                    About
Ellsberg, D. Secrets: a memoir of Vietnam and the
Pentagon papers   959.704
Elman, Natalie Madorsky
The unwritten rules of friendship   649
Elmore, Bartow J.
Citizen Coke   338.7
ELOCUTION *See* Public speaking
The **eloquent** president: a portrait of Lincoln through
his words. White, R. C.   92
Elphick, Chris
(ed) Sibley, D. The Sibley guide to bird life & be-
havior   598
Elphick, Jonathan
(ed) The atlas of bird migration   598
The World of Birds   598
Elsa Schiaparelli. Secrest, M.   92
Elser, Johann Georg, 1903-1945
                    About
The lone assassin   943.086
Elsewhere. Russo, R.   92
Elshtain, Jean Bethke
Just war against terror   363.32
Eltis, David
Atlas of the transatlantic slave trade   381
Elton, Chester
All in   658.3
ELVES
        See also Folklore
Elvis and Ginger. Alden, G.   92

The **Elvis** encyclopedia. Victor, A.   781.66
Elvis Presley. Mason, B. A.   92
Ely, James W.
(ed) The Oxford guide to United States Supreme
Court decisions   342
Ely, Melvin Patrick
The adventures of Amos 'n' Andy   791.44
Elytes, Odysseus
The collected poems of Odysseus Elytis   889
EMAIL *See* E-mail
EMANCIPATION *See* Freedom
EMANCIPATION OF SLAVES *See* Slaves --
Emancipation
EMANCIPATION OF WOMEN *See* Women's
rights
EMANCIPATION PROCLAMATION (1863)
Brewster, T. Lincoln's Gamble   973.7
McPherson, J. M. Drawn with the sword   973.7
Slotkin, R. Long Road to Antietam   973.7
Emanuel, Kerry A.
Divine wind   551.55
The **embarrassment** of riches. Schama, S.   949.2
Embers of War. Logevall, F.   959.704
EMBLEMS *See* Decorations of honor; Heraldry;
Insignia; Mottoes; National emblems; Seals (Nu-
mismatics); Signs and symbols
Embracing defeat. Dower, J. W.   952.04
Embroideries. Satrapi, M.   741
Embroidery. Ganderton, L.   746.44
EMBROIDERY
A-z of Ribbon Embroidery   746.44
A-Z of Whitework   746.44
Ganderton, L. Embroidery   746.44
Prain, L. Hoopla   746.44
Rebecca Ringquist's embroidery workshops   746.44
Shimoda, N. Artfully embroidered   746.44
Watson, S. Pen to thread   746.44
EMBROIDERY
        See also Decoration and ornament; Needle-
work; Sewing
EMBRYOLOGY
Nilsson, L. A child is born   612.6
EMBRYOLOGY
        See also Biology; Zoology
EMERGENCIES *See* Accidents; Disasters; First
aid
EMERGENCY ASSISTANCE *See* Helping behav-
ior
EMERGENCY MANAGEMENT -- HAND-
BOOKS, MANUALS, ETC
Kostigen, T. M. National Geographic extreme
weather survival guide   613.6
EMERGENCY MEDICINE
Robbins, A. The nurses   362.17
Emerson. Richardson, R. D.   814
Emerson, Ken

Doo-dah!: Stephen Foster and the rise of American popular culture **92**

Emerson, Ralph Waldo
Collected poems & translations **811**
About
Kazin, A. An American procession **810**
Matthiessen, F. O. American renaissance **810**
Richardson, R. D. Emerson **814**
Wayne, T. K. Critical companion to Ralph Waldo Emerson **818**

Emery, Fred
Watergate **973.924**

Emet, Joseph
Finding the blue sky **294.3**

EMIGRANTS *See* Immigrants

EMIGRATION *See* Immigration and emigration

Emily Post's etiquette. Post, P. **395**

Emily Post's The etiquette advantage in business. Post, P. **395**

Emily Post's wedding etiquette. **395.2**

EMINENT DOMAIN
Benedict, J. Little pink house **343**

EMINENT DOMAIN
See also Constitutional law; Land use; Property

Eminent lives [series]
Armstrong, K. Muhammad **297**
Bryson, B. Shakespeare **822.3**
Epstein, J. Alexis De Tocqueville **92**
Gottlieb, R. A. George Balanchine: the ballet maker **92**
Hitchens, C. Thomas Jefferson: author of America **92**
Johnson, P. George Washington: the Founding Father **92**
Korda, M. Ulysses S. Grant: the unlikely hero **92**
Morris, E. Beethoven: the universal composer **92**
Prose, F. Caravaggio **92**
Ridley, M. Francis Crick **92**

Eminent outlaws. Bram, C. **810.9**

Emlen, Douglas J.
Animal weapons **591.47**

Emling, Shelley
Marie Curie and her daughters **920**

Emma Lazarus. Lazarus, E. **811**

Emmerson, Charles
1913 **909.82**
The future history of the Arctic **998**

Emmett Till. Anderson, D. S. **364.1**

Emmons, Henry
(jt. auth) Alter, D. Staying sharp **612.8**

EMMY AWARDS
See also Television broadcasting

Emotional freedom. Orloff, J. **152.4**
Emotional intelligence. Goleman, D. **152.4**
Emotional resilience. Viscott, D. S. **158**

EMOTIONAL STRESS *See* Stress (Psychology)

EMOTIONALLY DISTURBED CHILDREN
Brazelton, T. B. To listen to a child **155.4**
Glickman, E. R. Your kid's a brat and it's all your fault **649.1**
Goleman, D. Emotional intelligence **152.4**

EMOTIONALLY DISTURBED CHILDREN
See also Exceptional children; Mentally ill

EMOTIONS
Appignanesi, L. Trials of passion **364.152**
Damasio, A. R. The feeling of what happens **153**
Damasio, A. R. Looking for Spinoza **152.4**
Goleman, D. Emotional intelligence **152.4**
Goleman, D. Primal Leadership **658.4**
Goleman, D. Social intelligence **158**
Greene, J. Moral tribes **170**
Orloff, J. Emotional freedom **152.4**
Paterniti, M. Love and Other Ways of Dying **814**
Pinker, S. How the mind works **153**

EMOTIONS
See also Psychology; Psychophysiology

EMOTIONS -- PHYSIOLOGICAL ASPECTS
Linden, D. J. Touch **612.8**

EMOTIONS -- POETRY
Brock-Broido, L. Stay, Illusion **811**
Gizzi, P. In defense of nothing **811**
Nadelberg, A. Bright brave phenomena **811**

EMOTIONS IN CHILDREN
Konner, M. The evolution of childhood **305.23**

EMOTIONS IN CHILDREN
See also Child psychology; Emotions

EMPATHY
The age of empathy **152.4**
Borba, M. Unselfie **649.7**
Jamison, L. The empathy exams **814**
Kolko, J. Well-designed **658.5**
Ofri, D. What doctors feel **610.69**

EMPATHY
See also Attitude (Psychology); Emotions; Social psychology

The **empathy** exams. Jamison, L. **814**

The **emperor** of all maladies. Mukherjee, S. **616.99**

Emperor of Japan: Meiji and His world, 1852-1912. Keene, D. **952.03**

EMPERORS
Bix, H. P. Hirohito and the making of modern Japan **92**
Bulfinch, T. Bulfinch's mythology **398.2**
Carter, M. George, Nicholas, and Wilhelm **940.3**
Cerami, C. A. Jefferson's great gamble **973.4**
Clay, C. King, Kaiser, Tsar **920**
Coote, S. Napoleon and the Hundred Days **940.2**
De Madariaga, I. Ivan the Terrible **92**
Esdaile, C. J. Napoleon's wars **940.2**
Everitt, A. Augustus **92**
Everitt, A. Hadrian and the triumph of Rome **92**

Faber, T. Faberge's eggs **739.2**
Ferro, M. Nicholas II **92**
Johnson, P. Napoleon **944.05**
Keene, D. Emperor of Japan: Meiji and His world, 1852-1912 **952.03**
Kissinger, H. Diplomacy **327.2**
Kurth, P. Tsar: the lost world of Nicholas and Alexandra **947.08**
Lieven, D. C. B. Russia against Napoleon **940.2**
Massie, R. K. Nicholas and Alexandra **92**
Massie, R. K. The Romanovs **947.08**
Pocock, T. The terror before Trafalgar **940.2**
Remnick, D. Reporting **814**
Reston, J. Defenders of the faith **940.2**
Romanov riches **891.7**
Schom, A. Napoleon Bonaparte **92**
Schom, A. One hundred days **944.05**
Seagrave, S. The Yamato dynasty **952.03**
Strathern, P. Napoleon in Egypt **962**
Talty, S. The illustrious dead **940.2**
The twelve Caesars **878**
Wilson, D. A. Charlemagne **92**

EMPERORS
See also Kings and rulers

EMPERORS -- FRANCE -- BIOGRAPHY
Gueniffey, P. Bonaparte **92**
Johnson, P. Napoleon **944.05**
Schom, A. Napoleon Bonaparte **92**

EMPERORS -- ROME
Goldsworthy, A. Augustus **92**

EMPERORS -- ROME -- BIOGRAPHY
Goldsworthy, A. Augustus **92**
The **emperors** of chocolate. Brenner, J. G. **338.7**
Empire express. Bain, D. H. **385**
Empire of cotton. Beckert, S. **338.4**
Empire of deception. Jobb, D. **92**
Empire of dreams. Eyman, S. **92**
An **empire** of ice. Larson, E. J. **919**
Empire of liberty. Wood, G. S. **973.4**
Empire of self. Parini, J. **92**
Empire of shadows. Black, G. **978.7**
Empire of sin. Krist, G. **976.3**
Empire of the stars. Miller, A. I. **520**
Empire of the summer moon. Gwynne, S. C. **92**
An **empire** on the edge. Bunker, N. **973.3**
Empire's Crossroads. Gibson, C. **972.9**
Empire: the rise and demise of the British world order and the lessons for global power. Ferguson, N. **909**
Empires at war. Fowler, W. M. **973.2**
Empires of the sea. Crowley, R. **359**
Empires, nations, and families. Hyde, A. F. **978**

EMPIRICISM
Morrissey, S. Parallax **821**

EMPIRICISM
See also Philosophy; Rationalism; Theory of knowledge

EMPLOYEE ASSISTANCE PROGRAMS
See also Personnel management

EMPLOYEE BENEFITS
See also Salaries, wages, etc.

EMPLOYEE MORALE
Kelly, M. The dream manager **658.3**
Tracy, B. Full engagement! **658.3**

EMPLOYEE MORALE
See also Applied psychology; Morale; Personnel management

EMPLOYEE MOTIVATION
Elton, C. All in **658.3**

EMPLOYEE OWNERSHIP
Abrams, J. Companies we keep **338.7**

EMPLOYEE RIGHTS
Sack, S. M. The employee rights handbook **344**

EMPLOYEE RIGHTS
See also Civil rights; Labor laws and legislation

The **employee** rights handbook. Sack, S. M. **344**

EMPLOYEES
Chapman, B. Everybody matters **658.4**

EMPLOYEES
See also Labor

EMPLOYEES -- TRAINING
Berger, L. All work, no pay **650.14**

EMPLOYEES -- TRAINING
See also Occupational training; Personnel management; Vocational education

EMPLOYEES -- TRAINING OF
Sarillo, N. A slice of the pie **658.02**

EMPLOYEES AND OFFICIALS *See* Civil service

The **employer's** legal handbook. Steingold, F. S. **344**

EMPLOYER-EMPLOYEE RELATIONS *See* Industrial relations

EMPLOYMENT
Garson, B. Down the up escalator **339.2**
Johnson, J. Where did the jobs go-- and how do we get them back? **331.1**
Wildsmith, S. Joining the United States Air Force **358.4**

EMPLOYMENT
See also Economics; Labor

EMPLOYMENT AGENCIES
See also Labor; Labor turnover; Personnel management; Recruiting of employees; Unemployment

EMPLOYMENT INTERVIEWING
Kay, A. This is how to get your next job **650.14**
Port, M. Steal the show **658.4**
Empress Dowager Cixi. Jung Chang **92**
The **Empress** of Art. Jaques, S. **92**
Empress of Fashion. Stuart, A. M. **92**

EMPRESSES

Catherine The memoirs of Catherine the Great **92**
Erickson, C. Great Catherine **947**
Faber, T. Faberge's eggs **739.2**
Freisenbruch, A. Caesars' wives **937**
Jung Chang Empress Dowager Cixi **92**
Kurth, P. Tsar: the lost world of Nicholas and Alexandra **947.08**
Massie, R. K. Catherine the Great **947**
Massie, R. K. Nicholas and Alexandra **92**
Massie, R. K. The Romanovs **947.08**
Remnick, D. Reporting **814**
Romanov riches **891.7**
Rounding, V. Catherine the Great **92**
Williams, K. Ambition and desire **92**

EMPRESSES -- CHINA -- BIOGRAPHY

Jung Chang Empress Dowager Cixi **92**

EMPRESSES -- FRANCE -- BIOGRAPHY

Williams, K. Ambition and desire **92**
Empson, William Sir, 1906-1984
About
Kermode, F. An appetite for poetry **801**
Empty mansions. Dedman, B. **92**
The **empty** ocean. Ellis, R. **577.7**
The **empty** space. Brook, P. **792**
Emrys, Barbara
The Toltec art of life and death **299.7**
Emswiler, James P.
Emswiler, M. A. Guiding your child through grief **155.9**
Emswiler, Mary Ann
Guiding your child through grief **155.9**
Enabling acts. Davis, L. J. **342.73**
ENAMEL AND ENAMELING
See also Decoration and ornament; Decorative arts
Enayati, Amanda
Seeking serenity **155.9**
ENCEPHALITIS
Cahalan, S. Brain on fire **616.8**
Crosby, M. C. Asleep **362.1**
Encore Provence. Mayle, P. **944.083**
Encounter. Kundera, M. **809**
Encounter on the narrow ridge: a life of Martin Buber. Friedman, M. S. **92**
Encounters at the heart of the world. Fenn, E. A. **305.897**
ENCOURAGEMENT
See also Courage; Helping behavior
ENCYCLOPAEDIA BRITANNICA
Jacobs, A. J. The know-it-all **031**
Encyclopaedia Britannica, Inc.
Getty Images Inc. History of the world in photographs **909.8**
Encyclopaedia Judaica. **296**
Encyclopedia of abortion in the United States.

Palmer, L. J. **363.46**
The **Encyclopedia** of African and African-American religions. **299.6**
Encyclopedia of African-American writing. **810**
Encyclopedia of American business. **338**
Encyclopedia of American ethnic literature [series]
Encyclopedia of American Indian literature **810**
Encyclopedia of American folk art. **745**
Encyclopedia of American folklife. **398**
Encyclopedia of American historical documents. **973**
Encyclopedia of American history. **973**
Encyclopedia of American Indian literature. **810**
Encyclopedia of American literature. Facts on File, I. **810**
Encyclopedia of American military history. **355**
Encyclopedia of American poetry, the twentieth century. **811**
Encyclopedia of American women in business. Krismann, C. **920.003**
Encyclopedia of ancient Egypt. Bunson, M. R. **932**
Encyclopedia of ancient Rome. Bunson, M. **937**
Encyclopedia of animal behavior. **591.5**
Encyclopedia of artists. **709**
Encyclopedia of Associations. **060.4**
Encyclopedia of biodiversity. Rice, S. A. **578.7**
Encyclopedia of Business Information Sources. **330**
Encyclopedia of careers and vocational guidance. J.G. Ferguson Publishing Company **331.7**
Encyclopedia of conflicts since World War II. **909.82**
Encyclopedia of constitutional amendments, proposed amendments, and amending issues, 1789-2010. Vile, J. R. **342**
The **Encyclopedia** of Country Music. **781.64**
Encyclopedia of crime and punishment. **346**
Encyclopedia of Cuba. Martinez-Fernandez, L. **972.91**
The **encyclopedia** of cults, sects, and new religions. **200**
The **encyclopedia** of demons and demonology. Guiley, R. E. **133.4**
Encyclopedia of dog breeds. Coile, D. C. **636.7**
The **encyclopedia** of Earth. Allaby, M. **910**
Encyclopedia of earthquakes and volcanoes. Gates, A. E. **551.2**
Encyclopedia of Exercise Anatomy. Liebman, H. L. **613.7**
Encyclopedia of exploration. Waldman, C. **910.3**
Encyclopedia of forensic science. Bell, S. **363.2**
The **encyclopedia** of furniture. Aronson, J. **749.03**
Encyclopedia of German literature. **830**
The **encyclopedia** of ghosts and spirits. Guiley, R. E. **133.1**
Encyclopedia of global resources. **333.7**
Encyclopedia of global warming & climate change. **363.738**

The **encyclopedia** of herbs. Tucker, A. O.   635

The **encyclopedia** of HIV and AIDS. Stratton, S. E.   362.196

Encyclopedia of insects.   595.7

Encyclopedia of Irish history and culture.   941.5

Encyclopedia of Islam. Campo, J. E.   297

Encyclopedia of Islam and the Muslim world.   909

Encyclopedia of Jewish folklore and traditions.   398.2

Encyclopedia of Jewish life before and during the Holocaust.   940.53

Encyclopedia of Latin American & Caribbean art.   709

The **encyclopedia** of literary and cultural theory.   801

Encyclopedia of marine science. Nichols, C. R.   551.46

Encyclopedia of mathematics. Tanton, J. S.   510

Encyclopedia of mathematics and society.   303.48

The **encyclopedia** of Middle East wars.   355

Encyclopedia of Native American tribes. Waldman, C.   970.004

Encyclopedia of Native American wars and warfare.   970.004

Encyclopedia of native tribes of North America. Johnson, M.   970.004

Encyclopedia of native tribes of North America.   970.004

The **encyclopedia** of natural medicine. Murray, M. T.   615.5

Encyclopedia of pasta. Pasta, a. d. p. t.   641.8

Encyclopedia of plague and pestilence.   614.4

Encyclopedia of pollution. Gates, A. E.   363.7

Encyclopedia of public health.   362.1

Encyclopedia of religion.   200

Encyclopedia of religious rites, rituals, and festivals.   200

Encyclopedia of rural America.   973

The **encyclopedia** of saints. Guiley, R. E.   282

The **Encyclopedia** of science and technology.   503

Encyclopedia of science, technology, and ethics.   503

The **encyclopedia** of sewing machine techniques. Bednar, N.   646.2

The **encyclopedia** of superheroes on film and television. Muir, J. K.   791.43

The **encyclopedia** of survival techniques. Stilwell, A.   613.6

Encyclopedia of terrorism.   363.32

The **encyclopedia** of the American armed forces. Axelrod, A.   355

Encyclopedia of the American Civil War.   973.7

Encyclopedia of the ancient Maya.   972.81

Encyclopedia of the ancient world.   930

Encyclopedia of the Cold War.   909.82

Encyclopedia of the crusades. Andrea, A. J.   909.07

The **Encyclopedia** of the Dead Sea scrolls.   296.1

Encyclopedia of the developing world.   909

Encyclopedia of the Enlightenment. Wilson, E.

J.   940.2

Encyclopedia of the First Amendment.   342

Encyclopedia of the industrial revolution in America. Olson, J. S.   973

Encyclopedia of the Lewis and Clark Expedition. Woodger, E.   917

Encyclopedia of the medieval world. English, E. D.   940.1

Encyclopedia of the new American nation.   973

Encyclopedia of the Renaissance.   940.2

Encyclopedia of the scientific revolution.   509

Encyclopedia of the U.S. Census.   304.6

Encyclopedia of the U.S. presidency.   352.23

Encyclopedia of the United Nations. Moore, J. A.   341.23

Encyclopedia of the United Nations and international agreements. Osmanczyk, E. J.   341.23

Encyclopedia of the United States Constitution. Schultz, D. A.   342

Encyclopedia of the Victorian era.   941.081

The **encyclopedia** of the Vietnam War. Tucker, S. C.   959.704

Encyclopedia of U.S. political history.   973

Encyclopedia of vampire mythology. Bane, T.   398

The **encyclopedia** of vampires & werewolves. Guiley, R. E.   398

Encyclopedia of water garden plants. Speichert, C. G.   635

The **encyclopedia** of weather and climate change. Fry, J. L.   551.6

The **encyclopedia** of witches, witchcraft, and Wicca. Guiley, R. E.   133.4

Encyclopedia of women and American politics.   973

Encyclopedia of women's autobiography.   920.003

The **Encyclopedia** of wood.   674

Encyclopedia of world religions [series]
Campo, J. E. Encyclopedia of Islam   297

The **Encyclopedia** of World War I.   940.3

Encyclopedia of World War II.   940.53

ENCYCLOPEDIAS *See* Encyclopedias and dictionaries

ENCYCLOPEDIAS AND DICTIONARIES

The American Heritage dictionary of the English language   423

Balick, M. J. Rodale's 21st-century herbal   635

Brain, M. The engineering book   620.009

Comprehensive Yiddish-English Dictionary   439

Encyclopedia of Associations   060.4

Encyclopedia of global warming & climate change   363.738

Famous first facts, international edition   031.02

The New York Public Library desk reference   031.02

The World Book Encyclopedia   031

ENCYCLOPEDIAS AND DICTIONARIES
See also Reference books

The **end.** De Villiers, M.   363.34

The **End** of absence. Harris, M.   **302.23**

The **End** of Alchemy. King, M. A.   **330.122**

The **end** of country. McGraw, S.   **333.79**

End of Days. Swanson, J. L.   **973.922**

The **end** of discovery. Stannard, R.   **501**

The **end** of education. Postman, N.   **370.9**

The **end** of empire. Kelly, C.   **92**

The **end** of heart disease. Fuhrman, J.   **616.12**

The **end** of leadership. Kellerman, B.   **303.3**

The **End** of Memory. Ingram, J.   **616.8**

The **end** of men. Rosin, H.   **305.42**

The **end** of night. Bogard, P.   **551.56**

The **end** of power. Naím, M.   **303.3**

The **end** of sex. Freitas, D.   **176**

The **end** of suffering. Cairns, S.   **231**

The **end** of the certain world. Greenspan, N. T.   **92**

The **End** of the Cold War, 1985-1991. Service, R.   **909.82**

End of the earth. Matthiessen, P.   **508**

END OF THE EARTH *See* End of the world

The **end** of the game. Beard, P. H.   **967.6**

The **end** of the line. Clover, C.   **333**

The **end** of the long summer. Dumanoski, D.   **551.6**

The **end** of the peace process. Said, E. W.   **956.05**

The **end** of the west. Dickman, M.   **811**

END OF THE WORLD

  Childs, C. Apocalyptic planet   **550**

  Plait, P. C. Death from the skies!   **520**

  Tevis, J. The world is on fire   **814**

  Weber, E. Apocalypses   **200**

END OF THE WORLD

   See also Eschatology

END OF THE WORLD (ASTRONOMY) *See* End of the world

The **end** of Wall Street. Lowenstein, R.   **332.6**

The **end** of your life book club. Schwalbe, W.   **616.99**

End this depression now! Krugman, P. R.   **330.9**

END-OF-THE-WORLD FICTION *See* Apocalyptic fiction

ENDANGERED SPECIES

  Ackerman, D. The rarest of the rare   **578.68**

  Barrow, M. V. Nature's ghosts   **333.95**

  Chadwick, D. H. The company we keep   **333.95**

  Ellis, R. The empty ocean   **577.7**

  Ellis, R. Tuna   **333.95**

  Fraser, C. Rewilding the world   **333.95**

  Matthiessen, P. Tigers in the snow   **599.756**

  McNamee, T. The return of the wolf to Yellowstone   **333.95**

  Montaigne, F. Fraser's penguins   **577.2**

  Neme, L. A. Animal investigators   **363.2**

  Owens, D. The eye of the elephant   **333.95**

  Quammen, D. Monster of God   **591.6**

  Smith, D. W. Decade of the wolf   **599.77**

  Stanford, C. B. Planet without apes   **599.88**

  Voigt, E. The dragon behind the glass   **597.176**

  Wilson, E. O. The future of life   **333.95**

  The world's rarest birds   **598**

ENDANGERED SPECIES

   See also Environmental protection; Nature conservation

ENDANGERED SPECIES -- HAWAII

  Williams, T. M. The odyssey of KP2   **599.79**

ENDANGERED SPECIES -- LAOS -- NAKAI-NAM THEUN NATIONAL BIODIVERSITY CONSERVATION AREA

  DeBuys, W. The last unicorn   **591.68**

ENDANGERED SPECIES -- LAW AND LEGISLATION

  Barrow, M. V. Nature's ghosts   **333.95**

ENDANGERED SPECIES -- RESEARCH

  Rigney, M. In pursuit of giants   **597**

ENDANGERED SPECIES -- UNITED STATES

  Mooallem, J. Wild ones   **333.95**

  Neme, L. A. Animal investigators   **363.2**

ENDANGERED SPECIES -- UNITED STATES -- PSYCHOLOGICAL ASPECTS

  Mooallem, J. Wild ones   **333.95**

The **endangered** species road trip. Macdonald, C.   **974**

Ende, Werner

  (ed) Islam in der Gegenwart./English. Islam in the world today   **297**

Endersby, Jim

  A guinea pig's history of biology   **576.5**

Endgame. Rohde, D.   **949.7**

Endgame. Brady, F.   **92**

The **endgame.** Gordon, M. R.   **956.7**

Ending the Vietnam War. Kissinger, H.   **959.704**

Endless forms most beautiful. Carroll, S. B.   **571.8**

ENDOCRINOLOGY

   See also Medicine

ENDOWED CHARITIES *See* Charities; Endowments

ENDOWMENTS

   See also Finance

ENDOWMENTS -- DIRECTORIES

  The Foundation directory   **061**

ENDOWMENTS -- UNITED STATES -- HISTORY

  Zunz, O. Philanthropy in America   **361.7**

The **ends** of the earth.   **998**

The **Endurance.** Alexander, C.   **998**

ENDURANCE (SHIP)

  Alexander, C. The Endurance   **998**

ENDURANCE SPORTS -- PHYSIOLOGICAL ASPECTS

  Fitzgerald, M. How bad do you want it?   **612.044**

ENDURANCE SPORTS -- PSYCHOLOGICAL ASPECTS

  Fitzgerald, M. How bad do you want it?   **612.044**

ENDURANCE, PHYSICAL *See* Physical fitness

Enemies. Weiner, T.   **363.25**

Enemies of the people. Marton, K.   **92**

Enemy of the state. Newton, M. A.   **345**

ENERGY *See* Energy resources; Force and energy

ENERGY AND STATE *See* Energy policy

ENERGY CONSERVATION
   Feynman, R. P. Six easy pieces   **530**
   Newton, D. E. World energy crisis   **333.79**

ENERGY CONSERVATION
   See also Conservation of natural resources;
   Energy resources

ENERGY CONSUMPTION
   See also Energy resources

ENERGY CONSUMPTION -- UNITED STATES
   Koerth-Baker, M. Before the lights go out   **333.79**

ENERGY CONVERSION, MICROBIAL *See*
   Biomass energy

ENERGY DEVELOPMENT
   Alley, R. B. Earth   **621**
   Muller, R. A. Energy for future presidents   **333.79**
   Renewable energy   **333**

ENERGY DEVELOPMENT
   See also Energy resources

Energy for future presidents. Muller, R. A.   **333.79**

ENERGY INDUSTRY EXECUTIVES
   Bruni, F. Ambling into history: the unlikely odyssey of George W. Bush   **973.931**
   Burrough, B. The big rich   **338.2**
   Chernow, R. Titan: the life of John D. Rockefeller, Sr.   **92**
   Farmer, J. J. The ground truth   **973.931**
   Hersh, S. M. Chain of command   **973.931**
   Schlesinger, A. M. War and the American presidency   **327.1**
   Walsh, J. The J. Paul Getty Museum and its collections   **708.1**
   Woodward, B. The commanders   **973.928**
   Woodward, B. Plan of attack   **956.7**
   Woodward, B. State of denial   **973.931**

ENERGY INTAKE -- PHYSIOLOGY
   Nesheim, M. Why calories count   **613.2**

ENERGY POLICY
   Helm, D. The carbon crunch   **333.79**
   McGraw, S. The end of country   **333.79**
   Newton, D. E. World energy crisis   **333.79**
   Renewable energy   **333**
   Yergin, D. The quest   **333.79**

ENERGY POLICY
   See also Energy resources; Industrial policy

ENERGY RESOURCES
   Friedman, T. L. Hot, flat, and crowded   **363.7**
   Levi, M. Power surge   **333.79**
   McGraw, S. The end of country   **333.79**
   Muller, R. A. Energy for future presidents   **333.79**
   Yergin, D. The quest   **333.79**
   Zuckerman, G. The frackers   **338.2**

ENFIELD (LONDON, ENGLAND) -- HISTORY
   Brown, P. Shakespeare's Pub   **647.9**

Engard, Nicole C.
   (ed) Library mashups   **020**

Engel, Beverly
   The nice girl syndrome   **155.6**

Engel, Richard, 1973-
       About
   Engel, R. And then all hell broke loose   **956.05**

Engelberg, Stephen
   Germs   **358**

Engels, Friedrich, 1820-1895
   Marx, K. The Communist manifesto   **335.4**
       About
   Heilbroner, R. L. The worldly philosophers   **330.1**
   Hunt, T. Marx's general   **92**

Engine empire. Hong, C. P.   **811**

ENGINEERING
   Brain, M. The engineering book   **620.009**
   Molotch, H. L. Where stuff comes from   **620**
   Petroski, H. To forgive design   **620**
   Petroski, H. The essential engineer   **620**
   Petroski, H. Success through failure   **620**
   Train   **625.1**
   Waldman, J. Rust   **620.1**

ENGINEERING
   See also Industrial arts; Technology

ENGINEERING -- STUDY AND TEACHING
   Poe, M. Learning to communicate in science and engineering   **501**

The engineering book. Brain, M.   **620.009**

ENGINEERING INSTRUMENTS
   See also Scientific apparatus and instruments

ENGINEERING MATERIALS *See* Materials

Engineering the financial crisis. Friedman, J.   **330.9**

ENGINEERING, GENETIC *See* Genetic engineering

ENGINEERS
   Burleigh, N. Unholy business   **933**

Engineers of victory. Kennedy, P. M.   **940.54**

ENGINES
   See also Machinery

Engines of change. Ingrassia, P.   **629.222**

ENGLAND
   Ackroyd, P. Tudors   **942.05**
   Stewart, R. The Marches   **941.3**

ENGLAND
   See also Great Britain

ENGLAND -- ANTIQUITIES
   Pearson, M. P. Stonehenge   **936.2**

ENGLAND -- CHURCH HISTORY -- 16TH CENTURY
   Ronald, S. Heretic queen   **942.05**

ENGLAND -- DESCRIPTION AND TRAVEL
   Macfarlane, R. The old ways   **914.2**
   Raymo, C. Walking zero   **526**

ENGLAND -- DRAMA.
Bennett, A. The history boys   **822**
ENGLAND -- ETHNIC RELATIONS
Walsh, M. Gypsy boy   **92**
ENGLAND -- HISTORY *See* Great Britain -- History
ENGLAND -- HISTORY, MILITARY -- 19TH CENTURY -- SOURCES
Crane, D. Went the day well?   **940.2**
ENGLAND -- INTELLECTUAL LIFE -- 16TH CENTURY
Nuttall, A. D. Shakespeare the thinker   **822.3**
ENGLAND -- SOCIAL CONDITIONS -- 16TH CENTURY
MacGregor, N. Shakespeare's restless world   **942.055**
Mortimer, I. The time traveler's guide to Elizabethan England   **942.05**
ENGLAND -- SOCIAL CONDITIONS -- 19TH CENTURY -- SOURCES
Crane, D. Went the day well?   **940.2**
ENGLAND -- SOCIAL LIFE AND CUSTOMS
MacColl, G. To marry an English Lord   **974.7**
Walsh, M. Gypsy boy   **92**
Engle, Charlie
Running Man   **796.42**
Englehart, Murray
AC/DC   **920**
Englert, Rod
Blood secrets   **363.2**
ENGLISH
Tombs, R. The English and their history   **942**
The **English** and their history. Tombs, R.   **942**
English as a global language. Crystal, D.   **420**
ENGLISH AS A SECOND LANGUAGE -- BIBLIOGRAPHY
Riechel, R. Easy information sources for ESL, adult learners, & new readers   **016**
ENGLISH AUTHORS
Campbell, H. The art of Neil Gaiman   **92**
The history of British women's writing   **820**
Orwell, G. Diaries   **828**
ENGLISH AUTHORS
See also Authors
ENGLISH AUTHORS -- BIOGRAPHY
Ker, I. G. K. Chesterton   **828**
ENGLISH AUTHORS -- HOMES
See also Literary landmarks
ENGLISH DRAMA
Critical survey of drama   **809**
ENGLISH DRAMA
See also Drama; English literature
ENGLISH DRAMA -- COLLECTIONS
Christie, A. The mousetrap and other plays   **822**
ENGLISH DRAMA -- DICTIONARIES
Critical survey of drama   **809**

ENGLISH DRAMA -- HISTORY AND CRITICISM
Baker, W. The facts on file companion to Shakespeare   **822.3**
ENGLISH ESSAYS
See also English literature; Essays
ENGLISH FICTION
Herald, D. T. Genreflecting   **016**
ENGLISH FICTION
See also English literature; Fiction
ENGLISH FICTION -- HISTORY AND CRITICISM
The Columbia history of the British novel   **823**
The Facts on File companion to the British novel   **823**
Head, D. The Cambridge introduction to modern British fiction, 1950-2000   **823**
ENGLISH FICTION -- STORIES, PLOTS, ETC
Herald, D. T. Genreflecting   **016**
ENGLISH GRAMMAR *See* English language -- Grammar
ENGLISH HISTORY *See* Great Britain -- History
ENGLISH LANGUAGE
Crystal, D. The Cambridge encyclopedia of the English language   **420**
Garner, B. A. Garner's modern American usage   **423**
Macfarlane, R. Landmarks   **914.1**
Simpson, J. The word detective   **423.092**
ENGLISH LANGUAGE
See also Language and languages
ENGLISH LANGUAGE -- AMERICANISMS
See Americanisms
ENGLISH LANGUAGE -- BUSINESS ENGLISH
Pollack, J. Shortcut   **808**
ENGLISH LANGUAGE -- COMPOSITION AND EXERCISES
Glenn, C. Hodges' Harbrace handbook   **808**
ENGLISH LANGUAGE -- DIALECTS
Crystal, D. By hook or by crook   **427**
Do you speak American ?(Television program) Do you speak American?   **427**
ENGLISH LANGUAGE -- DICTIONARIES
Merriam-Webster's visual dictionary   **423**
ENGLISH LANGUAGE -- ERRORS IN USAGE
Norris, M. Between you & me   **428**
ENGLISH LANGUAGE -- ETYMOLOGY
Crystal, D. The story of English in 100 words   **422**
Forsyth, M. The etymologicon   **422**
Fowler, H. W. A dictionary of modern English usage   **428**
ENGLISH LANGUAGE -- ETYMOLOGY
See also English language -- History
ENGLISH LANGUAGE -- ETYMOLOGY -- DICTIONARIES
Hendrickson, R. The Facts on File encyclopedia of

word and phrase origins **422**

**ENGLISH LANGUAGE -- FOREIGN ELE-
MENTS**

Crystal, D. The story of English in 100 words **422**

**ENGLISH LANGUAGE -- FOREIGN WORDS
AND PHRASES -- DICTIONARIES**

From bonbon to cha-cha **422**

Manser, M. H. The Facts on File dictionary of foreign words and phrases **422**

ENGLISH LANGUAGE -- GRAMMAR

Dunn, P. A. Grammar rants **428**

Garner, B. A. Garner's Modern English Usage **808**

Hult, C. A. The Handy English grammar answer
book **428**

Norris, M. Between you & me **428**

Pinker, S. The sense of style **808**

ENGLISH LANGUAGE -- GRAMMAR

See also Grammar

**ENGLISH LANGUAGE -- GRAMMAR --
HANDBOOKS, MANUALS, ETC**

Hult, C. A. The Handy English grammar answer
book **428**

ENGLISH LANGUAGE -- HISTORY

Bailey, R. W. Speaking American **427**

Crystal, D. The story of English in 100 words **422**

Nunberg, G. The ascent of the A-word **427**

ENGLISH LANGUAGE -- IDIOMS

Fowler, H. W. A dictionary of modern English usage **428**

ENGLISH LANGUAGE -- LEXICOGRAPHY

Simpson, J. The word detective **423.092**

**ENGLISH LANGUAGE -- LEXICOGRAPHY --
HISTORY -- 19TH CENTURY**

Winchester, S. The professor and the madman **423**

**ENGLISH LANGUAGE -- LEXICOGRAPHY --
UNITED STATES**

Bailey, R. W. Speaking American **427**

ENGLISH LANGUAGE -- OBSCENE WORDS

Nunberg, G. The ascent of the A-word **427**

**ENGLISH LANGUAGE -- ORTHOGRAPHY
AND SPELLING**

Crystal, D. Spell It Out **421**

ENGLISH LANGUAGE -- PUNCTUATION *See*
Punctuation

ENGLISH LANGUAGE -- RHETORIC *See*
Rhetoric

ENGLISH LANGUAGE -- RHYME

Espy, W. R. Words to rhyme with **423**

Upton, C. Oxford rhyming dictionary **423**

ENGLISH LANGUAGE -- SLANG

Axelrod, A. Whiskey tango foxtrot **427**

Nunberg, G. The ascent of the A-word **427**

**ENGLISH LANGUAGE -- SLANG -- DICTION-
ARIES**

The new Partridge dictionary of slang and unconventional English **427**

Spears, R. A. McGraw-Hill's dictionary of American slang and colloquial expressions **427**

ENGLISH LANGUAGE -- SOCIAL ASPECTS

Crystal, D. English as a global language **420**

ENGLISH LANGUAGE -- STYLE

Garvey, M. Stylized **808**

Pinker, S. The sense of style **808**

Strunk, W. The elements of style **808**

**ENGLISH LANGUAGE -- SYNONYMS AND
ANTONYMS**

Concise Oxford American thesaurus **423**

Dictionary of confusable words **423**

Historical thesaurus of the Oxford English dictionary **423**

Little, B. &. C. I. Bartlett's Roget's thesaurus **423**

Merriam-Webster Inc. Merriam-Webster's collegiate thesaurus **423**

Oxford American writer's thesaurus **423**

Roget's 21st century thesaurus in dictionary
form **423**

Roget's international thesaurus **423**

**ENGLISH LANGUAGE -- TERMS AND PHRAS-
ES**

Jurafsky, D. The language of food **641.3**

**ENGLISH LANGUAGE -- UNITED STATES --
HISTORY**

Bailey, R. W. Speaking American **427**

Lepore, J. A is for American **306.44**

**ENGLISH LANGUAGE -- UNITED STATES --
SLANG -- DICTIONARIES**

Axelrod, A. Whiskey tango foxtrot **427**

**ENGLISH LANGUAGE -- UNITED STATES --
USAGE**

Bailey, R. W. Speaking American **427**

Peters, P. The Cambridge guide to English usage **428**

ENGLISH LANGUAGE -- USAGE

Fowler, H. W. A dictionary of modern English usage **428**

Hult, C. A. The Handy English grammar answer
book **428**

ENGLISH LANGUAGE -- USAGE

See also English language -- Grammar

**ENGLISH LANGUAGE -- USAGE -- DICTION-
ARIES**

The American Heritage dictionary of the English
language **423**

**ENGLISH LANGUAGE -- VARIATION -- UNIT-
ED STATES**

Bailey, R. W. Speaking American **427**

ENGLISH LANGUAGE -- VOCABULARY *See*
Vocabulary

ENGLISH LETTERS

See also English literature; Letters

ENGLISH LITERATURE

The Cambridge guide to literature in English **820**

The Continuum encyclopedia of British literature   **810**

Macfarlane, R. Landmarks   **914.1**

The New Oxford book of literary anecdotes   **828**

Orwell, G. Diaries   **828**

The Oxford companion to English literature   **820**

Sanders, A. The short Oxford history of English literature   **820**

ENGLISH LITERATURE

  See also Literature

ENGLISH LITERATURE -- 20TH CENTURY

The history of British women's writing   **820**

ENGLISH LITERATURE -- ANECDOTES

The New Oxford book of literary anecdotes   **828**

ENGLISH LITERATURE -- BIO-BIBLIOGRAPHY

The Cambridge guide to literature in English   **820**

The Oxford companion to English literature   **820**

ENGLISH LITERATURE -- BLACK AUTHORS -- HISTORY AND CRITICISM

Black literature criticism   **809**

ENGLISH LITERATURE -- COLLECTIONS

The Norton anthology of English literature   **820**

ENGLISH LITERATURE -- DICTIONARIES

The Cambridge guide to literature in English   **820**

The Oxford companion to English literature   **820**

ENGLISH LITERATURE -- ENCYCLOPEDIAS

The Continuum encyclopedia of British literature   **810**

ENGLISH LITERATURE -- HISTORY AND CRITICISM

Coles, R. Handing one another along   **820**

Donoghue, D. Speaking of beauty   **801**

Donoghue, E. Inseparable   **809**

The Oxford companion to English literature   **820**

Sanders, A. The short Oxford history of English literature   **820**

ENGLISH LITERATURE -- WOMEN AUTHORS

The history of British women's writing   **820**

ENGLISH LITERATURE -- WOMEN AUTHORS -- DICTIONARIES

The Cambridge guide to women's writing in English   **820**

ENGLISH LITERATURE -- WOMEN AUTHORS -- HISTORY AND CRITICISM

The history of British women's writing   **820**

Pierpont, C. R. Passionate minds   **810**

ENGLISH NOVELISTS

Orwell, G. Diaries   **828**

ENGLISH NOVELISTS

  See also Novelists

ENGLISH PERIODICALS

  See also Periodicals

ENGLISH POETRY

The Best poems of the English language   **821**

The complete poems   **811**

Good poems   **811**

The Making of a poem   **821**

The Oxford book of English verse   **821**

Poems to read   **808.81**

ENGLISH POETRY

  See also English literature; Poetry

ENGLISH POETRY -- 20TH CENTURY

Contemporary poets   **821**

Davie, D. Collected poems   **821**

ENGLISH POETRY -- 20TH CENTURY -- HISTORY AND CRITICISM

Contemporary poets   **821**

Swift, D. Bomber County   **821**

ENGLISH POETRY -- COLLECTIONS

100 essential modern poems   **821**

100 great poems of the twentieth century   **821**

The Best poems of the English language   **821**

Christmas poems   **821**

The Columbia anthology of British poetry   **821**

Good poems   **811**

The Making of a poem   **821**

The Norton anthology of modern and contemporary poetry   **821**

The Oxford book of comic verse   **821**

The Oxford book of English verse   **821**

The Oxford book of sonnets   **821**

The Penguin book of the sonnet   **821**

Poetry speaks expanded   **811**

ENGLISH POETRY -- HISTORY AND CRITICISM

The complete poems   **811**

ENGLISH POETRY -- IRISH AUTHORS

An anthology of modern Irish poetry   **821**

The New Oxford book of Irish verse   **821**

ENGLISH POETRY -- WOMEN AUTHORS -- COLLECTIONS

British women poets of the Romantic era   **821**

ENGLISH POETS

  See also Poets

ENGLISH POETS -- BIOGRAPHY

Hollis, M. Now all roads lead to France   **821**

ENGLISH TEACHERS

Nafisi, A. The Republic of Imagination   **819**

ENGLISH TEACHERS -- PENNSYLVANIA -- LEVITTOWN -- BIOGRAPHY

Sokolove, M. Drama high   **92**

ENGLISH WIT AND HUMOR

The Oxford book of humorous prose   **827**

ENGLISH WIT AND HUMOR

  See also English literature; Wit and humor

English, Ashley

Home dairy with Ashley English   **637**

English, Bella

Last lion   **92**

English, Edward D.

Encyclopedia of the medieval world **940.1**

The **Englishman** who posted himself and other curious objects. Tingey, J. **92**

Englund, Peter
The beauty and the sorrow **940.3**

ENGRAVERS
Bentley, G. E. The stranger from paradise: a biography of William Blake **821**

ENGRAVERS
See also Artists

ENGRAVING
Hauptman, J. Degas **709**

ENGRAVING
See also Art; Graphic arts; Illustration of books; Pictures

ENGRAVINGS *See* Engraving

Enigma: the battle for the code. Sebag-Montefiore, H. **940.54**

ENIGMAS *See* Curiosities and wonders; Riddles

The **enjoyment** of music. Forney, K. **780**

The **enlightened** cyclist. Bike Snob **796.6**

Enlightened journey. Thondup, T. **294.3**

Enlightening the world. Khan, Y. S. **974.7**

The **Enlightenment.** Pagden, A. **940.2**

ENLIGHTENMENT
See also Modern civilization; Modern philosophy; Rationalism

ENLIGHTENMENT
Gay, P. The rise of modern paganism **190**
Gay, P. The science of freedom **190**
Himmelfarb, G. The roads to modernity **190**
Pagden, A. The Enlightenment **940.2**
Staloff, D. Hamilton, Adams, Jefferson **973.4**

ENLIGHTENMENT -- ENCYCLOPEDIAS
Wilson, E. J. Encyclopedia of the Enlightenment **940.2**

ENLIGHTENMENT -- GERMANY -- PRUSSIA
Blanning, T. Frederick the Great **92**

ENLIGHTENMENT -- SCOTLAND
Boswell's enlightenment **828**
Zaretsky, R. Boswell's enlightenment **92**

The **Enlightenment: an interpretation** [series]
Gay, P. The rise of modern paganism **190**
Gay, P. The science of freedom **190**

Enough. Davis, W. **241**

Enough. Giffords, G. D. **363.33**

Enriched classics series
Heyerdahl, T. Kon-Tiki **910.4**

Enright, D. J.
(ed) The Oxford book of death **808.88**

ENSEMBLES (MATHEMATICS) *See* Set theory

ENSEMBLES (MUSIC)
See also Music; Musical form; Musicians

ENSIGNS *See* Flags

Enss, Chris
Mochi's war **978.8**

Enter Helen. Hauser, B. **92**

Enterprise [series]
Parks, T. Medici money **332.1**

ENTERPRISES *See* Business enterprises

ENTERTAINERS
Carter, R. A. Buffalo Bill Cody **978**
Hirschfeld, A. Hirschfeld on line **741.5**
Holmes, R. African queen **92**
Warren, L. S. Buffalo Bill's America **92**

ENTERTAINERS -- UNITED STATES -- BIOGRAPHY
Angelou, M. Mom & me & mom **818**
Ball, L. Love, Lucy **92**
MacLaine, S. Above the line **92**
Poole, W. S. Vampira **92**

ENTERTAINING
Anderson, P. Perfect one-dish dinners **641.8**
Anderson, P. Perfect recipes for having people over **641.5**
Bayless, R. Fiesta at Rick's **641.5**
Charlie Palmer's American fare **641.59**
Colwin, L. More home cooking **642**
Davies, K. Q. What Katie Ate on the Weekend
The Eat Like a Man Guide to Feeding a Crowd **641.5**
Home **641.5**
Jamison, C. A. The big book of outdoor cooking and entertaining **641.5**
Julia Reed's south **642.4**
Martha's entertaining
Mozza at home **641.5**
Pepin, J. Jacques Pepin celebrates **641.5**
Rosenstrach, J. How to celebrate everything **641.568**
Schuman, E. Cupcakes and cashmere at home **746.9**
Sedaris, A. I like you **793.2**
Stewart, M. Martha Stewart's cooking school **641.5**
Tanis, D. Heart of the artichoke and other kitchen journeys **641.5**
Tanis, D. A platter of figs and other recipes **641.5**

ENTERTAINING
See also Etiquette; Home economics

ENTERTAINMENTS *See* Amusements

Entice with spice. Ramineni, S. **641.5**

An **entirely** synthetic fish. Halverson, A. **639.3**

ENTOMOLOGISTS
Fraser, K. Ornament and silence **809**
Heinrich, B. Summer world **591.7**

ENTOZOA *See* Parasites

ENTRANCE REQUIREMENTS FOR COLLEGES AND UNIVERSITIES *See* Colleges and universities -- Entrance requirements

Entrelac. Drysdale, R. **746.432**

ENTREPRENEURS
Burleigh, N. Unholy business **933**
Kidder, D. S. The Startup playbook **658.1**
Stabiner, K. Generation chef **641.5**

ENTREPRENEURS

See also Businesspeople; Self-employed

ENTREPRENEURSHIP

Barringer, B. Launching a Business — **658.1**

Buelow, B. L. The Introvert Entrepreneur — **658.11**

Casnocha, B. My start-up life — **338.7**

Duffy, S. Launch! — **658.1**

Grant, A. Originals — **153.3**

Guillebeau, C. The $100 startup — **658.1**

Hewitt, B. The town that food saved — **338.1**

Hill, N. Think and grow rich — **650.1**

Ivanko, J. D. Homemade for Sale — **664**

Jerrard, J. Crisis in employment — **025.5**

Kidder, D. S. The Startup playbook — **658.1**

Nalebuff, B. Mission in a bottle — **338.7**

Pimsleur, J. Million Dollar Women — **658.4**

Sarillo, N. A slice of the pie — **658.02**

Wasserman, N. The founder's dilemmas — **658.1**

ENTREPRENEURSHIP

See also Business; Capitalism; Small business

ENTREPRENEURSHIP -- UNITED STATES -- ANECDOTES

Stone, B. Things a little bird told me — **006.7**

ENTREPRENEURSHIP -- UNITED STATES -- BIOGRAPHY

Ping Fu Bend, not break — **92**

Entrepreneurship and small business management collection [series]

Barringer, B. Launching a Business — **658.1**

ENTROPY

Muller, R. A. Now — **530.11**

ENTROPY

See also Thermodynamics

ENVIRONMENT

Park, C. A dictionary of environment and conservation — **333.7**

ENVIRONMENT -- GOVERNMENT POLICY

See Environmental policy

ENVIRONMENT AND STATE *See* Environmental policy

ENVIRONMENTAL DEGRADATION

Blackwell, A. Visit sunny Chernobyl — **363.73**

Ladd, B. Autophobia — **303.4**

McKibben, B. Eaarth — **253**

Novacek, M. J. Terra — **576.8**

Safina, C. The view from Lazy Point — **508**

Wilcove, D. S. No way home — **591.56**

Wilson, E. O. The future of life — **333.95**

ENVIRONMENTAL DEGRADATION

See also Environment; Natural disasters

ENVIRONMENTAL DESTRUCTION *See* Environmental degradation

ENVIRONMENTAL DETERIORATION *See* Environmental degradation

ENVIRONMENTAL DISASTERS

Kolbert, E. The sixth extinction — **576.8**

ENVIRONMENTAL ECONOMICS

Klein, N. This changes everything — **363.738**

ENVIRONMENTAL ENGINEERING -- UNITED STATES

Humes, E. Garbology — **628.4**

ENVIRONMENTAL ETHICS

See also Ethics

ENVIRONMENTAL ETHICS -- UNITED STATES -- HISTORY

Souder, W. On a farther shore — **92**

ENVIRONMENTAL HEALTH

Shulman, S. Cooler smarter — **363.7**

Smith, R. Toxin toxout — **613**

Sustaining life — **333.95**

Terry, B. Plastic-free — **363.738**

ENVIRONMENTAL HEALTH

See also Environmental influence on humans; Public health

ENVIRONMENTAL HEALTH -- NEW YORK CITY -- PERSONAL NARRATIVES

Farley, T. Saving Gotham — **362.1**

ENVIRONMENTAL INFLUENCE ON HUMANS

Diamond, J. M. Guns, germs, and steel — **303.4**

Hansen, J. E. Storms of my grandchildren — **363.7**

Louv, R. The nature principle — **128**

Louv, R. Last child in the woods — **155.4**

Lynas, M. Six degrees — **551.6**

McPhee, J. The control of nature — **304.2**

ENVIRONMENTAL INFLUENCE ON HUMANS

See also Adaptation (Biology); Human ecology; Human geography

ENVIRONMENTAL LAW

See also Environmental policy; Environmental protection; Law

ENVIRONMENTAL LAWYERS -- UNITED STATES -- BIOGRAPHY

Barrett, P. M. Law of the jungle — **344**

ENVIRONMENTAL LOBBY *See* Environmental movement

ENVIRONMENTAL MONITORING -- HUDSON RIVER VALLEY (N.Y. AND N.J.)

Busch, A. The incidental steward — **363.7**

ENVIRONMENTAL MOVEMENT

American earth — **333.72**

Friedman, T. L. Hot, flat, and crowded — **363.7**

Lytle, M. H. The gentle subversive — **92**

McKibben, B. Oil and Honey — **363.7**

Pipher, M. The green boat — **303.4**

Potter, W. Green is the new red — **320.5**

ENVIRONMENTAL MOVEMENT

See also Environment; Social movements

ENVIRONMENTAL POLICY

Diamond, J. M. Collapse: how societies choose to

fail or succeed **304.2**

Gore, A. Our choice **363.7**

Klein, N. This changes everything **363.738**

Pooley, E. The climate war **363.7**

Speth, J. G. The bridge at the end of the world **333.7**

ENVIRONMENTAL POLICY

See also Environment

ENVIRONMENTAL POLICY -- CHINA

Kelly, W. J. The People's Republic of Chemicals **363.739**

ENVIRONMENTAL POLICY -- ECONOMIC ASPECTS

Klein, N. This changes everything **363.738**

ENVIRONMENTAL POLICY -- UNITED STATES

Chadwick, D. H. The company we keep **333.95**

Friedman, T. L. Hot, flat, and crowded **363.7**

Gore, A. An inconvenient truth **363.7**

Jones, V. The green-collar economy **363.7**

Speth, J. G. America the possible **338.9**

ENVIRONMENTAL POLLUTION See Pollution

ENVIRONMENTAL PROTECTION

American earth **333.72**

Beavan, C. No impact man **333.72**

Brinkley, D. The quiet world **333.72**

Busch, A. The incidental steward **363.7**

Goleman, D. Ecological intelligence **333.7**

Gore, A. An inconvenient truth **363.7**

Gore, A. Our choice **363.7**

Hoekstra, J. M. The atlas of global conservation **333.95**

Jones, V. The green-collar economy **363.7**

Leopold, A. A Sand County almanac & other writings on ecology & conservation **508**

Logan, W. B. Air **551.5**

Mary, B. An American River

McKibben, B. The Bill McKibben reader **333.72**

McPhee, J. The control of nature **304.2**

Prud'homme, A. Hydrofracking **622**

Wilson, D. An unreasonable woman **92**

Wohlforth, C. The fate of nature **304.2**

ENVIRONMENTAL PROTECTION

See also Ecology; Environment

ENVIRONMENTAL PROTECTION -- ARCTIC REGIONS

Stewart, B. Don't trust, don't fear, don't beg **363.738**

ENVIRONMENTAL PROTECTION -- UNITED STATES

Brinkley, D. Rightful heritage **92**

ENVIRONMENTAL PROTECTION -- UNITED STATES -- CITIZEN PARTICIPATION

Shulman, S. Cooler smarter **363.7**

ENVIRONMENTAL QUALITY -- GOVERNMENT POLICY See Environmental policy

ENVIRONMENTAL RESPONSIBILITY --

UNITED STATES

Jenkins, M. Poison spring **363.73**

Sachs, J. The price of civilization **330.9**

ENVIRONMENTAL SCIENCE

Ball, P. Patterns in nature **500.2**

ENVIRONMENTAL SCIENCES

The global warming reader **363.738**

McDaniel, C. N. Wisdom for a livable planet **333.72**

ENVIRONMENTAL SCIENCES

See also Science

ENVIRONMENTAL SCIENCES -- DICTIONARIES

Park, C. A dictionary of environment and conservation **333.7**

ENVIRONMENTAL TECHNOLOGY See Green technology

ENVIRONMENTAL TOURISM See Ecotourism

ENVIRONMENTAL TOXICOLOGY -- UNITED STATES -- CASE STUDIES

Lerner, S. Sacrifice zones **363.738**

ENVIRONMENTALISM See Environmental movement; Environmental protection

ENVIRONMENTALISM -- APPALACHIAN REGION, SOUTHERN

House, S. Something's rising **338.2**

ENVIRONMENTALISM -- HISTORY

Lytle, M. H. The gentle subversive **92**

ENVIRONMENTALISM -- UNITED STATES

McKibben, B. Oil and Honey **363.7**

ENVIRONMENTALISM -- UNITED STATES -- HISTORY

Souder, W. On a farther shore **92**

Sullivan, R. The Thoreau you don't know **92**

ENVIRONMENTALISTS

Humes, E. Eco Barons **363.7**

Kuipers, D. Operation Bite Back **92**

Maathai, W. Unbowed **92**

McKibben, B. Oil and Honey **363.7**

ENVIRONMENTALISTS

See also Activists; Scientists

ENVIRONMENTALISTS -- UNITED STATES -- BIOGRAPHY

McKibben, B. Oil and Honey **363.7**

Souder, W. On a farther shore **92**

ENVIRONMENTALLY FRIENDLY ARCHITECTURE See Sustainable architecture

ENVIRONMENTALLY INDUCED DISEASES

See also Diseases -- Causes; Environmental health

ENVIRONMENTALLY INDUCED DISEASES -- NUTRITIONAL ASPECTS

Smith, R. Toxin toxout **613**

Envisioning emancipation. Krauthamer, B. **973.7**

EOLITHIC PERIOD See Stone Age

Éon de Beaumont, Charles Geneviève Louis Au-

guste André Timothée d', 1728-1810
About
Paul, J. R. Unlikely allies   **973.3**

Ephron, Dan
Killing a king   **956.94**

Ephron, Nora, 1941-2012
I feel bad about my neck   **814**
The Most of Nora Ephron   **814**

Ephrussi family
About
De Waal, E. The hare with amber eyes   **920**

Ephrussi, Charles, 1849-1905
About
De Waal, E. The hare with amber eyes   **920**

EPIC FILMS
   See also Motion pictures

EPIC LITERATURE
   See also Literature

EPIC POETRY
Carson, A. Red doc>   **811**
Jenkyns, R. Classical literature   **880**
Manguel, A. Homer's The Iliad and The Odyssey   **883**
Nicolson, A. Why Homer matters   **883**

EPIC POETRY
   See also Epic literature; Narrative poetry

EPIC POETRY, GREEK -- ADAPTATIONS
Carson, A. Red doc>   **811**

EPIC POETRY, GREEK -- HISTORY AND CRITICISM
Nicolson, A. Why Homer matters   **883**

Epic tomatoes. LeHoullier, C.   **635**
An **Epidemic** of Absence. Velasquez-Manoff, M.   **616.97**

EPIDEMICS
Crosby, M. C. Asleep   **362.1**
Garrett, L. The coming plague   **614.4**
Iweala, U. Our kind of people   **362.196**
Khan, A. S. The next pandemic   **362.1**
Oldstone, M. B. A. Viruses, plagues, and history   **614.4**
Quammen, D. Spillover   **614.4**

EPIDEMICS
   See also Diseases; Public health

EPIDEMICS -- ENCYCLOPEDIAS
Encyclopedia of plague and pestilence   **614.4**

EPIDEMICS -- HISTORY
McNeill, W. H. Plagues and peoples   **614.4**

EPIDEMIOLOGY
Kolata, G. Flu   **614.5**

EPIDEMIOLOGY
   See also Public health

EPIDEMIOLOGY -- AFRICA -- HISTORY
Halperin, D. Tinderbox   **614.5**

Epigenetics. Francis, R. C.   **572.8**
Epigrams. Martial   **878**

EPIGRAMS
   See also Wit and humor

EPIGRAMS
Martial Epigrams   **878**

EPILEPSY
Fadiman, A. The spirit catches you and you fall down   **306.4**

EPILEPSY
   See also Nervous system -- Diseases

EPILEPSY -- GRAPHIC NOVELS
B., D. Epileptic   **741.5**

EPILEPSY -- SURGERY
Dittrich, L. Patient H.M.   **616.85**

EPILEPSY IN CHILDREN
Fadiman, A. The spirit catches you and you fall down   **306.4**

Epileptic. B., D.   **741.5**
Epilogue. Roiphe, A. R.   **92**

EPIPHYTES
Air plants   **628.5**

Episcopal Church
Episcopal Church/Book of common prayer The Book of common prayer and administration of the sacraments and other rites and ceremonies of the church   **264**

Episcopal Church/Book of common prayer
The Book of common prayer and administration of the sacraments and other rites and ceremonies of the church   **264**

EPISCOPAL CHURCH -- CLERGY -- BIOGRAPHY
Bell-Scott, P. The firebrand and the First Lady   **92**

The **episodic** career. Chideya, F.   **650.1**
EPISTEMOLOGY *See* Theory of knowledge
The **epistles** of Horace. Horace   **871**

EPISTOLARY FICTION
   See also Fiction

EPISTOLARY POETRY
   See also Poetry

EPITAPHS
   See also Biography; Cemeteries; Inscriptions; Tombs

EPITHETS *See* Names; Nicknames
EPIZOA *See* Parasites

Epping, Randy Charles
The 21st century economy   **330.9**

Epstein, Daniel Mark
Nat King Cole   **92**
Sister Aimee: the life of Aimee Semple McPherson   **92**

Epstein, David
The sports gene   **613.7**

Epstein, Edward Jay
The annals of unsolved crime   **364.152**

Epstein, Joseph, 1937-
Snobbery   **305.5**

Alexis De Tocqueville 92
(ed) The Norton book of personal essays 808.84
Epstein, Lawrence J.
The basic beliefs of Judaism 296.3
Epstein, Nicky
Nicky Epstein's essential edgings collection
Epstein, Randi Hutter
Get me out 618.2
Equal. Strebeigh, F. 342
EQUAL EMPLOYMENT OPPORTUNITY *See*
Affirmative action programs; Discrimination in
employment
EQUAL OPPORTUNITY IN EMPLOYMENT
See Affirmative action programs; Discrimination
in employment
EQUAL PAY FOR EQUAL WORK
See also Discrimination in employment; Sala-
ries, wages, etc.; Women -- Employment
EQUAL RIGHTS AMENDMENTS
See also Constitutions; Sex discrimination
EQUAL TIME RULE (BROADCASTING)
See also Broadcasting; Television and politics
EQUALITY
Capital in the twenty-first century 332
The divide 303.3
The great divergence 339.2
Hayes, C. Twilight of the elites 305.5
Murray, C. Coming apart 305.8
Pickett, K. The spirit level 306
Tough, P. How children succeed 372.21
EQUALITY
See also Political science; Sociology
EQUALITY -- ECONOMIC ASPECTS
The economics of inequality 339.2
**EQUALITY -- ECONOMIC ASPECTS -- UNIT-
ED STATES -- HISTORY -- 19TH CENTURY**
Holzer, H. A just and generous nation 973.7
EQUALITY -- UNITED STATES
Carville, J. It's the middle class, stupid! 320.51
Stiglitz, J. E. The price of inequality 305.5
**EQUALITY -- UNITED STATES -- HISTORY --
21ST CENTURY**
Garson, B. Down the up escalator 339.2
The **equation** that couldn't be solved. Livio, M. 512
EQUATIONS
Crease, R. P. The great equations 509
Mackenzie, D. The universe in zero words 512.9
EQUATIONS
See also Mathematics
Equiano, Olaudah, 1745-1797
About
Carretta, V. Equiano, the African 92
Equiano, the African. Carretta, V. 92
EQUILIBRIUM (ECONOMICS)
See also Economics
Equus. Shaffer, P. 822

Erasmus, Desiderius, 1466?-1536
Praise of folly 877
About
Russell, B. A history of Western philosophy 109
Eratosthenes, 3rd cent. B.C.
About
Nicastro, N. Circumference 526
Erdman, David V.
(ed) Blake, W. The complete poetry and prose of
William Blake 821
Erdman, Sarah
Nine hills to Nambonkaha 966.68
Erdrich, Louise
Original fire 811
About
Erdrich, L. Books and islands in Ojibwe country 92
ERGONOMICS
See also Applied psychology; Engineering;
Industrial design; Psychophysiology
Erickson, Carolly
Great Catherine 947
Her little majesty: the life of Queen Victoria 92
Erickson, Renee
A boat, a whale, and a walrus 641.597
Erickson-Schroth, Laura
(ed) Trans bodies, trans selves 306.76
Ericsson, Anders
Peak 153.9
ERIE CANAL (N.Y.) -- HISTORY
Bernstein, P. L. Wedding of the waters 386
Kelly, J. Heaven's ditch 386
Erikson, Erik H.
Young man Luther 92
ERIS (DWARF PLANET)
Brown, M. How I killed Pluto and why it had it
coming 523.4
Erlich, Reese
Inside Syria 956.91
Ernie Pyle's war. Tobin, J. E. 070.4
Ernst, Carl H.
Snakes of the United States and Canada 597.96
Venomous reptiles of the United States, Canada,
and northern Mexico 597.9
Ernst, Carl W.
Following Muhammad 297
The Shambhala guide to Sufism 297.4
Ernst, Evelyn M.
(jt. auth) Ernst, C. H. Venomous reptiles of the
United States, Canada, and northern Mexico 597.9
Ernst, C. H. Snakes of the United States and Cana-
da 597.96
Ernsthausen, David G.
Strauss's handbook of business information 016
EROSION
See also Geology
ERRORS

Boller, P. F. They never said it **808.88**

Goldacre, B. Bad science **500**

Hallinan, J. T. Why we make mistakes **153**

Posamentier, A. S. Magnificent mistakes in mathematics **510**

Reinhart, A. Statistics done wrong **519.5**

ERRORS -- PSYCHOLOGICAL ASPECTS

Dobelli, R. The art of thinking clearly **153.4**

Schulz, K. Being wrong **153**

ERRORS, SCIENTIFIC

Ohanian, H. C. Einstein's mistakes **530**

Posamentier, A. S. Magnificent mistakes in mathematics **510**

ERUDITION *See* Learning and scholarship

Eruptions that shook the world. Oppenheimer, C. **551.2**

Erway, Cathy

The food of Taiwan **641.595**

Escape from Davao. Lukacs, J. D. **940.54**

Escape from the deep. Kershaw, A. **940.54**

Escape Points. Weldon, M. **362.196**

ESCAPES

Felton, M. Zero Night **940.54**

Wright, R. A. Our man in Tehran **955**

ESCAPES

See also Adventure and adventurers; Prisons

ESCAPES -- ARMENIA -- HISTORY -- 20TH CENTURY

MacKeen, D. A. The hundred-year walk **92**

ESCAPES -- BOSNIA AND HERCEGOVINA -- HISTORY -- 20TH CENTURY

Shapiro, S. The Bosnia list **92**

ESCAPES -- GERMANY (EAST) -- HISTORY

Mitchell, G. The tunnels **943.155**

ESCAPES -- KOREA (NORTH) -- HISTORY -- 20TH CENTURY

Weintraub, S. A Christmas far from home **951.904**

ESCAPES -- VIETNAM -- CENTRAL HIGHLANDS -- HISTORY -- 20TH CENTURY

Wolf, M. J. Abandoned in hell **959.704**

Escaping the delta. Wald, E. **92**

ESCHATOLOGY

Wright, N. T. Surprised by hope **236**

ESCHATOLOGY

See also Theology

Escott, Colin

Hank Williams **92**

Esdaile, Charles J.

Napoleon's wars **940.2**

Esfandiari, Haleh, 1940-

About

Esfandiari, H. My prison, my home **92**

Eshkenazi, Dalia

About

Tolan, S. The lemon tree **956.94**

Eskilson, Stephen J.

Graphic design **740**

ESKIMO LEADERS

Hensley, W. L. Fifty miles from tomorrow **92**

ESKIMOS *See* Inuit

Eslanda. Ransby, B. **92**

Esmonde-White, Miranda

Aging backwards **613.2**

ESP *See* Extrasensory perception

ESPERANTO

Okrent, A. In the land of invented languages **499**

Espinoza, Roberta

Pivotal moments **371.102**

ESPIONAGE

Downing, T. Secret Warriors **940.4**

Hastings, M. The secret war **940.54**

Hoffman, D. E. The Billion Dollar Spy **327.12**

Javers, E. Broker, trader, lawyer, spy **364.1**

Le Carré, J. The Pigeon Tunnel **823**

Williams, S. Spies in the congo **553.4**

Wise, D. Spy: the inside story of how the FBI's Robert Hanssen betrayed America **327.12**

ESPIONAGE

See also Intelligence service; Secret service; Subversive activities

ESPIONAGE -- EUROPE -- HISTORY -- 20TH CENTURY

Macintyre, B. Double cross **940.54**

ESPIONAGE -- GREAT BRITAIN -- HISTORY -- 19TH CENTURY

Dickey, C. Our Man in Charleston **92**

ESPIONAGE -- UNITED STATES -- HISTORY -- 18TH CENTURY

Nagy, J. A. George Washington's secret spy war **973.385**

ESPIONAGE -- UNITED STATES -- HISTORY -- 20TH CENTURY

Weiner, T. Enemies **363.25**

ESPIONAGE, AMERICAN *See* American espionage

ESPIONAGE, AMERICAN -- EUROPE -- HISTORY -- 20TH CENTURY

Blum, H. The Last Goodnight **940.54**

ESPIONAGE, AMERICAN -- HISTORY

Crist, D. The twilight war **327**

ESPIONAGE, AMERICAN -- HISTORY -- 20TH CENTURY

Lichtblau, E. The Nazis next door **324.1**

ESPIONAGE, IRANIAN -- HISTORY

Crist, D. The twilight war **327**

ESPIONAGE, SOVIET -- GREAT BRITAIN -- HISTORY

Macintyre, B. A Spy Among Friends **327.12**

ESPN, INC.

Miller, J. A. Those guys have all the fun **791.45**

Esposito, John L.

Esposito, J. L. Islam **297**

Unholy war **322.4**

What everyone needs to know about Islam **297**

(ed) The Oxford dictionary of Islam **297**

(ed) The Oxford history of Islam **297**

Espy, Willard R.

Words to rhyme with **423**

ESQUIMAUX *See* Inuit

ESSAY

See also Literature

ESSAY -- AUTHORSHIP

D'Agata, J. The lifespan of a fact **808.02**

An **essay** concerning human understanding. Locke, J. **121**

ESSAYISTS

Achebe, C. The education of a British-protected child **92**

Achebe, C. Home and exile **823**

Ackroyd, P. Poe **92**

Adams, H. The education of Henry Adams **92**

Adams, M. B. Shaggy muses **920**

Addams, J. Twenty years at Hull-House **361.7**

Alice Walker **813**

Alice Walker's The color purple **813**

Amis, M. Experience **92**

Angelou, M. Letter to my daughter **92**

Angelou, M. I know why the caged bird sings **92**

Angelou, M. A song flung up to heaven **818**

Angier, C. The double bond: Primo Levi, a biography **92**

Archibald MacLeish: reflections **92**

Armstrong, J. Love, life, Goethe **92**

Bailey, E. T. The sound of a wild snail eating **92**

Bair, D. Simone de Beauvoir **848**

Baker, J. H. Margaret Sanger **92**

Baker, R. Growing up **92**

Bakewell, S. How to live, or, A life of Montaigne in one question and twenty attempts at an answer **92**

Baraka, I. A. The LeRoi Jones/Amiri Baraka reader **818**

Barnes, J. Nothing to be frightened of **92**

Bass, R. Why I came West **92**

Bayley, J. Elegy for Iris **823**

Bechdel, A. Fun home **741.5**

Becker, C. The Declaration of Independence **973.3**

Bell, E. T. Men of mathematics **920**

Benfey, C. E. G. A summer of hummingbirds **920**

Bernstein, R. B. Thomas Jefferson **92**

Biss, E. Notes from no man's land **305.8**

Black women writers (1950-1980) **810**

Blight, D. W. American oracle **973.7**

Bloom, H. The Western canon **809**

Boyd, B. Vladimir Nabokov: the American years **813**

Boyd, B. Vladimir Nabokov: the Russian years **813**

Bradford, R. Lucky him: the life of Kingsley Amis **92**

Briggs, J. Virginia Woolf: an inner life **92**

Broadwater, J. George Mason, forgotten founder **92**

Brodsky, J. Less than one **809.1**

Brookhiser, R. America's first dynasty **973.4**

Brown, C. Chance and circumstance **92**

Brown, C. Manchild in the promised land **92**

Bryson, B. The life and times of the thunderbolt kid **92**

Burana, L. I love a man in uniform **92**

Burstein, A. Madison and Jefferson **973.4**

Butcher, T. Chasing the Devil **916**

Callow, P. From noon to starry night: a life of Walt Whitman **811**

Campbell, G. John Milton **92**

Camus, A. The rebel **303.6**

Carter, W. C. Marcel Proust **843**

Cerami, C. A. Jefferson's great gamble **973.4**

Chadha, Y. Gandhi **954.03**

Cohen, I. B. Science and the founding fathers **973.3**

Collins, P. The trouble with Tom: the strange afterlife and times of Thomas Paine **92**

Connors, P. Fire season **634.9**

Conradi, P. Iris Murdoch **823**

Conversations with Nadine Gordimer **823**

Culkin, J. A final arc of sky **92**

Damasio, A. R. Looking for Spinoza **152.4**

Danticat, E. Brother, I'm dying **92**

Danticat, E. Create dangerously **92**

Dearborn, M. V. Mailer **813**

Didion, J. The year of magical thinking **92**

Dillard, A. The writing life **818**

Dillard, A. An American childhood **92**

Doty, M. Dog years **92**

Downing, D. C. Into the region of awe **248.2**

Eco, U. Confessions of a young novelist **808.3**

Elie, P. The life you save may be your own **810**

Elledge, S. E. B. White **92**

Ellis, J. J. American sphinx: the character of Thomas Jefferson **92**

Ellison, R. The collected essays of Ralph Ellison **814**

Ellison, R. Going to the territory **818**

Erdrich, L. Books and islands in Ojibwe country **92**

Existentialism from Dostoevsky to Sartre **142**

Feldman, B. 112 Mercer Street **920**

Ford, P. F. Companion to Narnia **823**

Frampton, S. When I am playing with my cat, how do I know she is not playing with me? **844**

Fraser, K. Ornament and silence **809**

Frazier, I. Travels in Siberia **957**

French, P. The world is what it is **92**

Friedman, M. S. Encounter on the narrow ridge: a life of Martin Buber **92**

Gandhi, M. An autobiography **92**

Garton-Ash, T. The file **327.12**

Garvey, M. Stylized **808**

Gates, H. L. The future of the race **305.896**

Gates, H. L. Thirteen ways of looking at a black man **920.71**

George, being George **92**

Giddings, P. Ida: a sword among lions **92**

Gillespie, C. Critical companion to Alice Walker **813**

Gillespie, C. Critical companion to Toni Morrison **813**

Gillespie, M. A. Maya Angelou **92**

Glendinning, V. Leonard Woolf **92**

Gordon, L. T.S. Eliot **92**

Gordon, L. Vindication **92**

Gordon-Reed, A. The Hemingses of Monticello **920**

Gordon-Reed, A. Thomas Jefferson and Sally Hemings **973.4**

Greene, G. Graham Greene **92**

Hague, W. J. William Wilberforce **92**

Hansberry, L. To be young, gifted, and Black **92**

Hare, R. M. Plato **184**

Havel, V. To the castle and back **92**

Hawkes, D. John Milton **92**

Heaney, S. Finders keepers **821**

Heat Moon, W. L. Roads to Quoz **917**

Hertog, S. Anne Morrow Lindbergh **92**

Hitchens, C. Hitch-22 **92**

Hitchens, C. Thomas Jefferson: author of America **92**

Hofstadter, R. The American political tradition, and the men who made it **973**

Hogan, L. The woman who watches over the world **818**

Hollis, L. London rising **942**

Hollis, M. Now all roads lead to France **821**

Hooks, B. Belonging **92**

Hooks, B. Wounds of passion **92**

Hughes, K. George Eliot **823**

Jarrell, R. No other book **809**

Karr, M. Lit **92**

Kazin, A. An American procession **810**

Keene, D. Five modern Japanese novelists **895.6**

Kellman, S. G. Redemption: the life of Henry Roth **92**

Ker, I. G. K. Chesterton **828**

Kermode, F. An appetite for poetry **801**

Kermode, F. Concerning E.M. Forster **823**

Kiernan, F. Seeing Mary plain: a life of Mary McCarthy **818**

Knight, L. W. Jane Addams **92**

Kurzke, H. Thomas Mann **92**

Langer, L. L. Admitting the Holocaust **940.53**

Larson, E. J. A magnificent catastrophe **324**

Leader, Z. The life of Kingsley Amis **92**

Lee, H. Virginia Woolf **823**

Lee, H. Virginia Woolf's nose **820**

Leibowitz, H. A. Something urgent I have to say to you: the life and works of William Carlos Williams **92**

Lelyveld, J. Great soul **92**

Lepore, J. A is for American **306.44**

Lessing, D. M. Under my skin **92**

Levi, P. The periodic table **92**

Lewis, D. L. W.E.B. Du Bois **92**

Life stories **920**

Lindbergh, R. Under a wing **92**

Loving, J. Mark Twain **92**

Mackall, J. Plain secrets **289.7**

Mailer, N. C. A ticket to the circus **92**

Malcolm, J. Two lives **92**

Malone, J. W. It doesn't take a rocket scientist **920**

Marshall, P. Triangular road **92**

Marton, K. The great escape **920**

Matthiessen, F. O. American renaissance **810**

McCall, N. Makes me wanna holler **305.38**

McCalman, I. Darwin's armada **576.8**

McCracken, E. An exact replica of a figment of my imagination **92**

McMurtry, L. Books **92**

McMurtry, L. Walter Benjamin at the Dairy Queen **818**

Meade, M. Dorothy Parker **92**

Meyers, J. Orwell **828**

Mill, J. S. Autobiography **92**

Miller, J. C. The Federalist era, 1789-1801 **973.4**

Miller, L. The magician's book **823**

Milosz, C. Legends of modernity **891.8**

Milosz, C. To begin where I am **891.8**

Moffat, W. A great unrecorded history **92**

Mohandas Gandhi **92**

Molesworth, C. Marianne Moore **92**

Morris, R. Ambrose Bierce **92**

Murphy, M. M. Scout, Atticus, and Boo **813**

Murphy, R. E. Critical companion to T.S. Eliot **811**

My life as author and editor **818**

Nabokov, V. V. Lectures on literature **808.3**

Nabokov, V. V. Speak, memory **813**

Nadler, S. M. The best of all possible worlds **190**

Naipaul, V. S. Between father and son **823**

Naipaul, V. S. Reading & writing **92**

Oates, J. C. A widow's story **92**

Oates, J. C. The journal of Joyce Carol Oates: 1973-1982 **92**

O'Driscoll, D. Stepping stones **821**

Oliver, C. M. Critical companion to Walt Whitman **811**

O'Rourke, M. The long goodbye **92**

Orwell, G. Diaries **828**

The Oxford companion to Mark Twain **818**

Oz, A. A tale of love and darkness **92**

Parini, J. The art of teaching **371.1**

Pearson, R. Voltaire almighty 92
Peters, S. Bernard Shaw 822
Pick, H. Simon Wiesenthal 940.53
Pierpont, C. R. Passionate minds 810
Pirsig, R. M. Zen and the art of motorcycle maintenance 92
Playwrights at work 812
Poundstone, W. Carl Sagan 92
Powers, R. Mark Twain 92
Price, R. Ardent spirits 92
Quinn, E. Critical companion to George Orwell 828
Rampersad, A. Ralph Ellison 92
Remnick, D. Reporting 814
Richardson, R. D. Emerson 814
Rodgers, M. E. Mencken 92
Rodriguez, R. Hunger of memory 92
Roiphe, A. R. Art and madness 92
Roiphe, A. R. Epilogue 92
Rollyson, C. E. Susan Sontag 818
Roper, R. Now the drum of war 973.7
Rosenblatt, R. Making toast 92
Rowley, H. Richard Wright 813
Rudahl, S. A dangerous woman 335
Russell, B. A history of Western philosophy 109
Safranski, R. Nietzsche 193
Said, E. W. Out of place 92
Salamon, J.   Wendy and the lost boys 92
Sanders, S. R. A private history of awe 92
Sartre, J. P. The words 92
Scammell, M. Koestler 92
Sebald, W. G. On the natural history of destruction 833
Segev, T. Simon Wiesenthal 92
Severin, T. In search of Robinson Crusoe 996
Shattuck, R. Proust's way 843
Shelden, M. Mark Twain 92
Silverman, K. Begin again 92
Silverman, K. Edgar A. Poe 92
Simon, J. F. What kind of nation 342
Singer, I. B.   More stories from my father's court 839
Slaughter, T. P. The beautiful soul of John Woolman, apostle of abolition 92
Solomon, R. C. What Nietzsche really said 193
Sontag, S. Reborn 92
Sova, D. B. Critical companion to Edgar Allan Poe 818
Soyinka, W. You must set forth at dawn 92
Spurling, H. Pearl Buck in China 92
Staloff, D. Hamilton, Adams, Jefferson 973.4
Stashower, D. The beautiful cigar girl 364.152
Steffens, L. The autobiography of Lincoln Steffens 92
Stein, G. The autobiography of Alice B. Toklas 92
Stewart, D. O. American emperor 973.4
Styron, W. Darkness visible 616.85

Sullivan, R. The Thoreau you don't know 92
Sutherland, J. Stephen Spender 92
Tan, A. The opposite of fate 814
Taylor, D. J. Orwell: the life 92
Teachout, T. The skeptic: the life of H.L. Mencken 92
Thursby, J. S. Critical companion to Maya Angelou 818
Todd, O. Albert Camus 848
Trillin, C. Quite enough of Calvin Trillin 817
Trillin, C. About Alice 92
Ulrich, L. Well-behaved women seldom make history 305.4
Unger, H. G. The last founding father 92
Vendler, H. H. Coming of age as a poet 820
Vidal, G. Inventing a nation: Washington, Adams, Jefferson 973.4
Vidal, G. Point to point navigation 92
Volkov, S. St. Petersburg 947
Vowell, S. Assassination vacation 973
Walker, A. The same river twice 813
Wall, C. A. Women of the Harlem Renaissance 810
Walsh, J. E. Midnight dreary 818
Wayne, T. K. Critical companion to Ralph Waldo Emerson 818
White, E. B. Letters of E.B. White 92
Williamson, E. Borges, a life 92
Wills, G. 'Negro president' 326
Wills, G. Outside looking in 92
Wilson, A. N. C.S. Lewis 823
Wilson, E. Patriotic gore 810
Winters, K. C. Anne Morrow Lindbergh 92
Wolpert, S. A. Gandhi's passion 954.03
Woolf, V. A moment's liberty: the shorter diary 92
Woolf, V. Moments of being 823
Worthen, J. D.H. Lawrence 92
Worthen, J. D.H. Lawrence, the early years, 1885-1912 92
Wright, R. Black boy 92
Zacks, R. The pirate coast 973.4
Essays. Orwell, G. 824
ESSAYS
The Art of the personal essay 808.84
Calvino, I. Collection of Sand 854
Count on me 177
Flannery, T. An explorer's notebook 304.2
Frazier, I. Hogs wild 814.54
Gaiman, N. The view from the cheap seats 824
Hall, D. Essays After Eighty 814
Hart, H. Buffering 792.702
Holroyd, M. A book of secrets 306.874
Jamison, L. The empathy exams 814
Let me tell you 818
The Norton book of personal essays 808.84
Read Harder 814
Styron, W. My generation 814

Things that are **508**

Walker, A. The cushion in the road **814**

Essays After Eighty. Hall, D. **814**

Essays and reviews. Poe, E. A. **809**

Essays of E.B. White. White, E. B. **814**

The **essence** of style. DeJean, J. E. **391**

Essence total makeover. **646.7**

ESSENCES AND ESSENTIAL OILS

    See also Distillation; Oils and fats

ESSENES

    See also Jews

Essential car care for women. McCormick, D. **629.28**

The **essential** Chaplin. **92**

The **essential** credit repair handbook. McNaughton, D. **332.024**

The **essential** cuisines of Mexico. Kennedy, D. **641.59**

The **essential** diabetes cookbook. Worrall-Thompson, A. **641.5**

Essential Emeril. Lagasse, E. **641.5**

The **essential** engineer. Petroski, H. **620**

The **essential** feminist reader. **305.4**

Essential first steps for parents of children with autism. Harris, S. L. **618.92**

The **essential** first year. Leach, P. **649**

The **essential** guide to cultivating mushrooms. Russell, S. **635**

The **essential** guide to hysterectomy. Streicher, L. F. **618.1**

The **essential** Gwendolyn Brooks. Brooks, G. **811**

The **essential** James Beard cookbook. Rodgers, R. **641.597**

Essential Judaism. Robinson, G. **296**

The **essential** Jung. **150.19**

The **essential** New York Times cook book. Hesser, A. **641.5**

The **essential** New York times grilling cookbook. **641.5**

The **Essential** Oyster. Jacobsen, R. **641.694**

Essential Pepin. Pepin, J. **641.5**

Essential perennials. Christopher, T. **635.9**

Essential road bike maintenance handbook. Downs, T. **629.28**

The **essential** Rumi. Selections/English **891**

The **essential** transcendentalists. **141**

The **essential** vegetarian cookbook. Shaw, D. **641.5**

The **essential** writings of James Weldon Johnson. Johnson, J. W. **818**

Essentialism. McKeown, G. **153.8**

ESSENTIALISM (PHILOSOPHY)

    McKeown, G. Essentialism **153.8**

The **essentials.** Arnold, J. **791.43**

Essentials of Asian cuisine. Trang, C. **641.5**

Essentials of classic Italian cooking. Hazan, M. **641.59**

Essinger, James

    Ada's algorithm **92**

Estabrook, Barry

    Pig tales **636.4**

ESTATE PLANNING

    Clifford, D. Make your own living trust **346.05**

    Clifford, D. Plan your estate **346.05**

ESTATE PLANNING

    See also Personal finance; Planning

Estep, Preston

    The mindspan diet **616.8**

Estes, Angie

    Tryst **811**

Estevan, d. 1539

    About

    Abdul-Jabbar, K. Black profiles in courage **920**

ESTHETICS *See* Aesthetics

ESTIMATION (MATHEMATICS) *See* Approximate computation

ESTONIA -- DESCRIPTION AND TRAVEL

    Theroux, A. Estonia: a ramble through the periphery **947.98**

Estonia: a ramble through the periphery. Theroux, A. **947.98**

ESTRANGEMENT (SOCIAL PSYCHOLOGY) *See* Alienation (Social psychology)

Estreich, George

    About

    Estreich, G. The Shape of the Eye **618.92**

Estreich, Laura Regina

    About

    Estreich, G. The Shape of the Eye **618.92**

Estrine, Darryl

    Harvest to heat **641.5**

Esty, Mary Lee

    Conquering Concussion **617.4**

Etched in Sand. Calcaterra, R. **92**

ETCHERS

    Blackburn, J. Old man Goya **92**

    Hughes, R. Goya **760**

    Schama, S. Rembrandt's eyes **92**

ETCHERS

    See also Artists; Engravers

ETCHING

    See also Art; Pictures

Eteraz, Ali

    About

    Eteraz, A. Children of dust **92**

The **eternal** city. Graber, K. **811**

The **eternal** darkness. Ballard, R. D. **551.46**

Eternal enemies. **891.8**

The **eternal** frontier. Flannery, T. F. **508**

Eternal life. Spong, J. S. **236**

ETERNAL LIFE *See* Eternity; Future life; Immortality

ETERNAL PUNISHMENT *See* Hell

ETERNITY
Eire, C. M. N. A very brief history of eternity 236
Spong, J. S. Eternal life 236
Ethics. 170
ETHICS
  See also Philosophy
ETHICS
Aristotle Nicomachean ethics 170
Armstrong, K. Twelve steps to a compassionate life 177
Churchland, P. S. Braintrust 612.8
Cicero, M. T. On the good life 878
Coles, R. Lives of moral leadership 170
Comte-Sponville, A. A small treatise on the great virtues 170
Covey, S. M. R. Smart trust 174
Edelman, M. W. The measure of our success 170
Ethics 170
Fair, E. Consequence 956.704
Greene, J. Moral tribes 170
Marcus Aurelius Meditations 188
National Geographic concise history of world religions 200
Peterson, D. The moral lives of animals 156
Piaget, J. The moral judgment of the child 155.4
Sandel, M. J. Justice 172
Wolfe, A. Moral freedom 170
ETHICS -- ENCYCLOPEDIAS
Ethics 170
ETHICS -- PSYCHOLOGICAL ASPECTS
Haidt, J. The righteous mind 201
ETHIOPIA -- DESCRIPTION AND TRAVEL
Shah, T. In search of King Solomon's mines 963
ETHNIC CONFLICT -- CHINA
Platt, S. R. Autumn in the Heavenly Kingdom 951
ETHNIC RELATIONS
Berger, J. The pious ones 973
Buruma, I. Murder in Amsterdam 364.152
Curtis, E. E. Muslims in America 305.8
ETHNIC RELATIONS
  See also Acculturation; Ethnology; Sociology
ETHNICITY
Toumani, M. There was and there was not 327
ETHNOLOGISTS
King, J. Farley: the life of Farley Mowat 92
Mowat, F. Born naked 92
ETHNOLOGY
Diamond, J. M. Guns, germs, and steel 303.4
Gibbon, P. Tribe 305.8
Linden, E. The ragged edge of the world 303.4
ETHNOLOGY
  See also Human beings
ETHNOLOGY -- NEW GUINEA
Flannery, T. F. Throwim way leg 995.3
ETHNOLOGY -- POLYNESIA

Heyerdahl, T. Kon-Tiki 910.4
ETHNOPSYCHOLOGY
Levi-Strauss, C. The savage mind 155.8
ETHNOPSYCHOLOGY
  See also Anthropology; Ethnology; Psychology; Sociology
ETHNOZOOLOGY
  See also Animals -- Folklore; Ethnobiology; Ethnology
ETIQUETTE
Baldrige, L. Letitia Baldrige's new manners for new times 395
Dresser, N. Multicultural manners 395
Emily Post's wedding etiquette 395.2
Forni, P. M. The civility solution 395
How to be a perfect stranger 203
Martin, J. Miss Manners' guide to excruciatingly correct behavior 395
Post, P. Emily Post's etiquette 395
ETIQUETTE
  See also Human behavior
ETIQUETTE FOR CHILDREN AND TEENAGERS
  See also Children -- Conduct of life; Teenagers -- Conduct of life
ETRUSCAN ART
  See also Art
Etty, Thomas
  (jt. auth) Harrison, L. Heirloom Plants 635
The **etymologicon.** Forsyth, M. 422
Euchner, Charles
Nobody turn me around 323.1
Euclid
    About
Berlinski, D. The king of infinite space 516.2
Rudman, P. S. The Babylonian theorem 510
Eudora. Waldron, A. 92
Eudora Welty: a biography. Marrs, S. 92
Eudoxus, of Cnidus, ca. 400-ca. 350 B.C.
    About
Bell, E. T. Men of mathematics 920
Eugene O'Neill. Dowling, R. M. 92
Eugene Onegin and other poems. Pushkin, A. S. 891.7
EUGENICS
Bruinius, H. Better for all the world 363.9
Lombardo, P. A. Three generations, no imbeciles 344
Moreno, J. D. The body politic 303.48
Nourse, V. F. In reckless hands 344
EUGENICS
  See also Genetics; Population
EUGENICS -- GERMANY -- HISTORY -- 20TH CENTURY
Tate, T. Hitler's forgotten children 940.53
EUGENICS -- UNITED STATES -- HISTORY --

20TH CENTURY
Lombardo, P. A. Three generations, no imbeciles 344
Nourse, V. F. In reckless hands 344
Euler, Leonhard, 1707-1783
        About
Bell, E. T. Men of mathematics 920
EULOGIES
The Book of eulogies 808.8
Remembrances and celebrations 808.8
EUPHEMISM -- DICTIONARIES
Holder, R. W. How not to say what you mean 427
EUPHRATES RIVER
Kriwaczek, P. Babylon 935
The **Eureka** factor. Kounios, J. 612.8
Eureka man. Hirshfeld, A. 92
Eureka! Orzel, C. 500
Euripides. Euripides 882
Euripides
Euripides 882
Euripides [2] 882
Euripides [2] Euripides 882
EURO
    See also Capital market; Money
The **Europa** world year book 2014. 310
EUROPE -- CHURCH HISTORY
Bainton, R. H. Here I stand: a life of Martin Luther 92
Erikson, E. H. Young man Luther 92
Oberman, H. A. Luther: man between God and the Devil 92
Phillips, J. Holy warriors 909.07
Wilson, D. A. Out of the storm 92
EUROPE -- CHURCH HISTORY -- ENCYCLO-PEDIAS
Andrea, A. J. Encyclopedia of the crusades 909.07
EUROPE -- CIVILIZATION
Barzun, J. From dawn to decadence 940.2
Blanning, T. C. W. The pursuit of glory 940.2
Europe 1789 to 1914 940.2
The revolt of the masses 901
EUROPE -- CIVILIZATION -- 20TH CENTURY
Blom, P. The vertigo years 940.2
EUROPE -- CIVILIZATION -- ENCYCLOPE-DIAS
Europe 1789 to 1914 940.2
EUROPE -- COLONIES -- AMERICA
Dolin, E. J. Fur, fortune, and empire 381
EUROPE -- COMMERCE
Bown, S. R. Merchant kings 338.8
EUROPE -- DESCRIPTION AND TRAVEL
The fault line 914
EUROPE -- EMIGRATION AND IMMIGRA-TION -- GOVERNMENT POLICY
Carr, M. Fortress Europe 363.28
EUROPE-- ETHNIC RELATIONS

Nirenberg, D. Anti-Judaism 305.892
EUROPE -- FOREIGN RELATIONS -- UNITED STATES
De Grazia, V. Irresistible empire 306
EUROPE -- HISTORY
Edsel, R. M. The monuments men 940.53
EUROPE -- HISTORY -- 1492-1789
Blanning, T. C. W. The pursuit of glory 940.2
Pettegree, A. The book in the Renaissance 070.5
EUROPE -- HISTORY -- 1789-1815
Blanning, T. C. W. The pursuit of glory 940.2
Esdaile, C. J. Napoleon's wars 940.2
Fraser, F. Pauline Bonaparte 92
King, D. Vienna, 1814 940.2
Lieven, D. C. B. Russia against Napoleon 940.2
O'Brien, M. Mrs. Adams in winter 940.2
Pocock, T. The terror before Trafalgar 940.2
Talty, S. The illustrious dead 940.2
Winik, J. The great upheaval 909.7
Zamoyski, A. Rites of peace 940.2
EUROPE -- HISTORY -- 1789-1900
Europe 1789 to 1914 940.2
Hobsbawm, E. J. The age of revolution 1789-1848 940.2
Mostert, N. The line upon a wind 940.2
EUROPE -- HISTORY -- 1789-1900 -- ENCY-CLOPEDIAS
Europe 1789 to 1914 940.2
EUROPE -- HISTORY -- 17TH CENTURY
Grayling, A. C. The Age of Genius 940.2
EUROPE -- HISTORY -- 1871-1918
Clark, C. The sleepwalkers 940.3
Hastings, M. Catastrophe 1914 940.3
EUROPE -- HISTORY -- 1871-1918 -- ENCY-CLOPEDIAS
Europe 1789 to 1914 940.2
EUROPE -- HISTORY -- 1918-1945
Beevor, A. The Second World War 940.54
Kershaw, I. To Hell and Back 940.5
EUROPE -- HISTORY -- 1945-
Lowe, K. Savage continent 940.55
EUROPE -- HISTORY -- 20TH CENTURY
Celan, P. Breathturn into timestead 635.9
Jarausch, K. H. Out of ashes 940.5
Kaplan, R. D. In Europe's shadow 949.8
EUROPE -- HISTORY -- 20TH CENTURY -- BI-OGRAPHY
Prochnik, G. The Impossible Exile 92
EUROPE -- HISTORY -- 476-1492
Pye, M. The Edge of the World 940.1
EUROPE -- HISTORY -- ENCYCLOPEDIAS
Ancient Europe 8000 B.C.-A.D. 1000 936
EUROPE -- HISTORY -- JULY CRISIS, 1914
Hastings, M. Catastrophe 1914 940.3
McMeekin, S. July 1914 940.3
EUROPE -- IMMIGRATION AND EMIGRA-

TION
Carr, M. Fortress Europe   363.28
EUROPE -- INTELLECTUAL LIFE
Grayling, A. C. The Age of Genius   940.2
EUROPE -- NAVAL HISTORY
Crowley, R. Empires of the sea   359
EUROPE -- POLITICS AND GOVERNMENT
King, D. Vienna, 1814   940.2
EUROPE -- POLITICS AND GOVERNMENT --
   1871-1918
Carter, M. George, Nicholas, and Wilhelm   940.3
Clark, C. The sleepwalkers   940.3
EUROPE -- POLITICS AND GOVERNMENT --
   1918-1945
Cornwell, J. Hitler's pope: the secret history of
   Pius XII   92
Faber, D. Munich, 1938   940.53
EUROPE -- POLITICS AND GOVERNMENT --
   20TH CENTURY
Jarausch, K. H. Out of ashes   940.5
Paxton, R. O. The anatomy of fascism   321.9
EUROPE -- RELIGION
Levack, B. P. The Devil within   133.4
EUROPE -- SOCIAL CONDITIONS
Tuchman, B. W. The proud tower   909.82
EUROPE -- SOCIAL CONDITIONS -- 20TH
   CENTURY
Jarausch, K. H. Out of ashes   940.5
Europe 1789 to 1914.   940.2
EUROPE, EASTERN See Eastern Europe
EUROPEAN FEDERATION
   See also Europe -- Politics and government;
   Federal government; International economic
   integration; International organization
European tapestries in the Art Institute of Chicago.
Brosens, K.   746.3
EUROPEAN WAR, 1914-1918 See World War,
   1914-1918
EUROPEAN WAR, 1939-1945 See World War,
   1939-1945
EUROPEANS -- CHINA -- HISTORY
Platt, S. R. Autumn in the Heavenly Kingdom 951
EUTHANASIA
Humphry, D. Final exit   179.7
Peck, M. S. Denial of the soul   179.7
Wanzer, S. H. To die well   179.7
Yount, L. Right to die and euthanasia   179.7
EUTHANASIA
   See also Homicide; Medical ethics
EUTHANASIA -- LAW AND LEGISLATION --
   UNITED STATES
Ball, H. At liberty to die   344
EUTHANASIA -- MORAL AND ETHICAL AS-
   PECTS
Butler, K. Knocking on Heaven's Door   616.02
Eva Braun. Gortemaker, H. B.   92

EVACUATION AND RELOCATION OF JAPA-
   NESE AMERICANS, 1942-1945 See Japanese
   Americans -- Evacuation and relocation, 1942-
   1945
EVACUATION OF CIVILIANS
   See also Civil defense; Disaster relief
Evaluating teen services and programs. Flowers,
   S.   027.62
EVANGELICALISM -- SOUTHERN CALIFOR-
   NIA
Dochuk, D. From Bible belt to sunbelt   277
EVANGELICALISM -- UNITED STATES
Joyce, K. The child catchers   362.734
Sutton, M. A. American apocalypse   277.3
EVANGELISTIC HEALING See Spiritual healing
EVANGELISTIC WORK
   See also Church work
EVANGELISTS
Epstein, D. M. Sister Aimee: the life of Aimee
   Semple McPherson   92
Graham, B. Just as I am   92
Hillenbrand, L. Unbroken   940.54
Martin, W. C. With God on our side   261.8
Tomkins, S. John Wesley   287
Evans, Arthur V.
An inordinate fondness for beetles   595.7
Evans, Dave
Designing your life   650.1
Evans, G. Edward
Collection management basics   025.2
Introduction to library public services   025.5
Evans, Harold
They made America   920
Evans, Mari
(ed) Black women writers (1950-1980)   810
Evans, Martin
Algeria   965
Evans, R. Tripp
Grant Wood   92
Evans, Rachel Held
Searching for Sunday   248
Evans, Richard J.
The coming of the Third Reich   943.08
The Third Reich at war   940.53
The Third Reich in power, 1933-1939   943.086
Evans, Sid
(ed) Southern living 50 years   975
Evans, Stewart
(comp) The Ultimate Jack the Ripper compan-
   ion   364.15
Evans, Walker, 1903-1975
Agee, J. Cotton Tenants   976.1
Agee, J. Let us now praise famous men   976.1
American photographs   779
Evanzz, Karl
The messenger: the rise and fall of Elijah Muham-

mad **297.8**

Eve of a Hundred Midnights. Lascher, B. **070.449**

The eve of destruction. Patterson, J. T. **973.923**

Evelyn, John, 1620-1706

About

Hollis, L. London rising **942**

Even the hollow my body made is gone. Harrington, J. N. **811**

Even This I Get to Experience. Lear, N. **92**

EVENING AND CONTINUATION SCHOOLS

See also Compulsory education; Continuing education; Education; Public schools; Schools; Secondary education; Technical education

EVEREST, MOUNT (CHINA AND NEPAL) *See* Mount Everest (China and Nepal)

Everest: mountain without mercy. Coburn, B. **796.522**

Everett, Daniel L.

Don't sleep, there are snakes **305.8**

Language **400**

The Everglades. Douglas, M. S. **577.6**

EVERGLADES (FLA.)

Perez, L. Snake in the grass **597.96**

EVERGLADES (FLA.) -- ENVIRONMENTAL CONDITIONS

Davis, J. E. An Everglades providence **92**

An Everglades providence. Davis, J. E. **92**

An Evergreen bk [series]

Mamet, D. Speed-the-plow **812**

EVERGREENS

See also Landscape gardening; Shrubs; Trees

Everitt, Anthony

Augustus **92**

Cicero **92**

Hadrian and the triumph of Rome **92**

The rise of Rome **937**

Everitt, Brian

The Cambridge dictionary of statistics **519.5**

EVERLEIGH CLUB (CHICAGO, ILL.)

Abbott, K. Sin in the Second City **977.3**

Everleigh, Ada, 1876-1960

About

Abbott, K. Sin in the Second City **977.3**

Everleigh, Minna, 1878-1948

About

Abbott, K. Sin in the Second City **977.3**

Evers, Medgar Wiley, 1925-1963

About

Evers, M. W. The autobiography of Medgar Evers: a hero's life and legacy revealed through his writings, letters, and speeches **92**

Evers-Williams, Myrlie

(ed) Evers, M. W. The autobiography of Medgar Evers: a hero's life and legacy revealed through his writings, letters, and speeches **92**

Everson, Landis

Everything preserved: poems, 1955-2005 **811**

Evert, Chris

About

Howard, J. The rivals **92**

Every book its reader. Basbanes, N. A. **028**

Every drop for sale. Rothfeder, J. **333.91**

Every grain of rice. Dunlop, F. **641.59**

Every landlord's legal guide. Stewart, M. **346.04**

Every living thing. Herriot, J. **636.089**

Every love story is a ghost story. Max, D. T. c. **92**

Every man in this village is a liar. Stack, M. **956.05**

Every patient tells a story. Sanders, L. **616.07**

Every shut eye ain't asleep. **811**

Every step you take. Marshall, L. **92**

Every tenant's legal guide. Portman, J. **346.04**

Everybody behaves badly. Blume, L. M. M. **813**

Everybody loves our town. Yarm, M. **781.66**

Everybody matters. Chapman, B. **658.4**

Everybody was so young. Vaill, A. **759.13**

Everybody's brother. Cee-Lo **782.421**

Everybody's guide to small claims court. Warner, R. E. **347**

The everyday baker. Dodge, A. J. **641.815**

The everyday DASH diet cookbook. Heller, M. **613.2**

Everyday greatness. Reader's Digest Association **170**

Everyday life in America [series]

Hawke, D. F. Everyday life in early America **973.2**

Schlereth, T. J. Victorian America **973.8**

Everyday life in early America. Hawke, D. F. **973.2**

The everyday meat guide. **641.36**

The Everyday Parenting Toolkit. Kazdin, A. E. **649**

Everydaycook. Brown, A. **641.5**

Everyman's library [series]

Boswell, J. The life of Samuel Johnson **92**

Dante Alighieri The divine comedy **851**

The Iliad **883**

Machiavelli, N. The prince **320.1**

Odyssey The Odyssey **883**

Orwell, G. Essays **824**

Tocqueville, A. d. Democracy in America **973.5**

Virgil The Aeneid **873**

Everyman's library pocket poets [series]

Baudelaire, C. Poems **841**

Beat poets **811**

Blues poems **811**

Burns, R. Burns **821**

Christmas poems **821**

Donne, J. Poems and prose **821**

Herbert, G. Herbert: poems **821**

Hopkins, G. M. Poems and prose **821**

Jazz poems **811**

Keats, J. Poems **821**

Marvell, A. Poems **821**

Persian poets **891**

Pushkin, A. S. Eugene Onegin and other poems **891.7**

Rimbaud, A. Poems **841**

Robinson, E. A. Poems **821**

Selections./English. Poems **891.7**

Shelley, P. B. Poems **821**

Tennyson, A. T. Poems **821**

Everyman, and medieval miracle plays. **822**

Everyone is Italian on Sunday. Ray, R. **641.59**

Everyone loves you when you're dead. Strauss, N. **920**

Everything is an afterthought. Avery, K. **92**

Everything is broken. Larkin, E. **959.1**

Everything is obvious. Watts, D. J. **153.4**

Everything preserved: poems, 1955-2005. Everson, L. **811**

Everything to gain. Carter, J. **92**

Everything you wanted to know about Indians but were afraid to ask. Treuer, A. **909**

Evicted. Desmond, M. c. **339.4**

EVICTION -- UNITED STATES

Desmond, M. c. Evicted **339.4**

EVIDENCE

Nelson, M. The red parts **362.88**

Evidence explained. Mills, E. S. **907**

EVIL *See* Good and evil

The **evil** hours. Morris, D. J. **616.85**

EVIL SPIRITS *See* Demonology

Evolution. **576.8**

EVOLUTION

Alvarez, W. A Most Improbable Journey **508**

Ayala, F. J. Darwin's gift to science and religion **576.8**

Ball, P. Nature's patterns **500.2**

Barash, D. P. Homo mysterious **303.4**

Birkhead, T. Ten thousand birds **598**

Bloom, H. The Lucifer principle **128**

Boyd, B. On the origin of stories **809**

Byrne, E. Darwin **576.8**

Carroll, S. B. Endless forms most beautiful **571.8**

Carroll, S. B. The making of the fittest **572.8**

Carroll, S. B. Remarkable creatures **508**

Coyne, J. A. Why evolution is true **576.8**

Darwin, C. The Beagle letters **576.8**

Darwin, C. The Darwin reader **576.8**

Darwin, C. On the origin of species **576.8**

Darwin, C. The origin of species by means of natural selection, or, The preservation of favored races in the struggle for life **576.8**

Dawkins, R. A devil's chaplain **500**

Dawkins, R. The greatest show on Earth **576.8**

Dawkins, R. The selfish gene **576**

Dennett, D. C. Darwin's dangerous idea **146**

DeSalle, R. The brain **612.8**

Dunn, R. The wild life of our bodies **579**

Eiseley, L. C. The immense journey **576.8**

Eldredge, N. Extinction and Evolution **560**

Eldredge, N. Why we do it **155.3**

Evolution **576.8**

Evolution, the whole story **576.8**

Finkel, E. The Genome Generation **572**

Flannery, T. Here on Earth **551**

Fortey, R. A. Life **576.8**

Fortey, R. A. Trilobite! **560**

Francis, R. C. Domesticated **636**

Gould, S. J. The structure of evolutionary theory **576.8**

Gould, S. J. Hen's teeth and horse's toes **576.8**

Gould, S. J. The richness of life **508**

Greenspan, S. I. The first idea **153.7**

Harari, Y. N. Sapiens **909**

Hazen, R. M. The story of Earth **550**

Horner, J. R. How to build a dinosaur **567.9**

Johnson, P. Darwin **576.8**

Jolly, A. Lucy's legacy **599.93**

Jones, S. Darwin's ghost **576.8**

Keller, M. Charles Darwin's On the Origin of Species **576.8**

Kenneally, C. The first word **400**

Kirschvink, J. A new history of life **576.8**

Konner, M. The evolution of childhood **305.23**

Kurzweil, R. The singularity is near **153.9**

Leakey, R. E. The origin of humankind **599.93**

Leakey, R. E. Origins reconsidered **599.93**

Lieberman, D. The story of the human body **612**

Maestripieri, D. Games primates play **155.7**

Margulis, L. Symbiotic planet **576.8**

Marks, J. What it means to be 98[percent] chimpanzee **599.93**

Martin, R. How we do it **612.6**

Mayr, E. What evolution is **576.8**

McCalman, I. Darwin's armada **576.8**

Mesler, B. A Brief History of Creation **576.8**

Mithen, S. J. The singing neanderthals **780.9**

Mlodinow, L. The upright thinkers **509**

Moalem, S. Survival of the sickest **616**

Nielsen, C. Animal evolution **591.3**

Novacek, M. J. Terra **576.8**

Pagel, M. Wired for culture **303.4**

Pinker, S. How the mind works **153**

Prothero, D. R. The story of life in 25 fossils **560**

Ridley, M. The evolution of everything **303.48**

Sarmiento, E. The last human **569.9**

Shlain, L. Sex, time, and power **306.7**

Shubin, N. Your inner fish **611**

Switek, B. Written in stone **576.8**

Tattersall, I. The fossil trail **599.93**

Tattersall, I. Masters of the planet **599.93**

Taylor, P. D. A history of life in 100 fossils **560**

Taylor, T. The artificial ape **599.93**

Teilhard de Chardin, P. The phenomenon of

man **113**

Trivers, R. The folly of fools **153.4**

Tyson, N. d. Origins: fourteen billion years of cosmic evolution **523.1**

Wade, N. Before the dawn **599.93**

Wagner, A. Arrival of the fittest **572.8**

Walker, A. The wisdom of the bones **599.93**

Watson, L. Dark nature **111**

Wilkinson, M. Restless creatures **591.47**

Wills, C. Green Equilibrium **577**

Wilson, D. S. Evolution for everyone **576.8**

Young, C. C. Evolution and creationism **576.8**

EVOLUTION -- COMIC BOOKS, STRIPS, ETC

Byrne, E. Darwin **576.8**

EVOLUTION -- ENCYCLOPEDIAS

Rice, S. A. Encyclopedia of biodiversity **578.7**

EVOLUTION -- GRAPHIC NOVELS

Keller, M. Charles Darwin's On the Origin of Species **576.8**

EVOLUTION -- HISTORY

Carroll, S. B. Remarkable creatures **508**

Dawkins, R. The ancestor's tale **576.8**

Flannery, T. Here on Earth **551**

Stott, R. Darwin's ghosts **576.8**

EVOLUTION -- MATHEMATICAL MODELS

Highfield, R. Supercooperators **519.3**

EVOLUTION -- PHILOSOPHY

Dawkins, R. The ancestor's tale **576.8**

Larson, E. J. Evolution: the remarkable history of a scientific theory **576.8**

Wilson, E. O. The social conquest of earth **599.93**

EVOLUTION -- POPULAR WORKS

Evolution, the whole story **576.8**

Nye, B. Undeniable **576.8**

EVOLUTION -- SIMULATION METHODS

Long, J. Darwin's devices **629.8**

EVOLUTION -- STUDY AND TEACHING

Long, J. Darwin's devices **629.8**

EVOLUTION -- STUDY AND TEACHING -- DRAMA

Lawrence, J. Inherit the wind **812**

EVOLUTION AND CHRISTIANITY See Creationism

Evolution and creationism. Young, C. C. **576.8**

Evolution for everyone. Wilson, D. S. **576.8**

The **evolution** of childhood. Konner, M. **305.23**

The **evolution** of everything. Ridley, M. **303.48**

The **evolution** of physics. Einstein, A. **530**

Evolution of the Word. Borg, M. J. **225**

Evolution, the whole story. **576.8**

Evolution: the remarkable history of a scientific theory. Larson, E. J. **576.8**

EVOLUTIONARY GENETICS

Pagel, M. Wired for culture **303.4**

Wagner, A. Arrival of the fittest **572.8**

EVOLUTIONARY PALEOBIOLOGY

Horner, J. R. How to build a dinosaur **567.9**

Taylor, P. D. A history of life in 100 fossils **560**

EVOLUTIONARY PSYCHOLOGY

Dunbar, R. Human evolution **155.7**

EVOLUTIONARY PSYCHOLOGY

See also Psychology

EVOLUTIONARY ROBOTICS

Long, J. Darwin's devices **629.8**

EVREĬSKAĬA AVTONOMNAĬA OBLAST' (RUSSIA) -- HISTORY

Gessen, M. Where the Jews aren't **957.7**

Ewans, Martin

Afghanistan **958.1**

Ewer, Cynthia Townley

Cut the Clutter **648.5**

Ewing, Heather P.

The lost world of James Smithson **92**

Ewing, Rex A.

Got sun? go solar **697**

Ewing, William A.

Brandow, T. Edward Steichen **779**

EX-NUNS

See also Nuns

EX-PRESIDENTS -- UNITED STATES -- HISTORY

Duffy, M. The presidents club **973.92**

EX-PRIESTS

See also Catholic Church -- Clergy; Priests

An **exact** replica of a figment of my imagination. McCracken, E. **92**

EXAMINATIONS

See also Questions and answers; Teaching

EXAMINATIONS -- STUDY GUIDES

The official guide to the HiSET exam **373.126**

Examined lives. Miller, J. **190**

EXCAVATIONS (ARCHAEOLOGY) -- EGYPT

Hawass, Z. A. Hidden treasures of ancient Egypt **932**

Noël Hume, I. Belzoni **92**

EXCAVATIONS (ARCHAEOLOGY) -- NEW YORK (STATE) -- LONG ISLAND

Griswold, M. The Manor **974.7**

EXCAVATIONS (ARCHEOLOGY)

Pearson, M. P. Stonehenge **936.2**

EXCAVATIONS (ARCHEOLOGY)

See also Archeology

EXCAVATIONS (ARCHAEOLOGY) -- EGYPT

Hawass, Z. A. Hidden treasures of ancient Egypt **932**

Ryan, D. P. Beneath the sands of Egypt **92**

EXCAVATIONS (ARCHEOLOGY) -- GREECE

Great moments in Greek archaeology **938**

EXCAVATIONS (ARCHEOLOGY) -- ITALY

Pellegrino, C. R. Ghosts of Vesuvius **937**

EXCEPTIONAL CHILDREN

Bowers, M. 8 keys to raising the quirky child **649**

EXCEPTIONAL CHILDREN
See also Children; Elementary education
EXCEPTIONAL CHILDREN -- UNITED STATES -- PSYCHOLOGY
Solomon, A. Far from the tree   **362.4**
EXCHANGE OF PRISONERS OF WAR *See* Prisoners of war
EXCHANGE RATES *See* Foreign exchange
The **excruciating** history of dentistry. Wynbrandt, J.   **617.6**
EXCUSES
See also Etiquette; Manners and customs
EXECUTIONS AND EXECUTIONERS
Harrington, J. F. The faithful executioner   **364.66**
EXECUTIONS AND EXECUTIONERS -- GERMANY -- NUREMBERG -- BIOGRAPHY
Harrington, J. F. The faithful executioner   **364.66**
EXECUTIONS AND EXECUTIONERS -- UNITED STATES -- HISTORY -- 19TH CENTURY
Berg, S. W. 38 nooses   **973.7**
EXECUTIVE ABILITY
Chan, R. W. Behind the Berkshire Hathaway curtain   **658.4**
Covey, S. The 4 disciplines of execution   **658.4**
Elton, C. All in   **658.3**
Horstman, M. The effective manager   **658**
Kouzes, J. M. The truth about leadership   **658.4**
EXECUTIVE ABILITY
See also Ability
EXECUTIVE ABILITY IN CHILDREN
Dawson, P. Smart but scattered   **649**
EXECUTIVE AGENCIES *See* Administrative agencies
EXECUTIVE DEPARTMENTS
See also Administrative agencies
EXECUTIVE FUNCTIONS (NEUROPSYCHOLOGY)
Richey, M. A. The impulsive, disorganized child   **649**
EXECUTIVE POWER
Moynihan, D. P. Secrecy   **352.3**
Simon, J. F. What kind of nation   **342**
Tuchman, B. W. Practicing history   **907**
EXECUTIVE POWER
See also Constitutional law; Political science
EXECUTIVE POWER -- UNITED STATES
Raphael, R. Mr. president   **352.23**
EXECUTIVE POWER -- UNITED STATES -- HISTORY
McPherson, J. M. Tried by war   **92**
Simon, J. F. What kind of nation   **342**
EXECUTIVE POWER -- UNITED STATES -- HISTORY -- 20TH CENTURY
Simon, J. F. FDR and Chief Justice Hughes **973.917**
EXECUTIVES
Isaacson, W. Steve Jobs   **92**

EXECUTORS AND ADMINISTRATORS
See also Inheritance and succession
The **exegesis** of Philip K. Dick. Dick, P. K.   **818**
EXERCISE
Abbott, C. The Badass Body Diet   **613.2**
Brewer, S. C. The Canyon Ranch guide to men's health   **613**
Broad, W. J. The science of yoga   **613.7**
Complete guide to fitness & health   **613.7**
Contreras, B. Strong curves   **613.7**
Fitness and exercise sourcebook   **613.7**
Flippin, R. The diabetes reset   **616.4**
Liebman, H. L. Encyclopedia of Exercise Anatomy   **613.7**
Schuler, L. Strong   **613.7**
EXERCISE
See also Health; Hygiene
EXERCISE -- POPULAR WORKS
Reynolds, G. The first 20 minutes   **613.7**
EXERCISE -- SOCIAL ASPECTS
Kunitz, D. Lift   **613.7**
EXERCISE ADDICTION
See also Compulsive behavior
EXERCISE FOR WOMEN
Pagano, J. Strength training exercises for women   **613.7**
Schuler, L. Strong   **613.7**
EXERCISE MOVEMENT TECHNIQUES -- POPULAR WORKS
Aaronson, N. Pilates for breast cancer survivors   **616.99**
EXHIBIT DESIGNERS
Albrecht, D. The Work of Charles and Ray Eames   **745.4**
EXHIBITIONS
Prentice, C. The lost tribe of Coney Island   **305.8**
Tirella, J. Tomorrow-land   **607**
EXHIBITS *See* Exhibitions
EXHUMATION
Kammen, M. G. Digging up the dead   **393**
EXILES
See also Persons; Political refugees
EXISTENTIALISM
Barrett, W. Irrational man   **142**
Existentialism from Dostoevsky to Sartre   **142**
Ferry, L. A brief history of thought   **100**
May, R. The discovery of being   **150.19**
Sartre, J. P. Being and nothingness   **142**
Sartre, J. P. Existentialism and human emotions **142**
Tillich, P. The courage to be   **179**
EXISTENTIALISM
See also Metaphysics; Modern philosophy; Phenomenology
Existentialism and human emotions. Sartre, J. P.   **142**
Existentialism from Dostoevsky to Sartre.   **142**

Exit the colonel. Chorin, E. **961.204**

Exmouth, Edward Pellew, Viscount, 1757-1833
About
Taylor, S. Commander **92**

EXOBIOLOGY
Sasselov, D. The life of super-Earths **576.8**
Tyson, N. d. Death by black hole **523.8**

Exodus. Feldman, D. **92**

Exorcising Hitler. Taylor, F. **943.087**

EXORCISM
See also Supernatural

EXORCISM -- EUROPE -- HISTORY
Levack, B. P. The Devil within **133.4**

EXOTIC ANIMALS
Belozerskaya, M. The Medici giraffe **636**

The **expectant** father. Brott, A. A. **649**

EXPECTATION (PSYCHOLOGY)
Berdik, C. Mind over mind **153.4**

EXPEDITIONS, SCIENTIFIC *See* Scientific expeditions

Experience. Amis, M. **92**

EXPERIENCE *See* Empiricism

EXPERIENCE (RELIGION)
Wathey, J. C. The illusion of God's presence **204**

Experiment central. **507.8**

EXPERIMENTAL AUTOMOBILES -- EXHIBITIONS
Gross, K. Dream cars **629.222**

Experimental drawing. Kaupelis, R. **741.2**

EXPERIMENTAL MUSIC
Moore, T. No wave **781.66**

Experimenting with babies. Gallagher, S. **306.874**

EXPERIMENTS, SCIENTIFIC *See* Science -- Experiments

EXPERT SYSTEMS (COMPUTER SCIENCE)
See also Artificial intelligence; Data processing; Information systems

EXPERTISE
Ericsson, A. Peak **153.9**
Schulz, K. Being wrong **153**

EXPERTS *See* Specialists

Explaining Hitler. Rosenbaum, R. **943.086**

EXPLANATION
This explains everything **500**

Exploding the Phone. Lapsley, P. **384**

EXPLOITATION
Prentice, C. The lost tribe of Coney Island **305.8**

EXPLORATION
Adams, M. Meet Me in Atlantis **398.23**
Fagan, B. Beyond the blue horizon **910.4**
Macleod, A. Explorers **910.4**
Man, J. Marco Polo **915**
The Oxford companion to world exploration **910.3**
Polo, M. The travels of Marco Polo **915**
Waldman, C. Encyclopedia of exploration **910.3**

EXPLORATION
See also Adventure and adventurers; Geography; History

EXPLORATION -- ATLASES
Foer, J. Atlas Obscura **910.41**

EXPLORATION OF SPACE *See* Outer space -- Exploration

EXPLORATIONS *See* Exploration

An **explorer's** notebook. Flannery, T. **304.2**

Explorers. Macleod, A. **910.4**

EXPLORERS
See also Adventure and adventurers; Heroes and heroines

EXPLORERS
Abdul-Jabbar, K. Black profiles in courage **920**
Adams, M. Turn right at Machu Picchu **985**
Alexander, C. The Bounty: the true story of the mutiny on the Bounty **996**
Alexander, C. The Endurance **998**
Ambrose, S. E. Undaunted courage **917**
Bellec, F. Unknown lands **910.4**
Bergreen, L. Marco Polo **92**
Bergreen, L. Over the edge of the world **910.4**
Blainey, G. Sea of dangers **92**
Brandt, A. The man who ate his boots **910.4**
Carlsen, W. Jungle of Stone **972.81**
Cliff, N. Holy war **909**
Cookman, S. Ice blink **919**
Croke, V. The lady and the panda **599.78**
Dolnick, E. Down the great unknown **979.1**
Fernandez-Armesto, F. Amerigo **92**
Fischer, D. H. Champlain's dream **92**
Gifford, B. Ledyard **92**
Grann, D. The lost city of Z **918**
Grant, R. Crazy river **916**
Heaney, C. Cradle of gold **92**
Horwitz, T. A voyage long and strange **970.01**
Hough, R. A. Captain James Cook **92**
Howell, G. Gertrude Bell **92**
Jeal, T. Explorers of the Nile **962**
Jeal, T. Stanley **92**
Larson, E. J. An empire of ice **919**
Lovell, M. S. A rage to live: a biography of Richard and Isabel Burton **92**
Macleod, A. Explorers **910.4**
Manchester, W. A world lit only by fire **940.2**
Mann, C. C. 1493 **909**
McGoogan, K. Race to the Polar Sea **92**
Millard, C. The river of doubt **973.91**
Morison, S. E. Admiral of the ocean sea: a life of Christopher Columbus **92**
Niven, J. Ada Blackjack **92**
Points unknown **910**
Prescott, W. H. History of the conquest of Mexico **972**
Preston, D. A first rate tragedy **919**
Ridley, G. The discovery of Jeanne Baret **92**

Riffenburgh, B. Shackleton's forgotten expedition **998**

Schneider, P. Brutal journey: the epic story of the first crossing of North America **970.01**

Slaughter, T. P. Exploring Lewis and Clark **978**

Solomon, S. The coldest March **919**

Tabor, J. M. Blind descent **796.52**

Thomas, N. Cook **910**

Turney, C. 1912 **998**

Waldman, C. Encyclopedia of exploration **910.3**

Wallach, J. Desert queen **956**

Williams, G. Arctic labyrinth **910.4**

EXPLORERS -- DICTIONARIES

World explorers and discoverers **920.003**

EXPLORERS -- NORWAY -- BIOGRAPHY

Bown, S. R. The last Viking **92**

EXPLORERS -- UNITED STATES -- BIOGRAPHY

Dolnick, E. Down the great unknown **979.1**

Explorers of the Nile. Jeal, T. **962**

Exploring Lewis and Clark. Slaughter, T. P. **978**

Exploring Mars. Hubbard, S. **523.43**

Exploring wine. Kolpan, S. **641.2**

EXPLOSIONS

MacDonald, L. M. Curse of the Narrows **971**

EXPLOSIVES

Castner, B. All the ways we kill and die **958.104**

EXPLOSIVES

See also Chemistry

EXPO 92 (SEVILLE, SPAIN)

See also Exhibitions; Fairs

EXPORTS

See also International trade

EXPOSED CHILDREN *See* Abandoned children

EXPOSITION (RHETORIC)

Gutkind, L. You can't make this stuff up **808**

Jager-Hyman, J. B+ grades, A+ college application **378.1**

EXPOSITION UNIVERSELLE DE 1889 (PARIS, FRANCE)

Jonnes, J. Eiffel's tower **944**

The **exquisite** book of paper flowers. Cetti, L. **745.594**

EXTINCT ANIMALS

Barrow, M. V. Nature's ghosts **333.95**

Lister, A. Mammoths **569**

EXTINCT ANIMALS

See also Animals

EXTINCT ANIMALS -- SOMALIA

Girling, R. The Hunt for the Golden Mole **591.68**

EXTINCT BIRDS

The world's rarest birds **598**

EXTINCT CITIES

Hunt, P. Ten discoveries that rewrote history **930.1**

EXTINCT CITIES

See also Archeology; Cities and towns

EXTINCTION (BIOLOGY)

Eldredge, N. Extinction and Evolution **560**

Kolbert, E. The sixth extinction **576.8**

Newitz, A. Scatter, adapt, and remember **576.8**

O'Connor, M. R. Resurrection Science **591.68**

Shapiro, B. How to Clone a Mammoth **591.68**

EXTINCTION (BIOLOGY)

See also Biology

Extinction and Evolution. Eldredge, N. **560**

EXTINCTION OF SPECIES *See* Extinction (Biology)

EXTINCTION OF SPECIES, MASS *See* Mass extinctions

Extra lives. Bissell, T. **794.8**

Extra Sensory. Clegg, B. **133.8**

Extra virginity. Mueller, T. **664**

EXTRAGALACTIC NEBULAE *See* Galaxies

EXTRAMARITAL RELATIONSHIPS *See* Adultery

Extraordinary everyday photography. Manwaring, J. **778.71**

Extraordinary, ordinary people. Rice, C. **92**

EXTRASENSORY PERCEPTION

Clegg, B. Extra Sensory **133.8**

Sheldrake, R. Dogs that know when their owners are coming home **133.8**

Sheldrake, R. The sense of being stared at **133.8**

EXTRASOLAR PLANETS

Sasselov, D. The life of super-Earths **576.8**

EXTRASOLAR PLANETS

See also Planets

EXTRATERRESTRIAL BEINGS

Davies, P. C. W. The eerie silence **576.8**

EXTRATERRESTRIAL BEINGS

See also Life on other planets

EXTRATERRESTRIAL LIFE *See* Life on other planets

EXTRAVEHICULAR ACTIVITY (MANNED SPACE FLIGHT)

Anderson, C. The ordinary spaceman **92**

EXTRAVEHICULAR ACTIVITY (SPACE FLIGHT)

See also Space flight

EXTREME ENVIRONMENTS

Baker, D. The 50 most extreme places in our solar system **523.2**

Toomey, D. Weird Life **571**

The **Extreme** Searcher's Internet Handbook. Hock, R. **025.042**

EXTREME SPORTS

O'Brien, K. Catching the Sky **796.94**

EXTREME SPORTS

See also Sports

Extreme stars. Kaler, J. B. **523.8**

EXTREME WEATHER

Kostigen, T. M. National Geographic extreme

weather survival guide   **613.6**
EXTREMISM (POLITICAL SCIENCE)   *See*
   Radicalism
EXTREMITIES (ANATOMY) -- EVOLUTION
   Wilkinson, M. Restless creatures   **591.47**
Exuberance. Jamison, K. R.   **152.4**
The **exultant** ark. Balcombe, J.   **591.5**
EXXON CORPORATION
   Coll, S. Private empire   **338.7**
EXXON MOBIL CORPORATION
   Coll, S. Private empire   **338.7**
EYE -- WOUNDS AND INJURIES -- PATIENTS
-- UNITED STATES -- BIOGRAPHY
   Axelrod, H. The point of vanishing   **92**
Eye against eye. Gander, F.   **811**
Eye of the beholder. Snyder, L. J.   **701**
The **eye** of the elephant. Owens, D.   **333.95**
Eye of the sixties. Stein, J. E.   **92**
Eye on the Struggle. Morris, J. M.   **92**
Eyes of the nation. Virga, V.   **973**
The **eyes** of Willie McGee. Heard, A.   **364.66**
The **Eyes** on the prize civil rights reader.   **323.1**
Eyes on the prize: America's civil rights years, 1954-
   1965. Williams, J.   **323.1**
Eyes on the street. Kanigel, R.   **92**
Eyewitness history [series]
   Purcell, S. J. The early national period   **973.4**
   Schwartz, R. A. The 1990s   **909.82**
Eyewitness to America.   **973**
Eyewitness Travel Malaysia & Singapore.   **915.9**
Eyman, Scott
   Empire of dreams   **92**
   John Wayne: the life and legend   **92**
   Lion of Hollywood   **92**
Ezekiel, Raphael S.
   The racist mind   **320.5**
Ezra Pound. Tytell, J.   **92**
Ezzo, Gary
   On becoming baby wise   **649**

F

F.D.R. and his enemies. Fried, A.   **92**
Fab. Sounes, H.   **92**
Faber, Adele
   How to Talk So Kids Will Listen and Listen So Kids
   Will Talk   **649.1**
Faber, David
   Munich, 1938   **940.53**
Faber, Toby
   Faberge's eggs   **739.2**
Faberge revealed. Von Habsburg, G.   **739.2**
FABERGÉ (FIRM) -- CATALOGS
   Von Habsburg, G. Faberge revealed   **739.2**
Fabergé, Peter Carl, 1846-1920
           About
   Faber, T. Faberge's eggs   **739.2**

Von Habsburg, G. Faberge revealed   **739.2**
Faberge's eggs. Faber, T.   **739.2**
Fabian, Ann
   The skull collectors   **599.9**
FABLES
   See also Fiction; Literature
FABRIC DESIGN *See* Textile design
The **fabric** of the cosmos. Greene, B. R.   **523.1**
FABRICS
   The Mood guide to fabric and fashion   **746.9**
   Schoeser, M. World textiles: a concise history   **677**
   White, C. Uniquely felt   **746**
Face. Alexie, S.   **811**
FACE IN ART
   Parks, C. S. Secrets to drawing realistic fac-
   es   **743.42**
Face paint. Eldridge, L.   **391.6**
FACE PAINTING
   See also Painting
FACE PERCEPTION
   Sacks, O. The mind's eye   **616.85**
Face value. Whitefield-Madrano, A.   **111.85**
FACEBOOK (WEB SITE)
   See also Social networking; Web sites
The **Facebook** effect. Kirkpatrick, D.   **338.7**
FACEBOOK INC.
   Kirkpatrick, D. The Facebook effect   **338.7**
FACETIAE *See* Anecdotes; Wit and humor
Facing east from Indian country. Richter, D.
   K.   **970.004**
Facing the wave. Ehrlich, G.   **363.34**
FACTORIALS
   See also Number theory; Sequences (Math-
   ematics)
FACTORIES
   Von Drehle, D. Triangle: the fire that changed
   America   **974.7**
FACTORY AND TRADE WASTE *See* Industrial
   waste
FACTORY FARMS
   Genoways, T. The chain   **338.7**
Factory girls. Chang, L. T.   **331.4**
Factory man. Macy, B.   **338.7**
FACTORY MANAGEMENT
   See also Management
FACTORY WASTE *See* Industrial waste
FACTORY WORKERS
   Bragg, R. Ava's man   **975**
   Nuland, S. B. Lost in America   **92**
FACTORY WORKERS *See* Labor; Working class
The **facts.** Roth, P.   **813**
Facts about the presidents. Kane, J. N.   **920**
The **Facts** on File companion to classical drama.
   Thorburn, J. E.   **880**
The **facts** on file companion to Shakespeare. Baker,
   W.   **822.3**

The **Facts** on File companion to the American novel. **813**

The **Facts** on File companion to the British novel. **823**

The **Facts** on File companion to the British short story. Maunder, A. **823**

Facts on File crime library [series]
Rosen, F. The historical atlas of American crime **364**
Sifakis, C. The mafia encyclopedia **364.1**

The **Facts** on File dictionary of allusions. Manser, M. H. **422**

The **Facts** on File dictionary of foreign words and phrases. Manser, M. H. **422**

The **Facts** on File dictionary of proverbs. Manser, M. H. **398.9**

The **Facts** on File encyclopedia of word and phrase origins. Hendrickson, R. **422**

Facts on File library of American history [series]
Axelrod, A. The encyclopedia of the American armed forces **355**
Carey, C. W. American inventors, entrepreneurs & business visionaries **920**
Congress investigates **328**
Encyclopedia of American business **338**
Encyclopedia of American historical documents **973**
Encyclopedia of American history **973**
Hamilton, N. A. Presidents **920.003**
Leiter, R. A. Landmark Supreme Court cases **347**
My fellow citizens **352.23**
Schneider, D. First ladies **920.003**
Schultz, D. A. Encyclopedia of the United States Constitution **342**
Waldman, C. Atlas of the North American Indian **970.004**
Waldman, C. Encyclopedia of Native American tribes **970.004**
Woodger, E. Encyclopedia of the Lewis and Clark Expedition **917**

Facts on File library of American literature [series]
Abbotson, S. C. W. Critical companion to Arthur Miller **812**
Dowling, R. M. Critical companion to Eugene O'Neill **812**
The **Facts** on File companion to the American novel **813**
Facts on File, I. Encyclopedia of American literature **810**
Fargnoli, A. N. Critical companion to William Faulkner **813**
Farrell, S. E. Critical companion to Kurt Vonnegut **813**
Gillespie, C. Critical companion to Alice Walker **813**

Gillespie, C. Critical companion to Toni Morrison **813**
Haralson, E. L. Critical companion to Henry James **813**
Heintzelman, G. Critical companion to Tennessee Williams **812**
Jones, S. L. Critical companion to Zora Neale Hurston **813**
Kirk, C. A. Critical companion to Flannery O'Connor **813**
Murphy, R. E. Critical companion to T.S. Eliot **811**
Nadel, I. B. Critical companion to Philip Roth **813**
Oliver, C. M. Critical companion to Ernest Hemingway **813**
Oliver, C. M. Critical companion to Walt Whitman **811**
Schultz, J. D. Critical companion to John Steinbeck **813**
Sova, D. B. Critical companion to Edgar Allan Poe **818**
Tate, M. J. Critical companion to F. Scott Fitzgerald **813**
Thursby, J. S. Critical companion to Maya Angelou **818**
Wayne, T. K. Critical companion to Ralph Waldo Emerson **818**
Wright, S. B. Critical companion to Nathaniel Hawthorne **813**

Facts on File library of language and literature [series]
Espy, W. R. Words to rhyme with **423**
Hendrickson, R. The Facts on File encyclopedia of word and phrase origins **422**
Manser, M. H. The Facts on File dictionary of allusions **422**
Manser, M. H. The Facts on File dictionary of foreign words and phrases **422**
Manser, M. H. The Facts on File dictionary of proverbs **398.9**

Facts on File library of religion and mythology [series]
Jordan, M. Dictionary of gods and goddesses **201**

Facts on File library of world history [series]
David, A. R. Handbook to life in ancient Egypt **932**
Dictionary of wars **355**
Encyclopedia of plague and pestilence **614.4**
English, E. D. Encyclopedia of the medieval world **940.1**
Kuhlman, E. A. A to Z of women in world history **920.003**
Moore, J. A. Encyclopedia of the United Nations **341.23**
Waldman, C. Encyclopedia of exploration **910.3**

Facts on File library of world literature [series]
Baker, W. Critical companion to Jane Austen **823**
Boyce, C. Critical companion to William Shake-

speare **822.3**

Davis, P. B. Critical companion to Charles Dickens **823**

DeGategno, P. J. Critical companion to Jonathan Swift **828**

The Facts on File companion to the British novel **823**

Fargnoli, A. N. Critical companion to James Joyce **823**

Manser, M. H. Critical companion to the Bible **220.6**

Maunder, A. The Facts on File companion to the British short story **823**

Quinn, E. Critical companion to George Orwell **828**

Ross, D. A. Critical companion to William Butler Yeats **821**

Ruud, J. Critical companion to Dante **850**

Thorburn, J. E. The Facts on File companion to classical drama **880**

Facts on File science library [series]

Bell, S. Encyclopedia of forensic science **363.2**

Gates, A. E. Encyclopedia of earthquakes and volcanoes **551.2**

Gates, A. E. Encyclopedia of pollution **363.7**

Nichols, C. R. Encyclopedia of marine science **551.46**

Tanton, J. S. Encyclopedia of mathematics **510**

Facts on File, Inc.

The Facts on File companion to the American novel **813**

Encyclopedia of American literature **810**

Maunder, A. The Facts on File companion to the British short story **823**

FACTS, MISCELLANEOUS See Books of lists; Curiosities and wonders

FACULTY (EDUCATION) See Colleges and universities -- Faculty; Educators; Teachers

Faderman, Lillian, 1940-

The gay revolution **306.76**

Fadiman, Anne

The spirit catches you and you fall down **306.4**

Fadiman, Clifton

(ed) World poetry **808.81**

Fading echoes. Sielski, M. **92**

FADS

Bissonnette, Z. The great Beanie Baby bubble **338.7**

FADS

See also Manners and customs; Popular culture

The **faerie** queene. Spenser, E. **821**

Faerm, Steven

Fashion: design course **746.9**

Fagan, Brian

Beyond the blue horizon **910.4**

Elixir **553.7**

The intimate bond **591.5**

The long summer: how climate changed civilization **551.6**

Fagan, Deirdre

Critical companion to Robert Frost **811**

Fagin, Dan

Toms River **363.72**

Fahey, Anne Marie

About

Rule, A. --and never let her go **364.1**

FAIENCE See Pottery

Faigman, David L.

Laboratory of justice **347**

Failing law schools. Tamanaha, B. Z. **340**

FAILURE (PSYCHOLOGY)

Beilock, S. L. Choke **153.9**

Hallinan, J. T. Why we make mistakes **153**

Lahey, J. The gift of failure **649**

Riess, J. Flunking sainthood **248.4**

Very good lives **158**

FAILURE IN BUSINESS See Bankruptcy; Business failures

Failure is impossible. **92**

Failure is not an option. Kranz, E. F. **629.45**

FAILURE OF BANKS See Bank failures

FAILURES, STRUCTURAL See Structural failures

Fainaru, Steve

League of Denial **617.1**

Fainaru-Wada, Mark

(jt. auth) Fainaru, S. League of Denial **617.1**

Fair food. Hesterman, O. B. **338.1**

FAIR HOUSING See Discrimination in housing

The **fair** society. Corning, P. **303.3**

FAIR TRADE (TARIFF) See Free trade

FAIR TRIAL

See also Civil rights; Due process of law

FAIR TRIAL -- UNITED STATES

Leamer, L. The price of justice **346.730**

FAIR USE (COPYRIGHT)

Butler, R. P. Copyright for teachers & librarians in the 21st century **346**

Crews, K. D. Copyright law for librarians and educators **346.04**

Gasaway, L. N. Copyright questions and answers for information professionals **346.73**

FAIR USE (COPYRIGHT)

See also Copyright

FAIR USE (COPYRIGHT) -- UNITED STATES

Crews, K. D. Copyright law for librarians and educators **346.04**

Gasaway, L. N. Copyright questions and answers for information professionals **346.73**

Fair, Eric

About

Fair, E. Consequence **956.704**

Fairbank, John King
China 951
The great Chinese revolution: 1800-1985 951
Fairbanks, Douglas, 1883-1939
About
Goessel, T. The first king of Hollywood 92
Fairchild, Barbara
The Bon appetit cookbook 641.5
The Bon appetit fast easy fresh cookbook 641.5
FAIRIES
See also Folklore
FAIRNESS
Corning, P. The fair society 303.3
FAIRNESS
See also Conduct of life
FAIRNESS DOCTRINE (BROADCASTING)
See also Broadcasting; Television and politics
FAIRY TALES
Del Negro, J. M. Folktales aloud 027.62
Favorite folktales from around the world 398.2
Haase, D. The Greenwood encyclopedia of folktales and fairy tales 398.2
The Original Folk and Fairy Tales of the Brothers Grimm 398.2
The turnip princess 398.209
FAIRY TALES
See also Children's literature; Fiction
FAIRY TALES -- ENCYCLOPEDIAS
Haase, D. The Greenwood encyclopedia of folktales and fairy tales 398.2
FAIRY TALES -- GERMANY
The Original Folk and Fairy Tales of the Brothers Grimm 398.2
FAIRY TALES -- HISTORY AND CRITICISM
Orenstein, C. Little Red Riding Hood uncloaked 398.2
Zipes, J. The irresistible fairy tale 398.209
FAIRY TALES -- SOCIAL ASPECTS
Zipes, J. The irresistible fairy tale 398.209
Fairyland. Abbott, A. 813
FAITH
Barnes, J. Falling in love with Joseph Smith 92
Believer, beware 200.9
John Paul Crossing the threshold of hope 282
Keller, T. J. The reason for God 239
Sacks, J. The great partnership 201.65
Terkel, S. Will the circle be unbroken? 128
Wathey, J. C. The illusion of God's presence 204
FAITH
See also Religion; Salvation; Spiritual life; Theology; Virtue
FAITH -- PSYCHOLOGY
Barrett, J. L. Born believers 200.1
FAITH -- PSYCHOLOGY
See also Psychology of religion
Faith and treason. Fraser, A. 942.06

FAITH CURE See Spiritual healing
FAITH HEALING See Spiritual healing
Faith of my fathers. McCain, J. S. 92
Faithful and virtuous night. Glück, L. 811
The faithful executioner. Harrington, J. F. 364.66
FALCONRY
Hines, R. No Way but Gentlenesse 92
MacDonald, H. H is for Hawk 598.9
FALCONRY
See also Game and game birds; Hunting
Faleiro, Sonia
Beautiful thing 792.7
Falk, Beverly
Teaching matters 370.9
Falk, Daina
The hungry fan's game day cookbook 641.5
Falk, Dan
In search of time 529
The Science of Shakespeare 822.3
Falkner, David
Great time coming: the life of Jackie Robinson, from baseball to Birmingham 92
The fall. 92
The fall line. Vinton, N. 796.935
The fall of Berlin. Read, A. 940.54
The fall of Berlin 1945. Beevor, A. 940.54
The fall of heaven. Cooper, A. S. 955.05
The fall of the house of Dixie. Levine, B. 973.7
FALLACIES See Errors; Logic
The fallen sky. Cokinos, C. 523.5
Falletti, Sébastien
(jt. auth) Kim, E. A Thousand Miles to Freedom 92
FALLIBILITY
Schulz, K. Being wrong 153
Falling in love with Joseph Smith. Barnes, J. 92
Falling into the fire. Montross, C. 92
Falling leaves. Mah, A. Y. 305.48
Falling to Earth. Worden, A. 92
Falling upwards. Holmes, R. 387.7
Fallows, James M.
China airborne 387.7
Looking at the sun 950
Postcards from Tomorrow Square 951.05
FALSE ACCUSATION
Burns, S. The Central Park Five 364.1
FALSE IMPRISONMENT -- UNITED STATES
Echols, D. Life after death 364.66
FALSE MEMORIES See False memory syndrome
FALSE MEMORY SYNDROME
Schacter, D. L. Searching for memory 153.1
FALSE MEMORY SYNDROME
See also Memory
FALSEHOOD See Truthfulness and falsehood
Faludi, Susan
In the Darkroom 818.603

FAME
Boorstin, D. J. The image 973.9
Common One day it'll all make sense 92
Mann, W. J. Hello, gorgeous 92

FAME -- PSYCHOLOGICAL ASPECTS
Kalb, C. Andy Warhol was a hoarder 616.89

FAME -- SOCIAL ASPECTS -- UNITED STATES
Burr, T. Gods like us 306.4

FAMILIES
Blair, G. S. Design mom 747
Jackson, R. The learning habit 371.3
Rosenstrach, J. Dinner 642
Rosenstrach, J. How to celebrate every-
thing 641.568
Sandler, L. One and only 306.874
Schwartz, J. Oddly normal 306.76
Seek, A. God and Jetfire 92

FAMILIES -- ECONOMIC ASPECTS
Economides, A. The moneysmart family system 332.024

**FAMILIES -- ECONOMIC ASPECTS -- UNITED
STATES**
Carbone, J. Marriage markets 306.85

**FAMILIES -- ECONOMIC ASPECTS -- UNITED
STATES -- HISTORY**
Hochschild, A. R. The outsourced self 306.85

FAMILIES -- HEALTH AND HYGIENE
The America's Test Kitchen healthy family cook-
book 641.5
Willingham, E. The informed parent 649.1

FAMILIES -- HISTORY
Ross, T. A cancer in the family 616.99

FAMILIES -- ITALY -- NAPLES
Wilson, K. Only in Naples 945.731

FAMILIES -- LEBANON
Shadid, A. House of stone 306

FAMILIES -- NUTRITION
The family cooks 641.3

FAMILIES -- UNITED STATES
Levs, J. All in 306.3
Nutt, A. E. Becoming Nicole 306.76

**FAMILIES -- WEST (U.S.) -- HISTORY -- 19TH
CENTURY**
Hyde, A. F. Empires, nations, and families 978
Families like mine. Garner, A. 306.8

**FAMILIES OF MILITARY PERSONNEL --
UNITED STATES**
Bannerman, S. Homefront 911 362.86
Poole, R. M. Section 60 975.5
Sheeler, J. Final salute 956.7

**FAMILIES OF MILITARY PERSONNEL --
UNITED STATES -- HANDBOOKS, MANU-
ALS, ETC**
Scott, J. Raising children in the military 355.1

FAMILIES OF TERMINALLY ILL
Coutts, M. The Iceberg 92

Schwalbe, W. The end of your life book club 616.99
Sederer, L. I. The family guide to mental health
care 616.89

**FAMILIES OF THE MENTALLY ILL -- COUN-
SELING OF**
Sederer, L. I. The family guide to mental health
care 616.89
The **Family.** Laskin, D. 92

FAMILY
Abu-Jaber, D. Life Without a Recipe 92
Besh, J. My family table 641.59
De Laurentiis, G. Happy cooking 641.5
Flinn, K. Burnt toast makes you sing good 641.597
Hernández, D. A cup of water under my bed 920.009
Lewis, O. The children of Sanchez 972.08
Nathans, S. To free a family 306.3
Nutt, A. E. Becoming Nicole 306.76
Omar, Q. A. A fort of nine towers 958.104
Robicelli, A. Robicelli's 641.86
Tannen, D. I only say this because I love you 306.87
Toffler, A. Future shock 303.4
Van't Hul, J. The artful year 745.594

FAMILY
See also Interpersonal relations; Sociology
Family & friends' guide to domestic violence.
Weiss, E. 362.82

FAMILY -- ECONOMIC ASPECTS
Carbone, J. Marriage markets 306.85
Hochschild, A. R. The outsourced self 306.85

FAMILY -- HUMOR
Barry, D. You can date boys when you're forty 306.85

FAMILY -- RELIGIOUS LIFE
See also Religious life

FAMILY -- UNITED STATES
Clinton, H. R. It takes a village 305.23
Family affair. 305.8

FAMILY AND WORK *See* Work and family
Family Britain, 1951-1957. Kynaston, D. 941.085
FAMILY BUDGET *See* Household budgets
The **family** calendar cookbook. Banfield, K. 641.5
FAMILY CAREGIVERS *See* Caregivers
The **family** cooks. 641.3
FAMILY DEVOTIONS *See* Devotional exercises;
Family -- Religious life
FAMILY FARMS
Berry, W. Bringing it to the table 630
FAMILY FARMS
See also Farms
FAMILY FINANCE *See* Personal finance
The **family** guide to mental health care. Sederer, L.
I. 616.89

Family Handyman
Refresh your home 643
FAMILY HISTORIES *See* Genealogy
FAMILY LIFE

See also Family

FAMILY LIFE -- ANECDOTES
Roberts, D. Been there, done that   92

FAMILY LIFE -- GRAPHIC NOVELS
Small, D. Stitches   **741.5**

FAMILY PLANNING ADVOCATES
Baker, J. H. Margaret Sanger   92
Rudahl, S. A dangerous woman   335

FAMILY PRAYERS *See* Devotional exercises;
Family -- Religious life
Family properties. Satter, B.   **363.5**

FAMILY RECREATION
Handy dad   **745.592**
Louv, R. Vitamin N   **155.9**
Van't Hul, J. The artful year   **745.594**

FAMILY RELATIONS *See* Domestic relations;
Family life

FAMILY REUNIONS
Williams, H. A. Help me to find my people   **306.3**

**FAMILY REUNIONS -- MASSACHUSETTS
-- CAMBRIDGE -- HISTORY -- 19TH CEN-
TURY**
Nathans, S. To free a family   **306.3**

FAMILY SECRETS
Brannan, K. The Family Tree   **364.134**

**FAMILY SECRETS -- COMIC BOOKS, STRIPS,
ETC**
Georges, N. J. Calling Dr. Laura   **92**

FAMILY SIZE
Sandler, L. One and only   **306.874**
The **Family** Tree. Brannan, K.   **364.134**
Family trees. Well, F.   **929.2**

FAMILY TREES *See* Genealogy

FAMILY VIOLENCE *See* Domestic violence

FAMILY-OWNED BUSINESS ENTERPRISES
Denton, S. The Profiteers   **338.7**
Handwerker, L. Famous Nathan   **92**

FAMINES
Kim, J. Under the same sky   **92**

FAMINES
See also Food supply; Starvation

FAMINES -- CHINA
Dikötter, F. Mao's great famine   **951.05**

**FAMINES -- IRELAND -- HISTORY -- 19TH
CENTURY**
Kelly, J. The graves are walking   **941.5**
Famous first facts, international edition.   **031.02**
Famous Nathan. Handwerker, L.   **92**

FAMOUS PEOPLE *See* Celebrities

FAN FICTION
See also Fiction

FAN MAGAZINES *See* Fanzines

FANATICISM
See also Emotions

FANCY WORK
Butler, A. Amy Butler's style stitches   **646.4**

The **Fannie** Farmer baking book. Cunningham,
M.   **641.7**
The **Fannie** Farmer cookbook. Cunningham,
M.   **641.5**

FANNIE MAE
Acharya, V. V. Guaranteed to fail   **332.7**
Morgenson, G. Reckless endangerment   **332.7**

Fannin, Caroline M.
Gubert, B. K. Distinguished African Americans in
aviation and space science   **629.13**

Fanon, Frantz, 1925-1961
About
Macey, D. Frantz Fanon   **92**

FANS (DRESS ACCESSORIES)
See also Clothing and dress; Costume; Fashion accessories

FANTASTIC FICTION *See* Fantasy fiction

**FANTASTIC FOUR (FICTIONAL CHARAC-
TERS)**
Lee, S. Stan Lee's How to draw comics   **741.5**
The **fantastic** laboratory of Dr. Weigl. Allen,
A.   **614.5**

FANTASTIC, THE, IN LITERATURE
Saler, M. As if   **823**

FANTASY
Jones, G. Killing monsters   **302.23**

FANTASY
See also Dreams; Imagination

FANTASY FICTION
See also Fiction

FANTASY FICTION -- BIBLIOGRAPHY
Buker, D. M. The science-fiction and fantasy read-
ers' advisory   **025.5**
Herald, D. T. Fluent in fantasy   **016**
Hollands, N. Fellowship in a ring   **809**
Hollands, N. Read on . . . fantasy fiction   **016**
Kallio, J. Read on ... speculative fiction for
teens   **016**

FANTASY FICTION -- DICTIONARIES
Manguel, A. The dictionary of imaginary places   **809**

**FANTASY FICTION -- HISTORY AND CRITI-
CISM**
Walton, J. What Makes This Book So Great   **813**

**FANTASY FICTION, AMERICAN -- BIBLIOG-
RAPHY**
Kallio, J. Read on ... speculative fiction for
teens   **016**

FANZINES
The riot grrrl collection   **781.64**

FANZINES
See also Periodicals
Far from the tree. Solomon, A.   **362.4**

FAR NORTH *See* Arctic regions
Far out. Benson, M.   **778.3**

Fara, Patricia

Newton: the making of genius 92
Science **509**
Farabee, Charles R.
National park ranger **363.6**
Faraday, Michael, 1791-1867
About
Hirshfeld, A. The electric life of Michael Faraday 92
Malone, J. W. It doesn't take a rocket scientist 920
Faragher, John Mack
Daniel Boone 92
Farah, Empress, consort of Mohammad Reza Pahlavi, Shah of Iran, 1938-
About
Cooper, A. S. The fall of heaven **955.05**
The **Faraway** Nearby. Solnit, R. **814**
Farber, David R.
(ed) The Columbia guide to America in the 1960s **973.923**
Farfour, Gadi
(ed) The cat encyclopedia **636.8**
Fargnoli, A. Nicholas
Critical companion to James Joyce **823**
Critical companion to William Faulkner **813**
Fargues, Philippe
The atlas of the Arab world **909**
Farinella, Matteo
(jt. auth) Ros, H. Neurocomic **612.82**
Farley, Tom
Saving Gotham **362.1**
Farley: the life of Farley Mowat. King, J. **92**
FARM FAMILY -- ALABAMA -- HISTORY -- 20TH CENTURY
Agee, J. Cotton Tenants **976.1**
FARM IMPLEMENTS See Agricultural machinery
FARM LABORERS See Agricultural laborers
FARM LIFE
Animal, vegetable, miracle **641**
Katz, J. Dog days **636**
FARM LIFE
See also Country life; Farmers
FARM LIFE -- ENGLAND -- LAKE DISTRICT
Rebanks, J. The shepherd's life **92**
FARM LIFE -- NEW YORK (STATE)
Katz, J. Dog days **636**
Kimball, K. The dirty life **92**
FARM LIFE -- NEW YORK (STATE) -- UPSTATE NEW YORK
Ridge, B. The Beekman 1802 heirloom dessert cookbook **641.5**
FARM MACHINERY See Agricultural machinery
FARM MANAGEMENT
Levatino, A. Woman-powered farm **630**
FARM MANAGEMENT
See also Farms; Management

FARM MECHANICS See Agricultural engineering; Agricultural machinery
FARM PRODUCE
Acheson, H. The broad fork **641.597**
America--farm to table **641.597**
Genetically modified foods **363.1**
Montgomery, D. R. The hidden half of nature **579**
Pringle, P. Food, inc **363.1**
Saltsman, A. The Santa Monica Farmers' Market Cookbook **641.5**
Tomlinson, S. Agricola cookbook **641.564**
FARM PRODUCE
See also Food; Raw materials
FARM PRODUCE -- MARKETING
See also Marketing; Prices
FARM PRODUCE -- NEW YORK (STATE) -- UPSTATE NEW YORK
Ridge, B. The Beekman 1802 heirloom dessert cookbook **641.5**
Farm Sanctuary. Baur, G. **179**
FARM TENANCY
Agee, J. Let us now praise famous men **976.1**
FARM TENANCY
See also Farms; Land tenure
FARM TENANCY -- ALABAMA -- HISTORY -- 20TH CENTURY
Agee, J. Cotton Tenants **976.1**
Farm, fork, food. Skokan, E.
Farmer, David Hugh
The Oxford dictionary of saints **920.003**
Farmer, John J.
The ground truth **973.931**
FARMERS
Bryan, P. L. Midnight assassin **364.152**
Hamilton, L. M. Deeply rooted **338.1**
Kimball, K. The dirty life **92**
Lamb, C. House of stone **968.91**
Lawrence, S. River house **92**
Link, M. Bootstrapper **92**
FARMERS
See also Agriculture
FARMERS -- ENGLAND -- LAKE DISTRICT -- BIOGRAPHY
Rebanks, J. The shepherd's life **92**
FARMERS -- GEORGIA -- ECONOMIC CONDITIONS
Sherrod, S. The courage to hope **975.8**
The **Farmette** cookbook. McDonnell, I. **641.5**
FARMHOUSES -- FRANCE -- MÉDOC
Thorisson, M. A kitchen in France **641.594**
FARMING See Agriculture
FARMING, ORGANIC See Organic farming
FARMS
America--farm to table **641.597**
Goulson, D. A Buzz in the Meadow **638**
Markham, B. L. Mini farming **635**

FARMS, SMALL -- UNITED STATES
America--farm to table   641.597
Farquhar, Michael
Behind the palace doors   941
Farrakhan, Louis, 1933-
      About
Gardell, M. In the name of Elijah Muhammad 297
Gates, H. L. Thirteen ways of looking at a black man   920.71
Levinsohn, F. H. Looking for Farrakhan   297.8
Farrand, John
Bull, J. L. The National Audubon Society field guide to North American birds, Eastern region 598
Udvardy, M. D. F. National Audubon Society field guide to North American birds, Western region   598
Farrar, Christi Showman
(ed) Sears List of Subject Headings   025.4
Farrell, Greg
Crash of the titans   332.1
Farrell, John A.
Clarence Darrow   92
Farrell, Patrick
Paper to petal   745.54
Farrell, Susan Elizabeth
Critical companion to Kurt Vonnegut   813
Farrington, Lisa E.
Creating their own image   709
Farris, Scott
Almost president   920
Farrow & Ball How to Decorate. Studholme, J.   747.94
Farrow, Joanna
Gingerbread Houses, Animals and Decorations   641.865
Farther away. Franzen, J.   814
Farther traveler. Wilson, R. V.   818
Farthest field. Karnad, R.   940.54
Faruqi, Sonia
Project Animal Farm   338.1
Farwell, Byron
Over there   940.4
FASCISM
Bosworth, R. J. B. Mussolini   945.091
Paxton, R. O. The anatomy of fascism   321.9
FASCISM
     See also Totalitarianism
FASCISM -- FRANCE
Kaplan, A. The collaborator: the trial & execution of Robert Brasillach   848
FASCISM -- ITALY -- HISTORY
Bosworth, R. J. B. Mussolini   945.091
Corner, P. The Fascist Party and popular opinion in Mussolini's Italy   945.091
FASCISM -- ITALY -- HISTORY -- 20TH CENTURY

Hughes-Hallett, L. Gabriele d'Annunzio   858
FASCISM AND THE CATHOLIC CHURCH -- ITALY
Kertzer, D. I. The Pope and Mussolini   322
The **Fascist** Party and popular opinion in Mussolini's Italy. Corner, P.   945.091
Fashion. Stevenson, N. J.   391.009
FASHION
Bowles, H. Vogue and the Metropolitan Museum of Art Costume Institute   391
Eldridge, L. Face paint   391.6
Halbreich, B. I'll drink to that   92
Hirsch, G. A modern guide to sportswear styles of the 1940s and 1950s   646.4
Linett, A. The cool factor   746.92
The Mood guide to fabric and fashion   746.9
Moses, S. The art of dressing curves   746.92
Stanley, S. H. DIY wardrobe makeovers   646
Stuart, A. M. Empress of Fashion   92
FASHION
     See also Clothing and dress
FASHION -- FRANCE -- HISTORY -- 20TH CENTURY
Grumbach, D. History of international fashion   746.9
FASHION -- HISTORY
Dirix, E. Dressing the Decades   391.009
Grumbach, D. History of international fashion   746.9
FASHION -- HISTORY -- 19TH CENTURY
Stevenson, N. J. Fashion   391.009
FASHION -- UNITED STATES
Cleveland, P. Walking with the muses   92
FASHION ACCESSORIES
Doh, J. Signature styles   646.4
FASHION ACCESSORIES
     See also Clothing and dress
FASHION DESIGN
Crowe, L. G. The towering world of Jimmy Choo   391
Faerm, S. Fashion: design course   746.9
Garelick, R. K. Mademoiselle   92
Grumbach, D. History of international fashion   746.9
FASHION DESIGN
     See also Clothing industry; Commercial art; Design
FASHION DESIGN -- HISTORY
Grumbach, D. History of international fashion   746.9
Stevenson, N. J. Fashion   391.009
FASHION DESIGNERS
Ali, K. Fighting weight   92
Dirix, E. Dressing the Decades   391.009
Fraser, K. Ornament and silence   809
Garelick, R. K. Mademoiselle   92

Grumbach, D. History of international fashion **746.9**
Hazan, M. Amarcord, Marcella remembers **92**
Hilfiger, T. American dreamer **92**
Lowit, R. Yves Saint Laurent **746.9**
Mazzeo, T. J. The secret of Chanel No. 5 **338.7**
Secrest, M. Elsa Schiaparelli **92**
Thomas, D. Gods and Kings **92**
Tynan, T. Wear and tear **92**
Vaughan, H. Sleeping with the enemy **92**
Von Furstenberg, D. The woman I wanted to be **92**

**FASHION DESIGNERS -- FRANCE -- PARIS --
BIOGRAPHY**
Volk, P. Shocked **92**

**FASHION DESIGNERS -- UNITED STATES --
BIOGRAPHY**
Hilfiger, T. American dreamer **92**
Tynan, T. Wear and tear **92**
Von Furstenberg, D. The woman I wanted to be **92**

FASHION INDUSTRY See Clothing industry

**FASHION MERCHANDISING -- SOCIAL AS-
PECTS**
Givhan, R. The Battle of Versailles **746.9**
Gross, M. Focus **770.92**

**FASHION MERCHANDISING -- UNITED
STATES**
Ziegler, M. Wild company **381**

FASHION MODELS
See also Advertising

FASHION PHOTOGRAPHERS -- BIOGRAPHY
Gross, M. Focus **770.92**

FASHION SHOWS
Givhan, R. The Battle of Versailles **746.9**

FASHION SHOWS
See also Exhibitions
Fashion: design course. Faerm, S. **746.9**

FASHIONABLE SOCIETY See Upper class
Fassett, Kaffe
Kaffe Fassett's Bold Blooms **746**
Fast food nation. Schlosser, E. **394.1**

FAST FOOD RESTAURANTS
See also Convenience foods; Restaurants

**FAST FOOD RESTAURANTS -- NEW YORK
(STATE) -- HISTORY**
Handwerker, L. Famous Nathan **92**
Fast Food, Good Food. Weil, A. **641.563**

FAST FOODS See Convenience foods
Fast forward. Verveer, M. **650.1**
Faster, higher, stronger. McClusky, M. **613.7**
Fastest Things on Wings. Masear, T. **598**

FASTING
See also Asceticism; Diet

FASTS AND FEASTS See Religious holidays

FASTS AND FEASTS -- JUDAISM
Axelrod, M. Your guide to the Jewish holidays **296.4**

Goldman, A. L. Being Jewish **296.4**

FASTS AND FEASTS -- JUDAISM See Jewish
holidays
Fasulo, Linda M.
An insider's guide to the UN **341.23**
Fat kid got fit. Baroni, B. **362.196**
The fat man and infinity. Antunes, A. L. **869**
Fat witch bake sale. Baker, L. **641.81**

FAT WITCH BAKERY
Baker, L. Fat witch bake sale **641.81**
Fatal invention. Roberts, D. **305.8**
Fatal risk. Boyd, R. **368**
The fatal shore. Hughes, R. **994**
Fatal vision. McGinniss, J. **364.1**

FATALLY ILL CHILDREN See Terminally ill
children

FATALLY ILL PATIENTS See Terminally ill

FATE AND FATALISM
May, R. Freedom and destiny **158**

FATE AND FATALISM
See also Philosophy

**FATE AND FATALISM -- RELIGIOUS AS-
PECTS -- CHRISTIANITY**
Jakes, T. D. Destiny **248.4**
The fate of nature. Wohlforth, C. **304.2**

FATHER AND CHILD See Father-child relationship
The father of us all. Hanson, V. D. **355**

FATHER'S DAY
See also Holidays

FATHER-CHILD RELATIONSHIP
Austin, P. Beautiful eyes **92**
Edgerton, C. Papadaddy's book for new fathers **649**
Handy dad **745.592**
Levs, J. All in **306.3**

FATHER-CHILD RELATIONSHIP
See also Children; Fathers; Parent-child relationship

**FATHER AND CHILD -- CALIFORNIA -- LOS
ANGELES**
Leap, J. Project Fatherhood **306.874**

FATHER-DAUGHTER RELATIONSHIP
Anderson, S. The Hostage's Daughter **92**
Faludi, S. In the Darkroom **818.603**
Foreman, T. My year of running dangerously **92**
Shaw, B. Major Barbara **822**
Tyler, C. Soldier's heart **741.5**
Wickersham, J. The suicide index **155.9**

FATHER-DAUGHTER RELATIONSHIP
See also Daughters; Father-child relationship;
Fathers

FATHER-SON RELATIONSHIP
Abad, H. Oblivion **868**
Bragg, R. The prince of Frogtown **92**
Burns, E. The Golden Lad **92**
Cockburn, H. Henry's demons **92**

Denmead, K. Geek dad **790**

Dorris, M. The broken cord **362.292**

Edmundson, M. Why football matters **92**

The fall **92**

Giraldi, W. The Hero's Body **92**

Kozol, J. The theft of memory **92**

Molina, B. Molina **92**

Ollestad, N. Crazy for the storm **92**

Phillips, P. Elegy for a broken machine **811**

Thomson, D. Try to tell the story **92**

FATHER-SON RELATIONSHIP

   See also Father-child relationship; Fathers; Sons

FATHERHOOD

Edgerton, C. Papadaddy's book for new fathers **649**

When I first held you **306.874**

FATHERHOOD

   See also Parenthood

FATHERHOOD -- CALIFORNIA -- LOS ANGELES

Leap, J. Project Fatherhood **306.874**

FATHERHOOD -- POETRY

Fay-LeBlanc, G. Death of a ventriloquist **811**

FATHERS

Brott, A. A. The expectant father **649**

Chabon, M. Manhood for amateurs **92**

Leap, J. Project Fatherhood **306.874**

FATHERS

   See also Family; Men

FATHERS -- POETRY

Berry, W. New collected poems **811**

FATHERS -- PUERTO RICO

Molina, B. Molina **92**

FATHERS AND DAUGHTERS *See* Father-daughter relationship

Fathers and sons. Waugh, A. **920**

FATHERS AND SONS *See* Father-son relationship

FATHERS AND SONS

Iyer, P. The man within my head **809**

Taseer, A. Stranger to history **915.6**

FATHERS AND SONS -- BIOGRAPHY

The fall **92**

Kozol, J. The theft of memory **92**

FATHERS OF THE CHURCH

   See also Christian biography

FATIGUE

   See also Physiology

FATNESS *See* Obesity

FATWAS -- PERSONAL NARRATIVES

Rushdie, S. Joseph Anton **92**

Fauchald, Nick

   (jt. auth) Carroll, J. Feeding the fire **641.7**

Death & Co **641.87**

Faulkner, Steven

Bitterroot **978**

Faulkner, William, 1897-1962

About

Fargnoli, A. N. Critical companion to William Faulkner **813**

Kazin, A. An American procession **810**

Parini, J. One matchless time **92**

William Faulkner **813**

The **fault** line. **914**

Fault lines. Rajan, R. G. **330.9**

FAULTS (GEOLOGY)

Dvorak, J. Earthquake Storms **551.22**

FAULTS (GEOLOGY)

   See also Geology

FAUNA *See* Animals; Zoology

FAUNA FOUNDATION

Westoll, A. The chimps of Fauna Sanctuary **636.9**

FAUNE MARINE

Hoyt, E. Creatures of the deep **591.7**

Fauset, Jessie Redmon, 1882-1961

About

Wall, C. A. Women of the Harlem Renaissance **810**

Faust, Drew Gilpin

Faust, D. G. This republic of suffering **973.7**

Mothers of invention **973.7**

This republic of suffering **973.7**

The **Faustian** bargain. Petropoulos, J. **709**

Favorite folktales from around the world. **398.2**

Favorite Poem Project

Americans' favorite poems **808.81**

Favreau, Marc

   (ed) Remembering slavery **326**

Fawcett, P. H. (Percy Harrison), 1867-1925

About

Grann, D. The lost city of Z **918**

Fawkes, Guy, 1570-1606

About

Fraser, A. Faith and treason **942.06**

FAX TRANSMISSION

   See also Data transmission systems; Telecommunication

Fay-LeBlanc, Gibson

Death of a ventriloquist **811**

FBI AGENTS

Wise, D. Spy: the inside story of how the FBI's Robert Hanssen betrayed America **327.12**

FBI OFFICIALS

Geary, R. J. Edgar Hoover **363.2**

Gentry, C. J. Edgar Hoover **353**

FDR. Smith, J. E. **92**

FDR and Chief Justice Hughes. Simon, J. F. **973.917**

FÉDÉRATION INTERNATIONALE DE FOOTBALL ASSOCIATION

Thompson, T. American huckster **796.334**

FEAR

   See also Emotions

FEAR

Berger, J. The better to eat you with **591.5**

Clark, T. Nerve **152.4**
Gardner, D. The science of fear **152.4**
Jeffers, S. J. Feel the fear--and do it anyway **152.4**
Molotch, H. Against security **363.325**
FEAR -- RELIGIOUS ASPECTS
Lucado, M. Fearless **248**
Nussbaum, M. C. The new religious intolerance **201**
Fear and loathing at Rolling Stone. Thompson, H. S.
Fear and loathing in America. Thompson, H. S. **070**
FEAR IN CHILDREN
See also Child psychology; Fear
Fear itself. Katznelson, I. **973.917**
FEAR OF OPEN SPACES See Agoraphobia
Fear of physics. Krauss, L. M. **530**
FEAR OF THE DARK
See also Fear; Fear in children
Fearing, Kenneth
Selected poems **811**
Fearless. Lucado, M. **248**
Fearless genius. Menuez, D. **979.4**
Fearnley-Whittingstall, Hugh
River Cottage every day **641.5**
River Cottage Veg **641.5**
FEAST DAYS See Religious holidays
FEAST OF DEDICATION See Hanukkah
FEAST OF LIGHTS See Hanukkah
Feather, Leonard
The biographical encyclopedia of jazz **781.65**
From Satchmo to Miles **920**
Feathers. Hanson, T. **598**
FEATHERS
Hanson, T. Feathers **598**
Featherstone, Liza
Selling women short **331.4**
Feature writing for newspapers and magazines.
Friedlander, E. J. **070.4**
Feaver, Peter
(jt. auth) Crossman, A. Getting the best out of college **378.1**
FECES
George, R. The big necessity **363.7**
FEDERAL AID
See also Public finance
FEDERAL AID TO EDUCATION
See also Education -- Government policy;
Federal aid
FEDERAL BUDGET See Budget -- United States
FEDERAL GOVERNMENT
Boorstin, D. J. The Americans: The national experience **973**
Fredrickson, G. M. Big enough to be inconsistent **973.7**
FEDERAL GOVERNMENT
See also Constitutional law; Political science;
Republics

FEDERAL GOVERNMENT -- UNITED STATES -- HISTORY -- 18TH CENTURY
Ellis, J. J. The Quartet **973.3**
FEDERAL HOME LOAN MORTGAGE CORPORATION
Acharya, V. V. Guaranteed to fail **332.7**
FEDERAL NATIONAL MORTGAGE ASSOCIATION
Howard, T. The mortgage wars **332.7**
FEDERAL PARTY (U.S.)
Miller, J. C. The Federalist era, 1789-1801 **973.4**
FEDERAL REPUBLIC OF GERMANY See Germany; Germany (West)
FEDERAL RESERVE BANKS
Lowenstein, R. America's Bank **332.1**
Meltzer, A. H. A history of the Federal Reserve **332.1**
FEDERAL RESERVE BANKS
See also Banks and banking
FEDERAL RESERVE SYSTEM (U.S.)
Wessel, D. In Fed we trust **332.1**
FEDERAL RESERVE SYSTEM (U.S.) -- BOARD OF GOVERNORS
Meltzer, A. H. A history of the Federal Reserve **332.1**
Overtveldt, J. v. Bernanke's test **332.1**
Wessel, D. In Fed we trust **332.1**
Woodward, B. Maestro: Greenspan's Fed and the American boom **331.1**
FEDERAL SPENDING POLICY See United States -- Appropriations and expenditures
FEDERAL-CITY RELATIONS
See also Federal government; Municipal government
FEDERAL-STATE RELATIONS
See also Federal government; State governments
FEDERALISM See Federal government
The **Federalist.** **342**
The **Federalist** era, 1789-1801. Miller, J. C. **973.4**
Federico Garcia Lorca: a life. Gibson, I. **92**
The **feed** zone cookbook. Lim, A. **641.5**
Feed zone portables. Lim, A. **641.5**
FEEDBACK (PSYCHOLOGY)
Bright, D. The truth doesn't have to hurt **158.2**
FEEDBACK (PSYCHOLOGY)
See also Psychology of learning
Feeding the fire. Carroll, J. **641.7**
Feel the fear--and do it anyway. Jeffers, S. J. **152.4**
The **Feel** Trio. Moten, F. **811**
FEELING See Perception; Touch
Feeling good. Burns, D. D. **158**
The **feeling** of what happens. Damasio, A. R. **153**
FEELINGS See Emotions
FEES See Salaries, wages, etc.
Feifer, Gregory

The great gamble   **958.1**

Feiffer, Jules
> *About*
> Feiffer, J. Backing into forward   **92**

Feige, David
> *About*
> Feige, D. Indefensible   **345**

Feiler, Bruce S.
> Walking the Bible   **915**

Feiling, Tom
> Cocaine nation   **362.29**

Feinberg, Andrew
> (jt. auth) Clark, M. Franny's   **641.594**

Feinberg, Kenneth R.
> What is life worth?   **362.88**

Feingold, Russ, 1953-
> While America sleeps   **327**

Feinman, Jay M.
> Law 101   **340**

Feinstein, Adam
> Pablo Neruda   **92**

Feinstein, Elaine
> Anna of all the Russias   **92**
> Ted Hughes   **821**
> (tr) Tsvetaeva, M. I. Selected poems   **891.7**

Feinstein, John
> A good walk spoiled   **796.352**
> Last dance   **796.323**
> The legends club   **796.323**
> A march to madness   **796.323**
> Next man up   **796.332**
> Where nobody knows your name   **796.357**

Feinstein, Michael
> *About*
> Feinstein, M. The Gershwins and me   **92**

Felch, Jason
> (jt. auth) Frammolino, R. Chasing Aphrodite   **930**

Feldman, Burton
> 112 Mercer Street   **920**
> The Nobel Prize   **001.4**

Feldman, Deborah, 1986-
> *About*
> Feldman, D. Exodus   **92**
> Feldman, D. Unorthodox   **92**

Feldman, Jay
> When the Mississippi ran backwards   **551.2**

Feldman, Noah
> Scorpions   **920**

Feldman, Paula R.
> (ed) British women poets of the Romantic era   **821**

Feldstein, Mark
> Poisoning the press   **973.924**

FELIDAE
> Sunquist, F. The wild cat book   **599.75**

FELIDAE *See* Wild cats

FELINES *See* Cats

Felisbret, Eric
> Graffiti New York   **751.7**

Fellman, Michael
> Citizen Sherman   **92**
> The making of Robert E. Lee   **92**

Fellow citizens.   **352.23**

Fellowship in a ring. Hollands, N.   **809**

FELONY *See* Crime

FELT CRAFT
> Sheldon, K. Felt-o-ween   **745.594**

FELT WORK
> Adams, L. Needle felting   **746**

Felt, Hali
> Soundings   **526**

Felt-o-ween. Sheldon, K.   **745.594**

Felton, Mark
> Zero Night   **940.54**

FEMALE ACTORS *See* Actresses

FEMALE CLIMACTERIC *See* Menopause

FEMALE FRIENDSHIP
> Donoghue, E. Inseparable   **809**
> Goodman, E. I know just what you mean   **158.2**
> Lerner, B. The bridge ladies   **92**
> Link, M. J. The Drummond Girls   **92**
> Quinn, S. Eleanor and Hick   **92**

FEMALE FRIENDSHIP
> *See also* Friendship

FEMALE FRIENDSHIP -- UNITED STATES
> Bell-Scott, P. The firebrand and the First Lady   **92**
> Count on me   **177**
> Lerner, B. The bridge ladies   **92**

The female gaze.   **704**

FEMALE IDENTITY *See* Women -- Identity

FEMALE OFFENDERS -- MASSACHUSETTS -- BOSTON -- SOCIAL CONDITIONS
> Sered, S. S. Can't catch a break   **362.83**

FEMALE ROLE *See* Gender role

FEMALE SUPERHERO GRAPHIC NOVELS
> *See also* Graphic novels

FEMALE-MALE RELATIONSHIP *See* Man-woman relationship

FEMALE-TO-MALE TRANSSEXUALS -- UNITED STATES -- BIOGRAPHY
> McBee, T. P. Man alive   **92**

FEMININE BEAUTY (AESTHETICS) -- SOCIAL ASPECTS
> Whitefield-Madrano, A. Face value   **111.85**

FEMININE IDENTITY *See* Women -- Identity

The feminine mystique. Friedan, B.   **305.4**

FEMININE PSYCHOLOGY *See* Women -- Psychology

FEMININITY
> Orenstein, P. Cinderella ate my daughter   **305.23**
> Wolf, N. The beauty myth   **305.4**
> Wolf, N. Vagina   **305.42**

FEMININITY

See also Sex -- Psychological aspects

FEMININITY (PSYCHOLOGY) *See* Femininity

FEMININITY OF GOD

   See also God

FEMINISM

  Adichie, C. N. We Should All Be Feminists **305.42**

  Armstrong, J. K. Sexy feminism **305.42**

  The essential feminist reader **305.4**

  Failure is impossible **92**

  Friedan, B. The feminine mystique **305.4**

  Friedan, B. Life so far **92**

  Gay, R. Bad Feminist **814**

  Ginzberg, L. D. Elizabeth Cady Stanton **92**

  Goldsmith, B. Other powers **92**

  Heilbrun, C. G. The education of a woman **92**

  Lewis, R. C. Voyage of the Sable Venus and other poems **811**

  Matteson, J. The lives of Margaret Fuller **920**

  Moran, C. How to be a woman **92**

  Murphy, C. The Word according to Eve **220.8**

  Painter, N. I. Sojourner Truth **305.5**

  Rich, A. Arts of the possible **811**

  Scanlon, J. Bad girls go everywhere: the life of Helen Gurley Brown **92**

  Scroggins, D. Wanted women **305.48**

  Sigerman, H. The Columbia documentary history of American women since 1941 **305.4**

  Spar, D. L. Wonder Women **305.42**

  Steinem, G. Moving beyond words **305.42**

  Steinem, G. Outrageous acts and everyday rebellions **305.42**

  Traister, R. Big girls don't cry **324**

  Ulrich, L. Well-behaved women seldom make history **305.4**

  Valenti, J. Full Frontal Feminism **305.42**

  Valenti, J. Sex object **92**

FEMINISM -- HISTORY

  Encyclopedia of women and American politics **973**

FEMINISM -- POETRY

  Clifton, L. The collected poems of Lucille Clifton 1965-2010 **811**

FEMINISM -- UNITED STATES

  Steinem, G. My life on the road **92**

FEMINISM -- UNITED STATES -- HISTORY -- 20TH CENTURY

  Brownmiller, S. In our time **305.42**

  Collins, G. When everything changed **305.4**

  Coontz, S. A strange stirring **305.42**

FEMINISM IN LITERATURE

  Lepore, J. The Secret History of Wonder Woman **741.5**

FEMINIST CRITICISM

  Gay, R. Bad Feminist **814**

FEMINISTS

  Bair, D. Simone de Beauvoir **848**

  Baker, J. H. Margaret Sanger **92**

Berkin, C. Civil War wives **920**

Fraser, K. Ornament and silence **809**

Friedan, B. Life so far **92**

Furmansky, D. Z. Rosalie Edge, hawk of mercy **92**

Goldsmith, B. Other powers **92**

Gordon, L. Vindication **92**

Heilbrun, C. G. The education of a woman **92**

Hirsi Ali, A. Infidel **92**

Hooks, B. Belonging **92**

Hooks, B. Wounds of passion **92**

McKillop, A. B. The spinster & the prophet **941.08**

Pierpont, C. R. Passionate minds **810**

Shulman, A. K. To love what is **92**

Steinem, G. Moving beyond words **305.42**

Steinem, G. Outrageous acts and everyday rebellions **305.42**

Von Mehren, J. Minerva and the muse: a life of Margaret Fuller **92**

Woo, I. The great divorce **92**

FEMINISTS -- UNITED STATES -- BIOGRAPHY

  Friedan, B. Life so far **92**

  Matteson, J. The lives of Margaret Fuller **920**

  Steinem, G. My life on the road **92**

The **fence.** Lehr, D. **364.1**

Fences. Wilson, A. **812**

FENCING

  Cohen, R. By the sword **796.8**

FENG SHUI

  See also Divination

Feniger, Susan

  (jt. auth) Alger, K. Susan Feniger's street food **641.59**

Fenn, Elizabeth A. (Elizabeth Anne), 1959-

  Encounters at the heart of the world **305.897**

Fenn, Lisa

  Carry on **920**

Fenton, James

  Selected poems **811**

Fenton, William Nelson

  The Great Law and the Longhouse **970.004**

Fenway 1912. Stout, G. **796.357**

FENWAY PARK (BOSTON, MASS.)

  Stout, G. Fenway 1912 **796.357**

Fenwick, George H.

  Lebbin, D. J. The American Bird Conservancy guide to bird conservation **333.95**

FERAL ANIMALS *See* Wildlife

FERAL CATS *See* Wild cats

Ferguson Publishing

  The top 100 **331.7**

Ferguson, Charles

  Predator nation **330.973**

Ferguson, Charles D.

  Nuclear energy **333.79**

Ferguson, Gary

Smith, D. W. Decade of the wolf   599.77

Ferguson, Niall
The ascent of money   330
Empire: the rise and demise of the British world or-
  der and the lessons for global power   909
Kissinger   92

Ferguson, Robert
The Vikings   948
(tr) Norwegian wood   634.9

Fergusson, James
The world's most dangerous place   967.73

Fergusson, Rosalind
(ed) Manser, M. H. The Facts on File dictionary of
  proverbs   398.9

Ferling, John
Whirlwind   973.3

Ferlinghetti, Lawrence
City lights pocket poets anthology   808.81
These are my rivers   811
        About
Writing Across the Landscape   92

Fermat's enigma. Singh, S.   512

Fermat, Pierre de, 1601-1665
        About
Bell, E. T. Men of mathematics   920
Devlin, K. J. The unfinished game   519.2

FERMENTATION
Katz, S. E. The art of fermentation   664

FERMENTATION
    See also Chemical engineering; Chemistry;
    Microbiology

FERMENTED FOODS
Katz, S. E. The art of fermentation   664

FERMENTED FOODS
    See also Food

FERMENTS *See* Fermentation

Fernald, Anya
Home cooked   641.5

Fernández Revuelta, Alina
        About
Gimbel, W. Havana dreams   972.91

Fernandez-Armesto, Felipe
Amerigo   92
Near a thousand tables   394.1

Ferngren, Gary B.
(ed) The History of science and religion in the
  western tradition   201

FERNS
    See also Plants

FERRARI SPA
Baime, A. J. Go like hell   796.72

Ferrari, G. R. F.
(ed) Plato The republic   888

Ferrari, Michelle
(comp) Reporting America at war   070.4

Ferrazzi, Keith

Never eat alone and other secrets to success   658.4

Ferreira, Pedro G.
The perfect theory   530.11

Ferreiro, Larrie D.
Measure of the Earth   526

Ferrell, Lori Anne
The Bible and the people   220.5

Ferris, Gary W.
Presidential places   917

Ferris, Timothy
The science of liberty   303.4
Seeing in the dark   520

Ferris, William
Give my poor heart ease   781.643

Ferriter, Diarmaid
The transformation of Ireland   941.5

Ferro, Jeffrey
Prisons   365

Ferro, Marc
Nicholas II   92

Ferry, David
Bewilderment   811

Ferry, Georgina
Sulston, J. The common thread   572.8

Ferry, Luc
A brief history of thought   100

Fertel, Rien
The one true barbecue   641.5

Fertig, Beth
Why cant U teach me 2 read?   372.4

Fertig, Judith
The back in the swing cookbook   641.5

Fertik, Michael
(jt. auth) Thompson, D. C. The reputation economy   302.23

FERTILIZATION IN VITRO
Whitehouse, B. The match   92

Fessler, Ann
The girls who went away   362.82

Fest, Joachim C.
Speer: the final verdict   92

FESTIVALS
Holiday symbols and customs   394.26
Rajtar, S. United States holidays and observanc-
  es   394.26

FESTIVALS
    See also Manners and customs

FESTIVALS -- DICTIONARIES
Holidays, festivals, and celebrations of the world
  dictionary   394.26

FETAL ALCOHOL SYNDROME
    See also Social problems

FETAL DEATH *See* Miscarriage

Fetherling, Dale
Woodhouse, V. Divorce & money   346.01

FETISHISM (SEXUAL BEHAVIOR)

See also Sex

Fetterman, Bonny V.
Wiesenthal, S. The sunflower   **179.7**

Fetterolf, Monty L.
Cobb, C. The joy of chemistry   **540**

FETUS
Your pregnancy week by week   **618.2**

FETUS
See also Embryology; Reproduction

FEUDALISM
Gies, J. Life in a medieval castle   **940.2**
Linklater, A. Owning the earth   **333.3**

FEUDALISM
See also Land tenure; Medieval civilization

The **fever.** Shah, S.   **614.5**

FEVER
See also Pathology

A **fever** in Salem. Carlson, L. M.   **133.4**

A **few** good books. Maatta, S. L.   **028**

Fey, Tina, 1970-
About
Fey, T. Bossypants   **92**

Feynman.   **92**

Feynman's lost lecture. Goodstein, D. L.   **521**

Feynman, Richard Phillips, 1918-1988
The meaning of it all   **500**
The pleasure of finding things out   **500**
QED   **539.7**
Six easy pieces   **530**
About
Feynman   **92**
Goodstein, D. L. Feynman's lost lecture   **521**
Krauss, L. M. Quantum man   **92**

FIANCÉES -- SOVIET UNION -- CORRESPON-DENCE
Figes, O. Just send me word   **365**

Fiasco: the American military adventure in Iraq. Ricks, T. E.   **956.7**

FIBER OPTICS
See also Optics

FIBROMYALGIA
Murphree, R. H. Treating and beating fibromyalgia and chronic fatigue syndrome   **616**

FICTION
See also Literature

FICTION -- 21ST CENTURY
Dilevko, J. Contemporary world fiction   **016**

FICTION -- AUTHORSHIP
Boyd, B. On the origin of stories   **809**
Eco, U. Confessions of a young novelist   **808.3**
Koch, S. The modern library writer's workshop   **808.3**
Maass, D. Writing the breakout novel   **808.3**
MFA vs NYC   **808.02**
Stein, S. How to grow a novel   **808.3**
Wood, J. How fiction works   **808.3**

FICTION -- BIO-BIBLIOGRAPHY
Beacham's encyclopedia of popular fiction   **809**

FICTION -- HISTORY AND CRITICISM
Boyd, B. On the origin of stories   **809**
Kundera, M. The curtain   **801**
Moore, S. The novel   **809**
Nabokov, V. V. Lectures on literature   **808.3**
Smiley, J. Thirteen ways of looking at the novel   **813**

FICTION -- PUBLISHING -- UNITED STATES
MFA vs NYC   **808.02**

FICTION -- TECHNIQUE
Bingham, H. The writers' and artists' yearbook guide to how to write   **808.3**

FICTION -- TECHNIQUE
See also Authorship

FICTION GENRES -- BIBLIOGRAPHY
Herald, D. T. Genreflecting   **016**
Schall, L. Teen talkback with interactive booktalks!   **021.7**

FICTION IN LIBRARIES -- UNITED STATES
Baker, J. S. The readers' advisory guide to historical fiction   **026**
Buker, D. M. The science-fiction and fantasy readers' advisory   **025.5**
Charles, J. A. The mystery readers' advisory **025.2**
Herald, D. T. Strictly science fiction   **016**
Honig, M. Urban grit   **016**
Kallio, J. Read on ... speculative fiction for teens   **016**
Morris, V. I. The readers' advisory guide to street literature   **016**
Pulliam, J. M. Read on . . . horror fiction   **025**
Saricks, J. G. The readers' advisory guide to genre fiction   **025.5**
Spratford, B. S. The horror readers' advisory **025.5**
Torres-Roman, S. A. Read on-- science fiction **016**
Vnuk, R. Women's fiction   **016**

FIDDLE *See* Violins

Fidel. Szulc, T.   **92**

Fidel Castro: my life. Castro, F.   **92**

Fideler, Elizabeth F.
Men still at work   **331.3**
Women still at work   **331.4**

Fiedler on the roof. Fiedler, L. A.   **814**

Fiedler, Leslie A.
Fiedler on the roof   **814**

FIEFS *See* Feudalism; Land tenure

A **field** guide to American houses. McAlester, V. S.   **728**

Field guide to edible wild plants. Angier, B. **581.6**
The **field** guide to fleece. Ekarius, C.   **677**
The **field** guide to geology. Lambert, D.   **551**
A **field** guide to germs. Biddle, W.   **616**
Field guide to grasshoppers, crickets, and katydids of the United States. Capinera, J. L.   **595.7**

A **field** guide to hawks of North America. Clark, W. S. **598**

A **field** guide to hummingbirds of North America. Williamson, S. L. **598**

A **field** guide to lies. Levitin, D. J. **153.4**

A **field** guide to mushrooms, North America. McKnight, K. H. **579.6**

A **field** guide to reptiles & amphibians. Conant, R. **597.9**

A **field** guide to rocks and minerals. Pough, F. H. **549**

Field guide to stains. Friedman, V. M. **648**

A **field** guide to Western reptiles and amphibians. Stebbins, R. C. **597.9**

FIELD HOCKEY
　　See also Sports

Field notes from a catastrophe. Kolbert, E. **363.7**

Field poetry series
　　Estes, A. Tryst **811**

FIELD RECORDINGS -- UNITED STATES -- HISTORY
　　Wade, S. The beautiful music all around us **781.62**

Field, Rick
　　The Art of preserving **641.4**

Field, Syd
　　Screenplay **808.2**

Fielding, George
　　Ali, K. Fighting weight **92**

Fields of battle. Curtis, B. **940.54**

Fields of battle. Keegan, J. **355.009**

Fields of Blood. Armstrong, K. **201**

Fiennes, Ranulph, 1944-
　　Agincourt **944**

A **fierce** discontent. McGerr, M. E. **324.2**

A **fiery** peace in a cold war. Sheehan, N. **92**

The **fiery** trial. Foner, E. **973.7**

Fiesta at Rick's. Bayless, R. **641.5**

FIESTAS *See* Festivals

FIFTEENTH CENTURY *See* World history -- 15th century

Fifth Avenue, 5 AM. Wasson, S. **791.43**

FIFTH COLUMN *See* Subversive activities; World War, 1939-1945 -- Collaborationists

The **fifties.** Halberstam, D. **973.92**

Fifty miles from tomorrow. Hensley, W. L. **92**

Fifty minerals that changed the course of history. Chaline, E. **549**

Fifty Weapons That Changed the Course of History. Levy, J. **355.8**

A **fifty-year** silence. Richmond Mouillot, M. **940.53**

Figes, Orlando, 1959-
　　Figes, O. The Crimean War **947**
　　Just send me word **365**
　　A people's tragedy **947.084**
　　The whisperers **947.084**

Fight like a girl-- and win. Gervasi, L. H. **613.6**

The **fight** to save Juárez. Ainslie, R. C. **363.45**

The **Fight** to Vote. Waldman, M. **324.6**

FIGHTER PILOTS -- UNITED STATES -- BIOGRAPHY
　　Hynes, S. The unsubstantial air **940.4**

FIGHTING *See* Battles; Boxing; Bullfights; Dueling; Fencing; Gladiators; Military art and science; Naval art and science; Self-defense; Self-defense for women; War

A **fighting** chance. Warren, E. **92**

Fighting chance. Dudden, F. E. **324.6**

Fighting the devil in Dixie. Greenhaw, W. **323.1**

Fighting the Great War. Neiberg, M. **940.4**

Fighting to serve. Nicholson, A. **355**

Fighting weight. Ali, K. **92**

FIGURE DRAWING
　　Bradley, B. Drawing people **743.4**
　　Hart, C. Human anatomy made amazingly easy **743.4**
　　Lester, T. Da Vinci's ghost **741.092**
　　Loomis, A. Figure drawing for all it's worth **743.4**
　　Ryder, A. The artist's complete guide to figure drawing **743.4**
　　Vanderpoel, J. H. The human figure **743.4**

FIGURE DRAWING
　　See also Artistic anatomy; Drawing

FIGURE DRAWING -- TECHNIQUE
　　Loomis, A. Figure drawing for all it's worth **743.4**
　　Ryder, A. The artist's complete guide to figure drawing **743.4**
　　Winslow, V. L. Classic human anatomy **743.49**

Figure drawing for all it's worth. Loomis, A. **743.4**

Figure drawing for artists. Huston, S. **743.4**

FIGURE PAINTING
　　See also Artistic anatomy; Painting

The **figured** wheel. Pinsky, R. **811**

Figurehead & other poems. Hollander, J. **811**

FIGURES OF SPEECH
　　See also Rhetoric; Symbolism

The **file.** Garton-Ash, T. **327.12**

Filipovic, Zlata
　　(ed) Stolen voices **920**

Filiu, Jean-Pierre
　　Gaza **953**

Filkins, Dexter
　　　　　　　　About
　　Filkins, D. The forever war **956.7**

Fillmore, Millard, 1800-1874
　　　　　　　　About
　　Finkelman, P. Millard Fillmore **92**

FILM ADAPTATIONS
　　See also Motion pictures

FILM CRITICISM
　　Schickel, R. Keepers **791.43**

FILM CRITICISM
　　See also Criticism

FILM CRITICS -- UNITED STATES -- BIOGRA-PHY
Gleiberman, O. Movie freak   **791.43**
FILM HISTORIANS
Schiavi, M. Celluloid activist   **92**
Thomson, D. Try to tell the story   **92**
FILM INDUSTRY (MOTION PICTURES) *See* Motion picture industry
Film noir.   **791.43**
FILM NOIR
    See also Motion pictures
FILM POSTERS
    See also Posters
FILM PRODUCERS *See* Motion picture producers and directors
FILM PRODUCTION *See* Motion pictures -- Production and direction
The **filmmaker's** handbook. Ascher, S.   **777**
FILMMAKING *See* Motion pictures -- Production and direction
FILMS *See* Filmstrips; Motion pictures
FILMSTRIPS
    See also Audiovisual materials; Photography
The **filter** bubble. Pariser, E.   **025.04**
A **final** arc of sky. Culkin, J.   **92**
The **final** days. Woodward, B.   **973.924**
Final exam. Chen, P. W.   **92**
Final exit. Humphry, D.   **179.7**
Final Frontier. Clegg, B.   **629.4**
Final Jeopardy. Baker, S.   **006.3**
Final salute. Sheeler, J.   **956.7**
Final Solution. Cesarani, D.   **940.53**
Finamore, Roy
Moonen, R. Fish without a doubt   **641.6**
Finan, Christopher M.
Alfred E. Smith, the happy warrior   **92**
FINANCE
Chang Economics   **330**
Smith, G. S. Cost control for nonprofits in crisis   **025.1**
Weatherall, J. O. The physics of Wall Street   **332.63**
FINANCE
    See also Economics
FINANCE -- UNITED STATES
Stiglitz, J. E. The price of inequality   **305.5**
White, S. Prince of darkness   **92**
FINANCE -- UNITED STATES -- HISTORY -- 21ST CENTURY
Lewis, M. Flash boys   **332.6**
Finance and investment handbook. Downes, J. **332.6**
FINANCE, HOUSEHOLD *See* Household budgets
FINANCE, PERSONAL *See* Personal finance
FINANCE, PUBLIC *See* Public finance
FINANCE, PUBLIC -- UNITED STATES -- HISTORY
McCraw, T. K. The founders and finance **330.973**

FINANCIAL ACCOUNTING *See* Accounting
FINANCIAL AID TO STUDENTS *See* Student aid
FINANCIAL ANALYSTS
Shen, A. J. A tiger's heart   **92**
FINANCIAL CRASHES *See* Financial crises
FINANCIAL CRISES
Acharya, V. V. Guaranteed to fail   **332.7**
Boeckh, J. A. The great reflation   **332.6**
Boyd, R. Fatal risk   **368**
Cassidy, J. How markets fail   **381**
Grind, K. The lost bank   **332.3**
Lanchester, J. I.O.U.   **330.9**
Panic   **338.5**
Perino, M. A. The hellhound of Wall Street   **330.9**
Reinhart, C. M. This time is different   **338.5**
Rickards, J. Currency wars   **332.4**
Shiller, R. J. Irrational exuberance   **332.63**
Smith, G. S. Cost control for nonprofits in crisis   **025.1**
Sorkin, A. R. Too big to fail   **330.9**
FINANCIAL CRISES
    See also Finance
FINANCIAL CRISES -- UNITED STATES
Blinder, A. S. After the music stopped   **330.973**
Ferguson, C. Predator nation   **330.973**
Johnson, S. 13 bankers   **332.1**
Kelly, K. Street fighters   **332.6**
Lewis, M. The big short   **330.9**
Lowenstein, R. The end of Wall Street   **332.6**
McGee, S. Chasing Goldman Sachs   **332.6**
McLean, B. All the devils are here   **330.9**
Paulson, H. M. On the brink   **330.9**
Sorkin, A. R. Too big to fail   **330.9**
Tett, G. Fool's gold   **332.6**
Wessel, D. In Fed we trust   **332.1**
FINANCIAL CRISES -- UNITED STATES -- 21ST CENTURY
Morgenson, G. Reckless endangerment   **332.7**
FINANCIAL CRISES -- UNITED STATES -- HISTORY
Gasparino, C. The sellout   **332**
Madrick, J. G. Age of greed   **330.9**
FINANCIAL CRISES -- UNITED STATES -- HISTORY -- 19TH CENTURY
Ward, G. C. A disposition to be rich   **974.7**
FINANCIAL CRISES -- UNITED STATES -- HISTORY -- 21ST CENTURY
Friedman, J. Engineering the financial crisis **330.9**
Krugman, P. R. End this depression now!   **330.9**
FINANCIAL SERVICES INDUSTRY
Lewis, M. Flash boys   **332.6**
FINANCIAL SERVICES INDUSTRY
    See also Industries
FINANCIAL SERVICES INDUSTRY -- LAW AND LEGISLATION -- UNITED STATES

Kaiser, R. G. Act of Congress **346.73**

FINANCIERS

Ahamed, L. Lords of finance **332.1**

Buffett, M. Warren Buffett and the art of stock arbitrage **332.6**

Burrough, B. The big rich **338.2**

Cannadine, D. Mellon **92**

Chan, R. W. Behind the Berkshire Hathaway curtain **658.4**

Gordon, J. S. A thread across the ocean **384.1**

Leamer, L. The Kennedy men **920**

Mahoney, R. D. Sons and brothers: the days of Jack and Bobby Kennedy **92**

Partnoy, F. The match king **92**

Renehan, E. J. Commodore **92**

Schroeder, A. D. The snowball: Warren Buffett and the business of life **92**

Strouse, J. Morgan **92**

Tuchman, B. W. Practicing history **907**

FINANCIERS *See* Capitalists and financiers

Finch, Christopher

Chuck Close **92**

Fincher, David, 1962-

About

Waxman, S. Rebels on the backlot **920**

Find a way. Nyad, D. **92**

Find Me Unafraid. Posner, J. **92**

Finder, Henry

(ed) The 40s **973.917**

(ed) The 50s **973**

Finders keepers. Heaney, S. **821**

Finders keepers. Childs, C. L. **930.1**

Finding beauty in a broken world. Williams, T. T. **814**

Finding Florida. Allman, T. D. **975.9**

Finding Fontainebleau. Carhart, T. **944.36**

Finding the answers to legal questions. Tucker, V. **340**

Finding the blue sky. Emet, J. **294.3**

Finding zero. Aczel, A. D. **513.5**

Fine cooking appetizers. **641.8**

Fine Cooking Magazine

(comp) Fine cooking appetizers **641.8**

(comp) Fine cooking roasting **641.7**

Fine cooking roasting. **641.7**

A fine romance. Bergen, C. **92**

A fine romance. Lehman, D. **782.42**

Fine, Doug

Hemp bound **633.5**

Too high to fail **338.4**

Fine, Marshall

Accidental genius **791**

The finer edge. Omdahl, K. **746.43**

The Finer Things. Lemieux, C. **747**

Fingal, Jim

(jt. auth) D'Agata, J. The lifespan of a fact **808.02**

The **finger.** Trumble, A. **306.4**

FINGER PAINTING

See also Child artists; Painting

FINGER PLAY

See also Play

FINGER WEAVING

Weil, A. Knitting without needles **746.432**

Fingeroth, Danny J.

(ed) 101 outstanding graphic novels **741.5**

FINGERPRINTS

See also Anthropometry; Criminal investigation; Criminals -- Identification; Identification

FINGERS

Trumble, A. The finger **306.4**

FINISHES AND FINISHING

See also Materials

Finishing school. Newton, D. **746.43**

Finishing the hat. Sondheim, S. **92**

Fink, Donald G., 1911-1996

(ed) Standard Handbook for Electrical Engineers **621.3**

Fink, Sheri

Five days at memorial **362.11**

Finkel, Caroline

Osman's dream **956**

Finkel, David

The good soldiers **956.7**

Thank You for Your Service **362.86**

Finkel, Elizabeth

The Genome Generation **572**

Finkelman, Paul

(ed) Encyclopedia of the new American nation **973**

Landmark decisions of the United States Supreme Court **347**

Millard Fillmore **92**

Finlay, B. Brett

Let Them Eat Dirt **616.9**

Finn, Adharanand

The Way of the Runner **796.42**

Finn, Peter

The Zhivago affair **891.73**

Finnanger, Tone, 1973-

Tilda Homemade & Happy **746.4**

Tilda's toy box **745.592**

Finnegan, William

About

Finnegan, W. Barbarian Days **92**

Finneran, Richard J.

(ed) Yeats, W. B. The collected poems of W.B. Yeats **821**

Finney, Nikky

Head off & split **811**

FINNO-RUSSIAN WAR, 1939-1940 *See* Russo-Finnish War, 1939-1940

Fiore's summer library reading program handbook. Fiore, C. D. **027.62**

Fiore, Carole D.

Fiore's summer library reading program handbook **027.62**

Fiorina, Carly

About

Burrows, P. Backfire: Carly Fiorina's high-stakes battle for the soul of Hewlett-Packard **338.7**

Firdawsi

Shahnameh **891**

Fire. Junger, S. **909.82**

FIRE

Hillman, B. Seasonal works with letters on fire **811**

Streever, B. Heat **551.41**

Thurkettle, V. The Wood Fire Handbook **697.1**

Wrangham, R. W. Catching fire **641.3**

FIRE

See also Chemistry

Fire and ashes. Maclean, J. N. **363.3**

Fire and rain. Browne, D. **781.66**

FIRE BASE KATE (VIETNAM)

Wolf, M. J. Abandoned in hell **959.704**

FIRE ECOLOGY

See also Ecology

FIRE ECOLOGY -- YELLOWSTONE NATIONAL PARK

Henry, J. The year Yellowstone burned **634.9**

FIRE FIGHTERS

Dickman, K. On the burning edge **363.37**

Halberstam, D. Firehouse **363.34**

MacLean, N. Young men & fire **634.9**

Smith, D. Report from ground zero **363.34**

Smith, J. Smokejumper **92**

FIRE FIGHTING

See also Fire prevention; Fires

FIRE IN MYTHOLOGY

See also Mythology

Fire in the ashes. Kozol, J. **362.7**

Fire in the lake. FitzGerald, F. **959.704**

FIRE INSURANCE

See also Insurance

FIRE LOOKOUT STATIONS

Connors, P. Fire season **634.9**

FIRE LOOKOUTS

Connors, P. Fire season **634.9**

FIRE PREVENTION

Fire protection handbook **628.9**

FIRE PREVENTION

See also Fires

Fire protection handbook. **628.9**

Fire season. Connors, P. **634.9**

The **fire** smart home handbook. Soles, C. **643**

The **Fire** This Time. **305.896**

Fire to fire. Doty, M. **811**

The **fire** within the eye. Park, D. **535**

Firearms. **683.4**

FIREARMS *See* Guns

FIREARMS -- CONTROL *See* Gun control

FIREARMS -- LAW AND LEGISLATION *See* Gun control

FIREARMS -- SOCIAL ASPECTS -- UNITED STATES

Baum, D. Gun guys **683.4**

FIREARMS CONTROL *See* Gun control

FIREARMS INDUSTRY

Baum, D. Gun guys **683.4**

Firearms **683.4**

Gun digest 2015 **623.4**

FIREARMS INDUSTRY

See also Industries

FIREARMS OWNERSHIP -- UNITED STATES

Baum, D. Gun guys **683.4**

Diaz, T. The last gun **338.4**

Giffords, G. D. Enough **363.33**

FIREARMS TRADE *See* Firearms industry

The **firebrand** and the First Lady. Bell-Scott, P. **92**

Firebrand of liberty. Ash, S. V. **973.7**

Firefly Encyclopedia of Reptiles and Amphibians. **597.9**

Firefly guide to gems. Oldershaw, C. **553.8**

Firehouse. Halberstam, D. **363.34**

FIREMEN AND FIREWOMEN *See* Fire fighters

FIREPLACES

See also Architecture -- Details; Buildings; Heating; Space heaters

FIREPROOFING

See also Fire insurance; Fire prevention

FIRES

Von Drehle, D. Triangle: the fire that changed America **974.7**

FIRES

See also Accidents; Disasters; Fire

The **fires** of spring. Culbertson, S. **909**

The **fires** of Vesuvius. Beard, M. **937**

The **fireside** cook book. Beard, J. **641.5**

Firestein, Stuart

Ignorance **501**

FIREWORKS

See also Amusements

The **Firm:** the troubled life of the House of Windsor. Junor, P. **941.085**

Firmage, George James

(ed) Cummings, E. E. Complete poems, 1904-1962 **811**

FIRMS *See* Business enterprises

FIRST (ORGANIZATION)

Bascomb, N. The new cool **629.8**

The **first** 1,000 days. Thurow, R. **618.92**

The **first** 20 minutes. Reynolds, G. **613.7**

FIRST AID

First aid manual **616.02**

FIRST AID

See also Health self-care; Home accidents;

Medicine; Nursing; Rescue work; Sick

**FIRST AID IN ILLNESS AND INJURY -- HAND-
BOOKS, MANUALS, ETC**

First aid manual   **616.02**

First aid manual.   **616.02**

The first Americans. Adovasio, J. M.   **970.01**

First as tragedy, then as farce. Zizek, S.   **337**

First bite.   **641.01**

First bites. White, D. A.   **641.3**

The first collection of criticism by a living female rock critic. Hopper, J.

The First Congress. Bordewich, F. M.   **327.73**

First contact. Kaufman, M.   **576.8**

First dads. Kendall, J. C.   **973**

The first emancipator. Levy, A.   **92**

First families. Angelo, B.   **920**

The first family. Dash, M.   **364.1**

First fire, then birds. Hix, H. L.   **811**

FIRST GENERATION CHILDREN See Children
of immigrants

First great triumph. Zimmermann, W.   **973**

The first heroes. Nelson, C.   **940.54**

The first idea. Greenspan, S. I.   **153.7**

First in. Schroen, G. C.   **958.1**

The first king of Hollywood. Goessel, T.   **92**

First ladies. Schneider, D.   **920.003**

First ladies. Caroli, B. B.   **920**

FIRST LADIES -- UNITED STATES See Presidents' spouses -- United States

FIRST LOVES -- FRANCE -- BIOGRAPHY

Maitland, L. Crossing the borders of time   **940.53**

The First Muslim. Hazleton, L.   **297.6**

FIRST NAMES See Personal names

FIRST NATIONS AUTHORS

See also Canadian authors

First over there. Davenport, M. J.   **940.4**

The first Paul. Borg, M. J.   **227**

First person: an astonishingly frank self-portrait.   **92**

First prize pies. Kave, A.   **641.86**

A first rate tragedy. Preston, D.   **919**

The first salute. Tuchman, B. W.   **973.3**

First they killed my father. Ung, L.   **959.6**

First things first. Covey, S. R.   **158**

First time sewing.   **646.2**

First to Fly. Flood, C. B.

The first tycoon. Stiles, T. J.   **92**

The first war of physics. Baggott, J. E.   **355.8**

First women. Brower, K. A.   **973.099**

The first word. Kenneally, C.   **400**

The First World War. Gilbert, M.   **940.3**

FIRST WORLD WAR See World War, 1914-1918

The First World War. Strachan, H.   **940.3**

The First World War in 100 objects. Hughes-Wilson, J.   **940.3**

Firstbrook, Peter

A Man Most Driven   **975.5**

FISCAL POLICY

Reinhart, C. M. This time is different   **338.5**

FISCAL POLICY

See also Economic policy; Public finance

FISCAL POLICY -- UNITED STATES

Kleinbard, E. D. We are better than this   **336.3**

Kramer, M. A people's guide to the federal budget   **352.4**

**FISCAL POLICY -- UNITED STATES -- HIS-
TORY**

McCraw, T. K. The founders and finance   **330.973**

Fischer, Bobby, 1943-2008

Bobby Fischer teaches chess   **794.1**

About

Brady, F. Endgame   **92**

Fischer, Chris

The Beetlebung Farm cookbook   **641**

Fischer, David Hackett

Champlain's dream   **92**

Liberty and freedom   **323.44**

Paul Revere's ride   **973.3**

Washington's crossing   **973.3**

Fischer, Klaus P.

Nazi Germany   **943.086**

Fischer, Paul

A Kim Jong-Il production   **791.43**

Fischer, Stefan

Hieronymus Bosch   **759.94**

FISH See Fish as food; Fishes

FISH AS FOOD

See also Cooking; Fishes; Food

A fish caught in time. Weinberg, S.   **597.3**

FISH CULTURE

Greenberg, P. Four fish   **333.95**

FISH FARMING See Fish culture

FISH HATCHERIES See Fish culture

FISH POPULATIONS -- RESEARCH

Rigney, M. In pursuit of giants   **597**

The fish that ate the whale. Cohen, R.   **338.7**

FISH TRADE

Greenberg, P. American catch   **333.95**

Fish without a doubt. Moonen, R.   **641.6**

Fisher investments series

Fisher, K. L. How to smell a rat   **364.1**

Fisher, Carrie

About

Fisher, C. Wishful drinking   **92**

Fisher, David

Read, A. The fall of Berlin   **940.54**

Fisher, Edwin B.

Goldfarb, T. L. American Lung Association 7 steps
to a smoke-free life   **616.86**

Fisher, Helen, 1942-

Anatomy of Love   **302.3**

Fisher, James Maxwell McConnell, 1912-1970

About

Weidensaul, S. Return to wild America   **578**

Fisher, James Terence
On the Irish waterfront   **331.7**

Fisher, John H.
Chaucer, G. The complete poetry and prose of Geoffrey Chaucer   **821**

Fisher, Kathleen
Taylor's guide to shrubs   **635.9**

Fisher, Kenneth L.
How to smell a rat   **364.1**

Fisher, M. F. K. (Mary Frances Kennedy), 1908-1992
The art of eating   **641**
A stew or a story   **641**
About
Barr, L. Provence, 1970   **641.59**

Fisher, Marshall
A terrible splendor   **796.342**

Fisher, Robin Gaby
Choosing hope   **371.7**

Fisher, Roy
Selected poems   **821**

FISHERIES *See* Commercial fishing

FISHERIES -- ENVIRONMENTAL ASPECTS
Hilborn, R. Overfishing   **338.3**

FISHERIES -- HISTORY
Rigney, M. In pursuit of giants   **597**

FISHERIES -- MEXICO -- CHIAPAS -- HISTORY
Franklin, J. 438 days   **910.916**

FISHERIES -- UNITED STATES
Halverson, A. An entirely synthetic fish   **639.3**

FISHERMEN
Wilson, D. An unreasonable woman   **92**

FISHES
Bailey, M. The Ultimate Encyclopedia of Aquarium Fish & Fish Care   **639.34**
Balcombe, J. What a Fish Knows   **597.15**
Mills, D. Aquarium fish   **639.34**
Pepperell, J. G. Fishes of the open ocean   **597**
Rigney, M. In pursuit of giants   **597**
Schultz, K. Ken Schultz's field guide to saltwater fish   **597**
Voigt, E. The dragon behind the glass   **597.176**

FISHES -- CONSERVATION -- UNITED STATES
Greenberg, P. American catch   **333.95**

FISHES -- ECOLOGY
See also Ecology

FISHES -- GEOGRAPHICAL DISTRIBUTION
See also Biogeography

FISHES -- NORTH AMERICA
Gilbert, C. R. National Audubon Society field guide to fishes, North America   **597**
Page, L. M. Peterson field guide to freshwater fishes of North America north of Mexico   **597**
Fishes of the open ocean. Pepperell, J. G.   **597**

FISHING
Bourne, W. Basic fishing   **799.1**
Cermele, J. The total fishing manual   **799.1**
Ellis, R. The empty ocean   **577.7**
Gierach, J. All Fishermen Are Liars   **799.12**
Greenlaw, L. The hungry ocean   **639.2**
Rosenbauer, T. The Orvis guide to the essential American flies   **799.1**
Talleur, R. W. L.L. Bean ultimate book of fly fishing   **799.1**

FISHING
See also Sports

FISHING -- HISTORY
Rigney, M. In pursuit of giants   **597**

FISHING BOATS -- MEXICO -- CHIAPAS
Franklin, J. 438 days   **910.916**

Fishman, Charles
The big thirst   **333.91**

Fishman, Stephen
The copyright handbook   **346.04**
The public domain   **346**
Working for yourself   **343**

Fisk, Carlton, 1947-
About
Wilson, D. Pudge   **92**

Fiske guide to colleges. Fiske, E. B.   **378**
Fiske Guide to Getting Into The Right College. Fiske, E. B.   **378.1**

Fiske, Brian D.
(jt. auth) Downs, T. Essential road bike maintenance handbook   **629.28**

Fiske, Edward B.
Fiske guide to colleges   **378**
Fiske Guide to Getting Into The Right College   **378.1**

Fist, stick, knife, gun. Canada, G.   **305.23**

Fitch, Noel Riley
Appetite for life   **92**

FITNESS *See* Physical fitness

Fitness and exercise sourcebook.   **613.7**
Fitness swimming. Hines, E. W.   **613.7**

Fitzgerald, Cathy
Cullinane, J. The new retirement   **646.7**

Fitzgerald, Ella
About
Feather, L. From Satchmo to Miles   **920**

Fitzgerald, F. Scott (Francis Scott), 1896-1940
About
Fitzgerald, F. S. A life in letters   **813**
Kazin, A. An American procession   **810**
Miller, N. New world coming   **973.91**
Tate, M. J. Critical companion to F. Scott Fitzgerald   **813**

FitzGerald, Frances
Fire in the lake   **959.704**
Way out there in the blue   **973.927**

Fitzgerald, Matt

How bad do you want it?   612.044

FitzGerald, Michael C.
Picasso and American art   709

Fitzgerald, Zelda, 1900-1948
About
Mackrell, J. Flappers   920

Fitzhugh, George, 1806-1881
About
Wilson, E. Patriotic gore   810

Fitzhugh, William W.
(ed) Vikings: the North Atlantic saga   970.01

The **five** biggest unsolved problems in science. Wiggins, A. W.   500

Five billion years of solitude. Billings, L.   576.8

The **five** books of Moses. Bible/O.T./Pentateuch   222

The **five** books of Moses. Bible/O.T./Pentateuch   222

Five Came Back. Harris, M.   791.43

Five days at memorial. Fink, S.   362.11

Five days in London, May 1940. Lukacs, J.   940.53

Five days in November. Hill, C.   973.922

Five easy theses. Stone, J. M.   330.973

Five families. Raab, S.   364.1

Five Germanys I have known. Stern, F. R.   943.08

Five lessons.   796.352

Five lives in music. Porter, C. H.   780.92

Five modern Japanese novelists. Keene, D.   895.6

Five myths about nuclear weapons. Wilson, W.   355.02

Five nights in Paris. Baxter, J.   914.4

Five plays. Hughes, L.   812

Five presidents. Hill, C.   363.28

Five sisters. Fox, J.   975.5

FIXED IDEAS *See* Obsessive-compulsive disorder

Fixing the sky. Fleming, J. R.   551.6

Flag: an American biography. Leepson, M.   929.9

Flagrant conduct. Carpenter, D.   342.73

FLAGS
Znamierowski, A. The World Encyclopedia of Flags   929.9

FLAGS -- UNITED STATES
Leepson, M. Flag: an American biography   929.9
Miller, M. R. Betsy Ross and the making of America   92
Shearer, B. F. State names, seals, flags, and symbols   929.9
Testi, A. Capture the flag   929.9

Flags of our fathers. Bradley, J.   940.54

Flaherty, Francis
The elements of story   808.5

Flais, Shelly Vaziri
(ed) The big book of symptoms   618.92

The **flame** of Miletus. Freely, J.   509

A **flame** of pure fire: Jack Dempsey and the roaring '20s. Kahn, R.   92

The **flame** trees of Thika. Huxley, E.   828

The **flamingo's** smile. Gould, S. J.   500

Flanagan, Caitlin
Girl land   305.235

Flanagan, Shalane
Run fast, eat slow   641.563

Flanders, Judith
A circle of sisters   920
The invention of murder   364.152
The Victorian city   942.1
Victorian house Inside the Victorian home   306

The **flaneur.** White, E.   944.083

Flannery. Gooch, B.   92

Flannery O'Connor: a life. Cash, J. W.   92

Flannery, Tim F.
Chasing kangaroos   599.2
The eternal frontier   508
An explorer's notebook   304.2
Here on Earth   551
Throwim way leg   995.3
The weather makers   363.7
Flannery, T. Here on Earth   551

Flapper. Zeitz, J.   305.4

Flappers. Mackrell, J.   920

Flash boys. Lewis, M.   332.6

FLASH MOBS
See also Crowds; Performance art

Flatbreads and flavors. Alford, J.   641.8

FLATS *See* Apartments

Flaubert. Brown, F.   92

Flaubert, Gustave, 1821-1880
About
Brown, F. Flaubert   92
Nabokov, V. V. Lectures on literature   808.3

The **flavor** bible. Page, K.   641.5

Flavor flours.   641.3

Flavorful. Boyle, T.   641.86

FLAVORING ESSENCES
See also Cooking; Essences and essential oils; Food

Flawless. Selby, S. A.   364.1

Flay, Bobby, 1964-
Brunch @ Bobby's   641.5

Flea market fabulous. Spencer, L.   747

FLEA MARKETS
Lee, V. Kitchenalia   747
Spencer, L. Flea market fabulous   747
Stanton, M. Killer stuff and tons of money   381

FLEA MARKETS
See also Markets; Secondhand trade

Fleck, Ludwik, 1896-1961
About
Allen, A. The fantastic laboratory of Dr. Weigl   614.5

Fleming, Fergus
Ninety degrees North   919

Fleming, Gerald
Hitler and the final solution   943.086

Fleming, James Rodger
Fixing the sky **551.6**
Fleming, Thomas J.
Washington's secret war **973.3**
Fleming, Victor, 1883-1949
About
Sragow, M. Victor Fleming **92**
Flesch, Rudolf Franz
Why Johnny can't read--and what you can do about it **372.4**
Fletcher, Anne M.
Inside rehab **362.29**
Fletcher, Catherine
The divorce of Henry VIII **942.05**
Fletcher, Colin, 1922-2007
About
Fletcher, C. The man who walked through time **917**
Fletcher, Joann
Cleopatra the great **92**
The Story of Egypt **932**
Fletcher, Seth
Bottled lightning **621.31**
Flexner, James Thomas
George Washington and the new nation, 1783-1793 **92**
George Washington: anguish and farewell 1793-1799 **92**
George Washington: the forge of experience, 1732-1775 **92**
FLIES
See also Household pests; Insects; Pests
FLIES, ARTIFICIAL
Gathercole, P. Fly tying for beginners **688.7**
Gathercole, P. The fly-tying bible **688.7**
FLIES, ARTIFICIAL *See* Artificial flies
FLIES, ARTIFICIAL -- HISTORY
The history of fly fishing in fifty flies **799.124**
FLIGHT
Higgins, M. Bird dream **797.5**
Holmes, R. Falling upwards **387.7**
Flight 232. Gonzales, L. **363.12**
FLIGHT ATTENDANTS
See also Airlines
Flight from Monticello. Kranish, M. **973.4**
The **flight** of the century. Kessner, T. **92**
FLIGHT TO THE MOON *See* Space flight to the moon
FLIGHT TRAINING *See* Aeronautics -- Study and teaching; Airplanes -- Piloting
Flight: 100 years of aviation. Grant, R. G. **629.13**
Flink, David
Thinking Differently **371.9**
Flinn, Caryl
Brass diva **92**
Flinn, Kathleen
About

Flinn, K. Burnt toast makes you sing good **641.597**
The kitchen counter cooking school **641.5**
FLIPPED CLASSROOMS
See also Teaching
Flippin, Royce
The diabetes reset **616.4**
Floating collections. Bartlett, W. K. **025.2**
FLOOD CONTROL
See also Hydraulic engineering
FLOODS
Clark, R. Dark water **945**
FLOODS
See also Meteorology; Natural disasters; Rain; Water
FLOODS -- MISSISSIPPI RIVER
Barry, J. M. Rising tide **977**
Welky, D. The thousand-year flood **363.34**
FLOODS -- OHIO RIVER VALLEY
Welky, D. The thousand-year flood **363.34**
FLOORS
Bollinger, D. Hardwood floors **690**
FLOORS
See also Architecture -- Details; Buildings
FLORA *See* Botany; Plants
Flora illustrata. **016**
Flora, Joseph M.
(ed) The Companion to southern literature **810**
Flora: a gardener's encyclopedia. **635.9**
FLORAL DECORATION *See* Flower arrangement
Florence. **759.5**
FLORENCE (ITALY) -- HISTORY
Florence **759.5**
Strathern, P. The Medici **945.51**
FLORENCE (ITALY) -- HISTORY -- 1421-1737
Hales, D. Mona Lisa **759.5**
Strathern, P. Death in Florence **945**
FLORENCE (ITALY) -- HISTORY -- 1421-1737 -- BIOGRAPHY
Unger, M. J. Machiavelli **92**
Florence Nightingale. Bostridge, M. **92**
Flores, Dan
Coyote America **599.77**
Flores, Eva Kosmas
Adventures in chicken **641.665**
Florey, Kitty Burns
Sister Bernadette's barking dog **428**
FLORICULTURE *See* Flower gardening
FLORIDA -- DESCRIPTION AND TRAVEL
Schneider, P. Brutal journey: the epic story of the first crossing of North America **970.01**
White, E. B. Essays of E.B. White **814**
FLORIDA -- HISTORY
Allman, T. D. Finding Florida **975.9**
FLORIDA -- RACE RELATIONS
King, G. Devil in the grove **305.896**
FLORISTS' DESIGNS *See* Flower arrangement

Flottum, Kim
The backyard beekeeper   **638.1**
Flour. Matheson, C.   **641.8**
FLOUR
Flavor flours   **641.3**
Matheson, C. Flour   **641.8**
FLOUR BAKERY + CAFE
Matheson, C. Flour   **641.8**
Flour water salt yeast. Forkish, K.   **641.81**
Flow. Kim, S.   **612.6**
FLOW CHARTS *See* Graphic methods; System analysis
Flow: the psychology of optimal experience. Csikszentmihalyi, M.   **155.2**
FLOWCHARTING *See* Graphic methods; System analysis
FLOWER ARRANGEMENT
Chezar, A. The flower workshop   **745.92**
Cylinder, C. The flower chef   **745.92**
Harampolis, A. The flower recipe book   **745.92**
Heffernan, C. Flowers A to Z   **635.9**
FLOWER ARRANGEMENT
See also Decoration and ornament; Flowers; Table setting and decoration
The **flower** chef. Cylinder, C.   **745.92**
FLOWER GARDENING
Christopher, T. Essential perennials   **635.9**
Ellis, B. W. Taylor's guide to annuals   **635.9**
Ellis, B. W. Taylor's guide to perennials   **635.9**
Heffernan, C. Flowers A to Z   **635.9**
FLOWER GARDENING
See also Gardening; Horticulture
The **flower** of empire. Holway, T.   **727**
FLOWER PAINTING AND ILLUSTRATION
See Botanical illustration; Flowers in art
FLOWER PRINTS *See* Flowers in art
The **flower** recipe book. Harampolis, A.   **745.92**
FLOWER SHOWS
See also Exhibitions
The **flower** workshop. Chezar, A.   **745.92**
Flowering plant families of the world. Heywood, V. H.   **582.13**
FLOWERING SHRUBS -- ENCYCLOPEDIAS
Gardiner, J. The Timber Press encyclopedia of flowering shrubs   **635.9**
FLOWERS
Flora: a gardener's encyclopedia   **635.9**
Heffernan, C. Flowers A to Z   **635.9**
Heywood, V. H. Flowering plant families of the world   **582.13**
Wells, D. 100 flowers and how they got their names   **582.13**
FLOWERS
See also Plants
FLOWERS -- ARRANGEMENT *See* Flower arrangement

FLOWERS -- DRYING
See also Plants -- Collection and preservation
Flowers A to Z. Heffernan, C.   **635.9**
FLOWERS IN ART
Fassett, K. Kaffe Fassett's Bold Blooms   **746**
Peacock, M. The paper garden   **92**
Flowers, Arthur
I see the promised land   **92**
FLOWERS, ARTIFICIAL *See* Artificial flowers
Flowers, Sarah
Evaluating teen services and programs   **027.62**
Floyd Patterson. Levy, A. H.   **92**
Floyd Patterson. Stratton, W. K.   **92**
Floyd, Ted
Smithsonian field guide to the birds of North America   **598**
Flu. Kolata, G.   **614.5**
FLU *See* Influenza
Fluent in fantasy. Herald, D. T.   **016**
FLUGELHORNISTS
Cook, R. It's about that time   **92**
Davis, M. Miles, the autobiography   **92**
Feather, L. From Satchmo to Miles   **920**
Lees, G. You can't steal a gift   **781.65**
Fluke. Mazur, J.   **519.2**
Flunking sainthood. Riess, J.   **248.4**
FLUORESCENT LIGHTING
See also Electric lighting
FLUTISTS
Dance, S. The world of Count Basie   **920**
Wilson, E. Patriotic gore   **810**
FLY CASTING
Deeter, K. The little red book of fly fishing **799.124**
Gathercole, P. Fly tying for beginners   **688.7**
The history of fly fishing in fifty flies   **799.124**
The Orvis fly-fishing guide   **799.124**
Talleur, R. W. L.L. Bean ultimate book of fly fishing   **799.1**
FLY CASTING
See also Fishing
FLY FISHING
Deeter, K. The little red book of fly fishing **799.124**
Gathercole, P. Fly tying for beginners   **688.7**
The Orvis fly-fishing guide   **799.124**
FLY FISHING *See* Fly casting
FLY FISHING -- ANECDOTES
Gierach, J. All Fishermen Are Liars   **799.12**
FLY FISHING -- HISTORY
The history of fly fishing in fifty flies   **799.124**
FLY TYING
Gathercole, P. Fly tying for beginners   **688.7**
Gathercole, P. The fly-tying bible   **688.7**
Fly tying for beginners. Gathercole, P.   **688.7**
The **fly-tying** bible. Gathercole, P.   **688.7**
FLYING *See* Flight
Flying at night. Kooser, T.   **811**

FLYING SAUCERS *See* Unidentified flying objects

Flynn, Kevin
Dwyer, J. 102 minutes **974.7**

Flynn, Nick, 1960-
About
Flynn, N. Another bullshit night in Suck City **92**

Flynn, Raymond
John Paul II **92**

FOALS *See* Horses; Ponies

Focus. Goleman, D. **153.7**

Focus. Gross, M. **770.92**

FOCUS GROUPS
See also Research; Social groups

Fodor's Germany. **914.3**

Fodor's Rio de Janeiro & Sao Paulo. Rigby, C. **918.15**

Fodor's Travel Publications Inc.
(comp) Fodor's Germany **914.3**

Foege, William H., 1936-
House on fire **614.5**

Foer, Franklin
How soccer explains the world **303.482**

Foer, Jonathan Safran, 1977-
Eating animals **641.3**
(ed) New American Haggadah **296.4**

Foer, Joshua
Atlas Obscura **910.41**
Moonwalking with Einstein **153.1**

Foerstel, Herbert N.
Banned in the U.S.A **025.2**

FOG
See also Atmosphere; Meteorology

Fogerty, John, 1945-
About
Fogerty, J. Fortunate son **92**

Fogle, Bruce
Dog owner's manual **636.7**

Fogler, Janet
Improving your memory **153.1**

Foley, Charles
(ed) Doyle, A. C. Arthur Conan Doyle **92**

Foley, Jeana Kae
Panzer, M. Mathew Brady and the image of history **770.92**

Folger, Henry Clay, 1857-1930
About
Mays, A. E. The millionaire and the bard **822.33**

Folger, Tim
(ed) The best American science and nature writing 2012 **810.8**
(ed) The best American science and nature writing 2014 **810.8**

FOLK MUSIC
Gioia, T. Work songs **782.42**
Roden, S. ... i listen to the wind that obliterates my traces **781.64**
Szwed, J. F. Alan Lomax **92**

FOLK MUSIC
See also Music

FOLK MUSIC -- GREAT BRITAIN
Young, R. Electric Eden **781.62**

FOLK MUSIC -- UNITED STATES
The Encyclopedia of Country Music **781.64**
Wade, S. The beautiful music all around us **781.62**

FOLK MUSIC -- UNITED STATES -- HISTORY AND CRITICISM
Wade, S. The beautiful music all around us **781.62**

FOLK MUSICIANS
Adler, W. M. The man who never died **92**
Dunaway, D. K. How can I keep from singing? **92**
Dylan, B. Chronicles **92**
Gray, M. The Bob Dylan encyclopedia **782.42**
Klein, J. Woody Guthrie **92**
Kruth, J. To live's to fly **92**
Weller, S. Girls like us **920**
Wilkinson, A. The protest singer **92**

FOLK POETRY, PUSHTO -- TRANSLATIONS INTO ENGLISH
I am the beggar of the world **891**

FOLK PSYCHOLOGY *See* Ethnopsychology

FOLK SONGS
See also Folklore; Songs; Vocal music

FOLK SONGS -- UNITED STATES
Polenberg, R. Hear my sad story **782.42**

FOLK SONGS -- UNITED STATES
See also American songs

FOLK SONGS, ENGLISH -- UNITED STATES -- HISTORY AND CRITICISM
Polenberg, R. Hear my sad story **782.42**

FOLK TALES *See* Folklore; Legends

Folkens, Pieter A.
National Audubon Society guide to marine mammals of the world **599.5**

FOLKLORE
Encyclopedia of American folklife **398**
Favorite folktales from around the world **398.2**
Haase, D. The Greenwood encyclopedia of folktales and fairy tales **398.2**
World folklore for storytellers **398**

FOLKLORE
See also Ethnology; Fiction; Manners and customs

FOLKLORE -- ENCYCLOPEDIAS
Encyclopedia of Jewish folklore and traditions **398.2**

FOLKLORE -- EUROPE
Bulfinch, T. Bulfinch's mythology **398.2**

FOLKLORE -- GERMANY
The Original Folk and Fairy Tales of the Brothers Grimm **398.2**

FOLKLORE -- HAWAII

Moore, S. Paradise of the Pacific   **996.9**

FOLKLORE -- IRELAND

  McMahon, S. Brewer's dictionary of Irish phrase & fable   **427**

FOLKLORE -- UNITED STATES

  Polenberg, R. Hear my sad story   **782.42**

FOLKLORE -- UNITED STATES -- ENCYCLO-PEDIAS

  Encyclopedia of American folklife   **398**

Folklore, memoirs, and other writings.   **398**

FOLKLORISTS

  Boyd, V. Wrapped in rainbows   **92**

  Folklore, memoirs, and other writings   **398**

  Hurston, Z. N. Dust tracks on a road   **92**

  Jones, S. L. Critical companion to Zora Neale Hurston   **813**

  Pierpont, C. R. Passionate minds   **810**

  Szwed, J. F. Alan Lomax   **92**

  Wall, C. A. Women of the Harlem Renaissance   **810**

  Zora Neale Hurston   **813**

  Zora Neale Hurston: a life in letters   **92**

Folktales aloud. Del Negro, J. M.   **027.62**

FOLKWAYS *See* Manners and customs

Follain, John

  Zoya Zoya's story   **958.1**

Follett, Ken

  On wings of eagles   **955**

Following Muhammad. Ernst, C. W.   **297**

Following the path. Chittister, J.   **248.4**

The **folly** of fools. Trivers, R.   **153.4**

Folsom, W. Davis

  (ed) Encyclopedia of American business   **338**

Fonda, Jane, 1937-

     About

  Williams, M. The lost daughter   **979.4**

Fondin, Michelle S.

  The wheel of healing with ayurveda   **615.5**

Foner, Eric, 1943-

  The fiery trial   **973.7**

  Forever free   **973.8**

  Reconstruction   **973.8**

  The story of American freedom   **323.44**

  Gateway to Freedom   **973.7**

  (ed) Our Lincoln   **92**

  Wallace, A. F. C. The long bitter trail   **323.1**

Foner, Moe, 1915-2002

     About

  Foner, M. Not for bread alone   **92**

Foner, Philip S.

  Douglass, F. Frederick Douglass: selected speeches and writings   **326**

Fong, Henry

  Nom nom paleo   **641.5**

Fonseca, Anthony J.

  Hooked on horror III   **016**

  Pulliam, J. M. Read on . . . horror fiction   **025**

Fonseca, Christine

  Raising the shy child   **649**

FONTAINEBLEAU (FRANCE) -- BIOGRAPHY

  Carhart, T. Finding Fontainebleau   **944.36**

Fontes, Lisa Aronson

  Invisible chains   **158.2**

FONTS

  Garfield, S. Just my type   **686.2**

FOOD

  Abu-Jaber, D. Life Without a Recipe   **92**

  Anthony, J. C. Hoosh   **394.1**

  Bittman, M. The food matters cookbook   **641.3**

  Blount, R. Save room for pie   **641.3**

  Bourdain, A. A cook's tour   **641**

  Davidson, A. The Oxford companion to food   **641**

  Fisher, M. F. K. A stew or a story   **641**

  Gibney, M. Something to chew on   **616.02**

  López-Alt, J. K. The food lab   **664**

  The Oxford encyclopedia of food and drink in America   **641.3**

  The science of good cooking   **641.3**

  Srulovich, I. Honey & Co the Baking Book   **641**

  Standage, T. An edible history of humanity   **394.1**

  Sunset kitchen gypsy   **641.5**

FOOD

     See also Home economics

Food & Wine Annual Cookbook 2015. Cowin, D.   **641**

FOOD -- ANALYSIS

  López-Alt, J. K. The food lab   **664**

FOOD -- ANECDOTES

  Blount, R. Save room for pie   **641.3**

FOOD -- BIBLIOGRAPHY

  Stoeger, M. B. Food lit   **016.6**

FOOD -- BIOTECHNOLOGY

  Adamchak, R. W. Tomorrow's table   **664**

  Genetically modified foods   **363.1**

  Pringle, P. Food, inc   **363.1**

FOOD -- CALORIC CONTENT

  Nesheim, M. Why calories count   **613.2**

FOOD -- COMPOSITION -- TABLES

  Netzer, C. T. The complete book of food counts   **613.2**

FOOD -- ENCYCLOPEDIAS

  Larousse gastronomique   **641.3**

  The Oxford encyclopedia of food and drink in America   **641.3**

FOOD -- EXPERIMENTS

  López-Alt, J. K. The food lab   **664**

FOOD -- GREECE -- IKARIA (MUNICIPALITY)

  Kochilas, D. Ikaria   **641.594**

FOOD -- HISTORY

  Dewitt, D. Precious Cargo   **306.3**

  Le, S. One hundred million years of food   **641.3**

FOOD -- LAW AND LEGISLATION

  Hilts, P. J. Protecting America's health   **353.9**

FOOD -- LAW AND LEGISLATION
 See also Law; Legislation
FOOD -- MYANMAR
 Duguid, N. Burma   **641.59**
FOOD -- NEW YORK (STATE) -- NEW YORK
 Red Rooster Cookbook   **641.5**
FOOD -- PICTORIAL WORKS
 Vibrant food   **641.5**
FOOD -- POETRY
 The Hungry Ear   **811**
FOOD -- PRESERVATION
 Field, R. The Art of preserving   **641.4**
FOOD -- PSYCHOLOGICAL ASPECTS
 Christensen, K. Blue plate special   **92**
FOOD -- PURCHASING *See* Grocery shopping
FOOD -- QUALITY -- POPULAR WORKS
 Olmsted, L. Real food/fake food   **641.3**
FOOD -- RELIGIOUS ASPECTS -- ISLAM
 Maffei, Y. My halal kitchen   **641.595**
FOOD -- SAFETY MEASURES
 Peacock, K. W. Food security   **338.1**
FOOD -- SOCIAL ASPECTS
 Ciezadlo, A. Day of honey   **92**
 Tye, D. Baking as biography   **92**
FOOD -- SODIUM CONTENT
 Sodium girls limitless low-salt cookbook   **641.5**
FOOD -- TAIWAN
 Erway, C. The food of Taiwan   **641.595**
FOOD -- TERMS AND PHRASES
 Jurafsky, D. The language of food   **641.3**
FOOD -- UNITED STATES
 Price, C. Vitamania   **612.3**
FOOD -- UNITED STATES -- HISTORY -- 19TH CENTURY
 Food in the Civil War era   **641.597**
FOOD -- UNITED STATES -- PSYCHOLOGICAL ASPECTS
 Price, C. Vitamania   **612.3**
FOOD ADDITIVES
 Sacks, S. What the fork are you eating?   **641.3**
FOOD ADDITIVES
 See also Food -- Analysis; Food -- Preservation
FOOD ADDITIVES -- DICTIONARIES
 Winter, R. A consumer's dictionary of food additives   **664**
FOOD ADDITIVES -- POPULAR WORKS
 Olmsted, L. Real food/fake food   **641.3**
FOOD ADULTERATION AND INSPECTION
 Hilts, P. J. Protecting America's health   **353.9**
 Mueller, T. Extra virginity   **664**
FOOD ADULTERATION AND INSPECTION
 See also Consumer protection; Public health
Food allergies. Sicherer, S. H.   **616.97**
FOOD ALLERGIES *See* Food allergy
FOOD ALLERGY

Beasley, S. Don't kill the birthday girl   **92**
Pascal, C. The whole foods allergy cookbook **641.5**
Sears, W. The allergy book   **618.92**
Sicherer, S. H. Food allergies   **616.97**
Sicherer, S. H. Understanding and managing your child's food allergies   **618.92**
FOOD ALLERGY
 See also Allergy
FOOD ALLERGY -- DIET THERAPY
 Sicherer, S. H. Food allergies   **616.97**
FOOD AND BEER PAIRING
 Beer bites   **641.5**
The **Food** and Wine of France. Behr, E.   **641.5**
FOOD AND WINE PAIRING
 Morgan, J. The covenant kitchen   **641.5**
FOOD ASSISTANCE PROGRAMS *See* Food relief
FOOD BANKS
 See also Food relief
FOOD BUYING *See* Grocery shopping
FOOD CALORIES *See* Food -- Caloric content
FOOD CHAINS (ECOLOGY)
 See also Animals -- Food; Ecology
FOOD CONSERVATION
 Vinton, S. B. Eat it up!   **641.5**
FOOD CONSUMPTION -- UNITED STATES
 Pollan, M. The omnivore's dilemma   **394.1**
FOOD CONTAMINATION
 Nestle, M. Pet food politics   **363.1**
 Wilson, B. Swindled   **363.1**
FOOD CONTAMINATION
 See also Food adulteration and inspection
FOOD CONTAMINATION -- PRESS COVERAGE
 See also Mass media
FOOD CONTROL *See* Food supply
FOOD CRITICS
 Bittman, M. Food matters   **613.2**
 Bruni, F. Born round   **92**
 Fisher, M. F. K. A stew or a story   **641**
 Hazan, M. Amarcord, Marcella remembers   **92**
 A homemade life   **92**
 Reichl, R. Comfort me with apples   **92**
 Reichl, R. Garlic and sapphires   **92**
 Sheehan, J. Cooking dirty   **92**
FOOD CROPS
 Jabbour, N. Groundbreaking food gardens   **635**
 Joy, L. Start a community food garden   **635**
FOOD CROPS -- IDENTIFICATION
 Madison, D. Vegetable literacy   **641.6**
FOOD CUSTOMS *See* Eating customs
FOOD FOR INVALIDS *See* Cooking for the sick
FOOD FOR SCHOOL CHILDREN *See* School children -- Food
Food from many Greek kitchens. Kiros, T.   **641.5**
Food gift love. Battista, M.   **642**

FOOD HABITS

Altmann, T. R. What to feed your baby **649.3**

Bittman, M. Food matters **613.2**

Porto, A. The pediatrician's guide to feeding babies and toddlers **618.92**

FOOD HABITS *See* Eating customs

FOOD HABITS -- ANTARCTICA

Anthony, J. C. Hoosh **394.1**

FOOD HABITS -- CHINA

Richardson, A. The breath of a wok **641.59**

FOOD HABITS -- ECONOMIC ASPECTS

Cowen, T. An economist gets lunch **394.1**

FOOD HABITS -- ECONOMIC ASPECTS -- UNITED STATES

McMillan, T. The American way of eating **338.4**

Moss, M. Salt, sugar, fat **613.2**

FOOD HABITS -- FRANCE

Loomis, S. H. In a French kitchen **641.594**

My Paris kitchen **641.59**

FOOD HABITS -- GREECE

Hoffman, S. The olive and the caper **641.594**

Kochilas, D. The glorious foods of Greece **641.59**

FOOD HABITS -- HISTORY

Jurafsky, D. The language of food **641.3**

Wrangham, R. W. Catching fire **641.3**

FOOD HABITS -- HISTORY -- 20TH CENTURY

Collingham, L. The taste of war **940.53**

FOOD HABITS -- JAPAN

Goulding, M. Rice, noodle, fish **394.12**

FOOD HABITS -- POPULAR WORKS

The whole30 **613.2**

FOOD HABITS -- RUSSIA (FEDERATION)

Jones, C. C. A year of Russian feasts **641.59**

FOOD HABITS -- SOVIET UNION

Von Bremzen, A. Mastering the art of Soviet cooking **641.59**

FOOD HABITS -- UNITED STATES

Obama, M. American grown **635**

FOOD HABITS -- UNITED STATES -- HISTORY -- 19TH CENTURY

Food in the Civil War era **641.597**

FOOD IN LITERATURE

Stoeger, M. B. Food lit **016.6**

Food in the Civil War era. **641.597**

FOOD INDUSTRY

Bittman, M. Food matters **613.2**

Bloom, J. American wasteland **363.7**

Cowen, T. An economist gets lunch **394.1**

Faruqi, S. Project Animal Farm **338.1**

Foer, J. S. Eating animals **641.3**

Genoways, T. The chain **338.7**

Hesterman, O. B. Fair food **338.1**

Hewitt, B. The town that food saved **338.1**

Lappé, A. Diet for a hot planet **641**

McWilliams, J. E. Just food **394.1**

Nesheim, M. Why calories count **613.2**

Schlosser, E. Fast food nation **394.1**

Shetreat-Klein, M. The Dirt Cure **618.92**

Spurlock, M. Don't eat this book **614.5**

Stuart, T. Waste **363.8**

Wilson, B. Swindled **363.1**

FOOD INDUSTRY -- UNITED STATES

Bittman, M. A bone to pick **338.1**

Kurlansky, M. Birdseye **338.7**

McMillan, T. The American way of eating **338.4**

Moss, M. Salt, sugar, fat **613.2**

Pollan, M. Cooked **641.5**

Schatzker, M. The Dorito effect **641.3**

FOOD INDUSTRY EXECUTIVES

Brenner, J. G. The emperors of chocolate **338.7**

Cohen, R. Sweet and low **920**

FOOD INSPECTION *See* Food adulteration and inspection

The **food** lab. López-Alt, J. K. **664**

Food lit. Stoeger, M. B. **016.6**

The **food** lover's cleanse. Dickerman, S. **641.5**

The **Food** Lover's Guide to Paris. **914.4**

Food matters. Bittman, M. **613.2**

The **food** matters cookbook. Bittman, M. **641.3**

The **food** of a younger land. **394.1**

FOOD OF ANIMAL ORIGIN

Rinella, S. Meat eater **799.29**

FOOD OF ANIMAL ORIGIN

See also Food

The **food** of Morocco. **641.59**

The **food** of Portugal. Anderson, J. **641.5**

The **food** of Spain. Roden, C. **641.5**

The **food** of Taiwan. Erway, C. **641.595**

The **food** of Vietnam. Nguyen, L. **641.59**

FOOD PLANTS *See* Edible plants

Food plants of the world. Van Wyk **581.6**

FOOD POISONING

See also Poisons and poisoning

FOOD PORTIONS

Schatzker, M. The Dorito effect **641.3**

FOOD PREFERENCES

First bite **641.01**

FOOD PREFERENCES -- ECONOMIC ASPECTS

Cowen, T. An economist gets lunch **394.1**

FOOD PREPARATION *See* Cooking; Food industry

FOOD PREPARATION INDUSTRY *See* Food industry

FOOD PROCESSING PLANTS -- UNITED STATES

Genoways, T. The chain **338.7**

FOOD RELIEF

Astyk, S. A nation of farmers **338.1**

FOOD RELIEF

See also Charities; Disaster relief; Public welfare; Unemployed

Food security. Peacock, K. W. **338.1**
FOOD SECURITY
Ackerman-Leist, P. Rebuilding the foodshed **338.1**
Peacock, K. W. Food security **338.1**
FOOD SECURITY -- HISTORY -- 20TH CENTURY
Collingham, L. The taste of war **940.53**
FOOD SERVICE
See also Food industry; Service industries
FOOD STAMPS
See also Food relief
FOOD SUBSTITUTES -- POPULAR WORKS
Olmsted, L. Real food/fake food **641.3**
FOOD SUPPLEMENTS *See* Dietary supplements
FOOD SUPPLY
Astyk, S. A nation of farmers **338.1**
Bloom, J. American wasteland **363.7**
Diamond, J. M. Guns, germs, and steel **303.4**
Dikötter, F. Mao's great famine **951.05**
Hesterman, O. B. Fair food **338.1**
Hewitt, B. The town that food saved **338.1**
Kotler, S. Abundance **303.48**
Lappé, A. Diet for a hot planet **641**
Peacock, K. W. Food security **338.1**
FOOD SUPPLY -- CHINA
Dikötter, F. Mao's great famine **951.05**
FOOD SUPPLY -- HISTORY -- 20TH CENTURY
Collingham, L. The taste of war **940.53**
FOOD SUPPLY -- UNITED STATES
McMillan, T. The American way of eating **338.4**
Pollan, M. The omnivore's dilemma **394.1**
FOOD SUPPLY -- UNITED STATES -- HISTORY -- 20TH CENTURY
Coe, A. A square meal **641.5**
FOOD TOURISM -- JAPAN
Goulding, M. Rice, noodle, fish **394.12**
FOOD TRADE *See* Food industry
FOOD WASTE -- PREVENTION
Vinton, S. B. Eat it up! **641.5**
FOOD WRITERS -- GERMANY -- BIOGRAPHY
Mosler, L. Driving hungry **92**
FOOD WRITERS -- UNITED STATES -- BIOGRAPHY
Mosler, L. Driving hungry **92**
Von Bremzen, A. Mastering the art of Soviet cooking **641.59**
Wizenberg, M. Delancey **647.95**
FOOD WRITING
Best food writing 2014 **641.3**
Christensen, K. How to cook a moose **641.597**
Consider the fork **643**
Will write for food **808**
FOOD, CANNED *See* Canning and preserving
FOOD, COST OF *See* Cost and standard of living
Food, inc. Pringle, P. **363.1**
Food52 baking. **641.81**

Food52 genius recipes. Miglore, K. **641.5**
Fool for love, and other plays. Shepard, S. **812**
Fool me twice. Otto, S. **303.4**
Fool's gold. Tett, G. **332.6**
Fool's paradise. Gaines, S. S. **975.9**
Fooling Houdini. Stone, A. **793.8**
Fooling ourselves. Triandis, H. C. **155.2**
Foolproof preserving. **641.4**
FOOLS AND JESTERS
See also Comedians; Courts and courtiers; Entertainers
Foose, Martha Hall
Screen doors and sweet tea **641.5**
A southerly course **641.59**
FOOT
See also Anatomy
FOOTBALL
Anderson, L. Carlisle vs. Army **796.332**
Bissinger, H. G. Friday night lights **796.332**
Cosell, G. The games that changed the game **796.332**
Dawidoff, N. Collision Low Crossers **796.3**
Feinstein, J. Next man up **796.332**
Football's greatest stars **796.332**
St. John, W. Rammer jammer yellow hammer **796.332**
FOOTBALL
See also Ball games; Sports
FOOTBALL -- BIOGRAPHY
Harris, D. The genius **92**
Lewis, M. The blind side **92**
Peter, J. Hero of the underground **92**
Sielski, M. Fading echoes **92**
FOOTBALL -- COACHING
Gwynne, S. C. The Perfect Pass **796.332**
Walsh, B. The score takes care of itself **658.4**
FOOTBALL -- COACHING
See also Coaching (Athletics)
FOOTBALL -- CORRUPT PRACTICES -- UNITED STATES
Benedict, J. The System **796.332**
FOOTBALL -- HISTORY
Roberts, D. Tribal **796.332**
Ross, C. K. Mavericks, money, and men **796.332**
FOOTBALL -- UNITED STATES
Dawidoff, N. Collision Low Crossers **796.3**
FOOTBALL -- UNITED STATES -- HISTORY
Gwynne, S. C. The Perfect Pass **796.332**
Myers, G. Brady vs Manning **92**
Roberts, D. Tribal **796.332**
FOOTBALL COACHES
Gwynne, S. C. The Perfect Pass **796.332**
Parcells, B. Parcells **796.332**
Ribowsky, M. The last cowboy **92**
FOOTBALL COACHES -- UNITED STATES -- BIOGRAPHY

Burke, M. Saban   796.332
Maraniss, D. When pride still mattered: a life of
    Vince Lombardi   92
Parcells, B. Parcells   796.332
Ribowsky, M. The last cowboy   92
Robinson, R. Rockne of Notre Dame   92
FOOTBALL COMMISSIONERS -- UNITED
    STATES -- BIOGRAPHY
Izenberg, J. Rozelle   92
FOOTBALL INJURIES -- UNITED STATES
Fainaru, S. League of Denial   617.1
FOOTBALL PLAYERS
Curtis, B. Fields of Battle   940.54
Dent, J. Courage beyond the game   796.332
Football's greatest stars   796.332
Gates, H. L. Thirteen ways of looking at a black
    man   920.71
Lewis, M. The blind side   92
Peter, J. Hero of the underground   92
Robeson, P. Here I stand   92
Robeson, P. The undiscovered Paul Robeson   92
Toobin, J. The run of his life   345.73
FOOTBALL PLAYERS -- UNITED STATES --
    BIOGRAPHY
Anderson, L. The Mannings   796.332
Benedict, J. QB   92
Dunnavant, K. Montana   92
Edmundson, M. Why football matters   92
Myers, G. Brady vs Manning   92
Football's greatest stars.   796.332
Foote, Horton, 1916-2009
Collected plays   812
                    About
Foote, H. Beginnings   812
Foote, Shelby
The Civil War   973.7
The Civil War, a narrative   973.7
Stars in their courses   973.7
Footnotes in Gaza. Sacco, J.   956.04
FOOTWEAR See Shoes
For a song and one hundred songs. Liao Yiwu   365
For all the tea in China. Rose, S.   382
For cause and comrades. McPherson, J. M.   973.7
For cod and country. Seaver, B.   641.6
--For dummies [series]
Hoving, T. Art for dummies   709
For goodness sex. Vernacchio, A.   613.9
For liberty and glory. Gaines, J. R.   92
For love of insects. Eisner, T.   595.7
For Tamara. Lang, S.   C
For the Glory. Hamilton, D.   92
For the glory of God. Stark, R.   201
For the love of a dog. McConnell, P.   636.7
For the love of animals. Shevelow, K.   179
For the love of physics. Goldstein, W.   92
For the prevention of cruelty. Beers, D. L.   179

For the soul of France. Brown, F.   944.081
FORAGE PLANTS
    See also Economic botany; Feeds; Plants
Forbes, Bruce David
Christmas   394.26
Forbes, Peter
Dazzled and deceived   578.4
Forbush, Edward Howe, 1858-1929
                    About
White, E. B. Essays of E.B. White   814
FORCE AND ENERGY
Bodanis, D. E   530.1
Bodanis, D. Electric universe   537
A force of nature. Reeves, R.   92
FORCED INDOCTRINATION See Brainwashing
FORCED LABOR
    See also Crimes against humanity; Labor
FORCED MIGRATION
    See also Internal migration
FORCED STERILIZATION
Lombardo, P. A. Three generations, no imbe-
    ciles   344
Forces of habit. Courtwright, D. T.   362.29
Forche, Carolyn
Blue hour   811
Forcing the spring. Becker, J.   346.73
FORD AUTOMOBILE
    See also Automobiles
FORD MOTOR CO.
Baime, A. J. Go like hell   796.72
Brinkley, D. Wheels for the world   338.7
Grandin, G. Fordlandia   307.7
Vlasic, B. Once upon a car   338.4
Ford, Charlotte
Crash course in reference   025.5
Ford, Gerald R., 1913-2006
                    About
Woodward, B. Shadow   973.92
Ford, Henry, 1863-1947
                    About
Baldwin, N. Henry Ford and the Jews   305
Brinkley, D. Wheels for the world   338.7
Grandin, G. Fordlandia   307.7
Watts, S. The people's tycoon   92
Ford, Katie
Blood lyrics   811
Ford, Kenneth W.
101 quantum questions   530.1
Ford, Lacy K.
Deliver us from evil   973.7
Ford, Lynne E.
(ed) Encyclopedia of women and American poli-
    tics   973
Ford, Mark
(ed) Ashbery, J. Collected poems 1956-1987   811
Ford, Paul F.

Companion to Narnia **823**

Ford, Richard T.

Rights gone wrong **342**

Fordlandia. Grandin, G. **307.7**

FORDLANDIA PLANTATION (BRAZIL)

Grandin, G. Fordlandia **307.7**

FORECASTING

Cullen, H. The weather of the future **551.63**

Gore, A. The future **303.4**

Jacques, M. When China rules the world **327**

Jenkins, P. The new faces of Christianity **270**

Kaku, M. Physics of the future **303.49**

Klosterman, C. But What If We're Wrong? **909.83**

Milo, P. Your flying car awaits **909.82**

Popular mechanics magazine. The wonderful future that never was **609**

Smith, L. C. The world in 2050 **304.2**

Taleb, N. N. The black swan **003**

This will change everything **501**

FORECASTING -- HISTORY

Silver, N. The signal and the noise **519.5**

FORECASTING -- METHODOLOGY

Silver, N. The signal and the noise **519.5**

FORECASTS See Forecasting

FORECLOSURE

Elias, S. The foreclosure survival guide **346**

The **foreclosure** survival guide. Elias, S. **346**

FOREIGN AFFAIRS See International relations

FOREIGN AID

Banerjee, A. V. Poor economics **339.4**

FOREIGN AID

See also Economic policy; International cooperation; International economic relations

FOREIGN AID PROGRAM See Foreign aid; Military assistance; Technical assistance

FOREIGN ASSISTANCE See Foreign aid

FOREIGN AUTOMOBILES

See also Automobiles

Foreign babes in Beijing. DeWoskin, R. **951**

FOREIGN COMMERCE See International trade

FOREIGN CORRESPONDENTS -- UNITED STATES -- BIOGRAPHY

Engel, R. And then all hell broke loose **956.05**

FOREIGN CORRESPONDENTS -- YEMEN (REPUBLIC) -- BIOGRAPHY

Kasinof, L. Don't be afraid of the bullets **953.305**

FOREIGN ECONOMIC RELATIONS See International economic relations

FOREIGN ECONOMIC RELATIONS -- UNITED STATES See United States -- Foreign economic relations

FOREIGN EXCHANGE

Rickards, J. Currency wars **332.4**

FOREIGN EXCHANGE

See also Banks and banking; Exchange; Finance; Money

FOREIGN INVESTMENTS

See also Investments; Multinational corporations

FOREIGN LANGUAGE PHRASES See English language -- Foreign words and phrases; Modern languages -- Conversation and phrase books

FOREIGN PESTS See Nonindigenous pests

FOREIGN POLICY See International relations

Foreign policy begins at home. Haass, R. N. **327.73**

FOREIGN POPULATION See Immigrants; Immigration and emigration; Minorities; Noncitizens; Population

FOREIGN RELATIONS See International relations

FOREIGN STUDENTS

Beyond the asterisk **378.1**

Ripley, A. The smartest kids in the world **370.9**

FOREIGN STUDENTS

See also Students

FOREIGN STUDENTS -- FRANCE

Kaplan, A. Dreaming in French **944**

FOREIGN STUDY

See also Education

FOREIGN TRADE See International trade

FOREIGNERS See Immigrants; Noncitizens

Foreman, Amanda

Georgiana, Duchess of Devonshire **941.07**

A world on fire **973.7**

Foreman, Tom

About

Foreman, T. My year of running dangerously **92**

FORENSIC ANTHROPOLOGY

Bass, W. M. Death's acre **614**

Maples, W. R. Dead men do tell tales **614**

Massie, R. K. The Romanovs **947.08**

Pringle, H. A. The mummy congress **393**

FORENSIC ANTHROPOLOGY

See also Anthropology; Forensic sciences

FORENSIC ARCHAEOLOGY -- JAPAN -- HIROSHIMA-SHI

Pellegrino, C. To hell and back **940.54**

FORENSIC MEDICINE See Medical jurisprudence

FORENSIC PATHOLOGISTS -- NEW YORK (STATE) -- NEW YORK -- BIOGRAPHY

Mitchell, T. J. Working stiff **614**

FORENSIC PATHOLOGY -- LOUISIANA -- NEW ORLEANS -- CASE STUDIES

Fink, S. Five days at memorial **362.11**

FORENSIC SCIENCE See Forensic sciences

FORENSIC SCIENCES

Bell, S. Encyclopedia of forensic science **363.2**

Blum, D. The poisoner's handbook **614**

Colmez, C. Math on trial **345**

Englert, R. Blood secrets **363.2**

Hempel, S. The inheritor's powder **364.152**

McCrery, N. Silent witnesses **363.25**
Mitchell, T. J. Working stiff **614**
Neme, L. A. Animal investigators **363.2**
Paradis, C. The measure of madness **364.3**
Starr, D. The killer of little shepherds **364.152**
Wagner, E. J. The science of Sherlock Holmes **363.2**
FORENSIC SCIENCES
See also Science
FORENSIC SCIENCES -- CASE STUDIES
McCrery, N. Silent witnesses **363.25**
FORENSIC SCIENCES -- ENCYCLOPEDIAS
Bell, S. Encyclopedia of forensic science **363.2**
FORENSIC SCIENCES -- HISTORY
Blum, D. The poisoner's handbook **614**
McCrery, N. Silent witnesses **363.25**
Starr, D. The killer of little shepherds **364.152**
Wagner, E. J. The science of Sherlock Holmes **363.2**
FORENSIC STATISTICS
Colmez, C. Math on trial **345**
FORENSIC TOXICOLOGY
Blum, D. The poisoner's handbook **614**
Hempel, S. The inheritor's powder **364.152**
FOREST ANIMALS
See also Animals
FOREST CONSERVATION
Egan, T. The big burn **973.91**
FOREST CONSERVATION
See also Conservation of natural resources
FOREST ECOLOGY
See also Ecology
FOREST FIRES
Brown, D. Under a flaming sky **634.9**
Connors, P. Fire season **634.9**
Egan, T. The big burn **973.91**
MacLean, N. Young men & fire **634.9**
FOREST FIRES
See also Fires
FOREST FIRES -- UNITED STATES -- HISTORY
Egan, T. The big burn **973.91**
FOREST FIRES -- YELLOWSTONE NATIONAL PARK
Henry, J. The year Yellowstone burned **634.9**
FOREST INFLUENCES
See also Climate; Water supply
FOREST PLANTS
Darke, R. The American woodland garden **635.9**
The forest unseen. Haskell, D. G. **577.3**
Foresta, Merry A.
Irving Penn **770**
FORESTERS
Egan, T. The big burn **973.91**
Miller, C. Gifford Pinchot and the making of modern environmentalism **333.7**
FORESTRY See Forests and forestry
FORESTS AND FORESTRY

Wohlleben, P. The Hidden Life of Trees **582.16**
FORESTS AND FORESTRY
See also Agriculture; Natural resources
FORESTS AND FORESTRY -- TENNESSEE
Haskell, D. G. The forest unseen **577.3**
Forever blue. D'Antonio, M. **92**
Forever free. Foner, E. **973.8**
The forever war. Filkins, D. **956.7**
Forgan, James W.
(jt. auth) Richey, M. A. The impulsive, disorganized child **649**
FORGERS
Worrall, S. The poet and the murderer **364.15**
FORGERY
Burleigh, N. Unholy business **933**
Worrall, S. The poet and the murderer **364.15**
FORGERY
See also Crime; Fraud; Impostors and imposture
FORGIVENESS
Bettencourt, M. F. Triumph of the heart **155.9**
The book of forgiving **179**
Kushner, H. S. How good do we have to be? **296.7**
Wiesenthal, S. The sunflower **179.7**
FORGIVENESS
See also Virtue
FORGIVENESS -- RELIGIOUS ASPECTS -- CHRISTIANITY
Kraybill, D. B. Amish grace **364.152**
Forgotten. Hervieux, L. **940.54**
Forgotten founder, drunken prophet. Kauffman, B. **92**
The forgotten man. **973.91**
A forgotten sisterhood. McCluskey, A. T. **370.922**
Forked. Jayaraman, S. **331.2**
Forkish, Ken
The elements of pizza **641.82**
Flour water salt yeast **641.81**
FORMAL GARDENS See Gardens
Former people. Smith, D. **305.5**
FORMOSA See Taiwan
Forney, Kristine
The enjoyment of music **780**
Forni, Pier Massimo
The civility solution **395**
Forrest, Edwin, 1806-1872
About
Cliff, N. The Shakespeare riots **974.4**
Forrest, Emma
About
Forrest, E. Your voice in my head **362.196**
Forrester, James
The Heart Healers **616.1**
Forshaw, Jeff
(jt. auth) Cox, B. The quantum universe **530.12**
Forster, E. M. (Edward Morgan), 1879-1970

About

Kermode, F. Concerning E.M. Forster   **823**

Moffat, W. A great unrecorded history   **92**

FORSYTH COUNTY (GA.) -- RACE RELATIONS -- HISTORY

Phillips, P. Blood at the root   **305.8**

Forsyth, Mark

The etymologicon   **422**

A **fort** of nine towers. Omar, Q. A.   **958.104**

FORT SUMTER (CHARLESTON, S.C.)

Detzer, D. Allegiance   **973.7**

FORT TICONDEROGA (N.Y.) -- CAPTURE, 1775

Phillips, K. 1775   **973.3**

Fort, Charles, 1874-1932

About

Steinmeyer, J. Charles Fort   **92**

Forte, Eric

(ed) The basic business library   **016**

Forte, Sara

The sprouted kitchen   **641.3**

The sprouted kitchen bowl and spoon   **641.3**

Fortey, Richard

Earth   **551.7**

Fossils   **560**

Horseshoe crabs and velvet worms   **595**

Life   **576.8**

Trilobite!   **560**

FORTIFICATION

See also Military art and science

FORTIFICATION -- ENGLAND -- LONDON -- HISTORY

Jones, N. Tower   **942.1**

Fortnow, Lance

The golden ticket   **511.3**

Fortress Europe. Carr, M.   **363.28**

Fortunate son. Fogerty, J.   **92**

Fortunate sons. Leibovitz, L.   **951.05**

Fortunato, Alfred

Rabiner, S. Thinking like your editor   **808**

FORTUNE *See* Fate and fatalism; Probabilities; Success

FORTUNE TELLING

See also Amusements; Divination

Fortune's Fool. Alford, T.   **92**

Fortune, Brandon Brame

Elaine de kooning   **759.13**

Fortune, Robert, 1813-1880

About

Rose, S. For all the tea in China   **382**

FORTUNES *See* Income; Wealth

The **fortunes** of Africa. Meredith, M.   **960**

Fortuny, Mariano, 1871-1949

About

Byatt, A. S. Peacock & vine   **700.92**

Forty-one false starts. Malcolm, J.   **808.02**

Forty-seven days. Yockelson, M. A.   **940.4**

FORUMS (DISCUSSIONS) *See* Discussion groups

Forward. Wambach, A.   **92**

Fosdick, Sarah Graves, 1825-1871

About

Brown, D. The indifferent stars above   **92**

Foss, Ben

The dyslexia empowerment plan   **618.92**

Fosse. Wasson, S.   **92**

Fosse, Bob, 1927-1987

About

Wasson, S. Fosse   **92**

Fossey, Dian

Gorillas in the mist   **599.88**

FOSSIL HOMINIDS

Johanson, D. C. From Lucy to language   **599.93**

Pyne, L. Seven skeletons   **569.9**

Sarmiento, E. The last human   **569.9**

Swisher, C. C. Java Man   **599.93**

Switek, B. Written in stone   **576.8**

Walker, A. The wisdom of the bones   **599.93**

FOSSIL HOMINIDS

See also Archeology; Fossils

FOSSIL MAMMALS

Johanson, D. C. Lucy: the beginnings of humankind   **599.93**

The **fossil** trail. Tattersall, I.   **599.93**

Fossils. Fortey, R. A.   **560**

FOSSILS

Coenraads, R. R. Rocks and fossils   **552**

Dinosaurs the grand tour   **567.9**

Fortey, R. A. Fossils   **560**

Fortey, R. A. Trilobite!   **560**

Larson, P. L. Rex appeal   **567.9**

Poinar, G. O. The quest for life in amber   **560**

Prothero, D. R. The story of life in 25 fossils   **560**

Rea, T. Bone wars   **560**

Sampson, S. D. Dinosaur odyssey   **567.9**

Switek, B. Written in stone   **576.8**

Tattersall, I. The fossil trail   **599.93**

Taylor, P. D. A history of life in 100 fossils   **560**

Thompson, I. The Audubon Society field guide to North American fossils   **560**

Travels with the fossil hunters   **560**

FOSSILS

See also Biology; Natural history; Stratigraphic geology

FOSSILS -- PICTORIAL WORKS

Taylor, P. D. A history of life in 100 fossils   **560**

FOSTER CHILDREN

Calcaterra, R. Etched in Sand   **92**

DeGarmo, J. The foster parenting manual   **306.874**

FOSTER CHILDREN

See also Children

FOSTER GRANDPARENTS

See also Grandparents; Volunteer work

FOSTER HOME CARE
Beam, C. To the end of June **362.73**
Bernstein, N. The lost children of Wilder **362.73**
DeGarmo, J. The foster parenting manual **306.874**
FOSTER HOME CARE
See also Child welfare
FOSTER HOME CARE -- UNITED STATES
Beam, C. To the end of June **362.73**
The **foster** parenting manual. DeGarmo, J. **306.874**
FOSTER PARENTS
DeGarmo, J. The foster parenting manual **306.874**
Foster, Charles
Being a Beast **591.5**
Foster, David K.
Angier, B. Field guide to edible wild plants **581.6**
Foster, Jeremy
(jt. auth) Kuhn, C. Buzzed **615.7**
Foster, Joanne
Beyond intelligence **649**
Foster, Lynn V.
A brief history of Mexico **972**
Foster, R. F.
Foster, R. F. W.B. Yeats: a life **821**
W.B. Yeats: a life **821**
Foster, Rick
How we choose to be happy **158**
Foster, Russell G.
Rhythms of life **571.7**
Foster, Stephen Collins, 1826-1864
About
Emerson, K. Doo-dah!: Stephen Foster and the rise
of American popular culture **92**
Foster, Steven
Peterson field guide to medicinal plants and herbs
of eastern and central North America **581.6**
Fothergill, Alastair
Planet Earth **508**
FOTONOVELAS
See also Comic books, strips, etc.
Foucault, Michel, 1926-1984
About
Said, E. W. Reflections on exile and other es-
says **814**
Foulds, Adam
The broken word **821**
The **Foundation** directory. **061**
Foundation for the National Archives
Center for the National Archives Experience Dis-
covering the Civil War **973.7**
FOUNDATION OFFICIALS
Gregorian, V. The road to home **92**
Halberstam, D. The best and the brightest **973.922**
FOUNDATIONS
See also Architecture -- Details; Buildings;
Structural engineering
The **founder's** dilemmas. Wasserman, N. **658.1**

The **founders** and finance. McCraw, T. K. **330.973**
Founders' son. Brookhiser, R. **92**
Founders' son. **92**
FOUNDING
See also Manufacturing processes; Metalwork
Founding brothers. Ellis, J. J. **973.4**
Founding faith. Waldman, S. **342**
Founding father: rediscovering George Washington.
Brookhiser, R. **92**
**FOUNDING FATHERS OF THE UNITED
STATES**
Broadwater, J. James Madison **92**
Ellis, J. J. American creation **973.3**
Ellis, J. J. The Quartet **973.3**
Ellis, J. J. Revolutionary summer **973.3**
Raphael, R. Constitutional myths **342.73**
Raphael, R. Mr. president **352.23**
Sehat, D. The Jefferson rule **306.2**
Signer, M. Becoming Madison **92**
Stewart, D. O. Madison's Gift **92**
**FOUNDING FATHERS OF THE UNITED
STATES**
See also Statesmen -- United States
**FOUNDING FATHERS OF THE UNITED
STATES -- RELIGIOUS LIFE**
Waldman, S. Founding faith **342**
Founding gardeners. Wulf, A. **712**
Founding mothers. Roberts, C. **920**
Foung, Jessica Goldman
Sodium girls limitless low-salt cookbook **641.5**
The **four** books on architecture. Palladio, A. **720**
Four centuries of quilts. Baumgarten, L. **746.46**
Four fish. Greenberg, P. **333.95**
Four kings. Kimball, G. **920**
The **four** pillars of investing. Bernstein, W. **332.6**
Four tragedies, and Octavia. Seneca, L. A. **882**
Fourier, Jean-Baptiste-Joseph, baron, 1768-1830
About
Bell, E. T. Men of mathematics **920**
Fourquet, Emile
About
Starr, D. The killer of little shepherds **364.152**
The **fourteenth** day. Coleman, D. G. **73.922**
FOURTH DIMENSION
Nadis, S. The shape of inner space **530.1**
FOURTH DIMENSION
See also Mathematics
The **fourth** dimension of a poem. Abrams, M.
H. **808.1**
FOURTH OF JULY
See also Holidays; United States -- History
-- 1775-1783, Revolution
The **fourth** part of the world. Lester, T. **912**
Fouts, Roger
Next of kin **156**
Fowler, Brenda

Iceman **937**

Fowler, H. W. (Henry Watson), 1858-1933
A dictionary of modern English usage **428**

Fowler, Loretta
The Columbia guide to American Indians of the Great Plains **970.004**

Fowler, Sarah
(jt. auth) Ebert, D. A. A pocket guide to sharks of the world **597.3**

Fowler, Sarah L.
Compagno, L. J. V. Sharks of the world **597**

Fowler, William M.
American crisis **973.3**
Empires at war **973.2**

Fox, Everett
Bible/O.T./Pentateuch The five books of Moses **222**

Fox, Gustavus Vasa, 1821-1883
About
Symonds, C. L. Lincoln and his admirals **92**

Fox, James
Five sisters **975.5**
Richards, K. Life **92**

Fox, Justin
The myth of the rational market **332.6**

Fox, Margalit
The Riddle of the Labyrinth **487**

Fox, MeiMei
(jt. auth) Ping Fu Bend, not break **92**

Fox, Michael J.
About
Fox, M. J. Always looking up **92**
Fox, M. J. Lucky man **92**

Fox, Mindy
DeMasco, K. The craft of baking **641.8**

Fox, Richard T.
(jt. auth) Clark, C. A. Read on...sports **016**

Fox, William Price
Satchel Paige's America **92**

Foxfire 40th anniversary book. **975.8**

Foxman, Abraham H., 1940-
Viral hate **364.15**

The **frackers.** Zuckerman, G. **338.2**

FRACKING (ENGINEERING) *See* Hydraulic fracturing

FRACTAL GEOMETRY *See* Fractals

FRACTALS
Ball, P. Patterns in nature **500.2**

Fragrant. Aftel, M. **612.8**

FRAGRANT GARDENS
Keville, K. The aromatherapy garden **635.9**

FRAGRANT GARDENS
See also Gardens

Fraioli, James O.
The Canon Cocktail Book **641**
Culinary birds **641.6**

Fraistat, Neil
(ed) Shelley's poetry and prose **821**

FRAMING OF PICTURES *See* Picture frames and framing

Frammolino, Ralph
Chasing Aphrodite **930**

Frampton, Saul
When I am playing with my cat, how do I know she is not playing with me? **844**

France. **914.4**

FRANCE
Goulson, D. A Buzz in the Meadow **638**

FRANCE -- ARMÉE
Philpott, W. Three armies on the Somme **940.4**

FRANCE -- COLONIES
Logevall, F. Embers of War **959.704**

FRANCE -- DESCRIPTION AND TRAVEL
Baxter, J. The perfect meal **641.59**
Carhart, T. Finding Fontainebleau **944.36**
France **914.4**

FRANCE -- FOREIGN RELATIONS -- 1945-
Evans, M. Algeria **965**

FRANCE -- FOREIGN RELATIONS -- GREAT BRITAIN
Barr, J. A line in the sand **956**
Green, D. The Hundred Years War **944**

FRANCE -- FOREIGN RELATIONS -- UNITED STATES
Khan, Y. S. Enlightening the world **974.7**

FRANCE -- HISTORY
Horne, A. La belle France **944**

FRANCE -- HISTORY -- 1328-1589, HOUSE OF VALOIS
Goldstone, N. The rival queens **944**
Green, D. The Hundred Years War **944**

FRANCE -- HISTORY -- 1589-1789, BOURBONS
Fiennes, R. Agincourt **944**

FRANCE -- HISTORY -- 1789-1799, REVOLUTION
McPhee, P. Liberty or death **944.04**

FRANCE -- HISTORY -- 1789-1799, REVOLUTION
See also Revolutions

FRANCE -- HISTORY -- 1799-1815
Gueniffey, P. Bonaparte **92**

FRANCE -- HISTORY -- 1815-1914
Read, P. P. The Dreyfus affair **944.081**

FRANCE -- HISTORY -- 1940-1945, GERMAN OCCUPATION
King, D. Death in the city of light

FRANCE -- HISTORY -- CHARLES VII, 1422-1461
Castor, H. Joan of Arc **92**
Gordon, M. Joan of Arc **944**

FRANCE -- HISTORY -- CONSULATE AND FIRST EMPIRE, 1799-1815

Esdaile, C. J. Napoleon's wars   **940.2**
Gueniffey, P. Bonaparte   **92**
Schom, A. Napoleon Bonaparte   **92**
**FRANCE -- HISTORY -- GERMAN OCCUPA-
TION, 1940-1945**
Beevor, A. D-day   **940.54**
Kershaw, A. Avenue of spies   **940.53**
**FRANCE -- HISTORY -- GERMAN OCCUPA-
TION, 1940-1945 -- BIOGRAPHY**
Kaiser, C. The cost of courage   **92**
**FRANCE -- HISTORY -- REVOLUTION, 1789-
1799**
Gaines, J. R. For liberty and glory   **92**
McPhee, P. Liberty or death   **944.04**
McPhee, P. Robespierre   **92**
**FRANCE -- HISTORY -- THIRD REPUBLIC,
1870-1940**
Brown, F. For the soul of France   **944.081**
Read, P. P. The Dreyfus affair   **944.081**
FRANCE -- HISTORY, MILITARY -- 1328-1589
Green, D. The Hundred Years War   **944**
FRANCE -- HISTORY, MILITARY -- 1789-1815
Barbero, A. The Battle   **940.2**
The Black Count   **944.04**
**FRANCE -- INTELLECTUAL LIFE -- 20TH
CENTURY**
Carroll, S. B. Brave genius   **920**
Kaplan, A. The collaborator: the trial & execution
of Robert Brasillach   **848**
FRANCE -- KINGS AND RULERS
Johnson, P. Napoleon   **944.05**
Schom, A. Napoleon Bonaparte   **92**
FRANCE -- POLITICS AND GOVERNMENT
Chirac, J. My life in politics   **944.084**
**FRANCE -- POLITICS AND GOVERNMENT --
1789-1799**
McPhee, P. Robespierre   **92**
**FRANCE -- POLITICS AND GOVERNMENT --
1815-1914**
Bredin The affair   **944.081**
Derfler, L. The Dreyfus affair   **944.081**
FRANCE -- SOCIAL CONDITIONS
Sante, L. The other Paris   **944**
FRANCE -- SOCIAL LIFE AND CUSTOMS
DeJean, J. E. The essence of style   **391**
Mayle, P. French lessons   **394.1**
Moorehead, C. Dancing to the precipice: Lucie de
la Tour du Pin and the French Revolution   **92**
Riding, A. And the show went on   **944**
Sciolino, E. La seduction   **302.3**
**FRANCE --HISTORY --GERMAN OCCUPA-
TION, 1940-1945.**
Moorehead, C. A train in winter
France, John
Perilous glory   **355**
France, Peter

(ed) The Oxford guide to literature in English
translation   **820**
FRANCE. ARMÉE -- BIOGRAPHY
Auricchio, L. The marquis   **92**
The Black Count   **944.04**
Frances, Allen
Saving Normal   **616.89**
FRANCHISE *See* Citizenship; Elections; Suffrage
FRANCHISES (RETAIL TRADE)
Bond's Top 100 Franchises, 2015   **381**
FRANCHISES (RETAIL TRADE)
See also Retail trade
FRANCHISING *See* Franchises (Retail trade)
Francis Bacon in Your Blood. Peppiatt, M.   **759.2**
Francis Crick. Ridley, M.   **92**
Francis, a new world pope. Cool, M.   **92**
Francis, Gavin
Adventures in human being   **612**
Francis, of Assisi, Saint, 1182-1226
        About
The little flowers of St. Francis of Assisi   **242**
Martin, V. Salvation: scenes from the life of St.
Francis   **92**
Francis, Pope, 1936-
The church of mercy   **282**
Walking with Jesus   **282**
Wills, G. The Future of the Catholic Church With
Pope Francis   **282**
        About
Cool, M. Francis, a new world pope   **92**
Pope Francis among the wolves   **282**
Francis, Richard C.
Domesticated   **636**
Epigenetics   **572.8**
FRANCISCANS
Russell, B. A history of Western philosophy   **109**
FRANCISCANS
See also Monasticism and religious orders
Francisco, Jane
(ed) Burgers   **641.66**
Frank. Kaplan, J.   **92**
Frank. Frank, B.   **92**
Frank family
        About
Gies, M. Anne Frank remembered   **92**
Frank Lloyd Wright. Secrest, M.   **92**
Frank Lloyd Wright. Huxtable, A. L.   **92**
The **Frank** Lloyd Wright companion. Storrer, W.
A.   **720.9**
Frank, Adam
About time   **523.1**
The constant fire   **201**
Frank, Anne, 1929-1945
Barnouw, D. The diary of Anne Frank: the critical
edition   **92**
The diary of a young girl: the definitive edition   **92**

About

Anne Frank **92**

Barnouw, D. The diary of Anne Frank: the critical
edition **92**

Frank, A. The diary of a young girl: the definitive
edition **92**

Jacobson, S. Anne Frank **92**

Ozick, C. Quarrel & quandary **814**

Prose, F. Anne Frank **839.3**

Frank, Barney, 1940-

About

Frank, B. Frank **92**

Frank, Jeffrey

Ike and Dick **973.921**

Frank, Joseph

Dostoevsky **92**

Frank, Joshua

The people's pension **368.4**

Frank, Katherine

Crusoe **823**

Frank, Otto

Frank, A. The diary of a young girl: the definitive
edition **92**

Frank, Richard B.

Downfall **940.54**

MacArthur **92**

Frank, Robert, 1924-

The Americans **779.997**

Frank, Thomas

What's the matter with Kansas? **978.1**

Frankel, Felice

On the surface of things **530.4**

Frankel, Haskel

Hagen, U. Respect for acting **792**

Frankenstein's cat. Anthes, E. **616.02**

Frankenstein's monster (Fictional character)

About

Montillo, R. The lady and her monsters **823**

Frankfurter, Felix, 1882-1965

About

Feldman, N. Scorpions **920**

**FRANKFURTERS -- NEW YORK (STATE) --
HISTORY**

Handwerker, L. Famous Nathan **92**

FRANKINCENSE

Aftel, M. Fragrant **612.8**

Frankl, Viktor E.

About

Frankl, V. E. Man's search for meaning **92**

Franklin and Lucy. Persico, J. E. **920**

Franklin barbecue. Mackay, J. **641.7**

Franklin D. Roosevelt and the New Deal, 1932-
1940. Leuchtenburg, W. E. **973.917**

Franklin, Aaron

(jt. auth) Mackay, J. Franklin barbecue **641.7**

Franklin, Aretha

About

Ritz, D. Respect **92**

Franklin, Benjamin, 1706-1790

Autobiography, Poor Richard, and later writings **818**

About

Cohen, I. B. Science and the founding fathers **973.3**

Ellis, J. J. Founding brothers **973.4**

Franklin, B. The autobiography of Benjamin
Franklin **92**

Isaacson, W. Benjamin Franklin **92**

Lepore, J. Book of ages **92**

Pasles, P. C. Benjamin Franklin's numbers **510**

Franklin, John Hope, 1915-2009

From slavery to freedom **305.8**

In search of the promised land **929**

Reconstruction after the Civil War **973.8**

Franklin, John Sir, 1786-1847

About

Cookman, S. Ice blink **919**

Geiger, J. Frozen in time **919**

Franklin, Jon

The wolf in the parlor **636.7**

Franklin, Jonathan

438 days **910.916**

Franklin, R. W.

(ed) The poems of Emily Dickinson **811**

Franklin, Rosalind, 1920-1958

About

Maddox, B. Rosalind Franklin: the dark lady of
DNA **92**

Franklin, Ruth

Shirley Jackson **92**

Franklin, Wayne

James Fenimore Cooper **92**

Frankopan, Peter

The Silk Roads **909**

Franks, Tommy, 1945-

About

Franks, T. American soldier **973.931**

Franny's. Clark, M. **641.594**

Franscell, Ron

Morgue **616.07**

Frantz Fanon. Macey, D. **92**

Franzen, Jonathan, 1959-

Farther away **814**

Franzen, Jonathan

About

Franzen, J. The discomfort zone **92**

Fraser's penguins. Montaigne, F. **577.2**

Fraser, Antonia

Faith and treason **942.06**

Love and Louis XIV **92**

Marie Antoinette **944**

Mary Queen of Scots **92**

Must you go? **92**

The wives of Henry VIII   920

Fraser, Bill

About

Montaigne, F. Fraser's penguins   577.2

Fraser, Caroline

Rewilding the world   333.95

Fraser, Flora

Pauline Bonaparte   92

Princesses   920

The Washingtons   92

Fraser, Kennedy

Ornament and silence   809

Fraser, Laura

(jt. auth) Pouillon, N. My organic life   92

Fraser, Rebecca

The story of Britain   941

Fraser, Steve, 1945-

The age of acquiescence   973.91

Fraser, Susan M.

(ed) Flora illustrata   016

FRATERNITIES AND SORORITIES

    See also Colleges and universities; Students -- Societies

FRAUD

Fisher, K. L. How to smell a rat   364.1

Goodman, M. The Sun and the moon   974.7

Mueller, T. Extra virginity   664

Park, R. L. Voodoo science   500

FRAUD

    See also Commercial law; Crime; Offenses against property; White collar crimes

FRAUD -- POPULAR WORKS

Olmsted, L. Real food/fake food   641.3

FRAUD IN SCIENCE

Reich, E. S. Plastic fantastic   92

FRAUD IN SCIENCE

    See also Science

Fraud of the century. Morris, R.   324.9

FRAUD, COMPUTER *See* Computer crimes

FRAUDS, LITERARY *See* Literary forgeries

Frauenfelder, Mark

Maker dad   745.5

Frayn, Michael

The human touch   128

Frazier, Ian

Great Plains   917

Hogs wild   814.54

Travels in Siberia   957

Frazier, Joe, 1944-

About

Kram, M. The ghosts of Manila   796.83

Frazier, Nancy

The Penguin concise dictionary of art history   703

Frazier, Nishani

(ed) Freedom on my mind   305.8

FRBR. Maxwell, R. L.   025.3

FRBR (CONCEPTUAL MODEL)

Maxwell, R. L. FRBR   025.3

Freakonomics. Dubner, S. J.   330

Freaks, geeks and asperger syndrome. Jackson, L.   618.92

Fred Jones Jr. Museum of Art -- Catalogs

The James T. Bialac Native American Art Collection   704.03

The **Frederic** Remington Art Museum collection. Dippie, B. W.   709

Frederick Douglass and the Fourth of July. Colaiaco, J. A.   973.7

Frederick Douglass: selected speeches and writings. Douglass, F.   326

Frederick II, King of Prussia, 1712-1786

About

Blanning, T. Frederick the Great   92

MacDonogh, G. Frederick the Great   943

Frederick the Great. MacDonogh, G.   943

Frederick the Great. Blanning, T.   92

Frederick, Jim

Black hearts   956.7

Fredrickson, George M.

Big enough to be inconsistent   973.7

Fredriksen, John C.

American military leaders   355

Civil War almanac   973.7

Fredriksen, Paula

Jesus of Nazareth, King of the Jews   232.9

Fredston, Jill A.

Rowing to latitude   797.1

About

Fredston, J. A. Snowstruck   551.3

FREE AFRICAN AMERICANS

Davis, D. B. The problem of slavery in the age of emancipation   306.3

FREE ENTERPRISE

Burgin, A. The great persuasion   330.12

Hochschild, A. R. The outsourced self   306.85

Patel, R. The value of nothing   330.1

Sandel, M. J. What money can't buy   330.1

FREE ENTERPRISE

    See also Economic policy

Free for all. Turan, K.   92

FREE MARKETS *See* Free enterprise

FREE MATERIAL

    See also Gifts

FREE PRESS *See* Freedom of the press

FREE SPEECH *See* Freedom of speech

Free speech in its forgotten years. Rabban, D. M.   342

FREE TRADE

Friedman, T. L. The Lexus and the olive tree   337

Goldstein, N. Globalization and free trade   382

FREE TRADE

    See also Commercial policy; International

trade

FREE TRADE -- CASE STUDIES
Goldstein, N. Globalization and free trade   **382**

FREE TRADE AND PROTECTION See Free trade; Protectionism

FREE UNIVERSITIES
   See also Colleges and universities

FREE VERSE
Glück, L. Poems 1962-2012   **811**

FREE VERSE
   See also Poetry

FREE WILL AND DETERMINISM
Dennett, D. C. Freedom evolves   **153.8**
May, R. Freedom and destiny   **158**

FREE WILL AND DETERMINISM
   See also Philosophy

Free world. Garton Ash, T.   **909.08**

Freeberg, Ernest
The Age of Edison   **303.48**

FreeDarko presents the macrophenomenal pro basketball almanac.   **796.323**

Freedman, David Noel
(ed) Eerdmans dictionary of the Bible   **220.3**

Freedman, Eric
(ed) Presidents and Black America   **973.09**

Freedman, Estelle B.
(ed) The essential feminist reader   **305.4**

Freedman, Harry
The Talmud   **296.1**

Freedman, Lawrence
Kennedy's wars   **973.922**

Freedman, Samuel G.
Jew vs. Jew   **296**

FREEDMEN -- UNITED STATES
Ward, A. The slaves' war   **973.7**

FREEDOM
Allen, D. Our Declaration   **973.3**
Fischer, D. H. Liberty and freedom   **323.44**
Foner, E. The story of American freedom   **323.44**
Scott, R. J. Freedom papers   **305.896**

FREEDOM
   See also Democracy; Political science

FREEDOM (PSYCHOLOGY) See Autonomy (Psychology)

Freedom and destiny. May, R.   **158**
Freedom evolves. Dennett, D. C.   **153.8**
Freedom from fear. Kennedy, D. M.   **973.91**
Freedom from fear, and other writings. Aung San Suu Kyi   **959.1**
Freedom in exile. Bstan-'dzin-rgya-mtsho, D. L. X.   **92**

FREEDOM MARCHES FOR CIVIL RIGHTS
   See Civil rights demonstrations

Freedom national. Oakes, J.   **973.7**

FREEDOM OF INFORMATION
Morozov, E. The net delusion   **303.48**

FREEDOM OF INFORMATION
   See also Civil rights; Intellectual freedom

FREEDOM OF MOVEMENT
   See also Civil rights; Freedom

FREEDOM OF RELIGION
Berlinerblau, J. How to be secular   **211**
Nussbaum, M. C. The new religious intolerance   **201**
Nussbaum, M. C. Liberty of conscience   **342**
Waldman, S. Founding faith   **342**
Wexler, J. Holy hullabaloos   **342**

FREEDOM OF RELIGION
   See also Civil rights; Freedom; Toleration

Freedom of speech. Shipler, D. K.   **323.44**

FREEDOM OF SPEECH
Bawer, B. Surrender   **297**
Bezanson, R. P. How free can the press be?   **342**
Burn this book   **814**
Healy, T. The great dissent   **342.73**
Mersky, R. M. Landmark Supreme Court cases   **347.73**
Rabban, D. M. Free speech in its forgotten years   **342**
Stone, G. R. Perilous times   **323.44**

FREEDOM OF SPEECH
   See also Censorship; Civil rights; Freedom; Intellectual freedom

FREEDOM OF SPEECH -- UNITED STATES
Shipler, D. K. Freedom of speech   **323.44**

FREEDOM OF THE PRESS
Kluger, R. Indelible ink   **686.209**
Mersky, R. M. Landmark Supreme Court cases   **347.73**
Simon, J. The new censorship   **363.31**

FREEDOM OF THE PRESS
   See also Civil rights; Freedom; Intellectual freedom; Press

FREEDOM OF THE PRESS -- HISTORY -- 21ST CENTURY
Simon, J. The new censorship   **363.31**

FREEDOM OF THE PRESS -- UNITED STATES -- HISTORY -- 18TH CENTURY
Kluger, R. Indelible ink   **686.209**

Freedom on my mind.   **305.8**
Freedom papers. Scott, R. J.   **305.896**
Freedom riders. Arsenault, R.   **323**
Freedom summer. Watson, B.   **323.1**
Freedom's battle. Bass, G. J.   **341.5**
Freedom's cap. Gugliotta, G.   **975.3**
Freedom's forge. Herman, A.   **940.53**
Freedom's prophet. Newman, R. S.   **92**
Freehand.   **741.2**
Freeing the natural voice. Linklater, K.   **808.5**
Freeing your child from anxiety. Chansky, T. E.   **618.92**

FREELANCERS See Self-employed

Freeland, Chrystia, 1968-
Plutocrats **305.5**
Freeland, David
Automats, taxi dances, and vaudeville
Freely, John
The flame of Miletus **509**
Freeman, Charles
The closing of the Western mind **940.1**
Egypt, Greece, and Rome **909**
Freeman, Douglas Southall, 1886-1953
Lee **92**
Freeman, Joshua B., 1949-
Affairs of honor **306.2**
American empire, 1945-2000 **973.92**
Freeman, Michael
The photographer's mind **775**
The **Freemasons.** Ridley, J. G. **366**
FREEMASONS
Ridley, J. G. The Freemasons **366**
FREEZING See Cryobiology; Frost; Ice; Refrigeration
FREIGHT
McPhee, J. A. Uncommon carriers **388**
FREIGHT
See also Maritime law; Materials handling;
Railroads; Transportation
FREIGHT AND FREIGHTAGE See Freight
Freimiller, Jane
Ellington, E. A year of reading **011**
Freinkel, Susan
Plastic **620.1**
Freisenbruch, Annelise
Caesars' wives **937**
Freitas, Donna
The end of sex **176**
FRENCH ART
King, R. The judgment of Paris **759**
FRENCH AS A SECOND LANGUAGE
Collins, L. When in French **92**
The **French** beauty solution. Thomas, M. **646.7**
FRENCH CANADIANS
See also Canadians
The **French** chef in America. Prud'homme,
A. **641.509**
FRENCH COOKERY See French cooking
FRENCH COOKING
Bard, E. Lunch in Paris **92**
Barr, L. Provence, 1970 **641.59**
Baxter, J. The perfect meal **641.59**
Behr, E. The Food and Wine of France **641.5**
Child, J. From Julia Child's kitchen **641.5**
Child, J. Julia and Jacques cooking at home **641.59**
Child, J. Mastering the art of French cooking **641.5**
The country cooking of France **641.59**
David, E. French provincial cooking **641.5**
Dusoulier, C. The French market cookbook **641.5**

The Food Lover's Guide to Paris **914.4**
The French kitchen cookbook **641.594**
Friedman, A. One souffle at a time **92**
Goin, S. Sunday suppers at Lucques **641.5**
Greenspan, D. Around my French table **641.5**
Greenspan, D. Baking chez moi **641.86**
Grigson, J. Charcuterie and French pork cookery **641.6**
Hamilton, G. Prune **641.3**
Larousse gastronomique **641.3**
Loomis, S. H. In a French kitchen **641.594**
Moulle, J. P. French roots **641.594**
My Paris kitchen **641.59**
Nathan, J. Quiches, kugels, and couscous **641.5**
Olney, R. Lulu's Provencal table **641.59**
Olney, R. Simple French food **641.59**
Patricia Wells at home in Provence **641.59**
Payard, F. Payard cookies **641.86**
Peltre, B. My French family table **641.5**
Pepin, J. Essential Pepin **641.5**
Peterson, J. Glorious French food **641.5**
Roux, M. The French kitchen **641.5**
Shulman, M. R. The art of French pastry **641.86**
Spieler, M. Paris **641.5**
Spitz, B. Dearie **92**
Thorisson, M. A kitchen in France **641.594**
Wells, P. The Provence cookbook **641.5**
FRENCH COOKING
See also Cooking
FRENCH COOKING -- PROVENCAL STYLE
Patricia Wells at home in Provence **641.59**
The **French** kitchen. Roux, M. **641.5**
The **French** kitchen cookbook. **641.594**
FRENCH LANGUAGE
Nadeau The story of French **440**
FRENCH LANGUAGE
See also Language and languages; Romance
languages
FRENCH LANGUAGE -- DICTIONARIES
Correard The Oxford-Hachette French dictionary **443**
**FRENCH LANGUAGE -- DICTIONARIES --
ENGLISH**
See also Encyclopedias and dictionaries
**FRENCH LANGUAGE -- STUDY AND TEACH-
ING AS A SECOND LANGUAGE** See French
as a second language
French lessons. Mayle, P. **394.1**
FRENCH LITERATURE
Yalom, M. How the French invented love **944**
FRENCH LITERATURE
See also Literature; Romance literature
**FRENCH LITERATURE -- HISTORY AND
CRITICISM**
Donoghue, E. Inseparable **809**
Severson, M. S. Masterpieces of French litera-

ture **843**

The **French** market cookbook. Dusoulier, C. **641.5**

FRENCH NATIONAL CHARACTERISTICS

Brown, F. For the soul of France **944.081**

Karnow, S. Paris in the fifties **944**

FRENCH PAINTING

Danchev, A. Cézanne **759.4**

Kelder, D. The great book of French impressionism **759**

King, R. Mad enchantment **759.4**

FRENCH POETRY

See also French literature; Poetry

FRENCH POETRY -- COLLECTIONS

French poetry, 1820-1950, with prose translations **841**

The Random House book of twentieth-century French poetry **841**

French poetry, 1820-1950, with prose translations. **841**

French provincial cooking. David, E. **641.5**

The **French** Revolution. Lefebvre, G. **944.04**

FRENCH REVOLUTION *See* France -- History -- 1789-1799, Revolution

French roots. Moulle, J. P. **641.594**

French women don't get facelifts. Guiliano, M. **613**

French, Francis

(jt. auth) Worden, A. Falling to Earth **92**

French, Kelley

(jt. auth) French, T. Juniper **618.92**

French, Patrick

India **954.04**

The world is what it is **92**

French, Thomas

Juniper **618.92**

Zoo story **590.73**

FRENCH-ALGERIAN WAR, 1954-1962

Camus, A. Algerian chronicles **965**

FRESCO PAINTING *See* Mural painting and decoration

Fresh Fish. Thompson, J. T. **641.692**

Fresh water. Pielou, E. C. **551.48**

FRESHWATER BIOLOGY

See also Biology

FRESHWATER ECOLOGY

See also Ecology

FRESHWATER PLANTS

Speichert, C. G. Encyclopedia of water garden plants **635**

FRESHWATER PLANTS

See also Freshwater biology; Plants

Freud. Gay, P. **92**

Freud and man's soul. Bettelheim, B. **150.19**

The **Freud** reader. **150.19**

Freud, Lucian

About

Smee, S. The art of rivalry **700.92**

Freud, Sigmund, 1856-1939

The basic writings of Sigmund Freud **150.19**

The Freud reader **150.19**

Interpretation of dreams **154.6**

About

Bettelheim, B. Freud and man's soul **150.19**

Bloom, H. The Western canon **809**

Gay, P. Freud **92**

Gay, P. A Godless Jew **150.19**

Freudenburg, William R.

Blowout in the Gulf **363.7**

Freudenheim, Ellen

The Brooklyn experience **917.47**

Frey, Julia

Toulouse-Lautrec **92**

Frey, Kate

The bee-friendly garden **595.799**

Frida Kahlo. Lozano **759.9**

Frida Kahlo : 1907-1954. Kettenmann, A. **709**

Frida: a biography of Frida Kahlo. Herrera, H. **709**

Friday night lights. Bissinger, H. G. **796.332**

Friday, Nancy

My mother/my self **155.6**

Fried twinkies, buckle bunnies & bull riders. Peter, J. **791.8**

Fried, Albert

F.D.R. and his enemies **92**

Frieda, Leonie

The Deadly Sisterhood **945**

Friedan, Betty, 1921-2006

The feminine mystique **305.4**

About

Friedan, B. Life so far **92**

Friedan, Betty. Feminine mystique

About

Coontz, S. A strange stirring **305.42**

Friedlander, Edward Jay

Feature writing for newspapers and magazines **070.4**

Friedlander, Saul

Nazi Germany and the Jews **940.53**

The years of extermination **940.53**

Friedman, Amy

One souffle at a time **92**

Friedman, Andrew, 1967-

Classico e moderno **641.59**

Knives at dawn **641.5**

Friedman, Anita

Rywka's Diary **940.53**

Friedman, Barry

The will of the people **347**

Friedman, Elias Weiss

The Dogist **779**

Friedman, Howard S.

The longevity project **613.2**

Friedman, Ian C.

Carey, C. W. American inventors, entrepreneurs & business visionaries **920**

Latino athletes **920.003**

Hamilton, N. A. Presidents **920.003**

Friedman, Jaclyn

(ed) Yes means yes! **306.7**

Friedman, Jeffrey

Engineering the financial crisis **330.9**

Friedman, Lawrence Meir

American law in the 20th century **349**

Friedman, Leon

(ed) Justices of the United States Supreme Court **347.73**

Friedman, Leonard H.

(ed) 101 careers in healthcare management **362.106**

Friedman, Matti

About

Friedman, M. Pumpkinflowers **956.92**

Friedman, Maurice S.

Encounter on the narrow ridge: a life of Martin Buber **92**

Friedman, Thomas L.

From Beirut to Jerusalem **956**

Hot, flat, and crowded **363.7**

The Lexus and the olive tree **337**

Friedman, Virginia M.

Field guide to stains **648**

Friedwald, Will

A biographical guide to the great jazz and pop singers **920.003**

Sinatra! the song is you **92**

Friend, David

(ed) Bohemians, bootleggers, flappers, and swells **810.8**

Watching the world change **974.7**

Friend, Tim

Animal talk **591.59**

FRIENDLY FIRE (MILITARY SCIENCE)

See also Military art and science

FRIENDS *See* Friendship

Friends, followers, and the future. O'Connor, R. **302.3**

FRIENDS, SOCIETY OF *See* Society of Friends

FRIENDSHIP

Alvarez, J. A wedding in Haiti **818**

Braude, J. The honored dead **364.152**

Caldwell, G. Let's take the long way home **92**

Elman, N. M. The unwritten rules of friendship **649**

Goodman, E. I know just what you mean **158.2**

Jahren, H. Lab girl **92**

Kidder, T. Good prose **808.02**

Power, C. If the oceans were ink **297**

Shanahan, T. Runnng with the champ **796.830**

Tuck, S. Getting from me to we **155.4**

FRIENDSHIP

See also Human behavior

FRIENDSHIP -- GRAPHIC NOVELS

My friend Dahmer **741.5**

FRIENDSHIP -- POLITICAL ASPECTS -- UNITED STATES -- HISTORY

Stewart, D. O. Madison's Gift **92**

FRIENDSHIP -- PSYCHOLOGICAL ASPECTS

Vincent, I. Dinner with Edward **158.1**

FRIENDSHIP BETWEEN WOMEN *See* Female friendship

FRIENDSHIP IN WOMEN *See* Female friendship

FRIGATES -- GREAT BRITAIN -- HISTORY -- 18TH CENTURY

Taylor, S. Commander **92**

FRIGATES -- GREAT BRITAIN -- HISTORY -- 19TH CENTURY

Taylor, S. Commander **92**

Frisch, Michael B.

Miller, C. A. Creating your best life **158**

Frisoni, Christine-Lea

The Big Book of a Miniature House **745**

Fritzsche, Peter

Life and death in the Third Reich **943.086**

FROGS

Moore, R. In search of lost frogs **597.8**

FROGS

See also Amphibians

FROGS -- DISSECTION

See also Dissection

Frolund, Tina

Genrefied classics **016**

Read on...history **016**

From airline reservations to Sonic the Hedgehog. Campbell-Kelly, M. **005**

From alchemy to chemistry in picture and story. Greenberg, A. **540**

From Bauhaus to our house. Wolfe, T. **720.9**

From Beirut to Jerusalem. Friedman, T. L. **956**

From Bible belt to sunbelt. Dochuk, D. **277**

From bonbon to cha-cha. **422**

From colony to superpower. Herring, G. C. **327**

From dawn to decadence. Barzun, J. **940.2**

From Emeril's kitchens. Lagasse, E. **641.5**

From eternity to here. Carroll, S. M. **530.1**

From Frontiers to Football. Brown, M. **980**

From Gutenberg to Zuckerberg. Naughton, J. **004.67**

From here to infinity. Rees, M. J. **500**

From Julia Child's kitchen. Child, J. **641.5**

From Lucy to language. Johanson, D. C. **599.93**

From Midnight to Dawn. Tobin, J. **322**

From my Mexican kitchen. Kennedy, D. **641.5**

From noon to starry night: a life of Walt Whitman. Callow, P. **811**

From Satchmo to Miles. Feather, L. **920**

From slavery to freedom. Franklin, J. H. **305.8**

From spirituals to symphonies. Walker-Hill, H. **780**

From the folks who brought you the weekend. Murolo, P.   **331**

From the Marine Corps to college. Ventrone, J.   **378.1**

From the New World. Graham, J.   **811**

From the ruins of empire. Mishra, P.   **950**

From the shadows. Gates, R. M.   **327**

From totems to hip-hop.   **811**

From vines to wines. Cox, J.   **634.8**

From where you dream. Butler, R. O.   **808.3**

Fromartz, Samuel
  In search of the perfect loaf   **641.81**

Fromm, Erich
  The art of loving   **152.4**
  On being human   **150.19**

Frommer's Rio de Janeiro day By day. De Vries, A.   **918.15**

Frommer, Harvey
  (ed) It happened in the Catskills   **974.7**

Frommer, Myrna Katz
  (ed) It happened in the Catskills   **974.7**

FRONTAL LOBES -- DISEASES -- PATIENTS -- UNITED STATES -- BIOGRAPHY
  Cahalan, S. Brain on fire   **616.8**

FRONTIER AND PIONEER LIFE
  Faragher, J. M. Daniel Boone   **92**
  Means, H. B. Johnny Appleseed   **92**
  Milner, C. A. As big as the West   **92**
  Morgan, R. Boone   **92**
  Osborn, W. M. The wild frontier   **970.004**
  Pioneer girl   **92**
  Sandburg, C. Abraham Lincoln: The prairie years and The war years   **92**
  Warren, L. S. Buffalo Bill's America   **92**

FRONTIER AND PIONEER LIFE
  See also Adventure and adventurers

FRONTIER AND PIONEER LIFE -- AUSTRA- LIA
  Keneally, T. A commonwealth of thieves   **994**

FRONTIER AND PIONEER LIFE -- CALIFOR- NIA
  Brown, D. The indifferent stars above   **92**

FRONTIER AND PIONEER LIFE -- KANSAS
  Stratton, J. L. Pioneer women   **978.1**

FRONTIER AND PIONEER LIFE -- KEN- TUCKY
  Morgan, R. Boone   **92**

FRONTIER AND PIONEER LIFE -- KLOND- IKE RIVER VALLEY (YUKON)
  Gray, C. Gold diggers   **971**

FRONTIER AND PIONEER LIFE -- NORTH AMERICA
  Dolin, E. J. Fur, fortune, and empire   **381**

FRONTIER AND PIONEER LIFE -- NORTH DAKOTA
  DiSilvestro, R. L. Theodore Roosevelt in the Bad- lands   **92**

FRONTIER AND PIONEER LIFE -- UNITED STATES
  Osborn, W. M. The wild frontier   **970.004**
  Pioneer girl   **92**

FRONTIER AND PIONEER LIFE -- WEST (U.S.)
  Buck, R. The Oregon Trail   **978**

FRONTIER AND PIONEER LIFE -- WEST (U.S.) -- POETRY
  Hong, C. P. Engine empire   **811**

FRONTIER AND PIONEER LIFE -- WESTERN STATES
  Dary, D. The Oregon Trail   **978**
  Gwynne, S. C. Empire of the summer moon   **92**
  Warren, L. S. Buffalo Bill's America   **92**

FRONTIERS *See* Boundaries

FROST
  See also Meteorology; Water

Frost, David
About
  Reston, J. The conviction of Richard Nixon   **973.924**

Frost, Mark
  The match   **796.352**

Frost, Randy O.
  Stuff   **616.85**

Frost, Robert, 1874-1963
  Collected poems, prose, & plays   **811**
About
  Fagan, D. Critical companion to Robert Frost   **811**
  Hollis, M. Now all roads lead to France   **821**
  Jarrell, R. No other book   **809**
  Kendall, T. The art of Robert Frost   **811**
  Parini, J. Robert Frost   **811**

Frozen earth. Macdougall, J. D.   **551.7**

FROZEN EMBRYOS
  See also Cryobiology; Embryology

FROZEN FOODS
  Kurlansky, M. Birdseye   **338.7**

FROZEN FOODS
  See also Food

FROZEN FOODS INDUSTRY -- UNITED STATES -- HISTORY
  Kurlansky, M. Birdseye   **338.7**

Frozen in Time. Zuckoff, M.   **940.54**

Frozen in time. Geiger, J.   **919**

FROZEN STARS *See* Black holes (Astronomy)

The **frugal** librarian.   **025.1**

FRUIT
  Apples of uncommon character   **634**
  Dunn Chace, T. Seeing seeds   **581.4**
  Jabbour, N. Groundbreaking food gardens   **635**
  Kirk, M. The ultimate book of modern juicing   **663**

FRUIT -- DISEASES AND PESTS -- CONTROL
  Deardorff, D. What's wrong with my fruit gar- den?   **634**

FRUIT -- PRESERVATION

The all new ball book of canning and preserving 641.42

Complete book of home preserving 641.4

West, K. Saving the season 641.4

FRUIT -- PRESERVATION
See also Canning and preserving; Food -- Preservation

FRUIT GROWERS

Brenner, M. Apples and oranges 92

Means, H. B. Johnny Appleseed 92

FRUIT PAINTING AND ILLUSTRATION See Botanical illustration

FRUIT TREES -- PRUNING

Ralph, A. Grow a little fruit tree 634

Fruitless fall. Jacobsen, R. 638

Frum, David

How we got here 973.92

FRUSTRATION
See also Attitude (Psychology); Emotions

Fry, Juliane L.

The encyclopedia of weather and climate change 551.6

Fry, Laura F.

(jt. auth) Hassrick, P. H. Art of the American West 709

Frye, Northrop

Northrop Frye on Shakespeare 822.3

FRYING

Kaminsky, P. Mallmann on fire 641.598

FSL See French as a second language

Fu, Ping, 1958-

About

Ping Fu Bend, not break 92

Fuegi, John

Brecht and company 92

FUEL

Shulman, S. Cooler smarter 363.7

FUEL
See also Combustion; Energy resources; Engines; Fire; Home economics

FUEL CELLS
See also Electric batteries; Electrochemistry

Fuentes, Carlos

Myself with others 864

A new time for Mexico 972.08

Fuentes, Laura

The best homemade kids' lunches on the planet 641.5

The best homemade kids' snacks on the planet 641.5

Fugard, Athol

Blood knot and other plays 822

Master Harold-- and the boys 822

Fugitive denim. Snyder, R. L. 382

FUGITIVE SLAVES

Foner, E. Gateway to Freedom 973.7

Nathans, S. To free a family 306.3

FUGITIVE SLAVES
See also Slaves

FUGITIVE SLAVES -- UNITED STATES -- HISTORY

Walters, K. The Underground Railroad 973.7

FUGITIVES FROM JUSTICE

Cullen, K. Whitey Bulger 364.1

Nagorski, A. The Nazi hunters 940.53

FUGITIVES FROM JUSTICE
See also Criminals

FUGITIVES FROM JUSTICE -- NOVA SCOTIA -- HALIFAX -- BIOGRAPHY

Jobb, D. Empire of deception 92

FUGITIVES FROM JUSTICE -- UNITED STATES

Bergen, P. L. Manhunt 363.325

FUGUE
See also Counterpoint; Musical form

Fuhrer, Margaret

American dance 792.8

Fuhrman, Joel

The end of heart disease 616.12

Fukuhara, Frank, 1924-2015

About

Sakamoto, P. R. Midnight in broad daylight 940.53

Fukuhara, Harry K., 1920-2015

About

Sakamoto, P. R. Midnight in broad daylight 940.53

Fukuhara, Pierce, 1922-2008

About

Sakamoto, P. R. Midnight in broad daylight 940.53

Fukuoka, Masanobu

Sowing seeds in the desert 631.6

Fukushima. Lyman, E. 363.17

FUKUSHIMA NUCLEAR ACCIDENT, FUKUSHIMA, JAPAN, 2011

Ehrlich, G. Facing the wave 363.34

Lyman, E. Fukushima 363.17

Mockett, M. M. Where the Dead Pause, and the Japanese Say Goodbye 952

Fukuyama, Francis, 1952-

The origins of political order 320

Political Order and Political Decay 320.1

Fulbrook, Mary

A concise history of Germany 943

FULFILLMENT, SELF See Self-realization

Full bloom. Drohojowska-Philp, H. 92

Full body burden. Iversen, K. 363.17

Full engagement! Tracy, B. 658.3

Full Frontal Feminism. Valenti, J. 305.42

A full life. Carter, J. 92

Fullbright, Colleen Dolan

How to help your friend with cancer 616.99

Fuller, Alexandra, 1969-

About

Fuller, A. Leaving Before the Rains Come 305.409

Fuller, A. Don't let's go to the dogs tonight   **92**

Fuller, Gary
   The trivia lover's guide to the world   **910**

Fuller, Graham E., 1937-
   A world without Islam   **297**

Fuller, Jack, 1946-2016
   What is happening to news   **070.4**

Fuller, John
   (ed) The Oxford book of sonnets   **821**

Fuller, Margaret, 1810-1850
         About
   Matteson, J. The lives of Margaret Fuller   **920**
   Von Mehren, J. Minerva and the muse: a life of Margaret Fuller   **92**

Fuller, Nicolle Rager
   Keller, M. Charles Darwin's On the Origin of Species   **576.8**

Fullilove, Michael
   Rendezvous with destiny   **973.917**

Fully alive. Shriver, T.   **796.087**

FUMIGATION
     See also Communicable diseases; Insecticides

Fun home. Bechdel, A.   **741.5**

The **Fun** of it.   **814**

FUNCTIONAL COMPETENCIES *See* Life skills

FUNCTIONAL EQUATIONS
     See also Equations; Functions

FUNCTIONAL FOODS
   Buettner, D. The Blue Zones solution   **613.2**

FUND RAISING
   Gerding, S. K. Winning grants   **025.1**
   Johnson, V. M. Grant writing 101   **658.1**

FUND RAISING
     See also Finance

FUNDACIÓN DEL ESTADO PARA EL SISTEMA NACIONAL DE LAS ORQUESTAS JUVENILES E INFANTILES DE VENEZUELA -- HISTORY
   Tunstall, T. Changing lives   **780.7**

FUNDAMENTAL FYSIKS GROUP (BERKELEY, CALIF.)
   Kaiser, D. How the hippies saved physics **530.092**

FUNDAMENTALISTS -- ALASKA -- MCCARTHY -- BIOGRAPHY
   Pilgrim's wilderness   **92**

Fundamentals of Collection Development and Management. Johnson, P.   **025.2**

Fundamentals of library supervision. Giesecke, J.   **023**

Fundamentals of Managing Reference Collections. Singer, C. A.   **025.2**

Fundamentals of reference. Mulac, C. M.   **025.5**

FUNDING *See* Finance

FUNDS *See* Finance

Fundukian, Laurie J.
   (ed) The Gale encyclopedia of alternative medicine   **615.5**

FUNERAL CUSTOMS AND RITES *See* Funeral rites and ceremonies

FUNERAL DIRECTORS *See* Undertakers and undertaking

FUNERAL RITES AND CEREMONIES
   Jokinen, T. Curtains   **393**
   Kammen, M. G. Digging up the dead   **393**
   Mitford, J. The American way of death revisited   **338.4**
   Wieseltier, L. Kaddish   **296.4**

FUNERAL RITES AND CEREMONIES
     See also Manners and customs; Rites and ceremonies

FUNGI
   Hudler, G. W. Magical mushrooms, mischievous molds   **579.5**

FUNGI
     See also Agricultural pests; Pests; Plants

FUNGICIDES
     See also Pesticides

FUNK (MUSIC)
   Smith, R. J. The one   **92**

FUNK (MUSIC)
     See also Popular music

FUNNIES *See* Comic books, strips, etc.

FUR TRADE -- NORTH AMERICA -- HISTORY
   Dolin, E. J. Fur, fortune, and empire   **381**

FUR TRADE -- SOCIAL ASPECTS
   Hyde, A. F. Empires, nations, and families   **978**

FUR TRADE -- WESTERN STATES -- HISTORY
   Dolin, E. J. Fur, fortune, and empire   **381**

Fur, fortune, and empire. Dolin, E. J.   **381**

FURBEARING ANIMALS
     See also Animals; Economic zoology

Furedi, Frank
   Paranoid parenting   **649**

Furgurson, Ernest B.
   Ashes of glory   **975.5**
   Chancellorsville, 1863   **973.7**

Furious cool. Henry, D.   **92**

Furious love. Kashner, S.   **92**

Furiously happy. Lawson, J.   **92**

Furmansky, Dyana Z.
   Rosalie Edge, hawk of mercy   **92**

Furniture. Miller, J.   **749**

FURNITURE
     See also Decoration and ornament; Decorative arts; Interior design

FURNITURE
   Aronson, J. The encyclopedia of furniture **749.03**
   Handmade interiors   **646.2**
   Miller, J. Furniture   **749**

FURNITURE -- CONSERVATION AND RESTORATION *See* Furniture -- Repairing; Furniture finishing

FURNITURE -- REFINISHING *See* Furniture finishing

FURNITURE -- REPAIRING
New fix-it-yourself manual **643**
Pourny, C. The furniture bible **684.1**

FURNITURE -- REPAIRING
See also Furniture making
The **furniture** bible. Pourny, C. **684.1**

FURNITURE BUILDING *See* Furniture making

FURNITURE DESIGNERS
Albrecht, D. The Work of Charles and Ray Eames **745.4**
Weber, N. F. The Bauhaus group **920**

FURNITURE FINISHING
Blair, B. Furniture Makeovers **684.1**
Blair, B. Furniture makes the room **684.1**
Bruno, I. Reinventing Ikea **684.1**
Hingley, B. D. Furniture repair & restoration **684.1**
Jones, S. Upstyle your furniture **684.1**
Pourny, C. The furniture bible **684.1**
Sloan, A. Color recipes for painted furniture and more

FURNITURE FINISHING
See also Furniture making; Handicraft; Wood finishing
Furniture Makeovers. Blair, B. **684.1**
Furniture makes the room. Blair, B. **684.1**

FURNITURE MAKING
Bruno, I. Reinventing Ikea **684.1**
Macy, B. Factory man **338.7**
Paolini, G. Arts & crafts furniture projects **684.1**

FURNITURE MAKING
See also Furniture; Woodwork
Furniture repair & restoration. Hingley, B. D. **684.1**

FURNITURE, AMERICAN *See* American furniture

Fursenko, A. V.
One hell of a gamble **973.922**

Further along the road less traveled. Peck, M. S. **158**

Fury, Shawn
Rise & fire **796.323**

Fussell, Paul
(ed) The Norton book of modern war **808.8**
The **future**. Gore, A. **303.4**
Future Chefs. Ganeshram, R. **641.3**
The **future** history of the Arctic. Emmerson, C. **998**

FUTURE LIFE
Klosterman, C. But What If We're Wrong? **909.83**
Miller, L. Heaven **236**
Moody, R. A. Life after life **133.9**
Roach, M. Spook **133.9**
Spong, J. S. Eternal life **236**
Wintz, J. Will I see my dog in heaven? **231.7**
Wright, N. T. Surprised by hope **236**

FUTURE LIFE
See also Death; Eschatology

FUTURE LIFE -- POETRY
Ferry, D. Bewilderment **811**
The **future** of ideas. Lessig, L. **004.67**
The **future** of life. Wilson, E. O. **333.95**
The **Future** of the Catholic Church With Pope Francis. Wills, G. **282**
The **future** of the mind. Kaku, M. **612.8**
The **future** of the race. Gates, H. L. **305.896**
Future perfect. Johnson, S. **303.48**
Future shock. Toffler, A. **303.4**

FUTURE SHOCK *See* Culture conflict

FUTURES
See also Investments; Securities

FUTURISM (ART)
See also Art

FUTUROLOGY *See* Forecasting

FUZZY SYSTEMS
See also System analysis

G

G. K. Chesterton. Ker, I. **828**

Gabler, Neal
Walt Disney **92**

Gabriel Garcia Marquez. Martin, G. **92**

Gabriel, Mary
Love and capital **92**

Gabriele d'Annunzio. Hughes-Hallett, L. **858**

Gaddis, John Lewis, 1941-
George F. Kennan **327**

GAELS *See* Celts

Gage, Beverly
The day Wall Street exploded **974.7**

GAIA CONCEPT *See* Gaia hypothesis

GAIA HYPOTHESIS
Lovelock, J. The ages of Gaia **570.1**
Margulis, L. Symbiotic planet **576.8**

GAIA HYPOTHESIS
See also Biology; Earth; Ecology; Life (Biology)

Gaiman, Neil, 1960-
The view from the cheap seats **824**

Gaines, James R.
For liberty and glory **92**

Gaines, Steven S.
Fool's paradise **975.9**

Galassi, Peter
Ansel Adams in Yosemite Valley

GALAXIE 500 (MUSICAL GROUP)
Wareham, D. Black postcards **92**

GALAXIES
Geach, J. Galaxy **523.1**

GALAXIES
See also Astronomy; Stars

GALAXIES -- ATLASES
Trefil, J. Space atlas **520**
Galaxy. Geach, J. **523.1**

Galaxy, Jackson
Catification   **636**
Galba, Servius Sulpicius, Emperor of Rome, 3 B.C.-69
About
The twelve Caesars   **878**
Galbraith, John Kenneth
The great crash, 1929   **338.5**
Name-dropping   **973.9**
Gale Cengage Learning (Company)
(comp) What Do I Read Next?   **020**
Gale critical companion collection [series]
The Beat generation   **810**
Gale directory of databases.   **025.04**
The **Gale** encyclopedia of alternative medicine.   **615.5**
Gale encyclopedia of American law.   **349**
Gale encyclopedia of everyday law.   **349**
Gale Gand's brunch! Gand, G.   **641.5**
Galeano, Eduardo H.
Mirrors   **909**
Soccer in sun and shadow   **796.334**
Galen
About
Mattern, S. P. Prince of medicine   **610.9**
Galens, David
(ed) Literary movements for students   **809**
Galfard, Christophe
The Universe in Your Hand   **523.1**
Galilei, Galileo, 1564-1642
About
Heilbron, J. L. Galileo   **92**
Hofstadter, D. The Earth moves   **509**
Sobel, D. Galileo's daughter   **92**
Galileo. Heilbron, J. L.   **92**
Galileo's daughter. Sobel, D.   **92**
Galileo's middle finger. Dreger, A.   **174.2**
Galimberti, Gabriele
In her kitchen   **641.59**
GALIMBERTI, GABRIELE -- TRAVEL
Galimberti, G. In her kitchen   **641.59**
Galison, Peter Louis
Einstein's clocks and Poincare's maps   **529**
Galitz, Kathryn Calley
The Metropolitan Museum of Art   **700**
Gall, Carlotta
The wrong enemy   **958.104**
Gall, Gilbert J.
Zieger, R. H. American workers, American unions   **331.8**
Gallagher, Gary W.
The Confederate War   **973.7**
The union war   **973.7**
Gallagher, Shaun
Experimenting with babies   **306.874**
Gallagher, Tess

Dear ghosts,   **811**
Gallagher, Tim
About
Gallagher, T. Imperial Dreams   **598.7**
Gallagher, Winifred
How the Post Office Created America   **383.49**
Gallatin, Albert, 1761-1849
About
McCraw, T. K. The founders and finance **330.973**
The **Gallaudet** dictionary of American Sign Language.   **419**
Gallaudet University
The Gallaudet dictionary of American Sign Language   **419**
Sacks, O. W. Seeing voices   **362.4**
Gallaudet, T. H. (Thomas Hopkins), 1787-1851
About
Lepore, J. A is for American   **306.44**
Gallaway, Beth
Game on!   **025.2**
Gallen, David
Carson, C. Malcolm X: the FBI file   **92**
The **Gallic** War. Caesar, J.   **878**
Gallo, Carmine
Talk like TED   **658.4**
Gallo, Phil
Calamar, G. Record store days   **780.2**
Galloway, Joseph L.
Moore, H. G. We are soldiers still   **959.704**
Moore, H. G. We were soldiers once--and young   **959.704**
Gallun, Lucy
(jt. auth) Bajac, Q. Photography at MOMA   **770**
Gallwey, W. Timothy
The inner game of tennis   **796.342**
Galois, Évariste, 1811-1832
About
Bell, E. T. Men of mathematics   **920**
Livio, M. The equation that couldn't be solved **512**
Galuszka, Peter A.
Thunder on the Mountain   **363.11**
GALVESTON (TEX.) -- HISTORY -- 20TH CENTURY
Roker, A. The storm of the century   **976.4**
Galvin, Brendan
Habitat   **811**
Gambaro, Jill, 1959-
The truth about carpal tunnel syndrome   **616.85**
Gambito, Sarah Verdes
Delivered   **811**
GAMBLING
Ainslie, T. Ainslie's complete guide to thoroughbred racing   **798.401**
Denton, S. The money and the power   **979.3**
GAMBLING
See also Games

GAMBLING -- NEVADA -- LAS VEGAS
Schüll, N. D. Addiction by design   362.2
A **gambling** man. Uglow, J. S.   92
The **game.** Pessah, J.
GAME AND GAME BIRDS
   See also Animals; Birds; Wildlife
GAME AND GAME-BIRDS, DRESSING OF
   The complete guide to hunting, butchering, and
   cooking big game   799.2
   Danforth, A. Butchering poultry, rabbit, lamb, goat,
   and pork   664
The **game** makers. Orbanes, P.   338.7
The **game** of boxes. Barnett, C.   811
Game of crowns. Andersen, C.   941.085
Game on! Gallaway, B.   025.2
GAME PRESERVES *See* Game reserves
GAME PROTECTION
   See also Game and game birds; Hunting;
   Wildlife conservation
GAME RESERVES
   Varty, B. Cathedral of the wild   639.9
GAME RESERVES
   See also Hunting; Wildlife conservation
GAME SHOW HOSTS
   Kanfer, S. Groucho: the life and times of Julius
   Henry Marx   92
   Life stories   920
The **game** theorist's guide to parenting. Raeburn,
P.   641.1
GAME THEORY
   Devlin, K. J. The unfinished game   519.2
   Highfield, R. Supercooperators   519.3
   Raeburn, P. The game theorist's guide to parent-
   ing   641.1
   Roth, A. E. Who gets what--and why   330.01
GAME THEORY
   See also Mathematical models; Mathematics;
   Probabilities
GAME THEORY -- SOCIAL ASPECTS
   Raeburn, P. The game theorist's guide to parent-
   ing   641.1
The **Games.** Goldblatt, D.   796.48
GAMES
   See also Entertaining; Physical education;
   Recreation
GAMES
   Cohen, L. J. Playful parenting   649
   Conner, B. Unplugged play   790.1
   Games primates play. Maestripieri, D.   155.7
The **games** that changed the game. Cosell,
G.   796.332
Gammage, Jeff
                  About
   Gammage, J. China ghosts   362.7
Gamow, George, 1904-1968
                  About

Segrè, G. Ordinary geniuses   572.8
Gand, Gale
   Gale Gand's brunch!   641.5
Gander, Forrest
   Core samples from the world   811
   Eye against eye   811
   (tr) Then come back   861
   Torn awake   811
Ganderton, Lucinda
   Embroidery   746.44
Gandhi. Chadha, Y.   954.03
Gandhi. Mohandas   92
Gandhi before India. Guha, R.   92
Gandhi on non-violence. Gandhi, M.   322.4
Gandhi's passion. Wolpert, S. A.   954.03
Gandhi, Mahatma, 1869-1948
   An autobiography   92
   Gandhi on non-violence   322.4
                  About
   Chadha, Y. Gandhi   954.03
   Gandhi, M. An autobiography   92
   Guha, R. Gandhi before India   92
   Lelyveld, J. Great soul   92
   Mohandas Gandhi   92
   Wolpert, S. A. Gandhi's passion   954.03
Gandhi, Rajmohan
   Mohandas Gandhi   92
Ganeshram, Ramin
   Future Chefs   641.3
GANG MEMBERS
   Meeink, F. Autobiography of a recovering skin-
   head   92
GANGS
   Common One day it'll all make sense   92
   Grillo, I. Gangster Warlords   364.106
   Queen, W. Under and alone   364.1
   Seligman, S. D. Tong wars   364.106
   Urschel, J. The Year of Fear   364.152
GANGS
   See also Criminals; Juvenile delinquency;
   Organized crime
GANGS -- GRAPHIC NOVELS
   Ghetto Brother   92
GANGSTER FILMS
   See also Motion pictures
Gangster Warlords. Grillo, I.   364.106
GANGSTERS *See* Gangs
Gann, Alexander
   (ed) The annotated and illustrated double he-
   lix   572.8
Ganon, Jill Alison
   Agnew, C. L. Twins!   649
Gans, Joe
                  About
   Gildea, W. The longest fight   796.83
Ganz, Nicholas

Graffiti world **751**

The **gap.** Suddendorf, T. **156**

Gaquin, Deirdre A.

(ed) The who, what, and where of America **317.3**

GARBAGE See Refuse and refuse disposal

GARBAGE DISPOSAL See Refuse and refuse disposal

Garbage land. Royte, E. **363.7**

Garber, Marjorie

Shakespeare after all **822.3**

Shakespeare and modern culture **822.3**

The use and abuse of literature **801**

Garbology. Humes, E. **628.4**

Garbutt, Glenda

(jt. auth) Dilevko, J. Contemporary world fiction **016**

García Márquez, Gabriel, 1928-
    About

Martin, G. Gabriel Garcia Marquez **92**

Garcia. Jackson, B. **92**

García Lorca, Federico, 1898-1936

Collected poems **861**

Poet in New York **861**
    About

Gibson, I. Federico Garcia Lorca: a life **92**

García Márquez, Gabriel, 1928-

News of a kidnapping **364.15**

The story of a shipwrecked sailor **910.4**
    About

Garcia Marquez, G. Living to tell the tale **92**

Garcia, Jerry
    About

Brightman, C. Sweet chaos **920**

Jackson, B. Garcia **92**

García, Lorena

Lorena Garcia's new taco classics **641.84**

Gardell, Mattias

In the name of Elijah Muhammad **297**

GARDEN ARCHITECTURE See Garden structures

Garden Design. Majerus, M. **712**

GARDEN DESIGN

Gardiner, J. The Timber Press encyclopedia of flowering shrubs **635.9**

Greayer, R. Cultivating garden style **636.8**

Karsten, J. Straw bale gardens complete **635**

The layered garden design lessons for year-round beauty from Brandywine Cottage **635**

Majerus, M. Garden Design **712**

Nagel, V. G. Understanding garden design **712**

GARDEN DESIGN

See also Design; Gardening

GARDEN ECOLOGY

See also Ecology

GARDEN FURNITURE See Garden ornaments and furniture

The **garden** of invention. Smith, J. S. **92**

A **Garden** of Marvels. Kassinger, R. **580**

GARDEN ORNAMENTS AND FURNITURE

Color concrete garden projects **721**

The **garden** party and other plays. Havel, V. **891.8**

Garden perennials

Armitage's garden perennials **635.9**

GARDEN PESTS See Agricultural pests; Insect pests; Plant diseases

GARDEN PESTS -- BIOLOGICAL CONTROL

Gardiner, M. M. Good garden bugs **635**

Walliser, J. Attracting beneficial bugs to your garden **628.9**

The **garden** primer. Damrosch, B. **635**

Garden revolution. Christopher, T. **577**

GARDEN ROOMS

See also Houses; Rooms

GARDEN STRUCTURES

Stiles, D. Backyard Building **690**

GARDEN STRUCTURES

See also Buildings; Landscape architecture

GARDEN STRUCTURES -- DESIGN AND CONSTRUCTION -- AMATEURS' MANUALS

The complete outdoor builder **690**

The **gardener** and the carpenter. Gopnik, A. **155.4**

The **Gardener's** Garden. Cox, M. **712**

The **gardener's** guide to weather and climate. **635**

The **gardener's** guide to weather and climate. Allaby, M. **635**

The **gardener's** year. **635**

GARDENING

Allaby, M. The gardener's guide to weather and climate **635**

Armitage, A. M. Armitage's native plants for North American gardens **635.9**

Biodynamic gardening **635**

Black, S. H. Gardening for butterflies **638**

Bowling, B. L. Homegrown berries **634**

Campbell, S. How to mulch **635**

Christopher, T. Garden revolution **577**

Citizen farmers **635**

Cox, M. The Gardener's Garden **712**

Damrosch, B. The garden primer **635**

Darke, R. The American woodland garden **635.9**

Deardorff, D. What's wrong with my fruit garden? **634**

Druse, K. The new shade garden

Duffield, M. R. Plants for dry climates **635.9**

Frey, K. The bee-friendly garden **595.799**

The gardener's year **635**

Gardiner, J. The Timber Press encyclopedia of flowering shrubs **635.9**

Grasses **635.9**

Grow All You Can Eat in Three Square Feet **635**

Hanson, D. Breaking through concrete **630**

Harrison, L. Heirloom Plants **635**

Hutchinson, C. Time-saving gardener **635**

Kassinger, R. A Garden of Marvels **580**

Keville, K. The aromatherapy garden **635.9**

Kukielski, P. E. Roses without chemicals **635.9**

The layered garden design lessons for year-round beauty from Brandywine Cottage **635**

Lowe, J. Pruning **631.5**

McIndoe, A. The creative shrub garden **635.9**

The New Southern Living Garden Book **635.9**

Pember, M. The Little Veggie Patch Co. DIY Garden Projects **712.6**

Penick, P. The water-saving garden **635.9**

The plant finder **635.9**

Pleasant, B. The complete compost gardening guide **631.8**

Pruning plant by plant **635**

Ripe **641.6**

The seed garden

Springer, L. Passionate gardening **635**

Walliser, J. Attracting beneficial bugs to your garden **628.9**

Wiley, K. Designing and planting a woodland garden **635.9**

Wulf, A. The brother gardeners **635**

Wulf, A. Founding gardeners **712**

GARDENING

    See also Agriculture

GARDENING -- ENCYCLOPEDIAS

Wyman, D. Wyman's gardening encyclopedia **635**

GARDENING -- EQUIPMENT AND SUPPLIES -- MAINTENANCE AND REPAIR

Small engines and outdoor power equipment **621.43**

GARDENING -- UNITED STATES

Obama, M. American grown **635**

Gardening for butterflies. Black, S. H. **638**

GARDENING FOR CHILDREN

Bartholomew, M. All new square foot gardening **635**

GARDENING IN THE SHADE

    See also Gardening

GARDENING TO ATTRACT WILDLIFE

Frey, K. The bee-friendly garden **595.799**

Gardening with less water. Bainbridge, D. A. **635.9**

GARDENS

The bold dry garden **635.9**

Bunny Williams' on garden style

Cox, M. The Gardener's Garden **712**

Graham, W. American Eden **712**

Greayer, R. Cultivating garden style **636.8**

Karsten, J. Straw bale gardens complete **635**

Kassinger, R. A Garden of Marvels **580**

Kristal, M. At home in the garden **635.09**

The layered garden design lessons for year-round beauty from Brandywine Cottage **635**

Majerus, M. Garden Design **712**

McDowell, M. All the presidents' gardens **635.09**

Moss, C. Charlotte Moss **747**

Swift, V. Gardens of awe and folly **635**

Wulf, A. The brother gardeners **635**

Wulf, A. Founding gardeners **712**

GARDENS -- DESIGN *See* Garden design

GARDENS -- PENNSYLVANIA -- DESIGN

The layered garden design lessons for year-round beauty from Brandywine Cottage **635**

GARDENS -- STYLES

Greayer, R. Cultivating garden style **636.8**

GARDENS -- WASHINGTON (D.C.) -- HISTORY

McDowell, M. All the presidents' gardens **635.09**

Gardens of awe and folly. Swift, V. **635**

GARDENS, SHADE *See* Gardening in the shade

Gardiner, Jim

The Timber Press encyclopedia of flowering shrubs **635.9**

Gardiner, John Eliot

Bach **92**

Gardiner, Mary M.

Good garden bugs **635**

Gardiner, Wendy

The sewing machine accessory bible **646.2**

Gardner's art through the ages. Gardner, H. **709**

Gardner, Chris

    About

Gardner, C. The pursuit of happyness **92**

Gardner, Daniel

The science of fear **152.4**

Gardner, Helen

Gardner's art through the ages **709**

Gardner, John

The art of fiction **808.3**

On becoming a novelist **808.3**

On moral fiction **801**

Gardner, Mark L.

To hell on a fast horse **92**

Gardner, Mark Lee

Rough Riders **973.91**

Gardner, Martin, 1914-2010

The colossal book of short puzzles and problems **793.8**

Did Adam and Eve have navels? **500**

Gardner, Sue

(ed) A to Z of crochet **746.434**

Gardoqui, Dan

(ed) What the robin knows **598.8**

Gardullo, Paul

(ed) The Scurlock Studio and Black Washington **779**

Garelick, Rhonda K.

Mademoiselle **92**

Garfield, James A. (James Abram), 1831-1881

    About

Millard, C. The destiny of the republic **973.8**

Perry, J. M. Touched with fire **973.7**

Garfield, Simon
Just my type **686.2**
Mauve **667**
Garfinkle, Norton
(jt. auth) Holzer, H. A just and generous nation **973.7**
Gargan, Edward A.
A river's tale **915**
Garland encyclopedias in the history of science [series]
Instruments of science **502.8**
Garland reference library of social science [series]
Native America in the twentieth century **970.004**
Garland reference library of the humanities [series]
Archaeology of prehistoric native America **970.01**
Encyclopedia of the scientific revolution **509**
The History of science and religion in the western tradition **201**
The United States in the First World War **940.3**
Garland, Judy
About
Clarke, G. Get happy: the life of Judy Garland **92**
Garland, Madge, 1896-1990
About
Cohen, L. All we know **920.72**
Garlic and sapphires. Reichl, R. **92**
Garlick, Hattie
Born to Be Wild **796.083**
GARMENTS *See* Clothing and dress
Garnar, Martin
Intellectual Freedom Manual **025.2**
Garner's modern American usage. Garner, B. A. **423**
Garner's Modern English Usage. Garner, B. A. **808**
Garner, Abigail
Families like mine **306.8**
Garner, Bryan A.
Garner's Modern American usage **423**
Garner's Modern English Usage **808**
Garraty, John Arthur
American national biography **920.003**
Garrels, Anne, 1951-
About
Garrels, A. Putin country **947.43**
Garrelts, Colby
Made in america
Garrelts, Megan
(jt. auth) Garrelts, C. Made in america
Garrett, Brandon L.
Too big to jail **345.73**
Garrett, Laurie
Betrayal of trust **362.1**
The coming plague **614.4**
Garrett, Pat F. (Pat Floyd), 1850-1908
About

Gardner, M. L. To hell on a fast horse **92**
Garrison, Lucy McKim
Ware, C. P. Slave songs of the United States **781.62**
Garro, Elena
About
Biron, R. E. Elena Garro and Mexico's modern dreams **868**
Garson, Barbara
Down the up escalator **339.2**
Garson, Paul
(comp) Album of the damned **943.086**
Garten, Ina, 1948-
Barefoot Contessa at home **641**
Barefoot Contessa family style **641.5**
Barefoot Contessa, how easy is that? **641.5**
Barefoot in Paris **641**
Cooking for Jeffrey **641.5**
Make it ahead **641.5**
Gartland, Ashley
Heartlandia **641.597**
Garton Ash, Timothy
Free world **909.08**
About
Garton-Ash, T. The file **327.12**
Garvey, Mark
Stylized **808**
Gary Cooper. **92**
Garza, Anabel
About
Brick, M. Saving the school **373.22**
GAS
See also Fuel
GAS INDUSTRY
See also Industries
GAS WARFARE *See* Chemical warfare
GAS WELLS -- HYDRAULIC FRACTURING -- POPULAR WORKS
Prud'homme, A. Hydrofracking **622**
Gasaway, Laura N., 1945-
Copyright questions and answers for information professionals **346.73**
Gascoyne, Kevin
(ed) Tea **641.3**
GASES
See also Fluid mechanics; Hydrostatics; Physics
Gaskell, Elizabeth Cleghorn
The life of Charlotte Bronte **92**
Gaskin, Ina May
Ina May's guide to childbirth **618.4**
Gaskin, J. C. A.
(ed) Hobbes, T. Leviathan **320.1**
GASOLINE
See also Fuel; Petroleum
Gasparino, Charles
The sellout **332**

Gaspipe. Carlo, P. 92

Gasser, Urs
  Palfrey, J. Born digital 302.23

GASTROINTESTINAL SYSTEM -- POPULAR WORKS
  Roach, M. Gulp 612.3

GASTRONOMY
  Bourdain, A. Medium raw 92
  First bite 641.01
  Kamp, D. The United States of Arugula 641

GASTRONOMY
  See also Diet

Gatcum, Chris
  The Beginner's photography guide 770

The gate. Bizot, F. 959.604

The gatekeepers. Steinberg, J. 378.1

Gates, Alexander E.
  Encyclopedia of earthquakes and volcanoes 551.2
  Encyclopedia of pollution 363.7
  A to Z of earth scientists 920.003

Gates, Erin
  Elements of style 747

Gates, Henry Louis
  (ed) African American lives 920
  (ed) The African American national biography 920.003
  (ed) Africana: the encyclopedia of the African and African American experience 909
  The African-American century 305
  (jt. auth) Burke, K. M. And Still I Rise 973
  Colored people 92
  The future of the race 305.896
  In search of our roots 305.8
  Life upon these shores 305.8
  Thirteen ways of looking at a black man 920.71
  (ed) The Norton anthology of African American literature 810
  (ed) Twelve years a slave 92
    About
  Gates, H. L. Colored people 92

Gates, Robert Michael, 1943-
  From the shadows 327
    About
  Gates, R. M. A passion for leadership 92

Gateway to Freedom. Foner, E. 973.7

Gather at the table. DeWolf, T. N. 306.3

Gathercole, Peter
  Fly tying for beginners 688.7
  The fly-tying bible 688.7

The gathering storm. Churchill, W. 940.53

GAUCHOS *See* Cowhands

Gaughan, Norah
  Norah Gaughan's Knitted Cable Sourcebook 746.432

GAUL -- GEOGRAPHY
  See also Ancient geography; Historical geography

Gaul, Gilbert M., 1951-
  Billion-Dollar Ball 796.332

Gaulle, Charles de, 1890-1970
    About
  Kissinger, H. Diplomacy 327.2
  Williams, C. The last great Frenchman 944

Gauss, Carl Friedrich, 1777-1855
    About
  Bell, E. T. Men of mathematics 920

Gaustad, Edwin S. (Edwin Scott)
  (jt. auth) Schmidt, L. E. The religious history of America 200.973
  Roger Williams 92

Gautama Buddha
    About
  Armstrong, K. Buddha 294.3

Gavin, James
  Stormy weather 92

Gawain, Shakti
  Creative visualization 153.3

Gawande, Atul
  Being mortal 362.17
  Better 616
  The checklist manifesto 610.28
  Complications: a young surgeon's notes on an imperfect science 617

GAY ACTIVISTS
  Schiavi, M. Celluloid activist 92

GAY AND LESBIAN ALLIANCE AGAINST DEFAMATION
  Schiavi, M. Celluloid activist 92

GAY AND LESBIAN RIGHTS *See* Gay rights

GAY ARTISTS -- UNITED STATES -- BIOGRAPHY
  Duberman, M. B. Hold tight gently 920

GAY ATHLETES -- UNITED STATES -- BIOGRAPHY
  Marcus, E. Coming out to play 92

GAY AUTHORS
  See also Authors; Gay men

Gay Berlin. Beachy, R. 306.76

GAY COUPLES
  Rosswood, E. Journey to Same-sex Parenthood 306.874

GAY COUPLES -- LEGAL STATUS, LAWS, ETC.
  Hertz, F. A legal guide for lesbian and gay couples 346.01
  Yoshino, K. Speak now 346.73

GAY COUPLES -- LEGAL STATUS, LAWS, ETC. -- UNITED STATES
  Dickey, L. Then comes marriage 346

GAY LEGISLATORS -- UNITED STATES -- BIOGRAPHY
  Frank, B. Frank 92

GAY LIBERATION MOVEMENT
See also Homosexuality

GAY LIBERATION MOVEMENT -- UNITED STATES -- HISTORY
Faderman, L.   The gay revolution   **306.76**
Hirshman, L.   Victory   **306.76**

GAY LIFESTYLE *See* Homosexuality

GAY MARRIAGE *See* Same-sex marriage

GAY MEN
Beachy, R.   Gay Berlin   **306.76**
Blanco, R.   The Prince of Los Cocuyos   **92**
Carter, D.   Stonewall   **306.76**
Chu, J.   Does Jesus Really Love Me?   **261.8**
Duberman, M. B.   Hold tight gently   **920**
Faderman, L.   The gay revolution   **306.76**
Isherwood, C.   Liberation   **809**
Marcus, E.   Coming out to play   **92**
White, E.   City boy   **92**

GAY MEN
See also Gays; LGBT people; Men

GAY MEN -- BIOGRAPHY
Bram, C.   Eminent outlaws   **810.9**
Walsh, M.   Gypsy boy   **92**

GAY MEN -- POETRY
Powell, D. A.   Repast   **811**
Powell, D. A.   Useless landscape   **811**

GAY MEN -- UNITED STATES -- BIOGRAPHY
Hammer, L.   James Merrill   **92**
Savage, D.   American Savage   **306.76**

GAY MILITARY PERSONNEL -- GOVERNMENT POLICY -- UNITED STATES
Nicholson, A.   Fighting to serve   **355**

GAY PARENTS
Abbott, A.   Fairyland   **813**
Garner, A.   Families like mine   **306.8**
Lev, A. I.   The complete lesbian & gay parenting guide   **649**

GAY PARENTS
See also Gay men; Lesbians; Parents
The **gay** revolution. Faderman, L.   **306.76**

GAY RIGHTS
Carter, D.   Stonewall   **306.76**

GAY RIGHTS
See also Civil rights

GAY RIGHTS -- UNITED STATES
Carpenter, D.   Flagrant conduct   **342.73**

GAY RIGHTS -- UNITED STATES -- HISTORY
Duberman, M. B.   The Martin Duberman reader   **306.76**
Faderman, L.   The gay revolution   **306.76**

GAY RIGHTS -- UNITED STATES -- HISTORY -- 21ST CENTURY
Nicholson, A.   Fighting to serve   **355**

GAY RIGHTS ACTIVISTS
Schiavi, M.   Celluloid activist   **92**

GAY STUDENTS -- UNITED STATES
Cahill, S.   LGBT youth in America's schools   **371.82**

GAY TEENAGERS
Anderson, T.   Sweet Tooth   **92**
Schwartz, J.   Oddly normal   **306.76**

GAY TEENAGERS
See also Gay youth; Teenagers

GAY TEENAGERS -- COUNSELING OF -- NEW YORK (STATE) -- NEW YORK
Berg, R.   No house to call my home   **362.786**

GAY WOMEN *See* Lesbians

GAY WOMEN'S WRITINGS *See* Lesbians' writings

GAY YOUTH
Cahill, S.   LGBT youth in America's schools   **371.82**

GAY YOUTH
See also Youth

Gay, John
The beggar's opera   **822**

Gay, lesbian, bisexual, and transgendered literature.
Bosman, E.   **016**

Gay, Peter, 1923-
(ed) The Freud reader   **150.19**
Freud   **92**
A Godless Jew   **150.19**
The rise of modern paganism   **190**
The science of freedom   **190**

About
Gay, P.   My German question   **943**

Gay, Ross, 1974-
Catalog of Unabashed Gratitude   **811.6**

Gay, Roxane
Bad Feminist   **814**

Gay, Ruth
The Jews of Germany   **943**

Gay, Timothy M.
Tris Speaker   **92**

Gaydosik, Victoria
(ed) The Facts on File companion to the British novel   **823**

Gaye, Jan
(jt. auth) Ritz, D.   After the Dance   **782.42**

Gaylard, Linda
The tea book   **641.3**

GAYS -- CRIMES AGAINST -- UNITED STATES
Jimenez, S.   The Book of Matt   **364.1**

GAYS -- LEGAL STATUS, LAWS, ETC. -- UNITED STATES
Carpenter, D.   Flagrant conduct   **342.73**
Hirshman, L.   Victory   **306.76**

GAYS -- UNITED STATES
Savage, D.   American Savage   **306.76**

GAYS -- UNITED STATES -- HISTORY
Duberman, M. B.   The Martin Duberman reader   **306.76**
Faderman, L.   The gay revolution   **306.76**

GAYS AND LESBIANS IN THE MILITARY

Faderman, L. The gay revolution **306.76**

GAYS AND LESBIANS IN THE MILITARY
  See also Gays; Military personnel
GAYS IN THE MILITARY *See* Gays and lesbians
  in the military
**GAYS' WRITINGS, AMERICAN -- HISTORY
  AND CRITICISM**
  Bram, C. Eminent outlaws **810.9**
GAYS, FEMALE *See* Lesbians
GAYS, MALE *See* Gay men
Gaza. Filiu **953**
GAZA -- HISTORY
  Filiu Gaza **953**
Gazella, Karolyn A.
  The definitive guide to thriving after cancer **616.99**
GAZETTEERS
  The Columbia gazetteer of the world **910.3**
GAZETTEERS
  See also Geography
Gazit, Shlomo
  Herzog, C. The Arab-Israeli wars **956**
Gazzaniga, Michael S.
  Tales from Both Sides of the Brain **92**
Gazzaniga, Michael S.
  Human **612.8**
Geach, James
  Galaxy **523.1**
GEARING
  See also Machinery; Power transmission;
  Wheels
Geary, Rick
  J. Edgar Hoover **363.2**
  The Lindbergh child **364.1**
Geary, Theresa Flores
  The illustrated bead bible **745.594**
Geck, Martin
  Johann Sebastian Bach **92**
  Robert Schumann **92**
Gedeon, Jade
  Beautiful bracelets by hand **745.594**
Gediman, Dan
  (ed) This I believe **170**
  (ed) This I believe II **170**
Geek dad. Denmead, K. **790**
A geek in Thailand. Houton, J. **915.9**
The geeks shall inherit the Earth. Robbins, A.
GEESE
  See also Birds; Poultry
Gehrig, Lou, 1903-1941
  About
  Robinson, R. Iron horse: Lou Gehrig in his time **92**
Gehring, Wes D.
  James Dean: rebel with a cause **92**
Gehrman, Elizabeth
  Rare birds **598**
Gehry, Frank O., 1929-

  About
  Goldberger, P. Building art **92**
  Isenberg, B. Conversations with Frank Gehry **92**
Geiger, Chris
  The Cancer Survivors' Club **362.196**
Geiger, John
  Frozen in time **919**
GEISHAS
  Downer, L. Women of the pleasure quarters **792.7**
GEISHAS
  See also Entertainers
Geist, Bill
  Little League confidential **796.357**
Gelb, Arthur, 1924-2014
  About
  Gelb, A. City room **92**
Gelb, Donna
  (jt. auth) Kaminsky, P. Mallmann on fire **641.598**
Gelber, Teri
  Goin, S. Sunday suppers at Lucques **641.5**
Geldard, Richard G.
  (ed) The essential transcendentalists **141**
Gelfant, Blanche H.
  (ed) The Columbia companion to the twentieth-
  century American short story **813**
Gellately, Robert
  Stalin's curse **947.084**
Gellman, Irwin F.
  The President and the Apprentice **973.921**
Gem. **553.8**
GEMINI PROJECT
  See also Orbital rendezvous (Space flight);
  Space flight
GEMS
  Gem **553.8**
  Harlow, G. E. Gems & Crystals **549**
  Oldershaw, C. Firefly guide to gems **553.8**
GEMS
  See also Archeology; Art; Decoration and or-
  nament; Engraving; Minerals
Gems & Crystals. Harlow, G. E. **549**
GEMSTONES *See* Precious stones
GENDER AND POLITICS
  Schnall, M. What will it take to make a woman
  president? **305.4**
GENDER IDENTITY
  Trans bodies, trans selves **306.76**
GENDER IDENTITY
  See also Identity (Psychology)
GENDER IDENTITY -- AFGHANISTAN
  Nordberg, J. The underground girls of Kabul **305.42**
GENDER IDENTITY -- GERMANY -- BERLIN
  Beachy, R. Gay Berlin **306.76**
GENDER IDENTITY -- POETRY
  Salah, T. Wanting in Arabic **811**
GENDER IDENTITY -- UNITED STATES

McBee, T. P. Man alive   **92**

GENDER IDENTITY -- UNITED STATES -- CASE STUDIES
Mock, J. Redefining Realness   **306.76**

GENDER MAINSTREAMING
Bohnet, I. What works   **331.4**

GENDER ROLE
Als, H. White Girls   **814**
Angier, N. Woman   **612.6**
Annis, B. Work with me   **306.3**
Bohnet, I. What works   **331.4**
Brown, C. S. Parenting beyond pink and blue   **649**
Duron, L. Raising my rainbow   **306.87**
Nordberg, J. The underground girls of Kabul **305.42**
Senior, J. All Joy and No Fun   **306.874**
Williams, J. What works for women at work **650.1**
Wolf, N. The beauty myth   **305.4**
Yes means yes!   **306.7**

GENDER ROLE
   See also Sex; Sex differences (Psychology); Social role

GENDER STUDIES
   See also Education
The **gene**. Mukherjee, S.   **616.042**

GENE MAPPING
   See also Genetics

GENE SPLICING *See* Genetic engineering

GENE THERAPY
Wapner, J. The Philadelphia chromosome **616.99**

GENE THERAPY
   See also Genetic engineering; Therapeutics

GENE THERAPY -- GERMANY -- BERLIN -- HISTORY
Holt, N. Cured   **614.5**

GENE TRANSFER *See* Genetic engineering
The **genealogist's** address book. Bentley, E. P. **929**
The **genealogist's** companion and sourcebook. Croom, E. A.   **929**

GENEALOGY
Baxter, A. In search of your European roots **929**
Bentley, E. P. Directory of family associations **929**
Bentley, E. P. The genealogist's address book **929**
Croom, E. A. The genealogist's companion and sourcebook   **929**
Gates, H. L. In search of our roots   **305.8**
Greenwood, V. D. The researcher's guide to American genealogy   **929**
Kemp, T. J. Virtual roots 2.0   **929**
Laskin, D. The Family   **92**
Mann, S. Hold Still   **92**
Marshall, S. Reunited   **362.82**
Swarns, R. L. American tapestry   **92**
Sykes, B. DNA USA   **559.9**

GENEALOGY
   See also History

GENEALOGY -- ANECDOTES

McCarthy, A. Journeys home   **929.1**

GENEALOGY -- BIBLIOGRAPHY
Printed sources   **016**

GENEALOGY -- SOCIAL ASPECTS -- UNITED STATES
Well, F. Family trees   **929.2**

GENEALOGY -- UNITED STATES -- HISTORY
Well, F. Family trees   **929.2**

General Mills Inc.
(comp) Betty Crocker cookbook   **641.5**

GENERAL MOTORS CORP.
Vlasic, B. Once upon a car   **338.4**

GENERAL MOTORS CORP. -- BANKRUPTCY
Lutz, B. Car guys vs. bean counters   **338.7**
General Patton: a soldier's life. Hirshson, S. P. **92**

GENERAL RELATIVITY (PHYSICS)
Greene, B. The hidden reality   **530.1**
Susskind, L. The black hole war   **530.1**

GENERAL STORES
   See also Retail trade; Stores

GENERAL SURGERY -- PENNSYLVANIA -- BIOGRAPHY
Aptowicz, C. O. Dr. Mütter's Marvels   **92**
The **general** theory of employment, interest and money. Keynes, J. M.   **330.1**
A **general** theory of love. Lewis, T.   **152.4**
The **General** Vs. the President. Brands, H. W.   **973.918**
The **generalissimo**. Taylor, J.   **92**
The **generals**. Groom, W.   **940.54**

GENERALS
Ambrose, S. E. Eisenhower   **92**
Ambrose, S. E. The victors   **940.54**
Anderson, L. Carlisle vs. Army   **796.332**
Atkinson, R. The guns at last light   **940.54**
Barry, J. M. Rising tide   **977**
Bell, M. S. Toussaint Louverture   **92**
Brands, H. W. Andrew Jackson   **92**
Brighton, T. Patton, Montgomery, Rommel **920**
Brookhiser, R. Founding father: rediscovering George Washington   **92**
Brown, D. A. Bury my heart at Wounded Knee   **970.004**
Bunting, J. Ulysses S. Grant   **92**
Connell, E. S. Son of the Morning Star **973.8**
Davis, B. Sherman's march   **973.7**
De Young, K. Soldier: the life of Colin Powell **92**
Donovan, J. A terrible glory   **973.8**
Duke, L. Mandela, Mobutu, and me   **968.06**
Ellis, J. J. His Excellency   **92**
Fellman, M. Citizen Sherman   **92**
Fellman, M. The making of Robert E. Lee   **92**
Fischer, D. H. Washington's crossing   **973.3**
Fleming, T. J. Washington's secret war **973.3**
Flexner, J. T. George Washington and the new nation, 1783-1793   **92**

Flexner, J. T.   George Washington: anguish and farewell 1793-1799   **92**

Flexner, J. T.   George Washington: the forge of experience, 1732-1775   **92**

Fowler, W. M.   American crisis   **973.3**

Frank, R. B.   MacArthur   **92**

Franks, T.   American soldier   **973.931**

Freeman, D. S.   Lee   **92**

Gaines, J. R.   For liberty and glory   **92**

Gates, H. L.   Thirteen ways of looking at a black man   **920.71**

Geary, R.   The Lindbergh child   **364.1**

Goldsworthy, A. K.   Antony and Cleopatra   **92**

Grant, U. S.   Memoirs and selected letters   **973.8**

Groom, W.   The generals   **940.54**

Groom, W.   Kearny's march   **979**

Groom, W.   Patriotic fire   **973.5**

Groom, W.   Vicksburg, 1863   **973.7**

Halberstam, D.   The best and the brightest **973.922**

Hanson, V. D.   The soul of battle   **355**

Hibbert, C.   Wellington   **92**

Hirshson, S. P.   General Patton: a soldier's life   **92**

Hofstadter, R.   The American political tradition, and the men who made it   **973**

Johnson, P.   George Washington: the Founding Father   **92**

Jordan, J. W.   American warlords   **973.917**

Keneally, T.   American scoundrel: the life of the notorious Civil War General Dan Sickles   **92**

Kennett, L. B.   Sherman   **92**

Kessner, T.   The flight of the century   **92**

Kissinger, H.   Diplomacy   **327.2**

Kluger, R.   The bitter waters of Medicine Creek   **979.7**

Korda, M.   Ulysses S. Grant: the unlikely hero   **92**

Langguth, A. J.   Driven West   **973.5**

Lemann, N.   Redemption: the last battle of the Civil War   **975**

Lindbergh, C.   The spirit of St. Louis   **629.13**

Lindbergh, R.   Under a wing   **92**

Linklater, A.   An artist in treason   **92**

Lockhart, P. D.   The whites of their eyes   **973.3**

McPherson, J. M.   Drawn with the sword   **973.7**

Meacham, J.   American lion   **92**

Moore, H. G.   We are soldiers still   **959.704**

Morris, R.   Fraud of the century   **324.9**

Nelson, C.   The first heroes   **940.54**

Norris, R. S.   Racing for the bomb: General Leslie R. Groves, the Manhattan Project's indispensable man   **92**

O'Connell, R. L.   The ghosts of Cannae   **937**

Pakula, H.   The last empress   **92**

Palmer, J.   The bloody white baron   **92**

Parssinen, T. M.   The Oster conspiracy of 1938   **943.086**

Perry, J. M.   Touched with fire   **973.7**

Perry, M.   The most dangerous man in America   **92**

Philbrick, N.   The last stand   **973.8**

Powell, C. L.   My American journey   **92**

Randall, W. S.   George Washington   **92**

Remini, R. V.   Andrew Jackson   **92**

Reynolds, D. S.   Waking giant   **973.5**

Rice, A.   The teeth may smile but the heart does not forget   **967.6**

Ricks, T. E.   The generals   **355.009**

Roberts, A.   Masters and commanders   **940.54**

Sandoz, M.   The Battle of the Little Bighorn **973.8**

Sears, S. W.   Chancellorsville   **973.7**

Sears, S. W.   George B. McClellan   **92**

Sheehan, N.   A fiery peace in a cold war   **92**

Showalter, D. E.   Patton and Rommel   **92**

Smith, J. E.   Grant   **92**

Spencer, C. E. M. S.   Prince Rupert   **92**

Tacitus, C.   Complete works of Tacitus   **878**

Taylor, J.   The generalissimo   **92**

Thomas, E. M.   Robert E. Lee   **92**

Thomas, E.   Ike's bluff   **973.92**

Tuchman, B. W.   Stilwell and the American experience in China, 1911-45   **327**

Unger, H. G.   The last founding father   **92**

Vidal, G.   Inventing a nation: Washington, Adams, Jefferson   **973.4**

Von Tunzelmann, A.   Red heat   **972.9**

Wallace, A. F. C.   The long bitter trail   **323.1**

Warner, E. J.   Generals in blue   **920**

Warner, E. J.   Generals in gray   **920**

Weintraub, S.   15 stars   **920**

Wert, J. D.   Cavalryman of the lost cause   **92**

Wert, J. D.   Custer   **92**

Wicker, T.   Dwight D. Eisenhower   **973.921**

Wiencek, H.   An imperfect god   **973.4**

Wilentz, S.   Andrew Jackson   **92**

Williams, C.   The last great Frenchman   **944**

Wilson, E.   Patriotic gore   **810**

Woodward, B.   The commanders   **973.928**

Woodworth, S. E.   Sherman   **92**

The **generals.** Ricks, T. E.   **355.009**

GENERALS

See also Military personnel

GENERALS -- CONFEDERATE STATES OF AMERICA -- BIOGRAPHY

Blount, R.   Robert E. Lee   **92**

Davis, W. C.   Crucible of commmand   **920**

GENERALS -- FRANCE -- BIOGRAPHY

Auricchio, L.   The marquis   **92**

The Black Count   **944.04**

GENERALS -- ISRAEL

Landau, D.   Arik   **92**

GENERALS -- ISRAEL -- BIOGRAPHY

Bar-On, M.   Moshe Dayan   **956.940**

GENERALS -- UNITED STATES -- BIOGRAPHY

Herman, A. Douglas MacArthur **92**

White, R. C. American Ulysses **92**

GENERALS -- UNITED STATES -- HISTORY -- 20TH CENTURY

Ricks, T. E. The generals **355.009**

Generals in blue. Warner, E. J. **920**

Generals in gray. Warner, E. J. **920**

GENERALS' SPOUSES -- UNITED STATES -- BIOGRAPHY

Fraser, F. The Washingtons **92**

The **generals'** war. Gordon, M. R. **956.7**

Generation chef. Stabiner, K. **641.5**

Generation kill. Wright, E. **956.7**

GENERATION X

See also Population

GENERATION Y

See also Population

Generations of captivity. Berlin, I. **326**

GENERATIVE ORGANS *See* Reproductive system

GENERIC DRUGS

See also Drugs; Generic products

GENERIC PRODUCTS

See also Commercial products; Manufactures

GENEROSITY

Santi, J. The giving way to happiness **179**

GENES

Eldredge, N. Why we do it **155.3**

Mukherjee, S. The gene **616.042**

Shenk, D. The genius in all of us **155.2**

GENES *See* Heredity

GENES -- POPULAR WORKS

Tanzi, R. E. Super genes **613**

Genes, girls, and Gamow. Watson, J. D. **92**

Genesis: a living conversation. Moyers, B. **222**

Genet, Jean

The blacks: a clown show **842**

The maids [and] Deathwatch **842**

GENETIC CODE

Cobb, M. Life's Greatest Secret **572.8**

GENETIC CODE

The annotated and illustrated double helix **572.8**

GENETIC COUNSELING

See also Medical genetics; Prenatal diagnosis

GENETIC ENGINEERING

Adamchak, R. W. Tomorrow's table **664**

Rutherford, A. Creation **576.8**

Shapiro, B. How to Clone a Mammoth **591.68**

Stock, G. Redesigning humans **176**

Genetic rounds. Marion, R. **92**

GENETIC SCREENING

Collins, F. S. The language of life **616**

GENETIC SURGERY *See* Genetic engineering

Genetically modified foods. **363.1**

GENETICALLY MODIFIED FOODS

Adamchak, R. W. Tomorrow's table **664**

Genetically modified foods **363.1**

Pringle, P. Food, inc **363.1**

Shetterly, C. Modified **664**

GENETICISTS

Henig, R. M. The monk in the garden: how Gregor Mendel and his pea plants solved the mystery of inheritance **576.5**

Malone, J. W. It doesn't take a rocket scientist **920**

GENETICS

Arney, K. Herding Hemingway's Cats **572.8**

Dawkins, R. The selfish gene **576**

Endersby, J. A guinea pig's history of biology **576.5**

Epstein, D. The sports gene **613.7**

Francis, R. C. Epigenetics **572.8**

Henderson, M. 100 most important science ideas **500**

Kean, S. The violinist's thumb **572.8**

Kurzweil, R. The singularity is near **153.9**

Marks, J. What it means to be 98[percent] chimpanzee **599.93**

Moalem, S. Survival of the sickest **616**

Raine, A. The anatomy of violence **616.85**

Ridley, M. The agile gene **155.7**

Ridley, M. Francis Crick **92**

Ridley, M. Genome **599.93**

Ross, T. A cancer in the family **616.99**

Sagan, C. The dragons of Eden **153**

Stock, G. Redesigning humans **176**

Sykes, B. Adam's curse **599.93**

Sykes, B. DNA USA **559.9**

GENETICS

See also Biology; Embryology; Life (Biology); Mendel's law; Reproduction

Genetics & inherited conditions. Knight, J. A. **576.5**

GENETICS -- ENCYCLOPEDIAS

Knight, J. A. Genetics & inherited conditions **576.5**

GENETICS -- HISTORY

Kenneally, C. The invisible history of the human race **616**

Mukherjee, S. The gene **616.042**

GENETICS AND ENVIRONMENT *See* Nature and nurture

Genghis Khan and the making of the modern world. Weatherford, J. M. **92**

Genghis Khan and the Quest for God. Weatherford, J. **950**

Genghis Khan, 1162-1227

About

Weatherford, J. M. Genghis Khan and the making of the modern world **92**

GENITALIA *See* Reproductive system

Genius. Bloom, H. **153.9**

GENIUS

See also Psychology

GENIUS

Barnett, K. The spark **618.92**

Bloom, H. Genius   **153.9**

Stephens, K. The Prodigy's Cousin   **155.45**

The **genius.** Harris, D.   **92**

The **genius** in all of us. Shenk, D.   **155.2**

The **Genius** of Birds. Ackerman, J.   **598**

GENOCIDE

Akcam, T. A shameful act   **956.6**

Alvarez, A. Native America and the question of genocide   **973**

Gourevitch, P. We wish to inform you that tomorrow we will be killed with our families   **967.571**

Hatzfeld, J. The antelope's strategy   **967.571**

Hatzfeld, J. Machete season   **967.571**

Kidder, T. Strength in what remains   **92**

Sands, P. East West Street   **345**

Stearns, J. K. Dancing in the glory of monsters   **967.51**

Ureneck, L. The Great Fire   **956.1**

Wiesenthal, S. The sunflower   **179.7**

GENOCIDE -- ARMENIA

MacKeen, D. A. The hundred-year walk   **92**

GENOCIDE -- ARMENIA -- PSYCHOLOGICAL ASPECTS

Toumani, M. There was and there was not   **327**

GENOCIDE -- BANGLADESH

Bass, G. J. The Blood telegram   **327.73**

GENOCIDE -- EUROPE

Snyder, T. D. Bloodlands   **940.54**

GENOCIDE -- PSYCHOLOGICAL ASPECTS

Goldhagen, D. J. Worse than war   **364.1**

GENOCIDE -- TURKEY

Armenian Golgotha   **956**

Balakian, P. The burning Tigris   **956.6**

Genome. Ridley, M.   **599.93**

GENOME See Genomes

The **Genome** Generation. Finkel, E.   **572**

GENOMES

Finkel, E. The Genome Generation   **572**

Ridley, M. Genome   **599.93**

Venter, J. C. Life at the Speed of Light   **303.48**

GENOMES

See also Genetics

GENOMICS

Roberts, D. Fatal invention   **305.8**

Venter, J. C. Life at the Speed of Light   **303.48**

Genoways, Ted

The chain   **338.7**

GENRE PAINTING

See also Painting

Genrefied classics. Frolund, T.   **016**

Genreflecting. Herald, D. T.   **016**

Genreflecting advisory series

Bosman, E. Gay, lesbian, bisexual, and transgendered literature   **016**

Cords, S. S. The real story   **025.5**

Fonseca, A. J. Hooked on horror III   **016**

Frolund, T. Genrefied classics   **016**

Herald, D. T. Fluent in fantasy   **016**

Herald, D. T. Genreflecting   **016**

Herald, D. T. Strictly science fiction   **016**

Johnson, S. L. Historical fiction II   **016**

Vnuk, R. Women's fiction   **016**

Gentile, Gian P.

Wrong turn   **355.02**

Gentile, Mary C.

Giving voice to values   **174**

Gentile, Olivia

Life list   **92**

The **gentle** subversive. Lytle, M. H.   **92**

Gentleman spy. Grose, P.   **92**

Gentry, Ann

The Real Food Daily cookbook   **641.5**

Gentry, Curt

Bugliosi, V. Helter skelter   **364.1**

J. Edgar Hoover   **353**

GEOBIOLOGY -- RESEARCH -- ANECDOTES

Jahren, H. Lab girl   **92**

GEOCHEMISTRY

See also Chemistry; Earth sciences; Petrology

GEOCHEMISTS

Maddox, B. Rosalind Franklin: the dark lady of DNA   **92**

GEOCHRONOMETRY

Macdougall, J. D. Nature's clocks   **551.7**

GEODESY

See also Earth; Measurement

GEODESY -- EUROPE -- HISTORY

Ferreiro, L. D. Measure of the Earth   **526**

GEODETIC ASTRONOMY -- HISTORY -- 18TH CENTURY

Wulf, A. Chasing Venus   **523.9**

Geoffrey Chaucer's The Canterbury tales.   **821**

GEOGRAPHERS

Nicastro, N. Circumference   **526**

GEOGRAPHIC INFORMATION SYSTEMS -- HISTORY

Bray, H. You are here   **910.285**

GEOGRAPHIC NAMES

See also Names

GEOGRAPHIC NAMES -- ENCYCLOPEDIAS

Home ground   **917**

GEOGRAPHIC NAMES -- UNITED STATES

Beatty, M. A. County name origins of the United States   **917**

Shearer, B. F. State names, seals, flags, and symbols   **929.9**

GEOGRAPHICAL ATLASES See Atlases

GEOGRAPHICAL DISTRIBUTION OF ANIMALS AND PLANTS See Biogeography

GEOGRAPHICAL MYTHS

See also Mythology

GEOGRAPHY
Alder, K. The measure of all things **526**
Atlas A-Z **912**
The World Almanac and Book of Facts 2015 **030**
GEOGRAPHY
See also Earth; Earth sciences; World history
GEOGRAPHY -- DICTIONARIES
See also Encyclopedias and dictionaries
GEOGRAPHY -- MAPS
Oxford new concise world atlas **912**
GEOGRAPHY -- MISCELLANEA
Fuller, G. The trivia lover's guide to the world **910**
GEOGRAPHY -- PICTORIAL WORKS
Hitchcock, S. T. National geographic rarely seen **779**
GEOGRAPHY, HISTORICAL *See* Historical geography
GEOGRAPHY, POLITICAL *See* Geopolitics
GEOLOGICAL TIME
Macdougall, J. D. Nature's clocks **551.7**
Richet, P. A natural history of time **551.7**
Stager, C. Deep future **363.7**
GEOLOGISTS
Bass, R. Why I came West **92**
Dennett, D. C. Darwin's dangerous idea **146**
Dolnick, E. Down the great unknown **979.1**
Ewing, H. P. The lost world of James Smithson **92**
Sandweiss, M. A. Passing strange **92**
Winchester, S. The map that changed the world **526**
GEOLOGISTS
See also Scientists
GEOLOGY
Alvarez, W. A Most Improbable Journey **508**
Bjornerud, M. Reading the rocks **551.7**
Lambert, D. The field guide to geology **551**
Montgomery, D. R. The rocks don't lie **551.48**
Shubin, N. H. The universe within **550**
Welland, M. Sand **553.6**
Whitehouse, D. Into the Heart of Our World **551**
GEOLOGY
See also Earth sciences; Science
GEOLOGY -- MAPS
See also Maps
GEOLOGY, STRATIGRAPHIC *See* Stratigraphic geology
GEOMAGIC (FIRM)
Ping Fu Bend, not break **92**
GEOMETRIC PATTERNS *See* Patterns (Mathematics)
GEOMETRICAL DRAWING
See also Drawing; Geometry
GEOMETRY
Alexander, A. Infinitesimal **511**
Apostol, T. M. New Horizons in Geometry **516**
Lehmann, I. The secrets of triangles **516**
Livio, M. The golden ratio **516.2**

Nadis, S. The shape of inner space **530.1**
GEOMETRY
See also Mathematics
GEOMETRY -- HISTORY
Berlinski, D. The king of infinite space **516.2**
GEOMETRY IN NATURE
Ball, P. Patterns in nature **500.2**
GEOMORPHOLOGISTS -- UNITED STATES -- BIOGRAPHY
Felt, H. Soundings **526**
GEOPHYSICS
See also Earth sciences; Physics
GEOPOLITICS
The CIA World Factbook **028**
Emmerson, C. The future history of the Arctic **998**
Kaplan, R. D. In Europe's shadow **949.8**
McMeekin, S. The Berlin-Baghdad express **940.3**
GEOPOLITICS
See also International relations; Political science
GEOPOLITICS -- HISTORY -- 21ST CENTURY -- FORECASTING
Brzezinski, Z. Strategic vision **327.1**
Georgano, G. N.
(ed) The Beaulieu encyclopedia of the automobile **629.222**
George B. McClellan. Sears, S. W. **92**
George Balanchine: the ballet maker. Gottlieb, R. A. **92**
George Bush. Parmet, H. S. **92**
George Eliot. Hughes, K. **823**
George F. Kennan. Gaddis, J. L. **327**
George Frideric Handel. Harris, E. T. **92**
George Gershwin. Hyland, W. G. **92**
George Gershwin. Pollack, H. **92**
George Harrison. Thomson, G. **92**
George III, King of Great Britain, 1738-1820
About
Fraser, F. Princesses **920**
Hadlow, J. A royal experiment **92**
Tillyard, S. K. A royal affair **920**
GEORGE INN (ENFIELD, LONDON, ENGLAND) -- HISTORY
Brown, P. Shakespeare's Pub **647.9**
George Marshall. Unger, I. **92**
George Mason, forgotten founder. Broadwater, J. **92**
George Philip & Son
New Concise World Atlas **912**
George Sand. Harlan, E. **92**
George Sand. Jack, B. E. **843**
George V, King of Great Britain, 1865-1936
About
Carter, M. George, Nicholas, and Wilhelm **940.3**
Clay, C. King, Kaiser, Tsar **920**
George Washington. Randall, W. S. **92**
George Washington and the new nation, 1783-1793.

Flexner, J. T.   **92**

George Washington's journey. Breen, T. H.   **92**

George Washington's secret six. Yaeger, D.   **973.4**

George Washington's secret spy war. Nagy, J. A.   **973.385**

George Washington: anguish and farewell 1793-1799. Flexner, J. T.   **92**

George Washington: the forge of experience, 1732-1775. Flexner, J. T.   **92**

George Washington: the Founding Father. Johnson, P.   **92**

George, being George.   **92**

George, Don
   (ed) An Innocent Abroad   **910.4**

George, Henry, 1839-1897
About
   Heilbroner, R. L. The worldly philosophers   **330.1**

George, John H.
   Boller, P. F. They never said it   **808.88**

George, Nicholas, and Wilhelm. Carter, M.   **940.3**

George, Rose
   The big necessity   **363.7**

George-Warren, Holly
   Public cowboy no. 1   **92**
   Lang, M. The road to Woodstock   **781.66**

Georges, Nicole J.
About
   Georges, N. J. Calling Dr. Laura   **92**

Georges-Picot, Charles Francois, b. 1870
About
   Barr, J. A line in the sand   **956**

GEORGETOWN (WASHINGTON, D.C.) -- BIOGRAPHY
   Herken, G. The Georgetown set   **975.3**

The **Georgetown** set. Herken, G.   **975.3**

GEORGIA -- HISTORY
   Pressly, P. M. On the rim of the Caribbean   **975.8**

GEORGIA -- RURAL CONDITIONS
   Sherrod, S. The courage to hope   **975.8**

GEORGIA -- SOCIAL LIFE AND CUSTOMS
   Carter, J. An hour before daylight   **92**

Georgia O'Keeffe: a life. Robinson, R.   **709**

Georgiana, Duchess of Devonshire. Foreman, A.   **941.07**

The **Georgics** of Virgil. Virgil   **872**

GEOSCIENCE *See* Earth sciences; Geology

GEOSPATIAL DATA
   Bray, H. You are here   **910.285**

GEOTHERMAL RESOURCES
   See also Geochemistry; Ocean energy resources; Renewable energy resources

Geraghty, Tony
   Soldiers of fortune   **355.3**

Gerald, Gloria E.
   (jt. auth) Gerald, M. C. The Biology Book   **570.9**

Gerald, Michael C.

The Biology Book   **570.9**

Gerardi, Juan, 1922-1998
About
   Goldman, F. The art of political murder   **972.81**

Gerding, Stephanie K.
   Winning grants   **025.1**

Gerdts, William H.
   American impressionism   **759.13**

Gerhartsreiter, Christian, 1961-
About
   Kirn, W. Blood will out   **364.152**

Gering, Jacquie
   Quilting modern   **746.46**

The **Germ** Files. Tetro, J.   **579.3**

GERM THEORY *See* Life -- Origin

GERM THEORY OF DISEASE
   Biddle, W. A field guide to germs   **616**
   Tetro, J. The Germ Files   **579.3**

GERM THEORY OF DISEASE
   See also Communicable diseases

GERM WARFARE *See* Biological warfare

GERMAN COOKING
   Nolen, J. German cooking now   **641.594**

German cooking now. Nolen, J.   **641.594**

GERMAN ESPIONAGE
   Vaughan, H. Sleeping with the enemy   **92**

The **German** genius. Watson, P.   **943**

GERMAN LANGUAGE
   See also Language and languages

GERMAN LANGUAGE -- DICTIONARIES
   Random House Webster's German-English, English-German dictionary   **433**

German library [series]
   Lessing, G. E. Nathan the Wise, Minna von Barnhelm, and other plays and writings   **832**

GERMAN LITERATURE
   Encyclopedia of German literature   **830**

GERMAN LITERATURE
   See also Literature

GERMAN LITERATURE -- ENCYCLOPEDIAS
   Encyclopedia of German literature   **830**

GERMAN LITERATURE -- HISTORY AND CRITICISM
   Sebald, W. G. On the natural history of destruction   **833**

GERMAN OCCUPATION OF FRANCE, 1940-1945 *See* France -- History -- 1940-1945, German occupation

GERMAN POETRY
   Celan, P. Breathturn into timestead   **635.9**

GERMAN POETRY -- COLLECTIONS
   Across the land and the water   **831**

GERMAN SCIENTISTS
   Jacobsen, A. Operation Paperclip   **940.54**

German voices. Tubach, F. C.   **943.086**

The **German** War. Stargardt, N.   **943.086**

German, Bill
About
German, B. Under their thumb   **781.66**
German, Roger
Remodeling a basement   **643**
GERMANIC PEOPLES
Pagden, A. Peoples and empires   **909**
Germano, William P.
Getting it published   **070.5**
Germany.   **914.304**
GERMANY
Harding, T. The House by the Lake   **943**
Honigstein, R. Das Reboot   **796.334**
Germany. MacGregor, N.   **943**
GERMANY (EAST)
See also Germany
**GERMANY (EAST) -- MINISTERIUM FÜR
STAATSSICHERHEIT**
Garton-Ash, T. The file   **327.12**
**GERMANY (EAST) -- POLITICS AND GOV-
ERNMENT**
Sarotte, M. E. The collapse   **943.087**
**GERMANY (EAST) -- POLITICS AND GOV-
ERNMENT -- 1989-1990**
Sarotte, M. E. The collapse   **943.087**
GERMANY (WEST) *See* Germany
**GERMANY -- ARMED FORCES -- HISTORY --
20TH CENTURY -- SOURCES**
Soldaten   **940.54**
**GERMANY -- ARMED FORCES -- HISTORY --
WORLD WAR, 1939-1945**
Kennedy, P. M. Engineers of victory   **940.54**
**GERMANY -- ARMED FORCES -- WEAPONS
SYSTEMS -- HISTORY -- 20TH CENTURY**
Preston, D. A higher form of killing   **940.4**
GERMANY -- CIVILIZATION
MacGregor, N. Germany   **943**
**GERMANY -- CIVILIZATION -- AMERICAN
INFLUENCES**
Urwand, B. The collaboration   **791.43**
GERMANY -- DESCRIPTION AND TRAVEL
Fodor's Germany   **914.3**
Germany   **914.304**
GERMANY -- ETHNIC RELATIONS
Dwork, D. Holocaust: a history   **940.53**
Fritzsche, P. Life and death in the Third
Reich   **943.086**
**GERMANY -- FOREIGN RELATIONS -- SO-
VIET UNION**
Kinney, D. The devil's diary   **940.53**
**GERMANY -- FOREIGN RELATIONS -- TUR-
KEY**
McMeekin, S. The Berlin-Baghdad express   **940.3**
**GERMANY -- FOREIGN RELATIONS -- UNIT-
ED STATES**
Beschloss, M. R. The conquerors: Roosevelt, Tru-
man, and the destruction of Hitler's Germany,
1941-1945   **940.53**
GERMANY -- HEER
Philpott, W. Three armies on the Somme   **940.4**
**GERMANY -- HEER -- BAYERISCHES RE-
SERVE-INFANTERIE-REGIMENT 16**
Weber, T. Hitler's first war   **940.4**
GERMANY -- HISTORY
Beachy, R. Gay Berlin   **306.76**
MacGregor, N. Germany   **943**
GERMANY -- HISTORY -- 0-1517
Tacitus, C. Complete works of Tacitus   **878**
GERMANY -- HISTORY -- 1517-1740
Robisheaux, T. The last witch of Langenburg **133.4**
GERMANY -- HISTORY -- 1918-1933
Evans, R. J. The coming of the Third Reich **943.08**
Goebbels   **92**
Haffner, S. Defying Hitler   **943.085**
MacMillan, M. Paris 1919   **940.3**
GERMANY -- HISTORY -- 1918-1945
Mazower, M. Hitler's empire   **940.53**
GERMANY -- HISTORY -- 1933-1945
Goebbels   **92**
Marsh, C. Strange glory   **92**
Stargardt, N. The German War   **943.086**
Urwand, B. The collaboration   **791.43**
**GERMANY -- HISTORY -- 1933-1945 -- BIOG-
RAPHY**
Gortemaker, H. B. Eva Braun   **92**
GERMANY -- HISTORY -- 1945-1955
Bessel, R. Germany 1945   **943.087**
Taylor, F. Exorcising Hitler   **943.087**
GERMANY -- HISTORY -- UNIFICATION, 1990
Service, R.   The End of the Cold War, 1985-
1991   **909.82**
GERMANY -- INTELLECTUAL LIFE
Watson, P. The German genius   **943**
GERMANY -- KRIEGSMARINE
Blair, C. Hitler's U-boat war   **940.54**
Massie, R. K. Castles of steel   **940.4**
**GERMANY -- POLITICS AND GOVERNMENT
-- 1866-1918**
Steinberg, J. Bismarck   **92**
**GERMANY -- POLITICS AND GOVERNMENT
-- 1918-1933**
Hitler, A. Mein Kampf   **92**
Turner, H. A. Hitler's thirty days to power **943.086**
**GERMANY -- POLITICS AND GOVERNMENT
-- 1933-1945**
Orbach, D. The plots against Hitler   **940.53**
**GERMANY -- POLITICS AND GOVERNMENT
-- 1945-1990**
Taylor, F. Exorcising Hitler   **943.087**
GERMANY -- SOCIAL CONDITIONS
Aycoberry, P. The social history of the Third
Reich   **943.086**

GERMANY -- SOCIAL LIFE AND CUSTOMS
Tubach, F. C. German voices   **943.086**
Germany 1945. Bessel, R.   **943.087**
Germany, 1866-1945. Craig, G. A.   **943.08**
Germs. Engelberg, S.   **358**
GERMS *See* Bacteria; Germ theory of disease; Microorganisms
Geronimo. Utley, R. M.   **92**
Geronimo, Apache Chief, 1829-1909
        About
Brown, D. A. The American West   **978**
Brown, D. A. Bury my heart at Wounded Knee   **970.004**
Roberts, D. Once they moved like the wind **970.004**
Utley, R. M. Geronimo   **92**
GERONTOLOGY
    See also Social sciences
Geroux, William
The Mathews Men   **940.54**
Gershwin, George, 1898-1937
        About
Feinstein, M. The Gershwins and me   **92**
Gilbert, S. E. The music of Gershwin   **780**
Hyland, W. G. George Gershwin   **92**
Pollack, H. George Gershwin   **92**
Gershwin, Ira, 1896-1983
        About
Feinstein, M. The Gershwins and me   **92**
The **Gershwins** and me. Feinstein, M.   **92**
Gerson, Fany
My sweet Mexico   **641.5**
Gerson, Stéphane
Nostradamus   **92**
Gerstler, Amy
Scattered at sea   **811**
Gerth, Karl
As China goes, so goes the world   **339.4**
Gertie's ultimate dress book. Hirsch, G.   **646.4**
Gertner, Jon
The idea factory   **384**
Gertrude Bell. Howell, G.   **92**
Gervasi, Lori Hartman
Fight like a girl-- and win   **613.6**
Gesell Institute of Child Development
Ames, L. B. Your five-year-old   **649**
Gessen, Masha
Perfect rigor   **92**
Where the Jews aren't   **957.7**
Gessner, David
All the Wild That Remains   **363.7**
GESTALT PSYCHOLOGY
    See also Consciousness; Perception; Psychology; Senses and sensation; Theory of knowledge
Get a financial life. Kobliner, B.   **332.024**
Get Capone. Eig, J.   **92**

Get cooking. Katzen, M.   **641.5**
Get happy: the life of Judy Garland. Clarke, G. **92**
Get me out. Epstein, R. H.   **618.2**
Get set, sew. Bull, J.   **646.2**
Get what's yours. Solman, P.   **368.4**
Getting a life with Asperger's. Saperstein, J. A. **92**
Getting financial aid.   **378.3**
Getting from me to we. Tuck, S.   **155.4**
Getting in by standing out. Bedor, D.   **371**
Getting it published.   **070.5**
Getting it wrong. Campbell, W. J.   **071**
Getting past no. Ury, W.   **158**
Getting Schooled. Keizer, G.   **373.1**
Getting smart. Vander Ark, T.   **371.33**
Getting the best out of college. Crossman, A. **378.1**
Getting what we deserve. Sommer, A.   **362.1**
GETTY CENTER (LOS ANGELES, CALIF.)
Meier, R. Building the Getty   **708**
Getty Images Inc.
History of the world in photographs   **909.8**
Getty, J. Paul, 1892-1976
        About
Walsh, J. The J. Paul Getty Museum and its collections   **708.1**
Getty, Sarah
Bring me her heart   **811**
Gettysburg. Sears, S. W.   **973.7**
Gettysburg. Guelzo, A. C.   **973.7**
GETTYSBURG (PA.), BATTLE OF, 1863
Foote, S. Stars in their courses   **973.7**
Guelzo, A. C. Gettysburg   **973.7**
McPherson, J. M. Hallowed ground   **973.7**
Sears, S. W. Gettysburg   **973.7**
GETTYSBURG (PA.), BATTLE OF, 1863
    See also Battles; United States -- History -- 1861-1865, Civil War -- Campaigns
The **Gettysburg** gospel. Boritt, G. S.   **973.7**
Gevisser, Mark
        About
Gevisser, M. Lost and Found in Johannesburg, a memoir   **92**
Gevisser, Mark
A legacy of liberation   **92**
Gewanter, David
(ed) Lowell, R. Collected poems   **811**
GEYSERS
    See also Geology; Geothermal resources; Physical geography; Water
GHANA -- BIOGRAPHY
Mahama, J. D. My first coup d'etat and other true stories from the lost decades of Africa **966.705**
GHANA -- DESCRIPTION AND TRAVEL
Hartman, S. V. Lose your mother   **323**
Ghayour, Sabrina
Persiana   **641.595**
Ghetto Brother.   **92**

GHETTOS, INNER CITY *See* Inner cities

Ghettoside. Leovy, J.   364.152

Ghettostadt. Horwitz, G. J.   940.53

Ghez, Didier
  They drew as they pleased   741.58

Ghose, Aruna
  (ed) Eyewitness Travel Malaysia & Singapore   915.9

Ghosh, Amitav, 1956-
  The great derangement   809

Ghost. Ramsland, K. M.   133.1

Ghost hunters. Blum, D.   133.9

Ghost in the wires. Mitnick, K. D.   364.16

The **ghost** map. Johnson, S.   614.5

Ghost soldiers. Sides, H.   940.54

GHOST STORIES
  See also Fantasy fiction; Horror fiction; Paranormal fiction

GHOST TOWNS
  See also Extinct cities

Ghost wars. Coll, S.   958.1

Ghostland. Dickey, C.   133.1

GHOSTS
  Aykroyd, P. A history of ghosts   133.1
  Boylan, J. F. I'm looking through you   92
  Dickey, C. Ghostland   133.1
  Norman, M. Haunted America   133.1
  Ramsland, K. M. Ghost   133.1

GHOSTS
  See also Apparitions; Folklore; Spirits

GHOSTS -- ENCYCLOPEDIAS
  Guiley, R. E. The encyclopedia of ghosts and spirits   133.1

The **ghosts** of Cannae. O'Connell, R. L.   937

Ghosts of empire. Kwarteng, K.   909

The **Ghosts** of K2. Conefrey, M.   796.522

The **ghosts** of Manila. Kram, M.   796.83

Ghosts of Spain. Tremlett, G.   946

Ghosts of Vesuvius. Pellegrino, C. R.   937

Ghoting, Saroj Nadkarni
  STEP into storytime   027.62

Ghouri, Nadene
  The lightless sky   958.104

GI brides. Barrett, D.   940.53

Giangreco, D. M.
  Hell to pay   940.54

The **giant** of the French Revolution. Lawday, D.   92

GIANT PANDA
  Croke, V. The lady and the panda   599.78
  Nicholls, H. The way of the panda   599.7

GIANTS
  See also Folklore; Monsters

Gibbon, Edward
  The decline and fall of the Roman empire   937

Gibbon, Guy E.
  (ed) Archaeology of prehistoric native America   970.01

Gibbon, Piers
  Tribe   305.8

Gibbons, Euell
  Stalking the wild asparagus   581.6

Gibbons, Reginald
  Creatures of a day   811
  It's time: poems   811

GIBBS & COX -- HISTORY -- 20TH CENTURY
  Ujifusa, S. A man and his ship   623.8

Gibbs, Nancy
  (jt. auth) Duffy, M. The presidents club   973.92

Gibbs, William F. (William Francis), 1886-1967
        About
  Ujifusa, S. A man and his ship   623.8

Gibler, John
  To die in Mexico   363.45

Gibney, Mike
  Something to chew on   616.02

Gibran, Kahlil
  The collected works   818
  The Prophet   811

Gibson family
        About
  Sharfstein, D. J. The invisible line   305.8

Gibson, Carrie
  Empire's Crossroads   972.9

Gibson, Ian
  Federico Garcia Lorca: a life   92

Gibson, Larry S.
  Young Thurgood   347.73

Gibson, Walter Brown
  Hoyle's modern encyclopedia of card games   795.4

Gibson, William
  The miracle worker   812

Giddings, Paula
  Ida: a sword among lions   92

Giddins, Gary
  Bing Crosby: a pocketful of dreams: the early years, 1903-1940   92
  Jazz   781.65
  Visions of jazz   781.65
  Weather bird   781.65

Gideon's trumpet. Lewis, A.   345

Gideon, Clarence Earl
        About
  Lewis, A. Gideon's trumpet   345

Gielgud, John Sir, 1904-2000
        About
  Gielgud, J. An actor and his time   92

Gienapp, William E.
  Abraham Lincoln and Civil War America   973.7

Gierach, John
  All Fishermen Are Liars   799.12

Gies, David Thatcher
  (ed) The Cambridge history of Spanish litera-

ture   860
Gies, Frances
  Life in a medieval village   940.1
  Gies, J. Life in a medieval castle   940.2
  Gies, J. Life in a medieval city   940.1
Gies, Joseph
  Gies, F. Life in a medieval village 940.1
  Life in a medieval castle   940.2
  Life in a medieval city   940.1
Gies, Miep
  Anne Frank remembered   92
Giesecke, Joan
  Fundamentals of library supervision   023
Gifford Pinchot and the making of modern environ-
  mentalism. Miller, C.   333.7
Gifford, Bill
  Ledyard   92
Gifford, Justin
  Street poison   813
Giffords, Gabrielle D. (Gabrielle Dee), 1970-
  Enough   363.33
The **gift**. Hafiz   891
GIFT BASKETS
  Battista, M. Food gift love   642
The **gift** of failure. Lahey, J.   649
The **gift** of Southern cooking. Lewis, E.   641.59
The **gift** of thanks. Visser, M.   394
The **gift** of years. Chittister, J.   200
GIFT WRAPPING
  See also Packaging; Paper crafts
Gifted children. Winner, E.   155.45
GIFTED CHILDREN
  See also Exceptional children; Gifted people
GIFTED CHILDREN
  Nugent, B. American nerd   305.9
  Winner, E. Gifted children   155.45
GIFTED WOMEN
  Holroyd, M. A book of secrets   306.874
GIFTS
  Battista, M. Food gift love   642
  Shore, D. Half yard gifts   646.2
  Waldfogel, J. Scroogenomics   339.4
GIFTS
  See also Manners and customs
Gifts differing. Myers, I. B.   155.2
The **gifts** of the Jews. Cahill, T.   909
Gig posters volume 1. Hayes, C.   741.6
Gigante, Denise
  The Keats brothers   920
GILA NATIONAL FOREST (N.M.)
  Connors, P. Fire season   634.9
Gilbert, Carter Rowell
  National Audubon Society field guide to fishes,
  North America   597
Gilbert, Daniel
  Stumbling on happiness   158

Gilbert, Elizabeth, 1969-
  Big magic   153.3
        About
  Gilbert, E. Eat, pray, love   92
Gilbert, Jack, 1925-2012
  Collected poems   811
  The dance most of all   811
  Refusing heaven   811
Gilbert, Martin
  The First World War   940.3
  History of the twentieth century   909.82
  Jerusalem in the twentieth century   956.94
  Kristallnacht   940.53
  The Routledge atlas of the Holocaust   940.53
  The Second World War   940.53
Gilbert, Sandra M.
  Death's door   155.9
Gilbert, Steven E.
  The music of Gershwin   780
Gildea, William
  The longest fight   796.83
Gilder, Louisa
  The age of entanglement   530.1
Gilding, Paul
  The great disruption   304.2
Gilgamesh. Gilgamesh   892
GILGAMESH
  Damrosch, D. The buried book   809
Gilgamesh
  Gilgamesh   892
Gill, A. A., 1954-
        About
  Gill, A. A. To America with love   917.3
Gill, Anton
  Art lover   92
Gill, Jonathan
  Harlem   974.7
Gilleland, Diane
  All points patchwork   746.46
Gillespie, Carmen
  Critical companion to Alice Walker   813
  Critical companion to Toni Morrison   813
Gillespie, Dizzy, 1917-1993
        About
  Feather, L. From Satchmo to Miles   920
  Lees, G. You can't steal a gift   781.65
Gillespie, Marcia Ann
  Maya Angelou   92
Gillespie, Michael Patrick
  Fargnoli, A. N. Critical companion to James
  Joyce   823
Gillette, J. Michael
  Designing With Light: An Introduction to Stage
  Lighting   792
  Theatrical design and production   792.02
Gillette, Michael L.

Lady Bird Johnson **92**

Gillies, Andrea

About

Gillies, A. Keeper **616.8**

Gilligan, Carol

The birth of pleasure **152.4**

Gillingham, Sara Kate

The Kitchn cookbook **641.5**

Gilmore, Glenda Elizabeth

These United States **973.9**

Gilmour, David

The long recessional: the imperial life of Rudyard Kipling **92**

Gimbel, Wendy

Havana dreams **972.91**

Gimlette, John

Theatre of fish **917**

GINGERBREAD

Beddall, C. The magic of gingerbread **641.86**

Farrow, J. Gingerbread Houses, Animals and Decorations **641.865**

Samuell, K. A year of gingerbread houses **745.5**

Gingerbread Houses, Animals and Decorations. Farrow, J. **641.865**

Ginsberg, Allen, 1926-1997

Collected poems, 1947-1997 **811**

Deliberate prose **814**

Howl, and other poems **811**

About

Ginsberg, A. The letters of Allen Ginsberg **92**

Morgan, B. I celebrate myself **92**

Spontaneous mind **811**

Ginsburg, Ruth Bader

About

Hirshman, L. Sisters in law **347.73**

Ginzberg, Lori D.

Elizabeth Cady Stanton **92**

Ginzler, Elinor

Delehanty, H. Caring for your parents **362.6**

Gioia, Dana

Can poetry matter? **809.1**

Disappearing ink **811**

(ed) Twentieth-century American poetry **811**

Gioia, Ted

Delta blues **781.643**

The history of jazz **781.65**

Work songs **782.42**

Gionfriddo, Paul

Losing Tim **92**

Gionfriddo, Tim

About

Gionfriddo, P. Losing Tim **92**

Giovanni, Nikki

Bicycles **811**

Blues **811**

The collected poetry of Nikki Giovanni, 1968-

1998 **811**

Quilting the black-eyed pea **811**

About

Black women writers (1950-1980) **810**

Chasing Utopia **811**

GIPSIES See Gypsies

GIRAFFE

Giraffe reflections **599.638**

Giraffe reflections. **599.638**

Giraldi, William

The Hero's Body **92**

Giramonti, Lisa Borgnes

Novel interiors **747**

Giridharadas, Anand

About

Giridharadas, A. India calling **954.05**

A **Girl** and Her Greens. Bloomfield, A. **641.65**

The **girl** from foreign. Shepard, S. **92**

Girl land. Flanagan, C. **305.235**

Girl sleuth. Rehak, M. **813**

Girl Unbroken. Calcaterra, R. **306**

The **girl** who escaped ISIS. **956.7**

The **Girl** Who Fell to Earth. Al-Maria, S. **92**

The **girl's** guide to absolutely everything. Kirsch, M. **646.7**

The **girl's** guide to homelessness. Karp, B. **92**

Girling, Richard

The Hunt for the Golden Mole **591.68**

GIRLS

Deak, J. Girls will be girls **649**

Flanagan, C. Girl land **305.235**

Simmons, R. Odd girl out **305.23**

GIRLS

See also Children

GIRLS -- AFGHANISTAN

Nordberg, J. The underground girls of Kabul **305.42**

GIRLS -- EDUCATION

Lamb, C. I am Malala **92**

GIRLS -- EDUCATION

See also Education

GIRLS -- EMPLOYMENT See Women -- Employment; Youth -- Employment

GIRLS -- NEW YORK (STATE) -- NEW YORK -- BIOGRAPHY

Rips, N. Trying to float **974.7**

GIRLS -- PSYCHOLOGY

Orenstein, P. Cinderella ate my daughter **305.23**

Simmons, R. Odd girl out **305.23**

GIRLS -- SEXUAL BEHAVIOR

Durham, M. G. The Lolita effect **302.23**

Wolf, N. Promiscuities **306.7**

Girls and Sex. Orenstein, P. **306.7**

Girls like us. Weller, S. **920**

The **girls** of atomic city. Kiernan, D. **976.8**

Girls of tender age. Tirone Smith **92**

The **girls** who went away. Fessler, A. **362.82**

Girls will be girls. Deak, J.   **649**

GIRLS, TEENAGE *See* Teenage girls

Gironimo! Moore, T.   **796.6**

Giroux, Robert
   Bishop, E. Poems, prose, and letters   **818**

Girzone, Joseph F.
   Never alone   **248.4**
   A portrait of Jesus   **232.9**

GIS *See* Soldiers -- United States

Gislason, Gunnar Karl
   (jt. auth) Eddy, J. North   **641.59**

Gitler, Ira
   Feather, L. The biographical encyclopedia of jazz   **781.65**

Gitlin, Todd
   The sixties   **973.922**

Giuliani, Rudolph W.
   About
   Siegel, F. F. The prince of the city   **92**

Give and take. Grant, A.   **158.2**

Give my poor heart ease. Ferris, W.   **781.643**

Give us the ballot. Berman, A.   **324.6**

Given. Berry, W.   **811**

Givens, Terryl
   By the hand of Mormon   **289.3**

Givhan, Robin
   The Battle of Versailles   **746.9**

GIVING *See* Generosity

Giving voice to values. Gentile, M. C.   **174**

The **giving** way to happiness. Santi, J.   **179**

Gizzi, Peter
   Archeophonics   **811.54**
   In defense of nothing   **811**
   (ed) Spicer, J. My vocabulary did this to me   **811**

GLACIERS
   Heacox, K. John Muir and the ice that started a fire   **92**
   Pollack, H. N. A world without ice   **551.3**

GLACIERS
   See also Geology; Ice; Physical geography

GLACIERS -- ALASKA
   Heacox, K. John Muir and the ice that started a fire   **92**

GLADIATORS
   Amidon, S. Something like the gods   **306.4**

GLADNESS *See* Happiness

Gladstone, Brooke
   About
   Gladstone, B. The influencing machine   **302.23**

Gladwell, Malcolm, 1963-
   Blink: the power of thinking without thinking   **153.4**
   David and Goliath   **155.2**
   Outliers   **302**
   The tipping point   **302**

The **glamour** of strangeness. James, J.   **700.19**

Glancey, Jonathan

The story of architecture   **720.9**

GLANDS
   See also Anatomy; Physiology

Glantz, Stephen
   Kramer, C. Clara's war   **92**

Glare, P. G. W.
   (ed) Oxford Latin dictionary   **473**

Glasberg, Beth A.
   (jt. auth) Harris, S. L. Siblings of Children With Autism   **618.92**

Glaser, Gabrielle
   Her best-kept secret   **362.292**

Glaser, Michael S.
   (ed) Clifton, L. The collected poems of Lucille Clifton 1965-2010   **811**

GLASS
   Macfarlane, A. Glass: a world history   **666**

GLASS
   See also Building materials; Ceramics

The **glass** castle. Walls, J.   **92**

The **Glass** Closet. Browne, J.   **331.5**

GLASS CONSTRUCTION
   See also Building materials

GLASS CRAFT
   Stevenson, C. Creative stained glass   **748.5**

GLASS FIBERS
   See also Fibers; Glass

GLASS GARDENS
   Colletti, M. Terrariums   **635.9**

GLASS PAINTING AND STAINING
   Rich, C. Stained glass basics   **748.5**
   Stevenson, C. Creative stained glass   **748.5**

GLASS PAINTING AND STAINING
   See also Decoration and ornament; Painting

The **glass** universe. Sobel, D.   **522.197**

Glass, Alison
   Alison Glass Appliqué   **746**

Glass, Brent D.
   50 great American places   **973**

Glass, Charles
   The deserters   **940.54**

Glass, Philip
   About
   Glass, P. Words Without Music   **92**

GLASS, STAINED *See* Glass painting and staining

Glass: a world history. Macfarlane, A.   **666**

Glassé, Cyril
   The new encyclopedia of Islam   **297**

Glasser, Joshua M.
   The eighteen-day running mate   **973.924**

Glasser, Ronald J.
   365 days   **959.704**

Glasser, Susan
   Baker, P. Kremlin rising   **947.086**

Glasser, William
   Choice theory   **150**

GLASSWARE -- TRADEMARKS
See also Trademarks
Glavan, James
Corson, R. Stage makeup **792**
Glaysher, Frederick
(ed) Hayden, R. E. Collected poems **811**
Glaze. Taylor, B. **738.1**
GLAZES
Taylor, B. Glaze **738.1**
GLAZES
See also Ceramics; Pottery
Glazier, Stephen D.
(ed) The Encyclopedia of African and African-American religions **299.6**
GLAZING (CERAMICS)
Burnett, J. B. Graphic clay **738.1**
Gleeson, Matthew
(ed) Writing Across the Landscape **92**
Glei, Jocelyn K.
(ed) Manage your day-to-day **153.4**
Gleiberman, Owen
About
Gleiberman, O. Movie freak **791.43**
Gleick, James, 1954-
The information **020**
Isaac Newton **92**
Time travel **530.11**
Glendinning, Victoria
Leonard Woolf **92**
Glengarry Glen Ross. Mamet, D. **812**
Glenmullen, Joseph
Wanzer, S. H. To die well **179.7**
Glenn, Cheryl
Hodges' Harbrace handbook **808**
Glenny, Misha
McMafia **364.1**
Glickman, Elaine Rose
Your kid's a brat and it's all your fault **649.1**
Glidden, Sarah
How to understand Israel in 60 days or less **741.5**
GLIDERS (AERONAUTICS)
See also Aeronautics; Airplanes
GLIDING AND SOARING
See also Aeronautics
Glitter and Glue. Corrigan, K. **92**
Glitterville's handmade Christmas. Brown, S. **745.594**
Glitterville's handmade Halloween. Brown, S. **745.594**
Global crisis. Parker, G. **909**
GLOBAL ENVIRONMENTAL CHANGE
Cullen, H. The weather of the future **551.63**
Ellis, R. On thin ice **599.78**
Global weirdness **577.2**
Gore, A. The future **303.4**
Hertsgaard, M. Hot **304.2**

Kolbert, E. Field notes from a catastrophe **363.7**
Macdougall, J. D. Frozen earth **551.7**
Montaigne, F. Fraser's penguins **577.2**
GLOBAL ENVIRONMENTAL CHANGE -- ECONOMIC ASPECTS
Klein, N. This changes everything **363.738**
GLOBAL FINANCIAL CRISIS, 2008-2009
Bartiromo, M. The weekend that changed Wall Street **330.9**
Bernanke, B. The Courage to Act **92**
Blinder, A. S. After the music stopped **330.973**
Friedman, J. Engineering the financial crisis **330.9**
Garson, B. Down the up escalator **339.2**
Gasparino, C. The sellout **332**
Hudson, M. The monster **332.6**
Lanchester, J. I.O.U. **330.9**
Lewis, M. The big short **330.9**
Lowenstein, R. The end of Wall Street **332.6**
McGee, S. Chasing Goldman Sachs **332.6**
McLean, B. All the devils are here **330.9**
Morgenson, G. Reckless endangerment **332.7**
Paulson, H. M. On the brink **330.9**
Rajan, R. G. Fault lines **330.9**
Sorkin, A. R. Too big to fail **330.9**
Stiglitz, J. E. The price of inequality **305.5**
Taibbi, M. Griftopia **973.932**
Wessel, D. In Fed we trust **332.1**
A **global** history of architecture. Jarzombek, M. **720.9**
GLOBAL POSITIONING SYSTEM
Bray, H. You are here **910.285**
GLOBAL POSITIONING SYSTEM
See also Navigation
Global studies [series]
Hanks, R. R. Central Asia **958**
The **global** village. McLuhan, M. **302.2**
GLOBAL WARMING
Alley, R. B. Earth **621**
Berners-Lee, M. How bad are bananas? **363.7**
Braasch, G. Earth under fire **363.7**
Climate change **363.738**
Coll, S. Private empire **338.7**
Ellis, R. On thin ice **599.78**
Encyclopedia of global warming & climate change **363.738**
Flannery, T. F. The weather makers **363.7**
Fleming, J. R. Fixing the sky **551.6**
The global warming reader **363.738**
Global weirdness **577.2**
Goodell, J. How to cool the planet **551.6**
Gore, A. An inconvenient truth **363.7**
Hansen, J. E. Storms of my grandchildren **363.7**
Hertsgaard, M. Hot **304.2**
Kolbert, E. Field notes from a catastrophe **363.7**
Lappé, A. Diet for a hot planet **641**
Lynas, M. Six degrees **551.6**

McKibben, B. Eaarth   253
Mooney, C. Storm world   363.7
Pearce, F. With speed and violence   551.6
Pilkey, O. H. The rising sea   363.34
Pollack, H. N. A world without ice   551.3
Stager, C. Deep future   363.7
Walker, G. The hot topic   363.7
Weart, S. R. The discovery of global warming   551.6

GLOBAL WARMING
   See also Climate; Solar radiation

GLOBAL WARMING -- ENCYCLOPEDIAS
Encyclopedia of global warming & climate
   change   363.738
The **global** warming reader.   363.738
Global weirdness.   577.2

GLOBALIZATION
Borzutzky, D. The performance of becoming hu-
   man   811.6
Deb, S. The beautiful and the damned   954.05
Epping, R. C. The 21st century economy   330.9
Foer, F. How soccer explains the world   303.482
Hoekstra, J. M. The atlas of global conserva-
   tion   333.95
Jacques, M. When China rules the world   327
Novogratz, J. The blue sweater   339.4
Saunders, D. Arrival city   307.24
Stiglitz, J. E. Globalization and its discontents   337
Yergin, D. The quest   333.79
Zizek, S. First as tragedy, then as farce   337

GLOBALIZATION
   See also International relations

GLOBALIZATION -- ECONOMIC ASPECTS
Newman, K. S. The accordion family   306.874

GLOBALIZATION -- ECONOMIC ASPECTS --
   CASE STUDIES
Goldstein, N. Globalization and free trade   382

GLOBALIZATION -- SOCIAL ASPECTS
Bacon, D. Illegal people   331.6
Glenny, M. McMafia   364.1
Goldhagen, D. J. The Devil That Never
   Dies   305.892
Globalization and free trade. Goldstein, N.   382
Globalization and its discontents. Stiglitz, J. E.   337
Globe Newspaper Co.
(comp) Betrayal   282
English, B. Last lion   92

GLOBES
   See also Maps
Glockner, Andy
Chasing perfection   796.323
The **glorious** cause. Middlekauff, R.   973.3
A **glorious** enterprise.   508
The **glorious** foods of Greece. Kochilas, D.   641.59
Glorious French food. Peterson, J.   641.5
The **glorious** pasta of Italy. Marchetti, D.   641.82

GLORY (MOTION PICTURE)

McPherson, J. M. Drawn with the sword   973.7
The **glory** of the tree.   582.16
The **glory** of their times. Ritter, L. S.   920
Glory road. Haskins, D.   796
GLOSSARIES *See* Encyclopedias and dictionaries
A **glossary** of literary terms. Abrams, M. H.   803
GLOUCESTER (MASS.)
Kurlansky, M. The last fish tale   639.2
GLOVERSVILLE (N.Y.) -- BIOGRAPHY
Russo, R. Elsewhere   92
GLOW-IN-THE-DARK BOOKS
   See also Picture books for children; Toy and
   movable books
Glück, Louise, 1943-
Averno   811
Faithful and virtuous night   811
Poems 1962-2012   811
A village life   811
Gluck, Sandy
(jt. auth) Ridge, B. The Beekman 1802 heirloom
   dessert cookbook   641.5
GLUTEN
Yafa, S. Grain of truth   633.1
Gluten-free & vegan pie.   641.3
GLUTEN-FREE DIET
Ahern, S. J. Gluten-Free Girl American classics re-
   invented   641.597
Ahern, S. J. Gluten-free girl every day   641.5
Devlin, N. River Cottage Gluten Free   641.5
Gluten-free & vegan pie   641.3
Gluten-free wish list   641.5
Perlmutter, D. The grain brain cookbook   641.563
Walker, D. Danielle Walker's against all
   grain   641.563
Yafa, S. Grain of truth   633.1
GLUTEN-FREE DIET -- RECIPES
Ahern, S. J. Gluten-Free Girl American classics re-
   invented   641.597
Ahern, S. J. Gluten-free girl every day   641.5
Fong, H. Nom nom paleo   641.5
Gluten-free & vegan pie   641.3
Gluten-Free Girl American classics reinvent-
   ed   641.597
Gluten-free wish list   641.5
Gluten-Free Girl American classics reinvented.
   Ahern, S. J.   641.597
Gluten-Free Girl American classics reinvent-
   ed.   641.597
Gluten-free girl every day. Ahern, S. J.   641.5
Gluten-free wish list.   641.5
Gnaulati, Enrico
Back to normal   618.92
GNOMES
   See also Folklore
The **Gnostic** Bible.   299
The **Gnostic** Gospels. Pagels, E. H.   299

GNOSTICISM

The Gnostic Bible   **299**

Pagels, E. H. The Gnostic Gospels   **299**

GNOSTICISM

    See also Church history -- 30-600, Early church; Philosophy; Religions

The **Go** ask Alice book of answers. Columbia University/Health Service   **613**

Go down together. Guinn, J.   **364.1**

Go like hell. Baime, A. J.   **796.72**

Göth, Amon, 1908-1946

    About

My grandfather would have shot me   **929.2**

GOAL -- PSYCHOLOGY

Covey, S. The 4 disciplines of execution   **658.4**

GOAL SETTING IN PERSONNEL MANAGEMENT

Covey, S. The 4 disciplines of execution   **658.4**

Goalen, Kaitlyn

The craft cocktail party   **641.87**

GOBLINS

    See also Folklore

GOD

Armstrong, K. The case for God   **211**

Armstrong, K. A history of God   **200**

Buber, M. I and thou   **181**

Dawkins, R. The God delusion   **200**

Kushner, H. S. The book of Job   **223**

Nadler, S. M. The best of all possible worlds   **190**

Overman, D. L. A case for the existence of God **212**

Sagan, C. Broca's brain   **500**

Strobel, L. The Case for Grace   **234**

Wathey, J. C. The illusion of God's presence   **204**

GOD -- CHRISTIANITY

Bass, D. B. Grounded   **231**

GOD -- CHRISTIANITY

    See also Christianity -- Doctrines

GOD -- JUDAISM

Kushner, H. S. Who needs God   **296.7**

GOD -- PROVIDENCE AND GOVERNMENT

    See Providence and government of God

GOD -- SOVEREIGNTY *See* Providence and government of God

God and Jetfire. Seek, A.   **92**

The **God** delusion. Dawkins, R.   **200**

God is not great. Hitchens, C.   **200**

God Is Not Here. Edmonds, B. R.   **956.704**

God is not one. Prothero, S. R.   **200**

God is red.   **275.1**

God Is Round.   **796.334**

The **god** machine. Chiles, J. R.   **629.133**

The **God** problem. Bloom, H.   **500**

God'll Cut You Down. Safran, J.   **364.152**

God's almost chosen peoples. Rable, G. C.   **973.7**

God's Bankers. Posner, G.   **364.16**

God's Chinese son. Spence, J. D.   **951**

God's equation. Aczel, A. D.   **523.1**

God's hotel. Sweet, V.   **610.92**

Goddard, Jolyon

    (ed) Concise history of science & invention   **509**

Goddard, Robert Hutchings, 1882-1945

    About

Clary, D. A. Rocket man   **92**

GODDESS RELIGION

    See also Paganism

GODDESSES *See* Gods and goddesses

Goddesses never age. Northrup, C.   **613**

Gödel, Kurt

    About

Feldman, B. 112 Mercer Street   **920**

Goldstein, R. Incompleteness   **92**

Godfrey, Tony

Painting today   **759.06**

Godfrey-Nicholls, Gaye

Mastering calligraphy   **745.6**

Godin des Odonais, Isabelle de Grandmaison, 1728-1792

    About

Whitaker, R. The mapmaker's wife   **981**

A **Godless** Jew. Gay, P.   **150.19**

A **godly** hero. Kazin, M.   **92**

GODS *See* Gods and goddesses

GODS AND GODDESSES

Wilkinson, R. H. The complete gods and goddesses of ancient Egypt   **299**

GODS AND GODDESSES -- DICTIONARIES

Jordan, M. Dictionary of gods and goddesses   **201**

Gods and heroes in art. Impelluso, L.   **700**

Gods and Kings. Thomas, D.   **92**

Gods like us. Burr, T.   **306.4**

Gods, graves, and scholars. Ceram, C. W.   **930.1**

Goebbels, Joseph, 1897-1945

    About

Goebbels   **92**

Goessel, Tracey

The first king of Hollywood   **92**

Goethe's Faust. Goethe, J. W. v.   **832**

Goethe, Johann Wolfgang von, 1749-1832

Goethe's Faust   **832**

Selected poetry   **831**

    About

Armstrong, J. Love, life, Goethe   **92**

Bloom, H. The Western canon   **809**

Goetzmann, William H.

Beyond the Revolution   **973.2**

Gogh, Theo van

    About

Buruma, I. Murder in Amsterdam   **364.152**

Gogh, Vincent van, 1853-1890

    About

Naifeh, S. Van Gogh   **92**

Thomson, B. Van Gogh paintings   **759.9**

Gogol, Nikola Vasilevich, 1809-1852
          About
  Nabokov, V. V. Lectures on Russian literature **891.7**
Gohr, Siegfried
  Magritte   **759.94**
Goin, Suzanne
  Sunday suppers at Lucques   **641.5**
Going beyond Google again. Devine, J. **025.042**
Going Clear. Wright, L.   **299**
Going Into the City. Christgau, R.   **92**
Going places. Burgin, R.   **910.4**
Going solo. Klinenberg, E.   **306.81**
Going to Tehran. Leverett, F.   **327.73**
Going to the territory. Ellison, R.   **818**
Goins, Wayne Everett
  Blues all day long   **92**
Golan, Oded
          About
  Burleigh, N. Unholy business   **933**
Golant, Susan K.
  Carter, R. Helping yourself help others **649.8**
Golay, Michael
  America 1933   **973.917**
Golay, Michael
  Fargnoli, A. N. Critical companion to William
    Faulkner   **813**
Golb, Norman
  Who wrote the Dead Sea scrolls? **296.1**
GOLD
    See also Chemical elements; Precious metals
Gold diggers. Gray, C.   **971**
Gold in the water. Mullen, P. H.   **797.2**
GOLD MINES AND MINING
  Gray, C. Gold diggers   **971**
  Tobar, H. Deep down dark   **363.11**
Gold, Alison Leslie
  Gies, M. Anne Frank remembered   **92**
Gold, Tammy
  Secrets of the nanny whisperer   **649**
Goldacre, Ben
  Bad Pharma   **615.107**
  Bad science   **500**
Goldbarth, Albert
  The kitchen sink   **811**
Goldberg, Dan
  Cuba!   **641.5**
Goldberg, Dave
  A user's guide to the universe   **530**
  The Universe in the Rearview Mirror **539.7**
Goldberg, Paul
  (jt. auth) Brawley, O. W. How we do harm **362.109**
Goldberg, Philip
  American Veda   **294.5**
  Bloomfield, H. H. Making peace with your past **158**
Goldberg, Rita
  Motherland   **940.531**

Goldberger, Paul
  Building art   **92**
Goldblatt, David
  The Games   **796.48**
GOLDEN FLEECE (SHIP)
  Kurson, R. Pirate hunters   **910.91**
GOLDEN GATE BRIDGE (SAN FRANCISCO,
  CALIF.)
    See also Bridges
Golden holocaust. Proctor, R. N. **362.29**
The Golden Lad. Burns, E.   **92**
GOLDEN MOLES -- SOMALIA
  Girling, R. The Hunt for the Golden Mole **591.68**
The golden ratio. Livio, M.   **516.2**
GOLDEN RULE
    See also Ethics
The golden ticket. Fortnow, L.   **511.3**
Golden, Alisa
  Making handmade books   **686.3**
Goldensohn, Lorrie
  (ed) American war poetry   **811**
Goldfarb, Toni L.
  American Lung Association 7 steps to a smoke-free
    life   **616.86**
Goldfayn, Alex
  The revenue growth habit   **658.15**
Goldfield, David R.
  America aflame   **973.7**
The goldfinches of Baghdad. Adamson, R. **821**
GOLDFISH
    See also Fishes
Goldhaber, Alfred Scharff
  (jt. auth) Crease, R. P. The quantum moment **530.12**
Goldhagen, Daniel Jonah
  The Devil That Never Dies   **305.892**
  Hitler's willing executioners   **940.53**
  Worse than war   **364.1**
GOLDMAN SACHS & CO.
  Cohan, W. D. Money and power   **332.6**
  McGee, S. Chasing Goldman Sachs   **332.6**
GOLDMAN SACHS GROUP, INC.
  Cohan, W. D. Money and power   **332.6**
Goldman, Ari L.
  Being Jewish   **296.4**
Goldman, Bob
  Brain fitness   **153.1**
Goldman, Duff
  Duff Bakes   **641.81**
Goldman, Emma, 1869-1940
          About
  Avrich, K. Sasha and Emma   **335**
  Rudahl, S. A dangerous woman   **335**
Goldman, Francisco
  The art of political murder   **972.81**
Goldman, Merle
  Fairbank, J. K. China   **951**

Goldman, Seth
(jt. auth) Nalebuff, B. Mission in a bottle **338.7**
Goldman, William
Adventures in the screen trade **791.43**
Goldman, William, 1931-
About
Goldman, W. Adventures in the screen trade **791.43**
Goldman, W. Which Lie Did I Tell? **791.43**
Goldsby, Robert W.
Molière on stage **842**
Goldsmith, Barbara
Other powers **92**
Goldsmith, Donald
Tyson, N. d. Origins: fourteen billion years of cosmic evolution **523.1**
Goldsmith, Francisca
The readers' advisory guide to graphic novels **025.2**
Goldsmith, George
About
Goldsmith, M. The inextinguishable symphony **940.53**
Goldsmith, Marshall
Triggers **155.2**
Goldsmith, Martin
The inextinguishable symphony **940.53**
Goldsmith, Rosemarie, 1917-1984
About
Goldsmith, M. The inextinguishable symphony **940.53**
Goldstein, Donald M.
The Vietnam War: the story and photographs **959.704**
Prange, G. W. At dawn we slept **940.54**
Goldstein, Joyce
The new Mediterranean Jewish table **641.5**
Goldstein, Martin
The nature of animal healing **636.089**
Goldstein, Nancy
Jackie Ormes **741.5**
Goldstein, Natalie
Globalization and free trade **382**
Goldstein, Rebecca
Incompleteness **92**
Goldstein, Sam
Brooks, R. B. Raising resilient children **649**
Goldstein, Warren
For the love of physics **92**
The Goldstein-Goren series in American Jewish history [series]
Ashton, D. Hanukkah in America **296.4**
Goldstone, Lawrence
Birdmen **629.13**
Drive! **338.4**
Goldstone, Nancy
The rival queens **944**
Goldsworthy, Adrian Keith
Antony and Cleopatra **92**
Augustus **92**
Caesar **92**
Pax romana **937.06**
Goldwag, Arthur
The new hate **306.2**
Goldwhite, Harold
Cobb, C. Creations of fire **540**
GOLDWORK
See also Art metalwork; Gold; Metalwork
Goldwyn, Meathead
Blonder, G. Meathead **641.7**
Goleman, Daniel
Ecological intelligence **333.7**
Emotional intelligence **152.4**
Focus **153.7**
Primal Leadership **658.4**
Social intelligence **158**
Golembesky, Michael
About
Bruning, J. R. Level zero heroes **958.104**
GOLF
Cook, K. Tommy's honor **92**
Cullen, B. Golf is not a game of perfect **796.352**
Feinstein, J. A good walk spoiled **796.352**
Five lessons **796.352**
Nicklaus, J. Jack Nicklaus **796.352**
Sampson, C. Masters **796.352**
GOLF
See also Sports
GOLF -- CALIFORNIA -- PEBBLE BEACH -- HISTORY.
Frost, M. The match **796.352**
GOLF -- COACHING
Haney, H. The big miss **796.352**
GOLF -- PSYCHOLOGICAL ASPECTS
Cullen, B. Golf is not a game of perfect **796.352**
GOLF COACHES -- UNITED STATES
Haney, H. The big miss **796.352**
Golf is not a game of perfect. Cullen, B. **796.352**
A **golfer's** life. Palmer, A. **92**
GOLFERS
Poulter, I. No Limits **920**
GOLFERS -- UNITED STATES -- BIOGRAPHY
Haney, H. The big miss **796.352**
Palmer, A. A life well played **92**
Golitsyn family
About
Smith, D. Former people **305.5**
Gollaher, David
Circumcision **392**
Golper, Zachary
(jt. auth) Kaminsky, P. Bien Cuit **641.815**
Golub, Leon
Nearest star **523.7**
Golway, Terry

Dallek, R. Let every nation know 92
(ed) Fellow citizens 352.23
Gombrich, E. H.
The story of art 709
Gomorrah. Saviano, R. 364.1
Gompertz, Will
What Are You Looking at? 709
Gone 'til November. Lil Wayne 782.421
Gone tomorrow. Rogers, H. 363.7
Gonzales, Laurence, 1947-
Flight 232 363.12
Surviving survival 155.9
Gonzales, Sara
(jt. auth) Goldman, D. Duff Bakes 641.81
Gonzalez Echevarria, Roberto
The Cambridge history of Latin American litera-
ture 860
Gonzalez, Juan, 1969-
News for all the people 302.23
Gonzo. Wenner, J. S. 92
Gooch, Brad, 1952-
Flannery 92
About
Gooch, B. Smash Cut 92
Good and cheap. Brown, L. 641.5
GOOD AND EVIL
Bloom, H. The Lucifer principle 128
Kushner, H. S. How good do we have to be? 296.7
Made for goodness 170
Nadler, S. M. The best of all possible worlds 190
Watson, L. Dark nature 111
GOOD AND EVIL
See also Ethics; Philosophy; Theology
The **good** dog. 636.7
GOOD FRIDAY
See also Christian holidays; Holy Week; Lent
Good garden bugs. Gardiner, M. M. 635
The **good** girls revolt. Povich, L. 331.4
The **good** good pig. Montgomery, S. 636.4
GOOD GROOMING *See* Personal grooming
Good housekeeping (Periodical)
The Good Housekeeping cookbook 641.5
The **Good** Housekeeping cookbook. Good house-
keeping (Periodical) 641.5
The **Good** Housekeeping step-by-step cook-
book. 641.4
A **good** month for murder. Wilber, D. Q. 363.25
Good morning blues: the autobiography of Count
Basie. Basie, C. 92
The **good** neighbor cookbook. Quessenberry,
S. 641.5
The **good** nurse. Graeber, C. 364.152
Good poems. 811
Good prose. Kidder, T. 808.02
The **good** sleeper. Kennedy, J. K. 649
The **good** soldiers. Finkel, D. 956.7

The **good** son. Anderson, C. 92
The **Good** Spy. Bird, K. 92
Good to great. Collins, J. C. 658
A **good** walk spoiled. Feinstein, J. 796.352
The **good** war. 940.54
The **good,** the bad, and me. Wallach, E. 92
Goodall, Jane, 1934-
In the shadow of man 599.8
The ten trusts 333.95
Through a window 599.8
About
Goodall, J. Seeds of Hope 580
Goodall, J. Beyond innocence 92
Peterson, D. Jane Goodall: the woman who rede-
fined man 92
Goodall, Tiffany
The ultimate student cookbook 641.5
Goodavage, Maria
Secret Service Dogs 363.283
Goodbody, Mary
Barrenechea, T. The Basque table 641.59
Lobel, S. The meat bible 641.6
Goodbye, darkness. Manchester, W. 940.54
Goodchild, Peter
Edward Teller, the real Dr Strangelove 92
Goode, J. J.
(jt. auth) Bloomfield, A. A Girl and Her
Greens 641.65
Lang, A. P. Serious barbecue 641.5
(jt. auth) Santibañez, R. Truly Mexican 641.59
Goodell, Jeff
How to cool the planet 551.6
Goodheart, Adam
1861 973.7
Goodman family
About
Goodman, S. The Orpheus Clock 940.53
Goodman, Ellen
I know just what you mean 158.2
Goodman, Jordan Elliot
Downes, J. Finance and investment handbook 332.6
Goodman, Linda
Linda Goodman's star signs 130
Linda Goodman's sun signs 133.5
Goodman, Martin
Rome and Jerusalem 933
Goodman, Matthew
The Sun and the moon 974.7
Goodman, Ruth
How to be a Tudor 942.05
Goodman, Simon, 1948-
The Orpheus Clock 940.53
Goodrich, Frances
The diary of Anne Frank 812
Goodstein, David L.
Feynman's lost lecture 521

Out of gas   333.8
Goodstein, Judith R.
  Goodstein, D. L. Feynman's lost lecture   **521**
Goodwin, Doris Kearns, 1943-
  No ordinary time   **92**
About
  The Bully Pulpit   **973.91**
  Goodwin, D. K. Wait till next year   **796.357**
  Team of rivals   **92**
Goodwin, Jason
  Lords of the horizons   **956.1**
Goodwin, Robert
  Spain   **946**
GOOGLE (FIRM)
  Bock, L. Work rules!   **658.4**
GOOGLE (FIRM)
  See also Web search engines; Web sites
GOOGLE (FIRM) -- MANAGEMENT
  Bock, L. Work rules!   **658.4**
  Work rules!   **658.4**
Google hacks. Dornfest, R.   **025.04**
GOOGLE, INC.
  Auletta, K. Googled   **338.7**
  Dornfest, R. Google hacks   **025.04**
  Levy, S. In the plex   **338.7**
  Stross, R. Planet Google   **338.7**
  Vaidhyanathan, S. The Googlization of every-
  thing   **338.7**
Googled. Auletta, K.   **338.7**
The **Googlization** of everything. Vaidhyanathan,
  S.   **338.7**
Gopal, Anand, 1980-
  No good men among the living   **958.104**
Gopnik, Adam
About
  Gopnik, A. Through the children's gate   **974.71**
Gopnik, Adam
  Angels and ages   **973.7**
  Through the children's gate   **974.71**
Gopnik, Alison
  The gardener and the carpenter   **155.4**
  The scientist in the crib   **155.4**
Gorbachev, Mikhail
  On my country and the world   **947.085**
About
  Kissinger, H. Diplomacy   **327.2**
  Mann, J. The rebellion of Ronald Reagan   **973.927**
  Ratnesar, R. Tear down this wall   **973.927**
  Tolstaia, T. Pushkin's children   **891.7**
Gordimer, Nadine, 1923-
About
  Conversations with Nadine Gordimer   **823**
Gordin, Michael D.
  Red cloud at dawn   **355**
  A well-ordered thing: Dmitrii Mendeleev and the
  shadow of the periodic table   **92**

Gordon Ramsay's fast food. Ramsay, G.   **641.5**
Gordon, Andrew
  The modern history of Japan   **952.03**
Gordon, Charlotte
  Mistress Bradstreet   **92**
  Romantic outlaws   **92**
Gordon, Deborah
  Sperling, D. Two billion cars   **388.3**
Gordon, Elisabeth
  Keller, L. The lives of ants   **595.7**
Gordon, Joanne
  Schultz, H. Onward   **647.9**
Gordon, John S., 1944-
  Washington's monument   **975.3**
Gordon, John Steele
  A thread across the ocean   **384.1**
Gordon, Linda
  Dorothea Lange   **92**
Gordon, Lois G.
  The world of Samuel Beckett, 1906-1946   **848**
Gordon, Lyndall
  Charlotte Bronte   **92**
  Lives like loaded guns   **92**
  T.S. Eliot   **92**
  Vindication   **92**
Gordon, Mary
  Joan of Arc   **944**
  Reading Jesus   **232**
Gordon, Matthew
  Understanding Islam   **297**
Gordon, Michael R., 1951-
  The endgame   **956.7**
  The generals' war   **956.7**
Gordon, Robert
  Respect yourself   **384**
Gordon, W. Terrence
  (ed) Understanding media   **302.23**
Gordon-Reed, Annette
  Andrew Johnson   **92**
  The Hemingses of Monticello   **920**
  Most Blessed of the Patriarchs   **92**
  Thomas Jefferson and Sally Hemings   **973.4**
Gore, Al, 1948-
  An inconvenient truth   **363.7**
  The future   **303.4**
  Our choice   **363.7**
About
  Remnick, D. Reporting   **814**
  Zelnick, B. Gore: a political life   **92**
Gore: a political life. Zelnick, B.   **92**
Goreham, Gary
  (ed) Encyclopedia of rural America   **973**
Gorenberg, Gershom
  The accidental empire   **956.94**
Gorey, Edward, 1925-2000
About

Ross, C. The world of Edward Gorey   700.92
Gorgas, William Crawford, 1854-1920
                    About
McCullough, D. G. The path between the
seas   972.87
GORGE-PURGE SYNDROME See Bulimia
GORILLAS
Fossey, D. Gorillas in the mist   599.88
GORILLAS
        See also Apes
Gorillas in the mist. Fossey, D.   599.88
Gorky, Maksim, 1868-1936
                    About
Nabokov, V. V. Lectures on Russian literature 891.7
Gorman, Gerard
Woodpeckers of the World   598.7
Gorman, Hugh S.
The story of N   547
Gorman, James
Horner, J. R. How to build a dinosaur   567.9
Gorman, Robert F.
(ed) Great events from history: The 20th century,
  1901-1940   909.82
(ed) Great events from history: The 20th century,
  1941-1970   909.82
(ed) Great events from history: The 20th century,
  1971-2000   909.82
(ed) Great lives from history: the 20th century,
  1901-2000   920.003
Gormley, Ken
The death of American virtue   973.929
Gorn, Elliott J.
Mother Jones   331.88
Gorra, Michael Edward
The bells in their silence   943
Gorst, Brian
The complete oil painter   751.45
Gortemaker, Heike B.
Eva Braun   92
Goscha, Christopher
Vietnam   959.7
Gosling, Sam
Snoop   155.9
Gosnell, Mariana
Ice   551.3
GOSPEL MUSIC
Ward-Royster, W. How I got over   920
GOSPEL MUSIC
        See also African American music; Church
  music; Popular music
**GOSPEL MUSICIANS -- UNITED STATES -- BI-
  OGRAPHY**
Kot, G. I'll take you there   92
Gospel of freedom. Rieder, J.   323.1
GOSPEL OF THOMAS
Pagels, E. H. Beyond belief   229

GOSSIP
        See also Journalism; Libel and slander
GOSSIP COLUMNISTS
Walls, J. The glass castle   92
Gostick, Adrian
(jt. auth) Elton, C. All in   658.3
Got milked? Hamilton, A.   641.5
Got sun? go solar. Ewing, R. A.   697
Gotham. Burrows, E. G.   974.7
Gotham unbound. Steinberg, T.   508
Gotsch, Gwen
(ed) The Womanly art of breastfeeding   649
Gott, J. Richard
Welcome to the universe   523.1
Gott, Richard
Britain's empire   942
Gottfried, Martin
Arthur Miller   92
Gottheimer, Josh
Berry, M. F. Power in words   973.932
Gottlieb, Anthony
The dream of enlightenment   190
The dream of reason   180
Gottlieb, Daniel
Learning from the heart   170
Gottlieb, Robert Adams
George Balanchine: the ballet maker   92
Lives and letters   814
Gottman, John
The man's guide to women   155.3
Gottman, Julie Schwartz
(jt. auth) Gottman, J. The man's guide to wom-
  en   155.3
Gottschalk, Louis Moreau, 1829-1869
                    About
Schonberg, H. C. The great pianists   920
Goudsouzian, Aram
Sidney Poitier   92
Gould, Eliga H.
Among the powers of the earth   973.3
Gould, Glenn, 1932-1982
                    About
Hafner, K. A romance on three legs   92
Schonberg, H. C. The great pianists   920
Gould, Jonathan
Can't buy me love   920
Gould, Lewis L.
Grand Old Party   324.273
Gould, Stephen Jay
The flamingo's smile   500
Hen's teeth and horse's toes   576.8
The mismeasure of man   153.9
The richness of life   508
                    About
Dennett, D. C. Darwin's dangerous idea 146
Goulding, Matt

About

Goulding, M. Rice, noodle, fish   **394.12**

Goulson, Dave

A Buzz in the Meadow   **638**

Goulston, Mark

Just listen   **650.1**

Gourevitch, Philip

Standard operating procedure   **956.7**

We wish to inform you that tomorrow we will be killed with our families   **967.571**

The **gourmet** cookbook.   **641.5**

The **Gourmet** cookie book.   **641.8**

Gourmet today.   **641.5**

Govenar, Alan B.

Lightnin' Hopkins   **92**

Texas blues   **781.64**

GOVERNESSES

Landon, M. Anna and the King of Siam   **92**

GOVERNMENT BUSINESS ENTERPRISES

See also Business enterprises

GOVERNMENT CONTRACTORS -- UNITED STATES -- BIOGRAPHY

Fair, E. Consequence   **956.704**

GOVERNMENT EMPLOYEES *See* Civil service

GOVERNMENT INFORMATION

The WikiLeaks files   **327.73**

GOVERNMENT INFORMATION -- UNITED STATES

The WikiLeaks files   **327.73**

GOVERNMENT LENDING

See also Domestic economic assistance; Economic policy; Loans; Public finance

GOVERNMENT OFFICIALS

Alexander, C. The Bounty: the true story of the mutiny on the Bounty   **996**

Ambrose, S. E. The wild blue   **940.54**

Bernstein, J. Oppenheimer   **92**

Beschloss, M. R. The conquerors: Roosevelt, Truman, and the destruction of Hitler's Germany, 1941-1945   **940.53**

Bird, K. American Prometheus   **92**

Bremer, F. J. John Winthrop   **974.4**

Brown, D. A. Bury my heart at Wounded Knee   **970.004**

Cleland, M. Heart of a patriot   **92**

Edwards, B. Edward R. Murrow and the birth of broadcast journalism   **92**

Ellsberg, D. Secrets: a memoir of Vietnam and the Pentagon papers   **959.704**

Feinberg, K. R. What is life worth?   **362.88**

Feldman, N. Scorpions   **920**

Gevisser, M. A legacy of liberation   **92**

Gormley, K. The death of American virtue **973.929**

Greenhouse, L. Becoming Justice Blackmun   **92**

Greenspan, A. The age of turbulence   **92**

Grose, P. Gentleman spy   **92**

Halberstam, D. The best and the brightest **973.922**

Harris, J. W. The hanging of Thomas Jeremiah   **92**

Kushner, T. Angels in America   **812**

Lee, H. Virginia Woolf's nose   **820**

Long, J. The plot against Pepys   **941.06**

Lukacs, J. Five days in London, May 1940 **940.53**

Meredith, M. Diamonds, gold, and war   **968.04**

Millman, C. The detonators   **940.4**

Olson, L. Citizens of London   **940.54**

Overtveldt, J. v. Bernanke's test   **332.1**

Pepys, S. The diary of Samuel Pepys   **941.06**

Rice, A. The teeth may smile but the heart does not forget   **967.6**

Rice, C. Extraordinary, ordinary people   **92**

Sandweiss, M. A. Passing strange   **92**

Schlesinger, A. M. Journals: 1952-2000   **92**

Schlesinger, A. M. A life in the twentieth century   **92**

Schneider, P. Brutal journey: the epic story of the first crossing of North America   **970.01**

Sorensen, T. C. Counselor   **92**

Sperber, A. M. Murrow, his life and times   **92**

Symonds, C. L. Lincoln and his admirals   **92**

Thompson, N. The hawk and the dove   **92**

Tomalin, C. Samuel Pepys   **941.06**

Varmus, H. The art and politics of science   **92**

Wessel, D. In Fed we trust   **332.1**

Woodward, B. Maestro: Greenspan's Fed and the American boom   **331.1**

Woodward, B. The commanders   **973.928**

GOVERNMENT OWNERSHIP

See also Economic policy; Industrial policy; Socialism

GOVERNMENT POLICY *See* Buy national policy; Commercial policy; Cultural policy; Economic policy; Energy policy; Environmental policy; Fiscal policy; Industrial policy; Labor policy; Medical policy; Military policy; Monetary policy; Social policy; Wage-price policy

GOVERNMENT PROGRAMS -- HISTORY -- UNITED STATES

Masterson, K. M. The malaria project   **616.9**

GOVERNMENT PUBLICATIONS

See also Library resources

GOVERNMENT PUBLICATIONS -- UNITED STATES -- HANDBOOKS, MANUALS, ETC

Ernsthausen, D. G. Strauss's handbook of business information   **016**

GOVERNMENT RECORDS -- PRESERVATION

See Archives

GOVERNMENT REGULATION -- HISTORY -- UNITED STATES

Proctor, R. N. Golden holocaust   **362.29**

GOVERNMENT REGULATION OF INDUSTRY

See Industrial policy

GOVERNMENT SERVICE *See* Civil service

GOVERNMENT SPENDING POLICY *See* United States -- Appropriations and expenditures

GOVERNMENT SPENDING POLICY -- UNITED STATES

Johnson, S. White House burning   **336.3**

Kleinbard, E. D. We are better than this   **336.3**

Kramer, M. A people's guide to the federal budget   **352.4**

GOVERNMENT, RESISTANCE TO -- GREAT BRITAIN -- COLONIES -- HISTORY

Gott, R. Britain's empire   **942**

GOVERNMENT, RESISTANCE TO -- UNITED STATES

Urofsky, M. I. Dissent and the Supreme Court   **342.73**

GOVERNMENTAL INVESTIGATIONS

See also Administration of justice

GOVERNMENTAL INVESTIGATIONS -- UNITED STATES

Willman, D. The mirage man   **363.325**

GOVERNORS

Adams, M. Turn right at Machu Picchu   **985**

Algeo, M. The president is a sick man   **973.8**

Berthon, S. Warlords   **940.53**

Beschloss, M. R. The conquerors: Roosevelt, Truman, and the destruction of Hitler's Germany, 1941-1945   **940.53**

Borneman, W. R. Polk   **92**

Brackett, E. Pay to play   **92**

Branch, T. The Clinton tapes   **92**

Brands, H. W. Traitor to his class   **92**

Brands, H. W. Woodrow Wilson   **92**

Bruni, F. Ambling into history: the unlikely odyssey of George W. Bush   **973.931**

Buckley, W. F. The Reagan I knew   **92**

Burns, J. M. The three Roosevelts   **973.91**

Bush, G. W. Decision points   **92**

Carter, J. Everything to gain   **92**

Carter, J. An hour before daylight   **92**

Carter, J. Keeping faith: memoirs of a president   **92**

Carter, J. Sharing good times   **92**

Clinton, B. My life   **92**

Cooper, J. M. The warrior and the priest: Woodrow Wilson and Theodore Roosevelt   **92**

Cooper, J. M. Woodrow Wilson   **92**

Cordery, S. A. Alice   **92**

Crapol, E. P. John Tyler   **92**

DiSilvestro, R. L. Theodore Roosevelt in the Badlands   **92**

D'Souza, D. Ronald Reagan   **973.927**

Egan, T. The big burn   **973.91**

Farmer, J. J. The ground truth   **973.931**

Feldman, N. Scorpions   **920**

Finan, C. M. Alfred E. Smith, the happy warrior   **92**

FitzGerald, F. Way out there in the blue   **973.927**

Fried, A. F.D.R. and his enemies   **92**

Goodwin, D. K. Team of rivals   **92**

Goodwin, D. K. No ordinary time   **92**

Gordon-Reed, A. Andrew Johnson   **92**

Gormley, K. The death of American virtue   **973.929**

Graff, H. F. Grover Cleveland   **92**

Hair, W. I. The Kingfish and his realm: the life and times of Huey P. Long   **92**

Heaney, C. Cradle of gold   **92**

Hersh, S. M. Chain of command   **973.931**

Hofstadter, R. The American political tradition, and the men who made it   **973**

Johnson, H. B. Sleepwalking through history   **973.927**

Karabell, Z. The last campaign   **324.9**

Kennedy, J. F. Profiles in courage   **920**

Kissinger, H. Diplomacy   **327.2**

Lemann, N. Redemption: the last battle of the Civil War   **975**

Leuchtenburg, W. E. Franklin D. Roosevelt and the New Deal, 1932-1940   **973.917**

MacMillan, M. Paris 1919   **940.3**

Mann, J. The rebellion of Ronald Reagan   **973.927**

May, G. John Tyler   **92**

McCullough, D. G. Mornings on horseback   **92**

McCullough, D. G. The path between the seas   **972.87**

McDougal, S. The woman who wouldn't talk   **973.929**

McKean, D. Suspected of independence   **92**

Merry, R. W. A country of vast designs   **92**

Millard, C. The river of doubt   **973.91**

Miller, C. Gifford Pinchot and the making of modern environmentalism   **333.7**

Miller, S. The President and the assassin   **973.8**

Morris, E. The rise of Theodore Roosevelt   **92**

Morris, E. Theodore Rex   **92**

Morris, R. Fraud of the century   **324.9**

Olson, L. Citizens of London   **940.54**

O'Toole, P. When trumpets call   **92**

Perry, J. M. Touched with fire   **973.7**

Persico, J. E. Franklin and Lucy   **920**

Phillips, K. P. William McKinley   **92**

Ratnesar, R. Tear down this wall   **973.927**

Rauchway, E. Murdering McKinley   **973.8**

Reagan, R. Reagan   **92**

Reagan, R. My father at 100   **92**

Reeves, R. President Reagan: the triumph of imagination   **973.927**

Roberts, A. Masters and commanders   **940.54**

Roosevelt, C. Too close to the sun   **92**

Schlesinger, A. M. The coming of the New Deal, 1933-1935   **973.917**

Schlesinger, A. M. The crisis of the old order, 1919-1933   **973.91**

Schlesinger, A. M. The politics of upheaval, 1935-1936   **973.917**

Schlesinger, A. M. War and the American presidency **327.1**

Sears, S. W. George B. McClellan **92**

Shesol, J. Supreme power **347**

Smith, J. E. FDR **92**

Stephanopoulos, G. All too human **973.929**

Taylor, N. American-made **331.1**

Thomas, E. The war lovers **973.8**

Toobin, J. R. A vast conspiracy **973.929**

Traister, R. Big girls don't cry **324**

Tuchman, B. W. Practicing history **907**

Wilson, E. Patriotic gore **810**

Woodward, B. Plan of attack **956.7**

Woodward, B. Shadow **973.92**

Woodward, B. State of denial **973.931**

Zimmermann, W. First great triumph **973**

GOVERNORS

    See also State governments

GOVERNORS -- INDIANA -- BIOGRAPHY

Collins, G. William Henry Harrison **92**

GOVERNORS -- MONTANA -- BIOGRAPHY

Egan, T. The immortal Irishman **92**

GOVERNORS -- PENNSYLVANIA -- BIOGRA-PHY

McKean, D. Suspected of independence **92**

GOVERNORS -- VIRGINIA -- BIOGRAPHY

Kranish, M. Flight from Monticello **973.4**

Gowing, Lawrence

  (ed) Biographical encyclopedia of artists **920.003**

Gowon, Yusuf

        About

Rice, A. The teeth may smile but the heart does not forget **967.6**

Goya. Hughes, R. **760**

Goya, Francisco, 1746-1828

        About

Blackburn, J. Old man Goya **92**

Hughes, R. Goya **760**

GPS (NAVIGATION SYSTEM) *See* Global Positioning System

Graber, Kathleen

The eternal city **811**

GRACE

Lamott, A. Small victories **248**

GRACE (AESTHETICS)

Kaufman, S. L. The art of grace **302.1**

GRACE (THEOLOGY)

Strobel, L. The Case for Grace **234**

GRACE (THEOLOGY)

    See also Doctrinal theology; Salvation

Grace Hopper and the invention of the information age. Beyer, K. W. **92**

The **grace** of silence. Norris, M. **92**

Grace without God. Ozment, K. **200.973**

GRADING AND MARKING (EDUCATION)

    See also Educational tests and measurements

GRADUATE STUDENTS -- FICTION

Howley, K. Thrown **796.8**

GRADUATES, COLLEGE *See* College graduates

GRADUATION *See* Commencements

Graeber, Charles

The good nurse **364.152**

Graebner, Clark, 1943-

        About

McPhee, J. Levels of the game **796.34**

GRAF ZEPPELIN (AIRSHIP)

Botting, D. Dr. Eckener's dream machine **629.133**

Graff, Garrett M.

The threat matrix **363.325**

Graff, Henry F.

Grover Cleveland **92**

GRAFFITI

Ganz, N. Graffiti world **751**

GRAFFITI -- NEW YORK (N.Y.) -- HISTORY

Felisbret, E. Graffiti New York **751.7**

Graffiti New York. Felisbret, E. **751.7**

Graffiti world. Ganz, N. **751**

GRAFT IN POLITICS *See* Political corruption

GRAFTING

    See also Plant propagation

Grafton, Anthony

Cartographies of time **902**

Graham Greene. Greene, G. **92**

Graham, Billy, 1918-

        About

Graham, B. Just as I am **92**

Martin, W. C. With God on our side **261.8**

Wacker, G. America's pastor **92**

Graham, Jorie

The dream of the unified field **811**

From the New World **811**

Overlord **811**

Graham, Katharine

  (comp) Katharine Graham's Washington **975.3**

        About

Remnick, D. Reporting **814**

Graham, Mark (Mark A.)

        About

Dreazen, Y. The invisible front **92**

Graham, Martha

        About

Ware, S. Letter to the world **920.72**

Graham, Wade

American Eden **712**

Graham-Dixon, Andrew

Caravaggio **92**

GRAIL

    See also Folklore

GRAIN

Ancient grains for modern meals **641.59**

Simply ancient grains **641.6**

The **grain** brain cookbook. Perlmutter, D. **641.563**

Grain of truth. Yafa, S.   633.1
Gramling, Robert
(jt. auth) Freudenburg, W. R. Blowout in the
Gulf   363.7
Gramm, Jeff
Dear chairman   659.2
GRAMMAR
Dunn, P. A. Grammar rants   428
Pinker, S. Words and rules   401
GRAMMAR
See also Language and languages; Linguistics
The **grammar** bible. Strumpf, M.   428
Grammar rants. Dunn, P. A.   428
GRAMMAR SCHOOLS *See* Elementary educa-
tion
GRAMMY AWARDS
See also Sound recordings
Gran cocina latina.   641.597
The **grand** alliance. Churchill, W.   940.53
GRAND CANYON (ARIZ.)
Fletcher, C. The man who walked through time 917
A **grand** delusion. Mann, R.   959.704
The **grand** design. Hawking, S.   530.1
Grand expectations. Patterson, J. T.   973.92
Grand Old Party. Gould, L. L.   324.273
Grandbaby cakes. Adams, J. D.   641.86
**GRANDCHILDREN OF WAR CRIMINALS --
GERMANY -- BIOGRAPHY**
My grandfather would have shot me   929.2
Grande, Reyna
About
Grande, R. The distance between us   92
GRANDFATHERS
My grandfather would have shot me   929.2
GRANDFATHERS
See also Grandparents
Grandin, Greg
Fordlandia   307.7
Kissinger's Shadow   327.2
Grandin, Temple, 1947-
Animals in translation   591.5
Animals make us human   636
The autistic brain   616.85
Grandison, Alice
(ed) Manser, M. H. The Facts on File dictionary of
foreign words and phrases   422
Grandmaster Flash
The adventures of Grandmaster Flash   92
Grandmaster Flash, 1958-
About
Grandmaster Flash The adventures of Grandmas-
ter Flash   92
GRANDMOTHERS
Galimberti, G. In her kitchen   641.59
GRANDMOTHERS
See also Grandparents

GRANDPARENT AND CHILD *See* Grandparent-
grandchild relationship
**GRANDPARENT-GRANDCHILD RELATION-
SHIP**
Roosevelt, C. Too close to the sun   92
Rosenblatt, R. Making toast   92
GRANDPARENTS -- BIOGRAPHY
Richmond Mouillot, M. A fifty-year silence   940.53
GRANDPARENTS AS PARENTS
Rosenblatt, R. Making toast   92
GRANDPARENTS AS PARENTS
See also Grandparents; Parenting
Grange, Kevin
Beneath blossom rain   915
Granger, Edith
The Columbia Granger's index to poetry in antholo-
gies   808.81
GRANITE
See also Rocks; Stone
Grann, David
The lost city of Z   918
The **granny** square book. Hubert, M.   746.43
Grant. Smith, J. E.   92
Grant family
About
Grant, G. M. At the elbows of my elders   920
Grant Wood. Evans, R. T.   92
Grant writing 101. Johnson, V. M.   658.1
Grant, Adam
Give and take   158.2
Originals   153.3
Grant, Colin
The natural mystics   920
Grant, Edward
Science and religion, 400 B.C. to A.D. 1550   261.5
Grant, Gail Milissa
At the elbows of my elders   920
Grant, James
John Adams   92
Grant, Julia Dent, 1826-1902
About
Berkin, C. Civil War wives   920
Grant, Michael, 1954-
(tr) Cicero, M. T. On the good life   878
A guide to the ancient world   913
Grant, R. G.
Battle at sea   359
Flight: 100 years of aviation   629.13
World War I   940.3
Grant, Richard
Crazy river   916
Grant, Ulysses S. (Ulysses Simpson), 1822-1885
Memoirs and selected letters   973.8
About
Brands, H. W. The man who saved the union   355.009
Bunting, J. Ulysses S. Grant   92

Davis, W. C. Crucible of commmand **920**
Grant, U. S. Memoirs and selected letters **973.8**
Korda, M. Ulysses S. Grant: the unlikely hero **92**
McPherson, J. M. Drawn with the sword **973.7**
Perry, J. M. Touched with fire **973.7**
Smith, J. E. Grant **92**
Ward, G. C. A disposition to be rich **974.7**
White, R. C. American Ulysses **92**
Wilson, E. Patriotic gore **810**
GRANTS See Grants-in-aid; Subsidies
GRANTS-IN-AID
Gerding, S. K. Winning grants **025.1**
Johnson, V. M. Grant writing 101 **658.1**
GRANTS-IN-AID
  See also Public finance
Granz, Norman, 1918-2001
About
Feather, L. From Satchmo to Miles **920**
GRAPES
Robinson, J. Wine grapes **664**
GRAPES
  See also Fruit
GRAPES -- FRANCE -- BURGUNDY -- HERBI-
  CIDE INJURIES -- CASE STUDIES
Potter, M. Shadows in the vineyard **364.16**
GRAPES -- VARIETIES
Robinson, J. Wine grapes **664**
GRAPH THEORY
  See also Algebra; Mathematical analysis; To-
  pology
GRAPHIC ARTS
Heller, S. Becoming a graphic & digital design-
  er **741.6**
GRAPHIC ARTS
  See also Art
GRAPHIC ARTS -- HISTORY
Eskilson, S. J. Graphic design **740**
Graphic clay. Burnett, J. B. **738.1**
Graphic design. Eskilson, S. J. **740**
GRAPHIC DESIGN
Spiekermann, E. Stop Stealing Sheep and Find out
  How Type Works **686.2**
GRAPHIC DESIGN (TYPOGRAPHY)
Lupton, E. Thinking with type **686.2**
GRAPHIC FICTION See Graphic novels
GRAPHIC MEDICINE
  See also Graphic novels; Medicine
GRAPHIC METHODS
  See also Drawing; Geometrical drawing; Me-
  chanical drawing
GRAPHIC METHODS -- HISTORY
Lima, M. The book of trees **001.2**
GRAPHIC NOVELS
101 outstanding graphic novels **741.5**
Andelman, B. Will Eisner: A Spirited Life **741.5**
B., D. Epileptic **741.5**

Bechdel, A. Fun home **741.5**
Crumb, R. The book of Genesis **741.5**
Delisle, G. Pyongyang: a journey in North Ko-
  rea **741.5**
Geary, R. J. Edgar Hoover **363.2**
Geary, R. The Lindbergh child **364.1**
Glidden, S. How to understand Israel in 60 days or
  less **741.5**
Goldsmith, F. The readers' advisory guide to graph-
  ic novels **025.2**
Guibert, E. Alan's war **741.5**
Guibert, E. The photographer **958.1**
Hennessey, J. The United States Constitution **342**
I see the promised land **92**
Jacobson, S. The 9/11 report **741.5**
Jacobson, S. Anne Frank **92**
Keller, M. Charles Darwin's On the Origin of Spe-
  cies **576.8**
Kleist, R. Johnny Cash **92**
Lee, S. Stan Lee's How to draw comics **741.5**
Neufeld, J. A.D. **976.3**
O'Neil, D. Batman unauthorized **741.5**
Rudahl, S. A dangerous woman **335**
Sacco, J. Footnotes in Gaza **956.04**
Santiago, W. 21 **92**
Satrapi, M. The complete Persepolis **741.5**
Satrapi, M. Embroideries **741**
Small, D. Stitches **741.5**
Spiegelman, A. MetaMaus **940.53**
Spiegelman, A. In the shadow of no towers **973.931**
Spiegelman, A. Maus **940.53**
Students for a Democratic Society **378.1**
Torres, A. American widow **741.5**
Tran, G. B. Vietnamerica **741.5**
GRAPHIC NOVELS
  See also Comic books, strips, etc.; Fiction
GRAPHIC NOVELS -- ADMINISTRATION
Serchay, D. S. The librarian's guide to graphic nov-
  els for adults **025.2**
GRAPHIC NOVELS -- AUTHORSHIP
Abel, J. Drawing words & writing pictures **741.5**
Eisner, W. Comics and sequential art **741.5**
GRAPHIC NOVELS -- BIBLIOGRAPHY
Alpert, A. Read on-- graphic novels **016**
Karp, J. Graphic novels in your school library **741.5**
Martin, W. P. Wonderfully wordless **011.62**
GRAPHIC NOVELS -- DRAWING
McCloud, S. Making comics **741.5**
GRAPHIC NOVELS -- HISTORY AND CRITI-
  CISM
Graphic novels beyond the basics **025.2**
Graphic novels beyond the basics. **025.2**
GRAPHIC NOVELS IN EDUCATION -- UNIT-
  ED STATES
Karp, J. Graphic novels in your school library **741.5**
Graphic novels in your school library. Karp, J. **741.5**

GRAPHICS, COMPUTER *See* Computer graphics
GRAPHITE
    See also Carbon
GRAPHOLOGY
    See also Handwriting; Writing
GRASS (DRUG) *See* Marijuana
Grasses.   **635.9**
GRASSES
    See also Plants
GRASSES
    Ellis, B. W. Covering ground   **635.9**
    Grasses   **635.9**
    Greenlee, J. The American meadow garden   **635.9**
    Michener, D. Taylor's guide to ground covers **635.9**
GRASSHOPPERS
    Capinera, J. L. Field guide to grasshoppers, crickets, and katydids of the United States   **595.7**
GRASSLAND ECOLOGY
    See also Ecology
GRATEFUL DEAD (MUSICAL GROUP)
    Richardson, P. No simple highway   **781.66**
GRATEFULNESS *See* Gratitude
GRATITUDE
    Visser, M. The gift of thanks   **394**
GRATITUDE
    See also Emotions; Virtue
Graubart, Cynthia
    (jt. auth) Dupree, N. Mastering the art of Southern cooking   **641.59**
Grave of light. Notley, A.   **811**
GRAVE ROBBING
    Craughwell, T. J. Stealing Lincoln's body   **973.7**
Graver, Dennis
    Scuba diving   **797.2**
GRAVES *See* Burial; Cemeteries; Epitaphs; Funeral rites and ceremonies; Mounds and mound builders; Tombs
The **graves** are walking. Kelly, J.   **941.5**
Graves, Robert
    The Greek myths   **292**
    (tr) The twelve Caesars   **878**
Graves, Robert, 1895-1985
    About
    Jarrell, R. No other book   **809**
GRAVITATION
    Darling, D. J. Gravity's arc   **530**
    Feynman, R. P. Six easy pieces   **530**
GRAVITATION
    See also Physics
GRAVITY
    Darling, D. J. Gravity's arc   **530**
    Rovelli, C. Seven Brief Lessons on Physics   **530**
    Scharf, C. Gravity's engines   **523.8**
GRAVITY
    See also Gravitation
Gravity's arc. Darling, D. J.   **530**

Gravity's engines. Scharf, C.   **523.8**
The **Gray** Notebook.   **849**
Gray's anatomy.   **611**
Gray, Charlotte
    Gold diggers   **971**
    Reluctant genius   **92**
Gray, Douglas
    (ed) The Oxford companion to Chaucer   **821**
Gray, Elisha, 1835-1901
    About
    Shulman, S. The telephone gambit   **621.3**
Gray, John, 1951-
    (jt. auth) Annis, B. Work with me   **306.3**
Gray, Michael
    The Bob Dylan encyclopedia   **782.42**
    Hand me my travelin' shoes   **92**
Gray, Theodore
    The elements   **546**
    Molecules   **541**
Grayling, A. C.
    The Age of Genius   **940.2**
    Among the dead cities   **940.54**
Grayson, Gabriel
    Talking with your hands, listening with your eyes   **419**
Grealy, Lucy, 1963-2002
    About
    Patchett, A. Truth & beauty   **92**
A **Great** & Terrible King. Morris, M.   **92**
The **Great** Acceleration. Colvile, R.   **303.483**
The **great** american documents. Ashby, R.   **973**
The **great** American history fact-finder. Cornelison, P.   **973**
The **great** American railroad war. Drabelle, D. **385**
Great American trials.   **347**
The **great** Arab conquests. Kennedy, H.   **909**
A **great** aridness. DeBuys, W. E.   **551.6**
GREAT BASIN
    Durham, M. S. Desert between the mountains **979**
Great battles of history series
    Sandoz, M. The Battle of the Little Bighorn **973.8**
The **great** Beanie Baby bubble. Bissonnette, Z.   **338.7**
The **Great** Big Pressure Cooker Book.   **641.5**
The **great** book of French impressionism. Kelder, D.   **759**
GREAT BOOKS OF THE WESTERN WORLD
    Adler, M. J. How to think about the great ideas **080**
GREAT BOOKS OF THE WESTERN WORLD (FRANKLIN CENTER, PA.)
    Beam, A. A great idea at the time   **973.91**
GREAT BOOKS PROGRAM *See* Discussion groups
GREAT BRITAIN
    Macfarlane, R. Landmarks   **914.1**
GREAT BRITAIN -- ANTIQUITIES

Higgins, C. Under another sky   **936**

GREAT BRITAIN -- ARMED FORCES -- RE-CRUITING AND ENLISTMENT -- BIOGRA-PHY

Hollis, M. Now all roads lead to France   **821**

GREAT BRITAIN -- ARMY

Philpott, W. Three armies on the Somme   **940.4**

GREAT BRITAIN -- BIOGRAPHY

Thompson, L. The six   **92**

Weintraub, S. Charlotte and Lionel   **92**

GREAT BRITAIN -- BIOGRAPHY -- DICTION-ARIES

Who's who 2008   **920.003**

Who's who in British history   **920.003**

GREAT BRITAIN -- CIVILIZATION

Tombs, R. The English and their history   **942**

GREAT BRITAIN -- CIVILIZATION -- 21ST CENTURY

Bryson, B. The road to Little Dribbling   **914**

GREAT BRITAIN -- COLONIES

Gott, R. Britain's empire   **942**

Hunt, T. Cities of empire   **941**

Kwarteng, K. Ghosts of empire   **909**

GREAT BRITAIN -- COLONIES

    See also Colonies

GREAT BRITAIN -- COLONIES -- ADMINIS-TRATION -- HISTORY -- 20TH CENTURY

Howell, G. Gertrude Bell   **92**

GREAT BRITAIN -- COLONIES -- AFRICA

Anderson, D. M. Histories of the hanged   **967.62**

Meredith, M. Diamonds, gold, and war   **968.04**

GREAT BRITAIN -- COLONIES -- AMERICA

Bailyn, B. The barbarous years   **973.2**

GREAT BRITAIN -- COLONIES -- AUSTRALIA

Clendinnen, I. Dancing with strangers   **994**

GREAT BRITAIN -- COLONIES -- HISTORI-OGRAPHY

Bailyn, B. Sometimes an art, never a science, always a craft   **907.2**

GREAT BRITAIN -- COLONIES -- HISTORY

Ferguson, N. Empire: the rise and demise of the British world order and the lessons for global power   **909**

Gott, R. Britain's empire   **942**

Kwarteng, K. Ghosts of empire   **909**

GREAT BRITAIN -- COLONIES -- HISTORY -- CASE STUDIES

Hunt, T. Cities of empire   **941**

GREAT BRITAIN -- DESCRIPTION AND TRAVEL

Bryson, B. The road to Little Dribbling   **914**

Lipscomb, S. A Journey Through Tudor England   **942.05**

GREAT BRITAIN -- FOREIGN RELATIONS

Fletcher, C. The divorce of Henry VIII   **942.05**

GREAT BRITAIN -- FOREIGN RELATIONS --

20TH CENTURY

Manchester, W. The last lion, Winston Spencer Churchill   **92**

GREAT BRITAIN -- FOREIGN RELATIONS -- CATHOLIC CHURCH

Fletcher, C. The divorce of Henry VIII   **942.05**

GREAT BRITAIN -- FOREIGN RELATIONS -- CONFEDERATE STATES OF AMERICA

Dickey, C. Our Man in Charleston   **92**

GREAT BRITAIN -- FOREIGN RELATIONS -- FRANCE

Barr, J. A line in the sand   **956**

Green, D. The Hundred Years War   **944**

GREAT BRITAIN -- FOREIGN RELATIONS -- IRAN

Abrahamian, E. The coup   **955.05**

GREAT BRITAIN -- FOREIGN RELATIONS -- UNITED STATES

Bunker, N. An empire on the edge   **973.3**

GREAT BRITAIN -- HISTORY

Ekin, D. The Last Armada   **941.505**

Jones, N. Tower   **942.1**

Jordan, D. The king's revenge   **941.062**

MacColl, G. To marry an English Lord   **974.7**

Manchester, W. The last lion, Winston Spencer Churchill   **92**

Phillips, K. 1775   **973.3**

Tombs, R. The English and their history   **942**

GREAT BRITAIN -- HISTORY -- 0-1066

Charles-Edwards, T. M. Wales and the Britons, 350-1064   **942.901**

Higgins, C. Under another sky   **936**

Morris, M. A Great & Terrible King   **92**

GREAT BRITAIN -- HISTORY -- 1066-1154, NORMAN PERIOD

Morris, M. The Norman Conquest   **942.02**

Thomas Becket   **92**

GREAT BRITAIN -- HISTORY -- 1066-1485, ME-DIEVAL PERIOD

Green, D. The Hundred Years War   **944**

GREAT BRITAIN -- HISTORY -- 1154-1399, PLANTAGENETS

Jones, D. The Plantagenets   **942.03**

Seward, D. The Demon's Brood   **942.03**

GREAT BRITAIN -- HISTORY -- 1455-1485, WARS OF THE ROSES

Gristwood, S. Blood sisters   **942.04**

Jones, D. The Wars of the Roses   **942.04**

Jones, M. K. Bosworth 1485   **942.04**

Weir, A. The Wars of the Roses   **942.04**

GREAT BRITAIN -- HISTORY -- 1485-1603, TU-DORS

Ackroyd, P. Tudors   **942.05**

Borman, T. Thomas Cromwell   **92**

Goodman, R. How to be a Tudor   **942.05**

Guy, J. The Children of Henry VIII   **941**

Lipscomb, S.   A Journey Through Tudor England **942.05**

Norton, E.   The Temptation of Elizabeth Tudor   **92**

Ronald, S.   Heretic queen   **942.05**

Starmore, A.   Tudor roses   **746.432**

Weir, A.   The lost Tudor princess   **92**

GREAT BRITAIN -- HISTORY -- 1485-1603, TUDORS -- DRAMA

Bolt, R.   A man for all seasons   **822**

GREAT BRITAIN -- HISTORY -- 1558-1603, ELIZABETH

Castor, H.   She-wolves   **920**

Guy, J.   Elizabeth   **92**

Hilton, L.   Elizabeth   **92**

Mortimer, I.   The time traveler's guide to Elizabethan England   **942.05**

Ronald, S.   Heretic queen   **942.05**

Weir, A.   The life of Elizabeth I   **942.05**

GREAT BRITAIN -- HISTORY -- 1603-1714, STUARTS

Ackroyd, P.   Rebellion   **941.06**

GREAT BRITAIN -- HISTORY -- 1660-1688, RESTORATION

Uglow, J. S.   A gambling man   **92**

GREAT BRITAIN -- HISTORY -- 1853-1856, CRIMEAN WAR *See* Crimean War, 1853-1856

GREAT BRITAIN -- HISTORY -- 18TH CENTURY

Byrne, P.   Belle   **92**

GREAT BRITAIN -- HISTORY -- 1945-1952

Kynaston, D.   Austerity Britain   **941.085**

GREAT BRITAIN -- HISTORY -- 1952-

Kynaston, D.   Family Britain, 1951-1957   **941.085**

GREAT BRITAIN -- HISTORY -- 19TH CENTURY

Denlinger, E. C.   Before Victoria   **920**

Encyclopedia of the Victorian era   **941.081**

Erickson, C.   Her little majesty: the life of Queen Victoria   **92**

Hibbert, C.   Queen Victoria   **92**

Hibbert, C.   Wellington   **92**

Vallone, L.   Becoming Victoria   **941.08**

Victorian house   Inside the Victorian home   **306**

Wilson, A. N.   The Victorians   **941.081**

GREAT BRITAIN -- HISTORY -- 20TH CENTURY

Cadbury, D.   Princes at war   **941.084**

Crosby, M. C.   The great pearl heist   **364.16**

GREAT BRITAIN -- HISTORY -- ANNE, 1702-1714

Somerset, A.   Queen Anne   **92**

GREAT BRITAIN -- HISTORY -- CHARLES II, 1660-1685

Jordan, D.   The king's revenge   **941.062**

Pepys, S.   The diary of Samuel Pepys   **941.06**

Spencer, C. E. M. S.   Prince Rupert   **92**

GREAT BRITAIN -- HISTORY -- EDWARD I, 1272-1307

Morris, M.   A Great & Terrible King   **92**

GREAT BRITAIN -- HISTORY -- EDWARD III, 1327-1377

Ormrod, W. M.   Edward III   **92**

GREAT BRITAIN -- HISTORY -- EDWARD VII, 1901-1910

Ridley, J.   The heir apparent   **92**

GREAT BRITAIN -- HISTORY -- GEORGE III, 1760-1820

Fraser, F.   Princesses   **920**

Hadlow, J.   A royal experiment   **92**

GREAT BRITAIN -- HISTORY -- GEORGE III, 1760-1820 -- BIOGRAPHY

Foreman, A.   Georgiana, Duchess of Devonshire   **941.07**

GREAT BRITAIN -- HISTORY -- HENRY II, 1154-1189 -- BIOGRAPHY

Thomas Becket   **92**

Weir, A.   Eleanor of Aquitaine   **92**

GREAT BRITAIN -- HISTORY -- HENRY VII, 1485-1509

Gristwood, S.   Blood sisters   **942.04**

GREAT BRITAIN -- HISTORY -- HENRY VIII, 1509-1547

Porter, L.   Katherine the queen   **92**

Weir, A.   Henry VIII   **942.05**

Weir, A.   The lady in the tower   **92**

GREAT BRITAIN -- HISTORY -- LANCASTER AND YORK, 1399-1485

Jones, D.   The Wars of the Roses   **942.04**

GREAT BRITAIN -- HISTORY -- PURITAN REVOLUTION, 1642-1660

Jordan, D.   The king's revenge   **941.062**

GREAT BRITAIN -- HISTORY -- STUARTS, 1603-1714

Campbell, G.   John Milton   **92**

GREAT BRITAIN -- HISTORY -- VICTORIA, 1837-1901

Flanders, J.   The invention of murder   **364.152**

Summerscale, K.   Mrs. Robinson's disgrace   **941.081**

GREAT BRITAIN -- HISTORY, LOCAL

Higgins, C.   Under another sky   **936**

GREAT BRITAIN -- HISTORY, MILITARY -- 1066-1485

Green, D.   The Hundred Years War   **944**

GREAT BRITAIN -- HISTORY, NAVAL -- 18TH CENTURY

Taylor, S.   Commander   **92**

GREAT BRITAIN -- INTELLECTUAL LIFE

Brewer, J.   The pleasures of the imagination   **941.07**

Sanders, A.   The short Oxford history of English literature   **820**

Snyder, L. J.   The philosophical breakfast club   **509**

GREAT BRITAIN -- KINGS AND RULERS

Andersen, C. Game of crowns 941.085
Cadbury, D. Princes at war 941.084
Hadlow, J. A royal experiment 92
Jones, D. The Plantagenets 942.03
Morris, M. A Great & Terrible King 92
Morris, M. King John 92
Ridley, J. The heir apparent 92
Somerset, A. Queen Anne 92
Wilson, A. N. Victoria 92

GREAT BRITAIN -- KINGS AND RULERS
   See also Kings and rulers
GREAT BRITAIN -- KINGS AND RULERS -- BIOGRAPHY
Hadlow, J. A royal experiment 92
Jones, D. The Plantagenets 942.03
Ormrod, W. M. Edward III 92
Ridley, J. The heir apparent 92
Weir, A. Henry VIII 942.05

GREAT BRITAIN -- KINGS AND RULERS -- FICTION.
Ackroyd, P. The death of King Arthur 398.2
GREAT BRITAIN -- KINGS, QUEENS, RULERS, ETC. *See* Great Britain -- Kings and rulers
GREAT BRITAIN -- LOCAL HISTORY
Bathurst, B. The wreckers 910.4
GREAT BRITAIN -- MI5
Andrew, C. M. Defend the realm 327.12
GREAT BRITAIN -- MI6
Dorril, S. MI6 327.12
GREAT BRITAIN -- MILITARY HISTORY
Sacco, J. The Great War 940.4
GREAT BRITAIN -- POLITICS AND GOVERNMENT
Moore, C. Margaret Thatcher 92
GREAT BRITAIN -- POLITICS AND GOVERNMENT -- 1154-1399
Jones, D. The Plantagenets 942.03
GREAT BRITAIN -- POLITICS AND GOVERNMENT -- 1327-1377
Ormrod, W. M. Edward III 92
GREAT BRITAIN -- POLITICS AND GOVERNMENT -- 1509-1547
Fletcher, C. The divorce of Henry VIII 942.05
GREAT BRITAIN -- POLITICS AND GOVERNMENT -- 1760-1820
Hague, W. J. William Wilberforce 92
Norman, J. Edmund Burke 92
GREAT BRITAIN -- POLITICS AND GOVERNMENT -- 1789-1820
Foreman, A. Georgiana, Duchess of Devonshire 941.07
GREAT BRITAIN -- POLITICS AND GOVERNMENT -- 1936-1945
Lukacs, J. Five days in London, May 1940 940.53
GREAT BRITAIN -- PRIME MINISTERS *See* Prime ministers -- Great Britain

GREAT BRITAIN -- QUEENS *See* Queens -- Great Britain
GREAT BRITAIN -- RACE RELATIONS
Byrne, P. Belle 92
GREAT BRITAIN -- RELATIONS -- UNITED STATES
Maier, T. When lions roar 941.084
GREAT BRITAIN -- ROYAL AIR FORCE
Korda, M. With wings like eagles 940.54
Swift, D. Bomber County 821
GREAT BRITAIN -- ROYAL NAVY
Massie, R. K. Castles of steel 940.4
GREAT BRITAIN -- SOCIAL CONDITIONS
Jordan, D. White cargo 326
Kynaston, D. Austerity Britain 941.085
Kynaston, D. Family Britain, 1951-1957 941.085
Nicolson, J. The perfect summer 942
GREAT BRITAIN -- SOCIAL CONDITIONS -- 16TH CENTURY
Goodman, R. How to be a Tudor 942.05
GREAT BRITAIN -- SOCIAL CONDITIONS -- HISTORY
MacGregor, N. Shakespeare's restless world 942.055
Mortimer, I. The time traveler's guide to Elizabethan England 942.05
GREAT BRITAIN -- SOCIAL LIFE AND CUSTOMS -- 18TH CENTURY
Foreman, A. Georgiana, Duchess of Devonshire 941.07
GREAT BRITAIN -- SOCIAL LIFE AND CUSTOMS -- 20TH CENTURY
Byrne, P. Kick 92
Leaming, B. Kick Kennedy 92
Nicolson, J. The perfect summer 942
GREAT BRITAIN -- SPECIAL OPERATIONS EXECUTIVE
Helm, S. A life in secrets 92
GREAT BRITAIN -- WAR CABINET
Roberts, A. Masters and commanders 940.54
GREAT BRITAIN. ARMY -- BIOGRAPHY
Anderson, S. Lawrence in Arabia 940.4
GREAT BRITAIN. ARMY. BRITISH INDIAN ARMY -- BIOGRAPHY
Karnad, R. Farthest field 940.54
GREAT BRITAIN. GOVERNMENT COMMUNICATIONS HEADQUARTERS -- HISTORY
McKay, S. The secret lives of codebreakers 940.54
GREAT BRITAIN. ROYAL NAVY. OFFICERS -- BIOGRAPHY
Taylor, S. Commander 92
Great Catherine. Erickson, C. 947
The **great** Chinese revolution: 1800-1985. Fairbank, J. K. 951
Great Christian thinkers. Kung, H. 230
The **great** circle. Philip, N. 970.004

The **great** cook. Briscione, J.   641.5

Great cookies. Walter, C.   641.8

The **great** crash, 1929. Galbraith, J. K.   338.5

The **great** deluge. Brinkley, D.   976.3

GREAT DEPRESSION, 1929-1939

   Coe, A. A square meal   641.5

   Dickstein, M. Dancing in the dark   973.91

   Egan, T. The worst hard time   978

   The forgotten man   973.91

   Galbraith, J. K. The great crash, 1929   338.5

   Golay, M. America 1933   973.917

   Gup, T. A secret gift   977.1

   Snyder, J. Hill of Beans   92

   Terkel, S. Hard times   973.91

   Urschel, J. The Year of Fear   364.152

GREAT DEPRESSION, 1929-1939

   See also Depressions; Economic conditions

The **great** derangement. Ghosh, A.   809

Great discoveries [series]

   Goldstein, R. Incompleteness   92

   Johnson, G. Miss Leavitt's stars   92

   Krauss, L. M. Quantum man   92

   Leavitt, D. The man who knew too much   92

   Nuland, S. B. The doctors' plague   92

   Reeves, R. A force of nature   92

   Vollmann, W. T. Uncentering the Earth   92

Great displays for your library step by step. Phillips, S. P.   021.7

The **great** disruption. Gilding, P.   304.2

The **great** dissent. Healy, T.   342.73

The **great** divergence.   339.2

The **great** divide. Watson, P.   909

The **great** divorce. Woo, I.   92

The **great** emergence. Tickle, P.   270

The **great** enigma.   839.7

The **great** equations. Crease, R. P.   509

The **great** escape. Marton, K.   920

Great events from history, The 17th century, 1601-1700.   909

Great events from history, The 18th century, 1701-1800.   909.7

Great events from history, The 19th century, 1801-1900.   909.81

Great events from history, The ancient world, prehistory-476 C.E.   930

Great events from history, The Middle Ages, 477-1453.   909.07

Great events from history, The Renaissance & early modern era, 1454-1600.   909

Great events from history: The 20th century, 1901-1940.   909.82

Great events from history: The 20th century, 1941-1970.   909.82

Great events from history: The 20th century, 1971-2000.   909.82

Great expectations. Neifert, M. R.   649

The **Great** Fire. Ureneck, L.   956.1

The **great** gamble. Feifer, G.   958.1

Great generals series

   Frank, R. B. MacArthur   92

   Remini, R. V. Andrew Jackson   92

   Woodworth, S. E. Sherman   92

The **great** hurricane-1938. Burns, C.   974.7

A **great** idea at the time. Beam, A.   973.91

The **great** influenza. Barry, J. M.   614.5

GREAT LAKES

   Dennis, J. The living Great Lakes   977

The **great** lakes of Africa. Chretien   967.6

GREAT LAKES REGION

   McDonnell, M. A. Masters of Empire   977.4

The **Great** Law and the Longhouse. Fenton, W. N.   970.004

The **Great** Leader and the Fighter Pilot. Harden, B.   92

Great lives from history.   920.009

Great lives from history, The 17th century, 1601-1700.   920.003

Great lives from history, The 18th century, 1701-1800. Powell, J.   920.003

Great lives from history, The 19th century, 1801-1900.   920.003

Great lives from history, The ancient world, prehistory-476 C.E.   920.003

Great lives from history, the Middle Ages, 477-1453.   920.003

Great lives from history, the Renaissance & early modern era, 1454-1600.   920.003

Great lives from history: Notorious lives.   920.003

Great lives from history: the 20th century, 1901-2000.   920.003

Great maps. Brotton, J.   912.09

The **great** match race. Eisenberg, J.   798.4

Great moments in Greek archaeology.   938

The **great** mortality. Kelly, J.   614.5

The **Great** Oom. Love, R.   92

The **great** partnership. Sacks, J.   201.65

The **great** pearl heist. Crosby, M. C.   364.16

The **great** persuasion. Burgin, A.   330.12

The **great** pianists. Schonberg, H. C.   920

The **great** pictorial history of world crime. Nash, J. R.   364

Great Plains. Frazier, I.   917

GREAT PLAINS -- DESCRIPTION

   Frazier, I. Great Plains   917

GREAT PLAINS -- HISTORY

   Egan, T. The worst hard time   978

GREAT PLAINS -- HISTORY -- MAPS

   Lavin, S. J. Atlas of the great plains   912

GREAT PLAINS -- SOCIAL CONDITIONS -- 20TH CENTURY

   Egan, T. The worst hard time   978

GREAT PLAINS -- SOCIAL LIFE AND CUS-

TOMS

Frazier, I. Great Plains   **917**

The **great** railway bazaar. Theroux, P.   **915**

The **great** reflation. Boeckh, J. A.   **332.6**

The **great** republic. Churchill, W.   **973**

The **great** shark hunt. Thompson, H. S.   **818**

Great soul. Lelyveld, J.   **92**

Great Soul of Siberia. Sooyong Park   **599.756**

Great stars [series]

Gary Cooper   **92**

Thomson, D. Bette Davis   **92**

Thomson, D. Humphrey Bogart   **92**

Thomson, D. Ingrid Bergman   **92**

The **great** starvation experiment. Tucker, T.   **174.2**

The **great** swim. Mortimer, G.   **920**

Great tales from English history. Lacey, R.   **941**

Great tales from English history [2] Lacey, R.   **941**

Great tales from English history [3] Lacey, R.   **941**

Great time coming: the life of Jackie Robinson, from baseball to Birmingham. Falkner, D.   **92**

The **great** transformation. Armstrong, K.   **200.9**

A **great** unrecorded history. Moffat, W.   **92**

The **great** upheaval. Winik, J.   **909.7**

The **Great** War. Sacco, J.   **940.4**

The **great** war of our time. Morell, M. J.   **363.325**

The **greater** journey. McCullough, D. G.   **920.009**

The **greatest** benefit to mankind. Porter, R.   **610**

The **Greatest** Knight. Asbridge, T.   **92**

The **greatest** show on Earth. Dawkins, R.   **576.8**

Greayer, Rochelle

Cultivating garden style   **636.8**

Grebe, Anja

Florence   **759.5**

GREECE -- ANTIQUITIES

Fox, M. The Riddle of the Labyrinth   **487**

GREECE -- ANTIQUITIES

See also Classical antiquities

GREECE -- BIOGRAPHY

Plutarch: the lives of the noble Grecians and Romans   **920**

GREECE -- BIOGRAPHY

See also Biography

GREECE -- CIVILIZATION

Freely, J. The flame of Miletus   **509**

GREECE -- CIVILIZATION

See also Classical civilization

GREECE -- DESCRIPTION *See* Greece -- Description and travel

GREECE -- DESCRIPTION AND TRAVEL

Kochilas, D. Ikaria   **641.594**

GREECE -- GEOGRAPHY

See also Geography

GREECE -- HISTORICAL GEOGRAPHY

See also Ancient geography; Greece -- Geography; Historical geography

GREECE -- HISTORY

Green, P. The Hellenistic age   **938**

Herodotus, c. 4. B. B. C. The landmark Herodotus   **938**

GREECE -- HISTORY -- ENCYCLOPEDIAS

Ancient Greece   **938**

GREECE -- HISTORY -- PELOPONNESIAN WAR, 431-404 B.C.

Kagan, D. The Peloponnesian War   **938**

Kagan, D. Thucydides   **938**

The Landmark Xenophon's Hellenika   **938**

Thucydides The landmark Thucydides   **938**

GREECE -- HISTORY -- TO 146 B.C.

Cartledge, P. Ancient Greece   **938**

Herodotus, c. 4. B. B. C. The landmark Herodotus   **938**

The Landmark Xenophon's Hellenika   **938**

GREECE -- INTELLECTUAL LIFE -- TO 146 B.C

Freely, J. The flame of Miletus   **509**

GREECE -- POLITICS AND GOVERNMENT -- TO 146 B.C

Cartledge, P. Democracy   **321.8**

GREECE -- SOCIAL LIFE AND CUSTOMS

Hoffman, S. The olive and the caper   **641.594**

GREECE, ANCIENT *See* Greece -- History -- 0-323

Greek art. Boardman, J.   **709.3**

GREEK ART

See also Ancient art; Art; Classical antiquities

GREEK ART

Boardman, J. Greek art   **709.3**

GREEK CIVILIZATION *See* Greece -- Civilization

GREEK COOKING

Hoffman, S. The olive and the caper   **641.594**

Kiros, T. Food from many Greek kitchens   **641.5**

Kochilas, D. The glorious foods of Greece   **641.59**

Kochilas, D. Ikaria   **641.594**

Psilakis, M. How to roast a lamb   **641.5**

GREEK DRAMA

See also Drama; Greek literature

GREEK LANGUAGE

See also Language and languages

GREEK LITERATURE

The Odyssey   **883**

GREEK LITERATURE

See also Literature

GREEK LITERATURE -- COLLECTIONS

7 Greeks   **881**

The Norton book of classical literature   **880**

GREEK MYTHOLOGY

Wroe, A. Orpheus   **398.2**

GREEK MYTHOLOGY

See also Classical mythology

The **Greek** myths. Graves, R.   **292**

GREEK ORTHODOX CHURCH

See also Christian sects; Orthodox Eastern Church

GREEK PHILOSOPHY *See* Ancient philosophy

GREEK POETRY -- HISTORY AND CRITICISM
Nicolson, A. Why Homer matters   **883**

GREEK SCULPTURE
See also Sculpture

The Greek tragedy in new translations [series]
Aeschylus The Oresteia   **882**

Greek, C. Ray
Sacred cows and golden geese   **179**

Greek, Jean Swingle
Greek, C. R. Sacred cows and golden geese   **179**

The **Greeks** and Greek civilization. Burckhardt, J.   **938**

Greeley, Alexandra
Nong's Thai kitchen   **641.595**

GREEN ARCHITECTURE *See* Sustainable architecture

GREEN BAY PACKERS (FOOTBALL TEAM)
Maraniss, D. When pride still mattered: a life of Vince Lombardi   **92**

GREEN BELT MOVEMENT (KENYA)
Maathai, W. Unbowed   **92**

The **green** boat. Pipher, M.   **303.4**

Green Equilibrium. Wills, C.   **577**

Green is the new red. Potter, W.   **320.5**

GREEN MARKETING
See also Marketing

Green metropolis. Owen, D.   **304.2**

GREEN MOVEMENT *See* Environmental movement

GREEN TECHNOLOGY
Owen, D. Green metropolis   **304.2**
Standard Handbook for Electrical Engineers   **621.3**

GREEN TECHNOLOGY
See also Technology

GREEN TOURISM *See* Ecotourism

Green volunteers.   **333.72**

Green, Aliza
Making artisan pasta   **641.82**

Green, Bill, 1942-
About
Green, B. Boltzmann's tomb   **509**

Green, David
The Hundred Years War   **944**

Green, Elizabeth Shippen, 1871-1954
About
Carter, A. A. The Red Rose girls   **759.13**

Green, Hardy
The company town   **307.7**

Green, Kristen
Something Must Be Done About Prince Edward County   **379.26**

Green, Lisa

On Your Case   **344**

Green, Michael D.
Perdue, T. The Columbia guide to American Indians of the Southeast   **970.004**

Green, Peter
(tr.) Catullus, G. V. The poems of Catullus   **874**
The Hellenistic age   **938**

Green, Susan E.
(jt. auth) Butler, P. M. Joint libraries   **027**

The **green-collar** economy. Jones, V.   **363.7**

Greenawalt, Kent
Does God belong in public schools?   **379**

Greenbaum, Jessica
The two Yvonnes   **811**

Greenberg, Arthur
From alchemy to chemistry in picture and story   **540**

Greenberg, David
Republic of spin   **973.099**

Greenberg, Karen J.
(ed) The torture papers   **973.931**

Greenberg, Keith Elliot
December 8, 1980   **92**

Greenberg, Maurice R.
About
Boyd, R. Fatal risk   **368**

Greenberg, Paul
American catch   **333.95**

Greenberg, Paul
Four fish   **333.95**

Greenberg, Stan
(jt. auth) Carville, J. It's the middle class, stupid!   **320.51**

Greenberger, Dennis
Mind over mood   **616.89**

Greenblat, Musho Rodney Alan
Dharma Delight   **294.3**

Greenblatt, Stephen
The swerve   **940.2**
Will in the world   **822.3**
(ed) The Norton anthology of English literature **820**

Greenburg, Zack O'Malley, 1985-
Michael Jackson, Inc   **92**

Greene, B. (Brian), 1963-
The hidden reality   **530.1**
The elegant universe   **539.7**
The fabric of the cosmos   **523.1**

Greene, David, 1976-
About
Greene, D. Midnight in Siberia   **914.7**

Greene, Donald
(ed) Samuel Johnson   **828**

Greene, Graham, 1904-1991
About
Butcher, T. Chasing the Devil   **916**
Greene, G. Graham Greene   **92**
Iyer, P. The man within my head   **809**

Greene, Joshua
Moral tribes   170

Greene, Richard
(ed) Greene, G.   Graham Greene   92

Greene, Ross W.
Raising human beings   306.874

Greenfield, Amy Butler
A perfect red   667

Greenfield, Robert
Timothy Leary   92

Greenfield, Susan, 1950-
Mind change   155.9

Greenhaw, Wayne
Fighting the devil in Dixie   323.1

GREENHOUSE EFFECT *See* Global warming

GREENHOUSE GAS MITIGATION
Helm, D.   The carbon crunch   333.79

GREENHOUSE GASES -- ENVIRONMENTAL ASPECTS
Global weirdness   577.2

Greenhouse, Linda
Becoming Justice Blackmun   92

GREENHOUSES
Coleman, E.   Winter harvest handbook   635
McGowan, A.   Bulbs in the basement, geraniums on the windowsill   635.9

GREENHOUSES
See also Flower gardening; Gardening; Horticulture

Greenhow, Rose O'Neal, 1814-1864
About
Abbott, K.   Liar, Temptress, Soldier, Spy   973.7

GREENLAND
Ehrlich, G.   This cold heaven   998

Greenlaw, Linda
The hungry ocean   639.2
The lobster chronicles   639

Greenlee, John
The American meadow garden   635.9

Greenman, Ben
Mo' meta blues   92

Greenough, Horatio, 1805-1852
About
Matthiessen, F. O.   American renaissance   810

Greenough, Sarah
Stieglitz, A.   Alfred Stieglitz: the key set   770

GREENPEACE INTERNATIONAL
Stewart, B.   Don't trust, don't fear, don't beg   363.738

Greenspan, Alan
About
Greenspan, A.   The age of turbulence   92
Grind, K.   The lost bank   332.3
Overtveldt, J. v.   Bernanke's test   332.1
Woodward, B.   Maestro: Greenspan's Fed and the American boom   331.1

Greenspan, Dorie
Around my French table   641.5
Baking chez moi   641.86
Child, J.   Baking with Julia   641.7
Dorie's cookies   641.86

Greenspan, Nancy Thorndike
The end of the certain world   92

Greenspan, Stanley I.
Brazelton, T. B.   The irreducible needs of children   155.4
The first idea   153.7

Greenstein, Elaine
A Jewish baker's pastry secrets   641.86

Greenstein, George
(jt. auth) Greenstein, E.   A Jewish baker's pastry secrets   641.86

Greenstein, Julia
(jt. auth) Greenstein, E.   A Jewish baker's pastry secrets   641.86

Greenwald, Glenn, 1967-
No place to hide   327.12

Greenwald, Richard A.
(ed) Labor rising   331.88

GREENWICH VILLAGE (NEW YORK, N.Y.) -- HISTORY
Carter, D.   Stonewall   306.76
Reid, D.   The brazen age   974.7
Strausbaugh, J.   The Village   974.7

The **Greenwood** companion to Shakespeare.   822.3

The **Greenwood** encyclopedia of African American folklore. Prahlad, A.   398

The **Greenwood** encyclopedia of folktales and fairy tales. Haase, D.   398.2

The **Greenwood** encyclopedia of homes through American history.   728

Greenwood guides to historic events, 1500-1900 [series]
Derfler, L.   The Dreyfus affair   944.081
Postma, J.   The Atlantic slave trade   306.3

Greenwood guides to science and religion [series]
Grant, E.   Science and religion, 400 B.C. to A.D. 1550   261.5
Olson, R.   Science and religion, 1450-1900   261.5

The Greenwood Histories of the Modern Nations [series]
Clarke, F. G.   The history of Australia   994
Johanneson, G. T.   The history of Iceland   949.12
Kirkwood, B.   The history of Mexico   972
McLeod, J.   The history of India   954
Perez, L. G.   The history of Japan   952

Greenwood introduces literary masterpieces [series]
Severson, M. S.   Masterpieces of French literature   843

Greenwood, Val D.
The researcher's guide to American genealogy   929

Greer, Germaine
The Cambridge guide to women's writing in English   **820**
The change   **618.1**
     About
Fraser, K. Ornament and silence   **809**
GREETING CARDS
Watanabe, J. The Complete Photo Guide to Cardmaking   **745.594**
Greetings from Utopia Park. Hoffman, C.   **92**
Gregg, Linda
All of it singing   **811**
Gregorian, Vartan
     About
Gregorian, V. The road to home   **92**
Gregory, R. L.
(ed) The Oxford companion to the mind   **128**
Gregory, Ross
Cold War America, 1946 to 1990   **973.92**
Greitens, Eric, 1974-
Resilience   **155.2**
Grendler, Paul F.
(ed) Encyclopedia of the Renaissance   **940.2**
Grene, David
(ed) Aeschylus Aeschylus   **882**
(ed) Euripides Euripides   **882**
(ed) Euripides Euripides [2]   **882**
(ed) Sophocles Sophocles   **882**
Grenier, Robert (Robert L.)
     About
Grenier, R. L. 88 days to Kandahar   **958.104**
Grenier, Robert L.
88 days to Kandahar   **958.104**
Grenny, Joseph
(jt. auth) McMillan, R. Crucial conversations   **153.6**
Grescoe, Taras
Bottomfeeder   **641.6**
Shanghai grand   **951.132**
Gresko, Brian
(ed) When I first held you   **306.874**
GREY MARKET *See* Black market
Grey, Jane Lady, 1537-1554
     About
De Lisle, L. The sisters who would be queen   **920**
Grey, Zane, 1872-1939
     About
Pauly, T. H. Zane Grey   **92**
Gribbin, John
13.8   **523.1**
Almost everyone's guide to science   **500**
Einstein's Masterwork   **530.11**
In search of Schrodinger's cat   **530.1**
Schrodinger's kittens and the search for reality   **530.1**
The scientists   **509**
Gribbin, Mary

Gribbin, J. R. Almost everyone's guide to science   **500**
Gribbon, Deborah Ann
Walsh, J. The J. Paul Getty Museum and its collections   **708.1**
GRIEF
Barnes, J. Levels of life   **823**
The Book of eulogies   **808.8**
Deraniyagala, S. Wave   **954.93**
Doka, K. J. Grief is a journey   **155.9**
Gilbert, S. M. Death's door   **155.9**
MacDonald, H. H is for Hawk   **598.9**
Mockett, M. M. Where the Dead Pause, and the Japanese Say Goodbye   **952**
Paterniti, M. Love and Other Ways of Dying   **814**
Rosenblatt, R. Kayak morning   **300**
Ward, J. Men We Reaped   **92**
Wieseltier, L. Kaddish   **296.4**
GRIEF
     See also Emotions
GRIEF -- POETRY
Gilbert, J. Collected poems   **811**
Grief is a journey. Doka, K. J.   **155.9**
Grierson, Francis, 1848-1927
     About
Wilson, E. Patriotic gore   **810**
Grieve, Michael
(ed) MacDiarmid, H. Selected poetry   **821**
Grieve, Paul
A brief guide to Islam   **297**
Griffin, Brooke
Skinny suppers   **641.5**
Griffin, Donald Redfield
Animal minds   **591.5**
Griffin, Jasper
(ed) The Oxford history of the Roman world   **937**
Griffin, John Howard
Black like me   **305.8**
Griffith, D. W. (David Wark), 1875-1948
     About
Lehr, D. The Birth of a Nation   **305.8**
Griffith, H. Winter
Complete Guide to Prescription & Nonprescription Drugs   **615**
Griffiths, Tom
Slicing the silence   **998**
Griftopia. Taibbi, M.   **973.932**
Griggs, John
     About
Schou, N. Orange sunshine   **363.45**
Grigore, Adina
Skin cleanse   **613**
Grigson, Jane
Charcuterie and French pork cookery   **641.6**
GRILL COOKING *See* Barbecue cooking
GRILLING *See* Barbecue cooking

The **grilling** book. **641.5**

Grillo, Ioan
Gangster Warlords **364.106**

Grimes, Dixie
The B.T.C. old-fashioned grocery cookbook **641.59**

Grimes, Jill
(ed) Sexually transmitted disease **616.95**

Grimké, Angelina Emily, 1805-1879
About
Berkin, C. Civil War wives **920**

The **grind.** Svrluga, B. **796.357**

Grind, Kirsten
The lost bank **332.3**

Grinker, Roy Richard, 1961-
Unstrange minds **616.85**

Gristwood, Sarah
Blood sisters **942.04**

Griswold, Eliza
The tenth parallel **297**

Griswold, Mac
The Manor **974.7**

Grit. Duckworth, A. **158.1**

Grob's basic electronics. Schultz, M. E. **621.381**

GROCERIES -- PURCHASING *See* Grocery
shopping

GROCERY SHOPPING
Hazan, M. Ingredienti **641.5**
My pantry **641.594**
Sacks, S. What the fork are you eating? **641.3**

GROCERY SHOPPING
See also Home economics; Shopping

GROCERY SHOPPING -- ITALY -- ROME
Minchilli, E. Eating Rome **641.594**

GROCERY TRADE
See also Food industry

Groom, Winston
1942 **940.53**
The aviators **920**
The generals **940.54**
Kearny's march **979**
Patriotic fire **973.5**
Shiloh, 1862 **973.7**
Vicksburg, 1863 **973.7**

GROOMING, PERSONAL *See* Personal grooming

Groopman, Jerome E.
The anatomy of hope **616**
How doctors think **610**
Your medical mind **610**

Groove interrupted. Spera, K. **920**

Gropius, Walter
The new architecture and the Bauhaus **724**
About
Weber, N. F. The Bauhaus group **920**

Grose, Peter
Gentleman spy **92**

GROSS NATIONAL PRODUCT
See also Economics; Statistics; Wealth

Gross, John J.
(ed) The New Oxford book of literary anecdotes **828**
(ed) The Oxford book of aphorisms **808.88**
(ed) The Oxford book of comic verse **821**

Gross, Ken
Dream cars **629.222**

Gross, Michael
Focus **770.92**
Rogues' gallery **920**

Gross, Robert
(jt. auth) Ash, A. Elliptic tales **515**

GROSSINGER (N.Y.)
Grossinger, T. Growing up at Grossinger's **917.4**

Grossinger, Tania
About
Grossinger, T. Growing up at Grossinger's **917.4**

Grossman, Allen R.
Descartes' loneliness **811**

Grossman, David
The yellow wind **956.95**

Grossman, Edith
Garcia Marquez, G. Living to tell the tale **92**
Why translation matters **418**

Grossman, Gail Boorstein
Restorative yoga for life **613.7**

GROTTOES *See* Caves

Groucho: the life and times of Julius Henry Marx.
Kanfer, S. **92**

The **ground** truth. Farmer, J. J. **973.931**

Groundbreaking food gardens. Jabbour, N. **635**

Grounded. Bass, D. B. **231**

GROUNDS MAINTENANCE
See also Gardening

GROUNDWATER
See also Water

**GROUNDWATER -- POLLUTION -- HEALTH
ASPECTS -- TOMS RIVER REGION**
Fagin, D. Toms River **363.72**

GROUP DECISION MAKING
See also Decision making

GROUP DISCUSSION *See* Discussion groups

GROUP DYNAMICS *See* Social groups

Group f.64. Alinder, M. S. **770.92**

GROUP F.64 -- HISTORY
Alinder, M. S. Group f.64 **770.92**

GROUP HOMES
See also Institutional care; Social work

**GROUP HOMES FOR YOUTH -- NEW YORK
(STATE) -- NEW YORK**
Berg, R. No house to call my home **362.786**

GROUP IDENTITY
Robbins, A. The geeks shall inherit the Earth

GROUP IDENTITY

See also Identity (Psychology)

GROUP IDENTITY -- POLITICAL ASPECTS

Bishop, B. The big sort   **305.8**

GROUP IDENTITY -- POLITICAL ASPECTS -- UNITED STATES

Bawer, B. The victims' revolution   **320**

GROUP IDENTITY -- SOUTHERN STATES

Thompson, T. The new mind of the South   **305.8**

GROUP IDENTITY -- UNITED STATES

Biss, E. Notes from no man's land   **305.8**

GROUP IDENTITY IN LITERATURE

Prothero, S. The American Bible   **973**

GROUP THEORY

Livio, M. The equation that couldn't be solved **512**

GROUP THEORY

   See also Algebra; Mathematics; Number theory

GROUP TRAVEL *See* Travel

GROUP VALUES *See* Social values

GROUPON (FIRM)

Sennett, F. Groupon's biggest deal ever   **381**

Groupon's biggest deal ever. Sennett, F.   **381**

GROUPS, SOCIAL *See* Social groups

GROUPS, THEORY OF *See* Group theory

Grout, Donald Jay

   (jt. auth) Palisca, C. V. A history of Western music   **780.9**

The **Grove** book of opera singers.   **920**

The **Grove** book of operas. Sadie, S.   **792.5**

The **Grove** encyclopedia of American art.   **709**

Grove library of world art [series]

   Encyclopedia of Latin American & Caribbean art   **709**

Grove, Andrew S., 1936-

     About

Tedlow, R. S. Andy Grove   **92**

GROVELAND (FLA.) -- RACE RELATIONS

King, G. Devil in the grove   **305.896**

Grover Cleveland. Graff, H. F.   **92**

Grover, Sharon

Listening to learn   **372.4**

Groves, Leslie R., 1896-1970

     About

Norris, R. S. Racing for the bomb: General Leslie R. Groves, the Manhattan Project's indispensable man   **92**

Grow a little fruit tree. Ralph, A.   **634**

Grow a living wall. Coronado, S.   **635**

Grow All You Can Eat in Three Square Feet.   **635**

Grow your money! Pond, J. D.   **332.024**

Growing a garden city. Smith, J. N.   **635**

Growing up. Baker, R.   **92**

Growing up again. Moore, M. T.   **92**

Growing up at Grossinger's. Grossinger, T.   **917.4**

GROWN-UP ABUSED CHILDREN *See* Adult child abuse victims

GROWTH

   See also Physiology

GROWTH DISORDERS

   See also Metabolism

The **growth** of the American Republic. Morison, S. E.   **973**

Groza, Victor

Adopting older children   **362.7**

Gruber, Jonathan, 1965-

Health care reform   **362.1**

Gruen, Bob

New York Dolls   **781.66**

Grumbach, Didier

History of international fashion   **746.9**

Grumet, Bridget Hall

Reconstruction era: primary sources   **973.8**

Grummer, Arnold E.

Trash-to-treasure papermaking   **676**

Grun, Bernard

The timetables of history   **902**

GRUNDY (VA.) -- BIOGRAPHY

Smith, L. Dimestore   **92**

GRUNDY (VA.) -- SOCIAL LIFE AND CUS-TOMS

Smith, L. Dimestore   **92**

Grundy, Valerie

   (ed) Correard The Oxford-Hachette French dictionary   **443**

Grunstein, Michael

Clark, W. R. Are we hardwired?   **155.7**

Grunt. Roach, M.   **355.07**

Grunwald, Lisa

Women's letters   **305.4**

Grunwald, Michael

Douglas, M. S. The Everglades   **577.6**

The swamp   **975.9**

Grymes, James A.

Violins of hope   **92**

Guadalupi, Gianni

Manguel, A. The dictionary of imaginary places   **809**

GUANTANAMO BAY DETENTION CAMP

Craig, W. Yankee come home   **917.2**

Guantanamo diary   **958.104**

Hickman, J. Murder at Camp Delta   **355.1**

The Senate Intelligence Committee report on torture

GUANTÁNAMO BAY NAVAL BASE (CUBA)

Khan, M. R. My Guantanamo diary   **909.83**

Guantanamo diary.   **958.104**

GUAPORE RIVER VALLEY (BRAZIL AND BO-LIVIA)

Reel, M. The last of the tribe   **981**

GUARANTEED ANNUAL INCOME

   See also Income

Guaranteed to fail. Acharya, V. V.   **332.7**

The **guardian** of all things. Malone, M. S.   **153.1**

Guare, John
Six degrees of separation **812**
   About
Playwrights at work **812**
Guare, Richard
(jt. auth) Dawson, P. Smart but scattered **649**
GUATEMALA -- POLITICS AND GOVERN-MENT
Goldman, F. The art of political murder **972.81**
Gubar, Susan
Judas **92**
   About
Gubar, S. Memoir of a debulked woman **616.99**
Gubert, Betty Kaplan
Distinguished African Americans in aviation and space science **629.13**
Gubnitskaia, Vera
(ed) Marketing your library **021.7**
Guelzo, Allen C.
Gettysburg **973.7**
Lincoln and Douglas **973.6**
Gueniffey, Patrice
Bonaparte **92**
GUERILLAS See Guerrillas
GUERRILLA WARFARE
Kilcullen, D. The accidental guerrilla **355.4**
GUERRILLA WARFARE
 See also Insurgency; Military art and science; Tactics; War
GUERRILLAS
Roy, A. Walking with the comrades **954**
GUERRILLAS -- FRANCE -- BIOGRAPHY
Kaiser, C. The cost of courage **92**
Guesdon, Jean-Michel
(jt. auth) Margotin, P. All the Songs **781.66**
(jt. auth) Margotin, P. Bob Dylan **782.42**
Guest of honor. Davis, D. **973.91**
Guest, Barbara
The collected poems of Barbara Guest **811**
Guest, Hadley Haden
(ed) Guest, B. The collected poems of Barbara Guest **811**
Guest, Robert
Borderless economics **303.48**
GUESTS See Entertaining
Guevara March, Aleida, 1960-
Remembering Che **972.91**
Guevara, Che, 1928-1967
   About
Anderson, J. L. Che Guevara **92**
Casey, M. Che's afterlife **980**
Diary of a combatant **92**
Remembering Che **972.91**
Von Tunzelmann, A. Red heat **972.9**
Guggenheim, Peggy, 1898-1979
   About

Gill, A. Art lover **92**
Guggiana, Marissa
Primal cuts **641.6**
Gugliotta, Guy
Freedom's cap **975.3**
Guha, Ramachandra
Gandhi before India **92**
India after Gandhi **954.04**
Guibert, Emmanuel
Alan's war **741.5**
The photographer **958.1**
GUIDANCE See Counseling
GUIDANCE, VOCATIONAL See Vocational guidance
Guidara, Will, 1980-
(jt. auth) Humm, D. I love New York **641.59**
(jt. auth) Humm, D. The NoMad cookbook **641.597**
A **guide** book of United States coins. Yeoman, R. S. **737.4**
GUIDE DOGS
 See also Animals and people with disabilities; Working dogs
A **guide** to amphibians and reptiles. **597.9**
The **guide** to good health for teens & adults with Down syndrome. Chicoine, B. **618.92**
Guide to literary agents. **070.5**
The **guide** to period styles for interiors. Gura, J. **747**
Guide to reference. **011**
Guide to reference books. **011**
Guide to Reference in Business and Economics. **016**
Guide to reference in medicine and health. **025.06**
Guide to reference materials for school library media centers. Safford, B. R. **011.6**
A **guide** to the ancient world. Grant, M. **913**
Guide to the presidency and the executive branch. **352.23**
GUIDED MISSILES
 See also Bombs; Projectiles; Rocketry; Rockets (Aeronautics)
GUIDES (PERSONS)
Clark, E. E. Sacagawea of the Lewis and Clark expedition **92**
Hari, D. The translator **92**
Slaughter, T. P. Exploring Lewis and Clark **978**
Guiding your child through grief. Emswiler, M. A. **155.9**
Guiley, Rosemary Ellen
The encyclopedia of demons and demonology **133.4**
The encyclopedia of ghosts and spirits **133.1**
The encyclopedia of saints **282**
The encyclopedia of vampires & werewolves **398**
The encyclopedia of witches, witchcraft, and Wicca **133.4**
Guiliano, Mireille
French women don't get facelifts **613**
GUILLAIN-BARRÉ SYNDROME

Manguso, S. The two kinds of decay 362
Guillebeau, Chris, 1979-
The $100 startup **658.1**
Guillemin, Jeanne
Biological weapons **358**
Guillermoprieto, Alma
Dancing with Cuba **972.91**
Guilloux, Louis, 1899-1980
About
Kaplan, A. Y. The interpreter **940.54**
GUILT
Kushner, H. S. How good do we have to be? **296.7**
GUILT
See also Conscience; Emotions; Ethics; Good and evil; Sin
A **guinea** pig's history of biology. Endersby, J. 576.5
Guinn, Jeff
Go down together **364.1**
Manson **364.152**
Guinness world records 2015. **031**
Guinness World Records Ltd.
(comp) Guinness world records 2015 **031**
GUITAR *See* Guitars
Guitar All-in-one for Dummies. Chappell, J. **787.87**
GUITARISTS
Albertine, V. Clothes, Clothes, Clothes. Music, Music, Music. Boys, Boys, Boys **92**
The Beatles anthology **782.421**
Brightman, C. Sweet chaos **920**
Clapton, E. Clapton **92**
Cross, C. R. Heavier than heaven: a biography of Kurt Cobain **92**
Cross, C. R. Room full of mirrors **92**
Dance, S. The world of Count Basie **920**
Dregni, M. Django: the life and music of a Gypsy legend **92**
Govenar, A. B. Lightnin' Hopkins **92**
Gray, M. Hand me my travelin' shoes **92**
Jackson, B. Garcia **92**
King, B. B. Blues all around me **781.643**
Kruth, J. To live's to fly **92**
Murray, C. S. Crosstown traffic: Jimi Hendrix and the post-war rock'n'roll revolution **787.87**
Richards, K. Life **92**
Schumacher, M. Crossroads **92**
Spitz, B. The Beatles: the biography **920**
Wald, E. Escaping the delta **92**
Wareham, D. Black postcards **92**
Wolfe, C. K. The life and legend of Leadbelly **92**
Zappa, F. The real Frank Zappa book **92**
GUITARISTS -- UNITED STATES -- BIOGRA-PHY
Goins, W. E. Blues all day long **92**
GUITARS
Chapman, R. The new complete guitarist **787.87**
Chappell, J. Guitar All-in-one for Dummies **787.87**

GUITARS -- METHODS (JAZZ)
See also Jazz music
GUITARS -- METHODS -- SELF INSTRUC-TION
Chappell, J. Guitar All-in-one for Dummies **787.87**
Guiteau, Charles Julius, 1841-1882
About
Millard, C. The destiny of the republic **973.8**
Guittard Chocolate cookbook. **641.6**
Guittard, Amy
Guittard Chocolate cookbook **641.6**
Gulag. Applebaum, A. **365**
Gulag. Kizny, T. **365**
The **Gulag** Archipelago, 1918-1956 v1. Solzhenitsyn, A. **365**
The **Gulag** Archipelago, 1918-1956 v2. Solzhenitsyn, A. **365**
The **Gulag** Archipelago, 1918-1956 v3. Solzhenitsyn, A. **365**
Gulbrandsen, Don
Edward Sheriff Curtis **770**
GULF COAST (U.S.)
Ulanski, S. L. The Gulf Stream **551.46**
Zebrowski, E. Category 5 **363.34**
GULF COAST (U.S.) -- HISTORY, MILITARY -- 18TH CENTURY
DuVal, K. Independence Lost **973.3**
GULF STATES (U.S.)
See also United States
The **Gulf** Stream. Ulanski, S. L. **551.46**
GULF WAR, 1991 *See* Persian Gulf War, 1991
Gull, Imtiaz
The most dangerous place **954.91**
Gullberg, Maria
Tapestry crochet and more **746.434**
Gulp. Roach, M. **612.3**
GUMS AND RESINS
See also Forest products; Industrial chemistry; Plastics
GUN CONTROL
See also Law; Legislation
GUN CONTROL -- UNITED STATES -- ENCY-CLOPEDIAS
Guns in American society **363.33**
Gun digest 2015. **623.4**
Gun guys. Baum, D. **683.4**
Gunn, James E.
Isaac Asimov **813**
Gunn, Thom
Boss Cupid **821**
Collected poems **821**
Gunnels, Claire B.
(jt. auth) Butler, P. M. Joint libraries **027**
GUNPOWDER
See also Explosives; Guns
GUNPOWDER PLOT, 1605

Fraser, A. Faith and treason   **942.06**
GUNS
  Firearms   **683.4**
  Gun digest 2015   **623.4**
GUNS
  See also Weapons
GUNS -- CONTROL *See* Gun control
The **guns** at last light. Atkinson, R.   **940.54**
Guns in American society.   **363.33**
The **guns** of August. Tuchman, B. W.   **940.3**
Guns, germs, and steel. Diamond, J. M.   **303.4**
GUNSMITHING *See* Firearms industry
Gunton, Mike
  (jt. auth) Barrington, R. Life   **578.4**
Gup, Ted
  Book of honor   **327.12**
  A secret gift   **977.1**
Guppy, Joe
           About
  Guppy, J. My fluorescent God   **92**
Gur, Janna
  The book of New Israeli food   **641.5**
Gura, Judith
  The guide to period styles for interiors **747**
Gura, Philip F., 1950-
  The life of William Apess, Pequot   **92**
Guralnick, Peter
  Careless love: the unmaking of Elvis Presley **92**
  Dream boogie   **92**
  Sam Phillips   **92**
Gurney, A. R.
  Love letters and two other plays: The golden age
  and What I did last summer   **812**
Gussow, Mel
  Edward Albee   **92**
Gustave Caillebotte. Shackelford, G. T. M. **759.4**
Guth, Dorothy Lobrano
  (ed) White, E. B. Letters of E.B. White   **92**
Guthrie, Julian
  How to make a spaceship   **629.47**
Guthrie, Woody, 1912-1967
           About
  Klein, J. Woody Guthrie   **92**
Gutierrez, Eduardo, 1978-1999
           About
  Breslin, J. The short sweet dream of Eduardo Guti-
  errez   **331.6**
Gutjahr, Paul C.
  The Book of Mormon   **289.3**
Gutkind, Lee
  (ed) Twelve breaths a minute   **616**
  You can't make this stuff up   **808**
Gutman, Huck
  (jt. auth) Sanders, B. Outsider in the White
  House   **92**
Gutman, Robert W.

Mozart   **92**
Gutmann family
           About
  Goodman, S. The Orpheus Clock   **940.53**
Gutmann, Amy
  (ed) The lives of animals   **179**
Guttenplan, D. D.
  American radical   **92**
  The Holocaust on trial   **940.53**
Gutting, Gary
  What philosophy can do   **100**
  (ed) Talking God   **210**
Guy, John
  The Children of Henry VIII   **941**
  Elizabeth   **92**
  Thomas Becket   **92**
Guy, Richard K.
  Conway, J. H. The book of numbers   **512.7**
Guzman, Andrew T.
  Overheated   **363.738**
Gwynne, S. C.
  Empire of the summer moon   **92**
  The Perfect Pass   **796.332**
  Rebel Yell   **92**
GYMNASTICS
  See also Athletics; Exercise; Sports
GYNECOLOGISTS
  Press, E. Absolute convictions   **363.46**
**GYNECOLOGISTS -- SOMALIA -- BIOGRA-
PHY**
  Abdi, H. Keeping hope alive   **92**
GYNECOLOGY *See* Women -- Diseases; Women
-- Health and hygiene
GYPSIES
  Lewy, G. The Nazi persecution of the gyp-
  sies   **940.53**
GYPSIES -- ENGLAND -- BIOGRAPHY
  Walsh, M. Gypsy boy   **92**
GYPSUM
  See also Minerals
Gypsy boy. Walsh, M.   **92**

H

H is for Hawk. MacDonald, H.   **598.9**
H. D. Collected poems, 1912-1944 811
H. M., 1926-2008
           About
  Dittrich, L. Patient H.M.   **616.85**
Ha, Robin
  Cook Korean!   **641.595**
Haab, Sherri
  The art of metal clay   **739.27**
Haag, Michael
  The Tragedy of the Templars   **271**
Haas, Robert B.
  Through the eyes of the Vikings   **779**

Haase, Donald
  The Greenwood encyclopedia of folktales and fairy
    tales   **398.2**
Haase, Ynez D.
  Beck, W. A. Historical atlas of the American
    West   **911**
Haass, Richard
  Foreign policy begins at home   **327.73**
  War of necessity: war of choice   **956.7**
HABEAS CORPUS
    See also Civil rights; Constitutional law;
    Criminal procedure; Martial law
Haber, Carol Chase
  Ames, L. B. Your eight-year-old   **649**
  Ames, L. B. Your one-year-old   **649**
  Ames, L. B. Your seven-year-old   **649**
HABIT
  The power of habit   **158.1**
  Rubin, G. Better than before   **158.1**
HABIT
    See also Human behavior; Psychology
HABIT -- SOCIAL ASPECTS
  The power of habit   **158.1**
The **habit** of being. O'Connor, F.   **92**
Habitat. Galvin, B.   **811**
HABITAT (ECOLOGY)
  Fothergill, A. Planet Earth   **508**
  Welcome to subirdia   **598**
HABITAT (ECOLOGY)
    See also Ecology
HABITATIONS OF DOMESTIC ANIMALS *See*
  Animal housing
HABITATIONS, HUMAN *See* Housing
HABITS OF ANIMALS *See* Animal behavior
Habsburg, House of
          About
  Wawro, G. A mad catastrophe   **940.4**
Hacker, Andrew
  (jt. auth) Dreifus, C. Higher education?   **378**
Hacker, Marilyn
  Selected poems   **811**
  Squares and courtyards   **811**
  A stranger's mirror   **811**
Hackett classics [series]
  Russell, B. The problems of philosophy   **100**
Hackett, Albert
  Goodrich, F. The diary of Anne Frank   **812**
Hackett, David A.
  The Buchenwald report   **940.53**
Hacking the Future. Stryker, C.   **004.67**
HACKTIVISM
  Olson, P. We are Anonymous   **005.8**
Had I Known. Lunden, J.   **791.450**
Haden, Jeff
  The complete dictionary of real estate terms ex-
    plained simply   **333.3**

HADES *See* Hell
Hadfield, Chris, 1959-
          About
  Hadfield, C. An astronaut's guide to life on earth **92**
Hadland, Tony
  (jt. auth) Lessing Bicycle design   **629.2**
Hadlow, Janice
  A royal experiment   **92**
Hadrian and the triumph of Rome. Everitt, A.   **92**
Hadrian, Emperor of Rome, 76-138
          About
  Everitt, A. Hadrian and the triumph of Rome   **92**
Haedrich, Ken
  Pie: 300 tried-and-true recipes for delicious home-
    made pie   **641.8**
Haelle, Tara
  (jt. auth) Willingham, E. The informed par-
    ent   **649.1**
Haffner, Sebastian
          About
  Haffner, S. Defying Hitler   **943.085**
Hafiz
  The gift   **891**
Hafner, Katie
  A romance on three legs   **92**
Hagedorn, Ann
  The invisible soldiers   **355**
  Savage peace   **973.91**
Hagen, Uta
  Respect for acting   **792**
HAGGADAH
  New American Haggadah   **296.4**
Hagler, Marvin, 1954-
          About
  Kimball, G. Four kings   **920**
Hagopian, Jesse
  (ed) More Than a Score   **371.26**
Hagstrom, Robert G., 1956-
  The Warren Buffett Way   **332.6**
Hague, William Jefferson
  William Wilberforce   **92**
Hahn, Emily, 1905-1997
          About
  Grescoe, T. Shanghai grand   **951.132**
Hahn, Harry, b. 1897
          About
  Brewer, J. The American Leonardo   **759**
Hahn, Steven
  A nation under our feet   **305.8**
  A Nation Without Borders   **973.5**
Haidt, Jonathan
  The happiness hypothesis   **170**
  The righteous mind   **201**
HAIKU
  Berry, W. New collected poems   **811**
  Haiku before haiku   **895.6**

Higginson, W. J. The haiku handbook **808.1**

HAIKU

 See also Poetry

Haiku before haiku. **895.6**

The **haiku** handbook. Higginson, W. J. **808.1**

Hainsworth, Peter

 (ed) The Oxford companion to Italian literature **850**

HAIR

 See also Head; Personal grooming

Hair, Jaden

 The steamy kitchen cookbook **641.5**

Hair, William Ivy

 The Kingfish and his realm: the life and times of Huey P. Long **92**

Hairston family

   About

 Wiencek, H. The Hairstons **920**

The **Hairstons**. Wiencek, H. **920**

HAIRSTYLISTS

 Rodriguez, D. Kabul Beauty School **305.4**

Haiti. Dubois, L. **972.94**

HAITI -- HISTORY

 Dubois, L. Haiti **972.94**

 Von Tunzelmann, A. Red heat **972.9**

HAITI -- SOCIAL CONDITIONS

 Danticat, E. Create dangerously **92**

HAITI EARTHQUAKE, HAITI, 2010

 Alvarez, J. A wedding in Haiti **818**

 Katz, J. M. The big truck that went by **363.34**

 McClelland, M. Irritable hearts **92**

 The World Is Moving Around Me **972.94**

Hajdu, David

 The ten-cent plague **741.5**

Hakkakiyan, Ru'ya

 Assassins of the Turquoise Palace **364.152**

Halaby, Laila

 My name on his tongue **811**

Halber, Deborah

 The skeleton crew **363.25**

Halberstam, David

 The amateurs **797.1**

 (ed) The Best American sports writing of the century **796**

 The best and the brightest **973.922**

 The children **323.1**

 The coldest winter **951.9**

 The fifties **973.92**

 Firehouse **363.34**

 Summer of '49 **796.357**

 The teammates **796**

Halbreich, Betty, 1927-

   About

 Halbreich, B. I'll drink to that **92**

Hale, Robert (Robert Allen), 1941-2008

   About

 Pilgrim's wilderness **92**

Hale, Sheila

 Titian **92**

Hales, Dianne

 Mona Lisa **759.5**

Halevi, Yossi Klein

 Like dreamers **356**

Haley family

   About

 Haley, A. Roots **920**

Haley, Alex

 Roots **920**

 Malcolm X The autobiography of Malcolm X **92**

   About

 Norrell, R. J. Alex Haley and the books that changed a nation **92**

Haley, James L.

 Captive paradise **996.9**

The **half** has never been told. Baptist, E. E. **306.3**

Half the sky. Kristof, N. D. **362.83**

Half yard gifts. Shore, D. **646.2**

The **half-life** of facts. Arbesman, S. **501**

Halfway to Hollywood. Palin, M. **92**

HALIFAX (N.S.)

 MacDonald, L. M. Curse of the Narrows **971**

Halifax, Edward Frederick Lindley Wood, 1st Earl of, 1881-1959

   About

 Lukacs, J. Five days in London, May 1940 **940.53**

Hall, Donald, 1928-

 The back chamber **811**

 Essays After Eighty **814**

 The selected poems of Donald Hall **811.54**

 White apples and the taste of stone **811**

Hall, James, III

   About

 Herrington, S. A. Traitors among us **327.12**

Hall, Jean-Blaise

 Spieler, M. Paris **641.5**

Hall, Kermit

 (ed) The Oxford companion to American law **349**

 (ed) The Oxford companion to the Supreme Court of the United States **347**

 (ed) The Oxford guide to United States Supreme Court decisions **342**

Hall, Stephen S.

 Wisdom **179**

Hall, Timothy L.

 (ed) U.S. laws, acts, and treaties **348**

Hall, Trevor

 (ed) Coles, R. Handing one another along **820**

Hallelujah junction. Adams, J. **92**

Hallett, Richard

 Bike deconstructed **629.227**

Hallett, Tracy

 Digital photography complete course **770**

HALLEY'S COMET

Sagan, C. Comet   **523.6**

HALLEY'S COMET
> *See also* Comets

Halliday, Jon
> Chang, J. Mao: the unknown story   **92**

Halligan, Karen
> Doc Halligan's What every pet owner should know   **636**

Hallinan, Joseph T.
> Why we make mistakes   **153**

Hallman, J. C.
> The chess artist   **794.1**
> (ed) The story about the story   **809**

Halloran, Andrew R.
> ### About
> Halloran, A. R. The song of the ape   **599.885**

Hallowed ground. McPherson, J. M.   **973.7**

HALLOWEEN
> Brown, S. Glitterville's handmade Halloween   **745.594**
> Morton, L. Trick or Treat   **394.264**
> Sheldon, K. Felt-o-ween   **745.594**

HALLOWEEN
> *See also* Holidays

HALLOWEEN DECORATIONS
> Brown, S. Glitterville's handmade Halloween   **745.594**
> Sheldon, K. Felt-o-ween   **745.594**

Hallowell, Edward M.
> Driven to Distraction   **616.85**
> Shine   **658.3**

HALLUCINATIONS AND ILLUSIONS
> Hustvedt, S. Living, thinking, looking   **814**

HALLUCINOGENS
> Lattin, D. The Harvard Psychedelic Club   **920**
> Shroder, T. Acid test   **615.7**

HALLUCINOGENS
> *See also* Drugs; Psychotropic drugs; Stimulants

Halm, Brad
> (jt. auth) McCrate, C. High-yield vegetable gardening   **635**

Halperin, Daniel
> Tinderbox   **614.5**

Halperin, Mark
> Double Down   **324.9**

Halpern, Jake
> Bad paper   **332.7**

Halpern, Paul
> Edge of the universe   **523.1**
> Einstein's dice and Schrödinger's cat   **530.13**

Halsey, William Frederick, 1882-1959
> ### About
> Borneman, W. R. The admirals   **920**

Halsted, Deborah D.
> Disaster planning   **025.8**

Halverson, Anders
> An entirely synthetic fish   **639.3**

Ham radio for dummies. Silver, H. W.   **621.384**

HAM RADIO STATIONS *See* Amateur radio stations

Ham, Paul
> Hiroshima Nagasaki   **940.54**

HAMAS
> Remnick, D. Reporting   **814**

Hamberger, Lars
> Nilsson, L. A child is born   **612.6**

Hamblin, Robert W.
> Fargnoli, A. N. Critical companion to William Faulkner   **813**

Hamblyn, Richard
> The invention of clouds   **551.57**

HAMBURGERS
> Burgers   **641.66**

Hamid, Mohsin, 1971-
> Discontent and its civilizations   **814**

Hamill, Sam
> (ed) Carruth, H. Toward the distant islands   **811**

Hamilton. McCarter, J.   **782.1**

Hamilton, Adams, Jefferson. Staloff, D.   **973.4**

Hamilton, Alexander, 1757-1804
> Writings   **973.4**
> ### About
> Chernow, R. Alexander Hamilton   **92**
> Ellis, J. J. Founding brothers   **973.4**
> Larson, E. J. A magnificent catastrophe   **324**
> McCraw, T. K. The founders and finance   **330.973**
> Miller, J. C. The Federalist era, 1789-1801   **973.4**
> Sedgwick, J. War of two   **973.4**
> Staloff, D. Hamilton, Adams, Jefferson   **973.4**

Hamilton, Alissa
> Got milked?   **641.5**

Hamilton, Duncan
> For the Glory   **92**

Hamilton, Edith
> (ed) Plato The collected dialogues of Plato, including the letters   **888**

Hamilton, Gabrielle
> Prune   **641.3**
> ### About
> Hamilton, G. Blood, bones & butter   **92**

Hamilton, Garry
> Super species   **578.6**

Hamilton, Jeremiah G., -1875
> ### About
> White, S. Prince of darkness   **92**

Hamilton, Lisa M.
> Deeply rooted   **338.1**

Hamilton, Martha M.
> (ed) The best business writing 2013   **330.9**

Hamilton, Melissa
> Barrow, C. Mrs. Wheelbarrow's practical pan-

try 641.4

Bayless, R. More Mexican everyday 641.597

(jt. auth) Hirsheimer, C. Canal house cooks every day 641.5

Hamilton, Neil A.

Presidents 920.003

Hamilton, Nigel

Biography 907

Commander in chief 940.53

The mantle of command 940.54

Hamilton, Tyler

The Secret Race 796.62

Hamilton, William Rowan Sir, 1805-1865

About

Bell, E. T. Men of mathematics 920

Hamilton-Paterson, James

Marked for death 940.44

Hamlet: poem unlimited. Bloom, H. 822.3

Hamm, Thomas D.

The Quakers in America 289.6

Hammarskjold, Dag

Markings 839.7

Hammel, Bob

Knight, B. Knight: my story 92

Hammer, Joshua

The bad-ass librarians of Timbuktu 025.8

Hammer, Langdon

James Merrill 92

Hammond, Bruce G.

(jt. auth) Fiske, E. B. Fiske Guide to Getting Into The Right College 378.1

Hammond, Scott John

(jt. auth) Roberts, R. N. Campaigning for president in America, 1788-2016 324.709

Hample, Zack

Watching baseball smarter 796.357

Hampton, Dan

The hunter killers 959.704

Hamshaw, Gena

Choosing raw 641.3

Han, Lori Cox

Handbook to American democracy 320.4

Han, Tomislav

(jt. auth) Han, L. C. Handbook to American democracy 320.4

Hanagarne, Joshua, 1977-

About

Hanagarne, J. The world's strongest librarian 92

Hancock, Graham

Underworld: the mysterious origins of civilization 551.7

HAND

Reid, L. The art of hand reading 133.6

Hand drawn jokes for smart attractive people. Diffee, M. 741.5

Hand dyeing yarn and fleece. Callahan, G. 746.6

Hand me my travelin' shoes. Gray, M. 92

HAND SPINNING

Anderson, S. The spinner's book of yarn designs 746.14

Boggs, J. Spin art 746.12

Hand to mouth. Tirado, L. 362.5

HAND WEAVING

Mitchell, S. Inventive weavng on a little loom 746.1

Murphy, M. Woven to wear 746.1

HAND WEAVING See Weaving

Hand, Diana

Draw Horses in 15 Minutes 743.6

Handal, Nathalie

(ed) Language for a new century 808.81

(ed) The Poetry of Arab women 892.7

HANDBAGS

Butler, A. Amy Butler's style stitches 646.4

Kim, S. Boutique bags 646.4

Mallalieu, N. The better bag maker 646.4

Handbook of Chinese mythology. Yang Lihui 299.5

Handbook of denominations in the United States. Atwood, C. D. 280

The **handbook** of knots. Pawson, D. 623.88

Handbook of United States coins. Yeoman, R. S. 737.4

Handbook to American democracy. Han, L. C. 320.4

Handbook to life in ancient Egypt. David, A. R. 932

Handbooks of world mythology [series]

Yang Lihui Handbook of Chinese mythology 299.5

The **handbuilt** home. White, A. 684.1

Handel, George Frideric, 1685-1759

About

Harris, E. T. George Frideric Handel 92

HANDGUN CONTROL See Gun control

HANDGUNS

See also Guns

HANDICAPPED See People with disabilities

HANDICAPPED CHILDREN See Children with disabilities

HANDICRAFT

Adams, L. Needle felting 746

Adarme, A. The year of cozy 641.3

Akiyama, L. Rubber band engineer 745

Bardwell, S. Sewing Basics 746

Bassetti, A. Arm knitting 746.43

Bernard, W. Up, down, all-around stitch dictionary 746.43

Bibliocraft 745.5

Bluhm, L. Creative soldered jewelry & accessories 745.594

Bried, E. How to sew a button 640

Brown, C. The new Christmas tree 745.594

Brown, S. Glitterville's handmade christmas 745.594

Brown, S. Glitterville's handmade Halloween 745.594

Bull, J. Get set, sew **646.2**

Chapin, K. The handmade marketplace **745.5**

Chapman, E. A beautiful mess happy handmade home **747**

Combs, R. A. Kumihimo : basics & beyond **745.594**

Corwin, L. Lena Corwin's made by hand **746.6**

Corwin, L. Printing by hand **745.5**

Ellis, C. Home sewn **646.21**

Finnanger, T. Tilda Homemade & Happy **746.4**

Foxfire 40th anniversary book **975.8**

Frauenfelder, M. Maker dad **745.5**

Gedeon, J. Beautiful bracelets by hand **745.594**

Handy dad **745.592**

Kim, S. Boutique bags **646.4**

Martha Stewart living Martha Stewart's encyclopedia of crafts **745.5**

Omdahl, K. The finer edge **746.43**

The paper playhouse **745.54**

Pember, M. The Little Veggie Patch Co. DIY Garden Projects **712.6**

Pester, S. Supercraft **745.5**

Sheldon, K. Felt-o-ween **745.594**

Stewart, M. Martha Stewart's encyclopedia of sewing and fabric crafts **746**

Watanabe, J. The Complete Photo Guide to Cardmaking **745.594**

White, C. Uniquely felt **746**

Yaker, R. Little one-yard wonders **646.2**

HANDICRAFT

See also Arts

HANDICRAFT -- DESIGN

Handy dad **745.592**

HANDICRAFT FOR CHILDREN

Anderson, S. B. Susan B. Anderson's kids' knitting workshop **746.43**

Neuburger, E. K. Show me a story **741.6**

Van't Hul, J. The artful parent **745.5**

HANDICRAFT FOR GIRLS

Frauenfelder, M. Maker dad **745.5**

HANDICRAFT INDUSTRIES -- MANAGEMENT -- HANDBOOKS, MANUALS, ETC

Lindsay, V. Sewing to sell **646.2**

Handing one another along. Coles, R. **820**

Handley, Ann

Content rules **658.8**

Handlin, Oscar

The uprooted **325**

Handling the truth. Kephart, B. **808.06**

HANDLOOMS

Mitchell, S. Inventive weavng on a little loom **746.1**

Handmade interiors. **646.2**

The handmade marketplace. Chapin, K. **745.5**

Hands of my father. Uhlberg, M. **92**

The handweaver's pattern directory. Dixon, A. **746.1**

Handwerker, Lloyd

Famous Nathan **92**

Handwerker, Nathan, 1892-1974

About

Handwerker, L. Famous Nathan **92**

HANDWRITING

Trubek, A. The History and Uncertain Future of Handwriting **652.1**

HANDWRITING

See also Writing

The **handy** anatomy answer book. Balaban, N. E. **611**

Handy dad. **745.592**

The **Handy** English grammar answer book. Hult, C. A. **428**

The **handy** Islam answer book. Renard, J. **297**

The **handy** science answer book. **500**

Handy, W. C. (William Christopher), 1873-1958

About

Robertson, D. W.C. Handy **92**

Hanel, Marnie

The picnic **642**

Haney, Eric L.

Inside Delta Force **356**

Haney, Hank

About

Haney, H. The big miss **796.352**

HANGING *See* Capital punishment

Hanging man. Martin, B. **709**

The **hanging** of Thomas Jeremiah. Harris, J. W. **92**

Hanin, Jennifer S.

(jt. auth) Potter, D. A. What to do when you can't get pregnant **618.1**

Reuben, S. C. Becoming Jewish **296.7**

Hank Williams. Escott, C. **92**

Hanks, Patrick

(ed) Dictionary of American family names **929.4**

Hanks, Reuel R.

Central Asia **958**

Hanlan, James P.

(ed) Historical encyclopedia of American labor **331.8**

Hannah, Susan

(jt. auth) Smith, R. G. ASD, the complete autism spectrum disorder health & diet guide **616.85**

Hannaway, Dorian

(jt. auth) Reynolds, D. Make 'em Laugh **92**

Hannay, Alastair

(tr) The concept of anxiety **233**

Hannegan, Lizette D.

(jt. auth) Grover, S. Listening to learn **372.4**

Hannemann, Robert E.

(ed) Caring for your baby and young child **618.92**

Hannibal, 247-183 B.C.

About

O'Connell, R. L. The ghosts of Cannae **937**

Hanoch, Doron

The yoga lifestyle 613.7

Hans Christian Andersen. Wullschlager, J. 839.8

Hans Christian Andersen: a new life. Andersen, J. 92

Hansberry, Lorraine, 1930-1965
A raisin in the sun 812
About
Hansberry, L. To be young, gifted, and Black 92

HANSEN'S DISEASE *See* Leprosy

Hansen, Eric
Orchid fever 635.9

Hansen, James E.
Storms of my grandchildren 363.7

Hanson, David
Breaking through concrete 630

Hanson, Thor
Feathers 598
The triumph of seeds 581.4

Hanson, Victor Davis
Carnage and culture 904
The father of us all 355
The soul of battle 355

Hanssen, Robert Philip
About
Wise, D. Spy: the inside story of how the FBI's Robert Hanssen betrayed America 327.12

HANUKKAH
See also Jewish holidays
Hanukkah in America. Ashton, D. 296.4

HAPPENING (ART) *See* Performance art

The **happiest** baby guide to great sleep. Karp, H. 649

The **happiest** baby on the block. Karp, H. 649

Happiness. 152.4

HAPPINESS
See also Emotions

HAPPINESS
Achor, S. Before happiness 158
Csikszentmihalyi, M. Flow: the psychology of optimal experience 155.2
De Graaf, J. What's the economy for, anyway? 330.9
Edelman, S. The happiness of pursuit 153
Ehrenreich, B. Bright-sided 155.2
Enayati, A. Seeking serenity 155.9
Foster, R. How we choose to be happy 158
Gilbert, D. Stumbling on happiness 158
Haidt, J. The happiness hypothesis 170
Happiness 152.4
Heller, R. Secular meditation 158.1
Hurley, K. The happy kid handbook 649
Jacobs, B. Life is good 650.1
Jamison, K. R. Exuberance 152.4
Miller, C. A. Creating your best life 158
Nettle, D. Happiness 152.4
Pillemer, K. A. 30 lessons for living 305.26

Prager, D. Happiness is a serious problem 158
Santi, J. The giving way to happiness 179
Saviuc, L. D. 15 things you should give up to be happy 152.4
Senior, J. All Joy and No Fun 306.874
Sugar, L. Power your happy 158
Walsh, P. Lighten up 332.024
Happiness. Nettle, D. 152.4

HAPPINESS -- RELIGIOUS ASPECTS -- BUDDHISM
Emet, J. Finding the blue sky 294.3

HAPPINESS -- SOCIAL ASPECTS
Davies, W. The happiness industry 304

HAPPINESS -- SOCIAL ASPECTS -- UNITED STATES -- HISTORY
Lepore, J. The mansion of happiness 973
The **happiness** hypothesis. Haidt, J. 170

HAPPINESS IN CHILDREN
Hurley, K. The happy kid handbook 649
The **happiness** industry. Davies, W. 304
Happiness is a serious problem. Prager, D. 158
The **happiness** of pursuit. Edelman, S. 153
Happy cooking. De Laurentiis, G. 641.5
Happy home. 646.2
The **happy** isles of Oceania. Theroux, P. 919
The **happy** kid handbook. Hurley, K. 649
Happy life. Budbill, D. 811
The **happy** sleeper. 649

Haralson, Eric L.
(ed) Encyclopedia of American poetry, the twentieth century 811
Critical companion to Henry James 813

Harampolis, Alethea
The flower recipe book 745.92

Harari, Yuval Noah
Sapiens 909

Harasewych, M. G.
The book of shells 594

HARASSMENT, SEXUAL *See* Sexual harassment

Harbach, Chad
(ed) MFA vs NYC 808.02

Harbison, Lawrence
The Best Men's Stage Monologues 2016 792
(ed) 2010: the best women's stage monologues and scenes 808.82
(ed) The best stage scenes of 2007 808.82

HARBORS
See also Civil engineering; Hydraulic structures; Merchant marine; Navigation; Shipping; Transportation

Harbutt, Juliet
(ed) World cheese book 641.3
Hard choices. Clinton, H. R. 92
Hard driving: the Wendell Scott story. Donovan, B. 92
Hard times. Terkel, S. 973.91

The **hard** times guide to retirement security. Miller, M. **332.024**

Hard times require furious dancing. Walker, A. **811**

HARD-OF-HEARING *See* Hearing impaired

HARDANGER NEEDLEWORK

    See also Drawn work; Embroidery; Needlework

Harden, Blaine

  The Great Leader and the Fighter Pilot **92**

  A river lost **333.91**

The **hardest** working man. Sullivan, J. **92**

Hardesty, Von

  Black wings **920**

HARDIN HIGH SCHOOL (HARDIN, MONT.) -- BASKETBALL

  Colton, L. Counting coup **796.323**

Harding, James M.

  Crist, D. T. World ocean census **578.7**

Harding, Julia

  (ed) The Oxford companion to wine **641.22**

  (jt. auth) Robinson, J. Wine grapes **664**

Harding, Stephen

  Last to die **940.54**

Harding, Thomas

  The House by the Lake **943**

Hardouin-Fugier, Elisabeth

  Baratay, E. Zoo: a history of zoological gardens in the West **590.73**

Hardwick, Elizabeth

  Herman Melville **813**

Hardwood floors. Bollinger, D. **690**

Hardy succulents. Kelaidis, G. M. **635.9**

Hardy, Grahame H.

    About

  Kanigel, R. The man who knew infinity **510**

Hardy, Grant

  Understanding the Book of Mormon **289.3**

Hardy, Justine

  In the valley of mist **954**

Hardy, Thomas, 1840-1928

    About

  Thomas Hardy **821**

  Tomalin, C. Thomas Hardy **92**

The **hare** with amber eyes. De Waal, E. **920**

Hare, R. M.

  Plato **184**

Harel, Yair

  (jt. auth) Rotman, J. L. The last fisherman **778.7**

Harford, Tim

  Messy **153.35**

Hargittai, Istvan

  The Martians of science **920**

Hargraves, Orin

  Espy, W. R. Words to rhyme with **423**

Hargreaves, Anne

  Cannon, J. The kings & queens of Britain **920**

Hargreaves, Ian

  Journalism **070.4**

Hargrove, John

  Beneath the surface **599.53**

Hari, Daoud

    About

  Hari, D. The translator **92**

Harjo, Joy

  A map to the next world **811**

Harker, Richard J. W.

  (ed) Beyond Rosie **940**

Harkness, Ruth

    About

  Croke, V. The lady and the panda **599.78**

Harlan, Elizabeth

  George Sand **92**

Harlan, Louis R.

  Booker T. Washington: the making of a black leader, 1856-1901 **92**

  Booker T. Washington: the wizard of Tuskegee, 1901-1915 **92**

Harlem. Gill, J. **974.7**

HARLEM (NEW YORK, N.Y.)

  Red Rooster Cookbook **641.5**

HARLEM (NEW YORK, N.Y.) -- ECONOMIC CONDITIONS

  Tough, P. Whatever it takes **362.7**

HARLEM (NEW YORK, N.Y.) -- INTELLECTUAL LIFE -- 20TH CENTURY

  Bernard, E. Carl Van Vechten and the Harlem Renaissance **92**

HARLEM RENAISSANCE

  Abdul-Jabbar, K. On the shoulders of giants **92**

  Bernard, E. Carl Van Vechten and the Harlem Renaissance **92**

  Kaplan, C. Miss Anne in Harlem **700.92**

  The Portable Harlem Renaissance reader **810**

  Ransby, B. Eslanda **92**

  The visual blues **704.03**

  Wall, C. A. Women of the Harlem Renaissance **810**

HARLEM RENAISSANCE

    See also African American art; African American music; American literature -- African American authors

Harleston family

    About

  Ball, E. The sweet hell inside **920**

Harley-Davidson. **629.22**

HARLEY-DAVIDSON MOTORCYCLE

  Harley-Davidson **629.22**

Harlow, George E.

  Gems & Crystals **549**

Harman, Claire

  Jane's fame **92**

Harman, Jay

  The shark's paintbrush **600**

HARMFUL INSECTS *See* Insect pests

Harmon, Alexandra

Indians in the making   **970.004**

Harmon, William

(ed) Classic writings on poetry   **809.1**

Harmony.   **781.2**

HARMONY

    See also Composition (Music); Music; Music
    -- Theory

HARMONY

Harmony   **781.2**

Harms, Roger W.

(ed) Mayo Clinic guide to a healthy pregnancy   **618.2**

Harper's anthology of 20th century Native American poetry.   **811**

Harper, Judith E.

Women during the Civil War   **973.7**

Harper, Michael S.

(ed) Every shut eye ain't asleep   **811**

(ed) The Vintage book of African American poetry   **811**

The **HarperCollins** Bible dictionary.   **220.3**

The **HarperCollins** encyclopedia of Catholicism.   **282**

HarperCollins Publishers Ltd.

(comp) The Times comprehensive atlas of the world   **912**

**HARPERS FERRY (W. VA.) -- HISTORY --
JOHN BROWN'S RAID, 1859**

Horwitz, T. Midnight rising   **92**

Harries, Meirion

The last days of innocence   **940.4**

Harries, Susie

Harries, M. The last days of innocence   **940.4**

Harriet Beecher Stowe. Hedrick, J. D.   **92**

Harriet Jacobs: a life. Yellin, J. F.   **92**

Harriet Tubman. Humez, J. M.   **92**

Harriet Tubman: the road to freedom. Clinton, C.   **92**

Harriman, Averell, 1891-1986

          About

Galbraith, J. K. Name-dropping   **973.9**

Olson, L. Citizens of London   **940.54**

Harriman, W. Averell (William Averell), 1891-1986

          About

Fullilove, M. Rendezvous with destiny   **973.917**

Harrington, Janice N.

Even the hollow my body made is gone   **811**

Harrington, Joel F.

The faithful executioner   **364.66**

Harrington, Walt

(ed) The beholder's eye   **814**

Harris, Alton B.

(jt. auth) Kramer, A. S. Breaking through bias   **650.101**

Harris, Blake J.

Console wars   **338.7**

Harris, Carla A.

Strategize to win   **650.1**

Harris, Dan

10% happier   **158.1**

Harris, David

The genius   **92**

Harris, Doll, 1913-2001

          About

Reeder, L. Dust bowl girls   **796.323**

Harris, Ellen T.

George Frideric Handel   **92**

Harris, J. William

The hanging of Thomas Jeremiah   **92**

Harris, Jill Werman

(ed) Remembrances and celebrations   **808.8**

Harris, Judith Rich

No two alike   **155.2**

Harris, Mark

Five Came Back   **791.43**

Pictures at a revolution   **791.43**

Harris, Michael

The End of absence   **302.23**

Harris, Miriam

Magpie   **641.86**

Harris, Neil Patrick, 1973-

          About

Harris, N. P. Neil Patrick Harris   **92**

Harris, Pat

McDougal, S. The woman who wouldn't talk   **973.929**

Harris, Sam, 1967-

Islam and the future of tolerance   **297.2**

Harris, Sandra L.

Essential first steps for parents of children with autism   **618.92**

Siblings of Children With Autism   **618.92**

Harris, Shane

@WAR   **355.3**

The watchers   **363.32**

Harrison, Benjamin, 1833-1901

          About

Calhoun, C. W. Benjamin Harrison   **92**

Perry, J. M. Touched with fire   **973.7**

Harrison, George,1943-2001

          About

The Beatles anthology   **782.421**

Spitz, B. The Beatles: the biography   **920**

Thomson, G. George Harrison   **92**

Harrison, Hazel, 1883-1969

          About

Ellison, R. The collected essays of Ralph Ellison   **814**

Harrison, Jim

Harrison, J. Songs of unreason   **811**

In search of small gods 811
The shape of the journey 811
Harrison, John, 1693-1776
About
Sobel, D. Longitude 526
Harrison, Kathryn
About
Harrison, K. The kiss 813
Harrison, Kathryn, 1961-
The kiss 813
Harrison, Lorraine
Heirloom Plants 635
Harrison, William Henry, 1773-1841
About
Collins, G. William Henry Harrison 92
Harrison-Hall, Jessica
(ed) Ming 951
Harrod, Kerol
(ed) Marketing your library 021.7
Harry Ransom Humanities Research Center [series]
Burnshaw, S. The collected poems and selected prose 811
Harry S. Truman. Dallek, R. 92
HARRY S. TRUMAN LIBRARY (INDEPENDENCE, MO.)
See also Presidents -- United States -- Archives
Harryhausen, Ray
The art of Ray Harryhausen 778.5
Harshav, Benjamin
Kruk, H. The last days of the Jerusalem of Lithuania 940.53
Hart, Benjamin L.
Your ideal cat 636.8
Hart, Carl
High Price 362.29
Hart, Christopher
Cartooning for the beginner 741.5
Human anatomy made amazingly easy 743.4
Hart, Gary, 1936-
About
Bai, M. All the truth is out 328.73
Hart, Hannah
Buffering 792.702
Hart, James David
The Oxford companion to American literature 810
Hart, Lynette A.
(jt. auth) Hart, B. L. Your ideal cat 636.8
Hart, Matthew
Diamond: a journey to the heart of an obsession 553.8
Hart, Patrick
(ed) Merton, T. Intimate Merton 271
Hart, Peter
The Somme 940.4

Hart-Davis, Adam
(ed) History 909
Harter, Penny
Higginson, W. J. The haiku handbook 808.1
Hartman, Elizabeth
Modern patchwork 746.46
Hartman, Saidiya V.
Lose your mother 323
Hartmann, Kat
Hot knots 746.42
Hartwell, Frederic P., 1947-
(ed) American electricians' handbook 621.3
(jt. auth) Richter, H. P. Wiring simplified 621.319
Hartwig, Dallas
The whole30 613.2
Hartwig, Melissa
The whole30 613.2
Hartwood. Werner, E. 641.597
HARTWOOD (RESTAURANT : TULUM, MEXICO)
Werner, E. Hartwood 641.597
Hartzband, Pamela
Groopman, J. E. Your medical mind 610
The **Harvard** biographical dictionary of music. 780
HARVARD COLLEGE OBSERVATORY
Sobel, D. The glass universe 522.197
The **Harvard** concise dictionary of music and musicians. 780
The **Harvard** dictionary of music. 780
The **Harvard** Psychedelic Club. Lattin, D. 920
HARVARD UNIVERSITY
Lattin, D. The Harvard Psychedelic Club 920
Harvard University Press reference library [series]
The Harvard dictionary of music 780
A new literary history of America 810
Harvest to heat. Estrine, D. 641.5
HARVESTING MACHINERY
See also Agricultural machinery
Harvey, Eleanor Jones
The Civil War and American art 709
Harvey, Giles
(ed) The 40s 973.917
Harvey, Paul
(jt. auth) Blum, E. J. The color of Christ 232
HASHISH *See* Marijuana
HASIDIM -- NEW YORK (STATE) -- NEW YORK -- SOCIAL CONDITIONS
Berger, J. The pious ones 973
Feldman, D. Unorthodox 92
HASIDISM
Feldman, D. Exodus 92
HASIDISM
See also Judaism
Haskell, Barbara
The American century 709

Haskell, David George

The forest unseen   **577.3**

About

Haskell, D. G. The forest unseen   **577.3**

Haskins, Don, 1930-2008

About

Haskins, D. Glory road   **796**

Haskins, James

African American religious leaders   **920**

Hass, Robert

The apple trees at Olema   **811**

Time and materials   **811**

(ed) Into the garden   **808.8**

Hassan, Hassan

(jt. auth) Weiss, M. Isis   **956.05**

Hasselbrink, Kimberley

Vibrant food   **641.5**

HASSIDISM See Hasidism

Hassig, Ralph C.

The hidden people of North Korea   **951.93**

Hassrick, Peter H.

Art of the American West   **709**

HASTINGS (EAST SUSSEX, ENGLAND), BATTLE OF, 1066

Morris, M. The Norman Conquest   **942.02**

HASTINGS (EAST SUSSEX, ENGLAND), BATTLE OF, 1066

See also Battles; Great Britain -- History -- 1066-1154, Norman period

Hastings, Adrian

(ed) Oxford companion to Christian thought   **230**

Hastings, Max

Armageddon: the battle for Germany, 1944-45   **940.54**

Catastrophe 1914   **940.3**

Inferno   **940.54**

Retribution   **940.54**

The secret war   **940.54**

Warriors   **355**

Hastings, Selina

The secret lives of Somerset Maugham   **92**

Hatch, Peter J.

A rich spot of earth   **635**

Hatch, Shari Dorantes

(ed) Encyclopedia of African-American writing   **810**

Hatch, Thom

The Last Outlaws   **364.15**

Hatching Twitter. Bilton, N.   **006.7**

HATE

See also Emotions

HATE CRIMES

Citron, D. K. Hate crimes in cyberspace   **364.15**

McConnell, D. American honor killings   **364.15**

HATE CRIMES

See also Crime; Discrimination; Violence

HATE CRIMES -- MISSISSIPPI

Anderson, D. S. Emmett Till   **364.1**

HATE CRIMES -- PREVENTION

Foxman, A. H. Viral hate   **364.15**

HATE CRIMES -- UNITED STATES -- PUBLIC OPINION

Jimenez, S. The Book of Matt   **364.1**

Hate crimes in cyberspace. Citron, D. K.   **364.15**

HATE GROUPS -- POLITICAL ASPECTS -- UNITED STATES

Goldwag, A. The new hate   **306.2**

HATE SPEECH

Foxman, A. H. Viral hate   **364.15**

HATHA YOGA

Broad, W. J. The science of yoga   **613.7**

Grossman, G. B. Restorative yoga for life   **613.7**

Hanoch, D. The yoga lifestyle   **613.7**

Lacerda, D. 2,100 Asanas   **613.7**

HATHA YOGA

See also Exercise; Yoga

Hathaway, Sandee Eisenberg

Murkoff, H. E. What to expect the first year   **649**

HATS

See also Clothing and dress; Costume

Hatshepsut, Queen of Egypt

About

Cooney, K. The woman who would be king   **92**

Hatshepsut: from queen to Pharaoh   **932**

Mertz, B. Temples, tombs, & hieroglyphs   **932**

Ryan, D. P. Beneath the sands of Egypt   **92**

Hatshepsut: from queen to Pharaoh.   **932**

Hattie McDaniel. Watts, J.   **92**

Hattie: the life of Hattie McDaniel. Jackson, C.   **92**

Hattis, Shana Hertz

(ed) Vital Statistics of the United States 2014   **310**

Hatzfeld, Jean

The antelope's strategy   **967.571**

Machete season   **967.571**

Haub, Erivan, 1932-

About

Hassrick, P. H. Art of the American West   **709**

Haub, Helga

About

Hassrick, P. H. Art of the American West   **709**

Hauge, Michael

Writing screenplays that sell   **808.2**

Haunted America. Norman, M.   **133.1**

HAUNTED HOUSES

See also Houses

HAUNTED HOUSES -- UNITED STATES

Dickey, C. Ghostland   **133.1**

The haunted wood. Weinstein, A.   **327.12**

Hauptman, Jodi

Degas   **709**

(ed) Henri Matisse   **709.2**

HAUSA (AFRICAN PEOPLE) -- NIGER -- NIA-

MEY -- ECONOMIC CONDITIONS

Youngstedt, S. M. Surviving with dignity **362.84**

Hauser, Brooke

Enter Helen **92**

Hauser, Peter C.

How deaf children learn **371.91**

Hauser, Thomas

Boxing is-- **796.8**

Hausman, Kalani Kirk

(jt. auth) Horne, R. 3d printing for dummies **621.9**

HAVANA (CUBA) -- BIOGRAPHY

Cooke, J. The other side of paradise **972.91**

Eire, C. M. N. Waiting for snow in Havana **92**

Havana dreams. Gimbel, W. **972.91**

Havel. Zantovsky, M. **943.704**

Havel, Václav, 1936-2011

The garden party and other plays **891.8**

Spontaneous mind **811**

About

Havel, V. To the castle and back **92**

Remnick, D. Reporting **814**

The **haves** and the have-nots. Milanović, B. **339.2**

Havil, Julian

The irrationals **512**

Having been an accomplice. Cronk, L. **811**

Having our say. Delany, S. **92**

Havlice, Patricia Pate

Index to artistic biography **920.003**

Havrilesky, Heather

How to be a person in the world **070.444**

Hawa Abdi, 1947-

About

Abdi, H. Keeping hope alive **92**

HAWAII -- ANNEXATION TO THE UNITED STATES

Haley, J. L. Captive paradise **996.9**

Vowell, S. Unfamiliar fishes **996.9**

HAWAII -- BIOGRAPHY

Maraniss, D. Barack Obama **92**

HAWAII -- DESCRIPTION AND TRAVEL

Moore, S. Paradise of the Pacific **996.9**

HAWAII -- HISTORY

Haley, J. L. Captive paradise **996.9**

Moore, S. Paradise of the Pacific **996.9**

Hawaiian dictionary. Pukui, M. K. **499**

HAWAIIAN LANGUAGE -- DICTIONARIES

Pukui, M. K. Hawaiian dictionary **499**

HAWAIIAN MONK SEAL -- CONSERVATION

Williams, T. M. The odyssey of KP2 **599.79**

Hawass, Zahi A.

Hidden treasures of ancient Egypt **932**

Tutankhamun and the golden age of the pharaohs **932**

The **hawk** and the dove. Thompson, N. **92**

Hawke, David Freeman

Everyday life in early America **973.2**

John Milton **92**

HAWKING See Falconry

Hawking, Stephen, 1942-

Black holes and baby universes and other essays **523.1**

(ed) Einstein, A. A stubbornly persistent illusion **530.1**

The nature of space and time **530.1**

The universe in a nutshell **530.1**

Black holes and baby universes and other essays **523.1**

A brief history of time **523.1**

A briefer history of time **523.1**

The grand design **530.1**

About

My brief history **92**

Susskind, L. The black hole war **530.1**

HAWKS

Clark, W. S. A field guide to hawks of North America **598**

MacDonald, H. H is for Hawk **598.9**

Hawley, Samuel Jay

Speed duel **796.72**

Haws, Barbara B.

Bernstein, B. Leonard Bernstein **92**

Hawthorne, Nathaniel, 1804-1864

About

Kazin, A. An American procession **810**

Matthiessen, F. O. American renaissance **810**

Wineapple, B. Hawthorne: a life **92**

Wright, S. B. Critical companion to Nathaniel Hawthorne **813**

Hawthorne: a life. Wineapple, B. **92**

Haxton, Brooks

They lift their wings to cry **811**

HAY

See also Farm produce; Forage plants

HAY FEVER

See also Allergy

Hay, Donna

Life in Balance **641.563**

Hay, John Milton, 1838-1905

About

Zimmermann, W. First great triumph **973**

Hay, Louise L.

You can heal your life **158**

Hayakawa, Hiroshi

Kirigami menagerie **736**

Haycock, David Boyd

Mortal coil **571.8**

Hayden, Jennifer

The Story of My Tits **741.5**

Hayden, Robert Earl

Collected poems **811**

Hayden, Tom

The long sixties **973.92**

Hayden, Torey L.
Twilight children   **618.92**

Haydn.   **92**

Haydn, Joseph, 1732-1809
About
Haydn   **92**
Rosen, C. The classical style   **780.9**

Hayes, Christopher
Twilight of the elites   **305.5**

Hayes, Clay
Gig posters volume 1   **741.6**

Hayes, Derek
Historical atlas of the American West   **911**
Historical atlas of the North American railroad **385**
Historical atlas of the United States   **911**

Hayes, Paddy
Queen of Spies   **327.12**

Hayes, Rutherford B., 1822-1893
About
Morris, R. Fraud of the century   **324.9**
Perry, J. M. Touched with fire   **973.7**

Hayes, Terrance
How to be drawn   **811**
Lighthead   **811**

Haygood, Wil
Showdown   **347.73**
Sweet thunder   **92**

Hayman, Ronald
A life of Jung   **150.19**

The **Haynes** bicycle book. Henderson, B.   **629.28**

Haynes, Fred
The lions of Iwo Jima   **940.54**

Haynes, John Earl
Spies   **327.12**
Venona   **327.12**

Haynsworth, Leslie
Amelia Earhart's daughters   **629.13**

Hayward, Gordon
Stone in the garden   **712**

Hayward, Neil
Lost among the birds   **598.072**

Hazan, Marcella. 1924-2013
Essentials of classic Italian cooking   **641.59**
Ingredienti   **641.5**
Marcella cucina   **641.59**
Marcella says . . .   **641.5**
About
Hazan, M. Amarcord, Marcella remembers   **92**

Hazan, Victor
(jt. auth) Hazan, M. Ingredienti   **641.5**

HAZARDOUS OCCUPATIONS
See also Occupations

HAZARDOUS SUBSTANCES
See also Materials

HAZARDOUS SUBSTANCES -- HEALTH AS-
PECTS -- UNITED STATES -- CASE STUD-

IES
Lerner, S. Sacrifice zones   **363.738**

HAZARDOUS WASTE SITES
Lerner, S. Sacrifice zones   **363.738**

Hazen, Edith P.
(ed) The Columbia Granger's dictionary of poetry
quotations   **808.81**

Hazen, Robert M., 1948-
(jt. auth) Hazen, R. M. The story of Earth   **550**

Hazleton, Lesley, 1945-
After the prophet   **297**
Agnostic   **211**
The First Muslim   **297.6**
Mary: a flesh-and-blood biography of the Virgin
Mother   **92**

Hazzard, Shirley
The ancient shore   **945**

Heacox, Kim
John Muir and the ice that started a fire   **92**
National Geographic the national parks   **363.6**

HEAD
See also Anatomy

HEAD -- WOUNDS AND INJURIES
Laskas, J. M. Concussion   **617.5**
The **Head** Game. Mudd, P.   **153.4**
Head off & split. Finney, N.   **811**

Head, Anthony
Gentry, A. The Real Food Daily cookbook   **641.5**

Head, Dominic
(ed) The Cambridge guide to literature in English   **820**
The Cambridge introduction to modern British fiction, 1950-2000   **823**

HEADACHE
See also Pain

Heade, Martin Johnson, 1819-1904
About
Benfey, C. E. G. A summer of hummingbirds   **920**

HEADS OF STATE
Amis, M. Koba the dread   **947.084**
Berthon, S. Warlords   **940.53**
Bosworth, R. J. B. Mussolini   **945.091**
Bosworth, R. J. B. Mussolini's Italy   **945**
Brent, J. Inside the Stalin archives   **947.086**
Brent, J. Stalin's last crime   **947.084**
Brinkley, J. Cambodia's curse   **959.6**
Carlson, P. K blows top   **947.085**
Chang, J. Mao: the unknown story   **92**
Conquest, R. Stalin   **92**
Cornwell, J. Hitler's pope: the secret history of
Pius XII   **92**
Dikötter, F. Mao's great famine   **951.05**
Dobbs, M. One minute to midnight   **973.922**
Duiker, W. J. Ho Chi Minh   **959.704**
Fischer, K. P. Nazi Germany   **943.086**
Fleming, G. Hitler and the final solution   **943.086**

Fulbrook, M. A concise history of Germany   **943**

Gordin, M. D. Red cloud at dawn   **355**

Hassig, R. C. The hidden people of North Korea   **951.93**

Hochschild, A. The unquiet ghost   **947.084**

Kershaw, I. Hitler   **92**

Kershaw, I. Hitler, 1936-1945: nemesis   **943.086**

Kissinger, H. Diplomacy   **327.2**

Medvedev, R. A. Let history judge   **947.084**

Montefiore, S. Stalin: the court of the red tsar   **92**

Montefiore, S. Young Stalin   **92**

Nikita Khrushchev   **92**

Orbach, D. The plots against Hitler   **940.53**

Parssinen, T. M. The Oster conspiracy of 1938   **943.086**

Pipes, R. Russia under the Bolshevik regime   **947.084**

Pleshakov, K. Stalin's folly   **940.54**

Pomper, P. Lenin's brother   **92**

Pringle, P. The murder of Nikolai Vavilov   **92**

Radzinsky, E. Stalin   **92**

Rosenbaum, R. Explaining Hitler   **943.086**

Ryback, T. W. Hitler's private library   **027**

Service, R. Lenin--a biography   **947.084**

Service, R. Stalin   **92**

Shirer, W. L. The rise and fall of the Third Reich   **943.086**

Short, P. Mao   **951.05**

Snyder, T. D. Bloodlands   **940.54**

Speer, A. Inside the Third Reich   **943.086**

Spence, J. D. Mao Zedong   **951.05**

Strathern, P. The artist, the philosopher, and the warrior   **920**

Sun Shuyun The Long March   **951.04**

Taubman, W. Khrushchev   **92**

Taylor, F. Exorcising Hitler   **943.087**

Turner, H. A. Hitler's thirty days to power   **943.086**

Volkogonov, D. A. Lenin   **947.084**

Weber, T. Hitler's first war   **940.4**

West, R. Tito   **949.7**

HEADS OF STATE

 See also Executive power; Statesmen

HEADS OF STATE -- CHINA -- BIOGRAPHY

Levine, S. I. Mao   **951.05**

Short, P. Mao   **951.05**

Spence, J. D. Mao Zedong   **951.05**

HEADS OF STATE -- FRANCE -- BIOGRAPHY

Gueniffey, P. Bonaparte   **92**

HEADS OF STATE -- GERMANY -- BIOGRAPHY

Hitler   **92**

Orbach, D. The plots against Hitler   **940.53**

HEADS OF STATE -- SOUTH AMERICA -- BIOGRAPHY

Arana, M. Bolivar   **92**

HEADS OF STATE -- SOVIET UNION -- BIOG-

RAPHY

Kotkin, S. Stalin   **92**

Montefiore, S. Stalin: the court of the red tsar   **92**

Service, R. Lenin--a biography   **947.084**

Stalin   **92**

Taubman, W. Khrushchev   **92**

Healey, Steve

10 Mississippi   **811**

HEALING

Kaur, R. Milk and honey   **811.6**

HEALING

 See also Therapeutics

The **healing** of America. Reid, T. R.   **362.1**

HEALING, MENTAL See Mental healing

HEALING, SPIRITUAL See Spiritual healing

HEALTH

Bittman, M. The food matters cookbook   **641.3**

Budig, K. Aim true   **613.7**

Buettner, D. The Blue Zones solution   **613.2**

Collen, A. 10% human   **612.3**

Complete guide to fitness & health   **613.7**

Dietert, R. The human superorganism   **613**

Enayati, A. Seeking serenity   **155.9**

Gazella, K. A. The definitive guide to thriving after cancer   **616.99**

Grigore, A. Skin cleanse   **613**

Hanoch, D. The yoga lifestyle   **613.7**

Helwig, J. Smoothie-licious   **641.87**

Leake, L. 100 days of real food   **613.2**

The longevity kitchen   **612.6**

Montgomery, D. R. The hidden half of nature   **579**

Pacheco, R. Do your om thing   **181**

Patalsky, K. Healthy happy vegan kitchen   **641.5**

Reynolds, G. The first 20 minutes   **613.7**

Roizen, M. F. This is your do-over   **613**

Velasquez-Manoff, M. An Epidemic of Absence   **616.97**

Weil, A. Fast Food, Good Food   **641.563**

HEALTH

 See also Medicine; Physiology; Preventive medicine

HEALTH & FITNESS -- CHILDREN

Porto, A. The pediatrician's guide to feeding babies and toddlers   **618.92**

Health care for some. Hoffman, B.   **362.1**

HEALTH CARE PERSONNEL

Foner, M. Not for bread alone   **92**

Health care reform. Gruber, J.   **362.1**

HEALTH CARE REFORM -- UNITED STATES

Gruber, J. Health care reform   **362.1**

Hoffman, B. Health care for some   **362.1**

Makary, M. Unaccountable   **610.730**

HEALTH CARE, SELF See Health self-care

HEALTH COMMUNICATION

Topol, E. The creative destruction of medicine   **610.28**

HEALTH COUNSELING
 See also Counseling; Health education

HEALTH EDUCATION
 See also Education; Health

HEALTH FACILITIES
 Cosgrove, T. The Cleveland Clinic way **362.11**

HEALTH FACILITIES
 See also Medical care; Public health

HEALTH FACILITIES -- LOUISIANA -- AD-MINISTRATION -- CASE STUDIES
 Fink, S. Five days at memorial **362.11**

HEALTH FACILITIES -- PUBLIC RELATIONS
 Makary, M. Unaccountable **610.730**

HEALTH FACILITIES -- STANDARDS -- UNIT-ED STATES -- OHIO
 Cosgrove, T. The Cleveland Clinic way **362.11**

HEALTH FOODS *See* Natural foods

HEALTH INSURANCE
 Nather, D. The new health care system **344**
 Starr, P. Remedy and reaction **362.1**

HEALTH INSURANCE
 See also Insurance

HEALTH INSURANCE -- UNITED STATES
 Atlas, S. W. In excellent health **362.109**

HEALTH MAINTENANCE ORGANIZATIONS
 See also Health insurance; Medical practice

HEALTH PERSONNEL *See* Medical personnel

HEALTH POLICY *See* Medical policy

HEALTH POLICY -- NEW YORK CITY -- PER-SONAL NARRATIVES
 Farley, T. Saving Gotham **362.1**

HEALTH PROFESSIONS *See* Medical personnel

HEALTH PROMOTION
 Montgomery, D. R. The hidden half of nature **579**

HEALTH RECORDS *See* Medical records

Health reference series
 Domestic violence sourcebook **362.82**
 Fitness and exercise sourcebook **613.7**

HEALTH RESORTS
 See also Resorts

HEALTH SCIENCES PERSONNEL *See* Medical personnel

HEALTH SELF-CARE
 Artemis, N. Holistic dental care **617.6**
 Beattie, M. Codependent no more **616.86**
 Blum, S. Your immune system recovery plan **616.97**
 Hay, L. L. You can heal your life **158**
 Kosik, K. S. Outsmarting alzheimer's **616.8**
 Low Dog, T. Healthy at home **615.5**
 Mercola, J. M. Effortless healing **613.2**
 Tanzi, R. E. Super genes **613**
 Thomas, M. The French beauty solution **646.7**
 Weil, A. Eight weeks to optimum health **613**

HEALTH SERVICES ADMINISTRATION -- UNITED STATES
 101 careers in healthcare management **362.106**

HEALTH SERVICES PERSONNEL *See* Medical personnel

HEALTH, INDUSTRIAL *See* Occupational health and safety

HEALTHS, DRINKING OF *See* Toasts

Healthy aging. Weil, A. **612.6**
Healthy at home. Low Dog, T. **615.5**
Healthy happy vegan kitchen. Patalsky, K. **641.5**
The **healthy** kitchen. Weil, A. **641.5**
Healthy pasta. Bastianich, J. **641.82**
The **healthy** pregnancy book. Sears, W. **618.2**

Healy, Thomas
 The great dissent **342.73**

Heaney, Christopher
 Cradle of gold **92**

Heaney, Seamus
 The burial at Thebes **822**
 District and circle **821**
 Electric light **821**
 Finders keepers **821**
 Human chain **821**
 Opened ground **821**
    About
 O'Driscoll, D. Stepping stones **821**

Hear my sad story. Polenberg, R. **782.42**

Heard, Alex
 The eyes of Willie McGee **364.66**

HEARING
 See also Senses and sensation; Sound

HEARING EAR DOGS
 See also Animals and people with disabilities; Deaf -- Means of communication; Working dogs

HEARING IMPAIRED
 Bouton, K. Shouting won't help **617.8**

HEARING IMPAIRED
 See also People with physical disabilities

HEARING IMPAIRED -- LEGAL STATUS, LAWS, ETC. -- UNITED STATES
 Legal rights **346.73**

HEARING IN ANIMALS
 See also Hearing; Senses and sensation in animals

Hearn, Maxwell K.
 Splendors of Imperial China **709**

Hearne, Julie Kramis
 (jt. auth) Bevill, A. World spice at home **641.6**

Hearns, Thomas, 1958-
    About
 Kimball, G. Four kings **920**

Hearst, Patricia, 1954-
    About
 Toobin, J. American Heiress **322.4**

Hearst, William Randolph, 1863-1951
    About
 Nasaw, D. The chief: the life of William Randolph

Hearst **070.5**

Thomas, E. The war lovers **973.8**

Whyte, K. The uncrowned king **92**

HEART

Amidon, S. The sublime engine **612.1**

Heart & soul in the kitchen. **641.5**

HEART -- ANATOMY

See also Anatomy

HEART -- DISEASES *See* Heart diseases

HEART -- TRANSPLANTATION -- PATIENTS -- UNITED STATES -- BIOGRAPHY

Fair, E. Consequence **956.704**

HEART ATTACK

See also Heart diseases

HEART DISEASE *See* Heart diseases

HEART DISEASES

Brewer, S. C. The Canyon Ranch guide to men's health **613**

De Richemond, J. The Medical Library Association guide to finding out about heart disease **016**

Forrester, J. The Heart Healers **616.1**

Khan, J. The whole heart solution **616.1**

HEART DISEASES

See also Diseases

HEART DISEASES -- DIET THERAPY

New American Heart Association cookbook The new American Heart Association cookbook **641.5**

HEART DISEASES -- PREVENTION

Fuhrman, J. The end of heart disease **616.12**

HEART DISEASES -- PREVENTION

See also Preventive medicine

The **Heart** Healers. Forrester, J. **616.1**

HEART MOUNTAIN RELOCATION CENTER (WYO.) -- PICTORIAL WORKS

Colors of confinement **940.53**

Heart of a patriot. Cleland, M. **92**

Heart of darkness. Mitton, S. **523.1**

The **heart** of everything that is. Drury, B. **92**

The **heart** of power. Blumenthal, D. **362.1**

Heart of the artichoke and other kitchen journeys. Tanis, D. **641.5**

The **heart** of the plate. **641.5**

HEART RESUSCITATION *See* Cardiac resuscitation

A **heart,** a cross & a flag. Noonan, P. **973.931**

Heartbreak House. Shaw, B. **822**

Hearth, Amy Hill

Delany, S. Having our say **92**

Pelosi, N. Know your power **92**

Heartlandia. Gartland, A. **641.597**

The **heartless** stone. Zoellner, T. **553.8**

Hearts touched by fire. **973.7**

Heaser, Sue

The polymer clay techniques book **745.572**

Heat. Streever, B. **551.41**

Heat. Buford, B. **641.5**

HEAT

Streever, B. Heat **551.41**

HEAT ENGINES

See also Engines; Thermodynamics

Heat Moon, William Least

Blue highways **917**

Here, there, elsewhere **910.4**

Roads to Quoz **917**

HEAT PUMPS

See also Pumping machinery; Thermodynamics

Heat wave. Bogle, D. **92**

Heath, Chip

Switch **303.4**

Heath, Dan, 1973-

(jt. auth) Heath, C. Switch **303.4**

HEATING

See also Home economics

Heatter, Maida

Maida Heatter's book of great desserts **641.8**

Maida Heatter's brand-new book of great cookies **641.8**

Maida Heatter's cookies **641.8**

Heaven. Phillips, R. R. **811**

Heaven. Miller, L. **236**

HEAVEN

See also Eschatology; Future life

HEAVEN

Miller, L. Heaven **236**

Phillips, R. R. Heaven **811**

Heaven & earth holding company. Hodgen, J. **811**

Heaven cracks, earth shakes. Palmer, J. **951**

Heaven Is Beautiful. Panagore, P. B. **231.7**

Heaven's bride. Schmidt, L. E. **92**

Heaven's ditch. Kelly, J. **386**

Heavenly bodies. Huntington, C. **811**

Heavier than heaven: a biography of Kurt Cobain. Cross, C. R. **92**

HEAVY METAL (MUSIC)

Turman, K. Louder Than Hell **781.66**

Waksman, S. This ain't the summer of love **781.66**

HEAVY METAL (MUSIC)

See also Rock music

Hébrard, Jean M.

(jt. auth) Scott, R. J. Freedom papers **305.896**

HEBREW LANGUAGE

See also Language and languages

HEBREW LANGUAGE -- DICTIONARIES

Zilkha, A. Modern English-Hebrew dictionary **492.4**

HEBREW LITERATURE

See also Literature

HEBREW POETRY -- COLLECTIONS

Music of a distant drum **808.81**

Hebrew Union College Press

Gay, P. A Godless Jew **150.19**

HEBREWS *See* Jews
HEBRIDES (SCOTLAND) -- DESCRIPTION
Boswell, J. The journal of a tour to the Hebrides with Samuel Johnson **914**
HEBRIDES (SCOTLAND) -- SOCIAL LIFE AND CUSTOMS
Nicolson, A. Sea room: an island life in the Hebrides **941.1**
Hecht, Anthony
Collected later poems **811**
Hecht, Jennifer Michael
Doubt: a history **121**
Hedges, Chris
Days of destruction, days of revolt **305.5**
Wages of rebellion **303.48**
War is a force that gives us meaning **355.02**
Hedrick, Joan D.
Harriet Beecher Stowe **92**
Hedy's folly. Rhodes, R. **92**
Heen, Sheila
Stone, D. Difficult conversations **158**
Heffernan, Cecelia
Flowers A to Z **635.9**
Heffernan, Virginia
Magic and Loss **303.48**
Hefner, Hugh
About
Watts, S. Mr. Playboy **92**
Hegel, Georg Wilhelm Friedrich
About
Camus, A. The rebel **303.6**
Durant, W. J. The story of philosophy **109**
The philosophy of Hegel **193**
Russell, B. A history of Western philosophy **109**
Heibel, Tara
Rooted in design **635.9**
Heidegger, Martin
Basic writings **193**
Being and time **111**
About
Existentialism from Dostoevsky to Sartre **142**
The **Heidi** chronicles and other plays. Wasserstein, W. **812**
Heidler, David Stephen
(ed) Encyclopedia of the American Civil War **973.7**
Henry Clay **92**
Heidler, Jeanne T.
(ed) Encyclopedia of the American Civil War **973.7**
Heidler, D. S. Henry Clay **92**
Heil, Alan L.
Voice of America **384.54**
Heilbron, J. L.
Galileo **92**
(ed) The Oxford companion to the history of modern science **509**
Heilbroner, Robert L.

The worldly philosophers **330.1**
Heilbrun, Carolyn G.
The education of a woman **92**
Heilemann, John
(jt. auth) Halperin, M. Double Down **324.9**
Heilpern, John
John Osborne **92**
Heim, Tami
@stickyjesus **248.4**
Heinrich, Bernd
Life everlasting **591.7**
Summer world **591.7**
Heintzelman, Greta
Critical companion to Tennessee Williams **812**
The **heir** apparent. Ridley, J. **92**
HEIRESSES -- UNITED STATES -- BIOGRAPHY
Dedman, B. Empty mansions **92**
Heirloom Plants. Harrison, L. **635**
HEIRLOOM VARIETIES (PLANTS)
Simply ancient grains **641.6**
HEIRS *See* Inheritance and succession
Heisenberg, Werner, 1901-1976
About
Cassidy, D. C. Beyond uncertainty **92**
Helbig, Alethea
Dictionary of American young adult fiction, 1997-2001 **028.5**
Helding, Patricia
(jt. auth) Baker, L. Fat witch bake sale **641.81**
A **Helen** Adam reader. Adam, H. **811**
Helen Keller. Herrmann, D. **92**
Helen Keller: selected writings. Keller, H. **92**
Helfand, Jessica
Scrapbooks: an American history **745.54**
Helga's diary. **940.53**
Helgoe, Laurie A.
Introvert power **155.2**
HELICOPTERS
Chiles, J. R. The god machine **629.133**
HELICOPTERS
See also Aeronautics; Airplanes
HELICOPTERS -- PILOTING
See also Airplanes -- Piloting
HELIUM
See also Chemical elements; Gases
HELL
Turner, A. K. The history of hell **200**
HELL
See also Eschatology; Future life
Hell and Good Company. Rhodes, R. **946.081**
Hell from the heavens. Wukovits, J. F. **940.54**
Hell to pay. Giangreco, D. M. **940.54**
Hellbeck, Jochen
(ed) Stalingrad **940.54**
HELLENISM

The Cambridge history of Judaism 296
Freeman, C. The closing of the Western mind 940.1
Green, P. The Hellenistic age 938
Waterfield, R. Why Socrates died 183
HELLENISM
See also Greece -- Civilization
The **Hellenistic** age. Green, P. 938
Heller, Anne Conover
Ayn Rand and the world she made 92
Heller, Joseph
About
Daugherty, T. Just one catch 92
Heller, Marla
The everyday DASH diet cookbook 613.2
Heller, Nancy
Women artists 920
Heller, Rick
Secular meditation 158.1
Heller, Steven, 1950-
Becoming a graphic & digital designer 741.6
The **hellhound** of Wall Street. Perino, M. A. 330.9
Hellhound on his trail. Sides, H. 364.152
Hellige, Hendrick
(ed) A Map of the World 912
Hellman, Lillian, 1906-1984
About
Hellman, L. Pentimento 92
Martinson, D. Lillian Hellman 92
Playwrights at work 812
Hellmann, Paul T.
Historical gazetteer of the United States 911
Hellmich, Mittie, 1960-
Ultimate bar book 641.8
Hello, gorgeous. Mann, W. J. 92
Hello, my name is awesome. Watkins, A. 658.8
Helm, Bennett
The water gardener's bible 635.9
Helm, Dieter
The carbon crunch 333.79
Helm, Sarah
A life in secrets 92
Ravensbruck 940.53
Helman, Scott
(jt. auth) Russell, J. Long mile home 363.325
HELODERMA -- NORTH AMERICA
Ernst, C. H. Venomous reptiles of the United States,
Canada, and northern Mexico 597.9
Heloise
About
Life stories 920
Helou, Anissa
Mediterranean street food 641.59
Help me to find my people. Williams, H. A. 306.3
Help Your Dog Fight Cancer. Kaplan, L. 636.7
Help your teenager beat an eating disorder. Lock,
J. 616.85

Helper, Hinton Rowan, 1829-1909
About
Wilson, E. Patriotic gore 810
HELPFUL INSECTS *See* Beneficial insects
HELPFULNESS *See* Helping behavior
HELPING BEHAVIOR
Fullbright, C. D. How to help your friend with can-
cer 616.99
Keltner, D. Born to be good 155.2
Pogrebin, L. C. How to be a friend to a friend who's
sick 610
HELPING BEHAVIOR
See also Human behavior; Interpersonal rela-
tions
Helping Children Succeed. Tough, P. 372.1
Helping yourself help others. Carter, R. 649.8
HELPLESSNESS (PSYCHOLOGY)
See also Emotions
Helter skelter. Bugliosi, V. 364.1
Helwig, Jenna
Smoothie-licious 641.87
Hely, Steve
The wonder trail 917.28
About
Hely, S. The wonder trail 917.28
Hemings family
About
Gordon-Reed, A. The Hemingses of Monticel-
lo 920
Hemings, Sally, 1773-1835
About
Gordon-Reed, A. The Hemingses of Monticel-
lo 920
Gordon-Reed, A. Thomas Jefferson and Sally
Hemings 973.4
The **Hemingses** of Monticello. Gordon-Reed,
A. 920
Hemingway. Lynn, K. S. 92
Hemingway, Ernest
The dangerous summer 791.8
Death in the afternoon 791.8
About
Blume, L. M. M. Everybody behaves badly 813
Kazin, A. An American procession 810
Life stories 920
Lynn, K. S. Hemingway 92
Murray, A. The blue devils of Nada 780.89
Oliver, C. M. Critical companion to Ernest Heming-
way 813
Reynolds, M. S. Hemingway: the Paris years 92
Hemingway, Ernest, 1899-1961. Sun also rises
About
Blume, L. M. M. Everybody behaves badly 813
Hemingway: the Paris years. Reynolds, M. S. 92
Heminsley, Alexandra, 1976-
About

Heminsley, A. Running like a girl   **796.420**

The **hemlock** cup. Hughes, B.   **92**

Hemming, Henry

    The ingenious Mr. Pyke   **327.12**

HEMODIALYSIS -- PATIENTS

    Snyder, R. d. 1. What you must know about dialysis   **617.4**

Hemon, Aleksandar, 1964-

    The book of my lives   **814**

HEMORRHAGIC FEVER, EBOLA -- HISTORY -- POPULAR WORKS

    Quammen, D. Ebola   **614.5**

HEMP

    Fine, D. Hemp bound   **633.5**

Hemp bound. Fine, D.   **633.5**

HEMP INDUSTRY

    Fine, D. Hemp bound   **633.5**

Hempel, Sandra

    The inheritor's powder   **364.152**

Hemphill, Essex

    About

    Duberman, M. B. Hold tight gently   **920**

Hemphill, Ian

    The spice & herb bible   **641.3**

Hemphill, Kate

    (jt. auth) Hemphill, I. The spice & herb bible **641.3**

Hemphill, Paul

    Lovesick blues   **92**

Hen's teeth and horse's toes. Gould, S. J.   **576.8**

Henbest, Nigel

    Couper, H. The history of astronomy   **520**

Henderson, Bill

    (ed) Pushcart Prize XXXVI: best of the small presses 2012   **810**

Henderson, Bob

    The Haynes bicycle book   **629.28**

Henderson, Bruce B., 1946-

    Rescue at Los Banos   **940.53**

Henderson, Emily

    (jt. auth) Borsics, A. Styled   **747**

Henderson, Helene

    (ed) Holiday symbols and customs   **394.26**

Henderson, Mark

    100 most important science ideas   **500**

Henderson, Russell

    About

    Jimenez, S. The Book of Matt   **364.1**

Henderson, Timothy J.

    The Mexican Wars for Independence   **972**

Hendey, Lisa M.

    A book of saints for Catholic moms   **248.8**

Hendricks, James E.

    About

    Kaplan, A. Y. The interpreter   **940.54**

Hendricks, Steve

    The unquiet grave   **970.004**

Hendrickson, Paul

    The living and the dead   **959.704**

    Sons of Mississippi   **305.8**

Hendrickson, Robert

    The Facts on File encyclopedia of word and phrase origins   **422**

Hendrickson, Susan

    About

    Malone, J. W. It doesn't take a rocket scientist **920**

Hendrix, Amanda R.

    (jt. auth) Wohlforth, C. Beyond Earth   **629.455**

Hendrix, Jimi

    About

    Cross, C. R. Room full of mirrors   **92**

    Murray, C. S. Crosstown traffic: Jimi Hendrix and the post-war rock'n'roll revolution   **787.87**

Hendrix, Scott H.

    Martin Luther   **92**

Henican, Ellis

    Worth dying for   **359.984**

Henig, Robin Marantz

    The monk in the garden: how Gregor Mendel and his pea plants solved the mystery of inheritance   **576.5**

Henion, Leigh Ann

    About

    Henion, L. A. Phenomenal   **910.4**

Henkenius, Merle

    Plumbing: complete projects for the home   **696**

Hennessey, Jonathan

    The United States Constitution   **342**

Hennessey, Maureen Hart

    Norman Rockwell   **759.13**

Hennessy, Kathryn

    (ed) Car   **629.222**

    (ed) Natural history   **508**

Henri Matisse.   **709.2**

Henry Clay. Heidler, D. S.   **92**

Henry Ford and the Jews. Baldwin, N.   **305**

Henry Miller on writing. Miller, H.   **818**

Henry VIII. Weir, A.   **942.05**

Henry VIII, King of England, 1491-1547

    About

    Fletcher, C. The divorce of Henry VIII   **942.05**

    Fraser, A. The wives of Henry VIII   **920**

    Weir, A. Henry VIII   **942.05**

    Weir, A. The lost Tudor princess   **92**

    Weir, A. The six wives of Henry VIII   **942.05**

Henry's demons. Cockburn, H.   **92**

Henry, David

    Furious cool   **92**

Henry, Diana

    A Bird in the Hand   **641.665**

    A Change of Appetite   **641.5**

    Roast figs, sugar snow   **641.5**

    Simple   **641.5**

Henry, Emile, 1872-1894
About
Merriman, J. M. The dynamite club **363.32**
Henry, Jeff
The year Yellowstone burned **634.9**
Henry, Joe
(jt. auth) Henry, D. Furious cool **92**
Henry, John
A short history of scientific thought **501**
Henry, Mya
(jt. auth) Werner, E. Hartwood **641.597**
Henry, Patrick, 1736-1799
About
Kranish, M. Flight from Monticello **973.4**
Hensley, William L., 1941-
About
Hensley, W. L. Fifty miles from tomorrow **92**
Henson, Jim
About
Jones, B. J. Jim Henson **92**
Hensperger, Beth
The best quick breads **641.8**
Hepburn, Audrey, 1929-1993
About
Walker, A. Audrey **92**
Wasson, S. Fifth Avenue, 5 AM **791.43**
Hepburn, Katharine, 1907-2003
About
Berg, A. S. Kate remembered **92**
Hepburn, K. Me **92**
Mann, W. J. Kate: the woman who was Hepburn **92**
Ware, S. Letter to the world **920.72**
HEPTATHLETES
Joyner-Kersee, J. A kind of grace **796.42**
Her. Parravani, C. **92**
Her best-kept secret. Glaser, G. **362.292**
Her last death. Sonnenberg, S. **92**
Her little majesty: the life of Queen Victoria. Erickson, C. **92**
HERA (GREEK DEITY)
See also Gods and goddesses
Herald, Diana Tixier
Fluent in fantasy **016**
Genreflecting **016**
Strictly science fiction **016**
HERALDRY
See also Archeology; Signs and symbols; Symbolism
HERB GARDENING
Orr, S. The new American herbal **615.3**
HERB GARDENING
See also Gardening
HERB REMEDIES *See* Herbs -- Therapeutic use
The **herbal** apothecary. **615.3**
HERBAL MEDICINE *See* Herbs -- Therapeutic use; Medical botany

HERBALS
Balick, M. J. Rodale's 21st-century herbal **635**
Orr, S. The new American herbal **615.3**
HERBALS *See* Herbs; Materia medica
HERBARIA *See* Plants -- Collection and preservation
Herbert Hoover in the White House. Rappleye, C. **92**
Herbert von Karajan. Osborne, R. **92**
Herbert, Brian
Dreamer of Dune **813**
Herbert, Frank, 1920-1986
About
Herbert, B. Dreamer of Dune **813**
Herbert, George
Herbert: poems **821**
Herbert, Wray
On second thought **153.4**
Herbert, Zbigniew
The collected poems, 1956-1998 **891.8**
About
Heaney, S. Finders keepers **821**
Milosz, C. To begin where I am **891.8**
Herbert: poems. Herbert, G. **821**
HERBICIDES
See also Agricultural chemicals; Pesticides
Herbivoracious. Natkin, M. **641.5**
HERBIVORES
See also Animals
HERBS
Hemphill, I. The spice & herb bible **641.3**
Orr, S. The new American herbal **615.3**
HERBS
See also Plants
HERBS -- ENCYCLOPEDIAS
Tucker, A. O. The encyclopedia of herbs **635**
HERBS -- HANDBOOKS, MANUALS, ETC
Orr, S. The new American herbal **615.3**
HERBS -- THERAPEUTIC USE
Balick, M. J. Rodale's 21st-century herbal **635**
Cervantes, J. The Cannabis Encyclopedia **633.79**
HERBS -- THERAPEUTIC USE
See also Therapeutics
HERBS -- THERAPEUTIC USE -- HANDBOOKS, MANUALS, ETC
The herbal apothecary **615.3**
HERBS -- UTILIZATION -- HANDBOOKS, MANUALS, ETC
Orr, S. The new American herbal **615.3**
HERCULES (LEGENDARY CHARACTER)
Huber, M. R. Mythematics **510**
Hercules, Olias
Mamushka **641.594**
Herding Hemingway's Cats. Arney, K. **572.8**
Here Comes Exterminator! McGraw, E. **798.4**
Here I Am. Huffman, A. **770.92**

Here I stand. Robeson, P.   **92**

Here I stand: a life of Martin Luther. Bainton, R. H.   **92**

Here on Earth. Flannery, T.   **551**

Here we are now. Cross, C. R.   **92**

Here's looking at Euclid. Bellos, A.   **513**

Here, there, elsewhere. Heat-Moon, W. L.   **910.4**

HEREDITARY DISEASES *See* Medical genetics

HEREDITARY SUCCESSION *See* Inheritance and succession

HEREDITY

   Darwin, C. On the origin of species   **576.8**

   Darwin, C. The origin of species by means of natural selection, or, The preservation of favored races in the struggle for life   **576.8**

   Endersby, J. A guinea pig's history of biology **576.5**

   Estreich, G. The Shape of the Eye   **618.92**

   Mukherjee, S. The gene   **616.042**

   Shenk, D. The genius in all of us   **155.2**

   Tanzi, R. E. Super genes   **613**

HEREDITY

   See also Biology; Breeding

HEREDITY -- GRAPHIC NOVELS

   Keller, M. Charles Darwin's On the Origin of Species   **576.8**

HEREDITY AND ENVIRONMENT *See* Nature and nurture

HEREDITY OF DISEASES *See* Medical genetics

HEREFORD CATTLE

   See also Beef cattle

Hérelle, Félix d', 1873-1949

         About

   Malone, J. W. It doesn't take a rocket scientist **920**

HERESIES *See* Heresy

HERESIES, CHRISTIAN *See* Christian heresies

HERESY

   Dreger, A. Galileo's middle finger   **174.2**

HERESY

   See also Religion

HERESY IN SCIENCE

   Dreger, A. Galileo's middle finger   **174.2**

The **heretic** in Darwin's court. Slotten, R. A.   **92**

Heretic queen. Ronald, S.   **942.05**

Heritage. Brock, S.   **641.59**

HERITAGE PROPERTY *See* Cultural property

HERITAGE TOURISM *See* Cultural tourism

Herken, Gregg

   The Georgetown set   **975.3**

Herlihy, David

   The black death and the transformation of the west   **940.1**

The lost cyclist   **92**

Herman Melville. Parker, H.   **813**

Herman Melville. Hardwick, E.   **813**

Herman Melville. Parker, H.   **813**

Herman, Amy E.

Visual intelligence   **152.14**

Herman, Arthur

   Douglas MacArthur   **92**

   Freedom's forge   **940.53**

   How the Scots invented the modern world   **941.1**

   The idea of decline in Western history   **909.08**

Herman, Gabriela

   The Beetlebung Farm cookbook   **641**

Herman, Jeff

   Jeff Herman's guide to book publishers, editors, & literary agents   **070.5**

Hermes, Will

   Love goes to buildings on fire   **781.64**

HERMETIC ART AND PHILOSOPHY *See* Alchemy; Astrology; Occultism

Hermite, Charles, 1822-1901

         About

   Bell, E. T. Men of mathematics   **920**

HERMITS

   Armstrong, K. Visions of God   **248.2**

HERMITS

   See also Eccentrics and eccentricities

Hernández, Daisy

         About

   Hernández, D. A cup of water under my bed **920.009**

Hernon, Peter

   Assessing service quality   **025.5**

Hero. Korda, M.   **92**

Hero of the empire. Millard, C.   **968.04**

Hero of the underground. Peter, J.   **92**

The **Hero's** Body. Giraldi, W.   **92**

Herodotus, ca. 484 B.C.-425 B.C.

   The Histories   **938**

   The landmark Herodotus   **938**

   Travels with Herodotus   **930**

HEROES

   Morrison, G. Supergods   **741.5**

HEROES -- UNITED STATES -- BIOGRAPHY

   Egan, T. The immortal Irishman   **92**

   Groom, W. The aviators   **920**

   Sadler, A. The 15:17 to Paris   **363.325**

   Wolf, M. J. Abandoned in hell   **959.704**

HEROES AND HEROINES

   Boorstin, D. J. The Americans: The national experience   **973**

   Ellis, S. How to Be a Heroine   **809.3**

   Henican, E. Worth dying for   **359.984**

   McDougall, C. Natural Born Heroes   **940.53**

   Morgan, E. S. American heroes   **920**

HEROES AND HEROINES

   See also Adventure and adventurers

HEROES AND HEROINES -- POETRY

   Zapruder, M. Come on all you ghosts   **811**

HEROIN

   Peter, J. Hero of the underground   **92**

HEROIN

See also Morphine; Narcotics
**HEROIN -- NEVADA -- LAS VEGAS -- HISTO-
RY -- 20TH CENTURY**
Assael, S. The murder of Sonny Liston   **796.83**
HEROIN ABUSE
Assael, S. The murder of Sonny Liston   **796.83**
Quinones, S. Dreamland   **362.29**
HEROIN ABUSE -- UNITED STATES
Quinones, S. Dreamland   **362.29**
HEROINES *See* Heroes and heroines
Heroines of Mercy Street. Toler, P. D.   **973.775**
HEROISM *See* Courage; Heroes and heroines
HERPETOLOGISTS
James, J. The snake charmer   **92**
Herrera, Hayden
Frida: a biography of Frida Kahlo   **709**
Listening to stone   **92**
Herridge, Catherine
The next wave   **363.32**
Herring, George C., 1936-
From colony to superpower   **327**
Herrington, Sarah
(jt. auth) Krasno, J. Wanderlust   **613.7**
Herrington, Stuart A.
Traitors among us   **327.12**
Herriot, James
All creatures great and small   **92**
James Herriot's animal stories   **636.089**
James Herriot's cat stories   **636.8**
James Herriot's dog stories   **636.7**
James Herriot's favorite dog stories   **636.7**
Herrmann, Dorothy
Helen Keller   **92**
Herschel, John Frederick William Sir, 1792-1871
      About
Snyder, L. J. The philosophical breakfast club   **509**
Hersey, John
Hiroshima   **940.54**
Hersh, Seymour M.
Chain of command   **973.931**
      About
Miraldi, R. Seymour Hersh   **92**
The killing of Osama Bin Laden   **327.73**
HERSHEY FOODS CORP.
Brenner, J. G. The emperors of chocolate   **338.7**
Hershey, Milton Snavely, 1857-1945
      About
Brenner, J. G. The emperors of chocolate   **338.7**
**Hertford, Catherine Grey Seymour, Countess of,
ca. 1538-1568**
      About
De Lisle, L. The sisters who would be queen   **920**
Hertog, Susan
Anne Morrow Lindbergh   **92**
Hertsgaard, Mark
Hot   **304.2**

Hertz, Frederick
A legal guide for lesbian and gay couples   **346.01**
Hertz, Zygmunt
      About
Milosz, C. To begin where I am   **891.8**
Hervieux, Linda
Forgotten   **940.54**
Herwig, Holger H.
The Marne, 1914   **940.4**
Herz, Rachel S.
The scent of desire   **152.1**
Herzing, Denise L.
Dolphin diaries   **599.5**
Herzl's vision. Avineri, S.   **320.54**
Herzog, Amy
Knit to flatter   **746.43**
Knit wear love   **746.432**
You can knit that   **746.432**
Herzog, Chaim
The Arab-Israeli wars   **956**
Hess, Paul
(ed) Floyd, T. Smithsonian field guide to the birds
of North America   **598**
Hessenbruch, Arne
(ed) Reader's guide to the history of science   **509**
Hesser, Amanda
The essential New York Times cook book   **641.5**
Hessler, Peter
Country driving   **303.4**
Oracle bones   **951**
Hesson, James L.
Weight training for life   **613.7**
Hester, Beth Landis
(ed) Car   **629.222**
Hesterman, Oran B.
Fair food   **338.1**
HETEROSEXUALITY -- HISTORY
Blank, H. Straight   **306.76**
Heuser, Charles W.
(jt. auth) Dirr, M. A. The Reference Manual of
Woody Plant Propagation   **631.5**
Hever, Julieanna
The Vegiterranean Diet   **613.2**
Hewitt, Ben
The town that food saved   **338.1**
Hewitt, Terry
The complete book of cacti & succulents   **635.9**
HEWLETT-PACKARD CO.
Burrows, P. Backfire: Carly Fiorina's high-stakes
battle for the soul of Hewlett-Packard   **338.7**
Hexham, Irving
Understanding world religions   **200**
Heyerdahl, Thor
Kon-Tiki   **910.4**
Heylin, Clinton
So long as men can breathe   **822.3**

Heywood, V. H.
 Flowering plant families of the world   **582.13**
Heywood, W.
 (ed) The little flowers of St. Francis of Assisi   **242**
HI-LO BOOKS
 Riechel, R.   Easy information sources for ESL, adult learners, & new readers   **016**
Hibbert, Christopher
 The Borgias and their enemies   **945**
 The House of Medici   **920**
 Nelson   **92**
 Queen Victoria   **92**
 Redcoats and rebels   **973.3**
 Wellington   **92**
HIBERNATION
 See also Animal behavior
HIBOUX
 Mikkola, H. Owls of the world   **598.9**
HIBOUX -- OUVRAGES ILLUSTRÉS
 Mikkola, H. Owls of the world   **598.9**
HICCUPS
 Provine, R. R. Curious behavior   **152.3**
Hickam, Homer H., 1943-
　　　　About
 Hickam, H. H. Rocket boys   **629.1**
Hickey, Michael
 The Korean War   **951.904**
Hickey, Michael C.
 (ed) Competing voices from the Russian Revolution   **947.084**
Hickman, Joseph
 Murder at Camp Delta   **355.1**
　　　　About
 Hickman, J. Murder at Camp Delta   **355.1**
Hickock, Richard, 1931-1965
　　　　About
 Capote, T. In cold blood   **364.1**
Hickok, Lorena A
　　　　About
 Golay, M. America 1933   **973.917**
Hicks, George
 The comfort women   **940.54**
Hicks, Greg
 Foster, R. How we choose to be happy   **158**
Hicok, Bob, 1960-
 Elegy owed   **811**
Hidden America. Laskas, J. M.   **305.5**
The **hidden** brain. Vedantam, S.   **154.2**
HIDDEN CHILDREN (HOLOCAUST)
 See also Jewish children in the Holocaust
Hidden Figures. Lee Shetterly, M.   **510.92**
The **hidden** half of nature. Montgomery, D. R.   **579**
Hidden harmonies. Kaplan, E.   **516.2**
Hidden history. Boorstin, D. J.   **973**
Hidden in plain view. Tobin, J.   **973.7**
The **hidden** life of dogs. Thomas, E. M.   **599.77**

The **Hidden** Life of Trees. Wohlleben, P.   **582.16**
Hidden minds. Tallis, F.   **154.2**
The **hidden** people of North Korea. Hassig, R. C.   **951.93**
Hidden power. Marton, K.   **920**
The **hidden** reality. Greene, B.   **530.1**
The **hidden** room. Page, P. K.   **811**
Hidden treasures of ancient Egypt. Hawass, Z. A.   **932**
The **hidden** Wordsworth. Johnston, K. R.   **821**
Hide & seek. Aron, W.   **92**
Hider, James
 The spiders of Allah   **956.05**
Hiding man. Daugherty, T.   **92**
HIDING PLACES -- UNITED STATES -- HISTORY
 Puleo, S. American treasures   **973**
Hiebert, Helen, 1965-
 The papermaker's companion   **676**
HIEROGLYPHICS
 Ceram, C. W. Gods, graves, and scholars   **930.1**
 Mertz, B. Temples, tombs, & hieroglyphs   **932**
 Robinson, A. Cracking the Egyptian code   **493**
HIEROGLYPHICS
 See also Inscriptions; Writing
Hieronymus Bosch. Fischer, S.   **759.94**
Higashi, Chris
 Pearl, N. Now read this   **016**
Higashida, Naoki, 1992-
　　　　About
 The reason I jump   **92**
Higginbotham, Evelyn Brooks
 (ed) African American lives   **920**
 (ed) The African American national biography   **920.003**
 Franklin, J. H. From slavery to freedom   **305.8**
Higgins, Charlotte
 It's all Greek to me   **938**
 Under another sky   **936**
Higgins, Kathleen Marie
 Solomon, R. C. A passion for wisdom   **109**
 Solomon, R. C. What Nietzsche really said   **193**
Higgins, Katie
 Chocolate-covered Katie   **641.6**
Higgins, Matt
 Bird dream   **797.5**
Higginson, William J.
 The haiku handbook   **808.1**
HIGGS BOSONS
 Carroll, S. The particle at the end of the Universe   **539.7**
 Lincoln, D. The large hadron collider   **539.7**
Higgs discovery. Randall, L.   **539.72**
High financier. Ferguson, N.   **92**
HIGH INCOME PEOPLE *See* Rich
HIGH   INTEREST-LOW   VOCABULARY

BOOKS *See* Hi-Lo books

HIGH INTEREST-LOW VOCABULARY BOOKS -- BIBLIOGRAPHY

Riechel, R. Easy information sources for ESL, adult learners, & new readers 016

HIGH JUMPERS

Ware, S. Letter to the world 920.72

High latitudes. Mowat, F. 971

HIGH MUSEUM OF ART -- CATALOGS

Gross, K. Dream cars 629.222

High Price. Hart, C. 362.29

HIGH RISK STUDENTS *See* At risk students

HIGH SCHOOL -- GRAPHIC NOVELS

My friend Dahmer 741.5

HIGH SCHOOL EDUCATION *See* Secondary education

HIGH SCHOOL EQUIVALENCY EXAMINATIONS

The official guide to the HiSET exam 373.126

HIGH SCHOOL LIBRARIES

See also School libraries

HIGH SCHOOL LIBRARIES -- BOOK LISTS

Keane, N. J. 101 great, ready-to-use book lists for teens 028.5

HIGH SCHOOL LIFE *See* High school students

HIGH SCHOOL STUDENTS

Abrams, J. Boys among men 796.323

McCullough, D. J. You Are Not Special 170

Robbins, A. The geeks shall inherit the Earth

HIGH SCHOOL STUDENTS

See also Students

HIGH SCHOOL TEACHERS

McCourt, F. Angela's ashes 92

McCourt, F. Teacher man 92

McCourt, F. 'Tis 92

HIGH SCHOOL TEACHERS -- PENNSYLVANIA -- LEVITTOWN -- BIOGRAPHY

Sokolove, M. Drama high 92

HIGH SCHOOLS

Brick, M. Saving the school 373.22

Keizer, G. Getting Schooled 373.1

HIGH SCHOOLS

See also Public schools; Schools

HIGH SCHOOLS -- RHODE ISLAND -- PROVIDENCE

Reynolds, B. Hope 796.323

HIGH TECHNOLOGY INDUSTRY

Menuez, D. Fearless genius 979.4

Piscione, D. P. Secrets of Silicon Valley 330.9

HIGH TECHNOLOGY INDUSTRY

See also Industries

HIGH-PROTEIN DIET -- RECIPES

Fong, H. Nom nom paleo 641.5

Well fed 641.5

High-yield vegetable gardening. McCrate, C. 635

HIGHER EDUCATION

Bloom, A. D. The closing of the American mind 973.92

Boorstin, D. J. The Americans: The democratic experience 973

Delbanco, A. College 378.73

Dreifus, C. Higher education? 378

Espinoza, R. Pivotal moments 371.102

Levine, L. W. The opening of the American mind 001.1

Martin, R. H. Racing Odysseus 92

Mettler, S. Degrees of inequality 378.73

Rose, M. Back to school 374

Selingo, J. J. College (un)bound 378

Wilder, C. S. Ebony and Ivy 379.26

HIGHER EDUCATION

See also Education

Higher education? Dreifus, C. 378

A higher form of killing. Preston, D. 940.4

Higher gossip. 818

HIGHER NERVOUS ACTIVITY -- MEASUREMENT

Kounios, J. The Eureka factor 612.8

Highfield, Roger

Supercooperators 519.3

Wilmut, I. After Dolly 176

Highsmith, Patricia, 1921-1995

About

Schenkar, J. The talented Miss Highsmith 92

HIGHWAY CONSTRUCTION *See* Roads

HIGHWAY ENGINEERING

See also Civil engineering; Engineering

HIGHWAY TRANSPORTATION

Hessler, P. Country driving 303.4

HIJACKING OF AIRPLANES

Koerner, B. I. The skies belong to us 364.15

Longman, J. Among the heroes 364.1

HIJACKING OF AIRPLANES

See also Offenses against public safety

Hikayati sharhun yatul./English

The locust and the bird 92

HIKERS -- UNITED STATES -- BIOGRAPHY

Davis, J. P. Called again 92

HIKING

Berger, K. America's great hiking trails 796.51

Marquis, S. Wild by nature 613.6

Solnit, R. Wanderlust 796.51

Stafford, E. Walking the Amazon 918.1

Strayed, C. Wild 92

HIKING

See also Outdoor life

HIKING -- AMAZON RIVER REGION

Stafford, E. Walking the Amazon 918.1

HIKING -- APPALACHIAN REGION, SOUTHERN -- GUIDEBOOKS

Spira, T. P. Waterfalls and wildflowers in the Southern Appalachians 796.51

HIKING -- RUSSIA (FEDERATION) -- URAL MOUNTAINS REGION
Eichar, D. Dead Mountain   **914.7**
Hilborn, Ray
Overfishing   **338.3**
Hilborn, Ulrike
(jt. auth) Hilborn, R. Overfishing   **338.3**
Hilburn, Robert
Johnny Cash   **92**
Hildy, Franklin J.
Brockett, O. G. History of the theatre   **792.09**
Hilfiger, Tommy
About
Hilfiger, T. American dreamer   **92**
Hilfiger, Tommy, 1951-
American dreamer   **92**
HILL DISTRICT (PITTSBURGH, PA.) -- DRAMA.
Wilson, A. Two trains running   **812**
Hill of Beans. Snyder, J.   **92**
Hill, Anita, 1956-
Reimagining equality   **305.8**
Hill, Barbara Albers
(jt. auth) Stoler, D. R. Coping with concussion and mild traumatic brain injury   **617.4**
Hill, Cherry
How to think like a horse   **636.1**
Hill, Christopher T.
(jt. auth) Lederman, L. Beyond the god particle   **539.7**
Hill, Chrystie
Inside, outside, and online   **021.2**
Hill, Clint
Five days in November   **973.922**
Five presidents   **363.28**
Mrs. Kennedy and me   **973.922**
Hill, Geoffrey
The orchards of Syon   **821**
Selected poems   **821**
The triumph of love   **821**
Without title   **821**
Hill, Joe, 1879-1915
About
Adler, W. M. The man who never died   **92**
Hill, McKel
Nutrition Stripped   **641.302**
Hill, Napoleon
Think and grow rich   **650.1**
Hill, Pamela Smith, 1954-
(ed) Pioneer girl   **92**
Hill, Rosemary
Stonehenge   **936.2**
Hill, Samuel S.
Atwood, C. D. Handbook of denominations in the United States   **280**
Hill, Winfield

(jt. auth) Horowitz, P. The art of electronics   **621.381**
Hillbilly elegy. Vance, J. D.   **92**
HILLBILLY MUSIC *See* Country music
Hilleman, Maurice R., 1919-2005
About
Offit, P. A. Vaccinated   **92**
Hillenbrand, Laura
Seabiscuit   **798.4**
Unbroken   **940.54**
Hillerman, Tony
About
Hillerman, T. Seldom disappointed   **813**
The **Hillier** gardener's guide to trees & shrubs. **635.9**
Hillman, Brenda
Cascadia   **811**
Pieces of air in the epic   **811**
Seasonal works with letters on fire   **811**
Hillstrom, Kevin
(ed) Contemporary women artists   **920.003**
The Cold War   **909.82**
Hillstrom, Laurie
(ed) Contemporary women artists   **920.003**
The Thanksgiving book   **394.26**
Hilton, Lisa
Elizabeth   **92**
Hilton, Walter, 1340-1396
About
Armstrong, K. Visions of God   **248.2**
Hilts, Philip J.
Protecting America's health   **353.9**
Hiltzik, Michael A.
Colossus   **627**
Him, Chanrithy, 1965-
About
Him, C. When broken glass floats   **959.604**
HIMALAYA MOUNTAINS
Khanna, V. Return to the rivers   **641.59**
Himelstein, Shmuel
(ed) The New encyclopedia of Judaism   **296**
Himes, Chester, 1909-1984
About
Sallis, J. Chester Himes   **813**
Himmelfarb, Gertrude
The moral imagination   **190**
The roads to modernity   **190**
Himmelman, John
Cricket radio   **595.7**
Himmler, Heinrich, 1900-1945
About
Breitman, R. The architect of genocide   **92**
Hinden, Stan
How to retire happy   **646.7**
HINDI LANGUAGE
See also Indian languages; Language and languages

HINDI POETRY
    See also Hindi literature; Indian poetry
Hinds, P. Mignon
    (ed) Essence total makeover   **646.7**
HINDU HOLIDAYS
    See also Religious holidays
HINDU PHILOSOPHY
    See also Philosophy
HINDUISM
    Calasso, R. Ardor   **294.5**
    Davis, R. H. The Bhagavad Gita   **294.5**
    Doniger, W. On Hinduism   **294.5**
    Eastern religions   **200.9**
    Goldberg, P. American Veda   **294.5**
HINDUISM
    See also Religions
Hine, Darlene Clark
    (ed) Black women in America   **920.003**
Hine, Robert S.
    (ed) A dictionary of biology   **570**
Hine, Thomas
    The rise and fall of the American teenager **305.235**
Hines, Emmett W.
    Fitness swimming   **613.7**
Hines, Richard, 1945-
        About
    Hines, R. No Way but Gentlenesse   **92**
Hiney, Tom
    Raymond Chandler   **813**
The **hinge** of fate. Churchill, W.   **940.53**
Hinges of history [series]
    Cahill, T. The gifts of the Jews   **909**
    Cahill, T. Sailing the wine-dark sea   **909**
Hingley, Brian D.
    Furniture repair & restoration   **684.1**
Hinton, Milt, 1910-2000
        About
    Lees, G. You can't steal a gift   **781.65**
Hip hop matters. Watkins, S. C.   **781.64**
HIP-HOP
    Chang, J. Can't stop, won't stop   **781.64**
    Charnas, D. The big payback   **781.64**
    Dyson, M. E. Holler if you hear me: searching for
      Tupac Shakur   **92**
    Grandmaster Flash The adventures of Grandmas-
      ter Flash   **92**
    Watkins, S. C. Hip hop matters   **781.64**
HIP-HOP -- ENCYCLOPEDIAS
    Edwards, P. The concise guide to hip-hop mu-
      sic   **782.42**
HIP-HOP -- UNITED STATES -- HISTORY
    Austen, J. Darkest America   **791**
HIPPIES
    MacLean, R. Magic bus   **915**
HIPPIES
    See also Bohemianism

Hirigoyen, Gerald
    Pintxos   **641.8**
Hirohito and the making of modern Japan. Bix, H.
    P.   **92**
Hirohito, Emperor of Japan, 1901-1989
        About
    Bix, H. P. Hirohito and the making of modern Ja-
      pan   **92**
    Seagrave, S. The Yamato dynasty   **952.03**
Hiroko Shimbo
    Hiroko's American kitchen   **641.59**
Hiroko's American kitchen. Hiroko Shimbo **641.59**
Hiroshima. Hersey, J.   **940.54**
Hiroshima. Takaki, R. T.   **940.54**
**HIROSHIMA (JAPAN) -- BOMBARDMENT,
1945**
    Ham, P. Hiroshima Nagasaki   **940.54**
    Pellegrino, C. To hell and back   **940.54**
Hiroshima in America. Lifton, R. J.   **940.54**
Hiroshima Nagasaki. Ham, P.   **940.54**
HIROSHIMA (JAPAN) -- BIOGRAPHY
    Pellegrino, C. To hell and back   **940.54**
**HIROSHIMA (JAPAN) -- HISTORY -- BOM-
BARDMENT, 1945 -- MORAL AND ETHI-
CAL ASPECTS**
    Ham, P. Hiroshima Nagasaki   **940.54**
Hirsch, E. D.
    The schools we need and why we don't have
      them   **370.9**
Hirsch, Edward
    Earthly measures   **811**
    How to read a poem   **808.1**
    The living fire   **811**
    On love   **811**
    Poet's choice   **809.1**
    A Poet's Glossary   **808.1**
    Special orders   **811**
Hirsch, Gretchen
    Gertie's ultimate dress book   **646.4**
    A modern guide to sportswear styles of the 1940s
      and 1950s   **646.4**
Hirsch, James S.
    Riot and remembrance   **976.6**
    Willie Mays   **92**
Hirsch, Lee
    (ed) Bully   **371.5**
The **Hirschfeld** century. Leopold, D.   **741.5**
Hirschfeld on line. Hirschfeld, A.   **741.5**
Hirschfeld, Al
    Hirschfeld on line   **741.5**
        About
    Leopold, D. The Hirschfeld century   **741.5**
Hirschfeld, Erik
    The world's rarest birds   **598**
Hirshberg, Charles
    Zwonitzer, M. Will you miss me when I'm

gone? **781.642**

Hirsheimer, Christopher

Barrow, C. Mrs. Wheelbarrow's practical pantry **641.4**

Bastianich, L. M. Lidia's family table **641.5**

Bayless, R. Authentic Mexican **641.597**

Bayless, R. Mexican everyday **641.597**

Bayless, R. More Mexican everyday **641.597**

Canal house cooks every day **641.5**

Mozza at home **641.5**

Hirshey, Gerri

Not pretty enough **92**

Hirshfeld, Alan

The electric life of Michael Faraday **92**

Eureka man **92**

Starlight Detectives **523.1**

Hirshfield, Jane

After **811**

The beauty **811**

Ten windows **808.1**

Hirshman, Linda

Sisters in law **347.73**

Victory **306.76**

Hirshman, Susan L.

Does this make my assets look fat? **332.024**

Hirshson, Stanley

(jt. auth) Unger, I. George Marshall **92**

Hirshson, Stanley P.

General Patton: a soldier's life **92**

Hirsi Ali, Ayaan, 1969-

About

Hirsi Ali, A. Infidel **92**

Scroggins, D. Wanted women **305.48**

Hirst, Michael

Michelangelo **709.2**

Hirtle, Sheila

De Villiers, M. Sahara: a natural history **508**

His Excellency. Ellis, J. J. **92**

His final battle. Lelyveld, J. **92**

His George Washington [series]

Flexner, J. T. George Washington and the new nation, 1783-1793 **92**

Flexner, J. T. George Washington: anguish and farewell 1793-1799 **92**

Flexner, J. T. George Washington: the forge of experience, 1732-1775 **92**

Hischak, Thomas

The Oxford companion to the American musical **792.6**

HISPANIC AMERICAN ART

St. James guide to Hispanic artists **920.003**

HISPANIC AMERICAN ATHLETES

Ruck, R. Raceball **796.357**

HISPANIC AMERICAN LITERATURE (SPANISH)

Latino literature **016**

HISPANIC AMERICAN WOMEN

Count on me **177**

Sotomayor, S. My beloved world **92**

Thorpe, H. Just like us **305.8**

HISPANIC AMERICAN WOMEN -- BIOGRAPHY

Count on me **177**

Sotomayor, S. My beloved world **92**

HISPANIC AMERICANS

Monterrey, M. Americanos **305.8**

Morales, E. Living in Spanglish **305.868**

HISPANIC AMERICANS See Latinos (U.S.)

HISPANIC AMERICANS -- BIOGRAPHY

Pawel, M. The Crusades of Cesar Chavez **92**

HISPANIC AMERICANS -- BIOGRAPHY -- ENCYCLOPEDIAS

Great lives from history **920.009**

HISPANIC AMERICANS -- DICTIONARIES

Friedman, I. C. Latino athletes **920.003**

Martinez Wood, J. Latino writers and journalists **920.003**

Newton, D. E. Latinos in science, math, and professions **920.003**

Otfinoski, S. Latinos in the arts **920.003**

HISPANIC AMERICANS -- EDUCATION (HIGHER) -- HANDBOOKS, MANUALS, ETC

The Latino student's guide to college success **378.1**

HISPANIC AMERICANS -- HISTORY

Pawel, M. The Crusades of Cesar Chavez **92**

HISPANIC AMERICANS AND LIBRARIES

Moller, S. C. Library service to Spanish speaking patrons **027.6**

HISPANIC AMERICANS IN LITERATURE

Latino and Latina writers **810**

Hiss, Alger

About

Haynes, J. E. Venona **327.12**

Hissing cousins. Peyser, M. **92**

HISTORIANS

See also Authors

HISTORIANS -- UNITED STATES

Schlesinger, A. M. Journals: 1952-2000 **92**

Schlesinger, A. M. A life in the twentieth century **92**

HISTORIANS -- UNITED STATES -- BIOGRAPHY

Brookhiser, R. America's first dynasty **973.4**

Crais, C. History lessons **92**

Duberman, M. Howard Zinn **92**

HISTORIC BUILDINGS

World Heritage sites **910.2**

HISTORIC BUILDINGS

See also Buildings; Historic sites; Monuments

HISTORIC BUILDINGS -- NEW YORK (N.Y.)

Freeland, D. Automats, taxi dances, and vaudeville

HISTORIC BUILDINGS -- UNITED STATES
Gugliotta, G. Freedom's cap   975.3

HISTORIC HOUSES *See* Historic buildings

Historic lives [series]
Brown, M. T.E. Lawrence   92

HISTORIC PRESERVATION
Puleo, S. American treasures   973

HISTORIC PRESERVATIONISTS
Wilson, A. N. Betjeman   92

HISTORIC SITES
Caro, I. Paris to the past   914
Curtis, N. C. Black heritage sites   973
Hunt, P. Ten discoveries that rewrote history 930.1
Loewen, J. W. Lies across America   973
World Heritage sites   910.2

HISTORIC SITES
See also Archeology; History

HISTORIC SITES -- UNITED STATES --
   GUIDEBOOKS
Ferris, G. W. Presidential places   917
Glass, B. D. 50 great American places   973

The **historic** unfullfilled promise. Zinn, H. 973.924

The **historical** atlas of American crime. Rosen,
F.   364

Historical atlas of Central Europe. Magocsi, P.
R.   911

Historical atlas of the American West. Hayes,
D.   911

Historical atlas of the American West. Beck, W.
A.   911

A **Historical** atlas of the Jewish people.   909

Historical atlas of the North American railroad.
Hayes, D.   385

Historical atlas of the United States. Hayes, D. 911

HISTORICAL ATLASES
Atlas of the Civil War   973.7
Beck, W. A. Historical atlas of the American
West   911
Hayes, D. Historical atlas of the American West 911
Hayes, D. Historical atlas of the North American
railroad   385
Smithsonian atlas of world aviation   629.13
Swanson, M. Atlas of the Civil War, month by
month   973.7
Woodworth, S. E. Atlas of the Civil War   973.7

HISTORICAL ATLASES
See also Atlases

HISTORICAL CHRONOLOGY
Grafton, A. Cartographies of time   902
Grun, B. The timetables of history   902
National Geographic concise history of the
world   909
The timetables of American history   902

HISTORICAL CHRONOLOGY
See also Chronology; History

Historical dictionaries of religions, philosophies,
   and movements [series]
Olson, C. Historical dictionary of Buddhism 294.3

Historical dictionaries of war, revolution, and civil
   unrest [series]
Anderson, S. Historical dictionary of terrorism   363.32

Historical dictionary of Buddhism. Olson, C. 294.3

Historical dictionary of terrorism. Anderson,
S.   363.32

HISTORICAL DRAMA
McCarter, J. Hamilton   782.1

HISTORICAL DRAMA
See also Drama

Historical encyclopedia of American labor.   331.8

HISTORICAL FICTION
Baker, J. S. The readers' advisory guide to histori-
cal fiction   026
Johnson, S. L. Historical fiction II   016

HISTORICAL FICTION
See also Fiction

HISTORICAL FICTION -- BIBLIOGRAPHY
Hooper, B. Read on....historical fiction   016
Historical fiction II. Johnson, S. L.   016
Historical gazetteer of the United States. Hellmann,
P. T.   911

HISTORICAL GEOGRAPHY
Riffenburgh, B. Mapping the world   912

HISTORICAL GEOGRAPHY
See also Geography; History

HISTORICAL GEOGRAPHY -- MAPS *See* Historical atlases

HISTORICAL GEOLOGY
Stager, C. Deep future   363.7

HISTORICAL SITES *See* Historic sites

Historical thesaurus of the Oxford English dictionary.   423

HISTORICAL TOURISM *See* Cultural tourism

The **Histories.** Herodotus, c. 4. B. B. C.   938

Histories of the hanged. Anderson, D. M.   967.62

HISTORIOGRAPHERS *See* Historians

HISTORIOGRAPHY
Hobsbawm, E. J. On history   901
Kagan, D. Thucydides   938
MacMillan, M. Dangerous games   901
McKillop, A. B. The spinster & the prophet 941.08
Tuchman, B. W. Practicing history   907

HISTORIOGRAPHY
See also Authorship; History

HISTORIOGRAPHY -- PHILOSOPHY
Bailyn, B. Sometimes an art, never a science, always a craft   907.2

HISTORIOGRAPHY AND PHOTOGRAPHY --
   UNITED STATES
Krauthamer, B. Envisioning emancipation   973.7

History.   909

HISTORY
See also Humanities; Social sciences

HISTORY
Crapol, E. P. John Tyler 92
Galeano, E. H. Mirrors 909

HISTORY -- ATLASES *See* Historical atlases

HISTORY -- BIBLIOGRAPHY
Frolund, T. Read on...history 016

HISTORY -- EUROPE -- GREAT BRITAIN
Brown, P. Shakespeare's Pub 647.9

HISTORY -- GENERAL
Lind, M. Land of promise 330.973

HISTORY -- HISTORIOGRAPHY *See* Historiography

HISTORY -- PHILOSOPHY
Bailyn, B. Sometimes an art, never a science, always a craft 907.2
Black, J. Other pasts, different presents, alternative futures 900
Kreeft, P. Philosophy 101 by Socrates 183

HISTORY -- PHILOSOPHY
See also Philosophy

HISTORY -- POETRY
Schutt, W. Westerly 811

HISTORY -- RESEARCH
Mills, E. S. Evidence explained 907

HISTORY -- SOURCES
Competing voices from the Russian Revolution 947.084
History of the world in 1,000 objects 909
The Penguin Book of Witches 133.4

HISTORY -- SOURCES
See also Historiography

HISTORY -- STUDY AND TEACHING
Lefkowitz, M. R. Not out of Africa 960
The History and Uncertain Future of Handwriting. Trubek, A. 652.1
The history book. 909
The history boys. Bennett, A. 822
History lessons. Crais, C. 92
A history of ancient Egypt. Romer, J. 932
A history of art in Africa. Visona, M. B. 709
The history of astronomy. Couper, H. 520
The history of Australia. Clarke, F. G. 994
History of beauty. Eco, U. 111
A history of Britain. Schama, S. 941
The history of British women's writing. 820
History of communication [series]
Bezanson, R. P. How free can the press be? 342
History of computing [series]
Campbell-Kelly, M. From airline reservations to Sonic the Hedgehog 005
History of disability series
Keller, H. Helen Keller: selected writings 92
History of East Central Europe [series]
Magocsi, P. R. Historical atlas of Central Eu-
rope 911
History of England [series]
Ackroyd, P. Tudors 942.05
The history of fly fishing in fifty flies. 799.124
A history of ghosts. Aykroyd, P. 133.1
A history of God. Armstrong, K. 200
The history of hell. Turner, A. K. 200
The history of Iceland. Johanneson, G. T. 949.12
The history of India. McLeod, J. 954
History of international fashion. Grumbach, D. 746.9
A history of Iraq. Tripp, C. 956.7
A history of Israel. Sachar, H. M. 956.94
A history of Israel. Bregman, A. 956.94
The history of Japan. Perez, L. G. 952
History of Japanese literature [series]
Keene, D. Seeds in the heart 895.6
The history of jazz. Gioia, T. 781.65
A history of life in 100 fossils. Taylor, P. D. 560
A history of mathematics. Boyer, C. B. 510
The history of Mexico. Kirkwood, B. 972
History of modern art. Arnason, H. H. 709.04
History of modern science and mathematics. 500
The history of music in fifty instruments. Wilkinson, P. 784.19
A history of opera. Abbate, C. 782.1
The history of pirates. Konstam, A. 910.4
A History of private life. Aries, P. 909
A History of private life. Aries, P. 909
A history of psychiatry. Shorter, E. 616.89
A history of Russia. Riasanovsky, N. V. 947
A history of Russian literature. Terras, V. 891.7
The History of science and religion in the western tradition. 201
The History of Television 1880 to 1941. Abramson, A. 621.388
The history of television, 1942 to 2000. Abramson, A. 621.388
History of the American West [series]
Calloway, C. G. One vast winter count 978
A history of the Arab peoples. Hourani, A. H. 909
History of the conquest of Mexico. Prescott, W. H. 972
A history of the Federal Reserve. Meltzer, A. H. 332.1
A history of the Jews. Johnson, P. 909
A history of the Jews in the modern world. Sachar, H. M. 909
A history of the Ostrogoths. Burns, T. S. 909.07
History of the theatre. Brockett, O. G. 792.09
History of the twentieth century. Gilbert, M. 909.82
A history of the wife. Yalom, M. 306.872
History of the world in 1,000 objects. 909
A history of the world in 100 objects. MacGregor, N. 930.1
A history of the world in 6 glasses. Standage,

T.   394.1
History of the world in photographs. Getty Images
Inc.   909.8
The history of Wales [series]
    Charles-Edwards, T. M. Wales and the Britons,
    350-1064   942.901
A history of Western architecture. Watkin, D.   720
A history of Western music. Palisca, C. V.   780.9
A history of Western philosophy. Russell, B.   109
The history of White people. Painter, N. I.   305.8
A history of Zionism. Laqueur, W.   956.94
History on trial. Lipstadt, D. E.   940.53
HISTORY PLAYS See Historical drama
HISTORY TOURISM See Cultural tourism
History's People. MacMillan, M.   920
HISTORY, 19TH CENTURY -- PENNSYLVANIA
    Aptowicz, C. O. Dr. Mütter's Marvels   92
HISTORY, ANCIENT
    Herodotus, c. 4. B. B. C. The landmark Herodo-
    tus   938
    Mattern, S. P. Prince of medicine   610.9
HISTORY, MODERN
    Mann, C. C. 1493   909
HISTORY, MODERN See Modern history
HISTORY, MODERN -- 17TH CENTURY
    Parker, G. Global crisis   909
HISTORY, MODERN -- 17TH CENTURY See
    World history -- 17th century
HISTORY, MODERN -- 1945- See World history
    -- 1945-
HISTORY, MODERN -- 1945-1989
    Kurlansky, M. 1968   909.82
HISTORY, MODERN -- 19TH CENTURY See
    World history -- 19th century
HISTORY, MODERN -- 20TH CENTURY
    The Columbia history of the 20th century   909.82
    Encyclopedia of World War II   940.53
    Great lives from history: the 20th century, 1901-
    2000   920.003
    National Geographic Society (U.S.) National Geo-
    graphic eyewitness to the 20th century   909.82
    The Oxford history of the twentieth century 909.82
    Stepan, P. Photos that changed the world   779
HISTORY, MODERN -- 20TH CENTURY See
    World history -- 20th century
HISTORY, MODERN -- 21ST CENTURY See
    World history -- 21st century
HISTORY, MODERN -- 21ST CENTURY -- PIC-
    TORIAL WORKS
    Reuters   909.83
Hitch-22. Hitchens, C.   92
HITCH-HIKING See Hitchhiking
Hitchcock, Alfred, 1899-1980
                    About
    Chandler, C. It's only a movie   92
    Spoto, D. The dark side of genius   791.43

Hitchcock, Susan Tyler
    National geographic rarely seen   779
Hitchens, Christopher
    Arguably   814
    (ed) The best American essays 2010   814
    Hitch-22   92
    God is not great   200
    Thomas Jefferson: author of America   92
                    About
    Hitchens, C. Mortality   304.6
HITCHHIKING
    See also Hiking
HITCHHIKING -- UNITED STATES
    Waters, J. Carsick   92
Hitchings, Henry
    The language wars   420
    The secret life of words   422
Hitler. Kershaw, I.   92
Hitler.   92
Hitler and the final solution. Fleming, G.   943.086
Hitler's empire. Mazower, M.   940.53
Hitler's first war. Weber, T.   940.4
Hitler's forgotten children. Tate, T.   940.53
Hitler's philosophers. Sherratt, Y.   193
Hitler's pope: the secret history of Pius XII. Corn-
    well, J.   92
Hitler's private library. Ryback, T. W.   027
Hitler's thirty days to power. Turner, H. A.   943.086
Hitler's U-boat war. Blair, C.   940.54
Hitler's willing executioners. Goldhagen, D.   940.53
Hitler, 1936-1945: nemesis. Kershaw, I.   943.086
Hitler, Adolf, 1889-1945
                    About
    Berthon, S. Warlords   940.53
    Breitman, R. The architect of genocide   92
    Cornwell, J. Hitler's pope: the secret history of
    Pius XII   92
    Fischer, K. P. Nazi Germany   943.086
    Fleming, G. Hitler and the final solution   943.086
    Fulbrook, M. A concise history of Germany   943
    Gortemaker, H. B. Eva Braun   92
    Hitler   92
    Hitler, A. Mein Kampf   92
    Kershaw, I. Hitler   92
    Kershaw, I. Hitler, 1936-1945: nemesis   943.086
    Kinney, D. The devil's diary   940.53
    Kissinger, H. Diplomacy   327.2
    The lone assassin   943.086
    Orbach, D. The plots against Hitler   940.53
    Parssinen, T. M. The Oster conspiracy of
    1938   943.086
    Rosenbaum, R. Explaining Hitler   943.086
    Ryback, T. W. Hitler's private library   027
    Sherratt, Y. Hitler's philosophers   193
    Shirer, W. L. The rise and fall of the Third
    Reich   943.086

Snyder, T. D. Bloodlands   **940.54**
Speer, A. Inside the Third Reich   **943.086**
Taylor, F. Exorcising Hitler   **943.087**
Turner, H. A. Hitler's thirty days to power **943.086**
Weber, T. Hitler's first war   **940.4**
Hitter: the life and turmoils of Ted Williams. Linn,
E.   **92**

HITTITES
    See also Ancient history

HIV DISEASE *See* AIDS (Disease)

HIV INFECTIONS
  Holt, N. Cured   **614.5**
  Stratton, S. E. The encyclopedia of HIV and
    AIDS   **362.196**

**HIV INFECTIONS -- EPIDEMIOLOGY -- AF-
  RICA**
  Halperin, D. Tinderbox   **614.5**

**HIV INFECTIONS -- SOCIAL ASPECTS -- NI-
  GERIA**
  Iweala, U. Our kind of people   **362.196**

**HIV INFECTIONS -- TREATMENT -- GERMA-
  NY -- BERLIN**
  Holt, N. Cured   **614.5**

**HIV-POSITIVE PERSONS -- UNITED STATES
  -- BIOGRAPHY**
  Duberman, M. B. Hold tight gently   **920**

Hively, Will
  Ballard, R. D. The eternal darkness   **551.46**

Hix, H. L.
  First fire, then birds   **811**

HMONG (ASIAN PEOPLE)
  Fadiman, A. The spirit catches you and you fall
    down   **306.4**

HMONG (ASIAN PEOPLE)
    See also Indigenous peoples

Ho Chi Minh. Duiker, W. J.   **959.704**

Ho, Chí Minh, 1890-1969
                  About
  Duiker, W. J. Ho Chi Minh   **959.704**

Ho, Oliver
  The Ultimate Book of Family Card Games   **795.4**

Hoadley, R. Bruce
  Understanding wood   **684**

Hoagland, Tony
  Unincorporated persons in the late Honda dynas-
    ty   **811**
  What narcissism means to me   **811**

Hoare, Philip
  The whale   **599.5**

Hoban, Phoebe
  Alice Neel   **92**

HOBART (TAS.) -- BIOGRAPHY
  Brierley, S. A long way home   **92**

Hobbes, Thomas
  Leviathan   **320.1**
                  About

Russell, B. A history of Western philosophy   **109**

HOBBIES
  Jenkins, J. K. All the time in the world   **390**

HOBBIES
    See also Amusements; Leisure; Recreation

Hobbs, Jeff
  The short and tragic life of Robert Peace   **92**

Hobsbawm, E. J.
  The age of revolution 1789-1848   **940.2**
  On history   **901**

Hobson, Jake
  The art of creative pruning   **715**

Hobson, John Atkinson, 1858-1940
                  About
  Heilbroner, R. L. The worldly philosophers   **330.1**

Hochschild, Adam
  Bury the chains   **326**
  King Leopold's ghost   **967.5**
  Spain in our hearts   **946.081**
  To end all wars   **940.3**
  The unquiet ghost   **947.084**

Hochschild, Arlie Russell
  The outsourced self   **306.85**
  Strangers in their own land   **320.52**

Hochtritt, Lisa
  (ed) Art and social justice education   **372.5**

Hock, Randolph
  The Extreme Searcher's Internet Handbook **025.042**

HOCKEY
  McKinley, M. Hockey: a people's history **796.962**

HOCKEY -- HISTORY
  Hockey Hall of Fame Book of Players   **796.962**
  Hockey Hall of Fame Book of Players.   **796.962**

HOCKEY PLAYERS
  Hockey Hall of Fame Book of Players   **796.962**
  Howe, G. Mr. Hockey   **92**
  Hockey: a people's history. McKinley, M. **796.962**

Hockney, David
                  About
  Sykes, C. S. David Hockney   **92**
  Sykes, C. S. David Hockney   **92**

Hodes, Martha
  Mourning Lincoln   **973.7**

Hodge, Nathan
  A nuclear family vacation   **623.4**

Hodgen, John
  Heaven & earth holding company   **811**
  Hodges' Harbrace handbook. Glenn, C.   **808**

Hodges, Ben
  (ed) The play that changed my life   **812**

HODGKIN'S DISEASE
  Jamison, K. R. Nothing was the same   **92**

Hodgman, George
                  About
  Hodgman, G. Bettyville   **306.874**

Hodgson, Larry

Perennials for every purpose   **635.9**

Hodson, Sara S.
(jt. auth) Adam, P. Jack London, photographer **92**

Hoekstra, Jonathan M.
The atlas of global conservation   **333.95**

Hoffa, Jimmy, b. 1913
About
Russell, T. Out of the jungle   **92**

Hoffer, Peter Charles
The Salem witchcraft trials   **345**
Hull, N. E. H. Roe v. Wade   **344**

Hoffer, Richard
Something in the air   **796.4**

Hoffman, Adina
(jt. auth) Cole, P. Sacred trash   **296.09**
Till we have built Jerusalem   **956.94**
My happiness bears no relation to happiness   **92**

Hoffman, Beatrix
Health care for some   **362.1**

Hoffman, Bruce
Anonymous soldiers   **956.94**

Hoffman, Carl
The lunatic express   **910.4**
A Savage Harvest   **995**

Hoffman, Claire
About
Hoffman, C. Greetings from Utopia Park   **92**

Hoffman, Daniel
Beyond silence   **811**

Hoffman, David E., 1953-
The Billion Dollar Spy   **327.12**

Hoffman, Donald D.
Visual intelligence   **152.14**

Hoffman, Eva
After such knowledge   **940.53**

Hoffman, Miles
The NPR classical music companion   **780**

Hoffman, Susanna
The olive and the caper   **641.594**

Hoffman, Terry Paula
(jt. auth) De Richemond, J. The Medical Library Association guide to finding out about heart disease   **016**

Hoffmann, Andrea C.
The girl who escaped ISIS   **956.7**

Hoffmann, James
The world atlas of coffee   **641.3**

Hoffmans, Lara
Fisher, K. L. How to smell a rat   **364.1**

Hofmann, Josef, 1876-1957
About
Schonberg, H. C. The great pianists   **920**

Hofmann, Mark
About
Worrall, S. The poet and the murderer   **364.15**

Hofstadter, Dan

The Earth moves   **509**

Hofstadter, Douglas
Surfaces and essences   **169**

Hofstadter, Douglas R.
I am a strange loop   **153**

Hofstadter, Richard
The age of reform from Bryan to F.D.R.   **973.91**
The American political tradition, and the men who made it   **973**

Hogan, Lawrence D.
Shades of glory   **796.357**

Hogan, Linda
About
Hogan, L. The woman who watches over the world   **818**

Hogan, Lori
Hogan, P. R. Stages of senior care   **362.6**

Hogan, Margaret A.
(ed) Adams, J. My dearest friend   **92**

Hogan, Paul Ross
Stages of senior care   **362.6**

Hogan, Sean
(ed) Flora: a gardener's encyclopedia   **635.9**

Hogeland, William
Declaration   **973.3**
The Whiskey Rebellion   **973.4**

HOGS See Pigs
Hogs wild. Frazier, I.   **814.54**

Hohn, Donovan
Moby-Duck   **551.46**

HOISTING MACHINERY
See also Machinery

Hoke, Mateo
(ed) Palestine Speaks   **956.94**
Hold Still. Mann, S.   **92**
Hold tight gently. Duberman, M. B.   **920**

Holden, Alan
Crystals and crystal growing   **548**

Holden, Wendy
Born Survivors   **940.531**

Holder, R. W.
How not to say what you mean   **427**
Holding company. Jackson, M.   **811**
Holding on upside down. Leavell, L.   **92**
The hole in the universe. Cole, K. C.   **530.01**
Hole in the wall. Pickard, T.   **821**
Holiday cookies.   **641.86**

HOLIDAY COOKING
Holiday cookies   **641.86**
Rosenstrach, J. How to celebrate everything   **641.568**
Vegan holiday cooking from Candle Cafe   **641.5**

HOLIDAY COOKING
See also Cooking

HOLIDAY DECORATIONS
Van't Hul, J. The artful year   **745.594**

HOLIDAY DECORATIONS
 See also Decoration and ornament
Holiday symbols and customs. **394.26**
Holiday, Billie, 1915-1959
  About
 Feather, L. From Satchmo to Miles **920**
 Holiday, B. Lady sings the blues **92**
HOLIDAYS
 Holiday symbols and customs **394.26**
 Rajtar, S. United States holidays and observanc-
 es **394.26**
HOLIDAYS
 See also Days; Manners and customs
HOLIDAYS -- DICTIONARIES
 Holidays, festivals, and celebrations of the world
 dictionary **394.26**
Holidays, festivals, and celebrations of the world
 dictionary. **394.26**
HOLIDAYS, JEWISH *See* Jewish holidays
Holifield, E. Brooks
 Theology in America **230**
Holistic dental care. Artemis, N. **617.6**
HOLISTIC HEALTH *See* Holistic medicine
HOLISTIC HEALTH -- POPULAR WORKS
 Artemis, N. Holistic dental care **617.6**
HOLISTIC MEDICINE
 Hay, L. L. You can heal your life **158**
 Khan, J. The whole heart solution **616.1**
HOLISTIC MEDICINE
 See also Alternative medicine; Medicine
HOLISTIC MEDICINE -- UNITED STATES
 Rankin, L. The anatomy of a calling **92**
Holladay, Wilhelmina Cole
 A museum of their own **704**
Holland, James
 Battle of Britain **940.54**
 The rise of Germany 1939-1941 **940.54**
Hollander, John
 (ed) American wits **811**
 (ed) Christmas poems **821**
 A draft of light **811**
 Figurehead & other poems **811**
 (ed) Lazarus, E. Emma Lazarus **811**
Hollands, Neil
 Fellowship in a ring **809**
 Read on . . . fantasy fiction **016**
Holldobler, Bert
 The ants **595.79**
 Journey to the ants **595.79**
 The leafcutter ants **595.7**
 The superorganism **595.7**
Holler if you hear me: searching for Tupac Shakur.
 Dyson, M. E. **92**
Hollingsworth, Dennis, 1967-
    About
 Becker, J. Forcing the spring **346.73**

 Yoshino, K. Speak now **346.73**
Hollis, Edward
 The secret lives of buildings **720.9**
Hollis, Leo
 London rising **942**
Hollis, Matthew
 Now all roads lead to France **821**
HOLLYWOOD (CALIF.)
 Longworth, K. Hollywood frame by frame **791.43**
**HOLLYWOOD (LOS ANGELES, CALIF.)--HIS-
 TORY.**
 Goldman, W. Adventures in the screen trade **791.43**
Hollywood frame by frame. Longworth, K. **791.43**
Hollywood's copyright wars. Decherney, P. **346.73**
Holman, James, 1786-1857
    About
 Roberts, J. A sense of the world **92**
Holmes, Martha
 (jt. auth) Barrington, R. Life **578.4**
Holmes, Oliver Wendell, 1841-1935
    About
 Commager, H. S. The American mind **973**
 Healy, T. The great dissent **342.73**
 Menand, L. The Metaphysical Club **973.9**
 Wilson, E. Patriotic gore **810**
Holmes, Rachel
 African queen **92**
Holmes, Richard, 1945-
 The age of wonder **509**
 Falling upwards **387.7**
Holmes, Sherlock (Fictional character)
    About
 Konnikova, M. Mastermind **153.4**
**HOLMES, SHERLOCK (FICTITIOUS CHAR-
 ACTER)**
 Wagner, E. J. The science of Sherlock Holmes **363.2**
Holmstrom, Darwin
 (ed) Harley-Davidson **629.22**
The Holocaust and history. **940.53**
HOLOCAUST DENIAL
 See also Holocaust, 1939-1945
The Holocaust on trial. Guttenplan, D. D. **940.53**
Holocaust poetry. Schiff, H. **808.81**
HOLOCAUST SURVIVORS
 Angier, C. The double bond: Primo Levi, a biogra-
 phy **92**
 Goldberg, R. Motherland **940.531**
 Kirshenblatt, M. They called me Mayer July **92**
 Klemperer, V. I will bear witness **943.086**
 Kramer, C. Clara's war **92**
 Levi, P. The periodic table **92**
 Pick, H. Simon Wiesenthal **940.53**
 Scheyer, M. Asylum **940.53**
 Segev, T. Simon Wiesenthal **92**
 Wiesel, E. All rivers run to the sea **813**
 Wiesel, E. Night **92**

HOLOCAUST SURVIVORS
See also Holocaust, 1939-1945
HOLOCAUST SURVIVORS -- BIOGRAPHY
Kurtz, G. Three minutes in Poland   947.7
Richmond Mouillot, M. A fifty-year silence 940.53
Wiesel, E. And the sea is never full   813
HOLOCAUST SURVIVORS -- GRAPHIC NOVELS
Spiegelman, A. MetaMaus   940.53
HOLOCAUST SURVIVORS -- NETHERLANDS -- BIOGRAPHY
Goldberg, R. Motherland   940.531
HOLOCAUST VICTIMS
Barnouw, D. The diary of Anne Frank: the critical edition   92
Frank, A. The diary of a young girl: the definitive edition   92
Jacobson, S. Anne Frank   92
Ozick, C. Quarrel & quandary   814
Prose, F. Anne Frank   839.3
HOLOCAUST VICTIMS -- BIOGRAPHY
Grymes, J. A. Violins of hope   92
HOLOCAUST, 1933-1945
Ackerman, D. The zookeeper's wife   940.53
Barnouw, D. The diary of Anne Frank: the critical edition   92
Berenbaum, M. The world must know   940.53
Breitman, R. Official secrets   940.54
The Chronicle of the Lodz ghetto, 1941-1944 943.8
Cohen, R. The avengers   940.53
Dawidowicz, L. S. The war against the Jews, 1933-1945   940.53
Dwork, D. Holocaust: a history   940.53
Fleming, G. Hitler and the final solution   943.086
Frank, A. The diary of a young girl: the definitive edition   92
Friedlander, S. Nazi Germany and the Jews 940.53
Friedlander, S. The years of extermination 940.53
Fritzsche, P. Life and death in the Third Reich   943.086
Gies, M. Anne Frank remembered   92
Goldhagen, D. Hitler's willing executioners 940.53
Goldsmith, M. The inextinguishable symphony   940.53
Hoffman, E. After such knowledge   940.53
The Holocaust and history   940.53
Horwitz, G. J. Ghettostadt   940.53
Johnson, E. A. What we knew   943.086
Kruk, H. The last days of the Jerusalem of Lithuania   940.53
Langer, L. L. Admitting the Holocaust   940.53
Lifton, R. J. The Nazi doctors   940.53
Lipstadt, D. E. The Eichmann trial   345
Mendelsohn, D. The lost   92
Rees, L. Auschwitz: a new history   940.53
Silver, D. B. Refuge in hell   362.1

Snyder, T. D. Bloodlands   940.54
Wiesel, E. And the sea is never full   813
The World reacts to the Holocaust   940.53
Zuccotti, S. Under his very windows   940.53
HOLOCAUST, 1933-1945 *See* Holocaust, 1939-1945
HOLOCAUST, 1933-1945 -- ENCYCLOPEDIAS
Encyclopedia of Jewish life before and during the Holocaust   940.53
HOLOCAUST, 1933-1945 -- GRAPHIC NOVELS
Jacobson, S. Anne Frank   92
Spiegelman, A. MetaMaus   940.53
Spiegelman, A. Maus   940.53
HOLOCAUST, 1933-1945 -- HISTORIOGRAPHY
Clendinnen, I. Reading the Holocaust   940.53
Guttenplan, D. D. The Holocaust on trial 940.53
Langer, L. L. Admitting the Holocaust   940.53
Lipstadt, D. E. Denying the Holocaust   940.53
Lipstadt, D. E. History on trial   940.53
HOLOCAUST, 1933-1945 -- MAPS
Gilbert, M. The Routledge atlas of the Holocaust   940.53
HOLOCAUST, 1933-1945 -- PERSONAL NARRATIVES
Frankl, V. E. Man's search for meaning   92
Hackett, D. A. The Buchenwald report   940.53
Kramer, C. Clara's war   92
Langer, L. L. Art from the ashes   940.53
Levi, P. Survival in Auschwitz   940.53
Prose, F. Anne Frank   839.3
Rosenfeld, O. In the beginning was the ghetto   940.53
Smith, L. Remembering: voices of the holocaust   940.53
Wiesel, E. All rivers run to the sea   813
Wiesel, E. And the sea is never full   813
Wiesel, E. Night   92
Wiesenthal, S. The sunflower   179.7
HOLOCAUST, 1933-1945 -- POETRY
Schiff, H. Holocaust poetry   808.81
HOLOCAUST, 1933-1945, IN LITERATURE
Langer, L. L. Admitting the Holocaust   940.53
Langer, L. L. Art from the ashes   940.53
HOLOCAUST, 1939-1945
Cesarani, D. Final Solution   940.53
Eisner, P. The Pope's Last Crusade   940.53
Goldberg, R. Motherland   940.531
Grymes, J. A. Violins of hope   92
Helm, S. Ravensbruck   940.53
Joukowsky, A. Defying the Nazis   940.53
Kinney, D. The devil's diary   940.53
Kurtz, G. Three minutes in Poland   947.7
Nagorski, A. The Nazi hunters   940.53
Pivnik, S. Survivor   940.53
Snyder, T. D. Black Earth   940.53

Szegedy-Maszák, M. I kiss your hands many
times **920**
Underground in Berlin **940.531**
HOLOCAUST, 1939-1945
See also Antisemitism; Germany -- History
-- 1933-1945; Jews -- Persecutions
**HOLOCAUST, 1939-1945 -- PERSONAL NAR-
RATIVES**
Friedman, A. Rywka's Diary **940.53**
**HOLOCAUST, 1939-1945 -- PERSONAL NAR-
RATIVES**
See also Autobiographies
HOLOCAUST, 1939-1945, IN LITERATURE
Langer, L. L. Admitting the Holocaust **940.53**
Langer, L. L. Art from the ashes **940.53**
HOLOCAUST, JEWISH (1939-1945) *See* Holo-
caust, 1939-1945
HOLOCAUST, JEWISH (1939-1945) -- FRANCE
Richmond Mouillot, M. A fifty-year silence **940.53**
**HOLOCAUST, JEWISH (1939-1945) -- FRANCE
-- MARSEILLE**
Zuccotti, S. Père Marie-Benoît and Jewish res-
cue **940.53**
**HOLOCAUST, JEWISH (1939-1945) -- GER-
MANY**
Fritzsche, P. Life and death in the Third
Reich **943.086**
Goodman, S. The Orpheus Clock **940.53**
**HOLOCAUST, JEWISH (1939-1945) -- HUN-
GARY**
Szegedy-Maszák, M. I kiss your hands many
times **920**
**HOLOCAUST, JEWISH (1939-1945) -- NETH-
ERLANDS -- AMSTERDAM -- BIOGRAPHY**
Anne Frank **92**
**HOLOCAUST, JEWISH (1939-1945) -- PHILOS-
OPHY**
Kinney, D. The devil's diary **940.53**
HOLOCAUST, JEWISH (1939-1945) -- POLAND
Kurtz, G. Three minutes in Poland **947.7**
Mazzeo, T. J. Irena's children **940.53**
Mendelsohn, D. The lost **92**
**HOLOCAUST, JEWISH (1939-1945) -- POLAND
-- LÓDZ**
Horwitz, G. J. Ghettostadt **940.53**
Holocaust: a history. Dwork, D. **940.53**
HOLOGRAPHY
See also Laser recording; Photography
Holohan, William V
About
Lulushi, A. Donovan's Devils **940.54**
Holroyd, Michael
A book of secrets **306.874**
Holstein, Amara
(ed) Cylinder, C. The flower chef **745.92**
Holstein, Katharine

A Different Kind of Daughter **92**
HOLSTEIN-FRIESIAN CATTLE
See also Dairy cattle
Holt, Jim
Why does the world exist? **113**
Holt, Nathalia
Cured **614.5**
Rise of the Rocket Girls **629.4**
Holt, Saxon
Greenlee, J. The American meadow garden **635.9**
Holton, Woody
Abigail Adams **92**
Holtz, Allan
American newspaper comics **741.5**
Holway, Tatiana
The flower of empire **727**
HOLY DAYS *See* Religious holidays
Holy hullabaloos. Wexler, J. **342**
HOLY LAND *See* Palestine
HOLY OFFICE *See* Inquisition
Holy people of the world. **920.003**
HOLY ROMAN EMPIRE
Reston, J. Defenders of the faith **940.2**
HOLY SEE *See* Papacy; Popes
HOLY SPIRIT
See also God -- Christianity; Trinity
Holy war. Cliff, N. **909**
HOLY WAR (ISLAM) *See* Jihad
Holy warriors. Phillips, J. **909.07**
HOLY WEEK
Benedict XVI, P. Jesus of Nazareth. part two **232.9**
Holzer, Harold
The Civil War in 50 objects **973.7**
A just and generous nation **973.7**
(ed) Hearts touched by fire **973.7**
(ed) The Lincoln anthology **92**
Lincoln and the power of the press **973.7**
Lincoln president-elect **92**
Holzman, Jac
About
Houghton, M. Becoming Elektra **781.64**
Homans, Jennifer
Apollo's angels **792.8**
Homburg, Cornelia
Neo-impressionism and the dream of reali-
ties **709.04**
Home. **641.5**
HOME
Hooks, B. Belonging **92**
Raboteau, E. Searching for Zion **305.896**
Home. DeGeneres, E. **747**
Home. Andrews, J. **92**
HOME -- LEBANON -- HISTORY
Shadid, A. House of stone **306**
HOME -- PSYCHOLOGICAL ASPECTS
Smith, T. K. Ordinary light **92**

HOME -- RELIGIOUS ASPECTS -- CHRISTIANITY

Smith, M. The nesting place   **248.4**

HOME -- SOCIAL ASPECTS -- NEW YORK (STATE) -- NEW YORK.

Gopnik, A. Through the children's gate   **974.71**

Home and exile. Achebe, C.   **823**

HOME CARE SERVICES

Carter, R. Helping yourself help others   **649.8**

HOME CARE SERVICES

See also Medical care

Home comforts. Mendelson, C.   **640**

HOME COMPUTERS See Personal computers

HOME CONSTRUCTION See House construction

Home cooked. Fernald, A.   **641.5**

Home cooking. Colwin, L.   **641.5**

Home cooking with Jean-Georges. Ko, G.   **641.5**

Home dairy with Ashley English. English, A.   **637**

HOME DECORATION See Interior design

Home Depot, Inc.

Home improvement 1-2-3   **643**

HOME ECONOMICS

Alink, M. Little house living   **640**

Bartholomew, M. Square foot gardening high-value veggies   **635**

Bried, E. How to sew a button   **640**

Laundry   **648**

The life-changing magic of tidying up   **648**

Mendelson, C. Home comforts   **640**

The perfectly imperfect home   **747**

Senior, J. All Joy and No Fun   **306.874**

Stewart, M. Martha Stewart's Homekeeping Handbook   **640**

Walsh, P. How to organize just about everything   **640**

HOME ECONOMICS -- ACCOUNTING See Household budgets

HOME ECONOMICS -- UNITED STATES -- HISTORY -- 20TH CENTURY

Coe, A. A square meal   **641.5**

HOME EDUCATION See Correspondence schools and courses; Home schooling; Self-instruction

HOME EQUITY LOANS

See also Loans

Home ground.   **917**

HOME HEALTH CARE See Home care services

Home improvement 1-2-3. Home Depot, I.   **643**

Home is burning. Marshall, D.   **92**

Home sewn. Ellis, C.   **646.21**

HOME SHARING See Shared housing

HOME STORAGE See Storage in the home

HOME STUDY COURSES See Correspondence schools and courses; Self-instruction

Home town. Kidder, T.   **974.4**

HOME-BASED BUSINESS

Arden, L. The work-at-home sourcebook   **338.7**

Ivanko, J. D. Homemade for Sale   **664**

HOME-BASED BUSINESS

See also Business; Self-employed; Small business

HOME-BASED BUSINESSES -- MANAGEMENT -- HANDBOOKS, MANUALS, ETC

Lindsay, V. Sewing to sell   **646.2**

Homefront 911. Bannerman, S.   **362.86**

Homegrown berries. Bowling, B. L.   **634**

Homegrown harvest.   **635**

HOMELESS

Cadillac Man Land of the lost souls   **92**

Karp, B. The girl's guide to homelessness   **92**

LeMieux, R. Breakfast at Sally's   **92**

Lopez, S. The soloist   **92**

Murray, L. Breaking night   **92**

HOMELESS See Homeless persons; Homelessness

HOMELESS PEOPLE See Homeless persons

HOMELESS PERSONS

Cadillac Man Land of the lost souls   **92**

Hanson, D. Breaking through concrete   **630**

Karp, B. The girl's guide to homelessness   **92**

Kozol, J. Rachel and her children   **362.5**

LeMieux, R. Breakfast at Sally's   **92**

Lopez, S. The soloist   **92**

Murray, L. Breaking night   **92**

Padilla Peralta Undocumented   **92**

HOMELESSNESS

Moran, R. Paid for   **306.74**

HOMELESSNESS

See also Housing; Poverty; Social problems

Homemade for Sale. Ivanko, J. D.   **664**

A **homemade** life.   **92**

Homemade living [series]

English, A. Home dairy with Ashley English   **637**

HOMEMAKERS

Bryan, P. L. Midnight assassin   **364.152**

Levinson, D. J. The seasons of a woman's life **155.6**

Life stories   **920**

Mallon, T. Mrs. Paine's garage and the murder of John F. Kennedy   **364.1**

Rule, A. Too late to say goodbye   **364.152**

Ryan, T. The prize winner of Defiance, Ohio **977.1**

Schiller, L. Perfect murder, perfect town   **364.15**

Skloot, R. The immortal life of Henrietta Lacks **92**

Tye, D. Baking as biography   **92**

Ung, L. Lucky child   **92**

HOMEMAKING See Home economics

HOMEOPATHIC PHYSICIANS

Larson, E. Thunderstruck   **364.152**

HOMEOPATHY

See also Alternative medicine; Pharmacy

The **homeowner's** complete tree & shrub handbook. O'Sullivan, P.   **635.9**

The **homeowner's** guide to managing a renovation. Solakian, S. E.   **643**

Homer

About

Alexander, C. The war that killed Achilles   **883**

Manguel, A. Homer's The Iliad and The Odyssey   **883**

Nicolson, A. Why Homer matters   **883**

Homer's odyssey. Cooper, G.   **636.8**

Homer's The Iliad and The Odyssey. Manguel, A.   **883**

Homer, Winslow, 1836-1910

About

Cikovsky, N. Winslow Homer   **759.13**

HOMES *See* Houses

HOMES (INSTITUTIONS) *See* Charities; Institutional care; Orphanages

HOMEWORK

Jackson, R. The learning habit   **371.3**

HOMICIDE

Bowden, C. Murder city   **364.152**

Braude, J. The honored dead   **364.152**

Brown, E. Shake the devil off   **364.152**

Bugliosi, V. Helter skelter   **364.1**

Burke, T. M. The Paradiso files   **364.152**

Capote, T. In cold blood   **364.1**

Chaudry, R. Adnan's Story   **364.152**

Collins, P. The murder of the century   **364.152**

Douglas, J. E. The cases that haunt us   **364.1**

Flanders, J. The invention of murder   **364.152**

James, B. Popular crime   **364.1**

Jimenez, S. The Book of Matt   **364.1**

Kushner, D. Alligator candy   **362.88**

Larson, E. Thunderstruck   **364.152**

Leovy, J. Ghettoside   **364.152**

Matthews, J. Bringing Adam home   **364.1**

McConnell, D. American honor killings   **364.15**

McGinniss, J. Fatal vision   **364.1**

Olsen, J. I: the creation of a serial killer   **364.1**

Parry, R. L. People who eat darkness   **364.152**

Presley, J. The Phantom Killer   **364.152**

Robisheaux, T. The last witch of Langenburg **133.4**

Rule, A. --and never let her go   **364.1**

Rule, A. Too late to say goodbye   **364.152**

Safran, J. God'll Cut You Down   **364.152**

Schechter, H. Psycho USA   **364.152**

Schiller, L. Perfect murder, perfect town   **364.15**

Starr, D. The killer of little shepherds   **364.152**

Stashower, D. The beautiful cigar girl   **364.152**

Stewart, J. B. Blind eye   **364.1**

Summerscale, K. The suspicions of Mr. Whicher   **364.152**

Toobin, J. The run of his life   **345.73**

The Ultimate Jack the Ripper companion   **364.15**

Wilber, D. Q. A good month for murder   **363.25**

Worrall, S. The poet and the murderer   **364.15**

Zacharias, K. S. A silence of mockingbirds **364.152**

HOMICIDE

See also Crime; Criminal law; Offenses against the person

HOMICIDE -- GRAPHIC NOVELS

Geary, R. The Lindbergh child   **364.1**

HOMICIDE TRIALS *See* Trials (Homicide)

HOMICIDES -- WASHINGTON METROPOLITAN AREA

Wilber, D. Q. A good month for murder   **363.25**

HOMINIDS *See* Human origins

HOMINIDS, FOSSIL *See* Fossil hominids

Homo mysterious. Barash, D. P.   **303.4**

HOMO SAPIENS *See* Human beings

HOMOSEXUAL MARRIAGE *See* Same-sex marriage

HOMOSEXUAL PARENTS *See* Gay parents

HOMOSEXUALITY

Bagemihl, B. Biological exuberance   **591.56**

Garner, A. Families like mine   **306.8**

Kugle, S. S. Living out Islam   **297**

Robb, G. Strangers: homosexual love in the nineteenth century   **306.76**

HOMOSEXUALITY

See also Sex

HOMOSEXUALITY -- HISTORY

Blank, H. Straight   **306.76**

Parkinson, R. B. A little gay history   **306.76**

HOMOSEXUALITY -- LAW AND LEGISLATION -- TEXAS

Carpenter, D. Flagrant conduct   **342.73**

HOMOSEXUALITY -- POLITICAL ASPECTS -- UNITED STATES -- HISTORY -- 21ST CENTURY

Nicholson, A. Fighting to serve   **355**

HOMOSEXUALITY -- RELIGIOUS ASPECTS -- CHRISTIANITY

Chu, J. Does Jesus Really Love Me?   **261.8**

HOMOSEXUALITY -- RELIGIOUS ASPECTS -- ISLAM

Kugle, S. S. Living out Islam   **297**

HOMOSEXUALITY -- UNITED STATES -- HISTORY

Bram, C. Eminent outlaws   **810.9**

HOMOSEXUALITY AND EDUCATION -- UNITED STATES

Cahill, S. LGBT youth in America's schools **371.82**

HOMOSEXUALITY IN LITERATURE

Bosman, E. Gay, lesbian, bisexual, and transgendered literature   **016**

HOMOSEXUALITY IN MOTION PICTURES

Mann, W. J. Behind the screen   **791.43**

Schiavi, M. Celluloid activist   **92**

HOMOSEXUALS, FEMALE *See* Lesbians

HOMOSEXUALS, MALE *See* Gay men

Honan, Park

Christopher Marlowe **92**

Honderich, Ted

(ed) The Oxford companion to philosophy **103**

Hone, David

The Tyrannosaur Chronicles **567.91**

Honemann, Daniel H.

(jt. auth) Robert, H. M. Robert's rules of order newly revised **060.4**

(jt. auth) Robert, H. M. Robert's rules of order, newly revised, in brief **060.4**

HONEST TEA (FIRM) -- HISTORY -- COMIC BOOKS, STRIPS, ETC

Nalebuff, B. Mission in a bottle **338.7**

The **honest** truth about dishonesty. Ariely, D. **177**

HONESTY

Ariely, D. The honest truth about dishonesty **177**

HONESTY

See also Ethics; Human behavior

HONEY

See also Food

Honey & Co the Baking Book. Srulovich, I. **641**

Honey & Co. **641.595**

HONEY PLANTS

Frey, K. The bee-friendly garden **595.799**

HONEYBEE

The bee book **595.799**

Ellis, H. Sweetness & light **595.7**

Flottum, K. The backyard beekeeper **638.1**

Jacobsen, R. Fruitless fall **638**

HONEYBEE -- BEHAVIOR

Seeley, T. D. Honeybee democracy **595.799**

HONEYBEE CULTURE *See* Beekeeping

Honeybee democracy. Seeley, T. D. **595.799**

Honeymoon in Tehran. Moaveni, A. **92**

Hong, Cathy Park, 1976-

Engine empire **811**

Honig, Megan

Urban grit **016**

Honigstein, Raphael

Das Reboot **796.334**

HONOR

Nordland, R. The Lovers **958.104**

HONOR

See also Conduct of life

Honor in the dust. Jones, G. **959.9**

An **honorable** defeat. Davis, W. C. **973.7**

The **honored** dead. Braude, J. **364.152**

HONOUR *See* Honor

Hood, Bruce

The self illusion **155.2**

Hooded Americanism: the history of the Ku Klux Klan. Chalmers, D. M. **322.4**

Hooke, Robert, 1635-1703

About

Hollis, L. London rising **942**

Hooked on horror III. Fonseca, A. J. **016**

HOOKED RUGS

See also Handicraft; Rugs and carpets

Hooker, Joseph Dalton, 1817-1911

About

McCalman, I. Darwin's armada **576.8**

Hooker, Joseph, 1814-1879

About

Sears, S. W. Chancellorsville **973.7**

Hooks, Bell

Belonging **92**

Remembered rapture **808**

Wounds of passion **92**

Hoop roots. Wideman, J. E. **813**

Hooper, Brad

Read on....historical fiction **016**

The short story readers' advisory **028**

Hooper, John

The Italians **945.093**

Hoopla. Prain, L. **746.44**

Hoops. Jackson, M. **811**

Hoosh. Anthony, J. C. **394.1**

HOOVER DAM (ARIZ. AND NEV.)

Denton, S. The Profiteers **338.7**

Hiltzik, M. A. Colossus **627**

Hoover, Herbert, 1874-1964

About

Hofstadter, R. The American political tradition, and the men who made it **973**

Rappleye, C. Herbert Hoover in the White House **92**

Hoover, J. Edgar (John Edgar), 1895-1972

About

Geary, R. J. Edgar Hoover **363.2**

Gentry, C. J. Edgar Hoover **353**

Reavill, G. Mafia summit **364.106**

Weiner, T. Enemies **363.25**

Hoover, Paul

(ed) Postmodern American poetry **811**

Hope. Zoglin, R. **92**

HOPE

See also Emotions; Spiritual life; Virtue

HOPE

Fisher, R. G. Choosing hope **371.7**

Groopman, J. E. The anatomy of hope **616**

Lamott, A. Small victories **248**

Wright, N. T. Surprised by hope **236**

Hope. Reynolds, B. **796.323**

Hope against hope. Mandelstam, N. **891.71**

Hope in a jar. Peiss, K. L. **391.6**

Hope in hell. Bortolotti, D. **610**

Hope, Bob, 1903-2003

About

Quirk, L. J. Bob Hope: the road well-traveled **92**

Zoglin, R. Hope **92**

Hopelain, Allison

(jt. auth) Moore, R. This is Camino **641.5**

Hopkins, Edward J.

Buckley, B. Weather: a visual guide **551.5**

Hopkins, Gerard Manley
Poems and prose **821**

Hopkins, Harry L. (Harry Lloyd), 1890-1946
About
Fullilove, M. Rendezvous with destiny **973.917**

Hopkins, Jerry
No one here gets out alive **92**

Hopkins, Lightnin', 1912-1982
About
Govenar, A. B. Lightnin' Hopkins **92**

Hopler, Jay
The Abridged History of Rainfall **811.6**

Hopp, Steven L.
Animal, vegetable, miracle **641**

Hopper, Grace, 1906-1992
About
Beyer, K. W. Grace Hopper and the invention of the information age **92**

Hopwood, Shon
About
Burke, D. Law man **92**

Horace
The epistles of Horace **871**
The odes of Horace **874**

Horbury, William
(ed) The Cambridge history of Judaism **296.09**

Horenstein, Henry
Digital photography **770**

Horgan, David
(jt. auth) Block, S. When Your Parent Moves in **306.874**

HORMEL FOODS CORPORATION
Genoways, T. The chain **338.7**

Horn, James P. P.
A land as God made it **975.5**
Horn, J. A kingdom strange **975.6**

Horn, Jonathan
The Man Who Would Not Be Washington **92**

Hornbacher, Marya
Wasted: a memoir of anorexia and bulimia **616.85**

Hornblower, Simon
(ed) The Oxford classical dictionary **938**

Horne, Alistair
La belle France **944**
Seven ages of Paris **944**

Horne, Jed
Breach of faith **976.3**

Horne, Jennifer, 1960-
(ed) Circling faith **200.8**

Horne, Lena
About
Gavin, J. Stormy weather **92**

Horne, Richard
3d printing for dummies **621.9**

Horner, John R.

How to build a dinosaur **567.9**

Hornet's sting. Ryan, M. **92**

Hornfischer, James D.
Service **956.704**
Ship of ghosts **940.54**

HOROLOGY *See* Clocks and watches; Sundials; Time

HOROSCOPES
See also Astrology

Horovitz, David Phillip
A little too close to God **956.940**
(ed) Shalom, friend: the life and legacy of Yitzhak Rabin **92**

Horowitz, Alexandra
Inside of a dog **636.7**

Horowitz, Joseph
Classical music in America **781.6**

Horowitz, Paul
The art of electronics **621.381**

Horowitz, Richard I.
Why can't I get better? **616.9**

HORROR
See also Emotions; Fear

HORROR FICTION
See also Fiction

HORROR FICTION -- BIBLIOGRAPHY
Fonseca, A. J. Hooked on horror III **016**

HORROR FICTION -- HISTORY AND CRITICISM
Horror: another 100 best books **823**
Spratford, B. S. The horror readers' advisory **025.5**

HORROR FILMS
Fonseca, A. J. Hooked on horror III **016**
The **horror** readers' advisory. Spratford, B. S. **025.5**

HORROR TALES -- BIBLIOGRAPHY.
Pulliam, J. M. Read on . . . horror fiction **025**

HORROR TELEVISION PROGRAMS
See also Television programs
Horror: another 100 best books. **823**

HORS D'OEUVRES *See* Appetizers
The **horse.** Williams, W. **636.1**
Horse latitudes. Muldoon, P. **821**
Horse of a different color. Squires, J. D. **798.4**

HORSE RACING
Ainslie, T. Ainslie's complete guide to thoroughbred racing **798.401**
Drape, J. American Pharoah **798.4**
Eisenberg, J. The great match race **798.4**
Hillenbrand, L. Seabiscuit **798.4**
Mitchell, E. Three strides before the wire **798.4**
Nack, W. Secretariat **798.4**
Ours, D. Man o' War **798.4**
Squires, J. D. Horse of a different color **798.4**

HORSE RACING -- UNITED STATES -- HISTORY
McGraw, E. Here Comes Exterminator! **798.4**

HORSE TRAINERS
Trzebinski, E. The lives of Beryl Markham **629.13**
HORSEMANSHIP
Hill, C. How to think like a horse **636.1**
HORSES
Hutton, R. Sgt. Reckless **951.904**
Letts, E. The eighty-dollar champion **798.2**
Letts, E. The perfect horse **940.54**
Richards, S. Chosen by a horse **636.1**
Storey's horse-lover's encyclopedia **636.1**
Williams, W. The horse **636.1**
HORSES
See also Mammals
HORSES -- BEHAVIOR
Hill, C. How to think like a horse **636.1**
HORSES -- DISEASES
See also Animals -- Diseases
HORSES -- EVOLUTION
Williams, W. The horse **636.1**
HORSES -- HISTORY
Williams, W. The horse **636.1**
Horses where the answers should have been.
Twichell, C. **811**
Horseshoe crabs and velvet worms. Fortey, R. **595**
Horstman, Mark
The effective manager **658**
HORTICULTURE
See also Agriculture; Plants
**HORTICULTURE -- WASHINGTON (D.C.) --
HISTORY**
McDowell, M. All the presidents' gardens **635.09**
HORTICULTURISTS
Rose, S. For all the tea in China **382**
Smith, J. S. The garden of invention **92**
Wulf, A. The brother gardeners **635**
Horton, James Oliver
Slavery and the making of America **326**
Horton, Lois E.
Horton, J. O. Slavery and the making of America **326**
Horwitz, Debra
(ed) Decoding Your Dog **636.7**
Horwitz, Gordon J.
Ghettostadt **940.53**
Horwitz, Joshua
War of the Whales **333.95**
Horwitz, Tony
Baghdad without a map, and other misadventures in Arabia **915**
Confederates in the attic **973.7**
Midnight rising **92**
A voyage long and strange **970.01**
HOSIERY
See also Clothing and dress; Textile industry
Hosking, Geoffrey A.
Russia and the Russians **947**

Russia: people and empire, 1552-1917 **947**
Hoskins, Patricia
One-yard wonders **646.2**
(jt. auth) Yaker, R. Little one-yard wonders **646.2**
Hoskyns, Barney
Lowside of the road **92**
HOSPICES
Gawande, A. Being mortal **362.17**
HOSPICES
See also Hospitals; Social medicine; Terminal care
HOSPITAL ADMINISTRATORS
Traister, R. Big girls don't cry **324**
**HOSPITAL CARE -- CALIFORNIA -- SAN
FRANCISCO -- ANECDOTES**
Sweet, V. God's hotel **610.92**
**HOSPITAL CARE -- NEW YORK (STATE) --
NEW YORK -- CASE STUDIES**
Manheimer, E. Twelve patients **362.11**
HOSPITALIZATION INSURANCE
See also Health insurance
HOSPITALS
Fink, S. Five days at Memorial **362.11**
Manheimer, E. Twelve patients **362.11**
Sweet, V. God's hotel **610.92**
Hossack, Margaret, 1843-1916
About
Bryan, P. L. Midnight assassin **364.152**
HOSTAGE ESCAPES *See* Escapes
HOSTAGE NEGOTIATION
See also Hostages; Negotiation
The **Hostage's** Daughter. Anderson, S. **92**
HOSTAGES
Anderson, S. The Hostage's Daughter **92**
Corbett, S. A house in the sky **92**
David, S. Operation Thunderbolt **967.61**
Garcia Marquez, G. News of a kidnapping **364.15**
HOSTAGES
See also Terrorism
HOSTAGES -- SOMALIA -- BIOGRAPHY
Corbett, S. A house in the sky **92**
Hostetler, John A.
Amish society **289.7**
Hostetter, David
(ed) Congress investigates **328**
Hot. Hertsgaard, M. **304.2**
The **Hot** Bread Kitchen cookbook. Rodriguez, J. W. **641.59**
The **hot** chicken cookbook. Davis, T. C. **641.7**
**HOT DOG STANDS -- NEW YORK (STATE) --
HISTORY**
Handwerker, L. Famous Nathan **92**
HOT DOGS
Handwerker, L. Famous Nathan **92**
Hot knots. Hartmann, K. **746.42**
The **hot** topic. Walker, G. **363.7**

The **hot** zone. Preston, R.   **614.5**

Hot, flat, and crowded. Friedman, T. L.   **363.7**

Hot, sour, salty, sweet. Alford, J.   **641.59**

Hotel. Sandoval-Strausz, A. K.   **917**

HOTEL EXECUTIVES
  Singer, M. Character studies   **920**
  Slater, R. No such thing as over-exposure   **92**

HOTELS AND MOTELS
  Sandoval-Strausz, A. K. Hotel   **917**

HOTELS AND MOTELS -- UNITED STATES
  Rips, N. Trying to float   **974.7**

HOTHOUSES *See* Greenhouses

HOTLINES (TELEPHONE COUNSELING)
  Ackerman, D. A slender thread   **362.28**

HOTLINES (TELEPHONE COUNSELING)
  See also Counseling; Information services; Social work

Hotta, Eri
  Japan 1941   **940.54**

Houbein, Lolo
  One Magic Square Vegetable Gardening   **635**

Houdini, Harry, 1874-1926
      About
  Jaher, D. The witch of Lime Street   **92**

Hough, Nigel
      About
  Lamb, C. House of stone   **968.91**

Hough, Richard Alexander, 1922-1999
  Captain James Cook   **92**

Hough, Susan Elizabeth
  Richter's scale   **92**

Houghton Mifflin Co.
  The American Heritage guide to contemporary usage and style   **423**
  The Concise American Heritage Spanish dictionary   **463**

Houghton Mifflin Harcourt Publishing Co.
  (comp) The American Heritage dictionary of the English language   **423**

Houghton, Mick
  Becoming Elektra   **781.64**

Hound dog. Leiber, J.   **92**

Houppert, Karen
  Chasing Gideon   **345.73**

An **hour** before daylight. Carter, J.   **92**

The **hour** of sunlight. Al Jundi, S.   **92**

Hourani, Albert Habib
  A history of the Arab peoples   **909**

HOURS OF LABOR
  See also Labor

Housden, Roger
  Saved by beauty   **955**

House. Kidder, T.   **690**

The **house** at Sugar Beach. Cooper, H.   **92**

HOUSE BUYING
  Scott, D. Dream home   **643.12**

HOUSE BUYING *See* Houses -- Buying and selling

The **House** by the Lake. Harding, T.   **943**

HOUSE CLEANING
  Ewer, C. T. Cut the Clutter   **648.5**
  Kerr, J. My boyfriend barfed in my handbag ... and other things you can't ask Martha   **648**
  The life-changing magic of tidying up   **648**
  Platt, S. What's a disorganized person to do?   **648**

HOUSE CLEANING
    See also Cleaning; Home economics; Household sanitation

HOUSE CONSTRUCTION
  The Art of natural building   **690**
  The best homes from This old house   **643**
  Complete do-it-yourself manual   **643**
  Johnston, A. What your contractor can't tell you   **690**
  Kidder, T. House   **690**

HOUSE CONSTRUCTION
    See also Building; Domestic architecture

HOUSE DECORATION *See* Interior design

HOUSE FOR ALL SINNERS AND SAINTS (DENVER, COLO.) -- BIOGRAPHY
  Bolz-Weber, N. Accidental saints   **284.1**

HOUSE FURNISHING *See* Interior design

HOUSE FURNISHINGS
  Chapman, E. A beautiful mess happy handmade home   **747**
  Crochet at home   **746.43**
  Happy home   **646.2**
  Lemieux, C. The Finer Things   **747**
  One-yard wonders   **646.2**
  Staples, H. Sew organized for the busy girl   **646.2**

House Guests, House Pests. Jones, R.   **590**

A **house** in the sky. Corbett, S.   **92**

House of hits. Bradley, A.   **781.64**

House of Lost Worlds. Conniff, R.   **069**

The **House** of Medici. Hibbert, C.   **920**

House of Medici
      About
  Hibbert, C. The House of Medici   **920**
  Parks, T. Medici money   **332.1**

House of nails. Dykstra, L.   **796.357**

House of rain. Childs, C. L.   **978.9**

House of Romanov
      About
  Faber, T. Faberge's eggs   **739.2**
  Massie, R. K. The Romanovs   **947.08**
  Remnick, D. Reporting   **814**
  Romanov riches   **891.7**

House of stone. Shadid, A.   **306**

House of stone. Lamb, C.   **968.91**

House of Tudor
      About
  Meyer, G. J. The Tudors   **942.05**

House of war. Carroll, J.   **355**
House of Windsor
      About
  Junor, P. The Firm: the troubled life of the House of
  Windsor   **941.085**
The **house** of wisdom. Al-Khalili, J.   **509**
The **House** of Wittgenstein. Waugh, A.   **920**
House on fire. Foege, W. H.   **614.5**
HOUSE PAINTERS
  Eggers, D. Zeitoun   **92**
HOUSE PAINTING
  Santos, B. Painting and wallpapering secrets from
  Brian Santos, the Wall Wizard   **698**
HOUSE PAINTING
    See also House construction
HOUSE PLANTS
  Air plants   **628.5**
  Deardorff, D. What's wrong with my house-
  plant?   **635.9**
  Heibel, T. Rooted in design   **635.9**
  Pleasant, B. The complete houseplant survival
  manual   **635.9**
  The unexpected houseplant   **635.9**
The **house** tells the story. Van Doren, A.   **728**
The **house** that George built.   **975.3**
The **house** that Trane built. Kahn, A.   **781.65**
A **house** unlocked. Lively, P.   **92**
The **house** with sixteen handmade doors.   **728**
House, Callie, 1861-1928
      About
  Berry, M. F. My face is black is true   **92**
House, Edward Mandell, 1858-1938
      About
  Neu, C. E. Colonel House   **92**
House, Karen Elliott
  On Saudi Arabia   **953.8**
House, Silas
  Something's rising   **338.2**
HOUSEBOATS
    See also Boats and boating
**HOUSEHOLD APPLIANCES -- MAINTE-
NANCE AND REPAIR -- AMATEURS' MAN-
UALS**
  New fix-it-yourself manual   **643**
HOUSEHOLD BUDGETS
  Alink, M. Little house living   **640**
  Brown, L. Good and cheap   **641.5**
  Economides, A. The moneysmart family sys-
  tem   **332.024**
HOUSEHOLD BUDGETS
    See also Cost and standard of living; Personal
  finance
HOUSEHOLD EMPLOYEES
    See also Home economics; Labor
**HOUSEHOLD EMPLOYEES -- WASHINGTON
(D.C.) -- SOCIAL LIFE AND CUSTOMS --**

ANECDOTES
  Brower, K. A. The residence   **975.3**
HOUSEHOLD EQUIPMENT AND SUPPLIES
    See also Home economics; Implements, uten-
  sils, etc.
**HOUSEHOLD EQUIPMENT AND SUPPLIES --
MAINTENANCE AND REPAIR**
  Small engines and outdoor power equipment **621.43**
HOUSEHOLD FINANCES *See* Cost and standard
  of living; Household budgets
HOUSEHOLD LINENS
  Crochet at home   **746.43**
  New complete guide to sewing   **646.2**
HOUSEHOLD MANAGEMENT *See* Home eco-
  nomics
HOUSEHOLD MOVING *See* Moving
HOUSEHOLD PESTS
  Jones, R. House Guests, House Pests   **590**
HOUSEHOLD PESTS
    See also Home economics; Household sanita-
  tion; Pests
**HOUSEHOLD PRODUCTS INDUSTRY EXEC-
UTIVES**
  Kealing, B. Tupperware, unsealed   **338.7**
HOUSEKEEPING
  Alink, M. Little house living   **640**
  The life-changing magic of tidying up   **648**
HOUSEKEEPING *See* Home economics
HOUSEKEEPING -- MISCELLANEA
  Petersik, S. Young house love   **747**
HOUSES
  Bryson, B. At home   **643**
  Diedricksen, D. Microshelters   **690**
  Harding, T. The House by the Lake   **943**
  Kidder, T. House   **690**
  Petersik, S. Lovable livable home   **645**
  Van der Meer, A. Coastal living beach house hap-
  py   **747**
  Van Doren, A. The house tells the story   **728**
  Woodford, C. Atoms Under the Floorboards   **502**
HOUSES
    See also Buildings
HOUSES -- BUYING AND SELLING
  Scott, D. Dream home   **643.12**
HOUSES -- BUYING AND SELLING
    See also Real estate business
HOUSES -- MAINTENANCE AND REPAIR
  The book of home how-to   **643**
  The complete guide to wiring   **621.319**
  Petersik, S. Young house love   **747**
  Pierce, D. The accessible home   **728.087**
  Richter, H. P. Wiring simplified   **621.319**
  Wing, C. How Your House Works   **643**
HOUSES -- REMODELING
  101 Saturday morning projects   **643**
  Carlson, J. Remodelista   **747**

The complete guide to finishing basements **643**

The complete guide to plumbing **696**

The complete guide to roofing & siding **695**

Johnston, A. What your contractor can't tell you **690**

Litchfield, M. W. Renovation **643**

Scott, D. Dream home **643.12**

Shadid, A. House of stone **306**

Susanka, S. Not so big remodeling **643.7**

HOUSES -- REMODELING

  See also House construction

HOUSES -- SAFETY MEASURES

Soles, C. The fire smart home handbook **643**

HOUSEWIVES *See* Homemakers

HOUSING

Acharya, V. V. Guaranteed to fail **332.7**

Dedman, B. Empty mansions **92**

Klinenberg, E. Going solo **306.81**

Kobliner, B. Get a financial life **332.024**

HOUSING

  See also Houses; Landlord and tenant

HOUSING -- UNITED STATES -- HISTORY

Howard, T. The mortgage wars **332.7**

HOUSING NEEDS *See* Housing

Housman, A. E. (Alfred Edward), 1859-1936

The collected poems of A. E. Housman **821**

About

Stoppard, T. The invention of love **822**

HOUSTON (CRUISER)

Hornfischer, J. D. Ship of ghosts **940.54**

HOUSTON ASTROS (BASEBALL TEAM)

Dierker, L. This ain't brain surgery **796**

HOUSTON ASTROS (BASEBALL TEAM)

  See also Baseball teams

Houston, Jane

Gibbon, P. Tribe **305.8**

Houston, Keith

The Book **002.09**

Shady characters **411**

Houston, Samuel, 1793-1863

About

Kennedy, J. F. Profiles in courage **920**

Houton, Jody

A geek in Thailand **915.9**

Houts, Peter S.

(ed) American Cancer Society complete guide to family caregiving **649.8**

Hoving, Thomas

Art for dummies **709**

Wyeth, A. Andrew Wyeth **92**

How about never--is never good for you? Mankoff, B. **92**

How bad are bananas? Berners-Lee, M. **363.7**

How bad do you want it? Fitzgerald, M. **612.044**

How can I keep from singing? Dunaway, D. K. **92**

How champions think in sports and in life. Rotella,

B. **796.01**

How children succeed. Tough, P. **372.21**

How Computers Work. White, R. **004**

How deaf children learn. Hauser, P. C. **371.91**

How doctors think. Groopman, J. E. **610**

How does it feel to be a problem? Bayoumi, M. **305.8**

How fiction works. Wood, J. **808.3**

How free can the press be? Bezanson, R. P. **342**

How good do we have to be? Kushner, H. S. **296.7**

How great leaders think. Bolman, L. G. **658.4**

How I got over. Ward-Royster, W. **920**

How I killed Pluto and why it had it coming. Brown, M. **523.4**

How it happens. Kipfer, B. A. **500**

How language works. Crystal, D. **401**

How Lincoln learned to read. Wolff, D. **920**

How many licks? Santos, A. **519.2**

How markets fail. Cassidy, J. **381**

How Music Works. Byrne, D. **781.1**

How not to be wrong. Ellenberg, J. **510**

How not to say what you mean. Holder, R. W. **427**

How old is the universe? Weintraub, D. A. **523.1**

How pleasure works. Bloom, P. **152.4**

How soccer explains the world. Foer, F. **303.482**

How the Beatles destroyed rock 'n' roll. Wald, E. **781.64**

How the body knows its mind. Beilock, S. **153.7**

How the French invented love. Yalom, M. **944**

How the hippies saved physics. Kaiser, D. **530.092**

How the Irish saved civilization. Cahill, T. **941.501**

How the mind works. Pinker, S. **153**

How the Post Office Created America. Gallagher, W. **383.49**

How the Scots invented the modern world. Herman, A. **941.1**

How the World Moves. Nabokov, P. **970.3**

How to Bake Everything. Bittman, M. **641.86**

How to bake pi. Cheng, E. **510.1**

How to be a domestic goddess. Lawson, N. **641.815**

How to be a friend to a friend who's sick. Pogrebin, L. C. **610**

How to Be a Heroine. Ellis, S. **809.3**

How to be a perfect stranger. **203**

How to be a person in the world. Havrilesky, H. **070.444**

How to be a Tudor. Goodman, R. **942.05**

How to be a woman. Moran, C. **92**

How to Be an Illustrator. **741.6**

How to be compassionate. **294.3**

How to be drawn. Hayes, T. **811**

How to be secular. Berlinerblau, J. **211**

How to be your dog's best friend. Monks of New Skete **636.7**

How to become a scandal. Kipnis, L. **306.7**

How to break up with anyone. Waxman, J. **158.2**

How to build a dinosaur. Horner, J. R. **567.9**

How to build an android. Dufty, D. F.   **629.8**

How to build chicken coops. Johnson, S.   **636.5**

How to celebrate everything. Rosenstrach, J. **641.568**

How to Clone a Mammoth. Shapiro, B.   **591.68**

How to cook a moose. Christensen, K.   **641.597**

How to cook everything. Bittman, M.   **641.5**

How to Cook Everything Fast. Bittman, M.   **641.5**

How to cook everything vegetarian. Bittman, M.   **641.5**

How to cook without a book. Anderson, P.   **641.5**

How to cool the planet. Goodell, J.   **551.6**

How to create a mind. Kurzweil, R.   **612.8**

How to create the perfect wife. Moore, W.   **823**

How to crochet.   **746.43**

How to defeat your own clone. Kurpinski, K.   **660.6**

How to draw what you see. De Reyna, R.   **741.2**

How to Eat. Lawson, N.   **641.5**

How to eataly.   **641.594**

How to file for Chapter 7 bankruptcy. Elias, S. **346.07**

How to find out anything. MacLeod, D.   **001.4**

How to fold it. O'Rourke, J.   **516**

How to Get a Green Card. Lewis, L. N.   **342**

How to grow a novel. Stein, S.   **808.3**

How to guard an art gallery and other discrete mathematical adventures. Michael, T. S.   **511**

How to have a good day. Webb, C.   **650.1**

How to help your friend with cancer. Fullbright, C. D.   **616.99**

How to live, or, A life of Montaigne in one question and twenty attempts at an answer. Bakewell, S. **92**

How to make a spaceship. Guthrie, J.   **629.47**

How to meditate. Chödrön, P.   **294.3**

How to mulch. Campbell, S.   **635**

How to organize just about everything. Walsh, P. **640**

How to play the 5-string banjo. Seeger, P.   **787.8**

How to raise a puppy you can live with. Rutherford, C.   **636.7**

How to raise a wild child. Sampson, S. D.   **508**

How to raise an adult. Lythcott-Haims, J.   **306.874**

How to read a poem. Hirsch, E.   **808.1**

How to read Islamic carpets. Denny, W. B.   **746.7**

How to read series

Denny, W. B. How to read Islamic carpets   **746.7**

How to read the Bible. Kugel, J. L.   **221**

How to Read the Solar System. North, C.   **523.2**

How to retire happy. Hinden, S.   **646.7**

How to retire happy. Hinden, S.   **646.7**

How to roast a lamb. Psilakis, M.   **641.5**

How to see. Salle, D.   **709.04**

How to sew a button. Bried, E.   **640**

How to slice an onion. Crumpacker, B.   **641.5**

How to smell a rat. Fisher, K. L.   **364.1**

How to speak money. Velshi, A.   **332.024**

How to Speak Money. Lanchester, J.   **330.1**

HOW TO START A BUSINESS *See* New business enterprises

How to Talk So Kids Will Listen and Listen So Kids Will Talk.   **649.1**

How to think about the great ideas. Adler, M. J. **080**

How to think like a horse. Hill, C.   **636.1**

How to travel practically anywhere. Stellin, S. **910.2**

How to travel with a salmon & other essays. Eco, U.   **854**

How to understand Israel in 60 days or less. Glidden, S.   **741.5**

How to watch a movie. Thomson, D.   **791.43**

How to win friends and influence people. Carnegie, D.   **158**

How to work a room. RoAne, S.   **650.1**

How to write & give a speech.   **808.5**

How to write a business plan.   **658.15**

How to write a children's book and get it published. Seuling, B.   **808.06**

How to write anything. Brown, L.   **808**

How to write killer fiction. Wheat, C.   **808.3**

How wars end. Rose, G.   **355**

How we choose to be happy. Foster, R.   **158**

How we decide. Lehrer, J.   **153.8**

How we die. Nuland, S. B.   **616.07**

How we do harm. Brawley, O. W.   **362.109**

How we do it. Martin, R.   **612.6**

How we got here. Frum, D.   **973.92**

How we invented the airplane. Wright, O.   **92**

How we learn. Carey, B.   **153.1**

How women decide. Huston, T.   **155.333**

How Your House Works. Wing, C.   **643**

How-to-do-it manuals [series]

Laguardia, C. Marketing your library's electronic resources   **025.2**

How-to-do-it manuals for librarians [series]

Gerding, S. K. Winning grants   **025.1**

Halsted, D. D. Disaster planning   **025.8**

John, L. Z. Running book discussion groups   **374**

Mitchell, A. M. Cataloging and organizing digital resources   **025.3**

Nilsen, K. Conducting the reference interview   **025.5**

Lavender, K. Book repair   **025.7**

Stanley, M. J. Managing library employees   **023**

Tucker, V. Finding the answers to legal questions   **340**

HOW-TO-STOP-SMOKING PROGRAMS *See* Smoking cessation programs

Howard Cosell. Ribowsky, M.   **92**

Howard Zinn. Duberman, M.   **92**

Howard, David

Lost rights   **973.7**

Howard, Hugh

Architecture's odd couple   **720.973**

Howard, Jason

(jt. auth) House, S. Something's rising   **338.2**

Howard, Johnette

The rivals 92

Howard, Judith A.
Zebrowski, E. Category 5 363.34

Howard, Luke, 1772-1864
About
Hamblyn, R. The invention of clouds 551.57

Howard, Michael Eliot
(ed) The Oxford history of the twentieth century 909.82

Howard, Richard
(tr) Baudelaire, C. Les fleurs du mal 841
Inner voices 811
The silent treatment 811
Without saying 811

Howard, Timothy
The mortgage wars 332.7

Howatson, M. C.
(ed) The Oxford companion to classical literature 880

Howcroft, Heidi
(jt. auth) Majerus, M. Garden Design 712

Howe, Ben Ryder
About
Howe, B. R. My Korean deli 92

Howe, Daniel Walker, 1937-
What hath God wrought 973.5

Howe, Fanny, 1940-
Second childhood 811

Howe, Gordie, 1928-2016
Mr. Hockey 92

Howe, Katherine
(ed) The Penguin Book of Witches 133.4

Howe, Sean
Marvel Comics 741.5

Howe, Susan
Souls of the Labadie tract 811
That this 811

Howell, Georgina
Gertrude Bell 92

Howes, Kelly King
Reconstruction era: almanac 973.8

Howl, and other poems. Ginsberg, A. 811

Howley, Kerry
Thrown 796.8

Hoxie, Frederick E.
This Indian country 323.1

Hoy, Brandon
(jt. auth) Parachini, C. Roberta's 641.82

Hoyer, Daniel
Mayan cuisine 641.59

Hoyle's modern encyclopedia of card games. Gibson, W. B. 795.4

Hoyle's rules of games. Hoyle, E. 795.4

Hoyle, Edmond
Hoyle's rules of games 795.4

Hoyt, Erich

Creatures of the deep 591.7

Hoyt, Mike
(ed) Reporting Iraq 070

Hrabovsky, George
The theoretical minimum 530

Hubbard, L. Ron (La Fayette Ron), 1911-1986
About
Wright, L. Going Clear 299

Hubbard, Scott
Exploring Mars 523.43

Hubbell, Sue
A book of bees 638

Hubble. Kerrod, R. 522

HUBBLE SPACE TELESCOPE
Kerrod, R. Hubble 522
Zimmerman, R. The universe in a mirror 629.43

HUBBLE SPACE TELESCOPE (SPACECRAFT) -- MAINTENANCE AND REPAIR -- HISTORY
Massimino, M. Spaceman 92

Huber, Jeffrey T.
(ed) Introduction to reference sources in the health sciences 016.6

Huber, Michael R.
Mythematics 510

Hubert, Margaret
10 Granny Squares 30 Blankets 746.43
The complete photo guide to crochet 746.43
The granny square book 746.43

Huck Finn's America. Levy, A. 813

Huck's raft. Mintz, S. 305.23

Huckelbridge, Dane
The United States of beer 641.23

HUCKLEBERRY (RESTAURANT)
Breakfast at Huckleberry 641.5

Huddleston, Rodney D.
The Cambridge grammar of the English language 425

Hudler, George W.
Magical mushrooms, mischievous molds 579.5

HUDSON RIVER (N.Y. AND N.J.) -- HISTORY
Daughan, G. C. Revolution on the Hudson 974.73

Hudson, David L.
(ed) Encyclopedia of the First Amendment 342

Hudson, Gail
(jt. auth) Goodall, J. Seeds of Hope 580

Hudson, Mark
Titian 92

Hudson, Michael
The monster 332.6

Huey, Glen D.
Shaker furniture projects

Huey, John
Walton, S. Sam Walton, made in America 92

Huffington, Arianna Stassinopoulos, 1950-
The sleep revolution 613.794

Third World America   **330.9**

Huffman, Alan
Here I Am   **770.92**

HUGGING
    See also Manners and customs; Nonverbal communication; Touch

Huggins, Kathleen
The nursing mother's companion   **649**

Hughes, Bettany
The hemlock cup   **92**

Hughes, Charles Evans, 1862-1948
       About
Simon, J. F. FDR and Chief Justice Hughes **973.917**

Hughes, Charles W.
Christ-Janer, A. American hymns old and new   **782.27**

Hughes, Holly, 1955-
(ed) Best food writing 2014   **641.3**

Hughes, Howard C.
Sensory exotica   **573.8**

Hughes, Kathryn
George Eliot   **823**

Hughes, Ken
Chasing shadows   **973.924**

Hughes, Langston, 1902-1967
Five plays   **812**
I wonder as I wander   **818**
Selected poems of Langston Hughes   **811**
       About
Marshall, P. Triangular road   **92**
Rampersad, A. The life of Langston Hughes Volume I: 1902-1941   **92**
Rampersad, A. The life of Langston Hughes Volume II: 1941-1967   **818**

Hughes, Robert
American visions   **709**
The fatal shore   **994**
Goya   **760**
Rome   **945**

Hughes, Ted, 1930-1998
Collected poems   **821**
(tr) Ovid Tales from Ovid   **873**
       About
Feinstein, E. Ted Hughes   **821**

Hughes-Hallett, Lucy
Gabriele d'Annunzio   **858**

Hughes-Wilson, John
The First World War in 100 objects   **940.3**

HUGO AWARD
    See also Literary prizes; Science fiction

Hugo, Nancy Ross
Seeing trees   **582.16**

Hugo, Richard, 1923-1982
Making certain it goes on   **811**

HUGUENOTS
    See also Christian sects; Reformation

Huling, Jim
(jt. auth) Covey, S. The 4 disciplines of execution   **658.4**

HULL HOUSE (CHICAGO, ILL.)
Addams, J. Twenty years at Hull-House   **361.7**
Knight, L. W. Jane Addams   **92**

Hull, N. E. H.
Roe v. Wade   **344**

Hull, Raymond
The Peter principle   **817**

Hulse, Michael
(ed) The 20th Century in Poetry   **808.81**

Hult, Christine A.
The Handy English grammar answer book   **428**

Hult-Lewis, Christine
Watkins, C. E. Carleton Watkins: the complete mammoth photographs   **778.9**

Hum. May, J.   **811**

Human. Gazzaniga, M. S.   **612.8**

HUMAN ANATOMY
Balaban, N. E. The handy anatomy answer book   **611**
Carter, R. The human brain book   **612.82**
Francis, G. Adventures in human being   **612**
The Human body   **612**
Roebuck, J. Anatomy 360 degrees
Shubin, N. Your inner fish   **611**
Winslow, V. L. Classic human anatomy   **743.49**

HUMAN ANATOMY
    See also Anatomy

HUMAN ANATOMY -- ATLASES
    See also Atlases

HUMAN ANATOMY IN ART *See* Artistic anatomy; Nude in art

Human anatomy made amazingly easy. Hart, C.   **743.4**

HUMAN ARTIFICIAL INSEMINATION
    See also Artificial insemination; Reproduction

HUMAN BEHAVIOR
Aiken, M. The cyber effect   **155.9**
Cannadine, D. The undivided past   **128**
Edelman, M. W. The measure of our success   **170**
Goldsmith, M. Triggers   **155.2**
Greenberger, D. Mind over mood   **616.89**
Miller, P. The smart swarm   **156**
Mlodinow, L. Subliminal   **154.2**
Montross, C. Falling into the fire   **92**
Piaget, J. The moral judgment of the child   **155.4**
Provine, R. R. Curious behavior   **152.3**
Rudder, C. Dataclysm   **155.2**
Smoller, J. The other side of normal   **591.5**
Thaler, R. H. Misbehaving   **330.01**
Viscott, D. S. Emotional resilience   **158**
Waal, F. d. Our inner ape   **156**
Wilson, E. O. The social conquest of earth **599.93**

HUMAN BEHAVIOR
   See also Character; Psychology; Social sciences
HUMAN BEINGS
Barash, D. P. Homo mysterious   **303.4**
Bloom, H. The Lucifer principle   **128**
Christian, B. The most human human   **128**
Gazzaniga, M. S. Human   **612.8**
Harari, Y. N. Sapiens   **909**
Kenneally, C. The invisible history of the human race   **616**
Marks, J. What it means to be 98[percent] chimpanzee   **599.93**
Newitz, A. Scatter, adapt, and remember   **576.8**
Olson, S. Mapping human history   **599.9**
Sarmiento, E. The last human   **569.9**
Startalk   **523.1**
Suddendorf, T. The gap   **156**
Teilhard de Chardin, P. The phenomenon of man   **113**
Watson, L. Dark nature   **111**
Wilson, E. O. The Meaning of Human Existence   **128**
Wilson, E. O. In search of nature   **113**
HUMAN BEINGS
   See also Primates
HUMAN BEINGS (THEOLOGY)
   See also Doctrinal theology
HUMAN BEINGS -- ATTITUDE AND MOVEMENT
Streb, E. Streb   **92**
HUMAN BEINGS -- EFFECT OF CLIMATE ON
Flannery, T. An explorer's notebook   **304.2**
Hertsgaard, M. Hot   **304.2**
HUMAN BEINGS -- EFFECT OF ENVIRONMENT ON
Flannery, T. An explorer's notebook   **304.2**
Wills, C. Green Equilibrium   **577**
HUMAN BEINGS -- SEXUAL BEHAVIOR *See* Sex
HUMAN BIOLOGY
Provine, R. R. Curious behavior   **152.3**
The **Human** body   **612**
HUMAN BODY
Francis, G. Adventures in human being   **612**
Herzog, A. Knit to flatter   **746.43**
Lieberman, D. The story of the human body   **612**
Provine, R. R. Curious behavior   **152.3**
Shinner, P. You feel so mortal   **814**
Shubin, N. H. The universe within   **550**
Spierenburg, P. Violence and punishment   **364.67**
HUMAN BODY
   See also Human beings; Self
HUMAN BODY -- FOLKLORE
Shinner, P. You feel so mortal   **814**
HUMAN BODY -- POETRY

Powell, D. A. Useless landscape   **811**
Sinclair, S. Cannibal   **811.6**
The **human** brain book. Carter, R.   **612.82**
HUMAN CAPITAL
   See also Capital
Human chain. Heaney, S.   **821**
HUMAN CLONING
Kurpinski, K. How to defeat your own clone **660.6**
Wilmut, I. After Dolly   **176**
HUMAN CLONING
   See also Cloning
HUMAN CLONING -- ETHICAL ASPECTS
   See also Ethics
Human dark with sugar. Shaughnessy, B.   **811**
HUMAN ECOLOGY
Barnosky, A. D. Dodging extinction   **576.8**
Brown, C. S. A big history   **909**
De Villiers, M. The end   **363.34**
Dunn, R. The wild life of our bodies   **579**
Fagan, B. Elixir   **553.7**
Gilding, P. The great disruption   **304.2**
Gore, A. An inconvenient truth   **363.7**
Gore, A. Our choice   **363.7**
Guzman, A. T. Overheated   **363.738**
McPhee, J. The control of nature   **304.2**
Owen, D. Green metropolis   **304.2**
Roberts, C. The ocean of life   **551.46**
Safina, C. The view from Lazy Point   **508**
Williams, F. Breasts   **612.6**
Wilson, E. O. In search of nature   **113**
Wohlforth, C. The fate of nature   **304.2**
Worster, D. Shrinking the Earth   **304.2**
Zuk, M. Riddled with life   **616.07**
HUMAN ECOLOGY
   See also Sociology
HUMAN ECOLOGY -- ALASKA
Wohlforth, C. The fate of nature   **304.2**
HUMAN ENGINEERING
Norman, D. The design of everyday things   **745.2**
Human evolution. Dunbar, R.   **155.7**
HUMAN EVOLUTION
Barash, D. P. Homo mysterious   **303.4**
Eldredge, N. Why we do it   **155.3**
Johanson, D. C. From Lucy to language   **599.93**
Jolly, A. Lucy's legacy   **599.93**
Konner, M. The evolution of childhood   **305.23**
Marks, J. What it means to be 98[percent] chimpanzee   **599.93**
Martin, R. How we do it   **612.6**
Pagel, M. Wired for culture   **303.4**
Pyne, L. Seven skeletons   **569.9**
Sarmiento, E. The last human   **569.9**
Shlain, L. Sex, time, and power   **306.7**
Shubin, N. Your inner fish   **611**
Switek, B. Written in stone   **576.8**
Taylor, T. The artificial ape   **599.93**

Wade, N. Before the dawn **599.93**
Walter, C. Last ape standing **569.9**
Wrangham, R. W. Catching fire **641.3**
Zuk, M. Riddled with life **616.07**

HUMAN EVOLUTION -- PHILOSOPHY
Wilson, E. O. The social conquest of earth **599.93**

HUMAN EXPERIMENTATION -- HISTORY -- UNITED STATES
Masterson, K. M. The malaria project **616.9**

HUMAN EXPERIMENTATION IN MEDICINE
Masterson, K. M. The malaria project **616.9**
Roach, M. Stiff **611**
Skloot, R. The immortal life of Henrietta Lacks **92**
Tucker, T. The great starvation experiment **174.2**
Washington, H. A. Medical apartheid **174.2**

HUMAN EXPERIMENTATION IN MEDICINE
  See also Medical ethics; Medicine -- Research
A **human** eye. Rich, A. **814**

HUMAN FERTILITY
Martin, R. How we do it **612.6**
Weschler, T. Taking charge of your fertility **613.9**

HUMAN FERTILITY
  See also Birth rate; Fertility; Population
The **human** figure. Vanderpoel, J. H. **743.4**

HUMAN FIGURE IN ART
Bradley, B. Drawing people **743.4**
Hart, C. Human anatomy made amazingly easy **743.4**

HUMAN FIGURE IN ART *See* Artistic anatomy; Figure drawing; Figure painting; Nude in art

HUMAN FOSSILS *See* Fossil hominids

HUMAN GENETICS
Epstein, D. The sports gene **613.7**
Marks, J. What it means to be 98[percent] chimpanzee **599.93**

HUMAN GENETICS -- POPULAR WORKS
Ridley, M. Genome **599.93**
Sykes, B. DNA USA **559.9**

HUMAN GENOME
Kean, S. The violinist's thumb **572.8**

HUMAN GENOME
  See also Genetics

HUMAN GENOME PROJECT
Sulston, J. The common thread **572.8**

HUMAN GEOGRAPHY
  See also Anthropology; Ethnology; Geography; Human ecology; Immigration and emigration

HUMAN INFLUENCE ON NATURE
Barnosky, A. D. Dodging extinction **576.8**
Cousteau, J. Y. The human, the orchid, and the octopus **333.95**
Earle, S. A. The world is blue **551.46**
Fleming, J. R. Fixing the sky **551.6**
The **global** warming reader **363.738**
Goodall, J. The ten trusts **333.95**

Kolbert, E. The sixth extinction **576.8**
McKibben, B. Eaarth **253**
McPhee, J. The control of nature **304.2**
Meyer, J. L. The spirit of Yellowstone **978.7**
Montaigne, F. Fraser's penguins **577.2**
Nicholls, S. Paradise found **508**
Novacek, M. J. Terra **576.8**
Roberts, C. The unnatural history of the sea **909**
Weisman, A. The world without us **304.2**
Worster, D. Shrinking the Earth **304.2**

HUMAN INFLUENCE ON NATURE
  See also Human ecology

HUMAN INFORMATION PROCESSING
Hoffman, D. D. Visual intelligence **152.14**
Medina, J. Brain rules **153**

HUMAN LOCOMOTION
Cordoza, G. Becoming a supple leopard **613.7**
Streb, E. Streb **92**
Wilkinson, M. Restless creatures **591.47**

HUMAN LOCOMOTION
  See also Locomotion; Physiology

HUMAN MECHANICS *See* Human locomotion

HUMAN MIGRATION -- HISTORY
Kenneally, C. The invisible history of the human race **616**

HUMAN MOVEMENT *See* Human locomotion

HUMAN ORIGINS
Darwin, C. On the origin of species **576.8**
Darwin, C. The origin of species by means of natural selection, or, The preservation of favored races in the struggle for life **576.8**
Eiseley, L. C. The immense journey **576.8**
Johanson, D. C. From Lucy to language **599.93**
Johanson, D. C. Lucy: the beginnings of humankind **599.93**
Johanson, D. C. Lucy's legacy **569.9**
Leakey, R. E. The origin of humankind **599.93**
Leakey, R. E. Origins reconsidered **599.93**
Meredith, M. Born in Africa **960**
Pyne, L. Seven skeletons **569.9**
Swisher, C. C. Java Man **599.93**
Tattersall, I. The fossil trail **599.93**
Tattersall, I. Masters of the planet **599.93**
Taylor, T. The artificial ape **599.93**
Walker, A. The wisdom of the bones **599.93**
Walter, C. Last ape standing **569.9**
Wilson, E. O. The social conquest of earth **599.93**

HUMAN ORIGINS
  See also Physical anthropology

HUMAN ORIGINS -- GRAPHIC NOVELS
Keller, M. Charles Darwin's On the Origin of Species **576.8**

HUMAN PALEONTOLOGY *See* Fossil hominids

HUMAN PHYSIOLOGY
Ashcroft, F. The spark of life **612**
Francis, G. Adventures in human being **612**

Palca, J. Annoying **612.8**

HUMAN PHYSIOLOGY *See* Physiology

HUMAN POPULATION GENETICS

  Olson, S. Mapping human history **599.9**

  Roberts, D. Fatal invention **305.8**

HUMAN POPULATION GENETICS -- UNITED STATES -- POPULAR WORKS

  Sykes, B. DNA USA **559.9**

HUMAN RACE *See* Anthropology; Human beings

HUMAN REPRODUCTION

  Martin, R. How we do it **612.6**

HUMAN REPRODUCTIVE TECHNOLOGY -- POPULAR WORKS

  Potter, D. A. What to do when you can't get pregnant **618.1**

HUMAN RESOURCE MANAGEMENT *See* Personnel management

HUMAN RIGHTS

  Balakian, P. The burning Tigris **956.6**

  Dershowitz, A. M. Rights from wrongs **323**

  Ebadi, S. Until We Are Free **92**

  Schulz, W. F. In our own best interest **323**

  The unfinished revolution **305.42**

HUMAN RIGHTS -- KOREA (NORTH)

  Kim, J. Under the same sky **92**

HUMAN RIGHTS -- POETRY

  Liu, X. June fourth elegies **811**

HUMAN RIGHTS ACTIVISTS

  Baiev, K. The Oath **947.5**

  Bolkovac, K. The whistleblower **92**

  Carlin, J. Playing the enemy **968.06**

  Duke, L. Mandela, Mobutu, and me **968.06**

  Goldman, F. The art of political murder **972.81**

  In his own words **92**

  Johnson, H. M. Too late to die young **92**

  Mandela, N. Conversations with myself **92**

  Mandela, N. Long walk to freedom: the autobiography of Nelson Mandela **92**

  Mandela, N. Mandela **968.06**

  Remnick, D. Reporting **814**

  Sampson, A. Nelson Mandela **92**

  Smith, D. J. Young Mandela **92**

  Wiesel, E. All rivers run to the sea **813**

  Wiesel, E. And the sea is never full **813**

  Wiesel, E. Night **92**

  Wintle, J. Perfect hostage **92**

HUMAN RIGHTS ADVOCACY

  Ebadi, S. Until We Are Free **92**

HUMAN RIGHTS WORKERS -- SOMALIA -- BIOGRAPHY

  Abdi, H. Keeping hope alive **92**

HUMAN SETTLEMENTS

  See also Human ecology; Human geography; Population; Sociology

HUMAN SEXUALITY *See* Sex

The **human** spark. Kagan, J. **155**

The **human** superorganism. Dietert, R. **613**

HUMAN SURVIVAL SKILLS *See* Survival skills

The **human** touch. Frayn, M. **128**

HUMAN TRAFFICKING

  Faleiro, S. Beautiful thing **792.7**

HUMAN TRAFFICKING

  See also Crimes against humanity; Sex crimes

HUMAN TRAFFICKING -- UNITED STATES

  Keefe, P. R. The snakehead **364.1**

HUMAN VALUES *See* Values

HUMAN ZOOS -- UNITED STATES -- HISTORY -- 20TH CENTURY

  Newkirk, P. Spectacle **92**

The **human,** the orchid, and the octopus. Cousteau, J. Y. **333.95**

HUMAN-ANIMAL COMMUNICATION

  Hill, C. How to think like a horse **636.1**

  Link, T. Talking with dogs and cats **636.088**

  Morell, V. Animal wise **591.5**

HUMAN-ANIMAL RELATIONSHIP

  Barilla, J. My Backyard Jungle **577.5**

  Blackwell, L. The life and love of dogs **636.7**

  Boston, S. Lucky Dog **636.089**

  Bradshaw, J. Dog sense **636.7**

  Casey, S. Voices in the Ocean **599.53**

  Do unto animals **590**

  Francis, R. C. Domesticated **636**

  The good dog **636.7**

  Hill, C. How to think like a horse **636.1**

  Lawler, A. Why did the chicken cross the world? **636.5**

  Mooallem, J. Wild ones **333.95**

  Neiwert, D. Of orcas and men **599.53**

  Patchett, A. This Is the Story of a Happy Marriage **92**

  Pierce, J. Run, Spot, run **636.08**

  Rosenfelt, D. Dogtripping **636.7**

  Strycker, N. The thing with feathers **598**

  Weintraub, R. No better friend **304.2**

  Zickefoose, J. The bluebird effect **598**

HUMAN-ANIMAL RELATIONSHIPS -- ANECDOTES

  The good dog **636.7**

HUMAN-ANIMAL RELATIONSHIPS -- HISTORY

  Fagan, B. The intimate bond **591.5**

  Foster, C. Being a Beast **591.5**

  Williams, W. The horse **636.1**

HUMAN-ANIMAL RELATIONSHIPS -- MORAL AND ETHICAL ASPECTS

  Pierce, J. Run, Spot, run **636.08**

HUMAN-COMPUTER INTERACTION

  Zarkadakis, G. In Our Own Image **006.3**

HUMAN-PLANT RELATIONSHIPS

  Goodall, J. Seeds of Hope **580**

  Marder, M. The philosopher's plant **580**

Pollan, M. The botany of desire **306.4**

Weisman, A. The world without us **304.2**

HUMANE SOCIETY OF THE UNITED STATES

Kirby, D. Death at SeaWorld **599.53**

HUMANE TREATMENT OF ANIMALS *See* Animal welfare

HUMANISM

Berlinerblau, J. How to be secular **211**

Fromm, E. On being human **150.19**

Rogers, C. R. A way of being **150.19**

HUMANITARIAN INTERVENTION

Bass, G. J. Freedom's battle **341.5**

Katz, J. M. The big truck that went by **363.34**

Mortenson, G. Three cups of tea **371.82**

HUMANITARIAN INTERVENTION

See also Social action

HUMANITARIANISM

Rieff, D. A bed for the night **361.2**

HUMANITARIANISM -- HISTORY

Zunz, O. Philanthropy in America **361.7**

HUMANITARIANS *See* Philanthropists

HUMANITIES

Bawer, B. The victims' revolution **320**

HUMANITIES

See also Humanism; Learning and scholarship

HUMANITIES -- BIBLIOGRAPHY

Frolund, T. Genrefied classics **016**

Perrault, A. H. Information resources in the humanities and the arts **016**

HUMANS IN SPACE *See* Space flight

Humans of New York. Stanton, B. **974.7**

Humans of New York: stories. Stanton, B. **974.7**

Humbert, Agnès, 1894-1963

About

Humbert, A. Resistance **92**

Humboldt, Alexander von, 1769-1859

About

Wulf, A. The invention of nature **92**

Humbug. **741.5**

Hume, David, 1711-1776

About

Russell, B. A history of Western philosophy **109**

Humes, Edward

Eco Barons **363.7**

Garbology **628.4**

Humez, Jean McMahon

Harriet Tubman **92**

HUMIDITY

See also Meteorology; Weather

Humm, Daniel

I love New York **641.59**

The NoMad cookbook **641.597**

Hummingbirds. **598.7**

HUMMINGBIRDS

Hummingbirds **598.7**

Masear, T. Fastest Things on Wings **598**

Williamson, S. L. A field guide to hummingbirds of North America **598**

HUMOR *See* Wit and humor

HUMORISTS

Almond, S. Candyfreak: a journey through the chocolate underbelly of America **338.4**

Almond, S. Rock and roll will save your life **781.66**

Amis, M. Experience **92**

Baker, R. Growing up **92**

Becker, S. I had brain surgery, what's your excuse? **92**

Benfey, C. E. G. A summer of hummingbirds **920**

Bradford, R. Lucky him: the life of Kingsley Amis **92**

Buckley, C. T. Losing Mum and Pup **92**

Elledge, S. E. B. White **92**

Frazier, I. Travels in Siberia **957**

Garvey, M. Stylized **808**

Jacobs, A. J. The know-it-all **031**

Kazin, A. An American procession **810**

Leader, Z. The life of Kingsley Amis **92**

Loving, J. Mark Twain **92**

Mayle, P. Encore Provence **944.083**

McCrum, R. Wodehouse **92**

Meade, M. Dorothy Parker **92**

Morgan, J. Dr. Seuss & Mr. Geisel **92**

The Oxford companion to Mark Twain **818**

Palin, M. Halfway to Hollywood **92**

Parker, D. M. Ogden Nash **92**

Powers, R. Mark Twain **92**

Rooney, A. A. My war **940.54**

Rudnick, P. I shudder **92**

Shelden, M. Mark Twain **92**

Trillin, C. Quite enough of Calvin Trillin **817**

Trillin, C. About Alice **92**

White, E. B. Letters of E.B. White **92**

HUMORISTS

See also Wit and humor

HUMORISTS, AMERICAN -- 21ST CENTURY -- BIOGRAPHY

Lawson, J. Furiously happy **92**

HUMOROUS POETRY -- COLLECTIONS

American wits **811**

The Oxford book of comic verse **821**

Humphrey Bogart. Thomson, D. **92**

Humphreys, Andrew A. (Andrew Atkinson), 1810-1883

About

Barry, J. M. Rising tide **977**

Humphry, Derek

Final exit **179.7**

A **hundred** and one days. Seierstad, A. **956.7**

The **Hundred** Years War. Green, D. **944**

HUNDRED YEARS' WAR, 1339-1453

Green, D. The Hundred Years War **944**

HUNDRED YEARS' WAR, 1339-1453
   See also Europe -- History -- 476-1492;
   France -- History -- 1328-1589, House of
   Valois; Great Britain -- History -- 1066-1485,
   Medieval period
The **hundred-year** walk. MacKeen, D. A.   **92**
Hunefeldt, Christine
   A brief history of Peru   **985**
Hung, Hsiu-chüan, 1814-1864
       About
   Spence, J. D. God's Chinese son   **951**
HUNGARIAN REFUGEES
   Michener, J. A. The bridge at Andau   **943.9**
HUNGARIANS -- UNITED STATES -- BIOGRA-
   PHY
   Szegedy-Maszák, M. I kiss your hands many
   times   **920**
HUNGARY -- HISTORY
   The burning of the world   **92**
   Wawro, G. A mad catastrophe   **940.4**
HUNGARY -- HISTORY -- 1867-1918 -- BIOG-
   RAPHY
   The burning of the world   **92**
HUNGARY -- HISTORY -- 1956, REVOLUTION
   Von Tunzelmann, A. Blood and Sand   **973.92**
HUNGARY -- HISTORY -- 1956, REVOLUTION
   See also Revolutions
HUNGER
   Ludwig, D. Always hungry?   **613.2**
Hunger Makes Me a Modern Girl. Brownstein,
   C.   **92**
Hunger of memory. Rodriguez, R.   **92**
HUNGER STRIKES
   See also Demonstrations; Fasting; Nonvio-
   lence; Passive resistance; Resistance to gov-
   ernment
The **Hungry** Ear.   **811**
The **hungry** fan's game day cookbook. Falk,
   D.   **641.5**
Hungry girl clean & hungry. Lillien, L.   **641.302**
Hungry heart. Weiner, J.   **92**
The **hungry** ocean. Greenlaw, L.   **639.2**
Hunn, Peter
   (ed) Small engines and outdoor power equip-
   ment   **621.43**
HUNS
   Kelly, C. The end of empire   **92**
The **hunt** for KSM. McDermott, T.   **363.325**
The **Hunt** for the Golden Mole. Girling, R.   **591.68**
The **hunt** for Vulcan. Levenson, T.   **523.4**
Hunt, Patrick
   Ten discoveries that rewrote history   **930.1**
Hunt, Tim
   (ed) Jeffers, R. The selected poetry of Robinson
   Jeffers   **811**
Hunt, Tristram, 1974-

   Cities of empire   **941**
   Marx's general   **92**
Hunt, Truman Knight
       About
   Prentice, C. The lost tribe of Coney Island   **305.8**
Hunter Killer. Maurer, K.   **92**
The **hunter** killers. Hampton, D.   **959.704**
Hunter, Luke
   Wild cats of the world   **599.75**
Hunter, Michael
   Boyle   **92**
HUNTERS
   Carter, R. A. Buffalo Bill Cody   **978**
   Rinella, S. American buffalo   **599.64**
   Warren, L. S. Buffalo Bill's America   **92**
HUNTERS -- UNITED STATES -- BIOGRAPHY
   Rinella, S. Meat eater   **799.29**
HUNTING
   Beard, P. H. The end of the game   **967.6**
   The Complete Guide to Hunting, Butchering, and
   Cooking Wild Game   **799.2**
   Girling, R. The Hunt for the Golden Mole   **591.68**
   Rinella, S. Meat eater   **799.29**
HUNTING -- GREAT BRITAIN
   Gies, J. Life in a medieval castle   **940.2**
HUNTING -- HANDBOOKS, MANUALS, ETC
   Canterbury, D. The Bushcraft field guide to trap-
   ping, gathering, and cooking in the wild   **641.691**
HUNTING -- MORAL AND ETHICAL ASPECTS
   Girling, R. The Hunt for the Golden Mole   **591.68**
HUNTING -- UNITED STATES
   The complete guide to hunting, butchering, and
   cooking big game   **799.2**
Hunting Eichmann. Bascomb, N.   **943.086**
HUNTING STORIES, AMERICAN
   Rinella, S. Meat eater   **799.29**
Huntington, Cynthia
   Heavenly bodies   **811**
Huntington, Samuel P.
   The clash of civilizations and the remaking of world
   order   **909.82**
HURDLERS
   Ware, S. Letter to the world   **920.72**
Hurley, Dan
   Diabetes rising   **362.1**
Hurley, Katie
   The happy kid handbook   **649**
HURRICANE KATRINA, 2005
   Baum, D. Nine lives   **976.3**
   Brinkley, D. The great deluge   **976.3**
   Dyson, M. E. Come hell or high water   **976.3**
   Eggers, D. Zeitoun   **92**
   Horne, J. Breach of faith   **976.3**
   Remnick, D. Reporting   **814**
   Rivlin, G. Katrina   **976.3**
   Spera, K. Groove interrupted   **920**

Trethewey, N. D. Beyond Katrina   **818**
Van Heerden, I. L. The storm   **976.3**
HURRICANE KATRINA, 2005
  See also Hurricanes
HURRICANE KATRINA, 2005 -- GRAPHIC NOVELS
Neufeld, J. A.D.   **976.3**
HURRICANE KATRINA, 2005 -- PERSONAL NARRATIVES
Voices rising   **976.3**
HURRICANE KATRINA, 2005 -- SOCIAL ASPECTS
Eggers, D. Zeitoun   **92**
HURRICANE SANDY, 2012
Miles, K. Superstorm   **551.55**
Sobel, A. Storm surge   **551.55**
HURRICANES
Burns, C. The great hurricane-1938   **974.7**
Emanuel, K. A. Divine wind   **551.55**
Mooney, C. Storm world   **363.7**
Sobel, A. Storm surge   **551.55**
Zebrowski, E. Category 5   **363.34**
HURRICANES
  See also Cyclones; Storms; Winds
HURRICANES -- TEXAS -- GALVESTON -- HISTORY -- 20TH CENTURY
Roker, A. The storm of the century   **976.4**
HURRICANES -- UNITED STATES -- HISTORY -- 21ST CENTURY
Miles, K. Superstorm   **551.55**
Hurston, Zora Neale, 1891-1960
Dust tracks on a road   **92**
Folklore, memoirs, and other writings   **398**
Novels and stories   **813**
    About
Boyd, V. Wrapped in rainbows   **92**
Folklore, memoirs, and other writings   **398**
Hurston, Z. N. Dust tracks on a road   **92**
Jones, S. L. Critical companion to Zora Neale Hurston   **813**
Pierpont, C. R. Passionate minds   **810**
Wall, C. A. Women of the Harlem Renaissance   **810**
Zora Neale Hurston   **813**
Zora Neale Hurston: a life in letters   **92**
HUSBAND ABUSE
  See also Domestic violence
HUSBAND AND WIFE
Kalanithi, P. When breath becomes air   **616.99**
Husband, Janet
Sequels   **016**
Husband, Jonathan F.
Husband, J. Sequels   **016**
HUSBANDS
Silver, M. Breast cancer husband   **616.99**
HUSBANDS
  See also Family; Marriage; Married people;

Men
Hussein, King of Jordan, 1935-1999
    About
Ashton, N. King Hussein of Jordan   **92**
Hussein, Saddam
    About
Newton, M. A. Enemy of the state   **345**
The **hustle.** Merlino, D.   **796.323**
Huston, Anjelica
    About
Huston, A. Watch me   **92**
Huston, John, 1906-1987
    About
Meyers, J. John Huston   **92**
Huston, Steve
Figure drawing for artists   **743.4**
Huston, Therese
How women decide   **155.333**
Hustvedt, Siri
Living, thinking, looking   **814**
Hutchinson, Carolyn
Time-saving gardener   **635**
Hutchinson, George
In search of Nella Larsen   **92**
Hutchison, Kay Bailey
American heroines   **920**
Hutchison, William R.
Religious pluralism in America   **200**
HUTTERIAN BRETHREN
Kraybill, D. B. Concise encyclopedia of Amish, Brethren, Hutterites, and Mennonites   **289.7**
Kraybill, D. B. On the backroad to heaven   **289.7**
Hutton, Andrea
Bald Is Better With Earrings   **616.99**
Hutton, Paul Andrew
The Apache wars   **979**
Hutton, Robin
Sgt. Reckless   **951.904**
Hutton, Ronald
The triumph of the moon   **133.4**
HUTU (AFRICAN PEOPLE)
Hatzfeld, J. The antelope's strategy   **967.571**
Hatzfeld, J. Machete season   **967.571**
Huxley, Aldous
Brave new world revisited   **303.3**
The perennial philosophy   **210**
Huxley, Elspeth, 1907-1997
    About
Huxley, E. The flame trees of Thika   **828**
Huxley, Thomas Henry, 1825-1895
    About
McCalman, I. Darwin's armada   **576.8**
Huxtable, Ada Louise
Frank Lloyd Wright   **92**
On architecture   **724**
HYBRID AUTOMOBILES

See also Automobiles

HYBRIDIZATION *See* Plant breeding

Hyde, Anne F.

Empires, nations, and families **978**

Hyde, H. Montgomery (Harford Montgomery), 1907-1989

About

Blum, H. The Last Goodnight **940.54**

Hyde, Lewis

(ed) Aleixandre, V. A longing for the light **861**

Hyde, L. Common as air **346.04**

HYDRAULIC ENGINEERING

Ward, D. R. Water wars **333.91**

HYDRAULIC ENGINEERING

See also Civil engineering; Engineering; Fluid mechanics; Water power

HYDRAULIC FRACTURING

Prud'homme, A. Hydrofracking **622**

Wilber, T. Under the surface **333.8**

Zuckerman, G. The frackers **338.2**

HYDRAULIC FRACTURING

See also Hydraulic engineering

HYDRAULIC FRACTURING -- POPULAR WORKS

Prud'homme, A. Hydrofracking **622**

Hydrofracking. Prud'homme, A. **622**

HYDROFRACKING *See* Hydraulic fracturing

Hydrogen. Rigden, J. S. **546**

HYDROGEN

See also Chemical elements

HYDROGEN

Rigden, J. S. Hydrogen **546**

HYGIENE

George, R. The big necessity **363.7**

Hyland, William G.

George Gershwin **92**

Hylton, Keith N.

Laws of creation **346.04**

Hyman, Gwen

Urban Italian **641.5**

Hyman, Laurence Jackson

(ed) Let me tell you **818**

HYMNALS

See also Hymns; Songbooks

HYMNOLOGY *See* Hymns

HYMNS

Christ-Janer, A. American hymns old and new **782.27**

HYMNS

See also Church music; Liturgies; Songs; Vocal music

Hynde, Chrissie.

About

Hynde, C. Reckless **92**

Hynes, Samuel

The unsubstantial air **940.4**

Hyper. Denevi, T. **92**

HYPERACTIVE CHILDREN

See also Children with disabilities

HYPERACTIVE CHILDREN -- UNITED STATES

Schwarz, A. ADHD nation **618.92**

HYPERACTIVITY

Saul, R. ADHD does not exist **618.92**

Hyperspace. Kaku, M. **530.1**

HYPERSPACE

Nadis, S. The shape of inner space **530.1**

HYPERSPACE *See* Fourth dimension

HYPERTENSION -- DIET THERAPY -- RECIPES

Heller, M. The everyday DASH diet cookbook **613.2**

HYPNOTISTS

O'Dell, C. Miss O'Dell **92**

The Hypo. Van Sciver, N. **92**

Hysell, Shannon Graff

(ed) Recommended reference books for small and medium-sized libraries and media centers, Vol. 34 **011**

Hyslop, Stephen G.

Atlas of the Civil War **973.7**

Currie, R. The letter and the scroll **220.9**

HYSTERECTOMY

Streicher, L. F. The essential guide to hysterectomy **618.1**

I

I am a strange loop. Hofstadter, D. R. **153**

I am Brian Wilson. Wilson, B. **92**

I am Malala. Lamb, C. **92**

I Am Not a Slut. Tanenbaum, L. **305.23**

I am Nujood, age 10 and divorced. Ali, N. **92**

I am Ozzy. Osbourne, O. **92**

I am the beggar of the world. **891**

I and thou. Buber, M. **181**

I blame Dennis Hopper. Douglas, I. **792.02**

I celebrate myself. Morgan, B. **92**

I ching

The classic of changes **299.5**

I Contain Multitudes. Yong, E. **579**

I don't wish nobody to have a life like mine. Chura, D. **371.9**

I feel bad about my neck. Ephron, N. **814**

I had brain surgery, what's your excuse? Becker, S. **92**

The I hate to cook book. Bracken, P. **641.5**

I have a name. Ignatow, D. **811**

I kiss your hands many times. Szegedy-Maszák, M. **920**

I know just what you mean. Goodman, E. **158.2**

I know why the caged bird sings. Angelou, M. **92**

I like you. Sedaris, A. **793.2**

. . . i listen to the wind that obliterates my traces. Roden, S. **781.64**

I love a man in uniform. Burana, L. **92**

I love New York. Humm, D. **641.59**

I may not get there with you: the true Martin Luther King, Jr. Dyson, M. E. **323**

I must say. Short, M. **92**

I never had it made. Robinson, J. **92**

I only say this because I love you. Tannen, D. **306.87**

I see the promised land. **92**

I shall not be moved. Angelou, M. **811**

I shudder. Rudnick, P. **92**

I thought my father was God and other true tales from the National Story Project. **810**

I want to thank my brain for remembering me. Breslin, J. **92**

I will bear witness. Klemperer, V. **943.086**

I Will Find You. Connors, J. **364.15**

I wonder as I wander. Hughes, L. **818**

I'd hate myself in the morning. Lardner, R. **813**

I'll drink to that. Halbreich, B. **92**

I'll find a way or make one. Williams, J. **378**

I'll sleep when I'm dead. Zevon, C. **92**

I'll take you there. Kot, G. **92**

I'm a stranger here myself. Bryson, B. **818**

I'm fascinated by sacrifice flies. Kurkjian, T. **796.357**

I'm looking through you. Boylan, J. F. **92**

I'm not a terrorist, but I've played one on tv. Jobrani, M. **92**

I'm off then. Kerkeling, H. **914**

I'm supposed to protect you from all this. Spiegelman, N. **741.5**

I'm your man. Simmons, S. **92**

I've got a home in glory land. Smardz Frost, K. **92**

I, Tina. Turner, T. **92**

I.O.U. Lanchester, J. **330.9**

I: the creation of a serial killer. Olsen, J. **364.1**

Iacoboni, Marco
Mirroring people **573.8**

Ian, Janis, 1951-
About
Ian, J. Society's child **92**

Ibrahima, Abd al-Rahman, 1762-1829
About
Lepore, J. A is for American **306.44**

Ibsen, Henrik, 1828-1906
The complete major prose plays **839.8**
About
Bloom, H. The Western canon **809**

ICBM *See* Intercontinental ballistic missiles

Ice. Ice-T **92**

ICE
Gosnell, M. Ice **551.3**
Pollack, H. N. A world without ice **551.3**

ICE
See also Cold; Frost; Physical geography; Water

Ice. Gosnell, M. **551.3**

ICE AGE
Macdougall, J. D. Frozen earth **551.7**

ICE AGE
See also Earth

The **ice** balloon. Wilkinson, A. **910.91**

Ice blink. Cookman, S. **919**

ICE CREAM, ICES, ETC
A la mode **641.865**
Bauer, J. B. Jeni's splendid ice creams at home **641.8**
Bilderback, L. No-churn ice cream **641.86**
The perfect scoop **641.8**
Roden, N. Ice Pops!
Van Leeuwen Artisan Ice Cream **641**

ICE CREAM, ICES, ETC.
See also Desserts; Frozen foods

ICE FISHING
See also Fishing; Winter sports

ICE HOCKEY *See* Hockey

The **ice** museum. Kavenna, J. **998**

Ice-T
About
Ice-T Ice **92**

The **Iceberg.** Coutts, M. **92**

Iceberg Slim, 1918-1992
About
Gifford, J. Street poison **813**
Street poison **813**

ICEBERGS
Seaman, C. Melting away **910.91**

ICEBERGS
See also Ice; Ocean; Physical geography

ICEBERGS -- POLAR REGIONS -- PICTORIAL WORKS
Seaman, C. Melting away **910.91**

ICEBOATS
See also Boats and boating

ICED TEA -- UNITED STATES -- COMIC BOOKS, STRIPS, ETC
Nalebuff, B. Mission in a bottle **338.7**

ICELAND
Eddy, J. North **641.59**
Solnit, R. The Faraway Nearby **814**

ICELAND -- HISTORY
Johanneson, G. T. The history of Iceland **949.12**

ICELANDIC LANGUAGE
See also Language and languages; Scandinavian languages

ICELANDIC LITERATURE
See also Literature; Scandinavian literature

Iceman. Fowler, B. **937**

The **iconic** interior. Bradbury, D. **747**

Icons [series]
Beller, T. J.D. Salinger **92**

ICONS (COMPUTER GRAPHICS)
    See also Computer graphics
Ida: a sword among lions. Giddings, P.   **92**
The **idea** factory.
The **idea** factory. Gertner, J.   **384**
The **idea** of decline in Western history. Herman, A.   **909.08**
An **idea** whose time has come. Purdum, T. S. **342.73**
IDEAL STATES *See* Utopian fiction; Utopias
IDEALISM
    See also Philosophy
The **Idealist.** Peters, J.   **004.67**
Ideas. Watson, P.   **909**
Ideas in food. Kamozawa, A.   **641.5**
IDENTITY *See* Identity (Psychology); Individuality; Personality
IDENTITY (PSYCHOLOGY)
  Faludi, S. In the Darkroom   **818.603**
  James, J. The glamour of strangeness   **700.19**
  Mock, J. Redefining Realness   **306.76**
  The Poetry of Derek Walcott 1948-2013   **811**
  Wright, I. T. Darling Days   **92**
IDENTITY (PSYCHOLOGY)
    See also Personality; Psychology; Self
IDENTITY (PSYCHOLOGY) -- COMIC BOOKS, STRIPS, ETC
  Georges, N. J. Calling Dr. Laura   **92**
IDENTITY (PSYCHOLOGY) -- UNITED STATES
  Hernández, D. A cup of water under my bed **920.009**
  Smith, T. K. Ordinary light   **92**
  Solomon, A. Far from the tree   **362.4**
IDENTITY (PSYCHOLOGY) IN ART
  Nguyen, V. T. Nothing ever dies   **959.704**
IDENTITY POLITICS -- UNITED STATES
  Bawer, B. The victims' revolution   **320**
IDENTITY THEFT
    See also Offenses against the person; Theft
IDEOLOGY
    See also Philosophy; Political science; Psychology; Theory of knowledge; Thought and thinking
Idiot brain. Burnett, D.   **612.8**
IDITAROD TRAIL SLED DOG RACE, ALASKA
  Paulsen, G. Winterdance   **798.8**
If I am missing or dead. Latus, J.   **92**
If I were another. Darwish, M.   **892.7**
If it's not one thing, it's your mother. Sweeney, J.   **362.734**
If not, winter. Sappho   **884**
If the oceans were ink. Power, C.   **297**
Ifill, Sherrilyn A.
  On the courthouse lawn   **364.1**
Iggy Pop. Trynka, P.   **92**
IGLOOS
    See also Houses; Inuit

Ignatius, Adi
  (tr) Prisoner of the state   **92**
Ignatius, of Loyola, Saint, 1491-1556
    About
  Martin, J. The Jesuit guide to almost everything   **248.4**
Ignatow, David
  I have a name   **811**
  Shadowing the ground   **811**
Igniting the American Revolution.   **973.3**
Ignorance. Firestein, S.   **501**
IGNORANCE
  Firestein, S. Ignorance   **501**
Ignotofsky, Rachel
  Women in science   **509.252**
IGUANODON
    See also Dinosaurs
Ikaria. Kochilas, D.   **641.594**
IKARIA (GREECE : MUNICIPALITY)
  Kochilas, D. Ikaria   **641.594**
Ike and Dick. Frank, J.   **973.921**
Ike's bluff. Thomas, E.   **973.92**
IKEA (COMPANY)
  Bruno, I. Reinventing Ikea   **684.1**
Il viaggio di Vetri. Vetri, M.   **641.5**
Ilasco, Meg Mateo
  (ed) Congdon, L. Art, Inc.   **702**
Ilg, Frances Lillian
  Ames, L. B. Your five-year-old   **649**
  Ames, L. B. Your four-year-old   **649**
  Ames, L. B. Your one-year-old   **649**
  Ames, L. B. Your six-year-old   **649**
  Ames, L. B. Your two-year-old   **649**
  Your three-year-old   **649**
The **Iliad.** Homer   **883**
The **Iliad.**   **883**
Iliad.   **883**
ILLEGAL ALIEN CHILDREN -- GOVERNMENT POLICY -- UNITED STATES
  Truax, E. Dreamers   **325**
ILLEGAL ALIENS
  Bacon, D. Illegal people   **331.6**
  Keefe, P. R. The snakehead   **364.1**
  Perez, W. We are Americans   **371.82**
  Thorpe, H. Just like us   **305.8**
ILLEGAL ALIENS *See* Unauthorized immigrants
ILLEGAL ALIENS -- CRIMES AGAINST -- MEXICAN-AMERICAN BORDER REGION
  Urrea, L. A. The devil's highway   **325**
ILLEGAL ALIENS -- GOVERNMENT POLICY -- EUROPE
  Carr, M. Fortress Europe   **363.28**
ILLEGAL ALIENS -- MEXICO -- BIOGRAPHY
  Franklin, J. 438 days   **910.916**
Illegal people. Bacon, D.   **331.6**
ILLEGITIMACY

Holroyd, M. A book of secrets   **306.874**

The **illuminated** Kaddish. Bolsta, H. S.   **296.4**

ILLUMINATED MANUSCRIPTS *See* Illumination of books and manuscripts

ILLUMINATION *See* Lighting

ILLUMINATION OF BOOKS AND MANU-SCRIPTS

Bolsta, H. S. The illuminated Kaddish   **296.4**

ILLUMINATION OF BOOKS AND MANU-SCRIPTS

See also Art; Books; Decoration and ornament; Illustration of books; Manuscripts; Medieval art

The **illusion** of God's presence. Wathey, J. C.   **204**

ILLUSIONS *See* Hallucinations and illusions; Optical illusions

The **illustrated** art of war. Sun-tzu   **355**

The **illustrated** atlas of wildlife. Bambaradeniya, C. N. B.   **591.9**

The **illustrated** bead bible. Geary, T. F.   **745.594**

ILLUSTRATED CHILDREN'S BOOKS

Neuburger, E. K. Show me a story   **741.6**

The **illustrated** guide to cows. Lewis, C.   **636.2**

An **illustrated** history of 151 video games. Parkin, S.   **794.8**

The **illustrated** Jesus through the centuries. Pelikan, J. J.   **232.9**

The **illustrated** kitchen bible.   **641.5**

Illustrating children's books. Salisbury, M.   **741.6**

ILLUSTRATION OF BOOKS

Salisbury, M. Children's Picturebooks   **741**

Salisbury, M. Illustrating children's books   **741.6**

ILLUSTRATION OF BOOKS

See also Art; Books; Color printing; Decoration and ornament

ILLUSTRATORS

Adams, H. Tom and Jack   **92**

Becker, S. I had brain surgery, what's your excuse?   **92**

Bentley, G. E. The stranger from paradise: a biography of William Blake   **821**

Carter, A. A. The Red Rose girls   **759.13**

Ellis, R. Tuna   **333.95**

Feiffer, J. Backing into forward   **92**

Hennessey, M. H. Norman Rockwell   **759.13**

How to Be an Illustrator   **741.6**

King, R. The judgment of Paris   **759**

Lear, L. J. Beatrix Potter   **92**

Mankoff, B. How about never--is never good for you?   **92**

Michaelis, D. N.C. Wyeth   **92**

Morgan, J. Dr. Seuss & Mr. Geisel   **92**

Ross, C. The world of Edward Gorey   **700.92**

Salisbury, M. Illustrating children's books   **741.6**

Small, D. Stitches   **741.5**

Steinberg, S. Steinberg at the New Yorker   **741.5**

Tran, G. B. Vietnamerica   **741.5**

Uglow, J. S. Nature's engraver   **92**

Weidensaul, S. Return to wild America   **578**

ILLUSTRATORS

See also Artists

ILLUSTRATORS -- INTERVIEWS

Neuburger, E. K. Show me a story   **741.6**

ILLUSTRATORS -- UNITED STATES

Solomon, D. American mirror   **92**

The **illustrious** dead. Talty, S.   **940.2**

Ilse, Sherokee

The prenatal bombshell   **618.3**

The **image**. Boorstin, D. J.   **973.9**

IMAGE CONSULTANTS -- UNITED STATES -- BIOGRAPHY

Halbreich, B. I'll drink to that   **92**

IMAGE OF GOD

Winner, L. F. Wearing God   **231.7**

IMAGINARY ANIMALS *See* Mythical animals

IMAGINARY CREATURES *See* Mythical animals

IMAGINARY HISTORIES

Black, J. Other pasts, different presents, alternative futures   **900**

IMAGINARY HISTORIES (FICTION) *See* Alternative histories

IMAGINARY PLACES

Saler, M. As if   **823**

IMAGINARY PLAYMATES

See also Child psychology; Imagination; Play

IMAGINARY SOCIETIES IN LITERATURE

Saler, M. As if   **823**

IMAGINARY VOYAGES

See also Fantasy fiction; Science fiction

IMAGINATION

Gawain, S. Creative visualization   **153.3**

Linn, S. The case for make believe   **155.4**

Nafisi, A. The Republic of Imagination   **819**

Very good lives   **158**

IMAGINATION

See also Educational psychology; Intellect; Psychology

IMAGINATION -- POETRY

Raine, K. The collected poems of Kathleen Raine   **821**

Imagination in place. Berry, W.   **814**

IMAMS

Hazleton, L. After the prophet   **297**

Imbeciles. Cohen, A.   **344**

Imhoff, Kathleen R.

Library contests   **021.7**

The **imitation** of Christ. Imitation of Christ   **242**

Imitation of Christ

The imitation of Christ   **242**

The **immense** journey. Eiseley, L. C.   **576.8**

IMMIGRANTS

Nabokov, P. How the World Moves **970.3**

IMMIGRANTS
See also Minorities

IMMIGRANTS -- NEW YORK (STATE) -- NEW YORK -- HISTORY
Anbinder, T. City of Dreams **974.71**

IMMIGRANTS -- NORTH AMERICA -- HISTORY -- 17TH CENTURY
Bailyn, B. The barbarous years **973.2**

IMMIGRANTS -- UNITED STATES
Grande, R. The distance between us **92**
Kim, J. Under the same sky **92**
Min, A. The Cooked Seed **92**
Truax, E. Dreamers **325**

IMMIGRANTS -- UNITED STATES -- BIOGRAPHY
Maitland, L. Crossing the borders of time **940.53**

IMMIGRANTS -- UNITED STATES -- HISTORY
Cannato, V. J. American passage **325**

IMMIGRATION AND EMIGRATION
Bailyn, B. The barbarous years **973.2**
Pagden, A. Peoples and empires **909**

IMMIGRATION AND EMIGRATION
See also Population

IMMIGRATION LAW
See also Law

IMMIGRATION LAW -- UNITED STATES
Bray, I. M. U.S. Immigration Made Easy **342**
Miller, T. Border patrol nation **363.28**
The **immortal** Irishman. Egan, T. **92**
The **immortal** life of Henrietta Lacks. Skloot, R. **92**

IMMORTALITY
See also Eschatology; Soul; Theology

IMMORTALITY (PHILOSOPHY)
Haycock, D. B. Mortal coil **571.8**

IMMUNE SYSTEM
Blum, S. Your immune system recovery plan **616.97**
Velasquez-Manoff, M. An Epidemic of Absence **616.97**

IMMUNE SYSTEM
See also Anatomy; Physiology

IMMUNIZATION
Biss, E. On immunity **616.07**
Conis, E. Vaccine nation **614.4**

IMMUNIZATION
See also Immunity; Public health

IMMUNIZATION OF CHILDREN
Sears, R. W. The vaccine book **614.4**

Impelluso, Lucia
Gods and heroes in art **700**
Imperfect control. Viorst, J. **158.1**
An **imperfect** god. Wiencek, H. **973.4**
An **imperfect** offering. Orbinski, J. **610**
Imperial Dreams. Gallagher, T. **598.7**
Imperial grunts. Kaplan, R. D. **973.931**
Imperial life in the emerald city. Chandrasekaran, R. **956.704**

IMPERIAL TRANS-ANTARCTIC EXPEDITION (1914-1917)
Alexander, C. The Endurance **998**

IMPERIAL WOODPECKER
Gallagher, T. Imperial Dreams **598.7**

IMPERIALISM
Arendt, H. Origins of totalitarianism **321.9**
Ferguson, N. Empire: the rise and demise of the British world order and the lessons for global power **909**
Gould, E. H. Among the powers of the earth **973.3**
Halperin, D. Tinderbox **614.5**
Heilbroner, R. L. The worldly philosophers **330.1**
Karsh, E. Islamic imperialism **297**

IMPERIALISM
See also Political science

IMPERIALISM -- HISTORY
Crowley, R. Conquerors **909**
Frankopan, P. The Silk Roads **909**
Gott, R. Britain's empire **942**
Kwarteng, K. Ghosts of empire **909**
Rogan, E. The Arabs **909**

IMPERIALISM -- HISTORY -- CASE STUDIES
Hunt, T. Cities of empire **941**
The **importance** of being earnest and other plays. Wilde, O. **822**
The **Importance** of Being Little. Christakis, E. **372.21**

IMPORTS
See also International trade
The **Impossible** Exile. Prochnik, G. **92**

IMPOSTORS
Massie, R. K. The Romanovs **947.08**

IMPOSTORS AND IMPOSTURE
See also Crime; Criminals

IMPOSTORS AND IMPOSTURE -- UNITED STATES -- CASE STUDIES
Kirn, W. Blood will out **364.152**

IMPOTENCE
See also Diseases
Impresario. Maguire, J. **92**

IMPRESSIONISM (ART)
Baillio, J. Claude Monet, 1840-1926 **759**
Gerdts, W. H. American impressionism **759.13**
Homburg, C. Neo-impressionism and the dream of realities **709.04**
Kelder, D. The great book of French impressionism **759**
King, R. The judgment of Paris **759**
Roe, S. The private lives of the impressionists **759**

IMPRESSIONISM (ART)
See also Art

IMPRISONMENT *See* Prisons

IMPRISONMENT -- SOVIET UNION
Figes, O. Just send me word **365**

Improbable libraries. Johnson, A. 027

Improv handbook for modern quilters. 746.46

Improving your memory. Fogler, J. 153.1

IMPROVISED EXPLOSIVE DEVICES -- DE-TECTION -- AFGHANISTAN

Castner, B. All the ways we kill and die 958.104

An **improvised** life. Arkin, A. 92

IMPULSE RECORDS (FIRM)

Kahn, A. The house that Trane built 781.65

The **impulsive,** disorganized child. Richey, M. A. 649

In a different key. Donvan, J. 616.85

In a French kitchen. Loomis, S. H. 641.594

In a sunburned country. Bryson, B. 919

In cold blood. Capote, T. 364.1

In command of history. Reynolds, D. 940.53

In defense of food. Pollan, M. 613

In defense of nothing. Gizzi, P. 811

In Europe. Mak, G. 940.5

In Europe's shadow. Kaplan, R. D. 949.8

In excellent health. Atlas, S. W. 362.109

In Fed we trust. Wessel, D. 332.1

In focus. National Geographic Society (U.S.) 779

In Hanuman's hands. Rao, C. 92

In harmony. 704

In heaven as it is on earth. Brown, S. M. 236

In her kitchen. Galimberti, G. 641.59

In his own words. 92

In Montgomery, and other poems. Brooks, G. 811

In Montmartre. Roe, S. 809

In other worlds. Atwood, M. 809

In our image. Karnow, S. 959.9

In our own best interest. Schulz, W. F. 323

In Our Own Image. Zarkadakis, G. 006.3

In our time. Brownmiller, S. 305.42

In Patagonia. Chatwin, B. 918

In praise of science. Bais, S. 500

In pursuit of giants. Rigney, M. 597

In reckless hands. Nourse, V. F. 344

In retrospect. McNamara, R. S. 959.704

In search of King Solomon's mines. Shah, T. 963

In search of lost frogs. Moore, R. 597.8

In search of memory. Kandel, E. R. 153

In search of nature. Wilson, E. O. 113

In search of Nella Larsen. Hutchinson, G. 92

In search of our roots. Gates, H. L. 305.8

In search of Robinson Crusoe. Severin, T. 996

In search of Schrodinger's cat. Gribbin, J. R. 530.1

In search of small gods. Harrison, J. 811

In search of the perfect loaf. Fromartz, S. 641.81

In search of the promised land. Franklin, J. H. 929

In search of the Trojan War. Wood, M. 939

In search of Tiger. Callahan, T. 92

In search of time. Falk, D. 529

In search of your European roots. Baxter, A. 929

In Siberia. Thubron, C. 957

In spite of myself. Plummer, C. 92

In such good company. Burnett, C. 791.45

In the absence of sun. Lee, H. 979.4

In the balance. Tushnet, M. 347.73

In the beginning was the ghetto. Rosenfeld, O. 940.53

In the belly of the beast. Abbott, J. H. 365

In the Catskills. 974.7

In the company of soldiers. Atkinson, R. 956.7

In the crevice of time. Jacobsen, J. 811

In the dark before dawn. Merton, T. 811

In the Darkroom. Faludi, S. 818.603

In the footsteps of Marco Polo. Belliveau, D. 915

In the green kitchen. Waters, A. 641.5

In the house of the interpreter. Ngugi wa Thiong'o 823

In the kingdom of ice. Sides, H. 910.4

In the kitchen with a good appetite. Clark, M. 641.5

In the land of invented languages. Okrent, A. 499

In the name of Elijah Muhammad. Gardell, M. 297

In the pines. Notley, A. 811

In the place of justice. Rideau, W. 92

In the plex. Levy, S. 338.7

In the room of never grieve. Waldman, A. 811

In the shadow of man. Goodall, J. 599.8

In the shadow of no towers. Spiegelman, A. 973.931

In the shadow of the Oval Office. Daalder, I. H. 355

In the sweet kitchen. Daley, R. 641.8

In the valley of mist. Hardy, J. 954

In the wake of the plague. Cantor, N. F. 614.5

In the water they can't see you cry. Beard, A. 797.2

In these girls, hope is a muscle. Blais, M. 796.323

In this house. Altman, H. 811

IN VITRO FERTILIZATION *See* Fertilization in vitro

IN-SERVICE TRAINING *See* Employees -- Training

Ina May's guide to childbirth. Gaskin, I. M. 618.4

Inaba, Mitsutoshi, 1964-

Willie Dixon 92

Incarnadine. Szybist, M. 811

INCAS

Bingham, H. Lost city of the Incas 985

Heaney, C. Cradle of gold 92

Moseley, M. E. The Incas and their ancestors 985

Thomson, H. The white rock 985

The **Incas** and their ancestors. Moseley, M. E. 985

INCENDIARY WEAPONS

See also Chemical warfare

INCENTIVE (PSYCHOLOGY) *See* Motivation (Psychology)

INCEST

See also Sex crimes

INCEST -- ALASKA -- MCCARTHY

Pilgrim's wilderness 92

The **incidental** steward. Busch, A. 363.7

INCINERATION *See* Cremation; Refuse and refuse disposal

INCLUSION, SOCIAL *See* Social integration

INCLUSIVE EDUCATION
See also Exceptional children

Incognito. Eagleman, D. **153**

INCOME
Adler, M. Economics for the rest of us **330**
The economics of inequality **339.2**
Fraser, S. The age of acquiescence **973.91**

INCOME
See also Economics; Finance; Property;
Wealth

INCOME DISTRIBUTION
Capital in the twenty-first century **332**
The economics of inequality **339.2**
Milanović, B. The haves and the have-nots **339.2**

**INCOME DISTRIBUTION -- SOCIAL ASPECTS
-- UNITED STATES**
Stiglitz, J. E. The price of inequality **305.5**

INCOME DISTRIBUTION -- UNITED STATES
The divide **303.3**
The great divergence **339.2**
Reich, R. B. Saving capitalism **330.973**
Smith, H. Who stole the American dream? **973.91**

**INCOME DISTRIBUTION -- UNITED STATES
-- HISTORY**
Fraser, S. The age of acquiescence **973.91**
Rajan, R. G. Fault lines **330.9**

**INCOME DISTRIBUTION -- UNITED STATES
-- HISTORY -- 21ST CENTURY**
Garson, B. Down the up escalator **339.2**

INCOME GAP -- UNITED STATES
Shaefer, H. L. $2.00 a Day **339.4**

INCOME TAX
J.K. Lasser's your income tax **336.2**
Weltman, B. J.K. Lasser's guide for tough
times **332.024**

INCOME TAX
See also Internal revenue; Taxation

Incompleteness. Goldstein, R. **92**

An **inconvenient** truth. Gore, A. **363.7**

Increase, decrease. Durant, J. **746.43**

INCUNABULA
See also Books

INDEBTEDNESS *See* Debt

Indefensible. Feige, D. **345**

Indelible ink. Kluger, R. **686.209**

Indentured. Nocera, J. **796.04**

INDENTURED SERVANTS *See* Contract labor

INDEPENDENCE (PSYCHOLOGY) *See* Autonomy (Psychology)

Independence Lost. DuVal, K. **973.3**

INDEPENDENT FILMS
See also Motion pictures

The **indestructible** houseplant. **635.9**

INDETERMINISM *See* Free will and determinism

INDEX LIBRORUM PROHIBITORUM *See*
Books -- Censorship

Index to artistic biography. Havlice, P. P. **920.003**

India. Tharoor, S. **954.04**

India. French, P. **954.04**

INDIA -- CIVILIZATION
Collingham, E. M. Curry **394.1**
Giridharadas, A. India calling **954.05**
Sen, A. K. The argumentative Indian **954**
Tharoor, S. India **954.04**

INDIA -- CIVILIZATION -- 21ST CENTURY
Deb, S. The beautiful and the damned **954.05**

INDIA -- DESCRIPTION AND TRAVEL
Giridharadas, A. India calling **954.05**
MacLean, R. Magic bus **915**

INDIA -- FOREIGN RELATIONS -- MYANMAR
Thant Myint-U Where China meets India **959.1**

INDIA -- FOREIGN RELATIONS -- PAKISTAN
Halperin, D. Tinderbox **614.5**

INDIA -- HISTORY
Tharoor, S. India **954.04**
Walsh, J. E. A brief history of India **954**

**INDIA -- HISTORY -- 1765-1947, BRITISH OC-
CUPATION**
Karnad, R. Farthest field **940.54**

INDIA -- HISTORY -- 1947-
French, P. India **954.04**
Guha, R. India after Gandhi **954.04**
McLeod, J. The history of India **954**

INDIA -- HISTORY -- 20TH CENTURY
Guha, R. Gandhi before India **92**
Raghavan, S. India's war **940.53**

INDIA -- HISTORY -- 21ST CENTURY
Levy, A. The siege **363.325**

INDIA -- HISTORY -- PARTITION, 1947
Halperin, D. Tinderbox **614.5**

INDIA -- HISTORY -- TO 324 B.C. -- POETRY
Satyamurti, C. Mahabharata **821**

INDIA -- POLITICS AND GOVERNMENT
Chadha, Y. Gandhi **954.03**
Gandhi, M. Gandhi on non-violence **322.4**
Lelyveld, J. Great soul **92**
Mohandas Gandhi **92**
Roy, A. Walking with the comrades **954**
Wolpert, S. A. Gandhi's passion **954.03**

**INDIA -- POLITICS AND GOVERNMENT --
1919-1947**
Lelyveld, J. Great soul **92**
Mohandas Gandhi **92**

**INDIA -- POLITICS AND GOVERNMENT --
21ST CENTURY**
Deb, S. The beautiful and the damned **954.05**

INDIA -- RELIGION
Dalrymple, W. Nine lives **294**

INDIA -- SOCIAL LIFE AND CUSTOMS

Made in India **641.595**
India after Gandhi. Guha, R. **954.04**
India calling. Giridharadas, A. **954.05**
India's war. Raghavan, S. **940.53**
INDIAN ART
   Russell, K. K. Shapeshifting **704.03**
   Schobinger, J. The ancient Americans **970.01**
INDIAN ART
   See also Art
INDIAN ART -- CATALOGS
   The James T. Bialac Native American Art Collection **704.03**
INDIAN BALLERINAS -- UNITED STATES -- BIOGRAPHY
   Tallchief, M. Maria Tallchief **92**
INDIAN CHIEFS
   Brown, D. A. The American West **978**
   Eckert, A. W. A sorrow in our heart: the life of Tecumseh **977**
   Gwynne, S. C. Empire of the summer moon **92**
   Kluger, R. The bitter waters of Medicine Creek **979.7**
   Mankiller, W. Mankiller: a chief and her people **92**
   McLoughlin, W. G. After the Trail of Tears **970.004**
   McMurtry, L. Crazy Horse **92**
   Philbrick, N. The last stand **973.8**
   Powers, T. The killing of Crazy Horse **92**
   Roberts, D. Once they moved like the wind **970.004**
   Taylor, A. The divided ground **974.7**
   Utley, R. M. Sitting Bull: the life and times of an American patriot **92**
   West, E. The last Indian war **973.8**
   Yenne, B. Sitting Bull **92**
INDIAN COOKING
   Iyer, R. 660 curries **641.5**
   Iyer, R. Indian cooking unfolded **641.59**
   Jaffrey, M. An invitation to Indian cooking **641.59**
   Jaffrey, M. Vegetarian India **641.595**
   Made in India **641.595**
   Makan, C. The Cardamom Trail **641.5**
INDIAN COOKING
   See also Cooking
Indian cooking unfolded. Iyer, R. **641.59**
INDIAN LEADERS
   Hendricks, S. The unquiet grave **970.004**
   Lepore, J. A is for American **306.44**
   Price, D. Love and hate in Jamestown **975.5**
   Steltenkamp, M. F. Black Elk, holy man of the Oglala **92**
INDIAN LITERATURE
   See also Literature
INDIAN OCEAN
   See also Ocean
INDIAN OCEAN EARTHQUAKE AND TSUNAMI, 2004
   Deraniyagala, S. Wave **954.93**

INDIAN OCEAN REGION -- FOREIGN RELATIONS -- UNITED STATES
   Kaplan, R. D. Monsoon **327**
INDIAN OCEAN TSUNAMI, 2004
   Deraniyagala, S. Wave **954.93**
INDIAN PAINTING
   See also Indian art; Painting
INDIAN PHILOSOPHY
   See also Philosophy
INDIAN POETRY
   Satyamurti, C. Mahabharata **821**
INDIAN SCULPTURE
   See also Indian art; Sculpture
Indian war sites. Rajtar, S. **970.004**
Indiana biography series
   Gehring, W. D. James Dean: rebel with a cause **92**
INDIANA STATE UNIVERSITY
   Davis, S. When March went mad **796.323**
INDIANA. NATIONAL GUARD -- BIOGRAPHY
   Thorpe, H. Soldier girls **956.704**
Indians in the making. Harmon, A. **970.004**
INDIANS OF NORTH AMERICA -- RELIGION
   Blum, E. J. The color of Christ **232**
   Nabokov, P. Where the lightning strikes **299.7**
INDIANS OF NORTH AMERICA -- SOCIAL LIFE AND CUSTOMS *See* Native Americans -- Social life and customs
INDIANS, TREATMENT OF -- NEW ENGLAND -- HISTORY
   Gura, P. F. The life of William Apess, Pequot **92**
INDIC ART *See* Indian art
INDIC COOKING
   Ramineni, S. Entice with spice **641.5**
INDIC COOKING *See* Indian cooking
INDIC POETRY *See* Indian poetry
The indifferent stars above. Brown, D. **92**
INDIGENOUS PEOPLES
   Before they pass away **305.8**
INDIGENOUS PEOPLES
   See also Ethnology
INDIGENOUS PEOPLES -- AMERICA *See* Native Americans
INDIGENOUS PEOPLES -- PICTORIAL WORKS
   Before they pass away **305.8**
An indigenous peoples' history of the United States. Dunbar-Ortiz, R. **970.004**
INDIGENOUS PLANTS *See* Native plants
The indispensable librarian. **025.1**
INDIVIDUAL RETIREMENT ACCOUNTS
   See also Pensions; Retirement income
INDIVIDUALISM
   See also Economics; Equality; Political science; Sociology
INDIVIDUALISM -- CHINA
   Osnos, E. Age of ambition **951.06**

INDIVIDUALITY
  Harris, J. R. No two alike   155.2
INDIVIDUALITY
  See also Consciousness; Psychology
INDIVIDUALIZED INSTRUCTION
  Siegel, L. M. The complete IEP guide   371.9
**INDIVIDUALS WITH DISABILITIES EDUCA-
  TION ACT**
  Siegel, L. M. The complete IEP guide   371.9
INDOCHINESE WAR, 1946-1954
  Logevall, F. Embers of War   959.704
  Morgan, T. Valley of death   959.704
INDOCTRINATION, FORCED *See* Brainwash-
  ing
INDONESIA
  Taylor, J. G. Indonesia: peoples and histories **959.8**
Indonesia: peoples and histories. Taylor, J. G. **959.8**
INDOOR AIR POLLUTION
  See also Air pollution
INDOOR GAMES
  Botermans, J. The book of games   794
INDOOR GAMES
  See also Games
INDOOR GARDENING
  Bender, R. W. Bountiful bonsai   635.9
  Colletti, M. Terrariums   635.9
  Deardorff, D. What's wrong with my house-
    plant?   635.9
  Heibel, T. Rooted in design   635.9
  The unexpected houseplant   635.9
INDUSTRIAL ACCIDENTS
  Puleo, S. Dark tide   363.1
**INDUSTRIAL ARTS -- HANDBOOKS, MANU-
  ALS, ETC.**
  Horne, R. 3d printing for dummies   621.9
**INDUSTRIAL DESIGN -- PSYCHOLOGICAL
  ASPECTS**
  Norman, D. The design of everyday things 745.2
INDUSTRIAL DESIGNERS
  Albrecht, D. The Work of Charles and Ray
    Eames   745.4
INDUSTRIAL MANAGEMENT
  Sarillo, N. A slice of the pie   658.02
INDUSTRIAL MANAGEMENT *See* Management
**INDUSTRIAL MANAGEMENT -- UNITED
  STATES**
  Cox, H. H. American drive   338
**INDUSTRIAL MANAGEMENT -- UNITED
  STATES -- HISTORY -- 20TH CENTURY**
  Herman, A. Freedom's forge   940.53
**INDUSTRIAL MOBILIZATION -- UNITED
  STATES -- HISTORY -- 20TH CENTURY**
  Herman, A. Freedom's forge   940.53
  Klein, M. A call to arms   940.53
INDUSTRIAL ORGANIZATION *See* Manage-
  ment

INDUSTRIAL PLANTS *See* Factories
INDUSTRIAL POLICY
  Power, Inc.   322
  Tobbell, D. A. Pills, power, and policy   338.4
INDUSTRIAL POLICY
  See also Economic policy
INDUSTRIAL POLICY -- UNITED STATES
  Liveris, A. Make it in America   330.9
INDUSTRIAL PSYCHOLOGY
  Kerpen, D. The art of people   650.1
  Webb, C. How to have a good day   650.1
INDUSTRIAL PSYCHOLOGY
  See also Applied psychology
INDUSTRIAL RELATIONS
  Goleman, D. Emotional intelligence   152.4
  Green, H. The company town   307.7
INDUSTRIAL RELATIONS
  See also Labor; Management
INDUSTRIAL RELATIONS -- UNITED STATES
  Tobbell, D. A. Pills, power, and policy   338.4
**INDUSTRIAL RELATIONS -- UNITED STATES
  -- HISTORY**
  Green, H. The company town   307.7
  Historical encyclopedia of American labor 331.8
INDUSTRIAL RESEARCH
  See also Research
INDUSTRIAL REVOLUTION
  Mann, C. C. 1493   909
INDUSTRIAL REVOLUTION
  See also Economic conditions; Industries --
  History
**INDUSTRIAL REVOLUTION -- ENCYCLOPE-
  DIAS**
  Olson, J. S. Encyclopedia of the industrial revolu-
  tion in America   973
**INDUSTRIAL REVOLUTION -- UNITED
  STATES -- HISTORY -- 19TH CENTURY**
  Leach, W. Butterfly people   595.78
INDUSTRIAL ROBOTS
  See also Automation; Industrial equipment;
  Robots
INDUSTRIAL SAFETY
  Genoways, T. The chain   338.7
**INDUSTRIAL SAFETY -- GOVERNMENT POL-
  ICY -- UNITED STATES -- CASE STUDIES**
  Brown, K. Plutopia   363.17
INDUSTRIAL TRUSTS
  See also Capital; Commerce; Economics
INDUSTRIAL WASTE
  Fagin, D. Toms River   363.72
INDUSTRIAL WORKERS OF THE WORLD
  Adler, W. M. The man who never died   92
INDUSTRIALIZATION
  See also Economic policy; Industries
**INDUSTRIALIZATION -- UNITED STATES --
  HISTORY**

Dray, P. There is power in a union **331.8**

INDUSTRIES

Goleman, D. Ecological intelligence **333.7**

INDUSTRIES

See also Economics

INDUSTRIES -- GOVERNMENT POLICY *See* Industrial policy

INDUSTRIES -- HISTORY

Hobsbawm, E. J. The age of revolution 1789-1848 **940.2**

INDUSTRIES -- ORGANIZATION, CONTROL, ETC. *See* Industrial policy

INDUSTRIES -- SOCIAL RESPONSIBILITY *See* Social responsibility of business

The **Inevitable.** **814**

The **inextinguishable** symphony. Goldsmith, M. **940.53**

Infamous scribblers. Burns, E. **071**

Infamy. Reeves, R. **940.53**

INFANT CARE *See* Infants -- Care

INFANTILE PARALYSIS *See* Poliomyelitis

INFANTS

DeSouza, L. Eat, Play, Sleep **649.122**

Gallagher, S. Experimenting with babies **306.874**

McConville, B. On Becoming a Mother **306.874**

Murkoff, H. E. What to expect the first year **649**

The pregnancy encyclopedia **618.2**

Watch my baby grow **649.122**

INFANTS

See also Children

INFANTS -- CARE

Caring for your baby and young child **618.92**

Ezzo, G. On becoming baby wise **649**

Kennedy, J. K. The good sleeper **649**

Linden, D. W. Preemies **618.92**

Murkoff, H. What to Expect the First Year **649**

Sears, W. The baby book **649**

INFANTS -- DEVELOPMENT

Sears, W. The baby book **649**

INFANTS -- DISEASES

See also Diseases

INFANTS -- EDUCATION *See* Preschool education

INFANTS -- HEALTH AND HYGIENE

Jassey, J. The newborn sleep book **618.92**

Linden, D. W. Preemies **618.92**

White, D. A. First bites **641.3**

INFANTS -- HEALTH AND HYGIENE

See also Health; Hygiene

INFANTS -- HEALTH AND HYGIENE -- CASE STUDIES

Thurow, R. The first 1,000 days **618.92**

INFANTS -- HYGIENE *See* Infants -- Health and hygiene

INFANTS -- NUTRITION

Altmann, T. R. What to feed your baby **649.3**

Porto, A. The pediatrician's guide to feeding babies and toddlers **618.92**

Thurow, R. The first 1,000 days **618.92**

White, D. A. First bites **641.3**

INFANTS -- NUTRITION

See also Nutrition

INFANTS -- NUTRITION -- CASE STUDIES

Thurow, R. The first 1,000 days **618.92**

INFANTS -- SLEEP

The happy sleeper **649**

Jassey, J. The newborn sleep book **618.92**

Karp, H. The happiest baby on the block **649**

Kennedy, J. K. The good sleeper **649**

INFANTS' CLOTHING

Crochet one-skein wonders for babies **746.434**

One-skein wonders for babies **746.43**

INFANTS' CLOTHING

See also Children's clothing; Clothing and dress; Infants' supplies

INFECTION AND INFECTIOUS DISEASES *See* Communicable diseases

Infectious madness. Washington, H. A. **616.89**

Infeld, Leopold

Einstein, A. The evolution of physics **530**

The **Inferno.** Dante Alighieri **851**

Inferno. Hastings, M. **940.54**

INFERTILITY

Boggs, B. The art of waiting **618.178**

Potter, D. A. What to do when you can't get pregnant **618.1**

INFERTILITY

See also Reproduction

INFERTILITY -- TREATMENT -- POPULAR WORKS

Potter, D. A. What to do when you can't get pregnant **618.1**

INFERTILITY, FEMALE -- DIET THERAPY

The kind mama **618.1**

Infidel. Hirsi Ali, A. **92**

Infidel kings and unholy warriors. Catlos, B. A. **909.07**

INFINITE

Barrow, J. D. The infinite book **111**

Close, F. E. The infinity puzzle **530.1**

Cole, K. C. The hole in the universe **530.01**

Deutsch, D. The beginning of infinity **501**

Stillwell, J. Roads to infinity **511.3**

INFINITE

See also Mathematics

The **infinite** book. Barrow, J. D. **111**

The **infinite** gift. Yang, C. **401**

Infinitesimal. Alexander, A. **511**

INFINITY *See* Infinite

The **infinity** puzzle. Close, F. E. **530.1**

INFIRMARIES *See* Hospitals

INFLAMMATORY BOWEL DISEASES

Reiner, J. The man who couldn't eat **92**

INFLATION (FINANCE)
   See also Finance

INFLUENCE (LITERARY, ARTISTIC, ETC.)
  Bloom, H. The anatomy of influence **801**

INFLUENCE (PSYCHOLOGY)
  Berger, J. Invisible Influence **302.13**
  Karlins, M. The like switch **158.2**
Influence: the psychology of persuasion. Cialdini,
  R. B. **153.8**
The **influencing** machine. Gladstone, B. **302.23**

INFLUENZA
  Barry, J. M. The great influenza **614.5**
  Kolata, G. Flu **614.5**

INFLUENZA
   See also Communicable diseases; Diseases

INFLUENZA -- HISTORY -- 20TH CENTURY
  Kolata, G. Flu **614.5**

INFLUENZA VACCINES -- HISTORY
  Jacobs, C. D. Jonas Salk **92**
  Jonas Salk **92**
The **information.** Gleick, J. **020**

INFORMATION COMMONS
  Hyde, L. Common as air **346.04**

INFORMATION DESIGN
   See also Graphic arts
The **information** diet. Johnson, C. **303.48**

INFORMATION HIGHWAY
  Blum, A. Tubes **384.3**

INFORMATION LITERACY
  Seife, C. Virtual unreality **025.04**

INFORMATION LITERACY
   See also Literacy

INFORMATION NETWORKS
  Blum, A. Tubes **384.3**
  Johnson, S. Future perfect **303.48**

INFORMATION NETWORKS
   See also Information systems

INFORMATION ORGANIZATION
  Pariser, E. The filter bubble **025.04**
  Stross, R. Planet Google **338.7**

INFORMATION ORGANIZATION -- HISTORY
  Wright, A. Cataloging the world **020.9**

INFORMATION RESOURCES
  Cukier, K. Big data **306.46**
  MacLeod, D. How to find out anything **001.4**
  Seife, C. Virtual unreality **025.04**

INFORMATION RESOURCES
   See also Information science
Information resources in the humanities and the
  arts. Perrault, A. H. **016**

INFORMATION RETRIEVAL
   See also Documentation; Information science

INFORMATION SCIENCE
  Gleick, J. The information **020**
  Levitin, D. J. A field guide to lies **153.4**

INFORMATION SCIENCE
   See also Communication

INFORMATION SCIENCE -- DICTIONARIES
  ALA glossary of library and information science **020**

INFORMATION SCIENTISTS
  Defending professionalism **020**

INFORMATION SOCIETY
  Fuller, J. What is happening to news **070.4**
  Harris, M. The End of absence **302.23**
  Johnson, C. The information diet **303.48**
  Lessig, L. The future of ideas **004.67**
  Palfrey, J. Born digital **302.23**
  Shirky, C. Cognitive surplus **303.4**

**INFORMATION SUPERHIGHWAY -- SECURI-
TY MEASURES -- UNITED STATES**
  Mitnick, K. D. Ghost in the wires **364.16**

INFORMATION SYSTEMS
  Mitchell, A. M. Cataloging and organizing digital
  resources **025.3**
  Pariser, E. The filter bubble **025.04**

INFORMATION SYSTEMS
   See also Bibliographic control; Computers;
  Information science

INFORMATION SYSTEMS -- DIRECTORIES
  Gale directory of databases **025.04**

INFORMATION SYSTEMS -- MANAGEMENT
   See also Management

INFORMATION TECHNOLOGY
  Blum, A. Tubes **384.3**
  Bolan, K. Technology made simple **025**
  Burke, J. J. Neal-Schuman library technology
  companion **025**
  Carr, N. G. The big switch **303.4**
  Cohn, J. M. The complete library technology plan-
  ner **025**
  Core technology competencies for librarians and
  library staff **020**
  Greenfield, S. Mind change **155.9**
  Lanier, J. You are not a gadget **303.4**
  MacKellar, P. H. Writing successful technology
  grant proposals **025.1**
  Palfrey, J. Born digital **302.23**
  Siegel, D. Pull **658.8**
  Tapscott, D. Macrowikinomics **303.4**
  Turkle, S. Alone together **303.4**
  Weinberger, D. Too big to know **303.48**

INFORMATION TECHNOLOGY
   See also Technology

INFORMATION TECHNOLOGY -- HISTORY
  Wu, T. c. The master switch **384**

**INFORMATION TECHNOLOGY -- MANAGE-
MENT**
  Arora, P. To the cloud **004.67**

**INFORMATION TECHNOLOGY -- MORAL
AND ETHICAL ASPECTS**

Angwin, J. Dragnet nation   **323.44**

INFORMATION TECHNOLOGY -- PSYCHO-LOGICAL ASPECTS

Greenfield, S. Mind change   **155.9**

Thompson, C. Smarter Than You Think   **303.48**

INFORMATION TECHNOLOGY -- SOCIAL ASPECTS

Boyd, D. It's complicated   **004.67**

Harris, M. The End of absence   **302.23**

Johnson, S. Future perfect   **303.48**

Rushkoff, D. Present Shock   **303.48**

INFORMATION TECHNOLOGY EXECU-TIVES

Auletta, K. Googled   **338.7**

INFORMATION THEORY

    See also Communication

INFORMATION VISUALIZATION

Rendgen, S. Understanding the world   **741.6**

INFORMATION VISUALIZATION

    See also Information science

INFORMATION WARFARE -- UNITED STATES

Harris, S. @WAR   **355.3**

INFORMATION, FREEDOM OF *See* Freedom of information

The **informed** parent. Willingham, E.   **649.1**

INFORMERS

Carlo, P. Gaspipe   **92**

INFRARED RADIATION

    See also Electromagnetic waves; Radiation

INFRASTRUCTURE (ECONOMICS)

Fishman, C. The big thirst   **333.91**

INFRASTRUCTURE (ECONOMICS)

    See also Economic development; Public works

Ingall, Marjorie

Mamaleh knows best   **649.1**

Inge, William

4 plays   **812**

The **ingenious** Mr. Pyke. Hemming, H.   **327.12**

Ingram, Jay

The End of Memory   **616.8**

Ingrassia, Paul

Engines of change   **629.222**

Ingredienti. Hazan, M.   **641.5**

Ingrid Bergman. Thomson, D.   **92**

Inherit the wind. Lawrence, J.   **812**

The **inheritance** of Rome. Wickham, C.   **940.1**

Inheriting the Holy Land. Miller, J.   **956.94**

Inheriting the revolution. Appleby, J. O.   **973**

The **inheritor's** powder. Hempel, S.   **364.152**

INITIATION RITES

    See also Rites and ceremonies

INJUNCTIONS

    See also Constitutional law; Labor unions

INJURIES *See* Accidents; First aid; Wounds and injuries

INJURIOUS INSECTS *See* Insect pests

The **injustice** system. Smith, C. S.   **345.73**

INLAND NAVIGATION

    See also Navigation; Shipping; Transportation

INNER CITIES

Kozol, J. Amazing grace   **362.7**

The **inner** game of tennis. Gallwey, W. T.   **796.342**

INNER PEACE

Enayati, A. Seeking serenity   **155.9**

Inner voices. Howard, R.   **811**

An **Innocent** Abroad.   **910.4**

INNOVATIONS, TECHNOLOGICAL *See* Technological innovations

The **innovators.** Isaacson, W.   **004**

INNS *See* Hotels and motels

INNUIT *See* Inuit

INOCULATION *See* Vaccination

An **inordinate** fondness for beetles. Evans, A. V.   **595.7**

INORGANIC CHEMISTRY

    See also Chemistry

INQUISITION

Kamen, H. The Spanish Inquisition   **272**

Perez, J. The Spanish Inquisition   **272**

INQUISITION

    See also Catholic Church

INQUISITION -- ITALY

Hofstadter, D. The Earth moves   **509**

INSANE *See* Mentally ill

INSANITY -- JURISPRUDENCE -- UNITED STATES

Lombardo, P. A. Three generations, no imbeciles   **344**

The **insanity** offense. Torrey, E. F.   **362.1**

INSCRIPTIONS

    See also Ancient history; Archeology

INSCRIPTIONS, CUNEIFORM *See* Cuneiform inscriptions

INSECT PESTS

Schmidt, J. O. The sting of the wild   **595.7**

Stewart, A. Wicked bugs   **632**

INSECT PESTS

    See also Economic zoology; Insects; Pests

INSECTICIDES

    See also Agricultural chemicals; Pesticides

INSECTICIDES -- TOXICOLOGY

    See also Poisons and poisoning

Insectopedia. Raffles, H.   **595.7**

INSECTS

Eisner, T. For love of insects   **595.7**

Eisner, T. Secret weapons   **595.7**

Goulson, D. A Buzz in the Meadow   **638**

Holldobler, B. The superorganism   **595.7**

Milne, L. J. The Audubon Society field guide to North American insects and spiders   **595.7**

Raffles, H. Insectopedia **595.7**
Waldbauer, G. What good are bugs? **595.7**
Zuk, M. Sex on six legs **595.7**
INSECTS
 See also Animals
INSECTS -- ENCYCLOPEDIAS
 Encyclopedia of insects **595.7**
INSECTS AS CARRIERS OF DISEASE
 Lockwood, J. A. Six-legged soldiers **358**
INSECTS AS CARRIERS OF DISEASE
 See also Animals as carriers of disease; Insect
  pests
Inseminating the elephant. Perillo, L. M. **811**
Inseparable. Donoghue, E. **809**
INSERVICE TRAINING *See* Employees -- Train-
 ing
Inside Apple. Lashinsky, A. **338.7**
Inside Delta Force. Haney, E. L. **356**
Inside of a dog. Horowitz, A. **636.7**
**INSIDE PASSAGE -- DESCRIPTION AND
 TRAVEL**
 Raban, J. Passage to Juneau **979.8**
Inside rehab. Fletcher, A. M. **362.29**
Inside Scientology. Reitman, J. **299**
Inside Syria. Erlich, R. **956.91**
Inside the Kingdom. Lacey, R. **953.8**
Inside the not so big house. **728.37**
Inside the Pentagon papers. **959.704**
Inside the red mansion. August, O. **951.05**
Inside the room. **808.2**
Inside the Stalin archives. Brent, J. **947.086**
Inside the Third Reich. Speer, A. **943.086**
Inside the Victorian home. Victorian house **306**
Inside, outside, and online. Hill, C. **021.2**
INSIDER TRADING
 See also Commercial law; Securities; Stock
  exchanges
An **insider's** guide to the UN. Fasulo, L. M. **341.23**
INSIGHT
 Kounios, J. The Eureka factor **612.8**
Insight Guide Explore Rio. **918**
Insight Guides (Company)
 (comp) Insight Guide Explore Rio **918**
Inskeep, Steve
 Instant city **954.91**
 Jacksonland **973.5**
INSOLVENCY *See* Bankruptcy
INSOMNIA
 See also Sleep
INSOMNIA -- BIOGRAPHY
 Mutch, M. Know the night **92**
INSPECTION OF FOOD *See* Food adulteration
 and inspection
INSPECTION OF SCHOOLS *See* School supervi-
 sion; Schools -- Administration
INSPIRATION

Bloomston, C. The little spark **153.3**
Gilbert, E. Big magic **153.3**
INSPIRATION *See* Creation (Literary, artistic, etc.)
INSPIRATIONAL WRITERS
 Gibson, W. The miracle worker **812**
 Graham, B. Just as I am **92**
 Herrmann, D. Helen Keller **92**
 Keller, H. Helen Keller: selected writings **92**
 Keller, H. The story of my life **92**
 Martin, W. C. With God on our side **261.8**
 Norris, K. Acedia & me **92**
Inspired baby names from around the world. Shane,
 N. **929.4**
INSTALLATIONS (ART) -- EXHIBITIONS
 Ai weiwei **709.5**
INSTALLMENT PLAN
 See also Business; Consumer credit; Credit;
  Purchasing
Instant city. Inskeep, S. **954.91**
The **instant** economist. Taylor, T. **330**
Instinct. Jakes, T. D. **248.4**
INSTINCT
 See also Animal behavior; Psychology
INSTINCT
 Jakes, T. D. Instinct **248.4**
INSTRUCTIONAL MATERIALS CENTERS
 Safford, B. R. Guide to reference materials for
  school library media centers **011.6**
INSTRUMENTATION AND ORCHESTRATION
 Piston, W. Orchestration **784**
INSTRUMENTATION AND ORCHESTRATION
 See also Bands (Music); Composition (Mu-
  sic); Music; Orchestra
Instruments of science. **502.8**
INSTRUMENTS, MUSICAL *See* Musical instru-
 ments
INSTRUMENTS, SCIENTIFIC *See* Scientific ap-
 paratus and instruments
INSURANCE
 Boyd, R. Fatal risk **368**
INSURANCE
 See also Estate planning; Finance; Personal
  finance
INSURANCE EXECUTIVES
 Boyd, R. Fatal risk **368**
 Gioia, D. Can poetry matter? **809.1**
 Jarrell, R. No other book **809**
 Kermode, F. An appetite for poetry **801**
INSURGENCY
 Crutchfield, J. A. Revolt at Taos **972**
 Kurlansky, M. 1968 **909.82**
INSURGENCY
 See also Revolutions
INSURGENCY -- IRAQ
 Gordon, M. R. The endgame **956.7**
INTEGRATIVE MEDICINE

Cosgrove, T. The Cleveland Clinic way 362.11

INTEL CORP.
Tedlow, R. S. Andy Grove 92

INTELLECT
Alter, D. Staying sharp 612.8
Brogaard, B. The superhuman mind 153.9
Everett, D. L. Language 400
Foster, J. Beyond intelligence 649
Goleman, D. Emotional intelligence 152.4
Goleman, D. Social intelligence 158
Hofstadter, D. R. I am a strange loop 153
Jolly, A. Lucy's legacy 599.93
Kandel, E. R. The age of insight 154.2
Pinker, S. How the mind works 153
Sagan, C. The dragons of Eden 153
Shenk, D. The genius in all of us 155.2
Surowiecki, J. The wisdom of crowds 303.3

INTELLECT
See also Psychology

INTELLECTUAL FREEDOM
Intellectual Freedom Manual 025.2
Pinnell-Stephens, J. Protecting intellectual freedom in your public library 025.2

INTELLECTUAL FREEDOM
See also Freedom
Intellectual Freedom Manual. 025.2

INTELLECTUAL LIFE
Dawkins, R. Brief Candle in the Dark 570
James, C. Cultural amnesia 920

INTELLECTUAL LIFE
See also Culture

INTELLECTUAL LIFE -- HISTORY
Watson, P. Ideas 909

INTELLECTUAL PROPERTY
Baldwin, P. The copyright wars 346
Gasaway, L. N. Copyright questions and answers for information professionals 346.73
Hyde, L. Common as air 346.04
Hylton, K. N. Laws of creation 346.04
Lessig, L. The future of ideas 004.67

INTELLECTUALS
Becker, D. L. Many subtle channels 840.9
James, C. Cultural amnesia 920
Ker, I. G. K. Chesterton 828
Mishra, P. From the ruins of empire 950

INTELLECTUALS
See also Persons; Social classes

INTELLECTUALS -- ALGERIA -- BIOGRAPHY
Macey, D. Frantz Fanon 92

INTELLECTUALS -- FRANCE -- POLITICAL ACTIVITY
Kaplan, A. The collaborator: the trial & execution of Robert Brasillach 848

INTELLECTUALS -- ITALY -- BIOGRAPHY
Unger, M. J. Machiavelli 92

INTELLECTUALS -- UNITED STATES

McCullough, D. G. The greater journey 920.009

INTELLIGENCE OFFICERS -- UNITED STATES -- BIOGRAPHY
Grenier, R. L. 88 days to Kandahar 958.104
Woods, R. B. Shadow warrior 92

INTELLIGENCE SERVICE
Bamford, J. The shadow factory 327.12
Conant, J. A covert affair 940.54
Hastings, M. The secret war 940.54
Hoffman, D. E. The Billion Dollar Spy 327.12
Johnson, L. K. National Security Intelligence
Le Carré, J. The Pigeon Tunnel 823
Theoharis, A. G. Abuse of power 363.325
Willner, N. Forty Autumns

INTELLIGENCE SERVICE
See also Public administration; Research

INTELLIGENCE SERVICE -- GERMANY (EAST)
Garton-Ash, T. The file 327.12

INTELLIGENCE SERVICE -- GREAT BRITAIN
Hayes, P. Queen of Spies 327.12

INTELLIGENCE SERVICE -- ISRAEL
Pedahzur, A. The Israeli secret services and the struggle against terrorism 363.32

INTELLIGENCE SERVICE -- SOVIET UNION -- HISTORY
Draitser, E. Stalin's Romeo spy 92

INTELLIGENCE SERVICE -- UNITED STATES
Bird, K. The Good Spy 92
Greenwald, G. No place to hide 327.12
Grenier, R. L. 88 days to Kandahar 958.104
Weiner, T. Enemies 363.25
Weiner, T. Legacy of ashes 327.12

INTELLIGENCE SERVICE -- UNITED STATES -- HISTORY -- 21ST CENTURY
Scahill, J. Dirty wars 355.02

INTELLIGENCE SERVICE AGENTS
Dickey, C. Securing the city 363.32
Helm, S. A life in secrets 92
Macintyre, B. Agent Zigzag 92
Macintyre, B. Operation Mincemeat 940.54
Schroen, G. C. First in 958.1
Smyth, D. Deathly deception 940.54

INTELLIGENCE SERVICE OFFICIALS
Grose, P. Gentleman spy 92

INTELLIGENCE TESTING *See* Intelligence tests
INTELLIGENCE TESTS
Gould, S. J. The mismeasure of man 153.9
Murdoch, S. IQ 153.9

INTELLIGENCE TESTS
See also Child psychology; Educational psychology

INTELLIGENT BUILDINGS
See also Buildings

INTELLIGENT DESIGN (TELEOLOGY)
Ayala, F. J. Darwin's gift to science and reli-

gion   **576.8**

INTENSIVE CARE UNITS -- PENNSYLVANIA -- POPULAR WORKS
Brown, T. The shift   **616.02**

INTENTIONALISM
Dyer, W. W. The power of intention   **158**

INTERAGENCY COORDINATION -- UNITED STATES
Mazzetti, M. The way of the knife   **356**

INTERCONTINENTAL BALLISTIC MISSILES
Sheehan, N. A fiery peace in a cold war   **92**

INTERCOUNTRY ADOPTION -- INDIA
Brierley, S. A long way home   **92**

INTERCOUNTRY MARRIAGE
Fuller, A. Leaving Before the Rains Come **305.409**

INTERCULTURAL COMMUNICATION
Alexander, L. Access to Asia   **395.5**
Fadiman, A. The spirit catches you and you fall down   **306.4**
Friedman, T. L. The Lexus and the olive tree   **337**

INTERCULTURAL STUDIES *See* Cross-cultural studies

INTERDENOMINATIONAL COOPERATION
See also Christian sects; Church work

INTEREST (ECONOMICS)
Keynes, J. M. The general theory of employment, interest and money   **330.1**

INTEREST (ECONOMICS)
See also Banks and banking; Business mathematics; Capital; Finance; Loans

INTEREST GROUPS *See* Lobbying; Political action committees

Interesting times. Packer, G.   **814**

INTERFAITH RELATIONS
Karabell, Z. Peace be upon you   **201**
Niebuhr, G. Beyond tolerance   **201**
Power, C. If the oceans were ink   **297**

INTERGENERATIONAL RELATIONS
Lerner, B. The bridge ladies   **92**

INTERGOVERNMENTAL TAX RELATIONS
See also Taxation

INTERIOR ARCHITECTURE
The elements of style   **728**
Inside the not so big house   **728.37**
Susanka, S. Not so big solutions for your home **728**

INTERIOR DECORATION *See* Interior design

INTERIOR DECORATION -- AMATEURS' MANUALS
Bonney, G. Design*Sponge at home   **747**
Chapman, E. A beautiful mess happy handmade home   **747**

INTERIOR DECORATION -- CANADA
Richardson, S. Sarah style   **747**

INTERIOR DECORATION -- HANDBOOKS, MANUALS, ETC
The book of decorating   **747**

Borsics, A. Styled   **747**
Roney, C. [The nest] home design handbook

INTERIOR DECORATION -- HISTORY -- 20TH CENTURY -- THEMES, MOTIVES
Bradbury, D. The iconic interior   **747**

INTERIOR DECORATION -- HUMAN FACTORS
Blair, G. S. Design mom   **747**

INTERIOR DECORATION -- MISCELLANEA
Petersik, S. Young house love   **747**

INTERIOR DECORATION IN LITERATURE
Giramonti, L. B. Novel interiors   **747**

INTERIOR DESIGN
Atwood, R. Living with pattern   **701.85**
Becker, H. Decorate   **747**
Blair, B. Furniture makes the room   **684.1**
Blair, G. S. Design mom   **747**
Bonney, G. Design*Sponge at home   **747**
The book of decorating   **747**
Borsics, A. Styled   **747**
Bradbury, D. The iconic interior   **747**
Bruno, I. Reinventing Ikea   **684.1**
Carlson, J. Remodelista   **747**
Chapman, E. A beautiful mess happy handmade home   **747**
Crochet at home   **746.43**
Crochet, T. Bungalow style   **747**
DeGeneres, E. Home   **747**
Domino : your guide to a stylish home   **747**
Finnanger, T. Tilda Homemade & Happy   **746.4**
Frisoni The Big Book of a Miniature House   **745**
Galaxy, J. Catification   **636**
Gates, E. Elements of style   **747**
Giramonti, L. B. Novel interiors   **747**
Handmade interiors   **646.2**
Happy home   **646.2**
Home Depot, I. Home improvement 1-2-3   **643**
The indestructible houseplant   **635.9**
Inside the not so big house   **728.37**
Jenkins, A. 300 tips for painting & decorating **698**
Lee, V. Kitchenalia   **747**
Lemieux, C. The Finer Things   **747**
Montano, M. The big-ass book of home decor **645**
Moss, C. Charlotte Moss   **747**
New decorating book   **747**
Novel living   **002.075**
One-yard wonders   **646.2**
The perfectly imperfect home   **747**
Petersik, S. Lovable livable home   **645**
Richardson, S. Sarah style   **747**
Roney, C. [The nest] home design handbook
Schuman, E. Cupcakes and cashmere at home **746.9**
Smith, M. The nesting place   **248.4**
Spencer, L. Flea market fabulous   **747**
Studholme, J. Farrow & Ball How to Decorate   **747.94**

Susanka, S. Creating the not so big house **728**

Susanka, S. Not so big solutions for your home **728**

Wilhide, E. Scandinavian Home **728**

INTERIOR DESIGN

See also Art; Decoration and ornament; Design; Home economics

INTERIOR DESIGN -- HISTORY

Gura, J. The guide to period styles for interiors **747**

INTERIOR DESIGNERS

Albrecht, D. The Work of Charles and Ray Eames **745.4**

INTERMENT *See* Burial

The **internal** enemy. Taylor, A. **975.5**

INTERNAL MEDICINE -- ENCYCLOPEDIAS

The Gale encyclopedia of alternative medicine **615.5**

INTERNAL MIGRATION

Berlin, I. The making of African America **305.8**

Saunders, D. Arrival city **307.24**

Wilkerson, I. The warmth of other suns **307**

Youngstedt, S. M. Surviving with dignity **362.84**

INTERNAL SECURITY -- AFGHANISTAN

Gopal, A. No good men among the living **958.104**

INTERNATIONAL ADOPTION

Brierley, S. A long way home **92**

INTERNATIONAL ADOPTION

See also Adoption

INTERNATIONAL AGENCIES

Rieff, D. A bed for the night **361.2**

INTERNATIONAL ARBITRATION

See also International cooperation; International law; International relations; International security; Treaties

INTERNATIONAL ASSOCIATIONS *See* International agencies

INTERNATIONAL BROTHERHOOD OF TEAMSTERS, CHAUFFEURS, WAREHOUSEMEN AND HELPERS OF AMERICA

Russell, T. Out of the jungle **92**

INTERNATIONAL BUSINESS ENTERPRISES

See Multinational corporations

INTERNATIONAL COMPETITION

Nolan, P. Is China buying the world? **332.67**

INTERNATIONAL COMPETITION

See also International relations; International trade

International Conference on Relocation and Redress

Japanese Americans, from relocation to redress **940.53**

INTERNATIONAL COOKING

Alford, J. Flatbreads and flavors **641.8**

Alger, K. Susan Feniger's street food **641.59**

Carruthers, J. Eat street **641.76**

Classic home desserts **641.8**

Galimberti, G. In her kitchen **641.59**

Ghayour, S. Persiana **641.595**

The heart of the plate **641.5**

The illustrated kitchen bible **641.5**

Marks, G. The world of Jewish cooking **641.5**

Phillips, M. The Chelsea Market cookbook **641.59**

Red Rooster Cookbook **641.5**

Robertson, R. Vegan planet **641.5**

Rodriguez, J. W. The Hot Bread Kitchen cookbook **641.59**

Swanson, H. Near & far **641.59**

INTERNATIONAL COOPERATION

See also Cooperation; International law; International relations

INTERNATIONAL COPYRIGHT *See* Copyright

INTERNATIONAL ECONOMIC INTEGRATION

See also International economic relations; International finance

INTERNATIONAL ECONOMIC RELATIONS

Friedman, T. L. The Lexus and the olive tree **337**

Goldstein, N. Globalization and free trade **382**

Stiglitz, J. E. Globalization and its discontents **337**

INTERNATIONAL FINANCE

Conway, E. The Summit **339.5**

Epping, R. C. The 21st century economy **330.9**

Ferguson, N. The ascent of money **330**

Lanchester, J. I.O.U. **330.9**

McLean, B. All the devils are here **330.9**

Reinhart, C. M. This time is different **338.5**

Rhodes, W. R. Banker to the world **92**

Stiglitz, J. E. Globalization and its discontents **337**

INTERNATIONAL FINANCE

See also Finance

INTERNATIONAL FINANCE -- HISTORY -- 20TH CENTURY

Ahamed, L. Lords of finance **332.1**

Steil, B. The battle of Bretton Woods **339.5**

INTERNATIONAL LAW

Moynihan, D. P. On the law of nations **327**

INTERNATIONAL LAW

See also Law

INTERNATIONAL MONETARY FUND

Stiglitz, J. E. Globalization and its discontents **337**

INTERNATIONAL ORGANIZATION

See also International relations; International security

INTERNATIONAL ORGANIZATION OFFICIALS

Ellison, R. The collected essays of Ralph Ellison **814**

Halberstam, D. The best and the brightest **973.922**

Hendrickson, P. The living and the dead **959.704**

Millman, C. The detonators **940.4**

INTERNATIONAL ORGANIZATIONS *See* International agencies

INTERNATIONAL POLICE

See also International cooperation; International organization; International relations; International security

INTERNATIONAL POLITICS *See* World politics

INTERNATIONAL RELATIONS
Burgis, T. The looting machine **338.2**
Cold War **909.82**
Eichenwald, K. 500 days **973.931**
Feingold, R. While America sleeps **327**
Kaplan, R. D. Warrior politics **320**
Kissinger, H. World Order **327**
Lewis, B. Notes on a century **956**
Starobin, P. After America **973.91**

INTERNATIONAL RELATIONS -- ENCYCLO-PEDIAS
Moore, J. A. Encyclopedia of the United Nations **341.23**
Osmanczyk, E. J. Encyclopedia of the United Nations and international agreements **341.23**

INTERNATIONAL RELATIONS -- HISTORY -- 20TH CENTURY
Encyclopedia of conflicts since World War II **909.82**
Tooze, A. The deluge **940.3**

INTERNATIONAL RELATIONS -- HISTORY -- 21ST CENTURY -- FORECASTING
Brzezinski, Z. Strategic vision **327.1**

INTERNATIONAL RELATIONS -- RELIGIOUS ASPECTS
Preston, A. Sword of the spirit, shield of faith **322**

INTERNATIONAL RELATIONS SPECIALISTS
Dallek, R. Nixon and Kissinger **92**
Kissinger, H. Years of renewal **973.924**
Stern, J. Denial **92**

INTERNATIONAL RELIEF
Rieff, D. A bed for the night **361.2**

INTERNATIONAL SECURITY
Chayes, S. Thieves of state **364.1**

INTERNATIONAL SECURITY
See also International relations

INTERNATIONAL SPACE STATION
Anderson, C. The ordinary spaceman **92**

INTERNATIONAL STANDARD BIBLIO-GRAPHIC DESCRIPTION
See also Cataloging

INTERNATIONAL TRADE
Epping, R. C. The 21st century economy **330.9**
Nabhan, G. P. Cumin, camels, and caravans **382**
Pressly, P. M. On the rim of the Caribbean **975.8**
Snyder, R. L. Fugitive denim **382**

INTERNATIONAL TRADE
See also Commerce; International economic relations

International vital records handbook. Kemp, T. J. **929**

INTERNATIONALITY
Khan, A. S. The next pandemic **362.1**

INTERNATIONALIZATION *See* Globalization

INTERNET
Aiken, M. The cyber effect **155.9**
Bartlett, J. The Dark Net **302.23**
Blum, A. Tubes **384.3**
Carr, N. G. The big switch **303.4**
Citron, D. K. Hate crimes in cyberspace **364.15**
Heffernan, V. Magic and Loss **303.48**
Keen, A. The Internet Is Not the Answer **302.23**
Krebs, B. Spam nation **364.16**
Lessig, L. The future of ideas **004.67**
Martinez, A. G. Chaos Monkeys **338.4**
McClure, C. R. Public libraries and internet service roles **025.04**
Naughton, J. From Gutenberg to Zuckerberg **004.67**
Peters, J. The Idealist **004.67**
Weinberger, D. Too big to know **303.48**
Zuckerman, E. Rewire **302.23**

INTERNET
See also Computer networks; Information networks

INTERNET (COMPUTER NETWORK) *See* Internet

INTERNET -- CENSORSHIP
Pariser, E. The filter bubble **025.04**

INTERNET -- HISTORY
Isaacson, W. The innovators **004**

INTERNET -- HOME SHOPPING SERVICES
See Internet marketing; Internet shopping

INTERNET -- MISCELLANA
Pogue, D. Pogue's basics **004**

INTERNET -- MORAL AND ETHICAL AS-PECTS
Foxman, A. H. Viral hate **364.15**

INTERNET -- POLITICAL ASPECTS
McChesney, R. W. Digital disconnect **302.23**
Morozov, E. The net delusion **303.48**

INTERNET -- PSYCHOLOGICAL ASPECTS
Carr, N. G. The shallows **612.8**
Thompson, C. Smarter Than You Think **303.48**

INTERNET -- PUBLIC LIBRARIES
McClure, C. R. Public libraries and internet service roles **025.04**

INTERNET -- SAFETY MEASURES
Moore, A. Cyber self-defense **613.6**

INTERNET -- SECURITY MEASURES
Davis, M. Digital assassination **005**

INTERNET -- SOCIAL ASPECTS
Cukier, K. Big data **306.46**
Foxman, A. H. Viral hate **364.15**
Heim, T. @stickyjesus **248.4**
Steiner-Adair, C. The Big Disconnect **303.48**
Stryker, C. Hacking the Future **004.67**
Tanenbaum, L. I Am Not a Slut **305.23**
Thompson, C. Smarter Than You Think **303.48**
Wellman, B. Networked **006.7**

Zuckerman, E. Rewire   302.23

INTERNET ADDRESSES
  See also Internet

INTERNET ADVERTISING
  Miles, J. YouTube marketing power   658.8
  Sennett, F. Groupon's biggest deal ever   381

INTERNET AND CHILDREN
  Palfrey, J. Born digital   302.23

INTERNET AND CHILDREN
  See also Children

INTERNET AND FAMILIES
  Clark, L. S. The parent app   302.23

INTERNET AND RELIGION
  Nasr, A. A. My Isl@m   297.09

INTERNET AND TEENAGERS
  Boyd, D. It's complicated   004.67
  Moreno, M. Sex, drugs 'n Facebook   004.67
  Obee, J. Social networking   004.67
  Palfrey, J. Born digital   302.23
  Sales, N. J. American girls   004.67

INTERNET ENTERTAINMENT
  Rose, F. The art of immersion   306.4

INTERNET EXECUTIVES
  Auletta, K. Googled   338.7
  Kirkpatrick, D. The Facebook effect   338.7

INTERNET FRAUD -- PREVENTION
  Seife, C. Virtual unreality   025.04

INTERNET FRAUD -- UNITED STATES
  Krebs, B. Spam nation   364.16

INTERNET GAMBLING
  See also Gambling

INTERNET IN EDUCATION
  Devine, J. Going beyond Google again   025.042
  Vander Ark, T. Getting smart   371.33

INTERNET IN EDUCATION
  See also Education

INTERNET IN LIBRARY REFERENCE SERVICES
  Mulac, C. M. Fundamentals of reference   025.5
  Reference reborn   025.5

INTERNET IN PUBLICITY
  Thompson, D. C. The reputation economy   302.23

INTERNET INDUSTRY
  Angwin, J. Stealing MySpace   338.7
  Auletta, K. Googled   338.7
  Bartlett, J. The Dark Net   302.23
  Keen, A. The Internet Is Not the Answer   302.23
  Kirkpatrick, D. The Facebook effect   338.7
  Sennett, F. Groupon's biggest deal ever   381
  Stone, B. Things a little bird told me   006.7
  Stross, R. Planet Google   338.7
  Vaidhyanathan, S. The Googlization of everything   338.7

INTERNET INDUSTRY
  See also Industries

INTERNET INDUSTRY -- UNITED STATES

Bilton, N. Hatching Twitter   006.7
Dwyer, J. More awesome than money   384.3
The **Internet** Is Not the Answer. Keen, A.   302.23

INTERNET JOURNALISM *See* Online journalism

INTERNET LITERACY
  Seife, C. Virtual unreality   025.04

INTERNET MARKETING
  Chapin, K. The handmade marketplace   745.5
  Handley, A. Content rules   658.8
  Miles, J. YouTube marketing power   658.8
  Rose, F. The art of immersion   306.4
  Schaefer, M. W. Return on influence   658.8
  Sennett, F. Groupon's biggest deal ever   381
  Siegel, D. Pull   658.8
  Turow, J. The daily you   659.1

INTERNET MARKETING
  See also Electronic commerce; Marketing

INTERNET RESEARCH
  Hock, R. The Extreme Searcher's Internet Handbook   025.042

INTERNET RESOURCES
  Library mashups   020

INTERNET RESOURCES
  See also Information resources; Internet

INTERNET SEARCHING
  Auletta, K. Googled   338.7
  Bell, S. S. Librarian's guide to online searching   025.04
  Dornfest, R. Google hacks   025.04
  Hock, R. The Extreme Searcher's Internet Handbook   025.042
  MacLeod, D. How to find out anything   001.4
  Stross, R. Planet Google   338.7

INTERNET SEARCHING -- STUDY AND TEACHING
  Devine, J. Going beyond Google again   025.042

INTERNET SERVICE PROVIDERS
  See also Internet industry

INTERNET SHOPPING
  See also Electronic commerce; Shopping

INTERNET SOFTWARE INDUSTRY -- UNITED STATES
  Casnocha, B. My start-up life   338.7

INTERNET TELEVISION
  See also Internet; Television broadcasting

INTERNET USERS -- PSYCHOLOGY
  Aiken, M. The cyber effect   155.9

INTERNET VIDEOS
  Miles, J. YouTube marketing power   658.8

INTERNET-BASED COMPUTING *See* Cloud computing

INTERNISTS
  Malcolm, J. Iphigenia in Forest Hills   345

INTERNMENT CAMPS *See* Concentration camps

INTERNMENT OF JAPANESE AMERICANS,

1942-1945 *See* Japanese Americans -- Evacuation and relocation, 1942-1945

INTERNS

Gormley, K. The death of American virtue **973.929**

INTERNSHIP PROGRAMS

Berger, L. All work, no pay **650.14**

INTERNSHIP PROGRAMS

See also Employees -- Training

INTERNSHIP PROGRAMS -- NEW YORK (STATE)

Chertavian, G. A Year Up **331.25**

INTERNSHIP PROGRAMS -- UNITED STATES

Chertavian, G. A Year Up **331.25**

INTERNSHIPS *See* Internship programs

INTERPERSONAL ATTRACTION

Karlins, M. The like switch **158.2**

INTERPERSONAL COMMUNICATION

Kerpen, D. The art of people **650.1**

McMillan, R. Crucial conversations **153.6**

Meyers, P. As we speak **808.5**

Port, M. Steal the show **658.4**

INTERPERSONAL RELATIONS

Atik, C. Modern Dating **646.7**

Becker-Phelps, L. Love **646.7**

Borba, M. Unselfie **649.7**

Bright, D. The truth doesn't have to hurt **158.2**

Brown, T. The shift **616.02**

Burroughs, A. Lust and Wonder **92**

Cain, S. Quiet **155.2**

Duffy, M. The presidents club **973.92**

Ferrazzi, K. Never eat alone and other secrets to success **658.4**

Fontes, L. A. Invisible chains **158.2**

Gilligan, C. The birth of pleasure **152.4**

Glasser, W. Choice theory **150**

Goleman, D. Social intelligence **158**

Goulston, M. Just listen **650.1**

Grant, A. Give and take **158.2**

Hallowell, E. M. Shine **658.3**

Jensen, D. Queen of the air **791.3**

Keltner, D. Born to be good **155.2**

Kerpen, D. The art of people **650.1**

Lerner, H. G. The dance of intimacy **155.6**

Levine, R. The power of persuasion **153.8**

Maestripieri, D. Games primates play **155.7**

McMillan, R. Crucial conversations **153.6**

Miller, D. Scary close **158.2**

Peck, M. S. The road less traveled **158**

RoAne, S. How to work a room **650.1**

Ronk, M. Transfer of Qualities **811**

Ronson, J. So you've been publicly shamed **152.4**

Rosenblatt, R. The book of love **152.4**

Smith, D. Monkey mind **616.85**

Stone, D. Difficult conversations **158**

Toffler, A. Future shock **303.4**

Turkle, S. Alone together **303.4**

Wellman, B. Networked **006.7**

Wright, J. It Ended Badly **302**

INTERPERSONAL RELATIONS

See also Social psychology

INTERPERSONAL RELATIONS -- NEW YORK (STATE) -- NEW YORK

Martin, W. Primates of Park Avenue **974.7**

INTERPERSONAL RELATIONS -- PSYCHOLOGICAL ASPECTS

Aiken, M. The cyber effect **155.9**

INTERPERSONAL RELATIONS -- RELIGIOUS ASPECTS

Chapman, G. D. Love as a way of life **241**

INTERPERSONAL RELATIONS AND CULTURE -- UNITED STATES -- HISTORY

Hochschild, A. R. The outsourced self **306.85**

INTERPERSONAL RELATIONS IN LITERATURE

Franzen, J. Farther away **814**

INTERPLANETARY VISITORS *See* Extraterrestrial beings

INTERPLANETARY VOYAGES

Piantadosi, C. A. Mankind beyond Earth **629.45**

Wohlforth, C. Beyond Earth **629.455**

INTERPLANETARY VOYAGES

See also Astronautics; Fiction

INTERPLANETARY VOYAGES -- POPULAR WORKS

Clegg, B. Final Frontier **629.4**

Interpretation of dreams. Freud, S. **154.6**

The **interpreter.** Kaplan, A. Y. **940.54**

INTERPRETERS

Clark, E. E. Sacagawea of the Lewis and Clark expedition **92**

Him, C. When broken glass floats **959.604**

Slaughter, T. P. Exploring Lewis and Clark **978**

INTERPRETING AND TRANSLATING *See* Translating and interpreting

INTERPRETIVE DANCE *See* Modern dance

INTERPROFESSIONAL RELATIONS -- PENNSYLVANIA -- PERSONAL NARRATIVES

Brown, T. The shift **616.02**

INTERPROFESSIONAL RELATIONS -- PERSONAL NARRATIVES

Ofri, D. What doctors feel **610.69**

INTERRACIAL ADOPTION

See also Adoption; Race relations

INTERRACIAL MARRIAGE

Pascoe, P. What comes naturally **346**

INTERRACIAL MARRIAGE -- ENGLAND -- LONDON

Seth, V. Two lives **92**

The **interstellar** age. Bell, J. **919**

INTERSTELLAR COMMUNICATION

See also Life on other planets; Telecommunication

INTERSTELLAR TRAVEL *See* Interplanetary voyages
INTERVENTION (INTERNATIONAL LAW)
  See also International law; War
INTERVENTION (INTERNATIONAL LAW) -- HISTORY -- 20TH CENTURY
  Olson, L. Those angry days   **940.53**
Interventions. Annan, K. A.   **341.23**
INTERVIEWING
  See also Social psychology
INTERVIEWING FOR EMPLOYMENT *See* Job interviews
INTERVIEWING IN JOURNALISM
  See also Interviewing; Journalism
INTERVIEWS
  Jacqueline Kennedy   **973.922**
INTERVIEWS
  See also Conversation
INTERVIEWS -- NEW YORK (STATE) -- NEW YORK
  Stanton, B. Humans of New York: stories   **974.7**
INTERVIEWS -- RUSSIA (FEDERATION)
  Greene, D. Midnight in Siberia   **914.7**
  Pomerantsev, P. Nothing is true and everything is possible   **306**
INTERVIEWS -- RUSSIA (FEDERATION) -- CHELIABINSK
  Garrels, A. Putin country   **947.43**
INTESTACY *See* Inheritance and succession
INTESTINES -- MICROBIOLOGY
  Collen, A. 10% human   **612.3**
INTIFADA, 1987-1992
  See also Israel-Arab conflicts
INTIFADA, 2000-
  Tolan, S. Children of the stone   **780**
INTIFADA, 2000-
  See also Israel-Arab conflicts
INTIMACY (PSYCHOLOGY)
  Gilligan, C. The birth of pleasure   **152.4**
  Miller, D. Scary close   **158.2**
INTIMACY (PSYCHOLOGY)
  See also Emotions; Interpersonal relations; Love; Psychology
The **intimate** bond. Fagan, B.   **591.5**
An **intimate** look at the night sky. Raymo, C.   **520**
Intimate Merton. Merton, T.   **271**
INTIMATE PARTNER VIOLENCE
  Fontes, L. A. Invisible chains   **158.2**
INTIMIDATION
  Fontes, L. A. Invisible chains   **158.2**
Into the Black. White, R.   **629.44**
Into the classroom. McKeown, R.   **370.71**
Into the garden.   **808.8**
Into the Heart of Our World. Whitehouse, D.   **551**
Into the Magic Shop. Doty, J. R.   **92**
Into the region of awe. Downing, D. C.   **248.2**

Into the story. Maraniss, D.   **92**
Into the wild. Krakauer, J.   **917**
Into thin air. Krakauer, J.   **796.522**
Into Tibet. Laird, T.   **327.12**
INTOLERANCE *See* Fanaticism; Toleration
INTOXICANTS *See* Alcohol; Alcoholic beverages; Liquors
INTOXICATION *See* Alcoholism; Temperance
INTRODUCED FISHES -- UNITED STATES
  Halverson, A. An entirely synthetic fish   **639.3**
Introducing RDA. Oliver, C.   **025.3**
Introduction to library public services. Evans, G. E.   **025.5**
Introduction to logic. Copi, I. M.   **160**
Introduction to public librarianship. McCook, K. d. l. P.   **027.4**
Introduction to reference sources in the health sciences.   **016.6**
An **introduction** to the New Testament. Brown, R. E.   **225**
INTROVERSION AND EXTROVERSION
  Cain, S. Quiet   **155.2**
  Helgoe, L. A. Introvert power   **155.2**
The **Introvert** Entrepreneur. Buelow, B. L.   **658.11**
Introvert power. Helgoe, L. A.   **155.2**
INTROVERTS
  Cain, S. Quiet   **155.2**
INTUITION
  Gladwell, M. Blink: the power of thinking without thinking   **153.4**
  Kahneman, D. Thinking, fast and slow   **153.4**
  Kounios, J. The Eureka factor   **612.8**
INTUITION
  See also Philosophy; Psychology; Rationalism; Theory of knowledge
Intuition Pumps and Other Tools for Thinking. Dennett, D. C.   **121**
INUIT
  Ehrlich, G. This cold heaven   **998**
  Wohlforth, C. The whale and the supercomputer   **305.897**
INUIT
  See also Indigenous peoples
INUIT -- CANADA -- SOCIAL CONDITIONS
  Winter, K. Boundless   **910.9**
INUIT -- FOLKLORE
  See also Folklore
INUPIAT
  Hensley, W. L. Fifty miles from tomorrow   **92**
INVALID COOKING *See* Cooking for the sick; Diet therapy
INVALIDS
  See also Sick
INVASION OF PRIVACY *See* Right of privacy
INVASIONS, BIOLOGICAL *See* Biological invasions

INVECTIVE

    See also Satire

Inventing a nation: Washington, Adams, Jefferson. Vidal, G.   **973.4**

Inventing Japan, 1853-1964. Buruma, I.   **952.03**

Inventing Wyatt Earp. Barra, A.   **92**

The **invention** of air. Johnson, S.   **92**

The **invention** of clouds. Hamblyn, R.   **551.57**

The **invention** of love. Stoppard, T.   **822**

The **invention** of murder. Flanders, J.   **364.152**

The **invention** of nature. Wulf, A.   **92**

The **Invention** of Russia. Ostrovsky, A.   **947.086**

The **Invention** of Science. Wootton, D.   **509**

INVENTIONS

  Doorley, R. Tinkerlab   **600**

  Evans, H. They made America   **920**

  Macaulay, D. The Way Things Work Now   **600**

  Pressman, D. Patent it yourself   **346**

INVENTIONS

    See also Technology

INVENTIONS -- HISTORY

  Abramson, A. The History of Television 1880 to 1941   **621.388**

  Degraaf, L. Edison and the rise of innovation   **92**

INVENTIONS -- HISTORY -- CHRONOLOGY

  Concise history of science & invention   **509**

Inventions of the March Hare.   **811**

Inventive weavng on a little loom. Mitchell, S. **746.1**

INVENTORS

  Abdul-Jabbar, K. Black profiles in courage   **920**

  Carey, C. W. American inventors, entrepreneurs & business visionaries   **920**

  Cohen, I. B. Science and the founding fathers **973.3**

  Evans, H. They made America   **920**

  Franklin, B. The autobiography of Benjamin Franklin   **92**

  Gray, C. Reluctant genius   **92**

  Hemming, H. The ingenious Mr. Pyke   **327.12**

  Isaacson, W. Benjamin Franklin   **92**

  Israel, P. Edison   **92**

  Klein, S. Leonardo's legacy   **709**

  Larson, E. Thunderstruck   **364.152**

  Lepore, J. A is for American   **306.44**

  Pasles, P. C. Benjamin Franklin's numbers   **510**

  Shulman, S. The telephone gambit   **621.3**

  Smiley, J. The man who invented the computer   **92**

  Wright, O. How we invented the airplane   **92**

INVENTORS -- UNITED STATES -- BIOGRA-PHY

  Carlson, W. B. Tesla   **92**

  Degraaf, L. Edison and the rise of innovation   **92**

  Kendall, J. America's obsessives   **609.2**

  Kurlansky, M. Birdseye   **338.7**

INVENTORS -- UNITED STATES -- HISTORY -- 20TH CENTURY

  Gertner, J. The idea factory   **384**

INVENTORY CONTROL

    See also Management; Retail trade

INVERTEBRATES

  Attenborough, D. Life in the undergrowth   **592**

  Naskrecki, P. The smaller majority   **591.7**

INVERTEBRATES

    See also Animals

INVERTEBRATES -- CONSERVATION

  Fortey, R. Horseshoe crabs and velvet worms **595**

INVESTIGATIVE REPORTING -- UNITED STATES -- HISTORY -- 20TH CENTURY

  Golay, M. America 1933   **973.917**

INVESTMENT ANALYSIS

  Dreman, D. Contrarian investment strate-gies   **332.601**

INVESTMENT BANKERS

  Burns, S. The Central Park Five   **364.1**

  Paulson, H. M. On the brink   **330.9**

INVESTMENTS

  Bernstein, W. The four pillars of investing **332.6**

  Bernstein, W. The investor's manifesto   **332.6**

  Boeckh, J. A. The great reflation   **332.6**

  Bogle, J. C. The clash of the cultures   **332.6**

  Buffett, M. Warren Buffett and the art of stock ar-bitrage   **332.6**

  Cohan, W. D. Money and power   **332.6**

  Cortese, A. Locavesting   **332.6**

  Downes, J. Finance and investment handbook **332.6**

  Fisher, K. L. How to smell a rat   **364.1**

  Hagstrom, R. G. The Warren Buffett Way   **332.6**

  Hirshman, S. L. Does this make my assets look fat?   **332.024**

  Kelly, K. Street fighters   **332.6**

  Malkiel, B. G. A random walk down Wall Street   **332.6**

  Pond, J. D. Grow your money!   **332.024**

  Quinn, J. B. Making the most of your money now   **332.024**

  Schwab-Pomerantz, C. It pays to talk   **332.024**

  Solin, D. R. The smartest retirement book you'll ever read   **332.024**

  Tengler, N. The women's guide to successful in-vesting   **332.6**

  Tett, G. Fool's gold   **332.6**

  Tobias, A. P. The only investment guide you'll ever need   **332.024**

  Weltman, B. J.K. Lasser's guide for tough times   **332.024**

  Where are the customers' yachts?   **332.64**

INVESTMENTS

    See also Banks and banking; Capital; Finance

INVESTMENTS -- PSYCHOLOGICAL AS-PECTS

  Dreman, D. Contrarian investment strate-gies   **332.601**

  Panic   **338.5**

Pepper, C. The seven pearls of financial wisdom   **332.024**
The **investor's** manifesto. Bernstein, W. **332.6**
INVISIBILITY
Ball, P. Invisible   **535**
Invisible. Ball, P.   **535**
The **Invisible** Bridge. Perlstein, R.   **973.924**
Invisible chains. Fontes, L. A.   **158.2**
Invisible City.   **779**
The **invisible** front. Dreazen, Y.   **92**
The **invisible** gorilla. Chabris, C.   **153.7**
The **invisible** history of the human race. Kenneally, C.   **616**
Invisible Influence. Berger, J.   **302.13**
The **invisible** kingdom. Ben-Barak, I.   **579**
The **invisible** line. Sharfstein, D. J.   **305.8**
The **invisible** soldiers. Hagedorn, A.   **355**
INVISIBLE WEB
Pariser, E. The filter bubble   **025.04**
An **invitation** to Indian cooking. Jaffrey, M.   **641.59**
Ionesco, Eugène, 1912-1994
Rhinoceros, and other plays   **842**
                            About
Playwrights at work   **812**
IOWA
Hoffman, C. Greetings from Utopia Park   **92**
IOWA -- BIOGRAPHY
Blair, J. By the Iowa Sea   **977.7**
Iphigenia in Forest Hills. Malcolm, J.   **345**
IQ. Murdoch, S.   **153.9**
IQ TESTS *See* Intelligence tests
IRAN
Moaveni, A. Lipstick jihad   **92**
IRAN -- DESCRIPTION AND TRAVEL
Elliot, J. Mirrors of the unseen   **915**
Housden, R. Saved by beauty   **955**
Jubber, N. Drinking arak off an ayatollah's beard   **915**
IRAN -- FOREIGN RELATIONS -- CANADA
Baglio, M. Argo   **955.05**
IRAN -- FOREIGN RELATIONS -- GREAT BRITAIN
Abrahamian, E. The coup   **955.05**
IRAN -- FOREIGN RELATIONS -- UNITED STATES
Leverett, F. Going to Tehran   **327.73**
Pollack, K. M. Unthinkable   **355.8**
IRAN -- GRAPHIC NOVELS
Satrapi, M. The complete Persepolis   **741.5**
Satrapi, M. Embroideries   **741**
IRAN -- HISTORY
Baglio, M. Argo   **955.05**
Cooper, A. S. The fall of heaven   **955.05**
IRAN -- HISTORY -- 1941-1979
Abrahamian, E. The coup   **955.05**
Andalibian, R. The rose hotel   **92**

IRAN -- HISTORY -- 1979-
Buchan, J. Days of God   **955.05**
Crist, D. The twilight war   **327**
Secor, L. Children of Paradise   **955.05**
IRAN -- HISTORY -- 1979-1997
Buchan, J. Days of God   **955.05**
IRAN -- HISTORY -- MOHAMMAD REZA PAHLAVI, 1941-1979
Cooper, A. S. The fall of heaven   **955.05**
IRAN -- HISTORY -- REVOLUTION, 1979
Buchan, J. Days of God   **955.05**
IRAN -- HISTORY -- REVOLUTION, 1979 -- INFLUENCE
Buchan, J. Days of God   **955.05**
IRAN -- HISTORY -- REVOLUTION, 1979 -- PERSONAL NARRATIVES
Andalibian, R. The rose hotel   **92**
IRAN -- MILITARY RELATIONS -- UNITED STATES
Crist, D. The twilight war   **327**
IRAN -- POLITICS AND GOVERNMENT
Crist, D. The twilight war   **327**
Morozov, E. The net delusion   **303.48**
Secor, L. Children of Paradise   **955.05**
IRAN -- POLITICS AND GOVERNMENT -- 1941-1979
Abrahamian, E. The coup   **955.05**
IRAN -- POLITICS AND GOVERNMENT -- 20TH CENTURY
Buchan, J. Days of God   **955.05**
IRAN -- POLITICS AND GOVERNMENT -- 21ST CENTURY
Pollack, K. M. Unthinkable   **355.8**
IRAN -- SOCIAL CONDITIONS
Ebadi, S. Until We Are Free   **92**
IRAN -- SOCIAL LIFE AND CUSTOMS
Housden, R. Saved by beauty   **955**
Moaveni, A. Lipstick jihad   **92**
IRAN HOSTAGE CRISIS, 1979-1981
Follett, K. On wings of eagles   **955**
Wright, R. A. Our man in Tehran   **955**
IRAN HOSTAGE CRISIS, 1979-1981
Baglio, M. Argo   **955.05**
IRAN HOSTAGE CRISIS, 1979-1981
See also American hostages -- Iran; Iran -- Foreign relations -- United States; United States -- Foreign relations -- Iran
IRAN-CONTRA AFFAIR, 1985-1990
The Iran-Contra scandal   **973.927**
The **Iran-Contra** scandal.   **973.927**
IRANIAN AMERICAN WOMEN
Nafisi, A. The Republic of Imagination   **819**
IRANIAN AMERICANS
Andalibian, R. The rose hotel   **92**
Jobrani, M. I'm not a terrorist, but I've played one on tv   **92**

Moaveni, A. Honeymoon in Tehran   **92**

The **Iranians.** Mackey, S.   **955**

Iraq. Robertson, J.   **956.7**

IRAQ

Chandrasekaran, R. Imperial life in the emerald city   **956.704**

Weiss, M. Isis   **956.05**

IRAQ -- CIVILIZATION

Robertson, J. Iraq   **956.7**

IRAQ -- CIVILIZATION -- TO 634

Kriwaczek, P. Babylon   **935**

IRAQ -- COALITION PROVISIONAL AUTHORITY

Chandrasekaran, R. Imperial life in the emerald city   **956.704**

IRAQ -- DESCRIPTION AND TRAVEL

Stewart, R. The prince of the marshes   **956.7**

IRAQ -- HISTORY

Kriwaczek, P. Babylon   **935**

Robertson, J. Iraq   **956.7**

IRAQ -- HISTORY -- 2003-2011 , ANGLO-AMERICAN INVASION *See* Iraq War, 2003-2011

IRAQ -- HISTORY -- TO 634

Kriwaczek, P. Babylon   **935**

IRAQ -- POLITICS AND GOVERNMENT

Gordon, M. R. The endgame   **956.7**

IRAQ -- REFUGEES -- BIOGRAPHY

The girl who escaped ISIS   **956.7**

IRAQ -- SOCIAL CONDITIONS

Seierstad, A. A hundred and one days   **956.7**

Stewart, R. The prince of the marshes   **956.7**

The **Iraq** war. Murray, W.   **956.7**

IRAQ WAR, 2003- -- ART AND THE WAR

Bilal, W. Shoot an Iraqi   **92**

IRAQ WAR, 2003- -- ATROCITIES

Frederick, J. Black hearts   **956.7**

IRAQ WAR, 2003- -- CAUSES

Haass, R. War of necessity: war of choice   **956.7**

IRAQ WAR, 2003- -- ENCYCLOPEDIAS

The encyclopedia of Middle East wars   **355**

IRAQ WAR, 2003- -- PERSONAL NARRATIVES

Brownfield, C. J. My nuclear family   **92**

Filkins, D. The forever war   **956.7**

Mansoor, P. R. Baghdad at sunrise   **956.7**

Mills, D. Sniper one   **956.7**

Raddatz, M. The long road home   **956.7**

Reporting Iraq   **070**

Seierstad, A. A hundred and one days   **956.7**

Weisskopf, M. Blood brothers   **92**

Wright, E. Generation kill   **956.7**

IRAQ WAR, 2003- -- POLITICAL ASPECTS

Haass, R. War of necessity: war of choice   **956.7**

IRAQ WAR, 2003-2011

Allawi, A. A. The occupation of Iraq   **956.7**

Atkinson, R. In the company of soldiers   **956.7**

Bannerman, S. Homefront 911   **362.86**

Bergen, P. L. The longest war   **909.83**

Bolger, D. P. Why We Lost   **956.704**

Busch, B. Dust to dust   **92**

Chandrasekaran, R. Imperial life in the emerald city   **956.704**

Coll, S. Private empire   **338.7**

Dower, J. W. Cultures of war   **355**

Fair, E. Consequence   **956.704**

Filkins, D. The forever war   **956.7**

Finkel, D. The good soldiers   **956.7**

Gentile, G. P. Wrong turn   **355.02**

Gordon, M. R. The endgame   **956.7**

Gourevitch, P. Standard operating procedure   **956.7**

Hersh, S. M. Chain of command   **973.931**

Koltz, T. It worked for me   **92**

Murray, W. The Iraq war   **956.7**

Packer, G. The assassins' gate   **956.7**

Poole, R. M. Section 60   **975.5**

Ricks, T. E. Fiasco: the American military adventure in Iraq   **956.7**

Robertson, J. Iraq   **956.7**

Schlesinger, A. M. War and the American presidency   **327.1**

Shadid, A. Night draws near   **956.7**

Sheeler, J. Final salute   **956.7**

Sielski, M. Fading echoes   **92**

Sky, E. The Unraveling   **956.7**

Thorpe, H. Soldier girls   **956.704**

The torture papers   **973.931**

Van Buren, P. We meant well   **956.7**

Willman, D. The mirage man   **363.325**

Woodward, B. Plan of attack   **956.7**

Woodward, B. State of denial   **973.931**

IRAQ WAR, 2003-2011 -- ATROCITIES

Fair, E. Consequence   **956.704**

IRAQ WAR, 2003-2011 -- BIOGRAPHY

Busch, B. Dust to dust   **92**

IRAQ WAR, 2003-2011 -- CAMPAIGNS

Bolger, D. P. Why We Lost   **956.704**

Hornfischer, J. D. Service   **956.704**

Thorpe, H. Soldier girls   **956.704**

IRAQ WAR, 2003-2011 -- CASUALTIES -- UNITED STATES

Poole, R. M. Section 60   **975.5**

IRAQ WAR, 2003-2011 -- PERSONAL NARRATIVES

Castner, B. The long walk   **956.704**

Edmonds, B. R. God Is Not Here   **956.704**

Sites, K. The things they cannot say   **355**

IRAQ WAR, 2003-2011 -- PERSONAL NARRATIVES, AMERICAN

Bolger, D. P. Why We Lost   **956.704**

Busch, B. Dust to dust   **92**

Castner, B. The long walk   **956.704**

Fair, E. Consequence   **956.704**

Hornfischer, J. D. Service   956.704
Rodriguez, D. Rise   92
IRAQ WAR, 2003-2011 -- VETERANS -- UNITED STATES
Bannerman, S. Homefront 911   362.86
Finkel, D. Thank You for Your Service   362.86
IRAQ WAR, 2003-2011 -- VETERANS -- UNITED STATES -- BIOGRAPHY
Castner, B. The long walk   956.704
IRAQ WAR, 2003-2011 -- WOMEN -- UNITED STATES -- BIOGRAPHY
Thorpe, H. Soldier girls   956.704
IRELAND
McDonnell, I. The Farmette cookbook   641.5
IRELAND -- CIVILIZATION
Cahill, T. How the Irish saved civilization 941.501
Encyclopedia of Irish history and culture 941.5
IRELAND -- DESCRIPTION AND TRAVEL
Macfarlane, R. The wild places   914
IRELAND -- EMIGRATION AND IMMIGRATION -- HISTORY -- 19TH CENTURY
Kelly, J. The graves are walking   941.5
IRELAND -- ENCYCLOPEDIAS
Encyclopedia of Irish history and culture 941.5
IRELAND -- HISTORY -- 1910-1921
Walsh, M. Bitter freedom   941.508
IRELAND -- HISTORY -- 20TH CENTURY
Nic Dhiarmada, B. The 1916 Irish Rebellion 941.5
Walsh, M. Bitter freedom   941.508
IRELAND -- HISTORY -- EASTER RISING, 1916
Nic Dhiarmada, B. The 1916 Irish Rebellion 941.5
IRELAND -- HISTORY -- FAMINE, 1845-1852
Egan, T. The immortal Irishman   92
Irena's children. Mazzeo, T. J.   940.53
Iris Murdoch. Conradi, P.   823
IRISH AMERICANS
Fisher, J. T. On the Irish waterfront   331.7
McCourt, A. A long stone's throw   92
McCourt, F. Angela's ashes   92
McCourt, F. Teacher man   92
McCourt, F. 'Tis   92
McCourt, J. Lasting City   92
Nic Dhiarmada, B. The 1916 Irish Rebellion 941.5
IRISH AMERICANS -- BIOGRAPHY
Egan, T. The immortal Irishman   92
IRISH COOKING
Andrews, C. Country cooking of Ireland   641.5
McDonnell, I. The Farmette cookbook   641.5
IRISH LITERATURE
See also Literature
IRISH LITERATURE -- DICTIONARIES
McMahon, S. Brewer's dictionary of Irish phrase & fable   427
The Oxford companion to Irish literature   820
IRISH POETRY

Morrissey, S. Parallax   821
The New Oxford book of Irish verse   821
IRISH POETRY -- COLLECTIONS
An anthology of modern Irish poetry   821
The New Oxford book of Irish verse   821
IRISH QUESTION
Nic Dhiarmada, B. The 1916 Irish Rebellion 941.5
Irmscher, Christoph
Louis Agassiz   92
IRON
See also Chemical elements; Metals
Iron & silk. Salzman, M.   951.05
IRON AGE
See also Civilization
Iron curtain. Applebaum, A.   947
Iron horse: Lou Gehrig in his time. Robinson, R. 92
IRON INDUSTRY
See also Industries
Iron John. Bly, R.   305.31
Iron tears. Weintraub, S.   973.3
The iron wall. Shlaim, A.   956.04
Iron-Georges, Tracy
Masterplots II, poetry series   809.1
IRONING See Laundry
Irons in the fire. McPhee, J. A.   081
Ironwood American classics [series]
Alcott, L. M. The sketches of Louisa May Alcott   818
IRONWORK
See also Decoration and ornament; Iron; Metalwork
IROQUOIS INDIANS
Taylor, A. The divided ground   974.7
IROQUOIS INDIANS -- HISTORY
Fenton, W. N. The Great Law and the Longhouse   970.004
Taylor, A. The divided ground   974.7
Irrational exuberance. Shiller, R. J.   332.63
Irrational man. Barrett, W.   142
IRRATIONAL NUMBERS
Havil, J. The irrationals   512
The irrationals. Havil, J.   512
The irreducible needs of children. Brazelton, T. B.   155.4
The irregulars. Conant, J.   940.54
Irrepressible. Bingham, E.   306.76
Irresistible empire. De Grazia, V.   306
The irresistible fairy tale. Zipes, J.   398.209
IRREVERSIBLE COMA See Brain death
IRRIGATION
See also Agricultural engineering; Hydraulic engineering; Water resources development; Water supply
IRRITABLE BOWEL SYNDROME
Lacy, B. E. Making sense of IBS   616.3
IRRITABLE COLON -- DIET THERAPY --

RECIPES

Shepherd, S. The 2-step low-FODMAP eating plan **641.5**

Irritable hearts. McClelland, M. **92**

Irvine, William Braxton
On desire **128**

Irving Penn. Foresta, M. A. **770**

Irving, David John Cawdell, 1938-
About
Guttenplan, D. D. The Holocaust on trial **940.53**
Lipstadt, D. E. History on trial **940.53**

Irving, Shae
(ed) Nolo's encyclopedia of everyday law **340**

Irwin, Robert
Tips & traps for negotiating real estate **333.3**
(ed) Night and horses and the desert **892.7**

IS (ORGANIZATION)

The girl who escaped ISIS **956.7**
Warrick, J. Black flags **956.91**
Wright, L. The terror years **363.325**

Is China buying the world? Nolan, P. **332.67**

Is everyone hanging out without me? (and other concerns) Kaling, M. **818**

Is it a big problem or a little problem? Egan, A. **649**

Is Pluto a planet? Weintraub, D. A. **523.4**

Isaac Asimov. Gunn, J. E. **813**

Isaac Newton. Gleick, J. **92**

Isaac Newton Institute series of lectures [series]
Hawking, S. W. The nature of space and time **530.1**

Isaacs, Ronald H.
Kosher living **296.7**

Isaacson, Walter
Benjamin Franklin **92**
Einstein: his life and universe **92**
The innovators **004**
Steve Jobs **92**

Isabella. Downey, K. **92**

Isabella I, Queen of Spain, 1451-1504
About
Downey, K. Isabella **92**

Isacoff, Stuart
A natural history of the piano **786.2**

Isacowitz, Rael
Pilates **613.7**

Isak Dinesen. Thurman, J. **92**

Isay, Dave
Callings **920.073**

Isenberg, Barbara
Conversations with Frank Gehry **92**

Isenberg, Nancy
Burstein, A. Madison and Jefferson **973.4**

Isherwood, Christopher, 1904-1986
Liberation **809**

Ishi
About
Kroeber, T. Ishi in two worlds **92**

Ishi in two worlds. Kroeber, T. **92**

Ishida, Sanae
About
Ishida, S. Sewing happiness **646.2**

Isis. Weiss, M. **956.05**

Islam. Armstrong, K. **297**

Islam. Esposito, J. L. **297**

ISLAM
See also Religions

ISLAM
Armstrong, K. A history of God **200**
Armstrong, K. Islam **297**
Armstrong, K. Muhammad **297**
Aslan, R. No god but God **297**
Barrett, P. M. American Islam **920**
Ben Jelloun, T. Islam explained **297**
Campo, J. E. Encyclopedia of Islam **297**
Encyclopedia of Islam and the Muslim world **909**
Ernst, C. W. Following Muhammad **297**
Esposito, J. L. Islam **297**
Esposito, J. L. What everyone needs to know about Islam **297**
Glassé, C. The new encyclopedia of Islam **297**
Gordon, M. Understanding Islam **297**
Grieve, P. A brief guide to Islam **297**
Harris, S. Islam and the future of tolerance **297.2**
The Many faces of Islam **297**
Nasr, S. H. Islam: religion, history, and civilization **297**
The Oxford history of Islam **297**
Renard, J. The handy Islam answer book **297**
Smith, J. I. Islam in America **297.092**
Taseer, A. Stranger to history **915.6**

ISLAM -- APPRECIATION
Ben Jelloun, T. Islam explained **297**
The Many faces of Islam **297**
Power, C. If the oceans were ink **297**

ISLAM -- CUSTOMS AND PRACTICES
Kugle, S. S. Living out Islam **297**
Nawaz, Z. Laughing All the Way to the Mosque **92**

ISLAM -- CUSTOMS AND PRACTICES
See also Rites and ceremonies

ISLAM -- DICTIONARIES
The Oxford dictionary of Islam **297**

ISLAM -- DIETARY LAWS
See also Islam -- Customs and practices

ISLAM -- ENCYCLOPEDIAS
Campo, J. E. Encyclopedia of Islam **297**
Encyclopedia of Islam and the Muslim world **909**

ISLAM -- ESSENCE, GENIUS, NATURE
Ben Jelloun, T. Islam explained **297**
Esposito, J. L. What everyone needs to know about Islam **297**
The Many faces of Islam **297**
Power, C. If the oceans were ink **297**

ISLAM -- HISTORY

Hazleton, L. The First Muslim **297.6**

ISLAM -- MIDDLE EAST

Bhutto, B. Reconciliation **92**

Taseer, A. Stranger to history **915.6**

ISLAM -- POLITICAL ASPECTS *See* Islam and politics

ISLAM -- PUBLIC OPINION

Bawer, B. Surrender **297**

Power, C. If the oceans were ink **297**

ISLAM -- RELATIONS

Three Testaments **208**

Zafar, H. Demystifying Islam **297**

ISLAM -- RELATIONS -- CHRISTIANITY

Crowley, R. Empires of the sea **359**

Griswold, E. The tenth parallel **297**

Saldana, S. The bread of angels **92**

ISLAM -- RELATIONS -- CHRISTIANITY -- HISTORY -- TO 1500

Cobb, P. M. The race for paradise **909.07**

ISLAM -- RELATIONS -- JUDAISM

See also Islam; Judaism

ISLAM -- UNITED STATES

Abdul Rauf, F. Moving the mountain **297.09**

Smith, J. I. Islam in America **297.092**

ISLAM -- UNITED STATES -- HISTORY

Curtis, E. E. Muslims in America **305.8**

ISLAM AND LITERATURE

Rushdie, S. Joseph Anton **92**

ISLAM AND POLITICS

Bhutto, B. Reconciliation **92**

Buchan, J. Days of God **955.05**

Esposito, J. L. Unholy war **322.4**

Johnson, I. A mosque in Munich **297**

Karsh, E. Islamic imperialism **297**

Kepel, G. Jihad **297**

Kimball, C. When religion becomes lethal **201**

Lewis, B. The crisis of Islam **297**

Nasr, V. The Shia revival **297**

Rashid, A. Taliban **958.1**

ISLAM AND POLITICS

See also Political science

Islam and the future of tolerance. Harris, S. **297.2**

Islam explained. Ben Jelloun, T. **297**

Islam in America. Smith, J. I. **297.092**

Islam in der Gegenwart./English.

Islam in the world today **297**

Islam in the world today. Islam in der Gegenwart./English. **297**

Islam: religion, history, and civilization. Nasr, S. H. **297**

ISLAMIC ARCHITECTURE

See also Architecture

ISLAMIC ART

Denny, W. B. How to read Islamic carpets **746.7**

Khalili, N. D. Islamic art and culture **709**

O'Kane, B. Treasures of Islam **709.1**

ISLAMIC ART

See also Art

ISLAMIC ART -- EXHIBITIONS

In harmony **704**

Islamic art and culture. Khalili, N. D. **709**

ISLAMIC BROTHERHOOD

Johnson, I. A mosque in Munich **297**

ISLAMIC CIVILIZATION

Ansary, M. T. West of Kabul, East of New York **958.1**

Fuller, G. E. A world without Islam **297**

Islam in der Gegenwart./English. Islam in the world today **297**

Kennedy, H. The great Arab conquests **909**

Kennedy, H. When Baghdad ruled the Muslim world **956.7**

Khalili, N. D. Islamic art and culture **709**

Nasr, S. H. Islam: religion, history, and civilization **297**

O'Kane, B. Treasures of Islam **709.1**

Taseer, A. Stranger to history **915.6**

ISLAMIC CIVILIZATION

See also Civilization

Islamic civilization & Muslim networks [series]

Ernst, C. W. Following Muhammad **297**

ISLAMIC COOKING

Maffei, Y. My halal kitchen **641.595**

ISLAMIC COUNTRIES -- FOREIGN RELATIONS -- UNITED STATES

Nasr, V. The dispensable nation **327.73**

ISLAMIC COUNTRIES -- HISTORY

The Cambridge illustrated history of the Islamic world **909**

ISLAMIC COUNTRIES -- POLITICS AND GOVERNMENT

The Many faces of Islam **297**

ISLAMIC FUNDAMENTALISM

Armstrong, K. The battle for God **200.9**

Elshtain, J. B. Just war against terror **363.32**

Eteraz, A. Children of dust **92**

Herridge, C. The next wave **363.32**

Johnson, I. A mosque in Munich **297**

Lewis, B. The crisis of Islam **297**

Nasr, A. A. My Isl@m **297.09**

Rashid, A. Taliban **958.1**

Warrick, J. Black flags **956.91**

ISLAMIC FUNDAMENTALISM

See also Islam; Religious fundamentalism

ISLAMIC FUNDAMENTALISM -- GERMANY

Johnson, I. A mosque in Munich **297**

ISLAMIC GARDENS

See also Gardens

ISLAMIC HOLIDAYS

See also Religious holidays

ISLAMIC HOLY WAR *See* Jihad

Islamic imperialism. Karsh, E. **297**

ISLAMIC LAW
Abdul Rauf, F. Moving the mountain   **297.09**
Nordland, R. The Lovers   **958.104**
ISLAMIC LAW
    See also Law
ISLAMIC LEADERS
Armstrong, K. Muhammad   **297**
Hazleton, L. After the prophet   **297**
Qazwini, H. American crescent   **92**
ISLAMIC LEARNING AND SCHOLARSHIP --
    MALI -- TOMBOUCTOU
Hammer, J.   The bad-ass librarians of Timbuk-
    tu   **025.8**
ISLAMIC LITERATURE
Hammer, J.   The bad-ass librarians of Timbuk-
    tu   **025.8**
ISLAMIC MUSIC
    See also Music; Religious music
ISLAMIC POETRY
    See also Islamic literature; Poetry
ISLAMIC RUGS -- HISTORY
Denny, W. B. How to read Islamic carpets   **746.7**
ISLAMIC SERMONS
    See also Islamic literature; Sermons
ISLAMIC WOMEN *See* Muslim women
ISLAMOPHOBIA
Zafar, H. Demystifying Islam   **297**
ISLAMOPHOBIA
    See also Prejudices
ISLAMOPHOBIA -- EUROPE
Power, C. If the oceans were ink   **297**
ISLAMOPHOBIA -- UNITED STATES
Nussbaum, M. C.   The new religious intoler-
    ance   **201**
ISLAND ECOLOGY
    See also Ecology
The **island** of the colorblind. Sacks, O. W.   **617.7**
Islands of the damned. Burgin, R. V.   **940.54**
ISLANDS OF THE PACIFIC
Michener, J. A. Return to paradise   **990**
Sacks, O. W. The island of the colorblind   **617.7**
ISLE AU HAUT (MAINE)
Greenlaw, L. The lobster chronicles   **639**
. . . isms: understanding art. Little, S.   **709**
ISOLATIONISM
    See also International relations
ISOLATIONISM -- UNITED STATES -- HISTO-
    RY -- 20TH CENTURY
Olson, L. Those angry days   **940.53**
ISOTOPES
    See also Atoms
Israel. Rubin, B.   **956.940**
ISRAEL
Cohen, R. Israel   **956.940**
Rubin, B. Israel   **956.940**
ISRAEL

    See also Middle East
Israel. Cohen, R.   **956.940**
ISRAEL -- ANTIQUITIES
Burleigh, N. Unholy business   **933**
ISRAEL -- DESCRIPTION AND TRAVEL
Cohen, R. Israel is real   **956.94**
ISRAEL -- DESCRIPTION AND TRAVEL --
    GRAPHIC NOVELS
Glidden, S. How to understand Israel in 60 days or
    less   **741.5**
ISRAEL -- FOREIGN RELATIONS
Shlaim, A. The iron wall   **956.04**
ISRAEL -- FOREIGN RELATIONS -- ARAB
    COUNTRIES
Mitchell, G. J. A Path to Peace   **956.94**
ISRAEL -- FOREIGN RELATIONS -- UNITED
    STATES
Ross, D. B. Doomed to succeed   **327.73**
ISRAEL -- HISTORY
Ephron, D. Killing a king   **956.94**
Halevi, Y. K. Like dreamers   **356**
Hoffman, B. Anonymous soldiers   **956.94**
Landau, D. Arik   **92**
Shavit, A. My promised land   **956.05**
ISRAEL -- MILITARY HISTORY
Karpin, M. I. The bomb in the basement   **355**
ISRAEL -- POLITICS AND GOVERNMENT
Bar-On, M. Moshe Dayan   **956.940**
Landau, D. Arik   **92**
Menachem Begin   **956.940**
O'Malley, P. The two-state delusion   **956.94**
Shavit, A. My promised land   **956.05**
ISRAEL -- POLITICS AND GOVERNMENT --
    1993-
Ephron, D. Killing a king   **956.94**
ISRAEL -- POLITICS AND GOVERNMENT --
    20TH CENTURY
Menachem Begin   **956.940**
ISRAEL -- SOCIAL CONDITIONS
Horovitz, D. P. A little too close to God   **956.940**
Shipler, D. K. Arab and Jew   **956.94**
Israel is real. Cohen, R.   **956.94**
Israel, Fred L.
(ed) Justices of the United States Supreme
    Court   **347.73**
(ed) My fellow citizens   **352.23**
Israel, Paul
Edison   **92**
ISRAEL-ARAB CONFLICTS
Al Jundi, S. The hour of sunlight   **92**
Chesler, P. The new anti-semitism   **305.8**
David, A. Once upon a country   **92**
Hoffman, B. Anonymous soldiers   **956.94**
La Guardia, A. War without end   **956.940**
LeBor, A. City of oranges   **956.94**
Lozowick, Y. Right to exist   **956.940**

Miller, A. D. The much too promised land **956.05**

Miller, J. Inheriting the Holy Land **956.94**

Mitchell, G. J. A Path to Peace **956.94**

Morris, B. Righteous victims **956**

O'Malley, P. The two-state delusion **956.94**

Rice, C. No higher honor **327.73**

Said, E. W. The end of the peace process **956.05**

Shavit, A. My promised land **956.05**

Shipler, D. K. Arab and Jew **956.94**

Shlaim, A. The iron wall **956.04**

Tolan, S. The lemon tree **956.94**

ISRAEL-ARAB CONFLICTS

See also Arab countries -- Foreign relations -- Israel; Israel -- Foreign relations -- Arab countries

ISRAEL-ARAB CONFLICTS -- GRAPHIC NOVELS

Glidden, S. How to understand Israel in 60 days or less **741.5**

Sacco, J. Footnotes in Gaza **956.04**

ISRAEL-ARAB RELATIONS *See* Arab countries -- Foreign relations -- Israel; Israel -- Foreign relations -- Arab countries

ISRAEL-ARAB WAR, 1948-1949

Collins, L. O Jerusalem! **956.94**

ISRAEL-ARAB WAR, 1948-1949

See also Israel-Arab conflicts

ISRAEL-ARAB WAR, 1967

Bregman, A. Cursed victory

Halevi, Y. K. Like dreamers **356**

Oren, M. Six days of war **956.04**

ISRAEL-ARAB WAR, 1967

See also Israel-Arab conflicts

ISRAEL-ARAB WAR, 1973

See also Israel-Arab conflicts

ISRAEL-ARAB WAR, 1973 -- PEACE

Wright, L. Thirteen Days in September **956.04**

ISRAELI COOKING

Cook, S. Zahav **641.59**

Gur, J. The book of New Israeli food **641.5**

Ottolenghi, Y. Jerusalem **641.5**

ISRAELI NATIONAL CHARACTERISTICS

Horovitz, D. P. A little too close to God **956.940**

La Guardia, A. War without end **956.940**

The **Israeli** secret services and the struggle against terrorism. Pedahzur, A. **363.32**

Isserman, Maurice

(jt. auth) Cronkite, W. Cronkite's war **070.4**

Continental divide **796.52**

Istanbul. Pamuk, O. **949.6**

ISTANBUL (TURKEY)

Pamuk, O. Istanbul **949.6**

ISTITUTO PER LE OPERE DI RELIGIONE -- CORRUPT PRACTICES

Posner, G. God's Bankers **364.16**

It doesn't take a rocket scientist. Malone, J. W. **920**

It Ended Badly. Wright, J. **302**

It happened in the Catskills. **974.7**

It pays to talk. Schwab-Pomerantz, C. **332.024**

It takes a village. Clinton, H. R. **305.23**

It worked for me. Koltz, T. **92**

It's a jungle in there. Rosenbaum, D. A. **153**

It's about that time. Cook, R. **92**

It's all easy. **641.5**

It's all Greek to me. Higgins, C. **938**

It's complicated. Boyd, D. **004.67**

It's never too late to begin again. Cameron, J. B. **155.67**

It's not about the money. Kessel, B. **332.024**

It's only a movie. Chandler, C. **92**

It's our day. Jellison, K. **392**

It's the middle class, stupid! Carville, J. **320.51**

It's the pictures that got small. **92**

It's time: poems. Gibbons, R. **811**

It's What I Do. Addario, L. **92**

ITALIAN AMERICANS -- WISCONSIN -- MIL-WAUKEE -- HISTORY -- 20TH CENTURY

Strang, D. A. Worse than the devil **345**

ITALIAN ART

Adams, L. Italian Renaissance art **709.02**

Florence **759.5**

Hirst, M. Michelangelo **709.2**

ITALIAN AUTHORS

The Oxford companion to Italian literature **850**

Tuck, L. Woman of Rome: a life of Elsa Morante **92**

Italian Comfort Food. **641.594**

Italian food. David, E. **641.5**

Italian grill. Batali, M. **641.5**

ITALIAN PAINTING

See also Painting

ITALIAN POETRY

The collected poems of Eugenio Montale 1925-1977 **851**

Italian Renaissance art. Adams, L. **709.02**

Italian ways. Parks, T. **941.5**

The **Italians.** Hooper, J. **945.093**

ITALIANS

Hooper, J. The Italians **945.093**

ITALY

Saviano, R. Gomorrah **364.1**

ITALY -- ANTIQUITIES

Fowler, B. Iceman **937**

ITALY -- ANTIQUITIES

See also Antiquities

ITALY -- CIVILIZATION

Hooper, J. The Italians **945.093**

ITALY -- CIVILIZATION -- 1268-1559

Lee, A. The ugly Renaissance **945**

ITALY -- DESCRIPTION AND TRAVEL

Caggiano, B. Biba's Italy **641.59**

Parks, T. Italian ways **941.5**

The rough guide to Italy   **914.504**

ITALY -- HISTORY
Crowley, R. City of fortune   **945**
Norwich, J. J. Sicily   **945.8**

ITALY -- HISTORY -- 0-1559
Frieda, L. The Deadly Sisterhood   **945**
Lee, A. The ugly Renaissance   **945**

ITALY -- HISTORY -- 1492-1559 -- BIOGRAPHY
Unger, M. J. Machiavelli   **92**

ITALY -- HISTORY -- 1914-1945
Bosworth, R. J. B. Mussolini's Italy   **945**
Zuccotti, S. Under his very windows   **940.53**

ITALY -- HISTORY -- 19TH CENTURY
Wills, G. Verdi's Shakespeare   **822.3**

ITALY -- INTELLECTUAL LIFE
Heilbron, J. L. Galileo   **92**

ITALY -- POLITICS AND GOVERNMENT -- 1268-1559
King, R. Leonardo and the Last supper   **759**

ITALY -- POLITICS AND GOVERNMENT -- 1914-1945
Hughes-Hallett, L. Gabriele d'Annunzio   **858**

ITCHING -- POPULAR WORKS
Yosipovitch, G. Living with itch   **616.5**

Ito, Michiyo
Simply sewn   **646.4**

Ivan IV, the Terrible, Czar of Russia, 1530-1584
About
De Madariaga, I. Ivan the Terrible   **92**
Ivan the Terrible. De Madariaga, I.   **92**
Ivan's war. Merridale, C.   **940.54**

Ivanko, John D.
Homemade for Sale   **664**

Iversen, Kristen
About
Iversen, K. Full body burden   **363.17**

Iverson, Peter
We are still here   **970.004**

Ives, Charles Edward, 1874-1954
About
Swafford, J. Charles Ives   **92**

Ivey, Kimberly Smith
(jt. auth) Baumgarten, L. Four centuries of quilts   **746.46**

IVORIES, ROMANESQUE -- SCOTLAND -- LEWIS WITH HARRIS ISLAND
Brown, N. M. Ivory Vikings   **736**

IVORY
Orenstein, R. Ivory, horn and blood   **333.95**

IVORY COAST
Erdman, S. Nine hills to Nambonkaha   **966.68**
Ivory Vikings. Brown, N. M.   **736**
Ivory, horn and blood. Orenstein, R.   **333.95**

Iweala, Uzodinma
Our kind of people   **362.196**
Iwo Jima.   **940.54**

IWO JIMA, BATTLE OF, 1945
Bradley, J. Flags of our fathers   **940.54**
Haynes, F. The lions of Iwo Jima   **940.54**
Iwo Jima   **940.54**

Iyengar, B. K. S.
Light on life   **294**

Iyengar, Sheena
The art of choosing   **153.8**

Iyer, Pico
The Art of Stillness   **302.23**
The man within my head   **809**
The open road   **92**

Iyer, Raghavan
660 curries   **641.5**
Indian cooking unfolded   **641.59**

Izenberg, Jerry
Rozelle   **92**

J

J. Edgar Hoover. Geary, R.   **363.2**
J. Edgar Hoover. Gentry, C.   **353**
J. M. Coetzee and the Life of Writing. Attwell, D.   **823**

J. Paul Getty Museum
Frammolino, R. Chasing Aphrodite   **930**
Walsh, J. The J. Paul Getty Museum and its collections   **708.1**
Watkins, C. E. Carleton Watkins: the complete mammoth photographs   **778.9**
The **J.** Paul Getty Museum and its collections. Walsh, J.   **708.1**
J.D. Salinger. Slawenski, K.   **92**
J.D. Salinger. Beller, T.   **92**
J.D. Salinger.   **813**

J.G. Ferguson Publishing Company
Encyclopedia of careers and vocational guidance   **331.7**

J.K. Lasser Tax Institute
Weltman, B. J.K. Lasser's guide for tough times   **332.024**
J.K. Lasser's guide for tough times. Weltman, B.   **332.024**
J.K. Lasser's your income tax.   **336.2**
J.m.w.   turner.

Jabbour, Niki
Groundbreaking food gardens   **635**
Jack and other new poems. Kumin, M.   **811**
Jack be nimble. O'Brien, J.   **92**
Jack Johnson, rebel sojourner. Runstedtler, T.   **796.83**
Jack London. Labor, E.   **92**
Jack London, photographer. Adam, P.   **92**
Jack Nicklaus. Nicklaus, J.   **796.352**
Jack the Ripper
About
The Ultimate Jack the Ripper companion   **364.15**
JACK THE RIPPER MURDERS, LONDON,

ENGLAND, 1888

See also Serial killers

Jack, Belinda Elizabeth

George Sand   843

Jackie and Campy. Kashatus, W. C.   92

Jackie Ormes. Goldstein, N.   741.5

Jackling, Daniel Cowan, 1869-1956

     About

LeCain, T. J. Mass destruction   338.2

Jackman, Ian

(jt. auth) Feinstein, M. The Gershwins and me 92

Jackson Pollock. Solomon, D.   92

Jackson, Albert

Popular mechanics complete home how-to   643

Jackson, Andrew P.

(ed) The 21st-century black librarian in America   020

Jackson, Andrew, 1767-1845

     About

Brands, H. W. Andrew Jackson   92

Groom, W. Patriotic fire   973.5

Hofstadter, R. The American political tradition, and the men who made it   973

Langguth, A. J. Driven West   973.5

Meacham, J. American lion   92

Remini, R. V. Andrew Jackson   92

Reynolds, D. S. Waking giant   973.5

Wallace, A. F. C. The long bitter trail   323.1

Wilentz, S. Andrew Jackson   92

Jackson, Blair

Garcia   92

Jackson, Carlton

Hattie: the life of Hattie McDaniel   92

Jackson, Jesse L., 1941-

     About

Baraka, I. A. The LeRoi Jones/Amiri Baraka reader   818

Jackson, Joe

Atlantic fever   629.130

Jackson, Kenneth T.

(ed) The Scribner encyclopedia of American lives   920.003

Jackson, Luke, 1988-

     About

Jackson, L. Freaks, geeks and asperger syndrome   618.92

Jackson, L. Sex, drugs and Asperger's syndrome (ASD)   618.92

Jackson, Major

Holding company   811

Hoops   811

Jackson, Michael, 1958-2009

     About

Greenburg, Z. O. Michael Jackson, Inc   92

Jackson, Pamela

(ed) Dick, P. K. The exegesis of Philip K. Dick 818

Jackson, Rebecca

The learning habit   371.3

Jackson, Robert Houghwout, 1892-1954

     About

Feldman, N. Scorpions   920

Jackson, Sally

Brunch @ Bobby's   641.5

Jackson, Shirley, 1916-1965

Let me tell you   818

     About

Franklin, R. Shirley Jackson   92

Jackson, Stonewall

     About

Gwynne, S. C. Rebel Yell   92

Robertson, J. I. Stonewall Jackson   92

Jackson, Sumner Waldron

     About

Kershaw, A. Avenue of spies   940.53

Jackson, Tom

Chilled   621.56

Jackson, Troy

Becoming King   92

Jacksonland. Inskeep, S.   973.5

Jacob, Dianne

Will write for food   808

Jacob, Kathryn Allamong

King of the lobby   92

Jacobi, C. G. J. (Carl Gustav Jakob), 1804-1851

     About

Bell, E. T. Men of mathematics   920

Jacobs, A. J.

(jt. auth) Bike Snob The enlightened cyclist 796.6

The know-it-all   031

Jacobs, Alan

Original sin   233

Jacobs, Bert, 1964-

     About

Jacobs, B. Life is good   650.1

Jacobs, Charlotte DeCroes

Jonas Salk   92

Jacobs, Chip

Chemicals   363.739

(jt. auth) Kelly, W. J. The People's Republic of Smogtown   363.7

Jacobs, Harriet A., 1813-1897

     About

Yellin, J. F. Harriet Jacobs: a life   92

Jacobs, Hollye

     About

Jacobs, H. The Silver Lining   616.99

Jacobs, Jane, 1916-2006

     About

Kanigel, R. Eyes on the street   92

Jacobs, John, 1968-

     About

Jacobs, B. Life is good   650.1

Jacobsen, Annie
Area 51   **358.4**
Operation Paperclip   **940.54**
The Pentagon's Brain   **355**
Jacobsen, Josephine
In the crevice of time   **811**
Jacobsen, Rolf
The roads have come to an end now   **839.8**
Jacobsen, Rowan
Apples of uncommon character   **634**
The Essential Oyster   **641.694**
Fruitless fall   **638**
The living shore   **639.9**
Jacobson, Howard
Proteinaholic   **613.2**
Jacobson, Sidney
The 9/11 report   **741.5**
Anne Frank   **92**
Jacobsthal, Hilde
About
Goldberg, R. Motherland   **940.531**
Jacoby, Karl
The strange career of William Ellis   **92**
Jacoby, Kate
Vedge   **641.6**
Jacoby, Susan
Never say die   **305.26**
Jacqueline Bouvier. Davis, J. H.   **92**
Jacqueline Bouvier Kennedy Onassis. Leaming, B.   **92**
Jacqueline Kennedy. Bowles, H.   **92**
Jacqueline Kennedy.   **973.922**
Jacques Cousteau. Matsen, B.   **92**
Jacques Pepin celebrates. Pepin, J.   **641.5**
Jacques, Juliet
Trans   **306.76**
Jacques, Martin
When China rules the world   **327**
Jacquet de La Guerre, Elisabeth-Claude, 1665-1729
About
Porter, C. H. Five lives in music   **780.92**
Jadhav, Narendra
Untouchables   **305.5**
Jaeger, Paul T.
(jt. auth) McClure, C. R. Public libraries and internet service roles   **025.04**
Jaffe, Aniela
Jung, C. G. Memories, dreams, reflections   **150.19**
Jaffe, Harry
(jt. auth) Giffords, G. D. Enough   **363.33**
Jaffe, Marc
(ed) The longest trail   **970.004**
Jaffrey, Madhur
An invitation to Indian cooking   **641.59**
At home with Madhur Jaffrey   **641.5**
Climbing the mango trees   **92**
Madhur Jaffrey's world vegetarian   **641.5**
Ultimate curry bible   Madhur Jaffrey's ultimate curry bible   **641.5**
Vegetarian India   **641.595**
Jager-Hyman, Joie
B+ grades, A+ college application   **378.1**
Jaglom, Henry, 1939-
About
My Lunches With Orson   **791.43**
Jaher, David
The witch of lime street   **92**
Jahren, Hope
About
Jahren, H. Lab girl   **92**
JAILHOUSE LAWYERS -- NEBRASKA -- BIOGRAPHY
Burke, D. Law man   **92**
JAILS *See* Prisons
JAINISM
     See also Religions
Jakes, T. D., 1957-
Destiny   **248.4**
Instinct   **248.4**
Jalal al-Din Rumi
Barks, C. Rumi: the big red book   **891**
JAM
Foolproof preserving   **641.4**
JAMAICA -- RELIGION
Chevannes, B. Rastafari: roots and ideology   **299.6**
JAMAICAN POETRY
Sinclair, S. Cannibal   **811.6**
James Beard's American cookery. Beard, J.   **641.5**
James Brown, the godfather of soul. Brown, J.   **92**
James Dean: rebel with a cause. Gehring, W. D.   **92**
James Fenimore Cooper. Franklin, W.   **92**
James Herriot's animal stories. Herriot, J.   **636.089**
James Herriot's cat stories. Herriot, J.   **636.8**
James Herriot's dog stories. Herriot, J.   **636.7**
James Herriot's favorite dog stories. Herriot, J.   **636.7**
James Joyce. Bowker, G.   **823**
James Joyce. Ellmann, R.   **92**
James Joyce. O'Brien, E.   **823**
James Madison. Cheney, L. V.   **92**
James Madison. Wills, G.   **92**
James Madison. Broadwater, J.   **92**
James Merrill. Hammer, L.   **92**
The **James** T. Bialac Native American Art Collection.   **704.03**
James Tiptree, Jr. Phillips, J.   **813**
James, Bill, 1949-
Popular crime   **364.1**
James, Chris
The complete serger handbook   **646.2**
James, Clive, 1939-

As of this writing | 824
Cultural amnesia | 920
Latest readings | 828
James, Eloisa
    About
James, E. Paris in love | 92
James, Etta, 1938-2012
    About
James, E. Rage to survive | 92
James, Henry, 1843-1916
Literary criticism | 809
    About
Haralson, E. L. Critical companion to Henry James | 813
Kazin, A. An American procession | 810
Ozick, C. Quarrel & quandary | 814
James, Jamie
The glamour of strangeness | 700.19
The snake charmer | 92
James, Jesse, 1847-1882
    About
Stiles, T. J. Jesse James | 364.15
James, P. D.
James, P. D. Talking about detective fiction | 823
    About
James, P. D. Time to be in earnest | 823
James, Vaughn E.
The Alzheimer's advisor | 344
James, William
The varieties of religious experience | 210
    About
Blum, D. Ghost hunters | 133.9
Commager, H. S. The American mind | 973
Durant, W. J. The story of philosophy | 109
Menand, L. The Metaphysical Club | 973.9
Richardson, R. D. William James | 92
James, Wilmot
(ed) In his own words | 92
Jameson, Marni
Downsizing the family home | 346.04
JAMESTOWN (VA.) -- HISTORY
Horn, J. P. P. A land as God made it | 975.5
Price, D. Love and hate in Jamestown | 975.5
Jamie Oliver's comfort food. | 641.5
Jamie's dinners. Oliver, J. | 641
Jamie's Italy. | 641.59
Jamieson, Dave
Mint condition | 796.357
Jamieson, Michael
(ed) Jonson, B. Volpone and other plays | 822
Jamison, Bill
The border cookbook | 641.59
Jamison, C. A. The big book of outdoor cooking and entertaining | 641.5
Jamison, Cheryl Alters
The big book of outdoor cooking and entertain-

ing | 641.5
Jamison, B. The border cookbook | 641.59
Jamison, Kay R.
Exuberance | 152.4
Nothing was the same | 92
Jamison, Leslie
The empathy exams | 814
Jamison, Steve
Walsh, B. The score takes care of itself | 658.4
Jamling Tenzing Norgay
Touching my father's soul | 796.522
JAMMU AND KASHMIR (INDIA)
Hardy, J. In the valley of mist | 954
Jane Addams. Knight, L. W. | 92
Jane Austen. Tomalin, C. | 823
Jane Austen. Nokes, D. | 823
Jane Austen. Shields, C. | 823
Jane Brody's guide to the great beyond. Brody, J. E. | 616.02
Jane Goodall: the woman who redefined man. Peterson, D. | 92
Jane Seymour, Queen, consort of Henry VIII, King of England, 1509?-1537
    About
Fraser, A. The wives of Henry VIII | 920
Starkey, D. Six wives: the queens of Henry VIII | 942.05
Jane's fame. Harman, C. | 92
Janes, Andrew
Maps | 912.09
Jang, Jin-sung
    About
Jang Jin-sung Dear Leader | 92
Jang, Lucia
(jt. auth) McClelland, S. Stars Between the Sun and Moon | 92
Janowitz, Tama
    About
Janowitz, T. Scream | 92
Jansen, Marius B.
The making of modern Japan | 952
Janson's history of art. Janson, H. W. | 709
Janson, H. W.
Janson's history of art | 709
Janssen, Peter A.
(ed) Chapman piloting & seamanship | 623.88
Janssen, Sarah
(ed) The World Almanac and Book of Facts 2015 | 030
Jantsch, John
The referral engine | 658.8
JAPAN
Finn, A. The Way of the Runner | 796.42
JAPAN -- FOREIGN RELATIONS -- UNITED STATES
Nimura, J. P. Daughters of the Samurai | 920.72

JAPAN -- HISTORY

Dower, J. W. Ways of forgetting, ways of remembering **940.53**

JAPAN -- HISTORY -- 1868-1945

Frank, R. B. Downfall **940.54**

Keene, D. Emperor of Japan: Meiji and His world, 1852-1912 **952.03**

JAPAN -- HISTORY -- 1945-1952, ALLIED OCCUPATION

Morris, S. Supreme Commander **327.73**

JAPAN -- KINGS AND RULERS

Seagrave, S. The Yamato dynasty **952.03**

JAPAN -- MILITARY POLICY -- HISTORY -- 20TH CENTURY

Hotta, E. Japan 1941 **940.54**

JAPAN -- RELATIONS -- UNITED STATES

Sakamoto, P. R. Midnight in broad daylight **940.53**

JAPAN -- SOCIAL LIFE AND CUSTOMS

Downer, L. Women of the pleasure quarters **792.7**

Japan 1941. Hotta, E. **940.54**

Japan, a modern history. McClain, J. L. **952**

JAPAN. KAIGUN. KAMIKAZE TOKUBETSU KŌGEKITAI

Wukovits, J. F. Hell from the heavens **940.54**

JAPANESE -- UNITED STATES

Reeves, R. Infamy **940.53**

JAPANESE AESTHETICS

See also Aesthetics

JAPANESE AMERICAN FAMILIES -- WASHINGTON -- SEATTLE

Sakamoto, P. R. Midnight in broad daylight **940.53**

JAPANESE AMERICAN SCULPTORS -- BIOGRAPHY

Herrera, H. Listening to stone **92**

JAPANESE AMERICAN WOMEN

Nimura, J. P. Daughters of the Samurai **920.72**

JAPANESE AMERICANS

Checkoway, J. The three-year swim club **797.2**

JAPANESE AMERICANS -- EVACUATION AND RELOCATION, 1942-1945

Colors of confinement **940.53**

Sakamoto, P. R. Midnight in broad daylight **940.53**

Sone, M. Nisei daughter **979.7**

JAPANESE AMERICANS -- WASHINGTON (STATE) -- SEATTLE -- BIOGRAPHY

Sone, M. Nisei daughter **979.7**

Japanese Americans, from relocation to redress. **940.53**

JAPANESE ART

101 top tips from professional manga artists **741.5**

JAPANESE COOKING

Cole, T. Uchi: the cookbook **641.6**

Goulding, M. Rice, noodle, fish **394.12**

Hiroko Shimbo Hiroko's American kitchen **641.59**

Olivier, M. Little Bento **641.53**

JAPANESE LANGUAGE

See also Language and languages

JAPANESE LITERATURE -- HISTORY AND CRITICISM

Keene, D. Five modern Japanese novelists **895.6**

Keene, D. The pleasures of Japanese literature **895.6**

Keene, D. Seeds in the heart **895.6**

Modern Japanese writers **895.6**

JAPANESE PAPER FOLDING *See* Origami

JAPANESE POETRY

Haiku before haiku **895.6**

JAPANESE POETRY -- COLLECTIONS

One hundred poems from the Japanese **895.6**

Jaques Cattell Press

Who's who in American politics 2007-2008 **920.003**

Jaques, Susan

The Empress of Art **92**

Jarausch, Konrad H.

Out of ashes **940.5**

Jarden Corp.

(comp) The all new ball book of canning and preserving **641.42**

Jarhead: a Marine's chronicle of the Gulf War and other battles. Swofford, A. **956.704**

Jarolim, Edith

(ed) Blackburn, P. The collected poems of Paul Blackburn **811**

Jaronsky, Shelly

The cookies & cups cookbook **641.86**

Jarrell, Randall

The complete poems **811**

No other book **809**

Jarzombek, Mark

A global history of architecture **720.9**

Jasanoff, Maya

Edge of empire **909.08**

Liberty's exiles **973.3**

JASMINE

Aftel, M. Fragrant **612.8**

Jason, Dan

(jt. auth) Malone, H. The Power of Pulses **635.65**

Jason, Julie

The AARP Retirement Survival Guide **332.024**

Jason, Philip K.

(ed) Masterplots II, poetry series **809.1**

Jasper, Richard P.

Halsted, D. D. Disaster planning **025.8**

Jaspers, Karl, 1883-1969

About

Existentialism from Dostoevsky to Sartre **142**

Jassey, Jonathan

The newborn sleep book **618.92**

Jassey, Lewis

(jt. auth) Jassey, J. The newborn sleep book **618.92**

Jauhar, Sandeep, 1968-

About

Jauhar, S. Doctored **92**

Java Man. Swisher, C. C. **599.93**

JAVELIN THROWERS

Ware, S. Letter to the world **920.72**

Javers, Eamon

Broker, trader, lawyer, spy **364.1**

Jaworski, Ron

Cosell, G. The games that changed the game **796.332**

Jay, Antony

(ed) Lend me your ears **808.88**

Jay, Ricky

About

Singer, M. Character studies **920**

Jayaraman, Saru

Forked **331.2**

Jayyusi, Salma Khadra

(ed) Anthology of modern Palestinian literature **892.7**

Jazz. **781.65**

Jazz. Ward, G. C. **781.65**

Jazz covers. Paulo, J. **781.65**

The jazz ear. Ratliff, B. **781.65**

JAZZ ENSEMBLES

Cooke, M. The chronicle of jazz **781.65**

JAZZ MUSIC

Ellison, R. The collected essays of Ralph Ellison **814**

Giddins, G. Visions of jazz **781.65**

Kahn, A. The house that Trane built **781.65**

Morgenstern, D. Living with jazz **781.65**

Paulo, J. Jazz covers **781.65**

Seibert, B. What the eye hears **792.7**

Ward, G. C. Jazz **781.65**

JAZZ MUSIC

See also Music

JAZZ MUSIC -- CHRONOLOGY

Cooke, M. The chronicle of jazz **781.65**

JAZZ MUSIC -- DICTIONARIES

Friedwald, W. A biographical guide to the great jazz and pop singers **920.003**

JAZZ MUSIC -- DISCOGRAPHY

Cook, R. The Penguin guide to jazz recordings **781.65**

JAZZ MUSIC -- HISTORY AND CRITICISM

Armstrong, L. Louis Armstrong, in his own words **92**

Cooke, M. The chronicle of jazz **781.65**

Jazz **781.65**

Myers, M. Why jazz happened **781.65**

Teachout, T. Pops **92**

The visual blues **704.03**

JAZZ MUSIC -- POETRY

Jazz poems **811**

JAZZ MUSIC -- SOCIAL ASPECTS -- LOUISIANA -- NEW ORLEANS -- HISTORY -- 20TH

CENTURY

Krist, G. Empire of sin **976.3**

JAZZ MUSICIANS

Armstrong, L. Louis Armstrong, in his own words **92**

Basie, C. Good morning blues: the autobiography of Count Basie **92**

Berlin, E. A. King of ragtime: Scott Joplin and his era **92**

Cohodas, N. Princess Noire **92**

Cook, R. It's about that time **92**

Cooke, M. The chronicle of jazz **781.65**

Dance, S. The world of Count Basie **920**

Davis, M. Miles, the autobiography **92**

Dregni, M. Django: the life and music of a Gypsy legend **92**

Ellison, R. Going to the territory **818**

Epstein, D. M. Nat King Cole **92**

Feather, L. The biographical encyclopedia of jazz **781.65**

Feather, L. From Satchmo to Miles **920**

Giddins, G. Visions of jazz **781.65**

Kahn, A. The house that Trane built **781.65**

Kelley, R. D. G. Thelonious Monk **92**

Lees, G. You can't steal a gift **781.65**

Murray, A. The blue devils of Nada **780.89**

Nolan, T. Three chords for beauty's sake: the life of Artie Shaw **92**

Ratliff, B. Coltrane **92**

Teachout, T. Pops **92**

JAZZ MUSICIANS -- BIOGRAPHY

Brothers, T. Louis Armstrong, master of modernism **92**

JAZZ MUSICIANS -- UNITED STATES -- BIOG-

RAPHY

Crouch, S. Kansas City lightning **92**

De Barros, P. Shall we play that one together? **92**

Goins, W. E. Blues all day long **92**

Strayhorn **781.650**

Teachout, T. Duke **92**

Jazz poems. **811**

Jeal, Tim

Explorers of the Nile **962**

Stanley **92**

JEALOUSY

See also Emotions

Jean-Jacques Rousseau. Damrosch, L. **848**

Jean-Jacques: the early life and work of Jean-Jacques Rousseau, 1712-1754. Cranston, M. **92**

JEANNETTE (STEAMER) -- HISTORY

Sides, H. In the kingdom of ice **910.4**

JEANS (CLOTHING)

Snyder, R. L. Fugitive denim **382**

Jeff Herman's guide to book publishers, editors, & literary agents. Herman, J. **070.5**

Jeff Koons. Rothkopf, S. **709.2**

Jeffers, Robinson, 1887-1962
The selected poetry of Robinson Jeffers   **811**
About
Gioia, D. Can poetry matter?   **809.1**
Jeffers, Susan J.
Feel the fear--and do it anyway   **152.4**
JEFFERSON COUNTY (COLORADO) -- BIOG-RAPHY
Iversen, K. Full body burden   **363.17**
Jefferson Davis, American. Cooper, W. J.   **92**
The **Jefferson** rule. Sehat, D.   **306.2**
Jefferson's great gamble. Cerami, C. A.   **973.4**
Jefferson, Jon
Bass, W. M. Death's acre   **614**
Jefferson, Julius
(ed) The 21st-century black librarian in Ameri-ca   **020**
Jefferson, Margo, 1947-
About
Jefferson, M. Negroland   **92**
Jefferson, Thomas, 1743-1826
Writings   **818**
About
Becker, C. The Declaration of Independence **973.3**
Bernstein, R. B. Thomas Jefferson   **92**
Burstein, A. Madison and Jefferson   **973.4**
Cerami, C. A. Jefferson's great gamble   **973.4**
Cohen, I. B. Science and the founding fathers **973.3**
Ellis, J. J. American sphinx: the character of Thom-as Jefferson   **92**
Ellis, J. J. Founding brothers   **973.4**
Gordon-Reed, A. The Hemingses of Monticel-lo   **920**
Gordon-Reed, A. Most Blessed of the Patriarchs **92**
Gordon-Reed, A. Thomas Jefferson and Sally Hemings   **973.4**
Hatch, P. J. A rich spot of earth   **635**
Hitchens, C. Thomas Jefferson: author of Ameri-ca   **92**
Hofstadter, R. The American political tradition, and the men who made it   **973**
Kranish, M. Flight from Monticello   **973.4**
Larson, E. J. A magnificent catastrophe   **324**
Malone, J. W. It doesn't take a rocket scientist **920**
Meacham, J. Thomas Jefferson   **92**
Miller, J. C. The Federalist era, 1789-1801 **973.4**
Simon, J. F. What kind of nation   **342**
Staloff, D. Hamilton, Adams, Jefferson   **973.4**
Stewart, D. O. American emperor   **973.4**
Vidal, G. Inventing a nation: Washington, Adams, Jefferson   **973.4**
Wiencek, H. Master of the mountain   **973.4**
Wills, G. 'Negro president'   **326**
Zacks, R. The pirate coast   **973.4**
Jeffery, Keith
1916   **909.82**

Jeffs, Warren
About
Brower, S. Prophet's prey   **306.8**
Jellison, Katherine
It's our day   **392**
Jeni's splendid ice creams at home. Bauer, J. B.   **641.8**
Jenike, Michael A.
Murphy, T. W. Life in rewind   **92**
Jenkins, Alison
300 tips for painting & decorating   **698**
Jenkins, Jeffrey Eric
(ed) The best plays of 2006-2007   **808.82**
Jenkins, Jessica Kerwin
All the time in the world   **390**
Jenkins, McKay
Poison spring   **363.73**
Jenkins, Nancy Harmon
The new Mediterranean diet cookbook   **641.5**
Jenkins, Peter
Looking for Alaska   **979.8**
A walk across America   **917**
Jenkins, Philip
The new faces of Christianity   **270**
Jenkyns, Richard
Classical literature   **880**
Jennings, Dana Andrew
Sing me back home   **781.642**
Jensen, Dean
Queen of the air   **791.3**
Jensen, Derrick
What we leave behind   **304.2**
Jensen, Frances E.
The teenage brain   **612.6**
Jensen, Joel
Steam: an enduring legacy   **625.2**
JEOPARDY (TELEVISION PROGRAM)
Baker, S. Final Jeopardy   **006.3**
Jeremiah, Thomas, d. 1775
About
Harris, J. W. The hanging of Thomas Jeremiah **92**
Jerrard, Jane
Crisis in employment   **025.5**
Jerry West. Lazenby, R.   **92**
Jerusalem. Ottolenghi, Y.   **641.5**
Jerusalem. Armstrong, K.   **956.94**
JERUSALEM
Hoffman, A. Till we have built Jerusalem   **956.94**
Jerusalem. Montefiore, S.   **956.94**
JERUSALEM -- DESCRIPTION AND TRAVEL
Ottolenghi, Y. Jerusalem   **641.5**
JERUSALEM -- HISTORY
Armstrong, K. Jerusalem   **956.94**
Goodman, M. Rome and Jerusalem   **933**
Montefiore, S. Jerusalem   **956.94**
JERUSALEM -- HISTORY -- 1948, SIEGE

Collins, L. O Jerusalem! **956.94**

Jerusalem in the twentieth century. Gilbert, M. **956.94**

Jerusalem, Jerusalem. Carroll, J. **956.94**

Jesperson, Keith Hunter
About
Olsen, J. I: the creation of a serial killer **364.1**

Jesse James. Stiles, T. J. **364.15**

Jestice, Phyllis G.
(ed) Holy people of the world **920.003**

The **Jesuit** guide to almost everything. Martin, J. **248.4**

Jesus. Wilson, A. N. **232.9**

JESUS CHRIST
See also God -- Christianity

Jesus Christ
About
Benedict XVI, P. Jesus of Nazareth. part two **232.9**
Bible/N.T./Gospels The three Gospels **226.3**
Blum, E. J. The color of Christ **232**
Fredriksen, P. Jesus of Nazareth, King of the Jews **232.9**
Girzone, J. F. A portrait of Jesus **232.9**
Gordon, M. Reading Jesus **232**
Heim, T. @stickyjesus **248.4**
Kline, F. R. Leonardo's holy child **741.945**
McKnight, S. Kingdom conspiracy **231.7**
Meier, J. P. A marginal Jew **232.9**
Pelikan, J. J. The illustrated Jesus through the centuries **232.9**
Price, R. A serious way of wondering **241**
Short stories by Jesus **226.8**
Spong, J. S. Biblical literalism **226.2**
Wilson, A. N. Jesus **232.9**

Jesus of Nazareth, King of the Jews. Fredriksen, P. **232.9**

Jesus of Nazareth. part two. Benedict XVI, P. **232.9**

JET LAG
See also Aviation medicine; Biological rhythms; Fatigue

JET PLANES
See also Airplanes

JET PROPULSION
Holt, N. Rise of the Rocket Girls **629.4**

Jetton, Tamara L.
(ed) Adolescent literacy in the academic disciplines **428**

Jew vs. Jew. Freedman, S. G. **296**

Jewel, 1974-
About
Jewel Never broken **92**

JEWELERS
Faber, T. Faberge's eggs **739.2**

Jewell, Andrew
(ed) Cather, W. The selected letters of Willa Cather **813**

JEWELRY
Bluhm, L. Creative soldered jewelry & accessories **745.594**
Codina, C. The complete book of jewelry making **739.27**
Combs, R. A. Kumihimo : basics & beyond **745.594**
DeCoster, M. Marcia DeCoster's beaded opulence **739.27**
Deeb, M. The beader's color palette **745.594**
Haab, S. The art of metal clay **739.27**
Katz, A. Seed bead chic **745.594**
Michaels, C. F. Teach yourself visually jewelry making & beading **745.59**
Miller, J. Miller's costume jewelry **739.27**
Wiseman, J. Jill Wiseman's beautiful beaded ropes **745.594**
Young, A. The workbench guide to jewelry techniques **739.27**

JEWELRY
See also Clothing and dress; Costume; Decorative arts; Fashion accessories

JEWELRY -- RUSSIA -- CATALOGS
Von Habsburg, G. Faberge revealed **739.2**

JEWELRY MAKING
Crowther, J. Make a statement **745.594**
Kan, L. Bead metamorphosis **745.594**
Karon, K. Advanced chain maille jewelry workshop **745.594**
McGrath, J. The complete jewelry making course **739.27**
Papp, C. Sensational soutache jewelry making **745.594**

JEWELRY THEFT -- HISTORY
Crosby, M. C. The great pearl heist **364.16**

JEWELS *See* Gems; Jewelry; Precious stones

Jewish American literature. **810**

JEWISH ART AND SYMBOLISM
Levine, L. I. Visual Judaism in late antiquity **704.9**

JEWISH ARTISTS -- POLAND -- BIOGRAPHY
Rynecki, E. Chasing portraits **700.92**

JEWISH AUTHORS -- 20TH CENTURY -- BIOGRAPHY
Prochnik, G. The Impossible Exile **92**

A **Jewish** baker's pastry secrets. Greenstein, E. **641.86**

JEWISH BANKERS -- GERMANY -- BIOGRAPHY
Goodman, S. The Orpheus Clock **940.53**

The **Jewish** Bible. **221**

JEWISH BUSINESSPEOPLE -- LOUISIANA -- NEW ORLEANS -- BIOGRAPHY
Cohen, R. The fish that ate the whale **338.7**

JEWISH CHILDREN IN THE HOLOCAUST
Friedman, A. Rywka's Diary **940.53**

JEWISH CHILDREN IN THE HOLOCAUST
See also Holocaust, 1939-1945

**JEWISH CHILDREN IN THE HOLOCAUST --
BIOGRAPHY**
Anne Frank   **92**
JEWISH CIVILIZATION
Cultures of the Jews   **909**
Nirenberg, D. Anti-Judaism   **305.892**
Roden, C. The book of Jewish food   **641.5**
JEWISH CIVILIZATION
See also Civilization
JEWISH COOKING
Goldstein, J. The new Mediterranean Jewish table   **641.5**
Greenstein, E. A Jewish baker's pastry secrets   **641.86**
Koenig, L. Modern Jewish cooking   **641.5**
Marks, G. The world of Jewish cooking   **641.5**
Morgan, J. The covenant kitchen   **641.5**
Nathan, J. Jewish cooking in America   **641.5**
Nathan, J. Quiches, kugels, and couscous   **641.5**
The New York Times Jewish cookbook   **641.5**
The New York Times Passover cookbook   **641.5**
Ottolenghi, Y. Jerusalem   **641.5**
Roden, C. The book of Jewish food   **641.5**
Rose, E. 100 Best Jewish Recipes   **641.5**
Wex, M. Rhapsody in schmaltz   **641.5**
Jewish cooking in America. Nathan, J.   **641.5**
JEWISH CUSTOMS *See* Jews -- Social life and customs; Judaism -- Customs and practices
JEWISH DIASPORA
Brenner, F. Diaspora: homelands in exile   **909**
Freedman, H. The Talmud   **296.1**
JEWISH DIASPORA
See also Human geography; Jews
Jewish encounters [series]
Century, D. Barney Ross   **92**
Lehman, D. A fine romance   **782.42**
Lipstadt, D. E. The Eichmann trial   **345**
Pinsky, R. The life of David   **92**
JEWISH ETHICS
Telushkin, J. Biblical literacy   **221**
Telushkin, J. Jewish wisdom   **296.3**
JEWISH ETHICS
See also Ethics
**JEWISH FAMILIES -- CZECH REPUBLIC --
PRAGUE -- BIOGRAPHY**
Woodward, B. Prague winter   **943.71**
JEWISH FOLK LITERATURE
Encyclopedia of Jewish folklore and traditions   **398.2**
JEWISH FOLK LITERATURE
See also Folk literature; Jewish literature
JEWISH HOLIDAYS
Axelrod, M. Your guide to the Jewish holidays   **296.4**
Goldman, A. L. Being Jewish   **296.4**
JEWISH HOLIDAYS
See also Judaism; Religious holidays
JEWISH HOLOCAUST (1933-1945) *See* Holocaust, 1939-1945
**JEWISH ILLUMINATION OF BOOKS AND
MANUSCRIPTS**
Bolsta, H. S. The illuminated Kaddish   **296.4**
JEWISH LANGUAGE *See* Hebrew language; Yiddish language
JEWISH LEADERS
Pick, H. Simon Wiesenthal   **940.53**
Segev, T. Simon Wiesenthal   **92**
JEWISH LIFE *See* Jews -- Social life and customs; Judaism -- Customs and practices
JEWISH LITERATURE
Kirsch, A. The people and the books   **809.889**
JEWISH LITERATURE
See also Literature; Religious literature
**JEWISH LITERATURE -- HISTORY AND
CRITICISM**
Kirsch, A. The people and the books   **809.889**
Jewish lives [series]
Cohen-Solal, A. Mark Rothko   **759.13**
Shawn, A. Leonard Bernstein   **92**
JEWISH MEN
Cohen-Solal, A. Mark Rothko   **759.13**
JEWISH MUSICIANS -- EUROPE -- BIOGRAPHY
Grymes, J. A. Violins of hope   **92**
Jewish people in America [series]
Diner, H. R. A time for gathering   **305.8**
JEWISH PHILOSOPHY
Buber, M. I and thou   **181**
Friedman, M. S. Encounter on the narrow ridge: a life of Martin Buber   **92**
Nirenberg, D. Anti-Judaism   **305.892**
Jewish Publication Society
Eisenberg, R. L. The JPS guide to Jewish traditions   **296.4**
JEWISH REFUGEES
Marton, K. The great escape   **920**
JEWISH REFUGEES -- BIOGRAPHY
Maitland, L. Crossing the borders of time   **940.53**
JEWISH RELIGION *See* Judaism
JEWISH RELIGIOUS FICTION
See also Fiction; Jewish literature; Religious fiction
JEWISH WAY OF LIFE
Bronfman, E. M. Why be Jewish?   **296**
Epstein, L. J. The basic beliefs of Judaism   **296.3**
Goldman, A. L. Being Jewish   **296.4**
Levy, N. To begin again   **296.7**
Jewish wisdom. Telushkin, J.   **296.3**
JEWISH WIT AND HUMOR
See also Wit and humor
JEWISH WOMEN
Diamant, A. Pitching my tent   **296.7**

Prose, F. Peggy Guggenheim   92
Vincent, L. Cut me loose   **305.892**

JEWISH WOMEN
   See also Women

JEWISH WOMEN -- NEW YORK (STATE) -- NEW YORK -- BIOGRAPHY
Vincent, L. Cut me loose   **305.892**

JEWISH-ARAB RELATIONS
Friedman, T. L. From Beirut to Jerusalem   **956**
Grossman, D. The yellow wind   **956.95**
Herzog, C. The Arab-Israeli wars   **956**
Morris, B. Righteous victims   **956**
Said, E. W. The end of the peace process   **956.05**
Shipler, D. K. Arab and Jew   **956.94**
Shlaim, A. The iron wall   **956.04**

JEWISH-ARAB RELATIONS
   See also Arabs; Jews

JEWS
Encyclopaedia Judaica   **296**
Laskin, D. The Family   **92**

JEWS -- ANTIQUITIES
   See also Antiquities

JEWS -- AUSTRIA
O'Connor The lady in gold   **759.36**

JEWS -- BELARUS -- BIOGRAPHY
Laskin, D. The Family   **92**

JEWS -- BIOGRAPHY
At the edge of the abyss   **940.53**

JEWS -- CIVILIZATION *See* Jewish civilization

JEWS -- CUSTOMS *See* Jews -- Social life and customs; Judaism -- Customs and practices

JEWS -- CZECH REPUBLIC -- PRAGUE
Helga's diary   **940.53**

JEWS -- EUROPE -- HISTORY -- 20TH CENTURY
Sachar, H. M. Dreamland   **940.5**
Wasserstein, B. On the eve   **305.892**

JEWS -- FESTIVALS *See* Jewish holidays

JEWS -- FOLKLORE
   See also Folklore

JEWS -- FOLKLORE -- ENCYCLOPEDIAS
Encyclopedia of Jewish folklore and traditions   **398.2**

JEWS -- FOOD
Wex, M. Rhapsody in schmaltz   **641.5**

JEWS -- FRANCE
Maitland, L. Crossing the borders of time   **940.53**

JEWS -- FRANCE -- BIOGRAPHY
Richmond Mouillot, M. A fifty-year silence   **940.53**

JEWS -- FRANCE -- MARSEILLE -- HISTORY -- 20TH CENTURY
Zuccotti, S. Père Marie-Benoît and Jewish rescue   **940.53**

JEWS -- GERMANY
Goodman, S. The Orpheus Clock   **940.53**
Underground in Berlin   **940.531**

JEWS -- HISTORY
Cohen, R. Israel   **956.940**
Cole, P. Sacred trash   **296.09**
It happened in the Catskills   **974.7**
Judt, T. Thinking the twentieth century   **320.092**
New American Haggadah   **296.4**
Schama, S. The story of the Jews   **909**

JEWS -- HISTORY -- MAPS
A Historical atlas of the Jewish people   **909**

JEWS -- HUNGARY
Marton, K. The great escape   **920**

JEWS -- HUNGARY -- BIOGRAPHY
Szegedy-Maszák, M. I kiss your hands many times   **920**

JEWS -- IDENTITY
Bronfman, E. M. Why be Jewish?   **296**

JEWS -- INDIA
Shepard, S. The girl from foreign   **92**

JEWS -- IRAQ
Sabar, A. My father's paradise   **305.8**

JEWS -- ITALY
Zuccotti, S. Under his very windows   **940.53**

JEWS -- LANGUAGE *See* Hebrew language; Yiddish language

JEWS -- LITERATURE *See* Hebrew literature; Jewish literature

JEWS -- LITHUANIA
Kruk, H. The last days of the Jerusalem of Lithuania   **940.53**

JEWS -- NETHERLANDS
Goldberg, R. Motherland   **940.531**

JEWS -- NETHERLANDS -- GRAPHIC NOVELS
Jacobson, S. Anne Frank   **92**

JEWS -- NETHERLANDS -- SOCIAL CONDITIONS -- 20TH CENTURY
Goldberg, R. Motherland   **940.531**

JEWS/RECREATION/NEW YORK (STATE)/ CATSKILL MOUNTAINS REGION
In the Catskills   **974.7**

JEWS -- PERSECUTIONS
Brent, J. Stalin's last crime   **947.084**
Friedlander, S. Nazi Germany and the Jews   **940.53**
Friedlander, S. The years of extermination   **940.53**
Gay, P. My German question   **943**
Gilbert, M. Kristallnacht   **940.53**
Horwitz, G. J. Ghettostadt   **940.53**

JEWS -- PERSECUTIONS
   See also Antisemitism; Persecution

JEWS -- PERSECUTIONS -- EUROPE -- HISTORY -- 20TH CENTURY
Wasserstein, B. On the eve   **305.892**

JEWS -- PERSECUTIONS -- POLAND -- LÓDZ -- HISTORY
Horwitz, G. J. Ghettostadt   **940.53**

JEWS -- PICTORIAL WORKS

Brenner, F. Diaspora: homelands in exile **909**

JEWS -- POLAND

Kurtz, G. Three minutes in Poland **947.7**

JEWS -- ROME

Goodman, M. Rome and Jerusalem **933**

JEWS -- RUSSIA

Gessen, M. Where the Jews aren't **957.7**

JEWS -- SOCIAL CONDITIONS

Wasserstein, B. On the eve **305.892**

JEWS -- SOCIAL CONDITIONS

See also Social conditions

JEWS -- SOCIAL LIFE AND CUSTOMS

Epstein, L. J. The basic beliefs of Judaism **296.3**

Wex, M. Rhapsody in schmaltz **641.5**

JEWS -- SOCIAL LIFE AND CUSTOMS

See also Manners and customs

JEWS -- SOCIAL LIFE AND CUSTOMS -- EN-CYCLOPEDIAS

Encyclopedia of Jewish folklore and traditions **398.2**

JEWS -- SPAIN

Kamen, H. The Spanish Inquisition **272**

JEWS -- UKRAINE

King, C. Odessa **947.7**

JEWS -- UNITED STATES

Ashton, D. Hanukkah in America **296.4**

In the Catskills **974.7**

Sarna, J. D. Lincoln and the Jews **973.7**

JEWS -- UNITED STATES -- BIOGRAPHY

Richmond Mouillot, M. A fifty-year silence **940.53**

JEWS -- UNITED STATES -- HISTORY

Diner, H. R. A time for gathering **305.8**

Sarna, J. D. American Judaism **296**

JEWS IN ART

Rynecki, E. Chasing portraits **700.92**

JEWS IN LITERATURE

Fiedler, L. A. Fiedler on the roof **814**

The **Jews** of Germany. Gay, R. **943**

JEWS, BELARUSIAN -- PALESTINE -- BIOG-RAPHY

Laskin, D. The Family **92**

JFK's last hundred days. Clarke, T. **92**

JFK, conservative. Stoll, I. **973.922**

JIGSAW PUZZLES

See also Puzzles

Jihad. Kepel, G. **297**

JIHAD

Di Giovanni, J. The Morning They Came For Us **956.91**

Esposito, J. L. Unholy war **322.4**

Karsh, E. Islamic imperialism **297**

Kepel, G. Jihad **297**

Lewis, B. The crisis of Islam **297**

McMeekin, S. The Berlin-Baghdad express **940.3**

JIHAD

See also International relations; Islam

Jill Wiseman's beautiful beaded ropes. Wiseman, J. **745.594**

Jim Henson. Jones, B. J. **92**

Jimenez, Stephen

The Book of Matt **364.1**

JIMMY CHOO (FIRM)

Crowe, L. G. The towering world of Jimmy Choo **391**

JINGLES (ADVERTISING SONGS)

See also Songs

Jinich, Pati

Mexican today **641.5**

Jitney. Wilson, A. **812**

JIU-JITSU

See also Martial arts; Self-defense

The **jive** talker. Kambalu, S. **92**

Joachim, David

Cooking light global kitchen **641.59**

Mastering pasta **641.82**

Rustic Italian food **641.59**

Vetri, M. Il viaggio di Vetri **641.5**

Joan Mitchell. Albers, P. **92**

Joan of Arc. Gordon, M. **944**

Joan of Arc. Castor, H. **92**

Joan of Arc: her story. Pernoud, R. **92**

Joan Palevsky imprint in classical literature [series]

Catullus, G. V. The poems of Catullus **874**

Joan, of Arc, Saint, 1412-1431

About

Castor, H. Joan of Arc **92**

Gordon, M. Joan of Arc **944**

Pernoud, R. Joan of Arc: her story **92**

Shaw, B. Saint Joan **822**

Joannou, Maroula

(ed) The history of British women's writing **820**

The **job.** Osborne, S. **92**

JOB ANALYSIS

See also Factory management; Industrial efficiency; Management; Occupations; Personnel management; Salaries, wages, etc.

JOB APPLICATIONS *See* Applications for positions

JOB CREATION -- UNITED STATES

Cox, H. H. American drive **338**

JOB HUNTING

Berger, L. All work, no pay **650.14**

Citrin, J. M. The career playbook **650.14**

Jerrard, J. Crisis in employment **025.5**

Kay, A. This is how to get your next job **650.14**

Mackay, H. Use your head to get your foot in the door **650.14**

Post, P. Emily Post's The etiquette advantage in business **395**

Raskin, D. The dirty little secrets of getting your dream job **650.14**

What color is your parachute? 2017   **650.1**

Yate, M. Knock 'em dead 2015   **158**

Yate, M. Knock 'em dead cover letters   **650.14**

JOB HUNTING

  See also Employment agencies; Vocational guidance

JOB HUNTING -- UNITED STATES -- HISTORY -- 21ST CENTURY

  Chideya, F. The episodic career   **650.1**

JOB INTERVIEWS

  Port, M. Steal the show   **658.4**

  Yate, M. Knock 'em dead 2015   **158**

JOB INTERVIEWS

  See also Applications for positions; Interviewing

JOB PLACEMENT GUIDANCE *See* Vocational guidance

JOB SATISFACTION

  Chapman, B. Everybody matters   **658.4**

  Hallowell, E. M. Shine   **658.3**

JOB SATISFACTION

  See also Attitude (Psychology); Employee morale; Personnel management; Work

JOB SATISFACTION -- PSYCHOLOGICAL ASPECTS

  Webb, C. How to have a good day   **650.1**

Jobb, Dean

  Empire of deception   **92**

JOBLESSNESS *See* Unemployment

Jobrani, Maz, 1972-

    About

  Jobrani, M. I'm not a terrorist, but I've played one on tv   **92**

JOBS *See* Occupations; Professions

Jobs, Steve, 1955-2011

    About

  Isaacson, W. Steve Jobs   **92**

  Tetzeli, R. Becoming Steve Jobs   **92**

JOCKEYS

  Drape, J. Black maestro   **92**

Joe DiMaggio. Cramer, R. B.   **796.357**

Joe Louis. Roberts, R.   **92**

Joffe, Daron

  Citizen farmers   **635**

JOGGING

  See also Running

Johann Sebastian Bach. Geck, M.   **92**

Johann Sebastian Bach. Wolff, C.   **92**

Johannes Brahms. Swafford, J.   **92**

JOHANNESBURG (SOUTH AFRICA) -- BIOGRAPHY

  Gevisser, M. Lost and Found in Johannesburg, a memoir   **92**

Johanneson, Gudni Thorlacius

  The history of Iceland   **949.12**

Johansen, Bruce E.

The Native peoples of North America   **970.004**

Johanson, Donald C.

  From Lucy to language   **599.93**

  Lucy: the beginnings of humankind   **599.93**

  Lucy's legacy   **569.9**

John Adams. Grant, J.   **92**

John Adams. McCullough, D. G.   **92**

John and Robin Diskson series in Texas music [series]

  Govenar, A. B. Texas blues   **781.64**

JOHN BIRCH SOCIETY

  Conner, C. Wrapped in the flag   **322.4**

John Brown, abolitionist. Reynolds, D. S.   **92**

John Clare: a biography. Bate, J.   **92**

John Dryden. Dryden, J.   **821**

John F. Kennedy. Brinkley, A.   **92**

JOHN H. REAGAN HIGH SCHOOL (AUSTIN, TEX.)

  Brick, M. Saving the school   **373.22**

John Huston. Meyers, J.   **92**

John James Audubon. Rhodes, R.   **92**

John Lennon. Norman, P.   **92**

John Marshall. Smith, J. E.   **347**

John Marshall. Unger, H. G.   **92**

John Milton. Hawkes, D.   **92**

John Milton. Campbell, G.   **92**

John Muir. Wilkins, T.   **92**

John Muir and the ice that started a fire. Heacox, K.   **92**

John Osborne. Heilpern, J.   **92**

John Paul II. Flynn, R.   **92**

John Paul II, Pope, 1920-2005

  Crossing the threshold of hope   **282**

    About

  Buttiglione, R. Karol Wojtyla   **282**

  Flynn, R. John Paul II   **92**

  O'Connor, G. Universal Father: a life of John Paul II   **92**

John Paul Jones. Morison, S. E.   **92**

John Paul Jones. Thomas, E.   **92**

John Quincy Adams. Nagel, P. C.   **92**

John Quincy Adams. Kaplan, F.   **92**

John Quincy Adams. Remini, R. V.   **92**

John Quincy Adams. Traub, J.   **92**

John Quincy Adams. Giles Unger, H.   **92**

John Shaw's nature photography field guide. Shaw, J.   **778.9**

John Steinbeck.   **813**

John Tyler. Crapol, E. P.   **92**

John Tyler. May, G.   **92**

John Wayne: the life and legend. Eyman, S.   **92**

John Wesley. Tomkins, S.   **287**

John Winthrop. Bremer, F. J.   **974.4**

John, Catherine Rachel

  Attwater, D. The Penguin dictionary of saints   **920.003**

John, King of England, 1167-1216
About
Morris, M. King John — 92
John, Lauren Z.
Running book discussion groups — 374
Johnny Appleseed. Means, H. B. — 92
Johnny Cash. Kleist, R. — 92
Johnny Cash. Streissguth, M. — 92
Johnny Cash. Hilburn, R. — 92
The **Johns** Hopkins guide to diabetes. Rubin, R. R. — 616.4
Johns Hopkins patients' guide to colon and rectal cancer. Ahuja, N. — 616.99
Johns Hopkins Press health book [series]
Mace, N. L. The 36-hour day — 618.97
Thomas, D. E. The lupus encyclopedia — 616.7
Yosipovitch, G. Living with itch — 616.5
Johns Hopkins, poetry and fiction [series]
Jacobsen, J. In the crevice of time — 811
Johnsen, Gregory D.
The last refuge — 363.325
Johnsen, Ole
Minerals of the world — 549
Johnson, Alex
Improbable libraries — 027
Johnson, Andrew, 1808-1875
About
Gordon-Reed, A. Andrew Johnson — 92
Johnson, Catherine
Grandin, T. Animals in translation — 591.5
Grandin, T. Animals make us human — 636
Johnson, Clay
The information diet — 303.48
Johnson, Daniel
(jt. auth) Johnson, S. How to build chicken coops — 636.5
Johnson, Doug
The indispensable librarian — 025.1
Johnson, Elaine
(ed) Sunset the great outdoors cookbook — 641.5
Johnson, Eric A.
What we knew — 943.086
Johnson, George
Miss Leavitt's stars — 92
A shortcut through time — 004.1
The ten most beautiful experiments — 507.8
Johnson, Greg
(ed) Oates, J. C. The journal of Joyce Carol Oates: 1973-1982 — 92
Johnson, Gus, 1913-2000
About
Dance, S. The world of Count Basie — 920
Johnson, Harriet McBryde
About
Johnson, H. M. Too late to die young — 92
Johnson, Haynes Bonner

Balz, D. J. The battle for America, 2008 — 973.932
The age of anxiety — 973.921
Sleepwalking through history — 973.927
Johnson, Hugh
The world of trees — 582.16
Johnson, Ian
A mosque in Munich — 297
Johnson, Jack, 1878-1946
About
Runstedtler, T. Jack Johnson, rebel sojourner — 796.83
Ward, G. C. Unforgivable blackness — 92
Johnson, James Weldon
Complete poems — 811
The essential writings of James Weldon Johnson — 818
Johnson, Jean
Where did the jobs go-- and how do we get them back? — 331.1
Johnson, Joyce, 1935-
The voice is all — 818
Johnson, Kendall
Haralson, E. L. Critical companion to Henry James — 813
Johnson, Lady Bird, 1912-2007
About
Caroli, B. B. Lady Bird and Lyndon — 92
Gillette, M. L. Lady Bird Johnson — 92
Johnson, Loch K.
National Security Intelligence
Johnson, Lyndon B. (Lyndon Baines), 1908-1973
About
Busby, H. W. The thirty-first of March — 973.923
Caro, R. A. The passage of power — 92
Caro, R. A. The path to power — 92
Caroli, B. B. Lady Bird and Lyndon — 92
Galbraith, J. K. Name-dropping — 973.9
Gillette, M. L. Lady Bird Johnson — 92
Halberstam, D. The best and the brightest — 973.922
Kaiser, D. E. American tragedy — 959.704
Kotz, N. Judgment days — 323
Morrow, L. The best year of their lives — 920
Peters, C. Lyndon B. Johnson — 92
Pietrusza, D. 1960: LBJ vs. JFK vs. Nixon — 973.92
Taking charge — 973.923
Woods, R. B. Prisoners of hope — 973.923
Johnson, Marilyn
Lives in ruins — 930.1
This book is overdue! — 020
Johnson, Michael
Encyclopedia of native tribes of North America — 970.004
Johnson, Michael G.
Encyclopedia of native tribes of North America — 970.004
Johnson, Paul, 1928-

Art: a new history   709
    Churchill   92
    Darwin   576.8
    Eisenhower   92
    George Washington: the Founding Father   92
    A history of the Jews   909
    Napoleon   944.05
    Socrates   92
Johnson, Peggy
    Developing and managing electronic collections   025.2
    Fundamentals of Collection Development and Management   025.2
Johnson, Peter
    Rants and raves   811
Johnson, Philip, 1906-2005
    About
    Howard, H. Architecture's odd couple   720.973
Johnson, Robert, 1911-1938
    About
    Wald, E. Escaping the delta   92
Johnson, Ronald
    The shrubberies   811
Johnson, Samantha
    How to build chicken coops   636.5
Johnson, Samuel
    Samuel Johnson   828
    About
    Bloom, H. The Western canon   809
    Boswell, J. The journal of a tour to the Hebrides with Samuel Johnson   914
    Boswell, J. The life of Samuel Johnson   92
    Martin, P. Samuel Johnson   92
    Meyers, J. Samuel Johnson   92
    Starr, W. W. Whisky, kilts, and the Loch Ness Monster   914
Johnson, Sarah L.
    Historical fiction II   016
Johnson, Simon
    13 bankers   332.1
    White House burning   336.3
Johnson, Steven
    Future perfect   303.48
    The ghost map   614.5
    The invention of air   92
Johnson, Terry D.
    Kurpinski, K. How to defeat your own clone   660.6
Johnson, Tim
    Tragedy in crimson   294.3
Johnson, Victoria M.
    Grant writing 101   658.1
Johnson, Walter
    River of dark dreams   305.8
    Soul by soul   326
Johnson, Whitney
    Disrupt yourself   658.4

Johnston, Amy
    What your contractor can't tell you   690
Johnston, Andrew K.
    Launius, R. D. Smithsonian atlas of space exploration   500.5
Johnston, Ann Dowsett
    Drink   362.292
Johnston, David Cay
    The making of Donald Trump   973.932
Johnston, Devin
    Traveler   811
Johnston, Kenneth R.
    The hidden Wordsworth   821
Johnstone, Christi Farr
    Smart cookie   641.865
Join the club. Rosenberg, T.   303.3
Joining the military [series]
    Wildsmith, S. Joining the United States Air Force   358.4
Joining the United States Air Force. Wildsmith, S.   358.4
JOINT CUSTODY OF CHILDREN See Child custody; Part-time parenting
Joint libraries. Butler, P. M.   027
JOINT VENTURES
    See also Business enterprises; Partnership
JOINT-USE LIBRARIES -- UNITED STATES
    Butler, P. M. Joint libraries   027
JOKE BOOKS See Jokes
JOKES
    Diffee, M. Hand drawn jokes for smart attractive people   741.5
JOKES
    See also Wit and humor
Jokinen, Tom
    Curtains   393
Joliot-Curie, Irène, 1897-1956
    About
    Emling, S. Marie Curie and her daughters   920
Jolly, Alison
    Lucy's legacy   599.93
Jonas Salk.   92
Jonas Salk. Jacobs, C. D.   92
Jonathan Edwards. Marsden, G. M.   92
Jonathan Swift. Damrosch, L.   92
Jones, Anna
    A modern way to eat   641.5
Jones, Barbara
    Mandela   92
Jones, Bill T., 1954-
    About
    Gates, H. L. Thirteen ways of looking at a black man   920.71
    Story/Time   814
Jones, Brian Jay
    Jim Henson   92

Jones, Carey
The Brooklyn bartender   **641.874**
Jones, Catherine Cheremeteff
A year of Russian feasts   **641.59**
Jones, Colin
Paris   **944**
Jones, Dan
The Plantagenets   **942.03**
The Wars of the Roses   **942.04**
Jones, Denna
(ed) Architecture   **720.9**
Jones, Gayl, 1949-
          About
Black women writers (1950-1980)   **810**
Jones, Genevieve (Genevieve Estelle), 1847-1879
          About
Kiser, J. M. America's other Audubon   **598**
Jones, Gerard
Killing monsters   **302.23**
Men of tomorrow   **741.5**
Jones, Gregg
Honor in the dust   **959.9**
Jones, Hettie
Tobin, J. From Midnight to Dawn   **322**
Jones, Jacqueline
A dreadful deceit   **305.8**
Saving Savannah   **975.8**
Jones, Jo, 1911-1985
          About
Dance, S. The world of Count Basie   **920**
Jones, John Paul, 1747-1792
          About
Morison, S. E. John Paul Jones   **92**
Thomas, E. John Paul Jones   **92**
Jones, Judith
Cameron, A. The L.L. Bean game and fish cook-
book   **641.6**
The pleasures of cooking for one   **641.5**
          About
Barr, L. Provence, 1970   **641.59**
Jones, Lindsay
(ed) Encyclopedia of religion   **200**
Jones, Malcolm, 1952-
          About
Jones, M. Little boy blues   **92**
Jones, Mark
Penguins   **598.47**
Jones, Michael
After Hitler   **940.53**
Bosworth 1485   **942.04**
The retreat   **940.54**
Jones, Michael, Jr.
          About
Spence, G. The smoking gun   **345**
Jones, Mother, 1830-1930
          About

Gorn, E. J. Mother Jones   **331.88**
Jones, Nigel
Tower   **942.1**
Jones, Quincy, 1933-
          About
Jones, Q. Q: the autobiography of Quincy Jones **92**
Jones, Richard, 1790-1855
House Guests, House Pests   **590**
          About
Snyder, L. J. The philosophical breakfast club **509**
Jones, Saeed
Prelude to bruise   **811**
Jones, Sandy
          About
Spence, G. The smoking gun   **345**
Jones, Sharon L.
Critical companion to Zora Neale Hurston   **813**
Jones, Stephanie
Upstyle your furniture   **684.1**
Jones, Stephen
(ed) Horror: another 100 best books   **823**
Jones, Stephen A.
(ed) Presidents and Black America   **973.09**
Jones, Steve
Darwin's ghost   **576.8**
Jones, Van
The green-collar economy   **363.7**
Jones, Warren D.
Duffield, M. R. Plants for dry climates   **635.9**
Jong, Cees de
(ed) The poster   **741.6**
Jong, Erica
(ed) Sugar in my bowl   **306.7**
Jonnes, Jill
Eiffel's tower   **944**
Jonson, Ben
The complete poems   **821**
Volpone and other plays   **822**
Jonze, Spike
          About
Waxman, S. Rebels on the backlot   **920**
Joo, Judy
Korean food made simple   **641.595**
Joplin, Janis
          About
Cooke, J. B. On the road with Janis Joplin   **92**
Joplin, Scott, 1868-1917
          About
Berlin, E. A. King of ragtime: Scott Joplin and his
era   **92**
JORDAN -- HISTORY
Ashton, N. King Hussein of Jordan   **92**
JORDAN -- KINGS AND RULERS
Ashton, N. King Hussein of Jordan   **92**
Jordan, Brian Matthew, 1986-
Marching Home   **973.7**

Jordan, Christy
Sweetness 641
Jordan, Don
The king's revenge 941.062
White cargo 326
Jordan, Jonathan W.
American warlords 973.917
Jordan, June
Directed by desire 811
Jordan, Mary
The prison angel 92
Jordan, Michael
Dictionary of gods and goddesses 201
Jordan, Michael, 1963-
About
Lazenby, R. Michael Jordan 92
Jordan, Wendy Adler
Universal design for the home 728
Jorgensen, Timothy J.
Strange glow 539.2
Joris, Pierre
(ed) Poems for the millennium 808.81
Joseph Anton. Rushdie, S. 92
JOSEPH PAPP PUBLIC THEATER (NEW YORK, N.Y.)
Turan, K. Free for all 92
Joseph Roth. 92
Joseph Smith. Remini, R. V. 92
Joseph Smith. Bushman, R. L. 92
Joseph Smith and the beginnings of Mormonism.
Bushman, R. L. 289.3
Joseph, Charles M.
Stravinsky inside out 92
Joseph, Nez Percé Chief, 1840-1904
About
Brown, D. A. The American West 978
West, E. The last Indian war 973.8
Joseph, Peniel E.
Waiting 'til the midnight hour 323.1
Josephine, Empress, consort of Napoleon I, Emperor of the French, 1763-1814
About
Williams, K. Ambition and desire 92
Josephson, Barney, 1902-1988
About
Josephson, B. Cafe Society 792.7
Josephy, Alvin M., 1915-2005
America in 1492 970.004
The longest trail 970.004
The Nez Perce Indians and the opening of the Northwest 970.004
Jost, Kenneth
The Supreme Court A to Z 347.73
Joukowsky, Artemis
Defying the Nazis 940.53
Joulwan, Melissa

Well fed 641.5
The **journal** of a tour to the Hebrides with Samuel Johnson. Boswell, J. 914
The **journal** of Joyce Carol Oates: 1973-1982. Oates, J. C. 92
JOURNALING
See also Authorship; Diaries
Journalism. 070.4
JOURNALISM
Algeo, M. The president is a sick man 973.8
The best business writing 2013 330.9
Braude, J. The honored dead 364.152
Burns, E. Infamous scribblers 071
Collins, P. The murder of the century 364.152
Commager, H. S. The American mind 973
Deb, S. The beautiful and the damned 954.05
Friedlander, E. J. Feature writing for newspapers and magazines 070.4
Fuller, J. What is happening to news 070.4
Gonzales, L. Flight 232 363.12
Goodman, M. The Sun and the moon 974.7
Hohn, D. Moby-Duck 551.46
Journalism 070.4
Knight, R. M. Journalistic writing 070
The New new journalism 071
Remnick, D. Reporting 814
Reporting civil rights 323.1
Reuters 909.83
Ross, L. Reporting always 070.4
Shepard, S. B. Deadlines and disruption 070.5
Simon, J. The new censorship 363.31
Sundaram, A. Stringer 967.51
Written into history 071
JOURNALISM
See also Authorship; Literature
JOURNALISM -- AUTHORSHIP
Knight, R. M. Journalistic writing 070
JOURNALISM -- ETHICAL ASPECTS See Journalistic ethics
JOURNALISM -- GRAPHIC NOVELS
Gladstone, B. The influencing machine 302.23
JOURNALISM -- OBJECTIVITY
Campbell, W. J. Getting it wrong 071
Kovach, B. Blur 070
JOURNALISM -- OBJECTIVITY
See also Journalistic ethics
JOURNALISM -- POLITICAL ASPECTS -- HISTORY -- 21ST CENTURY
Simon, J. The new censorship 363.31
JOURNALISM -- TECHNOLOGICAL INNOVATIONS
Shepard, S. B. Deadlines and disruption 070.5
JOURNALISM -- UNITED STATES
Kovach, B. The elements of journalism 071
Miraldi, R. Seymour Hersh 92
JOURNALISM -- UNITED STATES -- HISTORY

Goodwin, D. K. The Bully Pulpit   **973.91**
Sheehy, G. Daring   **92**
Journalistas.   **808.8**
JOURNALISTIC ETHICS
  Campbell, W. J. Getting it wrong   **071**
  Fuller, J. What is happening to news   **070.4**
  Kovach, B. The elements of journalism   **071**
JOURNALISTIC ETHICS
  See also Professional ethics
JOURNALISTIC PHOTOGRAPHY *See* Photo-
  journalism
Journalistic writing. Knight, R. M.   **070**
JOURNALISTS
  Algeo, M. The president is a sick man   **973.8**
  Allende, I. My invented country   **863**
  Allende, I. Paula   **92**
  Allende, I. The sum of our days   **92**
  Almond, S. Candyfreak: a journey through the
    chocolate underbelly of America   **338.4**
  Almond, S. Rock and roll will save your life **781.66**
  Aron, W. Hide & seek   **92**
  Avery, K. Everything is an afterthought   **92**
  Bageant, J. Deer hunting with Jesus   **305.5**
  Baker, R. Growing up   **92**
  Bard, E. Lunch in Paris   **92**
  Beavan, C. No impact man   **333.72**
  Blight, D. W. American oracle   **973.7**
  Boyd, G. M. My Times in black and white   **92**
  Bragg, R. The prince of Frogtown   **92**
  Brenner, M. Apples and oranges   **92**
  Brinkley, A. The publisher   **92**
  Brokaw, T. A Lucky Life Interrupted   **92**
  Brokaw, T. A long way from home   **070**
  Brookhiser, R. Right time, right place   **92**
  Brown, C. Manchild in the promised land   **92**
  Bryson, B. The life and times of the thunderbolt
    kid   **92**
  Buk-Swienty, T. The other half   **92**
  Caldwell, G. Let's take the long way home   **92**
  Carr, D. The night of the gun   **92**
  Chadha, Y. Gandhi   **954.03**
  Chambers, W. Witness   **92**
  Ciezadlo, A. Day of honey   **92**
  Conover, T. The routes of man   **388.1**
  Cooper, H. The house at Sugar Beach   **92**
  D'Agata, J. The lifespan of a fact   **808.02**
  Di Giovanni, J. Madness visible   **949.7**
  Dickinson, A. The mighty queens of Freeville   **92**
  Didion, J. The year of magical thinking   **92**
  Edwards, B. Edward R. Murrow and the birth of
    broadcast journalism   **92**
  Ehrenreich, B. The Way to the Spring   **956.95**
  Elie, P. The life you save may be your own   **810**
  Ellison, R. The collected essays of Ralph Elli-
    son   **814**
  Engel, R. And then all hell broke loose   **956.05**

Eteraz, A. Children of dust   **92**
Farrell, S. E. Critical companion to Kurt Vonne-
  gut   **813**
Fenn, L. Carry on   **920**
Filkins, D. The forever war   **956.7**
Forrest, E. Your voice in my head   **362.196**
French, P. The world is what it is   **92**
Gammage, J. China ghosts   **362.7**
Gandhi, M. An autobiography   **92**
Garcia Marquez, G. Living to tell the tale   **92**
George, being George   **92**
Giddings, P. Ida: a sword among lions   **92**
Gilbert, E. Eat, pray, love   **92**
Gillies, A. Keeper   **616.8**
Giridharadas, A. India calling   **954.05**
Gopnik, A. Through the children's gate   **974.71**
Guillermoprieto, A. Dancing with Cuba   **972.91**
Guttenplan, D. D. American radical   **92**
Hardy, J. In the valley of mist   **954**
Heilbroner, R. L. The worldly philosophers   **330.1**
Heilbrun, C. G. The education of a woman   **92**
Hessler, P. Country driving   **303.4**
Hillerman, T. Seldom disappointed   **813**
Hitchens, C. Hitch-22   **92**
Jacobs, A. J. The know-it-all   **031**
Jeal, T. Stanley   **92**
Johnson, T. Tragedy in crimson   **294.3**
Jones, M. Little boy blues   **92**
Joseph Roth   **92**
Kaplan, A. The collaborator: the trial & execution
  of Robert Brasillach   **848**
Katz, J. Dog days   **636**
Kavenna, J. The ice museum   **998**
Kimball, K. The dirty life   **92**
Kurson, R. Crashing through   **92**
Lascher, B. Eve of a Hundred Midnights   **070.449**
Latus, J. If I am missing or dead   **92**
Lelyveld, J. Great soul   **92**
Life stories   **920**
Lobdell, W. Losing my religion   **92**
Lunden, J. Had I Known   **791.450**
Lynn, K. S. Hemingway   **92**
MacFarquhar, N. The media relations department
  of Hizbollah wishes you a happy birthday   **956.04**
Mackall, J. Plain secrets   **289.7**
MacPherson, M. All governments lie   **92**
Maraniss, D. Into the story   **92**
Martin, G. Gabriel Garcia Marquez   **92**
Marton, K. Enemies of the people   **92**
Marton, K. The great escape   **920**
Mayer, J. Dark money   **320.52**
McBride, J. The color of water   **92**
McCall, N. Makes me wanna holler   **305.38**
McClelland, M. Irritable hearts   **92**
McKeen, W. Outlaw journalist   **92**
Meier, A. Black earth   **947.086**

Mendelsohn, D. The lost 92
Moaveni, A. Honeymoon in Tehran 92
Moaveni, A. Lipstick jihad 92
Mohandas Gandhi 92
Montgomery, S. Birdology 598
Moore, H. G. We are soldiers still 959.704
Morgan, T. My battle of Algiers 965
Morris, J. M. Eye on the Struggle 92
Morris, J. M. Pulitzer 92
Morris, J. Contact! 910.4
Morris, R. Ambrose Bierce 92
Moser, B. Why this world 92
Moyers, W. C. Broken: my story of addiction and redemption 92
Naipaul, V. S. Between father and son 823
Naipaul, V. S. Reading & writing 92
Norris, M. The grace of silence 92
O'Reilly, B. A bold fresh piece of humanity 92
O'Shea, J. The deal from hell 92
Politkovskaya, A. A Russian diary 947.086
Proulx, A. Bird cloud 92
Remnick, D. Reporting 814
Reynolds, M. S. Hemingway: the Paris years 92
Rideau, W. In the place of justice 92
Rinella, S. American buffalo 599.64
Rooney, A. A. My war 940.54
Rosenblatt, R. Making toast 92
Sabar, A. My father's paradise 305.8
Sabbag, R. Down around midnight 92
Scammell, M. Koestler 92
Scheyer, M. Asylum 940.53
Schmidle, N. To live or to perish forever 954.91
Seierstad, A. The angel of Grozny 947.5
Seierstad, A. A hundred and one days 956.7
Shields, C. J. And so it goes: Kurt Vonnegut: a life 92
Singer, I. B. More stories from my father's court 839
Smith, D. Monkey mind 616.85
Smith, G. The Dogs Are Eating Them Now 958.104
Sonnenberg, S. Her last death 92
Sperber, A. M. Murrow, his life and times 92
Stack, M. Every man in this village is a liar 956.05
Steffens, L. The autobiography of Lincoln Steffens 92
Steinberg, N. Drunkard 92
Steinem, G. Moving beyond words 305.42
Steinem, G. Outrageous acts and everyday rebellions 305.42
Thompson, H. S. Fear and loathing in America 070
Thompson, H. S. The kingdom of fear 92
Timerman, J. Prisoner without a name, cell without a number 92
Tobin, J. E. Ernie Pyle's war 070.4
Tofel, R. J. Restless genius 92
Travels with Herodotus 930

Wainaina, B. One day I will write about this place 823
Ware, S. Letter to the world 920.72
Weisskopf, M. Blood brothers 92
Wenner, J. S. Gonzo 92
Wiesel, E. All rivers run to the sea 813
Wiesel, E. And the sea is never full 813
Wiesel, E. Night 92
Wills, G. Outside looking in 92
Wilson, E. Patriotic gore 810
Wolpert, S. A. Gandhi's passion 954.03
JOURNALISTS
    See also Authors
JOURNALISTS -- BIOGRAPHY
Aitkenhead, D. All at sea 92
Cooper, A. The rainbow comes and goes 92
Lanzmann, C. The Patagonian hare 791.43
JOURNALISTS -- CANADA -- BIOGRAPHY
Corbett, S. A house in the sky 92
JOURNALISTS -- ENGLAND -- BIOGRAPHY
Moran, C. How to be a woman 92
JOURNALISTS -- FRANCE -- BIOGRAPHY
Lanzmann, C. The Patagonian hare 791.43
JOURNALISTS -- GREAT BRITAIN -- BIOGRAPHY
Aitkenhead, D. All at sea 92
Meyers, J. Orwell 828
JOURNALISTS -- MICHIGAN -- DETROIT -- BIOGRAPHY
LeDuff, C. Detroit 977.4
JOURNALISTS -- UNITED STATES -- BIOGRAPHY
Brinkley, D. Cronkite 92
Caldwell, G. New life, no instructions 92
JOURNALISTS -- VIOLENCE AGAINST
Simon, J. The new censorship 363.31
JOURNALS See Periodicals
JOURNALS (DIARIES) See Diaries
Journals of Ayn Rand. Rand, A. 92
Journals: 1952-2000. Schlesinger, A. M. 92
A journey. Blair, T. 92
Journey of the pink dolphins. Montgomery, S. 599.53
A Journey Through Tudor England. Lipscomb, S. 942.05
Journey to Same-sex Parenthood. Rosswood, E. 306.874
Journey to the ants. Holldobler, B. 595.79
Journey: new and selected poems, 1969-1999. Norris, K. 811
JOURNEYS See Travel; Voyages and travels
Journeys home. McCarthy, A. 929.1
Joy. Santamaria, A. 92
JOY
Jamison, K. R. Exuberance 152.4
Lamott, A. Small victories 248

JOY AND SORROW
See also Emotions
The **joy** of chemistry. Cobb, C.   **540**
Joy of cooking. Rombauer, I. v. S.   **641.5**
The **joy** of origami. Van Sicklen, M.   **736**
The **joy** of sex. Comfort, A.   **613.9**
The **joy** of X. Strogatz, S.   **510**
Joy ride. Lahr, J.   **792.02**
Joy, LaManda
Start a community food garden   **635**
Joyce, Anna
Stamp stencil paint   **745.5**
Joyce, David
Pruning & training
Joyce, James, 1882-1941
About
Bloom, H. The Western canon   **809**
Bowker, G. James Joyce   **823**
Ellmann, R. James Joyce   **92**
Fargnoli, A. N. Critical companion to James Joyce   **823**
Kiberd, D. Ulysses and us   **823**
Nabokov, V. V. Lectures on literature   **808.3**
O'Brien, E. James Joyce   **823**
Joyce, Kathryn
The child catchers   **362.734**
JPS guide [series]
The Jewish Bible   **221**
The **JPS** guide to Jewish traditions. Eisenberg, R. L.   **296.4**
Juan, Don
About
Castaneda, C. The teachings of Don Juan   **299.7**
Jubber, Nicholas
Drinking arak off an ayatollah's beard   **915**
Jubilant thicket. Williams, J.   **811**
Jubilee city. Andoe, J.   **92**
JUDAISM
See also Religions
JUDAISM -- CUSTOMS AND PRACTICES
Bolsta, H. S. The illuminated Kaddish   **296.4**
JUDAISM -- CUSTOMS AND PRACTICES
See also Rites and ceremonies
JUDAISM -- DICTIONARIES
The Oxford dictionary of the Jewish religion   **296**
JUDAISM -- DIETARY LAWS
See also Judaism -- Customs and practices
JUDAISM -- DOCTRINES
See also Doctrinal theology
JUDAISM -- ENCYCLOPEDIAS
Encyclopedia of Jewish folklore and traditions   **398.2**
The Oxford dictionary of the Jewish religion   **296**
JUDAISM -- ESSENCE, GENIUS, NATURE
Bronfman, E. M. Why be Jewish?   **296**
JUDAISM -- HISTORY -- SOURCES

Cole, P. Sacred trash   **296.09**
JUDAISM -- LITURGY
Wagner, J. L. The synagogue survival kit   **296.4**
JUDAISM -- LITURGY -- TEXTS
Bolsta, H. S. The illuminated Kaddish   **296.4**
New American Haggadah   **296.4**
JUDAISM -- PRAYERS
See also Prayers
JUDAISM -- RELATIONS
Three Testaments   **208**
JUDAISM -- RELATIONS -- CHRISTIANITY
See also Christianity and other religions; Judaism
JUDAISM -- RELATIONS -- ISLAM
See also Islam; Judaism
JUDAISM -- UNITED STATES -- HISTORY -- 21ST CENTURY
Ashton, D. Hanukkah in America   **296.4**
JUDAISM AND POLITICS
Kimball, C. When religion becomes lethal   **201**
Judas. Gubar, S.   **92**
Judas Iscariot
About
Gubar, S. Judas   **92**
JUDEA AND SAMARIA *See* West Bank
JUDGES
Bakewell, S. How to live, or, A life of Montaigne in one question and twenty attempts at an answer   **92**
Bloom, H. The Western canon   **809**
Feldman, N. Scorpions   **920**
Frampton, S. When I am playing with my cat, how do I know she is not playing with me?   **844**
Gormley, K. The death of American virtue   **973.929**
Greenhouse, L. Becoming Justice Blackmun   **92**
Haygood, W. Showdown   **347.73**
Kennedy, J. F. Profiles in courage   **920**
LaPlante, E. Salem witch judge   **92**
Perino, M. A. The hellhound of Wall Street   **330.9**
Rowan, C. T. Dream makers, dream breakers   **92**
Urofsky, M. I. Louis D. Brandeis   **92**
Wilson, E. Patriotic gore   **810**
JUDGES
See also Lawyers
JUDGES -- BIOGRAPHY
Justices of the United States Supreme Court   **347.73**
The Supreme Court justices   **347.73**
Unger, H. G. John Marshall   **92**
JUDGES -- RECUSAL -- UNITED STATES
Leamer, L. The price of justice   **346.730**
JUDGES -- SELECTION AND APPOINTMENT -- UNITED STATES -- HISTORY -- 20TH CENTURY
Haygood, W. Showdown   **347.73**
JUDGES -- UNITED STATES
Feldman, N. Scorpions   **920**
Tushnet, M. In the balance   **347.73**

JUDGES -- UNITED STATES -- BIOGRAPHY
Gibson, L. S. Young Thurgood   **347.73**
Hirshman, L. Sisters in law   **347.73**
Justices of the United States Supreme Court **347.73**
Marshall, T. Thurgood Marshall   **347**
Murphy, B. A. Scalia   **92**
Sotomayor, S. My beloved world   **92**
The Supreme Court justices   **347.73**
Unger, H. G. John Marshall   **92**
Williams, J. Thurgood Marshall   **92**
JUDGMENT DAY
    See also End of the world; Second Advent
Judgment days. Kotz, N.   **323**
The **judgment** of Paris. King, R.   **759**
JUDICIAL ERROR
Colmez, C. Math on trial   **345**
Strang, D. A. Worse than the devil   **345**
JUDICIAL OPINION -- UNITED STATES
Urofsky, M. I. Dissent and the Supreme Court   **342.73**
JUDICIAL POWER
Tushnet, M. In the balance   **347.73**
JUDICIAL PROCESS -- UNITED STATES -- PUBLIC OPINION
Friedman, B. The will of the people   **347**
JUDICIAL REVIEW -- UNITED STATES
Breyer, S. G. Making our democracy work   **347**
Toobin, J. R. The nine   **347**
JUDICIAL REVIEW -- UNITED STATES -- HISTORY
Breyer, S. G. Making our democracy work   **347**
JUDICIARY *See* Courts
JÜDISCHES KRANKENHAUS (BERLIN, GERMANY)
Silver, D. B. Refuge in hell   **362.1**
Judith, Anodea
Eastern body, Western mind   **150.19**
JUDO
    See also Martial arts; Self-defense
Judt, Tony
Postwar   **940.55**
Reappraisals   **909.82**
Thinking the twentieth century   **320.092**
       About
Judt, T. Thinking the twentieth century   **320.092**
JUGGLING
    See also Amusements; Tricks
Julavits, Heidi
(ed) Read Harder   **814**
Julia and Jacques cooking at home. Child, J. **641.59**
Julia Reed's south.   **642.4**
Julian, of Norwich, b. 1343
       About
Armstrong, K. Visions of God   **248.2**
July 1914. McMeekin, S.   **940.3**
Jump, Anne

(ed) Sontag, S. At the same time   **814**
June fourth elegies. Liu, X.   **811**
Jung Chang, 1952-
Empress Dowager Cixi   **92**
Jung, C. G. (Carl Gustav), 1875-1961
The essential Jung   **150.19**
The basic writings of C. G. Jung   **150.19**
Man and his symbols   **150.19**
The portable Jung   **150.19**
       About
Hayman, R. A life of Jung   **150.19**
Jung, C. G. Memories, dreams, reflections **150.19**
Jung-Beeman, Mark
(jt. auth) Kounios, J. The Eureka factor   **612.8**
Junger, Sebastian
Fire   **909.82**
The perfect storm   **910.4**
Tribe   **302.3**
War   **958.1**
JUNGLE ANIMALS
    See also Animals; Forest animals
JUNGLE ECOLOGY
    See also Ecology; Forest ecology
Jungle of snakes. Arnold, J. R.   **355**
Jungle of Stone. Carlsen, W.   **972.81**
JUNGLES
    See also Forests and forestry
JUNIOR COLLEGES
Peterson's two-year colleges 2015   **378.73**
JUNIOR COLLEGES
    See also Colleges and universities; Higher education
JUNIOR HIGH SCHOOLS
    See also High schools; Public schools; Schools
Juniper. French, T.   **618.92**
JUNK FOOD
Schatzker, M. The Dorito effect   **641.3**
JUNK FOOD -- MARKETING
Moss, M. Salt, sugar, fat   **613.2**
Junor, Penny
The Firm: the troubled life of the House of Windsor   **941.085**
JUPITER (PLANET)
    See also Planets
Jurafsky, Dan
The language of food   **641.3**
JURISPRUDENCE *See* Law
JURISPRUDENCE, MEDICAL *See* Medical jurisprudence
JURISTS *See* Lawyers
JURY
    See also Courts; Criminal law
A **jury** of her peers. Showalter, E.   **810**
A **just** and generous nation. Holzer, H.   **973.7**
Just as I am. Graham, B.   **92**

Just food. McWilliams, J. E.   **394.1**
Just kids. Smith, P.   **92**
Just like us. Thorpe, H.   **305.8**
Just listen. Goulston, M.   **650.1**
Just Mercy. Stevenson, B.   **353.4**
Just my type. Garfield, S.   **686.2**
Just one catch. Daugherty, T.   **92**
Just one of the kids. Palmer, S.   **649**
Just ride. Petersen, G.   **796.6**
Just send me word. Figes, O.   **365**
Just six numbers. Rees, M. J.   **523.1**
Just war against terror. Elshtain, J. B.   **363.32**
JUST WAR DOCTRINE -- HISTORY -- 20TH CENTURY
  Preston, D. A higher form of killing   **940.4**
Just, Tim
  (ed) U.S. Chess Federation's official rules of chess   **794.1**
Justice. Sandel, M. J.   **172**
JUSTICE
  Sandel, M. J. Justice   **172**
JUSTICE
  See also Ethics; Law; Virtue
JUSTICE LEAGUE (FICTIONAL CHARACTERS)
  See also Fictional characters; Superheroes
JUSTICE, ADMINISTRATION OF *See* Administration of justice
Justice, Donald Rodney, 1925-2004
  Collected poems   **811**
      About
  Gioia, D. Can poetry matter?   **809.1**
Justices of the United States Supreme Court. **347.73**
Juvenal
  The sixteen satires   **877**
JUVENILE CORRECTIONS -- UNITED STATES
  Sweeney, J. Literacy   **027.62**
JUVENILE COURTS
  See also Courts
JUVENILE DELINQUENCY
  Bernstein, N. Burning down the house   **365**
  Chura, D. I don't wish nobody to have a life like mine   **371.9**
  Salzman, M. True notebooks   **371.9**
JUVENILE PROSTITUTION
  Bolkovac, K. The whistleblower   **92**
  Moran, R. Paid for   **306.74**
  Phelps, C. Runaway girl   **362.74**
JUVENILE PROSTITUTION
  See also Juvenile delinquency; Prostitution

      K

K blows top. Carlson, P.   **947.085**
K-food. West   **641.595**
Ka-ching! Duhamel, D.   **811**

Kaag, John
  American philosophy   **191**
Kaatz, Kevin W.
  (ed) Voices of early Christianity   **270.1**
Kabul Beauty School. Rodriguez, D.   **305.4**
KABUL BEAUTY SCHOOL (AFGHANISTAN)
  Rodriguez, D. Kabul Beauty School   **305.4**
Kaddish. Wieseltier, L.   **296.4**
KADDISH
  Bolsta, H. S. The illuminated Kaddish   **296.4**
  Wieseltier, L. Kaddish   **296.4**
Kadri, Sadakat
  The trial   **345**
Kael, Pauline, 1919-2001
  The age of movies   **791.43**
      About
  Kellow, B. Pauline Kael   **92**
Kaffe Fassett's Bold Blooms. Fassett, K.   **746**
Kafka. Murray, N.   **92**
Kafka, Barbara
  Vegetable love   **641.6**
Kafka, die Jahre der Entscheidungen/English
  Kafka, the decisive years   **92**
Kafka, Franz, 1883-1924
      About
  Bloom, H. The Western canon   **809**
  Existentialism from Dostoevsky to Sartre   **142**
  Kafka, d. J. d. E. Kafka, the decisive years   **92**
  Kafka, the years of insight   **833**
  Langer, L. L. Admitting the Holocaust   **940.53**
  Murray, N. Kafka   **92**
  Nabokov, V. V. Lectures on literature   **808.3**
Kafka, the decisive years. Kafka, d. J. d. E.   **92**
Kafka, the years of insight.   **833**
Kagan, Donald
  The Peloponnesian War   **938**
  Thucydides   **938**
Kagan, Jerome
  The human spark   **155**
Kagan, Neil
  (ed) Atlas of the Civil War   **973.7**
  (ed) National Geographic concise history of the world   **909**
Kaganovich family
      About
  Laskin, D. The Family   **92**
Kagarise, Leon
  Pure country   **781.642**
Kahlo, Frida, 1907-1954
      About
  Herrera, H. Frida: a biography of Frida Kahlo   **709**
  Kahlo, F. The diary of Frida Kahlo   **92**
  Lozano Frida Kahlo   **759.9**
Kahn, Ashley
  The house that Trane built   **781.65**
Kahn, Cynthia M.

(ed) The Merck veterinary manual   636.089

Kahn, Miriam B.
Disaster response and planning for libraries   025.8

Kahn, Roger
A flame of pure fire: Jack Dempsey and the roaring '20s   92

Kahneman, Daniel, 1934-
Thinking, fast and slow   153.4

Kaiser, Charles
The cost of courage   92

Kaiser, David E.
American tragedy   959.704
How the hippies saved physics   530.092
The road to Dallas   973.922

Kaiser, Robert G.
Act of Congress   346.73
So damn much money   328

Kakalios, James
The amazing story of quantum mechanics   530.1

Kaku, Michio
The future of the mind   612.8
Hyperspace   530.1
Parallel worlds   523.1
Physics of the future   303.49

Kalanithi, Paul, 1977-2015
About
Kalanithi, P. When breath becomes air   616.99

Kalb, Claudia
Andy Warhol was a hoarder   616.89

Kale, Tessa
(ed) The Columbia Granger's index to poetry in anthologies   808.81

Kaler, James B.
Extreme stars   523.8

Kaling, Mindy, 1979-
About
Kaling, M. Is everyone hanging out without me? (and other concerns)   818
Kaling, M. Why not me?   92

Kallio, Jamie
Read on ... speculative fiction for teens   016

Kamal, Eric Djiva
White, A. C. E-metrics for library and information professionals   025.2

KAMASUTRA
McConnachie, J. The book of love   306.7

Kambalu, Samson, 1975-
About
Kambalu, S. The jive talker   92

KAMDESH, BATTLE OF, AFGHANISTAN, 2009
Romesha, C. L. Red platoon   958.1

Kamel, Basem
About
Cambanis, T. Once upon a revolution   962.05

Kamen, Henry
Philip of Spain   946

The Spanish Inquisition   272

Kamensky, Jane
A revolution in color   759.13

KAMIKAZE AIRPLANES
Sheftall, M. G. Blossoms in the wind   940.54

KAMIKAZE PILOTS -- JAPAN
Wukovits, J. F. Hell from the heavens   940.54

Kaminsky, Peter
(ed) The essential New York times grilling cookbook   641.5
Bien Cuit   641.815
Charred & scruffed   641.7
Mallmann on fire   641.598
Mallmann, F. Seven fires   641.5

Kamkwamba, William, 1987-
About
Kamkwamba, W. The boy who harnessed the wind   92

Kammen, Michael G.
Digging up the dead   393

Kamozawa, Aki
Ideas in food   641.5

Kamp, David
The United States of Arugula   641

KAMPUCHEA See Cambodia

Kan, Lisa
Bead metamorphosis   745.594

Kandel, Eric R., 1929-
About
The age of insight   154.2
Kandel, E. R. In search of memory   153

Kandel, Robert S.
Water from heaven   553.7

Kandinsky, Wassily, 1866-1944
About
Weber, N. F. The Bauhaus group   920

Kane, Elisha Kent, 1820-1857
About
McGoogan, K. Race to the Polar Sea   92

Kane, Joseph Nathan
Facts about the presidents   920

Kanfer, Stefan
Groucho: the life and times of Julius Henry Marx   92

Kang, Mandip S.
The doctor's kidney diets   616.6

KANGAROOS
Flannery, T. F. Chasing kangaroos   599.2

Kanigel, Robert
Eyes on the street   92
The man who knew infinity   510

KANSAS
Frank, T. What's the matter with Kansas?   978.1

KANSAS -- HISTORY
Stratton, J. L. Pioneer women   978.1
Kansas City lightning. Crouch, S.   92

Kant, Immanuel, 1724-1804

Basic writings of Kant   **193**
Critique of pure reason   **193**
About
Durant, W. J. The story of philosophy   **109**
Russell, B. A history of Western philosophy   **109**
Kantor, Jodi
The Obamas   **973.932**
Kantrowitz, Stephen
More than freedom   **323.1**
Kanzanjian, Howard
(jt. auth) Enss, C. Mochi's war   **978.8**
Kaplan, Alice
(ed) Camus, A. Algerian chronicles   **965**
The collaborator: the trial & execution of Robert Brasillach   **848**
Dreaming in French   **944**
The interpreter   **940.54**
Kaplan, Carla
Miss Anne in Harlem   **700.92**
(ed) Zora Neale Hurston: a life in letters   **92**
Kaplan, David
(jt. auth) Fauchald, N. Death & Co   **641.87**
Kaplan, Ellen
Hidden harmonies   **516.2**
Kaplan, Fred, 1937-
Dark territory   **363.325**
John Quincy Adams   **92**
Kaplan, Gary
Total recovery   **616**
Kaplan, James, 1951-
Kaplan, J. Frank   **92**
Lewis, J. Dean & me   **92**
McEnroe, J. You cannot be serious   **796.342**
Sinatra   **92**
Kaplan, Larry
Tallchief, M. Maria Tallchief   **92**
Kaplan, Laurie
Help Your Dog Fight Cancer   **636.7**
Kaplan, Matt
Medusa's gaze and vampire's bite   **001.944**
Kaplan, Richard
(ed) Building and managing e-book collections   **025.2**
Kaplan, Robert
(jt. auth) Kaplan, E. Hidden harmonies   **516.2**
Kaplan, Robert D., 1952-
Imperial grunts   **973.931**
Monsoon   **327**
Warrior politics   **320**
About
Kaplan, R. D. In Europe's shadow   **949.8**
Kaplan, Roberta
(jt. auth) Dickey, L. Then comes marriage   **346**
Kaplanian-Buller, Lynn
Keuning-Tichelaar, A. Passing on the comfort   **940.54**

Kapuscinski, Ryszard, 1932-2007
About
Travels with Herodotus   **930**
Karabell, Zachary
The last campaign   **324.9**
Parting the desert   **386**
Peace be upon you   **201**
KARACHI (PAKISTAN) -- DESCRIPTION AND TRAVEL
Inskeep, S. Instant city   **954.91**
Karajan, Herbert von
About
Osborne, R. Herbert von Karajan   **92**
Karasik, Paul
(ed) Masters of American comics   **741.5**
KARATE
    See also Judo; Martial arts; Self-defense
Karem, Abraham, 1937-
About
Whittle, R. Predator   **623.74**
Karinch, Maryann
(jt. auth) Biever, J. A. The wandering mind   **612.8**
Karl Marx. Sperber, J.   **92**
Karl Marx. Wheen, F.   **335.4**
Karlgaard, Rich
Team Genius   **658.1**
Karlins, Marvin
The like switch   **158.2**
Karlsen, Carol F.
The devil in the shape of a woman   **133.4**
Karlson, Kevin T.
Birding by Impression   **598**
Karnad, Raghu
Farthest field   **940.54**
Karnazes, Dean
The legend of Marathon   **938.03**
Karnow, Stanley, 1925-2013
Karnow, S. In our image   **959.9**
Paris in the fifties   **944**
Vietnam   **959.704**
Karol Wojtyla. Buttiglione, R.   **282**
Karon, Karen
Advanced chain maille jewelry workshop   **745.594**
Karp, Brianna, 1985-
About
Karp, B. The girl's guide to homelessness   **92**
Karp, Harvey
The happiest baby guide to great sleep   **649**
The happiest baby on the block   **649**
Karp, Jesse
Graphic novels in your school library   **741.5**
Karp, Josh
Orson Welles's last movie   **791.43**
Karpin, Michael I.
The bomb in the basement   **355**
Karr, Mary

About

Karr, M. Lit   **92**

Karr-Morse, Robin

Scared sick   **155.9**

Karsh, Efraim

Islamic imperialism   **297**

Karski, Jan, 1914-2000

About

Karski, J. Story of a secret state   **940.53**

Karsten, Joel

Straw bale gardens complete   **635**

KARTS AND KARTING

See also Automobile racing

Karzai, Hamid, 1957-

About

Partlow, J. A kingdom of their own   **958.104**

Kashatus, William C.

Jackie and Campy   **92**

KASHMIR (TROOPSHIP)

Scott, R. N. Many were held by the sea   **940.4**

Kashner, Sam

Furious love   **92**

Kashuk, Sonia

Real beauty   **646.7**

Kasinof, Laura

About

Kasinof, L. Don't be afraid of the bullets   **953.305**

Kasischke, Laura

Space, in chains   **811**

Kasper, Lynne Rossetto

(jt. auth) Swift, S. The Splendid table's how to eat supper   **641.5**

Kasper, Shirl

Annie Oakley   **92**

Kass, Leon

The beginning of wisdom   **222**

Kassinger, Ruth, 1954-

About

Kassinger, R. A Garden of Marvels   **580**

Kastin, David

Nica's dream   **92**

Kataoka, Mami

(ed) Ai weiwei   **709.5**

Kate remembered. Berg, A. S.   **92**

Kate: the woman who was Hepburn. Mann, W. J. **92**

Katharine Graham's Washington.   **975.3**

Katherine the queen. Porter, L.   **92**

Katlama, Jacqueline Boulloche, 1918-1994

About

Kaiser, C. The cost of courage   **92**

Katrina. Rivlin, G.   **976.3**

KATRINA, HURRICANE, 2005 *See* Hurricane Katrina, 2005

KATYDIDS

Capinera, J. L. Field guide to grasshoppers, crickets, and katydids of the United States   **595.7**

Himmelman, J. Cricket radio   **595.7**

Katz on dogs. Katz, J.   **636.7**

Katz, Amy

Seed bead chic   **745.594**

Katz, Daniel

(ed) Labor rising   **331.88**

Katz, Friedrich

The life and times of Pancho Villa   **972.08**

Katz, Harry L.

Civil War sketch book   **973.7**

Katz, Jon

Dog days   **636**

Katz on dogs   **636.7**

The new work of dogs   **636.7**

About

Katz, J. Saving Simon   **636.1**

Katz, Jonathan M.

The big truck that went by   **363.34**

Katz, Rebecca

The cancer-fighting kitchen   **641.5**

The longevity kitchen   **612.6**

Katz, Robert

The battle for Rome   **940.54**

Katz, Sandor Ellix

The art of fermentation   **664**

Katz, Victor J.

(ed) Sherlock Holmes in Babylon   **510**

Katzen, Mollie

Get cooking   **641.5**

The heart of the plate   **641.5**

The Moosewood Cookbook   **641.5**

Katzinger, Jennifer

Gluten-free & vegan pie   **641.3**

Katznelson, Ira

Fear itself   **973.917**

When affirmative action was white   **323.1**

Kauffman, Bill

Forgotten founder, drunken prophet   **92**

Kaufman field guide to birds of North America. Kaufman, K.   **598**

Kaufman field guide to butterflies of North America. Brock, J. P.   **595.7**

Kaufman, David

Doris Day   **92**

Some enchanted evenings   **92**

Kaufman, Kenn

Brock, J. P. Kaufman field guide to butterflies of North America   **595.7**

Kaufman field guide to birds of North America **598**

Kaufman, Marc

First contact   **576.8**

Kaufman, Sarah L.

The art of grace   **302.1**

Kaufman, Sharon R.

--And a time to die   **362.1**

Kaufmann, Walter

(ed) Existentialism from Dostoevsky to Sartre 142

(tr) Goethe, J. W. v. Goethe's Faust 832

(ed) Nietzsche, F. W. Basic writings of Nietzsche 193

Kaupelis, Robert
Experimental drawing 741.2

Kaur, Rupi
Milk and honey 811.6

Kavanagh, Julie
Nureyev 92

Kavanagh, Patrick, 1904-1967
About
Heaney, S. Finders keepers 821

Kave, Allison
First prize pies 641.86

Kavenna, Joanna
The ice museum 998

Kavin, Kim
The Dog Merchants 636.7

Kawa, Abraham
Democracy 741.5

Kawasaki, Guy
The art of the start 2.0 658.1

Kay, Andrea
This is how to get your next job 650.14

Kay, Christian
(ed) Historical thesaurus of the Oxford English dictionary 423

Kayak morning. Rosenblatt, R. 300

Kayaking. 797.1

KAYAKING
See also Canoes and canoeing

KAYAKS AND KAYAKING
Rosenblatt, R. Kayak morning 300

Kaye, Megan
(jt. auth) Becker-Phelps, L. Love 646.7

Kazan, Elia
About
Schickel, R. Elia Kazan 92

Kazdin, Alan E.
The Everyday Parenting Toolkit 649

Kazin, Alfred
An American procession 810
Cook, R. M. Alfred Kazin's journals 92

Kazin, Alfred, 1915-1998
About
Cook, R. M. Alfred Kazin's journals 92

Kazin, Michael
A godly hero 92

Keach, William
(ed) Coleridge, S. T. The complete poems 821

Keahey, John
Seeking Sicily 945

Kealing, Bob
Tupperware, unsealed 338.7

Kean, Sam
The disappearing spoon 546
The tale of the dueling neurosurgeons 617.4
The violinist's thumb 572.8

Keane, Nancy J.
101 great, ready-to-use book lists for teens 028.5

Kearney, Kirsten
Block city 794

Kearns, Emily
(ed) The Oxford dictionary of classical myth and religion 292

Kearny's march. Groom, W. 979

Kearny, Stephen Watts, 1794-1848
About
Groom, W. Kearny's march 979

Keaton, Buster, 1895-1966
About
Meade, M. Buster Keaton 92

Keats. Motion, A. 821

The **Keats** brothers. Gigante, D. 920

Keats, John, 1795-1821
The complete poems of John Keats 821
Poems 821
About
Motion, A. Keats 821
Vendler, H. H. Coming of age as a poet 820

Kee, Howard Clark
The Cambridge companion to the Bible 220.9

Keefe, Patrick Radden
The snakehead 364.1

Keegan, John
(ed) The Book of war 355
The American Civil War 973.7
Fields of battle 355.009

Keegan, Paul
(ed) Hughes, T. Collected poems 821

Keen, Andrew
The Internet Is Not the Answer 302.23

Keenan, George F. (George Frost), 1904-2005
About
Gaddis, J. L. George F. Kennan 327

Keene, Carolyn
About
Rehak, M. Girl sleuth 813

Keene, Donald
Emperor of Japan: Meiji and His world, 1852-1912 952.03
Five modern Japanese novelists 895.6
The pleasures of Japanese literature 895.6
Seeds in the heart 895.6

Keene, Nancy
Your Child in the Hospital 362.1

Keep watching the skies! Warren, B. 791.43

Keeper. Gillies, A. 616.8

Keepers. Schickel, R. 791.43

Keepers. Brennan, K. 641.5

Keeping an eye open. Barnes, J. 709.04

Keeping faith: memoirs of a president. Carter, J. **92**
Keeping hope alive. Abdi, H. **92**
Kees, Weldon
      About
 Gioia, D. Can poetry matter? **809.1**
Keflezighi, Meb, 1975-
 (jt. auth) Douglas, S. Meb for mortals **796.42**
Keiler, Allan
 Marian Anderson **92**
Keillor, Garrison
 (comp) Good poems **811**
Keim, Cecily
 Teach yourself visually crochet **746.43**
Keizer, Garret
 Getting Schooled **373.1**
 The unwanted sound of everything we want **363.7**
Kelaidis, Gwen Moore
 Hardy succulents **635.9**
Kelder, Diane
 The great book of French impressionism **759**
Keller, Cathleen A.
 (ed) Hatshepsut: from queen to Pharaoh **932**
Keller, Helen, 1880-1968
      About
 Gibson, W. The miracle worker **812**
 Herrmann, D. Helen Keller **92**
 Keller, H. Helen Keller: selected writings **92**
 Keller, H. The story of my life **92**
Keller, Joe
      About
 Dohrmann, G. Play their hearts out **796.323**
Keller, Laurent
 The lives of ants **595.7**
Keller, Michael
 Charles Darwin's On the Origin of Species **576.8**
Keller, Thomas, 1955-
 Ad Hoc at home **641.5**
 Bouchon Bakery **641.59**
Keller, Timothy J.
 The reason for God **239**
Kellerman, Barbara
 The end of leadership **303.3**
Kelley, Kitty
 Let Freedom Ring **323.1**
Kelley, Robin D. G., 1962-
 Thelonious Monk **92**
Kellman, Steven G.
 Redemption: the life of Henry Roth **92**
 (ed) Magill's survey of American literature **810**
 (ed) Magill's survey of world literature **809**
Kellow, Brian
 Pauline Kael **92**
Kelly, Christopher
 The end of empire **92**
Kelly, Denis
 Aidells, B. The complete meat cookbook **641.6**

Kelly, Franklin
 Cikovsky, N. Winslow Homer **759.13**
Kelly, J. N. D.
 The Oxford dictionary of Popes **920.003**
Kelly, Jack
 Heaven's ditch **386**
Kelly, John
 The graves are walking **941.5**
Kelly, John
 (ed) The Hillier gardener's guide to trees & shrubs **635.9**
 The great mortality **614.5**
Kelly, Joseph
 America's longest siege **305.896**
Kelly, Kate
 Street fighters **332.6**
Kelly, Mark E., 1964-
 (jt. auth) Giffords, G. D. Enough **363.33**
Kelly, Matthew
 The dream manager **658.3**
Kelly, Megyn, 1970-
 Settle for More **791.45**
Kelly, Robert
 Lapis **811**
 Red actions **811**
Kelly, William J.
 Jacobs, C. Smogtown **363.7**
 The People's Republic of Chemicals **363.739**
Kelo, Susette
      About
 Benedict, J. Little pink house **343**
Kelsey, Ann L.
 (jt. auth) Cohn, J. M. The complete library technology planner **025**
Kelsey, Elin
 Watching giants **599.5**
Kelsey, John
 Woodworking **684**
Keltner, Dacher
 Born to be good **155.2**
Kemp, Barry
 The city of Akhenaten and Nefertiti **930**
Kemp, E. G., 1860-1939
      About
 Morris-Suzuki, T. To the Diamond Mountains **915**
Kemp, Thomas Jay
 International vital records handbook **929**
 Virtual roots 2.0 **929**
Kempis, Thomas
 Imitation of Christ The imitation of Christ **242**
 Selected writings **189**
Kempner, Vitka
      About
 Cohen, R. The avengers **940.53**
Ken Schultz's field guide to saltwater fish. Schultz, K. **597**

Kendall, Joshua
America's obsessives   **609.2**
Kendall, Joshua C.
First dads   **973**
Kendall, Tim
The art of Robert Frost   **811**
Kendi, Ibram X.
Stamped from the beginning   **305.8**
Kendo. Bennett, A. C.   **796.86**
KENDO
Bennett, A. C. Kendo   **796.86**
Keneally, Thomas
Abraham Lincoln   **92**
American scoundrel: the life of the notorious Civil
War General Dan Sickles   **92**
A commonwealth of thieves   **994**
Kenji Yoshino
A thousand times more fair   **822.3**
KENKEN
See also Puzzles
Kennan, George Frost, 1904-2005
About
Kennan, G. F. Sketches from a life   **92**
Thompson, N. The hawk and the dove   **92**
Kenneally, Christine
The first word   **400**
The invisible history of the human race   **616**
Kennedy & Nixon. Matthews, C.   **973.922**
KENNEDY FAMILY
Brinkley, A. John F. Kennedy   **92**
Byrne, P. Kick   **92**
Larson, K. C. Rosemary   **92**
Leamer, L. The Kennedy men   **920**
Leaming, B. Kick Kennedy   **92**
Maier, T. When lions roar   **941.084**
Taraborrelli, J. R. After Camelot   **920**
The **Kennedy** men. Leamer, L.   **920**
Kennedy's wars. Freedman, L.   **973.922**
Kennedy, Caroline, 1957-
Jacqueline Kennedy   **973.922**
Kennedy, David M.
Freedom from fear   **973.91**
Kennedy, Dennis
(ed) The Oxford companion to theatre and perfor-
mance   **792**
Kennedy, Diana
The essential cuisines of Mexico   **641.59**
From my Mexican kitchen   **641.5**
Kennedy, Edward Moore, 1932-2009
About
English, B. Last lion   **92**
Kennedy, E. M. True compass   **92**
Kennedy, Hugh
The great Arab conquests   **909**
When Baghdad ruled the Muslim world   **956.7**
Kennedy, James R.

(ed) Our new public, a changing clientele   **025.1**
Kennedy, Janet Krone
The good sleeper   **649**
Kennedy, John F. (John Fitzgerald), 1917-1963
Profiles in courage   **920**
About
Brinkley, A. John F. Kennedy   **92**
Bugliosi, V. Reclaiming history   **973.922**
Clarke, T. JFK's last hundred days   **92**
Coleman, D. G. The fourteenth day   **73.922**
Dallek, R. Let every nation know   **92**
Dallek, R. An unfinished life: John F. Kennedy,
1917-1963   **92**
Doyle, W. PT 109   **940.54**
Freedman, L. Kennedy's wars   **973.922**
Galbraith, J. K. Name-dropping   **973.9**
Halberstam, D. The best and the brightest **973.922**
Hill, C. Five days in November   **973.922**
Jacqueline Kennedy   **973.922**
Kaiser, D. E. American tragedy   **959.704**
Kaiser, D. E. The road to Dallas   **973.922**
Leamer, L. The Kennedy men   **920**
Mahoney, R. D. Sons and brothers: the days of Jack
and Bobby Kennedy   **92**
Maier, T. When lions roar   **941.084**
Mallon, T. Mrs. Paine's garage and the murder of
John F. Kennedy   **364.1**
Matthews, C. Kennedy & Nixon   **973.922**
Mitchell, G. The tunnels   **943.155**
Morrow, L. The best year of their lives   **920**
Pietrusza, D. 1960: LBJ vs. JFK vs. Nixon **973.92**
Posner, G. L. Case closed   **973.922**
Rasenberger, J. The brilliant disaster   **972.91**
Reeves, R. President Kennedy   **973.922**
Shenon, P. A cruel and shocking act   **973.922**
Sorensen, T. C. Counselor   **92**
Stoll, I. JFK, conservative   **973.922**
KENNEDY, JOHN F. (JOHN FITZGERALD),
1917-1963 -- ASSASSINATION
Hill, C. Five days in November   **973.922**
Minutaglio, B. Dallas 1963   **973.922**
Shenon, P. A cruel and shocking act   **973.922**
Swanson, J. L. End of Days   **973.922**
Kennedy, John F. Jr., 1960-1999
About
Anderson, C. The good son   **92**
Kennedy, Joseph F.
(ed) The Art of natural building   **690**
Kennedy, Joseph P. (Joseph Patrick), 1888-1969
About
Leamer, L. The Kennedy men   **920**
Mahoney, R. D. Sons and brothers: the days of Jack
and Bobby Kennedy   **92**
Nasaw, D. The patriarch   **92**
Kennedy, Kathleen, 1920-1948
About

Byrne, P. Kick 92
Leaming, B. Kick Kennedy 92
Kennedy, Kostya
56 92
Pete Rose 92
Kennedy, Marie R.
(jt. auth) Laguardia, C. Marketing your library's electronic resources 025.2
Kennedy, Max
Kennedy, R. F. Make gentle the life of this world 973.922
Kennedy, Michael
(jt. auth) Bourne, J. The Oxford Dictionary of Music 780.3
Kennedy, Paul M., 1945-
Engineers of victory 940.54
The rise and fall of the great powers 909.08
Kennedy, Robert F., 1925-1968
Make gentle the life of this world 973.922
Thirteen days 973.922
About
Clarke, T. The last campaign 92
Mahoney, R. D. Sons and brothers: the days of Jack and Bobby Kennedy 92
Reavill, G. Mafia summit 364.106
Schlesinger, A. M. Robert Kennedy and his times 92
Thomas, E. Robert Kennedy 92
Tye, L. Bobby Kennedy 92
Kennedy, Vicki
(ed) Coles, R. Handing one another along 820
Kennedy-Moore, Eileen, 1964-
Elman, N. M. The unwritten rules of friendship 649
Smart parenting for smart kids 649
Kennefick, Daniel
(jt. auth) Schulmann, R. An Einstein encyclopedia 530.092
Kenner, Hugh
The Pound era 811
Kennett, Lee B.
Sherman 92
Kenney, David Ngaruri, 1973-
About
Kenney, D. N. Asylum denied 92
Kenny, Anthony John Patrick
(ed) The Oxford history of Western philosophy 190
Kenny, Brian
Ahead of the curve 796.357
KENTUCKY
Hooks, B. Belonging 92
KENTUCKY DERBY
Squires, J. D. Horse of a different color 798.4
KENYA
Anderson, D. M. Histories of the hanged 967.62
Dinesen, I. Out of Africa and Shadows on the grass 967.62

Huxley, E. The flame trees of Thika 828
Kenney, D. N. Asylum denied 92
Maathai, W. Unbowed 92
KENYA -- DESCRIPTION AND TRAVEL
Adamson, J. Born free 599.75
KENYA -- POETRY
Foulds, A. The broken word 821
Kenyon, Jane
Collected poems 811
Keown, Damien
A dictionary of Buddhism 294.3
Kepel, Gilles
Jihad 297
Kephart, Beth
Handling the truth 808.06
Ker, Ian
G. K. Chesterton 828
Kerasote, Ted
Merle's door 636.7
Pukka's Promise 636.7
Kerkeling, Hape
I'm off then 914
Kermode, Frank
An appetite for poetry 801
Concerning E.M. Forster 823
Pieces of my mind 824
Shakespeare's language 822.3
Kern, M. Kathleen
Virtual reference best practices 025.5
Kerouac, Jack, 1922-1969
Book of blues 811
Book of sketches, 1952-53 811
Pomes all sizes 811
Scattered poems 811
Some of the dharma 294.3
About
Johnson, J. The voice is all 818
Kerouac, J. Selected letters, 1940-1956 92
Kerouac, J. Selected letters, 1957-1969 813
Kerpen, Dave
The art of people 650.1
Kerr, Hillary
(jt. auth) Power, K. The career code 650.1
Kerr, Jolie
My boyfriend barfed in my handbag ... and other things you can't ask Martha 648
Kerr, Kelsie
Streiff, F. The art of simple food 641.5
Kerrigan, Anthony
(tr) The revolt of the masses 901
Kerrod, Robin
Hubble 522
Kersey, Geoff
Painting successful watercolours from photographs 751.42
Kershaw, Alex

Avenue of spies 940.53
Escape from the deep 940.54
Kershaw, Ian
To Hell and Back 940.5
Hitler 92
Hitler, 1936-1945: nemesis 943.086
Kersten, Jason
The art of making money 92
Kertész, André
About
Marton, K. The great escape 920
Kertzer, David I.
The Popes against the Jews 261.2
The Pope and Mussolini 322
Kessel, Brent
It's not about the money 332.024
Kessel, William B.
(ed) Encyclopedia of Native American wars and warfare 970.004
Kesselman, Wendy Ann
Goodrich, F. The diary of Anne Frank 812
Kessler, Andrew
Martian summer 523.4
Kessler, David
Kubler-Ross, E. Life lessons 170
Kessler, Lauren
Dancing with Rose 362.1
Kessler, Ronald
The CIA at war 973.931
Kessler-Harris, Alice
Out to work 331.4
Kessner, Ellen Zelda
Crompton, V. Saving beauty from the beast 362.88
Kessner, Thomas
The flight of the century 92
Ketcham, Katherine
Moyers, W. C. Broken: my story of addiction and redemption 92
O'Dell, C. Miss O'Dell 92
Ketchum, Richard M.
Saratoga 973.3
Keteyian, Armen
(jt. auth) Benedict, J. The System 796.332
Kettenmann, Andrea
Frida Kahlo : 1907-1954 709
Kettl, Donald F.
The next government of the United States 351
Kettmann, Steve
Baseball maverick 92
Keuning-Tichelaar, An
Passing on the comfort 940.54
Keville, Kathi
The aromatherapy garden 635.9
Key, Francis Scott, 1779-1843
About
Vogel, S. Through the perilous fight 973.5

KEYBOARDS (MUSICAL INSTRUMENTS)
See also Organs (Musical instruments); Pianos
Keynes, John Maynard, 1883-1946
The general theory of employment, interest and money 330.1
About
Heilbroner, R. L. The worldly philosophers 330.1
Steil, B. The battle of Bretton Woods 339.5
Keys, Ancel, 1904-2004
About
Tucker, T. The great starvation experiment 174.2
Keys, Mary Grey Lady, ca. 1540-1578
About
De Lisle, L. The sisters who would be queen 920
KGB
Haynes, J. E. Spies 327.12
Khalaf, Farida
About
The girl who escaped ISIS 956.7
Khalil, Ashraf
Liberation Square 962.05
Khalili, Nasser D.
Islamic art and culture 709
Khan family
About
Seierstad, A. The bookseller of Kabul 958.1
Khan, Ali S.
The next pandemic 362.1
Khan, Joel
The whole heart solution 616.1
Khan, Mahvish Rukhsana
My Guantanamo diary 909.83
Khan, Yasmin Sabina
Enlightening the world 974.7
Khanna, Vikas
Return to the rivers 641.59
Khetarpal, Roma
The perfect parent 306.874
Khlevniuk, Oleg V.
Stalin 92
Khomeini, Ruhollah
About
Buchan, J. Days of God 955.05
Khrushchev. Taubman, W. 92
Khrushchev, Nikita Sergeevich, 1894-1971
About
Carlson, P. K blows top 947.085
Coleman, D. G. The fourteenth day 73.922
Kissinger, H. Diplomacy 327.2
Nikita Khrushchev 92
Taubman, W. Khrushchev 92
Kian Lam Kho
Phoenix claws and jade trees 641.595
Kiberd, Declan
Ulysses and us 823

Kick. Byrne, P. 92
Kick Kennedy. Leaming, B. 92
The kid. Bradlee, B. C. 92
Kidder, David S.
The Startup playbook 658.1
Kidder, Tracy
Good prose 808.02
Home town 974.4
House 690
Strength in what remains 92
KIDNAPPING
Fischer, P. A Kim Jong-Il production 791.43
Garcia Marquez, G. News of a kidnapping 364.15
Macy, B. Truevine 791.3
Matthews, J. Bringing Adam home 364.1
Toobin, J. American Heiress 322.4
KIDNAPPING -- GRAPHIC NOVELS
Geary, R. The Lindbergh child 364.1
KIDNAPPING, PARENTAL See Parental kidnapping
KIDNEYS
Rose, D. A. Larry's kidney 915
KIDNEYS -- DISEASES
Kang, M. S. The doctor's kidney diets 616.6
Snyder, R. d. 1. What you must know about dialysis 617.4
Kierkegaard, Søren, 1813-1855
The concept of anxiety 233
About
Existentialism from Dostoevsky to Sartre 142
Kiernan, Ben
The Pol Pot regime 959.6
Kiernan, Denise
The girls of atomic city 976.8
D'Agnese, J. The money book for freelancers, part-time, and the self-employed 332.024
Kiernan, Frances
Seeing Mary plain: a life of Mary McCarthy 818
Kiernan, Stephen P.
Last rights 179.7
Kijac, Maria Baez
The South American table 641.59
Kiki de Montparnasse. Bocquet 759.4
Kiki, 1901-1953
About
Bocquet Kiki de Montparnasse 759.4
Kilcullen, David
The accidental guerrilla 355.4
Kilgore, Bernard, 1908-1967
About
Tofel, R. J. Restless genius 92
Kill 'em and leave. McBride, J. 92
Kill Chain. Cockburn, A. 623.7
Kill or cure. Parker, S. 610
Killen, Andreas
1973 nervous breakdown 973.924

The killer of little shepherds. Starr, D. 364.152
Killer stuff and tons of money. Stanton, M. 381
KILLER WHALE
Hargrove, J. Beneath the surface 599.53
Kirby, D. Death at SeaWorld 599.53
Neiwert, D. Of orcas and men 599.53
Killian, Kevin
(ed) Spicer, J. My vocabulary did this to me 811
Killing a king. Ephron, D. 956.94
Killing Custer. Welch, J. 973.8
Killing monsters. Jones, G. 302.23
The killing of Crazy Horse. Powers, T. 92
The killing of Osama Bin Laden. Hersh, S. 327.73
Kilmeade, Brian
(jt. auth) Yaeger, D. George Washington's secret six 973.4
Kilmer-Purcell, Josh
(jt. auth) Ridge, B. The Beekman 1802 heirloom dessert cookbook 641.5
A Kim Jong-Il production. Fischer, P. 791.43
Kim, Eunsun, 1986-
A Thousand Miles to Freedom 92
Kim, Jong Il, 1942-2011
Fischer, P. A Kim Jong-Il production 791.43
About
Hassig, R. C. The hidden people of North Korea 951.93
Jang Jin-sung Dear Leader 92
Kim, Joseph
Under the same sky 92
Kim, Sue
Boutique bags 646.4
Kim, Susan
Flow 612.6
Kimball, Charles
When religion becomes lethal 201
Kimball, George, 1943-2011
At the fights 796.8
Four kings 920
Kimball, Kristin
About
Kimball, K. The dirty life 92
Kimball, Robert
(ed) Porter, C. Selected lyrics 782.42
Kincaid, Jamaica, 1946-
A small place 972.9
The kind mama. 618.1
A kind of grace. Joyner-Kersee, J. 796.42
KINDERGARTEN
See also Elementary education; Schools
KINDNESS
Pierson, M. H. The secret history of kindness 636.7
The kindness of strangers: the life of Tennessee Williams. Spoto, D. 92
Kindred spirits. Schoen, A. M. 636.089
Kindred, Dave

Sound and fury **796**

Kindsvatter, Peter S.

American soldiers **355**

KINESIOLOGY

See also Human locomotion; Physical fitness

KINETIC ART

See also Art

KINETIC SCULPTURE

See also Kinetic art; Sculpture

The **King** and Queen of Malibu. Randall, D. K. **979.4**

King Arthur in legend and history. **942.01**

King Hussein of Jordan. Ashton, N. **92**

King John. Morris, M. **92**

King legacy series

King, M. L. The trumpet of conscience **973.92**

King, M. L. Where do we go from here **323.1**

King Leopold's ghost. Hochschild, A. **967.5**

King of infinite space. Roberts, S. **92**

The **king** of infinite space. Berlinski, D. **516.2**

King of ragtime: Scott Joplin and his era. Berlin, E. A. **92**

King of the lobby. Jacob, K. A. **92**

King of the world: Muhammad Ali and the rise of an American hero. Remnick, D. **92**

King Philip's War. Schultz, E. B. **973.2**

KING PHILIP'S WAR, 1675-1676

Lepore, J. The name of war **973.2**

Schultz, E. B. King Philip's War **973.2**

KING PHILIP'S WAR, 1675-1676

See also Native Americans -- Wars; United States -- History -- 1600-1775, Colonial period

The **king's** revenge. Jordan, D. **941.062**

King, B. B.

About

King, B. B. Blues all around me **781.643**

King, Carole

About

Weller, S. Girls like us **920**

King, Charles

Odessa **947.7**

King, Clarence, 1842-1901

About

Sandweiss, M. A. Passing strange **92**

King, David

Death in the city of light

Red star over Russia **947**

Vienna, 1814 **940.2**

Walker, G. The hot topic **363.7**

King, Dean

Patrick O'Brian **823**

King, Ernest Joseph, 1878-1956

About

Borneman, W. R. The admirals **920**

King, George L.

(jt. auth) Flippin, R. The diabetes reset **616.4**

King, Gilbert, 1962-

Devil in the grove **305.896**

King, Greg, 1964-

(jt. auth) Wilson, P. Lusitania **910.4**

King, James

Farley: the life of Farley Mowat **92**

King, Kaiser, Tsar. Clay, C. **920**

King, Martin Luther, Jr., 1929-1968

The autobiography of Martin Luther King, Jr **323**

Strength to love **252**

A testament of hope **323.1**

Thou, dear God **242**

The trumpet of conscience **973.92**

Where do we go from here **323.1**

Why we can't wait **323.1**

About

Branch, T. At Canaan's edge **973.923**

Branch, T. Pillar of fire **973.922**

Branch, T. Parting the waters: America in the King years, 1954-63 **973.921**

Burns, R. Burial for a King **92**

Cornel West on Black prophetic fire **92**

Dyson, M. E. I may not get there with you: the true Martin Luther King, Jr **323**

I see the promised land **92**

Jackson, T. Becoming King **92**

King, M. L. The autobiography of Martin Luther King, Jr **323**

Kotz, N. Judgment days **323**

Pepper, W. F. An act of state **364.1**

The radical King **323**

Risen, C. A nation on fire **973.923**

Sides, H. Hellhound on his trail **364.152**

Young, A. An easy burden **92**

King, Martin Luther, Jr., 1929-1968

Letter from Birmingham jail

About

Rieder, J. Gospel of freedom **323.1**

King, Mervyn A., 1948-

The End of Alchemy **330.122**

King, Ross

Art: over 2,500 works from cave to contemporary **709**

Brunelleschi's dome **726**

Florence **759.5**

The judgment of Paris **759**

Leonardo and the Last supper **759**

Mad enchantment **759.4**

Michelangelo & the Pope's ceiling **759**

King, Stephen, 1947-

About

King, S. On writing **813**

Kingdom conspiracy. McKnight, S. **231.7**

The **kingdom** of fear. Thompson, H. S. **92**

KINGDOM OF GOD

McKnight, S. Kingdom conspiracy **231.7**

The **kingdom** of rarities. Dinerstein, E. 596

A **kingdom** of their own. Partlow, J. 958.104

A **kingdom** strange. Horn, J. 975.6

The **Kingfish** and his realm: the life and times of Huey P. Long. Hair, W. I. 92

Kingma, Daphne Rose
The ten things to do when your life falls apart 155.9

Kingmakers. Meyer, K. E. 956

Kingry, Judi
(ed) Complete book of home preserving 641.4

KINGS
Ackroyd, P. The death of King Arthur 398.2
Ashton, N. King Hussein of Jordan 92
Brier, B. The murder of Tutankhamen 932
Buckley, V. The secret wife of Louis XIV 944
Carter, M. George, Nicholas, and Wilhelm 940.3
Ceram, C. W. Gods, graves, and scholars 930.1
DeJean, J. E. The essence of style 391
Fraser, A. Love and Louis XIV 92
Fraser, A. The wives of Henry VIII 920
Fraser, F. Princesses 920
Hawass, Z. A. Tutankhamun and the golden age of the pharaohs 932
Hibbert, C. The Borgias and their enemies 945
Junor, P. The Firm: the troubled life of the House of Windsor 941.085
Kamen, H. Philip of Spain 946
King Arthur in legend and history 942.01
Landon, M. Anna and the King of Siam 92
Lever, E. Madame de Pompadour 944
MacDonogh, G. Frederick the Great 943
Malory, T. Le morte Darthur, or, The hoole book of Kyng Arthur and of his noble knyghtes of the Rounde Table 398.2
Mertz, B. Temples, tombs, & hieroglyphs 932
Meyer, G. J. The Tudors 942.05
Pinsky, R. The life of David 92
Starkey, D. Six wives: the queens of Henry VIII 942.05
Tillyard, S. K. A royal affair 920
Uglow, J. S. A gambling man 92
Weatherford, J. M. Genghis Khan and the making of the modern world 92
Weir, A. Henry VIII 942.05
Weir, A. The lady in the tower 92
Weir, A. The six wives of Henry VIII 942.05

The **kings** & queens of Britain. Cannon, J. 920

KINGS AND RULERS
Clay, C. King, Kaiser, Tsar 920
Mayor, A. The Poison King 92
Penman, M. Robert the Bruce 92
Wilson, D. A. Charlemagne 92

KINGS AND RULERS
See also Heads of state

KINGS, QUEENS, RULERS, ETC. *See* Kings and rulers

Kingsbury, Noël
The glory of the tree 582.16

Kingsolver, Barbara, 1955-
About
Animal, vegetable, miracle 641

Kingsolver, Camille
Animal, vegetable, miracle 641

Kingston, Maxine Hong
China men 920
About
Kingston, M. H. The woman warrior 92

Kinnell, Galway
A new selected poems 811
Strong is your hold 811

Kinney, David
The devil's diary 940.53

Kinsella, Thomas
(ed) The New Oxford book of Irish verse 821
(tr) Tain bo Cuailnge The Tain 891.6

Kinsella, Tim
(ed) Hopper, J. The first collection of criticism by a living female rock critic

KINSHIP
See also Ethnology; Family

Kinsley, Michael, 1951-
About
Kinsley, M. Old age 814.54

Kinte family
About
Haley, A. Roots 920

Kintpuash, Modoc Chief, 1837?-1873
About
Brown, D. A. Bury my heart at Wounded Knee 970.004

Kinzer, Stephen
All the Shah's men 327
Crescent and star 956.1

KIOWA INDIANS
Brown, D. A. The American West 978

Kipfer, Barbara Ann
How it happens 500
(ed) Roget's 21st century thesaurus in dictionary form 423
(ed) Roget's international thesaurus 423

Kiple, Kenneth F.
(ed) The Cambridge world history of food 641.3

Kipling, Alice, 1837-1910
About
Flanders, J. A circle of sisters 920

Kipling, Rudyard, 1865-1936
Complete verse 821
About
Gilmour, D. The long recessional: the imperial life of Rudyard Kipling 92
Jarrell, R. No other book 809
Ricketts, H. Rudyard Kipling 92

Kipnis, Laura
How to become a scandal   **306.7**
Kirby, David
Animal factory   **363.7**
Death at SeaWorld   **599.53**
Talking about movies with Jesus   **811**
Kirby, Richard R.
Ocean drifters   **578.7**
Kirigami menagerie. Hayakawa, H.   **736**
Kirk, Connie Ann
Critical companion to Flannery O'Connor   **813**
Kirk, Mimi
The ultimate book of modern juicing   **663**
Kirkpatrick, David
The Facebook effect   **338.7**
Kirkpatrick, James Achilles, 1764-1805
         About
Dalrymple, W. White Mughals   **954**
Kirkpatrick, Rob
1969   **973.92**
Kirkpatrick, Sidney
Edgar Cayce   **92**
Kirkwood, Burton
The history of Mexico   **972**
Kirn, Walter, 1962-
         About
Kirn, W. Blood will out   **364.152**
Kiros, Tessa
Food from many Greek kitchens   **641.5**
Kirsch, Adam
The people and the books   **809.889**
Kirsch, Melissa
The girl's guide to absolutely everything   **646.7**
Kirschbaum, Erik
Soccer without borders   **796.334**
Kirschvink, Joseph
A new history of life   **576.8**
Kirshenblatt, Mayer, 1916-
         About
Kirshenblatt, M. They called me Mayer July   **92**
Kirshenblatt-Gimblett, Barbara
(jt. auth) Kirshenblatt, M. They called me Mayer July   **92**
Kiser, Joy M.
America's other Audubon   **598**
The **kiss**. Harrison, K.   **813**
Kiss, bow, or shake hands. Morrison, T.   **395**
Kissinger. Ferguson, N.   **92**
Kissinger's Shadow. Grandin, G.   **327.2**
Kissinger, Henry, 1923-
Diplomacy   **327.2**
Ending the Vietnam War   **959.704**
World Order   **327**
Years of renewal   **973.924**
         About
Bass, G. J. The Blood telegram   **327.73**

Dallek, R. Nixon and Kissinger   **92**
Ferguson, N. Kissinger   **92**
Kistler, Vivian Carli
The complete photo guide to framing & displaying artwork   **749**
Kitano, Harry
(ed) Japanese Americans, from relocation to redress   **940.53**
Kitchen confidential. Bourdain, A.   **92**
The **kitchen** counter cooking school. Flinn, K.   **641.5**
KITCHEN GARDENS
Houbein, L. One Magic Square Vegetable Gardening   **635**
KITCHEN GARDENS *See* Vegetable gardening
KITCHEN GARDENS -- WASHINGTON (D.C.)
Obama, M. American grown   **635**
A **kitchen** in France. Thorisson, M.   **641.594**
Kitchen simple. Peterson, J.   **641.5**
The **kitchen** sink. Goldbarth, A.   **811**
KITCHEN UTENSILS -- HISTORY
Consider the fork   **643**
Kitchen, Denis
The art of Harvey Kurtzman   **741.5**
Kitchenalia. Lee, V.   **747**
KITCHENS
Besh, J. My family table   **641.59**
Do it yourself kitchens   **643**
The Kitchn cookbook   **641.5**
Lee, V. Kitchenalia   **747**
Perelman, D. The smitten kitchen cookbook   **641.5**
KITCHENS
         See also Houses; Rooms
KITCHENS -- MANAGEMENT
Atlas, N. Plant power   **641.5**
Brennan, K. Keepers   **641.5**
The **Kitchn** cookbook.   **641.5**
KITES
         See also Aeronautics
KITSCH
         See also Aesthetics
KITTENS *See* Cats
Kittredge, William
(ed) The Portable Western reader   **810**
Kivirist, Lisa
(jt. auth) Ivanko, J. D. Homemade for Sale   **664**
Kiyosaki, Robert T., 1947-
Why "A" Students Work for "C" Students and Why "B" Students Work for the Government   **332.024**
Kizer, Carolyn
Cool, calm & collected   **811**
Kizny, Tomasz
Gulag   **365**
Kizzia, Tom
Pilgrim's wilderness   **92**
Kjellberg, Ann
Brodsky, J. Collected poems in English, 1972-

1999   **891.7**

Kl. Wachsmann, N.   **940.53**

Klanten, Robert
  (ed) A Map of the World   **912**

Klatt, Kathy Fling
  (jt. auth) Ghoting, S. N. STEP into storytime **027.62**

Klatz, Ronald
  Goldman, B. Brain fitness   **153.1**

Klauser, Henriette Anne
  Write it down, make it happen   **158**

Klebold, Dylan, 1981-1999
      About
  Klebold, S. A mother's reckoning   **373**

Klebold, Sue
      About
  Klebold, S. A mother's reckoning   **373**

Klee, Paul, 1879-1940
      About
  Weber, N. F. The Bauhaus group   **920**

Klehr, Harvey
  Haynes, J. E. Spies   **327.12**
  Haynes, J. E. Venona   **327.12**

Klein, Alan H.
  Agnew, C. L. Twins!   **649**

Klein, Cornelis
  Manual of mineral science   **549**

Klein, Joe
  Woody Guthrie   **92**

Klein, Maury
  A call to arms   **940.53**
  Days of defiance   **973.7**

Klein, Maya
  Flavor flours   **641.3**

Klein, Naomi
  This changes everything   **363.738**

Klein, Stefan
  Leonardo's legacy   **709**

Kleinbard, Edward D.
  We are better than this   **336.3**

Kleiner, Fred S.
  Gardner, H. Gardner's art through the ages   **709**

Kleinzahler, August
  (ed) Fisher, R. Selected poems   **821**
  Sleeping it off in Rapid City   **811**

Kleist, Heinrich von
  Selected writings   **838**

Kleist, Reinhard
  Johnny Cash   **92**

Klemp, Nathaniel J.
  (jt. auth) Langshur, E. Start here   **158**

Klemperer, Victor, 1881-1960
      About
  Klemperer, V. I will bear witness   **943.086**

KLEZMER MUSIC
  Strom, Y. The book of Klezmer   **781.62**

KLEZMER MUSIC

See also Jewish music; Popular music

Klezmer, Deborah
  (ed) Women in world history   **920.003**

Klimchuk, A. B.
      About
  Tabor, J. M. Blind descent   **796.52**

Klimt, Gustav, 1862-1918. Adele Bloch-Bauer I
      About
  O'Connor The lady in gold   **759.36**

Kline, Fred
      About
  Kline, F. R. Leonardo's holy child   **741.945**

Klinenberg, Eric
  Going solo   **306.81**

Klink, Joanna
  Raptus   **811**

Klinsmann, Jurgen
      About
  Kirschbaum, E. Soccer without borders   **796.334**

Klipper, Miriam Z.
  Benson, H. The relaxation response   **155.9**

KLONDIKE RIVER VALLEY (YUKON) -- GOLD DISCOVERIES
  Gray, C. Gold diggers   **971**

Kloosterboer, Lorena, 1962-
  Kloosterboer, L. Painting in acrylics   **751.426**

Kloppenborg, John S.
  Q, the earliest Gospel   **226**

Klosterman, Chuck, 1972-
  But What If We're Wrong?   **909.83**
  Eating the dinosaur   **973.92**

Klubeck, Martin
  Why organizations struggle so hard to improve so little   **658.4**

Kluger, Jeffrey
  The Narcissist Next Door   **616.85**
  Splendid solution: Jonas Salk and the conquest of polio   **92**

Kluger, Richard
  The bitter waters of Medicine Creek   **979.7**
  Indelible ink   **686.209**

Knapp, Caroline
      About
  Caldwell, G. Let's take the long way home   **92**

Knapp, Jake
  (jt. auth) Kowitz, B. Sprint   **658.4**

Knappe, Martha
  Pearl, N. Now read this   **016**

Knappman, Edward W.
  (ed) Great American trials   **347**

Knauer, Kelly
  TIME History's Greatest Images   **909.82**

Kneece, Mark
  The art of comic book writing   **741.5**

Knight, Bobby
      About

Knight, B. Knight: my story 92

Knight, Erika
500 crochet stitches 746.43
750 knitting stitches 746.432

Knight, Jeffrey A.
Genetics & inherited conditions 576.5

Knight, Lorna
Gardiner, W. The sewing machine accessory bible 646.2

Knight, Louise W.
Jane Addams 92

Knight, Molly
The best team money can buy 796.357

Knight, Philip H., 1938-
About
Knight, P. H. Shoe dog 92

Knight, Robert M., 1948-
Journalistic writing 070

Knight: my story. Knight, B. 92

KNIGHTHOOD *See* Knights and knighthood

Knights. 940.1

KNIGHTS AND KNIGHTHOOD
Amidon, S. Something like the gods 306.4
Asbridge, T. The Greatest Knight 92
Gies, J. Life in a medieval castle 940.2
Knights 940.1

KNIGHTS AND KNIGHTHOOD
See also Middle Ages; Nobility

KNIGHTS AND KNIGHTHOOD -- GREAT BRITAIN -- FICTION.
Ackroyd, P. The death of King Arthur 398.2

KNIGHTS OF THE ROUND TABLE *See* Arthurian romances

Knit to flatter. Herzog, A. 746.43
Knit wear love. Herzog, A. 746.432
The **knitter's** book of yarn. Parkes, C. 677
The **knitter's** companion. Square, V. 746.43
The **knitter's** handy book of patterns. Budd, A. 746.43
Knitter's handy book of top-down sweaters. Budd, A. 746.432

KNITTING
Anderson, S. B. Susan B. Anderson's kids' knitting workshop 746.43
Bassetti, A. Arm knitting 746.43
Bernard, W. Up, down, all-around stitch dictionary 746.43
Bestor, L. A. Cast on, bind off 746.43
Budd, A. The knitter's handy book of patterns 746.43
Budd, A. Knitter's handy book of top-down sweaters 746.432
Budd, A. New directions in sock knitting 746.432
Budd, A. Sock knitting master class 746.432
Circular knitting workshop 746.43
Dosen, S. Woodland knits 746.43

Drysdale, R. Entrelac 746.432
Durant, J. Cable left, cable right 746.432
Durant, J. Increase, decrease 746.43
Epstein, N. Nicky Epstein's essential edgings collection
Herzog, A. Knit to flatter 746.43
Herzog, A. Knit wear love 746.432
Herzog, A. You can knit that 746.432
Knitting fabric rugs 746.7
Knitting masterclass 746.432
Lavold, E. Viking knits and ancient ornaments
Marchant, N. Knitting brioche 746.43
Marchant, N. Knitting fresh brioche 746.43
Newton, D. Finishing school 746.43
Nico, B. More Lovely Knitted Lace 746.432
Norah Gaughan's Knitted Cable Sourcebook 746.432
One-skein wonders for babies 746.43
Parkes, C. The knitter's book of yarn 677
Radcliffe, M. The knitting answer book 746.43
Radcliffe, M. The knowledgeable knitter 746.43
Righetti, M. Knitting in plain English 746.43
Square, V. The knitter's companion 746.43
Starmore, A. Alice Starmore's book of Fair Isle knitting 746.43
Starmore, A. Tudor roses 746.432
Stitch 'n bitch superstar knitting 746.43
Stoller, D. Stitch 'n bitch 746.43
Turner, S. Teach yourself visually knitting 746.43
Vogue knitting 746.43
Weil, A. Knitting without needles 746.432
Wood, J. Refined knits 746.432
Zimmermann, E. Knitting without tears 746.4

KNITTING
See also Needlework

KNITTING -- MISCELLANEA
Radcliffe, M. The knitting answer book 746.43

KNITTING -- NETHERLANDS
Marchant, N. Knitting brioche 746.43

KNITTING -- PATTERNS
Budd, A. The knitter's handy book of patterns 746.43
Budd, A. Knitter's handy book of top-down sweaters 746.432
Budd, A. Sock knitting master class 746.432
Circular knitting workshop 746.43
Dosen, S. Woodland knits 746.43
Drysdale, R. Entrelac 746.432
Durant, J. Increase, decrease 746.43
Herzog, A. Knit to flatter 746.43
Knitting fabric rugs 746.7
Marchant, N. Knitting brioche 746.43
Marchant, N. Knitting fresh brioche 746.43
Melville, S. Knitting pattern essentials 746.43
Newton, D. Finishing school 746.43
One-skein wonders for babies 746.43

Radcliffe, M. The knowledgeable knitter   **746.43**
Weil, A. Knitting without needles   746.432
Wood, J. Refined knits   746.432
**KNITTING -- PATTERNS -- JUVENILE LIT-
ERATURE**
Anderson, S. B. Susan B. Anderson's kids' knitting
workshop   **746.43**
**KNITTING -- SCOTLAND -- FAIR ISLE -- PAT-
TERNS**
Starmore, A. Alice Starmore's book of Fair Isle
knitting   **746.43**
KNITTING -- TECHNIQUE
Knight, E. 750 knitting stitches   746.432
The **knitting** answer book. Radcliffe, M.   **746.43**
Knitting brioche. Marchant, N.   **746.43**
Knitting fabric rugs.   746.7
Knitting fresh brioche. Marchant, N.   **746.43**
Knitting in plain English. Righetti, M.   **746.43**
Knitting masterclass.   746.432
Knitting pattern essentials. Melville, S.   **746.43**
Knitting without needles. Weil, A.   746.432
Knitting without tears. Zimmermann, E.   746.4
KNITWEAR -- PATTERN DESIGN
Melville, S. Knitting pattern essentials   **746.43**
KNIVES
See also Hardware; Weapons
Knives at dawn. Friedman, A.   **641.5**
Knobler, Peter
(jt. auth) Hilfiger, T. American dreamer   92
Knock 'em dead 2015. Yate, M.   158
Knock 'em dead cover letters. Yate, M.   650.14
Knock 'em dead cover letters.   650.14
Knock 'em dead resumes. Yate, M.   650.14
Knocking on Heaven's Door. Butler, K.   616.02
Knocking on heaven's door. Randall, L.   500
Knoedelseder, William
Bitter brew   338.7
Knopper, Steve
Appetite for self-destruction   384
KNOTS AND SPLICES
Bigon, M. The Morrow guide to knots   623.88
Pawson, D. The handbook of knots   623.88
KNOTS AND SPLICES
See also Navigation; Rope
Knott, Bill
The unsubscriber   811
Know the night. Mutch, M.   92
Know your power. Pelosi, N.   92
The **know-it-all**. Jacobs, A. J.   031
KNOWLEDGE MANAGEMENT
Johnson, M. This book is overdue!   020
KNOWLEDGE MANAGEMENT
See also Management
**KNOWLEDGE REPRESENTATION (INFOR-
MATION THEORY)**
Domingos, P. The master algorithm   003

**KNOWLEDGE WORKERS -- PROFESSIONAL
ETHICS**
Defending professionalism   020
KNOWLEDGE WORKERS -- TRAINING OF
Defending professionalism   020
KNOWLEDGE, SOCIOLOGY OF
Weinberger, D. Too big to know   303.48
KNOWLEDGE, THEORY OF *See* Theory of
knowledge
KNOWLEDGE, THEORY OF -- HISTORY
Lima, M. The book of trees   001.2
The **knowledgeable** knitter. Radcliffe, M.   746.43
Knowles, Elizabeth M.
(ed) Oxford dictionary of modern quotations   808.88
(ed) Oxford dictionary of phrase and fable   803
(ed) Oxford dictionary of quotations   082
Knox, Bernard MacGregor Walker
(ed) The Norton book of classical literature   880
Knox, Jennifer L.
The mystery of the hidden driveway   811
Knox, Paul
(ed) The atlas of cities   912
Knox, Robert, 1640?-1720
About
Frank, K. Crusoe   823
Knutson, Ann
Hennessey, M. H. Norman Rockwell   759.13
Ko, Genevieve
Home cooking with Jean-Georges   641.5
Koba the dread. Amis, M.   947.084
Kobliner, Beth
Get a financial life   332.024
Koch, Kenneth
The collected poems of Kenneth Koch   811
Making your own days   809.1
On the edge   811
Koch, Stephen
The modern library writer's workshop   808.3
Kochendorfer, Kelly
Estrine, D. Harvest to heat   641.5
Kochilas, Diane
The glorious foods of Greece   641.59
Ikaria   641.594
Kodansha globe [series]
Mead, M. Blackberry winter   92
Koegel, Lynn Kern
(jt. auth) Lazebnik, C. Overcoming Autism   618.92
Koehler, Jeff
Spain   641.59
Koenig, Leah
Modern Jewish cooking   641.5
**Koenigswarter, Pannonica de, Baroness, 1913-
1988**
About
Kastin, D. Nica's dream   92
Koerner, Brendan I.

The skies belong to us | **364.15**

Koertge, Noretta
(ed) New dictionary of scientific biography **920.003**

Koertge, Ron
The ogre's wife | **811**

Koerth-Baker, Maggie
Before the lights go out | **333.79**

Koestler. Scammell, M. | **92**

Koestler, Arthur, 1905-1983
About
Marton, K. The great escape | **920**
Scammell, M. Koestler | **92**

Kogan, Lee
(ed) Encyclopedia of American folk art | **745**

Kohl, Herbert R.
(ed) The muses go to school | **700**

Kohlenberger, John R.
Strong, J. The strongest Strong's exhaustive concordance of the Bible | **220.5**

Kohn, George C.
(ed) Dictionary of wars | **355**
(ed) Encyclopedia of plague and pestilence | **614.4**

Koker, David, 1921-1945
About
At the edge of the abyss | **940.53**

Kolata, Gina
Flu | **614.5**
(ed) The New York Times book of mathematics | **510**

Kolbert, Elizabeth
(ed) The ends of the earth | **998**
Field notes from a catastrophe | **363.7**
The sixth extinction | **576.8**

KOLKATA (INDIA) -- BIOGRAPHY
Brierley, S. A long way home | **92**

Kolker, Robert
Lost Girls | **364.152**

Kolko, Jon
Well-designed | **658.5**

Kolodiejchuk, Brian
(ed) A call to mercy | **234.5**

Kolpan, Steven
Exploring wine | **641.2**
Winewise | **641.2**

Koltz, Tony
It worked for me | **92**

Komara, Edward
(ed) A basic music library | **016**

Komunyakaa, Yusef
The chameleon couch | **811**
Talking dirty to the gods | **811**
Thieves of paradise | **811**
Warhorses | **811**

Kon-Tiki. Heyerdahl, T. | **910.4**

KON-TIKI EXPEDITION (1947)
Heyerdahl, T. Kon-Tiki | **910.4**

Kondo, Marie

The life-changing magic of tidying up | **648**

Konner, Melvin
The evolution of childhood | **305.23**

Konnikova, Maria, 1987-
The Confidence Game | **364.163**
Mastermind | **153.4**

Konstam, Angus
The history of pirates | **910.4**

Kookooland. Norris, G. | **92**

Koons, Jeff, 1955-
About
Rothkopf, S. Jeff Koons | **709.2**

Kooser, Ted
Delights & shadows | **811**
Flying at night | **811**
The poetry home repair manual | **808.1**
About
Gioia, D. Can poetry matter? | **809.1**

Kopecky, Elyse
(jt. auth) Flanagan, S. Run fast, eat slow | **641.563**

Koppel, Lily
The Astronaut Wives Club | **629.45**

Koppel, Ted, 1940-
About
Koppel, T. Off camera | **92**

Kopper, Philip
Holladay, W. C. A museum of their own | **704**

KORAN -- CRITICISM
Wagner, W. H. Opening the Qur'an | **297.1**

KORAN -- ENCYCLOPEDIAS
The Qur'an: an encyclopedia | **297.1**

Korb, Scott
Life in year one | **933**

Korczak-Marla, Rozka, 1921-1988
About
Cohen, R. The avengers | **940.53**

Kord, Tyler
A super upsetting cookbook about sandwiches | **641.84**

Korda, Alberto, 1928-2001
About
Casey, M. Che's afterlife | **980**

Korda, Alexander Sir, 1893-1956
About
Marton, K. The great escape | **920**

Korda, Michael, 1933-
Clouds of Glory | **92**
Korda, M. Hero | **92**
Ulysses S. Grant: the unlikely hero | **92**
With wings like eagles | **940.54**

Kore. | **610**

KOREA (DEMOCRATIC PEOPLE'S REPUBLIC) See Korea (North)

KOREA (NORTH)
Fischer, P. A Kim Jong-Il production | **791.43**
Kim, E. A Thousand Miles to Freedom | **92**

Sweeney, J. North Korea undercover

KOREA (NORTH) -- DESCRIPTION AND TRAVEL

Delisle, G. Pyongyang: a journey in North Korea   **741.5**

Morris-Suzuki, T. To the Diamond Mountains **915**

Sweeney, J. North Korea undercover

KOREA (NORTH) -- ECONOMIC CONDITIONS

Demick, B. Nothing to envy   **951.93**

Hassig, R. C. The hidden people of North Korea   **951.93**

KOREA (NORTH) -- FOREIGN RELATIONS

Lankov, A. The real North Korea   **951.93**

KOREA (NORTH) -- POLITICS AND GOVERNMENT

Lankov, A. The real North Korea   **951.93**

McClelland, S. Stars Between the Sun and Moon **92**

KOREA (SOUTH) -- SOCIAL LIFE AND CUSTOMS

Morris-Suzuki, T. To the Diamond Mountains **915**

KOREA -- HISTORY

Breen, M. The Koreans   **951.9**

Cumings, B. Korea's place in the sun   **951.9**

Oberdorfer, D. The two Koreas   **951.9**

Peterson, M. A brief history of Korea   **951.9**

Korea's place in the sun. Cumings, B.   **951.9**

KOREAN AMERICANS

Deuki Hong Koreatown   **641.59**

Howe, B. R. My Korean deli   **92**

Lee, H. In the absence of sun   **979.4**

KOREAN COOKING

Chattman, L. Maangchi's real Korean cooking   **641.595**

Deuki Hong Koreatown   **641.59**

Ha, R. Cook Korean!   **641.595**

Korean food made simple   **641.595**

Lee, C. Quick and easy Korean cooking   **641.5**

West K-food   **641.595**

Korean food made simple.   **641.595**

KOREAN LANGUAGE -- DICTIONARIES

Berlitz Korean compact dictionary   **495.7**

KOREAN NATIONAL CHARACTERISTICS

Breen, M. The Koreans   **951.9**

The **Korean** War. Hickey, M.   **951.904**

The **Korean** War. Cumings, B.   **951.9**

KOREAN WAR, 1950-1953

Cumings, B. The Korean War   **951.9**

Hickey, M. The Korean War   **951.904**

Weintraub, S. A Christmas far from home **951.904**

KOREAN WAR, 1950-1953 -- CAMPAIGNS

Halberstam, D. The coldest winter   **951.9**

Hutton, R. Sgt. Reckless   **951.904**

KOREAN WAR, 1950-1953 -- PERSONAL NARRATIVES

Brady, J. The coldest war   **951.9**

KOREAN WAR, 1950-1953 -- REGIMENTAL HISTORIES -- UNITED STATES

Weintraub, S. A Christmas far from home **951.904**

KOREAN WAR, 1950-1953 -- UNITED STATES

Cumings, B. The Korean War   **951.9**

Halberstam, D. The coldest winter   **951.9**

The **Koreans.** Breen, M.   **951.9**

KOREANS

Demick, B. Nothing to envy   **951.93**

Koreatown. Deuki Hong   **641.59**

Koretz, Leo, 1879-1925

About

Jobb, D. Empire of deception   **92**

Korn, Larry

(ed) Fukuoka, M. Sowing seeds in the desert **631.6**

Kornbluh, Peter

(ed) The Iran-Contra scandal   **973.927**

Kort, Michael

The Columbia guide to the Cold War   **973.92**

KOSHER FOOD

Morgan, J. The covenant kitchen   **641.5**

Kosher living. Isaacs, R. H.   **296.7**

Kosik, Kenneth S.

Outsmarting alzheimer's   **616.8**

Koslow, J. Anthony

The silent deep   **578.7**

KOSOVO (SERBIA)

Di Giovanni, J. Madness visible   **949.7**

KOSOVO (SERBIA) -- HISTORY

Clark, W. K. Waging modern war   **949.703**

McAllester, M. Beyond the Mountains of the Damned   **949.71**

Kostigen, Thomas M.

National Geographic extreme weather survival guide   **613.6**

Kostow, Christopher, 1976-

A new Napa cuisine   **641.59**

Kot, Greg

I'll take you there   **92**

Ripped   **780.2**

Kotkin, Stephen

Stalin   **92**

Uncivil society   **947**

Kotler, Steven, 1967-

Abundance   **303.48**

Kotlikoff, Laurence J.

(jt. auth) Solman, P. Get what's yours   **368.4**

Kotter, John P., 1947-

Buy-in   **650.1**

Kotz, Nick

Judgment days   **323**

Koufax, Sandy, 1935-

About

Leavy, J. Sandy Koufax   **796.357**

Koufopoulos, Michelle

(ed) Eat Pray Love Made Me Do It   **910.4**

Kounios, John, 1956-
The Eureka factor   **612.8**
Kouzes, James M.
The truth about leadership   **658.4**
Kovach, Bill
Blur   **070**
The elements of journalism   **071**
The **Kovacs** guide to electronic library collection development. Kovacs, D. K.   **025**
Kovacs, Diane K.
The Kovacs guide to electronic library collection development   **025**
Kovalevskaia, S. V. (Sofia Vasil'evna), 1850-1891
About
Bell, E. T. Men of mathematics   **920**
Kovel, Ralph M.
Kovels' dictionary of marks: pottery and porcelain   **738**
Kovels' new dictionary of marks   **738**
Kovel, Terry H.
Kovel, R. M. Kovels' dictionary of marks: pottery and porcelain   **738**
Kovel, R. M. Kovels' new dictionary of marks **738**
Kovels' dictionary of marks: pottery and porcelain. Kovel, R. M.   **738**
Kovels' new dictionary of marks. Kovel, R. M. **738**
Kovner, Abba, 1918-1987
About
Cohen, R. The avengers   **940.53**
Kovner, Anthony R.
(ed) 101 careers in healthcare management **362.106**
Kowalski, Robin M.
Cyberbullying   **302.34**
Kowitz, Braden
Sprint   **658.4**
Kozol, Harry L., 1906-
About
Kozol, J. The theft of memory   **92**
Kozol, Jonathan, 1936-
Amazing grace   **362.7**
Fire in the ashes   **362.7**
Letters to a young teacher   **371.1**
Ordinary resurrections   **305.23**
Rachel and her children   **362.5**
Savage inequalities   **371.9**
The shame of the nation   **379**
The theft of memory   **92**
Kragh, Helge
Quantum generations   **530**
Krakatoa: the day the world exploded, August 27, 1883. Winchester, S.   **551.2**
Krakauer, Jon, 1954-
Into the wild   **917**
Into thin air   **796.522**
Missoula   **362.883**
Kraken. Williams, W.   **594**

Kram, Mark
The ghosts of Manila   **796.83**
Kramer, Andrea S.
Breaking through bias   **650.101**
Kramer, Clara, 1927-
About
Kramer, C. Clara's war   **92**
Kramer, Mattea
A people's guide to the federal budget   **352.4**
Kramer, Peter D.
Listening to Prozac   **616.85**
Ordinarily well   **615.7**
Krane, Jim
City of gold   **953**
Kranish, Michael
Flight from Monticello   **973.4**
Kranz, Eugene F.
Failure is not an option   **629.45**
Krapp, Kristine M.
(ed) Notable black American scientists   **509**
Krasner, Lee, 1908-1984
About
Levin, G. Lee Krasner   **92**
Krasno, Jeff
Wanderlust   **613.7**
Krass, Peter
Carnegie   **338.7**
Kraus, Wladimir
(jt. auth) Friedman, J. Engineering the financial crisis   **330.9**
Krause, Chester L.
Standard catalog of world coins   **737.4**
Krauss, Erich
Wave of destruction   **959.3**
Krauss, Lawrence M.
Fear of physics   **530**
Quantum man   **92**
A universe from nothing   **523.1**
Krauthamer, Barbara
Envisioning emancipation   **973.7**
Kraybill, Donald B.
Amish grace   **364.152**
Concise encyclopedia of Amish, Brethren, Hutterites, and Mennonites   **289.7**
Kraybill, Donald B.
Amish grace   **364.152**
Concise encyclopedia of Amish, Brethren, Hutterites, and Mennonites   **289.7**
On the backroad to heaven   **289.7**
The riddle of Amish culture   **289.7**
Kreamer, Anne
Risk/reward   **650.1**
Krebs, Brian
Spam nation   **364.16**
Kreeft, Peter
Philosophy 101 by Socrates   **183**

Kreisler, Harry
Political awakenings   **920**

Kreitzman, Leon
Foster, R. G. Rhythms of life   **571.7**

Kremlin rising. Baker, P.   **947.086**

KREUGER & TOLL, INC.
Partnoy, F. The match king   **92**

Kreuger, Ivar, 1880-1932
    About
Partnoy, F. The match king   **92**

Kriegel, Mark
Pistol   **92**

Krieger, Ellie
You have it made!   **641.5**

Kriegsman, Kay Harris
(jt. auth) Palmer, S. Just one of the kids   **649**

Krismann, Carol
Encyclopedia of American women in business   **920.003**

Krissoff, Liana
Canning for a New Generation   **641**

Krist, Gary
Empire of sin   **976.3**
The white cascade   **979.7**

Kristal, Marc
At home in the garden   **635.09**

Kristallnacht. Gilbert, M.   **940.53**

KRISTALLNACHT, 1938
    See also Germany -- History -- 1933-1945;
    Jews -- Persecutions

Kristeller, Paul Oskar
(ed) The Renaissance philosophy of man   **189**

Kristof, Nicholas D., 1959-
Half the sky   **362.83**

Kritzer, Herbert M.
(ed) Legal systems of the world   **340**

Kriwaczek, Paul
Babylon   **935**

Kroeber, Theodora
Ishi in two worlds   **92**

Kronecker, Leopold, 1823-1891
    About
Bell, E. T. Men of mathematics   **920**

Kronski, Tadeusz, 1907-1958
    About
Milosz, C. To begin where I am   **891.8**

Kroodsma, Donald E.
The singing life of birds   **598**

Kroski, Ellusa
Web 2.0 for librarians and information professionals   **020**

Krstovic, Jelena O.
(ed) Black literature criticism   **809**

Krug, Louise
Louise   **617.4**

Krug, Steve

Don't make me think, revisited   **006.7**

Krugman, Paul R., 1953-
End this depression now!   **330.9**

Kruk, Herman
The last days of the Jerusalem of Lithuania   **940.53**

Krulos, Tea
Monster hunters   **001.94**

Kruse, Kevin M.
One nation under God   **322**

Kruth, John
To live's to fly   **92**

KU KLUX KLAN
Chalmers, D. M. Hooded Americanism: the history of the Ku Klux Klan   **322.4**
Ezekiel, R. S. The racist mind   **320.5**
Greenhaw, W. Fighting the devil in Dixie   **323.1**
Leamer, L. The Lynching   **364.134**

Kubler-Ross, Elisabeth
Life lessons   **170**
On children and death   **155.9**
On death and dying   **155.9**
    About
Kubler-Ross, E. The wheel of life   **150**

Kubrick, Stanley
    About
D'Alessandro, E. Stanley Kubrick and me   **791.43**
LoBrutto, V. Stanley Kubrick   **92**

Kugel, James L.
How to read the Bible   **221**

Kugle, Scott Siraj al-Haqq
Living out Islam   **297**

Kuhl, Patricia K.
Gopnik, A. The scientist in the crib   **155.4**

Kuhlman, Erika A.
A to Z of women in world history   **920.003**

Kuhn, Andrea
(jt. auth) Goldberg, D. Cuba!   **641.5**

Kuhn, Cynthia
Buzzed   **615.7**

Kuhn, Daniel
Alzheimer's early stages   **616.8**

Kuipers, Dean
Operation Bite Back   **92**

Kujawski, Jennifer
(jt. auth) Campbell, S. How to mulch   **635**

Kukielski, Peter E.
Roses without chemicals   **635.9**

Kukil, Karen V.
Plath, S. The unabridged journals of Sylvia Plath, 1950-1962   **818**

Kukla, Jon
A wilderness so immense   **973.4**

Kulaga, Agatha
Ovenly   **641.81**

Kulik, Peter H.
(ed) Van Nostrand's scientific encyclopedia   **503**

Kumar, Manjit
Quantum   **530.1**
Kumihimo : basics & beyond. Combs, R. A. **745.594**
Kumin, Maxine
Connecting the dots   **811**
Jack and other new poems   **811**
The long marriage   **811**
The Pawnbroker's Daughter   **92**
Selected poems, 1960-1990   **811**
Kummer, Ernst Edward, 1810-1893
    About
Bell, E. T. Men of mathematics   **920**
Kundera, Milan
The curtain   **801**
Encounter   **809**
KUNG FU
    See also Martial arts
Kung, Hans
Great Christian thinkers   **230**
Kunhardt, Peter W.
Kunhardt, P. B. Looking for Lincoln   **92**
Kunhardt, Philip B.
Looking for Lincoln   **92**
Kunitz, Daniel
Lift   **613.7**
Kunitz, Stanley
The collected poems   **811**
Wakeman, J. World authors, 1970-1975   **920.003**
Kunstler, James Howard
Too much magic   **303.48**
Kunth, Wolfgang
(ed) Terra Maxima   **902.2**
Kunzel, Bonnie Lenderman
Herald, D. T. Fluent in fantasy   **016**
Herald, D. T. Strictly science fiction   **016**
Kuralt, Charles
Charles Kuralt's America   **973.92**
On the road with Charles Kuralt   **973.92**
Kurian, George Thomas
Timetables of world literature   **809**
Kurkjian, Tim
I'm fascinated by sacrifice flies   **796.357**
Kurlansky, Mark, 1948-
1968   **909.82**
The Basque history of the world   **946**
Birdseye   **338.7**
Cod   **333.95**
The Eastern stars   **796.357**
The last fish tale   **639.2**
Paper   **676.09**
Salt: a world history   **553.6**
Kurosawa, Akira, 1910-1998
    About
Kurosawa, A. Something like an autobiography **92**
Kurpinski, Kyle
How to defeat your own clone   **660.6**

Kurson, Robert
Pirate hunters   **910.91**
    About
Kurson, R. Crashing through   **92**
Kurt Vonnegut. Vonnegut, K.   **813**
Kurt Weill. Schebera, J.   **92**
Kurth, Peter
Tsar: the lost world of Nicholas and Alexandra   **947.08**
Kurtz, Glenn
    About
Kurtz, G. Three minutes in Poland   **947.7**
Kurtzman, Harvey, 1924-1993
(ed) Humbug   **741.5**
    About
Kitchen, D. The art of Harvey Kurtzman   **741.5**
Kurzke, Hermann
Thomas Mann   **92**
Kurzweil, Allen
Whipping Boy   **92**
Kurzweil, Ray, 1948-
How to create a mind   **612.8**
The singularity is near   **153.9**
Kushner, David, 1968-
    About
Kushner, D. Alligator candy   **362.88**
Kushner, Harold S., 1935-
The book of Job   **223**
How good do we have to be?   **296.7**
When bad things happen to good people   **296.3**
Who needs God   **296.7**
Kushner, Jonathan Mark, 1962-1973
    About
Kushner, D. Alligator candy   **362.88**
Kushner, Tony
Angels in America   **812**
Kutler, Stanley I.
(ed) Abuse of power   **973.924**
Kwak, James
(jt. auth) Johnson, S. White House burning **336.3**
Johnson, S. 13 bankers   **332.1**
KWANZAA
    See also Holidays
Kwarteng, Kwasi
Ghosts of empire   **909**
Kwatra, Shawn G.
(jt. auth) Yosipovitch, G. Living with itch   **616.5**
Kyger, Joanne
About now   **811**
Kynaston, David
Austerity Britain   **941.085**
Family Britain, 1951-1957   **941.085**

L

L'OREAL SA
Brandon, R. Ugly beauty   **646.7**

The **L.L.** Bean game and fish cookbook. Cameron, A. **641.6**

L.L. Bean ultimate book of fly fishing. Talleur, R. W. **799.1**

La belle France. Horne, A. **944**

La Guardia, Anton
War without end **956.940**

La Leche League International
The Womanly art of breastfeeding **649**

A **la** mode. **641.865**

La Place, Viana
Verdura **641.6**

La seduction. Sciolino, E. **302.3**

La Tour du Pin Gouvernet, Henriette Lucie Dillon, marquise de, 1770-1853
About
Moorehead, C. Dancing to the precipice: Lucie de la Tour du Pin and the French Revolution **92**

Lab girl. Jahren, H. **92**

LABOR -- HISTORY
Beckert, S. Empire of cotton **338.4**
Murolo, P. From the folks who brought you the weekend **331**

LABOR -- HOUSING
See also Housing

LABOR -- LAW AND LEGISLATION
Steingold, F. S. The employer's legal handbook **344**

LABOR -- SONGS
Gioia, T. Work songs **782.42**

LABOR -- UNITED STATES
Dubofsky, M. Labor in America **331.8**
Ehrenreich, B. Nickel and dimed **305.5**
Lichtenstein, N. State of the Union: a century of American labor **331**
Murolo, P. From the folks who brought you the weekend **331**
Reef, C. Working in America **305**
Shulman, B. The betrayal of work **331.2**
Stepan-Norris, J. Left out **331.8**
Terkel, S. Working **331.2**
Zieger, R. H. American workers, American unions **331.8**

LABOR -- UNITED STATES -- DICTIONARIES
Murray, R. E. The lexicon of labor **331**

LABOR -- UNITED STATES -- ENCYCLOPE-DIAS
Historical encyclopedia of American labor **331.8**

LABOR CAMPS -- RUSSIA (FEDERATION) -- PECHORA (KOMI)
Figes, O. Just send me word **365**

LABOR CONTRACT
See also Contracts; Industrial relations

LABOR DISPUTES
See also Industrial relations

LABOR ECONOMICS
Labor rising **331.88**

LABOR ECONOMICS
See also Economics

Labor in America. Dubofsky, M. **331.8**

Labor in crisis [series]
Russell, T. Out of the jungle **92**

LABOR LEADERS
Foner, M. Not for bread alone **92**
Gorn, E. J. Mother Jones **331.88**
Russell, T. Out of the jungle **92**
Shaw, R. Beyond the fields **331.8**

LABOR MOVEMENT
Bacon, D. Illegal people **331.6**
Foner, E. The story of American freedom **323.44**
Murolo, P. From the folks who brought you the weekend **331**

LABOR MOVEMENT
See also Social movements

LABOR MOVEMENT -- ENCYCLOPEDIAS
Historical encyclopedia of American labor **331.8**
St. James encyclopedia of labor history world-wide **331.8**

LABOR MOVEMENT -- HISTORY
Labor rising **331.88**

LABOR MOVEMENT -- UNITED STATES
Pawel, M. The Crusades of Cesar Chavez **92**

LABOR MOVEMENT -- UNITED STATES -- HISTORY
Dray, P. There is power in a union **331.8**
Historical encyclopedia of American labor **331.8**
Labor rising **331.88**
Murolo, P. From the folks who brought you the weekend **331**

LABOR ORGANIZATIONS *See* Labor unions

LABOR OUTPUT *See* Labor productivity

LABOR POLICY
Bacon, D. Illegal people **331.6**

LABOR POLICY
See also Economic policy

LABOR PRODUCTIVITY
Vaden, R. Procrastinate on purpose **650.1**

LABOR RELATIONS *See* Industrial relations

LABOR RIGHTS *See* Employee rights

Labor rising. **331.88**

LABOR SUPPLY
See also Economic conditions; Employment; Labor

LABOR TURNOVER
See also Personnel management

LABOR UNIONS
Dubofsky, M. Labor in America **331.8**
Lichtenstein, N. State of the Union: a century of American labor **331**
Zieger, R. H. American workers, American unions **331.8**

LABOR UNIONS
See also Industrial relations; Labor; Societies

LABOR UNIONS -- UNITED STATES
Stepan-Norris, J. Left out   **331.8**
LABOR UNIONS -- UNITED STATES -- HISTORY
Dray, P. There is power in a union   **331.8**
Labor, Earle
Jack London   **92**
LABOR-MANAGEMENT RELATIONS See Industrial relations
LABORATORIES
Pagana, T. J. Mosby's diagnostic and laboratory test reference   **616.07**
The labyrinth of solitude. Paz, O.   **864**
Lacassagne, Alexandre, 1843-1924
About
Starr, D. The killer of little shepherds   **364.152**
LACE AND LACE MAKING
Nico, B. More Lovely Knitted Lace   **746.432**
LACE AND LACE MAKING
See also Crocheting; Needlework; Weaving
Lacerda, Daniel
2,100 Asanas   **613.7**
Lacey, Paul A.
(ed) Levertov, D. Selected poems   **811**
Lacey, Robert
Great tales from English history   **941**
Great tales from English history [2]   **941**
Great tales from English history [3]   **941**
Inside the Kingdom   **953.8**
Lachman, Liz
(jt. auth) Alger, K. Susan Feniger's street food   **641.59**
Lachs, Mark
Treat me, not my age   **612.6**
Lacks, Henrietta
About
Skloot, R. The immortal life of Henrietta Lacks **92**
LACROSSE
See also Ball games; Sports
LACROSSE PLAYERS
Cohan, W. D. The price of silence   **364.15**
Lacy, Brian E.
Autophobia   **303.4**
Making sense of IBS   **616.3**
Ladd, Dana L.
The Medical Library Association guide to finding out about diabetes   **016**
Laderman, Gary
(ed) Religion and American cultures   **200.9**
Ladies of liberty. Roberts, C.   **920**
The lady and her monsters. Montillo, R.   **823**
The lady and the panda. Croke, V.   **599.78**
Lady Bird and Lyndon. Caroli, B. B.   **92**
Lady Bird Johnson. Gillette, M. L.   **92**
Lady Byron and Her Daughters. Markus, J.   **92**
The lady in gold. O'Connor   **759.36**

The lady in the tower. Weir, A.   **92**
Lady sings the blues. Holiday, B.   **92**
The lady upstairs. Nissenson, M.   **92**
Laeter, J. R. de
Bevan, A. W. R. Meteorites: a journey through space and time   **523.5**
Lafayette in the Somewhat United States. Vowell, S.   **973.3**
Lafayette, Bernard, 1940-
About
Halberstam, D. The children   **323.1**
Lafayette, Marie Joseph Paul Yves Roch Gilbert Du Motier, marquis de, 1757-1834
About
Auricchio, L. The marquis   **92**
Gaines, J. R. For liberty and glory   **92**
Laferrière, Dany
About
The World Is Moving Around Me   **972.94**
LAFFEY (SHIP)
Wukovits, J. F. Hell from the heavens   **940.54**
Laffite, Jean, 1780?-1825?
About
Groom, W. Patriotic fire   **973.5**
LaFrieda, Pat
(jt. auth) Carreño, C. Meat   **641.6**
Lagasse, Emeril, 1959-
Essential Emeril   **641.5**
From Emeril's kitchens   **641.5**
The lagoon.   **570.1**
Lagrange, Joseph Louis, comte de, 1736-1813
About
Bell, E. T. Men of mathematics   **920**
Laguardia, Cheryl
Marketing your library's electronic resources **025.2**
LAGUNA HONDA HOSPITAL (SAN FRANCISCO, CALIF.) -- HISTORY
Sweet, V. God's hotel   **610.92**
Lahey, Jessica
The gift of failure   **649**
Lahr, John
Joy ride   **792.02**
Tennessee Williams   **92**
Lai Changxing
About
August, O. Inside the red mansion   **951.05**
Laing, Olivia
The Trip to Echo Spring   **810.9**
Laird, Rebecca J.
(jt. auth) Nouwen, H. Discernment   **248.4**
Laird, Thomas
Into Tibet   **327.12**
LAISSEZ-FAIRE See Free enterprise
LAITY
See also Church
LAITY -- CATHOLIC CHURCH

See also Catholic Church

Lake Antiquity. Downing, B.   **811**

LAKE ECOLOGY

    See also Ecology

LAKES

    See also Physical geography; Water; Water-ways

LAKESIDE SCHOOL (SEATTLE, WASH.)

Merlino, D. The hustle   **796.323**

Laki, Duncan

    About

Rice, A. The teeth may smile but the heart does not forget   **967.6**

Laki, Eliphaz, d. 1972

    About

Rice, A. The teeth may smile but the heart does not forget   **967.6**

Lakshmi, Padma

    About

Lakshmi, P. Love, loss, and what we ate   **92**

Lalleman, Pieter J.

(ed) Manser, M. H. Critical companion to the Bible   **220.6**

Lamar, Lucius Quintus Cincinnatus, 1825-1893

    About

Kennedy, J. F. Profiles in courage   **920**

Lamar, William W.

Campbell, J. The venomous reptiles of the Western Hemisphere   **597.96**

LaMarche, Una

    About

Lamarche, U. Unabrow   **92**

Lamarr, Hedy, 1913-2000

    About

Rhodes, R. Hedy's folly   **92**

Shearer, S. M. Beautiful   **92**

LAMAZE METHOD OF CHILDBIRTH *See* Natural childbirth

Lamb, Brian

(comp) Booknotes (Television program) Booknotes: life stories   **920**

Lamb, Charles

Tales from Shakespeare   **822.3**

Lamb, Christina

House of stone   **968.91**

I am Malala   **92**

Lamb, David

The Arabs   **909**

Lamb, Mary

Lamb, C. Tales from Shakespeare   **822.3**

Lambert, David

The field guide to geology   **551**

Lambert, Megan Dowd

Reading picture books with children   **372.133**

Lamm, Lawrence W.

(ed) The World's great speeches   **808.85**

Lamothe, Matt

The where, the why, and the how   **502**

Lamott, Anne

Bird by bird   **808**

    About

Lamott, A. Small victories   **248**

LAMPS

    See also Lighting

Lampson, Marc

Tucker, V. Finding the answers to legal questions   **340**

Lamson, Laurie

(ed) Now write! screenwriting   **808.2**

Lancaster, Burt, 1913-1994

    About

Buford, K. Burt Lancaster   **92**

Lance, Peter

Deal With the Devil   **363.25**

Lanchester, John

How to Speak Money   **330.1**

I.O.U.   **330.9**

A **land** as God made it. Horn, J. P. P.   **975.5**

LAND GRANTS

    See also Colonization; Public lands

LAND MINES

    See also Explosives; Ordnance

Land of fish and rice. Dunlop, F.   **641.5**

Land of promise. Lind, M.   **330.973**

Land of the firebird. Massie, S.   **947**

Land of the lost souls. Cadillac Man   **92**

LAND QUESTION *See* Land tenure

LAND REFORM

    See also Economic policy; Land use; Social policy

LAND SETTLEMENT

    See also Colonies; Land use

LAND SETTLEMENT -- GAZA

Filiu Gaza   **953**

LAND SETTLEMENT -- UNITED STATES

Inskeep, S. Jacksonland   **973.5**

LAND TENURE -- HISTORY

Linklater, A. Owning the earth   **333.3**

LAND USE

    See also Economics

The **land** where the blues began. Lomax, A.   **781.643**

Landau, David

Arik   **92**

Landau, Herbert B.

The small public library survival guide   **025.1**

Landau, Rich

(jt. auth) Jacoby, K. Vedge   **641.6**

LANDFORMS

    See also Earth -- Surface; Geology

LANDLORD AND TENANT

Linklater, A. Owning the earth   **333.3**

Portman, J. Every tenant's legal guide   **346.04**

Stewart, M. Every landlord's legal guide **346.04**

LANDLORD AND TENANT
   See also Commercial law; Land tenure; Real estate

Landmark decisions of the United States Supreme Court. Finkelman, P. **347**

The **landmark** Herodotus. Herodotus, c. 4. B. B. C. **938**

Landmark law cases & American society [series]
   Hoffer, P. C. The Salem witchcraft trials **345**
   Hull, N. E. H. Roe v. Wade **344**

Landmark legislation, 1774-2002. Stathis, S. W. **348**

Landmark Supreme Court cases. Leiter, R. A. **347**

Landmark Supreme Court cases. Mersky, R. M. **347.73**

The **landmark** Thucydides. Thucydides **938**

The **Landmark** Xenophon's Hellenika. **938**

Landmarks. Macfarlane, R. **914.1**

Landmarks of the American mosaic [series]
   Davis, T. J. Plessy v. Ferguson **342**

LANDMARKS, LITERARY *See* Literary landmarks

LANDMARKS, PRESERVATION OF *See* National monuments; Natural monuments

Landon, Margaret
   Anna and the King of Siam **92**

Landry, Tom
             About
   Ribowsky, M. The last cowboy **92**

Landsberg, Brian K.
   (ed) Major acts of Congress **348**

LANDSCAPE ARCHITECTS
   Rybczynski, W. A clearing in the distance: Frederick Law Olmsted and America in the nineteenth century **712**

LANDSCAPE ARCHITECTURE
   Graham, W. American Eden **712**

LANDSCAPE ECOLOGY
   Christopher, T. Garden revolution **577**

LANDSCAPE GARDENING
   Buchanan, R. Taylor's master guide to landscaping **712**
   Bunny Williams' on garden style **712**
   Dirr, M. A. Manual of woody landscape plants **635.9**
   Dirr, M. Dirr's Hardy trees and shrubs **635.9**
   Dirr, M. Dirr's trees and shrubs for warm climates **635.9**
   Greenlee, J. The American meadow garden **635.9**
   Hayward, G. Stone in the garden **712**
   The plant finder **635.9**
   Speichert, C. G. Encyclopedia of water garden plants **635**

LANDSCAPE GARDENING
   See also Gardening; Horticulture

LANDSCAPE GARDENING -- WATER CON-SERVATION
   The bold dry garden **635.9**

LANDSCAPE PAINTING
   Wilton, A. American sublime **759.13**

LANDSCAPE PAINTING
   See also Painting

LANDSCAPE PHOTOGRAPHY
   Hitchcock, S. T. National geographic rarely seen **779**

LANDSCAPE PROTECTION
   House, S. Something's rising **338.2**

LANDSCAPE PROTECTION
   See also Environmental protection; Nature conservation

LANDSCAPE PROTECTION -- ALASKA -- DENALI NATIONAL PARK AND PRESERVE (ALASKA)
   Heacox, K. Rhythm of the wild **979.8**

LANDSCAPE PROTECTION -- APPALACHIAN REGION, SOUTHERN -- CITIZEN PARTICIPATION
   House, S. Something's rising **338.2**

Landscape turned red. Sears, S. W. **973.7**

LANDSCAPES
   Macfarlane, R. The old ways **914.2**

LANDSCAPES -- EUROPE
   Nicolson, A. Why Homer matters **883**

LANDSCAPES -- GREAT BRITAIN
   Higgins, C. Under another sky **936**

LANDSLIDES
   See also Natural disasters

Lane Fox, Robin
   The classical world **938**

Lane, Anthony
   Nobody's perfect **791.43**

Lane, Carl
   A Nation Wholly Free **336.3**

Lane, Charles
   The day freedom died **976.3**

Lane, Christina
   Dessert for Two **641.86**

Lane, Stewart F.
   Black Broadway **792**

Lang, Adam Perry
   (jt. auth) Kaminsky, P. Charred & scruffed **641.7**
   Serious barbecue **641.5**

Lang, Anthony E.
   Parkinson's disease **616.8**

Lang, Avis
   (ed) Space chronicles **629.4**

Lang, Josephine, 1815-1880
             About
   Porter, C. H. Five lives in music **780.92**

Lang, Kenneth R.
   The Cambridge guide to the solar system **523.2**

Lang, Michael

The road to Woodstock 781.66

Lang, Rebecca

The Southern vegetable book 641.65

Lang, Sarah

For Tamara C

Langdon, Helen

Caravaggio 709

Lange's handbook of chemistry. 540

Lange, Dorothea, 1895-1965

About

Gordon, L. Dorothea Lange 92

Langer, Lawrence L.

Admitting the Holocaust 940.53

Art from the ashes 940.53

Langewiesche, William

American ground, unbuilding the World Trade Center 974.7

The atomic bazaar 355

Sahara unveiled 916

Langguth, A. J., 1933-2014

After Lincoln 973.8

Driven West 973.5

Our Vietnam 959.704

Langhorne family

About

Fox, J. Five sisters 975.5

Langland, William

Piers Plowman 821

Langley, Jacqueline D.

Swanson, M. Atlas of the Civil War, month by month 973.7

Langlois, Jill

(jt. auth) Rigby, C. Fodor's Rio de Janeiro & Sao Paulo 918.15

Langmuir, Irving, 1881-1957

About

Coffey, P. Cathedrals of science 540

Langshur, Eric

Start here 158

Langthorne, Michael

(jt. auth) Klubeck, M. Why organizations struggle so hard to improve so little 658.4

Language. Everett, D. L. 400

LANGUAGE See Language and languages

LANGUAGE ACQUISITION

See also Language and languages

LANGUAGE AND CULTURE

Everett, D. L. Language 400

LANGUAGE AND CULTURE

See also Culture; Language and languages

LANGUAGE AND CULTURE -- UNITED STATES

Prothero, S. The American Bible 973

LANGUAGE AND LANGUAGES

Crystal, D. The Cambridge encyclopedia of language 400

Crystal, D. How language works 401

Deutscher, G. Through the language glass 410

Dorren, G. Lingo 306.44

Kenneally, C. The first word 400

Pagel, M. Wired for culture 303.4

Pinker, S. The language instinct 400

Pinker, S. The stuff of thought 401

Pinker, S. Words and rules 401

Pollack, J. Shortcut 808

Rosen, M. Alphabetical 421

Stevens, C. Written in Stone 422

Yang, C. The infinite gift 401

LANGUAGE AND LANGUAGES

See also Anthropology; Communication; Ethnology

LANGUAGE AND LANGUAGES -- COMPARATIVE PHILOLOGY See Linguistics

LANGUAGE AND LANGUAGES -- DICTIONARIES

Crystal, D. A dictionary of language 410

LANGUAGE AND LANGUAGES -- ENCYCLOPEDIAS

Crystal, D. The Cambridge encyclopedia of language 400

LANGUAGE AND SOCIETY See Sociolinguistics

LANGUAGE ARTS

Lambert, M. D. Reading picture books with children 372.133

LANGUAGE ARTS

See also Communication

LANGUAGE ARTS (SECONDARY)

Adolescent literacy in the academic disciplines 428

LANGUAGE DISORDERS IN CHILDREN -- DIAGNOSIS

Camarata, S. M. Late-talking children 618.92

Language for a new century. 808.81

The language instinct. Pinker, S. 400

The language of food. Jurafsky, D. 641.3

The language of life. Collins, F. S. 616

The language of passion. Vargas Llosa, M. 864

The language wars. Hitchings, H. 420

LANGUAGES See Language and languages

LANGUAGES -- VOCABULARY See Vocabulary

LANGUAGES, ARTIFICIAL

Okrent, A. In the land of invented languages 499

Lanier, Jaron

You are not a gadget 303.4

Lanier, Sidney, 1842-1881

About

Wilson, E. Patriotic gore 810

Lankes, R. David

The atlas of new librarianship 020

(ed) Virtual reference service 025.5

Lankov, Andrei

The real North Korea 951.93

Lannon, Richard

Lewis, T. A general theory of love **152.4**

Lansky, Aaron, 1955-
About
Lansky, A. Outwitting history **002.07**

Lanterne Rouge. Leonard, M. **796.62**

Lanterns. Edelman, M. W. **92**

Lanting, Frans
Waal, F. d. Bonobo **599.88**

Lanzmann, Claude, 1925-
About
Lanzmann, C. The Patagonian hare **791.43**

Lao-tzu
Tao te ching **299.5**

LAOS -- DESCRIPTION AND TRAVEL
DeBuys, W. The last unicorn **591.68**
DK Eyewitness Travel Cambodia & Laos **915.9**

Lapidus, Lenora M.
American Civil Liberties Union The rights of women **346.01**

Lapierre, Dominique
Collins, L. O Jerusalem! **956.94**
The City of Joy **954**

Lapis. Kelly, R. **811**

Laplace, Pierre Simon, 1749-1827
About
Bell, E. T. Men of mathematics **920**

LAPLAND
Beach, H. A year in Lapland **948.97**

LaPlante, Eve
Salem witch judge **92**

LaPlantz, Shereen, 1947-2003
Cover to cover **686.3**

Lappé, Anna, 1973-
Diet for a hot planet **641**

Lapsley, Phil
Exploding the Phone **384**

Laqueur, Walter
A history of Zionism **956.94**

LARCENY See Theft

Lardner, Ring, 1915-2000
About
Lardner, R. I'd hate myself in the morning **813**

LARGE AND SMALL See Size

LARGE DATA SETS See Big data

The **large** hadron collider. Lincoln, D. **539.7**

LARGE HADRON COLLIDER (FRANCE AND SWITZERLAND)
Aczel, A. D. Present at the creation **539.7**
Lincoln, D. The large hadron collider **539.7**

LARGE PRINT BOOKS
Berendt, J. Midnight in the garden of good and evil **975.8**
Brokaw, T. An album of memories **940.54**
Bruni, F. Ambling into history: the unlikely odyssey of George W. Bush **973.931**
Bryson, B. I'm a stranger here myself **818**

Bryson, B. In a sunburned country **919**
Carter, J. The virtues of aging **305.26**
Churchill, W. The great republic **973**
Dolnick, E. Down the great unknown **979.1**
Fraser, A. Marie Antoinette **944**
Hepburn, K. Me **92**
Herriot, J. Every living thing **636.089**
Herriot, J. James Herriot's animal stories **636.089**
Herriot, J. James Herriot's favorite dog stories **636.7**
Hillerman, T. Seldom disappointed **813**
Johnson, P. Napoleon **944.05**
Leaming, B. Mrs. Kennedy **973.922**
Martin, S. Pure drivel **814**
McCullough, D. G. John Adams **92**
McMurtry, L. Crazy Horse **92**
McMurtry, L. Roads **917**
McMurtry, L. Walter Benjamin at the Dairy Queen **818**
Milford, N. Savage beauty: the life of Edna St. Vincent Millay **92**
Miller, J. The cell: inside the 9/11 plot and why the FBI and CIA failed to stop it **973.931**
Palmer, A. A golfer's life **92**
Quirk, L. J. Bob Hope: the road well-traveled **92**
Reeve, C. Still me **92**
Roach, M. Stiff **611**
Sacks, O. W. Uncle Tungsten **616.8**
Schlosser, E. Fast food nation **394.1**
Sedaris, D. Me talk pretty one day **814**
Shields, C. Jane Austen **823**
Sides, H. Ghost soldiers **940.54**
Smiley, J. Charles Dickens **823**
Thomas, E. M. The social lives of dogs **636.7**
Tuchman, B. W. The first salute **973.3**
Von Drehle, D. Triangle: the fire that changed America **974.7**
White, E. The flaneur **944.083**
Wills, G. Lincoln at Gettysburg **973.7**
Winchester, S. Krakatoa: the day the world exploded, August 27, 1883 **551.2**

LARGE TYPE BOOKS See Large print books

Largent, Mark A.
Young, C. C. Evolution and creationism **576.8**

Lark jewelry & beading bead inspirations [series]
Katz, A. Seed bead chic **745.594**

Larkin, Emma
Everything is broken **959.1**

Larkin, Philip
About
Heaney, S. Finders keepers **821**

LaRocque, Paula, 1937-
The book on writing **808**

Larousse gastronomique. **641.3**

Larry's kidney. Rose, D. A. **915**

Larsen, Laura

Drug abuse sourcebook **362.29**

Larsen, Nella
    About
Hutchinson, G. In search of Nella Larsen **92**
Wall, C. A. Women of the Harlem Renaissance **810**

Larson, Edward
The Return of George Washington **92**

Larson, Edward J.
(ed) The History of science and religion in the western tradition **201**
Larson, E. J. An empire of ice **919**
Evolution: the remarkable history of a scientific theory **576.8**
A magnificent catastrophe **324**
(ed) Madison, J. The Constitutional Convention **342**

Larson, Edward J. (Edward John), 1953-
An empire of ice **919**

Larson, Elsie
(jt. auth) Chapman, E. A beautiful mess happy handmade home **747**

Larson, Erik
Dead wake **940.4**
The devil in the white city **364.15**
Thunderstruck **364.152**

Larson, Jeanette C.
The public library policy writer **025.1**

Larson, Kate Clifford
Bound for the promised land **92**
Rosemary **92**

Larson, Kay
Where the heart beats **700.1**

Larson, Peter L.
Rex appeal **567.9**

LaRussa, Tony
    About
Bissinger, H. G. Three nights in August **796.357**

LAS COMADRES PARA LAS AMERICAS
Count on me **177**

Las Comadres para las Americas (Organization)
(comp) Count on me **177**

LAS VEGAS (NEV.)
Schüll, N. D. Addiction by design **362.2**

LAS VEGAS (NEV.) -- HISTORY
Assael, S. The murder of Sonny Liston **796.83**

LAS VEGAS METROPOLITAN AREA (NEV.) -- SOCIAL LIFE AND CUSTOMS
D'Agata, J. About a mountain **979.3**

Lascher, Bill
Eve of a Hundred Midnights **070.449**

LASERS
    See also Light

LASERS IN AERONAUTICS
    See also Aeronautics; Lasers

Lashinsky, Adam
Inside Apple **338.7**

Lask, Bryan
Can I tell you about eating disorders? **616.85**
Eating disorders **616.85**

Laskas, Jeanne Marie, 1958-
Concussion **617.5**
Hidden America **305.5**

Laskin, David, 1953-
The children's blizzard **977**
The long way home **920**
    About
Laskin, D. The Family **92**

Laslow, Caroline
(jt. auth) Peacock, J. The soup club cookbook **641.81**

Last ape standing. Walter, C. **569.9**
The last apocalypse. Reston, J. **940.1**
The Last Armada. Ekin, D. **941.505**
The last bohemia. Anasi, R. **974.7**
The last boy. Leavy, J. **92**
Last call. Okrent, D. **363.4**
The last campaign. Karabell, Z. **324.9**
The last campaign. Clarke, T. **92**
Last chain on Billie. Bradley, C. **639.97**
Last child in the woods. Louv, R. **155.4**
The last cowboy. Ribowsky, M. **92**
Last dance. Feinstein, J. **796.323**
The last days of innocence. Harries, M. **940.4**
The last days of old Beijing. Meyer, M. J. **951**
The last days of the Jerusalem of Lithuania. Kruk, H. **940.53**
The last dive. Chowdhury, B. **363.14**
The last empress. Pakula, H. **92**
The last empty places. Stark, P. **973**
The last fish tale. Kurlansky, M. **639.2**
The last fisherman. Rotman, J. L. **778.7**
The last founding father. Unger, H. G. **92**
The last full measure. Stephenson, M. **305.9**
The Last Goodnight. Blum, H. **940.54**
The last great Frenchman. Williams, C. **944**
The last gun. Diaz, T. **338.4**
The last hero. Bryant, H. **92**
The last holiday. Scott-Heron, G. **920**
The last human. Sarmiento, E. **569.9**
The last Indian war. West, E. **973.8**
Last lion. English, B. **92**
The last lion, Winston Spencer Churchill. Manchester, W. **92**
The last lion, Winston Spencer Churchill. Manchester, W. **92**
The last lion, Winston Spencer Churchill. Manchester, W. **92**
The Last Love Song. Daugherty, T. **92**
Last man off. Lewis, M. **910.91**
The last of his mind. Thorndike, J. **92**
The last of the tribe. Reel, M. **981**
The Last Outlaws. Hatch, T. **364.15**

The last outlaws [series]
  Hatch, T. The Last Outlaws   364.15
The **last** refuge. Johnsen, G. D.   363.325
The **last** resort. Rogers, D.   968.91
Last rights. Kiernan, S. P.   179.7
The **last** stand. Philbrick, N.   973.8
LAST SUPPER IN ART
  King, R. Leonardo and the Last supper   759
LAST THINGS (THEOLOGY) *See* Eschatology
Last to die. Harding, S.   940.54
Last train to Zona Verde. Theroux, P.   916
The **last** unicorn. DeBuys, W.   591.68
The **last** Viking. Bown, S. R.   92
The **Last** Voyageurs. Boissoneault, L.   977
The **last** wild wolves. McAllister, I.   599.77
The **last** witch of Langenburg. Robisheaux, T.   133.4
Lasting City. McCourt, J.   92
Late-talking children. Camarata, S. M.   618.92
LATERALITY
  Edwards, B. Drawing on the Right Side of the Brain   741.2
Latest readings. James, C.   828
Latham, Alison
  (ed) The Oxford companion to music   780
Latham, Edward
  A dictionary of names, nicknames, and surnames of persons, places, and things   929.4
Latimer, Lewis Howard, 1848-1928
About
  Abdul-Jabbar, K. Black profiles in courage   920
LATIN AMERICA -- HISTORY
  Brown, M. From Frontiers to Football   980
LATIN AMERICA -- POLITICS AND GOVERN-MENT
  Grillo, I. Gangster Warlords   364.106
LATIN AMERICA -- POLITICS AND GOVERN-MENT
  See also Politics
Latin American and Caribbean artists of the modern era. Shipp, S.   920.003
Latin American art. Scott, J. F.   709
LATIN AMERICAN ART
  Barnitz, J. Twentieth-century art of Latin America   709
  Scott, J. F. Latin American art   709
  Shipp, S. Latin American and Caribbean artists of the modern era   920.003
LATIN AMERICAN ART
  See also Art
LATIN AMERICAN ART -- ENCYCLOPEDIAS
  Encyclopedia of Latin American & Caribbean art   709
LATIN AMERICAN COOKING
  García, L. Lorena Garcia's new taco classics   641.84
  Gran cocina latina   641.597
  Kijac, M. B. The South American table   641.59
    New World kitchen   641.59
Latin American histories [series]
  Perez, L. A. Cuba   972.91
LATIN AMERICAN LITERATURE
  Concise encyclopedia of Latin American literature   860
LATIN AMERICAN LITERATURE -- HISTORY AND CRITICISM
  Gonzalez Echevarria, R. The Cambridge history of Latin American literature   860
LATIN AMERICAN POETRY -- COLLECTIONS
  Twentieth century Latin American poetry   861
Latin for the illiterati. Stone, J. R.   473
LATIN LANGUAGE
  Ostler, N. Ad infinitum   470
LATIN LANGUAGE
  See also Language and languages
LATIN LANGUAGE -- DICTIONARIES
  Oxford Latin dictionary   473
  Stone, J. R. Latin for the illiterati   473
LATIN LITERATURE
  See also Literature
LATIN LITERATURE -- COLLECTIONS
  The Portable Roman reader   870
LATIN POETRY
  Catullus, G. V. The poems of Catullus   874
Latino and Latina writers.   810
Latino athletes. Friedman, I. C.   920.003
LATINO AUTHORS
  See also American authors
Latino literature.   016
LATINO LITERATURE (ENGLISH) *See* American literature -- Latino authors
LATINO LITERATURE (SPANISH) *See* American literature (Spanish)
The **Latino** student's guide to college success.   378.1
Latino writers and journalists. Martinez Wood, J.   920.003
LATINOS (U.S.)
  Great lives from history   920.009
  Monterrey, M. Americanos   305.8
  Morales, E. Living in Spanglish   305.868
Latinos in science, math, and professions. Newton, D. E.   920.003
Latinos in the arts. Otfinoski, S.   920.003
LATITUDE
  See also Earth; Geodesy; Nautical astronomy
LATTER-DAY SAINTS *See* Church of Jesus Christ of Latter-day Saints
Lattimore, Richmond Alexander
  (ed) Aeschylus Aeschylus   882
  (ed) Euripides Euripides   882
  (ed) Euripides Euripides [2]   882
  (ed) Sophocles Sophocles   882
Lattin, Don

The Harvard Psychedelic Club **920**

Latus, Amy, 1965-2002
>About
Latus, J. If I am missing or dead **92**

Latus, Janine, 1959-
>About
Latus, J. If I am missing or dead **92**

Lau, Jamie
(jt. auth) Abousteit, N. BurdaStyle sewing vintage modern **646.4**

Laughing All the Way to the Mosque. Nawaz, Z. **92**

Laughlin, James
The collected poems of James Laughlin **811**
The secret room **811**

Laughlin, Sara
The quality library **025.1**

LAUGHTER
>See also Emotions

Launch! Duffy, S. **658.1**
Launching a Business. Barringer, B. **658.1**
Laundry. **648**

LAUNDRY
>See also Cleaning; Home economics; Household sanitation

LAUNDRY
Laundry **648**

LAUNDRY WORKERS
Berry, M. F. My face is black is true **92**

Launius, Roger D.
Smithsonian atlas of space exploration **500.5**

Lauper, Cyndi, 1953-
>About
Lauper, C. Cyndi Lauper **92**

Laura Ingalls Wilder country. Anderson, W. T. **92**

Laurence, Dan H.
(ed) Shaw, B. Arms and the man **822**
(ed) Shaw, B. Heartbreak House **822**
(ed) Shaw, B. Man and Superman **822**
(ed) Shaw, B. Saint Joan **822**

Laurens, Henry, 1724-1792
>About
Harris, J. W. The hanging of Thomas Jeremiah **92**

Laursen, Eric
(jt. auth) Frank, J. The people's pension **368.4**

Lauterbach, Ann
(jt. auth) Brainard, J. The Nancy book **759**
Or to begin again **811**

Lauterbach, Preston
Beale Street Dynasty **976.8**

Laux, Dorianne
Addonizio, K. The poet's companion **808.1**

Laveau, Marie, 1794-1881
>About
Ward, M. C. Voodoo queen **92**

Lavender, Kenneth
Book repair **025.7**

Lavers, Chris
The natural history of unicorns **398.2**

Lavin, Stephen J.
Atlas of the great plains **912**

Lavold, Elsebeth
Viking knits and ancient ornaments

LAW
Green, L. On Your Case **344**
Witt, J. F. Lincoln's code **343**

LAW
>See also Political science

LAW -- ENCYCLOPEDIAS
Legal systems of the world **340**

LAW -- GENERAL
Raine, A. The anatomy of violence **616.85**

LAW -- POLITICAL ASPECTS -- UNITED STATES
Tushnet, M. In the balance **347.73**

LAW -- RESEARCH
Tucker, V. Finding the answers to legal questions **340**

LAW -- STUDY AND TEACHING -- UNITED STATES
Tamanaha, B. Z. Failing law schools **340**

LAW -- UNITED STATES
Guns in American society **363.33**

LAW -- UNITED STATES -- CASES
Mersky, R. M. Landmark Supreme Court cases **347.73**

LAW -- UNITED STATES -- DICTIONARIES
Black's law dictionary **340**

LAW -- UNITED STATES -- ENCYCLOPEDIAS
Gale encyclopedia of American law **349**
Major acts of Congress **348**
The Oxford companion to American law **349**

LAW -- UNITED STATES -- HISTORY
O'Connor, S. D. Out of order **347.73**

LAW -- VOCATIONAL GUIDANCE
>See also Professions; Vocational guidance

Law 101. Feinman, J. M. **340**

LAW ENFORCEMENT
Shipler, D. K. The rights of the people **323**

LAW ENFORCEMENT
>See also Administration of criminal justice

LAW ENFORCEMENT -- HISTORY
Thompson, H. A. Blood in the water **365**

LAW ENFORCEMENT -- MEXICO
Ainslie, R. C. The fight to save Juárez **363.45**

LAW ENFORCEMENT OFFICIALS
Kauffman, B. Forgotten founder, drunken prophet **92**
Starr, D. The killer of little shepherds **364.152**

LAW IN LITERATURE
Kenji Yoshino A thousand times more fair **822.3**
Law man. Burke, D. **92**
LAW OF NATIONS See International law

LAW OF SUPPLY AND DEMAND *See* Supply and demand

Law of the jungle. Barrett, P. M.   **344**

LAW REFORM
   See also Law

LAW SCHOOLS
   See also Colleges and universities

LAW SCHOOLS -- UNITED STATES -- FINANCE
   Tamanaha, B. Z. Failing law schools   **340**

LAW TEACHERS
   Chua, A. Battle hymn of the tiger mother **306.874**
   Commager, H. S. The American mind   **973**
   Gormley, K. The death of American virtue **973.929**

Law, Jonathan
   (ed) A dictionary of chemistry   **540**

Lawday, David
   The giant of the French Revolution   **92**

Lawhorne-Scott, Cheryl
   Military mental health care   **355.3**
   (jt. auth) Scott, J. Raising children in the military   **355.1**

Lawler, Andrew
   Why did the chicken cross the world?   **636.5**

LAWMAKERS *See* Legislators

LAWN TENNIS *See* Tennis

LAWNS
   See also Landscape gardening

Lawrence in Arabia. Anderson, S.   **940.4**

Lawrence, D. H. (David Herbert), 1885-1930
   The complete poems   **821**
   About
   Worthen, J. D.H. Lawrence   **92**
   Worthen, J. D.H. Lawrence, the early years, 1885-1912   **92**

Lawrence, Jerome
   Inherit the wind   **812**

Lawrence, John Geddes
   About
   Carpenter, D. Flagrant conduct   **342.73**

Lawrence, Mark Atwood
   (ed) The Vietnam War   **959.704**

Lawrence, Sarahlee
   River house   **92**
   About
   Lawrence, S. River house   **92**

Lawrence, T. E. (Thomas Edward), 1888-1935
   Seven pillars of wisdom   **940.4**
   About
   Anderson, S. Lawrence in Arabia   **940.4**
   Brown, M. T.E. Lawrence   **92**
   Korda, M. Hero   **92**
   Sattin, A. The Young T. E. Lawrence   **92**

Lawrence-Lightfoot, Sara
   The third chapter   **305.26**

LAWS *See* Law; Legislation

The **Laws** of Cooking. Warner, J.   **641.502**
Laws of creation. Hylton, K. N.   **346.04**
The **laws** of medicine. Mukherjee, S.   **610**

Lawson, James M., 1928-
   About
   Halberstam, D. The children   **323.1**

Lawson, Jenny, 1979-
   About
   Lawson, J. Furiously happy   **92**

Lawson, Nigella, 1960-
   How to be a domestic goddess   **641.815**
   How to Eat   **641.5**
   Nigella express   **641.5**
   Simply Nigella   **641.5**

LAWYERS
   Alter, J. The promise   **92**
   Balz, D. J. The battle for America, 2008   **973.932**
   Bernstein, C. A woman in charge   **92**
   Blum, H. American lightning   **364.152**
   Boritt, G. S. The Gettysburg gospel   **973.7**
   Boyle, K. Arc of justice   **345**
   Brenner, M. Apples and oranges   **92**
   Burlingame, M. Abraham Lincoln   **92**
   Carwardine, R. Lincoln: a life of purpose and power   **92**
   Chen, D. Colors of the mountain   **92**
   Chen, D. Sounds of the river   **951.05**
   Chua, A. Battle hymn of the tiger mother **306.874**
   Clinton, C. Mrs. Lincoln   **92**
   Clinton, H. R. Living history   **92**
   Commager, H. S. The American mind   **973**
   Craughwell, T. J. Stealing Lincoln's body   **973.7**
   Davis, W. C. Three roads to the Alamo   **976.4**
   Donald, D. H. Lincoln   **92**
   Farrell, J. A. Clarence Darrow   **92**
   Feige, D. Indefensible   **345**
   Feinberg, K. R. What is life worth?   **362.88**
   Feldman, N. Scorpions   **920**
   Foner, E. The fiery trial   **973.7**
   Fredrickson, G. M. Big enough to be inconsistent   **973.7**
   Gienapp, W. E. Abraham Lincoln and Civil War America   **973.7**
   Gimlette, J. Theatre of fish   **917**
   Gioia, D. Can poetry matter?   **809.1**
   Goodwin, D. K. Team of rivals   **92**
   Gopnik, A. Angels and ages   **973.7**
   Gormley, K. The death of American virtue **973.929**
   Grose, P. Gentleman spy   **92**
   Guelzo, A. C. Lincoln and Douglas   **973.6**
   Hayden, T. The long sixties   **973.92**
   Haynes, J. E. Venona   **327.12**
   Hofstadter, R. The American political tradition, and the men who made it   **973**
   Holzer, H. Lincoln president-elect   **92**
   Jarrell, R. No other book   **809**

Johnson, H. M. Too late to die young 92

Kauffman, B. Forgotten founder, drunken prophet 92

Kazin, M. A godly hero 92

Keneally, T. Abraham Lincoln 92

Kennedy, J. F. Profiles in courage 920

Kermode, F. An appetite for poetry 801

Khan, M. R. My Guantanamo diary 909.83

Kindred, D. Sound and fury 796

Korda, M. Ulysses S. Grant: the unlikely hero 92

Kunhardt, P. B. Looking for Lincoln 92

Kushner, T. Angels in America 812

The Lincoln anthology 92

Lind, M. What Lincoln believed 92

Macintyre, B. Operation Mincemeat 940.54

Marshall, T. Thurgood Marshall 347

Martin, P. A life of James Boswell 828

McPherson, J. M. Tried by war 92

McPherson, J. M. Abraham Lincoln 92

McPherson, J. M. Abraham Lincoln and the second American Revolution 973.7

McPherson, J. M. Drawn with the sword 973.7

McPherson, J. M. This mighty scourge 973.7

Mendell, D. Obama 92

Millman, C. The detonators 940.4

Morris, R. Fraud of the century 324.9

Norgren, J. Belva Lockwood 92

Obama, B. Dreams from my father 92

Our Lincoln 92

Paludan, P. S. The presidency of Abraham Lincoln 973.7

Perino, M. A. The hellhound of Wall Street 330.9

Pierpont, C. R. Passionate minds 810

Pinsker, M. Lincoln's sanctuary 92

Pooley, E. The climate war 363.7

Remini, R. V. Daniel Webster 328

Remnick, D. The bridge 92

Ribowsky, M. Howard Cosell 92

Rowan, C. T. Dream makers, dream breakers 92

Rule, A. --and never let her go 364.1

Sandburg, C. Abraham Lincoln: The prairie years and The war years 92

Sands, P. East West Street 345

Satter, B. Family properties 363.5

Shenk, J. W. Lincoln's melancholy 92

Siegel, F. F. The prince of the city 92

Sisman, A. Boswell's presumptuous task 828

Smyth, D. Deathly deception 940.54

Sorensen, T. C. Counselor 92

Starr, W. W. Whisky, kilts, and the Loch Ness Monster 914

Stevenson, B. Just Mercy 353.4

Swanson, J. L. Manhunt 364.152

Symonds, C. L. Lincoln and his admirals 92

Traister, R. Big girls don't cry 324

Urofsky, M. I. Louis D. Brandeis 92

Walsh, J. E. Moonlight 345

White, R. C. A. Lincoln 92

White, R. C. The eloquent president: a portrait of Lincoln through his words 92

Williams, J. Thurgood Marshall 92

Wills, G. Lincoln at Gettysburg 973.7

Wilson, E. Patriotic gore 810

Zimmermann, W. First great triumph 973

LAWYERS

See also Law

LAWYERS -- BIOGRAPHY

Burke, D. Law man 92

Vance, J. D. Hillbilly elegy 92

LAWYERS -- ILLINOIS -- CHICAGO -- BIOGRAPHY

Jobb, D. Empire of deception 92

LAWYERS -- SALARIES, WAGES, ETC.

See also Salaries, wages, etc.

LAWYERS -- UNITED STATES

Tamanaha, B. Z. Failing law schools 340

Lax, Robert

Love had a compass 811

A thing that is 811

LAY MINISTRY

See also Church work

LAYDEN, JOSEPH, 1959-

Rodriguez, D. Rise 92

The **layered** garden design lessons for year-round beauty from Brandywine Cottage. 635

Lazarus, Emma

Emma Lazarus 811

Lazebnik, Claire

Overcoming Autism 618.92

Lazenby, Roland

Jerry West 92

Michael Jordan 92

LAZINESS

See also Personality

LE BERNARDIN (NEW YORK, N.Y.: RESTAURANT)

Ripert, E. On the line 647

Le Carré, John, 1931-

The Pigeon Tunnel 823

Le Coultre, Martijn F.

(ed) The poster 741.6

Le Gallienne, Richard

(ed) Pepys, S. The diary of Samuel Pepys 941.06

Le Grange, Daniel

(jt. auth) Lock, J. Help your teenager beat an eating disorder 616.85

Le morte Darthur, or, The hoole book of Kyng Arthur and of his noble knyghtes of the Rounde Table.

Malory, T. 398.2

Le, Stephanie

Easy Gourmet 641.5

Le, Stephen

One hundred million years of food **641.3**

Leach, Amy
Things that are **508**

Leach, Mike, 1961-
About
Gwynne, S. C. The Perfect Pass **796.332**

Leach, Penelope
Child care today **362.7**
The essential first year **649**
Your baby & child **649**
Your Baby and Child From Birth to Age Five **618.92**

Leach, William
Butterfly people **595.78**

LEAD POISONING
See also Occupational diseases; Poisons and poisoning

Leadbelly, 1885-1949
About
Wolfe, C. K. The life and legend of Leadbelly **92**

Leader, Zachary
The life of Kingsley Amis **92**
The Life of Saul Bellow **92**

Leaders of the American Civil War. **973.7**

LEADERSHIP
See also Ability; Executive ability; Social groups; Success

LEADERSHIP -- CASE STUDIES.
Wills, G. Certain trumpets **303.3**

LEADERSHIP -- MORAL AND ETHICAL ASPECTS
Covey, S. M. R. Smart trust **174**

LEADERSHIP -- UNITED STATES
Bolger, D. P. Why We Lost **956.704**
Gates, R. M. A passion for leadership **92**
Koltz, T. It worked for me **92**

LEADERSHIP -- UNITED STATES -- CASE STUDIES
Century, D. Making a difference **303.3**

Leaf, Clifton
The truth in small doses **616.99**

The **leafcutter** ants. Holldobler, B. **595.7**

League of Denial. Fainaru, S. **617.1**

Leahy, Christopher W.
The birdwatcher's companion to North American birdlife **598**

Leahy, William D
About
Borneman, W. R. The admirals **920**

Leake, Lisa
100 days of real food **613.2**

Leakey, Richard E.
The origin of humankind **599.93**
Origins reconsidered **599.93**

LEAKS (DISCLOSURE OF INFORMATION)
The WikiLeaks files **327.73**

Leal, Brigitte
The ultimate Picasso **759**

Leaman, Oliver
(ed) The Qur'an: an encyclopedia **297.1**

Leamer, Laurence
The Kennedy men **920**
The Lynching **364.134**
The price of justice **346.730**

Leaming, Barbara
Jacqueline Bouvier Kennedy Onassis **92**
Kick Kennedy **92**
Mrs. Kennedy **973.922**

Lean in. Sandberg, S. **658.4**

Leap, Jorja
Project Fatherhood **306.874**

Lear, Edward
The complete verse and other nonsense **821**

Lear, Linda J.
Beatrix Potter **92**

Lear, Norman
About
Lear, N. Even This I Get to Experience **92**

Learn calligraphy. Shepherd, M. **745.6**

LEARNED INSTITUTIONS AND SOCIETIES
See Learning and scholarship

Learned optimism. Seligman, M. E. P. **155.2**

LEARNING
Carey, B. How we learn **153.1**
Levine, M. D. A mind at a time **370.15**

LEARNING AND SCHOLARSHIP
Bawer, B. The victims' revolution **320**
Cahill, T. How the Irish saved civilization **941.501**
Otto, S. Fool me twice **303.4**

LEARNING AND SCHOLARSHIP
See also Civilization; Intellectual life

LEARNING AND SCHOLARSHIP -- HISTORY
Lima, M. The book of trees **001.2**

LEARNING DISABILITIES
Flink, D. Thinking Differently **371.9**
Levine, M. D. A mind at a time **370.15**

LEARNING DISABILITIES
See also Psychology of learning; Slow learning children

Learning from the heart. Gottlieb, D. **170**

The **learning** habit. Jackson, R. **371.3**

LEARNING RESOURCE CENTERS See Instructional materials centers

Learning to communicate in science and engineering. Poe, M. **501**

Learning to die in Miami. Eire, C. M. N. **92**

Learning to see creatively. Peterson, B. **770.1**

LEARNING, PSYCHOLOGY OF
Carey, B. How we learn **153.1**
Gopnik, A. The scientist in the crib **155.4**

LEARNING, PSYCHOLOGY OF See Psychology of learning

Lears, T. J. Jackson

Rebirth of a nation **973.8**

Leary, Timothy, 1920-1996
About
Greenfield, R. Timothy Leary **92**
Lattin, D. The Harvard Psychedelic Club **920**

LEATHER GARMENTS
See also Clothing and dress; Leather work

LEATHER INDUSTRY
See also Industries

LEATHER WORK
See also Decoration and ornament; Decorative arts; Handicraft

Leave Your Mark. Licht, A. **650.1**

Leavell, Linda
Holding on upside down **92**

LEAVES
Vogel, S. The life of a leaf **575.5**

LEAVES
See also Plants

LEAVES -- GROWTH
Vogel, S. The life of a leaf **575.5**

LEAVES -- PHYSIOLOGY
Vogel, S. The life of a leaf **575.5**

Leaves of grass. Whitman, W. **811**
Leaving Before the Rains Come. Fuller, A. **305.409**
Leaving orbit. Dean, M. L. **629.4**

Leavitt, David
The man who knew too much **92**

Leavitt, Henrietta Swan, 1868-1921
About
Johnson, G. Miss Leavitt's stars **92**
Malone, J. W. It doesn't take a rocket scientist **920**

Leavitt, Sarah
Tangles **362.196**

Leavy, Jane
The last boy **92**
Sandy Koufax **796.357**

LEBANESE
Anderson, S. The Hostage's Daughter **92**

LEBANESE COOKING
Massaad, B. A. Man'oushé **641.5**
Roden, C. Arabesque: a taste of Morocco, Turkey, and Lebanon **641.5**

LEBANON -- EMIGRATION AND IMMIGRATION -- SOCIAL ASPECTS
Shadid, A. House of stone **306**

LEBANON -- HISTORY
Friedman, T. L. From Beirut to Jerusalem **956**

LEBANON -- SOCIAL LIFE AND CUSTOMS
Ciezadlo, A. Day of honey **92**

Lebbin, Daniel J.
The American Bird Conservancy guide to bird conservation **333.95**

LEBENSBORN E.V. (GERMANY)
Tate, T. Hitler's forgotten children **940.53**

LeBlanc, Adrian Nicole

Random family **305.5**

Lebo, Kate
Pie school **909**

LeBor, Adam
City of oranges **956.94**

Lebovitz, David
My Paris kitchen **641.59**
The perfect scoop **641.8**

Leboyer, Frédérick, 1918-
Birth without violence **618.4**

Lebrecht, Norman
Why Mahler? **92**

Lebsock, Suzanne
A murder in Virginia **364.1**

LeBuhn, Gretchen
(jt. auth) Frey, K. The bee-friendly garden **595.799**

Leca, Benedict
(ed) The World Is an Apple **759.4**

LeCain, Timothy J.
Mass destruction **338.2**

Leckie, Robert, 1920-
Okinawa **940.54**

LECTURERS
Ellmann, R. Oscar Wilde **92**
Grant, G. M. At the elbows of my elders **920**
Norgren, J. Belva Lockwood **92**

LECTURES AND LECTURING
See also Public speaking; Rhetoric; Teaching
Lectures on literature. Nabokov, V. V. **808.3**
Lectures on Russian literature. Nabokov, V. V. **891.7**

Lederer, Roger J.
Beaks, bones, and bird songs **598**

Lederman, Leon
Beyond the god particle **539.7**

LeDuff, Charlie
About
LeDuff, C. Detroit **977.4**

Ledyard. Gifford, B. **92**

Ledyard, John, 1751-1789
About
Gifford, B. Ledyard **92**

Lee. Freeman, D. S. **92**
The **Lee** Bros. Charleston kitchen. Lee, M. **641.59**
The **Lee** Bros. southern cookbook. Lee, M. **641.5**

Lee family
About
Lee, H. In the absence of sun **979.4**

Lee Krasner. Levin, G. **92**
Lee Miller. Burke, C. **92**

Lee Shetterly, Margot
Hidden Figures **510.92**

Lee, Alexander
The ugly Renaissance **945**

Lee, Bruce
Marching orders **940.54**

Lee, Cecilia Hae-Jin

Quick and easy Korean cooking **641.5**

Lee, Erika
The making of Asian America **973**

Lee, Gypsy Rose, 1914-1970
About
Abbott, K. American rose **92**

Lee, Harper, 1926-2016
About
Mills, M. The Mockingbird Next Door **92**
Murphy, M. M. Scout, Atticus, and Boo **813**

Lee, Helie
In the absence of sun **979.4**

Lee, Hermione
Edith Wharton **92**
Virginia Woolf **823**
Virginia Woolf's nose **820**
Willa Cather **92**

Lee, Janet
The supplement handbook **613.2**

Lee, Jennifer Tyler
The 52 new foods challenge **641.5**

Lee, Jerry
(ed) Gun digest 2015 **623.4**

Lee, John
Friedlander, E. J. Feature writing for newspapers
  and magazines **070.4**

Lee, Li-Young
Behind my eyes **811**

Lee, Linda
Sewing edges and corners **646.2**

Lee, Marshall
Bookmaking: editing, design, production **686**

Lee, Matt
The Lee Bros. Charleston kitchen **641.59**

Lee, Matthew
The Lee Bros. southern cookbook **641.5**

Lee, Robert E. (Robert Edward), 1807-1870
About
Blount, R. Robert E. Lee **92**
Davis, W. C. Crucible of commmand **920**
Fellman, M. The making of Robert E. Lee **92**
Freeman, D. S. Lee **92**
Korda, M. Clouds of Glory **92**
Thomas, E. M. Robert E. Lee **92**

Lee, Robert Edwin
Lawrence, J. Inherit the wind **812**

Lee, Stan, 1922-
Stan Lee's How to draw comics **741.5**

Lee, Ted
(jt. auth) Lee, M. The Lee Bros. Charleston kitch-
  en **641.59**

Lee, Ted
Lee, M. The Lee Bros. southern cookbook **641.5**

Lee, Vinny
Kitchenalia **747**

Leeds, Regina
Rightsize . . . right now! **648**

Leeming, David Adams
The Oxford companion to world mythology **201**

Leepson, Marc
Flag: an American biography **929.9**

Leerhsen, Charles
Ty Cobb **92**

Lees, Gene
You can't steal a gift **781.65**

Leeuwenhoek, Antoni van, 1632-1723
About
Snyder, L. J. Eye of the beholder **701**

Lefebvre, Georges
The French Revolution **944.04**

Lefebvre, Henri, 1901-1991
Critique of everyday life **301**

Lefer, David
Evans, H. They made America **920**

Lefevre, Didier
Guibert, E. The photographer **958.1**

Lefevre, John
Straight to Hell **332.1**

Lefkowitz, Ilene N.
(jt. auth) Quillen, C. L. Read on... romance **016**

Lefkowitz, Mary R.
Not out of Africa **960**

LEFT (POLITICAL SCIENCE) *See* Liberalism;
  Right and left (Political science)

LEFT AND RIGHT (DIRECTION)
  See also Direction sense

Left out. Stepan-Norris, J. **331.8**

LEGACIES *See* Inheritance and succession; Wills

Legacies: a Chinese mosaic. Lord, B. B. 951.05

Legacy of ashes. Weiner, T. **327.12**

A **legacy** of liberation. Gevisser, M. **92**

LEGAL AID
Houppert, K. Chasing Gideon **345.73**

LEGAL ASSISTANCE TO THE POOR *See* Legal
  aid

LEGAL DRAMA (FILMS)
  See also Motion pictures

LEGAL DRAMA (TELEVISION PROGRAMS)
  See also Television programs

LEGAL ETHICS
  See also Professional ethics

A **legal** guide for lesbian and gay couples. Hertz,
  F. **346.01**

Legal history of North America [series]
Documents of American Indian diplomacy **970.004**

Legal rights. **346.73**

LEGAL SERVICES FOR THE POOR *See* Legal
  aid

LEGAL STORIES
  See also Fiction

Legal systems of the world. **340**

LEGAL TENDER *See* Money

Legend. Blehm, E.   **959.7**

The **legend** of Marathon. Karnazes, D.   **938.03**

LEGENDARY CHARACTERS
   See also Legends; Mythology

LEGENDS
   See also Fiction; Literature

LEGENDS -- HAWAII
  Moore, S. Paradise of the Pacific   **996.9**

LEGENDS -- UNITED STATES
  Brunvand, J. H. The vanishing hitchhiker   **398.2**
  Shenkman, R. Legends, lies & cherished myths of
    American history   **973**

The **legends** club. Feinstein, J.   **796.323**

Legends of modernity. Milosz, C.   **891.8**

Legends, lies & cherished myths of American history. Shenkman, R.   **973**

LEGERDEMAIN *See* Juggling; Magic tricks

LEGIBILITY OF HANDWRITING *See* Handwriting

LEGISLATION
  Stathis, S. W. Landmark legislation, 1774-2002 **348**

LEGISLATION
   See also Political science

LEGISLATION -- UNITED STATES
  Davis, L. J. Enabling acts   **342.73**

LEGISLATIVE BODIES
   See also Constitutional law; Legislation;
   Representative government and representation

LEGISLATORS
  Stahr, W. Seward   **92**

LEGISLATORS
   See also Statesmen

LEGISLATORS -- UNITED STATES
  Lewis, J. March   **92**

**LEGISLATORS -- UNITED STATES -- BIOG-
RAPHY**
  Frank, B. Frank   **92**
  Tye, L. Bobby Kennedy   **92**

LEGITIMACY (LAW) *See* Illegitimacy

LEGO KONCERNEN (DENMARK)
  Breen, B. Brick by brick   **338.7**

LEGO TOYS -- HISTORY
  Breen, B. Brick by brick   **338.7**

The **legs** are the last to go. Carroll, D.   **92**

LeHand, Missy, 1898-1944
About
  Persico, J. E. Franklin and Lucy   **920**

Lehman, David, 1948-
  (ed) The best American poetry   **811**
  (ed) Best of the Best American Poetry   **811**
  A fine romance   **782.42**
  (ed) The Oxford book of American poetry   **811**

Lehmann, Chris
  The money cult   **261.8**

Lehmann, Ingmar
  The secrets of triangles   **516**

  (jt. auth) Posamentier, A. S. Magnificent mistakes
   in mathematics   **510**

LeHoullier, Craig
  Epic tomatoes   **635**

Lehr, Dick
  The Birth of a Nation   **305.8**
  The fence   **364.1**

Lehrer, Jonah
  How we decide   **153.8**

Lehu, Pierre A.
  (jt. auth) Westheimer, R. K. The Doctor Is in

Leiber, Jerry, 1933-2011
About
  Leiber, J. Hound dog   **92**

**Leibniz, Gottfried Wilhelm, Freiherr von, 1646-
1716**
About
  Bell, E. T. Men of mathematics   **920**
  Nadler, S. M. The best of all possible worlds   **190**
  Russell, B. A history of Western philosophy   **109**

Leibovich, Lori
  (ed) Maybe baby   **306.8**

Leibovitz, Annie
  Annie Leibovitz at work   **779**
  A photographer's life, 1990-2005   **779**
  Women   **779**

Leibovitz, Liel
  Fortunate sons   **951.05**

Leibowitz, Herbert A.
  Something urgent I have to say to you: the life and
   works of William Carlos Williams   **92**

Leider, Emily W.
  Myrna Loy   **92**

Leidich, Shari Koolik
  Two Moms in the Raw   **641.5**

Leifer, John
  After you hear it's cancer   **616.99**

Leifer, Neil
  Neil Leifer: Ballet in the dirt   **796.357**

Leigh, Mitch
  Cervantes Saavedra, M. d. Man of La Mancha **812**

Leininger, Phillip
  Hart, J. D. The Oxford companion to American literature   **810**

Leite, David
  The new Portuguese table   **641.5**

Leiter, Richard A.
  (jt. auth) Mersky, R. M. Landmark Supreme Court
   cases   **347.73**

Leiter, Richard A.
  Landmark Supreme Court cases   **347**
  (ed) National survey of state laws   **349**
  (jt. auth) Mersky, R. M. Landmark Supreme Court
   cases   **347.73**

Leiter, Sharon
  Critical companion to Emily Dickinson   **811**

Leithauser, Brad
Jarrell, R. No other book **809**
Leitzel, Lillian
About
Jensen, D. Queen of the air **791.3**
Lellenberg, Jon L.
(ed) Doyle, A. C. Arthur Conan Doyle **92**
Lelyveld, Joseph
Great soul **92**
His final battle **92**
Lemann, Nicholas
Redemption: the last battle of the Civil War **975**
Lemay, J. A. Leo
(ed) Franklin, B. Autobiography, Poor Richard,
and later writings **818**
**Lemelson Center studies in invention and innova-
tion** [series]
Beyer, K. W. Grace Hopper and the invention of the
information age **92**
Lemercier, Frederic
Guibert, E. The photographer **958.1**
Lemieux, Christiane
The Finer Things **747**
LeMieux, Richard
About
LeMieux, R. Breakfast at Sally's **92**
Lemmon, Gayle Tzemach
Ashley's war **92**
The dressmaker of Khair Khana **92**
The **lemon** tree. Tolan, S. **956.94**
Lempicka, Tamara de, 1898-1980
About
Mackrell, J. Flappers **920**
Lena Corwin's made by hand. Corwin, L. **746.6**
Lend me your ears. **808.88**
LENDING See Loans
LENDING OF LIBRARY MATERIALS See Li-
brary circulation
Leni Riefenstahl. Trimborn, J. **92**
Leni: the life and work of Leni Riefenstahl. Bach,
S. **92**
Lenin. Volkogonov, D. A. **947.084**
Lenin's brother. Pomper, P. **92**
Lenin's tomb. Remnick, D. **947.085**
Lenin, Vladimir Il¿ich, 1870-1924
About
Pipes, R. Russia under the Bolshevik re-
gime **947.084**
Pomper, P. Lenin's brother **92**
Service, R. Lenin--a biography **947.084**
Volkogonov, D. A. Lenin **947.084**
Lenin--a biography. Service, R. **947.084**
Leningrad. Reid, A.
Leningrad. Moynahan, B. **940.54**
Lennon. Riley, T. **92**
Lennon, J. Michael

Norman Mailer **92**
Lennon, John, 1940-1980
About
The Beatles anthology **782.421**
Greenberg, K. E. December 8, 1980 **92**
Norman, P. John Lennon **92**
Riley, T. Lennon **92**
Spitz, B. The Beatles: the biography **920**
**Lennox, Margaret Douglas, Countess of, 1515-
1578**
About
Weir, A. The lost Tudor princess **92**
Lenoir, Frédéric
Happiness **152.4**
LENT -- MEDITATIONS
See also Meditations
LENTEN SERMONS
See also Lent; Sermons
Lenya, Lotte
About
Mordden, E. Love song **920**
Lenz, Frank, d. 1894
About
Herlihy, D. V. The lost cyclist **92**
Leo & his circle. Cohen-Solal, A. **92**
Leon, Donna
My Venice and Other Essays **945**
Leon, Luis D.
Religion and American cultures **200.9**
Leonard Bernstein. Bernstein, B. **92**
Leonard Bernstein.
Leonard Bernstein. Shawn, A. **92**
Leonard Cohen on Leonard Cohen. **92**
Leonard Woolf. Glendinning, V. **92**
Leonard, Annie
The story of stuff **306.4**
Leonard, Elisabeth
(ed) Guide to Reference in Business and Econom-
ics **016**
Leonard, Elizabeth D.
All the daring of the soldier **973.7**
Leonard, Glen M.
Walker, R. W. Massacre at Mountain Mead-
ows **979.2**
Leonard, Max
Lanterne Rouge **796.62**
Leonard, Robin
Credit repair **332.7**
Elias, S. Chapter 13 bankruptcy **346**
Elias, S. How to file for Chapter 7 bankrupt-
cy **346.07**
Solve your money troubles **346**
Leonard, Sugar Ray, 1956-
About
Kimball, G. Four kings **920**
Leonard, Thomas M.

(ed) Encyclopedia of the developing world   **909**

Leonardo. White, M.   **92**

Leonardo. Bramly, S.   **709**

Leonardo and the Last supper. King, R.   **759**

Leonardo Da Vinci. Aquino, L.   **92**

Leonardo da Vinci. Nuland, S. B.   **709**

Leonardo da Vinci. Brown, D. A.   **759**

Leonardo's holy child. Kline, F. R.   **741.945**

Leonardo's legacy. Klein, S.   **709**

Leonardo, da Vinci, 1452-1519

About

Aquino, L.   Leonardo Da Vinci   **92**

Bramly, S.   Leonardo   **709**

Brewer, J.   The American Leonardo   **759**

Brown, D. A.   Leonardo da Vinci   **759**

Klein, S.   Leonardo's legacy   **709**

Kline, F. R.   Leonardo's holy child   **741.945**

Lester, T.   Da Vinci's ghost   **741.092**

Nuland, S. B.   Leonardo da Vinci   **709**

Sassoon, D.   Becoming Mona Lisa   **759**

Scotti, R. A.   Vanished smile   **759**

Strathern, P.   The artist, the philosopher, and the warrior   **920**

White, M.   Leonardo   **92**

Leonardo, da Vinci, 1452-1519. Last supper

About

King, R.   Leonardo and the Last supper   **759**

Leonardo, da Vinci, 1452-1519. Mona Lisa

About

Hales, D.   Mona Lisa   **759.5**

Leonardo, da Vinci, 1452-1519. Vitruvian man

About

Lester, T.   Da Vinci's ghost   **741.092**

Leonowens, Anna Harriette, 1831-1915

About

Landon, M.   Anna and the King of Siam   **92**

Leopold, Aldo, 1886-1948

A Sand County almanac & other writings on ecology & conservation   **508**

Leopold, David

The Hirschfeld century   **741.5**

Leovy, Jill

Ghettoside   **364.152**

LEPIDOPTERA See Butterflies; Moths

Lepore, Jill

A is for American   **306.44**

Book of ages   **92**

The mansion of happiness   **973**

The name of war   **973.2**

New York burning   **974.7**

The Secret History of Wonder Woman   **741.5**

The story of America   **973**

LEPROSY

Tayman, J.   The Colony   **614.5**

LEPROSY

See also Diseases

Lerner, Alan Jay

Shaw, B.   Pygmalion . . . and My fair lady   **822**

Lerner, Ben

About

Angle of yaw   **811**

Lerner, Betsy

About

Lerner, B.   The bridge ladies   **92**

Lerner, Harriet Goldhor

The dance of anger   **152.4**

The dance of deception   **155.3**

The dance of intimacy   **155.6**

Lerner, Neal

Poe, M.   Learning to communicate in science and engineering   **501**

Lerner, Steve

Sacrifice zones   **363.738**

The **LeRoi** Jones/Amiri Baraka reader. Baraka, I. A.   **818**

Leroi, Armand Marie

The lagoon   **570.1**

Les fleurs du mal. Baudelaire, C.   **841**

LESBIAN AUTHORS -- UNITED STATES -- BIOGRAPHY

Borich, B. J.   Body geographic   **818**

LESBIAN MARRIAGE See Same-sex marriage

LESBIAN RIGHTS See Gay rights

LESBIAN STUDENTS -- UNITED STATES

Cahill, S.   LGBT youth in America's schools **371.82**

LESBIANISM

See also Homosexuality

LESBIANISM IN LITERATURE

Donoghue, E.   Inseparable   **809**

LESBIANS

Carter, D.   Stonewall   **306.76**

Cooper, A.   Saving Alex   **92**

Faderman, L.   The gay revolution   **306.76**

LESBIANS

See also Gays; LGBT people; Women

LESBIANS -- CIVIL RIGHTS See Gay rights

LESBIANS -- UNITED STATES -- BIOGRAPHY

Bingham, E.   Irrepressible   **306.76**

LESBIANS AND GAYS IN THE MILITARY See Gays and lesbians in the military

LESBIANS IN THE MILITARY See Gays and lesbians in the military

LESBIANS' WRITINGS

Georges, N. J.   Calling Dr. Laura   **92**

LESBIANS' WRITINGS

See also Literature

Leschi, Nisqually chief, d. 1858

About

Kluger, R.   The bitter waters of Medicine Creek   **979.7**

Leslie, Clare Walker

The Curious Nature Guide   **508**

Less than one. Brodsky, J.   **809.1**

Lesseps, Ferdinand Marie de, vicomte, 1805-1894
              About
  Karabell, Z. Parting the desert   **386**
  McCullough, D. G. The path between the
    seas   **972.87**
Lessig, Lawrence
  The future of ideas   **004.67**
  Remix   **346**
Lessing, Doris May, 1919-
              About
  Lessing, D. M. Under my skin   **92**
  Pierpont, C. R. Passionate minds   **810**
Lessing, Gotthold Ephraim
  Nathan the Wise, Minna von Barnhelm, and other
    plays and writings   **832**
Lessing, Hans-Erhard
  Bicycle design   **629.2**
Lessons in realistic watercolor. Robinson, M.
  A.   **751.422**
The **lessons** of terror. Carr, C.   **303.6**
Lester, Toby
  Da Vinci's ghost   **741.092**
  The fourth part of the world   **912**
Let every nation know. Dallek, R.   **92**
Let Freedom Ring. Kelley, K.   **323.1**
Let history judge. Medvedev, R. A.   **947.084**
Let it bleed. Russell, E. A.   **781.66**
Let me tell you.   **818**
Let the swords encircle me. Peterson, S.   **955**
Let Them Eat Dirt. Finlay, B. B.   **616.9**
Let us now praise famous men. Agee, J.   **976.1**
Let's explore diabetes with owls. Sedaris, D.   **814**
Let's start the music. Brown, A.   **027.62**
Let's take the long way home. Caldwell, G.   **92**
Lethem, Jonathan
  (ed) Dick, P. K. The exegesis of Philip K. Dick **818**
  The ecstasy of influence   **814**
Letitia Baldrige's new manners for new times. Bal-
  drige, L.   **395**
The **letter** and the scroll. Currie, R.   **220.9**
Letter from America, 1946-2004. Cooke, A. **973.9**
Letter to an imaginary friend. McGrath, T.   **811**
Letter to my daughter. Angelou, M.   **92**
Letter to the world. Ware, S.   **920.72**
LETTER WRITING
    See also Etiquette; Literary style; Rhetoric
LETTERING
  Doh, J. Creative lettering   **745.6**
  Doh, J. More creative lettering   **745.6**
LETTERING
    See also Decoration and ornament; Industrial
    painting; Mechanical drawing
LETTERS
  Auster, P. Report from the interior   **92**
  Burroughs, W. S. Rub out the words   **813**
  The Collected Letters of Thomas Hardy   **823**

  Cronkite, W. Cronkite's war   **070.4**
  Mallon, T. Yours ever   **808.86**
  Suitable accommodations   **92**
Letters from Black America.   **305.8**
The **letters** of Allen Ginsberg. Ginsberg, A.   **92**
Letters of Ayn Rand. Rand, A.   **813**
LETTERS OF CREDIT *See* Credit; Negotiable
  instruments
Letters of E.B. White. White, E. B.   **92**
LETTERS OF RECOMMENDATION *See* Ap-
  plications for positions
The **letters** of Sylvia Beach.   **92**
LETTERS OF THE ALPHABET *See* Alphabet
Letters of the century.   **816**
Letters to a Young Scientist. Wilson, E. O.   **570**
Letters to a young teacher. Kozol, J.   **371.1**
Letters to Malcolm: chiefly on prayer. Lewis, C.
  S.   **248**
LETTERS, COVER *See* Cover letters
Letts, Elizabeth
  The eighty-dollar champion   **798.2**
  The perfect horse   **940.54**
Leuchtenburg, William Edward
  Franklin D. Roosevelt and the New Deal, 1932-
    1940   **973.917**
  Morison, S. E. The growth of the American Repub-
    lic   **973**
LEUKEMIA
    See also Blood -- Diseases; Cancer
Leung, Cecilia
  (jt. auth) Moore, C. Little Flower baking **641.815**
Lev, Arlene Istar
  The complete lesbian & gay parenting guide **649**
Levack, Brian P.
  The Devil within   **133.4**
LEVANT *See* Middle East
Levatino, Audrey
  Woman-powered farm   **630**
Level zero heroes. Bruning, J. R.   **958.104**
Levels of life. Barnes, J.   **823**
Levels of the game. McPhee, J.   **796.34**
Levenson, J. C.
  (ed) Crane, S. Prose and poetry   **813**
Levenson, Thomas
  The hunt for Vulcan   **523.4**
  Newton and the counterfeiter   **92**
Lever, Evelyne
  Madame de Pompadour   **944**
  Marie Antoinette   **92**
Lever, Maurice
  Beaumarchais   **92**
LEVERAGED BUYOUTS
    See also Corporate mergers and acquisitions
Leverett, Flynt
  Going to Tehran   **327.73**
Leverett, Hillary Mann

(jt. auth) Leverett, F. Going to Tehran 327.73

Leverich, Lyle
Tom 92

Levertov, Denise
Selected poems 811

Levi, Jan Heller
(ed) Jordan, J. Directed by desire 811

Levi, Mark
Why cats land on their feet 530

Levi, Michael
Power surge 333.79

Levi, Primo, 1919-1987
Survival in Auschwitz 940.53

About
Angier, C. The double bond: Primo Levi, a biography 92
Levi, P. The periodic table 92

Levi-Strauss, Claude
The savage mind 155.8

Leviathan. Dolin, E. J. 639.2

Leviathan. Hobbes, T. 320.1

Levin Becker, Daniel

About
Becker, D. L. Many subtle channels 840.9

Levin, Gail, 1948-
Lee Krasner 92

Levin, Phillis
(ed) The Penguin book of the sonnet 821

Levine, Adam, 1958-
The layered garden design lessons for year-round beauty from Brandywine Cottage 635

Levine, Bruce
The fall of the house of Dixie 973.7

Levine, Judith
Not buying it 640.73

Levine, Lawrence W.
The opening of the American mind 001.1

Levine, Lee I.
Visual Judaism in late antiquity 704.9

Levine, Lisbeth
Weiss, M. The wedding book 395

Levine, Madeline G.
(tr) Milosz, C. Milosz's ABCs 891.8
(ed) Milosz, C. To begin where I am 891.8

Levine, Marvin J.
Children for hire 331.3

Levine, Melvin D.
A mind at a time 370.15

Levine, Philip
Breath 811
The mercy 811
New selected poems 811
News of the world 811
The simple truth 811
What work is 811

Levine, Robert

The power of persuasion 153.8

Levine, Sarabeth
Sarabeth's good morning cookbook 641.5

Levine, Steven I.
Deng Xiaoping 951.05
Mao 951.05

Levine-Clark, Michael, 1969-
(ed) ALA glossary of library and information science 020

Levinsohn, Florence Hamlish
Looking for Farrakhan 297.8

Levinson, Daniel J.
The seasons of a man's life 155.6
The seasons of a woman's life 155.6

Levinson, David
(ed) Encyclopedia of crime and punishment 346

Levinson, Judy D.
Levinson, D. J. The seasons of a woman's life 155.6

Levitin, Daniel J.
A field guide to lies 153.4

Levitt, Len
NYPD confidential 364.1

Levitt, Steven D., 1967-
Dubner, S. J. Freakonomics 330
Superfreakonomics 330

Levs, Josh
All in 306.3

Levy, Adrian
Scott-Clark, C. The Amber Room 940.54
The siege 363.325

Levy, Alan Howard
Floyd Patterson 92

Levy, Alexander
The orphaned adult 152.4

Levy, Andrew
The first emancipator 92
Huck Finn's America 813

Levy, David H., 1948-

About
Malone, J. W. It doesn't take a rocket scientist 920

Levy, Emanuel
Vincente Minnelli 92

Levy, Joel
Fifty Weapons That Changed the Course of History 355.8

Levy, Matthys
Why buildings fall down 690

Levy, Naomi
To begin again 296.7

Levy, Reynold

About
Levy, R. They told me not to take that job 792.09

Levy, Shawn
Paul Newman 92

Levy, Steven
In the plex 338.7

Lewin, Roger
  Leakey, R. E. Origins reconsidered **599.93**
  Swisher, C. C. Java Man **599.93**
Lewin, W. H. G. (Walter H. G.)
                About
  Goldstein, W. For the love of physics **92**
Lewin, Walter
  (jt. auth) Goldstein, W. For the love of physics 92
Lewinsky, Monica
                About
  Gormley, K. The death of American virtue **973.929**
Lewis & Clark. Duncan, D. **917**
The **Lewis** & Clark Trail. Schmidt, T. **978**
LEWIS AND CLARK EXPEDITION (1804-1806)
  Ambrose, S. E. Undaunted courage **917**
  Clark, E. E. Sacagawea of the Lewis and Clark ex-
    pedition **92**
  Duncan, D. Lewis & Clark **917**
  Faulkner, S. Bitterroot **978**
  Schmidt, T. The Lewis & Clark Trail **978**
  Slaughter, T. P. Exploring Lewis and Clark **978**
  Woodger, E. Encyclopedia of the Lewis and Clark
    Expedition **917**
LEWIS AND CLARK EXPEDITION (1804-1806)
      See also United States -- Exploring expedi-
      tions; United States -- History -- 1783-1815
Lewis Carroll. Cohen, M. N. **92**
LEWIS CHESSMEN
  Brown, N. M. Ivory Vikings **736**
**The Lewis Walpole Series in Eighteenth-Century
  Culture and History** [series]
  Damrosch, L. Jonathan Swift **92**
  Eltis, D. Atlas of the transatlantic slave trade **381**
**LEWIS WITH HARRIS ISLAND (SCOTLAND)
  -- ANTIQUITIES**
  Brown, N. M. Ivory Vikings **736**
Lewis, Andrew B.
  The shadows of youth **323.1**
Lewis, Anthony
  Gideon's trumpet **345**
  (ed) Written into history **071**
Lewis, Bernard, 1916-
  The crisis of Islam **297**
  The Middle East **956**
  (ed) Music of a distant drum **808.81**
                About
  Lewis, B. Notes on a century **956**
Lewis, C. S. (Clive Staples), 1898-1963
  Letters to Malcolm: chiefly on prayer **248**
  Mere Christianity **230**
  Miracles **231.7**
  The Screwtape letters **248**
                About
  Downing, D. C. Into the region of awe **248.2**
  Ford, P. F. Companion to Narnia **823**
  McGrath, A. E. C. S. Lewis **92**

  Miller, L. The magician's book **823**
  Wilson, A. N. C.S. Lewis **823**
Lewis, Catherine M.
  (ed) Beyond Rosie **940**
Lewis, Celia
  The illustrated guide to cows **636.2**
Lewis, Damien
  The Dog Who Could Fly **940.54**
Lewis, David Levering
  W.E.B. Du Bois **92**
  (ed) The Portable Harlem Renaissance reader **810**
Lewis, Edna, 1916-2006
  Lewis, E. The gift of Southern cooking **641.59**
  The taste of country cooking **641.5**
Lewis, Gilbert Newton, 1875-1946
                About
  Coffey, P. Cathedrals of science **540**
Lewis, James R.
  (ed) The encyclopedia of cults, sects, and new reli-
    gions **200**
  The astrology book **133.5**
  The dream encyclopedia **154.6**
Lewis, Jerry, 1926-
                About
  Lewis, J. Dean & me **92**
Lewis, John R., 1940-
  March **92**
  (jt. auth) Lewis, J. March **92**
Lewis, John, 1940-
                About
  Halberstam, D. The children **323.1**
Lewis, Julia M.
  Wallerstein, J. S. The unexpected legacy of di-
    vorce **306.89**
Lewis, Lennox
                About
  Remnick, D. Reporting **814**
Lewis, Linda K.
  The complete guide to acquisitions manage-
    ment **025.2**
Lewis, Loida Nicolas
  How to Get a Green Card **342**
Lewis, Matt, 1974-
                About
  Lewis, M. Last man off **910.91**
Lewis, Meriwether, 1774-1809
                About
  Ambrose, S. E. Undaunted courage **917**
  Slaughter, T. P. Exploring Lewis and Clark **978**
Lewis, Michael D., 1960-
  The big short **330.9**
  The blind side **92**
  Flash boys **332.6**
  Lewis, M. D. The new new thing **338.4**
  Moneyball **796.357**
  (ed) Panic **338.5**

The Undoing Project **153**

Lewis, Moshe
Understanding pain **616**

Lewis, Norman
The tomb in Seville **946.081**

Lewis, Oscar
The children of Sanchez **972.08**

Lewis, Robin Coste
Voyage of the Sable Venus and other poems **811**

Lewis, Sinclair, 1885-1951. Babbitt
About
Nafisi, A. The Republic of Imagination **819**

Lewis, Thomas
A general theory of love **152.4**

Lewis-Jones, Huw
Conquest of Everest **796.522**

Lewy, Guenter
The Nazi persecution of the gypsies **940.53**

LEXICOGRAPHERS
Simpson, J. The word detective **423.092**

LEXICOGRAPHY
See also Encyclopedias and dictionaries

The **lexicon** of labor. Murray, R. E. **331**

LEXINGTON (MASS.), BATTLE OF, 1775
Fischer, D. H. Paul Revere's ride **973.3**

LEXINGTON (MASS.), BATTLE OF, 1775
See also Battles; United States -- History -- 1775-1783, Revolution -- Campaigns

LEXINGTON, BATTLE OF, LEXINGTON, MASS., 1775
Phillips, K. 1775 **973.3**

The **Lexus** and the olive tree. Friedman, T. L. **337**

LEYTE GULF, BATTLE OF, PHILIPPINES, 1944
Prados, J. Storm over Leyte **940.54**

LGBT COMIC BOOKS, STRIPS, ETC.
See also Comic books, strips, etc.

LGBT LITERATURE
See also Literature

LGBT PEOPLE
Browne, J. The Glass Closet **331.5**
Duberman, M. B. The Martin Duberman reader **306.76**
Savage, D. American Savage **306.76**

LGBT PEOPLE -- LEGAL STATUS, LAWS, ETC.
Hirshman, L. Victory **306.76**
Nicholson, A. Fighting to serve **355**

LGBT YOUTH
Cooper, A. Saving Alex **92**
Duron, L. Raising my rainbow **306.87**
Speaking Out **306.76**

LGBT YOUTH -- NEW YORK (STATE) -- NEW YORK
Berg, R. No house to call my home **362.786**

LGBT youth in America's schools. Cahill, S. **371.82**

Li, Charles N.
The bitter sea **92**

Li, Charles N., 1940-
About
Li, C. N. The bitter sea **92**

Li, Laura Tyson
Madame Chiang Kai-Shek **92**

Li, Leslie, 1945-
About
Li, L. Daughter of heaven **92**

Li, Luchen
Schultz, J. D. Critical companion to John Steinbeck **813**

LIABILITY (LAW)
See also Contracts

LIABILITY FOR OIL POLLUTION DAMAGES -- ECUADOR
Barrett, P. M. Law of the jungle **344**

Liao, Yiwu, 1958-
God is red **275.1**
About
Liao Yiwu For a song and one hundred songs **365**

The **liar's** tale. Campbell, J. **177**

Liar, Temptress, Soldier, Spy. Abbott, K. **973.7**

LIBEL AND SLANDER
See also Journalism

LIBERALISM
Shorto, R. Amsterdam **949.2**

LIBERALISM
See also Political science; Social sciences

LIBERALISM -- NETHERLANDS -- AMSTERDAM -- HISTORY
Shorto, R. Amsterdam **949.2**

LIBERALISM -- UNITED STATES
Hochschild, A. R. Strangers in their own land **320.52**

LIBERALISM -- UNITED STATES -- HISTORY -- 20TH CENTURY
Woods, R. B. Prisoners of hope **973.923**

LIBERALISM -- UNITED STATES -- HISTORY -- 21ST CENTURY
Hochschild, A. R. Strangers in their own land **320.52**

Liberation. Isherwood, C. **809**

Liberation Square. Khalil, A. **962.05**

LIBERATION THEOLOGY
See also Christianity -- Doctrines; Church and social problems; Theology

The **liberation trilogy** [series]
Atkinson, R. An army at dawn **940.54**
Atkinson, R. The guns at last light **940.54**
Atkinson, R. The day of battle **940.54**

LIBERIA
Cooper, H. The house at Sugar Beach **92**

LIBERIA -- DESCRIPTION AND TRAVEL
Butcher, T. Chasing the Devil **916**

LIBERIA -- HISTORY -- CIVIL WAR, 1989-1996 -- ATROCITIES

Dwyer, J. American warlord   **966.62**

Libertarianism. Brennan, J.   **320.51**

LIBERTARIANISM

Brennan, J. Libertarianism   **320.51**

LIBERTARIANISM -- UNITED STATES

Brennan, J. Libertarianism   **320.51**

LIBERTY *See* Freedom

LIBERTY -- HISTORY

Ferris, T. The science of liberty   **303.4**

Liberty and freedom. Fischer, D. H.   **323.44**

Liberty of conscience. Nussbaum, M. C.   **342**

LIBERTY OF SPEECH *See* Freedom of speech

LIBERTY OF THE PRESS *See* Freedom of the press

LIBERTY OF THE WILL *See* Free will and determinism

Liberty or death. McPhee, P.   **944.04**

Liberty's blueprint. Meyerson, M.   **342**

Liberty's exiles. Jasanoff, M.   **973.3**

The **librarian's** guide to graphic novels for adults. Serchay, D. S.   **025.2**

Librarian's guide to online searching. Bell, S. S.   **025.04**

Librarian's guide to passive programming. Wichman, E. T.   **025.5**

The **librarian's** nitty-gritty guide to social media. Solomon, L.   **006.7**

LIBRARIANS

Defending professionalism   **020**

Eagle, M. Answering teens' tough questions **027.62**

Heaney, S. Finders keepers   **821**

The indispensable librarian   **025.1**

Johnson, M. This book is overdue!   **020**

Lavender, K. Book repair   **025.7**

McCracken, E. An exact replica of a figment of my imagination   **92**

Solomon, L. The librarian's nitty-gritty guide to social media   **006.7**

Wichman, E. T. Librarian's guide to passive programming   **025.5**

LIBRARIANS -- EDUCATION *See* Library education

LIBRARIANS -- EFFECT OF TECHNOLOGICAL INNOVATIONS ON

Woodward, J. The transformed library   **020**

LIBRARIANS -- ETHICS

See also Professional ethics

LIBRARIANS -- IN-SERVICE TRAINING

Core technology competencies for librarians and library staff   **020**

LIBRARIANS -- IN-SERVICE TRAINING

See also Library education

LIBRARIANS -- MALI -- TOMBOUCTOU

Hammer, J. The bad-ass librarians of Timbuk-

tu   **025.8**

LIBRARIANS -- PROFESSIONAL ETHICS

Defending professionalism   **020**

LIBRARIANS -- TRAINING *See* Library education

LIBRARIANS -- TRAINING OF

Bell, S. S. Librarian's guide to online searching   **025.04**

LIBRARIANS -- UNITED STATES -- HANDBOOKS, MANUALS, ETC

Crews, K. D. Copyright law for librarians and educators   **346.04**

LIBRARIANS -- UTAH -- SALT LAKE CITY -- BIOGRAPHY

Hanagarne, J. The world's strongest librarian   **92**

Librarians as community partners.   **021.2**

LIBRARIANS OF CONGRESS

Archibald MacLeish: reflections   **92**

LIBRARIANS' UNIONS

See also Labor unions

LIBRARIANSHIP

Lankes, R. D. The atlas of new librarianship   **020**

LIBRARIANSHIP *See* Library science

LIBRARIANSHIP -- SOCIAL ASPECTS

McClure, C. R. Public libraries and internet service roles   **025.04**

LIBRARIES

Basbanes, N. A. Patience & fortitude   **002**

Petroski, H. The book on the bookshelf   **022**

LIBRARIES -- ACQUISITIONS

Lewis, L. K. The complete guide to acquisitions management   **025.2**

Rethinking collection development and management   **025.2**

LIBRARIES -- ACQUISITIONS

See also Libraries -- Collection development; Library technical processes

LIBRARIES -- ACTIVITY PROGRAMS -- UNITED STATES

Wichman, E. T. Librarian's guide to passive programming   **025.5**

LIBRARIES -- ADMINISTRATION

Johnson, P. Fundamentals of Collection Development and Management   **025.2**

MacKellar, P. H. Writing successful technology grant proposals   **025.1**

Mosley, P. A. The challenge of library management   **025.1**

LIBRARIES -- AIMS AND OBJECTIVES

Woodward, J. The transformed library   **020**

LIBRARIES -- AUTOMATION

Bolan, K. Technology made simple   **025**

Burke, J. J. Neal-Schuman library technology companion   **025**

Cohn, J. M. The complete library technology planner   **025**

LIBRARIES -- AUTOMATION -- UNITED STATES -- FINANCE
MacKellar, P. H. Writing successful technology grant proposals **025.1**

LIBRARIES -- CATALOGING See Cataloging

LIBRARIES -- CENSORSHIP
Foerstel, H. N. Banned in the U.S.A **025.2**

LIBRARIES -- CENSORSHIP
See also Censorship

LIBRARIES -- CIRCULATION, LOANS See Library circulation

LIBRARIES -- COLLECTION DEVELOPMENT
American reference books annual 2016 **011**
Bartlett, W. K. Floating collections **025.2**
A basic music library **016**
Building and managing e-book collections **025.2**
Disher, W. Crash Course in Collection Development **025.2**
Evans, G. E. Collection management basics **025.2**
Johnson, P. Developing and managing electronic collections **025.2**
Johnson, P. Fundamentals of Collection Development and Management **025.2**
Karp, J. Graphic novels in your school library **741.5**
Laguardia, C. Marketing your library's electronic resources **025.2**
Managing Electronic Resources **025.1**
Rethinking collection development and management **025.2**
Vnuk, R. The weeding handbook **025.2**

LIBRARIES -- COOPERATION See Library cooperation

LIBRARIES -- COST CONTROL
Smith, G. S. Cost control for nonprofits in crisis **025.1**

LIBRARIES -- COST EFFECTIVENESS
Smith, G. S. Cost control for nonprofits in crisis **025.1**

LIBRARIES -- CULTURAL PROGRAMS
The artist's library **021.2**

LIBRARIES -- DESTRUCTION AND PILLAGE
Báez, F. A universal history of the destruction of books **900**

LIBRARIES -- DESTRUCTION AND PILLAGE -- MALI -- TOMBOUCTOU
Hammer, J. The bad-ass librarians of Timbuktu **025.8**

LIBRARIES -- EQUIPMENT AND SUPPLIES
See also Furniture

LIBRARIES -- EVALUATION
Hill, C. Inside, outside, and online **021.2**

LIBRARIES -- EXHIBITIONS
Phillips, S. P. Great displays for your library step by step **021.7**

LIBRARIES -- FINANCE See Library finance

LIBRARIES -- FORECASTING

LIBRARIES --
Woodward, J. The transformed library **020**

LIBRARIES -- GOVERNMENT POLICY
See also Social policy

LIBRARIES -- HANDBOOKS, MANUALS, ETC.
Stanley, M. J. Managing library employees **023**

LIBRARIES -- INFORMATION TECHNOLOGY
Woodward, J. The transformed library **020**

LIBRARIES -- INFORMATION TECHNOLOGY -- UNITED STATES -- FINANCE
MacKellar, P. H. Writing successful technology grant proposals **025.1**

LIBRARIES -- INFORMATION TECHNOLOGY.
More technology for the rest of us **025**

LIBRARIES -- LAW AND LEGISLATION
See also Law; Legislation

LIBRARIES -- LIGHTING
See also Lighting

LIBRARIES -- MANAGEMENT
Laughlin, S. The quality library **025.1**

LIBRARIES -- MARKETING
Marketing your library **021.7**

LIBRARIES -- MISCELLANEA
Johnson, A. Improbable libraries **027**

LIBRARIES -- ORDER DEPARTMENT See Libraries -- Acquisitions

LIBRARIES -- PICTORIAL WORKS
Johnson, A. Improbable libraries **027**

LIBRARIES -- PROBLEMS, EXERCISES, ETC
The artist's library **021.2**

LIBRARIES -- PUBLIC RELATIONS
Marketing your library **021.7**

LIBRARIES -- PUBLIC RELATIONS
See also Libraries and community

LIBRARIES -- SAFETY MEASURES
Kahn, M. B. Disaster response and planning for libraries **025.8**

LIBRARIES -- SAFETY MEASURES -- PLANNING
Kahn, M. B. Disaster response and planning for libraries **025.8**

LIBRARIES -- SOCIAL ASPECTS
The artist's library **021.2**

LIBRARIES -- SPECIAL COLLECTIONS
Evans, G. E. Collection management basics **025.2**
Pattee, A. S. Developing library collections for today's young adults **027.62**
Singer, C. A. Fundamentals of Managing Reference Collections **025.2**

LIBRARIES -- SPECIAL COLLECTIONS -- AUDIOBOOKS
Grover, S. Listening to learn **372.4**
Saricks, J. G. Read on--audiobooks **011**

LIBRARIES -- SPECIAL COLLECTIONS -- ELECTRONIC BOOKS
Building and managing e-book collections **025.2**

Johnson, P. Developing and managing electronic collections **025.2**

Laguardia, C. Marketing your library's electronic resources **025.2**

LIBRARIES -- SPECIAL COLLECTIONS -- ELECTRONIC BOOKS

Building and managing e-book collections **025.2**

No shelf required 2 **070.5**

LIBRARIES -- SPECIAL COLLECTIONS -- ELECTRONIC INFORMATION RESOURCES

Evans, G. E. Collection management basics **025.2**

Johnson, P. Developing and managing electronic collections **025.2**

Laguardia, C. Marketing your library's electronic resources **025.2**

Managing Electronic Resources **025.1**

LIBRARIES -- SPECIAL COLLECTIONS -- GRAPHIC NOVELS

Alpert, A. Read on-- graphic novels **016**

Brenner, R. E. Understanding manga and anime **025.2**

Goldsmith, F. The readers' advisory guide to graphic novels **025.2**

Graphic novels beyond the basics **025.2**

Karp, J. Graphic novels in your school library **741.5**

Serchay, D. S. The librarian's guide to graphic novels for adults **025.2**

LIBRARIES -- SPECIAL COLLECTIONS -- POPULAR CULTURE

Brookover, S. Pop goes the library **021.2**

LIBRARIES -- SPECIAL COLLECTIONS -- REFERENCE SOURCES

Singer, C. A. Fundamentals of Managing Reference Collections **025.2**

LIBRARIES -- SPECIAL COLLECTIONS -- SEXUAL MINORITIES

Naidoo, J. C. Rainbow family collections **028.1**

LIBRARIES -- STATISTICS

See also Statistics

LIBRARIES -- TECHNOLOGICAL INNOVATIONS.

More technology for the rest of us **025**

LIBRARIES -- UNITED STATES

Flowers, S. Evaluating teen services and programs **027.62**

LIBRARIES -- UNITED STATES -- MARKETING -- CASE STUDIES

Laguardia, C. Marketing your library's electronic resources **025.2**

LIBRARIES -- UNITED STATES -- SPECIAL COLLECTIONS -- HISTORICAL FICTION

Baker, J. S. The readers' advisory guide to historical fiction **026**

LIBRARIES AND AFRICAN AMERICANS

See also African Americans; Library services

LIBRARIES AND CHILDREN *See* Children's libraries

LIBRARIES AND COMMUNITY

The artist's library **021.2**

Brookover, S. Pop goes the library **021.2**

The frugal librarian **025.1**

Hill, C. Inside, outside, and online **021.2**

Imhoff, K. R. Library contests **021.7**

Jerrard, J. Crisis in employment **025.5**

Landau, H. B. The small public library survival guide **025.1**

Lankes, R. D. The atlas of new librarianship **020**

Librarians as community partners **021.2**

Ross, C. S. The pleasures of reading **028**

LIBRARIES AND COMMUNITY

See also Libraries

LIBRARIES AND COMMUNITY.

Ross, C. S. Reading matters **028**

LIBRARIES AND ELECTRONIC PUBLISHING

Building and managing e-book collections **025.2**

Johnson, P. Developing and managing electronic collections **025.2**

LIBRARIES AND ELECTRONIC PUBLISHING

See also Electronic publishing; Libraries and publishers

LIBRARIES AND HISPANIC AMERICANS

Moller, S. C. Library service to Spanish speaking patrons **027.6**

LIBRARIES AND JUVENILE DELINQUENTS -- UNITED STATES

Sweeney, J. Literacy **027.62**

LIBRARIES AND PRESCHOOL CHILDREN -- UNITED STATES

Ghoting, S. N. STEP into storytime **027.62**

LIBRARIES AND PRISONS -- UNITED STATES

Sweeney, J. Literacy **027.62**

LIBRARIES AND PUBLISHERS

See also Publishers and publishing

LIBRARIES AND READERS *See* Library services

LIBRARIES AND SCHOOLS

See also Libraries; Schools

LIBRARIES AND SEXUAL MINORITIES

Naidoo, J. C. Rainbow family collections **028.1**

LIBRARIES AND SEXUAL MINORITIES -- UNITED STATES

Naidoo, J. C. Rainbow family collections **028.1**

LIBRARIES AND SOCIETY

Defending professionalism **020**

Johnson, M. This book is overdue! **020**

Woodward, J. The transformed library **020**

LIBRARIES AND STUDENTS

Our new public, a changing clientele **025.1**

Vaillancourt, R. J. Bare bones young adult services **027.62**

LIBRARIES AND TEENAGERS -- UNITED

STATES

Eagle, M. Answering teens' tough questions **027.62**

Flowers, S. Evaluating teen services and programs **027.62**

Pattee, A. S. Developing library collections for today's young adults **027.62**

LIBRARIES AND THE INTERNET

Johnson, M. This book is overdue! **020**

McClure, C. R. Public libraries and internet service roles **025.04**

More technology for the rest of us **025**

Woodward, J. The transformed library **020**

Libraries Unlimited library and information science text series

Perrault, A. H. Information resources in the humanities and the arts **016**

Libraries Unlimited library management collection [series]

Our new public, a changing clientele **025.1**

LIBRARY ADMINISTRATION

Hill, C. Inside, outside, and online **021.2**

Laughlin, S. The quality library **025.1**

Matthews, J. R. Scorecards for results **027.4**

Our new public, a changing clientele **025.1**

LIBRARY ADMINISTRATION See Libraries -- Administration

LIBRARY ADMINISTRATION -- DECISION MAKING

Smith, G. S. Cost control for nonprofits in crisis **025.1**

LIBRARY ADMINISTRATION -- PROBLEMS, EXERCISES, ETC

Mosley, P. A. The challenge of library management **025.1**

Library and information science text series

Berard, G. L. Science and technology resources **025.5**

Evans, G. E. Collection management basics **025.2**

Evans, G. E. Introduction to library public services **025.5**

LIBRARY CIRCULATION

Evans, G. E. Introduction to library public services **025.5**

LIBRARY CIRCULATION

See also Library services

LIBRARY CLASSIFICATION

See also Cataloging; Classification; Library technical processes

LIBRARY CONSORTIA See Library cooperation

Library contests. Imhoff, K. R. **021.7**

LIBRARY COOPERATION

Butler, P. M. Joint libraries **027**

LIBRARY COOPERATION

See also Libraries

LIBRARY DIRECTORS

Gregorian, V. The road to home **92**

LIBRARY EDUCATION

Core technology competencies for librarians and library staff **020**

Lewis, L. K. The complete guide to acquisitions management **025.2**

Reference reborn **025.5**

LIBRARY EDUCATION

See also Education; Professional education

LIBRARY EDUCATION -- CURRICULA

See also Education -- Curricula

LIBRARY EXTENSION

See also Library services

LIBRARY FINANCE

The frugal librarian **025.1**

Landau, H. B. The small public library survival guide **025.1**

Wichman, E. T. Librarian's guide to passive programming **025.5**

LIBRARY FINANCE

See also Finance; Libraries -- Administration

LIBRARY FINANCE -- UNITED STATES

Smith, G. S. Cost control for nonprofits in crisis **025.1**

Library in a book [series]

Ferro, J. Prisons **365**

Yount, L. Right to die and euthanasia **179.7**

LIBRARY INFORMATION NETWORKS

See also Information networks; Library cooperation

Library mashups. **020**

LIBRARY MATERIALS See Library resources

LIBRARY MATERIALS -- CONSERVATION AND RESTORATION

Rethinking collection development and management **025.2**

LIBRARY MATERIALS -- CONSERVATION AND RESTORATION -- PLANNING

Kahn, M. B. Disaster response and planning for libraries **025.8**

Library of African-American biography [series]

Smock, R. W. Booker T. Washington **92**

Library of America [series]

American earth **333.72**

Leopold, A. A Sand County almanac & other writings on ecology & conservation **508**

Liebling, A. J. World War II writings **940.54**

O'Neil, E. Complete plays **812**

Library of Black America [series]

Marshall, T. Thurgood Marshall **347**

Library of Congress

Conaway, J. America's library **027.5**

Virga, V. Eyes of the nation **973**

LIBRARY OF CONGRESS

Conaway, J. America's library **027.5**

LIBRARY OF CONGRESS

See also Libraries

Library of contemporary thought [series]

Carter, J. The virtues of aging   **305.26**

LIBRARY POLICIES *See* Libraries -- Administration

LIBRARY REFERENCE SERVICES *See* Reference services (Libraries)

LIBRARY RESOURCES

Bibliocraft   **745.5**

Laguardia, C. Marketing your library's electronic resources   **025.2**

No shelf required 2   **070.5**

LIBRARY RESOURCES

    See also Libraries

LIBRARY RESOURCES -- CONSERVATION AND RESTORATION

Kahn, M. B. Disaster response and planning for libraries   **025.8**

LIBRARY RESOURCES -- PRESERVATION

    See Library resources -- Conservation and restoration

LIBRARY SCHOOLS

    See also Library education

LIBRARY SCIENCE

The 21st-century black librarian in America   **020**

Intellectual Freedom Manual   **025.2**

Johnson, M. This book is overdue!   **020**

Lankes, R. D. The atlas of new librarianship   **020**

Pinnell-Stephens, J. Protecting intellectual freedom in your public library   **025.2**

Reference reborn   **025.5**

Sears List of Subject Headings   **025.4**

LIBRARY SCIENCE

    See also Documentation; Information science

LIBRARY SCIENCE -- DICTIONARIES

ALA glossary of library and information science   **020**

LIBRARY SCIENCE -- PHILOSOPHY

Woodward, J. The transformed library   **020**

LIBRARY SCIENCE -- STUDY AND TEACHING *See* Library education

Library service to Spanish speaking patrons. Moller, S. C.   **027.6**

LIBRARY SERVICES

Braafladt, K. Technology and literacy   **027.62**

Eagle, M. Answering teens' tough questions   **027.62**

Evans, G. E. Introduction to library public services   **025.5**

Flowers, S. Evaluating teen services and programs   **027.62**

Hernon, P. Assessing service quality   **025.5**

Orr, C. Crash course in readers' advisory   **025.5**

Pattee, A. S. Developing library collections for today's young adults   **027.62**

Wichman, E. T. Librarian's guide to passive programming   **025.5**

LIBRARY USERS -- CASE STUDIES

The artist's library   **021.2**

The **library's** crisis communications planner. Thenell, J.   **021.7**

LIBRETTISTS

Rose, M. The birth of an opera   **782.1**

LIBRETTOS

    See also Books

LIBYA -- HISTORY -- CIVIL WAR, 2011-

Chorin, E. Exit the colonel   **961.204**

LICENSES

    See also Commercial law; Public administration

Licht, Aliza

Leave Your Mark   **650.1**

Lichtblau, Eric

The Nazis next door   **324.1**

Lichtenstein, Nelson

State of the Union: a century of American labor   **331**

Lichtman, Flora

Palca, J. Annoying   **612.8**

Liddell, Eric, 1902-1945.
About
Hamilton, D. For the Glory   **92**

Liddon, Angela

The oh she glows cookbook   **641.5**

Lidia cooks from the heart of Italy. Bastianich, L.   **641.5**

Lidia's commonsense Italian cooking. Bastianich, L. M.   **641.59**

Lidia's family table. Bastianich, L. M.   **641.5**

Lidia's favorite recipes. Bastianich, L. M.   **641.594**

Lidia's Italian-American kitchen. Bastianich, L.   **641.59**

Lidia's mastering the art of Italian cuisine. Bastianich, L. M.   **641.594**

LIE DETECTORS AND DETECTION

    See also Criminal investigation; Medical jurisprudence; Truthfulness and falsehood

Lieber, Ron

The Opposite of Spoiled   **332.024**

Lieberman, Daniel, 1964-

The story of the human body   **612**

Lieberman, Jeffrey A.

Shrinks   **616.89**

Lieberman, Matthew D., 1970-

Social   **302**

Liebling, A. J. (Abbott Joseph), 1904-1963

Liebling, A. J. The sweet science   **796.83**

World War II writings   **940.54**

Liebman, Hollis Lance

Encyclopedia of Exercise Anatomy   **613.7**

Liebman, James S.

The wrong Carlos   **364.152**

Liedtke, Walter A.

Vermeer and the Delft school   **759.9**

Lies across America. Loewen, J. W.   **973**

Lieven, Anatol
Chechnya 947.086
Pakistan 954.91
Lieven, D. C. B.
Russia against Napoleon 940.2
Life. Richards, K. 92
Life. Fortey, R. A. 576.8
Life. Barrington, R. 578.4
LIFE
Egan, K. On living 170.44
Kinsley, M. Old age 814.54
Lepore, J. The mansion of happiness 973
Tippett, K. Becoming Wise 158.1
Toomey, D. Weird Life 571
We Have Only This Life to Live 848
Life & times [series]
Dry, S. Curie 92
LIFE (BIOLOGY)
Lovelock, J. The ages of Gaia 570.1
Margulis, L. What is life? 570.1
Ward, P. D. Life as we do not know it 576.8
LIFE (BIOLOGY)
 See also Biology
**LIFE (BIOLOGY) -- SOCIAL ASPECTS -- UNIT-
ED STATES -- HISTORY**
Lepore, J. The mansion of happiness 973
LIFE -- ORIGIN
Billings, L. Five billion years of solitude 576.8
Cobb, M. Life's Greatest Secret 572.8
Kirschvink, J. A new history of life 576.8
McFadden, J. Life on the Edge 572
Rutherford, A. Creation 576.8
Scharf, C. The Copernicus complex 523.1
LIFE -- ORIGIN
 See also Evolution
**LIFE -- RELIGIOUS ASPECTS -- CHRISTIAN-
ITY**
Lamott, A. Small victories 248
**LIFE -- SOCIAL ASPECTS -- UNITED STATES
-- HISTORY**
Lepore, J. The mansion of happiness 973
Life after college. Blake, J. 646.7
Life after death. Echols, D. 364.66
LIFE AFTER DEATH *See* Future life; Immortal-
ity
Life after life. Moody, R. A. 133.9
Life and death in Shanghai. Cheng, N. 92
Life and death in the Third Reich. Fritzsche,
P. 943.086
The **life** and legend of Leadbelly. Wolfe, C. K. 92
The **life** and love of dogs. Blackwell, L. 636.7
The **life** and times of Little Richard. White, C. 92
The **life** and times of Pancho Villa. Katz, F. 972.08
The **life** and times of the thunderbolt kid. Bryson,
B. 92
Life as we do not know it. Ward, P. D. 576.8

Life at the Speed of Light. Venter, J. C. 303.48
Life at the zoo: behind the scenes with the animal
doctors. Robinson, P. T. 590.73
LIFE CHANGE EVENTS
James, E. Paris in love 92
**LIFE CHANGE EVENTS -- PSYCHOLOGICAL
ASPECTS**
Kinsley, M. Old age 814.54
LIFE CYCLE, HUMAN
Pepper, C. The seven pearls of financial wis-
dom 332.024
**LIFE CYCLE, HUMAN -- SOCIAL ASPECTS --
UNITED STATES -- HISTORY**
Lepore, J. The mansion of happiness 973
LIFE CYCLES *See* Life cycles (Biology)
LIFE CYCLES (BIOLOGY)
Heinrich, B. Life everlasting 591.7
LIFE CYCLES (BIOLOGY)
 See also Biology; Cycles; Life (Biology)
Life everlasting. Heinrich, B. 591.7
LIFE EXPECTANCY
 See also Age; Life; Vital statistics
Life from scratch. Martin, S. 92
LIFE HISTORIES *See* Biography
Life in a medieval castle. Gies, J. 940.2
Life in a medieval city. Gies, J. 940.1
Life in a medieval village. Gies, F. 940.1
Life in Balance. Hay, D. 641.563
Life in cold blood. Attenborough, D. 597.9
A **life** in letters. Fitzgerald, F. S. 813
Life in motion. Copeland, M. 92
Life in photographs. McCartney, L. 779
Life in rewind. Murphy, T. W. 92
A **life** in secrets. Helm, S. 92
Life in the treetops. Lowman, M. 577.34
A **life** in the twentieth century. Schlesinger, A.
M. 92
Life in the undergrowth. Attenborough, D. 592
Life in year one. Korb, S. 933
LIFE INSURANCE
Schultz, E. Retirement heist 331.2
LIFE INSURANCE
 See also Insurance
Life is good. Jacobs, B. 650.1
LIFE IS GOOD (FIRM)
Jacobs, B. Life is good 650.1
Life is not an accident. Williams, J. 92
Life itself. Ebert, R. 92
Life lessons. Kubler-Ross, E. 170
Life list. Gentile, O. 92
The **life** of a leaf. Vogel, S. 575.5
The **life** of Billy Yank. Wiley, B. I. 973.7
The **life** of birds. Attenborough, D. 598
The **life** of Charlotte Bronte. Gaskell, E. C. 92
The **life** of David. Pinsky, R. 92
The **life** of Elizabeth I. Weir, A. 942.05

The **life** of Isaac Newton. Westfall, R. S.   **92**

A **life** of James Boswell. Martin, P.   **828**

The **life** of Johnny Reb. Wiley, B. I.   **973.7**

A **life** of Jung. Hayman, R.   **150.19**

The **life** of Kingsley Amis. Leader, Z.   **92**

The **life** of Langston Hughes Volume I: 1902-1941. Rampersad, A.   **92**

The **life** of Langston Hughes Volume II: 1941-1967. Rampersad, A.   **818**

The **life** of Mendelssohn. Mercer-Taylor, P. J.   **92**

The **life** of Samuel Johnson. Boswell, J.   **92**

The **Life** of Saul Bellow. Leader, Z.   **92**

The **life** of super-Earths. Sasselov, D.   **576.8**

The **life** of the automobile. Parissien, S.   **629.222**

The **life** of the drama. Bentley, E.   **809**

The **life** of W.B. Yeats. Brown, T.   **821**

The **life** of William Apess, Pequot. Gura, P. F.   **92**

Life on Mars. Smith, T. K.   **811**

LIFE ON OTHER PLANETS

   Catling, D. C. Astrobiology   **576.8**

   Davies, P. C. W. The eerie silence   **576.8**

   Kaufman, M. First contact   **576.8**

   Sasselov, D. The life of super-Earths   **576.8**

   Ward, P. D. Life as we do not know it   **576.8**

LIFE ON OTHER PLANETS

   See also Astronomy; Planets; Universe

Life on the Edge. McFadden, J.   **572**

Life on the ice. Smith, R.   **998**

LIFE QUALITY *See* Quality of life

LIFE SCIENCES

   Kirschvink, J. A new history of life   **576.8**

   Lamothe, M. The where, the why, and the how **502**

LIFE SCIENCES

   See also Science

LIFE SKILLS

   Bried, E. How to sew a button   **640**

   Covey, S. R. First things first   **158**

   Dawson, P. Smart but scattered   **649**

   Ellenberg, J. How not to be wrong   **510**

   Greitens, E. Resilience   **155.2**

   Lang, S. For Tamara   **C**

LIFE SKILLS

   See also Interpersonal relations; Success

LIFE SKILLS -- HANDBOOKS, MANUALS, ETC.

   Bernard, W. Up, down, all-around stitch dictionary   **746.43**

   Bigon, M. The Morrow guide to knots   **623.88**

   Blake, J. Life after college   **646.7**

   Morgan, G. Undecided   **371.4**

   Richardson, S. Sarah style   **747**

   Robert, H. M. Robert's rules of order newly revised   **060.4**

   Robert, H. M. Robert's rules of order, newly revised, in brief   **060.4**

   Stiles, D. Backyard Building   **690**

LIFE SKILLS GUIDES *See* Life skills

Life so far. Friedan, B.   **92**

LIFE SPAN PROLONGATION *See* Longevity

Life stories.   **920**

Life strategies. McGraw, P. C.   **158**

LIFE STYLES *See* Lifestyles

LIFE SUPPORT SYSTEMS (MEDICAL ENVIRONMENT)

   See also Hospitals; Terminal care

Life upon these shores. Gates, H. L.   **305.8**

A **life** well played. Palmer, A.   **92**

Life Without a Recipe. Abu-Jaber, D.   **92**

The **life** you save may be your own. Elie, P.   **810**

Life's a dream. Calderon de la Barca, P.   **862**

Life's Greatest Secret. Cobb, M.   **572.8**

A **life's** work. Cusk, R.   **306.874**

Life, animated. Suskind, R.   **618.92**

LIFE, FUTURE *See* Future life

Life, myth, and art in Ancient Rome. Allan, T.   **937**

The **life-changing** magic of tidying up.   **648**

Life: World War 2.   **779**

LIFEGUARDS

   See also Water safety

LIFELONG EDUCATION *See* Adult education; Continuing education

LIFESAVING

   See also Rescue work

The **lifespan** of a fact. D'Agata, J.   **808.02**

LIFESTYLES

   Fondin, M. S. The wheel of healing with ayurveda   **615.5**

   Wann, D. The new normal   **306**

LIFESTYLES

   See also Human behavior; Manners and customs

Lift. Kunitz, D.   **613.7**

Lift every voice. Sullivan, P.   **323.1**

LIFT-THE-FLAP BOOKS

   See also Picture books for children; Toy and movable books

Lifton, Robert Jay

   Hiroshima in America   **940.54**

   The Nazi doctors   **940.53**

LIGHT

   Feynman, R. P. QED   **539.7**

   Gribbin, J. R. Schrodinger's kittens and the search for reality   **530.1**

   Park, D. The fire within the eye   **535**

LIGHT

   See also Electromagnetic waves; Physics

Light & shade. Clark, T.   **811**

The **light** of the world. Alexander, E.   **92**

Light on life. Iyengar, B. K. S.   **294**

LIGHT POLLUTION

   Bogard, P. The end of night   **551.56**

LIGHT, ELECTRIC *See* Electric lighting

Light, Michael
100 suns, 1945-1962 **355.8**
Lighten up. Walsh, P. **332.024**
Lighthead. Hayes, T. **811**
LIGHTHOUSES
See also Navigation
LIGHTING
Brox, J. Brilliant **621.32**
LIGHTING
See also Interior design; Light
LIGHTING -- PHYSIOLOGICAL ASPECTS
Bogard, P. The end of night **551.56**
Lighting the way. Schiff, K. G. **920**
The **lightless** sky. Ghouri, N. **958.104**
Lightman, Alan P., 1948-
The discoveries **509**
About
Lightman, A. P. Screening room **92**
Lightman, Marjorie
Yans-McLaughlin, V. Ellis Island and the peopling
of America **325**
Lightnin' Hopkins. Govenar, A. B. **92**
LIGHTNING
See also Electricity; Meteorology; Thunder-
storms
The **lights** of Pointe-Noire. Mabanckou, A. **848**
Like a lampshade in a whorehouse. Diller, P. **92**
Like dreamers. Halevi, Y. K. **356**
Like men of war. Trudeau, N. A. **973.7**
The **like** switch. Karlins, M. **158.2**
Lil Wayne, 1982-
Gone 'til November **782.421**
Lilienfeld, Scott O.
Brainwashed **612.8**
Lillian Hellman. Martinson, D. **92**
Lillien, Lisa
Hungry girl clean & hungry **641.302**
Lim, Allen
The feed zone cookbook **641.5**
Feed zone portables **641.5**
Lima, Manuel
The book of trees **001.2**
Limber, Susan P.
(jt. auth) Kowalski, R. M. Cyberbullying **302.34**
**LIMBIC SYSTEM -- DISEASES -- PATIENTS --
UNITED STATES -- BIOGRAPHY**
Cahalan, S. Brain on fire **616.8**
LIME
See also Fertilizers; Minerals
LIMITATION OF ARMAMENT *See* Arms con-
trol
LIMITED LIABILITY COMPANIES
See also Corporation law; Corporations
Limón, Ada, 1976-
Limon, A. Bright dead things **811**
LIMULUS POLYPHEMUS -- CONSERVATION

Fortey, R. Horseshoe crabs and velvet worms **595**
Lincoln. Donald, D. H. **92**
Lincoln and Douglas. Guelzo, A. C. **973.6**
Lincoln and his admirals. Symonds, C. L. **92**
Lincoln and the Jews. Sarna, J. D. **973.7**
Lincoln and the power of the press. Holzer, H. **973.7**
The **Lincoln** anthology. **92**
Lincoln at Gettysburg. Wills, G. **973.7**
**LINCOLN CENTER FOR THE PERFORMING
ARTS**
Levy, R. They told me not to take that job **792.09**
Lincoln president-elect. Holzer, H. **92**
Lincoln's autocrat. Marvel, W. **92**
LINCOLN'S BIRTHDAY
See also Holidays
Lincoln's code. Witt, J. F. **343**
Lincoln's Gamble. Brewster, T. **973.7**
Lincoln's Greatest Case. McGinty, B. **346**
Lincoln's melancholy. Shenk, J. W. **92**
Lincoln's sanctuary. Pinsker, M. **92**
Lincoln, Abraham
Speeches and writings, 1832-1858 **973.5**
Speeches and writings, 1859-1865 **973.7**
LINCOLN, ABRAHAM, 1809-1865
See also Presidents -- United States
Lincoln, Abraham, 1809-1865
About
Berg, S. W. 38 nooses **973.7**
Blumenthal, S. A self-made man **92**
Boritt, G. S. The Gettysburg gospel **973.7**
Brewster, T. Lincoln's Gamble **973.7**
Brookhiser, R. Founders' son **92**
Burlingame, M. Abraham Lincoln **92**
Carwardine, R. Lincoln: a life of purpose and pow-
er **92**
Craughwell, T. J. Stealing Lincoln's body **973.7**
Donald, D. H. Lincoln **92**
Egerton, D. R. Year of meteors **973.7**
Foner, E. The fiery trial **973.7**
Founders' son **92**
Fredrickson, G. M. Big enough to be inconsis-
tent **973.7**
Gienapp, W. E. Abraham Lincoln and Civil War
America **973.7**
Goodwin, D. K. Team of rivals **92**
Gopnik, A. Angels and ages **973.7**
Guelzo, A. C. Lincoln and Douglas **973.6**
Hodes, M. Mourning Lincoln **973.7**
Hofstadter, R. The American political tradition, and
the men who made it **973**
Holzer, H. A just and generous nation **973.7**
Holzer, H. Lincoln and the power of the press **973.7**
Holzer, H. Lincoln president-elect **92**
Keneally, T. Abraham Lincoln **92**
Kunhardt, P. B. Looking for Lincoln **92**
The Lincoln anthology **92**

Lind, M. What Lincoln believed   92
Marvel, W. Lincoln's autocrat   92
McGinty, B. Lincoln's Greatest Case   346
McPherson, J. M. Tried by war   92
McPherson, J. M. Abraham Lincoln   92
McPherson, J. M. Abraham Lincoln and the second American Revolution   973.7
McPherson, J. M. Drawn with the sword   973.7
McPherson, J. M. This mighty scourge   973.7
Our Lincoln   92
Paludan, P. S. The presidency of Abraham Lincoln   973.7
Pinsker, M. Lincoln's sanctuary   92
Sandburg, C. Abraham Lincoln: The prairie years and The war years   92
Sarna, J. D. Lincoln and the Jews   973.7
Shenk, J. W. Lincoln's melancholy   92
Slotkin, R. Long Road to Antietam   973.7
Swanson, J. L. Manhunt   364.152
Symonds, C. L. Lincoln and his admirals   92
Van Sciver, N. The Hypo   92
Walsh, J. E. Moonlight   345
White, R. C. A. Lincoln   92
White, R. C. The eloquent president: a portrait of Lincoln through his words   92
Wills, G. Lincoln at Gettysburg   973.7
Wilson, E. Patriotic gore   810
Witt, J. F. Lincoln's code   343

Lincoln, Abraham, 1809-1865. Gettysburg address
About
Puleo, S. American treasures   973

Lincoln, Don
The large hadron collider   539.7

Lincoln, Mary Todd, 1818-1882
About
Baker, J. H. Mary Todd Lincoln   92
Clinton, C. Mrs. Lincoln   92

LINCOLN-DOUGLAS DEBATES, 1858
Guelzo, A. C. Lincoln and Douglas   973.6
Lincoln, A. Speeches and writings, 1832-1858   973.5
Lincoln: a life of purpose and power. Carwardine, R.   92

Lind, Michael, 1962-
Land of promise   330.973
Vietnam, the necessary war   959.704
What Lincoln believed   92

Linda Goodman's star signs. Goodman, L.   130
Linda Goodman's sun signs. Goodman, L.   133.5

Lindberg, Christine A.
(ed) New Oxford American dictionary   423
(comp) Oxford American writer's thesaurus   423
The **Lindbergh** child. Geary, R.   364.1

Lindbergh, Anne Morrow, 1906-2001
About
Hertog, S. Anne Morrow Lindbergh   92

Lindbergh, R. Under a wing   92
Winters, K. C. Anne Morrow Lindbergh   92

Lindbergh, Ben
(jt. auth) Miller, S. The Only Rule Is It Has to Work   796.357

Lindbergh, Charles A. (Charles Augustus), 1902-1974
About
Geary, R. The Lindbergh child   364.1
Groom, W. The aviators   920
Jackson, J. Atlantic fever   629.130
Kessner, T. The flight of the century   92
Lindbergh, C. The spirit of St. Louis   629.13
Lindbergh, R. Under a wing   92
Olson, L. Those angry days   940.53

Lindbergh, Reeve
About
Lindbergh, R. Under a wing   92

Lindblom, Ken
(jt. auth) Dunn, P. A. Grammar rants   428

Linden, Dana Wechsler
Preemies   618.92

Linden, David J.
Touch   612.8

Linden, Eugene
The ragged edge of the world   303.4
The winds of change   551.6

Lindhout, Amanda
About
Corbett, S. A house in the sky   92

Lindner, Lawrence
Ali, K. Fighting weight   92

Lindsay, Sarah
Twigs & knucklebones   811

Lindsay, Virginia
Sewing to sell   646.2

Lindsey, Robert
(ed) Plays The complete plays   822

Lindström, Martin
Small Data   658.8

Lindstrom, Nicole
(jt. auth) Krasno, J. Wanderlust   613.7

LINE ENGRAVING *See* Engraving
A **line** in the sand. Barr, J.   956
The **line** upon a wind. Mostert, N.   940.2

Line, Scott
(ed) The Merck veterinary manual   636.089

LINEAR ALGEBRA
   See also Algebra; Mathematical analysis

LINEAR EQUATIONS
   See also Equations

LINEAR SYSTEM THEORY *See* System analysis

Lineberry, Cate
The secret rescue   940.54

LINEN
   See also Fabrics; Fibers

Linett, Andrea
The cool factor   **746.92**
Ling, Kate
(jt. auth) Cross, C. The baby book   **649.122**
Lingo. Dorren, G.   **306.44**
LINGUISTIC INFORMANTS
Kroeber, T. Ishi in two worlds   **92**
LINGUISTIC SCIENCE *See* Linguistics
LINGUISTICS
Barlow, J. The story of Spanish   **460**
Crystal, D. The Cambridge encyclopedia of language   **400**
Crystal, D. How language works   **401**
Deutscher, G. Through the language glass   **410**
Jurafsky, D. The language of food   **641.3**
LINGUISTICS
See also Language and languages
LINGUISTS
Bryson, B. The life and times of the thunderbolt kid   **92**
Chen, D. Colors of the mountain   **92**
Chen, D. Sounds of the river   **951.05**
Everett, D. L. Don't sleep, there are snakes   **305.8**
Li, C. N. The bitter sea   **92**
Sabar, A. My father's paradise   **305.8**
LINGUISTS -- IRAQ -- BIOGRAPHY
Fair, E. Consequence   **956.704**
Link, Donald
(jt. auth) Disbrowe, P. Down south   **641.59**
Real Cajun   **641.5**
Link, Greg
(jt. auth) Covey, S. M. R. Smart trust   **174**
Link, Mardi Jo
The Drummond Girls   **92**
(jt. auth) Link, M. Bootstrapper   **92**
Link, Tim
Talking with dogs and cats   **636.088**
Linklater, Andro
An artist in treason   **92**
Owning the earth   **333.3**
Linklater, Kristin
Freeing the natural voice   **808.5**
Linn, Edward
Hitter: the life and turmoils of Ted Williams   **92**
Linn, Susan
The case for make believe   **155.4**
Linnaeus, the compleat naturalist. Blunt, W.   **92**
Linné, Carl von, 1707-1778
About
Blunt, W. Linnaeus, the compleat naturalist   **92**
LINOLEUM BLOCK PRINTING
See also Printing; Prints
LINOTYPE
See also Printing; Type and type-founding; Typesetting
Lintala, Janet

The un-prescription for Autism   **616.85**
Linus Pauling in his own words. Pauling, L. C. **081**
Lion of Hollywood. Eyman, S.   **92**
LIONS
Adamson, J. Born free   **599.75**
The **lions** of Iwo Jima. Haynes, F.   **940.54**
Lions of the West. Morgan, R.   **920**
LIPIZZANER HORSE -- AUSTRIA -- HISTORY -- 20TH CENTURY
Letts, E. The perfect horse   **940.54**
Lippincott, Jenifer Marshall
7 things your teenager won't tell you   **649**
Lipscomb, Suzannah
A Journey Through Tudor England   **942.05**
Lipsky, David
Absolutely American   **355**
Lipstadt, Deborah E.
The Eichmann trial   **345**
About
Denying the Holocaust   **940.53**
Guttenplan, D. D. The Holocaust on trial   **940.53**
History on trial   **940.53**
Lipstick jihad. Moaveni, A.   **92**
Lipton, Judith Eve
Barash, D. P. The myth of monogamy   **306.7**
LIQUEURS
Jones, C. The Brooklyn bartender   **641.874**
LIQUEURS *See* Liquors
Liquid intelligence. Arnold, D.   **641.87**
LIQUIDS
See also Fluid mechanics; Physics
LIQUOR PROBLEM *See* Alcoholism; Drinking of alcoholic beverages
LIQUORS
Watman, M. Chasing the white dog   **363.4**
LIQUORS
See also Alcoholic beverages; Beverages
LIQUORS AND LIQUEURS *See* Liquors
Lispector, Clarice, 1925-1977
About
Moser, B. Why this world   **92**
Listen to this. Ross, A.   **780**
Listen! Mayakovsky, V.   **891.7**
LISTENING
See also Attention; Educational psychology
Listening to learn. Grover, S.   **372.4**
Listening to Prozac. Kramer, P. D.   **616.85**
Listening to stone. Herrera, H.   **92**
Lister, Adrian
Mammoths   **569**
Liston, Sonny, 1932-1970
About
Assael, S. The murder of Sonny Liston   **796.83**
LISTS
Gawande, A. The checklist manifesto   **610.28**
Liszt, Franz, 1811-1886

About

Schonberg, H. C. The great pianists   **920**

Lit. Karr, M.   **92**

Litchfield, Michael W.
Renovation   **643**

Litchfield, Michael W.
Renovation   **643**

Literacy. Sweeney, J.   **027.62**

LITERACY
Adolescent literacy in the academic disciplines **428**

Grover, S. Listening to learn   **372.4**

Newman, N. Raising passionate readers   **649.58**

Sweeney, J. Literacy   **027.62**

LITERACY
See also Education

LITERACY -- SOCIAL ASPECTS -- UNITED STATES
Sweeney, J. Literacy   **027.62**

LITERACY -- STUDY AND TEACHING -- UNITED STATES
Grover, S. Listening to learn   **372.4**

LITERACY PROGRAMS
Braafladt, K. Technology and literacy   **027.62**

LITERARY AGENTS -- UNITED STATES -- BIOGRAPHY
Lerner, B. The bridge ladies   **92**

Ninety days   **362.29**

LITERARY CHARACTERS *See* Characters and characteristics in literature

LITERARY COLLECTIONS *See* Anthologies; Literature -- Collections

Literary conversations series
Conversations with Nadine Gordimer   **823**

Literary criticism. James, H.   **809**

LITERARY CRITICISM *See* Criticism; Literature -- History and criticism

LITERARY CRITICS
Amis, M. Experience   **92**

Arana, M. American chica   **92**

As always, Julia   **92**

Bayley, J. Elegy for Iris   **823**

Black women writers (1950-1980)   **810**

Blight, D. W. American oracle   **973.7**

Bloom, H. The anatomy of influence   **801**

Bloom, H. The Western canon   **809**

Boswell, J. The journal of a tour to the Hebrides with Samuel Johnson   **914**

Boswell, J. The life of Samuel Johnson   **92**

Boyd, B. Vladimir Nabokov: the American years   **813**

Boyd, B. Vladimir Nabokov: the Russian years **813**

Bradford, R. Lucky him: the life of Kingsley Amis   **92**

Caldwell, G. Let's take the long way home   **92**

Carter, W. C. Marcel Proust   **843**

Coupland, D. Marshall McLuhan   **92**

Dillard, A. The writing life   **818**

Dillard, A. An American childhood   **92**

Downing, D. C. Into the region of awe   **248.2**

Eco, U. Confessions of a young novelist   **808.3**

Ellison, R. Going to the territory   **818**

Ford, P. F. Companion to Narnia   **823**

Fraser, K. Ornament and silence   **809**

Gates, H. L. Colored people   **92**

Gates, H. L. Thirteen ways of looking at a black man   **920.71**

Gillespie, C. Critical companion to Toni Morrison   **813**

Gioia, D. Can poetry matter?   **809.1**

Gordon, L. T.S. Eliot   **92**

Hartman, S. V. Lose your mother   **323**

Heaney, S. Finders keepers   **821**

Kazin, A. An American procession   **810**

Kenner, H. The Pound era   **811**

Ker, I. G. K. Chesterton   **828**

Kermode, F. An appetite for poetry   **801**

Kermode, F. Concerning E.M. Forster   **823**

Kiernan, F. Seeing Mary plain: a life of Mary McCarthy   **818**

Leader, Z. The life of Kingsley Amis   **92**

Life stories   **920**

Malcolm, J. Two lives   **92**

Martin, P. Samuel Johnson   **92**

Mendelsohn, D. The lost   **92**

Meyers, J. Samuel Johnson   **92**

Miller, L. The magician's book   **823**

Milosz, C. Legends of modernity   **891.8**

Milosz, C. To begin where I am   **891.8**

Moffat, W. A great unrecorded history   **92**

Murphy, R. E. Critical companion to T.S. Eliot **811**

My life as author and editor   **818**

Nabokov, V. V. Lectures on literature   **808.3**

Nabokov, V. V. Speak, memory   **813**

Nafisi, A. Reading Lolita in Tehran   **92**

Nafisi, A. Things I've been silent about   **92**

Parini, J. The art of teaching   **371.1**

Pierpont, C. R. Passionate minds   **810**

Rampersad, A. Ralph Ellison   **92**

Rodgers, M. E. Mencken   **92**

Rollyson, C. E. Susan Sontag   **818**

Rubin, L. D. My father's people   **920**

Said, E. W. Out of place   **92**

Said, E. W. Reflections on exile and other essays   **814**

Samet, E. D. Soldier's heart   **810**

Shattuck, R. Proust's way   **843**

Sontag, S. Reborn   **92**

Starr, W. W. Whisky, kilts, and the Loch Ness Monster   **914**

Stein, G. The autobiography of Alice B. Toklas **92**

Sutherland, J. Stephen Spender   **92**

Teachout, T. The skeptic: the life of H.L. Menck-

en 92
Treglown, J. V.S. Pritchett: a working life 92
Tytell, J. Ezra Pound 92
Vendler, H. H. Coming of age as a poet 820
Wall, C. A. Women of the Harlem Renaissance 810
Williamson, E. Borges, a life 92
Wilson, A. N. C.S. Lewis 823
Literary essays and reviews of the 1920s & 30s.
Wilson, E. 814
Literary essays and reviews of the 1930s & 40s.
Wilson, E. 814

LITERARY FORGERIES
Boller, P. F. They never said it 808.88

LITERARY FORGERIES
   See also Counterfeits and counterfeiting;
   Forgery

LITERARY FORM
Becker, D. L. Many subtle channels 840.9
The Making of a poem 821

LITERARY LANDMARKS
Bass, R. Why I came West 92
Cyclopedia of literary places 809

LITERARY LANDMARKS
   See also Historic buildings; Literature -- History and criticism

LITERARY LANDMARKS -- UNITED STATES
Anderson, W. T. Laura Ingalls Wilder country 92
Literary market place. 070.5
Literary movements for students. 809

LITERARY PROPERTY *See* Copyright; Intellectual property

LITERARY RECREATIONS
   See also Amusements

LITERARY STYLE
Becker, D. L. Many subtle channels 840.9
Max, D. T. c. Every love story is a ghost story 92

LITERARY STYLE
   See also Literature

LITERATURE
Frolund, T. Genrefied classics 016
Giramonti, L. B. Novel interiors 747
Morris, E. This living hand 814
Reference guide to world literature 809
Rich, M. World authors, 2000-2005 920.003
We Have Only This Life to Live 848

LITERATURE
   See also Humanities; Language arts

LITERATURE -- 21ST CENTURY
Oliver, M. A thousand mornings 811

LITERATURE -- ADAPTATIONS
Carson, A. Red doc> 811

LITERATURE -- APPRECIATION
Bloom, H. The anatomy of influence 801
Garber, M. The use and abuse of literature 801
Mendelsohn, D. Waiting for the barbarians 801

LITERATURE -- BIO-BIBLIOGRAPHY

Colby, V. World authors, 1975-1980 920.003
Colby, V. World authors, 1980-1985 809
Colby, V. World authors, 1985-1990 809
Drew, B. A. 100 most popular nonfiction au-
   thors 920.003
Magill's survey of American literature 810
Magill's survey of world literature 809
Reference guide to world literature 809
Rich, M. World authors, 2000-2005 920.003
Thompson, C. World authors, 1990-1995 809
Thompson, C. World authors, 1995-2000 809
Wakeman, J. World authors, 1950-1970 920.003
Wakeman, J. World authors, 1970-1975 920.003

LITERATURE -- BIOGRAPHY
Andelman, B. Will Eisner: A Spirited Life 741.5

LITERATURE -- CHRONOLOGY
Kurian, G. T. Timetables of world literature 809

LITERATURE -- COLLECTIONS
American earth 333.72
The Art of the personal essay 808.84
Journalistas 808.8
The Norton book of modern war 808.8
The Paris review book of heartbreak, madness, sex,
   love, betrayal, outsiders, intoxication, war, whim-
   sy, horrors, God, death, dinner, baseball, travels,
   the art of writing, and everything else in the world
   since 1953 808.8

LITERATURE -- COMPETITIONS
   See also Contests; Literary prizes

LITERATURE -- CRITICISM *See* Literature --
   History and criticism

LITERATURE -- DICTIONARIES
Abrams, M. H. A glossary of literary terms 803
Ayto, J. Brewer's dictionary of modern phrase &
   fable 803
Benet's reader's encyclopedia 803
Cuddon, J. A. The Penguin dictionary of literary
   terms and literary theory 803
Cyclopedia of literary characters 803
Manser, M. H. The Facts on File dictionary of allu-
   sions 422
Oxford dictionary of phrase and fable 803
Rockwood, C. Brewer's dictionary of phrase &
   fable 803

LITERATURE -- DICTIONARIES
   See also Encyclopedias and dictionaries

LITERATURE -- ENCYCLOPEDIAS
Cyclopedia of literary places 809

LITERATURE -- EVALUATION *See* Best books;
   Book reviewing; Books and reading; Criticism;
   Literature -- History and criticism

LITERATURE -- HISTORY AND CRITICISM
The encyclopedia of literary and cultural theory 801
Franzen, J. Farther away 814
Hitchens, C. Arguably 814
Mendelsohn, D. Waiting for the barbarians 801

Moretti, F. Distant reading **801**
Morris, E. This living hand **814**
Turner, F. Renegade **813**
Wroe, A. Orpheus **398.2**
**LITERATURE -- HISTORY AND CRITICISM --
    THEORY, ETC**
Jarrell, R. No other book **809**
LITERATURE -- PHILOSOPHY
Bloom, H. The anatomy of influence **801**
Garber, M. The use and abuse of literature **801**
Gardner, J. On moral fiction **801**
Kundera, M. The curtain **801**
Weinstein, A. A scream goes through the house **801**
LITERATURE -- STUDY AND TEACHING
Samet, E. D. Soldier's heart **810**
LITERATURE -- TRANSLATIONS
Grossman, E. Why translation matters **418**
LITERATURE -- WOMEN AUTHORS
Showalter, E. A jury of her peers **810**
LITERATURE AND COMMUNISM See Communism and literature
Literature and its times. **809**
LITERATURE AND SCIENCE
Falk, D. The Science of Shakespeare **822.3**
**LITERATURE AND SOCIETY -- UNITED
    STATES**
Gioia, D. Can poetry matter? **809.1**
Lepore, J. The Secret History of Wonder Woman **741.5**
Parini, J. Promised land **810**
**LITERATURE AND SOCIETY -- UNITED
    STATES -- HISTORY**
Prothero, S. The American Bible **973**
LITERATURE AND TECHNOLOGY
Braafladt, K. Technology and literacy **027.62**
Literature of travel and exploration. **910.4**
**LITERATURE   PUBLISHING -- UNITED
    STATES -- HISTORY -- 21ST CENTURY**
Smith Rakoff, J. My Salinger year **92**
LITERATURE, EXPERIMENTAL
Jones, B. T. Story/Time **814**
LITERATURE, MODERN -- 20TH CENTURY
Bohemians, bootleggers, flappers, and swells **810.8**
Lithgow, John, 1945-
    About
Lithgow, J. Drama **92**
LITHIUM
Fletcher, S. Bottled lightning **621.31**
LITHOGRAPHERS
Adams, H. Tom and Jack **92**
Frey, J. Toulouse-Lautrec **92**
LITHOGRAPHERS
    See also Artists
LITHOGRAPHY
    See also Color printing; Printing; Prints
LITIGATION

See also Law
LITTERING See Refuse and refuse disposal
Little Bento. Olivier, M. **641.53**
The **little** big things. Peters, T. J. **658.4**
LITTLE BIGHORN, BATTLE OF THE, 1876
Brown, D. A. The American West **978**
Connell, E. S. Son of the Morning Star **973.8**
Donovan, J. A terrible glory **973.8**
McMurtry, L. Custer **92**
Philbrick, N. The last stand **973.8**
Sandoz, M. The Battle of the Little Bighorn **973.8**
Stiles, T. J. Custer's trials **92**
Welch, J. Killing Custer **973.8**
Little bites. **641.5**
Little book of book making. Rivers, C. **686**
The **little** book of lunch. Craig, C. **641.5**
Little boy blues. Jones, M. **92**
Little Crow, Sioux Chief, d. 1863
    About
Berg, S. W. 38 nooses **973.7**
Brown, D. A.   Bury my heart at Wounded Knee **970.004**
Little failure. Shteyngart, G. **92**
LITTLE FLOWER (RESTAURANT)
Moore, C. Little Flower baking **641.815**
Little Flower baking. Moore, C. **641.815**
The **little** flowers of St. Francis of Assisi. **242**
A **little** gay history. Parkinson, R. B. **306.76**
Little house living. Alink, M. **640**
LITTLE LEAGUE BASEBALL
    See also Baseball
LITTLE LEAGUE BASEBALL, INC.
Geist, B. Little League confidential **796.357**
Little League confidential. Geist, B. **796.357**
LITTLE MAGAZINES
    See also Periodicals
Little one-yard wonders. Yaker, R. **646.2**
Little pink house. Benedict, J. **343**
The **little** red book of fly fishing. Deeter, K. **799.124**
LITTLE RED RIDING HOOD
Orenstein, C.   Little Red Riding Hood uncloaked **398.2**
Little Red Riding Hood uncloaked. Orenstein, C. **398.2**
Little Richard
    About
White, C. The life and times of Little Richard **92**
LITTLE ROCK (ARK.) -- RACE RELATIONS
Margolick, D. Elizabeth and Hazel **92**
The **little** spark. Bloomston, C. **153.3**
LITTLE THEATER MOVEMENT
    See also Theater
A **little** too close to God. Horovitz, D. P. **956.940**
The **Little** Veggie Patch Co. DIY Garden Projects. Pember, M. **712.6**
Little, Brown & Co. Inc.

Bartlett's Roget's thesaurus   **423**

Little, Elbert Luther

The Audubon Society field guide to North American trees   **582.16**

Little, Felicia M.

Halsted, D. D. Disaster planning   **025.8**

Little, Jamie

(jt. auth) McCormick, D. Essential car care for women   **629.28**

Little, Stephen

. . . isms: understanding art   **709**

Littlefield history of the Civil War era [series]

Rable, G. C. God's almost chosen peoples   **973.7**

LITURGIES

    See also Public worship; Rites and ceremonies

Liu, Charles, 1968 April 5-

(ed) Startalk   **523.1**

Liu, Xiaobo, 1955-

          About

Liu, X. June fourth elegies   **811**

Live & learn [series]

Diehn, G. Real life journals: designing & using handmade books   **686.3**

Live from New York. Shales, T.   **791.45**

LIVE POLIOVIRUS VACCINE *See* Poliomyelitis vaccine

Live, love, eat! Puck, W.   **641.5**

Lived through this.   **362.883**

Lively, Emma

(jt. auth) Cameron, J. B. It's never too late to begin again   **155.67**

Lively, Penelope, 1933-

          About

Lively, P. A house unlocked   **92**

Liveris, Andrew

Make it in America   **330.9**

Lives and legacies [series]

Gaustad, E. S. Roger Williams   **92**

Lives and letters. Gottlieb, R. A.   **814**

Lives in ruins. Johnson, M.   **930.1**

Lives like loaded guns. Gordon, L.   **92**

The lives of a cell. Thomas, L.   **570.1**

The lives of animals.   **179**

The lives of ants. Keller, L.   **595.7**

The lives of Beryl Markham. Trzebinski, E.   **629.13**

Lives of great religious books [series]

Davis, R. H. The Bhagavad Gita   **294.5**

The lives of Margaret Fuller. Matteson, J.   **920**

Lives of moral leadership. Coles, R.   **170**

Lives of the artists. Tomkins, C.   **920**

The lives of the great composers. Schonberg, H. C.   **780**

Lives of the poets. Schmidt, M.   **821**

Lives of the popes. McBrien, R. P.   **920**

LIVESTOCK

Do unto animals   **590**

LIVESTOCK *See* Domestic animals; Livestock industry

LIVESTOCK BREEDING

    See also Breeding; Livestock industry

LIVESTOCK INDUSTRY

Baur, G. Farm Sanctuary   **179**

Faruqi, S. Project Animal Farm   **338.1**

Kirby, D. Animal factory   **363.7**

Rebanks, J. The shepherd's life   **92**

LIVESTOCK INDUSTRY

    See also Agriculture; Economic zoology

LIVESTOCK JUDGING

    See also Livestock industry

LIVING ALONE -- UNITED STATES

Klinenberg, E. Going solo   **306.81**

The living and the dead. Hendrickson, P.   **959.704**

LIVING EARTH THEORY *See* Gaia hypothesis

The living fire. Hirsch, E.   **811**

The living Great Lakes. Dennis, J.   **977**

Living history. Clinton, H. R.   **92**

Living in Spanglish. Morales, E.   **305.868**

The living Mass. Lucatero, H.   **264**

Living on the wind. Weidensaul, S.   **598**

Living out Islam. Kugle, S. S.   **297**

The living shore. Jacobsen, R.   **639.9**

LIVING SKILLS *See* Life skills

Living the Secular Life. Zuckerman, P.   **211**

Living to tell the tale. Garcia Marquez, G.   **92**

Living with itch. Yosipovitch, G.   **616.5**

Living with jazz. Morgenstern, D.   **781.65**

Living with pattern. Atwood, R.   **701.85**

Living with Shakespeare.   **822.3**

Living, thinking, looking. Hustvedt, S.   **814**

Livingston, Jane

The paintings of Joan Mitchell   **759.13**

Livingstone, Marco

Pop art   **709.04**

Livingstone, Natalie

The mistresses of Cliveden   **942.009**

Livio, Mario

The equation that couldn't be solved   **512**

The golden ratio   **516.2**

LIZARDS

    See also Reptiles

Llewellyn's complete book of chakras. Dale, C.   **131**

Lloyd, Carli, 1982-

          About

Coffey, W. When nobody was watching   **796.334**

Lloyd, Seth

Programming the universe   **530.1**

Lo, Eileen Yin-Fei

Mastering the art of Chinese cooking   **641.59**

LOAN ASSOCIATIONS *See* Savings and loan associations

LOAN FUNDS, STUDENT *See* Student loan funds

LOANS

Mayer, R. Quick cash   **332**

LOANS

See also Finance

Lobachevsky, N. I. (Nikolai Ivanovich), 1792-1856

About

Bell, E. T. Men of mathematics   **920**

LOBBYING

Jacob, K. A. King of the lobby   **92**

Kaiser, R. G. So damn much money   **328**

LOBBYING

See also Politics; Propaganda

LOBBYING AND LOBBYISTS *See* Lobbying

LOBBYISTS

Jacob, K. A. King of the lobby   **92**

Kaiser, R. G. So damn much money   **328**

LOBBYISTS *See* Lobbying

Lobdell, William

About

Lobdell, W. Losing my religion   **92**

Lobel, Stanley

The meat bible   **641.6**

Lobo, Julio, 1898-1983

About

Rathbone, J. P. The sugar king of Havana   **92**

LoBrutto, Vincent

Stanley Kubrick   **92**

The **lobster** chronicles. Greenlaw, L.   **639**

LOBSTER FISHERIES

Greenlaw, L. The lobster chronicles   **639**

LOCAL AREA NETWORKS

See also Computer networks

LOCAL FOODS

Ackerman-Leist, P. Rebuilding the foodshed **338.1**

Humm, D. I love New York   **641.59**

LOCAL FOODS -- UNITED STATES

America--farm to table   **641.597**

Greenberg, P. American catch   **333.95**

Mario Batali Big American cookbook   **641.597**

LOCAL GOVERNMENT

See also Administrative law; Community organization; Political science

LOCAL GOVERNMENT OFFICIALS

Caro, R. A. The power broker: Robert Moses and the fall of New York   **92**

Dickey, C. Securing the city   **363.32**

Halberstam, D. The children   **323.1**

LOCAL HISTORY

Taylor, B. Naples declared   **945**

LOCAL HISTORY

See also Historiography; History

LOCAL TRAFFIC *See* City traffic

LOCAL TRANSIT

See also Traffic engineering; Transportation

Local visitations. Dunn, S.   **811**

Locavesting. Cortese, A.   **332.6**

LOCH NESS MONSTER

See also Monsters

Lochbaum, David L.

(jt. auth) Lyman, E. Fukushima   **363.17**

Lock, James

Help your teenager beat an eating disorder   **616.85**

Locke, John, 1632-1704

An essay concerning human understanding   **121**

About

Hollis, L. London rising   **942**

Russell, B. A history of Western philosophy   **109**

Locked in the cabinet. Reich, R. B.   **973.929**

Lockhart, Paul Douglas

The whites of their eyes   **973.3**

Lockwood, Belva Ann, 1830-1917

About

Norgren, J. Belva Lockwood   **92**

Lockwood, Jeffrey A.

Six-legged soldiers   **358**

Lockwood, Lewis

Beethoven: the music and the life   **780**

LOCOMOTIVES

See also Railroads

LOCOMOTIVES -- JUVENILE LITERATURE

Bewes, D. Slow Train to Switzerland   **914.94**

LOCUS STANDI -- UNITED STATES -- CASES

Becker, J. Forcing the spring   **346.73**

The **locust** and the bird. Hikayati sharhun yatul./ English   **92**

LOCUSTS

See also Insect pests; Insects

Loder, Kurt

Turner, T. I, Tina   **92**

Lodge, Henry Cabot, 1850-1924

About

Thomas, E. The war lovers   **973.8**

Zimmermann, W. First great triumph   **973**

Lodgings. Poems./English./Selections   **891.8**

LODZ (POLAND) -- ETHNIC RELATIONS

Horwitz, G. J. Ghettostadt   **940.53**

LODZ (POLAND) -- SOCIAL CONDITIONS

The Chronicle of the Lodz ghetto, 1941-1944   **943.8**

Loewen, James W.

Lies across America   **973**

Sundown towns   **363.5**

Lofas, Jeannette

Stepparenting   **646.7**

Lofgren, Mike

The party is over   **324.273**

Loftsgordon, Amy

(jt. auth) Elias, S. The foreclosure survival guide   **346**

(jt. auth) Leonard, R. Credit repair   **332.7**

(jt. auth) Leonard, R. Solve your money troubles   **346**

LOG CABINS AND HOUSES

Diedricksen, D. Microshelters **690**

LOG CABINS AND HOUSES
   See also House construction; Houses

Logan, M. David
   Mat, mount and frame it yourself **749**

Logan, William
   Our savage art **811**

Logan, William Bryant
   Air **551.5**

Logevall, Fredrik, 1963-
   Embers of War **959.704**

LOGGING
   See also Forests and forestry

LOGIC
   Copi, I. M. Introduction to logic **160**

LOGIC
   See also Intellect; Philosophy; Science --
   Methodology

LOGIC, SYMBOLIC AND MATHEMATICAL
   Stillwell, J. Roads to infinity **511.3**

LOGIC, SYMBOLIC AND MATHEMATICAL
   See Symbolic logic

LOGICIANS
   Bell, E. T. Men of mathematics **920**
   Edmonds, D. Wittgenstein's poker **192**
   Feldman, B. 112 Mercer Street **920**
   Menand, L. The Metaphysical Club **973.9**
   Waugh, A. The House of Wittgenstein **920**

The **Lolita** effect. Durham, M. G. **302.23**

Lomax, Alan, 1915-2002
   (comp) American ballads and folk songs **781.62**
   The land where the blues began **781.643**
   (comp) Our singing country **781.62**
      About
   Szwed, J. F. Alan Lomax **92**

Lomax, John Avery
   (comp) American ballads and folk songs **781.62**
   (comp) Our singing country **781.62**

Lombardi, Vince
      About
   Maraniss, D. When pride still mattered: a life of
   Vince Lombardi **92**

Lombardo, Paul A.
   Three generations, no imbeciles **344**

**LONDOLOZI GAME RESERVE (SOUTH AF-
RICA) -- HISTORY**
   Varty, B. Cathedral of the wild **639.9**

LONDON (ENGLAND)
   Summerscale, K. The suspicions of Mr. Whicher **364.152**

LONDON (ENGLAND) -- BIOGRAPHY
   Seth, V. Two lives **92**

**LONDON (ENGLAND) -- BUILDINGS, STRUC-
TURES, ETC**
   Jones, N. Tower **942.1**

LONDON (ENGLAND) -- BUILDINGS, STRUC-

TURES, ETC. -- HISTORY
   Brown, P. Shakespeare's Pub **647.9**

LONDON (ENGLAND) -- HISTORY
   Flanders, J. The Victorian city **942.1**

**LONDON (ENGLAND) -- INTELLECTUAL
LIFE -- 17TH CENTURY**
   Mays, A. E. The millionaire and the bard **822.33**

London rising. Hollis, L. **942**

London, Jack, 1876-1916
      About
   Adam, P. Jack London, photographer **92**
   Labor, E. Jack London **92**

London: the biography. Ackroyd, P. **942**

**LONDONDERRY (NORTHERN IRELAND) --
HISTORY -- 20TH CENTURY**
   Campbell, J. Setting the truth free **941.6**

The **lone** assassin. **943.086**

Lone survivor. Luttrell, M. **92**

LONELINESS
   See also Emotions

LONELINESS -- UNITED STATES
   Olds, J. The lonely American **302.5**

The **lonely** American. Olds, J. **302.5**

Lonely Planet (Company)
   (comp) Ultimate travel **910.2**
   (comp) Lonely Planet Rio De Janeiro **918.15**
   (comp) The World **910.2**

Lonely Planet Rio De Janeiro. **918.15**

Lonelyhearts. Meade, M. **92**

The **long** bitter trail. Wallace, A. F. C. **323.1**

LONG DISTANCE RUNNING *See* Marathon running

LONG DISTANCE SWIMMING *See* Marathon
swimming

LONG DISTANCE TELEPHONE SERVICE
   See also Telephone

The **long** emancipation. Berlin, I. **326.8**

The **long** goodbye. O'Rourke, M. **92**

LONG ISLAND (N.Y.) -- BIOGRAPHY
   Griswold, M. The Manor **974.7**

LONG ISLAND (N.Y.) -- HISTORY
   Griswold, M. The Manor **974.7**

LONG LIFE *See* Longevity

The **Long** March. Sun Shuyun **951.04**

The **long** marriage. Kumin, M. **811**

Long mile home. Russell, J. **363.325**

The **long** recessional: the imperial life of Rudyard
   Kipling. Gilmour, D. **92**

The **long** road home. Raddatz, M. **956.7**

The **long** road home. Shephard, B. **940.53**

Long Road to Antietam. Slotkin, R. **973.7**

The **long** sixties. Hayden, T. **973.92**

A **long** stone's throw. McCourt, A. **92**

A **long** strange trip. McNally, D. **782.421**

The **long** summer: how climate changed civilization.
   Fagan, B. M. **551.6**

Long time leaving. Blount, R. 975

The **long** walk. Castner, B. 956.704

Long walk to freedom: the autobiography of Nelson Mandela. Mandela, N. 92

A **long** way from home. Brokaw, T. 070

A **long** way gone. Beah, I. 92

A **long** way home. Brierley, S. 92

The **long** way home. Laskin, D. 920

Long, Ben

Long, J. The plot against Pepys 941.06

Long, Huey Pierce, 1893-1935

About

Hair, W. I. The Kingfish and his realm: the life and times of Huey P. Long 92

Long, James

The plot against Pepys 941.06

Long, John

Darwin's devices 629.8

Long, Richard A.

Gillespie, M. A. Maya Angelou 92

Long, Robert Emmet

Truman Capote, enfant terrible 92

LONG-DISTANCE RUNNERS

Engle, C. Running Man 796.42

LONG-DISTANCE RUNNERS -- UNITED STATES -- BIOGRAPHY

Foreman, T. My year of running dangerously 92

LONG-TERM CARE FACILITIES

See also Hospitals; Medical care

Longerich, Peter

Goebbels 92

The **longest** afternoon. Simms, B. 940.2

The **longest** fight. Gildea, W. 796.83

The **longest** night. Eicher, D. J. 973.7

The **longest** night. Mortimer, G. 940.53

The **longest** road. Caputo, P. 973.93

The **longest** trail. 970.004

The **longest** war. Bergen, P. L. 909.83

LONGEVITY

Esmonde-White, M. Aging backwards 613.2

Friedman, H. S. The longevity project 613.2

Haycock, D. B. Mortal coil 571.8

Kochilas, D. Ikaria 641.594

The longevity kitchen 612.6

Stipp, D. The youth pill 612.6

LONGEVITY -- NUTRITIONAL ASPECTS

The **longevity** kitchen 612.6

The **longevity** kitchen. 612.6

The **longevity** project. Friedman, H. S. 613.2

Longfellow, Henry Wadsworth

Poems and other writings 811

A **longing** for the light. Aleixandre, V. 861

Longing to tell. 306.7

Longitude. Sobel, D. 526

LONGITUDE

Raymo, C. Walking zero 526

Sobel, D. Longitude 526

LONGITUDE

See also Earth; Geodesy; Nautical astronomy

LONGITUDINAL STUDIES

Vaillant, G. E. Triumphs of experience 305.31

Longman, Jere

Among the heroes 364.1

Longworth, Alice Roosevelt, 1884-1980

About

Cordery, S. A. Alice 92

Peyser, M. Hissing cousins 92

Longworth, Karina

Hollywood frame by frame 791.43

Look. Sharif, S. 811.6

Look back in anger. Osborne, J. 822

Look me in the eye. Robison, J. E. 92

The **look** of architecture. Rybczynski, W. 721

Look, I made a hat. Sondheim, S. 782.1

Looking at Mindfulness. André, C. 158.1

Looking at the sun. Fallows, J. M. 950

Looking for a ship. McPhee, J. A. 910.4

Looking for Alaska. Jenkins, P. 979.8

Looking for Farrakhan. Levinsohn, F. H. 297.8

Looking for Lincoln. Kunhardt, P. B. 92

Looking for Spinoza. Damasio, A. R. 152.4

The **looking** glass brother. Von Ziegesar, P. 92

LOOKING GLASSES *See* Mirrors

The **looming** tower. Wright, L. 973.931

Loomis, Andrew, 1892-1959

Figure drawing for all it's worth 743.4

Loomis, Susan Herrmann

In a French kitchen 641.594

LOOMS

Mitchell, S. Inventive weaving on a little loom 746.1

Loop-d-loop crochet. 746.43

Loosestrife. Dunn, S. 811

The **looting** machine. Burgis, T. 338.2

Lopate, Phillip

(ed) The Art of the personal essay 808.84

Lopez, Adriana V.

(ed) Count on me 177

Lopez, Barry Holstun

(ed) Home ground 917

Of wolves and men 599.77

Lopez, Steve

The soloist 92

López-Alt, J. Kenji

The food lab 664

LORAN

See also Navigation

LORD'S DAY *See* Sabbath

Lord, Bette Bao

Legacies: a Chinese mosaic 951.05

Lord, Macauley

Talleur, R. W. L.L. Bean ultimate book of fly fishing 799.1

Lord, Walter
A night to remember **910.4**
Lorde, Audre
The collected poems of Audre Lorde **811**
About
Black women writers (1950-1980) **810**
Lords of finance. Ahamed, L. **332.1**
Lords of the horizons. Goodwin, J. **956.1**
Lorena Garcia's new taco classics. García, L. **641.84**
Loret, John
(ed) Experiment central **507.8**
LOS ANGELES (CALIF.)
Leovy, J. Ghettoside **364.152**
LOS ANGELES (CALIF.) -- BIOGRAPHY
Grande, R. The distance between us **92**
McCourt, M. Singing my him song **974.7**
Stein, J. West of Eden **979.4**
LOS ANGELES (CALIF.) -- HISTORY
Roman, J. Chronicles of old los angeles
The **Los** Angeles diaries. Brown, J. **92**
LOS ANGELES DODGERS (BASEBALL TEAM)
D'Antonio, M. Forever blue **92**
Knight, M. The best team money can buy **796.357**
LOS ANGELES LAKERS (BASKETBALL TEAM)
Lazenby, R. Jerry West **92**
LOS ANGELES TIMES
Blum, H. American lightning **364.152**
O'Shea, J. The deal from hell **92**
LOS BAÑOS INTERNMENT CAMP
Henderson, B. B. Rescue at Los Banos **940.53**
Lose your mother. Hartman, S. V. **323**
Losing Mum and Pup. Buckley, C. T. **92**
Losing my religion. Lobdell, W. **92**
Losing the race. McWhorter, J. H. **305.8**
Losing the signal. McNish, J. **338.4**
Losing Tim. Gionfriddo, P. **92**
LOSS (PSYCHOLOGY)
Brizendine, J. Stunned by grief **248**
Doka, K. J. Grief is a journey **155.9**
Edelman, H. Motherless daughters **155.9**
Edelman, H. Motherless mothers **155.9**
Emswiler, M. A. Guiding your child through grief **155.9**
Levy, A. The orphaned adult **152.4**
Oates, J. C. A widow's story **92**
Parravani, C. Her **92**
LOSS (PSYCHOLOGY)
See also Psychology
LOSS (PSYCHOLOGY) -- POETRY
Rekdal, P. Animal eye **811**
The **loss** of a pet. Sife, W. **155.9**
The **lost.** Mendelsohn, D. **92**
Lost among the birds. Hayward, N. **598.072**
Lost and Found in Johannesburg, a memoir. Gevisser, M. **92**

Lost and found in Russia. Richards, S. **947.086**
LOST ARCHITECTURE
See also Architecture
The **lost** bank. Grind, K. **332.3**
Lost battalions. Slotkin, R. **940.3**
The **Lost** Book of Moses. Tigay, C.
LOST CHILDREN *See* Missing children
The **lost** children of Wilder. Bernstein, N. **362.73**
Lost city of the Incas. Bingham, H. **985**
The **lost** city of Z. Grann, D. **918**
The **lost** cyclist. Herlihy, D. V. **92**
The **lost** daughter. Williams, M. **979.4**
Lost discoveries. Teresi, D. **509**
Lost for words. Mugglestone, L. **423**
Lost Girls. Kolker, R. **364.152**
The **lost** girls. Baggett, J. **910.4**
Lost in America. Nuland, S. B. **92**
Lost in Shangri-la. Zuckoff, M. **940.54**
Lost in Yonkers. Simon, N. **812**
The **Lost** Landscape. Oates, J. C. **92**
Lost lives, lost art. Muller, M. **709**
The **lost** peace. Dallek, R. **909.82**
Lost puritan: a life of Robert Lowell. Mariani, P. L. **811**
Lost rights. Howard, D. **973.7**
Lost to the West. Brownworth, L. **949.5**
The **lost** tribe of Coney Island. Prentice, C. **305.8**
LOST TRIBES OF ISRAEL
See also Jews
The **lost** Tudor princess. Weir, A. **92**
The **lost** world of James Smithson. Ewing, H. P. **92**
LOTTERIES
See also Gambling
Lottman, Herbert R.
Man Ray's Montparnasse **709**
Loucks, James F.
(ed) Browning, R. Robert Browning's poetry **821**
Louder Than Hell. Turman, K. **781.66**
Louis Agassiz. Irmscher, C. **92**
Louis Armstrong, in his own words. Armstrong, L. **92**
Louis Armstrong, master of modernism. Brothers, T. **92**
Louis D. Brandeis. Urofsky, M. I. **92**
Louis XIV, King of France, 1638-1715
About
Buckley, V. The secret wife of Louis XIV **944**
DeJean, J. E. The essence of style **391**
Fraser, A. Love and Louis XIV **92**
Louis, Jenn
Pasta by hand **641.82**
Louis, Joe, 1914-1981
About
Margolick, D. Beyond glory **796.8**
Roberts, R. Joe Louis **92**
Louis, Wm. Roger

(ed) The Oxford history of the twentieth century   **909.82**

Louisa. Thomas, L.   **92**

Louisa May Alcott. Reisen, H.   **92**

Louise. Krug, L.   **617.4**

LOUISIANA -- POLITICS AND GOVERNMENT

Hair, W. I. The Kingfish and his realm: the life and times of Huey P. Long   **92**

LOUISIANA -- RACE RELATIONS

Lane, C. The day freedom died   **976.3**

The **Louisiana** Purchase.   **973.4**

LOUISIANA PURCHASE

Cerami, C. A. Jefferson's great gamble   **973.4**

Kukla, J. A wilderness so immense   **973.4**

The Louisiana Purchase   **973.4**

LOUISIANA PURCHASE

See also United States -- History -- 1783-1815

LOUISIANA STATE PENITENTIARY

Rideau, W. In the place of justice   **92**

LOUISVILLE REGION (KY.) -- BIOGRAPHY

Bingham, E. Irrepressible   **306.76**

Lourie, Bruce

(jt. auth) Smith, R. Toxin toxout   **613**

Louv, Richard, 1949-

Last child in the woods   **155.4**

The nature principle   **128**

Vitamin N   **155.9**

Louvin, Charlie, 1927-2011

Satan is real   **920**

Louvish, Simon

Monkey business   **920**

Lovable livable home. Petersik, S.   **645**

Love. Becker-Phelps, L.   **646.7**

LOVE

See also Emotions; Human behavior

LOVE

Ackerman, D. A natural history of love   **152.4**

Appignanesi, L. Trials of passion   **364.152**

Burroughs, A. Lust and Wonder   **92**

Collins, L. When in French   **92**

Fromm, E. The art of loving   **152.4**

Gilligan, C. The birth of pleasure   **152.4**

Graham, J. From the New World   **811**

Lewis, T. A general theory of love   **152.4**

Nordland, R. The Lovers   **958.104**

Peck, M. S. The road less traveled   **158**

Rosenblatt, R. The book of love   **152.4**

Shulman, A. K. To love what is   **92**

Westheimer, R. K. The Doctor Is in

LOVE -- PSYCHOLOGICAL ASPECTS

Becker-Phelps, L. Love   **646.7**

LOVE -- RELIGIOUS ASPECTS

Chapman, G. D. Love as a way of life   **241**

LOVE -- SOCIAL ASPECTS

Posner, J. Find Me Unafraid   **92**

Love and capital. Gabriel, M.   **92**

Love and hate in Jamestown. Price, D.   **975.5**

The **Love** and Lemons Cookbook. Donofrio, J.   **641.5**

Love and Louis XIV. Fraser, A.   **92**

Love and Other Ways of Dying. Paterniti, M.   **814**

Love as a way of life. Chapman, G. D.   **241**

LOVE CANAL CHEMICAL WASTE LANDFILL (NIAGARA FALLS, N.Y.)

See also Hazardous waste sites; Landfills

Love goes to buildings on fire. Hermes, W.   **781.64**

Love had a compass.   **811**

LOVE IN LITERATURE

Yalom, M. How the French invented love   **944**

Love letters and two other plays: The golden age and What I did last summer. Gurney, A. R.   **812**

LOVE POETRY

Amichai, Y. Poems of Jerusalem; and, Love poems   **892**

A Book of love poetry   **808.81**

Cronk, L. Having been an accomplice   **811**

Gilbert, J. Collected poems   **811**

Rekdal, P. Animal eye   **811**

LOVE POETRY

See also Poetry

Love song. Mordden, E.   **920**

Love soup. Thomas, A.   **641.5**

LOVE STORIES

Ephron, N. The Most of Nora Ephron   **814**

Figes, O. Just send me word   **365**

Maitland, L. Crossing the borders of time   **940.53**

LOVE STORIES

See also Fiction

LOVE STORIES -- BIBLIOGRAPHY

Quillen, C. L. Read on... romance   **016**

LOVE STORIES -- HISTORY AND CRITICISM

Bouricius, A. The romance readers' advisory   **016**

Quillen, C. L. Read on... romance   **016**

Ramsdell, K. Romance fiction   **016**

LOVE STORIES -- TECHNIQUE

See also Authorship

Love thy neighbor. Maass, P.   **949.702**

Love warrior. Melton, G. D.   **92**

Love, life, Goethe. Armstrong, J.   **92**

Love, loss, and what we ate. Lakshmi, P.   **92**

Love, Lucy. Ball, L.   **92**

Love, Preston

About

Dance, S. The world of Count Basie   **920**

Love, Reggie, 1981-

About

Love, R. Power forward   **320.092**

Love, Robert

The Great Oom   **92**

Love, Susan M.

Dr. Susan Love's Breast Book   **618.1**

LOVE-LETTERS -- UNITED STATES

Cronkite, W. Cronkite's war   **070.4**

Lovejoy, Bess
Rest in pieces   **306.9**

Lovelace, Ada King, Countess of, 1815-1852
     About
Essinger, J. Ada's algorithm   **92**

Lovell, Mary S.
A rage to live: a biography of Richard and Isabel Burton   **92**

Lovelock, James
The ages of Gaia   **570.1**

The **Lovers.** Nordland, R.   **958.104**

Lovesick blues. Hemphill, P.   **92**

Loving Our Addicted Daughters Back to Life. Dahl, L.   **362.29**

Loving, Jerome
Mark Twain   **92**

LOW BUDGET COOKING
Brennan, K. Keepers   **641.5**
Brown, L. Good and cheap   **641.5**

Low Dog, Tieraona
Healthy at home   **615.5**

LOW TEMPERATURES -- RESEARCH
Shachtman, T. Absolute zero and the conquest of cold   **536**

LOW-CALORIE DIET
DiSpirito, R. Now eat this!   **641.5**
Griffin, B. Skinny suppers   **641.5**
Netzer, C. T. The complete book of food counts   **613.2**

LOW-CALORIE DIET
   See also Diet

LOW-CALORIE DIET -- RECIPES
Griffin, B. Skinny suppers   **641.5**

LOW-CARBOHYDRATE DIET
Taubes, G. Why we get fat and what to do about it   **613.7**

LOW-CARBOHYDRATE DIET
   See also Diet

LOW-CHOLESTEROL DIET
New American Heart Association cookbook The new American Heart Association cookbook   **641.5**

LOW-CHOLESTEROL DIET
   See also Diet

LOW-FAT DIET
Jenkins, N. H. The new Mediterranean diet cookbook   **641.5**

LOW-FAT DIET
   See also Diet

LOW-INCOME HOUSING -- UNITED STATES
Desmond, M. c. Evicted   **339.4**

Lowe, George
(jt. auth) Lewis-Jones, H. Conquest of Everest   **796.522**

Lowe, Jaime
Digging for dirt   **92**

Lowe, Judy
Pruning   **631.5**

Lowe, Keith
Savage continent   **940.55**

Lowe, Paul
(jt. auth) Hallett, T. Digital photography complete course   **770**

Lowe, Shelly C.
(ed) Beyond the asterisk   **378.1**

Lowell, Amy
Selected poems   **811**

Lowell, Robert, 1917-1977
Collected poems   **811**
Selected poems   **811**
     About
Heaney, S. Finders keepers   **821**
Mariani, P. L. Lost Puritan: a life of Robert Lowell   **811**

Lowen, Cynthia
(ed) Bully   **371.5**

Lowenstein, Roger
America's Bank   **332.1**
The end of Wall Street   **332.6**
While America aged   **331.2**

Lowenthal, Mark S.
(jt. auth) Kennedy-Moore, E. Smart parenting for smart kids   **649**

Lowit, Roxanne
Yves Saint Laurent   **746.9**

Lowman, Margaret
     About
Lowman, M. Life in the treetops   **577.34**

Lowney, Chris
A vanished world   **946**

LOWRY PARK ZOO
French, T. Zoo story   **590.73**

Lowside of the road. Hoskyns, B.   **92**

Loxton, Daniel
(jt. auth) Prothero, D. R. Abominable science!   **001.944**

Loy, Myrna
     About
Leider, E. W. Myrna Loy   **92**

LOYALISTS, AMERICAN *See* American Loyalists

LOYALTY
   See also Ethics; Virtue

Lozano, Luis-Martin
Frida Kahlo   **759.9**

Lozowick, Yaacov
Right to exist   **956.940**

LSD (DRUG)
Shroder, T. Acid test   **615.7**

LSD (DRUG)
   See also Hallucinogens

Lubas, Rebecca L.

(jt. auth) Lewis, L. K. The complete guide to acquisitions management **025.2**

Lubben, Kristen
(ed) Magnum contact sheets **779.092**

Lubow, Arthur
Diane Arbus **92**

LUBRICATION AND LUBRICANTS
See also Machinery

Lucado, Max
Before amen **248.3**
Fearless **248**

Lucas, Dave
Weather **811**

Lucatero, Heliodoro
The living Mass **264**

Luce, Clare Boothe, 1903-1987
About
Morris, S. J. Rage for fame: the ascent of Clare Boothe Luce **92**

Luce, Henry Robinson, 1898-1967
About
Brinkley, A. The publisher **92**
Life stories **920**

Lucero, Claudia
One-hour cheese **637**

Lucey, Donna M.
Wiencek, H. National Geographic guide to America's great houses **728.8**

The **Lucifer** effect. Zimbardo, P. **155.9**
The **Lucifer** principle. Bloom, H. **128**
Luck. Dolnick, B. **130**
Lucky. Sebold, A. **362.883**
Lucky child. Ung, L. **92**
Lucky Dog. Boston, S. **636.089**
Lucky him: the life of Kingsley Amis. Bradford, R. **92**
A **Lucky** Life Interrupted. Brokaw, T. **92**
Lucky man. Fox, M. J. **92**
Lucky Peach 101 easy Asian recipes. Meehan, P. **641.595**

Lucretius Carus, Titus
About
Greenblatt, S. The swerve **940.2**
Lucrezia Borgia. Bradford, S. **92**
Lucy's legacy. Jolly, A. **599.93**
Lucy's legacy. Johanson, D. C. **569.9**

Lucy, Liza Prior
(jt. auth) Fassett, K. Kaffe Fassett's Bold Blooms **746**
Lucy: the beginnings of humankind. Johanson, D. C. **599.93**

Ludlum, David M.
The Audubon Society field guide to North American weather **551.6**

Ludwig, David
Always hungry? **613.2**

LUGGAGE
See also Containers

Luhr, James F.
(ed) Earth **550**

Lukács, György, 1885-1971
About
Said, E. W. Reflections on exile and other essays **814**

Lukacs, John D.
Escape from Davao **940.54**

Lukacs, John, 1924-
Five days in London, May 1940 **940.53**
A short history of the twentieth century **909.82**

Lukas, J. Anthony
Common ground **305.8**

Lukeman, Noah
The plot thickens **808.3**

Lukins, Sheila
The Silver Palate cookbook **641.5**

LULLABIES
See also Bedtime; Children's poetry; Children's songs; Songs

Lulu's Provencal table. Olney, R. **641.59**

Lulushi, Albert
Donovan's Devils **940.54**

LULZSEC (GROUP)
Olson, P. We are Anonymous **005.8**

LUMBER AND LUMBERING
See also Forest products; Forests and forestry; Trees; Wood

Lumet, Sidney
Making movies **791.43**

LUMINESCENCE
See also Light; Radiation

LUNA (MUSICAL GROUP)
Wareham, D. Black postcards **92**

LUNAR ECLIPSES
See also Astronomy

LUNAR EXPEDITIONS *See* Space flight to the moon

The **Lunatic.** Simic, C. **811**
The **lunatic** express. Hoffman, C. **910.4**
Lunch in Paris. Bard, E. **92**
The **lunch-box** chronicles. Winik, M. **306.85**

LUNCHBOX COOKING
Fuentes, L. The best homemade kids' lunches on the planet **641.5**

LUNCHEONS
Craig, C. The little book of lunch **641.5**

LUNCHEONS
See also Cooking; Menus

LUNCHROOMS *See* Restaurants

Lunde, Darrin
The naturalist **973.91**

Lunden, Joan, 1950-
Had I Known **791.450**

Lundy, Ronni
Victuals   **641.5**
Lung cancer. Scott, W. J.   **616.99**
LUNG CANCER
Ali, N. Understanding lung cancer   **616.99**
Kalanithi, P. When breath becomes air   **616.99**
Scott, W. J. Lung cancer   **616.99**
LUNG CANCER
See also Cancer; Lungs -- Diseases
Lupton, Ellen
Thinking with type   **686.2**
The **lupus** encyclopedia. Thomas, D. E.   **616.7**
LUPUS ERYTHEMATOSUS
See also Autoimmune diseases
Lusane, Clarence
The Black history of the White House   **975.3**
Lusitania. Wilson, P.   **910.4**
LUSITANIA (STEAMSHIP)
Larson, E. Dead wake   **940.4**
Wilson, P. Lusitania   **910.4**
Lussu, Emilio, 1890-1975
A soldier on the southern front   **940.4**
Lust and Wonder. Burroughs, A.   **92**
Luther, Martin, 1483-1546
About
Bainton, R. H. Here I stand: a life of Martin Luther   **92**
Erikson, E. H. Young man Luther   **92**
Hendrix, S. H. Martin Luther   **92**
Kung, H. Great Christian thinkers   **230**
Oberman, H. A. Luther: man between God and the Devil   **92**
Wilson, D. A. Out of the storm   **92**
Luther: man between God and the Devil. Oberman, H. A.   **92**
Luthra, Namita
American Civil Liberties Union The rights of women   **346.01**
Lutnick, Howard
On top of the world   **332.6**
Luttrell, Marcus, 1975-
About
Hornfischer, J. D. Service   **956.704**
Luttrell, M. Lone survivor   **92**
Lutz, Robert A.
About
Lutz, B. Car guys vs. bean counters   **338.7**
Luxenberg, Steve
About
Luxenberg, S. Annie's ghosts   **92**
LUXURIES
Noonan, M. L. The coat route   **338.4**
Lycett, Andrew
Dylan Thomas: a new life   **92**
Lydersen, Kari
Bilal, W. Shoot an Iraqi   **92**

LYING *See* Truthfulness and falsehood
Lyman, Edwin
Fukushima   **363.17**
Lyman, Kennie
(ed) Bigon, M. The Morrow guide to knots   **623.88**
LYME DISEASE
See also Diseases
LYMPHATIC SYSTEM
See also Physiology
Lynas, Mark
Six degrees   **551.6**
The **Lynching.** Leamer, L.   **364.134**
LYNCHING
Brannan, K. The Family Tree   **364.134**
Dray, P. At the hands of persons unknown   **364.1**
Giddings, P. Ida: a sword among lions   **92**
Ifill, S. A. On the courthouse lawn   **364.1**
Leamer, L. The Lynching   **364.134**
LYNCHING
See also Crime
LYNCHING -- MISSISSIPPI -- HISTORY -- 20TH CENTURY
Anderson, D. S. Emmett Till   **364.1**
LYNCHING -- UNITED STATES -- HISTORY
Ifill, S. A. On the courthouse lawn   **364.1**
Lyndon B. Johnson. Peters, C.   **92**
Lynn, Cari
Bolkovac, K. The whistleblower   **92**
Lynn, Kenneth S.
Hemingway   **92**
Lynn, Loretta
About
Lynn, L. Still woman enough   **92**
Lynskey, Dorian
33 revolutions per minute   **782.42**
Lyon, Danny
The bikeriders   **796.7**
Memories of myself   **779**
Lyons, Patricia, -2013
About
Simon, S. Unforgettable   **92**
LYRICISTS
Hischak, T. The Oxford companion to the American musical   **792.6**
Lehman, D. A fine romance   **782.42**
Leiber, J. Hound dog   **92**
McBrien, W. Cole Porter   **92**
Sondheim, S. Finishing the hat   **92**
Sondheim, S. Look, I made a hat   **782.1**
LYRICISTS
See also Poets
LYRICS *See* Popular song lyrics
LYSERGIC ACID DIETHYLAMIDE *See* LSD (Drug)
Lythcott-Haims, Julie
How to raise an adult   **306.874**

Lytle, Mark Hamilton
The gentle subversive 92
Lyttle, Bethany
Denyse Schmidt quilts 746.46

M

M train. Smith, P. 92
M: the man who became Caravaggio. Robb, P. 759
Ma Jian
Red dust 951.05
Ma Rainey's black bottom. Wilson, A. 812
Maangchi (Cookbook writer)
Chattman, L. Maangchi's real Korean cooking 641.595
Maangchi's real Korean cooking. Chattman, L. 641.595
Maass, Donald
Writing the breakout novel 808.3
Maass, Peter
Crude world 338.2
Love thy neighbor 949.702
Maathai, Wangari, 1940-2001
About
Maathai, W. Unbowed 92
Maatta, Stephanie L.
A few good books 028
Mabanckou, Alain, 1966-
About
Mabanckou, A. The lights of Pointe-Noire 848
Mabbott, Thomas Ollive
(ed) Poe, E. A. Complete poems 811
Mabey, Richard
The cabaret of plants 580
Weeds 632
MABINOGION
Bulfinch, T. Bulfinch's mythology 398.2
MacArthur. Frank, R. B. 92
Macarthur at war. Borneman, W. R. 92
About
MacArthur, Douglas, 1880-1964
About
Borneman, W. R. Macarthur at war 92
Duffy, J. P. War at the end of the world 940.54
Frank, R. B. MacArthur 92
Groom, W. The generals 940.54
Herman, A. Douglas MacArthur 92
Morris, S. Supreme Commander 327.73
Perry, M. The most dangerous man in America 92
Weintraub, S. 15 stars 920
Macaulay, David
The Way Things Work Now 600
MacColl, Gail
To marry an English Lord 974.7
MacCulloch, Diarmaid
Christianity 270
The Reformation 270.6

MacDiarmid, Hugh, 1892-1978
Selected poetry 821
About
Heaney, S. Finders keepers 821
Macdonald, Cameron
The endangered species road trip 974
Macdonald, David W.
(ed) The Princeton encyclopedia of mammals 599
Macdonald, Emma
Artisan Preserving 641.4
Macdonald, Helen, 1970-
About
MacDonald, H. H is for Hawk 598.9
MacDonald, Hugh
Bizet 92
MacDonald, Jeffrey R., 1943-
About
McGinniss, J. Fatal vision 364.1
Morris, E. A wilderness of error 364.152
MacDonald, Laura M.
Curse of the Narrows 971
Macdonald, Ross, 1915-1983
About
Meanwhile there are letters 92
MacDonogh, Giles
Frederick the Great 943
Macdougall, J. D.
Frozen earth 551.7
Nature's clocks 551.7
A short history of planet earth 551.7
Mace, Nancy L.
The 36-Hour Day 616.8
MACEDONIA (REPUBLIC) -- FOLKLORE -- POETRY
pH neutral history 891.8
Maceira de Rosen, Sagra
Crowe, L. G. The towering world of Jimmy Choo 391
MacEwen, William
Escott, C. Hank Williams 92
Macey, David
Frantz Fanon 92
Macfarlane, Alan
Glass: a world history 666
Macfarlane, Robert
Landmarks 914.1
The wild places 914
About
Macfarlane, R. The old ways 914.2
MacFarquhar, Neil
The media relations department of Hizbollah wishes you a happy birthday 956.04
MacGibbon, James
(ed) Smith, S. Collected poems 821
MacGowan, Christopher J.
Twentieth-century American poetry 811

(ed) Williams, W. C. Paterson **811**

MacGregor, Neil, 1946-
Germany **943**
A history of the world in 100 objects **930.1**
Shakespeare's restless world **942.055**

Machete season. Hatzfeld, J. **967.571**

Machiavelli. Unger, M. J. **92**

Machiavelli, Niccolo, 1469-1527
The prince **320.1**

About
Strathern, P. The artist, the philosopher, and the warrior **920**
Unger, M. J. Machiavelli **92**
Viroli, M. Niccolo's smile: a biography of Machiavelli **92**

MACHINE DESIGN
See also Design; Machinery

MACHINE INTELLIGENCE *See* Artificial intelligence

MACHINE QUILTING -- PATTERNS
Gering, J. Quilting modern **746.46**

MACHINE READABLE BIBLIOGRAPHIC DATA
See also Cataloging; Information services; Information systems; Libraries -- Automation

MACHINE READABLE DICTIONARIES
See also Encyclopedias and dictionaries

MACHINE SEWING
First time sewing **646.2**
Happy home **646.2**
Ishida, S. Sewing happiness **646.2**
One-yard wonders **646.2**
Yaker, R. Little one-yard wonders **646.2**

MACHINE TOOLS
See also Machinery; Tools

MACHINERY
Macaulay, D. The Way Things Work Now **600**
Sagan, C. Broca's brain **500**

MACHINERY
See also Manufactures; Mechanical engineering; Power (Mechanics); Technology; Tools

MACHINERY IN THE WORKPLACE
See also Work environment

MACHINES *See* Machinery

Machlis, Joseph
(jt. auth) Forney, K. The enjoyment of music **780**

MACHU PICCHU (PERU)
Adams, M. Turn right at Machu Picchu **985**
Bingham, H. Lost city of the Incas **985**
Heaney, C. Cradle of gold **92**

MACINTOSH (COMPUTER)
See also Computers

MacIntosh, Julie
Dethroning the king **338.8**

Macintyre, Ben, 1963-
Agent Zigzag **92**

Double cross **940.54**
Operation Mincemeat **940.54**
Rogue Heroes **940.54**
A Spy Among Friends **327.12**

Mackall, Joe
About
Mackall, J. Plain secrets **289.7**

Mackay, Harvey
Use your head to get your foot in the door **650.14**

Mackay, James A.
Allan Pinkerton **363.28**

Mackay, Jordan
Franklin barbecue **641.7**

MacKeen, Dawn Anahid
About
MacKeen, D. A. The hundred-year walk **92**

MacKellar, Pamela H.
(jt. auth) Gerding, S. K. Winning grants **025.1**
Writing successful technology grant proposals **025.1**

Mackenzie, Dana
The universe in zero words **512.9**

Mackenzie, Jennifer
The complete book of pickling **641.4**

MacKethan, Lucinda Hardwick
(ed) The Companion to southern literature **810**

Mackey, John, 1954-
Conscious capitalism **174**

Mackey, Nathaniel
Splay anthem **811**

Mackey, Sandra
The Iranians **955**

Mackrell, Judith
Flappers **920**
Craine, D. The Oxford dictionary of dance **792.8**

MacLaine, Shirley, 1934-
About
MacLaine, S. Above the line **92**

Maclean, John N.
Fire and ashes **363.3**

MacLean, Norman
Young men & fire **634.9**

MacLean, Rory
Magic bus **915**

MacLeish, Archibald, 1892-1982
Collected poems, 1917-1982 **811**
About
Archibald MacLeish: reflections **92**

Macleod, Alasdair
Explorers **910.4**

Macleod, D. Peter
Northern Armageddon **971.01**

MacLeod, Don
How to find out anything **001.4**

MacMillan, Margaret
Dangerous games **901**

History's People 920
Paris 1919 940.3
MacNeil, Neil
(jt. auth) Baker, R. A. The American Senate 328.73
MacNeil, Robert
Do you speak American ?(Television program) Do you speak American? 427
McCrum, R. The story of English 420
MacPherson, Myra
All governments lie 92
MACRAME
Hartmann, K. Hot knots 746.42
Macready, William Charles, 1793-1873
About
Cliff, N. The Shakespeare riots 974.4
MACROECONOMICS
See also Economics
Macrowikinomics. Tapscott, D. 303.4
Macumber, William, 1935-
About
Siegel, B. Manifest injustice 364.152
Macy, Beth
Factory man 338.7
Truevine 791.3
Macy, Laura Williams
(ed) The Grove book of opera singers 920
Sadie, S. The Grove book of operas 792.5
A **mad** catastrophe. Wawro, G. 940.4
Mad enchantment. King, R. 759.4
Mad forest. Churchill, C. 822
Madame Chiang Kai-Shek. Li, L. T. 92
Madame de Pompadour. Lever, E. 944
MADAMS
Abbott, K. Sin in the Second City 977.3
Madden, Matt
(jt. auth) Abel, J. Drawing words & writing pictures 741.5
(jt. auth) Abel, J. Mastering comics 741.5
Madden, Thomas F.
Venice 945
Maddex, Robert L.
The U.S. Constitution A to Z 342
Maddow, Rachel, 1973-
Drift 306.2
Maddox, Brenda
Rosalind Franklin: the dark lady of DNA 92
Made for goodness. 170
Made in america. Garrelts, C.
Made in America. Bryson, B. 420
Made in India. 641.595
Mademoiselle. Garelick, R. K. 92
Madhur Jaffrey's ultimate curry bible. Ultimate curry bible 641.5
Madhur Jaffrey's world vegetarian. Jaffrey, M. 641.5
Madigan, Carleen

(ed) The backyard homestead 641
Madison and Jefferson. Burstein, A. 973.4
MADISON COUNTY (N.Y.) -- BIOGRAPHY
Busch, B. Dust to dust 92
Madison's Gift. Stewart, D. O. 92
Madison, Deborah
The new vegetarian cooking for everyone 641.5
Vegetable literacy 641.6
Vegetarian cooking for everyone 641.5
Vegetarian suppers from Deborah Madison's kitchen 641.5
Madison, Dolley, 1768-1849
About
Allgor, C. A perfect union 92
Madison, James, 1751-1836
The Constitutional Convention 342
About
Broadwater, J. James Madison 92
Burstein, A. Madison and Jefferson 973.4
Cheney, L. V. James Madison 92
Cohen, I. B. Science and the founding fathers 973.3
Ellis, J. J. Founding brothers 973.4
Signer, M. Becoming Madison 92
Stewart, D. O. Madison's Gift 92
Wills, G. James Madison 92
Madness. Porter, R. 616.89
Madness in civilization. Scull, A. 616.89
Madness visible. Di Giovanni, J. 949.7
Madrick, Jeffrey G.
Age of greed 330.9
Maestripieri, Dario
Games primates play 155.7
Maestro: Greenspan's Fed and the American boom. Woodward, B. 331.1
Maffei, Yvonne
My halal kitchen 641.595
MAFIA
Balsamo, W. Young Al Capone 92
Carlo, P. Gaspipe 92
Dash, M. The first family 364.1
Lance, P. Deal With the Devil 363.25
Raab, S. Five families 364.1
Reavill, G. Mafia summit 364.106
MAFIA -- DICTIONARIES
Sifakis, C. The mafia encyclopedia 364.1
MAFIA -- HISTORY
Dash, M. The first family 364.1
The **mafia** encyclopedia. Sifakis, C. 364.1
Mafia summit. Reavill, G. 364.106
MAGAZINE EDITORS
Baggett, J. The lost girls 910.4
Blight, D. W. American oracle 973.7
Brinkley, A. The publisher 92
Brookhiser, R. Right time, right place 92
Buckley, C. T. Losing Mum and Pup 92
Buckley, W. F. Miles gone by 92

Buckley, W. F. Nearer, my God **282**

Buckley, W. F. The Reagan I knew **92**

Buford, B. Heat **641.5**

Fraser, K. Ornament and silence **809**

George, being George **92**

German, B. Under their thumb **781.66**

Gioia, D. Can poetry matter? **809.1**

Guttenplan, D. D. American radical **92**

Heilbrun, C. G. The education of a woman **92**

Jones, M. Little boy blues **92**

Life stories **920**

MacPherson, M. All governments lie **92**

Oates, J. C. A widow's story **92**

O'Rourke, M. The long goodbye **92**

Rapoport, R. Citizen Moore **92**

Reichl, R. Comfort me with apples **92**

Reichl, R. Garlic and sapphires **92**

Scanlon, J. Bad girls go everywhere: the life of
  Helen Gurley Brown **92**

Steinem, G. Moving beyond words **305.42**

Steinem, G. Outrageous acts and everyday rebellions **305.42**

Thorndike, J. The last of his mind **92**

What there is to say we have said **92**

MAGAZINE EXECUTIVES

Brinkley, A. The publisher **92**

Buford, B. Heat **641.5**

De Waal, E. The hare with amber eyes **920**

Life stories **920**

Watts, S. Mr. Playboy **92**

MAGAZINES See Periodicals

Magee, Bryan

The story of philosophy **190**

Magellan, Ferdinand, 1480?-1521

About

Bergreen, L. Over the edge of the world **910.4**

Manchester, W. A world lit only by fire **940.2**

Maggot. Muldoon, P. **821**

Magi, Trina

Intellectual Freedom Manual **025.2**

MAGIC

See also Occultism

MAGIC -- PSYCHOLOGICAL ASPECTS

Stone, A. Fooling Houdini **793.8**

MAGIC -- SOCIAL ASPECTS

Stone, A. Fooling Houdini **793.8**

Magic and Loss. Heffernan, V. **303.48**

Magic bus. MacLean, R. **915**

The **magic** of gingerbread. Beddall, C. **641.86**

The **Magic** of Math. Benjamin, A. **510**

The **magic** of reality. Dawkins, R. **501**

The **magic** of thinking big. Schwartz, D. J. **158**

MAGIC REALISM (LITERATURE)

See also Fantasy fiction; Surrealism

MAGIC TRICKS

Miles, B. 101 magic tricks **793.8**

Stone, A. Fooling Houdini **793.8**

MAGIC TRICKS

See also Amusements; Tricks

Magical mushrooms, mischievous molds. Hudler,
  G. W. **579.5**

MAGICAL THINKING

Gilbert, E. Big magic **153.3**

The **magician's** book. Miller, L. **823**

MAGICIANS

Singer, M. Character studies **920**

Magida, Arthur J.

(ed) How to be a perfect stranger **203**

Magill's choice [series]

Ancient Greece **938**

Salem Press Inc. Notable Latino writers **810**

Short story writers **809**

U.S. laws, acts, and treaties **348**

Magill's encyclopedia of science. **580**

Magill's guide to military history. **355**

Magill's medical guide. **610.3**

Magill's medical guide. **610**

Magill's survey of American literature. **810**

Magill's survey of world literature. **809**

Magill, Frank Northen

(ed) Cyclopedia of literary characters **803**

Magill, R. Jay

Sincerity **179**

MAGNA CARTA

See also Charters; Great Britain -- History --
  1154-1399, Plantagenets

Magner, Mike

Poisoned legacy **338.7**

MAGNET SCHOOLS

See also Public schools; School integration;
  Schools

MAGNETIC NEEDLE See Compass

The **magnetic** north. Wheeler, S. **910.4**

MAGNETIC RECORDERS AND RECORDING

See also Electronic apparatus and appliances

MAGNETIC RESONANCE IMAGING

See also Diagnosis

MAGNETISM

See also Physics

A **magnificent** catastrophe. Larson, E. J. **324**

Magnificent mistakes in mathematics. Posamentier,
  A. S. **510**

Magnum contact sheets. **779.092**

Magnum Photos, Inc.

New York September 11 **770**

Magocsi, Paul R.

Historical atlas of Central Europe **911**

Magpie. Harris, M. **641.86**

Magritte. Gohr, S. **759.94**

Magritte. Paquet, M. **709**

Magritte, René, 1898-1967

About

Gohr, S. Magritte 759.94

Magueijo, Joao
A brilliant darkness 92

Maguire, James
American bee 372.6
Impresario 92

Mah, Adeline Yen, 1937-
About
Mah, A. Y. Falling leaves 305.48

Mahabharata. Satyamurti, C. 821

Mahabharata/Bhagavadgita
Bhagavad Gita 294.5

Mahajan, Sanjoy
Street-fighting mathematics 510

Mahama, John Dramani, 1958-
About
Mahama, J. D. My first coup d'etat and other true
stories from the lost decades of Africa 966.705

Mahan, A. T. (Alfred Thayer), 1840-1914
About
Zimmermann, W. First great triumph 973

Mahar, Maggie
Bull!: a history of the boom, 1982-1999 332.6

Maharaj, Kris
About
Smith, C. S. The injustice system 345.73

Mahler, Gustav, 1860-1911
About
Lebrecht, N. Why Mahler? 92

Mahoney, Richard D.
Sons and brothers: the days of Jack and Bobby Kennedy 92

MAIASAURA
See also Dinosaurs

Maida Heatter's book of great desserts. Heatter,
M. 641.8

Maida Heatter's brand-new book of great cookies.
Heatter, M. 641.8

Maida Heatter's cakes. Heatter, M. 641.8

Maida Heatter's cookies. Heatter, M. 641.8

The **maids** [and] Deathwatch. Genet, J. 842

Maier, Karl
This house has fallen 966.905

Maier, Pauline, 1938-2013
American scripture 973.3
Ratification 342

Maier, Thomas
When lions roar 941.084

MAIL-ORDER BUSINESS
See also Business; Direct selling; Selling

Mailer. Dearborn, M. V. 813

Mailer, Norman, 1923-2007
Dearborn, M. V. Mailer 813
Lennon, J. M. Norman Mailer 92
Mailer, N. C. A ticket to the circus 92
Of a fire on the moon 629.45

Schultz, K. M. Buckley and Mailer 973.92

Mailer, Norris Church
About
Mailer, N. C. A ticket to the circus 92

Mainardi, Diogo, 1962-
About
The fall 92

MAINE
The house with sixteen handmade doors 728

MAINE -- DESCRIPTION AND TRAVEL
Thoreau, H. D. The Maine woods 917
The **Maine** woods. Thoreau, H. D. 917

MAINSTREAMING IN EDUCATION
See also Children with disabilities; Education; Exceptional children

MAINTENANCE OF BIODIVERSITY *See* Biodiversity conservation

MAINTENANCE SERVICES EXECUTIVES
St. John, W. Outcasts united 796.334

Maintenon, Madame de, 1635-1719
About
Buckley, V. The secret wife of Louis XIV 944

Mair, Victor H.
(ed) The Columbia history of Chinese literature 895.1

Maitland, Leslie
Crossing the borders of time 940.53

Majerus, Marianne
Garden Design 712

Major. Balf, T. 92

Major acts of Congress. 348

Major Barbara. Shaw, B. 822

MAJOR LEAGUE BASEBALL
Kennedy, K. Pete Rose 92
Pessah, J. The game
Sawchik, T. Big data baseball 796.357
Svrluga, B. The grind 796.357

**MAJOR LEAGUE BASEBALL (ORGANIZA-
TION)**
Ruck, R. Raceball 796.357

Major, John S.
(ed) World poetry 808.81

Majorana, Ettore
About
Magueijo, J. A brilliant darkness 92

Mak, Geert
In Europe 940.5

Makan, Chetna
The Cardamom Trail 641.5

Makary, Marty
Unaccountable 610.730

Make. Platt, C. 621.381

Make 'em Laugh. Reynolds, D. 92

Make a statement. Crowther, J. 745.594

Make gentle the life of this world. Kennedy, R.
F. 973.922

Make it ahead.   **641.5**

Make it in America. Liveris, A.   **330.9**

Make mine a mystery. Niebuhr, G. W.   **809**

Make mine a mystery II. Niebuhr, G. W.   **016**

Make the bread, buy the butter. Reese, J.   **641.3**

Make your own living trust. Clifford, D.   **346.05**

The **make-ahead** cook.   **641.5**

MAKE-AHEAD COOKING

  Make it ahead   **641.5**

  The make-ahead cook   **641.5**

  You have it made!   **641.5**

Maker dad. Frauenfelder, M.   **745.5**

Makes me wanna holler. McCall, N.   **305.38**

MAKEUP (COSMETICS) *See* Cosmetics

MAKEUP, THEATRICAL *See* Theatrical makeup

Maki, Allan

  Football's greatest stars   **796.332**

Making a difference. Century, D.   **303.3**

Making an elephant. Swift, G.   **828**

Making artisan pasta. Green, A.   **641.82**

Making certain it goes on. Hugo, R.   **811**

Making comics. McCloud, S.   **741.5**

Making handmade books. Golden, A.   **686.3**

Making haste from Babylon. Bunker, N.   **974.4**

Making history [series]

  Gilbert, M. Kristallnacht   **940.53**

  Roberts, A. Waterloo: June 18, 1815   **940.2**

Making movies. Lumet, S.   **791.43**

The **Making** of a poem.   **821**

The **making** of African America. Berlin, I.   **305.8**

The **making** of Asian America. Lee, E.   **973**

The **making** of Donald Trump. Johnston, D. C.   **973.932**

The **making** of modern Japan. Jansen, M. B.   **952**

The **making** of Robert E. Lee. Fellman, M.   **92**

The **making** of the fittest. Carroll, S. B.   **572.8**

Making our democracy work. Breyer, S. G.   **347**

Making peace with your past. Bloomfield, H. H.   **158**

Making saints. Woodward, K. L.   **235**

Making sense of IBS. Lacy, B. E.   **616.3**

Making the most of your money now. Quinn, J. B.   **332.024**

Making toast. Rosenblatt, R.   **92**

Making your own days. Koch, K.   **809.1**

MAKING-CHOICES STORIES *See* Plot-your-own stories

Makos, Adam

  Devotion   **951.904**

MALABSORPTION SYNDROMES -- DIET THERAPY -- RECIPES

Shepherd, S. The 2-step low-FODMAP eating plan   **641.5**

MALADJUSTED CHILDREN *See* Emotionally disturbed children

MALADJUSTMENT (PSYCHOLOGY) *See* Adjustment (Psychology)

Malakov, Daniel, d. 2007

     About

  Malcolm, J. Iphigenia in Forest Hills   **345**

Malamud, Bernard, 1914-1986

     About

  Langer, L. L. Admitting the Holocaust   **940.53**

  Smith, J. M. My father is a book   **92**

MALARIA

  See also Diseases

The **malaria** project. Masterson, K. M.   **616.9**

MALAWI -- RURAL CONDITIONS

Kamkwamba, W. The boy who harnessed the wind   **92**

MALAYSIA -- DESCRIPTION AND TRAVEL

Eyewitness Travel Malaysia & Singapore   **915.9**

Malcolm. Perry, B.   **92**

Malcolm X. Marable, M.   **92**

Malcolm X, 1925-1965

     About

  Carson, C. Malcolm X: the FBI file   **92**

  Cornel West on Black prophetic fire   **92**

  Malcolm X The autobiography of Malcolm X   **92**

  Marable, M. Malcolm X   **92**

  Perry, B. Malcolm   **92**

  Smith, J. Blood brothers   **92**

Malcolm X: the FBI file. Carson, C.   **92**

Malcolm, Janet

  Forty-one false starts   **808.02**

  Iphigenia in Forest Hills   **345**

  Reading Chekhov   **891.7**

  Two lives   **92**

MALE FRIENDSHIP -- UNITED STATES

Kashatus, W. C. Jackie and Campy   **92**

MALE IMPERSONATORS -- AFGHANISTAN

Nordberg, J. The underground girls of Kabul   **305.42**

MALE ROLE *See* Gender role

MALE-FEMALE RELATIONSHIP *See* Man-woman relationship

Malebranche, Nicolas, 1638-1715

     About

  Nadler, S. M. The best of all possible worlds   **190**

Malek, Alia

  A country called Amreeka   **305.8**

Malek, Cate

  (ed) Palestine Speaks   **956.94**

MALFEASANCE IN OFFICE *See* Misconduct in office

MALI -- HISTORY -- TUAREG REBELLION, 2012- -- DESTRUCTION AND PILLAGE

Hammer, J. The bad-ass librarians of Timbuktu   **025.8**

MALICIOUS ACCUSATION

Cohan, W. D. The price of silence   **364.15**

MALIGNANT TUMORS *See* Cancer

Malin, Gray

  Beaches   **779.37**

Malin, Jo
(ed) Encyclopedia of women's autobiography **920.003**
Malinowski, Sharon
(ed) Notable native Americans **920.003**
Malkiel, Burton Gordon, 1932-
A random walk down Wall Street **332.6**
Mallalieu, Nicole
The better bag maker **646.4**
Mallarme, Stephane
Collected poems and other verse **841**
Mallayev, Mikhail
About
Malcolm, J. Iphigenia in Forest Hills **345**
Malle, Chloe
(ed) Bowles, H. Vogue and the Metropolitan Museum of Art Costume Institute **391**
Mallegg, Kristin
(ed) Almanac of Famous People **920**
Malley, Marjorie Caroline
Radioactivity **539.7**
Mallmann on fire. Kaminsky, P. **641.598**
Mallmann, Francis
(jt. auth) Kaminsky, P. Mallmann on fire **641.598**
Seven fires **641.5**
Mallon, Thomas
Mrs. Paine's garage and the murder of John F. Kennedy **364.1**
Yours ever **808.86**
MALLS, SHOPPING See Shopping centers and malls
MALNUTRITION
See also Nutrition
Malone, Hilary
The Power of Pulses **635.65**
Malone, John Williams
It doesn't take a rocket scientist **920**
Malone, Michael S.
(jt. auth) Karlgaard, R. Team Genius **658.1**
The guardian of all things **153.1**
Maloney, Elbert S.
(ed) Chapman piloting & seamanship **623.88**
Malory, Thomas Sir, 15th cent.
Ackroyd, P. The death of King Arthur **398.2**
Le morte Darthur, or, The hoole book of Kyng Arthur and of his noble knyghtes of the Rounde Table **398.2**
MALPRACTICE INSURANCE
See also Insurance
Malthus, T. R. (Thomas Robert), 1766-1834
About
Heilbroner, R. L. The worldly philosophers **330.1**
Mama doc medicine. Swanson, W. S. **649.1**
Mamaleh knows best. Ingall, M. **649.1**
Mamet, David
Glengarry Glen Ross **812**

Speed-the-plow **812**
True and false **792**
About
Playwrights at work **812**
Mammal tracks & sign. Elbroch, M. **599**
MAMMALS
Elbroch, M. Mammal tracks & sign **599**
Nowak, R. M. Walker's mammals of the world **599**
The Princeton encyclopedia of mammals **599**
Whitaker, J. O. National Audubon Society field guide to North American mammals **599**
MAMMALS
See also Animals
MAMMALS -- ENCYCLOPEDIAS
The Princeton encyclopedia of mammals **599**
MAMMALS, FOSSIL See Fossil mammals
Mammoths. Lister, A. **569**
MAMMOTHS
Lister, A. Mammoths **569**
MAMMOTHS
See also Fossil mammals
Mamushka. Hercules, O. **641.594**
Man alive. McBee, T. P. **92**
A **man** and his ship. Ujifusa, S. **623.8**
Man and his symbols. Jung, C. G. **150.19**
Man and Superman. Shaw, B. **822**
A **man** for all seasons. Bolt, R. **822**
MAN IN SPACE See Space flight
A **Man** Most Driven. Firstbrook, P. **975.5**
Man o' War. Ours, D. **798.4**
MAN O' WAR (RACE HORSE)
Ours, D. Man o' War **798.4**
Man of blessing. Butcher, C. A. **271**
Man of constant sorrow. Stanley, R. **92**
A **man** of good hope. Steinberg, J. **92**
Man of La Mancha. Cervantes Saavedra, M. d. **812**
Man Ray's Montparnasse. Lottman, H. R. **709**
The **man** who ate his boots. Brandt, A. **910.4**
The **man** who couldn't eat. Reiner, J. **92**
The **man** who couldn't stop. Adam, D. **616.85**
The **man** who counted. Tahan, M. **793.74**
The **man** who invented the computer. Smiley, J. **92**
The **man** who knew infinity. Kanigel, R. **510**
The **man** who knew too much. Leavitt, D. **92**
The **man** who loved China. Winchester, S. **92**
The **man** who mistook his wife for a hat and other clinical tales. Sacks, O. W. **616.8**
The **man** who never died. Adler, W. M. **92**
The **man** who owns the news. Wolff, M. **92**
The **man** who saved the union. Brands, H. W. **355.009**
The **man** who walked through time. Fletcher, C. **917**
The **Man** Who Would Not Be Washington. Horn, J. **92**
The **man** within my head. Iyer, P. **809**
A **man** without a country. Vonnegut, K. **814**

Man'oushé. Massaad, B. A.   **641.5**

The **man's** guide to women. Gottman, J.   **155.3**

Man's search for meaning. Frankl, V. E.   **92**

Man, John

   Marco Polo   **915**

   Ninja   **355.5**

MAN, PREHISTORIC *See* Fossil hominids; Prehistoric peoples

MAN, PRIMITIVE *See* Primitive societies

Man-made catastrophes. Davis, L. A.   **904**

MAN-WOMAN RELATIONSHIP

   Collins, L. When in French   **92**

   Fisher, H. Anatomy of Love   **302.3**

   Gottman, J. The man's guide to women   **155.3**

   Rosin, H. The end of men   **305.42**

MAN-WOMAN RELATIONSHIP

   See also Interpersonal relations

MAN-WOMAN RELATIONSHIP -- POETRY

   Nadelberg, A. Bright brave phenomena   **811**

MAN-WOMAN RELATIONSHIPS

   Gilligan, C. The birth of pleasure   **152.4**

   McClelland, M. Irritable hearts   **92**

   Roiphe, K. Uncommon arrangements   **920**

MAN-WOMAN RELATIONSHIPS -- PSYCHOLOGICAL ASPECTS

   Gottman, J. The man's guide to women   **155.3**

Manage your day-to-day.   **153.4**

MANAGEMENT

   Abrams, J. Companies we keep   **338.7**

   Barringer, B. Launching a Business   **658.1**

   Bock, L. Work rules!   **658.4**

   Chan, R. W. Behind the Berkshire Hathaway curtain   **658.4**

   Collins, J. C. Good to great   **658**

   Covert, J. The 100 best business books of all time   **016.6**

   Drucker, P. F. The Drucker lectures   **658**

   Goldfayn, A. The revenue growth habit   **658.15**

   Goleman, D. Primal Leadership   **658.4**

   Hallowell, E. M. Shine   **658.3**

   Horstman, M. The effective manager   **658**

   Karlgaard, R. Team Genius   **658.1**

   Kowitz, B. Sprint   **658.4**

   Laughlin, S. The quality library   **025.1**

   McCormack, M. H. What they don't teach you at Harvard Business School   **650.1**

   Mudd, P. The Head Game   **153.4**

   Peters, T. J. The little big things   **658.4**

   Wall Street journal The Wall Street Journal essential guide to management   **658**

   Walsh, B. The score takes care of itself   **658.4**

   Wasserman, N. The founder's dilemmas   **658.1**

   Wooldridge, A. Masters of management   **658**

MANAGEMENT

   See also Business; Industries

MANAGEMENT -- ANECDOTES

Hull, R. The Peter principle   **817**

MANAGEMENT -- ASIA

   Alexander, L. Access to Asia   **395.5**

Managing Electronic Resources.   **025.1**

Managing library employees. Stanley, M. J.   **023**

Managing prostate cancer. Roth, A. J.   **616.99**

Manbo, Bill T., 1908-1992

About

   Colors of confinement   **940.53**

Manchild in the promised land. Brown, C.   **92**

MANCHUS

   Platt, S. R. Autumn in the Heavenly Kingdom   **951**

Manco, Tristan

   (ed) Ganz, N. Graffiti world   **751**

MANDAN INDIANS

   Fenn, E. A. Encounters at the heart of the world   **305.897**

MANDATES

   See also International law; International organization; International relations

Mandel, David

   Who's who in the Jewish Bible   **920.003**

Mandela. Mandela, N.   **968.06**

Mandela. Jones, B.   **92**

Mandela, Mobutu, and me. Duke, L.   **968.06**

Mandela, Nelson, 1918-2013

About

   Carlin, J. Playing the enemy   **968.06**

   Duke, L. Mandela, Mobutu, and me   **968.06**

   Jones, B. Mandela   **92**

   In his own words   **92**

   Mandela, N. Conversations with myself   **92**

   Mandela, N. Long walk to freedom: the autobiography of Nelson Mandela   **92**

   Mandela, N. Mandela   **968.06**

   Sampson, A. Nelson Mandela   **92**

   Smith, D. J. Young Mandela   **92**

Mandelstam, Nadezhda, 1899-1980

About

   Mandelstam, N. Hope against hope   **891.71**

Mandelstam, Osip

   The selected poems of Osip Mandelstam   **891.7**

Mandery, Evan J.

   A wild justice   **345.73**

Manegold, Catherine

   Ten Hills Farm   **974.4**

Manet, Édouard, 1832-1883

About

   Brombert, B. A. Edouard Manet   **92**

   King, R. The judgment of Paris   **759**

   Smee, S. The art of rivalry   **700.92**

Manfield, Christine

   Dessert Divas   **641**

MANGA

   See also Graphic novels

MANGA -- STUDY AND TEACHING

101 top tips from professional manga artists **741.5**
Mangini, Cara
The Vegetable Butcher **641.65**
Mango, Andrew
Osmanczyk, E. J. Encyclopedia of the United Nations and international agreements **341.23**
The Turks today **956.1**
Manguel, Alberto
The dictionary of imaginary places **809**
Homer's The Iliad and The Odyssey **883**
A reader on reading **818**
Manguso, Sarah, 1974-
About
Manguso, S. The two kinds of decay **362**
MANHATTAN (NEW YORK, N.Y.)
Calhoun, A. St. Marks Is Dead **974.7**
Miller, D. L. Supreme city **974.7**
MANHATTAN PROJECT
Norris, R. S. Racing for the bomb: General Leslie R. Groves, the Manhattan Project's indispensable man **92**
Manheimer, Eric
Twelve patients **362.11**
Manhood for amateurs. Chabon, M. **92**
Manhunt. Bergen, P. L. **363.325**
Manhunt. Swanson, J. L. **364.152**
MANIA See Manic-depressive illness
MANIC DEPRESSION See Manic-depressive illness
MANIC-DEPRESSIVE ILLNESS
Jamison, K. R. Nothing was the same **92**
Manifest injustice. Siegel, B. **364.152**
Mankiller: a chief and her people **92**
Mankiller, Wilma
About
Mankiller, W. Mankiller: a chief and her people **92**
Mankiller: a chief and her people. Mankiller, W. **92**
Mankind beyond Earth. Piantadosi, C. A. **629.45**
Mankoff, Robert
(ed) The complete cartoons of the New Yorker **741.5**
About
Mankoff, B. How about never--is never good for you? **92**
Mann, Charles C.
1491 **970.01**
1493 **909**
Mann, James
The rebellion of Ronald Reagan **973.927**
Mann, Robert
A grand delusion **959.704**
Mann, Sally, 1951-
About
Mann, S. Hold Still **92**
Mann, Thomas, 1875-1955
About

Kurzke, H. Thomas Mann **92**
Mann, Traci
Secrets from the eating lab **613.2**
Mann, William J.
Behind the screen **791.43**
Hello, gorgeous **92**
Kate: the woman who was Hepburn **92**
Tinseltown **364.152**
MANNED SPACE FLIGHT
Wohlforth, C. Beyond Earth **629.455**
MANNED SPACE FLIGHT See Space flight
MANNED SPACE FLIGHT -- HISTORY -- POPULAR WORKS
Piantadosi, C. A. Mankind beyond Earth **629.45**
MANNERS AND CUSTOMS -- HISTORY
Jenkins, J. K. All the time in the world **390**
MANNERS AND CUSTOMS -- HISTORY -- SOURCES
Daily life through world history in primary documents **909**
Mannes, Elena
The power of music **781**
Manning family
About
Anderson, L. The Mannings **796.332**
Manning, Archie, 1949-
About
Anderson, L. The Mannings **796.332**
Manning, Chandra
Troubled refuge **973.711**
Manning, Eli, 1981-
About
Anderson, L. The Mannings **796.332**
Manning, Maurice
The common man **811**
Manning, Peyton
About
Anderson, L. The Mannings **796.332**
Myers, G. Brady vs Manning **92**
Manning, Rob
Mars Rover Curiosity **629.295**
The **Mannings.** Anderson, L. **796.332**
The **Manor.** Griswold, M. **974.7**
MANPOWER POLICY See Labor policy
Manseau, Peter
(ed) Believer, beware **200.9**
Manser, Martin H.
Critical companion to the Bible **220.6**
The Facts on File dictionary of allusions **422**
The Facts on File dictionary of foreign words and phrases **422**
The Facts on File dictionary of proverbs **398.9**
Mansfield, Elizabeth
Arnason, H. H. History of modern art **709.04**
Mansfield, William Murray, Earl of, 1705-1793
About

Byrne, P. Belle 92
The **mansion** of happiness. Lepore, J. 973
MANSIONS -- UNITED STATES -- HISTORY
Dedman, B. Empty mansions 92
MANSLAUGHTER *See* Homicide
Manson. Guinn, J. 364.152
Manson, Charles, 1934-
         About
Bugliosi, V. Helter skelter 364.1
Guinn, J. Manson 364.152
Manson, Mark
The subtle art of not giving a fu*k 158.1
Mansoor, Peter R., 1960-
         About
Mansoor, P. R. Baghdad at sunrise 956.7
The **mantle** of command. Hamilton, N. 940.54
Mantle, Mickey, 1931-1995
         About
Leavy, J. The last boy 92
A **manual** for writers of research papers, theses, and
  dissertations. 808.06
Manual of mineral science. Klein, C. 549
Manual of woody landscape plants. Dirr, M.
A. 635.9
Manual of Zen Buddhism. Suzuki, D. T. 294.3
**MANUAL WORK -- SOCIAL ASPECTS -- UNIT-
ED STATES**
Laskas, J. M. Hidden America 305.5
MANUAL WORKERS *See* Labor; Working class
Manuali, Tanya Bastianich
(jt. auth) Bastianich, J. Healthy pasta 641.82
(jt. auth) Bastianich, L. M. Lidia's commonsense
  Italian cooking 641.59
(jt. auth) Bastianich, L. M. Lidia's favorite reci-
  pes 641.594
(jt. auth) Bastianich, L. M. Lidia's mastering the
  art of Italian cuisine 641.594
Bastianich, L. Lidia cooks from the heart of Ita-
  ly 641.5
MANUFACTURES
Liveris, A. Make it in America 330.9
MANUFACTURES
    See also Commercial products; Industries
MANUFACTURES -- DEFECTS *See* Product re-
call
MANUFACTURES RECALL *See* Product recall
MANUFACTURING EXECUTIVES
Crowe, D. Oskar Schindler 92
Kurson, R. Crashing through 92
Partnoy, F. The match king 92
MANUFACTURING INDUSTRIES
Chang, L. T. Factory girls 331.4
MANUFACTURING INDUSTRIES
    See also Industries
**MANUFACTURING INDUSTRIES -- MILI-
TARY ASPECTS -- UNITED STATES -- HIS-**

TORY -- 20TH CENTURY
Herman, A. Freedom's forge 940.53
**MANUFACTURING INDUSTRIES -- UNITED
STATES**
Ferguson, C. Predator nation 330.973
Herman, A. Freedom's forge 940.53
MANUSCRIPTS
Cole, P. Sacred trash 296.09
Howard, D. Lost rights 973.7
MANUSCRIPTS
    See also Archives; Bibliography; Books
**MANUSCRIPTS -- COLLECTION AND PRES-
ERVATION -- UNITED STATES -- HISTORY**
Puleo, S. American treasures 973
**MANUSCRIPTS, ARABIC -- MALI -- TOM-
BOUCTOU**
Hammer, J. The bad-ass librarians of Timbuk-
tu 025.8
MANUSCRIPTS, ILLUMINATED *See* Illumina-
tion of books and manuscripts
Manwaring, Jed
Extraordinary everyday photography 778.71
Manweller, Mathew
(ed) Chronology of the U.S. presidency 973.09
The **Many** faces of Islam. 297
Many subtle channels. Becker, D. L. 840.9
Many were held by the sea. Scott, R. N. 940.4
Manzione, Gianmarc
Pin Action 794.6
Mao. Levine, S. I. 951.05
Mao. Short, P. 951.05
Mao Zedong. Spence, J. D. 951.05
Mao Zedong, 1893-1976
         About
Bernstein, R. China 1945 327.73
Chang, J. Mao: the unknown story 92
Dikötter, F. Mao's great famine 951.05
Levine, S. I. Mao 951.05
Short, P. Mao 951.05
Spence, J. D. Mao Zedong 951.05
Sun Shuyun The Long March 951.04
Mao's great famine. Dikötter, F. 951.05
Mao: the unknown story. Chang, J. 92
MAORIS
    See also Indigenous peoples
Map. 891.8
MAP DRAWING
Brotton, J. Great maps 912.09
Janes, A. Maps 912.09
Lester, T. The fourth part of the world 912
A **Map** of the World 912
Reinhartz, D. The Art of the Map 526
MAP DRAWING
    See also Drawing
The **map** of my dead pilots. Mondor, C. C. 387.7
A **Map** of the World. 912

The **map** that changed the world. Winchester, S. 526

A **map** to the next world. Harjo, J. 811

MAPLE SUGAR

    See also Sugar

Maple, Amanda

  (ed) A basic music library 016

Maples, William R., 1937-1997

        About

  Maples, W. R. Dead men do tell tales 614

The **mapmaker's** wife. Whitaker, R. 981

Mapping Census 2010. Peake, R. 304.6

Mapping human history. Olson, S. 599.9

Mapping Mars. Morton, O. 523.43

Mapping the world. Riffenburgh, B. 912

Mapplethorpe, Robert

        About

  Smith, P. Just kids 92

Maps. Janes, A. 912.09

MAPS

  Benson, M. Cosmigraphics 523.1

  Brotton, J. Great maps 912.09

  Janes, A. Maps 912.09

  A Map of the World 912

  Oxford new concise world atlas 912

  Rand McNally Goodes World Atlas 912

  Reinhartz, D. The Art of the Map 526

  Riffenburgh, B. Mapping the world 912

MAPS

    See also Geography

MAPS -- DESIGN

  Rendgen, S. Understanding the world 741.6

MAPS -- PSYCHOLOGICAL ASPECTS

  Borich, B. J. Body geographic 818

Maps and legends. Chabon, M. 814

MAPS, HISTORICAL *See* Historical atlases

Mar, Alex

  Witches of America 299

Marable, Manning

  (ed) Evers, M. W. The autobiography of Medgar Evers: a hero's life and legacy revealed through his writings, letters, and speeches 92

  (ed) Freedom on my mind 305.8

  Malcolm X 92

Maraniss, Andrew

  Strong inside 92

Maraniss, David

  Barack Obama 92

  Clemente 92

  Once in a great city 977.4

  They marched into sunlight 959.704

  When pride still mattered: a life of Vince Lombardi 92

        About

  Maraniss, D. Into the story 92

MARATHON RUNNING

  Bede, P. N. The Runner's world big book of marathon and half-marathon training 796.425

  Caesar, E. Two hours 796.42

  Douglas, S. Meb for mortals 796.42

  Engle, C. Running Man 796.42

  Finn, A. The Way of the Runner 796.42

  Karnazes, D. The legend of Marathon 938.03

  McDougall, C. Born to run 796.42

  Robbins, L. A race like no other 796.42

  Wade, B. Run the World 796.42

  What I talk about when I talk about running 92

MARATHON RUNNING

    See also Running

MARATHON RUNNING -- PSYCHOLOGICAL ASPECTS

  Foreman, T. My year of running dangerously 92

MARATHON SWIMMING

  Mortimer, G. The great swim 920

MARATHON SWIMMING

    See also Swimming

MARATHON, BATTLE OF, 490 B.C.

  Karnazes, D. The legend of Marathon 938.03

Maravich, Pete, 1947-1988

        About

  Kriegel, M. Pistol 92

MARBLE

    See also Rocks; Stone

Marcel Proust. Carter, W. C. 843

Marcella cucina. Hazan, M. 641.59

Marcella says... Hazan, M. 641.5

MARCELLUS SHALE

  Wilber, T. Under the surface 333.8

March. Lewis, J. 92

March. Lewis, J. R. 92

March de la Torre, Aleida

        About

  Remembering Che 972.91

The **march** of folly. Tuchman, B. W. 909.08

MARCH ON WASHINGTON FOR JOBS AND FREEDOM (1963 : WASHINGTON, D.C.)

  Kelley, K. Let Freedom Ring 323.1

A **march** to madness. Feinstein, J. 796.323

Marchand, Francois

  (ed) Tea 641.3

Marchand, Leslie Alexis

  (ed) Byron, G. G. B. Selected poetry of Lord Byron 821

Marchant, Jo

  Cure 616.89

  Decoding the heavens 681.1

Marchant, Nancy

  Knitting brioche 746.43

  Knitting fresh brioche 746.43

The **Marches.** Stewart, R. 941.3

MARCHES (DEMONSTRATIONS) *See* Demonstrations

MARCHES FOR CIVIL RIGHTS *See* Civil rights

demonstrations

Marchetti, Domenica
The glorious pasta of Italy   **641.82**

MARCHING DRILLS
See also Physical education

Marching Home. Jordan, B. M.   **973.7**

Marching orders. Lee, B.   **940.54**

Marchione, Anthony James, 1925-1945
About
Harding, S. Last to die   **940.54**

Marcia DeCoster's beaded opulence. DeCoster, M.   **739.27**

Marco Polo. Man, J.   **915**

Marco Polo. Bergreen, L.   **92**

Marcoci, Roxana
(jt. auth) Bajac, Q. Photography at MOMA   **770**

Marconi. Raboy, M.   **92**

Marconi, Guglielmo, 1874-1937
About
Larson, E. Thunderstruck   **364.152**
Raboy, M. Marconi   **92**

Marcus Aurelius
Meditations   **188**

Marcus off duty.   **641.5**

Marcus, Eric
Coming out to play   **92**
Why suicide?   **179.7**

Marcus, Greil
(ed) A new literary history of America   **810**
The shape of things to come   **973**

Marcus, Leonard S., 1950-
(ed) Maurice Sendak   **741.6**

Marcus, W. Andrew
(ed) Atlas of Yellowstone   **912.09**

Marder, Michael
The philosopher's plant   **580**

Margaret Sanger. Baker, J. H.   **92**

Margaret Thatcher. Moore, C.   **92**

Margaret, of Anjou, Queen, consort of Henry VI, King of England, 1430-1482
About
Gristwood, S. Blood sisters   **942.04**

Margaret, of York, Duchess, consort of Charles the Bold, Duke of Burgundy, 1446-1503
About
Gristwood, S. Blood sisters   **942.04**

Margery, 1888-1941
About
Jaher, D. The witch of Lime Street   **92**

A **marginal** Jew. Meier, J. P.   **232.9**

Margolick, David
Beyond glory   **796.8**
Elizabeth and Hazel   **92**

Margonelli, Lisa
Oil on the brain   **338.2**

Margotin, Philippe

All the Songs   **781.66**
Bob Dylan   **782.42**

Peterson, M. A brief history of Korea   **951.9**

Margulies, Stuart
Fischer, B. Bobby Fischer teaches chess   **794.1**

Margulis, Jennifer
The business of baby   **649**

Margulis, Lynn
Symbiotic planet   **576.8**
What is life?   **570.1**

Mari, Angelica
(jt. auth) Rigby, C. Fodor's Rio de Janeiro & Sao Paulo   **918.15**

Maria Celeste, 1600-1634
About
Sobel, D. Galileo's daughter   **92**

Maria Tallchief. Tallchief, M.   **92**

Marian Anderson. Keiler, A.   **92**

Mariani, Paul L.
The broken tower: a life of Hart Crane   **811**
Lost puritan: a life of Robert Lowell   **811**

Marianne Moore. Molesworth, C.   **92**

Marie Antoinette. Fraser, A.   **944**

Marie Antoinette. Lever, E.   **92**

Marie Antoinette, Queen, consort of Louis XVI, King of France, 1755-1793
About
Fraser, A. Marie Antoinette   **944**
Lever, E. Marie Antoinette   **92**

Marie Curie and her daughters. Emling, S.   **920**

Marie-Benoît, de Bourg d'Iré, 1895-1990
About
Zuccotti, S. Père Marie-Benoît and Jewish rescue   **940.53**

MARIHUANA *See* Marijuana

MARIJUANA
Backes, M. Cannabis Pharmacy   **615.7**
Cervantes, J. The Cannabis Encyclopedia   **633.79**
Pollan, M. The botany of desire   **306.4**

MARIJUANA
See also Narcotics

MARIJUANA -- ECONOMIC ASPECTS
Fine, D. Too high to fail   **338.4**

MARIJUANA INDUSTRY
Fine, D. Too high to fail   **338.4**

Marin, Cheech
Chicano visions   **709**

Marinacci, Barbara
Pauling, L. C. Linus Pauling in his own words   **081**

MARINAS
See also Boats and boating; Harbors; Yachts and yachting

MARINE ACCIDENTS -- GREAT BRITAIN -- HISTORY -- 20TH CENTURY
Scott, R. N. Many were held by the sea   **940.4**

MARINE ANIMALS

Crist, D. T. World ocean census   **578.7**

MARINE AQUARIUMS

Blanchard, Z. Saltwater Fish and Reef Tanks   **639**

Hargrove, J. Beneath the surface   **599.53**

MARINE AQUARIUMS

See also Aquariums

MARINE BIOLOGISTS

Kirby, D. Death at SeaWorld   **599.53**

Lytle, M. H. The gentle subversive   **92**

Olson, R. Don't be such a scientist   **501**

Safina, C. The view from Lazy Point   **508**

MARINE BIOLOGISTS -- UNITED STATES -- BIOGRAPHY

Souder, W. On a farther shore   **92**

MARINE BIOLOGY

Carson, R. The edge of the sea   **577.7**

Carson, R. Under the sea wind   **578.7**

Cramer, D. Smithsonian ocean   **578.7**

Crist, D. T. World ocean census   **578.7**

Day, T. Oceans   **551.46**

Earle, S. A. The world is blue   **551.46**

Hoyt, E. Creatures of the deep   **591.7**

Plankton   **578.7**

Stow, D. A. V. Oceans: an illustrated reference   **551.46**

MARINE BIOLOGY

See also Biology; Oceanography

MARINE DISASTERS *See* Shipwrecks

MARINE DRILLING PLATFORMS *See* Drilling platforms

MARINE ECOLOGY

Cramer, D. Smithsonian ocean   **578.7**

Earle, S. A. The world is blue   **551.46**

Ellis, R. The empty ocean   **577.7**

Koslow, J. A. The silent deep   **578.7**

Pepperell, J. G. Fishes of the open ocean   **597**

Plankton   **578.7**

Roberts, C. The ocean of life   **551.46**

Safina, C. The view from Lazy Point   **508**

MARINE FISHES -- CONSERVATION

Rigney, M. In pursuit of giants   **597**

MARINE FISHES -- ECOLOGY

Rigney, M. In pursuit of giants   **597**

MARINE INSURANCE

See also Commerce; Insurance; Maritime law; Merchant marine; Shipping

MARINE MAMMALS

Folkens, P. A. National Audubon Society guide to marine mammals of the world   **599.5**

MARINE MAMMALS

See also Mammals; Marine animals

MARINE MAMMALS -- BEHAVIOR

Kirby, D. Death at SeaWorld   **599.53**

MARINE MINERAL RESOURCES

See also Marine resources; Mines and mineral resources; Ocean bottom; Ocean engineering

MARINE PAINTING

See also Painting

MARINE PHOTOGRAPHY

Rotman, J. L. The last fisherman   **778.7**

MARINE PLANKTON

Kirby, R. R. Ocean drifters   **578.7**

MARINE PLANTS

See also Marine biology; Plants

MARINE POLLUTION

Earle, S. A. The world is blue   **551.46**

Moore, C. Plastic ocean   **363.7**

MARINE POLLUTION

See also Oceanography; Water pollution

MARINE RESOURCES

Grescoe, T. Bottomfeeder   **641.6**

Koslow, J. A. The silent deep   **578.7**

MARINE RESOURCES

See also Commercial products; Marine biology; Natural resources; Oceanography

MARINE SALVAGE

Peffer, R. Where divers dare   **940.54**

MARINE SALVAGE

See also International law; Maritime law; Salvage

MARINE SCIENCES

Nichols, C. R. Encyclopedia of marine science   **551.46**

Marine, Carol

Daily painting   **751.4**

MARINELAND (FLA.)

See also Marine aquariums

MARINER'S COMPASS *See* Compass

MARINERS *See* Sailors

MARINES

Burgin, R. V. Islands of the damned   **940.54**

Sielski, M. Fading echoes   **92**

Swofford, A. Jarhead: a Marine's chronicle of the Gulf War and other battles   **956.704**

MARINES -- EDUCATION -- UNITED STATES

Ventrone, J. From the Marine Corps to college   **378.1**

MARINES -- UNITED STATES -- HISTORY -- 20TH CENTURY

Weintraub, S. A Christmas far from home   **951.904**

Mario Batali Big American cookbook.   **641.597**

Marion, Robert

About

Marion, R. Genetic rounds   **92**

MARIONETTES *See* Puppets and puppet plays

Maris, Roger, 1934-1985

About

Clavin, T. Roger Maris   **92**

MARITAL INFIDELITY *See* Adultery

MARITIME DISCOVERIES *See* Exploration

MARITIME LAW

See also International law; Law; Shipping

Mark Bittman's Kitchen express. Bittman, M. **641.5**

Mark Bittman's kitchen matrix. Bittman, M. **641.5**

Mark Rothko. Cohen-Solal, A. **759.13**

Mark Twain. Loving, J. **92**

Mark Twain. Powers, R. **92**

Mark Twain. Shelden, M. **92**

Mark Twain and the Colonel. McFarland, P. **973.8**

The Mark Twain papers [series]

    Autobiography of Mark Twain **92**

Mark Twain's library of humor. Twain, M. **817**

Marked for death. Hamilton-Paterson, J. **940.44**

MARKET SURVEYS

    See also Advertising; Surveys

MARKETING

    Burcher, N. Paid, owned, earned **658.8**

    Casey, M. Che's afterlife **980**

    Jantsch, J. The referral engine **658.8**

    Lindström, M. Small Data **658.8**

    Martinez, A. G. Chaos Monkeys **338.4**

    Parr, B. Captivology **153.7**

    Thompson, M. Now, build a great business! **658**

    Underhill, P. Why we buy **658.8**

    Watkins, A. Hello, my name is awesome **658.8**

MARKETING

    See also Business; Management

MARKETING (HOME ECONOMICS) *See* Grocery shopping; Shopping

MARKETING -- MANAGEMENT

    Burcher, N. Paid, owned, earned **658.8**

MARKETING -- SOCIAL ASPECTS

    Davies, W. The happiness industry **304**

MARKETING -- TECHNOLOGICAL INNOVATIONS

    Turow, J. The daily you **659.1**

MARKETING RESEARCH

    Kolko, J. Well-designed **658.5**

Marketing your library. **021.7**

Marketing your library's electronic resources. Laguardia, C. **025.2**

MARKETS

    Roth, A. E. Who gets what--and why **330.01**

    Saltsman, A. The Santa Monica Farmers' Market Cookbook **641.5**

MARKETS

    See also Business; Cities and towns; Commerce

Markham, Beryl, 1902-1986

    West with the night **92**

        About

    Trzebinski, E. The lives of Beryl Markham **629.13**

Markham, Brett L.

    Mini farming **635**

Markings. Hammarskjold, D. **839.7**

Markoe, Arnie

    (ed) The Scribner encyclopedia of American lives **920.003**

Markoe, Karen

    (ed) The Scribner encyclopedia of American lives **920.003**

Markoff, John

    What the dormouse said-- **004**

Markowitz, Harvey

    (ed) American Indians **970.004**

Marks' standard handbook for mechanical engineers. **621**

Marks, Gil

    The world of Jewish cooking **641.5**

Marks, Jonathan

    What it means to be 98[percent] chimpanzee **599.93**

MARKSMEN

    Kasper, S. Annie Oakley **92**

Markus, Julia

    Lady Byron and Her Daughters **92**

Marley, Bob

        About

    Grant, C. The natural mystics **920**

Marling, Karal Ann

    As seen on TV **973.92**

Marlow, Kristian

    (jt. auth) Brogaard, B. The superhuman mind **153.9**

Marlowe, Christopher, 1564-1593

    Plays The complete plays **822**

        About

    Heaney, S. Finders keepers **821**

    Honan, P. Christopher Marlowe **92**

    Nicholl, C. The reckoning **92**

Marlowe, Jen

    Al Jundi, S. The hour of sunlight **92**

The Marne, 1914. Herwig, H. H. **940.4**

Marnham, Patrick

    Dreaming with his eyes open **92**

The marquis. Auricchio, L. **92**

Marquis, Sarah, 1972-

        About

    Marquis, S. Wild by nature **613.6**

MARRIAGE

    Alexander, E. The light of the world **92**

    Barash, D. P. The myth of monogamy **306.7**

    Bergen, C. A fine romance **92**

    Cusk, R. Aftermath **823**

    Fisher, H. Anatomy of Love **302.3**

    Goleman, D. Emotional intelligence **152.4**

    MacColl, G. To marry an English Lord **974.7**

    Moore, W. How to create the perfect wife **823**

    Roiphe, A. R. Married **306.81**

    Roiphe, K. Uncommon arrangements **920**

    Rosenblatt, R. The book of love **152.4**

    Shulman, A. K. To love what is **92**

    Wizenberg, M. Delancey **647.95**

    Wright, J. It Ended Badly **302**

    Yalom, M. A history of the wife **306.872**

MARRIAGE

See also Family; Sacraments

MARRIAGE -- ECONOMIC ASPECTS -- UNITED STATES

Carbone, J. Marriage markets   **306.85**

MARRIAGE -- GREAT BRITAIN -- HISTORY -- 18TH CENTURY

Moore, W. How to create the perfect wife   **823**

MARRIAGE -- POETRY

Gilbert, J. Collected poems   **811**

MARRIAGE -- PSYCHOLOGICAL ASPECTS

Cusk, R. Aftermath   **823**

MARRIAGE CONTRACTS

See also Contracts; Marriage

MARRIAGE COUNSELING

See also Counseling; Family life education; Marriage

MARRIAGE CUSTOMS AND RITES

Jellison, K. It's our day   **392**

MARRIAGE CUSTOMS AND RITES

See also Manners and customs; Marriage; Rites and ceremonies; Weddings

MARRIAGE LAW -- UNITED STATES

Dickey, L. Then comes marriage   **346**

Marriage markets. Carbone, J.   **306.85**

MARRIAGE PROBLEMS

Blair, J. By the Iowa Sea   **977.7**

Married. Roiphe, A. R.   **306.81**

MARRIED LIFE *See* Marriage

MARRIED MEN *See* Husbands

MARRIED PEOPLE

Chafe, W. H. Bill and Hillary   **973.929**

Lascher, B. Eve of a Hundred Midnights   **070.449**

Wizenberg, M. Delancey   **647.95**

MARRIED PEOPLE

See also Family; Marriage

MARRIED PEOPLE -- UNITED STATES -- BIOGRAPHY

Caroli, B. B. Lady Bird and Lyndon   **92**

MARRIED PERSONS *See* Married people

MARRIED WOMEN *See* Wives

MARRIED WOMEN -- UNITED STATES -- HISTORY

Berkin, C. Civil War wives   **920**

Marriott, Susannah

(jt. auth) Cross, C. The baby book   **649.122**

Marrocco, Geraldine F.

(ed) Magill's medical guide   **610**

Marrs, Suzanne

Eudora Welty: a biography   **92**

(ed) Meanwhile there are letters   **92**

(ed) What there is to say we have said   **92**

MARS (PLANET)

Morton, O. Mapping Mars   **523.43**

MARS (PLANET)

See also Planets

MARS (PLANET) -- EXPLORATION

Aldrin, B. Mission to mars   **629.44**

Hubbard, S. Exploring Mars   **523.43**

Manning, R. Mars Rover Curiosity   **629.295**

Mars Rover Curiosity. Manning, R.   **629.295**

Mars, Forrest, Sr.

About

Brenner, J. G. The emperors of chocolate   **338.7**

MARS, INC.

Brenner, J. G. The emperors of chocolate   **338.7**

Marsalis, Wynton

Moving to higher ground   **781.65**

Marschark, Marc

(jt. auth) Hauser, P. C. How deaf children learn   **371.91**

Marsden, George M.

Jonathan Edwards   **92**

MARSEILLE (FRANCE) -- BIOGRAPHY

Zuccotti, S. Père Marie-Benoît and Jewish rescue   **940.53**

MARSH ECOLOGY

See also Ecology

Marsh, Charles

Strange glory   **92**

Marsh, Henry, 1954-

Do No Harm   **92**

Marshal, William

About

Asbridge, T. The Greatest Knight   **92**

Marshall McLuhan. Coupland, D.   **92**

MARSHALL PLAN *See* Reconstruction (1939-1951)

Marshall, Dan

About

Marshall, D. Home is burning   **92**

Marshall, George C. (George Catlett), 1880-1959

Don't Even Think About It   **551.6**

About

Groom, W. The generals   **940.54**

Halberstam, D. The best and the brightest   **973.922**

Jordan, J. W. American warlords   **973.917**

Roberts, A. Masters and commanders   **940.54**

Unger, I. George Marshall   **92**

Weintraub, S. 15 stars   **920**

Marshall, Jim

Trust   **781.66**

Marshall, John, 1755-1835

About

Simon, J. F. What kind of nation   **342**

Smith, J. E. John Marshall   **347**

Unger, H. G. John Marshall   **92**

Marshall, Leslie

Every step you take   **92**

Marshall, Paule, 1929-

About

Black women writers (1950-1980)   **810**

Marshall, P. Triangular road   **92**

Marshall, Samantha
  Reunited   **362.82**
Marshall, Thurgood, 1908-1993
    About
  Gibson, L. S. Young Thurgood   **347.73**
  Haygood, W. Showdown   **347.73**
  King, G. Devil in the grove   **305.896**
  Marshall, T. Thurgood Marshall   **347**
  Rowan, C. T. Dream makers, dream breakers   **92**
  Williams, J. Thurgood Marshall   **92**
MARSHALS
  Brighton, T. Patton, Montgomery, Rommel   **920**
  Millard, C. The river of doubt   **973.91**
  Roberts, A. Masters and commanders   **940.54**
  Showalter, D. E. Patton and Rommel   **92**
MARSHALS -- SOVIET UNION -- BIOGRAPHY
  Roberts, G. Stalin's general   **940.54**
Marshes. Burt, W.   **578.7**
MARSHES
  Burt, W. Marshes   **578.7**
The **marshmallow** test. Mischel, W.   **155.2**
Marston, Daniel
  (ed) The Pacific War   **940.54**
MARSUPIALS
  See also Mammals
Martelle, Scott
  Detroit   **977.4**
Marten, James
  Civil War America   **973.7**
Marter, Joan
  (ed) The Grove encyclopedia of American art **709**
Martha Stewart living
  Martha Stewart's encyclopedia of crafts   **745.5**
Martha Stewart Living Omnimedia Inc.
  (comp) One pot   **641.82**
Martha Stewart's cooking school. Stewart, M. **641.5**
Martha Stewart's encyclopedia of crafts. Martha
  Stewart living   **745.5**
Martha Stewart's encyclopedia of sewing and fabric
  crafts. Stewart, M.   **746**
Martha Stewart's Homekeeping Handbook. Stew-
  art, M.   **640**
Martha Washington. Brady, P.   **92**
Martha's   entertaining.
MARTHA'S VINEYARD (MASS.)
  The Beetlebung Farm cookbook   **641**
Martial
  Epigrams   **878**
MARTIAL ARTS
  Salzman, M. Iron & silk   **951.05**
  Wertheim, L. J. Blood in the cage   **92**
MARTIAL ARTS
  See also Athletics
MARTIAL ARTS -- FICTION
  Howley, K. Thrown   **796.8**
MARTIAL LAW

  See also Law
Martian summer. Kessler, A.   **523.4**
The **Martians** of science. Hargittai, I.   **920**
The **Martin** Duberman reader. Duberman, M.
  B.   **306.76**
Martin Luther. Hendrix, S. H.   **92**
MARTIN LUTHER KING DAY
  See also Holidays
Martin Van Buren. Widmer, E. L.   **92**
Martin, Barnaby
  Hanging man   **709**
Martin, Billy, 1928-1989
    About
  Billy Martin   **92**
  Pennington, B. Billy Martin   **92**
Martin, Brett
  Difficult men   **791.450**
Martin, Dean
    About
  Lewis, J. Dean & me   **92**
Martin, Deborah L.
  Pleasant, B. The complete compost gardening
  guide   **631.8**
Martin, Emily J.
  American Civil Liberties Union The rights of
  women   **346.01**
Martin, Gerald
  Gabriel Garcia Marquez   **92**
Martin, Gerry
  Macfarlane, A. Glass: a world history   **666**
Martin, Giles
  (ed) Dewey decimal classification and relative in-
  dex   **025.4**
Martin, James
  The Jesuit guide to almost everything   **248.4**
  My life with the saints   **920**
    About
  Martin, J. My life with the saints   **920**
Martin, John
  (ed) Bukowski, C. The pleasures of the damned **811**
Martin, Judith
  Miss Manners' guide to excruciatingly correct be-
  havior   **395**
Martin, Leslie R.
  (jt. auth) Friedman, H. S. The longevity proj-
  ect   **613.2**
Martin, Luther, 1744-1826
    About
  Kauffman, B. Forgotten founder, drunken proph-
  et   **92**
Martin, Mary, 1913-1990
    About
  Kaufman, D. Some enchanted evenings   **92**
Martin, Peter
  A life of James Boswell   **828**
  Samuel Johnson   **92**

Martin, Richard C.
(ed) Encyclopedia of Islam and the Muslim world   **909**
Martin, Robert
How we do it   **612.6**
Martin, Roger H., 1943-
    About
Martin, R. H. Racing Odysseus   **92**
Martin, Sasha
    About
Martin, S. Life from scratch   **92**
Martin, Steve, 1945-
Pure drivel   **814**
    About
Martin, S. Born standing up   **92**
Martin, Tovah
The indestructible houseplant   **635.9**
The new terrarium   **635.9**
The unexpected houseplant   **635.9**
Martin, Valerie
Salvation: scenes from the life of St. Francis   **92**
Martin, Wednesday
    About
Martin, W. Primates of Park Avenue   **974.7**
Martin, William C.
With God on our side   **261.8**
Martin, William Patrick
Wonderfully wordless   **011.62**
Martinez Wood, Jamie
Latino writers and journalists   **920.003**
Martinez, Antonio Garcia
Chaos Monkeys   **338.4**
Martínez, Rubén
Desert America   **330.9**
The new Americans   **305.9**
Martinez, Sara E.
(ed) Latino literature   **016**
Martinez-Fernandez, Luis
Encyclopedia of Cuba   **972.91**
Martinson, Deborah
Lillian Hellman   **92**
Marton, Endre, 1910-2005
    About
Marton, K. Enemies of the people   **92**
Marton, Ilona, 1912-2004
    About
Marton, K. Enemies of the people   **92**
Marton, Kati
The great escape   **920**
Hidden power   **920**
    About
Marton, K. Enemies of the people   **92**
Marty, Edwin
(jt. auth) Hanson, D. Breaking through concrete   **630**
Marty, Martin E.

Pilgrims in their own land   **277**
MARTYRS
Strathern, P. Death in Florence   **945**
MARTYRS
    See also Church history; Heroes and heroines
Martz, Louis Lohr
(ed) Collected poems, 1912-1944   **811**
Marvel Comics. Howe, S.   **741.5**
MARVEL COMICS GROUP
75 years of Marvel Comics   **741.5**
Marvel, William
Burgin, R. V. Islands of the damned   **940.54**
Lincoln's autocrat   **92**
Marvell, Andrew
Poems   **821**
MARVELOUS, THE, IN LITERATURE
Saler, M. As if   **823**
Marx Brothers
    About
Louvish, S. Monkey business   **920**
Marx's general. Hunt, T.   **92**
Marx, Groucho, 1891-1977
    About
Kanfer, S. Groucho: the life and times of Julius Henry Marx   **92**
Marx, Jenny
    About
Gabriel, M. Love and capital   **92**
Marx, Karl, 1818-1883
Capital: an abridged edition   **330.1**
The Communist manifesto   **335.4**
    About
Camus, A. The rebel   **303.6**
Gabriel, M. Love and capital   **92**
Heilbroner, R. L. The worldly philosophers   **330.1**
Sperber, J. Karl Marx   **92**
Wheen, F. Karl Marx   **335.4**
Marx, Rebecca Flint
The Basque book   **641.5**
MARXIAN THEORY *See* Marxism
MARXISM
Gabriel, M. Love and capital   **92**
Lefebvre, H. Critique of everyday life   **301**
Mary Cassatt. Mathews, N. M.   **759.13**
Mary Queen of Scots. Fraser, A.   **92**
Mary Shelley. Seymour, M.   **92**
Mary Thomas's dictionary of embroidery stitches. Thomas, M.   **746.44**
Mary through the centuries. Pelikan, J. J.   **232.91**
Mary Todd Lincoln. Baker, J. H.   **92**
Mary, Blessed Virgin, Saint
    About
Hazleton, L. Mary: a flesh-and-blood biography of the Virgin Mother   **92**
Pelikan, J. J. Mary through the centuries   **232.91**
Mary, Duchess of Gloucester, 1776-1857
    About

About
Fraser, F. Princesses   **920**

Mary, Queen of Scots, 1542-1587
About
Fraser, A. Mary Queen of Scots   **92**
Schiller, F. Don Carlos and Mary Stuart   **832**
Weir, A. The lost Tudor princess   **92**
Weir, A. Mary, Queen of Scots, and the murder of Lord Darnley   **92**

Mary, Queen of Scots, and the murder of Lord Darnley. Weir, A.   **92**

Mary: a flesh-and-blood biography of the Virgin Mother. Hazleton, L.   **92**

Maryam Jameelah, 1934-2012
About
Baker, D. The convert   **92**

MARYLAND -- HISTORY
Rudacille, D. Roots of steel   **338.4**

MARYLAND -- HISTORY -- WAR OF 1812 -- CAMPAIGNS
Snow, P. When Britain burned the White House   **975.3**
Vogel, S. Through the perilous fight   **973.5**

Marzluff, John M.
Welcome to subirdia   **598**

MASAI (AFRICAN PEOPLE)
See also Africans; Indigenous peoples

MASCULINITY
Giraldi, W. The Hero's Body   **92**
McBee, T. P. Man alive   **92**
Wiseman, R. Masterminds and wingmen   **649**

MASCULINITY
See also Sex -- Psychological aspects

MASCULINITY (PSYCHOLOGY) See Masculinity

Masear, Terry
Fastest Things on Wings   **598**

MASKS (PLAYS)
See also Drama; Pageants; Theater

MASKS (SCULPTURE)
See also Sculpture

The masks of God [series]
Campbell, J. Creative mythology   **201**
Campbell, J. Occidental mythology   **201**
Campbell, J. Oriental mythology   **201**
Campbell, J. Primitive mythology   **201**

Maslin, Ruthie
Imhoff, K. R. Library contests   **021.7**

Maslon, Laurence
Broadway   **792.6**

Mason, Andrew, 1981-
About
Sennett, F. Groupon's biggest deal ever   **381**

Mason, Bobbie Ann
Elvis Presley   **92**

Mason, David

(ed) Twentieth-century American poetry   **811**

Mason, George, 1725-1792
About
Broadwater, J. George Mason, forgotten founder   **92**

Mason, Julian D.
(ed) The poems of Phillis Wheatley   **811**

Mason, Shirley Ardell
About
Nathan, D. Sybil exposed   **616.85**

MASONRY
The complete outdoor builder   **690**

MASONRY
See also Building; Stone

MASONRY -- AMATEURS' MANUALS
The complete outdoor builder   **690**

Masquerade: the life and times of Deborah Sampson, Continental soldier. Young, A. F.   **92**

MASS COMMUNICATION See Communication; Mass media; Telecommunication

MASS CULTURE See Popular culture

Mass destruction. LeCain, T. J.   **338.2**

MASS EXTINCTIONS
Alvarez, W. T. rex and the Crater of Doom   **551.7**
Barnosky, A. D. Dodging extinction   **576.8**

MASS MEDIA
Burcher, N. Paid, owned, earned   **658.8**
Carpini, M. X. D. After broadcast news   **071**
Coupland, D. Marshall McLuhan   **92**
Durham, M. G. The Lolita effect   **302.23**
Gladstone, B. The influencing machine   **302.23**
Gonzalez, J. News for all the people   **302.23**
Jones, G. Killing monsters   **302.23**
Journalism   **070.4**
McLuhan, M. The global village   **302.2**
O'Connor, R. Friends, followers, and the future   **302.3**
Postman, N. Amusing ourselves to death   **302.23**
Understanding media   **302.23**
Wolff, M. The man who owns the news   **92**

MASS MEDIA
See also Communication

MASS MEDIA -- ECONOMIC ASPECTS
Elberse, A. Blockbusters   **384**

MASS MEDIA -- HISTORY
Wu, T. c. The master switch   **384**

MASS MEDIA -- OBJECTIVITY -- UNITED STATES
Sherrod, S. The courage to hope   **975.8**

MASS MEDIA -- POLITICAL ASPECTS -- UNITED STATES
Carpini, M. X. D. After broadcast news   **071**

MASS MEDIA -- POLITICAL ASPECTS -- UNITED STATES -- HISTORY -- 20TH CENTURY
Bai, M. All the truth is out   **328.73**

MASS MEDIA -- SOCIAL ASPECTS

Rushkoff, D. Present Shock **303.48**

MASS MEDIA -- UNITED STATES -- HISTORY

Understanding media **302.23**

MASS MEDIA -- UNITED STATES -- INFLUENCE

Jimenez, S. The Book of Matt **364.1**

MASS MURDER

Goldhagen, D. J. Worse than war **364.1**

MASS POLITICAL BEHAVIOR *See* Political participation; Political psychology

MASS PSYCHOLOGY *See* Social psychology

MASS SURVEILLANCE

See also Intelligence service

Massaad, Barbara Abdeni

Man'oushé **641.5**

MASSACHUSETTS -- HISTORY

Fischer, D. H. Paul Revere's ride **973.3**

Manegold, C. Ten Hills Farm **974.4**

MASSACHUSETTS -- HISTORY -- 1600-1775, COLONIAL PERIOD

Bradford, W. Of Plymouth Plantation, 1620-1647 **974.4**

Bunker, N. Making haste from Babylon **974.4**

Demos, J. The unredeemed captive **973.2**

LaPlante, E. Salem witch judge **92**

Philbrick, N. Mayflower **973.2**

MASSACHUSETTS -- HISTORY -- REVOLUTION, 1775-1783

Raphael, R. The spirit of 74 **973.3**

Massacre at Mountain Meadows. Walker, R. W. **979.2**

MASSACRES

Lane, C. The day freedom died **976.3**

Snyder, T. D. Bloodlands **940.54**

Stearns, J. K. Dancing in the glory of monsters **967.51**

MASSACRES

See also Atrocities; History; Persecution

MASSACRES -- CONGO (DEMOCRATIC REPUBLIC)

Stearns, J. K. Dancing in the glory of monsters **967.51**

MASSACRES -- GRAPHIC NOVELS

Sacco, J. Footnotes in Gaza **956.04**

MASSACRES -- NORTHERN IRELAND -- LONDONDERRY -- HISTORY -- 20TH CENTURY

Campbell, J. Setting the truth free **941.6**

Massery, Hazel Bryan, 1942-

About

Margolick, D. Elizabeth and Hazel **92**

MASSEY ENERGY (FIRM)

Galuszka, P. A. Thunder on the Mountain **363.11**

MASSEY ENERGY (FIRM) -- TRIALS, LITIGATION, ETC

Leamer, L. The price of justice **346.730**

Massey, Lorraine

Curly girl **646.7**

Massie, Robert K., 1929-

Catherine the Great **947**

Nicholas and Alexandra **92**

Massie, R. K. Castles of steel **940.4**

The Romanovs **947.08**

Massie, Suzanne

Land of the firebird **947**

Massimino, Mike, 1962-

About

Massimino, M. Spaceman **92**

MASSIVE OPEN ONLINE COURSES

See also Internet in education; University extension

Masson, J. Moussaieff

When elephants weep **591.5**

Massov, Olga

Van Leeuwen Artisan Ice Cream **641**

Mast Brothers Chocolate. **641.6**

MAST BROTHERS CHOCOLATE

Mast Brothers Chocolate **641.6**

Mast, Michael

Mast Brothers Chocolate **641.6**

Mast, Rick

Mast Brothers Chocolate **641.6**

MASTECTOMY

Stark, L. Pandora's DNA **616.99**

The **master** algorithm. Domingos, P. **003**

Master Harold-- and the boys. Fugard, A. **822**

Master of the grill. **641.578**

Master of the mountain. Wiencek, H. **973.4**

The **master** switch. Wu, T. c. **384**

Mastering artisan cheesemaking. Caldwell, G. **637**

Mastering calligraphy. Godfrey-Nicholls, G. **745.6**

Mastering comics. Abel, J. **741.5**

Mastering My Mistakes in the Kitchen. Cowin, D. **641.5**

Mastering pasta. **641.82**

Mastering Sauces. Volland, S. **641.81**

Mastering the art of Chinese cooking. **641.59**

Mastering the art of French cooking. Child, J. **641.5**

Mastering the art of Southern cooking. Dupree, N. **641.59**

Mastering the art of Soviet cooking. Von Bremzen, A. **641.59**

Mastermind. Konnikova, M. **153.4**

Masterminds and wingmen. Wiseman, R. **649**

Masterpieces of French literature. Severson, M. S. **843**

Masterplots II, drama series. **809**

Masterplots II, poetry series. **809.1**

Masters. Sampson, C. **796.352**

Masters and commanders. Roberts, A. **940.54**

Masters of American comics. **741.5**

Masters of Empire. McDonnell, M. A. **977.4**

Masters of management. Wooldridge, A.   658
Masters of the planet. Tattersall, I.   599.93
Masters, Jarvis
             About
  Masters, J. That bird has my wings   92
Masterson, Karen M.
  The malaria project   616.9
MASTODON
      See also Extinct animals; Fossil mammals
Masur, Louis P.
  The Civil War: a concise history   973.7
  The soiling of Old Glory   974.4
Mat, mount and frame it yourself. Logan, M. D. 749
The match. Whitehouse, B.   92
The match. Frost, M.   796.352
The match king. Partnoy, F.   92
MATCHING THEORY
  Roth, A. E. Who gets what--and why   330.01
MATERIA MEDICA
      See also Medicine; Therapeutics
MATERIA MEDICA -- DICTIONARIES
  O'Neil, M. J. The Merck index   615
**MATERIA MEDICA, VEGETABLE -- HAND-
  BOOKS, MANUALS, ETC**
  The herbal apothecary   615.3
MATERIAL CULTURE
  History of the world in 1,000 objects   909
  Leonard, A. The story of stuff   306.4
  MacGregor, N. A history of the world in 100 ob-
    jects   930.1
  Weisman, A. The world without us   304.2
MATERIAL CULTURE
      See also Culture
MATERIAL CULTURE -- HISTORY
  History of the world in 1,000 objects   909
MATERIALISM
  Gosling, S. Snoop   155.9
MATERIALISM
      See also Philosophy; Positivism
MATERIALISM -- UNITED STATES
  Roberts, J. A. Shiny objects   339.4
MATERIALS
  Miodownik, M. Stuff matters   620.1
MATERIALS HANDLING
      See also Management
The math book. Pickover, C. A.   510
Math on trial. Colmez, C.   345
MATHEMATICAL ABILITY
      See also Ability
MATHEMATICAL ANALYSIS
  Adam, J. A. A mathematical nature walk   510
  Anderson, C. The numbers game   796.334
  Michael, T. S. How to guard an art gallery and oth-
    er discrete mathematical adventures   511
MATHEMATICAL MODELS
  Baker, S. The numerati   303.4

MATHEMATICAL MODELS
      See also Mathematics
A mathematical nature walk. Adam, J. A.   510
MATHEMATICAL RECREATIONS
  Gardner, M. The colossal book of short puzzles
    and problems   793.8
  Tahan, M. The man who counted   793.74
The mathematical universe. Dunham, W.   510
MATHEMATICIANS
  Aczel, A. D. The artist and the mathematician 500
  Bell, E. T. Men of mathematics   920
  The Cambridge companion to Newton   530
  Cohen, M. N. Lewis Carroll   92
  Connor, J. A. Pascal's wager   92
  Dennett, D. C. Darwin's dangerous idea   146
  Derbyshire, J. Prime obsession   512.7
  Devlin, K. J. The unfinished game   519.2
  Dolnick, E. The clockwork universe   509
  Dunham, W. The mathematical universe   510
  Fara, P. Newton: the making of genius   92
  Feldman, B. 112 Mercer Street   920
  Galison, P. L. Einstein's clocks and Poincare's
    maps   529
  Gessen, M. Perfect rigor   92
  Gleick, J. Isaac Newton   92
  Goldstein, R. Incompleteness   92
  Hargittai, I. The Martians of science   920
  Havil, J. The irrationals   512
  Hirshfeld, A. Eureka man   92
  Kanigel, R. The man who knew infinity   510
  Leavitt, D. The man who knew too much   92
  Levenson, T. Newton and the counterfeiter   92
  Life stories   920
  Livio, M. The equation that couldn't be solved 512
  Marton, K. The great escape   920
  Miller, A. I. Empire of the stars   520
  Nadler, S. M. The best of all possible worlds   190
  Remnick, D. Reporting   814
  Roberts, S. King of infinite space   92
  Rudman, P. S. The Babylonian theorem   510
  Russell, B. A history of Western philosophy   109
  Singh, S. Fermat's enigma   512
  Smiley, J. The man who invented the computer 92
  Snyder, L. J. The philosophical breakfast club 509
  Szpiro, G. G. Poincare's prize   510
  Watson, R. A. Cogito ergo sum: the life of Rene
    Descartes   92
  Westfall, R. S. The life of Isaac Newton   92
MATHEMATICIANS
      See also Scientists
MATHEMATICIANS -- BIOGRAPHY
  Schewe, P. F. Maverick Genius   92
MATHEMATICIANS -- DICTIONARIES
  Newton, D. E. Latinos in science, math, and profes-
    sions   920.003
MATHEMATICIANS -- FRANCE -- BIOGRA-

PHY
Birth of a theorem 92
MATHEMATICIANS -- GREAT BRITAIN -- BI-OGRAPHY
Copeland, B. J. Turing 92
Essinger, J. Ada's algorithm 92
MATHEMATICS
Adam, J. A. A mathematical nature walk 510
Alexander, A. Infinitesimal 511
Barrow, J. D. 100 essential things you didn't know you didn't know 510
Benjamin, A. The Magic of Math 510
Boyer, C. B. A history of mathematics 510
Colmez, C. Math on trial 345
Dunham, W. The mathematical universe 510
Ellenberg, J. How not to be wrong 510
Henderson, M. 100 most important science ideas 500
The New York Times book of mathematics 510
O'Rourke, J. How to fold it 516
Ouellette, J. The calculus diaries 515
Parker, M. Things to make and do in the fourth dimension 510
Pasles, P. C. Benjamin Franklin's numbers 510
Posamentier, A. S. Magnificent mistakes in mathematics 510
Seife, C. Proofiness 510
Singh, S. The Simpsons and their mathematical secrets 510
Stewart, I. Visions of Infinity 510
Strogatz, S. The joy of X 510
Szpiro, G. G. Numbers rule 510
Szpiro, G. G. Poincare's prize 510
Tammet, D. Thinking in numbers 510
Tegmark, M. Our mathematical universe 523.1
Thaller, B. Numbers 513.5
Tymony, C. Sneaky math 510
Winston, W. L. Mathletics 796
MATHEMATICS
See also Science
MATHEMATICS -- COMPUTER-ASSISTED INSTRUCTION
See also Computer-assisted instruction
MATHEMATICS -- ENCYCLOPEDIAS
Encyclopedia of mathematics and society 303.48
MATHEMATICS -- HISTORY
Dyson, G. Turing's cathedral 004
Encyclopedia of mathematics and society 303.48
Havil, J. The irrationals 512
Mackenzie, D. The universe in zero words 512.9
Pickover, C. A. The math book 510
MATHEMATICS -- MISCELLANEA
Stewart, I. Professor Stewart's casebook of mathematical mysteries 510
MATHEMATICS -- POPULAR WORKS
Cheng, E. How to bake pi 510.1

Mazur, J. Fluke 519.2
MATHEMATICS -- SOCIAL ASPECTS
Encyclopedia of mathematics and society 303.48
MATHEMATICS TEACHERS
Hargittai, I. The Martians of science 920
Marton, K. The great escape 920
MATHEMATICS, GREEK
Berlinski, D. The king of infinite space 516.2
Nicastro, N. Circumference 526
Matheson, Christie
Flour 641.8
Mathew Brady. Wilson, R. 770.92
Mathew Brady and the image of history. Panzer, M. 770.92
Mathewes-Green, Frederica
Welcome to the Orthodox Church 281.9
The **Mathews** Men. Geroux, W. 940.54
Mathews, Nancy Mowll
Mary Cassatt 759.13
Mathletics. Winston, W. L. 796
MATING BEHAVIOR *See* Animal courtship; Sexual behavior in animals
Matisse the master. Spurling, H. 92
Matisse, Henri, 1869-1954
About
Fraser, K. Ornament and silence 809
Henri Matisse 709.2
Smee, S. The art of rivalry 700.92
Spurling, H. Matisse the master 92
Spurling, H. The unknown Matisse 92
Matlen, Terry
The queen of distraction 616.85
Matlins, Stuart M.
(ed) How to be a perfect stranger 203
Matos, Michaelangelo
The underground is massive 781.648
MATRIMONY *See* Marriage
Matsen, Bradford
Jacques Cousteau 92
Matson, Tim, 1943-
Earth ponds 627
MATTER
Lederman, L. Beyond the god particle 539.7
Ronk, M. Transfer of Qualities 811
MATTER
See also Dynamics; Physics
Matter, Jordan
About
Matter, J. Dancers among us 770
Mattera, John (Wreck diver)
About
Kurson, R. Pirate hunters 910.91
Mattern, Susan P.
Prince of medicine 610.9
Matteson, John
Eden's outcasts 92

The lives of Margaret Fuller   **920**

Matthews, Chris
Kennedy & Nixon   **973.922**

Matthews, Dona
(jt. auth) Foster, J. Beyond intelligence   **649**

Matthews, Joe
Bringing Adam home   **364.1**

Matthews, Joseph L.
Social security, Medicare & government pensions   **344**

Matthews, Joseph R.
Scorecards for results   **027.4**

Matthews, William
After all   **811**
Selected poems and translations, 1969-1991   **811**

Matthews, Winton E.
(ed) Dewey decimal classification and relative index   **025.4**

Matthiessen, F. O.
American renaissance   **810**

Matthiessen, Peter
African silences   **916**
End of the earth   **508**
Tigers in the snow   **599.756**

Mattison, Chris
(ed) Firefly Encyclopedia of Reptiles and Amphibians   **597.9**
What reptile?   **639.3**

Mattison, Christopher
The new encyclopedia of snakes   **597.96**
Snakes of the world   **597.96**

MATURATION (PSYCHOLOGY)
    See also Developmental psychology

Matuz, Roger
Reconstruction era: biographies   **920**

Matz, Joshua
(jt. auth) Tribe, L. H. Uncertain justice   **342.73**

MAU MAU
Anderson, D. M. Histories of the hanged   **967.62**

MAU MAU -- POETRY
Foulds, A. The broken word   **821**

Maugham, W. Somerset (William Somerset), 1874-1965
    About
Hastings, S. The secret lives of Somerset Maugham   **92**

Mauldin, Bill, 1921-2003
    About
DePastino, T. Bill Mauldin   **92**

Mault, Natalie A.
(ed) The visual blues   **704.03**

Maunder, Andrew
The Facts on File companion to the British short story   **823**

Maurer, Christopher
(ed) Garcia Lorca, F. Collected poems   **861**

(ed) Garcia Lorca, F. Poet in New York   **861**

Maurer, Kevin
Hunter Killer   **92**
No easy day   **958.104**

Maurice Sendak.   **741.6**

MAURITANIANS -- CUBA -- GUANTÁNAMO BAY NAVAL BASE -- DIARIES
Guantanamo diary   **958.104**

Maus. Spiegelman, A.   **940.53**

Mauve. Garfield, S.   **667**

MAUVE
Garfield, S. Mauve   **667**

Maverick Genius. Schewe, P. F.   **92**

Mavericks, money, and men. Ross, C. K.   **796.332**

Mawson, Douglas, Sir, 1882-1958
    About
Roberts, D. Alone on the ice   **919**

Max, D. T., ca. 1962-
Every love story is a ghost story   **92**

Maxfield, Katherine
Starting up Silicon Valley   **338.7**

MAXIMS *See* Proverbs

Maximum city. Mehta, S.   **954**

The **Maximum** Security Book Club. Brottman, M.   **365.66**

The **Maximus** poems. Olson, C.   **811**

Maxwell's handbook for RDA, resource description & access. Maxwell, R. L.   **025.3**

Maxwell, Glyn, 1962-
One thousand nights and counting   **821**
(ed) The Poetry of Derek Walcott 1948-2013   **811**

Maxwell, Robert L.
FRBR   **025.3**
Maxwell's handbook for RDA, resource description & access   **025.3**

Maxwell, William, 1908-2000
    About
What there is to say we have said   **92**

Maxwell-Stuart, P. G.
Chronicle of the popes   **282**

May, Charles E.
(ed) Short story writers   **809**

May, Elaine Tyler, 1947-
America and the pill   **363.9**

May, Gary
John Tyler   **92**

May, Jamaal
Hum   **811**

May, Mike
Kurson, R. Crashing through   **92**

May, Rollo
The courage to create   **153.3**
The discovery of being   **150.19**
Freedom and destiny   **158**

The **Maya.** Coe, M. D.   **972**

Maya Angelou. Gillespie, M. A.   **92**

MAYA ARCHITECTURE
Royal cities of the ancient Maya   972.81
MAYA COOKING
Sterling, D. Yucatán   641.59
Mayakovsky, Vladimir, 1893-1930
Listen!   891.7
About
Night wraps the sky   92
MAYAN COOKING
Hoyer, D. Mayan cuisine   641.59
Mayan cuisine. Hoyer, D.   641.59
MAYAS
Ceram, C. W. Gods, graves, and scholars   930.1
Coe, M. D. The Maya   972
Encyclopedia of the ancient Maya   972.81
MAYAS -- ANTIQUITIES
Carlsen, W. Jungle of Stone   972.81
MAYAS -- HISTORY
Royal cities of the ancient Maya   972.81
MAYAS -- RELIGION
Popol vuh   Popol vuh   299.7
MAYAS -- SOCIAL LIFE AND CUSTOMS
Sterling, D. Yucatán   641.59
Maybe baby.   306.8
Maybrick, Florence Elizabeth, 1862-1941
About
Colquhoun, K. Did she kill him?   364.152
Maybrick, James, 1838-1889
About
Colquhoun, K. Did she kill him?   364.152
Mayer, Bernadette
Scarlet tanager   811
Mayer, Catherine
Born to be king   92
Mayer, Jane
Dark money   320.52
The dark side   973.931
Mayer, Louis B. (Louis Burt), 1885-1957
About
Eyman, S. Lion of Hollywood   92
Mayer, Robert
Quick cash   332
Mayer-Schonberger, Viktor
(jt. auth) Cukier, K. Big data   306.46
Mayer-Thurman, Christa C.
(ed) Brosens, K. European tapestries in the Art Institute of Chicago   746.3
Mayes, Frances
About
Mayes, F. Under magnolia   92
Mayes, F. Under the Tuscan sun   945
A year in the world   914
Mayes, Linda C.
The Yale Child Study Center guide to understanding your child   649
Mayfield, Katherine, 1958-

About
Mayfield, K. The undertaker's daughter   92
Mayflower. Philbrick, N.   973.2
MAYFLOWER (SHIP)
Bunker, N. Making haste from Babylon   974.4
Mayle, Peter
Encore Provence   944.083
French lessons   394.1
A year in Provence   944.083
Mayo Clinic guide to a healthy pregnancy.   618.2
Mayo Clinic, the essential diabetes book.   616.4
Mayor, Adrienne
The Poison King   92
MAYORS
Algeo, M. The president is a sick man   973.8
Baraka, I. A. The LeRoi Jones/Amiri Baraka reader   818
Cohen, A. American pharaoh: Mayor Richard J. Daley: his battle for Chicago and the nation   977.3
Graff, H. F. Grover Cleveland   92
Halberstam, D. The children   323.1
Siegel, F. F. The prince of the city   92
Traister, R. Big girls don't cry   324
Young, A. An easy burden   92
Mayr, Ernst
What evolution is   576.8
Mays, Andrea E.
The millionaire and the bard   822.33
Mays, Willie, 1931-
About
Hirsch, J. S. Willie Mays   92
MAZE GARDENS
See also Gardens
MAZE PUZZLES
See also Puzzles
Mazel, Sharon
(jt. auth) Murkoff, H. What to Expect the First Year   649
(jt. auth) Murkoff, H. What to expect when you're expecting   618.2
Murkoff, H. E. What to expect the second year   649
Mazer, Ben
(ed) Everson, L. Everything preserved: poems, 1955-2005   811
Mazlish, Elaine
How to Talk So Kids Will Listen and Listen So Kids Will Talk   649.1
Mazor, Barry
Meeting Jimmie Rodgers   92
Mazower, Mark
Dark continent: Europe's twentieth century   940.55
Hitler's empire   940.53
Salonica, city of ghosts   949.5
Mazur, Joseph
Fluke   519.2
Mazzarella, Mark

Dimitrius Reading people 155.2

Mazzeo, Tilar J.
Irena's children 940.53
The secret of Chanel No. 5 338.7

Mazzetti, Mark
The way of the knife 356

Mbeki, Thabo, 1942-
About
Gevisser, M. A legacy of liberation 92

MCA INC.
Bruck, C. When Hollywood had a king 338.7

McAlester, Virginia Savage
A field guide to American houses 728

McAllester, Matthew
Beyond the Mountains of the Damned 949.71

McAllister, Ian
The last wild wolves 599.77

McAuliffe, Kathleen
This is your brain on parasites 612.8

McBay, Aric
Jensen, D. What we leave behind 304.2

McBee, Thomas Page
About
McBee, T. P. Man alive 92

McBride, Anne E.
(jt. auth) Payard, F. Payard cookies 641.86

McBride, James, 1957-
About
McBride, J. The color of water 92
Kill 'em and leave 92

McBride, Karyl
Will I ever be good enough? 616.85

McBride-Jordan, Ruth, 1921-2010
About
McBride, J. The color of water 92

McBrien, Richard P.
(ed) The HarperCollins encyclopedia of Catholicism 282
Lives of the popes 920

McBrien, William
Cole Porter 92

McCabe, Gerard B.
(ed) Our new public, a changing clientele 025.1

McCabe, John
Cagney 92

McCain, John S.
Faith of my fathers 92
Why courage matters 179

McCall, Nathan
About
McCall, N. Makes me wanna holler 305.38

McCallum, Jack
(jt. auth) Boeheim, J. Bleeding Orange 92
Dream team 796.323

McCalman, Iain, 1947-
Darwin's armada 576.8

McCandless, Christopher
About
Krakauer, J. Into the wild 917

McCarter, Jeremy
Hamilton 782.1

MCCARTHY (ALASKA) -- BIOGRAPHY
Pilgrim's wilderness 92

McCarthy, Andrew
Journeys home 929.1

McCarthy, David Matzko
Sharing God's Good Company 235

McCarthy, Joseph, 1908-1957
About
Conant, J. A covert affair 940.54
Johnson, H. B. The age of anxiety 973.921
Morgan, T. Reds: McCarthyism in twentieth-century America 973.9
Wicker, T. Shooting star: the brief arc of Joe McCarthy 92

McCarthy, Mary, 1912-1989
About
Kiernan, F. Seeing Mary plain: a life of Mary McCarthy 818
Pierpont, C. R. Passionate minds 810

McCarthy, Susan
Masson, J. M. When elephants weep 591.5
Becoming a tiger 591.5

McCarthy, Timothy Patrick
(ed) The Radical reader 303.4

McCartney, Linda
Life in photographs 779

McCartney, Paul
About
The Beatles anthology 782.421
Sounes, H. Fab 92
Spitz, B. The Beatles: the biography 920

McCaughan, Mac
Cook, J. Our noise 338

McChesney, Chris
(jt. auth) Covey, S. The 4 disciplines of execution 658.4

McChesney, Robert Waterman, 1952-
Digital disconnect 302.23

McClain, James L.
Japan, a modern history 952

McClatchy, J. D.
(ed) Christmas poems 821
(ed) Merrill, J. The collected poems of James Merrill 811
(ed) Poets of the Civil War 811
(ed) The Vintage book of contemporary world poetry 808.81

McClellan, George Brinton, 1826-1885
About
Sears, S. W. George B. McClellan 92

McClelland, Mac

About

McClelland, M. Irritable hearts   **92**

McClelland, Susan

Stars Between the Sun and Moon   **92**

McClinton-Temple, Jennifer

(ed) Encyclopedia of American Indian literature   **810**

McCloud, Scott

Making comics   **741.5**

Reinventing comics   **741.5**

Understanding comics   **741.5**

McClure, Charles R.

Public libraries and internet service roles   **025.04**

McClure, Michael

Of indigo and saffron   **811**

McCluskey, Audrey Thomas

A forgotten sisterhood   **370.922**

McClusky, Mark

Faster, higher, stronger   **613.7**

McCommons, James

The book of love   **306.7**

Waiting on a train   **385**

McConnell, David

American honor killings   **364.15**

McConnell, Malcolm

Franks, T. American soldier   **973.931**

McConnell, Patricia

For the love of a dog   **636.7**

McConville, Brigid

On Becoming a Mother   **306.874**

McCook, Kathleen de la Peña

Introduction to public librarianship   **027.4**

McCormack, Mark H.

What they don't teach you at Harvard Business School   **650.1**

McCormick, Danielle

Essential car care for women   **629.28**

McCormick, Katherine Dexter, 1876-1967

About

Eig, J. The birth of the pill   **618.1**

McCormick, Malcolm

Reynolds, N. No fixed points   **792.8**

McCorvey, Norma

About

Hull, N. E. H. Roe v. Wade   **344**

McCourt family

About

McCourt, F. Angela's ashes   **92**

McCourt, Alphie

About

McCourt, A. A long stone's throw   **92**

McCourt, Frank

About

Angela's ashes   **92**

Teacher man   **92**

'Tis   **92**

McCourt, James, 1941-

About

McCourt, J. Lasting City   **92**

McCourt, Malachy, 1931-

About

McCourt, M. A monk swimming   **974.7**

McCourt, M. Singing my him song   **974.7**

McCoy, Alfred W.

A question of torture   **323.4**

McCracken, Elizabeth

About

McCracken, E. An exact replica of a figment of my imagination   **92**

McCrate, Colin

High-yield vegetable gardening   **635**

McCraw, Thomas K., 1940-2012

The founders and finance   **330.973**

McCray, W. Patrick

The visioneers   **509**

McCrery, Nigel

Silent witnesses   **363.25**

McCrum, Robert

The story of English   **420**

Wodehouse   **92**

McCubbin, Lisa

(jt. auth) Hill, C. Five days in November   **973.922**

(jt. auth) Hill, C. Five presidents   **363.28**

(jt. auth) Hill, C. Mrs. Kennedy and me   **973.922**

McCullers, Carson, 1917-1967

About

Savigneau, J. Carson McCullers   **813**

McCullers, Carson, 1917-1967. Heart is a lonely hunter

About

Nafisi, A. The Republic of Imagination   **819**

McCullough, David

McCullough, D. G. 1776   **973.3**

McCullough, D. G. The greater journey   **920.009**

McCullough, D. G. John Adams   **92**

McCullough, D. G. Truman   **92**

Mornings on horseback   **92**

The path between the seas   **972.87**

(jt. auth) McCullough, D. J. You Are Not Special   **170**

The Wright brothers   **92**

McCullough, David, Jr.

You Are Not Special   **170**

McCullough, Frances Monson

(ed) The 150 best American recipes   **641.5**

McCumber, David

Playing off the rail   **794.7**

McCurley, T. Mark

(jt. auth) Maurer, K. Hunter Killer   **92**

McCutcheon, Chuck

(jt. auth) Barone, M. The almanac of American politics 2012   **328**

McDaniel, Carl N.
Wisdom for a livable planet   **333.72**

McDaniel, Hattie, 1895-1952
About
Jackson, C. Hattie: the life of Hattie McDaniel   92
Watts, J. Hattie McDaniel   92

McDermott, Kate
Art of the pie   **641.86**

McDermott, Terry
The hunt for KSM   **363.325**

McDonald family
About
Flanders, J. A circle of sisters   920

McDonnell, Duggan
Drinking the devil's acre   **641.87**

McDonnell, Imen
The Farmette cookbook   **641.5**

McDonnell, Michael A.
Masters of Empire   **977.4**

McDonough, Jimmy
Tammy Wynette   92

McDougal, Susan
About
McDougal, S. The woman who wouldn't talk   **973.929**

McDougall, Christopher
(ed) The Best American Sports Writing 2014   814
Born to run   **796.42**
Natural Born Heroes   **940.53**

McDowell, Marta
All the presidents' gardens   **635.09**

McEnroe, John
About
McEnroe, J. You cannot be serious   **796.342**

McFadden, Johnjoe
Life on the Edge   **572**

McFarland, Philip
Mark Twain and the Colonel   **973.8**

McFarlane, Rodger
The complete bedside companion   **649.8**

McGarr, Paul
(ed) Gould, S. J. The richness of life   508

McGarry, Jack
The Dead Rabbit drinks manual   **641.87**

McGee, Suzanne
Chasing Goldman Sachs   **332.6**

McGee, William J.
Attention all passengers   **387.7**

McGee, Willie, d. 1951
About
Heard, A. The eyes of Willie McGee   **364.66**

McGerr, Michael E.
A fierce discontent   **324.2**

McGilligan, Patrick
Oscar Micheaux   92
Young Orson   92

McGinniss, Joe
Fatal vision   **364.1**

McGinty, Brian
Lincoln's Greatest Case   346

McGirr, Lisa
The war on alcohol   **363.4**

McGonigal, David
Antarctica   998

McGonigal, Jane
Reality is broken   **306.4**

McGoogan, Kenneth
Race to the Polar Sea   92

McGovern, George S. (George Stanley), 1922-
About
Ambrose, S. E. The wild blue   **940.54**
Glasser, J. M. The eighteen-day running mate   **973.924**

McGowan, Alice
Bulbs in the basement, geraniums on the windowsill   **635.9**

McGowan, Bill
Pitch Perfect   **658.452**

McGowan, Brian
McGowan, A. Bulbs in the basement, geraniums on the windowsill   **635.9**

McGrath, Alister E., 1953-
C. S. Lewis   92

McGrath, Jinks
The complete jewelry making course   **739.27**

McGrath, Thomas
Letter to an imaginary friend   **811**

McGraw, Eliza
Here Comes Exterminator!   **798.4**

McGraw, Phillip C.
Life strategies   **158**

McGraw, Seamus
Betting the farm on a drought   **363.738**
The end of country   **333.79**

McGraw-Hill concise encyclopedia of science & technology. McGraw-Hill Publishing Company   **503**

McGraw-Hill dictionary of scientific and technical terms.   **503**

McGraw-Hill Publishing Company
McGraw-Hill concise encyclopedia of science & technology   **503**

McGraw-Hill's dictionary of American slang and colloquial expressions. Spears, R. A.   **427**

McGregor, James H.
Paris from the ground up   **914**
Rome from the ground up   **711**

McGregor, Richard
The Party   **324.2**

McGregor, Robert Kuhn, 1952-
A Calculus of Color   **796.357**

McGuckin, Maryanne

(jt. auth) Goldfarb, T. L. The patient survival guide
McGuire, Bill
Waking the giant **551.5**
McGuire, Danielle L.
At the dark end of the street **323.1**
McGuire, Dennis Eugene
Chicoine, B. The guide to good health for teens &
adults with Down syndrome **618.92**
McHugh, Heather
Upgraded to serious **811**
McIndoe, Andy
The creative shrub garden **635.9**
McInerny, Ralph M.
(ed) Thomas Selected writings **189**
McKay, Nellie Y.
(ed) The Norton anthology of African American
literature **810**
McKay, Sinclair
The secret lives of codebreakers **940.54**
McKean, David
Suspected of independence **92**
McKean, Thomas, 1734-1817
About
McKean, D. Suspected of independence **92**
McKechnie, Lynne
Ross, C. S. Reading matters **028**
McKee, Annie
(jt. auth) Goleman, D. Primal Leadership **658.4**
McKeen, William
Outlaw journalist **92**
McKeever, Mike
How to write a business plan **658.15**
McKenna, Amy
Nontraditional careers for women and men **331.702**
McKenna, Maryn
Superbug **616.9**
McKenna, Stephen J.
(ed) The World's great speeches **808.85**
McKenney, Eileen, d. 1940
About
Meade, M. Lonelyhearts **92**
McKeown, Greg
Essentialism **153.8**
McKeown, Rosalyn
Into the classroom **370.71**
McKibben, Bill, 1960-
(ed) American earth **333.72**
The Bill McKibben reader **333.72**
Eaarth **253**
(ed) The global warming reader **363.738**
About
McKibben, B. Oil and Honey **363.7**
McKillop, A. B.
The spinster & the prophet **941.08**
McKinley, Michael
Hockey: a people's history **796.962**

McKinley, Richard
Pastel pointers **741.235**
McKinley, William, 1843-1901
About
Miller, S. The President and the assassin **973.8**
Perry, J. M. Touched with fire **973.7**
Phillips, K. P. William McKinley **92**
Rauchway, E. Murdering McKinley **973.8**
Thomas, E. The war lovers **973.8**
McKinney, Aaron James
About
Jimenez, S. The Book of Matt **364.1**
McKnight, Kent H.
A field guide to mushrooms, North America **579.6**
McKnight, Scot
Kingdom conspiracy **231.7**
McKnight, Vera B.
McKnight, K. H. A field guide to mushrooms,
North America **579.6**
McLagan, Jennifer
Bitter **664**
Odd bits **641.3**
McLane, Maureen N., 1967-
My poets **811**
This Blue **811**
McLaughlin, Michael, 1954-
The Silver Palate cookbook **641.5**
McLean, Bethany
All the devils are here **330.9**
McLellan, David
(ed) Marx, K. Capital: an abridged edition **330.1**
McLeod, John
The history of India **954**
McLoughlin, William Gerald
After the Trail of Tears **970.004**
McLuhan, Marshall
The global village **302.2**
Understanding media **302.23**
About
Coupland, D. Marshall McLuhan **92**
McLynn, Frank
1759: the year Britain became master of the
world **941.07**
Wagons west **978**
McMafia. Glenny, M. **364.1**
McMahon, Sean
Brewer's dictionary of Irish phrase & fable **427**
McManus, James
Cowboys full **795.4**
Positively Fifth Street **795.4**
McMaster, Juliet
(ed) The Cambridge companion to Jane Austen **823**
McMeekin, Sean
The Berlin-Baghdad express **940.3**
July 1914 **940.3**
McMichael, James

Capacity **811**

McMillan, John
Reinventing the bazaar **330.12**

McMillan, Ron
Crucial conversations **153.6**

McMillan, Tracie
The American way of eating **338.4**

McMillian, John Campbell
(ed) Freedom on my mind **305.8**
(ed) The Radical reader **303.4**

McMullen, William, 1824-1901
About
Biddle, D. R. Tasting freedom **92**

McMurray, Jacob
Taking punk to the masses **781.66**

McMurtry, Larry
Books **92**
Crazy Horse **92**
Custer **92**
Roads **917**
Walter Benjamin at the Dairy Queen **818**

McNally, Dennis
A long strange trip **782.421**

McNamara, Kevin J.
Dreams of a great small nation **943.703**

McNamara, Michael J.
(jt. auth) Gillette, J. M. Designing With Light: An
Introduction to Stage Lighting **792**

McNamara, Robert S., 1916-2009
In retrospect **959.704**
About
Halberstam, D. The best and the brightest **973.922**
Hendrickson, P. The living and the dead **959.704**

McNamee, Gregory
(ed) Burns, M. The only one living to tell **305.897**

McNamee, Thomas
The return of the wolf to Yellowstone **333.95**

McNaughton, Deborah
The essential credit repair handbook **332.024**

McNeil, Beth
(jt. auth) Giesecke, J. Fundamentals of library supervision **023**

McNeill, William H. (William Hardy), 1917-2016
Plagues and peoples **614.4**

McNish, Jacquie
Losing the signal **338.4**

McPartland, James C.
(jt. auth) Dawson, G. A parent's guide to high-
functioning autism spectrum disorder **618.92**

McPartland, Marian
About
De Barros, P. Shall we play that one together? **92**

McPhee, John, 1931-
Coming into the country **979.8**
Irons in the fire **081**
Looking for a ship **910.4**

The ransom of Russian art **709**
Uncommon carriers **388**

McPhee, J. The control of nature **304.2**
Levels of the game **796.34**

McPhee, Peter
Liberty or death **944.04**
Robespierre **92**

McPhee, Stephen
(ed) Current medical diagnosis and treatment **610**

McPherson, Aimee Semple, 1890-1944
About
Epstein, D. M. Sister Aimee: the life of Aimee
Semple McPherson **92**

McPherson, James M.
Abraham Lincoln **92**
Abraham Lincoln and the second American Revo-
lution **973.7**
Battle cry of freedom **973.7**
Drawn with the sword **973.7**
For cause and comrades **973.7**
Hallowed ground **973.7**
This mighty scourge **973.7**
Tried by war **92**
The war that forged a nation **973.7**

McReynolds, Edwin C.
The Seminoles **970.004**

McShann, Jay
About
Dance, S. The world of Count Basie **920**

McSweeney, Kerry
(ed) Carlyle, T. Sartor resartus **824**

McTell, Blind Willie, 1898?-1959
About
Gray, M. Hand me my travelin' shoes **92**

McWhorter, Diane
Carry me home **976.1**

McWhorter, John H.
Losing the race **305.8**

McWilliam, Candia
About
McWilliam, C. What to look for in winter **92**

McWilliams, James E.
Just food **394.1**

McWilliams, Mary
(ed) In harmony **704**

Mda, Zakes
About
Mda, Z. Sometimes there is a void **828**

Me. Hepburn, K. **92**
Me talk pretty one day. Sedaris, D. **814**

MÉDOC (FRANCE) -- BIOGRAPHY
Thorisson, M. A kitchen in France **641.594**

Meacham, Jon
American lion **92**
Destiny and Power **92**
Thomas Jefferson **92**

(ed) Voices in our blood **323.1**

Mead, Frank Spencer
Atwood, C. D. Handbook of denominations in the United States **280**

Mead, Jane
World of made and unmade **811.54**

Mead, Margaret, 1901-1978
Coming of age in Samoa **306**

About
Mead, M. Blackberry winter **92**
Ware, S. Letter to the world **920.72**

Mead, Rebecca
One perfect day **392**

About
Mead, R. My life in Middlemarch **823**

Meade, Marion
Buster Keaton **92**
Dorothy Parker **92**
Lonelyhearts **92**

Meade, Teresa
A brief history of Brazil **981**

Meagher, Thomas Francis, 1823-1867
About
Egan, T. The immortal Irishman **92**

MEAL PLANNING See Menus; Nutrition

Mealer, Bryan
Kamkwamba, W. The boy who harnessed the wind **92**

MEALS FOR SCHOOL CHILDREN See School children -- Food

MEALS ON WHEELS PROGRAMS
See also Food relief

MEANING (PHILOSOPHY)
Isay, D. Callings **920.073**
Tippett, K. Becoming Wise **158.1**
Wilson, E. O. The Meaning of Human Existence **128**

MEANING (PSYCHOLOGY)
Kinsley, M. Old age **814.54**
The **Meaning** of Human Existence. Wilson, E. O. **128**
The **meaning** of it all. Feynman, R. P. **500**
The **meaning** of relativity. Einstein, A. **530.1**
The **meaning** of the glorious Koran. **297.1**

Means, Howard B.
Johnny Appleseed **92**
Meanwhile there are letters. **92**
The **measure** of a man. Poitier, S. **92**
The **measure** of all things. Alder, K. **526**
The **measure** of madness. Paradis, C. **364.3**
The **measure** of our success. Edelman, M. W. **170**
Measure of the Earth. Ferreiro, L. D. **526**
Measure twice, cut once. Abram, N. **684**

MEASUREMENT
Barrow, J. D. The constants of nature **530.8**
Blatner, D. Spectrums **539.2**

Nicastro, N. Circumference **526**
Robinson, A. The story of measurement **530.8**

MEASUREMENT
See also Mathematics

MEASURES See Weights and measures

MEASURING INSTRUMENTS
Arnold, D. Liquid intelligence **641.87**

MEASURING INSTRUMENTS
See also Measurement; Weights and measures

Meat. Peterson, J. **641.6**
Meat. Carreño, C. **641.6**

MEAT
Danforth, A. Butchering poultry, rabbit, lamb, goat, and pork **664**
The everyday meat guide **641.36**

MEAT
See also Food
Meat eater. Rinella, S. **799.29**

MEAT INDUSTRY
Carreño, C. Meat **641.6**
Estabrook, B. Pig tales **636.4**
Genoways, T. The chain **338.7**

MEAT INDUSTRY
See also Food industry

MEAT INDUSTRY AND TRADE See Meat industry

MEAT INSPECTION
See also Food adulteration and inspection; Meat industry; Public health
Meat on the side. Dinki, N. **641.35**

MEAT PACKING INDUSTRY See Meat industry

MEATCUTTING -- UNITED STATES
Guggiana, M. Primal cuts **641.6**
Meathead. Blonder, G. **641.7**
Meb for mortals. Douglas, S. **796.42**

Méchain, Pierre-Fran¿cois-André, 1744-1804
About
Alder, K. The measure of all things **526**

MECHANICAL DRAWING
See also Drawing; Engineering; Machinery; Patternmaking

MECHANICAL ENGINEERING -- HAND-BOOKS, MANUALS, ETC.
Marks' standard handbook for mechanical engineers **621**

MECHANICAL ENGINEERS
Sobel, D. Longitude **526**

MECHANICAL ENGINEERS -- MALAWI -- BI-OGRAPHY
Kamkwamba, W. The boy who harnessed the wind **92**

MECHANICAL MUSICAL INSTRUMENTS
See also Musical instruments

MECHANICS
See also Physics

MECHANICS (PERSONS)

Crawford, M. B. Shop class as soulcraft **331**

Robison, J. E. Look me in the eye **92**

Mecom, Jane, 1712-1794

About

Lepore, J. Book of ages **92**

MÉDECINS SANS FRONTIÈRES (ORGANIZA-TION)

Bortolotti, D. Hope in hell **610**

Orbinski, J. An imperfect offering **610**

MÉDECINS SANS FRONTIÈRES (ORGANIZA-TION) -- GRAPHIC NOVELS

Guibert, E. The photographer **958.1**

MEDIA *See* Mass media

MEDIA CENTERS (EDUCATION) *See* Instructional materials centers

MEDIA LITERACY

See also Literacy

Media man. Auletta, K. **92**

The **media** relations department of Hizbollah wishes you a happy birthday. MacFarquhar, N. **956.04**

MEDICAID

Nather, D. The new health care system **344**

MEDICAL -- ESSAYS

Sweet, V. God's hotel **610.92**

Medical apartheid. Washington, H. A. **174.2**

MEDICAL ASSISTANCE

Orbinski, J. An imperfect offering **610**

MEDICAL BOTANY

The herbal apothecary **615.3**

Peterson field guide to medicinal plants and herbs of eastern and central North America **581.6**

Sumner, J. The natural history of medicinal plants **581.6**

MEDICAL BOTANY

See also Botany; Medicine; Pharmacy

MEDICAL CARE

Brawley, O. W. How we do harm **362.109**

Brown, T. The shift **616.02**

Cosgrove, T. The Cleveland Clinic way **362.11**

Fadiman, A. The spirit catches you and you fall down **306.4**

Garrett, L. Betrayal of trust **362.1**

Gruber, J. Health care reform **362.1**

Michelson, L. D. The patient's playbook **610.69**

Taber's cyclopedic medical dictionary **610.3**

MEDICAL CARE

See also Public health

MEDICAL CARE -- ACCESS *See* Access to health care

MEDICAL CARE -- COSTS

Gruber, J. Health care reform **362.1**

Hoffman, B. Health care for some **362.1**

MEDICAL CARE -- ETHICAL ASPECTS *See* Medical ethics

MEDICAL CARE -- GOVERNMENT POLICY

Blumenthal, D. The heart of power **362.1**

Nather, D. The new health care system **344**

Reid, T. R. The healing of America **362.1**

Sommer, A. Getting what we deserve **362.1**

Starr, P. Remedy and reaction **362.1**

MEDICAL CARE -- GOVERNMENT POLICY

See Medical policy

MEDICAL CARE -- QUALITY CONTROL

Gawande, A. The checklist manifesto **610.28**

Makary, M. Unaccountable **610.730**

MEDICAL CARE -- SOCIAL ASPECTS *See* Social medicine

MEDICAL CARE -- UNITED STATES

Atlas, S. W. In excellent health **362.109**

Jauhar, S. Doctored **92**

MEDICAL ERRORS

Makary, M. Unaccountable **610.730**

MEDICAL ERRORS *See* Errors; Medical personnel -- Malpractice; Physicians -- Malpractice

MEDICAL ERRORS -- PREVENTION

Michelson, L. D. The patient's playbook **610.69**

MEDICAL ETHICS

Gawande, A. Better **616**

Peck, M. S. Denial of the soul **179.7**

Shah, S. The body hunters **362.1**

Teresi, D. The undead **610**

Washington, H. A. Deadly monopolies **338.4**

MEDICAL ETHICS

See also Bioethics; Ethics; Professional ethics

MEDICAL ETHICS -- UNITED STATES

Elliott, C. White coat, black hat **174.2**

MEDICAL EXAMINERS (LAW) -- NEW YORK (STATE) -- NEW YORK -- BIOGRAPHY

Mitchell, T. J. Working stiff **614**

MEDICAL EXPERIMENTATION ON HUMANS *See* Human experimentation in medicine

Medical firsts. Adler, R. E. **610**

MEDICAL GENETICS

Collins, F. S. The language of life **616**

Marion, R. Genetic rounds **92**

MEDICAL GENETICS

See also Genetics; Pathology

MEDICAL GENETICS -- ENCYCLOPEDIAS

Knight, J. A. Genetics & inherited conditions **576.5**

Medical humanities [series]

Twelve breaths a minute **616**

MEDICAL ILLUSTRATION -- HISTORY

Anderson, J. The art of medicine **610**

MEDICAL INFORMATICS

Wachter, R. The digital doctor **610.28**

MEDICAL INFORMATICS APPLICATIONS

Topol, E. The creative destruction of medicine **610.28**

MEDICAL INSTRUMENTS AND APPARATUS -- UNITED STATES -- HISTORY -- 19TH CENTURY

Millard, C. The destiny of the republic **973.8**

MEDICAL INSURANCE *See* Health insurance

MEDICAL JURISPRUDENCE
Mitchell, T. J. Working stiff **614**

MEDICAL JURISPRUDENCE
  See also Forensic sciences

The **Medical** Library Association guide to finding out about diabetes. Ladd, D. L. **016**

The **Medical** Library Association guide to finding out about heart disease. De Richemond, J. **016**

Medical Library Association Guides [series]
  Introduction to reference sources in the health sciences **016.6**

MEDICAL MISCONCEPTIONS
  Goldacre, B. Bad science **500**

MEDICAL PERSONNEL
  Montross, C. Falling into the fire **92**

MEDICAL PERSONNEL
  See also Employees

MEDICAL PERSONNEL -- EMPLOYMENT
  101 careers in healthcare management **362.106**

MEDICAL PERSONNEL AND PATIENT
  Makary, M. Unaccountable **610.730**

MEDICAL PHOTOGRAPHY
  See also Photography; Photography -- Scientific applications

MEDICAL POLICY
  Garrett, L. Betrayal of trust **362.1**

MEDICAL POLICY
  See also Social policy

MEDICAL POLICY -- UNITED STATES
  Brawley, O. W. How we do harm **362.109**
  The economists' voice 2.0 **330.9**
  Gruber, J. Health care reform **362.1**

MEDICAL PRACTICE
  See also Medicine

MEDICAL PROFESSION *See* Medical personnel; Medical practice; Medicine

MEDICAL RECORDS
  Makary, M. Unaccountable **610.730**

MEDICAL TECHNOLOGY
  Callahan, D. Taming the beloved beast **338.4**
  Finkel, E. The Genome Generation **572**
  Topol, E. The creative destruction of medicine **610.28**
  Wachter, R. The digital doctor **610.28**

MEDICARE
  Matthews, J. L. Social security, Medicare & government pensions **344**
  Nather, D. The new health care system **344**

MEDICARE
  See also Elderly -- Medical care; National health insurance; State medicine

MEDICATION ABUSE
  See also Drug abuse; Substance abuse

The **Medici.** Strathern, P. **945.51**

The **Medici** giraffe. Belozerskaya, M. **636**

Medici money. Parks, T. **332.1**

MEDICI, HOUSE OF
  Strathern, P. The Medici **945.51**

Medici, Lorenzo de', 1449-1492
                About
  Strathern, P. Death in Florence **945**

MEDICINAL HERBS *See* Herbs -- Therapeutic use; Medical botany

MEDICINAL PLANTS *See* Medical botany

MEDICINE
  Bowers, K. Zoobiquity **636.089**
  Current medical diagnosis and treatment **610**
  Doherty, G. M. Current Diagnosis and Treatment Surgery **617**
  Gawande, A. Better **616**
  Goleman, D. Emotional intelligence **152.4**
  Groopman, J. E. How doctors think **610**
  Groopman, J. E. Your medical mind **610**
  Kore **610**
  Mosby's medical dictionary **610.3**
  Mukherjee, S. The laws of medicine **610**
  Pagana, T. J. Mosby's diagnostic and laboratory test reference **616.07**
  Sweet, V. God's hotel **610.92**

MEDICINE
  See also Life sciences; Therapeutics

MEDICINE -- BIBLIOGRAPHY
  Guide to reference in medicine and health **025.06**

MEDICINE -- BIOGRAPHY
  See also Biography

MEDICINE -- COST OF MEDICAL CARE *See* Medical care -- Costs

MEDICINE -- DECISION MAKING
  Groopman, J. E. How doctors think **610**
  Michelson, L. D. The patient's playbook **610.69**

MEDICINE -- DICTIONARIES
  Mosby's medical dictionary **610.3**
  Taber's cyclopedic medical dictionary **610.3**

MEDICINE -- ENCYCLOPEDIAS
  Magill's medical guide **610.3**

MEDICINE -- ETHICAL ASPECTS *See* Medical ethics

MEDICINE -- HANDBOOKS, MANUALS, ETC.
  First aid manual **616.02**

MEDICINE -- HISTORY
  Burns, T. Our Necessary Shadow **616.89**
  Kore **610**
  Mattern, S. P. Prince of medicine **610.9**

MEDICINE -- HISTORY -- PICTORIAL WORKS
  Anderson, J. The art of medicine **610**

MEDICINE -- HISTORY -- POPULAR WORKS
  Parker, S. Kill or cure **610**

MEDICINE -- INFORMATION SERVICES
  Guide to reference in medicine and health **025.06**
  Introduction to reference sources in the health sci-

ences   **016.6**

MEDICINE -- LAW AND LEGISLATION

James, V. E. The Alzheimer's advisor   **344**

MEDICINE -- LAW AND LEGISLATION

See also Law; Legislation

MEDICINE -- MISCELLANEA

See also Curiosities and wonders

MEDICINE -- PHILOSOPHY

Haycock, D. B. Mortal coil   **571.8**

Pollack, R. The missing moment   **610**

MEDICINE -- PHYSIOLOGICAL EFFECT *See*
Pharmacology

**MEDICINE -- REFERENCE BOOKS -- BIBLI-
OGRAPHY**

Guide to reference in medicine and health   **025.06**

Introduction to reference sources in the health sciences   **016.6**

MEDICINE -- RESEARCH

Forrester, J. The Heart Healers   **616.1**

Leaf, C. The truth in small doses   **616.99**

MEDICINE -- RESEARCH

See also Research

MEDICINE -- SOCIAL ASPECTS *See* Social
medicine

MEDICINE -- UNITED STATES

Tweedy, D. Black Man in a White Coat   **92**

**MEDICINE -- UNITED STATES -- HISTORY --
19TH CENTURY**

Millard, C. The destiny of the republic   **973.8**

MEDICINE AND PSYCHOLOGY

Brewer, S. C. The Canyon Ranch guide to men's
health   **613**

Pollack, R. The missing moment   **610**

MEDICINE AND STATE *See* Medical policy

MEDICINE IN ART

Anderson, J. The art of medicine   **610**

MEDICINE MEN *See* Shamans

MEDICINE, AYURVEDIC

Hanoch, D. The yoga lifestyle   **613.7**

**MEDICINE, AYURVEDIC -- POPULAR
WORKS**

Fondin, M. S. The wheel of healing with ayurveda   **615.5**

MEDICINE, POPULAR *See* Popular medicine

MEDICINE, PREVENTIVE *See* Preventive medicine

**Medicine, science, and religion in historical con-
text** [series]

Schoepflin, R. B. Christian Science on trial   **289.5**

MEDIEVAL ARCHITECTURE

See also Architecture; Medieval civilization

MEDIEVAL ART

See also Art; Medieval civilization

MEDIEVAL CIVILIZATION

Al-Khalili, J. The house of wisdom   **509**

Aries, P. A History of private life   **909**

Asbridge, T. The crusades   **909.07**

Burns, T. S. A history of the Ostrogoths   **909.07**

Cahill, T. How the Irish saved civilization **941.501**

Castor, H. Joan of Arc   **92**

Crowley, R. City of fortune   **945**

Gies, F. Life in a medieval village   **940.1**

Gies, J. Life in a medieval city   **940.1**

Great events from history, The Middle Ages, 477-
1453   **909.07**

Herlihy, D. The black death and the transformation
of the west   **940.1**

The New Cambridge medieval history   **940.1**

Tuchman, B. W. A distant mirror   **944**

Weinberg, S. To explain the world   **509**

Wickham, C. The inheritance of Rome   **940.1**

MEDIEVAL CIVILIZATION

See also Civilization

MEDIEVAL LITERATURE

See also Literature; Medieval civilization

MEDIEVAL PHILOSOPHY

The Renaissance philosophy of man   **189**

Rubenstein, R. E. Aristotle's children   **189**

MEDIEVAL PHILOSOPHY

See also Medieval civilization; Philosophy

MEDIEVAL TOURNAMENTS

See also Chivalry; Medieval civilization;
Pageants

Medina, John, 1956-

Brain rules   **153**

Brain rules for baby   **649**

Meditate your weight. Cruikshank, T.   **613.25**

MEDITATION

Chödrön, P. How to meditate   **294.3**

Cruikshank, T. Meditate your weight   **613.25**

Harris, D. 10% happier   **158.1**

Nichtern, E. The road home   **294.3**

Salzberg, S. Real happiness   **158**

Siff, J. Thoughts are not the enemy   **294.3**

Wellings, N. Why can't I meditate?   **158.12**

MEDITATION

See also Devotional exercises; Spiritual life

MEDITATION -- BUDDHISM

Nichtern, E. The road home   **294.3**

Siff, J. Thoughts are not the enemy   **294.3**

MEDITATION -- PSYCHOLOGICAL ASPECTS

Heller, R. Secular meditation   **158.1**

Meditations. Marcus Aurelius   **188**

MEDITATIONS

See also Devotional literature; Prayers

MEDITATIONS

Angelou, M. Wouldn't take nothing for my journey
now   **814**

Carter, J. Sources of strength   **248.4**

MEDITERRANEAN CIVILIZATION

Freeman, C. Egypt, Greece, and Rome   **909**

Mediterranean clay pot cooking. Wolfert, P. **641.59**

MEDITERRANEAN COOKING

Acquista, A. The Mediterranean Family Table   **641.59**

David, E. A book of Mediterranean food   **641.5**

Goldstein, J. The new Mediterranean Jewish table   **641.5**

Helou, A. Mediterranean street food   **641.59**

Hever, J. The Vegiterranean Diet   **613.2**

Jenkins, N. H. The new Mediterranean diet cookbook   **641.5**

Ottolenghi   **641.5**

Ottolenghi, Y. Nopi   **641.5**

Psilakis, M. How to roast a lamb   **641.5**

Wadi, S. The new mediterranean cookbook **641.59**

Wolfert, P. Mediterranean clay pot cooking **641.59**

Wolfert, P. The slow Mediterranean kitchen **641.5**

The **Mediterranean** Family Table. Acquista, A.   **641.59**

Mediterranean harvest. Shulman, M. R.   **641.5**

MEDITERRANEAN REGION -- COMMERCE -- HISTORY

Crowley, R. City of fortune   **945**

MEDITERRANEAN REGION -- GAZETTEERS

Grant, M. A guide to the ancient world   **913**

MEDITERRANEAN REGION -- HISTORY

Catlos, B. A. Infidel kings and unholy warriors   **909.07**

Mediterranean street food. Helou, A.   **641.59**

Medium raw. Bourdain, A.   **92**

Medrich, Alice

Chewy gooey crispy crunchy melt-in-your-mouth cookies   **641.8**

Flavor flours   **641.3**

Medusa's gaze and vampire's bite. Kaplan, M.   **001.944**

Medvedev, Roy Aleksandrovich, 1925-

Let history judge   **947.084**

Meehan, Peter

Lucky Peach 101 easy Asian recipes   **641.595**

Chang, D. Momofuku   **641.5**

Meeink, Frank, 1975-

About

Meeink, F. Autobiography of a recovering skinhead   **92**

Meet Me in Atlantis. Adams, M.   **398.23**

Meet the Beatles. Stark, S. D.   **920**

Meeting Jimmie Rodgers. Mazor, B.   **92**

MEGALITHIC MONUMENTS

See also Antiquities; Archeology; Monuments

MEGALITHIC MONUMENTS -- ENGLAND

Hill, R. Stonehenge   **936.2**

Pearson, M. P. Stonehenge   **936.2**

Mehr, Bob

Trouble boys   **782.42**

Mehta, Suketu

Maximum city   **954**

Meier, Andrew

Black earth   **947.086**

Meier, John J.

(ed) Dinosaurs   **567.9**

Meier, John P.

A marginal Jew   **232.9**

Meier, Richard

Building the Getty   **708**

Meiji, Emperor of Japan, 1852-1912

About

Keene, D. Emperor of Japan: Meiji and His world, 1852-1912   **952.03**

Seagrave, S. The Yamato dynasty   **952.03**

Meili, Trisha

About

Burns, S. The Central Park Five   **364.1**

Mein Kampf. Hitler, A.   **92**

Meine, Curt

(ed) Leopold, A. A Sand County almanac & other writings on ecology & conservation   **508**

Meissonier, Jean-Louis-Ernest, 1815-1891

About

King, R. The judgment of Paris   **759**

MELANCHOLIA *See* Depression (Psychology); Manic-depressive illness

MELANCHOLY

Norris, K. Acedia & me   **92**

MELANCHOLY

See also Emotions; Mood (Psychology)

Melendez, Benjy

About

Ghetto Brother   **92**

Melina, Vesanto

(jt. auth) Davis, B. Becoming vegan   **613.2**

Melinek, Judy

About

Mitchell, T. J. Working stiff   **614**

Mellon. Cannadine, D.   **92**

Mellon, Andrew William, 1855-1937

About

Cannadine, D. Mellon   **92**

Mellon, Tamara

About

Crowe, L. G. The towering world of Jimmy Choo   **391**

Mellor, Don

Trailside (Television program) Rock climbing   **796.522**

MELODRAMA

See also Drama

Melting away. Seaman, C.   **910.91**

Melton's encyclopedia of American religions. Melton, J. G.   **200.9**

Melton, Glennon Doyle, 1976-

About

Melton, G. D. Love warrior   **92**

Melton, J. Gordon

Melton's encyclopedia of American religions **200.9**

The vampire book   **398**

Meltzer, Allan H.

A history of the Federal Reserve   **332.1**

Meltzoff, Andrew N.

Gopnik, A. The scientist in the crib   **155.4**

Melville. Delbanco, A.   **92**

Melville, Herman

The poems of Herman Melville   **811**

About

Parker, H. Herman Melville   **813**

Philbrick, N. Why read Moby-Dick?   **813**

Melville, Sally

Knitting pattern essentials   **746.43**

MEMBERS OF CONGRESS

Abuse of power   **973.924**

Ambrose, S. E. The wild blue   **940.54**

Baker, N. The World on Sunday   **071**

Balz, D. J. The battle for America, 2008   **973.932**

Black, C. M. Richard M. Nixon   **92**

Boritt, G. S. The Gettysburg gospel   **973.7**

Borneman, W. R. Polk   **92**

Brackett, E. Pay to play   **92**

Brookhiser, R. America's first dynasty   **973.4**

Bugliosi, V. Reclaiming history   **973.922**

Burlingame, M. Abraham Lincoln   **92**

Burstein, A. Madison and Jefferson   **973.4**

Busby, H. W. The thirty-first of March   **973.923**

Bush, G. All the best, George Bush   **92**

Caro, R. A. The path to power   **92**

Carwardine, R. Lincoln: a life of purpose and power   **92**

Clinton, C. Mrs. Lincoln   **92**

Cohen, I. B. Science and the founding fathers **973.3**

Crapol, E. P. John Tyler   **92**

Craughwell, T. J. Stealing Lincoln's body   **973.7**

Dallek, R. Let every nation know   **92**

Dallek, R. Nixon and Kissinger   **92**

Dallek, R. An unfinished life: John F. Kennedy, 1917-1963   **92**

Davis, W. C. Three roads to the Alamo   **976.4**

Dobbs, M. One minute to midnight   **973.922**

Donald, D. H. Lincoln   **92**

Emery, F. Watergate   **973.924**

Finkelman, P. Millard Fillmore   **92**

Foner, E. The fiery trial   **973.7**

Franklin, B. The autobiography of Benjamin Franklin   **92**

Fredrickson, G. M. Big enough to be inconsistent   **973.7**

Freedman, L. Kennedy's wars   **973.922**

Gienapp, W. E. Abraham Lincoln and Civil War America   **973.7**

Goodwin, D. K. Team of rivals   **92**

Gopnik, A. Angels and ages   **973.7**

Gordon-Reed, A. Andrew Johnson   **92**

Guelzo, A. C. Lincoln and Douglas   **973.6**

Halberstam, D. The best and the brightest **973.922**

Halberstam, D. The children   **323.1**

Heidler, D. S. Henry Clay   **92**

Hofstadter, R. The American political tradition, and the men who made it   **973**

Holzer, H. Lincoln president-elect   **92**

Isaacson, W. Benjamin Franklin   **92**

Kaiser, D. E. American tragedy   **959.704**

Kaiser, D. E. The road to Dallas   **973.922**

Kauffman, B. Forgotten founder, drunken prophet   **92**

Keneally, T. Abraham Lincoln   **92**

Keneally, T. American scoundrel: the life of the notorious Civil War General Dan Sickles   **92**

Kennedy, J. F. Profiles in courage   **920**

Kissinger, H. Diplomacy   **327.2**

Kotz, N. Judgment days   **323**

Kunhardt, P. B. Looking for Lincoln   **92**

Leamer, L. The Kennedy men   **920**

The Lincoln anthology   **92**

Lind, M. What Lincoln believed   **92**

Mahoney, R. D. Sons and brothers: the days of Jack and Bobby Kennedy   **92**

Mallon, T. Mrs. Paine's garage and the murder of John F. Kennedy   **364.1**

Matthews, C. Kennedy & Nixon   **973.922**

May, G. John Tyler   **92**

McCain, J. S. Faith of my fathers   **92**

McPherson, J. M. Tried by war   **92**

McPherson, J. M. Abraham Lincoln   **92**

McPherson, J. M. Abraham Lincoln and the second American Revolution   **973.7**

McPherson, J. M. Drawn with the sword   **973.7**

McPherson, J. M. This mighty scourge   **973.7**

Merry, R. W. A country of vast designs   **92**

Meyerson, M. Liberty's blueprint   **342**

Miller, S. The President and the assassin   **973.8**

Miller, W. L. Arguing about slavery   **973.5**

Morris, J. M. Pulitzer   **92**

Morris, S. J. Rage for fame: the ascent of Clare Boothe Luce   **92**

Morrow, L. The best year of their lives   **920**

Nagel, P. C. John Quincy Adams   **92**

O'Brien, M. Mrs. Adams in winter   **940.2**

Our Lincoln   **92**

Paludan, P. S. The presidency of Abraham Lincoln   **973.7**

Parmet, H. S. George Bush   **92**

Pasles, P. C. Benjamin Franklin's numbers   **510**

Pelosi, N. Know your power   **92**

Perlstein, R. Nixonland   **973.924**

Perry, J. M. Touched with fire   **973.7**

Peters, C. Lyndon B. Johnson   **92**

Phillips, K. P. William McKinley   92
Pietrusza, D. 1960: LBJ vs. JFK vs. Nixon **973.92**
Pinsker, M. Lincoln's sanctuary   92
Pooley, E. The climate war   **363.7**
Posner, G. L. Case closed   **973.922**
Rasenberger, J. The brilliant disaster   **972.91**
Rauchway, E. Murdering McKinley   **973.8**
Reeves, R. President Kennedy   **973.922**
Reeves, R. President Nixon   **973.924**
Remini, R. V. John Quincy Adams   92
Remnick, D. Reporting   **814**
Reston, J. The conviction of Richard Nixon **973.924**
Sandburg, C. Abraham Lincoln: The prairie years
   and The war years   92
Shenk, J. W. Lincoln's melancholy   92
Sorensen, T. C. Counselor   92
Swanson, J. L. Manhunt   **364.152**
Symonds, C. L. Lincoln and his admirals   92
Taking charge   **973.923**
Thomas, E. The war lovers   **973.8**
Unger, H. G. The last founding father   92
Walsh, J. E. Moonlight   **345**
Wheen, F. Strange days indeed   **973.92**
White, R. C. A. Lincoln   92
White, R. C. The eloquent president: a portrait of
   Lincoln through his words   92
Wills, G. James Madison   92
Wills, G. Lincoln at Gettysburg   **973.7**
Wilson, E. Patriotic gore   **810**
Woodward, B. The commanders   **973.928**
Woodward, B. The final days   **973.924**
Woodward, B. Shadow   **973.92**
Young, A. An easy burden   92
Zelnick, B. Gore: a political life   92
MEMBERS OF PARLIAMENT *See* Legislators
Memoir. Yagoda, B.   **809**
Memoir of a debulked woman. Gubar, S.   **616.99**
Memoirs. Teller, E.   92
MEMOIRS *See* Autobiographies; Autobiography;
  Biography
Memoirs. Rockefeller, D.   **332.1**
Memoirs and selected letters. Grant, U. S.   **973.8**
The **memoirs** of Catherine the Great. Catherine 92
MEMORIAL DAY
Poole, R. M. Section 60   **975.5**
MEMORIAL DAY
   See also Holidays
MEMORIAL MEDICAL CENTER (NEW OR-
   LEANS, LA.)
Fink, S. Five days at memorial   **362.11**
Memories.   92
Memories of myself. Lyon, D.   **779**
Memories, dreams, reflections. Jung, C. G. **150.19**
MEMORY
Buonomano, D. Brain bugs   **612.8**
Chabris, C. The invisible gorilla   **153.7**

Dittrich, L. Patient H.M.   **616.85**
Dyer, G. The missing of the Somme   **940.4**
Foer, J. Moonwalking with Einstein   **153.1**
Goldman, B. Brain fitness   **153.1**
Hoffman, E. After such knowledge   **940.53**
Kandel, E. R. In search of memory   **153**
Malone, M. S. The guardian of all things   **153.1**
Schacter, D. L. Searching for memory   **153.1**
Schacter, D. L. The seven sins of memory   **153.1**
MEMORY
   See also Brain; Educational psychology;
   Intellect; Psychology; Psychophysiology;
   Thought and thinking
MEMORY -- AGE FACTORS
Fogler, J. Improving your memory   **153.1**
Goldman, B. Brain fitness   **153.1**
MEMORY -- POPULAR WORKS
Burnett, D. Idiot brain   **612.8**
MEMORY -- SOCIOLOGICAL ASPECTS
Nguyen, V. T. Nothing ever dies   **959.704**
MEMORY DISORDERS
Dittrich, L. Patient H.M.   **616.85**
MEMORY DISORDERS
Schacter, D. L. The seven sins of memory   **153.1**
MEMORY DISORDERS -- TREATMENT
Foer, J. Moonwalking with Einstein   **153.1**
MEMORY IN OLD AGE
Fogler, J. Improving your memory   **153.1**
MEMORY, LONG-TERM
Dittrich, L. Patient H.M.   **616.85**
MEMPHIS (TENN.) -- HISTORY
Lauterbach, P. Beale Street Dynasty   **976.8**
Lightman, A. P. Screening room   92
MEN -- ATTITUDES
Annis, B. Work with me   **306.3**
MEN -- EMPLOYMENT -- UNITED STATES --
   JUVENILE LITERATURE
McKenna, A. Nontraditional careers for women
   and men   **331.702**
MEN -- HEALTH AND HYGIENE
Brewer, S. C. The Canyon Ranch guide to men's
   health   **613**
Roth, A. J. Managing prostate cancer   **616.99**
MEN -- PSYCHOLOGY
Bly, R. Iron John   **305.31**
Chabon, M. Manhood for amateurs   92
Levinson, D. J. The seasons of a man's life **155.6**
MEN -- UNITED STATES -- LONGITUDINAL
   STUDIES
Vaillant, G. E. Triumphs of experience   **305.31**
Men and women of the Bible. Tischler, N. M. **220.9**
MEN IN BUSINESS *See* Businessmen
Men in the off hours. Carson, A.   **811**
Men of mathematics. Bell, E. T.   **920**
Men of salt. Benanav, M.   **916**
Men of tomorrow. Jones, G.   **741.5**

Men still at work. Fideler, E. F. **331.3**

Men We Reaped. Ward, J. **92**

MEN'S CLOTHING

Noonan, M. L. The coat route **338.4**

MEN'S CLOTHING

See also Clothing and dress

MEN-WOMEN RELATIONSHIP See Man-woman relationship

Menachem Begin. **956.940**

Menand, Louis

The Metaphysical Club **973.9**

Menashe, Samuel

New and selected poems **811**

Mencken. Rodgers, M. E. **92**

Mencken, F. Carson

(jt. auth) Bader, C. D. Paranormal America **133.8**

Mencken, H. L.

My life as author and editor **818**

Mencken, H. L. (Henry Louis), 1880-1956

About

My life as author and editor **818**

Rodgers, M. E. Mencken **92**

Teachout, T. The skeptic: the life of H.L. Mencken **92**

Mendel, Gregor, 1822-1884

About

Henig, R. M. The monk in the garden: how Gregor Mendel and his pea plants solved the mystery of inheritance **576.5**

Malone, J. W. It doesn't take a rocket scientist **920**

Mendeleev, Dmitri I.

About

Gordin, M. D. A well-ordered thing: Dmitrii Mendeleev and the shadow of the periodic table **92**

Mendell, David

Obama **92**

Mendelsohn, Daniel

Waiting for the barbarians **801**

(ed & tr) Cavafy, C. P. Collected poems **889**

(ed & tr) Cavafy, C. P. The unfinished poems **889**

The lost **92**

About

Mendelsohn, D. The lost **92**

Mendelson, Cheryl

Home comforts **640**

Laundry **648**

Mendelssohn, Felix, 1809-1847

About

Mercer-Taylor, P. J. The life of Mendelssohn **92**

Mendelsund, Peter

What we see when we read **028**

Mendez, Antonio J

About

Baglio, M. Argo **955.05**

Mengele, Josef

About

Lifton, R. J. The Nazi doctors **940.53**

MENNONITES

Kraybill, D. B. Concise encyclopedia of Amish, Brethren, Hutterites, and Mennonites **289.7**

Kraybill, D. B. On the backroad to heaven **289.7**

MENOPAUSE

Greer, G. The change **618.1**

Sheehy, G. The silent passage: menopause **618.1**

MENOPAUSE

See also Aging

MENSTRUATION

Kim, S. Flow **612.6**

MENSTRUATION

See also Reproduction

MENTAL CALCULATORS

Tammet, D. Born on a blue day **92**

MENTAL DEPRESSION See Depression (Psychology)

MENTAL DISEASES See Abnormal psychology; Mental illness

MENTAL DISORDERS -- PSYCHOLOGY -- PERSONAL NARRATIVES

Montross, C. Falling into the fire **92**

MENTAL EFFICIENCY

Duhigg, C. Smarter faster better **158**

MENTAL HEALING

Marchant, J. Cure **616.89**

MENTAL HEALING

See also Alternative medicine

MENTAL HEALTH

Donvan, J. In a different key **616.85**

Frances, A. Saving Normal **616.89**

Gnaulati, E. Back to normal **618.92**

Guppy, J. My fluorescent God **92**

Kalb, C. Andy Warhol was a hoarder **616.89**

Saul, R. ADHD does not exist **618.92**

Wax, R. Sane new world **158.1**

MENTAL HEALTH

See also Happiness; Health

MENTAL HEALTH CARE See Mental health services

MENTAL HEALTH PERSONNEL

See also Medical personnel

MENTAL HEALTH POLICY -- UNITED STATES

Gionfriddo, P. Losing Tim **92**

MENTAL HEALTH SERVICES

Lawhorne-Scott, C. Military mental health care **355.3**

Sederer, L. I. The family guide to mental health care **616.89**

MENTAL HEALTH SERVICES

See also Medical care

MENTAL HEALTH SERVICES -- UNITED STATES

Gionfriddo, P. Losing Tim **92**

MENTAL HYGIENE See Mental health

MENTAL ILLNESS
Adamec, C. When your adult child breaks your
heart **616.89**
Bailey, B. The Splendid Things We Planned **92**
Biever, J. A. The wandering mind **612.8**
Braitman, L. Animal madness **591.5**
Frances, A. Saving Normal **616.89**
Montross, C. Falling into the fire **92**
Naifeh, S. Van Gogh **92**
Porter, R. Madness **616.89**
Shroder, T. Acid test **615.7**
Slater, L. Prozac diary **616.89**
Smoller, J. The other side of normal **591.5**
Washington, H. A. Infectious madness **616.89**
Whitaker, R. Anatomy of an epidemic **616.89**
MENTAL ILLNESS
See also Abnormal psychology; Diseases
MENTAL ILLNESS -- DRUG THERAPY
See also Drug therapy
MENTAL ILLNESS -- HISTORY
Scull, A. Madness in civilization **616.89**
MENTAL ILLNESS -- HUMOR
Lawson, J. Furiously happy **92**
**MENTAL ILLNESS -- PHYSIOLOGICAL AS-
PECTS**
See also Physiology
MENTAL ILLNESS -- TREATMENT
Shroder, T. Acid test **615.7**
MENTAL ILLNESS -- UNITED STATES
Sederer, L. I. The family guide to mental health
care **616.89**
Whitaker, R. Anatomy of an epidemic **616.89**
MENTAL WORK
Newport, C. Deep work **650.1**
MENTALLY ILL
Montross, C. Falling into the fire **92**
Murphy, T. W. Life in rewind **92**
Nathan, D. Sybil exposed **616.85**
Smith, T. A balanced life **362.1**
Torrey, E. F. Surviving schizophrenia **616.89**
Von Ziegesar, P. The looking glass brother **92**
Winchester, S. The professor and the madman **423**
MENTALLY ILL
See also Sick
MENTALLY ILL -- FAMILY RELATIONSHIPS
Earley, P. Resilience **616.89**
MENTALLY ILL -- INSTITUTIONAL CARE
Ronson, J. The psychopath test **616.85**
**MENTALLY ILL -- UNITED STATES -- BIOG-
RAPHY**
Shroder, T. Acid test **615.7**
Smith, D. Monkey mind **616.85**
**MENTALLY ILL -- WASHINGTON (STATE) --
SEATTLE -- BIOGRAPHY**
Guppy, J. My fluorescent God **92**
MENTALLY ILL CHILDREN *See* Emotionally
disturbed children
**MENTALLY ILL PERSONS -- PSYCHOLOGY
-- PERSONAL NARRATIVES**
Montross, C. Falling into the fire **92**
MENTALLY RETARDED *See* People with mental
disabilities
MENTALLY RETARDED CHILDREN *See* Chil-
dren with mental disabilities
MENTORING
Chertavian, G. A Year Up **331.25**
Edelman, M. W. Lanterns **92**
MENTORING
See also Counseling
Menuez, Doug
Fearless genius **979.4**
MENUS
Bayless, R. Fiesta at Rick's **641.5**
Brennan, K. Keepers **641.5**
Tanis, D. Heart of the artichoke and other kitchen
journeys **641.5**
Tanis, D. A platter of figs and other recipes **641.5**
MENUS
See also Cooking; Diet
MENUS.
Garten, I. Barefoot Contessa at home **641**
MERCANTILE LAW *See* Commercial law
MERCEDES AUTOMOBILES
Michelli, J. A. Driven to delight **658**
MERCENARY SOLDIERS
Geraghty, T. Soldiers of fortune **355.3**
MERCENARY SOLDIERS
See also Military personnel; Soldiers
MERCENARY TROOPS *See* Mercenary soldiers
Mercer-Taylor, Peter Jameson
The life of Mendelssohn **92**
MERCHANDISING *See* Marketing; Retail trade
Merchant kings. Bown, S. R. **338.8**
MERCHANT MARINE
See also Maritime law; Sailors; Ships; Trans-
portation
MERCHANT MARINE -- UNITED STATES
Geroux, W. The Mathews Men **940.54**
MERCHANTS
Bown, S. R. Merchant kings **338.8**
Hardy, J. In the valley of mist **954**
Harris, J. W. The hanging of Thomas Jeremiah **92**
Milner, C. A. As big as the West **92**
MERCHANTS
See also Businesspeople
MERCHANTS -- ITALY -- VENICE -- HISTORY
Crowley, R. City of fortune **945**
Merchants of doubt. Conway, E. M. **174**
The **Merck** index. O'Neil, M. J. **615**
The **Merck** veterinary manual. **636.089**
Mercola, Joseph M., 1954-
Effortless healing **613.2**

MERCURY

   See also Chemical elements; Metals

MERCURY (PLANET)

   See also Planets

The **Mercury** 13: the untold story of thirteen American women and the dream of space flight. Ackmann, M.   **629.45**

Mercy. Clifton, L.   **811**

The **mercy.** Levine, P.   **811**

MERCY

   A call to mercy   **234.5**

MERCY KILLING *See* Euthanasia

Mere Christianity. Lewis, C. S.   **230**

Meredith, Martin

   Born in Africa   **960**

   Diamonds, gold, and war   **968.04**

   The fortunes of Africa   **960**

Meredith, William

   Effort at speech   **811**

Merewether, Charles

   (ed) Ai weiwei   **709.5**

MERGE RECORDS (CHAPEL HILL, N.C.: FIRM)

   Cook, J. Our noise   **338**

MERGERS *See* Corporate mergers and acquisitions

Merle's door. Kerasote, T.   **636.7**

Merleau-Ponty, Maurice, 1908-1961

   About

   Said, E. W. Reflections on exile and other essays   **814**

Merlino, Doug

   The hustle   **796.323**

A Merloyd Lawrence book [series]

   Martin, J. Rebel Souls   **92**

MERMAIDS AND MERMEN

   See also Mythical animals

Merman, Ethel, 1908 or 9-1984

   About

   Flinn, C. Brass diva   **92**

Merriam-Webster Inc.

   (comp) Merriam-Webster's visual dictionary   **423**

   Merriam-Webster's collegiate dictionary   **423**

   Merriam-Webster's collegiate thesaurus   **423**

Merridale, Catherine

   Ivan's war   **940.54**

MERRILL LYNCH & CO., INC.

   Farrell, G. Crash of the titans   **332.1**

Merrill, A. Roger

   Covey, S. R. First things first   **158**

Merrill, James, 1926-1995

   The changing light at Sandover   **811**

   The collected poems of James Merrill   **811**

   About

   Hammer, L. James Merrill   **92**

Merrill, Rebecca R.

   (jt. auth) Covey, S. M. R. Smart trust   **174**

Covey, S. R. First things first   **158**

Merriman, John M.

   (ed) Europe 1789 to 1914   **940.2**

   The dynamite club   **363.32**

Merritt, George

   Escott, C. Hank Williams   **92**

Merry, Robert W., 1946-

   A country of vast designs   **92**

Mersky, Roy M.

   Leiter, R. A. Landmark Supreme Court cases   **347**

   Landmark Supreme Court cases   **347.73**

Merton, Thomas

   (ed) Gandhi, M. Gandhi on non-violence   **322.4**

   In the dark before dawn   **811**

   About

   Elie, P. The life you save may be your own   **810**

   Merton, T. The seven storey mountain   **92**

   Merton, T. Intimate Merton   **271**

Mertz, Barbara

   Temples, tombs, & hieroglyphs   **932**

Merwin, W. S.

   (tr) Chanson de Roland The song of Roland   **841**

   (tr) Mandelstam, O. The selected poems of Osip Mandelstam   **891.7**

   Migration   **811**

   (tr) Selected translations 1948-2010   **808.81**

Merzbach, Uta C.

   (jt. auth) Boyer, C. B. A history of mathematics   **510**

Mesler, Bill

   A Brief History of Creation   **576.8**

Message from an unknown Chinese mother. Xinran   **305.4**

Messenger, Charles

   (ed) Reader's guide to military history   **355.009**

The **messenger:** the rise and fall of Elijah Muhammad. Evanzz, K.   **297.8**

Messick, Kendall

   The projectionist   **92**

MESSINESS

   See also Human behavior

Messori, Vittorio

   (ed) John Paul Crossing the threshold of hope   **282**

Messy. Harford, T.   **153.35**

METABOLIC DISORDERS

   See also Diseases

METABOLISM

   See also Biochemistry

METABOLISM -- REGULATION

   Cruikshank, T. Meditate your weight   **613.25**

   Ludwig, D. Always hungry?   **613.2**

METAFICTION

   See also Fiction

METAL (MUSIC) *See* Heavy metal (Music)

METAL INDUSTRY EXECUTIVES

   Krass, P. Carnegie   **338.7**

Nasaw, D. Andrew Carnegie   92
Rea, T. Bone wars   560
Wall, J. F. Andrew Carnegie   92
Waugh, A. The House of Wittgenstein   920
METAL WORK See Metalwork
METALS -- FINISHING
 See also Finishes and finishing; Metalwork
METALWORK
Haab, S. The art of metal clay   739.27
Karon, K. Advanced chain maille jewelry work-
 shop   745.594
METALWORK
 See also Decoration and ornament
METALWORKERS
Faber, T. Faberge's eggs   739.2
Fischer, D. H. Paul Revere's ride   973.3
Lepore, J. A is for American   306.44
METALWORKING MACHINERY
 See also Machinery
MetaMaus. Spiegelman, A.   940.53
Metamorphoses. Ovid   873
The **Metaphysical** Club. Menand, L.   973.9
Metaphysical dog. Bidart, F.   811
METAPHYSICS
Menand, L. The Metaphysical Club   973.9
METAPHYSICS
 See also Philosophy
METAPHYSICS -- POETRY
Bidart, F. Metaphysical dog   811
Metaxas, Eric
Bonhoeffer   92
Metcalf, Allan A.
Predicting new words   420
METEORITES
Bevan, A. W. R. Meteorites: a journey through
 space and time   523.5
Cokinos, C. The fallen sky   523.5
METEORITES
 See also Astronomy; Meteors
Meteorites: a journey through space and time. Be-
 van, A. W. R.   523.5
METEOROLOGICAL INSTRUMENTS
 See also Scientific apparatus and instruments
METEOROLOGISTS
Hamblyn, R. The invention of clouds   551.57
METEOROLOGY
Buckley, B. Weather: a visual guide   551.5
 Global weirdness   577.2
Hamblyn, R. The invention of clouds   551.57
Monmonier, M. S. Air apparent   551.63
Redniss, L. Thunder & Lightning   551.6
Williams, J. The AMS weather book   551.5
METEOROLOGY
 See also Earth sciences
METEOROLOGY -- ENCYCLOPEDIAS
Fry, J. L. The encyclopedia of weather and climate

change   551.6
METHAMPHETAMINE ABUSE
Reding, N. Methland   362.29
**METHICILLIN-RESISTANT STAPHYLOCOC-
 CUS AUREUS**
McKenna, M. Superbug   616.9
Methland. Reding, N.   362.29
METHODIST CHURCH
Tomkins, S. John Wesley   287
METRIC SYSTEM
Alder, K. The measure of all things   526
METROPOLITAN AREAS -- CASE STUDIES
Hunt, T. Cities of empire   941
METROPOLITAN FINANCE
 See also Municipal finance; Public finance
The **Metropolitan** Museum of Art. Galitz, K. C. 700
Metropolitan Museum of Art (New York, N.Y.)
Cikovsky, N. Winslow Homer   759.13
Liedtke, W. A. Vermeer and the Delft school 759.9
Thomas Eakins   759.13
**METROPOLITAN MUSEUM OF ART (NEW
 YORK, N.Y.)**
Denny, W. B. How to read Islamic carpets 746.7
Gross, M. Rogues' gallery   920
METROPOLITAN OPERA (NEW YORK, N.Y.)
Volpe, J. The toughest show on earth   92
METROPOLITAN PLANNING See Regional
 planning
Mettler, Suzanne
Degrees of inequality   378.73
Metzger, Bruce Manning
(ed) The Oxford companion to the Bible   220.3
Mevoli, Nick, 1981-2013
      About
Skolnick, A. One breath   797.2
**MEXICAN AMERICAN BOYS -- EDUCATION
 -- UNITED STATES**
Davis, J. Spare parts   629.8
MEXICAN AMERICAN COOKING
Jinich, P. Mexican today   641.5
Tausend, M. Cocina de la familia   641.5
MEXICAN AMERICAN WOMEN
 See also Mexican Americans; Women
MEXICAN AMERICANS
Marin, C. Chicano visions   709
Quiñones-Hinojosa, A. Becoming Dr. Q   92
Thorpe, H. Just like us   305.8
MEXICAN AMERICANS
 See also Americans; Ethnic groups; Immi-
  grants -- United States; Latinos (U.S.); Mi-
  norities
MEXICAN AMERICANS -- BIOGRAPHY
Grande, R. The distance between us   92
Rodriguez, R. Hunger of memory   92
**MEXICAN AMERICANS -- ECONOMIC CON-
 DITIONS**

Davis, J. Spare parts   **629.8**

MEXICAN COOKING

Bayless, R. Authentic Mexican   **641.597**

Bayless, R. Mexican everyday   **641.597**

Bayless, R. Mexico: one plate at a time   **641.597**

Bayless, R. More Mexican everyday   **641.597**

Bayless, R. Fiesta at Rick's   **641.5**

Bayless, R. Rick Bayless's Mexican kitchen **641.59**

Carrillo Arronte, M. Mexico   **641.59**

Cramby, J. Tex-Mex from Scratch   **641.59**

García, L. Lorena Garcia's new taco classics **641.84**

Gerson, F. My sweet Mexico   **641.5**

Jamison, B. The border cookbook   **641.59**

Jinich, P. Mexican today   **641.5**

Kennedy, D. The essential cuisines of Mexico   **641.59**

Kennedy, D. From my Mexican kitchen **641.5**

Santibañez, R. Truly Mexican   **641.59**

Stupak, A. Tacos   **641.84**

Tellez, L. Eat Mexico   **641.597**

Werner, E. Hartwood   **641.597**

Mexican everyday. Bayless, R.   **641.597**

MEXICAN LITERATURE

    See also Latin American literature; Literature

MEXICAN NATIONAL CHARACTERISTICS

Paz, O. The labyrinth of solitude   **864**

MEXICAN POETRY

Paz, O. The poems of Octavio Paz   **861**

MEXICAN POETRY -- COLLECTIONS

Torre, M. d. l. Reversible monuments   **861**

Mexican today. Jinich, P.   **641.5**

MEXICAN WAR, 1846-1848

Hahn, S. A Nation Without Borders   **973.5**

MEXICAN WAR, 1846-1848

    See also United States -- History -- 1815-1861

The **Mexican** Wars for Independence. Henderson, T. J.   **972**

MEXICAN-AMERICAN BORDER REGION -- BIOGRAPHY

Jacoby, K. The strange career of William Ellis **92**

MEXICAN-AMERICAN BORDER REGION -- ECONOMIC CONDITIONS

Miller, T. Border patrol nation   **363.28**

MEXICANS -- UNITED STATES

Davis, J. Spare parts   **629.8**

MEXICANS -- UNITED STATES

    See also Minorities; Noncitizens -- United States

Mexico. Carrillo Arronte, M.   **641.59**

MEXICO -- ANTIQUITIES

Coe, M. D. The Maya   **972**

Smith, M. E. The Aztecs   **972**

MEXICO -- CIVILIZATION

Biron, R. E. Elena Garro and Mexico's modern dreams   **868**

MEXICO -- EMIGRATION AND IMMIGRA-

TION -- SOCIAL ASPECTS

Grande, R. The distance between us   **92**

Urrea, L. A. The devil's highway   **325**

MEXICO -- HISTORY

Diaz del Castillo, B. The discovery and conquest of Mexico, 1517-1521   **972**

Foster, L. V. A brief history of Mexico   **972**

Henderson, T. J. The Mexican Wars for Independence   **972**

Katz, F. The life and times of Pancho Villa **972.08**

Kirkwood, B. The history of Mexico   **972**

Meyer, M. C. The course of Mexican history **972**

The Oxford history of Mexico   **972**

Prescott, W. H. History of the conquest of Mexico   **972**

Womack, J. Zapata and the Mexican Revolution   **972.08**

MEXICO -- POLITICS AND GOVERNMENT

Fuentes, C. A new time for Mexico   **972.08**

MEXICO CITY (MEXICO)

Tellez, L. Eat Mexico   **641.597**

MEXICO CITY (MEXICO) -- SOCIAL CONDITIONS

Lewis, O. The children of Sanchez   **972.08**

Mexico: one plate at a time. Bayless, R.   **641.597**

Meyer, G. J.

The Tudors   **942.05**

Meyer, Jennifer

Decision quality   **658.4**

Meyer, Josh

(jt. auth) McDermott, T. The hunt for KSM **363.325**

Meyer, Joyce

Seize the day   **248.4**

Meyer, Judith L.

The spirit of Yellowstone   **978.7**

Meyer, Karl E.

(jt. auth) Brysac, S. B. The China collectors **709.5**

Kingmakers   **956**

Meyer, Marvin W.

(ed) The Gnostic Bible   **299**

Meyer, Michael C.

The course of Mexican history   **972**

(ed) The Oxford history of Mexico   **972**

Meyer, Michael J.

The last days of old Beijing   **951**

Meyer, Sheldon

(ed) Morgenstern, D. Living with jazz   **781.65**

Meyerink, Kory L.

(ed) Printed sources   **016**

Meyerowitz, Rick

Drunk stoned brilliant dead   **051**

Meyers, Charlie

(jt. auth) Deeter, K. The little red book of fly fishing   **799.124**

Meyers, Jeffrey

John Huston   **92**

Orwell   828
Samuel Johnson   92
Meyers, Peter
As we speak   808.5
Meyerson, Michael
Liberty's blueprint   342
Mezrich, Ben
The 37th parallel   001.942
Once Upon a Time in Russia   330
MEZZOTINT ENGRAVING
See also Engraving
MFA vs NYC.   808.02
MI6. Dorril, S.   327.12
MIAMI (FLA.)
Eire, C. M. N. Learning to die in Miami   92
MICE
See also Mammals
Michael Jackson, Inc. Greenburg, Z. O.   92
Michael Jordan. Lazenby, R.   92
Michael Symon's 5 in 5 for every season.   641.81
Michael Thompson: Portraits. Thompson, M.   779
Michael, T. S.
How to guard an art gallery and other discrete mathematical adventures   511
Michaeli, Ethan
The defender   071
Michaelis, David
N.C. Wyeth   92
Schulz and Peanuts   92
Michaels, Chris Franchetti
Teach yourself visually jewelry making & beading   745.59
Michaels, J. Ramsey
Passing by the dragon   813
Michaels, Julie
(jt. auth) Chezar, A. The flower workshop   745.92
Micheaux, Oscar, 1884-1951
About
McGilligan, P. Oscar Micheaux   92
Michelangelo. Unger, M. J.   92
Michelangelo. Hirst, M.   709.2
Michelangelo & the Pope's ceiling. King, R.   759
Michelangelo Buonarroti, 1475-1564
About
Hirst, M. Michelangelo   709.2
King, R. Michelangelo & the Pope's ceiling   759
Unger, M. J. Michelangelo   92
Michelle Obama. Slevin, P.   92
Michelli, Joseph A.
Driven to delight   658
Michels, Barry, 1954-
The tools   158
Michelson, Leslie D.
The patient's playbook   610.69
Michener, Charles
Volpe, J. The toughest show on earth   92

Michener, David
Taylor's guide to ground covers   635.9
Michener, James A.
The bridge at Andau   943.9
Return to paradise   990
MICHIGAN STATE UNIVERSITY
Davis, S. When March went mad   796.323
Micklethwait, John
The company   338.7
Micklewright, Keith
Drawing: mastering the language of visual expression   741.2
MICROBES *See* Bacteria; Germ theory of disease; Microorganisms; Viruses
Microbes and people: an A-Z of microorganisms in our lives. Sankaran, N.   579
MICROBIAL ENERGY CONVERSION *See* Biomass energy
MICROBIAL METABOLISM
Collen, A. 10% human   612.3
MICROBIOLOGISTS
Kluger, J. Splendid solution: Jonas Salk and the conquest of polio   92
Malone, J. W. It doesn't take a rocket scientist   920
Offit, P. A. Vaccinated   92
Varmus, H. The art and politics of science   92
MICROBIOLOGY
Ben-Barak, I. The invisible kingdom   579
Biddle, W. A field guide to germs   616
Dietert, R. The human superorganism   613
McAuliffe, K. This is your brain on parasites   612.8
Tetro, J. The Germ Files   579.3
Yong, E. I Contain Multitudes   579
Zimmer, C. Microcosm   579.3
MICROBIOLOGY
See also Biology
MICROBIOLOGY -- DICTIONARIES
Sankaran, N. Microbes and people: an A-Z of microorganisms in our lives   579
MICROBIOTA
Finlay, B. B. Let Them Eat Dirt   616.9
MICROBIOTA -- PHYSIOLOGY
Montgomery, D. R. The hidden half of nature   579
MICROBREWERIES
Acitelli, T. The audacity of hops   641.2
MICROCHEMISTRY
See also Chemistry
MICROCOMPUTERS
Lloyd, S. Programming the universe   530.1
MICROCOMPUTERS *See* Personal computers
Microcosm. Zimmer, C.   579.3
MICROECONOMICS
See also Economics
MICROELECTRONICS
Menuez, D. Fearless genius   979.4
MICROELECTRONICS

See also Electronics; Semiconductors
**MICROELECTRONICS INDUSTRY -- CALI-
FORNIA -- SANTA CLARA VALLEY (SANTA
CLARA COUNTY) -- HISTORY**
Menuez, D. Fearless genius   **979.4**
MICROFINANCE
Novogratz, J. The blue sweater   **339.4**
MICROORGANISMS
Dunn, R. The wild life of our bodies   **579**
Finlay, B. B. Let Them Eat Dirt   **616.9**
Tetro, J. The Germ Files   **579.3**
Yong, E. I Contain Multitudes   **579**
MICROORGANISMS -- THERAPEUTIC USE
Collen, A. 10% human   **612.3**
Microshelters. Diedricksen, D.   **690**
MIDDLE AGE
Cameron, J. B. It's never too late to begin
again   **155.67**
Levinson, D. J. The seasons of a man's life   **155.6**
Levinson, D. J. The seasons of a woman's life **155.6**
Sheehy, G. New passages   **305.24**
MIDDLE AGE
See also Age; Life (Biology)
MIDDLE AGE -- PSYCHOLOGICAL ASPECTS
Bulik, C. M. Midlife eating disorders   **616.85**
MIDDLE AGED MEN
See also Middle aged persons
MIDDLE AGED MEN -- BIOGRAPHY
Blair, J. By the Iowa Sea   **977.7**
MIDDLE AGED PERSONS
Bulik, C. M. Midlife eating disorders   **616.85**
MIDDLE AGED WOMEN
Levinson, D. J. The seasons of a woman's life **155.6**
MIDDLE AGED WOMEN
See also Middle aged persons
MIDDLE AGES
Gies, F. Life in a medieval village   **940.1**
Gies, J. Life in a medieval castle   **940.2**
Gies, J. Life in a medieval city   **940.1**
Great events from history, The Middle Ages, 477-
1453   **909.07**
Morris, M. King John   **92**
The New Cambridge medieval history   **940.1**
Wickham, C. The inheritance of Rome   **940.1**
MIDDLE AGES
See also World history
MIDDLE AGES -- BIOGRAPHY
Great lives from history, the Middle Ages, 477-
1453   **920.003**
MIDDLE AGES -- DICTIONARIES
Dictionary of the Middle Ages   **909.07**
MIDDLE AGES -- ENCYCLOPEDIAS
English, E. D. Encyclopedia of the medieval
world   **940.1**
MIDDLE AGES -- HISTORY *See* Middle Ages
MIDDLE CLASS

Carville, J. It's the middle class, stupid!   **320.51**
Whitaker, J. Service and style   **381**
MIDDLE CLASS
See also Social classes
MIDDLE CLASS -- UNITED STATES
Barlett, D. L. The betrayal of the American
dream   **330.973**
Smith, H. Who stole the American dream? **973.91**
Warren, E. A fighting chance   **92**
Middle earth. Cole, H.   **811**
The **Middle** East. Lewis, B.   **956**
The **Middle** East. Congressional Quarterly, I. **956**
MIDDLE EAST
Barr, J. A line in the sand   **956**
MIDDLE EAST -- CIVILIZATION
Civilizations of the Ancient Near East   **939**
MIDDLE EAST -- CIVILIZATION -- TO 622
Levine, L. I. Visual Judaism in late antiquity **704.9**
MIDDLE EAST -- DESCRIPTION
Feiler, B. S. Walking the Bible   **915**
O'Neill, Z. All strangers are kin   **910.917**
Taseer, A. Stranger to history   **915.6**
**MIDDLE EAST -- FOREIGN RELATIONS --
20TH CENTURY**
Barr, J. A line in the sand   **956**
**MIDDLE EAST -- FOREIGN RELATIONS --
UNITED STATES**
Bacevich, A. J. America's war for the greater Mid-
dle East   **956.054**
Haass, R. War of necessity: war of choice   **956.7**
Miller, A. D. The much too promised land   **956.05**
Nasr, V. The dispensable nation   **327.73**
MIDDLE EAST -- HISTORY
Bacevich, A. J. America's war for the greater Mid-
dle East   **956.054**
MIDDLE EAST -- HISTORY -- 1914-1923
Anderson, S. Lawrence in Arabia   **940.4**
MIDDLE EAST -- HISTORY -- 1979-
Wright, L. The terror years   **363.325**
MIDDLE EAST -- HISTORY -- 20TH CENTURY
Brown, M. T.E. Lawrence   **92**
Howell, G. Gertrude Bell   **92**
Lewis, B. Notes on a century   **956**
Meyer, K. E. Kingmakers   **956**
**MIDDLE EAST -- MILITARY HISTORY -- EN-
CYCLOPEDIAS**
The encyclopedia of Middle East wars   **355**
**MIDDLE EAST -- POLITICS AND GOVERN-
MENT**
Lewis, B. Notes on a century   **956**
Owen, R. The rise and fall of Arab presidents for
life   **352.23**
Worth, R. F. A rage for order   **909**
Wright, L. The terror years   **363.325**
**MIDDLE EAST -- POLITICS AND GOVERN-
MENT -- 1914-1945**

Barr, J. A line in the sand   **956**

MIDDLE EAST -- POLITICS AND GOVERN-MENT -- 21ST CENTURY

Engel, R. And then all hell broke loose   **956.05**

Warrick, J. Black flags   **956.91**

MIDDLE EAST -- SOCIAL CONDITIONS

Anderson, S. The Hostage's Daughter   **92**

Sattouf, R. The Arab of the Future 2   **92**

MIDDLE EAST -- STRATEGIC ASPECTS

    See also Military geography; Strategy

MIDDLE EAST WAR, 1991 *See* Persian Gulf War, 1991

MIDDLE EASTERN COOKING

Abood, M. Rose water and orange blossoms

Bishara, R. Olives, lemons & za'atar   **641.59**

Duguid, N. Taste of Persia   **641.5**

Ghayour, S. Persiana   **641.595**

Henry, D. A Change of Appetite   **641.5**

Honey & Co.   **641.595**

Maffei, Y. My halal kitchen   **641.595**

Ottolenghi, Y. Nopi   **641.5**

Roden, C. The new book of Middle Eastern food   **641.59**

MIDDLE EASTERN STUDIES SPECIALISTS

Esfandiari, H. My prison, my home   **92**

Grant, R. Crazy river   **916**

Lovell, M. S. A rage to live: a biography of Richard and Isabel Burton   **92**

The **middle** of everywhere. Pipher, M. B.   **305.9**

Middle passages. Campbell, J. T.   **916**

The **middle** place. Corrigan, K.   **92**

MIDDLE WEST

    See also Mississippi River Valley; United States

MIDDLE WEST -- BIOGRAPHY

Borich, B. J. Body geographic   **818**

MIDDLE-AGED MEN -- UNITED STATES -- BIOGRAPHY

Foreman, T. My year of running dangerously   **92**

MIDDLE-AGED PERSONS

Bulik, C. M. Midlife eating disorders   **616.85**

Middlebrook, Diane Wood

Anne Sexton   **811**

Middlekauff, Robert

The glorious cause   **973.3**

MIDLIFE CRISIS

Blair, J. By the Iowa Sea   **977.7**

MIDLIFE CRISIS

    See also Middle age

Midlife eating disorders. Bulik, C. M.   **616.85**

Midnight assassin. Bryan, P. L.   **364.152**

Midnight dreary. Walsh, J. E.   **818**

Midnight in broad daylight. Sakamoto, P. R. **940.53**

Midnight in Siberia. Greene, D.   **914.7**

Midnight in the garden of good and evil. Berendt, J.   **975.8**

Midnight rising. Horwitz, T.   **92**

MIDWAY, BATTLE OF, 1942

Ballard, R. D. Return to Midway   **940.54**

MIDWESTERN COOKING

Thielen, A. The New Midwestern table   **641.59**

MIDWIFERY *See* Midwives

MIDWIVES

Vincent, P. Baby catcher   **618.2**

MIDWIVES

    See also Childbirth; Natural childbirth; Nurses

Mies van der Rohe, Ludwig, 1886-1969

      About

Weber, N. F. The Bauhaus group   **920**

Mightier than the sword. Reynolds, D. S.   **813**

The **mighty** queens of Freeville. Dickinson, A.   **92**

Miglore, Kristen

Food52 genius recipes   **641.5**

MIGRANT LABOR

Bacon, D. Illegal people   **331.6**

Chang, L. T. Factory girls   **331.4**

Laskas, J. M. Hidden America   **305.5**

Quiñones-Hinojosa, A. Becoming Dr. Q   **92**

MIGRANT LABOR

    See also Employees; Labor

Migration. Merwin, W. S.   **811**

MIGRATION *See* Animals -- Migration; Immigration and emigration

MIGRATION, INTERNAL *See* Internal migration

MIGRATION, INTERNAL -- UNITED STATES -- HISTORY

Berlin, I. The making of African America   **305.8**

MIGRATION, INTERNAL -- UNITED STATES -- HISTORY -- 20TH CENTURY

Wilkerson, I. The warmth of other suns   **307**

MIGRATORY WORKERS *See* Migrant labor

Mihailescu, Calin-Andrei

(ed) Borges, J. L. This craft of verse   **809.1**

Mihalkanin, Edward S.

(ed) American statesmen   **920.003**

Mikkola, Heimo

Owls of the world   **598.9**

Mikolajski, Andrew

Pruning plant by plant   **635**

Milanović, Branko

The haves and the have-nots   **339.2**

Mildon, Emma

The soul searcher's handbook   **131**

Miles gone by. Buckley, W. F.   **92**

Miles, Barry

Call Me Burroughs   **92**

Miles, Bryan

101 magic tricks   **793.8**

Miles, Jason

YouTube marketing power   **658.8**

Miles, Kathryn

Superstorm 551.55

Miles, Lera
(ed) World atlas of great apes and their conservation 599.8

Miles, Sara
(ed) Jordan, J. Directed by desire 811

Miles, the autobiography. Davis, M. 92

Milestones of space. 629.4

Miletich, Patrick Jay, 1968-
About
Wertheim, L. J. Blood in the cage 92

Milford, Nancy
Savage beauty: the life of Edna St. Vincent Millay 92

Milgrom, Melissa
Still life 590.75

MILITARISM -- ITALY -- HISTORY -- 20TH CENTURY
Hughes-Hallett, L. Gabriele d'Annunzio 858

MILITARISM -- UNITED STATES
Maddow, R. Drift 306.2

MILITARY AERONAUTICS
See also Aeronautics; Military art and science; War

MILITARY AIRPLANES
See also Airplanes; Military aeronautics

MILITARY ART AND SCIENCE
Boot, M. War made new 355
Carney, J. T. No room for error 356
Clausewitz, C. v. On war 355
Cockburn, A. Kill Chain 623.7
Cotterell, A. Chariot 357
Emlen, D. J. Animal weapons 591.47
Harris, S. @WAR 355.3
Maurer, K. Hunter Killer 92
Scahill, J. Dirty wars 355.02
Singer, P. W. Wired for war 355
Sun-tzu The illustrated art of war 355
Walker, W. T. Betrayal at Little Gibraltar 940.436
Weapons & warfare 623.4
The West Point History of the Civil War 973.7
Whittle, R. Predator 623.74

MILITARY ART AND SCIENCE -- HISTORY
France, J. Perilous glory 355
Hastings, M. Inferno 940.54
Stephenson, M. The last full measure 305.9

MILITARY ART AND SCIENCE -- UNITED STATES -- DICTIONARIES
Axelrod, A. Whiskey tango foxtrot 427

MILITARY ATROCITIES *See* Atrocities; War crimes

MILITARY BASES
Paglen, T. Blank spots on the map 355.3

MILITARY CAMPS
See also Military art and science

MILITARY CONSCRIPTION *See* Draft

MILITARY DESERTERS -- HISTORY -- 20TH CENTURY
Glass, C. The deserters 940.54

MILITARY ENGINEERS
Barry, J. M. Rising tide 977

MILITARY FACILITIES *See* Military bases

MILITARY GEOGRAPHY
See also Geography

MILITARY GEOGRAPHY -- UNITED STATES
Keegan, J. The American Civil War 973.7

MILITARY HEALTH *See* Military personnel -- Health and hygiene

MILITARY HISTORY
Arnold, J. R. Jungle of snakes 355
Beevor, A. The Second World War 940.54
The Book of war 355
Boot, M. War made new 355
Clark, L. Blitzkrieg 940.54
De Pauw, L. G. Battle cries and lullabies 355
Hanson, V. D. Carnage and culture 904
Hanson, V. D. The father of us all 355
Hanson, V. D. The soul of battle 355
Hastings, M. Inferno 940.54
Hastings, M. Warriors 355
Levy, J. Fifty Weapons That Changed the Course of History 355.8
Magill's guide to military history 355
Morris, I. War! What is it good for? 303.6
Reader's guide to military history 355.009

MILITARY HISTORY
See also History

MILITARY HISTORY -- 17TH CENTURY
Parker, G. Global crisis 909

MILITARY HISTORY -- DICTIONARIES
Dictionary of wars 355
Magill's guide to military history 355

MILITARY HISTORY -- ENCYCLOPEDIAS
War: from ancient Egypt to Iraq 355

MILITARY HISTORY, MODERN
Boot, M. War made new 355
Kennedy, P. M. The rise and fall of the great powers 909.08

MILITARY HOSPITALS
See also Hospitals; Military medicine

MILITARY INSTALLATIONS *See* Military bases

MILITARY INTELLIGENCE
Scahill, J. Dirty wars 355.02

MILITARY INTELLIGENCE
See also Intelligence service

MILITARY INTERROGATION -- IRAQ
Fair, E. Consequence 956.704

MILITARY INTERROGATION -- UNITED STATES
Fair, E. Consequence 956.704

MILITARY LAW
See also International law; Law

MILITARY LAW -- UNITED STATES -- HISTORY

Witt, J. F. Lincoln's code   **343**

MILITARY LIFE *See* Military personnel

Military life [series]

Lawhorne-Scott, C. Military mental health care   **355.3**

Scott, J. Raising children in the military   **355.1**

MILITARY MEDICINE

See also Medicine

Military mental health care. Lawhorne-Scott, C.   **355.3**

MILITARY MUSIC

See also Music

MILITARY OCCUPATION

Allawi, A. A. The occupation of Iraq   **956.7**

Bregman, A. Cursed victory

Palestine Speaks   **956.94**

MILITARY OCCUPATION

See also War

MILITARY OFFICIALS

Lee, H. Virginia Woolf's nose   **820**

Long, J. The plot against Pepys   **941.06**

Pepys, S. The diary of Samuel Pepys   **941.06**

Symonds, C. L. Lincoln and his admirals   **92**

Tomalin, C. Samuel Pepys   **941.06**

MILITARY PENSIONS

See also Pensions

MILITARY PERSONNEL

Taylor, S. Commander   **92**

MILITARY PERSONNEL

See also Armed forces; War

MILITARY PERSONNEL -- HEALTH AND HYGIENE

Lawhorne-Scott, C. Military mental health care   **355.3**

MILITARY PERSONNEL -- HEALTH AND HYGIENE

See also Hygiene

MILITARY PERSONNEL -- UNITED STATES

Bolger, D. P. Why We Lost   **956.704**

Castner, B. All the ways we kill and die   **958.104**

Henican, E. Worth dying for   **359.984**

Moore, W. The work   **92**

Rodriguez, D. Rise   **92**

Scott, J. Raising children in the military   **355.1**

Wildsmith, S. Joining the United States Air Force   **358.4**

MILITARY PLANNING -- JAPAN -- HISTORY -- 20TH CENTURY

Hotta, E. Japan 1941   **940.54**

MILITARY PLANNING -- UNITED STATES

Rose, G. How wars end   **355**

MILITARY POLICY

See also Military history

MILITARY POLICY -- UNITED STATES

Glass, C. The deserters   **940.54**

Grandin, G. Kissinger's Shadow   **327.2**

Henican, E. Worth dying for   **359.984**

Maddow, R. Drift   **306.2**

Mazzetti, M. The way of the knife   **356**

Nicholson, A. Fighting to serve   **355**

Preston, A. Sword of the spirit, shield of faith   **322**

Zinn, H. The historic unfullfilled promise   **973.924**

MILITARY POSTS *See* Military bases

MILITARY POWER *See* Armies; Military art and science; Navies; Sea power

MILITARY READINESS -- ECONOMIC ASPECTS

Kennedy, P. M. The rise and fall of the great powers   **909.08**

MILITARY RESEARCH

Horwitz, J. War of the Whales   **333.95**

MILITARY SPOUSES

Barrett, D. GI brides   **940.53**

Burana, L. I love a man in uniform   **92**

MILITARY WEAPONS

Klein, M. A call to arms   **940.53**

Singer, P. W. Wired for war   **355**

Weapons & warfare   **623.4**

MILITARY WEAPONS

See also Ordnance; Weapons

MILITIA MOVEMENTS

See also Radicalism; Social movements

MILK

Hamilton, A. Got milked?   **641.5**

MILK

See also Dairy products; Dairying; Food

Milk and honey. Kaur, R.   **811.6**

Milk Bar Life.   **641.86**

Milk Bar Life.   **641.86**

Mill, John Stuart, 1806-1873

About

Mill, J. S. Autobiography   **92**

Millar, David

The Cambridge dictionary of scientists   **920.003**

Millard Fillmore. Finkelman, P.   **92**

Millard, Candice

The destiny of the republic   **973.8**

Hero of the empire   **968.04**

The river of doubt   **973.91**

Millay, Edna St. Vincent

Collected poems   **811**

Selected poems   **811**

Millay, Edna St. Vincent, 1892-1950

About

Milford, N. Savage beauty: the life of Edna St. Vincent Millay   **92**

MILLENARIANISM *See* Millennium

MILLENNIALISM *See* Millennium

MILLENNIUM

Weber, E. Apocalypses   **200**

MILLENNIUM
   See also Eschatology
Miller's antiques handbook & price guide. Miller, J.   **745.1**
Miller's arts & crafts. Miller, J.   **745.4**
Miller's costume jewelry. Miller, J.   **739.27**
Miller, Aaron David
   The much too promised land   **956.05**
Miller, Adrian
   Soul food   **641.59**
Miller, Arthur I.
   Empire of the stars   **520**
Miller, Arthur, 1915-2005
   Collected plays, 1944-1961   **812**
         About
   Abbotson, S. C. W. Critical companion to Arthur Miller   **812**
   Bigsby, C. Arthur Miller   **92**
   Gottfried, M. Arthur Miller   **92**
   Playwrights at work   **812**
Miller, Caroline Adams
   Creating your best life   **158**
Miller, Char
   Gifford Pinchot and the making of modern environmentalism   **333.7**
Miller, Christine Marie
   Ancell, R. M. The biographical dictionary of World War II generals and flag officers   **920.003**
Miller, Cristanne
   (ed) Words for the hour   **811**
Miller, Donald
   Scary close   **158.2**
Miller, Donald L.
   City of the century   **977.3**
   Supreme city   **974.7**
Miller, Donald, 1971-
         About
   Miller, D. Blue like jazz   **92**
Miller, Edward
   Misalliance   **959.704**
Miller, Geoffrey F.
   Spent   **339.4**
Miller, Henry, 1891-1980
   Henry Miller on writing   **818**
         About
   Turner, F. Renegade   **813**
Miller, James Andrew
   Those guys have all the fun   **791.45**
   (jt. auth) Shales, T. Live from New York   **791.45**
Miller, Jan
   (ed) Better Homes and Gardens New Cook Book   **641.5**
Miller, Jennifer
   Inheriting the Holy Land   **956.94**
Miller, Jim
   Examined lives   **190**

Miller, John
   The cell: inside the 9/11 plot and why the FBI and CIA failed to stop it   **973.931**
Miller, John
         About
   Nordhaus, H. The beekeeper's lament   **638**
Miller, John Chester
   The Federalist era, 1789-1801   **973.4**
Miller, Judith
   Engelberg, S. Germs   **358**
   Furniture   **749**
   Miller's antiques handbook & price guide   **745.1**
   Miller's costume jewelry   **739.27**
Miller, Judith, 1951-
   Miller's arts & crafts   **745.4**
Miller, Kimberly Rae
         About
   Miller, K. R. Coming clean   **92**
Miller, Laura
   The magician's book   **823**
   Raw, vegan, not gross   **641.5**
Miller, Lee, 1907-1977
         About
   Burke, C. Lee Miller   **92**
Miller, Lisa
   Heaven   **236**
   The Spiritual Child   **649**
Miller, Mark
   The hard times guide to retirement security **332.024**
Miller, Marla R.
   Betsy Ross and the making of America   **92**
Miller, Matthew
   (jt. auth) Leibovitz, L. Fortunate sons   **951.05**
Miller, Nathan
   New world coming   **973.91**
   War at sea   **940.54**
Miller, Peter
   The smart swarm   **156**
Miller, Randall M.
   (ed) Daily life through American history in primary documents   **973**
   (ed) Pennsylvania: a history of the Commonwealth   **974.8**
Miller, Sam
   Delhi   **954**
   The Only Rule Is It Has to Work   **796.357**
Miller, Scott
   The President and the assassin   **973.8**
Miller, Stephen G.
   Ancient Greek athletics   **796**
Miller, Steven F.
   (ed) Remembering slavery   **326**
Miller, Sue
         About
   Miller, S. The story of my father   **92**
Miller, Susan

Planets and possibilities   **133.5**

Miller, Todd
Border patrol nation   **363.28**

Miller, William Lee
Arguing about slavery   **973.5**

Millgate, Michael
(ed) The Collected Letters of Thomas Hardy   **823**

MILLINERY *See* Hats

Million Dollar Women. Pimsleur, J.   **658.4**

The **millionaire** and the bard. Mays, A. E.   **822.33**

MILLIONAIRES
See also Rich

MILLIONAIRES -- MEXICO -- BIOGRAPHY
Jacoby, K. The strange career of William Ellis   **92**

**MILLIONAIRES -- NEW YORK (STATE) --
NEW YORK -- BIOGRAPHY**
Mays, A. E. The millionaire and the bard   **822.33**

**MILLIONAIRES -- UNITED STATES -- BIOG-
RAPHY**
White, S. Prince of darkness   **92**

Millman, Chad
The detonators   **940.4**

MILLS
See also Manufactures; Technology

Mills, Dan, 1968-
About
Mills, D. Sniper one   **956.7**

Mills, Dick
Aquarium fish   **639.34**

Mills, Eleanor
(ed) Journalistas   **808.8**

Mills, Elizabeth S.
Evidence explained   **907**

Mills, J. A.
Blood of the tiger   **639.97**

Mills, Marja
About
Mills, M. The Mockingbird Next Door   **92**

Mills, Stephen Tukel
Fouts, R. Next of kin   **156**

Milne, Lorus Johnson
The Audubon Society field guide to North American insects and spiders   **595.7**

Milne, Margery Joan Greene
Milne, L. J. The Audubon Society field guide to
North American insects and spiders   **595.7**

Milner, Clyde A.
As big as the West   **92**

Milner, Greg
Perfecting sound forever   **781.49**

Milo, Paul
Your flying car awaits   **909.82**

Milosz's ABCs. Milosz, C.   **891.8**

Milosz, Czeslaw
A Book of lumininous things   **808.81**
Legends of modernity   **891.8**

Milosz's ABCs   **891.8**
New and collected poems 1931-2001   **891.8**
A roadside dog   **891.8**
To begin where I am   **891.8**
About
Milosz, C. Legends of modernity   **891.8**

Milton, Giles
Big Chief Elizabeth   **970.004**

Milton, John, 1608-1674
About
Bloom, H. The Western canon   **809**
Campbell, G. John Milton   **92**
Hawkes, D. John Milton   **92**
Kermode, F. An appetite for poetry   **801**
Vendler, H. H. Coming of age as a poet   **820**

**MILWAUKEE (WIS.) -- HISTORY -- 20TH CEN-
TURY**
Strang, D. A. Worse than the devil   **345**

MIME
See also Acting

Min, Anchee, 1957-
About
Min, A. The Cooked Seed   **92**
Min, A. Red Azalea   **92**

Minahan, James
The complete guide to national symbols and emblems   **929.9**

Minchilli, Elizabeth
Eating Rome   **641.594**

MIND *See* Intellect; Psychology

MIND AND BODY
André, C. Looking at Mindfulness   **158.1**
Beilock, S. How the body knows its mind   **153.7**
Berdik, C. Mind over mind   **153.4**
Brown, J. The Runner's Brain   **796.42**
Doty, J. R. Into the Magic Shop   **92**
Harris, D. 10% happier   **158.1**
Hay, L. L. You can heal your life   **158**
Kaku, M. The future of the mind   **612.8**
Lilienfeld, S. O. Brainwashed   **612.8**
Parks, T. Teach us to sit still   **616**
Raine, A. The anatomy of violence   **616.85**

MIND AND BODY
See also Brain; Medicine; Parapsychology;
Philosophy

MIND AND BODY THERAPIES
Marchant, J. Cure   **616.89**

A **mind** at a time. Levine, M. D.   **370.15**

Mind change. Greenfield, S.   **155.9**

MIND CONTROL *See* Brainwashing

MIND CURE *See* Mental healing

The **mind** of the South. Cash, W. J.   **975**

Mind over mind. Berdik, C.   **153.4**

Mind over mood. Greenberger, D.   **616.89**

The **mind's** eye. Sacks, O.   **616.85**

MIND-BODY RELATIONS, METAPHYSICAL

Edelman, S. The happiness of pursuit **153**

Mindell, David A.
Our Robots, Ourselves **629.8**

Minden, Eliza Gaynor
The ballet companion **792.8**

MINDFULNESS (PSYCHOLOGY)
Wellings, N. Why can't I meditate? **158.12**

**MINDFULNESS-BASED COGNITIVE THERA-
PY**
Wax, R. Sane new world **158.1**

Mindless eating. Wansink, B. **616.85**

The **mindspan** diet. Estep, P. **616.8**

Mindware. Nisbett, R. E. **153.4**

MINERALS
Bonewitz, R. Rocks and minerals **549**
Chaline, E. Fifty minerals that changed the course
of history **549**
Chesterman, C. W. The Audubon Society field
guide to North American rocks and minerals **549**
Coenraads, R. R. Rocks and fossils **552**
Johnsen, O. Minerals of the world **549**
Klein, C. Manual of mineral science **549**
Pellant, C. Rocks and Minerals **552**
Pough, F. H. A field guide to rocks and miner-
als **549**

Minerals of the world. Johnsen, O. **549**

MINERS
Milner, C. A. As big as the West **92**

MINERS
See also Labor

Minerva and the muse: a life of Margaret Fuller.
Von Mehren, J. **92**

MINES AND MINERAL RESOURCES
Chaline, E. Fifty minerals that changed the course
of history **549**

MINES AND MINERAL RESOURCES
See also Economic geology; Natural resources; Raw materials

**MINES AND MINERAL RESOURCES -- UNIT-
ED STATES**
Hedges, C. Days of destruction, days of re-
volt **305.5**

Ming. **951**

Mini farming. Markham, B. L. **635**

MINIATURE GARDENS
See also Gardens; Miniature objects

MINIATURE OBJECTS
Frisoni The Big Book of a Miniature House **745**

MINIMUM WAGE
Ehrenreich, B. Nickel and dimed **305.5**
Shulman, B. The betrayal of work **331.2**

MINIMUM WAGE
See also Salaries, wages, etc.

MINING *See* Mines and mineral resources; Mining
engineering

MINING ENGINEERING

LeCain, T. J. Mass destruction **338.2**

Minnelli, Vincente, 1910-1986
About
Levy, E. Vincente Minnelli **92**

MINNESOTA
Borich, B. J. Body geographic **818**

Minois, Georges
The atheist's Bible **200**

MINOR LEAGUE BASEBALL
Feinstein, J. Where nobody knows your
name **796.357**

MINOR LEAGUE BASEBALL
See also Baseball

**MINOR LEAGUE BASEBALL -- UNITED
STATES -- HISTORY**
Barry, D. Bottom of the 33rd **796.357**
Feinstein, J. Where nobody knows your
name **796.357**

MINOR PLANETS *See* Asteroids

Minor, William C., d. 1920
About
Winchester, S. The professor and the madman **423**

MINORITIES
Bishop, B. The big sort **305.8**
Peake, R. Mapping Census 2010 **304.6**

**MINORITIES -- EDUCATION (HIGHER) --
UNITED STATES -- HISTORY**
Wilder, C. S. Ebony and Ivy **379.26**

MINORITIES -- SUFFRAGE -- UNITED STATES
Berman, A. Give us the ballot **324.6**

MINORITIES -- UNITED STATES
Bishop, B. The big sort **305.8**
Slotkin, R. Lost battalions **940.3**

**MINORITIES -- UNITED STATES -- POPULA-
TION -- STATISTICS -- MAPS**
Peake, R. Mapping Census 2010 **304.6**

Minoui, Delphine
Ali, N. I am Nujood, age 10 and divorced **92**

**MINSTREL SHOWS -- UNITED STATES -- HIS-
TORY**
Austen, J. Darkest America **791**

MINSTRELS
See also Poets

Mint condition. Jamieson, D. **796.357**

MINTS
See also Money

MINTS (PLANTS)
Aftel, M. Fragrant **612.8**

Mintz, Steven
Huck's raft **305.23**

Minutaglio, Bill
Dallas 1963 **973.922**

Miodownik, Mark
Stuff matters **620.1**

Miotke, Jim
BetterPhoto basics **771**

Miracle dogs.   636.7

Miracle in the Andes. Parrado, N.   982

MIRACLE PLAYS *See* Mysteries and miracle plays

The **miracle** worker. Gibson, W.   812

Miracles. Lewis, C. S.   231.7

MIRACLES
> Lewis, C. S. Miracles   231.7
> Woodward, K. L. The book of miracles   231.7

Miracles of life. Ballard, J. G.   823

The **mirage** man. Willman, D.   363.325

Miraldi, Robert
> Seymour Hersh   92

Miranda, Lin-Manuel, 1980-
> (jt. auth) McCarter, J. Hamilton   782.1

Mirarchi, Carlo
> (jt. auth) Parachini, C. Roberta's   641.82

Mires, Charlene
> Capital of the world   341.23

Mirror mirror. Pendergrast, M.   535

Mirroring people. Iacoboni, M.   573.8

Mirrors. Galeano, E. H.   909

MIRRORS
> *See also* Furniture

MIRRORS
> Pendergrast, M. Mirror mirror   535

Mirrors of the unseen. Elliot, J.   915

Mirth of a nation.   817

Misalliance. Miller, E.   959.704

The **misanthrope** and other plays. Moliere   842

Misbehaving. Thaler, R. H.   330.01

MISCARRIAGE
> McCracken, E. An exact replica of a figment of my imagination   92

MISCARRIAGE
> *See also* Pregnancy

MISCARRIAGE OF JUSTICE
> Siegel, B. Manifest injustice   364.152

MISCEGENATION -- UNITED STATES -- HISTORY
> Pascoe, P. What comes naturally   346
> Sharfstein, D. J. The invisible line   305.8

MISCELLANEA *See* Books of lists; Curiosities and wonders

MISCELLANEOUS FACTS *See* Books of lists; Curiosities and wonders

Mischel, Walter
> The marshmallow test   155.2

MISCONDUCT IN OFFICE -- UNITED STATES
> Gormley, K. The death of American virtue   973.929

Mishchenko, Lev
> **About**
> Figes, O. Just send me word   365

Mishchenko, Svetlana
> **About**
> Figes, O. Just send me word   365

Mishler, Clifford
> Krause, C. L. Standard catalog of world coins   737.4

Mishra, Pankaj
> From the ruins of empire   950
> Temptations of the West   954.05

Miskjian, Stepan, 1886-1974
> **About**
> MacKeen, D. A. The hundred-year walk   92

The **mismeasure** of man. Gould, S. J.   153.9

Miss Anne in Harlem. Kaplan, C.   700.92

Miss Leavitt's stars. Johnson, G.   92

Miss Manners' guide to excruciatingly correct behavior. Martin, J.   395

Miss O'Dell. O'Dell, C.   92

MISSILES, BALLISTIC *See* Ballistic missiles

MISSING CHILDREN
> Brierley, S. A long way home   92

MISSING CHILDREN
> *See also* Children; Missing persons

MISSING IN ACTION
> *See also* Prisoners of war; Soldiers

Missing microbes. Blaser, M. J.   615.7

The **missing** moment. Pollack, R.   610

MISSING OBSERVATIONS (STATISTICS)
> Reinhart, A. Statistics done wrong   519.5

The **missing** of the Somme. Dyer, G.   940.4

MISSING PERSONS
> Butler, S. East to the dawn   629.13
> Hoffman, C. A Savage Harvest   995
> Rule, A. --and never let her go   364.1
> Russell, T. Out of the jungle   92
> Winters, K. C. Amelia Earhart   92

MISSING PERSONS
> *See also* Criminal investigation

Missing, Sophie
> (jt. auth) Craig, C. The little book of lunch   641.5

The **Mission** Chinese Food Cookbook. Ying, C.   641.595

Mission in a bottle. Nalebuff, B.   338.7

MISSION OF THE CHURCH
> McKnight, S. Kingdom conspiracy   231.7

Mission to mars. Aldrin, B.   629.44

MISSIONARIES
> Spink, K. Mother Teresa   271
> Taylor, A. The divided ground   974.7

MISSIONARIES, CHRISTIAN *See* Christian missionaries

MISSIONS -- INDIA
> Spink, K. Mother Teresa   92

MISSISSIPPI -- PICTORIAL WORKS
> Welty, E. One time, one place   976.2

MISSISSIPPI -- RACE RELATIONS
> Anderson, D. S. Emmett Till   364.1
> Heard, A. The eyes of Willie McGee   364.66
> Hendrickson, P. Sons of Mississippi   305.8
> Watson, B. Freedom summer   323.1

MISSISSIPPI RIVER
Boissoneault, L. The Last Voyageurs   977
MISSISSIPPI RIVER VALLEY
Feldman, J. When the Mississippi ran backwards   551.2
MISSISSIPPI RIVER VALLEY
See also United States
MISSISSIPPI RIVER VALLEY -- COMMERCE -- HISTORY -- 19TH CENTURY
Johnson, W. River of dark dreams   305.8
MISSISSIPPI RIVER VALLEY -- HISTORY
Barry, J. M. Rising tide   977
Feldman, J. When the Mississippi ran backwards   551.2
Johnson, W. River of dark dreams   305.8
MISSISSIPPI STATE PENITENTIARY
Oshinsky, D. M. Worse than slavery   365
Missoula. Krakauer, J.   362.883
MISSOULA (MONT.)
Krakauer, J. Missoula   362.883
MISTAKES *See* Errors
Mistaking each other for ghosts. Raab, L.   811
Mistress Bradstreet. Gordon, C.   92
MISTRESSES
Gimbel, W. Havana dreams   972.91
Gordon-Reed, A. The Hemingses of Monticello   920
Gordon-Reed, A. Thomas Jefferson and Sally Hemings   973.4
MISTRESSES -- GERMANY -- BIOGRAPHY
Gortemaker, H. B. Eva Braun   92
The **mistresses** of Cliveden. Livingstone, N.   942.009
Mitcham, Carl
(ed) Encyclopedia of science, technology, and ethics   503
Mitchell, Andie
Eating in the middle   641.3
Mitchell, Anne M.
Cataloging and organizing digital resources   025.3
Mitchell, Chris
Miller, J. The cell: inside the 9/11 plot and why the FBI and CIA failed to stop it   973.931
Mitchell, Elizabeth
Three strides before the wire   798.4
Mitchell, George J. (George John), 1933-
A Path to Peace   956.94
Mitchell, Greg
Lifton, R. J. Hiroshima in America   940.54
The tunnels   943.155
Mitchell, Joan
About
Albers, P. Joan Mitchell   92
Livingston, J. The paintings of Joan Mitchell   759.13
Mitchell, Joan S.
(ed) Dewey decimal classification and relative index   025.4

Mitchell, Joni
About
Weller, S. Girls like us   920
Mitchell, Margaret, 1900-1949
About
Pierpont, C. R. Passionate minds   810
Mitchell, Martha
Rich, C. Stained glass basics   748.5
Mitchell, Melanie
Complexity   501
Mitchell, Rose
(jt. auth) Janes, A. Maps   912.09
Mitchell, Ryan
Tiny house living   728
Mitchell, Stacy
Big-box swindle   381
Mitchell, Stephen
(ed & tr) Amichai, Y. The selected poetry of Yehuda Amichai   892
(tr) Gilgamesh Gilgamesh   892
(ed) Into the garden   808.8
(tr) Mahabharata/Bhagavadgita Bhagavad Gita   294.5
Mitchell, Syne
Inventive weavng on a little loom   746.1
Mitchell, T. J.
Working stiff   614
Mitenbuler, Reid
Bourbon empire   663
MITES
Beccaloni, J. Arachnids   595.4
Stewart, A. Wicked bugs   632
Mitford family
About
The Mitfords   920
Thompson, L. The six   92
Mitford, Jessica
The American way of death revisited   338.4
Mitford, Jessica, 1917-1996
About
Thompson, L. The six   92
Mitford, Nancy, 1904-1973
About
Thompson, L. The six   92
Mitford, Pamela, 1907-1994
About
Thompson, L. The six   92
Mitford, Unity, 1914-1948
About
Thompson, L. The six   92
The **Mitfords.**   920
Mithen, Steven J.
The singing neanderthals   780.9
Mithridates VI Eupator, King of Pontus, ca. 132-63 B.C.

About

Mayor, A. The Poison King   92

Mitnick, Kevin

About

Mitnick, K. D. Ghost in the wires   364.16

Mitnick, Sarai

The Colette sewing handbook   646.4

Mitteldorf, Josh

(jt. auth) Sagan, D. Cracking the aging code 612.67

Mittendorf, Bradley C.

(ed) The Oxford book of the American South 810

Mitton, Simon

Heart of darkness   523.1

Mix + Match Cakes. Wright, C.   641.86

Mix shake stir.   641.8

MIXED MARTIAL ARTS

Rousey, R. My fight / your fight   92

MIXED MEDIA PAINTING

See also Painting

MIXED RACE PEOPLE *See* Racially mixed people

Mixerman

(comp) Zen and the art of recording   621.389

MIXOLOGY *See* Bartending

MLA handbook for writers of research papers. Modern Language Association of America   808

MLA style manual and guide to scholarly publishing.   808

Mlodinow, Leonard

The Drunkard's walk   519.2

Hawking, S. A briefer history of time   523.1

(jt. auth) Hawking, S. The grand design 530.1

Subliminal   154.2

The upright thinkers   509

Mnatsakanian, Mamikon A.

(jt. auth) Apostol, T. M. New Horizons in Geometry   516

MNEMONICS

Fogler, J. Improving your memory   153.1

Mo' meta blues. Greenman, B.   92

Moalem, Sharon

Survival of the sickest   616

Moaveni, Azadeh, 1976-

About

Moaveni, A. Honeymoon in Tehran   92

Moaveni, A. Lipstick jihad   92

Mobley, Gregory

Wray, T. J. The birth of Satan   235

MOBS *See* Crowds; Riots

MOBSTERS

Balsamo, W. Young Al Capone   92

Bergreen, L. Capone   364.1

Carlo, P. Gaspipe   92

Dash, M. The first family   364.1

Eig, J. Get Capone   92

Mobutu Sese Seko, 1930-1997

About

Duke, L. Mandela, Mobutu, and me   968.06

Moby-Duck. Hohn, D.   551.46

Mochi's war. Enss, C.   978.8

Mochi, approximately 1841-1881

About

Enss, C. Mochi's war   978.8

Mock, Janet, 1983-

About

Mock, J. Redefining Realness   306.76

MOCK-HEROIC LITERATURE

See also Literature; Wit and humor

Mockett, Marie Mutsuki

Where the Dead Pause, and the Japanese Say Goodbye   952

The **Mockingbird** Next Door. Mills, M.   92

MODELING

Heaser, S. The polymer clay techniques book   745.572

Pavelka, L. The complete book of polymer clay   738.1

MODELING

See also Clay; Sculpture

MODELS *See* Artists' models; Fashion models; Mathematical models; Models and modelmaking

MODELS (PERSONS)

Ali, K. Fighting weight   92

Burke, C. Lee Miller   92

MODELS (PERSONS) *See* Artists' models; Fashion models

MODELS (PERSONS) -- BIOGRAPHY

Gross, M. Focus   770.92

Modern American memoirs.   810

MODERN ARCHITECTURE *See* Modernism in architecture

Modern architecture since 1900. Curtis, W. J. R. 724

MODERN ART

Arnason, H. H. History of modern art   709.04

MODERN ART -- ENCYCLOPEDIAS

Dempsey, A. Art in the modern era   709.04

MODERN ART -- EXHIBITIONS

Bajac, Q. Photography at MOMA   770

Modern calligraphy.   745.6

MODERN CIVILIZATION

Bloom, H. The Lucifer principle   128

Gopnik, A. Angels and ages   973.7

Greenblatt, S. The swerve   940.2

Milo, P. Your flying car awaits   909.82

Morris, I. Why the West rules--for now   909

Winik, J. The great upheaval   909.7

MODERN CIVILIZATION

See also Civilization

MODERN CIVILIZATION -- 1950-

Huntington, S. P. The clash of civilizations and the remaking of world order   909.82

Toffler, A. Future shock   303.4

Modern critical interpretations [series]
Alice Walker's The color purple 813
Geoffrey Chaucer's The Canterbury tales 821
Samuel Beckett's Waiting for Godot 842
Modern critical views [series]
Alice Walker 813
J.D. Salinger 813
John Steinbeck 813
William Faulkner 813
Zora Neale Hurston 813
MODERN DANCE
Reynolds, N. No fixed points 792.8
MODERN DANCE
See also Dance
MODERN DANCE -- UNITED STATES -- HISTORY
Fuhrer, M. American dance 792.8
Modern Dating. Atik, C. 646.7
Modern English-Hebrew dictionary. Zilkha, A. 492.4
MODERN GREEK LANGUAGE
See also Language and languages
MODERN GREEK LITERATURE
See also Literature
A **modern** guide to sportswear styles of the 1940s and 1950s. Hirsch, G. 646.4
MODERN HISTORY
Bailyn, B. Sometimes an art, never a science, always a craft 907.2
Judt, T. Reappraisals 909.82
Kennedy, P. M. The rise and fall of the great powers 909.08
Kwarteng, K. Ghosts of empire 909
MacMillan, M. History's People 920
Mann, C. C. 1493 909
Tuchman, B. W. The march of folly 909.08
Tuchman, B. W. Practicing history 907
Winik, J. The great upheaval 909.7
MODERN HISTORY
See also World history
MODERN HISTORY -- PICTORIAL WORKS
Getty Images Inc. History of the world in photographs 909.8
The **modern** history of Japan. Gordon, A. 952.03
Modern Japanese writers. 895.6
Modern Jewish cooking. Koenig, L. 641.5
Modern Language Association of America
MLA handbook for writers of research papers 808
MODERN LANGUAGES
See also Language and languages
Modern Library chronicles [series]
Byron, G. G. B. Selected poetry of Lord Byron 821
Cumings, B. The Korean War 951.9
Green, P. The Hellenistic age 938
Kotkin, S. Uncivil society 947
Larson, E. J. Evolution: the remarkable history of a

scientific theory 576.8
Micklethwait, J. The company 338.7
Modern library classics [series]
Johnson, J. W. The essential writings of James Weldon Johnson 818
Modern Library classics [series]
Martial Epigrams 878
The **modern** library writer's workshop. Koch, S. 808.3
MODERN LITERATURE *See* Literature; Modernism in literature
Modern patchwork. Hartman, E. 746.46
MODERN PHILOSOPHY
Gay, P. The rise of modern paganism 190
Gay, P. The science of freedom 190
Gottlieb, A. The dream of enlightenment 190
Himmelfarb, G. The moral imagination 190
Lefebvre, H. Critique of everyday life 301
Nadler, S. M. The best of all possible worlds 190
Sedgwick, P. Descartes to Derrida 190
We Have Only This Life to Live 848
MODERN PHILOSOPHY
See also Philosophy
Modern physics and ancient faith. Barr, S. M. 201
Modern war studies [series]
Inside the Pentagon papers 959.704
Kindsvatter, P. S. American soldiers 355
A **modern** way to eat. Jones, A. 641.5
MODERNISM *See* Modernism (Aesthetics); Modernism (Theology)
MODERNISM (AESTHETICS)
Alinder, M. S. Group f.64 770.92
Roe, S. In Montmartre
Wilson, E. Literary essays and reviews of the 1920s & 30s 814
Wilson, E. Literary essays and reviews of the 1930s & 40s 814
MODERNISM (AESTHETICS)
See also Aesthetics
MODERNISM (AESTHETICS) -- HISTORY -- 20TH CENTURY
Cohen, L. All we know 920.72
MODERNISM (ART) -- WEST (U.S.) -- HISTORY
Alinder, M. S. Group f.64 770.92
MODERNISM (ARTS) *See* Modernism (Aesthetics)
MODERNISM (LITERATURE) *See* Modernism in literature
MODERNISM (LITERATURE) -- MEXICO
Biron, R. E. Elena Garro and Mexico's modern dreams 868
MODERNISM (THEOLOGY)
See also Christianity -- Doctrines
MODERNISM IN ARCHITECTURE
Wilhide, E. Scandinavian Home 728

MODERNISM IN ARCHITECTURE
See also Architecture; Modernism (Aesthetics)

MODERNISM IN ART
See also Art; Modernism (Aesthetics)

MODERNISM IN LITERATURE
Biron, R. E. Elena Garro and Mexico's modern dreams   **868**
The collected poems of Eugenio Montale 1925-1977   **851**
Modified. Shetterly, C.   **664**
Modigliani. Secrest, M.   **92**
Modigliani, Amedeo, 1884-1920
About
Secrest, M. Modigliani   **92**
Modschiedler, Christa
(ed) Guide to reference in medicine and health   **025.06**
Moe, Richard
Roosevelt's second act   **973.917**
Moebes, Deborah
Stitch Savvy   **646**
Moeller, Philip
(jt. auth) Solman, P. Get what's yours   **368.4**
Moffat, Wendy
A great unrecorded history   **92**
Moffett, Kay
Not your mother's divorce   **306.89**
Moffett, Mark W.
Adventures among ants   **595.7**
Moglia, Paul
(ed) Magill's medical guide   **610**
MOGUL EMPIRE
McLeod, J. The history of India   **954**
Wolpert, S. A. A new history of India   **954**
Mohammad Reza Pahlavi, Shah of Iran, 1919-1980
About
Cooper, A. S. The fall of heaven   **955.05**
Mohammed, Khalid Shaikh, 1965-
About
McDermott, T. The hunt for KSM   **363.325**
Mohandas
Gandhi   **92**
MOHAWK INDIANS
Demos, J. The unredeemed captive   **973.2**
Mohr, Tara
Playing big   **650.1**
MOJAVE DESERT (CALIF.)
Stillman, D. Desert reckoning   **363.2**
Moker, Molly
(ed) The official guide to America's national parks   **917**
Mokyr, Joel
(ed) The Oxford encyclopedia of economic history   **330**

MOLDS (FUNGI)
See also Fungi

MOLECULAR BIOLOGISTS
Watson, J. D. Avoid boring people   **92**
Watson, J. D. Genes, girls, and Gamow   **92**

MOLECULAR BIOLOGISTS -- FRANCE -- BIOGRAPHY
Carroll, S. B. Brave genius   **920**

MOLECULAR BIOLOGISTS -- UNITED STATES -- BIOGRAPHY
Segrè, G. Ordinary geniuses   **572.8**
Watson, J. D. Genes, girls, and Gamow   **92**

MOLECULAR BIOLOGY
The annotated and illustrated double helix   **572.8**

MOLECULAR BIOLOGY
See also Biochemistry; Biophysics

MOLECULAR CLONING
See also Cloning; Genetic engineering

MOLECULAR TECHNOLOGY See Nanotechnology

Molecules. Gray, T.   **541**

MOLECULES
Gray, T. Molecules   **541**

MOLES (ANIMALS)
Girling, R. The Hunt for the Golden Mole   **591.68**

MOLESTING OF CHILDREN See Child sexual abuse

Molesworth, Charles
Marianne Moore   **92**

Molière, 1622-1673
About
Goldsby, R. W. Molière on stage   **842**
The misanthrope and other plays   **842**
Tartuffe and other plays   **842**
Molière on stage. Goldsby, R. W.   **842**
Molina. Molina, B.   **92**
Molina, Bengie, 1974-
About
Molina, B. Molina   **92**
Molina, Benjamin
About
Molina, B. Molina   **92**
Moller, Sharon Chickering
Library service to Spanish speaking patrons   **027.6**
MOLLUSKS
Harasewych, M. G. The book of shells   **594**
Molnar, Jennifer L.
(ed) Hoekstra, J. M. The atlas of global conservation   **333.95**
Molotch, Harvey
Against security   **363.325**
Where stuff comes from   **620**
Molotov's magic lantern. Polonsky, R.   **947**
Molotov, Vyacheslav, 1890-1986
About
Polonsky, R. Molotov's magic lantern   **947**

Mom & me & mom. Angelou, M. **818**

The **mom** & pop store. Spector, R. **381**

The **mom** 100 cookbook. **641.5**

Mom in the movies. Corliss, R. **791.43**

The **moment.** **818**

A **moment's** liberty: the shorter diary. Woolf, V. **92**

Moments. Buell, H. **070.4**

Moments of being. Woolf, V. **823**

The **mommy** docs' ultimate guide to pregnancy and birth. **618.2**

Momofuku. Chang, D. **641.5**

Momofuku Milk Bar. Tosi, C. **641.8**

Mona Lisa. Hales, D. **759.5**

MONA LISA (PAINTING)
> Hales, D. Mona Lisa **759.5**

MONARCH BUTTERFLIES
> The monarch butterfly **595.7**

The **monarch** butterfly. **595.7**

MONARCHS *See* Kings and rulers

MONARCHY
> *See also* Constitutional history; Constitutional law; Executive power; Political science

MONARCHY -- ARAB COUNTRIES
> Owen, R. The rise and fall of Arab presidents for life **352.23**

MONARCHY -- GREAT BRITAIN -- HISTORY
> Castor, H. She-wolves **920**

MONASTICISM AND RELIGIOUS ORDERS
> Norris, K. Acedia & me **92**
> Norris, K. The cloister walk **255**

MONASTICISM AND RELIGIOUS ORDERS FOR MEN
> *See also* Monasticism and religious orders

MONASTICISM AND RELIGIOUS ORDERS FOR WOMEN
> *See also* Convents; Monasticism and religious orders

Mondor, Colleen Catherine
> The map of my dead pilots **387.7**

Monet, Claude, 1840-1926
> **About**
> Baillio, J. Claude Monet, 1840-1926 **759**
> King, R. Mad enchantment **759.4**

MONETARY POLICY
> Cassidy, J. How markets fail **381**
> Conway, E. The Summit **339.5**
> Rickards, J. Currency wars **332.4**

MONETARY POLICY
> *See also* Economic policy

MONETARY POLICY -- HISTORY -- 20TH CENTURY
> Steil, B. The battle of Bretton Woods **339.5**

MONETARY POLICY -- UNITED STATES
> Overtveldt, J. v. Bernanke's test **332.1**
> Wessel, D. In Fed we trust **332.1**
> Woodward, B. Maestro: Greenspan's Fed and the

American boom **331.1**

MONETARY POLICY -- UNITED STATES -- HISTORY
> McCraw, T. K. The founders and finance **330.973**

MONETARY UNIONS
> *See also* Money

Monette, Paul
> **About**
> Monette, P. Borrowed time **362.1**

MONEY
> Ferguson, N. The ascent of money **330**
> Kessel, B. It's not about the money **332.024**
> Keynes, J. M. The general theory of employment, interest and money **330.1**
> King, M. A. The End of Alchemy **330.122**
> Kobliner, B. Get a financial life **332.024**
> Velshi, A. How to speak money **332.024**

MONEY
> *See also* Economics; Exchange; Finance

MONEY -- POLITICAL ASPECTS
> Yergin, D. The quest **333.79**

Money and power. Cohan, W. D. **332.6**

Money and Soccer. Szymanski, S. **796.334**

The **money** and the power. Denton, S. **979.3**

The **money** book for freelancers, part-time, and the self-employed. D'Agnese, J. **332.024**

The **money** class. Orman, S. **332.024**

The **money** cult. Lehmann, C. **261.8**

MONEY RAISING *See* Fund raising

MONEY SUPPLY
> *See also* Money

MONEY-MAKING PROJECTS FOR CHILDREN
> *See also* Business enterprises

Moneyball. Lewis, M. **796.357**

The **moneysmart** family system. Economides, A. **332.024**

Monge, Gaspard, 1746-1818
> **About**
> Bell, E. T. Men of mathematics **920**

Mongkut, King of Siam, 1804-1868
> **About**
> Landon, M. Anna and the King of Siam **92**

MONGOLS -- HSITORY
> Polo, M. The travels of Marco Polo **915**

Moniz, Gil
> (ed) National electrical code handbook 2014 **621.3**

The **monk** in the garden: how Gregor Mendel and his pea plants solved the mystery of inheritance. Henig, R. M. **576.5**

A **monk** swimming. McCourt, M. **974.7**

Monk, Jane
> Tangle stitches for quilters + fabric artists

Monk, Ray
> Robert Oppenheimer **92**

Monk, Thelonious, 1917-1982

About

Kelley, R. D. G. Thelonious Monk   **92**

Monkey business. Louvish, S.   **920**

Monkey mind. Smith, D.   **616.85**

MONKEYS

   See also Primates

MONKEYS -- BEHAVIOR

   See also Animal behavior

Monkman, Betty C.

   The White House   **975.3**

MONKS

   Butcher, C. A. Man of blessing   **271**

   Elie, P. The life you save may be your own   **810**

   Massie, R. K. Nicholas and Alexandra   **92**

   Merton, T. The seven storey mountain   **92**

   Merton, T. Intimate Merton   **271**

Monks of New Skete

   (comp) The art of raising a puppy   **636.7**

   How to be your dog's best friend   **636.7**

Monmonier, Mark S.

   Air apparent   **551.63**

Monod, Jacques

About

   Carroll, S. B. Brave genius   **920**

MONOGRAMS

   See also Alphabets; Decoration and ornament; Lettering

Monologue and scene study series

   2010: the best women's stage monologues and scenes   **808.82**

Monologue audition series

   The Ultimate audition book   **808.82**

Monologue of a dog.   **891.8**

MONOLOGUES

   2010: the best women's stage monologues and scenes   **808.82**

   The Best Men's Stage Monologues 2016   **792**

   The Best Women's Stage Monologues 2016   **792**

   The Ultimate audition book   **808.82**

MONOPOLIES

   See also Commerce; Economics

MONORAIL RAILROADS

   See also Railroads

Monosson, Emily

   Unnatural selection   **576.5**

MONOTHEISM

   Stark, R. For the glory of God   **201**

MONOTHEISM

   See also Religion; Theism

MONOTYPE (ENGRAVING) -- 19TH CENTU-RY -- EXHIBITIONS

   Hauptman, J. Degas   **709**

Monro, Alexander

   The paper trail   **676**

MONROE DOCTRINE

   See also International relations; Intervention

(International law); United States -- Foreign relations

Monroe, James, 1758-1831

About

   Unger, H. G. The last founding father   **92**

Monroe, Marilyn, 1926-1962

About

   Taraborrelli, J. R. The secret life of Marilyn Monroe   **92**

Monsoon. Kaplan, R. D.   **327**

MONSOONS

   See also Meteorology

The **monster.** Hudson, M.   **332.6**

MONSTER FILMS *See* Horror films

Monster hunters. Krulos, T.   **001.94**

Monster of God. Quammen, D.   **591.6**

MONSTERS

   Asma, S. T. On monsters   **398.2**

   Krulos, T. Monster hunters   **001.94**

MONSTERS

   See also Animals -- Folklore; Curiosities and wonders; Folklore; Mythology

MONSTERS -- ENCYCLOPEDIAS

   Guiley, R. E. The encyclopedia of vampires & werewolves   **398**

MONSTERS -- POETRY

   Carson, A. Red doc>   **811**

Montagu, Ewen, 1901-1985

About

   Macintyre, B. Operation Mincemeat   **940.54**

   Smyth, D. Deathly deception   **940.54**

Montaigne, Fen

   Fraser's penguins   **577.2**

Montaigne, Michel de, 1533-1592

About

   Bakewell, S. How to live, or, A life of Montaigne in one question and twenty attempts at an answer **92**

   Bloom, H. The Western canon   **809**

   Frampton, S. When I am playing with my cat, how do I know she is not playing with me?   **844**

Montaldo, Jonathan

   (ed) Merton, T. Intimate Merton   **271**

Montale, Eugenio

   The collected poems of Eugenio Montale 1925-1977   **851**

   Collected poems, 1920-1954   **851**

Montalvan, Luis Carlos, 1973-

About

   Witter, B. Until Tuesday   **362.4**

Montana. Dunnavant, K.   **92**

MONTANA

   Milner, C. A. As big as the West   **92**

Montana, Joe, 1956-

About

   Dunnavant, K. Montana   **92**

Montano, Mark

The big-ass book of home decor 645

Montero, Eder
The Basque book 641.5

Monterrey, Manuel
Americanos 305.8

The **Montessori** method. Montessori, M. 371.3

MONTESSORI METHOD OF EDUCATION
Montessori, M. The Montessori method 371.3

MONTESSORI METHOD OF EDUCATION
See also Elementary education; Kindergarten; Teaching

Montessori, Maria
The Montessori method 371.3

MONTFAUCON (MEUSE, FRANCE) -- HISTO-RY, MILITARY -- 20TH CENTURY
Walker, W. T. Betrayal at Little Gibraltar 940.436

Montgomerie, Bob
(jt. auth) Birkhead, T. Ten thousand birds 598

MONTGOMERY (ALA.) -- RACE RELATIONS
Brinkley, D. Rosa Parks 92
Jackson, T. Becoming King 92
Theoharis, J. The rebellious life of Mrs. Rosa Parks 92

Montgomery of Alamein, Bernard Law Montgom-ery, Viscount, 1887-1976
About
Brighton, T. Patton, Montgomery, Rommel 920

Montgomery, David R.
The hidden half of nature 579
The rocks don't lie 551.48

Montgomery, Denise L.
Ottemiller's index to plays in collections 016

Montgomery, Sy
Birdology 598
The good good pig 636.4
Journey of the pink dolphins 599.53
The soul of an octopus 594

The **monthly** sky guide. Ridpath, I. 523.8

MONTICELLO (VA.)
Hatch, P. J. A rich spot of earth 635

MONTICELLO (VA.) -- HISTORY
Wiencek, H. Master of the mountain 973.4

Montillo, Roseanne
The lady and her monsters 823

Montross, Christine
Falling into the fire 92

MONTY PYTHON (COMEDY TROUPE)
Palin, M. Halfway to Hollywood 92

MONUMENTS
Gordon, J. S. Washington's monument 975.3
Loewen, J. W. Lies across America 973

MONUMENTS
See also Architecture; Sculpture

MONUMENTS -- GREAT BRITAIN
Higgins, C. Under another sky 936

MONUMENTS -- UNITED STATES

Carlson, B. Dead presidents 973.09

The **monuments** men. Edsel, R. M. 940.53

Monush, Barry
Screen world presents the encyclopedia of Holly-wood film actors 920.003

Mooallem, Jon
Wild ones 333.95

MOOD (PSYCHOLOGY)
Greenberger, D. Mind over mood 616.89

MOOD (PSYCHOLOGY)
See also Psychology

Mood Designer Fabrics (Company)
(comp) The Mood guide to fabric and fashion 746.9

The **Mood** guide to fabric and fashion. 746.9

Moody, Raymond A.
Life after life 133.9

Moody, Rick
On celestial music 780.9

MOON
Goodman, M. The Sun and the moon 974.7

Moon Rio De Janeiro. Sommers, M. 918.15

MOON WORSHIP
See also Religion

Moon, Rachel Y.
(ed) Sleep 618.92

MOON, VOYAGES TO *See* Space flight to the moon

Moondust. Smith, A. 920

Moonen, Rick
Fish without a doubt 641.6

Mooney, Chris
Storm world 363.7

Mooney, Jonathan
About
Mooney, J. The short bus 92

Mooney, Paul
About
Mooney, P. Black is the new white 92

Moonlight. Walsh, J. E. 345

MOONS *See* Satellites

Moonwalking with Einstein. Foer, J. 153.1

Moore, Albert Joseph, 1841-1893
About
Asleson, R. Albert Moore 759.2

Moore, Alexis
Cyber self-defense 613.6

Moore, Christine
Little Flower baking 641.815

Moore, Colten
(jt. auth) O'Brien, K. Catching the Sky 796.94

Moore, Dorothy Rudd, 1940-
About
Walker-Hill, H. From spirituals to symphonies 780

Moore, Gerald
(ed) The Penguin book of modern African poet-ry 896

Moore, Harold G.
We are soldiers still   **959.704**
We were soldiers once--and young   **959.704**
Moore, Honor
(ed) Lowell, A. Selected poems   **811**
(ed) Poems from the women's movement   **811**
Moore, John Allphin
Encyclopedia of the United Nations   **341.23**
Moore, Kathy
Delicious dump cakes   **641.86**
Moore, Kenneth
(ed) The revolt of the masses   **901**
Moore, Lucy
Anything goes   **973.91**
Moore, Marianne, 1887-1972
The poems of Marianne Moore   **811**
About
Jarrell, R. No other book   **809**
Leavell, L. Holding on upside down   **92**
Molesworth, C. Marianne Moore   **92**
Moore, Mary Tyler
About
Moore, M. T. Growing up again   **92**
Moore, Michael
About
Rapoport, R. Citizen Moore   **92**
Moore, Rachel S.
The artist's compass   **791.023**
Moore, Robin
In search of lost frogs   **597.8**
Moore, Russell
Onward   **230**
This is Camino   **641.5**
Moore, Sonia
The Stanislavski system   **792**
Moore, Stephen W.
(jt. auth) Griffith, H. W. Complete Guide to Prescription & Nonprescription Drugs   **615**
Moore, Steven, 1978-
The novel   **809**
Moore, Susanna, 1948-
Paradise of the Pacific   **996.9**
Moore, Thurston
No wave   **781.66**
Moore, Tim
Gironimo!   **796.6**
Moore, Undine Smith, 1904-1989
About
Walker-Hill, H. From spirituals to symphonies **780**
Moore, Wendy
How to create the perfect wife   **823**
Moore, Wes, 1978-
The other Wes Moore   **92**
The work   **92**
Moorehead, Caroline
Dancing to the precipice: Lucie de la Tour du Pin

and the French Revolution   **92**
Village of Secrets   **944**
Moorhouse, Roger
Berlin at war   **943**
The Devils' Alliance   **940.53**
MOORS *See* Muslims
Moose, Christina J.
(ed) Great events from history, The Renaissance & early modern era, 1454-1600   **909**
(ed) Great lives from history, the Renaissance & early modern era, 1454-1600   **920.003**
Moosewood Collective
Moosewood restaurant favorites   **641.5**
The **Moosewood** Cookbook. Katzen, M.   **641.5**
Moosewood Foods (Company)
(comp) Moosewood Restaurant cooks at home   **641.5**
(comp) Moosewood restaurant favorites   **641.5**
MOOSEWOOD RESTAURANT
Moosewood Restaurant cooks at home   **641.5**
Moosewood restaurant favorites   **641.5**
Moosewood Restaurant cooks at home.   **641.5**
Moosewood restaurant favorites.   **641.5**
Moral combat. Burleigh, M.   **940.54**
MORAL CONDITIONS
See also Social conditions
MORAL DEVELOPMENT
See also Child psychology; Moral education
MORAL EDUCATION
See also Education; Ethics
Moral freedom. Wolfe, A.   **170**
The **moral** imagination. Himmelfarb, G.   **190**
The **moral** judgment of the child. Piaget, J.   **155.4**
The **moral** lives of animals. Peterson, D.   **156**
MORAL MOTIVATION
Peterson, D. The moral lives of animals   **156**
MORAL PHILOSOPHY *See* Ethics
MORAL THEOLOGY, CHRISTIAN *See* Christian ethics
Moral tribes. Greene, J.   **170**
MORALE
See also Courage
Morales, Ed
Living in Spanglish   **305.868**
Moran, Caitlin, 1975-
About
Moran, C. How to be a woman   **92**
Moran, Rachel
Paid for   **306.74**
Morante, Elsa, d. 1985
About
Tuck, L. Woman of Rome: a life of Elsa Morante   **92**
Mordden, Ethan
Anything goes   **782.1**
Love song   **920**

Ziegfeld   **92**

More awesome than money. Dwyer, J.   **384.3**

More book lust. Pearl, N.   **025**

More creative lettering. Doh, J.   **745.6**

More home cooking. Colwin, L.   **642**

More Lovely Knitted Lace. Nico, B.   **746.432**

More Mexican everyday. Bayless, R.   **641.597**

The **more** of less. Becker, J.   **241.68**

A **more** perfect heaven. Sobel, D.   **520**

More stories from my father's court. Singer, I. B.   **839**

More technology for the rest of us.   **025**

More Than a Score.   **371.26**

More than freedom. Kantrowitz, S.   **323.1**

More word histories and mysteries.   **422**

More, Thomas Sir, Saint, 1478-1535
About
Bolt, R. A man for all seasons   **822**

Russell, B. A history of Western philosophy   **109**

Morehead, Albert H.
(ed) Hoyle, E. Hoyle's rules of games   **795.4**

Morehead, Philip D.
(ed) Hoyle, E. Hoyle's rules of games   **795.4**

Morell, Michael J
About
Morell, M. J. The great war of our time   **363.325**

Morell, Virginia
Animal wise   **591.5**

Morello, Giuseppe, 1870-1930
About
Dash, M. The first family   **364.1**

Moreno, Jonathan D.
The body politic   **303.48**

Moreno, Megan
Sex, drugs 'n Facebook   **004.67**

Moreno, Megan Andreas
(jt. auth) Moreno, M. Sex, drugs 'n Facebook   **004.67**

Moretti, Franco
Distant reading   **801**

Moretzsohn, Fabio
Harasewych, M. G. The book of shells   **594**

Morgan. Strouse, J.   **92**

Morgan, Bill
(ed) Burroughs, W. S. Rub out the words   **813**

(ed) Ginsberg, A. The letters of Allen Ginsberg   **92**

I celebrate myself   **92**

The typewriter is holy   **810**

Morgan, David Leon
(jt. auth) Abousteit, N. BurdaStyle sewing vintage modern   **646.4**

Morgan, Edmund Sears
American heroes .   **920**

The birth of the Republic, 1763-89   **973.3**

Morgan, Genevieve
Undecided   **371.4**

Morgan, J. Pierpont (John Pierpont), 1837-1913
About
Strouse, J. Morgan   **92**

Morgan, Jeff
The covenant kitchen   **641.5**

Morgan, Jodie
(jt. auth) Morgan, J. The covenant kitchen   **641.5**

Morgan, Judith
Dr. Seuss & Mr. Geisel   **92**

Morgan, Kenneth O.
(ed) The Oxford history of Britain   **941**

Morgan, Neil Bowen
Morgan, J. Dr. Seuss & Mr. Geisel   **92**

Morgan, Robert, 1944-
Boone   **92**

Lions of the West   **920**

Morgan, Sharon Leslie
(jt. auth) DeWolf, T. N. Gather at the table   **306.3**

Morgan, Ted, 1932-
Reds: McCarthyism in twentieth-century America   **973.9**

Valley of death   **959.704**

Wilderness at dawn   **970**
About
Morgan, T. My battle of Algiers   **965**

Morgan, William, 1928-1961
About
Weiss, M. The Yankee comandante   **92**

Morgenson, Gretchen
Reckless endangerment   **332.7**

Morgenstern, Dan
Living with jazz   **781.65**

Morgenthaler, Jeffrey
Bar Book   **641.87**

Morgenthau, Henry, 1856-1946
About
Tuchman, B. W. Practicing history   **907**

Morgue. Franscell, R.   **616.07**

Morike, Eduard Friedrich
Mozart's journey to Prague and a selection of poems   **831**

Morison, Samuel Eliot
Admiral of the ocean sea: a life of Christopher Columbus   **92**

The growth of the American Republic   **973**

John Paul Jones   **92**

Morkes, Andrew
(jt. auth) McKenna, A. Nontraditional careers for women and men   **331.702**

Morley, Paul
The age of Bowie   **92**

Mormando, Franco
Bernini   **92**

MORMON CHURCH
Barnes, J. Falling in love with Joseph Smith   **92**

Bushman, R. L. Mormonism   **289.3**

MORMON CHURCH *See* Church of Jesus Christ of Latter-day Saints

MORMON GAYS -- UNITED STATES -- BIOGRAPHY
Cooper, A. Saving Alex   92

MORMON LEADERS
Brower, S. Prophet's prey   306.8
Bushman, R. L. Joseph Smith   92
Bushman, R. L. Joseph Smith and the beginnings of Mormonism   289.3
Bushman, R. L. Mormonism   289.3
Remini, R. V. Joseph Smith   92

Mormonism. Bushman, R. L.   289.3

MORMONS
Barnes, J. Falling in love with Joseph Smith   92
Beam, A. American crucifixion   289.3
Book of Mormon The Book of Mormon   289.3
Bushman, R. L. Joseph Smith   92
Cooper, A. Saving Alex   92
Durham, M. S. Desert between the mountains   979
Gutjahr, P. C. The Book of Mormon   289.3
Remini, R. V. Joseph Smith   92
Wariner, R. The sound of gravel   92

The **Morning** They Came For Us. Di Giovanni, J.   956.91

Mornings on horseback. McCullough, D. G.   92

MOROCCAN COOKING
Couscous and other good food from Morocco   641.59
The food of Morocco   641.59
Roden, C. Arabesque: a taste of Morocco, Turkey, and Lebanon   641.5

MOROCCO
Braude, J. The honored dead   364.152

MOROCCO -- DESCRIPTION AND TRAVEL
Shah, T. The Caliph's house   964

Morone, James A.
Blumenthal, D. The heart of power   362.1

Morozov, Evgeny
The net delusion   303.48

MORPHINE
See also Narcotics

Morrell, Jessica Page
Thanks, but this isn't for us   808.3

Morris, Aldon D.
The scholar denied   301

Morris, Benny
Righteous victims   956

Morris, David J., 1971-
About
Morris, D. J. The evil hours   616.85

Morris, Desmond
Planet ape   599.8

Morris, Edmund
Beethoven: the universal composer   92
Colonel Roosevelt   92

The rise of Theodore Roosevelt   92
Theodore Rex   92
This living hand   814

Morris, Errol
Gourevitch, P. Standard operating procedure   956.7
Believing is seeing   770.9
A wilderness of error   364.152

Morris, Ian
War! What is it good for?   303.6
Why the West rules--for now   909

Morris, James McGrath
Eye on the Struggle   92

Morris, James McGrath
Pulitzer   92

Morris, Jan
Contact!   910.4
A writer's house in Wales   942.9

Morris, Julie
Superfood Kitchen   641.5

Morris, Lawrence
(ed) Daily life through world history in primary documents   909

Morris, Marc
A Great & Terrible King   92
King John   92
The Norman Conquest   942.02

Morris, Patrick
(jt. auth) Barrington, R. Life   578.4

Morris, Roger
Denton, S. The money and the power   979.3

Morris, Roy
Ambrose Bierce   92
Fraud of the century   324.9

Morris, Seymour
Supreme Commander   327.73

Morris, Sylvia Jukes
Rage for fame: the ascent of Clare Boothe Luce   92

Morris, Tom, 1821-1908
About
Cook, K. Tommy's honor   92

Morris, Tom, 1851-1875
About
Cook, K. Tommy's honor   92

Morris, Vanessa Irvin
The readers' advisory guide to street literature   016

Morris, William, 1834-1896
About
Byatt, A. S. Peacock & vine   700.92

Morris-Suzuki, Tessa
To the Diamond Mountains   915

Morrison, Dan
The black Nile   962

Morrison, Grant
Supergods   741.5

Morrison, Jim, 1943-1971
About

Hopkins, J. No one here gets out alive   92

Riordan, J. Break on through: the life and death of
   Jim Morrison   92

Morrison, Joanna
   Charles, J. A. The mystery readers' advisory **025.2**

Morrison, Phylis
   Holden, A. Crystals and crystal growing   **548**

Morrison, Terri
   Kiss, bow, or shake hands   **395**

Morrison, Toni, 1931-
   (ed) Burn this book   **814**
                        About
   Black women writers (1950-1980)   **810**
   Gillespie, C. Critical companion to Toni Morri-
      son   **813**

Morrissey, Sinéad
   Parallax   **821**

The **Morrow** guide to knots. Bigon, M.   **623.88**

Morrow, Bradford
   (ed) The Inevitable   **814**

Morrow, Lance
   The best year of their lives   **920**
   Second drafts of history   **973.92**

Morrow-Cribbs, Briony
   Stewart, A. Wicked bugs   **632**

Morse, Samuel Finley Breese, 1791-1872
                        About
   Lepore, J. A is for American   **306.44**

Mort, Terry
   Thieves' Road   **978.3**

Mortal coil. Haycock, D. B.   **571.8**

Mortal Sins. D'Antonio, M.   **261.8**

Mortality. Hitchens, C.   **304.6**

MORTALITY
   Hitchens, C. Mortality   **304.6**

MORTALITY
   See also Population; Vital statistics

Mortenson, Greg, 1957-
                        About
   Mortenson, G. Three cups of tea   **371.82**

**MORTGAGE BANKS -- UNITED STATES --
   HISTORY**
   Howard, T. The mortgage wars   **332.7**

The **mortgage** wars. Howard, T.   **332.7**

MORTGAGE-BACKED SECURITIES
   McLean, B. All the devils are here   **330.9**

MORTGAGES
   Acharya, V. V. Guaranteed to fail   **332.7**
   Howard, T. The mortgage wars   **332.7**
   Hudson, M. The monster   **332.6**
   McLean, B. All the devils are here   **330.9**
   Morgenson, G. Reckless endangerment   **332.7**

MORTGAGES
   See also Loans; Securities

MORTICIANS *See* Undertakers and undertaking

Mortimer, Gavin

Chasing Icarus   **629.13**
   The great swim   **920**
   The longest night   **940.53**

Mortimer, Ian
   The time traveler's guide to Elizabethan Eng-
      land   **942.05**

Morton, Andrew
   17 carnations   **941.084**

Morton, Brian
   Cook, R. The Penguin guide to jazz record-
      ings   **781.65**

Morton, Ella
   (jt. auth) Foer, J. Atlas Obscura   **910.41**

Morton, Laura
   (jt. auth) Roberts, D. Been there, done that   **92**

Morton, Lisa
   Trick or Treat   **394.264**

Morton, Mary
   (jt. auth) Shackelford, G. T. M. Gustave Caille-
      botte   **759.4**

Morton, Oliver
   Eating the sun   **572**
   Mapping Mars   **523.43**

Morton, Samuel George, 1799-1851
                        About
   Fabian, A. The skull collectors   **599.9**

MORTUARY CUSTOMS *See* Cremation; Funeral
   rites and ceremonies

MORTUARY STATISTICS *See* Mortality; Vital
   statistics

Mosaddeq, Mohammad, 1880-1967
                        About
   Kinzer, S. All the Shah's men   **327**

MOSAICS
   See also Decoration and ornament; Decora-
      tive arts

Mosby's diagnostic and laboratory test reference.
   Pagana, T. J.   **616.07**

Mosby's medical dictionary.   **610.3**

Mosby's Rangers. Wert, J. D.   **973.7**

Mosby, John Singleton, 1833-1916
                        About
   Wilson, E. Patriotic gore   **810**

Mosby, Rebekah Presson
   (ed) Poetry speaks expanded   **811**

MOSCOW (RUSSIA) -- BIOGRAPHY
   Von Bremzen, A. Mastering the art of Soviet cook-
      ing   **641.59**

**MOSCOW (RUSSIA) -- DESCRIPTION AND
   TRAVEL**
   Polonsky, R. Molotov's magic lantern   **947**

Moseley, Michael Edward
   The Incas and their ancestors   **985**

Mosenfelder, Donn
   Fischer, B. Bobby Fischer teaches chess   **794.1**

Moser, Benjamin

Why this world **92**
Moser, Charles A.
  (ed) The Cambridge history of Russian literature **891.7**
Moses, Kate
  (ed) Because I said so **306.8**
Moses, Robert, 1888-1981
         About
  Caro, R. A. The power broker: Robert Moses and the fall of New York **92**
Moses, Sam
  At all costs **940.54**
Moses, Susan
  The art of dressing curves **746.92**
Moshe Dayan. Bar-On, M. **956.940**
Mosier, John
  The myth of the Great War **940.4**
Moskowitz, Isa Chandra
  Vegan pie in the sky **641.5**
MOSLEMS *See* Muslims
Mosler, Layne
         About
  Mosler, L. Driving hungry **92**
Mosley, Charlotte
  (ed) The Mitfords **920**
Mosley, Diana, 1910-2003
         About
  Thompson, L. The six **92**
Mosley, Pixey Anne
  The challenge of library management **025.1**
Mosley, Shelley
  Tucker, D. C. Crash course in library supervision **023**
A **mosque** in Munich. Johnson, I. **297**
MOSQUE OFFICERS
  See also Muslims
MOSQUES
  Johnson, I. A mosque in Munich **297**
MOSQUES
  See also Islamic architecture; Religious institutions; Temples
MOSQUES -- GERMANY
  Johnson, I. A mosque in Munich **297**
Mosquito. Spielman, A. **595.77**
MOSQUITOES
  Spielman, A. Mosquito **595.77**
MOSQUITOES
  See also Insects
Moss, Charlotte
  Charlotte Moss **747**
Moss, Howard, 1922-1987
         About
  Gioia, D. Can poetry matter? **809.1**
Moss, Joyce
  (ed) Literature and its times **809**
Moss, Michael

Salt, sugar, fat **613.2**
Moss, Rita W.
  (jt. auth) Ernsthausen, D. G. Strauss's handbook of business information **016**
Moss, Steven
  (jt. auth) Paul, R. We could not fail **920**
MOSSES
      See also Plants
The **most** beautiful walk in the world. Baxter, J. **914**
Most Blessed of the Patriarchs. Gordon-Reed, A. **92**
The **most** dangerous man in America. Perry, M. **92**
The **most** dangerous place. Gull, I. **954.91**
The **most** famous man in America. Applegate, D. **92**
The **most** human human. Christian, B. **128**
A **Most** Improbable Journey. Alvarez, W. **508**
The **Most** of Nora Ephron. Ephron, N. **814**
The **Most** Perfect Thing. Birkhead, T. **598**
Mostert, Noel
  The line upon a wind **940.2**
MOTELS *See* Hotels and motels
Moten, Fred
  The Feel Trio **811**
MOTHER AND CHILD *See* Mother-child relationship
Mother Jones. Gorn, E. J. **331.88**
Mother Teresa. Spink, K. **271**
Mother Teresa. Spink, K. **92**
MOTHER'S DAY
      See also Holidays
A **mother's** reckoning. Klebold, S. **373**
MOTHER-CHILD RELATIONSHIP
  McConville, B. On Becoming a Mother **306.874**
  Swanson, W. S. Mama doc medicine **649.1**
MOTHER-CHILD RELATIONSHIP
      See also Children; Mothers; Parent-child relationship
MOTHER-DAUGHTER RELATIONSHIP
  Angelou, M. Mom & me & mom **818**
  Anselmo, L. My (part-time) Paris life **944.361**
  Corrigan, K. Glitter and Glue **92**
  Edelman, H. Motherless daughters **155.9**
  Edelman, H. Motherless mothers **155.9**
  Friday, N. My mother/my self **155.6**
  Leavell, L. Holding on upside down **92**
  Lerner, B. The bridge ladies **92**
  McBride, K. Will I ever be good enough? **616.85**
  Orenstein, P. Cinderella ate my daughter **305.23**
  O'Rourke, M. The long goodbye **92**
  Stuart, S. P. Perfectly miserable **92**
  Tassler, N. What I Told My Daughter **155.433**
  Winterson, J. Why be happy when you could be normal? **823**
MOTHER-DAUGHTER RELATIONSHIP
      See also Daughters; Mother-child relationship; Mothers
MOTHER-DAUGHTER RELATIONSHIP --

GRAPHIC NOVELS

Bechdel, A. Are you my mother? **741.5**

MOTHER-SON RELATIONSHIP

Adams, R. Raising Henry **92**

Cooper, A. The rainbow comes and goes **92**

Schwalbe, W. The end of your life book club **616.99**

Simon, S. Unforgettable **92**

MOTHER-SON RELATIONSHIP

See also Mother-child relationship; Mothers; Sons

MOTHERHOOD

Boggs, B. The art of waiting **618.178**

Bowman, D. Bottled **362.292**

Cleage, P. Things I Should Have Told My Daughter **92**

Cusk, R. A life's work **306.874**

Hendey, L. M. A book of saints for Catholic moms **248.8**

Mulgrew, K. Born With Teeth **791.45**

Seek, A. God and Jetfire **92**

Warner, J. Perfect madness **306.8**

MOTHERHOOD

See also Parenthood

MOTHERHOOD -- CALIFORNIA

Sweeney, J. If it's not one thing, it's your mother **362.734**

MOTHERHOOD -- POETRY

Greenbaum, J. The two Yvonnes **811**

Lang, S. For Tamara **C**

Motherland. Goldberg, R. **940.531**

Motherless daughters. Edelman, H. **155.9**

Motherless mothers. Edelman, H. **155.9**

MOTHERS

Because I said so **306.8**

Boland, E. A woman without a country **821**

Chua, A. Battle hymn of the tiger mother **306.874**

Corliss, R. Mom in the movies **791.43**

Cusk, R. A life's work **306.874**

Friday, N. My mother/my self **155.6**

Holden, W. Born Survivors **940.531**

Karr-Morse, R. Scared sick **155.9**

Lamarche, U. Unabrow **92**

Martin, W. Primates of Park Avenue **974.7**

Warner, J. Perfect madness **306.8**

Weldon, M. Escape Points **362.196**

Xinran Message from an unknown Chinese mother **305.4**

MOTHERS

See also Family; Women

MOTHERS -- COLORADO -- LITTLETON -- BIOGRAPHY

Klebold, S. A mother's reckoning **373**

MOTHERS -- EMPLOYMENT *See* Working mothers

MOTHERS -- LIFE SKILLS GUIDES

Matlen, T. The queen of distraction **616.85**

MOTHERS -- NEW YORK (STATE) -- NEW YORK -- BIOGRAPHY

Martin, W. Primates of Park Avenue **974.7**

MOTHERS -- NEW YORK (STATE) -- NEW YORK -- SOCIAL LIFE AND CUSTOMS

Martin, W. Primates of Park Avenue **974.7**

MOTHERS -- POETRY

Ford, K. Blood lyrics **811**

MOTHERS -- PRAYERS AND DEVOTIONS

Hendey, L. M. A book of saints for Catholic moms **248.8**

MOTHERS -- UNITED STATES -- BIOGRAPHY

Lamarche, U. Unabrow **92**

MOTHERS -- UNITED STATES -- DEATH

Anselmo, L. My (part-time) Paris life **944.361**

Smith, T. K. Ordinary light **92**

MOTHERS AND DAUGHTERS

Chua, A. Battle hymn of the tiger mother **306.874**

Corrigan, K. Glitter and Glue **92**

Emling, S. Marie Curie and her daughters **920**

Orenstein, P. Cinderella ate my daughter **305.23**

O'Rourke, M. The long goodbye **92**

MOTHERS AND DAUGHTERS *See* Mother-daughter relationship

MOTHERS AND DAUGHTERS -- CALIFORNIA -- BIOGRAPHY

Williams, M. The lost daughter **979.4**

MOTHERS AND DAUGHTERS -- UNITED STATES

Anselmo, L. My (part-time) Paris life **944.361**

Christensen, K. Blue plate special **92**

Lerner, B. The bridge ladies **92**

Marshall, D. Home is burning **92**

Smith, T. K. Ordinary light **92**

Volk, P. Shocked **92**

MOTHERS AND SONS *See* Mother-son relationship

MOTHERS AND SONS -- BIOGRAPHY

Mutch, M. Know the night **92**

MOTHERS AND SONS -- UNITED STATES

Hodgman, G. Bettyville **306.874**

Marshall, D. Home is burning **92**

MOTHERS AND SONS -- UNITED STATES -- CORRESPONDENCE

Cooper, A. The rainbow comes and goes **92**

MOTHERS IN MOTION PICTURES

Corliss, R. Mom in the movies **791.43**

MOTHERS OF AUTISTIC CHILDREN -- CASE STUDIES

Barnett, K. The spark **618.92**

Mothers of invention. Faust, D. G. **973.7**

MOTHERS-IN-LAW -- ITALY -- NAPLES -- BIOGRAPHY

Wilson, K. Only in Naples **945.731**

MOTHS

See also Insects

MOTION PICTURE ACTORS AND ACTRESSES *See* Actors

MOTION PICTURE ACTORS AND ACTRESSES -- GERMANY -- BIOGRAPHY
Dietrich & Riefenstahl   **791.43**

MOTION PICTURE ACTORS AND ACTRESSES -- GREAT BRITAIN -- BIOGRAPHY
Cleese, J. So, anyway...   **92**

MOTION PICTURE ACTORS AND ACTRESSES -- UNITED STATES -- BIOGRAPHY
Douglas, I. I blame Dennis Hopper   **792.02**

MOTION PICTURE ACTORS AND ACTRESSES -- UNITED STATES -- INTERVIEWS
Apatow, J. Sick in the head   **792.7**

MOTION PICTURE AUTHORSHIP
Goldman, W. Which Lie Did I Tell?   **791.43**

MOTION PICTURE CRITICS
Butcher, T. Chasing the Devil   **916**
Ebert, R. Life itself   **92**
Greene, G. Graham Greene   **92**
Kellow, B. Pauline Kael   **92**
Schiavi, M. Celluloid activist   **92**
Wranovics, J. Chaplin and Agee   **92**

MOTION PICTURE DIRECTION *See* Motion pictures -- Production and direction

MOTION PICTURE DIRECTORS
Bach, S. Leni: the life and work of Leni Riefenstahl   **92**
Biskind, P. Star   **92**
Black women writers (1950-1980)   **810**
Blum, H. American lightning   **364.152**
Buruma, I. Murder in Amsterdam   **364.152**
Callow, S. Orson Welles   **92**
Chandler, C. It's only a movie   **92**
The essential Chaplin   **92**
Eyman, S. Empire of dreams   **92**
Fine, M. Accidental genius   **791**
Goudsouzian, A. Sidney Poitier   **92**
Kurosawa, A. Something like an autobiography **92**
Levy, E. Vincente Minnelli   **92**
Levy, S. Paul Newman   **92**
Lewis, J. Dean & me   **92**
LoBrutto, V. Stanley Kubrick   **92**
Marton, K. The great escape   **920**
McGilligan, P. Oscar Micheaux   **92**
Meade, M. Buster Keaton   **92**
Meyers, J. John Huston   **92**
Olson, R. Don't be such a scientist   **501**
Playwrights at work   **812**
Poitier, S. The measure of a man   **92**
Rapoport, R. Citizen Moore   **92**
Said, E. W. Reflections on exile and other essays   **814**
Scherman, T. Pop   **92**
Schickel, R. Elia Kazan   **92**
Shepard, S. The girl from foreign   **92**

Sikov, E. On Sunset Boulevard: the life and times of Billy Wilder   **92**
Singer, M. Character studies   **920**
Spoto, D. The dark side of genius   **791.43**
Sragow, M. Victor Fleming   **92**
Thomson, H. The white rock   **985**
Trimborn, J. Leni Riefenstahl   **92**
Waters, J. Role models   **92**
Waxman, S. Rebels on the backlot   **920**
Wranovics, J. Chaplin and Agee   **92**
Zuckoff, M. Robert Altman   **92**

MOTION PICTURE DIRECTORS *See* Motion picture producers and directors

MOTION PICTURE EXECUTIVES
Bruck, C. When Hollywood had a king   **338.7**
Bullock-Prado, G. Confections of a closet master baker   **92**
Eyman, S. Lion of Hollywood   **92**
Wolff, M. The man who owns the news   **92**

MOTION PICTURE INDUSTRY
Bruck, C. When Hollywood had a king   **338.7**
Conversations at the American Film Institute with the great moviemakers   **791.43**
Decherney, P. Hollywood's copyright wars **346.73**
Ebert, R. Life itself   **92**
Goldman, W. Which Lie Did I Tell?   **791.43**
Goldman, W. Adventures in the screen trade **791.43**
Harris, M. Five Came Back   **791.43**
Harris, M. Pictures at a revolution   **791.43**
Kurosawa, A. Something like an autobiography **92**
Longworth, K. Hollywood frame by frame **791.43**
Mann, W. J. Behind the screen   **791.43**
Masear, T. Fastest Things on Wings   **598**
Reynolds, D. Make 'em Laugh   **92**

MOTION PICTURE INDUSTRY
See also Industries

MOTION PICTURE INDUSTRY -- CALIFORNIA -- LOS ANGELES -- HISTORY
Eyman, S. Empire of dreams   **92**
Harris, M. Five Came Back   **791.43**
Thomson, D. The whole equation   **791.43**

MOTION PICTURE INDUSTRY -- HISTORY
Dixon, W. W. A Short History of Film   **791.43**
Mann, W. J. Tinseltown   **364.152**
Urwand, B. The collaboration   **791.43**

MOTION PICTURE PHOTOGRAPHY *See* Cinematography

MOTION PICTURE PLAYS -- TECHNIQUE
Field, S. Screenplay   **808.2**
Hauge, M. Writing screenplays that sell   **808.2**
Now write! screenwriting   **808.2**

MOTION PICTURE PLAYS -- TECHNIQUE
See also Drama -- Technique

MOTION PICTURE PRODUCER AND DIRECTORS -- UNITED STATES -- BIOGRAPHY
Goessel, T. The first king of Hollywood   **92**

MOTION PICTURE PRODUCERS

Albrecht, D.   The Work of Charles and Ray Eames   **745.4**

Bach, S.   Leni: the life and work of Leni Riefenstahl   **92**

Biskind, P.   Star   **92**

Buford, K.   Burt Lancaster   **92**

Callow, S.   Orson Welles   **92**

The essential Chaplin   **92**

Eyman, S.   Empire of dreams   **92**

Marton, K.   The great escape   **920**

Trimborn, J.   Leni Riefenstahl   **92**

Wranovics, J.   Chaplin and Agee   **92**

Zuckoff, M.   Robert Altman   **92**

MOTION PICTURE PRODUCERS *See* Motion picture producers and directors

MOTION PICTURE PRODUCERS AND DI-RECTORS

See also Motion picture industry

MOTION PICTURE PRODUCERS AND DI-RECTORS -- BIOGRAPHY

Callow, S.   Orson Welles   **92**

D'Alessandro, E.   Stanley Kubrick and me   **791.43**

Lanzmann, C.   The Patagonian hare   **791.43**

MOTION PICTURE PRODUCERS AND DI-RECTORS -- BIOGRAPHY -- DICTIONAR-IES

Rough Guides (Firm)   The Rough Guide to film   **791.43**

MOTION PICTURE PRODUCERS AND DI-RECTORS -- CRIMES AGAINST -- UNITED STATES

Mann, W. J.   Tinseltown   **364.152**

MOTION PICTURE PRODUCERS AND DI-RECTORS -- FRANCE -- BIOGRAPHY

Lanzmann, C.   The Patagonian hare   **791.43**

MOTION PICTURE PRODUCERS AND DI-RECTORS -- KOREA (SOUTH) -- BIOGRA-PHY

Fischer, P.   A Kim Jong-Il production   **791.43**

MOTION PICTURE PRODUCERS AND DI-RECTORS -- UNITED STATES

Harris, M.   Five Came Back   **791.43**

Mann, W. J.   Tinseltown   **364.152**

My Lunches With Orson   **791.43**

MOTION PICTURE PRODUCERS AND DI-RECTORS -- UNITED STATES -- BIOGRA-PHY

D'Alessandro, E.   Stanley Kubrick and me   **791.43**

Waters, J.   Carsick   **92**

MOTION PICTURE PRODUCERS AND DI-RECTORS -- UNITED STATES -- DIARIES

It's the pictures that got small   **92**

MOTION PICTURE PRODUCERS AND DI-RECTORS -- UNITED STATES -- INTER-VIEWS

Allen, W.   Woody Allen on Woody Allen   **791.43**

Conversations at the American Film Institute with the great moviemakers   **791.43**

MOTION PICTURE PRODUCTION *See* Motion pictures -- Production and direction

MOTION PICTURE PROJECTIONISTS

Messick, K.   The projectionist   **92**

MOTION PICTURE SERIALS

See also Motion pictures

MOTION PICTURE THEATERS

Messick, K.   The projectionist   **92**

MOTION PICTURES

1001 Movies You Must See Before You Die **791.43**

Biskind, P.   Easy riders, raging bulls   **791.43**

Conversations at the American Film Institute with the great moviemakers   **791.43**

Film noir   **791.43**

Harris, M.   Pictures at a revolution   **791.43**

Kellow, B.   Pauline Kael   **92**

Rabin, N.   My year of flops   **791.43**

MOTION PICTURES

See also Audiovisual materials; Mass media; Performing arts

MOTION PICTURES -- APPRECIATION

Arnold, J.   The essentials   **791.43**

Thomson, D.   How to watch a movie   **791.43**

MOTION PICTURES -- BIOGRAPHY

See also Biography

MOTION PICTURES -- BIOGRAPHY -- DIC-TIONARIES

Monush, B.   Screen world presents the encyclopedia of Hollywood film actors   **920.003**

MOTION PICTURES -- CENSORSHIP

See also Censorship

MOTION PICTURES -- ETHICAL ASPECTS

See also Ethics

MOTION PICTURES -- EVALUATION

Rabin, N.   My year of flops   **791.43**

Schickel, R.   Keepers   **791.43**

MOTION PICTURES -- HISTORY AND CRITI-CISM

Burr, T.   Gods like us   **306.4**

Ebert, R.   Life itself   **92**

Gleiberman, O.   Movie freak   **791.43**

Turan, K.   Not to be missed   **791.43**

MOTION PICTURES -- HISTORY.

Dixon, W. W.   A Short History of Film   **791.43**

MOTION PICTURES -- KOREA (NORTH) -- HISTORY -- 20TH CENTURY

Fischer, P.   A Kim Jong-Il production   **791.43**

MOTION PICTURES -- PRODUCTION AND DIRECTION

Ascher, S.   The filmmaker's handbook   **777**

It's the pictures that got small   **92**

Karp, J.   Orson Welles's last movie   **791.43**

MacLaine, S.   Above the line   **92**

MOTION PICTURES -- PRODUCTION AND DIRECTION
  See also Motion picture industry

MOTION PICTURES -- PRODUCTION AND DIRECTION -- HANDBOOKS, MANUALS, ETC
  Ascher, S. The filmmaker's handbook   **777**

MOTION PICTURES -- PRODUCTION AND DIRECTION -- UNITED STATES -- HISTORY -- 20TH CENTURY
  It's the pictures that got small   **92**

MOTION PICTURES -- REVIEWS
  Arnold, J. The essentials   **791.43**
  Kael, P. The age of movies   **791.43**
  Lane, A. Nobody's perfect   **791.43**

MOTION PICTURES -- SOCIAL ASPECTS
  Thomson, D. The big screen   **791.43**

MOTION PICTURES -- UNITED STATES
  Lehr, D. The Birth of a Nation   **305.8**

MOTION PICTURES -- UNITED STATES -- HISTORY
  Harris, M. Five Came Back   **791.43**
  Sragow, M. Victor Fleming   **92**
  Thomson, D. The big screen   **791.43**

MOTION PICTURES -- UNITED STATES -- PICTORIAL WORKS
  Longworth, K. Hollywood frame by frame   **791.43**

Motion, Andrew
  Keats   **821**

MOTIVATION (PSYCHOLOGY)
  Duhigg, C. Smarter faster better   **158**
  Hallowell, E. M. Shine   **658.3**
  Kelly, M. The dream manager   **658.3**
  Osteen, J. The power of I am   **248.4**
  Pink, D. H. Drive   **153.1**
  Tracy, B. Full engagement!   **658.3**
  Vedantam, S. The hidden brain   **154.2**

MOTIVATION (PSYCHOLOGY)
  See also Psychology

MOTIVATION (PSYCHOLOGY) -- UNITED STATES -- CASE STUDIES
  Kendall, J. America's obsessives   **609.2**

MOTIVATION IN ANIMALS
  Bekoff, M. Wild justice   **591.5**

MOTIVATIONAL SPEAKERS
  Meeink, F. Autobiography of a recovering skinhead   **92**
  Mooney, J. The short bus   **92**
  Murray, L. Breaking night   **92**

Motley, Isolde
  Caughman, S. You can adopt   **362.7**

MOTOR VEHICLES -- SAFETY APPLIANCES -- RESEARCH -- UNITED STATES -- HISTORY -- 20TH CENTURY
  Ryan, C. Sonic wind   **92**

MOTORBOATS
  See also Boats and boating

MOTORCYCLES
  Harley-Davidson   **629.22**

MOTORCYCLES
  See also Bicycles

MOTORCYCLISTS -- UNITED STATES
  Lyon, D. The bikeriders   **796.7**

MOTORING *See* Automobile travel

Mott-Smith, Geoffrey
  (ed) Hoyle, E. Hoyle's rules of games   **795.4**

Moullé, Denise Lurton
      About
  Moulle, J. P. French roots   **641.594**

Moullé, Jean-Pierre
      About
  Moulle, J. P. French roots   **641.594**

Moulton, Sara
  Sara Moulton's Home Cooking 101   **641.5**

MOUNDS AND MOUND BUILDERS
  See also Archeology; Burial; Tombs

MOUNT EVEREST (CHINA AND NEPAL)
  Lewis-Jones, H. Conquest of Everest   **796.522**

MOUNT EVEREST (CHINA AND NEPAL)
  See also Mountains

MOUNT EVEREST EXPEDITION (1996)
  Boukreev, A. The climb   **796.522**
  Coburn, B. Everest: mountain without mercy   **796.522**
  Jamling Tenzing Norgay Touching my father's soul   **796.522**
  Krakauer, J. Into thin air   **796.522**

MOUNT RAINIER (WASH.)
  See also Mountains

MOUNT SAINT HELENS (WASH.)
  Thompson, D. Volcano cowboys   **551.21**

Mountain home.   **895.1**

MOUNTAIN LIFE
  See also Country life

MOUNTAIN MEADOWS MASSACRE, 1857
  Walker, R. W. Massacre at Mountain Meadows   **979.2**

MOUNTAIN PEOPLE
  See also Ethnology

MOUNTAIN PLANTS
  See also Plant ecology; Plants

MOUNTAINEERING
  Boukreev, A. The climb   **796.522**
  Coburn, B. Everest: mountain without mercy   **796.522**
  Conefrey, M. The Ghosts of K2   **796.522**
  Cordes, K. The tower   **796**
  Denny, G. Valley walls   **796.52**
  Eichar, D. Dead Mountain   **914.7**
  Grange, K. Beneath blossom rain   **915**
  Isserman, M. Continental divide   **796.52**
  Jamling Tenzing Norgay Touching my father's

soul **796.522**
Krakauer, J. Into thin air **796.522**
Sieberson, S. The naked mountaineer **92**
Taylor, J. E. Pilgrims of the vertical **796.52**
Trailside (Television program) Rock climbing **796.522**
Zuckerman, P. Buried in the sky **796.522**
MOUNTAINEERING
 See also Outdoor life
MOUNTAINEERING -- ANECDOTES
Sieberson, S. The naked mountaineer **92**
MOUNTAINEERING -- PAKISTAN -- K2 (MOUNTAIN)
Zuckerman, P. Buried in the sky **796.522**
MOUNTAINEERING -- PERSONAL NARRATIVES
Krakauer, J. Into thin air **796.522**
MOUNTAINEERING -- UNITED STATES -- HISTORY
Isserman, M. Continental divide **796.52**
MOUNTAINEERING ACCIDENTS -- PAKISTAN -- K2 (MOUNTAIN)
Zuckerman, P. Buried in the sky **796.522**
MOUNTAINEERING ACCIDENTS -- RUSSIA (FEDERATION) -- URAL MOUNTAINS REGION -- 20TH CENTURY
Eichar, D. Dead Mountain **914.7**
MOUNTAINEERS
Fredston, J. A. Snowstruck **551.3**
Jamling Tenzing Norgay Touching my father's soul **796.522**
Mortenson, G. Three cups of tea **371.82**
MOUNTAINEERS -- PAKISTAN -- K2 (MOUNTAIN)
Zuckerman, P. Buried in the sky **796.522**
MOUNTAINEERS -- UNITED STATES -- BIOGRAPHY
Sieberson, S. The naked mountaineer **92**
MOUNTAINS
Isserman, M. Continental divide **796.52**
MOUNTAINS
 See also Landforms; Physical geography
MOUNTAINS -- NORTH AMERICA
Strayed, C. Wild **92**
MOUNTAINS -- PAKISTAN
Conefrey, M. The Ghosts of K2 **796.522**
Zuckerman, P. Buried in the sky **796.522**
MOUNTAINTOP MINING
House, S. Something's rising **338.2**
MOUNTAINTOP REMOVAL MINING -- ENVIRONMENTAL ASPECTS -- APPALACHIAN REGION, SOUTHERN
House, S. Something's rising **338.2**
MOURNING *See* Bereavement
MOURNING CUSTOMS *See* Funeral rites and ceremonies

Mourning Lincoln. Hodes, M. **973.7**
Mousavizadeh, Nader
 (jt. auth) Annan, K. A. Interventions **341.23**
The **mousetrap** and other plays. Christie, A. **822**
MOVEMENT, PSYCHOLOGY OF
 Streb, E. Streb **92**
MOVEMENTS OF ANIMALS *See* Animal locomotion
Movie freak. Gleiberman, O. **791.43**
MOVIE NOVELS
 See also Fiction
MOVIE THEATERS *See* Motion picture theaters
MOVIES *See* Motion pictures
MOVING
 Jameson, M. Downsizing the family home **346.04**
 Leeds, R. Rightsize . . . right now! **648**
 Rosenfelt, D. Dogtripping **636.7**
 Warnick, M. This Is Where You Belong **155.94**
MOVING
 See also Home economics
Moving beyond words. Steinem, G. **305.42**
Moving the mountain. Abdul Rauf, F. **297.09**
Moving to higher ground. Marsalis, W. **781.65**
MOVING, HOUSEHOLD
 Leeds, R. Rightsize . . . right now! **648**
MOVING, HOUSEHOLD *See* Moving
Mowat, Farley
 High latitudes **971**
 About
 King, J. Farley: the life of Farley Mowat **92**
 Mowat, F. Born naked **92**
Moyad, Mark
 (jt. auth) Lee, J. The supplement handbook **613.2**
Moyer, Jessica E.
 The readers' advisory handbook **025.5**
 Research-based readers' advisory **025.5**
Moyers, Bill
 Campbell, J. The power of myth **201**
 Genesis: a living conversation **222**
Moyers, William C.
 About
 Moyers, W. C. Broken: my story of addiction and redemption **92**
Moynahan, Brian
 Leningrad **940.54**
Moynihan, Daniel Patrick
 On the law of nations **327**
 Secrecy **352.3**
Mozart. Einstein, A. **92**
Mozart. Solomon, M. **92**
Mozart. Gutman, R. W. **92**
Mozart's journey to Prague and a selection of poems. Morike, E. F. **831**
Mozart, Wolfgang Amadeus, 1756-1791
 About
 Einstein, A. Mozart **92**

Gutman, R. W. Mozart   92
Osborne, C. The complete operas of Mozart   792.5
Rosen, C. The classical style   780.9
Schonberg, H. C. The great pianists   920
Shaffer, P. Peter Shaffer's Amadeus   822
Solomon, M. Mozart   92
Mozza at home.   641.5
Mr. Churchill's profession. Clarke, P.   941.084
Mr. Hockey. Howe, G.   92
Mr. Playboy. Watts, S.   92
Mr. president. Raphael, R.   352.23
Mr. Wilkinson's vegetables. Wilkinson, M.   641.65
Mrs. Adams in winter. O'Brien, M.   940.2
Mrs. Dred Scott. VanderVelde, L.   92
Mrs. Kennedy. Leaming, B.   973.922
Mrs. Kennedy and me. Hill, C.   973.922
Mrs. Lincoln. Clinton, C.   92
Mrs. Paine's garage and the murder of John F. Kennedy. Mallon, T.   364.1
Mrs. Robinson's disgrace. Summerscale, K.   941.081
Mrs. Wheelbarrow's practical pantry. Barrow, C.   641.4
The **much** too promised land. Miller, A. D.   956.05
Mudd, Philip
  The Head Game   153.4
Mudgett, Herman W., 1861-1896
About
  Larson, E. The devil in the white city   364.15
Mueller, Hans-Friedrich
  (ed) Gibbon, E. The decline and fall of the Roman empire   937
Mueller, James R.
  (ed) Bible The Oxford study Bible   220.5
Mueller, Scott
  Upgrading and repairing PCs   004.16
Mueller, Tom
  Extra virginity   664
Mufleh, Luma
About
  St. John, W. Outcasts united   796.334
Mugabe, Robert Gabriel, 1924-
About
  Godwin, P. The fear
Mugaseth, Bobby, 1919-1944
About
  Karnad, R. Farthest field   940.54
Mugglestone, Lynda
  Lost for words   423
Muḥammad, Prophet, d. 632
About
  Armstrong, K. Muhammad   297
  Hazleton, L. After the prophet   297
  Hazleton, L. The First Muslim   297.6
Muhammad. Armstrong, K.   297
Muhlke, Christine
  Ripert, E. On the line   647

Muir, Edwin, 1887-1959
About
  Heaney, S. Finders keepers   821
Muir, Frank
  (ed) The Oxford book of humorous prose   827
Muir, John, 1838-1914
  The encyclopedia of superheroes on film and television   791.43
  The Yosemite   979.4
About
  Heacox, K. John Muir and the ice that started a fire   92
  Muir, J. Nature writings   508
  Muir, J. The story of my boyhood and youth   92
  Wilkins, T. John Muir   92
  Worster, D. A passion for nature   92
Mukherjee, Siddhartha
  The emperor of all maladies   616.99
  The gene   616.042
  The laws of medicine   610
Mulac, Carolyn M.
  Fundamentals of reference   025.5
MULATTOES See Racially mixed people
MULCHING
  Campbell, S. How to mulch   635
Muldoon, Paul
  Horse latitudes   821
  Maggot   821
  Poems, 1968-1998   821
Muldoon, Sean
  The Dead Rabbit drinks manual   641.87
Mulgrew, Kate, 1955-
  Born With Teeth   791.45
Mullainathan, Sendhil
  (jt. auth) Shafir, E. Scarcity   338.5
Mullane, Deirdre
  (ed) Crossing the danger water   810
Mullen, P. H.
  Gold in the water   797.2
Muller, Eric L.
  (ed) Colors of confinement   940.53
Muller, Kristin
  The potter's studio handbook   738.1
Muller, Melissa, 1967-
  Anne Frank   92
  Lost lives, lost art   709
Muller, Richard A., 1944-
  Dauber, P. M. The three big bangs   523.1
  Energy for future presidents   333.79
  Now   530.11
Mulley, Clare
  The Spy Who Loved   940.54
Mullin, Glenn H.
  The second Dalai Lama   92
MULTICULTURAL EDUCATION
  See also Acculturation; Education; Multicul-

turalism

MULTICULTURAL LITERATURE
  See also Literature; Multiculturalism
Multicultural manners. Dresser, N.   **395**
MULTICULTURALISM
  Levine, L. W. The opening of the American
  mind   **001.1**
  Patel, E. Acts of faith   **92**
  Postman, N. The end of education   **370.9**
  Woodard, C. American nations   **970.004**
MULTICULTURALISM
  See also Culture; Social policy
MULTILINGUALISM
  See also Language and languages
MULTIMEDIA
  Pattee, A. S. Developing library collections for to-
  day's young adults   **027.62**
MULTIMEDIA LIBRARY SERVICES
  Gallaway, B. Game on!   **025.2**
**MULTIMEDIA LIBRARY SERVICES -- UNIT-
ED STATES**
  Pattee, A. S. Developing library collections for to-
  day's young adults   **027.62**
MULTIMEDIA SYSTEMS *See* Multimedia
MULTINATIONAL CORPORATIONS
  Bown, S. R. Merchant kings   **338.8**
MULTIPLE MYELOMA -- TREATMENT
  Brokaw, T. A Lucky Life Interrupted   **92**
MULTIPLE PERSONALITIES *See* Multiple per-
  sonality
MULTIPLE PERSONALITY
  Nathan, D. Sybil exposed   **616.85**
  Schreiber, F. R. Sybil   **616.85**
MULTIPLE SCLEROSIS -- TREATMENT
  Bowling, A. C. Optimal health with multiple scle-
  rosis   **616.8**
MULTIRACIAL PEOPLE *See* Racially mixed
  people
**MUMBAI TERRORIST ATTACKS, MUMBAI,
INDIA, 2008**
  Levy, A. The siege   **363.325**
Mumford, Lewis
  The city in history   **307.7**
  The culture of cities   **307.7**
Mumme, Hal
  About
  Gwynne, S. C. The Perfect Pass   **796.332**
MUMMIES
  Fowler, B. Iceman   **937**
  Pringle, H. A. The mummy congress   **393**
MUMMIES
  See also Archeology; Burial; Human remains
  (Archeology)
The **mummy** congress. Pringle, H. A.   **393**
Munch, Edvard, 1863-1944
  About

Dolnick, E. The rescue artist   **364.1**
Prideaux, S. Edvard Munch   **92**
MUNDANEUM -- HISTORY
  Wright, A. Cataloging the world   **020.9**
MUNICH (GERMANY)
  Johnson, I. A mosque in Munich   **297**
**MUNICH (GERMANY) -- DESCRIPTION AND
TRAVEL**
  Dk Eyewitness Munich & the Bavarian
  Alps   **914.336**
MUNICH FOUR-POWER AGREEMENT (1938)
  Faber, D. Munich, 1938   **940.53**
Munich, 1938. Faber, D.   **940.53**
MUNICIPAL OFFICIALS AND EMPLOYEES
  Nagle, R. Picking up   **331.7**
Munroe, Randall, 1984-
  Thing Explainer   **500**
  What if?   **500**
MUPPET SHOW (TELEVISION PROGRAM)
  Jones, B. J. Jim Henson   **92**
Murakami, Haruki
  Underground   **364.1**
  What I talk about when I talk about running   **92**
MURAL PAINTING AND DECORATION
  Ganz, N. Graffiti world   **751**
  Hirst, M. Michelangelo   **709.2**
  King, R. Michelangelo & the Pope's ceiling   **759**
MURAL PAINTING AND DECORATION
  See also Decoration and ornament; Interior
  design; Painting
**MURAL PAINTING AND DECORATION,
  AMERICAN -- NEW YORK (STATE) -- NEW
  YORK**
  Felisbret, E. Graffiti New York   **751.7**
MURDER *See* Homicide
MURDER -- ENGLAND -- CASE STUDIES
  Colquhoun, K. Did she kill him?   **364.152**
MURDER -- GERMANY -- HISTORY
  Robisheaux, T. The last witch of Langenburg **133.4**
**MURDER -- GREAT BRITAIN -- HISTORY --
  19TH CENTURY**
  Flanders, J. The invention of murder   **364.152**
  Hempel, S. The inheritor's powder   **364.152**
**MURDER -- INVESTIGATION -- CALIFORNIA
  -- LOS ANGELES -- CASE STUDIES**
  Mann, W. J. Tinseltown   **364.152**
**MURDER -- INVESTIGATION -- JAPAN -- TO-
  KYO**
  Parry, R. L. People who eat darkness   **364.152**
**MURDER -- LOUISIANA -- NEW ORLEANS --
  HISTORY -- 20TH CENTURY**
  Krist, G. Empire of sin   **976.3**
**MURDER -- NORTH CAROLINA -- CASE
  STUDIES**
  Morris, E. A wilderness of error   **364.152**
MURDER -- OREGON -- CASE STUDIES

Zacharias, K. S. A silence of mockingbirds **364.152**

MURDER -- UNITED STATES

Leovy, J. Ghettoside **364.152**

MURDER -- UNITED STATES -- CASE STUDIES

McConnell, D. American honor killings **364.15**

Schechter, H. Psycho USA **364.152**

Murder at Camp Delta. Hickman, J. **355.1**

Murder city. Bowden, C. **364.152**

Murder in Amsterdam. Buruma, I. **364.152**

A **murder** in Virginia. Lebsock, S. **364.1**

MURDER MYSTERIES *See* Mystery and detective plays; Mystery fiction; Mystery films; Mystery radio programs; Mystery television programs

The **murder** of Nikolai Vavilov. Pringle, P. **92**

The **murder** of Sonny Liston. Assael, S. **796.83**

The **murder** of the century. Collins, P. **364.152**

The **murder** of Tutankhamen. Brier, B. **932**

MURDER TRIALS *See* Trials (Homicide)

MURDER VICTIMS

Abdul-Jabbar, K. Black profiles in courage **920**

Brown, E. Shake the devil off **364.152**

Goldman, F. The art of political murder **972.81**

Herlihy, D. V. The lost cyclist **92**

Latus, J. If I am missing or dead **92**

Malcolm, J. Iphigenia in Forest Hills **345**

Matthews, J. Bringing Adam home **364.1**

Rice, A. The teeth may smile but the heart does not forget **967.6**

Rule, A. --and never let her go **364.1**

Rule, A. Too late to say goodbye **364.152**

Schiller, L. Perfect murder, perfect town **364.15**

Stashower, D. The beautiful cigar girl **364.152**

Summerscale, K. The suspicions of Mr. Whicher **364.152**

MURDER VICTIMS -- FLORIDA -- TAMPA -- BIOGRAPHY

Kushner, D. Alligator candy **362.88**

MURDER VICTIMS' FAMILIES -- FLORIDA -- TAMPA -- BIOGRAPHY

Kushner, D. Alligator candy **362.88**

MURDERERS

Brown, E. Shake the devil off **364.152**

Bugliosi, V. Helter skelter **364.1**

Bugliosi, V. Reclaiming history **973.922**

Burke, T. M. The Paradiso files **364.152**

Capote, T. In cold blood **364.1**

Guinn, J. Go down together **364.1**

King, D. Death in the city of light **364.1**

Larson, E. The devil in the white city **364.15**

Larson, E. Thunderstruck **364.152**

Lifton, R. J. The Nazi doctors **940.53**

Malcolm, J. Iphigenia in Forest Hills **345**

Mallon, T. Mrs. Paine's garage and the murder of John F. Kennedy **364.1**

McGinniss, J. Fatal vision **364.1**

Miller, S. The President and the assassin **973.8**

Moore, W. The other Wes Moore **92**

Olsen, J. I: the creation of a serial killer **364.1**

Posner, G. L. Case closed **973.922**

Prejean, H. The death of innocents **364.66**

Rauchway, E. Murdering McKinley **973.8**

Rice, A. The teeth may smile but the heart does not forget **967.6**

Rideau, W. In the place of justice **92**

Rule, A. --and never let her go **364.1**

Rule, A. The stranger beside me **92**

Sides, H. Hellhound on his trail **364.152**

Starr, D. The killer of little shepherds **364.152**

Stewart, J. B. Blind eye **364.1**

Summerscale, K. The suspicions of Mr. Whicher **364.152**

Swanson, J. L. Manhunt **364.152**

The Ultimate Jack the Ripper companion **364.15**

Winchester, S. The professor and the madman **423**

Worrall, S. The poet and the murderer **364.15**

MURDERERS -- UNITED STATES -- BIOGRAPHY

Guinn, J. Manson **364.152**

Schechter, H. Psycho USA **364.152**

MURDERERS -- UNITED STATES -- CASE STUDIES

Kirn, W. Blood will out **364.152**

McConnell, D. American honor killings **364.15**

Morris, E. A wilderness of error **364.152**

Murdering McKinley. Rauchway, E. **973.8**

Murdoch, Iris

About

Bayley, J. Elegy for Iris **823**

Conradi, P. Iris Murdoch **823**

Murdoch, Rupert

About

Wolff, M. The man who owns the news **92**

Murdoch, Stephen

IQ **153.9**

MURGAB RIVER REGION (AFGHANISTAN AND TURKMENISTAN) -- HISTORY, MILITARY

Bruning, J. R. Level zero heroes **958.104**

Murie, Olaus Johan

Elbroch, M. The Peterson field guide to animal tracks **599**

Muriel Spark. Stannard, M. **92**

Murkoff, Heidi

What to Expect the First Year **649**

What to expect the second year **649**

What to expect when you're expecting **618.2**

Murolo, Priscilla

From the folks who brought you the weekend **331**

Murphree, Rodger H.

Treating and beating fibromyalgia and chronic fatigue syndrome **616**

Murphy, Brian, 1959-
81 days below zero   **940.54**

Murphy, Bruce
(ed) Benet's reader's encyclopedia   **803**

Murphy, Bruce Allen
Scalia   **92**

Murphy, Cullen
The Word according to Eve   **220.8**

Murphy, Curtis
      About
Halberstam, D. The children   **323.1**

Murphy, Esther, 1898-1962
      About
Cohen, L. All we know   **920.72**

Murphy, Gerald, 1888-1964
      About
Vaill, A. Everybody was so young   **759.13**

Murphy, Marilyn
Woven to wear   **746.1**

Murphy, Martha W.
(jt. auth) Lintala, J. The un-prescription for Autism   **616.85**

Murphy, Mary McDonagh
Scout, Atticus, and Boo   **813**

Murphy, Monica, 1970-
Rabid   **614.5**

Murphy, Paul Thomas
Shooting Victoria   **941.081**

Murphy, Russell E.
Critical companion to T.S. Eliot   **811**

Murphy, Sara, 1883-1975
      About
Vaill, A. Everybody was so young   **759.13**

Murphy, Shelley
(jt. auth) Cullen, K. Whitey Bulger   **364.1**

Murphy, T. J.
(jt. auth) Starrett, K. Ready to run   **613.7**

Murphy, Terry Weible
Life in rewind   **92**

Murphy-O'Connor, J.
Paul   **225.9**

Murray, Alan S.
Wall Street journal The Wall Street Journal essential guide to management   **658**

Murray, Alan V.
(ed) The Crusades   **909.07**

Murray, Albert
Basie, C. Good morning blues: the autobiography of Count Basie   **92**
The blue devils of Nada   **780.89**
      About
Gates, H. L. Thirteen ways of looking at a black man   **920.71**

Murray, Charles Shaar
Crosstown traffic: Jimi Hendrix and the post-war rock'n'roll revolution   **787.87**

Murray, Charles, 1943-
Coming apart   **305.8**

Murray, Erin Byers
(jt. auth) Sewall, J. The New England kitchen   **641.597**

Murray, James Augustus Henry Sir, 1837-1915
      About
Winchester, S. The professor and the madman   **423**

Murray, Les A.
The biplane houses   **821**
Conscious and verbal   **821**
Poems the size of photographs   **821**
Murray, L. Taller when prone   **821**

Murray, Liz
      About
Murray, L. Breaking night   **92**

Murray, Michael T.
The encyclopedia of natural medicine   **615.5**

Murray, Nicholas
Kafka   **92**

Murray, Oswyn
(ed) The Oxford history of the Roman world   **937**

Murray, Pauli, 1910-1985
      About
Bell-Scott, P. The firebrand and the First Lady   **92**

Murray, R. Emmett
The lexicon of labor   **331**

Murray, Williamson
The Iraq war   **956.7**

Murrow, Edward R.
      About
Edwards, B. Edward R. Murrow and the birth of broadcast journalism   **92**
Olson, L. Citizens of London   **940.54**
Sperber, A. M. Murrow, his life and times   **92**

Murrow, his life and times. Sperber, A. M.   **92**

MUSCLE STRENGTH
Pagano, J. Strength training exercises for women   **613.7**

MUSCULOSKELETAL SYSTEM
     See also Anatomy; Physiology

Musee d'Orsay (Paris, France)
Thomas Eakins   **759.13**
The **muses** go to school.   **700**

MUSEUM ADMINISTRATORS
Carter, M. Anthony Blunt: his lives   **92**
Cole, K. C. Something incredibly wonderful happens   **92**

MUSEUM EXHIBITS -- MORAL AND ETHICAL ASPECTS
Crais, C. C. Sara Baartman and the Hottentot Venus   **92**

Museum of Fine Arts (Boston, Mass.)
Cikovsky, N. Winslow Homer   **759.13**

Museum of Modern Art (New York, N.Y.)
Dickerman, L. Dada   **709.04**

A **museum** of their own. Holladay, W. C.   **704**

MUSEUMS
Museums of the World   **069**

MUSEUMS -- CURATORSHIP
Obrist Ways of curating   **707.5**

MUSEUMS -- HISTORY
Conniff, R. House of Lost Worlds   **069**

MUSEUMS -- HISTORY -- PENNSYLVANIA
Aptowicz, C. O. Dr. Mütter's Marvels   **92**

MUSEUMS AND SCHOOLS
     See also Museums; Schools

Museums of the World.   **069**

Musgrave, Toby
(jt. auth) Cox, M. The Gardener's Garden   **712**

Mushet, Cindy
The art and soul of baking   **641.8**

The **mushroom** hunter's field guide. Smith, A. H.   **579.6**

MUSHROOMS
McKnight, K. H. A field guide to mushrooms, North America   **579.6**
Russell, S. The essential guide to cultivating mushrooms   **635**
Smith, A. H. The mushroom hunter's field guide   **579.6**
Turner, N. J. The North American guide to common poisonous plants and mushrooms   **581.6**

MUSHROOMS
     See also Plants

Music.   **780.9**

MUSIC
     See also Humanities

MUSIC
Bourne, J. The Oxford Dictionary of Music   **780.3**
The complete classical music guide   **780**
The Harvard concise dictionary of music and musicians   **780**
Mithen, S. J. The singing neanderthals   **780.9**

MUSIC -- BIBLIOGRAPHY
A basic music library   **016**

MUSIC -- BIO-BIBLIOGRAPHY
The Harvard biographical dictionary of music   **780**
The Harvard concise dictionary of music and musicians   **780**
Musicians & composers of the 20th century **920.003**
The New Grove dictionary of music and musicians   **780**
The Norton/Grove dictionary of women composers   **780.92**
The Oxford companion to music   **780**

MUSIC -- COMPOSITION See Composition (Music)

MUSIC -- COMPUTER PROGRAMS
Milner, G. Perfecting sound forever   **781.49**

MUSIC -- CRITICISM See Music -- History and criticism

MUSIC -- DICTIONARIES
Bourne, J. The Oxford Dictionary of Music   **780.3**

MUSIC -- DISCOGRAPHY
All music guide to classical music   **016**

MUSIC -- HISTORY AND CRITICISM
Bostridge, I. Schubert's winter journey   **782.4**
Forney, K. The enjoyment of music   **780**
Hopper, J. The first collection of criticism by a living female rock critic
Music   **780.9**
Norton Anthology of Western Music   **780**
Palisca, C. V. A history of Western music   **780.9**
Wilkinson, P. The history of music in fifty instruments   **784.19**

MUSIC -- HUMOR
     See also Wit and humor

MUSIC -- INSTRUCTION AND STUDY See Music -- Study and teaching

MUSIC -- INSTRUCTION AND STUDY -- UNITED STATES
Brown, A. Let's start the music   **027.62**
Tunstall, T. Changing lives   **780.7**

MUSIC -- INSTRUCTION AND STUDY -- VENEZUELA
Tunstall, T. Changing lives   **780.7**

MUSIC -- INSTRUCTION AND STUDY -- WEST BANK
Tolan, S. Children of the stone   **780**

MUSIC -- INTERNET RESOURCES
Kot, G. Ripped   **780.2**

MUSIC -- METHODS
     See also Music -- Study and teaching

MUSIC -- NEW ORLEANS (LA.)
Spera, K. Groove interrupted   **920**

MUSIC -- NEW YORK (N.Y.)
Hermes, W. Love goes to buildings on fire   **781.64**

MUSIC -- POLITICAL ASPECTS
Sachs, H. The Ninth   **785**

MUSIC -- PSYCHOLOGICAL ASPECTS
Mannes, E. The power of music   **781**

MUSIC -- PSYCHOLOGICAL ASPECTS
     See also Psychology

MUSIC -- PUBLISHING
2015 songwriter's market   **338.4**

MUSIC -- PUBLISHING
     See also Publishers and publishing

MUSIC -- SOCIAL ASPECTS
Forney, K. The enjoyment of music   **780**

MUSIC -- STUDY AND TEACHING
Brown, A. Let's start the music   **027.62**
Tolan, S. Children of the stone   **780**
Tunstall, T. Changing lives   **780.7**

MUSIC -- THERAPEUTIC USE See Music therapy

MUSIC -- UNITED STATES -- HISTORY AND CRITICISM

Crawford, R. America's musical life 780.9

Horowitz, J. Classical music in America 781.6

Suisman, D. Selling sounds 338.4

Walker-Hill, H. From spirituals to symphonies 780

MUSIC ADMINISTRATORS

Volpe, J. The toughest show on earth 92

MUSIC AND LITERATURE

See also Literature; Music

MUSIC AND SCIENCE

Mannes, E. The power of music 781

MUSIC APPRECIATION

Forney, K. The enjoyment of music 780

Moody, R. On celestial music 780.9

Norton Anthology of Western Music 780

Siblin, E. The cello suites 787.3

Stanley, B. Yeah! Yeah! Yeah! 781.64

Steinberg, M. The symphony 784.2

MUSIC APPRECIATION

See also Music -- Study and teaching

MUSIC ARRANGERS

Brown, M. Tearing down the wall of sound 92

Jones, Q. Q: the autobiography of Quincy Jones 92

MUSIC COLLECTIONS

Norton Anthology of Western Music 780

MUSIC CONDUCTORS See Conductors (Music)

MUSIC CRITICS

Avery, K. Everything is an afterthought 92

German, B. Under their thumb 781.66

MUSIC EDUCATION See Music -- Study and teaching

MUSIC FESTIVALS

See also Festivals

MUSIC FESTIVALS -- RHODE ISLAND -- NEWPORT

Wald, E. Dylan Goes Electric! 781.66

Music for chameleons. Capote, T. 818

MUSIC HISTORIANS

Gates, H. L. Thirteen ways of looking at a black man 920.71

Music in American life [series]

Goins, W. E. Blues all day long 92

Josephson, B. Cafe Society 792.7

Wade, S. The beautiful music all around us 781.62

MUSIC INDUSTRY

Bradley, A. House of hits 781.64

Broven, J. Record makers and breakers 781.64

Calamar, G. Record store days 780.2

Charnas, D. The big payback 781.64

The Encyclopedia of Country Music 781.64

Greenburg, Z. O. Michael Jackson, Inc 92

Houghton, M. Becoming Elektra 781.64

Knopper, S. Appetite for self-destruction 384

Kot, G. Ripped 780.2

O'Dell, C. Miss O'Dell 92

Scott-Heron, G. The last holiday 920

Seabrook, J. The song machine 781.64

Suisman, D. Selling sounds 338.4

MUSIC INDUSTRY -- VOCATIONAL GUIDANCE

Cutler, D. The savvy musician 780.2

MUSIC LIBRARIES -- COLLECTION DEVELOPMENT

A basic music library 016

Music of a distant drum. 808.81

The music of Gershwin. Gilbert, S. E. 780

MUSIC PUBLISHERS

Robertson, D. W.C. Handy 92

MUSIC TEACHERS

Ellison, R. The collected essays of Ralph Ellison 814

MUSIC THERAPY

Lopez, S. The soloist 92

MUSIC THERAPY

See also Therapeutics

MUSIC TRADE

Elberse, A. Blockbusters 384

MUSIC TRADE -- UNITED STATES

Suisman, D. Selling sounds 338.4

MUSIC, CHORAL See Choral music

Music, Debra

Theo Chocolate 641.6

MUSICAL ANALYSIS

Norton Anthology of Western Music 780

MUSICAL CRITICISM

Ross, A. Listen to this 780

The musical instrument desk reference. Pagliaro, M. 784.192

MUSICAL INSTRUMENTS

The complete classical music guide 780

Pagliaro, M. The musical instrument desk reference 784.192

Piston, W. Orchestration 784

Wilkinson, P. The history of music in fifty instruments 784.19

MUSICAL INSTRUMENTS -- MAINTENANCE AND REPAIR -- HISTORY -- 20TH CENTURY

Grymes, J. A. Violins of hope 92

MUSICAL INSTRUMENTS -- PICTORIAL WORKS

Roden, S. . . . i listen to the wind that obliterates my traces 781.64

Musical lives [series]

Mercer-Taylor, P. J. The life of Mendelssohn 92

MUSICAL NOTATION

See also Music

MUSICAL PERCEPTION

Milner, G. Perfecting sound forever 781.49

MUSICAL REVUES, COMEDIES, ETC. See Musicals

MUSICAL THEATER -- HISTORY

Sondheim, S. Finishing the hat 92

MUSICAL THERAPY *See* Music therapy

MUSICALS
- Bloom, K. Broadway musicals **792.6**
- Mordden, E. Anything goes **782.1**
- Riedel, M. Razzle Dazzle **792.09**
- Sondheim, S. Finishing the hat **92**
- Sondheim, S. Look, I made a hat **782.1**
- Stempel, L. Showtime **792.6**

MUSICALS
> *See also* Theater

MUSICALS -- DICTIONARIES
- Hischak, T. The Oxford companion to the American musical **792.6**

MUSICALS -- NEW YORK (N.Y.)
- Stempel, L. Showtime **792.6**

MUSICALS -- PRODUCTION AND DIRECTION
- Boland, R. Musicals! **792.6**

MUSICALS -- UNITED STATES
- Lane, S. F. Black Broadway **792**
- Maslon, L. Broadway **792.6**

MUSICALS -- UNITED STATES -- HISTORY AND CRITICISM
- Mordden, E. Anything goes **782.1**
- Viertel, J. The secret life of the American musical **792.6**

Musicals! Boland, R. **792.6**

MUSICALS--EXCERPTS--LIBRETTOS.
- Sondheim, S. Look, I made a hat **782.1**

MUSICIANS
- Bernstein, B. Leonard Bernstein **92**
- Blanning, T. C. W. The triumph of music **780.9**
- Fogerty, J. Fortunate son **92**
- Grandmaster Flash The adventures of Grandmaster Flash **92**
- Greenman, B. Mo' meta blues **92**
- James, C. Cultural amnesia **920**
- Louvin, C. Satan is real **920**
- Schonberg, H. C. The great pianists **920**
- Spera, K. Groove interrupted **920**
- Starr, R. Photograph **782.4**
- Strouse, C. Put on a happy face **92**
- Terkel, S. And they all sang **780.9**
- Thomson, G. George Harrison **92**

MUSICIANS
> *See also* Music

Musicians & composers of the 20th century. **920.003**

MUSICIANS -- BIOGRAPHY
- Costello, E. Unfaithful Music & Disappearing Ink **92**
- Feynman **92**
- Glass, P. Words Without Music **92**

MUSICIANS -- BIOGRAPHY
> *See also* Biography

MUSICIANS -- DICTIONARIES
- Musicians & composers of the 20th century **920.003**

- Otfinoski, S. Latinos in the arts **920.003**
- The Oxford companion to music **780**

MUSICIANS -- UNITED STATES
- Bell, I. Once upon a time **92**
- Brown, D. Bob Dylan **92**
- Greenburg, Z. O. Michael Jackson, Inc **92**
- Hilburn, R. Johnny Cash **92**
- McBride, J. Kill 'em and leave **92**
- Shawn, A. Leonard Bernstein **92**

Musicians in Their Own Words [series]
- Leonard Cohen on Leonard Cohen **92**

MUSICIANS, BLACK *See* Black musicians

MUSICIANS, BLACK -- UNITED STATES -- BIOGRAPHY
- Smith, J. E. Becoming Belafonte **92**

MUSICOLOGISTS
- Szwed, J. F. Alan Lomax **92**

MUSICOLOGY
> *See also* Research

MUSLIM ART *See* Islamic art

MUSLIM CIVILIZATION *See* Islamic civilization

MUSLIM CONVERTS -- BIOGRAPHY
- Power, C. If the oceans were ink **297**

MUSLIM MEN -- UNITED STATES -- BIOGRAPHY
- All-American **297.092**

MUSLIM WOMEN
- Baker, D. The convert **92**
- Hikayati sharhun yatul./English The locust and the bird **92**
- Hirsi Ali, A. Infidel **92**
- Scroggins, D. Wanted women **305.48**

MUSLIM WOMEN
> *See also* Muslims; Women

MUSLIM WOMEN -- POLITICAL ACTIVITY
- Scroggins, D. Wanted women **305.48**

MUSLIM WOMEN -- SOCIAL CONDITIONS
- Scroggins, D. Wanted women **305.48**

MUSLIMS
- Cliff, N. Holy war **909**
- Curtis, E. E. Muslims in America **305.8**
- Eteraz, A. Children of dust **92**
- Glassé, C. The new encyclopedia of Islam **297**
- Shapiro, S. The Bosnia list **92**

MUSLIMS -- HISTORY
- Cobb, P. M. The race for paradise **909.07**

MUSLIMS -- MALAYSIA -- BIOGRAPHY
- Nasr, A. A. My Isl@m **297.09**

MUSLIMS -- MEDITERRANEAN REGION -- HISTORY -- TO 15000
- Cobb, P. M. The race for paradise **909.07**

MUSLIMS -- RITES AND CEREMONIES *See* Islam -- Customs and practices

MUSLIMS -- UNITED STATES
- Abdul Rauf, F. Moving the mountain **297.09**

All-American **297.092**

MUSLIMS -- UNITED STATES -- HISTORY
Curtis, E. E.   Muslims in America   **305.8**
Muslims in America. Curtis, E. E.   **305.8**
Musser, George
Spooky action at a distance   **530.11**
Mussolini. Bosworth, R. J. B.   **945.091**
Mussolini's Italy. Bosworth, R. J. B.   **945**
Mussolini, Benito, 1883-1945
About
Bosworth, R. J. B. Mussolini   **945.091**
Bosworth, R. J. B. Mussolini's Italy   **945**
Kertzer, D. I. The Pope and Mussolini   **322**
Must you go? Fraser, A.   **92**
MUTATION (BIOLOGY) See Evolution; Variation (Biology)
Mutch, Maria
About
Mutch, M. Know the night   **92**
MUTINEERS
Alexander, C. The Bounty: the true story of the mutiny on the Bounty   **996**
MUTTER MUSEUM
Aptowicz, C. O. Dr. Mütter's Marvels   **92**
Mutter, Thomas D. (Thomas Dent), 1811-1859
About
Aptowicz, C. O. Dr. Mütter's Marvels   **92**
MUTUAL FUNDS
Bogle, J. C. The clash of the cultures   **332.6**
MUTUAL FUNDS
See also Investments
MUTUAL SUPPORT GROUPS See Self-help groups
MUTUALISM (BIOLOGY) See Symbiosis
My (part-time) Paris life. Anselmo, L.   **944.361**
My age of anxiety. Stossel, S.   **616.85**
My American century. Terkel, S.   **920**
My American journey. Powell, C. L.   **92**
My appeal to the world. Tenzin Gyatso, D. L. X.   **951**
My Backyard Jungle. Barilla, J.   **577.5**
My battle of Algiers. Morgan, T.   **965**
My beloved world. Sotomayor, S.   **92**
My bondage and my freedom. Douglass, F.   **92**
My boyfriend barfed in my handbag ... and other things you can't ask Martha. Kerr, J.   **648**
My brief history. Hawking, S.   **92**
My brother's book. Sendak, M.   **811**
My dearest friend. Adams, J.   **92**
My dyslexia. Schultz, P.   **92**
My face is black is true. Berry, M. F.   **92**
My family table. Besh, J.   **641.59**
My father at 100. Reagan, R.   **92**
My father is a book. Smith, J. M.   **92**
My father's paradise. Sabar, A.   **305.8**
My father's people. Rubin, L. D.   **920**
My fellow citizens.   **352.23**

My fight / your fight. Rousey, R.   **92**
My first coup d'etat and other true stories from the lost decades of Africa. Mahama, J. D.   **966.705**
My fluorescent God. Guppy, J.   **92**
My French family table. Peltre, B.   **641.5**
My friend Dahmer.   **741.5**
My generation. Styron, W.   **814**
My German question. Gay, P.   **943**
My grandfather would have shot me.   **929.2**
My Guantanamo diary. Khan, M. R.   **909.83**
My halal kitchen. Maffei, Y.   **641.595**
My happiness bears no relation to happiness. Hoffman, A.   **92**
My invented country. Allende, I.   **863**
My Isl@m. Nasr, A. A.   **297.09**
My kitchen year. Reichl, R.   **641.5**
My Korean deli. Howe, B. R.   **92**
My life. Duncan, I.   **92**
My life. Clinton, B.   **92**
My life as author and editor.   **818**
My life in France. Child, J.   **92**
My life in Middlemarch. Mead, R.   **823**
My life in politics. Chirac, J.   **944.084**
My life on the road. Steinem, G.   **92**
My life with Pablo Neruda. Urrutia, M.   **92**
My life with the saints. Martin, J.   **920**
My lives. White, E.   **813**
My losing season. Conroy, P.   **796.323**
My Lunches With Orson.   **791.43**
My mother/my self. Friday, N.   **155.6**
My name on his tongue. Halaby, L.   **811**
My New Orleans. Besh, J.   **641.59**
My new roots. Britton, S.   **641.3**
My nuclear family. Brownfield, C. J.   **92**
My organic life. Pouillon, N.   **92**
My pantry.   **641.594**
My Paris kitchen.   **641.59**
My perfect pantry.   **641.5**
My poets. McLane, M. N.   **811**
My prison, my home. Esfandiari, H.   **92**
My promised land. Shavit, A.   **956.05**
My Salinger year. Smith Rakoff, J.   **92**
My sister, guard your veil; my brother guard, your eyes. Azam Zanganeh, L.   **305**
My song. Belafonte, H.   **92**
My start-up life. Casnocha, B.   **338.7**
My stroke of insight. Taylor, J. B.   **362.19**
My sweet Mexico. Gerson, F.   **641.5**
My Tibet. Bstan-'dzin-rgya-mtsho, D. L. X.   **951**
My Times in black and white. Boyd, G. M.   **92**
My Venice and Other Essays. Leon, D.   **945**
My vocabulary did this to me. Spicer, J.   **811**
My war. Rooney, A. A.   **940.54**
My year of flops. Rabin, N.   **791.43**
My year of running dangerously. Foreman, T.   **92**
MYANMAR

Duguid, N. Burma **641.59**

MYANMAR -- DESCRIPTION AND TRAVEL

Thant Myint-U Where China meets India **959.1**

MYANMAR -- POLITICS AND GOVERNMENT

Aung San Suu Kyi Freedom from fear, and other writings **959.1**

Wintle, J. Perfect hostage **92**

MYCOLOGY See Fungi

Myer, Valerie Grosvenor

(ed) The Continuum encyclopedia of British literature **810**

Myers, Allen C.

(ed) Eerdmans dictionary of the Bible **220.3**

Myers, Amy

The autoimmune solution **616.97**

Myers, Gary

Brady vs Manning **92**

Myers, Isabel Briggs

Gifts differing **155.2**

Myers, Marc

Why jazz happened **781.65**

Myers, Peter B.

Myers, I. B. Gifts differing **155.2**

Myerson, Joel

(ed) Transcendentalism **810**

Myne. Presley, F. **821**

Myrdal, Gunnar, 1898-1987

About

Ellison, R. The collected essays of Ralph Ellison **814**

Myrna Loy. Leider, E. W. **92**

Myron, Vicki

Dewey **636.8**

Myself with others. Fuentes, C. **864**

MYSPACE (WEB SITE)

Angwin, J. Stealing MySpace **338.7**

MYSPACE (WEB SITE)

See also Social networking; Web sites

MYSTERIES See Mysteries and miracle plays; Mystery and detective plays; Mystery fiction; Mystery films; Mystery radio programs; Mystery television programs

MYSTERIES AND MIRACLE PLAYS

Everyman, and medieval miracle plays **822**

MYSTERIES AND MIRACLE PLAYS

See also Bible plays; English drama; Pageants; Religious drama; Theater

Mysteries of the mall. Rybczynski, W. **720**

MYSTERIOUS DEATHS

Eichar, D. Dead Mountain **914.7**

Mystery and suspense writers. **809**

MYSTERY COMIC BOOKS, STRIPS, ETC.

See also Comic books, strips, etc.

MYSTERY FICTION

See also Fiction

MYSTERY FICTION -- BIBLIOGRAPHY

Bleiler, R. Reference and research guide to mystery and detective fiction **016**

Charles, J. A. The mystery readers' advisory **025.2**

Niebuhr, G. W. Make mine a mystery **809**

Trott, B. Read on . . . crime fiction **016**

MYSTERY FICTION -- DICTIONARIES

Mystery and suspense writers **809**

MYSTERY FICTION -- HISTORY AND CRITICISM

Critical survey of mystery and detective fiction **809**

James, P. D. Talking about detective fiction **823**

Niebuhr, G. W. Make mine a mystery **809**

Symons, J. Bloody murder **809**

MYSTERY FICTION -- TECHNIQUE

Roberts, G. You can write a mystery **808.3**

Wheat, C. How to write killer fiction **808.3**

MYSTERY FILMS

Film noir **791.43**

MYSTERY FILMS

See also Motion pictures

MYSTERY GRAPHIC NOVELS

Geary, R. The Lindbergh child **364.1**

MYSTERY GRAPHIC NOVELS

See also Graphic novels

The **mystery** of capital. Soto, H. d. **330.12**

The **mystery** of the hidden driveway. Knox, J. L. **811**

MYSTERY PLAYS See Mysteries and miracle plays; Mystery and detective plays

The **mystery** readers' advisory. Charles, J. A. **025.2**

MYSTERY STORIES See Mystery fiction

MYSTERY TELEVISION PROGRAMS

See also Television programs

MYSTERY WRITERS

Barr, N. Seeking enlightenment--hat by hat **92**

Dirda, M. On Conan Doyle; or, The whole art of storytelling **823**

Doyle, A. C. Arthur Conan Doyle **92**

Hillerman, T. Seldom disappointed **813**

Hiney, T. Raymond Chandler **813**

James, P. D. Time to be in earnest **823**

Life stories **920**

Rehak, M. Girl sleuth **813**

Sallis, J. Chester Himes **813**

Schenkar, J. The talented Miss Highsmith **92**

MYSTICAL THEOLOGY See Mysticism

MYSTICISM

Armstrong, K. Visions of God **248.2**

Downing, D. C. Into the region of awe **248.2**

James, W. The varieties of religious experience **210**

Schmidt, L. E. Heaven's bride **92**

MYSTICS

Armstrong, K. Visions of God **248.2**

Castaneda, C. The teachings of Don Juan **299.7**

The **myth** and mystery of UFOs. Bullard, T. E. **001.9**

The **myth** of monogamy. Barash, D. P. **306.7**

The **myth** of Sisyphus, and other essays. Camus, A.   **844**

The **myth** of the Great War. Mosier, J.   **940.4**

The **myth** of the rational market. Fox, J.   **332.6**

Mythematics. Huber, M. R.   **510**

MYTHICAL ANIMALS

  Prothero, D. R. Abominable science!   **001.944**

MYTHICAL ANIMALS

  See also Mythology

MYTHOLOGY

  Armstrong, K. A short history of myth   **398.2**

  Bulfinch, T. Bulfinch's mythology   **398.2**

  Campbell, J. Occidental mythology   **201**

  Campbell, J. The power of myth   **201**

  Campbell, J. Primitive mythology   **201**

  Leeming, D. A. The Oxford companion to world mythology   **201**

MYTHOLOGY -- DICTIONARIES

  Leeming, D. A. The Oxford companion to world mythology   **201**

  Rockwood, C. Brewer's dictionary of phrase & fable   **803**

MYTHOLOGY IN LITERATURE

  Campbell, J. Creative mythology   **201**

Mytting, Lars, 1968-

  Norwegian wood   **634.9**

N

N.C. Wyeth. Michaelis, D.   **92**

Nabhan, Gary Paul, 1952-

  Cumin, camels, and caravans   **382**

Nabokov, Peter

  How the World Moves   **970.3**

  (ed) Native American testimony   **970.004**

  Where the lightning strikes   **299.7**

Nabokov, Vladimir Vladimirovich

  Lectures on literature   **808.3**

  Lectures on Russian literature   **891.7**

  Speak, memory   **813**

      About

  Boyd, B. Vladimir Nabokov: the American years   **813**

  Boyd, B. Vladimir Nabokov: the Russian years   **813**

  Nabokov, V. V. Speak, memory   **813**

  Pitzer, A. The Secret History of Vladimir Nabokov   **891.73**

Nack, William

  Secretariat   **798.4**

Nadeau, Jean-Benoît

  (jt. auth) Barlow, J. The story of Spanish   **460**

  The story of French   **440**

Nadel, Dan

  Art in time   **741.5**

Nadel, Ira Bruce

  Critical companion to Philip Roth   **813**

Nadelberg, Amanda

  Bright brave phenomena   **811**

Nader, Ralph

  Told you so   **303.3**

Nadis, Steve

  The shape of inner space   **530.1**

Nadkarni, Nalini

  Between earth and sky   **582.16**

Nadler, Steven M.

  The best of all possible worlds   **190**

Naef, Weston J.

  Watkins, C. E. Carleton Watkins: the complete mammoth photographs   **778.9**

Nafisi, Azar

      About

  Nafisi, A. Reading Lolita in Tehran   **92**

  Nafisi, A. The Republic of Imagination   **819**

  Nafisi, A. Things I've been silent about   **92**

Naftali, Timothy J.

  Fursenko, A. V. One hell of a gamble   **973.922**

NAGASAKI (JAPAN) -- BOMBARDMENT, 1945

  Ham, P. Hiroshima Nagasaki   **940.54**

Nagel, Paul C.

  John Quincy Adams   **92**

Nagel, Vanessa Gardner

  Understanding garden design   **712**

Nagelschneider, Mieshelle

  The cat whisperer   **636.8**

Nagle, Robin

  Picking up   **331.7**

Nagorski, Andrew

  The Nazi hunters   **940.53**

Nagoski, Emily

  Come as you are   **613.9**

Nagy, John A.

  George Washington's secret spy war   **973.385**

Naidoo, Jamie Campbell

  Rainbow family collections   **028.1**

Naifeh, Steven

  Van Gogh   **92**

Naím, Moisés, 1952-

  The end of power   **303.3**

Naipaul, V. S. (Vidiadhar Surajprasad), 1932-

      About

  French, P. The world is what it is   **92**

  Naipaul, V. S. Between father and son   **823**

  Naipaul, V. S. Reading & writing   **92**

Naish, Darren

  (jt. auth) Barrett, P. Dinosaurs   **567.9**

NAKAI-NAM THEUN NATIONAL BIODIVER-SITY CONSERVATION AREA (LAOS)

  DeBuys, W. The last unicorn   **591.68**

The **naked** cookbook.   **641.302**

Naked in the marketplace. Eisler, B.   **92**

The **naked** mountaineer. Sieberson, S.   **92**

Naked statistics. Wheelan, C.   **519.5**

Nalebuff, Barry, 1958-

Mission in a bottle **338.7**

The **name** of war. Lepore, J. **973.2**

Name-dropping. Galbraith, J. K. **973.9**

NAMES

Yoon, C. K. Naming nature **570.1**

NAMES -- DICTIONARIES

Latham, E. A dictionary of names, nicknames, and surnames of persons, places, and things **929.4**

NAMES, PERSONAL See Personal names

NAMIBIA -- DESCRIPTION AND TRAVEL

Theroux, P. Last train to Zona Verde **916**

Naming nature. Yoon, C. K. **570.1**

NANCY (FICTITIOUS CHARACTER)

Brainard, J. The Nancy book **759**

The **Nancy** book. Brainard, J. **759**

NANJING (JIANGSU PROVINCE, CHINA) MASSACRE, 1937

Chang, I. The rape of Nanking **951.04**

NANJING HANG KONG HANG TIAN DA XUE -- BIOGRAPHY

Ping Fu Bend, not break **92**

NANNIES

Corrigan, K. Glitter and Glue **92**

Lamb, C. House of stone **968.91**

NANNIES

See also Child care

NANNIES -- EMPLOYMENT -- UNITED STATES

Gold, T. Secrets of the nanny whisperer **649**

NANOTECHNOLOGY

Kurzweil, R. The singularity is near **153.9**

McCray, W. P. The visioneers **509**

NANOTECHNOLOGY

See also Technology

Naoki Higashida

The reason I jump **92**

Napalm & silly putty. Carlin, G. **817**

NAPLES (ITALY)

Taylor, B. Naples declared **945**

NAPLES (ITALY) -- DESCRIPTION AND TRAVEL

Hazzard, S. The ancient shore **945**

Taylor, B. Naples declared **945**

NAPLES (ITALY) -- SOCIAL LIFE AND CUS-TOMS

Taylor, B. Naples declared **945**

Wilson, K. Only in Naples **945.731**

Naples declared. Taylor, B. **945**

Napoleon. Broers, M. **92**

Napoleon. Johnson, P. **944.05**

Napoleon. Roberts, A. **92**

Napoleon and the Hundred Days. Coote, S. **940.2**

Napoleon Bonaparte. Schom, A. **92**

Napoleon I, Emperor of the French, 1769-1821
About

Cerami, C. A. Jefferson's great gamble **973.4**

Coote, S. Napoleon and the Hundred Days **940.2**

Esdaile, C. J. Napoleon's wars **940.2**

Gueniffey, P. Bonaparte **92**

Johnson, P. Napoleon **944.05**

Kissinger, H. Diplomacy **327.2**

Lieven, D. C. B. Russia against Napoleon **940.2**

Pocock, T. The terror before Trafalgar **940.2**

Roberts, A. Napoleon **92**

Schom, A. Napoleon Bonaparte **92**

Schom, A. One hundred days **944.05**

Strathern, P. Napoleon in Egypt **962**

Talty, S. The illustrious dead **940.2**

Williams, K. Ambition and desire **92**

Napoleon in Egypt. Strathern, P. **962**

Napoleon's wars. Esdaile, C. J. **940.2**

NAPOLEONIC WARS, 1800-1815

Esdaile, C. J. Napoleon's wars **940.2**

Roberts, A. Napoleon **92**

NAPOLEONIC WARS, 1800-1815

See also Europe -- History -- 1789-1815; France -- History -- 1799-1815

NAPOLEONIC WARS, 1800-1815 -- CAM-PAIGNS -- RUSSIA

Lieven, D. C. B. Russia against Napoleon **940.2**

Napoli, Lisa

Radio Shangri-La **954.9**

Napoli, Philip F.

Bringing it all back home **959.704**

NAPS (SLEEP)

Kennedy, J. K. The good sleeper **649**

Naranjo, Ralph

The Art of Seamanship **623.8**

Narayan, R. K.

The Ramayana **891**

NARCISSISM

Kluger, J. The Narcissist Next Door **616.85**

McBride, K. Will I ever be good enough? **616.85**

NARCISSISM

See also Neuroses; Personality disorders

The **Narcissist** Next Door. Kluger, J. **616.85**

NARCOTICS

Quinones, S. Dreamland **362.29**

NARCOTICS

See also Drugs; Materia medica; Psychotro-pic drugs

NARCOTICS -- UNITED STATES

Quinones, S. Dreamland **362.29**

NARCOTICS AND CRIME See Drugs and crime

NARCOTICS DEALERS

Schou, N. Orange sunshine **363.45**

NARNIA (IMAGINARY PLACE)

See also Imaginary places

NARRATION (RHETORIC) -- PSYCHOLOGI-CAL ASPECTS

Solnit, R. The Faraway Nearby **814**

NARRATIONS See Monologues; Recitations

Narrative of the life of Frederick Douglass, an American slave. Douglass, F.   **92**

NARRATIVE POETRY
Halaby, L. My name on his tongue   **811**

NARRATIVE POETRY
   See also Poetry

Narrowing the nation's power: the Supreme Court sides with the states. Noonan, J. T.   **342**

Narth, Angela
Aykroyd, P. A history of ghosts   **133.1**

Narváez, Pánfilo de, d. 1528
        About
Schneider, P. Brutal journey: the epic story of the first crossing of North America   **970.01**

NASA OFFICIALS
Biddle, W. Dark side of the moon   **92**
Neufeld, M. J. Von Braun   **92**

Nasaw, David
Andrew Carnegie   **92**
The chief: the life of William Randolph Hearst **070.5**
The patriarch   **92**

Nash, Diane, 1938-
        About
Halberstam, D. The children   **323.1**

Nash, Gary B.
(ed) Encyclopedia of American history   **973**

Nash, Jay Robert
The great pictorial history of world crime   **364**

Nash, Ogden, 1902-1971
        About
Parker, D. M. Ogden Nash   **92**

NASHVILLE (TENN.)
Davis, T. C. The hot chicken cookbook   **641.7**

NASIELSK (POLAND) -- BIOGRAPHY
Kurtz, G. Three minutes in Poland   **947.7**

Naskrecki, Piotr
The smaller majority   **591.7**

Nasr, Amir Ahmad
        About
Nasr, A. A. My Isl@m   **297.09**

Nasr, Seyyed Hossein
Islam: religion, history, and civilization   **297**

Nasr, Vali
The dispensable nation   **327.73**
The Shia revival   **297**

Nat King Cole. Epstein, D. M.   **92**

The Nathan I. Huggins lectures [series]
Berlin, I. The long emancipation   **326.8**

Nathan the Wise, Minna von Barnhelm, and other plays and writings. Lessing, G. E.   **832**

NATHAN'S FAMOUS
Handwerker, L. Famous Nathan   **92**

Nathan, Debbie
Sybil exposed   **616.85**

Nathan, Joan
Jewish cooking in America   **641.5**

Quiches, kugels, and couscous   **641.5**

Nathan, Zoe
Breakfast at Huckleberry   **641.5**

Nathans, Sydney
To free a family   **306.3**

Nather, David
The new health care system   **344**

A **nation** of farmers. Astyk, S.   **338.1**

NATION OF ISLAM *See* Black Muslims

A **nation** on fire. Risen, C.   **973.923**

A **nation** under our feet. Hahn, S.   **305.8**

A **Nation** Wholly Free. Lane, C.   **336.3**

A **Nation** Without Borders. Hahn, S.   **973.5**

National Air and Space Museum (U.S.)
Hardesty, V. Black wings   **920**

NATIONAL AIR AND SPACE MUSEUM -- CATALOGS
Milestones of space   **629.4**

NATIONAL ANTHEMS *See* National songs

National anthems of the world.   **782.42**

NATIONAL ASSOCIATION FOR THE ADVANCEMENT OF COLORED PEOPLE
King, G. Devil in the grove   **305.896**
Rowan, C. T. Dream makers, dream breakers   **92**
Sullivan, P. Lift every voice   **323.1**

NATIONAL ASSOCIATION FOR THE ADVANCEMENT OF COLORED PEOPLE -- HISTORY
Sullivan, P. Lift every voice   **323.1**

National Association of the Deaf
(comp) Legal rights   **346.73**

National Audubon Society
Bull, J. L. The National Audubon Society field guide to North American birds, Eastern region **598**
Chesterman, C. W. The Audubon Society field guide to North American rocks and minerals **549**
Folkens, P. A. National Audubon Society guide to marine mammals of the world   **599.5**
Little, E. L. The Audubon Society field guide to North American trees   **582.16**
Ludlum, D. M. The Audubon Society field guide to North American weather   **551.6**
McKnight, K. H. A field guide to mushrooms, North America   **579.6**
Milne, L. J. The Audubon Society field guide to North American insects and spiders   **595.7**
Bird   **598**
Pyle, R. M. The Audubon Society field guide to North American butterflies   **595.7**
Sibley, D. The Sibley guide to bird life & behavior   **598**
Sibley, D. The Sibley guide to birds   **598**
Smith, C. L. National Audubon Society field guide to tropical marine fishes of the Caribbean, the Gulf of Mexico, Florida, the Bahamas, and Bermuda   **597**

Thompson, I. The Audubon Society field guide to North American fossils **560**

Udvardy, M. D. F. National Audubon Society field guide to North American birds, Western region **598**

Whitaker, J. O. National Audubon Society field guide to North American mammals **599**

National Audubon Society field guide series

Thieret, J. W. National Audubon Society field guide to North American wildflowers: eastern region **582.13**

National Audubon Society field guide to fishes, North America. Gilbert, C. R. **597**

The **National** Audubon Society field guide to North American birds, Eastern region. Bull, J. L. **598**

National Audubon Society field guide to North American birds, Western region. Udvardy, M. D. F. **598**

National Audubon Society field guide to North American mammals. Whitaker, J. O. **599**

National Audubon Society field guide to North American wildflowers, western region. Spellenberg, R. **582.13**

National Audubon Society field guide to North American wildflowers: eastern region. Thieret, J. W. **582.13**

National Audubon Society field guide to tropical marine fishes of the Caribbean, the Gulf of Mexico, Florida, the Bahamas, and Bermuda. Smith, C. L. **597**

National Audubon Society guide to marine mammals of the world. Folkens, P. A. **599.5**

NATIONAL BASEBALL HALL OF FAME AND MUSEUM

Stanton, T. Road to Cooperstown **92**

NATIONAL BASKETBALL ASSOCIATION

Abrams, J. Boys among men **796.323**

Glockner, A. Chasing perfection **796.323**

Williams, J. Life is not an accident **92**

NATIONAL BASKETBALL ASSOCIATION

See also Basketball

NATIONAL BASKETBALL ASSOCIATION -- FORECASTING -- STATISTICS

Glockner, A. Chasing perfection **796.323**

NATIONAL BOOK WEEK

See also Books and reading

NATIONAL BROADCASTING COMPANY -- HISTORY

Mitchell, G. The tunnels **943.155**

NATIONAL CHARACTERISTICS

Appy, C. G. American Reckoning **959.704**

NATIONAL CHARACTERISTICS

See also Anthropology; Nationalism; Social psychology

NATIONAL CHARACTERISTICS -- ENCYCLOPEDIAS

Minahan, J. The complete guide to national symbols and emblems **929.9**

NATIONAL CHARACTERISTICS IN LITERATURE

Nafisi, A. The Republic of Imagination **819**

NATIONAL CHARACTERISTICS, AMERICAN

Boorstin, D. J. The image **973.9**

Brokaw, T. A long way from home **070**

Caputo, P. The longest road **973.93**

Commager, H. S. The American mind **973**

Ellis, J. J. American creation **973.3**

Fischer, D. H. Liberty and freedom **323.44**

Marcus, G. The shape of things to come **973**

Menand, L. The Metaphysical Club **973.9**

Noonan, P. A heart, a cross & a flag **973.931**

Prothero, S. The American Bible **973**

Rinella, S. American buffalo **599.64**

Walker, J. The United States of paranoia **973**

Well, F. Family trees **929.2**

White, R. Railroaded **385**

Wood, G. S. Empire of liberty **973.4**

NATIONAL CHARACTERISTICS, AMERICAN

See American national characteristics

NATIONAL CHARACTERISTICS, AMERICAN -- HISTORY

Lepore, J. A is for American **306.44**

McPherson, J. M. The war that forged a nation **973.7**

NATIONAL CHARACTERISTICS, AMERICAN, IN LITERATURE

Parini, J. Promised land **810**

Prothero, S. The American Bible **973**

NATIONAL CHARACTERISTICS, EAST INDIAN

Giridharadas, A. India calling **954.05**

NATIONAL CHARACTERISTICS, MEXICAN, IN LITERATURE

Biron, R. E. Elena Garro and Mexico's modern dreams **868**

NATIONAL COLLEGIATE ATHLETIC ASSOCIATION

Nocera, J. Indentured **796.04**

National Commission on Terrorist Attacks Upon the United States

Jacobson, S. The 9/11 report **741.5**

The 9/11 Commission report **973.931**

NATIONAL CONSCIOUSNESS *See* Nationalism

National electrical code handbook 2014. **621.3**

NATIONAL EMBLEMS

See also Signs and symbols

NATIONAL EMBLEMS -- ENCYCLOPEDIAS

Minahan, J. The complete guide to national symbols and emblems **929.9**

National Fire Protection Association

Fire protection handbook **628.9**

National five digit zip code and post office directory. **383**

NATIONAL FOOTBALL LEAGUE
Dawidoff, N. Collision Low Crossers **796.3**
Fainaru, S. League of Denial **617.1**
Football's greatest stars **796.332**
Izenberg, J. Rozelle **92**
Laskas, J. M. Concussion **617.5**
Myers, G. Brady vs Manning **92**

NATIONAL FOOTBALL LEAGUE
See also Football

NATIONAL FOOTBALL LEAGUE -- HISTORY
Ross, C. K. Mavericks, money, and men **796.332**

National Gallery (Great Britain)
Liedtke, W. A. Vermeer and the Delft school **759.9**

National Gallery of Art. National Gallery of Art (U.S.) **708**

National Gallery of Art (U.S.)
Cikovsky, N. Winslow Homer **759.13**
Dickerman, L. Dada **709.04**
Edouard Vuillard **759**
National Gallery of Art **708**
Stieglitz, A. Alfred Stieglitz: the key set **770**

National geographic (Periodical)
National Geographic Society (U.S.) Through the lens **779**

National Geographic birding essentials. Alderfer, J. **598**

National Geographic complete birds of North America. **598**

National Geographic concise history of the world. **909**

National Geographic concise history of world religions. **200**

National Geographic directions [series]
Erdrich, L. Books and islands in Ojibwe country **92**
Morris, J. A writer's house in Wales **942.9**

National Geographic extreme weather survival guide. Kostigen, T. M. **613.6**

National Geographic eyewitness to the 20th century. National Geographic Society (U.S.) **909.82**

National Geographic guide to America's great houses. Wiencek, H. **728.8**

National Geographic guide to the national parks of the United States. National Geographic Society (U.S.) **917**

National Geographic Guide to the State Parks of the United States. **917.3**

National Geographic Maps (Firm)
Atlas of the World **912**

National geographic rarely seen. Hitchcock, S. T. **779**

National Geographic Society (U.S.)
(comp) Abroad at home **917.3**
(comp) Atlas of the World **912**
(comp) Women of vision **770.82**
(comp) World's best travel experiences **910.4**

Alderfer, J. National Geographic birding essentials **598**
Atlas of the Civil War **973.7**
Ballard, R. D. Return to Midway **940.54**
Chadwick, D. H. The company we keep **333.95**
Hawass, Z. A. Hidden treasures of ancient Egypt **932**
National Geographic complete birds of North America **598**
In focus **779**
National Geographic eyewitness to the 20th century **909.82**
National Geographic guide to the national parks of the United States **917**
National Geographic visual history of the world **902.2**
Through the lens **779**
Schmidt, T. The Lewis & Clark Trail **978**
Wiencek, H. National Geographic guide to America's great houses **728.8**

National Geographic the national parks. Heacox, K. **363.6**

National Geographic visual atlas of the world. **912**

National Geographic visual history of the world. National Geographic Society (U.S.) **902.2**

National Geographic, the photographs. **778**

NATIONAL INSTITUTES OF HEALTH (U.S.)
Varmus, H. The art and politics of science **92**

NATIONAL LAMPOON (PERIODICAL)
Meyerowitz, R. Drunk stoned brilliant dead **051**

NATIONAL LANDMARKS See National monuments

NATIONAL LEAGUE FOR DEMOCRACY (BURMA)
Wintle, J. Perfect hostage **92**

NATIONAL LIBERATION MOVEMENTS
See also Nationalism; Revolutions

NATIONAL MONUMENTS
Khan, Y. S. Enlightening the world **974.7**

NATIONAL MONUMENTS
See also Monuments; National parks and reserves

National Museum of Natural History (U.S.)
Vikings: the North Atlantic saga **970.01**

NATIONAL MUSEUM OF WOMEN IN THE ARTS (U.S.)
Holladay, W. C. A museum of their own **704**

NATIONAL PALACE MUSEUM (TAIPEI, TAIWAN)
Hearn, M. K. Splendors of Imperial China **709**

National park ranger. Farabee, C. R. **363.6**
The **national** parks. Duncan, D. **333.7**

NATIONAL PARKS AND RESERVES -- ALASKA
Heacox, K. Rhythm of the wild **979.8**

NATIONAL PARKS AND RESERVES -- UNIT-

ED STATES

Duncan, D. The national parks **333.7**

Egan, T. The big burn **973.91**

Farabee, C. R. National park ranger **363.6**

National Geographic Society (U.S.) National Geographic guide to the national parks of the United States **917**

The official guide to America's national parks **917**

NATIONAL PARKS AND RESERVES -- UNITED STATES -- HISTORY

Egan, T. The big burn **973.91**

Heacox, K. National Geographic the national parks **363.6**

NATIONAL PATRIMONY *See* Cultural property

NATIONAL PLANNING *See* Economic policy; Social policy

National Priorities Project (Organization)

(comp) Kramer, M. A people's guide to the federal budget **352.4**

NATIONAL PSYCHOLOGY *See* Ethnopsychology; National characteristics

National Public Radio (U.S.)

Hoffman, M. The NPR classical music companion **780**

NATIONAL RESOURCES *See* Economic conditions; Natural resources; United States -- Economic conditions

NATIONAL REVIEW

Brookhiser, R. Right time, right place **92**

NATIONAL SECURITY

Johnson, L. K. National Security Intelligence

NATIONAL SECURITY -- INDIAN OCEAN REGION

Kaplan, R. D. Monsoon **327**

NATIONAL SECURITY -- MORAL AND ETHICAL ASPECTS

Angwin, J. Dragnet nation **323.44**

NATIONAL SECURITY -- UNITED STATES

Cockburn, A. Kill Chain **623.7**

Graff, G. M. The threat matrix **363.325**

Hagedorn, A. The invisible soldiers **355**

Maddow, R. Drift **306.2**

Weiner, T. Enemies **363.25**

NATIONAL SECURITY -- UNITED STATES -- DECISION MAKING

Mazzetti, M. The way of the knife **356**

NATIONAL SECURITY -- UNITED STATES -- HISTORY -- 20TH CENTURY

Thomas, E. Ike's bluff **973.92**

Thompson, N. The hawk and the dove **92**

NATIONAL SECURITY COUNCIL (U.S.) -- BIOGRAPHY

Rice, C. No higher honor **327.73**

National Security Intelligence. Johnson, L. K.

NATIONAL SELF-DETERMINATION

See also Nationalism

NATIONAL SOCIALISM

Aycoberry, P. The social history of the Third Reich **943.086**

Breitman, R. The architect of genocide **92**

Evans, R. J. The coming of the Third Reich **943.08**

Evans, R. J. The Third Reich in power, 1933-1939 **943.086**

Fest, J. C. Speer: the final verdict **92**

Fischer, K. P. Nazi Germany **943.086**

Fisher, M. A terrible splendor **796.342**

Fritzsche, P. Life and death in the Third Reich **943.086**

Fulbrook, M. A concise history of Germany **943**

Gay, P. My German question **943**

Goldhagen, D. Hitler's willing executioners **940.53**

Hitler, A. Mein Kampf **92**

Kershaw, I. Hitler, 1936-1945: nemesis **943.086**

Kinney, D. The devil's diary **940.53**

Lewy, G. The Nazi persecution of the gypsies **940.53**

Mazower, M. Hitler's empire **940.53**

Nelson, A. Red Orchestra **943.086**

Petropoulos, J. The Faustian bargain **709**

Roberts, G. Stalin's general **940.54**

Rosenbaum, R. Explaining Hitler **943.086**

Sereny, G. Albert Speer **92**

Tubach, F. C. German voices **943.086**

Turner, H. A. Hitler's thirty days to power **943.086**

Urwand, B. The collaboration **791.43**

NATIONAL SOCIALISM

Weale, A. Army of evil **940.54**

NATIONAL SOCIALISM

See also Fascism; World War, 1939-1945 -- Causes

NATIONAL SOCIALISM -- HISTORY

Goebbels **92**

NATIONAL SOCIALISM -- PHILOSOPHY

Kinney, D. The devil's diary **940.53**

NATIONAL SOCIALISM AND MOTION PICTURES

Urwand, B. The collaboration **791.43**

NATIONAL SOCIALISTS

Jacobsen, A. Operation Paperclip **940.54**

Kinney, D. The devil's diary **940.53**

Lichtblau, E. The Nazis next door **324.1**

My grandfather would have shot me **929.2**

NATIONAL SONGS

National anthems of the world **782.42**

NATIONAL SONGS

See also Songs

NATIONAL SONGS -- UNITED STATES

See also American songs

National Story Project (U.S.)

I thought my father was God and other true tales from the National Story Project **810**

National survey of state laws. **349**

NATIONAL TREASURE *See* Cultural property
National Wildlife Federation
  McKnight, K. H. A field guide to mushrooms,
    North America **579.6**
NATIONAL YIDDISH BOOK CENTER
  Lansky, A. Outwitting history **002.07**
NATIONALISM
  Boland, E. A woman without a country **821**
  The Causes of the Civil War **973.7**
  Evans, M. Algeria **965**
  Said, E. W. Reflections on exile and other es-
    says **814**
NATIONALISM
  See also International relations; Political sci-
    ence
**NATIONALISM -- ARAB COUNTRIES -- HIS-
  TORY**
  Rogan, E. The Arabs **909**
NATIONALISM -- FRANCE
  Brown, F. For the soul of France **944.081**
NATIONALISM -- UNITED STATES
  Marcus, G. The shape of things to come **973**
  Zeskind, L. Blood and politics **305.8**
**NATIONALISM AND LITERATURE -- UNITED
  STATES**
  Prothero, S. The American Bible **973**
NATIONALIST CHINA *See* Taiwan
NATIONALISTS -- ITALY -- BIOGRAPHY
  Hughes-Hallett, L. Gabriele d'Annunzio **858**
**NATIONALSOZIALISTISCHE DEUTSCHE
  ARBEITER-PARTEI. SCHUTZSTAFFEL**
  Weale, A. Army of evil **940.54**
NATIONS
  Acemoglu, D. Why nations fail **330**
NATIONS
  See also Political science
Native America and the question of genocide. Alva-
  rez, A. **973**
Native America in the twentieth century. **970.004**
NATIVE AMERICAN ARCHITECTURE
  See also Architecture
NATIVE AMERICAN ART
  Berlo, J. C. Native North American art **709.01**
  Hassrick, P. H. Art of the American West **709**
  The James T. Bialac Native American Art Collec-
    tion **704.03**
  Russell, K. K. Shapeshifting **704.03**
  Schobinger, J. The ancient Americans **970.01**
  A **Native** American encyclopedia. Pritzker,
    B. **970.004**
**NATIVE AMERICAN LITERATURE -- ENCY-
  CLOPEDIAS**
  Encyclopedia of American Indian literature **810**
**NATIVE AMERICAN LITERATURE -- HISTO-
  RY AND CRITICISM**
  The Cambridge companion to Native American lit-

    erature **897**
NATIVE AMERICAN POLITICAL ACTIVISTS
  Hoxie, F. E. This Indian country **323.1**
NATIVE AMERICAN SIGN LANGUAGE
  See also Sign language
Native American son. Buford, K. **92**
Native American testimony. **970.004**
NATIVE AMERICAN WOMEN
  Sifters: Native American women's lives **920**
NATIVE AMERICAN WOMEN
  See also Women
NATIVE AMERICANS
  Bragdon, K. J. The Columbia guide to American
    Indians of the Northeast **970.004**
  Deloria, V. Custer died for your sins **970.004**
  Dorris, M. The broken cord **362.292**
  Gulbrandsen, D. Edward Sheriff Curtis **770**
  Hogan, L. The woman who watches over the
    world **818**
  Iverson, P. We are still here **970.004**
  Milton, G. Big Chief Elizabeth **970.004**
  Philip, N. The great circle **970.004**
  Reséndez, A. The other slavery **306.3**
  Richter, D. K. Facing east from Indian coun-
    try **970.004**
  Waldman, C. Atlas of the North American Indi-
    an **970.004**
  Weatherford, J. M. Native roots **970.004**
  Wilson, J. The earth shall weep **970.004**
NATIVE AMERICANS -- ANTIQUITIES
  Josephy, A. M. America in 1492 **970.004**
  Schobinger, J. The ancient Americans **970.01**
NATIVE AMERICANS -- ANTIQUITIES
  See also Antiquities
**NATIVE AMERICANS -- ANTIQUITIES -- EN-
  CYCLOPEDIAS**
  Archaeology of prehistoric native America **970.01**
NATIVE AMERICANS -- ART
  Raban, J. Passage to Juneau **979.8**
NATIVE AMERICANS -- BIOGRAPHY
  Black Elk Black Elk speaks **92**
  Buford, K. Native American son **92**
  Crawford, B. All American **92**
  Gulbrandsen, D. Edward Sheriff Curtis **770**
  McMurtry, L. Crazy Horse **92**
NATIVE AMERICANS -- BRAZIL
  Reel, M. The last of the tribe **981**
NATIVE AMERICANS -- CAPTIVITIES
  Demos, J. The unredeemed captive **973.2**
NATIVE AMERICANS -- CAPTIVITIES
  See also Frontier and pioneer life
NATIVE AMERICANS -- CUSTOMS *See* Native
  Americans -- Social life and customs
NATIVE AMERICANS -- DICTIONARIES
  Notable native Americans **920.003**
NATIVE AMERICANS -- ECONOMIC CONDI-

TIONS
See also Economic conditions

NATIVE AMERICANS -- EDUCATION
Beyond the asterisk   378.1

NATIVE AMERICANS -- EDUCATION
See also Education

NATIVE AMERICANS -- ENCYCLOPEDIAS
American Indians   970.004
Encyclopedia of native tribes of North America   970.004
Johnson, M. Encyclopedia of native tribes of North America   970.004
Native America in the twentieth century 970.004
Pritzker, B. A Native American encyclopedia   970.004
Waldman, C. Encyclopedia of Native American tribes   970.004

NATIVE AMERICANS -- FIRST CONTACT WITH EUROPEANS
See also Native Americans -- History

NATIVE AMERICANS -- FOLKLORE
Raban, J. Passage to Juneau   979.8

NATIVE AMERICANS -- FOLKLORE
See also Folklore

NATIVE AMERICANS -- GOVERNMENT RELATIONS
Documents of American Indian diplomacy 970.004
Donovan, J. A terrible glory   973.8
Hendricks, S. The unquiet grave   970.004
Native American testimony   970.004
Osborn, W. M. The wild frontier   970.004
Schultz, E. B. King Philip's War   973.2
Wallace, A. F. C. The long bitter trail 323.1

NATIVE AMERICANS -- GOVERNMENT RELATIONS -- HISTORY
Berg, S. W. 38 nooses   973.7

NATIVE AMERICANS -- GREAT PLAINS
Fowler, L. The Columbia guide to American Indians of the Great Plains   970.004

NATIVE AMERICANS -- HISTORY
Cardozo, C. Edward S. Curtis   770
Egan, T. Short nights of the Shadow Catcher 770.92
Fenn, E. A. Encounters at the heart of the world   305.897
Hoxie, F. E. This Indian country   323.1
The longest trail   970.004
Treuer, A. Everything you wanted to know about Indians but were afraid to ask 909
Wheelan, J. Terrible swift sword   355.009

NATIVE AMERICANS -- HISTORY -- SOURCES
Native American testimony   970.004

NATIVE AMERICANS -- MEXICO -- ENCYCLOPEDIAS
American Indians   970.004

NATIVE AMERICANS -- NORTH AMERICA

Encyclopedia of native tribes of North America   970.004
Russell, K. K. Shapeshifting   704.03
Treuer, A. Atlas of Indian nations   970.004

NATIVE AMERICANS -- NORTHWEST COAST OF NORTH AMERICA
Harmon, A. Indians in the making   970.004

NATIVE AMERICANS -- ORIGIN
Adovasio, J. M. The first Americans   970.01

NATIVE AMERICANS -- PICTORIAL WORKS
Egan, T. Short nights of the Shadow Catcher 770.92
Gulbrandsen, D. Edward Sheriff Curtis   770

NATIVE AMERICANS -- POLITICS AND GOVERNMENT
Hoxie, F. E. This Indian country   323.1

NATIVE AMERICANS -- RELIGION
Nabokov, P. Where the lightning strikes 299.7
Popol vuh Popol vuh   299.7

NATIVE AMERICANS -- RELIGION
See also Religion

NATIVE AMERICANS -- RELOCATION
Enss, C. Mochi's war   978.8
Langguth, A. J. Driven West   973.5

NATIVE AMERICANS -- RITES AND CEREMONIES
See also Rites and ceremonies

NATIVE AMERICANS -- SOCIAL CONDITIONS
Colton, L. Counting coup   796.323

NATIVE AMERICANS -- SOCIAL CONDITIONS
See also Social conditions

NATIVE AMERICANS -- SOCIAL LIFE AND CUSTOMS
Treuer, A. Everything you wanted to know about Indians but were afraid to ask 909

NATIVE AMERICANS -- SOCIAL LIFE AND CUSTOMS
See also Manners and customs

NATIVE AMERICANS -- SOUTHERN STATES
Perdue, T. The Columbia guide to American Indians of the Southeast   970.004

NATIVE AMERICANS -- TRIBAL GOVERNMENT *See* Native Americans -- Politics and government

NATIVE AMERICANS -- UNITED STATES
Alvarez, A. Native America and the question of genocide   973
Dunbar-Ortiz, R. An indigenous peoples' history of the United States   970.004
McDonnell, M. A. Masters of Empire   977.4

NATIVE AMERICANS -- WARS
Berg, S. W. 38 nooses   973.7
Mort, T. Thieves' Road   978.3

NATIVE AMERICANS -- WARS
See also Native Americans -- History

NATIVE AMERICANS -- WARS -- ENCYCLO-PEDIAS
Encyclopedia of Native American wars and warfare   **970.004**

NATIVE AMERICANS -- WASHINGTON (STATE)
Kluger, R.   The bitter waters of Medicine Creek   **979.7**

NATIVE AMERICANS -- WEST (U.S.)
Brown, D. A.   Bury my heart at Wounded Knee   **970.004**
Calloway, C. G.   One vast winter count   **978**

NATIVE AMERICANS -- WEST (U.S.) -- HISTORY
Black, G.   Empire of shadows   **978.7**

NATIVE AMERICANS -- WOMEN See Native American women

NATIVE AMERICANS IN ART
Eisler, B.   The Red Man's Bones   **92**

NATIVE AMERICANS IN LITERATURE -- ENCYCLOPEDIAS
Encyclopedia of American Indian literature   **810**
Native North American art. Berlo, J. C.   **709.01**

NATIVE PEOPLES See Indigenous peoples

NATIVE PEOPLES -- CANADA
See also Canadians
The **Native** peoples of North America. Johansen, B. E.   **970.004**

NATIVE PLANTS
Cullina, W.   Native trees, shrubs & vines   **635.9**

NATIVE PLANTS
See also Plants
Native roots. Weatherford, J. M.   **970.004**
Native trees, shrubs & vines. Cullina, W.   **635.9**

NATIVES See Indigenous peoples

Natkin, Michael
Herbivoracious   **641.5**

Natterson-Horowitz, Barbara
(jt. auth) Bowers, K.   Zoobiquity   **636.089**
Natural beauty. DuPriest, L.   **646.7**

NATURAL BEAUTY CONSERVATION See Landscape protection

Natural Born Heroes. McDougall, C.   **940.53**

NATURAL CHILDBIRTH
Birth without violence   **618.4**
Gaskin, I. M.   Ina May's guide to childbirth   **618.4**

NATURAL CHILDBIRTH
See also Childbirth

NATURAL DISASTERS
De Villiers, M.   The end   **363.34**
McGuire, B.   Waking the giant   **551.5**
The World Is Moving Around Me   **972.94**

NATURAL DISASTERS
See also Disasters

NATURAL DISASTERS -- UNITED STATES
Cross, K.   What Stands in a Storm   **363.34**

Roker, A.   The storm of the century   **976.4**

NATURAL FOOD COOKING See Cooking -- Natural foods

NATURAL FOODS
Barber, D.   The third plate   **641.3**
Helwig, J.   Smoothie-licious   **641.87**
Leake, L.   100 days of real food   **613.2**
The longevity kitchen   **612.6**
McWilliams, J. E.   Just food   **394.1**
Robinson, J.   Eating on the wild side   **306.4**
Sacks, S.   What the fork are you eating?   **641.3**
Weil, A.   The healthy kitchen   **641.5**

NATURAL FOODS
See also Food

NATURAL FOODS -- PROCESSING
Reese, J.   Make the bread, buy the butter   **641.3**

NATURAL FOODS -- RECIPES
The longevity kitchen   **612.6**

NATURAL GARDENING See Organic gardening

NATURAL GAS
Wilber, T.   Under the surface   **333.8**

NATURAL GAS
See also Fuel; Gases

Natural history.   **508**

NATURAL HISTORY
The best American science and nature writing 2012   **810.8**
Conniff, R.   House of Lost Worlds   **069**
Darwin, C.   The voyage of the Beagle   **508**
Fisher, H.   Anatomy of Love   **302.3**
A glorious enterprise   **508**
Gould, S. J.   The flamingo's smile   **500**
Gould, S. J.   The richness of life   **508**
Leslie, C. W.   The Curious Nature Guide   **508**
National Geographic Society (U.S.)   National Geographic eyewitness to the 20th century   **909.82**
Natural history   **508**
Nye, B.   Undeniable   **576.8**
Rudwick, M. J. S.   Earth's deep history   **550**
Shunk, S. A.   Peterson Reference Guide to Woodpeckers of North America   **598.7**
Taylor, P. D.   A history of life in 100 fossils   **560**
Things that are   **508**

NATURAL HISTORY
See also Science

NATURAL HISTORY -- AFRICA
De Villiers, M.   Sahara: a natural history   **508**
Matthiessen, P.   African silences   **916**

NATURAL HISTORY -- ALASKA
Brinkley, D.   The quiet world   **333.72**
Wohlforth, C.   The fate of nature   **304.2**

NATURAL HISTORY -- ALASKA -- DENALI NATIONAL PARK AND PRESERVE
Heacox, K.   Rhythm of the wild   **979.8**

NATURAL HISTORY -- APPALACHIAN REGION, SOUTHERN -- GUIDEBOOKS

Spira, T. P. Waterfalls and wildflowers in the Southern Appalachians **796.51**

NATURAL HISTORY -- CANADA

Mowat, F. High latitudes **971**

NATURAL HISTORY -- HISTORY

Henry, J. A short history of scientific thought **501**

Rudwick, M. J. S. Earth's deep history **550**

NATURAL HISTORY -- MAINE

Shetterly, S. H. Settled in the wild **508**

NATURAL HISTORY -- MEXICO

Gallagher, T. Imperial Dreams **598.7**

NATURAL HISTORY -- MOZAMBIQUE -- PARQUE NACIONAL DA GORONGOSA

A window on eternity **333.95**

NATURAL HISTORY -- NEW JERSEY

What the robin knows **598.8**

NATURAL HISTORY -- NEW YORK (STATE) -- NEW YORK

Steinberg, T. Gotham unbound **508**

NATURAL HISTORY -- NORTH AMERICA

Flannery, T. F. The eternal frontier **508**

Nicholls, S. Paradise found **508**

Weidensaul, S. Return to wild America **578**

NATURAL HISTORY -- PHILOSOPHY -- POPULAR WORKS

Nye, B. Undeniable **576.8**

NATURAL HISTORY -- POLAR REGIONS -- PICTORIAL WORKS

Seaman, C. Melting away **910.91**

NATURAL HISTORY -- RESEARCH -- PENNSYLVANIA -- PHILADELPHIA

A glorious enterprise **508**

NATURAL HISTORY -- STUDY AND TEACHING

Sampson, S. D. How to raise a wild child **508**

NATURAL HISTORY -- TENNESSEE

Haskell, D. G. The forest unseen **577.3**

NATURAL HISTORY -- VIRGINIA

Dillard, A. Pilgrim at Tinker Creek **818**

NATURAL HISTORY -- WYOMING

Proulx, A. Bird cloud **92**

NATURAL HISTORY LITERATURE

Things that are **508**

NATURAL HISTORY MUSEUMS -- UNITED STATES

Lunde, D. The naturalist **973.91**

A **natural** history of love. Ackerman, D. **152.4**

The **natural** history of medicinal plants. Sumner, J. **581.6**

A **natural** history of the piano. Isacoff, S. **786.2**

A **natural** history of the senses. Ackerman, D. **152.1**

A **natural** history of time. Richet, P. **551.7**

The **natural** history of unicorns. Lavers, C. **398.2**

NATURAL LANGUAGE PROCESSING (COMPUTER SCIENCE)

Baker, S. Final Jeopardy **006.3**

NATURAL LAW

See also Ethics; Law

NATURAL MONUMENTS

See also Landscape protection; Monuments; Nature conservation

The **natural** mystics. Grant, C. **920**

NATURAL PESTICIDES

Deardorff, D. C. What's wrong with my plant (and how do I fix it?) **635**

NATURAL PESTICIDES

See also Pesticides

The **natural** pregnancy book. Romm, A. J. **618.2**

NATURAL RESOURCES

Burgis, T. The looting machine **338.2**

Kotler, S. Abundance **303.48**

NATURAL RESOURCES

See also Economic conditions

NATURAL RESOURCES -- ENCYCLOPEDIAS

Encyclopedia of global resources **333.7**

NATURAL RESOURCES -- MANAGEMENT

See also Management

NATURAL SATELLITES *See* Satellites

NATURAL SELECTION

Ayala, F. J. Darwin's gift to science and religion **576.8**

Darwin, C. The Darwin reader **576.8**

Darwin, C. On the origin of species **576.8**

Darwin, C. The origin of species by means of natural selection, or, The preservation of favored races in the struggle for life **576.8**

Dennett, D. C. Darwin's dangerous idea **146**

Jones, S. Darwin's ghost **576.8**

Keller, M. Charles Darwin's On the Origin of Species **576.8**

Moalem, S. Survival of the sickest **616**

Monosson, E. Unnatural selection **576.5**

Pinker, S. How the mind works **153**

Wagner, A. Arrival of the fittest **572.8**

Wilson, E. O. The social conquest of earth **599.93**

NATURAL SELECTION

See also Genetics; Variation (Biology)

NATURAL SELECTION -- COMIC BOOKS, STRIPS, ETC

Byrne, E. Darwin **576.8**

NATURAL SELECTION -- GRAPHIC NOVELS

Keller, M. Charles Darwin's On the Origin of Species **576.8**

NATURAL THEOLOGY

See also Apologetics; Theology

NATURAL THERAPY *See* Naturopathy

NATURALISM IN ART *See* Realism in art

The **naturalist.** Lunde, D. **973.91**

NATURALISTS

See also Scientists

NATURALISTS -- BIOGRAPHY

Wulf, A. The invention of nature **92**

NATURALISTS -- ENGLAND -- BIOGRAPHY
Johnson, P. Darwin   **576.8**
NATURALISTS -- GERMANY -- BIOGRAPHY
Wulf, A. The invention of nature   **92**
**NATURALISTS -- UNITED STATES -- BIOG-
RAPHY**
Irmscher, C. Louis Agassiz   **92**
Lunde, D. The naturalist   **973.91**
Souder, W. On a farther shore   **92**
**NATURALISTS -- UNITED STATES -- CORRE-
SPONDENCE**
Wilson, E. O. Letters to a Young Scientist   **570**
NATURALIZATION
   See also Immigration and emigration; Inter-
      national law; Suffrage
Naturally sweet.   **641.86**
Naturally, delicious. Seo, D.   **641.302**
Nature. Swenson, M.   **811**
NATURE
Ball, P. Patterns in nature   **500.2**
The best American science and nature writing
   2014   **810.8**
Dawkins, R. The magic of reality   **501**
Leslie, C. W. The Curious Nature Guide   **508**
Louv, R. The nature principle   **128**
McLane, M. N. This Blue   **811**
NATURE -- EFFECT OF HUMAN BEINGS ON
Cousteau, J. Y. The human, the orchid, and the oc-
   topus   **333.95**
Earle, S. A. The world is blue   **551.46**
Gorman, H. S. The story of N   **547**
Weisman, A. Countdown   **304.2**
Weisman, A. The world without us   **304.2**
Wills, C. Green Equilibrium   **577**
NATURE -- EFFECT OF HUMAN BEINGS ON
See Human influence on nature
NATURE -- POETRY *See* Nature poetry
NATURE -- PSYCHOLOGICAL ASPECTS
Louv, R. The nature principle   **128**
Louv, R. Vitamin N   **155.9**
Louv, R. Last child in the woods   **155.4**
Nature anatomy. Rothman, J.   **508**
NATURE AND NURTURE
Clark, W. R. Are we hardwired?   **155.7**
Pinker, S. The blank slate   **155.2**
Ridley, M. The agile gene   **155.7**
Tanzi, R. E. Super genes   **613**
Wright, L. Twins   **155.44**
NATURE AND NURTURE
   See also Genetics; Heredity
NATURE CONSERVATION
American earth   **333.72**
Brinkley, D. The quiet world   **333.72**
Brinkley, D. The wilderness warrior   **92**
Cousteau, J. Y. The human, the orchid, and the oc-
   topus   **333.95**

Davis, J. E. An Everglades providence   **92**
Duncan, D. The national parks   **333.7**
Egan, T. The big burn   **973.91**
Heacox, K. John Muir and the ice that started a
   fire   **92**
Leopold, A. A Sand County almanac & other writ-
   ings on ecology & conservation   **508**
Wilson, E. O. The diversity of life   **333.95**
Wilson, E. O. The future of life   **333.95**
NATURE CONSERVATION
   See also Conservation of natural resources
NATURE CONSERVATION -- ALASKA
Heacox, K. John Muir and the ice that started a
   fire   **92**
NATURE CONSERVATION -- DIRECTORIES
Green volunteers   **333.72**
**NATURE CONSERVATION -- MOZAMBIQUE
-- PARQUE NACIONAL DA GORONGOSA**
A window on eternity   **333.95**
NATURE CONSERVATION -- SOUTH AFRICA
Girling, R. The Hunt for the Golden Mole   **591.68**
NATURE CONSERVATION -- UNITED STATES
Lunde, D. The naturalist   **973.91**
NATURE CRAFT
   See also Handicraft
NATURE OBSERVATION
What the robin knows   **598.8**
NATURE OBSERVATION -- TENNESSEE
Haskell, D. G. The forest unseen   **577.3**
The **nature** of animal healing. Goldstein, M. **636.089**
Nature of human society series
Levi-Strauss, C. The savage mind   **155.8**
The **nature** of space and time. Hawking, S. W. **530.1**
NATURE PHOTOGRAPHY
Shaw, J. John Shaw's nature photography field
   guide   **778.9**
NATURE PHOTOGRAPHY
   See also Natural history; Photography
NATURE POETRY
Black nature   **808**
Doty, M. Deep lane   **811**
Oliver, M. A thousand mornings   **811**
The Poetry of Derek Walcott 1948-2013   **811**
NATURE POETRY
   See also Poetry
The **nature** principle. Louv, R.   **128**
NATURE PRINTS
   See also Printing; Prints
NATURE PROTECTION *See* Nature conservation
NATURE STUDY
Haskell, D. G. The forest unseen   **577.3**
Kiser, J. M. America's other Audubon   **598**
Sullivan, R. The Thoreau you don't know   **92**
NATURE STUDY
   See also Education; Science -- Study and
      teaching

NATURE TELEVISION PROGRAMS
   See also Television programs
NATURE TOURISM *See* Ecotourism
Nature writings. Muir, J.   **508**
Nature's clocks. Macdougall, J. D.   **551.7**
Nature's engraver. Uglow, J. S.   **92**
Nature's ghosts. Barrow, M. V.   **333.95**
Nature's patterns. Ball, P.   **500.2**
NATUROPATHY
   Low Dog, T. Healthy at home   **615.5**
NATUROPATHY
   See also Alternative medicine; Therapeutics
NATUROPATHY -- ENCYCLOPEDIAS
   Murray, M. T. The encyclopedia of natural medi-
   cine   **615.5**
Naughton, John
   From Gutenberg to Zuckerberg   **004.67**
Naumov, Vladimir P.
   Brent, J. Stalin's last crime   **947.084**
NAVAJO INDIANS
   Pasternak, J. Yellow dirt   **979.1**
   Sides, H. Blood and thunder   **978**
NAVAJO WOMEN
   See also Native American women; Navajo
   Indians
NAVAL ADMINISTRATION *See* Naval art and
   science
NAVAL ARCHITECTS -- UNITED STATES -- BI-
   OGRAPHY
   Ujifusa, S. A man and his ship   **623.8**
NAVAL ARCHITECTURE
   See also Architecture
NAVAL ART AND SCIENCE
   Grant, R. G. Battle at sea   **359**
NAVAL ART AND SCIENCE -- ENCYCLOPE-
   DIAS
   Naval warfare   **359**
NAVAL ART AND SCIENCE -- HISTORY --
   20TH CENTURY
   Borneman, W. R. The admirals   **920**
NAVAL BATTLES
   Crowley, R. Empires of the sea   **359**
   Ekin, D. The Last Armada   **941.505**
NAVAL BATTLES
   See also Battles
NAVAL CONVOYS -- ATLANTIC OCEAN --
   HISTORY -- 20TH CENTURY
   Kennedy, P. M. Engineers of victory   **940.54**
NAVAL EDUCATION
   See also Education
NAVAL HISTORY
   Grant, R. G. Battle at sea   **359**
   Mostert, N. The line upon a wind   **940.2**
NAVAL HISTORY
   See also History
NAVAL OFFICERS

Alexander, C. The Bounty: the true story of the mu-
   tiny on the Bounty   **996**
Blainey, G. Sea of dangers   **92**
Brandt, A. The man who ate his boots   **910.4**
Brownfield, C. J. My nuclear family   **92**
Cookman, S. Ice blink   **919**
Cousteau, J. Y. The human, the orchid, and the oc-
   topus   **333.95**
Hough, R. A. Captain James Cook   **92**
Matsen, B. Jacques Cousteau   **92**
Morison, S. E. John Paul Jones   **92**
Roberts, J. A sense of the world   **92**
Thomas, E. John Paul Jones   **92**
Thomas, N. Cook   **910**
Naval warfare.   **359**
NAVIGATION
   Bray, H. You are here   **910.285**
   Cutler, T. J. Dutton's nautical navigation   **623.89**
   Naranjo, R. The Art of Seamanship   **623.8**
   Rousmaniere, J. The Annapolis Book of Seaman-
   ship   **623.88**
   Sleight, S. The complete sailing manual   **797.124**
NAVIGATION (AERONAUTICS)
   See also Aeronautics
NAVIGATION (ASTRONAUTICS)
   See also Astrodynamics; Astronautics
NAVIGATION -- HANDBOOKS, MANUALS,
   ETC.
   Chapman piloting & seamanship   **623.88**
NAVIGATION, PREHISTORIC
   Fagan, B. Beyond the blue horizon   **910.4**
NAVIGATORS *See* Explorers; Sailors
Navratilova, Martina, 1956-
            About
   Howard, J. The rivals   **92**
NAVY *See* Naval art and science; Navies; Sea
   power
NAVY YARDS AND NAVAL STATIONS
   See also Naval art and science
Nawaz, Maajid, 1978-
   (jt. auth) Harris, S. Islam and the future of toler-
   ance   **297.2**
Nawaz, Zarqa.
            About
   Nawaz, Z. Laughing All the Way to the Mosque **92**
The **Nazi** doctors. Lifton, R. J.   **940.53**
Nazi Germany. Fischer, K. P.   **943.086**
Nazi Germany and the Jews. Friedlander, S. **940.53**
The **Nazi** hunters. Nagorski, A.   **940.53**
NAZI HUNTERS
   Pick, H. Simon Wiesenthal   **940.53**
   Segev, T. Simon Wiesenthal   **92**
NAZI HUNTERS -- HISTORY
   Nagorski, A. The Nazi hunters   **940.53**
NAZI LEADERS
   Ahamed, L. Lords of finance   **332.1**

Bascomb, N. Hunting Eichmann **943.086**
Berthon, S. Warlords **940.53**
Breitman, R. The architect of genocide **92**
Cornwell, J. Hitler's pope: the secret history of Pius XII **92**
Fest, J. C. Speer: the final verdict **92**
Fischer, K. P. Nazi Germany **943.086**
Fleming, G. Hitler and the final solution **943.086**
Fulbrook, M. A concise history of Germany **943**
Hitler, A. Mein Kampf **92**
Kershaw, I. Hitler **92**
Kershaw, I. Hitler, 1936-1945: nemesis **943.086**
Kissinger, H. Diplomacy **327.2**
Lifton, R. J. The Nazi doctors **940.53**
Lipstadt, D. E. The Eichmann trial **345**
Parssinen, T. M. The Oster conspiracy of 1938 **943.086**
Rosenbaum, R. Explaining Hitler **943.086**
Ryback, T. W. Hitler's private library **027**
Sereny, G. Albert Speer **92**
Shirer, W. L. The rise and fall of the Third Reich **943.086**
Snyder, T. D. Bloodlands **940.54**
Speer, A. Inside the Third Reich **943.086**
Taylor, F. Exorcising Hitler **943.087**
Turner, H. A. Hitler's thirty days to power **943.086**
Weber, T. Hitler's first war **940.4**
The **Nazi** persecution of the gypsies. Lewy, G. **940.53**

NAZIS *See* National socialists

NAZIS -- BIOGRAPHY
Goebbels **92**

NAZIS -- DIARIES
Kinney, D. The devil's diary **940.53**

NAZIS -- FAMILY RELATIONSHIPS
My grandfather would have shot me **929.2**

NAZIS -- UNITED STATES -- HISTORY -- 20TH CENTURY
Lichtblau, E. The Nazis next door **324.1**
The **Nazis** next door. Lichtblau, E. **324.1**

NAZISM *See* National socialism

NBA FINALS (BASKETBALL)
 See also Basketball; Sports tournaments
Neal Cassady. Sandison, D. **92**
Neal-Schuman library technology companion. Burke, J. J. **025**

NEANDERTHALS
 See also Fossil hominids
Near & far. Swanson, H. **641.59**
Near a thousand tables. Fernandez-Armesto, F. **394.1**

NEAR EAST *See* Middle East

NEAR-DEATH EXPERIENCES
Emrys, B. The Toltec art of life and death **299.7**
Moody, R. A. Life after life **133.9**
Panagore, P. B. Heaven Is Beautiful **231.7**

NEAR-DEATH EXPERIENCES
 See also Death

NEAR-EARTH OBJECTS
 See also Solar system
Nearer, my God. Buckley, W. F. **282**
Nearest star. Golub, L. **523.7**

NEATNESS *See* Cleanliness; Orderliness

NEBRASKA -- LITERARY COLLECTIONS
Cather, W. Stories, poems, and other writings **818**

NEBULA AWARD
 See also Literary prizes; Science fiction

NEBULAE, EXTRAGALACTIC *See* Galaxies
A **necessary** evil. Wills, G. **973**

NECROLOGIES *See* Obituaries

NECROMANCY *See* Divination; Magic
Needham, Joseph, 1900-1995
  About
Winchester, S. The man who loved China **92**
Needle felting. Adams, L. **746**
Needleman, Deborah
(ed) The book of decorating **747**
The perfectly imperfect home **747**

NEEDLEPOINT
Christensen, J. I. The needlepoint book **746.44**

NEEDLEPOINT
 See also Embroidery; Needlework
The **needlepoint** book. Christensen, J. I. **746.44**

NEEDLEWORK
A-Z of Whitework **746.44**
Ganderton, L. Embroidery **746.44**
Marchant, N. Knitting brioche **746.43**
Todhunter, T. Crochet **746.434**

NEEDLEWORK
 See also Decoration and ornament; Decorative arts

NEEDLEWORK -- PATTERNS
Budd, A. New directions in sock knitting **746.432**
Eckman, E. Connect-the-shapes crochet motifs **746.43**
Marchant, N. Knitting fresh brioche **746.43**
Nico, B. More Lovely Knitted Lace **746.432**
Radcliffe, M. The knowledgeable knitter **746.43**
Shimoda, N. Artfully embroidered **746.44**
Watson, S. Pen to thread **746.44**

NEEDLEWORKERS
Berry, M. F. My face is black is true **92**
Miller, M. R. Betsy Ross and the making of America **92**
Neel, Alice, 1900-1984
  About
Hoban, P. Alice Neel **92**
Neely, Gina
Neely, P. Down home with the Neelys **641.5**
Neely, Pat
Down home with the Neelys **641.5**
Neff, James

Vendetta **973.922**

Negative blue. Wright, C. **811**

NEGOTIABLE INSTRUMENTS
> *See also* Banks and banking; Commercial law; Contracts; Credit

NEGOTIATION
Davidds, Y. Your own terms **658.4**
Irwin, R. Tips & traps for negotiating real estate **333.3**
Morrison, T. Kiss, bow, or shake hands **395**
Powell, J. Terrorists at the table **363.325**
Raeburn, P. The game theorist's guide to parenting **641.1**
Ury, W. Getting past no **158**
Wheeler, M. The art of negotiation **658.4**

NEGOTIATION
> *See also* Applied psychology

NEGOTIATION IN BUSINESS
Davidds, Y. Your own terms **658.4**
Wheeler, M. The art of negotiation **658.4**

NEGRITUDE *See* Blacks -- Race identity

NEGRO LEAGUES
Hogan, L. D. Shades of glory **796.357**

NEGRO LEAGUES
> *See also* Baseball

NEGRO LEAGUES -- HISTORY
Hogan, L. D. Shades of glory **796.357**
Tye, L. Satchel **92**

'Negro president' Wills, G. **326**

NEGROES *See* African Americans; Blacks

Negroland. Jefferson, M. **92**

Nehru, Jawaharlal, 1889-1964
> **About**

Brown, J. M. Nehru: a political life **92**
Galbraith, J. K. Name-dropping **973.9**
Tharoor, S. Nehru: the invention of India **954.04**
Nehru: a political life. Brown, J. M. **92**
Nehru: the invention of India. Tharoor, S. **954.04**

Neiberg, Michael
The blood of free men **940.54**
Fighting the Great War **940.4**
Potsdam **940.53**

Neifert, Marianne R.
Great expectations **649**

The **neighborhood** project. Wilson, D. S. **307.7**

NEIGHBORHOODS -- CHINA -- SHANGHAI
Schmitz, R. Street of Eternal Happiness **951.132**

NEIGHBORHOODS -- FRANCE -- PARIS -- GUIDEBOOKS
Baxter, J. Five nights in Paris **914.4**

Neihardt, John Gneisenau
Black Elk Black Elk speaks **92**

Neil Armstrong. Barbree, J. **92**

Neil Leifer: Ballet in the dirt. Leifer, N. **796.357**

Neil Patrick Harris. Harris, N. P. **92**

Neil, David H.

Rutherford, C. How to raise a puppy you can live with **636.7**

Neitzel, Sönke, 1968-
Soldaten **940.54**

Neiwert, David
Of orcas and men **599.53**

Nellie Taft. Anthony, C. S. **92**

Nelson. Hibbert, C. **92**

Nelson Mandela. Sampson, A. **92**

Nelson, Anne
Red Orchestra **943.086**

Nelson, Craig
The age of radiance **539.7**
The first heroes **940.54**
Pearl Harbor **940.54**
Rocket men **629.45**

Nelson, Glenn C.
Ceramics: a potter's handbook **738.1**

Nelson, Horatio Nelson, Viscount, 1758-1805
> **About**

Adkin, M. The Trafalgar companion **940.2**
Hibbert, C. Nelson **92**
Pocock, T. The terror before Trafalgar **940.2**
Sugden, J. Nelson: a dream of glory, 1758-1797 **92**

Nelson, James Carl
The remains of Company D **920**

Nelson, James L.
With fire & sword **973.3**

Nelson, Jennifer
(jt. auth) Braafladt, K. Technology and literacy **027.62**

Nelson, John, 1892-1993
> **About**

Nelson, J. C. The remains of Company D **920**

Nelson, Maggie
The red parts **362.88**

Nelson, Michael
(ed) Guide to the presidency and the executive branch **352.23**

Nelson, Paul
> **About**

Avery, K. Everything is an afterthought **92**

Nelson, Willie
> **About**

Patoski, J. N. Willie Nelson **92**

Nelson: a dream of glory, 1758-1797. Sugden, J. **92**

Nemat, Marina
> **About**

Nemat, M. Prisoner of Tehran **92**

Neme, Laurel A.
Animal investigators **363.2**

Nemerov, Howard
The selected poems of Howard Nemerov **811**

Nemiroff, Robert
Hansberry, L. To be young, gifted, and Black **92**

NEO-FASCISM *See* Fascism; Neo-Nazis

NEO-IMPRESSIONISM (ART) *See* Impressionism (Art)

Neo-impressionism and the dream of realities. Homburg, C. **709.04**

NEO-NAZIS
See also Fascism

NEOLIBERALISM -- SOCIAL ASPECTS
Davies, W. The happiness industry **304**

NEOLITHIC PERIOD *See* Stone Age

NEOPAGANISM
Hutton, R. The triumph of the moon **133.4**

NEOPAGANISM
See also Religions

NEOPAGANISM -- UNITED STATES
Mar, A. Witches of America **299**

Neporent, Liz
(jt. auth) Brown, J. The Runner's Brain **796.42**

NEPTUNE (PLANET)
See also Planets

Néret, Gilles
(jt. auth) Descharnes, R. Salvador Dalí, 1904-1989 **759.6**

NERO, 37-68 (EMPEROR OF ROME)
See also Emperors -- Rome

Nero, Emperor of Rome, 37-68
About
The twelve Caesars **878**

Neruda, Pablo, 1904-1973
The poetry of Pablo Neruda **861**
About
Bloom, H. The Western canon **809**
Feinstein, A. Pablo Neruda **92**
Then come back **861**
Urrutia, M. My life with Pablo Neruda **92**

Nerve. Clark, T. **152.4**

NERVES
See also Nervous system

NERVES -- DISEASES *See* Nervous system -- Diseases

NERVOUS SYSTEM
DeSalle, R. The brain **612.8**
Doty, J. R. Into the Magic Shop **92**
Iacoboni, M. Mirroring people **573.8**
Kandel, E. R. In search of memory **153**
Kosik, K. S. Outsmarting alzheimer's **616.8**
Ramachandran, V. S. The tell-tale brain **616.8**
Ropper, A. H. Reaching down the rabbit hole **616.8**
Sacks, O. The mind's eye **616.85**
Wolf, N. Vagina **305.42**

NERVOUS SYSTEM
See also Anatomy; Physiology

NERVOUS SYSTEM -- DISEASES
McAuliffe, K. This is your brain on parasites **612.8**

NERVOUS SYSTEM -- DISEASES
See also Diseases

Nesheim, Malden

Why calories count **613.2**

Ness, Bryan D.
(ed) Magill's encyclopedia of science **580**

NEST BUILDING
Zickefoose, J. Baby Birds **598**

NEST BUILDING
See also Animal behavior; Animals -- Habitations

Nesteroff, Kliph
The Comedians **792.7**

The nesting place. Smith, M. **248.4**

Nestle, Marion
(jt. auth) Nesheim, M. Why calories count **613.2**
Pet food politics **363.1**

Nestor, James
Deep **797.2**

The net delusion. Morozov, E. **303.48**

Netanyahu, Benjamin
About
Remnick, D. Reporting **814**

NETHERLANDS
Buruma, I. Murder in Amsterdam **364.152**

NETHERLANDS -- CIVILIZATION
Schama, S. The embarrassment of riches **949.2**

NETHERLANDS -- HISTORY
Shorto, R. Amsterdam **949.2**

NETHERLANDS -- HISTORY -- 1940-1945, GERMAN OCCUPATION
Barnouw, D. The diary of Anne Frank: the critical edition **92**
Frank, A. The diary of a young girl: the definitive edition **92**
Gies, M. Anne Frank remembered **92**

NETHERLANDS -- HISTORY -- 1940-1945, GERMAN OCCUPATION -- DRAMA
Goodrich, F. The diary of Anne Frank **812**

Netherlands State Institute for War Documentation
Barnouw, D. The diary of Anne Frank: the critical edition **92**

Nettle, Daniel
Happiness **152.4**

Nettles, Brenda S.
(jt. auth) Ahuja, N. Johns Hopkins patients' guide to colon and rectal cancer **616.99**

NETWORK THEORY *See* System analysis

Networked. Wellman, B. **006.7**

Netzer, Corinne T.
The complete book of food counts **613.2**

Neu, Charles E.
Colonel House **92**

Neubauer, Alexander
(ed) Poetry in person **809.1**

Neubauer, Linda
(ed) The complete photo guide to window treatments **646.2**

Neuburger, Emily K.
Show me a story **741.6**
Neufeld, Josh
Gladstone, B. The influencing machine **302.23**
A.D. **976.3**
Neufeld, Michael J.
(ed) Milestones of space **629.4**
Von Braun **92**
NEURASTHENIA
See also Mental illness
NEUROANATOMY
Taylor, J. B. My stroke of insight **362.19**
NEUROBIOLOGY
Churchland, P. S. Braintrust **612.8**
Neurocomic. Ros, H. **612.82**
**NEUROLOGIC MANIFESTATIONS -- POPU-
LAR WORKS**
Kean, S. The tale of the dueling neurosur-
geons **617.4**
NEUROLOGICAL SCIENCES *See* Neurosci-
ences
NEUROLOGISTS
Quiñones-Hinojosa, A. Becoming Dr. Q **92**
Sacks, O. W. Uncle Tungsten **616.8**
NEUROLOGISTS -- BIOGRAPHY
Kozol, J. The theft of memory **92**
NEUROLOGISTS -- ENGLAND -- BIOGRAPHY
Sacks, O. W. Uncle Tungsten **616.8**
Sacks, O. On the move **92**
**NEUROLOGISTS -- MASSACHUSETTS -- BOS-
TON -- BIOGRAPHY**
Ropper, A. H. Reaching down the rabbit hole **616.8**
NEUROPATHOLOGY *See* Nervous system -- Dis-
eases
NEUROPHYSIOLOGY
Carr, N. G. The shallows **612.8**
DeSalle, R. The brain **612.8**
The Oxford companion to the mind **128**
NEUROPLASTICITY
Doidge, N. The brain that changes itself **612.8**
Doidge, N. The brain's way of healing **612.8**
NEUROPSYCHOLOGY
Carr, N. G. The shallows **612.8**
Churchland, P. S. Braintrust **612.8**
Gazzaniga, M. S. Human **612.8**
Hall, S. S. Wisdom **179**
Hoffman, D. D. Visual intelligence **152.14**
Kaku, M. The future of the mind **612.8**
Palca, J. Annoying **612.8**
Webb, C. How to have a good day **650.1**
NEUROSCIENCES
Burnett, D. Idiot brain **612.8**
Gazzaniga, M. S. Tales from Both Sides of the
Brain **92**
Grandin, T. The autistic brain **616.85**
Jensen, F. E. The teenage brain **612.6**
Kaku, M. The future of the mind **612.8**
Kean, S. The tale of the dueling neurosur-
geons **617.4**
Lieberman, M. D. Social **302**
Lilienfeld, S. O. Brainwashed **612.8**
Ropper, A. H. Reaching down the rabbit hole **616.8**
Ros, H. Neurocomic **612.82**
NEUROSCIENCES
See also Medicine
**NEUROSCIENCES -- HISTORY -- POPULAR
WORKS**
Kean, S. The tale of the dueling neurosur-
geons **617.4**
NEUROSCIENCES -- POPULAR WORKS
Burnett, D. Idiot brain **612.8**
NEUROSCIENTISTS
Kandel, E. R. In search of memory **153**
Weiner, J. Time, love, memory **591.5**
NEUROSES
See also Abnormal psychology
NEUROSURGEONS
Quiñones-Hinojosa, A. Becoming Dr. Q **92**
NEUROSURGEONS -- BIOGRAPHY
Kalanithi, P. When breath becomes air **616.99**
Never alone. Girzone, J. F. **248.4**
Never broken. Jewel **92**
Never eat alone and other secrets to success. Fer-
razzi, K. **658.4**
Never say die. Jacoby, S. **305.26**
Never Trust a Skinny Italian Chef. Bottura,
M. **641.594**
New & selected poems, 1974-1994. Dunn, S. **811**
NEW AGE MOVEMENT
Goodman, L. Linda Goodman's star signs **130**
NEW AGE MOVEMENT
See also Cults; Occultism; Social movements
The **New** American Bible. **220.5**
New American Haggadah. **296.4**
The **new** American Heart Association cookbook.
New American Heart Association cookbook **641.5**
New American Heart Association cookbook
The new American Heart Association cook-
book **641.5**
The **new** American herbal. Orr, S. **615.3**
New American nation series
Leuchtenburg, W. E. Franklin D. Roosevelt and the
New Deal, 1932-1940 **973.917**
The **new** American plate cookbook. American Insti-
tute for Cancer Research **641.5**
The **new** Americans. Martinez, R. **305.9**
New and collected poems 1931-2001. Milosz,
C. **891.8**
New and collected poems, 1966-2006. Reed, I. **811**
New and selected poems. Menashe, S. **811**
New and selected poems. Oliver, M. **811**
New and selected poems (1965-2006) Shapiro,

D.   811
New and selected poems 1962-2012. Simic, C. 811
The **new** anti-semitism. Chesler, P.   305.8
The **New** Arabs. Cole, J.   909
The **new** architecture and the Bauhaus. Gropius, W.   724
The **new** atlas of the Arab world.   912
The **new** best recipe. Cook's illustrated (Periodical)   641.5
The **new** black. Shockley, E.   811
The **new** Bohemians. Blakeney, J.   747
The **new** book of Middle Eastern food. Roden, C.   641.59

NEW BUSINESS ENTERPRISES
  Barringer, B. Launching a Business   658.1
  Downs, P. Boss Life   92
  Duffy, S. Launch!   658.1
  Guillebeau, C. The $100 startup   658.1
  How to write a business plan   658.15
  Maxfield, K. Starting up Silicon Valley   338.7
NEW BUSINESS ENTERPRISES
  See also Business enterprises
NEW BUSINESS ENTERPRISES -- MANAGEMENT
  Guillebeau, C. The $100 startup   658.1
  Kidder, D. S. The Startup playbook   658.1
  Wasserman, N. The founder's dilemmas   658.1
NEW BUSINESS ENTERPRISES -- PLANNING
  Pinson, L. Anatomy of a business plan   658.4
NEW BUSINESS ENTERPRISES -- UNITED STATES
  Dwyer, J. More awesome than money   384.3
  Strauss, S. D. The small business bible   658.02
NEW BUSINESS ENTERPRISES -- UNITED STATES -- MANAGEMENT
  Casnocha, B. My start-up life   338.7
  Downs, P. Boss Life   92
New California poetry [series]
  Waldrop, K. Transcendental studies   811
The **New** Cambridge medieval history.   940.1
New Catholic encyclopedia.   282
The **new** censorship. Simon, J.   363.31
The **new** Christmas tree. Brown, C.   745.594
New collected poems. Oppen, G.   811
New collected poems. Boland, E.   821
New collected poems. Berry, W.   811
The **new** complete dog book.   636.7
New complete guide to sewing. Reader's Digest Association, I.   646.2
New complete guide to sewing.   646.2
The **new** complete guitarist. Chapman, R.   787.87
New Concise World Atlas.   912
The **new** cool. Bascomb, N.   629.8
NEW DEAL, 1933-1939
  Brands, H. W. Traitor to his class   92
  Downey, K. The woman behind the New Deal   92

The forgotten man   973.91
Katznelson, I. Fear itself   973.917
Kruse, K. M. One nation under God   322
Leuchtenburg, W. E. Franklin D. Roosevelt and the New Deal, 1932-1940   973.917
Schlesinger, A. M. The coming of the New Deal, 1933-1935   973.917
Schlesinger, A. M. The politics of upheaval, 1935-1936   973.917
Simon, J. F. FDR and Chief Justice Hughes 973.917
Taylor, N. American-made   331.1
Welky, D. The thousand-year flood   363.34
NEW DEAL, 1933-1939 -- PUBLIC OPINION
  Kruse, K. M. One nation under God   322
New decorating book.   747
New dictionary of scientific biography.   920.003
The **New** Directions anthology of classical chinese poetry.   895.1
New directions in sock knitting. Budd, A.   746.432
A **new** earth. Tolle, E.   158
The **new** encyclopedia of Islam. Glassé, C.   297
The **New** encyclopedia of Judaism.   296
The **new** encyclopedia of snakes. Mattison, C.   597.96
NEW ENGLAND
  Christensen, K. How to cook a moose   641.597
  Sewall, J. The New England kitchen   641.597
NEW ENGLAND
  See also United States
NEW ENGLAND -- HISTORY -- 1600-1775, COLONIAL PERIOD
  Karlsen, C. F. The devil in the shape of a woman   133.4
  Schultz, E. B. King Philip's War   973.2
  Vowell, S. The wordy shipmates   974
NEW ENGLAND -- INTELLECTUAL LIFE
  Transcendentalism   810
New England Bound. Warren, W.   306.362
The **New** England cookbook. Dojny, B.   641.5
The **New** England kitchen. Sewall, J.   641.597
NEW ENGLISH DICTIONARY ON HISTORICAL PRINCIPLES
  Winchester, S. The professor and the madman   423
The **new** faces of Christianity. Jenkins, P.   270
The **new** first three years of life. White, B. L. 155.4
New fix-it-yourself manual.   643
NEW FRANCE *See* Canada -- History -- 0-1763 (New France); Mississippi River Valley -- History
The **new** generation breast cancer book. Port, E.   616.99
The **New** Grove dictionary of music and musicians.   780
NEW GUINEA
  Hoffman, C. A Savage Harvest   995
NEW GUINEA -- DESCRIPTION
  Flannery, T. F. Throwim way leg   995.3

The **new** hate. Goldwag, A. **306.2**

The **new** health care system. Nather, D. **344**

A **new** history of India. Wolpert, S. A. **954**

A **new** history of life. Kirschvink, J. **576.8**

The **new** history of the world. Roberts, J. M. **909**

New Horizons in Geometry. Apostol, T. M. **516**

The **new** Jerusalem Bible. **220.5**

The **new** joys of Yiddish. Rosten, L. **422**

New life, no instructions. Caldwell, G. **92**

A **new** literary history of America. **810**

The **new** mediterranean cookbook. Wadi, S. **641.59**

The **new** Mediterranean diet cookbook. Jenkins, N. H. **641.5**

The **new** Mediterranean Jewish table. Goldstein, J. **641.5**

NEW MEXICO

Connors, P. Fire season **634.9**

NEW MEXICO -- ECONOMIC CONDITIONS -- 21ST CENTURY

Martínez, R. Desert America **330.9**

The **New** Midwestern table. Thielen, A. **641.59**

The **new** mind of the South. Thompson, T. **305.8**

A **new** Napa cuisine. Kostow, C. **641.59**

New narratives in American history [series]

Franklin, J. H. In search of the promised land **929**

NEW NEGRO MOVEMENT *See* Harlem Renaissance

The **New** new journalism. **071**

The **new** new thing. Lewis, M. D. **338.4**

The **new** normal. Wann, D. **306**

NEW ORLEANS (LA.)

Rivlin, G. Katrina **976.3**

NEW ORLEANS (LA.) -- BIOGRAPHY

Baum, D. Nine lives **976.3**

Crais, C. History lessons **92**

NEW ORLEANS (LA.) -- DESCRIPTION AND TRAVEL

Horne, J. Breach of faith **976.3**

NEW ORLEANS (LA.) -- GRAPHIC NOVELS

Neufeld, J. A.D. **976.3**

NEW ORLEANS (LA.) -- HISTORY

Krist, G. Empire of sin **976.3**

NEW ORLEANS (LA.) -- RACE RELATIONS

Johnson, W. Soul by soul **326**

Rasmussen, D. American uprising **976.3**

NEW ORLEANS (LA.) -- SOCIAL LIFE AND CUSTOMS

Besh, J. My New Orleans **641.59**

NEW ORLEANS (LA.), BATTLE OF, 1815

Groom, W. Patriotic fire **973.5**

New Orleans, mon amour. Codrescu, A. **814**

New Oxford American dictionary. **423**

The **New** Oxford book of Irish verse. **821**

The **New** Oxford book of literary anecdotes. **828**

The **new** Partridge dictionary of slang and unconventional English. **427**

New passages. Sheehy, G. **305.24**

A **new** path to the waterfall. Carver, R. **811**

New poems. Rilke, R. M. **831**

The **new** Portuguese table. Leite, D. **641.5**

NEW PRODUCT DEVELOPMENT *See* New products

NEW PRODUCTS

Duffy, S. Launch! **658.1**

Kolko, J. Well-designed **658.5**

NEW PRODUCTS

See also Commercial products; Industrial research; Marketing

The **new** religious intolerance. Nussbaum, M. C. **201**

The **new** retirement. Cullinane, J. **646.7**

New rules of social media series

Handley, A. Content rules **658.8**

New selected poems. Levine, P. **811**

A **new** selected poems. Kinnell, G. **811**

The **new** sewing essentials. **646.2**

The **new** shade garden. Druse, K. **635.9**

The **new** solar system. Daniels, P. **523.2**

The **New** Southern Living Garden Book. **635.9**

The **new** stokes field guide to birds. Stokes, D. **598**

The **new** stokes field guide to birds. Stokes, D. **598**

The **new** terrarium. Martin, T. **635.9**

NEW THOUGHT

James, W. The varieties of religious experience **210**

A **new** time for Mexico. Fuentes, C. **972.08**

The **new** time travelers. Toomey, D. M. **530.1**

A **New** Turn in the South. Acheson, H. **641.59**

The **new** vegetarian cooking for everyone. Madison, D. **641.5**

NEW WORDS

Metcalf, A. A. Predicting new words **420**

NEW WORDS

See also Vocabulary

The **new** work of dogs. Katz, J. **636.7**

New world coming. Miller, N. **973.91**

New World kitchen. **641.59**

NEW YEAR

See also Holidays

NEW YORK (N.Y.)

Christgau, R. Going Into the City **92**

Gooch, B. Smash Cut **92**

Invisible City **779**

Martin, W. Primates of Park Avenue **974.7**

Ninety days **362.29**

Rips, N. Trying to float **974.7**

Stanton, B. Humans of New York **974.7**

Winder, E. Pain, Parties, Work **811**

NEW YORK (N.Y.) -- 20TH CENTURY

McCourt, J. Lasting City **92**

NEW YORK (N.Y.) -- BIOGRAPHY

Feldman, D. Exodus **92**

Mariani, P. L. The broken tower: a life of Hart

Crane   **811**

Martin, W. Primates of Park Avenue   **974.7**

McCourt, M. A monk swimming   **974.7**

McCourt, M. Singing my him song   **974.7**

Napoli, P. F. Bringing it all back home   **959.704**

Rips, N. Trying to float   **974.7**

Vincent, I. Dinner with Edward   **158.1**

Ward, G. C. A disposition to be rich   **974.7**

NEW YORK (N.Y.) -- BOARD OF EDUCATION

Fertig, B. Why cant U teach me 2 read?   **372.4**

NEW YORK (N.Y.) -- BUILDINGS, STRUCTURES, ETC

Mires, C. Capital of the world   **341.23**

NEW YORK (N.Y.) -- CIVILIZATION

Reid, D. The brazen age   **974.7**

NEW YORK (N.Y.) -- COMMERCE -- HISTORY

Mays, A. E. The millionaire and the bard   **822.33**

NEW YORK (N.Y.) -- DESCRIPTION AND TRAVEL

Freudenheim, E. The Brooklyn experience   **917.47**

NEW YORK (N.Y.) -- EMIGRATION AND IMMIGRATION -- HISTORY

Anbinder, T. City of Dreams   **974.71**

NEW YORK (N.Y.) -- ETHNIC RELATIONS

Berger, J. The pious ones   **973**

NEW YORK (N.Y.) -- FIRE DEPT.

Halberstam, D. Firehouse   **363.34**

Smith, D. Report from ground zero   **363.34**

NEW YORK (N.Y.) -- GUIDEBOOKS

Freudenheim, E. The Brooklyn experience   **917.47**

NEW YORK (N.Y.) -- HARLEM

Gill, J. Harlem   **974.7**

NEW YORK (N.Y.) -- HISTORY

The 60s   **909.826**

Miller, D. L. Supreme city   **974.7**

Reid, D. The brazen age   **974.7**

Seligman, S. D. Tong wars   **364.106**

NEW YORK (N.Y.) -- HISTORY, MILITARY

New York at war   **355.009**

NEW YORK (N.Y.) -- POETRY

Garcia Lorca, F. Poet in New York   **861**

NEW YORK (N.Y.) -- POLICE DEPT.

Dickey, C. Securing the city   **363.32**

Levitt, L. NYPD confidential   **364.1**

NEW YORK (N.Y.) -- POLITICS AND GOVERNMENT

Siegel, F. F. The prince of the city   **92**

NEW YORK (N.Y.) -- SOCIAL CONDITIONS

Anasi, R. The last bohemia   **974.7**

Canada, G. Fist, stick, knife, gun   **305.23**

LeBlanc, A. N. Random family   **305.5**

NEW YORK (N.Y.) -- SOCIAL LIFE AND CUSTOMS

Anasi, R. The last bohemia   **974.7**

Clancy, T. The Clancys of Queens   **974.7**

Cliff, N. The Shakespeare riots   **974.4**

Freeland, D. Automats, taxi dances, and vaudeville

Martin, W. Primates of Park Avenue   **974.7**

Rips, N. Trying to float   **974.7**

Rudnick, P. I shudder   **92**

NEW YORK (N.Y.) -- SOCIAL LIFE AND CUSTOMS -- 20TH CENTURY

The Fun of it   **814**

Miller, D. L. Supreme city   **974.7**

NEW YORK (N.Y.) -- SOCIAL LIFE AND CUSTOMS -- PICTORIAL WORKS

Stanton, B. Humans of New York: stories   **974.7**

NEW YORK (N.Y.) -- SOCIAL LIFE AND CUSTOMS.

Gopnik, A. Through the children's gate   **974.71**

NEW YORK (N.Y.). POLICE DEPARTMENT -- OFFICIALS AND EMPLOYEES -- BIOGRAPHY

Osborne, S. The job   **92**

NEW YORK (STATE)

Humm, D. I love New York   **641.59**

NEW YORK (STATE) -- HISTORY -- 1775-1865

Kelly, J. Heaven's ditch   **386**

Taylor, A. The divided ground   **974.7**

NEW YORK (STATE) -- HISTORY -- REVOLUTION, 1775-1783 -- SECRET SERVICE

Yaeger, D. George Washington's secret six   **973.4**

New York at war.   **355.009**

New York burning. Lepore, J.   **974.7**

New York Dolls. Gruen, B.   **781.66**

NEW YORK DOLLS (MUSICAL GROUP)

Gruen, B. New York Dolls   **781.66**

NEW YORK GIANTS (BASEBALL TEAM)

Hirsch, J. S. Willie Mays   **92**

NEW YORK GIANTS (FOOTBALL TEAM)

Parcells, B. Parcells   **796.332**

NEW YORK HARBOR (N.Y. AND N.J.)

Fisher, J. T. On the Irish waterfront   **331.7**

NEW YORK JETS (FOOTBALL TEAM)

Dawidoff, N. Collision Low Crossers   **796.3**

NEW YORK KNICKS (BASKETBALL TEAM)

See also Basketball teams

NEW YORK PHILHARMONIC

Bernstein, B. Leonard Bernstein   **92**

NEW YORK POST

Nissenson, M. The lady upstairs   **92**

New York Public Library

Denlinger, E. C. Before Victoria   **920**

The **New** York Public Library desk reference. **031.02**

New York Review Books classics [series]

The burning of the world   **92**

David, E. A book of Mediterranean food   **641.5**

David, E. Summer cooking   **641.5**

The Gray Notebook   **849**

Mandelstam, O. The selected poems of Osip Mandelstam   **891.7**

New York September 11. Magnum Photos, I.   **770**

NEW YORK SUN (NEWSPAPER: 1833-1950)
Goodman, M. The Sun and the moon   **974.7**
NEW YORK TIMES
Boyd, G. M. My Times in black and white   **92**
Gelb, A. City room   **92**
New York Times 20th century in review [series]
The Vietnam War   **959.704**
The **New** York Times book of mathematics.   **510**
NEW YORK TIMES COMPANY
Gelb, A. City room   **92**
The **New** York Times complete World War II, 1939-1945.   **940.53**
The **New** York Times disunion.   **973.7**
The **New** York Times Jewish cookbook.   **641.5**
New York Times living history [series]
World War II   **940.53**
The **New** York times manual of style and usage. Siegal, A.   **808**
The **New** York Times Passover cookbook.   **641.5**
NEW YORK WORLD (NEWSPAPER)
Baker, N. The World on Sunday   **071**
NEW YORK YANKEES (BASEBALL TEAM)
Pennington, B. Billy Martin   **92**
NEW YORK YANKEES (BASEBALL TEAM) -- HISTORY
Billy Martin   **92**
Pennington, B. Billy Martin   **92**
NEW YORKER (NEW YORK, N.Y. : 1925)
The 40s   **973.917**
Mankoff, B. How about never--is never good for you?   **92**
NEW YORKER (PERIODICAL)
The complete cartoons of the New Yorker   **741.5**
Fraser, K. Ornament and silence   **809**
The Fun of it   **814**
Lane, A. Nobody's perfect   **791.43**
Steinberg, S. Steinberg at the New Yorker   **741.5**
New Yorker Magazine Inc.
(comp) The 60s   **909.826**
NEW YORKER MAGAZINE, INC.
The complete cartoons of the New Yorker   **741.5**
Steinberg, S. Steinberg at the New Yorker   **741.5**
New, Gregory R.
(ed) Dewey decimal classification and relative index   **025.4**
NEW-YORK HISTORICAL SOCIETY
Holzer, H. The Civil War in 50 objects   **973.7**
NEWBERY MEDAL
   See also Children's literature; Literary prizes
NEWBORN INFANTS -- CARE
Sears, W. The baby book   **649**
NEWBORN INFANTS -- POPULAR WORKS
The pregnancy encyclopedia   **618.2**
The **newborn** sleep book. Jassey, J.   **618.92**
Newell, Paul Clark
(jt. auth) Dedman, B. Empty mansions   **92**

Newitz, Annalee
Scatter, adapt, and remember   **576.8**
Newkirk, Pamela
(ed) Letters from Black America   **305.8**
Spectacle   **92**
Newlin, Keith
(ed) A Theodore Dreiser encyclopedia   **813**
Newman, Joseph Dwight
   About
Dance, S. The world of Count Basie   **920**
Newman, Katherine S., 1953-
The accordion family   **306.874**
Newman, Kim
(ed) Horror: another 100 best books   **823**
Newman, Nancy
Raising passionate readers   **649.58**
Newman, Paul, 1925-2008
   About
Levy, S. Paul Newman   **92**
Newman, Richard S.
Freedom's prophet   **92**
Newport, Cal
Deep work   **650.1**
Newquist, H. P.
(jt. auth) Gruber, J. Health care reform   **362.1**
NEWS AGENCIES
   See also Press
News for all the people. Gonzalez, J.   **302.23**
News of a kidnapping. Garcia Marquez, G.   **364.15**
News of the world. Levine, P.   **811**
NEWS PHOTOGRAPHY *See* Photojournalism
The **News** Sorority. Weller, S.   **070.1**
NEWSLETTERS
   See also Journalism; Newspapers
NEWSPAPER ADVERTISING
   See also Advertising; Newspapers
NEWSPAPER EDITORS
Boyd, G. M. My Times in black and white   **92**
Connors, P. Fire season   **634.9**
Elie, P. The life you save may be your own   **810**
Ellison, R. The collected essays of Ralph Ellison   **814**
Gelb, A. City room   **92**
Hansberry, L. To be young, gifted, and Black   **92**
Luxenberg, S. Annie's ghosts   **92**
My life as author and editor   **818**
Nasaw, D. The chief: the life of William Randolph Hearst   **070.5**
O'Shea, J. The deal from hell   **92**
Rodgers, M. E. Mencken   **92**
Teachout, T. The skeptic: the life of H.L. Mencken   **92**
Thomas, E. The war lovers   **973.8**
Whyte, K. The uncrowned king   **92**
NEWSPAPER EXECUTIVES
Baker, N. The World on Sunday   **071**

Giddings, P. Ida: a sword among lions   **92**
Kennedy, J. F. Profiles in courage   **920**
Morris, J. M. Pulitzer   **92**
Nasaw, D. The chief: the life of William Randolph Hearst   **070.5**
Nissenson, M. The lady upstairs   **92**
O'Shea, J. The deal from hell   **92**
Remnick, D. Reporting   **814**
Symonds, C. L. Lincoln and his admirals   **92**
Thomas, E. The war lovers   **973.8**
Timerman, J. Prisoner without a name, cell without a number   **92**
Tofel, R. J. Restless genius   **92**
Whyte, K. The uncrowned king   **92**
Wolff, M. The man who owns the news   **92**
NEWSPAPER PUBLISHING -- TECHNOLOGICAL INNOVATIONS
Shepard, S. B. Deadlines and disruption   **070.5**
NEWSPAPER WORK *See* Reporters and reporting
NEWSPAPERS
    See also Mass media; Serial publications
NEWSPAPERS -- SECTIONS, COLUMNS, ETC. -- COMICS
Holtz, A. American newspaper comics   **741.5**
NEWSPAPERS -- UNITED STATES
Collins, P. The murder of the century   **364.152**
Michaeli, E. The defender   **071**
The New York Times complete World War II, 1939-1945   **940.53**
NEWSWEEK
Povich, L. The good girls revolt   **331.4**
Newton and the counterfeiter. Levenson, T.   **92**
Newton, Aaron
Astyk, S. A nation of farmers   **338.1**
Newton, David E.
Latinos in science, math, and professions   **920.003**
World energy crisis   **333.79**
Newton, Deborah
Finishing school   **746.43**
Newton, Isaac Sir, 1642-1727
    About
Bell, E. T. Men of mathematics   **920**
The Cambridge companion to Newton   **530**
Dolnick, E. The clockwork universe   **509**
Fara, P. Newton: the making of genius   **92**
Gleick, J. Isaac Newton   **92**
Levenson, T. Newton and the counterfeiter   **92**
Westfall, R. S. The life of Isaac Newton   **92**
Newton, Michael A.
Enemy of the state   **345**
Newton: the making of genius. Fara, P.   **92**
The **next** government of the United States. Kettl, D. F.   **351**
Next man up. Feinstein, J.   **796.332**
Next of kin. Fouts, R.   **156**
The **next** pandemic. Khan, A. S.   **362.1**

The **next** wave. Herridge, C.   **363.32**
Nexus: small worlds and the groundbreaking science of networks. Buchanan, M.   **530**
NEZ PERCÉ INDIANS -- HISTORY -- 19TH CENTURY
West, E. The last Indian war   **973.8**
NEZ PERCE INDIANS
Brown, D. A. The American West   **978**
Josephy, A. M. The Nez Perce Indians and the opening of the Northwest   **970.004**
The **Nez** Perce Indians and the opening of the Northwest. Josephy, A. M.   **970.004**
Ngô, Đình Diệm, 1901-1963
    About
Miller, E. Misalliance   **959.704**
Ngũgĩ wa Thiong'o, 1938-
    About
Ngugi wa Thiong'o In the house of the interpreter   **823**
Nguyen, Andrea
Asian dumplings   **641.59**
Nguyen, Luke
The food of Vietnam   **641.59**
Nguyen, Viet Thanh, 1971-
Nothing ever dies   **959.704**
Nic Dhiarmada, Bríona
The 1916 Irish Rebellion   **941.5**
Nica's dream. Kastin, D.   **92**
NICARAGUA -- POLITICS AND GOVERNMENT
Unferth, D. O. Revolution   **920**
Nicastro, Nicholas
Circumference   **526**
Niccolo's smile: a biography of Machiavelli. Viroli, M.   **92**
The **nice** girl syndrome. Engel, B.   **155.6**
Nice, David
Prokofiev: from Russia to the West, 1891-1935   **92**
Nicholas and Alexandra. Massie, R. K.   **92**
Nicholas II. Ferro, M.   **92**
Nicholas II, Emperor of Russia, 1868-1918
    About
Carter, M. George, Nicholas, and Wilhelm   **940.3**
Clay, C. King, Kaiser, Tsar   **920**
Ferro, M. Nicholas II   **92**
Kurth, P. Tsar: the lost world of Nicholas and Alexandra   **947.08**
Massie, R. K. Nicholas and Alexandra   **92**
Massie, R. K. The Romanovs   **947.08**
Rappaport, H. The Romanov sisters   **920**
Nicholl, Charles
The reckoning   **92**
Nicholls, Henry
The way of the panda   **599.7**
Nicholls, Steve
Paradise found   **508**

Nichols, C. Reid
Encyclopedia of marine science   **551.46**
Nichols, Lew
(jt. auth) Proulx, A. Cider   **641.2**
Nicholson, Alexander
Fighting to serve   **355**
Nichter, Luke A.
(ed) The Nixon tapes   **973.924**
Nichtern, Ethan
The road home   **294.3**
Nickel and dimed. Ehrenreich, B.   **305.5**
Nicklaus, Jack
About
Nicklaus, J. Jack Nicklaus   **796.352**
NICKNAMES
Delahunty, A. Oxford dictionary of nick-
names   **929.4**
Latham, E. A dictionary of names, nicknames, and
surnames of persons, places, and things   **929.4**
NICKNAMES
See also Personal names
Nicky Epstein's essential edgings collection. Epstein, N.
Nico, Brooke
More Lovely Knitted Lace   **746.432**
Nicolson, Adam, 1957-
Sea room: an island life in the Hebrides   **941.1**
About
Nicolson, A. Why Homer matters   **883**
Nicolson, Juliet
The perfect summer   **942**
Nicomachean ethics. Aristotle   **170**
NICOTINE HABIT *See* Tobacco habit
Niebuhr, Gary Warren
Caught up in crime   **016**
Make mine a mystery   **809**
Make mine a mystery II   **016**
Niebuhr, Gustav
Beyond tolerance   **201**
Niedecker, Lorine
Collected works   **811**
Nielsen, Claus
Animal evolution   **591.3**
Nielsen, Kim E.
A disability history of the United States   **362.4**
(ed) Keller, H. Helen Keller: selected writings   **92**
Nietzsche. Safranski, R.   **193**
Nietzsche, Friedrich Wilhelm, 1844-1900
Basic writings of Nietzsche   **193**
The portable Nietzsche   **193**
Thus spoke Zarathustra   **193**
The will to power   **193**
About
Camus, A. The rebel   **303.6**
Durant, W. J. The story of philosophy   **109**
Existentialism from Dostoevsky to Sartre   **142**
Russell, B. A history of Western philosophy   **109**

Safranski, R. Nietzsche   **193**
Solomon, R. C. What Nietzsche really said   **193**
Nigella express. Lawson, N.   **641.5**
NIGERIA -- COLONIZATION
Achebe, C. The education of a British-protected
child   **92**
NIGERIA -- POLITICS AND GOVERNMENT
Maier, K. This house has fallen   **966.905**
Nigge, Klaus
Whooping crane   **598**
Night. Wiesel, E.   **92**
NIGHT
See also Chronology; Time
NIGHT
Brassaï Brassai   **944.361**
Ekirch, A. R. At day's close   **306.4**
NIGHT -- PSYCHOLOGICAL ASPECTS
Bogard, P. The end of night   **551.56**
NIGHT -- SOCIAL ASPECTS
Ekirch, A. R. At day's close   **306.4**
The **night** Abraham called to the stars. Bly, R.   **811**
Night and horses and the desert.   **892.7**
Night draws near. Shadid, A.   **956.7**
The **night** of the gun. Carr, D.   **92**
A **night** to remember. Lord, W.   **910.4**
Night wraps the sky.   **92**
Nightingale, Florence, 1820-1910
About
Bostridge, M. Florence Nightingale   **92**
NIGHTINGALES
Birkhead, T. Bird sense   **598**
**NIGHTLIFE -- FRANCE -- PARIS -- GUIDE-
BOOKS**
Baxter, J. Five nights in Paris   **914.4**
NightWatch: a practical guide to viewing the uni-
verse. Dickinson, T.   **520**
NIHILISM
Camus, A. The rebel   **303.6**
NIKE (FIRM)
Knight, P. H. Shoe dog   **92**
Nikita Khrushchev.   **92**
NILE RIVER -- DESCRIPTION AND TRAVEL
Wood, L. Walking the Nile   **916.2**
NILE RIVER -- EXPLORATION
Jeal, T. Explorers of the Nile   **962**
NILE RIVER -- SOCIAL CONDITIONS
Morrison, D. The black Nile   **962**
Nilsen, Kirsti
Conducting the reference interview   **025.5**
Nilsson, Lennart
A child is born   **612.6**
Nimitz, Chester W. (Chester William), 1885-1966
About
Borneman, W. R. The admirals   **920**
Nimura, Janice P.
Daughters of the Samurai   **920.72**

Nin, Anaïs, 1903-1977
About
Pierpont, C. R. Passionate minds   **810**
The **nine.** Toobin, J. R.   **347**
Nine hills to Nambonkaha. Erdman, S.   **966.68**
Nine horses. Collins, B.   **811**
Nine lives. Dalrymple, W.   **294**
Nine lives. Baum, D.   **976.3**
Nine plays of the modern theater.   **808.82**
NINETEEN EIGHTIES
Sirota, D. Back to our future   **973.92**
NINETEEN EIGHTIES
See also World history -- 20th century
NINETEEN FIFTIES
The 50s   **973**
NINETEEN FIFTIES
See also World history -- 20th century
NINETEEN FORTIES
The 40s   **973.917**
Weisbrode, K. The Year of Indecision, 1946 **973.918**
NINETEEN SEVENTIES
Frum, D. How we got here   **973.92**
Killen, A. 1973 nervous breakdown   **973.924**
Wheen, F. Strange days indeed   **973.92**
NINETEEN SEVENTIES
See also World history -- 20th century
NINETEEN SIXTIES
The 60s   **909.826**
Huntington, C. Heavenly bodies   **811**
Markoff, J. What the dormouse said--   **004**
Savage, J. 1966   **781.66**
Schultz, K. M. Buckley and Mailer   **973.92**
Stone, R. Prime green   **92**
NINETEEN SIXTIES
See also World history -- 20th century
NINETEEN SIXTIES -- DRAMA
Wilson, A. Two trains running   **812**
NINETEEN THIRTEEN, A.D
Emmerson, C. 1913   **909.82**
NINETEEN THIRTIES
See also World history -- 20th century
NINETEEN TWENTIES
Burns, E. 1920   **973.91**
Mackrell, J. Flappers   **920**
NINETEEN TWENTIES
See also World history -- 20th century
NINETEENTH CENTURY *See* World history --
19th century
Ninety days.   **362.29**
Ninety degrees North. Fleming, F.   **919**
Ninja. Man, J.   **355.5**
NINJA
Man, J. Ninja   **355.5**
The **Ninth.** Sachs, H.   **785**
Niose, David
Nonbeliever nation   **211**

Nirenberg, David
Anti-Judaism   **305.892**
NIRVANA (MUSICAL GROUP)
Cross, C. R. Heavier than heaven: a biography of
Kurt Cobain   **92**
Cross, C. R. Here we are now   **92**
Nisbett, Richard E.
Mindware   **153.4**
NISEI *See* Japanese Americans
Nisei daughter. Sone, M.   **979.7**
**NISQUALLI INDIANS -- GOVERNMENT RE-
LATIONS**
Kluger, R. The bitter waters of Medicine
Creek   **979.7**
NISQUALLI INDIANS -- HISTORY
Kluger, R. The bitter waters of Medicine
Creek   **979.7**
Nissenson, Marilyn
The lady upstairs   **92**
Nissley, Tom
A reader's book of days   **809**
NITRATES
See also Chemicals; Fertilizers
NITROGEN -- ENVIRONMENTAL ASPECTS
Gorman, H. S. The story of N   **547**
NITROGEN CYCLE
Gorman, H. S. The story of N   **547**
Nitze, Paul H.
About
Thompson, N. The hawk and the dove   **92**
Niven, Jennifer
Ada Blackjack   **92**
Niven, Penelope, 1939-2014
Thornton Wilder   **809**
Nix, Lacy Hunter
(ed) Foxfire 40th anniversary book   **975.8**
Nix, Shann
(jt. auth) Meyers, P. As we speak   **808.5**
Nixon and Kissinger. Dallek, R.   **92**
The **Nixon** Defense. Dean, J. W.   **973.924**
The **Nixon** tapes.   **973.924**
**NIXON, RICHARD M. (RICHARD MILHOUS),
1913-1994**
About
Abuse of power   **973.924**
Bass, G. J. The Blood telegram   **327.73**
Black, C. M. Richard M. Nixon   **92**
Dallek, R. Nixon and Kissinger   **92**
Dean, J. W. The Nixon Defense   **973.924**
Emery, F. Watergate   **973.924**
Feldstein, M. Poisoning the press   **973.924**
Frank, J. Ike and dick   **973.921**
Gellman, I. F. The President and the Appren-
tice   **973.921**
Hughes, K. Chasing shadows   **973.924**
Kissinger, H. Diplomacy   **327.2**

Matthews, C. Kennedy & Nixon   **973.922**
Morrow, L. The best year of their lives   **920**
The Nixon tapes   **973.924**
Perlstein, R. Nixonland   **973.924**
Pietrusza, D. 1960: LBJ vs. JFK vs. Nixon   **973.92**
Reeves, R. President Nixon   **973.924**
Reston, J. The conviction of Richard Nixon   **973.924**
Thomas, E. Being Nixon   **92**
Weiner, T. One man against the world   **973.924**
Wheen, F. Strange days indeed   **973.92**
Woodward, B. The final days   **973.924**
Woodward, B. Shadow   **973.92**
Nixonland. Perlstein, R.   **973.924**
Niyizonkiza, Deogratias, 1970-
                    About
Kidder, T. Strength in what remains   **92**
No applause, just throw money; or, The book that
  made vaudeville famous. Trav S. D.   **792.7**
No better friend. Weintraub, R.   **304.2**
No crueler tyrannies. Rabinowitz, D.   **345**
No dream is too high. Aldrin, B.   **92**
No easy day. Maurer, K.   **958.104**
No exit, and three other plays. Sartre, J. P.   **842**
No fears, no excuses. Smith, L. R.   **650.1**
No fixed points. Reynolds, N.   **792.8**
No future without forgiveness. Tutu, D.   **968.06**
No god but God. Aslan, R.   **297**
No good men among the living. Gopal, A.   **958.104**
No heaven. Ostriker, A.   **811**
No higher honor. Rice, C.   **327.73**
No house to call my home. Berg, R.   **362.786**
No impact man. Beavan, C.   **333.72**
No Limits. Poulter, I.   **920**
No nature. Snyder, G.   **811**
No one here gets out alive. Hopkins, J.   **92**
No ordinary time. Goodwin, D. K.   **92**
No other book. Jarrell, R.   **809**
No place to hide. Greenwald, G.   **327.12**
NO PLAYS
  Waley, A. The No plays of Japan   **895.6**
The **No** plays of Japan. Waley, A.   **895.6**
No quarter. Slotkin, R.   **973.7**
No regrets. Burke, C.   **92**
No room for error. Carney, J. T.   **356**
No shelf required.   **025.17**
No shelf required 2.   **070.5**
No simple highway. Richardson, P.   **781.66**
No small courage.   **305.4**
No such thing as over-exposure. Slater, R.   **92**
No two alike. Harris, J. R.   **155.2**
No wave. Moore, T.   **781.66**
No Way but Gentlenesse. Hines, R.   **92**
No way home. Wilcove, D. S.   **591.56**
No-churn ice cream. Bilderback, L.   **641.86**
No-drama discipline. Siegel, D. J.   **649**
NOAH'S ARK

Montgomery, D. R. The rocks don't lie   **551.48**
Noah, Timothy
The great divergence   **339.2**
Noakes, Vivien
(ed) Lear, E. The complete verse and other non-
  sense   **821**
NOBEL LAUREATES FOR CHEMISTRY
Coffey, P. Cathedrals of science   **540**
Pauling, L. C. Linus Pauling in his own words   **081**
Reeves, R. A force of nature   **92**
**NOBEL LAUREATES FOR ECONOMIC SCI-
  ENCES**
Ellison, R. The collected essays of Ralph Elli-
  son   **814**
NOBEL LAUREATES FOR PEACE
Addams, J. Twenty years at Hull-House   **361.7**
Alter, J. The promise   **92**
Balz, D. J. The battle for America, 2008   **973.932**
Bloom, H. The Western canon   **809**
Branch, T. At Canaan's edge   **973.923**
Branch, T. Pillar of fire   **973.922**
Branch, T. Parting the waters: America in the King
  years, 1954-63   **973.921**
Brands, H. W. Woodrow Wilson   **92**
Bstan-'dzin-rgya-mtsho, D. L. X. Freedom in ex-
  ile   **92**
Burns, J. M. The three Roosevelts   **973.91**
Burns, R. Burial for a King   **92**
Carlin, J. Playing the enemy   **968.06**
Carter, J. Everything to gain   **92**
Carter, J. An hour before daylight   **92**
Carter, J. Keeping faith: memoirs of a president   **92**
Carter, J. Sharing good times   **92**
Cooper, J. M. The warrior and the priest: Woodrow
  Wilson and Theodore Roosevelt   **92**
Cooper, J. M. Woodrow Wilson   **92**
Cordery, S. A. Alice   **92**
Dallek, R. Nixon and Kissinger   **92**
DiSilvestro, R. L. Theodore Roosevelt in the Bad-
  lands   **92**
Duke, L. Mandela, Mobutu, and me   **968.06**
Dyson, M. E. I may not get there with you: the true
  Martin Luther King, Jr   **323**
Egan, T. The big burn   **973.91**
Feinstein, A. Pablo Neruda   **92**
Halberstam, D. The best and the brightest   **973.922**
Hayden, T. The long sixties   **973.92**
Hofstadter, R. The American political tradition, and
  the men who made it   **973**
I see the promised land   **92**
In his own words   **92**
Iyer, P. The open road   **92**
Jackson, T. Becoming King   **92**
Johnson, T. Tragedy in crimson   **294.3**
King, M. L. The autobiography of Martin Luther
  King, Jr   **323**

Kissinger, H. Diplomacy **327.2**
Kissinger, H. Years of renewal **973.924**
Knight, L. W. Jane Addams **92**
Kotz, N. Judgment days **323**
Maathai, W. Unbowed **92**
MacMillan, M. Paris 1919 **940.3**
Mandela, N. Conversations with myself **92**
Mandela, N. Long walk to freedom: the autobiography of Nelson Mandela **92**
Mandela, N. Mandela **968.06**
Mann, J. The rebellion of Ronald Reagan **973.927**
McCullough, D. G. Mornings on horseback **92**
McCullough, D. G. The path between the seas **972.87**
Mendell, D. Obama **92**
Millard, C. The river of doubt **973.91**
Morris, E. The rise of Theodore Roosevelt **92**
Morris, E. Theodore Rex **92**
Neruda, P. The poetry of Pablo Neruda **861**
Obama, B. Dreams from my father **92**
O'Toole, P. When trumpets call **92**
Pauling, L. C. Linus Pauling in his own words **081**
Pepper, W. F. An act of state **364.1**
Pooley, E. The climate war **363.7**
Ratnesar, R. Tear down this wall **973.927**
Rauchway, E. Murdering McKinley **973.8**
Remnick, D. The bridge **92**
Remnick, D. Reporting **814**
Risen, C. A nation on fire **973.923**
Roberts, A. Masters and commanders **940.54**
Sampson, A. Nelson Mandela **92**
Shalom, friend: the life and legacy of Yitzhak Rabin **92**
Sides, H. Hellhound on his trail **364.152**
Smith, D. J. Young Mandela **92**
Spink, K. Mother Teresa **271**
Thomas, E. The war lovers **973.8**
Thurman, R. A. F. Why the Dalai Lama matters **294.3**
Tolstaia, T. Pushkin's children **891.7**
Tuchman, B. W. Practicing history **907**
Urrutia, M. My life with Pablo Neruda **92**
Weintraub, S. 15 stars **920**
Wiesel, E. All rivers run to the sea **813**
Wiesel, E. And the sea is never full **813**
Wiesel, E. Night **92**
Wintle, J. Perfect hostage **92**
Woodward, B. Shadow **973.92**
Young, A. An easy burden **92**
Zelnick, B. Gore: a political life **92**
Zimmermann, W. First great triumph **973**

NOBEL LAUREATES FOR PHYSICS
Aczel, A. D. God's equation **523.1**
Bodanis, D. E **530.1**
Bolles, E. B. Einstein defiant **530.1**
Brian, D. The Curies **92**

Cassidy, D. C. Beyond uncertainty **92**
Dry, S. Curie **92**
Einstein, A. Einstein on politics **92**
Einstein, A. A stubbornly persistent illusion **530.1**
Feldman, B. 112 Mercer Street **920**
Galison, P. L. Einstein's clocks and Poincare's maps **529**
Goodstein, D. L. Feynman's lost lecture **521**
Greenspan, N. T. The end of the certain world **92**
Gribbin, J. R. Schrodinger's kittens and the search for reality **530.1**
Hargittai, I. The Martians of science **920**
Isaacson, W. Einstein: his life and universe **92**
Krauss, L. M. Quantum man **92**
Larson, E. Thunderstruck **364.152**
Marton, K. The great escape **920**
Miller, A. I. Empire of the stars **520**
Ohanian, H. C. Einstein's mistakes **530**
Rigden, J. S. Einstein 1905 **530.1**
Sagan, C. Broca's brain **500**

NOBEL LAUREATES FOR PHYSIOLOGY OR MEDICINE
Kandel, E. R. In search of memory **153**
Ridley, M. Francis Crick **92**
Varmus, H. The art and politics of science **92**
Watson, J. D. Avoid boring people **92**
Watson, J. D. Genes, girls, and Gamow **92**
The Nobel Prize. Feldman, B. **001.4**

NOBEL PRIZE WINNERS -- FRANCE -- BIOGRAPHY
Carroll, S. B. Brave genius **920**

NOBEL PRIZES
Feldman, B. The Nobel Prize **001.4**
Feynman **92**
Spink, K. Mother Teresa **92**
Varmus, H. The art and politics of science **92**

NOBILITY
MacColl, G. To marry an English Lord **974.7**

NOBILITY
See also Upper class

NOBILITY -- ENGLAND -- BIOGRAPHY
Byrne, P. Belle **92**
Livingstone, N. The mistresses of Cliveden **942.009**

NOBILITY -- GREAT BRITAIN -- BIOGRAPHY
Foreman, A. Georgiana, Duchess of Devonshire **941.07**
Weir, A. The lost Tudor princess **92**

NOBILITY -- RUSSIA
Smith, D. Former people **305.5**

Noble, Bill
(jt. auth) Cox, M. The Gardener's Garden **712**

Nobody turn me around. Euchner, C. **323.1**

Nobody's perfect. Lane, A. **791.43**

Nocera, Joe
(jt. auth) McLean, B. All the devils are here **330.9**
Indentured **796.04**

Noël Hume, Ivor
Belzoni 92
Nofi, Albert A.
Dunnigan, J. F. The Pacific War encyclopedia 940.54
Noguchi, Isamu, 1904-1988
About
Herrera, H. Listening to stone 92
NOISE
See also Public health; Sound
NOISE -- PSYCHOLOGICAL ASPECTS
Keizer, G. The unwanted sound of everything we want 363.7
NOISE POLLUTION
See also Pollution
Nokes, David
Jane Austen 823
Nolan, Peter
Is China buying the world? 332.67
Nolan, Tom
(ed) Meanwhile there are letters 92
Three chords for beauty's sake: the life of Artie Shaw 92
Nolen, Jeremy
German cooking now 641.594
Nolen, Jessica
(jt. auth) Nolen, J. German cooking now 641.594
Nolo (Firm)
Nolo's encyclopedia of everyday law 340
Nolo's encyclopedia of everyday law. 340
Nolo's essential guide to buying your first home. Bray, I. M. 643
Nolo's essential guide to divorce. Doskow, E. 346.01
Nolo's quick reference series
Stim, R. Contracts 346
Nolt, Steven M.
(jt. auth) Kraybill, D. B. Amish grace 364.152
Nom de plume. Ciuraru, C. 929.4
Nom nom paleo. Fong, H. 641.5
The **NoMad** cookbook. Humm, D. 641.597
NOMAD HOTEL (NEW YORK, N.Y.)
Humm, D. The NoMad cookbook 641.597
Nomad's hotel. Nootebooms hotel./English 910.4
NOMADIC PEOPLES See Nomads
NOMADS
Badkhen, A. Walking With Abel 305.896
Badkhen, A. The world is a carpet 958.1
Sattouf, R. The Arab of the Future 92
NOMADS
See also Primitive societies
NON-INSULIN-DEPENDENT DIABETES -- ALTERNATIVE TREATMENT
Flippin, R. The diabetes reset 616.4
NON-PROLIFERATION OF NUCLEAR WEAPONS See Arms control
Nonbeliever nation. Niose, D. 211

NONCITIZENS
See also Minorities
NONCITIZENS -- UNITED STATES
Lewis, L. N. How to Get a Green Card 342
NONCONFORMITY See Conformity; Counter culture; Dissent
NONFICTION WRITERS
Abdul-Jabbar, K. On the shoulders of giants 92
Abuse of power 973.924
Adams, M. B. Shaggy muses 920
Applegate, D. The most famous man in America 92
Armstrong, J. Love, life, Goethe 92
Bair, D. Simone de Beauvoir 848
Becker, S. I had brain surgery, what's your excuse? 92
Benfey, C. E. G. A summer of hummingbirds 920
Berkin, C. Civil War wives 920
Black, C. M. Richard M. Nixon 92
Bloom, H. The Western canon 809
Bostridge, M. Florence Nightingale 92
Branch, T. At Canaan's edge 973.923
Branch, T. Pillar of fire 973.922
Branch, T. Parting the waters: America in the King years, 1954-63 973.921
Breslin, J. I want to thank my brain for remembering me 92
Brown, J. M. Nehru: a political life 92
Bryson, B. The life and times of the thunderbolt kid 92
Burns, R. Burial for a King 92
Buzbee, L. The yellow-lighted bookshop 002
Capote, T. Portraits and observations 814
Capote, T. Too brief a treat 92
Chace, J. Acheson 92
Commager, H. S. The American mind 973
Conover, T. The routes of man 388.1
Coupland, D. Marshall McLuhan 92
Cousteau, J. Y. The human, the orchid, and the octopus 333.95
Dallek, R. Nixon and Kissinger 92
Delany, S. Having our say 92
Didion, J. The year of magical thinking 92
Dyson, M. E. I may not get there with you: the true Martin Luther King, Jr 323
Edmonds, D. Wittgenstein's poker 192
Elie, P. The life you save may be your own 810
Ellison, R. The collected essays of Ralph Ellison 814
Ellison, R. Going to the territory 818
Ellsberg, D. Secrets: a memoir of Vietnam and the Pentagon papers 959.704
Emery, F. Watergate 973.924
Existentialism from Dostoevsky to Sartre 142
Feldman, B. 112 Mercer Street 920
Fraser, K. Ornament and silence 809
Frazier, I. Travels in Siberia 957

French, P. The world is what it is **92**
Friedan, B. Life so far **92**
Garton-Ash, T. The file **327.12**
Garvey, M. Stylized **808**
Gates, H. L. Colored people **92**
Gates, H. L. The future of the race **305.896**
Gay, P. My German question **943**
Giddings, P. Ida: a sword among lions **92**
Goodall, J. Beyond innocence **92**
Goodwin, D. K. Wait till next year **796.357**
Halberstam, D. The best and the brightest **973.922**
Hansberry, L. To be young, gifted, and Black **92**
Harlan, L. R. Booker T. Washington: the making of a black leader, 1856-1901 **92**
Harlan, L. R. Booker T. Washington: the wizard of Tuskegee, 1901-1915 **92**
Hedrick, J. D. Harriet Beecher Stowe **92**
Heilbroner, R. L. The worldly philosophers **330.1**
Heller, A. C. Ayn Rand and the world she made **92**
Hooks, B. Belonging **92**
Hooks, B. Wounds of passion **92**
Hunter, M. Boyle **92**
Huxtable, A. L. Frank Lloyd Wright **92**
I see the promised land **92**
Jackson, T. Becoming King **92**
Judt, T. Thinking the twentieth century **320.092**
Katz, J. Dog days **636**
Kazin, A. An American procession **810**
Kennan, G. F. Sketches from a life **92**
King, J. Farley: the life of Farley Mowat **92**
King, M. L. The autobiography of Martin Luther King, Jr **323**
Kissinger, H. Diplomacy **327.2**
Kissinger, H. Years of renewal **973.924**
Kotz, N. Judgment days **323**
Kozol, J. Letters to a young teacher **371.1**
Kurson, R. Crashing through **92**
Lattin, D. The Harvard Psychedelic Club **920**
Lee, H. Edith Wharton **92**
Lewis, D. L. W.E.B. Du Bois **92**
Long, R. E. Truman Capote, enfant terrible **92**
Manguel, A. A reader on reading **818**
Marton, K. Enemies of the people **92**
Matsen, B. Jacques Cousteau **92**
Matteson, J. Eden's outcasts **92**
Matthews, C. Kennedy & Nixon **973.922**
Matthiessen, F. O. American renaissance **810**
Mayle, P. Encore Provence **944.083**
McKeen, W. Outlaw journalist **92**
McPherson, J. M. Drawn with the sword **973.7**
Merton, T. The seven storey mountain **92**
Merton, T. Intimate Merton **271**
Morgan, T. My battle of Algiers **965**
Morrow, L. The best year of their lives **920**
Mowat, F. Born naked **92**
Naipaul, V. S. Between father and son **823**

Naipaul, V. S. Reading & writing **92**
Norrell, R. J. Up from history **92**
Pepper, W. F. An act of state **364.1**
Perlstein, R. Nixonland **973.924**
Peters, S. Bernard Shaw **822**
Peterson, D. Jane Goodall: the woman who redefined man **92**
Pierpont, C. R. Passionate minds **810**
Pietrusza, D. 1960: LBJ vs. JFK vs. Nixon **973.92**
Plimpton, G. Truman Capote **813**
Proulx, A. Bird cloud **92**
Rand, A. Journals of Ayn Rand **92**
Rand, A. Letters of Ayn Rand **813**
Rapoport, R. Citizen Moore **92**
Reeves, R. President Nixon **973.924**
Remnick, D. Reporting **814**
Reston, J. The conviction of Richard Nixon **973.924**
Reynolds, D. S. Mightier than the sword **813**
Risen, C. A nation on fire **973.923**
Rosenblatt, R. Making toast **92**
Rowley, H. Richard Wright **813**
Sartre, J. P. The words **92**
Scanlon, J. Bad girls go everywhere: the life of Helen Gurley Brown **92**
Schlesinger, A. M. Journals: 1952-2000 **92**
Schlesinger, A. M. A life in the twentieth century **92**
Schroen, G. C. First in **958.1**
Sebald, W. G. On the natural history of destruction **833**
Secrest, M. Frank Lloyd Wright **92**
Service, R. Trotsky **92**
Shah, T. The Caliph's house **964**
Sides, H. Hellhound on his trail **364.152**
Smock, R. W. Booker T. Washington **92**
Spiegelman, A. MetaMaus **940.53**
Steinberg, N. Drunkard **92**
Stewart, R. The prince of the marshes **956.7**
Storrer, W. A. The Frank Lloyd Wright companion **720.9**
Sullivan, R. The Thoreau you don't know **92**
Tharoor, S. Nehru: the invention of India **954.04**
Thompson, H. S. Fear and loathing in America **070**
Thompson, H. S. The kingdom of fear **92**
Thompson, N. The hawk and the dove **92**
Tolstaia, T. Pushkin's children **891.7**
Travels with Herodotus **930**
Uncle Tom or new Negro **370**
Vowell, S. Assassination vacation **973**
Washington, B. T. Up from slavery **92**
Wenner, J. S. Gonzo **92**
What I talk about when I talk about running **92**
Wheen, F. Strange days indeed **973.92**
Wideman, J. E. Hoop roots **813**
Wilson, E. Patriotic gore **810**
Wintle, J. Perfect hostage **92**

Wolff, T. This boy's life: a memoir **92**

Woodward, B. The final days **973.924**

Woodward, B. Shadow **973.92**

Wranovics, J. Chaplin and Agee **92**

Wright, R. Black boy **92**

Young, A. An easy burden **92**

Nong's Thai kitchen. Greeley, A. **641.595**

NONGRADED SCHOOLS

    See also Ability grouping in education; Education -- Experimental methods; Schools

NONINDIGENOUS PESTS

    Hamilton, G. Super species **578.6**

NONPRESCRIPTION DRUGS

    PDR for nonprescription drugs **615**

NONPRESCRIPTION DRUGS

    See also Drugs

NONPROFIT CORPORATIONS *See* Nonprofit organizations

NONPROFIT ORGANIZATIONS -- UNITED STATES -- HISTORY

    Zunz, O. Philanthropy in America **361.7**

NONPROFIT SECTOR *See* Nonprofit organizations

NONPROFITS *See* Nonprofit organizations

Nonrequired reading. Szymborska, W. **028.1**

NONSENSE VERSES

    Lear, E. The complete verse and other nonsense **821**

NONSENSE VERSES

    See also Children's poetry; Humorous poetry; Wit and humor

Nontraditional careers for women and men. McKenna, A. **331.702**

NONVERBAL COMMUNICATION

    Dimitrius Reading people **155.2**

    Pease, A. The definitive book of body language **153.6**

NONVERBAL COMMUNICATION

    See also Communication

NONVIOLENCE

    Gandhi, M. Gandhi on non-violence **322.4**

    Rieder, J. Gospel of freedom **323.1**

    A testament of hope **323.1**

NONVIOLENT NONCOOPERATION *See* Passive resistance

NOODLES

    Green, A. Making artisan pasta **641.82**

Noonan, John Thomas

    Narrowing the nation's power: the Supreme Court sides with the states **342**

Noonan, Meg Lukens

    The coat route **338.4**

Noonan, Peggy

    A heart, a cross & a flag **973.931**

The **noonday** demon. Solomon, A. **616.85**

Nooteboom, Cees

    Nomad's hotel **910.4**

Nooteboms hotel./English

    Nomad's hotel **910.4**

Nopi. Ottolenghi, Y. **641.5**

NOPI (RESTAURANT)

    Ottolenghi, Y. Nopi **641.5**

Norah Gaughan's Knitted Cable Sourcebook. **746.432**

Norcross, Beverly Gore

    Corson, R. Stage makeup **792**

Nordberg, Jenny

    The underground girls of Kabul **305.42**

Nordhaus, Hannah

    The beekeeper's lament **638**

NORDIC PEOPLES *See* Teutonic peoples

Nordland, Rod

    The Lovers **958.104**

Norgaard, Mette

    (jt. auth) Conant, D. R. Touchpoints **658.4**

Norgren, Jill

    Belva Lockwood **92**

Norling, Ernest R.

    Perspective made easy **742**

NORM (PHILOSOPHY)

    Smoller, J. The other side of normal **591.5**

The **Norman** Conquest. Morris, M. **942.02**

Norman Mailer. Lennon, J. M. **92**

Norman Rockwell. Hennessey, M. H. **759.13**

Norman, Don

    The design of everyday things **745.2**

Norman, Elizabeth M.

    Tears in the darkness **940.54**

Norman, Jesse

    Edmund Burke **92**

Norman, Marsha

    Collected plays **812**

Norman, Michael

    (jt. auth) Norman, E. M. Tears in the darkness **940.54**

    Haunted America **133.1**

Norman, Philip

    John Lennon **92**

NORMANDY (FRANCE), ATTACK ON, 1944

    Ambrose, S. E. D-Day, June 6, 1944 **940.54**

    Beevor, A. D-day **940.54**

    Hervieux, L. Forgotten **940.54**

    Macintyre, B. Double cross **940.54**

    Talty, S. Agent Garbo **940.5**

NORMANDY (FRANCE), ATTACK ON, 1944

    See also World War, 1939-1945 -- Campaigns

NORMANS

    See also Great Britain -- History -- 1066-1154, Norman period

Norrell, Robert J.

    Alex Haley and the books that changed a nation **92**

    Up from history **92**

Norris, Frank, 1870-1902

About

Drabelle, D. The great American railroad war **385**

Norris, George William, 1861-1944

About

Kennedy, J. F. Profiles in courage **920**

Norris, Gloria

About

Norris, G. Kookooland **92**

Norris, Kathleen, 1947-

The cloister walk **255**

Journey: new and selected poems, 1969-1999 **811**

About

Norris, K. Acedia & me **92**

Norris, Mary

Between you & me **428**

Norris, Michele

The grace of silence **92**

Norris, Michele, 1961-

About

Norris, M. The grace of silence **92**

Norris, Robert S.

Racing for the bomb: General Leslie R. Groves, the Manhattan Project's indispensable man **92**

NORSE LITERATURE *See* Old Norse literature; Scandinavian literature

NORSE MYTHOLOGY

See also Mythology

NORSEMEN *See* Vikings

North. Eddy, J. **641.59**

NORTH AFRICA

See also Africa

NORTH AFRICA -- HISTORY

Tinniswood, A. Pirates of Barbary **909**

NORTH AMERICA

Abroad at home **917.3**

NORTH AMERICA -- ANTIQUITIES -- ENCY-CLOPEDIAS

Archaeology of prehistoric native America **970.01**

NORTH AMERICA -- CIVILIZATION -- 17TH CENTURY

Bailyn, B. The barbarous years **973.2**

NORTH AMERICA -- GAZETTEERS

The Columbia gazetteer of North America **917**

NORTH AMERICA -- HISTORICAL GEOGRA-PHY

Hayes, D. Historical atlas of the North American railroad **385**

NORTH AMERICA -- HISTORY

Keegan, J. Fields of battle **355.009**

Morgan, T. Wilderness at dawn **970**

NORTH AMERICA -- RACE RELATIONS

Woodard, C. American nations **970.004**

The **North** American guide to common poisonous plants and mushrooms. Turner, N. J. **581.6**

NORTH CAROLINA STATE UNIVERSITY -- BASKETBALL -- HISTORY

Feinstein, J. The legends club **796.323**

NORTH KOREA *See* Korea (North)

North Korea undercover. Sweeney, J.

NORTH LUANGWA NATIONAL PARK (ZAMBIA)

Owens, D. The eye of the elephant **333.95**

NORTH POLE

Fleming, F. Ninety degrees North **919**

NORTH POLE -- DISCOVERY AND EXPLORATION -- NORWEIGIAN

Bown, S. R. The last Viking **92**

NORTH SEA

Pye, M. The Edge of the World **940.1**

North, Chris

How to Read the Solar System **523.2**

North, Dan

Foner, M. Not for bread alone **92**

NORTHAMPTON (MASS.)

Kidder, T. Home town **974.4**

NORTHEAST AFRICA

See also Africa

NORTHEAST PASSAGE

See also Arctic regions; Exploration; Voyages and travels

NORTHEASTERN STATES

Burns, C. The great hurricane-1938 **974.7**

NORTHEASTERN STATES -- POLITICS AND GOVERNMENT

Sokol, J. All eyes are upon us **323.1**

NORTHEASTERN STATES -- RACE RELATIONS

Sugrue, T. J. Sweet land of liberty **323**

Northern Armageddon. Macleod, D. P. **971.01**

NORTHERN BOUNDARY OF THE UNITED STATES -- HISTORY

Taylor, A. The civil war of 1812 **973.5**

Taylor, A. The divided ground **974.7**

NORTHERN IRELAND

Conroy, J. Unspeakable acts, ordinary people **323.4**

Coogan, T. P. The troubles **941.6**

NORTHERN IRELAND -- HISTORY

Campbell, J. Setting the truth free **941.6**

NORTHMEN *See* Vikings

Northrop Frye on Shakespeare. Frye, N. **822.3**

Northrup, Christiane

Goddesses never age **613**

Northup, Solomon, 1808-

About

Twelve years a slave **92**

NORTHWEST COAST OF NORTH AMERICA -- DESCRIPTION AND TRAVEL

Raban, J. Passage to Juneau **979.8**

NORTHWEST PASSAGE

Brandt, A. The man who ate his boots **910.4**

Cookman, S. Ice blink **919**

Geiger, J. Frozen in time **919**

Williams, G. Arctic labyrinth 910.4
Winter, K. Boundless 910.9
NORTHWEST PASSAGE
   See also America -- Exploration; Arctic regions
NORTHWEST PASSAGE -- DESCRIPTION AND TRAVEL
   Winter, K. Boundless 910.9
NORTHWEST, PACIFIC *See* Pacific Northwest
NORTHWEST, PACIFIC -- DESCRIPTION AND TRAVEL
   Raban, J. Passage to Juneau 979.8
The **Norton** anthology of African American literature. 810
The **Norton** anthology of English literature. 820
The **Norton** anthology of Latino literature. 810
The **Norton** anthology of modern and contemporary poetry. 821
Norton Anthology of Western Music. 780
The **Norton** book of American autobiography. 920
The **Norton** book of classical literature. 880
The **Norton** book of modern war. 808.8
The **Norton** book of personal essays. 808.84
A **Norton critical edition** [series]
   Browning, R. Robert Browning's poetry 821
   Malory, T. Le morte Darthur, or, The hoole book of Kyng Arthur and of his noble knyghtes of the Rounde Table 398.2
Norton, Elizabeth
   The Temptation of Elizabeth Tudor 92
Norton-Hawk, Maureen
   (jt. auth) Sered, S. S. Can't catch a break 362.83
The **Norton/Grove** dictionary of women composers. 780.92
NORWEGIAN LANGUAGE
   See also Language and languages; Scandinavian languages
NORWEGIAN LITERATURE
   See also Literature; Scandinavian literature
Norwegian wood. 634.9
Norwich, John Julius
   Byzantium: the apogee 949.5
   Byzantium: the decline and fall 949.5
   Byzantium: the early centuries 949.5
   Shakespeare's kings 822.3
   Sicily 945.8
Nosakhere, Akilah S.
   (ed) The 21st-century black librarian in America 020
NOSOCOMIAL INFECTIONS -- PREVENTION
   Goldfarb, T. L. The patient survival guide
NOSTALGIA -- POETRY
   pH neutral history 891.8
Nostradamus. Gerson, S. 92
Nostradamus, 1503-1566
       About
   Gerson, S. Nostradamus 92

Not buying it. Levine, J. 640.73
Not for bread alone. Foner, M. 92
Not for specialists. Snodgrass, W. D. 811
Not out of Africa. Lefkowitz, M. R. 960
Not pretty enough. Hirshey, G. 92
Not quite adults. Ray, B. E. 306.8
The **not** so big house. Susanka, S. 728
Not so big remodeling. Susanka, S. 643.7
Not so big solutions for your home. Susanka, S. 728
Not to be missed. Turan, K. 791.43
Not your mother's divorce. Moffett, K. 306.89
NOT-FOR-PROFIT ORGANIZATIONS *See* Nonprofit organizations
Notable American women. Ware, S. 920.003
Notable American women: the modern period. 920.003
Notable black American men, book I. 920.003
Notable black American men, book II. 920.003
Notable black American scientists. 509
Notable black American women, book I. 920.003
Notable black American women, Book III. 920.003
Notable Latino writers. Salem Press Inc. 810
Notable native Americans. 920.003
Notable scientists [series]
   Gates, A. E. A to Z of earth scientists 920.003
Notable voices [series]
   Cording, R. Walking with Ruskin 811
Notable women in American history. Adamson, L. G. 016
Notable women in world history. Adamson, L. G. 016
NOTE-TAKING
   See also Reporters and reporting; Study skills
NOTEBOOKS
   See also Books
Notes from a small island. Bryson, B. 914
Notes from no man's land. Biss, E. 305.8
Notes from the air. Ashbery, J. 811
Notes on a century. Lewis, B. 956
Nothing. Close, F. E. 530
Nothing. 501
NOTHING (PHILOSOPHY)
   Barrow, J. D. The book of nothing 111
   Close, F. E. Nothing 530
   Nothing 501
Nothing but the blues. 781.643
Nothing ever dies. Nguyen, V. T. 959.704
Nothing is true and everything is possible. Pomerantsev, P. 306
Nothing like it in the world. Ambrose, S. E. 385
Nothing to be frightened of. Barnes, J. 92
Nothing to envy. Demick, B. 951.93
Nothing was the same. Jamison, K. R. 92
Notley, Alice
   Grave of light 811
   In the pines 811

(ed) Poems/Selections The collected poems of Ted Berrigan **811**

Notorious. Spoto, D. **92**

NOTRE DAME FIGHTING IRISH (FOOTBALL TEAM)

Robinson, R. Rockne of Notre Dame **92**

Nourse, Victoria F.

In reckless hands **344**

Nouwen, Henri

Discernment **248.4**

Novacek, Michael J.

Terra **576.8**

About

Novacek, M. J. Time traveler **92**

The **novel.** Moore, S. **809**

Novel interiors. Giramonti, L. B. **747**

Novel living. **002.075**

NOVELISTS

See also Authors

NOVELISTS, AMERICAN

Wilson, E. Patriotic gore **810**

NOVELISTS, AMERICAN *See* American novelists

NOVELISTS, AMERICAN -- 20TH CENTURY -- BIOGRAPHY

Atlas, J. Bellow **813**

Burroughs, A. Running with scissors **813**

Conroy, P. My losing season **796.323**

Harrison, K. The kiss **813**

Hillerman, T. Seldom disappointed **813**

Lamott, A. Small victories **248**

Leader, Z. The Life of Saul Bellow **92**

Max, D. T. c. Every love story is a ghost story **92**

Miles, B. Call Me Burroughs **92**

Sallis, J. Chester Himes **813**

NOVELISTS, AMERICAN -- 20TH CENTURY -- CORRESPONDENCE

Cather, W. The selected letters of Willa Cather **813**

NOVELISTS, AMERICAN -- BIOGRAPHY

Russo, R. Elsewhere **92**

NOVELISTS, ENGLISH -- 20TH CENTURY -- BIOGRAPHY

Ballard, J. G. Miracles of life **823**

Bayley, J. Elegy for Iris **823**

Conradi, P. Iris Murdoch **823**

Iyer, P. The man within my head **809**

King, D. Patrick O'Brian **823**

NOVELS *See* Fiction

Novels and stories. Hurston, Z. N. **813**

Novogratz, Jacqueline

The blue sweater **339.4**

Now. Muller, R. A. **530.11**

Now all roads lead to France. Hollis, M. **821**

Now eat this! DiSpirito, R. **641.5**

Now I sit me down. Rybczynski, W. **749.32**

Now read this. Pearl, N. **016**

Now read this II. Pearl, N. **016**

Now read this III. Pearl, N. **016**

Now the drum of war. Roper, R. **973.7**

Now write! screenwriting. **808.2**

Now, build a great business! Thompson, M. **658**

Nowak, M. A. (Martin A.)

(jt. auth) Highfield, R. Supercooperators **519.3**

Nowak, Ronald M.

Walker's mammals of the world **599**

Nowlan, Robert A.

Born this day **808.88**

Nox. Carson, A. **811**

NP-COMPLETE PROBLEMS

Fortnow, L. The golden ticket **511.3**

The **NPR** classical music companion. Hoffman, M. **780**

NUCLEAR ARMS CONTROL -- GOVERNMENT POLICY -- UNITED STATES

Pollack, K. M. Unthinkable **355.8**

Nuclear energy. Ferguson, C. D. **333.79**

NUCLEAR ENERGY

See also Nuclear physics

NUCLEAR ENERGY

Ferguson, C. D. Nuclear energy **333.79**

Nelson, C. The age of radiance **539.7**

Smith, G. Nuclear roulette **621.48**

NUCLEAR ENGINEERING

Hodge, N. A nuclear family vacation **623.4**

NUCLEAR ENGINEERING

See also Engineering; Nuclear energy; Nuclear physics

A **nuclear** family vacation. Hodge, N. **623.4**

NUCLEAR FUSION

Seife, C. Sun in a bottle **539.7**

NUCLEAR NONPROLIFERATION -- IRAN

Pollack, K. M. Unthinkable **355.8**

NUCLEAR PARTICLES *See* Particles (Nuclear physics)

NUCLEAR PHYSICS

Magueijo, J. A brilliant darkness **92**

Nelson, C. The age of radiance **539.7**

NUCLEAR PHYSICS

See also Physics

NUCLEAR POWER *See* Nuclear energy

NUCLEAR POWER PLANTS

Ferguson, C. D. Nuclear energy **333.79**

NUCLEAR POWER PLANTS -- ACCIDENTS

Smith, G. Nuclear roulette **621.48**

NUCLEAR POWER PLANTS -- ACCIDENTS -- JAPAN -- FUKUSHIMA-KEN

Lyman, E. Fukushima **363.17**

Nuclear roulette. Smith, G. **621.48**

NUCLEAR SUBMARINES

Brownfield, C. J. My nuclear family **92**

NUCLEAR SUBMARINES

See also Nuclear propulsion; Submarines

Nuclear terrorism. Allison, G. T. **363.32**
NUCLEAR TEST BAN *See* Arms control
NUCLEAR WARFARE
Allison, G. T. Nuclear terrorism **363.32**
Rees, M. J. From here to infinity **500**
Sheinkin, S. Bomb **623.4**
Wilson, W. Five myths about nuclear weapons **355.02**
NUCLEAR WARFARE
See also War
NUCLEAR WARFARE -- GOVERNMENT POLICY -- UNITED STATES -- HISTORY -- 20TH CENTURY
Thomas, E. Ike's bluff **973.92**
NUCLEAR WEAPONS
Gordin, M. D. Red cloud at dawn **355**
Hodge, N. A nuclear family vacation **623.4**
Iversen, K. Full body burden **363.17**
Karpin, M. I. The bomb in the basement **355**
Langewiesche, W. The atomic bazaar **355**
Leverett, F. Going to Tehran **327.73**
Nelson, C. The age of radiance **539.7**
Pollack, K. M. Unthinkable **355.8**
Rhodes, R. Arsenals of folly **355**
Sheehan, N. A fiery peace in a cold war **92**
Weapons of mass destruction **358**
Wilson, W. Five myths about nuclear weapons **355.02**
NUCLEAR WEAPONS
See also Military weapons
NUCLEAR WEAPONS -- ACCIDENTS -- ARKANSAS -- HISTORY
Schlosser, E. Command and control **363.17**
NUCLEAR WEAPONS -- GOVERNMENT POLICY -- UNITED STATES -- HISTORY -- 20TH CENTURY
Thomas, E. Ike's bluff **973.92**
NUCLEAR WEAPONS -- HISTORY
Gordin, M. D. Red cloud at dawn **355**
NUCLEAR WEAPONS -- IRAN
Pollack, K. M. Unthinkable **355.8**
NUCLEAR WEAPONS -- PICTORIAL WORKS
Light, M. 100 suns, 1945-1962 **355.8**
NUCLEAR WEAPONS -- PSYCHOLOGICAL ASPECTS
Wilson, W. Five myths about nuclear weapons **355.02**
NUCLEAR WEAPONS -- UNITED STATES -- HISTORY
Brands, H. W. The General Vs. the President **973.918**
Schlosser, E. Command and control **363.17**
NUCLEAR WEAPONS PLANTS -- HEALTH ASPECTS -- COLORADO
Iversen, K. Full body burden **363.17**
NUCLEIC ACIDS

See also Biochemistry
NUCLEONS *See* Particles (Nuclear physics)
Nudelman, Meyer
About
Nuland, S. B. Lost in America **92**
Nugent, Benjamin
American nerd **305.9**
Nuland, Sherwin B.
Nuland, S. B. The doctors' plague **92**
How we die **616.07**
Leonardo da Vinci **709**
About
Nuland, S. B. Lost in America **92**
Nuland, Sherwin B., 1930-2014
The doctors' plague **92**
NUMBER CONCEPT
Bellos, A. Here's looking at Euclid **513**
NUMBER THEORY
Ash, A. Elliptic tales **515**
Conway, J. H. The book of numbers **512.7**
Derbyshire, J. Prime obsession **512.7**
Singh, S. Fermat's enigma **512**
NUMBER THEORY
See also Algebra; Mathematics; Set theory
Numbers. Thaller, B. **513.5**
NUMBERS
Tammet, D. Thinking in numbers **510**
Thaller, B. Numbers **513.5**
The **numbers** game. Anderson, C. **796.334**
Numbers rule. Szpiro, G. G. **510**
NUMERALS
Aczel, A. D. Finding zero **513.5**
The **numerati.** Baker, S. **303.4**
Nunberg, Geoffrey
The ascent of the A-word **427**
NUNS
See also Women
NUREMBERG TRIAL OF MAJOR GERMAN WAR CRIMINALS, 1945-1946
Nagorski, A. The Nazi hunters **940.53**
Nureyev. Kavanagh, J. **92**
Nureyev, Rudolf, 1938-1993
About
Kavanagh, J. Nureyev **92**
NURSE-PATIENT RELATIONS -- PENNSYLVANIA -- POPULAR WORKS
Brown, T. The shift **616.02**
NURSE-PATIENT RELATIONS -- UNITED STATES -- PERSONAL NARRATIVES
Robbins, A. The nurses **362.17**
NURSERY RHYMES -- DICTIONARIES
The Oxford dictionary of nursery rhymes **398.8**
NURSERY SCHOOLS
See also Elementary education; Schools
The **nurses.** **362.17**
NURSES

Baker, J. H. Margaret Sanger   92
Benedict, J. Little pink house   **343**
Bostridge, M. Florence Nightingale   92
Brown, T. The shift   **616.02**
Culkin, J. A final arc of sky   92
Hutchinson, G. In search of Nella Larsen   92
Lineberry, C. The secret rescue   **940.54**
Robbins, A. The nurses   **362.17**
Summerscale, K. The suspicions of Mr. Whicher   **364.152**
Toler, P. D. Heroines of Mercy Street   **973.775**
Wall, C. A. Women of the Harlem Renaissance **810**
The **nurses.** Robbins, A.   **362.17**

NURSES
     See also Medical personnel

NURSES -- UNITED STATES -- BIOGRAPHY
Graeber, C. The good nurse   **364.152**

NURSING
Culkin, J. A final arc of sky   92
Robbins, A. The nurses   **362.17**

NURSING
     See also Medicine; Therapeutics

NURSING HOMES
     See also Hospitals; Institutional care; Long-term care facilities
The **nursing** mother's companion. Huggins, K. **649**
The **nursing** mother's companion. Huggins, K. **649**

NURSING SERVICE, HOSPITAL -- UNITED STATES -- PERSONAL NARRATIVES
Robbins, A. The nurses   **362.17**

NURTURE AND NATURE *See* Nature and nurture
Nussbaum, David
Bastianich, L. Lidia cooks from the heart of Italy   **641.5**
Child, J. Julia and Jacques cooking at home **641.59**
Nussbaum, Martha Craven, 1947-
Liberty of conscience   **342**
The new religious intolerance   **201**
Nusseibeh, Sari
     About
David, A. Once upon a country   92

NUTRITION
Bittman, M. Food matters   **613.2**
Bittman, M. The food matters cookbook   **641.3**
Brewer, S. C. The Canyon Ranch guide to men's health   **613**
The Cambridge world history of food   **641.3**
Davis, B. Becoming vegan   **613.2**
Duyff, R. L. American Dietetic Association complete food and nutrition guide   **613.2**
The family cooks   **641.3**
Flanagan, S. Run fast, eat slow   **641.563**
Gibney, M. Something to chew on   **616.02**
Le, S. One hundred million years of food   **641.3**
Mercola, J. M. Effortless healing   **613.2**
Morris, J. Superfood Kitchen   **641.5**

Natkin, M. Herbivoracious   **641.5**
Nesheim, M. Why calories count   **613.2**
Peacock, K. W. Food security   **338.1**
Pollan, M. In defense of food   **613**
Price, C. Vitamania   **612.3**
Robinson, J. Eating on the wild side   **306.4**
Ruggiero, T. The truly healthy family cookbook   **641.5**
Sacks, S. What the fork are you eating?   **641.3**
Schatzker, M. The Dorito effect   **641.3**
Weil, A. Eight weeks to optimum health   **613**
The whole30   **613.2**

NUTRITION
     See also Health; Physiology; Therapeutics

NUTRITION -- ECONOMIC ASPECTS -- UNITED STATES
Moss, M. Salt, sugar, fat   **613.2**

NUTRITION -- POPULAR WORKS
The whole30   **613.2**

NUTRITION -- TABLES
Netzer, C. T. The complete book of food counts   **613.2**

NUTRITION -- UNITED STATES -- PSYCHOLOGICAL ASPECTS
Price, C. Vitamania   **612.3**

NUTRITION POLICY -- HISTORY -- 20TH CENTURY
Collingham, L. The taste of war   **940.53**

NUTRITION POLICY -- UNTIED STATES
Bittman, M. A bone to pick   **338.1**
Nutrition Stripped. Hill, M.   **641.302**

NUTRITION. -- POPULAR WORKS
Olmsted, L. Real food/fake food   **641.3**

NUTRITIONAL SUPPLEMENTS *See* Dietary supplements

NUTS
     See also Food; Seeds
Nutt, Amy Ellis
     (jt. auth) Jensen, F. E. The teenage brain   **612.6**
     Becoming Nicole   **306.76**
Nuttall, A. D.
     Shakespeare the thinker   **822.3**
Nyad, Diana
     About
     Nyad, D. Find a way   92
Nyberg, Amanda Jean
     (jt. auth) Arkison, C. Sunday morning quilts **746.46**
Nye, Bill, 1955-
     Undeniable   **576.8**
Nye, Naomi Shihab
     You & yours: poems   **811**
NYPD confidential. Levitt, L.   **364.1**

O

O Jerusalem! Collins, L.   **956.94**
O'Brady, Tara

Seven spoons **641.597**

O'Brian, Patrick
About
King, D. Patrick O'Brian **823**

O'Brien, David M.
Storm center **347**

O'Brien, Edna
James Joyce **823**
About
O'Brien, E. Country Girl **92**

O'Brien, Geoffrey
Bartlett's familiar quotations **808.88**

O'Brien, Jack, 1939-
About
O'Brien, J. Jack be nimble **92**
Swidey, N. The assist **796.323**

O'Brien, Keith
Catching the Sky **796.94**

O'Brien, Michael
Mrs. Adams in winter **940.2**

O'Brien, Patricia
Goodman, E. I know just what you mean **158.2**

O'Clair, Robert
(ed) The Norton anthology of modern and contemporary poetry **821**

O'Connell, John
The Book of Spice **641.3**

O'Connell, Robert L.
The ghosts of Cannae **937**

O'Conner, Patricia T.
Woe is I **428**

O'Connor, Anne-Marie
The lady in gold **759.36**

O'Connor, Birgit
Watercolor essentials **751.42**

O'Connor, Carol A.
Milner, C. A. As big as the West **92**

O'Connor, Flannery
The habit of being **92**
About
Cash, J. W. Flannery O'Connor: a life **92**
Elie, P. The life you save may be your own **810**
Gooch, B. Flannery **92**
Kirk, C. A. Critical companion to Flannery O'Connor **813**
Michaels, J. R. Passing by the dragon **813**
O'Connor, F. The habit of being **92**

O'Connor, Garry
Universal Father: a life of John Paul II **92**

O'Connor, Kevin
The best homes from This old house **643**

O'Connor, M. R.
Resurrection Science **591.68**

O'Connor, Rory
Friends, followers, and the future **302.3**

O'Connor, Sandra Day
About
Biskupic, J. Sandra Day O'Connor **92**
Hirshman, L. Sisters in law **347.73**
Out of order **347.73**

O'Dea, Aaron
(jt. auth) Taylor, P. D. A history of life in 100 fossils **560**

O'Dell, Chris, 1947-
About
O'Dell, C. Miss O'Dell **92**

O'Donnell, Francis
Belliveau, D. In the footsteps of Marco Polo **915**

O'Donnell, Patrick K.
Washington's Immortals **973.3**

O'Donoghue, Jo
McMahon, S. Brewer's dictionary of Irish phrase & fable **427**

O'Driscoll, Dennis
Stepping stones **821**

O'Faolain, Nuala
Are you somebody **070**
A radiant life **824**

O'Gorman, Jack
Reference sources for small and medium-sized libraries **011**

O'Hara, Frank
The collected poems of Frank O'Hara **811**

O'Kane, Bernard
Treasures of Islam **709.1**

O'Keeffe, Georgia, 1887-1986
About
Drohojowska-Philp, H. Full bloom **92**
Robinson, R. Georgia O'Keeffe: a life **709**

O'Keeffe, Paul
Waterloo **940.2**

O'Leary, Peter
Johnson, R. The shrubberies **811**

O'Malley, Padraig
The two-state delusion **956.94**

O'Malley, Walter Francis, 1903-1979
About
D'Antonio, M. Forever blue **92**

O'Neil, Buck, 1911-2006
About
Posnanski, J. The soul of baseball **796.357**

O'Neil, Cathy
Weapons of math destruction **005.7**

O'Neil, Dennis
Batman unauthorized **741.5**
The DC comics guide to writing comics **741.5**

O'Neil, Eugene
Complete plays **812**

O'Neil, Maryadele J.
The Merck index **615**

O'Neill, Eugene, 1888-1953
About

Dowling, R. M.   Critical companion to Eugene
  O'Neill   **812**
Dowling, R. M. Eugene O'Neill   **92**
O'Neill, Laura
Van Leeuwen Artisan Ice Cream   **641**
O'Neill, Molly
(ed) American food writing   **641.5**
One big table   **641.5**
O'Neill, Tony
Peter, J. Hero of the underground   **92**
O'Neill, William L.
(ed) The Scribner encyclopedia of American lives,
  The 1960s   **920.003**
O'Neill, Zora
                        About
O'Neill, Z. All strangers are kin   **910.917**
O'Reilly, Bill
                        About
O'Reilly, B. A bold fresh piece of humanity   **92**
O'Rourke, Barbara Kelly, d. 2008
                        About
O'Rourke, M. The long goodbye   **92**
O'Rourke, Joseph
How to fold it   **516**
O'Rourke, Meghan
                        About
O'Rourke, M. The long goodbye   **92**
O'Shea, James
                        About
O'Shea, J. The deal from hell   **92**
O'Shea, Mark
Venomous snakes of the world   **597.96**
O'Sullivan, Penelope
The homeowner's complete tree & shrub hand-
  book   **635.9**
O'Toole, Marie
(ed) Mosby's medical dictionary   **610.3**
O'Toole, Patricia
When trumpets call   **92**
OAK
   See also Trees; Wood
**OAK RIDGE (TENN.) -- HISTORY -- 20TH
   CENTURY**
Kiernan, D. The girls of atomic city   **976.8**
Oakes, Elizabeth H.
American writers   **920.003**
A to Z of chemists   **920.003**
Oakes, James
Freedom national   **973.7**
Oakes, Ted
(jt. auth) Barrington, R. Life   **578.4**
OAKLAND (CALIF.) -- BIOGRAPHY
Williams, M. The lost daughter   **979.4**
Oakley, Annie, 1860-1926
                        About
Kasper, S. Annie Oakley   **92**

Oakley, Violet, 1874-1961
                        About
Carter, A. A. The Red Rose girls   **759.13**
Oates, Joyce Carol, 1938-
(ed) The Best American essays of the century **814**
The Lost Landscape   **92**
                        About
Oates, J. C. A widow's story   **92**
Oates, J. C. The journal of Joyce Carol Oates:
  1973-1982   **92**
Oates, Stephen B.
The approaching fury   **973.5**
The **oath**. Toobin, J.   **347.73**
The **Oath**. Baiev, K.   **947.5**
Obama. Mendell, D.   **92**
Obama, Barack, 1961-
Berry, M. F. Power in words   **973.932**
                        About
Dyson, M. E. The Black presidency   **305.8**
Halperin, M. Double Down   **324.9**
Hersh, S. The killing of Osama Bin Laden **327.73**
Kantor, J. The Obamas   **973.932**
Love, R. Power forward   **320.092**
Toobin, J. The oath   **347.73**
Alter, J. The promise   **92**
Hayden, T. The long sixties   **973.92**
Maraniss, D. Barack Obama   **92**
Mendell, D. Obama   **92**
Obama, B. Dreams from my father   **92**
Remnick, D. The bridge   **92**
Obama, Michelle, 1964-
                        About
Traister, R. Big girls don't cry   **324**
American grown   **635**
Swarns, R. L. American tapestry   **92**
Kantor, J. The Obamas   **973.932**
Slevin, P. Michelle Obama   **92**
The **Obamas**. Kantor, J.   **973.932**
Obara, Joji
                        About
Parry, R. L. People who eat darkness   **364.152**
OBEDIENCE
   See also Virtue
Obee, Jennifer
Social networking   **004.67**
OBELISKS
   See also Archeology; Architecture; Monu-
   ments
Oberdorfer, Don
The two Koreas   **951.9**
Oberhauser, Karen S.
(ed) The monarch butterfly   **595.7**
Oberman, Heiko Augustinus
Luther: man between God and the Devil   **92**
OBESITY
Bruni, F. Born round   **92**

Moss, M. Salt, sugar, fat **613.2**

Taubes, G. Why we get fat and what to do about it **613.7**

OBESITY

    See also Body weight

OBESITY -- PREVENTION

Nesheim, M. Why calories count **613.2**

OBITUARIES

Thomas, R. M. 52 McGs **920**

OBITUARIES

    See also Biography

OBJECTIVISM (PHILOSOPHY)

Heller, A. C. Ayn Rand and the world she made **92**

Rand, A. The virtue of selfishness **171**

Rand, A. The voice of reason; essays in objectivist thought **191**

OBJETS D'ART *See* Art objects

OBLIGATION *See* Responsibility

Oblivion. Abad, H. **868**

Obrist, Hans-Ulrich, 1968-

Ways of curating **707.5**

OBSERVATION (SCIENTIFIC METHOD)

Wilson, E. O. Letters to a Young Scientist **570**

Obsessed. Brzezinski, M. **362.196**

OBSESSION (PSYCHOLOGY) *See* Obsessive-compulsive disorder

OBSESSIVE-COMPULSIVE DISORDER

Adam, D. The man who couldn't stop **616.85**

Frost, R. O. Stuff **616.85**

Murphy, T. W. Life in rewind **92**

OBSESSIVE-COMPULSIVE NEUROSES *See* Obsessive-compulsive disorder

OBSTETRICS *See* Childbirth

OBSTETRICS -- POPULAR WORKS

The pregnancy encyclopedia **618.2**

Obstfeld, Raymond

Abdul-Jabbar, K. On the shoulders of giants **92**

Occhiogrosso, Peter

Zappa, F. The real Frank Zappa book **92**

Occhipinti, Lisa

Novel living **002.075**

OCCIDENTAL CIVILIZATION *See* Western civilization

Occidental mythology. Campbell, J. **201**

OCCULT SCIENCES *See* Occultism

OCCULTISM

Goodman, L. Linda Goodman's star signs **130**

Mar, A. Witches of America **299**

Mildon, E. The soul searcher's handbook **131**

OCCULTISM

    See also Religions; Supernatural

OCCULTISTS

Schmidt, L. E. Heaven's bride **92**

The **occupation** of Iraq. Allawi, A. A. **956.7**

OCCUPATIONAL DISEASES

    See also Diseases

OCCUPATIONAL GUIDANCE *See* Vocational guidance

OCCUPATIONAL HEALTH AND SAFETY

Gambaro, J. The truth about carpal tunnel syndrome **616.85**

Genoways, T. The chain **338.7**

Occupational outlook handbook. Bureau of Labor Statistics **331.7**

Occupational outlook handbook 2013-2014. **331.12**

OCCUPATIONAL TRAINING -- UNITED STATES

Chertavian, G. A Year Up **331.25**

OCCUPATIONS

Bureau of Labor Statistics Occupational outlook handbook **331.7**

Ferguson Publishing The top 100 **331.7**

McKenna, A. Nontraditional careers for women and men **331.702**

Occupational outlook handbook 2013-2014 **331.12**

OCCUPATIONS -- ENCYCLOPEDIAS

J.G. Ferguson Publishing Company Encyclopedia of careers and vocational guidance **331.7**

OCCUPIED TERRITORY *See* Military occupation

OCCUPY PROTEST MOVEMENTS

    See also Demonstrations; Protest movements

OCEAN

Carson, R. The sea around us **551.46**

Cramer, D. Smithsonian ocean **578.7**

Day, T. Oceans **551.46**

Nestor, J. Deep **797.2**

Pilkey, O. H. The rising sea **363.34**

Prager, E. J. Chasing science at sea **551.46**

Roberts, C. The ocean of life **551.46**

Roberts, C. The unnatural history of the sea **909**

Stow, D. A. V. Oceans: an illustrated reference **551.46**

OCEAN

    See also Earth; Physical geography; Water

OCEAN -- ECONOMIC ASPECTS *See* Marine resources; Shipping

OCEAN -- HISTORY

Roberts, C. The ocean of life **551.46**

OCEAN AND CIVILIZATION

Roberts, C. The ocean of life **551.46**

Winchester, S. Atlantic **551.46**

OCEAN BOTTOM

Hoyt, E. Creatures of the deep **591.7**

OCEAN BOTTOM

    See also Ocean; Submarine geology

OCEAN CABLES *See* Submarine cables

OCEAN CURRENTS

    See also Navigation; Ocean

Ocean drifters. Kirby, R. R. **578.7**

OCEAN LINERS -- UNITED STATES -- HISTORY -- 20TH CENTURY

Ujifusa, S. A man and his ship   **623.8**

OCEAN MINING

  Roberts, C. The ocean of life   **551.46**

OCEAN MINING

  See also Marine mineral resources; Mining engineering; Ocean engineering

The **ocean** of life. Roberts, C.   **551.46**

OCEAN TRAVEL

  Rackley, A. Salt, sweat, tears   **92**

OCEAN TRAVEL

  See also Transportation; Travel; Voyages and travels

OCEAN TRAVEL -- HISTORY

  Fagan, B. Beyond the blue horizon   **910.4**

OCEAN TRAVEL -- NORTH ATLANTIC OCEAN -- ANECDOTES

  Wilson, P. Lusitania   **910.4**

OCEAN WAVES

  Casey, S. The wave   **551.46**

OCEAN WAVES

  See also Ocean; Waves

OCEANIA -- DESCRIPTION AND TRAVEL

  Alexander, C. The Bounty: the true story of the mutiny on the Bounty   **996**

  Theroux, P. The happy isles of Oceania   **919**

OCEANIA -- EXPLORATION

  Blainey, G. Sea of dangers   **92**

OCEANOGRAPHERS

  Cousteau, J. Y. The human, the orchid, and the octopus   **333.95**

  Crane, K. Sea legs   **92**

  Matsen, B. Jacques Cousteau   **92**

OCEANOGRAPHY

  Carson, R. The sea around us   **551.46**

  Casey, S. The wave   **551.46**

  Cousteau, J. Y. The human, the orchid, and the octopus   **333.95**

  Crane, K. Sea legs   **92**

  Day, T. Oceans   **551.46**

  Earle, S. A. The world is blue   **551.46**

  Hohn, D. Moby-Duck   **551.46**

  Matsen, B. Jacques Cousteau   **92**

  Prager, E. J. Chasing science at sea   **551.46**

  Stow, D. A. V. Oceans: an illustrated reference   **551.46**

OCEANOGRAPHY

  See also Earth sciences

OCEANOGRAPHY -- HISTORY

  Felt, H. Soundings   **526**

OCEANOGRAPHY -- RESEARCH

  See also Research

OCEANOLOGY *See* Oceanography

Oceans. Day, T.   **551.46**

OCEANS *See* Ocean

Oceans: an illustrated reference. Stow, D. A. V.   **551.46**

OCTOPUSES -- BEHAVIOR

  Montgomery, S. The soul of an octopus   **594**

Odd bits. McLagan, J.   **641.3**

Odd girl out. Simmons, R.   **305.23**

ODDITIES *See* Curiosities and wonders

Oddly normal. Schwartz, J.   **306.76**

Odede, Kennedy

  (jt. auth) Posner, J. Find Me Unafraid   **92**

The **odes** of Horace. Horace   **874**

Odessa. King, C.   **947.7**

ODORS

  Aftel, M. Fragrant   **612.8**

ODYSSEUS (GREEK MYTHOLOGY)

  Manguel, A. Homer's The Iliad and The Odyssey   **883**

The **Odyssey.**   **883**

Odyssey. Homer   **883**

Odyssey

  The Odyssey   **883**

  The **Odyssey.** Odyssey   **883**

  The **Odyssey.** Homer   **883**

The **odyssey** of KP2. Williams, T. M.   **599.79**

Oelhafen, Ingrid von

                      About

  Tate, T. Hitler's forgotten children   **940.53**

Of a feather. Weidensaul, S.   **598**

Of a fire on the moon. Mailer, N.   **629.45**

Of Africa. Soyinka, W.   **960**

Of Arms and Artists. Staiti, P.   **759.13**

Of indigo and saffron. McClure, M.   **811**

Of orcas and men. Neiwert, D.   **599.53**

Of Plymouth Plantation, 1620-1647. Bradford, W.   **974.4**

Of wolves and men. Lopez, B. H.   **599.77**

Off camera. Koppel, T.   **92**

OFFENSES AGAINST PROPERTY

  See also Crime; Criminal law

OFFENSES AGAINST PUBLIC SAFETY

  Molotch, H. Against security   **363.325**

OFFICE WORKERS

  Karp, B. The girl's guide to homelessness   **92**

OFFICE WORKERS

  See also Employees

OFFICE WORKERS -- SALARIES, WAGES, ETC.

  See also Salaries, wages, etc.

The **official** guide to America's national parks.   **917**

The **official** guide to the HiSET exam.   **373.126**

OFFICIAL MISCONDUCT *See* Misconduct in office

Official red book series

  Yeoman, R. S. A guide book of United States coins   **737.4**

The **official** Scrabble players dictionary.   **793.7**

Official secrets. Breitman, R.   **940.54**

OFFICIAL SECRETS -- UNITED STATES

The WikiLeaks files 327.73

OFFICIALS AND EMPLOYEES *See* Civil service; Public officers

Offit, Paul A.
Deadly choices 614.4
Vaccinated 92

OFFSET PRINTING
See also Lithography; Printing

OFFSHORE GAS INDUSTRY -- ENVIRONMENTAL ASPECTS -- ARCTIC REGIONS
Stewart, B. Don't trust, don't fear, don't beg 363.738

OFFSHORE OIL INDUSTRY
See also Petroleum industry

OFFSHORE OIL INDUSTRY -- ENVIRONMENTAL ASPECTS -- ARCTIC REGIONS
Stewart, B. Don't trust, don't fear, don't beg 363.738

OFFSHORE OIL WELL DRILLING
Freudenburg, W. R. Blowout in the Gulf 363.7

OFFSHORE OIL WELL DRILLING -- SAFETY MEASURES
Magner, M. Poisoned legacy 338.7

OFFSHORE WATER POLLUTION *See* Marine pollution

OFLAG VI B (CONCENTRATION CAMP)
Felton, M. Zero Night 940.54

Ofri, Danielle
What doctors feel 610.69

Ogden Nash. Parker, D. M. 92

OGLALA INDIANS
Black Elk Black Elk speaks 92
Drury, B. The heart of everything that is 92
McMurtry, L. Crazy Horse 92
Powers, T. The killing of Crazy Horse 92
Steltenkamp, M. F. Black Elk, holy man of the Oglala 92

The **ogre's** wife. Koertge, R. 811

The **oh** she glows cookbook. Liddon, A. 641.5

Oh, Kong Dan
Hassig, R. C. The hidden people of North Korea 951.93

Ohanian, Hans C.
Einstein's mistakes 530

Oher, Michael, 1986-
About
Lewis, M. The blind side 92

OIL *See* Oils and fats; Petroleum

Oil and Honey. McKibben, B. 363.7

OIL DRILLING PLATFORMS *See* Drilling platforms

OIL INDUSTRY *See* Petroleum industry

Oil on the brain. Margonelli, L. 338.2

The **Oil** Painter's Bible. Scott, M. 751.45

OIL PAINTING
Gorst, B. The complete oil painter 751.45

Scott, M. The Oil Painter's Bible 751.45

OIL PAINTING
See also Painting

Oil painting for the absolute beginner. Willenbrink, M. 751.45

OIL POLLUTION OF WATER
See also Water pollution

OIL SPILLS
Freudenburg, W. R. Blowout in the Gulf 363.7

OIL SPILLS -- ENVIRONMENTAL ASPECTS
Magner, M. Poisoned legacy 338.7

OIL WELLS -- BLOWOUTS
Magner, M. Poisoned legacy 338.7

OIL WELLS -- HYDRAULIC FRACTURING -- POPULAR WORKS
Prud'homme, A. Hydrofracking 622

Ojakangas, Beatrice
The Best Casserole cookbook ever 641.8

OJIBWA INDIANS
Erdrich, L. Books and islands in Ojibwe country 92

Okinawa. Leckie, R. 940.54

OKLAHOMA PRESBYTERIAN COLLEGE -- BASKETBALL -- HISTORY
Reeder, L. Dust bowl girls 796.323

Oklahoma western biographies [series]
Wilkins, T. John Muir 92

Okrent, Arika
In the land of invented languages 499

Okrent, Daniel, 1948-
Last call 363.4

Ol' Dirty Bastard, 1969-2004
About
Lowe, J. Digging for dirt 92

Old age. Kinsley, M. 814.54

OLD AGE
Athill, D. Somewhere towards the end 92
Hall, D. Essays After Eighty 814
Jacoby, S. Never say die 305.26
Lawrence-Lightfoot, S. The third chapter 305.26
Pillemer, K. A. 30 lessons for living 305.26

OLD AGE PENSIONS
See also Pensions; Retirement income

OLD GROWTH FOREST ECOLOGY -- TENNESSEE
Haskell, D. G. The forest unseen 577.3

OLD GROWTH FORESTS -- TENNESSEE
Haskell, D. G. The forest unseen 577.3

Old man Goya. Blackburn, J. 92

OLD NORSE LANGUAGE
See also Language and languages; Scandinavian languages

OLD NORSE LITERATURE
The Sagas of Icelanders 839

OLD NORSE LITERATURE
See also Literature; Medieval literature

OLD NORTHWEST

See also United States

The **old** Patagonian express. Theroux, P. **918**

OLD SOUTHWEST

   See also United States

The **old** ways. Macfarlane, R. **914.2**

Old world, new world. Burk, K. **327**

Old, Marnie

  Wine **641.2**

OLDER MEN -- EMPLOYMENT -- UNITED STATES

  Fideler, E. F. Men still at work **331.3**

OLDER PEOPLE -- HEALTH AND HYGIENE

  The longevity kitchen **612.6**

OLDER PERSONS *See* Elderly

OLDER PERSONS -- RELIGIOUS LIFE

  Meyer, J. Seize the day **248.4**

OLDER WOMEN -- EMPLOYMENT -- UNITED STATES

  Fideler, E. F. Women still at work **331.4**

OLDER WOMEN -- FRANCE -- ATTITUDES

  Guiliano, M. French women don't get facelifts **613**

OLDER WOMEN -- HEALTH AND HYGIENE -- FRANCE

  Guiliano, M. French women don't get facelifts **613**

OLDER WOMEN -- UNITED STATES -- SOCIAL LIFE AND CUSTOMS

  Lerner, B. The bridge ladies **92**

Oldershaw, Cally

  Firefly guide to gems **553.8**

Olds, Jacqueline

  The lonely American **302.5**

Olds, Sharon, 1942-

  Stag's leap **811**

Oldstone, Michael B. A.

  Viruses, plagues, and history **614.4**

OLIGARCHY

  See also Political science

OLIVE -- FOLKLORE

  Mueller, T. Extra virginity **664**

OLIVE -- HISTORY

  Mueller, T. Extra virginity **664**

The **olive** and the caper. Hoffman, S. **641.594**

OLIVE OIL

  Mueller, T. Extra virginity **664**

OLIVE OIL -- HISTORY

  Mueller, T. Extra virginity **664**

OLIVE OIL INDUSTRY -- MORAL AND ETHICAL ASPECTS

  Mueller, T. Extra virginity **664**

Oliver, Charles M.

  Critical companion to Ernest Hemingway **813**

  Critical companion to Walt Whitman **811**

Oliver, Chris

  Introducing RDA **025.3**

Oliver, Evelyn Dorothy

  Lewis, J. R. The dream encyclopedia **154.6**

Oliver, Jamie, 1975-

  Cook with Jamie **641.5**

  Jamie Oliver's comfort food **641.5**

  Jamie's dinners **641**

  Jamie's Italy **641.59**

Oliver, Mary

  New and selected poems **811**

  A poetry handbook **808.1**

  A thousand mornings **811**

Oliver, Vicky

  301 smart answers to tough business etiquette questions **395**

Olives, lemons & za'atar. Bishara, R. **641.59**

Olivier, Michele

  Little Bento **641.53**

Oller, John

  American queen **92**

Ollestad, Norman, 1968-

        About

  Ollestad, N. Crazy for the storm **92**

Olmos, Edward James

  Monterrey, M. Americanos **305.8**

Olmsted, Frederick Law, 1822-1903

        About

  Rybczynski, W. A clearing in the distance: Frederick Law Olmsted and America in the nineteenth century **712**

Olmsted, Larry

  Real food/fake food **641.3**

Olney, Richard

  Lulu's Provencal table **641.59**

  Simple French food **641.59**

        About

  Barr, L. Provence, 1970 **641.59**

Olsen, Jack

  I: the creation of a serial killer **364.1**

Olsen, Kirstin

  All things Austen **823**

Olshaker, Mark

  Douglas, J. E. The cases that haunt us **364.1**

Olson, Carl

  Historical dictionary of Buddhism **294.3**

Olson, Charles

  The Maximus poems **811**

Olson, James Stuart

  Encyclopedia of the industrial revolution in America **973**

Olson, Keith W.

  Watergate **973.924**

Olson, Lynne

  Citizens of London **940.54**

  Those angry days **940.53**

Olson, Parmy

  We are Anonymous **005.8**

Olson, Randy

        About

Olson, R. Don't be such a scientist **501**

Olson, Richard
Science and religion, 1450-1900 **261.5**

Olson, Steve
Mapping human history **599.9**

OLYMPIC ATHLETES
Amidon, S. Something like the gods **306.4**
Beard, A. In the water they can't see you cry **797.2**
Goldblatt, D. The Games **796.48**

OLYMPIC ATHLETES
See also Athletes

OLYMPIC GAMES
Checkoway, J. The three-year swim club **797.2**
Goldblatt, D. The Games **796.48**
Halberstam, D. The amateurs **797.1**
McCallum, J. Dream team **796.323**
Miller, S. G. Ancient Greek athletics **796**
Spivey, N. J. The ancient Olympics **796.48**

OLYMPIC GAMES
See also Athletics; Contests; Games; Sports

OLYMPIC GAMES, 1936 (BERLIN, GER.)
Brown, D. J. The Boys in the Boat **797.12**
Schaap, J. Triumph **92**

OLYMPIC GAMES, 1968 (MEXICO CITY, MEX.)
Hoffer, R. Something in the air **796.4**

OLYMPIC GAMES, 1996 (ATLANTA, GA.)
See also Olympic games

OLYMPIC GAMES, 2000 (SYDNEY, AUSTRALIA)
Mullen, P. H. Gold in the water **797.2**

Omar, Qais Akbar
About
Omar, Q. A. A fort of nine towers **958.104**

Omdahl, Kristin
The finer edge **746.43**

Omeros. Walcott, D. **811**

The **omnivore's** dilemma. Pollan, M. **394.1**

On a farther shore. Souder, W. **92**
On architecture. Huxtable, A. L. **724**
On Becoming a Mother. McConville, B. **306.874**
On becoming a novelist. Gardner, J. **808.3**
On becoming baby wise. Ezzo, G. **649**
On being human. Fromm, E. **150.19**
On celestial music. Moody, R. **780.9**
On children and death. Kubler-Ross, E. **155.9**
On Conan Doyle; or, The whole art of storytelling. Dirda, M. **823**
On death and dying. Kubler-Ross, E. **155.9**
On desire. Irvine, W. B. **128**
On Hinduism. Doniger, W. **294.5**
On history. Hobsbawm, E. J. **901**
On immunity. Biss, E. **616.07**
On living. Egan, K. **170.44**
On love. Hirsch, E. **811**
On monsters. Asma, S. T. **398.2**

On moral fiction. Gardner, J. **801**
On my country and the world. Gorbachev, M. **947.085**
On paper. Basbanes, N. A. **676**
On politics. Ryan, A. **320.01**
On Saudi Arabia. House, K. E. **953.8**
On second thought. Herbert, W. **153.4**
On Sunset Boulevard: the life and times of Billy Wilder. Sikov, E. **92**
On the backroad to heaven. Kraybill, D. B. **289.7**
On the brink. Paulson, H. M. **330.9**
On the burning edge. Dickman, K. **363.37**
On the bus with Rosa Parks. Dove, R. **811**
On the courthouse lawn. Ifill, S. A. **364.1**
On the edge. Koch, K. **811**
On the eve. Wasserstein, B. **305.892**
On the good life. Cicero, M. T. **878**
On the Irish waterfront. Fisher, J. T. **331.7**
On the law of nations. Moynihan, D. P. **327**
On the line. Ripert, E. **647**
On the move. Sacks, O. **92**
On the natural history of destruction. Sebald, W. G. **833**
On the nature of things: De rerum natura. Lucretius Carus, T. **187**
On the origin of species. Darwin, C. **576.8**
On the origin of stories. Boyd, B. **809**
On the rim of the Caribbean. Pressly, P. M. **975.8**
On the road with Charles Kuralt. Kuralt, C. **973.92**
On the road with Janis Joplin. Cooke, J. B. **92**
On the shoulders of giants. Abdul-Jabbar, K. **92**
On the spectrum of possible deaths. Perillo, L. **811**
On the surface of things. Frankel, F. **530.4**
On the water. Stone, N. **917**

ON THE WATERFRONT (MOTION PICTURE)
Fisher, J. T. On the Irish waterfront **331.7**
On thin ice. Ellis, R. **599.78**
On top of the world. Lutnick, H. **332.6**
On ugliness. **111**
On war. Clausewitz, C. v. **355**
On wings of eagles. Follett, K. **955**
On writing. King, S. **813**
On Your Case. Green, L. **344**

Onassis, Jacqueline Kennedy, 1929-1994
About
Anderson, C. The good son **92**
Bowles, H. Jacqueline Kennedy **92**
Davis, J. H. Jacqueline Bouvier **92**
Galbraith, J. K. Name-dropping **973.9**
Hill, C. Five days in November **973.922**
Hill, C. Mrs. Kennedy and me **973.922**
Jacqueline Kennedy **973.922**
Kaplan, A. Dreaming in French **944**
Leaming, B. Jacqueline Bouvier Kennedy Onassis **92**
Leaming, B. Mrs. Kennedy **973.922**

Once in a great city. Maraniss, D.   **977.4**

Once they moved like the wind. Roberts, D. **970.004**

Once upon a car. Vlasic, B.   **338.4**

Once upon a country. David, A.   **92**

Once upon a revolution. Cambanis, T.   **962.05**

Once upon a time. Bell, I.   **92**

Once Upon a Time in Russia. Mezrich, B.   **330**

ONCOLOGISTS -- UNITED STATES -- BIOG-RAPHY

  DeVita-Raeburn, E. The death of cancer   **92**

  Ross, T. A cancer in the family   **616.99**

Ondra, Nancy J.

  Grasses   **635.9**

  Taylor's guide to roses   **635.9**

The **one**. Smith, R. J.   **92**

ONE ACT PLAYS

  The Best American short plays   **812**

ONE ACT PLAYS

    See also Amateur theater; Drama

One and only. Sandler, L.   **306.874**

One big table. O'Neill, M.   **641.5**

One breath. Skolnick, A.   **797.2**

One day I will write about this place. Wainaina, B.   **823**

One day it'll all make sense. Common   **92**

One doctor. Reilly, B.   **610.69**

One dough, ten breads. Black, S.   **641.81**

One good dish. Tanis, D.   **641.82**

One hell of a gamble. Fursenko, A. V.   **973.922**

One hundred days. Schom, A.   **944.05**

One hundred million years of food. Le, S.   **641.3**

One hundred poems from the Japanese.   **895.6**

One Magic Square Vegetable Gardening. Houbein, L.   **635**

One man against the world. Weiner, T.   **973.924**

One matchless time. Parini, J.   **92**

One minute to midnight. Dobbs, M.   **973.922**

One nation under God. Kruse, K. M.   **322**

One of Us.   **363.325**

ONE PARENT FAMILY *See* Single-parent families

The **one** percent doctrine. Suskind, R.   **973.931**

One perfect day. Mead, R.   **392**

One pot.   **641.82**

One souffle at a time. Friedman, A.   **92**

One sweet cookie. Zabar, T.   **641.8**

One thousand nights and counting. Maxwell, G. **831**

One time, one place. Welty, E.   **976.2**

The **one** true barbecue.   **641.5**

One vast winter count. Calloway, C. G.   **978**

One with others. Wright, C. D.   **811**

One writer's beginnings. Welty, E.   **92**

ONE-DISH COOKING

  Anderson, P. Perfect one-dish dinners   **641.8**

  The best one-dish suppers   **641.8**

  Peacock, J. The soup club cookbook   **641.81**

ONE-DISH MEALS

  Bowl   **641.81**

  One pot   **641.82**

  Tanis, D. One good dish   **641.82**

One-hour cheese. Lucero, C.   **637**

One-skein wonders for babies.   **746.43**

One-yard wonders.   **646.2**

One-yard wonders series

  Yaker, R. Little one-yard wonders   **646.2**

Onians, John

  (ed) Atlas of world art   **709**

ONLINE BOOKS *See* Electronic books

ONLINE CHAT GROUPS

    See also Conversation

ONLINE COMMERCE *See* Electronic commerce

ONLINE DATING

  Atik, C. Modern Dating   **646.7**

ONLINE DATING

    See also Dating (Social customs)

ONLINE ETIQUETTE

  Moreno, M. Sex, drugs 'n Facebook   **004.67**

ONLINE HATE SPEECH

  Foxman, A. H. Viral hate   **364.15**

ONLINE IDENTITIES -- SOCIAL ASPECTS

  Thompson, D. C. The reputation economy **302.23**

ONLINE IDENTITY THEFT -- PREVENTION

  Moore, A. Cyber self-defense   **613.6**

ONLINE JOURNALISM

  Carpini, M. X. D. After broadcast news   **071**

  Shepard, S. B. Deadlines and disruption   **070.5**

ONLINE SOCIAL NETWORKS

  Angwin, J. Stealing MySpace   **338.7**

  Boyd, D. It's complicated   **004.67**

  Heim, T. @stickyjesus   **248.4**

  Kirkpatrick, D. The Facebook effect   **338.7**

  Obee, J. Social networking   **004.67**

  Schaefer, M. W. Return on influence   **658.8**

  Tapscott, D. Macrowikinomics   **303.4**

  Wellman, B. Networked   **006.7**

ONLINE SOCIAL NETWORKS -- LIBRARY APPLICATIONS

  Solomon, L. The librarian's nitty-gritty guide to social media   **006.7**

ONLINE SOCIAL NETWORKS -- MISCELLA-NEA

  Pogue, D. Pogue's basics   **004**

ONLINE SOCIAL NETWORKS -- UNITED STATES

  Bilton, N. Hatching Twitter   **006.7**

  Dwyer, J. More awesome than money   **384.3**

  Stone, B. Things a little bird told me   **006.7**

ONLY CHILD

  Sandler, L. One and only   **306.874**

ONLY CHILD

    See also Children; Family size

Only in Naples. Wilson, K.   **945.731**

The **only** investment guide you'll ever need. Tobias, A. P. **332.024**

The **only** one living to tell. Burns, M. **305.897**

The **Only** Rule Is It Has to Work. Miller, S. **796.357**

The **only** way I know. Ripken, C. **92**

Only yesterday. Allen, F. L. **973.91**

ONTARIO -- HISTORY -- WAR OF 1812

Taylor, A. The civil war of 1812 **973.5**

ONTOLOGY

Buber, M. I and thou **181**

Heidegger, M. Being and time **111**

Tillich, P. The courage to be **179**

ONTOLOGY

See also Philosophy

Onuf, Peter S.

(jt. auth) Gordon-Reed, A. Most Blessed of the Patriarchs **92**

Onward. Moore, R. **230**

Onward. Schultz, H. **647.9**

Open. Agassi, A. **92**

Open access. Suber, P. **070.5**

OPEN ACCESS PUBLISHING

Peters, J. The Idealist **004.67**

OPEN ACCESS PUBLISHING

See also Electronic publishing

OPEN ADOPTION

Seek, A. God and Jetfire **92**

OPEN AND CLOSED SHOP

See also Labor; Labor contract; Labor unions

Open closed open. Amichai, Y. **892.4**

OPEN HOUSING *See* Discrimination in housing

Open media [series]

Gibler, J. To die in Mexico **363.45**

Open Media series

Lusane, C. The Black history of the White House **975.3**

OPEN PLAN SCHOOLS

See also Education -- Experimental methods

The **open** road. Iyer, P. **92**

The **open** road. **770**

Opened ground. Heaney, S. **821**

The **opening** of the American mind. Levine, L. W. **001.1**

Opening the Qur'an. Wagner, W. H. **297.1**

OPERA

Berger, W. Puccini without excuses **92**

The Grove book of opera singers **920**

Levy, R. They told me not to take that job **792.09**

Rose, M. The birth of an opera **782.1**

Wills, G. Verdi's Shakespeare **822.3**

OPERA

See also Drama; Musical form; Performing arts; Vocal music

OPERA -- ENCYCLOPEDIAS

Sadie, S. The Grove book of operas **792.5**

OPERA -- HISTORY

Abbate, C. A history of opera **782.1**

OPERA -- SOUND RECORDINGS

See also Sound recordings

OPERA -- STORIES, PLOTS, ETC.

Osborne, C. The complete operas of Mozart **792.5**

Osborne, C. The complete operas of Puccini **792.5**

Osborne, C. The complete operas of Richard Wagner **792.5**

OPERA SINGERS

Keiler, A. Marian Anderson **92**

Ware, S. Letter to the world **920.72**

OPERAS *See* Opera

OPERAS -- ANALYSIS, APPRECIATION

Rose, M. The birth of an opera **782.1**

Operation Bite Back. Kuipers, D. **92**

OPERATION DESERT STORM *See* Persian Gulf War, 1991

OPERATION FRESHMAN, 1942

Sheinkin, S. Bomb **623.4**

Operation Mincemeat. Macintyre, B. **940.54**

Operation Paperclip. Jacobsen, A. **940.54**

OPERATION PETER PAN

Eire, C. M. N. Waiting for snow in Havana **92**

Operation Thunderbolt. David, S. **967.61**

Opie, Iona Archibald

(ed) The Oxford dictionary of nursery rhymes **398.8**

Opie, Peter

(ed) The Oxford dictionary of nursery rhymes **398.8**

OPINION, PUBLIC *See* Public opinion

OPIUM

See also Narcotics

Oppen, George

New collected poems **811**

Oppenheim, Michael R.

(ed) The basic business library **016**

Oppenheim, Thomas

(ed) The muses go to school **700**

Oppenheimer. Bernstein, J. **92**

Oppenheimer, Betty

Candlemaker's companion **745.59**

Oppenheimer, Clive

Eruptions that shook the world **551.2**

Oppenheimer, Frank, 1912-1985

About

Cole, K. C. Something incredibly wonderful happens **92**

Oppenheimer, J. Robert, 1904-1967

About

Bernstein, J. Oppenheimer **92**

Bird, K. American Prometheus **92**

Monk, R. Robert Oppenheimer **92**

OPPORTUNITY

Gladwell, M. David and Goliath **155.2**

The **opposite** of fate. Tan, A. **814**

The **Opposite** of Spoiled. Lieber, R. **332.024**

OPPOSITION (POLITICAL SCIENCE) -- GER-

MANY -- HISTORY -- 20TH CENTURY
Orbach, D. The plots against Hitler   **940.53**

OPTICAL IMAGES
Frankel, F. On the surface of things   **530.4**

OPTICAL INSTRUMENTS
See also Scientific apparatus and instruments

OPTICS
Park, D. The fire within the eye   **535**

OPTICS
See also Physics

Optimal health with multiple sclerosis. Bowling, A.
C.   **616.8**

OPTIMISM
Ehrenreich, B. Bright-sided   **155.2**
Jacobs, B. Life is good   **650.1**
Ridley, M. The rational optimist   **339.2**
Or to begin again. Lauterbach, A.   **811**
Oracle bones. Hessler, P.   **951**

ORACLES
See also Occultism

ORAL CONTRACEPTIVES
Eig, J. The birth of the pill   **618.1**
May, E. T. America and the pill   **363.9**

**ORAL CONTRACEPTIVES -- SOCIAL AS-
PECTS**
May, E. T. America and the pill   **363.9**

ORAL HABITS
See also Habit; Mouth

ORAL HISTORY
Aleksievich, S. Secondhand time   **947.086**
Napoli, P. F. Bringing it all back home   **959.704**
Stein, J. West of Eden   **979.4**

ORAL HISTORY
See also History

**ORAL HISTORY -- CALIFORNIA -- LOS AN-
GELES**
Stein, J. West of Eden   **979.4**

ORAL HISTORY -- RUSSIA (FEDERATION)
Aleksievich, S. Secondhand time   **947.086**

ORAL HYGIENE -- POPULAR WORKS
Artemis, N. Holistic dental care   **617.6**

ORANGE COUNTY (N.C.) -- BIOGRAPHY
Nathans, S. To free a family   **306.3**
Orange sunshine. Schou, N.   **363.45**

ORATIONS *See* Speeches

ORATORS
Everitt, A. Cicero   **92**
Goldsworthy, A. K. Antony and Cleopatra   **92**
Hofstadter, R. The American political tradition, and
the men who made it   **973**
McPherson, J. M. Drawn with the sword   **973.7**

ORATORS -- GREAT BRITAIN -- BIOGRAPHY
Norman, J. Edmund Burke   **92**

ORATORS -- UNITED STATES -- BIOGRAPHY
Watts, S. Self-help Messiah   **92**

ORATORY *See* Public speaking

Orbach, Danny
The plots against Hitler   **940.53**

Orbach, Susie
Bodies   **362.1**

Orbanes, Philip
The game makers   **338.7**

Orbinski, James
About
Orbinski, J. An imperfect offering   **610**

ORBITAL RENDEZVOUS (SPACE FLIGHT)
See also Space flight; Space stations; Space
vehicles

ORCHARDS *See* Fruit culture
The **orchards** of Syon. Hill, G.   **821**

ORCHESTRAL MUSIC
See also Instrumental music; Music; Orchestra

Orchestration. Piston, W.   **784**

ORCHESTRATION *See* Instrumentation and orchestration

Orchid fever. Hansen, E.   **635.9**

ORCHIDS
Hansen, E. Orchid fever   **635.9**
Ordaining women. Chaves, M.   **262**

ORDER -- HISTORY
Fukuyama, F. Political Order and Political Decay   **320.1**

ORDERLINESS
Leeds, R. Rightsize . . . right now!   **648**

ORDERS, MONASTIC *See* Monasticism and re-
ligious orders
Ordinarily well. Kramer, P. D.   **615.7**
The **ordinary** acrobat. Wall, D.   **796.47**
Ordinary geniuses. Segrè, G.   **572.8**
Ordinary light. Smith, T. K.   **92**
Ordinary resurrections. Kozol, J.   **305.23**
The **ordinary** spaceman. Anderson, C.   **92**

ORDINATION
See also Rites and ceremonies; Sacraments

ORDINATION OF WOMEN
Chaves, M. Ordaining women   **262**

ORDNANCE
Stephenson, M. The last full measure   **305.9**

ORDNANCE
See also Military art and science

ORDNANCE DISPOSAL UNITS
Castner, B. The long walk   **956.704**

**ORDNANCE DISPOSAL UNITS -- AFGHANI-
STAN**
Castner, B. All the ways we kill and die   **958.104**

ORE DEPOSITS
See also Geology

OREGON COUNTRY *See* Pacific Northwest

OREGON NATIONAL HISTORIC TRAIL
Buck, R. The Oregon Trail   **978**
The Oregon Trail   **978**

The **Oregon** Trail. Dary, D.   **978**

The **Oregon** Trail.   **978**

OREGON TRAIL

    See also Overland journeys to the Pacific; United States

The **Oregon** Trail. Buck, R.   **978**

OREGON TRAIL

  Buck, R. The Oregon Trail   **978**

  Dary, D. The Oregon Trail   **978**

Oren, Michael

  Six days of war   **956.04**

Orenstein, Catherine

  Little Red Riding Hood uncloaked   **398.2**

Orenstein, Peggy

  Cinderella ate my daughter   **305.23**

  Girls and Sex   **306.7**

Orenstein, Ronald

  Butterflies   **595.78**

  Hummingbirds   **598.7**

  Ivory, horn and blood   **333.95**

ORES

    See also Minerals

Oreskes, Naomi

  (jt. auth) Conway, E. M. Merchants of doubt   **174**

The **Oresteia.** Aeschylus   **882**

ORGANIC FARMING

  Adamchak, R. W. Tomorrow's table   **664**

  Biodynamic gardening   **635**

  Coleman, E. Winter harvest handbook   **635**

  Kimball, K. The dirty life   **92**

  Pouillon, N. My organic life   **92**

ORGANIC FARMING

    See also Agriculture

ORGANIC FOODS *See* Natural foods

ORGANIC GARDENING

  Citizen farmers   **635**

  Deardorff, D. What's wrong with my vegetable garden?   **635**

  Houbein, L. One Magic Square Vegetable Gardening   **635**

  Smith, E. C. The vegetable gardener's bible   **635**

ORGANIC GARDENING

    See also Gardening; Horticulture

ORGANIC GARDENING -- ENCYCLOPEDIAS

  Rodale's ultimate encyclopedia of organic gardening   **635**

ORGANIC LIVING

  Pouillon, N. My organic life   **92**

ORGANICALLY GROWN FOODS *See* Natural foods

ORGANICULTURE *See* Organic farming; Organic gardening

ORGANISMS

  Toomey, D. Weird Life   **571**

ORGANIZATION

  Covey, S. The 4 disciplines of execution   **658.4**

Naím, M. The end of power   **303.3**

ORGANIZATION AND MANAGEMENT *See* Management

ORGANIZATION DEVELOPMENT *See* Organizational change

ORGANIZATION OFFICIALS

  Friedan, B. Life so far   **92**

  Patel, E. Acts of faith   **92**

  Tough, P. Whatever it takes   **362.7**

ORGANIZATIONAL BEHAVIOR

  Bohnet, I. What works   **331.4**

  Covey, S. M. R. Smart trust   **174**

  Duhigg, C. Smarter faster better   **158**

  Klubeck, M. Why organizations struggle so hard to improve so little   **658.4**

ORGANIZATIONAL BEHAVIOR

    See also Applied psychology; Management; Social psychology

ORGANIZATIONAL CHANGE

  Collins, J. C. Good to great   **658**

  Grant, A. Originals   **153.3**

  Johnson, W. Disrupt yourself   **658.4**

  Klubeck, M. Why organizations struggle so hard to improve so little   **658.4**

ORGANIZATIONAL CHANGE

    See also Management

ORGANIZATIONAL CHANGE -- MANAGEMENT

  Mosley, P. A. The challenge of library management   **025.1**

ORGANIZATIONAL CHANGE -- UNITED STATES

  Gates, R. M. A passion for leadership   **92**

ORGANIZED CRIME

  Carlo, P. Gaspipe   **92**

  Dash, M. The first family   **364.1**

  Denton, S. The money and the power   **979.3**

  Eig, J. Get Capone   **92**

  Glenny, M. McMafia   **364.1**

  Manzione, G. Pin Action   **794.6**

  Niebuhr, G. W. Caught up in crime   **016**

  Raab, S. Five families   **364.1**

  Saviano, R. Gomorrah   **364.1**

ORGANIZED CRIME

    See also Crime

ORGANIZED CRIME -- MASSACHUSETTS -- BOSTON -- CASE STUDIES

  Cullen, K. Whitey Bulger   **364.1**

ORGANIZED CRIME -- MEXICO

  Slater, D. Wolf Boys   **364**

ORGANIZED CRIME -- UNITED STATES

  Cullen, K. Whitey Bulger   **364.1**

ORGANIZED CRIME -- UNITED STATES -- HISTORY

  Dash, M. The first family   **364.1**

ORGANIZED LABOR *See* Labor unions

ORGANS (MUSICAL INSTRUMENTS)
Whitney, C. R. All the stops   **786.5**
ORGANS (MUSICAL INSTRUMENTS)
    See also Musical instruments
ORIENT *See* Asia; East Asia; Middle East
Oriental mythology. Campbell, J.   **201**
ORIENTAL MYTHOLOGY
Campbell, J. Oriental mythology   **201**
ORIENTAL RUGS
    See also Rugs and carpets
ORIENTALISM
    See also East and West
The **Orientalist.** Reiss, T.   **92**
ORIENTATION *See* Direction sense
ORIENTEERING
    See also Hiking; Racing; Running; Sports
ORIGAMI
Cetti, L. The exquisite book of paper flowers   **745.594**
O'Rourke, J. How to fold it   **516**
Van Sicklen, M. The joy of origami   **736**
ORIGAMI
    See also Paper crafts
Origami bridges. Ackerman, D.   **811**
Origen
         About
Kung, H. Great Christian thinkers   **230**
The **origin** of humankind. Leakey, R. E.   **599.93**
ORIGIN OF LIFE *See* Life -- Origin
ORIGIN OF MAN *See* Human origins
The **origin** of Satan. Pagels, E. H.   **235**
ORIGIN OF SPECIES *See* Evolution
The **origin** of species by means of natural selection, or, The preservation of favored races in the struggle for life. Darwin, C.   **576.8**
Original fire. Erdrich, L.   **811**
The **Original** Folk and Fairy Tales of the Brothers Grimm.   **398.2**
Original sin. Jacobs, A.   **233**
Originals. Grant, A.   **153.3**
The **origins** of political order. Fukuyama, F.   **320**
Origins of totalitarianism. Arendt, H.   **321.9**
Origins reconsidered. Leakey, R. E.   **599.93**
Origins: fourteen billion years of cosmic evolution. Tyson, N. d.   **523.1**
Orlando Furioso/The frenzy of Orlando, part 1. Ariosto, L.   **851**
Orlando Furioso/The frenzy of Orlando, part 2. Ariosto, L.   **851**
Orlean, Susan
Rin Tin Tin   **636.7**
Orloff, Judith
Emotional freedom   **152.4**
Ormal-Grenon, Jean-Benoit
(ed) Correard The Oxford-Hachette French dictionary   **443**

Orman, Suze
The money class   **332.024**
Ormes, Jackie, 1911-1985
         About
Goldstein, N. Jackie Ormes   **741.5**
Ormrod, W. Mark
Edward III   **92**
ORNAMENT *See* Decoration and ornament
Ornament and silence. Fraser, K.   **809**
ORNAMENTAL ALPHABETS *See* Alphabets; Illumination of books and manuscripts; Lettering
ORNAMENTAL BERRIES
Bowling, B. L. Homegrown berries   **634**
ORNAMENTAL GRASSES
Grasses   **635.9**
ORNAMENTAL PLANTS
Air plants   **628.5**
American Horticultural Society encyclopedia of plants & flowers   **635.9**
Armitage, A. M. Armitage's native plants for North American gardens   **635.9**
Armitage, A. M. Armitage's vines and climbers   **635.9**
Cullina, W. Native trees, shrubs & vines   **635.9**
Deardorff, D. C. What's wrong with my plant (and how do I fix it?)   **635**
Dirr, M. A. Dirr's encyclopedia of trees and shrubs   **635.9**
Dirr, M. A. Manual of woody landscape plants   **635.9**
Dirr, M. Dirr's trees and shrubs for warm climates   **635.9**
Ellis, B. W. Covering ground   **635.9**
Grasses   **635.9**
The Hillier gardener's guide to trees & shrubs   **635.9**
McGowan, A. Bulbs in the basement, geraniums on the windowsill   **635.9**
Michener, D. Taylor's guide to ground covers   **635.9**
O'Sullivan, P. The homeowner's complete tree & shrub handbook   **635.9**
The plant finder   **635.9**
ORNAMENTAL PLANTS
    See also Cultivated plants; Flower gardening; Landscape gardening
ORNAMENTAL PLANTS -- ENCYCLOPEDIAS
Flora: a gardener's encyclopedia   **635.9**
Wyman, D. Wyman's gardening encyclopedia   **635**
ORNAMENTAL SHRUBS
Fisher, K. Taylor's guide to shrubs   **635.9**
McIndoe, A. The creative shrub garden   **635.9**
ORNAMENTAL SHRUBS -- ENCYCLOPEDIAS
Dirr, M. A. Dirr's encyclopedia of trees and shrubs   **635.9**
ORNAMENTAL WOODY PLANTS -- UNITED STATES
Cullina, W. Native trees, shrubs & vines   **635.9**
Ornelas, Kriemhild Conee

The Cambridge world history of food   641.3
**ORNITHOLOGICAL   ILLUSTRATION --
    NORTH AMERICA**
    Kiser, J. M. America's other Audubon   598
ORNITHOLOGISTS
    Birkhead, T. Ten thousand birds   598
    Rhodes, R. John James Audubon   92
    Weidensaul, S. Return to wild America   578
    White, E. B. Essays of E.B. White   814
**ORNITHOLOGISTS -- UNITED STATES -- BI-
    OGRAPHY**
    Kiser, J. M. America's other Audubon   598
**ORNITHOLOGY -- HISTORY -- 19TH CEN-
    TURY**
    Birkhead, T. Ten thousand birds   598
ORPHANAGES
    See also Charities; Children -- Institutional
    care
The **orphaned** adult. Levy, A.   152.4
ORPHANS
    See also Children
Orpheus. Wroe, A.   398.2
ORPHEUS (GREEK MYTHOLOGY)
    Wroe, A. Orpheus   398.2
The **Orpheus** Clock. Goodman, S.   940.53
Orr, Cynthia
    (ed) Herald, D. T. Genreflecting   016
    Crash course in readers' advisory   025.5
Orr, David
    Beautiful & pointless   809.1
Orr, Stephen
    The new American herbal   615.3
Orson Welles. Callow, S.   92
Orson Welles. Callow, S.   92
Orson Welles. Callow, S.   92
Orson Welles's last movie. Karp, J.   791.43
Ortega y Gasset, Jose
    What is philosophy?   196
    The revolt of the masses   901
Ortega, Ines
    Ortega, S. 1080 recipes   641.5
Ortega, Jose
    The revolt of the masses   901
Ortega, Simone
    1080 recipes   641.5
ORTHODOX EASTERN CHURCH
    Mathewes-Green, F. Welcome to the Orthodox
    Church   281.9
ORTHOPEDICS
    See also Medicine; Surgery
Ortner, Helmut
    The lone assassin   943.086
Orton, Joe
    Plays The complete plays   822
Ortuzar, Sisha
    Colicchio, T. 'wichcraft   641.8

The **Orvis** fly-fishing guide.   799.124
The **Orvis** guide to the essential American flies.
    Rosenbauer, T.   799.1
Orwell. Meyers, J.   828
Orwell, George, 1903-1950
    Essays   824
                    About
    Meyers, J. Orwell   828
    Orwell, G. Diaries   828
    Quinn, E. Critical companion to George Orwell   828
    Taylor, D. J. Orwell: the life   92
Orwell: the life. Taylor, D. J.   92
Ory, Deborah
    (jt. auth) Browar, K. The art of movement   792
Orzel, Chad
    Eureka!   500
**OSAGE INDIANS -- UNITED STATES -- BIOG-
    RAPHY.**
    Tallchief, M. Maria Tallchief   92
Osama bin Laden. Scheuer, M.   92
Osama bin Laden
                    About
    Coll, S. Ghost wars   958.1
    Randal, J. C. Osama: the making of a terrorist   92
    Scheuer, M. Osama bin Laden   92
Osama: the making of a terrorist. Randal, J. C.   92
Osborn, William M.
    The wild frontier   970.004
Osborne, Charles
    The complete operas of Mozart   792.5
    The complete operas of Puccini   792.5
    The complete operas of Richard Wagner   792.5
Osborne, John, 1929-1994
    Look back in anger   822
                    About
    Heilpern, J. John Osborne   92
Osborne, Richard
    Herbert von Karajan   92
Osborne, Robert A.
    75 years of the Oscar   791.43
Osborne, Steve (Stephen T), 1960-
                    About
    Osborne, S. The job   92
Osbourne, Ozzy
                    About
    Osbourne, O. I am Ozzy   92
Oscar Micheaux. McGilligan, P.   92
Oscar Wilde. Ellmann, R.   92
OSCARS (MOTION PICTURES) *See* Academy
    Awards (Motion pictures)
Oseland, James
    Saveur   641.5
Oshinsky, David M.
    Worse than slavery   365
Oskar Schindler. Crowe, D.   92
Osman's dream. Finkel, C.   956

Osmanczyk, Edmund Jan
Encyclopedia of the United Nations and international agreements   **341.23**

Osnos, Evan
Age of ambition   **951.06**

Osteen, Joel, 1963-
The power of I am   **248.4**

OSTEOPATHIC MEDICINE
  See also Medicine

OSTEOPOROSIS
Pizzorno, L. Your bones   **616.7**
The **Oster** conspiracy of 1938. Parssinen, T. M.   **943.086**

Oster, Hans, 1888-1945
     About
Parssinen, T. M. The Oster conspiracy of 1938   **943.086**

Ostertag, Bob
People's movements, people's press   **071**

Ostler, Nicholas
Ad infinitum   **470**

Ostriker, Alicia
No heaven   **811**

Ostriker, Jeremiah P.
(jt. auth) Mitton, S. Heart of darkness   **523.1**

Ostrovsky, Arkady
The Invention of Russia   **947.086**

Oswald, Lee Harvey, 1939-1963
     About
Bugliosi, V. Reclaiming history   **973.922**
Mallon, T. Mrs. Paine's garage and the murder of John F. Kennedy   **364.1**
Posner, G. L. Case closed   **973.922**

Oswald, Marina
     About
Mallon, T. Mrs. Paine's garage and the murder of John F. Kennedy   **364.1**

Otfinoski, Steven
Latinos in the arts   **920.003**
Other colors. Pamuk, O.   **894**
The **other** half. Buk-Swienty, T.   **92**
The **other** Paris. Sante, L.   **944**
Other pasts, different presents, alternative futures. Black, J.   **900**
Other powers. Goldsmith, B.   **92**
The **other** side of desire. Bergner, D.   **306.7**
The **other** side of normal. Smoller, J.   **591.5**
The **other** side of paradise. Cooke, J.   **972.91**
OTHER SIDE OF THE WIND (MOTION PICTURE)
Karp, J. Orson Welles's last movie   **791.43**
The **other** slavery. Reséndez, A.   **306.3**
The **other** Wes Moore. Moore, W.   **92**
Otherwise known as the human condition. Dyer, G.   **824**
Otho, Marcus Salvius, Emperor of Rome, 32-69

     About
The twelve Caesars   **878**

Otlet, Paul, 1868-1944
     About
Wright, A. Cataloging the world   **020.9**

OTRANTO (TROOPSHIP)
Scott, R. N. Many were held by the sea   **940.4**

Ottaviani, Jim
Feynman   **92**

Ottemiller's index to plays in collections. Montgomery, D. L.   **016**

Otto, Shawn
Fool me twice   **303.4**

Ottolenghi.   **641.5**

OTTOLENGHI (RESTAURANT)
Ottolenghi   **641.5**
Ottolenghi, Y. Plenty   **647.9**
Ottolenghi, Y. Plenty more   **641.6**

Ottolenghi, Yotam
Jerusalem   **641.5**
Nopi   **641.5**
Ottolenghi   **641.5**
Plenty   **647.9**
Plenty more   **641.6**

Ouellette, Jennifer
The calculus diaries   **515**

OULIPO (ASSOCIATION)
Becker, D. L. Many subtle channels   **840.9**
Our babies, ourselves. Small, M. F.   **649**
Our bodies, ourselves. Boston Women's Health Book Collective   **613**
Our choice. Gore, A.   **363.7**
Our daily meds. Petersen, M.   **338.4**
Our Declaration. Allen, D.   **973.3**
Our hero. De Haven, T.   **741.5**
Our inner ape. Waal, F. d.   **156**
Our kind of people. Iweala, U.   **362.196**
Our Lincoln.   **92**
Our lives, our fortunes and our sacred honor. Beeman, R. R.   **973.3**
Our Man in Charleston. Dickey, C.   **92**
Our man in Tehran. Wright, R. A.   **955**
Our mathematical universe. Tegmark, M.   **523.1**
Our mothers' war. Yellin, E.   **940.53**
Our Necessary Shadow. Burns, T.   **616.89**
Our new public, a changing clientele.   **025.1**
Our noise. Cook, J.   **338**
Our own devices. Tenner, E.   **303.48**
Our Robots, Ourselves. Mindell, D. A.   **629.8**
Our savage art. Logan, W.   **811**
Our singing country.   **781.62**
Our stories remember. Bruchac, J.   **970.004**
Our Sunday Visitor Catholic almanac.   **282**
Our sustainable future [series]
Couch, J. Traveling the power line   **333.793**
Our town. Wilder, T.   **812**

Our Vietnam. Langguth, A. J.   **959.704**

Ours, Dorothy

Man o' War   **798.4**

Ousby, Ian

The road to Verdun   **940.4**

Out of Africa and Shadows on the grass. Dinesen, I.   **967.62**

Out of ashes. Jarausch, K. H.   **940.5**

Out of Eden. Burdick, A.   **577**

Out of gas. Goodstein, D. L.   **333.8**

Out of Mao's shadow. Pan, P. P.   **951.05**

Out of my life and thought. Schweitzer, A.   **900**

Out of order. O'Connor, S. D.   **347.73**

Out of place. Said, E. W.   **92**

Out of the blue. Bernstein, R.   **973.931**

Out of the jungle. Russell, T.   **92**

Out of the storm. Wilson, D. A.   **92**

Out to work. Kessler-Harris, A.   **331.4**

Out with it. Preston, K.   **92**

OUT-OF-DOORS EDUCATION See Outdoor education

OUTBUILDINGS

Diedricksen, D. Microshelters   **690**

OUTBUILDINGS -- DESIGN AND CONSTRUCTION -- AMATEURS' MANUALS

The complete outdoor builder   **690**

Outcalt, Todd

Your beautiful wedding on any budget   **395**

Outcasts united. St. John, W.   **796.334**

Outdoor adventures [series]

Canoeing   **797.1**

Kayaking   **797.1**

OUTDOOR COOKING

Kaminsky, P. Mallmann on fire   **641.598**

Mallmann, F. Seven fires   **641.5**

Master of the grill   **641.578**

Sunset the great outdoors cookbook   **641.5**

OUTDOOR COOKING

See also Camping; Cooking

OUTDOOR COOKING -- ANTARCTICA

Anthony, J. C. Hoosh   **394.1**

OUTDOOR EDUCATION

Sampson, S. D. How to raise a wild child   **508**

OUTDOOR EDUCATION

See also Education

OUTDOOR LIFE

White, D. Under the stars   **796.54**

OUTDOOR LIFE -- ACCIDENTS

Zuckerman, P. Buried in the sky   **796.522**

OUTDOOR LIFE -- HANDBOOKS, MANUALS, ETC

Canterbury, D. Advanced bushcraft   **613.69**

Canterbury, D. Bushcraft 101   **613.6**

OUTDOOR LIFE -- UNITED STATES

White, D. Under the stars   **796.54**

Outdoor lives [series]

Grange, K. Beneath blossom rain   **915**

OUTDOOR PHOTOGRAPHY

See also Photography

OUTDOOR PHOTOGRAPHY -- AMATEURS' MANUALS

Manwaring, J. Extraordinary everyday photography   **778.71**

OUTDOOR RECREATION

Citro, A. 150+ screen-free activities for kids   **796.5**

Louv, R. Vitamin N   **155.9**

OUTDOOR RECREATION -- HANDBOOKS, MANUALS, ETC

Canterbury, D. Advanced bushcraft   **613.69**

Canterbury, D. Bushcraft 101   **613.6**

OUTER SPACE

Randall, L. Dark Matter and the Dinosaurs   **523.1**

Schilling, G. Deep Space   **520**

OUTER SPACE

See also Astronautics; Astronomy; Space sciences

OUTER SPACE -- COLONIES See Space colonies

OUTER SPACE -- EXPLORATION

Aldrin, B. Mission to mars   **629.44**

Bell, J. The interstellar age   **919**

Clegg, B. Final Frontier   **629.4**

Hadfield, C. An astronaut's guide to life on earth   **92**

Piantadosi, C. A. Mankind beyond Earth   **629.45**

White, R. Into the Black   **629.44**

OUTER SPACE -- EXPLORATION

See also Exploration; Interplanetary voyages; Space flight

OUTER SPACE -- EXPLORATION -- PICTORIAL WORKS

Launius, R. D. Smithsonian atlas of space exploration   **500.5**

OUTER SPACE -- EXPLORATION -- POPULAR WORKS

Clegg, B. Final Frontier   **629.4**

Piantadosi, C. A. Mankind beyond Earth   **629.45**

OUTER SPACE -- JUVENILE LITERATURE

Munroe, R. Thing Explainer   **500**

Outlaw journalist. McKeen, W.   **92**

OUTLAWS

Brown, D. A. The American West   **978**

Gardner, M. L. To hell on a fast horse   **92**

Guinn, J. Go down together   **364.1**

Katz, F. The life and times of Pancho Villa   **972.08**

Stiles, T. J. Jesse James   **364.15**

Wallis, M. Billy the Kid   **92**

OUTLAWS See Criminals; Thieves

OUTLAWS -- WEST (U.S.) -- BIOGRAPHY

Hatch, T. The Last Outlaws   **364.15**

Stiles, T. J. Jesse James   **364.15**

Outliers. Gladwell, M.   **302**

Outrageous acts and everyday rebellions. Steinem,

G.   305.42
Outside looking in. Wills, G.   92
OUTSIDER ART
   See also Art
Outsider in the White House. Sanders, B.   92
Outsmarting alzheimer's. Kosik, K. S.   616.8
The **outsourced** self. Hochschild, A. R.   306.85
OUTSOURCING
  Hochschild, A. R. The outsourced self   306.85
  Macy, B. Factory man   338.7
OUTSOURCING
   See also Contracts
Outwitting history. Lansky, A.   002.07
Ovenly.   641.81
OVENLY (BAKERY)
  Ovenly   641.81
Over the edge of the world. Bergreen, L.   910.4
Over there. Farwell, B.   940.4
Over time. Deford, F.   92
OVER-THE-COUNTER DRUGS *See* Nonpre-
  scription drugs
Overbooked. Becker, E.   338.4
Overcoming Autism. Lazebnik, C.   618.92
Overdevelopment, Overpopulation, Over-
  shoot.   363.9
Overfishing. Hilborn, R.   338.3
OVERFISHING
  Hilborn, R. Overfishing   338.3
  Rigney, M. In pursuit of giants   597
  Rotman, J. L. The last fisherman   778.7
Overheated. Guzman, A. T.   363.738
OVERLAND JOURNEYS TO THE PACIFIC
  Brown, D. The indifferent stars above   92
  McLynn, F. Wagons west   978
OVERLAND JOURNEYS TO THE PACIFIC
   See also Frontier and pioneer life; Voyages
  and travels
Overlord. Graham, J.   811
Overman, Dean L.
  A case for the existence of God   212
OVERPOPULATION
  Overdevelopment, Overpopulation, Over-
  shoot   363.9
  Rees, M. J. From here to infinity   500
OVERPOPULATION
   See also Population
Overtveldt, Johan van
  Bernanke's test   332.1
OVERUSE INJURIES -- MISCELLANEA
  Gambaro, J. The truth about carpal tunnel syn-
  drome   616.85
OVERWEIGHT *See* Obesity
OVERWEIGHT PERSONS -- NEW JERSEY --
  BIOGRAPHY
  Baroni, B. Fat kid got fit   362.196
OVERWEIGHT PERSONS -- UNITED STATES

-- BIOGRAPHY
  Spiker, T. Down size   92
Overy, Richard
  (ed) The New York Times complete World War II,
  1939-1945   940.53
  Why the Allies won   940.53
Ovid
  Metamorphoses   873
  Tales from Ovid   873
Owen, David, 1955-
  Green metropolis   304.2
Owen, Mark, 1976?-
       About
  Maurer, K. No easy day   958.104
Owen, Roger
  The rise and fall of Arab presidents for life 352.23
Owen, Stephen
  (ed) An Anthology of Chinese literature   895.1
Owens, Delia
  The eye of the elephant   333.95
  Owens, M. Secrets of the savanna   599
Owens, Jesse, 1913-1980
       About
  Schaap, J. Triumph   92
Owens, Mark
  (jt. auth) Owens, D. The eye of the elephant 333.95
  Secrets of the savanna   599
Owls. Taylor, M.   598.9
OWLS
  Taylor, M. Owls   598.9
Owls of the world. Mikkola, H.   598.9
The **owner** of the house. Simpson, L. A. M. 811
Owning the earth. Linklater, A.   333.3
OXFORD (ENGLAND)
  Cartwright, J. Oxford revisited   942
The **Oxford** American book of great music writing.
  Smirnoff, M.   781.64
Oxford American writer's thesaurus.   423
The **Oxford** anthology of African-American poet-
  ry.   811
Oxford Atlas of the world.   912
Oxford Bible atlas. Curtis, A.   220.9
The **Oxford** book of American poetry.   811
The **Oxford** book of aphorisms.   808.88
The **Oxford** book of comic verse.   821
The **Oxford** book of death.   808.88
The **Oxford** book of English verse.   821
The **Oxford** book of humorous prose.   827
The **Oxford** book of sonnets.   821
The **Oxford** book of the American South.   810
The **Oxford** book of war poetry.   808.81
The **Oxford** book of women's writing in the United
  States.   810
The **Oxford** classical dictionary.   938
The **Oxford** companion to American law.   349
The **Oxford** companion to American literature.

Hart, J. D. **810**

The **Oxford** Companion to Archaeology. **930.1**

The **Oxford** companion to Chaucer. **821**

Oxford companion to Christian thought. **230**

The **Oxford** companion to classical literature. **880**

The **Oxford** companion to English literature. **820**

The **Oxford** companion to food. Davidson, A. **641**

The **Oxford** companion to Irish literature. **820**

The **Oxford** companion to Italian literature. **850**

The **Oxford** companion to Mark Twain. **818**

The **Oxford** companion to music. **780**

The **Oxford** companion to philosophy. **103**

The **Oxford** companion to Shakespeare. **822.3**

The **Oxford** companion to the American musical. Hischak, T. **792.6**

The **Oxford** companion to the Bible. **220.3**

The **Oxford** companion to the history of modern science. **509**

The **Oxford** companion to the mind. **128**

The **Oxford** companion to the Supreme Court of the United States. **347**

The **Oxford** companion to theatre and performance. **792**

The **Oxford** companion to wine. **641.22**

The **Oxford** companion to wine. **641.2**

The **Oxford** companion to world exploration. **910.3**

The **Oxford** companion to world mythology. Leeming, D. A. **201**

Oxford composer companions [series]

Haydn **92**

The **Oxford** dictionary of classical myth and religion. **292**

The **Oxford** dictionary of dance. Craine, D. **792.8**

Oxford dictionary of English idioms. **423**

Oxford dictionary of humorous quotations. **808.88**

The **Oxford** dictionary of Islam. **297**

Oxford dictionary of modern quotations. **808.88**

The **Oxford** Dictionary of Music. Bourne, J. **780.3**

Oxford dictionary of nicknames. Delahunty, A. **929.4**

The **Oxford** dictionary of nursery rhymes. **398.8**

The **Oxford** dictionary of philosophy. Blackburn, S. **103**

Oxford dictionary of phrase and fable. **803**

The **Oxford** dictionary of Popes. Kelly, J. N. D. **920.003**

Oxford dictionary of quotations. **082**

The **Oxford** dictionary of saints. Farmer, D. H. **920.003**

Oxford dictionary of scientific quotations. **500**

The **Oxford** dictionary of slang. Ayto, J. **427**

The **Oxford** dictionary of the Jewish religion. **296**

The **Oxford** encyclopedia of American literature. **810**

The **Oxford** encyclopedia of ancient Egypt. **932**

The **Oxford** encyclopedia of economic history. **330**

The **Oxford** encyclopedia of food and drink in America. **641.3**

The **Oxford** English dictionary. **423**

OXFORD ENGLISH DICTIONARY

Mugglestone, L. Lost for words **423**

Simpson, J. The word detective **423.092**

Winchester, S. The professor and the madman **423**

The **Oxford** guide to literature in English translation. **820**

The **Oxford** guide to United States Supreme Court decisions. **342**

Oxford history of art [series]

Berlo, J. C. Native North American art **709.01**

Craske, M. Art in Europe, 1700-1830 **709.03**

Patton, S. F. African-American art **704.03**

The **Oxford** history of Britain. **941**

The **Oxford** history of Islam. **297**

The **Oxford** history of Mexico. **972**

Oxford history of modern Europe [series]

Craig, G. A. Germany, 1866-1945 **943.08**

The **Oxford** history of the biblical world. **220.9**

The **Oxford** history of the Roman world. **937**

The **Oxford** history of the twentieth century. **909.82**

Oxford history of the United States [series]

Herring, G. C. From colony to superpower **327**

Howe, D. W. What hath God wrought **973.5**

Kennedy, D. M. Freedom from fear **973.91**

McPherson, J. M. Battle cry of freedom **973.7**

Middlekauff, R. The glorious cause **973.3**

Wood, G. S. Empire of liberty **973.4**

The **Oxford** history of Western philosophy. **190**

The **Oxford** illustrated history of the Crusades. **909.07**

The **Oxford** illustrated history of the Vikings. **948**

Oxford Latin dictionary. **473**

Oxford new concise world atlas. **912**

Oxford new concise world atlas. **912**

Oxford paperback reference [series]

Ayto, J. The Oxford dictionary of slang **427**

Cannon, J. The kings & queens of Britain **920**

Craine, D. The Oxford dictionary of dance **792.8**

Oxford dictionary of English idioms **423**

Park, C. A dictionary of environment and conservation **333.7**

The **Oxford** picture dictionary. Adelson-Goldstein, J. **423**

Oxford revisited. Cartwright, J. **942**

Oxford rhyming dictionary. Upton, C. **423**

The **Oxford** study Bible. Bible **220.5**

Oxford University Press

Calhoun, C. J. Dictionary of the social sciences **300**

(comp) New Concise World Atlas **912**

(comp) Oxford Atlas of the world **912**

(comp) Oxford new concise world atlas **912**

The Oxford companion to the Bible **220.3**

The Oxford encyclopedia of economic history **330**

The **Oxford** W. E. B. Du Bois reader. 305.896
Oxford world's classics [series]
  Aristotle Politics 320
  Augustine Confessions 242
  The Bible: Authorized King James Version 220.5
  Cicero, M. T. The republic; and, The laws 320.1
  Du Bois, W. E. B. The souls of Black folk 305.8
  Freud, S. Interpretation of dreams 154.6
  Gaskell, E. C. The life of Charlotte Bronte 92
  Hobbes, T. Leviathan 320.1
  Marx, K. Capital: an abridged edition 330.1
  Nietzsche, F. W. Thus spoke Zarathustra 193
  Pindar The complete odes of Pindar 884
  Pope, A. Selected poetry 821
  Samuel Johnson 828
  Veblen, T. The theory of the leisure class 305.5
  Vega, L. d. Three major plays 862
  Washington, B. T. Up from slavery 92
The **Oxford-Hachette** French dictionary. Correard 443
OXYCODONE -- UNITED STATES
  Quinones, S. Dreamland 362.29
OXYGEN
  See also Chemical elements; Gases
Oyen, Jeremy
  (ed) Canoeing 797.1
  (ed) Kayaking 797.1
OYSTERS
  Jacobsen, R. The Essential Oyster 641.694
  Jacobsen, R. The living shore 639.9
Oz, Amos
  About
  Oz, A. A tale of love and darkness 92
  Remnick, D. Reporting 814
OZËRSK (CHELIABINSKAIA OBLAST, RUS-SIA) -- HISTORY -- 20TH CENTURY
  Brown, K. Plutopia 363.17
Ozick, Cynthia
  The din in the head 809
  Quarrel & quandary 814
Ozment, Katherine
  Grace without God 200.973
Ozonoff, Sally
  (jt. auth) Dawson, G. A parent's guide to high-functioning autism spectrum disorder 618.92

P

P. T. Barnum: the legend and the man. Saxon, A. H. 338.7
Pablo Neruda. Feinstein, A. 92
Pacheco, Rebecca
  Do your om thing 181
PACHYCEPHALOSAURUS
  See also Dinosaurs
Pacific. Winchester, S. 909
PACIFIC COAST (NORTH AMERICA)

Winchester, S. Pacific 909
PACIFIC CREST TRAIL
  Strayed, C. Wild 92
  Pacific crucible. Toll, I. W. 940.54
PACIFIC NORTHWEST
  Faulkner, S. Bitterroot 978
PACIFIC NORTHWEST
  See also North America; United States; West (U.S.)
PACIFIC OCEAN
  Winchester, S. Pacific 909
PACIFIC OCEAN
  See also Ocean
PACIFIC REGION
  Winchester, S. Pacific 909
PACIFIC STATES
  See also West (U.S.)
The **Pacific** War. 940.54
The **Pacific** War. Costello, J. 940.54
The **Pacific** War encyclopedia. Dunnigan, J. F. 940.54
PACIFISM
  Hochschild, A. To end all wars 940.3
PACIFISM
  See also War -- Religious aspects
PACIFISTS
  Addams, J. Twenty years at Hull-House 361.7
  Al Jundi, S. The hour of sunlight 92
  Chadha, Y. Gandhi 954.03
  Ellsberg, D. Secrets: a memoir of Vietnam and the Pentagon papers 959.704
  Gandhi, M. An autobiography 92
  Kazin, A. An American procession 810
  Knight, L. W. Jane Addams 92
  Lelyveld, J. Great soul 92
  Matthiessen, F. O. American renaissance 810
  Mohandas Gandhi 92
  Sullivan, R. The Thoreau you don't know 92
  Wolpert, S. A. Gandhi's passion 954.03
PACK TRANSPORTATION *See* Backpacking
PACKAGING
  See also Advertising; Retail trade
Packard, Jerrold M.
  American nightmare 305.8
Packer, George
  The assassins' gate 956.7
  Interesting times 814
  The unwinding 973.924
Packer, Sarit
  Honey & Co. 641.595
  (jt. auth) Srulovich, I. Honey & Co the Baking Book 641
Packing for Mars. Roach, M. 571
PACKING INDUSTRY *See* Meat industry
Paddock, Lisa Olson
  Rollyson, C. E. Susan Sontag 818

Paderewski, Ignace Jan, 1860-1941
About
Schonberg, H. C. The great pianists **920**
Padesky, Christine A.
(jt. auth) Greenberger, D. Mind over mood **616.89**
Padgett, Donald
(jt. auth) Klubeck, M. Why organizations struggle so hard to improve so little **658.4**
Padgett, Jason
Struck by genius **155.9**
Padgett, Ron, 1942-
(jt. auth) Brainard, J. The Nancy book **759**
Collected Poems **811**
Padilla Peralta, Dan-el
About
Padilla Peralta Undocumented **92**
Padoan, Amanda
(jt. auth) Zuckerman, P. Buried in the sky **796.522**
Pagana, Kathleen Deska
(jt. auth) Pagana, T. J. Mosby's diagnostic and laboratory test reference **616.07**
Pagana, Theresa N.
(jt. auth) Pagana, T. J. Mosby's diagnostic and laboratory test reference **616.07**
Pagana, Timothy J.
Mosby's diagnostic and laboratory test reference **616.07**
Paganelli, Jennifer
Happy home **646.2**
PAGANISM
Adler, M. Drawing down the moon **133.4**
Mar, A. Witches of America **299**
PAGANISM
See also Religions
Pagano, Joan
Strength training exercises for women **613.7**
Strength training for women **613.7**
Pagden, Anthony
The Enlightenment **940.2**
Peoples and empires **909**
Page, Inman, 1852-1935
About
Ellison, R. The collected essays of Ralph Ellison **814**
Page, Jake
Adovasio, J. M. The first Americans **970.01**
Page, Karen
The flavor bible **641.5**
Page, Larry
About
Auletta, K. Googled **338.7**
Page, Lawrence M.
Peterson field guide to freshwater fishes of North America north of Mexico **597**
Page, P. K.
The hidden room **811**

Page, Thomas Nelson, 1853-1922
About
Wilson, E. Patriotic gore **810**
PAGEANTS
See also Acting
Pagel, Mark
Wired for culture **303.4**
Pagels, Elaine H.
Beyond belief **229**
The Gnostic Gospels **299**
The origin of Satan **235**
Paglen, Trevor, 1974-
Blank spots on the map **355.3**
Paglia, Camille
Break, blow, burn **809.1**
Pagliaro, Michael
The musical instrument desk reference **784.192**
Paice, Edward
World War I: the African Front **940.4**
Paid for. Moran, R. **306.74**
Paid, owned, earned. Burcher, N. **658.8**
Paige, Satchel, 1906-1982
About
Fox, W. P. Satchel Paige's America **92**
Tye, L. Satchel **92**
PAIN
Jamison, L. The empathy exams **814**
PAIN
See also Diagnosis; Emotions; Psychophysiology; Senses and sensation
PAIN -- TREATMENT
Lewis, M. Understanding pain **616**
Pain, Parties, Work. Winder, E. **811**
Paine, Jeffery
(ed) The Poetry of our world **808.81**
Paine, Ruth
About
Mallon, T. Mrs. Paine's garage and the murder of John F. Kennedy **364.1**
Paine, Thomas, 1737-1809
Rights of man; and, Common sense **320**
About
Collins, P. The trouble with Tom: the strange afterlife and times of Thomas Paine **92**
Phillips, K. 1775 **973.3**
PAINTED GLASS *See* Glass painting and staining
Painter, Nell Irvin
The history of White people **305.8**
Sojourner Truth **305.5**
PAINTERS
Adams, H. Tom and Jack **92**
Albers, P. Joan Mitchell **92**
Andoe, J. Jubilee city **92**
Aquino, L. Leonardo Da Vinci **92**
Asleson, R. Albert Moore **759.2**
Bailey, A. Velazquez: surrendering at Breda **759**

Baillio, J. Claude Monet, 1840-1926 **759**

Bell, J. Van Gogh **92**

Benfey, C. E. G. A summer of hummingbirds **920**

Biel, S. American Gothic **759.13**

Blackburn, J. Old man Goya **92**

Bocquet Kiki de Montparnasse **759.4**

Bramly, S. Leonardo **709**

Brewer, J. The American Leonardo **759**

Brombert, B. A. Edouard Manet **92**

Brown, D. A. Leonardo da Vinci **759**

Carter, A. A. The Red Rose girls **759.13**

Cikovsky, N. Winslow Homer **759.13**

Cockburn, H. Henry's demons **92**

Cohen-Solal, A. Mark Rothko **759.13**

Dippie, B. W. The Frederic Remington Art Museum collection **709**

Dolnick, E. The rescue artist **364.1**

Drohojowska-Philp, H. Full bloom **92**

Ebert-Schifferer, S. Caravaggio **92**

Edouard Vuillard **759**

Elderfield, J. De Kooning: a retrospective **759.13**

Evans, R. T. Grant Wood **92**

Finch, C. Chuck Close **92**

FitzGerald, M. C. Picasso and American art **709**

Fraser, K. Ornament and silence **809**

Frey, J. Toulouse-Lautrec **92**

Gioia, D. Can poetry matter? **809.1**

Graham-Dixon, A. Caravaggio **92**

Hennessey, M. H. Norman Rockwell **759.13**

Herrera, H. Frida: a biography of Frida Kahlo **709**

Hoban, P. Alice Neel **92**

Hudson, M. Titian **92**

Hughes, R. Goya **760**

Kahlo, F. The diary of Frida Kahlo **92**

King, R. The judgment of Paris **759**

King, R. Michelangelo & the Pope's ceiling **759**

Kirshenblatt, M. They called me Mayer July **92**

Klein, S. Leonardo's legacy **709**

Langdon, H. Caravaggio **709**

Leal, B. The ultimate Picasso **759**

Lepore, J. A is for American **306.44**

Levin, G. Lee Krasner **92**

Liedtke, W. A. Vermeer and the Delft school **759.9**

Livingston, J. The paintings of Joan Mitchell **759.13**

Lottman, H. R. Man Ray's Montparnasse **709**

Lozano Frida Kahlo **759.9**

Marnham, P. Dreaming with his eyes open **92**

Mathews, N. M. Mary Cassatt **759.13**

Michaelis, D. N.C. Wyeth **92**

Naifeh, S. Van Gogh **92**

Nathan, D. Sybil exposed **616.85**

Nuland, S. B. Leonardo da Vinci **709**

Penrose, R. Picasso: his life and work **709**

Prideaux, S. Edvard Munch **92**

Prose, F. Caravaggio **92**

Rhodes, R. John James Audubon **92**

Robb, P. M: the man who became Caravaggio **759**

Robinson, R. Georgia O'Keeffe: a life **709**

Sassoon, D. Becoming Mona Lisa **759**

Schama, S. Rembrandt's eyes **92**

Scotti, R. A. Vanished smile **759**

Sebald, W. G. On the natural history of destruction **833**

Solomon, D. Jackson Pollock **92**

Spurling, H. Matisse the master **92**

Spurling, H. The unknown Matisse **92**

Stanton, T. Road to Cooperstown **92**

Strathern, P. The artist, the philosopher, and the warrior **920**

Swan, A. De Kooning: an American master **92**

Tate, M. J. Critical companion to F. Scott Fitzgerald **813**

Thomas Eakins **759.13**

Thomson, B. Van Gogh paintings **759.9**

Tomkins, C. Duchamp **709**

Vaill, A. Everybody was so young **759.13**

Weber, N. F. The Bauhaus group **920**

White, M. Leonardo **92**

Wullschlager, J. Chagall **92**

Wyeth, A. Andrew Wyeth **92**

PAINTERS

See also Artists

PAINTERS -- BIOGRAPHY

Fortune, B. B. Elaine de kooning **759.13**

Hale, S. Titian **92**

J.m.w. Drawing down the moon turner

PAINTERS -- FRANCE -- BIOGRAPHY

Danchev, A. Cézanne **759.4**

PAINTERS -- UNITED STATES -- BIOGRAPHY

Solomon, D. American mirror **92**

PAINTING

Artist's painting techniques **751.4**

Jenkins, A. 300 tips for painting & decorating **698**

Marine, C. Daily painting **751.4**

Sloan, A. Color recipes for painted furniture and more

PAINTING

See also Art; Graphic arts

PAINTING -- 15TH AND 16TH CENTURIES

Capponi, N. The Day the Renaissance Was Saved **945**

PAINTING -- 21ST CENTURY

Godfrey, T. Painting today **759.06**

PAINTING -- ITALY -- FLORENCE

Florence **759.5**

PAINTING -- TECHNIQUE

Painting the great masters **751.45**

Painting and wallpapering secrets from Brian Santos, the Wall Wizard. Santos, B. **698**

Painting in acrylics. Kloosterboer, L. **751.426**

Painting successful watercolours from photographs. Kersey, G. **751.42**

Painting the great masters. **751.45**
Painting today. Godfrey, T. **759.06**
Painting with pastels. Price, M. **741.2**
PAINTING, AMERICAN *See* American painting
PAINTING, DECORATIVE *See* Decoration and
ornament
PAINTING, FRENCH
King, R. The judgment of Paris **759**
PAINTING, ITALIAN
Graham-Dixon, A. Caravaggio **92**
Hudson, M. Titian **92**
PAINTING, RENAISSANCE *See* Painting -- 15th
and 16th centuries
PAINTING, RENAISSANCE -- EXPERTISING
Brewer, J. The American Leonardo **759**
PAINTINGS *See* Painting
The **paintings** of Joan Mitchell. Livingston,
J. **759.13**
Paisner, Daniel
Darling, R. The complete game **92**
Pakenham, Thomas
The scramble for Africa **960**
Pakistan. Lieven, A. **954.91**
PAKISTAN -- DESCRIPTION AND TRAVEL
Schmidle, N. To live or to perish forever **954.91**
**PAKISTAN -- FOREIGN RELATIONS -- UNIT-
ED STATES**
Gall, C. The wrong enemy **958.104**
PAKISTAN -- HISTORY
Halperin, D. Tinderbox **614.5**
Lieven, A. Pakistan **954.91**
PAKISTAN -- POLITICS AND GOVERNMENT
Gall, C. The wrong enemy **958.104**
**PAKISTAN -- POLITICS AND GOVERNMENT
-- 1988-**
Bhutto, B. Reconciliation **92**
Lieven, A. Pakistan **954.91**
Rashid, A. Descent into chaos **954**
Schmidle, N. To live or to perish forever **954.91**
PAKISTAN -- RELATIONS -- UNITED STATES
Grenier, R. L. 88 days to Kandahar **958.104**
**PAKISTAN. INTER SERVICES INTELLI-
GENCE**
Gall, C. The wrong enemy **958.104**
Pakroo, Peri
The small business start-up kit **346**
Pakula, Hannah
The last empress **92**
PALACES
See also Buildings
Palakean, Grigoris, 1876-1934
About
Armenian Golgotha **956**
Palattella, John
(ed) Reporting Iraq **070**
Palca, Joe

Annoying **612.8**
Pale blue dot. Sagan, C. **520**
PALEO COOKING
Bryant, G. The paleo kitchen **641.5**
Fong, H. Nom nom paleo **641.5**
Paleo takeout **641.5**
Sanfilippo, D. Practical paleo **641.5**
Well fed **641.5**
The **paleo** kitchen. Bryant, G. **641.5**
Paleo takeout. **641.5**
PALEO-INDIANS
See also Native Americans -- History; Prehis-
toric peoples
PALEOHYDROLOGY
Montgomery, D. R. The rocks don't lie **551.48**
PALEOLITHIC PERIOD *See* Stone Age
PALEONTOLOGISTS
Dennett, D. C. Darwin's dangerous idea **146**
Larson, P. L. Rex appeal **567.9**
Novacek, M. J. Time traveler **92**
PALEONTOLOGY
Fortey, R. Horseshoe crabs and velvet worms **595**
Johanson, D. C. From Lucy to language **599.93**
Novacek, M. J. Time traveler **92**
Prothero, D. R. The story of life in 25 fossils **560**
Sampson, S. D. Dinosaur odyssey **567.9**
PALEONTOLOGY
See also Historical geology; Zoology
PALEOZOOLOGY *See* Paleontology
PALESTINE
Bregman, A. Cursed victory
Ehrenreich, B. The Way to the Spring **956.95**
Mitchell, G. J. A Path to Peace **956.94**
Palestine Speaks **956.94**
PALESTINE -- HISTORY
Hoffman, B. Anonymous soldiers **956.94**
PALESTINE LIBERATION ORGANIZATION
Remnick, D. Reporting **814**
Palestine Speaks. **956.94**
PALESTINIAN ARABS
Al Jundi, S. The hour of sunlight **92**
David, A. Once upon a country **92**
Ehrenreich, B. The Way to the Spring **956.95**
Grossman, D. The yellow wind **956.95**
La Guardia, A. War without end **956.940**
Said, E. W. Reflections on exile and other es-
says **814**
Shipler, D. K. Arab and Jew **956.94**
PALESTINIAN ARABS
See also Arabs
PALESTINIAN ARABS -- ETHNIC IDENTITY
La Guardia, A. War without end **956.940**
O'Malley, P. The two-state delusion **956.94**
**PALESTINIAN ARABS -- HISTORY -- 21ST
CENTURY**
O'Malley, P. The two-state delusion **956.94**

PALESTINIAN ARABS -- POLITICS AND GOV-ERNMENT -- 21ST CENTURY
O'Malley, P. The two-state delusion   **956.94**

PALESTINIAN TERRITORIES *See* Palestine

PALESTINIAN UPRISING, 2000- *See* Intifada, 2000-

PALESTINIAN-ISRAELI CONFLICT, 2000- *See* Intifada, 2000-

PALESTINIANS *See* Palestinian Arabs

Paley, Rebecca
(jt. auth) Beard, A. In the water they can't see you cry   **797.2**
(jt. auth) Halbreich, B. I'll drink to that   **92**

Palfreman, Jon
Brain storms   **616.8**

Palfrey, John
Born digital   **302.23**

Palgrave essential histories [series]
Bregman, A. A history of Israel   **956.94**

Palin, Michael
     About
Palin, M. Halfway to Hollywood   **92**

Palin, Sarah, 1964-
     About
Traister, R. Big girls don't cry   **324**

Palisca, Claude V.
(ed) Norton Anthology of Western Music   **780**
A history of Western music   **780.9**

Palladio, Andrea, 1508-1580
The four books on architecture   **720**
     About
Boucher, B. Andrea Palladio   **720.9**
Rybczynski, W. The perfect house: a journey with the Renaissance architect Andrea Palladio   **720.9**

PALLIATIVE TREATMENT
Volandes, A. E. The conversation   **616.02**

PALLIATIVE TREATMENT
     See also Therapeutics

Palmer, Arnold, 1929-2016
     About
Palmer, A. A life well played   **92**
Palmer, A. A golfer's life   **92**

Palmer, Charlie
Charlie Palmer's American fare   **641.59**

Palmer, James
The bloody white baron   **92**
Heaven cracks, earth shakes   **951**

Palmer, Louis J.
Encyclopedia of abortion in the United States **363.46**

Palmer, Sara
Just one of the kids   **649**

Palmer, Xueyan Z.
Palmer, L. J. Encyclopedia of abortion in the United States   **363.46**

Palmisano, Joseph M.
(ed) World of sociology   **301**

PALMISTRY
Reid, L. The art of hand reading   **133.6**

PALMISTRY
     See also Divination; Fortune telling; Occultism

PALSY *See* Parkinson's disease

Paltrow, Gwyneth, 1972-
It's all easy   **641.5**

Paludan, Phillip S.
The presidency of Abraham Lincoln   **973.7**

PAMPERED CHILD SYNDROME
Glickman, E. R. Your kid's a brat and it's all your fault   **649.1**

PAMPHLETEERS
Collins, P. The trouble with Tom: the strange afterlife and times of Thomas Paine   **92**
DeGategno, P. J. Critical companion to Jonathan Swift   **828**
Severin, T. In search of Robinson Crusoe   **996**

PAMPHLETS
     See also Press

PAMPHLETS -- DESIGN
     See also Design

Pamuk, Orhan
Istanbul   **949.6**
Other colors   **894**

Pan, Philip P.
Out of Mao's shadow   **951.05**

PAN-AFRICANISM
     See also Africa -- Politics and government

PAN-ARABISM
     See also Arab countries -- Politics and government

Panagore, Peter Baldwin
Heaven Is Beautiful   **231.7**

PANAMA -- DESCRIPTION
Royte, E. The Tapir's morning bath   **577.34**

PANAMA CANAL
McCullough, D. G. The path between the seas   **972.87**

PANDEMONIUM AVIARIES
Raffin, M. The birds of Pandemonium   **639.97**

Pandora's DNA. Stark, L.   **616.99**

Panek, Richard
(jt. auth) Grandin, T. The autistic brain   **616.85**

PANEL DISCUSSIONS *See* Discussion groups

Panic.   **338.5**

PANIC DISORDERS
     See also Abnormal psychology; Neuroses

PANICS (FINANCE) *See* Financial crises

Pankey, Eric
The pear as one example   **811**
Trace   **811**

PANTHEISM
     See also Philosophy; Religion

PANTOMIMES

See also Acting; Amateur theater; Drama; Theater

Pantsov, Alexander V.
  (jt. auth) Levine, S. I. Deng Xiaoping   **951.05**
  (jt. auth) Levine, S. I. Mao   **951.05**
Panzer, Mary
  Mathew Brady and the image of history   **770.92**
Paolini, Gregory
  Arts & crafts furniture projects   **684.1**
PAPACY
  Duffy, E. Saints & sinners   **282**
  Maxwell-Stuart, P. G. Chronicle of the popes   **282**
  McBrien, R. P. Lives of the popes   **920**
PAPACY
  See also Catholic Church; Church history
Papadaddy's book for new fathers. Edgerton, C.   **649**
Papadakis, Maxine
  (ed) Current medical diagnosis and treatment   **610**
Papadatos, Alecos
  Democracy   **741.5**
PAPAL ENCYCLICALS
  See also Christian literature
PAPAL VISITS
  See also Voyages and travels
Papenfuss, Mary
  (jt. auth) Thompson, T. American huckster **796.334**
Paper. Kurlansky, M.   **676.09**
PAPER
  Baker, N. Double fold   **025.2**
  Basbanes, N. A. On paper   **676**
  Grummer, A. E. Trash-to-treasure papermaking   **676**
  Monro, A. The paper trail   **676**
PAPER -- HISTORY
  Kurlansky, M. Paper   **676.09**
PAPER BOUND BOOKS *See* Paperback books
PAPER CRAFTS
  Hayakawa, H. Kirigami menagerie   **736**
  Helfand, J. Scrapbooks: an American history   **745.54**
  Henri Matisse   **709.2**
  The paper playhouse   **745.54**
PAPER CRAFTS
  See also Handicraft
PAPER FLOWERS
  Farrell, P. Paper to petal   **745.54**
PAPER FOLDING *See* Origami; Paper crafts
The **paper** garden. Peacock, M.   **92**
PAPER HANGING *See* Paperhanging
PAPER INDUSTRY
  Basbanes, N. A. On paper   **676**
  Monro, A. The paper trail   **676**
PAPER INDUSTRY
  See also Industries
PAPER INDUSTRY -- HISTORY

Basbanes, N. A. On paper   **676**
Kurlansky, M. Paper   **676.09**
The **paper** playhouse.   **745.54**
PAPER SCULPTURE *See* Paper crafts
Paper to petal. Farrell, P.   **745.54**
The **paper** trail. Monro, A.   **676**
PAPER WORK
  Gilleland, D. All points patchwork   **746.46**
PAPER WORK *See* Paper crafts
PAPER, HANDMADE
  Hiebert, H. The papermaker's companion   **676**
PAPERBACK BOOKS
  Lavender, K. Book repair   **025.7**
PAPERBACK BOOKS
  See also Books; Editions
PAPERHANGING
  Santos, B. Painting and wallpapering secrets from Brian Santos, the Wall Wizard   **698**
PAPERHANGING
  See also Interior design
The **papermaker's** companion. Hiebert, H.   **676**
PAPERMAKING
  Grummer, A. E. Trash-to-treasure papermaking   **676**
  Hiebert, H. The papermaker's companion   **676**
  Monro, A. The paper trail   **676**
PAPERMAKING
  See also Manufactures; Paper
PAPERMAKING -- HISTORY
  Basbanes, N. A. On paper   **676**
  Kurlansky, M. Paper   **676.09**
  Monro, A. The paper trail   **676**
PAPERMAKING INDUSTRY *See* Paper industry
PAPIER-MÂCHÉ *See* Paper crafts
Papp, Csilla
  Sensational soutache jewelry making   **745.594**
Papp, Joseph
About

  Turan, K. Free for all   **92**
Pappalardo, Joe
  Sunflowers   **583**
Paquet, Marcel, 1947-2014
  Paquet, M. Magritte   **709**
Paracelsus. Webster, C.   **92**
Paracelsus, 1493-1541
About

  Webster, C. Paracelsus   **92**
Parachini, Chris
  Roberta's   **641.82**
PARACHUTES
  See also Aeronautics
PARADES
  See also Festivals; Pageants
Paradis, Cheryl
  The measure of madness   **364.3**
Paradis, Thomas W.

(ed) The Greenwood encyclopedia of homes through American history **728**

PARADISE

See also Future life

A **paradise** built in hell. Solnit, R. **303.4**

Paradise found. Nicholls, S. **508**

Paradise of the Pacific. Moore, S. **996.9**

Paradiso. Dante Alighieri **851**

The **Paradiso** files. Burke, T. M. **364.152**

Paradiso, Leonard J., 1942-2008

About

Burke, T. M. The Paradiso files **364.152**

Parallax. Morrissey, S. **821**

Parallel worlds. Kaku, M. **523.1**

PARALYSIS

See also Nervous system -- Diseases

PARALYSIS, CEREBRAL *See* Cerebral palsy

PARALYSIS, SPASTIC, IN CHILDREN -- BIOG-RAPHY

The fall **92**

PARANOIA

Guppy, J. My fluorescent God **92**

Walker, J. The United States of paranoia **973**

Wheen, F. Strange days indeed **973.92**

Paranoid parenting. Furedi, F. **649**

Paranormal America. Bader, C. D. **133.8**

PARANORMAL FICTION

See also Fiction

PARANORMAL PHENOMENA *See* Parapsychology

PARAPROFESSIONALS

See also Occupations; Professions

PARAPSYCHOLOGISTS

Steinmeyer, J. Charles Fort **92**

PARAPSYCHOLOGY

Bader, C. D. Paranormal America **133.8**

Blum, D. Ghost hunters **133.9**

Clegg, B. Extra Sensory **133.8**

Goodman, L. Linda Goodman's star signs **130**

Guiley, R. E. The encyclopedia of ghosts and spirits **133.1**

Mezrich, B. The 37th parallel **001.942**

Shermer, M. Why people believe weird things **001.9**

Steinmeyer, J. Charles Fort **92**

PARAPSYCHOLOGY

See also Psychology; Research; Supernatural

PARAPSYCHOLOGY -- MISCELLANEA

Krulos, T. Monster hunters **001.94**

PARAPSYCHOLOGY -- SOUTHWESTERN STATES

Mezrich, B. The 37th parallel **001.942**

PARASAUROLOPHUS

See also Dinosaurs

PARASITES

Dunn, R. The wild life of our bodies **579**

McAuliffe, K. This is your brain on parasites **612.8**

Zuk, M. Riddled with life **616.07**

PARASITIC DISEASES

Velasquez-Manoff, M. An Epidemic of Absence **616.97**

PARASITOLOGY

McAuliffe, K. This is your brain on parasites **612.8**

Parcells. Parcells, B. **796.332**

Parcells, Bill, 1941-

About

Parcells, B. Parcells **796.332**

Pardlo, Gregory, 1968-

Digest **811**

PARDON

See also Administration of criminal justice; Executive power

PARENT AND ADULT CHILD

Adamec, C. When your adult child breaks your heart **616.89**

Newman, K. S. The accordion family **306.874**

PARENT AND CHILD

Bailey, R. A. Easy to love, difficult to discipline **155**

Brooks, R. B. Raising resilient children **649**

Clark, L. S. The parent app **302.23**

Dawson, P. Smart but scattered **649**

Furedi, F. Paranoid parenting **649**

Gallagher, S. Experimenting with babies **306.874**

Glickman, E. R. Your kid's a brat and it's all your fault **649.1**

Greene, R. W. Raising human beings **306.874**

Karp, H. The happiest baby on the block **649**

Keene, N. Your Child in the Hospital **362.1**

Kubler-Ross, E. On children and death **155.9**

Mayes, L. C. The Yale Child Study Center guide to understanding your child **649**

Roffman, D. Talk to me first **613.907**

Sears, W. Parenting the fussy baby and high-need child **649**

Van't Hul, J. The artful parent **745.5**

PARENT AND CHILD *See* Parent-child relationship

PARENT AND CHILD -- POPULAR WORKS

Trainor, K. Calming your anxious child **618.92**

PARENT AND CHILD -- UNITED STATES -- PSYCHOLOGICAL ASPECTS

Solomon, A. Far from the tree **362.4**

PARENT AND INFANT

Kennedy, J. K. The good sleeper **649**

PARENT AND TEENAGER

Jensen, F. E. The teenage brain **612.6**

Roffman, D. Talk to me first **613.907**

Schwartz, J. Oddly normal **306.76**

Vernacchio, A. For goodness sex **613.9**

Wiseman, R. Masterminds and wingmen **649**

The **parent** app. Clark, L. S. **302.23**

A **parent's** guide to high-functioning autism spectrum disorder. Dawson, G. **618.92**

PARENT-ADULT CHILD RELATIONSHIP

Hodgman, G. Bettyville   **306.874**

PARENT-CHILD RELATIONSHIP

Block, S. When Your Parent Moves in   **306.874**

Brazelton, T. B. To listen to a child   **155.4**

Brooks, R. B. Raising resilient children   **649**

Duron, L. Raising my rainbow   **306.87**

Ezzo, G. On becoming baby wise   **649**

Furedi, F. Paranoid parenting   **649**

Garner, A. Families like mine   **306.8**

Glickman, E. R. Your kid's a brat and it's all your fault   **649.1**

Greene, R. W. Raising human beings   **306.874**

How to Talk So Kids Will Listen and Listen So Kids Will Talk   **649.1**

Ingall, M. Mamaleh knows best   **649.1**

Karp, H. The happiest baby on the block   **649**

Kazdin, A. E. The Everyday Parenting Toolkit   **649**

Keene, N. Your Child in the Hospital   **362.1**

Kennedy-Moore, E. Smart parenting for smart kids   **649**

Khetarpal, R. The perfect parent   **306.874**

Lippincott, J. M. 7 things your teenager won't tell you   **649**

Lythcott-Haims, J. How to raise an adult   **306.874**

Mayes, L. C. The Yale Child Study Center guide to understanding your child   **649**

Medina, J. Brain rules for baby   **649**

Miller, K. R. Coming clean   **92**

Newman, K. S. The accordion family   **306.874**

Pipher, M. B. Another country   **306.874**

Russo, R. Elsewhere   **92**

Small, M. F. Our babies, ourselves   **649**

Steiner-Adair, C. The Big Disconnect   **303.48**

Suskind, D. Thirty Million Words   **612.8**

Swanson, W. S. Mama doc medicine   **649.1**

Trainor, K. Calming your anxious child   **618.92**

Van't Hul, J. The artful parent   **745.5**

PARENT-CHILD RELATIONSHIP

   See also Child-adult relationship; Children; Family; Parents

PARENTAL BEHAVIOR *See* Parenting

PARENTAL CUSTODY *See* Child custody

PARENTAL KIDNAPPING

Woo, I. The great divorce   **92**

PARENTAL KIDNAPPING

   See also Child custody

PARENTAL LEAVE -- UNITED STATES

Levs, J. All in   **306.3**

PARENTAL OVERPROTECTION

Lahey, J. The gift of failure   **649**

PARENTHOOD

Rosswood, E. Journey to Same-sex Parenthood   **306.874**

PARENTHOOD

   See also Family

PARENTHOOD -- ECONOMIC ASPECTS

Margulis, J. The business of baby   **649**

PARENTING

Bailey, R. A. Easy to love, difficult to discipline **155**

Bowers, M. 8 keys to raising the quirky child   **649**

Brown, C. S. Parenting beyond pink and blue   **649**

Bullard, S. Teaching tolerance   **649**

Christakis, E. The Importance of Being Little   **372.21**

Chua, A. Battle hymn of the tiger mother   **306.874**

Clinton, H. R. It takes a village   **305.23**

Cohen, L. J. Playful parenting   **649**

Crompton, V. Saving beauty from the beast **362.88**

Cross, C. The baby book   **649.122**

Cusk, R. A life's work   **306.874**

Dahl, L. Loving Our Addicted Daughters Back to Life   **362.29**

Dalpiaz, C. M. Breaking free, starting over **362.82**

Dawson, P. Smart but scattered   **649**

DeGarmo, J. The foster parenting manual **306.874**

DeSouza, L. Eat, Play, Sleep   **649.122**

Dunckley, V. L. Reset your child's brain   **004.67**

Durham, M. G. The Lolita effect   **302.23**

Edelman, H. Motherless mothers   **155.9**

Fonseca, C. Raising the shy child   **649**

Foster, J. Beyond intelligence   **649**

Furedi, F. Paranoid parenting   **649**

Garner, A. Families like mine   **306.8**

Glickman, E. R. Your kid's a brat and it's all your fault   **649.1**

Goleman, D. Emotional intelligence   **152.4**

Gopnik, A. The gardener and the carpenter   **155.4**

Greene, R. W. Raising human beings   **306.874**

Groza, V. Adopting older children   **362.7**

How to Talk So Kids Will Listen and Listen So Kids Will Talk   **649.1**

Hurley, K. The happy kid handbook   **649**

Ingall, M. Mamaleh knows best   **649.1**

Jensen, F. E. The teenage brain   **612.6**

Karp, H. The happiest baby guide to great sleep **649**

Karr-Morse, R. Scared sick   **155.9**

Khetarpal, R. The perfect parent   **306.874**

Lahey, J. The gift of failure   **649**

Leach, P. Your Baby and Child From Birth to Age Five   **618.92**

Leap, J. Project Fatherhood   **306.874**

Lee, J. T. The 52 new foods challenge   **641.5**

Lev, A. I. The complete lesbian & gay parenting guide   **649**

Lieber, R. The Opposite of Spoiled   **332.024**

Lippincott, J. M. 7 things your teenager won't tell you   **649**

Lock, J. Help your teenager beat an eating disorder   **616.85**

Lofas, J. Stepparenting   **646.7**

Lythcott-Haims, J. How to raise an adult   **306.874**

Maybe baby   **306.8**
Miller, L. The Spiritual Child   **649**
The mom 100 cookbook   **641.5**
Phelan, T. W. 1-2-3 magic   **649**
Pitman, T. Sweet sleep   **649**
Prosek, J. Raising Can-Do Kids   **649.7**
Raeburn, P. The game theorist's guide to parent-ing   **641.1**
Roberts, D. Been there, done that   **92**
Roffman, D. Talk to me first   **613.907**
Rosenblatt, R. Making toast   **92**
Sampson, S. D. How to raise a wild child   **508**
Sandler, L. One and only   **306.874**
Sears, W. Parenting the fussy baby and high-need child   **649**
Senior, J. All Joy and No Fun   **306.874**
Sicherer, S. H. Understanding and managing your child's food allergies   **618.92**
Siegel, D. J. No-drama discipline   **649**
Siegel, D. J. The whole-brain child   **649**
Sleep   **618.92**
Solomon, A. Far from the tree   **362.4**
Spock, B. Dr. Spock on parenting   **649**
Steiner-Adair, C. The Big Disconnect   **303.48**
Swanson, W. S. Mama doc medicine   **649.1**
Tough, P. Helping Children Succeed   **372.1**
Willingham, E. The informed parent   **649.1**
Winik, M. The lunch-box chronicles   **306.85**

PARENTING
    See also Parent-child relationship

PARENTING -- ANECDOTES
Roberts, D. Been there, done that   **92**

PARENTING -- CALIFORNIA
Sweeney, J. If it's not one thing, it's your moth-er   **362.734**

PARENTING -- CALIFORNIA -- LOS ANGE-LES
Leap, J. Project Fatherhood   **306.874**

PARENTING -- HUMOR
Barry, D. You can date boys when you're for-ty   **306.85**

PARENTING -- UNITED STATES
Clinton, H. R. It takes a village   **305.23**
Lahey, J. The gift of failure   **649**
Parenting beyond pink and blue. Brown, C. S. **649**

PARENTING BY GRANDPARENTS *See* Grand-parents as parents
Parenting the fussy baby and high-need child. Sears, W.   **649**

PARENTS
Bradford, S. L. The Wall Street Journal: financial guidebook for new parents   **332.024**
Foss, B. The dyslexia empowerment plan   **618.92**
French, T. Juniper   **618.92**

PARENTS
    See also Family

PARENTS -- DEATH
Budd, K. The voluntourist   **361.7**
Deraniyagala, S. Wave   **954.93**
Levy, A. The orphaned adult   **152.4**

PARENTS OF AUTISTIC CHILDREN
Barnett, K. The spark   **618.92**
Dawson, G. A parent's guide to high-functioning autism spectrum disorder   **618.92**
Harris, S. L. Essential first steps for parents of chil-dren with autism   **618.92**
Lazebnik, C. Overcoming Autism   **618.92**
Suskind, R. Life, animated   **618.92**

PARENTS OF AUTISTIC CHILDREN
    See also Parents of children with disabilities

PARENTS OF CHILDREN WITH DISABILI-TIES
Adams, R. Raising Henry   **92**
Mutch, M. Know the night   **92**
Palmer, S. Just one of the kids   **649**
Rapp, E. The still point of the turning world **618.92**

PARENTS OF CHILDREN WITH DISABILI-TIES
    See also Children with disabilities

PARENTS OF CHILDREN WITH DISABILI-TIES -- BIOGRAPHY
Austin, P. Beautiful eyes   **92**
Estreich, G. The Shape of the Eye   **618.92**

PARENTS OF CHILDREN WITH DISABILI-TIES -- UNITED STATES
Solomon, A. Far from the tree   **362.4**

PARENTS OF EXCEPTIONAL CHILDREN
Bowers, M. 8 keys to raising the quirky child **649**

PARENTS OF EXCEPTIONAL CHILDREN -- UNITED STATES
Solomon, A. Far from the tree   **362.4**

PARENTS OF GAYS
Schwartz, J. Oddly normal   **306.76**

PARENTS OF GAYS
    See also Parents

PARENTS OF GIFTED CHILDREN
Kennedy-Moore, E. Smart parenting for smart kids   **649**

PARENTS OF MENTALLY ILL CHILDREN -- PSYCHOLOGY
Adamec, C. When your adult child breaks your heart   **616.89**

PARENTS OF MURDERED CHILDREN
Schiller, L. Perfect murder, perfect town   **364.15**

PARENTS OF PRESIDENTS
Adams, J. My dearest friend   **92**
Bush, G. All the best, George Bush   **92**
Holton, W. Abigail Adams   **92**
Leamer, L. The Kennedy men   **920**
Mahoney, R. D. Sons and brothers: the days of Jack and Bobby Kennedy   **92**
Parmet, H. S. George Bush   **92**

Persico, J. E. Franklin and Lucy **920**
Woodward, B. The commanders **973.928**
Woodward, B. Shadow **973.92**
PARENTS OF PROMINENT PERSONS
Flanders, J. A circle of sisters **920**
Hikayati sharhun yatul./English The locust and the bird **92**
McBride, J. The color of water **92**
PARENTS' CHOICE OF SCHOOL *See* School choice
Parfitt, George A. E.
(ed) Jonson, B. The complete poems **821**
Parini, Jay
The art of teaching **371.1**
(ed) The Columbia history of American poetry **811**
Empire of self **92**
(ed) Essays/Selections The selected essays of Gore Vidal **814**
(ed) The Norton book of American autobiography **920**
(ed) The Oxford encyclopedia of American literature **810**
One matchless time **92**
Promised land **810**
Robert Frost **811**
Parini, Jay

About
Parini, J. The art of teaching **371.1**
Paris. Jones, C. **944**
Paris. Spieler, M. **641.5**
PARIS (FRANCE)
Brassaï Brassai **944.361**
Downie, D. A passion for Paris **944**
Sante, L. The other Paris **944**
PARIS (FRANCE) -- BIOGRAPHY
Anselmo, L. My (part-time) Paris life **944.361**
Baldwin, R. Paris, I love you but you're bringing me down **944**
PARIS (FRANCE) -- DESCRIPTION AND TRAVEL
Anselmo, L. My (part-time) Paris life **944.361**
Baldwin, R. Paris, I love you but you're bringing me down **944**
Baxter, J. Five nights in Paris **914.4**
The Food Lover's Guide to Paris **914.4**
James, E. Paris in love **92**
My Paris kitchen **641.59**
PARIS (FRANCE) -- HISTORY
Kaplan, A. Dreaming in French **944**
Kershaw, A. Avenue of spies **940.53**
McCullough, D. G. The greater journey **920.009**
PARIS (FRANCE) -- INTELLECTUAL LIFE
Bakewell, S. At the Existentialist Cafe **142**
McCullough, D. G. The greater journey **920.009**
PARIS (FRANCE) -- INTELLECTUAL LIFE -- 20TH CENTURY

The letters of Sylvia Beach **92**
Lottman, H. R. Man Ray's Montparnasse **709**
Riding, A. And the show went on **944**
PARIS (FRANCE) -- SOCIAL LIFE AND CUSTOMS
Anselmo, L. My (part-time) Paris life **944.361**
Baldwin, R. Paris, I love you but you're bringing me down **944**
Baxter, J. Five nights in Paris **914.4**
Karnow, S. Paris in the fifties **944**
My Paris kitchen **641.59**
White, E. The flaneur **944.083**
PARIS (FRANCE) -- SOCIAL LIFE AND CUSTOMS -- 20TH CENTURY
Riding, A. And the show went on **944**
Sante, L. The other Paris **944**
PARIS (FRANCE) -- TOURS
Baxter, J. Five nights in Paris **914.4**
Paris 1919. MacMillan, M. **940.3**
Paris from the ground up. McGregor, J. H. S. **914**
Paris in love. James, E. **92**
Paris in the fifties. Karnow, S. **944**
PARIS PEACE CONFERENCE (1919-1920)
MacMillan, M. Paris 1919 **940.3**
The **Paris** review book of heartbreak, madness, sex, love, betrayal, outsiders, intoxication, war, whimsy, horrors, God, death, dinner, baseball, travels, the art of writing, and everything else in the world since 1953. **808.8**
Paris to the past. Caro, I. **914**
Paris was ours. **944**
Paris, Barry
(ed) Adler, S. Stella Adler on America's master playwrights **812**
Paris, I love you but you're bringing me down. Baldwin, R. **944**
Pariser, Eli
The filter bubble **025.04**
PARISH REGISTERS *See* Registers of births, etc.
Parisi, Joseph
(ed) 100 essential modern poems **821**
(ed) The Poetry anthology, 1912-2002 **811**
Parisians. Robb, G. **944**
Parissien, Steven
The life of the automobile **629.222**
PARK RANGERS
Barr, N. Seeking enlightenment--hat by hat **92**
Park, Chris
A dictionary of environment and conservation **333.7**
Park, David
The fire within the eye **535**
Park, Ed
(ed) Read Harder **814**
Park, Robert L.
Voodoo science **500**
PARKER BROTHERS (FIRM)

Orbanes, P. The game makers   338.7
Parker, Barry R.
Quantum legacy   530.12
Parker, Charlie, 1920-1955
About
Crouch, S. Kansas City lightning   92
Feather, L. From Satchmo to Miles   920
Parker, Dorothy, 1893-1967
The portable Dorothy Parker   818
About
Meade, M. Dorothy Parker   92
Parker, Douglas M.
Ogden Nash   92
Parker, Ely Samuel, 1828-1895
About
Brown, D. A.   Bury my heart at Wounded
Knee   970.004
Parker, Geoffrey
Global crisis   909
Parker, Hershel
Herman Melville   813
Parker, Matt
Things to make and do in the fourth dimension 510
Parker, Quanah, Comanche Chief, 1845?-1911
About
Gwynne, S. C. Empire of the summer moon   92
Parker, Roger
(jt. auth) Abbate, C. A history of opera   782.1
Parker, Steve, 1952-
(ed) Evolution, the whole story   576.8
Kill or cure   610
Morris, D. Planet ape   599.8
Parkes, Clara
The knitter's book of yarn   677
Parkin, Simon
An illustrated history of 151 video games   794.8
Parkinson's disease. Lang, A. E.   616.8
PARKINSON'S DISEASE
See also Brain -- Diseases
PARKINSON'S DISEASE
Kinsley, M. Old age   814.54
Lang, A. E. Parkinson's disease   616.8
Palfreman, J. Brain storms   616.8
Sacks, O. W. The island of the colorblind   617.7
**PARKINSON'S DISEASE -- PATIENTS -- UNIT-
ED STATES -- BIOGRAPHY**
Kinsley, M. Old age   814.54
**PARKINSON'S DISEASE -- PERSONAL NAR-
RATIVES**
Fox, M. J. Always looking up   92
Fox, M. J. Lucky man   92
Palfreman, J. Brain storms   616.8
Parkinson, Peter
The artist blacksmith   682
Parkinson, R. B.
A little gay history   306.76

Parkinson, Robert G.
The common cause   973.31
PARKS
See also Cities and towns; Landscape archi-
tecture
PARKS -- UNITED STATES
National Geographic Guide to the State Parks of the
United States   917.3
Parks, Carrie Stuart
Secrets to drawing realistic faces   743.42
Parks, Rosa, 1913-2005
About
Abdul-Jabbar, K. Black profiles in courage   920
Brinkley, D. Rosa Parks   92
Theoharis, J. The rebellious life of Mrs. Rosa
Parks   92
Parks, Suzan-Lori
Topdog/underdog   812
Parks, Tim
Medici money   332.1
Teach us to sit still   616
About
Parks, T. Italian ways   941.5
Parkyn, Neil
(ed) The Seventy wonders of the modern
world   720.9
PARLIAMENTARY PRACTICE
American Institute of Parliamentarians standard
code of parliamentary procedure   060.4
Robert, H. M. Robert's rules of order newly re-
vised   060.4
Robert, H. M. Robert's rules of order, newly re-
vised, in brief   060.4
Webster's New World Robert's rules of order 060.4
PARLIAMENTARY PRACTICE
See also Debates and debating; Legislation;
Legislative bodies; Public meetings
Parmet, Herbert S.
George Bush   92
PARODY
See also Literature; Satire; Wit and humor
PAROLE
See also Administration of criminal justice;
Corrections; Punishment; Social case work
Paroli, Emma Trenti
(jt. auth) Linden, D. W. Preemies   618.92
**PARQUE NACIONAL DA GORONGOSA (MO-
ZAMBIQUE) -- DESCRIPTION AND TRAV-
EL**
A window on eternity   333.95
Parr, Ben
Captivology   153.7
Parr, Mike
Lebbin, D. J. The American Bird Conservancy
guide to bird conservation   333.95
Parrado, Nando, 1949-

About

Parrado, N. Miracle in the Andes   **982**

Parravani, Cara

About

Parravani, C. Her   **92**

Parravani, Christa, 1978-

About

Parravani, C. Her   **92**

Parrish, Thomas

The submarine   **359.9**

Parry, Richard Lloyd

People who eat darkness   **364.152**

Parshley, Howard M.

(ed) Beauvoir, S. d. The second sex   **305.4**

Parsons, Brad Thomas

Amaro   **641.874**

Bitters   **641.8**

Parsons, Jack, 1914-1952

About

Pendle, G. Strange angel   **92**

Parssinen, Terry M.

The Oster conspiracy of 1938   **943.086**

The **particle** at the end of the Universe. Carroll, S.   **539.7**

PARTICLES (NUCLEAR PHYSICS)

Lederman, L. Beyond the god particle   **539.7**

Randall, L. Warped passages   **530**

PARTICLES (NUCLEAR PHYSICS)

See also Nuclear physics

PARTIES

See also Entertaining

The **parties** versus the people. Edwards, M.   **320**

PARTIES, POLITICAL See Political parties

Parting the desert. Karabell, Z.   **386**

Parting the waters: America in the King years, 1954-63. Branch, T.   **973.921**

PARTISANS See Guerrillas

PARTITO NAZIONALE FASCISTA (ITALY)

Corner, P. The Fascist Party and popular opinion in Mussolini's Italy   **945.091**

Partlow, Joshua

A kingdom of their own   **958.104**

PARTNERSHIP

See also Business enterprises

Partnoy, Frank

The match king   **92**

Wait   **153.8**

The **Party**. McGregor, R.   **324.2**

The **party** is over. Lofgren, M.   **324.273**

Pasachoff, Jay M., 1943-

(jt. auth) Golub, L. Nearest star   **523.7**

Pascal's wager. Connor, J. A.   **92**

Pascal, Blaise, 1623-1662

About

Bell, E. T. Men of mathematics   **920**

Connor, J. A. Pascal's wager   **92**

Devlin, K. J. The unfinished game   **519.2**

Pascal, Cybele

The whole foods allergy cookbook   **641.5**

Paschen, Elise

(ed) Poetry speaks expanded   **811**

Pascoe, Peggy

What comes naturally   **346**

Pasles, Paul C.

Benjamin Franklin's numbers   **510**

The **passage** of power. Caro, R. A.   **92**

Passage to Juneau. Raban, J.   **979.8**

Passan, Jeff

The Arm   **796.357**

Passarlay, Gulwali

(jt. auth) Ghouri, N. The lightless sky   **958.104**

Passero, Kathy

Englert, R. Blood secrets   **363.2**

PASSING (FOOTBALL)

Gwynne, S. C. The Perfect Pass   **796.332**

PASSING (IDENTITY)

Sandweiss, M. A. Passing strange   **92**

PASSING (IDENTITY) -- UNITED STATES -- HISTORY

Jacoby, K. The strange career of William Ellis   **92**

Passing by the dragon. Michaels, J. R.   **813**

Passing on the comfort. Keuning-Tichelaar, A.   **940.54**

Passing strange. Sandweiss, M. A.   **92**

A **passion** for leadership. Gates, R. M.   **92**

A **passion** for nature. Worster, D.   **92**

A **passion** for Paris. Downie, D.   **944**

A **passion** for wisdom. Solomon, R. C.   **109**

PASSION PLAYS

See also Bible plays; Mysteries and miracle plays; Religious drama; Theater

Passionate gardening. Springer, L.   **635**

Passionate minds. Pierpont, C. R.   **810**

PASSIONS See Emotions

PASSIVE RESISTANCE

Gandhi, M. Gandhi on non-violence   **322.4**

PASSIVE RESISTANCE

See also Resistance to government

PASSOVER

The New York Times Passover cookbook   **641.5**

PASSOVER

See also Jewish holidays

Past masters series

Hare, R. M. Plato   **184**

Pasta. Carluccio, A.   **641.82**

Pasta by hand.   **641.82**

Pasta modern.   **641.82**

PASTA PRODUCTS -- ENCYCLOPEDIAS

Pasta, a. d. p. t. Encyclopedia of pasta   **641.8**

Pasta, atlante dei prodotti tipici/English

Encyclopedia of pasta   **641.8**

The **pastel** book. Creevy, B.   **751.235**

PASTEL DRAWING
  Creevy, B. The pastel book   **751.235**
  Eagle, E. Pastel painting atelier   **741.235**
  McKinley, R. Pastel pointers   **741.235**
  Price, M. Painting with pastels   **741.2**
PASTEL DRAWING
  See also Drawing
Pastel painting atelier. Eagle, E.   **741.235**
Pastel pointers. McKinley, R.   **741.235**
Pasternak, Boris Leonidovich, 1890-1960
               About
  Milosz, C. To begin where I am   **891.8**
Pasternak, Boris Leonidovich, 1890-1960. Doktor Zhivago
            About
  Finn, P. The Zhivago affair   **891.73**
Pasternak, Judy
  Yellow dirt   **979.1**
PASTORAL PSYCHOLOGY
  Peale, N. V. The power of positive living   **248**
PASTORAL PSYCHOLOGY
  See also Applied psychology; Church work; Psychology of religion
PASTORAL THEOLOGY
  McKnight, S. Kingdom conspiracy   **231.7**
PASTORAL THEOLOGY
  See also Theology
PASTORAL WORK *See* Pastoral theology
Pastorelles. Taggart, J.   **811**
PASTORS *See* Clergy; Priests
PASTRY
  Ansel, D. Dominique Ansel   **641.86**
  Bouchon Bakery   **641.59**
  Goldman, D. Duff Bakes   **641.81**
  Greenstein, E. A Jewish baker's pastry secrets   **641.86**
  Robertson, C. Tartine   **641.8**
  Shulman, M. R. The art of French pastry   **641.86**
PASTRY
  See also Baking; Cooking
PASTURES
  See also Agriculture; Land use
PATAGONIA (ARGENTINA AND CHILE) -- DESCRIPTION AND TRAVEL
  Chatwin, B. In Patagonia   **918**
The **Patagonian** hare. Lanzmann, C.   **791.43**
Patai, Raphael
  (ed) Encyclopedia of Jewish folklore and traditions   **398.2**
Patalsky, Kathy
  Healthy happy vegan kitchen   **641.5**
Patchett, Ann
  Truth & beauty   **92**
            About
Patchett, A. This Is the Story of a Happy Marriage   **92**

PATCHWORK
  Arkison, C. Sunday morning quilts   **746.46**
  Denyse Schmidt quilts   **746.46**
  Gering, J. Quilting modern   **746.46**
  Gilleland, D. All points patchwork   **746.46**
  Hartman, E. Modern patchwork   **746.46**
PATCHWORK
  See also Needlework
PATCHWORK -- PATTERNS
  Arkison, C. Sunday morning quilts   **746.46**
  Denyse Schmidt quilts   **746.46**
  Gering, J. Quilting modern   **746.46**
  Gilleland, D. All points patchwork   **746.46**
PATCHWORK QUILTS *See* Quilts
Patel, Eboo, 1975-
            About
  Patel, E. Acts of faith   **92**
Patel, Raj
  The value of nothing   **330.1**
Patell, Cyrus R. K.
  (ed) The Cambridge history of American literature   **810**
Patent it yourself. Pressman, D.   **346**
PATENT MEDICINES *See* Nonprescription drugs
Patent, copyright & trademark. Stim, R.   **346**
Patent, Greg
  Baking in America   **641.8**
Patently female. Vare, E. A.   **609.2**
PATENTS
  Hyde, L. Common as air   **346.04**
  Pressman, D. Patent it yourself   **346**
  Stim, R. Patent, copyright & trademark   **346**
PATENTS
  See also Manufactures
Paterniti, Michael
  Love and Other Ways of Dying   **814**
Paterson. Williams, W. C.   **811**
Paterson, Don
  Rain   **821**
Paterson, Katherine
            About
  Paterson, K. Stories of my life   **92**
The **path** between the seas. McCullough, D. G.   **972.87**
A **Path** to Peace. Mitchell, G. J.   **956.94**
The **path** to power. Caro, R. A.   **92**
PATHOLOGICAL PSYCHOLOGY *See* Abnormal psychology
PATHOLOGISTS -- NEW YORK (STATE) -- BROOKLYN -- BIOGRAPHY
  Franscell, R. Morgue   **616.07**
PATHOLOGY
  Bowers, K. Zoobiquity   **636.089**
  Zuk, M. Riddled with life   **616.07**
PATHOLOGY
  See also Medicine

PATHOLOGY -- HISTORY -- PENNSYLVANIA
Aptowicz, C. O. Dr. Mütter's Marvels **92**
PATHOLOGY, VETERINARY
Bowers, K. Zoobiquity **636.089**
PATIENCE
Partnoy, F. Wait **153.8**
PATIENCE
See also Human behavior; Virtue
Patience & fortitude. Basbanes, N. A. **002**
PATIENT ADVOCACY
Michelson, L. D. The patient's playbook **610.69**
PATIENT CARE RECORDS *See* Medical records
PATIENT EDUCATION
Goldfarb, T. L.   The patient survival guide
Makary, M. Unaccountable **610.730**
Michelson, L. D. The patient's playbook **610.69**
Streicher, L. F.   The essential guide to hysterectomy **618.1**
Patient H.M. Dittrich, L. **616.85**
PATIENT PARTICIPATION
Berger, Z. Talking to your doctor **610.69**
The **patient** survival guide. Goldfarb, T. L.
The **patient's** playbook. Michelson, L. D. **610.69**
PATIENTS
Brown, T. The shift **616.02**
Goldfarb, T. L.   The patient survival guide
Groopman, J. E. The anatomy of hope **616**
Manheimer, E. Twelve patients **362.11**
Patinkin, Erin
Ovenly **641.81**
PATIOS
Black & Decker Corp. The complete guide to patios & walkways **690**
PATIOS
See also Landscape architecture
Patoski, Joe Nick
Willie Nelson **92**
The **patriarch**. Nasaw, D. **92**
Patricia Wells at home in Provence. **641.59**
Patricia Wells' trattoria. Wells, P. **641.5**
Patrick O'Brian. King, D. **823**
Patrick, Jane
The weaver's idea book **746.1**
Patrick, Wiliam
(jt. auth) Khan, A. S. The next pandemic **362.1**
Patriotic fire. Groom, W. **973.5**
Patriotic gore. Wilson, E. **810**
PATRIOTIC POETRY
See also Poetry
PATRIOTIC SONGS *See* National songs
PATRIOTISM
Testi, A. Capture the flag **929.9**
PATRIOTISM
See also Citizenship; Human behavior; Loyalty
PATRONS OF THE ARTS

Bradford, S. Lucrezia Borgia **92**
Brewer, J. The American Leonardo **759**
De Waal, E. The hare with amber eyes **920**
Fraser, F. Pauline Bonaparte **92**
Gill, A. Art lover **92**
Heilbroner, R. L. The worldly philosophers **330.1**
Kastin, D. Nica's dream **92**
Strathern, P. Death in Florence **945**
Vaill, A. Everybody was so young **759.13**
Pattee, Amy S.
Developing library collections for today's young adults **027.62**
PATTERN FORMATION (BIOLOGY)
Ball, P. Nature's patterns **500.2**
Ball, P. Patterns in nature **500.2**
PATTERN PERCEPTION
This explains everything **500**
PATTERN PERCEPTION
See also Perception
PATTERN RECOGNITION *See* Pattern perception
PATTERNMAKING
Joyce, A. Stamp stencil paint **745.5**
Veblen, S. The complete photo guide to perfect fitting **646.4**
Patternmaking for fashion design. Armstrong, H. J. **646.4**
PATTERNS (MATHEMATICS)
Ball, P. Nature's patterns **500.2**
Ball, P. Patterns in nature **500.2**
Buchanan, M. Nexus: small worlds and the groundbreaking science of networks **530**
PATTERNS (MATHEMATICS)
See also Mathematics
Patterns in nature. Ball, P. **500.2**
Patterson, Floyd
About
Levy, A. H. Floyd Patterson **92**
Life stories **920**
Stratton, W. K. Floyd Patterson **92**
Patterson, James T.
The eve of destruction **973.923**
Grand expectations **973.92**
Restless giant **973.92**
Patterson, Kerry
(jt. auth) McMillan, R. Crucial conversations **153.6**
Patterson, Pat, 1941-
About
Patterson, P. Accepted **92**
Patti Smith Collected Lyrics, 1970-2015. Smith, P. **782.42**
Pattison, John
Slow church **253**
Patton and Rommel. Showalter, D. E. **92**
Patton, Bruce
Stone, D. Difficult conversations **158**

Patton, George S. (George Smith), 1885-1945
War as I knew it 940.54
About
Brighton, T. Patton, Montgomery, Rommel 920
Groom, W. The generals 940.54
Hanson, V. D. The soul of battle 355
Hirshson, S. P. General Patton: a soldier's life 92
Showalter, D. E. Patton and Rommel 92
Patton, Montgomery, Rommel. Brighton, T. 920
Patton, Sharon F.
African-American art 704.03
Paul. Murphy-O'Connor, J. 225.9
Paul among the people. Ruden, S. 225.9
Paul Newman. Levy, S. 92
Paul Revere's ride. Fischer, D. H. 973.3
Paul, Gregory S.
The Princeton field guide to dinosaurs 567.9
Paul, Joel R.
Unlikely allies 973.3
Paul, Richard
We could not fail 920
Paul, the Apostle, Saint
About
Borg, M. J. The first Paul 227
Kung, H. Great Christian thinkers 230
Murphy-O'Connor, J. Paul 225.9
Ruden, S. Paul among the people 225.9
Paula. Allende, I. 92
Pauli, Wolfgang, 1900-1958
About
Feldman, B. 112 Mercer Street 920
Pauline Bonaparte. Fraser, F. 92
Pauline Kael. Kellow, B. 92
Pauling, Linus C., 1901-1994
About
Pauling, L. C. Linus Pauling in his own words 081
Paulo, Joaquim
Jazz covers 781.65
Paulsen, Gary, 1939-
About
Paulsen, G. Winterdance 798.8
Paulsen, Luke
(jt. auth) Paulsen, M. S. The Constitution 342.73
Paulsen, Michael Stokes
The Constitution 342.73
Paulson, Henry M.
On the brink 330.9
Pauly, Thomas H.
Zane Grey 92
PAUPERISM *See* Poverty
Pavelka, Lisa
The complete book of polymer clay 738.1
Pavlac, Brian Alexander
(ed) Great events from history, The Middle Ages,
477-1453 909.07
Pavord, Anna

Bulb 635.9
Pawel, Miriam
The Crusades of Cesar Chavez 92
The **Pawnbroker's** Daughter. Kumin, M. 92
Pawson, Des
The handbook of knots 623.88
PAWTUCKET RED SOX (BASEBALL TEAM)
Barry, D. Bottom of the 33rd 796.357
Pax romana. Goldsworthy, A. 937.06
Paxton, Robert O.
The anatomy of fascism 321.9
Pay to play. Brackett, E. 92
Payard cookies. Payard, F. 641.86
Payard, Francois
Payard cookies 641.86
Payback. Atwood, M. 332.7
Paz, Octavio
The collected poems of Octavio Paz, 1957-1987 861
The labyrinth of solitude 864
About
Paz, O. The poems of Octavio Paz 861
PDR Network, LLC
PDR for nonprescription drugs 615
Père Marie-Benoît and Jewish rescue. Zuccotti,
S. 940.53
Peace. Conoley, G. 811
PEACE
Goldsworthy, A. Pax romana 937.06
Tenzin Gyatso, D. L. X. My appeal to the world 951
PEACE
See also International relations
Peace be upon you. Karabell, Z. 201
PEACE CORPS (U.S.)
Erdman, S. Nine hills to Nambonkaha 966.68
PEACE MOVEMENTS
Ghetto Brother 92
PEACE MOVEMENTS
See also Social movements
Peace, Robert, 1980-2010
About
Hobbs, J. The short and tragic life of Robert
Peace 92
PEACE-BUILDING -- AFGHANISTAN
Gopal, A. No good men among the living 958.104
**PEACE-BUILDING -- CHINA -- TIBET AUTON-
OMOUS REGION**
Tenzin Gyatso, D. L. X. My appeal to the world 951
PEACEFUL COEXISTENCE *See* International
relations
Peacock & vine. Byatt, A. S. 700.92
Peacock, Julie
The soup club cookbook 641.81
Peacock, Kathy Wilson
Food security 338.1
Peacock, Molly, 1947-
The paper garden 92

Peacock, Scott
(jt. auth) Lewis, E. The gift of Southern cooking 641.59
PEACOCKS
See also Birds
Peak. Ericsson, A. 153.9
Peake, Riley
Mapping Census 2010 304.6
Peale, Norman Vincent
The power of positive living 248
PEANUTS (COMIC STRIP)
Michaelis, D. Schulz and Peanuts 92
The **pear** as one example. Pankey, E. 811
Pearce, Fred
With speed and violence 551.6
Pearl Buck in China. Spurling, H. 92
PEARL FISHERIES
See also Commercial fishing
Pearl Harbor. Nelson, C. 940.54
PEARL HARBOR (OAHU, HAWAII), ATTACK ON, 1941
Hotta, E. Japan 1941 940.54
Nelson, C. Pearl Harbor 940.54
Prange, G. W. At dawn we slept 940.54
Toll, I. W. Pacific crucible 940.54
PEARL HARBOR (OAHU, HAWAII), ATTACK ON, 1941
See also World War, 1939-1945 -- Campaigns
Pearl, Nancy
Book lust 011
More book lust 025
Now read this 016
Now read this II 016
Now read this III 016
Pearson, Joanne
(ed) Belief beyond boundaries 209
Pearson, Mike Parker
Stonehenge 936.2
Pearson, Roger
Voltaire almighty 92
Peary, Danny
Clavin, T. Roger Maris 92
PEASANTRY
See also Feudalism; Labor
Pease, Allan
The definitive book of body language 153.6
Pease, Barbara
Pease, A. The definitive book of body language 153.6
Peck, Abraham J.
(ed) The Holocaust and history 940.53
Peck, M. Scott
Denial of the soul 179.7
Further along the road less traveled 158
The road less traveled 158
The road less traveled and beyond 158

Peck, Robert McCracken
A glorious enterprise 508
Pecora, Ferdinand, 1882-1971
About
Perino, M. A. The hellhound of Wall Street 330.9
PEDAGOGY *See* Education; Education -- Study and teaching; Teaching
Pedahzur, Ami
The Israeli secret services and the struggle against terrorism 363.32
PEDDLERS AND PEDDLING
See also Direct selling; Sales personnel
Pedersen, Katie
(jt. auth) Gering, J. Quilting modern 746.46
The **pediatrician's** guide to feeding babies and toddlers. Porto, A. 618.92
PEDIATRICIANS
Marion, R. Genetic rounds 92
PEDIATRICS *See* Children -- Diseases; Children -- Health and hygiene; Infants -- Diseases; Infants -- Health and hygiene
PEDIGREE
Kenneally, C. The invisible history of the human race 616
PEDIGREES *See* Genealogy; Heraldry
PEDODONTICS
Best-Boss, A. Your child's teeth 617.6
PEER PRESSURE
Rosenberg, T. Join the club 303.3
PEER PRESSURE
See also Socialization
PEER PRESSURE IN ADOLESCENCE
See also Peer pressure
PEERAGE *See* Nobility
Peffer, Randall
Where divers dare 940.54
Peggy Guggenheim. Prose, F. 92
Peikoff, Leonard
Rand, A. The voice of reason; essays in objectivist thought 191
Peirce, Charles S. (Charles Sanders), 1839-1914
About
Menand, L. The Metaphysical Club 973.9
Peiss, Kathy Lee
Hope in a jar 391.6
Pekar, Harvey
Students for a Democratic Society 378.1
Pelaez, Ana Sofia
The Cuban table 641.59
Pelczar, Rita
(ed) Homegrown harvest 635
Pelikan, Jaroslav Jan
The illustrated Jesus through the centuries 232.9
Mary through the centuries 232.91
Pell, Arthur R.
Hill, N. Think and grow rich 650.1

Pellant, Chris
  Rocks and Minerals   **552**
Pellant, Helen
  (jt. auth) Pellant, C. Rocks and Minerals   **552**
Pellegrino, Charles
  Ghosts of Vesuvius   **937**
  To hell and back   **940.54**
The **Peloponnesian** War. Kagan, D.   **938**
Pelosi, Nancy, 1940-
                    About
  Pelosi, N. Know your power   **92**
Peltre, Beatrice
  My French family table   **641.5**
Pember, Mat
  The Little Veggie Patch Co. DIY Garden Proj-
  ects   **712.6**
PEN DRAWING
      See also Drawing
PEN NAMES *See* Pseudonyms
Pen to thread. Watson, S.   **746.44**
PENAL COLONIES
  Hughes, R. The fatal shore   **994**
  Keneally, T. A commonwealth of thieves   **994**
PENAL COLONIES
      See also Colonies; Correctional institutions
PENAL INSTITUTIONS *See* Correctional institu-
  tions; Prisons; Reformatories
Penberthy, Jenny Lynn
  (ed) Niedecker, L. Collected works   **811**
Pencak, William
  (ed) Pennsylvania: a history of the Common-
  wealth   **974.8**
The **pencil.** Petroski, H.   **674**
PENCIL DRAWING
      See also Drawing
PENCILS
  Petroski, H. The pencil   **674**
Pendergast, Sara
  (ed) Encyclopedia of the Victorian era   **941.081**
  (ed) Reference guide to world literature   **809**
  (ed) St. James encyclopedia of popular cul-
  ture   **973.9**
Pendergast, Tom
  (ed) Encyclopedia of the Victorian era   **941.081**
  (ed) Reference guide to world literature   **809**
  (ed) St. James encyclopedia of popular cul-
  ture   **973.9**
Pendergrast, Mark
  Mirror mirror   **535**
Pendle, George
  Strange angel   **92**
The **Penguin** anthology of twentieth-century Ameri-
  can poetry.   **811**
The **Penguin** anthology of twentieth-century Ameri-
  can poetry.   **811**
The **Penguin** book of modern African poetry. **896**

The **Penguin** book of Spanish verse.   **861**
The **Penguin** book of the sonnet.   **821**
The **Penguin** Book of Witches.   **133.4**
Penguin Classics [series]
  Apollonius   The voyage of Argo: the Argonauti-
  ca   **881**
  Ariosto, L. Orlando Furioso/The frenzy of Orlan-
  do, part 1   **851**
  Ariosto, L. Orlando Furioso/The frenzy of Orlan-
  do, part 2   **851**
  Carson, R. Under the sea wind   **578.7**
  Chatwin, B. In Patagonia   **918**
  Cicero, M. T. On the good life   **878**
  Coleridge, S. T. The complete poems   **821**
  De civitate Dei./English   Concerning the city of
  God against the pagans   **239**
  Douglass, F. My bondage and my freedom   **92**
  Erasmus, D. Praise of folly   **877**
  French poetry, 1820-1950, with prose transla-
  tions   **841**
  Goethe, J. W. v. Selected poetry   **831**
  Jonson, B. The complete poems   **821**
  Jonson, B. Volpone and other plays   **822**
  Juvenal   The sixteen satires   **877**
  Kant, I. Critique of pure reason   **193**
  Lamb, C. Tales from Shakespeare   **822.3**
  Morike, E. F. Mozart's journey to Prague and a se-
  lection of poems   **831**
  Narayan, R. K. The Ramayana   **891**
  Plays   The complete plays   **822**
  Plautus, T. M. The pot of gold, and other plays **872**
  Plautus, T. M. The rope, and other plays   **872**
  Reed, J. Ten days that shook the world   **947.084**
  Rose, R. Twelve angry men   **812**
  Rossetti, C. G. Christina Rossetti   **821**
  Schiller, F. The robbers [and] Wallenstein   **832**
  Seneca, L. A. Four tragedies, and Octavia   **882**
  Shaw, B. Arms and the man   **822**
  Shaw, B. Heartbreak House   **822**
  Shaw, B. Major Barbara   **822**
  Shaw, B. Man and Superman   **822**
  Shaw, B. Saint Joan   **822**
  Sheridan, R. B. The school for scandal and other
  plays   **822**
  Spenser, E. The faerie queene   **821**
  Tagore, R. Selected poems   **891**
  Twelve years a slave   **92**
  Yevtushenko, Y. A. Selected poems   **891.7**
The **Penguin** concise dictionary of art history. Fra-
  zier, N.   **703**
The **Penguin** dictionary of literary terms and literary
  theory. Cuddon, J. A.   **803**
The **Penguin** dictionary of saints. Attwater,
  D.   **920.003**
The **Penguin** guide to jazz recordings. Cook,
  R.   **781.65**

The Penguin history of American life [series]
  Campbell, J. T. Middle passages **916**
The Penguin history of Europe [series]
  Blanning, T. C. W. The pursuit of glory **940.2**
  Wickham, C. The inheritance of Rome **940.1**
The **Penguin** history of Latin America. Williamson, E. **980**
Penguin lives series
  Armstrong, K. Buddha **294.3**
  Blount, R. Robert E. Lee **92**
  Breslin, J. Branch Rickey **92**
  Brinkley, D. Rosa Parks **92**
  Gordon, M. Joan of Arc **944**
  Hardwick, E. Herman Melville **813**
  Huxtable, A. L. Frank Lloyd Wright **92**
  Johnson, P. Napoleon **944.05**
  Keneally, T. Abraham Lincoln **92**
  Mason, B. A. Elvis Presley **92**
  McMurtry, L. Crazy Horse **92**
  Nuland, S. B. Leonardo da Vinci **709**
  O'Brien, E. James Joyce **823**
  Remini, R. V. Joseph Smith **92**
  Shields, C. Jane Austen **823**
  Smiley, J. Charles Dickens **823**
  Spence, J. D. Mao Zedong **951.05**
  Wills, G. Saint Augustine **270.2**
Penguin nature library [series]
  Thoreau, H. D. The Maine woods **917**
Penguin Plays [series]
  Osborne, J. Look back in anger **822**
Penguin poets [series]
  Dorn, E. Way more West **811**
  Foulds, A. The broken word **821**
  Gerstler, A. Scattered at sea **811**
  Hayes, T. Lighthead **811**
  Kerouac, J. Book of blues **811**
  Kerouac, J. Book of sketches, 1952-53 **811**
  Klink, J. Raptus **811**
  Lauterbach, A. Or to begin again **811**
  Notley, A. In the pines **811**
Penguin reference [series]
  Cuddon, J. A. The Penguin dictionary of literary terms and literary theory **803**
Penguin twentieth-century classics [series]
  Lawrence, D. H. The complete poems **821**
  Tsvetaeva, M. I. Selected poems **891.7**
Penguins. Jones, M. **598.47**
PENGUINS
  See also Birds
PENGUINS
  Montaigne, F. Fraser's penguins **577.2**
PENICILLIN
  See also Antibiotics
Penick, Pam
  The water-saving garden **635.9**
PENINSULAR CAMPAIGN, 1862

  Sears, S. W. To the gates of Richmond **973.7**
PENITENTIARIES *See* Prisons
Penman, Michael
  Robert the Bruce **92**
PENMANSHIP *See* Handwriting
Pennington, Bill
  Billy Martin **92**
PENNSYLVANIA
  McGraw, S. The end of country **333.79**
PENNSYLVANIA -- HISTORY
  Pennsylvania: a history of the Commonwealth **974.8**
PENNSYLVANIA -- RACE RELATIONS
  Biddle, D. R. Tasting freedom **92**
PENNSYLVANIA ACADEMY OF THE FINE ARTS -- EXHIBITIONS
  The female gaze **704**
Pennsylvania: a history of the Commonwealth. **974.8**
Pennyweight windows. Revell, D. **811**
PENOLOGY *See* Corrections; Punishment
Penrose, Roger
  Hawking, S. W. The nature of space and time **530.1**
  About
  Dennett, D. C. Darwin's dangerous idea **146**
Penrose, Roland
  Picasso: his life and work **709**
PENSIONS
  Jason, J. The AARP Retirement Survival Guide **332.024**
  Lowenstein, R. While America aged **331.2**
  Matthews, J. L. Social security, Medicare & government pensions **344**
  Schultz, E. Retirement heist **331.2**
PENSIONS
  See also Annuities; Retirement income
The **Pentagon.** Vogel, S. **355.6**
PENTAGON (ARLINGTON, VA.: BUILDING)
  Carroll, J. House of war **355**
  Vogel, S. The Pentagon **355.6**
PENTAGON (VA.) TERRORIST ATTACK, 2001
  See September 11 terrorist attacks, 2001
PENTAGON PAPERS
  Ellsberg, D. Secrets: a memoir of Vietnam and the Pentagon papers **959.704**
  Inside the Pentagon papers **959.704**
The **Pentagon's** Brain. Jacobsen, A. **355**
PENTATHLETES
  Anderson, L. Carlisle vs. Army **796.332**
  Crawford, B. All American **92**
PENTECOSTAL CHURCHES
  See also Christian sects; Protestantism
PENTECOSTALISM
  See also Christianity
Pentimento. Hellman, L. **92**
PEOPLE *See* Ethnic groups; Indigenous peoples; Persons
The **people** and the books. Kirsch, A. **809.889**

PEOPLE IN SPACE *See* Space flight

People who eat darkness. Parry, R. L.   **364.152**

PEOPLE WITH AUTISM *See* Autistic people

PEOPLE WITH DISABILITIES

Berthon, S. Warlords   **940.53**

Beschloss, M. R. The conquerors: Roosevelt, Truman, and the destruction of Hitler's Germany, 1941-1945   **940.53**

Brands, H. W. Traitor to his class   **92**

Burns, J. M. The three Roosevelts   **973.91**

Feldman, N. Scorpions   **920**

Fenn, L. Carry on   **920**

Fried, A. F.D.R. and his enemies   **92**

Goodwin, D. K. No ordinary time   **92**

Hofstadter, R. The American political tradition, and the men who made it   **973**

Kissinger, H. Diplomacy   **327.2**

Leuchtenburg, W. E. Franklin D. Roosevelt and the New Deal, 1932-1940   **973.917**

Persico, J. E. Franklin and Lucy   **920**

Reeve, C. Still me   **92**

Roberts, A. Masters and commanders   **940.54**

Roosevelt, C. Too close to the sun   **92**

Schlesinger, A. M. The coming of the New Deal, 1933-1935   **973.917**

Schlesinger, A. M. The crisis of the old order, 1919-1933   **973.91**

Schlesinger, A. M. The politics of upheaval, 1935-1936   **973.917**

Senator, S. Autism Adulthood   **616.85**

Shesol, J. Supreme power   **347**

Smith, J. E. FDR   **92**

Susskind, L. The black hole war   **530.1**

Taylor, N. American-made   **331.1**

PEOPLE WITH DISABILITIES -- CLOTHING

See also Clothing and dress

PEOPLE WITH MENTAL DISABILITIES

See also People with disabilities

PEOPLE WITH PHYSICAL DISABILITIES

Reeve, C. Still me   **92**

PEOPLE WITH VISUAL DISABILITIES -- UNITED STATES -- BIOGRAPHY

Axelrod, H. The point of vanishing   **92**

PEOPLE'S BANKS *See* Cooperative banks

A **people's** guide to the federal budget. Kramer, M.   **352.4**

A **people's** history of the American Revolution. Raphael, R.   **973.3**

A **people's** history of the United States. Zinn, H.   **973**

People's movements, people's press. Ostertag, B.   **071**

The **people's** pension. Frank, J.   **368.4**

The **People's** Republic of Chemicals. Kelly, W. J.   **363.739**

A **people's** tragedy. Figes, O.   **947.084**

The **people's** tycoon. Watts, S.   **92**

Peoples and empires. Pagden, A.   **909**

Peoples of America [series]

Smith, M. E. The Aztecs   **972**

The **peopling** of British North America. Bailyn, B.   **973.2**

Pepin, Claudine

Pepin, J. Jacques Pepin celebrates   **641.5**

Pepin, Jacques

The apprentice: my life in the kitchen   **641.5**

Child, J. Julia and Jacques cooking at home   **641.59**

Essential Pepin   **641.5**

Jacques Pepin celebrates   **641.5**

Heart & soul in the kitchen   **641.5**

Pepper, Carol

The seven pearls of financial wisdom   **332.024**

Pepper, William F.

An act of state   **364.1**

Pepperell, Julian G.

Fishes of the open ocean   **597**

Peppiatt, Michael

Francis Bacon in Your Blood   **759.2**

Pepys, Samuel, 1633-1703

About

Lee, H. Virginia Woolf's nose   **820**

Long, J. The plot against Pepys   **941.06**

Pepys, S. The diary of Samuel Pepys   **941.06**

Tomalin, C. Samuel Pepys   **941.06**

PEQUOT INDIANS -- BIOGRAPHY

Gura, P. F. The life of William Apess, Pequot   **92**

PERCEPTION

Berdik, C. Mind over mind   **153.4**

Chabris, C. The invisible gorilla   **153.7**

Edelman, S. The happiness of pursuit   **153**

Hoffman, D. D. Visual intelligence   **152.14**

Kandel, E. R. The age of insight   **154.2**

Konnikova, M. Mastermind   **153.4**

Sacks, O. The mind's eye   **616.85**

Stone, A. Fooling Houdini   **793.8**

Vedantam, S. The hidden brain   **154.2**

PERCEPTION

See also Intellect; Psychology; Senses and sensation; Theory of knowledge; Thought and thinking

PERCUSSION INSTRUMENTS

See also Musical instruments

PERCUSSIONISTS

Grant, C. The natural mystics   **920**

Percy, Walker, 1916-1990

About

Elie, P. The life you save may be your own   **810**

Perdue, Theda

The Columbia guide to American Indians of the Southeast   **970.004**

(ed) Sifters: Native American women's lives   **920**

Perelman, Deb

The smitten kitchen cookbook **641.5**

Perelman, Grigori

　　　　　About

Gessen, M. Perfect rigor **92**

Szpiro, G. G. Poincare's prize **510**

The **perennial** philosophy. Huxley, A. **210**

PERENNIALS

Christopher, T. Essential perennials **635.9**

Cullina, W. Understanding perennials **635.9**

DiSabato-Aust, T. The well-tended perennial garden **635.9**

Ellis, B. W. Taylor's guide to perennials **635.9**

Hodgson, L. Perennials for every purpose **635.9**

McGowan, A. Bulbs in the basement, geraniums on the windowsill **635.9**

PERENNIALS

　　See also Cultivated plants; Flower gardening; Flowers

PERENNIALS -- ENCYCLOPEDIAS

Garden perennials Armitage's garden perennials **635.9**

PERENNIALS -- HANDBOOKS, MANUALS, ETC

Christopher, T. Essential perennials **635.9**

Perennials for every purpose. Hodgson, L. **635.9**

Perez, Joseph

The Spanish Inquisition **272**

Perez, Larry

Snake in the grass **597.96**

Perez, Louis A.

Cuba **972.91**

Perez, Louis G.

The history of Japan **952**

Perez, William

We are Americans **371.82**

Perez-Brignoli, Hector

A brief history of Central America **972.8**

The **perfect** horse. Letts, E. **940.54**

Perfect hostage. Wintle, J. **92**

The **perfect** house: a journey with the Renaissance architect Andrea Palladio. Rybczynski, W. **720.9**

Perfect madness. Warner, J. **306.8**

The **perfect** meal. Baxter, J. **641.59**

Perfect murder, perfect town. Schiller, L. **364.15**

Perfect one-dish dinners. Anderson, P. **641.8**

The **perfect** parent. Khetarpal, R. **306.874**

The **Perfect** Pass. Gwynne, S. C. **796.332**

Perfect recipes for having people over. Anderson, P. **641.5**

A **perfect** red. Greenfield, A. B. **667**

Perfect rigor. Gessen, M. **92**

The **perfect** scoop. **641.8**

The **perfect** storm. Junger, S. **910.4**

The **perfect** summer. Nicolson, J. **942**

The **perfect** theory. Ferreira, P. G. **530.11**

A **perfect** union. Allgor, C. **92**

Perfecting sound forever. Milner, G. **781.49**

PERFECTION

　　See also Philosophy

The **perfection** deception. Bluestein, J. **155.2**

PERFECTIONISM (PERSONALITY TRAIT)

Bluestein, J. The perfection deception **155.2**

PERFECTIONISM (PERSONALITY TRAIT)

　　See also Personality

The **perfectly** imperfect home. **747**

Perfectly miserable. Stuart, S. P. **92**

PERFORMANCE

Brown, J. The Runner's Brain **796.42**

Duhigg, C. Smarter faster better **158**

PERFORMANCE

　　See also Work

PERFORMANCE -- PSYCHOLOGICAL ASPECTS

Ericsson, A. Peak **153.9**

Webb, C. How to have a good day **650.1**

PERFORMANCE ART

Fuhrer, M. American dance **792.8**

PERFORMANCE ART

　　See also Art; Performing arts

PERFORMANCE ARTISTS

Bilal, W. Shoot an Iraqi **92**

The **performance** of becoming human. Borzutzky, D. **811.6**

PERFORMANCE STANDARDS

　　See also Performance

PERFORMING ARTS

Giddins, G. Weather bird **781.65**

Reynolds, D. Make 'em Laugh **92**

PERFORMING ARTS

　　See also Arts

PERFORMING ARTS -- ECONOMIC ASPECTS

Moore, R. S. The artist's compass **791.023**

PERFORMING ARTS -- ENCYCLOPEDIAS

The Oxford companion to theatre and performance **792**

PERFORMING ARTS -- NEW YORK (STATE) -- NEW YORK -- MANAGEMENT

Levy, R. They told me not to take that job **792.09**

PERFORMING ARTS -- STUDY AND TEACHING

Sokolove, M. Drama high **92**

PERFORMING ARTS -- VOCATIONAL GUIDANCE

Moore, R. S. The artist's compass **791.023**

PERFUMERS

Mazzeo, T. J. The secret of Chanel No. 5 **338.7**

Vaughan, H. Sleeping with the enemy **92**

PERFUMES

Aftel, M. Fragrant **612.8**

Mazzeo, T. J. The secret of Chanel No. 5 **338.7**

Turin, L. The secret of scent **668**

PERFUMES

See also Cosmetics; Essences and essential oils

Peri, Camille
(ed) Because I said so   **306.8**

Perillo, Lucia Maria
Inseminating the elephant   **811**
On the spectrum of possible deaths   **811**

Perilous glory. France, J.   **355**
Perilous times. Stone, G. R.   **323.44**

Perino, Michael A.
The hellhound of Wall Street   **330.9**

PERIODIC HEALTH EXAMINATIONS
     See also Medicine

PERIODIC LAW
Aldersey-Williams, H. Periodic tales   **546**
The elements   **546**
Gordin, M. D. A well-ordered thing: Dmitrii Mendeleev and the shadow of the periodic table   **92**
The **periodic** table. Levi, P.   **92**
Periodic tales. Aldersey-Williams, H.   **546**

PERIODICAL EDITORS -- UNITED STATES -- BIOGRAPHY
Hirshey, G. Not pretty enough   **92**
Mankoff, B. How about never--is never good for you?   **92**

PERIODICALS
Bohemians, bootleggers, flappers, and swells **810.8**
Read Harder   **814**

PERIODICALS
     See also Mass media; Serial publications

Perkin, William Henry, 1838-1907
About
Garfield, S. Mauve   **667**

Perkins, Agnes
Helbig, A. Dictionary of American young adult fiction, 1997-2001   **028.5**

Perkins, Frances, 1882-1965
About
Downey, K. The woman behind the New Deal   **92**

Perlmutter, David
The grain brain cookbook   **641.563**

Perlstein, Rick
The Invisible Bridge   **973.924**
Nixonland   **973.924**

PERMIAN HIGH SCHOOL (ODESSA, TEX.)
Bissinger, H. G. Friday night lights   **796.332**

Pernick, Ron
Clean Tech Nation   **333.794**

Pernoud, Regine
Joan of Arc: her story   **92**

Perper, Timothy
(ed) Graphic novels beyond the basics   **025.2**

Perrault, Anna H.
Information resources in the humanities and the arts   **016**

Perrins, Christopher M.
(ed) The Princeton encyclopedia of birds   **598**

Perry, Alex
The Rift   **320.9**

Perry, Bruce
Malcolm   **92**

Perry, Grayson, 1960-
Playing to the gallery   **709.05**

Perry, James M.
Touched with fire   **973.7**

Perry, Julia, 1924-1979
About
Walker-Hill, H. From spirituals to symphonies **780**

Perry, Kristin
About
Becker, J. Forcing the spring   **346.73**
Yoshino, K. Speak now   **346.73**

Perry, Mark
The most dangerous man in America   **92**

PERSECUTION
Conroy, J. Unspeakable acts, ordinary people **323.4**
God is red   **275.1**

PERSEVERANCE (ETHICS)
Duckworth, A. Grit   **158.1**

PERSIAN GULF WAR, 1991
Atkinson, R. Crusade   **956.7**
Gordon, M. R. The generals' war   **956.7**
Woodward, B. The commanders   **973.928**

PERSIAN GULF WAR, 1991 -- CAUSES
Haass, R. War of necessity: war of choice   **956.7**

PERSIAN GULF WAR, 1991 -- ENCYCLOPEDIAS
The encyclopedia of Middle East wars   **355**

PERSIAN GULF WAR, 1991 -- PERSONAL NARRATIVES
Swofford, A. Jarhead: a Marine's chronicle of the Gulf War and other battles   **956.704**

PERSIAN POETRY -- COLLECTIONS
Music of a distant drum   **808.81**
Persian poets   **891**
Persian poets.   **891**

Persiana. Ghayour, S.   **641.595**

Persico, Joseph E.
Franklin and Lucy   **920**
Powell, C. L. My American journey   **92**

PERSISTENCE
     See also Personality

PERSISTENT PAIN *See* Chronic pain

PERSISTENT VEGETATIVE STATE
Teresi, D. The undead   **610**

PERSONAL APPEARANCE
Berg, R. Beauty: the new basics   **646.7**
Brandon, R. Ugly beauty   **646.7**
DuPriest, L. Natural beauty   **646.7**
Essence total makeover   **646.7**
Halbreich, B. I'll drink to that   **92**
Kashuk, S. Real beauty   **646.7**

Peiss, K. L. Hope in a jar **391.6**
Thomas, M. The French beauty solution **646.7**
Whitefield-Madrano, A. Face value **111.85**
Wolf, N. The beauty myth **305.4**

PERSONAL BELONGINGS
Jameson, M. Downsizing the family home **346.04**

PERSONAL CLEANLINESS *See* Hygiene

PERSONAL COMPUTERS
Upgrading and repairing PCs **004.16**
White, R. How Computers Work **004**

PERSONAL FINANCE
Armstrong, F. The retirement challenge--will you sink or swim? **332.024**
Blake, J. Life after college **646.7**
Boeckh, J. A. The great reflation **332.6**
Bradford, S. L. The Wall Street Journal: financial guidebook for new parents **332.024**
D'Agnese, J. The money book for freelancers, part-time, and the self-employed **332.024**
Downes, J. Finance and investment handbook **332.6**
Economides, A. The moneysmart family system **332.024**
Halpern, J. Bad paper **332.7**
Hirshman, S. L. Does this make my assets look fat? **332.024**
Jason, J. The AARP Retirement Survival Guide **332.024**
Kessel, B. It's not about the money **332.024**
Kobliner, B. Get a financial life **332.024**
Lanchester, J. How to Speak Money **330.1**
Lieber, R. The Opposite of Spoiled **332.024**
McNaughton, D. The essential credit repair handbook **332.024**
Orman, S. The money class **332.024**
Quinn, J. B. Making the most of your money now **332.024**
Schwab-Pomerantz, C. It pays to talk **332.024**
Solin, D. R. The smartest retirement book you'll ever read **332.024**
Solman, P. Get what's yours **368.4**
Tobias, A. P. The only investment guide you'll ever need **332.024**
Velshi, A. How to speak money **332.024**
Walsh, P. Lighten up **332.024**
Weltman, B. J.K. Lasser's guide for tough times **332.024**
Yeager, J. The cheapskate next door **332.024**

PERSONAL FINANCE
See also Finance

PERSONAL FREEDOM *See* Freedom

PERSONAL GROOMING
Thomas, M. The French beauty solution **646.7**

PERSONAL NAMES
See also Names

PERSONAL NAMES -- DICTIONARIES
Dictionary of American family names **929.4**

Latham, E. A dictionary of names, nicknames, and surnames of persons, places, and things **929.4**
Shane, N. Inspired baby names from around the world **929.4**

PERSONALITY
Brooks, D. B. The Road to Character **170**
Dimitrius Reading people **155.2**
Harris, J. R. No two alike **155.2**
Karlins, M. The like switch **158.2**
Myers, I. B. Gifts differing **155.2**

PERSONALITY
See also Consciousness; Psychology

PERSONALITY -- CASE STUDIES
Hitler **92**

PERSONALITY DISORDERS
Kramer, P. D. Listening to Prozac **616.85**

PERSONALITY DISORDERS
See also Abnormal psychology

PERSONALITY, MULTIPLE *See* Multiple personality

PERSONNEL ADMINISTRATION *See* Personnel management

PERSONNEL MANAGEMENT
Elton, C. All in **658.3**
Giesecke, J. Fundamentals of library supervision **023**
Horstman, M. The effective manager **658**
Kelly, M. The dream manager **658.3**
Mosley, P. A. The challenge of library management **025.1**
Stanley, M. J. Managing library employees **023**
Tracy, B. Full engagement! **658.3**

PERSONNEL MANAGEMENT
See also Industrial relations; Management

PERSONS
See also Human beings

PERSPECTIVE
Brehm, M. Drawing perspective **742**
Norling, E. R. Perspective made easy **742**

PERSPECTIVE
See also Descriptive geometry; Geometrical drawing; Optics; Painting

Perspective made easy. Norling, E. R. **742**

PERSUASION (PSYCHOLOGY)
Cialdini, R. B. Influence: the psychology of persuasion **153.8**
Dutton, K. Split-second persuasion **153.8**
Levine, R. The power of persuasion **153.8**

PERSUASION (PSYCHOLOGY)
See also Communication; Conformity

PERSUASION (RHETORIC)
Sehat, D. The Jefferson rule **306.2**

PERSUASION (RHETORIC) *See* Public speaking; Rhetoric

PERSUASIVE COMMUNICATION -- UNITED STATES

Proctor, R. N. Golden holocaust **362.29**
Peru. Acurio, G. **641.598**
PERU
  Acurio, G. Peru **641.598**
PERU -- ANTIQUITIES
  Adams, M. Turn right at Machu Picchu **985**
  Bingham, H. Lost city of the Incas **985**
  Heaney, C. Cradle of gold **92**
  Moseley, M. E. The Incas and their ancestors **985**
PERU -- HISTORY
  Hunefeldt, C. A brief history of Peru **985**
PESACH See Passover
Peshawaria, Rajeev
  Too many bosses, too few leaders **658.4**
Pesky, Johnny, 1919-
      About
  Halberstam, D. The teammates **796**
Pessah, Jon
  The game
Pessoa, Fernando, 1888-1935
      About
  Bloom, H. The Western canon **809**
PEST CONTROL
    See also Agricultural pests; Economic zoology; Pests
Pester, Sophie
  Supercraft **745.5**
PESTICIDES
  Smith, R. Toxin toxout **613**
PESTICIDES
    See also Agricultural chemicals; Pest control; Poisons and poisoning
PESTICIDES -- ENVIRONMENTAL ASPECTS
    See also Environment; Pollution
PESTICIDES -- ENVIRONMENTAL ASPECTS -- UNITED STATES -- HISTORY
  Souder, W. On a farther shore **92**
PESTICIDES AND WILDLIFE
  Carson, R. Silent spring **363.7**
  Monosson, E. Unnatural selection **576.5**
PESTICIDES AND WILDLIFE
    See also Pesticides -- Environmental aspects; Wildlife conservation
PESTILENCES See Epidemics
Pet food politics. Nestle, M. **363.1**
PET THERAPY
    See also Animals and people with disabilities; Therapeutics
Pete Dunne on bird watching. Dunne, P. **598**
Pete Dunne's essential field guide companion. Dunne, P. **598**
Pete Rose. Kennedy, K. **92**
The **Peter** principle. Hull, R. **817**
Peter Shaffer's Amadeus. Shaffer, P. **822**
Peter, Jason, 1974-
      About

Peter, J. Hero of the underground **92**
Peter, Josh
  Fried twinkies, buckle bunnies & bull riders **791.8**
Peter, Laurence J., 1919-1990
  (jt. auth) Hull, R. The Peter principle **817**
Peternell, Cal
  A Recipe for Cooking **641.5**
  Twelve Recipes **641.5**
Peters, Charles
  Lyndon B. Johnson **92**
Peters, Gerhard
  (ed) The presidency A to Z **973.09**
Peters, Justin
  The Idealist **004.67**
Peters, Pam
  The Cambridge guide to English usage **428**
Peters, Sally
  Bernard Shaw **822**
Peters, Thomas J.
  The little big things **658.4**
PETERSBURG (VA.) -- HISTORY -- SIEGE, 1864-1865
  Slotkin, R. No quarter **973.7**
Petersen, Grant
  Just ride **796.6**
Petersen, Melody
  Our daily meds **338.4**
Petersik, John
  (jt. auth) Petersik, S. Lovable livable home **645**
  (jt. auth) Petersik, S. Young house love **747**
Petersik, Sherry
  Lovable livable home **645**
  Young house love **747**
The Peterson field guide series
  Conant, R. A field guide to reptiles & amphibians **597.9**
  Elbroch, M. The Peterson field guide to animal tracks **599**
  Peterson, R. T. Peterson field guide to birds of North America **598**
  Peterson, R. T. Peterson field guide to birds of Eastern and Central North America **598**
  Peterson, R. T. Peterson field guide to birds of Western North America **598**
  Peterson field guide to medicinal plants and herbs of eastern and central North America **581.6**
  Stebbins, R. C. A field guide to Western reptiles and amphibians **597.9**
The **Peterson** field guide to animal tracks. Elbroch, M. **599**
Peterson field guide to birds of Eastern and Central North America. Peterson, R. T. **598**
Peterson field guide to birds of North America. Peterson, R. T. **598**
Peterson field guide to birds of Western North America. Peterson, R. T. **598**

Peterson field guide to freshwater fishes of North America north of Mexico. Page, L. M. **597**

Peterson field guide to medicinal plants and herbs of eastern and central North America. **581.6**

Peterson Reference Guide to Woodpeckers of North America. Shunk, S. A. **598.7**

Peterson's
Peterson's four-year colleges 2015 **378.73**

Peterson's four-year colleges 2015. **378.73**

Peterson's how to get money for college 2015. **378.3**

Peterson's Nelnet LLC
(comp) Peterson's four-year colleges 2015 **378.73**
(comp) Peterson's how to get money for college 2015 **378.3**
(comp) Peterson's two-year colleges 2015 **378.73**

Peterson's two-year colleges 2015. **378.73**

Peterson, Bryan
Learning to see creatively **770.1**
Understanding exposure **771**

Peterson, Dale
Ammann, K. Elephant reflections **599.67**
Giraffe reflections **599.638**
Goodall, J. Beyond innocence **92**
Jane Goodall: the woman who redefined man **92**
The moral lives of animals **156**

Peterson, James
Baking **641.8**
Cooking **641.5**
Glorious French food **641.5**
Kitchen simple **641.5**
Meat **641.6**
Sauces **641.81**

Peterson, Mark
A brief history of Korea **951.9**

Peterson, Merrill D.
(ed) Writings **818**

Peterson, Oscar, 1925-2007
About
Feather, L. From Satchmo to Miles **920**

Peterson, Roger Tory, 1908-1996
Peterson, R. T. Peterson field guide to birds of North America **598**
Peterson field guide to birds of Eastern and Central North America **598**
Peterson field guide to birds of Western North America **598**
About
Weidensaul, S. Return to wild America **578**

Peterson, Scott
Let the swords encircle me **955**

Petiot, Marcel, 1897-1946
About
King, D. Death in the city of light

Petrarca, Francesco, 1304-1374
About
The Renaissance philosophy of man **189**

Petrich, Mike
(jt. auth) Wilkinson, K. The Art of tinkering **500**

PETROCHEMICALS
See also Chemicals

PETROGLYPHS *See* Rock drawings, paintings, and engravings

PETROLEUM
Goodstein, D. L. Out of gas **333.8**

PETROLEUM AS FUEL
See also Fuel

PETROLEUM INDUSTRY
Barrett, P. M. Law of the jungle **344**
Burrough, B. The big rich **338.2**
Coll, S. Private empire **338.7**
Maass, P. Crude world **338.2**
Margonelli, L. Oil on the brain **338.2**
Yergin, D. The prize **338.2**

PETROLEUM INDUSTRY
See also Industries

PETROLEUM INDUSTRY -- ETHICAL ASPECTS
Magner, M. Poisoned legacy **338.7**

PETROLEUM INDUSTRY -- ENVIRONMENTAL ASPECTS
Margonelli, L. Oil on the brain **338.2**
McKibben, B. Oil and Honey **363.7**

PETROLEUM INDUSTRY -- ENVIRONMENTAL ASPECTS -- ARCTIC REGIONS
Stewart, B. Don't trust, don't fear, don't beg **363.738**

PETROLEUM INDUSTRY -- POLITICAL ASPECTS -- UNITED STATES -- HISTORY -- 20TH CENTURY
Abrahamian, E. The coup **955.05**

PETROLEUM INDUSTRY -- UNITED STATES -- BIOGRAPHY
Zuckerman, G. The frackers **338.2**

PETROLEUM INDUSTRY AND TRADE *See* Petroleum industry

PETROLEUM INDUSTRY AND TRADE -- POLITICAL ASPECTS -- UNITED STATES
Coll, S. Private empire **338.7**
McKibben, B. Oil and Honey **363.7**

PETROLOGY
Shubin, N. H. The universe within **550**

PETROLOGY
See also Science

Petropoulos, Jonathan
The Faustian bargain **709**

Petroski, Catherine
About
The house with sixteen handmade doors **728**

Petroski, Henry
The book on the bookshelf **022**
The essential engineer **620**
The pencil **674**

Success through failure   **620**
     About
The house with sixteen handmade doors   **728**
To forgive design   **620**
Petrusewicz, Mary
   (ed) Frank, J. Dostoevsky   **92**
PETS
Bradshaw, J. Cat sense   **636.8**
The complete cat breed book   **636.8**
Goldstein, M. The nature of animal healing **636.089**
The good dog   **636.7**
Mattison, C. What reptile?   **639.3**
Miracle dogs   **636.7**
Montgomery, S. The good good pig   **636.4**
Schoen, A. M. Kindred spirits   **636.089**
Sheldrake, R. Dogs that know when their owners
   are coming home   **133.8**
Sife, W. The loss of a pet   **155.9**
PETS
   See also Animals
PETS -- BEHAVIOR
Link, T. Talking with dogs and cats   **636.088**
PETS -- ETHICAL ASPECTS
Pierce, J. Run, Spot, run   **636.08**
PETS -- FOOD
Nestle, M. Pet food politics   **363.1**
PETS -- HEALTH AND HYGIENE
Halligan, K. Doc Halligan's What every pet owner
   should know   **636**
Pettegree, Andrew
The book in the Renaissance   **070.5**
PETTING ZOOS
   See also Zoos
Pettit, Brandon
     About
Wizenberg, M. Delancey   **647.95**
Peynaud, Emile
The taste of wine   **641.2**
Peyser, Marc
Hissing cousins   **92**
Pfeiffer, Jacquy
   (jt. auth) Shulman, M. R. The art of French pas-
   try   **641.86**
PGA TOUR INC.
Feinstein, J. A good walk spoiled   **796.352**
pH neutral history.   **891.8**
Phaidon Press
   (comp) The Art Book   **709**
   (comp) The Silver Spoon   **641.59**
Pham, Andrew X.
The eaves of heaven   **92**
Pham, Thong Van
     About
Pham, A. X. The eaves of heaven   **92**
Phan, Charles
The slanted door   **641.59**

Vietnamese home cooking   **641.59**
The **Phantom** Killer. Presley, J.   **364.152**
PHANTOMS *See* Apparitions; Ghosts
PHARAOHS -- BIOGRAPHY
Cooney, K. The woman who would be king   **92**
PHARMACEUTICAL CHEMISTRY
   See also Chemistry
**PHARMACEUTICAL INDUSTRY -- UNITED
STATES**
Elliott, C. White coat, black hat   **174.2**
Petersen, M. Our daily meds   **338.4**
**PHARMACEUTICAL INDUSTRY -- UNITED
STATES -- HISTORY -- 20TH CENTURY**
Tobbell, D. A. Pills, power, and policy   **338.4**
**PHARMACEUTICAL INDUSTRY --MORAL
AND ETHICAL ASPECTS**
Goldacre, B. Bad Pharma   **615.107**
PHARMACEUTICALS *See* Drugs
PHARMACODYNAMICS *See* Pharmacology
PHARMACOLOGY
Griffith, H. W. Complete Guide to Prescription &
   Nonprescription Drugs   **615**
PDR for nonprescription drugs   **615**
Physicians' desk reference   **615**
PHARMACOLOGY
   See also Medicine
PHARMACOTHERAPY *See* Drug therapy
PHARMACY
   See also Chemistry; Medicine
PHEASANTS
   See also Birds; Game and game birds
Phelan, Thomas W.
1-2-3 magic   **649**
Phelps, Carissa
     About
Phelps, C. Runaway girl   **362.74**
Phenomenal. Henion, L. A.   **910.4**
PHENOMENOLOGY
Heidegger, M. Being and time   **111**
Mendelsund, P. What we see when we read   **028**
PHENOMENOLOGY
   See also Modern philosophy
The **phenomenon** of man. Teilhard de Chardin,
P.   **113**
**PHILADELPHIA (PA.) -- HISTORY -- 18TH
CENTURY**
Miller, M. R. Betsy Ross and the making of Amer-
   ica   **92**
**PHILADELPHIA (PA.) -- RACE RELATIONS --
HISTORY**
Biddle, D. R. Tasting freedom   **92**
The **Philadelphia** chromosome. Wapner, J. **616.99**
**PHILADELPHIA CHROMOSOME -- UNITED
STATES**
Wapner, J. The Philadelphia chromosome   **616.99**
Philadelphia Museum of Art

Thomas Eakins **759.13**

Philander, George S.

(ed) Encyclopedia of global warming & climate change **363.738**

PHILANTHROPISTS

Addams, J. Twenty years at Hull-House **361.7**

Auletta, K. Media man **92**

Baldwin, N. Henry Ford and the Jews **305**

Brinkley, D. Wheels for the world **338.7**

Buckley, C. T. Losing Mum and Pup **92**

Burrough, B. The big rich **338.2**

Cannadine, D. Mellon **92**

Chernow, R. Titan: the life of John D. Rockefeller, Sr. **92**

Ewing, H. P. The lost world of James Smithson **92**

Grandin, G. Fordlandia **307.7**

Gup, T. A secret gift **977.1**

Hague, W. J. William Wilberforce **92**

Hofstadter, R. The American political tradition, and the men who made it **973**

Knight, L. W. Jane Addams **92**

Krass, P. Carnegie **338.7**

Meredith, M. Diamonds, gold, and war **968.04**

Nasaw, D. Andrew Carnegie **92**

Rea, T. Bone wars **560**

Rockefeller, D. Memoirs **332.1**

Wall, J. F. Andrew Carnegie **92**

Walsh, J. The J. Paul Getty Museum and its collections **708.1**

Watts, S. The people's tycoon **92**

PHILANTHROPISTS -- PERSONAL NARRATIVES

Novogratz, J. The blue sweater **339.4**

PHILANTHROPY -- HISTORY

Zunz, O. Philanthropy in America **361.7**

PHILANTHROPY -- UNITED STATES

Zunz, O. Philanthropy in America **361.7**

Philanthropy in America. Zunz, O. **361.7**

Philbrick, Nathaniel

Bunker Hill **973.3**

The last stand **973.8**

Mayflower **973.2**

Valiant Ambition **973.3**

Why read Moby-Dick? **813**

Philby, Kim, 1912-1988

About

Macintyre, B. A Spy Among Friends **327.12**

Philip II, King of Spain, 1527-1598

About

Kamen, H. Philip of Spain **946**

Philip of Spain. Kamen, H. **946**

Philip, Neil

The great circle **970.004**

PHILIPPENES -- HISTORY -- PHILIPPINE AMERICAN WAR, 1899-1902

Jones, G. Honor in the dust **959.9**

PHILIPPINES -- HISTORY

Karnow, S. In our image **959.9**

Phillip, Arthur, 1738-1814

About

Keneally, T. A commonwealth of thieves **994**

Phillips, Carolyn

All under heaven **641.5**

Phillips, Cassandra

(jt. auth) Moore, C. Plastic ocean **363.7**

Phillips, Ellen

(ed) Rodale's ultimate encyclopedia of organic gardening **635**

Phillips, Jonathan

Holy warriors **909.07**

Phillips, Julie

James Tiptree, Jr. **813**

Phillips, Kevin P.

William McKinley **92**

Phillips, Kevin, 1940-

1775 **973.3**

Phillips, Michael

The Chelsea Market cookbook **641.59**

Phillips, Patrick

Blood at the root **305.8**

Elegy for a broken machine **811**

Phillips, Rowan Ricardo

Heaven **811**

Phillips, Ruth B.

Berlo, J. C. Native North American art **709.01**

Phillips, Sam, 1923-2003

About

Guralnick, P. Sam Phillips **92**

Phillips, Susan P.

Great displays for your library step by step **021.7**

Phillips, Wendell, 1811-1884

About

Hofstadter, R. The American political tradition, and the men who made it **973**

PHILOLOGISTS

Gates, H. L. Colored people **92**

Hartman, S. V. Lose your mother **323**

My life as author and editor **818**

Rodgers, M. E. Mencken **92**

Samet, E. D. Soldier's heart **810**

Teachout, T. The skeptic: the life of H.L. Mencken **92**

PHILOLOGY *See* Language and languages; Linguistics

PHILOLOGY, COMPARATIVE *See* Linguistics

The **philosopher's** plant. Marder, M. **580**

PHILOSOPHERS

Adler, M. J. Aristotle for everybody **185**

Armstrong, K. Buddha **294.3**

Bair, D. Simone de Beauvoir **848**

Bayley, J. Elegy for Iris **823**

Bell, E. T. Men of mathematics **920**

Blum, D. Ghost hunters **133.9**

Camus, A. The rebel **303.6**

Commager, H. S. The American mind **973**

Conradi, P. Iris Murdoch **823**

Crawford, M. B. Shop class as soulcraft **331**

Damasio, A. R. Looking for Spinoza **152.4**

Damrosch, L. Jean-Jacques Rousseau **848**

David, A. Once upon a country **92**

Edmonds, D. Wittgenstein's poker **192**

Everitt, A. Cicero **92**

Existentialism from Dostoevsky to Sartre **142**

Feldman, B. 112 Mercer Street **920**

Friedman, M. S. Encounter on the narrow ridge: a life of Martin Buber **92**

Greenblatt, S. The swerve **940.2**

Hare, R. M. Plato **184**

Heller, A. C. Ayn Rand and the world she made **92**

Herman, A. The idea of decline in Western history **909.08**

Hollis, L. London rising **942**

Hughes, B. The hemlock cup **92**

James, C. Cultural amnesia **920**

Johnson, P. Socrates **92**

Kaag, J. American philosophy **191**

Kazin, A. An American procession **810**

Kreeft, P. Philosophy 101 by Socrates **183**

Kung, H. Great Christian thinkers **230**

Matteson, J. Eden's outcasts **92**

Matthiessen, F. O. American renaissance **810**

Menand, L. The Metaphysical Club **973.9**

Mill, J. S. Autobiography **92**

Miller, J. Examined lives **190**

Milosz, C. To begin where I am **891.8**

Nadler, S. M. The best of all possible worlds **190**

The Oxford companion to philosophy **103**

Pearson, R. Voltaire almighty **92**

Pierpont, C. R. Passionate minds **810**

Rand, A. Journals of Ayn Rand **92**

Rand, A. Letters of Ayn Rand **813**

The Renaissance philosophy of man **189**

Richardson, R. D. Emerson **814**

Richardson, R. D. William James **92**

Rubenstein, R. E. Aristotle's children **189**

Rudman, P. S. The Babylonian theorem **510**

Russell, B. A history of Western philosophy **109**

Safranski, R. Nietzsche **193**

Said, E. W. Reflections on exile and other essays **814**

Sartre, J. P. The words **92**

Sebald, W. G. On the natural history of destruction **833**

Shields, C. J. Aristotle **185**

Snyder, L. J. The philosophical breakfast club **509**

Solomon, R. C. What Nietzsche really said **193**

Stone, I. F. The trial of Socrates **183**

Unger, M. J. Machiavelli **92**

Waterfield, R. Why Socrates died **183**

Watson, R. A. Cogito ergo sum: the life of Rene Descartes **92**

Waugh, A. The House of Wittgenstein **920**

Wayne, T. K. Critical companion to Ralph Waldo Emerson **818**

Wills, G. Saint Augustine **270.2**

World philosophers and their works **109**

PHILOSOPHERS -- BIOGRAPHY

James, C. Cultural amnesia **920**

Miller, J. Examined lives **190**

PHILOSOPHERS -- FRANCE -- BIOGRAPHY

Bakewell, S. At the Existentialist Cafe **142**

Watson, R. A. Cogito ergo sum: the life of Rene Descartes **92**

PHILOSOPHERS -- GERMANY

Sherratt, Y. Hitler's philosophers **193**

PHILOSOPHERS -- GERMANY -- BIOGRAPHY

Sperber, J. Karl Marx **92**

PHILOSOPHERS -- GERMANY -- HISTORY -- 20TH CENTURY

Sherratt, Y. Hitler's philosophers **193**

PHILOSOPHERS' STONE *See* Alchemy

The **philosophical** breakfast club. Snyder, L. J. **509**

PHILOSOPHY

Blackburn, S. Think: a compelling introduction to philosophy **100**

Churchland, P. S. Braintrust **612.8**

Einstein, A. A stubbornly persistent illusion **530.1**

Ferry, L. A brief history of thought **100**

Frayn, M. The human touch **128**

Gutting, G. What philosophy can do **100**

Happiness **152.4**

Kant, I. Basic writings of Kant **193**

Magee, B. The story of philosophy **190**

Nirenberg, D. Anti-Judaism **305.892**

Ortega y Gasset, J. What is philosophy? **196**

The Oxford companion to philosophy **103**

The Oxford companion to the mind **128**

Russell, B. The problems of philosophy **100**

Sagan, C. Broca's brain **500**

Wilson, E. O. Consilience **121**

Wilson, E. J. Encyclopedia of the Enlightenment **940.2**

PHILOSOPHY

See also Humanities

PHILOSOPHY -- DICTIONARIES

Blackburn, S. The Oxford dictionary of philosophy **103**

The Cambridge dictionary of philosophy **103**

PHILOSOPHY -- ENCYCLOPEDIAS

The Oxford companion to philosophy **103**

Wilson, E. J. Encyclopedia of the Enlightenment **940.2**

PHILOSOPHY -- ENCYCLOPEDIAS

See also Encyclopedias and dictionaries

PHILOSOPHY -- HISTORIOGRAPHY

See also Historiography

PHILOSOPHY -- HISTORY

Judt, T. Thinking the twentieth century **320.092**

PHILOSOPHY -- INTRODUCTIONS

Kreeft, P. Philosophy 101 by Socrates **183**

PHILOSOPHY -- MISCELLANEA

Dennett, D. C. Intuition Pumps and Other Tools for Thinking **121**

PHILOSOPHY -- PSYCHOLOGICAL ASPECTS

Miller, J. Examined lives **190**

PHILOSOPHY -- UNITED STATES

Romano, C. America the philosophical **191**

Philosophy 101 by Socrates. Kreeft, P. **183**

PHILOSOPHY AND RELIGION

Huxley, A. The perennial philosophy **210**

Talking God **210**

Zaretsky, R. Boswell's enlightenment **92**

PHILOSOPHY AND RELIGION

See also Philosophy; Religion

PHILOSOPHY AND RELIGION -- SCOTLAND -- HISTORY -- 18TH CENTURY

Boswell's enlightenment **828**

Zaretsky, R. Boswell's enlightenment **92**

The **philosophy** of Hegel. Hegel, G. W. F. **193**

PHILOSOPHY OF HISTORY *See* History -- Philosophy

PHILOSOPHY OF NATURE

Goodall, J. Seeds of Hope **580**

Haskell, D. G. The forest unseen **577.3**

Watson, L. Dark nature **111**

What the robin knows **598.8**

Wilson, E. O. In search of nature **113**

PHILOSOPHY OF RELIGION *See* Religion -- Philosophy

PHILOSOPHY, AMERICAN

Robinson, M. When I was a child I read books **814**

PHILOSOPHY, AMERICAN *See* American philosophy

PHILOSOPHY, AMERICAN -- MISCELLANEA

Kaag, J. American philosophy **191**

PHILOSOPHY, ANCIENT

Marcus Aurelius Meditations **188**

Waterfield, R. Why Socrates died **183**

PHILOSOPHY, ANCIENT *See* Ancient philosophy

PHILOSOPHY, GERMAN -- 20TH CENTURY

Sherratt, Y. Hitler's philosophers **193**

PHILOSOPHY, MEDICAL

Kore **610**

PHILOSOPHY, MEDIEVAL *See* Medieval philosophy

PHILOSOPHY, MODERN *See* Modern philosophy

PHILOSOPHY, MODERN -- 20TH CENTURY"||PHILOSOPHY -- FRANCE -- HISTORY -- 20TH CENTURY

Bakewell, S. At the Existentialist Cafe **142**

PHILOSOPHY, RENAISSANCE

Greenblatt, S. The swerve **940.2**

Philpott, Don

(jt. auth) Lawhorne-Scott, C. Military mental health care **355.3**

(jt. auth) Scott, J. Raising children in the military **355.1**

Philpott, William

Three armies on the Somme **940.4**

Phinney, Robert Edgar, 1915-1989

About

The house with sixteen handmade doors **728**

PHISHING

Krebs, B. Spam nation **364.16**

PHOBIAS

Shawn, A. Wish I could be there **92**

PHOBIAS

See also Fear; Neuroses

PHOENICIANS

See also Ancient history

PHOENIX (ARIZ.) -- SOCIAL LIFE AND CUSTOMS

Davis, J. Spare parts **629.8**

PHOENIX (MYTHICAL BIRD)

See also Mythical animals

Phoenix claws and jade trees. **641.595**

PHOENIX MARS MISSION (U.S.)

Kessler, A. Martian summer **523.4**

PHONETICS

See also Language and languages; Sound

PHONETICS -- STUDY AND TEACHING

Flesch, R. F. Why Johnny can't read--and what you can do about it **372.4**

PHONOGRAPH RECORDS *See* Sound recordings

PHOSPHORESCENCE

See also Luminescence; Radioactivity

PHOTO JOURNALISM *See* Photojournalism

PHOTO-REALISM

Crilley, M. The realism challenge **751.4**

PHOTOCOPYING -- FAIR USE(COPYRIGHT) -- UNITED STATES

Gasaway, L. N. Copyright questions and answers for information professionals **346.73**

PHOTODOCUMENTATION *See* Documentary photography

PHOTOENGRAVING

See also Engraving

Photograph. Starr, R. **782.4**

The **photographer.** Guibert, E. **958.1**

A **photographer's** life, 1990-2005. Leibovitz, A. **779**

The **photographer's** mind. Freeman, M. **775**

PHOTOGRAPHERS

Adam, P. Jack London, photographer 92
Addario, L. It's What I Do 92
Alinder, M. S. Ansel Adams 92
Ang, T. Photography 770.9
Brandow, T. Edward Steichen 779
Burke, C. Lee Miller 92
Casey, M. Che's afterlife 980
Connolly, K. M. Double take 92
Egan, T. Short nights of the Shadow Catcher 770.92
Foresta, M. A. Irving Penn 770
Herlihy, D. V. The lost cyclist 92
Lees, G. You can't steal a gift 781.65
Leibovitz, A. Annie Leibovitz at work 779
Leibovitz, A. A photographer's life, 1990-2005 779
Lottman, H. R. Man Ray's Montparnasse 709
Marton, K. The great escape 920
Min, A. Red Azalea 92
Panzer, M. Mathew Brady and the image of history 770.92
Robison, J. E. Look me in the eye 92
Smith, J. Edward Steichen: the early years 779
Snyder, L. J. The philosophical breakfast club 509
Stieglitz, A. Alfred Stieglitz: the key set 770

PHOTOGRAPHERS

See also Artists

PHOTOGRAPHERS -- UNITED STATES -- BIOGRAPHY

Alinder, M. S. Group f.64 770.92
Cardozo, C. Edward S. Curtis 770
Egan, T. Short nights of the Shadow Catcher 770.92
Szarkowski, J. Ansel Adams at 100 770
White, E. The Tastemaker 92
Wilson, R. Mathew Brady 770.92

PHOTOGRAPHIC CHEMISTRY

See also Chemistry

PHOTOGRAPHIC CRITICISM

The open road 770

PHOTOGRAPHS FROM SPACE *See* Space photography

Photography. Ang, T. 770.9

PHOTOGRAPHY

See also Graphic arts

PHOTOGRAPHY

Alinder, M. S. Group f.64 770.92
Arbus, D. Diane Arbus 779.2
Brassaï Brassai 944.361
Edward weston 770
Evans, W. American photographs 779
Gatcum, C. The Beginner's photography guide 770
Gross, M. Focus 770.92
Hallett, T. Digital photography complete course 770
Hitchcock, S. T. National geographic rarely seen 779
Invisible City 779
Lubow, A. Diane Arbus 92

Magnum contact sheets 779.092
Manwaring, J. Extraordinary everyday photography 778.71
Miotke, J. BetterPhoto basics 771
Peterson, B. Learning to see creatively 770.1
Peterson, B. Understanding exposure 771
Roman vishniac rediscovered 779.092
Stanton, B. Humans of New York 974.7
Steve McCurry 779.092
Watkins, C. E. Carleton Watkins: the complete mammoth photographs 778.9

PHOTOGRAPHY -- AESTHETICS *See* Artistic photography

PHOTOGRAPHY -- AMATEURS' MANUALS

Miotke, J. BetterPhoto basics 771

PHOTOGRAPHY -- DIGITAL TECHNIQUES

Hallett, T. Digital photography complete course 770
Horenstein, H. Digital photography 770

PHOTOGRAPHY -- DIGITAL TECHNIQUES

See Digital photography

PHOTOGRAPHY -- EXHIBITIONS

Bajac, Q. Photography at MOMA 770

PHOTOGRAPHY -- EXPOSURE

Peterson, B. Understanding exposure 771

PHOTOGRAPHY -- HISTORY

Ang, T. Photography 770.9

PHOTOGRAPHY -- HISTORY -- UNITED STATES

Gordon, L. Dorothea Lange 92

PHOTOGRAPHY -- PROCESSING

Ang, T. Digital photography masterclass 775

PHOTOGRAPHY -- TECHNIQUE -- AMATEURS' MANUALS

Manwaring, J. Extraordinary everyday photography 778.71

PHOTOGRAPHY -- UNITED STATES -- HISTORY

Alinder, M. S. Group f.64 770.92
Photography at MOMA. Bajac, Q. 770

PHOTOGRAPHY IN ASTRONAUTICS *See* Space photography

PHOTOGRAPHY IN ETHNOLOGY

Cardozo, C. Edward S. Curtis 770

PHOTOGRAPHY OF ANIMALS

McAllister, I. The last wild wolves 599.77
The new complete dog book 636.7
Sunquist, F. The wild cat book 599.75

PHOTOGRAPHY OF SPORTS -- HISTORY

Buckland, G. Who shot sports 779.97

PHOTOGRAPHY, ARTISTIC

Arbus, D. Diane Arbus 779.2
Brandow, T. Edward Steichen 779
Evans, W. American photographs 779
Leibovitz, A. Annie Leibovitz at work 779
The open road 770
Smith, J. Edward Steichen: the early years 779

Stanton, B. Humans of New York **974.7**

Szarkowski, J. William Eggleston's Guide **779**

PHOTOGRAPHY, ARTISTIC *See* Artistic photography

PHOTOGRAPHY, ARTISTIC -- 20TH CENTURY

Cartier-Bresson, H. The Decisive Moment **770**

PHOTOGRAPHY, ARTISTIC -- EXHIBITIONS

Szarkowski, J. Ansel Adams at 100 **770**

PHOTOGRAPHY, COMBAT *See* War photography

PHOTOGRAPHY, DOCUMENTARY *See* Documentary photography

PHOTOGRAPHY, WAR *See* War photography

PHOTOJOURNALISM

Addario, L. It's What I Do **92**

Buell, H. Moments **070.4**

Knauer, K. TIME History's Greatest Images **909.82**

Lyon, D. The bikeriders **796.7**

Masur, L. P. The soiling of Old Glory **974.4**

National Geographic, the photographs **778**

Sontag, S. Regarding the pain of others **303.6**

Stepan, P. Photos that changed the world **779**

Women of vision **770.82**

PHOTOJOURNALISM

See also Commercial photography; Journalism; Photography

PHOTOJOURNALISM -- GRAPHIC NOVELS

Guibert, E. The photographer **958.1**

PHOTOJOURNALISM -- UNITED STATES -- AWARDS

Buell, H. Moments **070.4**

PHOTOJOURNALISTS

Bradley, J. Flags of our fathers **940.54**

Buk-Swienty, T. The other half **92**

Burrows, L. Vietnam **770.92**

Marton, K. The great escape **920**

Masur, L. P. The soiling of Old Glory **974.4**

PHOTOMECHANICAL PROCESSES

See also Illustration of books; Photography

PHOTOMETRISTS

Johnson, G. Miss Leavitt's stars **92**

Malone, J. W. It doesn't take a rocket scientist **920**

PHOTOMETRY

See also Measurement

PHOTOMICROGRAPHY

See also Photography

Photos that changed the world. Stepan, P. **779**

PHOTOSYNTHESIS

Morton, O. Eating the sun **572**

PHOTOVOLTAIC POWER GENERATION

Ewing, R. A. Got sun? go solar **697**

PHOTOVOLTAIC POWER GENERATION

See also Solar energy

PHRENOLOGY

See also Brain; Head; Psychology

PHYLOGENY

Nielsen, C. Animal evolution **591.3**

PHYSICAL ANTHROPOLOGY

Johanson, D. C. From Lucy to language **599.93**

Olson, S. Mapping human history **599.9**

Pringle, H. A. The mummy congress **393**

Roberts, D. Fatal invention **305.8**

PHYSICAL EDUCATION

Afremow, J. The champion's mind **796.01**

Cordoza, G. Becoming a supple leopard **613.7**

PHYSICAL EDUCATION AND TRAINING -- PHYSIOLOGICAL ASPECTS

Reynolds, G. The first 20 minutes **613.7**

PHYSICAL EDUCATION AND TRAINING -- SOCIAL ASPECTS

Kunitz, D. Lift **613.7**

PHYSICAL FITNESS

Baroni, B. Fat kid got fit **362.196**

Complete guide to fitness & health **613.7**

Durant, J. Spartan Fit **613.7**

Esmonde-White, M. Aging backwards **613.2**

Fitness and exercise sourcebook **613.7**

Fitzgerald, M. How bad do you want it? **612.044**

Hines, E. W. Fitness swimming **613.7**

Kunitz, D. Lift **613.7**

The longevity kitchen **612.6**

Pagano, J. Strength training for women **613.7**

PHYSICAL FITNESS

See also Exercise; Health; Health self-care; Physical education

PHYSICAL FITNESS FOR WOMEN

Pagano, J. Strength training exercises for women **613.7**

PHYSICAL GEOGRAPHY

Oxford Atlas of the world **912**

PHYSICAL GEOGRAPHY

See also Geography; Geology

PHYSICAL GEOGRAPHY -- YELLOWSTONE NATIONAL PARK -- MAPS

Atlas of Yellowstone **912.09**

PHYSICAL SCIENCES

Ball, P. Patterns in nature **500.2**

Miodownik, M. Stuff matters **620.1**

PHYSICIAN AND PATIENT

Berger, Z. Talking to your doctor **610.69**

Brokaw, T. A Lucky Life Interrupted **92**

Roth, A. J. Managing prostate cancer **616.99**

PHYSICIAN-ASSISTED SUICIDE *See* Assisted suicide

PHYSICIAN-NURSE RELATIONS -- UNITED STATES -- PERSONAL NARRATIVES

Robbins, A. The nurses **362.17**

PHYSICIAN-PATIENT RELATIONSHIP

Berger, Z. Talking to your doctor **610.69**

Groopman, J. E. The anatomy of hope **616**

Groopman, J. E. Your medical mind **610**

Kore **610**

Montross, C. Falling into the fire **92**

Ofri, D. What doctors feel **610.69**

Reilly, B. One doctor **610.69**

Volandes, A. E. The conversation **616.02**

Wachter, R. The digital doctor **610.28**

PHYSICIANS

Anderson, J. L. Che Guevara **92**

Boyle, K. Arc of justice **345**

Brock, P. Charlatan **92**

Callow, P. Chekhov, the hidden ground **891.7**

Casey, M. Che's afterlife **980**

Chekhov, A. P. Anton Chekhov's life and thought **92**

Gawande, A. Better **616**

Groopman, J. E. How doctors think **610**

Halberstam, D. The children **323.1**

Hollis, L. London rising **942**

Jarrell, R. No other book **809**

Jauhar, S. Doctored **92**

Johnson, S. The ghost map **614.5**

Kean, S. The tale of the dueling neurosurgeons **617.4**

Kluger, J. Splendid solution: Jonas Salk and the
conquest of polio **92**

Lattin, D. The Harvard Psychedelic Club **920**

Leibowitz, H. A. Something urgent I have to say
to you: the life and works of William Carlos Williams **92**

Lifton, R. J. The Nazi doctors **940.53**

Mah, A. Y. Falling leaves **305.48**

Malcolm, J. Reading Chekhov **891.7**

Marion, R. Genetic rounds **92**

McCullough, D. G. The path between the
seas **972.87**

McGoogan, K. Race to the Polar Sea **92**

Nabokov, V. V. Lectures on Russian literature **891.7**

Nuland, S. B. The doctors' plague **92**

Ofri, D. What doctors feel **610.69**

Orbinski, J. An imperfect offering **610**

Sacks, O. W. Uncle Tungsten **616.8**

Sagan, C. Broca's brain **500**

Starr, D. The killer of little shepherds **364.152**

Stewart, J. B. Blind eye **364.1**

Sweet, V. God's hotel **610.92**

Tweedy, D. Black Man in a White Coat **92**

Von Tunzelmann, A. Red heat **972.9**

Webster, C. Paracelsus **92**

PHYSICIANS

See also Medical personnel

PHYSICIANS -- ATTITUDES

Teresi, D. The undead **610**

PHYSICIANS -- BIOGRAPHY

Aptowicz, C. O. Dr. Mütter's Marvels **92**

Franscell, R. Morgue **616.07**

Kershaw, A. Avenue of spies **940.53**

Manheimer, E. Twelve patients **362.11**

PHYSICIANS -- COLOMBIA -- BIOGRAPHY

Abad, H. Oblivion **868**

**PHYSICIANS -- HISTORY -- POPULAR
WORKS**

Kean, S. The tale of the dueling neurosurgeons **617.4**

**PHYSICIANS -- PENNSYLVANIA -- BIOGRA-
PHY**

Aptowicz, C. O. Dr. Mütter's Marvels **92**

PHYSICIANS -- PSYCHOLOGY

Ofri, D. What doctors feel **610.69**

**PHYSICIANS -- UNITED STATES -- AUTOBI-
OGRAPHY**

Jauhar, S. Doctored **92**

**PHYSICIANS -- UNITED STATES -- BIOGRA-
PHY**

Rankin, L. The anatomy of a calling **92**

Stewart, J. B. Blind eye **364.1**

Physicians' desk reference. **615**

PHYSICISTS

Aczel, A. D. God's equation **523.1**

Bell, E. T. Men of mathematics **920**

Bernstein, J. Oppenheimer **92**

Bird, K. American Prometheus **92**

Bodanis, D. E **530.1**

Bolles, E. B. Einstein defiant **530.1**

Brian, D. The Curies **92**

The Cambridge companion to Newton **530**

Cassidy, D. C. Beyond uncertainty **92**

Clary, D. A. Rocket man **92**

Cole, K. C. Something incredibly wonderful happens **92**

Dolnick, E. The clockwork universe **509**

Dry, S. Curie **92**

Einstein, A. Einstein on politics **92**

Einstein, A. A stubbornly persistent illusion **530.1**

Fara, P. Newton: the making of genius **92**

Feldman, B. 112 Mercer Street **920**

Galison, P. L. Einstein's clocks and Poincare's
maps **529**

Gleick, J. Isaac Newton **92**

Goldstein, W. For the love of physics **92**

Goodchild, P. Edward Teller, the real Dr Strangelove **92**

Goodstein, D. L. Feynman's lost lecture **521**

Greenspan, N. T. The end of the certain world **92**

Gribbin, J. R. Schrodinger's kittens and the search
for reality **530.1**

Hargittai, I. The Martians of science **920**

Hirshfeld, A. The electric life of Michael Faraday **92**

Hollis, L. London rising **942**

Hunter, M. Boyle **92**

Isaacson, W. Einstein: his life and universe **92**

Krauss, L. M. Fear of physics **530**

Krauss, L. M. Quantum man **92**

Levenson, T. Newton and the counterfeiter 92

Magueijo, J. A brilliant darkness 92

Malone, J. W. It doesn't take a rocket scientist 920

Marton, K. The great escape 920

Ohanian, H. C. Einstein's mistakes 530

Raymo, C. Walking zero 526

Reeves, R. A force of nature 92

Reich, E. S. Plastic fantastic 92

Rigden, J. S. Einstein 1905 530.1

Sagan, C. Broca's brain 500

Schulmann, R. An Einstein encyclopedia 530.092

Smiley, J. The man who invented the computer 92

Susskind, L. The black hole war 530.1

Teller, E. Memoirs 92

Westfall, R. S. The life of Isaac Newton 92

PHYSICISTS

See also Scientists

PHYSICISTS -- BIOGRAPHY

Ferreira, P. G. The perfect theory 530.11

Hawking, S. My brief history 92

Kaiser, D. How the hippies saved physics 530.092

Monk, R. Robert Oppenheimer 92

Schewe, P. F. Maverick Genius 92

PHYSICISTS -- BIOGRAPHY -- ENCYCLOPE-DIAS

Schulmann, R. An Einstein encyclopedia 530.092

PHYSICISTS -- GERMANY -- BIOGRAPHY

Cassidy, D. C. Beyond uncertainty 92

PHYSICISTS -- GRAPHIC NOVELS

Feynman 92

PHYSICISTS -- UNITED STATES -- BIOGRA-PHY

Bernstein, J. Oppenheimer 92

Hargittai, I. The Martians of science 920

Monk, R. Robert Oppenheimer 92

Segrè, G. Ordinary geniuses 572.8

PHYSICISTS -- UNITED STATES -- INTEL-LECTUAL LIFE -- 20TH CENTURY

Monk, R. Robert Oppenheimer 92

PHYSICS

Ananthaswamy, A. The edge of physics 530

Balibar, S. The atom and the apple 530

Barr, S. M. Modern physics and ancient faith 201

Cole, K. C. The hole in the universe 530.01

Cox, B. The quantum universe 530.12

A cultural history of physics 530

Eckstut, A. The Secret Language of Color 535.6

Feynman, R. P. Six easy pieces 530

Goldberg, D. The Universe in the Rearview Mirror 539.7

Goldberg, D. A user's guide to the universe 530

Henderson, M. 100 most important science ideas 500

Hrabovsky, G. The theoretical minimum 530

Krauss, L. M. Fear of physics 530

Lamothe, M. The where, the why, and the how 502

Ohanian, H. C. Einstein's mistakes 530

Randall, L. Higgs discovery 539.72

Randall, L. Knocking on heaven's door 500

Rovelli, C. Seven Brief Lessons on Physics 530

Stannard, R. The end of discovery 501

Tegmark, M. Our mathematical universe 523.1

This explains everything 500

Weatherall, J. O. The physics of Wall Street 332.63

Wertheim, M. Physics on the fringe 530.1

PHYSICS

See also Physical sciences; Science

PHYSICS -- DICTIONARIES

Pickover, C. A. The physics book 530

PHYSICS -- HISTORY

Pickover, C. A. The physics book 530

PHYSICS -- HISTORY -- 20TH CENTURY -- EN-CYCLOPEDIAS

Schulmann, R. An Einstein encyclopedia 530.092

PHYSICS -- PHILOSOPHY

Krauss, L. M. A universe from nothing 523.1

Muller, R. A. Now 530.11

PHYSICS -- POPULAR WORKS

Crease, R. P. The quantum moment 530.12

PHYSICS -- STUDY AND TEACHING

Goldstein, W. For the love of physics 92

PHYSICS -- TABLES

CRC Handbook of Chemistry and Physics 540

The **physics** book. Pickover, C. A. 530

Physics of the future. Kaku, M. 303.49

The **physics** of Wall Street. Weatherall, J. O. 332.63

Physics on the fringe. Wertheim, M. 530.1

PHYSIOGNOMY

Dimitrius Reading people 155.2

PHYSIOGNOMY

See also Psychology

PHYSIOLOGICAL CHEMISTRY *See* Biochem-istry

PHYSIOLOGICAL STRESS *See* Stress (Physiol-ogy)

PHYSIOLOGISTS

Tucker, T. The great starvation experiment 174.2

PHYSIOLOGY

Angier, N. Woman 612.6

Ashcroft, F. The spark of life 612

Balaban, N. E. The handy anatomy answer book 611

Francis, G. Adventures in human being 612

The Human body 612

Lewis, M. Understanding pain 616

Palca, J. Annoying 612.8

Roebuck, J. Anatomy 360 degrees

PHYSIOLOGY

See also Biology; Medicine; Science

PHYSIOLOGY, COMPARATIVE

Bowers, K. Zoobiquity 636.089

PHYSIOLOGY, COMPARATIVE *See* Comparative physiology

Piaf, Édith, 1915-1963
About
Burke, C. No regrets   92
Piaget, Jean
The moral judgment of the child   155.4
PIANISTS
Basie, C. Good morning blues: the autobiography of Count Basie   92
Berlin, E. A. King of ragtime: Scott Joplin and his era   92
Cohodas, N. Princess Noire   92
Coleman, R. Blue Monday   92
Dance, S. The world of Count Basie   920
Eisler, B. Chopin's funeral   92
Ellison, R. The collected essays of Ralph Ellison   814
Epstein, D. M. Nat King Cole   92
Feather, L. From Satchmo to Miles   920
Hafner, K. A romance on three legs   92
Kelley, R. D. G. Thelonious Monk   92
Lees, G. You can't steal a gift   781.65
Murray, A. The blue devils of Nada   780.89
Schonberg, H. C. The great pianists   920
Wilson, E. Patriotic gore   810
PIANISTS -- UNITED STATES -- BIOGRAPHY
De Barros, P. Shall we play that one together?   92
PIANO See Pianos
The **piano** lesson. Wilson, A.   812
PIANO MUSIC
See also Instrumental music; Music
PIANO MUSIC -- HISTORY AND CRITICISM
Isacoff, S. A natural history of the piano   786.2
PIANOS
Hafner, K. A romance on three legs   92
Isacoff, S. A natural history of the piano   786.2
Piantadosi, Claude A.
Mankind beyond Earth   629.45
Piatt, Julie
(jt. auth) Roll, R. The plantpower way   641.563
Piazza, Gina M.
(ed) First aid manual   616.02
PICARESQUE LITERATURE
See also Fiction; Literature
Picasso and American art. FitzGerald, M. C.   709
Picasso, Pablo, 1881-1973
About
FitzGerald, M. C. Picasso and American art   709
Leal, B. The ultimate Picasso   759
Penrose, R. Picasso: his life and work   709
Smee, S. The art of rivalry   700.92
Picasso: his life and work. Penrose, R.   709
Pick, Hella
Simon Wiesenthal   940.53
Pickard, Tom
Hole in the wall   821

Pickering, David
(ed) Manser, M. H. The Facts on File dictionary of allusions   422
(ed) Manser, M. H. The Facts on File dictionary of foreign words and phrases   422
(ed) Manser, M. H. The Facts on File dictionary of proverbs   398.9
Pickett, Kate
The spirit level   306
Pickford. Whitfield, E.   92
Pickford, Mary, 1893-1979
About
Whitfield, E. Pickford   92
Picking up. Nagle, R.   331.7
Pickles, pigs & whiskey. Currence, J.   641.59
PICKLING See Canning and preserving
Pickover, Clifford A.
The math book   510
The physics book   530
The **picnic.** Hanel, M.   642
PICNICKING See Picnics
PICNICS
Hanel, M. The picnic   642
PICNICS
See also Dining; Dinners; Luncheons; Outdoor recreation
PICTURE BOOKS -- BIBLIOGRAPHY
Martin, W. P. Wonderfully wordless   011.62
PICTURE BOOKS FOR CHILDREN
Lambert, M. D. Reading picture books with children   372.133
Salisbury, M. Children's Picturebooks   741
Salisbury, M. Illustrating children's books   741.6
Shulevitz, U. Writing with pictures   808.06
PICTURE DICTIONARIES
Adelson-Goldstein, J. The Oxford picture dictionary   423
PICTURE DICTIONARIES
See also Encyclopedias and dictionaries
PICTURE FRAMES AND FRAMING
Kistler, V. C. The complete photo guide to framing & displaying artwork   749
Logan, M. D. Mat, mount and frame it yourself   749
Pictures at a revolution. Harris, M.   791.43
Picturing Frederick Douglass. Stauffer, J.   92
Pie school.   909
Pie: 300 tried-and-true recipes for delicious homemade pie. Haedrich, K.   641.8
Pieces of air in the epic. Hillman, B.   811
Pieces of my mind. Kermode, F.   824
Pielou, E. C.
Fresh water   551.48
Pierce, Deborah
The accessible home   728.087
Pierce, Jessica
(jt. auth) Bekoff, M. Wild justice   591.5

Run, Spot, run 636.08
Piercy, Marge
Colors passing through us 811
So you want to write 808.3
Pierpont, Claudia Roth
Passionate minds 810
Piers Plowman. Langland, W. 821
Pierson, Joy
Vegan holiday cooking from Candle Cafe 641.5
Pierson, Melissa Holbrook
The secret history of kindness 636.7
Pierson, Stephanie
The brisket book 641.3
PIES
Gluten-free & vegan pie 641.3
Harris, M. Magpie 641.86
Kave, A. First prize pies 641.86
A la mode 641.865
McDermott, K. Art of the pie 641.86
Moskowitz, I. C. Vegan pie in the sky 641.5
Pie school 909
PIES
See also Baking; Cooking
Pietrusza, David
1920: the year of the six presidents 973.91
1960: LBJ vs. JFK vs. Nixon 973.92
Pig tales. Estabrook, B. 636.4
The **Pigeon** Tunnel. Le Carré, J. 823
PIGS
Estabrook, B. Pig tales 636.4
Montgomery, S. The good good pig 636.4
PIGS
See also Domestic animals; Mammals
Pigza, Jessica
Bibliocraft 745.5
Piketty, Thomas, 1971-
Capital in the twenty-first century 332
The economics of inequality 339.2
Pilates. Isacowitz, R. 613.7
Pilates for breast cancer survivors. Aaronson, N. 616.99
PILATES METHOD
Aaronson, N. Pilates for breast cancer survivors 616.99
Isacowitz, R. Pilates 613.7
PILATES METHOD
See also Exercise
Pilgrim at Tinker Creek. Dillard, A. 818
Pilgrim's wilderness. 92
Pilgrimage. Shriver, M. 282.092
PILGRIMS (NEW ENGLAND COLONISTS)
Bradford, W. Of Plymouth Plantation, 1620-1647 974.4
Bunker, N. Making haste from Babylon 974.4
Philbrick, N. Mayflower 973.2
Vowell, S. The wordy shipmates 974

PILGRIMS (NEW ENGLAND COLONISTS)
See also Puritans; United States -- History -- 1600-1775, Colonial period
Pilgrims in their own land. Marty, M. E. 277
Pilgrims of the vertical. Taylor, J. E. 796.52
Pilkey, Orrin H., 1934-
The rising sea 363.34
Pillar of fire. Branch, T. 973.922
Pillemer, Karl A.
30 lessons for living 305.26
Pills, power, and policy. Tobbell, D. A. 338.4
Pillsbury best cookies cookbook. Pillsbury Co. 641.8
Pillsbury Co.
Pillsbury best cookies cookbook 641.8
Pim, Keiron
Dinosaurs the grand tour 567.9
PIMPS -- ILLINOIS -- CHICAGO -- BIOGRAPHY
Gifford, J. Street poison 813
Street poison 813
Pimsleur, Julia
Million Dollar Women 658.4
Pin Action. Manzione, G. 794.6
Pinchot, Gifford, 1865-1946
About
Egan, T. The big burn 973.91
Miller, C. Gifford Pinchot and the making of modern environmentalism 333.7
Pincott, J.
Do gentlemen really prefer blondes? 155.3
Pincus, Ed, 1938-2013
(jt. auth) Ascher, S. The filmmaker's handbook 777
Pincus, Gregory, 1903-1967
About
Eig, J. The birth of the pill 618.1
Pindar
The complete odes of Pindar 884
PINE RIDGE INDIAN RESERVATION (S.D.)
Hedges, C. Days of destruction, days of revolt 305.5
Pineda, Jorge
Vegan holiday cooking from Candle Cafe 641.5
Pinfield, Matt
(jt. auth) Cohen, M. All These Things That I've Done 781.66
Ping Fu
Bend, not break 92
Pink brain, blue brain. Eliot, L. 612.6
PINK FLOYD (MUSICAL GROUP)
Povey, G. Echoes: the complete history of Pink Floyd 920
Pink, Daniel H.
Drive 153.1
Pink, Tula
Quilts from the house of Tula Pink 746.46

Tula Pink's city sampler   **746.46**

Pinker, Steven
The better angels of our nature
The blank slate   **155.2**
How the mind works   **153**
The language instinct   **400**
The sense of style   **808**
The stuff of thought   **401**
Words and rules   **401**

Pinkerton, Allan, 1819-1884
      About
Mackay, J. A. Allan Pinkerton   **363.28**

Pinnell-Stephens, June
Protecting intellectual freedom in your public library   **025.2**

Pinsker, Matthew
Lincoln's sanctuary   **92**

Pinsky, Robert
(ed) Americans' favorite poems   **808.81**
(ed) Best of the Best American Poetry   **811**
Democracy, culture, and the voice of poetry   **811**
The figured wheel   **811**
The life of David   **92**
(ed) Poems to read   **808.81**
Singing School   **808.1**
The sounds of poetry   **808.5**

Pinson, Linda
Anatomy of a business plan   **658.4**

Pinter, Harold, 1930-2008
Complete works   **822**
      About
Fraser, A. Must you go?   **92**
Playwrights at work   **812**

Pintxos. Hirigoyen, G.   **641.8**

Pioneer girl.   **92**

PIONEER LIFE *See* Frontier and pioneer life

Pioneer women. Stratton, J. L.   **978.1**

PIONEERS
Brown, D. The indifferent stars above   **92**
Davis, W. C. Three roads to the Alamo   **976.4**
Faragher, J. M. Daniel Boone   **92**
Horwitz, T. Midnight rising   **92**
Means, H. B. Johnny Appleseed   **92**
Milner, C. A. As big as the West   **92**
Morgan, R. Boone   **92**
Sides, H. Blood and thunder   **978**

**PIONEERS -- ALASKA -- MCCARTHY -- BIOG-
RAPHY**
Pilgrim's wilderness   **92**

Piot, Christine
Leal, B. The ultimate Picasso   **759**

The **pious** ones. Berger, J.   **973**

PIPE ORGANS *See* Organs (Musical instruments)

PIPELINES
      See also Hydraulic structures; Transportation

Pipes, Richard

Communism: a history   **335.4**
A concise history of the Russian Revolution   **947.084**
Russia under the Bolshevik regime   **947.084**
The Russian Revolution   **947.08**

Pipher, Mary
Another country   **306.874**
The green boat   **303.4**
The middle of everywhere   **305.9**

PIRACY *See* Pirates

PIRAHÃ INDIANS
Everett, D. L. Don't sleep, there are snakes   **305.8**

The **pirate** coast. Zacks, R.   **973.4**

Pirate hunters. Kurson, R.   **910.91**

PIRATES
Cordingly, D. Under the black flag   **910.4**
Groom, W. Patriotic fire   **973.5**
Konstam, A. The history of pirates   **910.4**
Tinniswood, A. Pirates of Barbary   **909**

PIRATES
      See also Criminals; International law; Maritime law; Naval history

PIRATES -- HISTORY
Kurson, R. Pirate hunters   **910.91**

Pirates of Barbary. Tinniswood, A.   **909**

Pirsig, Robert M., 1928-
      About
Pirsig, R. M. Zen and the art of motorcycle maintenance   **92**

Pisani, Elizabeth
The wisdom of whores   **614.5**

Piscione, Deborah Perry
Secrets of Silicon Valley   **330.9**

Pistol. Kriegel, M.   **92**

Piston, Walter
Harmony   **781.2**
Counterpoint   **781.2**
Orchestration   **784**

Pit bull. Dickey, B.   **636.755**

PIT BULL TERRIERS
Dickey, B. Pit bull   **636.755**

Pitch Perfect. McGowan, B.   **658.452**

Pitching my tent. Diamant, A.   **296.7**

Pitman, Teresa
Sweet sleep   **649**
The womanly art of breastfeeding   **649**

Pitt poetry series
Duhamel, D. Ka-ching!   **811**
Hodgen, J. Heaven & earth holding company   **811**
Kooser, T. Flying at night   **811**
Ostriker, A. No heaven   **811**

PITTSBURGH PIRATES (BASEBALL TEAM)
Sawchik, T. Big data baseball   **796.357**

PITY *See* Sympathy

Pitzer, Andrea
The Secret History of Vladimir Nabokov   **891.73**

Pius XI, Pope, 1857-1939

About
Kertzer, D. I. The Pope and Mussolini 322
Pius XII, Pope, 1876-1958
About
Cornwell, J. Hitler's pope: the secret history of
Pius XII 92
Zuccotti, S. Under his very windows 940.53
Pivnik, Sam
Survivor 940.53
Pivotal moments. Espinoza, R. 371.102
Pivotal moments in American history [series]
Arsenault, R. Freedom riders 323
Fischer, D. H. Washington's crossing 973.3
Kessner, T. The flight of the century 92
West, E. The last Indian war 973.8
PIZZA
Forkish, K. The elements of pizza 641.82
Forkish, K. Flour water salt yeast 641.81
Parachini, C. Roberta's 641.82
PIZZERIA MOZZA
Mozza at home 641.5
**PIZZERIAS -- WASHINGTON (STATE) -- SE-
ATTLE**
Wizenberg, M. Delancey 647.95
Pizzorno, Joseph E.
(jt. auth) Murray, M. T. The encyclopedia of natu-
ral medicine 615.5
Pizzorno, Lara
Your bones 616.7
Pla, Josep, 1897-1981
About
The Gray Notebook 849
PLACES OF WORK *See* Work environment
PLAGIARISM
McKillop, A. B. The spinster & the prophet 941.08
PLAGIARISM
See also Authorship; Offenses against prop-
erty
PLAGUE
Cantor, N. F. In the wake of the plague 614.5
Chase, M. The Barbary plague 362.1
Herlihy, D. The black death and the transformation
of the west 940.1
Kelly, J. The great mortality 614.5
Tuchman, B. W. A distant mirror 944
PLAGUE
See also Communicable diseases; Epidemics
Plagues and peoples. McNeill, W. H. 614.4
Plain secrets. Mackall, J. 289.7
Plain, honest men. Beeman, R. 342
**PLAINS OF ABRAHAM, BATTLE OF THE,
QUÉBEC, 1759**
Macleod, D. P. Northern Armageddon 971.01
Plait, Philip C.
Death from the skies! 520
Plan of attack. Woodward, B. 956.7

Plan your estate. Clifford, D. 346.05
PLANE CRASHES *See* Aircraft accidents
PLANE GEOMETRY
See also Geometry
Planet ape. Morris, D. 599.8
Planet Earth. Fothergill, A. 508
Planet Google. Stross, R. 338.7
A **planet** of viruses. Zimmer, C. 362.196
Planet without apes. Stanford, C. B. 599.88
PLANETARIUMS
See also Astronomy
PLANETARY SATELLITES *See* Satellites
PLANETOIDS *See* Asteroids
The **planets.** 523
PLANETS
Brown, M. How I killed Pluto and why it had it
coming 523.4
Goodstein, D. L. Feynman's lost lecture 521
Ridpath, I. Stars and planets 520
Weintraub, D. A. Is Pluto a planet? 523.4
Whitehouse, D. Into the Heart of Our World 551
PLANETS
See also Astronomy; Solar system
PLANETS -- EXPLORATION
Bell, J. The interstellar age 919
PLANETS -- EXPLORATION
See also Outer space -- Exploration
PLANETS -- SATELLITES *See* Satellites
Planets and possibilities. Miller, S. 133.5
Planisphere. Ashbery, J. 811
Plankton. 578.7
PLANKTON -- PICTORIAL WORKS
Plankton 578.7
PLANNED COMMUNITIES
See also City planning
PLANNED COMMUNITIES -- BRAZIL
Grandin, G. Fordlandia 307.7
PLANNED PARENTHOOD *See* Birth control
PLANNING
Klauser, H. A. Write it down, make it happen 158
PLANNING
See also Creation (Literary, artistic, etc.); Ex-
ecutive ability; Management
PLANNING, LIBRARY
Cohn, J. M. The complete library technology plan-
ner 025
Laughlin, S. The quality library 025.1
PLANNING, NATIONAL *See* Social policy
PLANS *See* Geometrical drawing; Map drawing;
Maps; Mechanical drawing
PLANT BREEDING
Smith, J. S. The garden of invention 92
PLANT BREEDING
See also Agriculture; Breeding; Horticulture
PLANT COLLECTORS
Hansen, E. Orchid fever 635.9

Wulf, A. The brother gardeners **635**

PLANT CONSERVATION

Fortey, R. Horseshoe crabs and velvet worms **595**

PLANT CONSERVATION

See also Conservation of natural resources; Economic botany; Endangered species; Nature conservation

PLANT DISEASES

Deardorff, D. C. What's wrong with my plant (and how do I fix it?) **635**

PLANT DISEASES

See also Agricultural pests; Diseases; Fungi

PLANT ECOLOGY

See also Ecology

The **plant** finder. **635.9**

PLANT GENETICISTS

Pringle, P. The murder of Nikolai Vavilov **92**

Plant power. Atlas, N. **641.5**

PLANT PROPAGATION

Dirr, M. A. The Reference Manual of Woody Plant Propagation **631.5**

PLANT PROPAGATION

See also Fruit culture; Gardening; Nurseries (Horticulture)

PLANT SHUTDOWNS

See also Factories; Unemployment

Plantagenet, House of

About

Gristwood, S. Blood sisters **942.04**

Jones, D. The Plantagenets **942.03**

Jones, D. The Wars of the Roses **942.04**

The **Plantagenets**. Jones, D. **942.03**

PLANTATION LIFE

Baker, J. F. The Washingtons of Wessyngton Plantation **920**

Ball, E. Slaves in the family **975.7**

White, S. The sounds of slavery **326**

PLANTATION LIFE

See also Country life

PLANTATION LIFE -- LOUISIANA -- HISTORY -- 19TH CENTURY

Twelve years a slave **92**

PLANTATION LIFE -- VIRGINIA -- ALBEMARLE COUNTY -- HISTORY

Wiencek, H. Master of the mountain **973.4**

PLANTATION LIFE -- VIRGINIA -- TIDEWATER (REGION) -- HISTORY

Taylor, A. The internal enemy **975.5**

PLANTATION OWNERS

Ball, E. Slaves in the family **975.7**

Broadwater, J. George Mason, forgotten founder **92**

Harris, J. W. The hanging of Thomas Jeremiah **92**

Levy, A. The first emancipator **92**

PLANTATIONS

Grandin, G. Fordlandia **307.7**

Griswold, M. The Manor **974.7**

PLANTATIONS

See also Farms

PLANTATIONS -- GEORGIA -- HISTORY -- 18TH CENTURY

Pressly, P. M. On the rim of the Caribbean **975.8**

The **plantiful** table. Duclos, A. **641.5**

PLANTING *See* Agriculture; Gardening; Landscape gardening; Tree planting

The **plantpower** way. Roll, R. **641.563**

PLANTS

Britton, S. My new roots **641.3**

Goodall, J. Seeds of Hope **580**

The indestructible houseplant **635.9**

PLANTS -- ADAPTATION

Marder, M. The philosopher's plant **580**

PLANTS -- ANATOMY

See also Anatomy; Botany

PLANTS -- COLLECTION AND PRESERVATION

Flora illustrata **016**

PLANTS -- COLLECTION AND PRESERVATION

See also Collectors and collecting

PLANTS -- DISEASES *See* Plant diseases

PLANTS -- ENCYCLOPEDIAS

American Horticultural Society encyclopedia of plants & flowers **635.9**

PLANTS -- FOLKLORE

See also Folklore

PLANTS -- GEOGRAPHICAL DISTRIBUTION

See also Biogeography

PLANTS -- GREAT BRITAIN -- NOMENCLATURE -- DICTIONARIES

Coombes, A. J. The A to Z of plant names **635**

PLANTS -- IDENTIFICATION

Peterson field guide to medicinal plants and herbs of eastern and central North America **581.6**

PLANTS -- NAMES *See* Botany -- Nomenclature; Popular plant names

PLANTS -- NOMENCLATURE *See* Botany -- Nomenclature; Popular plant names

PLANTS -- NORTH AMERICA -- NOMENCLATURE -- DICTIONARIES

Coombes, A. J. The A to Z of plant names **635**

PLANTS -- NUTRITION

See also Nutrition; Plant physiology

PLANTS -- PROPAGATION *See* Plant propagation

PLANTS -- TRAINING -- HANDBOOKS, MANUALS, ETC

Joyce, D. Pruning & training

Plants for dry climates. Duffield, M. R. **635.9**

PLANTS, CULTIVATED *See* Cultivated plants

PLANTS, EDIBLE *See* Edible plants

PLANTS, FOSSIL

Taylor, P. D. A history of life in 100 fossils **560**

PLANTS, USEFUL

Stewart, A. The drunken botanist **581.6**

PLASTER AND PLASTERING

See also Masonry

PLASTER CASTS

See also Sculpture

Plastic. Freinkel, S. **620.1**

Plastic fantastic. Reich, E. S. **92**

PLASTIC MATERIALS *See* Plastics

Plastic ocean. Moore, C. **363.7**

PLASTIC SCRAP -- ENVIRONMENTAL AS-PECTS

Terry, B. Plastic-free **363.738**

PLASTIC SURGERY

Anstett, P. Breast cancer surgery and reconstruction **618.1**

PLASTIC SURGERY

See also Surgery

PLASTIC WASTE -- ENVIRONMENTAL AS-PECTS

Terry, B. Plastic-free **363.738**

Plastic-free. Terry, B. **363.738**

PLASTICS

Freinkel, S. Plastic **620.1**

Moore, C. Plastic ocean **363.7**

PLASTICS CRAFT

See also Handicraft

PLASZÓW (CONCENTRATION CAMP)

My grandfather would have shot me **929.2**

PLATE METALWORK

See also Metalwork; Sheet metalwork

PLATE TECTONICS

Whitehouse, D. Into the Heart of Our World **551**

Plater-Zyberk, Elizabeth

(jt. auth) Duany, A. Suburban nation **307.76**

PLATFORMS, DRILLING *See* Drilling platforms

Plath, Sylvia

Plath, S. Ariel **811**

The collected poems **811**

The unabridged journals of Sylvia Plath, 1950-1962 **818**

About

Heaney, S. Finders keepers **821**

Plath, S. The unabridged journals of Sylvia Plath, 1950-1962 **818**

Vendler, H. H. Coming of age as a poet **820**

Plato. Hare, R. M. **184**

Plato

The collected dialogues of Plato, including the letters **888**

The republic **888**

About

Durant, W. J. The story of philosophy **109**

Hare, R. M. Plato **184**

Russell, B. A history of Western philosophy **109**

Plato. Apology

About

Kreeft, P. Philosophy 101 by Socrates **183**

Platt, Charles

Make **621.381**

Platt, Stacey

What's a disorganized person to do? **648**

Platt, Stephen R.

Autumn in the Heavenly Kingdom **951**

A **platter** of figs and other recipes. Tanis, D. **641.5**

Plaut, David

Cosell, G. The games that changed the game **796.332**

Plautus, Titus Maccius

The pot of gold, and other plays **872**

The rope, and other plays **872**

PLAY

Cohen, L. J. Playful parenting **649**

Conner, B. Unplugged play **790.1**

Elkind, D. The power of play **155.4**

Linn, S. The case for make believe **155.4**

PLAY -- PSYCHOLOGICAL ASPECTS

Ackerman, D. Deep play **155.6**

Play baseball the Ripken way. Ripken, C. **796.357**

The **play** goes on. Simon, N. **812**

PLAY REVIEWS *See* Theater -- Reviews

The **play** that changed my life. **812**

Play their hearts out. Dohrmann, G. **796.323**

PLAY THERAPY

See also Therapeutics

PLAY WRITING *See* Drama -- Technique; Motion picture plays -- Technique; Radio plays -- Technique; Television plays -- Technique

Playful parenting. Cohen, L. J. **649**

Playing big. Mohr, T. **650.1**

Playing off the rail. McCumber, D. **794.7**

Playing the enemy. Carlin, J. **968.06**

Playing to the gallery. Perry, G. **709.05**

PLAYROOMS

Doorley, R. Tinkerlab **600**

PLAYS *See* Drama -- Collections; One act plays

Plays, 1937-1955. Williams, T. **812**

Plays, 1957-1980. Williams, T. **812**

PLAYWRIGHTS *See* Dramatists

Playwrights at work. **812**

PLAYWRITING *See* Drama -- Technique; Motion picture plays -- Technique; Radio plays -- Technique; Television plays -- Technique

Pleasant, Barbara

The complete compost gardening guide **631.8**

The complete houseplant survival manual **635.9**

Starter vegetable gardens **635**

Please Enjoy Your Happiness. Brinkley-Rogers, P. **070.92**

PLEASURE

Balcombe, J. The exultant ark **591.5**

Bloom, P. How pleasure works   **152.4**

PLEASURE

    See also Emotions; Joy and sorrow; Senses and sensation

The **pleasure** of finding things out. Feynman, R. P.   **500**

The **pleasures** and sorrows of work. De Botton, A.   **331**

The **pleasures** of cooking for one. Jones, J.   **641.5**

The **pleasures** of Japanese literature. Keene, D.   **895.6**

The **pleasures** of reading. Ross, C. S.   **028**

The **pleasures** of the damned. Bukowski, C.   **811**

The **pleasures** of the imagination. Brewer, J. **941.07**

Plenty. Ottolenghi, Y.   **647.9**

Plenty more. Ottolenghi, Y.   **641.6**

Pleshakov, Konstantin

    Stalin's folly   **940.54**

    There is no freedom without bread!   **947**

    The Tsar's last armada   **952.03**

Plessy v. Ferguson. Davis, T. J.   **342**

Plessy, Homer Adolph

About

    Davis, T. J. Plessy v. Ferguson   **342**

Plimpton, George

    (ed) Playwrights at work   **812**

    Truman Capote   **813**

About

    George, being George   **92**

Plokhy, S. M.

    Yalta   **940.53**

Plomp, Michiel

    Liedtke, W. A. Vermeer and the Delft school **759.9**

Ploof, John

    (ed) Art and social justice education   **372.5**

The **plot** against Pepys. Long, J.   **941.06**

The **plot** thickens. Lukeman, N.   **808.3**

PLOT-YOUR-OWN STORIES

    Harris, N. P. Neil Patrick Harris   **92**

PLOT-YOUR-OWN STORIES

    See also Children's literature; Fiction; Literary recreations

Plotinus

About

    Russell, B. A history of Western philosophy   **109**

Plotnik, Arthur

    Spunk & bite   **808**

The **plots** against Hitler. Orbach, D.   **940.53**

PLOWS

    See also Agricultural machinery

Plum, Camilla

    The Scandinavian Kitchen   **641.59**

PLUMBING

    Black & Decker Corp. The complete guide to plumbing   **696**

    The complete guide to plumbing   **696**

Henkenius, M. Plumbing: complete projects for the home   **696**

    Ultimate guide to plumbing

PLUMBING

    See also Building

PLUMBING -- AMATEURS' MANUALS

    The complete guide to plumbing   **696**

Plumbing: complete projects for the home. Henkenius, M.   **696**

Plume drama [series]

    Simon, N. Lost in Yonkers   **812**

Plummer, Christopher

About

    Plummer, C. In spite of myself   **92**

PLURALISM (SOCIAL SCIENCES)

    See also Culture

PLURALITY OF WORLDS

    Tegmark, M. Our mathematical universe   **523.1**

Pluriverse. Cardenal, E.   **861**

Plutarch

    Plutarch: the lives of the noble Grecians and Romans   **920**

Plutarch: the lives of the noble Grecians and Romans.   **920**

PLUTO (DWARF PLANET)

    Brown, M. How I killed Pluto and why it had it coming   **523.4**

    Weintraub, D. A. Is Pluto a planet?   **523.4**

PLUTO (DWARF PLANET)

    See also Planets

Plutocrats. Freeland, C.   **305.5**

Plutonium. Bernstein, J.   **546**

PLUTONIUM

    Bernstein, J. Plutonium   **546**

    Brown, K. Plutopia   **363.17**

PLUTONIUM -- HEALTH ASPECTS -- COLORADO

    Iversen, K. Full body burden   **363.17**

PLUTONIUM INDUSTRY -- SOCIAL ASPECTS -- WASHINGTON (STATE) -- RICHLAND -- HISTORY -- 20TH CENTURY

    Brown, K. Plutopia   **363.17**

Plutopia. Brown, K.   **363.17**

PLYWOOD

    See also Wood

PNEUMATICS

    See also Physics

POACHING

    Neme, L. A. Animal investigators   **363.2**

    Orenstein, R. Ivory, horn and blood   **333.95**

    Welch, C. Shell games   **364.1**

Pocahontas, d. 1617

About

    Price, D. Love and hate in Jamestown   **975.5**

POCKET BILLIARDS *See* Pool (Game)

A **pocket** guide to sharks of the world. Ebert, D.

A. **597.3**
POCKETBOOKS (HANDBAGS) *See* Handbags
Pocock, Tom
The terror before Trafalgar **940.2**
PODCASTING
See also Multimedia; Video recordings
Podell, Albert
Around the World in 50 Years **910.4**
Podell, Janet
(ed) Famous first facts, international edition **031.02**
Kane, J. N. Facts about the presidents **920**
Podhajsky, Alois
About
Letts, E. The perfect horse **940.54**
PODIATRY
See also Medicine
Poe. Ackroyd, P. **92**
Poe, Edgar Allan, 1809-1849
Complete poems **811**
Essays and reviews **809**
Poetry and tales **818**
About
Ackroyd, P. Poe **92**
Collins, P. Edgar Allan Poe **92**
Silverman, K. Edgar A. Poe **92**
Sova, D. B. Critical companion to Edgar Allan
Poe **818**
Stashower, D. The beautiful cigar girl **364.152**
Walsh, J. E. Midnight dreary **818**
Poe, Mya
Learning to communicate in science and engineer-
ing **501**
Poehler, Amy, 1971-
Yes please **92**
The **poem** of the Cid. Cid **861**
Poems. Keats, J. **821**
Poems. Shelley, P. B. **821**
Poems. Tennyson, A. T. **821**
Poems. Marvell, A. **821**
Poems. Baudelaire, C. **841**
Poems. Selections./English. **891.7**
Poems. Rimbaud, A. **841**
Poems. Robinson, E. A. **821**
Poems 1959-2009. Seidel, F. **811**
Poems 1960-2000. Adcock, F. **821**
Poems 1962-2012. Glück, L. **811**
Poems and other writings. Longfellow, H. W. **811**
Poems and prose. Hopkins, G. M. **821**
Poems and prose. Donne, J. **821**
Poems and translations. Pound, E. **811**
Poems for the millennium. **808.81**
Poems from the women's movement. **811**
The **poems** of Catullus. Catullus, G. V. **874**
The **poems** of Catullus. Catullus, G. V. **874**
The **poems** of Charles Reznikoff. Reznikoff, C. **811**
The **poems** of Dylan Thomas. Thomas, D. **821**

The **poems** of Emily Dickinson. **811**
The **poems** of Herman Melville. Melville, H. **811**
Poems of Jerusalem; and, Love poems. Amichai,
Y. **892**
The **poems** of Marianne Moore. Moore, M. **811**
The **poems** of Octavio Paz. Paz, O. **861**
Poems of Paul Celan. Celan, P. **831**
The **poems** of Phillis Wheatley. **811**
Poems seven. Dugan, A. **811**
Poems the size of photographs. Murray, L. A. **821**
Poems to read. **808.81**
Poems, 1955-2005. Stevenson, A. **821**
Poems, 1968-1998. Muldoon, P. **821**
Poems, new and collected, 1957-1997. Szymborska,
W. **891.8**
Poems, prose, and letters. Bishop, E. **818**
The **poet** and the murderer. Worrall, S. **364.15**
Poet in New York. Garcia Lorca, F. **861**
Poet's choice. Hirsch, E. **809.1**
The **poet's** companion. Addonizio, K. **808.1**
A **Poet's** Glossary. Hirsch, E. **808.1**
Poetical works [series]
Garcia Lorca, F. Collected poems **861**
POETICS
Abrams, M. H. The fourth dimension of a
poem **808.1**
Addonizio, K. The poet's companion **808.1**
Classic writings on poetry **809.1**
Hirsch, E. How to read a poem **808.1**
Kooser, T. The poetry home repair manual **808.1**
Oliver, M. A poetry handbook **808.1**
Poetry in person **809.1**
Till I end my song **808.81**
POETICS
See also Poetry
POETICS -- DICTIONARIES
Deutsch, B. Poetry handbook: a dictionary of
terms **808.1**
The Princeton encyclopedia of poetry and poet-
ics **808.1**
POETRY
Gizzi, P. In defense of nothing **811**
Graham, J. From the New World **811**
Howe, F. Second childhood **811**
Jones, S. Prelude to bruise **811**
Komunyakaa, Y. Warhorses **811**
Orr, D. Beautiful & pointless **809.1**
Pinsky, R. Singing School **808.1**
Pinsky, R. Democracy, culture, and the voice of po-
etry **811**
Pinsky, R. The sounds of poetry **808.5**
The Poetry of Derek Walcott 1948-2013 **811**
POETRY
See also Literature
POETRY -- AUTHORSHIP
Poetry in person **809.1**

Rich, A. Arts of the possible **811**
Spontaneous mind **811**
POETRY -- COLLECTIONS
The 20th Century in Poetry **808.81**
Berry, W. New collected poems **811**
The best American poetry **811**
Best of the Best American Poetry **811**
Bidart, F. Metaphysical dog **811**
Boland, E. A woman without a country **821**
Cloud, A. Sylph **811**
The collected poems of Eugenio Montale 1925-1977 **851**
The complete poems **811**
Conoley, G. Peace **811**
Cronk, L. Having been an accomplice **811**
Fay-LeBlanc, G. Death of a ventriloquist **811**
Ferry, D. Bewilderment **811**
Ford, K. Blood lyrics **811**
Gay, R. Catalog of Unabashed Gratitude **811.6**
Gilbert, J. Collected poems **811**
Giovanni, N. Chasing Utopia **811**
Gizzi, P. Archeophonics **811.54**
Glück, L. Poems 1962-2012 **811**
Greenbaum, J. The two Yvonnes **811**
Hacker, M. A stranger's mirror **811**
Halaby, L. My name on his tongue **811**
Hall, D. The selected poems of Donald Hall **811.54**
Hillman, B. Seasonal works with letters on fire **811**
Hirshfield, J. The beauty **811**
Hong, C. P. Engine empire **811**
Hopler, J. The Abridged History of Rainfall **811.6**
The Hungry Ear **811**
I am the beggar of the world **891**
Kaur, R. Milk and honey **811.6**
Koertge, R. The ogre's wife **811**
Limon, A. Bright dead things **811**
May, J. Hum **811**
McLane, M. N. This Blue **811**
Mead, J. World of made and unmade **811.54**
Merwin, W. S. Selected translations 1948-2010 **808.81**
Moten, F. The Feel Trio **811**
Nadelberg, A. Bright brave phenomena **811**
The Oxford book of war poetry **808.81**
Paz, O. The poems of Octavio Paz **861**
Phillips, P. Elegy for a broken machine **811**
Powell, D. A. Useless landscape **811**
Rasmussen, M. Black aperture **811**
Rekdal, P. Animal eye **811**
Schutt, W. Westerly **811**
Sendak, M. My brother's book **811**
Sharif, S. Look **811.6**
Simic, C. The Lunatic **811**
Simic, C. New and selected poems 1962-2012 **811**
Sinclair, S. Cannibal **811.6**
Sze, A. Compass Rose **811**

Then come back **861**
Wilson, R. V. Farther traveler **818**
Young, K. Blue laws **811.54**
Zapruder, M. Come on all you ghosts **811**
POETRY -- DICTIONARIES
The Princeton encyclopedia of poetry and poetics **808.1**
POETRY -- HISTORY AND CRITICISM
Abrams, M. H. The fourth dimension of a poem **808.1**
Hirsch, E. A Poet's Glossary **808.1**
Hirshfield, J. Ten windows **808.1**
McLane, M. N. My poets **811**
POETRY -- HISTORY AND CRITICISM -- 20TH CENTURY
The 20th Century in Poetry **808.81**
POETRY -- INDEXES
The Columbia Granger's index to poetry in anthologies **808.81**
The Columbia Granger's Index to poetry in collected and selected works **808.81**
POETRY -- INFLUENCE
McLane, M. N. My poets **811**
POETRY -- MARKETING
2009 poet's market **808.1**
POETRY -- MEMORIZING
See also Mnemonics
POETRY -- TERMINOLOGY
Deutsch, B. Poetry handbook: a dictionary of terms **808.1**
POETRY -- TRANSLATIONS INTO ENGLISH
Poems to read **808.81**
Selected translations 1948-2010 **808.81**
POETRY -- WOMEN AUTHORS -- COLLECTIONS
I am the beggar of the world **891**
Poetry 180. **811**
Poetry and tales. Poe, E. A. **818**
The **Poetry** anthology, 1912-2002. **811**
A **poetry** handbook. Oliver, M. **808.1**
Poetry handbook: a dictionary of terms. Deutsch, B. **808.1**
The **poetry** home repair manual. Kooser, T. **808.1**
Poetry in person. **809.1**
The **Poetry** of Arab women. **892.7**
The **Poetry** of Derek Walcott 1948-2013. **811**
The **Poetry** of our world. **808.81**
The **poetry** of Pablo Neruda. Neruda, P. **861**
Poetry pléiade [series]
Davie, D. Collected poems **821**
Poetry speaks expanded. **811**
POETS
Achebe, C. The education of a British-protected child **92**
Achebe, C. Home and exile **823**
Ackroyd, P. Chaucer **92**

Ackroyd, P. Poe 92

Adams, M. B. Shaggy muses 920

Adler, W. M. The man who never died 92

Alexander, C. The war that killed Achilles 883

Alice Walker 813

Alice Walker's The color purple 813

Amis, M. Experience 92

Angelou, M. Letter to my daughter 92

Angelou, M. I know why the caged bird sings 92

Angelou, M. A song flung up to heaven 818

Angier, C. The double bond: Primo Levi, a biography 92

Archibald MacLeish: reflections 92

Armstrong, J. Love, life, Goethe 92

Baraka, I. A. The LeRoi Jones/Amiri Baraka reader 818

Bate, J. John Clare: a biography 92

Bate, J. Soul of the age 822.3

Beasley, S. Don't kill the birthday girl 92

Benfey, C. E. G. A summer of hummingbirds 920

Bentley, G. E. The stranger from paradise: a biography of William Blake 821

Binyon, T. J. Pushkin: a biography 92

Biss, E. Notes from no man's land 305.8

Black women writers (1950-1980) 810

Blanco, R. The Prince of Los Cocuyos 92

Blight, D. W. American oracle 973.7

Bloom, H. Hamlet: poem unlimited 822.3

Bloom, H. Shakespeare: the invention of the human 822.3

Bloom, H. The Western canon 809

Boyce, C. Critical companion to William Shakespeare 822.3

Boyd, B. Vladimir Nabokov: the American years 813

Boyd, B. Vladimir Nabokov: the Russian years 813

Bradford, R. Lucky him: the life of Kingsley Amis 92

Brainard, J. The Nancy book 759

Brodsky, J. Less than one 809.1

Brown, C. Chance and circumstance 92

Bryson, B. Shakespeare 822.3

Butler, C. The practical Shakespeare 822.3

Callow, P. From noon to starry night: a life of Walt Whitman 811

Campbell, G. John Milton 92

Cliff, N. The Shakespeare riots 974.4

Cohen, R. The avengers 940.53

Collins, P. The book of William 822.3

Crane, H. Complete poems and selected letters 811

Crawford, R. The bard 92

DeGategno, P. J. Critical companion to Jonathan Swift 828

Dillard, A. The writing life 818

Dillard, A. An American childhood 92

Doty, M. Dog years 92

Eisler, B. Byron--child of passion, fool of fame 92

Elie, P. The life you save may be your own 810

Elledge, S. E. B. White 92

Ellmann, R. Oscar Wilde 92

Erdrich, L. Books and islands in Ojibwe country 92

Existentialism from Dostoevsky to Sartre 142

Fagan, D. Critical companion to Robert Frost 811

Fargnoli, A. N. Critical companion to James Joyce 823

Feinstein, A. Pablo Neruda 92

Feinstein, E. Anna of all the Russias 92

Feinstein, E. Ted Hughes 821

Flanders, J. A circle of sisters 920

Flynn, N. Another bullshit night in Suck City 92

Fraser, K. Ornament and silence 809

Frye, N. Northrop Frye on Shakespeare 822.3

Fuegi, J. Brecht and company 92

Garber, M. Shakespeare after all 822.3

Garber, M. Shakespeare and modern culture 822.3

Garvey, M. Stylized 808

Gaskell, E. C. The life of Charlotte Bronte 92

Geoffrey Chaucer's The Canterbury tales 821

Gibson, I. Federico Garcia Lorca: a life 92

Gillespie, C. Critical companion to Alice Walker 813

Gillespie, M. A. Maya Angelou 92

Gilmour, D. The long recessional: the imperial life of Rudyard Kipling 92

Gioia, D. Can poetry matter? 809.1

Gordon, C. Mistress Bradstreet 92

Gordon, L. G. The world of Samuel Beckett, 1906-1946 848

Gordon, L. Charlotte Bronte 92

Gordon, L. Lives like loaded guns 92

Greenblatt, S. J. Will in the world 822.3

Greenblatt, S. The swerve 940.2

The Greenwood companion to Shakespeare 822.3

Guest, B. The collected poems of Barbara Guest 811

Heaney, S. Finders keepers 821

Hertog, S. Anne Morrow Lindbergh 92

Heylin, C. So long as men can breathe 822.3

Hirst, M. Michelangelo 709.2

Hoffman, A. My happiness bears no relation to happiness 92

Hogan, L. The woman who watches over the world 818

Hooks, B. Belonging 92

Hooks, B. Wounds of passion 92

Jarrell, R. No other book 809

Johnston, K. R. The hidden Wordsworth 821

Kafka, d. J. d. E. Kafka, the decisive years 92

Kazin, A. An American procession 810

Kenji Yoshino A thousand times more fair 822.3

Kenner, H. The Pound era 811

Kermode, F. An appetite for poetry 801

Kermode, F. Shakespeare's language **822.3**

Kiberd, D. Ulysses and us **823**

Kumin, M. The Pawnbroker's Daughter **92**

Lamb, C. Tales from Shakespeare **822.3**

Langer, L. L. Admitting the Holocaust **940.53**

Leader, Z. The life of Kingsley Amis **92**

Lee, H. Virginia Woolf's nose **820**

Leibowitz, H. A. Something urgent I have to say to you: the life and works of William Carlos Williams **92**

Leiter, S. Critical companion to Emily Dickinson **811**

Levi, P. The periodic table **92**

Life stories **920**

Lindbergh, R. Under a wing **92**

Lowell, R. Collected poems **811**

Lycett, A. Dylan Thomas: a new life **92**

Lynn, K. S. Hemingway **92**

Malcolm, J. Two lives **92**

Mandelstam, N. Hope against hope **891.71**

Manguel, A. Homer's The Iliad and The Odyssey **883**

Manguso, S. The two kinds of decay **362**

Mariani, P. L. Lost puritan: a life of Robert Lowell **811**

Marshall, P. Triangular road **92**

Matthiessen, F. O. American renaissance **810**

Mayes, F. Under the Tuscan sun **945**

McLane, M. N. My poets **811**

Meade, M. Dorothy Parker **92**

Merton, T. The seven storey mountain **92**

Merton, T. Intimate Merton **271**

Milford, N. Savage beauty: the life of Edna St. Vincent Millay **92**

Milosz, C. Legends of modernity **891.8**

Milosz, C. To begin where I am **891.8**

Monette, P. Borrowed time **362.1**

Morgan, B. I celebrate myself **92**

Motion, A. Keats **821**

Murphy, R. E. Critical companion to T.S. Eliot **811**

Murray, A. The blue devils of Nada **780.89**

Murray, N. Kafka **92**

Nabokov, V. V. Lectures on literature **808.3**

Nabokov, V. V. Speak, memory **813**

Neruda, P. The poetry of Pablo Neruda **861**

Night wraps the sky **92**

Norris, K. Acedia & me **92**

Norwich, J. J. Shakespeare's kings **822.3**

Oates, J. C. A widow's story **92**

Oates, J. C. The journal of Joyce Carol Oates: 1973-1982 **92**

O'Brien, E. James Joyce **823**

O'Driscoll, D. Stepping stones **821**

Oliver, C. M. Critical companion to Ernest Hemingway **813**

Oliver, C. M. Critical companion to Walt Whitman **811**

The Oxford companion to Chaucer **821**

The Oxford companion to Shakespeare **822.3**

Parini, J. The art of teaching **371.1**

Parker, D. M. Ogden Nash **92**

Patchett, A. Truth & beauty **92**

Pearson, R. Voltaire almighty **92**

Pierpont, C. R. Passionate minds **810**

Pinsky, R. Singing School **808.1**

Plath, S. The unabridged journals of Sylvia Plath, 1950-1962 **818**

Playwrights at work **812**

Pomfret, J. Chinese lessons **951.05**

Pritchard, W. H. Updike **813**

Rasmussen, E. The Shakespeare thefts **822.3**

Remnick, D. Reporting **814**

The Renaissance philosophy of man **189**

Reynolds, M. S. Hemingway: the Paris years **92**

Richardson, R. D. Emerson **814**

Ricketts, H. Rudyard Kipling **92**

Rodriguez, R. Hunger of memory **92**

Roper, R. Now the drum of war **973.7**

Rosenbaum, R. The Shakespeare wars **822.3**

Ross, D. A. Critical companion to William Butler Yeats **821**

Rossignol, R. Critical companion to Chaucer **821**

Rostand, E. Cyrano de Bergerac **842**

Ruud, J. Critical companion to Dante **850**

Samuel Beckett's Waiting for Godot **842**

Sawyer-Laucanno, C. E.E. Cummings **92**

Seth, V. Two lives **92**

Shakespeare, W. The complete works **822.3**

Shapiro, J. Contested Will **822.3**

Shapiro, J. A year in the life of William Shakespeare, 1599 **822.3**

Silverman, K. Begin again **92**

Silverman, K. Edgar A. Poe **92**

Sklenicka, C. Raymond Carver **92**

Sova, D. B. Critical companion to Edgar Allan Poe **818**

Soyinka, W. You must set forth at dawn **92**

Spontaneous mind **811**

Stashower, D. The beautiful cigar girl **364.152**

Stein, G. The autobiography of Alice B. Toklas **92**

Stoppard, T. The invention of love **822**

Stoppard, T. Rosencrantz and Guildenstern are dead **822**

Sutherland, J. Stephen Spender **92**

Thursby, J. S. Critical companion to Maya Angelou **818**

Tolstaia, T. Pushkin's children **891.7**

Tomalin, C. Thomas Hardy **92**

Tuck, L. Woman of Rome: a life of Elsa Morante **92**

Tytell, J. Ezra Pound **92**

Ulrich, L. Well-behaved women seldom make history   **305.4**

Urrutia, M. My life with Pablo Neruda   **92**

Vendler, H. H. Coming of age as a poet   **820**

Volkov, S. St. Petersburg   **947**

Walker, A. The same river twice   **813**

Walker-Hill, H. From spirituals to symphonies **780**

Walsh, J. E. Midnight dreary   **818**

Wayne, T. K. Critical companion to Ralph Waldo Emerson   **818**

Wells, S. W. Shakespeare: for all time   **822.3**

West, R. Chaucer, 1340-1400   **821**

White, E. B. Letters of E.B. White   **92**

Williamson, E. Borges, a life   **92**

Wills, G. Verdi's Shakespeare   **822.3**

Wilson, A. N. Betjeman   **92**

Wilson, E. Patriotic gore   **810**

Wilson, F. The ballad of Dorothy Wordsworth   **92**

Winters, K. C. Anne Morrow Lindbergh   **92**

Worthen, J. D.H. Lawrence   **92**

Worthen, J. D.H. Lawrence, the early years, 1885-1912   **92**

Wranovics, J. Chaplin and Agee   **92**

Zimmermann, W. First great triumph   **973**

POETS

   See also Authors

POETS -- KOREA (NORTH) -- BIOGRAPHY

Jang Jin-sung Dear Leader   **92**

POETS -- PSYCHOLOGY

Smith, T. K. Ordinary light   **92**

POETS LAUREATE

Blight, D. W. American oracle   **973.7**

Bloom, H. The Western canon   **809**

Feinstein, E. Ted Hughes   **821**

Gioia, D. Can poetry matter?   **809.1**

Heaney, S. Finders keepers   **821**

Johnston, K. R. The hidden Wordsworth   **821**

Wilson, A. N. Betjeman   **92**

Wilson, F. The ballad of Dorothy Wordsworth   **92**

The **poets** laureate anthology.   **811**

Poets of the Civil War.   **811**

Poets of World War II.   **811**

POETS, AMERICAN

Berrigan, T. Dear Sandy, hello   **92**

Ginsberg, A. The letters of Allen Ginsberg   **92**

Gordon, L. Lives like loaded guns   **92**

Hughes, L. I wonder as I wander   **818**

Karr, M. Lit   **92**

Middlebrook, D. W. Anne Sexton   **811**

Molesworth, C. Marianne Moore   **92**

O'Rourke, M. The long goodbye   **92**

Poetry in person   **809.1**

Rampersad, A. The life of Langston Hughes Volume I: 1902-1941   **92**

Rampersad, A. The life of Langston Hughes Volume II: 1941-1967   **818**

Schultz, P. My dyslexia   **92**

Smith, P. Just kids   **92**

POETS, AMERICAN *See* American poets

POETS, AMERICAN -- 20TH CENTURY -- BIOGRAPHY

Crawford, R. Young Eliot   **92**

Gordon, L. T.S. Eliot   **92**

Hammer, L. James Merrill   **92**

Mariani, P. L. The broken tower: a life of Hart Crane   **811**

Parini, J. Robert Frost   **811**

POETS, AMERICAN -- DICTIONARIES

Contemporary poets   **821**

Encyclopedia of American poetry, the twentieth century   **811**

POETS, CANADIAN -- 20TH CENTURY -- INTERVIEWS

Leonard Cohen on Leonard Cohen   **92**

POETS, ENGLISH

Gigante, D. The Keats brothers   **920**

Hawkes, D. John Milton   **92**

Motion, A. Keats   **821**

POETS, ENGLISH -- 19TH CENTURY -- BIOGRAPHY

Johnston, K. R. The hidden Wordsworth   **821**

Motion, A. Keats   **821**

POETS, ENGLISH -- BIOGRAPHY

Schmidt, M. Lives of the poets   **821**

POETS, ENGLISH -- DICTIONARIES

Contemporary poets   **821**

POETS, IRISH

Brown, T. The life of W.B. Yeats   **821**

Foster, R. F. W.B. Yeats: a life   **821**

POETS, ITALIAN -- 20TH CENTURY -- BIOGRAPHY

Hughes-Hallett, L. Gabriele d'Annunzio   **858**

Pogrebin, Letty Cottin

How to be a friend to a friend who's sick   **610**

Pogue's basics. Pogue, D.   **004**

Pogue, David

Pogue's basics   **004**

Poinar, George O.

The quest for life in amber   **560**

Poinar, Roberta

Poinar, G. O. The quest for life in amber   **560**

Poincare's prize. Szpiro, G. G.   **510**

Poincaré, Henri, 1854-1912

    About

Bell, E. T. Men of mathematics   **920**

Galison, P. L. Einstein's clocks and Poincare's maps   **529**

Szpiro, G. G. Poincare's prize   **510**

The **point** of vanishing. Axelrod, H.   **92**

Point to point navigation. Vidal, G.   **92**

Points unknown.   **910**

POISON IVY

   See also Poisonous plants

The **Poison** King. Mayor, A.   **92**

Poison spring. Jenkins, M.   **363.73**

Poisoned legacy. Magner, M.   **338.7**

The **poisoner's** handbook. Blum, D.   **614**

POISONING

    Blum, D. The poisoner's handbook   **614**

POISONING -- ENGLAND -- CASE STUDIES

    Colquhoun, K. Did she kill him?   **364.152**

POISONING -- GREAT BRITAIN -- HISTORY
    -- 19TH CENTURY

    Hempel, S. The inheritor's powder   **364.152**

Poisoning the press. Feldstein, M.   **973.924**

POISONOUS ANIMALS

    Campbell, J. The venomous reptiles of the Western
    Hemisphere   **597.96**

    Ernst, C. H. Venomous reptiles of the United States,
    Canada, and northern Mexico   **597.9**

    O'Shea, M. Venomous snakes of the world **597.96**

    Schmidt, J. O. The sting of the wild   **595.7**

    Wilcox, C. Venomous   **572**

POISONOUS ANIMALS

    See also Animals; Dangerous animals; Eco-
    nomic zoology; Poisons and poisoning

POISONOUS ARTHROPODA

    Schmidt, J. O. The sting of the wild   **595.7**

POISONOUS GASES

    See also Gases; Poisons and poisoning

POISONOUS GASES -- WAR USE *See* Chemical
    warfare

POISONOUS PLANTS

    Turner, N. J. The North American guide to com-
    mon poisonous plants and mushrooms   **581.6**

POISONOUS PLANTS

    See also Economic botany; Plants; Poisons
    and poisoning

POISONOUS SNAKES -- NORTH AMERICA

    Ernst, C. H. Venomous reptiles of the United States,
    Canada, and northern Mexico   **597.9**

POISONOUS SUBSTANCES *See* Poisons and poi-
    soning

POISONS AND POISONING

    Blum, D. The poisoner's handbook   **614**

    Hempel, S. The inheritor's powder   **364.152**

POISONS AND POISONING

    See also Accidents; Hazardous substances;
    Homicide; Medical jurisprudence

Poitier, Sidney

    About

    Goudsouzian, A. Sidney Poitier   **92**

    Poitier, S. The measure of a man   **92**

POKER

    McManus, J. Cowboys full   **795.4**

    McManus, J. Positively Fifth Street   **795.4**

POKER

    See also Card games

Pol Pot

    About

    Brinkley, J. Cambodia's curse   **959.6**

The **Pol** Pot regime. Kiernan, B.   **959.6**

POLAND -- HISTORY -- 1918-1945

    Kurtz, G. Three minutes in Poland   **947.7**

**POLAND -- HISTORY -- OCCUPATION, 1939-
1945**

    Karski, J. Story of a secret state   **940.53**

POLAND -- POLITICS AND GOVERNMENT

    Pleshakov, K. There is no freedom without
    bread!   **947**

Polanka, Sue

    (ed) No shelf required   **025.17**

    (ed) No shelf required 2   **070.5**

POLAR BEAR

    Ellis, R. On thin ice   **599.78**

POLAR EXPEDITIONS *See* Antarctica -- Explo-
    ration; Arctic regions -- Exploration; Scientific
    expeditions

POLAR REGIONS

    The ends of the earth   **998**

**POLAR REGIONS -- DISCOVERY AND EX-
    PLORATION**

    Wilkinson, A. The ice balloon   **910.91**

POLAR REGIONS -- EXPLORATION

    Wilkinson, A. The ice balloon   **910.91**

POLAR REGIONS -- PICTORIAL WORKS

    Seaman, C. Melting away   **910.91**

**POLARIZATION (SOCIAL SCIENCES) --
    UNITED STATES**

    Edwards, M. The parties versus the people   **320**

    Smith, H. Who stole the American dream? **973.91**

Polenberg, Richard

    Hear my sad story   **782.42**

POLICE

    Queen, W. Under and alone   **364.1**

POLICE

    See also Administration of criminal justice;
    Law enforcement

POLICE -- COMPLAINTS AGAINST *See* Police
    brutality; Police corruption

POLICE -- CORRUPT PRACTICES *See* Police
    corruption

POLICE -- NEW YORK (N.Y.)

    Conway, J. N. The big policeman   **92**

    Dickey, C. Securing the city   **363.32**

    Levitt, L. NYPD confidential   **364.1**

    Osborne, S. The job   **92**

POLICE -- NEW YORK -- BIOGRAPHY

    Osborne, S. The job   **92**

POLICE BRUTALITY

    Conroy, J. Unspeakable acts, ordinary people **323.4**

    Hendrickson, P. Sons of Mississippi   **305.8**

    Lehr, D. The fence   **364.1**

POLICE BRUTALITY

    See also Police

POLICE CORRUPTION
Lehr, D. The fence   **364.1**
Levitt, L. NYPD confidential   **364.1**
POLICE CORRUPTION
   See also Misconduct in office; Police
POLICE CORRUPTION -- CALIFORNIA
Crooks, P. The setup   **363.28**
POLICE OFFICIALS
Conway, J. N. The big policeman   **92**
Dickey, C. Securing the city   **363.32**
POLIOMYELITIS
Kluger, J. Splendid solution: Jonas Salk and the conquest of polio   **92**
POLIOMYELITIS
   See also Diseases
POLIOMYELITIS -- UNITED STATES -- HISTORY
Jacobs, C. D. Jonas Salk   **92**
Jonas Salk   **92**
POLISH LITERATURE
Milosz, C. Legends of modernity   **891.8**
POLITENESS *See* Courtesy; Etiquette
Politi, Marco
Pope Francis among the wolves   **282**
POLITICAL ACTIVISTS
Biddle, D. R. Tasting freedom   **92**
Cambanis, T. Once upon a revolution   **962.05**
Kreisler, H. Political awakenings   **920**
Lewis, A. B. The shadows of youth   **323.1**
Liu, X. June fourth elegies   **811**
Martin, B. Hanging man   **709**
Mitchell, G. The tunnels   **943.155**
Potter, W. Green is the new red   **320.5**
POLITICAL ACTIVISTS -- COLOMBIA -- BIOGRAPHY
Abad, H. Oblivion   **868**
POLITICAL ACTIVISTS -- CRIMES AGAINST
Abad, H. Oblivion   **868**
POLITICAL ACTIVISTS -- EGYPT -- BIOGRAPHY
Cambanis, T. Once upon a revolution   **962.05**
POLITICAL ACTIVISTS -- GERMANY (WEST) -- BIOGRAPHY
Mitchell, G. The tunnels   **943.155**
POLITICAL ACTIVISTS -- UNITED STATES -- HISTORY
Hoxie, F. E. This Indian country   **323.1**
POLITICAL AND SOCIAL PHILOSOPHERS
Camus, A. The rebel   **303.6**
Collins, P. The trouble with Tom: the strange afterlife and times of Thomas Paine   **92**
Cranston, M. Jean-Jacques: the early life and work of Jean-Jacques Rousseau, 1712-1754   **92**
Cranston, M. The solitary self: Jean-Jacques Rousseau in exile and adversity   **92**
Damrosch, L. Jean-Jacques Rousseau   **848**

Gabriel, M. Love and capital   **92**
Heilbroner, R. L. The worldly philosophers   **330.1**
Hollis, L. London rising   **942**
Hunt, T. Marx's general   **92**
Macey, D. Frantz Fanon   **92**
Milosz, C. To begin where I am   **891.8**
Pierpont, C. R. Passionate minds   **810**
Rousseau Confessions   **92**
Russell, B. A history of Western philosophy   **109**
Strathern, P. The artist, the philosopher, and the warrior   **920**
Viroli, M. Niccolo's smile: a biography of Machiavelli   **92**
Wheen, F. Karl Marx   **335.4**
POLITICAL ASYLUM *See* Asylum
POLITICAL ATROCITIES -- CAMBODIA
Bizot, F. The gate   **959.604**
Him, C. When broken glass floats   **959.604**
Ung, L. First they killed my father   **959.6**
Political awakenings. Kreisler, H.   **920**
POLITICAL BALLADS AND SONGS
Lynskey, D. 33 revolutions per minute   **782.42**
POLITICAL CAMPAIGNS -- UNITED STATES -- HISTORY
Balz, D. J. The battle for America, 2008   **973.932**
Roberts, R. N. Campaigning for president in America, 1788-2016   **324.709**
POLITICAL CAMPAIGNS -- UNITED STATES -- HISTORY -- 21ST CENTURY
Halperin, M. Double Down   **324.9**
Johnston, D. C. The making of Donald Trump   **973.932**
POLITICAL COMMENTATORS
Goodwin, D. K. Wait till next year   **796.357**
Rosenblatt, R. Making toast   **92**
Schorr, D. Staying tuned   **070**
POLITICAL CONSULTANTS
Schoen, D. E. The power of the vote   **324**
POLITICAL CONSULTANTS -- UNITED STATES -- BIOGRAPHY
Greenberg, D. Republic of spin   **973.099**
POLITICAL CORRUPTION
Allman, T. D. Finding Florida   **975.9**
Boo, K. Behind the beautiful forevers   **305.5**
Brackett, E. Pay to play   **92**
Chandrasekaran, R. Imperial life in the emerald city   **956.704**
Chayes, S. Thieves of state   **364.1**
Denton, S. The money and the power   **979.3**
Great lives from history: Notorious lives   **920.003**
Jenkins, M. Poison spring   **363.73**
Kaiser, R. G. So damn much money   **328**
Khalil, A. Liberation Square   **962.05**
Lauterbach, P. Beale Street Dynasty   **976.8**
Morris, R. Fraud of the century   **324.9**
Pomerantsev, P. Nothing is true and everything is

possible 306
Posner, G. God's Bankers 364.16
Taibbi, M. Griftopia 973.932
POLITICAL CORRUPTION
    See also Conflict of interests; Political crimes
    and offenses; Political ethics; Politics
POLITICAL CORRUPTION -- CASE STUDIES
Chayes, S. Thieves of state 364.1
**POLITICAL CORRUPTION -- PRESS COVER-
    AGE -- CALIFORNIA**
Drabelle, D. The great American railroad war 385
**POLITICAL CORRUPTION -- RUSSIA (FED-
    ERATION)**
Dawisha, K. Putin's kleptocracy 947.086
POLITICAL CRIMES AND OFFENSES
Hakkakiyan, R. Assassins of the Turquoise Pal-
    ace 364.152
Medvedev, R. A. Let history judge 947.084
POLITICAL CRIMES AND OFFENSES
    See also Criminal law; Political ethics; Sub-
    versive activities
**POLITICAL CULTURE -- CALIFORNIA -- SAN
    FRANCISCO -- HISTORY -- 20TH CENTU-
    RY**
Talbot, D. Season of the witch 306
**POLITICAL CULTURE -- EUROPE, EASTERN
    -- HISTORY -- 20TH CENTURY**
Applebaum, A. Iron curtain 947
POLITICAL CULTURE -- KOREA (NORTH)
Hassig, R. C. The hidden people of North Ko-
    rea 951.93
**POLITICAL CULTURE -- RUSSIA (FEDERA-
    TION) -- CHELIABINSK**
Garrels, A. Putin country 947.43
**POLITICAL CULTURE -- SAN FRANCISCO
    (CALIF.)**
Talbot, D. Season of the witch 306
**POLITICAL CULTURE -- SOVIET UNION --
    HISTORY**
Kotkin, S. Stalin 92
POLITICAL CULTURE -- UNITED STATES
Bishop, B. The big sort 305.8
Maddow, R. Drift 306.2
Sehat, D. The Jefferson rule 306.2
Shorris, E. The politics of heaven 973.93
Sirota, D. Back to our future 973.92
Walker, J. The United States of paranoia 973
**POLITICAL CULTURE -- UNITED STATES --
    HISTORY -- 19TH CENTURY**
Larson, E. J. A magnificent catastrophe 324
Millard, C. The destiny of the republic 973.8
**POLITICAL CULTURE -- UNITED STATES --
    HISTORY -- 20TH CENTURY**
Feldstein, M. Poisoning the press 973.924
Katznelson, I. Fear itself 973.917
Kruse, K. M. One nation under God 322

Olson, L. Those angry days 940.53
Smith, H. Who stole the American dream? 973.91
Tirella, J. Tomorrow-land 607
**POLITICAL CULTURE -- UNITED STATES --
    HISTORY -- 21ST CENTURY**
Feingold, R. While America sleeps 327
Smith, H. Who stole the American dream? 973.91
POLITICAL CULTURE -- WASHINGTON (D.C.)
Feldstein, M. Poisoning the press 973.924
**POLITICAL CULTURE -- WASHINGTON (D.C.)
    -- HISTORY -- 20TH CENTURY**
Herken, G. The Georgetown set 975.3
POLITICAL DEFECTORS *See* Defectors
POLITICAL ECONOMY *See* Economics
POLITICAL ETHICS
Gormley, K. The death of American virtue 973.929
Kaplan, R. D. Warrior politics 320
Machiavelli, N. The prince 320.1
POLITICAL ETHICS
    See also Ethics; Political science; Politics;
    Social ethics
POLITICAL EXTREMISM *See* Radicalism
POLITICAL FICTION
    See also Fiction
POLITICAL GEOGRAPHY *See* Boundaries;
    Geopolitics
POLITICAL LEADERS
Amis, M. Koba the dread 947.084
Baraka, I. A. The LeRoi Jones/Amiri Baraka read-
    er 818
Berthon, S. Warlords 940.53
Bhutto, B. Reconciliation 92
Blair, T. A journey 92
Brent, J. Inside the Stalin archives 947.086
Brent, J. Stalin's last crime 947.084
Brinkley, J. Cambodia's curse 959.6
Brookhiser, R. America's first dynasty 973.4
Bstan-'dzin-rgya-mtsho, D. L. X. Freedom in ex-
    ile 92
Buruma, I. Murder in Amsterdam 364.152
Carlin, J. Playing the enemy 968.06
Carlson, P. K blows top 947.085
Chadha, Y. Gandhi 954.03
Chang, J. Mao: the unknown story 92
Conquest, R. Stalin 92
Cooper, W. J. Jefferson Davis, American 92
Costigliola, F. Roosevelt's lost alliances 940.53
David, A. Once upon a country 92
Davis, W. C. An honorable defeat 973.7
Dikötter, F. Mao's great famine 951.05
Dobbs, M. One minute to midnight 973.922
Duiker, W. J. Ho Chi Minh 959.704
Duke, L. Mandela, Mobutu, and me 968.06
Finan, C. M. Alfred E. Smith, the happy warrior 92
Gandhi, M. An autobiography 92
Gevisser, M. A legacy of liberation 92

Gordin, M. D. Red cloud at dawn **355**

Guelzo, A. C. Lincoln and Douglas **973.6**

Hibbert, C. The House of Medici **920**

Hochschild, A. The unquiet ghost **947.084**

Hofstadter, R. The American political tradition, and the men who made it **973**

In his own words **92**

Iyer, P. The open road **92**

Johnson, T. Tragedy in crimson **294.3**

Kazin, M. A godly hero **92**

Kennedy, J. F. Profiles in courage **920**

Kissinger, H. Diplomacy **327.2**

Leamer, L. The Kennedy men **920**

Lelyveld, J. Great soul **92**

Mandela, N. Conversations with myself **92**

Mandela, N. Long walk to freedom: the autobiography of Nelson Mandela **92**

Mandela, N. Mandela **968.06**

Medvedev, R. A. Let history judge **947.084**

Mohandas Gandhi **92**

Montefiore, S. Stalin: the court of the red tsar **92**

Montefiore, S. Young Stalin **92**

Morris, R. Fraud of the century **324.9**

Nikita Khrushchev **92**

Parks, T. Medici money **332.1**

Pipes, R. Russia under the Bolshevik regime **947.084**

Pleshakov, K. Stalin's folly **940.54**

Pomper, P. Lenin's brother **92**

Pringle, P. The murder of Nikolai Vavilov **92**

Radzinsky, E. Stalin **92**

Remnick, D. Reporting **814**

Sampson, A. Nelson Mandela **92**

Service, R. Trotsky **92**

Service, R. Lenin--a biography **947.084**

Service, R. Stalin **92**

Shalom, friend: the life and legacy of Yitzhak Rabin **92**

Short, P. Mao **951.05**

Smith, D. J. Young Mandela **92**

Snyder, T. D. Bloodlands **940.54**

Spence, J. D. Mao Zedong **951.05**

Strathern, P. Death in Florence **945**

Sun Shuyun The Long March **951.04**

Taubman, W. Khrushchev **92**

Thomas, E. The war lovers **973.8**

Thurman, R. A. F. Why the Dalai Lama matters **294.3**

Volkogonov, D. A. Lenin **947.084**

Von Tunzelmann, A. Red heat **972.9**

West, R. Tito **949.7**

Wilson, E. Patriotic gore **810**

Wintle, J. Perfect hostage **92**

Wolpert, S. A. Gandhi's passion **954.03**

POLITICAL LEADERSHIP -- UNITED STATES -- CASE STUDIES

Clarke, T. JFK's last hundred days **92**

POLITICAL LEADERSHIP -- UNITED STATES -- HISTORY -- 20TH CENTURY

Mann, J. The rebellion of Ronald Reagan **973.927**

Winik, J. 1944 **940.53**

Political Order and Political Decay. Fukuyama, F. **320.1**

POLITICAL PARTICIPATION

See also Politics

POLITICAL PARTIES

Wilentz, S. The Politicians and the Egalitarians **306.2**

POLITICAL PARTIES

See also Political science; Politics

POLITICAL PARTIES -- UNITED STATES

Edwards, M. The parties versus the people **320**

POLITICAL PARTIES -- UNITED STATES -- HISTORY -- 20TH CENTURY

Lofgren, M. The party is over **324.273**

POLITICAL PARTIES -- UNITED STATES -- HISTORY -- 21ST CENTURY

Lofgren, M. The party is over **324.273**

POLITICAL PARTY LEADERS

Cohen, A. American pharaoh: Mayor Richard J. Daley: his battle for Chicago and the nation **977.3**

POLITICAL PERSECUTION -- EUROPE, EASTERN -- HISTORY -- 20TH CENTURY

Applebaum, A. Iron curtain **947**

POLITICAL PHILOSOPHY

Norman, J. Edmund Burke **92**

The politics book **320.01**

Ryan, A. On politics **320.01**

Sehat, D. The Jefferson rule **306.2**

Sherratt, Y. Hitler's philosophers **193**

POLITICAL PHILOSOPHY

See also Philosophy; Political science

POLITICAL POETRY

See also Poetry

POLITICAL PRISONERS

Carlin, J. Playing the enemy **968.06**

Cheng, N. Life and death in Shanghai **92**

Duke, L. Mandela, Mobutu, and me **968.06**

Esfandiari, H. My prison, my home **92**

In his own words **92**

Jones, B. Mandela **92**

Mandela, N. Conversations with myself **92**

Mandela, N. Long walk to freedom: the autobiography of Nelson Mandela **92**

Mandela, N. Mandela **968.06**

Marton, K. Enemies of the people **92**

Milosz, C. To begin where I am **891.8**

Nemat, M. Prisoner of Tehran **92**

Remnick, D. Reporting **814**

Sampson, A. Nelson Mandela **92**

Smith, D. J. Young Mandela **92**

Solzhenitsyn, A. The Gulag Archipelago, 1918-

1956 v1 **365**

Solzhenitsyn, A. The Gulag Archipelago, 1918-1956 v2 **365**

Solzhenitsyn, A. The Gulag Archipelago, 1918-1956 v3 **365**

Timerman, J. Prisoner without a name, cell without a number **92**

Tolstaia, T. Pushkin's children **891.7**

Wintle, J. Perfect hostage **92**

POLITICAL PRISONERS

See also Political crimes and offenses; Prisoners

POLITICAL PRISONERS -- CHINA

Liao Yiwu For a song and one hundred songs **365**

POLITICAL PRISONERS -- CUBA -- GUANTÁNAMO BAY NAVAL BASE

Hickman, J. Murder at Camp Delta **355.1**

POLITICAL PRISONERS -- CUBA -- GUANTÁNAMO BAY NAVAL BASE -- DIARIES

Guantanamo diary **958.104**

POLITICAL PRISONERS -- RUSSIA

Figes, O. Just send me word **365**

POLITICAL PRISONERS -- RUSSIA

Stewart, B. Don't trust, don't fear, don't beg **363.738**

POLITICAL PRISONERS -- RUSSIA (FEDERATION)

Stewart, B. Don't trust, don't fear, don't beg **363.738**

POLITICAL PRISONERS -- RUSSIA (FEDERATION) -- PECHORA (KOMI)

Figes, O. Just send me word **365**

POLITICAL PRISONERS -- SOUTH AFRICA -- BIOGRAPHY

Jones, B. Mandela **92**

POLITICAL PRISONERS -- SOVIET UNION

Draitser, E. Stalin's Romeo spy **92**

Kizny, T. Gulag **365**

POLITICAL PRISONERS -- UNITED STATES -- DIARIES

Guantanamo diary **958.104**

POLITICAL PSYCHOLOGY

Haidt, J. The righteous mind **201**

Hochschild, A. R. Strangers in their own land **320.52**

POLITICAL PSYCHOLOGY

See also Political science; Psychology; Social psychology

POLITICAL QUESTIONS AND JUDICIAL POWER -- UNITED STATES

Breyer, S. G. Making our democracy work **347**

Toobin, J. R. The nine **347**

Tushnet, M. In the balance **347.73**

POLITICAL QUESTIONS AND JUDICIAL POWER -- UNITED STATES -- HISTORY

Shesol, J. Supreme power **347**

Simon, J. F. What kind of nation **342**

POLITICAL QUESTIONS AND JUDICIAL POWER -- UNITED STATES -- HISTORY -- 21ST CENTURY

Coyle, M. The Roberts court **347.73**

Toobin, J. The oath **347.73**

POLITICAL REFUGEES

Ghouri, N. The lightless sky **958.104**

Kenney, D. N. Asylum denied **92**

POLITICAL REFUGEES

See also Asylum; International law; International relations; Refugees

POLITICAL REFUGEES -- CAMBODIA

Him, C. When broken glass floats **959.604**

POLITICAL REFUGEES -- IRAN -- BIOGRAPHY

Andalibian, R. The rose hotel **92**

POLITICAL REFUGEES -- KOREA (NORTH) -- BIOGRAPHY

Jang Jin-sung Dear Leader **92**

POLITICAL REFUGEES -- UNITED STATES

Him, C. When broken glass floats **959.604**

POLITICAL REFUGEES -- UNITED STATES -- BIOGRAPHY

Andalibian, R. The rose hotel **92**

Ping Fu Bend, not break **92**

POLITICAL SATIRE

See also Satire

POLITICAL SCANDALS *See* Political corruption

POLITICAL SCIENCE

Aristotle Politics **320**

Cartledge, P. Democracy **321.8**

Cicero, M. T. The republic; and, The laws **320.1**

Cohen, I. B. Science and the founding fathers **973.3**

Einstein, A. Einstein on politics **92**

The Europa world year book 2014 **310**

Guide to the presidency and the executive branch **352.23**

Himmelfarb, G. The moral imagination **190**

Hobbes, T. Leviathan **320.1**

Judt, T. Thinking the twentieth century **320.092**

Machiavelli, N. The prince **320.1**

Nasr, V. The dispensable nation **327.73**

Paine, T. Rights of man; and, Common sense **320**

Plato The republic **888**

Robinson, M. When I was a child I read books **814**

Rousseau The social contract **320.1**

Ryan, A. On politics **320.01**

The statesman's yearbook **310**

Sunstein, C. R. Simpler **973.932**

Walker, A. The cushion in the road **814**

POLITICAL SCIENCE

See also Social sciences

POLITICAL SCIENCE -- ENCYCLOPEDIAS

Encyclopedia of U.S. political history **973**

POLITICAL SCIENCE -- PHILOSOPHY *See*

Political philosophy

POLITICAL SCIENCE -- PHILOSOPHY -- HISTORY
Ryan, A. On politics   **320.01**

POLITICAL SCIENCE -- POLITICAL PROCESS -- POLITICAL ADVOCACY
Niose, D. Nonbeliever nation   **211**

POLITICAL SCIENCE -- QUOTATIONS
Lend me your ears   **808.88**

POLITICAL SCIENCE -- RELIGIOUS ASPECTS See Religion and politics

POLITICAL SCIENCE -- UNITED STATES -- PHILOSOPHY
Robinson, M. When I was a child I read books **814**

POLITICAL SCIENTISTS
Brownfield, C. J. My nuclear family   **92**
Epstein, J. Alexis De Tocqueville   **92**
Halberstam, D. The best and the brightest **973.922**
Pierpont, C. R. Passionate minds   **810**
Rice, C. Extraordinary, ordinary people   **92**

POLITICAL SCIENTISTS -- GREAT BRITAIN -- BIOGRAPHY
Norman, J. Edmund Burke   **92**

POLITICAL SCIENTISTS -- ITALY -- BIOGRAPHY
Unger, M. J. Machiavelli   **92**
Political speeches. Cicero, M. T.   **875**

POLITICAL THEORY See Political science

POLITICAL VIOLENCE See Sabotage; Terrorism

POLITICAL VIOLENCE -- CONGO (DEMOCRATIC REPUBLIC)
Stearns, J. K. Dancing in the glory of monsters   **967.51**

POLITICAL VIOLENCE -- IRAN -- HISTORY -- 20TH CENTURY
Buchan, J. Days of God   **955.05**

POLITICAL VIOLENCE -- LIBERIA
Dwyer, J. American warlord   **966.62**

POLITICAL VIOLENCE -- SYRIA -- HISTORY -- 21ST CENTURY
Erlich, R. Inside Syria   **956.91**

POLITICIANS
See also Statesmen

POLITICIANS -- HUMOR
Trillin, C. Quite enough of Calvin Trillin   **817**

POLITICIANS -- MASSACHUSETTS -- BIOGRAPHY
Frank, B. Frank   **92**

POLITICIANS -- UNITED STATES
Blumenthal, S. A self-made man   **92**
Frank, B. Frank   **92**
Sanders, B. Outsider in the White House   **92**

POLITICIANS -- UNITED STATES -- ANECDOTES
Galbraith, J. K. Name-dropping   **973.9**

POLITICIANS -- UNITED STATES -- ATTITUDES
Schnall, M. What will it take to make a woman president?   **305.4**

POLITICIANS -- UNITED STATES -- BIOGRAPHY
Ellis, J. J. The Quartet   **973.3**
Nasaw, D. The patriarch   **92**
Packer, G. The unwinding   **973.924**

POLITICIANS -- UNITED STATES -- DICTIONARIES
Jaques Cattell Press Who's who in American politics 2007-2008   **920.003**
The **Politicians** and the Egalitarians. Wilentz, S.   **306.2**

POLITICIANS' SPOUSES -- WASHINGTON (D.C.) -- BIOGRAPHY
Roberts, C. Capital dames   **793.7**

POLITICIANS' WRITINGS
Clarke, P. Mr. Churchill's profession   **941.084**
Warren, E. A fighting chance   **92**
Politics. Aristotle   **320**

POLITICS
Allitt, P. The conservatives   **320.5**
As consciousness is harnessed to flesh   **818**
Einstein, A. Einstein on politics   **92**
Graham, J. From the New World   **811**

POLITICS AND CULTURE -- FRANCE -- HISTORY -- 20TH CENTURY
Carroll, S. B. Brave genius   **920**

POLITICS AND CULTURE -- UNITED STATES
Goldwag, A. The new hate   **306.2**

POLITICS AND CULTURE -- UNITED STATES -- HISTORY
Lepore, J. The mansion of happiness   **973**

POLITICS AND ISLAM See Islam and politics

POLITICS AND LITERATURE -- ITALY -- HISTORY -- 20TH CENTURY
Hughes-Hallett, L. Gabriele d'Annunzio   **858**

POLITICS AND LITERATURE -- SOVIET UNION -- HISTORY
Finn, P. The Zhivago affair   **891.73**

POLITICS AND LITERATURE -- UNITED STATES -- HISTORY -- 20TH CENTURY
Turner, F. Renegade   **813**

POLITICS AND RELIGION See Religion and politics

Politics and society in twentieth-century America [series]
Lichtenstein, N. State of the Union: a century of American labor   **331**
The **politics** book.   **320.01**

POLITICS IN LITERATURE
Said, E. W. Reflections on exile and other essays   **814**
The **politics** of heaven. Shorris, E.   **973.93**

The **politics** of upheaval, 1935-1936. Schlesinger, A. M.   **973.917**

POLITICS, PRACTICAL *See* Politics

POLITICS, PRACTICAL -- UNITED STATES
Carville, J. It's the middle class, stupid!   **320.51**

Politkovskaya, Anna
A Russian diary   **947.086**

Polito, Robert
(ed) Fearing, K. Selected poems   **811**

Polk. Borneman, W. R.   **92**

Polk, James K. (James Knox), 1795-1849
About
Borneman, W. R. Polk   **92**
Merry, R. W. A country of vast designs   **92**

Polk, William Roe
Understanding Iraq   **956.7**

Pollack, H. N.
A world without ice   **551.3**

Pollack, Howard
George Gershwin   **92**

Pollack, John
Shortcut   **808**

Pollack, Kenneth M.
Unthinkable   **355.8**

Pollack, Robert
The missing moment   **610**

Pollan, Michael, 1955-
The botany of desire   **306.4**
Cooked   **641.5**
In defense of food   **613**
The omnivore's dilemma   **394.1**

POLLEN AS FOOD
See also Food

Pollinger, Ben
School of fish   **641.6**

Pollitt, Katha, 1949-
Pro   **363.46**

Pollock, Jackson, 1912-1956
About
Adams, H. Tom and Jack   **92**
Smee, S. The art of rivalry   **700.92**
Solomon, D. Jackson Pollock   **92**

POLLSMOOR PRISON (SOUTH AFRICA) -- ANECDOTES
Jones, B. Mandela   **92**

POLLUTION
Blackwell, A. Visit sunny Chernobyl   **363.73**
Fagin, D. Toms River   **363.72**
Gates, A. E. Encyclopedia of pollution   **363.7**
Harden, B. A river lost   **333.91**
Humes, E. Garbology   **628.4**
Jensen, D. What we leave behind   **304.2**
Lerner, S. Sacrifice zones   **363.738**
Monosson, E. Unnatural selection   **576.5**
Terry, B. Plastic-free   **363.738**

POLLUTION
See also Environmental health; Human influence on nature; Public health; Sanitary engineering; Sanitation

POLLUTION -- ENCYCLOPEDIAS
Gates, A. E. Encyclopedia of pollution   **363.7**

POLLUTION -- MATHEMATICAL MODELS
See also Mathematical models

POLLUTION -- RESEARCH -- UNITED STATES
Jenkins, M. Poison spring   **363.73**

POLLUTION -- UNITED STATES -- CASE STUDIES
Lerner, S. Sacrifice zones   **363.738**

POLLUTION CONTROL INDUSTRY
See also Industries

POLLUTION OF AIR *See* Air pollution

POLLUTION OF WATER *See* Water pollution

Polo, Marco, 1254-1323?
About
Belliveau, D. In the footsteps of Marco Polo   **915**
Bergreen, L. Marco Polo   **92**
Polo, M. The travels of Marco Polo   **915**

Polonsky, Rachel
Molotov's magic lantern   **947**

POLTERGEISTS *See* Ghosts

POLYGAMY
Brower, S. Prophet's prey   **306.8**
Sheff, E. Stories from the Polycule   **306.84**
Wariner, R. The sound of gravel   **92**

POLYGAMY
See also Marriage

POLYGLOT DICTIONARIES
See also Encyclopedias and dictionaries

POLYMER CLAY CRAFT
See also Handicraft

The **polymer** clay techniques book. Heaser, S.   **745.572**

POLYTHEISM
See also Religion; Theism

Pomerantsev, Peter
Nothing is true and everything is possible   **306**

Pomes all sizes. Kerouac, J.   **811**

Pomfret, John
Chinese lessons   **951.05**

Pompadour, Jeanne Antoinette Poisson, marquise de, 1721-1764
About
Lever, E. Madame de Pompadour   **944**

POMPEII (EXTINCT CITY)
Beard, M. The fires of Vesuvius   **937**
Berry, J. The complete Pompeii   **937**
Pellegrino, C. R. Ghosts of Vesuvius   **937**

Pomper, Philip
Lenin's brother   **92**

Pomponazzi, Pietro, 1462-1525
About
The Renaissance philosophy of man   **189**

Poncelet, Jean Victor, 1788-1867
About
Bell, E. T. Men of mathematics   **920**
POND ECOLOGY
See also Ecology
Pond, Jonathan D.
Grow your money!   **332.024**
PONDS
Matson, T. Earth ponds   **627**
PONDS
See also Water
PONIES
See also Horses
Pontecorvo, Gillo
About
Said, E. W. Reflections on exile and other essays   **814**
PONTIAC'S CONSPIRACY, 1763-1765
See also Native Americans -- Wars; United States -- History -- 1600-1775, Colonial period
PONZI SCHEMES
Konnikova, M. The Confidence Game   **364.163**
PONZI SCHEMES -- ILLINOIS -- CHICAGO -- HISTORY -- 20TH CENTURY
Jobb, D. Empire of deception   **92**
PONZI SCHEMES -- NEW YORK (STATE) -- NEW YORK -- HISTORY -- 19TH CENTURY
Ward, G. C. A disposition to be rich   **974.7**
Ponzi's scheme. Zuckoff, M.   **364**
Ponzi, Charles, d. 1949
About
Zuckoff, M. Ponzi's scheme   **364**
POOL (GAME)
Byrne, R. Byrne's new standard book of pool and billiards   **794.7**
McCumber, D. Playing off the rail   **794.7**
POOL (GAME)
See also Billiards
POOL PLAYERS
McCumber, D. Playing off the rail   **794.7**
Pool, Robert
(jt. auth) Ericsson, A. Peak   **153.9**
Poole, Robert M.
Section 60   **975.5**
Poole, W. Scott
Vampira   **92**
Pooley, Eric
The climate war   **363.7**
POOR
Grande, R. The distance between us   **92**
Vollmann, W. T. Poor people   **362.5**
POOR
See also Poverty; Public welfare
POOR -- FRANCE -- PARIS -- HISTORY
Sante, L. The other Paris   **944**
POOR -- MEDICAL CARE

See also Medical care
POOR -- MEXICO CITY (MEXICO)
Lewis, O. The children of Sanchez   **972.08**
POOR -- NEW YORK (N.Y.)
Kozol, J. Amazing grace   **362.7**
LeBlanc, A. N. Random family   **305.5**
POOR -- SOCIAL CONDITIONS
Tough, P. Whatever it takes   **362.7**
POOR -- UNITED STATES
Hedges, C. Days of destruction, days of revolt   **305.5**
Kozol, J. Fire in the ashes   **362.7**
Tirado, L. Hand to mouth   **362.5**
Tough, P. How children succeed   **372.21**
POOR CHILDREN -- UNITED STATES
Kozol, J. Fire in the ashes   **362.7**
Poor economics. Banerjee, A. V.   **339.4**
POOR FAMILIES -- UNITED STATES
Kozol, J. Fire in the ashes   **362.7**
Poor people. Vollmann, W. T.   **362.5**
POOR YOUTH -- EDUCATION, HIGHER -- NEW YORK (STATE)
Chertavian, G. A Year Up   **331.25**
POOR YOUTH -- EMPLOYMENT -- NEW YORK (STATE)
Chertavian, G. A Year Up   **331.25**
POOR YOUTH -- VOCATIONAL EDUCATION -- NEW YORK (STATE)
Chertavian, G. A Year Up   **331.25**
Pop. Scherman, T.   **92**
Pop art. Livingstone, M.   **709.04**
POP ART
See also Art
POP ART
Livingstone, M. Pop art   **709.04**
Scherman, T. Pop   **92**
POP CULTURE *See* Popular culture
Pop goes the library. Brookover, S.   **021.2**
POP MUSIC *See* Popular music
POP MUSICIANS
Cole, N. Angel on my shoulder   **92**
Feather, L. From Satchmo to Miles   **920**
Pop, Iggy, 1947-
About
Trynka, P. Iggy Pop   **92**
The **Pope** and Mussolini. Kertzer, D. I.   **322**
Pope Francis. Vallely, P.   **92**
Pope Francis among the wolves.   **282**
The **Pope's** Last Crusade. Eisner, P.   **940.53**
Pope, Alexander
Selected poetry   **821**
Pope, Alice
(ed) Children's writer's & illustrator's market   **808**
Pope, Hugh
Dining with al-Qaeda   **956.05**
POPES

Brown, N. M. The abacus and the cross   92
Buttiglione, R. Karol Wojtyla   282
Cornwell, J. Hitler's pope: the secret history of
  Pius XII   92
Flynn, R. John Paul II   92
Francis, P. The church of mercy   282
Hofstadter, D. The Earth moves   509
Maxwell-Stuart, P. G. Chronicle of the popes   282
McBrien, R. P. Lives of the popes   920
O'Connor, G. Universal Father: a life of John Paul
  II   92
Tuchman, B. W. The march of folly   909.08
Zuccotti, S. Under his very windows   940.53
POPES
  See also Church history
POPES -- BIOGRAPHY
Shriver, M. Pilgrimage   282.092
POPES -- DICTIONARIES
Kelly, J. N. D.   The Oxford dictionary of
  Popes   920.003
POPES -- TEMPORAL POWER
  See also Church history
The **Popes** against the Jews. Kertzer, D. I. 261.2
Popkin, Richard Henry
  (ed) The Columbia history of Western philoso-
  phy   190
Popkin, Samuel L.
  The candidate   324.9
Popoff, Alexandra
  The wives   891.7
Popol vuh. Popol vuh   299.7
Popol vuh
  Popol vuh   299.7
Popper, Karl Raimund Sir, 1902-1994
                  About
Edmonds, D. Wittgenstein's poker   192
Pops. Teachout, T.   92
POPULAR ARTS *See* Popular culture
Popular authors series
  Drew, B. A.   100 most popular nonfiction au-
  thors   920.003
Popular crime. James, B.   364.1
POPULAR CULTURE
  Angell, R. This old man   92
  Capella, M. Barbie   688.722
  Christgau, R. Going Into the City   92
  Hamid, M. Discontent and its civilizations 814
  Lepore, J. The mansion of happiness   973
  Nunberg, G. The ascent of the A-word   427
  Savage, J. 1966   781.66
  The World Almanac and Book of Facts 2015   030
POPULAR CULTURE
  See also Communication; Culture; Intellec-
    tual life; Recreation
POPULAR CULTURE -- 21ST CENTURY
  Mendelsohn, D. Waiting for the barbarians   801

POPULAR CULTURE -- FRANCE
  Riding, A. And the show went on   944
**POPULAR CULTURE -- POLITICAL ASPECTS
  -- UNITED STATES**
  Carpini, M. X. D. After broadcast news   071
  Kunhardt, P. B. Looking for Lincoln   92
POPULAR CULTURE -- UNITED STATES
  Austen, J. Darkest America   791
  Boorstin, D. J. The image   973.9
  Cross, C. R. Here we are now   92
  Ingrassia, P. Engines of change   629.222
  Klosterman, C. But What If We're Wrong? 909.83
  Lamarche, U. Unabrow   92
  Matos, M. The underground is massive   781.648
  Mendelsohn, D. Waiting for the barbarians   801
  Poole, W. S. Vampira   92
  Romano, C. America the philosophical   191
  Turner, F. Renegade   813
**POPULAR CULTURE -- UNITED STATES --
  ENCYCLOPEDIAS**
  St. James encyclopedia of popular culture 973.9
**POPULAR CULTURE -- UNITED STATES --
  HISTORY**
  Beam, A. A great idea at the time   973.91
  Burr, T. Gods like us   306.4
  Lepore, J. The mansion of happiness   973
**POPULAR CULTURE -- UNITED STATES --
  HISTORY -- 19TH CENTURY**
  Gallagher, G. W. The union war   973.7
**POPULAR CULTURE -- UNITED STATES --
  HISTORY -- 20TH CENTURY**
  Beam, A. A great idea at the time   973.91
  Boorstin, D. J. The image   973.9
  Dickstein, M. Dancing in the dark   973.91
  Mackrell, J. Flappers   920
**POPULAR CULTURE -- UNITED STATES --
  MISCELLANEA**
  Lamarche, U. Unabrow   92
POPULAR GOVERNMENT *See* Democracy
**POPULAR LITERATURE -- STORIES, PLOTS,
  ETC**
  Herald, D. T. Genreflecting   016
POPULAR LITERATURE.
  Ross, C. S. Reading matters   028
Popular mechanics complete home how-to. Jack-
  son, A.   643
Popular mechanics magazine.
  The wonderful future that never was   609
POPULAR MEDICINE
  The Human body   612
  Myers, A. The autoimmune solution   616.97
  Parker, S. Kill or cure   610
POPULAR MEDICINE
  See also Medicine
POPULAR MUSIC
  Bradley, A. House of hits   781.64

Broven, J. Record makers and breakers   **781.64**

Crumb, R. R. Crumb: the complete record cover collection   **741.6**

Hermes, W. Love goes to buildings on fire   **781.64**

Houghton, M. Becoming Elektra   **781.64**

Roden, S. . . . i listen to the wind that obliterates my traces   **781.64**

POPULAR MUSIC

See also Music; Songs

POPULAR MUSIC -- 20TH CENTURY

Lynskey, D. 33 revolutions per minute   **782.42**

POPULAR MUSIC -- 21ST CENTURY

Lynskey, D. 33 revolutions per minute   **782.42**

POPULAR MUSIC -- BIO-BIBLIOGRAPHY

Friedwald, W. A biographical guide to the great jazz and pop singers   **920.003**

POPULAR MUSIC -- DICTIONARIES

Friedwald, W. A biographical guide to the great jazz and pop singers   **920.003**

POPULAR MUSIC -- ECONOMIC ASPECTS -- UNITED STATES

Greenburg, Z. O. Michael Jackson, Inc   **92**

POPULAR MUSIC -- HISTORY AND CRITICISM

Moody, R. On celestial music   **780.9**

Stanley, B. Yeah! Yeah! Yeah!   **781.64**

POPULAR MUSIC -- PRODUCTION AND DIRECTION

Seabrook, J. The song machine   **781.64**

Zen and the art of recording   **621.389**

POPULAR MUSIC -- TEXTS *See* Popular song lyrics

POPULAR MUSIC -- WRITING AND PUBLISHING

See also Composition (Music)

POPULAR MUSIC -- WRITING AND PUBLISHING -- UNITED STATES

Feinstein, M. The Gershwins and me   **92**

POPULAR PLANT NAMES

Coombes, A. J. The A to Z of plant names   **635**

Wells, D. 100 flowers and how they got their names   **582.13**

POPULAR PLANT NAMES

See also Plants

Popular psychology. Cordon, L. A.   **150**

POPULAR SONG LYRICS

Smith, P. Patti Smith Collected Lyrics, 1970-2015   **782.42**

Sondheim, S. Look, I made a hat   **782.1**

POPULATION

Kotler, S. Abundance   **303.48**

New Concise World Atlas   **912**

Weisman, A. Countdown   **304.2**

POPULATION

See also Economics; Human ecology; Sociology; Vital statistics

POPULATION -- STATISTICS

The CIA World Factbook   **028**

POPULATION BIOLOGY

See also Biology

POPULATION ECOLOGY

Weisman, A. Countdown   **304.2**

POPULATION EXPLOSION *See* Overpopulation

PORCELAIN

See also Decorative arts; Pottery; Tableware

PORCELAIN -- HISTORY

De Waal, E. The white road   **738.209**

PORCELAIN -- MARKS

Kovel, R. M. Kovels' dictionary of marks: pottery and porcelain   **738**

Kovel, R. M. Kovels' new dictionary of marks   **738**

PORCHES

Cory, S. Ultimate guide: porches   **690**

Port, Elisa

The new generation breast cancer book   **616.99**

Port, Michael

Steal the show   **658.4**

The **Portable** beat reader.   **810**

The **portable** Chekhov. Chekhov, A. P.   **891.7**

PORTABLE COMPUTERS

See also Computers

The **portable** Dante. Dante Alighieri   **851**

The **portable** Dorothy Parker. Parker, D.   **818**

The **Portable** Harlem Renaissance reader.   **810**

The **portable** Jung. Jung, C. G.   **150.19**

The **portable** Nietzsche. Nietzsche, F. W.   **193**

The **Portable** Roman reader.   **870**

The **Portable** sixties reader.   **810**

The **portable** Voltaire. Voltaire   **848**

The **Portable** Western reader.   **810**

Porter, Cecelia Hopkins

Five lives in music   **780.92**

Porter, Cole, 1891-1964

Selected lyrics   **782.42**

About

McBrien, W. Cole Porter   **92**

Porter, Joy

(ed) The Cambridge companion to Native American literature   **897**

Porter, Linda

Katherine the queen   **92**

Porter, Margaret Pratt

(ed) Inside the Pentagon papers   **959.704**

Porter, Roy

(ed) The Cambridge illustrated history of medicine   **610**

(ed) Oxford dictionary of scientific quotations   **500**

The greatest benefit to mankind   **610**

Madness   **616.89**

PORTLAND (ME.)

Christensen, K. How to cook a moose   **641.597**

PORTLAND (OR.)

Gartland, A. Heartlandia **641.597**

Portman, Janet
Every tenant's legal guide **346.04**
Stewart, M. Every landlord's legal guide **346.04**

Porto, Anthony
The pediatrician's guide to feeding babies and toddlers **618.92**

Portrait and dream. Berkson, B. **811**

A **portrait** of Jesus. Girzone, J. F. **232.9**

PORTRAIT PAINTING
O'Connor The lady in gold **759.36**

PORTRAIT PAINTING
See also Painting; Portraits

PORTRAIT PAINTING -- ATTRIBUTION
Cumming, L. The Vanishing Velazquez **759.6**

PORTRAIT PHOTOGRAPHY
All about Eve **770**
Carter, G. Vanity Fair, the portraits **779**
Cartier-Bresson, H. The Decisive Moment **770**
Casey, M. Che's afterlife **980**
Leibovitz, A. Annie Leibovitz at work **779**
Leibovitz, A. A photographer's life, 1990-2005 **779**
McCartney, L. Life in photographs **779**
National Geographic Society (U.S.) In focus **779**
Panzer, M. Mathew Brady and the image of history **770.92**
Stanton, B. Humans of New York: stories **974.7**

PORTRAIT PHOTOGRAPHY
See also Photography; Portraits

PORTRAITS
See also Art; Biography; Pictures

Portraits and observations. Capote, T. **814**

PORTRAITS, RENAISSANCE -- ITALY -- EXHIBITIONS
The Renaissance portrait **704.9**

PORTRAITURE *See* Portrait painting; Portrait photography

PORTUGAL -- COLONIES -- HISTORY -- 16TH CENTURY
Crowley, R. Conquerors **909**

PORTUGUESE COOKING
Anderson, J. The food of Portugal **641.5**
Leite, D. The new Portuguese table **641.5**

PORTUGUESE LITERATURE
See also Literature; Romance literature

Posamentier, Alfred S.
(jt. auth) Lehmann, I. The secrets of triangles **516**
Magnificent mistakes in mathematics **510**
(jt. auth) Thaller, B. Numbers **513.5**

POSITIVE PSYCHOLOGY
Pierson, M. H. The secret history of kindness **636.7**

Positively Fifth Street. McManus, J. **795.4**

POSITIVISM
See also Philosophy; Rationalism

Posnanski, Joe
The soul of baseball **796.357**

Posner, Barry Z.
Kouzes, J. M. The truth about leadership **658.4**

Posner, Gerald
Case closed **973.922**
God's Bankers **364.16**

Posner, Jessica
Find Me Unafraid **92**

The **possessed.** Batuman, E. **891.7**

Post, Anna
Emily Post's wedding etiquette **395.2**
(jt. auth) Post, P. Emily Post's etiquette **395**
(jt. auth) Post, P. Emily Post's The etiquette advantage in business **395**

Post, Lizzie
Emily Post's wedding etiquette **395.2**
(jt. auth) Post, P. Emily Post's etiquette **395**
(jt. auth) Post, P. Emily Post's The etiquette advantage in business **395**

Post, Peggy
Emily Post's etiquette **395**
Emily Post's The etiquette advantage in business **395**

Post, Peter
(jt. auth) Post, P. Emily Post's The etiquette advantage in business **395**

POST-APARTHEID ERA -- SOUTH AFRICA
Burge, K. The born frees **305.242**

POST-COMMUNISM -- RUSSIA (FEDERATION)
Aleksievich, S. Secondhand time **947.086**
Meier, A. Black earth **947.086**

POST-MODERNISM *See* Postmodernism

POST-TRAUMATIC STRESS DISORDER
Castner, B. The long walk **956.704**
McClelland, M. Irritable hearts **92**
Shroder, T. Acid test **615.7**

POST-TRAUMATIC STRESS DISORDER
See also Anxiety; Neuroses; Stress (Psychology)

POST-TRAUMATIC STRESS DISORDER -- PATIENTS -- BIOGRAPHY
Leaming, B. Jacqueline Bouvier Kennedy Onassis **92**

POST-TRAUMATIC STRESS DISORDER -- PATIENTS -- UNITED STATES -- BIOGRAPHY
McClelland, M. Irritable hearts **92**
Morris, D. J. The evil hours **616.85**
Shroder, T. Acid test **615.7**

POST-TRAUMATIC STRESS DISORDER -- TREATMENT
Shroder, T. Acid test **615.7**
Van der Kolk, B. A. The body keeps the score **616.85**

POST-TRAUMATIC STRESS DISORDER -- UNITED STATES
Dreazen, Y. The invisible front **92**

Finkel, D. Thank You for Your Service **362.86**

Morris, D. J. The evil hours **616.85**

POSTAL DELIVERY CODE *See* Zip code

POSTAL SERVICE

   See also Communication; Transportation

POSTAL SERVICE -- GREAT BRITAIN

   Tingey, J. The Englishman who posted himself and
other curious objects **92**

POSTAL SERVICE -- UNITED STATES -- HISTORY

   Gallagher, W. How the Post Office Created America **383.49**

Postcards from Tomorrow Square. Fallows, J.
M. **951.05**

POSTCOLONIALISM

   See also Political science

The **poster.** **741.6**

POSTERS

   Hayes, C. Gig posters volume 1 **741.6**

   The poster **741.6**

POSTERS

   See also Advertising; Commercial art

POSTIMPRESSIONISM (ART)

   See also Art

Postma, Johannes

   The Atlantic slave trade **306.3**

Postman, Neil

   Amusing ourselves to death **302.23**

   The end of education **370.9**

Postmodern American poetry. **811**

POSTMODERNISM

   Ferry, L. A brief history of thought **100**

   Larson, K. Where the heart beats **700.1**

   Postmodern American poetry **811**

POSTMODERNISM

   See also Aesthetics

POSTMODERNISM (LITERATURE) -- UNITED STATES

   Postmodern American poetry **811**

Postmus, Judy L.

   (ed) Sexual violence and abuse **364.15**

POSTPARTUM DEPRESSION

   See also Depression (Psychology)

POSTTRAUMATIC STRESS DISORDER *See*
Post-traumatic stress disorder

POSTURE

   Rybczynski, W. Now I sit me down **749.32**

POSTURE

   See also Physical fitness

Postwar. Judt, T. **940.55**

Postwar America. **973.92**

POSTWAR RECONSTRUCTION

   Sky, E. The Unraveling **956.7**

   Van Buren, P. We meant well

POT (DRUG) *See* Marijuana

The **pot** of gold, and other plays. Plautus, T. M. **872**

POTABLE WATER *See* Drinking water

POTATO CHIPS

   Burhans, D. E. Crunch! **338.4**

POTATOES

   Pollan, M. The botany of desire **306.4**

POTATOES

   See also Vegetables

POTPOURRI

   See also Herbs; Nature craft; Perfumes

Potsdam. Neiberg, M. **940.53**

The **potter's** bible. **738**

The **potter's** studio handbook. Muller, K. **738.1**

Potter, Beatrix, 1866-1943

   About

   Lear, L. J. Beatrix Potter **92**

Potter, Daniel A.

   What to do when you can't get pregnant **618.1**

Potter, Deborah

   Wenger, D. H. Advancing the story **070.1**

Potter, Maximillian

   Shadows in the vineyard **364.16**

Potter, Will

   Green is the new red **320.5**

POTTERS

   See also Artists

POTTERY

   Muller, K. The potter's studio handbook **738.1**

   Nelson, G. C. Ceramics: a potter's handbook **738.1**

   The potter's bible **738**

POTTERY

   See also Ceramics; Clay industry; Decoration
and ornament; Decorative arts; Tableware

POTTERY -- MARKS

   Kovel, R. M. Kovels' dictionary of marks: pottery
and porcelain **738**

   Kovel, R. M. Kovels' new dictionary of marks **738**

POTTERY CRAFT

   Burnett, J. B. Graphic clay **738.1**

Potts, Joanna

   Berthon, S. Warlords **940.53**

POTTSTOWN (PA.) -- BIOGRAPHY

   Harding, S. Last to die **940.54**

Pough, Frederick H.

   A field guide to rocks and minerals **549**

Pouillon, Nora

   About

   Pouillon, N. My organic life **92**

Poulter, Ian

   No Limits **920**

POULTRY

   Rude, E. Tastes Like Chicken **636.5**

POULTRY

   See also Birds; Domestic animals

The **Pound** era. Kenner, H. **811**

Pound, Ezra, 1885-1972

   The cantos of Ezra Pound **811**

Poems and translations **811**
About
Kazin, A. An American procession **810**
Kenner, H. The Pound era **811**
Tytell, J. Ezra Pound **92**
Pound, Roscoe, 1870-1964
About
Commager, H. S. The American mind **973**
Poundstone, William
Carl Sagan **92**
Pourny, Christophe
The furniture bible **684.1**
POVERTY
Banerjee, A. V. Poor economics **339.4**
Boo, K. Behind the beautiful forevers **305.5**
Ehrenreich, B. Nickel and dimed **305.5**
Faleiro, S. Beautiful thing **792.7**
The great divergence **339.2**
Martínez, R. Desert America **330.9**
McMillan, T. The American way of eating **338.4**
Milanović, B. The haves and the have-nots **339.2**
Sante, L. The other Paris **944**
Tough, P. Whatever it takes **362.7**
Vollmann, W. T. Poor people **362.5**
POVERTY
See also Economic conditions; Social problems
POVERTY -- DEVELOPING COUNTRIES
Acemoglu, D. Why nations fail **330**
Novogratz, J. The blue sweater **339.4**
POVERTY -- HISTORY
Milanović, B. The haves and the have-nots **339.2**
POVERTY -- PREVENTION
Banerjee, A. V. Poor economics **339.4**
Tough, P. Whatever it takes **362.7**
POVERTY -- UNITED STATES
Shaefer, H. L. $2.00 a Day **339.4**
Tirado, L. Hand to mouth **362.5**
Ward, J. Men We Reaped **92**
Povey, Glenn
Echoes: the complete history of Pink Floyd **920**
Povich, Lynn
The good girls revolt **331.4**
Powell, Colin L., 1937-
(jt. auth) Koltz, T. It worked for me **92**
Rice, C. No higher honor **327.73**
About
De Young, K. Soldier: the life of Colin Powell **92**
Gates, H. L. Thirteen ways of looking at a black man **920.71**
Powell, C. L. My American journey **92**
Powell, Corey S.
(ed) Nye, B. Undeniable **576.8**
Powell, D. A.
Repast **811**
Useless landscape **811**

Powell, Gloria J.
About
Halberstam, D. The children **323.1**
Powell, John
(ed) Great events from history, The 18th century, 1701-1800 **909.7**
(ed) Great events from history, The 19th century, 1801-1900 **909.81**
(ed) Great lives from history, The 19th century, 1801-1900 **920.003**
(ed) Magill's guide to military history **355**
Great lives from history, The 18th century, 1701-1800 **920.003**
(ed) Weapons & warfare **623.4**
Powell, John Wesley
About
Dolnick, E. Down the great unknown **979.1**
Powell, John Wesley, 1834-1902
About
Dolnick, E. Down the great unknown **979.1**
Powell, Jonathan
Terrorists at the table **363.325**
Powell, Mark Allan
(ed) The HarperCollins Bible dictionary **220.3**
Powell, Neil, 1948-
(ed) Davie, D. Collected poems **821**
Benjamin Britten **92**
Powell, Rodney
About
Halberstam, D. The children **323.1**
POWER (SOCIAL SCIENCES)
Fraser, S. The age of acquiescence **973.91**
Freeland, C. Plutocrats **305.5**
Naím, M. The end of power **303.3**
Wills, G. Certain trumpets **303.3**
POWER (SOCIAL SCIENCES)
See also Political science
POWER (SOCIAL SCIENCES) -- RUSSIA (FEDERATION)
Pomerantsev, P. Nothing is true and everything is possible **306**
POWER (SOCIAL SCIENCES) -- UNITED STATES -- HISTORY
Fraser, S. The age of acquiescence **973.91**
POWER (SOCIAL SCIENCES) -- UNITED STATES -- HISTORY -- 19TH CENTURY
Millard, C. The destiny of the republic **973.8**
The **power** broker: Robert Moses and the fall of New York. Caro, R. A. **92**
Power forward. Love, R. **320.092**
Power in words. Berry, M. F. **973.932**
The **power** of art. Schama, S. **709**
POWER OF ATTORNEY
See also Law
The **power** of habit. **158.1**
The **power** of I am. Osteen, J. **248.4**

The **power** of intention. Dyer, W. W.   158
The **power** of music. Mannes, E.   781
The **power** of myth. Campbell, J.   201
The **power** of now. Tolle, E.   158
The **power** of persuasion. Levine, R.   153.8
The **power** of play. Elkind, D.   155.4
The **power** of positive living. Peale, N. V.   248
The **Power** of Pulses. Malone, H.   635.65
The **power** of the vote. Schoen, D. E.   324
POWER PLANTS, NUCLEAR See Nuclear power plants
POWER POLITICS See Balance of power; Cold war
POWER RESOURCES See Energy resources
POWER RESOURCES -- POLITICAL ASPECTS
   Yergin, D. The quest   333.79
POWER RESOURCES -- SOCIAL ASPECTS
   Muller, R. A. Energy for future presidents 333.79
POWER RESOURCES -- UNITED STATES
   Couch, J. Traveling the power line   333.793
POWER RESOURCES CONSERVATION See Energy conservation
POWER RESOURCES DEVELOPMENT See Energy development
Power sewing step-by-step. Betzina, S.   646.4
POWER SUPPLY See Energy resources
Power surge. Levi, M.   333.79
POWER TOOLS
   Warner, P. The router book   684
Power your happy. Sugar, L.   158
Power, Carla
              About
   Power, C. If the oceans were ink   297
Power, Inc.   322
Power, Katherine
   The career code   650.1
Powers, Bruce R.
   McLuhan, M. The global village   302.2
Powers, J. F. (James Farl), 1917-1999
              About
   Suitable accommodations   92
Powers, Katherine A.
   (ed) Suitable accommodations   92
Powers, Ron
   Bradley, J. Flags of our fathers   940.54
   Mark Twain   92
POWERS, SEPARATION OF See Separation of powers
Powers, Thomas
   The killing of Crazy Horse   92
POWHATAN INDIANS
   Price, D. Love and hate in Jamestown   975.5
POWS See Prisoners of war
POWWOWS
   See also Festivals; Native Americans -- Rites and ceremonies; Native Americans -- Social
life and customs
Poynter, Agnes, 1843-1906
              About
   Flanders, J. A circle of sisters   920
Practical paleo. Sanfilippo, D.   641.5
PRACTICAL POLITICS See Politics
PRACTICAL PSYCHOLOGY See Applied psychology
The **practical** Shakespeare. Butler, C.   822.3
Practically radical. Taylor, W.   658.4
PRACTICE TEACHING See Student teaching
Practicing Catholic. Carroll, J.   92
Practicing history. Tuchman, B. W.   907
Prados, John
   Storm over Leyte   940.54
   (ed) Inside the Pentagon papers   959.704
Prager, Dennis
   Happiness is a serious problem   158
Prager, Ellen J.
   Chasing science at sea   551.46
PRAGMATISM
   Commager, H. S. The American mind   973
   Kaag, J. American philosophy   191
PRAGMATISM
   See also Philosophy; Positivism; Realism; Theory of knowledge
PRAGUE (CZECH REPUBLIC) -- BIOGRAPHY
   Helga's diary   940.53
   Woodward, B. Prague winter   943.71
PRAGUE (CZECH REPUBLIC) -- HISTORY
   Demetz, P. Prague in black and gold   943.71
Prague in black and gold. Demetz, P.   943.71
Prague winter. Woodward, B.   943.71
Prahlad, Anand
   The Greenwood encyclopedia of African American folklore   398
Prain, Leanne
   Hoopla   746.44
PRAIRIE ECOLOGY
   See also Ecology; Grassland ecology
Praise of folly. Erasmus, D.   877
Prakash, Vikramaditya
   (jt. auth) Jarzombek, M. A global history of architecture   720.9
Prange, Gordon William
   At dawn we slept   940.54
Pratchett, Terry, 1948-2015
   A slip of the keyboard   824
Pratt, Doug
   Ewing, R. A. Got sun? go solar   697
PRAYER
   Bolsta, H. S. The illuminated Kaddish   296.4
   Lewis, C. S. Letters to Malcolm: chiefly on prayer   248
   Lucado, M. Before amen   248.3
PRAYER -- JUDAISM

Wagner, J. L. The synagogue survival kit   **296.4**

PRAYERS

Hendey, L. M. A book of saints for Catholic moms   **248.8**

New American Haggadah   **296.4**

Thou, dear God   **242**

Precious Cargo. Dewitt, D.   **306.3**

PRECIOUS METAL CLAY

Haab, S. The art of metal clay   **739.27**

PRECIOUS STONES

Gem   **553.8**

Oldershaw, C. Firefly guide to gems   **553.8**

Predator. Whittle, R.   **623.74**

Predator nation. Ferguson, C.   **330.973**

PREDATORS See Predatory animals

PREDATORY ANIMALS

Quammen, D. Monster of God   **591.6**

PREDATORY ANIMALS

   See also Animals

PREDATORY INSECTS

Gardiner, M. M. Good garden bugs   **635**

PREDESTINATION

   See also Theology

The **prediabetes** diet plan. Wright, H.   **616.4**

PREDIABETIC STATE -- PATIENTS -- DIET THERAPY

Wright, H. The prediabetes diet plan   **616.4**

Predicting new words. Metcalf, A. A.   **420**

PREDICTIONS See Forecasting; Prophecies

Preemies. Linden, D. W.   **618.92**

PREFABRICATED BUILDINGS

   See also Buildings

PREFABRICATED HOUSES

   See also Domestic architecture; House construction; Houses; Prefabricated buildings

PREGNANCY

Brott, A. A. The expectant father   **649**

Cross, C. The baby book   **649.122**

Ilse, S. The prenatal bombshell   **618.3**

The kind mama   **618.1**

Maybe baby   **306.8**

Mayo Clinic guide to a healthy pregnancy   **618.2**

The mommy docs' ultimate guide to pregnancy and birth   **618.2**

Murkoff, H. What to expect when you're expecting   **618.2**

Nilsson, L. A child is born   **612.6**

The pregnancy encyclopedia   **618.2**

Sears, W. The healthy pregnancy book   **618.2**

Simkin, P. The Birth Partner   **618.2**

Your pregnancy week by week   **618.2**

PREGNANCY

   See also Reproduction

PREGNANCY -- COMPLICATIONS

Linden, D. W. Preemies   **618.92**

PREGNANCY -- ECONOMIC ASPECTS

Margulis, J. The business of baby   **649**

PREGNANCY -- NUTRITIONAL ASPECTS

The kind mama   **618.1**

PREGNANCY -- POPULAR WORKS

Pregnancy day by day   **618.2**

The pregnancy encyclopedia   **618.2**

Romm, A. J. The natural pregnancy book   **618.2**

Simkin, P. The Birth Partner   **618.2**

Pregnancy day by day.   **618.2**

The **pregnancy** encyclopedia.   **618.2**

PREHISTORIC ANIMALS

   See also Animals; Fossils

PREHISTORIC ART

   See also Art

PREHISTORIC MAN See Fossil hominids; Prehistoric peoples

PREHISTORIC PEOPLES

Fowler, B. Iceman   **937**

Hancock, G. Underworld: the mysterious origins of civilization   **551.7**

Leakey, R. E. The origin of humankind   **599.93**

Leakey, R. E. Origins reconsidered   **599.93**

Wrangham, R. W. Catching fire   **641.3**

PREHISTORIC PEOPLES

   See also Antiquities; Archeology; Human beings

PREHISTORIC PEOPLES -- FOOD

Le, S. One hundred million years of food   **641.3**

Wrangham, R. W. Catching fire   **641.3**

PREHISTORIC PEOPLES -- NUTRITION

Fong, H. Nom nom paleo   **641.5**

Well fed   **641.5**

PREHISTORY See Archeology; Fossil hominids; Prehistoric peoples

Prejean, Helen

The death of innocents   **364.66**

PREJUDICE See Prejudices

PREJUDICE-MOTIVATED CRIMES See Hate crimes

PREJUDICES

Bullard, S. Teaching tolerance   **649**

Goldhagen, D. J. Worse than war   **364.1**

Griffin, J. H. Black like me   **305.8**

PREJUDICES

   See also Attitude (Psychology); Emotions; Interpersonal relations

Prelude to bruise. Jones, S.   **811**

PREMATURE BURIAL

   See also Burial

PREMATURE INFANTS

French, T. Juniper   **618.92**

PREMENSTRUAL SYNDROME

   See also Menstruation

The **prenatal** bombshell. Ilse, S.   **618.3**

PRENATAL CARE

Ilse, S. The prenatal bombshell   **618.3**

Mayo Clinic guide to a healthy pregnancy **618.2**

PRENATAL CARE
 See also Pregnancy
PRENATAL DIAGNOSIS
 See also Diagnosis
PRENATAL DIAGNOSIS -- PSYCHOLOGY -- PERSONAL NARRATIVES
 Ilse, S. The prenatal bombshell **618.3**
Prentice, Claire
 The lost tribe of Coney Island **305.8**
Prentice, Rachel
 (jt. auth) Keene, N. Your Child in the Hospital **362.1**
PRESCHOOL EDUCATION
 Christakis, E. The Importance of Being Little **372.21**
PRESCHOOL EDUCATION
 See also Education
Prescott, William Hickling
 History of the conquest of Mexico **972**
Prescriptions for living. Siegel, B. S. **158**
Presence. Cuddy, A. **158.1**
Present at the creation. Aczel, A. D. **539.7**
Present Shock. Rushkoff, D. **303.48**
Presentation zen. Reynolds, G.
PRESERVING *See* Canning and preserving
The **presidency** A to Z. **973.09**
The **presidency** of Abraham Lincoln. Paludan, P. S. **973.7**
The **President** and the Apprentice. Gellman, I. F. **973.921**
The **President** and the assassin. Miller, S. **973.8**
The **president** is a sick man. Algeo, M. **973.8**
President Kennedy. Reeves, R. **973.922**
President Nixon. Reeves, R. **973.924**
President Reagan: the triumph of imagination. Reeves, R. **973.927**
PRESIDENTIAL ADVISERS
 Dallek, R. Nixon and Kissinger **92**
 Feldman, N. Scorpions **920**
 Greenspan, A. The age of turbulence **92**
 Halberstam, D. The best and the brightest **973.922**
 Kissinger, H. Years of renewal **973.924**
 Millman, C. The detonators **940.4**
 Overtveldt, J. v. Bernanke's test **332.1**
 Rice, C. Extraordinary, ordinary people **92**
 Sorensen, T. C. Counselor **92**
 Woodward, B. Maestro: Greenspan's Fed and the American boom **331.1**
 Woodward, B. The commanders **973.928**
PRESIDENTIAL AIDES
 Gormley, K. The death of American virtue **973.929**
PRESIDENTIAL AIDES *See* Presidents -- United States -- Staff
PRESIDENTIAL CAMPAIGNS -- UNITED STATES *See* Presidents -- United States -- Election

PRESIDENTIAL CANDIDATES
 Ambrose, S. E. The wild blue **940.54**
 Balz, D. J. The battle for America, 2008 **973.932**
 Baraka, I. A. The LeRoi Jones/Amiri Baraka reader **818**
 Bernstein, C. A woman in charge **92**
 Clarke, T. The last campaign **92**
 Clinton, H. R. Living history **92**
 Davis, W. C. An honorable defeat **973.7**
 English, B. Last lion **92**
 Finan, C. M. Alfred E. Smith, the happy warrior **92**
 Goldsmith, B. Other powers **92**
 Goodwin, D. K. Team of rivals **92**
 Gormley, K. The death of American virtue **973.929**
 Guelzo, A. C. Lincoln and Douglas **973.6**
 Hofstadter, R. The American political tradition, and the men who made it **973**
 Karabell, Z. The last campaign **324.9**
 Kazin, M. A godly hero **92**
 Kennedy, E. M. True compass **92**
 Kennedy, J. F. Profiles in courage **920**
 Mahoney, R. D. Sons and brothers: the days of Jack and Bobby Kennedy **92**
 McCain, J. S. Faith of my fathers **92**
 Morris, R. Fraud of the century **324.9**
 Norgren, J. Belva Lockwood **92**
 Pooley, E. The climate war **363.7**
 Remnick, D. Reporting **814**
 Schlesinger, A. M. Robert Kennedy and his times **92**
 Sears, S. W. George B. McClellan **92**
 Siegel, F. F. The prince of the city **92**
 Thomas, E. Robert Kennedy **92**
 Traister, R. Big girls don't cry **324**
 Zelnick, B. Gore: a political life **92**
PRESIDENTIAL CANDIDATES -- UNITED STATES
 Bai, M. All the truth is out **328.73**
 Popkin, S. L. The candidate **324.9**
 Schnall, M. What will it take to make a woman president? **305.4**
PRESIDENTIAL CANDIDATES -- UNITED STATES -- BIOGRAPHY
 Sanders, B. Outsider in the White House **92**
PRESIDENTIAL CANDIDATES -- UNITED STATES -- CASE STUDIES
 Popkin, S. L. The candidate **324.9**
PRESIDENTIAL CANDIDATES -- UNITED STATES -- HISTORY
 Roberts, R. N. Campaigning for president in America, 1788-2016 **324.709**
Presidential elections 1789-2008. Congressional Quarterly, I. **324.6**
PRESIDENTIAL LIBRARIES *See* Presidents -- United States -- Archives

Presidential places. Ferris, G. W. **917**

Presidential wives. Boller, P. F. **920**

Presidents. Hamilton, N. A. **920.003**

PRESIDENTS

Abuse of power **973.924**

Adams, J. My dearest friend **92**

Algeo, M. The president is a sick man **973.8**

Alter, J. The promise **92**

Ambrose, S. E. Eisenhower **92**

Ambrose, S. E. The victors **940.54**

Anderson, L. Carlisle vs. Army **796.332**

Baker, P. Kremlin rising **947.086**

Balz, D. J. The battle for America, 2008 **973.932**

Becker, C. The Declaration of Independence **973.3**

Bernstein, R. B. Thomas Jefferson **92**

Berthon, S. Warlords **940.53**

Beschloss, M. R. The conquerors: Roosevelt, Truman, and the destruction of Hitler's Germany, 1941-1945 **940.53**

Black, C. M. Richard M. Nixon **92**

Boritt, G. S. The Gettysburg gospel **973.7**

Borneman, W. R. Polk **92**

Branch, T. The Clinton tapes **92**

Brands, H. W. Andrew Jackson **92**

Brands, H. W. Traitor to his class **92**

Brands, H. W. Woodrow Wilson **92**

Brookhiser, R. America's first dynasty **973.4**

Brookhiser, R. Founding father: rediscovering George Washington **92**

Bruni, F. Ambling into history: the unlikely odyssey of George W. Bush **973.931**

Buckley, W. F. The Reagan I knew **92**

Bugliosi, V. Reclaiming history **973.922**

Bunting, J. Ulysses S. Grant **92**

Burlingame, M. Abraham Lincoln **92**

Burns, J. M. The three Roosevelts **973.91**

Burstein, A. Madison and Jefferson **973.4**

Busby, H. W. The thirty-first of March **973.923**

Bush, G. W. Decision points **92**

Bush, G. All the best, George Bush **92**

Calhoun, C. W. Benjamin Harrison **92**

Carlin, J. Playing the enemy **968.06**

Caro, R. A. The path to power **92**

Carter, J. Everything to gain **92**

Carter, J. An hour before daylight **92**

Carter, J. Keeping faith: memoirs of a president **92**

Carter, J. Sharing good times **92**

Carwardine, R. Lincoln: a life of purpose and power **92**

Castro, F. Fidel Castro: my life **92**

Cerami, C. A. Jefferson's great gamble **973.4**

Clinton, B. My life **92**

Clinton, C. Mrs. Lincoln **92**

Cohen, I. B. Science and the founding fathers **973.3**

Coltman, L. The real Fidel Castro **92**

Cooper, J. M. The warrior and the priest: Woodrow

Wilson and Theodore Roosevelt **92**

Cooper, J. M. Woodrow Wilson **92**

Cordery, S. A. Alice **92**

Crapol, E. P. John Tyler **92**

Craughwell, T. J. Stealing Lincoln's body **973.7**

Dallek, R. Harry S. Truman **92**

Dallek, R. Let every nation know **92**

Dallek, R. Nixon and Kissinger **92**

Dallek, R. An unfinished life: John F. Kennedy, 1917-1963 **92**

DiSilvestro, R. L. Theodore Roosevelt in the Badlands **92**

Dobbs, M. One minute to midnight **973.922**

Donald, D. H. Lincoln **92**

D'Souza, D. Ronald Reagan **973.927**

Duke, L. Mandela, Mobutu, and me **968.06**

Egan, T. The big burn **973.91**

Ellis, J. J. American sphinx: the character of Thomas Jefferson **92**

Ellis, J. J. His Excellency **92**

Emery, F. Watergate **973.924**

Farmer, J. J. The ground truth **973.931**

Feldman, N. Scorpions **920**

Finkelman, P. Millard Fillmore **92**

First person: an astonishingly frank self-portrait **92**

Fischer, D. H. Washington's crossing **973.3**

FitzGerald, F. Way out there in the blue **973.927**

Fleming, T. J. Washington's secret war **973.3**

Flexner, J. T. George Washington and the new nation, 1783-1793 **92**

Flexner, J. T. George Washington: anguish and farewell 1793-1799 **92**

Flexner, J. T. George Washington: the forge of experience, 1732-1775 **92**

Foner, E. The fiery trial **973.7**

Fowler, W. M. American crisis **973.3**

Fredrickson, G. M. Big enough to be inconsistent **973.7**

Freedman, L. Kennedy's wars **973.922**

Fried, A. F.D.R. and his enemies **92**

Gaines, J. R. For liberty and glory **92**

Gevisser, M. A legacy of liberation **92**

Gienapp, W. E. Abraham Lincoln and Civil War America **973.7**

Gimbel, W. Havana dreams **972.91**

Goodwin, D. K. Team of rivals **92**

Goodwin, D. K. No ordinary time **92**

Gopnik, A. Angels and ages **973.7**

Gordin, M. D. Red cloud at dawn **355**

Gordon-Reed, A. Andrew Johnson **92**

Gordon-Reed, A. The Hemingses of Monticello **920**

Gordon-Reed, A. Thomas Jefferson and Sally Hemings **973.4**

Gormley, K. The death of American virtue **973.929**

Graff, H. F. Grover Cleveland **92**

Grant, J. John Adams **92**

Grant, U. S. Memoirs and selected letters **973.8**

Groom, W. Patriotic fire **973.5**

Groom, W. Vicksburg, 1863 **973.7**

Guelzo, A. C. Lincoln and Douglas **973.6**

Halberstam, D. The best and the brightest **973.922**

Havel, V. To the castle and back **92**

Hayden, T. The long sixties **973.92**

Hersh, S. M. Chain of command **973.931**

Hitchens, C. Thomas Jefferson: author of America **92**

Hofstadter, R. The American political tradition, and the men who made it **973**

Holton, W. Abigail Adams **92**

Holzer, H. Lincoln president-elect **92**

In his own words **92**

Johnson, H. B. Sleepwalking through history **973.927**

Johnson, P. George Washington: the Founding Father **92**

Kaiser, D. E. American tragedy **959.704**

Kaiser, D. E. The road to Dallas **973.922**

Karabell, Z. The last campaign **324.9**

Keneally, T. Abraham Lincoln **92**

Kennedy, J. F. Profiles in courage **920**

Kissinger, H. Diplomacy **327.2**

Korda, M. Ulysses S. Grant: the unlikely hero **92**

Kotz, N. Judgment days **323**

Kranish, M. Flight from Monticello **973.4**

Kunhardt, P. B. Looking for Lincoln **92**

Langguth, A. J. Driven West **973.5**

Larson, E. J. A magnificent catastrophe **324**

Leamer, L. The Kennedy men **920**

Leuchtenburg, W. E. Franklin D. Roosevelt and the New Deal, 1932-1940 **973.917**

The Lincoln anthology **92**

Lind, M. What Lincoln believed **92**

Lockhart, P. D. The whites of their eyes **973.3**

MacMillan, M. Paris 1919 **940.3**

Mahoney, R. D. Sons and brothers: the days of Jack and Bobby Kennedy **92**

Mallon, T. Mrs. Paine's garage and the murder of John F. Kennedy **364.1**

Malone, J. W. It doesn't take a rocket scientist **920**

Mandela, N. Conversations with myself **92**

Mandela, N. Long walk to freedom: the autobiography of Nelson Mandela **92**

Mandela, N. Mandela **968.06**

Mann, J. The rebellion of Ronald Reagan **973.927**

Matthews, C. Kennedy & Nixon **973.922**

May, G. John Tyler **92**

McCullough, D. G. John Adams **92**

McCullough, D. G. Mornings on horseback **92**

McCullough, D. G. The path between the seas **972.87**

McDougal, S. The woman who wouldn't talk **973.929**

McPherson, J. M. Tried by war **92**

McPherson, J. M. Abraham Lincoln **92**

McPherson, J. M. Abraham Lincoln and the second American Revolution **973.7**

McPherson, J. M. Drawn with the sword **973.7**

McPherson, J. M. This mighty scourge **973.7**

Meacham, J. American lion **92**

Mendell, D. Obama **92**

Merry, R. W. A country of vast designs **92**

Meyerson, M. Liberty's blueprint **342**

Millard, C. The river of doubt **973.91**

Miller, J. C. The Federalist era, 1789-1801 **973.4**

Miller, S. The President and the assassin **973.8**

Miller, W. L. Arguing about slavery **973.5**

Morris, E. The rise of Theodore Roosevelt **92**

Morris, E. Theodore Rex **92**

Morris, R. Fraud of the century **324.9**

Morrow, L. The best year of their lives **920**

Nagel, P. C. John Quincy Adams **92**

Newton, M. A. Enemy of the state **345**

Obama, B. Dreams from my father **92**

O'Brien, M. Mrs. Adams in winter **940.2**

O'Toole, P. When trumpets call **92**

Our Lincoln **92**

Pakula, H. The last empress **92**

Paludan, P. S. The presidency of Abraham Lincoln **973.7**

Parmet, H. S. George Bush **92**

Perlstein, R. Nixonland **973.924**

Perry, J. M. Touched with fire **973.7**

Persico, J. E. Franklin and Lucy **920**

Peters, C. Lyndon B. Johnson **92**

Phillips, K. P. William McKinley **92**

Pietrusza, D. 1960: LBJ vs. JFK vs. Nixon **973.92**

Pinsker, M. Lincoln's sanctuary **92**

Politkovskaya, A. A Russian diary **947.086**

Posner, G. L. Case closed **973.922**

Randall, W. S. George Washington **92**

Rasenberger, J. The brilliant disaster **972.91**

Ratnesar, R. Tear down this wall **973.927**

Rauchway, E. Murdering McKinley **973.8**

Reagan, R. Reagan **92**

Reagan, R. My father at 100 **92**

Reeves, R. President Kennedy **973.922**

Reeves, R. President Nixon **973.924**

Reeves, R. President Reagan: the triumph of imagination **973.927**

Remini, R. V. Andrew Jackson **92**

Remini, R. V. John Quincy Adams **92**

Remnick, D. The bridge **92**

Remnick, D. Reporting **814**

Reston, J. The conviction of Richard Nixon **973.924**

Reynolds, D. S. Waking giant **973.5**

Rice, A. The teeth may smile but the heart does not forget **967.6**

Roberts, A. Masters and commanders **940.54**
Roosevelt, C. Too close to the sun **92**
Sampson, A. Nelson Mandela **92**
Sandburg, C. Abraham Lincoln: The prairie years
and The war years **92**
Schlesinger, A. M. The coming of the New Deal,
1933-1935 **973.917**
Schlesinger, A. M. The crisis of the old order,
1919-1933 **973.91**
Schlesinger, A. M. The politics of upheaval, 1935-
1936 **973.917**
Schlesinger, A. M. War and the American presi-
dency **327.1**
Shenk, J. W. Lincoln's melancholy **92**
Shesol, J. Supreme power **347**
Simon, J. F. What kind of nation **342**
Smith, D. J. Young Mandela **92**
Smith, J. E. FDR **92**
Smith, J. E. Grant **92**
Sorensen, T. C. Counselor **92**
Staloff, D. Hamilton, Adams, Jefferson **973.4**
Stephanopoulos, G. All too human **973.929**
Stewart, D. O. American emperor **973.4**
Swanson, J. L. Manhunt **364.152**
Symmes, P. The boys from Dolores **972.91**
Symonds, C. L. Lincoln and his admirals **92**
Szulc, T. Fidel **92**
Taking charge **973.923**
Taylor, J. The generalissimo **92**
Taylor, N. American-made **331.1**
Thomas, E. The war lovers **973.8**
Tolstaia, T. Pushkin's children **891.7**
Toobin, J. R. A vast conspiracy **973.929**
Tuchman, B. W. Practicing history **907**
Tuchman, B. W. Stilwell and the American experi-
ence in China, 1911-45 **327**
Unger, H. G. The last founding father **92**
Vidal, G. Inventing a nation: Washington, Adams,
Jefferson **973.4**
Von Tunzelmann, A. Red heat **972.9**
Wallace, A. F. C. The long bitter trail **323.1**
Walsh, J. E. Moonlight **345**
Weintraub, S. 15 stars **920**
Wheen, F. Strange days indeed **973.92**
White, R. C. A. Lincoln **92**
White, R. C. The eloquent president: a portrait of
Lincoln through his words **92**
Wicker, T. Dwight D. Eisenhower **973.921**
Widmer, E. L. Martin Van Buren **92**
Wiencek, H. An imperfect god **973.4**
Wilentz, S. Andrew Jackson **92**
Williams, C. The last great Frenchman **944**
Wills, G. James Madison **92**
Wills, G. Lincoln at Gettysburg **973.7**
Wills, G. 'Negro president' **326**
Wilson, E. Patriotic gore **810**

Woodward, B. The commanders **973.928**
Woodward, B. The final days **973.924**
Woodward, B. Plan of attack **956.7**
Woodward, B. Shadow **973.92**
Woodward, B. State of denial **973.931**
Zacks, R. The pirate coast **973.4**
Zimmermann, W. First great triumph **973**
PRESIDENTS
　　See also Heads of state
**PRESIDENTS -- ARAB COUNTRIES -- HIS-
TORY**
Owen, R. The rise and fall of Arab presidents for
life **352.23**
PRESIDENTS -- ATTITUDES
Presidents and Black America **973.09**
PRESIDENTS -- CHINA
Taylor, J. The generalissimo **92**
**PRESIDENTS -- DWELLINGS -- UNITED
STATES -- PICTORIAL WORKS**
Van Doren, A. The house tells the story **728**
**PRESIDENTS -- FAMILY RELATIONSHIPS --
UNITED STATES -- ANECDOTES**
Brower, K. A. The residence **975.3**
**PRESIDENTS -- FAMILY RELATIONSHIPS --
UNITED STATES -- HISTORY**
Kendall, J. C. First dads **973**
PRESIDENTS -- FRANCE -- BIOGRAPHY
Chirac, J. My life in politics **944.084**
Williams, C. The last great Frenchman **944**
**PRESIDENTS -- MEDICAL CARE -- UNITED
STATES -- HISTORY -- 19TH CENTURY**
Millard, C. The destiny of the republic **973.8**
PRESIDENTS -- MIDDLE EAST
Owen, R. The rise and fall of Arab presidents for
life **352.23**
**PRESIDENTS -- PROTECTION -- UNITED
STATES**
Hill, C. Five presidents **363.28**
**PRESIDENTS -- RELATIONS WITH AFRICAN
AMERICANS -- HISTORY -- SOURCES**
Presidents and Black America **973.09**
PRESIDENTS -- SOUTH AFRICA
Mandela, N. Conversations with myself **92**
PRESIDENTS -- TAIWAN
Taylor, J. The generalissimo **92**
**PRESIDENTS -- TERM OF OFFICE -- UNITED
STATES**
Moe, R. Roosevelt's second act **973.917**
**PRESIDENTS -- TRAVEL -- UNITED STATES --
HISTORY -- 18TH CENTURY**
Breen, T. H. George Washington's journey **92**
PRESIDENTS -- UNITED STATES
Berg, A. S. Wilson **92**
Brands, H. W. The man who saved the union **355.009**
Broadwater, J. James Madison **92**
Brookhiser, R. Founders' son **92**

Brower, K. A. The residence **975.3**
Cheney, L. V. James Madison **92**
Chronology of the U.S. presidency **973.09**
Duffy, M. The presidents club **973.92**
Greenberg, D. Republic of spin **973.099**
Guide to the presidency and the executive branch **352.23**
Hatch, P. J. A rich spot of earth **635**
Johnson, P. Eisenhower **92**
Kaplan, F. John Quincy Adams **92**
Maraniss, D. Barack Obama **92**
Presidents and Black America **973.09**
Ross, D. B. Doomed to succeed **327.73**
Simon, J. F. FDR and Chief Justice Hughes **973.917**
Smith, J. E. Bush **973.931**
Thomas, E. Being Nixon **92**
Thomas, E. Ike's bluff **973.92**
Weiner, T. One man against the world **973.924**
PRESIDENTS -- UNITED STATES -- ARCHIVES
The Nixon tapes **973.924**
PRESIDENTS -- UNITED STATES -- ARCHIVES
See also Archives
PRESIDENTS -- UNITED STATES -- ASSASSI-NATION
Hill, C. Mrs. Kennedy and me **973.922**
Millard, C. The destiny of the republic **973.8**
PRESIDENTS -- UNITED STATES -- ASSASSI-NATION
See also Assassination
PRESIDENTS -- UNITED STATES -- BIOGRA-PHY
Brands, H. W. Reagan **92**
Bush, G. W. 41 **92**
Caro, R. A. The passage of power **92**
Carter, J. A full life **92**
Collins, G. William Henry Harrison **92**
Davis, D. Guest of honor **973.91**
Frank, J. Ike and dick **973.921**
Giles Unger, H. John Quincy Adams **92**
Kendall, J. C. First dads **973**
Lunde, D. The naturalist **973.91**
Meacham, J. Destiny and Power **92**
Meacham, J. Thomas Jefferson **92**
The presidency A to Z **973.09**
Raphael, R. Mr. president **352.23**
Smith, J. E. Eisenhower **973.921**
Traub, J. John Quincy Adams **92**
White, R. C. American Ulysses **92**
PRESIDENTS -- UNITED STATES -- BIOGRA-PHY -- ANECDOTES
Brower, K. A. The residence **975.3**
PRESIDENTS -- UNITED STATES -- BROTH-ERS AND SISTERS -- BIOGRAPHY
Byrne, P. Kick **92**
Leaming, B. Kick Kennedy **92**
PRESIDENTS -- UNITED STATES -- BURIAL

See Presidents -- United States -- Death and burial
PRESIDENTS -- UNITED STATES -- CHIL-DREN
Burns, E. The Golden Lad **92**
Kendall, J. C. First dads **973**
PRESIDENTS -- UNITED STATES -- DEATH
Carlson, B. Dead presidents **973.09**
PRESIDENTS -- UNITED STATES -- DICTION-ARIES
Hamilton, N. A. Presidents **920.003**
PRESIDENTS -- UNITED STATES -- ELEC-TION
Popkin, S. L. The candidate **324.9**
PRESIDENTS -- UNITED STATES -- ELEC-TION -- 1800
Larson, E. J. A magnificent catastrophe **324**
Stewart, D. O. American emperor **973.4**
PRESIDENTS -- UNITED STATES -- ELEC-TION -- 1860
Egerton, D. R. Year of meteors **973.7**
PRESIDENTS -- UNITED STATES -- ELEC-TION -- 1920
Pietrusza, D. 1920: the year of the six presidents **973.91**
PRESIDENTS -- UNITED STATES -- ELEC-TION -- 1940
Moe, R. Roosevelt's second act **973.917**
PRESIDENTS -- UNITED STATES -- ELEC-TION -- 1948
Karabell, Z. The last campaign **324.9**
PRESIDENTS -- UNITED STATES -- ELEC-TION -- 1960
Pietrusza, D. 1960: LBJ vs. JFK vs. Nixon **973.92**
PRESIDENTS -- UNITED STATES -- ELEC-TION -- 1972
Glasser, J. M. The eighteen-day running mate **973.924**
PRESIDENTS -- UNITED STATES -- ELEC-TION -- 2008
Balz, D. J. The battle for America, 2008 **973.932**
Berry, M. F. Power in words **973.932**
Traister, R. Big girls don't cry **324**
PRESIDENTS -- UNITED STATES -- ELEC-TION -- 2012
Halperin, M. Double Down **324.9**
PRESIDENTS -- UNITED STATES -- ELEC-TION -- FINANCE
Vogel, K. P. Big money **324.7**
PRESIDENTS -- UNITED STATES -- ELEC-TION -- HISTORY
Roberts, R. N. Campaigning for president in America, 1788-2016 **324.709**
PRESIDENTS -- UNITED STATES -- ENCY-CLOPEDIAS
Encyclopedia of the U.S. presidency **352.23**
The presidency A to Z **973.09**

PRESIDENTS -- UNITED STATES -- ENCY-CLOPEDIAS, JUVENILE
Encyclopedia of the U.S. presidency 352.23

PRESIDENTS -- UNITED STATES -- FAMILY
Kantor, J. The Obamas 973.932
Nasaw, D. The patriarch 92
Taraborrelli, J. R. After Camelot 920

PRESIDENTS -- UNITED STATES -- FUNERAL AND MEMORIAL SERVICES See Presidents -- United States -- Death and burial

PRESIDENTS -- UNITED STATES -- HEALTH
Lelyveld, J. His final battle 92

PRESIDENTS -- UNITED STATES -- HISTORY
Duffy, M. The presidents club 973.92
Greenberg, D. Republic of spin 973.099
Kendall, J. C. First dads 973
Perry, J. M. Touched with fire 973.7

PRESIDENTS -- UNITED STATES -- HISTORY -- 18TH CENTURY
Raphael, R. Mr. president 352.23

PRESIDENTS -- UNITED STATES -- HISTORY -- CHRONOLOGY
Chronology of the U.S. presidency 973.09

PRESIDENTS -- UNITED STATES -- HISTORY -- ENCYCLOPEDIAS, JUVENILE
Encyclopedia of the U.S. presidency 352.23

PRESIDENTS -- UNITED STATES -- HISTORY -- JUVENILE LITERATURE
The house that George built 975.3

PRESIDENTS -- UNITED STATES -- HOMES
The house that George built 975.3
Van Doren, A. The house tells the story 728

PRESIDENTS -- UNITED STATES -- ILLNESS See Presidents -- United States -- Health

PRESIDENTS -- UNITED STATES -- INAUGU-RAL ADDRESSES
Fellow citizens 352.23
My fellow citizens 352.23
State of the union 352.23

PRESIDENTS -- UNITED STATES -- MESSAG-ES
State of the union 352.23

PRESIDENTS -- UNITED STATES -- POWER See Executive power -- United States

PRESIDENTS -- UNITED STATES -- PRESS RE-LATIONS
Holzer, H. Lincoln and the power of the press 973.7

PRESIDENTS -- UNITED STATES -- PUBLIC OPINION -- HISTORY
Greenberg, D. Republic of spin 973.099

PRESIDENTS -- UNITED STATES -- QUOTA-TIONS
See also Quotations

PRESIDENTS -- UNITED STATES -- RACIAL ATTITUDES -- SOURCES
Presidents and Black America 973.09

PRESIDENTS -- UNITED STATES -- SPOUSES
See Presidents' spouses -- United States

PRESIDENTS -- UNITED STATES -- STAFF
Hill, C. Five presidents 363.28
Love, R. Power forward 320.092

PRESIDENTS -- UNITED STATES -- TRAVEL
Breen, T. H. George Washington's journey 92

PRESIDENTS -- UNITED STATES -- VOYAGES AND TRAVELS See Presidents -- United States -- Travel

PRESIDENTS --UNITED STATES -- POLICIES
The forgotten man 973.91
Presidents and Black America. 973.09
The presidents club. Duffy, M. 973.92

PRESIDENTS' SPOUSES -- FAMILY RELA-TIONSHIPS -- UNITED STATES -- CASE STUDIES
Clinton, H. R. It takes a village 305.23

PRESIDENTS' SPOUSES -- PROTECTION -- UNITED STATES
Hill, C. Mrs. Kennedy and me 973.922

PRESIDENTS' SPOUSES -- UNITED STATES
Brower, K. A. First women 973.099
Clinton, H. R. It takes a village 305.23
Cook, B. W. Eleanor Roosevelt 973.917
Hill, C. Mrs. Kennedy and me 973.922
Jacqueline Kennedy 973.922
Leaming, B. Jacqueline Bouvier Kennedy Onas-sis 92
Peyser, M. Hissing cousins 92
Quinn, S. Eleanor and Hick 92
Slevin, P. Michelle Obama 92
Taraborrelli, J. R. After Camelot 920
Thomas, L. Louisa 92

PRESIDENTS' SPOUSES -- UNITED STATES -- BIOGRAPHY
Bell-Scott, P. The firebrand and the First Lady 92
Burns, J. M. The three Roosevelts 973.91
Caroli, B. B. Lady Bird and Lyndon 92
Chafe, W. H. Bill and Hillary 973.929
Clinton, H. R. Living history 92
Cook, J. H. American phoenix 973.5
Fraser, F. The Washingtons 92
Gillette, M. L. Lady Bird Johnson 92
Leaming, B. Jacqueline Bouvier Kennedy Onas-sis 92
Leaming, B. Mrs. Kennedy 973.922
Peyser, M. Hissing cousins 92
Slevin, P. Michelle Obama 92

PRESIDENTS' SPOUSES -- UNITED STATES -- BIOGRAPHY -- ANECDOTES
Brower, K. A. The residence 975.3

PRESIDENTS' SPOUSES -- UNITED STATES -- DICTIONARIES
Schneider, D. First ladies 920.003

PRESIDENTS' WIVES -- UNITED STATES See

Presidents' spouses -- United States

PRESIDENTS SPOUSES -- UNITED STATES -- INTERVIEWS

Jacqueline Kennedy   **973.922**

Presilla, Maricel E.

Gran cocina latina   **641.597**

Presley, Elvis, 1935-1977

About

Alden, G. Elvis and Ginger   **92**

Guralnick, P. Careless love: the unmaking of Elvis Presley   **92**

Mason, B. A. Elvis Presley   **92**

Victor, A. The Elvis encyclopedia   **781.66**

Presley, Frances

Myne   **821**

Presley, James

The Phantom Killer   **364.152**

PRESS

Holzer, H. Lincoln and the power of the press **973.7**

PRESS

See also Journalism; Propaganda; Publicity

PRESS -- GOVERNMENT POLICY

See also Freedom of information

PRESS AND POLITICS -- HISTORY -- 21ST CENTURY

Simon, J. The new censorship   **363.31**

PRESS AND POLITICS -- UNITED STATES

Carpini, M. X. D. After broadcast news   **071**

PRESS AND POLITICS -- UNITED STATES -- HISTORY -- 19TH CENTURY

Holzer, H. Lincoln and the power of the press **973.7**

PRESS AND POLITICS -- UNITED STATES -- HISTORY -- 20TH CENTURY

Bai, M. All the truth is out   **328.73**

Feldstein, M. Poisoning the press   **973.924**

Goodwin, D. K. The Bully Pulpit   **973.91**

PRESS CENSORSHIP *See* Freedom of the press

Press, Eyal

Absolute convictions   **363.46**

Press, Shalom, 1940-

About

Press, E. Absolute convictions   **363.46**

Pressler, Mirjam

Frank, A. The diary of a young girl: the definitive edition   **92**

Pressly, Paul M.

On the rim of the Caribbean   **975.8**

Pressman, David

Patent it yourself   **346**

Pressman, Robert M.

(jt. auth) Jackson, R. The learning habit   **371.3**

Pressner, Amanda

About

Baggett, J. The lost girls   **910.4**

PRESSURE COOKING

The Great Big Pressure Cooker Book   **641.5**

PRESSURE GROUPS *See* Lobbying; Political action committees

PRESTIDIGITATION *See* Magic tricks

Preston, Andrew

Sword of the spirit, shield of faith   **322**

Preston, Diana

A higher form of killing   **940.4**

Before the fallout   **355.8**

The Boxer Rebellion   **951**

A first rate tragedy   **919**

Preston, Katherine, 1984-

About

Preston, K. Out with it   **92**

Preston, Richard

The demon in the freezer   **616.9**

The hot zone   **614.5**

The wild trees   **577.3**

Pretty is what changes. Queller, J.   **92**

Prevallet, Kristin

(ed) Adam, H. A Helen Adam reader   **811**

PREVENTIVE HEALTH SERVICES -- NEW YORK CITY -- PERSONAL NARRATIVES

Farley, T. Saving Gotham   **362.1**

PREVENTIVE MEDICINE

Pizzorno, L. Your bones   **616.7**

Wright, H. The prediabetes diet plan   **616.4**

PREVENTIVE MEDICINE

See also Medicine

The **price** of civilization. Sachs, J.   **330.9**

The **price** of inequality. Stiglitz, J. E.   **305.5**

The **price** of justice. Leamer, L.   **346.730**

The **price** of silence. Cohan, W. D.   **364.15**

Price, Catherine

Vitamania   **612.3**

Price, David

Love and hate in Jamestown   **975.5**

Price, Maggie

Painting with pastels   **741.2**

Price, Reynolds

Bible/N.T./Gospels The three Gospels   **226.3**

Ardent spirits   **92**

A serious way of wondering   **241**

Price, Reynolds, 1933-2011

About

Price, R. Ardent spirits   **92**

Price, Simon

(ed) The Oxford dictionary of classical myth and religion   **292**

Priceless. Wittman, R.   **364.1**

PRICES

The value of a dollar   **338.5**

The value of a dollar: colonial era to the Civil War, 1600-1865   **338.5**

PRICES

See also Commerce; Consumption (Economics); Economics; Finance; Manufactures

PRIDE AND VANITY
See also Conduct of life; Sin
Prideaux, Sue
Strindberg 839.7
Edvard Munch 92
Priestland, David
The red flag 335.4
Priestley, Joseph, 1733-1804
About
Johnson, S. The invention of air 92
Malone, J. W. It doesn't take a rocket scientist 920
PRIESTS
Armenian Golgotha 956
Boyle, G. J. Tattoos on the heart 277
Carroll, J. Practicing Catholic 92
Fisher, J. T. On the Irish waterfront 331.7
Martin, J. The Jesuit guide to almost everything 248.4
Martin, J. My life with the saints 920
PRIESTS
See also Clergy
PRIESTS -- FRANCE -- MARSEILLE -- BIOGRAPHY
Zuccotti, S. Père Marie-Benoît and Jewish rescue 940.53
Prijatel, Patricia, 1945-
About
Prijatel, P. Surviving triple negative breast cancer 616.99
Primal cuts. Guggiana, M. 641.6
Primal Leadership. Goleman, D. 658.4
PRIMARIES
See also Elections; Political conventions; Politics
PRIMARY EDUCATION *See* Elementary education
Primary sourcebook series
Hillstrom, K. The Cold War 909.82
The **primate** family tree. Redmond, I. 599.8
A **primate's** memoir. Sapolsky, R. M. 599.8
PRIMATES
Redmond, I. The primate family tree 599.8
PRIMATES
See also Mammals
PRIMATES -- BEHAVIOR
Martin, W. Primates of Park Avenue 974.7
PRIMATES -- EVOLUTION
Walter, C. Last ape standing 569.9
Primates of Park Avenue. Martin, W. 974.7
PRIMATOLOGISTS
Goodall, J. Beyond innocence 92
Halloran, A. R. The song of the ape 599.885
Peterson, D. Jane Goodall: the woman who redefined man 92
Prime green. Stone, R. 92
PRIME MINISTERS

See also Cabinet officers; Executive power
PRIME MINISTERS -- GREAT BRITAIN
Clarke, P. Mr. Churchill's profession 941.084
Moore, C. Margaret Thatcher 92
PRIME MINISTERS -- INDIA
Brown, J. M. Nehru: a political life 92
Tharoor, S. Nehru: the invention of India 954.04
PRIME MINISTERS -- ISRAEL
Menachem Begin 956.940
PRIME MINISTERS -- ISRAEL -- BIOGRAPHY
Menachem Begin 956.940
PRIME MINISTERS -- PAKISTAN
Bhutto, B. Reconciliation 92
Prime obsession. Derbyshire, J. 512.7
PRIMITIVE CHRISTIANITY *See* Church history -- 30-600, Early church
PRIMITIVE MAN *See* Primitive societies
Primitive mythology. Campbell, J. 201
PRIMITIVE SOCIETIES
Zuckoff, M. Lost in Shangri-la 940.54
PRIMITIVE SOCIETIES
See also Civilization; Ethnology
PRIMITIVE SOCIETIES -- NEW GUINEA
Zuckoff, M. Lost in Shangri-la 940.54
PRIMITIVE SOCIETY *See* Primitive societies
The **prince.** Machiavelli, N. 320.1
Prince of darkness. White, S. 92
The **prince** of Frogtown. Bragg, R. 92
The **Prince** of Los Cocuyos. Blanco, R. 92
Prince of medicine. Mattern, S. P. 610.9
The **prince** of the city. Siegel, F. F. 92
The **prince** of the marshes. Stewart, R. 956.7
Prince Rupert. Spencer, C. E. M. S. 92
PRINCES
Fulbrook, M. A concise history of Germany 943
Kissinger, H. Diplomacy 327.2
Mayer, C. Born to be king 92
Schiller, F. Don Carlos and Mary Stuart 832
Spencer, C. E. M. S. Prince Rupert 92
Weir, A. Mary, Queen of Scots, and the murder of Lord Darnley 92
PRINCES
See also Courts and courtiers
PRINCES -- GREAT BRITAIN -- BIOGRAPHY
Mayer, C. Born to be king 92
PRINCES AND PRINCESSES *See* Princes; Princesses
Princes at war. Cadbury, D. 941.084
Princess Noire. Cohodas, N. 92
Princesses. Fraser, F. 920
PRINCESSES
Andersen, C. Game of crowns 941.085
Brown, T. The Diana chronicles 92
Fraser, F. Pauline Bonaparte 92
Fraser, F. Princesses 920
Price, D. Love and hate in Jamestown 975.5

Williams, K. Becoming Queen Victoria **92**

PRINCESSES

See also Courts and courtiers

PRINCESSES -- FICTION

The turnip princess **398.209**

PRINCESSES -- RUSSIA -- BIOGRAPHY -- SOURCES

Rappaport, H. The Romanov sisters **920**

The **Princeton** encyclopedia of birds. **598**

The **Princeton** encyclopedia of mammals. **599**

The **Princeton** encyclopedia of poetry and poetics. **808.1**

The **Princeton** field guide to dinosaurs. Paul, G. S. **567.9**

Princeton field guides [series]

Compagno, L. J. V. Sharks of the world **597**

Johnsen, O. Minerals of the world **549**

Paul, G. S. The Princeton field guide to dinosaurs **567.9**

Ridpath, I. Stars and planets **520**

Princeton Language Institute

Roget's 21st century thesaurus in dictionary form **423**

Princeton pocket guides [series]

Ebert, D. A. A pocket guide to sharks of the world **597.3**

Princeton series of contemporary poets [series]

Graber, K. The eternal city **811**

The **principles** of knitting. **746.9**

Pringle, Heather Anne

The mummy congress **393**

Pringle, Peter

Food, inc **363.1**

The murder of Nikolai Vavilov **92**

Printed sources. **016**

PRINTERS -- UNITED STATES -- BIOGRAPHY

Kluger, R. Indelible ink **686.209**

PRINTING

Garfield, S. Just my type **686.2**

Pettegree, A. The book in the Renaissance **070.5**

PRINTING

See also Bibliography; Book industry; Graphic arts; Industrial arts; Publishers and publishing

PRINTING -- EUROPE -- HISTORY -- 16TH CENTURY

Pettegree, A. The book in the Renaissance **070.5**

PRINTING -- EXHIBITIONS

See also Exhibitions

PRINTING -- NEW YORK (STATE) -- HISTORY -- 18TH CENTURY

Kluger, R. Indelible ink **686.209**

PRINTING -- SPECIMENS

See also Advertising; Initials

PRINTING -- STYLE MANUALS

The Chicago manual of style **808**

United States/Government Printing Office Style manual **808**

Printing by hand. Corwin, L. **745.5**

Printing on fabric. Swearington, J. **746.6**

PRINTMAKERS

Blackburn, J. Old man Goya **92**

Hughes, R. Goya **760**

Weber, N. F. The Bauhaus group **920**

PRINTS

See also Graphic arts

The **prison** angel. Jordan, M. **92**

PRISON LIBRARIES -- UNITED STATES

Sweeney, J. Literacy **027.62**

PRISON REFORM

See also Social problems

PRISON RIOTS -- NEW YORK (STATE)

Thompson, H. A. Blood in the water **365**

PRISON SCHOOLS *See* Prisoners -- Education

Prisoner of Tehran. Nemat, M. **92**

Prisoner of the state. **92**

Prisoner without a name, cell without a number. Timerman, J. **92**

PRISONER-OF-WAR ESCAPES -- GERMANY -- WARBURG -- HISTORY -- 20TH CENTURY

Felton, M. Zero Night **940.54**

PRISONERS

Abbott, J. H. In the belly of the beast **365**

Al Jundi, S. The hour of sunlight **92**

Bugliosi, V. Helter skelter **364.1**

Denham, W. Arrested **362.82**

Guantanamo diary **958.104**

Lil Wayne Gone 'til November **782.421**

Masters, J. That bird has my wings **92**

McDougal, S. The woman who wouldn't talk **973.929**

Moore, W. The other Wes Moore **92**

Nourse, V. F. In reckless hands **344**

Prejean, H. The death of innocents **364.66**

Rideau, W. In the place of justice **92**

PRISONERS

See also Criminals

PRISONERS -- BIOGRAPHY

Burke, D. Law man **92**

PRISONERS -- CHINA -- BIOGRAPHY

Liao Yiwu For a song and one hundred songs **365**

PRISONERS -- CIVIL RIGHTS

Thompson, H. A. Blood in the water **365**

PRISONERS -- CIVIL RIGHTS -- UNITED STATES

Hickman, J. Murder at Camp Delta **355.1**

PRISONERS -- EDUCATION

Brottman, M. The Maximum Security Book Club **365.66**

PRISONERS -- EDUCATION

See also Adult education; Prisons

PRISONERS -- TASMANIA -- BIOGRAPHY
Egan, T. The immortal Irishman   92
**PRISONERS -- UNITED STATES -- BIOGRA-
PHY**
Echols, D. Life after death   364.66
PRISONERS AND PRISONS *See* Prisoners; Pris-
oners of war; Prisons
PRISONERS OF CONSCIENCE *See* Political
prisoners
Prisoners of hope. Woods, R. B.   973.923
Prisoners of the Japanese. Daws, G.   940.54
PRISONERS OF WAR
Balz, D. J. The battle for America, 2008   973.932
Daws, G. Prisoners of the Japanese   940.54
Enss, C. Mochi's war   978.8
Gourevitch, P. Standard operating procedure 956.7
Hickman, J. Murder at Camp Delta   355.1
Hillenbrand, L. Unbroken   940.54
Khan, M. R. My Guantanamo diary   909.83
McCain, J. S. Faith of my fathers   92
Norman, E. M. Tears in the darkness   940.54
PRISONERS OF WAR
        See also War
**PRISONERS OF WAR -- FLORIDA -- CASTIL-
LO DE SAN MARCOS NATIONAL MONU-
MENT (SAINT AUGUSTINE) -- BIOGRA-
PHY**
Enss, C. Mochi's war   978.8
**PRISONERS OF WAR -- GERMANY -- ATTI-
TUDES -- SOURCES**
Soldaten   940.54
**PRISONERS OF WAR -- GERMANY -- WAR-
BURG -- HISTORY -- 20TH CENTURY**
Felton, M. Zero Night   940.54
**PRISONERS OF WAR -- NETHERLANDS -- BI-
OGRAPHY**
At the edge of the abyss   940.53
**PRISONERS OF WAR -- PHILIPPINES -- BATA-
AN (PROVINCE)**
Norman, E. M. Tears in the darkness   940.54
**PRISONERS OF WAR -- UNITED STATES --
DIARIES**
Guantanamo diary   958.104
Prisoners without trial. Daniels, R.   940.53
Prisons. Ferro, J.   365
PRISONS
Echols, D. Life after death   364.66
Ferro, J. Prisons   365
PRISONS
        See also Administration of criminal justice;
        Correctional institutions; Punishment
**PRISONS -- ENGLAND -- LONDON -- HISTO-
RY**
Jones, N. Tower   942.1
PRISONS -- UNITED STATES
Abbott, J. H. In the belly of the beast   365

Ferro, J. Prisons   365
Oshinsky, D. M. Worse than slavery   365
Pritchard, William H.
Updike   813
**Pritchett, V. S. (Victor Sawdon), 1900-1997
About**
Treglown, J. V.S. Pritchett: a working life   92
Pritzker, Barry
A Native American encyclopedia   970.004
PRIVACY
Martinez, A. G. Chaos Monkeys   338.4
PRIVACY
        See also Social psychology
PRIVACY, RIGHT OF *See* Right of privacy
PRIVACY, RIGHT OF -- UNITED STATES
Dwyer, J. More awesome than money   384.3
PRIVATE ART COLLECTIONS *See* Art collec-
tions
Private empire. Coll, S.   338.7
PRIVATE ENTERPRISE *See* Free enterprise
PRIVATE EYE STORIES *See* Mystery and detec-
tive plays; Mystery fiction; Mystery films; Mys-
tery radio programs; Mystery television programs
A **private** history of awe. Sanders, S. R.   92
PRIVATE INVESTIGATORS
Crooks, P. The setup   363.28
Halber, D. The skeleton crew   363.25
PRIVATE INVESTIGATORS -- CALIFORNIA
Crooks, P. The setup   363.28
The **private** lives of the impressionists. Roe, S. 759
PRIVATE MILITARY COMPANIES
Hagedorn, A. The invisible soldiers   355
PRIVATE PROPERTY, RIGHT OF *See* Right of
property
PRIVATE SECRETARIES
Malcolm, J. Two lives   92
Persico, J. E. Franklin and Lucy   920
Stein, G. The autobiography of Alice B. Toklas 92
PRIVITIZATION
Frank, J. The people's pension   368.4
Prizant, Barry M.
Uniquely human   618.92
The **prize.** Russakoff, D.   371.2
The **prize.** Yergin, D.   338.2
PRIZE CONTESTS IN ADVERTISING
Ryan, T. The prize winner of Defiance, Ohio 977.1
PRIZE FIGHTING *See* Boxing
The **prize** winner of Defiance, Ohio. Ryan, T. 977.1
PRIZEWINNERS
Ryan, T. The prize winner of Defiance, Ohio 977.1
Pro. Pollitt, K.   363.46
PRO-CHOICE ACTIVISTS
Hull, N. E. H. Roe v. Wade   344
PRO-CHOICE MOVEMENT
        See also Social movements
PRO-LIFE MOVEMENT

Pollitt, K. Pro **363.46**
Press, E. Absolute convictions **363.46**
PRO-LIFE MOVEMENT
    See also Social movements
PROBABILITIES
Arbesman, S. The half-life of facts **501**
Devlin, K. J. The unfinished game **519.2**
Mlodinow, L. The Drunkard's walk **519.2**
Santos, A. How many licks? **519.2**
**PROBLEM CHILDREN -- BEHAVIOR MODI-
    FICATION**
Dunckley, V. L. Reset your child's brain **004.67**
Glickman, E. R. Your kid's a brat and it's all your
    fault **649.1**
PROBLEM DRINKING *See* Alcoholism
The **problem** of slavery in the age of emancipation.
    Davis, D. B. **306.3**
PROBLEM SOLVING
Costa, R. D. The watchman's rattle **501**
Huber, M. R. Mythematics **510**
Kowitz, B. Sprint **658.4**
Mahajan, S. Street-fighting mathematics **510**
Nisbett, R. E. Mindware **153.4**
PROBLEM SOLVING
    See also Psychology
**PROBLEM YOUTH -- BOOKS AND READING
    -- UNITED STATES**
Sweeney, J. Literacy **027.62**
The **problems** of philosophy. Russell, B. **100**
PROCESSED FOODS -- COSTS
Reese, J. Make the bread, buy the butter **641.3**
Prochnicky, Jerry
Riordan, J. Break on through: the life and death of
    Jim Morrison **92**
Prochnik, George
The Impossible Exile **92**
Procrastinate on purpose. Vaden, R. **650.1**
PROCRASTINATION
Partnoy, F. Wait **153.8**
Tracy, B. Eat that frog! **640**
Proctor, Rob
Springer, L. Passionate gardening **635**
Proctor, Robert N.
Golden holocaust **362.29**
PROCUREMENT OF ORGANS, TISSUES, ETC.
Carney, S. The red market **364.1**
Whitehouse, B. The match **92**
The **Prodigy's** Cousin. Stephens, K. **155.45**
PRODUCT DESIGN
Kolko, J. Well-designed **658.5**
PRODUCT DESIGN -- EXHIBITIONS
Gross, K. Dream cars **629.222**
PRODUCT DEVELOPMENT *See* New products
PRODUCT RECALL
Nestle, M. Pet food politics **363.1**
PRODUCTION *See* Economics; Industries

PROFESSIONAL BULL RIDERS, INC.
Peter, J. Fried twinkies, buckle bunnies & bull rid-
    ers **791.8**
The **professional** chef. **641.5**
**PROFESSIONAL DEVELOPMEN -- HAND-
    BOOKS, MANUALS, ETC.**
Blake, J. Life after college **646.7**
PROFESSIONAL EDUCATION
    See also Education; Higher education; Learn-
    ing and scholarship
**PROFESSIONAL EMPLOYEES -- UNITED
    STATES**
Fideler, E. F. Men still at work **331.3**
PROFESSIONAL ETHICS
Defending professionalism **020**
PROFESSIONAL ETHICS
    See also Ethics
PROFESSIONAL SPORTS
    See also Sports
PROFESSIONS
McKenna, A. Nontraditional careers for women
    and men **331.702**
PROFESSIONS
    See also Occupations; Self-employed
The **professor** and the madman. Winchester, S. **423**
Professor Stewart's casebook of mathematical mys-
    teries. Stewart, I. **510**
PROFESSORS *See* Educators; Teachers
Profiles in courage. Kennedy, J. F. **920**
Profiles of American colleges 2015. **378.73**
PROFIT
Dreman, D. Contrarian investment strate-
    gies **332.601**
PROFIT
    See also Business; Capital; Economics;
    Wealth
PROFIT -- UNITED STATES
Desmond, M. c. Evicted **339.4**
PROFIT SHARING
    See also Commerce; Salaries, wages, etc.
The **Profiteers.** Denton, S. **338.7**
PROGNOSIS
Gawande, A. Being mortal **362.17**
Programming the universe. Lloyd, S. **530.1**
PROGRESS
Johnson, S. Future perfect **303.48**
PROGRESS
    See also Civilization
PROGRESSIVE EDUCATION *See* Education --
    Experimental methods
**PROGRESSIVISM (UNITED STATES POLI-
    TICS)**
Diner, S. J. A very different age **973.8**
McGerr, M. E. A fierce discontent **324.2**
**PROGRESSIVISM (UNITED STATES POLI-
    TICS)**

See also Political science

PROGRESSIVISM (UNITED STATES POLI-TICS) -- HISTORY -- 20TH CENTURY

Goodwin, D. K. The Bully Pulpit   **973.91**

PROGRESSIVISM (UNITED STATES POLI-TICS) -- HISTORY -- 21ST CENTURY

Feingold, R. While America sleeps   **327**

PROHIBITED BOOKS *See* Books -- Censorship

PROHIBITED BOOKS -- SOVIET UNION -- HISTORY

Finn, P. The Zhivago affair   **891.73**

PROHIBITED BOOKS -- UNITED STATES -- BIBLIOGRAPHY

Scales, P. R. Books under fire   **016**

PROHIBITION

McGirr, L. The war on alcohol   **363.4**

Okrent, D. Last call   **363.4**

Project Animal Farm. Faruqi, S.   **338.1**

PROJECT APOLLO

Nelson, C. Rocket men   **629.45**

Pyle, R. Destination moon   **629.45**

Smith, A. Moondust   **920**

PROJECT APOLLO *See* Apollo project

PROJECT APOLLO (U.S.)

Mailer, N. Of a fire on the moon   **629.45**

PROJECT APOLLO (U.S.) -- HISTORY

Barbree, J. Neil Armstrong   **92**

Project Fatherhood. Leap, J.   **306.874**

PROJECT MERCURY

Ackmann, M. The Mercury 13: the untold story of thirteen American women and the dream of space flight   **629.45**

PROJECT METHOD IN TEACHING

See also Teaching

Project smoke. Raichlen, S.   **641.6**

PROJECT VOYAGER

Bell, J. The interstellar age   **919**

Pyne, S. J. Voyager   **919**

PROJECT VOYAGER

See also Astronautics -- United States

The **projectionist**. Messick, K.   **92**

PROJECTIVE GEOMETRY

See also Geometry

Prokofiev, Sergey, 1891-1953

About

Nice, D. Prokofiev: from Russia to the West, 1891-1935   **92**

Prokofiev: from Russia to the West, 1891-1935. Nice, D.   **92**

PROLETARIAT

The revolt of the masses   **901**

PROLETARIAT

See also Labor; Socialism; Working class

PROLIFERATION OF ARMS *See* Arms race

Promiscuities. Wolf, N.   **306.7**

The **promise**. Alter, J.   **92**

Promised land. Parini, J.   **810**

PROMISES

See also Ethics

Proof. Rogers, A.   **663**

Proof. Auburn, D.   **812**

Proofiness. Seife, C.   **510**

PROOFREADING

See also Printing

PROPAGANDA

Dower, J. W. Ways of forgetting, ways of remembering   **940.53**

Huxley, A. Brave new world revisited   **303.3**

PROPAGANDA

See also Political psychology; Public opinion

PROPAGANDA -- KOREA (NORTH)

Jang Jin-sung Dear Leader   **92**

PROPAGATION OF PLANTS *See* Plant propagation

A **proper** drink. Simonson, R.   **641.87**

PROPHECIES

Gerson, S. Nostradamus   **92**

PROPHECIES

See also Occultism; Supernatural

PROPHECIES (OCCULT SCIENCES) *See* Prophecies

PROPHECIES (OCCULTISM)

Gerson, S. Nostradamus   **92**

PROPHECIES (OCCULTISM) *See* Prophecies

PROPHECY *See* Prophecies

The **Prophet**. Gibran, K.   **811**

Prophet's prey. Brower, S.   **306.8**

PROPHETS

Armstrong, K. Muhammad   **297**

Hazleton, L. After the prophet   **297**

PROPHETS

See also Religious biography

PROPHETS -- UNITED STATES -- BIOGRAPHY

Cornel West on Black prophetic fire   **92**

PROPORTIONAL REPRESENTATION

See also Constitutional law; Representative government and representation

PROPOSAL WRITING FOR GRANTS

MacKellar, P. H. Writing successful technology grant proposals   **025.1**

PROPRIETARY RIGHTS *See* Intellectual property

ProQuest LLC

(comp) Proquest Statistical Abstract of the United States 2015   **317.3**

Prose and poetry. Crane, S.   **813**

PROSE LITERATURE -- AUTHORSHIP

Kidder, T. Good prose   **808.02**

PROSE LITERATURE, AMERICAN *See* American prose literature

PROSE POETRY

See also Poetry

Prose, Francine

Anne Frank   **839.3**

Caravaggio   **92**

Peggy Guggenheim   **92**

Reading like a writer   **808**

PROSECUTION -- CORRUPT PRACTICES

Cohan, W. D. The price of silence   **364.15**

PROSECUTION -- UNITED STATES

Garrett, B. L. Too big to jail   **345.73**

Prosek, Jen

Raising Can-Do Kids   **649.7**

PROSPECTING

See also Gold mines and mining; Mines and mineral resources; Silver mines and mining

Prosper, David

(jt. auth) White, V. The Total Skywatcher's Manual   **523.8**

PROSTITUTES -- IRELAND -- DUBLIN -- BIOGRAPHY

Moran, R. Paid for   **306.74**

PROSTITUTION

Hicks, G. The comfort women   **940.54**

Kolker, R. Lost Girls   **364.152**

Krist, G. Empire of sin   **976.3**

PROSTITUTION

See also Sexual ethics; Social problems; Women -- Social conditions

PROSTITUTION -- CALIFORNIA

Phelps, C. Runaway girl   **362.74**

PROSTITUTION -- ILLINOIS -- CHICAGO

Abbott, K. Sin in the Second City   **977.3**

PROSTITUTION -- IRELAND

Moran, R. Paid for   **306.74**

Protecting America's health. Hilts, P. J.   **353.9**

Protecting intellectual freedom in your public library. Pinnell-Stephens, J.   **025.2**

PROTECTIVE CUSTODY

Rushdie, S. Joseph Anton   **92**

Proteinaholic. Jacobson, H.   **613.2**

PROTEINS

See also Biochemistry; Nutrition

PROTEINS IN HUMAN NUTRITION

Jacobson, H. Proteinaholic   **613.2**

PROTEST MARCHES AND RALLIES *See* Demonstrations

PROTEST MOVEMENTS

Hedges, C. Wages of rebellion   **303.48**

Kasinof, L. Don't be afraid of the bullets   **953.305**

Razsa, M. Bastards of Utopia   **303.48**

PROTEST MOVEMENTS

See also Social movements

PROTEST MOVEMENTS -- ARCTIC REGIONS

Stewart, B. Don't trust, don't fear, don't beg   **363.738**

PROTEST MOVEMENTS -- SYRIA -- HISTORY

-- 21ST CENTURY

Erlich, R. Inside Syria   **956.91**

PROTEST MOVEMENTS -- UNITED STATES -- HISTORY

Fraser, S. The age of acquiescence   **973.91**

Young, R. Dissent   **303.48**

PROTEST MOVEMENTS -- YEMEN (REPUBLIC) -- HISTORY -- 21ST CENTURY

Kasinof, L. Don't be afraid of the bullets   **953.305**

The **protest** singer. Wilkinson, A.   **92**

PROTEST SONGS -- HISTORY AND CRITICISM

Lynskey, D. 33 revolutions per minute   **782.42**

PROTESTANTISM

Preston, A. Sword of the spirit, shield of faith   **322**

PROTESTANTISM

See also Christianity; Church history

PROTESTS, DEMONSTRATIONS, ETC. *See* Demonstrations

Prothero, Donald R., 1954-

Abominable science!   **001.944**

The story of life in 25 fossils   **560**

Prothero, Stephen

The American Bible   **973**

God is not one   **200**

Religious literacy   **200**

PROTONS

See also Atoms; Particles (Nuclear physics)

PROTOPLASM

See also Biology; Life (Biology)

PROTOZOA

See also Microorganisms

The **proud** tower. Tuchman, B. W.   **909.82**

Proulx, Annie, 1935-

Bird cloud   **92**

Cider   **641.2**

Proust's way. Shattuck, R.   **843**

Proust, Marcel, 1871-1922

About

Bloom, H. The Western canon   **809**

Carter, W. C. Marcel Proust   **843**

Nabokov, V. V. Lectures on literature   **808.3**

Shattuck, R. Proust's way   **843**

PROVENCE (FRANCE)

Mayle, P. Encore Provence   **944.083**

PROVENCE (FRANCE) -- BIOGRAPHY

Barr, L. Provence, 1970   **641.59**

PROVENCE (FRANCE) -- DESCRIPTION

Patricia Wells at home in Provence   **641.59**

PROVENCE (FRANCE) -- SOCIAL LIFE AND CUSTOMS

Mayle, P. Encore Provence   **944.083**

A year in Provence   **944.083**

The **Provence** cookbook. Wells, P.   **641.5**

Provence, 1970. Barr, L.   **641.59**

PROVERBS

Manser, M. H. The Facts on File dictionary of proverbs **398.9**

PROVERBS

    See also Folklore; Quotations

PROVIDENCE AND GOVERNMENT OF GOD

Kushner, H. S. When bad things happen to good people **296.3**

PROVIDENCE AND GOVERNMENT OF GOD

    See also God

Provine, Robert R.

Curious behavior **152.3**

Prozac diary. Slater, L. **616.89**

Prud'homme, Alex

Child, J. My life in France **92**

The French chef in America **641.509**

Hydrofracking **622**

Prueitt, Elisabeth M.

(jt. auth) Robertson, C. Tartine **641.8**

Prune. Hamilton, G. **641.3**

PRUNE (RESTAURANT)

Hamilton, G. Prune **641.3**

Pruning. Lowe, J. **631.5**

PRUNING

    See also Forests and forestry; Fruit culture; Gardening; Trees

PRUNING

Hobson, J. The art of creative pruning **715**

Lowe, J. Pruning **631.5**

Pruning plant by plant **635**

Ralph, A. Grow a little fruit tree **634**

Pruning & training. Joyce, D.

PRUNING -- HANDBOOKS, MANUALS, ETC

Joyce, D. Pruning & training

Pruning plant by plant. **635**

PRUSSIA (GERMANY) -- HISTORY -- FRED-ERICK II, 1740-1786

Blanning, T. Frederick the Great **92**

MacDonogh, G. Frederick the Great **943**

PRUSSIA -- KINGS AND RULERS

Blanning, T. Frederick the Great **92**

Pryor, Richard, 1940-2005

    About

Henry, D. Furious cool **92**

Life stories **920**

Mooney, P. Black is the new white **92**

PSEUDONYMS

Ciuraru, C. Nom de plume **929.4**

PSEUDONYMS

    See also Names; Personal names

PSEUDOSCIENCE

Prothero, D. R. Abominable science! **001.944**

PSI (PARAPSYCHOLOGY) *See* Parapsychology

Psilakis, Michael

How to roast a lamb **641.5**

PSYCHIATRISTS

Halberstam, D. The children **323.1**

Hayman, R. A life of Jung **150.19**

Jamison, K. R. Nothing was the same **92**

Jung, C. G. Memories, dreams, reflections **150.19**

Kubler-Ross, E. The wheel of life **150**

Macey, D. Frantz Fanon **92**

Murphy, T. W. Life in rewind **92**

Saks, E. R. The center cannot hold **92**

PSYCHIATRISTS

    See also Psychologists

PSYCHIATRISTS -- ALGERIA -- BIOGRAPHY

Macey, D. Frantz Fanon **92**

PSYCHIATRY

Burns, T. Our Necessary Shadow **616.89**

Frances, A. Saving Normal **616.89**

Kramer, P. D. Listening to Prozac **616.85**

Lieberman, J. A. Shrinks **616.89**

Porter, R. Madness **616.89**

Shorter, E. A history of psychiatry **616.89**

Whitaker, R. Anatomy of an epidemic **616.89**

PSYCHIC TRAUMA

Karr-Morse, R. Scared sick **155.9**

Padgett, J. Struck by genius **155.9**

PSYCHICAL RESEARCH *See* Parapsychology

PSYCHICS

Kirkpatrick, S. Edgar Cayce **92**

PSYCHICS

    See also Parapsychology; Persons

Psycho USA. Schechter, H. **364.152**

PSYCHOACTIVE DRUGS *See* Psychotropic drugs

PSYCHOANALYSIS

The basic writings of Sigmund Freud **150.19**

Bettelheim, B. Freud and man's soul **150.19**

The essential Jung **150.19**

The Freud reader **150.19**

Freud, S. Interpretation of dreams **154.6**

Fromm, E. On being human **150.19**

Gay, P. A Godless Jew **150.19**

Jung, C. G. The basic writings of C. G. Jung **150.19**

Jung, C. G. The portable Jung **150.19**

Lieberman, J. A. Shrinks **616.89**

PSYCHOANALYSIS

    See also Psychology

PSYCHOANALYSTS

Bettelheim, B. Freud and man's soul **150.19**

Bloom, H. The Western canon **809**

Gay, P. Freud **92**

Gay, P. A Godless Jew **150.19**

PSYCHOBIOLOGY

Smoller, J. The other side of normal **591.5**

PSYCHOLOGISTS

Bjork, D. W. B.F. Skinner **92**

Blum, D. Ghost hunters **133.9**

Commager, H. S. The American mind **973**

Frankl, V. E. Man's search for meaning **92**

Greenfield, R. Timothy Leary **92**

Hayman, R. A life of Jung   **150.19**

Jamison, K. R. Nothing was the same   **92**

Jung, C. G. Memories, dreams, reflections **150.19**

Lattin, D. The Harvard Psychedelic Club   **920**

Menand, L. The Metaphysical Club   **973.9**

Richardson, R. D. William James   **92**

Sagan, C. Broca's brain   **500**

Said, E. W. Reflections on exile and other essays   **814**

Slater, L. Prozac diary   **616.89**

PSYCHOLOGISTS -- RESEARCH
Hustvedt, S. Living, thinking, looking   **814**

PSYCHOLOGY
Bluestein, J. The perfection deception   **155.2**

Boyes, A. The anxiety toolkit   **616.85**

Brogaard, B. The superhuman mind   **153.9**

Brotherton, R. Suspicious Minds   **153.4**

Colman, A. M. A dictionary of psychology   **150**

Crawford, M. B. The World Beyond Your Head   **155.2**

Edelman, S. The happiness of pursuit   **153**

Glasser, W. Choice theory   **150**

Gonzales, L. Surviving survival   **155.9**

James, W. The varieties of religious experience **210**

Judith, A. Eastern body, Western mind   **150.19**

Jung, C. G. Man and his symbols   **150.19**

Kagan, J. The human spark   **155**

Lewis, M. Understanding pain   **616**

The Oxford companion to the mind   **128**

Pink, D. H. Drive   **153.1**

Pinker, S. How the mind works   **153**

Pollack, R. The missing moment   **610**

Rogers, C. R. A way of being   **150.19**

Ros, H. Neurocomic   **612.82**

Saul, R. ADHD does not exist   **618.92**

Smoller, J. The other side of normal   **591.5**

Tallis, F. Hidden minds   **154.2**

Triandis, H. C. Fooling ourselves   **155.2**

Trivers, R. The folly of fools   **153.4**

Viorst, J. Imperfect control   **158.1**

Waal, F. B. M. d. Are We Smart Enough to Know How Smart Animals Are?   **591.5**

Washington, H. A. Infectious madness   **616.89**

Weber, R. J. The created self   **155.2**

PSYCHOLOGY
See also Brain; Philosophy; Soul

PSYCHOLOGY -- DICTIONARIES
Colman, A. M. A dictionary of psychology   **150**

The Oxford companion to the mind   **128**

PSYCHOLOGY -- ENCYCLOPEDIAS
Cordon, L. A. Popular psychology   **150**

PSYCHOLOGY AND RELIGION *See* Psychology of religion

PSYCHOLOGY OF LEARNING
Carey, B. How we learn   **153.1**

Ericsson, A. Peak   **153.9**

Gopnik, A. The scientist in the crib   **155.4**

Jackson, R. The learning habit   **371.3**

PSYCHOLOGY OF LEARNING
See also Animal intelligence; Child psychology; Education; Educational psychology; Memory

PSYCHOLOGY OF RELIGION
The concept of anxiety   **233**

Haidt, J. The righteous mind   **201**

Peck, M. S. Further along the road less traveled **158**

Triandis, H. C. Fooling ourselves   **155.2**

PSYCHOLOGY OF RELIGION
See also Psychology; Religion

PSYCHOLOGY, APPLIED *See* Applied psychology; Persuasion (Psychology)

PSYCHOLOGY, COMPARATIVE *See* Comparative psychology

PSYCHOLOGY, EVOLUTIONARY *See* Evolutionary psychology

PSYCHOLOGY, INDUSTRIAL
Kerpen, D. The art of people   **650.1**

Webb, C. How to have a good day   **650.1**

PSYCHOLOGY, INDUSTRIAL *See* Industrial psychology

PSYCHOLOGY, MILITARY -- HANDBOOKS, MANUALS, ETC
Lawhorne-Scott, C. Military mental health care   **355.3**

PSYCHOLOGY, PASTORAL *See* Pastoral psychology

PSYCHOLOGY, PATHOLOGICAL
Grandin, T. The autistic brain   **616.85**

PSYCHOLOGY, PATHOLOGICAL *See* Abnormal psychology

PSYCHOLOGY, RELIGIOUS
Barrett, J. L. Born believers   **200.1**

The concept of anxiety   **233**

Haidt, J. The righteous mind   **201**

PSYCHOLOGY, RELIGIOUS *See* Pastoral psychology; Psychology of religion

The **psychopath** test. Ronson, J.   **616.85**

PSYCHOPATHS
Ronson, J. The psychopath test   **616.85**

PSYCHOSES
Earley, P. Resilience   **616.89**

PSYCHOSES *See* Mental illness

PSYCHOSOMATIC MEDICINE
See also Abnormal psychology; Medicine; Mind and body; Psychoanalysis

PSYCHOTHERAPISTS -- UNITED STATES -- BIOGRAPHY
Smith, C. B. The rules of inheritance   **616.99**

PSYCHOTHERAPISTS -- WASHINGTON (STATE) -- SEATTLE -- BIOGRAPHY
Guppy, J. My fluorescent God   **92**

PSYCHOTHERAPY

Burns, D. D. Feeling good   **158**
Hayden, T. L. Twilight children   **618.92**
Kramer, P. D. Listening to Prozac   **616.85**
May, R. The discovery of being   **150.19**
Prizant, B. M. Uniquely human   **618.92**

PSYCHOTHERAPY
  See also Psychiatry; Therapeutics

PSYCHOTIC CHILDREN *See* Emotionally disturbed children

PSYCHOTICS *See* Mentally ill

PSYCHOTROPIC DRUGS
Courtwright, D. T. Forces of habit   **362.29**
Kramer, P. D. Listening to Prozac   **616.85**
Slater, L. Prozac diary   **616.89**
Whitaker, R. Anatomy of an epidemic   **616.89**

PSYCHOTROPIC DRUGS
  See also Drugs

PT 109. Doyle, W.   **940.54**

PT-109 (TORPEDO BOAT)
Doyle, W. PT 109   **940.54**

Ptacek, Greg
Vare, E. A. Patently female   **609.2**

Ptak, Claire
The Violet Bakery cookbook   **641.86**

Pubantz, Jerry
Moore, J. A. Encyclopedia of the United Nations   **341.23**

PUBLIC ADMINISTRATION
  See also Local government; Municipal government; Political science

PUBLIC ADMINISTRATION -- UNITED STATES -- ANECDOTES
Gates, R. M. A passion for leadership   **92**

PUBLIC BUILDINGS
  See also Buildings; Public works

PUBLIC BUILDINGS -- UNITED STATES
Vogel, S. The Pentagon   **355.6**
Public cowboy no. 1. George-Warren, H.   **92**

PUBLIC DEBTS
  See also Debt; Loans; Public finance

PUBLIC DEBTS -- UNITED STATES
Johnson, S. White House burning   **336.3**
Lane, C. A Nation Wholly Free   **336.3**

PUBLIC DEMONSTRATIONS *See* Demonstrations

The **public** domain. Fishman, S.   **346**

PUBLIC FIGURES *See* Celebrities

PUBLIC FINANCE
Kleinbard, E. D. We are better than this   **336.3**
Pond, J. D. Grow your money!   **332.024**

PUBLIC FINANCE
  See also Finance

PUBLIC HEALTH
Encyclopedia of public health   **362.1**
Farley, T. Saving Gotham   **362.1**
Garrett, L. Betrayal of trust   **362.1**

Quammen, D. Ebola   **614.5**

PUBLIC HEALTH
  See also Health; Human services; Social problems; State medicine

PUBLIC HEALTH -- ENCYCLOPEDIAS
Encyclopedia of public health   **362.1**

PUBLIC HEALTH -- GOVERNMENT POLICY
  See Medical policy

PUBLIC HEALTH -- METHODS -- NEW YORK CITY -- PERSONAL NARRATIVES
Farley, T. Saving Gotham   **362.1**

PUBLIC HEALTH -- UNITED STATES
Sommer, A. Getting what we deserve   **362.1**

PUBLIC HEALTH OFFICIALS
McCullough, D. G. The path between the seas   **972.87**
Varmus, H. The art and politics of science   **92**

PUBLIC INTEREST -- UNITED STATES
Smith, H. Who stole the American dream?   **973.91**

PUBLIC LANDS
  See also Colonization; Land use

PUBLIC LIBRARIANSHIP
McCook, K. d. l. P. Introduction to public librarianship   **027.4**

PUBLIC LIBRARIES
Butler, P. M. Joint libraries   **027**
Landau, H. B. The small public library survival guide   **025.1**
Larson, J. C. The public library policy writer   **025.1**
Matthews, J. R. Scorecards for results   **027.4**
Moller, S. C. Library service to Spanish speaking patrons   **027.6**
Saricks, J. G. Readers' advisory service in the public library   **025.5**
Vaillancourt, R. J. Bare bones young adult services   **027.62**
Wyatt, N. The readers' advisory guide to nonfiction   **025.5**

PUBLIC LIBRARIES
  See also Libraries

PUBLIC LIBRARIES -- AIMS AND OBJECTIVES
McClure, C. R. Public libraries and internet service roles   **025.04**

PUBLIC LIBRARIES -- BOOK SELECTION -- UNITED STATES
Foerstel, H. N. Banned in the U.S.A   **025.2**

PUBLIC LIBRARIES -- CENSORSHIP -- UNITED STATES
Foerstel, H. N. Banned in the U.S.A   **025.2**
Pinnell-Stephens, J. Protecting intellectual freedom in your public library   **025.2**

PUBLIC LIBRARIES -- COLLECTION DEVELOPMENT
Alabaster, C. Developing an outstanding core collection   **025.2**

PUBLIC LIBRARIES -- COLLECTION DEVELOPMENT -- UNITED STATES
Bartlett, W. K. Floating collections   **025.2**
Vnuk, R. The weeding handbook   **025.2**
PUBLIC LIBRARIES -- SOCIAL ASPECTS
McClure, C. R. Public libraries and internet service roles   **025.04**
PUBLIC LIBRARIES -- UNITED STATES
McCook, K. d. l. P. Introduction to public librarianship   **027.4**
PUBLIC LIBRARIES -- UNITED STATES -- BOOK LISTS
Alpert, A. Read on-- graphic novels   **016**
Frolund, T. Read on...history   **016**
Torres-Roman, S. A. Read on-- science fiction **016**
Vnuk, R. Women's fiction   **016**
PUBLIC LIBRARIES -- UNITED STATES -- BOOK LISTS.
Pulliam, J. M. Read on . . . horror fiction   **025**
PUBLIC LIBRARIES -- UTAH -- SALT LAKE CITY
Hanagarne, J. The world's strongest librarian   **92**
Public libraries and internet service roles. McClure, C. R.   **025.04**
Public Library Association
Vaillancourt, R. J. Bare bones young adult services   **027.62**
The **public** library policy writer. Larson, J. C. **025.1**
PUBLIC OPINION
Bai, M. All the truth is out   **328.73**
Corner, P. The Fascist Party and popular opinion in Mussolini's Italy   **945.091**
Davis, M. Digital assassination   **005**
Hodes, M. Mourning Lincoln   **973.7**
Wolfe, A. Moral freedom   **170**
PUBLIC OPINION
See also Freedom of conscience; Political psychology; Political science; Social psychology
PUBLIC OPINION -- ITALY -- HISTORY -- 20TH CENTURY
Corner, P. The Fascist Party and popular opinion in Mussolini's Italy   **945.091**
PUBLIC OPINION -- POLITICAL ASPECTS -- UNITED STATES -- HISTORY
Greenberg, D. Republic of spin   **973.099**
PUBLIC OPINION -- UNITED STATES
Friedman, B. The will of the people   **347**
Kunhardt, P. B. Looking for Lincoln   **92**
Wolfe, A. Moral freedom   **170**
PUBLIC OPINION -- UNITED STATES -- HISTORY -- 20TH CENTURY
Bai, M. All the truth is out   **328.73**
PUBLIC OPINION POLLS
See also Public opinion
PUBLIC RECORDS -- PRESERVATION *See* Archives

PUBLIC RELATIONS
Kotter, J. P. Buy-in   **650.1**
RoAne, S. How to work a room   **650.1**
Thompson, D. C. The reputation economy **302.23**
PUBLIC RELATIONS -- LIBRARIES *See* Libraries -- Public relations
PUBLIC RELATIONS AND POLITICS -- UNITED STATES -- HISTORY
Greenberg, D. Republic of spin   **973.099**
PUBLIC SAFETY, CRIMES AGAINST *See* Offenses against public safety
PUBLIC SCHOOLS
Kozol, J. Savage inequalities   **371.9**
PUBLIC SCHOOLS -- CENSORSHIP -- UNITED STATES
Foerstel, H. N. Banned in the U.S.A   **025.2**
PUBLIC SCHOOLS -- UNITED STATES
Reese, W. J. Testing wars in the public schools   **371.26**
Russakoff, D. The prize   **371.2**
PUBLIC SCHOOLS -- VERMONT -- CASE STUDIES
Keizer, G. Getting Schooled   **373.1**
PUBLIC SCHOOLS AND RELIGION *See* Religion in the public schools
PUBLIC SERVICE COMMISSIONS
See also Corporation law; Corporations; Industrial policy
PUBLIC SERVICES (LIBRARIES)
Evans, G. E. Introduction to library public services   **025.5**
Hernon, P. Assessing service quality   **025.5**
Ross, C. S. Reading matters   **028**
PUBLIC SERVICES (LIBRARIES) -- UNITED STATES
Reference reborn   **025.5**
PUBLIC SPEAKING
Duarte, N. Resonate   **658.452**
Gallo, C. Talk like TED   **658.4**
How to write & give a speech   **808.5**
Meyers, P. As we speak   **808.5**
Reynolds, G. Presentation zen
The **publisher.** Brinkley, A.   **92**
PUBLISHERS AND AUTHORS *See* Authors and publishers
PUBLISHERS AND PUBLISHING
Brewer, R. L. Writer's Market   **808**
Brinkley, A. The publisher   **92**
The Chicago manual of style   **808**
Children's writer's & illustrator's market   **808**
Getting it published   **070.5**
Herman, J. Jeff Herman's guide to book publishers, editors, & literary agents   **070.5**
Whyte, K. The uncrowned king   **92**
PUBLISHERS AND PUBLISHING -- DIRECTO-

RIES
American book trade directory   **070.5**
Literary market place   **070.5**
Publishers, distributors & wholesalers of the United States   **070.5**
PUBLISHERS AND PUBLISHING -- ENGLAND -- LONDON -- HISTORY -- 17TH CENTURY
Mays, A. E. The millionaire and the bard   **822.33**
PUBLISHERS AND PUBLISHING -- HANDBOOKS, MANUALS, ETC.
The Chicago manual of style   **808**
United States/Government Printing Office Style manual   **808**
PUBLISHERS AND PUBLISHING -- HISTORY -- 20TH CENTURY
Smith Rakoff, J. My Salinger year   **92**
PUBLISHERS AND PUBLISHING -- UNITED STATES -- BIOGRAPHY
Nasaw, D. The chief: the life of William Randolph Hearst   **070.5**
The tender hour of twilight   **070.5**
PUBLISHERS AND PUBLISHING -- UNITED STATES -- HISTORY -- 20TH CENTURY
Turner, F. Renegade   **813**
PUBLISHERS' CATALOGS
    See also Publishers and publishing
PUBLISHERS' STANDARD BOOK NUMBERS
    See also Publishers and publishing
Publishers, distributors & wholesalers of the United States.   **070.5**
PUBLISHING *See* Publishers and publishing
PUBLISHING EXECUTIVES
Brent, J. Inside the Stalin archives   **947.086**
Breslin, E. Drinking with Miss Dutchie   **92**
Glendinning, V. Leonard Woolf   **92**
Rubin, L. D. My father's people   **920**
Schumacher, M. Will Eisner   **92**
Wolff, M. The man who owns the news   **92**
PUBS *See* Bars
Puccini without excuses. Berger, W.   **92**
Puccini, Giacomo, 1858-1924
        About
Berger, W. Puccini without excuses   **92**
Osborne, C. The complete operas of Puccini **792.5**
Puck, Wolfgang
Live, love, eat!   **641.5**
Pudge. Wilson, D.   **92**
PUEBLO INDIANS
Childs, C. L. House of rain   **978.9**
Nabokov, P. How the World Moves   **970.3**
PUERPERAL SEPTICEMIA
Nuland, S. B. The doctors' plague   **92**
PUERTO RICANS -- NEW YORK (N.Y.)
Ghetto Brother   **92**
PUFFINS
    See also Birds

PUGET SOUND REGION (WASH.)
Jacobsen, R. The living shore   **639.9**
Kluger, R. The bitter waters of Medicine Creek   **979.7**
Welch, C. Shell games   **364.1**
Pugh-Gannon, JoAnn
Bednar, N. The encyclopedia of sewing machine techniques   **646.2**
PUGILISM *See* Boxing
Pujol, Juan
        About
Talty, S. Agent Garbo   **940.5**
Pukka's Promise. Kerasote, T.   **636.7**
Pukui, Mary Kawena
Hawaiian dictionary   **499**
Puleo, Stephen
American treasures   **973**
Dark tide   **363.1**
Pulitzer. Morris, J. M.   **92**
PULITZER PRIZES
Buell, H. Moments   **070.4**
Written into history   **071**
Pulitzer, Joseph, 1847-1911
        About
Morris, J. M. Pulitzer   **92**
Pull. Siegel, D.   **658.8**
Pulliam, June Michele
Fonseca, A. J. Hooked on horror III   **016**
Read on . . . horror fiction   **025**
Pullum, Geoffrey K.
Huddleston, R. D. The Cambridge grammar of the English language   **425**
PULSARS
    See also Astronomy
Pult, Jon, 1966-
Cooking my way back home   **641.5**
PUMPING MACHINERY
    See also Engines; Hydraulic engineering
Pumpkinflowers. Friedman, M.   **956.92**
PUNCTUALITY
    See also Time; Virtue
PUNCTUATED EQUILIBRIUM (EVOLUTION)
Gould, S. J. The structure of evolutionary theory   **576.8**
PUNCTUATION
Truss, L. Eats, shoots & leaves   **421**
PUNCTUATION
    See also Rhetoric
PUNCTUATION -- HISTORY
Houston, K. Shady characters   **411**
PUNIC WARS, 264 B.C.-146 B.C.
O'Connell, R. L. The ghosts of Cannae   **937**
PUNISHMENT
Spierenburg, P. Violence and punishment **364.67**
PUNISHMENT
    See also Administration of criminal justice;

Corrections

PUNK CULTURE

Punk rock   **781.66**

The riot grrrl collection   **781.64**

PUNK CULTURE

See also Counter culture

Punk rock.   **781.66**

PUNK ROCK MUSIC

Albertine, V. Clothes, Clothes, Clothes. Music, Music, Music. Boys, Boys, Boys   **92**

McMurray, J. Taking punk to the masses   **781.66**

Moore, T. No wave   **781.66**

Punk rock   **781.66**

Trynka, P. Iggy Pop   **92**

Waksman, S. This ain't the summer of love   **781.66**

PUNK ROCK MUSIC -- HISTORY AND CRITICISM

Punk rock   **781.66**

PUNK ROCK MUSIC -- PERIODICALS

The riot grrrl collection   **781.64**

PUNK ROCK MUSICIANS -- GREAT BRITAIN -- BIOGRAPHY

Albertine, V. Clothes, Clothes, Clothes. Music, Music, Music. Boys, Boys, Boys   **92**

PUNK ROCK MUSICIANS -- UNITED STATES -- BIOGRAPHY

Rufus, R. Die young with me   **92**

PUNS

See also Wit and humor

Pupo-Walker, Enrique

(ed) Gonzalez Echevarria, R. The Cambridge history of Latin American literature   **860**

PUPPETEERS -- UNITED STATES -- BIOGRAPHY

Jones, B. J. Jim Henson   **92**

Puppetry. Blumenthal, E.   **791.5**

PUPPETS AND PUPPET PLAYS

Blumenthal, E. Puppetry   **791.5**

PUPPETS AND PUPPET PLAYS

See also Drama; Folk drama; Theater

PUPPIES

The art of raising a puppy   **636.7**

PUPPIES *See* Dogs

PUPPIES -- TRAINING

The art of raising a puppy   **636.7**

Purcell, L. Edward

Burg, D. F. Almanac of World War I   **940.3**

Purcell, Sarah J.

The early national period   **973.4**

PURCHASING

See also Management

PURCHASING MANAGERS

Singer, M. Character studies   **920**

Purdum, Todd S., 1959-

An idea whose time has come   **342.73**

Pure country. Kagarise, L.   **781.642**

Pure drivel. Martin, S.   **814**

PURE FOOD *See* Food adulteration and inspection

Purgatorio. Dante Alighieri   **851**

PURGATORY

See also Eschatology

PURITANS

Barry, J. M. Roger Williams and the creation of the American soul   **974.5**

Boorstin, D. J. The Americans: The colonial experience   **973**

Gaustad, E. S. Roger Williams   **92**

Vowell, S. The wordy shipmates   **974**

Purnell, Sonia

Clementine   **92**

Pursell, J. J.

The herbal apothecary   **615.3**

PURSES *See* Handbags

The **pursuit** of glory. Blanning, T. C. W.   **940.2**

The **pursuit** of happyness. Gardner, C.   **92**

Purvis, Alston W.

(ed) The poster   **741.6**

Pushcart Prize XXXVI: best of the small presses 2012.   **810**

Pushkin's children. Tolstaia, T.   **891.7**

Pushkin, Aleksandr Sergeevich

Eugene Onegin and other poems   **891.7**

Pushkin, Aleksandr Sergeevich, 1799-1837

About

Binyon, T. J. Pushkin: a biography   **92**

Pushkin: a biography. Binyon, T. J.   **92**

PUSHTO POETRY -- 20TH CENTURY -- TRANSLATIONS INTO ENGLISH

I am the beggar of the world   **891**

Put 'em up! Vinton, S. B.   **641.6**

Put on a happy face. Strouse, C.   **92**

Putin country. Garrels, A.   **947.43**

Putin's kleptocracy. Dawisha, K.   **947.086**

Putin, Vladimir

About

First person: an astonishingly frank self-portrait   **92**

Politkovskaya, A. A Russian diary   **947.086**

Remnick, D. Reporting   **814**

Tolstaia, T. Pushkin's children   **891.7**

Dawisha, K. Putin's kleptocracy   **947.086**

Garrels, A. Putin country   **947.43**

PUYALLUP ASSEMBLY CENTER (PUYALLUP, WASH.)

Sone, M. Nisei daughter   **979.7**

PUZZLES

Levi, M. Why cats land on their feet   **530**

PUZZLES

See also Amusements

Pye, Michael

The Edge of the World   **940.1**

Pygmalion . . . and My fair lady. Shaw, B.   **822**

PYGMIES -- UNITED STATES -- BIOGRAPHY

Newkirk, P. Spectacle 92
Pyle, Ernie, 1900-1945
About
Tobin, J. E. Ernie Pyle's war **070.4**
Pyle, Robert Michael
The Audubon Society field guide to North American butterflies **595.7**
Pyle, Rod
Destination moon **629.45**
Pyne, Lydia
Seven skeletons **569.9**
Pyne, Stephen J.
Voyager **919**
Pyongyang: a journey in North Korea. Delisle, G. **741.5**
The **pyramids.** Verner, M. **932**
PYRAMIDS
Verner, M. The pyramids **932**
PYRAMIDS
See also Ancient architecture; Archeology; Monuments
PYROGRAPHY
See also Etching; Woodwork
Pythagoras
About
Rudman, P. S. The Babylonian theorem **510**
PYTHAGOREAN THEOREM
Kaplan, E. Hidden harmonies **516.2**
PYTHONS
Perez, L. Snake in the grass **597.96**

Q

Q HYPOTHESIS (SYNOPTICS CRITICISM)
Kloppenborg, J. S. Q, the earliest Gospel **226**
Q, the earliest Gospel. Kloppenborg, J. S. **226**
Q: the autobiography of Quincy Jones. Jones, Q. **92**
Qaddafi, Muammar
About
Chorin, E. Exit the colonel **961.204**
QAIDA (ORGANIZATION)
Bergen, P. L. The longest war **909.83**
Gull, I. The most dangerous place **954.91**
Herridge, C. The next wave **363.32**
Johnsen, G. D. The last refuge **363.325**
Soufan, A. H. The black banners **973.931**
Wright, L. The looming tower **973.931**
Wright, L. The terror years **363.325**
QAIDA (ORGANIZATION)
See also Terrorism
Qazwini, Hassan
About
Qazwini, H. American crescent **92**
QB. Benedict, J. **92**
QED. Feynman, R. P. **539.7**
QUACKS AND QUACKERY
Brock, P. Charlatan **92**

QUACKS AND QUACKERY
See also Impostors and imposture; Medicine; Swindlers and swindling
QUAKER LEADERS
Slaughter, T. P. The beautiful soul of John Woolman, apostle of abolition **92**
QUAKERS See Society of Friends
The **Quakers** in America. Hamm, T. D. **289.6**
QUALITY CONTROL
Cook, S. Customer care excellence **658.8**
The **quality** library. Laughlin, S. **025.1**
QUALITY OF LIFE
Becker, J. The more of less **241.68**
Chittister, J. Between the Dark and the Daylight **128**
Colvile, R. The Great Acceleration **303.483**
Evans, D. Designing your life **650.1**
Pickett, K. The spirit level **306**
Wann, D. The new normal **306**
QUALITY OF LIFE
See also Economic conditions; Social conditions
QUALITY OF LIFE -- FRANCE -- PARIS
James, E. Paris in love **92**
Quammen, David, 1948-
(ed) Darwin, C. On the origin of species **576.8**
Ebola **614.5**
Monster of God **591.6**
Spillover **614.4**
QUANTITY COOKERY See Quantity cooking
QUANTITY COOKING
The Eat Like a Man Guide to Feeding a Crowd **641.5**
QUANTITY COOKING
See also Cooking
Quantum. Kumar, M. **530.1**
QUANTUM CHAOS
Halpern, P. Einstein's dice and Schrödinger's cat **530.13**
Quantum generations. Kragh, H. **530**
Quantum legacy. Parker, B. R. **530.12**
Quantum man. Krauss, L. M. **92**
QUANTUM MECHANICS See Quantum theory
The **quantum** moment. Crease, R. P. **530.12**
The **quantum** story. Baggott, J. **530.1**
QUANTUM THEORY
Baggott, J. The quantum story **530.1**
Bolles, E. B. Einstein defiant **530.1**
Carroll, S. The Big Picture **577**
Close, F. E. The infinity puzzle **530.1**
Cole, K. C. The hole in the universe **530.01**
Cox, B. The quantum universe **530.12**
Einstein, A. The evolution of physics **530**
Feynman, R. P. QED **539.7**
Feynman, R. P. Six easy pieces **530**
Ford, K. W. 101 quantum questions **530.1**
Gilder, L. The age of entanglement **530.1**

Greene, B. The hidden reality **530.1**

Gribbin, J. R. In search of Schrödinger's cat **530.1**

Gribbin, J. R. Schrödinger's kittens and the search
for reality **530.1**

Gribbin, J. 13.8 **523.1**

Halpern, P. Einstein's dice and Schrödinger's
cat **530.13**

Hawking, S. W. The nature of space and time **530.1**

Hawking, S. W. The universe in a nutshell **530.1**

Hawking, S. The grand design **530.1**

Johnson, G. A shortcut through time **004.1**

Kaiser, D. How the hippies saved physics **530.092**

Kakalios, J. The amazing story of quantum mechanics **530.1**

Kumar, M. Quantum **530.1**

Lloyd, S. Programming the universe **530.1**

McFadden, J. Life on the Edge **572**

Parker, B. R. Quantum legacy **530.12**

Rigden, J. S. Einstein 1905 **530.1**

Rovelli, C. Seven Brief Lessons on Physics **530**

Susskind, L. The black hole war **530.1**

QUANTUM THEORY

See also Dynamics; Physics

QUANTUM THEORY -- HISTORY

Baggott, J. The quantum story **530.1**

Bolles, E. B. Einstein defiant **530.1**

Kumar, M. Quantum **530.1**

QUANTUM THEORY -- PHILOSOPHY

Halpern, P. Einstein's dice and Schrödinger's
cat **530.13**

QUANTUM THEORY -- POPULAR WORKS

Crease, R. P. The quantum moment **530.12**

The **quantum** universe. Cox, B. **530.12**

QUARANTINE *See* Communicable diseases

QUARKS

See also Particles (Nuclear physics)

Quarrel & quandary. Ozick, C. **814**

**QUARTERBACKS (FOOTBALL) -- UNITED
STATES -- BIOGRAPHY**

Anderson, L. The Mannings **796.332**

Dunnavant, K. Montana **92**

Myers, G. Brady vs Manning **92**

The **Quartet.** Ellis, J. J. **973.3**

QUARTZ

See also Crystals; Minerals

QUASARS

See also Astronomy; Radio astronomy

QUÉBEC CAMPAIGN, QUÉBEC, 1759

Macleod, D. P. Northern Armageddon **971.01**

Queen Anne. Somerset, A. **92**

The **queen** of distraction. Matlen, T. **616.85**

Queen of Spies. Hayes, P. **327.12**

Queen of the air. Jensen, D. **791.3**

Queen Victoria. Hibbert, C. **92**

Queen, William

Under and alone **364.1**

QUEENS

Andersen, C. Game of crowns **941.085**

Castor, H. She-wolves **920**

Cooney, K. The woman who would be king **92**

De Lisle, L. The sisters who would be queen **920**

Dryden, J. All for love **822**

Erickson, C. Her little majesty: the life of Queen
Victoria **92**

Fletcher, J. Cleopatra the great **92**

Fraser, A. Marie Antoinette **944**

Fraser, A. Mary Queen of Scots **92**

Fraser, A. The wives of Henry VIII **920**

Fraser, F. Princesses **920**

Goldsworthy, A. K. Antony and Cleopatra **92**

Hatshepsut: from queen to Pharaoh **932**

Hibbert, C. Queen Victoria **92**

Junor, P. The Firm: the troubled life of the House of
Windsor **941.085**

Lever, E. Marie Antoinette **92**

Mertz, B. Temples, tombs, & hieroglyphs **932**

Meyer, G. J. The Tudors **942.05**

Milton, G. Big Chief Elizabeth **970.004**

Porter, L. Katherine the queen **92**

Ryan, D. P. Beneath the sands of Egypt **92**

Schiff, S. Cleopatra **92**

Schiller, F. Don Carlos and Mary Stuart **832**

Starkey, D. Six wives: the queens of Henry
VIII **942.05**

Vallone, L. Becoming Victoria **941.08**

Waller, M. Sovereign ladies **920**

Weir, A. Eleanor of Aquitaine **92**

Weir, A. The lady in the tower **92**

Weir, A. The life of Elizabeth I **942.05**

Weir, A. Mary, Queen of Scots, and the murder of
Lord Darnley **92**

Williams, K. Becoming Queen Victoria **92**

QUEENS (NEW YORK, N.Y.)

Clancy, T. The Clancys of Queens **974.7**

QUEENS -- EGYPT -- BIOGRAPHY

Cooney, K. The woman who would be king **92**

QUEENS -- GREAT BRITAIN

Gristwood, S. Blood sisters **942.04**

Norton, E. The Temptation of Elizabeth Tudor **92**

Wilson, A. N. Victoria **92**

QUEENS -- GREAT BRITAIN -- BIOGRAPHY

Baird, J. Victoria **92**

Somerset, A. Queen Anne **92**

Starkey, D. Six wives: the queens of Henry
VIII **942.05**

Weir, A. Eleanor of Aquitaine **92**

Weir, A. The life of Elizabeth I **942.05**

QUEENS -- SPAIN -- BIOGRAPHY

Downey, K. Isabella **92**

A **queer** history of the United States. Bronski,
M. **306.76**

QUEER THEOLOGY

Edman, E. M.   Queer virtue   230
QUEER THEORY
   See also Criticism
Queer virtue. Edman, E. M.   230
Queller, Jessica, 1969-
        About
Queller, J.   Pretty is what changes   92
Quessenberry, Sara
   The good neighbor cookbook   641.5
The **quest.** Yergin, D.   333.79
The **quest** for life in amber. Poinar, G. O.   560
Quest, Penelope
   Reiki for life   615.8
A **question** of torture. McCoy, A. W.   323.4
Questions of science [series]
   Wilson, E. O.   The diversity of life   333.95
Questlove
        About
Greenman, B.   Mo' meta blues   92
Quiñones-Hinojosa, Alfredo
        About
Quiñones-Hinojosa, A.   Becoming Dr. Q   92
Quiches, kugels, and couscous. Nathan, J.   641.5
QUICK AND EASY COOKERY *See* Quick and
   easy cooking
QUICK AND EASY COOKING
   The best one-dish suppers   641.8
   Bittman, M.   Mark Bittman's Kitchen express 641.5
   Bracken, P.   The I hate to cook book   641.5
   Brennan, K.   Keepers   641.5
   Donofrio, J.   The Love and Lemons Cook-
     book   641.5
   Garten, I.   Cooking for Jeffrey   641.5
   Goodall, T.   The ultimate student cookbook   641.5
   The Great Big Pressure Cooker Book   641.5
   Griffin, B.   Skinny suppers   641.5
   Henry, D.   Simple   641.5
   It's all easy   641.5
   Le, S.   Easy Gourmet   641.5
   Olivier, M.   Little Bento   641.53
   One pot   641.82
   Spices of life   641.5
   Streiff, F.   The art of simple food   641.5
   Two Moms in the Raw   641.5
   You have it made!   641.5
QUICK AND EASY COOKING
   See also Cooking
Quick and easy Korean cooking. Lee, C.   641.5
Quick cash. Mayer, R.   332
QUICK-MEAL COOKING *See* Quick and easy
   cooking
Quiet. Cain, S.   155.2
The **quiet** world. Brinkley, D.   333.72
Quillen, C. L.
   Read on... romance   016
Quilliam, Susan

   (jt. auth)   Comfort, A.   The joy of sex   613.9
QUILT DESIGNING *See* Quilts -- Design
The **quilter's** album of patchwork patterns. Beyer,
   J.   746.46
QUILTING
   Beyer, J.   The quilter's album of patchwork pat-
     terns   746.46
   Gering, J.   Quilting modern   746.46
   Monk, J.   Tangle stitches for quilters + fabric artists
   Pink, T.   Quilts from the house of Tula Pink 746.46
   Pink, T.   Tula Pink's city sampler   746.46
QUILTING
   See also Needlework; Sewing
QUILTING -- HISTORY
   Baumgarten, L.   Four centuries of quilts   746.46
QUILTING -- PATTERNS
   Arkison, C.   Sunday morning quilts   746.46
   Denyse Schmidt   746.46
   Denyse Schmidt quilts   746.46
   Gilleland, D.   All points patchwork   746.46
   Hartman, E.   Modern patchwork   746.46
   Pink, T.   Quilts from the house of Tula Pink 746.46
Quilting modern. Gering, J.   746.46
Quilting the black-eyed pea. Giovanni, N.   811
QUILTS
   Arkison, C.   Sunday morning quilts   746.46
   Baumgarten, L.   Four centuries of quilts   746.46
   Fassett, K.   Kaffe Fassett's Bold Blooms   746
   Gering, J.   Quilting modern   746.46
   Hartman, E.   Modern patchwork   746.46
   Improv handbook for modern quilters   746.46
   Keuning-Tichelaar, A.   Passing on the com-
     fort   940.54
   Pink, T.   Quilts from the house of Tula Pink 746.46
   Pink, T.   Tula Pink's city sampler   746.46
   Tobin, J.   Hidden in plain view   973.7
QUILTS
   See also Interior design
QUILTS -- CATALOGS
   Baumgarten, L.   Four centuries of quilts   746.46
QUILTS -- DESIGN
   Denyse Schmidt   746.46
   Denyse Schmidt quilts   746.46
QUILTS -- DESIGN
   See also Design
QUILTS -- VIRGINIA -- WILLIAMSBURG --
     CATALOGS
   Baumgarten, L.   Four centuries of quilts   746.46
Quilts from the house of Tula Pink. Pink, T. 746.46
Quinion, Michael
   Ballyhoo, buckeroo, and spuds   422
Quinn, Alice
   (ed)   Bishop, E.   Edgar Allan Poe & the juke-
     box   811
Quinn, Edward
   Critical companion to George Orwell   828

Quinn, Jane Bryant
Making the most of your money now   **332.024**
Quinn, Susan
Eleanor and Hick   **92**
Quinn, Therese
(ed) Art and social justice education   **372.5**
QUINOA
Del Mar Sacasa, M. The quinoa [keen-wah] cook-
book   **641.3**
QUINOA
   See also Alternative grains; Farm produce
The **quinoa** [keen-wah] cookbook. Del Mar Sacasa,
M.   **641.3**
Quinones, Sam
Dreamland   **362.29**
Quiñones-Hinojosa, Alfredo
Becoming Dr. Q   **92**
Quirk, Lawrence J.
Bob Hope: the road well-traveled   **92**
QUIT-SMOKING PROGRAMS *See* Smoking
   cessation programs
Quite enough of Calvin Trillin. Trillin, C.   **817**
QUOTATIONS
Boller, P. F. They never said it   **808.88**
The Columbia Granger's dictionary of poetry quo-
tations   **808.81**
Einstein, A. The ultimate quotable Einstein   **530**
Kennedy, R. F. Make gentle the life of this
world   **973.922**
Nowlan, R. A. Born this day   **808.88**
O'Brien, G. Bartlett's familiar quotations   **808.88**
The Oxford book of aphorisms   **808.88**
Oxford dictionary of humorous quotations   **808.88**
Oxford dictionary of modern quotations   **808.88**
Oxford dictionary of scientific quotations   **500**
The Yale book of quotations   **082**
QUOTATIONS
   See also Epigrams
**QUOTATIONS -- TRANSLATIONS INTO ENG-
LISH**
Oxford dictionary of quotations   **082**
The **Qur'an.**   **297.1**
QUR'AN
   See also Islam; Sacred books
QUR'AN
The Qur'an   **297.1**
The Qur'an: an encyclopedia.   **297.1**
Qureshi, Anique
(jt. auth) Shim, J. K. Accounting handbook   **657**

R

R AND B MUSIC *See* Rhythm and blues music
RÉSUMÉS (EMPLOYMENT)
   See also Applications for positions; Job hunt-
   ing
R. Crumb: the complete record cover collection.

Crumb, R.   **741.6**
R.U.R. and The insect play. Capek, K.   **891.8**
Raab, Lawrence, 1946-
Mistaking each other for ghosts   **811**
Raab, Selwyn
Five families   **364.1**
Raban, Jonathan, 1942-
Bad land   **978**
Passage to Juneau   **979.8**
Rabban, David M.
Free speech in its forgotten years   **342**
RABBIS
Davidson, S. The December Project   **296.7**
Telushkin, J. Rebbe   **92**
RABBIS
   See also Clergy; Judaism
RABBITS
   See also Mammals
Rabid. Murphy, M.   **614.5**
RABIES
   See also Communicable diseases
RABIES -- TREATMENT -- HISTORY
Murphy, M. Rabid   **614.5**
Rabin, Nathan
My year of flops   **791.43**
Rabin, Yitzhak, 1922-1995
   About
Ephron, D. Killing a king   **956.94**
Shalom, friend: the life and legacy of Yitzhak
   Rabin   **92**
Rabiner, Susan
Thinking like your editor   **808**
Rabinowitz, Dorothy
No crueler tyrannies   **345**
Rabins, Peter V.
(jt. auth) Mace, N. L. The 36-hour day   **618.97**
Rable, George C.
God's almost chosen peoples   **973.7**
Raboteau, Emily
Searching for Zion   **305.896**
Rabow, Michael W.
(ed) Current medical diagnosis and treatment   **610**
Raboy, Marc
Marconi   **92**
RACE
Als, H. White Girls   **814**
Bonair-Agard, R. Bury my clothes   **811**
Roberts, D. Fatal invention   **305.8**
RACE
   See also Ethnology
RACE -- PHILOSOPHY
Jones, J. A dreadful deceit   **305.8**
**RACE -- POLITICAL ASPECTS -- UNITED
STATES**
Dyson, M. E. The Black presidency   **305.8**
RACE AWARENESS

Sharfstein, D. J. The invisible line   305.8

RACE AWARENESS

   See also Race relations

RACE AWARENESS -- UNITED STATES

Bayoumi, M. How does it feel to be a problem?   305.8

Sharfstein, D. J. The invisible line   305.8

RACE AWARENESS -- UNITED STATES -- HISTORY

Jones, J. A dreadful deceit   305.8

RACE DISCRIMINATION

Katznelson, I. When affirmative action was white   323.1

Marshall, T. Thurgood Marshall   347

Oshinsky, D. M. Worse than slavery   365

Phillips, P. Blood at the root   305.8

Rhoden, W. C. $40 million slaves   796

RACE DISCRIMINATION

   See also Discrimination; Race relations; Racism; Social problems

RACE DISCRIMINATION -- HISTORY

Norrell, R. J. Up from history   92

RACE DISCRIMINATION -- UNITED STATES

Wilder, C. S. Ebony and Ivy   379.26

RACE DISCRIMINATION -- UNITED STATES -- HISTORY -- 20TH CENTURY

Katznelson, I. When affirmative action was white   323.1

Paul, R. We could not fail   920

RACE DISCRIMINATION IN SPORTS -- HISTORY

Kashatus, W. C. Jackie and Campy   92

The **race** for paradise. Cobb, P. M.   909.07

RACE HORSES -- UNITED STATES -- BIOGRAPHY

Nack, W. Secretariat   798.4

RACE IDENTITY *See* Race awareness

A **race** like no other. Robbins, L.   796.42

RACE RELATIONS

Fabian, A. The skull collectors   599.9

Lauterbach, P. Beale Street Dynasty   976.8

Ruck, R. Raceball   796.357

Runstedtler, T. Jack Johnson, rebel sojourner   796.83

Sokol, J. All eyes are upon us   323.1

RACE RELATIONS

   See also Acculturation; Ethnology; Sociology

Race to the Polar Sea. McGoogan, K.   92

Raceball. Ruck, R.   796.357

RACES OF PEOPLE *See* Ethnology

Rachel and her children. Kozol, J.   362.5

Rachmaninoff, Sergei, 1873-1943

    About

Schonberg, H. C. The great pianists   920

RACIALLY MIXED PEOPLE

Byrne, P. Belle   92

Mendell, D. Obama   92

Mock, J. Redefining Realness   306.76

Morales, E. Living in Spanglish   305.868

My grandfather would have shot me   929.2

Obama, B. Dreams from my father   92

Pascoe, P. What comes naturally   346

Remnick, D. The bridge   92

Sharfstein, D. J. The invisible line   305.8

RACIALLY MIXED PEOPLE -- GERMANY -- BIOGRAPHY

My grandfather would have shot me   929.2

RACIALLY MIXED PEOPLE -- LEGAL STATUS, LAWS, ETC. -- UNITED STATES

Pascoe, P. What comes naturally   346

RACIALLY MIXED PEOPLE -- RACE IDENTITY

Sandweiss, M. A. Passing strange   92

RACIALLY MIXED PEOPLE -- UNITED STATES

Sharfstein, D. J. The invisible line   305.8

RACIALLY MIXED PEOPLE -- UNITED STATES -- BIOGRAPHY

Mock, J. Redefining Realness   306.76

Swarns, R. L. American tapestry   92

RACING *See* Bathtub racing; Chuckwagon racing

   See also Sports

Racing for the bomb: General Leslie R. Groves, the Manhattan Project's indispensable man. Norris, R. S.   92

Racing Odysseus. Martin, R. H.   92

RACISM

Achebe, C. The education of a British-protected child   92

Blum, E. J. The color of Christ   232

Brannan, K. The Family Tree   364.134

Dyson, M. E. The Black presidency   305.8

Ezekiel, R. S. The racist mind   320.5

The Fire This Time   305.896

Ford, R. T. Rights gone wrong   342

Goldhagen, D. J. Worse than war   364.1

King, M. L. Where do we go from here   323.1

Reed, I. Another day at the front   305.8

Touré Who's afraid of post-blackness?   305.8

Zeskind, L. Blood and politics   305.8

RACISM

   See also Attitude (Psychology); Prejudices; Race awareness; Race relations

RACISM -- GEORGIA

Phillips, P. Blood at the root   305.8

RACISM -- HISTORY

Kendi, I. X. Stamped from the beginning   305.8

Parkinson, R. G. The common cause   973.31

RACISM -- MISSISSIPPI -- HISTORY -- 20TH CENTURY

Anderson, D. S. Emmett Till   364.1

RACISM -- POETRY
Rankine, C. Citizen   **811**

RACISM -- POLITICAL ASPECTS -- NORTH-EASTERN STATES -- HISTORY
Sokol, J. All eyes are upon us   **323.1**

RACISM -- POLITICAL ASPECTS -- UNITED STATES
Dyson, M. E. The Black presidency   **305.8**

RACISM -- PSYCHOLOGICAL ASPECTS
Goldhagen, D. J. Worse than war   **364.1**

RACISM -- UNITED STATES
Blum, E. J. The color of Christ   **232**
Loewen, J. W. Sundown towns   **363.5**
Reed, I. Another day at the front   **305.8**
Takaki, R. T. Double victory   **940.53**

RACISM -- UNITED STATES -- HISTORY
Bruinius, H. Better for all the world   **363.9**
Fredrickson, G. M. Big enough to be inconsistent   **973.7**
Kendi, I. X. Stamped from the beginning   **305.8**
Lee, E. The making of Asian America   **973**

RACISM -- UNITED STATES -- HISTORY -- 18TH CENTURY
Parkinson, R. G. The common cause   **973.31**

RACISM IN EDUCATION -- UNITED STATES
Wilder, C. S. Ebony and Ivy   **379.26**

RACISM IN MUSEUM EXHIBITS
Crais, C. C. Sara Baartman and the Hottentot Venus   **92**

RACISM IN SPORTS
Runstedtler, T. Jack Johnson, rebel sojourner   **796.83**

RACISM IN SPORTS -- SOUTHERN STATES -- HISTORY -- 20 CENTURY
Maraniss, A. Strong inside   **92**

RACISM IN SPORTS -- UNITED STATES
Kashatus, W. C. Jackie and Campy   **92**
The **racist** mind. Ezekiel, R. S.   **320.5**

RACKETEERING
   See also Crime; Organized crime

RACKETEERING -- RUSSIA (FEDERATION)
Dawisha, K. Putin's kleptocracy   **947.086**

Rackley, Adam
Salt, sweat, tears   **92**

RACQUETBALL
   See also Ball games; Sports

Rad women worldwide. Schatz, K.   **920.72**

RADAR
   See also Navigation; Radio; Remote sensing

Radcliffe, Margaret
Circular knitting workshop   **746.43**
The knitting answer book   **746.43**
The knowledgeable knitter   **746.43**

Raddatz, Martha
     About
Raddatz, M. The long road home   **956.7**

Raden, Aja
Stoned   **739.27**

Radford, Marie L., 1951-
(jt. auth) Nilsen, K. Conducting the reference interview   **025.5**

A **radiant** life. O'Faolain, N.   **824**

RADIATION
Jorgensen, T. J. Strange glow   **539.2**
Nelson, C. The age of radiance   **539.7**

RADIATION
   See also Optics; Physics; Waves

RADIATION BIOLOGY *See* Radiobiology

Radical. Rhee, M. A.   **371.01**
The **radical** King.   **323**
The **Radical** reader.   **303.4**

RADICALISM
Eteraz, A. Children of dust   **92**
Kurlansky, M. 1968   **909.82**
The Radical reader   **303.4**
Ronson, J. Them: adventures with extremists **322.4**
Rudd, M. Underground   **92**

RADICALISM
   See also Political science; Revolutions; Right and left (Political science)

RADICALISM -- UNITED STATES
Goldwag, A. The new hate   **306.2**
The **radicalism** of the American Revolution. Wood, G. S.   **973.3**

RADICALS AND RADICALISM *See* Radicalism

Radin, Gary
(ed) What if it's not Alzheimer's?   **616.8**

Radin, Lisa
(ed) What if it's not Alzheimer's?   **616.8**

RADIO
Larson, E. Thunderstruck   **364.152**

RADIO
   See also Telecommunication

RADIO -- HANDBOOKS, MANUALS, ETC.
Silver, H. W. Ham radio for dummies   **621.384**

RADIO -- ITALY -- HISTORY
Raboy, M. Marconi   **92**

RADIO BROADCASTING
Heil, A. L. Voice of America   **384.54**
Schwartz, A. B. Broadcast hysteria   **791.44**

RADIO BROADCASTING
   See also Broadcasting; Mass media

RADIO REPORTERS
Cronkite, W. A reporter's life   **070**
Edwards, B. Edward R. Murrow and the birth of broadcast journalism   **92**
French, P. The world is what it is   **92**
Naipaul, V. S. Between father and son   **823**
Naipaul, V. S. Reading & writing   **92**
Norris, M. The grace of silence   **92**
Olson, L. Citizens of London   **940.54**
Sperber, A. M. Murrow, his life and times   **92**

Radio Shangri-La. Napoli, L.   **954.9**

RADIOACTIVE POLLUTION -- COLORADO -- JEFFERSON COUNTY

Iversen, K. Full body burden   **363.17**

RADIOACTIVE SUBSTANCES *See* Radioactivity

RADIOACTIVE WASTE DISPOSAL

See also Nuclear engineering; Nuclear power plants -- Environmental aspects; Radioactivity; Refuse and refuse disposal

RADIOACTIVE WASTE SITES -- CLEANUP -- COLORADO

Iversen, K. Full body burden   **363.17**

Radioactivity. Malley, M. C.   **539.7**

RADIOACTIVITY

Malley, M. C. Radioactivity   **539.7**

Nelson, C. The age of radiance   **539.7**

RADIOACTIVITY

See also Physics; Radiation

RADIOBIOLOGY

Jorgensen, T. J. Strange glow   **539.2**

RADIOBIOLOGY

See also Biology; Biophysics; Nuclear physics; Radioactivity

RADIOCARBON DATING

Macdougall, J. D. Nature's clocks   **551.7**

RADIOISOTOPES IN GEOLOGY

Macdougall, J. D. Nature's clocks   **551.7**

Radzinsky, Edvard

Stalin   **92**

Rae, Simon

(ed) The 20th Century in Poetry   **808.81**

Raeburn, Paul

The game theorist's guide to parenting   **641.1**

Raffin, Michele

The birds of Pandemonium   **639.97**

Raffles, Hugh

Insectopedia   **595.7**

RAFTING (SPORTS)

Lawrence, S. River house   **92**

RAGE *See* Anger

Rage for fame: the ascent of Clare Boothe Luce. Morris, S. J.   **92**

A **rage** for order. Worth, R. F.   **909**

A **rage** to live: a biography of Richard and Isabel Burton. Lovell, M. S.   **92**

Rage to survive. James, E.   **92**

The **ragged** edge of the world. Linden, E.   **303.4**

Raghavan, Srinath

India's war   **940.53**

The **Raging** Skillet. Rossi, C.   **92**

RAGING SKILLET (CATERING SERVICE)

Rossi, C. The Raging Skillet   **92**

Raichlen, Steven

The barbecue! bible   **641.5**

Project smoke   **641.6**

Raij, Alex

The Basque book   **641.5**

RAILROAD ACCIDENTS

Krist, G. The white cascade   **979.7**

RAILROAD ENGINEERING

Zoellner, T. Train   **385**

RAILROAD ENGINEERING

See also Civil engineering; Engineering; Railroads

RAILROAD EXECUTIVES

Renehan, E. J. Commodore   **92**

RAILROAD TRAVEL

Greene, D. Midnight in Siberia   **914.7**

Sadler, A. The 15:17 to Paris   **363.325**

RAILROAD TRAVEL

See also Transportation; Travel; Voyages and travels

RAILROAD TRAVEL -- HISTORY

Zoellner, T. Train   **385**

RAILROAD TRAVEL -- ITALY

Parks, T. Italian ways   **941.5**

RAILROAD TRAVEL -- RUSSIA (FEDERATION)

Greene, D. Midnight in Siberia   **914.7**

Railroaded. White, R.   **385**

RAILROADS

McMeekin, S. The Berlin-Baghdad express   **940.3**

Theroux, P. Riding the iron rooster   **915**

Train   **625.1**

Zoellner, T. Train   **385**

RAILROADS -- ASIA

Theroux, P. The great railway bazaar   **915**

RAILROADS -- CALIFORNIA -- HISTORY -- 19TH CENTURY

Drabelle, D. The great American railroad war   **385**

RAILROADS -- CANADA -- MAPS

Hayes, D. Historical atlas of the North American railroad   **385**

RAILROADS -- EMPLOYEES

See also Employees

RAILROADS -- FINANCE

See also Finance

RAILROADS -- FRANCE

Caro, I. Paris to the past   **914**

RAILROADS -- GOVERNMENT POLICY

See also Government ownership; Industrial policy

RAILROADS -- HISTORY

Stiles, T. J. The first tycoon   **92**

Train   **625.1**

Wolmar, C. Blood, iron, & gold   **385**

RAILROADS -- LATIN AMERICA

Theroux, P. The old Patagonian express   **918**

RAILROADS -- MERGERS

See also Corporate mergers and acquisitions

RAILROADS -- NORTH AMERICA -- HISTORY

Hayes, D. Historical atlas of the North American railroad **385**

RAILROADS -- PICTORIAL WORKS

Jensen, J. Steam: an enduring legacy **625.2**

Shaughnessy, J. The call of trains **779**

RAILROADS -- STATISTICS

See also Statistics

RAILROADS -- UNITED STATES

Bain, D. H. Empire express **385**

McCommons, J. Waiting on a train **385**

Schwantes, C. A. The West the railroads made **338**

Rain. Paterson, D. **821**

RAIN

Barnett, C. Rain **551.57**

Rain. Barnett, C. **551.57**

RAIN AND RAINFALL

Barnett, C. Rain **551.57**

RAIN AND RAINFALL *See* Rain

RAIN FOREST ANIMALS

McAllister, I. The last wild wolves **599.77**

RAIN FOREST ECOLOGY

Lowman, M. Life in the treetops **577.34**

Royte, E. The Tapir's morning bath **577.34**

The **rainbow** comes and goes. Cooper, A. **92**

Rainbow family collections. Naidoo, J. C. **028.1**

The **rainbow** people of God. Tutu, D. **968.06**

RAINBOW TROUT

Halverson, A. An entirely synthetic fish **639.3**

Raine, Adrian

The anatomy of violence **616.85**

Raine, Kathleen, 1908-2003

The collected poems of Kathleen Raine **821**

Raines, Ben

Cleland, M. Heart of a patriot **92**

RAINFALL *See* Rain

RAINFALL ANOMALIES

Barnett, C. Rain **551.57**

Rainie, Lee

(jt. auth) Wellman, B. Networked **006.7**

A **raisin** in the sun. Hansberry, L. **812**

Raising Can-Do Kids. Prosek, J. **649.7**

Raising children in the military. Scott, J. **355.1**

Raising Henry. Adams, R. **92**

Raising human beings. Greene, R. W. **306.874**

Raising my rainbow. Duron, L. **306.87**

Raising passionate readers. Newman, N. **649.58**

Raising resilient children. Brooks, R. B. **649**

Raising the shy child. Fonseca, C. **649**

Rajan, Raghuram G., 1963-

Fault lines **330.9**

Rajtar, Steve

Indian war sites **970.004**

United States holidays and observances **394.26**

Rakove, Jack

Revolutionaries **973.3**

(ed) The annotated U.S. Constitution and Declaration of Independence **342**

Rall, Ted

Bernie **92**

RALLIES (PROTEST) *See* Demonstrations

Ralph Ellison. Rampersad, A. **92**

Ralph, Ann

Grow a little fruit tree **634**

Ram Dass

About

Lattin, D. The Harvard Psychedelic Club **920**

Ramachandran, V. S.

The tell-tale brain **616.8**

Ramanujan Aiyangar, Srinivasa, 1887-1920

About

Kanigel, R. The man who knew infinity **510**

The **Ramayana.** Narayan, R. K. **891**

Ramazani, Jahan

(ed) The Norton anthology of modern and contemporary poetry **821**

Ramey, Gene

About

Dance, S. The world of Count Basie **920**

Ramineni, Shubhra

Entice with spice **641.5**

Ramm, David

Rich, M. World authors, 2000-2005 **920.003**

Rammer jammer yellow hammer. St. John, W. **796.332**

Ramo, Joshua Cooper

The age of the unthinkable **973.931**

Ramonet, Ignacio

Castro, F. Fidel Castro: my life **92**

Ramos, Angel, 1976-

Vegan holiday cooking from Candle Café **641.5**

Ramos, Jason A.

(jt. auth) Smith, J. Smokejumper **92**

Rampersad, Arnold

(ed) The Oxford anthology of African-American poetry **811**

The life of Langston Hughes Volume I: 1902-1941 **92**

The life of Langston Hughes Volume II: 1941-1967 **818**

Ralph Ellison **92**

Ramsay, Gordon, 1966-

Gordon Ramsay's fast food **641.5**

Ramsdell, Kristin

Romance fiction **016**

Ramses II, King of Egypt

About

Mertz, B. Temples, tombs, & hieroglyphs **932**

Ramsey, Dan

Teach yourself visually car care & maintenance **629.28**

Ramsey, John Bennett

About

Schiller, L. Perfect murder, perfect town **364.15**

Ramsey, JonBenet, d. 1996
About
Schiller, L. Perfect murder, perfect town **364.15**

Ramsey, Judy
Ramsey, D. Teach yourself visually car care & maintenance **629.28**

Ramsey, Patsy
About
Schiller, L. Perfect murder, perfect town **364.15**

Ramsland, Katherine M., 1953-
Ghost **133.1**

RANCH LIFE
Bell, L. Claiming ground **92**
DiSilvestro, R. L. Theodore Roosevelt in the Badlands **92**

RANCH LIFE
See also Farm life; Frontier and pioneer life

RANCH LIFE -- WEST (U.S.)
Rollins, K. A taste of cowboy **641.597**

RANCHERS
Blunt, J. Breaking clean **92**
Milner, C. A. As big as the West **92**

Rand McNally Goodes World Atlas. **912**

Rand, Ayn
The virtue of selfishness **171**
The voice of reason; essays in objectivist thought **191**
About
Heller, A. C. Ayn Rand and the world she made **92**
Pierpont, C. R. Passionate minds **810**
Rand, A. Journals of Ayn Rand **92**
Rand, A. Letters of Ayn Rand **813**

Randal, Jonathan C.
Osama: the making of a terrorist **92**

Randall, Alice
Soul food love **641.59**

Randall, David K.
Dreamland **612.8**
The King and Queen of Malibu **979.4**

Randall, John Herman
(ed) The Renaissance philosophy of man **189**

Randall, Lisa
Dark Matter and the Dinosaurs **523.1**
Higgs discovery **539.72**
Knocking on heaven's door **500**
Warped passages **530**

Randall, Willard Sterne
George Washington **92**

Randel, Don Michael
(ed) The Harvard biographical dictionary of music **780**
(ed) The Harvard concise dictionary of music and musicians **780**
(ed) The Harvard dictionary of music **780**

RANDOM ACCESS MEMORY

Dyson, G. Turing's cathedral **004**

Random family. LeBlanc, A. N. **305.5**

The **Random** House book of twentieth-century French poetry. **841**

Random House Webster's American Sign Language dictionary: unabridged. Costello, E. **419**

Random House Webster's German-English, English-German dictionary. **433**

Random House Webster's unabridged dictionary. **423**

A **random** walk down Wall Street. Malkiel, B. G. **332.6**

RANK *See* Social classes

Rankin, Lissa, 1969-
About
Rankin, L. The anatomy of a calling **92**

Rankine, Claudia, 1963-
Citizen **811**

Ransby, Barbara
Eslanda **92**

The **ransom** of Russian art. McPhee, J. A. **709**

Rants and raves. Johnson, P. **811**

Rao, Cheeni
About
Rao, C. In Hanuman's hands **92**

RAP MUSIC
Chang, J. Can't stop, won't stop **781.64**
Charnas, D. The big payback **781.64**
Common One day it'll all make sense **92**
Dyson, M. E. Holler if you hear me: searching for Tupac Shakur **92**
Ice-T Ice **92**
Lowe, J. Digging for dirt **92**
Watkins, S. C. Hip hop matters **781.64**
Westhoff, B. Dirty South **781.64**

RAP MUSIC
See also African American music; Popular music

RAP MUSICIANS
Cee-Lo Everybody's brother **782.421**
Lil Wayne Gone 'til November **782.421**

RAP MUSICIANS -- UNITED STATES -- BIOGRAPHY
Cee-Lo Everybody's brother **782.421**
Common One day it'll all make sense **92**
Dyson, M. E. Holler if you hear me: searching for Tupac Shakur **92**

RAP SONGS *See* Rap music

RAPE
Burns, S. The Central Park Five **364.1**
Cohan, W. D. The price of silence **364.15**
McGuire, D. L. At the dark end of the street **323.1**
Sebold, A. Lucky **362.883**
Surviving sexual violence **362.88**
Yes means yes! **306.7**

RAPE

See also Offenses against the person; Sex crimes

RAPE -- FLORIDA -- GROVELAND

King, G. Devil in the grove   **305.896**

RAPE -- MONTANA -- MISSOULA

Krakauer, J. Missoula   **362.883**

RAPE -- POLITICAL ASPECTS -- SOUTHERN STATES

McGuire, D. L. At the dark end of the street **323.1**

The **rape** of Nanking. Chang, I.   **951.04**

RAPE VICTIMS

Connors, J. I Will Find You   **364.15**

Lived through this   **362.883**

Parravani, C. Her   **92**

RAPE VICTIMS -- MONTANA -- MISSOULA

Krakauer, J. Missoula   **362.883**

Raphael, Marie

(jt. auth) Raphael, R. The spirit of 74 **973.3**

Raphael, Ray

Constitutional myths   **342.73**

Mr. president   **352.23**

A people's history of the American Revolution   **973.3**

The spirit of 74   **973.3**

RAPID PROTOTYPING

Rigsby, M. A beginner's guide to 3D printing **621.9**

Rapoport, Adam

(ed) The grilling book   **641.5**

Rapoport, Roger

Citizen Moore   **92**

Rapp, Emily

About

Rapp, E. The still point of the turning world **618.92**

Rappaport, Helen

The Romanov sisters   **920**

RAPPING (MUSIC) *See* Rap music

Rappleye, Charles

Herbert Hoover in the White House   **92**

RAPTOREX

See also Dinosaurs

Raptus. Klink, J.   **811**

RARE ANIMALS

Ackerman, D. The rarest of the rare   **578.68**

Dinerstein, E. The kingdom of rarities   **596**

Girling, R. The Hunt for the Golden Mole **591.68**

Macdonald, C. The endangered species road trip   **974**

Moore, R. In search of lost frogs   **597.8**

RARE ANIMALS

See also Animals

Rare birds. Gehrman, E.   **598**

RARE BIRDS

Gehrman, E. Rare birds   **598**

RARE BIRDS -- GEOGRAPHICAL DISTRIBUTION

The world's rarest birds   **598**

RARE BIRDS -- IDENTIFICATION

The world's rarest birds   **598**

RARE BOOKS

Collins, P. The book of William   **822.3**

Kaag, J. American philosophy   **191**

Rasmussen, E. The Shakespeare thefts   **822.3**

RARE BOOKS

See also Books

RARE FISHES -- CONSERVATION

Rigney, M. In pursuit of giants   **597**

RARE PLANTS

See also Plants

RARE REPTILES

Smith, J. E. Stolen world   **364.1**

RARE VERTEBRATES

Dinerstein, E. The kingdom of rarities   **596**

The **rarest** of the rare. Ackerman, D.   **578.68**

Rasenberger, Jim

The brilliant disaster   **972.91**

Rashid, Ahmed

Descent into chaos   **954**

Taliban   **958.1**

Rashke, Richard

Useful Enemies   **341.69**

Raskin, Donna

The dirty little secrets of getting your dream job   **650.14**

Rasmussen, Daniel

American uprising   **976.3**

Rasmussen, Eric

The Shakespeare thefts   **822.3**

Rasmussen, Matt

Black aperture   **811**

Rasmussen, R. Kent

(ed) Cyclopedia of literary places   **809**

Rasputin, Grigori Efimovich, 1871-1916

About

Massie, R. K. Nicholas and Alexandra   **92**

RASTAFARI MOVEMENT

Chevannes, B. Rastafari: roots and ideology **299.6**

Rastafari: roots and ideology. Chevannes, B. **299.6**

Ratcliff, Todd

(jt. auth) Baker, D. The 50 most extreme places in our solar system   **523.2**

RATE OF RETURN

Bartholomew, M. Square foot gardening high-value veggies   **635**

Siegel, J. J. Stocks for the long run   **332.63**

Ratey, John J.

(jt. auth) Hallowell, E. M. Driven to Distraction   **616.85**

Rathbone, John Paul

The sugar king of Havana   **92**

Rather outspoken. Diehl, D.   **92**

Rather, Dan

About

Diehl, D. Rather outspoken **92**

Ratification. Maier, P. **342**

Ratio. Ruhlman, M. **641.5**

RATIO AND PROPORTION
    See also Arithmetic; Geometry

RATIONAL EXPECTATIONS (ECONOMIC THEORY)
  Fox, J. The myth of the rational market **332.6**

The **rational** optimist. Ridley, M. **339.2**

RATIONALISM
    See also Philosophy; Religion; Secularism; Theory of knowledge

RATIONALISM -- HISTORY
  Minois, G. The atheist's Bible **200**

Ratliff, Ben
  Coltrane **92**
  The jazz ear **781.65**

Ratnesar, Romesh
  Tear down this wall **973.927**

Rattlesnake. Rubio, M. **597.96**

RATTLESNAKES
  Rubio, M. Rattlesnake **597.96**

RATTLESNAKES
    See also Poisonous animals; Snakes

Rauchway, Eric
  Murdering McKinley **973.8**

Rause, Vince
  Parrado, N. Miracle in the Andes **982**

Ravago, Miguel
  Tausend, M. Cocina de la familia **641.5**

RAVENSBRÜCK (CONCENTRATION CAMP)
  Helm, S. Ravensbruck **940.53**

Ravensbruck. Helm, S. **940.53**

Ravitch, Diane, 1938-
  The death and life of the great American school system **379**

Raw energy. Tourles, S. L. **641.5**

RAW FOOD DIET -- RECIPES
  Two Moms in the Raw **641.5**

RAW FOODS
  Raw, vegan, not gross **641.5**
  Two Moms in the Raw **641.5**

Raw, vegan, not gross. **641.5**

Rawlence, Ben
  City of thorns **967.73**

Rawles, James Wesley
  Tools for survival **613.6**

Ray, Barbara E.
  Not quite adults **306.8**

Ray, James Earl, 1928-1998
    About
  Sides, H. Hellhound on his trail **364.152**

Ray, Man, 1890-1976
    About
  Lottman, H. R. Man Ray's Montparnasse **709**

Ray, Rachael, 1968-

Everyone is Italian on Sunday **641.59**

Raymo, Chet
  An intimate look at the night sky **520**
  Walking zero **526**

Raymond Carver. Sklenicka, C. **92**

Raymond Chandler. Hiney, T. **813**

Raz, Tahl
  (jt. auth) Ferrazzi, K. Never eat alone and other secrets to success **658.4**

Razsa, Maple
  Bastards of Utopia **303.48**

Razzle Dazzle. Riedel, M. **792.09**

Rea, Tom
  Bone wars **560**

Reach for the skies. Branson, R. **629.1**

Reaching down the rabbit hole. Ropper, A. H. **616.8**

REACTION (POLITICAL SCIENCE) *See* Conservatism

Reactions. Atkins, P. W. **541**

REACTIONS, CHEMICAL *See* Chemical reactions

REACTORS (NUCLEAR PHYSICS) *See* Nuclear reactors

Read Harder. **814**

Read on . . . crime fiction. Trott, B. **016**

Read on . . . fantasy fiction. Hollands, N. **016**

Read on . . . horror fiction. Pulliam, J. M. **025**

Read on ... speculative fiction for teens. Kallio, J. **016**

Read on series
  Clark, C. A. Read on...sports **016**
  Frolund, T. Read on...history **016**
  Hollands, N. Read on . . . fantasy fiction **016**
  Kallio, J. Read on ... speculative fiction for teens **016**
  Pulliam, J. M. Read on . . . horror fiction **025**
  Saricks, J. G. Read on--audiobooks **011**
  Trott, B. Read on . . . crime fiction **016**

Read on-- biography. Roche, R. **016**

Read on-- graphic novels. Alpert, A. **016**

Read on-- life stories. Reisner, R. **016**

Read on-- science fiction. Torres-Roman, S. A. **016**

Read on-- women's fiction. Vnuk, R. **016**

Read on--audiobooks. Saricks, J. G. **011**

Read on... romance. Quillen, C. L. **016**

Read on....historical fiction. Hooper, B. **016**

Read on...history. Frolund, T. **016**

Read on...sports. Clark, C. A. **016**

Read, Anthony
  The fall of Berlin **940.54**

Read, Piers Paul
  Alive **910.4**
  The Dreyfus affair **944.081**

A **reader** on reading. Manguel, A. **818**

READER SERVICES (LIBRARIES) *See* Library services

A **reader's** book of days.   **809**

A **Reader's** companion to the short story in English.
Society for the Study of the Short Story   **809**

Reader's Digest Association
    (comp) 101 Saturday morning projects   **643**
    The big book of cross-stitch designs   **746.44**
    Complete do-it-yourself manual   **643**
    Everyday greatness   **170**
    (comp) New complete guide to sewing   **646.2**
    (comp) New fix-it-yourself manual   **643**

Reader's guide [series]
    Reader's guide to Judaism   **296**

Reader's guide to Judaism.   **296**

Reader's guide to military history.   **355.009**

Reader's guide to the history of science.   **509**

READERS AND LIBRARIES See Library services

Readers on American musicians [series]
    The Richard Rodgers reader   **782.1**

The **readers'** advisory guide to genre fiction. Saricks, J. G.   **025.5**

The **readers'** advisory guide to genre fiction. Saricks, J. G.   **025.5**

The **readers'** advisory guide to graphic novels. Goldsmith, F.   **025.2**

The **readers'** advisory guide to historical fiction. Baker, J. S.   **026**

The **readers'** advisory guide to nonfiction. Wyatt, N.   **025.5**

The **readers'** advisory guide to street literature. Morris, V. I.   **016**

The **readers'** advisory handbook. Moyer, J. E. **025.5**

Readers' advisory service in the public library. Saricks, J. G.   **025.5**

READERS' ADVISORY SERVICES -- UNITED STATES
    Alpert, A. Read on-- graphic novels   **016**
    Baker, J. S. The readers' advisory guide to historical fiction   **026**
    Buker, D. M. The science-fiction and fantasy readers' advisory   **025.5**
    Charles, J. A. The mystery readers' advisory **025.2**
    Frolund, T. Read on...history   **016**
    Herald, D. T. Strictly science fiction   **016**
    Honig, M. Urban grit   **016**
    Hooper, B. The short story readers' advisory   **028**
    Kallio, J. Read on ... speculative fiction for teens   **016**
    Morris, V. I. The readers' advisory guide to street literature   **016**
    Orr, C. Crash course in readers' advisory   **025.5**
    Pulliam, J. M. Read on . . . horror fiction   **025**
    Saricks, J. G. The readers' advisory guide to genre fiction   **025.5**
    Spratford, B. S. The horror readers' advisory **025.5**
    Torres-Roman, S. A. Read on-- science fiction **016**

Vnuk, R. Women's fiction   **016**

READERS' THEATER
    See also Theater

READINESS FOR SCHOOL
    See also Elementary education; Preschool education

READING
    Deheane, S. Reading in the brain   **418**
    Flesch, R. F. Why Johnny can't read--and what you can do about it   **372.4**
    Schall, L. Teen talkback with interactive booktalks!   **021.7**

READING
    See also Language arts

Reading & writing. Naipaul, V. S.   **92**

READING -- PHONETIC METHOD
    See also English language -- Pronunciation; Reading

READING -- REMEDIAL TEACHING
    Fertig, B. Why cant U teach me 2 read?   **372.4**
    Rosow, L. V. Accessing the classics   **011.6**

READING -- SOCIAL ASPECTS
    Dirda, M. Book by book   **028**
    Ross, C. S. The pleasures of reading   **028**

READING -- SOCIAL ASPECTS.
    Ross, C. S. Reading matters   **028**

READING -- STUDY AND TEACHING See Reading

READING -- UNITED STATES
    Grover, S. Listening to learn   **372.4**

Reading Chekhov. Malcolm, J.   **891.7**

READING COMPREHENSION
    See also Psychology of learning; Reading; Verbal learning

READING DISABILITY
    Fertig, B. Why cant U teach me 2 read?   **372.4**

READING DISABILITY
    See also Learning disabilities; Reading

Reading in the brain. Deheane, S.   **418**

READING INTERESTS
    Bouricius, A. The romance readers' advisory   **016**
    Herald, D. T. Genreflecting   **016**
    Quillen, C. L. Read on... romance   **016**
    Ross, C. S. The pleasures of reading   **028**
    Saricks, J. G. Readers' advisory service in the public library   **025.5**

READING INTERESTS See Books and reading

READING INTERESTS OF CHILDREN See Children -- Books and reading

READING INTERESTS.
    Ross, C. S. Reading matters   **028**

Reading Jesus. Gordon, M.   **232**

Reading like a writer. Prose, F.   **808**

Reading Lolita in Tehran. Nafisi, A.   **92**

READING MATERIALS
    See also Children's literature

Reading matters. Ross, C. S.   **028**

Reading people. Dimitrius   **155.2**

Reading picture books with children. Lambert, M. D.   **372.133**

READING PROMOTION -- UNITED STATES
Schall, L. Teen talkback with interactive book-talks!   **021.7**

READING PROMOTION.
Ross, C. S. Reading matters   **028**

READING READINESS
   See also Reading

Reading the Holocaust. Clendinnen, I.   **940.53**

Reading the rocks. Bjornerud, M.   **551.7**

READINGS (ANTHOLOGIES) *See* Anthologies

Ready reference [series]
   American Indians   **970.004**

Ready to run. Starrett, K.   **613.7**

Reagan. Reagan, R.   **92**

Reagan. Brands, H. W.   **92**

The **Reagan** diaries.   **92**

The **Reagan** I knew. Buckley, W. F.   **92**

Reagan, in his own hand.   **973.927**

Reagan, Leslie J.
   When abortion was a crime   **363.46**

Reagan, Ron
   My father at 100   **92**

Reagan, Ronald, 1911-2004
   The Reagan diaries   **92**
   Reagan, in his own hand   **973.927**
   About
   Brands, H. W. Reagan   **92**
   Buckley, W. F. The Reagan I knew   **92**
   D'Souza, D. Ronald Reagan   **973.927**
   FitzGerald, F. Way out there in the blue   **973.927**
   Johnson, H. B. Sleepwalking through history   **973.927**
   Kissinger, H. Diplomacy   **327.2**
   Mann, J. The rebellion of Ronald Reagan   **973.927**
   Ratnesar, R. Tear down this wall   **973.927**
   The Reagan diaries   **92**
   Reagan, R. Reagan   **92**
   Reagan, R. My father at 100   **92**
   Reeves, R. President Reagan: the triumph of imagination   **973.927**
   Rosenfeld, S. Subversives   **378.1**
   Woodward, B. Shadow   **973.92**

Real beauty. Kashuk, S.   **646.7**

Real Cajun. Link, D.   **641.5**

REAL ESTATE -- DICTIONARIES
Haden, J. The complete dictionary of real estate terms explained simply   **333.3**

REAL ESTATE BUSINESS
Irwin, R. Tips & traps for negotiating real estate   **333.3**

REAL ESTATE BUSINESS
   See also Business; Real estate

REAL ESTATE DEVELOPERS
Korda, M. Ulysses S. Grant: the unlikely hero   **92**
McDougal, S. The woman who wouldn't talk   **973.929**
Singer, M. Character studies   **920**
Slater, R. No such thing as over-exposure   **92**

REAL ESTATE DEVELOPERS -- UNITED STATES -- BIOGRAPHY
Johnston, D. C. The making of Donald Trump   **973.932**

REAL ESTATE DEVELOPMENT
   See also Real estate business

REAL ESTATE INVESTMENT
Corbett, M. Before you buy!   **643**
Crook, D. The Wall Street Journal complete home owner's guidebook   **643**
Irwin, R. Tips & traps for negotiating real estate   **333.3**

REAL ESTATE INVESTMENT
   See also Investments; Real estate; Speculation

REAL ESTATE INVESTMENT -- TAXATION
   See also Taxation

The **real** Fidel Castro. Coltman, L.   **92**

The **Real** Food Daily cookbook. Gentry, A.   **641.5**

Real food/fake food. Olmsted, L.   **641.3**

The **real** Frank Zappa book. Zappa, F.   **92**

Real happiness. Salzberg, S.   **158**

Real life journals: designing & using handmade books. Diehn, G.   **686.3**

The **real** North Korea. Lankov, A.   **951.93**

REAL PROPERTY -- PRICES -- UNITED STATES
Shiller, R. J. Irrational exuberance   **332.63**

REAL PROPERTY INVESTMENT *See* Real estate investment

Real stories [series]
   Stoeger, M. B. Food lit   **016.6**
   Burgin, R. Going places   **910.4**

The **real** story. Cords, S. S.   **025.5**

REALISM
   See also Philosophy

The **realism** challenge. Crilley, M.   **751.4**

REALISM IN ART
Crilley, M. The realism challenge   **751.4**
Robinson, M. A. Lessons in realistic watercolor   **751.422**

REALISM IN ART
   See also Art

REALISM IN LITERATURE
   See also Literature

REALITY
Dawkins, R. The magic of reality   **501**
Eagleman, D. The brain   **612.82**
Gribbin, J. R. In search of Schrodinger's cat   **530.1**
Gribbin, J. R. Schrodinger's kittens and the search

for reality **530.1**
REALITY
 See also Philosophy; Truth
Reality is broken. McGonigal, J. **306.4**
REALITY TELEVISION PROGRAMS
 See also Television programs
**REALITY TELEVISION PROGRAMS -- CALI-
 FORNIA**
 Crooks, P. The setup **363.28**
Ream, Anne K.
 Lived through this **362.883**
Reappraisals. Judt, T. **909.82**
Reardon, Joan
 (ed) As always, Julia **92**
 (ed) Fisher, M. F. K. A stew or a story **641**
REASON
 Kant, I. Critique of pure reason **193**
 Ridley, M. The rational optimist **339.2**
REASON
 See also Intellect; Rationalism
The **reason** for God. Keller, T. J. **239**
The **reason** I jump. **92**
REASONING
 Kahneman, D. Thinking, fast and slow **153.4**
 Pinker, S. How the mind works **153**
 Watts, D. J. Everything is obvious **153.4**
REASONING
 See also Psychology; Reason; Thought and
 thinking
REASONING (PSYCHOLOGY)
 Dobelli, R. The art of thinking clearly **153.4**
Reavill, Gil
 Mafia summit **364.106**
Rebanks, James
   About
 Rebanks, J. The shepherd's life **92**
Rebbe. Telushkin, J. **92**
Rebecca Ringquist's embroidery workshops. **746.44**
The **rebel.** Camus, A. **303.6**
Rebel Souls. Martin, J. **811**
Rebel Souls. Martin, J. **92**
Rebel Yell. Gwynne, S. C. **92**
Rebellion. Ackroyd, P. **941.06**
The **rebellion** of Ronald Reagan. Mann, J. **973.927**
REBELLIONS *See* Insurgency; Revolutions
The **rebellious** life of Mrs. Rosa Parks. Theoharis,
 J. **92**
REBELS (SOCIAL PSYCHOLOGY) *See* Alien-
 ation (Social psychology)
Rebels on the backlot. Waxman, S. **920**
Reber, Grote, 1911-2002
   About
 Malone, J. W. It doesn't take a rocket scientist **920**
Rebirth of a nation. Lears, T. J. J. **973.8**
Reborn. Sontag, S. **92**
Rebuilding the foodshed. Ackerman-Leist, P. **338.1**

REBUSES
 See also Literary recreations; Puzzles; Rid-
 dles
RECALL OF PRODUCTS *See* Product recall
**RECEIVING STOLEN GOODS -- ENGLAND --
 LONDON -- CASE STUDIES**
 Crosby, M. C. The great pearl heist **364.16**
RECESSIONS
 Krugman, P. R. End this depression now! **330.9**
RECESSIONS
 See also Business cycles
**RECESSIONS -- UNITED STATES -- HISTORY
 -- 21ST CENTURY**
 Krugman, P. R. End this depression now! **330.9**
A **Recipe** for Cooking. Peternell, C. **641.5**
Recipes. **641.5**
RECIPES *See* Cooking
Recipes from an Italian summer. **641.5**
Recipes from many kitchens. Rice, V. **641.5**
Reckless. Hynde, C. **92**
Reckless endangerment. Morgenson, G. **332.7**
The **reckoning.** Nicholl, C. **92**
Reckoning at Eagle Creek. Biggers, J. **333.73**
Reclaiming Conversation. Turkle, S. **302.23**
Reclaiming history. Bugliosi, V. **973.922**
Reclaiming the Dead Sea scrolls. Schiffman, L.
 H. **296.1**
RECLAMATION OF LAND
 See also Agriculture; Civil engineering; Hy-
 draulic engineering; Land use
RECLUSES *See* Hermits
RECLUSES -- UNITED STATES -- BIOGRAPHY
 Dedman, B. Empty mansions **92**
RECOLLECTION (PSYCHOLOGY)
 Schacter, D. L. The seven sins of memory **153.1**
RECOMBINANT DNA
 See also DNA; Genetic engineering; Genetic
 recombination
RECOMMENDATIONS FOR POSITIONS *See*
 Applications for positions
Recommended reference books for small and medi-
 um-sized libraries and media centers, Vol. 34. **011**
Reconciliation. Bhutto, B. **92**
RECONCILIATION
 The book of forgiving **179**
Reconstruction. Foner, E. **973.8**
RECONSTRUCTION (1865-1876)
 Dray, P. Capitol men **920**
 Dudden, F. E. Fighting chance **324.6**
 Foner, E. Forever free **973.8**
 Foner, E. Reconstruction **973.8**
 Grumet, B. H. Reconstruction era: primary sourc-
 es **973.8**
 Howes, K. K. Reconstruction era: almanac **973.8**
 Jacoby, K. The strange career of William Ellis **92**
 Kantrowitz, S. More than freedom **323.1**

Lane, C. The day freedom died   **976.3**

Langguth, A. J. After Lincoln   **973.8**

Marvel, W. Lincoln's autocrat   **92**

Matuz, R. Reconstruction era: biographies   **920**

Reconstruction after the Civil War   **973.8**

RECONSTRUCTION (1865-1876)

   See also United States -- History -- 1865-1898

RECONSTRUCTION (1939-1951)

Beschloss, M. R. The conquerors: Roosevelt, Truman, and the destruction of Hitler's Germany, 1941-1945   **940.53**

Bessel, R. Germany 1945   **943.087**

Lowe, K. Savage continent   **940.55**

RECONSTRUCTION (1939-1951) -- GERMANY

Beschloss, M. R. The conquerors: Roosevelt, Truman, and the destruction of Hitler's Germany, 1941-1945   **940.53**

Bessel, R. Germany 1945   **943.087**

Taylor, F. Exorcising Hitler   **943.087**

RECONSTRUCTION (U.S. HISTORY, 1865-1877)

Dray, P. Capitol men   **920**

Langguth, A. J. After Lincoln   **973.8**

Lemann, N. Redemption: the last battle of the Civil War   **975**

Wineapple, B. Ecstatic nation   **973.6**

RECONSTRUCTION (U.S. HISTORY, 1865-1877) -- BIOGRAPHY

Jacoby, K. The strange career of William Ellis   **92**

Marvel, W. Lincoln's autocrat   **92**

Roberts, C. Capital dames   **793.7**

Reconstruction after the Civil War.   **973.8**

Reconstruction Era reference library [series]

Grumet, B. H. Reconstruction era: primary sources   **973.8**

Howes, K. K. Reconstruction era: almanac   **973.8**

Matuz, R. Reconstruction era: biographies   **920**

Reconstruction era: almanac. Howes, K. K.   **973.8**

Reconstruction era: biographies. Matuz, R.   **920**

Reconstruction era: primary sources. Grumet, B. H.   **973.8**

RECONSTRUCTIVE SURGERY *See* Plastic surgery

Record makers and breakers. Broven, J.   **781.64**

RECORD PRODUCERS

Brown, M. Tearing down the wall of sound   **92**

Gordon, R. Respect yourself   **384**

Guralnick, P. Sam Phillips   **92**

Record store days. Calamar, G.   **780.2**

RECORD STORES

Calamar, G. Record store days   **780.2**

RECORDED BOOKS *See* Audiobooks

RECORDING INDUSTRY EXECUTIVES

Houghton, M. Becoming Elektra   **781.64**

RECORDING PRODUCERS

Brown, M. Tearing down the wall of sound   **92**

Feather, L. From Satchmo to Miles   **920**

Jones, Q. Q: the autobiography of Quincy Jones   **92**

Zappa, F. The real Frank Zappa book   **92**

RECOVERING ADDICTS -- PERSONAL NARRATIVES

Ninety days   **362.29**

RECYCLING

Pember, M. The Little Veggie Patch Co. DIY Garden Projects   **712.6**

Stuart, T. Waste   **363.8**

Terry, B. Plastic-free   **363.738**

White, B. Sewing green   **646.4**

RECYCLING

   See also Energy conservation; Pollution control industry; Salvage

RECYCLING (WASTE, ETC.) *See* Recycling

RED

   See also Color

Red actions. Kelly, R.   **811**

RED ARMY FACTION

Aust, S. Baader-Meinhof   **363.32**

Red Azalea. Min, A.   **92**

Red cloud at dawn. Gordin, M. D.   **355**

Red Cloud, Sioux Chief, 1822-1909

       About

Brown, D. A. The American West   **978**

Brown, D. A. Bury my heart at Wounded Knee   **970.004**

Drury, B. The heart of everything that is   **92**

Red doc>. Carson, A.   **811**

Red dust. Ma Jian   **951.05**

The **red** flag. Priestland, D.   **335.4**

Red heat. Von Tunzelmann, A.   **972.9**

RED HOOK (N.Y.) -- SOCIAL LIFE AND CUSTOMS

Sultan, T. Sunny's nights   **641.87**

The **Red** Man's Bones. Eisler, B.   **92**

The **red** market. Carney, S.   **364.1**

Red Orchestra. Nelson, A.   **943.086**

The **red** parts. Nelson, M.   **362.88**

Red platoon. Romesha, C. L.   **958.1**

RED ROOSTER (RESTAURANT)

Red Rooster Cookbook   **641.5**

Red Rooster Cookbook.   **641.5**

The **Red** Rose girls. Carter, A. A.   **759.13**

Red Smith on baseball. Smith, R.   **796.357**

Red star over Russia. King, D.   **947**

Redcoats and rebels. Hibbert, C.   **973.3**

Redding, Otis, 1941-1967

       About

Ribowsky, M. Dreams to remember   **92**

Redefining Realness. Mock, J.   **306.76**

Redemption: the last battle of the Civil War. Lemann, N.   **975**

Redemption: the life of Henry Roth. Kellman, S. G.   **92**

Redesigning humans. Stock, G.   **176**

Redford, Donald B.

(ed) The Oxford encyclopedia of ancient Egypt **932**

Rediker, Marcus

The Amistad rebellion   **326**

Reding, Nick

Methland   **362.29**

Redmond, Ian

The primate family tree   **599.8**

Redniss, Lauren

Thunder & Lightning   **551.6**

Reds: McCarthyism in twentieth-century America. Morgan, T.   **973.9**

REDUCING *See* Weight loss

REDUCING DIETS

Schatzker, M. The Dorito effect   **641.3**

Well fed   **641.5**

REDUCING DIETS -- EVALUATION

Brown, H. Body of truth   **613.2**

REDUCING DIETS -- PSYCHOLOGICAL ASPECTS

Mann, T. Secrets from the eating lab   **613.2**

REDUCING DIETS -- RECIPES

Heller, M. The everyday DASH diet cookbook   **613.2**

Ludwig, D. Always hungry?   **613.2**

The VB6 cookbook   **641.5**

REDWOOD

Preston, R. The wild trees   **577.3**

Reed, Charles Hancock, 1900-1980

About

Letts, E. The perfect horse   **940.54**

Reed, Ishmael

(ed) From totems to hip-hop   **811**

Another day at the front   **305.8**

New and collected poems, 1966-2006   **811**

Reed, John

Ten days that shook the world   **947.084**

Reed, Julia

Julia Reed's south   **642.4**

Reed, Thomas Brackett, 1839-1902

About

Thomas, E. The war lovers   **973.8**

Reed, Wendy

(ed) Circling faith   **200.8**

Reeder, Lydia

Dust bowl girls   **796.323**

REEF ECOLOGY

See also Ecology; Marine ecology

Reef, Catherine

Bader, P. African-American writers   **920.003**

Working in America   **305**

Reel to reel. Shapiro, A.   **811**

Reel, Monte

The last of the tribe   **981**

Rees, Darrell

How to Be an Illustrator   **741.6**

Rees, Laurence

Auschwitz: a new history   **940.53**

Rees, Martin J., 1942-

From here to infinity   **500**

Just six numbers   **523.1**

(ed) Universe   **523.1**

Reese, Jennifer

Make the bread, buy the butter   **641.3**

Reese, William J.

Testing wars in the public schools   **371.26**

Reesman, Jeanne Campbell

(jt. auth) Adam, P. Jack London, photographer **92**

Reeve, Christopher, 1952-2004

About

Reeve, C. Still me   **92**

Reeves, Bass, 1838-1910

About

Abdul-Jabbar, K. Black profiles in courage   **920**

Reeves, Randall R.

Folkens, P. A. National Audubon Society guide to marine mammals of the world   **599.5**

Reeves, Richard

Daring young men   **943.087**

A force of nature   **92**

Infamy   **940.53**

President Kennedy   **973.922**

President Nixon   **973.924**

President Reagan: the triumph of imagination   **973.927**

Reference and research guide to mystery and detective fiction. Bleiler, R.   **016**

REFERENCE BOOKS

Abrams, M. H. A glossary of literary terms   **803**

Acronyms, initialisms, & abbreviations dictionary   **421**

Adamson, L. G. Notable women in American history   **016**

Adamson, L. G. Notable women in world history   **016**

Adelson-Goldstein, J. The Oxford picture dictionary   **423**

Adonis to Zorro   **422**

The African American almanac   **305.8**

The African American national biography **920.003**

Africana: the encyclopedia of the African and African American experience   **909**

Alabaster, C. Developing an outstanding core collection   **025.2**

Allaby, M. The encyclopedia of Earth   **910**

Amazons to fighter pilots   **355**

American book trade directory   **070.5**

American foreign relations since 1600   **016**

The American Heritage dictionary of the English language   **423**

American Indians   **970.004**

American statesmen 920.003

American writers 920.003

Ancient Europe 8000 B.C.-A.D. 1000 936

Ancient Greece 938

Anderson, S. Historical dictionary of terrorism 363.32

Andrea, A. J. Encyclopedia of the crusades 909.07

Archaeology of prehistoric native America 970.01

Atlas of exploration 911

Atlas of the Civil War 973.7

Attwater, D. The Penguin dictionary of saints 920.003

Axelrod, A. The encyclopedia of the American armed forces 355

Ayto, J. Brewer's dictionary of modern phrase & fable 803

Bader, P. African-American writers 920.003

Bambaradeniya, C. N. B. The illustrated atlas of wildlife 591.9

Bane, T. Encyclopedia of vampire mythology 398

Beacham's encyclopedia of popular fiction 809

Beatty, S. The DC Comics encyclopedia 741.5

The Beaulieu encyclopedia of the automobile 629.222

Beck, W. A. Historical atlas of the American West 911

Bell, S. Encyclopedia of forensic science 363.2

Benet's reader's encyclopedia 803

Berkshire encyclopedia of China 951

Berlitz Korean compact dictionary 495.7

Biedermann, H. Dictionary of symbolism 302.2

Biographical encyclopedia of artists 920.003

Black women in America 920.003

Blackburn, S. The Oxford dictionary of philosophy 103

Bleiler, R. Reference and research guide to mystery and detective fiction 016

Boatner, M. M. The Civil War dictionary 973.7

Bouricius, A. The romance readers' advisory 016

Brave new words 809.3

Buker, D. M. The science-fiction and fantasy readers' advisory 025.5

Bureau of Labor Statistics Occupational outlook handbook 331.7

Burgess, M. Reference guide to science fiction, fantasy, and horror 016

Burt, D. S. The biography book 016

Butler's Lives of the saints 920.003

Calhoun, C. J. Dictionary of the social sciences 300

The Cambridge dictionary of classical civilization 938

The Cambridge dictionary of philosophy 103

The Cambridge guide to children's books in English 028.5

The Cambridge guide to literature in English 820

The Cambridge guide to women's writing in English 820

The Cambridge handbook of American literature 810

Campo, J. E. Encyclopedia of Islam 297

Cannon, J. The kings & queens of Britain 920

Carey, C. W. American inventors, entrepreneurs & business visionaries 920

Charles, J. A. The mystery readers' advisory 025.2

Cheng & Tsui English-Chinese lexicon of business terms with pinyin 495.1

Coile, D. C. Encyclopedia of dog breeds 636.7

Colby, V. World authors, 1975-1980 920.003

Colby, V. World authors, 1980-1985 809

Colby, V. World authors, 1985-1990 809

Colman, A. M. A dictionary of psychology 150

The Columbia companion to the twentieth-century American short story 813

The Columbia gazetteer of the world 910.3

The Columbia Granger's dictionary of poetry quotations 808.81

The Columbia Granger's index to poetry in anthologies 808.81

The Columbia Granger's Index to poetry in collected and selected works 808.81

The Companion to southern literature 810

Concise encyclopedia of Latin American literature 860

Concise Oxford American thesaurus 423

Congress investigates 328

Congressional Quarterly, I. Congress A to Z 328

Contemporary Jewish-American novelists 813

Contemporary poets 821

Contemporary women artists 920.003

The Continuum encyclopedia of British literature 810

Cordon, L. A. Popular psychology 150

Cornelison, P. The great American history factfinder 973

Correard The Oxford-Hachette French dictionary 443

Costello, E. Random House Webster's American Sign Language dictionary: unabridged 419

Counties USA 352.13

Craine, D. The Oxford dictionary of dance 792.8

CRC Handbook of Chemistry and Physics 540

Critical survey of drama 809

The Crusades 909.07

Crystal, D. The Cambridge encyclopedia of language 400

Crystal, D. A dictionary of language 410

Cuddon, J. A. The Penguin dictionary of literary terms and literary theory 803

Curtis, A. Oxford Bible atlas 220.9

Cyclopedia of literary characters 803

Cyclopedia of literary places 809

Daily life through world history in primary documents **909**

Darling, D. J. The universal book of mathematics **510**

Davidson, A. The Oxford companion to food **641**

Davidson, M. Right, wrong, and risky **423**

De Richemond, J. The Medical Library Association guide to finding out about heart disease **016**

Dempsey, A. Art in the modern era **709.04**

Deutsch, B. Poetry handbook: a dictionary of terms **808.1**

Dictionary of the Middle Ages **909.07**

Dictionary of wars **355**

Directory of special libraries and information centers **026**

Domestic violence sourcebook **362.82**

Dorland's illustrated medical dictionary **610**

Dow, K. The atlas of climate change **551.6**

Drew, B. A. 100 most popular nonfiction authors **920.003**

Dunnigan, J. F. The Pacific War encyclopedia **940.54**

Eerdmans dictionary of the Bible **220.3**

Eisenberg, R. L. The JPS guide to Jewish traditions **296.4**

Elie, P. The life you save may be your own **810**

Eltis, D. Atlas of the transatlantic slave trade **381**

Encyclopaedia Judaica **296**

The Encyclopedia of African and African-American religions **299.6**

Encyclopedia of African-American writing **810**

Encyclopedia of American business **338**

Encyclopedia of American folklife **398**

Encyclopedia of American history **973**

Encyclopedia of American Indian literature **810**

Encyclopedia of American military history **355**

Encyclopedia of American poetry, the twentieth century **811**

Encyclopedia of artists **709**

Encyclopedia of conflicts since World War II **909.82**

Encyclopedia of crime and punishment **346**

The encyclopedia of cults, sects, and new religions **200**

Encyclopedia of German literature **830**

Encyclopedia of global resources **333.7**

Encyclopedia of insects **595.7**

Encyclopedia of Irish history and culture **941.5**

Encyclopedia of Islam and the Muslim world **909**

Encyclopedia of Jewish life before and during the Holocaust **940.53**

Encyclopedia of Latin American & Caribbean art **709**

The encyclopedia of Middle East wars **355**

Encyclopedia of Native American wars and warfare **970.004**

Encyclopedia of plague and pestilence **614.4**

Encyclopedia of public health **362.1**

Encyclopedia of religion **200**

Encyclopedia of religious rites, rituals, and festivals **200**

Encyclopedia of rural America **973**

The Encyclopedia of science and technology **503**

Encyclopedia of science, technology, and ethics **503**

Encyclopedia of the American Civil War **973.7**

Encyclopedia of the ancient world **930**

Encyclopedia of the Cold War **909.82**

Encyclopedia of the developing world **909**

Encyclopedia of the First Amendment **342**

Encyclopedia of the new American nation **973**

Encyclopedia of the Renaissance **940.2**

Encyclopedia of the scientific revolution **509**

Encyclopedia of U.S. political history **973**

Encyclopedia of women's autobiography **920.003**

The Encyclopedia of wood **674**

The Encyclopedia of World War I **940.3**

Encyclopedia of World War II **940.53**

English, E. D. Encyclopedia of the medieval world **940.1**

Ernsthausen, D. G. Strauss's handbook of business information **016**

Ethics **170**

The Europa world year book 2014 **310**

Europe 1789 to 1914 **940.2**

Everitt, B. The Cambridge dictionary of statistics **519.5**

The Facts on File companion to the American novel **813**

Facts on File, I. Encyclopedia of American literature **810**

Famous first facts, international edition **031.02**

Farmer, D. H. The Oxford dictionary of saints **920.003**

Flora: a gardener's encyclopedia **635.9**

Fonseca, A. J. Hooked on horror III **016**

Ford, C. Crash course in reference **025.5**

The Foundation directory **061**

Frazier, N. The Penguin concise dictionary of art history **703**

Friedman, I. C. Latino athletes **920.003**

Friedwald, W. A biographical guide to the great jazz and pop singers **920.003**

Frolund, T. Genrefied classics **016**

From bonbon to cha-cha **422**

Fry, J. L. The encyclopedia of weather and climate change **551.6**

Gale directory of databases **025.04**

The Gale encyclopedia of alternative medicine **615.5**

Gale encyclopedia of American law **349**

The Gallaudet dictionary of American Sign Language **419**

Garden perennials Armitage's garden perennials **635.9**

Garner, B. A. Garner's modern American usage **423**

Garraty, J. A. American national biography **920.003**

Gates, A. E. Encyclopedia of earthquakes and volcanoes **551.2**

Gates, A. E. Encyclopedia of pollution **363.7**

Gates, A. E. A to Z of earth scientists **920.003**

Gilbert, M. The Routledge atlas of the Holocaust **940.53**

Grant, M. A guide to the ancient world **913**

Great events from history, The 17th century, 1601-1700 **909**

Great events from history, The 18th century, 1701-1800 **909.7**

Great events from history, The 19th century, 1801-1900 **909.81**

Great events from history, The ancient world, prehistory-476 C.E. **930**

Great events from history, The Middle Ages, 477-1453 **909.07**

Great events from history, The Renaissance & early modern era, 1454-1600 **909**

Great events from history: The 20th century, 1901-1940 **909.82**

Great events from history: The 20th century, 1941-1970 **909.82**

Great events from history: The 20th century, 1971-2000 **909.82**

Great lives from history, The 17th century, 1601-1700 **920.003**

Great lives from history, The 19th century, 1801-1900 **920.003**

Great lives from history, The ancient world, prehistory-476 C.E **920.003**

Great lives from history, the Middle Ages, 477-1453 **920.003**

Great lives from history, the Renaissance & early modern era, 1454-1600 **920.003**

Great lives from history: Notorious lives **920.003**

Great lives from history: the 20th century, 1901-2000 **920.003**

Green volunteers **333.72**

The Greenwood encyclopedia of homes through American history **728**

Guide to reference books **011**

Guiley, R. E. The encyclopedia of demons and demonology **133.4**

Guiley, R. E. The encyclopedia of ghosts and spirits **133.1**

Guiley, R. E. The encyclopedia of saints **282**

Guiley, R. E. The encyclopedia of vampires & werewolves **398**

Guiley, R. E. The encyclopedia of witches, witchcraft, and Wicca **133.4**

Haase, D. The Greenwood encyclopedia of folk-

tales and fairy tales **398.2**

Haden, J. The complete dictionary of real estate terms explained simply **333.3**

Hamilton, N. A. Presidents **920.003**

Harasewych, M. G. The book of shells **594**

Harper, J. E. Women during the Civil War **973.7**

The HarperCollins encyclopedia of Catholicism **282**

Hart, J. D. The Oxford companion to American literature **810**

The Harvard biographical dictionary of music **780**

The Harvard concise dictionary of music and musicians **780**

The Harvard dictionary of music **780**

Havlice, P. P. Index to artistic biography **920.003**

Hayes, D. Historical atlas of the American West **911**

Hayes, D. Historical atlas of the North American railroad **385**

Hayes, D. Historical atlas of the United States **911**

Helbig, A. Dictionary of American young adult fiction, 1997-2001 **028.5**

Hellmann, P. T. Historical gazetteer of the United States **911**

Hendrickson, R. The Facts on File encyclopedia of word and phrase origins **422**

Herald, D. T. Fluent in fantasy **016**

Herald, D. T. Genreflecting **016**

Herald, D. T. Strictly science fiction **016**

Hischak, T. The Oxford companion to the American musical **792.6**

Historical encyclopedia of American labor **331.8**

Historical thesaurus of the Oxford English dictionary **423**

Hoekstra, J. M. The atlas of global conservation **333.95**

Hoffman, M. The NPR classical music companion **780**

Holder, R. W. How not to say what you mean **427**

Holidays, festivals, and celebrations of the world dictionary **394.26**

Hollands, N. Read on . . . fantasy fiction **016**

Holy people of the world **920.003**

Home ground **917**

Houghton Mifflin Co. The Concise American Heritage Spanish dictionary **463**

Husband, J. Sequels **016**

Impelluso, L. Gods and heroes in art **700**

Instruments of science **502.8**

J.G. Ferguson Publishing Company Encyclopedia of careers and vocational guidance **331.7**

Jaques Cattell Press Who's who in American politics 2007-2008 **920.003**

Johnson, M. Encyclopedia of native tribes of North America **970.004**

Johnson, S. L. Historical fiction II **016**

Jordan, M. Dictionary of gods and goddesses **201**

Kane, J. N. Facts about the presidents **920**

Kelly, J. N. D. The Oxford dictionary of Popes **920.003**

King, R. Art: over 2,500 works from cave to contemporary **709**

Knight, J. A. Genetics & inherited conditions **576.5**

Krismann, C. Encyclopedia of American women in business **920.003**

Kuhlman, E. A. A to Z of women in world history **920.003**

Larousse gastronomique **641.3**

Latham, E. A dictionary of names, nicknames, and surnames of persons, places, and things **929.4**

Lavin, S. J. Atlas of the great plains **912**

Leaders of the American Civil War **973.7**

Leeming, D. A. The Oxford companion to world mythology **201**

Legal systems of the world **340**

Lend me your ears **808.88**

Lewis, J. R. The astrology book **133.5**

Lewis, J. R. The dream encyclopedia **154.6**

Literary market place **070.5**

Little, B. &. C. I. Bartlett's Roget's thesaurus **423**

Maddex, R. L. The U.S. Constitution A to Z **342**

Magill's encyclopedia of science **580**

Magill's guide to military history **355**

Magill's medical guide **610**

Magill's survey of American literature **810**

Magill's survey of world literature **809**

Magocsi, P. R. Historical atlas of Central Europe **911**

Major acts of Congress **348**

Mandel, D. Who's who in the Jewish Bible **920.003**

Manguel, A. The dictionary of imaginary places **809**

Manser, M. H. The Facts on File dictionary of allusions **422**

Manser, M. H. The Facts on File dictionary of foreign words and phrases **422**

Martinez Wood, J. Latino writers and journalists **920.003**

Martinez-Fernandez, L. Encyclopedia of Cuba **972.91**

Mattison, C. The new encyclopedia of snakes **597.96**

McGraw-Hill dictionary of scientific and technical terms **503**

McGraw-Hill Publishing Company McGraw-Hill concise encyclopedia of science & technology **503**

McMahon, S. Brewer's dictionary of Irish phrase & fable **427**

Melton, J. G. Melton's encyclopedia of American religions **200.9**

Melton, J. G. The vampire book **398**

Merriam-Webster Inc. Merriam-Webster's collegiate dictionary **423**

Merriam-Webster Inc. Merriam-Webster's collegiate thesaurus **423**

Millar, D. The Cambridge dictionary of scientists **920.003**

Minahan, J. The complete guide to national symbols and emblems **929.9**

Mitchell, A. M. Cataloging and organizing digital resources **025.3**

Monush, B. Screen world presents the encyclopedia of Hollywood film actors **920.003**

Moore, J. A. Encyclopedia of the United Nations **341.23**

More word histories and mysteries **422**

Muir, J. K. The encyclopedia of superheroes on film and television **791.43**

Murray, R. E. The lexicon of labor **331**

Musicians & composers of the 20th century **920.003**

Mystery and suspense writers **809**

Nash, J. R. The great pictorial history of world crime **364**

National Geographic visual atlas of the world **912**

Native America in the twentieth century **970.004**

Natural history **508**

Naval warfare **359**

The new atlas of the Arab world **912**

New Catholic encyclopedia **282**

New dictionary of scientific biography **920.003**

The New encyclopedia of Judaism **296**

The New Grove dictionary of music and musicians **780**

New Oxford American dictionary **423**

The new Partridge dictionary of slang and unconventional English **427**

The New York Public Library desk reference **031.02**

Newton, D. E. Latinos in science, math, and professions **920.003**

Nichols, C. R. Encyclopedia of marine science **551.46**

Niebuhr, G. W. Make mine a mystery **809**

The Norton/Grove dictionary of women composers **780.92**

Notable American women: the modern period **920.003**

Notable black American men, book I **920.003**

Notable black American men, book II **920.003**

Notable black American scientists **509**

Notable black American women, book I **920.003**

Notable black American women, Book III **920.003**

Notable native Americans **920.003**

Nowak, R. M. Walker's mammals of the world **599**

Oakes, E. H. American writers **920.003**

Oakes, E. H. A to Z of chemists **920.003**

Olsen, K. All things Austen **823**

Olson, C. Historical dictionary of Buddhism **294.3**

Olson, J. S. Encyclopedia of the industrial revolution in America **973**

Osmanczyk, E. J. Encyclopedia of the United Nations and international agreements **341.23**

Otfinoski, S. Latinos in the arts **920.003**

Oxford American writer's thesaurus **423**

Oxford companion to Christian thought **230**

The Oxford companion to classical literature **880**

The Oxford companion to English literature **820**

The Oxford companion to Irish literature **820**

The Oxford companion to Italian literature **850**

The Oxford companion to music **780**

The Oxford companion to philosophy **103**

The Oxford companion to Shakespeare **822.3**

The Oxford companion to the Bible **220.3**

The Oxford companion to the mind **128**

The Oxford companion to the Supreme Court of the United States **347**

The Oxford companion to theatre and performance **792**

The Oxford companion to wine **641.2**

The Oxford dictionary of classical myth and religion **292**

Oxford dictionary of English idioms **423**

Oxford dictionary of humorous quotations **808.88**

The Oxford dictionary of Islam **297**

Oxford dictionary of modern quotations **808.88**

The Oxford dictionary of nursery rhymes **398.8**

Oxford dictionary of phrase and fable **803**

The Oxford encyclopedia of American literature **810**

The Oxford encyclopedia of ancient Egypt **932**

The Oxford encyclopedia of economic history **330**

The Oxford encyclopedia of food and drink in America **641.3**

The Oxford English dictionary **423**

The Oxford guide to United States Supreme Court decisions **342**

Oxford Latin dictionary **473**

Oxford new concise world atlas **912**

Palmer, L. J. Encyclopedia of abortion in the United States **363.46**

Pasta, a. d. p. t. Encyclopedia of pasta **641.8**

Pearl, N. Now read this **016**

Pearl, N. Now read this II **016**

Pearl, N. Now read this III **016**

Perez, L. G. The history of Japan **952**

Perrault, A. H. Information resources in the humanities and the arts **016**

Peters, P. The Cambridge guide to English usage **428**

Postwar America **973.92**

Powell, J. Great lives from history, The 18th century, 1701-1800 **920.003**

Prahlad, A. The Greenwood encyclopedia of African American folklore **398**

The Princeton encyclopedia of birds **598**

The Princeton encyclopedia of mammals **599**

Printed sources **016**

Pritzker, B. A Native American encyclopedia **970.004**

Publishers, distributors & wholesalers of the United States **070.5**

Pukui, M. K. Hawaiian dictionary **499**

Pulliam, J. M. Read on . . . horror fiction **025**

The Qur'an: an encyclopedia **297.1**

Random House Webster's German-English, English-German dictionary **433**

Random House Webster's unabridged dictionary **423**

Reader's guide to Judaism **296**

Reader's guide to the history of science **509**

Recommended reference books for small and medium-sized libraries and media centers, Vol. 34 **011**

Reference guide to Russian literature **891.7**

Reference guide to world literature **809**

Religion and American cultures **200.9**

Required reading **301**

Rich, M. World authors, 2000-2005 **920.003**

Rockwood, C. Brewer's dictionary of phrase & fable **803**

Rodale's ultimate encyclopedia of organic gardening **635**

Roget's 21st century thesaurus in dictionary form **423**

Roget's international thesaurus **423**

Rough Guides (Firm) The Rough Guide to film **791.43**

Sadie, S. The Grove book of operas **792.5**

Sankaran, N. Microbes and people: an A-Z of microorganisms in our lives **579**

Saricks, J. G. The readers' advisory guide to genre fiction **025.5**

Schneider, D. First ladies **920.003**

Schultz, D. A. Encyclopedia of the United States Constitution **342**

The Scribner encyclopedia of American lives **920.003**

The Scribner encyclopedia of American lives, The 1960s **920.003**

Sexually transmitted disease **616.95**

Shearer, B. F. State names, seals, flags, and symbols **929.9**

Shipp, S. Latin American and Caribbean artists of the modern era **920.003**

Shorter Oxford English dictionary on historical principles **423**

Sifakis, C. The mafia encyclopedia **364.1**

Singer, C. A. Fundamentals of Managing Reference Collections **025.2**

Slatta, R. W. The cowboy encyclopedia **978**

Smithsonian atlas of world aviation **629.13**

Snodgrass, M. E. The Underground Railroad **973.7**

Spears, R. A. McGraw-Hill's dictionary of American slang and colloquial expressions   **427**

St. James encyclopedia of labor history world-wide   **331.8**

St. James encyclopedia of popular culture   **973.9**

Sternberg, M. L. A. American Sign Language   **419**

Stim, R. Contracts   **346**

Stone, J. R. Latin for the illiterati   **473**

Stratton, S. E. The encyclopedia of HIV and AIDS   **362.196**

Sutherland, J. African Americans at war   **355**

Sutton, R. B. Speech index   **808.85**

Swanson, M. Atlas of the Civil War, month by month   **973.7**

Tanton, J. S. Encyclopedia of mathematics   **510**

Thompson, C. World authors, 1990-1995   **809**

Thompson, C. World authors, 1995-2000   **809**

Thorburn, J. E. The Facts on File companion to classical drama   **880**

Trott, B. Read on . . . crime fiction   **016**

Tucker, A. O. The encyclopedia of herbs   **635**

Tucker, S. C. The encyclopedia of the Vietnam War   **959.704**

The United States in the First World War   **940.3**

Unwin, M. The atlas of birds   **598**

The value of a dollar   **338.5**

The value of a dollar: colonial era to the Civil War, 1600-1865   **338.5**

Van Nostrand's scientific encyclopedia   **503**

Vile, J. R. The Constitutional Convention of 1787   **342**

Vile, J. R. Encyclopedia of constitutional amendments, proposed amendments, and amending issues, 1789-2010   **342**

Wakeman, J. World authors, 1950-1970   **920.003**

Wakeman, J. World authors, 1970-1975   **920.003**

Waldman, C. Atlas of the North American Indian   **970.004**

Waldman, C. Encyclopedia of Native American tribes   **970.004**

War: from ancient Egypt to Iraq   **355**

Ware, S. Notable American women   **920.003**

Warren, B. Keep watching the skies!   **791.43**

Weapons & warfare   **623.4**

Who was who in America   **920.003**

Who's who 2008   **920.003**

Who's who among African Americans   **920.003**

Who's who in America, 2008   **920.003**

Who's who in American art, 2008   **920.003**

Who's who in British history   **920.003**

Who's who in finance and business 2008-2009   **920.003**

Who's who of American women 2007   **920.003**

Wilson, E. J. Encyclopedia of the Enlightenment   **940.2**

Winter, R. A consumer's dictionary of food additives   **664**

Women in world history   **920.003**

Woodward, D. R. World War I almanac   **940.3**

Woodworth, S. E. Atlas of the Civil War   **973.7**

Word histories and mysteries   **422**

World atlas of great apes and their conservation   **599.8**

The World Book Encyclopedia   **031**

World explorers and discoverers   **920.003**

World of sociology   **301**

Wyman, D. Wyman's gardening encyclopedia   **635**

Yeoman, R. S. A guide book of United States coins   **737.4**

Zilkha, A. Modern English-Hebrew dictionary   **492.4**

Zondervan dictionary of Christian spirituality   **248**

REFERENCE BOOKS

See also Bibliography; Books; Books and reading

REFERENCE BOOKS -- BIBLIOGRAPHY

American reference books annual 2016   **011**

Guide to reference   **011**

Guide to Reference in Business and Economics   **016**

Guide to reference in medicine and health   **025.06**

Mulac, C. M. Fundamentals of reference   **025.5**

Recommended reference books for small and medium-sized libraries and media centers, Vol. 34   **011**

Reference Sources for Small and Medium-Sized Libraries   **011**

REFERENCE BOOKS -- UNITED STATES

Singer, C. A. Fundamentals of Managing Reference Collections   **025.2**

REFERENCE BOOKS, MEDICAL -- RESOURCE GUIDES

Guide to reference in medicine and health   **025.06**

Reference guide to Russian literature.   **891.7**

Reference guide to science fiction, fantasy, and horror. Burgess, M.   **016**

Reference guide to world literature.   **809**

REFERENCE INTERVIEW

Nilsen, K. Conducting the reference interview   **025.5**

The **Reference** Manual of Woody Plant Propagation. Dirr, M. A.   **631.5**

Reference reborn.   **025.5**

REFERENCE SERVICES (LIBRARIES) -- UNITED STATES

Mulac, C. M. Fundamentals of reference   **025.5**

Reference reborn   **025.5**

REFERENCE SERVICES -- AUTOMATION

Kern, M. K. Virtual reference best practices   **025.5**

Nilsen, K. Conducting the reference interview   **025.5**

REFERENCE SERVICES -- HANDBOOKS, MANUALS, ETC.

Evans, G. E. Introduction to library public services   **025.5**

Ford, C. Crash course in reference **025.5**

Reference shelf [series]

Dinosaurs **567.9**

REFERENCE SOURCES -- BIBLIOGRAPHY

Guide to reference **011**

Mulac, C. M. Fundamentals of reference **025.5**

Reference sources for small and medium-sized libraries. O'Gorman, J. **011**

Reference Sources for Small and Medium-Sized Libraries. **011**

Reference sources in the humanities series

Bleiler, R. Reference and research guide to mystery and detective fiction **016**

Burgess, M. Reference guide to science fiction, fantasy, and horror **016**

REFERENCE WORK (LIBRARIES) See Reference services (Libraries)

REFERENDUM

See also Constitutional law; Democracy; Elections

The **referral** engine. Jantsch, J. **658.8**

REFINANCING

See also Finance

Refined knits. Wood, J. **746.432**

REFINISHING FURNITURE See Furniture finishing

Reflections in Black. Willis, D. **770.92**

Reflections on exile and other essays. Said, E. W. **814**

Reflections on the Revolution in France. Burke, E. **944.04**

The **Reformation**. MacCulloch, D. **270.6**

REFORMATION

See also Christianity; Church history -- 1500-, Modern period

REFORMATION

Bainton, R. H. Here I stand: a life of Martin Luther **92**

Erikson, E. H. Young man Luther **92**

MacCulloch, D. The Reformation **270.6**

Oberman, H. A. Luther: man between God and the Devil **92**

Stark, R. For the glory of God **201**

Tuchman, B. W. The march of folly **909.08**

Wilson, D. A. Out of the storm **92**

REFORMATION -- ENGLAND

Fletcher, C. The divorce of Henry VIII **942.05**

Ronald, S. Heretic queen **942.05**

REFORMATION -- EUROPE

Pettegree, A. The book in the Renaissance **070.5**

REFORMATION -- GERMANY -- BIOGRAPHY

Hendrix, S. H. Martin Luther **92**

REFORMATORIES

See also Children -- Institutional care; Correctional institutions; Prisons; Punishment

REFRACTION

See also Light; Optics

Refresh your home. Family Handyman **643**

REFRIGERATION

Jackson, T. Chilled **621.56**

Refuge in hell. Silver, D. B. **362.1**

REFUGEE CAMPS -- KENYA

Rawlence, B. City of thorns **967.73**

REFUGEE CHILDREN -- UNITED STATES -- BIOGRAPHY

Eire, C. M. N. Waiting for snow in Havana **92**

REFUGEES

Beah, I. A long way gone **92**

Deng, B. They poured fire on us from the sky **962.4**

The girl who escaped ISIS **956.7**

Hari, D. The translator **92**

Him, C. When broken glass floats **959.604**

Hirsi Ali, A. Infidel **92**

Jasanoff, M. Liberty's exiles **973.3**

Kenney, D. N. Asylum denied **92**

Kidder, T. Strength in what remains **92**

Kim, E. A Thousand Miles to Freedom **92**

McClelland, S. Stars Between the Sun and Moon **92**

Pham, A. X. The eaves of heaven **92**

Pipher, M. B. The middle of everywhere **305.9**

St. John, W. Outcasts united **796.334**

Tolan, S. The lemon tree **956.94**

REFUGEES

See also Homeless persons; Immigration and emigration; Noncitizens

REFUGEES -- GERMANY (EAST) -- BIOGRAPHY

Mitchell, G. The tunnels **943.155**

REFUGEES -- KENYA

Rawlence, B. City of thorns **967.73**

REFUGEES -- KOREA (NORTH) -- BIOGRAPHY

Kim, J. Under the same sky **92**

REFUGEES -- SOMALIA

Abdi, H. Keeping hope alive **92**

REFUGEES -- UNITED STATES -- HISTORY -- 20TH CENTURY

Lichtblau, E. The Nazis next door **324.1**

REFUGEES, PALESTINIAN ARAB -- WEST BANK -- EDUCATION

Tolan, S. Children of the stone **780**

REFUGEES, POLITICAL See Political refugees

REFUSE AND REFUSE DISPOSAL

Jensen, D. What we leave behind **304.2**

Rogers, H. Gone tomorrow **363.7**

Royte, E. Garbage land **363.7**

REFUSE AND REFUSE DISPOSAL

See also Municipal engineering; Pollution control industry; Public health; Sanitary engineering; Sanitation

REFUSE AND REFUSE DISPOSAL -- NEW YORK (N.Y.)

Nagle, R. Picking up   **331.7**

REFUSE AND REFUSE DISPOSAL -- UNITED STATES
Humes, E. Garbology   **628.4**

Refusing heaven. Gilbert, J.   **811**

Regarding the pain of others. Sontag, S.   **303.6**

Regazzoni, Guido
(jt. auth) Bigon, M. The Morrow guide to knots   **623.88**

REGENCY NOVELS
See also Historical fiction

REGENERATION (CHRISTIANITY)
See also Christianity -- Doctrines; Salvation

Regents Restoration drama series
Dryden, J. All for love   **822**
Gay, J. The beggar's opera   **822**

REGGAE MUSIC
Bradley, L. This is reggae music   **781.646**
Grant, C. The natural mystics   **920**

REGGAE MUSIC
See also Popular music

REGGAE MUSICIANS
Grant, C. The natural mystics   **920**

REGICIDES -- ENGLAND -- HISTORY -- 17TH CENTURY
Jordan, D. The king's revenge   **941.062**

REGIONAL PLANNING
Mumford, L. The culture of cities   **307.7**

REGIONALISM -- NORTH AMERICA
Woodard, C. American nations   **970.004**

REGIONALISM -- POLITICAL ASPECTS
Bishop, B. The big sort   **305.8**

REGISTERS OF BIRTHS, ETC.
Kemp, T. J. International vital records handbook   **929**

REGISTERS OF BIRTHS, ETC.
See also Genealogy

REGULATORY AGENCIES *See* Administrative agencies

REGULATORY AGENCY OFFICIALS
Feldman, N. Scorpions   **920**
Greenspan, A. The age of turbulence   **92**
Leamer, L. The Kennedy men   **920**
Mahoney, R. D. Sons and brothers: the days of Jack and Bobby Kennedy   **92**
Overtveldt, J. v. Bernanke's test   **332.1**
Perino, M. A. The hellhound of Wall Street   **330.9**
Wessel, D. In Fed we trust   **332.1**
Woodward, B. Maestro: Greenspan's Fed and the American boom   **331.1**

Rehak, Melanie
Girl sleuth   **813**

Rehnquist, William H.
All the laws but one   **342**

Reich, Eugenie Samuel
Plastic fantastic   **92**

Reich, Robert B.
Aftershock   **330.9**
Locked in the cabinet   **973.929**
Saving capitalism   **330.973**

Reichl, Ruth
(ed) The gourmet cookbook   **641.5**
(ed) Gourmet today   **641.5**
About
Reichl, R. Comfort me with apples   **92**
Reichl, R. Garlic and sapphires   **92**
My kitchen year   **641.5**

Reid, David
The brazen age   **974.7**

Reid, Lori
The art of hand reading   **133.6**

Reid, Paul
(jt. auth) Manchester, W. The last lion, Winston Spencer Churchill   **92**

Reid, T. R.
The healing of America   **362.1**

REIGN OF TERROR *See* France -- History -- 1789-1799, Revolution

REIKI (HEALING SYSTEM)
Quest, P. Reiki for life   **615.8**
Reiki for life. Quest, P.   **615.8**

Reill, Peter Hanns
(ed) Wilson, E. J. Encyclopedia of the Enlightenment   **940.2**

Reilly, Brendan
One doctor   **610.69**

Reimagining equality. Hill, A.   **305.8**

Reiman, Donald H.
(ed) Shelley's poetry and prose   **821**

REINDEER
See also Deer; Domestic animals; Mammals

Reiner, Jon
About
Reiner, J. The man who couldn't eat   **92**

Reiner, Julie
The craft cocktail party   **641.87**

REINFORCED CONCRETE
See also Building materials; Concrete

Reinhardt, Django, 1910-1953
About
Dregni, M. Django: the life and music of a Gypsy legend   **92**

Reinhart, Alex, 1991-
Statistics done wrong   **519.5**

Reinhart, Carmen M., 1955-
This time is different   **338.5**

Reinhartz, Dennis
The Art of the Map   **526**

Reinventing comics. McCloud, S.   **741.5**
Reinventing Ikea. Bruno, I.   **684.1**
Reinventing the bazaar. McMillan, J.   **330.12**

Reisen, Harriet

Louisa May Alcott   **92**

Reisner, Rosalind
Read on-- life stories   **016**

Reiss, Tom
The Black Count   **944.04**
The Orientalist   **92**

Reiter, Mark
(jt. auth) Goldsmith, M. Triggers   **155.2**

Reitman, Janet
Inside Scientology   **299**

REJECTION (PSYCHOLOGY)
    See also Psychology

Rejoicing in lament. Billings, J. T.   **248.8**

REJUVENATION
Esmonde-White, M. Aging backwards   **613.2**
Roizen, M. F. This is your do-over   **613**

Rejwan, Nissim
(ed) The Many faces of Islam   **297**

Rekdal, Paisley
Animal eye   **811**

RELATIONS AMONG ETHNIC GROUPS *See*
Ethnic relations

RELATIONSHIPS, MAN-WOMAN *See* Man-
woman relationship

RELATIVITY (PHYSICS)
Aczel, A. D. God's equation   **523.1**
Bodanis, D. E   **530.1**
Bolles, E. B. Einstein defiant   **530.1**
Einstein, A. The evolution of physics   **530**
Einstein, A. The meaning of relativity   **530.1**
Einstein, A. A stubbornly persistent illusion   **530.1**
Ferreira, P. G. The perfect theory   **530.11**
Galison, P. L. Einstein's clocks and Poincare's maps   **529**
Greene, B. The hidden reality   **530.1**
Gribbin, J. 13.8   **523.1**
Gribbin, J. Einstein's Masterwork   **530.11**
Kaku, M. Hyperspace   **530.1**
Levenson, T. The hunt for Vulcan   **523.4**
Musser, G. Spooky action at a distance   **530.11**
Rovelli, C. Seven Brief Lessons on Physics   **530**
Susskind, L. The black hole war   **530.1**
Wolfson, R. Simply Einstein   **530.1**

RELATIVITY (PHYSICS)
    See also Physics

**RELATIVITY (PHYSICS) -- HISTORY -- ENCY-
CLOPEDIAS**
Schulmann, R. An Einstein encyclopedia   **530.092**

RELATIVITY (PHYSICS) -- POPULAR WORKS
Gott, J. R. Welcome to the universe   **523.1**

RELAXATION
Grossman, G. B. Restorative yoga for life   **613.7**
Heller, R. Secular meditation   **158.1**

RELAXATION *See* Recreation; Rest
The **relaxation** response. Benson, H.   **155.9**

RELAXATION THERAPY -- POPULAR

WORKS
Aaronson, N. Pilates for breast cancer survi-
vors   **616.99**
The **relentless** revolution. Appleby, J.   **330.1**

RELIABILITY (ENGINEERING)
    See also Engineering; Probabilities; Systems
engineering

RELIGION
Bowker, J. World religions   **200**
Dawkins, R. The God delusion   **200**
Encyclopedia of religion   **200**
Feynman, R. P. The meaning of it all   **500**
Hazleton, L. Agnostic   **211**
Hitchens, C. God is not great   **200**
Rodríguez, R. Darling   **92**
Sagan, C. Broca's brain   **500**

RELIGION -- GOVERNMENT POLICY *See*
Church and state

RELIGION -- HISTORY
Voices of early Christianity   **270.1**

RELIGION -- HISTORY -- CHRONOLOGY
National Geographic concise history of world religions   **200**

RELIGION -- PHILOSOPHY
De Botton, A. Religion for atheists   **200**
Talking God   **210**

RELIGION -- POLITICAL ASPECTS *See* Religion and politics

RELIGION -- PSYCHOLOGICAL ASPECTS
See Psychology of religion

RELIGION -- SOCIAL ASPECTS *See* Religion
and sociology

Religion and American cultures.   **200.9**

RELIGION AND ART *See* Art and religion

RELIGION AND CIVILIZATION
Asbridge, T. The crusades   **909.07**
Phillips, J. Holy warriors   **909.07**

RELIGION AND ETHICS
National Geographic concise history of world religions   **200**

**RELIGION AND INTERNATIONAL RELA-
TIONS -- UNITED STATES -- HISTORY**
Preston, A. Sword of the spirit, shield of faith   **322**

RELIGION AND PHILOSOPHY *See* Philosophy
and religion

RELIGION AND POLITICS
Hider, J. The spiders of Allah   **956.05**
Kimball, C. When religion becomes lethal   **201**
Martin, W. C. With God on our side   **261.8**

RELIGION AND POLITICS
    See also Politics; Religion

**RELIGION AND POLITICS -- FRANCE -- HIS-
TORY -- 19TH CENTURY**
Read, P. P. The Dreyfus affair   **944.081**

RELIGION AND POLITICS -- UNITED STATES
Barry, J. M. Roger Williams and the creation of the

American soul **974.5**

Niose, D. Nonbeliever nation **211**

Preston, A. Sword of the spirit, shield of faith **322**

RELIGION AND PSYCHOLOGY *See* Psychology of religion

RELIGION AND SCIENCE

Barbour, I. G. When science meets religion **261.5**

Barr, S. M. Modern physics and ancient faith **201**

Bloom, H. The God problem **500**

Brown, N. M. The abacus and the cross **92**

Dawkins, R. Brief Candle in the Dark **570**

Dawkins, R. A devil's chaplain **500**

Ecklund, E. H. Science vs. religion **215**

Frank, A. The constant fire **201**

Grant, E. Science and religion, 400 B.C. to A.D. 1550 **261.5**

The History of science and religion in the western tradition **201**

Nye, B. Undeniable **576.8**

Olson, R. Science and religion, 1450-1900 **261.5**

Overman, D. L. A case for the existence of God **212**

Roach, M. Spook **133.9**

Rudwick, M. J. S. Earth's deep history **550**

Sacks, J. The great partnership **201.65**

Stark, R. For the glory of God **201**

Tyson, N. d. Death by black hole **523.8**

Wathey, J. C. The illusion of God's presence **204**

RELIGION AND SCIENCE

See also Religion; Science

RELIGION AND SCIENCE -- ENGLAND -- HISTORY -- 17TH CENTURY

Hunter, M. Boyle **92**

RELIGION AND SOCIETY *See* Religion and sociology

RELIGION AND SOCIOLOGY

Chaves, M. Ordaining women **262**

Pattison, J. Slow church **253**

RELIGION AND SOCIOLOGY

See also Religion; Sociology

RELIGION AND STATE *See* Church and state

RELIGION AND WAR *See* War -- Religious aspects

Religion for atheists. De Botton, A. **200**

Religion in American life [series]

Curtis, E. E. Muslims in America **305.8**

RELIGION IN LITERATURE

See also Literature; Religion

RELIGION IN THE PUBLIC SCHOOLS

Greenawalt, K. Does God belong in public schools? **379**

RELIGION IN THE PUBLIC SCHOOLS

See also Church and education; Church and state; Public schools; Religious education

Religion today [series]

Belief beyond boundaries **209**

RELIGIONS

Bowker, J. World religions **200**

The Cambridge illustrated history of religions **200.9**

Encyclopedia of religious rites, rituals, and festivals **200**

Hexham, I. Understanding world religions **200**

Prothero, S. R. God is not one **200**

Prothero, S. R. Religious literacy **200**

RELIGIONS

See also Civilization

RELIGIONS -- BIOGRAPHY *See* Religious biography

RELIGIONS -- ENCYCLOPEDIAS

National Geographic concise history of world religions **200**

RELIGIOUS ART

Campbell, J. The power of myth **201**

King, R. Leonardo and the Last supper **759**

RELIGIOUS BIOGRAPHY

Barthel, J. American saint **92**

RELIGIOUS BIOGRAPHY

See also Biography

RELIGIOUS BIOGRAPHY -- ENCYCLOPEDIAS

Holy people of the world **920.003**

RELIGIOUS DISCRIMINATION

Nussbaum, M. C. The new religious intolerance **201**

RELIGIOUS FUNDAMENTALISM

Almond, G. A. Strong religion **200.9**

Armstrong, K. The battle for God **200.9**

Hider, J. The spiders of Allah **956.05**

Kimball, C. When religion becomes lethal **201**

Martin, W. C. With God on our side **261.8**

RELIGIOUS FUNDAMENTALISM

See also Religion

RELIGIOUS GRAPHIC NOVELS

See also Graphic novels

RELIGIOUS HISTORY *See* Church history

The **religious** history of America. Schmidt, L. E. **200.973**

A **religious** history of the American people. Ahlstrom, S. E. **200**

RELIGIOUS HOLIDAYS

Jones, C. C. A year of Russian feasts **641.59**

RELIGIOUS HOLIDAYS

See also Holidays; Rites and ceremonies

RELIGIOUS INSTITUTIONS

National Geographic concise history of world religions **200**

RELIGIOUS INSTITUTIONS

See also Associations; Religion

RELIGIOUS LEADERS

Bainton, R. H. Here I stand: a life of Martin Luther **92**

Erikson, E. H. Young man Luther **92**

Kung, H. Great Christian thinkers **230**

Martin, J. The Jesuit guide to almost everything **248.4**

Oberman, H. A. Luther: man between God and the Devil **92**

Patel, E. Acts of faith **92**

Spence, J. D. God's Chinese son **951**

Wilson, D. A. Out of the storm **92**

RELIGIOUS LIBERTY *See* Freedom of religion

RELIGIOUS LIFE

Armstrong, K. The case for God **211**

De Botton, A. Religion for atheists **200**

How to be compassionate **294.3**

James, W. The varieties of religious experience **210**

Made for goodness **170**

Turner, J. G. Brigham Young, pioneer prophet **289.3**

RELIGIOUS LIFE

See also Religion

RELIGIOUS LIFE (CHRISTIAN) *See* Christian life

Religious literacy. Prothero, S. R. **200**

RELIGIOUS LITERATURE

See also Literature

RELIGIOUS MINORITIES

Wexler, J. Holy hullabaloos **342**

Religious pluralism in America. Hutchison, W. R. **200**

RELIGIOUS POETRY

American religious poems **811**

RELIGIOUS SCHOLARS

Armstrong, K. The spiral staircase **92**

Eire, C. M. N. Learning to die in Miami **92**

Eire, C. M. N. Waiting for snow in Havana **92**

Green, B. Boltzmann's tomb **509**

Lattin, D. The Harvard Psychedelic Club **920**

Taylor, B. B. An altar in the world **92**

RELIGIOUS SCULPTURE *See* Religious art

RELIGIOUS SOCIOLOGY *See* Religion and sociology

RELIGIOUS TOLERANCE

Abdul Rauf, F. Moving the mountain **297.09**

Harris, S. Islam and the future of tolerance **297.2**

Niebuhr, G. Beyond tolerance **201**

Nussbaum, M. C. The new religious intolerance **201**

Ronald, S. Heretic queen **942.05**

RELIGIOUS TOLERANCE

See also Toleration

Relin, David Oliver

Mortenson, G. Three cups of tea **371.82**

RELOCATION OF JAPANESE AMERICANS, 1942-1945 *See* Japanese Americans -- Evacuation and relocation, 1942-1945

Reluctant genius. Gray, C. **92**

The remains of Company D. Nelson, J. C. **920**

Remarkable creatures. Carroll, S. B. **508**

REMARRIAGE

See also Marriage

Rembrandt Harmenszoon van Rijn, 1606-1669

About

Schama, S. Rembrandt's eyes **92**

Rembrandt's eyes. Schama, S. **92**

Remedy and reaction. Starr, P. **362.1**

Remembered rapture. Hooks, B. **808**

Remembering Che. **972.91**

Remembering Jim Crow. **305.896**

Remembering slavery. **326**

Remembering, voices of the holocaust. Smith, L. **940.53**

Remembrances and celebrations. **808.8**

Remington, Frederic, 1861-1909

About

Dippie, B. W. The Frederic Remington Art Museum collection **709**

Remini, Robert Vincent

(ed) Fellow citizens **352.23**

Andrew Jackson **92**

Daniel Webster **328**

John Quincy Adams **92**

Joseph Smith **92**

Remix. Lessig, L. **346**

Remnick, David

The bridge **92**

King of the world: Muhammad Ali and the rise of an American hero **92**

Lenin's tomb **947.085**

(ed) Life stories **920**

Reporting **814**

Resurrection **947.086**

REMODELING (ARCHITECTURE) *See* Houses -- Remodeling

Remodeling a basement. German, R. **643**

REMODELING OF HOUSES *See* Houses -- Remodeling

Remodelista. Carlson, J. **747**

REMOTE SENSING

See also Aerial photography

REMOTE SUBMERSIBLES -- COMPETITIONS -- UNITED STATES

Davis, J. Spare parts **629.8**

REMOTELY PILOTED AIRCRAFT *See* Drone aircraft

Ren, Christine

Ali, K. Fighting weight **92**

RENAISSANCE

Aries, P. A History of private life **909**

Capponi, N. The Day the Renaissance Was Saved **945**

Frieda, L. The Deadly Sisterhood **945**

Great events from history, The Renaissance & early modern era, 1454-1600 **909**

Great lives from history, the Renaissance & early

modern era, 1454-1600 **920.003**

Greenblatt, S. The swerve **940.2**

Herlihy, D. The black death and the transformation of the west **940.1**

Lee, A. The ugly Renaissance **945**

Manchester, W. A world lit only by fire **940.2**

Pettegree, A. The book in the Renaissance **070.5**

Strathern, P. Death in Florence **945**

Strathern, P. The Medici **945.51**

Strathern, P. The artist, the philosopher, and the warrior **920**

RENAISSANCE

    See also Civilization

RENAISSANCE -- ENCYCLOPEDIAS

Encyclopedia of the Renaissance **940.2**

RENAISSANCE -- ITALY

Klein, S. Leonardo's legacy **709**

Lee, A. The ugly Renaissance **945**

RENAISSANCE ART *See* Art -- 15th and 16th centuries

RENAISSANCE PAINTING *See* Painting -- 15th and 16th centuries

The **Renaissance** philosophy of man. **189**

The **Renaissance** portrait. **704.9**

RENAISSANCE PORTRAIT PAINTING -- ITALY

Hales, D. Mona Lisa **759.5**

The Renaissance portrait **704.9**

Renaissance Society of America

Encyclopedia of the Renaissance **940.2**

Renard, John

The handy Islam answer book **297**

Renauer, Albin

Elias, S. How to file for Chapter 7 bankruptcy **346.07**

Rende, Richard

(jt. auth) Prosek, J. Raising Can-Do Kids **649.7**

Rendezvous with destiny. Fullilove, M. **973.917**

Rendgen, Sandra

Understanding the world **741.6**

Renegade. Turner, F. **813**

Renehan, Edward J.

Commodore **92**

Renewable energy. **333**

RENEWABLE ENERGY -- UNITED STATES

Levi, M. Power surge **333.79**

RENEWABLE ENERGY RESOURCES

Alley, R. B. Earth **621**

Helm, D. The carbon crunch **333.79**

Renewable energy **333**

RENEWABLE ENERGY RESOURCES

    See also Energy resources

RENEWABLE ENERGY SOURCES -- UNITED STATES

Friedman, T. L. Hot, flat, and crowded **363.7**

Koerth-Baker, M. Before the lights go out **333.79**

RENGA

Haiku before haiku **895.6**

Rennie, Richard

(ed) A dictionary of chemistry **540**

Renovation. Litchfield, M. W. **643**

RENOWN *See* Fame

RENTAL HOUSING

Smith, M. The nesting place **248.4**

Renzi, Jen

(jt. auth) Pourny, C. The furniture bible **684.1**

Repast. Powell, D. A. **811**

Repcheck, Jack

Copernicus' secret **92**

REPETITIVE PATTERNS (DECORATIVE ARTS) IN INTERIOR DECORATION

Atwood, R. Living with pattern **701.85**

REPLACEMENTS (MUSICAL GROUP)

Mehr, B. Trouble boys **782.42**

The **Replacements:** all over but the shouting. Walsh, J. **920**

Report from ground zero. Smith, D. **363.34**

Report from the interior. Auster, P. **92**

REPORT WRITING

Brown, L. How to write anything **808**

A manual for writers of research papers, theses, and dissertations **808.06**

Modern Language Association of America MLA handbook for writers of research papers **808**

Strunk, W. The elements of style **808**

Turabian, K. L. Student's guide to writing college papers **808**

REPORT WRITING

    See also Authorship

REPORTAGE LITERATURE -- TECHNIQUE

Gutkind, L. You can't make this stuff up **808**

A **reporter's** life. Cronkite, W. **070**

REPORTERS AND REPORTING

Reporting America at war **070.4**

Reporting Iraq **070**

Reporting World War II **940.53**

Ryan, B. Scribe **070.449**

REPORTERS AND REPORTING

    See also Journalism; Newspapers

REPORTERS AND REPORTING -- UNITED STATES

Hickman, J. Murder at Camp Delta **355.1**

Reporting. Remnick, D. **814**

Reporting always. Ross, L. **070.4**

Reporting America at war. **070.4**

Reporting civil rights. **323.1**

Reporting Iraq. **070**

Reporting World War II. **940.53**

REPORTS -- PREPARATION *See* Report writing

REPRODUCTION

Martin, R. How we do it **612.6**

REPRODUCTIVE SYSTEM

Wolf, N. Vagina   **305.42**

REPRODUCTIVE SYSTEM
> *See also* Anatomy; Physiology; Sex -- Physiological aspects

REPRODUCTIVE TECHNOLOGY
> Potter, D. A. What to do when you can't get pregnant   **618.1**
> Stock, G. Redesigning humans   **176**
> Wilmut, I. After Dolly   **176**

REPRODUCTIVE TECHNOLOGY
> *See also* Biotechnology

REPTILES
> Attenborough, D. Life in cold blood   **597.9**
> Campbell, J. The venomous reptiles of the Western Hemisphere   **597.96**
> Conant, R. A field guide to reptiles & amphibians   **597.9**
> Ernst, C. H. Venomous reptiles of the United States, Canada, and northern Mexico   **597.9**
> Firefly Encyclopedia of Reptiles and Amphibians   **597.9**
> A guide to amphibians and reptiles   **597.9**
> Mattison, C. What reptile?   **639.3**
> Smith, J. E. Stolen world   **364.1**
> Stebbins, R. C. A field guide to Western reptiles and amphibians   **597.9**

REPTILES
> *See also* Animals

REPTILES -- PHYSIOLOGY
> *See also* Physiology

The **republic**. Plato   **888**

REPUBLIC OF CHINA, 1949- *See* Taiwan

The **Republic** of Imagination. Nafisi, A.   **819**

Republic of spin. Greenberg, D.   **973.099**

REPUBLIC OF THE CONGO *See* Congo (Republic)

The **republic**; and, The laws. Cicero, M. T.   **320.1**

REPUBLICAN PARTY (U.S. : 1854-) -- HISTORY -- 20TH CENTURY
> Goodwin, D. K. The Bully Pulpit   **973.91**
> Lofgren, M. The party is over   **324.273**

REPUBLICAN PARTY (U.S.)
> Brennan, J. Libertarianism   **320.51**
> Edwards, M. The parties versus the people   **320**
> Gould, L. L. Grand Old Party   **324.273**

REPUBLICAN PARTY (U.S.)
> *See also* Political parties

REPUBLICS
> *See also* Constitutional history; Constitutional law; Political science

REPUTATION
> Davis, M. Digital assassination   **005**
> Thompson, D. C. The reputation economy   **302.23**

The **reputation** economy. Thompson, D. C.   **302.23**

Required reading.   **301**

Resch, John Phillips

   (ed) Americans at war   **973**

The **rescue** artist. Dolnick, E.   **364.1**

Rescue at Los Banos. Henderson, B. B.   **940.53**

RESCUE DOGS
> Miracle dogs   **636.7**

RESCUE DOGS
> *See also* Rescue work; Working dogs

RESCUE OF JEWS, 1939-1945 *See* World War, 1939-1945 -- Jews -- Rescue

Rescue road. Zheutlin, P.   **636.7**

RESCUE WORK
> Blehm, E. Legend   **959.7**
> Tobar, H. Deep down dark   **363.11**
> Tougias, M. Ten hours until dawn   **363.34**
> Toutonghi, P. Dog Gone   **636.7**
> Zuckoff, M. Frozen in Time   **940.54**

RESCUE WORK -- CHINA
> Kim, J. Under the same sky   **92**

RESCUES -- ANTARCTIC OCEAN
> Lewis, M. Last man off   **910.91**

RESEARCH
> Ronson, J. The psychopath test   **616.85**

RESEARCH -- METHODOLOGY
> MacLeod, D. How to find out anything   **001.4**

RESEARCH AND DEVELOPMENT *See* Research

RESEARCH BUILDINGS *See* Laboratories

RESEARCH PAPER WRITING *See* Report writing

Research-based readers' advisory. Moyer, J. E.   **025.5**

The **researcher's** guide to American genealogy. Greenwood, V. D.   **929**

Reséndez, Andrés
> The other slavery   **306.3**

Reset your child's brain. Dunckley, V. L.   **004.67**

Resh, Vincent H.
> (ed) Encyclopedia of insects   **595.7**

The **residence**. Brower, K. A.   **975.3**

RESIDENCE COUNSELORS -- NEW YORK (STATE) -- NEW YORK
> Berg, R. No house to call my home   **362.786**

RESIDENCES *See* Domestic architecture; Houses

Resilience. Earley, P.   **616.89**

Resilience. Greitens, E.   **155.2**

RESILIENCE (PERSONALITY TRAIT)
> Brown, B. Rising strong   **158**
> Greitens, E. Resilience   **155.2**
> Ping Fu Bend, not break   **92**
> Resistance. Humbert, A.   **92**

RESISTANCE TO GOVERNMENT
> Gott, R. Britain's empire   **942**
> Wills, G. A necessary evil   **973**

RESISTANCE TO GOVERNMENT
> *See also* Political ethics; Political science

Resistance, rebellion, and death. Camus, A.   **844**

Resonate. Duarte, N.   **658.452**
RESORTS
  Rogers, D. The last resort   **968.91**
RESOURCE DESCRIPTION AND ACCESS --
  HANDBOOKS, MANUALS, ETC.
  Maxwell, R. L. Maxwell's handbook for RDA, re-
    source description & access   **025.3**
  Oliver, C. Introducing RDA   **025.3**
RESOURCE MANAGEMENT *See* Conservation
  of natural resources
RESOURCEFULNESS
  Gonzales, L. Surviving survival   **155.9**
RESOURCES, MARINE *See* Marine resources
Respect. Ritz, D.   **92**
Respect for acting. Hagen, U.   **792**
Respect yourself. Gordon, R.   **384**
RESPONSIBILITY
  Covey, S. The 4 disciplines of execution **658.4**
RESPONSIBILITY
    See also Ethics
RESPONSIBILITY -- SOCIAL ASPECTS --
  MASSACHUSETTS -- BOSTON
  Sered, S. S. Can't catch a break   **362.83**
REST
  Benson, H. The relaxation response   **155.9**
  Grossman, G. B. Restorative yoga for life **613.7**
REST
    See also Health; Hygiene
REST -- RELIGIOUS ASPECTS
  Shulevitz, J. The Sabbath world   **296.4**
Rest in pieces. Lovejoy, B.   **306.9**
RESTAURANTS
  Balla, N. Bar Tartine   **641.59**
  Chambers, V. 32 yolks   **92**
  Cowen, T. An economist gets lunch   **394.1**
  Eddy, J. North   **641.59**
  The Food Lover's Guide to Paris   **914.4**
  Gartland, A. Heartlandia   **641.597**
  Honey & Co.   **641.595**
  Jayaraman, S. Forked   **331.2**
  Moore, R. This is Camino   **641.5**
  Mosler, L. Driving hungry   **92**
  Parachini, C. Roberta's   **641.82**
  The professional chef   **641.5**
  Red Rooster Cookbook   **641.5**
  Ripert, E. On the line   **647**
  Schlosser, E. Fast food nation   **394.1**
  Spurlock, M. Don't eat this book   **614.5**
  Stabiner, K. Generation chef   **641.5**
  Tomlinson, S. Agricola cookbook   **641.564**
  Wizenberg, M. Delancey   **647.95**
  Ying, C. The Mission Chinese Food Cook-
    book   **641.595**
RESTAURANTS -- ANECDOTES
  Mosler, L. Driving hungry   **92**
RESTAURANTS -- ITALY -- ROME

  Minchilli, E. Eating Rome   **641.594**
RESTAURANTS, BARS, ETC. *See* Bars; Res-
  taurants
RESTAURATEURS
  Buford, B. Heat   **641.5**
  Hamilton, G. Blood, bones & butter   **92**
  Josephson, B. Cafe Society   **792.7**
  McCourt, A. A long stone's throw   **92**
RESTAURATEURS -- FRANCE -- PARIS -- BI-
  OGRAPHY
  Chambers, V. 32 yolks   **92**
RESTAURATEURS -- UNITED STATES -- BI-
  OGRAPHY
  Wizenberg, M. Delancey   **647.95**
Restless creatures. Wilkinson, M.   **591.47**
Restless empire. Westad, O. A.   **327**
Restless genius. Tofel, R. J.   **92**
Restless giant. Patterson, J. T.   **973.92**
Reston, James
  The conviction of Richard Nixon   **973.924**
  Defenders of the faith   **940.2**
  The last apocalypse   **940.1**
RESTORATION ECOLOGY -- MOZAMBIQUE
  -- PARQUE NACIONAL DA GORONGOSA
  A window on eternity   **333.95**
RESTORATION OF FURNITURE *See* Furniture
  -- Repairing; Furniture finishing
Restorative yoga for life. Grossman, G. B. **613.7**
RESTORERS
  Robison, J. E. Look me in the eye   **92**
RESTRAINT OF TRADE
    See also Commerce; Commercial law
RESUMES (EMPLOYMENT)
  Knock 'em dead cover letters   **650.14**
  What color is your parachute? 2017   **650.1**
  Yate, M. Knock 'em dead 2015   **158**
  Yate, M. Knock 'em dead cover letters **650.14**
  Yate, M. Knock 'em dead resumes   **650.14**
Resurrection. Remnick, D.   **947.086**
RESURRECTION *See* Future life
Resurrection Science. O'Connor, M. R. **591.68**
RESUSCITATION -- POPULAR WORKS
  Casarett, D. Shocked   **616.02**
RESUSCITATION, HEART *See* Cardiac resusci-
  tation
RETAIL EXECUTIVES
  Walton, S. Sam Walton, made in America   **92**
RETAIL FRANCHISES *See* Franchises (Retail
  trade)
RETAIL PERSONNEL
  Herlihy, D. V. The lost cyclist   **92**
RETAIL TRADE
  Mitchell, S. Big-box swindle   **381**
RETARDED CHILDREN *See* Children with men-
  tal disabilities
Rethinking collection development and manage-

ment.   025.2
RETIREMENT
 See also Leisure; Old age
**RETIREMENT -- UNITED STATES -- PLAN-
 NING**
 Hinden, S. How to retire happy   646.7
RETIREMENT AGE -- UNITED STATES
 Fideler, E. F. Men still at work   331.3
The **retirement** challenge--will you sink or swim?
 Armstrong, F.   332.024
Retirement heist. Schultz, E.   331.2
RETIREMENT INCOME
 Jason, J.   The AARP Retirement Survival
 Guide   332.024
 Miller, M. The hard times guide to retirement secu-
 rity   332.024
 Pond, J. D. Grow your money!   332.024
 Solin, D. R. The smartest retirement book you'll
 ever read   332.024
RETIREMENT INCOME
 See also Income; Retirement
RETIREMENT INCOME -- UNITED STATES
 Hinden, S. How to retire happy   646.7
 Lowenstein, R. While America aged   331.2
 Solman, P. Get what's yours   368.4
RETIREMENT PLANNING
 See also Retirement
The **retreat.** Jones, M. K.   940.54
RETREATS
 See also Spiritual life
Retribution. Hastings, M.   940.54
The **return.** Treisman, D.   947.086
RETURN MIGRATION
 See also Immigration and emigration
Return of a king. Dalrymple, W.   958.1
The   **Return**   of   George   Washington.
The **Return** of George Washington. Larson, E. 92
The **return** of the wolf to Yellowstone. McNamee,
 T.   333.95
Return on influence. Schaefer, M. W.   658.8
Return to Midway. Ballard, R. D.   940.54
Return to paradise. Michener, J. A.   990
Return to the rivers. Khanna, V.   641.59
Return to wild America. Weidensaul, S. 578
Reuband, Karl-Heinz
 Johnson, E. A. What we knew   943.086
Reuben, Steven Carr
 Becoming Jewish   296.7
REUNIONS, FAMILY *See* Family reunions
Reunited. Marshall, S.   362.82
Reuters.   909.83
REVEGETATION
 Fukuoka, M. Sowing seeds in the desert 631.6
REVELATION
 See also God; Supernatural; Theology
Revell, Donald

Pennyweight windows   811
REVENUE *See* Tariff; Taxation
The **revenue** growth habit. Goldfayn, A. 658.15
REVENUE MANAGEMENT
 Goldfayn, A. The revenue growth habit 658.15
Revere, Paul, 1735-1818
                       About
 Fischer, D. H. Paul Revere's ride   973.3
Reversible monuments. Torre, M. d. l.   861
ReVisioning American history [series]
 Dunbar-Ortiz, R. An indigenous peoples' history of
 the United States   970.004
**REVISIONIST ZIONISTS -- ISRAEL -- BIOG-
 RAPHY**
 Menachem Begin   956.940
Revisiting New England [series]
 Baker, J. W. Thanksgiving   394.26
REVIVALS -- MUSIC *See* Gospel music
Revolt at Taos. Crutchfield, J. A.   972
The **revolt** of the masses.   901
Revolution. Unferth, D. O.   920
Revolution 1989. Sebestyen, V.   947
A **revolution** in color. Kamensky, J.   759.13
Revolution on the Hudson. Daughan, G. C. 974.73
REVOLUTION, AMERICAN *See* United States
 -- History -- 1775-1783, Revolution
REVOLUTION, FRENCH *See* France -- History
 -- 1789-1799, Revolution
Revolutionaries. Rakove, J.   973.3
REVOLUTIONARIES
 Burrough, B. Days of Rage   303.48
 Cambanis, T. Once upon a revolution 962.05
 Egan, T. The immortal Irishman   92
**REVOLUTIONARIES -- ALGERIA -- BIOGRA-
 PHY**
 Macey, D. Frantz Fanon   92
**REVOLUTIONARIES -- CUBA -- HISTORY --
 20TH CENTURY**
 Weiss, M. The Yankee comandante   92
**REVOLUTIONARIES -- EGYPT -- BIOGRA-
 PHY**
 Cambanis, T. Once upon a revolution 962.05
**REVOLUTIONARIES -- FRANCE -- BIOGRA-
 PHY**
 McPhee, P. Robespierre   92
**REVOLUTIONARIES -- GREAT BRITAIN -- BI-
 OGRAPHY**
 Johnston, K. R. The hidden Wordsworth 821
**REVOLUTIONARIES -- IRELAND -- BIOGRA-
 PHY**
 Egan, T. The immortal Irishman   92
**REVOLUTIONARIES -- KENYA -- BIOGRA-
 PHY**
 Ngugi wa Thiong'o In the house of the interpret-
 er   823
REVOLUTIONARIES -- LATIN AMERICA --

BIOGRAPHY
Remembering Che **972.91**

REVOLUTIONARIES -- UNITED STATES -- BIOGRAPHY
Beeman, R. R. Our lives, our fortunes and our sacred honor **973.3**
Cornel West on Black prophetic fire **92**

REVOLUTIONARIES -- UNITED STATES -- HISTORY -- 18TH CENTURY
Rakove, J. Revolutionaries **973.3**

REVOLUTIONARIES -- UNITED STATES -- HISTORY -- 20TH CENTURY
Weiss, M. The Yankee comandante **92**

REVOLUTIONARIES' SPOUSES -- LATIN AMERICA -- BIOGRAPHY
Remembering Che **972.91**

Revolutionary summer. Ellis, J. J. **973.3**

REVOLUTIONISTS See Revolutionaries

REVOLUTIONS
Camus, A. The rebel **303.6**
Hedges, C. Wages of rebellion **303.48**
Khalil, A. Liberation Square **962.05**
Mahama, J. D. My first coup d'etat and other true stories from the lost decades of Africa **966.705**
McNamara, K. J. Dreams of a great small nation **943.703**
Unferth, D. O. Revolution **920**
Walsh, M. Bitter freedom **941.508**

REVOLUTIONS
See also Political science

REVOLUTIONS -- ECONOMIC ASPECTS
Acemoglu, D. Why nations fail **330**

REVOLUTIONS -- HISTORY -- 17TH CENTURY
Parker, G. Global crisis **909**

REVOLUTIONS -- HISTORY -- 20TH CENTURY
Walsh, M. Bitter freedom **941.508**

REVOLUTIONS -- SOCIAL ASPECTS
Hedges, C. Wages of rebellion **303.48**

Revuelta, Natica
About
Gimbel, W. Havana dreams **972.91**

Rewilding the world. Fraser, C. **333.95**

Rewire. Zuckerman, E. **302.23**

Rewrites. Simon, N. **812**

Rex appeal. Larson, P. L. **567.9**

Rexroth, Kenneth
(ed) One hundred poems from the Japanese **895.6**
The complete poems of Kenneth Rexroth **811**

Reynolds, Bill
Hope **796.323**

Reynolds, David
America, empire of liberty **973**
In command of history **940.53**
Summits **909.82**

Reynolds, David S.
John Brown, abolitionist **92**
Mightier than the sword **813**
Waking giant **973.5**
(ed) Whitman, W. Leaves of grass **811**

Reynolds, David, 1952-
America, empire of liberty **973**

Reynolds, Debbie, 1932-2016
About
Reynolds, D. Make 'em Laugh **92**

Reynolds, Garr
Presentation zen

Reynolds, Gretchen
The first 20 minutes **613.7**

Reynolds, Michael S.
Hemingway: the Paris years **92**

Reynolds, Moira Davison
American women scientists **509**

Reynolds, Nancy
No fixed points **792.8**

Reznikoff, Charles
The poems of Charles Reznikoff **811**

Rhapsody in schmaltz. Wex, M. **641.5**

Rhee, Michelle
About
Rhee, M. A. Radical **371.01**

RHETORIC
Brown, L. How to write anything **808**
Flaherty, F. The elements of story **808.5**
Garvey, M. Stylized **808**
Plotnik, A. Spunk & bite **808**
Prose, F. Reading like a writer **808**
Strunk, W. The elements of style **808**

RHETORIC
See also Language and languages

RHETORIC -- POLITICAL ASPECTS -- UNITED STATES -- HISTORY
Prothero, S. The American Bible **973**

RHETORIC -- STUDY AND TEACHING
Turabian, K. L. Student's guide to writing college papers **808**
Zinsser, W. K. Writing to learn **808**

RHEUMATISM
See also Diseases

Rhinoceros, and other plays. Ionesco, E. **842**

RHINOCEROSES -- EFFECT OF POACHING ON
Orenstein, R. Ivory, horn and blood **333.95**

Rhodehamel, John H.
(ed) Washington, G. Writings **973.4**

Rhoden, William C.
$40 million slaves **796**

Rhodes, Richard
Arsenals of folly **355**
Hedy's folly **92**
Hell and Good Company **946.081**

John James Audubon   92
Why they kill   364.3
Rhodes, William Reginald
     About
Rhodes, W. R. Banker to the world   92
RHYTHM AND BLUES MUSIC
Govenar, A. B. Texas blues   781.64
RHYTHM AND BLUES MUSIC
     See also Popular music
RHYTHM AND BLUES MUSICIANS
Turner, T. I, Tina   92
Rhythm of the wild. Heacox, K.   979.8
Rhythms of life. Foster, R. G.   571.7
Riach, Alan
   (ed) MacDiarmid, H. Selected poetry   821
Riasanovsky, Nicholas V.
A history of Russia   947
RIBBON WORK
A-z of Ribbon Embroidery   746.44
RIBBON WORK
     See also Handicraft
Ribowsky, Mark
Dreams to remember   92
Howard Cosell   92
The last cowboy   92
Ricardo, David, 1772-1823
     About
Heilbroner, R. L. The worldly philosophers   330.1
Ricca, Brad
Super boys   92
Ricciardi, Holly
(jt. auth) Harris, M. Magpie   641.86
Rice, Andrew
The teeth may smile but the heart does not forget   967.6
Rice, Anne, 1941-
     About
Rice, A. Called out of darkness   92
Rice, Condoleezza, 1954-
     About
Rice, C. Extraordinary, ordinary people   92
Rice, C. No higher honor   327.73
Rice, noodle, fish. Goulding, M.   394.12
Rice, Stanley A.
Encyclopedia of biodiversity   578.7
Rice, Valentina
Recipes from many kitchens   641.5
RICH
Freeland, C. Plutocrats   305.5
Tough, P. How children succeed   372.21
RICH
     See also Social classes
RICH -- UNITED STATES
Mayer, J. Dark money   320.52
RICH PEOPLE See Rich
RICH PEOPLE -- CONDUCT OF LIFE

Freeland, C. Plutocrats   305.5
RICH PEOPLE -- ENGLAND -- BIOGRAPHY
Livingstone, N. The mistresses of Cliveden   942.009
RICH PEOPLE -- UNITED STATES
The divide   303.3
RICH PERSONS See Rich
A **rich** spot of earth. Hatch, P. J.   635
Rich, Adrienne, 1929-2012
Arts of the possible   811
Collected early poems, 1950-1970   811
A human eye   814
(ed) Rukeyser, M. Selected poems   811
The school among the ruins: poems, 2000-2004   811
Rich, Chris
Stained glass basics   748.5
Rich, Mari
World authors, 2000-2005   920.003
Thompson, C. World authors, 1995-2000   809
The Richard Ellmann lectures in modern literature [series]
Eco, U. Confessions of a young novelist   808.3
Richard M. Nixon. Black, C. M.   92
The **Richard** Rodgers reader.   782.1
Richard Wright. Rowley, H.   813
Richards, Dana
(ed) Gardner, M. The colossal book of short puzzles and problems   793.8
Richards, Keith
     About
Richards, K. Life   92
Richards, Leonard L.
Who freed the slaves?   342.73
Richards, Susan, 1949-
Lost and found in Russia   947.086
     About
Richards, S. Chosen by a horse   636.1
Richardson, Alan
Classic home desserts   641.8
Greenspan, D. Baking chez moi   641.86
The breath of a wok   641.59
Richardson, David
(jt. auth) Eltis, D. Atlas of the transatlantic slave trade   381
Richardson, John, 1924-
     About
Richardson, J. The sorcerer's apprentice   92
Richardson, Julie
Schreiber, C. Rustic fruit desserts   641.8
Vintage cakes   641.86
Richardson, Matthew
(jt. auth) Acharya, V. V. Guaranteed to fail   332.7
Richardson, Peter
No simple highway   781.66
Richardson, Robert D.
Emerson   814
William James   92

Richardson, Sarah, 1971-
    About
  Richardson, S. Sarah style **747**
Richelson, Jeffrey
  The wizards of Langley **327.12**
RICHES *See* Wealth
Richet, Pascal
  A natural history of time **551.7**
Richetti, John J.
  (ed) The Columbia history of the British novel **823**
Richey, Mary Anne
  The impulsive, disorganized child **649**
RICHLAND (WASH.) -- HISTORY -- 20TH CENTURY
  Brown, K. Plutopia **363.17**
RICHMOND (VA.) -- HISTORY
  Furgurson, E. B. Ashes of glory **975.5**
Richmond Mouillot, Miranda
    About
  Richmond Mouillot, M. A fifty-year silence **940.53**
The **richness** of life. Gould, S. J. **508**
Richter's scale. Hough, S. E. **92**
Richter, Charles F., 1900-1985
    About
  Hough, S. E. Richter's scale **92**
Richter, Daniel K.
  Facing east from Indian country **970.004**
Richter, H. P.
  Wiring simplified **621.319**
Richter, Sviatoslav, 1915-1997
    About
  Schonberg, H. C. The great pianists **920**
Rick Bayless's Mexican kitchen. Bayless, R. **641.59**
Rick Stein's complete seafood. **641.6**
Rickards, James
  Currency wars **332.4**
Rickenbacker, Eddie, 1890-1973
    About
  Groom, W. The aviators **920**
Ricketts, Harry
  Rudyard Kipling **92**
Rickey, Branch, 1881-1965
    About
  Breslin, J. Branch Rickey **92**
Rickford, Russell John
  Betty Shabazz: a remarkable story of survival and faith before and after Malcolm X **92**
Ricks, Christopher
  (ed) Inventions of the March Hare **811**
  (ed) Menashe, S. New and selected poems **811**
Ricks, Thomas E.
  Fiasco: the American military adventure in Iraq **956.7**
  The generals **355.009**
The **riddle** of Amish culture. Kraybill, D. B. **289.7**
The **riddle** of the compass. Aczel, A. D. **912**

The **Riddle** of the Labyrinth. Fox, M. **487**
Riddled with life. Zuk, M. **616.07**
RIDDLES
    See also Amusements; Literary recreations
Ride, Sally
    About
  Sherr, L. Sally Ride **92**
Rideau, Wilbert
    About
  Rideau, W. In the place of justice **92**
Ridge, Brent
  The Beekman 1802 heirloom dessert cookbook **641.5**
Riding the iron rooster. Theroux, P. **915**
Riding, Alan
  And the show went on **944**
Ridinger, Robert B. Marks
  Bosman, E. Gay, lesbian, bisexual, and transgendered literature **016**
Ridley, Glynis
  The discovery of Jeanne Baret **92**
Ridley, Jane
  The heir apparent **92**
Ridley, Jasper Godwin
  The Freemasons **366**
Ridley, Mark
  (ed) Darwin, C. The Darwin reader **576.8**
Ridley, Matt
  The agile gene **155.7**
  The evolution of everything **303.48**
  Francis Crick **92**
  Genome **599.93**
  The rational optimist **339.2**
Ridpath, Ian
  The monthly sky guide **523.8**
  Stars and planets **520**
Riechel, Rosemarie
  Easy information sources for ESL, adult learners, & new readers **016**
Riedel, Michael
  Razzle Dazzle **792.09**
Rieder, Jonathan
  Gospel of freedom **323.1**
Riefenstahl, Leni, 1902-2003
    About
  Bach, S. Leni: the life and work of Leni Riefenstahl **92**
  Dietrich & Riefenstahl **791.43**
  Trimborn, J. Leni Riefenstahl **92**
Rieff, David
  (ed) As consciousness is harnessed to flesh **818**
  A bed for the night **361.2**
  Slaughterhouse **949.7**
  (ed) Sontag, S. Reborn **92**
Riemann, Georg Friedrich Bernhard, 1826-1866
    About

Bell, E. T. Men of mathematics 920
Derbyshire, J. Prime obsession 512.7
Riendeau, Roger E.
A brief history of Canada 971
Riess, Jana
Flunking sainthood 248.4
Riffenburgh, Beau
Mapping the world 912
Shackleton's forgotten expedition 998
RIFLES
See also Guns
The **Rift.** Perry, A. 320.9
Rigby, Claire
Fodor's Rio de Janeiro & Sao Paulo 918.15
Rigden, John S.
Einstein 1905 530.1
Hydrogen 546
Riggs, Thomas
(ed) Contemporary poets 821
(ed) St. James guide to Hispanic artists 920.003
Righetti, Maggie
Crocheting in plain English 746.43
Knitting in plain English 746.43
RIGHT OF PRIVACY
Angwin, J. Dragnet nation 323.44
Baker, S. A. Skating on stilts 363.32
Stryker, C. Hacking the Future 004.67
RIGHT OF PRIVACY
See also Civil rights
RIGHT OF PRIVACY -- UNITED STATES
Carpenter, D. Flagrant conduct 342.73
RIGHT OF PROPERTY
Baldwin, P. The copyright wars 346
RIGHT OF PROPERTY
See also Civil rights; Property
The **right** stuff. Wolfe, T. 629.45
Right time, right place. Brookhiser, R. 92
RIGHT TO BEAR ARMS *See* Gun control
RIGHT TO COUNSEL
See also Civil rights
RIGHT TO COUNSEL -- UNITED STATES
Houppert, K. Chasing Gideon 345.73
RIGHT TO DIE
Butler, K. Knocking on Heaven's Door 616.02
Humphry, D. Final exit 179.7
Peck, M. S. Denial of the soul 179.7
Wanzer, S. H. To die well 179.7
Yount, L. Right to die and euthanasia 179.7
RIGHT TO DIE
See also Death; Medical ethics; Medicine --
Law and legislation
RIGHT TO DIE -- LAW AND LEGISLATION
Ball, H. At liberty to die 344
Right to die and euthanasia. Yount, L. 179.7
Right to exist. Lozowick, Y. 956.940
RIGHT TO HEALTH -- UNITED STATES -- HIS-

TORY
Hoffman, B. Health care for some 362.1
RIGHT TO HEALTH CARE
See also Human rights
RIGHT TO KNOW *See* Freedom of information
Right, wrong, and risky. Davidson, M. 423
RIGHT-TO-LIFE MOVEMENT (ANTI-ABOR-TION MOVEMENT) *See* Pro-life movement
RIGHT-WING EXTREMISTS -- UNITED STATES
Goldwag, A. The new hate 306.2
RIGHT-WING EXTREMISTS -- UNITED STATES -- HISTORY -- 20TH CENTURY
Conner, C. Wrapped in the flag 322.4
RIGHTEOUS GENTILES IN THE HOLO-CAUST
Ackerman, D. The zookeeper's wife 940.53
Joukowsky, A. Defying the Nazis 940.53
RIGHTEOUS GENTILES IN THE HOLO-CAUST
See also Holocaust, 1939-1945; World War, 1939-1945 -- Jews -- Rescue
RIGHTEOUS GENTILES IN THE HOLO-CAUST -- FRANCE -- MARSEILLE -- BIOG-RAPHY
Zuccotti, S. Père Marie-Benoît and Jewish rescue 940.53
RIGHTEOUS GENTILES IN THE HOLO-CAUST -- MASSACHUSETTS -- WELLES-LEY HILLS
Joukowsky, A. Defying the Nazis 940.53
RIGHTEOUS GENTILES IN THE HOLO-CAUST -- POLAND -- BIOGRAPHY
Mazzeo, T. J. Irena's children 940.53
The **righteous** mind. Haidt, J. 201
Righteous victims. Morris, B. 956
Rightful heritage. Brinkley, D. 92
Rights from wrongs. Dershowitz, A. M. 323
Rights gone wrong. Ford, R. T. 342
Rights of man; and, Common sense. Paine, T. 320
The **rights** of the people. Shipler, D. K. 323
The **rights** of women. American Civil Liberties Union 346.01
RIGHTS OF WOMEN *See* Women's rights
RIGHTS, HUMAN *See* Human rights
RIGHTS, PROPRIETARY *See* Intellectual property
Rightsize . . . right now! Leeds, R. 648
Rigney, Matt
In pursuit of giants 597
Rigsby, Mike
A beginner's guide to 3D printing 621.9
Riis, Jacob A. (Jacob August), 1849-1914
About
Buk-Swienty, T. The other half 92
RIJEKA (CROATIA) -- HISTORY -- 20TH CEN-

TURY
Hughes-Hallett, L. Gabriele d'Annunzio   **858**
Riley, Gregory J.
The river of God   **270.1**
Riley, Kathleen, 1974-
The Astaires   **92**
Riley, Tim
Lennon   **92**
Riley-Smith, Jonathan
(ed) The Oxford illustrated history of the Crusades   **909.07**
Rilke, Rainer Maria
Duino elegies   **831**
New poems   **831**
Sonnets to Orpheus   **831**
Uncollected poems   **831**
Rimbaud. Rimbaud, A.   **848**
Rimbaud, Arthur
Poems   **841**
Rimbaud   **848**
Rin Tin Tin. Orlean, S.   **636.7**
RIN-TIN-TIN (DOG)
Orlean, S. Rin Tin Tin   **636.7**
Rinella, Steven
American buffalo   **599.64**
The complete guide to hunting, butchering, and cooking big game   **799.2**
The Complete Guide to Hunting, Butchering, and Cooking Wild Game   **799.2**
About
Rinella, S. Meat eater   **799.29**
Ringquist, Rebecca
Rebecca Ringquist's embroidery workshops **746.44**
Rinzler, Lodro
The Buddha walks into a bar   **294.3**
RIO DE JANEIRO (BRAZIL) -- DESCRIPTION AND TRAVEL
De Vries, A. Frommer's Rio de Janeiro day By day   **918.15**
Dk Eyewitness Top 10 Rio De Janeiro   **918.15**
Insight Guide Explore Rio   **918**
Lonely Planet Rio De Janeiro   **918.15**
Rigby, C. Fodor's Rio de Janeiro & Sao Paulo   **918.15**
Sommers, M. Moon Rio De Janeiro   **918.15**
RIO DE JANEIRO (BRAZIL) -- ECONOMIC CONDITIONS
Barbassa, J. Dancing With the Devil in the City of God   **981.53**
Riordan, James
Break on through: the life and death of Jim Morrison   **92**
Riot and remembrance. Hirsch, J. S.   **976.6**
RIOT CONTROL
See also Crowds; Riots
The **riot** grrrl collection.   **781.64**

RIOT GRRRL MOVEMENT
Brownstein, C.   Hunger Makes Me a Modern Girl   **92**
The riot grrrl collection   **781.64**
RIOTS
Hirsch, J. S. Riot and remembrance   **976.6**
Risen, C. A nation on fire   **973.923**
RIOTS
See also Crime; Freedom of assembly; Offenses against public safety
RIOTS -- NEW YORK (N.Y.)
Cliff, N. The Shakespeare riots   **974.4**
Ripe.   **641.6**
Ripert, Eric, 1965-
On the line   **647**
About
Chambers, V. 32 yolks   **92**
Ripken, Billy
Ripken, C. Play baseball the Ripken way **796.357**
Ripken, Cal, Jr.
Play baseball the Ripken way   **796.357**
About
Ripken, C. The only way I know   **92**
Ripley, Amanda
The smartest kids in the world   **370.9**
The unthinkable   **155.9**
RIPOFFS See Fraud
Ripped. Kot, G.   **780.2**
Rips, Nicolaia
About
Rips, N. Trying to float   **974.7**
Rise. Rodriguez, D.   **92**
Rise & fire. Fury, S.   **796.323**
The **rise** and fall of ancient Egypt. Wilkinson, T. **932**
The **rise** and fall of Arab presidents for life. Owen, R.   **352.23**
The **rise** and fall of communism. Brown, A. **320.5**
The **rise** and fall of the American teenager. Hine, T.   **305.235**
The **rise** and fall of the great powers. Kennedy, P. M.   **909.08**
The **rise** and fall of the Third Reich. Shirer, W. L.   **943.086**
The **rise** of American democracy. Wilentz, S. **973.5**
The **rise** of Germany 1939-1941. Holland, J. **940.54**
The **rise** of modern paganism. Gay, P.   **190**
The **rise** of Rome. Everitt, A.   **937**
Rise of the Rocket Girls. Holt, N.   **629.4**
The **rise** of Theodore Roosevelt. Morris, E.   **92**
Rise to greatness. Black, C.   **971**
Risen, Clay
American Whiskey, Bourbon & Rye   **641.2**
The bill of the century   **342.73**
A nation on fire   **973.923**
Rising fire: volcanoes and our inner lives. Calderazzo, J.   **551.2**

The **rising** sea. Pilkey, O. H.   **363.34**

Rising strong. Brown, B.   **158**

Rising tide. Barry, J. M.   **977**

RISK
   Shiller, R. J.   Irrational exuberance   **332.63**

RISK
   See also Economics

RISK MANAGEMENT
   Kreamer, A.   Risk/reward   **650.1**

RISK-TAKING (PSYCHOLOGY)
   See also Psychology

Risk/reward. Kreamer, A.   **650.1**

RITALIN
   Schwarz, A.   ADHD nation   **618.92**

Ritchie, David
   Gates, A. E.   Encyclopedia of earthquakes and volcanoes   **551.2**

RITES AND CEREMONIES
   Encyclopedia of religious rites, rituals, and festivals   **200**
   How to be a perfect stranger   **203**
   New American Haggadah   **296.4**

Rites of peace. Zamoyski, A.   **940.2**

Ritter, Charles F.
   (ed) Leaders of the American Civil War   **973.7**

Ritter, Lawrence S.
   The glory of their times   **920**

RITUAL *See* Liturgies; Rites and ceremonies

Ritz, David
   After the Dance   **782.42**
   Respect   **92**

Ritz, David
   Grandmaster Flash   The adventures of Grandmaster Flash   **92**
   James, E.   Rage to survive   **92**
   King, B. B.   Blues all around me   **781.643**
   Leiber, J.   Hound dog   **92**

The **rival** queens. Goldstone, N.   **944**

The **rivals.** Howard, J.   **92**

Rivas, Mim Eichler
   Gardner, C.   The pursuit of happyness   **92**
   (jt. auth) Quiñones-Hinojosa, A.   Becoming Dr. Q   **92**

The **river** at the center of the world. Winchester, S.   **915**

River Cottage every day. Fearnley-Whittingstall, H.   **641.5**

River Cottage Gluten Free. Devlin, N.   **641.5**

River Cottage Veg. Fearnley-Whittingstall, H. **641.5**

RIVER ECOLOGY
   See also Ecology

River house. Lawrence, S.   **92**

A **river** lost. Harden, B.   **333.91**

River of dark dreams. Johnson, W.   **305.8**

The **river** of doubt. Millard, C.   **973.91**

The **river** of God. Riley, G. J.   **270.1**

The **river** of lost footsteps. Thant Myint-U   **959.1**

RIVER POLLUTION *See* Water pollution

A **river's** tale. Gargan, E. A.   **915**

Rivera, Diego, 1886-1957
   About
   Marnham, P.   Dreaming with his eyes open   **92**

Rivera, Mariano, 1969-
   About
   Rivera, M.   The closer   **92**

RIVERS
   Fagin, D.   Toms River   **363.72**
   Mary, B.   An American River

RIVERS
   See also Physical geography; Water; Waterways

Rivers of gold. Thomas, H.   **980**

Rivers, Charlotte
   Little book of book making   **686**

Rivlin, Gary
   Broke, USA   **339.4**
   Katrina   **976.3**

Rizzo, Jill
   (jt. auth) Harampolis, A.   The flower recipe book   **745.92**

Roach, Mary, 1959-
   Bonk   **612.6**
   Grunt   **355.07**
   Gulp   **612.3**
   Packing for Mars   **571**
   Roach, M.   Packing for Mars   **571**
   Spook   **133.9**
   Stiff   **611**

ROAD CONSTRUCTION *See* Roads

The **road** home. Nichtern, E.   **294.3**

The **road** less traveled. Peck, M. S.   **158**

The **road** less traveled and beyond. Peck, M. S. **158**

ROAD MAPS
   See also Maps

The **Road** to Character. Brooks, D. B.   **170**

Road to Cooperstown. Stanton, T.   **92**

The **road** to Dallas. Kaiser, D. E.   **973.922**

The **road** to home. Gregorian, V.   **92**

The **road** to Little Dribbling. Bryson, B.   **914**

The **road** to Verdun. Ousby, I.   **940.4**

The **road** to Woodstock. Lang, M.   **781.66**

Roads. McMurtry, L.   **917**

ROADS
   Conover, T.   The routes of man   **388.1**
   McMurtry, L.   Roads   **917**

ROADS
   See also Civil engineering; Transportation

The **roads** have come to an end now. Jacobsen, R.   **839.8**

Roads to infinity. Stillwell, J.   **511.3**

The **roads** to modernity. Himmelfarb, G.   **190**

Roads to Quoz. Heat Moon, W. L.   **917**

A **roadside** dog. Milosz, C.   **891.8**
ROADSIDE IMPROVEMENT
    See also Grounds maintenance; Landscape
    architecture; Roads
RoAne, Susan
  How to work a room   **650.1**
ROANOKE ISLAND (N.C.) -- HISTORY
  Horn, J. A kingdom strange   **975.6**
Roast figs, sugar snow. Henry, D.   **641.5**
ROASTING (COOKING)
  All about roasting   **641.7**
  Fine cooking roasting   **641.7**
Robb, Graham
  Balzac   **92**
  Parisians   **944**
  Strangers: homosexual love in the nineteenth cen-
  tury   **306.76**
Robb, John
  Punk rock   **781.66**
Robb, Peter
  M: the man who became Caravaggio   **759**
**ROBBEN ISLAND (SOUTH AFRICA) -- ANEC-
DOTES**
  Jones, B. Mandela   **92**
ROBBERS *See* Thieves
The **robbers** [and] Wallenstein. Schiller, F.   **832**
**ROBBERY INVESTIGATION -- ENGLAND --
  LONDON -- CASE STUDIES**
  Crosby, M. C. The great pearl heist   **364.16**
Robbins, Alexandra
  The geeks shall inherit the Earth
  The nurses   **362.17**
Robbins, Catherine C.
  All Indians do not live in teepees (or casi-
  nos)   **970.004**
Robbins, Jeffrey
  (ed) Feynman, R. P. The pleasure of finding things
  out   **500**
Robbins, Jerome
         About
  Vaill, A. Somewhere   **92**
Robbins, Liz
  A race like no other   **796.42**
Robbins, Martha M.
  (ed) Among African apes   **599.8**
Robbins, Tom, 1932-
         About
  Robbins, T. Tibetan Peach Pie   **92**
Robbins, Tony
  Unlimited power   **158**
Robert Altman. Zuckoff, M.   **92**
Robert Browning. Browning, R.   **821**
Robert Browning's poetry. Browning, R.   **821**
Robert C. Byrd Center for Legislative Studies
  Congress investigates   **328**
Robert E. Lee. Thomas, E. M.   **92**

Robert E. Lee. Blount, R.   **92**
Robert Frost. Parini, J.   **811**
Robert I, King of Scots, 1274-1329
         About
  Penman, M. Robert the Bruce   **92**
Robert Kennedy. Thomas, E.   **92**
Robert Kennedy and his times. Schlesinger, A.
M.   **92**
Robert McConnell Productions
  (comp) Webster's New World Robert's rules of or-
  der   **060.4**
Robert Oppenheimer. Monk, R.   **92**
Robert Schumann. Geck, M.   **92**
Robert the Bruce. Penman, M.   **92**
Robert's rules of order newly revised. Robert, H.
M.   **060.4**
Robert's rules of order, newly revised, in brief. Rob-
ert, H. M.   **060.4**
Robert, Henry M.
  Robert's rules of order newly revised   **060.4**
  Robert's rules of order, newly revised, in brief **060.4**
  Webster's New World Robert's rules of order **060.4**
Roberta's. Parachini, C.   **641.82**
ROBERTA'S (RESTAURANT)
  Parachini, C. Roberta's   **641.82**
The **Roberts** court. Coyle, M.   **347.73**
Roberts, Adam
  (ed) Browning, R. Robert Browning   **821**
Roberts, Andrew
  Roberts, A. Masters and commanders   **940.54**
  Napoleon   **92**
  The storm of war   **940.54**
  Waterloo: June 18, 1815   **940.2**
Roberts, Callum
  The ocean of life   **551.46**
  The unnatural history of the sea   **909**
Roberts, Cokie
  Capital dames   **793.7**
  Founding mothers   **920**
  Ladies of liberty   **920**
Roberts, David, 1943-
  Alone on the ice   **919**
  (ed) Points unknown   **910**
  Once they moved like the wind   **970.004**
Roberts, Deborah, 1960-
         About
  Roberts, D. Been there, done that   **92**
Roberts, Diane
  Tribal   **796.332**
Roberts, Dorothy
  Fatal invention   **305.8**
Roberts, Geoffrey
  Stalin's general   **940.54**
Roberts, Gillian
  You can write a mystery   **808.3**
Roberts, J. M.

The new history of the world 909
Roberts, James A.
  Shiny objects 339.4
Roberts, Jason
  A sense of the world 92
Roberts, John G., 1955-
  About
  Coyle, M. The Roberts court 347.73
  Toobin, J. The oath 347.73
  Tribe, L. H. Uncertain justice 342.73
  Tushnet, M. In the balance 347.73
Roberts, Priscilla Mary
  (ed) The encyclopedia of Middle East wars 355
  (ed) Encyclopedia of World War II 940.53
Roberts, Randy, 1951-
  Joe Louis 92
  (jt. auth) Smith, J. Blood brothers 92
Roberts, Robert North
  Campaigning for president in America, 1788-
  2016 324.709
Roberts, Siobhan
  King of infinite space 92
Robertson, Chad
  Balla, N. Bar Tartine 641.59
  Tartine 641.8
  Tartine Book No. 3 641.81
  Tartine bread 641.8
Robertson, David
  W.C. Handy 92
Robertson, David C.
  (jt. auth) Breen, B. Brick by brick 338.7
Robertson, Gil L.
  (ed) Family affair 305.8
Robertson, James I.
  Stonewall Jackson 92
Robertson, John
  Iraq 956.7
Robertson, Robin
  Robin Robertson's vegan without borders 641.5
  Vegan planet 641.5
Robeson, Eslanda Goode, 1896-1965
  About
  Ransby, B. Eslanda 92
Robeson, Paul, 1898-1976
  About
  Ransby, B. Eslanda 92
  Robeson, P. Here I stand 92
  Robeson, P. The undiscovered Paul Robeson 92
Robespierre. McPhee, P. 92
Robespierre, Maximilien, 1758-1794
  About
  McPhee, P. Robespierre 92
Robey, David
  (ed) The Oxford companion to Italian literature 850
Robicelli's. Robicelli, A. 641.86
Robicelli, Allison

Robicelli's 641.86
Robicelli, Matt
  (jt. auth) Robicelli, A. Robicelli's 641.86
Robillard, Douglas
  (ed) Melville, H. The poems of Herman Mel-
  ville 811
Robin Robertson's vegan without borders. 641.5
ROBINS
  See also Birds
Robins, Gay
  The art of ancient Egypt 709.3
Robinson, Alex.
  Dk Eyewitness Top 10 Rio De Janeiro 918.15
  The story of measurement 530.8
Robinson, Andrew, 1957-
  Cracking the Egyptian code 493
Robinson, Edwin Arlington
  Poems 821
Robinson, Eugene
  Disintegration 305.8
Robinson, Francis
  (ed) The Cambridge illustrated history of the Is-
  lamic world 909
Robinson, George
  Essential Judaism 296
Robinson, Jackie, 1919-1972
  About
  Falkner, D. Great time coming: the life of Jackie
  Robinson, from baseball to Birmingham 92
  I never had it made 92
  Kashatus, W. C. Jackie and Campy 92
  Tygiel, J. Baseball's great experiment 796.357
Robinson, James
  (jt. auth) Acemoglu, D. Why nations fail 330
Robinson, Jancis
  (ed) The Oxford companion to wine 641.22
  Wine grapes 664
Robinson, Jo
  Eating on the wild side 306.4
Robinson, Ken, 1950-
  (jt. auth) Aronica, L. Creative schools 371.2
Robinson, Marilynne, 1943-
  When I was a child I read books 814
Robinson, Mario Andres
  Lessons in realistic watercolor 751.422
Robinson, Peter
  (ed) Complete poetry: translations & selected
  prose 821
Robinson, Phillip T.
  Life at the zoo: behind the scenes with the animal
  doctors 590.73
Robinson, Ray
  Iron horse: Lou Gehrig in his time 92
  Rockne of Notre Dame 92
Robinson, Roxana
  Georgia O'Keeffe: a life 709

Robinson, Sugar Ray, 1921-1989
About
Haygood, W. Sweet thunder   92
ROBINSONADES
    See also Adventure fiction; Imaginary voyages
Robisheaux, Thomas
The last witch of Langenburg   133.4
Robison, John Elder, 1957-
About
Robison, J. E. Look me in the eye   92
Robison, J. E. Switched on   616.85
Robitschek, Leo
(jt. auth) Humm, D. The NoMad cookbook 641.597
ROBOTICISTS -- BIOGRAPHY
Dufty, D. F. How to build an android   629.8
ROBOTICS *See* Robots
ROBOTICS -- COMPETITIONS -- UNITED STATES
Davis, J. Spare parts   629.8
ROBOTICS -- POPULAR WORKS
Dufty, D. F. How to build an android   629.8
ROBOTS
Bascomb, N. The new cool   629.8
Bulletproof feathers   570.1
Dufty, D. F. How to build an android   629.8
Kurzweil, R. The singularity is near   153.9
Mindell, D. A. Our Robots, Ourselves   629.8
Singer, P. W. Wired for war   355
ROBOTS
    See also Machinery; Mechanical movements
ROBOTS -- COMPETITIONS
Davis, J. Spare parts   629.8
ROBOTS -- DESIGN AND CONSTRUCTION
Long, J. Darwin's devices   629.8
Robson, Deborah
(jt. auth) Ekarius, C. The field guide to fleece 677
Robson, John M.
(ed) Mill, J. S. Autobiography   92
Roche, Rick
Read on-- biography   016
ROCHESTER (N.Y.) -- BIOGRAPHY
Ward, G. C. A disposition to be rich   974.7
ROCHESTER RED WINGS (BASEBALL TEAM)
Barry, D. Bottom of the 33rd   796.357
ROCK AND ROLL MUSIC *See* Rock music
Rock and roll will save your life. Almond, S. 781.66
Rock climbing. Trailside (Television program)   796.522
ROCK CLIMBING *See* Mountaineering
ROCK DRAWINGS, PAINTINGS, AND ENGRAVINGS
Schobinger, J. The ancient Americans   970.01
ROCK MUSIC
Almond, S. Rock and roll will save your life 781.66

Browne, D. Fire and rain   **781.66**
Buckland, G. Who shot rock & roll   **781.66**
Cohen, M. All These Things That I've Done **781.66**
Cutler, S. You can't always get what you want   **781.66**
Hayes, C. Gig posters volume 1   **741.6**
Richardson, P. No simple highway   **781.66**
Smith, P. Patti Smith Collected Lyrics, 1970-2015   **782.42**
ROCK MUSIC
    See also Music; Popular music
ROCK MUSIC -- 1961-1970 -- HISTORY AND CRITICISM.
Savage, J. 1966   **781.66**
ROCK MUSIC -- 1991-2000 -- HISTORY AND CRITICISM
Cross, C. R. Here we are now   **92**
ROCK MUSIC -- HISTORY AND CRITICISM
Guralnick, P. Sam Phillips   **92**
ROCK MUSIC -- PICTORIAL WORKS
Buckland, G. Who shot rock & roll   **781.66**
Marshall, J. Trust   **781.66**
ROCK MUSIC -- SOCIAL ASPECTS
Richardson, P. No simple highway   **781.66**
ROCK MUSIC -- UNITED STATES
Cooke, J. B. On the road with Janis Joplin   **92**
ROCK MUSICIANS
The Beatles anthology   **782.421**
Brightman, C. Sweet chaos   **920**
Buckland, G. Who shot rock & roll   **781.66**
Byrne, D. Bicycle diaries   **796.6**
Clapton, E. Clapton   **92**
Coleman, R. Blue Monday   **92**
Cross, C. R. Heavier than heaven: a biography of Kurt Cobain   **92**
Cross, C. R. Room full of mirrors   **92**
Dylan, B. Chronicles   **92**
Englehart, M. AC/DC   **920**
Gould, J. Can't buy me love   **920**
Greenberg, K. E. December 8, 1980   **92**
Gruen, B. New York Dolls   **781.66**
Guralnick, P. Careless love: the unmaking of Elvis Presley   **92**
Hopkins, J. No one here gets out alive   **92**
Hoskyns, B. Lowside of the road   **92**
Jackson, B. Garcia   **92**
Mason, B. A. Elvis Presley   **92**
Murray, C. S. Crosstown traffic: Jimi Hendrix and the post-war rock'n'roll revolution   **787.87**
Norman, P. John Lennon   **92**
O'Dell, C. Miss O'Dell   **92**
Osbourne, O. I am Ozzy   **92**
Povey, G. Echoes: the complete history of Pink Floyd   **920**
Richards, K. Life   **92**
Riley, T. Lennon   **92**

Riordan, J. Break on through: the life and death of Jim Morrison **92**

Schumacher, M. Crossroads **92**

Smith, P. Just kids **92**

Sounes, H. Fab **92**

Spitz, B. The Beatles: the biography **920**

Stark, S. D. Meet the Beatles **920**

Strauss, N. Everyone loves you when you're dead **920**

Trynka, P. Iggy Pop **92**

Turman, K. Louder Than Hell **781.66**

Victor, A. The Elvis encyclopedia **781.66**

Walsh, J. The Replacements: all over but the shouting **920**

Wareham, D. Black postcards **92**

Weller, S. Girls like us **920**

White, C. The life and times of Little Richard **92**

Zappa, F. The real Frank Zappa book **92**

Zevon, C. I'll sleep when I'm dead **92**

ROCK MUSICIANS -- ANECDOTES
Punk rock **781.66**

ROCK MUSICIANS -- BIOGRAPHY
Carlin, P. A. Bruce **92**

ROCK MUSICIANS -- ENGLAND
Bowie on Bowie **92**

ROCK MUSICIANS -- ENGLAND -- BIOGRAPHY
Cohen, R. The Sun and the Moon and the Rolling Stones **782.42**

Morley, P. The age of Bowie **92**

ROCK MUSICIANS -- ENGLAND -- INTERVIEWS
Bowie on Bowie **92**

ROCK MUSICIANS -- UNITED STATES -- BIOGRAPHY
Brownstein, C. Hunger Makes Me a Modern Girl **92**

Cross, C. R. Here we are now **92**

Hynde, C. Reckless **92**

Mehr, B. Trouble boys **782.42**

Richardson, P. No simple highway **781.66**

Wilson, B. I am Brian Wilson **92**

ROCK PAINTINGS See Rock drawings, paintings, and engravings

Rock, John, 1890-1984
About
Eig, J. The birth of the pill **618.1**

Rockefeller, David, 1915-
About
Rockefeller, D. Memoirs **332.1**

Rockefeller, John D. (John Davison), 1839-1937
About
Chernow, R. Titan: the life of John D. Rockefeller, Sr. **92**

Rocket boys. Hickam, H. H. **629.1**

ROCKET FLIGHT See Space flight

Rocket man. Clary, D. A. **92**

Rocket men. Nelson, C. **629.45**

ROCKET PLANES
See also High speed aeronautics; Space vehicles

ROCKETRY
Biddle, W. Dark side of the moon **92**

Clary, D. A. Rocket man **92**

Neufeld, M. J. Von Braun **92**

ROCKETRY
See also Aeronautics; Astronautics

ROCKETS (AERONAUTICS)
Holt, N. Rise of the Rocket Girls **629.4**

ROCKETS (AERONAUTICS)
See also Aeronautics; High speed aeronautics; Projectiles; Rocketry

Rockne of Notre Dame. Robinson, R. **92**

Rockne, Knute, 1888-1931
About
Robinson, R. Rockne of Notre Dame **92**

ROCKS
Bonewitz, R. Rocks and minerals **549**

Chesterman, C. W. The Audubon Society field guide to North American rocks and minerals **549**

Coenraads, R. R. Rocks and fossils **552**

Pellant, C. Rocks and Minerals **552**

Pough, F. H. A field guide to rocks and minerals **549**

Rocks and fossils. Coenraads, R. R. **552**

Rocks and Minerals. Pellant, C. **552**

Rocks and minerals. Bonewitz, R. **549**

The rocks don't lie. Montgomery, D. R. **551.48**

Rockwell, Norman, 1894-1978
About
Hennessey, M. H. Norman Rockwell **759.13**

Solomon, D. American mirror **92**

Rockwood, Camilla
Brewer's dictionary of phrase & fable **803**

ROCKY FLATS PLANT (U.S.)
Iversen, K. Full body burden **363.17**

ROCKY FLATS PLANT (U.S.) -- ENVIRONMENTAL ASPECTS
Iversen, K. Full body burden **363.17**

ROCKY MOUNTAINS
See also Mountains

Rodabaugh, Katrina
The paper playhouse **745.54**

Rodale's 21st-century herbal. Balick, M. J. **635**

Rodale's ultimate encyclopedia of organic gardening. **635**

Rodale, Maria
Scratch **641.3**

Rodbard, Matt
(jt. auth) Deuki Hong Koreatown **641.59**

Rodd, Tony
(ed) The plant finder **635.9**

Roden, Cesar
(jt. auth) Roden, N. Ice Pops!

Roden, Claudia
Arabesque: a taste of Morocco, Turkey, and Lebanon **641.5**
The book of Jewish food **641.5**
The food of Spain **641.5**
The new book of Middle Eastern food **641.59**

Roden, Nadia
Ice Pops!

Roden, Steve
. . . i listen to the wind that obliterates my traces **781.64**

RODEOS
Brown, D. A. The American West **978**

RODEOS
See also Sports

Rodgers, Carolyn M., 1945-2010
 About
Black women writers (1950-1980) **810**

Rodgers, Jimmie, 1897-1933
 About
Mazor, B. Meeting Jimmie Rodgers **92**

Rodgers, Marion Elizabeth
Mencken **92**

Rodgers, Richard, 1902-1979
 About
The Richard Rodgers reader **782.1**

Rodgers, Rick
(jt. auth) Phillips, M. The Chelsea Market cookbook **641.59**
The essential James Beard cookbook **641.597**

Rodriguez, Ana Maria
Autism spectrum disorders **616.85**

Rodriguez, Daniel, 1988-
 About
Rodriguez, D. Rise **92**

Rodriguez, Deborah
Kabul Beauty School **305.4**

Rodriguez, Jessamyn Waldman
The Hot Bread Kitchen cookbook **641.59**

Rodriguez, Junius P.
(ed) The Louisiana Purchase **973.4**

Rodriguez, Richard, 1944-
 About
Rodríguez, R. Darling **92**
Rodríguez, R. Hunger of memory **92**
Roe v. Wade. Hull, N. E. H. **344**

ROE V. WADE
Hull, N. E. H. Roe v. Wade **344**

Roe, Sue
The private lives of the impressionists **759**

Roebuck, Jamie
Anatomy 360 degrees

Roehm, Carolyne
Kristal, M. At home in the garden **635.09**

Roehrig, Catharine
(ed) Hatshepsut: from queen to Pharaoh **932**

Roemer, Kenneth M.
(ed) The Cambridge companion to Native American literature **897**

Roesdahl, Else
The Vikings **948**

Roethke, Theodore
The collected poems of Theodore Roethke **811**

Roffman, Deborah
Talk to me first **613.907**

Rogan, Eugene
The Arabs **909**

Roger Maris. Clavin, T. **92**

Roger Williams. Gaustad, E. S. **92**

Roger Williams and the creation of the American soul. Barry, J. M. **974.5**

Rogers, Adam
Proof **663**

Rogers, Carl R.
A way of being **150.19**

Rogers, Clifford
(ed) The West Point History of the Civil War **973.7**

Rogers, Douglas
The last resort **968.91**

Rogers, Douglas, 1968-
 About
Rogers, D. The last resort **968.91**

Rogers, Heather
Gone tomorrow **363.7**

Rogers, Jimmy
 About
Goins, W. E. Blues all day long **92**

Rogers, Mary, 1820-1841
 About
Stashower, D. The beautiful cigar girl **364.152**

Rogers, Robbie
 About
Marcus, E. Coming out to play **92**

Roget's 21st century thesaurus in dictionary form. **423**

Roget's international thesaurus. **423**

Rogoff, Kenneth S., 1953-
(jt. auth) Reinhart, C. M. This time is different **338.5**

Rogue Heroes. Macintyre, B. **940.54**

Rogues' gallery. Gross, M. **920**

Rohde, David
Endgame **949.7**

Roig-DeBellis, Kaitlin
(jt. auth) Fisher, R. G. Choosing hope **371.7**

Roiphe, Anne Richardson, 1935-
Married **306.81**
 About
Roiphe, A. R. Art and madness **92**
Roiphe, A. R. Epilogue **92**

Roiphe, Katie
  Uncommon arrangements **920**
Roizen, Michael F.
  This is your do-over **613**
Roker, Al, 1954-
  (jt. auth) Roberts, D. Been there, done that **92**
  The storm of the century **976.4**
Roland (Legendary character)
        About
  Chanson de Roland The song of Roland **841**
ROLE CONFLICT
        See also Social conflict; Social role
Role models. Waters, J. **92**
Roll, Rich, 1972-
  The plantpower way **641.563**
Rollag, Keith
  What to do when you're new **158.2**
Rolle, Richard, of Hampole, 1290?-1349
        About
  Armstrong, K. Visions of God **248.2**
ROLLER COASTERS
        See also Amusements
ROLLER SKATING
        See also Outdoor recreation
Rollin, Nicholas
  (ed) Correard The Oxford-Hachette French dictionary **443**
ROLLING STONE (PERIODICAL)
  Thompson, H. S. Fear and loathing at Rolling Stone
ROLLING STONES
  Cohen, R. The Sun and the Moon and the Rolling Stones **782.42**
  Cutler, S. You can't always get what you want **781.66**
  German, B. Under their thumb **781.66**
  Richards, K. Life **92**
  Russell, E. A. Let it bleed **781.66**
Rollins, Kent
  A taste of cowboy **641.597**
Rollins, Shannon Keller
  Rollins, K. A taste of cowboy **641.597**
Rolls, Albert
  Rich, M. World authors, 2000-2005 **920.003**
Rollyson, Carl E.
  (ed) Critical survey of drama **809**
  (ed) Critical survey of mystery and detective fiction **809**
  Susan Sontag **818**
ROLM CORPORATION -- HISTORY
  Maxfield, K. Starting up Silicon Valley **338.7**
ROMAN ANTIQUITIES See Classical antiquities;
  Rome -- Antiquities; Rome (Italy) -- Antiquities
ROMAN ARCHITECTURE
        See also Ancient architecture; Architecture
ROMAN ART
  Allan, T. Life, myth, and art in Ancient Rome **937**

ROMAN MYTHOLOGY
  Allan, T. Life, myth, and art in Ancient Rome **937**
ROMAN MYTHOLOGY
        See also Classical mythology
ROMAN NUMERALS
        See also Numerals
ROMAN PHILOSOPHY See Ancient philosophy
Roman vishniac rediscovered. **779.092**
ROMAN WORLD
  Mattern, S. P. Prince of medicine **610.9**
Roman, James
  Chronicles of old los angeles
Romance fiction. Ramsdell, K. **016**
ROMANCE GRAPHIC NOVELS
        See also Graphic novels
ROMANCE LANGUAGES
        See also Language and languages
ROMANCE LITERATURE
  Jenkyns, R. Classical literature **880**
  Ramsdell, K. Romance fiction **016**
ROMANCE LITERATURE
        See also Literature
ROMANCE NOVELS See Love stories
A **romance** on three legs. Hafner, K. **92**
The **romance** readers' advisory. Bouricius, A. **016**
ROMANCES
  Ramsdell, K. Romance fiction **016**
ROMANCES
        See also Fiction; Literature
ROMANCES (LOVE STORIES) See Love stories
ROMANESQUE ARCHITECTURE
        See also Architecture; Medieval architecture
ROMANIA -- CIVILIZATION
  Kaplan, R. D. In Europe's shadow **949.8**
ROMANIES See Gypsies
ROMANIES -- ENGLAND
  Walsh, M. Gypsy boy **92**
Romano, Carlin
  America the philosophical **191**
Romanov riches. **891.7**
The **Romanov** sisters. Rappaport, H. **920**
Romanov, House of
        About
  Rappaport, H. The Romanov sisters **920**
  Sebag Montefiore, S. The Romanovs **920**
The **Romanovs.** Sebag Montefiore, S. **920**
The **Romanovs.** Massie, R. K. **947.08**
Romanowski, Perry
  Can you get hooked on lip balm? **646.7**
ROMANS À CLEF
        See also Fiction
ROMANS -- GREAT BRITAIN -- HISTORY
  Higgins, C. Under another sky **936**
Romans, Christine
  (jt. auth) Velshi, A. How to speak money **332.024**
ROMANTIC FICTION See Love stories

The **romantic** generation. Rosen, C.   **780.9**

Romantic outlaws. Gordon, C.   **92**

ROMANTIC STORIES *See* Love stories

ROMANTIC SUSPENSE NOVELS
   See also Adventure fiction

ROMANTICISM
   British women poets of the Romantic era   **821**
   Downie, D. A passion for Paris   **944**
   Rosen, C. The romantic generation   **780.9**

ROMANTICISM
   See also Aesthetics

ROMANTICISM -- HISTORY -- 18TH CENTURY
   Raban, J. Passage to Juneau   **979.8**

ROMANTICISM IN ART
   See also Art

ROMANTICISM IN MUSIC
   Sachs, H. The Ninth   **785**

Romany, Frank
   (ed) Plays The complete plays   **822**

Rombauer, Irma von Starkloff
   Joy of cooking   **641.5**

Rome. Hughes, R.   **945**

ROME
   Goldsworthy, A. Pax romana   **937.06**

ROME (ITALY)
   Minchilli, E. Eating Rome   **641.594**

ROME (ITALY) -- ANTIQUITIES
   See also Classical antiquities

ROME -- ANTIQUITIES
   Bunson, M. Encyclopedia of ancient Rome   **937**
   Higgins, C. Under another sky   **936**

ROME -- ANTIQUITIES
   See also Classical antiquities

ROME -- BIOGRAPHY
   Plutarch: the lives of the noble Grecians and Romans   **920**

ROME -- HISTORY -- AUGUSTUS, 30 B.C.-14 A.D
   Goldsworthy, A. Augustus   **92**

ROME -- HISTORY -- EMPIRE, 284-476
   Brown, P. Through the eye of a needle   **270.2**
   Everitt, A. The rise of Rome   **937**

ROME -- HISTORY -- EMPIRE, 30 B.C.-476 A.D
   Beard, M. SPQR   **937**

ROME -- HISTORY -- EMPIRE, 30 B.C.-476 A.D. -- ENCYCLOPEDIAS
   Bunson, M. Encyclopedia of ancient Rome   **937**

Rome and Jerusalem. Goodman, M.   **933**

Rome from the ground up. McGregor, J. H.   **711**

Romer, John
   A history of ancient Egypt   **932**

Romero, Terry Hope
   Moskowitz, I. C. Vegan pie in the sky   **641.5**
   Salad samurai   **641.83**

Romesha, Clinton L., 1981-

Red platoon   **958.1**

Romm, Aviva Jill
   The natural pregnancy book   **618.2**

Rommel, Erwin, 1891-1944
     About
   Brighton, T. Patton, Montgomery, Rommel   **920**
   Showalter, D. E. Patton and Rommel   **92**

Romney, Mitt
     About
   Halperin, M. Double Down   **324.9**

Ronald Reagan. D'Souza, D.   **973.927**

Ronald, Pamela C., 1961-
   (jt. auth) Adamchak, R. W. Tomorrow's table   **664**

Ronald, Susan
   Heretic queen   **942.05**

Ronda, James P.
   Schwantes, C. A. The West the railroads made   **338**

Roney, Carley
   [The nest] home design handbook

Ronk, Martha
   Transfer of Qualities   **811**

Ronnen, Tal
   Crossroads   **641.59**

Ronson, Jon
   The psychopath test   **616.85**
   So you've been publicly shamed   **152.4**
   Them: adventures with extremists   **322.4**

ROOFING -- HANDBOOKS, MANUALS, ETC
   The complete guide to roofing & siding   **695**

ROOFS
   Black & Decker Corp. The complete guide to roofing, siding & trim   **695**

ROOFS
   See also Architecture -- Details; Buildings

ROOKWOOD POTTERY
   See also Art pottery

Room full of mirrors. Cross, C. R.   **92**

ROOM LAYOUT (DWELLINGS)
   Inside the not so big house   **728.37**

Room, Adrian
   (ed) Dictionary of confusable words   **423**

ROOMING HOUSES *See* Hotels and motels

ROOMS
   Bryson, B. At home   **643**

ROOMS
   See also Buildings; Houses

Rooney, Andrew A.
     About
   Rooney, A. A. My war   **940.54**

Roosevelt family
     About
   McCullough, D. G. Mornings on horseback   **92**
   Peyser, M. Hissing cousins   **92**

Roosevelt's lost alliances. Costigliola, F.   **940.53**

Roosevelt's second act. Moe, R.   **973.917**

Roosevelt, Curtis

About

Roosevelt, C. Too close to the sun   92

Roosevelt, Eleanor, 1884-1962.

About

Quinn, S. Eleanor and Hick   92

Roosevelt, Franklin D. (Franklin Delano), 1882-1945

About

Berthon, S. Warlords   940.53

Beschloss, M. R. The conquerors: Roosevelt, Truman, and the destruction of Hitler's Germany, 1941-1945   940.53

Brands, H. W. Traitor to his class   92

Brinkley, D. Rightful heritage   92

Burns, J. M. The three Roosevelts   973.91

Costigliola, F. Roosevelt's lost alliances   940.53

Dobbs, M. Six months in 1945   940.53

Feldman, N. Scorpions   920

Fried, A. F.D.R. and his enemies   92

Fullilove, M. Rendezvous with destiny   973.917

Galbraith, J. K. Name-dropping   973.9

Goodwin, D. K. No ordinary time   92

Hamilton, N. Commander in chief   940.53

Hamilton, N. The mantle of command   940.54

Hofstadter, R. The American political tradition, and the men who made it   973

Jordan, J. W. American warlords   973.917

Kissinger, H. Diplomacy   327.2

Lelyveld, J. His final battle   92

Leuchtenburg, W. E. Franklin D. Roosevelt and the New Deal, 1932-1940   973.917

Moe, R. Roosevelt's second act   973.917

Olson, L. Those angry days   940.53

Persico, J. E. Franklin and Lucy   920

Roberts, A. Masters and commanders   940.54

Roosevelt, C. Too close to the sun   92

Schlesinger, A. M. The coming of the New Deal, 1933-1935   973.917

Schlesinger, A. M. The crisis of the old order, 1919-1933   973.91

Schlesinger, A. M. The politics of upheaval, 1935-1936   973.917

Shesol, J. Supreme power   347

Simon, J. F. FDR and Chief Justice Hughes   973.917

Smith, J. E. FDR   92

Winik, J. 1944   940.53

About

Roosevelt, Quentin, 1897-1918.

About

Burns, E. The Golden Lad   92

Roosevelt, Sara Delano

About

Persico, J. E. Franklin and Lucy   920

Roosevelt, Theodore, 1858-1919

About

Brinkley, D. The wilderness warrior   92

Burns, E. The Golden Lad   92

Burns, J. M. The three Roosevelts   973.91

Cooper, J. M. The warrior and the priest: Woodrow Wilson and Theodore Roosevelt   92

Davis, D. Guest of honor   973.91

DiSilvestro, R. L. Theodore Roosevelt in the Badlands   92

Egan, T. The big burn   973.91

Gardner, M. L. Rough Riders   973.91

Goodwin, D. K. The Bully Pulpit   973.91

Hofstadter, R. The American political tradition, and the men who made it   973

Jones, G. Honor in the dust   959.9

Kissinger, H. Diplomacy   327.2

Lunde, D. The naturalist   973.91

McCullough, D. G. Mornings on horseback   92

McCullough, D. G. The path between the seas   972.87

McFarland, P. Mark Twain and the Colonel   973.8

Millard, C. The river of doubt   973.91

Morris, E. Colonel Roosevelt   92

Morris, E. The rise of Theodore Roosevelt   92

Morris, E. Theodore Rex   92

O'Toole, P. When trumpets call   92

Rauchway, E. Murdering McKinley   973.8

Thomas, E. The war lovers   973.8

Zimmermann, W. First great triumph   973

ROOSEVELT-RONDON SCIENTIFIC EXPEDITION (1913-1914)

Millard, C. The river of doubt   973.91

The **Roosevelts.** Burns, K.   920

The **rooster's** wife. Edson, R.   811

ROOT CROPS

See also Vegetables

Root, Elihu, 1845-1937

About

Zimmermann, W. First great triumph   973

Rooted in design. Heibel, T.   635.9

Roots. Haley, A.   920

Roots of jazz [series]

Feather, L. From Satchmo to Miles   920

Roots of steel. Rudacille, D.   338.4

ROPE

Pawson, D. The handbook of knots   623.88

ROPE SKIPPING

See also Games

The **rope,** and other plays. Plautus, T. M. 872

Roper, Robert

Now the drum of war   973.7

Ropper, Allan H

About

Ropper, A. H. Reaching down the rabbit hole   616.8

Ros, Hana

Neurocomic   612.82

Rosa Parks. Brinkley, D.   92

Rosalie Edge, hawk of mercy. Furmansky, D. Z. 92

Rosalind Franklin: the dark lady of DNA. Maddox, B. **92**

The **rose** hotel. Andalibian, R. **92**

Rose water and orange blossoms. Abood, M.

Rose, Daniel Asa
Larry's kidney **915**

Rose, Evelyn
100 Best Jewish Recipes **641.5**

Rose, Frank
The art of immersion **306.4**

Rose, Gideon
How wars end **355**

Rose, Judi
(jt. auth) Rose, E. 100 Best Jewish Recipes **641.5**

Rose, Michael
The birth of an opera **782.1**

Rose, Mike
Back to school **374**

Rose, Naomi A
About
Kirby, D. Death at SeaWorld **599.53**

Rose, Pete, 1941-
About
Kennedy, K. Pete Rose **92**

Rose, Reginald
Twelve angry men **812**

Rose, Sarah
For all the tea in China **382**

Rose, Steven Peter Russell
(ed) Gould, S. J. The richness of life **508**

Rose, Toni
Ward-Royster, W. How I got over **920**

Rose, Tricia
(comp) Longing to tell **306.7**

Rosemary. Larson, K. C. **92**

Rosen, Charles
The classical style **780.9**
The romantic generation **780.9**

Rosen, Fred
The historical atlas of American crime **364**

Rosen, Michael J.
(ed) Mirth of a nation **817**

Rosen, Michael, 1946-
Alphabetical **421**

Rosenbauer, Tom
The Orvis fly-fishing guide **799.124**
The Orvis guide to the essential American flies **799.1**

Rosenbaum, David A., 1952-
It's a jungle in there **153**

Rosenbaum, Ron
Explaining Hitler **943.086**
The Shakespeare wars **822.3**
(ed) Those who forget the past **305.8**

Rosenberg, Alfred, 1893-1946
About

Kinney, D. The devil's diary **940.53**

Rosenberg, Daniel
(jt. auth) Grafton, A. Cartographies of time **902**

Rosenberg, Tina
Join the club **303.3**

Rosenblatt, Roger
The book of love **152.4**
Kayak morning **300**
About
Rosenblatt, R. Making toast **92**

Rosenblum, Joseph
(ed) The Greenwood companion to Shakespeare **822.3**

Rosenblum, Mort
Chocolate: a bittersweet saga of dark and light **641.3**

Rosencrantz and Guildenstern are dead. Stoppard, T. **822**

Rosenfeld, Oskar
In the beginning was the ghetto **940.53**

Rosenfeld, Seth, 1956-
Subversives **378.1**

Rosenfeld, Susan
(ed) Encyclopedia of American historical documents **973**

Rosenfelt, David
About
Rosenfelt, D. Dogtripping **636.7**

Rosengarten, Rafael D.
(ed) Plankton **578.7**

Rosengarten, Theodore
(ed) Plankton **578.7**

Rosenstiel, Tom
(jt. auth) Kovach, B. The elements of journalism **071**
Kovach, B. Blur **070**

Rosenstrach, Jenny
Dinner **642**
How to celebrate everything **641.568**

Rosenthal, Joe, 1911-2006
About
Bradley, J. Flags of our fathers **940.54**

Rosenthal, Mitchell
Cooking my way back home **641.5**

Rosenzveig, Charles H.
The World reacts to the Holocaust **940.53**

ROSES
Kukielski, P. E. Roses without chemicals **635.9**
Ondra, N. J. Taylor's guide to roses **635.9**

ROSES
See also Flowers

ROSES -- DISEASE AND PEST RESISTANCE -- NORTH AMERICA
Kukielski, P. E. Roses without chemicals **635.9**
Roses without chemicals. Kukielski, P. E. **635.9**

ROSETTA STONE
See also Hieroglyphics

ROSETTA STONE INSCRIPTION
Ceram, C. W. Gods, graves, and scholars   **930.1**
ROSH HA-SHANAH
   See also Jewish holidays
Rosin, Hanna
The end of men   **305.42**
Rosner, Joshua
(jt. auth) Morgenson, G. Reckless endangerment   **332.7**
Rosow, La Vergne
Accessing the classics   **011.6**
Ross, Alex
Listen to this   **780**
Ross, Angus
(ed) Swift, J. A tale of a tub, and other work   **823**
Ross, Barney, 1909-1967
    About
Century, D. Barney Ross   **92**
Ross, Betsy, 1752-1836
    About
Miller, M. R. Betsy Ross and the making of America   **92**
Ross, Catherine Sheldrick
(jt. auth) Nilsen, K. Conducting the reference interview   **025.5**
The pleasures of reading   **028**
Reading matters   **028**
Ross, Charles K.
Mavericks, money, and men   **796.332**
Ross, Clifford
The world of Edward Gorey   **700.92**
Ross, David A.
Critical companion to William Butler Yeats   **821**
Ross, Dennis, B., 1948-
Doomed to succeed   **327.73**
Ross, Edmund Gibson, 1826-1907
    About
Kennedy, J. F. Profiles in courage   **920**
Ross, John, Cherokee Chief, 1790-1866
    About
McLoughlin, W. G. After the Trail of Tears **970.004**
Ross, Lillian
(ed) The Fun of it   **814**
Reporting always   **070.4**
Ross, Theodora
    About
Ross, T. A cancer in the family   **616.99**
Rossabi, Morris
(ed) Polo, M. The travels of Marco Polo   **915**
Rosselet, Dale
(jt. auth) Karlson, K. T. Birding by Impression **598**
Rossetti, Christina Georgina
Christina Rossetti   **821**
Rossi, Chef
    About
Rossi, C. The Raging Skillet   **92**

Rossignol, Rosalyn
Critical companion to Chaucer   **821**
Rossini. Servadio, G.   **92**
Rossini, Gioacchino, 1792-1868
    About
Servadio, G. Rossini   **92**
Rosso, Julee
The Silver Palate cookbook   **641.5**
Rosswood, Eric
Journey to Same-sex Parenthood   **306.874**
Rostand, Edmond
Cyrano de Bergerac   **842**
Rosten, Leo
The new joys of Yiddish   **422**
Roston, Eric
The carbon age   **577**
ROTE KAPELLE (RESISTANCE GROUP)
Nelson, A. Red Orchestra   **943.086**
Rotella, Bob
(jt. auth) Cullen, B. Golf is not a game of perfect   **796.352**
How champions think in sports and in life   **796.01**
Rotella, Carlo
(jt. auth) Kazdin, A. E. The Everyday Parenting Toolkit   **649**
Roth, Alvin E., 1951-
Who gets what--and why   **330.01**
Roth, Andrew J.
Managing prostate cancer   **616.99**
Roth, Bernard
The Achievement Habit   **158.1**
Roth, Henry, 1906-1995
    About
Kellman, S. G. Redemption: the life of Henry Roth   **92**
Roth, John K.
(ed) Ethics   **170**
(ed) World philosophers and their works   **109**
Roth, Joseph, 1894-1939
    About
Joseph Roth   **92**
Roth, Philip
The facts   **813**
Shop talk   **809**
    About
Nadel, I. B. Critical companion to Philip Roth **813**
Remnick, D. Reporting   **814**
Rothbauer, Paulette M.
Ross, C. S. Reading matters   **028**
Rothenberg, David
Thousand mile song   **599.5**
Rothenberg, Jerome
(ed) Poems for the millennium   **808.81**
Rothenberg, Michael
(ed) Dorn, E. Way more West   **811**
Rothfeder, Jeffrey

Every drop for sale 333.91
Rothko, Mark, 1903-1970
About
Cohen-Solal, A. Mark Rothko 759.13
Rothkopf, Scott
Jeff Koons 709.2
Rothman, Jordana
(jt. auth) Stupak, A. Tacos 641.84
Rothman, Julia
(jt. auth) Lamothe, M. The where, the why, and the
how 502
Nature anatomy 508
Rothschild, Charlotte, 1819-1884
About
Weintraub, S. Charlotte and Lionel 92
Rothschild, Lionel Nathan, Baron, 1808-1879
About
Weintraub, S. Charlotte and Lionel 92
Rothschild, Miriam
About
Fraser, K. Ornament and silence 809
Rotman, Jeffrey L.
About
Rotman, J. L. The last fisherman 778.7
The **Rough** Guide to film. Rough Guides
(Firm) 791.43
The **rough** guide to Italy. 914.504
Rough Guides (Firm)
The Rough Guide to film 791.43
(comp) The rough guide to Italy 914.504
Rough Riders. Gardner, M. L. 973.91
The **roughest** riders. Tuccille, J. 973.8
Round about the earth. Chaplin, J. E. 910.4
Rounding, Virginia
Catherine the Great 92
Rouse, Chris
About
Chowdhury, B. The last dive 363.14
Rouse, Chrissy
About
Chowdhury, B. The last dive 363.14
Rousey, Ronda, 1987-
My fight / your fight 92
Rousmaniere, John
The Annapolis Book of Seamanship 623.88
Rousseau, Jean-Jacques, 1712-1778
Confessions 92
The social contract 320.1
About
Cranston, M. Jean-Jacques: the early life and work
of Jean-Jacques Rousseau, 1712-1754 92
Cranston, M. The solitary self: Jean-Jacques Rous-
seau in exile and adversity 92
Damrosch, L. Jean-Jacques Rousseau 848
Rousseau Confessions 92
Russell, B. A history of Western philosophy 109

Route 66: the mother road. Wallis, M. 917
The **router** book. Warner, P. 684
The **routes** of man. Conover, T. 388.1
ROUTES OF TRADE *See* Trade routes
The **Routledge** atlas of the Holocaust. Gilbert,
M. 940.53
Routledge encyclopedias of religion and society
[series]
Encyclopedia of religious rites, rituals, and festi-
vals 200
Routledge philosophers [series]
Shields, C. J. Aristotle 185
Routledge, Katherine, 1866-1935
About
Van Tilburg, J. Among stone giants 92
Roux, Michel
The French kitchen 641.5
Rouxel, Sebastien
Bouchon Bakery 641.59
Rovelli, Carlo
Seven Brief Lessons on Physics 530
Rowan, Carl Thomas
Dream makers, dream breakers 92
Rowe, David E.
(ed) Einstein, A. Einstein on politics 92
Rowell, Charles Henry
(ed) Angles of ascent 811
ROWERS -- BIOGRAPHY
Rackley, A. Salt, sweat, tears 92
ROWING
Halberstam, D. The amateurs 797.1
Rackley, A. Salt, sweat, tears 92
ROWING
See also Athletics; Boats and boating; Exer-
cise; Sports; Water sports
ROWING -- UNITED STATES -- HISTORY
Brown, D. J. The Boys in the Boat 797.12
Rowing to latitude. Fredston, J. A. 797.1
Rowland, Julia H.
(ed) Will my cancer come back? 616.99
Rowlands, Penelope
(ed) Paris was ours 944
Rowley, Hazel
Richard Wright 813
Rowling, J. K., 1965-
Very good lives 158
Roy, Arundhati
Walking with the comrades 954
Roy, Jody M.
Meeink, F. Autobiography of a recovering skin-
head 92
A **royal** affair. Tillyard, S. K. 920
Royal cities of the ancient Maya. 972.81
A **royal** experiment. Hadlow, J. 92
ROYAL FAVORITES
Buckley, V. The secret wife of Louis XIV 944

Lever, E. Madame de Pompadour   **944**
Royal Geographical Society (Great Britain)
Macleod, A. Explorers   **910.4**
ROYAL HOUSES *See* Kings and rulers; Monarchy
Royal Observatory, Greenwich
(comp) Astronomy photographer of the year   **520**
ROYAL PRETENDERS
Massie, R. K. The Romanovs   **947.08**
ROYAL SOCIETY (GREAT BRITAIN)
Dolnick, E. The clockwork universe   **509**
Seeing further   **506**
Royal, Marshall, 1912-1995
About
Dance, S. The world of Count Basie   **920**
ROYALTY *See* Kings and rulers; Monarchy;
Princes; Princesses; Queens
Royer, France, 1951-
(jt. auth) Dickinson, R. Weeds of North America   **632**
Royte, Elizabeth
Garbage land   **363.7**
The Tapir's morning bath   **577.34**
Rozelle. Izenberg, J.   **92**
Rozelle, Pete
About
Izenberg, J. Rozelle   **92**
Rub out the words. Burroughs, W. S.   **813**
Rubber band engineer. Akiyama, L.   **745**
RUBBER BANDS
Akiyama, L. Rubber band engineer   **745**
RUBBER STAMP PRINTING
Corwin, L. Printing by hand   **745.5**
RUBBER STAMP PRINTING
See also Handicraft; Printing
Rubel, David
(ed) World War II   **940.53**
Rubens family
About
Rubin, L. D. My father's people   **920**
Rubenstein, Richard E.
Aristotle's children   **189**
Rubin, Barry
Israel   **956.940**
Rubin, Gretchen
Better than before   **158.1**
Rubin, Jay
(ed) Modern Japanese writers   **895.6**
Rubin, Louis Decimus
My father's people   **920**
Rubin, Richard R.
The Johns Hopkins guide to diabetes   **616.4**
Rubinstein, Anton, 1829-1894
About
Schonberg, H. C. The great pianists   **920**
Rubinstein, Helena, 1870-1965
About

Brandon, R. Ugly beauty   **646.7**
Rubio, Manny
Rattlesnake   **597.96**
Ruck, Rob
Raceball   **796.357**
Rudacille, Deborah
Roots of steel   **338.4**
Rudahl, Sharon
A dangerous woman   **335**
Rudd, Mark, 1947-
About
Rudd, M. Underground   **92**
Rudder, Christian
Dataclysm   **155.2**
Rude, Emelyn
Tastes Like Chicken   **636.5**
Ruden, Sarah
Paul among the people   **225.9**
Rudman, Peter Strom
The Babylonian theorem   **510**
Rudnick, Paul
About
Rudnick, P. I shudder   **92**
Rudolph, Heather Wood
(jt. auth) Armstrong, J. K. Sexy feminism   **305.42**
Rudwick, Martin J. S.
Earth's deep history   **550**
Rudyard Kipling. Ricketts, H.   **92**
Ruefle, Mary
Selected poems   **811**
Rufus, Rob
About
Rufus, R. Die young with me   **92**
Rufus, Robert
Die young with me   **92**
RUGBY
Carlin, J. Playing the enemy   **968.06**
RUGBY *See* Rugby football
RUGBY FOOTBALL
Carlin, J. Playing the enemy   **968.06**
RUGBY FOOTBALL
See also Football
Ruger, Axel
Liedtke, W. A. Vermeer and the Delft school **759.9**
Ruggero, Ed
Duty first   **355**
Ruggiero, Tina
The truly healthy family cookbook   **641.5**
RUGS
Knitting fabric rugs   **746.7**
RUGS *See* Rugs and carpets
RUGS AND CARPETS
Denny, W. B. How to read Islamic carpets   **746.7**
Knitting fabric rugs   **746.7**
RUGS AND CARPETS
See also Decorative arts; Interior design

RUGS, ORIENTAL -- AFGHANISTAN
Badkhen, A. The world is a carpet   **958.1**
Ruhlman's how to braise. **641.7**
Ruhlman's twenty. **641.5**
Ruhlman, Michael
  Egg **641.675**
  Ratio **641.5**
  Ruhlman's how to braise **641.7**
  Ruhlman's twenty **641.5**
RUINS *See* Antiquities; Excavations (Archeology); Extinct cities
Ruiz, Don Miguel
  (jt. auth) Emrys, B. The Toltec art of life and death **299.7**
Ruiz, Miguel, 1952-
     About
  Emrys, B. The Toltec art of life and death **299.7**
Rukeyser, Muriel
  Selected poems **811**
RULE OF LAW
  See also Law
RULE OF LAW -- UNITED STATES
  Shipler, D. K. The rights of the people **323**
Rule, Ann
  --and never let her go **364.1**
  The stranger beside me **92**
  Too late to say goodbye **364.152**
Rule, Cheryl Sternman
  Yogurt culture **641.6**
RULERS *See* Emperors; Heads of state; Kings and rulers; Queens
The **rules** of inheritance. Smith, C. B. **616.99**
RULES OF ORDER *See* Parliamentary practice
Rumi: the big red book. Barks, C. **891**
Rumiz, Paolo
  The fault line **914**
A **rumor** of war. Caputo, P. **959.704**
Rump, Eric S.
  (ed) Sheridan, R. B. The school for scandal and other plays **822**
Rumspringa. Shachtman, T. **305.23**
Run fast, eat slow. Flanagan, S. **641.563**
The **run** of his life. Toobin, J. **345.73**
Run the World. Wade, B. **796.42**
Run, Spot, run. Pierce, J. **636.08**
RUNAWAY ADULTS
  See also Desertion and nonsupport; Missing persons
RUNAWAY CHILDREN
  See also Children; Homeless persons; Missing children
Runaway girl. Phelps, C. **362.74**
RUNAWAY SLAVES *See* Fugitive slaves
RUNAWAY TEENAGERS
  See also Homeless persons; Missing persons; Teenagers

The **Runner's** Brain. Brown, J. **796.42**
The **Runner's** world big book of marathon and half-marathon training. Bede, P. N. **796.425**
Runner's world complete book of running. Burfoot, A. **796.42**
RUNNERS (SPORTS)
  Hillenbrand, L. Unbroken **940.54**
  Hoffer, R. Something in the air **796.4**
  Schaap, J. Triumph **92**
RUNNERS (SPORTS) -- UNITED STATES -- BIOGRAPHY
  Heminsley, A. Running like a girl **796.420**
RUNNING
  Burfoot, A. Runner's world complete book of running **796.42**
  Finn, A. The Way of the Runner **796.42**
  Heminsley, A. Running like a girl **796.420**
  Starrett, K. Ready to run **613.7**
RUNNING -- PSYCHOLOGICAL ASPECTS
  Brown, J. The Runner's Brain **796.42**
Running away to home. Wilson, J. **305.8**
Running book discussion groups. John, L. Z. **374**
Running like a girl. Heminsley, A. **796.420**
Running Man. Engle, C. **796.42**
Running with scissors. Burroughs, A. **813**
Runnng with the champ. Shanahan, T. **796.830**
Runstedtler, Theresa
  Jack Johnson, rebel sojourner **796.83**
Rupert, Prince, Count Palatine, 1619-1682
     About
  Spencer, C. E. M. S. Prince Rupert **92**
RURAL CHURCHES
  See also Church work
RURAL COMMUNITY DEVELOPMENT *See* Rural development
RURAL DEVELOPMENT
  Sherrod, S. The courage to hope **975.8**
RURAL DEVELOPMENT
  See also Agriculture -- Government policy; Community development; Economic development; Regional planning
RURAL DEVELOPMENT -- GEORGIA
  Sherrod, S. The courage to hope **975.8**
RURAL EDUCATION *See* Rural schools
RURAL ELECTRIFICATION -- MALAWI
  Kamkwamba, W. The boy who harnessed the wind **92**
RURAL HIGH SCHOOLS *See* Rural schools
RURAL LIFE *See* Country life; Farm life; Outdoor life
RURAL POOR -- GEORGIA
  Sherrod, S. The courage to hope **975.8**
RURAL POOR -- MISSISSIPPI -- BIOGRAPHY
  Ward, J. Men We Reaped **92**
RURAL SCHOOLS
  Keizer, G. Getting Schooled **373.1**

RURAL-URBAN MIGRATION -- NIGER
Youngstedt, S. M. Surviving with dignity   362.84
RURAL-URBAN MIGRATION -- UNITED STATES -- HISTORY -- 20TH CENTURY
Wilkerson, I. The warmth of other suns   307
Ruse, Michael
(ed) Evolution   576.8
(ed) Genetically modified foods   363.1
Rushdie, Salman, 1947-
About
Rushdie, S. Joseph Anton   92
Rushdoony, Rousas John, 1916-2001
About
Christian reconstruction   230
Rushing, Jimmy, 1903-1972
About
Dance, S. The world of Count Basie   920
Rushkoff, Douglas
Present Shock   303.48
Rusk, Dean, 1909-1994
About
Halberstam, D. The best and the brightest   973.922
Russakoff, Dale
The prize   371.2
Russell, Bertrand, 1872-1970
A history of Western philosophy   109
The problems of philosophy   100
About
Durant, W. J. The story of philosophy   109
Feldman, B. 112 Mercer Street   920
Russell, David O.
About
Waxman, S. Rebels on the backlot   920
Russell, Ethan A.
Let it bleed   781.66
Russell, Jan Jarboe, 1951-
The Train to Crystal City   940.53
Russell, Jenna
Long mile home   363.325
Russell, Karen Kramer
Shapeshifting   704.03
Russell, Stephen
The essential guide to cultivating mushrooms   635
Russell, Thaddeus
Out of the jungle   92
Russell, Tony
Country music originals   781.642
RUSSIA
Brent, J. Inside the Stalin archives   947.086
Aleksievich, S. Secondhand time   947.086
Greene, D. Midnight in Siberia   914.7
Meier, A. Black earth   947.086
RUSSIA (FEDERATION) *See* Russia
RUSSIA -- DESCRIPTION AND TRAVEL
Greene, D. Midnight in Siberia   914.7
Meier, A. Black earth   947.086

Polonsky, R. Molotov's magic lantern   947
Richards, S. Lost and found in Russia   947.086
RUSSIA -- ECONOMIC CONDITIONS -- 1991-
Pomerantsev, P. Nothing is true and everything is possible   306
RUSSIA -- HISTORY -- 1991- *See* Russia -- History -- 1991-
RUSSIA -- POLITICS AND GOVERNMENT
Baker, P. Kremlin rising   947.086
Gorbachev, M. On my country and the world   947.085
Politkovskaya, A. A Russian diary   947.086
Remnick, D. Resurrection   947.086
Treisman, D. The return   947.086
RUSSIA -- POLITICS AND GOVERNMENT -- 1991-
Baker, P. Kremlin rising   947.086
Brent, J. Inside the Stalin archives   947.086
Dawisha, K. Putin's kleptocracy   947.086
Politkovskaya, A. A Russian diary   947.086
RUSSIA -- SOCIAL CONDITIONS
Greene, D. Midnight in Siberia   914.7
Von Bremzen, A. Mastering the art of Soviet cooking   641.59
RUSSIA -- SOCIAL LIFE AND CUSTOMS
Greene, D. Midnight in Siberia   914.7
Jones, C. C. A year of Russian feasts   641.59
Richards, S. Lost and found in Russia   947.086
RUSSIA -- CIVILIZATION
Massie, S. Land of the firebird   947
RUSSIA -- COMMUNISM *See* Communism -- Russia
RUSSIA -- DESCRIPTION AND TRAVEL
Garrels, A. Putin country   947.43
RUSSIA -- FOREIGN RELATIONS -- UNITED STATES
Cook, J. H. American phoenix   973.5
RUSSIA -- HISTORY
Gessen, M. Where the Jews aren't   957.7
Jaques, S. The Empress of Art   92
Smith, D. Former people   305.5
RUSSIA -- HISTORY -- 0-1917
Sebag Montefiore, S. The Romanovs   920
RUSSIA -- HISTORY -- 1613-1917
Sebag Montefiore, S. The Romanovs   920
RUSSIA -- HISTORY -- 1917-1921, REVOLUTION
Competing voices from the Russian Revolution   947.084
Memories   92
RUSSIA -- HISTORY -- 1917-1921, REVOLUTION
See also Revolutions
RUSSIA -- HISTORY -- 1917-1991, SOVIET UNION
Figes, O. Just send me word   365

Kotkin, S. Stalin **92**
Ostrovsky, A. The Invention of Russia **947.086**
Stalin **92**
Von Bremzen, A. Mastering the art of Soviet cooking **641.59**
RUSSIA -- HISTORY -- 1953-1991
Mezrich, B. Once Upon a Time in Russia **330**
RUSSIA -- HISTORY -- 1991-
Dawisha, K. Putin's kleptocracy **947.086**
Mezrich, B. Once Upon a Time in Russia **330**
RUSSIA -- INTELLECTUAL LIFE
Romanov riches **891.7**
RUSSIA -- KINGS AND RULERS
Sebag Montefiore, S. The Romanovs **920**
RUSSIA -- KINGS AND RULERS -- BIOGRAPHY
Sebag Montefiore, S. The Romanovs **920**
RUSSIA -- POLITICS AND GOVERNMENT
Ostrovsky, A. The Invention of Russia **947.086**
Russia against Napoleon. Lieven, D. C. B. **940.2**
Russia and the Russians. Hosking, G. A. **947**
Russia under the Bolshevik regime. Pipes, R. **947.084**
Russia: people and empire, 1552-1917. Hosking, G. A. **947**
RUSSIAN AMERICANS
Shteyngart, G. Little failure **92**
RUSSIAN AMERICANS -- BIOGRAPHY
Von Bremzen, A. Mastering the art of Soviet cooking **641.59**
RUSSIAN ART
King, D. Red star over Russia **947**
Massie, S. Land of the firebird **947**
McPhee, J. A. The ransom of Russian art **709**
RUSSIAN ARTS
Romanov riches **891.7**
RUSSIAN CHURCH See Russian Orthodox Church
RUSSIAN COMMUNISM See Communism -- Russia
RUSSIAN COOKING
Jones, C. C. A year of Russian feasts **641.59**
Von Bremzen, A. Mastering the art of Soviet cooking **641.59**
A **Russian** diary. Politkovskaya, A. **947.086**
RUSSIAN ESPIONAGE
Draitser, E. Stalin's Romeo spy **92**
Haynes, J. E. Spies **327.12**
Haynes, J. E. Venona **327.12**
Herrington, S. A. Traitors among us **327.12**
Weinstein, A. The haunted wood **327.12**
RUSSIAN FAR EAST (RUSSIA) -- DESCRIPTION AND TRAVEL
Vaillant, J. The tiger **599.75**
RUSSIAN LANGUAGE
See also Language and languages

RUSSIAN LITERATURE
See also Literature
RUSSIAN LITERATURE -- BIO-BIBLIOGRAPHY
Reference guide to Russian literature **891.7**
RUSSIAN LITERATURE -- DICTIONARIES
Reference guide to Russian literature **891.7**
RUSSIAN LITERATURE -- HISTORY AND CRITICISM
Batuman, E. The possessed **891.7**
Brodsky, J. Less than one **809.1**
The Cambridge history of Russian literature **891.7**
Nabokov, V. V. Lectures on Russian literature **891.7**
Romanov riches **891.7**
Terras, V. A history of Russian literature **891.7**
RUSSIAN NATIONAL CHARACTERISTICS
Hosking, G. A. Russia: people and empire, 1552-1917 **947**
RUSSIAN ORTHODOX CHURCH
Jones, C. C. A year of Russian feasts **641.59**
RUSSIAN ORTHODOX CHURCH
See also Christian sects; Orthodox Eastern Church
The **Russian** Revolution. Pipes, R. **947.08**
RUSSIAN REVOLUTION See Russia -- History -- 1917-1921, Revolution
RUSSIANS
See also Russia
Russo, Frank
The Cooperstown chronicles **92**
Russo, Julie
The Silver Palate cookbook **641.5**
Russo, Richard, 1949-
About
Russo, R. Elsewhere **92**
Russo, Vito, 1946-1990
About
Schiavi, M. Celluloid activist **92**
RUSSO-FINNISH WAR, 1939-1940
Edwards, R. The Winter War **948.97**
RUSSO-FINNISH WAR, 1939-1940
See also Europe -- History -- 1918-1945
RUSSO-JAPANESE WAR, 1904-1905
Pleshakov, K. The Tsar's last armada **952.03**
RUSSO-TURKISH WAR, 1853-1856 See Crimean War, 1853-1856
Rust. Waldman, J. **620.1**
RUST See Corrosion and anticorrosives
Rustic fruit desserts. Schreiber, C. **641.8**
Rustic Italian food. **641.59**
RUSTLESS COATINGS See Corrosion and anti-corrosives
Ruta, Domenica
With or without you **362.29**
RUTH BANCROFT GARDEN (WALNUT CREEK, CALIF.)

The bold dry garden **635.9**
Ruth, Babe, 1895-1948
    About
  Creamer, R. W. Babe **92**
Rutherford, Adam
  Creation **576.8**
Rutherford, Clarice
  How to raise a puppy you can live with **636.7**
Rutherford, Ernest, 1871-1937
    About
  Reeves, R. A force of nature **92**
Rutherford-Johnson, Tim
  (jt. auth) Bourne, J. The Oxford Dictionary of Music
  sic **780.3**
Rutherfurd, Lucy Mercer, 1891-1948
    About
  Persico, J. E. Franklin and Lucy **920**
Ruthsatz, Joanne
  (jt. auth) Stephens, K. The Prodigy's Cousin **155.45**
Ruud, Jay
  Critical companion to Dante **850**
RWANDA
  Chretien The great lakes of Africa **967.6**
  Hatzfeld, J. The antelope's strategy **967.571**
  Hatzfeld, J. Machete season **967.571**
RWANDA -- POLITICS AND GOVERNMENT
  Gourevitch, P. We wish to inform you that tomorrow we will be killed with our families **967.571**
Ryan family
    About
  Ryan, T. The prize winner of Defiance, Ohio **977.1**
Ryan, Alan
  On politics **320.01**
Ryan, Bob, 1946-
    About
  Ryan, B. Scribe **070.449**
Ryan, Craig
  Sonic wind **92**
Ryan, Donald P., 1957-
    About
  Ryan, D. P. Beneath the sands of Egypt **92**
Ryan, Evelyn
    About
  Ryan, T. The prize winner of Defiance, Ohio **977.1**
Ryan, Evelyn, d. 1998
    About
  Ryan, T. The prize winner of Defiance, Ohio **977.1**
Ryan, Kay
  The best of it **811**
Ryan, Mark
  Hornet's sting **92**
Ryan, Michael
  (ed) The encyclopedia of literary and cultural theory **801**
Ryan, Mike

Tennis' greatest stars **796.342**
Ryan, Terry
  The prize winner of Defiance, Ohio **977.1**
Ryback, Timothy W.
  Hitler's private library **027**
Rybczynski, Witold
  A clearing in the distance: Frederick Law Olmsted and America in the nineteenth century **712**
  The look of architecture **721**
  Mysteries of the mall **720**
  Now I sit me down **749.32**
  The perfect house: a journey with the Renaissance architect Andrea Palladio **720.9**
Ryckman, Pamela
  Stiletto network **331.4**
Ryder, Anthony
  The artist's complete guide to figure drawing **743.4**
Rynecki, Elizabeth
  Chasing portraits **700.92**
Rynecki, Moshe, 1881-1943
    About
  Rynecki, E. Chasing portraits **700.92**
Rywka's Diary. Friedman, A. **940.53**

S

Ṣiddīqī, 'Afiyah, 1972-
    About
  Scroggins, D. Wanted women **305.48**
S. Mark Taper Foundation imprint in Jewish studies [series]
  Kirshenblatt, M. They called me Mayer July **92**
Saba, Umberto
  Songbook **851**
Saban. Burke, M. **796.332**
Saban, Nick
    About
  Burke, M. Saban **796.332**
Sabar, Ariel
  My father's paradise **305.8**
Sabar, Yona
    About
  Sabar, A. My father's paradise **305.8**
Sabbag, Robert
    About
  Sabbag, R. Down around midnight **92**
SABBATH
  Shulevitz, J. The Sabbath world **296.4**
SABBATH
  See also Judaism
The **Sabbath** world. Shulevitz, J. **296.4**
SABIN VACCINE *See* Poliomyelitis vaccine
Sabor, Peter
  (ed) Carlyle, T. Sartor resartus **824**
SABOTAGE
  Millman, C. The detonators **940.4**
SABOTAGE

See also Offenses against public safety; Strikes; Subversive activities; Terrorism

SABOTAGE -- NORWAY -- HISTORY -- 20TH CENTURY
Bascomb, N. The winter fortress   **940.54**

Sacagawea of the Lewis and Clark expedition. Clark, E. E.   **92**

Sacagawea, b. 1786
    About
Clark, E. E. Sacagawea of the Lewis and Clark expedition   **92**
Slaughter, T. P. Exploring Lewis and Clark   **978**
Sacco and Vanzetti. Watson, B.   **345**

Sacco, Joe
Footnotes in Gaza   **956.04**
The Great War   **940.4**
(jt. auth) Hedges, C. Days of destruction, days of revolt   **305.5**

Sacco, Nicola, 1891-1927
    About
Watson, B. Sacco and Vanzetti   **345**
The **Sacco-Vanzetti** Affair. Temkin, M.   **345**

SACCO-VANZETTI TRIAL, DEDHAM, MASS., 1921
Temkin, M. The Sacco-Vanzetti Affair   **345**
Watson, B. Sacco and Vanzetti   **345**

Sachar, Howard Morley
Dreamland   **940.5**
A history of Israel   **956.94**
A history of the Jews in the modern world   **909**

Sachs, Harvey
The Ninth   **785**

Sachs, Jeffrey, 1954-
The age of sustainable development   **338.9**
The price of civilization   **330.9**

Sack, Steven Mitchell
The employee rights handbook   **344**

Sacks, Jonathan, 1948-
The great partnership   **201.65**

Sacks, Oliver W.
An anthropologist on Mars   **616.8**
The island of the colorblind   **617.7**
The man who mistook his wife for a hat and other clinical tales   **616.8**
Seeing voices   **362.4**
Sacks, O. The mind's eye   **616.85**
Sacks, O. On the move   **92**
    About
Sacks, O. W. Uncle Tungsten   **616.8**

Sacks, Stefanie
What the fork are you eating?   **641.3**

SACRAMENTS
    See also Church; Grace (Theology); Rites and ceremonies

SACRED ART *See* Religious art
SACRED BOOKS

Davis, R. H. The Bhagavad Gita   **294.5**
Gutjahr, P. C. The Book of Mormon   **289.3**
Tigay, C. The Lost Book of Moses
Sacred cows and golden geese. Greek, C. R.   **179**

SACRED SPACE
Nabokov, P. Where the lightning strikes   **299.7**
Sacred trash. Cole, P.   **296.09**
Sacrifice zones. Lerner, S.   **363.738**

Sadat, Anwar, 1918-1981
    About
Wright, L. Thirteen Days in September   **956.04**

Sade, marquis de, 1740-1814
    About
Camus, A. The rebel   **303.6**

Sadegh, Ali
(ed) Marks' standard handbook for mechanical engineers   **621**

Sadie, Julie Anne
(ed) The Norton/Grove dictionary of women composers   **780.92**

Sadie, Stanley
The Grove book of operas   **792.5**

Sadler, Anthony
    About
Sadler, A. The 15:17 to Paris   **363.325**

SAFARIS
    See also Adventure and adventurers; Outdoor recreation; Scientific expeditions; Travel
Safe kids, smart parents. Bailey, E.   **613.6**

SAFE SEX IN AIDS PREVENTION
    See also AIDS (Disease) -- Prevention; Sexual hygiene

SAFETY EDUCATION
Bailey, E. Safe kids, smart parents   **613.6**
Gervasi, L. H. Fight like a girl-- and win   **613.6**

SAFETY REGULATIONS
    See also Accidents -- Prevention; Law

SAFETY, INDUSTRIAL *See* Occupational health and safety

Safford, Barbara Ripp
Guide to reference materials for school library media centers   **011.6**

Safina, Carl
Beyond words   **591.56**
The view from Lazy Point   **508**
Voyage of the turtle   **597.92**

Safran, John
God'll Cut You Down   **364.152**

Safranski, Rudiger
Nietzsche   **193**

Sagan, Carl
Billions and billions   **500**
Broca's brain   **500**
Comet   **523.6**
Cosmos   **520**
The dragons of Eden   **153**

Pale blue dot 520

About

Poundstone, W. Carl Sagan 92

Sagan, Dorion

Cracking the aging code 612.67

Margulis, L. What is life? 570.1

SAGAS

The Sagas of Icelanders 839

SAGAS

See also Folklore; Literature; Old Norse literature; Scandinavian literature

The **Sagas** of Icelanders. 839

Sage, Lorna

(ed) The Cambridge guide to women's writing in English 820

SAHARA DESERT

De Villiers, M. Sahara: a natural history 508

Langewiesche, W. Sahara unveiled 916

SAHARA DESERT -- DESCRIPTION AND TRAVEL

Benanav, M. Men of salt 916

Sahara unveiled. Langewiesche, W. 916

Sahara: a natural history. De Villiers, M. 508

SAHEL -- DESCRIPTION AND TRAVEL

Tayler, J. Angry wind 916

Said, Edward W.

The end of the peace process 956.05

Out of place 92

Reflections on exile and other essays 814

Said, Kurban, 1905-1942

About

Reiss, T. The Orientalist 92

SAILING

Naranjo, R. The Art of Seamanship 623.8

Rousmaniere, J. The Annapolis Book of Seamanship 623.88

Sleight, S. The complete sailing manual 797.124

SAILING -- HANDBOOKS, MANUALS, ETC

Sleight, S. The complete sailing manual 797.124

Sailing alone around the room. Collins, B. 811

Sailing from Byzantium. Wells, C. M. 940.2

Sailing the wine-dark sea. Cahill, T. 909

SAILORS

Severin, T. In search of Robinson Crusoe 996

SAILORS

See also Military personnel; Naval art and science; Navies

SAILORS -- UNITED STATES -- LANGUAGE -- DICTIONARIES

Axelrod, A. Whiskey tango foxtrot 427

SAILORS' LIFE *See* Sailors; Seafaring life

Saint Augustine. Wills, G. 270.2

SAINT BARTHOLOMEW'S DAY, MASSACRE OF, 1572

See also France -- History -- 1328-1589, House of Valois; Huguenots; Massacres

Saint Joan. Shaw, B. 822

SAINT PETERSBURG (RUSSIA) -- HISTORY

Volkov, S. St. Petersburg 947

Saint-Just, 1767-1794

About

Camus, A. The rebel 303.6

SAINTS

Bolt, R. A man for all seasons 822

Borg, M. J. The first Paul 227

Butcher, C. A. Man of blessing 271

Davies, B. The thought of Thomas Aquinas 189

Gordon, M. Joan of Arc 944

Hazleton, L. Mary: a flesh-and-blood biography of the Virgin Mother 92

Kung, H. Great Christian thinkers 230

The little flowers of St. Francis of Assisi 242

Martin, J. The Jesuit guide to almost everything 248.4

Martin, V. Salvation: scenes from the life of St. Francis 92

Murphy-O'Connor, J. Paul 225.9

Pelikan, J. J. Mary through the centuries 232.91

Pernoud, R. Joan of Arc: her story 92

Ruden, S. Paul among the people 225.9

Russell, B. A history of Western philosophy 109

Shaw, B. Saint Joan 822

Wills, G. Saint Augustine 270.2

Woodward, K. L. Making saints 235

SAINTS

See also Religious biography

Saints & sinners. Duffy, E. 282

Sakamoto, Pamela Rotner, 1962-

Midnight in broad daylight 940.53

Sakenfeld, Katharine Doob

(ed) Bible The Oxford study Bible 220.5

Saks, Elyn R.

About

Saks, E. R. The center cannot hold 92

Salad as a meal. 641.8

Salad samurai. Romero, T. H. 641.83

SALADS

Alger, K. Susan Feniger's street food 641.59

Romero, T. H. Salad samurai 641.83

Salad as a meal 641.8

The sprouted kitchen bowl and spoon 641.3

SALADS

See also Cooking

Salah, Trish

Wanting in Arabic 811

SALAMANDERS

See also Amphibians

Salamon, Julie

Wendy and the lost boys

Salamone, Frank A.

(ed) Encyclopedia of religious rites, rituals, and festivals 200

SALARIES *See* Salaries, wages, etc.

SALARIES, WAGES, ETC.

Adler, M. Economics for the rest of us   **330**

Jayaraman, S. Forked   **331.2**

The value of a dollar   **338.5**

The value of a dollar: colonial era to the Civil War, 1600-1865   **338.5**

SALARIES, WAGES, ETC.

   See also Income

Saldana, Stephanie

About

Saldana, S. The bread of angels   **92**

SALEM (MASS.) -- HISTORY

Schiff, S. The Witches   **345**

Salem health [series]

Knight, J. A. Genetics & inherited conditions **576.5**

Magill's medical guide   **610**

Salem Press Inc.

Notable Latino writers   **810**

Salem witch judge. LaPlante, E.   **92**

SALEM WITCH TRIALS

Schiff, S. The Witches   **345**

The **Salem** witchcraft trials. Hoffer, P. C.   **345**

Saler, Michael

As if   **823**

SALES AGENTS *See* Sales personnel

SALES MANAGEMENT

   See also Management; Marketing; Selling

SALES PERSONNEL

Kealing, B. Tupperware, unsealed   **338.7**

SALES PERSONNEL

   See also Retail trade

SALES TAX

   See also Taxation

Sales, Nancy Jo

American girls   **004.67**

SALESMEN *See* Sales personnel

SALESWOMEN *See* Sales personnel

Salieri, Antonio, 1750-1825

About

Shaffer, P. Peter Shaffer's Amadeus   **822**

Salinger, J. D. (Jerome David), 1919-2010

About

Beller, T. J.D. Salinger   **92**

Slawenski, K. J.D. Salinger   **92**

Salisbury, Martin

Children's Picturebooks   **741**

Illustrating children's books   **741.6**

SALK VACCINE *See* Poliomyelitis vaccine

Salk, Jonas, 1914-1995

About

Jacobs, C. D. Jonas Salk   **92**

Jonas Salk   **92**

Kluger, J. Splendid solution: Jonas Salk and the conquest of polio   **92**

Sallah, Michael

(jt. auth) Weiss, M. The Yankee comandante   **92**

Tiger Force   **959.704**

Salle, David, 1952-

How to see   **709.04**

Salley, Columbus

The black 100   **920**

Sallis, James

Chester Himes   **813**

Sally Ride. Sherr, L.   **92**

Sally, David

(jt. auth) Anderson, C. The numbers game **796.334**

SALMON

Greenberg, P. Four fish   **333.95**

Trout and salmon of North America   **597**

SALMON

   See also Fishes

SALMON FISHING

Gathercole, P. The fly-tying bible   **688.7**

Salmon, Felix

(ed) The best business writing 2013   **330.9**

Salonica, city of ghosts. Mazower, M.   **949.5**

SALOONS *See* Bars

Salowey, Christina A.

(ed) Great lives from history, The ancient world, prehistory-476 C.E   **920.003**

SALT

Benanav, M. Men of salt   **916**

Kurlansky, M. Salt: a world history   **553.6**

SALT HOUSE (RESTAURANT)

Cooking my way back home   **641.5**

SALT WATER AQUARIUMS *See* Marine aquariums

Salt, sugar, fat. Moss, M.   **613.2**

Salt, sweat, tears. Rackley, A.   **92**

SALT-FREE DIET

   See also Cooking; Diet

SALT-FREE DIET -- RECIPES

Heller, M. The everyday DASH diet cookbook   **613.2**

Sodium girls limitless low-salt cookbook   **641.5**

Salt: a world history. Kurlansky, M.   **553.6**

Salter, Mark

McCain, J. S. Faith of my fathers   **92**

McCain, J. S. Why courage matters   **179**

Saltsman, Amelia

The Santa Monica Farmers' Market Cookbook   **641.5**

Saltwater Fish and Reef Tanks. Blanchard, Z. **639**

SALTWATER FISHING

   See also Fishing

SALTWATER FISHING -- PICTORIAL WORKS

Rotman, J. L. The last fisherman   **778.7**

SALUTATIONS *See* Etiquette

Salvador Dalí, 1904-1989. Descharnes, R.   **759.6**

SALVADORANS -- MEXICO -- CHIAPAS -- BIOGRAPHY

Franklin, J. 438 days   **910.916**

Salvadori, Mario George

Levy, M. Why buildings fall down   **690**

SALVAGE

Bloom, J. American wasteland   **363.7**

SALVAGE (WASTE, ETC.) *See* Salvage

SALVAGE (WASTE, ETC.) -- CHINA

Humes, E. Garbology   **628.4**

SALVAGE -- UNITED STATES -- HISTORY

Peffer, R. Where divers dare   **940.54**

SALVATION

   See also Doctrinal theology

SALVATION -- HISTORY OF DOCTRINES

   See also Doctrinal theology

SALVATION ARMY

Shaw, B. Major Barbara   **822**

Salvation: scenes from the life of St. Francis. Martin, V.   **92**

Salzberg, Sharon

Real happiness   **158**

Salzman, Jack

(ed) The Cambridge handbook of American literature   **810**

Salzman, Mark

Iron & silk   **951.05**

True notebooks   **371.9**

Sam Phillips. Guralnick, P.   **92**

Sam Walton, made in America. Walton, S.   **92**

The **same** river twice. Walker, A.   **813**

SAME-SEX MARRIAGE

Cleves, R. H. Charity and Sylvia   **306.84**

Faderman, L. The gay revolution   **306.76**

Yoshino, K. Speak now   **346.73**

SAME-SEX MARRIAGE

   See also Marriage

SAME-SEX MARRIAGE -- LAW AND LEGIS-LATION -- UNITED STATES

Dickey, L. Then comes marriage   **346**

SAME-SEX MARRIAGE -- LAW AND LEGIS-LATION -- UNITED STATES -- CASES

Becker, J. Forcing the spring   **346.73**

Yoshino, K. Speak now   **346.73**

SAME-SEX MARRIAGE -- UNITED STATES -- TO 1865

Cleves, R. H. Charity and Sylvia   **306.84**

Samet, Elizabeth D.

Soldier's heart   **810**

SAMI (EUROPEAN PEOPLE)

Beach, H. A year in Lapland   **948.97**

Samit, Jay

Disrupt you!   **650.1**

Sammataro, Diana

The beekeeper's handbook   **638.1**

SAMOAN ISLANDS -- SOCIAL LIFE AND CUS-TOMS

Mead, M. Coming of age in Samoa   **306**

SAMPLERS

   See also Needlework

SAMPLING (STATISTICS)

   See also Probabilities; Statistics

Sampson, Anthony

Nelson Mandela   **92**

Sampson, Curt

Masters   **796.352**

Sampson, Deborah, 1760-1827

     About

Young, A. F. Masquerade: the life and times of Deborah Sampson, Continental soldier   **92**

Sampson, Scott D.

Dinosaur odyssey   **567.9**

How to raise a wild child   **508**

Samuel Beckett's Waiting for Godot.   **842**

Samuel Beckett: the Grove centenary edition [series]

Beckett, S. Dramatic works   **842**

Samuel Johnson.   **828**

Samuel Johnson. Meyers, J.   **92**

Samuel Johnson. Martin, P.   **92**

Samuel Pepys. Tomalin, C.   **941.06**

Samuel, Rhian

(ed) The Norton/Grove dictionary of women composers   **780.92**

Samuell, Kristine

A year of gingerbread houses   **745.5**

Samuelsson, Marcus, 1970-

Red Rooster Cookbook   **641.5**

The soul of a new cuisine   **641.5**

     About

Chambers, V. Yes, chef   **92**

Marcus off duty   **641.5**

SAN FRANCISCO (CALIF.)

Drinking the devil's acre   **641.87**

SAN FRANCISCO (CALIF.) -- BIOGRAPHY

Talbot, D. Season of the witch   **306**

SAN FRANCISCO (CALIF.) -- EARTHQUAKE, 1906

Winchester, S. A crack in the edge of the world   **979.4**

SAN FRANCISCO 49ERS (FOOTBALL TEAM)

Benedict, J. QB   **92**

SAN JOSÉ MINE ACCIDENT, CHILE, 2010

Tobar, H. Deep down dark   **363.11**

SAN JUAN HILL, BATTLE OF, CUBA, 1898

Gardner, M. L. Rough Riders   **973.91**

SAN PEDRO DE MACORÍS (DOMINICAN RE-PUBLIC)

Kurlansky, M. The Eastern stars   **796.357**

SANA (YEMEN) -- BIOGRAPHY

Kasinof, L. Don't be afraid of the bullets   **953.305**

Sanchez, Sonia, 1934-

     About

Black women writers (1950-1980)   **810**

SANCTIONS (INTERNATIONAL LAW)
　　See also Economic policy; International economic relations; International law
SANCTUARY (LAW) *See* Asylum
SANCTUARY MOVEMENT
　　See also Asylum; Church and social problems; Social movements
Sand. Welland, M.　　　　　　　**553.6**
SAND
　Welland, M. Sand　　　　　　　**553.6**
A **Sand** County almanac & other writings on ecology & conservation. Leopold, A.　　**508**
SAND DUNES
　　See also Seashore
SAND SCULPTURE
　　See also Nature craft; Sculpture
Sand, George, 1804-1876
　　　　　　　About
　Eisler, B. Naked in the marketplace　　**92**
　Harlan, E. George Sand　　　　　　**92**
　Jack, B. E. George Sand　　　　　　**843**
Sandberg, Sheryl
　　　　　　　About
　Sandberg, S. Lean in　　　　　　　**658.4**
Sandburg, Carl
　Abraham Lincoln: The prairie years and The war years　　　　　　　　　　　　**92**
　The American songbag　　　　　　**781.62**
　The complete poems of Carl Sandburg　**811**
Sandel, Michael J., 1953-
　Justice　　　　　　　　　　　　**172**
　What money can't buy　　　　　　**330.1**
Sander, Emmanuel
　(jt. auth) Hofstadter, D. Surfaces and essences **169**
Sanders, Andrew
　The short Oxford history of English literature **820**
Sanders, Bernard, 1941-
　　　　　　　About
　Rall, T. Bernie　　　　　　　　**92**
　Sanders, B. Outsider in the White House　**92**
Sanders, Donald Theodore
　Zeilinga de Boer, J. Earthquakes in human history　　　　　　　　　　　**363.34**
Sanders, Ed
　Thirsting for peace in a raging century　**811**
Sanders, Lisa
　Every patient tells a story　　　　**616.07**
Sanders, Scott R. (Scott Russell), 1945-
　　　　　　　About
　Sanders, S. R. A private history of awe　**92**
Sandford, Gina
　(jt. auth) Bailey, M. The Ultimate Encyclopedia of Aquarium Fish & Fish Care　**639.34**
Sandison, David
　Neal Cassady　　　　　　　　**92**
Sandke, Randall

Where the dark and the light folks meet　**781.65**
Sandler, Lauren
　One and only　　　　　　　　**306.874**
Sandler, Robert
　(ed) Frye, N. Northrop Frye on Shakespeare **822.3**
Sandlin, Lee
　Storm kings　　　　　　　　**551.55**
Sandoval-Strausz, A. K.
　Hotel　　　　　　　　　　**917**
Sandoz, Mari
　The Battle of the Little Bighorn　　**973.8**
Sandra Day O'Connor. Biskupic, J.　**92**
Sands, Philippe
　East West Street　　　　　　　**345**
Sandweiss, Martha A.
　Passing strange　　　　　　　**92**
SANDWICHES
　Colicchio, T. 'wichcraft　　　　　**641.8**
　Kord, T. A super upsetting cookbook about sandwiches　　　　　　　　　　**641.84**
SANDWICHES
　　See also Cooking
Sandy Koufax. Leavy, J.　　　　**796.357**
Sane new world. Wax, R.　　　　**158.1**
Sanfilippo, Diane
　Practical paleo　　　　　　　**641.5**
Sanger, Margaret, 1879-1966
　　　　　　　About
　Baker, J. H. Margaret Sanger　　　**92**
　Eig, J. The birth of the pill　　　**618.1**
SANITARY AFFAIRS *See* Sanitary engineering; Sanitation
SANITARY ENGINEERING
　　See also Engineering
SANITATION
　George, R. The big necessity　　　**363.7**
SANITATION WORKERS -- NEW YORK (STATE) -- NEW YORK
　Nagle, R. Picking up　　　　　　**331.7**
Sankaran, Neeraja
　Microbes and people: an A-Z of microorganisms in our lives　　　　　　　　**579**
SANSKRIT LANGUAGE
　Satyamurti, C. Mahabharata　　　**821**
SANSKRIT LANGUAGE
　　See also Indian languages; Language and languages
SANTA CLARA VALLEY (SANTA CLARA COUNTY, CALIF.)
　Menuez, D. Fearless genius　　　**979.4**
SANTA CLARA VALLEY (SANTA CLARA COUNTY, CALIF.) -- ECONOMIC CONDITIONS
　Piscione, D. P. Secrets of Silicon Valley　**330.9**
SANTA CLARA VALLEY (SANTA CLARA COUNTY, CALIF.) -- HISTORY

Maxfield, K. Starting up Silicon Valley   338.7

SANTA CLAUS
    See also Christmas

SANTA MARIA DEL FIORE (CATHEDRAL: FLORENCE, ITALY)
    King, R. Brunelleschi's dome   726

SANTA MONICA (CALIF.)
    Saltsman, A. The Santa Monica Farmers' Market Cookbook   641.5

The **Santa** Monica Farmers' Market Cookbook. Saltsman, A.   641.5

Santamaria, Abigail
    Joy   92

Santana, Carlos
          About
    Santana, C. The universal tone   92

Santayana, George, 1863-1952
          About
    Durant, W. J. The story of philosophy   109

Sante, Luc
    The other Paris   944

SANTERIA
    See also Religion

Santi, Jenny
    The giving way to happiness   179

Santiago, Wilfred
    21   92

Santibañez, Roberto
    Truly Mexican   641.59

Santopietro, Tom
    Sinatra in Hollywood   92
    The sound of music story   791.43

Santorelli, Dina
    (ed) Bully   371.5

Santos, Aaron
    How many licks?   519.2

Santos, Brian
    Painting and wallpapering secrets from Brian Santos, the Wall Wizard   698

SAOLA
    DeBuys, W. The last unicorn   591.68

Saperstein, Jesse A.
    Getting a life with Asperger's   92

Sapiens. Harari, Y. N.   909

Sapolsky, Robert M.
          About
    Sapolsky, R. M. A primate's memoir   599.8

Saponaro, Margaret Zarnosky
    (jt. auth) Evans, G. E. Collection management basics   025.2

Sappho
    If not, winter   884

Sappington, Adam
    (jt. auth) Gartland, A. Heartlandia   641.597

Sappington, Jackie
    (jt. auth) Gartland, A. Heartlandia   641.597

Sara Baartman and the Hottentot Venus. Crais, C. C.   92

Sara Moulton's Home Cooking 101. Moulton, S.   641.5

Sarabeth's good morning cookbook.   641.5

Sarah style. Richardson, S.   747

SARAJEVO (BOSNIA AND HERCEGOVINA)
    Hemon, A. The book of my lives   814

Saratoga. Ketchum, R. M.   973.3

SARATOGA CAMPAIGN, 1777
    Ketchum, R. M. Saratoga   973.3
    Paul, J. R. Unlikely allies   973.3

SARCOSUCHUS IMPERATOR
    See also Dinosaurs

Sardet, Christian
    (tr) Plankton   578.7

Sarillo, Nick, 1963-
    A slice of the pie   658.02

Sarmiento, Esteban
    The last human   569.9

Sarna, Jonathan D.
    American Judaism   296
    Lincoln and the Jews   973.7

Sarotte, Mary Elise
    The collapse   943.087

Sarton, May
    Selected poems of May Sarton   811

Sartor resartus. Carlyle, T.   824

Sartore, Joel
    Chadwick, D. H. The company we keep   333.95

Sartre, Jean Paul, 1905-1980
    Being and nothingness   142
    No exit, and three other plays   842
    Truth and existence   121
          About
    Bair, D. Simone de Beauvoir   848
    Bakewell, S. At the Existentialist Cafe   142
    Existentialism from Dostoevsky to Sartre   142
    Sartre, J. P. The words   92
    We Have Only This Life to Live   848

SAS survival handbook. Wiseman, J.   613.6

Sasha and Emma. Avrich, K.   335

SASQUATCH
    See also Monsters; Mythical animals

Sasselov, Dimitar
    The life of super-Earths   576.8

Sasson, Jack M.
    (ed) Civilizations of the Ancient Near East   939

Sassoon, Donald
    Becoming Mona Lisa   759

Sassoon, Elias Victor, 1881-1961
          About
    Grescoe, T. Shanghai grand   951.132

SATAN *See* Devil

Satan is real. Louvin, C.   920

Satchel. Tye, L.   92

Satchel Paige's America. Fox, W. P.   92
Satel, Sally
  (jt. auth) Lilienfeld, S. O. Brainwashed   **612.8**
SATELLITES
  Holt, N. Rise of the Rocket Girls   **629.4**
SATELLITES
  See also Solar system
SATIRE
  Kitchen, D. The art of Harvey Kurtzman   **741.5**
  Lewis, C. S. The Screwtape letters   **248**
  Meyerowitz, R. Drunk stoned brilliant dead   **051**
SATIRE
  See also Literature; Rhetoric; Wit and humor
SATIRISTS
  Baker, R. Growing up   92
  Benfey, C. E. G. A summer of hummingbirds   920
  DeGategno, P. J. Critical companion to Jonathan Swift   **828**
  Downing, D. C. Into the region of awe   **248.2**
  Elledge, S. E. B. White   92
  Feiffer, J. Backing into forward   92
  Ford, P. F. Companion to Narnia   **823**
  Garvey, M. Stylized   **808**
  Kazin, A. An American procession   **810**
  Loving, J. Mark Twain   92
  McKeen, W. Outlaw journalist   **92**
  Miller, L. The magician's book   **823**
  The Oxford companion to Mark Twain   **818**
  Powers, R. Mark Twain   **92**
  Shelden, M. Mark Twain   **92**
  Thompson, H. S. Fear and loathing in America **070**
  Thompson, H. S. The kingdom of fear   **92**
  Wenner, J. S. Gonzo   **92**
  White, E. B. Letters of E.B. White   **92**
  Wilson, A. N. C.S. Lewis   **823**
  Wilson, A. N. Betjeman   **92**
SATISFACTION
  Langshur, E. Start here   **158**
  Shell, G. R. Springboard   **650.1**
Satrapi, Marjane
  Embroideries   **741**
      About
  Satrapi, M. The complete Persepolis   **741.5**
Satter, Beryl
  Family properties   **363.5**
Satter, David
  Age of delirium   **947.085**
Satter, Mark J., 1916-1965
      About
  Satter, B. Family properties   **363.5**
Satterly, Stephen
  (jt. auth) Dorn, M. Staying alive   **613.6**
Sattersten, Todd
  Covert, J. The 100 best business books of all time   **016.6**
Sattin, Anthony

  The Young T. E. Lawrence   **92**
Sattouf, Riad, 1978-
      About
  Sattouf, R. The Arab of the Future   **92**
  Sattouf, R. The Arab of the Future 2   **92**
SATURDAY NIGHT LIVE (TELEVISION PRO-GRAM)
  Shales, T. Live from New York   **791.45**
Saturday night widows. Aikman, B.   **306.88**
SATURN (PLANET)
  See also Planets
Satyamurti, Carole
  Mahabharata   **821**
SAUCERS, FLYING *See* Unidentified flying objects
Sauces. Peterson, J.   **641.81**
SAUCES
  See also Cooking
SAUCES
  Peterson, J. Sauces   **641.81**
  Rustic Italian food   **641.59**
  Volland, S. Mastering Sauces   **641.81**
Saudek, Christopher D.
  (jt. auth) Rubin, R. R. The Johns Hopkins guide to diabetes   **616.4**
SAUDI ARABIA -- CIVILIZATION
  House, K. E. On Saudi Arabia   **953.8**
SAUDI ARABIA -- SOCIAL CONDITIONS
  Lacey, R. Inside the Kingdom   **953.8**
Saul Bellow. Bellow, S.   **92**
Saul Steinberg. Bair, D.   **741.092**
Saul, Richard
  ADHD does not exist   **618.92**
Saunders, Doug
  Arrival city   **307.24**
SAUSAGES
  Ying, C. The wurst of Lucky peach   **641.3**
Sauvage, Jeanne
  Gluten-free wish list   **641.5**
Savage beauty: the life of Edna St. Vincent Millay. Milford, N.   **92**
Savage continent. Lowe, K.   **940.55**
A **Savage** Harvest. Hoffman, C.   **995**
Savage inequalities. Kozol, J.   **371.9**
The **savage** mind. Levi-Strauss, C.   **155.8**
Savage peace. Hagedorn, A.   **973.91**
Savage, Dan, 1964-
      About
  Savage, D. American Savage   **306.76**
Savage, Jon
  1966   **781.66**
SAVANNAH (GA.)
  Berendt, J. Midnight in the garden of good and evil   **975.8**
  Jones, J. Saving Savannah   **975.8**
SAVANTS (SAVANT SYNDROME)

Padgett, J. Struck by genius **155.9**
Tammet, D. Born on a blue day **92**
Save room for pie. Blount, R. **641.3**
Saved by beauty. Housden, R. **955**
Saveur. Oseland, J. **641.5**
Saveur Food Group (Company)
(comp) Italian Comfort Food **641.594**
Saviano, Roberto
Gomorrah **364.1**
Savigneau, Josyane
Carson McCullers **813**
Saving Alex. Cooper, A. **92**
SAVING AND INVESTMENT
See also Capital; Economics; Personal finance; Wealth
Saving beauty from the beast. Crompton, V. **362.88**
Saving capitalism. Reich, R. B. **330.973**
Saving Gotham. Farley, T. **362.1**
Saving Normal. Frances, A. **616.89**
Saving Savannah. Jones, J. **975.8**
Saving Simon. Katz, J. **636.1**
Saving the school. Brick, M. **373.22**
Saving the season. West, K. **641.4**
Saving vegetable seeds. Bradley, F. M. **635**
SAVINGS AND LOAN ASSOCIATIONS
Grind, K. The lost bank **332.3**
SAVINGS AND LOAN ASSOCIATIONS
See also Banks and banking; Cooperation; Cooperative societies; Investments; Loans; Personal loans; Saving and investment
SAVINGS BANKS *See* Banks and banking
Saviuc, Luminita D.
15 things you should give up to be happy **152.4**
Savonarola, Girolamo, 1452-1498
About
Strathern, P. Death in Florence **945**
Savoy, Lauret
Trace **917.3**
The **savvy** musician. Cutler, D. **780.2**
Sawchik, Travis
Big data baseball **796.357**
Sawyer, Miriam
Gubert, B. K. Distinguished African Americans in aviation and space science **629.13**
Sawyer, P. H.
(ed) The Oxford illustrated history of the Vikings **948**
Sawyer-Laucanno, Christopher
E.E. Cummings **92**
Sax, Richard
Classic home desserts **641.8**
Saxon, A. H.
P. T. Barnum: the legend and the man **338.7**
SAXOPHONISTS
Dance, S. The world of Count Basie **920**
Feather, L. From Satchmo to Miles **920**

Kahn, A. The house that Trane built **781.65**
Ratliff, B. Coltrane **92**
Saying goodbye to someone you love. Dresser, N. **155.9**
SAYINGS *See* Epigrams; Proverbs; Quotations
SBC WARBURG (FIRM)
Ferguson, N. High financier **92**
Scagell, Robin
Complete Guide to Stargazing **520**
Scahill, Jeremy, 1974-
Dirty wars **355.02**
Scalapino, Leslie
(ed) McClure, M. Of indigo and saffron **811**
Scales, Helen
Spirals in Time **594**
Scales, Pat R.
Books under fire **016**
Scales, Robert H.
Murray, W. The Iraq war **956.7**
Scalia. Murphy, B. A. **92**
Scalia, Antonin
About
Murphy, B. A. Scalia **92**
Scammell, Michael
Koestler **92**
SCANDALS
Bai, M. All the truth is out **328.73**
Kipnis, L. How to become a scandal **306.7**
Read, P. P. The Dreyfus affair **944.081**
Solomon, J. DSK **306.77**
SCANDALS
See also History
SCANDALS -- FRANCE -- HISTORY -- 19TH CENTURY
Read, P. P. The Dreyfus affair **944.081**
SCANDALS -- UNITED STATES -- HISTORY -- 20TH CENTURY
Bai, M. All the truth is out **328.73**
SCANDINAVIA -- CIVILIZATION
Booth, M. The Almost Nearly Perfect People **948**
SCANDINAVIAN ARCHITECTURE
Wilhide, E. Scandinavian Home **728**
SCANDINAVIAN COOKING
The Scandinavian Kitchen **641.59**
Scandinavian Home. Wilhide, E. **728**
The **Scandinavian** Kitchen. **641.59**
SCANDINAVIAN LANGUAGES
See also Language and languages
SCANDINAVIAN LITERATURE
See also Literature
Scanlon, Jennifer
Bad girls go everywhere: the life of Helen Gurley Brown **92**
Scarbrough, Mark
The Great Big Pressure Cooker Book **641.5**
A la mode **641.865**

Vegetarian dinner parties **641.5**

Weinstein, B. Cooking know-how **641.5**

Scarcity. Shafir, E. **338.5**

SCARCITY

Peacock, K. W. Food security **338.1**

Shafir, E. Scarcity **338.5**

SCARCITY

See also Supply and demand

Scared sick. Karr-Morse, R. **155.9**

Scarlet tanager. Mayer, B. **811**

Scarth, Alwyn

Vesuvius: a biography **551.2**

Scary close. Miller, D. **158.2**

Scatter, adapt, and remember. Newitz, A. **576.8**

Scattered at sea. Gerstler, A. **811**

Scattered poems. Kerouac, J. **811**

SCENE PAINTING

See also Painting; Theaters -- Stage setting and scenery

Scene study series

The best stage scenes of 2007 **808.82**

SCENERY *See* Landscape protection; Natural monuments; Views; Wilderness areas

SCENERY (STAGE) *See* Theaters -- Stage setting and scenery

SCENIC BYWAYS

See also Roads

SCENIC BYWAYS -- SOUTHERN STATES

Deep South **975**

The **scent** of desire. Herz, R. S. **152.1**

SCEPTICISM *See* Skepticism

Schön, Jan Hendrik

About

Reich, E. S. Plastic fantastic **92**

Schaaf, Fred

The 50 best sights in astronomy and how to see them **520**

Schaap, Jeremy

Cinderella Man **92**

Triumph **92**

Schaap, Rosie

About

Schaap, R. Drinking with men **92**

Schachter-Shalomi, Zalman, 1924-2014

About

Davidson, S. The December Project **296.7**

Schacter, Daniel L.

Searching for memory **153.1**

The seven sins of memory **153.1**

Schaefer, Mark W.

Return on influence **658.8**

Schafer, Jack

(jt. auth) Karlins, M. The like switch **158.2**

Schaffer, Ben

The Dead Rabbit drinks manual **641.87**

Schall, Lucy

Teen talkback with interactive booktalks! **021.7**

Schama, Chloe

Wild romance **92**

Schama, Simon, 1945-

The American future **973.93**

The embarrassment of riches **949.2**

A history of Britain **941**

The power of art **709**

Rembrandt's eyes **92**

The story of the Jews **909**

Scharf, Caleb

The Copernicus complex **523.1**

Gravity's engines **523.8**

Scharf, Michael P.

Newton, M. A. Enemy of the state **345**

Schatz, Kate

Rad women worldwide **920.72**

Schatzker, Mark

The Dorito effect **641.3**

Schebera, Jurgen

Kurt Weill **92**

Schechter, Abraham A.

Basic book repair methods **025.7**

Schechter, Harold

Psycho USA **364.152**

The whole death catalog **306.9**

Scheijen, Sjeng

Diaghilev **92**

Schein, Ann

About

Porter, C. H. Five lives in music **780.92**

Schell, Jonathan

Writing in time **973.928**

Schell, Orville

Wealth and power **951**

Schemmer, Benjamin F.

Carney, J. T. No room for error **356**

Schenkar, Joan

The talented Miss Highsmith **92**

Scherman, Tony

Pop **92**

Scheuer, Michael

Osama bin Laden **92**

Schewe, Phillip F.

Maverick Genius **92**

Scheyer, Moriz

Asylum **940.53**

Schiaparelli, Elsa, 1890-1973

About

Volk, P. Shocked **92**

Schiavi, Michael

Celluloid activist **92**

Schickel, Richard

(ed) The essential Chaplin **92**

Elia Kazan **92**

Schickel, Richard, 1933-

Keepers **791.43**

Schiefelbein, Susan
 Cousteau, J. Y. The human, the orchid, and the octopus **333.95**

Schiff, Dorothy, 1903-1989
 About
 Nissenson, M. The lady upstairs **92**

Schiff, Hilda
 Holocaust poetry **808.81**

Schiff, Karenna Gore
 Lighting the way **920**

Schiff, Stacy, 1961-
 Cleopatra **92**
 The Witches **345**

Schiffman, Lawrence H.
 (ed) The Encyclopedia of the Dead Sea scrolls **296.1**
 Reclaiming the Dead Sea scrolls **296.1**

Schiller, Friedrich
 Don Carlos and Mary Stuart **832**
 The robbers [and] Wallenstein **832**

Schiller, Lawrence
 Perfect murder, perfect town **364.15**

Schilling, Govert
 Deep Space **520**

Schindler, Oskar, 1908-1974
 About
 Crowe, D. Oskar Schindler **92**

SCHIZOPHRENIA
 Bollas, C. When the Sun Bursts **616.89**
 Cockburn, H. Henry's demons **92**
 Gionfriddo, P. Losing Tim **92**
 Saks, E. R. The center cannot hold **92**
 Torrey, E. F. Surviving schizophrenia **616.89**

SCHIZOPHRENIA
 See also Mental illness

SCHIZOPHRENIA IN CHILDREN -- PATIENTS -- UNITED STATES -- BIOGRAPHY
 Gionfriddo, P. Losing Tim **92**

SCHIZOPHRENICS
 Cockburn, H. Henry's demons **92**
 Lopez, S. The soloist **92**

Schlager, Neil
 (ed) St. James encyclopedia of labor history worldwide **331.8**

Schleiermacher, Friedrich, 1768-1834
 About
 Kung, H. Great Christian thinkers **230**

Schlender, Brent
 (jt. auth) Tetzeli, R. Becoming Steve Jobs **92**

Schlereth, Thomas J.
 Victorian America **973.8**

Schlesinger, Andrew
 (ed) Schlesinger, A. M. Journals: 1952-2000 **92**

Schlesinger, Arthur M. (Arthur Meier), 1917-2007
 (ed) Brinkley, A. John F. Kennedy **92**
 The coming of the New Deal, 1933-1935 **973.917**

The crisis of the old order, 1919-1933 **973.91**
 The cycles of American history **973**
 The politics of upheaval, 1935-1936 **973.917**
 Robert Kennedy and his times **92**
 War and the American presidency **327.1**
 About
 Schlesinger, A. M. Journals: 1952-2000 **92**
 Schlesinger, A. M. A life in the twentieth century **92**

Schlesinger, David
 (ed) Strayhorn **781.650**

Schlesinger, Stephen C.
 (ed) Schlesinger, A. M. Journals: 1952-2000 **92**

Schleuning, Sarah
 (jt. auth) Gross, K. Dream cars **629.222**

Schlosberg, Suzanne
 Quessenberry, S. The good neighbor cookbook **641.5**

Schlosser, Eric
 Command and control **363.17**
 Fast food nation **394.1**

Schmeling, Max, 1905-2005
 About
 Margolick, D. Beyond glory **796.8**

Schmidle, Nicholas
 To live or to perish forever **954.91**

Schmidt, Denyse
 Denyse Schmidt **746.46**
 Denyse Schmidt quilts **746.46**

Schmidt, Elizabeth
 (ed) The poets laureate anthology **811**

Schmidt, Franz, d. 1634
 About
 Harrington, J. F. The faithful executioner **364.66**

Schmidt, Justin O.
 The sting of the wild **595.7**

Schmidt, Leigh Eric
 Heaven's bride **92**
 The religious history of America **200.973**

Schmidt, Michael
 Lives of the poets **821**

Schmidt, Thomas
 The Lewis & Clark Trail **978**

Schmitz, Rob
 About
 Schmitz, R. Street of Eternal Happiness **951.132**

Schnabel, Artur, 1882-1951
 About
 Schonberg, H. C. The great pianists **920**

Schnall, Marianne
 What will it take to make a woman president? **305.4**

Schneerson, Menachem Mendel, 1902-1994
 About
 Telushkin, J. Rebbe **92**

Schneider, Carl J.
 Schneider, D. First ladies **920.003**

Schneider, Dorothy
First ladies **920.003**
Schneider, Howard
Backyard guide to the night sky **520**
Schneider, Paul
The Adirondacks **974.7**
Brutal journey: the epic story of the first crossing of North America **970.01**
Schneider, Steven Jay
(ed) 1001 Movies You Must See Before You Die **791.43**
Schneps, Leila
(jt. auth) Colmez, C. Math on trial **345**
Schobinger, Juan
The ancient Americans **970.01**
Schoen, Allen M.
Kindred spirits **636.089**
Schoen, Douglas E., 1953-
About
Schoen, D. E. The power of the vote **324**
Schoenberger, Nancy
Kashner, S. Furious love **92**
Schoepflin, Rennie B.
Christian Science on trial **289.5**
Schoerke, Meg
(ed) Twentieth-century American poetry **811**
Schoeser, Mary
World textiles: a concise history **677**
The scholar denied. Morris, A. D. **301**
SCHOLARS -- UNITED STATES -- BIOGRAPHY
Kendall, J. America's obsessives **609.2**
SCHOLARSHIP See Learning and scholarship
SCHOLARSHIPS
See also Education; Endowments; Student aid
SCHOLASTIC ACHIEVEMENT See Academic achievement
Scholl, John
(jt. auth) Carruthers, J. Eat street **641.76**
Schom, Alan
Napoleon Bonaparte **92**
One hundred days **944.05**
Schonberg, Harold C.
The great pianists **920**
The lives of the great composers **780**
Schönwerth, Franz Xaver von, 1809-1886
The turnip princess **398.209**
SCHOOL ADMINISTRATION AND ORGANIZATION See Schools -- Administration
SCHOOL ADMINISTRATORS
Halberstam, D. The children **323.1**
Rodriguez, D. Kabul Beauty School **305.4**
The school among the ruins: poems, 2000-2004. Rich, A. **811**
The school and society, and The child and the curriculum. Dewey, J. **372**
SCHOOL CHILDREN
Caring for your school-age child **649**
Kowalski, R. M. Cyberbullying **302.34**
SCHOOL CHILDREN
See also Children; Students
SCHOOL CHILDREN -- BOOKS AND READING
Lambert, M. D. Reading picture books with children **372.133**
SCHOOL CHILDREN -- FOOD
Fuentes, L. The best homemade kids' lunches on the planet **641.5**
SCHOOL CHOICE
Ravitch, D. The death and life of the great American school system **379**
The school for scandal and other plays. Sheridan, R. B. **822**
SCHOOL HYGIENE
See also Children -- Health and hygiene; Health education; Hygiene; Public health; Sanitation
SCHOOL IMPROVEMENT PROGRAMS -- TEXAS -- AUSTIN
Brick, M. Saving the school **373.22**
SCHOOL IMPROVEMENT PROGRAMS -- UNITED STATES
Aronica, L. Creative schools **371.2**
Brill, S. Class warfare
Rhee, M. A. Radical **371.01**
SCHOOL INSPECTION See School supervision; Schools -- Administration
SCHOOL INTEGRATION
Lukas, J. A. Common ground **305.8**
Margolick, D. Elizabeth and Hazel **92**
SCHOOL INTEGRATION
See also Race relations
SCHOOL LIBRARIAN PARTICIPATION IN CURRICULUM PLANNING
Grover, S. Listening to learn **372.4**
SCHOOL LIBRARIES
The indispensable librarian **025.1**
Karp, J. Graphic novels in your school library **741.5**
SCHOOL LIBRARIES
See also Instructional materials centers; Libraries
SCHOOL LIBRARIES -- ACTIVITY PROGRAMS -- UNITED STATES
Brown, A. Let's start the music **027.62**
SCHOOL LIBRARIES -- CATALOGS
Safford, B. R. Guide to reference materials for school library media centers **011.6**
SCHOOL LIBRARIES -- CENSORSHIP -- UNITED STATES
Scales, P. R. Books under fire **016**
SCHOOL LIBRARIES -- COLLECTION DE-

VELOPMENT -- UNITED STATES
Karp, J. Graphic novels in your school library **741.5**

SCHOOL LIBRARIES -- UNITED STATES -- ADMINISTRATION
The indispensable librarian **025.1**
School of fish. Pollinger, B. **641.6**

SCHOOL SHOOTINGS
Cullen, D. Columbine **364.152**
Fisher, R. G. Choosing hope **371.7**
Singular, S. The Spiral Notebook **364.152**

SCHOOL SHOOTINGS
See also Crime; School violence

SCHOOL SHOOTINGS -- COLORADO -- LITTLETON
Klebold, S. A mother's reckoning **373**

SCHOOL SONGBOOKS
See also Songbooks; Songs

SCHOOL SPORTS
Merlino, D. The hustle **796.323**
Sielski, M. Fading echoes **92**
Swidey, N. The assist **796.323**

SCHOOL SPORTS
See also Sports; Student activities

SCHOOL STORIES
See also Fiction

SCHOOL SUPERINTENDENTS AND PRINCIPALS
Brick, M. Saving the school **373.22**

SCHOOLS -- ADMINISTRATION
Brick, M. Saving the school **373.22**
Cahill, S. LGBT youth in America's schools **371.82**

SCHOOLS -- SELECTION *See* School choice
The schools we need and why we don't have them. Hirsch, E. D. **370.9**

Schopenhauer, Arthur, 1788-1860
About
Durant, W. J. The story of philosophy **109**

Schoppa, R. Keith
The Columbia guide to modern Chinese history **951.05**

Schor, Edward L.
(ed) Caring for your school-age child **649**

Schorr, Daniel, 1916-2010
About
Schorr, D. Staying tuned **070**

Schou, Nicholas
Orange sunshine **363.45**

Schrag, Philip G.
Kenney, D. N. Asylum denied **92**

Schreiber, Cory
Rustic fruit desserts **641.8**

Schreiber, Flora Rheta
Sybil **616.85**

Schreiner, Olive, 1855-1920
About
Pierpont, C. R. Passionate minds **810**

Schriever, Bernard A., 1910-2005
About
Sheehan, N. A fiery peace in a cold war **92**

Schrödinger, Erwin, 1887-1961
About
Gribbin, J. R. Schrodinger's kittens and the search for reality **530.1**
Halpern, P. Einstein's dice and Schrödinger's cat **530.13**

Schrodinger's kittens and the search for reality. Gribbin, J. R. **530.1**

Schroeder, Alayna
Bray, I. M. Nolo's essential guide to buying your first home **643**

Schroeder, Alice D.
The snowball: Warren Buffett and the business of life **92**

Schroeder, Keith
Cooking light mad delicious **641.5**

Schroen, Gary C.
First in **958.1**

Schrott, Allen
(ed) All music guide to classical music **016**

Schubert's winter journey. Bostridge, I. **782.4**

Schubert, Franz, 1797-1828. Winterreise
About
Bostridge, I. Schubert's winter journey **782.4**

Schueller, Eugene, 1881-1957
About
Brandon, R. Ugly beauty **646.7**

Schuler, Judith
Your pregnancy week by week **618.2**

Schuler, Lou
Strong **613.7**

Schulian, John
(ed) At the fights **796.8**

Schulkind, Jeanne
(ed) Woolf, V. Moments of being **823**

Schüll, Natasha Dow
Addiction by design **362.2**

Schulman, Bruce J.
The seventies **973.925**

Schulman, Grace
(ed) Moore, M. The poems of Marianne Moore **811**
Days of wonder **811**

Schulmann, Robert
An Einstein encyclopedia **530.092**
(ed) Einstein, A. Einstein on politics **92**

Schultz, David A.
(ed) Encyclopedia of the First Amendment **342**
Encyclopedia of the United States Constitution **342**

Schultz, Ellen
Retirement heist **331.2**

Schultz, Eric B.
King Philip's War **973.2**

Schultz, Howard

Onward   **647.9**

Schultz, Jeffrey D.
Critical companion to John Steinbeck   **813**

Schultz, Ken
Ken Schultz's field guide to saltwater fish   **597**

Schultz, Kevin M.
Buckley and Mailer   **973.92**

Schultz, Mitchel E.
Grob's basic electronics   **621.381**

Schultz, Philip, 1945-
About
Schultz, P. My dyslexia   **92**

Schulz and Peanuts. Michaelis, D.   **92**

Schulz, Charles M.
About
Michaelis, D. Schulz and Peanuts   **92**

Schulz, Kathryn
Being wrong   **153**

Schulz, William F.
In our own best interest   **323**

Schumacher, Michael
Crossroads   **92**
Will Eisner   **92**

Schuman, Emily
Cupcakes and cashmere at home   **746.9**

Schumann, Robert, 1810-1856
About
Geck, M. Robert Schumann   **92**

Schutt, Will
Westerly   **811**

Schuyler, James
Collected poems   **811**

Schwab, Charles
Schwab-Pomerantz, C. It pays to talk   **332.024**

Schwab-Pomerantz, Carrie
It pays to talk   **332.024**

Schwalbe, Will
The end of your life book club   **616.99**

Schwan, W. Creighton
(jt. auth) Richter, H. P. Wiring simplified   **621.319**

Schwantes, Carlos A.
The West the railroads made   **338**

Schwartz, A. Brad
Broadcast hysteria   **791.44**

Schwartz, David Joseph
The magic of thinking big   **158**

Schwartz, John
Oddly normal   **306.76**

Schwartz, Lloyd
Bishop, E. Poems, prose, and letters   **818**

Schwartz, Matthew, 1977-2012
About
Castner, B. All the ways we kill and die   **958.104**

Schwartz, Morris S.
About
Albom, M. Tuesdays with Morrie   **378.1**

Schwartz, Peter
Rand, A. The voice of reason; essays in objectivist thought   **191**

Schwartz, Richard Alan
The 1990s   **909.82**

Schwartz, Richard S.
(jt. auth) Olds, J. The lonely American   **302.5**

Schwartz, Sanford
Kael, P. The age of movies   **791.43**

Schwarz, Alan
ADHD nation   **618.92**

Schwed, Fred
Where are the customers' yachts?   **332.64**

Schweid, Richard
Consider the eel   **597**

Schweitzer, Albert, 1875-1965
Out of my life and thought   **900**

Schweitzer, Sharon
(jt. auth) Alexander, L. Access to Asia   **395.5**

Schweninger, Loren
Franklin, J. H. In search of the promised land   **929**

Science. Fara, P.   **509**

SCIENCE
Arbesman, S. The half-life of facts   **501**
Bais, S. In praise of science   **500**
The best American science and nature writing 2012   **810.8**
The best American science and nature writing 2014   **810.8**
Blatner, D. Spectrums   **539.2**
Bronowski, J. Science and human values   **500**
Brooks, M. 13 things that don't make sense   **500**
Bryson, B. A short history of nearly everything   **500**
Carroll, S. B. The Serengeti Rules   **570**
Clegg, B. Final Frontier   **629.4**
Dolnick, E. The clockwork universe   **509**
Dyson, F. J. Dreams of earth and sky   **500**
The Encyclopedia of science and technology   **503**
Feynman, R. P. The meaning of it all   **500**
Feynman, R. P. The pleasure of finding things out   **500**
Gardner, M. Did Adam and Eve have navels?   **500**
Gribbin, J. R. Almost everyone's guide to science   **500**
The handy science answer book   **500**
Kaku, M. Physics of the future   **303.49**
Kipfer, B. A. How it happens   **500**
López-Alt, J. K. The food lab   **664**
McGraw-Hill dictionary of scientific and technical terms   **503**
Moreno, J. D. The body politic   **303.48**
Nothing   **501**
Olson, R. Don't be such a scientist   **501**
Oxford dictionary of scientific quotations   **500**
Park, R. L. Voodoo science   **500**
Pauling, L. C. Linus Pauling in his own words   **081**

Randall, L. Knocking on heaven's door **500**
Reader's guide to the history of science **509**
Sagan, C. Billions and billions **500**
Sagan, C. Broca's brain **500**
Scientific American's ask the experts **500**
Seeing further **506**
Shermer, M. Why people believe weird things **001.9**
This will change everything **501**
Ward, P. D. Life as we do not know it **576.8**
Wiggins, A. W. The five biggest unsolved problems in science **500**

SCIENCE -- ARAB COUNTRIES
Al-Khalili, J. The house of wisdom **509**

SCIENCE -- BIBLIOGRAPHY -- METHODOL-OGY
Berard, G. L. Science and technology resources **025.5**

SCIENCE -- CHINA -- HISTORY
Winchester, S. The man who loved China **92**

SCIENCE -- DICTIONARIES
McGraw-Hill dictionary of scientific and technical terms **503**

SCIENCE -- ENCYCLOPEDIAS
The Encyclopedia of science and technology **503**
McGraw-Hill Publishing Company McGraw-Hill concise encyclopedia of science & technology **503**
Van Nostrand's scientific encyclopedia **503**

SCIENCE -- ETHICAL ASPECTS
Dreger, A. Galileo's middle finger **174.2**

SCIENCE -- ETHICAL ASPECTS -- ENCYCLO-PEDIAS
Encyclopedia of science, technology, and ethics **503**

SCIENCE -- EXHIBITIONS
See also Exhibitions

SCIENCE -- EXPERIMENTS
Gallagher, S. Experimenting with babies **306.874**

SCIENCE -- GOVERNMENTAL POLICY
Belfiore, M. The department of mad scientists **355**
Faigman, D. L. Laboratory of justice **347**

SCIENCE -- GREAT BRITAIN -- HISTORY
Holmes, R. The age of wonder **509**

SCIENCE -- GREECE -- HISTORY
Weinberg, S. To explain the world **509**

SCIENCE -- HISTORY
Bauer, S. W. The story of Western science **509**
A cultural history of physics **530**
Falk, D. The Science of Shakespeare **822.3**
A glorious enterprise **508**
Henry, J. A short history of scientific thought **501**
Mlodinow, L. The upright thinkers **509**
Munroe, R. Thing Explainer **500**
Weinberg, S. To explain the world **509**
Wootton, D. The Invention of Science **509**

SCIENCE -- HISTORY -- 21ST CENTURY
Kaku, M. Physics of the future **303.49**

SCIENCE -- HISTORY -- CHRONOLOGY
Concise history of science & invention **509**

SCIENCE -- HISTORY -- ENCYCLOPEDIAS
Encyclopedia of the scientific revolution **509**
Reader's guide to the history of science **509**

SCIENCE -- ITALY -- HISTORY
Heilbron, J. L. Galileo **92**

SCIENCE -- LIFE SCIENCES -- BIOLOGY -- GENERAL
Kean, S. The violinist's thumb **572.8**

SCIENCE -- LIFE SCIENCES -- GENETICS & GENOMICS
Kean, S. The violinist's thumb **572.8**

SCIENCE -- METHODOLOGY
Cox, B. The quantum universe **530.12**
Firestein, S. Ignorance **501**

SCIENCE -- METHODOLOGY -- HISTORY
Weinberg, S. To explain the world **509**

SCIENCE -- MISCELLANEA
Levi, M. Why cats land on their feet **530**
Munroe, R. What if? **500**

SCIENCE -- MORAL AND ETHICAL ASPECTS
Coffey, P. Cathedrals of science **540**
Dreger, A. Galileo's middle finger **174.2**
Mukherjee, S. The laws of medicine **610**
Preston, D. Before the fallout **355.8**

SCIENCE -- PHILOSOPHY -- HISTORY
Henry, J. A short history of scientific thought **501**

SCIENCE -- POLITICAL ASPECTS
Dreger, A. Galileo's middle finger **174.2**
Ferris, T. The science of liberty **303.4**

SCIENCE -- POPULAR WORKS
Casarett, D. Shocked **616.02**
Woodford, C. Atoms Under the Floorboards **502**

SCIENCE -- RELIGIOUS ASPECTS *See* Religion and science

SCIENCE -- SOCIAL ASPECTS
Bartusiak, M. Black hole **523.8**
Bloom, H. The God problem **500**
Kaku, M. Physics of the future **303.49**
Venter, J. C. Life at the Speed of Light **303.48**

SCIENCE -- STUDY AND TEACHING
Olson, R. Don't be such a scientist **501**
Otto, S. Fool me twice **303.4**
Poe, M. Learning to communicate in science and engineering **501**

SCIENCE -- UNITED STATES
Otto, S. Fool me twice **303.4**

SCIENCE -- UNITED STATES -- HISTORY
Cohen, I. B. Science and the Founding Fathers **973.3**
Ewing, H. P. The lost world of James Smithson **92**

SCIENCE -- VOCATIONAL GUIDANCE
Wilson, E. O. Letters to a Young Scientist **570**

SCIENCE AND CIVILIZATION
Dreger, A. Galileo's middle finger **174.2**

Falk, D. In search of time **529**
Fara, P. Science **509**
Ferris, T. The science of liberty **303.4**
Henry, J. A short history of scientific thought **501**
Rees, M. J. From here to infinity **500**

SCIENCE AND CIVILIZATION
See also Civilization; Progress; Science

SCIENCE AND CIVILIZATION -- HISTORY
Ferreira, P. G. The perfect theory **530.11**
Henry, J. A short history of scientific thought **501**
Science and health, with key to the Scriptures. Eddy, M. B. **289.5**
Science and human values. Bronowski, J. **500**

SCIENCE AND RELIGION *See* Religion and science

Science and religion, 1450-1900. Olson, R. **261.5**
Science and religion, 400 B.C. to A.D. 1550. Grant, E. **261.5**

SCIENCE AND SOCIETY *See* Science and civilization

SCIENCE AND SPACE *See* Space sciences

SCIENCE AND TECHNOLOGY LIBRARIES -- REFERENCE SERVICES
Berard, G. L. Science and technology resources **025.5**
Science and technology resources. Berard, G. L. **025.5**
Science and the City. Winkless, L. **307.76**
Science and the founding fathers. Cohen, I. B. **973.3**

SCIENCE AND THE HUMANITIES
The best American science and nature writing 2014 **810.8**
A cultural history of physics **530**

SCIENCE AND THE HUMANITIES
See also Humanities; Science

Science essentials [series]
Mitton, S. Heart of darkness **523.1**

SCIENCE EXPERIMENTS *See* Science -- Experiments

SCIENCE FICTION
Buker, D. M. The science-fiction and fantasy readers' advisory **025.5**
Herald, D. T. Strictly science fiction **016**
Hollands, N. Fellowship in a ring **809**
Kallio, J. Read on ... speculative fiction for teens **016**
Torres-Roman, S. A. Read on-- science fiction **016**

SCIENCE FICTION
See also Adventure fiction; Fiction

SCIENCE FICTION -- AUTHORSHIP
Atwood, M. In other worlds **809**
Dick, P. K. The exegesis of Philip K. Dick **818**

SCIENCE FICTION -- BIBLIOGRAPHY
Buker, D. M. The science-fiction and fantasy readers' advisory **025.5**
Burgess, M. Reference guide to science fiction,

fantasy, and horror **016**
Herald, D. T. Strictly science fiction **016**
Hollands, N. Fellowship in a ring **809**
Torres-Roman, S. A. Read on-- science fiction **016**

SCIENCE FICTION -- DICTIONARIES
Brave new words **809.3**

SCIENCE FICTION -- HISTORY AND CRITICISM
Walton, J. What Makes This Book So Great **813**

SCIENCE FICTION COMIC BOOKS, STRIPS, ETC.
See also Comic books, strips, etc.

SCIENCE FICTION FILMS
Warren, B. Keep watching the skies! **791.43**

SCIENCE FICTION FILMS
See also Motion pictures

SCIENCE FICTION FILMS -- CATALOGS
Barsanti, C. The science fiction movie guide **016**

SCIENCE FICTION GRAPHIC NOVELS
See also Graphic novels
The science fiction movie guide. Barsanti, C. **016**

SCIENCE FICTION PLAYS
See also Drama

SCIENCE FICTION POETRY
See also Poetry

SCIENCE FICTION RADIO PROGRAMS -- PSYCHOLOGICAL ASPECTS
Schwartz, A. B. Broadcast hysteria **791.44**

SCIENCE FICTION TELEVISION PROGRAMS
See also Television programs

SCIENCE FICTION WRITERS
Eller, J. R. Becoming Ray Bradbury **92**
Farrell, S. E. Critical companion to Kurt Vonnegut **813**
Gunn, J. E. Isaac Asimov **813**
Herbert, B. Dreamer of Dune **813**
King, S. On writing **813**
Malone, J. W. It doesn't take a rocket scientist **920**
McKillop, A. B. The spinster & the prophet **941.08**
Phillips, J. James Tiptree, Jr. **813**
Poundstone, W. Carl Sagan **92**
Shields, C. J. And so it goes: Kurt Vonnegut: a life **92**
Weller, S. The Bradbury chronicles **92**

SCIENCE FICTION, AMERICAN -- BIBLIOGRAPHY
Torres-Roman, S. A. Read on-- science fiction **016**

SCIENCE FICTION, AMERICAN -- HISTORY AND CRITICISM
Walton, J. What Makes This Book So Great **813**

SCIENCE FICTION, ENGLISH -- BIBLIOGRAPHY
Torres-Roman, S. A. Read on-- science fiction **016**

SCIENCE HISTORIANS
Winchester, S. The man who loved China **92**

SCIENCE IN MOTION PICTURES

Olson, R. Don't be such a scientist   **501**

SCIENCE LABORATORIES *See* Laboratories

Science masters series

Leakey, R. E. The origin of humankind   **599.93**

Margulis, L. Symbiotic planet   **576.8**

The **science** of fear. Gardner, D.   **152.4**

The **science** of freedom. Gay, P.   **190**

The **science** of good cooking.   **641.3**

The **science** of liberty. Ferris, T.   **303.4**

The **Science** of Shakespeare. Falk, D.   **822.3**

The **science** of Sherlock Holmes. Wagner, E. J.   **363.2**

The **science** of yoga. Broad, W. J.   **613.7**

SCIENCE TEACHERS

Delany, S. Having our say   **92**

Science vs. religion. Ecklund, E. H.   **215**

SCIENCE WRITERS -- UNITED STATES -- BIOGRAPHY

Souder, W. On a farther shore   **92**

SCIENCE, ANCIENT

Freely, J. The flame of Miletus   **509**

Teresi, D. Lost discoveries   **509**

Weinberg, S. To explain the world   **509**

SCIENCE, MEDIEVAL

Weinberg, S. To explain the world   **509**

SCIENCE, RENAISSANCE

Greenblatt, S. The swerve   **940.2**

Hofstadter, D. The Earth moves   **509**

The **science-fiction** and fantasy readers' advisory. Buker, D. M.   **025.5**

Scientific American's ask the experts.   **500**

SCIENTIFIC APPARATUS AND INSTRUMENTS

Lincoln, D. The large hadron collider   **539.7**

SCIENTIFIC APPARATUS AND INSTRUMENTS -- ENCYCLOPEDIAS

Instruments of science   **502.8**

SCIENTIFIC EXPEDITIONS

Anthony, J. C. Hoosh   **394.1**

Ferreiro, L. D. Measure of the Earth   **526**

Larson, E. J. An empire of ice   **919**

Stark, P. Astoria   **978**

Travels with the fossil hunters   **560**

Whitaker, R. The mapmaker's wife   **981**

SCIENTIFIC EXPEDITIONS

See also Voyages and travels

SCIENTIFIC EXPEDITIONS -- EUROPE -- HISTORY -- 18TH CENTURY

Ferreiro, L. D. Measure of the Earth   **526**

SCIENTIFIC EXPEDITIONS/ANTARCTIC REGIONS

Larson, E. J. An empire of ice   **919**

SCIENTIFIC LITERATURE -- BIBLIOGRAPHY -- METHODOLOGY

Berard, G. L. Science and technology resources   **025.5**

SCIENTIFIC RECREATIONS

Gardner, M. The colossal book of short puzzles and problems   **793.8**

SCIENTIFIC RECREATIONS

See also Amusements

The **scientist** in the crib. Gopnik, A.   **155.4**

The **scientists.** Gribbin, J. R.   **509**

SCIENTISTS

Aldrin, B. No dream is too high   **92**

Aquino, L. Leonardo Da Vinci   **92**

Biddle, W. Dark side of the moon   **92**

Bramly, S. Leonardo   **709**

Brewer, J. The American Leonardo   **759**

Brown, D. A. Leonardo da Vinci   **759**

Cohen, I. B. Science and the founding fathers **973.3**

Dawkins, R. Brief Candle in the Dark   **570**

Ewing, H. P. The lost world of James Smithson   **92**

Fara, P. Newton: the making of genius   **92**

Feldman, B. 112 Mercer Street   **920**

Flannery, T. An explorer's notebook   **304.2**

Franklin, B. The autobiography of Benjamin Franklin   **92**

Gleick, J. Isaac Newton   **92**

Green, B. Boltzmann's tomb   **509**

Gribbin, J. R. The scientists   **509**

Hart, C. High Price   **362.29**

Hirshfeld, A. Eureka man   **92**

Hough, S. E. Richter's scale   **92**

Hunter, M. Boyle   **92**

Isaacson, W. Benjamin Franklin   **92**

Johnson, S. The invention of air   **92**

Klein, S. Leonardo's legacy   **709**

Malone, J. W. It doesn't take a rocket scientist **920**

Millar, D. The Cambridge dictionary of scientists   **920.003**

Neufeld, M. J. Von Braun   **92**

Nuland, S. B. Leonardo da Vinci   **709**

Pasles, P. C. Benjamin Franklin's numbers   **510**

Pendle, G. Strange angel   **92**

Ridley, M. Francis Crick   **92**

Sassoon, D. Becoming Mona Lisa   **759**

Scotti, R. A. Vanished smile   **759**

Snyder, L. J. The philosophical breakfast club **509**

Strathern, P. The artist, the philosopher, and the warrior   **920**

Travels with the fossil hunters   **560**

Varmus, H. The art and politics of science   **92**

Watson, J. D. Avoid boring people   **92**

Westfall, R. S. The life of Isaac Newton   **92**

White, M. Leonardo   **92**

Winchester, S. The man who loved China   **92**

Wulf, A. Chasing Venus   **523.9**

SCIENTISTS -- ATTITUDES

Ecklund, E. H. Science vs. religion   **215**

SCIENTISTS -- BIOGRAPHY

Dawkins, R. An Appetite for Wonder   **92**

Sacks, O. On the move **92**

Stott, R. Darwin's ghosts **576.8**

Wulf, A. The invention of nature **92**

SCIENTISTS -- DICTIONARIES

Gates, A. E. A to Z of earth scientists **920.003**

Millar, D. The Cambridge dictionary of scientists **920.003**

New dictionary of scientific biography **920.003**

Newton, D. E. Latinos in science, math, and professions **920.003**

Notable black American scientists **509**

Oakes, E. H. A to Z of chemists **920.003**

SCIENTISTS -- GERMANY -- BIOGRAPHY

Wulf, A. The invention of nature **92**

SCIENTISTS -- GERMANY -- HISTORY

Jacobsen, A. Operation Paperclip **940.54**

SCIENTISTS -- GREAT BRITAIN -- HISTORY

Dolnick, E. The clockwork universe **509**

Snyder, L. J. The philosophical breakfast club **509**

SCIENTISTS -- POLAND -- BIOGRAPHY

Allen, A. The fantastic laboratory of Dr. Weigl **614.5**

SCIENTISTS -- PROFESSIONAL ETHICS

Dreger, A. Galileo's middle finger **174.2**

SCIENTISTS -- UNITED STATES -- HISTORY

Jacobsen, A. Operation Paperclip **940.54**

SCIENTOLOGY

Wright, L. Going Clear **299**

SCIENTOLOGY

See also Cults

Sciolino, Elaine

La seduction **302.3**

SCIPIONYX

See also Dinosaurs

SCLEROPAGES FORMOSUS

Voigt, E. The dragon behind the glass **597.176**

The **score** takes care of itself. Walsh, B. **658.4**

Scorecards for results. Matthews, J. R. **027.4**

Scorgie, Glen G.

(ed) Zondervan dictionary of Christian spirituality **248**

Scorpions. Feldman, N. **920**

Scorsese, Martin

About

Singer, M. Character studies **920**

SCOTLAND

Stewart, R. The Marches **941.3**

SCOTLAND -- CIVILIZATION

Herman, A. How the Scots invented the modern world **941.1**

SCOTLAND -- DESCRIPTION AND TRAVEL

Macfarlane, R. The old ways **914.2**

Starr, W. W. Whisky, kilts, and the Loch Ness Monster **914**

SCOTLAND -- HISTORY

Penman, M. Robert the Bruce **92**

SCOTLAND -- HISTORY -- 16TH CENTURY

Fraser, A. Mary Queen of Scots **92**

Weir, A. Mary, Queen of Scots, and the murder of Lord Darnley **92**

SCOTLAND -- HISTORY -- ROBERT I, 1306-1329

Penman, M. Robert the Bruce **92**

SCOTS -- EUROPE -- HISTORY -- 18TH CENTURY

Boswell's enlightenment **828**

Zaretsky, R. Boswell's enlightenment **92**

Scott, Beth

Norman, M. Haunted America **133.1**

Scott, Dred, ca. 1795-1858

About

VanderVelde, L. Mrs. Dred Scott **92**

Scott, Drew

Dream home **643.12**

Scott, George

(ed) Floyd, T. Smithsonian field guide to the birds of North America **598**

Scott, Harriet Robinson

About

VanderVelde, L. Mrs. Dred Scott **92**

Scott, James M., 1964-

Target Tokyo **940.54**

Scott, Jeff

Raising children in the military **355.1**

Scott, John F.

Latin American art **709**

Scott, Jonathan

(jt. auth) Scott, D. Dream home **643.12**

Scott, Marilyn

The potter's bible **738**

The Oil Painter's Bible **751.45**

Scott, Paul, 1920-1978

About

Fraser, K. Ornament and silence **809**

Scott, R. Neil

Many were held by the sea **940.4**

Scott, Ralph D.

Capinera, J. L. Field guide to grasshoppers, crickets, and katydids of the United States **595.7**

Scott, Rebecca J.

Freedom papers **305.896**

Scott, Robert Falcon, 1868-1912

About

Larson, E. J. An empire of ice **919**

Preston, D. A first rate tragedy **919**

Solomon, S. The coldest March **919**

Scott, Walter J.

Lung cancer **616.99**

Scott, Wendell, 1921-1990

About

Donovan, B. Hard driving: the Wendell Scott story **92**

Scott-Clark, Cathy
The Amber Room   **940.54**
(jt. auth) Levy, A. The siege   **363.325**
Scott-Heron, Gil, 1949-2011
The last holiday   **920**
Scotti, R. A.
Vanished smile   **759**
SCOTTISH NATIONAL CHARACTERISTICS
Herman, A. How the Scots invented the modern world   **941.1**
SCOTTISH PERSONAL NAMES
See also Personal names
Scout, Atticus, and Boo. Murphy, M. M.   **813**
SCOUTS
Carter, R. A. Buffalo Bill Cody   **978**
Faragher, J. M. Daniel Boone   **92**
Morgan, R. Boone   **92**
Sides, H. Blood and thunder   **978**
Warren, L. S. Buffalo Bill's America   **92**
SCOUTS AND SCOUTING
See also Clubs; Community life
Scoville, William Beecher, 1906-1984
About
Dittrich, L. Patient H.M.   **616.85**
Scowcroft, Gail
Crist, D. T. World ocean census   **578.7**
SCRABBLE (GAME) -- DICTIONARIES
The official Scrabble players dictionary   **793.7**
The **scramble** for Africa. Pakenham, T.   **960**
SCRAPBOOKING
See also Handicraft
SCRAPBOOKS
Helfand, J. Scrapbooks: an American history   **745.54**
Scrapbooks: an American history. Helfand, J.   **745.54**
Scratch. Rodale, M.   **641.3**
SCRATCH (COMPUTER PROGRAM LANGUAGE)
Braafladt, K. Technology and literacy   **027.62**
Scream. Janowitz, T.   **92**
A **scream** goes through the house. Weinstein, A. **801**
Screen doors and sweet tea. Foose, M. H.   **641.5**
SCREEN PRINTING *See* Silk screen printing
SCREEN PROCESS PRINTING
Corwin, L. Printing by hand   **745.5**
Screen world presents the encyclopedia of Hollywood film actors. Monush, B.   **920.003**
Screening room. Lightman, A. P.   **92**
Screenplay. Field, S.   **808.2**
SCREENPLAYS
See also Drama
SCREENWRITERS
Goldman, W. Which Lie Did I Tell?   **791.43**
SCREENWRITERS -- UNITED STATES -- DIARIES

It's the pictures that got small   **92**
The **Screwtape** letters. Lewis, C. S.   **248**
Scribe. Ryan, B.   **070.449**
The **Scribner** encyclopedia of American lives.   **920.003**
The **Scribner** encyclopedia of American lives, The 1960s.   **920.003**
Scribner library of modern Europe [series]
Europe 1789 to 1914   **940.2**
Scribner writers series
Latino and Latina writers   **810**
Supernatural fiction writers   **809**
Scroggins, Deborah
Wanted women   **305.48**
Scroogenomics. Waldfogel, J.   **339.4**
Scuba diving. Graver, D.   **797.2**
SCUBA DIVING
Chowdhury, B. The last dive   **363.14**
Skolnick, A. One breath   **797.2**
Scull, Andrew
Madness in civilization   **616.89**
SCULLING *See* Rowing
Scully, Pamela
(jt. auth) Crais, C. C. Sara Baartman and the Hottentot Venus   **92**
Scully, Ramael
(jt. auth) Ottolenghi, Y. Nopi   **641.5**
SCULPTORS
Dippie, B. W. The Frederic Remington Art Museum collection   **709**
Khan, Y. S. Enlightening the world   **974.7**
King, R. Brunelleschi's dome   **726**
King, R. The judgment of Paris   **759**
King, R. Michelangelo & the Pope's ceiling   **759**
Matthiessen, F. O. American renaissance   **810**
Mormando, F. Bernini   **92**
Thomas Eakins   **759.13**
SCULPTORS
See also Artists
SCULPTORS -- UNITED STATES -- BIOGRAPHY
Herrera, H. Listening to stone   **92**
SCULPTURE
Easter Island's silent sentinels   **990**
SCULPTURE
See also Art; Decoration and ornament
SCURLOCK STUDIO (FIRM)
The Scurlock Studio and Black Washington   **779**
The **Scurlock** Studio and Black Washington.   **779**
SDI (BALLISTIC MISSILE DEFENSE SYSTEM) *See* Strategic Defense Initiative
SEA ANIMALS *See* Marine animals
The **sea** around us. Carson, R.   **551.46**
SEA BED *See* Ocean bottom
SEA FISHERIES *See* Commercial fishing
SEA FOOD *See* Seafood

Sea legs. Crane, K. **92**

SEA LEVEL
  Pilkey, O. H. The rising sea **363.34**

SEA LIFE *See* Marine biology; Navies; Sailors; Seafaring life

Sea of dangers. Blainey, G. **92**

Sea of thunder. Thomas, E. **940.54**

SEA PEOPLES -- HISTORY
  Fagan, B. Beyond the blue horizon **910.4**

Sea room: an island life in the Hebrides. Nicolson, A. **941.1**

SEA STORIES -- HISTORY AND CRITICISM
  Philbrick, N. Why read Moby-Dick? **813**

SEA TRAVEL *See* Ocean travel

Sea turtles. Spotila, J. R. **597.92**

SEA TURTLES
  Sedaris, D. Let's explore diabetes with owls **814**
  Spotila, J. R. Sea turtles **597.92**

SEA WATER
  See also Water

SEA WATER AQUARIUMS *See* Marine aquariums

SEA WAVES *See* Ocean waves

SEA WORLD
  Hargrove, J. Beneath the surface **599.53**
  Kirby, D. Death at SeaWorld **599.53**

SEA-SHORE *See* Seashore

Seaberg, Maureen
  (jt. auth) Padgett, J. Struck by genius **155.9**

Seabiscuit. Hillenbrand, L. **798.4**

SEABISCUIT (RACE HORSE)
  Hillenbrand, L. Seabiscuit **798.4**

Seabrook, John
  The song machine **781.64**

SEAFARING LIFE
  Dana, R. H. Two years before the mast **910.4**
  McPhee, J. A. Looking for a ship **910.4**
  Mostert, N. The line upon a wind **940.2**

SEAFARING LIFE
  See also Adventure and adventurers; Manners and customs; Voyages and travels

SEAFARING LIFE -- HISTORY
  Fagan, B. Beyond the blue horizon **910.4**

SEAFOOD
  Grescoe, T. Bottomfeeder **641.6**

SEAFOOD
  See also Food; Marine resources

SEAFOOD INDUSTRY -- UNITED STATES
  Greenberg, P. American catch **333.95**

Seagrave, Peggy
  Seagrave, S. The Yamato dynasty **952.03**

Seagrave, Sterling
  The Yamato dynasty **952.03**

SEALS (ANIMALS)
  Williams, T. M. The odyssey of KP2 **599.79**

SEALS (ANIMALS)

  See also Mammals; Marine mammals

SEALS (NUMISMATICS)
  Shearer, B. F. State names, seals, flags, and symbols **929.9**

SEALS (NUMISMATICS)
  See also Heraldry; History; Inscriptions; Numismatics

Seaman, Camille, 1969-
  About
  Seaman, C. Melting away **910.91**

SEARCH DOGS -- ANECDOTES
  Warren, C. What the dog knows **636.7**

SEARCH ENGINES *See* Web search engines

The **search** for modern China. Spence, J. D. **951**

Search Press (Company)
  (comp) A-Z of Whitework **746.44**

Searching for memory. Schacter, D. L. **153.1**

Searching for Sunday. Evans, R. H. **248**

Searching for Zion. Raboteau, E. **305.896**

SEARCHING THE INTERNET *See* Internet searching

Searing, Susan E.
  (ed) Guide to reference **011**

Sears List of Subject Headings. **025.4**

Sears parenting library [series]
  Sears, R. W. The vaccine book **614.4**

Sears, James M.
  (jt. auth) Sears, W. The baby book **649**

Sears, Martha
  (jt. auth) Sears, W. The baby book **649**
  (jt. auth) Sears, W. The healthy pregnancy book **618.2**
  Sears, W. Parenting the fussy baby and high-need child **649**

Sears, Robert W.
  The vaccine book **614.4**
  (jt. auth) Sears, W. The allergy book **618.92**
  (jt. auth) Sears, W. The baby book **649**

Sears, Stephen W.
  Chancellorsville **973.7**
  (ed) The Civil War **973.7**
  George B. McClellan **92**
  Gettysburg **973.7**
  Landscape turned red **973.7**
  To the gates of Richmond **973.7**

Sears, William
  The allergy book **618.92**
  The baby book **649**
  The healthy pregnancy book **618.2**
  Parenting the fussy baby and high-need child **649**

SEAS
  See also Earth; Physical geography; Water

SEASHORE
  Carson, R. The edge of the sea **577.7**

SEASHORE ECOLOGY
  Dean, C. Against the tide **333.91**

SEASHORE ECOLOGY
   See also Ecology
Season of the witch. Talbot, D.   **306**
SEASONAL COOKING
  Acheson, H. The broad fork   **641.597**
  Bayless, R. More Mexican everyday   **641.597**
  Cowin, D.   Food & Wine Annual Cookbook 2015   **641**
  Reichl, R. My kitchen year   **641.5**
  Vibrant food   **641.5**
SEASONAL COOKING -- FRANCE -- MÉDOC
  Thorisson, M. A kitchen in France   **641.594**
Seasonal works with letters on fire. Hillman, B. **811**
SEASONS
  Michael Symon's 5 in 5 for every season   **641.81**
SEASONS
  See also Astronomy; Climate; Meteorology
SEASONS -- FRANCE -- MÉDOC
  Thorisson, M. A kitchen in France   **641.594**
SEASONS -- SOUTHERN STATES
  Deep South   **975**
SEASONS -- TENNESSEE
  Haskell, D. G. The forest unseen   **577.3**
The **seasons** of a man's life. Levinson, D. J. **155.6**
The **seasons** of a woman's life. Levinson, D. J. **155.6**
SEATTLE (WASH.) -- BIOGRAPHY
  Sone, M. Nisei daughter   **979.7**
Seaver, Barton
  For cod and country   **641.6**
  Two if by sea   **641.692**
Seaver, Jeannette, 1933-
  (ed) The tender hour of twilight   **070.5**
Seaver, Richard
             About
  The tender hour of twilight   **070.5**
Sebag Montefiore, Simon, 1965-
  Jerusalem   **956.94**
  The Romanovs   **920**
  Stalin: the court of the red tsar   **92**
  Young Stalin   **92**
Sebag-Montefiore, Hugh
  Enigma: the battle for the code   **940.54**
  Somme   **940.4**
Sebald, Winfried Georg, 1944-2001
  Across the land and the water   **831**
  On the natural history of destruction   **833**
Sebestyen, Victor
  1946   **909.82**
  Revolution 1989   **947**
Sebold, Alice
  Lucky   **362.883**
SECESSION -- SOUTHERN STATES
  Williams, D. Bitterly divided   **973.7**
SECESSION -- SOUTHERN STATES
  See also United States -- History -- 1861-1865, Civil War

SECLUSION *See* Solitude
SECOND ADVENT
  See also Eschatology
Second childhood. Howe, F.   **811**
The **second** Dalai Lama. Mullin, G. H.   **92**
Second drafts of history. Morrow, L.   **973.92**
Second nature. Balcombe, J.   **591.5**
The **second** sex. Beauvoir, S. d.   **305.4**
The **Second** World War. Beevor, A.   **940.54**
The **Second** World War. Gilbert, M.   **940.53**
Second World War [series]
  Churchill, W. Closing the ring   **940.53**
  Churchill, W. The gathering storm   **940.53**
  Churchill, W. The grand alliance   **940.53**
  Churchill, W. The hinge of fate   **940.53**
  Churchill, W. Their finest hour   **940.53**
  Churchill, W. Triumph and tragedy   **940.53**
SECOND WORLD WAR *See* World War, 1939-1945
SECONDARY EDUCATION
  Adolescent literacy in the academic disciplines **428**
SECONDARY EDUCATION
  See also Education
SECONDARY SCHOOLS *See* High schools; Junior high schools; Secondary education
Secondhand time. Aleksievich, S.   **947.086**
Secor, Laura
  Children of Paradise   **955.05**
Secrecy. Moynihan, D. P.   **352.3**
Secrest, Meryle
  Elsa Schiaparelli   **92**
  Frank Lloyd Wright   **92**
  Modigliani   **92**
A **secret** gift. Gup, T.   **977.1**
Secret historian. Spring, J.   **92**
The **secret** history of kindness. Pierson, M. H. **636.7**
The **Secret** History of Vladimir Nabokov. Pitzer, A.   **891.73**
The **Secret** History of Wonder Woman. Lepore, J.   **741.5**
The **secret** language of animals.   **591.5**
The **Secret** Language of Color. Eckstut, A.   **535.6**
The **secret** life of Marilyn Monroe. Taraborrelli, J. R.   **92**
The **secret** life of the American musical. Viertel, J.   **792.6**
The **secret** life of words. Hitchings, H.   **422**
The **secret** lives of buildings. Hollis, E.   **720.9**
The **secret** lives of codebreakers. McKay, S. **940.54**
The **secret** lives of Somerset Maugham. Hastings, S.   **92**
The **Secret** Lives of Sports Fans. Simons, E. **306.4**
The **secret** of Chanel No. 5. Mazzeo, T. J.   **338.7**
The **secret** of scent. Turin, L.   **668**
The **Secret** Race. Hamilton, T.   **796.62**
The **secret** rescue. Lineberry, C.   **940.54**

The **secret** room. Laughlin, J.   **811**

SECRET SERVICE
Johnson, L. K.   National Security Intelligence

SECRET SERVICE
See also Police

SECRET SERVICE -- GERMANY (EAST)
Garton-Ash, T.   The file   **327.12**

SECRET SERVICE -- ISRAEL
Bascomb, N.   Hunting Eichmann   **943.086**
Pedahzur, A.   The Israeli secret services and the struggle against terrorism   **363.32**

SECRET SERVICE -- UNITED STATES
Goodavage, M.   Secret Service Dogs   **363.283**
Hill, C.   Five presidents   **363.28**
Hill, C.   Mrs. Kennedy and me   **973.922**
Secret Service Dogs. Goodavage, M.   **363.283**

SECRET SOCIETIES
See also Rites and ceremonies; Societies
The **secret** war. Hastings, M.   **940.54**
The **secret** war against Hanoi. Shultz, R. H.   **959.704**
Secret Warriors. Downing, T.   **940.4**
Secret weapons. Eisner, T.   **595.7**
The **secret** wife of Louis XIV. Buckley, V.   **944**

SECRET WRITING *See* Cryptography
Secretariat. Nack, W.   **798.4**

SECRETARIAT (RACE HORSE)
Nack, W.   Secretariat   **798.4**

SECRETARIES
Rule, A.   --and never let her go   **364.1**

SECRETARIES OF COMMERCE
Hofstadter, R.   The American political tradition, and the men who made it   **973**

SECRETARIES OF DEFENSE
Halberstam, D.   The best and the brightest   **973.922**
Hendrickson, P.   The living and the dead   **959.704**
Roberts, A.   Masters and commanders   **940.54**
Weintraub, S.   15 stars   **920**
Woodward, B.   The commanders   **973.928**

SECRETARIES OF LABOR
Downey, K.   The woman behind the New Deal   **92**

SECRETARIES OF STATE
Balz, D. J.   The battle for America, 2008   **973.932**
Bernstein, C.   A woman in charge   **92**
Brookhiser, R.   America's first dynasty   **973.4**
Burstein, A.   Madison and Jefferson   **973.4**
Chace, J.   Acheson   **92**
Clinton, H. R.   Living history   **92**
Cohen, I. B.   Science and the founding fathers   **973.3**
Dallek, R.   Nixon and Kissinger   **92**
De Young, K.   Soldier: the life of Colin Powell   **92**
Gates, H. L.   Thirteen ways of looking at a black man   **920.71**
Goodwin, D. K.   Team of rivals   **92**
Gormley, K.   The death of American virtue   **973.929**
Halberstam, D.   The best and the brightest   **973.922**
Heidler, D. S.   Henry Clay   **92**

Hofstadter, R.   The American political tradition, and the men who made it   **973**
Kazin, M.   A godly hero   **92**
Kennedy, J. F.   Profiles in courage   **920**
Kissinger, H.   Years of renewal   **973.924**
McPherson, J. M.   Drawn with the sword   **973.7**
Meyerson, M.   Liberty's blueprint   **342**
Miller, W. L.   Arguing about slavery   **973.5**
Nagel, P. C.   John Quincy Adams   **92**
O'Brien, M.   Mrs. Adams in winter   **940.2**
Powell, C. L.   My American journey   **92**
Remini, R. V.   Daniel Webster   **328**
Remini, R. V.   John Quincy Adams   **92**
Rice, C.   Extraordinary, ordinary people   **92**
Roberts, A.   Masters and commanders   **940.54**
Simon, J. F.   What kind of nation   **342**
Smith, J. E.   John Marshall   **347**
Traister, R.   Big girls don't cry   **324**
Unger, H. G.   The last founding father   **92**
Weintraub, S.   15 stars   **920**
Widmer, E. L.   Martin Van Buren   **92**
Wills, G.   James Madison   **92**
Woodward, B.   The commanders   **973.928**
Zimmermann, W.   First great triumph   **973**

SECRETARIES OF THE INTERIOR
Kennedy, J. F.   Profiles in courage   **920**

SECRETARIES OF THE NAVY
Symonds, C. L.   Lincoln and his admirals   **92**
Thompson, N.   The hawk and the dove   **92**

SECRETARIES OF THE TREASURY
Beschloss, M. R.   The conquerors: Roosevelt, Truman, and the destruction of Hitler's Germany, 1941-1945   **940.53**
Cannadine, D.   Mellon   **92**
Chernow, R.   Alexander Hamilton   **92**
Goodwin, D. K.   Team of rivals   **92**
Hamilton, A.   Writings   **973.4**
Larson, E. J.   A magnificent catastrophe   **324**
Meyerson, M.   Liberty's blueprint   **342**
Miller, J. C.   The Federalist era, 1789-1801   **973.4**
Paulson, H. M.   On the brink   **330.9**
Staloff, D.   Hamilton, Adams, Jefferson   **973.4**

SECRETARIES OF WAR
Cooper, W. J.   Jefferson Davis, American   **92**
Davis, B.   Sherman's march   **973.7**
Davis, W. C.   An honorable defeat   **973.7**
Fellman, M.   Citizen Sherman   **92**
Hanson, V. D.   The soul of battle   **355**
Hofstadter, R.   The American political tradition, and the men who made it   **973**
Kennett, L. B.   Sherman   **92**
McPherson, J. M.   Drawn with the sword   **973.7**
Wilson, E.   Patriotic gore   **810**
Woodworth, S. E.   Sherman   **92**
Zimmermann, W.   First great triumph   **973**
Secrets from the eating lab. Mann, T.   **613.2**

Secrets of Silicon Valley. Piscione, D. P.   330.9
Secrets of the flesh: a life of Colette. Thurman, J. 92
Secrets of the nanny whisperer. Gold, T.   649
Secrets of the savanna. Owens, M.   599
The secrets of triangles. Lehmann, I.   516
Secrets to drawing realistic faces. Parks, C. S. 743.42
Secrets: a memoir of Vietnam and the Pentagon papers. Ellsberg, D.   959.704
Section 60. Poole, R. M.   975.5
SECTS
    Atwood, C. D. Handbook of denominations in the
    United States   280
SECTS
    See also Church history; Religions
SECTS -- ENCYCLOPEDIAS
    The encyclopedia of cults, sects, and new religions   200
    Melton, J. G. Melton's encyclopedia of American
    religions   200.9
SECULAR HUMANISM See Secularism
Secular meditation. Heller, R.   158.1
SECULARISM
    Zuckerman, P. Living the Secular Life   211
SECULARISM
    See also Ethics; Utilitarianism
SECULARISM -- 21ST CENTURY
    Heller, R. Secular meditation   158.1
SECULARISM -- UNITED STATES
    Niose, D. Nonbeliever nation   211
Securing the city. Dickey, C.   363.32
SECURITIES
    Bernstein, W. The investor's manifesto   332.6
    Cohan, W. D. Money and power   332.6
SECURITIES
    See also Finance; Investments; Stock exchanges
SECURITIES -- UNITED STATES
    Weatherall, J. O. The physics of Wall Street 332.63
SECURITIES BROKERS
    Gardner, C. The pursuit of happyness   92
    Torres, A. American widow   741.5
SECURITIES EXCHANGE See Stock exchanges
SECURITIES FRAUD
    Ferguson, C. Predator nation   330.973
SECURITIES FRAUD
    See also Fraud
SECURITY (PSYCHOLOGY)
    Molotch, H. Against security   363.325
SECURITY (PSYCHOLOGY)
    See also Emotions; Psychology
SECURITY TRADERS See Stockbrokers
SECURITY, INTERNATIONAL
    Haass, R. N. Foreign policy begins at home 327.73
    Kissinger, H. World Order   327
SECURITY, INTERNATIONAL See International
    security

SECURITY, INTERNATIONAL -- CASE STUDIES
    Chayes, S. Thieves of state   364.1
Sedaris, Amy
    I like you   793.2
Sedaris, David, 1956-
    Dress your family in corduroy and denim   814
    Let's explore diabetes with owls   814
    Me talk pretty one day   814
SEDER
    New American Haggadah   296.4
SEDER
    See also Judaism -- Customs and practices;
    Passover
SEDER -- LITURGY -- TEXTS
    New American Haggadah   296.4
Sederer, Lloyd I.
    The family guide to mental health care   616.89
Sedgwick, John
    War of two   973.4
Sedgwick, Peter
    Descartes to Derrida   190
Sediqi, Kamela, 1977-
                About
    Lemmon, G. T. The dressmaker of Khair Khana 92
SEDITION See Political crimes and offenses; Revolutions
SEDUCTION
    Sciolino, E. La seduction   302.3
Seed bead chic. Katz, A.   745.594
The seed garden.
SEEDS
    Bradley, F. M. Saving vegetable seeds   635
    Dunn Chace, T. Seeing seeds   581.4
    Hanson, T. The triumph of seeds   581.4
    The seed garden
SEEDS
    See also Plant propagation; Plants
Seeds in the heart. Keene, D.   895.6
Seeds of Hope. Goodall, J.   580
Seeger, Pete
    How to play the 5-string banjo   787.8
                About
    Dunaway, D. K. How can I keep from singing? 92
    Wilkinson, A. The protest singer   92
Seeger, Ruth Crawford
    (ed) Our singing country   781.62
Seeing further.   506
Seeing in the dark. Ferris, T.   520
Seeing Mary plain: a life of Mary McCarthy. Kiernan, F.   818
Seeing seeds. Dunn Chace, T.   581.4
Seeing trees. Hugo, N. R.   582.16
Seeing voices. Sacks, O. W.   362.4
Seek, Amy
    God and Jetfire   92

Seeking enlightenment--hat by hat. Barr, N.   92
Seeking serenity. Enayati, A.   155.9
Seeking Sicily. Keahey, J.   945
Seeley, Thomas D.
  Honeybee democracy   595.799
Segan, Francine
  Pasta modern   641.82
Segev, Tom
  Simon Wiesenthal   92
Segrè, Gino
  Ordinary geniuses   572.8
SEGREGATION
  Davis, T. J. Plessy v. Ferguson   342
SEGREGATION
  See also Race relations
SEGREGATION -- LAW AND LEGISLATION --
UNITED STATES -- HISTORY
  Davis, T. J. Plessy v. Ferguson   342
SEGREGATION -- UNITED STATES
  Bishop, B. The big sort   305.8
SEGREGATION IN EDUCATION
  Green, K. Something Must Be Done About Prince
  Edward County   379.26
  Kozol, J. Savage inequalities   371.9
  Kozol, J. The shame of the nation   379
SEGREGATION IN EDUCATION
  See also Segregation
SEGREGATION IN HOUSING *See* Discrimination in housing
SEGREGATION IN TRANSPORTATION
  Arsenault, R. Freedom riders   323
SEGREGATION IN TRANSPORTATION -- AL-
ABAMA -- MONTGOMERY -- HISTORY --
20TH CENTURY
  Brinkley, D. Rosa Parks   92
  Jackson, T. Becoming King   92
  Theoharis, J. The rebellious life of Mrs. Rosa
  Parks   92
SEGREGATION IN TRANSPORTATION --
LAW AND LEGISLATION -- LOUISIANA --
HISTORY
  Davis, T. J. Plessy v. Ferguson   342
Sehat, David
  The Jefferson rule   306.2
Seibert, Brian
  What the eye hears   792.7
Seidel, Frederick
  Poems 1959-2009   811
Seidule, Ty
  (ed) The West Point History of the Civil War 973.7
Seierstad, Asne
  The angel of Grozny   947.5
  The bookseller of Kabul   958.1
  A hundred and one days   956.7
  One of Us   363.325
Seife, Charles

Proofiness   510
Sun in a bottle   539.7
Virtual unreality   025.04
SEISMIC SEA WAVES *See* Tsunamis
SEISMOGRAPHY *See* Earthquakes
SEISMOLOGISTS
  Hough, S. E. Richter's scale   92
SEISMOLOGY *See* Earthquakes
Seitchik-Reardon, Dillon
  (jt. auth) Pember, M. The Little Veggie Patch Co.
  DIY Garden Projects   712.6
Seitz, Matt Zoller
  TV (the book)   791.45
Seiverling, Richard
       About
  Singer, M. Character studies   920
Seize the day. Meyer, J.   248.4
Selby, Scott Andrew
  Flawless   364.1
Seldom disappointed. Hillerman, T.   813
The **selected** essays of Gore Vidal. Essays/Selections   814
The **selected** letters of Willa Cather. Cather, W. 813
Selected letters, 1940-1956. Kerouac, J.   92
Selected letters, 1957-1969. Kerouac, J.   813
Selected lyrics. Porter, C.   782.42
Selected non-fictions. Borges, J. L.   864
Selected poems. Ashbery, J.   811
Selected poems.   811
Selected poems. Millay, E. S. V.   811
Selected poems. Borges, J. L.   861
Selected poems. Bronk, W.   811
Selected poems. Verlaine, P.   841
Selected poems. Zukofsky, L.   811
Selected poems. Rukeyser, M.   811
Selected poems. Levertov, D.   811
Selected poems. Tsvetaeva, M. I.   891.7
Selected poems. Lowell, A.   811
Selected poems. Tomlinson, C.   821
Selected poems. Duncan, R. E.   811
Selected poems. Lowell, R.   811
Selected poems. Tarn, N.   811
Selected poems. Sisson, C. H.   821
Selected poems. Fenton, J.   811
Selected poems. Yevtushenko, Y. A.   891.7
Selected poems. Fisher, R.   821
Selected poems. Fearing, K.   811
Selected poems. Van Duyn, M.   811
Selected poems. Hacker, M.   811
Selected poems. Tate, J.   811
Selected poems. Dove, R.   811
Selected poems. Tagore, R.   891
Selected poems. Hill, G.   821
Selected poems. Whittier, J. G.   811
Selected poems.   811
Selected poems and translations, 1969-1991. Mat-

thews, W.   **811**

The **selected** poems of Donald Hall. Hall, D. **811.54**

The **selected** poems of Howard Nemerov. Nemerov, H.   **811**

Selected poems of Langston Hughes. Hughes, L.   **811**

Selected poems of May Sarton. Sarton, M.   **811**

The **selected** poems of Osip Mandelstam. Mandelstam, O.   **891.7**

Selected poems, 1960-1990. Kumin, M.   **811**

Selected poetry. Pope, A.   **821**

Selected poetry. Goethe, J. W. v.   **831**

Selected poetry. MacDiarmid, H.   **821**

Selected poetry of Lord Byron. Byron, G. G. B. **821**

The **selected** poetry of Robinson Jeffers. Jeffers, R.   **811**

Selected poetry of William Wordsworth. Wordsworth, W.   **821**

The **selected** poetry of Yehuda Amichai. Amichai, Y.   **892**

Selected sonnets. Camoes, L. d.   **869**

Selected translations 1948-2010.   **808.81**

Selected writings. Kleist, H. v.   **838**

Selected writings. Thomas   **189**

Selected writings. Valery, P.   **848**

SELECTIVE SERVICE *See* Draft

Selengut, Becky
   Shroom   **641.658**

SELF
   Budig, K. Aim true   **613.7**
   Eagleman, D. The brain   **612.82**
   Eat Pray Love Made Me Do It   **910.4**
   Hofstadter, D. R. I am a strange loop   **153**
   Hood, B. The self illusion   **155.2**
   Judith, A. Eastern body, Western mind   **150.19**
   Jung, C. G. Man and his symbols   **150.19**
   Lerner, H. G. The dance of intimacy   **155.6**
   Weber, R. J. The created self   **155.2**

SELF
   See also Consciousness; Individuality; Personality

SELF HEALTH CARE *See* Health self-care

The **self** illusion. Hood, B.   **155.2**

SELF IMAGE *See* Personal appearance

SELF-ACCEPTANCE
   McBride, K. Will I ever be good enough? **616.85**

SELF-ACCEPTANCE
   See also Psychology

SELF-ACTUALIZATION *See* Self-realization

SELF-ACTUALIZATION (PSYCHOLOGY)
   Ackerman, D. Deep play   **155.6**
   Brogaard, B. The superhuman mind   **153.9**
   Brown, B. Rising strong   **158**
   James, E. Paris in love   **92**
   Michels, B. The tools   **158**
   Mohr, T. Playing big   **650.1**

Vincent, I. Dinner with Edward   **158.1**

Waxman, J. How to break up with anyone   **158.2**

SELF-ACTUALIZATION (PSYCHOLOGY) -- CASE STUDIES
   Mock, J. Redefining Realness   **306.76**

SELF-ACTUALIZATION (PSYCHOLOGY) -- RELIGIOUS ASPECTS -- CHRISTIANITY
   Jakes, T. D. Destiny   **248.4**

SELF-ACTUALIZATION (PSYCHOLOGY) -- RELIGIOUS ASPECTS -- JUDAISM
   Davidson, S. The December Project   **296.7**

SELF-ASSURANCE *See* Self-confidence; Self-reliance

SELF-AWARENESS *See* Self-perception

SELF-CARE, HEALTH
   Adamec, C. When your adult child breaks your heart   **616.89**
   Flippin, R. The diabetes reset   **616.4**
   Grigore, A. Skin cleanse   **613**
   Kang, M. S. The doctor's kidney diets   **616.6**
   Kosik, K. S. Outsmarting alzheimer's   **616.8**
   Ludwig, D. Always hungry?   **613.2**
   Michelson, L. D. The patient's playbook **610.69**
   Roizen, M. F. This is your do-over   **613**

SELF-CARE, HEALTH *See* Health self-care

SELF-CARE, HEALTH -- POPULAR WORKS
   The whole30   **613.2**

SELF-CARE, MEDICAL *See* Health self-care

SELF-CHANGE TECHNIQUES *See* Self-help techniques

SELF-CONCEPT *See* Self-perception

SELF-CONFIDENCE
   Ehrenreich, B. Bright-sided   **155.2**
   Engel, B. The nice girl syndrome   **155.6**
   Rollag, K. What to do when you're new   **158.2**
   Roth, B. The Achievement Habit   **158.1**

SELF-CONFIDENCE
   See also Emotions

SELF-CONFIDENCE -- RELIGIOUS ASPECTS -- CHRISTIANITY
   Osteen, J. The power of I am   **248.4**

SELF-CONSCIOUSNESS
   See also Psychology

SELF-CONSCIOUSNESS (AWARENESS)
   Kurzweil, R. How to create a mind   **612.8**

SELF-CONTROL
   Akst, D. We have met the enemy   **153.8**
   Bailey, R. A. Easy to love, difficult to discipline **155**
   Goleman, D. Focus   **153.7**
   Mischel, W. The marshmallow test   **155.2**

SELF-CONTROL
   See also Psychology

SELF-CONTROL IN CHILDREN
   Richey, M. A. The impulsive, disorganized child   **649**

SELF-CULTURE *See* Self-improvement; Self-instruction

SELF-DECEPTION
Triandis, H. C. Fooling ourselves **155.2**
Trivers, R. The folly of fools **153.4**

SELF-DEFENSE FOR WOMEN
Gervasi, L. H. Fight like a girl-- and win **613.6**
Zeisler, A. Weapons of fitness **613.6**

SELF-EMPLOYED
D'Agnese, J. The money book for freelancers, part-time, and the self-employed **332.024**
Fishman, S. Working for yourself **343**

SELF-EMPLOYED
See also Businesspeople

SELF-EMPLOYED WOMEN
See also Women -- Employment

SELF-ESTEEM
Engel, B. The nice girl syndrome **155.6**
Young-Eisendrath, P. The self-esteem trap **155.2**

SELF-ESTEEM
See also Psychology
The **self-esteem** trap. Young-Eisendrath, P. **155.2**

SELF-HELP GROUPS
Aikman, B. Saturday night widows **306.88**

SELF-HELP GROUPS
See also Counseling

SELF-HELP MEDICAL CARE See Health self-care

Self-help Messiah. Watts, S. **92**

SELF-HELP TECHNIQUES
Bluestein, J. The perfection deception **155.2**
Chittister, J. Following the path **248.4**
Duhigg, C. Smarter faster better **158**
Gladwell, M. David and Goliath **155.2**
Greitens, E. Resilience **155.2**
Jakes, T. D. Instinct **248.4**
Langshur, E. Start here **158**
Manson, M. The subtle art of not giving a fu*k **158.1**
Michels, B. The tools **158**
Mohr, T. Playing big **650.1**
Saviuc, L. D. 15 things you should give up to be happy **152.4**
Watts, S. Self-help Messiah **92**

SELF-HELP TECHNIQUES
See also Applied psychology; Life skills

SELF-IMPROVEMENT
Cardillo, J. Body intelligence **158.1**
Sandberg, S. Lean in **658.4**
Small, G. 2 weeks to a younger brain **616.8**

SELF-IMPROVEMENT
See also Life skills

SELF-INSTRUCTION
101 Saturday morning projects **643**
Complete do-it-yourself manual **643**
New fix-it-yourself manual **643**

SELF-INSTRUCTION

See also Education; Study skills

SELF-LOVE (PSYCHOLOGY) See Self-acceptance; Self-esteem

A **self-made** man. Blumenthal, S. **92**

SELF-MASTERY See Self-control

SELF-MEDICATION See Health self-care

SELF-MUTILATION
Forrest, E. Your voice in my head **362.196**

SELF-MUTILATION
See also Abnormal psychology

SELF-PERCEPTION
Cuddy, A. Presence **158.1**
Kessel, B. It's not about the money **332.024**
Krasno, J. Wanderlust **613.7**
Seligman, M. E. P. Learned optimism **155.2**

SELF-PERCEPTION
See also Psychology

SELF-PERCEPTION IN WOMEN
Borich, B. J. Body geographic **818**
Whitefield-Madrano, A. Face value **111.85**

SELF-PROTECTION IN ANIMALS See Animal defenses

SELF-PUBLISHING
See also Publishers and publishing

SELF-REALIZATION
Anselmo, L. My (part-time) Paris life **944.361**
Bloomfield, H. H. Making peace with your past **158**
Budd, K. The voluntourist **361.7**
Cardillo, J. Body intelligence **158.1**
Chittister, J. Between the Dark and the Daylight **128**
Covey, S. R. The 8th habit **158**
Cuddy, A. Presence **158.1**
Gawain, S. Creative visualization **153.3**
Greer, G. The change **618.1**
Havrilesky, H. How to be a person in the world **070.444**
Hay, L. L. You can heal your life **158**
Iyer, P. The man within my head **809**
Jakes, T. D. Destiny **248.4**
Manson, M. The subtle art of not giving a fu*k **158.1**
Mock, J. Redefining Realness **306.76**
Orloff, J. Emotional freedom **152.4**
Osteen, J. The power of I am **248.4**
Peck, M. S. Further along the road less traveled **158**
Peck, M. S. The road less traveled and beyond **158**
Roth, B. The Achievement Habit **158.1**
Santi, J. The giving way to happiness **179**
Siegel, B. S. Prescriptions for living **158**
Smith, C. B. The rules of inheritance **616.99**
Smith, L. R. No fears, no excuses **650.1**
Sugar, L. Power your happy **158**
Tolle, E. A new earth **158**
Tolle, E. The power of now **158**

SELF-REALIZATION

See also Psychology

SELF-REALIZATION IN WOMEN

Armstrong, J. K. Sexy feminism **305.42**

Cleage, P. Things I Should Have Told My Daughter **92**

SELF-RELIANCE

Markham, B. L. Mini farming **635**

Rawles, J. W. Tools for survival **613.6**

SELF-RELIANCE IN CHILDREN

Lahey, J. The gift of failure **649**

SELF-TALK -- RELIGIOUS ASPECTS -- CHRISTIANITY

Osteen, J. The power of I am **248.4**

The **selfish** gene. Dawkins, R. **576**

SELFISHNESS

See also Personality

Seligman, Martin E. P.

Learned optimism **155.2**

Seligman, Scott D.

Tong wars **364.106**

Selingo, Jeffrey J.

College (un)bound **378**

There Is Life After College **650.14**

Selkirk, Alexander, 1676-1721

About

Severin, T. In search of Robinson Crusoe **996**

Sellers, Vanessa Bezemer

(ed) Flora illustrata **016**

SELLING

See also Business; Retail trade

SELLING -- HANDBOOKS, MANUALS, ETC

Lindsay, V. Sewing to sell **646.2**

Selling sounds. Suisman, D. **338.4**

Selling women short. Featherstone, L. **331.4**

Sellmair, Nikola

My grandfather would have shot me **929.2**

The **sellout**. Gasparino, C. **332**

Selves. Booth, P. **811**

SEMANTIC WEB

Pariser, E. The filter bubble **025.04**

SEMANTIC WEB

See also Semantic networks (Information theory); World Wide Web

SEMANTICS

See also Language and languages; Linguistics

Sember, Brette McWhorter

Seniors' rights **346.01**

SEMICONDUCTORS

See also Electric conductors; Electronics

SEMINOLE INDIANS

McReynolds, E. C. The Seminoles **970.004**

The **Seminoles**. McReynolds, E. C. **970.004**

SEMIOTICS

The encyclopedia of literary and cultural theory **801**

SEMITIC PEOPLES

See also Ethnology

Semmelweis, Ignác Fülöp, 1818-1865

About

Nuland, S. B. The doctors' plague **92**

Sen, Amartya Kumar

The argumentative Indian **954**

The **senate** intelligence committee report on torture.

Senator, Susan

Autism Adulthood **616.85**

SENATORS

Abuse of power **973.924**

Adams, M. Turn right at Machu Picchu **985**

Alter, J. The promise **92**

Ambrose, S. E. The wild blue **940.54**

Balz, D. J. The battle for America, 2008 **973.932**

Bernstein, C. A woman in charge **92**

Beschloss, M. R. The conquerors: Roosevelt, Truman, and the destruction of Hitler's Germany, 1941-1945 **940.53**

Black, C. M. Richard M. Nixon **92**

Brookhiser, R. America's first dynasty **973.4**

Bugliosi, V. Reclaiming history **973.922**

Busby, H. W. The thirty-first of March **973.923**

Calhoun, C. W. Benjamin Harrison **92**

Caro, R. A. The path to power **92**

Clarke, T. The last campaign **92**

Cleland, M. Heart of a patriot **92**

Clinton, H. R. Living history **92**

Cohen, I. B. Science and the founding fathers **973.3**

Conant, J. A covert affair **940.54**

Cooper, W. J. Jefferson Davis, American **92**

Crapol, E. P. John Tyler **92**

Dallek, R. Harry S. Truman **92**

Dallek, R. Let every nation know **92**

Dallek, R. Nixon and Kissinger **92**

Dallek, R. An unfinished life: John F. Kennedy, 1917-1963 **92**

Davis, W. C. An honorable defeat **973.7**

Dobbs, M. One minute to midnight **973.922**

Emery, F. Watergate **973.924**

English, B. Last lion **92**

Feldman, N. Scorpions **920**

Freedman, L. Kennedy's wars **973.922**

Goodwin, D. K. Team of rivals **92**

Gordin, M. D. Red cloud at dawn **355**

Gormley, K. The death of American virtue **973.929**

Guelzo, A. C. Lincoln and Douglas **973.6**

Hair, W. I. The Kingfish and his realm: the life and times of Huey P. Long **92**

Halberstam, D. The best and the brightest **973.922**

Hayden, T. The long sixties **973.92**

Heaney, C. Cradle of gold **92**

Heidler, D. S. Henry Clay **92**

Johnson, H. B. The age of anxiety **973.921**

Kaiser, D. E. American tragedy **959.704**

Kaiser, D. E. The road to Dallas **973.922**

Karabell, Z. The last campaign **324.9**

Kennedy, E. M. True compass   **92**

Kennedy, J. F. Profiles in courage   **920**

Kissinger, H. Diplomacy   **327.2**

Kotz, N. Judgment days   **323**

Leamer, L. The Kennedy men   **920**

Lemann, N. Redemption: the last battle of the Civil War   **975**

Mahoney, R. D. Sons and brothers: the days of Jack and Bobby Kennedy   **92**

Mallon, T. Mrs. Paine's garage and the murder of John F. Kennedy   **364.1**

Matthews, C. Kennedy & Nixon   **973.922**

May, G. John Tyler   **92**

McCain, J. S. Faith of my fathers   **92**

McCullough, D. G. Truman   **92**

Mendell, D. Obama   **92**

Miller, W. L. Arguing about slavery   **973.5**

Morgan, T. Reds: McCarthyism in twentieth-century America   **973.9**

Morrow, L. The best year of their lives   **920**

Nagel, P. C. John Quincy Adams   **92**

Obama, B. Dreams from my father   **92**

O'Brien, M. Mrs. Adams in winter   **940.2**

Perlstein, R. Nixonland   **973.924**

Perry, J. M. Touched with fire   **973.7**

Peters, C. Lyndon B. Johnson   **92**

Pietrusza, D. 1960: LBJ vs. JFK vs. Nixon   **973.92**

Pooley, E. The climate war   **363.7**

Posner, G. L. Case closed   **973.922**

Rasenberger, J. The brilliant disaster   **972.91**

Reeves, R. President Kennedy   **973.922**

Reeves, R. President Nixon   **973.924**

Remini, R. V. John Quincy Adams   **92**

Remnick, D. The bridge   **92**

Remnick, D. Reporting   **814**

Reston, J. The conviction of Richard Nixon   **973.924**

Schlesinger, A. M. Robert Kennedy and his times   **92**

Sorensen, T. C. Counselor   **92**

Taking charge   **973.923**

Thomas, E. Robert Kennedy   **92**

Thomas, E. The war lovers   **973.8**

Traister, R. Big girls don't cry   **324**

Wheen, F. Strange days indeed   **973.92**

Wicker, T. Shooting star: the brief arc of Joe McCarthy   **92**

Woodward, B. The final days   **973.924**

Woodward, B. Shadow   **973.92**

Zelnick, B. Gore: a political life   **92**

Zimmermann, W. First great triumph   **973**

SENDAI EARTHQUAKE, JAPAN, 2011

Ehrlich, G. Facing the wave   **363.34**

Mockett, M. M. Where the Dead Pause, and the Japanese Say Goodbye   **952**

Sendak, Maurice, 1928-2012

         About

    Maurice Sendak   **741.6**

    My brother's book   **811**

    Parker, H. Herman Melville   **813**

    Spiegelman, A. Co-Mix   **741.5**

Sendlerowa, Irena, 1910-2008

         About

    Mazzeo, T. J. Irena's children   **940.53**

Seneca, Lucius Annaeus

    Four tragedies, and Octavia   **882**

Senelick, Laurence

    (ed) Chekhov, A. P. The complete plays   **891.7**

SENESCENCE *See* Aging

Seneviratne, Samantha

    Sugar and spice   **641.86**

Sengmueller, Elke

    (jt. auth) Smith, R. G. ASD, the complete autism spectrum disorder health & diet guide   **616.85**

Sengo, Zenaida

    Air plants   **628.5**

SENILE DEMENTIA

    See also Nervous system -- Diseases

SENIOR CITIZENS *See* Elderly

Senior, Jennifer

    All Joy and No Fun   **306.874**

Seniors' rights. Sember, B. M.   **346.01**

Sennett, Frank

    Groupon's biggest deal ever   **381**

Senning, Daniel Post

    (jt. auth) Post, P. Emily Post's etiquette   **395**

    (jt. auth) Post, P. Emily Post's The etiquette advantage in business   **395**

Sensational soutache jewelry making. Papp, C.   **745.594**

The **sense** of being stared at. Sheldrake, R.   **133.8**

SENSE OF DIRECTION *See* Direction sense

The **sense** of style. Pinker, S.   **808**

A **sense** of the world. Roberts, J.   **92**

SENSES AND SENSATION

    Ackerman, D. A natural history of the senses   **152.1**

    Hughes, H. C. Sensory exotica   **573.8**

SENSES AND SENSATION

    See also Intellect; Physiology; Psychology; Psychophysiology; Theory of knowledge

SENSES AND SENSATION IN ANIMALS

    Birkhead, T. Bird sense   **598**

SENSES AND SENSATION IN ANIMALS

    See also Senses and sensation

Sensory exotica. Hughes, H. C.   **573.8**

Seo, Danny

    Naturally, delicious   **641.302**

SEPARATION OF POWERS

    Simon, J. F. What kind of nation   **342**

SEPARATION OF POWERS

    See also Constitutional law; Executive power; Political science

SEPARATION OF POWERS -- UNITED STATES

Breyer, S. G. Making our democracy work   347

SEPARATIST MOVEMENTS

   See also Social movements

SEPHARDIM

Sabar, A. My father's paradise   305.8

Sepinwall, Alan, 1973-

(jt. auth) Seitz, M. Z. TV (the book)   791.45

SEPTEMBER 11 TERRORIST ATTACKS, 2001

Bernstein, R. Out of the blue   973.931

Chesler, P. The new anti-semitism   305.8

Dower, J. W. Cultures of war   355

Dwyer, J. 102 minutes   974.7

Eichenwald, K. 500 days   973.931

Elshtain, J. B. Just war against terror   363.32

Farmer, J. J. The ground truth   973.931

Feinberg, K. R. What is life worth?   362.88

Hersh, S. M. Chain of command   973.931

Langewiesche, W. American ground, unbuilding the World Trade Center   974.7

Longman, J. Among the heroes   364.1

Lutnick, H. On top of the world   332.6

Mayer, J. The dark side   973.931

McDermott, T. The hunt for KSM   363.325

Miller, J. The cell: inside the 9/11 plot and why the FBI and CIA failed to stop it   973.931

National Commission on Terrorist Attacks Upon the United States   The 9/11 Commission report   973.931

Noonan, P. A heart, a cross & a flag   973.931

Rice, C. No higher honor   327.73

Smith, D. Report from ground zero   363.34

Soufan, A. H. The black banners   973.931

Theoharis, A. G. Abuse of power   363.325

Wright, L. The looming tower   973.931

SEPTEMBER 11 TERRORIST ATTACKS, 2001

   See also Terrorism -- United States

SEPTEMBER 11 TERRORIST ATTACKS, 2001 -- GRAPHIC NOVELS

Jacobson, S. The 9/11 report   741.5

Spiegelman, A. In the shadow of no towers   973.931

Torres, A. American widow   741.5

SEPTEMBER 11 TERRORIST ATTACKS, 2001 -- PERSONAL NARRATIVES

After the fall   974.7

Smith, D. A decade of hope   974.7

Sequels. Husband, J.   016

SEQUENCES (MATHEMATICS)

Benjamin, A. The Magic of Math   510

SEQUENCES (MATHEMATICS)

   See also Algebra; Mathematics

Sequoyah, 1770?-1843

About

Lepore, J. A is for American   306.44

Serafin, Steven

(ed) The Continuum encyclopedia of British literature   810

Serani, Deborah

Depression in later life   618.97

Serchay, David S.

The librarian's guide to graphic novels for adults   025.2

Sered, Susan Starr

Can't catch a break   362.83

SERENDIPITY IN SCIENCE

Dyson, F. J. Dreams of earth and sky   500

The **Serengeti** Rules. Carroll, S. B.   570

Sereny, Gitta

Albert Speer   92

Sergeant Reckless (Horse), approximately 1948-1968

About

Hutton, R. Sgt. Reckless   951.904

SERIAL KILLERS

Graeber, C. The good nurse   364.152

King, D. Death in the city of light

Kolker, R. Lost Girls   364.152

SERIAL KILLERS

   See also Criminals; Homicide

SERIAL KILLERS -- HISTORY

Schechter, H. Psycho USA   364.152

SERIAL MURDERERS *See* Serial killers

SERIAL MURDERERS -- UNITED STATES -- BIOGRAPHY

Stewart, J. B. Blind eye   364.1

SERIAL PUBLICATIONS

   See also Bibliography; Publishers and publishing

SERIGRAPHY *See* Silk screen printing

Serious barbecue. Lang, A. P.   641.5

A **serious** way of wondering. Price, R.   241

SERMON ON THE MOUNT

Bonhoeffer, D. The cost of discipleship   226

SERMONS

American sermons   252

King, M. L. Strength to love   252

Tutu, D. The rainbow people of God   968.06

SERMONS

   See also Christian literature

Serota, Nicholas

(ed) Henri Matisse   709.2

SERPENTS *See* Snakes

Servadio, Gaia

Rossini   92

Service. Hornfischer, J. D.   956.704

SERVICE (IN INDUSTRY) *See* Customer services

Service and style. Whitaker, J.   381

SERVICE DOGS

Goodavage, M. Secret Service Dogs   363.283

Service, Robert, 1947-

The End of the Cold War, 1985-1991   909.82

Lenin--a biography   947.084

Stalin   92

Trotsky | 92

SERVICEMEMBERS UNITED (UNITED STATES)
Nicholson, A. Fighting to serve | 355

SESAME STREET (TELEVISION PROGRAM)
Jones, B. J. Jim Henson | 92

SET DESIGNERS
Brainard, J. The Nancy book | 759
Ross, C. The world of Edward Gorey | 700.92

SET THEORY
Stillwell, J. Roads to infinity | 511.3

SET THEORY
See also Mathematics

Seth, Vikram, 1952-
About
Seth, V. Two lives | 92

Seton, Elizabeth Ann, Saint, 1774-1821
About
Barthel, J. American saint | 92

SETS (MATHEMATICS) *See* Set theory

SETS OF FRACTIONAL DIMENSION *See* Fractals

SETS, FRACTAL *See* Fractals

Settersten, Richard
(jt. auth) Ray, B. E. Not quite adults | 306.8

Setting the truth free. Campbell, J. | 941.6

Settle for More. Kelly, M. | 791.45

Settled in the wild. Shetterly, S. H. | 508

The **settlement** of the Americas. Dillehay, T. D. | 970.01

The **setup.** Crooks, P. | 363.28

Seuling, Barbara
How to write a children's book and get it published | 808.06

Seuss, Dr.
About
Morgan, J. Dr. Seuss & Mr. Geisel | 92

Seven ages of Paris. Horne, A. | 944

Seven Brief Lessons on Physics. Rovelli, C. | 530

Seven days in the art world. Thornton, S. | 709.05

Seven fires. Mallmann, F. | 641.5

Seven guitars. Wilson, A. | 812

The **seven** pearls of financial wisdom. Pepper, C. | 332.024

Seven pillars of wisdom. Lawrence, T. E. | 940.4

The **seven** sins of memory. Schacter, D. L. | 153.1

Seven skeletons. Pyne, L. | 569.9

Seven spoons. O'Brady, T. | 641.597

The **seven** storey mountain. Merton, T. | 92

SEVEN YEARS' WAR, 1756-1763
Anderson, F. The crucible of war | 973.2
Macleod, D. P. Northern Armageddon | 971.01
McLynn, F. 1759: the year Britain became master of the world | 941.07

SEVENTEENTH CENTURY *See* World history -- 17th century

The **seventies.** Schulman, B. J. | 973.925

The **Seventy** wonders of the modern world. | 720.9

SEVERE STORMS
Kostigen, T. M. National Geographic extreme weather survival guide | 613.6

SEVERE STORMS -- ANTARCTIC OCEAN
Lewis, M. Last man off | 910.91

Severin, Timothy
In search of Robinson Crusoe | 996

Severson, Marilyn S.
Masterpieces of French literature | 843

Sew classic clothes for girls. Wilkes, L.

Sew organized for the busy girl. Staples, H. | 646.2

SEWAGE DISPOSAL
George, R. The big necessity | 363.7

SEWAGE DISPOSAL
See also Public health; Refuse and refuse disposal

Sewall, Jeremy
The New England kitchen | 641.597

Sewall, Samuel, 1652-1730
About
LaPlante, E. Salem witch judge | 92

Seward. Stahr, W. | 92

Seward, Desmond
The Demon's Brood | 942.03

Seward, William Henry, 1801-1872
About
Goodwin, D. K. Team of rivals | 92
Stahr, W. Seward | 92

Sewell, Darrel
(ed) Thomas Eakins | 759.13

SEWERAGE
See also House drainage; Municipal engineering; Plumbing; Sanitary engineering

SEWING
Abousteit, N. BurdaStyle sewing vintage modern | 646.4
Bardwell, S. Sewing Basics | 746
Bednar, N. The encyclopedia of sewing machine techniques | 646.2
Betzina, S. Power sewing step-by-step | 646.4
Bull, J. Get set, sew | 646.2
BurdaStyle modern sewing | 646.4
Butler, A. Amy Butler's style stitches | 646.4
Cheetham, K. Singer perfect plus | 646.2
Colgrove, D. Teach yourself visually sewing | 646.2
Creative Publishing International, I. The complete photo guide to sewing | 646.2
Doh, J. Signature styles | 646.4
Ellis, C. Home sewn | 646.21
Finnanger, T. Tilda Homemade & Happy | 746.4
First time sewing | 646.2
Happy home | 646.2
Hirsch, G. Gertie's ultimate dress book | 646.4
Hirsch, G. A modern guide to sportswear styles of

the 1940s and 1950s **646.4**

Ishida, S. Sewing happiness **646.2**

Ito, M. Simply sewn **646.4**

James, C. The complete serger handbook **646.2**

Knight, E. 500 crochet stitches **746.43**

Lee, L. Sewing edges and corners **646.2**

Lindsay, V. Sewing to sell **646.2**

Mallalieu, N. The better bag maker **646.4**

Mitnick, S. The Colette sewing handbook **646.4**

New complete guide to sewing **646.2**

The new sewing essentials **646.2**

One-yard wonders **646.2**

Reader's Digest Association, I. New complete guide to sewing **646.2**

Shore, D. Half yard gifts **646.2**

Smith, A. Dressmaking **646.4**

Smith, A. The sewing book **646.2**

Stanley, S. H. DIY wardrobe makeovers **646**

Staples, H. Sew organized for the busy girl **646.2**

Stewart, M. Martha Stewart's encyclopedia of sewing and fabric crafts **746**

Wilkes, L. Sew classic clothes for girls

SEWING

See also Home economics

SEWING -- TECHNIQUE

Knight, E. 750 knitting stitches **746.432**

Moebes, D. Stitch Savvy **646**

Sewing Basics. Bardwell, S. **746**

The **sewing** book. Smith, A. **646.2**

Sewing edges and corners. Lee, L. **646.2**

Sewing green. White, B. **646.4**

Sewing happiness. Ishida, S. **646.2**

The **sewing** machine accessory bible. Gardiner, W. **646.2**

SEWING MACHINES

Gardiner, W. The sewing machine accessory bible **646.2**

James, C. The complete serger handbook **646.2**

Sewing to sell. Lindsay, V. **646.2**

SEX

Angel, K. Unmastered **828**

Barash, D. P. Homo mysterious **303.4**

Berkowitz, E. The boundaries of desire **306.7**

Comfort, A. The joy of sex **613.9**

Eisner, S. Bi **306.76**

Eldredge, N. Why we do it **155.3**

Fisher, H. Anatomy of Love **302.3**

Jacques, J. Trans **306.76**

Roach, M. Bonk **612.6**

Rodríguez, R. Darling **92**

Savage, D. American Savage **306.76**

Shlain, L. Sex, time, and power **306.7**

Sugar in my bowl **306.7**

Sykes, B. Adam's curse **599.93**

SEX

See also Human behavior

SEX (PSYCHOLOGY) *See* Sex -- Psychological aspects

SEX -- PHYSIOLOGICAL ASPECTS

See also Biology

SEX -- PSYCHOLOGICAL ASPECTS

Bergner, D. What Do Women Want? **305**

Comfort, A. The joy of sex **613.9**

Freitas, D. The end of sex **176**

Gottman, J. The man's guide to women **155.3**

Moran, R. Paid for **306.74**

Orenstein, P. Girls and Sex **306.7**

SEX -- PSYCHOLOGICAL ASPECTS

See also Psychology

SEX -- RELIGIOUS ASPECTS -- CHRISTIAN-ITY

Edman, E. M. Queer virtue **230**

SEX -- SOCIAL ASPECTS

Berkowitz, E. The boundaries of desire **306.7**

Sex and the office. Berebitsky, J. **331.4**

SEX BIAS *See* Sexism

SEX CHANGE *See* Sex reassignment surgery

SEX CRIMES

Lived through this **362.883**

Sexual violence and abuse **364.15**

Solomon, J. DSK **306.77**

Surviving sexual violence **362.88**

SEX CRIMES

See also Crime; Sex

SEX CRIMES -- CASE STUDIES

Lived through this **362.883**

SEX CRIMES -- PREVENTION

Sexual violence and abuse **364.15**

SEX CUSTOMS

Barash, D. P. The myth of monogamy **306.7**

SEX CUSTOMS -- FRANCE -- HISTORY

Sciolino, E. La seduction **302.3**

SEX CUSTOMS -- HISTORY

Berkowitz, E. The boundaries of desire **306.7**

SEX CUSTOMS -- LOUISIANA -- NEW ORLEANS -- HISTORY -- 20TH CENTURY

Krist, G. Empire of sin **976.3**

SEX CUSTOMS -- UNITED STATES -- HISTORY -- 20TH CENTURY

Mackrell, J. Flappers **920**

SEX DIFFERENCES (PSYCHOLOGY)

Brown, C. S. Parenting beyond pink and blue **649**

Eliot, L. Pink brain, blue brain **612.6**

Mead, M. Coming of age in Samoa **306**

Tannen, D. You just don't understand **302.2**

Taylor, S. E. The tending instinct **304.5**

SEX DIFFERENCES (PSYCHOLOGY)

See also Sex -- Psychological aspects

SEX DISCRIMINATION

Featherstone, L. Selling women short **331.4**

SEX DISCRIMINATION

See also Discrimination; Sexism

**SEX DISCRIMINATION -- LAW AND LEGIS-
LATION**
Povich, L. The good girls revolt **331.4**
SEX DISCRIMINATION IN EMPLOYMENT
Bohnet, I. What works **331.4**
**SEX DISCRIMINATION IN EMPLOYMENT --
UNITED STATES**
Featherstone, L. Selling women short **331.4**
Povich, L. The good girls revolt **331.4**
SEX EDUCATION
Columbia University/Health Service The Go ask
Alice book of answers **613**
Comfort, A. The joy of sex **613.9**
Nagoski, E. Come as you are **613.9**
Roffman, D. Talk to me first **613.907**
Vernacchio, A. For goodness sex **613.9**
SEX IN MASS MEDIA
See also Mass media
SEX IN POPULAR CULTURE
See also Popular culture
SEX IN THE OFFICE *See* Sex in the workplace
SEX IN THE WORKPLACE
Berebitsky, J. Sex and the office **331.4**
SEX IN THE WORKPLACE
See also Sex
SEX INSTRUCTION *See* Sex education
SEX INSTRUCTION FOR CHILDREN
Roffman, D. Talk to me first **613.907**
SEX INSTRUCTION FOR TEENAGERS
Roffman, D. Talk to me first **613.907**
Vernacchio, A. For goodness sex **613.9**
SEX INSTRUCTION FOR WOMEN
Nagoski, E. Come as you are **613.9**
Sex object. Valenti, J. **92**
SEX OFFENDERS
Burke, T. M. The Paradiso files **364.152**
Sex on six legs. Zuk, M. **595.7**
SEX ORGANS *See* Reproductive system
SEX PRESELECTION
See also Reproduction
SEX REASSIGNMENT SURGERY
Faludi, S. In the Darkroom **818.603**
SEX REASSIGNMENT SURGERY
See also Surgery
SEX RESEARCHERS
Schmidt, L. E. Heaven's bride **92**
SEX ROLE *See* Gender role
**SEX ROLE -- UNITED STATES -- HISTORY --
20TH CENTURY**
Berebitsky, J. Sex and the office **331.4**
Mackrell, J. Flappers **920**
SEX ROLE IN THE WORK ENVIRONMENT
Annis, B. Work with me **306.3**
Williams, J. What works for women at work **650.1**
**SEX ROLE IN THE WORK ENVIRONMENT --
UNITED STATES**

Povich, L. The good girls revolt **331.4**
**SEX SCANDALS -- NEW YORK STATE -- NEW
YORK**
Solomon, J. DSK **306.77**
SEX THERAPY
See also Psychotherapy
SEX TRAFFICKING *See* Human trafficking
Sex, drugs 'n Facebook. Moreno, M. **004.67**
Sex, drugs and Asperger's syndrome (ASD) Jack-
son, L. **618.92**
Sex, time, and power. Shlain, L. **306.7**
SEXISM
Povich, L. The good girls revolt **331.4**
Yes means yes! **306.7**
SEXISM
See also Attitude (Psychology); Prejudices
Sexton, Anne
The complete poems **811**
About
Middlebrook, D. W. Anne Sexton **811**
SEXUAL ABSTINENCE
See also Asceticism; Sex
SEXUAL ABUSE *See* Child sexual abuse; Sex
crimes; Sexual harassment
SEXUAL ABUSE VICTIMS -- CASE STUDIES
Lived through this **362.883**
SEXUAL ABUSE VICTIMS -- PSYCHOLOGY
Surviving sexual violence **362.88**
**SEXUAL ABUSE VICTIMS -- REHABILITA-
TION**
Surviving sexual violence **362.88**
SEXUAL ASSAULT *See* Rape
SEXUAL ATTRACTION
Gottman, J. The man's guide to women **155.3**
Shlain, L. Sex, time, and power **306.7**
SEXUAL BEHAVIOR
Ackerman, D. A natural history of love **152.4**
Bader, M. J. Arousal, the secret logic of sexual fan-
tasies **306.7**
Barash, D. P. The myth of monogamy **306.7**
Bergner, D. The other side of desire **306.7**
McConnachie, J. The book of love **306.7**
Pincott, J. Do gentlemen really prefer
blondes? **155.3**
Pisani, E. The wisdom of whores **614.5**
Sugar in my bowl **306.7**
SEXUAL BEHAVIOR *See* Sex
SEXUAL BEHAVIOR IN ANIMALS
Barash, D. P. The myth of monogamy **306.7**
Bondar, C. Wild Sex **591.562**
Zuk, M. Sexual selections **591.56**
Zuk, M. Sex on six legs **595.7**
SEXUAL BEHAVIOR IN ANIMALS
See also Animal behavior; Sex -- Physiologi-
cal aspects
SEXUAL BEHAVIOR, PSYCHOLOGY OF *See*

Sex -- Psychological aspects

SEXUAL CRIMES *See* Sex crimes

SEXUAL DEVIATION

    See also Sex; Sexual disorders

SEXUAL ETHICS

Freitas, D. The end of sex   **176**

Vernacchio, A. For goodness sex   **613.9**

SEXUAL ETHICS

    See also Ethics

SEXUAL ETHICS FOR TEENAGERS

Roffman, D. Talk to me first   **613.907**

SEXUAL HARASSMENT

Berebitsky, J. Sex and the office   **331.4**

Sexual violence and abuse   **364.15**

Surviving sexual violence   **362.88**

SEXUAL HARASSMENT

    See also Sex; Sexual ethics

SEXUAL HARASSMENT -- PREVENTION

Strauss, S. L. Sexual harassment and bullying   **302.34**

Sexual harassment and bullying. Strauss, S. L.   **302.34**

SEXUAL HARASSMENT IN EDUCATION

Strauss, S. L. Sexual harassment and bullying   **302.34**

SEXUAL HEALTH

Nagoski, E. Come as you are   **613.9**

SEXUAL HYGIENE

    See also Hygiene

SEXUAL LIBERATION -- POETRY

Huntington, C. Heavenly bodies   **811**

SEXUAL MINORITIES -- EDUCATION

Cahill, S. LGBT youth in America's schools **371.82**

SEXUAL MINORITIES IN LITERATURE

Naidoo, J. C. Rainbow family collections   **028.1**

SEXUAL MINORITY YOUTH -- COUNSELING OF -- NEW YORK (STATE) -- NEW YORK

Berg, R. No house to call my home   **362.786**

Sexual selections. Zuk, M.   **591.56**

Sexual violence and abuse.   **364.15**

SEXUALITY *See* Sex; Sex -- Physiological aspects; Sex -- Psychological aspects

SEXUALLY ABUSED CHILDREN *See* Child sexual abuse

Sexually transmitted disease.   **616.95**

SEXUALLY TRANSMITTED DISEASES

    See also Communicable diseases

SEXUALLY TRANSMITTED DISEASES -- ENCYCLOPEDIAS

Sexually transmitted disease   **616.95**

SEXUALLY TRANSMITTED DISEASES -- PREVENTION

    See also Sexual hygiene

Sexy feminism. Armstrong, J. K.   **305.42**

Seymour Hersh. Miraldi, R.   **92**

Seymour, Corey

Wenner, J. S. Gonzo   **92**

Seymour, Marilyn Dallman

(ed) Conversations with Nadine Gordimer   **823**

Seymour, Miranda

Mary Shelley   **92**

Sgt. Reckless. Hutton, R.   **951.904**

Shāh Shujā', Amir of Afghanistan, 1780?-1842

    About

Dalrymple, W. Return of a king   **958.1**

Shabazz, Betty

    About

Rickford, R. J. Betty Shabazz: a remarkable story of survival and faith before and after Malcolm X   **92**

Shabtai, Aharon

War & love, love & war   **892.4**

Shachtman, Tom

Absolute zero and the conquest of cold   **536**

Airlift to America   **378.1**

Rumspringa   **305.23**

Shackelford, George T. M.

Gustave Caillebotte   **759.4**

Shackleton. Smith, M.   **92**

Shackleton's forgotten expedition. Riffenburgh, B.   **998**

Shackleton, Emma

(jt. auth) Anderson, J. The art of medicine   **610**

Shackleton, Ernest Henry Sir, 1874-1922

    About

Alexander, C. The Endurance   **998**

Larson, E. J. An empire of ice   **919**

Riffenburgh, B. Shackleton's forgotten expedition   **998**

SHADE GARDENS *See* Gardening in the shade

SHADE-TOLERANT PLANTS

Wiley, K. Designing and planting a woodland garden   **635.9**

SHADES AND SHADOWS

    See also Drawing

Shades of glory. Hogan, L. D.   **796.357**

Shadid, Anthony

House of stone   **306**

Night draws near   **956.7**

Shadow. Woodward, B.   **973.92**

The **shadow** factory. Bamford, J.   **327.12**

Shadow of the Silk Road. Thubron, C.   **911**

SHADOW PANTOMIMES AND PLAYS

    See also Amateur theater; Pantomimes; Puppets and puppet plays; Shadow pictures; Theater

SHADOW PICTURES

    See also Amusements

Shadow warrior. Woods, R. B.   **92**

Shadowing the ground. Ignatow, D.   **811**

SHADOWPACT (FICTIONAL CHARACTERS)

    See also Fictional characters; Superheroes

Shadows in the vineyard. Potter, M.   **364.16**

The **shadows** of youth. Lewis, A. B.   **323.1**

Shady characters. Houston, K.   **411**

SHADY GARDENS *See* Gardening in the shade

Shaefer, H. Luke
  $2.00 a Day   **339.4**

Shaffer, Peter
  Equus   **822**
  Peter Shaffer's Amadeus   **822**

Shafir, Eldar
  Scarcity   **338.5**

Shaggy muses. Adams, M. B.   **920**

Shah, Sonia
  The body hunters   **362.1**
  The fever   **614.5**
  The storyteller's daughter   **958.1**

Shah, Tahir
  In search of King Solomon's mines   **963**

        About
  Shah, T. The Caliph's house   **964**

Shahnameh. Firdawsi   **891**

SHAHNAMEH (EPIC POEM)
  Jubber, N. Drinking arak off an ayatollah's beard   **915**

Shake the devil off. Brown, E.   **364.152**

The **Shaker** experience in America. Stein, S. J. **289**

SHAKER FURNITURE
  Huey, G. D. Shaker furniture projects

Shaker furniture projects. Huey, G. D.

SHAKERS
  Stein, S. J. The Shaker experience in America **289**
  Woo, I. The great divorce   **92**

SHAKERS -- NEW YORK (STATE)
  Woo, I. The great divorce   **92**

Shakespeare. Bryson, B.   **822.3**

Shakespeare after all. Garber, M.   **822.3**

SHAKESPEARE AND COMPANY
  The letters of Sylvia Beach   **92**

Shakespeare and modern culture. Garber, M. **822.3**

The **Shakespeare** riots. Cliff, N.   **974.4**

Shakespeare the thinker. Nuttall, A. D.   **822.3**

The **Shakespeare** thefts. Rasmussen, E.   **822.3**

The **Shakespeare** wars. Rosenbaum, R.   **822.3**

Shakespeare's kings. Norwich, J. J.   **822.3**

Shakespeare's language. Kermode, F.   **822.3**

Shakespeare's Pub. Brown, P.   **647.9**

Shakespeare's restless world. MacGregor, N.   **942.055**

Shakespeare, Nicholas
  Bruce Chatwin   **823**
  Under the sun   **92**

Shakespeare, William, 1564-1616
  The complete works   **822.3**

        About
  Baker, W. The facts on file companion to Shakespeare   **822.3**

Bate, J. Soul of the age   **822.3**

Bloom, H. Hamlet: poem unlimited   **822.3**

Bloom, H. Shakespeare: the invention of the human   **822.3**

Bloom, H. The Western canon   **809**

Boyce, C. Critical companion to William Shakespeare   **822.3**

Bryson, B. Shakespeare   **822.3**

Butler, C. The practical Shakespeare   **822.3**

Cliff, N. The Shakespeare riots   **974.4**

Collins, P. The book of William   **822.3**

Falk, D. The Science of Shakespeare   **822.3**

Frye, N. Northrop Frye on Shakespeare   **822.3**

Garber, M. Shakespeare after all   **822.3**

Garber, M. Shakespeare and modern culture **822.3**

Greenblatt, S. J. Will in the world   **822.3**

The Greenwood companion to Shakespeare **822.3**

Heylin, C. So long as men can breathe   **822.3**

Kenji Yoshino A thousand times more fair **822.3**

Kermode, F. Shakespeare's language   **822.3**

Lamb, C. Tales from Shakespeare   **822.3**

Living with Shakespeare   **822.3**

MacGregor, N. Shakespeare's restless world   **942.055**

Mays, A. E. The millionaire and the bard **822.33**

Norwich, J. J. Shakespeare's kings   **822.3**

Nuttall, A. D. Shakespeare the thinker   **822.3**

The Oxford companion to Shakespeare   **822.3**

Rasmussen, E. The Shakespeare thefts   **822.3**

Rosenbaum, R. The Shakespeare wars   **822.3**

Shapiro, J. Contested Will   **822.3**

Shapiro, J. A year in the life of William Shakespeare, 1599   **822.3**

Stoppard, T. Rosencrantz and Guildenstern are dead   **822**

Wells, S. W. Shakespeare: for all time   **822.3**

Wills, G. Verdi's Shakespeare   **822.3**

Shakespeare: for all time. Wells, S. W.   **822.3**

Shakespeare: the invention of the human. Bloom, H.   **822.3**

Shakur, Tupac

        About
  Dyson, M. E. Holler if you hear me: searching for Tupac Shakur   **92**

SHALE GAS INDUSTRY
  Wilber, T. Under the surface   **333.8**
  Zuckerman, G. The frackers   **338.2**

SHALE GAS RESERVOIRS -- POPULAR WORKS
  Prud'homme, A. Hydrofracking   **622**

Shales, Tom
  (jt. auth) Miller, J. A. Those guys have all the fun   **791.45**
  Live from New York   **791.45**

Shall we play that one together? De Barros, P.   **92**

The **shallows.** Carr, N. G.   **612.8**

Shalom, friend: the life and legacy of Yitzhak Rabin. **92**

SHAMANISM
   See also Religions

SHAMANS
   Black Elk Black Elk speaks **92**
   Steltenkamp, M. F. Black Elk, holy man of the Oglala **92**
The **Shambhala** guide to Sufism. Ernst, C. W. **297.4**

SHAME
   Ronson, J. So you've been publicly shamed **152.4**
   Tanenbaum, L. I Am Not a Slut **305.23**

SHAME
   See also Emotions
The **shame** of the nation. Kozol, J. **379**
A **shameful** act. Akcam, T. **956.6**

Shanahan, Cynthia
   (ed) Adolescent literacy in the academic disciplines **428**

Shanahan, Tim
   Runnng with the champ **796.830**

Shane, Neala
   Inspired baby names from around the world **929.4**

SHANGHAI (CHINA) -- BIOGRAPHY
   Grescoe, T. Shanghai grand **951.132**
   Schmitz, R. Street of Eternal Happiness **951.132**
Shanghai grand. Grescoe, T. **951.132**
Shanghai, 1842-1949. Dong, S. **951**

Shankar, Ravi
   (ed) Language for a new century **808.81**

Shanker, Stuart G.
   Greenspan, S. I. The first idea **153.7**

Shannon, Joyce Brennfleck
   (ed) Domestic violence sourcebook **362.82**

Shannon, Lisa
   A thousand sisters **305.9**

SHAPE
   Ball, P. Nature's patterns **500.2**

SHAPE
   See also Concepts; Geometry; Perception
The **shape** of inner space. Nadis, S. **530.1**
The **Shape** of the Eye. Estreich, G. **618.92**
The **shape** of the journey. Harrison, J. **811**
The **shape** of things to come. Marcus, G. **973**

Shapell, Benjamin
   (jt. auth) Sarna, J. D. Lincoln and the Jews **973.7**

SHAPES *See* Shape
Shapeshifting. Russell, K. K. **704.03**

Shapiro, Alan, 1952-
   Reel to reel **811**

Shapiro, Beth
   How to Clone a Mammoth **591.68**

Shapiro, David
   New and selected poems (1965-2006) **811**

Shapiro, Ellen
   Psilakis, M. How to roast a lamb **641.5**

Shapiro, Fred R.
   (ed) The Yale book of quotations **082**

Shapiro, Harvey
   (ed) Poets of World War II **811**

Shapiro, James S.
   (ed) The Columbia anthology of British poetry **821**
   Contested Will **822.3**
A year in the life of William Shakespeare, 1599 **822.3**

Shapiro, Karl Jay
   Selected poems **811**

Shapiro, Norma
   Adelson-Goldstein, J. The Oxford picture dictionary **423**

Shapiro, Susan
   The Bosnia list **92**

Shapton, Leanne
         About
   Shapton, L. Swimming studies **797.2**

Sharansky, Natan
         About
   Remnick, D. Reporting **814**

SHARECROPPING
   See also Farm tenancy
SHARED CUSTODY *See* Child custody
SHARED HOUSING
   Block, S. When Your Parent Moves in **306.874**
SHARED HOUSING
   See also Housing
SHARES OF STOCK *See* Stocks

Sharfstein, Daniel J.
   The invisible line **305.8**

Sharif, Solmaz
   Look **811.6**

Sharing God's Good Company. McCarthy, D. M. **235**
Sharing good times. Carter, J. **92**
The **shark's** paintbrush. Harman, J. **600**

SHARKS
   Compagno, L. J. V. Sharks of the world **597**
   Ebert, D. A. A pocket guide to sharks of the world **597.3**
   Eilperin, J. Demon fish **597**
Sharks of the world. Compagno, L. J. V. **597**

Sharlet, Jeff
   (ed) Believer, beware **200.9**

Sharma, Ruchir
   Breakout nations **330.91**

Sharon, Ariel
         About
   Landau, D. Arik **92**

Sharp Cogan, Martha, 1905-1999
         About
   Joukowsky, A. Defying the Nazis **940.53**

Sharp, Waitstill, 1902-1984
         About

Joukowsky, A. Defying the Nazis   **940.53**

Shattuck, Roger
  Proust's way   **843**

Shatzky, Joel
  (ed) Contemporary Jewish-American novelists **813**

Shaughnessy, Brenda
  Human dark with sugar   **811**

Shaughnessy, Jim
  The call of trains   **779**

Shavit, Ari, 1957-
  My promised land   **956.05**

Shaw, Artie, 1910-2004
About
  Nolan, T. Three chords for beauty's sake: the life of
    Artie Shaw   **92**

Shaw, Bernard, 1856-1950
  Arms and the man   **822**
  Heartbreak House   **822**
  Major Barbara   **822**
  Man and Superman   **822**
  Pygmalion . . . and My fair lady   **822**
  Saint Joan   **822**
About
  Peters, S. Bernard Shaw   **822**

Shaw, Diana
  The essential vegetarian cookbook   **641.5**

Shaw, John
  John Shaw's nature photography field guide **778.9**

Shaw, Randy
  Beyond the fields   **331.8**

Shawn, Allen
  Leonard Bernstein   **92**
About
  Shawn, A. Wish I could be there   **92**

Shawn, William, 1907-1992
About
  Fraser, K. Ornament and silence   **809**

SHAWNEE INDIANS
  Eckert, A. W. A sorrow in our heart: the life of Te-
    cumseh   **977**

SHAWNEE NATIONAL FOREST REGION
(ILL.)
  Biggers, J. Reckoning at Eagle Creek   **333.73**

She-wolves. Castor, H.   **920**

Shearer, Barbara Smith
  Shearer, B. F. State names, seals, flags, and sym-
    bols   **929.9**

Shearer, Benjamin F.
  State names, seals, flags, and symbols   **929.9**

Shearer, Stephen Michael
  Beautiful   **92**

Sheedy, Chris
  Bond, J. Who the hell is Pansy O'Hara?   **920**

Sheehan, Jason
About
  Sheehan, J. Cooking dirty   **92**

Sheehan, Neil
  A bright shining lie: John Paul Vann and America in
    Vietnam   **959.704**
  A fiery peace in a cold war   **92**

Sheehan-Dean, Aaron
  (ed) The Civil War   **973.7**

Sheehy, Gail
  New passages   **305.24**
  The silent passage: menopause   **618.1**
About
  Sheehy, G. Daring   **92**

Sheeler, Jim
  Final salute   **956.7**

SHEEP
    See also Domestic animals; Mammals

SHEEP -- ENGLAND -- LAKE DISTRICT
  Rebanks, J. The shepherd's life   **92**

SHEET METALWORK
    See also Metalwork

SHEET MUSIC
    See also Music

Sheff, Elisabeth
  Stories from the Polycule   **306.84**

Sheftall, Mordecai G.
  Blossoms in the wind   **940.54**

Sheinkin, Steve
  Bomb   **623.4**

Shelden, Michael
  Mark Twain   **92**

Sheldon, Kathy
  Felt-o-ween   **745.594**

Sheldrake, Rupert
  Dogs that know when their owners are coming
    home   **133.8**
  The sense of being stared at   **133.8**

Shell games. Welch, C.   **364.1**

Shell, G. Richard
  Springboard   **650.1**

Shelley's poetry and prose.   **821**

Shelley, Fred M.
  Lavin, S. J. Atlas of the great plains   **912**
  Atlas of American politics, 1960-2000   **973.92**

Shelley, Mary Wollstonecraft, 1797-1851
About
  Gordon, C. Romantic outlaws   **92**
  Montillo, R. The lady and her monsters   **823**
  Seymour, M. Mary Shelley   **92**

Shelley, Percy Bysshe, 1792-1822
  Poems   **821**
  Shelley's poetry and prose   **821**
About
  Lee, H. Virginia Woolf's nose   **820**

SHELLS
  Harasewych, M. G. The book of shells   **594**
  Scales, H. Spirals in Time   **594**

Shelov, Steven P.

(ed) The big book of symptoms **618.92**

(ed) Caring for your baby and young child **618.92**

SHELTER ISLAND (N.Y.) -- HISTORY

Griswold, M. The Manor **974.7**

Shen, Aisling Juanjuan, 1974-

About

Shen, A. J. A tiger's heart **92**

Shenk, David

The genius in all of us **155.2**

Shenk, Joshua Wolf

Lincoln's melancholy **92**

Shenkman, Richard

Legends, lies & cherished myths of American history **973**

Shenon, Philip

A cruel and shocking act **973.922**

Shepard, Matthew, 1976-1998

About

Jimenez, S. The Book of Matt **364.1**

Shepard, Sadia

About

Shepard, S. The girl from foreign **92**

Shepard, Sam, 1943-

Fool for love, and other plays **812**

The unseen hand and other plays **812**

About

Playwrights at work **812**

Shepard, Stephen B.

Deadlines and disruption **070.5**

Shephard, Ben

The long road home **940.53**

The **shepherd's** life. Rebanks, J. **92**

Shepherd, Margaret

Learn calligraphy **745.6**

Shepherd, Sonayia

(jt. auth) Dorn, M. Staying alive **613.6**

Shepherd, Stephen H. A.

(ed) Malory, T. Le morte Darthur, or, The hoole book of Kyng Arthur and of his noble knyghtes of the Rounde Table **398.2**

Shepherd, Sue

The 2-step low-FODMAP eating plan **641.5**

SHEPHERDS

Bell, L. Claiming ground **92**

SHEPHERDS -- ENGLAND -- LAKE DISTRICT -- BIOGRAPHY

Rebanks, J. The shepherd's life **92**

Sheremetev family

About

Smith, D. Former people **305.5**

Sheridan, Philip Henry, 1831-1888

About

Wheelan, J. Terrible swift sword **355.009**

Sheridan, Richard Brinsley

The school for scandal and other plays **822**

SHERIFFS

Abdul-Jabbar, K. Black profiles in courage **920**

Barra, A. Inventing Wyatt Earp **92**

Gardner, M. L. To hell on a fast horse **92**

Tefertiller, C. Wyatt Earp **92**

SHERLOCK HOLMES FILMS

See also Motion pictures; Mystery films

Sherlock Holmes in Babylon. **510**

Sherman. Woodworth, S. E. **92**

Sherman. Kennett, L. B. **92**

Sherman's march. Davis, B. **973.7**

Sherman, Joan R.

(ed) African-American poetry of the nineteenth century **811**

Sherman, Josepha

(ed) World folklore for storytellers **398**

Sherman, William L.

Meyer, M. C. The course of Mexican history **972**

Sherman, William T. (William Tecumseh), 1820-1891

About

Davis, B. Sherman's march **973.7**

Fellman, M. Citizen Sherman **92**

Hanson, V. D. The soul of battle **355**

Kennett, L. B. Sherman **92**

Wilson, E. Patriotic gore **810**

Woodworth, S. E. Sherman **92**

Shermer, Michael

The believing brain **153.4**

Why people believe weird things **001.9**

SHERPA (NEPALESE PEOPLE)

Zuckerman, P. Buried in the sky **796.522**

Sherr, Lynn

(ed) Failure is impossible **92**

Sally Ride **92**

Sherratt, Yvonne

Hitler's philosophers **193**

Sherrin, Ned

(ed) Oxford dictionary of humorous quotations **808.88**

Sherrod, Shirley, 1948-

About

Sherrod, S. The courage to hope **975.8**

Sherwin, Martin J.

Bird, K. American Prometheus **92**

Shesol, Jeff

Supreme power **347**

Shestov, Lev, 1866-1938

About

Milosz, C. To begin where I am **891.8**

Shetreat-Klein, Maya

The Dirt Cure **618.92**

Shetterly, Caitlin

Modified **664**

Shetterly, Susan Hand

Settled in the wild **508**

Shevelow, Kathryn

For the love of animals **179**
SHI'AH
  Hazleton, L. After the prophet **297**
  Nasr, V. The Shia revival **297**
The **Shia** revival. Nasr, V. **297**
Shields, Carol
  Jane Austen **823**
Shields, Charles J.
  And so it goes: Kurt Vonnegut: a life **92**
Shields, David
  (ed) The Inevitable **814**
Shields, David S.
  (ed) American poetry: the seventeenth and eigh-
    teenth centuries **811**
Shifflett C. M.
  (jt. auth) Esty, M. L. Conquering Concussion **617.4**
Shiffman, John
  Wittman, R. Priceless **364.1**
The **shift.** Brown, T. **616.02**
Shiller, Robert J., 1946-
  Irrational exuberance **332.63**
Shiloh. Daniel, L. J. **973.7**
SHILOH (TENN.), BATTLE OF, 1862
  Daniel, L. J. Shiloh **973.7**
  Groom, W. Shiloh, 1862 **973.7**
Shiloh, 1862. Groom, W. **973.7**
Shilon, Avi
  Menachem Begin **956.940**
Shilts, Randy
  And the band played on **362.1**
Shim, Jae K.
  Accounting handbook **657**
Shimoda, Naoko
  Artfully embroidered **746.44**
Shine. Hallowell, E. M. **658.3**
Shing-Tung Yau
  (jt. auth) Nadis, S. The shape of inner space **530.1**
Shinner, Peggy
  You feel so mortal **814**
SHINTO
  Eastern religions **200.9**
SHINTO
  See also Religions
Shiny objects. Roberts, J. A. **339.4**
SHIP CAPTAINS
  Blainey, G. Sea of dangers **92**
  Harris, J. W. The hanging of Thomas Jeremiah **92**
Ship of ghosts. Hornfischer, J. D. **940.54**
SHIP PILOTS
  See also Sailors
SHIP SALVAGE *See* Marine salvage
Shipler, David K.
  Arab and Jew **956.94**
  Freedom of speech **323.44**
  The rights of the people **323**
Shipley, Graham

  (ed) The Cambridge dictionary of classical civiliza-
    tion **938**
Shipman, Pat
  Walker, A. The wisdom of the bones **599.93**
Shipp, Steve
  Latin American and Caribbean artists of the modern
    era **920.003**
SHIPPING
  See also Transportation
SHIPPING EXECUTIVES
  Millard, C. The river of doubt **973.91**
  Renehan, E. J. Commodore **92**
SHIPWRECK VICTIMS
  Wilson, P. Lusitania **910.4**
SHIPWRECK VICTIMS -- NORTH ATLANTIC
  OCEAN -- ANECDOTES
  Wilson, P. Lusitania **910.4**
SHIPWRECKS
  Ballard, R. D. Return to Midway **940.54**
  Bathurst, B. The wreckers **910.4**
  Beneath the seven seas **930.1**
  Chowdhury, B. The last dive **363.14**
  Junger, S. The perfect storm **910.4**
  Lord, W. A night to remember **910.4**
  Peffer, R. Where divers dare **940.54**
  Scott, R. N. Many were held by the sea **940.4**
  Tougias, M. Ten hours until dawn **363.34**
SHIPWRECKS
  See also Accidents; Adventure and adven-
    turers; Disasters; Navigation; Voyages and
    travels
SHIPWRECKS -- ANTARCTIC OCEAN
  Lewis, M. Last man off **910.91**
SHIPWRECKS -- ARCTIC OCEAN -- HISTORY
  -- 19TH CENTURY
  Sides, H. In the kingdom of ice **910.4**
SHIPWRECKS -- ATLANTIC COAST (U.S.)
  Chowdhury, B. The last dive **363.14**
SHIPWRECKS -- FICTION
  Kurson, R. Pirate hunters **910.91**
  Philbrick, N. Why read Moby-Dick? **813**
SHIPWRECKS -- MARSHALL ISLANDS
  Franklin, J. 438 days **910.916**
SHIPWRECKS -- NORTH ATLANTIC OCEAN
  Peffer, R. Where divers dare **940.54**
SHIPWRECKS -- SCOTLAND -- ISLAY
  Scott, R. N. Many were held by the sea **940.4**
Shirer, William L.
  The rise and fall of the Third Reich **943.086**
Shirky, Clay
  Cognitive surplus **303.4**
Shirley Jackson. Franklin, R. **92**
Shlaes, Amity
  The forgotten man **973.91**
  Coolidge **92**
Shlaim, Avi

The iron wall **956.04**

Shlain, Leonard

Sex, time, and power **306.7**

Shnayerson, Michael

Belafonte, H. My song **92**

Shocked. Casarett, D. **616.02**

Shocked. Volk, P. **92**

Shockley, Evie

The new black **811**

Shoe dog. Knight, P. H. **92**

SHOE INDUSTRY

See also Clothing industry; Leather industry

SHOES

Crowe, L. G. The towering world of Jimmy Choo **391**

SHOES

See also Clothing and dress

Shoolery, Judith

Teller, E. Memoirs **92**

Shoot an Iraqi. Bilal, W. **92**

Shooting star: the brief arc of Joe McCarthy. Wicker, T. **92**

Shooting Victoria. Murphy, P. T. **941.081**

SHOOTINGS IN SCHOOLS See School shootings

Shop class as soulcraft. Crawford, M. B. **331**

Shop talk. Roth, P. **809**

SHOPLIFTING

See also Theft

SHOPPERS' GUIDES See Consumer education; Shopping

SHOPPING

Levine, J. Not buying it **640.73**

Underhill, P. Why we buy **658.8**

SHOPPING

See also Home economics; Purchasing

SHOPPING CENTERS AND MALLS

Underhill, P. The call of the mall **306**

SHOPPING CENTERS AND MALLS

See also Commercial buildings; Retail trade

SHOPPING MALLS See Shopping centers and malls

Shore, Debbie

Half yard gifts **646.2**

Shore, Linda

(jt. auth) White, V. The Total Skywatcher's Manual **523.8**

Shorris, Earl

The politics of heaven **973.93**

The **short** and tragic life of Robert Peace. Hobbs, J. **92**

The **short** bus. Mooney, J. **92**

SHORT FILMS

See also Motion pictures

A **Short** History of Film. Dixon, W. W. **791.43**

A **short** history of myth. Armstrong, K. **398.2**

A **short** history of nearly everything. Bryson, B. **500**

A **short** history of planet earth. Macdougall, J. D. **551.7**

A **short** history of scientific thought. Henry, J. **501**

A **short** history of the twentieth century. Lukacs, J. **909.82**

Short nights of the Shadow Catcher. Egan, T. **770.92**

The **short** Oxford history of English literature. Sanders, A. **820**

SHORT PLAYS See One act plays

SHORT STORIES

Crane, S. Prose and poetry **813**

Hurston, Z. N. Novels and stories **813**

Tales of the Marvellous and News of the Strange **892.7**

SHORT STORIES

See also Fiction

Short stories by Jesus. **226.8**

SHORT STORY

See also Authorship; Fiction; Literature

The **short** story readers' advisory. Hooper, B. **028**

Short story writers. **809**

SHORT STORY -- HISTORY AND CRITICISM

The Columbia companion to the twentieth-century American short story **813**

Hooper, B. The short story readers' advisory **028**

Maunder, A. The Facts on File companion to the British short story **823**

Short story writers **809**

Society for the Study of the Short Story. A Reader's companion to the short story in English **809**

SHORT STORY WRITERS

Achebe, C. The education of a British-protected child **92**

Achebe, C. Home and exile **823**

Ackroyd, P. Poe **92**

Adam, P. Jack London, photographer **92**

Adams, M. B. Shaggy muses **920**

Alice Walker **813**

Alice Walker's The color purple **813**

Almond, S. Candyfreak: a journey through the chocolate underbelly of America **338.4**

Almond, S. Rock and roll will save your life **781.66**

Amis, M. Experience **92**

Andersen, J. Hans Christian Andersen: a new life **92**

Angier, C. The double bond: Primo Levi, a biography **92**

Athill, D. Somewhere towards the end **92**

Atlas, J. Bellow **813**

Bailey, B. Cheever **92**

Bailey, E. T. The sound of a wild snail eating **92**

Bair, D. Simone de Beauvoir **848**

Barnes, J. Nothing to be frightened of **92**

Bartlett, R. Tolstoy **891.7**

Bass, R. Why I came West 92

Bellow, S. Saul Bellow 92

Benfey, C. E. G. A summer of hummingbirds 920

Binyon, T. J. Pushkin: a biography 92

Black women writers (1950-1980) 810

Blight, D. W. American oracle 973.7

Bloom, H. The Western canon 809

Boyd, B. Vladimir Nabokov: the American years 813

Boyd, B. Vladimir Nabokov: the Russian years 813

Boyd, V. Wrapped in rainbows 92

Boylan, J. F. I'm looking through you 92

Bradford, R. Lucky him: the life of Kingsley Amis 92

Briggs, J. Virginia Woolf: an inner life 92

Brown, F. Flaubert 92

Brown, J. The Los Angeles diaries 92

Butcher, T. Chasing the Devil 916

Buzbee, L. The yellow-lighted bookshop 002

Callow, P. Chekhov, the hidden ground 891.7

Camus, A. The rebel 303.6

Capote, T. Portraits and observations 814

Capote, T. Too brief a treat 92

Cash, J. W. Flannery O'Connor: a life 92

Chabon, M. Manhood for amateurs 92

Chekhov, A. P. Anton Chekhov's life and thought 92

Conant, J. The irregulars 940.54

Conversations with Nadine Gordimer 823

Crane, H. Complete poems and selected letters 811

Danticat, E. Brother, I'm dying 92

Danticat, E. Create dangerously 92

Daugherty, T. Hiding man 92

Daugherty, T. Just one catch 92

Davis, J. E. An Everglades providence 92

Dubus, A. Townie 92

Elie, P. The life you save may be your own 810

Eller, J. R. Becoming Ray Bradbury 92

Ellison, R. The collected essays of Ralph Ellison 814

Ellison, R. Going to the territory 818

Ellmann, R. James Joyce 92

Erdrich, L. Books and islands in Ojibwe country 92

Existentialism from Dostoevsky to Sartre 142

Fargnoli, A. N. Critical companion to James Joyce 823

Fargnoli, A. N. Critical companion to William Faulkner 813

Farrell, S. E. Critical companion to Kurt Vonnegut 813

Fisher, C. Wishful drinking 92

Fisher, J. T. On the Irish waterfront 331.7

Fitzgerald, F. S. A life in letters 813

Flanders, J. A circle of sisters 920

Folklore, memoirs, and other writings 398

Frank, J. Dostoevsky 92

Fraser, K. Ornament and silence 809

French, P. The world is what it is 92

Garcia Marquez, G. Living to tell the tale 92

Gates, H. L. Thirteen ways of looking at a black man 920.71

Gilbert, E. Eat, pray, love 92

Gillespie, C. Critical companion to Alice Walker 813

Gilmour, D. The long recessional: the imperial life of Rudyard Kipling 92

Gioia, D. Can poetry matter? 809.1

Gooch, B. Flannery 92

Gordon, L. G. The world of Samuel Beckett, 1906-1946 848

Greene, G. Graham Greene 92

Gunn, J. E. Isaac Asimov 813

Hastings, S. The secret lives of Somerset Maugham 92

Hazzard, S. The ancient shore 945

Hedrick, J. D. Harriet Beecher Stowe 92

Heintzelman, G. Critical companion to Tennessee Williams 812

Hogan, L. The woman who watches over the world 818

Hughes, L. I wonder as I wander 818

Hurston, Z. N. Dust tracks on a road 92

Hutchinson, G. In search of Nella Larsen 92

J.D. Salinger 813

Jarrell, R. No other book 809

Jones, S. L. Critical companion to Zora Neale Hurston 813

Joseph Roth 92

Kafka, d. J. d. E. Kafka, the decisive years 92

Kazin, A. An American procession 810

Keene, D. Five modern Japanese novelists 895.6

Kellman, S. G. Redemption: the life of Henry Roth 92

Ker, I. G. K. Chesterton 828

Kermode, F. Concerning E.M. Forster 823

Kiberd, D. Ulysses and us 823

Kiernan, F. Seeing Mary plain: a life of Mary McCarthy 818

King, D. Patrick O'Brian 823

King, S. On writing 813

Kirk, C. A. Critical companion to Flannery O'Connor 813

Kurzke, H. Thomas Mann 92

Langer, L. L. Admitting the Holocaust 940.53

Leader, Z. The life of Kingsley Amis 92

Lee, H. Edith Wharton 92

Lee, H. Virginia Woolf 823

Lee, H. Virginia Woolf's nose 820

Lee, H. Willa Cather 92

Leibowitz, H. A. Something urgent I have to say to you: the life and works of William Carlos Williams 92

Lessing, D. M. Under my skin 92

Leverich, L. Tom   92

Levi, P. The periodic table   92

Life stories   920

Lively, P. A house unlocked   92

Long, R. E. Truman Capote, enfant terrible   92

Loving, J. Mark Twain   92

Lynn, K. S. Hemingway   92

Malcolm, J. Reading Chekhov   891.7

Malone, J. W. It doesn't take a rocket scientist 920

Mariani, P. L. The broken tower: a life of Hart Crane   811

Marrs, S. Eudora Welty: a biography   92

Marshall, P. Triangular road   92

Martin, G. Gabriel Garcia Marquez   92

Matthiessen, F. O. American renaissance   810

McCracken, E. An exact replica of a figment of my imagination   92

McCrum, R. Wodehouse   92

McMurtry, L. Books   92

McMurtry, L. Walter Benjamin at the Dairy Queen   818

McPherson, J. M. Drawn with the sword   973.7

Meade, M. Dorothy Parker   92

Miller, N. New world coming   973.91

Miller, S. The story of my father   92

Milosz, C. Legends of modernity   891.8

Milosz, C. To begin where I am   891.8

Moffat, W. A great unrecorded history   92

Morris, R. Ambrose Bierce   92

Moser, B. Why this world   92

Murphy, M. M. Scout, Atticus, and Boo   813

Murray, A. The blue devils of Nada   780.89

Murray, N. Kafka   92

Nabokov, V. V. Lectures on literature   808.3

Nabokov, V. V. Lectures on Russian literature 891.7

Nabokov, V. V. Speak, memory   813

Nadel, I. B. Critical companion to Philip Roth 813

Naipaul, V. S. Between father and son   823

Naipaul, V. S. Reading & writing   92

Oates, J. C. A widow's story   92

Oates, J. C. The journal of Joyce Carol Oates: 1973-1982   92

O'Brien, E. James Joyce   823

O'Connor, F. The habit of being   92

Oliver, C. M. Critical companion to Ernest Hemingway   813

The Oxford companion to Mark Twain   818

Oz, A. A tale of love and darkness   92

Ozick, C. Quarrel & quandary   814

Parini, J. One matchless time   92

Paulsen, G. Winterdance   798.8

Pierpont, C. R. Passionate minds   810

Playwrights at work   812

Plimpton, G. Truman Capote   813

Powers, R. Mark Twain   92

Price, R. Ardent spirits   92

Pritchard, W. H. Updike   813

Proulx, A. Bird cloud   92

Rampersad, A. The life of Langston Hughes Volume I: 1902-1941   92

Rampersad, A. The life of Langston Hughes Volume II: 1941-1967   818

Rampersad, A. Ralph Ellison   92

Rao, C. In Hanuman's hands   92

Remnick, D. Reporting   814

Reynolds, D. S. Mightier than the sword   813

Reynolds, M. S. Hemingway: the Paris years   92

Ricketts, H. Rudyard Kipling   92

Robb, G. Balzac   92

Rollyson, C. E. Susan Sontag   818

Roth, P. The facts   813

Rowley, H. Richard Wright   813

Said, E. W. Reflections on exile and other essays   814

Sallis, J. Chester Himes   813

Samuel Beckett's Waiting for Godot   842

Sanders, S. R. A private history of awe   92

Sartre, J. P. The words   92

Savigneau, J. Carson McCullers   813

Sebald, W. G. On the natural history of destruction   833

Shelden, M. Mark Twain   92

Shields, C. J. And so it goes: Kurt Vonnegut: a life   92

Silverman, K. Edgar A. Poe   92

Singer, I. B. More stories from my father's court   839

Sklenicka, C. Raymond Carver   92

Slawenski, K. J.D. Salinger   92

Smiley, J. Thirteen ways of looking at the novel   813

Smith, J. M. My father is a book   92

Smith, Z. Changing my mind   824

Sontag, S. Reborn   92

Sova, D. B. Critical companion to Edgar Allan Poe   818

Spoto, D. The kindness of strangers: the life of Tennessee Williams   92

Spring, J. Secret historian   92

Stannard, M. Muriel Spark   92

Stashower, D. The beautiful cigar girl   364.152

Sturrock, D. Storyteller   92

Sutherland, J. Stephen Spender   92

Tan, A. The opposite of fate   814

Tate, M. J. Critical companion to F. Scott Fitzgerald   813

Theroux, P. Dark star safari   916

Thomas, A. A three dog life   92

Thurman, J. Isak Dinesen   92

Tolstaia, T. Pushkin's children   891.7

Tomalin, C. Thomas Hardy   92

Treglown, J. V.S. Pritchett: a working life   92

Trillin, C. Quite enough of Calvin Trillin **817**

Trillin, C. About Alice **92**

Tuck, L. Woman of Rome: a life of Elsa Morante **92**

Ulrich, L. Well-behaved women seldom make history **305.4**

Unferth, D. O. Revolution **920**

Vollmann, W. T. Poor people **362.5**

Wainaina, B. One day I will write about this place **823**

Waldron, A. Eudora **92**

Walker, A. The same river twice **813**

Wall, C. A. Women of the Harlem Renaissance **810**

Walsh, J. E. Midnight dreary **818**

Weldon, F. Auto da Fay **823**

Weller, S. The Bradbury chronicles **92**

Welty, E. One writer's beginnings **92**

What I talk about when I talk about running **92**

What there is to say we have said **92**

White, E. City boy **92**

White, E. The flaneur **944.083**

White, E. My lives **813**

Wideman, J. E. Hoop roots **813**

William Faulkner **813**

Williamson, E. Borges, a life **92**

Wilson, E. Patriotic gore **810**

Wineapple, B. Hawthorne: a life **92**

Wolff, T. This boy's life: a memoir **92**

Woodress, J. L. Willa Cather **92**

Woolf, V. A moment's liberty: the shorter diary **92**

Woolf, V. Moments of being **823**

Worthen, J. D.H. Lawrence **92**

Worthen, J. D.H. Lawrence, the early years, 1885-1912 **92**

Wright, R. Black boy **92**

Wright, S. B. Critical companion to Nathaniel Hawthorne **813**

Wullschlager, J. Hans Christian Andersen **839.8**

Zora Neale Hurston **813**

Zora Neale Hurston: a life in letters **92**

The **short** sweet dream of Eduardo Gutierrez. Breslin, J. **331.6**

Short, Martin, 1950-
About
Short, M. I must say **92**

Short, Philip
Mao **951.05**

SHORTAGES See Scarcity

Shortall, Jessica
Work. Pump. Repeat. **649.33**

Shortcut. Pollack, J. **808**

A **shortcut** through time. Johnson, G. **004.1**

Shorter Oxford English dictionary on historical principles. **423**

Shorter, Edward
A history of psychiatry **616.89**

SHORTHAND
See also Business education; Office practice; Writing

Shorto, Russell
Amsterdam **949.2**

SHORTWAVE RADIO
See also Radio; Radio frequency modulation

Shostakovich, Dmitrii Dmitrievich, 1906-1975
About
Volkov, S. St. Petersburg **947**

SHOTGUNS
See also Guns

Shotton, Heather J.
(ed) Beyond the asterisk **378.1**

Shoulda been Jimi Savannah. Smith, P. **811**

Shouting won't help. Bouton, K. **617.8**

SHOW BUSINESS See Performing arts

Show me a story. Neuburger, E. K. **741.6**

SHOW WINDOWS
See also Advertising; Decoration and ornament; Windows

Showalter, Dennis E.
Patton and Rommel **92**

Showalter, Elaine
The Cambridge guide to women's writing in English **820**

A jury of her peers **810**

Showdown. Haygood, W. **347.73**

SHOWING OFF
See also Human behavior

Showtime. Stempel, L. **792.6**

Shrewsbury, Anna Maria Brudenell Talbot, Countess of, 1642-1702
About
Livingstone, N. The mistresses of Cliveden **942.009**

Shrinking the Earth. Worster, D. **304.2**

Shrinks. Lieberman, J. A. **616.89**

Shriver, Mark
Pilgrimage **282.092**

Shriver, Timothy
Fully alive **796.087**

Shroder, Tom
Acid test **615.7**

Shroom. **641.658**

The **shrub** identification book. Symonds, G. W. D. **582.1**

The **shrubberies.** Johnson, R. **811**

SHRUBS
Dirr, M. A. Dirr's encyclopedia of trees and shrubs **635.9**

Dirr, M. Dirr's Hardy trees and shrubs **635.9**

Dirr, M. Dirr's trees and shrubs for warm climates **635.9**

Fisher, K. Taylor's guide to shrubs **635.9**

Gardiner, J. The Timber Press encyclopedia of flowering shrubs **635.9**

The Hillier gardener's guide to trees & shrubs **635.9**

McIndoe, A. The creative shrub garden **635.9**

O'Sullivan, P. The homeowner's complete tree & shrub handbook **635.9**

Symonds, G. W. D. The shrub identification book **582.1**

SHRUBS

See also Plants; Trees

Shteyngart, Gary, 1972-

About

Shteyngart, G. Little failure **92**

Shubin, Neil H., 1960-

The universe within **550**

Your inner fish **611**

Shulevitz, Judith

The Sabbath world **296.4**

Shulevitz, Uri

Writing with pictures **808.06**

Shulman, Alix Kates

About

Shulman, A. K. To love what is **92**

Shulman, Beth

The betrayal of work **331.2**

Shulman, Lisa M.

Lang, A. E. Parkinson's disease **616.8**

Shulman, Martha Rose

The art of French pastry **641.86**

Mediterranean harvest **641.5**

The simple art of vegetarian cooking **641.5**

The very best of recipes for health **641.5**

Shulman, Seth

Cooler smarter **363.7**

The telephone gambit **621.3**

Shultz, Richard H.

The secret war against Hanoi **959.704**

Shunk, Stephen A.

Peterson Reference Guide to Woodpeckers of North America **598.7**

Shuster, Joe

About

Ricca, B. Super boys **92**

SHYNESS

Fonseca, C. Raising the shy child **649**

SHYNESS

See also Emotions

SIBERIA (RUSSIA) -- DESCRIPTION AND TRAVEL

Frazier, I. Travels in Siberia **957**

Thubron, C. In Siberia **957**

Vaillant, J. The tiger **599.75**

The **Sibley** field guide to birds of Eastern North America. Sibley, D. **598**

The **Sibley** field guide to birds of Western North America. Sibley, D. **598**

The **Sibley** guide to bird life & behavior. Sibley, D. **598**

The **Sibley** guide to birds. Sibley, D. **598**

The **Sibley** guide to trees. Sibley, D. **582.16**

Sibley's birding basics. Sibley, D. **598**

Sibley, David

The Sibley field guide to birds of Eastern North America **598**

The Sibley field guide to birds of Western North America **598**

The Sibley guide to bird life & behavior **598**

The Sibley guide to birds **598**

The Sibley guide to trees **582.16**

Sibley's birding basics **598**

Siblin, Eric

The cello suites **787.3**

SIBLING RIVALRY

See also Child psychology; Siblings

SIBLINGS

Harris, S. L. Siblings of Children With Autism **618.92**

SIBLINGS

See also Family

Siblings of Children With Autism. Harris, S. L. **618.92**

SIBLINGS OF PRESIDENTS

Clarke, T. The last campaign **92**

English, B. Last lion **92**

Kennedy, E. M. True compass **92**

Mahoney, R. D. Sons and brothers: the days of Jack and Bobby Kennedy **92**

Schlesinger, A. M. Robert Kennedy and his times **92**

Thomas, E. Robert Kennedy **92**

Sicherer, Scott H.

Food allergies **616.97**

Understanding and managing your child's food allergies **618.92**

Sicherman, Barbara

(ed) Notable American women: the modern period **920.003**

Sicile-Kira, Chantal

(jt. auth) Rodriguez, A. M. Autism spectrum disorders **616.85**

Sicily. Norwich, J. J. **945.8**

SICILY (ITALY)

Norwich, J. J. Sicily **945.8**

SICILY (ITALY) -- DESCRIPTION AND TRAVEL

Keahey, J. Seeking Sicily **945**

SICK

Kore **610**

Pogrebin, L. C. How to be a friend to a friend who's sick **610**

Reiner, J. The man who couldn't eat **92**

Whitehouse, B. The match **92**

SICK

See also People with disabilities

SICK -- PRAYERS
   See also Prayers
SICK CHILDREN -- PSYCHOLOGY
   Keene, N. Your Child in the Hospital   **362.1**
Sick in the head. Apatow, J.   **792.7**
Sickles, Daniel E., 1825-1914
         About
   Keneally, T. American scoundrel: the life of the no-
   torious Civil War General Dan Sickles   **92**
SICKNESS *See* Diseases
SIDDUR
   Wagner, J. L. The synagogue survival kit   **296.4**
SIDE DISHES (COOKING)
   Michael Symon's 5 in 5 for every season   **641.81**
Sides, Hampton
   Blood and thunder   **978**
   Ghost soldiers   **940.54**
   Hellhound on his trail   **364.152**
   In the kingdom of ice   **910.4**
SIDING (BUILDING MATERIALS)
   Black & Decker Corp. The complete guide to roof-
   ing, siding & trim   **695**
   The complete guide to roofing & siding   **695**
Sidney Poitier. Goudsouzian, A.   **92**
Sieberson, Steve
         About
   Sieberson, S. The naked mountaineer   **92**
Siegal, Allan
   The New York times manual of style and usage **808**
The **siege.** Levy, A.   **363.325**
Siegel, Barry
   Manifest injustice   **364.152**
Siegel, Bernie S.
   Prescriptions for living   **158**
Siegel, Daniel J.
   Brainstorm   **155.5**
   No-drama discipline   **649**
   The whole-brain child   **649**
Siegel, David
   Pull   **658.8**
Siegel, Frederick F.
   The prince of the city   **92**
Siegel, Harry
   Siegel, F. F. The prince of the city   **92**
Siegel, Jeremy J.
   Stocks for the long run   **332.63**
Siegel, Jerry, 1914-1996
         About
   Ricca, B. Super boys   **92**
Siegel, Joel G.
   (jt. auth) Shim, J. K. Accounting handbook   **657**
Siegel, Lawrence M.
   The complete IEP guide   **371.9**
Siegel, Shanyn
   (ed)   The   seed   garden
SIEGES *See* Battles

Siegler, Melody
   Eisner, T. Secret weapons   **595.7**
Sielski, Mike
   Fading echoes   **92**
Siems, Larry
   (ed) Guantanamo diary   **958.104**
Sienkewicz, Thomas J.
   (ed) Ancient Greece   **938**
   (ed) Encyclopedia of the ancient world   **930**
**SIERRA LEONE -- DESCRIPTION AND TRAV-
EL**
   Butcher, T. Chasing the Devil   **916**
**SIERRA LEONE -- HISTORY -- CIVIL WAR,
1991-2002**
   Beah, I. A long way gone   **92**
**SIERRA LEONEANS -- UNITED STATES --
HISTORY -- 19TH CENTURY**
   Rediker, M. The Amistad rebellion   **326**
SIERRA MADRE MOUNTAINS
   Gallagher, T. Imperial Dreams   **598.7**
Sifakis, Carl
   The mafia encyclopedia   **364.1**
Sife, Wallace
   The loss of a pet   **155.9**
Siff, Jason
   Thoughts are not the enemy   **294.3**
Sifters: Native American women's lives.   **920**
Sigerman, Harriet
   The Columbia documentary history of American
   women since 1941   **305.4**
SIGHT *See* Vision
SIGHT SAVING BOOKS *See* Large print books
SIGN LANGUAGE
   Grayson, G. Talking with your hands, listening
   with your eyes   **419**
   Sacks, O. W. Seeing voices   **362.4**
   Sternberg, M. L. A. American Sign Language **419**
SIGN LANGUAGE
   See also Language and languages
SIGN LANGUAGE -- DICTIONARIES
   Costello, E. Random House Webster's American
   Sign Language dictionary: unabridged   **419**
   The Gallaudet dictionary of American Sign Lan-
   guage   **419**
   Sternberg, M. L. A. American Sign Language **419**
   Tennant, R. A. The American Sign Language hand-
   shape dictionary   **419**
SIGN PAINTING
   See also Advertising; Industrial painting
The **signal** and the noise. Silver, N.   **519.5**
SIGNALS AND SIGNALING
   See also Communication; Military art and
   science; Naval art and science; Navigation;
   Signs and symbols
Signature styles. Doh, J.   **646.4**
Signer, Michael

Becoming Madison **92**

SIGNETS *See* Seals (Numismatics)

SIGNS AND SIGNBOARDS

> *See also* Advertising; Visual communication

SIGNS AND SYMBOLS

Biedermann, H. Dictionary of symbolism **302.2**

Minahan, J. The complete guide to national symbols and emblems **929.9**

SIGNS AND SYMBOLS

> *See also* Communication; Visual communication

SIGNS AND SYMBOLS -- HISTORY

Houston, K. Shady characters **411**

SIGNS AND SYMBOLS IN LITERATURE *See* Symbolism in literature

Signs of the zodiac. Snodgrass, M. E. **133.5**

SIKHISM

> *See also* Religions

The **Sikhs.** Singh, P. **294.6**

SIKHS

Singh, P. The Sikhs **294.6**

Sikka, Madhulika

A breast cancer alphabet **616.99**

Sikov, Ed

On Sunset Boulevard: the life and times of Billy Wilder **92**

Silberman, Neil Asher

(ed) The Oxford Companion to Archaeology **930.1**

Silcoff, Sean

(jt. auth) McNish, J. Losing the signal **338.4**

SILENCE

> *See also* Sound

A **silence** of mockingbirds. Zacharias, K. S. **364.152**

The **silent** deep. Koslow, J. A. **578.7**

SILENT FILMS

> *See also* Motion pictures

The **silent** passage: menopause. Sheehy, G. **618.1**

Silent spring. Carson, R. **363.7**

The **silent** treatment. Howard, R. **811**

Silent witnesses. McCrery, N. **363.25**

SILK

> *See also* Fabrics; Fibers

SILK ROAD -- HISTORY

Frankopan, P. The Silk Roads **909**

The **Silk** Roads. Frankopan, P. **909**

SILK SCREEN PRINTING

Corwin, L. Printing by hand **745.5**

SILK SCREEN PRINTING

> *See also* Color printing; Stencil work

Silko, Leslie

Storyteller **818**

SILKWORMS

> *See also* Beneficial insects; Insects; Moths

Sillett, Steve

> **About**

Preston, R. The wild trees **577.3**

SILVER

> *See also* Chemical elements; Precious metals

The **Silver** Lining. Jacobs, H. **616.99**

SILVER MINES AND MINING

> *See also* Mines and mineral resources

The **Silver** Palate cookbook. **641.5**

The **silver** spoon. **641.5**

The **Silver** Spoon. **641.59**

Silver, Alain

(ed) Film noir **791.43**

Silver, Daniel B.

Refuge in hell **362.1**

Silver, H. Ward

Ham radio for dummies **621.384**

Silver, Johanna

The bold dry garden **635.9**

Silver, Julie K.

(ed) Will my cancer come back? **616.99**

Silver, Marc

Breast cancer husband **616.99**

Silver, Nate

The signal and the noise **519.5**

Silverman, Kenneth

Begin again **92**

Edgar A. Poe **92**

Silverstone, Alicia, 1976-

The kind mama **618.1**

Silverton, Nancy

Mozza at home **641.5**

SILVERWORK

> *See also* Art metalwork; Metalwork; Silver

Simic, Charles, 1938-

The Lunatic **811**

New and selected poems 1962-2012 **811**

The voice at 3:00 a.m **811**

Simkin, Penny

The Birth Partner **618.2**

Simmons, Bill

The book of basketball **796.323**

Simmons, Marie

Whole world vegetarian **641.5**

Simmons, Rachel

Odd girl out **305.23**

Simmons, Sylvie

I'm your man **92**

Simms, Brendan

The longest afternoon **940.2**

Simon and Garfunkel

Browne, D. Fire and rain **781.66**

Simon Wiesenthal. Pick, H. **940.53**

Simon Wiesenthal. Segev, T. **92**

Simon, Carly, 1945-

> **About**

Simon, C. Boys in the trees **92**

Weller, S. Girls like us **920**

Simon, Daniel

(ed) Vonnegut, K. A man without a country **814**

Simon, James F.

FDR and Chief Justice Hughes **973.917**

What kind of nation **342**

Simon, Joel

The new censorship **363.31**

Simon, Marie Jalowicz

Underground in Berlin **940.531**

Simon, Neil

Brighton Beach memoirs **812**

The collected plays of Neil Simon **812**

Lost in Yonkers **812**

About

Playwrights at work **812**

Simon, N. The play goes on **812**

Simon, N. Rewrites **812**

Simon, Scott

About

Simon, S. Unforgettable **92**

Simon, William L.

(jt. auth) Manning, R. Mars Rover Curiosity **629.295**

(jt. auth) Mitnick, K. D. Ghost in the wires **364.16**

Simonds, Nina

Spices of life **641.5**

Simone de Beauvoir. Bair, D. **848**

Simone, Nina

About

Cohodas, N. Princess Noire **92**

Simons, Daniel

(jt. auth) Chabris, C. The invisible gorilla **153.7**

Simons, Eric

The Secret Lives of Sports Fans **306.4**

Simons, Jeffrey

(ed) Startalk **523.1**

Simonson, Robert

A proper drink **641.87**

Simonyi, Károly, 1916-2011

A cultural history of physics **530**

Simple. Henry, D. **641.5**

The **simple** art of vegetarian cooking. Shulman, M. R. **641.5**

Simple French food. Olney, R. **641.59**

SIMPLE MACHINES

See also Machinery; Mechanical movements; Mechanics

Simple Rules. Sull, D. **650.1**

The **simple** truth. Levine, P. **811**

Simpler. Sunstein, C. R. **973.932**

SIMPLICITY

Mitchell, R. Tiny house living **728**

SIMPLICITY

See also Conduct of life

SIMPLICITY -- RELIGIOUS ASPECTS -- CHRISTIANITY

Becker, J. The more of less **241.68**

Davis, W. Enough **241**

Soukup, R. Unstuffed **646.7**

Simply ancient grains. **641.6**

Simply Einstein. Wolfson, R. **530.1**

Simply Nigella. Lawson, N. **641.5**

Simply sewn. Ito, M. **646.4**

Simpson, Brooks D.

(ed) The Civil War **973.7**

Simpson, J. A.

(ed) The Oxford English dictionary **423**

About

Simpson, J. The word detective **423.092**

Simpson, John

The word detective **423.092**

Simpson, Louis Aston Marantz

The owner of the house **811**

Simpson, O. J., 1947-

About

Gates, H. L. Thirteen ways of looking at a black man **920.71**

SIMPSONS (TELEVISION PROGRAM)

Singh, S. The Simpsons and their mathematical secrets **510**

The **Simpsons** and their mathematical secrets. Singh, S. **510**

Sims, Michael

Apollo's fire **529**

SIMULATION GAMES

McGonigal, J. Reality is broken **306.4**

SIMULATION GAMES

See also Game theory

SIMULATION GAMES IN EDUCATION

See also Education; Educational games; Game theory

SIMULTANEITY (PHYSICS)

Mazur, J. Fluke **519.2**

SIN

The concept of anxiety **233**

Jacobs, A. Original sin **233**

SIN

See also Ethics; Good and evil; Theology

Sin in the Second City. Abbott, K. **977.3**

Sin, Sang-ok, 1926-2006

About

Fischer, P. A Kim Jong-Il production **791.43**

SINAI CAMPAIGN, 1956

See also Egypt -- History; Israel-Arab conflicts

Sinatra. Kaplan, J. **92**

Sinatra in Hollywood. Santopietro, T. **92**

Sinatra! the song is you. Friedwald, W. **92**

Sinatra, Frank, 1915-1998

About

Friedwald, W. Sinatra! the song is you **92**

Kaplan, J. Frank **92**

Kaplan, J. Sinatra **92**

Santopietro, T. Sinatra in Hollywood   92

Sincerity. Magill, R. J.   179

SINCERITY

Magill, R. J. Sincerity   179

Sinclair, Safiya

Cannibal   **811.6**

Sing me back home. Jennings, D. A.   **781.642**

SINGAPORE -- DESCRIPTION AND TRAVEL

Eyewitness Travel Malaysia & Singapore   **915.9**

Singer perfect plus. Cheetham, K.   **646.2**

Singer upholstery basics plus. Cone, S.   **684.1**

Singer, Carol A.

Fundamentals of Managing Reference Collections   **025.2**

Singer, Isaac Bashevis, 1904-1991

About

Singer, I. B. More stories from my father's court   839

Singer, Mark

Character studies   920

Singer, P. W.

Wired for war   355

SINGERS

Andrews, J. Home   92

Angelou, M. Letter to my daughter   92

Angelou, M. I know why the caged bird sings   92

Angelou, M. A song flung up to heaven   818

Armstrong, L. Louis Armstrong, in his own words   92

The Beatles anthology   **782.421**

Belafonte, H. My song   92

Black women writers (1950-1980)   **810**

Bogle, D. Heat wave   92

Brightman, C. Sweet chaos   920

Brown, J. James Brown, the godfather of soul   92

Browne, D. Fire and rain   **781.66**

Burke, C. No regrets   92

Byrne, D. Bicycle diaries   **796.6**

Carroll, D. The legs are the last to go   92

Cash, R. Composed   92

Clapton, E. Clapton   92

Clarke, G. Get happy: the life of Judy Garland   92

Cohodas, N. Princess Noire   92

Cole, N. Angel on my shoulder   92

Coleman, R. Blue Monday   92

Cross, C. R. Heavier than heaven: a biography of Kurt Cobain   92

Cross, C. R. Room full of mirrors   92

Crowell, R. Chinaberry sidewalks   92

Dance, S. The world of Count Basie   920

Davis, P. G. The American opera singer   920

Dunaway, D. K. How can I keep from singing?   92

Dylan, B. Chronicles   92

Epstein, D. M. Nat King Cole   92

Escott, C. Hank Williams   92

Feather, L. From Satchmo to Miles   920

Flinn, C. Brass diva   92

Friedwald, W. A biographical guide to the great jazz and pop singers   **920.003**

Friedwald, W. Sinatra! the song is you   92

Gates, H. L. Thirteen ways of looking at a black man   **920.71**

Gavin, J. Stormy weather   92

George-Warren, H. Public cowboy no. 1   92

Giddins, G. Bing Crosby: a pocketful of dreams: the early years, 1903-1940   92

Gillespie, M. A. Maya Angelou   92

Govenar, A. B. Lightnin' Hopkins   92

Grant, C. The natural mystics   920

Gray, M. The Bob Dylan encyclopedia   **782.42**

Gray, M. Hand me my travelin' shoes   92

Greenberg, K. E. December 8, 1980   92

The Grove book of opera singers   920

Guralnick, P. Careless love: the unmaking of Elvis Presley   92

Guralnick, P. Dream boogie   92

Hemphill, P. Lovesick blues   92

Hischak, T. The Oxford companion to the American musical   **792.6**

Holiday, B. Lady sings the blues   92

Hopkins, J. No one here gets out alive   92

Hoskyns, B. Lowside of the road   92

Ian, J. Society's child   92

Inaba, M. Willie Dixon   92

Jackson, B. Garcia   92

James, E. Rage to survive   92

Kaplan, J. Frank   92

Kaufman, D. Doris Day   92

King, B. B. Blues all around me   **781.643**

Klein, J. Woody Guthrie   92

Kleist, R. Johnny Cash   92

Kruth, J. To live's to fly   92

Lees, G. You can't steal a gift   **781.65**

Leonard Cohen on Leonard Cohen   92

Lewis, J. Dean & me   92

Lynn, L. Still woman enough   92

Mann, W. J. Hello, gorgeous   92

Mason, B. A. Elvis Presley   92

Mazor, B. Meeting Jimmie Rodgers   92

McDonough, J. Tammy Wynette   92

Murray, A. The blue devils of Nada   **780.89**

Murray, C. S. Crosstown traffic: Jimi Hendrix and the post-war rock'n'roll revolution   **787.87**

Norman, P. John Lennon   92

Osbourne, O. I am Ozzy   92

Patoski, J. N. Willie Nelson   92

Riley, T. Lennon   92

Riordan, J. Break on through: the life and death of Jim Morrison   92

Robeson, P. Here I stand   92

Robeson, P. The undiscovered Paul Robeson   92

Santopietro, T. Sinatra in Hollywood   92

Schumacher, M. Crossroads   92
Simon, C. Boys in the trees   92
Sounes, H. Fab   92
Spitz, B. The Beatles: the biography   920
Streissguth, M. Johnny Cash   92
Sullivan, J. The hardest working man   92
Trynka, P. Iggy Pop   92
Turner, T. I, Tina   92
Victor, A. The Elvis encyclopedia   781.66
Wald, E. Escaping the delta   92
Walker-Hill, H. From spirituals to symphonies 780
Wareham, D. Black postcards   92
Weller, S. Girls like us   920
White, C. The life and times of Little Richard 92
Wilkinson, A. The protest singer   92
Wolfe, C. K. The life and legend of Leadbelly 92
Zevon, C. I'll sleep when I'm dead   92
Zwonitzer, M. Will you miss me when I'm
    gone?   781.642
SINGERS
    See also Musicians
SINGERS -- BIOGRAPHY
    Brownstein, C. Hunger Makes Me a Modern
    Girl   92
    Jewel Never broken   92
    Kaufman, D. Some enchanted evenings   92
SINGERS -- CANADA -- INTERVIEWS
    Leonard Cohen on Leonard Cohen   92
SINGERS -- DICTIONARIES
    Friedwald, W. A biographical guide to the great
    jazz and pop singers   920.003
SINGERS -- UNITED STATES
    James, E. Rage to survive   92
    Robeson, P. The undiscovered Paul Robeson 92
SINGERS -- UNITED STATES -- BIOGRAPHY
    Bell, I. Once upon a time   92
    Brownstein, C. Hunger Makes Me a Modern
    Girl   92
    Cee-Lo Everybody's brother   782.421
    Clarke, G. Get happy: the life of Judy Garland 92
    Cole, N. Angel on my shoulder   92
    Jewel Never broken   92
    Kaplan, J. Sinatra   92
    Kaufman, D. Some enchanted evenings 92
    Lauper, C. Cyndi Lauper   92
    Mann, W. J. Hello, gorgeous   92
    Simon, C. Boys in the trees   92
Singh, Patwant
    The Sikhs   294.6
Singh, Simon
    Big bang: the origins of the universe 523.1
    Fermat's enigma   512
    The Simpsons and their mathematical secrets 510
SINGING
    See also Music
SINGING GAMES

    See also Games
The **singing** life of birds. Kroodsma, D. E.   598
Singing my him song. McCourt, M.   974.7
The **singing** neanderthals. Mithen, S. J.   780.9
Singing School. Pinsky, R.   808.1
SINGLE CHILD *See* Only child
**SINGLE MOTHERS -- UNITED STATES -- BI-
    OGRAPHY**
    Thorpe, H. Soldier girls   956.704
SINGLE PARENTS
    Markus, J. Lady Byron and Her Daughters   92
    Weldon, M. Escape Points   362.196
    Winik, M. The lunch-box chronicles   306.85
SINGLE PARENTS
    See also Parents; Unmarried couples
SINGLE WOMEN
    Bolick, K. Spinster   92
    Hauser, B. Enter Helen   92
Singular, Joyce
    (jt. auth) Singular, S. The Spiral Notebook 364.152
Singular, Stephen
    The Spiral Notebook   364.152
SINGULARITIES (MATHEMATICS)
    See also Geometry
The **singularity** is near. Kurzweil, R.   153.9
Sinha, Manisha
    The Slave's cause   973.711
SINO-JAPANESE CONFLICT, 1937-1945
    Chang, I. The rape of Nanking   951.04
    Hicks, G. The comfort women   940.54
    Tuchman, B. W. Stilwell and the American experi-
    ence in China, 1911-45   327
**SINO-JAPANESE WAR, 1937-1945 -- SOCIAL
    ASPECTS -- CHINA -- SHANGAHI**
    Grescoe, T. Shanghai grand   951.132
Sinton, Nan
    Michener, D. Taylor's guide to ground covers 635.9
Sir Gawain and the Green Knight.   398.2
Sirhan, Kamilah, d. 2001
                    About
    Hikayati sharhun yatul./English The locust and the
    bird   92
SIRIUS
    See also Stars
Sirota, David
    Back to our future   973.92
Sisman, Adam
    Boswell's presumptuous task   828
Sisodia, Raj
    (jt. auth) Chapman, B. Everybody matters 658.4
    (jt. auth) Mackey, J. Conscious capitalism 174
Sisson, C. H.
    Selected poems   821
Sister Aimee: the life of Aimee Semple McPherson.
    Epstein, D. M.   92
Sister Bernadette's barking dog. Florey, K. B.   428

Sister revolutions. Dunn, S.   **973.3**

Sister Wendy's American collection. Beckett, W.   **709**

SISTERS

Parravani, C. Her   **92**

Thompson, L. The six   **92**

SISTERS

See also Siblings; Women

SISTERS (RELIGIOUS) *See* Nuns

SISTERS -- GREAT BRITAIN -- BIOGRAPHY

Thompson, L. The six   **92**

SISTERS -- UNITED STATES -- BIOGRAPHY

Parravani, C. Her   **92**

SISTERS AND BROTHERS *See* Siblings

The **sisters** antipodes. Alison, J.   **92**

Sisters in law. Hirshman, L.   **347.73**

The **sisters** who would be queen. De Lisle, L.   **920**

SIT-INS FOR CIVIL RIGHTS *See* Civil rights demonstrations

SITCOMS *See* Comedy television programs

SITE-SPECIFIC INSTALLATIONS (ART) -- EX-HIBITIONS

Chihuly   **748.2**

Sites, Kevin

The things they cannot say   **355**

Sitting Bull. Yenne, B.   **92**

Sitting Bull, Dakota Chief, 1831-1890

About

Brown, D. A. The American West   **978**

Philbrick, N. The last stand   **973.8**

Utley, R. M. Sitting Bull: the life and times of an American patriot   **92**

Yenne, B. Sitting Bull   **92**

Sitting Bull: the life and times of an American patriot. Utley, R. M.   **92**

SITTING CUSTOMS -- HISTORY

Rybczynski, W. Now I sit me down   **749.32**

SITUATION COMEDIES *See* Comedy television programs

Sivan, Emmanuel

Almond, G. A. Strong religion   **200.9**

The **six.** Thompson, L.   **92**

SIX DAY WAR, 1967 *See* Israel-Arab War, 1967

Six days of war. Oren, M.   **956.04**

Six degrees. Lynas, M.   **551.6**

Six degrees of separation. Guare, J.   **812**

Six easy pieces. Feynman, R. P.   **530**

Six frigates. Toll, I. W.   **359**

Six months in 1945. Dobbs, M.   **940.53**

The **six** wives of Henry VIII. Weir, A.   **942.05**

Six wives: the queens of Henry VIII. Starkey, D.   **942.05**

Six-legged soldiers. Lockwood, J. A.   **358**

The **sixteen** satires. Juvenal   **877**

The **sixth** extinction. Kolbert, E.   **576.8**

The **sixties.** Gitlin, T.   **973.922**

SIZE

See also Concepts; Perception

SIZE AND SHAPE *See* Shape; Size

Sizwe's test. Steinberg, J.   **362.1**

Skal, David J.

Something in the Blood   **823.8**

Skarbek, Krystyna, 1908-1952

About

Mulley, C. The Spy Who Loved   **940.54**

Skarlatos, Alek

About

Sadler, A. The 15:17 to Paris   **363.325**

SKATEBOARDING

Connolly, K. M. Double take   **92**

Skating on stilts. Baker, S. A.   **363.32**

The **skeleton** crew. Halber, D.   **363.25**

The **skeptic:** the life of H.L. Mencken. Teachout, T.   **92**

SKEPTICISM

Davidson, S. The December Project   **296.7**

Keller, T. J. The reason for God   **239**

SKEPTICISM

See also Free thought; Philosophy; Rationalism

Sketches from a life. Kennan, G. F.   **92**

The **sketches** of Louisa May Alcott. Alcott, L. M.   **818**

SKETCHING *See* Drawing

SKETCHUP

Rigsby, M. A beginner's guide to 3D printing   **621.9**

Skidmore, Thomas E.

Brazil   **981**

SKIERS

Connolly, K. M. Double take   **92**

Kurson, R. Crashing through   **92**

SKIERS -- UNITED STATES

Vinton, N. The fall line   **796.935**

The **skies** belong to us. Koerner, B. I.   **364.15**

SKIING

Connolly, K. M. Double take   **92**

Vinton, N. The fall line   **796.935**

SKILL *See* Ability

SKILLED LABOR

See also Labor

SKILLET COOKING

Cook it in cast iron   **641.7**

SKIN -- CARE AND HYGIENE

DuPriest, L. Natural beauty   **646.7**

Grigore, A. Skin cleanse   **613**

Thomas, M. The French beauty solution   **646.7**

SKIN -- DISEASES

Yosipovitch, G. Living with itch   **616.5**

SKIN -- DISEASES

See also Diseases

SKIN -- DISEASES -- POPULAR WORKS

Yosipovitch, G. Living with itch   **616.5**

Skin cleanse. Grigore, A. **613**
SKIN DIVING
  Nestor, J. Deep **797.2**
Skin, Inc. Ellis, T. S. **811**
SKINHEADS *See* White supremacy movements
Skinner, B. F. (Burrhus Frederic), 1904-1990
  About behaviorism **150.19**
      About
  Bjork, D. W. B.F. Skinner **92**
Skinner, Jack T., d. 1977
      About
  Nourse, V. F. In reckless hands **344**
Skinner, Keith
  (comp) The Ultimate Jack the Ripper companion **364.15**
Skinner, Kiron K.
  (ed) Reagan, in his own hand **973.927**
  (ed) Reagan, R. Reagan **92**
Skinny suppers. Griffin, B. **641.5**
SKIS AND SKIING *See* Skiing
SKITS
     See also Amusements; Theater
Sklenicka, Carol
  Raymond Carver **92**
Skloot, Rebecca, 1972-
  The immortal life of Henrietta Lacks **92**
Skolnick, Adam
  One breath **797.2**
Skolnik, Fred
  (ed) Encyclopaedia Judaica **296**
  (ed) The New encyclopedia of Judaism **296**
Skrondal, Anders
  Everitt, B. The Cambridge dictionary of statistics **519.5**
SKULL
  Skulls **573.7**
The skull collectors. Fabian, A. **599.9**
Skulls. **573.7**
SKY
  Bogard, P. The end of night **551.56**
SKY
     See also Astronomy; Atmosphere
Sky, Emma
  The Unraveling **956.7**
SKYDIVING
     See also Aeronautical sports
Skyfaring. Vanhoenacker, M. **629.132**
Skyscrapers. Cornille, D. **720**
SKYSCRAPERS
  Cornille, D. Skyscrapers **720**
SKYSCRAPERS
     See also Buildings
SKYSCRAPERS -- EARTHQUAKE EFFECTS
     See also Buildings -- Earthquake effects; Earthquakes
Skywriting and other poems. Tomlinson, C. **821**

Slacks and calluses. **940.53**
Slade, Suzanne
  The house that George built **975.3**
Slahi, Mohamedou Ould
      About
  Guantanamo diary **958.104**
The slanted door. Phan, C. **641.59**
SLAPSTICK COMEDIES *See* Comedies; Comedy films; Comedy television programs
Slater, Dan
  Wolf Boys **364**
Slater, Lauren
      About
  Slater, L. Prozac diary **616.89**
Slater, Michael
  Charles Dickens **92**
Slater, Nigel
  Ripe **641.6**
Slater, Robert
  No such thing as over-exposure **92**
Slaton, Pamela
  (jt. auth) Marshall, S. Reunited **362.82**
Slatta, Richard W.
  The cowboy encyclopedia **978**
Slaughter, Thomas P.
  The beautiful soul of John Woolman, apostle of abolition **92**
  Exploring Lewis and Clark **978**
Slaughterhouse. Rieff, D. **949.7**
SLAUGHTERING AND SLAUGHTER-HOUSES
  Danforth, A. Butchering poultry, rabbit, lamb, goat, and pork **664**
  Foer, J. S. Eating animals **641.3**
SLAVE INSURRECTIONS -- LOUISIANA -- NEW ORLEANS
  Rasmussen, D. American uprising **976.3**
SLAVE INSURRECTIONS -- UNITED STATES
  Rediker, M. The Amistad rebellion **326**
SLAVE NARRATIVES
  Williams, H. A. Help me to find my people **306.3**
SLAVE NARRATIVES
     See also Autobiography; Slavery
Slave nation. Blumrosen, A. W. **973.3**
A slave no more. Blight, D. W. **326**
SLAVE REVOLTS
  Rediker, M. The Amistad rebellion **326**
SLAVE REVOLTS
     See also Revolutions
Slave songs of the United States. Ware, C. P. **781.62**
SLAVE TRADE
  Berlin, I. The making of African America **305.8**
  Hartman, S. V. Lose your mother **323**
  Johnson, W. Soul by soul **326**
  Reséndez, A. The other slavery **306.3**
SLAVE TRADE
     See also International law; Slavery

SLAVE TRADE -- MAPS
Eltis, D. Atlas of the transatlantic slave trade 381
SLAVE TRADE -- MASSACHUSETTS
Manegold, C. Ten Hills Farm 974.4
The **Slave's** cause. Sinha, M. 973.711
SLAVEHOLDERS
Ball, E. Slaves in the family 975.7
SLAVERY
Baker, J. F. The Washingtons of Wessyngton Plantation 920
Hochschild, A. Bury the chains 326
Miller, W. L. Arguing about slavery 973.5
Scott, R. J. Freedom papers 305.896
Stark, R. For the glory of God 201
Wise, S. M. Though the heavens may fall 342
SLAVERY -- BARBADOS -- HISTORY
Stuart, A. Sugar in the Blood 338.1
SLAVERY -- ECONOMIC ASPECTS
Baptist, E. E. The half has never been told 306.3
Beckert, S. Empire of cotton 338.4
SLAVERY -- EMANCIPATION *See* Slaves -- Emancipation
SLAVERY -- HISTORY
Davis, D. B. The problem of slavery in the age of emancipation 306.3
Reséndez, A. The other slavery 306.3
Stuart, A. Sugar in the Blood 338.1
Warren, W. New England Bound 306.362
SLAVERY -- LAW AND LEGISLATION -- UNITED STATES -- HISTORY -- 19TH CENTURY
Richards, L. L. Who freed the slaves? 342.73
SLAVERY -- LOUISIANA -- HISTORY -- 19TH CENTURY
Twelve years a slave 92
SLAVERY -- LOUISIANA -- NEW ORLEANS
Rasmussen, D. American uprising 976.3
SLAVERY -- MASSACHUSETTS
Manegold, C. Ten Hills Farm 974.4
SLAVERY -- MISSISSIPPI RIVER VALLEY -- HISTORY -- 19TH CENTURY
Johnson, W. River of dark dreams 305.8
SLAVERY -- NEW YORK (STATE) -- LONG ISLAND -- HISTORY
Griswold, M. The Manor 974.7
SLAVERY -- NORTH AMERICA -- HISTORY
Reséndez, A. The other slavery 306.3
SLAVERY -- POETRY
Young, K. Ardency 811
SLAVERY -- SOCIAL ASPECTS -- SOUTHERN STATES -- HISTORY -- 19TH CENTURY
Levine, B. The fall of the house of Dixie 973.7
SLAVERY -- SOCIAL ASPECTS -- UNITED STATES -- HISTORY
Williams, H. A. Help me to find my people 306.3
SLAVERY -- SOUTH CAROLINA -- CHARLESTON -- HISTORY

Kelly, J. America's longest siege 305.896
SLAVERY -- UNITED STATES
Baptist, E. E. The half has never been told 306.3
DeWolf, T. N. Gather at the table 306.3
Foner, E. Gateway to Freedom 973.7
Griswold, M. The Manor 974.7
Johnson, W. River of dark dreams 305.8
Kelly, J. America's longest siege 305.896
Krauthamer, B. Envisioning emancipation 973.7
Oakes, J. Freedom national 973.7
Rediker, M. The Amistad rebellion 326
Richards, L. L. Who freed the slaves? 342.73
Sinha, M. The Slave's cause 973.711
Smith, G. A. The slaves' gamble 973.5
Wiencek, H. Master of the mountain 973.4
SLAVERY -- UNITED STATES -- ENCYCLOPEDIAS
Snodgrass, M. E. The Underground Railroad 973.7
SLAVERY -- UNITED STATES -- HISTORY
Bordewich, F. M. America's great debate 973.6
Taylor, A. The internal enemy 975.5
Walters, K. The Underground Railroad 973.7
Wilder, C. S. Ebony and Ivy 379.26
Wineapple, B. Ecstatic nation 973.6
SLAVERY -- UNITED STATES -- SONGS
Ware, C. P. Slave songs of the United States 781.62
SLAVERY AND THE CHURCH -- SOCIETY OF FRIENDS
Slaughter, T. P. The beautiful soul of John Woolman, apostle of abolition 92
Slavery and the making of America. Horton, J. O. 326
Slavery by another name. Blackmon, D. A. 305.8
SLAVES
Abdul-Jabbar, K. Black profiles in courage 920
Blight, D. W. A slave no more 326
Carretta, V. Equiano, the African 92
Colaiaco, J. A. Frederick Douglass and the Fourth of July 973.7
Douglass, F. Autobiographies 92
Douglass, F. My bondage and my freedom 92
Douglass, F. Narrative of the life of Frederick Douglass, an American slave 92
Gordon-Reed, A. The Hemingses of Monticello 920
Gordon-Reed, A. Thomas Jefferson and Sally Hemings 973.4
Harlan, L. R. Booker T. Washington: the making of a black leader, 1856-1901 92
Harlan, L. R. Booker T. Washington: the wizard of Tuskegee, 1901-1915 92
Lepore, J. A is for American 306.44
Newman, R. S. Freedom's prophet 92
Norrell, R. J. Up from history 92
Smardz Frost, K. I've got a home in glory land 92
Smock, R. W. Booker T. Washington 92

Uncle Tom or new Negro **370**
VanderVelde, L. Mrs. Dred Scott **92**
Washington, B. T. Up from slavery **92**
Wise, S. M. Though the heavens may fall **342**
Yellin, J. F. Harriet Jacobs: a life **92**
SLAVES
    See also Slavery
SLAVES -- EMANCIPATION
Davis, D. B. The problem of slavery in the age of
    emancipation **306.3**
Jacoby, K. The strange career of William Ellis **92**
Kantrowitz, S. More than freedom **323.1**
Krauthamer, B. Envisioning emancipation **973.7**
Sinha, M. The Slave's cause **973.711**
SLAVES -- EMANCIPATION
    See also Freedom
**SLAVES -- EMANCIPATION -- UNITED
STATES**
Berlin, I. The long emancipation **326.8**
Manning, C. Troubled refuge **973.711**
Oakes, J. Freedom national **973.7**
Richards, L. L. Who freed the slaves? **342.73**
**SLAVES -- EMANCIPATION -- UNITED
STATES -- HISTORY -- 19TH CENTURY**
Richards, L. L. Who freed the slaves? **342.73**
SLAVES -- ENGLAND -- BIOGRAPHY
Byrne, P. Belle **92**
**SLAVES -- FAMILY RELATIONSHIPS -- UNIT-
ED STATES -- HISTORY**
Williams, H. A. Help me to find my people **306.3**
SLAVES -- LEGAL STATUS, LAWS, ETC.
VanderVelde, L. Mrs. Dred Scott **92**
SLAVES -- MASSACHUSETTS
Manegold, C. Ten Hills Farm **974.4**
**SLAVES -- SOUTH CAROLINA -- CHARLES-
TON -- HISTORY**
Kelly, J. America's longest siege **305.896**
**SLAVES -- SOUTHERN STATES -- BIOGRA-
PHY**
Ward, A. The slaves' war **973.7**
SLAVES -- TEXAS -- BIOGRAPHY
Jacoby, K. The strange career of William Ellis **92**
SLAVES -- UNITED STATES -- 19TH CENTURY
Twelve years a slave **92**
SLAVES -- UNITED STATES -- BIOGRAPHY
Clinton, C. Harriet Tubman: the road to freedom **92**
Twelve years a slave **92**
VanderVelde, L. Mrs. Dred Scott **92**
**SLAVES -- UNITED STATES -- SOCIAL CONDI-
TIONS -- 19TH CENTURY**
Douglass, F. Frederick Douglass: selected speech-
    es and writings **326**
**SLAVES -- VIRGINIA -- ALBEMARLE COUN-
TY -- HISTORY**
Wiencek, H. Master of the mountain **973.4**
SLAVES -- VIRGINIA -- TIDEWATER (RE-

GION) -- HISTORY
Taylor, A. The internal enemy **975.5**
Slaves in the family. Ball, E. **975.7**
The **slaves'** gamble. Smith, G. A. **973.5**
The **slaves'** war. Ward, A. **973.7**
SLAVES' WRITINGS, AMERICAN
Twelve years a slave **92**
Slavinski, Cindy Tate
Leiter, R. A. Landmark Supreme Court cases **347**
Slawenski, Kenneth
J.D. Salinger **92**
SLED DOG RACERS
Paulsen, G. Winterdance **798.8**
Sleep. **618.92**
SLEEP
    See also Health; Hygiene; Mind and body;
    Psychophysiology; Rest; Subconsciousness
SLEEP
Goldman, B. Brain fitness **153.1**
The happy sleeper **649**
Huffington, A. S. The sleep revolution **613.794**
Jassey, J. The newborn sleep book **618.92**
Karp, H. The happiest baby guide to great sleep **649**
Kennedy, J. K. The good sleeper **649**
Randall, D. K. Dreamland **612.8**
Sleep **618.92**
SLEEP -- HEALTH ASPECTS
Huffington, A. S. The sleep revolution **613.794**
SLEEP APNEA
    See also Sleep
SLEEP DEPRIVATION
Huffington, A. S. The sleep revolution **613.794**
The **sleep** revolution. Huffington, A. S. **613.794**
SLEEP THERAPY
Sleep **618.92**
SLEEPING BEAUTY (TALE)
    See also Fairy tales
SLEEPING CUSTOMS
Pitman, T. Sweet sleep **649**
Sleeping it off in Rapid City. Kleinzahler, A. **811**
Sleeping with the enemy. Vaughan, H. **92**
The **sleepwalkers.** Clark, C. **940.3**
SLEEPWALKING
Randall, D. K. Dreamland **612.8**
Sleepwalking through history. Johnson, H.
B. **973.927**
SLEIGHT OF HAND *See* Juggling; Magic tricks
Sleight, Steve
The complete sailing manual **797.124**
Slemrod, Joel
(jt. auth) Burman, L. Taxes in America **336.2**
A **slender** thread. Ackerman, D. **362.28**
Slevin, Peter
Michelle Obama **92**
A **slice** of the pie. Sarillo, N. **658.02**
Slicing the silence. Griffiths, T. **998**

Slide, Anthony
(ed) It's the pictures that got small   92
SLIDES (PHOTOGRAPHY)
See also Photography
Slim by design. Wansink, B.   613.2
A **slip** of the keyboard. Pratchett, T.   824
SLITS (MUSICAL GROUP)
Albertine, V. Clothes, Clothes, Clothes. Music,
Music, Music. Boys, Boys, Boys   92
Sloan, Annie
Color recipes for painted furniture and more
Sloan, Stephen
Anderson, S. Historical dictionary of terror-
ism   363.32
Slonecker, Andrea
Beer bites   641.5
(jt. auth) Hanel, M. The picnic   642
Slotkin, Richard, 1942-
Long Road to Antietam   973.7
Lost battalions   940.3
No quarter   973.7
Slotten, Ross A.
The heretic in Darwin's court   92
SLOVENIA
McNamara, K. J. Dreams of a great small na-
tion   943.703
Slow church. Pattison, J.   253
SLOW FOOD MOVEMENT
Waters, A. In the green kitchen   641.5
SLOW FOOD MOVEMENT
See also Gastronomy; Social movements
SLOW LEARNING CHILDREN
Solomon, A. Far from the tree   362.4
SLOW LEARNING CHILDREN
See also Exceptional children
The **slow** Mediterranean kitchen. Wolfert, P.   641.5
Slow Train to Switzerland. Bewes, D.   914.94
Slowinski, Joseph, 1962-2001
About
James, J. The snake charmer   92
SMALL BUSINESS
American Bar Association The American Bar As-
sociation legal guide for small business   346
Cortese, A. Locavesting   332.6
How to write a business plan   658.15
Mitchell, S. Big-box swindle   381
Pakroo, P. The small business start-up kit   346
Sarillo, N. A slice of the pie   658.02
Spector, R. The mom & pop store   381
SMALL BUSINESS
See also Business
**SMALL BUSINESS -- MANAGEMENT --
HANDBOOKS, MANUALS, ETC**
Lindsay, V. Sewing to sell   646.2
**SMALL BUSINESS -- UNITED STATES -- MAN-
AGEMENT**

Downs, P. Boss Life   92
Strauss, S. D. The small business bible   658.02
The **small** business bible. Strauss, S. D.   658.02
SMALL BUSINESS OWNERS
Howe, B. R. My Korean deli   92
The **small** business start-up kit. Pakroo, P.   346
SMALL CLAIMS COURT
Warner, R. E. Everybody's guide to small claims
court   347
SMALL CLAIMS COURTS
See also Civil procedure; Courts
Small Data. Lindström, M.   658.8
Small engines and outdoor power equipment.   621.43
SMALL FARMS
Bellamy, A. Small-space vegetable gardens   635
SMALL FARMS
See also Farms
**SMALL GASOLINE ENGINES -- MAINTE-
NANCE AND REPAIR**
Small engines and outdoor power equipment   621.43
SMALL HOUSES
Mitchell, R. Tiny house living   728
A **small** place. Kincaid, J.   972.9
The **small** public library survival guide. Landau, H.
B.   025.1
A **small** treatise on the great virtues. Comte-Spon-
ville, A.   170
Small victories. Lamott, A.   248
Small, David, 1945-
Stitches   741.5
Small, Gary
2 weeks to a younger brain   616.8
Small, Meredith F.
Our babies, ourselves   649
Small-space vegetable gardens. Bellamy, A.   635
The **smaller** majority. Naskrecki, P.   591.7
SMALLPOX
Foege, W. H. House on fire   614.5
Preston, R. The demon in the freezer   616.9
Smallwood, Carol
(ed) The frugal librarian   025.1
(ed) Librarians as community partners   021.2
(ed) Marketing your library   021.7
Smardz Frost, Karolyn
I've got a home in glory land   92
Smart but scattered. Dawson, P.   649
Smart cookie. Johnstone, C. F.   641.865
Smart parenting for smart kids. Kennedy-Moore,
E.   649
SMART PHONES See Smartphones
Smart pop series
O'Neil, D. Batman unauthorized   741.5
The **smart** swarm. Miller, P.   156
Smart trust. Covey, S. M. R.   174
Smarter faster better. Duhigg, C.   158
Smarter Than You Think. Thompson, C.   303.48

The **smartest** animals on the planet. Boysen, S. T. **591.5**

The **smartest** kids in the world. Ripley, A. **370.9**

The **smartest** retirement book you'll ever read. Solin, D. R. **332.024**

SMARTPHONES

McNish, J. Losing the signal **338.4**

Smash Cut. Gooch, B. **92**

Smee, Sebastian

The art of rivalry **700.92**

SMELL

Herz, R. S. The scent of desire **152.1**

Turin, L. The secret of scent **668**

SMELL

See also Senses and sensation

Smiley, Jane

Charles Dickens **823**

The man who invented the computer **92**

Thirteen ways of looking at the novel **813**

Smirnoff, Marc

The Oxford American book of great music writing **781.64**

Smith Howard, Alycia

Heintzelman, G. Critical companion to Tennessee Williams **812**

Smith Rakoff, Joanna, 1972-

About

Smith Rakoff, J. My Salinger year **92**

Smith, Adam, 1723-1790

The wealth of nations **330.1**

About

Heilbroner, R. L. The worldly philosophers **330.1**

Smith, Alexander Hanchett

The mushroom hunter's field guide **579.6**

Smith, Alfred Emanuel, 1873-1944

About

Finan, C. M. Alfred E. Smith, the happy warrior **92**

Smith, Alison

Dressmaking **646.4**

The sewing book **646.2**

Smith, Andrew

Moondust **920**

Smith, Andrew F.

(ed) The Oxford encyclopedia of food and drink in America **641.3**

Smith, Brian H.

(jt. auth) Kolpan, S. Exploring wine **641.2**

(jt. auth) Kolpan, S. Winewise **641.2**

Smith, C. Christopher

(jt. auth) Pattison, J. Slow church **253**

Smith, C. Lavett

National Audubon Society field guide to tropical marine fishes of the Caribbean, the Gulf of Mexico, Florida, the Bahamas, and Bermuda **597**

Smith, Charles Sprague

Christ-Janer, A. American hymns old and new **782.27**

Smith, Claire Bidwell, 1978-

About

Smith, C. B. The rules of inheritance **616.99**

Smith, Clive Stafford

The injustice system **345.73**

Smith, Daniel B., 1977-

About

Smith, D. Monkey mind **616.85**

Smith, Darren L.

(ed) Counties USA **352.13**

Smith, David James

Young Mandela **92**

Smith, Deirdre

Smith, D. A decade of hope **974.7**

Smith, Dennis

A decade of hope **974.7**

Report from ground zero **363.34**

Smith, Diane

(jt. auth) Brzezinski, M. Obsessed **362.196**

Smith, Douglas

Former people **305.5**

Smith, Douglas W.

Decade of the wolf **599.77**

Smith, Edward C.

The vegetable gardener's bible **635**

The vegetable gardener's container bible **635**

Smith, G. Stevenson

Cost control for nonprofits in crisis **025.1**

Smith, Gar

Nuclear roulette **621.48**

Smith, Gary

Standard deviations **519.5**

Smith, Gene Allen

The slaves' gamble **973.5**

Smith, George E.

(ed) The Cambridge companion to Newton **530**

Smith, Gordon T.

(ed) Zondervan dictionary of Christian spirituality **248**

Smith, Graeme

The Dogs Are Eating Them Now **958.104**

Smith, Gregory White, 1951-2014

(jt. auth) Naifeh, S. Van Gogh **92**

Smith, Hedrick

Who stole the American dream? **973.91**

Smith, Huston

About

Lattin, D. The Harvard Psychedelic Club **920**

Smith, Ian Haydn

(ed) 1001 Movies You Must See Before You Die **791.43**

Smith, Irene Britton, 1907-1999

About

Walker-Hill, H. From spirituals to symphonies **780**

Smith, James D.

(ed) Zondervan dictionary of Christian spirituality **248**

Smith, Jane Idleman
Islam in America **297.092**

Smith, Jane S.
The garden of invention **92**

Smith, Janna Malamud
My father is a book **92**

Smith, Jean Edward
Bush **973.931**
Eisenhower **973.921**
FDR **92**
Grant **92**
John Marshall **347**

Smith, Jennie Erin
Stolen world **364.1**

Smith, Jeremy N.
Growing a garden city **635**

Smith, Jessie Carney, 1930-
(ed) Black firsts **920**
(ed) Notable black American men, book II **920.003**
(ed) Notable black American women, book I **920.003**
(ed) Notable black American women, Book III **920.003**

Smith, Jessie Willcox, 1863-1935
About
Carter, A. A. The Red Rose girls **759.13**

Smith, Joel
Edward Steichen: the early years **779**

Smith, John David
(ed) Douglass, F. My bondage and my freedom **92**

Smith, John, 1580-1631
About
Price, D. Love and hate in Jamestown **975.5**

Smith, Johnny
Blood brothers **92**

Smith, Joseph, 1805-1844
About
Barnes, J. Falling in love with Joseph Smith **92**
Beam, A. American crucifixion **289.3**
Bushman, R. L. Joseph Smith **92**
Bushman, R. L. Joseph Smith and the beginnings of Mormonism **289.3**
Remini, R. V. Joseph Smith **92**

Smith, Judith E.
Becoming Belafonte **92**

Smith, Julian
Smokejumper **92**

Smith, Larry
(ed) The moment **818**
(ed) Iwo Jima **940.54**

Smith, Larry R., 1943-
No fears, no excuses **650.1**

Smith, Laurence C.
The world in 2050 **304.2**

Smith, Lee, 1944-
About
Smith, L. Dimestore **92**

Smith, Linda J.
(jt. auth) Pitman, T. Sweet sleep **649**

Smith, Lyn
Remembering, voices of the holocaust **940.53**

Smith, Michael
Shackleton **92**

Smith, Michael Ernest
The Aztecs **972**

Smith, Michael G.
(ed) The Art of natural building **690**

Smith, Myquillyn
The nesting place **248.4**

Smith, Nathan
Color concrete garden projects **721**

Smith, P. D.
City **307.76**

Smith, Patricia
Shoulda been Jimi Savannah **811**

Smith, Patti, 1946-
About
Just kids **92**
M train **92**
Patti Smith Collected Lyrics, 1970-2015 **782.42**

Smith, Perry, 1928-1965
About
Capote, T. In cold blood **364.1**

Smith, R. Garth
ASD, the complete autism spectrum disorder health & diet guide **616.85**

Smith, R. J.
The one **92**

Smith, Raymond J.
About
Oates, J. C. A widow's story **92**

Smith, Red
Red Smith on baseball **796.357**

Smith, Rick
Toxin toxout **613**

Smith, Roff
Life on the ice **998**

Smith, Stephen Drury
(ed) After the fall **974.7**

Smith, Stevie
Collected poems **821**

Smith, Tom
A balanced life **362.1**

Smith, Tony
(ed) The value of a dollar: colonial era to the Civil War, 1600-1865 **338.5**

Smith, Tracy K., 1972-
Life on Mars **811**
About
Smith, T.K. Ordinary light **92**

Smith, William, 1769-1839

About

Winchester, S. The map that changed the world **526**

Smith, Zadie, 1975-

Changing my mind **824**

Smithson, James, 1765-1829

About

Ewing, H. P. The lost world of James Smithson **92**

Smithsonian atlas of space exploration. Launius, R. D. **500.5**

Smithsonian atlas of world aviation. **629.13**

Smithsonian baseball. Wong, S. **796**

Smithsonian field guide to the birds of North America. Floyd, T. **598**

Smithsonian Institution

Launius, R. D. Smithsonian atlas of space exploration **500.5**

Macleod, A. Explorers **910.4**

SMITHSONIAN INSTITUTION -- HISTORY

Ewing, H. P. The lost world of James Smithson **92**

Smithsonian ocean. Cramer, D. **578.7**

The **smitten** kitchen cookbook. Perelman, D. **641.5**

Smock, Raymond

(ed) Congress investigates **328**

Smock, R. W. Booker T. Washington **92**

SMOCKING

See also Needlework

Smogtown. Jacobs, C. **363.7**

Smoke. Byres, T. **641.6**

Smoke gets in your eyes. Doughty, C. **92**

SMOKE PREVENTION

See also Sanitation

SMOKE-ENDING PROGRAMS *See* Smoking cessation programs

SMOKED FOODS

Raichlen, S. Project smoke **641.6**

Smokejumper. Smith, J. **92**

SMOKING (COOKING)

Raichlen, S. Project smoke **641.6**

SMOKING -- ADVERSE EFFECTS -- UNITED STATES

Proctor, R. N. Golden holocaust **362.29**

SMOKING CESSATION PROGRAMS

Goldfarb, T. L. American Lung Association 7 steps to a smoke-free life **616.86**

Proctor, R. N. Golden holocaust **362.29**

SMOKING CESSATION PROGRAMS

See also Tobacco habit

The **smoking** gun. Spence, G. **345**

Smolin, Lee

The trouble with physics **530.1**

Smoller, Jordan

The other side of normal **591.5**

Smoot, George

Wrinkles in time **523.1**

Smoothie-licious. Helwig, J. **641.87**

SMOOTHIES (BEVERAGES)

Helwig, J. Smoothie-licious **641.87**

Smuggler's Cove. Cate, M. **647.95**

SMUGGLERS

August, O. Inside the red mansion **951.05**

Keefe, P. R. The snakehead **364.1**

SMUGGLING

Keefe, P. R. The snakehead **364.1**

Smith, J. E. Stolen world **364.1**

Welch, C. Shell games **364.1**

SMUGGLING

See also Crime; Tariff

SMUGGLING OF DRUGS *See* Drug traffic

Smyth, Denis

Deathly deception **940.54**

SNACK FOODS

Battista, M. Food gift love **642**

Fuentes, L. The best homemade kids' snacks on the planet **641.5**

Little bites **641.5**

Tourles, S. L. Raw energy **641.5**

SNACK FOODS

See also Food

SNACKS *See* Snack foods

SNAILS

Bailey, E. T. The sound of a wild snail eating **92**

The **snake** charmer. James, J. **92**

Snake hips. Soffee, A. T. **793.3**

Snake in the grass. Perez, L. **597.96**

The **snakehead.** Keefe, P. R. **364.1**

SNAKES

Ernst, C. H. Snakes of the United States and Canada **597.96**

James, J. The snake charmer **92**

Mattison, C. Snakes of the world **597.96**

O'Shea, M. Venomous snakes of the world **597.96**

SNAKES

See also Reptiles

SNAKES -- ENCYCLOPEDIAS

Mattison, C. The new encyclopedia of snakes **597.96**

SNAKES -- FLORIDA -- EVERGLADES NATIONAL PARK

Perez, L. Snake in the grass **597.96**

SNAKES AS PETS

See also Pets; Snakes

Snakes of the United States and Canada. Ernst, C. H. **597.96**

Snakes of the world. Mattison, C. **597.96**

Snare, John

About

Cumming, L. The Vanishing Velazquez **759.6**

Sneaky math. Tymony, C. **510**

SNEEZING

Provine, R. R. Curious behavior **152.3**

Snetsinger, Phoebe, 1931-1999

About
Gentile, O. Life list **92**
Sneum, Thomas, 1917-2007
About
Ryan, M. Hornet's sting **92**
Sniper one. Mills, D. **956.7**
Snobbery. Epstein, J. **305.5**
Snodgrass, Mary Ellen
Signs of the zodiac **133.5**
The Underground Railroad **973.7**
Snodgrass, W. D.
Not for specialists **811**
Snoop. Gosling, S. **155.9**
Snow, John, 1813-1858
About
Johnson, S. The ghost map **614.5**
Snow, Peter
When Britain burned the White House **975.3**
The snowball: Warren Buffett and the business of life. Schroeder, A. D. **92**
SNOWBOARDING
Bennett, J. The complete snowboarder **796.9**
Snowman (Horse)
About
Letts, E. The eighty-dollar champion **798.2**
Snowstruck. Fredston, J. A. **551.3**
Snyder, Gary
No nature **811**
Snyder, John
About
Snyder, J. Hill of Beans **92**
Snyder, Laura J.
Eye of the beholder **701**
The philosophical breakfast club **509**
Snyder, Michael
Color concrete garden projects **721**
Snyder, Rachel Louise
Fugitive denim **382**
Snyder, Rich, d. 1993
What you must know about dialysis **617.4**
Snyder, Timothy D., 1969-
(jt. auth) Judt, T. Thinking the twentieth century **320.092**
Black Earth **940.53**
Bloodlands **940.54**
So damn much money. Kaiser, R. G. **328**
So long as men can breathe. Heylin, C. **822.3**
So you want to write. Piercy, M. **808.3**
So you've been publicly shamed. Ronson, J. **152.4**
So, anyway... Cleese, J. **92**
SOAP SCULPTURE
See also Modeling; Sculpture
Sobczak, A. J.
(ed) Cyclopedia of literary characters **803**
Sobel, Adam
Storm surge **551.55**

Street vegan **641.5**
Sobel, Dava
Galileo's daughter **92**
The glass universe **522.197**
Longitude **526**
A more perfect heaven **520**
SOBRIQUETS *See* Nicknames
SOCCER
Foer, F. How soccer explains the world **303.482**
God Is Round **796.334**
Soccer in sun and shadow **796.334**
St. John, W. Outcasts united **796.334**
Szymanski, S. Money and Soccer **796.334**
Vecsey, G. Eight world cups **796.334**
SOCCER
See also Ball games; Football; Sports
SOCCER -- MANAGEMENT -- CORRUPT PRACTICES
Thompson, T. American huckster **796.334**
SOCCER -- MATHEMATICAL MODELS
Anderson, C. The numbers game **796.334**
SOCCER COACHES -- GERMANY -- BIOGRAPHY
Kirschbaum, E. Soccer without borders **796.334**
Soccer in sun and shadow. **796.334**
SOCCER PLAYERS
Coffey, W. When nobody was watching **796.334**
God Is Round **796.334**
Szymanski, S. Money and Soccer **796.334**
SOCCER PLAYERS -- UNITED STATES -- BIOGRAPHY
Marcus, E. Coming out to play **92**
Wambach, A. Forward **92**
SOCCER TEAMS
God Is Round **796.334**
Honigstein, R. Das Reboot **796.334**
Szymanski, S. Money and Soccer **796.334**
SOCCER TEAMS -- UNITED STATES
Kirschbaum, E. Soccer without borders **796.334**
Soccer without borders. Kirschbaum, E. **796.334**
Social. Lieberman, M. D. **302**
SOCIAL ACTION
Budd, K. The voluntourist **361.7**
Shaw, R. Beyond the fields **331.8**
SOCIAL ACTION
See also Social policy
SOCIAL ACTION -- UNITED STATES -- HISTORY -- 20TH CENTURY
Shaw, R. Beyond the fields **331.8**
SOCIAL ACTIVISM *See* Social action
SOCIAL ADJUSTMENT
Daum, M. The unspeakable **814**
The **social** animal. Brooks, D. **305.5**
SOCIAL ANTHROPOLOGY *See* Ethnology
SOCIAL BEHAVIOR *See* Human behavior
SOCIAL BEHAVIOR IN ANIMALS

Balcombe, J. Second nature **591.5**

Bekoff, M. Wild justice **591.5**

SOCIAL CASE WORK

>*See also* Social work

SOCIAL CHANGE

Bram, C. Eminent outlaws **810.9**

Colvile, R. The Great Acceleration **303.483**

Diamond, J. M. Collapse: how societies choose to fail or succeed **304.2**

Diamond, J. M. Guns, germs, and steel **303.4**

Gilding, P. The great disruption **304.2**

Givhan, R. The Battle of Versailles **746.9**

Greene, D. Midnight in Siberia **914.7**

Hayden, T. The long sixties **973.92**

Johnson, S. Future perfect **303.48**

Kellerman, B. The end of leadership **303.3**

Linden, E. The winds of change **551.6**

Pagel, M. Wired for culture **303.4**

Rosenberg, T. Join the club **303.3**

Toffler, A. Future shock **303.4**

Toumani, M. There was and there was not **327**

Wade, N. Before the dawn **599.93**

SOCIAL CHANGE

>*See also* Anthropology; Social sciences; Sociology

SOCIAL CHANGE -- ARAB COUNTRIES

Cambanis, T. Once upon a revolution **962.05**

SOCIAL CHANGE -- CALIFORNIA -- SAN FRANCISCO -- HISTORY -- 20TH CENTURY

Talbot, D. Season of the witch **306**

SOCIAL CHANGE -- CHINA

Osnos, E. Age of ambition **951.06**

SOCIAL CHANGE -- CUBA -- HAVANA -- HISTORY -- 21ST CENTURY

Cooke, J. The other side of paradise **972.91**

SOCIAL CHANGE -- EGYPT -- HISTORY -- 21ST CENTURY

Cambanis, T. Once upon a revolution **962.05**

SOCIAL CHANGE -- EUROPE -- HISTORY -- 20TH CENTURY

Jarausch, K. H. Out of ashes **940.5**

SOCIAL CHANGE -- GERMANY -- PRUSSIA -- HISTORY -- 18TH CENTURY

Blanning, T. Frederick the Great **92**

SOCIAL CHANGE -- HAWAII -- HISTORY -- 18TH CENTURY

Moore, S. Paradise of the Pacific **996.9**

SOCIAL CHANGE -- INDIA

Karnad, R. Farthest field **940.54**

SOCIAL CHANGE -- JAPAN -- HISTORY -- 20TH CENTURY

Dower, J. W. Ways of forgetting, ways of remembering **940.53**

SOCIAL CHANGE -- NEW YORK (STATE) -- NEW YORK

Anasi, R. The last bohemia **974.7**

SOCIAL CHANGE -- PSYCHOLOGICAL ASPECTS

Pipher, M. The green boat **303.4**

SOCIAL CHANGE -- RUSSIA (FEDERATION)

Greene, D. Midnight in Siberia **914.7**

Pomerantsev, P. Nothing is true and everything is possible **306**

SOCIAL CHANGE -- TURKEY

Toumani, M. There was and there was not **327**

SOCIAL CHANGE -- UNITED STATES

Howe, D. W. What hath God wrought **973.5**

SOCIAL CHANGE -- UNITED STATES -- HISTORY

McPherson, J. M. The war that forged a nation **973.7**

SOCIAL CHANGE -- UNITED STATES -- HISTORY -- 20TH CENTURY

Tirella, J. Tomorrow-land **607**

SOCIAL CLASSES

Pickett, K. The spirit level **306**

Tough, P. How children succeed **372.21**

Veblen, T. The theory of the leisure class **305.5**

SOCIAL CLASSES

>*See also* Caste; Sociology

SOCIAL CLASSES -- UNITED STATES

Bageant, J. Deer hunting with Jesus **305.5**

Carbone, J. Marriage markets **306.85**

Hedges, C. Days of destruction, days of revolt **305.5**

Murray, C. Coming apart **305.8**

Tirado, L. Hand to mouth **362.5**

SOCIAL CONDITIONS

Daum, M. The unspeakable **814**

Gutting, G. What philosophy can do **100**

Hamid, M. Discontent and its civilizations **814**

Scull, A. Madness in civilization **616.89**

SOCIAL CONDITIONS

>*See also* Sociology

SOCIAL CONFLICT

Hedges, C. Days of destruction, days of revolt **305.5**

Murray, C. Coming apart **305.8**

Roy, A. Walking with the comrades **954**

Williams, D. Bitterly divided **973.7**

SOCIAL CONFLICT

>*See also* Social psychology; Sociology

SOCIAL CONFLICT -- GAZA STRIP -- HISTORY

Filiu Gaza **953**

SOCIAL CONFLICT -- SOUTHERN STATES -- HISTORY -- 19TH CENTURY

Williams, D. Bitterly divided **973.7**

SOCIAL CONFLICT -- SOVIET UNION -- HISTORY -- SOURCES

Competing voices from the Russian Revolution   947.084

SOCIAL CONFLICT -- UNITED STATES
Bishop, B. The big sort   305.8

SOCIAL CONFLICT -- UNITED STATES -- HISTORY
Fraser, S. The age of acquiescence   973.91

SOCIAL CONFLICT -- UNITED STATES -- HISTORY -- 20TH CENTURY
Kruse, K. M. One nation under God   322

SOCIAL CONFORMITY See Conformity
The **social** conquest of earth. Wilson, E. O.   599.93
The **social** contract. Rousseau   320.1

SOCIAL CONTRACT
Corning, P. The fair society   303.3

SOCIAL CONTRACT
    See also Political science; Sociology

SOCIAL CONTROL
Ronson, J. So you've been publicly shamed   152.4

SOCIAL CRITICS
Bageant, J. Deer hunting with Jesus   305.5
Commager, H. S. The American mind   973
Heilbroner, R. L. The worldly philosophers   330.1
Hooks, B. Belonging   92
Hooks, B. Wounds of passion   92
Kozol, J. Letters to a young teacher   371.1
My life as author and editor   818
Rapoport, R. Citizen Moore   92
Rodgers, M. E. Mencken   92
Said, E. W. Out of place   92
Teachout, T. The skeptic: the life of H.L. Mencken   92
Wills, G. Outside looking in   92

SOCIAL CUSTOMS See Manners and customs

SOCIAL DARWINISM
Johnson, P. Darwin   576.8

SOCIAL ETHICS
Callahan, D. The cheating culture   174
Corning, P. The fair society   303.3

SOCIAL ETHICS
    See also Ethics; Sociology

SOCIAL EVOLUTION
Barash, D. P. Homo mysterious   303.4
Jolly, A. Lucy's legacy   599.93
Pagel, M. Wired for culture   303.4
Shlain, L. Sex, time, and power   306.7
Wade, N. Before the dawn   599.93

SOCIAL EVOLUTION See Social change

SOCIAL EVOLUTION -- PHILOSOPHY
Wilson, E. O. The social conquest of earth   599.93

SOCIAL GROUP WORK
    See also Counseling; Social work

SOCIAL GROUPS
Robbins, A. The geeks shall inherit the Earth
Rosenberg, T. Join the club   303.3

SOCIAL GROUPS
    See also Sociology

SOCIAL HISTORY
Ekirch, A. R. At day's close   306.4
Encyclopedia of plague and pestilence   614.4

SOCIAL HISTORY See Social conditions
The **social** history of the Third Reich. Aycoberry, P.   943.086

SOCIAL HYGIENE See Public health; Sexual hygiene

SOCIAL IDENTITY See Group identity

SOCIAL INDICATORS -- MATHEMATICAL MODELS -- MORAL AND ETHICAL ASPECTS
O'Neil, C. Weapons of math destruction   005.7

SOCIAL INFLUENCE
Schaefer, M. W. Return on influence   658.8

SOCIAL INSURANCE See Social security

SOCIAL INTEGRATION
Warnick, M. This Is Where You Belong   155.94

SOCIAL INTEGRATION
    See also Interpersonal relations; Sociology
Social intelligence. Goleman, D.   158

SOCIAL INTERACTION
Lieberman, M. D. Social   302

SOCIAL ISOLATION See Loneliness

SOCIAL JUSTICE
Corning, P. The fair society   303.3

SOCIAL JUSTICE
    See also Equality; Justice

SOCIAL JUSTICE -- STUDY AND TEACHING
Art and social justice education   372.5

SOCIAL JUSTICE -- UNITED STATES
The divide   303.3
Nader, R. Told you so   303.3
Shaw, R. Beyond the fields   331.8
Speth, J. G. America the possible   338.9

SOCIAL LEARNING See Socialization

SOCIAL LEGISLATION -- UNITED STATES -- HISTORY -- 20TH CENTURY
Woods, R. B. Prisoners of hope   973.923

SOCIAL LIFE AND CUSTOMS See Manners and customs
The **social** lives of dogs. Thomas, E. M.   636.7

SOCIAL MEDIA
Bazelon, E. Sticks and stones   302.34
Burcher, N. Paid, owned, earned   658.8
Kowalski, R. M. Cyberbullying   302.34
Martinez, A. G. Chaos Monkeys   338.4
Moreno, M. Sex, drugs 'n Facebook   004.67
Rudder, C. Dataclysm   155.2
Sales, N. J. American girls   004.67
Solomon, L. The librarian's nitty-gritty guide to social media   006.7
Strauss, S. L. Sexual harassment and bullying   302.34

SOCIAL MEDIA -- ECONOMIC ASPECTS
O'Connor, R. Friends, followers, and the fu-

ture   **302.3**

SOCIAL MEDIA -- HISTORY
Standage, T. Writing on the wall   **302.23**

SOCIAL MEDIA -- MARKETING
Schaefer, M. W. Return on influence   **658.8**

SOCIAL MEDIA -- POLITICAL ASPECTS
O'Connor, R. Friends, followers, and the future   **302.3**

SOCIAL MEDICINE
Encyclopedia of plague and pestilence   **614.4**
Sommer, A. Getting what we deserve   **362.1**

SOCIAL MEDICINE
    See also Medicine; Public health; Public welfare; Sociology

SOCIAL MEDICINE -- HISTORY
Porter, R. The greatest benefit to mankind   **610**

SOCIAL MOBILITY
Vance, J. D. Hillbilly elegy   **92**

SOCIAL MOBILITY -- UNITED STATES
Murray, C. Coming apart   **305.8**

SOCIAL MOBILITY -- UNITED STATES -- HISTORY -- 19TH CENTURY
Holzer, H. A just and generous nation   **973.7**

SOCIAL MOVEMENTS
Hayden, T. The long sixties   **973.92**
Hedges, C. Wages of rebellion   **303.48**
Ostertag, B. People's movements, people's press   **071**

SOCIAL MOVEMENTS
    See also Social conditions; Social psychology

SOCIAL MOVEMENTS -- UNITED STATES -- ENCYCLOPEDIAS
Guns in American society   **363.33**
Social networking. Obee, J.   **004.67**

SOCIAL NETWORKING
    See also Communication

SOCIAL NETWORKING
Dwyer, J. More awesome than money   **384.3**
Grant, A. Give and take   **158.2**
Kirkpatrick, D. The Facebook effect   **338.7**
Lieberman, M. D. Social   **302**
Obee, J. Social networking   **004.67**
O'Connor, R. Friends, followers, and the future   **302.3**
Shirky, C. Cognitive surplus   **303.4**

SOCIAL NETWORKING -- HISTORY
Standage, T. Writing on the wall   **302.23**

SOCIAL NETWORKS
Johnson, S. Future perfect   **303.48**
Lieberman, M. D. Social   **302**
Wellman, B. Networked   **006.7**

SOCIAL NETWORKS *See* Social networking

SOCIAL NETWORKS -- AMERICA
Count on me   **177**

SOCIAL NETWORKS -- UNITED STATES
Count on me   **177**

SOCIAL PARTICIPATION -- CASE STUDIES.
Wills, G. Certain trumpets   **303.3**

SOCIAL PHOBIA
Fonseca, C. Raising the shy child   **649**

SOCIAL PHOBIA
    See also Phobias

SOCIAL PHOBIA IN CHILDREN
Fonseca, C. Raising the shy child   **649**

SOCIAL PLANNING *See* Social policy

SOCIAL POLICY
Corning, P. The fair society   **303.3**
Pickett, K. The spirit level   **306**

SOCIAL POLICY
    See also Planning; Social conditions

SOCIAL POLICY -- TEXAS
Collins, G. As Texas goes   **320.6**

SOCIAL POLICY -- UNITED STATES
The divide   **303.3**
Stone, J. M. Five easy theses   **330.973**
Woods, R. B. Prisoners of hope   **973.923**

SOCIAL PROBLEMS
Brokaw, T. The time of our lives   **973.927**
Nader, R. Told you so   **303.3**
Talbot, D. Season of the witch   **306**

SOCIAL PROBLEMS
    See also Social conditions; Sociology

SOCIAL PROBLEMS -- BRAZIL -- RIO DE JANEIRO
Barbassa, J. Dancing With the Devil in the City of God   **981.53**

SOCIAL PROBLEMS -- CALIFORNIA -- SAN FRANCISCO -- HISTORY -- 20TH CENTURY
Talbot, D. Season of the witch   **306**

SOCIAL PROBLEMS -- PSYCHOLOGICAL ASPECTS
Pipher, M. The green boat   **303.4**

SOCIAL PROBLEMS -- RUSSIA
Greene, D. Midnight in Siberia   **914.7**
Pomerantsev, P. Nothing is true and everything is possible   **306**

SOCIAL PROBLEMS -- UNITED STATES
Packer, G. The unwinding   **973.924**

SOCIAL PROBLEMS IN EDUCATION *See* Educational sociology

SOCIAL PROGRESS *See* Progress

SOCIAL PSYCHOLOGY
Aiken, M. The cyber effect   **155.9**
Davies, W. The happiness industry   **304**
Fromm, E. On being human   **150.19**
Gladwell, M. The tipping point   **302**
Gosling, S. Snoop   **155.9**
Greene, J. Moral tribes   **170**
Haidt, J. The righteous mind   **201**
Klinenberg, E. Going solo   **306.81**
Lieberman, M. D. Social   **302**

Robbins, A. The geeks shall inherit the Earth

Simons, E. The Secret Lives of Sports Fans **306.4**

Surowiecki, J. The wisdom of crowds **303.3**

Triandis, H. C. Fooling ourselves **155.2**

Zimbardo, P. The Lucifer effect **155.9**

SOCIAL PSYCHOLOGY

See also Human ecology; Psychology; Social groups; Sociology

SOCIAL PSYCHOLOGY -- UNITED STATES -- HISTORY

Fraser, S. The age of acquiescence **973.91**

SOCIAL REFORM See Social problems

SOCIAL REFORMERS

Ash, S. V. Firebrand of liberty **973.7**

Bainton, R. H. Here I stand: a life of Martin Luther **92**

Buk-Swienty, T. The other half **92**

Elie, P. The life you save may be your own **810**

Erikson, E. H. Young man Luther **92**

Fisher, J. T. On the Irish waterfront **331.7**

Greenfield, R. Timothy Leary **92**

Kozol, J. Letters to a young teacher **371.1**

Kung, H. Great Christian thinkers **230**

Lattin, D. The Harvard Psychedelic Club **920**

Oberman, H. A. Luther: man between God and the Devil **92**

Steffens, L. The autobiography of Lincoln Steffens **92**

Stevenson, B. Just Mercy **353.4**

Von Mehren, J. Minerva and the muse: a life of Margaret Fuller **92**

Wilson, D. A. Out of the storm **92**

SOCIAL REFORMERS -- UNITED STATES -- HISTORY

Young, R. Dissent **303.48**

SOCIAL RESPONSIBILITY OF BUSINESS

Auletta, K. Googled **338.7**

Elmore, B. J. Citizen Coke **338.7**

Mackey, J. Conscious capitalism **174**

SOCIAL RESPONSIBILITY OF BUSINESS

See also Business; Business ethics

SOCIAL RESPONSIBILITY OF BUSINESS -- UNITED STATES

Sachs, J. The price of civilization **330.9**

SOCIAL ROLE

See also Social psychology

SOCIAL SCIENCE -- ANTHROPOLOGY -- CULTURAL

Badkhen, A. The world is a carpet **958.1**

SOCIAL SCIENCES

Berger, J. Invisible Influence **302.13**

Calhoun, C. J. Dictionary of the social sciences **300**

Carr, N. G. Utopia is creepy **303.483**

Pagel, M. Wired for culture **303.4**

SOCIAL SCIENCES

See also Civilization

SOCIAL SCIENCES -- DICTIONARIES

Calhoun, C. J. Dictionary of the social sciences **300**

SOCIAL SCIENTISTS

Gates, H. L. Colored people **92**

SOCIAL SECURITY

Altman, N. J. The battle for Social Security **368.4**

Frank, J. The people's pension **368.4**

Matthews, J. L. Social security, Medicare & government pensions **344**

Social security handbook **368.4**

Solman, P. Get what's yours **368.4**

SOCIAL SECURITY

See also Pensions

Social security handbook. **368.4**

Social security, Medicare & government pensions. Matthews, J. L. **344**

SOCIAL SERVICE

Budd, K. The voluntourist **361.7**

SOCIAL STATUS

Brooks, D. The social animal **305.5**

SOCIAL STATUS

See also Social psychology

SOCIAL STATUS -- UNITED STATES

Epstein, J. Snobbery **305.5**

SOCIAL VALUES

Haidt, J. The righteous mind **201**

Wann, D. The new normal **306**

SOCIAL VALUES

See also Values

SOCIAL WELFARE See Charities; Public welfare; Social problems; Social work

SOCIAL WELFARE LEADERS

Addams, J. Twenty years at Hull-House **361.7**

Edelman, M. W. Lanterns **92**

Gibson, W. The miracle worker **812**

Herrmann, D. Helen Keller **92**

Keller, H. Helen Keller: selected writings **92**

Keller, H. The story of my life **92**

Knight, L. W. Jane Addams **92**

Tough, P. Whatever it takes **362.7**

SOCIAL WORK

Ackerman, D. A slender thread **362.28**

SOCIAL WORK WITH THE ELDERLY

See also Elderly; Social work

SOCIALISM

Tuchman, B. W. The proud tower **909.82**

SOCIALISM

See also Collectivism; Economics; Political science

SOCIALITES

Bowles, H. Jacqueline Kennedy **92**

Buckley, C. T. Losing Mum and Pup **92**

Cordery, S. A. Alice **92**

Davis, J. H. Jacqueline Bouvier **92**

Foreman, A. Georgiana, Duchess of Devonshire **941.07**

Gimbel, W. Havana dreams 972.91
Leaming, B. Mrs. Kennedy 973.922

**SOCIALITES -- UNITED STATES -- BIOGRA-
PHY**
Bingham, E. Irrepressible 306.76
Byrne, P. Kick 92
Cohen, L. All we know 920.72
Leaming, B. Kick Kennedy 92
Oller, J. American queen 92

SOCIALIZATION
Elman, N. M. The unwritten rules of friendship **649**
Sheehy, G. New passages 305.24

Society for the Study of the Short Story
A Reader's companion to the short story in English 809

SOCIETY OF FRIENDS
Boorstin, D. J. The Americans: The colonial expe-
rience 973
Hamm, T. D. The Quakers in America 289.6

Society's child. Ian, J. 92

SOCIETY, PRIMITIVE *See* Primitive societies

SOCIO-ECONOMIC STATUS *See* Social status

SOCIOBIOLOGY
Barash, D. P. Homo mysterious 303.4
Eldredge, N. Why we do it 155.3
Sykes, B. Adam's curse 599.93
Taylor, S. E. The tending instinct 304.5
Wilson, E. O. In search of nature 113

SOCIOBIOLOGY
See also Comparative psychology; Sociology

SOCIOECONOMICS
See also Economics; Sociology

SOCIOLINGUISTICS
Everett, D. L. Language 400
Lepore, J. A is for American 306.44

SOCIOLINGUISTICS
See also Language and languages; Linguistics; Sociology

SOCIOLOGISTS
Albom, M. Tuesdays with Morrie 378.1
Buruma, I. Murder in Amsterdam 364.152
Commager, H. S. The American mind 973
Coupland, D. Marshall McLuhan 92
Gates, H. L. The future of the race 305.896
Lewis, D. L. W.E.B. Du Bois 92
Patel, E. Acts of faith 92
Wilson, E. Patriotic gore 810

SOCIOLOGISTS -- UNITED STATES
Morris, A. D. The scholar denied 301

SOCIOLOGY
Cannadine, D. The undivided past 128
Commager, H. S. The American mind 973
Hochschild, A. R. The outsourced self 306.85

SOCIOLOGY
See also Social sciences

SOCIOLOGY -- BIBLIOGRAPHY

Required reading 301

SOCIOLOGY -- ENCYCLOPEDIAS
World of sociology 301

SOCIOLOGY -- HISTORY
Morris, A. D. The scholar denied 301

**SOCIOLOGY OF DISABILITY -- UNITED
STATES -- HISTORY**
Nielsen, K. E. A disability history of the United
States 362.4

SOCIOLOGY, MILITARY -- UNITED STATES
Dreazen, Y. The invisible front 92

SOCIOLOGY, URBAN *See* Urban sociology

SOCIOLOGY, URBAN -- HISTORY
Smith, P. D. City 307.76

SOCIOLOGY, URBAN -- PHILOSOPHY
Kanigel, R. Eyes on the street 92

Sock knitting master class. Budd, A. 746.432

SOCKS
Budd, A. New directions in sock knitting 746.432
Budd, A. Sock knitting master class 746.432

Socrates. Johnson, P. 92

Socrates
About
Hughes, B. The hemlock cup 92
Johnson, P. Socrates 92
Kreeft, P. Philosophy 101 by Socrates 183
Russell, B. A history of Western philosophy 109
Stone, I. F. The trial of Socrates 183
Waterfield, R. Why Socrates died 183

Soderbergh, Steven
About
Waxman, S. Rebels on the backlot 920

Sodha, Meera
Made in India 641.595

SODIUM CONTENT OF FOOD *See* Food -- Sodium content

Sodium girls limitless low-salt cookbook. 641.5

Soffee, Anne Thomas
Snake hips 793.3

Sofianides, Anna S.
(jt. auth) Harlow, G. E. Gems & Crystals 549

**SOFT DRINK INDUSTRY -- UNITED STATES
-- COMIC BOOKS, STRIPS, ETC**
Nalebuff, B. Mission in a bottle 338.7

SOFT TOY MAKING
Finnanger, T. Tilda's toy box 745.592

SOFT TOY MAKING
See also Sewing; Toy making

SOFTBALL
See also Ball games; Baseball; Sports

SOFTWARE FAILURES
Vamosi, R. When gadgets betray us 004

Sogyal
The Tibetan book of living and dying 294.3

SOIL CONSERVATION
See also Conservation of natural resources;

Environmental protection

SOIL ECOLOGY
Wolfe, D. W. Tales from the underground **578.7**

SOIL ECOLOGY
See also Ecology; Soils

SOIL FERTILITY See Soils

SOIL MICROBIOLOGY
Montgomery, D. R. The hidden half of nature **579**
Wolfe, D. W. Tales from the underground **578.7**

SOIL MICROBIOLOGY
Montgomery, D. R. The hidden half of nature **579**

SOIL MICROBIOLOGY
See also Microbiology; Sanitary engineering
The **soiling** of Old Glory. Masur, L. P. **974.4**

SOILS
Campbell, S. How to mulch **635**

SOILS
See also Agriculture; Economic geology

SOILS -- BACTERIOLOGY See Soil microbiology

Sojourner Truth. Painter, N. I. **305.5**

Sokol, Jason
All eyes are upon us **323.1**
There goes my everything **305.8**

Sokolove, Michael
Drama high **92**

Solakian, Susan E.
The homeowner's guide to managing a renovation **643**

SOLAR BATTERIES
See also Electric batteries; Photovoltaic power generation; Solar radiation

SOLAR CELLS See Photovoltaic power generation; Solar batteries

SOLAR ECLIPSES
See also Astronomy

SOLAR ENERGY
Barnham, K. The Burning Answer **333.79**
Ewing, R. A. Got sun? go solar **697**
Koerth-Baker, M. Before the lights go out **333.79**
Solar system. Chown, M. **523.2**

SOLAR SYSTEM
Baker, D. The 50 most extreme places in our solar system **523.2**
Brown, M. How I killed Pluto and why it had it coming **523.4**
Chown, M. Solar system **523.2**
Lang, K. R. The Cambridge guide to the solar system **523.2**
North, C. How to Read the Solar System **523.2**
Tyson, N. d. Death by black hole **523.8**
Ward, P. D. Life as we do not know it **576.8**
Weintraub, D. A. How old is the universe? **523.1**
Weintraub, D. A. Is Pluto a planet? **523.4**

SOLAR SYSTEM
See also Astronomy; Stars

SOLAR SYSTEM -- ATLASES
Trefil, J. Space atlas **520**
Soldaten. **940.54**

SOLDER AND SOLDERING
Bluhm, L. Creative soldered jewelry & accessories **745.594**

SOLDER AND SOLDERING See Soldering

SOLDERING
Bluhm, L. Creative soldered jewelry & accessories **745.594**

SOLDERING
See also Metals; Metalwork
Soldier girls. Thorpe, H. **956.704**
A **soldier** on the southern front. **940.4**
Soldier's heart. Samet, E. D. **810**
Soldier's heart. Tyler, C. **741.5**
Soldier: the life of Colin Powell. De Young, K. **92**

SOLDIERS
Atkinson, R. The guns at last light **940.54**
Beah, I. A long way gone **92**
Brown, E. Shake the devil off **364.152**
Brown, M. T.E. Lawrence **92**
Davis, W. C. Three roads to the Alamo **976.4**
Guibert, E. Alan's war **741.5**
Hastings, M. Warriors **355**
Herrington, S. A. Traitors among us **327.12**
Kindsvatter, P. S. American soldiers **355**
Korda, M. Hero **92**
Margolick, D. Beyond glory **796.8**
Mills, D. Sniper one **956.7**
Nelson, J. C. The remains of Company D **920**
Rostand, E. Cyrano de Bergerac **842**
Stephenson, M. The last full measure **305.9**
Young, A. F. Masquerade: the life and times of Deborah Sampson, Continental soldier **92**

SOLDIERS
See also Armies; Military personnel

SOLDIERS -- DRUG USE -- VIETNAM
Ulander, P. A. Walking point **959.704**

SOLDIERS -- FRANCE -- BIOGRAPHY
Castor, H. Joan of Arc **92**

SOLDIERS -- GERMANY
Weber, T. Hitler's first war **940.4**

SOLDIERS -- GERMANY -- ATTITUDES -- SOURCES
Soldaten **940.54**

SOLDIERS -- GRAPHIC NOVELS
Guibert, E. Alan's war **741.5**

SOLDIERS -- GREAT BRITAIN
Hochschild, A. To end all wars **940.3**
Korda, M. Hero **92**

SOLDIERS -- GREAT BRITAIN -- BIOGRAPHY
Anderson, S. Lawrence in Arabia **940.4**
Brown, M. T.E. Lawrence **92**
Sattin, A. The Young T. E. Lawrence **92**

SOLDIERS -- HUNGARY -- BIOGRAPHY

The burning of the world   **92**

SOLDIERS -- HYGIENE *See* Military personnel -- Health and hygiene

SOLDIERS -- INDIA -- BIOGRAPHY
Karnad, R. Farthest field   **940.54**

SOLDIERS -- ISRAEL
Bar-On, M. Moshe Dayan   **956.940**

SOLDIERS -- JAPAN -- BIOGRAPHY
Sakamoto, P. R. Midnight in broad daylight **940.53**

SOLDIERS -- LIBERIA
Dwyer, J. American warlord   **966.62**

SOLDIERS -- MENTAL HEALTH -- UNITED STATES
Dreazen, Y. The invisible front   **92**

SOLDIERS -- MENTAL HEALTH -- UNITED STATES -- HANDBOOKS, MANUALS, ETC
Lawhorne-Scott, C. Military mental health care   **355.3**

SOLDIERS -- PSYCHOLOGY
Roach, M. Grunt   **355.07**
Sites, K. The things they cannot say   **355**

SOLDIERS -- UNITED STATES
Hornfischer, J. D. Service   **956.704**
Ulander, P. A. Walking point   **959.704**
Weintraub, S. A Christmas far from home **951.904**

SOLDIERS -- UNITED STATES -- BIOGRAPHY
Ambrose, S. E. Citizen soldiers   **940.54**
Donald, A. D. Citizen soldier   **92**
Finkel, D. The good soldiers   **956.7**
Perry, J. M. Touched with fire   **973.7**
Rodriguez, D. Rise   **92**
Sadler, A. The 15:17 to Paris   **363.325**
Ulander, P. A. Walking point   **959.704**
Wolf, M. J. Abandoned in hell   **959.704**

SOLDIERS -- UNITED STATES -- HISTORY -- 20TH CENTURY
Weintraub, S. A Christmas far from home **951.904**

SOLDIERS -- UNITED STATES -- LANGUAGE -- DICTIONARIES
Axelrod, A. Whiskey tango foxtrot   **427**
Soldiers of fortune. Geraghty, T.   **355.3**
SOLDIERS OF FORTUNE *See* Mercenary soldiers
SOLDIERS' LIFE *See* Soldiers
Solensky, Michelle J.
(ed) The monarch butterfly   **595.7**
Soles, Clyde
The fire smart home handbook   **643**
SOLICITORS *See* Lawyers
SOLICITORS GENERAL
Marshall, T. Thurgood Marshall   **347**
Rowan, C. T. Dream makers, dream breakers **92**
Williams, J. Thurgood Marshall   **92**
SOLID GEOMETRY
See also Geometry
SOLID WASTE DISPOSAL *See* Refuse and refuse

disposal
SOLIDS
See also Physical chemistry; Physics
SOLILOQUIES
See also Drama; Monologues
Solin, Daniel R.
The smartest retirement book you'll ever read   **332.024**
SOLITAIRE (GAME)
See also Card games
The **solitary** self: Jean-Jacques Rousseau in exile and adversity. Cranston, M.   **92**
SOLITUDE
Axelrod, H. The point of vanishing   **92**
Connors, P. Fire season   **634.9**
SOLITUDE -- PSYCHOLOGICAL ASPECTS
Axelrod, H. The point of vanishing   **92**
Sollors, Werner
(ed) A new literary history of America   **810**
Solman, Paul
Get what's yours   **368.4**
Solnit, Rebecca
A paradise built in hell   **303.4**
Wanderlust   **796.51**
About
Solnit, R. The Faraway Nearby   **814**
The **soloist**. Lopez, S.   **92**
Solomon, Andrew
Far from the tree   **362.4**
The noonday demon   **616.85**
Solomon, Deborah, 1957-
American mirror   **92**
Jackson Pollock   **92**
Solomon, John
DSK   **306.77**
Solomon, Laura
The librarian's nitty-gritty guide to social media   **006.7**
Solomon, Maynard
Mozart   **92**
Solomon, Robert C.
A passion for wisdom   **109**
What Nietzsche really said   **193**
Solomon, Steven
Water   **553.7**
Solomon, Susan
The coldest March   **919**
Solomonov, Michael, 1978-
(jt. auth) Cook, S. Zahav   **641.59**
Solve your money troubles. Leonard, R.   **346**
SOLVENT ABUSE
See also Social problems; Substance abuse
Solzhenitsyn, Aleksandr, 1918-2008
The Gulag Archipelago, 1918-1956 v1   **365**
The Gulag Archipelago, 1918-1956 v2   **365**
The Gulag Archipelago, 1918-1956 v3   **365**

About

Remnick, D. Reporting **814**

Tolstaia, T. Pushkin's children **891.7**

SOMALI-ETHIOPIAN CONFLICT, 1979-

Rawlence, B. City of thorns **967.73**

SOMALIA -- BIOGRAPHY

Abdi, H. Keeping hope alive **92**

Steinberg, J. A man of good hope **92**

SOMALIA -- HISTORY -- 1991-

Corbett, S. A house in the sky **92**

SOMALIA -- SOCIAL CONDITIONS

Fergusson, J. The world's most dangerous place **967.73**

Steinberg, J. A man of good hope **92**

Some enchanted evenings. Kaufman, D. **92**

Some of the dharma. Kerouac, J. **294.3**

Somers Heidhues, Mary F.

Southeast Asia: a concise history **959**

Somerset, Anne

Queen Anne **92**

Somerset, James, fl. 1769-1772

About

Wise, S. M. Though the heavens may fall **342**

Something in the air. Hoffer, R. **796.4**

Something in the Blood. Skal, D. J. **823.8**

Something incredibly wonderful happens. Cole, K. C. **92**

Something like an autobiography. Kurosawa, A. **92**

Something like the gods. Amidon, S. **306.4**

Something Must Be Done About Prince Edward County. Green, K. **379.26**

Something to chew on. Gibney, M. **616.02**

Something urgent I have to say to you: the life and works of William Carlos Williams. Leibowitz, H. A. **92**

Something's rising. House, S. **338.2**

Sometimes an art, never a science, always a craft. Bailyn, B. **907.2**

Sometimes there is a void. Mda, Z. **828**

Somewhere. Vaill, A. **92**

Somewhere towards the end. Athill, D. **92**

The **Somme.** Hart, P. **940.4**

Somme. Sebag-Montefiore, H. **940.4**

SOMME, 1ST BATTLE OF THE, FRANCE, 1916

Sacco, J. The Great War **940.4**

Sebag-Montefiore, H. Somme **940.4**

Sommer, Alfred

Getting what we deserve **362.1**

Sommer, Jason

(ed) Hopper, J. The first collection of criticism by a living female rock critic

Sommers, Michael

Moon Rio De Janeiro **918.15**

Sommers, Sam

(jt. auth) Wertheim, L. J. This is your brain on sports **796**

Son of the Morning Star. Connell, E. S. **973.8**

Sondheim, Stephen, 1930-

About

Finishing the hat **92**

Look, I made a hat **782.1**

Sone, Monica Itoi, 1919-2011

About

Sone, M. Nisei daughter **979.7**

A **song** flung up to heaven. Angelou, M. **818**

SONG LYRICS See Popular song lyrics

The **song** machine. Seabrook, J. **781.64**

The **song** of Roland. Chanson de Roland **841**

The **song** of the ape. Halloran, A. R. **599.885**

SONG WRITING See Composition (Music); Popular music -- Writing and publishing

SONGBIRDS -- BEHAVIOR

What the robin knows **598.8**

Songbook. Saba, U. **851**

SONGBOOKS

See also Singing; Songs

The **songlines.** Chatwin, B. **919**

SONGS

Sondheim, S. Finishing the hat **92**

SONGS

See also Poetry; Vocal music

Songs of unreason. Harrison, J. **811**

SONGS, AFRICAN AMERICAN See African American music

SONGWRITERS

Adler, W. M. The man who never died **92**

The Beatles anthology **782.421**

Brown, M. Tearing down the wall of sound **92**

Browne, D. Fire and rain **781.66**

Byrne, D. Bicycle diaries **796.6**

Cash, R. Composed **92**

Cohodas, N. Princess Noire **92**

Crowell, R. Chinaberry sidewalks **92**

Dunaway, D. K. How can I keep from singing? **92**

Dylan, B. Chronicles **92**

Emerson, K. Doo-dah!: Stephen Foster and the rise of American popular culture **92**

Escott, C. Hank Williams **92**

Govenar, A. B. Lightnin' Hopkins **92**

Grant, C. The natural mystics **920**

Gray, M. The Bob Dylan encyclopedia **782.42**

Gray, M. Hand me my travelin' shoes **92**

Greenberg, K. E. December 8, 1980 **92**

Halberstam, D. The children **323.1**

Hemphill, P. Lovesick blues **92**

Hopkins, J. No one here gets out alive **92**

Hoskyns, B. Lowside of the road **92**

James, E. Rage to survive **92**

Klein, J. Woody Guthrie **92**

Kleist, R. Johnny Cash **92**

Kruth, J. To live's to fly **92**

Leiber, J. Hound dog **92**

Lynn, L. Still woman enough   92
Mazor, B. Meeting Jimmie Rodgers   92
Norman, P. John Lennon   92
Patoski, J. N. Willie Nelson   92
Riley, T. Lennon   92
Riordan, J. Break on through: the life and death of
  Jim Morrison   92
Sounes, H. Fab   92
Spitz, B. The Beatles: the biography   920
Streissguth, M. Johnny Cash   92
Trynka, P. Iggy Pop   92
Wald, E. Escaping the delta   92
Weller, S. Girls like us   920
Wilkinson, A. The protest singer   92
Wolfe, C. K. The life and legend of Leadbelly   92
Zappa, F. The real Frank Zappa book   92
Zevon, C. I'll sleep when I'm dead   92
Zwonitzer, M. Will you miss me when I'm
  gone?   781.642

SONGWRITERS *See* Composers; Lyricists
SONGWRITERS AND SONGWRITING
  2015 songwriter's market   338.4
  Lehman, D. A fine romance   782.42
SONGWRITING *See* Composition (Music); Popu-
  lar music -- Writing and publishing
Sonic wind. Ryan, C.   92
Sonnenberg, Susanna
About
  Sonnenberg, S. Her last death   92
SONNETS
    See also Poetry
Sonnets from the Portuguese. Browning, E. B.   821
Sonnets to Orpheus. Rilke, R. M.   831
SONS
    See also Family; Men
**SONS -- FAMILY RELATIONSHIPS -- UNITED
  STATES**
  Hodgman, G. Bettyville   306.874
SONS -- UNITED STATES -- DEATH
  Dreazen, Y. The invisible front   92
Sons and brothers: the days of Jack and Bobby Ken-
  nedy. Mahoney, R. D.   92
SONS AND FATHERS *See* Father-son relationship
SONS AND MOTHERS *See* Mother-son relation-
  ship
Sons of Mississippi. Hendrickson, P.   305.8
Sontag, Susan, 1933-2004
  At the same time   814
  Leibovitz, A. Women   779
  Regarding the pain of others   303.6
About
  As consciousness is harnessed to flesh   818
  Kaplan, A. Dreaming in French   944
  Rollyson, C. E. Susan Sontag   818
  Sontag, S. Reborn   92
SOOTHSAYING *See* Divination

Sooyong Park
  Great Soul of Siberia   599.756
Sophia. Anand, A.   92
Sophia, Princess, 1777-1848
About
  Fraser, F. Princesses   920
**Sophie Elisabeth, Duchess, consort of August,
  Duke of Braunschweig-Lüneburg, 1613-1676**
About
  Porter, C. H. Five lives in music   780.92
Sophocles. Sophocles   882
Sophocles
  Heaney, S. The burial at Thebes   822
  The Theban plays of Sophocles   882
  Sophocles   882
SOPORIFICS *See* Narcotics
The **sorcerer's** apprentice. Richardson, J.   92
SORCERY *See* Magic; Occultism; Witchcraft
Sorensen, Theodore C., 1928-2010
About
  Sorensen, T. C. Counselor   92
Sorkin, Andrew Ross
  Too big to fail   330.9
SORROW *See* Bereavement; Grief; Joy and sor-
  row
A **sorrow** in our heart: the life of Tecumseh. Eckert,
  A. W.   977
Sosnowski, Andrzej
  Lodgings   891.8
Soto, Hernando de
  The mystery of capital   330.12
Soto, Jock
About
  Marshall, L. Every step you take   92
Sotomayor, Sonia, 1954-
About
  Sotomayor, S. My beloved world   92
Souder, William
  On a farther shore   92
Soufan, Ali H.
  The black banners   973.931
Soukup, Ruth
  Unstuffed   646.7
SOUL
  Hofstadter, D. R. I am a strange loop   153
  Kore   610
  Roach, M. Spook   133.9
SOUL
    See also Future life; Human beings (Theol-
    ogy); Philosophy
Soul by soul. Johnson, W.   326
Soul food. Miller, A.   641.59
Soul food love.   641.59
Soul made flesh. Zimmer, C.   612.8
SOUL MUSIC
  Gordon, R. Respect yourself   384

Ribowsky, M. Dreams to remember   92
SOUL MUSIC -- HISTORY AND CRITICISM
Ribowsky, M. Dreams to remember   92
SOUL MUSICIANS
Brown, J. James Brown, the godfather of soul   92
Cohodas, N. Princess Noire   92
Guralnick, P. Dream boogie   92
James, E. Rage to survive   92
Ritz, D. Respect   92
Sullivan, J. The hardest working man   92
SOUL MUSICIANS -- UNITED STATES -- BI-
  OGRAPHY
Cee-Lo Everybody's brother   782.421
McBride, J. Kill 'em and leave   92
Ribowsky, M. Dreams to remember   92
Smith, R. J. The one   92
The **soul** of a new cuisine. Samuelsson, M.   641.5
The **soul** of an octopus. Montgomery, S.   594
The **soul** of baseball. Posnanski, J.   796.357
The **soul** of battle. Hanson, V. D.   355
Soul of the age. Bate, J.   822.3
The **soul** searcher's handbook. Mildon, E.   131
The **souls** of Black folk. Du Bois, W. E. B.   305.8
Souls of the Labadie tract. Howe, S.   811
SOUND
  See also Physics; Pneumatics; Radiation
SOUND -- PSYCHOLOGICAL ASPECTS
Keizer, G. The unwanted sound of everything we
want   363.7
SOUND -- RECORDING AND REPRODUCING
Milner, G. Perfecting sound forever   781.49
SOUND -- RECORDING AND REPRODUCING
  -- HISTORY
Day, T. A century of recorded music   780.26
Sound and fury. Kindred, D.   796
SOUND BOOKS
  See also Picture books for children; Toy and
  movable books
SOUND EFFECTS
  See also Sound
The **sound** of a wild snail eating. Bailey, E. T.   92
The **sound** of gravel. Wariner, R.   92
SOUND OF MUSIC (MOTION PICTURE)
Santopietro, T. The sound of music story   791.43
The **sound** of music story. Santopietro, T.   791.43
SOUND RECORDING EXECUTIVES AND
  PRODUCERS -- UNITED STATES -- BIOG-
  RAPHY
Guralnick, P. Sam Phillips   92
SOUND RECORDING INDUSTRY
Seabrook, J. The song machine   781.64
SOUND RECORDING INDUSTRY -- VOCA-
  TIONAL GUIDANCE
Zen and the art of recording   621.389
SOUND RECORDINGS
Crews, K. D. Copyright law for librarians and edu-

cators   346.04
Milner, G. Perfecting sound forever   781.49
The Nixon tapes   973.924
Wade, S. The beautiful music all around us   781.62
Zen and the art of recording   621.389
SOUND RECORDINGS -- ALBUM COVERS
Crumb, R. R. Crumb: the complete record cover
  collection   741.6
Paulo, J. Jazz covers   781.65
SOUND RECORDINGS -- HISTORY
Day, T. A century of recorded music   780.26
SOUND RECORDINGS -- REVIEWS
Cook, R. The Penguin guide to jazz record-
  ings   781.65
Soundings. Felt, H.   526
SOUNDPROOFING
  See also Architectural acoustics; Sound
SOUNDS
  See also Sound
The **sounds** of poetry. Pinsky, R.   808.5
The **sounds** of slavery. White, S.   326
Sounds of the river. Chen, D.   951.05
Sounes, Howard
  Fab   92
The **soup** club cookbook. Peacock, J.   641.81
SOUPS
  Bowl   641.81
  Broth   641.813
  Peacock, J. The soup club cookbook   641.81
  Thomas, A. Love soup   641.5
SOUPS
  See also Cooking
Sources of strength. Carter, J.   248.4
Soussan, Michael
  Backstabbing for beginners   363.8
SOUTH (U.S.) *See* Southern States
SOUTH AFRICA
Steinberg, J. Sizwe's test   362.1
SOUTH AFRICA
  See also Africa; Southern Africa
SOUTH AFRICA -- COMMISSION FOR TRUTH
  AND RECONCILIATION
Tutu, D. No future without forgiveness   968.06
SOUTH AFRICA -- DESCRIPTION AND TRAV-
  EL
Theroux, P. Last train to Zona Verde   916
SOUTH AFRICA -- HISTORY
Meredith, M. Diamonds, gold, and war   968.04
SOUTH AFRICA -- POLITICS AND GOVERN-
  MENT
Mda, Z. Sometimes there is a void   828
SOUTH AFRICA -- POLITICS AND GOVERN-
  MENT -- 1836-1909
Guha, R. Gandhi before India   92
SOUTH AFRICA -- POLITICS AND GOVERN-
  MENT -- 20TH CENTURY

Carlin, J. Playing the enemy **968.06**

Mandela, N. Conversations with myself **92**

SOUTH AFRICA -- POLITICS AND GOVERN-MENT -- ANECDOTES

Jones, B. Mandela **92**

SOUTH AFRICA -- RACE RELATIONS

Gevisser, M. Lost and Found in Johannesburg, a memoir **92**

SOUTH AFRICA -- RACE RELATIONS

See also Race relations

SOUTH AFRICA -- RACE RELATIONS -- AN-ECDOTES

Jones, B. Mandela **92**

SOUTH AFRICA -- RACE RELATIONS -- DRA-MA

Fugard, A. Master Harold-- and the boys **822**

SOUTH AFRICA -- SOCIAL LIFE AND CUS-TOMS

Burge, K. The born frees **305.242**

SOUTH AFRICAN WAR, 1899-1902

Meredith, M. Diamonds, gold, and war **968.04**

Millard, C. Hero of the empire **968.04**

SOUTH AMERICA -- HISTORY -- WARS OF IN-DEPENDENCE, 1806-1830

Arana, M. Bolivar **92**

SOUTH AMERICA -- SOCIAL LIFE AND CUS-TOMS

Hely, S. The wonder trail **917.28**

Kijac, M. B. The South American table **641.59**

SOUTH AMERICAN ART

See also Art

SOUTH AMERICAN LITERATURE *See* Latin American literature

The **South** American table. Kijac, M. B. **641.59**

SOUTH ASIA -- DESCRIPTION AND TRAVEL

Mishra, P. Temptations of the West **954.05**

SOUTH ASIA -- EMIGRATION AND IMMI-GRATION -- HISTORY

Lee, E. The making of Asian America **973**

SOUTH ASIA -- FOREIGN RELATIONS -- UNITED STATES

Bass, G. J. The Blood telegram **327.73**

SOUTH ASIA -- RELIGION

Eastern religions **200.9**

SOUTH BEACH (MIAMI BEACH, FLA.) -- SO-CIAL LIFE AND CUSTOMS

Gaines, S. S. Fool's paradise **975.9**

SOUTH CAROLINA

Ball, E. Slaves in the family **975.7**

SOUTH CAROLINA -- HISTORY

Lane, C. A Nation Wholly Free **336.3**

SOUTH CAROLINA -- RACE RELATIONS

Harris, J. W. The hanging of Thomas Jeremiah **92**

SOUTH POLE

Preston, D. A first rate tragedy **919**

Solomon, S. The coldest March **919**

SOUTHEAST ASIA -- DESCRIPTION AND TRAVEL

Gargan, E. A. A river's tale **915**

SOUTHEAST ASIA -- HISTORY

Somers Heidhues, M. F. Southeast Asia: a concise history **959**

Southeast Asia: a concise history. Somers Heidhues, M. F. **959**

SOUTHEAST ASIAN COOKING

Alford, J. Hot, sour, salty, sweet **641.59**

Meehan, P. Lucky Peach 101 easy Asian reci-pes **641.595**

A **southerly** course. Foose, M. H. **641.59**

SOUTHERN AFRICA

See also Africa

SOUTHERN COOKING

Acheson, H. The broad fork **641.597**

Acheson, H. A New Turn in the South **641.59**

Brock, S. Heritage **641.59**

Castle, S. The southern living community cookbook

Cooking my way back home **641.5**

Currence, J. Pickles, pigs & whiskey **641.59**

Dupree, N. Mastering the art of Southern cook-ing **641.59**

Foose, M. H. Screen doors and sweet tea **641.5**

Foose, M. H. A southerly course **641.59**

Grimes, D. The B.T.C. old-fashioned grocery cookbook **641.59**

Jordan, C. Sweetness **641**

Lang, R. The Southern vegetable book **641.65**

Lee, M. The Lee Bros. southern cookbook **641.5**

Lee, M. The Lee Bros. Charleston kitchen **641.59**

Lewis, E. The gift of Southern cooking **641.59**

Lewis, E. The taste of country cooking **641.5**

Neely, P. Down home with the Neelys **641.5**

The one true barbecue **641.5**

Southern living 50 years **975**

Terry, B. Vegan Soul kitchen **641.5**

Thompson-Anderson, T. Texas on the Ta-ble **641.597**

SOUTHERN COOKING

See also Cooking

Southern living 50 years. **975**

The **southern** living community cookbook. Castle, S.

Southern Living Magazine

(comp) The New Southern Living Garden Book **635.9**

(comp) Southern living 50 years **975**

Southern messenger poets [series]

Kirby, D. Talking about movies with Jesus **811**

SOUTHERN STATES

Deep South **975**

Disbrowe, P. Down south **641.59**

Mann, S. Hold Still **92**

Mayes, F. Under magnolia **92**

SOUTHERN STATES

See also United States

SOUTHERN STATES -- BIOGRAPHY

Bragg, R. Ava's man   **975**

Deep South   **975**

Savigneau, J. Carson McCullers   **813**

SOUTHERN STATES -- CIVILIZATION -- 21ST CENTURY

Thompson, T. The new mind of the South   **305.8**

SOUTHERN STATES -- DESCRIPTION AND TRAVEL

Southern living 50 years   **975**

SOUTHERN STATES -- ECONOMIC CONDITIONS

The Causes of the Civil War   **973.7**

SOUTHERN STATES -- HISTORY

Snyder, J. Hill of Beans   **92**

Williams, D. Bitterly divided   **973.7**

SOUTHERN STATES -- HISTORY

See also United States -- History

SOUTHERN STATES -- HUMOR

Blount, R. Long time leaving   **975**

SOUTHERN STATES -- INTELLECTUAL LIFE

The Companion to southern literature   **810**

SOUTHERN STATES -- RACE RELATIONS

Maraniss, A. Strong inside   **92**

McCluskey, A. T. A forgotten sisterhood   **370.922**

Safran, J. God'll Cut You Down   **364.152**

SOUTHERN STATES -- RACE RELATIONS -- HISTORY

Dray, P. Capitol men   **920**

Lemann, N. Redemption: the last battle of the Civil War   **975**

McCluskey, A. T. A forgotten sisterhood   **370.922**

Williams, D. Bitterly divided   **973.7**

SOUTHERN STATES -- RACE RELATIONS -- HISTORY -- 20TH CENTURY

Lewis, A. B. The shadows of youth   **323.1**

McGuire, D. L. At the dark end of the street   **323.1**

Sokol, J. There goes my everything   **305.8**

SOUTHERN STATES -- SOCIAL CONDITIONS

Bragg, R. The prince of Frogtown   **92**

Deep South   **975**

McCluskey, A. T. A forgotten sisterhood   **370.922**

SOUTHERN STATES -- SOCIAL LIFE AND CUSTOMS

Deep South   **975**

The one true barbecue   **641.5**

The **Southern** vegetable book. Lang, R.   **641.65**

SOUTHERN WOMEN -- RELIGIOUS LIFE

Circling faith   **200.8**

SOUTHWESTERN STATES

DeBuys, W. E. A great aridness   **551.6**

SOUTHWESTERN STATES

See also United States

SOUTHWESTERN STATES -- ANTIQUITIES

Childs, C. L. House of rain   **978.9**

Sova, Dawn B.

Critical companion to Edgar Allan Poe   **818**

Sovereign ladies. Waller, M.   **920**

SOVEREIGNS *See* Emperors; Kings and rulers; Monarchy; Queens

SOVEREIGNTY

See also International law; Political science

SOVIET COMMUNISM *See* Communism -- Russia

SOVIET UNION

Radzinsky, E. Stalin   **92**

SOVIET UNION *See* Russia -- History -- 1917-1991, Soviet Union

SOVIET UNION -- BIOGRAPHY

Aleksievich, S. Secondhand time   **947.086**

SOVIET UNION -- COMMUNISM *See* Communism -- Russia

SOVIET UNION -- FICTION

Hoffman, D. E. The Billion Dollar Spy   **327.12**

SOVIET UNION -- FOREIGN RELATIONS

Service, R. Trotsky   **92**

SOVIET UNION -- FOREIGN RELATIONS -- 1945-1991

Gordin, M. D. Red cloud at dawn   **355**

SOVIET UNION -- FOREIGN RELATIONS -- 1985-1991

Service, R. The End of the Cold War, 1985-1991   **909.82**

SOVIET UNION -- FOREIGN RELATIONS -- GERMANY

Moorhouse, R. The Devils' Alliance   **940.53**

SOVIET UNION -- FOREIGN RELATIONS -- UNITED STATES

Alperovitz, G. The decision to use the atomic bomb and the architecture of an American myth   **940.54**

Carlson, P. K blows top   **947.085**

Coleman, D. G. The fourteenth day   **73.922**

Costigliola, F. Roosevelt's lost alliances   **940.53**

Dobbs, M. Six months in 1945   **940.53**

Finn, P. The Zhivago affair   **891.73**

FitzGerald, F. Way out there in the blue   **973.927**

Fursenko, A. V. One hell of a gamble   **973.922**

Gates, R. M. From the shadows   **327**

Gordin, M. D. Red cloud at dawn   **355**

Kennedy, R. F. Thirteen days   **973.922**

Mann, J. The rebellion of Ronald Reagan   **973.927**

Ratnesar, R. Tear down this wall   **973.927**

Service, R. The End of the Cold War, 1985-1991   **909.82**

SOVIET UNION -- HISTORY

Hochschild, A. The unquiet ghost   **947.084**

Hosking, G. A. Russia and the Russians   **947**

Montefiore, S. Stalin: the court of the red tsar   **92**

Montefiore, S. Young Stalin   **92**

Pipes, R. Russia under the Bolshevik regime   **947.084**

Riasanovsky, N. V. A history of Russia **947**

Satter, D. Age of delirium **947.085**

Service, R. Trotsky **92**

Service, R. Stalin **92**

Snyder, T. D. Bloodlands **940.54**

Volkogonov, D. A. Lenin **947.084**

SOVIET UNION -- HISTORY *See* Russia -- History -- 1917-1991, Soviet Union

SOVIET UNION -- HISTORY -- 1917-1921, REVOLUTION

Figes, O. A people's tragedy **947.084**

Palmer, J. The bloody white baron **92**

Pomper, P. Lenin's brother **92**

Reed, J. Ten days that shook the world **947.084**

SOVIET UNION -- HISTORY -- 1917-1921, REVOLUTION *See* Russia -- History -- 1917-1921, Revolution

SOVIET UNION -- HISTORY -- 1917-1936

Snyder, T. D. Bloodlands **940.54**

SOVIET UNION -- HISTORY -- 1925-1953

Brent, J. Stalin's last crime **947.084**

Kizny, T. Gulag **365**

Kotkin, S. Stalin **92**

Montefiore, S. Stalin: the court of the red tsar **92**

Service, R. Stalin **92**

SOVIET UNION -- HISTORY -- 1925-1953 -- BIOGRAPHY

Sullivan, R. Stalin's daughter **92**

SOVIET UNION -- HISTORY -- 1939-1940, WAR WITH FINLAND *See* Russo-Finnish War, 1939-1940

SOVIET UNION -- HISTORY -- 1939-1945

Roberts, G. Stalin's general **940.54**

SOVIET UNION -- HISTORY -- 1953-1991 *See* Russia -- History -- 1953-1991

SOVIET UNION -- HISTORY -- PICTORIAL WORKS

King, D. Red star over Russia **947**

SOVIET UNION -- HISTORY -- REVOLUTION, 1917-1921 -- PERSONAL NARRATIVES

Competing voices from the Russian Revolution **947.084**

Memories **92**

SOVIET UNION -- INTELLECTUAL LIFE

Polonsky, R. Molotov's magic lantern **947**

SOVIET UNION -- POLITICS AND GOVERNMENT

Amis, M. Koba the dread **947.084**

Applebaum, A. Gulag **365**

Conquest, R. Stalin **92**

Gorbachev, M. On my country and the world **947.085**

Kizny, T. Gulag **365**

Kotkin, S. Uncivil society **947**

Medvedev, R. A. Let history judge **947.084**

Nikita Khrushchev **92**

Pleshakov, K. There is no freedom without bread! **947**

Remnick, D. Lenin's tomb **947.085**

Sebestyen, V. Revolution 1989 **947**

Solzhenitsyn, A. The Gulag Archipelago, 1918-1956 v1 **365**

Solzhenitsyn, A. The Gulag Archipelago, 1918-1956 v2 **365**

Solzhenitsyn, A. The Gulag Archipelago, 1918-1956 v3 **365**

SOVIET UNION -- POLITICS AND GOVERNMENT -- 1917-1936

Amis, M. Koba the dread **947.084**

Kotkin, S. Stalin **92**

Mandelstam, N. Hope against hope **891.71**

Service, R. Lenin--a biography **947.084**

SOVIET UNION -- POLITICS AND GOVERNMENT -- 1925-1953

Medvedev, R. A. Let history judge **947.084**

SOVIET UNION -- POLITICS AND GOVERNMENT -- 1936-1953

Amis, M. Koba the dread **947.084**

Gellately, R. Stalin's curse **947.084**

Kotkin, S. Stalin **92**

Mandelstam, N. Hope against hope **891.71**

Stalin **92**

SOVIET UNION -- POLITICS AND GOVERNMENT -- 1953-1985

Finn, P. The Zhivago affair **891.73**

Nikita Khrushchev **92**

SOVIET UNION -- RED ARMY

Merridale, C. Ivan's war **940.54**

SOVIET UNION -- RELATIONS -- EUROPE, EASTERN

Applebaum, A. Iron curtain **947**

SOVIET UNION -- SOCIAL CONDITIONS

Aleksievich, S. Secondhand time **947.086**

Applebaum, A. Iron curtain **947**

SOVIET UNION -- SOCIAL LIFE AND CUSTOMS

Von Bremzen, A. Mastering the art of Soviet cooking **641.59**

Sowards, Steven W.

(ed) Guide to Reference in Business and Economics **016**

Sowell, Thomas

Basic economics **330**

Sowing seeds in the desert. Fukuoka, M. **631.6**

Soyinka, Wole, 1934-

Of Africa **960**

About

Soyinka, W. You must set forth at dawn **92**

SPACE AND TIME

Bodanis, D. E **530.1**

Carroll, S. M. From eternity to here **530.1**

Frank, A. About time **523.1**

Gribbin, J. 13.8 — **523.1**

Hawking, S. W. The nature of space and time — **530.1**

Kaku, M. Hyperspace — **530.1**

Muller, R. A. Now — **530.11**

Susskind, L. The black hole war — **530.1**

Toomey, D. M. The new time travelers — **530.1**

SPACE AND TIME

    See also Fourth dimension; Metaphysics; Space sciences; Time

SPACE AND TIME -- PHILOSOPHY

Musser, G. Spooky action at a distance — **530.11**

SPACE AND TIME -- POPULAR WORKS

Gleick, J. Time travel — **530.11**

Space atlas. Trefil, J. — **520**

SPACE BIOLOGY

Catling, D. C. Astrobiology — **576.8**

Roach, M. Packing for Mars — **571**

Tyson, N. d. Death by black hole — **523.8**

SPACE BIOLOGY

    See also Biology; Space sciences

The **space** book. Bell, J. — **523.1**

SPACE CHEMISTRY

    See also Chemistry

Space chronicles. — **629.4**

SPACE COLONIES

McCray, W. P. The visioneers — **509**

Wohlforth, C. Beyond Earth — **629.455**

SPACE DEBRIS

    See also Pollution; Space environment

SPACE ENVIRONMENT

    See also Astronomy; Outer space

SPACE EXPLORATION (ASTRONAUTICS)

    See Outer space -- Exploration

SPACE FLIGHT

Guthrie, J. How to make a spaceship — **629.47**

Kranz, E. F. Failure is not an option — **629.45**

Massimino, M. Spaceman — **92**

Teitel, A. S. Breaking the Chains of Gravity — **629.4**

SPACE FLIGHT

    See also Aeronautics -- Flights; Astronautics

SPACE FLIGHT (FICTION) *See* Imaginary voyages; Science fiction

SPACE FLIGHT -- FORECASTING

Space chronicles — **629.4**

SPACE FLIGHT -- PHYSIOLOGICAL EFFECT

Wohlforth, C. Beyond Earth — **629.455**

SPACE FLIGHT TO MARS

Kessler, A. Martian summer — **523.4**

SPACE FLIGHT TO THE MOON

Aldrin, B. No dream is too high — **92**

Mailer, N. Of a fire on the moon — **629.45**

Nelson, C. Rocket men — **629.45**

Pyle, R. Destination moon — **629.45**

Worden, A. Falling to Earth — **92**

SPACE FLIGHT TO THE MOON

    See also Astronautics; Space flight

SPACE FLIGHT TO THE MOON -- HISTORY

Barbree, J. Neil Armstrong — **92**

Pyle, R. Destination moon — **629.45**

SPACE FLIGHTS -- UNITED STATES -- HISTORY

Massimino, M. Spaceman — **92**

SPACE PERCEPTION

Ellard, C. You are here — **153.7**

SPACE PHOTOGRAPHY

Astronomy photographer of the year — **520**

Benson, M. Far out — **778.3**

SPACE SCIENCES

Cole, K. C. The hole in the universe — **530.01**

SPACE VEHICLES

Manning, R. Mars Rover Curiosity — **629.295**

Space, in chains. Kasischke, L. — **811**

SPACE, OUTER *See* Outer space

SPACECRAFT *See* Space vehicles

Spaceman. Massimino, M. — **92**

Spaeth, Paul J.

    (ed) A thing that is — **811**

Spain. Koehler, J. — **641.59**

Spain. Goodwin, R. — **946**

SPAIN -- CIVILIZATION

Lowney, C. A vanished world — **946**

SPAIN -- COLONIES

Thomas, H. Rivers of gold — **980**

SPAIN -- DESCRIPTION

Dk Eyewitness Back Roads Spain — **914.6**

Hemingway, E. The dangerous summer — **791.8**

Stewart, C. Driving over lemons — **946.083**

SPAIN -- HISTORY

Downey, K. Isabella — **92**

Ekin, D. The Last Armada — **941.505**

Goodwin, R. Spain — **946**

SPAIN -- HISTORY -- 1898, WAR OF 1898 *See* Spanish-American War, 1898

SPAIN -- HISTORY -- 1936-1939, CIVIL WAR

Hochschild, A. Spain in our hearts — **946.081**

Rhodes, R. Hell and Good Company — **946.081**

SPAIN -- HISTORY -- FERDINAND AND ISABELLA, 1479-1516

Downey, K. Isabella — **92**

SPAIN -- SOCIAL LIFE AND CUSTOMS

Tremlett, G. Ghosts of Spain — **946**

Spain in our hearts. Hochschild, A. — **946.081**

SPAM (ELECTRONIC MAIL)

Krebs, B. Spam nation — **364.16**

Spam nation. Krebs, B. — **364.16**

SPANISCHE REITSCHULE (VIENNA, AUSTRIA) -- HISTORY -- 20TH CENTURY

Letts, E. The perfect horse — **940.54**

SPANISH AMERICAN LITERATURE *See* American literature (Spanish); Latin American literature

SPANISH ARMADA, 1588

See also Great Britain -- History -- 1485-1603, Tudors; Spain -- History

SPANISH COOKING

Andres, J. Tapas   **641.8**
Charcuteria   **641.594**
Koehler, J. Spain   **641:59**
Ortega, S. 1080 recipes   **641.5**
Roden, C. The food of Spain   **641.5**
The **Spanish** Inquisition. Perez, J.   **272**
The **Spanish** Inquisition. Kamen, H.   **272**

SPANISH LANGUAGE

See also Language and languages; Romance languages

SPANISH LANGUAGE -- DICTIONARIES

Houghton Mifflin Co. The Concise American Heritage Spanish dictionary   **463**

SPANISH LANGUAGE -- HISTORY

Barlow, J. The story of Spanish   **460**

SPANISH LITERATURE

See also Literature; Romance literature

SPANISH LITERATURE -- HISTORY AND CRITICISM

The Cambridge history of Spanish literature   **860**

SPANISH POETRY -- COLLECTIONS

The Penguin book of Spanish verse   **861**

SPANISH-AMERICAN WAR, 1898

Craig, W. Yankee come home   **917.2**
Thomas, E. The war lovers   **973.8**
Tuccille, J. The roughest riders   **973.8**
Zimmermann, W. First great triumph   **973**

SPANISH-AMERICAN WAR, 1898

See also Spain -- History; United States -- History -- 1865-1898; United States -- History -- 1898-1919

SPANISH-AMERICAN WAR, 1898 -- CAMPAIGNS

Tuccille, J. The roughest riders   **973.8**

SPANISH-AMERICAN WAR, 1898 -- CAMPAIGNS -- CUBA

Gardner, M. L. Rough Riders   **973.91**

SPANISH-AMERICAN WAR, 1898 -- CAUSES

Thomas, E. The war lovers   **973.8**

Spar, Debora L.

Wonder Women   **305.42**
Spare parts. Davis, J.   **629.8**
The **spark.** Barnett, K.   **618.92**
The **spark** of life. Ashcroft, F.   **612**

Spark, Muriel, 1918-2006

About

All the poems of Muriel Spark   **821**
Stannard, M. Muriel Spark   **92**

SPARRING *See* Boxing

Sparrow, Joshua D.

Brazelton, T. B. Touchpoints birth to 3   **649**

SPARTA (EXTINCT CITY)

Karnazes, D. The legend of Marathon   **938.03**

Spartan Fit. Durant, J.   **613.7**

Spawforth, Antony

(ed) The Oxford classical dictionary   **938**
Speak now. Yoshino, K.   **346.73**
Speak, memory. Nabokov, V. V.   **813**

Speake, Jennifer

(ed) Literature of travel and exploration   **910.4**

Speaker, Tris, 1888-1958

About

Gay, T. M. Tris Speaker   **92**

SPEAKERS OF THE HOUSE

Borneman, W. R. Polk   **92**
Heidler, D. S. Henry Clay   **92**
Merry, R. W. A country of vast designs   **92**
Pelosi, N. Know your power   **92**
Thomas, E. The war lovers   **973.8**

SPEAKING *See* Debates and debating; Lectures and lecturing; Preaching; Public speaking; Rhetoric; Speech; Voice

Speaking American. Bailey, R. W.   **427**
Speaking of beauty. Donoghue, D.   **801**
Speaking Out.   **306.76**

SPEAR FISHING

See also Fishing

Spears, Richard A.

McGraw-Hill's dictionary of American slang and colloquial expressions   **427**

SPECIAL COLLECTIONS IN LIBRARIES *See* Libraries -- Special collections

SPECIAL EDUCATION

Siegel, L. M. The complete IEP guide   **371.9**

SPECIAL EDUCATION

See also Education

SPECIAL FORCES (MILITARY SCIENCE)

Macintyre, B. Rogue Heroes   **940.54**

SPECIAL FORCES (MILITARY SCIENCE) -- ISRAEL

David, S. Operation Thunderbolt   **967.61**

SPECIAL FORCES (MILITARY SCIENCE) -- UNITED STATES

Bergen, P. L. Manhunt   **363.325**
Blehm, E. Legend   **959.7**
Bruning, J. R. Level zero heroes   **958.104**
Couch, D. Sua sponte   **356**
Lemmon, G. T. Ashley's war   **92**
Lineberry, C. The secret rescue   **940.54**
Maurer, K. No easy day   **958.104**

SPECIAL LIBRARIES

See also Libraries

SPECIAL LIBRARIES -- DIRECTORIES

Directory of special libraries and information centers   **026**

SPECIAL OLYMPICS

Shriver, T. Fully alive   **796.087**

SPECIAL OLYMPICS

See also Olympic games; Sports for people

with disabilities

SPECIAL OPERATIONS (MILITARY SCIENCE) -- UNITED STATES
Bergen, P. L. Manhunt   **363.325**

SPECIAL OPERATIONS (MILITARY SCIENCE) -- UNITED STATES -- HISTORY -- 21ST CENTURY
Scahill, J. Dirty wars   **355.02**
Special orders. Hirsch, E.   **811**

SPECIAL PROSECUTORS -- UNITED STATES
Gormley, K. The death of American virtue **973.929**

SPECIALISTS
Cohen, M. All These Things That I've Done **781.66**
SPECIE *See* Coins

SPECIES EXTINCTION *See* Extinction (Biology)

SPECIMENS, PRESERVATION OF *See* Plants -- Collection and preservation; Taxidermy; Zoological specimens -- Collection and preservation

Speck, Jeff
(jt. auth) Duany, A. Suburban nation   **307.76**

Speck, Maria
Ancient grains for modern meals   **641.59**
Simply ancient grains   **641.6**

Spectacle. Newkirk, P.   **92**

SPECTERS *See* Apparitions; Ghosts

Spector, Phil
About
Brown, M. Tearing down the wall of sound   **92**

Spector, Robert
The mom & pop store   **381**

Spector, Ronald
Eagle against the sun   **940.54**

Spector, Shmuel
(ed) Encyclopedia of Jewish life before and during the Holocaust   **940.53**

SPECTRUM ANALYSIS
Blatner, D. Spectrums   **539.2**

SPECTRUM ANALYSIS
See also Astronomy; Astrophysics; Chemistry; Optics; Radiation

Spectrum series
Sherlock Holmes in Babylon   **510**
Spectrums. Blatner, D.   **539.2**

SPECULATION
Bogle, J. C. The clash of the cultures   **332.6**

SPECULATION
See also Finance

SPECULATIVE FICTION, ENGLISH -- BIBLIOGRAPHY
Kallio, J. Read on ... speculative fiction for teens   **016**

SPEECH
See also Language arts

SPEECH DISORDERS
Preston, K. Out with it   **92**
SPEECH DISORDERS

See also Communicative disorders; Speech
Speech index. Sutton, R. B.   **808.85**

SPEECHES
Cicero, M. T. Political speeches   **875**
The World's great speeches   **808.85**

SPEECHES
See also Literature

SPEECHES -- INDEXES
Sutton, R. B. Speech index   **808.85**
Speeches and writings, 1832-1858. Lincoln, A.   **973.5**
Speeches and writings, 1859-1865. Lincoln, A.   **973.7**

SPEECHES, ADDRESSES, ETC. *See* Speeches

SPEECHES, ADDRESSES, ETC., AMERICAN
Douglass, F. Frederick Douglass: selected speeches and writings   **326**

SPEECHES, ADDRESSES, ETC., AMERICAN
See American speeches

SPEECHES, ADDRESSES, ETC., AMERICAN -- HISTORY AND CRITICISM
Prothero, S. The American Bible   **973**

SPEECHWRITERS
Buckley, C. T. Losing Mum and Pup   **92**

SPEED
Colvile, R. The Great Acceleration   **303.483**

SPEED (DRUG) *See* Methamphetamine
Speed duel. Hawley, S. J.   **796.72**

SPEED READING
See also Reading
Speed-the-plow. Mamet, D.   **812**

Speer, Albert, 1905-1981
Inside the Third Reich   **943.086**
About
Fest, J. C. Speer: the final verdict   **92**
Galbraith, J. K. Name-dropping   **973.9**
Sereny, G. Albert Speer   **92**
Speer: the final verdict. Fest, J. C.   **92**

Speerstra, Karen
(jt. auth) Anderson, H. The divine art of dying **202**

Speichert, C. Greg
Encyclopedia of water garden plants   **635**

Speichert, Sue
Speichert, C. G. Encyclopedia of water garden plants   **635**

Speid, Lorna
Clinical trials   **615.5**

Speight, James G.
(ed) Lange's handbook of chemistry   **540**

SPELEOLOGY *See* Caves
Spell It Out. Crystal, D.   **421**

Spellenberg, Richard
National Audubon Society field guide to North American wildflowers, western region **582.13**

SPELLERS
See also English language -- Spelling

SPELLING BEES

Maguire, J. American bee **372.6**

SPELLING BEES

See also Language and languages

SPELUNKERS

Tabor, J. M. Blind descent **796.52**

Spence, Gerry

The smoking gun **345**

Spence, Graham

(jt. auth) Anthony, L. The elephant whisperer **599.67**

Spence, Jonathan D.

The Chan's great continent **951**

God's Chinese son **951**

Mao Zedong **951.05**

The search for modern China **951**

Treason by the book **951**

Spencer family

About

Sharfstein, D. J. The invisible line **305.8**

Spencer Tracy. Curtis, J. **92**

Spencer, Bernard, 1909-1963

Complete poetry: translations & selected prose **821**

Spencer, Catherine

(ed) Chirac, J. My life in politics **944.084**

Spencer, Charles Edward Maurice Spencer

Prince Rupert **92**

Spencer, Herbert, 1820-1903

About

Durant, W. J. The story of philosophy **109**

Spencer, Lara

Flea market fabulous **747**

Spender, Stephen, 1909-1995

About

Sutherland, J. Stephen Spender **92**

Spengler, Oswald, 1880-1936

The decline of the West, volume one **901**

About

Herman, A. The idea of decline in Western history **909.08**

Spenser, Edmund

The faerie queene **821**

Spent. Miller, G. F. **339.4**

Spera, Keith

Groove interrupted **920**

Sperber, Ann M.

Murrow, his life and times **92**

Sperber, Jonathan

Karl Marx **92**

Sperling, Daniel

Two billion cars **388.3**

Speth, James Gustave, 1942-

America the possible **338.9**

The bridge at the end of the world **333.7**

Spetzler, Carl

(jt. auth) Meyer, J. Decision quality **658.4**

The **spice** & herb bible. Hemphill, I. **641.3**

SPICE TRADE -- HISTORY

Nabhan, G. P. Cumin, camels, and caravans **382**

Spicer, Jack

My vocabulary did this to me **811**

SPICES

Bevill, A. World spice at home **641.6**

Hemphill, I. The spice & herb bible **641.3**

Makan, C. The Cardamom Trail **641.5**

O'Connell, J. The Book of Spice **641.3**

SPICES

See also Food

SPICES -- HISTORY

Nabhan, G. P. Cumin, camels, and caravans **382**

O'Connell, J. The Book of Spice **641.3**

Spices of life. **641.5**

SPIDER-MAN (FICTIONAL CHARACTER)

See also Fictional characters; Superheroes

Spider-Man (Fictional character)

About

Lee, S. Stan Lee's How to draw comics **741.5**

SPIDERS

Beccaloni, J. Arachnids **595.4**

Eisner, T. Secret weapons **595.7**

Milne, L. J. The Audubon Society field guide to North American insects and spiders **595.7**

Stewart, A. Wicked bugs **632**

The **spiders** of Allah. Hider, J. **956.05**

Spiegelman, Art, 1948-

Co-Mix **741.5**

In the shadow of no towers **973.931**

Maus **940.53**

Spiegelman, A. MetaMaus **940.53**

Spiegelman, Nadja

I'm supposed to protect you from all this **741.5**

Spiegelman, Vladek

About

Spiegelman, A. Maus **940.53**

Spiekermann, Erik

Stop Stealing Sheep and Find out How Type Works **686.2**

Spieler, Marlena

Paris **641.5**

The U.S. House of Representatives **328.73**

Spielman, A.

Mosquito **595.77**

Spierenburg, Pieter

Violence and punishment **364.67**

Spies. Haynes, J. E. **327.12**

SPIES

Carter, M. Anthony Blunt: his lives **92**

Draitser, E. Stalin's Romeo spy **92**

Gup, T. Book of honor **327.12**

Hastings, M. The secret war **940.54**

Haynes, J. E. Spies **327.12**

Herrington, S. A. Traitors among us **327.12**

Kershaw, A. Avenue of spies **940.53**
Linklater, A. An artist in treason **92**
Metaxas, E. Bonhoeffer **92**
Paul, J. R. Unlikely allies **973.3**
Ryan, M. Hornet's sting **92**
Talty, S. Agent Garbo **940.5**
Weinstein, A. The haunted wood **327.12**
Wise, D. Spy: the inside story of how the FBI's
Robert Hanssen betrayed America **327.12**

SPIES
See also Espionage; Subversive activities

SPIES -- EUROPE -- BIOGRAPHY
Macintyre, B. Double cross **940.54**

SPIES -- FRANCE -- PARIS -- BIOGRAPHY
Kershaw, A. Avenue of spies **940.53**

SPIES -- GREAT BRITAIN -- BIOGRAPHY
Johnston, K. R. The hidden Wordsworth **821**
Macintyre, B. A Spy Among Friends **327.12**
Mulley, C. The Spy Who Loved **940.54**
Talty, S. Agent Garbo **940.5**

**SPIES -- GREAT BRITAIN -- HISTORY -- 19TH
CENTURY**
Dickey, C. Our Man in Charleston **92**

**SPIES -- NEW YORK (STATE) -- HISTORY --
18TH CENTURY**
Yaeger, D. George Washington's secret six **973.4**

SPIES -- UNITED STATES -- BIOGRAPHY
Gup, T. Book of honor **327.12**
Nagy, J. A. George Washington's secret spy
war **973.385**

**SPIES -- UNITED STATES -- HISTORY -- 18TH
CENTURY**
Yaeger, D. George Washington's secret six **973.4**

SPIES IN LITERATURE
Mystery and suspense writers **809**
Spies in the congo. Williams, S. **553.4**

Spiker, Ted
About
Spiker, T. Down size **92**

Spillman, Rob
All Tomorrow's Parties **070.4**

Spillover. Quammen, D. **614.4**

Spin art. Boggs, J. **746.12**

**SPIN DOCTORS -- UNITED STATES -- BIOG-
RAPHY**
Greenberg, D. Republic of spin **973.099**

Spink, Kathryn
Mother Teresa **92**
Mother Teresa **271**

The **spinner's** book of yarn designs. Anderson,
S. **746.14**

SPINNING
Boggs, J. Spin art **746.12**

SPINNING
See also Textile industry

SPINOSAURUS
See also Dinosaurs

Spinoza, Benedictus de, 1632-1677
About
Damasio, A. R. Looking for Spinoza **152.4**
Durant, W. J. The story of philosophy **109**
Russell, B. A history of Western philosophy **109**

Spinster. Bolick, K. **92**
The **spinster** & the prophet. McKillop, A. B. **941.08**

Spira, Timothy P.
Waterfalls and wildflowers in the Southern Appalachians **796.51**

The **Spiral** Notebook. Singular, S. **364.152**
The **spiral** staircase. Armstrong, K. **92**
Spirals in Time. Scales, H. **594**

SPIRES
See also Architecture; Church architecture

SPIRIT *See* Soul
The **spirit** catches you and you fall down. Fadiman,
A. **306.4**
The **spirit** level. Pickett, K. **306**
The **spirit** of 74. Raphael, R. **973.3**
The **spirit** of St. Louis. Lindbergh, C. **629.13**

SPIRIT OF ST. LOUIS (AIRPLANE)
Lindbergh, C. The spirit of St. Louis **629.13**
The **spirit** of Yellowstone. Meyer, J. L. **978.7**

SPIRITISM *See* Spiritualism

SPIRITS
See also Supernatural

SPIRITUAL BIOGRAPHY
Emrys, B. The Toltec art of life and death **299.7**
Henion, L. A. Phenomenal **910.4**
Ozment, K. Grace without God **200.973**
Saldana, S. The bread of angels **92**
The **Spiritual** Child. Miller, L. **649**

SPIRITUAL GIFTS
See also Grace (Theology)

SPIRITUAL HEALING
Brizendine, J. Stunned by grief **248**
James, W. The varieties of religious experience **210**

SPIRITUAL LIFE
The Art of Stillness **302.23**
The Bloomsbury Guide to Christian Spiritual-
ity **270**
Campbell, J. The power of myth **201**
Egan, K. On living **170.44**
Gibran, K. The collected works **818**
Girzone, J. F. Never alone **248.4**
Hammarskjold, D. Markings **839.7**
Henion, L. A. Phenomenal **910.4**
Jakes, T. D. Instinct **248.4**
Martin, J. The Jesuit guide to almost every-
thing **248.4**
Martin, J. My life with the saints **920**
Mildon, E. The soul searcher's handbook **131**
Miller, D. Blue like jazz **92**
Miller, L. The Spiritual Child **649**

Norris, K. Acedia & me **92**

Norris, K. The cloister walk **255**

Ozment, K. Grace without God **200.973**

Panagore, P. B. Heaven Is Beautiful **231.7**

Peck, M. S. Further along the road less traveled **158**

Peck, M. S. The road less traveled and beyond **158**

Phillips, R. R. Heaven **811**

Rice, A. Called out of darkness **92**

Riess, J. Flunking sainthood **248.4**

Siegel, B. S. Prescriptions for living **158**

Tolle, E. A new earth **158**

Tolle, E. The power of now **158**

SPIRITUAL LIFE

See also Religious life

SPIRITUAL LIFE -- BUDDHISM

Emet, J. Finding the blue sky **294.3**

Rinzler, L. The Buddha walks into a bar **294.3**

SPIRITUAL LIFE -- CHRISTIANITY

Taylor, B. B. An altar in the world **92**

Winner, L. F. Wearing God **231.7**

The **spiritual** life of children. Coles, R. **204**

SPIRITUAL WORKS OF MERCY

A call to mercy **234.5**

SPIRITUALISM

Aykroyd, P. A history of ghosts **133.1**

Blum, D. Ghost hunters **133.9**

Goldsmith, B. Other powers **92**

Jaher, D. The witch of Lime Street **92**

SPIRITUALISM

See also Occultism; Supernatural

SPIRITUALISTS -- UNITED STATES -- BIOGRAPHY

Jaher, D. The witch of Lime Street **92**

MacLaine, S. Above the line **92**

SPIRITUALITY

Circling faith **200.8**

Ozment, K. Grace without God **200.973**

Pacheco, R. Do your om thing **181**

Peck, M. S. The road less traveled **158**

SPIRITUALITY -- CHRISTIANITY

Bass, D. B. Grounded **231**

Winner, L. F. Wearing God **231.7**

SPIRITUALS (SONGS)

Ware, C. P. Slave songs of the United States **781.62**

SPIRITUALS (SONGS)

See also Folk songs -- United States; Hymns

Spitz, Bob

The Beatles: the biography **920**

Dearie **92**

Spivey, Nigel Jonathan

The ancient Olympics **796.48**

Splay anthem. Mackey, N. **811**

Splendid solution: Jonas Salk and the conquest of polio. Kluger, J. **92**

The **Splendid** table's how to eat supper. Swift, S. **641.5**

The **Splendid** Things We Planned. Bailey, B. **92**

Splendors of Imperial China. Hearn, M. K. **709**

Split-second persuasion. Dutton, K. **153.8**

Spock, Benjamin, 1903-1998

Dr. Spock on parenting **649**

Dr. Spock's baby and child care **649**

Dr. Spock's the first two years **649**

Dr. Spock's the school years **649**

SPOILS SYSTEM See Political corruption

Spong, John Shelby

Biblical literalism **226.2**

Eternal life **236**

Spontaneous mind. **811**

Spook. Roach, M. **133.9**

Spooky action at a distance. Musser, G. **530.11**

SPORT ASSOCIATION EXECUTIVES

White, B. Uppity **92**

SPORTING GOODS INDUSTRY -- UNITED STATES -- HISTORY

Knight, P. H. Shoe dog **92**

SPORTS

The Best American sports writing of the century **796**

Howley, K. Thrown **796.8**

Klosterman, C. Eating the dinosaur **973.92**

Rhoden, W. C. $40 million slaves **796**

Ribowsky, M. Howard Cosell **92**

SPORTS

See also Play; Recreation

SPORTS -- AUDIENCES See Sports spectators

SPORTS -- BIBLIOGRAPHY

Clark, C. A. Read on...sports **016**

SPORTS -- CORRUPT PRACTICES

Hamilton, T. The Secret Race **796.62**

Thompson, T. American huckster **796.334**

SPORTS -- ECONOMIC ASPECTS

Glockner, A. Chasing perfection **796.323**

Nocera, J. Indentured **796.04**

SPORTS -- GRAPHIC NOVELS

See also Graphic novels

SPORTS -- HISTORY

Buckland, G. Who shot sports **779.97**

Kunitz, D. Lift **613.7**

SPORTS -- MEDICAL ASPECTS See Sports medicine

SPORTS -- MISCELLANEA

Wertheim, L. J. This is your brain on sports **796**

SPORTS -- PHYSIOLOGICAL ASPECTS

Epstein, D. The sports gene **613.7**

SPORTS -- PSYCHOLOGICAL ASPECTS

Afremow, J. The champion's mind **796.01**

Fitzgerald, M. How bad do you want it? **612.044**

Rotella, B. How champions think in sports and in life **796.01**

Wertheim, L. J. This is your brain on sports **796**

SPORTS -- SOCIAL ASPECTS -- HISTORY

Amidon, S. Something like the gods **306.4**

Carlin, J. Playing the enemy **968.06**

SPORTS -- STATISTICS

Miller, S. The Only Rule Is It Has to Work **796.357**

SPORTS -- STATISTICS

See also Statistics

SPORTS BETTING

Kennedy, K. Pete Rose **92**

SPORTS BETTING

See also Gambling

SPORTS BROADCASTING *See* Radio broadcasting of sports; Television broadcasting of sports

SPORTS CARDS

See also Sports

SPORTS CARS

Baime, A. J. Go like hell **796.72**

SPORTS FOR PEOPLE WITH MENTAL DISABILITIES

Shriver, T. Fully alive **796.087**

SPORTS FOR WOMEN

Holstein, K. A Different Kind of Daughter **92**

SPORTS FOR WOMEN

See also Sports

The **sports** gene. Epstein, D. **613.7**

SPORTS HANDICAPPING *See* Sports betting

SPORTS IN TELEVISION *See* Television broadcasting of sports

SPORTS INJURIES

Laskas, J. M. Concussion **617.5**

Yaeger, D. Any given Monday **617.1**

SPORTS JOURNALISM

The Best American Sports Writing 2014 **814**

Deford, F. Over time **92**

Ryan, B. Scribe **070.449**

SPORTS MEDICINE

McClusky, M. Faster, higher, stronger **613.7**

Yaeger, D. Any given Monday **617.1**

SPORTS MEDICINE

See also Medical care; Medicine

SPORTS MEDICINE -- UNITED STATES

Fainaru, S. League of Denial **617.1**

SPORTS RECORDS

See also Sports

SPORTS RIVALRIES -- NORTH CAROLINA -- HISTORY

Feinstein, J. The legends club **796.323**

SPORTS RIVALRIES -- UNITED STATES

Myers, G. Brady vs Manning **92**

SPORTS SCANDALS *See* Sports -- Corrupt practices

SPORTS SCIENCE

McClusky, M. Faster, higher, stronger **613.7**

SPORTS SPECTATORS

Falk, D. The hungry fan's game day cookbook **641.5**

Simons, E. The Secret Lives of Sports Fans **306.4**

SPORTS STORIES *See* Sports -- Fiction

SPORTS TEAMS

See also Sports

SPORTS TOURNAMENTS

See also Contests; Sports

SPORTS TRAINERS

Atlas, T. Atlas **92**

Remnick, D. Reporting **814**

SPORTSCASTERS

Gates, H. L. Thirteen ways of looking at a black man **920.71**

Halberstam, D. The teammates **796**

Kindred, D. Sound and fury **796**

Life stories **920**

Ribowsky, M. Howard Cosell **92**

Toobin, J. The run of his life **345.73**

White, B. Uppity **92**

SPORTSCASTERS -- UNITED STATES -- BIOGRAPHY

Dierker, L. This ain't brain surgery **796**

Walton, B. Back from the dead **92**

Williams, J. Life is not an accident **92**

SPORTSMANSHIP

See also Human behavior; Sports

SPORTSWRITERS

George, being George **92**

Watman, M. Chasing the white dog **363.4**

Wertheim, L. J. Blood in the cage **92**

SPORTSWRITERS -- UNITED STATES -- BIOGRAPHY

Ryan, B. Scribe **070.449**

Spotila, James R.

Sea turtles **597.92**

Spoto, Donald

The dark side of genius **791.43**

The kindness of strangers: the life of Tennessee Williams **92**

Notorious **92**

Spotted Tail, Brulé Sioux Chief, 1823-1881

About

Brown, D. A. Bury my heart at Wounded Knee **970.004**

SPOUSES *See* Husbands; Wives

SPOUSES OF HEADS OF STATE -- GERMANY -- BIOGRAPHY

Gortemaker, H. B. Eva Braun **92**

SPOUSES OF PROMINENT PERSONS

Berkin, C. Civil War wives **920**

Buckley, C. T. Losing Mum and Pup **92**

Conant, J. A covert affair **940.54**

Flanders, J. A circle of sisters **920**

Foreman, A. Georgiana, Duchess of Devonshire **941.07**

Fox, J. Five sisters **975.5**

Gabriel, M. Love and capital **92**

Hazleton, L. After the prophet **297**

Hertog, S. Anne Morrow Lindbergh **92**

Life stories **920**

Lindbergh, R. Under a wing **92**

Mailer, N. C. A ticket to the circus **92**

Mallon, T. Mrs. Paine's garage and the murder of John F. Kennedy **364.1**

McDougal, S. The woman who wouldn't talk **973.929**

Meade, M. Lonelyhearts **92**

Oates, J. C. A widow's story **92**

Persico, J. E. Franklin and Lucy **920**

Rickford, R. J. Betty Shabazz: a remarkable story of survival and faith before and after Malcolm X **92**

Tate, M. J. Critical companion to F. Scott Fitzgerald **813**

Urrutia, M. My life with Pablo Neruda **92**

Vaill, A. Everybody was so young **759.13**

VanderVelde, L. Mrs. Dred Scott **92**

Weintraub, S. Charlotte and Lionel **92**

Wilson, E. Patriotic gore **810**

Winters, K. C. Anne Morrow Lindbergh **92**

SPOUSES OF THE PRESIDENTS

Baker, J. H. Mary Todd Lincoln **92**

SPQR. Beard, M. **937**

Sprague, Kate Chase, 1840-1899

      About

Oller, J. American queen **92**

Sprague, William, 1830-1915

      About

Oller, J. American queen **92**

Spratford, Becky Siegel

The horror readers' advisory **025.5**

SPRAYING AND DUSTING

   See also Agricultural pests; Fruit -- Diseases and pests

SPRING

   See also Seasons

Spring poems along the Rio Grande. Baca, J. S. **811**

Spring, Justin

Secret historian **92**

Springboard. Shell, G. R. **650.1**

Springer, Lauren

Passionate gardening **635**

Springsteen, Bruce

      About

Carlin, P. A. Bruce **92**

Sprint. Kowitz, B. **658.4**

The **sprouted** kitchen. **641.3**

The **sprouted** kitchen bowl and spoon. **641.3**

Spruce. Brown, A. **747**

Spufford, Francis

(ed) The ends of the earth **998**

SPUN YARNS

Anderson, S. The spinner's book of yarn designs **746.14**

Spungen, Susan

Recipes **641.5**

Spunk & bite. Plotnik, A. **808**

Spurling, Hilary

Matisse the master **92**

Pearl Buck in China **92**

The unknown Matisse **92**

Spurlock, Morgan

Don't eat this book **614.5**

A **Spy** Among Friends. Macintyre, B. **327.12**

SPY FILMS

   See also Motion pictures

SPY STORIES

   See also Adventure fiction

SPY TELEVISION PROGRAMS

   See also Television programs

The **Spy** Who Loved. Mulley, C. **940.54**

Spy: the inside story of how the FBI's Robert Hanssen betrayed America. Wise, D. **327.12**

SPYING *See* Espionage; Spies

SQUARE

   See also Geometry; Shape

SQUARE FOOT GARDENING

Bartholomew, M. All new square foot gardening **635**

Bartholomew, M. Square foot gardening high-value veggies **635**

Square foot gardening high-value veggies. Bartholomew, M. **635**

A **square** meal. Coe, A. **641.5**

Square, Vicki

The knitter's companion **746.43**

Squares and courtyards. Hacker, M. **811**

SQUIDS

Williams, W. Kraken **594**

Squires, James D.

Horse of a different color **798.4**

SQUIRRELS

   See also Mammals

Sragow, Michael

Victor Fleming **92**

SREBRENICA (BOSNIA AND HERCEGOVINA)

Rohde, D. Endgame **949.7**

Srulovich, Itamar

Honey & Co. **641.595**

Honey & Co the Baking Book **641**

St. James encyclopedia of labor history worldwide. **331.8**

St. James encyclopedia of popular culture. **973.9**

St. James guide to Hispanic artists. **920.003**

ST. JOHN'S COLLEGE (ANNAPOLIS, MD.)

Martin, R. H. Racing Odysseus **92**

St. John, Warren

Outcasts united **796.334**

Rammer jammer yellow hammer **796.332**

ST. LOUIS CARDINALS (BASEBALL TEAM)

Bissinger, H. G. Three nights in August **796.357**

St. Marks Is Dead. Calhoun, A. **974.7**

ST. PAUL'S CATHEDRAL (LONDON, ENG-LAND)

Hollis, L. London rising **942**

St. Petersburg. Volkov, S. **947**

STABILIZATION IN INDUSTRY *See* Business cycles

Stabiner, Karen

Generation chef **641.5**

Stach, Reiner

Kafka, the years of insight **833**

Kafka, d. J. d. E. Kafka, the decisive years **92**

Stack, Megan

About

Stack, M. Every man in this village is a liar **956.05**

Stafford, Ed

About

Stafford, E. Walking the Amazon **918.1**

Stafford, William Edgar

The way it is **811**

Stag's leap. Olds, S. **811**

STAGE *See* Acting; Drama; Theater

STAGE ADAPTATIONS

See also Drama

STAGE LIGHTING

Gillette, J. M. Designing With Light: An Introduction to Stage Lighting **792**

STAGE LIGHTING

See also Lighting

Stage makeup. Corson, R. **792**

STAGE MANAGEMENT.

Gillette, J. M. Theatrical design and production **792.02**

STAGE SCENERY *See* Theaters -- Stage setting and scenery

STAGE SETTING *See* Theaters -- Stage setting and scenery

Stager, Curt

Deep future **363.7**

Stages of senior care. Hogan, P. R. **362.6**

Stahr, Walter

Seward **92**

STAINED GLASS *See* Glass painting and staining

Stained glass basics. Rich, C. **748.5**

Staiti, Paul

Of Arms and Artists **759.13**

Stalin. Service, R. **92**

Stalin. Conquest, R. **92**

Stalin. Radzinsky, E. **92**

Stalin. Kotkin, S. **92**

Stalin. **92**

Stalin's curse. Gellately, R. **947.084**

Stalin's daughter. Sullivan, R. **92**

Stalin's folly. Pleshakov, K. **940.54**

Stalin's general. Roberts, G. **940.54**

Stalin's last crime. Brent, J. **947.084**

Stalin's Romeo spy. Draitser, E. **92**

Stalin, Joseph, 1879-1953

About

Amis, M. Koba the dread **947.084**

Berthon, S. Warlords **940.53**

Brent, J. Inside the Stalin archives **947.086**

Brent, J. Stalin's last crime **947.084**

Conquest, R. Stalin **92**

Costigliola, F. Roosevelt's lost alliances **940.53**

Dobbs, M. Six months in 1945 **940.53**

Gellately, R. Stalin's curse **947.084**

Gordin, M. D. Red cloud at dawn **355**

Hochschild, A. The unquiet ghost **947.084**

Kissinger, H. Diplomacy **327.2**

Kotkin, S. Stalin **92**

Medvedev, R. A. Let history judge **947.084**

Montefiore, S. Stalin: the court of the red tsar **92**

Montefiore, S. Young Stalin **92**

Pleshakov, K. Stalin's folly **940.54**

Pringle, P. The murder of Nikolai Vavilov **92**

Radzinsky, E. Stalin **92**

Service, R. Stalin **92**

Snyder, T. D. Bloodlands **940.54**

Stalin **92**

Sullivan, R. Stalin's daughter **92**

Stalin: the court of the red tsar. Montefiore, S. **92**

Stalingrad. **940.54**

Stalking the wild asparagus. Gibbons, E. **581.6**

Stallworthy, Jon, 1935-2014

(ed) A Book of love poetry **808.81**

The Oxford book of war poetry **808.81**

Staloff, Darren

Hamilton, Adams, Jefferson **973.4**

STAMINA, PHYSICAL *See* Physical fitness

STAMMERING *See* Speech disorders

STAMP COLLECTING

See also Collectors and collecting

Stamp stencil paint. Joyce, A. **745.5**

Stamped from the beginning. Kendi, I. X. **305.8**

Stampp, Kenneth M.

(ed) The Causes of the Civil War **973.7**

Stan Lee's How to draw comics. Lee, S. **741.5**

Stand Tall. Bozella, D. **365.6**

STAND-UP COMEDY -- UNITED STATES

Apatow, J. Sick in the head **792.7**

Standage, Tom

An edible history of humanity **394.1**

A history of the world in 6 glasses **394.1**

Writing on the wall **302.23**

Standard catalog of world coins. Krause, C. L. **737.4**

Standard deviations. Smith, G. **519.5**

STANDARD DEVIATIONS

Smith, G. Standard deviations **519.5**

Standard Handbook for Electrical Engineers. **621.3**

Standard operating procedure. Gourevitch, P. **956.7**

STANDARD TIME *See* Time

Standiford, Les
  (jt. auth) Matthews, J. Bringing Adam home **364.1**

Standing Bear, Ponca Chief, 1829?-1908
            About
  Brown, D. A. Bury my heart at Wounded
    Knee **970.004**

Standring, Susan
  (ed) Gray's anatomy **611**

Stanford, Craig B.
  Planet without apes **599.88**
  Bearzi, M. Beautiful minds **599.8**

Stanford, Frank
  What about this **811.54**

Stangneth, Bettina
  Eichmann before Jerusalem **92**

The **Stanislavski** system. Moore, S. **792**

Stanislavsky, Konstantin, 1863-1938
  An actor's work **792**
  Creating a role **792**
            About
  Moore, S. The Stanislavski system **792**

Stanley. Jeal, T. **92**

STANLEY CUP (HOCKEY)
    See also Awards; Hockey; Sports tourna-
    ments

Stanley Kubrick. LoBrutto, V. **92**

Stanley Kubrick and me. D'Alessandro, E. **791.43**

Stanley, Bob
  Yeah! Yeah! Yeah! **781.64**

Stanley, Henry M. (Henry Morton), 1841-1904
            About
  Jeal, T. Stanley **92**

Stanley, Mary J.
  Managing library employees **023**

Stanley, Ralph, 1927-
            About
  Stanley, R. Man of constant sorrow **92**

Stanley, Suzannah Hamlin
  DIY wardrobe makeovers **646**

Stanley, Tracy
  (ed) The complete outdoor builder **690**

Stannard, Martin
  Muriel Spark **92**

Stannard, Russell
  The end of discovery **501**

Stanton, Brandon
  Humans of New York **974.7**
  Humans of New York: stories **974.7**

Stanton, Edwin M. (Edwin McMasters), 1814-
  1869
            About
  Marvel, W. Lincoln's autocrat **92**

Stanton, Elizabeth Cady, 1815-1902
            About

Ginzberg, L. D. Elizabeth Cady Stanton **92**

Ulrich, L. Well-behaved women seldom make history **305.4**

Stanton, Maureen
  Killer stuff and tons of money **381**

Stanton, Tom
            About
  Stanton, T. Road to Cooperstown **92**

STAPLE SINGERS
  Kot, G. I'll take you there **92**

Staples, Heidi
  Sew organized for the busy girl **646.2**

Staples, Mavis
            About
  Kot, G. I'll take you there **92**

Stapp, John P. (John Paul), 1910-1999
            About
  Ryan, C. Sonic wind **92**

Star. Biskind, P. **92**

Star dust. Bidart, F. **811**

STAR WARS (BALLISTIC MISSILE DEFENSE
  SYSTEM) *See* Strategic Defense Initiative

STAR WARS FILMS
  Szostak, P. The art of Star Wars **791.43**
  Wallace, D. Ultimate Star wars

STAR WARS FILMS
    See also Motion pictures; Science fiction films

Starbucked. Clark, T. **338**

STARBUCKS COFFEE INTERNATIONAL
  (FIRM)
  Schultz, H. Onward **647.9**

STARBUCKS CORPORATION
  Clark, T. Starbucked **338**

Stargardt, Nicholas
  The German War **943.086**
  Witnesses of war **940.53**

Stark, Lizzie
            About
  Stark, L. Pandora's DNA **616.99**

Stark, Peter
  Astoria **978**
  The last empty places **973**

Stark, Rodney
  For the glory of God **201**

Stark, Steven D.
  Meet the Beatles **920**

Starkey, David
  Six wives: the queens of Henry VIII **942.05**

Starkman, Dean
  (ed) The best business writing 2013 **330.9**

Starlight Detectives. Hirshfeld, A. c. **523.1**

Starmore, Alice
  Alice Starmore's book of Fair Isle knitting **746.43**
  Tudor roses **746.432**

Starobin, Paul
  After America **973.91**

Starr, Douglas
The killer of little shepherds   364.152
Starr, Kenneth W., 1946-
          About
Gormley, K. The death of American virtue 973.929
Starr, Paul
Remedy and reaction   362.1
Starr, Ringo, 1940-
Photograph   782.4
          About
The Beatles anthology   782.421
Spitz, B. The Beatles: the biography   920
Starr, William W.
Whisky, kilts, and the Loch Ness Monster   914
Starrett, Kelly
(jt. auth) Cordoza, G. Becoming a supple leop-
ard   613.7
Ready to run   613.7
The **Stars.**   523.8
STARS
Gott, J. R. Welcome to the universe   523.1
Kaler, J. B. Extreme stars   523.8
Ridpath, I. Stars and planets   520
Tirion, W. The Cambridge star atlas   523.8
STARS -- ATLASES
     See also Atlases
STARS -- IDENTIFICATION
Ridpath, I. The monthly sky guide   523.8
STARS -- POPULAR WORKS
Gott, J. R. Welcome to the universe   523.1
Stars and planets. Ridpath, I.   520
Stars Between the Sun and Moon. McClelland,
S.   92
Stars in their courses. Foote, S.   973.7
Start a community food garden. Joy, L.   635
Start here. Langshur, E.   158
Startalk.   523.1
Starter vegetable gardens. Pleasant, B.   635
STARTING A BUSINESS *See* New business en-
terprises
Starting up Silicon Valley. Maxfield, K.   338.7
Starting your career as a freelance web designer.
Tortorella, N.   006.7
The **Startup** playbook. Kidder, D. S.   658.1
STARVATION
Tucker, T. The great starvation experiment   174.2
STARVATION -- HISTORY -- 20TH CENTURY
Collingham, L. The taste of war   940.53
Stashower, Daniel
(ed) Doyle, A. C. Arthur Conan Doyle   92
The beautiful cigar girl   364.152
Stat-spotting. Best, J.   301
STATE AND AGRICULTURE *See* Agriculture --
Government policy
STATE AND ENVIRONMENT *See* Environmen-
tal policy

STATE BIRDS
     See also Birds; State emblems
State by state.   973
STATE EMBLEMS
     See also Signs and symbols
STATE FLOWERS
     See also Flowers; State emblems
STATE GOVERNMENT EMPLOYEES
Rule, A. --and never let her go   364.1
STATE GOVERNMENT OFFICIALS
Caro, R. A. The power broker: Robert Moses and
the fall of New York   92
Cleland, M. Heart of a patriot   92
Downey, K. The woman behind the New Deal   92
Hair, W. I. The Kingfish and his realm: the life and
times of Huey P. Long   92
Kauffman, B. Forgotten founder, drunken proph-
et   92
Symonds, C. L. Lincoln and his admirals   92
STATE GOVERNMENTS
The book of the states   352.13
Noonan, J. T. Narrowing the nation's power: the
Supreme Court sides with the states   342
STATE GOVERNMENTS
     See also Political science
STATE LEGISLATORS
Alter, J. The promise   92
Balz, D. J. The battle for America, 2008   973.932
Blum, H. American lightning   364.152
Boritt, G. S. The Gettysburg gospel   973.7
Boyle, K. Arc of justice   345
Brackett, E. Pay to play   92
Burlingame, M. Abraham Lincoln   92
Cawardine, R. Lincoln: a life of purpose and pow-
er   92
Clinton, C. Mrs. Lincoln   92
Craughwell, T. J. Stealing Lincoln's body   973.7
Donald, D. H. Lincoln   92
Farrell, J. A. Clarence Darrow   92
Finan, C. M. Alfred E. Smith, the happy warrior 92
Foner, E. The fiery trial   973.7
Fredrickson, G. M. Big enough to be inconsis-
tent   973.7
Gienapp, W. E. Abraham Lincoln and Civil War
America   973.7
Goodwin, D. K. Team of rivals   92
Gopnik, A. Angels and ages   973.7
Guelzo, A. C. Lincoln and Douglas   973.6
Hayden, T. The long sixties   973.92
Hensley, W. L. Fifty miles from tomorrow   92
Hofstadter, R. The American political tradition, and
the men who made it   973
Holzer, H. Lincoln president-elect   92
Keneally, T. Abraham Lincoln   92
Kennedy, J. F. Profiles in courage   920
Kunhardt, P. B. Looking for Lincoln   92

The Lincoln anthology 92

Lind, M. What Lincoln believed 92

McPherson, J. M. Tried by war 92

McPherson, J. M. Abraham Lincoln 92

McPherson, J. M. Abraham Lincoln and the second American Revolution 973.7

McPherson, J. M. Drawn with the sword 973.7

McPherson, J. M. This mighty scourge 973.7

Mendell, D. Obama 92

Obama, B. Dreams from my father 92

Our Lincoln 92

Paludan, P. S. The presidency of Abraham Lincoln 973.7

Pinsker, M. Lincoln's sanctuary 92

Remnick, D. The bridge 92

Sandburg, C. Abraham Lincoln: The prairie years and The war years 92

Shenk, J. W. Lincoln's melancholy 92

Swanson, J. L. Manhunt 364.152

Symonds, C. L. Lincoln and his admirals 92

Walsh, J. E. Moonlight 345

White, R. C. A. Lincoln 92

White, R. C. The eloquent president: a portrait of Lincoln through his words 92

Wills, G. Lincoln at Gettysburg 973.7

Wilson, E. Patriotic gore 810

STATE MEDICINE

See also Medicine

State names, seals, flags, and symbols. Shearer, B. F. 929.9

State of denial. Woodward, B. 973.931

State of the union. 352.23

State of the Union: a century of American labor. Lichtenstein, N. 331

STATE PLANNING *See* Economic policy; Regional planning; Social policy

STATE POLICE

See also Police

STATE REGULATION OF INDUSTRY *See* Industrial policy

STATE RIGHTS

The Causes of the Civil War 973.7

STATE SONGS

See also Songs

STATE, HEADS OF *See* Heads of state

State, Paul F.

A brief history of Ireland 941.5

STATE, THE

Cicero, M. T. The republic; and, The laws 320.1

Fukuyama, F. The origins of political order 320

Hobbes, T. Leviathan 320.1

STATE, THE -- HISTORY

Fukuyama, F. Political Order and Political Decay 320.1

Fukuyama, F. The origins of political order 320

STATE-LOCAL RELATIONS

See also Local government; Municipal government; State governments

STATES' RIGHTS

See also Political science

The **statesman's** yearbook. 310

STATESMEN -- FRANCE

Solomon, J. DSK 306.77

STATESMEN -- FRANCE -- BIOGRAPHY

Solomon, J. DSK 306.77

STATESMEN -- GERMANY -- BIOGRAPHY

Steinberg, J. Bismarck 92

STATESMEN -- GHANA -- BIOGRAPHY

Annan, K. A. Interventions 341.23

STATESMEN -- GREAT BRITAIN -- BIOGRAPHY

Norman, J. Edmund Burke 92

Thomas Becket 92

STATESMEN -- INDIA

Lelyveld, J. Great soul 92

Wolpert, S. A. Gandhi's passion 954.03

STATESMEN -- INDIA -- BIOGRAPHY

Guha, R. Gandhi before India 92

STATESMEN -- ISRAEL -- BIOGRAPHY

Bar-On, M. Moshe Dayan 956.940

STATESMEN -- ITALY -- BIOGRAPHY

Unger, M. J. Machiavelli 92

STATESMEN -- UNITED STATES

McKean, D. Suspected of independence 92

Stahr, W. Seward 92

STATESMEN -- UNITED STATES -- BIOGRAPHY

Cheney, L. V. James Madison 92

Giles Unger, H. John Quincy Adams 92

Marvel, W. Lincoln's autocrat 92

STATESMEN -- UNITED STATES -- DICTIONARIES

American statesmen 920.003

STATESWOMEN -- UNITED STATES -- BIOGRAPHY

Rice, C. No higher honor 327.73

Stathis, Stephen W.

Landmark legislation, 1774-2002 348

STATICS

See also Mechanics; Physics

STATISTICAL DIAGRAMS *See* Statistics -- Graphic methods

STATISTICAL INFERENCE *See* Probabilities

STATISTICS

Best, J. Stat-spotting 301

The Europa world year book 2014 310

Silver, N. The signal and the noise 519.5

Smith, G. Standard deviations 519.5

Tammet, D. Thinking in numbers 510

STATISTICS

See also Economics

STATISTICS -- DICTIONARIES

Everitt, B. The Cambridge dictionary of statistics **519.5**

STATISTICS -- GRAPHIC METHODS
Lima, M. The book of trees **001.2**

STATISTICS -- METHODOLOGY
Reinhart, A. Statistics done wrong **519.5**
Statistics done wrong. Reinhart, A. **519.5**

STATUE OF LIBERTY (NEW YORK, N.Y.)
Khan, Y. S. Enlightening the world **974.7**

Statue of Liberty-Ellis Island Foundation
Yans-McLaughlin, V. Ellis Island and the peopling of America **325**

STATUES See Monuments; Sculpture

STATUS, SOCIAL See Social status

STATUTES See Law

Stauffer, Andrew M.
(ed) Browning, R. Robert Browning's poetry **821**

Stauffer, John
Picturing Frederick Douglass **92**

Stavans, Ilan
(ed) Neruda, P. The poetry of Pablo Neruda **861**
(ed) The Norton anthology of Latino literature **810**

Stavrinides, Liz
Miracle dogs **636.7**

STAX RECORDS -- HISTORY
Gordon, R. Respect yourself **384**

STAY AT HOME FATHERS -- BIOGRAPHY
Estreich, G. The Shape of the Eye **618.92**
Stay, Illusion. Brock-Broido, L. **811**
Staying alive. Dorn, M. **613.6**
Staying sharp. Alter, D. **612.8**
Staying tuned. Schorr, D. **070**
Stead, Christina, 1902-1983
About
Jarrell, R. No other book **809**
Steal away. Wright, C. D. **811**
Steal the show. Port, M. **658.4**
STEALING See Theft
Stealing history. Atwood, R. **364.1**
Stealing Lincoln's body. Craughwell, T. J. **973.7**
Stealing MySpace. Angwin, J. **338.7**
STEAM
See also Heat; Power (Mechanics); Water
STEAM ENGINEERING
See also Engineering
STEAM ENGINES
Jensen, J. Steam: an enduring legacy **625.2**
Steam: an enduring legacy. Jensen, J. **625.2**
STEAMBOATS
See also Boats and boating; Naval architecture; Ocean travel; Shipbuilding; Ships
STEAMBOATS -- HISTORY
Stiles, T. J. The first tycoon **92**
STEAMPUNK CULTURE
See also Counter culture
STEAMPUNK FICTION

See also Science fiction
The **steamy** kitchen cookbook. Hair, J. **641.5**
Stearns, Jason K.
Dancing in the glory of monsters **967.51**
Steavenson, Wendell, 1970-
Circling the Square **962.05**
Stebbins, Robert C.
A field guide to Western reptiles and amphibians **597.9**
Steegmuller, Francis
Hazzard, S. The ancient shore **945**
Steele, James B.
(jt. auth) Barlett, D. L. The betrayal of the American dream **330.973**
STEERS See Beef cattle
Steffens, Lincoln, 1866-1936
About
Steffens, L. The autobiography of Lincoln Steffens **92**
STEGOSAURUS
See also Dinosaurs
Steichen, Edward, 1879-1973
About
Brandow, T. Edward Steichen **779**
Smith, J. Edward Steichen: the early years **779**
Steil, Benn
The battle of Bretton Woods **339.5**
Stein on writing. Stein, S. **808**
Stein, Elissa
(jt. auth) Kim, S. Flow **612.6**
Stein, Gertrude, 1874-1946
Writings, 1903-1932 **818**
Writings, 1932-1946 **818**
About
Malcolm, J. Two lives **92**
Pierpont, C. R. Passionate minds **810**
Stein, G. The autobiography of Alice B. Toklas **92**
Stein, Howard
(ed) The Best American short plays **812**
Stein, Jean
West of Eden **979.4**
Stein, Judith E.
Eye of the sixties **92**
Stein, Rick
Rick Stein's complete seafood **641.6**
Stein, Sol
How to grow a novel **808.3**
Stein on writing **808**
Stein, Stephen J.
The Shaker experience in America **289**
Steinbach, Udo
(ed) Islam in der Gegenwart./English. Islam in the world today **297**
Steinbeck, John, 1902-1968
Travels with Charley **973**
About

John Steinbeck   **813**

Schultz, J. D.   Critical companion to John Steinbeck   **813**

Steinberg at the New Yorker. Steinberg, S.   **741.5**

Steinberg, Alan
  Abdul-Jabbar, K.   Black profiles in courage   **920**

Steinberg, Jacques
  The gatekeepers   **378.1**

Steinberg, Jonathan
  Bismarck   **92**

Steinberg, Jonny
  A man of good hope   **92**
  Sizwe's test   **362.1**

Steinberg, Julius
  (ed) Manser, M. H.   Critical companion to the Bible   **220.6**

Steinberg, Mark D.
  Riasanovsky, N. V.   A history of Russia   **947**

Steinberg, Michael
  Choral masterworks   **782.5**
  The symphony   **784.2**

Steinberg, Neil
        About
  Steinberg, N.   Drunkard   **92**

Steinberg, Saul, 1914-1999
        About
  Bair, D.   Saul Steinberg   **741.092**
  Steinberg at the New Yorker   **741.5**

Steinberg, Ted
  Gotham unbound   **508**

Steinem, Gloria
        About
  Heilbrun, C. G.   The education of a woman   **92**
  Steinem, G.   My life on the road   **92**
  Steinem, G.   Moving beyond words   **305.42**
  Steinem, G.   Outrageous acts and everyday rebellions   **305.42**

Steiner-Adair, Catherine
  The Big Disconnect   **303.48**

Steingold, Fred S.
  The employer's legal handbook   **344**

Steinhart, A. Hillary
  Crohn's & colitis diet guide   **616.3**

Steinmark, Freddie Joe, 1949-1971
        About
  Dent, J.   Courage beyond the game   **796.332**

Steinmeyer, Jim
  Charles Fort   **92**

STEINWAY & SONS
  Hafner, K.   A romance on three legs   **92**

Steketee, Gail
  (jt. auth) Frost, R. O.   Stuff   **616.85**

Stekler, Paul
  Welch, J.   Killing Custer   **973.8**

Stella Adler on America's master playwrights. Adler, S.   **812**

Stella Adler: the art of acting. Adler, S.   **792**

STELLA LYKES (FREIGHTER)
  McPhee, J. A.   Looking for a ship   **910.4**

Stellin, Susan
  How to travel practically anywhere   **910.2**

Steltenkamp, Michael F.
  Black Elk, holy man of the Oglala   **92**

Stelter, Brian
  Top of the morning   **791.45**

STEM CELL RESEARCH
  Moreno, J. D.   The body politic   **303.48**

STEM CELL RESEARCH
  See also Medical technology; Medicine -- Research

STEM EDUCATION
  See also Education

Stempel, Larry
  Showtime   **792.6**

STENCIL WORK
  Corwin, L.   Printing by hand   **745.5**
  Joyce, A.   Stamp stencil paint   **745.5**

STENCIL WORK
  See also Decoration and ornament; Painting

Stengel. Creamer, R. W.   **796.357**

Stengel, Casey
        About
  Creamer, R. W.   Stengel   **796.357**

STEP DANCING
  See also Dance

STEP into storytime. Ghoting, S. N.   **027.62**

STEP-PARENTS *See* Stepparents

Stepan, Peter
  Photos that changed the world   **779**

Stepan-Norris, Judith
  Left out   **331.8**

STEPCHILDREN
  Lofas, J.   Stepparenting   **646.7**

STEPCHILDREN
  See also Children; Parent-child relationship

STEPFAMILIES
  See also Family

STEPFATHERS
  Bragg, R.   The prince of Frogtown   **92**

STEPFATHERS
  See also Fathers; Stepparents

Stephanopoulos, George
  All too human   **973.929**

Stephen Spender. Sutherland, J.   **92**

Stephens, Alexander Hamilton, 1812-1883
        About
  Wilson, E.   Patriotic gore   **810**

Stephens, Francine
  (jt. auth) Clark, M.   Franny's   **641.594**

Stephens, Kimberly
  The Prodigy's Cousin   **155.45**

Stephenson, Michael

The last full measure **305.9**

STEPMOTHERS

See also Mothers; Stepparents

Stepparenting. Lofas, J. **646.7**

STEPPARENTS

Lofas, J. Stepparenting **646.7**

STEPPARENTS

See also Parents

Stepping stones. O'Driscoll, D. **821**

Steptoe, Sonja

Joyner-Kersee, J. A kind of grace **796.42**

STEREOTYPE (SOCIAL PSYCHOLOGY)

Brown, C. S. Parenting beyond pink and blue **649**

Jobrani, M. I'm not a terrorist, but I've played one on tv **92**

Tanenbaum, L. I Am Not a Slut **305.23**

STEREOTYPE (SOCIAL PSYCHOLOGY)

See also Attitude (Psychology); Social psychology; Thought and thinking

STEREOTYPED BEHAVIOR *See* Stereotype (Social psychology)

STEREOTYPES (SOCIAL PSYCHOLOGY)

Kramer, A. S. Breaking through bias **650.101**

Nugent, B. American nerd **305.9**

STEREOTYPES (SOCIAL PSYCHOLOGY) -- UNITED STATES

Jobrani, M. I'm not a terrorist, but I've played one on tv **92**

STERILITY IN ANIMALS *See* Infertility

STERILITY IN HUMANS *See* Infertility

STERILIZATION (BIRTH CONTROL)

Bruinius, H. Better for all the world **363.9**

Cohen, A. Imbeciles **344**

Lombardo, P. A. Three generations, no imbeciles **344**

Nourse, V. F. In reckless hands **344**

STERILIZATION (BIRTH CONTROL)

See also Birth control

STERILIZATION, EUGENIC

Lombardo, P. A. Three generations, no imbeciles **344**

Nourse, V. F. In reckless hands **344**

Sterling, David

Yucatán **641.59**

Sterling, Evelina Weidman

(jt. auth) Best-Boss, A. Your child's teeth **617.6**

Stern, Fritz Richard

Five Germanys I have known **943.08**

Stern, Gerald

This time **811**

Stern, Jeffrey E.

(jt. auth) Sadler, A. The 15:17 to Paris **363.325**

Stern, Jessica, 1958-

About

Stern, J. Denial **92**

Stern, Lynn, 1949-

(jt. auth) Fogler, J. Improving your memory **153.1**

Sternberg, Martin L. A.

American Sign Language **419**

STEROIDS

See also Biochemistry; Drugs

Stesichorus. Geryoneis

About

Carson, A. Red doc> **811**

Steve Jobs. Isaacson, W. **92**

Steve McCurry. **779.092**

STEVEDORES

Fisher, J. T. On the Irish waterfront **331.7**

Stevens, Christopher

Written in Stone **422**

Stevens, George, Jr., 1932-

(ed) Conversations at the American Film Institute with the great moviemakers **791.43**

Stevens, Isaac Ingalls, 1818-1862

About

Kluger, R. The bitter waters of Medicine Creek **979.7**

Stevens, John F. (John Frank), 1853-1943

About

McCullough, D. G. The path between the seas **972.87**

Stevens, Mark

Swan, A. De Kooning: an American master **92**

Stevens, Molly

(ed) The 150 best American recipes **641.5**

All about braising **641.7**

All about roasting **641.7**

Stevens, Scott Manning

(jt. auth) Hassrick, P. H. Art of the American West **709**

Stevens, Wallace, 1879-1955

Collected poetry and prose **811**

About

Gioia, D. Can poetry matter? **809.1**

Jarrell, R. No other book **809**

Kermode, F. An appetite for poetry **801**

Stevenson, Adlai E. (Adlai Ewing), 1900-1965

About

Galbraith, J. K. Name-dropping **973.9**

Stevenson, Amy

My perfect pantry **641.5**

Stevenson, Angus

(ed) New Oxford American dictionary **423**

(ed) Shorter Oxford English dictionary on historical principles **423**

Stevenson, Anne

Poems, 1955-2005 **821**

Stevenson, Bryan

Just Mercy **353.4**

Stevenson, Christine

Creative stained glass **748.5**

Stevenson, Jen

(jt. auth) Hanel, M. The picnic   **642**

Stevenson, Lorna
  (ed) Roebuck, J. Anatomy 360 degrees

Stevenson, N. J.
  Fashion   **391.009**

Stevenson, Robert Louis, 1850-1894
        About
  Nabokov, V. V. Lectures on literature   **808.3**

A **stew** or a story. Fisher, M. F. K.   **641**

Steward, Samuel M., 1909-1993
        About
  Spring, J. Secret historian   **92**

Stewart, Amy
  The drunken botanist   **581.6**
  The earth moved   **592**
  Wicked bugs   **632**

Stewart, Ben
  Don't trust, don't fear, don't beg   **363.738**

Stewart, Bruce
  The Oxford companion to Irish literature   **820**

Stewart, Chris
  Driving over lemons   **946.083**

Stewart, David O.
  American emperor   **973.4**
  Madison's Gift   **92**

Stewart, Ian
  Professor Stewart's casebook of mathematical mysteries   **510**
  Visions of Infinity   **510**
  Why beauty is truth   **539.7**

Stewart, James B.
  Blind eye   **364.1**

Stewart, Marcia
  Bray, I. M. Nolo's essential guide to buying your first home   **643**
  (ed) Pakroo, P. The small business start-up kit **346**
  Portman, J. Every tenant's legal guide   **346.04**
  Every landlord's legal guide   **346.04**

Stewart, Martha, 1941-
  Martha Stewart's cooking school   **641.5**
  Martha Stewart living Martha Stewart's encyclopedia of crafts   **745.5**
  Martha Stewart's encyclopedia of sewing and fabric crafts   **746**
  Stewart, M. Martha Stewart's Homekeeping Handbook   **640**

Stewart, Rory
  The Marches   **941.3**
        About
  Stewart, R. The prince of the marshes   **956.7**

Stewart, Tracey
  Do unto animals   **590**

STEWS
  Broth   **641.813**

Sticks and stones. Bazelon, E.   **302.34**

Stieglitz, Alfred

Alfred Stieglitz: the key set   **770**

Stiff. Roach, M.   **611**

Stiglitz, Joseph E., 1943-
  (ed) The economists' voice 2.0   **330.9**
  Globalization and its discontents   **337**
  The price of inequality   **305.5**

Stiles, David
  Backyard Building   **690**

Stiles, Jeanie
  (jt. auth) Stiles, D. Backyard Building   **690**

Stiles, T. J.
  Custer's trials   **92**
  The first tycoon   **92**
  Jesse James   **364.15**

Stiletto network. Ryckman, P.   **331.4**

Still foolin' 'em. Crystal, B.   **92**

Still life. Milgrom, M.   **590.75**

Still me. Reeve, C.   **92**

The **still** point of the turning world. Rapp, E. **618.92**

Still woman enough. Lynn, L.   **92**

Still, Robert
  The world's rarest birds   **598**

STILL-LIFE PAINTING
  The World Is an Apple   **759.4**

STILL-LIFE PAINTING
    See also Painting

Stillman, Deanne
  Desert reckoning   **363.2**

A **stillness** at Appomattox. Catton, B.   **973.7**

STILLS *See* Distillation

STILLS (MOTION PICTURES) -- UNITED STATES
  Longworth, K. Hollywood frame by frame **791.43**

Stillwell, John
  Roads to infinity   **511.3**

Stilwell and the American experience in China, 1911-45. Tuchman, B. W.   **327**

Stilwell, Alexander
  The encyclopedia of survival techniques   **613.6**

Stilwell, Joseph Warren, 1883-1946
        About
  Tuchman, B. W. Stilwell and the American experience in China, 1911-45   **327**

Stilwell, Victoria
  Train your dog positively   **636.7**

Stim, Richard
  Elias, S. Trademark   **346.04**
  Contracts   **346**
  Patent, copyright & trademark   **346**

Stimson, Henry L. (Henry Lewis), 1867-1950
        About
  Jordan, J. W. American warlords   **973.917**

STIMULANTS
    See also Drugs; Psychotropic drugs

The **sting** of the wild. Schmidt, J. O.   **595.7**

Stipp, David

The youth pill 612.6
Stitch 'n bitch. Stoller, D. 746.43
Stitch 'n bitch superstar knitting. 746.43
Stitch Savvy. Moebes, D. 646
Stitches. Small, D. 741.5
STITCHES (SEWING)
Knight, E. 750 knitting stitches 746.432
STOCK EXCHANGES
Cassidy, J. How markets fail 381
Dreman, D. Contrarian investment strategies 332.601
Perino, M. A. The hellhound of Wall Street 330.9
STOCK EXCHANGES
See also Finance; Markets
STOCK EXCHANGES -- UNITED STATES
Shiller, R. J. Irrational exuberance 332.63
STOCK MARKET CRASH, 1929
Perino, M. A. The hellhound of Wall Street 330.9
Stock, Gregory
Redesigning humans 176
STOCKBROKERS
Cramer, J. J. Confessions of a street addict 332.6
STOCKBROKERS -- UNITED STATES
Lewis, M. Flash boys 332.6
STOCKHOLDERS
Gramm, J. Dear chairman 659.2
STOCKS
Bernstein, W. The investor's manifesto 332.6
Cramer, J. J. Confessions of a street addict 332.6
Dreman, D. Contrarian investment strategies 332.601
Malkiel, B. G. A random walk down Wall Street 332.6
Siegel, J. J. Stocks for the long run 332.63
Where are the customers' yachts? 332.64
STOCKS
See also Commerce; Securities
STOCKS -- PRICES
Tengler, N. The women's guide to successful investing 332.6
STOCKS -- PRICES -- UNITED STATES
Shiller, R. J. Irrational exuberance 332.63
STOCKS -- UNITED STATES
Shiller, R. J. Irrational exuberance 332.63
Stocks for the long run. Siegel, J. J. 332.63
STOCKYARDS
See also Meat industry
Stoeger, Melissa Brackney
Food lit 016.6
STOICS
Marcus Aurelius Meditations 188
Russell, B. A history of Western philosophy 109
STOICS
See also Ancient philosophy; Ethics
Stokes, Donald W.
(ed) A guide to amphibians and reptiles 597.9

The bird feeder book 598
The butterfly book 595.7
Stokes, Gale
The walls came tumbling down 947.085
Stokes, Lillian Q.
(ed) A guide to amphibians and reptiles 597.9
Stokes, D. W. The bird feeder book 598
Stokes, D. W. The butterfly book 595.7
Stolen voices. 920
Stolen world. Smith, J. E. 364.1
Stoler, Diane Roberts
Coping with concussion and mild traumatic brain injury 617.4
Stoll, Ira
JFK, conservative 973.922
Stoller, Debbie
Stitch 'n bitch 746.43
Stitch 'n bitch superstar knitting 746.43
Stoller, Mike, 1933-
About
Leiber, J. Hound dog 92
Stolley, Richard B.
(ed) Life: World War 2 779
STOMACH
See also Anatomy
STOMACH -- SURGERY
Ali, K. Fighting weight 92
STONE
See also Building materials; Economic geology
STONE AGE
Stevens, C. Written in Stone 422
STONE AGE
See also Civilization
Stone in the garden. Hayward, G. 712
Stone, Alex
About
Stone, A. Fooling Houdini 793.8
Stone, Bill, 1952-
About
Tabor, J. M. Blind descent 796.52
Stone, Biz
About
Stone, B. Things a little bird told me 006.7
Stone, Douglas
Difficult conversations 158
Stone, Geoffrey R.
Perilous times 323.44
Stone, I. F. (Isidor Feinstein), 1907-1989
The trial of Socrates 183
About
Guttenplan, D. D. American radical 92
MacPherson, M. All governments lie 92
Stone, James M.
Five easy theses 330.973
Stone, Jon R.

Latin for the illiterati **473**

Stone, Michael

Miller, J. The cell: inside the 9/11 plot and why the FBI and CIA failed to stop it **973.931**

Stone, Nathaniel

On the water **917**

Stone, Norman

World War One **940.3**

Stone, Robert, 1937-

About

Stone, R. Prime green **92**

Stone, Ruth

What love comes to **811**

Stone, Samuel, 1887-1981

About

Gup, T. A secret gift **977.1**

STONECUTTING

See also Masonry; Stone

Stoned. Raden, A. **739.27**

Stonehenge. Hill, R. **936.2**

Stonehenge. Pearson, M. P. **936.2**

STONEHENGE (ENGLAND)

Pearson, M. P. Stonehenge **936.2**

STONEHENGE (ENGLAND)

See also Great Britain -- Antiquities

Stonewall. Carter, D. **306.76**

Stonewall Jackson. Robertson, J. I. **92**

STONEWALL RIOTS, NEW YORK, N.Y., 1969

Carter, D. Stonewall **306.76**

STONEWARE *See* Pottery

Stop Stealing Sheep and Find out How Type Works. Spiekermann, E. **686.2**

Stoppard, Tom

Arcadia **822**

The invention of love **822**

Rosencrantz and Guildenstern are dead **822**

Travesties **822**

About

Playwrights at work **812**

STORAGE IN THE HOME

101 Saturday morning projects **643**

Platt, S. What's a disorganized person to do? **648**

STORAGE IN THE HOME

See also Home economics

STORAGE IN THE HOME -- AMATEURS' MANUALS

101 Saturday morning projects **643**

STORES

See also Commercial buildings; Retail trade

Storey basics [series]

Campbell, S. How to mulch **635**

Storey's horse-lover's encyclopedia. **636.1**

STORIES *See* Anecdotes; Bible stories; Fairy tales; Fiction; Legends; Romances; Short stories; Stories in rhyme; Stories without words; Storytelling

Stories from the Polycule. Sheff, E. **306.84**

STORIES IN RHYME

See also Narrative poetry; Rhyme

Stories in stone. Williams, D. B. **550**

The **stories** of English. Crystal, D. **427**

Stories of my life. Paterson, K. **92**

STORIES WITHOUT WORDS

See also Picture books for children

STORIES, PLOTS, ETC.

See also Literature

Stories, poems, and other writings. Cather, W. **818**

The **storm.** Van Heerden, I. L. **976.3**

Storm center. O'Brien, D. M. **347**

STORM CHASERS

Sandlin, L. Storm kings **551.55**

Storm kings. Sandlin, L. **551.55**

The **storm** of the century. Roker, A. **976.4**

The **storm** of war. Roberts, A. **940.54**

Storm over Leyte. Prados, J. **940.54**

Storm surge. Sobel, A. **551.55**

Storm world. Mooney, C. **363.7**

STORMS

Cross, K. What Stands in a Storm **363.34**

Junger, S. The perfect storm **910.4**

Roker, A. The storm of the century **976.4**

STORMS

See also Meteorology; Natural disasters; Weather

Storms of my grandchildren. Hansen, J. E. **363.7**

Stormy weather. Gavin, J. **92**

Storr, Anthony

(ed) The essential Jung **150.19**

Storrer, William Allin

The Frank Lloyd Wright companion **720.9**

The **story** about the story. **809**

A **story** larger than my own. **810.9**

Story of a secret state. Karski, J. **940.53**

The **story** of a shipwrecked sailor. Garcia Marquez, G. **910.4**

The **story** of America. Lepore, J. **973**

The **story** of American freedom. Foner, E. **323.44**

The **story** of architecture. Glancey, J. **720.9**

The **story** of art. Gombrich, E. H. **709**

The **story** of Britain. Fraser, R. **941**

The **story** of Earth. Hazen, R. M. **550**

The **Story** of Egypt. Fletcher, J. **932**

The **story** of English. McCrum, R. **420**

The **story** of English in 100 words. Crystal, D. **422**

The **story** of French. Nadeau **440**

The **story** of life in 25 fossils. Prothero, D. R. **560**

The **story** of measurement. Robinson, A. **530.8**

The **story** of my boyhood and youth. Muir, J. **92**

The **story** of my father. Miller, S. **92**

The **story** of my life. Keller, H. **92**

The **Story** of My Tits. Hayden, J. **741.5**

The **story** of N. Gorman, H. S. **547**

The **story** of philosophy. Durant, W. J. **109**

The **story** of philosophy. Magee, B.   **190**

The **story** of Spanish. Barlow, J.   **460**

The **story** of stuff. Leonard, A.   **306.4**

The **story** of the human body. Lieberman, D.   **612**

The **story** of the Jews. Schama, S.   **909**

The **story** of Western science. Bauer, S. W.   **509**

Story/Time. Jones, B. T.   **814**

Storyteller. Sturrock, D.   **92**

Storyteller. Silko, L.   **818**

The **storyteller's** daughter. Shah, S.   **958.1**

STORYTELLING

  Bruchac, J. Our stories remember   **970.004**

  Del Negro, J. M. Folktales aloud   **027.62**

  Flaherty, F. The elements of story   **808.5**

  Ghoting, S. N. STEP into storytime   **027.62**

  Lambert, M. D. Reading picture books with children   **372.133**

  Neuburger, E. K. Show me a story   **741.6**

  World folklore for storytellers   **398**

STORYTELLING

  See also Children's literature

STORYTELLING -- UNITED STATES

  Ghoting, S. N. STEP into storytime   **027.62**

STORYVILLE (NEW ORLEANS, LA.) -- HISTORY -- 20TH CENTURY

  Krist, G. Empire of sin   **976.3**

Stossel, Scott

          About

  Stossel, S. My age of anxiety   **616.85**

Stothard, Peter

  Alexandria   **962**

Stott, Carole

  Kerrod, R. Hubble   **522**

Stott, Rebecca

  Darwin's ghosts   **576.8**

Stout, Glenn

  Fenway 1912   **796.357**

Stout, Harry S.

  Upon the altar of the nation : a moral history of the American Civil War   **973.7**

Stout, Janis

  (ed) Cather, W. The selected letters of Willa Cather   **813**

Stover, Kaite Mediatore

  (jt. auth) Moyer, J. E. The readers' advisory handbook   **025.5**

Stow, Dorrik A. V.

  Oceans: an illustrated reference   **551.46**

Stowe, Calvin Ellis, 1802-1886

          About

  Wilson, E. Patriotic gore   **810**

Stowe, Harriet Beecher, 1811-1896

          About

  Benfey, C. E. G. A summer of hummingbirds   **920**

  Hedrick, J. D. Harriet Beecher Stowe   **92**

  McPherson, J. M. Drawn with the sword   **973.7**

Reynolds, D. S. Mightier than the sword   **813**

Wilson, E. Patriotic gore   **810**

Strachan, Hew

  The First World War   **940.3**

Straight. Blank, H.   **306.76**

Straight to Hell. Lefevre, J.   **332.1**

STRAIN (PSYCHOLOGY) *See* Stress (Psychology)

Stranahan, Susan Q.

  (jt. auth) Lyman, E. Fukushima   **363.17**

Strand, Mark, 1934-2014

  (ed) 100 great poems of the twentieth century **821**

  (ed) The Making of a poem   **821**

  Collected poems   **811**

Strang, Dean A.

  Worse than the devil   **345**

Strange angel. Pendle, G.   **92**

The **strange** career of Jim Crow. Woodward, C. V.   **305.8**

The **strange** career of William Ellis. Jacoby, K.   **92**

Strange days indeed. Wheen, F.   **973.92**

Strange glory. Marsh, C.   **92**

Strange glow. Jorgensen, T. J.   **539.2**

A **strange** stirring. Coontz, S.   **305.42**

The **stranger** beside me. Rule, A.   **92**

The **stranger** from paradise: a biography of William Blake. Bentley, G. E.   **821**

Stranger to history. Taseer, A.   **915.6**

A **stranger's** mirror. Hacker, M.   **811**

Strangers in their own land. Hochschild, A. R.   **320.52**

Strangers: homosexual love in the nineteenth century. Robb, G.   **306.76**

Strassler, Robert B.

  (ed) Herodotus, c. 4. B. B. C. The landmark Herodotus   **938**

  (ed) The Landmark Xenophon's Hellenika   **938**

STRATEGIC ALLIANCES

  Ryckman, P. Stiletto network   **331.4**

STRATEGIC CULTURE -- UNITED STATES

  Bolger, D. P. Why We Lost   **956.704**

STRATEGIC DEFENSE INITIATIVE

  FitzGerald, F. Way out there in the blue   **973.927**

STRATEGIC DEFENSE INITIATIVE

  See also Military policy -- United States; Space warfare; United States -- Defenses

STRATEGIC MANAGEMENT *See* Strategic planning

STRATEGIC MATERIALS *See* Materials

STRATEGIC PLANNING

  Collins, J. C. Good to great   **658**

  Goldfayn, A. The revenue growth habit   **658.15**

  Johnson, W. Disrupt yourself   **658.4**

  Matthews, J. R. Scorecards for results   **027.4**

STRATEGIC PLANNING

  See also Planning

Strategic vision. Brzezinski, Z.   **327.1**

Strategize to win. Harris, C. A.   **650.1**

STRATEGY

   Collingham, L. The taste of war   **940.53**

   D'Este, C. Warlord   **92**

   Hamilton, N. The mantle of command   **940.54**

   Overy, R. Why the Allies won   **940.53**

   Preston, D. A higher form of killing   **940.4**

STRATEGY

   See also Military art and science; Naval art and science

STRATEGY -- HISTORY

   Clark, L. Blitzkrieg   **940.54**

STRATEGY -- HISTORY -- 20TH CENTURY

   Roberts, A. Masters and commanders   **940.54**

Stratemeyer, Edward, 1862-1930

     About

   Rehak, M. Girl sleuth   **813**

Strathern, Paul, 1940-

   The artist, the philosopher, and the warrior   **920**

   Death in Florence   **945**

   The Medici   **945.51**

   Napoleon in Egypt   **962**

STRATIGRAPHIC GEOLOGY

   Fortey, R. A. Earth   **551.7**

   Hancock, G. Underworld: the mysterious origins of civilization   **551.7**

   Macdougall, J. D. A short history of planet earth   **551.7**

   Winchester, S. The map that changed the world **526**

STRATIGRAPHIC GEOLOGY

   See also Geology

Stratton, Joanna L.

   Pioneer women   **978.1**

Stratton, Stephen E.

   The encyclopedia of HIV and AIDS   **362.196**

Stratton, W. K.

   Floyd Patterson   **92**

Strausbaugh, John

   The Village   **974.7**

Strauss's handbook of business information. Ernsthausen, D. G.   **016**

Strauss, Barry

   The death of Caesar   **937**

Strauss, Ben

   (jt. auth) Nocera, J. Indentured   **796.04**

Strauss, Michael A.

   (jt. auth) Gott, J. R. Welcome to the universe **523.1**

Strauss, Neil

   Everyone loves you when you're dead   **920**

Strauss, Richard, 1864-1949

     About

   Tuchman, B. W. The proud tower   **909.82**

Strauss, Steven D.

   The small business bible   **658.02**

Strauss, Susan L.

Sexual harassment and bullying   **302.34**

Strauss-Kahn, Dominique

     About

   Solomon, J. DSK   **306.77**

Stravinsky inside out. Joseph, C. M.   **92**

Stravinsky, Igor, 1882-1971

     About

   Joseph, C. M. Stravinsky inside out   **92**

   Walsh, S. Stravinsky: a creative spring   **92**

   Walsh, S. Stravinsky: the second exile   **92**

Stravinsky: a creative spring. Walsh, S.   **92**

Stravinsky: the second exile. Walsh, S.   **92**

Straw bale gardens complete. Karsten, J.   **635**

STRAWBERRIES

   See also Berries

Strayed, Cheryl, 1968-

   (ed) The Best American essays 2013   **814**

     About

   Strayed, C. Wild   **92**

Strayer, Joseph Reese

   (ed) Dictionary of the Middle Ages   **909.07**

Strayhorn.   **781.650**

Strayhorn, Billy

     About

   Strayhorn   **781.650**

STREAM ANIMALS

   See also Animals; Rivers

STREAM ECOLOGY

   See also Ecology; Freshwater ecology

Streatfeild, Dominic

   Cocaine   **362.29**

Streb. Streb, E.   **92**

Streb, Elizabeth

     About

   Streb, E. Streb   **92**

Strebeigh, Fred

   Equal   **342**

STREET ART

   Felisbret, E. Graffiti New York   **751.7**

   Ganz, N. Graffiti world   **751**

STREET ART

   See also Art

STREET ART -- NEW YORK (STATE) -- NEW YORK

   Felisbret, E. Graffiti New York   **751.7**

STREET CLEANING

   See also Cleaning; Municipal engineering; Public health; Roads; Sanitary engineering; Streets

STREET ENTERTAINERS

   Lopez, S. The soloist   **92**

Street fighters. Kelly, K.   **332.6**

STREET FOOD

   Alger, K. Susan Feniger's street food   **641.59**

STREET FOOD -- NEW YORK (STATE) -- NEW YORK

Street vegan **641.5**

STREET FOOD -- UNITED STATES
Carruthers, J. Eat street **641.76**

STREET GANGS *See* Gangs

STREET LIFE
Stanton, B. Humans of New York **974.7**

STREET LIFE
See also City and town life

STREET LIFE -- FICTION -- BIBLIOGRAPHY
Morris, V. I. The readers' advisory guide to street
literature **016**

STREET LIFE -- MARYLAND -- BALTIMORE
Coates The beautiful struggle
Street of Eternal Happiness. Schmitz, R. **951.132**

STREET PEOPLE *See* Homeless persons

**STREET PHOTOGRAPHY -- NEW YORK
(STATE) -- NEW YORK**
Stanton, B. Humans of New York: stories **974.7**

Street poison. **813**

Street poison. Gifford, J. **813**

STREET RAILROADS
See also Local transit; Railroads

STREET TRAFFIC *See* City traffic; Traffic engineering

Street vegan. **641.5**

Street-fighting mathematics. Mahajan, S. **510**

A **streetcar** named desire. Williams, T. **812**

STREETS
See also Cities and towns; Civil engineering;
Transportation

STREETS -- CHINA -- SHANGHAI
Schmitz, R. Street of Eternal Happiness **951.132**

STREETS -- LIGHTING
See also Lighting

Streever, Bill
Cold **998**
Heat **551.41**

Streicher, Lauren F., 1956-
The essential guide to hysterectomy **618.1**

Streiff, Fritz
The art of simple food **641.5**

Streisand, Barbra
About
Mann, W. J. Hello, gorgeous **92**

Streissguth, Michael
Johnny Cash **92**

Strength in what remains. Kidder, T. **92**

Strength to love. King, M. L. **252**

STRENGTH TRAINING *See* Weight lifting

Strength training exercises for women. Pagano,
J. **613.7**

Strength training for women. Pagano, J. **613.7**

STRESS (PHYSIOLOGY)
Benson, H. The relaxation response **155.9**
Gambaro, J. The truth about carpal tunnel syn-
drome **616.85**

Goldman, B. Brain fitness **153.1**

STRESS (PHYSIOLOGY)
See also Adaptation (Biology); Physiology

STRESS (PSYCHOLOGY)
Benson, H. The relaxation response **155.9**
Taylor, S. E. The tending instinct **304.5**
Van der Kolk, B. A. The body keeps the
score **616.85**

STRESS (PSYCHOLOGY)
See also Mental health; Psychology

STRESS MANAGEMENT
Goldman, B. Brain fitness **153.1**
Hanoch, D. The yoga lifestyle **613.7**
Harris, D. 10% happier **158.1**
Langshur, E. Start here **158**

STRESS MANAGEMENT
See also Health

STRETCHING EXERCISES
See also Exercise

Strickland, Bill
Tour de Lance **92**

Strictly science fiction. Herald, D. T. **016**

STRIKES
See also Industrial relations; Labor disputes

Strindberg. Prideaux, S. **839.7**

Strindberg, August, 1849-1912
Strindberg: five plays **839.7**
About
Prideaux, S. Strindberg **839.7**

Strindberg: five plays. Strindberg, A. **839.7**

STRING FIGURES
See also Amusements

STRING MODELS
Nadis, S. The shape of inner space **530.1**
Randall, L. Warped passages **530**
Smolin, L. The trouble with physics **530.1**

STRING MODELS *See* String theory

String theory. Wallace, D. F. **796.342**

STRING THEORY
See also Particles (Nuclear physics)

STRING THEORY
Greene, B. R. The elegant universe **539.7**
Hawking, S. The grand design **530.1**
Kaku, M. Parallel worlds **523.1**
Nadis, S. The shape of inner space **530.1**
Smolin, L. The trouble with physics **530.1**

STRINGED INSTRUMENTS
See also Musical instruments

Stringer. Sundaram, A. **967.51**

STRIPTEASERS
Abbott, K. American rose **92**
Burana, L. I love a man in uniform **92**

Strobel, Lee
The Case for Grace **234**

Strogatz, Steven, 1959-
Strogatz, S. The joy of X **510**

STROKE

See also Brain -- Diseases

STROKE PATIENTS

Taylor, J. B. My stroke of insight   **362.19**

Strom, Yale

The book of Klezmer   **781.62**

Strong. Schuler, L.   **613.7**

Strong curves. Contreras, B.   **613.7**

Strong inside. Maraniss, A.   **92**

Strong Is the New Beautiful. Vonn, L.   **613.042**

Strong is your hold. Kinnell, G.   **811**

Strong religion. Almond, G. A.   **200.9**

Strong, James

The strongest Strong's exhaustive concordance of the Bible   **220.5**

Stronger. Witter, B.   **92**

The **strongest** Strong's exhaustive concordance of the Bible. Strong, J.   **220.5**

Stroom, Gerrold van der

Barnouw, D. The diary of Anne Frank: the critical edition   **92**

Stross, Randall

Planet Google   **338.7**

Stroud, Patricia Tyson

A glorious enterprise   **508**

Strouse, Charles

About

Strouse, C. Put on a happy face   **92**

Strouse, Jean

Morgan   **92**

Struck by genius. Padgett, J.   **155.9**

STRUCTURAL ENGINEERING

See also Civil engineering; Engineering

STRUCTURAL ENGINEERS

Jonnes, J. Eiffel's tower   **944**

Tabor, J. M. Blind descent   **796.52**

STRUCTURAL FAILURES

Levy, M. Why buildings fall down   **690**

Petroski, H. To forgive design   **620**

STRUCTURAL MATERIALS *See* Building materials

STRUCTURAL STEEL

Waldman, J. Rust   **620.1**

STRUCTURAL STEEL

See also Building materials; Civil engineering; Steel

The **structure** of evolutionary theory. Gould, S. J.   **576.8**

STRUCTURES *See* Buildings

STRUCTURES, GARDEN *See* Garden structures

STRUGGLE -- PSYCHOLOGICAL ASPECTS

Gladwell, M. David and Goliath   **155.2**

Strumpf, Michael

The grammar bible   **428**

Strunk, William, 1869-1946

The elements of style   **808**

About

Garvey, M. Stylized   **808**

Strycker, Noah

The thing with feathers   **598**

Stryker, Cole

Hacking the Future   **004.67**

Stuart family

About

Stuart, A. Sugar in the Blood   **338.1**

Stuart, Amanda Mackenzie

Empress of Fashion   **92**

Stuart, Andrea

Sugar in the Blood   **338.1**

Stuart, Granville, 1834-1918

About

Milner, C. A. As big as the West   **92**

Stuart, House of

About

Ackroyd, P. Rebellion   **941.06**

Stuart, Jeb, 1833-1864

About

Wert, J. D. Cavalryman of the lost cause   **92**

Stuart, Sarah Payne

About

Stuart, S. P. Perfectly miserable   **92**

Stuart, Tristram

Waste   **363.8**

Stubblefield, R. Jay

DeGategno, P. J. Critical companion to Jonathan Swift   **828**

A **stubbornly** persistent illusion. Einstein, A. **530.1**

STUDENT AID

Jager-Hyman, J. B+ grades, A+ college application   **378.1**

Peterson's how to get money for college 2015 **378.3**

STUDENT LOAN FUNDS

Collinge, A. The student loan scam   **378.3**

Getting financial aid   **378.3**

STUDENT LOAN FUNDS

See also College costs; Student aid

The **student** loan scam. Collinge, A.   **378.3**

STUDENT MOVEMENTS -- CALIFORNIA -- BERKELEY -- HISTORY

Rosenfeld, S. Subversives   **378.1**

STUDENT NONVIOLENT COORDINATING COMMITTEE

Lewis, A. B. The shadows of youth   **323.1**

Watson, B. Freedom summer   **323.1**

Zellner, R. The wrong side of Murder Creek   **92**

STUDENT TEACHING

See also Teachers -- Training; Teaching

Student's guide to writing college papers. Turabian, K. L.   **808**

STUDENTS

Kidder, T. Strength in what remains   **92**

Murray, L. Breaking night   **92**

STUDENTS -- LIBRARY SERVICES
  See also Libraries and schools; Library services; School libraries
STUDENTS -- POLITICAL ACTIVITY
  Gitlin, T. The sixties   973.922
STUDENTS -- UNITED STATES
  Beyond the asterisk   378.1
Students for a Democratic Society.   378.1
STUDENTS FOR A DEMOCRATIC SOCIETY
  Rudd, M. Underground   92
**STUDENTS FOR A DEMOCRATIC SOCIETY --
  GRAPHIC NOVELS -- HISTORY**
  Students for a Democratic Society   378.1
STUDENTS WITH DISABILITIES
  Fertig, B. Why cant U teach me 2 read?   372.4
  Flink, D. Thinking Differently   371.9
  Mooney, J. The short bus   92
STUDENTS WITH PROBLEMS *See* At risk students*
STUDENTS' SONGS
  See also Songs
STUDENTS, FOREIGN *See* Foreign students
**STUDENTS, FOREIGN -- FRANCE -- PARIS --
  BIOGRAPHY**
  Kaplan, A. Dreaming in French   944
Studholme, Joa
  Farrow & Ball How to Decorate   747.94
**Studies in genocide: religion, history, and human
  rights** [series]
  Alvarez, A. Native America and the question of
  genocide   973
Studies in jazz [series]
  Sandke, R. Where the dark and the light folks
  meet   781.65
**Studies in modern science, technology, and the en-
  vironment** [series]
  Gorman, H. S. The story of N   547
STUDIO POTTERY *See* Art pottery
STUDY AND TEACHING *See* Education
STUDY GUIDES FOR EXAMINATIONS *See*
  Examinations -- Study guides
STUDY SKILLS
  Jackson, R. The learning habit   371.3
STUDY SKILLS
  See also Education; Life skills; Teaching
Stuff. Frost, R. O.   616.85
Stuff matters. Miodownik, M.   620.1
The **stuff** of thought. Pinker, S.   401
STUFFED BEARS (TOYS) *See* Teddy bears
STUFFED TOY MAKING *See* Soft toy making
Stumbling on happiness. Gilbert, D.   158
Stump, Al
  Cobb   796.357
Stunned by grief. Brizendine, J.   248
STUNT FLYING
  See also Airplanes -- Piloting

STUNT PERFORMERS
  See also Actors
Stuntz, William J.
  The collapse of American criminal justice   364.4
Stupak, Alex
  Tacos   641.84
Sturdy, John
  (ed) The Cambridge history of Judaism   296.09
Sturgeon, Alison
  (ed) World War II   940.54
Sturrock, Donald
  Storyteller   92
STUTTERERS -- BIOGRAPHY
  Preston, K. Out with it   92
STUTTERING *See* Speech disorders
Stutz, Phil, 1947-
  (jt. auth) Michels, B. The tools   158
STYLE IN DRESS *See* Clothing and dress; Costume; Fashion
STYLE MANIKINS *See* Fashion models
Style manual. United States/Government Printing
  Office   808
Style your perfect wedding.   392.5
STYLE, LITERARY *See* Literary style
Styled. Borsics, A.   747
Styler, Christopher
  Kafka, B. Vegetable love   641.6
Stylized. Garvey, M.   808
Styron, William, 1925-2006
  My generation   814
                      About
  Langer, L. L. Admitting the Holocaust   940.53
  Styron, W. Darkness visible   616.85
Sua sponte. Couch, D.   356
SUB-SAHARAN AFRICA
  See also Africa
SUBCONSCIOUSNESS
  Eagleman, D. Incognito   153
  Mlodinow, L. Subliminal   154.2
  Tallis, F. Hidden minds   154.2
  Vedantam, S. The hidden brain   154.2
SUBCONSCIOUSNESS
  See also Parapsychology; Psychology
SUBCONSCIOUSNESS IN ART
  Kandel, E. R. The age of insight   154.2
SUBCULTURE *See* Counter culture
**SUBCULTURE -- RUSSIA (FEDERATION) --
  CHELIABINSK**
  Garrels, A. Putin country   947.43
SUBCULTURE -- UNITED STATES
  Laskas, J. M. Hidden America   305.5
Suber, Peter
  Open access   070.5
SUBJECT DICTIONARIES *See* Encyclopedias
  and dictionaries
SUBJECT HEADINGS

Sears List of Subject Headings **025.4**
SUBJECT HEADINGS
    See also Cataloging; Indexes; Subject catalogs
The **sublime** engine. Amidon, S. **612.1**
Subliminal. Mlodinow, L. **154.2**
The **submarine.** Parrish, T. **359.9**
SUBMARINE BOATS *See* Submarines
SUBMARINE CABLES
  Gordon, J. S. A thread across the ocean **384.1**
SUBMARINE TOPOGRAPHY
  Felt, H. Soundings **526**
SUBMARINE WARFARE
    See also Naval art and science; War
SUBMARINES
  Parrish, T. The submarine **359.9**
  Peffer, R. Where divers dare **940.54**
SUBPRIME MORTGAGE LOANS
  Morgenson, G. Reckless endangerment **332.7**
SUBPRIME MORTGAGE LOANS -- UNITED STATES
  Howard, T. The mortgage wars **332.7**
SUBSTANCE ABUSE
  Adamec, C. When your adult child breaks your heart **616.89**
  Fletcher, A. M. Inside rehab **362.29**
  Ruta, D. With or without you **362.29**
SUBSTANCE ABUSE
    See also Social problems
SUBSTANCE ABUSE -- TREATMENT
  Fletcher, A. M. Inside rehab **362.29**
SUBTERFUGE *See* Deception
The **subtle** art of not giving a fu*k. Manson, M. **158.1**
SUBURBAN AREAS *See* Suburbs
SUBURBAN LIFE
  DeStefano, S. Coyote at the kitchen door **578.7**
SUBURBAN LIFE
    See also Suburbs
Suburban nation. Duany, A. **307.76**
SUBURBS
    See also Cities and towns -- Growth; City planning; Metropolitan areas
SUBURBS -- UNITED STATES
  Duany, A. Suburban nation **307.76**
SUBURBS AND ENVIRONS *See* Suburbs
SUBVERSIVE ACTIVITIES
  Shultz, R. H. The secret war against Hanoi **959.704**
SUBVERSIVE ACTIVITIES
    See also Insurgency
SUBVERSIVE ACTIVITIES -- CALIFORNIA -- BERKELEY -- HISTORY
  Rosenfeld, S. Subversives **378.1**
Subversives. Rosenfeld, S. **378.1**
SUBWAYS
    See also Local transit; Railroads

SUCCESS
  Beilock, S. L. Choke **153.9**
  Canfield, J. The success principles **158**
  Carnegie, D. How to win friends and influence people **158**
  Chan, R. W. Behind the Berkshire Hathaway curtain **658.4**
  Covey, S. R. The 7 habits of highly effective people **158**
  Covey, S. R. The 8th habit **158**
  Ehrenreich, B. Bright-sided **155.2**
  Gladwell, M. David and Goliath **155.2**
  Gladwell, M. Outliers **302**
  Grant, A. Give and take **158.2**
  Hill, N. Think and grow rich **650.1**
  Kendall, J. America's obsessives **609.2**
  Kowitz, B. Sprint **658.4**
  Licht, A. Leave Your Mark **650.1**
  McCormack, M. H. What they don't teach you at Harvard Business School **650.1**
  McGraw, P. C. Life strategies **158**
  Miller, C. A. Creating your best life **158**
  Mohr, T. Playing big **650.1**
  Moore, R. S. The artist's compass **791.023**
  Nyad, D. Find a way **92**
  Peale, N. V. The power of positive living **248**
  Pimsleur, J. Million Dollar Women **658.4**
  Riess, J. Flunking sainthood **248.4**
  Robbins, T. Unlimited power **158**
  Rollag, K. What to do when you're new **158.2**
  Rotella, B. How champions think in sports and in life **796.01**
  Schwartz, D. J. The magic of thinking big **158**
  Shell, G. R. Springboard **650.1**
  Sugar, L. Power your happy **158**
  Verveer, M. Fast forward **650.1**
  Wasmund, S. Do less, get more **650.1**
SUCCESS
    See also Business ethics; Wealth
SUCCESS -- PSYCHOLOGICAL ASPECTS
  McGraw, P. C. Life strategies **158**
  McWhorter, J. H. Losing the race **305.8**
  Rotella, B. How champions think in sports and in life **796.01**
SUCCESS IN BUSINESS
  The art of the start 2.0 **658.1**
  Buelow, B. L. The Introvert Entrepreneur **658.11**
  Citrin, J. M. The career playbook **650.14**
  Duckworth, A. Grit **158.1**
  Grant, A. Give and take **158.2**
  Johnson, W. Disrupt yourself **658.4**
  Kreamer, A. Risk/reward **650.1**
  Post, P. Emily Post's The etiquette advantage in business **395**
  Power, K. The career code **650.1**
  Stone, B. Things a little bird told me **006.7**

Sugar, L. Power your happy   158
SUCCESS IN BUSINESS -- CALIFORNIA --
   SANTA CLARA COUNTY
   Maxfield, K. Starting up Silicon Valley   338.7
SUCCESS IN BUSINESS -- UNITED STATES
   Lashinsky, A. Inside Apple   338.7
The **success** principles. Canfield, J.   158
Success through failure. Petroski, H.   620
SUCCESSFUL PEOPLE -- UNITED STATES --
   BIOGRAPHY
   Kendall, J. America's obsessives   609.2
SUCCULENT PLANTS
   Baldwin, D. L. Succulents simplified   635.9
   Hewitt, T. The complete book of cacti & succu-
      lents   635.9
   Kelaidis, G. M. Hardy succulents   635.9
SUCCULENT PLANTS -- VARIETIES
   Baldwin, D. L. Succulents simplified   635.9
Succulents simplified. Baldwin, D. L.   635.9
Suchet, John
   Beethoven   92
Suchlicki, Jaime
   Cuba   972.91
Suckley, Margaret L., 1891-1991
            About
   Persico, J. E. Franklin and Lucy   920
SUDAN
   Deng, B. They poured fire on us from the sky 962.4
SUDAN -- HISTORY -- DARFUR CONFLICT,
   2003-
   Hari, D. The translator   92
Suddendorf, Thomas
   The gap   156
SUDOKU
      See also Puzzles
SUDUR HAVID (FISHING BOAT)
   Lewis, M. Last man off   910.91
Suetonius Tranquillus, C.
   The twelve Caesars   878
SUEZ CANAL (EGYPT)
   Karabell, Z. Parting the desert   386
SUFFERING
   Cairns, S. The end of suffering   231
   Kingma, D. R. The ten things to do when your life
      falls apart   155.9
   Kushner, H. S. When bad things happen to good
      people   296.3
   Trachtenberg, P. The book of calamities   128
SUFFERING -- RELIGIOUS ASPECTS
   Billings, J. T. Rejoicing in lament   248.8
   Kushner, H. S. The book of Job   223
   Williamson, M. Tears to triumph   299.93
SUFFERING -- RELIGIOUS   ASPECTS --
   CHRISTIANITY
   Billings, J. T. Rejoicing in lament   248.8
   Cairns, S. The end of suffering   231

SUFFERING -- RELIGIOUS ASPECTS -- JUDA-
   ISM
   Kushner, H. S. The book of Job   223
SUFFRAGE
   Waldman, M. The Fight to Vote   324.6
SUFFRAGE
      See also Citizenship; Constitutional law; De-
      mocracy; Elections; Political science
SUFFRAGE -- UNITED STATES -- HISTORY --
   20TH CENTURY
   Berman, A. Give us the ballot   324.6
SUFFRAGE -- UNITED STATES -- HISTORY --
   21ST CENTURY
   Berman, A. Give us the ballot   324.6
SUFFRAGETTES See Suffragists
SUFFRAGISTS
   Anand, A. Sophia   92
   Failure is impossible   92
   Furmansky, D. Z. Rosalie Edge, hawk of mercy 92
   Ginzberg, L. D. Elizabeth Cady Stanton   92
   Goldsmith, B. Other powers   92
   Norgren, J. Belva Lockwood   92
   Ulrich, L. Well-behaved women seldom make his-
      tory   305.4
SUFISM
   Ernst, C. W. The Shambhala guide to Sufism 297.4
SUGAR
   Rathbone, J. P. The sugar king of Havana   92
SUGAR
      See also Food
Sugar and spice.   641.86
Sugar in my bowl.   306.7
Sugar in the Blood. Stuart, A.   338.1
The **sugar** king of Havana. Rathbone, J. P.   92
SUGAR SUBSTITUTES
   Cohen, R. Sweet and low   920
SUGAR TRADE -- BARBADOS -- HISTORY
   Stuart, A. Sugar in the Blood   338.1
Sugar, Lisa
   Power your happy   158
SUGAR-FREE DIET
   Naturally sweet   641.86
SUGAR-FREE DIET -- RECIPES
   The sprouted kitchen   641.3
SUGARCANE INDUSTRY -- BARBADOS --
   HISTORY
   Stuart, A. Sugar in the Blood   338.1
SUGARHILL RECORDING STUDIOS (FIRM)
   Bradley, A. House of hits   781.64
Sugden, John
   Nelson: a dream of glory, 1758-1797   92
Sugerman, Daniel
   Hopkins, J. No one here gets out alive   92
SUGGESTIVE THERAPEUTICS
      See also Therapeutics
Suggs, M. Jack

(ed) Bible The Oxford study Bible 220.5

Sugrue, Thomas J.

(jt. auth) Gilmore, G. E. These United States 973.9

Sweet land of liberty 323

SUICIDE

Ackerman, D. A slender thread 362.28

Durkheim, E. Suicide, a study in sociology 179.7

Humphry, D. Final exit 179.7

Marcus, E. Why suicide? 179.7

Max, D. T. c. Every love story is a ghost story 92

Peck, M. S. Denial of the soul 179.7

Rasmussen, M. Black aperture 811

Wickersham, J. The suicide index 155.9

SUICIDE

See also Medical jurisprudence; Social problems

SUICIDE -- POETRY

pH neutral history 891.8

SUICIDE -- PSYCHOLOGICAL ASPECTS

See also Human behavior

SUICIDE -- UNITED STATES

Dreazen, Y. The invisible front 92

SUICIDE ATTEMPTS *See* Suicide

SUICIDE BOMBERS

See also Terrorism

The suicide index. Wickersham, J. 155.9

Suicide, a study in sociology. Durkheim, E. 179.7

Suisman, David

Selling sounds 338.4

Suitable accommodations. 92

Süleyman I, Sultan of the Turks, 1495-1566

About

Reston, J. Defenders of the faith 940.2

Sulfaro, Valerie A.

(jt. auth) Roberts, R. N. Campaigning for president in America, 1788-2016 324.709

SULFONAMIDES

See also Drugs

Sull, Donald

Simple Rules 650.1

Sullenberger, Chesley, 1951-

(jt. auth) Century, D. Making a difference 303.3

Sullivan, Anne, 1866-1936

About

Gibson, W. The miracle worker 812

Sullivan, Ed, 1902-1974

About

Maguire, J. Impresario 92

Sullivan, James

The hardest working man 92

Sullivan, John Jeremiah

(ed) The best American essays 2014 814

Sullivan, Karen

(jt. auth) Cross, C. The baby book 649.122

Sullivan, Kevin

Jordan, M. The prison angel 92

Sullivan, Patricia

Lift every voice 323.1

Sullivan, Robert

The Thoreau you don't know 92

Sullivan, Rosemary

Stalin's daughter 92

SULPHUR

See also Chemical elements

Sulston, John

The common thread 572.8

Sultan, Tim

About

Sultan, T. Sunny's nights 641.87

SULTANS

Reston, J. Defenders of the faith 940.2

The sum of our days. Allende, I. 92

SUMMER

Heinrich, B. Summer world 591.7

SUMMER

See also Seasons

Summer cocktails. Del Mar Sacasa, M. 641.87

Summer cooking. David, E. 641.5

SUMMER EMPLOYMENT

See also Employment

Summer of '49. Halberstam, D. 796.357

A summer of hummingbirds. Benfey, C. E. G. 920

SUMMER RESORTS

See also Resorts

SUMMER SCHOOLS

See also Public schools; Schools

SUMMER THEATER

See also Theater

Summer world. Heinrich, B. 591.7

Summers, John

(ed) Agee, J. Cotton Tenants 976.1

Summers, Wilford I.

(ed) American electricians' handbook 621.3

Summerscale, Kate

Mrs. Robinson's disgrace 941.081

The suspicions of Mr. Whicher 364.152

The Summit. Conway, E. 339.5

Summits. Reynolds, D. 909.82

Sumner, Judith

The natural history of medicinal plants 581.6

SUN

Golub, L. Nearest star 523.7

SUN

See also Astronomy; Solar system

The Sun and the moon. Goodman, M. 974.7

The Sun and the Moon and the Rolling Stones. Cohen, R. 782.42

Sun in a bottle. Seife, C. 539.7

Sun Shuyun

The Long March 951.04

SUN WORSHIP

See also Religion

Sun-tzu

The illustrated art of war 355

Sundance Kid

About

Hatch, T. The Last Outlaws 364.15

Sundaram, Anjan

About

Sundaram, A. Stringer 967.51

Sunday morning quilts. Arkison, C. 746.46

SUNDAY SCHOOLS

See also Church work; Religious education

Sunday suppers at Lucques. Goin, S. 641.5

SUNDIALS

See also Clocks and watches; Garden ornaments and furniture; Time

Sundown towns. Loewen, J. W. 363.5

Sundquist, Eric J.

(ed) The Oxford W. E. B. Du Bois reader 305.896

The **sunflower.** Wiesenthal, S. 179.7

Sunflowers. Pappalardo, J. 583

SUNFLOWERS

Pappalardo, J. Sunflowers 583

SUNKEN CITIES *See* Extinct cities

SUNNIS

Hazleton, L. After the prophet 297

SUNNITES *See* Sunnis

Sunny's nights. Sultan, T. 641.87

Sunquist, Fiona

The wild cat book 599.75

Sunquist, Mel

(jt. auth) Sunquist, F. The wild cat book 599.75

Sunset kitchen gypsy. 641.5

Sunset the great outdoors cookbook. 641.5

SUNSPOTS

See also Meteorology; Solar radiation; Sun

Sunstein, Cass R. (Cass Robert), 1954–

Simpler 973.932

Suny, Ronald Grigor

They Can Live in the Desert but Nowhere Else 956.6

SUPER BOWL (GAME)

See also Football; Sports tournaments

Super boys. Ricca, B. 92

Super genes. Tanzi, R. E. 613

Super natural every day. Swanson, H. 641.5

Super species. Hamilton, G. 578.6

A **super** upsetting cookbook about sandwiches. Kord, T. 641.84

Superbug. McKenna, M. 616.9

SUPERCOMPUTERS

See also Computers

SUPERCONDUCTORS

See also Electric conductors; Electronics

Supercooperators. Highfield, R. 519.3

Supercraft. Pester, S. 745.5

Superfood Kitchen. Morris, J. 641.5

Superfreakonomics. Levitt, S. D. 330

Supergods. Morrison, G. 741.5

SUPERHERO COMIC BOOKS, STRIPS, ETC.

Howe, S. Marvel Comics 741.5

SUPERHERO COMIC BOOKS, STRIPS, ETC.

See also Comic books, strips, etc.

SUPERHERO COMIC BOOKS, STRIPS, ETC. -- HISTORY AND CRITICISM

75 years of Marvel Comics 741.5

SUPERHERO FILMS -- ENCYCLOPEDIAS

Muir, J. K. The encyclopedia of superheroes on film and television 791.43

SUPERHERO GRAPHIC NOVELS

Wednesday comics 741.5

SUPERHERO GRAPHIC NOVELS

See also Graphic novels

SUPERHERO TELEVISION PROGRAMS -- ENCYCLOPEDIAS

Muir, J. K. The encyclopedia of superheroes on film and television 791.43

SUPERHEROES

Morrison, G. Supergods 741.5

The **superhuman** mind. Brogaard, B. 153.9

Superintelligence. Bostrom, N. 006.3

SUPERINTENDENTS OF SCHOOLS *See* School superintendents and principals

SUPERMAN (FICTIONAL CHARACTER)

See also Fictional characters; Superheroes

SUPERMAN (FICTIONAL CHARACTER)

About

De Haven, T. Our hero 741.5

Morrison, G. Supergods 741.5

Ricca, B. Super boys 92

SUPERNATURAL

Dickey, C. Ghostland 133.1

Steinmeyer, J. Charles Fort 92

SUPERNATURAL

See also Religion

SUPERNATURAL -- MISCELLANEA

Krulos, T. Monster hunters 001.94

Supernatural fiction writers. 809

SUPERNATURAL GRAPHIC NOVELS

See also Graphic novels

SUPERNATURAL IN LITERATURE

Supernatural fiction writers 809

SUPERNOVAE *See* Supernovas

SUPERNOVAS

Dauber, P. M. The three big bangs 523.1

SUPERNOVAS

See also Stars

The **superorganism.** Holldobler, B. 595.7

SUPERSTITION

Dolnick, B. Luck 130

SUPERSTITION

See also Folklore

Superstorm. Miles, K. 551.55

SUPPERS

Madison, D. Vegetarian suppers from Deborah Madison's kitchen **641.5**

The **supplement** handbook. Lee, J. **613.2**

SUPPLEMENTARY EMPLOYMENT

    See also Labor; Part-time employment

SUPPLY AND DEMAND

  Akst, D. We have met the enemy **153.8**

SUPPLY AND DEMAND

    See also Economics

SUPPORT GROUPS *See* Self-help groups

Supreme city. Miller, D. L. **974.7**

Supreme Commander. Morris, S. **327.73**

The **Supreme** Court A to Z. Jost, K. **347.73**

SUPREME COURT JUSTICE

  Feldman, N. Scorpions **920**

The **Supreme** Court justices. **347.73**

SUPREME COURT JUSTICES

  Biskupic, J. Sandra Day O'Connor **92**

  Commager, H. S. The American mind **973**

  Feldman, N. Scorpions **920**

  Goodwin, D. K. Team of rivals **92**

  Greenhouse, L. Becoming Justice Blackmun **92**

  Kennedy, J. F. Profiles in courage **920**

  Marshall, T. Thurgood Marshall **347**

  Menand, L. The Metaphysical Club **973.9**

  Rowan, C. T. Dream makers, dream breakers **92**

  Simon, J. F. What kind of nation **342**

  Smith, J. E. John Marshall **347**

  Urofsky, M. I. Louis D. Brandeis **92**

  Williams, J. Thurgood Marshall **92**

  Wilson, E. Patriotic gore **810**

Supreme power. Shesol, J. **347**

Sur La Table (Firm)

  Mushet, C. The art and soul of baking **641.8**

Suratwala, Zahra T.

  (ed) All-American **297.092**

SURF *See* Ocean waves

SURF RIDING *See* Surfing

SURFACES (PHYSICS)

  Frankel, F. On the surface of things **530.4**

Surfaces and essences. Hofstadter, D. **169**

SURFBOARDING *See* Surfing

SURFING

  Casey, S. The wave **551.46**

  Finnegan, W. Barbarian Days **92**

SURFING -- SONGS

    See also Songs

SURGEONS

  Baiev, K. The Oath **947.5**

  Chen, P. W. Final exam **92**

  Doty, J. R. Into the Magic Shop **92**

  Kalanithi, P. When breath becomes air **616.99**

  Marsh, H. Do No Harm **92**

  McGinniss, J. Fatal vision **364.1**

  Nuland, S. B. Lost in America **92**

  Quiñones-Hinojosa, A. Becoming Dr. Q **92**

  Winchester, S. The professor and the madman **423**

SURGEONS

    See also Physicians

SURGERY

  Current surgical diagnosis & treatment **617**

  Doherty, G. M. Current Diagnosis and Treatment Surgery **617**

  Gawande, A. Complications: a young surgeon's notes on an imperfect science **617**

SURGERY

    See also Medicine

SURGERY -- HISTORY

  Aptowicz, C. O. Dr. Mütter's Marvels **92**

SURGERY, PLASTIC *See* Plastic surgery

SURGICAL PATIENTS

  Queller, J. Pretty is what changes **92**

SURGICAL TRANSPLANTATION *See* Transplantation of organs, tissues, etc.

SURNAMES *See* Personal names

Surowiecki, James

  The wisdom of crowds **303.3**

Surprised by hope. Wright, N. T. **236**

Surratt, Brian E.

  Mitchell, A. M. Cataloging and organizing digital resources **025.3**

Surreal lives. Brandon, R. **709.04**

SURREALISM

  Brandon, R. Surreal lives **709.04**

  Descharnes, R. Salvador Dalí, 1904-1989 **759.6**

  Gohr, S. Magritte **759.94**

SURREALISM

    See also Arts

SURREALISM -- BELGIUM

  Gohr, S. Magritte **759.94**

Surrender. Bawer, B. **297**

SURROGATE MOTHERS

    See also Mothers

SURVEILLANCE, ELECTRONIC *See* Electronic surveillance

SURVEYING

  Danson, E. Weighing the world **526**

SURVEYING

    See also Civil engineering; Geography; Measurement

SURVEYS

    See also Research

Surville, Jean François de, 1717-1770

    About

  Blainey, G. Sea of dangers **92**

SURVIVAL

  Dorn, M. Staying alive **613.6**

  Newitz, A. Scatter, adapt, and remember **576.8**

  Rawles, J. W. Tools for survival **613.6**

SURVIVAL -- KOREA (NORTH) -- HISTORY -- 20TH CENTURY

  Weintraub, S. A Christmas far from home **951.904**

SURVIVAL AFTER AIRPLANE ACCIDENTS, SHIPWRECKS, ETC.
Garcia Marquez, G. The story of a shipwrecked sailor   **910.4**
Krauss, E. Wave of destruction   **959.3**
Murphy, B. 81 days below zero   **940.54**
Parrado, N. Miracle in the Andes   **982**
Read, P. P. Alive   **910.4**
Sabbag, R. Down around midnight   **92**
Severin, T. In search of Robinson Crusoe   **996**
Zuckoff, M. Lost in Shangri-la   **940.54**
SURVIVAL AT SEA -- ANTARCTIC OCEAN
Lewis, M. Last man off   **910.91**
SURVIVAL AT SEA -- PACIFIC OCEAN
Franklin, J. 438 days   **910.916**
Survival in Auschwitz. Levi, P.   **940.53**
SURVIVAL OF THE FITTEST *See* Natural selection
Survival of the sickest. Moalem, S.   **616**
SURVIVAL SKILLS
Dorn, M. Staying alive   **613.6**
Fredston, J. A. Snowstruck   **551.3**
Holden, W. Born Survivors   **940.531**
Kostigen, T. M. National Geographic extreme weather survival guide   **613.6**
Murphy, B. 81 days below zero   **940.54**
Newitz, A. Scatter, adapt, and remember   **576.8**
Rawles, J. W. Tools for survival   **613.6**
Ripley, A. The unthinkable   **155.9**
Stilwell, A. The encyclopedia of survival techniques   **613.6**
Wiseman, J. SAS survival handbook   **613.6**
SURVIVAL SKILLS
See also Civil defense; Environmental influence on humans; Human ecology; Life skills
SURVIVALISM
See also Social movements
Surviving domestic violence. Weiss, E.   **362.82**
Surviving schizophrenia. Torrey, E. F.   **616.89**
Surviving sexual violence.   **362.88**
Surviving survival. Gonzales, L.   **155.9**
Surviving triple negative breast cancer. Prijatel, P.   **616.99**
Surviving with dignity. Youngstedt, S. M.   **362.84**
Survivor. Pivnik, S.   **940.53**
Susan B. Anderson's kids' knitting workshop. Anderson, S. B.   **746.43**
Susan Feniger's street food. Alger, K.   **641.59**
Susan Sontag. Rollyson, C. E.   **818**
Susanka, Sarah
Creating the not so big house   **728**
Inside the not so big house   **728.37**
The not so big house   **728**
Not so big solutions for your home   **728**
SUSHI
Cole, T. Uchi: the cookbook   **641.6**

Suskind, Beth
(jt. auth) Suskind, D. Thirty Million Words   **612.8**
Suskind, Dana
Thirty Million Words   **612.8**
Suskind, Owen
About
Suskind, R. Life, animated   **618.92**
Suskind, Ron
About
Suskind, R. Life, animated   **618.92**
The one percent doctrine   **973.931**
Suspected of independence. McKean, D.   **92**
SUSPENSE FICTION -- TECHNIQUE
Wheat, C. How to write killer fiction   **808.3**
SUSPENSE FILMS *See* Adventure films; Mystery films; Spy films
SUSPENSE NOVELS *See* Adventure fiction; Mystery fiction; Romantic suspense novels
The **suspicions** of Mr. Whicher. Summerscale, K.   **364.152**
Suspicious Minds. Brotherton, R.   **153.4**
Susskind, Leonard
The black hole war   **530.1**
(jt. auth) Hrabovsky, G. The theoretical minimum   **530**
Sussman, Julie
Dare to repair   **643**
SUSTAINABILITY
Gorman, H. S. The story of N   **547**
Weisman, A. Countdown   **304.2**
SUSTAINABLE AGRICULTURE
Berry, W. Bringing it to the table   **630**
Bittman, M. Food matters   **613.2**
Citizen farmers   **635**
Fukuoka, M. Sowing seeds in the desert   **631.6**
Hesterman, O. B. Fair food   **338.1**
Hewitt, B. The town that food saved   **338.1**
Skokan, E. Farm, fork, food   **338.1**
SUSTAINABLE ARCHITECTURE
Owen, D. Green metropolis   **304.2**
SUSTAINABLE DEVELOPMENT
Elmore, B. J. Citizen Coke   **338.7**
Harman, J. The shark's paintbrush   **600**
Pernick, R. Clean Tech Nation   **333.794**
Sachs, J. The age of sustainable development **338.9**
SUSTAINABLE FISHERIES
Hilborn, R. Overfishing   **338.3**
SUSTAINABLE LIVING
Citizen farmers   **635**
SUSTAINABLE LIVING -- UNITED STATES
Shulman, S. Cooler smarter   **363.7**
Sustaining life.   **333.95**
Sutherland, Harriet Elizabeth Georgiana Leveson-Gower, Duchess of, 1806-1868
About
Livingstone, N. The mistresses of Cliveden **942.009**

Sutherland, John
  Stephen Spender   **92**
Sutherland, Jonathan
  African Americans at war   **355**
Sutin, Lawrence
  All is change   **294.3**
Sutton, Amy L.
  (ed) Fitness and exercise sourcebook   **613.7**
Sutton, Judith
  Batali, M. Italian grill   **641.5**
Sutton, Matthew Avery
  American apocalypse   **277.3**
Sutton, Roberta Briggs
  Speech index   **808.85**
Suzuki, Daisetz Teitaro
  Manual of Zen Buddhism   **294.3**
Svrluga, Barry
  The grind   **796.357**
Swafford, Jan
  Beethoven   **92**
  Charles Ives   **92**
  Johannes Brahms   **92**
Swain, Dwight V.
  Creating characters   **808.3**
  Techniques of the selling writer   **808.3**
The **swamp.** Grunwald, M.   **975.9**
SWAMP ANIMALS
  See also Animals
SWAMP ECOLOGY
  See also Ecology; Wetland ecology
Swan, Annalyn
  De Kooning: an American master   **92**
Swango, Michael
        About
  Stewart, J. B. Blind eye   **364.1**
Swanson, Heidi
  Near & far   **641.59**
  Super natural every day   **641.5**
Swanson, James A.
  Strong, J. The strongest Strong's exhaustive concordance of the Bible   **220.5**
Swanson, James L.
  End of Days   **973.922**
  Manhunt   **364.152**
Swanson, Mark
  Atlas of the Civil War, month by month   **973.7**
Swanson, Wendy Sue
  Mama doc medicine   **649.1**
Swarns, Rachel L.
  American tapestry   **92**
Swartzwelder, Scott
  (jt. auth) Kuhn, C. Buzzed   **615.7**
Swash, Andy
  The world's rarest birds   **598**
SWASHBUCKLERS *See* Adventure fiction; Adventure films

Swearington, Jen
  Printing on fabric   **746.6**
SWEATERS
  Herzog, A. You can knit that   **746.432**
  Melville, S. Knitting pattern essentials   **746.43**
SWEDISH AMERICANS -- BIOGRAPHY
  Chambers, V. Yes, chef   **92**
SWEDISH LANGUAGE
    See also Language and languages; Scandinavian languages
SWEDISH LITERATURE
    See also Literature; Scandinavian literature
Sweeney, Jennifer
  Literacy   **027.62**
Sweeney, John
  North Korea undercover
Sweeney, Julia
  If it's not one thing, it's your mother   **362.734**
Sweet and low. Cohen, R.   **920**
Sweet chaos. Brightman, C.   **920**
The **sweet** hell inside. Ball, E.   **920**
Sweet land of liberty. Sugrue, T. J.   **323**
The **sweet** science. Liebling, A. J.   **796.83**
Sweet sleep. Pitman, T.   **649**
Sweet thunder. Haygood, W.   **92**
Sweet Tooth. Anderson, T.   **92**
Sweet, Ossian, d. 1960
          About
  Boyle, K. Arc of justice   **345**
Sweet, Victoria
          About
  Sweet, V. God's hotel   **610.92**
Sweetness. Jordan, C.   **641**
Sweetness & light. Ellis, H.   **595.7**
SWEETNESS (TASTE)
  Amaro   **641.874**
SWEETS *See* Candy; Confectionery
SWELL *See* Ocean waves
Swenson, May
  Nature   **811**
The **swerve.** Greenblatt, S.   **940.2**
Swidey, Neil
  The assist   **796.323**
Swift, Daniel
  Bomber County   **821**
Swift, Earl
  Auto Biography   **629.222**
Swift, Graham
  Making an elephant   **828**
Swift, Jonathan, 1667-1745
  A tale of a tub, and other work   **823**
          About
  Damrosch, L. Jonathan Swift   **92**
  DeGategno, P. J. Critical companion to Jonathan Swift   **828**
Swift, Sally

The Splendid table's how to eat supper **641.5**

Swift, Vivian
Gardens of awe and folly **635**

SWIMMERS
Cox, L. Swimming to Antarctica **92**

SWIMMERS -- UNITED STATES -- BIOGRA-PHY
Beard, A. In the water they can't see you cry **797.2**
Nyad, D. Find a way **92**

SWIMMING
Checkoway, J. The three-year swim club **797.2**
Hines, E. W. Fitness swimming **613.7**
Mullen, P. H. Gold in the water **797.2**
Sedaris, D. Let's explore diabetes with owls **814**
Shapton, L. Swimming studies **797.2**
Swimming studies. Shapton, L. **797.2**
Swimming to Antarctica. Cox, L. **92**
Swindled. Wilson, B. **363.1**

SWINDLERS
Brock, P. Charlatan **92**
Zuckoff, M. Ponzi's scheme **364**

SWINDLERS AND SWINDLING
Fisher, K. L. How to smell a rat **364.1**
Konnikova, M. The Confidence Game **364.163**
Partnoy, F. The match king **92**

SWINDLERS AND SWINDLING -- UNITED STATES -- HISTORY
Jobb, D. Empire of deception **92**
Ward, G. C. A disposition to be rich **974.7**

SWINE See Pigs

Swisher, Carl C.
Java Man **599.93**
Switch. Heath, C. **303.4**

SWITCHBOARD HOTLINES See Hotlines (Telephone counseling)
Switched on. Robison, J. E. **616.85**

Switek, Brian
Written in stone **576.8**

Switzer, Janet
Canfield, J. The success principles **158**

SWITZERLAND -- DESCRIPTION AND TRAVEL
Bewes, D. Slow Train to Switzerland **914.94**

Switzler, Al
(jt. auth) McMillan, R. Crucial conversations **153.6**

Swofford, Anthony
Jarhead: a Marine's chronicle of the Gulf War and other battles **956.704**

Swogger, Susan
(ed) Introduction to reference sources in the health sciences **016.6**
Sword of the spirit, shield of faith. Preston, A. **322**

SWORDPLAY -- JAPAN
Bennett, A. C. Kendo **796.86**

SWORDS
See also Weapons

Sybil. Schreiber, F. R. **616.85**
Sybil exposed. Nathan, D. **616.85**

SYDNEY (N.S.W.) -- BIOGRAPHY
Corrigan, K. Glitter and Glue **92**

Sykes, Bryan
Adam's curse **599.93**
DNA USA **559.9**

Sykes, Chrisopher Simon
David Hockney, 1937-1975 **92**
David Hockney, 1975-2012 **92**

Sykes, Mark Sir, 1879-1919
About
Barr, J. A line in the sand **956**

SYKES-PICOT AGREEMENT
Barr, J. A line in the sand **956**
Sylph. Cloud, A. **811**

Sylvester II, Pope, ca. 945-1003
About
Brown, N. M. The abacus and the cross **92**

SYLVESTER MANOR PLANTATION SITE (N.Y.)
Griswold, M. The Manor **974.7**

Sylvester, James Joseph, 1814-1897
About
Bell, E. T. Men of mathematics **920**

SYMBIOSIS
Margulis, L. Symbiotic planet **576.8**

SYMBIOSIS
See also Biology; Ecology
Symbiotic planet. Margulis, L. **576.8**

SYMBOLIC LOGIC
Dyson, G. Turing's cathedral **004**
Stillwell, J. Roads to infinity **511.3**

SYMBOLIC LOGIC
See also Logic; Mathematics

SYMBOLISM
Jung, C. G. Man and his symbols **150.19**

SYMBOLISM
See also Art; Mythology

SYMBOLISM IN LITERATURE
Homburg, C. Neo-impressionism and the dream of realities **709.04**

Symmes, Patrick
The boys from Dolores **972.91**

SYMMETRY
Livio, M. The equation that couldn't be solved **512**
Stewart, I. Why beauty is truth **539.7**

Symonds, Craig L.
Lincoln and his admirals **92**

Symonds, George W. D.
The shrub identification book **582.1**

Symons, Julian
Bloody murder **809**

SYMPATHY
Armstrong, K. Twelve steps to a compassionate life **177**

SYMPATHY
    See also Conduct of life; Emotions
SYMPHONIES *See* Symphony
The **symphony.** Steinberg, M.   **784.2**
SYMPHONY
    Moynahan, B. Leningrad   **940.54**
    Steinberg, M. The symphony   **784.2**
SYMPTOMS
    Horowitz, R. I. Why can't I get better?   **616.9**
SYMPTOMS *See* Diagnosis
SYNAGOGUE ETIQUETTE
    Wagner, J. L. The synagogue survival kit   **296.4**
The **synagogue** survival kit. Wagner, J. L.   **296.4**
SYNAGOGUES
    Wagner, J. L. The synagogue survival kit   **296.4**
SYNAGOGUES
    See also Buildings; Religious institutions;
    Temples
SYNCHRONIZED SWIMMING
    See also Swimming
Synge, J. M.
    The complete plays   **822**
SYNTHESIZER MUSIC *See* Electronic music
SYNTHETIC BIOLOGY
    Sasselov, D. The life of super-Earths   **576.8**
SYNTHETIC FABRICS
    See also Fabrics; Synthetic products
SYRIA
    Di Giovanni, J. The Morning They Came For
    Us   **956.91**
    Hersh, S. The killing of Osama Bin Laden **327.73**
    Weiss, M. Isis   **956.05**
SYRIA -- HISTORY -- CIVIL WAR, 2011-
    Erlich, R. Inside Syria   **956.91**
The **System.** Benedict, J.   **796.332**
SYSTEM ANALYSIS
    Buchanan, M. Nexus: small worlds and the ground-
    breaking science of networks   **530**
SYSTEM ANALYSIS
    See also Cybernetics; Mathematical models;
    System theory
SYSTEM DESIGN
    See also System analysis
SYSTEM FAILURES (ENGINEERING)
    Petroski, H. To forgive design   **620**
    Petroski, H. Success through failure   **620**
**SYSTEMIC LUPUS ERYTHEMATOSUS -- EN-
CYCLOPEDIAS**
    Thomas, D. E. The lupus encyclopedia   **616.7**
Szabo, Lynn
    (ed) Merton, T. In the dark before dawn   **811**
Szarkowski, John
    Ansel Adams at 100   **770**
    William Eggleston's Guide   **779**
Szczeklik, Andrzej
    Kore   **610**

Sze, Arthur
    Compass Rose   **811**
Szegedy-Maszak, Marianne, 1955-
                About
    Szegedy-Maszák, M. I kiss your hands many
    times   **920**
Szilard, Leo
                About
    Hargittai, I. The Martians of science   **920**
    Marton, K. The great escape   **920**
Szostak, Phil
    The art of Star Wars   **791.43**
Szpiro, George G.
    Numbers rule   **510**
    Poincare's prize   **510**
Szulc, Tad
    Fidel   **92**
Szwed, John F.
    Alan Lomax   **92**
Szybist, Mary
    Incarnadine   **811**
Szymanski, Stefan
    Money and Soccer   **796.334**
Szymborska, Wislawa, 1923-2012
    Map   **891.8**
    Monologue of a dog   **891.8**
    Nonrequired reading   **028.1**
    Poems, new and collected, 1957-1997   **891.8**

T

T'ai chi for seniors. Bonifonte, P.   **613.7**
T-SHIRTS
    See also Clothing and dress
T. rex and the Crater of Doom. Alvarez, W.   **551.7**
T.E. Lawrence. Brown, M.   **92**
T.S. Eliot. Gordon, L.   **92**
Taber's cyclopedic medical dictionary.   **610.3**
**TABLOID NEWSPAPERS -- UNITED STATES
-- HISTORY -- 20TH CENTURY**
    Bai, M. All the truth is out   **328.73**
TABOO
    See also Manners and customs
Tabor, James M.
    Blind descent   **796.52**
Tacitus, Cornelius
    Complete works of Tacitus   **878**
Tackett, Michael
    The Baseball Whisperer   **796.357**
TACOMA ART MUSEUM -- CATALOGS
    Hassrick, P. H. Art of the American West   **709**
Tacos. Stupak, A.   **641.84**
TACOS
    García, L. Lorena Garcia's new taco classics **641.84**
    Stupak, A. Tacos   **641.84**
TACTICS
    See also Military art and science; Strategy

TADPOLES *See* Frogs

TAE KWON DO

    See also Karate; Martial arts; Self-defense

Tafolla, Carmen

  (ed) Great lives from history   **920.009**

Taft, Helen Herron, 1861-1943

         About

  Anthony, C. S. Nellie Taft   **92**

Taft, Robert A., 1889-1953

         About

  Kennedy, J. F. Profiles in courage   **920**

Taft, William H. (William Howard), 1857-1930

         About

  Goodwin, D. K. The Bully Pulpit   **973.91**

Taggart, John

  Pastorelles   **811**

Tagore, Rabindranath

  Selected poems   **891**

Tahan, Malba

  The man who counted   **793.74**

TAI CHI

  Bonifonte, P. T'ai chi for seniors   **613.7**

TAI CHI

    See also Exercise; Martial arts

TAI JI QUAN *See* Tai chi

Taibbi, Matt, 1970-

  The divide   **303.3**

  Griftopia   **973.932**

TAICHI *See* Tai chi

TAILORING

  Cheetham, K. Singer perfect plus   **646.2**

  New complete guide to sewing   **646.2**

TAILORING

    See also Clothing and dress; Clothing industry

TAILORING (WOMEN'S)

  Betzina, S. Power sewing step-by-step   **646.4**

  BurdaStyle modern sewing   **646.4**

  Smith, A. Dressmaking   **646.4**

The **Tain**. Tain bo Cuailnge   **891.6**

Tain bo Cuailnge

  The Tain   **891.6**

Taisho, Emperor of Japan, 1879-1926

         About

  Seagrave, S. The Yamato dynasty   **952.03**

Taiwan. Copper, J. F.   **951.249**

TAIWAN

  Copper, J. F. Taiwan   **951.249**

TAIWAN -- DESCRIPTION AND TRAVEL

  Erway, C. The food of Taiwan   **641.595**

TAIWAN -- HISTORY -- 1945-

  Bernstein, R. China 1945   **327.73**

  Pakula, H. The last empress   **92**

  Taylor, J. The generalissimo   **92**

TAJ MAHAL PALACE HOTEL

  Levy, A. The siege   **363.325**

Takaki, Ronald T.

  Double victory   **940.53**

  Hiroshima   **940.54**

Take your shirt off and cry. Balbirer, N.   **92**

TAKEOVERS, CORPORATE *See* Corporate mergers and acquisitions

Taking charge.   **973.923**

Taking Charge of ADHD. Barkley, R. A.   **618.92**

Taking charge of ADHD. Barkley, R. A.   **618.92**

Taking charge of your fertility. Weschler, T.   **613.9**

Taking punk to the masses. McMurray, J.   **781.66**

Talbot, David

  The Devil's Chessboard   **92**

  Season of the witch   **306**

Talbot, H. Alexander

  Kamozawa, A. Ideas in food   **641.5**

Talbott, Harold

  Thondup, T. Enlightened journey   **294.3**

A **tale** of a tub, and other work. Swift, J.   **823**

A **tale** of love and darkness. Oz, A.   **92**

The **tale** of the dueling neurosurgeons. Kean, S.   **617.4**

Taleb, Nassim Nicholas

  The black swan   **003**

TALENT *See* Ability; Genius

TALENT AGENTS

  Bruck, C. When Hollywood had a king   **338.7**

The **talented** Miss Highsmith. Schenkar, J.   **92**

TALENTS *See* Ability

TALES *See* Fables; Fairy tales; Folklore; Legends

TALES -- GERMANY

  The Original Folk and Fairy Tales of the Brothers Grimm   **398.2**

Tales from Both Sides of the Brain. Gazzaniga, M. S.   **92**

Tales from Ovid. Ovid   **873**

Tales from Shakespeare. Lamb, C.   **822.3**

Tales from the underground. Wolfe, D. W.   **578.7**

Tales of a new Jerusalem [series]

  Kynaston, D. Austerity Britain   **941.085**

Tales of the Marvellous and News of the Strange.   **892.7**

Taliban. Rashid, A.   **958.1**

TALIBAN

    See also Islamic fundamentalism

TALIBAN

  Ghouri, N. The lightless sky   **958.104**

  Gopal, A. No good men among the living   **958.104**

  Grenier, R. L. 88 days to Kandahar   **958.104**

  Holstein, K. A Different Kind of Daughter   **92**

Talk like TED. Gallo, C.   **658.4**

TALK SHOW HOSTS

  Ali, K. Fighting weight   **92**

  Baraka, I. A. The LeRoi Jones/Amiri Baraka reader   **818**

  Life stories   **920**

O'Reilly, B. A bold fresh piece of humanity 92
Reston, J. The conviction of Richard Nixon 973.924
Terkel, S. Touch and go 92
Walters, B. Audition 92
TALK SHOWS
    See also Interviewing; Radio programs; Television programs
Talk to me first. Roffman, D. 613.907
TALKING *See* Conversation
Talking about detective fiction. James, P. D. 823
Talking about movies with Jesus. Kirby, D. 811
TALKING BOOKS *See* Audiobooks
Talking dirty to the gods. Komunyakaa, Y. 811
Talking God. 210
Talking to your doctor. Berger, Z. 610.69
Talking with dogs and cats. Link, T. 636.088
Talking with your hands, listening with your eyes. Grayson, G. 419
TALL TALES
    See also Folklore; Legends; Wit and humor
Tallchief, Maria
          About
  Tallchief, M. Maria Tallchief 92
Taller when prone. Murray, L. 821
Talleur, Richard W.
  L.L. Bean ultimate book of fly fishing 799.1
The **Talley** trilogy. Wilson, L. 812
Tallis, Frank
  Hidden minds 154.2
The **Talmud.** Freedman, H. 296.1
TALMUD
    See also Hebrew literature; Jewish literature; Judaism
TALMUD -- BIOGRAPHY
  Freedman, H. The Talmud 296.1
Talty, Stephan
  Agent Garbo 940.5
  The illustrious dead 940.2
Tam, Michelle
  (jt. auth) Fong, H. Nom nom paleo 641.5
Tamanaha, Brian Z.
  Failing law schools 340
Tamimi, Sami
  Ottolenghi 641.5
  (jt. auth) Ottolenghi, Y. Jerusalem 641.5
Taming the beloved beast. Callahan, D. 338.4
Tammet, Daniel, 1979-
  Born on a blue day 92
  Thinking in numbers 510
Tammy Wynette. McDonough, J. 92
Tan, Amy
  The opposite of fate 814
Tan, Amy
          About
  Tan, A. The opposite of fate 814
Tanacredi, John T.

  (ed) Experiment central 507.8
Tanakh. Bible/O.T. 221
Tanenbaum, Leora
  I Am Not a Slut 305.23
TANG (SHIP)
  Kershaw, A. Escape from the deep 940.54
Tangle stitches for quilters + fabric artists. Monk, J.
Tangles. Leavitt, S. 362.196
Tanguay, Paul
  The Tippling bros. 641.87
Tanis, David
  Heart of the artichoke and other kitchen journeys 641.5
  One good dish 641.82
  A platter of figs and other recipes 641.5
TANK WARFARE
    See also War
Tannen, Deborah
  I only say this because I love you 306.87
  You just don't understand 302.2
Tanton, James S.
  Encyclopedia of mathematics 510
TANZANIA -- DESCRIPTION AND TRAVEL
  Grant, R. Crazy river 916
Tanzi, Rudolph E.
  Super genes 613
TAO
    See also Philosophy
The **Tao** of vegetable gardening. Deppe, C. 635
Tao te ching. Lao-tzu 299.5
TAOISM
  Eastern religions 200.9
TAOISM
    See also Religions
TAOS (N.M.) -- HISTORY
  Crutchfield, J. A. Revolt at Taos 972
TAP DANCING
    See also Dance
TAP WATER *See* Drinking water
Tapas. Andres, J. 641.8
TAPE RECORDINGS, AUDIO *See* Sound recordings
Tape, Ken
          About
  Tape, K. D. The changing arctic landscape 551.69
TAPESTRY
  Brosens, K. European tapestries in the Art Institute of Chicago 746.3
TAPESTRY
    See also Decoration and ornament; Decorative arts; Interior design; Needlework
Tapestry crochet and more. Gullberg, M. 746.434
The **Tapir's** morning bath. Royte, E. 577.34
Tapscott, Don, 1947-
  Macrowikinomics 303.4
Tapscott, Stephen

(ed) Twentieth century Latin American poetry **861**

Taraborrelli, J. Randy
After Camelot **920**
The secret life of Marilyn Monroe **92**

TARAHUMARA INDIANS
McDougall, C. Born to run **796.42**

Tarantino, Quentin
About
Waxman, S. Rebels on the backlot **920**

Tardi, Alan
Champagne, uncorked **641.2**

TARGET MARKETING
See also Marketing
Target Tokyo. Scott, J. M. **940.54**
Target zero. Cleaver, E. **323**

TARGETED KILLING -- UNITED STATES -- HISTORY -- 21ST CENTURY
Scahill, J. Dirty wars **355.02**

TARIFF
See also Commercial policy; Economic policy; Public finance

Tarlow, Andrew
Dinner at the Long Table **641.5**

Tarn, Nathaniel
Selected poems **811**

TAROT
Crispin, J. The creative tarot **133.3**

TAROT
See also Card games; Fortune telling; Playing cards

TAROT (GAME) *See* Tarot

Tarr-Whelan, Linda
Women lead the way **658.4**

Tartine. Robertson, C. **641.8**

TARTINE (BAKERY)
Robertson, C. Tartine **641.8**
Robertson, C. Tartine Book No. 3 **641.81**
Tartine Book No. 3. Robertson, C. **641.81**
Tartine bread. Robertson, C. **641.8**
Tartuffe and other plays. Moliere **842**

Taseer, Aatish, 1980-
About
Taseer, A. Stranger to history **915.6**

Tassler, Nina
What I Told My Daughter **155.433**

TASTE
Bitter **664**
Centamore, A. Tasting wine & cheese

TASTE
See also Senses and sensation

TASTE (AESTHETICS) *See* Aesthetics
The taste of country cooking. Lewis, E. **641.5**
A taste of cowboy. Rollins, K. **641.597**
Taste of Persia. Duguid, N. **641.5**
The taste of war. Collingham, L. **940.53**
The taste of wine. Peynaud, E. **641.2**

The **Tastemaker.** White, E. **92**
Tastes Like Chicken. Rude, E. **636.5**
Tasting freedom. Biddle, D. R. **92**
Tasting whiskey. Bryson, L. **663**
Tasting wine & cheese. Centamore, A.
Tate, Buddy, 1913-2001
About
Dance, S. The world of Count Basie **920**

Tate, James
Selected poems **811**

Tate, Mary Jo
Critical companion to F. Scott Fitzgerald **813**

Tate, Tim
Hitler's forgotten children **940.53**

Tattersall, Ian
(jt. auth) DeSalle, R. The brain **612.8**
The fossil trail **599.93**
Masters of the planet **599.93**

TATTING
See also Lace and lace making

TATTOO ARTISTS
Spring, J. Secret historian **92**

TATTOOING
See also Manners and customs; Personal appearance
Tattoos on the heart. Boyle, G. J. **277**

Tatzkow, Monika
Muller, M. Lost lives, lost art **709**

Taub, Michael
(ed) Contemporary Jewish-American novelists **813**

The Tauber Institute for the Study of European Jewry [series]
Breitman, R. The architect of genocide **92**

Taubes, Gary
Why we get fat and what to do about it **613.7**

Taubman, William
Khrushchev **92**

Taunton's build like a pro [series]
German, R. Remodeling a basement **643**

Tausend, Marilyn
Cocina de la familia **641.5**

TAVERNS *See* Bars

Tavris, Carol
Anger **152.4**

TAXATION
Weltman, B. J.K. Lasser's guide for tough times **332.024**

TAXATION
See also Political science; Public finance

TAXATION -- UNITED STATES
Burman, L. Taxes in America **336.2**

TAXES *See* Taxation
Taxes in America. Burman, L. **336.2**

TAXICAB DRIVERS -- ANECDOTES
Mosler, L. Driving hungry **92**

TAXIDERMY

Milgrom, M. Still life **590.75**

TAY-SACHS DISEASE

Rapp, E. The still point of the turning world **618.92**

Tayler, Jeffrey

Angry wind **916**

Taylor's guide to annuals. Ellis, B. W. **635.9**

Taylor's guide to gardening [series]

Ellis, B. W. Taylor's guide to perennials **635.9**

Taylor's guide to ground covers. Michener, D. **635.9**

Taylor's guide to perennials. Ellis, B. W. **635.9**

Taylor's guide to roses. Ondra, N. J. **635.9**

Taylor's guide to shrubs. Fisher, K. **635.9**

Taylor's guides to gardening [series]

Ellis, B. W. Taylor's guide to annuals **635.9**

Fisher, K. Taylor's guide to shrubs **635.9**

Michener, D. Taylor's guide to ground covers **635.9**

Ondra, N. J. Taylor's guide to roses **635.9**

Taylor's master guide to landscaping. Buchanan, R. **712**

Taylor, Alan

American Revolutions **973.3**

The civil war of 1812 **973.5**

The divided ground **974.7**

The internal enemy **975.5**

Taylor, Barbara Brown

About

Taylor, B. B. An altar in the world **92**

Taylor, Benjamin, 1952-

(ed) Bellow, S. Saul Bellow **92**

About

Taylor, B. Naples declared **945**

Taylor, Brian

Glaze **738.1**

Taylor, C. James

(ed) Adams, J. My dearest friend **92**

Taylor, Charles Ghankay

About

Dwyer, J. American warlord **966.62**

Taylor, Chucky, 1977-

About

Dwyer, J. American warlord **966.62**

Taylor, David

(jt. auth) Hallett, T. Digital photography complete course **770**

Taylor, David J.

Orwell: the life **92**

Taylor, Elizabeth

Cohen, A. American pharaoh: Mayor Richard J. Daley: his battle for Chicago and the nation **977.3**

Taylor, Elizabeth, 1932-2011

About

Kashner, S. Furious love **92**

Taylor, Frederick

Exorcising Hitler **943.087**

Taylor, Gary

(ed) Shakespeare, W. The complete works **822.3**

Taylor, James, 1948-

About

Browne, D. Fire and rain **781.66**

Taylor, Jay

The generalissimo **92**

Taylor, Jean Gelman

Indonesia: peoples and histories **959.8**

Taylor, Jill Bolte

About

Taylor, J. B. My stroke of insight **362.19**

Taylor, Joseph E.

Pilgrims of the vertical **796.52**

Taylor, Kenneth, 1934-

About

Wright, R. A. Our man in Tehran **955**

Taylor, Larissa

(ed) Great events from history, The 17th century, 1601-1700 **909**

(ed) Great lives from history, The 17th century, 1601-1700 **920.003**

Taylor, Lindsey

(jt. auth) Cox, M. The Gardener's Garden **712**

Taylor, Major, 1878-1932

About

Balf, T. Major **92**

Taylor, Marianne

Owls **598.9**

Taylor, Marvin J.

(ed) 101 classic cookbooks **641**

Taylor, Maxwell D., 1901-1987

About

Halberstam, D. The best and the brightest **973.922**

Taylor, Nick

American-made **331.1**

Taylor, Paul D.

A history of life in 100 fossils **560**

Taylor, Sandra C.

(ed) Japanese Americans, from relocation to redress **940.53**

Taylor, Shelley E.

The tending instinct **304.5**

Taylor, Stephen

Commander **92**

Taylor, Timothy

The artificial ape **599.93**

The instant economist **330**

Taylor, Todd W.

The Companion to southern literature **810**

Walker, J. R. The Columbia guide to online style **808**

Taylor, William

Practically radical **658.4**

Taylor, William Desmond, 1877-1922

About

Mann, W. J. Tinseltown **364.152**

Taylor, Yuval

(jt. auth) Austen, J. Darkest America **791**

Douglass, F. Frederick Douglass: selected speeches and writings **326**

Tayman, John

The Colony **614.5**

Těffi, N. A. (Nadezhda Aleksandrovna), 1872-1952

About

Memories **92**

Tea. **641.3**

TEA

See also Beverages

TEA

Rose, S. For all the tea in China **382**

Tea **641.3**

TEA -- HISTORY

Standage, T. A history of the world in 6 glasses **394.1**

Tea **641.3**

The **tea** book. **641.3**

TEA INDUSTRY

Tea **641.3**

TEA TRADE -- UNITED STATES -- COMIC BOOKS, STRIPS, ETC

Nalebuff, B. Mission in a bottle **338.7**

Teach us to sit still. Parks, T. **616**

TEACH YOURSELF COURSES See Self-instruction

Teach yourself visually car care & maintenance. Ramsey, D. **629.28**

Teach yourself visually crochet. Keim, C. **746.43**

Teach yourself visually jewelry making & beading. Michaels, C. F. **745.59**

Teach yourself visually knitting. Turner, S. **746.43**

Teach yourself visually sewing. Colgrove, D. **646.2**

Teacher man. McCourt, F. **92**

TEACHER-STUDENT RELATIONSHIPS

See also Child-adult relationship; Interpersonal relations; Teaching

TEACHER-STUDENT RELATIONSHIPS -- DRAMA

Bennett, A. The history boys **822**

TEACHER-STUDENT RELATIONSHIPS -- UNITED STATES -- CASE STUDIES

Albom, M. Tuesdays with Morrie **378.1**

TEACHERS

Boissoneault, L. The Last Voyageurs **977**

Keizer, G. Getting Schooled **373.1**

Parini, J. The art of teaching **371.1**

Rudd, M. Underground **92**

Walker-Hill, H. From spirituals to symphonies **780**

TEACHERS

See also Educators

Teachers & Writers Collaborative

The Art of the personal essay **808.84**

TEACHERS -- PRACTICE TEACHING See Student teaching

TEACHERS -- TRAINING

See also Education -- Study and teaching; Teaching

TEACHERS -- UNITED STATES -- BIOGRAPHY

Watts, S. Self-help Messiah **92**

TEACHERS -- UNITED STATES -- CASE STUDIES

Falk, B. Teaching matters **370.9**

TEACHERS -- UNITED STATES -- HANDBOOKS, MANUALS, ETC

Crews, K. D. Copyright law for librarians and educators **346.04**

TEACHERS COLLEGES

See also Colleges and universities; Education -- Study and teaching

TEACHERS OF THE DEAF

Gibson, W. The miracle worker **812**

Gray, C. Reluctant genius **92**

Lepore, J. A is for American **306.44**

Shulman, S. The telephone gambit **621.3**

TEACHING

Falk, B. Teaching matters **370.9**

Hauser, P. C. How deaf children learn **371.91**

Keizer, G. Getting Schooled **373.1**

Kozol, J. Letters to a young teacher **371.1**

Kreeft, P. Philosophy 101 by Socrates **183**

McKeown, R. Into the classroom **370.71**

Parini, J. The art of teaching **371.1**

TEACHING -- SOCIAL ASPECTS -- UNITED STATES

Art and social justice education **372.5**

Teaching matters. Falk, B. **370.9**

TEACHING TEAMS

See also Teaching

Teaching tolerance. Bullard, S. **649**

The **teachings** of Don Juan. Castaneda, C. **299.7**

Teachout, Terry

All in the dances: a brief life of George Balanchine **92**

Duke **92**

Pops **92**

The skeptic: the life of H.L. Mencken **92**

TEAHOUSES See Tearooms

Team Genius. Karlgaard, R. **658.1**

Team of rivals. Goodwin, D. K. **92**

The **teammates.** Halberstam, D. **796**

TEAMS IN THE WORKPLACE

Karlgaard, R. Team Genius **658.1**

Tear down this wall. Ratnesar, R. **973.927**

Tearing down the wall of sound. Brown, M. **92**

TEAROOMS

Tea **641.3**

TEAROOMS

See also Restaurants; Tea industry

Tears in the darkness. Norman, E. M. **940.54**

Tears to triumph. Williamson, M.   **299.93**

**TECHNICAL LITERATURE -- BIBLIOGRA-
PHY -- METHODOLOGY**

Berard, G. L.   Science and technology resources   **025.5**

TECHNICAL SERVICE *See* Customer services

TECHNICAL WRITING

See also Authorship; Technology -- Language

Techniques of the selling writer. Swain, D. V. **808.3**

TECHNOLOGICAL CHANGE *See* Technological innovations

TECHNOLOGICAL FORECASTING

Kotler, S.   Abundance   **303.48**

Long, J.   Darwin's devices   **629.8**

TECHNOLOGICAL INNOVATIONS

Atlas, S. W.   In excellent health   **362.109**

Burke, J. J.   Neal-Schuman library technology companion   **025**

Carr, N. G.   The big switch   **303.4**

Core technology competencies for librarians and library staff   **020**

Keen, A.   The Internet Is Not the Answer   **302.23**

Kunstler, J. H.   Too much magic   **303.48**

Mindell, D. A.   Our Robots, Ourselves   **629.8**

Munroe, R.   Thing Explainer   **500**

Naughton, J. From Gutenberg to Zuckerberg **004.67**

Pernick, R.   Clean Tech Nation   **333.794**

Petroski, H.   The essential engineer   **620**

Popular mechanics magazine. The wonderful future that never was   **609**

Tapscott, D.   Macrowikinomics   **303.4**

Tenner, E.   Our own devices   **303.48**

Terra Maxima   **902.2**

Topol, E.   The creative destruction of medicine   **610.28**

Winkless, L.   Science and the City   **307.76**

Woodward, J.   The transformed library   **020**

TECHNOLOGICAL INNOVATIONS

See also Inventions; Technology

**TECHNOLOGICAL INNOVATIONS -- CALI-
FORNIA -- SANTA CLARA COUNTY**

Piscione, D. P. Secrets of Silicon Valley   **330.9**

**TECHNOLOGICAL INNOVATIONS -- CALI-
FORNIA -- SANTA CLARA COUNTY -- HIS-
TORY**

Maxfield, K.   Starting up Silicon Valley   **338.7**

**TECHNOLOGICAL INNOVATIONS -- ECO-
NOMIC ASPECTS**

Friedman, T. L. The Lexus and the olive tree   **337**

Samit, J. Disrupt you!   **650.1**

**TECHNOLOGICAL INNOVATIONS -- FORE-
CASTING**

Long, J.   Darwin's devices   **629.8**

**TECHNOLOGICAL INNOVATIONS -- HIS-
TORY**

Freeberg, E.   The Age of Edison   **303.48**

Gertner, J. The idea factory   **384**

Lind, M.   Land of promise   **330.973**

**TECHNOLOGICAL INNOVATIONS -- SOCIAL
ASPECTS**

Bray, H.   You are here   **910.285**

Thompson, C. Smarter Than You Think   **303.48**

**TECHNOLOGICAL INNOVATIONS -- UNITED
STATES -- HISTORY -- 20TH CENTURY**

Gertner, J. The idea factory   **384**

Tirella, J. Tomorrow-land   **607**

TECHNOLOGICAL LITERACY

See also Literacy

**TECHNOLOGICAL LITERACY -- STUDY AND
TEACHING**

Braafladt, K. Technology and literacy   **027.62**

TECHNOLOGY

Clegg, B.   Final Frontier   **629.4**

The handy science answer book   **500**

Harris, S. @WAR   **355.3**

Macaulay, D. The Way Things Work Now   **600**

Maxfield, K. Starting up Silicon Valley   **338.7**

Thompson, D. C. The reputation economy **302.23**

**TECHNOLOGY -- BIBLIOGRAPHY -- METH-
ODOLOGY**

Berard, G. L.   Science and technology resources   **025.5**

TECHNOLOGY -- DICTIONARIES

McGraw-Hill dictionary of scientific and technical terms   **503**

TECHNOLOGY -- DICTIONARIES

See also Encyclopedias and dictionaries

TECHNOLOGY -- ENCYCLOPEDIAS

The Encyclopedia of science and technology   **503**

Encyclopedia of science, technology, and ethics   **503**

McGraw-Hill Publishing Company McGraw-Hill concise encyclopedia of science & technology **503**

TECHNOLOGY -- HISTORY

Jackson, T. Chilled   **621.56**

TECHNOLOGY -- MISCELLANEA

Pogue, D. Pogue's basics   **004**

TECHNOLOGY -- PHILOSOPHY

Rushkoff, D. Present Shock   **303.48**

**TECHNOLOGY -- PSYCHOLOGICAL AS-
PECTS**

Greenfield, S. Mind change   **155.9**

TECHNOLOGY -- SOCIAL ASPECTS

Harris, M. The End of absence   **302.23**

Kotler, S. Abundance   **303.48**

McLuhan, M. The global village   **302.2**

Rushkoff, D. Present Shock   **303.48**

Tenner, E. Our own devices   **303.48**

TECHNOLOGY AND CIVILIZATION

Carr, N. G. Utopia is creepy   **303.483**

Diamond, J. M. Guns, germs, and steel   **303.4**

Dick, P. K. The exegesis of Philip K. Dick   **818**

Johnson, S. Future perfect   **303.48**

Kunstler, J. H. Too much magic   **303.48**

Lanier, J. You are not a gadget   **303.4**

Malone, M. S. The guardian of all things   **153.1**

McLuhan, M. The global village   **302.2**

Petroski, H. The essential engineer   **620**

Postman, N. The end of education   **370.9**

Tenner, E. Our own devices   **303.48**

Toffler, A. Future shock   **303.4**

Winkless, L. Science and the City   **307.76**

TECHNOLOGY AND CIVILIZATION

   See also Civilization; Technology

Technology and literacy. Braafladt, K.   **027.62**

TECHNOLOGY AND STATE

  Muller, R. A. Energy for future presidents **333.79**

Technology made simple. Bolan, K.   **025**

TECHNOLOGY TRANSFER

   See also Inventions; Technology

Tecumseh, Shawnee Chief, 1768-1813

    About

  Eckert, A. W. A sorrow in our heart: the life of Tecumseh   **977**

Ted Hughes. Feinstein, E.   **821**

TEDDY BEARS

  Bissonnette, Z. The great Beanie Baby bubble   **338.7**

Tedlow, Richard S.

  Andy Grove   **92**

Teege, Jennifer, 1970-

    About

  My grandfather would have shot me   **929.2**

TEEN AGE *See* Adolescence

Teen talkback with interactive booktalks! Schall, L.   **021.7**

TEENAGE BEHAVIOR *See* Adolescent psychology; Etiquette for children and teenagers; Teenagers -- Conduct of life

TEENAGE BOYS

   See also Boys; Teenagers

TEENAGE BOYS -- PSYCHOLOGY

  Wiseman, R. Masterminds and wingmen   **649**

The **teenage** brain. Jensen, F. E.   **612.6**

TEENAGE COOKS -- UNITED STATES

  Ganeshram, R. Future Chefs   **641.3**

TEENAGE FATHERS

   See also Fathers; Teenage parents

TEENAGE GANGS *See* Gangs

TEENAGE GIRLS

  Orenstein, P. Girls and Sex   **306.7**

  Sales, N. J. American girls   **004.67**

TEENAGE GIRLS

   See also Girls; Teenagers

TEENAGE GIRLS -- UNITED STATES

  Flanagan, C. Girl land   **305.235**

TEENAGE MOTHERS

  Hanson, D. Breaking through concrete   **630**

TEENAGERS

  Deak, J. Girls will be girls   **649**

  Hine, T. The rise and fall of the American teenager   **305.235**

  Lippincott, J. M. 7 things your teenager won't tell you   **649**

TEENAGERS

   See also Age; Youth

TEENAGERS -- ATTITUDES

  Eagle, M. Answering teens' tough questions **027.62**

TEENAGERS -- ATTITUDES

   See also Attitude (Psychology)

TEENAGERS -- BOOKS AND READING

   See also Books and reading

TEENAGERS -- BOOKS AND READING -- UNITED STATES

  Kallio, J. Read on ... speculative fiction for teens   **016**

  Keane, N. J. 101 great, ready-to-use book lists for teens   **028.5**

  Schall, L. Teen talkback with interactive booktalks!   **021.7**

TEENAGERS -- CONDUCT OF LIFE

   See also Conduct of life

TEENAGERS -- DEVELOPMENT *See* Adolescence

TEENAGERS -- EMPLOYMENT

  Levine, M. J. Children for hire   **331.3**

TEENAGERS -- RELIGIOUS LIFE

  Shachtman, T. Rumspringa   **305.23**

TEENAGERS -- RELIGIOUS LIFE

   See also Religious life; Youth -- Religious life

TEENAGERS -- SERVICES FOR -- UNITED STATES

  Eagle, M. Answering teens' tough questions **027.62**

TEENAGERS -- SEXUAL BEHAVIOR

  Orenstein, P. Girls and Sex   **306.7**

  Vernacchio, A. For goodness sex   **613.9**

TEENAGERS -- SOCIAL LIFE AND CUSTOMS -- 21ST CENTURY

  Boyd, D. It's complicated   **004.67**

TEENAGERS -- SUICIDE

   See also Suicide

TEENAGERS -- UNITED STATES

  Ganeshram, R. Future Chefs   **641.3**

TEENAGERS -- UNITED STATES

   See also Youth -- United States

TEENAGERS -- UNITED STATES -- ATTITUDES

  Eagle, M. Answering teens' tough questions **027.62**

The **teeth** may smile but the heart does not forget. Rice, A.   **967.6**

Tefertiller, Casey

  Wyatt Earp   **92**

Teffi, N. A. (Nadezhda Aleksandrovna), 1872-1952

  Memories   **92**

Tegmark, Max
Our mathematical universe **523.1**
Teilhard de Chardin, Pierre
The divine milieu **230**
The phenomenon of man **113**
Teitel, Amy Shira
Breaking the Chains of Gravity **629.4**
TELECOMMUNICATION
Wu, T. c. The master switch **384**
TELECOMMUNICATION
See also Communication
TELECOMMUNICATION -- HISTORY
Gertner, J. The idea factory **384**
Lapsley, P. Exploding the Phone **384**
Raboy, M. Marconi **92**
TELECOMMUNICATION SYSTEMS
Blum, A. Tubes **384.3**
TELECOMMUNICATIONS EXECUTIVES
Burrows, P. Backfire: Carly Fiorina's high-stakes
battle for the soul of Hewlett-Packard **338.7**
Gray, C. Reluctant genius **92**
Lepore, J. A is for American **306.44**
Shulman, S. The telephone gambit **621.3**
TELECOMMUTING
See also Automation; Telecommunication
TELECONFERENCING
See also Telephone
TELEGRAPH
Gordon, J. S. A thread across the ocean **384.1**
TELEGRAPH
See also Public utilities; Telecommunication
TELEGRAPH, WIRELESS -- HISTORY
Larson, E. Thunderstruck **364.152**
Raboy, M. Marconi **92**
**TELEGRAPH, WIRELESS -- MARCONI SYS-
TEM**
Raboy, M. Marconi **92**
TELEPHONE
Shulman, S. The telephone gambit **621.3**
TELEPHONE
See also Public utilities; Telecommunication
TELEPHONE COUNSELING *See* Hotlines (Tele-
phone counseling)
The **telephone** gambit. Shulman, S. **621.3**
TELEPHOTOGRAPHY
See also Photography
TELEVANGELISTS
See also Clergy; Television personalities
TELEVISION -- CENSORSHIP
See also Censorship
TELEVISION -- HISTORY
Abramson, A. The History of Television 1880 to
1941 **621.388**
Martin, B. Difficult men **791.450**
**TELEVISION ACTORS AND ACTRESSES --
CANADA -- BIOGRAPHY**

Short, M. I must say **92**
**TELEVISION ACTORS AND ACTRESSES --
UNITED STATES -- INTERVIEWS**
Apatow, J. Sick in the head **792.7**
TELEVISION AUTHORSHIP
Inside the room **808.2**
TELEVISION AUTHORSHIP
See also Authorship
TELEVISION BROADCASTING
Inside the room **808.2**
Marling, K. A. As seen on TV **973.92**
Postman, N. Amusing ourselves to death **302.23**
TELEVISION BROADCASTING
See also Broadcasting; Mass media; Televi-
sion
**TELEVISION BROADCASTING -- SOCIAL AS-
PECTS -- UNITED STATES**
Martin, B. Difficult men **791.450**
**TELEVISION BROADCASTING -- VOCA-
TIONAL GUIDANCE**
See also Vocational guidance
TELEVISION BROADCASTING OF NEWS
Brinkley, D. Cronkite **92**
Diehl, D. Rather outspoken **92**
Stelter, B. Top of the morning **791.45**
TELEVISION BROADCASTING OF NEWS
See also Broadcast journalism; Television
broadcasting
TELEVISION BROADCASTING OF SPORTS
Miller, J. A. Those guys have all the fun **791.45**
Williams, J. Life is not an accident **92**
TELEVISION CRITICS
Barnes, J. Nothing to be frightened of **92**
Coupland, D. Marshall McLuhan **92**
TELEVISION DIRECTORS
Thomson, H. The white rock **985**
Zuckoff, M. Robert Altman **92**
**TELEVISION JOURNALISTS -- UNITED
STATES -- BIOGRAPHY**
Brinkley, D. Cronkite **92**
Brokaw, T. A long way from home **070**
Cooper, A. The rainbow comes and goes **92**
Diehl, D. Rather outspoken **92**
TELEVISION MODERATORS
Koppel, T. Off camera **92**
O'Reilly, B. A bold fresh piece of humanity **92**
Terkel, S. Touch and go **92**
TELEVISION MOVIES
See also Motion pictures; Television programs
TELEVISION NEWS *See* Television broadcasting
of news
TELEVISION NEWS ANCHORS
Brokaw, T. A long way from home **070**
Cronkite, W. A reporter's life **070**
Edwards, B. Edward R. Murrow and the birth of
broadcast journalism **92**

Koppel, T. Off camera 92

Olson, L. Citizens of London **940.54**

Sperber, A. M. Murrow, his life and times 92

Walters, B. Audition 92

TELEVISION PERSONALITIES

As always, Julia 92

Baraka, I. A. The LeRoi Jones/Amiri Baraka reader 818

Bourdain, A. Kitchen confidential 92

Bourdain, A. Medium raw 92

Buford, B. Heat **641.5**

Child, J. My life in France 92

Conant, J. A covert affair **940.54**

Fitch, N. R. Appetite for life 92

Kanfer, S. Groucho: the life and times of Julius Henry Marx 92

Kindred, D. Sound and fury **796**

Lewis, J. Dean & me 92

Life stories **920**

Maguire, J. Impresario 92

Pepin, J. The apprentice: my life in the kitchen **641.5**

Ribowsky, M. Howard Cosell 92

Rodriguez, R. Hunger of memory 92

TELEVISION PERSONALITIES

See also Celebrities

TELEVISION PERSONALITIES -- BIOGRAPHY

Kelly, M. Settle for More **791.45**

TELEVISION PERSONALITIES -- UNITED STATES -- BIOGRAPHY

Johnston, D. C. The making of Donald Trump **973.932**

TELEVISION PLAYS

See also Drama; Television programs

TELEVISION PLAYS -- TECHNIQUE

See also Drama -- Technique; Television authorship

TELEVISION PRODUCERS

Buruma, I. Murder in Amsterdam **364.152**

Katz, J. Dog days 636

Life stories 920

Parrado, N. Miracle in the Andes 982

Reston, J. The conviction of Richard Nixon **973.924**

Trillin, C. About Alice 92

TELEVISION PRODUCERS AND DIRECTORS -- UNITED STATES -- BIOGRAPHY

Jones, B. J. Jim Henson 92

O'Brien, J. Jack be nimble 92

TELEVISION PROGRAM GENRES -- UNITED STATES

Martin, B. Difficult men **791.450**

TELEVISION PROGRAMS

Seitz, M. Z. TV (the book) **791.45**

Singh, S. The Simpsons and their mathematical secrets **510**

TELEVISION PROGRAMS

See also Television broadcasting

TELEVISION REPORTERS

Edwards, B. Edward R. Murrow and the birth of broadcast journalism 92

Norris, M. The grace of silence 92

Olson, L. Citizens of London **940.54**

O'Reilly, B. A bold fresh piece of humanity 92

Raddatz, M. The long road home **956.7**

Schorr, D. Staying tuned **070**

Sperber, A. M. Murrow, his life and times 92

TELEVISION SCRIPTS

See also Television broadcasting

TELEVISION SCRIPTWRITERS

Aron, W. Hide & seek 92

Fey, T. Bossypants 92

Foote, H. Beginnings 812

Life stories 920

Manguel, A. A reader on reading 818

Mooney, P. Black is the new white 92

Palin, M. Halfway to Hollywood 92

Playwrights at work 812

Queller, J. Pretty is what changes 92

Salamon, J. Wendy and the lost boys 812

Simon, N. The play goes on 812

Simon, N. Rewrites 812

TELEVISION SERIES -- UNITED STATES

Martin, B. Difficult men **791.450**

TELEVISION SERIES -- UNITED STATES -- HISTORY AND CRITICISM

Seitz, M. Z. TV (the book) **791.45**

TELEVISION SPORTS *See* Television broadcasting of sports

TELEVISION STATIONS

See also Television broadcasting

TELEVISION SUPPLIES INDUSTRY

Decherney, P. Hollywood's copyright wars **346.73**

TELEVISION WRITING *See* Television authorship

TELL EL-AMARNA (EGYPT)

Kemp, B. The city of Akhenaten and Nefertiti 930

The **tell-tale** brain. Ramachandran, V. S. **616.8**

Teller, Edward, 1908-2003

About

Goodchild, P. Edward Teller, the real Dr Strangelove 92

Hargittai, I. The Martians of science 920

Marton, K. The great escape 920

Teller, E. Memoirs 92

Tellez, Lesley

Eat Mexico **641.597**

Telushkin, Joseph, 1948-

Biblical literacy **221**

Jewish wisdom **296.3**

Rebbe 92

Temkin, Moshik, 1971-

The Sacco-Vanzetti Affair 345
TEMPER TANTRUMS
See also Emotions; Human behavior
TEMPERAMENT
Goleman, D. Emotional intelligence **152.4**
TEMPERAMENT
See also Mind and body; Psychology; Psychophysiology
TEMPERANCE
See also Virtue
TEMPLARS -- HISTORY
Haag, M. The Tragedy of the Templars **271**
TEMPLES
See also Buildings; Religious institutions
Temples, tombs, & hieroglyphs. Mertz, B. **932**
Tempo : a Rowman & Littlefield music series on rock, pop, and culture [series]
Brown, D. Bob Dylan **92**
TEMPORARY EMPLOYMENT
See also Employment
The **Temptation** of Elizabeth Tudor. Norton, E. **92**
Temptations of the West. Mishra, P. **954.05**
Ten days that shook the world. Reed, J. **947.084**
Ten discoveries that rewrote history. Hunt, P. **930.1**
Ten Hills Farm. Manegold, C. **974.4**
Ten hours until dawn. Tougias, M. **363.34**
The **ten** most beautiful experiments. Johnson, G. **507.8**
The **ten** things to do when your life falls apart. Kingma, D. R. **155.9**
Ten thousand birds. Birkhead, T. **598**
The **ten** trusts. Goodall, J. **333.95**
Ten windows. Hirshfield, J. **808.1**
The **ten-cent** plague. Hajdu, D. **741.5**
TENANT AND LANDLORD *See* Landlord and tenant
TENANT FARMING *See* Farm tenancy
The **tender** hour of twilight. **070.5**
The **tending** instinct. Taylor, S. E. **304.5**
Tenet, Stephanie
Sussman, J. Dare to repair **643**
Tengler, Nancy
The women's guide to successful investing **332.6**
Tennant, Richard A.
The American Sign Language handshape dictionary **419**
Tenner, Edward
Our own devices **303.48**
TENNESSEE -- HISTORY -- 1861-1865, CIVIL WAR
Groom, W. Shiloh, 1862 **973.7**
Tennessee Williams. Lahr, J. **92**
Tenney, Merrill C.
(ed) Zondervan illustrated Bible dictionary **220.3**
TENNIS
Agassi, A. Open **92**

Fisher, M. A terrible splendor **796.342**
Gallwey, W. T. The inner game of tennis **796.342**
McPhee, J. Levels of the game **796.34**
Wallace, D. F. String theory **796.342**
TENNIS
See also Sports
TENNIS -- BIOGRAPHY
Agassi, A. Open **92**
Howard, J. The rivals **92**
TENNIS -- PSYCHOLOGICAL ASPECTS
Gallwey, W. T. The inner game of tennis **796.342**
TENNIS -- TOURNAMENTS
Ryan, M. Tennis' greatest stars **796.342**
TENNIS LITERATURE
Wallace, D. F. String theory **796.342**
TENNIS PLAYERS
Ryan, M. Tennis' greatest stars **796.342**
Tennis' greatest stars. Ryan, M. **796.342**
Tennyson, Alfred Tennyson
Poems **821**
TENPINS *See* Bowling
TENSION (PHYSIOLOGY) *See* Stress (Physiology)
TENSION (PSYCHOLOGY) *See* Stress (Psychology)
The **tenth** parallel. Griswold, E. **297**
Tenzing Norgay, 1914-1986
About
Jamling Tenzing Norgay Touching my father's soul **796.522**
Terence
Terence, the comedies **872**
Terence, the comedies. Terence **872**
Teresi, Dick
Lost discoveries **509**
The undead **610**
TEREZIN (CZECHOSLOVAKIA: CONCENTRATION CAMP)
Helga's diary **940.53**
TEREZIN (CZECHOSLOVAKIA: CONCENTRATION CAMP)
See also Concentration camps
Terkel, Studs, 1912-2008
(ed) The good war **940.54**
And they all sang **780.9**
Hard times **973.91**
My American century **920**
Touch and go **92**
Will the circle be unbroken? **128**
Working **331.2**
Terkel, Studs, 1912-2008
About
Terkel, S. Touch and go **92**
TERM PAPER WRITING *See* Report writing
TERMINAL CARE
Brody, J. E. Jane Brody's guide to the great be-

yond **616.02**

Gawande, A. Being mortal **362.17**

Kaufman, S. R. --And a time to die **362.1**

Kiernan, S. P. Last rights **179.7**

Kubler-Ross, E. On death and dying **155.9**

McFarlane, R. The complete bedside companion **649.8**

Twelve breaths a minute **616**

Volandes, A. E. The conversation **616.02**

TERMINAL CARE

See also Medical care

TERMINAL CARE -- DECISION MAKING

Butler, K. Knocking on Heaven's Door **616.02**

TERMINAL CARE -- ETHICAL ASPECTS

Chen, P. W. Final exam **92**

Kaufman, S. R. --And a time to die **362.1**

Wanzer, S. H. To die well **179.7**

TERMINALLY ILL

Brody, J. E. Jane Brody's guide to the great beyond **616.02**

Egan, K. On living **170.44**

Schwalbe, W. The end of your life book club **616.99**

Twelve breaths a minute **616**

TERMINALLY ILL

See also Sick

TERMINALLY ILL -- UNITED STATES -- BIOGRAPHY

Hitchens, C. Mortality **304.6**

TERMINALLY ILL CHILDREN

Kubler-Ross, E. On children and death **155.9**

TERMINALLY ILL CHILDREN

See also Terminally ill

TERMINATION OF PREGNANCY See Abortion

TERMS AND PHRASES

See also Names

TERNS

See also Birds; Water birds

Terra. Novacek, M. J. **576.8**

TERRA COTTA

See also Building materials; Decoration and ornament; Pottery

Terra Maxima. **902.2**

TERRAPINS See Turtles

Terrariums. Colletti, M. **635.9**

TERRARIUMS

Colletti, M. Terrariums **635.9**

Martin, T. The new terrarium **635.9**

TERRARIUMS

See also Indoor gardening

Terras, Victor

A history of Russian literature **891.7**

A **terrible** glory. Donovan, J. **973.8**

A **terrible** splendor. Fisher, M. **796.342**

Terrible swift sword. Wheelan, J. **355.009**

TERRITORIAL GOVERNORS

Ambrose, S. E. Undaunted courage **917**

Kennedy, J. F. Profiles in courage **920**

Kluger, R. The bitter waters of Medicine Creek **979.7**

Linklater, A. An artist in treason **92**

Slaughter, T. P. Exploring Lewis and Clark **978**

TERRITORIAL LEGISLATORS

Kluger, R. The bitter waters of Medicine Creek **979.7**

TERROIR -- TEXAS

Thompson-Anderson, T. Texas on the Table **641.597**

Terror and consent. Bobbitt, P. **363.32**

The **terror** before Trafalgar. Pocock, T. **940.2**

The **terror** years. Wright, L. **363.325**

TERROR, REIGN OF See France -- History -- 1789-1799, Revolution

TERRORISM

Allison, G. T. Nuclear terrorism **363.32**

Aust, S. Baader-Meinhof **363.32**

Baker, S. A. Skating on stilts **363.32**

Bergen, P. L. The longest war **909.83**

Bernstein, R. Out of the blue **973.931**

Blum, H. American lightning **364.152**

Bobbitt, P. Terror and consent **363.32**

Carr, C. The lessons of terror **303.6**

Dershowitz, A. M. Why terrorism works **303.6**

Dickey, C. Securing the city **363.32**

Elshtain, J. B. Just war against terror **363.32**

Esposito, J. L. Unholy war **322.4**

Farmer, J. J. The ground truth **973.931**

Gage, B. The day Wall Street exploded **974.7**

The girl who escaped ISIS **956.7**

Great lives from history: Notorious lives **920.003**

Gull, I. The most dangerous place **954.91**

Harris, S. The watchers **363.32**

Junger, S. Fire **909.82**

Lamb, C. I am Malala **92**

Levy, A. The siege **363.325**

Lewis, B. The crisis of Islam **297**

Mazzetti, M. The way of the knife **356**

Merriman, J. M. The dynamite club **363.32**

Miller, J. The cell: inside the 9/11 plot and why the FBI and CIA failed to stop it **973.931**

Murakami, H. Underground **364.1**

National Commission on Terrorist Attacks Upon the United States The 9/11 Commission report **973.931**

Pedahzur, A. The Israeli secret services and the struggle against terrorism **363.32**

Preston, R. The demon in the freezer **616.9**

Randal, J. C. Osama: the making of a terrorist **92**

Roy, A. Walking with the comrades **954**

Scroggins, D. Wanted women **305.48**

Soufan, A. H. The black banners **973.931**

Suskind, R. The one percent doctrine **973.931**

Weiss, M. Isis **956.05**

Wright, L. The looming tower   **973.931**
Wright, L. The terror years   **363.325**
TERRORISM
   See also Insurgency; Political crimes and offenses; Subversive activities
TERRORISM -- DICTIONARIES
Anderson, S. Historical dictionary of terrorism   **363.32**
TERRORISM -- ENCYCLOPEDIAS
Encyclopedia of terrorism   **363.32**
TERRORISM -- GOVERNMENT POLICY
Powell, J. Terrorists at the table   **363.325**
TERRORISM -- GOVERNMENT POLICY -- UNITED STATES
Bobbitt, P. Terror and consent   **363.32**
Hersh, S. M. Chain of command   **973.931**
Johnson, H. B. The age of anxiety   **973.921**
Miller, J. The cell: inside the 9/11 plot and why the FBI and CIA failed to stop it   **973.931**
Wright, L. The looming tower   **973.931**
TERRORISM -- GOVERNMENT POLICY -- UNITED STATES -- HISTORY -- 21ST CENTURY
Feingold, R. While America sleeps   **327**
TERRORISM -- IRAQ
Warrick, J. Black flags   **956.91**
TERRORISM -- MASSACHUSETTS -- BOSTON -- CASE STUDIES
Russell, J. Long mile home   **363.325**
TERRORISM -- MIDDLE EAST
Warrick, J. Black flags   **956.91**
TERRORISM -- NEW YORK (N.Y.)
Gage, B. The day Wall Street exploded   **974.7**
TERRORISM -- PERSIAN GULF REGION -- PREVENTION
Johnsen, G. D. The last refuge   **363.325**
TERRORISM -- PREVENTION
Eichenwald, K. 500 days   **973.931**
Graff, G. M. The threat matrix   **363.325**
Morell, M. J. The great war of our time   **363.325**
Sadler, A. The 15:17 to Paris   **363.325**
Scahill, J. Dirty wars   **355.02**
Van Buren, P. We meant well
TERRORISM -- PREVENTION -- EUROPEAN UNION COUNTRIES -- HISTORY -- 21ST CENTURY
Sadler, A. The 15:17 to Paris   **363.325**
TERRORISM -- PREVENTION -- GOVERNMENT POLICY -- UNITED STATES
Molotch, H. Against security   **363.325**
TERRORISM -- PREVENTION -- UNITED STATES -- GOVERNMENT POLICY -- HISTORY -- 21ST CENTURY
Scahill, J. Dirty wars   **355.02**
TERRORISM -- RELIGIOUS ASPECTS
Esposito, J. L. Unholy war   **322.4**

Herridge, C. The next wave   **363.32**
Hider, J. The spiders of Allah   **956.05**
Lewis, B. The crisis of Islam   **297**
TERRORISM -- RELIGIOUS ASPECTS -- ISLAM
Esposito, J. L. Unholy war   **322.4**
Lewis, B. The crisis of Islam   **297**
Warrick, J. Black flags   **956.91**
Wright, L. The terror years   **363.325**
TERRORISM -- UNITED STATES
Russell, J. Long mile home   **363.325**
TERRORISM -- UNITED STATES -- HISTORY
Gage, B. The day Wall Street exploded   **974.7**
TERRORISM -- UNITED STATES -- PREVENTION
Bergen, P. L. The longest war   **909.83**
Bergen, P. L. Manhunt   **363.325**
Graff, G. M. The threat matrix   **363.325**
Harris, S. The watchers   **363.32**
McDermott, T. The hunt for KSM   **363.325**
Miller, J. The cell: inside the 9/11 plot and why the FBI and CIA failed to stop it   **973.931**
Morell, M. J. The great war of our time   **363.325**
Soufan, A. H. The black banners   **973.931**
Suskind, R. The one percent doctrine   **973.931**
Wright, L. The terror years   **363.325**
TERRORISM -- YEMEN (REPUBLIC)
Johnsen, G. D. The last refuge   **363.325**
TERRORISM VICTIMS
Witter, B. Stronger   **92**
TERRORIST ACTS *See* Terrorism
TERRORIST ATTACKS, SEPTEMBER 11, 2001
   See September 11 terrorist attacks, 2001
TERRORIST BOMBINGS *See* Bombings
TERRORISTS
Bergen, P. L. Manhunt   **363.325**
Coll, S. The Bin Ladens   **920**
Coll, S. Ghost wars   **958.1**
Great lives from history: Notorious lives   **920.003**
Herridge, C. The next wave   **363.32**
McDermott, T. The hunt for KSM   **363.325**
Randal, J. C. Osama: the making of a terrorist   **92**
Scheuer, M. Osama bin Laden   **92**
Wright, L. The terror years   **363.325**
TERRORISTS
   See also Criminals
TERRORISTS -- ISLAMIC COUNTRIES
McDermott, T. The hunt for KSM   **363.325**
TERRORISTS -- SAUDI ARABIA
Bergen, P. L. Manhunt   **363.325**
Terrorists at the table. Powell, J.   **363.325**
Terry, Beth
Plastic-free   **363.738**
Terry, Bryant
Afro-vegan   **641.59**
Vegan Soul kitchen   **641.5**

Terry, Clark, 1920-
About
Lees, G. You can't steal a gift   **781.65**
Terry, Michael
(ed) Reader's guide to Judaism   **296**
Tesla. Carlson, W. B.   **92**
Tesla, Nikola, 1856-1943
About
Carlson, W. B. Tesla   **92**
A **testament** of hope.   **323.1**
Testi, Arnaldo
Capture the flag   **929.9**
Testing wars in the public schools. Reese, W.
J.   **371.26**
TESTS See Educational tests and measurements;
Examinations
Tetro, Jason
The Germ Files   **579.3**
Tett, Gillian
Fool's gold   **332.6**
Tetzeli, Rick
Becoming Steve Jobs   **92**
TEUTONIC PEOPLES
Burns, T. S. A history of the Ostrogoths   **909.07**
TEUTONIC RACE See Teutonic peoples
Tevis, Joni
The world is on fire   **814**
Tex-Mex from Scratch. Cramby, J.   **641.59**
TEXAS
Thompson-Anderson, T. Texas on the Ta-
ble   **641.597**
TEXAS -- HISTORY
Collins, G. As Texas goes   **320.6**
Donovan, J. The blood of heroes   **976.4**
Presley, J. The Phantom Killer   **364.152**
TEXAS -- TRIALS, LITIGATION, ETC.
Carpenter, D. Flagrant conduct   **342.73**
**TEXAS A & M UNIVERSITY SYSTEM -- BIOG-
RAPHY**
Gates, R. M. A passion for leadership   **92**
Texas blues. Govenar, A. B.   **781.64**
Texas on the Table. Thompson-Anderson, T. **641.597**
Texas Pan American series
Twentieth century Latin American poetry   **861**
TEXTBOOKS
Dunn, P. A. Grammar rants   **428**
TEXTBOOKS
See also Books
**TEXTBOOKS -- CENSORSHIP -- UNITED
STATES**
Foerstel, H. N. Banned in the U.S.A   **025.2**
TEXTILE ARTISTS
Weber, N. F. The Bauhaus group   **920**
TEXTILE CHEMISTRY
See also Industrial chemistry; Textile industry
TEXTILE CRAFTS

Adams, L. Needle felting   **746**
Corwin, L. Lena Corwin's made by hand   **746.6**
Stewart, M. Martha Stewart's encyclopedia of
sewing and fabric crafts   **746**
TEXTILE DESIGN
Swearington, J. Printing on fabric   **746.6**
TEXTILE DESIGN
See also Commercial art; Decoration and or-
nament; Design
TEXTILE INDUSTRY
Beckert, S. Empire of cotton   **338.4**
Schoeser, M. World textiles: a concise history   **677**
TEXTILE PRINTING
Swearington, J. Printing on fabric   **746.6**
TEXTILE PRINTING
See also Printing; Textile industry
TEXTILE WORKERS
Beckert, S. Empire of cotton   **338.4**
TEXTILES See Fabrics
TEXTURE IN INTERIOR DECORATION
Atwood, R. Living with pattern   **701.85**
TGS (TRANSGENDER PEOPLE) See Transgen-
der people
THAI COOKING
Greeley, A. Nong's Thai kitchen   **641.595**
Thompson, D. Thai food   **641.5**
Thai food. Thompson, D.   **641.5**
THAILAND
Krauss, E. Wave of destruction   **959.3**
THAILAND -- HISTORY
Wyatt, D. K. Thailand: a short history   **959.3**
THAILAND -- SOCIAL LIFE AND CUSTOMS
Houton, J. A geek in Thailand   **915.9**
Thailand: a short history. Wyatt, D. K.   **959.3**
Thalberg, Sigismond, 1812-1871
About
Schonberg, H. C. The great pianists   **920**
Thaler, Richard H., 1945-
Misbehaving   **330.01**
Thaller, Bernd
Numbers   **513.5**
Thames. Ackroyd, P.   **942**
THAMES RIVER (ENGLAND)
Ackroyd, P. Thames   **942**
Thank You for Your Service. Finkel, D.   **362.86**
THANKFULNESS See Gratitude
Thanks, but this isn't for us. Morrell, J. P.   **808.3**
Thanksgiving. Baker, J. W.   **394.26**
The **Thanksgiving** book. Hillstrom, L.   **394.26**
THANKSGIVING DAY
Baker, J. W. Thanksgiving   **394.26**
Hillstrom, L. The Thanksgiving book   **394.26**
THANKSGIVING DAY
See also Holidays
Thant Myint-U
The river of lost footsteps   **959.1**

Where China meets India **959.1**

Tharoor, Shashi
India **954.04**
Nehru: the invention of India **954.04**

Tharp, Brenda
(jt. auth) Manwaring, J. Extraordinary everyday photography **778.71**

Tharp, Marie
About
Felt, H. Soundings **526**

That bird has my wings. Masters, J. **92**

That this. Howe, S. **811**

THEATER
Brook, P. The empty space **792**
Riedel, M. Razzle Dazzle **792.09**

THEATER
See also Amusements; Performing arts

THEATER -- ENCYCLOPEDIAS
The Oxford companion to theatre and performance **792**

THEATER -- HISTORY
Brockett, O. G. History of the theatre **792.09**

THEATER -- JAPAN
Keene, D. The pleasures of Japanese literature **895.6**

THEATER -- PRODUCERS AND DIRECTORS -- PENNSYLVANIA -- LEVITTOWN -- BIOGRAPHY
Sokolove, M. Drama high **92**

THEATER -- REVIEWS
Lahr, J. Joy ride **792.02**

THEATER -- UNITED STATES
The best plays of 2006-2007 **808.82**

THEATER -- UNITED STATES -- HISTORY
Mordden, E. Anything goes **782.1**

THEATER--PRODUCTION AND DIRECTION
Gillette, J. M. Theatrical design and production **792.02**
Theatre of fish. Gimlette, J. **917**
Theatrical design and production. Gillette, J. M. **792.02**

THEATRICAL DIRECTORS
Arkin, A. An improvised life **92**
Black women writers (1950-1980) **810**
Callow, S. Orson Welles **92**
Fuegi, J. Brecht and company **92**
Gibson, I. Federico Garcia Lorca: a life **92**
Gielgud, J. An actor and his time **92**
Moore, S. The Stanislavski system **792**
Playwrights at work **812**
Schickel, R. Elia Kazan **92**
Vaill, A. Somewhere **92**

THEATRICAL DIRECTORS *See* Theatrical producers and directors

THEATRICAL MAKEUP
Corson, R. Stage makeup **792**

THEATRICAL MAKEUP
See also Cosmetics; Costume

THEATRICAL PRODUCERS
Diaghilev **92**
Gielgud, J. An actor and his time **92**

THEATRICAL PRODUCERS *See* Theatrical producers and directors

THEATRICAL PRODUCERS AND DIRECTORS
Mordden, E. Ziegfeld **92**
O'Brien, J. Jack be nimble **92**
Turan, K. Free for all **92**

THEATRICAL PRODUCERS AND DIRECTORS -- UNITED STATES -- BIOGRAPHY
Lahr, J. Joy ride **792.02**
O'Brien, J. Jack be nimble **92**

THEATRICAL SCENERY *See* Theaters -- Stage setting and scenery

The **Theban** plays of Sophocles. Selections./English **882**

THEBES (EGYPT: EXTINCT CITY)
Mertz, B. Temples, tombs, & hieroglyphs **932**

THEFT
Howard, D. Lost rights **973.7**
Rasmussen, E. The Shakespeare thefts **822.3**
Selby, S. A. Flawless **364.1**

THEFT
See also Crime; Offenses against property

The **theft** of memory. Kozol, J. **92**

Their finest hour. Churchill, W. **940.53**

THEISM
See also Philosophy; Religion; Theology

Thelonious Monk. Kelley, R. D. G. **92**

Them: adventures with extremists. Ronson, J. **322.4**

THEMATIC MAPS
A Map of the World **912**

THEME PARKS *See* Amusement parks

Then come back. **861**

Then comes marriage. Dickey, L. **346**

Thenell, Jan
The library's crisis communications planner **021.7**

Theo Chocolate. **641.6**

THEO CHOCOLATE
Theo Chocolate **641.6**

THEOCRACY
See also Church and state; Political science

A **Theodore** Dreiser encyclopedia. **813**

Theodore Rex. Morris, E. **92**

Theodore Roosevelt in the Badlands. DiSilvestro, R. L. **92**

Theoharis, Athan G.
Abuse of power **363.325**

Theoharis, Jeanne
The rebellious life of Mrs. Rosa Parks **92**

THEOLOGIANS
Bainton, R. H. Here I stand: a life of Martin Lu-

ther 92
Bell, E. T. Men of mathematics 920
Connor, J. A. Pascal's wager 92
Davies, B. The thought of Thomas Aquinas 189
Devlin, K. J. The unfinished game 519.2
Downing, D. C. Into the region of awe 248.2
Erikson, E. H. Young man Luther 92
Ford, P. F. Companion to Narnia 823
Kung, H. Great Christian thinkers 230
Marsden, G. M. Jonathan Edwards 92
Marsh, C. Strange glory 92
Metaxas, E. Bonhoeffer 92
Miller, L. The magician's book 823
Nadler, S. M. The best of all possible worlds 190
Oberman, H. A. Luther: man between God and the
   Devil 92
Russell, B. A history of Western philosophy 109
Tomkins, S. John Wesley 287
Wills, G. Saint Augustine 270.2
Wilson, A. N. C.S. Lewis 823
Wilson, D. A. Out of the storm 92

THEOLOGY
Kung, H. Great Christian thinkers 230
Mesler, B. A Brief History of Creation 576.8
Nouwen, H. Discernment 248.4
Oxford companion to Christian thought 230
Robinson, M. When I was a child I read books 814

THEOLOGY -- DICTIONARIES
Oxford companion to Christian thought 230

THEOLOGY -- UNITED STATES
Robinson, M. When I was a child I read books 814
Theology in America. Holifield, E. B. 230

THEOLOGY, DOCTRINAL See Doctrinal theology

**THEOLOGY, DOCTRINAL -- POPULAR
   WORKS**
Allen, J. L. The Catholic church 282
The theoretical minimum. Hrabovsky, G. 530

THEORY OF GAMES See Game theory

THEORY OF KNOWLEDGE
Arbesman, S. The half-life of facts 501
Bostrom, N. Superintelligence 006.3
Greenspan, S. I. The first idea 153.7
Hood, B. The self illusion 155.2
Kant, I. Critique of pure reason 193
Locke, J. An essay concerning human understand-
   ing 121
Sartre, J. P. Truth and existence 121
Shermer, M. The believing brain 153.4
Silver, N. The signal and the noise 519.5
Stannard, R. The end of discovery 501
Weinberger, D. Too big to know 303.48
Wilson, E. O. Consilience 121

THEORY OF KNOWLEDGE
   See also Consciousness; Logic; Metaphysics;
   Philosophy

THEORY OF NUMBERS See Number theory
The theory of the leisure class. Veblen, T. 305.5

THEOSOPHY
   See also Mysticism; Religions

THERAPEUTIC SYSTEMS See Alternative medicine

THERAPEUTICS
Rubin, R. R. The Johns Hopkins guide to diabe-
   tes 616.4
There are words. Turnbull, G. 821
There goes my everything. Sokol, J. 305.8
There Is Life After College. Selingo, J. J. 650.14
There is no freedom without bread! Pleshakov,
   K. 947
There is power in a union. Dray, P. 331.8
There was a country. Achebe, C. 823
There was and there was not. Toumani, M. 327

**THERESIENSTADT (CONCENTRATION
   CAMP)**
Helga's diary 940.53

THERMODYNAMICS
Shachtman, T. Absolute zero and the conquest of
   cold 536

THERMODYNAMICS
   See also Dynamics; Physical chemistry;
   Physics

THERMOMETERS
   See also Heat; Meteorological instruments

Theroux, Alexander
Estonia: a ramble through the periphery 947.98

Theroux, Jessica
Cooking with Italian grandmothers 641.5

Theroux, Paul, 1941-
Dark star safari 916
The great railway bazaar 915
The happy isles of Oceania 919
The old Patagonian express 918
Riding the iron rooster 915
                    About
Deep South 975
Theroux, P. Last train to Zona Verde 916

Theroux, Phyllis
(ed) The Book of eulogies 808.8

THESAURI See Subject headings
These are my rivers. Ferlinghetti, L. 811
These United States. Gilmore, G. E. 973.9

THESES See Dissertations

THESSALONIKE (GREECE)
Mazower, M. Salonica, city of ghosts 949.5
They called me Mayer July. Kirshenblatt, M. 92
They Can Live in the Desert but Nowhere Else.
   Suny, R. G. 956.6
They drew as they pleased. Ghez, D. 741.58
They fought like demons. Blanton, D. 973.7
They lift their wings to cry. Haxton, B. 811
They made America. Evans, H. 920

They marched into sunlight. Maraniss, D.   **959.704**

They never said it. Boller, P. F.   **808.88**

They poured fire on us from the sky. Deng, B.   **962.4**

They told me not to take that job. Levy, R.   **792.09**

Thielen, Amy

The New Midwestern table   **641.59**

Thieret, John W.

National Audubon Society field guide to North American wildflowers: eastern region   **582.13**

THIEVES

Macintyre, B. Agent Zigzag   **92**

Mitnick, K. D. Ghost in the wires   **364.16**

Nourse, V. F. In reckless hands   **344**

Rideau, W. In the place of justice   **92**

Scotti, R. A. Vanished smile   **759**

Stiles, T. J. Jesse James   **364.15**

THIEVES

See also Criminals

Thieves of paradise. Komunyakaa, Y.   **811**

Thieves of state. Chayes, S.   **364.1**

Thieves' Road. Mort, T.   **978.3**

Thing Explainer. Munroe, R.   **500**

A **thing** that is.   **811**

The **thing** with feathers. Strycker, N.   **598**

Things a little bird told me. Stone, B.   **006.7**

Things I Should Have Told My Daughter. Cleage, P.   **92**

Things I've been silent about. Nafisi, A.   **92**

Things that are.   **508**

The **things** they cannot say. Sites, K.   **355**

Things to make and do in the fourth dimension. Parker, M.   **510**

Think and grow rich. Hill, N.   **650.1**

Think: a compelling introduction to philosophy. Blackburn, S.   **100**

THINKING *See* Thought and thinking

Thinking about architecture. Davies, C.   **720**

Thinking Differently. Flink, D.   **371.9**

Thinking in numbers. Tammet, D.   **510**

Thinking like your editor. Rabiner, S.   **808**

Thinking the twentieth century. Judt, T.   **320.092**

Thinking with type. Lupton, E.   **686.2**

Thinking, fast and slow. Kahneman, D.   **153.4**

The **third** chapter. Lawrence-Lightfoot, S.   **305.26**

The **third** coast. Dyja, T.   **977.3**

THIRD PARTIES (UNITED STATES POLITICS)

See also Political parties; United States -- Politics and government

The **third** plate. Barber, D.   **641.3**

The **Third** Reich. Burleigh, M.   **943.086**

The **Third** Reich at war. Evans, R. J.   **940.53**

The **Third** Reich in power, 1933-1939. Evans, R. J.   **943.086**

Third World America. Huffington, A.   **330.9**

Thirsting for peace in a raging century. Sanders, E.   **811**

Thirteen days. Kennedy, R. F.   **973.922**

Thirteen Days in September. Wright, L.   **956.04**

Thirteen ways of looking at a black man. Gates, H. L.   **920.71**

Thirteen ways of looking at the novel. Smiley, J.   **813**

Thirty Million Words. Suskind, D.   **612.8**

The **Thirty** Years War. Wilson, P. H.   **940.2**

THIRTY YEARS' WAR, 1618-1648

Wilson, P. H. The Thirty Years War   **940.2**

The **thirty-first** of March. Busby, H. W.   **973.923**

This ain't brain surgery. Dierker, L.   **796**

This ain't the summer of love. Waksman, S.   **781.66**

This Blue. McLane, M. N.   **811**

This book is overdue! Johnson, M.   **020**

This boy's life: a memoir. Wolff, T.   **92**

This changes everything. Klein, N.   **363.738**

This cold heaven. Ehrlich, G.   **998**

This craft of verse. Borges, J. L.   **809.1**

This explains everything.   **500**

This far by faith. Williams, J.   **200**

This house has fallen. Maier, K.   **966.905**

This I believe.   **170**

This I believe II.   **170**

This Indian country. Hoxie, F. E.   **323.1**

This is Camino. Moore, R.   **641.5**

This is how to get your next job. Kay, A.   **650.14**

This is reggae music. Bradley, L.   **781.646**

This Is the Story of a Happy Marriage. Patchett, A.   **92**

This Is Where You Belong. Warnick, M.   **155.94**

This is your brain on parasites. McAuliffe, K.   **612.8**

This is your brain on sports. Wertheim, L. J.   **796**

This is your do-over. Roizen, M. F.   **613**

This living hand. Morris, E.   **814**

This mighty scourge. McPherson, J. M.   **973.7**

This old man. Angell, R.   **92**

This republic of suffering. Faust, D. G.   **973.7**

This time. Stern, G.   **811**

This time is different. Reinhart, C. M.   **338.5**

This will change everything.   **501**

Thomas Becket.   **92**

Thomas Cromwell. Borman, T.   **92**

Thomas Eakins.   **759.13**

Thomas Hardy. Tomalin, C.   **92**

Thomas Hardy. Hardy, T.   **821**

Thomas Jefferson. Bernstein, R. B.   **92**

Thomas Jefferson. Meacham, J.   **92**

Thomas Jefferson and Sally Hemings. Gordon-Reed, A.   **973.4**

Thomas Jefferson: author of America. Hitchens, C.   **92**

Thomas Mann. Kurzke, H.   **92**

Thomas, a Becket, Saint, 1118?-1170

About

Thomas Becket   **92**

Thomas, Abigail, 1941-
A three dog life   92
What Comes Next and How to Like It   92
Thomas, Anna
Love soup   **641.5**
Vegan, vegetarian, omnivore   **641.5**
Thomas, Aquinas, Saint, 1225?-1274
About
Davies, B. The thought of Thomas Aquinas   **189**
Kung, H. Great Christian thinkers   **230**
Russell, B. A history of Western philosophy   **109**
Thomas, Biju
(jt. auth) Lim, A. The feed zone cookbook   **641.5**
(jt. auth) Lim, A. Feed zone portables   **641.5**
Thomas, Dana
Gods and Kings   92
Thomas, Donald E.
The lupus encyclopedia   **616.7**
Thomas, Dylan, 1914-1953
A child's Christmas in Wales   **828**
The poems of Dylan Thomas   **821**
Under milk wood   **822**
About
Lycett, A. Dylan Thomas: a new life   92
Thomas, Edward, 1878-1917
About
Hollis, M. Now all roads lead to France   **821**
Thomas, Elizabeth Marshall, 1931-
The hidden life of dogs   **599.77**
The social lives of dogs   **636.7**
Thomas, Emory M.
Robert E. Lee   92
Thomas, Evan
Being Nixon   92
Ike's bluff   **973.92**
John Paul Jones   92
Robert Kennedy   92
Sea of thunder   **940.54**
The war lovers   **973.8**
Thomas, Heather
Broth   **641.813**
Thomas, Hugh
Rivers of gold   **980**
Thomas, Lewis
The lives of a cell   **570.1**
Thomas, Lisa
(ed) Moore, R. In search of lost frogs   **597.8**
Thomas, Louisa
Louisa   92
Thomas, Mary
Mary Thomas's dictionary of embroidery stitches   **746.44**
Thomas, Mathilde
The French beauty solution   **646.7**
Thomas, Nicholas
Cook   **910**

Thomas, Robert McG.
52 McGs   **920**
Thomas, Roy
75 years of Marvel Comics   **741.5**
Thompson, Cliff
World authors, 1990-1995   **809**
World authors, 1995-2000   **809**
Thompson, Clive
Smarter Than You Think   **303.48**
Thompson, David
Thai food   **641.5**
Thompson, David C.
The reputation economy   **302.23**
Thompson, Dick
Volcano cowboys   **551.21**
Thompson, Dorothy
About
Ware, S. Letter to the world   **920.72**
Thompson, Gary Richard
(ed) Poe, E. A. Essays and reviews   **809**
Thompson, Heather Ann
Blood in the water   **365**
Thompson, Hunter S., 1937-2005
Fear and loathing in America   **070**
The great shark hunt   **818**
The kingdom of fear   92
About
McKeen, W. Outlaw journalist   92
Thompson, H. S. Fear and loathing in America **070**
Thompson, H. S. The kingdom of fear   92
Wenner, J. S. Gonzo   92
Thompson, Ida
The Audubon Society field guide to North American fossils   **560**
Thompson, Jennifer Trainer
Fresh Fish   **641.692**
Thompson, Laura
The six   92
Thompson, Mark
Now, build a great business!   **658**
The white war   **940.4**
Thompson, Michael
Michael Thompson: Portraits   **779**
Thompson, Nicholas
The hawk and the dove   92
Thompson, Susan
(ed) Core technology competencies for librarians and library staff   **020**
Thompson, Teri
American huckster   **796.334**
Thompson, Tracy
The new mind of the South   **305.8**
Thompson-Anderson, Terry, 1946-
Texas on the Table   **641.597**
Thomsen, Josh
(jt. auth) Tomlinson, S. Agricola cookbook **641.564**

Thomson Reuters Corp.
(comp) Reuters **909.83**
Thomson, Belinda
Van Gogh paintings **759.9**
Thomson, David, 1941-
Bette Davis **92**
The big screen **791.43**
Gary Cooper **92**
How to watch a movie **791.43**
Humphrey Bogart **92**
Ingrid Bergman **92**
Try to tell the story **92**
The whole equation **791.43**
Thomson, Graeme
George Harrison **92**
Thomson, Hugh
The white rock **985**
Thomson, Jess
(jt. auth) Erickson, R. A boat, a whale, and a walrus **641.597**
Thondup, Tulku
Enlightened journey **294.3**
THOR (NORSE DEITY)
    See also Gods and goddesses
Thorburn, John E.
The Facts on File companion to classical drama **880**
The **Thoreau** you don't know. Sullivan, R. **92**
Thoreau, Henry David, 1817-1862
Cape Cod **917**
Collected essays and poems **818**
The Maine woods **917**
Walden, or, Life in the woods **818**
A week on the Concord and Merrimack rivers; Walden, or, Life in the woods; The Maine woods; Cape Cod **818**
    About
Kazin, A. An American procession **810**
Matthiessen, F. O. American renaissance **810**
Sullivan, R. The Thoreau you don't know **92**
Thorisson, Mimi
    About
Thorisson, M. A kitchen in France **641.594**
Thorn, John
Baseball in the Garden of Eden **796.357**
Thornburgh, Nathan
(ed) Goulding, M. Rice, noodle, fish **394.12**
Thornbury, Charles
(ed) Berryman, J. Collected poems, 1937-1971 **811**
Thorndike, Joseph Jacobs, 1913-2005
    About
Thorndike, J. The last of his mind **92**
Thornton Wilder. Niven, P. **809**
Thornton, Sarah
Seven days in the art world **709.05**
Thornton, William, 1759-1828
    About

Lepore, J. A is for American **306.44**
THOROUGHFARES *See* Roads; Streets
Thorpe, Helen
Just like us **305.8**
Soldier girls **956.704**
Thorpe, Jim, 1888-1953
    About
Anderson, L. Carlisle vs. Army **796.332**
Buford, K. Native American son **92**
Crawford, B. All American **92**
Thorpe, Molly Suber
Modern calligraphy **745.6**
Those angry days. Olson, L. **940.53**
Those guys have all the fun. Miller, J. A. **791.45**
Those who forget the past. **305.8**
Thou, dear God. **242**
Though the heavens may fall. Wise, S. M. **342**
THOUGHT AND THINKING
Beilock, S. How the body knows its mind **153.7**
Bolman, L. G. How great leaders think **658.4**
Chabris, C. The invisible gorilla **153.7**
Crawford, M. B. The World Beyond Your Head **155.2**
Dobelli, R. The art of thinking clearly **153.4**
Edelman, S. The happiness of pursuit **153**
Herbert, W. On second thought **153.4**
Hofstadter, D. Surfaces and essences **169**
Kahneman, D. Thinking, fast and slow **153.4**
Kounios, J. The Eureka factor **612.8**
Locke, J. An essay concerning human understanding **121**
Morell, V. Animal wise **591.5**
Nisbett, R. E. Mindware **153.4**
Partnoy, F. Wait **153.8**
Pinker, S. The stuff of thought **401**
Ridley, M. The evolution of everything **303.48**
Roth, B. The Achievement Habit **158.1**
Watts, D. J. Everything is obvious **153.4**
THOUGHT AND THINKING
    See also Educational psychology; Psychology
The **thought** of Thomas Aquinas. Davies, B. **189**
Thoughts are not the enemy. Siff, J. **294.3**
Thousand mile song. Rothenberg, D. **599.5**
A **Thousand** Miles to Freedom. Kim, E. **92**
A **thousand** mornings. Oliver, M. **811**
A **thousand** sisters. Shannon, L. **305.9**
A **thousand** times more fair. Kenji Yoshino **822.3**
The **thousand-year** flood. Welky, D. **363.34**
A **thread** across the ocean. Gordon, J. S. **384.1**
The **threat** matrix. Graff, G. M. **363.325**
THREATENED SPECIES *See* Endangered species
Three armies on the Somme. Philpott, W. **940.4**
The **three** big bangs. Dauber, P. M. **523.1**
Three chords for beauty's sake: the life of Artie Shaw. Nolan, T. **92**
Three cups of tea. Mortenson, G. **371.82**

A **three** dog life. Thomas, A. **92**

Three generations, no imbeciles. Lombardo, P. A. **344**

The **three** Gospels. Bible/N.T./Gospels **226.3**

Three major plays. Vega, L. d. **862**

Three minutes in Poland. Kurtz, G. **947.7**

Three nights in August. Bissinger, H. G. **796.357**

Three plays. Coward, N. **822**

Three roads to the Alamo. Davis, W. C. **976.4**

The **three** Roosevelts. Burns, J. M. **973.91**

THREE STOOGES FILMS

    See also Comedy films; Motion pictures

Three strides before the wire. Mitchell, E. **798.4**

Three Testaments. **208**

THREE-DIMENSIONAL PHOTOGRAPHY

    See also Photography

THREE-DIMENSIONAL PRINTING

    Horne, R. 3d printing for dummies **621.9**

    Rigsby, M. A beginner's guide to 3D printing **621.9**

THREE-DIMENSIONAL PRINTING

    See also Printing

The **three-year** swim club. Checkoway, J. **797.2**

THRILLERS *See* Adventure fiction; Adventure films

THROAT

    See also Anatomy

Through a window. Goodall, J. **599.8**

Through the children's gate. Gopnik, A. **974.71**

Through the eye of a needle. Brown, P. **270.2**

Through the eyes of the Vikings. Haas, R. B. **779**

Through the language glass. Deutscher, G. **410**

Through the lens. National Geographic Society (U.S.) **779**

Through the perilous fight. Vogel, S. **973.5**

Throwim way leg. Flannery, T. F. **995.3**

Thrown. Howley, K. **796.8**

Thubron, Colin

    In Siberia **957**

    Shadow of the Silk Road **911**

    To a mountain in Tibet **915**

    About

    Thubron, C. To a mountain in Tibet **915**

Thucydides. Kagan, D. **938**

Thucydides

    The landmark Thucydides **938**

    About

    Kagan, D. Thucydides **938**

Thug Kitchen. **641.5**

Thug Kitchen LLC

    (comp) Thug Kitchen **641.5**

Thunder & Lightning. Redniss, L. **551.6**

Thunder on the Mountain. Galuszka, P. A. **363.11**

THUNDERSTORMS

    See also Meteorology; Storms

Thunderstruck. Larson, E. **364.152**

Thuras, Dylan

    (jt. auth) Foer, J. Atlas Obscura **910.41**

Thurgood Marshall. Williams, J. **92**

Thurgood Marshall. Marshall, T. **347**

Thurkettle, Vincent

    The Wood Fire Handbook **697.1**

Thurman, Judith

    Isak Dinesen **92**

    Secrets of the flesh: a life of Colette **92**

Thurman, Robert A. F.

    Why the Dalai Lama matters **294.3**

Thurow, Roger

    The first 1,000 days **618.92**

Thursby, Jacqueline S.

    Critical companion to Maya Angelou **818**

Thurston, Herbert

    (ed) Butler's Lives of the saints **920.003**

Thus spoke Zarathustra. Nietzsche, F. W. **193**

Thuss, Rebecca

    (jt. auth) Farrell, P. Paper to petal **745.54**

Thutmose III, King of Egypt, ca. 1504-1450 B.C.

    About

    Mertz, B. Temples, tombs, & hieroglyphs **932**

TIANANMEN SQUARE INCIDENT, BEIJING (CHINA), 1989 -- POETRY

    Liao Yiwu For a song and one hundred songs **365**

    Liu, X. June fourth elegies **811**

Tiberius, Emperor of Rome, 42 B.C.-37 A.D.

    About

    The twelve Caesars **878**

TIBET (CHINA)

    Tenzin Gyatso, D. L. X. My appeal to the world **951**

TIBET (CHINA) -- DESCRIPTION AND TRAVEL

    Alford, J. Beyond the Great Wall **641.5**

    Johnson, T. Tragedy in crimson **294.3**

    Thubron, C. To a mountain in Tibet **915**

TIBET (CHINA) -- PICTORIAL WORKS

    Bstan-'dzin-rgya-mtsho, D. L. X. My Tibet **951**

TIBET AUTONOMOUS REGION (CHINA) -- HISTORY

    Tenzin Gyatso, D. L. X. My appeal to the world **951**

The **Tibetan** book of living and dying. Sogyal **294.3**

Tibetan Peach Pie. Robbins, T. **92**

TIBETANS -- SOCIAL CONDITIONS

    Tenzin Gyatso, D. L. X. My appeal to the world **951**

A **ticket** to the circus. Mailer, N. C. **92**

Tickle, Phyllis, 1934-2015

    The great emergence **270**

TICKS

    Beccaloni, J. Arachnids **595.4**

    Stewart, A. Wicked bugs **632**

TIDAL WAVES *See* Tsunamis

The **tide.** Aldersey-Williams, H. **551.464**

TIDE POOL ECOLOGY

    See also Ecology

TIDES

Aldersey-Williams, H.   The tide **551.464**

Tiede, Karen
  Knitting fabric rugs **746.7**

Tigay, Chanan
  The   Lost   Book   of   Moses
The **tiger**. Vaillant, J. **599.75**
Tiger Force. Sallah, M. **959.704**
TIGER HUNTING
  Vaillant, J. The tiger **599.75**
TIGER TRADE -- CHINA
  Mills, J. A. Blood of the tiger **639.97**
A **tiger's** heart. Shen, A. J. **92**
TIGERS
  Matthiessen, P. Tigers in the snow **599.756**
  Sooyong Park Great Soul of Siberia **599.756**
Tigers in the snow. Matthiessen, P. **599.756**
TIGRIS RIVER
  Kriwaczek, P. Babylon **935**
Tilda Homemade & Happy. Finnanger, T. **746.4**
Tilda's toy box. Finnanger, T. **745.592**
Tilden, Bill, 1893-1953
            About
  Fisher, M. A terrible splendor **796.342**
Tilden, Samuel J., 1814-1886
            About
  Morris, R. Fraud of the century **324.9**
TILES
  See also Building materials; Ceramics
Till I end my song. **808.81**
Till we have built Jerusalem. Hoffman, A. **956.94**
Till, Emmett, 1941-1955
            About
  Abdul-Jabbar, K. Black profiles in courage **920**
  Anderson, D. S. Emmett Till **364.1**
Till-Mobley, Mamie, 1921-2003
            About
  Anderson, D. S. Emmett Till **364.1**
TILLANDSIA
  Air plants **628.5**
Tillich, Paul
  The courage to be **179**
Tillyard, Stella K.
  A royal affair **920**
TIMBER *See* Forests and forestry; Lumber and
  lumbering; Trees; Wood
The **Timber** Press encyclopedia of flowering shrubs.
  Gardiner, J. **635.9**
Timber Press Inc.
  (comp) Bowling, B. L. Homegrown berries **634**
A **timbered** choir. Berry, W. **811**
Timberg, Craig
  (jt. auth) Halperin, D. Tinderbox **614.5**
TIME
  Falk, D. In search of time **529**
  Galison, P. L.   Einstein's clocks and Poincare's
    maps **529**

  Sims, M. Apollo's fire **529**
TIME -- RELIGIOUS ASPECTS
  Shulevitz, J. The Sabbath world **296.4**
Time and materials. Hass, R. **811**
TIME AND SPACE *See* Space and time
A **time** for gathering. Diner, H. R. **305.8**
TIME History's Greatest Images. Knauer, K. **909.82**
TIME MANAGEMENT
  Covey, S. R. First things first **158**
  Staples, H. Sew organized for the busy girl **646.2**
  Tracy, B. Eat that frog! **640**
  Vaden, R. Procrastinate on purpose **650.1**
  Wasmund, S. Do less, get more **650.1**
TIME MANAGEMENT
      See also Management; Time
The **time** of our lives. Brokaw, T. **973.927**
The **time** paradox. Zimbardo, P. G. **153.7**
TIME PERCEPTION
  Zimbardo, P. G. The time paradox **153.7**
TIME SAVING COOKING *See* Quick and easy
  cooking
TIME STUDY
      See also Factory management; Industrial effi-
      ciency; Job analysis; Personnel management;
      Production standards
Time to be in earnest. James, P. D. **823**
Time travel. Gleick, J. **530.11**
TIME TRAVEL
  Gleick, J. Time travel **530.11**
TIME TRAVEL
      See also Fourth dimension; Space and time
Time traveler. Novacek, M. J. **92**
The **time** traveler's guide to Elizabethan England.
  Mortimer, I. **942.05**
Time, love, memory. Weiner, J. **591.5**
Time-saving gardener. Hutchinson, C. **635**
Timerman, Jacobo, 1923-1999
            About
  Timerman, J. Prisoner without a name, cell without
    a number **92**
The **Times** comprehensive atlas of the world. **912**
The **Times** were a changin' **973.923**
TIMESHARING (REAL ESTATE)
      See also Condominiums; Housing; Property;
      Real estate business
The **timetables** of American history. **902**
The **timetables** of history. Grun, B. **902**
Timetables of world literature. Kurian, G. T. **809**
Timothy Leary. Greenfield, R. **92**
TIN
      See also Chemical elements; Metals
Tinchant family
            About
  Scott, R. J. Freedom papers **305.896**
Tinderbox. Halperin, D. **614.5**
Tingey, John

The Englishman who posted himself and other curious objects   **92**

Tinkerlab. Doorley, R.   **600**

TINKERS -- UNITED STATES
   Wilkinson, K. The Art of tinkering   **500**

Tinniswood, Adrian
   Pirates of Barbary   **909**
   The Verneys   **920**

Tinseltown. Mann, W. J.   **364.152**

Tintori, Karen
   Trapped: the 1909 Cherry Mine disaster   **973.9**

TINWORK
   See also Metalwork

Tiny house living. Mitchell, R.   **728**

TINY OBJECTS *See* Miniature objects

Tippett, Krista
   Becoming Wise   **158.1**

The **tipping** point. Gladwell, M.   **302**

The **Tippling** bros. Tanguay, P.   **641.87**

Tips & traps for negotiating real estate. Irwin, R.   **333.3**

Tips & traps series
   Irwin, R. Tips & traps for negotiating real estate   **333.3**

Tiptree, James, 1916-1987
       About
   Phillips, J. James Tiptree, Jr.   **813**

Tirado, Linda
   Hand to mouth   **362.5**

Tirella, Joseph
   Tomorrow-land   **607**

Tirion, Wil
   Ridpath, I. The monthly sky guide   **523.8**
   The Cambridge star atlas   **523.8**

Tirone Smith, Mary-Ann, 1944-
       About
   Tirone Smith Girls of tender age   **92**

'Tis. McCourt, F.   **92**

Tischler, Nancy M.
   Men and women of the Bible   **220.9**

TISSUE AND ORGAN HARVESTING
   Teresi, D. The undead   **610**

TISSUES -- TRANSPLANTATION *See* Transplantation of organs, tissues, etc.

TITAN (MISSILE) -- HISTORY
   Schlosser, E. Command and control   **363.17**

TITAN (SATELLITE)
   Wohlforth, C. Beyond Earth   **629.455**

Titan: the life of John D. Rockefeller, Sr. Chernow, R.   **92**

TITANIC (STEAMSHIP)
   Lord, W. A night to remember   **910.4**
   Turner, S. The band that played on   **910.4**

TITHES
   See also Church finance; Ecclesiastical law; Taxation

Titian. Hale, S.   **92**

Titian. Hudson, M.   **92**

Titian, approximately 1488-1576
       About
   Hale, S. Titian   **92**

Tito. West, R.   **949.7**

Tito, 2000-
       About
   The fall   **92**

Tito, Josip Broz, 1892-1980
       About
   West, R. Tito   **949.7**

Titus, Emperor of Rome, 40-81
       About
   The twelve Caesars   **878**

To a mountain in Tibet. Thubron, C.   **915**

To America with love. Gill, A. A.   **917.3**

To Appomattox. Davis, B.   **973.7**

To be young, gifted, and Black. Hansberry, L.   **92**

To begin again. Levy, N.   **296.7**

To begin where I am. Milosz, C.   **891.8**

To die in Mexico. Gibler, J.   **363.45**

To die well. Wanzer, S. H.   **179.7**

To end all wars. Hochschild, A.   **940.3**

To explain the world. Weinberg, S.   **509**

To forgive design. Petroski, H.   **620**

To free a family. Nathans, S.   **306.3**

To hell and back. Pellegrino, C.   **940.54**

To Hell and Back. Kershaw, I.   **940.5**

To hell on a fast horse. Gardner, M. L.   **92**

To listen to a child. Brazelton, T. B.   **155.4**

To live or to perish forever. Schmidle, N.   **954.91**

To live's to fly. Kruth, J.   **92**

To love what is. Shulman, A. K.   **92**

To marry an English Lord. MacColl, G.   **974.7**

To the actor. Chekhov, M.   **792**

To the castle and back. Havel, V.   **92**

To the cloud. Arora, P.   **004.67**

To the Diamond Mountains. Morris-Suzuki, T.   **915**

To the end of June. Beam, C.   **362.73**

To the gates of Richmond. Sears, S. W.   **973.7**

TOADSTOOLS *See* Mushrooms

Toasts.   **808.88**

TOASTS
       See also Epigrams; Speeches

TOASTS
   Toasts   **808.88**

TOBACCO
   See also Plants

TOBACCO HABIT
   Goldfarb, T. L. American Lung Association 7 steps to a smoke-free life   **616.86**
   Proctor, R. N. Golden holocaust   **362.29**

Tobar, Héctor
   Deep down dark   **363.11**

Tobbell, Dominique A.

Pills, power, and policy   **338.4**

Tobias, Andrew P.

The only investment guide you'll ever need **332.024**

Tobin, Jacqueline

From Midnight to Dawn   **322**

Hidden in plain view   **973.7**

Tobin, James

Reporting America at war   **070.4**

Ernie Pyle's war   **070.4**

Tocqueville, Alexis de

Democracy in America   **973.5**

About

Epstein, J. Alexis De Tocqueville   **92**

Todd, Olivier

Albert Camus   **848**

Todd, Richard

(jt. auth) Kidder, T. Good prose   **808.02**

TODDLERS

Murkoff, H. E. What to expect the second year **649**

White, D. A. First bites   **641.3**

Todhunter, Tracey

Crochet   **746.434**

Tofel, Richard J.

Restless genius   **92**

Toffler, Alvin

Future shock   **303.4**

TOHOKU EARTHQUAKE AND TSUNAMI, JAPAN, 2011

Ehrlich, G. Facing the wave   **363.34**

TOILET TRAINING

See also Child rearing

TOILETRIES

See also Personal grooming

Toklas, Alice B.

About

Malcolm, J. Two lives   **92**

Stein, G. The autobiography of Alice B. Toklas **92**

TOKYO (JAPAN) -- HISTORY -- BOMBARDMENT, 1942

Nelson, C. The first heroes   **940.54**

Scott, J. M. Target Tokyo   **940.54**

Tolan, Sandy

Children of the stone   **780**

The lemon tree   **956.94**

Told you so. Nader, R.   **303.3**

Toler, Pamela D.

Heroines of Mercy Street   **973.775**

TOLERANCE *See* Toleration

TOLERATION

Bullard, S. Teaching tolerance   **649**

Buruma, I. Murder in Amsterdam   **364.152**

TOLERATION

See also Interpersonal relations

TOLERATION -- RELIGIOUS ASPECTS -- ISLAM

Harris, S. Islam and the future of tolerance   **297.2**

Toll, Ian W.

The conquering tide   **940.54**

Pacific crucible   **940.54**

Six frigates   **359**

Tolle, Eckhart

A new earth   **158**

The power of now   **158**

Tolstaia, Tat'iana

Pushkin's children   **891.7**

Tolstoy. Bartlett, R.   **891.7**

Tolstoy, Leo, graf, 1828-1910

About

Bartlett, R. Tolstoy   **891.7**

Bloom, H. The Western canon   **809**

Nabokov, V. V. Lectures on Russian literature **891.7**

The **Toltec** art of life and death. Emrys, B.   **299.7**

Tom. Leverich, L.   **92**

Tom and Jack. Adams, H.   **92**

Tomalin, Claire

Charles Dickens   **92**

Jane Austen   **823**

Samuel Pepys   **941.06**

Thomas Hardy   **92**

TOMATOES

LeHoullier, C. Epic tomatoes   **635**

The **tomb** in Seville. Lewis, N.   **946.081**

TOMBS

See also Archeology; Architecture; Burial; Monuments; Shrines

Tombs, Robert

The English and their history   **942**

Tomkins, Calvin

Duchamp   **709**

Lives of the artists   **920**

Tomkins, Stephen

John Wesley   **287**

Tomlinson, Charles

Selected poems   **821**

Skywriting and other poems   **821**

Tomlinson, Steve

Agricola cookbook   **641.564**

Tommy's honor. Cook, K.   **92**

Tomorrow's table. Adamchak, R. W.   **664**

Tomorrow-land. Tirella, J.   **607**

Toms River. Fagin, D.   **363.72**

TOMS RIVER WATERSHED (N.J.) -- ENVIRONMENTAL CONDITIONS

Fagin, D. Toms River   **363.72**

Tone, Andrea

Devices and desires   **363.9**

Tong wars. Seligman, S. D.   **364.106**

TONGUE TWISTERS

See also Children's poetry; Folklore; Nonsense verses

Toni Morrison lecture series

Danticat, E. Create dangerously   **92**

Jones, B. T. Story/Time   **814**

Too big to fail. Sorkin, A. R.   **330.9**

Too big to jail. Garrett, B. L.   **345.73**

Too big to know. Weinberger, D.   **303.48**

Too brief a treat. Capote, T.   **92**

Too close to the sun. Roosevelt, C.   **92**

Too high to fail. Fine, D.   **338.4**

Too late to die young. Johnson, H. M.   **92**

Too late to say goodbye. Rule, A.   **364.152**

Too many bosses, too few leaders. Peshawaria, R.   **658.4**

Too much magic. Kunstler, J. H.   **303.48**

Too soon to tell. Trillin, C.   **814**

Toobin, Jeffrey
American Heiress   **322.4**
The oath   **347.73**
The nine   **347**
A vast conspiracy   **973.929**
Toobin, J. The run of his life   **345.73**

The **tools.** Michels, B.   **158**

Tools for survival. Rawles, J. W.   **613.6**

Toomey, David
Weird Life   **571**

Toomey, David M.
Haynsworth, L. Amelia Earhart's daughters   **629.13**
The new time travelers   **530.1**

Toorpakai, Maria, 1990-
About
Holstein, K. A Different Kind of Daughter   **92**

Tooze, Adam
The deluge   **940.3**

The **top** 100. Ferguson Publishing   **331.7**

Top of the morning. Stelter, B.   **791.45**

Topdog/underdog. Parks   **812**

TOPIARY WORK
Hobson, J. The art of creative pruning   **715**

Topics in autism [series]
Harris, S. L. Essential first steps for parents of children with autism   **618.92**

TOPOGRAPHICAL DRAWING
See also Drawing; Surveying

Topol, Eric
The creative destruction of medicine   **610.28**

TOPOLOGY
See also Geometry; Set theory

Topsy. Daly, M.   **791.3**

The **Torah:** the five books of Moses.   **222**

Torgus, Judy
(ed) The Womanly art of breastfeeding   **649**

TORIES, AMERICAN *See* American Loyalists

Torn awake. Gander, F.   **811**

TORNADOES
Cross, K. What Stands in a Storm   **363.34**
Sandlin, L. Storm kings   **551.55**

TORNADOES
See also Meteorology; Storms; Winds

Toropov, Brandon
Woodger, E. Encyclopedia of the Lewis and Clark Expedition   **917**

TORPEDOES
See also Explosives; Naval art and science; Submarine warfare

TORRE MOUNTAIN (ARGENTINA)
Cordes, K. The tower   **796**

Torre, Joe, 1940-
About
Torre, J. The Yankee years   **92**

Torre, Monica de la
Reversible monuments   **861**

Torrenzano, Richard
(jt. auth) Davis, M. Digital assassination   **005**

Torres, Alissa
About
Torres, A. American widow   **741.5**

Torres, Joseph
(jt. auth) Gonzalez, J. News for all the people   **302.23**

Torres-Roman, Steven A.
Read on-- science fiction   **016**

Torrey, E. Fuller (Edwin Fuller), 1937-
The insanity offense   **362.1**
Surviving schizophrenia   **616.89**

TORT LIABILITY OF CORPORATIONS -- UNITED STATES
Garrett, B. L. Too big to jail   **345.73**

TORTILLAS
Stupak, A. Tacos   **641.84**

TORTOISES *See* Turtles

Tortorella, Neil
Starting your career as a freelance web designer   **006.7**

TORTURE
Conroy, J. Unspeakable acts, ordinary people   **323.4**
Evans, M. Algeria   **965**
Guantanamo diary   **958.104**
McCoy, A. W. A question of torture   **323.4**
Morgan, T. My battle of Algiers   **965**
The Senate Intelligence Committee report on torture
The torture papers   **973.931**

TORTURE
See also Criminal procedure; Cruelty; Punishment

TORTURE -- IRAQ
Fair, E. Consequence   **956.704**
The torture papers   **973.931**

The **torture** papers.   **973.931**

Tosh, Peter, 1944-1987
About
Grant, C. The natural mystics   **920**

Tosi, Christina
Milk Bar Life   **641.86**
Momofuku Milk Bar   **641.8**

The **total** fishing manual. Cermele, J.   **799.1**
**TOTAL HIP REPLACEMENT -- PATIENTS --
 BIOGRAPHY**
 Caldwell, G. New life, no instructions   **92**
TOTAL QUALITY MANAGEMENT
 Laughlin, S. The quality library   **025.1**
Total recovery. Kaplan, G.   **616**
The **Total** Skywatcher's Manual. White, V.   **523.8**
TOTALITARIANISM
 Arendt, H. Origins of totalitarianism   **321.9**
 Huxley, A. Brave new world revisited   **303.3**
TOTALITARIANISM
 See also Political science
TOTEMS AND TOTEMISM
 See also Ethnology; Mythology
Totten, Herman L.
 Larson, J. C. The public library policy writer   **025.1**
Touborg, Sarah
 Moffett, K. Not your mother's divorce   **306.89**
Touch. Linden, D. J.   **612.8**
TOUCH
 See also Senses and sensation
Touch and go. Terkel, S.   **92**
Touched with fire. Perry, J. M.   **973.7**
Touching my father's soul. Jamling Tenzing Nor-
 gay   **796.522**
Touchpoints. Conant, D. R.   **658.4**
Touchpoints birth to 3. Brazelton, T. B.   **649**
A Touchstone book [series]
 Karlins, M. The like switch   **158.2**
Tough, Paul
 Helping Children Succeed   **372.1**
 How children succeed   **372.21**
 Whatever it takes   **362.7**
The **toughest** show on earth. Volpe, J.   **92**
Tougias, Mike
 Schultz, E. B. King Philip's War   **973.2**
 Ten hours until dawn   **363.34**
Toulouse-Lautrec. Frey, J.   **92**
Toulouse-Lautrec, Henri de, 1864-1901
 About
 Frey, J. Toulouse-Lautrec   **92**
Toumani, Meline
 About
 Toumani, M. There was and there was not   **327**
TOUR DE FRANCE (BICYCLE RACE)
 Leonard, M. Lanterne Rouge   **796.62**
Tour de Lance. Strickland, B.   **92**
Touré, 1971-
 About
 Who's afraid of post-blackness?
TOURETTE SYNDROME
 Hanagarne, J. The world's strongest librarian   **92**
Tourgée, Albion Winegar, 1838-1905
 About
 Wilson, E. Patriotic gore   **810**

TOURISM -- CROSS CULTURAL STUDIES
 Becker, E. Overbooked   **338.4**
TOURISM -- ENVIRONMENTAL ASPECTS
 Blackwell, A. Visit sunny Chernobyl   **363.73**
Tourles, Stephanie L.
 Raw energy   **641.5**
Toussaint Louverture. Bell, M. S.   **92**
Toussaint Louverture, 1743?-1803
 About
 Bell, M. S. Toussaint Louverture   **92**
Toutonghi, Pauls
 Dog Gone   **636.7**
Toward the distant islands. Carruth, H.   **811**
Tower. Jones, N.   **942.1**
The **tower.** Cordes, K.   **796**
**TOWER OF LONDON (LONDON, ENGLAND)
 -- HISTORY**
 Jones, N. Tower   **942.1**
The **towering** world of Jimmy Choo. Crowe, L.
 G.   **391**
**TOWN HALL (RESTAURANT : SAN FRANCIS-
 CO, CALIF.)**
 Cooking my way back home   **641.5**
TOWN LIFE *See* City and town life
TOWN OFFICERS *See* Municipal officials and
 employees
TOWN PLANNING *See* City planning
The **town** that food saved. Hewitt, B.   **338.1**
Townie. Dubus, A.   **92**
TOWNS *See* Cities and towns
Townsend, Richard F.
 The Aztecs   **972**
Townsend, Robert, 1753-1838
 About
 Yaeger, D. George Washington's secret six   **973.4**
TOXICOLOGY
 Blum, D. The poisoner's handbook   **614**
TOXICOLOGY
 See also Medicine; Pharmacology
**TOXICOLOGY -- GREAT BRITAIN -- HISTO-
 RY -- 19TH CENTURY**
 Hempel, S. The inheritor's powder   **364.152**
Toxin toxout. Smith, R.   **613**
TOY AND MOVABLE BOOKS
 See also Picture books for children
TOY INDUSTRY
 Breen, B. Brick by brick   **338.7**
**TOY INDUSTRY -- UNITED STATES -- HIS-
 TORY**
 Bissonnette, Z. The great Beanie Baby bub-
 ble   **338.7**
TOY MAKING
 Handy dad   **745.592**
TOY MAKING
 See also Handicraft
Toye, Richard

Churchill's empire   92

Toynbee, Arnold, 1852-1883
     About
Herman, A. The idea of decline in Western history   **909.08**

TOYS
     See also Amusements

Trace. Pankey, E.   **811**

Trace. Savoy, L.   **917.3**

Trachtenberg, Peter
The book of calamities   **128**

TRACK ATHLETICS
     See also Athletics; Sports

TRACKING AND TRAILING
     See also Hunting

TRACKS OF ANIMALS *See* Animal tracks

Tractor.   **629.225**

TRACTORS
     See also Agricultural machinery

TRACTORS -- HISTORY
Tractor   **629.225**

TRACTORS -- PICTORIAL WORKS
Tractor   **629.225**

Tracy, Brian
Eat that frog!   **640**
Full engagement!   **658.3**
Thompson, M. Now, build a great business!   **658**

Tracy, Spencer, 1900-1967
     About
Curtis, J. Spencer Tracy   **92**

Tracy, Steven C.
(ed) Writers of the Black Chicago renaissance **810.9**

TRADE *See* Business; Commerce

TRADE AND PROFESSIONAL ASSOCIATIONS
     See also Associations

TRADE MARKS *See* Trademarks

TRADE ROUTES
Cliff, N. Holy war   **909**

TRADE ROUTES
     See also Commerce; Commercial geography; Transportation

TRADE ROUTES -- CENTRAL ASIA
Frankopan, P. The Silk Roads   **909**

TRADE ROUTES -- HISTORY
Frankopan, P. The Silk Roads   **909**

Trademark. Elias, S.   **346.04**

TRADEMARKS
Elias, S. Trademark   **346.04**
Stim, R. Patent, copyright & trademark   **346**

TRAFALGAR (SPAIN), BATTLE OF, 1805
Adkin, M. The Trafalgar companion   **940.2**
The **Trafalgar** companion. Adkin, M.   **940.2**

Traffic. Vanderbilt, T.   **629.28**

Tragedy in crimson. Johnson, T.   **294.3**
The **Tragedy** of the Templars. Haag, M.   **271**

TRAGICOMEDY

     See also Drama

TRAIL OF TEARS, 1838-1839
Langguth, A. J. Driven West   **973.5**

TRAILS
Macfarlane, R. The old ways   **914.2**

TRAILS
     See also Roads

TRAILS -- APPALACHIAN REGION, SOUTHERN -- GUIDEBOOKS
Spira, T. P. Waterfalls and wildflowers in the Southern Appalachians   **796.51**

Trailside (Television program)
Rock climbing   **796.522**

Trailside series guide [series]
Trailside (Television program)   Rock climbing   **796.522**

Train.   **625.1**

Train. Zoellner, T.   **385**

The **Train** to Crystal City. Russell, J. J.   **940.53**

TRAIN WRECKS *See* Railroad accidents

Train your dog positively. Stilwell, V.   **636.7**

The **trainable** cat. Bradshaw, J.   **636.8**

TRAINING OF CHILDREN *See* Child rearing

TRAINING OF EMPLOYEES *See* Employees -- Training

Trainor, Bernard E.
(jt. auth) Gordon, M. R. The endgame   **956.7**
Gordon, M. R. The generals' war   **956.7**

Trainor, Kathleen
Calming your anxious child   **618.92**

TRAINS *See* Railroads

Traister, Rebecca
Big girls don't cry   **324**

Traitor to his class. Brands, H. W.   **92**

Traitors among us. Herrington, S. A.   **327.12**

TRAMPS
     See also Homeless persons; Poor

Tran, G. B., 1976-
     About
Tran, G. B. Vietnamerica   **741.5**

Trang, Corinne
Essentials of Asian cuisine   **641.5**

TRANQUILIZING DRUGS -- SOCIAL ASPECTS
Stossel, S. My age of anxiety   **616.85**

Trans. Jacques, J.   **306.76**

Trans bodies, trans selves.   **306.76**

TRANSACTIONAL ANALYSIS
     See also Psychotherapy

TRANSATLANTIC FLIGHTS -- HISTORY -- 20TH CENTURY
Jackson, J. Atlantic fever   **629.130**

TRANSCENDENTAL MEDITATION
Hoffman, C. Greetings from Utopia Park   **92**

TRANSCENDENTAL MEDITATION
     See also Meditation

Transcendental studies. Waldrop, K.   811
Transcendentalism.   810
TRANSCENDENTALISM
The essential transcendentalists   141
TRANSCENDENTALISM
See also Philosophy
TRANSCENDENTALISM -- COLLECTIONS
Transcendentalism   810
Transcircularities. Troupe, Q.   811
TRANSCONTINENTAL JOURNEYS (AMERI-
CAN CONTINENT) See Overland journeys to
the Pacific
TRANSCULTURAL MEDICAL CARE -- CALI-
FORNIA -- CASE STUDIES
Fadiman, A. The spirit catches you and you fall
down   306.4
TRANSCULTURAL STUDIES See Cross-cultural
studies
Transfer of Qualities. Ronk, M.   811
TRANSFER PAYMENTS
See also Domestic economic assistance; Eco-
nomic policy; Subsidies
TRANSFER PRINTING
Burnett, J. B. Graphic clay   738.1
Transfigurations. Wright, J.   811
The transformation of Ireland. Ferriter, D.   941.5
The transformed library. Woodward, J.   020
TRANSGENDER PEOPLE
Jacques, J. Trans   306.76
Mock, J. Redefining Realness   306.76
Nutt, A. E. Becoming Nicole   306.76
Trans bodies, trans selves   306.76
TRANSGENDER PEOPLE
See also LGBT people
TRANSGENDER PEOPLE -- UNITED STATES
-- BIOGRAPHY
McBee, T. P. Man alive   92
Mock, J. Redefining Realness   306.76
TRANSGENDER TEENAGERS
Nutt, A. E. Becoming Nicole   306.76
TRANSGENDER TEENAGERS
See also Teenagers; Transgender people
TRANSGENDER YOUTH -- EDUCATION --
UNITED STATES
Cahill, S. LGBT youth in America's schools 371.82
TRANSGENDER YOUTH -- UNITED STATES
Nutt, A. E. Becoming Nicole   306.76
TRANSGENIC ANIMALS
Anthes, E. Frankenstein's cat   616.02
TRANSLATING AND INTERPRETING
Dilevko, J. Contemporary world fiction   016
Grossman, E. Why translation matters   418
The Oxford guide to literature in English transla-
tion   820
Remnick, D. Reporting   814
Selected translations 1948-2010   808.81

TRANSLATING AND INTERPRETING
See also Language and languages
Translations from the Asian classics [series]
Haiku before haiku   895.6
I ching The classic of changes   299.5
Translations from the Oriental classics [series]
The Columbia book of Chinese poetry   895.1
The translator. Hari, D.   92
TRANSLATORS
Athill, D. Somewhere towards the end   92
Bloom, H. The Western canon   809
Boyd, B. Vladimir Nabokov: the American
years   813
Boyd, B. Vladimir Nabokov: the Russian years 813
Draitser, E. Stalin's Romeo spy   92
Friedman, M. S. Encounter on the narrow ridge: a
life of Martin Buber   92
Gioia, D. Can poetry matter?   809.1
Heaney, S. Finders keepers   821
Jarrell, R. No other book   809
Mandelstam, N. Hope against hope   891.71
Manguel, A. A reader on reading   818
Milosz, C. To begin where I am   891.8
Nabokov, V. V. Speak, memory   813
O'Driscoll, D. Stepping stones   821
Seth, V. Two lives   92
Williamson, E. Borges, a life   92
TRANSLATORS -- UNITED STATES -- BIOG-
RAPHY
Sakamoto, P. R. Midnight in broad daylight 940.53
The tender hour of twilight   070.5
TRANSPLANTATION OF ORGANS, TISSUES,
ETC.
Rose, D. A. Larry's kidney   915
TRANSPLANTATION OF ORGANS, TISSUES,
ETC.
See also Surgery
TRANSPLANTATION OF ORGANS, TISSUES,
ETC. -- ETHICAL ASPECTS
Teresi, D. The undead   610
TRANSPLANTATION OF ORGANS, TISSUES,
ETC. -- MORAL AND RELIGIOUS ASPECTS
See Transplantation of organs, tissues, etc. -- Ethi-
cal aspects
TRANSPORTATION
Bike Snob The enlightened cyclist   796.6
Hoffman, C. The lunatic express   910.4
McCommons, J. Waiting on a train   385
McPhee, J. A. Uncommon carriers   388
TRANSPORTATION -- ENVIRONMENTAL AS-
PECTS
Shulman, S. Cooler smarter   363.7
TRANSPORTATION -- HISTORY
Chaplin, J. E. Round about the earth   910.4
TRANSPORTATION -- SECURITY MEASURES
-- UNITED STATES

Molotch, H. Against security **363.325**

TRANSPORTATION OF CRIMINALS *See* Penal colonies

TRANSPORTATION, AUTOMOTIVE -- CHINA
Hessler, P. Country driving **303.4**

TRANSPORTATION, AUTOMOTIVE -- UNITED STATES
Ladd, B. Autophobia **303.4**

TRANSPORTATION, HIGHWAY *See* Highway transportation

TRANSPORTS -- GREAT BRITAIN -- HISTORY -- 20TH CENTURY
Scott, R. N. Many were held by the sea **940.4**

TRANSSEXUALISM
Boylan, J. F. I'm looking through you **92**
McBee, T. P. Man alive **92**

TRANSSEXUALISM
See also Gender role

TRANSSEXUALITY *See* Transsexualism

TRANSSEXUALS
Boylan, J. F. I'm looking through you **92**

TRANSSEXUALS -- UNITED STATES -- BIOGRAPHY
McBee, T. P. Man alive **92**

Tranströmer, Tomas, 1931-2015
The great enigma **839.7**

TRANSVESTITES *See* Cross-dressers

Trapped: the 1909 Cherry Mine disaster. Tintori, K. **973.9**

Trash-to-treasure papermaking. Grummer, A. E. **676**

Trattner, Douglas
Michael Symon's 5 in 5 for every season **641.81**

Traub, James
John Quincy Adams **92**

TRAUMATIC STRESS SYNDROME *See* Post-traumatic stress disorder

Trav S. D.
No applause, just throw money; or, The book that made vaudeville famous **792.7**

TRAVEL
Abroad at home **917.3**
Becker, E. Overbooked **338.4**
Corrigan, K. Glitter and Glue **92**
Fodor's Germany **914.3**
Heat-Moon, W. L. Here, there, elsewhere **910.4**
An Innocent Abroad **910.4**
Iyer, P. The man within my head **809**
Macdonald, C. The endangered species road trip **974**
Podell, A. Around the World in 50 Years **910.4**
The rough guide to Italy **914.504**
Stellin, S. How to travel practically anywhere **910.2**
Ultimate travel **910.2**
The World **910.2**

TRAVEL

See also Manners and customs

TRAVEL -- AUTHORSHIP *See* Travel writing

TRAVEL -- HISTORY
Chaplin, J. E. Round about the earth **910.4**

TRAVEL BOOKS *See* Voyages and travels; Voyages around the world

TRAVEL IN LITERATURE
See also Literature -- Themes; Travel

TRAVEL PHOTOGRAPHY
Hitchcock, S. T. National geographic rarely seen **779**
National Geographic Society (U.S.) Through the lens **779**

TRAVEL TRAILERS AND CAMPERS
See also Camping; Recreational vehicles

TRAVEL WRITERS -- UNITED STATES -- BIOGRAPHY
O'Neill, Z. All strangers are kin **910.917**

TRAVEL WRITING
Burgin, R. Going places **910.4**
Capote, T. Portraits and observations **814**
Caputo, P. The longest road **973.93**
Hely, S. The wonder trail **917.28**
The open road **770**
Writing Across the Landscape **92**

TRAVEL WRITING
See also Authorship

Traveler. Johnston, D. **811**

TRAVELERS
Belliveau, D. In the footsteps of Marco Polo **915**
Bergreen, L. Marco Polo **92**
Howell, G. Gertrude Bell **92**
Wallach, J. Desert queen **956**
Whitaker, R. The mapmaker's wife **981**
Zaretsky, R. Boswell's enlightenment **92**

TRAVELERS
See also Voyages and travels

TRAVELERS -- EUROPE -- HISTORY -- 18TH CENTURY
Boswell's enlightenment **828**
Zaretsky, R. Boswell's enlightenment **92**

TRAVELERS' WRITINGS, AMERICAN
The best American travel writing 2012 **808**

TRAVELING SALES PERSONNEL *See* Sales personnel

Traveling the power line. Couch, J. **333.793**

TRAVELS *See* Voyages and travels

Travels in Siberia. Frazier, I. **957**
Travels in Vermeer. White, M. **92**
The **travels** of Marco Polo. Polo, M. **915**
Travels with Charley. Steinbeck, J. **973**
Travels with Herodotus. **930**
Travels with the fossil hunters. **560**
Travesties. Stoppard, T. **822**
Travis, Joseph
(ed) Evolution **576.8**

Travis, William Barret, 1809-1836
About
Davis, W. C. Three roads to the Alamo   **976.4**
TREASON
Read, P. P. The Dreyfus affair   **944.081**
TREASON
See also Crime; Political crimes and offenses; Subversive activities
Treason by the book. Spence, J. D.   **951**
TREASURE TROVES
Kurson, R. Pirate hunters   **910.91**
Treasure, G. R. R.
(ed) Who's who in British history   **920.003**
Treasures of Islam. O'Kane, B.   **709.1**
Treasury of XXth century murder [series]
Geary, R. The Lindbergh child   **364.1**
Treat me, not my age. Lachs, M.   **612.6**
TREATIES
Documents of American Indian diplomacy   **970.004**
TREATIES
See also Diplomacy; International law; International relations
Treating and beating fibromyalgia and chronic fatigue syndrome. Murphree, R. H.   **616**
TREATMENT *See* Therapeutics
TREATMENT OF DISEASES *See* Therapeutics
TREATY OF VERSAILLES (1919)
MacMillan, M. Paris 1919   **940.3**
Neu, C. E. Colonel House   **92**
Trebincevic, Kenan, 1980-
About
Shapiro, S. The Bosnia list   **92**
Trebing, Katie, 2002-
About
Whitehouse, B. The match   **92**
TREE PLANTING
See also Forests and forestry
TREES
Dirr, M. A. Dirr's encyclopedia of trees and shrubs   **635.9**
Dirr, M. Dirr's Hardy trees and shrubs   **635.9**
Dirr, M. Dirr's trees and shrubs for warm climates   **635.9**
The glory of the tree   **582.16**
The Hillier gardener's guide to trees & shrubs   **635.9**
Hugo, N. R. Seeing trees   **582.16**
Johnson, H. The world of trees   **582.16**
Nadkarni, N. Between earth and sky   **582.16**
O'Sullivan, P. The homeowner's complete tree & shrub handbook   **635.9**
Wohlleben, P. The Hidden Life of Trees   **582.16**
TREES
See also Plants
TREES -- NOMENCLATURE (POPULAR)
See also Popular plant names
TREES -- NORTH AMERICA

Little, E. L. The Audubon Society field guide to North American trees   **582.16**
Sibley, D. The Sibley guide to trees   **582.16**
TREES -- SYMBOLIC ASPECTS -- HISTORY
Lima, M. The book of trees   **001.2**
Trefil, James
Space atlas   **520**
Trefil, James S.
(ed) The Encyclopedia of science and technology   **503**
Tregear, Mary
Chinese art   **709**
Treglown, Jeremy
V.S. Pritchett: a working life   **92**
Treisman, Daniel
The return   **947.086**
Treister, Kenneth
Easter Island's silent sentinels   **990**
Tremlett, Giles
Ghosts of Spain   **946**
Trethewey, Natasha D., 1966-
Beyond Katrina   **818**
Tretick, Stanley
About
Kelley, K. Let Freedom Ring   **323.1**
Treuer, Anton
Atlas of Indian nations   **970.004**
Everything you wanted to know about Indians but were afraid to ask   **909**
The **trial**. Kadri, S.   **345**
The **trial** of Socrates. Stone, I. F.   **183**
TRIALS
Barrett, P. M. Law of the jungle   **344**
Bredin The affair   **944.081**
Great American trials   **347**
Guttenplan, D. D. The Holocaust on trial   **940.53**
Heard, A. The eyes of Willie McGee   **364.66**
Hoffer, P. C. The Salem witchcraft trials   **345**
Kadri, S. The trial   **345**
Lipstadt, D. E. History on trial   **940.53**
Long, J. The plot against Pepys   **941.06**
McGinty, B. Lincoln's Greatest Case   **346**
Newton, M. A. Enemy of the state   **345**
Rabinowitz, D. No crueler tyrannies   **345**
Strang, D. A. Worse than the devil   **345**
Strebeigh, F. Equal   **342**
Toobin, J. The run of his life   **345.73**
Walsh, J. E. Moonlight   **345**
Waterfield, R. Why Socrates died   **183**
Weiner, M. S. Black trials   **342**
Wise, S. M. Though the heavens may fall   **342**
TRIALS (ANARCHY) -- NEW YORK (STATE) -- NEW YORK -- HISTORY -- 20TH CENTURY
Healy, T. The great dissent   **342.73**
TRIALS (HOMICIDE)
Anderson, D. S. Emmett Till   **364.1**

Boyle, K. Arc of justice **345**

Bryan, P. L. Midnight assassin **364.152**

Collins, P. Duel With the Devil **364.152**

Colquhoun, K. Did she kill him? **364.152**

Goldman, F. The art of political murder **972.81**

Hakkakiyan, R. Assassins of the Turquoise Palace **364.152**

Kaplan, A. Y. The interpreter **940.54**

Lane, C. The day freedom died **976.3**

Lebsock, S. A murder in Virginia **364.1**

Liebman, J. S. The wrong Carlos **364.152**

Malcolm, J. Iphigenia in Forest Hills **345**

Nelson, M. The red parts **362.88**

Parry, R. L. People who eat darkness **364.152**

Rule, A. --and never let her go **364.1**

Smith, C. S. The injustice system **345.73**

Spence, G. The smoking gun **345**

Starr, D. The killer of little shepherds **364.152**

Temkin, M. The Sacco-Vanzetti Affair **345**

Toobin, J. The run of his life **345.73**

Watson, B. Sacco and Vanzetti **345**

TRIALS (HOMICIDE)

See also Homicide; Trials

TRIALS (MURDER) *See* Trials (Homicide)

TRIALS (MURDER) -- ARIZONA -- MARICOPA COUNTY

Siegel, B. Manifest injustice **364.152**

TRIALS (MURDER) -- FLORIDA

Smith, C. S. The injustice system **345.73**

TRIALS (MURDER) -- MASSACHUSETTS -- DEDHAM

Temkin, M. The Sacco-Vanzetti Affair **345**

TRIALS (MURDER) -- MISSISSIPPI -- SUMNER

Anderson, D. S. Emmett Till **364.1**

TRIALS (MURDER) -- QUEENS (NEW YORK, N.Y.)

Malcolm, J. Iphigenia in Forest Hills **345**

TRIALS (MURDER) -- TEXAS

Liebman, J. S. The wrong Carlos **364.152**

TRIALS (RAPE)

Krakauer, J. Missoula **362.883**

TRIALS (RIOTS) -- WISCONSIN -- MILWAUKEE -- HISTORY -- 20TH CENTURY

Strang, D. A. Worse than the devil **345**

TRIALS (SEDITIOUS LIBEL) -- NEW YORK (STATE)

Kluger, R. Indelible ink **686.209**

TRIALS (SODOMY) -- TEXAS

Carpenter, D. Flagrant conduct **342.73**

TRIALS (TREASON) -- POLITICAL ASPECTS -- FRANCE

Read, P. P. The Dreyfus affair **944.081**

Trials of passion. Appignanesi, L. **364.152**

Triandis, Harry C.

Fooling ourselves **155.2**

TRIANGLE

Lehmann, I. The secrets of triangles **516**

TRIANGLE

See also Geometry; Shape

TRIANGLE SHIRTWAIST COMPANY, INC.

Von Drehle, D. Triangle: the fire that changed America **974.7**

Triangle: the fire that changed America. Von Drehle, D. **974.7**

Triangular road. Marshall, P. **92**

TRIATHLETES

Dixon, M. The well-built triathlete **796.42**

TRIATHLETES

See also Athletes

TRIATHLON

See also Sports

Tribal. Roberts, D. **796.332**

TRIBAL GOVERNMENT

See also Political science; Tribes

TRIBAL LEADERS

Kelly, C. The end of empire **92**

Tribe. Gibbon, P. **305.8**

Tribe. Junger, S. **302.3**

Tribe, Laurence H., 1941-

Uncertain justice **342.73**

TRIBES

Junger, S. Tribe **302.3**

TRIBES

See also Clans; Family

TRIBES AND TRIBAL SYSTEM *See* Tribes

Tribune Tower (Chicago, Ill.)

(comp) Holiday cookies **641.86**

TRICERATOPS

See also Dinosaurs

Trick or Treat. Morton, L. **394.264**

Tried by war. McPherson, J. M. **92**

Triggers. Goldsmith, M. **155.2**

TRIGONOMETRY

Lehmann, I. The secrets of triangles **516**

TRIGONOMETRY

See also Geometry; Mathematics

Trillin, Alice, 1938-2001

About

Trillin, C. About Alice **92**

Trillin, Calvin

About Alice **92**

Quite enough of Calvin Trillin **817**

Too soon to tell **814**

Trilling-Josephson, Terry

Josephson, B. Cafe Society **792.7**

Trilobite! Fortey, R. A. **560**

Trimborn, Jurgen

Leni Riefenstahl **92**

Trinidad, David

Dear Prudence **811**

TRINITY

See also Christianity -- Doctrines; God --
Christianity

The **trip**. Davis, D.   **700.92**

The **Trip** to Echo Spring. Laing, O.   **810.9**

Tripp, Charles

  A history of Iraq   **956.7**

Tris Speaker. Gay, T. M.   **92**

Triumph. Schaap, J.   **92**

Triumph and tragedy. Churchill, W.   **940.53**

The **triumph** of love. Hill, G.   **821**

The **triumph** of music. Blanning, T. C. W.   **780.9**

The **triumph** of seeds. Hanson, T.   **581.4**

Triumph of the heart. Bettencourt, M. F.   **155.9**

The **triumph** of the moon. Hutton, R.   **133.4**

Triumphs of experience. Vaillant, G. E.   **305.31**

Trivers, Robert

  The folly of fools   **153.4**

TRIVIA *See* Curiosities and wonders; Questions
and answers

The **trivia** lover's guide to the world. Fuller, G. **910**

Trodd, Zoe

  (jt. auth) Stauffer, J. Picturing Frederick Douglass   **92**

TROJAN WAR

  Alexander, C. The war that killed Achilles   **883**

  Homer The Iliad   **883**

  Tuchman, B. W. The march of folly   **909.08**

  Wood, M. In search of the Trojan War   **939**

TROJAN WAR

  See also Greek mythology; Troy (Extinct city)

TROMBONISTS

  Dance, S. The world of Count Basie   **920**

TROODON

  See also Dinosaurs

TROPICAL FISH

  Smith, C. L. National Audubon Society field guide
to tropical marine fishes of the Caribbean, the
Gulf of Mexico, Florida, the Bahamas, and Bermuda   **597**

TROPICAL FISH

  See also Fishes

TROPICAL MEDICINE

  See also Medicine

TROPICS

  Naskrecki, P. The smaller majority   **591.7**

TROPICS

  See also Earth

Trotsky. Service, R.   **92**

Trotsky, Leon, 1879-1940

           About

  Service, R. Trotsky   **92**

Trott, Barry

  Read on . . . crime fiction   **016**

Trotta, Roberto

  The edge of the sky   **520**

Trotter, William Monroe, 1872-1934

           About

  Lehr, D. The Birth of a Nation   **305.8**

TROUBADOURS

  See also French poetry; Minstrels; Poets

Trouble boys. Mehr, B.   **782.42**

The **trouble** with physics. Smolin, L.   **530.1**

The **trouble** with poetry and other poems. Collins,
B.   **811**

The **trouble** with Tom: the strange afterlife and
times of Thomas Paine. Collins, P.   **92**

Troubled refuge. Manning, C.   **973.711**

The **troubles**. Coogan, T. P.   **941.6**

Troupe, Quincy

  Davis, M. Miles, the autobiography   **92**

  Gardner, C. The pursuit of happyness   **92**

  Transcircularities   **811**

TROUT

  Trout and salmon of North America   **597**

Trout and salmon of North America.   **597**

TROUT FISHING

  Gathercole, P. The fly-tying bible   **688.7**

TROUT FISHING

  See also Fishing

TROY (EXTINCT CITY)

  Wood, M. In search of the Trojan War   **939**

Truax, Eileen

  Dreamers   **325**

Trubek, Anne

  The History and Uncertain Future of Handwriting   **652.1**

TRUCK FARMING

  See also Agriculture; Gardening; Horticulture

TRUCKING

  See also Freight; Transportation

TRUCKING EXECUTIVES

  Russell, T. Out of the jungle   **92**

TRUCKS

  See also Automobiles; Highway transportation; Motor vehicles

Trudeau, Noah Andre

  Like men of war   **973.7**

True and false. Mamet, D.   **792**

True compass. Kennedy, E. M.   **92**

True north. Conway, J. K.   **92**

True notebooks. Salzman, M.   **371.9**

True, Margo

  (ed) Sunset the great outdoors cookbook   **641.5**

Truevine. Macy, B.   **791.3**

Trujillo Molina, Rafael Leónidas, 1891-1961

           About

  Von Tunzelmann, A. Red heat   **972.9**

The **truly** healthy family cookbook. Ruggiero,
T.   **641.5**

Truly Mexican. Santibañez, R.   **641.59**

Truman. McCullough, D. G.   **92**

Truman Capote. Plimpton, G.   **813**

Truman Capote, enfant terrible. Long, R. E.　　**92**

Truman, Harry S., 1884-1972
About
Beschloss, M. R. The conquerors: Roosevelt, Truman, and the destruction of Hitler's Germany, 1941-1945　　**940.53**

Dallek, R. Harry S. Truman　　**92**

Dobbs, M. Six months in 1945　　**940.53**

Donald, A. D. Citizen soldier　　**92**

Galbraith, J. K. Name-dropping　　**973.9**

Gordin, M. D. Red cloud at dawn　　**355**

Karabell, Z. The last campaign　　**324.9**

McCullough, D. G. Truman　　**92**

Trumble, Angus
The finger　　**306.4**

Trump, Donald J.
About
Johnston, D. C. The making of Donald Trump　　**973.932**

Singer, M. Character studies　　**920**

Slater, R. No such thing as over-exposure　　**92**

The **trumpet** of conscience. King, M. L.　　**973.92**

TRUMPET PLAYERS
Armstrong, L. Louis Armstrong, in his own words　　**92**

Cook, R. It's about that time　　**92**

Dance, S. The world of Count Basie　　**920**

Davis, M. Miles, the autobiography　　**92**

Feather, L. From Satchmo to Miles　　**920**

Lees, G. You can't steal a gift　　**781.65**

Murray, A. The blue devils of Nada　　**780.89**

Truss, Lynne
Eats, shoots & leaves　　**421**

Trust. Marshall, J.　　**781.66**

TRUST
Covey, S. M. R. Smart trust　　**174**

TRUST
See also Attitude (Psychology); Emotions

TRUST COMPANIES
See also Business; Corporations

TRUSTS AND TRUSTEES
See also Contracts

Truth. Blackburn, S.　　**121**

TRUTH
Blackburn, S. Truth　　**121**

TRUTH
See also Belief and doubt; Philosophy

Truth & beauty. Patchett, A.　　**92**

The **truth** about carpal tunnel syndrome. Gambaro, J.　　**616.85**

The **truth** about leadership. Kouzes, J. M.　　**658.4**

Truth and existence. Sartre, J. P.　　**121**

The **truth** doesn't have to hurt. Bright, D.　　**158.2**

The **truth** in small doses. Leaf, C.　　**616.99**

A **truth** universally acknowledged.　　**823**

Truth, Sojourner, d. 1883
About
Painter, N. I. Sojourner Truth　　**305.5**

TRUTHFULNESS AND FALSEHOOD
Ariely, D. The honest truth about dishonesty　　**177**

Campbell, J. The liar's tale　　**177**

Lerner, H. G. The dance of deception　　**155.3**

Levitin, D. J. A field guide to lies　　**153.4**

TRUTHFULNESS AND FALSEHOOD
See also Human behavior; Truth

Try to tell the story. Thomson, D.　　**92**

Trying to float. Rips, N.　　**974.7**

Trynka, Paul
Iggy Pop　　**92**

Tryst. Estes, A.　　**811**

Trzebinski, Errol
The lives of Beryl Markham　　**629.13**

Tsai, Ming
Blue Ginger　　**641.5**

The **Tsar's** last armada. Pleshakov, K.　　**952.03**

Tsar: the lost world of Nicholas and Alexandra. Kurth, P.　　**947.08**

Tseng, Chung, 1568-1650
About
Spence, J. D. Treason by the book　　**951**

Tsering Shakya
The dragon in the land of snows　　**951**

TSUNAMIS
Ehrlich, G. Facing the wave　　**363.34**

Krauss, E. Wave of destruction　　**959.3**

Lyman, E. Fukushima　　**363.17**

TSUNAMIS
See also Natural disasters; Ocean waves

Tsvetaeva, Marina Ivanovna, 1892-1941
Selected poems　　**891.7**
About
Brodsky, J. Less than one　　**809.1**

Pierpont, C. R. Passionate minds　　**810**

Tubach, Frederic C.
German voices　　**943.086**

Tubach, Sally P.
Tubach, F. C. German voices　　**943.086**

TUBERCULOSIS
Kafka, the years of insight　　**833**

Tubes. Blum, A.　　**384.3**

Tubman, Harriet, 1820?-1913
About
Abdul-Jabbar, K. Black profiles in courage　　**920**

Clinton, C. Harriet Tubman: the road to freedom　　**92**

Humez, J. M. Harriet Tubman　　**92**

Larson, K. C. Bound for the promised land　　**92**

Tuccille, Jerome
The roughest riders　　**973.8**

Tuchman, Barbara Wertheim
A distant mirror　　**944**

The first salute　　**973.3**

The guns of August　　**940.3**

The march of folly   **909.08**
Practicing history   **907**
The proud tower   **909.82**
Stilwell and the American experience in China,
1911-45   **327**
The Zimmermann telegram   **940.3**
Tuck, Lily
Woman of Rome: a life of Elsa Morante   **92**
Tuck, Shonna
Getting from me to we   **155.4**
Tucker, Arthur O.
The encyclopedia of herbs   **635**
Tucker, Bruce
Brown, J. James Brown, the godfather of soul   **92**
Tucker, Dennis C.
Crash course in library supervision   **023**
Tucker, Spencer C.
(ed) Encyclopedia of American military histo-
ry   **355**
(ed) The encyclopedia of Middle East wars   355
(ed) Encyclopedia of the Cold War   **909.82**
(ed) The Encyclopedia of World War I   **940.3**
(ed) Encyclopedia of World War II   **940.53**
(ed) Naval warfare   **359**
The encyclopedia of the Vietnam War   **959.704**
Tucker, Todd
The great starvation experiment   **174.2**
Tucker, Virginia
Finding the answers to legal questions   **340**
Tudge, Colin
The bird   **598**
Tudor roses. Starmore, A.   **746.432**
Tudor, House of
                      About
Ackroyd, P. Tudors   **942.05**
Jones, D. The Wars of the Roses   **942.04**
The **Tudors**. Meyer, G. J.   **942.05**
Tudors. Ackroyd, P.   **942.05**
Tuesdays with Morrie. Albom, M.   **378.1**
Tufte, Edward R., 1942-
The visual display of quantitative information **001.4**
TUGBOATS
      See also Boats and boating
TUITION See College costs; Colleges and univer-
sities -- Finance; Education -- Finance
Tula Pink's city sampler. Pink, T.   **746.46**
Tulipomania. Dash, M.   **635.9**
TULIPS
Dash, M. Tulipomania   **635.9**
Pollan, M. The botany of desire   **306.4**
TULSA (OKLA.) -- RACE RELATIONS
Hirsch, J. S. Riot and remembrance   **976.6**
TUMBLING
      See also Acrobats and acrobatics
Tuna. Ellis, R.   **333.95**
TUNA

Ellis, R. Tuna   **333.95**
Greenberg, P. Four fish   **333.95**
TUNDRA ECOLOGY
      See also Ecology
The **tunnels.** Mitchell, G.   **943.155**
**TUNNELS -- GERMANY -- BERLIN -- HISTO-
RY -- 20TH CENTURY**
Mitchell, G. The tunnels   **943.155**
Tunstall, Tricia
Changing lives   **780.7**
Tupper, Earl S., 1907-1983
                      About
Kealing, B. Tupperware, unsealed   **338.7**
TUPPERWARE CORP.
Kealing, B. Tupperware, unsealed   **338.7**
Tupperware, unsealed. Kealing, B.   **338.7**
Turabian, Kate L.
A manual for writers of research papers, theses, and
dissertations   **808.06**
Student's guide to writing college papers   **808**
Turan, Kenneth
Free for all   **92**
Not to be missed   **791.43**
Turbo, Richard
Caring for your baby and young child   **618.92**
Turgenev, Ivan Sergeevich, 1818-1883
                      About
Nabokov, V. V. Lectures on Russian literature   **891.7**
Turgeon, Heather
The happy sleeper   **649**
Turin, Luca
The secret of scent   **668**
Turing. Copeland, B. J.   **92**
TURING MACHINES
Dyson, G. Turing's cathedral   **004**
Turing's cathedral. Dyson, G.   **004**
Turing, Alan Mathison, 1912-1954
                      About
Copeland, B. J. Turing   **92**
Dyson, G. Turing's cathedral   **004**
Leavitt, D. The man who knew too much   **92**
TURKEY -- ANTIQUITIES
Wood, M. In search of the Trojan War   **939**
TURKEY -- ANTIQUITIES
      See also Antiquities
TURKEY -- FOREIGN RELATIONS
Toumani, M. There was and there was not   **327**
**TURKEY -- FOREIGN RELATIONS -- GER-
MANY**
McMeekin, S. The Berlin-Baghdad express   **940.3**
TURKEY -- HISTORY
Finkel, C. Osman's dream   **956**
Mango, A. The Turks today   **956.1**
**TURKEY -- HISTORY -- OTTOMAN EMPIRE,
1288-1918**
Finkel, C. Osman's dream   **956**

Goodwin, J. Lords of the horizons **956.1**

Reston, J. Defenders of the faith **940.2**

TURKEY -- POLITICS AND GOVERNMENT

Kinzer, S. Crescent and star **956.1**

TURKEYS

See also Birds; Poultry

TURKISH COOKING

Algar, A. E. Classical Turkish cooking **641.59**

Roden, C. Arabesque: a taste of Morocco, Turkey, and Lebanon **641.5**

TURKISH POETRY -- COLLECTIONS

Music of a distant drum **808.81**

Turkle, Sherry

Alone together **303.4**

Reclaiming Conversation **302.23**

The **Turks** today. Mango, A. **956.1**

Turley, Richard E.

Walker, R. W. Massacre at Mountain Meadows **979.2**

Turman, Katherine

Louder Than Hell **781.66**

Turn left at Orion. Consolmagno, G. **520**

Turn right at Machu Picchu. Adams, M. **985**

Turnage, Wallace, d. 1916

About

Blight, D. W. A slave no more **326**

Turnbull, Gael

There are words **821**

TURNCOATS *See* Defectors

Turner, Alice K.

The history of hell **200**

Turner, Frederick

Renegade **813**

Turner, Henry Ashby

Hitler's thirty days to power **943.086**

Turner, Jane Shoaf

(ed) Encyclopedia of Latin American & Caribbean art **709**

Turner, Jessica Anderson

Yang Lihui Handbook of Chinese mythology **299.5**

Turner, John G.

Brigham Young, pioneer prophet **289.3**

Turner, Kristy

But I could never go **641.5**

Turner, Nancy J.

The North American guide to common poisonous plants and mushrooms **581.6**

Turner, Sharon

Teach yourself visually knitting **746.43**

Turner, Steve

The band that played on **910.4**

Turner, Ted, 1938-

About

Auletta, K. Media man **92**

Turner, Tina

About

Turner, T. I, Tina **92**

Turney, Chris

1912 **998**

Turney, Jon

(ed) Seeing further **506**

TURNING

See also Carpentry; Manufacturing processes

Turning points [series]

Edwards, B. Edward R. Murrow and the birth of broadcast journalism **92**

The **turnip** princess. **398.209**

Turo, Ann Marie

(jt. auth) Aaronson, N. Pilates for breast cancer survivors **616.99**

Turow, Joseph

The daily you **659.1**

Turow, Scott

Ultimate punishment **345**

Turshen, Julia

(jt. auth) Rodriguez, J. W. The Hot Bread Kitchen cookbook **641.59**

TURTLES

Safina, C. Voyage of the turtle **597.92**

TURTLES

See also Reptiles

TUSCANY (ITALY) -- SOCIAL LIFE AND CUSTOMS

Mayes, F. Under the Tuscan sun **945**

Tushnet, Mark

In the balance **347.73**

Tushnet, Mark V.

(ed) Marshall, T. Thurgood Marshall **347**

TUSKEGEE INSTITUTE

Harlan, L. R. Booker T. Washington: the making of a black leader, 1856-1901 **92**

Harlan, L. R. Booker T. Washington: the wizard of Tuskegee, 1901-1915 **92**

Norrell, R. J. Up from history **92**

Smock, R. W. Booker T. Washington **92**

Uncle Tom or new Negro **370**

Washington, B. T. Up from slavery **92**

Tusman, Jordana

(ed) Johnstone, C. F. Smart cookie **641.865**

Tutankhamen, King of Egypt

About

Brier, B. The murder of Tutankhamen **932**

Ceram, C. W. Gods, graves, and scholars **930.1**

Hawass, Z. A. Tutankhamun and the golden age of the pharaohs **932**

Tutankhamun and the golden age of the pharaohs. Hawass, Z. A. **932**

TUTKA BAY LODGE (ALASKA)

Dixon, K. The Tutka Bay Lodge cookbook **641.59**

The **Tutka** Bay Lodge cookbook. Dixon, K. **641.59**

TUTSI (AFRICAN PEOPLE)

Hatzfeld, J. The antelope's strategy **967.571**

Hatzfeld, J. Machete season   **967.571**

TUTSI (AFRICAN PEOPLE)
>*See also* Africans; Indigenous peoples

Tutu, Desmond, 1931-
>The book of forgiving   **179**
>Made for goodness   **170**
>No future without forgiveness   **968.06**
>The rainbow people of God   **968.06**

Tutu, Mpho A., 1963-
>The book of forgiving   **179**
>Made for goodness   **170**

TV (the book) Seitz, M. Z.   **791.45**

TV PERSONALITIES *See* Television personalities

Twain, Mark, 1835-1910
>Autobiography of Mark Twain   **92**
>Mark Twain's library of humor   **817**
>The wit and wisdom of Mark Twain   **818**

Twain, Mark, 1835-1910. Adventures of Huckleberry Finn
>#### About
>Nafisi, A. The Republic of Imagination   **819**

Tweedy, Damon
>Black Man in a White Coat   **92**

Twelve angry men. Rose, R.   **812**

Twelve breaths a minute.   **616**

The **twelve** Caesars.   **878**

Twelve patients. Manheimer, E.   **362.11**

Twelve Recipes. Peternell, C.   **641.5**

TWELVE STEPS (SELF-HELP) *See* Twelve-step programs

Twelve steps to a compassionate life. Armstrong, K.   **177**

Twelve years a slave.   **92**

TWELVE-STEP PROGRAMS
>Armstrong, K. Twelve steps to a compassionate life   **177**

TWELVE-STEP PROGRAMS
>*See also* Behavior modification

TWENTIETH CENTURY *See* World history -- 20th century

TWENTIETH CENTURY -- FORECASTS
>Gerson, S. Nostradamus   **92**

Twentieth century Latin American poetry.   **861**

Twentieth-century American poetry.   **811**

Twentieth-century American poetry. MacGowan, C. J.   **811**

Twentieth-century art of Latin America. Barnitz, J.   **709**

Twenty years at Hull-House. Addams, J.   **361.7**

Twenty-eight artists and two saints. Acocella, J. R.   **920**

TWENTY-FIRST CENTURY *See* World history -- 21st century

Twichell, Chase
>Horses where the answers should have been   **811**

Twigs & knucklebones. Lindsay, S.   **811**

Twilight children. Hayden, T. L.   **618.92**

Twilight of the elites. Hayes, C.   **305.5**

The **twilight** war. Crist, D.   **327**

Twins. Wright, L.   **155.44**

TWINS
>*See also* Multiple birth; Siblings

TWINS
>Agnew, C. L. Twins!   **649**
>Parravani, C. Her   **92**
>Wright, L. Twins   **155.44**

TWINS -- UNITED STATES -- BIOGRAPHY
>Parravani, C. Her   **92**

Twins! Agnew, C. L.   **649**

TWISTERS (TORNADOES) *See* Tornadoes

TWITTER (WEB SITE)
>Bilton, N. Hatching Twitter   **006.7**
>Simon, S. Unforgettable   **92**
>Stone, B. Things a little bird told me   **006.7**

TWITTER (WEB SITE)
>*See also* Social networking; Web sites

Two billion cars. Sperling, D.   **388.3**

Two days in June. Cohen, A.   **973.922**

Two hours. Caesar, E.   **796.42**

Two if by sea. Seaver, B.   **641.692**

The **two** kinds of decay. Manguso, S.   **362**

The **two** Koreas. Oberdorfer, D.   **951.9**

Two lives. Seth, V.   **92**

Two lives. Malcolm, J.   **92**

Two Moms in the Raw.   **641.5**

TWO MOMS IN THE RAW (FIRM)
>Two Moms in the Raw   **641.5**

Two trains running. Wilson, A.   **812**

Two years before the mast. Dana, R. H.   **910.4**

The **two** Yvonnes. Greenbaum, J.   **811**

TWO-PARTY SYSTEMS -- UNITED STATES
>Edwards, M. The parties versus the people   **320**

The **two-state** delusion. O'Malley, P.   **956.94**

TWO-YEAR COLLEGES *See* Junior colleges

Ty Cobb. Leerhsen, C.   **92**

TY, INC. -- HISTORY
>Bissonnette, Z. The great Beanie Baby bubble   **338.7**

Tye, Diane
>Baking as biography   **92**

Tye, Larry
>Bobby Kennedy   **92**
>Satchel   **92**

Tye, Laurene, 1931-1989
>#### About
>Tye, D. Baking as biography   **92**

Tygiel, Jules
>Baseball's great experiment   **796.357**

Tyler, Carol
>#### About
>Tyler, C. Soldier's heart   **741.5**

Tyler, John, 1790-1862

About

Crapol, E. P. John Tyler   92

May, G. John Tyler   92

Tyler, Peter

(ed) The Bloomsbury Guide to Christian Spirituality   270

Tymony, Cy

Sneaky math   510

Tynan, Tracy

About

Tynan, T. Wear and tear   92

Tyning, Thomas F.

A guide to amphibians and reptiles   597.9

TYPE AND TYPE FOUNDING See Type and
type-founding

TYPE AND TYPE-FOUNDING

Lupton, E. Thinking with type   686.2

Spiekermann, E. Stop Stealing Sheep and Find out
How Type Works   686.2

TYPE AND TYPE-FOUNDING

See also Founding; Printing

TYPE AND TYPE-FOUNDING -- HISTORY

Garfield, S. Just my type   686.2

Houston, K. Shady characters   411

The **typewriter** is holy. Morgan, B.   810

TYPHUS

Allen, A. The fantastic laboratory of Dr. Weigl   614.5

Talty, S. The illustrious dead   940.2

TYPHUS FEVER -- POLAND -- HISTORY

Allen, A. The fantastic laboratory of Dr. Wei-
gl   614.5

TYPOGRAPHY

Houston, K. Shady characters   411

Lupton, E. Thinking with type   686.2

Spiekermann, E. Stop Stealing Sheep and Find out
How Type Works   686.2

TYPOGRAPHY

See also Graphic arts; Printing

TYPOLOGY (PSYCHOLOGY)

See also Personality; Psychology; Temperament

The **Tyrannosaur** Chronicles. Hone, D.   567.91

TYRANNOSAURUS REX

See also Dinosaurs

Tyson, Mike, 1966-

About

Remnick, D. Reporting   814

Tyson, Neil deGrasse

Death by black hole   523.8

(jt. auth) Gott, J. R. Welcome to the universe   523.1

Origins: fourteen billion years of cosmic evolution   523.1

Space chronicles   629.4

(ed) Startalk   523.1

Tytell, John

Ezra Pound   92

U

U-550 (SUBMARINE)

Peffer, R. Where divers dare   940.54

U.S. Chess Federation's official rules of chess.   794.1

The **U.S.** Constitution A to Z. Maddex, R. L.   342

U.S. Department of Labor

Occupational outlook handbook 2013-2014   331.12

**U.S. FISH AND WILDLIFE SERVICE -- FO-
RENSICS LABORATORY**

Neme, L. A. Animal investigators   363.2

The **U.S.** House of Representatives. Spieler,
M.   328.73

U.S. Immigration Made Easy. Bray, I. M.   342

U.S. laws, acts, and treaties.   348

UAVS (UNMANNED AERIAL VEHICLES) *See*
Drone aircraft

UCHI (AUSTIN, TEX.: RESTAURANT)

Cole, T. Uchi: the cookbook   641.6

Uchi: the cookbook. Cole, T.   641.6

Udvardy, Miklos D. F.

National Audubon Society field guide to North
American birds, Western region   598

Uebbing, James J.

(ed) Love had a compass   811

UFOS *See* Unidentified flying objects

UGANDA

Chretien The great lakes of Africa   967.6

Rice, A. The teeth may smile but the heart does not
forget   967.6

Uglow, Jennifer S.

A gambling man   92

Nature's engraver   92

Ugly beauty. Brandon, R.   646.7

The **ugly** Renaissance. Lee, A.   945

Uhlberg, Myron

About

Uhlberg, M. Hands of my father   92

Uhlenbroek, Charlotte

(ed) Animal life   591.5

Ujifusa, Steven

A man and his ship   623.8

UKRAINE

Hercules, O. Mamushka   641.594

Ulander, Perry A., 1948-

About

Ulander, P. A. Walking point   959.704

Ulanski, Stan L.

The Gulf Stream   551.46

Ulianov, Aleksandr, 1886-1887

About

Pomper, P. Lenin's brother   92

Ullrich, Volker

Hitler   92

Ulrich, Laurel

Well-behaved women seldom make history   305.4

The **Ultimate** audition book.   808.82

Ultimate bar book. Hellmich, M. **641.8**

The **ultimate** bicycle owner's manual. Weiss, E. **796.6**

The **Ultimate** Book of Family Card Games. Ho, O. **795.4**

The **ultimate** book of modern juicing. Kirk, M. 663

Ultimate crochet bible. Crowfoot, J. **746.43**

Ultimate curry bible

Madhur Jaffrey's ultimate curry bible **641.5**

The **Ultimate** Encyclopedia of Aquarium Fish & Fish Care. Bailey, M. **639.34**

ULTIMATE FIGHTING CHAMPIONSHIP (ORGANIZATION)

Wertheim, L. J. Blood in the cage **92**

The **ultimate** guide to dog training. Anderson, T. **636.7**

Ultimate guide to plumbing.

Ultimate guide: home repair and improvement. **643**

Ultimate guide: porches. Cory, S. **690**

The **Ultimate** Jack the Ripper companion. **364.15**

The **ultimate** Picasso. Leal, B. **759**

Ultimate punishment. Turow, S. **345**

The **ultimate** quotable Einstein. Einstein, A. **530**

Ultimate Star wars. Wallace, D.

The **ultimate** student cookbook. Goodall, T. **641.5**

Ultimate travel. **910.2**

ULTRA-ORTHODOX JEWS -- NEW YORK (STATE) -- NEW YORK -- BIOGRAPHY

Vincent, L. Cut me loose **305.892**

ULTRASONICS

See also Sound

ULTRAVIOLET RAYS

See also Electromagnetic waves; Radiation

Ulysses and us. Kiberd, D. **823**

Ulysses S. Grant. Bunting, J. **92**

Ulysses S. Grant: the unlikely hero. Korda, M. **92**

Umbrell, Colby, 1981-2007

About

Sielski, M. Fading echoes **92**

UMBRELLAS AND PARASOLS

See also Clothing and dress

The **un-prescription** for Autism. Lintala, J. **616.85**

The **unabridged** journals of Sylvia Plath, 1950-1962. Plath, S. **818**

Unabrow. Lamarche, U. **92**

Unaccountable. Makary, M. **610.730**

UNAUTHORIZED IMMIGRANTS

Bacon, D. Illegal people **331.6**

Carr, M. Fortress Europe **363.28**

Keefe, P. R. The snakehead **364.1**

Padilla Peralta Undocumented **92**

Perez, W. We are Americans **371.82**

Thorpe, H. Just like us **305.8**

Truax, E. Dreamers **325**

Urrea, L. A. The devil's highway **325**

UNAUTHORIZED IMMIGRANTS

See also Immigration and emigration; Noncitizens

UNBELIEF *See* Skepticism

UNBORN CHILD *See* Fetus

Unbowed. Maathai, W. **92**

Unbroken. Hillenbrand, L. **940.54**

Uncentering the Earth. Vollmann, W. T. **92**

Uncertain justice. Tribe, L. H. **342.73**

Uncivil society. Kotkin, S. **947**

Uncle Tom or new Negro. **370**

Uncle Tungsten. Sacks, O. W. **616.8**

UNCLES

See also Family

Uncollected poems. Rilke, R. M. **831**

Uncommon arrangements. Roiphe, K. **920**

Uncommon carriers. McPhee, J. A. **388**

UNCONVENTIONAL WARFARE *See* Guerrilla warfare

The **uncrowned** king. Whyte, K. **92**

Undaunted courage. Ambrose, S. E. **917**

The **undead.** Teresi, D. **610**

Undecided. Morgan, G. **371.4**

Undeniable. Nye, B. **576.8**

Under a flaming sky. Brown, D. **634.9**

Under a wing. Lindbergh, R. **92**

Under and alone. Queen, W. **364.1**

Under another sky. Higgins, C. **936**

Under his very windows. Zuccotti, S. **940.53**

Under magnolia. Mayes, F. **92**

Under milk wood. Thomas, D. **822**

Under my skin. Lessing, D. M. **92**

Under the black flag. Cordingly, D. **910.4**

Under the same sky. Kim, J. **92**

Under the sea wind. Carson, R. **578.7**

Under the stars. White, D. **796.54**

Under the sun. **92**

Under the surface. Wilber, T. **333.8**

Under the Tuscan sun. Mayes, F. **945**

Under their thumb. German, B. **781.66**

UNDERACHIEVERS

See also Students

UNDERGRADUATES *See* College students

Underground. Rudd, M. **92**

Underground. Murakami, H. **364.1**

UNDERGROUND ARCHITECTURE

See also Architecture

UNDERGROUND ECONOMY

See also Economics; Small business

The **underground** girls of Kabul. Nordberg, J. **305.42**

Underground in Berlin. **940.531**

The **underground** is massive. Matos, M. **781.648**

UNDERGROUND LEADERS

Cohen, R. The avengers **940.53**

Humbert, A. Resistance **92**

Parssinen, T. M. The Oster conspiracy of

1938 **943.086**

UNDERGROUND LITERATURE *See* Alternative press

UNDERGROUND PRESS *See* Alternative press

The **Underground** Railroad. Walters, K. **973.7**

UNDERGROUND RAILROAD
Bordewich, F. M. Bound for Canaan **973.7**
Clinton, C. Harriet Tubman: the road to freedom **92**
Foner, E. Gateway to Freedom **973.7**
Humez, J. M. Harriet Tubman **92**
Larson, K. C. Bound for the promised land **92**
Smardz Frost, K. I've got a home in glory land **92**
Tobin, J. From Midnight to Dawn **322**
Tobin, J. Hidden in plain view **973.7**
The **Underground** Railroad. Snodgrass, M. E. **973.7**

UNDERGROUND RAILROAD -- ENCYCLOPE-DIAS
Walters, K. The Underground Railroad **973.7**

Underhill, Paco
The call of the mall **306**
Why we buy **658.8**

Understanding and managing your child's food allergies. Sicherer, S. H. **618.92**
Understanding celiac disease. Ali, N. **616.3**
Understanding comics. **741.5**
Understanding exposure. Peterson, B. **771**
Understanding garden design. Nagel, V. G. **712**
Understanding Iraq. Polk, W. R. **956.7**
Understanding Islam. Gordon, M. **297**
Understanding lung cancer. Ali, N. **616.99**
Understanding manga and anime. Brenner, R. E. **025.2**
Understanding media. **302.23**
Understanding pain. Lewis, M. **616**
Understanding perennials. Cullina, W. **635.9**
Understanding the Book of Mormon. Hardy, G. **289.3**
Understanding the world. Rendgen, S. **741.6**
Understanding wood. Hoadley, R. B. **684**
Understanding world religions. Hexham, I. **200**
The **undertaker's** daughter. Mayfield, K. **92**

UNDERTAKERS AND UNDERTAKING
Doughty, C. Smoke gets in your eyes **92**
Grant, G. M. At the elbows of my elders **920**
Jokinen, T. Curtains **393**
Mayfield, K. The undertaker's daughter **92**
Mitford, J. The American way of death revisited **338.4**

UNDERTAKERS AND UNDERTAKING -- AN-ECDOTES
Doughty, C. Smoke gets in your eyes **92**

UNDERWATER ARCHAEOLOGY -- NORTH ATLANTIC OCEAN
Peffer, R. Where divers dare **940.54**

UNDERWATER DRILLING (PETROLEUM)
See Offshore oil well drilling

UNDERWATER EXPLORATION
Ballard, R. D. The eternal darkness **551.46**
Beneath the seven seas **930.1**

UNDERWATER EXPLORATION
See also Exploration; Oceanography

UNDERWATER PHOTOGRAPHY
Rotman, J. L. The last fisherman **778.7**

UNDERWATER PHOTOGRAPHY
See also Photography

UNDERWATER SWIMMING *See* Skin diving

Underworld: the mysterious origins of civilization. Hancock, G. **551.7**

The **undiscovered** Paul Robeson. Robeson, P. **92**
The **undivided** past. Cannadine, D. **128**
Undocumented. Padilla Peralta **92**

UNDOCUMENTED ALIENS *See* Unauthorized immigrants

The **Undoing** Project. Lewis, M. **153**

Unell, Barbara C.
(jt. auth) Fertig, J. The back in the swing cookbook **641.5**

UNEMPLOYED
See also Labor supply; Poor; Unemployment

UNEMPLOYMENT
Jerrard, J. Crisis in employment **025.5**
Krugman, P. R. End this depression now! **330.9**

UNEMPLOYMENT -- UNITED STATES
Johnson, J. Where did the jobs go-- and how do we get them back? **331.1**

UNEMPLOYMENT -- UNITED STATES -- HIS-TORY -- 21ST CENTURY
Krugman, P. R. End this depression now! **330.9**

UNEMPLOYMENT INSURANCE
See also Insurance

UNESCO
(comp) World Heritage sites **910.2**

Unexpected afghans. Chachula, R. **746.43**
The **unexpected** houseplant. **635.9**
The **unexpected** legacy of divorce. Wallerstein, J. S. **306.89**
An **unexpected** light. Elliot, J. **958.1**
Unfair. Benforado, A. **364.3**

UNFAIR COMPETITION
See also Commercial law

Unfaithful Music & Disappearing Ink. Costello, E. **92**
Unfamiliar fishes. Vowell, S. **996.9**

Unferth, Deb Olin
About
Unferth, D. O. Revolution **920**

The **unfinished** game. Devlin, K. J. **519.2**
An **unfinished** life: John F. Kennedy, 1917-1963. Dallek, R. **92**
The **unfinished** poems. Cavafy, C. P. **889**
The **unfinished** revolution. **305.42**
Unforgettable. Simon, S. **92**

Unforgivable blackness. Ward, G. C.　**92**

Ung, Chou
About
Ung, L. Lucky child　**92**

Ung, Loung
First they killed my father　**959.6**
Lucky child　**92**

Unger, Debi
(jt. auth) Unger, I. George Marshall　**92**
(ed) The Times were a changin'　**973.923**

Unger, Harlow G.
The last founding father　**92**
Unger, H. G. American tempest　**973.3**

Unger, Harlow Giles
Giles Unger, H. John Quincy Adams　**92**
American tempest　**973.3**
John Marshall　**92**

Unger, Irwin
George Marshall　**92**
(ed) The Times were a changin'　**973.923**

Unger, Leonard
(ed) American writers　**920.003**

Unger, Miles J.
Machiavelli　**92**
Michelangelo　**92**

Ungern-Sternberg, Roman, 1885-1921
About
Palmer, J. The bloody white baron　**92**

Unholy business. Burleigh, N.　**933**

Unholy war. Esposito, J. L.　**322.4**

UNICELLULAR ORGANISMS
Nielsen, C. Animal evolution　**591.3**

UNICORNS
Lavers, C. The natural history of unicorns　**398.2**

UNICORNS
See also Mythical animals

UNIDENTIFIED FLYING OBJECTS
Bullard, T. E. The myth and mystery of UFOs　**001.9**
Davies, P. C. W. The eerie silence　**576.8**

UNIDENTIFIED FLYING OBJECTS
See also Aeronautics; Astronautics

UNIFIED FIELD THEORIES
Halpern, P. Einstein's dice and Schrödinger's cat　**530.13**

UNIFORMS
See also Clothing and dress; Costume

Unincorporated persons in the late Honda dynasty. Hoagland, T.　**811**

Union of Concerned Scientists
(comp) Shulman, S. Cooler smarter　**363.7**

UNION OF SOVIET SOCIALIST REPUBLICS
See Russia -- History -- 1917-1991, Soviet Union

UNION PACIFIC RAILROAD COMPANY
Ambrose, S. E. Nothing like it in the world　**385**
Bain, D. H. Empire express　**385**
The **union** war. Gallagher, G. W.　**973.7**

UNIONS, LABOR *See* Labor unions

Uniquely felt. White, C.　**746**

Uniquely human. Prizant, B. M.　**618.92**

UNITARIANISM
See also Christian sects; Congregationalism

UNITED FARM WORKERS OF AMERICA
Shaw, R. Beyond the fields　**331.8**

UNITED FRUIT COMPANY -- BIOGRAPHY
Cohen, R. The fish that ate the whale　**338.7**

UNITED NATIONS
Fasulo, L. M. An insider's guide to the UN　**341.23**
Mires, C. Capital of the world　**341.23**
Moore, J. A. Encyclopedia of the United Nations　**341.23**
Osmanczyk, E. J. Encyclopedia of the United Nations and international agreements　**341.23**

UNITED NATIONS -- ARMED FORCES -- KOREA
Hickey, M. The Korean War　**951.904**

UNITED NATIONS -- BIOGRAPHY
Annan, K. A. Interventions　**341.23**

UNITED NATIONS -- HEADQUARTERS
Mires, C. Capital of the world　**341.23**

UNITED NATIONS -- OFFICE OF IRAQ PROGRAMME -- OIL-FOR-FOOD PROGRAMME
Soussan, M. Backstabbing for beginners　**363.8**

UNITED NATIONS EMPLOYEES
Bolkovac, K. The whistleblower　**92**

UNITED NATIONS RELIEF AND REHABILITATION ADMINISTRATION
Shephard, B. The long road home　**940.53**

UNITED PRESS INTERNATIONAL -- BIOGRAPHY
Cronkite, W. Cronkite's war　**070.4**

UNITED STATES
Lerner, S. Sacrifice zones　**363.738**
Moreno, J. D. The body politic　**303.48**

UNITED STATES (STEAMSHIP)
Ujifusa, S. A man and his ship　**623.8**

UNITED STATES -- ADVANCED RESEARCH PROJECTS AGENCY
Belfiore, M. The department of mad scientists　**355**

UNITED STATES -- ANTIQUITIES
Holzer, H. The Civil War in 50 objects　**973.7**

UNITED STATES -- ANTIQUITIES
See also Antiquities

UNITED STATES -- ANTIQUITIES -- COLLECTION AND PRESERVATION -- HISTORY
Puleo, S. American treasures　**973**

UNITED STATES -- APPROPRIATIONS AND EXPENDITURES
Johnson, S. White House burning　**336.3**
Kleinbard, E. D. We are better than this　**336.3**
Kramer, M. A people's guide to the federal budget　**352.4**

UNITED STATES -- ARMED FORCES
Axelrod, A. Whiskey tango foxtrot **427**
Klein, M. A call to arms **940.53**
Wildsmith, S. Joining the United States Air Force **358.4**
UNITED STATES -- ARMED FORCES -- AP-PROPRIATIONS AND EXPENDITURES
Maddow, R. Drift **306.2**
UNITED STATES -- ARMED FORCES -- ENCY-CLOPEDIAS
Axelrod, A. The encyclopedia of the American armed forces **355**
Sutherland, J. African Americans at war **355**
UNITED STATES -- ARMED FORCES -- GAYS
See Gays and lesbians in the military
UNITED STATES -- ARMED FORCES -- IRAQ -- HISTORY
Gordon, M. R. The endgame **956.7**
UNITED STATES -- ARMED FORCES -- MILI-TARY LIFE
Voices of war **355**
UNITED STATES -- ARMED FORCES -- MILI-TARY LIFE
See also Military personnel
UNITED STATES -- ARMED FORCES -- MILI-TARY LIFE -- HANDBOOKS, MANUALS, ETC
Scott, J. Raising children in the military **355.1**
UNITED STATES -- ARMED FORCES -- MOBI-LIZATION -- HISTORY -- 20TH CENTURY
Klein, M. A call to arms **940.53**
UNITED STATES -- ARMY AIR FORCES
Nelson, C. The first heroes **940.54**
UNITED STATES -- BIOGRAPHY
Cooper, A. Saving Alex **92**
Fraser, F. The Washingtons **92**
Kendall, J. America's obsessives **609.2**
Ward, G. C. A disposition to be rich **974.7**
UNITED STATES -- BIOGRAPHY
See also Biography
UNITED STATES -- BIOGRAPHY -- DICTION-ARIES
Garraty, J.A. American national biography **920.003**
Notable American women: the modern period **920.003**
Notable black American men, book I **920.003**
Notable black American men, book II **920.003**
Notable black American women, book I **920.003**
Notable black American women, Book III **920.003**
The Scribner encyclopedia of American lives **920.003**
The Scribner encyclopedia of American lives, The 1960s **920.003**
Ware, S. Notable American women **920.003**
Who was who in America **920.003**
Who's who in America, 2008 **920.003**

Who's who of American women 2007 **920.003**
UNITED STATES -- BOUNDARIES
See also Boundaries
UNITED STATES -- BUDGET *See* Budget -- United States
UNITED STATES -- CENSUS
Peake, R. Mapping Census 2010 **304.6**
The who, what, and where of America **317.3**
UNITED STATES -- CENSUS -- ENCYCLOPE-DIAS
Encyclopedia of the U.S. Census **304.6**
UNITED STATES -- CENSUS, 23RD, 2010 -- MAPS
Peake, R. Mapping Census 2010 **304.6**
UNITED STATES -- CHURCH AND STATE *See* Church and state -- United States
UNITED STATES -- CHURCH HISTORY
Ahlstrom, S. E. A religious history of the American people **200**
Blum, E. J. The color of Christ **232**
Schmidt, L. E. The religious history of America **200.973**
Yancey, P. Vanishing grace **277**
UNITED STATES -- CHURCH HISTORY
See also Church history
UNITED STATES -- CHURCH HISTORY -- 20TH CENTURY
Sutton, M. A. American apocalypse **277.3**
UNITED STATES -- CITIES AND TOWNS *See* Cities and towns -- United States
UNITED STATES -- CIVILIZATION
Cheever, S. Drinking in America **394.1**
Huckelbridge, D. The United States of beer **641.23**
Robinson, M. When I was a child I read books **814**
UNITED STATES -- CIVILIZATION
See also Civilization
UNITED STATES -- CIVILIZATION -- 1783-1865
Brands, H. W. The Age of Gold **979.4**
Wood, G. S. Empire of liberty **973.4**
UNITED STATES -- CIVILIZATION -- 17TH CENTURY
Barry, J. M. Roger Williams and the creation of the American soul **974.5**
UNITED STATES -- CIVILIZATION -- 1865-1918
Lears, T. J. J. Rebirth of a nation **973.8**
McFarland, P. Mark Twain and the Colonel **973.8**
UNITED STATES -- CIVILIZATION -- 1945-
The 50s **973**
UNITED STATES -- CIVILIZATION -- 1970-
Burrough, B. Days of Rage **303.48**
Klosterman, C. But What If We're Wrong? **909.83**
UNITED STATES -- CIVILIZATION -- 20TH CENTURY -- LITERARY COLLECTIONS
Bohemians, bootleggers, flappers, and swells **810.8**
UNITED STATES -- CIVILIZATION -- ENCY-CLOPEDIAS

Postwar America   **973.92**

St. James encyclopedia of popular culture   **973.9**

UNITED STATES -- CIVILIZATION -- FRENCH INFLUENCES

Kaplan, A. Dreaming in French   **944**

UNITED STATES -- CIVILIZATION -- PHILOSOPHY

Robinson, M. When I was a child I read books **814**

UNITED STATES -- CLIMATE

See also Climate

UNITED STATES -- COLONIZATION

Dunbar-Ortiz, R. An indigenous peoples' history of the United States   **970.004**

UNITED STATES -- COMMERCE -- CHINA -- HISTORY -- 18TH CENTURY

Dolin, E. J. When America first met China   **382**

UNITED STATES -- COMMERCE -- CHINA -- HISTORY -- 19TH CENTURY

Dolin, E. J. When America first met China   **382**

UNITED STATES -- CONSTITUTIONAL CONVENTION (1787)

Beeman, R. Plain, honest men   **342**

Berkin, C. A brilliant solution   **342**

Kauffman, B. Forgotten founder, drunken prophet   **92**

Madison, J. The Constitutional Convention   **342**

UNITED STATES -- CONSTITUTIONAL HISTORY *See* Constitutional history -- United States

UNITED STATES -- CONSTITUTIONAL LAW *See* Constitutional law -- United States

UNITED STATES -- CONTINENTAL ARMY

Fleming, T. J. Washington's secret war   **973.3**

Lockhart, P. D. The whites of their eyes   **973.3**

UNITED STATES -- CONTINENTAL CONGRESS

Hogeland, W. Declaration   **973.3**

UNITED STATES -- DECLARATION OF INDEPENDENCE

The annotated U.S. Constitution and Declaration of Independence   **342**

Becker, C. The Declaration of Independence **973.3**

Hogeland, W. Declaration   **973.3**

Maier, P. American scripture   **973.3**

UNITED STATES -- DESCRIPTION *See* United States -- Description and travel

UNITED STATES -- DESCRIPTION AND TRAVEL

Deep South   **975**

Glass, B. D. 50 great American places   **973**

The open road   **770**

UNITED STATES -- DESCRIPTION AND TRAVEL

See also Geography

UNITED STATES -- DESCRIPTION AND TRAVEL -- GUIDEBOOKS *See* United States -- Guidebooks

UNITED STATES -- DESCRIPTION AND TRAVEL -- PICTORIAL WORKS

The open road   **770**

UNITED STATES -- ECONOMIC CONDITIONS

Barlett, D. L. The betrayal of the American dream   **330.973**

Bernanke, B. The Courage to Act   **92**

Blinder, A. S. After the music stopped   **330.973**

Carbone, J. Marriage markets   **306.85**

Cox, H. H. American drive   **338**

The economists' voice 2.0   **330.9**

Garson, B. Down the up escalator   **339.2**

The great divergence   **339.2**

Johnson, J. Where did the jobs go-- and how do we get them back?   **331.1**

Krugman, P. R. End this depression now!   **330.9**

Kunstler, J. H. Too much magic   **303.48**

Lind, M. Land of promise   **330.973**

Packer, G. The unwinding   **973.924**

Patterson, J. T. Grand expectations   **973.92**

Zinn, H. The historic unfullfilled promise **973.924**

UNITED STATES -- ECONOMIC CONDITIONS

See also Economic conditions

UNITED STATES -- ECONOMIC CONDITIONS -- 1918-1945

Dickstein, M. Dancing in the dark   **973.91**

Golay, M. America 1933   **973.917**

UNITED STATES -- ECONOMIC CONDITIONS -- 1919-1933

Katznelson, I. Fear itself   **973.917**

Shlaes, A. Coolidge   **92**

UNITED STATES -- ECONOMIC CONDITIONS -- 1933-1945

Herman, A. Freedom's forge   **940.53**

UNITED STATES -- ECONOMIC CONDITIONS -- 1945-

American empire, 1945-2000   **973.92**

Greenspan, A. The age of turbulence   **92**

Murray, C. Coming apart   **305.8**

UNITED STATES -- ECONOMIC CONDITIONS -- 2001-2009

Lewis, M. The big short   **330.9**

UNITED STATES -- ECONOMIC CONDITIONS -- 2009-

Stone, J. M. Five easy theses   **330.973**

UNITED STATES -- ECONOMIC CONDITIONS -- 20TH CENTURY

American empire, 1945-2000   **973.92**

Burgin, A. The great persuasion   **330.12**

UNITED STATES -- ECONOMIC CONDITIONS -- 21ST CENTURY

Hayes, C. Twilight of the elites   **305.5**

Rajan, R. G. Fault lines   **330.9**

Sachs, J. The price of civilization   **330.9**

Stiglitz, J. E. The price of inequality   **305.5**

UNITED STATES -- ECONOMIC POLICY

Ferguson, C. Predator nation 330.973
McCraw, T. K. The founders and finance 330.973
Reich, R. B. Aftershock 330.9
Speth, J. G. America the possible 338.9

UNITED STATES -- ECONOMIC POLICY See
Economic policy -- United States

**UNITED STATES -- ECONOMIC POLICY --
1933-1945**
Dickstein, M. Dancing in the dark 973.91
Herman, A. Freedom's forge 940.53
Klein, M. A call to arms 940.53

**UNITED STATES -- ECONOMIC POLICY --
1961-1971**
Woods, R. B. Prisoners of hope 973.923

**UNITED STATES -- ECONOMIC POLICY --
2001-2009**
Lowenstein, R. The end of Wall Street 332.6
Madrick, J. G. Age of greed 330.9
Sorkin, A. R. Too big to fail 330.9

**UNITED STATES -- ECONOMIC POLICY --
2009-**
Blinder, A. S. After the music stopped 330.973
Sachs, J. The price of civilization 330.9
Stone, J. M. Five easy theses 330.973
Sunstein, C. R. Simpler 973.932

**UNITED STATES -- ECONOMIC POLICY --
20TH CENTURY**
Madrick, J. G. Age of greed 330.9

**UNITED STATES -- ECONOMIC POLICY --
21ST CENTURY**
Nader, R. Told you so 303.3

**UNITED STATES -- EMIGRATION AND IMMI-
GRATION**
Keefe, P. R. The snakehead 364.1

**UNITED STATES -- EMIGRATION AND IMMI-
GRATION** See United States -- Immigration and
emigration

**UNITED STATES -- EMIGRATION AND IMMI-
GRATION -- HISTORY**
Berlin, I. The making of African America 305.8
Cannato, V. J. American passage 325
Lee, E. The making of Asian America 973

**UNITED STATES -- EMIGRATION AND IMMI-
GRATION -- SOCIAL ASPECTS**
Grande, R. The distance between us 92
Truax, E. Dreamers 325

**UNITED STATES -- ENVIRONMENTAL CON-
DITIONS**
McGraw, S. Betting the farm on a drought 363.738

**UNITED STATES -- ENVIRONMENTAL CON-
DITIONS -- HISTORY -- 20TH CENTURY**
Coe, A. A square meal 641.5

UNITED STATES -- ETHNIC RELATIONS
Barrett, P. M. American Islam 920
Morales, E. Living in Spanglish 305.868
Slotkin, R. Lost battalions 940.3

**UNITED STATES -- ETHNIC RELATIONS --
HISTORY**
Goldwag, A. The new hate 306.2

UNITED STATES -- EXECUTIVE POWER See
Executive power -- United States

UNITED STATES -- EXPLORATION
See also America -- Exploration; Exploration

**UNITED STATES -- EXPLORING EXPEDI-
TIONS**
Sides, H. In the kingdom of ice 910.4
Stark, P. Astoria 978

**UNITED STATES -- EXPLORING EXPEDI-
TIONS**
See also Explorers

**UNITED STATES -- FOREIGN ECONOMIC
RELATIONS**
Dolin, E. J. When America first met China 382

**UNITED STATES -- FOREIGN ECONOMIC
RELATIONS**
See also International economic relations

UNITED STATES -- FOREIGN OPINION
Esposito, J. L. Unholy war 322.4

UNITED STATES -- FOREIGN OPINION
See also Public opinion

UNITED STATES -- FOREIGN POLICY See
United States -- Foreign relations

UNITED STATES -- FOREIGN POPULATION
See Immigrants -- United States; Noncitizens --
United States

**UNITED STATES -- FOREIGN PUBLIC OPIN-
ION, EUROPEAN -- HISTORY**
Temkin, M. The Sacco-Vanzetti Affair 345

UNITED STATES -- FOREIGN RELATIONS
Clinton, H. R. Hard choices 92
Feingold, R. While America sleeps 327
Gaddis, J. L. George F. Kennan 327
Grandin, G. Kissinger's Shadow 327.2
Haass, R. N. Foreign policy begins at home 327.73
Preston, A. Sword of the spirit, shield of faith 322
Simon, J. F. FDR and Chief Justice Hughes 973.917
Wright, L. The terror years 363.325

UNITED STATES -- FOREIGN RELATIONS
See also Diplomacy; International relations;
World politics

**UNITED STATES -- FOREIGN RELATIONS --
1775-1783**
Gould, E. H. Among the powers of the earth 973.3

**UNITED STATES -- FOREIGN RELATIONS --
1783-1865**
Traub, J. John Quincy Adams 92

**UNITED STATES -- FOREIGN RELATIONS --
1815-1861**
Howe, D. W. What hath God wrought 973.5

**UNITED STATES -- FOREIGN RELATIONS --
1861-1865**
Stahr, W. Seward 92

UNITED STATES -- FOREIGN RELATIONS -- 1913-1921

Neu, C. E.   Colonel House   92

UNITED STATES -- FOREIGN RELATIONS -- 1933-1945

Beschloss, M. R.   The conquerors: Roosevelt, Truman, and the destruction of Hitler's Germany, 1941-1945   940.53

Fullilove, M.   Rendezvous with destiny   973.917

Lelyveld, J.   His final battle   92

Moe, R.   Roosevelt's second act   973.917

Olson, L.   Those angry days   940.53

UNITED STATES -- FOREIGN RELATIONS -- 1945-1953

Gordin, M. D.   Red cloud at dawn   355

UNITED STATES -- FOREIGN RELATIONS -- 1945-1989

American empire, 1945-2000   973.92

Dallek, R.   Nixon and Kissinger   92

Lichtblau, E.   The Nazis next door   324.1

Miraldi, R.   Seymour Hersh   92

Ross, D. B.   Doomed to succeed   327.73

Thompson, N.   The hawk and the dove   92

UNITED STATES -- FOREIGN RELATIONS -- 1953-1961

Thomas, E.   Ike's bluff   973.92

UNITED STATES -- FOREIGN RELATIONS -- 1961-1963

Coleman, D. G.   The fourteenth day   73.922

Freedman, L.   Kennedy's wars   973.922

UNITED STATES -- FOREIGN RELATIONS -- 1969-1974

Bass, G. J.   The Blood telegram   327.73

Kissinger, H.   Years of renewal   973.924

UNITED STATES -- FOREIGN RELATIONS -- 1969-1974 -- SOURCES

The Nixon tapes   973.924

UNITED STATES -- FOREIGN RELATIONS -- 1977-1981

Wright, L.   Thirteen Days in September   956.04

UNITED STATES -- FOREIGN RELATIONS -- 1981-1989

Crist, D.   The twilight war   327

FitzGerald, F.   Way out there in the blue   973.927

Reeves, R.   President Reagan: the triumph of imagination   973.927

Service, R.   The End of the Cold War, 1985-1991   909.82

Zinn, H.   The historic unfullfilled promise   973.924

UNITED STATES -- FOREIGN RELATIONS -- 1989-

American empire, 1945-2000   973.92

Crist, D.   The twilight war   327

Maddow, R.   Drift   306.2

Miraldi, R.   Seymour Hersh   92

Ross, D. B.   Doomed to succeed   327.73

Zinn, H.   The historic unfullfilled promise   973.924

UNITED STATES -- FOREIGN RELATIONS -- 2001-

Bobbitt, P.   Terror and consent   363.32

Leverett, F.   Going to Tehran   327.73

Ramo, J. C.   The age of the unthinkable   973.931

UNITED STATES -- FOREIGN RELATIONS -- 2001-2009

Rice, C.   No higher honor   327.73

The WikiLeaks files   327.73

UNITED STATES -- FOREIGN RELATIONS -- 2009-

Hersh, S.   The killing of Osama Bin Laden   327.73

The WikiLeaks files   327.73

UNITED STATES -- FOREIGN RELATIONS -- 21ST CENTURY -- FORECASTING

Brzezinski, Z.   Strategic vision   327.1

UNITED STATES -- FOREIGN RELATIONS -- AFGHANISTAN

Partlow, J.   A kingdom of their own   958.104

UNITED STATES -- FOREIGN RELATIONS -- BIBLIOGRAPHY

American foreign relations since 1600   016

UNITED STATES -- FOREIGN RELATIONS -- CARIBBEAN REGION

Von Tunzelmann, A.   Red heat   972.9

UNITED STATES -- FOREIGN RELATIONS -- CENTRAL ASIA

Rashid, A.   Descent into chaos   954

UNITED STATES -- FOREIGN RELATIONS -- CHINA

Bernstein, R.   China 1945   327.73

Laird, T.   Into Tibet   327.12

Tuchman, B. W.   Practicing history   907

Tuchman, B. W.   Stilwell and the American experience in China, 1911-45   327

UNITED STATES -- FOREIGN RELATIONS -- CUBA

Craig, W.   Yankee come home   917.2

UNITED STATES -- FOREIGN RELATIONS -- DECISION MAKING

Bacevich, A. J.   Washington rules   355

UNITED STATES -- FOREIGN RELATIONS -- EAST AFRICA

Shachtman, T.   Airlift to America   378.1

UNITED STATES -- FOREIGN RELATIONS -- EUROPE

De Grazia, V.   Irresistible empire   306

UNITED STATES -- FOREIGN RELATIONS -- FRANCE

Khan, Y. S.   Enlightening the world   974.7

UNITED STATES -- FOREIGN RELATIONS -- GERMANY

Beschloss, M. R.   The conquerors: Roosevelt, Truman, and the destruction of Hitler's Germany, 1941-1945   940.53

Zinn, H.   The historic unfullfilled promise   973.924

UNITED STATES -- FOREIGN RELATIONS -- GREAT BRITAIN

Barr, N. Eisenhower's Armies   **940.53**

Bunker, N. An empire on the edge   **973.3**

Phillips, K. 1775   **973.3**

Snow, P. When Britain burned the White House   **975.3**

UNITED STATES -- FOREIGN RELATIONS -- INDIAN OCEAN REGION

Kaplan, R. D. Monsoon   **327**

UNITED STATES -- FOREIGN RELATIONS -- IRAN

Baglio, M. Argo   **955.05**

Crist, D. The twilight war   **327**

Pollack, K. M. Unthinkable   **355.8**

UNITED STATES -- FOREIGN RELATIONS -- IRAQ

Gordon, M. R. The endgame   **956.7**

UNITED STATES -- FOREIGN RELATIONS -- ISLAMIC COUNTRIES

Nasr, V. The dispensable nation   **327.73**

UNITED STATES -- FOREIGN RELATIONS -- ISRAEL

Ross, D. B. Doomed to succeed   **327.73**

UNITED STATES -- FOREIGN RELATIONS -- JAPAN

Nimura, J. P. Daughters of the Samurai   **920.72**

UNITED STATES -- FOREIGN RELATIONS -- KOREA (NORTH)

Harden, B. The Great Leader and the Fighter Pilot   **92**

UNITED STATES -- FOREIGN RELATIONS -- MIDDLE EAST

Bacevich, A. J. America's war for the greater Middle East   **956.054**

Haass, R. War of necessity: war of choice   **956.7**

Miller, A. D. The much too promised land   **956.05**

Nasr, V. The dispensable nation   **327.73**

UNITED STATES -- FOREIGN RELATIONS -- PAKISTAN

Gall, C. The wrong enemy   **958.104**

UNITED STATES -- FOREIGN RELATIONS -- PHILIPPINES

Karnow, S. In our image   **959.9**

UNITED STATES -- FOREIGN RELATIONS -- RELIGIOUS ASPECTS

Preston, A. Sword of the spirit, shield of faith   **322**

UNITED STATES -- FOREIGN RELATIONS -- RUSSIA

Cook, J. H. American phoenix   **973.5**

UNITED STATES -- FOREIGN RELATIONS -- SOUTH ASIA

Bass, G. J. The Blood telegram   **327.73**

UNITED STATES -- FOREIGN RELATIONS -- SOVIET UNION

Coleman, D. G. The fourteenth day   **73.922**

Service, R. The End of the Cold War, 1985-1991   **909.82**

UNITED STATES -- FOREIGN RELATIONS -- TREATIES

U.S. laws, acts, and treaties   **348**

UNITED STATES -- FOREIGN RELATIONS -- TREATIES

See also Treaties

UNITED STATES -- FOREIGN RELATIONS -- VIETNAM

Logevall, F. Embers of War   **959.704**

UNITED STATES -- FOREIGN RELATIONS -- VIETNAM (REPUBLIC)

Miller, E. Misalliance   **959.704**

UNITED STATES -- GAZETTEERS

Hellmann, P. T. Historical gazetteer of the United States   **911**

UNITED STATES -- GAZETTEERS

See also Gazetteers

UNITED STATES -- GENEALOGY -- ANECDOTES

McCarthy, A. Journeys home   **929.1**

UNITED STATES -- GENEALOGY -- HANDBOOKS, MANUALS, ETC

Croom, E. A. The genealogist's companion and sourcebook   **929**

McCarthy, A. Journeys home   **929.1**

UNITED STATES -- GEOGRAPHY

See also Geography

UNITED STATES -- GEOGRAPHY -- ENCYCLOPEDIAS

Encyclopedia of rural America   **973**

UNITED STATES -- GOVERNMENT *See* United States -- Politics and government

UNITED STATES -- GOVERNMENTAL INVESTIGATIONS *See* Governmental investigations -- United States

UNITED STATES -- GUIDEBOOKS

National Geographic Guide to the State Parks of the United States   **917.3**

UNITED STATES -- HISTORIC BUILDINGS *See* Historic buildings -- United States

UNITED STATES -- HISTORICAL GEOGRAPHY

See also Historical geography

UNITED STATES -- HISTORICAL GEOGRAPHY -- DICTIONARIES

Hellmann, P. T. Historical gazetteer of the United States   **911**

UNITED STATES -- HISTORICAL GEOGRAPHY -- MAPS

Hayes, D. Historical atlas of the United States   **911**

UNITED STATES -- HISTORIOGRAPHY

Bailyn, B. Sometimes an art, never a science, always a craft   **907.2**

UNITED STATES -- HISTORIOGRAPHY

See also Historiography

UNITED STATES -- HISTORY

Baglio, M. Argo   **955.05**

Beeman, R. R. Our lives, our fortunes and our sacred honor   **973.3**

Chronology of the U.S. presidency   **973.09**

Dolin, E. J. When America first met China   **382**

Gilmore, G. E. These United States   **973.9**

Haley, J. L. Captive paradise   **996.9**

Han, L. C. Handbook to American democracy   **320.4**

Koppel, L. The Astronaut Wives Club   **629.45**

Lepore, J. The story of America   **973**

Lind, M. Land of promise   **330.973**

Mires, C. Capital of the world   **341.23**

Nielsen, K. E. A disability history of the United States   **362.4**

Randall, D. K. The King and Queen of Malibu   **979.4**

Turner, F. Renegade   **813**

Warren, W. New England Bound   **306.362**

Wineapple, B. Ecstatic nation   **973.6**

Young, R. Dissent   **303.48**

UNITED STATES -- HISTORY -- 1600-1775, COLONIAL PERIOD

Bailyn, B. The barbarous years   **973.2**

Barry, J. M. Roger Williams and the creation of the American soul   **974.5**

Bunker, N. An empire on the edge   **973.3**

Dunbar-Ortiz, R. An indigenous peoples' history of the United States   **970.004**

Pressly, P. M. On the rim of the Caribbean   **975.8**

Taylor, A. American Revolutions   **973.3**

UNITED STATES -- HISTORY -- 1600-1775, COLONIAL PERIOD -- ENCYCLOPEDIAS

Encyclopedia of the new American nation   **973**

UNITED STATES -- HISTORY -- 1755-1763, FRENCH AND INDIAN WAR

Cohen, E. A. Conquered into liberty   **355**

Fowler, W. M. Empires at war   **973.2**

UNITED STATES -- HISTORY -- 1755-1763, FRENCH AND INDIAN WAR

   See also Native Americans -- Wars; Seven Years' War, 1756-1763; United States -- History -- 1600-1775, Colonial period

UNITED STATES -- HISTORY -- 1775-1783, REVOLUTION

Beck, D. W. The war before independence, 1775-1776   **973.3**

Borneman, W. R. American spring   **973.3**

Daughan, G. C. Revolution on the Hudson   **974.73**

DuVal, K. Independence Lost   **973.3**

Ellis, J. J. Revolutionary summer   **973.3**

Ferling, J. Whirlwind   **973.3**

Gordon-Reed, A. Most Blessed of the Patriarchs   **92**

Gould, E. H. Among the powers of the earth   **973.3**

Kamensky, J. A revolution in color   **759.13**

McKean, D. Suspected of independence   **92**

Nagy, J. A. George Washington's secret spy war   **973.385**

O'Donnell, P. K. Washington's Immortals   **973.3**

Parkinson, R. G. The common cause   **973.31**

Philbrick, N. Bunker Hill   **973.3**

Philbrick, N. Valiant Ambition   **973.3**

Phillips, K. 1775   **973.3**

Raphael, R. The spirit of 74   **973.3**

Staiti, P. Of Arms and Artists   **759.13**

Taylor, A. American Revolutions   **973.3**

Vowell, S. Lafayette in the Somewhat United States   **973.3**

Yaeger, D. George Washington's secret six   **973.4**

UNITED STATES -- HISTORY -- 1775-1783, REVOLUTION

   See also Revolutions

UNITED STATES -- HISTORY -- 1775-1783, REVOLUTION -- CAMPAIGNS

Fischer, D. H. Washington's crossing   **973.3**

Fleming, T. J. Washington's secret war   **973.3**

UNITED STATES -- HISTORY -- 1775-1783, REVOLUTION -- CAUSES

Bunker, N. An empire on the edge   **973.3**

UNITED STATES -- HISTORY -- 1775-1783, REVOLUTION -- ENCYCLOPEDIAS

Encyclopedia of the new American nation   **973**

UNITED STATES -- HISTORY -- 1775-1865

Berg, S. W. 38 nooses   **973.7**

Wiencek, H. Master of the mountain   **973.4**

UNITED STATES -- HISTORY -- 1783-1809

Ellis, J. J. American creation   **973.3**

Ellis, J. J. Founding brothers   **973.4**

The Louisiana Purchase   **973.4**

Miller, J. C. The Federalist era, 1789-1801   **973.4**

Morgan, E. S. American heroes   **920**

Morgan, E. S. The birth of the Republic, 1763-89   **973.3**

Winik, J. The great upheaval   **909.7**

UNITED STATES -- HISTORY -- 1783-1809 *See* United States -- History -- 1783-1815

UNITED STATES -- HISTORY -- 1783-1815

Taylor, A. The internal enemy   **975.5**

UNITED STATES -- HISTORY -- 1783-1865

Kelly, J. Heaven's ditch   **386**

Nathans, S. To free a family   **306.3**

UNITED STATES -- HISTORY -- 1783-1865 -- ENCYCLOPEDIAS

Encyclopedia of the new American nation   **973**

UNITED STATES -- HISTORY -- 17TH CENTURY

Barry, J. M. Roger Williams and the creation of the American soul   **974.5**

UNITED STATES -- HISTORY -- 1801-1805, TRIPOLITAN WAR

Zacks, R. The pirate coast **973.4**

UNITED STATES -- HISTORY -- 1812-1815, WAR OF 1812 See War of 1812

UNITED STATES -- HISTORY -- 1815-1861
Gugliotta, G. Freedom's cap **975.3**

UNITED STATES -- HISTORY -- 1815-1861 -- BIOGRAPHY
Roberts, C. Capital dames **793.7**
Roberts, C. Ladies of liberty **920**

UNITED STATES -- HISTORY -- 1845-1848, WAR WITH MEXICO See Mexican War, 1846-1848

UNITED STATES -- HISTORY -- 1849-1877
Gugliotta, G. Freedom's cap **975.3**
Wineapple, B. Ecstatic nation **973.6**

UNITED STATES -- HISTORY -- 1861-1865, CIVIL WAR -- BIOGRAPHY
Horn, J. The Man Who Would Not Be Washington **92**
Marvel, W. Lincoln's autocrat **92**

UNITED STATES -- HISTORY -- 1861-1865, CIVIL WAR -- BIOGRAPHY
See also Biography

UNITED STATES -- HISTORY -- 1861-1865, CIVIL WAR -- BIOGRAPHY -- DICTIONARIES
Leaders of the American Civil War **973.7**

UNITED STATES -- HISTORY -- 1861-1865, CIVIL WAR -- CAMPAIGNS
Groom, W. Shiloh, 1862 **973.7**
Wheelan, J. Terrible swift sword **355.009**

UNITED STATES -- HISTORY -- 1861-1865, CIVIL WAR -- CAUSES
The Causes of the Civil War **973.7**
Detzer, D. Allegiance **973.7**
Egerton, D. R. Year of meteors **973.7**
Goldfield, D. R. America aflame **973.7**
Goodheart, A. 1861 **973.7**
Klein, M. Days of defiance **973.7**
Oates, S. B. The approaching fury **973.5**

UNITED STATES -- HISTORY -- 1861-1865, CIVIL WAR -- CAUSES
See also Secession -- Southern States

UNITED STATES -- HISTORY -- 1861-1865, CIVIL WAR -- ENCYCLOPEDIAS
Boatner, M. M. The Civil War dictionary **973.7**
Encyclopedia of the American Civil War **973.7**

UNITED STATES -- HISTORY -- 1861-1865, CIVIL WAR -- HISTORIOGRAPHY
Blight, D. W. American oracle **973.7**
Gallagher, G. W. The Confederate War **973.7**

UNITED STATES -- HISTORY -- 1861-1865, CIVIL WAR -- HISTORIOGRAPHY
See also Historiography

UNITED STATES -- HISTORY -- 1861-1865, CIVIL WAR -- MAPS

Atlas of the Civil War **973.7**
Swanson, M. Atlas of the Civil War, month by month **973.7**
Woodworth, S. E. Atlas of the Civil War **973.7**

UNITED STATES -- HISTORY -- 1861-1865, CIVIL WAR -- MEDICAL CARE
See also Medical care

UNITED STATES -- HISTORY -- 1861-1865, CIVIL WAR -- NAVAL OPERATIONS
Symonds, C. L. Lincoln and his admirals **92**

UNITED STATES -- HISTORY -- 1861-1865, CIVIL WAR -- PERSONAL NARRATIVES
Katz, H. L. Civil War sketch book **973.7**

UNITED STATES -- HISTORY -- 1861-1865, CIVIL WAR -- PHOTOGRAPHY
Wilson, R. Mathew Brady **770.92**

UNITED STATES -- HISTORY -- 1861-1865, CIVIL WAR -- PICTORIAL WORKS
Harvey, E. J. The Civil War and American art **709**
Katz, H. L. Civil War sketch book **973.7**

UNITED STATES -- HISTORY -- 1861-1865, CIVIL WAR -- POETRY
Poets of the Civil War **811**
Wilson, E. Patriotic gore **810**
Words for the hour **811**

UNITED STATES -- HISTORY -- 1861-1865, CIVIL WAR -- PRISONERS AND PRISONS
See also Prisoners of war; Prisons

UNITED STATES -- HISTORY -- 1861-1865, CIVIL WAR -- RECONSTRUCTION See Reconstruction (1865-1876)

UNITED STATES -- HISTORY -- 1861-1865, CIVIL WAR -- RELIGIOUS ASPECTS
Goldfield, D. R. America aflame **973.7**
Rable, G. C. God's almost chosen peoples **973.7**

UNITED STATES -- HISTORY -- 1861-1865, CIVIL WAR -- SOURCES
The Causes of the Civil War **973.7**
The Civil War **973.7**

UNITED STATES -- HISTORY -- 1861-1865, CIVIL WAR -- WOMEN
Roberts, C. Capital dames **793.7**

UNITED STATES -- HISTORY -- 1861-1865, CIVIL WAR -- WOMEN -- ENCYCLOPEDIAS
Harper, J. E. Women during the Civil War **973.7**

UNITED STATES -- HISTORY -- 1865-1898
Millard, C. The destiny of the republic **973.8**
Reconstruction after the Civil War **973.8**

UNITED STATES -- HISTORY -- 1898, WAR OF 1898 See Spanish-American War, 1898

UNITED STATES -- HISTORY -- 1898-1919
Lears, T. J. J. Rebirth of a nation **973.8**
Zimmermann, W. First great triumph **973**

UNITED STATES -- HISTORY -- 1914-1918, WORLD WAR See World War, 1914-1918 -- United States

UNITED STATES -- HISTORY -- 1919-1933

Golay, M. America 1933   **973.917**

Shlaes, A. Coolidge   **92**

UNITED STATES -- HISTORY -- 1933-1945

The 40s   **973.917**

Brokaw, T. An album of memories   **940.54**

Dickstein, M. Dancing in the dark   **973.91**

Golay, M. America 1933   **973.917**

Goodwin, D. K. No ordinary time   **92**

Kennedy, D. M. Freedom from fear   **973.91**

Leuchtenburg, W. E. Franklin D. Roosevelt and the New Deal, 1932-1940   **973.917**

Schlesinger, A. M. The coming of the New Deal, 1933-1935   **973.917**

Schlesinger, A. M. The politics of upheaval, 1935-1936   **973.917**

Weinstein, A. The haunted wood   **327.12**

UNITED STATES -- HISTORY -- 1939-1945, WORLD WAR *See* World War, 1939-1945 -- United States

UNITED STATES -- HISTORY -- 1945-

American empire, 1945-2000   **973.92**

Patterson, J. T. Grand expectations   **973.92**

Patterson, J. T. Restless giant   **973.92**

Weiner, T. Legacy of ashes   **327.12**

UNITED STATES -- HISTORY -- 1945-1953

King, G. Devil in the grove   **305.896**

UNITED STATES -- HISTORY -- 1953-1961

Jacqueline Kennedy   **973.922**

UNITED STATES -- HISTORY -- 1961-1969

Branch, T. At Canaan's edge   **973.923**

Branch, T. Pillar of fire   **973.922**

The Columbia guide to America in the 1960s   **973.923**

Patterson, J. T. The eve of destruction   **973.923**

Schultz, K. M. Buckley and Mailer   **973.92**

UNITED STATES -- HISTORY -- 1961-1974

Coleman, D. G. The fourteenth day   **73.922**

Patterson, J. T. The eve of destruction   **973.923**

UNITED STATES -- HISTORY -- 1969-

Packer, G. The unwinding   **973.924**

Patterson, J. T. Restless giant   **973.92**

Zinn, H. The historic unfullfilled promise   **973.924**

UNITED STATES -- HISTORY -- 1974-1989

Johnson, H. B. Sleepwalking through history   **973.927**

UNITED STATES -- HISTORY -- 1989-

Schwartz, R. A. The 1990s   **909.82**

UNITED STATES -- HISTORY -- 19TH CENTURY

Black, G. Empire of shadows   **978.7**

Hahn, S. A Nation Without Borders   **973.5**

UNITED STATES -- HISTORY -- 20TH CENTURY

Burns, E. 1920   **973.91**

Coe, A. A square meal   **641.5**

Egan, T. The worst hard time   **978**

Howe, S. Marvel Comics   **741.5**

McGirr, L. The war on alcohol   **363.4**

Perlstein, R. The Invisible Bridge   **973.924**

Shenon, P. A cruel and shocking act   **973.922**

Weiner, T. Enemies   **363.25**

Weisbrode, K. The Year of Indecision, 1946 **973.918**

Worster, D. Shrinking the Earth   **304.2**

UNITED STATES -- HISTORY -- BIBLIOGRAPHY

Frolund, T. Read on...history   **016**

Printed sources   **016**

UNITED STATES -- HISTORY -- CHRONOLOGY

Daily life through American history in primary documents   **973**

UNITED STATES -- HISTORY -- CIVIL WAR, 1861-1865

Foote, S. The Civil War, a narrative   **973.7**

Fredriksen, J. C. Civil War almanac   **973.7**

Gallagher, G. W. The union war   **973.7**

Holzer, H. Lincoln president-elect   **92**

Keegan, J. The American Civil War   **973.7**

Lehr, D. The Birth of a Nation   **305.8**

McMurtry, L. Custer   **92**

McPherson, J. M. Tried by war   **92**

The New York Times disunion   **973.7**

Oakes, J. Freedom national   **973.7**

Our Lincoln   **92**

Stiles, T. J. Custer's trials   **92**

Stout, H. S. Upon the altar of the nation : a moral history of the American Civil War   **973.7**

Wineapple, B. Ecstatic nation   **973.6**

Witt, J. F. Lincoln's code   **343**

UNITED STATES -- HISTORY -- CIVIL WAR, 1861-1865 -- AFRICAN AMERICANS

Manning, C. Troubled refuge   **973.711**

Ward, A. The slaves' war   **973.7**

UNITED STATES -- HISTORY -- CIVIL WAR, 1861-1865 -- AFRICAN AMERICANS -- PICTORIAL WORKS

Krauthamer, B. Envisioning emancipation   **973.7**

UNITED STATES -- HISTORY -- CIVIL WAR, 1861-1865 -- ANECDOTES

Holzer, H. The Civil War in 50 objects   **973.7**

UNITED STATES -- HISTORY -- CIVIL WAR, 1861-1865 -- ART AND THE WAR -- EXHIBITIONS

Harvey, E. J. The Civil War and American art   **709**

UNITED STATES -- HISTORY -- CIVIL WAR, 1861-1865 -- BIOGRAPHY

Davis, W. C. Crucible of commmand   **920**

Egan, T. The immortal Irishman   **92**

Marvel, W. Lincoln's autocrat   **92**

Perry, J. M. Touched with fire   **973.7**

White, R. C. American Ulysses   **92**

UNITED STATES -- HISTORY -- CIVIL WAR, 1861-1865 -- CAMPAIGNS

Blount, R. Robert E. Lee — 92
Eicher, D. J. The longest night — 973.7
Goldfield, D. R. America aflame — 973.7
Groom, W. Shiloh, 1862 — 973.7
Keegan, J. The American Civil War — 973.7
Kennett, L. B. Sherman — 92
Perry, J. M. Touched with fire — 973.7
Wheelan, J. Terrible swift sword — 355.009

UNITED STATES -- HISTORY -- CIVIL WAR, 1861-1865 -- CAUSES

Egerton, D. R. Year of meteors — 973.7
Goldfield, D. R. America aflame — 973.7
Holzer, H. A just and generous nation — 973.7
Wineapple, B. Ecstatic nation — 973.6

UNITED STATES -- HISTORY -- CIVIL WAR, 1861-1865 -- COLLECTIBLES

Holzer, H. The Civil War in 50 objects — 973.7

UNITED STATES -- HISTORY -- CIVIL WAR, 1861-1865 -- ECONOMIC ASPECTS

Holzer, H. A just and generous nation — 973.7
Levine, B. The fall of the house of Dixie — 973.7

UNITED STATES -- HISTORY -- CIVIL WAR, 1861-1865 -- FOREIGN PUBLIC OPINION, BRITISH

Foreman, A. A world on fire — 973.7

UNITED STATES -- HISTORY -- CIVIL WAR, 1861-1865 -- INFLUENCE

Faust, D. G. This republic of suffering — 973.7
Goldfield, D. R. America aflame — 973.7
McPherson, J. M. The war that forged a nation — 973.7

UNITED STATES -- HISTORY -- CIVIL WAR, 1861-1865 -- JEWS

Sarna, J. D. Lincoln and the Jews — 973.7

UNITED STATES -- HISTORY -- CIVIL WAR, 1861-1865 -- PERSONAL NARRATIVES

Roper, R. Now the drum of war — 973.7
Ward, A. The slaves' war — 973.7

UNITED STATES -- HISTORY -- CIVIL WAR, 1861-1865 -- PICTORIAL WORKS

Katz, H. L. Civil War sketch book — 973.7

UNITED STATES -- HISTORY -- CIVIL WAR, 1861-1865 -- PRESS COVERAGE

Holzer, H. Lincoln and the power of the press — 973.7

UNITED STATES -- HISTORY -- CIVIL WAR, 1861-1865 -- PSYCHOLOGICAL ASPECTS

McPherson, J. M. The war that forged a nation — 973.7

UNITED STATES -- HISTORY -- CIVIL WAR, 1861-1865 -- SOCIAL ASPECTS

Faust, D. G. This republic of suffering — 973.7
Food in the Civil War era — 641.597
Goldfield, D. R. America aflame — 973.7
Harper, J. E. Women during the Civil War — 973.7

Holzer, H. A just and generous nation — 973.7
Levine, B. The fall of the house of Dixie — 973.7
Manning, C. Troubled refuge — 973.711
McPherson, J. M. The war that forged a nation — 973.7
Ward, A. The slaves' war — 973.7
Williams, D. Bitterly divided — 973.7

UNITED STATES -- HISTORY -- CIVIL WAR, 1861-1865 -- SOURCES

The Civil War — 973.7

UNITED STATES -- HISTORY -- CIVIL WAR, 1861-1865 -- VETERANS -- BIOGRAPHY

Winchester, S. The professor and the madman — 423

UNITED STATES -- HISTORY -- CIVIL WAR, 1861-1865 -- WOMEN

Berkin, C. Civil War wives — 920
Blanton, D. They fought like demons — 973.7
Harper, J. E. Women during the Civil War — 973.7
Leonard, E. D. All the daring of the soldier — 973.7
Roberts, C. Capital dames — 793.7

UNITED STATES -- HISTORY -- COLONIAL PERIOD, CA. 1600-1775

Encyclopedia of the new American nation — 973
Jordan, D. White cargo — 326

UNITED STATES -- HISTORY -- DICTIONARIES

Cornelison, P. The great American history factfinder — 973

UNITED STATES -- HISTORY -- DRAMA

See also Historical drama

UNITED STATES -- HISTORY -- ENCYCLOPEDIAS

Encyclopedia of American history — 973

UNITED STATES -- HISTORY -- PICTORIAL WORKS

Virga, V. Eyes of the nation — 973

UNITED STATES -- HISTORY -- REVOLUTION, 1775-1783

Brookhiser, R. What would the Founders do? — 320
Ellis, J. J. American creation — 973.3
Encyclopedia of the new American nation — 973
Ferling, J. Whirlwind — 973.3
Fischer, D. H. Washington's crossing — 973.3
Gaines, J. R. For liberty and glory — 92
Jasanoff, M. Liberty's exiles — 973.3
McCraw, T. K. The founders and finance — 330.973
Paul, J. R. Unlikely allies — 973.3
Phillips, K. 1775 — 973.3
Rakove, J. Revolutionaries — 973.3

UNITED STATES -- HISTORY -- REVOLUTION, 1775-1783 -- BIOGRAPHY

Auricchio, L. The marquis — 92
Beeman, R. R. Our lives, our fortunes and our sacred honor — 973.3
DuVal, K. Independence Lost — 973.3
Fraser, F. The Washingtons — 92

Kamensky, J. A revolution in color **759.13**

McKean, D. Suspected of independence **92**

Morgan, E. S. American heroes **920**

UNITED STATES -- HISTORY -- REVOLUTION, 1775-1783 -- CAMPAIGNS

Beck, D. W. The war before independence, 1775-1776 **973.3**

Ferling, J. Whirlwind **973.3**

UNITED STATES -- HISTORY -- REVOLUTION, 1775-1783 -- CAUSES

Igniting the American Revolution **973.3**

Raphael, R. The spirit of 74 **973.3**

UNITED STATES -- HISTORY -- REVOLUTION, 1775-1783 -- COMMITTEES OF SAFETY

Breen, T. H. American insurgents, American patriots **973.3**

UNITED STATES -- HISTORY -- REVOLUTION, 1775-1783 -- INFLUENCE

Gould, E. H. Among the powers of the earth **973.3**

UNITED STATES -- HISTORY -- REVOLUTION, 1775-1783 -- PARTICIPATION, FRENCH

Auricchio, L. The marquis **92**

UNITED STATES -- HISTORY -- REVOLUTION, 1775-1783 -- PROPAGANDA

Parkinson, R. G. The common cause **973.31**

UNITED STATES -- HISTORY -- REVOLUTION, 1775-1783 -- SECRET SERVICE

Nagy, J. A. George Washington's secret spy war **973.385**

Yaeger, D. George Washington's secret six **973.4**

UNITED STATES -- HISTORY -- REVOLUTION, 1775-1783 -- SOCIAL ASPECTS

Breen, T. H. American insurgents, American patriots **973.3**

DuVal, K. Independence Lost **973.3**

Kamensky, J. A revolution in color **759.13**

Parkinson, R. G. The common cause **973.31**

UNITED STATES -- HISTORY -- SOURCES

Ashby, R. The great American documents **973**

UNITED STATES -- HISTORY -- WAR OF 1812

Taylor, A. The civil war of 1812 **973.5**

UNITED STATES -- HISTORY -- WAR OF 1812 -- BIOGRAPHY

Cook, J. H. American phoenix **973.5**

UNITED STATES -- HISTORY -- WAR OF 1812 -- CAMPAIGNS

Snow, P. When Britain burned the White House **975.3**

Vogel, S. Through the perilous fight **973.5**

UNITED STATES -- HISTORY -- WAR OF 1812 -- DIPLOMATIC HISTORY

Cook, J. H. American phoenix **973.5**

UNITED STATES -- HISTORY -- WAR OF 1812 -- NAVAL OPERATIONS, BRITISH

Taylor, A. The internal enemy **975.5**

UNITED STATES -- HISTORY, MILITARY --

20TH CENTURY

Dower, J. W. Cultures of war **355**

Groom, W. The aviators **920**

Herman, A. Douglas MacArthur **92**

Kindsvatter, P. S. American soldiers **355**

Rose, G. How wars end **355**

UNITED STATES -- HISTORY, MILITARY -- 20TH CENTURY -- CASE STUDIES

Ricks, T. E. The generals **355.009**

UNITED STATES -- HISTORY, MILITARY -- 21ST CENTURY

Rose, G. How wars end **355**

Scahill, J. Dirty wars **355.02**

UNITED STATES -- HISTORY, MILITARY -- RELIGIOUS ASPECTS

Preston, A. Sword of the spirit, shield of faith **322**

UNITED STATES -- IMMIGRATION AND EMIGRATION

Bray, I. M. U.S. Immigration Made Easy **342**

Lewis, L. N. How to Get a Green Card **342**

Padilla Peralta Undocumented **92**

Rashke, R. Useful Enemies **341.69**

Urrea, L. A. The devil's highway **325**

UNITED STATES -- IMMIGRATION AND EMIGRATION

See also Americanization; Immigration and emigration

UNITED STATES -- IN LITERATURE

The 40s **973.917**

UNITED STATES -- INTELLECTUAL LIFE

Bawer, B. The victims' revolution **320**

Romano, C. America the philosophical **191**

UNITED STATES -- INTELLECTUAL LIFE

See also Intellectual life

UNITED STATES -- INTELLECTUAL LIFE -- 18TH CENTURY

Rakove, J. Revolutionaries **973.3**

Staloff, D. Hamilton, Adams, Jefferson **973.4**

UNITED STATES -- INTELLIGENCE SERVICE

See Intelligence service -- United States

UNITED STATES -- INTERNATIONAL STATUS -- HISTORY

Gould, E. H. Among the powers of the earth **973.3**

UNITED STATES -- LAND SETTLEMENT *See* Land settlement -- United States

UNITED STATES -- LAW *See* Law -- United States

UNITED STATES -- LOCAL HISTORY

Beatty, M. A. County name origins of the United States **917**

Cronkite, W. Around America **917**

Duncan, D. The national parks **333.7**

Stark, P. The last empty places **973**

Vowell, S. Assassination vacation **973**

UNITED STATES -- LOCAL HISTORY

See also Local history

UNITED STATES -- LOCAL HISTORY -- DIC-

TIONARIES

Hellmann, P. T. Historical gazetteer of the United States **911**

UNITED STATES -- MAPS
See also Atlases; Maps

UNITED STATES -- MILITARY ASSISTANCE COMMAND, VIETNAM -- STUDIES AND OBSERVATIONS GROUP

Shultz, R. H. The secret war against Hanoi **959.704**

UNITED STATES -- MILITARY HISTORY

Bacevich, A. J. America's war for the greater Middle East **956.054**

Bolger, D. P. Why We Lost **956.704**

Maddow, R. Drift **306.2**

Nelson, C. Pearl Harbor **940.54**

Perry, M. The most dangerous man in America **92**

Ricks, T. E. The generals **355.009**

Tuccille, J. The roughest riders **973.8**

Ujifusa, S. A man and his ship **623.8**

Yockelson, M. A. Forty-seven days **940.4**

UNITED STATES -- MILITARY HISTORY
See also Military history

UNITED STATES -- MILITARY HISTORY -- ENCYCLOPEDIAS

Encyclopedia of American military history **355**

UNITED STATES -- MILITARY PERSONNEL
See Military personnel -- United States

UNITED STATES -- MILITARY POLICY

Carroll, J. House of war **355**

Dower, J. W. Cultures of war **355**

Freedman, L. Kennedy's wars **973.922**

Gopal, A. No good men among the living **958.104**

Haass, R. War of necessity: war of choice **956.7**

Hagedorn, A. The invisible soldiers **355**

Hersh, S. The killing of Osama Bin Laden **327.73**

Johnsen, G. D. The last refuge **363.325**

Kaplan, R. D. Imperial grunts **973.931**

Kilcullen, D. The accidental guerrilla **355.4**

Maddow, R. Drift **306.2**

Olson, L. Those angry days **940.53**

Ramo, J. C. The age of the unthinkable **973.931**

Rose, G. How wars end **355**

UNITED STATES -- MILITARY POLICY *See* Military policy -- United States

UNITED STATES -- MILITARY POLICY -- DECISION MAKING

Bacevich, A. J. Washington rules **355**

Mazzetti, M. The way of the knife **356**

UNITED STATES -- MILITARY POLICY -- HISTORY -- 21ST CENTURY

Scahill, J. Dirty wars **355.02**

UNITED STATES -- MILITARY POLICY -- RELIGIOUS ASPECTS

Preston, A. Sword of the spirit, shield of faith **322**

UNITED STATES -- MILITARY RELATIONS -- IRAN

Crist, D. The twilight war **327**

UNITED STATES -- MILITIA -- HISTORY -- REVOLUTION, 1775-1783

Breen, T. H. American insurgents, American patriots **973.3**

UNITED STATES -- MORAL CONDITIONS

Edelman, M. W. The measure of our success **170**

Wolfe, A. Moral freedom **170**

UNITED STATES -- NATIONAL CHARACTERISTICS *See* American national characteristics

UNITED STATES -- NATIONAL GUARD

Thorpe, H. Soldier girls **956.704**

UNITED STATES -- NATIONAL SECURITY *See* National security -- United States

UNITED STATES -- NAVAL HISTORY

Toll, I. W. Pacific crucible **940.54**

UNITED STATES -- NAVAL HISTORY
See also Naval history

UNITED STATES -- NAVY -- SEA AIR LAND TEAM

Couch, D. The warrior elite **359.9**

UNITED STATES -- OFFICE OF STRATEGIC SERVICES

Conant, J. A covert affair **940.54**

UNITED STATES -- OFFICIALS AND EMPLOYEES

Thompson, N. The hawk and the dove **92**

UNITED STATES -- PICTORIAL WORKS

Evans, W. American photographs **779**

UNITED STATES -- POLITICIANS *See* Politicians -- United States

UNITED STATES -- POLITICS *See* United States -- Politics and government

UNITED STATES -- POLITICS AND GOVERNMENT

Appy, C. G. American Reckoning **959.704**

Beeman, R. R. Our lives, our fortunes and our sacred honor **973.3**

Bogus, C. T. Buckley **92**

Brinkley, A. John F. Kennedy **92**

Chandrasekaran, R. Imperial life in the emerald city **956.704**

Edwards, M. The parties versus the people **320**

Gilmore, G. E. These United States **973.9**

Goldwag, A. The new hate **306.2**

Greenberg, D. Republic of spin **973.099**

Han, L. C. Handbook to American democracy **320.4**

Jacobsen, A. The Pentagon's Brain **355**

Lepore, J. The story of America **973**

Lofgren, M. The party is over **324.273**

Mayer, J. Dark money **320.52**

Prothero, S. The American Bible **973**

Raphael, R. The spirit of 74 **973.3**

Rice, C. No higher honor **327.73**

Sehat, D. The Jefferson rule **306.2**

Smith, H. Who stole the American dream? **973.91**

Speth, J. G. America the possible **338.9**

Traub, J. John Quincy Adams **92**

Vogel, K. P. Big money **324.7**

Waldman, M. The Fight to Vote **324.6**

Wilentz, S. The Politicians and the Egalitarians **306.2**

Witcover, J. America's vice presidents **352.23**

Zinn, H. The historic unfullfilled promise **973.924**

UNITED STATES -- POLITICS AND GOVERNMENT

See also Political science; Politics; Public administration

UNITED STATES -- POLITICS AND GOVERNMENT -- 1775-1783

Becker, C. The Declaration of Independence **973.3**

Burstein, A. Madison and Jefferson **973.4**

Beeman, R. R. Our lives, our fortunes and our sacred honor **973.3**

Chernow, R. Washington **92**

Cohen, I. B. Science and the founding fathers **973.3**

Ellis, J. J. American creation **973.3**

Hamilton, A. Writings **973.4**

Hogeland, W. Declaration **973.3**

Maier, P. American scripture **973.3**

McCullough, D. G. John Adams **92**

Paine, T. Rights of man; and, Common sense **320**

Phillips, K. 1775 **973.3**

Rakove, J. Revolutionaries **973.3**

Stewart, D. O. Madison's Gift **92**

Washington, G. Writings **973.4**

Wood, G. S. The radicalism of the American Revolution **973.3**

UNITED STATES -- POLITICS AND GOVERNMENT -- 1783-1789

Berkin, C. A brilliant solution **342**

Ellis, J. J. American creation **973.3**

Ellis, J. J. The Quartet **973.3**

UNITED STATES -- POLITICS AND GOVERNMENT -- 1783-1809

Bordewich, F. M. The First Congress **327.73**

Ellis, J. J. The Quartet **973.3**

Meacham, J. Thomas Jefferson **92**

Raphael, R. Mr. president **352.23**

Sedgwick, J. War of two **973.4**

UNITED STATES -- POLITICS AND GOVERNMENT -- 1783-1865

Cheney, L. V. James Madison **92**

Larson, E. The Return of George Washington **92**

UNITED STATES -- POLITICS AND GOVERNMENT -- 1789-1797

Breen, T. H. George Washington's journey **92**

UNITED STATES -- POLITICS AND GOVERNMENT -- 1789-1815

Broadwater, J. James Madison **92**

Freeman, J. B. Affairs of honor **306.2**

Giles Unger, H. John Quincy Adams **92**

Remini, R. V. John Quincy Adams **92**

UNITED STATES -- POLITICS AND GOVERNMENT -- 1797-1801

Larson, E. J. A magnificent catastrophe **324**

McCullough, D. G. John Adams **92**

UNITED STATES -- POLITICS AND GOVERNMENT -- 1801-1809

Sedgwick, J. War of two **973.4**

UNITED STATES -- POLITICS AND GOVERNMENT -- 1809-1817

Broadwater, J. James Madison **92**

Wills, G. James Madison **92**

UNITED STATES -- POLITICS AND GOVERNMENT -- 1815-1861

Blumenthal, S. A self-made man **92**

Bordewich, F. M. America's great debate **973.6**

Egerton, D. R. Year of meteors **973.7**

Finkelman, P. Millard Fillmore **92**

Guelzo, A. C. Lincoln and Douglas **973.6**

Heidler, D. S. Henry Clay **92**

Howe, D. W. What hath God wrought **973.5**

Lincoln, A. Speeches and writings, 1832-1858 **973.5**

Lincoln, A. Speeches and writings, 1859-1865 **973.7**

Merry, R. W. A country of vast designs **92**

Miller, W. L. Arguing about slavery **973.5**

Remini, R. V. Daniel Webster **328**

Reynolds, D. S. Waking giant **973.5**

UNITED STATES -- POLITICS AND GOVERNMENT -- 1825-1829

Giles Unger, H. John Quincy Adams **92**

Remini, R. V. John Quincy Adams **92**

UNITED STATES -- POLITICS AND GOVERNMENT -- 1841-1845

Collins, G. William Henry Harrison **92**

Crapol, E. P. John Tyler **92**

Merry, R. W. A country of vast designs **92**

UNITED STATES -- POLITICS AND GOVERNMENT -- 1857-1861

Egerton, D. R. Year of meteors **973.7**

Guelzo, A. C. Lincoln and Douglas **973.6**

UNITED STATES -- POLITICS AND GOVERNMENT -- 1861-1865

Bordewich, F. M. America's great debate **973.6**

Brookhiser, R. Founders' son **92**

UNITED STATES -- POLITICS AND GOVERNMENT -- 1865-1869

Marvel, W. Lincoln's autocrat **92**

UNITED STATES -- POLITICS AND GOVERNMENT -- 1865-1877

Langguth, A. J. After Lincoln **973.8**

UNITED STATES -- POLITICS AND GOVERNMENT -- 1869-1877

White, R. C. American Ulysses **92**

UNITED STATES -- POLITICS AND GOVERN-MENT -- 1881-1885

Millard, C. The destiny of the republic   973.8

UNITED STATES -- POLITICS AND GOVERN-MENT -- 1897-1901

Miller, S. The President and the assassin   973.8

Rauchway, E. Murdering McKinley   973.8

Thomas, E. The war lovers   973.8

UNITED STATES -- POLITICS AND GOVERN-MENT -- 1901-1909

Davis, D. Guest of honor   973.91

Goodwin, D. K. The Bully Pulpit   973.91

Morris, E. Theodore Rex   92

Zimmermann, W. First great triumph   973

UNITED STATES -- POLITICS AND GOVERN-MENT -- 1909-1913

Goodwin, D. K. The Bully Pulpit   973.91

Morris, E. Colonel Roosevelt   92

O'Toole, P. When trumpets call   92

UNITED STATES -- POLITICS AND GOVERN-MENT -- 1913-1921

Berg, A. S. Wilson   92

Brands, H. W. Woodrow Wilson   92

Cooper, J. M. Woodrow Wilson   92

Morris, E. Colonel Roosevelt   92

Neu, C. E. Colonel House   92

O'Toole, P. When trumpets call   92

UNITED STATES -- POLITICS AND GOVERN-MENT -- 1919-1933

Cooper, J. M. Woodrow Wilson   92

UNITED STATES -- POLITICS AND GOVERN-MENT -- 1923-1929

Shlaes, A. Coolidge   92

UNITED STATES -- POLITICS AND GOVERN-MENT -- 1929-1933

Rappleye, C. Herbert Hoover in the White House   92

UNITED STATES -- POLITICS AND GOVERN-MENT -- 1933-1945

Wortman, M. 1941 : Fighting the Shadow War   973.917

UNITED STATES -- POLITICS AND GOVERN-MENT -- 1945-

American empire, 1945-2000   973.92

Brands, H. W. The General Vs. the President   973.918

Caro, R. A. The passage of power   92

Crist, D. The twilight war   327

Duffy, M. The presidents club   973.92

Patterson, J. T. Grand expectations   973.92

Patterson, J. T. Restless giant   973.92

Ross, D. B. Doomed to succeed   327.73

UNITED STATES -- POLITICS AND GOVERN-MENT -- 1945-1953

Conant, J. A covert affair   940.54

Donald, A. D. Citizen soldier   92

Morrow, L. The best year of their lives   920

UNITED STATES -- POLITICS AND GOVERN-MENT -- 1945-1989

American empire, 1945-2000   973.92

Cohen, A. American pharaoh: Mayor Richard J. Daley: his battle for Chicago and the nation   977.3

Conner, C. Wrapped in the flag   322.4

Frank, B. Frank   92

Frank, J. Ike and Dick   973.921

Gillette, M. L. Lady Bird Johnson   92

Kruse, K. M. One nation under God   322

Lichtblau, E. The Nazis next door   324.1

Miraldi, R. Seymour Hersh   92

Smith, H. Who stole the American dream?   973.91

Tye, L. Bobby Kennedy   92

UNITED STATES -- POLITICS AND GOVERN-MENT -- 1953-1961

Smith, J. E. Eisenhower   973.921

Wicker, T. Dwight D. Eisenhower   973.921

UNITED STATES -- POLITICS AND GOVERN-MENT -- 1961-1963

Brinkley, A. John F. Kennedy   92

Clarke, T. JFK's last hundred days   92

Coleman, D. G. The fourteenth day   73.922

Hughes, K. Chasing shadows   973.924

Jacqueline Kennedy   973.922

Kaiser, D. E. American tragedy   959.704

Leaming, B. Mrs. Kennedy   973.922

Purdum, T. S. An idea whose time has come   342.73

Stoll, I. JFK, conservative   973.922

UNITED STATES -- POLITICS AND GOVERN-MENT -- 1961-1974

Clarke, T. JFK's last hundred days   92

Glasser, J. M. The eighteen-day running mate   973.924

Logevall, F. Embers of War   959.704

Patterson, J. T. The eve of destruction   973.923

Purdum, T. S. An idea whose time has come   342.73

Stoll, I. JFK, conservative   973.922

UNITED STATES -- POLITICS AND GOVERN-MENT -- 1963-1969

Caro, R. A. The passage of power   92

Hughes, K. Chasing shadows   973.924

Kaiser, D. E. American tragedy   959.704

Patterson, J. T. The eve of destruction   973.923

Pepper, W. F. An act of state   364.1

Purdum, T. S. An idea whose time has come   342.73

Taking charge   973.923

Woods, R. B. Prisoners of hope   973.923

UNITED STATES -- POLITICS AND GOVERN-MENT -- 1969-1974

Abuse of power   973.924

Feldstein, M. Poisoning the press   973.924

Glasser, J. M. The eighteen-day running mate   973.924

Hughes, K. Chasing shadows   973.924

Perlstein, R. Nixonland   973.924

Reeves, R. President Nixon **973.924**

Thomas, E. Being Nixon **92**

Weiner, T. One man against the world **973.924**

UNITED STATES -- POLITICS AND GOVERN-MENT -- 1969-1974 -- SOURCES

The Nixon tapes **973.924**

UNITED STATES -- POLITICS AND GOVERN-MENT -- 1974-1977

Perlstein, R. Nixonland **973.924**

UNITED STATES -- POLITICS AND GOVERN-MENT -- 1974-1989

Carter, J. White House diary **92**

D'Souza, D. Ronald Reagan **973.927**

FitzGerald, F. Way out there in the blue **973.927**

Johnson, H. B. Sleepwalking through history **973.927**

The Reagan diaries **92**

Reeves, R. President Reagan: the triumph of imagination **973.927**

Woodward, B. Shadow **973.92**

UNITED STATES -- POLITICS AND GOVERN-MENT -- 1977-1981

Carter, J. A full life **92**

Carter, J. White House diary **92**

UNITED STATES -- POLITICS AND GOVERN-MENT -- 1981-1989

Brands, H. W. Reagan **92**

FitzGerald, F. Way out there in the blue **973.927**

The Reagan diaries **92**

Reagan, in his own hand **973.927**

Reeves, R. President Reagan: the triumph of imagination **973.927**

Zinn, H. The historic unfullfilled promise **973.924**

UNITED STATES -- POLITICS AND GOVERN-MENT -- 1989-

Axelrod, D. Believer **92**

UNITED STATES -- POLITICS AND GOVERN-MENT -- 1993-2001

Branch, T. The Clinton tapes **92**

Chafe, W. H. Bill and Hillary **973.929**

Clinton, H. R. Living history **92**

UNITED STATES -- POLITICS AND GOVERN-MENT -- 1993-2001 -- QUOTATIONS, MAX-IMS, ETC

Koltz, T. It worked for me **92**

UNITED STATES -- POLITICS AND GOVERN-MENT -- 19TH CENTURY

Marvel, W. Lincoln's autocrat **92**

Oller, J. American queen **92**

UNITED STATES -- POLITICS AND GOVERN-MENT -- 2001-

Barone, M. The almanac of American politics 2012 **328**

Frank, J. The people's pension **368.4**

Maddow, R. Drift **306.2**

UNITED STATES -- POLITICS AND GOVERN-

MENT -- 2001-2009

Bamford, J. The shadow factory **327.12**

Carville, J. It's the middle class, stupid! **320.51**

Chandrasekaran, R. Imperial life in the emerald city **956.704**

Love, R. Power forward **320.092**

Remnick, D. The bridge **92**

Smith, J. E. Bush **973.931**

Taibbi, M. Griftopia **973.932**

UNITED STATES -- POLITICS AND GOVERN-MENT -- 2009-

Dyson, M. E. The Black presidency **305.8**

Toobin, J. The oath **347.73**

UNITED STATES -- POLITICS AND GOVERN-MENT -- 20TH CENTURY

Frank, B. Frank **92**

Judt, T. Thinking the twentieth century **320.092**

Neff, J. Vendetta **973.922**

Tirella, J. Tomorrow-land **607**

Unger, I. George Marshall **92**

UNITED STATES -- POLITICS AND GOVERN-MENT -- CHRONOLOGY

Chronology of the U.S. presidency **973.09**

UNITED STATES -- POLITICS AND GOVERN-MENT -- ENCYCLOPEDIAS

Encyclopedia of U.S. political history **973**

Encyclopedia of women and American politics **973**

UNITED STATES -- POLITICS AND GOVERN-MENT -- ENCYCLOPEDIAS, JUVENILE

Encyclopedia of the U.S. presidency **352.23**

UNITED STATES -- POLITICS AND GOVERN-MENT -- HANDBOOKS, MANUALS, ETC

Han, L. C. Handbook to American democracy **320.4**

UNITED STATES -- POLITICS AND GOVERN-MENT -- MAPS

Shelley, F. M. Atlas of American politics, 1960-2000 **973.92**

UNITED STATES -- POLITICS AND GOVERN-MENT -- SOURCES

Ashby, R. The great american documents **973**

UNITED STATES -- POLITICS AND GOVERN-MENT -- TO 1775

Beeman, R. R. Our lives, our fortunes and our sacred honor **973.3**

Lepore, J. The name of war **973.2**

Richter, D. K. Facing east from Indian country **970.004**

UNITED STATES -- POPULAR CULTURE *See* Popular culture -- United States

UNITED STATES -- POPULATION

Peake, R. Mapping Census 2010 **304.6**

Sykes, B. DNA USA **559.9**

UNITED STATES -- RACE RELATIONS

Burke, K. M. And Still I Rise **973**

Coates Between the World and Me **305.8**

DeWolf, T. N. Gather at the table   306.3
Dunbar-Ortiz, R. An indigenous peoples' history of
   the United States   970.004
The Fire This Time   305.896
Kendi, I. X. Stamped from the beginning   305.8
Leamer, L. The Lynching   364.134
Lehr, D. The Birth of a Nation   305.8
Rankine, C. Citizen   811
Savoy, L. Trace   917.3
Sherrod, S. The courage to hope   975.8
Swarns, R. L. American tapestry   92

UNITED STATES -- RACE RELATIONS
   See also Race relations

**UNITED STATES -- RACE RELATIONS -- HIS-
   TORY**
Davis, T. J. Plessy v. Ferguson   342
Jones, J. A dreadful deceit   305.8
Parkinson, R. G. The common cause   973.31
Phillips, P. Blood at the root   305.8
Presidents and Black America   973.09

**UNITED STATES -- RACE RELATIONS -- HIS-
   TORY -- 19TH CENTURY**
White, S. Prince of darkness   92

**UNITED STATES -- RACE RELATIONS -- HIS-
   TORY -- 20TH CENTURY**
Anderson, D. S. Emmett Till   364.1
Davis, D. Guest of honor   973.91
Lewis, A. B. The shadows of youth   323.1
Masur, L. P. The soiling of Old Glory   974.4
Sugrue, T. J. Sweet land of liberty   323
Sullivan, P. Lift every voice   323.1

**UNITED STATES -- RACE RELATIONS -- PO-
   LITICAL ASPECTS**
Dray, P. Capitol men   920
Dyson, M. E. The Black presidency   305.8

**UNITED STATES -- RELATIONS -- GREAT
   BRITAIN**
Maier, T. When lions roar   941.084

UNITED STATES -- RELATIONS -- IRAQ
Gordon, M. R. The endgame   956.7

UNITED STATES -- RELATIONS -- JAPAN
Sakamoto, P. R. Midnight in broad daylight 940.53

UNITED STATES -- RELATIONS -- PAKISTAN
Grenier, R. L. 88 days to Kandahar   958.104

UNITED STATES -- RELIGION
Ahlstrom, S. E. A religious history of the American
   people   200
Ozment, K. Grace without God   200.973
Schmidt, L. E. The religious history of Ameri-
   ca   200.973
Sutton, M. A. American apocalypse   277.3
Zuckerman, P. Living the Secular Life   211

UNITED STATES -- RELIGION
   See also Religion

**UNITED STATES -- RELIGION -- 20TH CEN-
   TURY**

Kruse, K. M. One nation under God   322

**UNITED STATES -- RELIGION -- ENCYCLO-
   PEDIAS**
The encyclopedia of cults, sects, and new reli-
   gions   200
Melton, J. G. Melton's encyclopedia of American
   religions   200.9
Religion and American cultures   200.9

UNITED STATES -- RELIGION -- HISTORY
Waldman, S. Founding faith   342

UNITED STATES -- RELIGIOUS HISTORY *See*
   United States -- Church history

**UNITED STATES -- RELIGIOUS LIFE AND
   CUSTOMS**
Curtis, E. E. Muslims in America   305.8

**UNITED STATES -- RURAL CONDITIONS --
   ENCYCLOPEDIAS**
Encyclopedia of rural America   973

UNITED STATES -- SECRET SERVICE *See* Secret service -- United States

UNITED STATES -- SOCIAL CONDITIONS
Baum, D. Gun guys   683.4
Beam, C. To the end of June   362.73
Carville, J. It's the middle class, stupid! 320.51
Duberman, M. B.   The Martin Duberman read-
   er   306.76
Ford, R. T. Rights gone wrong   342
Fraser, S. The age of acquiescence   973.91
Jefferson, M. Negroland   92
Leovy, J. Ghettoside   364.152
O'Neil, C. Weapons of math destruction   005.7
Savoy, L. Trace   917.3
Shaefer, H. L. $2.00 a Day   339.4
Stone, J. M. Five easy theses   330.973
Well, F. Family trees   929.2

UNITED STATES -- SOCIAL CONDITIONS
   See also Social conditions

**UNITED STATES -- SOCIAL CONDITIONS --
   1865-1918**
Davis, D. Guest of honor   973.91
Miller, S. The President and the assassin 973.8

**UNITED STATES -- SOCIAL CONDITIONS --
   1918-1932 -- PICTORIAL WORKS**
Evans, W. American photographs   779

**UNITED STATES -- SOCIAL CONDITIONS --
   1918-1945**
Golay, M. America 1933   973.917

**UNITED STATES -- SOCIAL CONDITIONS --
   1933-1945**
Coe, A. A square meal   641.5
Dickstein, M. Dancing in the dark   973.91

**UNITED STATES -- SOCIAL CONDITIONS --
   1933-1945 -- PICTORIAL WORKS**
Evans, W. American photographs   779

**UNITED STATES -- SOCIAL CONDITIONS --
   1960-1980**

The Columbia guide to America in the 1960s **973.923**
Lattin, D. The Harvard Psychedelic Club **920**
Murray, C. Coming apart **305.8**
Patterson, J. T. The eve of destruction **973.923**
Schultz, K. M. Buckley and Mailer **973.92**

UNITED STATES -- SOCIAL CONDITIONS -- 1980-
Bageant, J. Deer hunting with Jesus **305.5**
Bishop, B. The big sort **305.8**
Cohen, L. A consumer's republic **339.4**
Friedman, T. L. Hot, flat, and crowded **363.7**
Hernández, D. A cup of water under my bed **920.009**
Laskas, J. M. Hidden America **305.5**
Murray, C. Coming apart **305.8**
Packer, G. The unwinding **973.924**
Sirota, D. Back to our future **973.92**
Stone, J. M. Five easy theses **330.973**

UNITED STATES -- SOCIAL CONDITIONS -- 19TH CENTURY
Reynolds, D. S. Waking giant **973.5**
White, S. Prince of darkness **92**

UNITED STATES -- SOCIAL CONDITIONS -- 20TH CENTURY
Burns, J. M. The three Roosevelts **973.91**
Hedges, C. Days of destruction, days of revolt **305.5**
Tirella, J. Tomorrow-land **607**

UNITED STATES -- SOCIAL CONDITIONS -- 21ST CENTURY
Caputo, P. The longest road **973.93**
Hayes, C. Twilight of the elites **305.5**
Hirshman, L. Victory **306.76**
Nader, R. Told you so **303.3**
O'Neil, C. Weapons of math destruction **005.7**
Rajan, R. G. Fault lines **330.9**
Robinson, E. Disintegration **305.8**
Stiglitz, J. E. The price of inequality **305.5**

UNITED STATES -- SOCIAL CONDITIONS -- FORECASTING
Reich, R. B. Aftershock **330.9**

UNITED STATES -- SOCIAL CONDITIONS -- SOURCES
Young, R. Dissent **303.48**

UNITED STATES -- SOCIAL CONDITIONS -- TO 1865
Brands, H. W. The Age of Gold **979.4**
Freeman, J. B. Affairs of honor **306.2**

UNITED STATES -- SOCIAL CUSTOMS -- 1933-1945
The 40s **973.917**

UNITED STATES -- SOCIAL LIFE AND CUSTOMS
Daily life through American history in primary documents **973**
Humes, E. Garbology **628.4**

Warnick, M. This Is Where You Belong **155.94**

UNITED STATES -- SOCIAL LIFE AND CUSTOMS
See also Manners and customs

UNITED STATES -- SOCIAL LIFE AND CUSTOMS -- 1945-1970
Frank, R. The Americans **779.997**

UNITED STATES -- SOCIAL LIFE AND CUSTOMS -- 1971-
Frum, D. How we got here **973.92**
Laskas, J. M. Hidden America **305.5**

UNITED STATES -- SOCIAL LIFE AND CUSTOMS -- 20TH CENTURY
The 40s **973.917**
Brokaw, T. A long way from home **070**
Byrne, P. Kick **92**
Tirella, J. Tomorrow-land **607**

UNITED STATES -- SOCIAL LIFE AND CUSTOMS -- 21ST CENTURY
Caputo, P. The longest road **973.93**

UNITED STATES -- SOCIAL LIFE AND CUSTOMS -- 21ST CENTURY -- HUMOR
Waters, J. Carsick **92**

UNITED STATES -- SOCIAL LIFE AND CUSTOMS -- ENCYCLOPEDIAS
Encyclopedia of American folklife **398**

UNITED STATES -- SOCIAL LIFE AND CUSTOMS -- PICTORIAL WORKS
The open road **770**

UNITED STATES -- SOCIAL POLICY
Alvarez, A. Native America and the question of genocide **973**

UNITED STATES -- SOCIAL POLICY See Social policy -- United States

UNITED STATES -- SOCIAL POLICY -- 1993-
Stone, J. M. Five easy theses **330.973**

UNITED STATES -- SOCIAL POLICY -- 20TH CENTURY
Woods, R. B. Prisoners of hope **973.923**

UNITED STATES -- SOCIAL POLICY -- 21ST CENTURY
Nader, R. Told you so **303.3**

UNITED STATES -- SOLDIERS See Soldiers -- United States

UNITED STATES -- SPECIAL ASSISTANT TO THE PRESIDENT FOR NATIONAL SECURITY AFFAIRS
Daalder, I. H. In the shadow of the Oval Office **355**

UNITED STATES -- STATE GOVERNMENTS
See State governments

UNITED STATES -- STATISTICS
Proquest Statistical Abstract of the United States 2015 **317.3**

UNITED STATES -- STATISTICS
See also Statistics

UNITED STATES -- TAXATION See Taxation --

United States

UNITED STATES -- TERRITORIAL EXPANSION

Anderson, F. The dominion of war 973.2

Cerami, C. A. Jefferson's great gamble 973.4

Gould, E. H. Among the powers of the earth 973.3

Merry, R. W. A country of vast designs 92

Morgan, R. Lions of the West 920

Sides, H. Blood and thunder 978

Thomas, E. The war lovers 973.8

Vowell, S. Unfamiliar fishes 996.9

UNITED STATES -- TERRITORIAL EXPANSION -- HISTORY

Merry, R. W. A country of vast designs 92

UNITED STATES -- TERRITORIAL EXPANSION -- HISTORY -- 19TH CENTURY

Miller, S. The President and the assassin 973.8

Wineapple, B. Ecstatic nation 973.6

UNITED STATES -- TRAVEL *See* United States -- Description and travel

UNITED STATES -- UNITED STATES

Zuckerman, P. Living the Secular Life 211

UNITED STATES -- VICE-PRESIDENTS *See* Vice-presidents -- United States

UNITED STATES -- WORKS PROGRESS ADMINISTRATION

Taylor, N. American-made 331.1

UNITED STATES -- WORLD WAR, 1914-1918 *See* World War, 1914-1918 -- United States

UNITED STATES -- WORLD WAR, 1939-1945 *See* World War, 1939-1945 -- United States

UNITED STATES CAPITOL (WASHINGTON, D.C.) -- HISTORY

Gugliotta, G. Freedom's cap 975.3

The **United** States Constitution. Hennessey, J. 342

United States holidays and observances. Rajtar, S. 394.26

United States Holocaust Memorial Museum

Berenbaum, M. The world must know 940.53

The Holocaust and history 940.53

The **United** States in the First World War. 940.3

UNITED STATES INDIAN SCHOOL (CARLISLE, PA.)

Anderson, L. Carlisle vs. Army 796.332

United States Military Academy

(comp) The West Point History of the Civil War 973.7

(comp) West Point History of World War II 940.53

UNITED STATES MILITARY ACADEMY

See also Colleges and universities

UNITED STATES MILITARY ACADEMY

Lipsky, D. Absolutely American 355

Ruggero, E. Duty first 355

Samet, E. D. Soldier's heart 810

The West Point History of the Civil War 973.7

West Point History of World War II 940.53

The **United** States of Arugula. Kamp, D. 641

The **United** States of beer. Huckelbridge, D. 641.23

The **United** States of paranoia. Walker, J. 973

UNITED STATES SOLDIERS' AND AIRMEN'S HOME (WASHINGTON, D.C.)

Pinsker, M. Lincoln's sanctuary 92

UNITED STATES. AIR FORCE -- OFFICERS -- BIOGRAPHY

Castner, B. All the ways we kill and die 958.104

Castner, B. The long walk 956.704

Ryan, C. Sonic wind 92

UNITED STATES. AIR FORCE -- VOCATIONAL GUIDANCE

Wildsmith, S. Joining the United States Air Force 358.4

UNITED STATES. AIR FORCE. STRATEGIC AIR COMMAND. STRATEGIC MISSILE WING, 308TH

Schlosser, E. Command and control 363.17

UNITED STATES. AMERICANS WITH DISABILITIES ACT OF 1990

Davis, L. J. Enabling acts 342.73

UNITED STATES. ARMY

Ambrose, S. E. The victors 940.54

Couch, D. Sua sponte 356

Eisenhower, J. S. D. Yanks: the epic story of the American Army in World War I 940.4

Finkel, D. The good soldiers 956.7

Franks, T. American soldier 973.931

Kennett, L. B. Sherman 92

Leonard, E. D. All the daring of the soldier 973.7

McPherson, J. M. For cause and comrades 973.7

Thorpe, H. Soldier girls 956.704

Ulander, P. A. Walking point 959.704

Weintraub, S. A Christmas far from home 951.904

UNITED STATES. ARMY -- AIRBORNE BRIGADE, 173RD

Junger, S. War 958.1

UNITED STATES. ARMY -- AIRBORNE DIVISION, 101ST

Atkinson, R. In the company of soldiers 956.7

Frederick, J. Black hearts 956.7

UNITED STATES. ARMY -- BIOGRAPHY

Davis, W. C. Crucible of commmand 920

Dreazen, Y. The invisible front 92

Herman, A. Douglas MacArthur 92

McMurtry, L. Custer 92

Perry, M. The most dangerous man in America 92

Rodriguez, D. Rise 92

Smith, J. E. Eisenhower 973.921

Stiles, T. J. Custer's trials 92

Unger, I. George Marshall 92

Wheelan, J. Terrible swift sword 355.009

UNITED STATES. ARMY -- CAVALRY, 1ST

Raddatz, M. The long road home 956.7

UNITED STATES. ARMY -- COMMANDO

TROOPS -- TRAINING OF

Couch, D. Sua sponte   356

UNITED STATES. ARMY -- DELTA FORCE

Haney, E. L. Inside Delta Force   356

UNITED STATES. ARMY -- GAYS -- BIOGRA-PHY

Nicholson, A. Fighting to serve   355

UNITED STATES. ARMY -- MILITARY LIFE -- HISTORY -- 20TH CENTURY

Ulander, P. A. Walking point   959.704

UNITED STATES. ARMY -- OFFICERS -- BIOGRAPHY

Egan, T. The immortal Irishman   92

UNITED STATES. ARMY -- WOMEN -- BIOGRAPHY

Thorpe, H. Soldier girls   956.704

UNITED STATES. ARMY AIR FORCES -- AERIAL GUNNERS -- BIOGRAPHY

Harding, S. Last to die   940.54

UNITED STATES. ARMY AIR FORCES. PHOTO RECONNAISSANCE SQUADRON, 20TH -- BIOGRAPHY

Harding, S. Last to die   940.54

UNITED STATES. ARMY OF THE POTOMAC. IRISH BRIGADE

Egan, T. The immortal Irishman   92

UNITED STATES. ARMY. AIRBORNE BRIGADE, 173RD. BRAVO COMPANY

Ulander, P. A. Walking point   959.704

UNITED STATES. ARMY. AMERICAN EXPEDITIONARY FORCES

Yockelson, M. A. Forty-seven days   940.4

UNITED STATES. ARMY. ANTI-ARICRAFT BARRAGE BALLOON BATTALION, 320TH -- HISTORY

Hervieux, L. Forgotten   940.54

UNITED STATES. ARMY. CAVALRY REGIMENT, MECHANIZED, 2ND -- HISTORY

Letts, E. The perfect horse   940.54

UNITED STATES. ARMY. CORPS, 10TH -- HISTORY -- 20TH CENTURY

Weintraub, S. A Christmas far from home 951.904

UNITED STATES. ARMY -- INFANTRY

Kindsvatter, P. S. American soldiers   355

UNITED STATES. ARMY. INFANTRY DIVISION, 1ST

Davenport, M. J. First over there   940.4

UNITED STATES. ARMY -- INFANTRY DIVISION, 77TH -- JOINT ASSAULT SIGNAL COMPANY, 292ND

Slotkin, R. Lost battalions   940.3

UNITED STATES. ARMY. INFANTRY DIVISION, 79TH -- HISTORY -- WORLD WAR, 1914-1918

Walker, W. T. Betrayal at Little Gibraltar 940.436

UNITED STATES. ARMY -- INFANTRY REGIMENT, 28TH

Nelson, J. C. The remains of Company D 920

UNITED STATES. ARMY -- INFANTRY REGIMENT, 327TH -- BATTALION, 1ST

Sallah, M. Tiger Force   959.704

UNITED STATES. ARMY -- INFANTRY REGIMENT, 369TH

Slotkin, R. Lost battalions   940.3

UNITED STATES. ARMY -- MILITARY LIFE

Wiley, B. I. The life of Billy Yank   973.7

UNITED STATES. ARMY -- PARACHUTE INFANTRY REGIMENT, 506TH -- COMPANY E

Alexander, L. Biggest brother   92

Ambrose, S. E. Band of brothers   940.54

UNITED STATES. ARMY -- RANGER BATTALION, 6TH

Sides, H. Ghost soldiers   940.54

UNITED STATES. ARMY. RANGER REGIMENT, 75TH

Couch, D. Sua sponte   356

UNITED STATES. ARMY -- SOUTH CAROLINA VOLUNTEERS, 1ST

Ash, S. V. Firebrand of liberty   973.7

UNITED STATES. ARMY -- SOUTH CAROLINA VOLUNTEERS, 2ND (1863-1864)

Ash, S. V. Firebrand of liberty   973.7

UNITED STATES. ARMY -- SPECIAL FORCES

Carney, J. T. No room for error   356

UNITED STATES. ARMY. SPECIAL FORCES -- OFFICERS -- BIOGRAPHY

Wolf, M. J. Abandoned in hell   959.704

UNITED STATES. ARMY -- TASK FORCE RANGER

Bowden, M. Black Hawk down   967.73

UNITED STATES. ARMY. VOLUNTEER CAVALRY, 1ST

Gardner, M. L. Rough Riders   973.91

United States. Bureau of Labor Statistics

(comp) Occupational outlook handbook 2013-2014   331.12

UNITED STATES. CENTRAL INTELLIGENCE AGENCY

Abrahamian, E. The coup   955.05

Bird, K. The Good Spy   92

Coll, S. Ghost wars   958.1

Grenier, R. L. 88 days to Kandahar   958.104

Grose, P. Gentleman spy   92

Gup, T. Book of honor   327.12

Johnson, I. A mosque in Munich   297

Kessler, R. The CIA at war   973.931

McCoy, A. W. A question of torture   323.4

Miller, J. The cell: inside the 9/11 plot and why the FBI and CIA failed to stop it   973.931

Morell, M. J. The great war of our time 363.325

Richelson, J. The wizards of Langley   327.12

Schroen, G. C. First in **958.1**

Talbot, D. The Devil's Chessboard **92**

Weiner, T. Legacy of ashes **327.12**

Woods, R. B. Shadow warrior **92**

UNITED STATES. CENTRAL INTELLIGENCE AGENCY -- BIOGRAPHY

Grenier, R. L. 88 days to Kandahar **958.104**

Woods, R. B. Shadow warrior **92**

UNITED STATES. CENTRAL INTELLIGENCE AGENCY -- HISTORY

Weiner, T. Legacy of ashes **327.12**

UNITED STATES. CENTRAL INTELLIGENCE AGENCY -- HISTORY -- 20TH CENTURY

Abrahamian, E. The coup **955.05**

Finn, P. The Zhivago affair **891.73**

Lichtblau, E. The Nazis next door **324.1**

UNITED STATES. CENTRAL INTELLIGENCE AGENCY -- OFFICIALS AND EMPLOYEES -- BIOGRAPHY

Gates, R. M. A passion for leadership **92**

Morell, M. J. The great war of our time **363.325**

UNITED STATES. CIVIL RIGHTS ACT OF 1964

Purdum, T. S. An idea whose time has come **342.73**

Risen, C. The bill of the century **342.73**

UNITED STATES. CONGRESS

Congressional Quarterly, I. Congress A to Z **328**

Dray, P. Capitol men **920**

Heidler, D. S. Henry Clay **92**

Kaiser, R. G. Act of Congress **346.73**

Kaiser, R. G. So damn much money **328**

Kramer, M. A people's guide to the federal budget **352.4**

Miller, W. L. Arguing about slavery **973.5**

Pooley, E. The climate war **363.7**

UNITED STATES. CONGRESS -- ELECTIONS -- FINANCE

Vogel, K. P. Big money **324.7**

UNITED STATES. CONGRESS. HOUSE

Dray, P. Capitol men **920**

Spieler, M. The U.S. House of Representatives **328.73**

UNITED STATES. CONGRESS. HOUSE -- BIOGRAPHY

Frank, B. Frank **92**

Sanders, B. Outsider in the White House **92**

UNITED STATES. CONGRESS. SENATE

Cleland, M. Heart of a patriot **92**

Clinton, H. R. Living history **92**

English, B. Last lion **92**

Kennedy, E. M. True compass **92**

Kennedy, J. F. Profiles in courage **920**

Mendell, D. Obama **92**

Sanders, B. Outsider in the White House **92**

The senate intelligence committee report on torture

Thomas, E. Robert Kennedy **92**

UNITED STATES. CONGRESS. SENATE -- BI-

OGRAPHY

Bai, M. All the truth is out **328.73**

Tye, L. Bobby Kennedy **92**

Warren, E. A fighting chance **92**

UNITED STATES. CONGRESS. SENATE -- HISTORY

Baker, R. A. The American Senate **328.73**

United States. Congress. Senate. Select Committee on Intelligence

(comp) The senate intelligence committee report on torture

UNITED STATES. CONSTITUTION

Amar, A. R. America's constitution **342**

The annotated U.S. Constitution and Declaration of Independence **342**

The Federalist **342**

Puleo, S. American treasures **973**

UNITED STATES. CONSTITUTION. 13TH AMENDMENT -- HISTORY

Richards, L. L. Who freed the slaves? **342.73**

UNITED STATES. CONSTITUTION. 1ST AMENDMENT

Shipler, D. K. Freedom of speech **323.44**

UNITED STATES. CONSTITUTION. 1ST-10TH AMENDMENTS

The annotated U.S. Constitution and Declaration of Independence **342**

Howard, D. Lost rights **973.7**

UNITED STATES. CONSTITUTION. 1ST-10TH AMENDMENTS. ENCYCLOPEDIAS

Encyclopedia of the First Amendment **342**

UNITED STATES. CONSTITUTION. 2ND AMENDMENT

Giffords, G. D. Enough **363.33**

UNITED STATES. CONSTITUTION. GRAPHIC NOVELS

Hennessey, J. The United States Constitution **342**

UNITED STATES. CONTINENTAL CONGRESS

Phillips, K. 1775 **973.3**

UNITED STATES. CONTINENTAL CONGRESS -- BIOGRAPHY

McKean, D. Suspected of independence **92**

UNITED STATES. CONTINENTAL CONGRESS -- HISTORY

Beeman, R. R. Our lives, our fortunes and our sacred honor **973.3**

UNITED STATES. CONTINENTAL CONGRESS, 1774

Beeman, R. R. Our lives, our fortunes and our sacred honor **973.3**

McKean, D. Suspected of independence **92**

UNITED STATES. DECLARATION OF INDEPENDENCE

Puleo, S. American treasures **973**

UNITED STATES. DECLARATION OF INDEPENDENCE -- CRITICISM, TEXTUAL

Allen, D. Our Declaration **973.3**

UNITED STATES. DECLARATION OF INDE-PENDENCE -- SIGNERS -- BIOGRAPHY

McKean, D. Suspected of independence **92**

UNITED STATES. DEFENSE OF MARRIAGE ACT

Becker, J. Forcing the spring **346.73**

Dickey, L. Then comes marriage **346**

Yoshino, K. Speak now **346.73**

UNITED STATES. DEPARTMENT OF DEFENSE -- OFFICIALS AND EMPLOYEES -- BIOGRAPHY

Gates, R. M. A passion for leadership **92**

UNITED STATES. DEPT. OF AGRICULTURE -- OFFICIALS AND EMPLOYEES -- BIOGRAPHY

Sherrod, S. The courage to hope **975.8**

UNITED STATES. DEPT. OF DEFENSE

Carroll, J. House of war **355**

Jacobsen, A. The Pentagon's Brain **355**

Vogel, S. The Pentagon **355.6**

Woodward, B. The commanders **973.928**

UNITED STATES. DEPT. OF HOMELAND SECURITY

Baker, S. A. Skating on stilts **363.32**

UNITED STATES. DEPT. OF LABOR

Downey, K. The woman behind the New Deal **92**

Reich, R. B. Locked in the cabinet **973.929**

UNITED STATES. DEPT. OF STATE -- BIOGRAPHY

Rice, C. No higher honor **327.73**

Stahr, W. Seward **92**

Unger, I. George Marshall **92**

UNITED STATES. DEPT. OF THE TREASURY -- HISTORY

McCraw, T. K. The founders and finance **330.973**

UNITED STATES. DODD-FRANK WALL STREET REFORM AND CONSUMER PROTECTION ACT

Kaiser, R. G. Act of Congress **346.73**

UNITED STATES. ENVIRONMENTAL PROTECTION AGENCY

Jenkins, M. Poison spring **363.73**

UNITED STATES. FEDERAL BUREAU OF INVESTIGATION

Burrough, B. Days of Rage **303.48**

Carson, C. Malcolm X: the FBI file **92**

Gentry, C. J. Edgar Hoover **353**

Graff, G. M. The threat matrix **363.325**

Hendricks, S. The unquiet grave **970.004**

Miller, J. The cell: inside the 9/11 plot and why the FBI and CIA failed to stop it **973.931**

Rosenfeld, S. Subversives **378.1**

Wise, D. Spy: the inside story of how the FBI's Robert Hanssen betrayed America **327.12**

UNITED STATES. FEDERAL BUREAU OF IN-

VESTIGATION -- GRAPHIC NOVELS

Geary, R. J. Edgar Hoover **363.2**

UNITED STATES. FEDERAL BUREAU OF INVESTIGATION -- HISTORY -- 20TH CENTURY

Lichtblau, E. The Nazis next door **324.1**

Weiner, T. Enemies **363.25**

UNITED STATES. FEDERAL BUREAU OF INVESTIGATION -- OFFICIALS AND EMPLOYEES -- BIOGRAPHY

Kinney, D. The devil's diary **940.53**

UNITED STATES. FOOD AND DRUG ADMINISTRATION

Hilts, P. J. Protecting America's health **353.9**

UNITED STATES. FOREST SERVICE

Egan, T. The big burn **973.91**

MacLean, N. Young men & fire **634.9**

UNITED STATES. IMMIGRATION BORDER PATROL -- HISTORY

Miller, T. Border patrol nation **363.28**

UNITED STATES. MARINE CORPS

Bradley, J. Flags of our fathers **940.54**

Kindsvatter, P. S. American soldiers **355**

Swofford, A. Jarhead: a Marine's chronicle of the Gulf War and other battles **956.704**

Ventrone, J. From the Marine Corps to college **378.1**

UNITED STATES -- MARINE CORPS -- MARINES, 28TH

Haynes, F. The lions of Iwo Jima **940.54**

UNITED STATES. MARINE CORPS -- HISTORY -- 20TH CENTURY

Hutton, R. Sgt. Reckless **951.904**

UNITED STATES. MARINE CORPS -- NON-COMMISSIONED OFFICERS -- BIOGRAPHY

Bruning, J. R. Level zero heroes **958.104**

UNITED STATES. MARINE CORPS -- OFFICERS

Hickman, J. Murder at Camp Delta **355.1**

UNITED STATES. MARINE CORPS -- OFFICERS -- BIOGRAPHY

Busch, B. Dust to dust **92**

UNITED STATES. MARINE CORPS. MARINE REGIMENT, 5TH -- BIOGRAPHY

Hutton, R. Sgt. Reckless **951.904**

UNITED STATES. NATIONAL AERONAUTICS AND SPACE ADMINISTRATION

Dean, M. L. Leaving orbit **629.4**

Hubbard, S. Exploring Mars **523.43**

Kranz, E. F. Failure is not an option **629.45**

Lee Shetterly, M. Hidden Figures **510.92**

Manning, R. Mars Rover Curiosity **629.295**

Milestones of space **629.4**

Paul, R. We could not fail **920**

Space chronicles **629.4**

Teitel, A. S. Breaking the Chains of Gravity 629.4

UNITED STATES. NATIONAL AERONAUTICS AND SPACE ADMINISTRATION -- BIOGRAPHY

Anderson, C. The ordinary spaceman 92

UNITED STATES. NATIONAL AERONAUTICS AND SPACE ADMINISTRATION -- OFFICIALS AND EMPLOYEES -- BIOGRAPHY

Paul, R. We could not fail 920

UNITED STATES. NATIONAL PARK SERVICE

Farabee, C. R. National park ranger 363.6

UNITED STATES. NATIONAL PARK SERVICE -- HISTORY

Duncan, D. The national parks 333.7

Farabee, C. R. National park ranger 363.6

UNITED STATES. NATIONAL SECURITY AGENCY

Bamford, J. The shadow factory 327.12

Harris, S. @WAR 355.3

UNITED STATES. NAVY

Berman, L. Zumwalt 92

Horwitz, J. War of the Whales 333.95

Symonds, C. L. Lincoln and his admirals 92

Thomas, E. John Paul Jones 92

Thomas, E. Sea of thunder 940.54

Toll, I. W. Six frigates 359

UNITED STATES. NAVY -- BIOGRAPHY

Borneman, W. R. The admirals 920

UNITED STATES. NAVY -- COMMANDO TROOPS

Henican, E. Worth dying for 359.984

UNITED STATES. NAVY -- COMMANDO TROOPS -- BIOGRAPHY

Maurer, K. No easy day 958.104

UNITED STATES. NAVY -- HISTORY -- 20TH CENTURY

Borneman, W. R. The admirals 920

UNITED STATES. NAVY -- OFFICERS -- BIOGRAPHY

Berman, L. Zumwalt 92

UNITED STATES. NAVY. SEALS

Daughan, G. C. 1812: the Navy's war 973.5

Symonds, C. L. Lincoln and his admirals 92

Luttrell, M. Lone survivor 92

UNITED STATES. NAVY. SEALS -- BIOGRAPHY

Maurer, K. No easy day 958.104

UNITED STATES. NAVY. SEALS -- OFFICERS -- BIOGRAPHY

Hornfischer, J. D. Service 956.704

UNITED STATES. OFFICE OF STRATEGIC SERVICES -- HISTORY

Lulushi, A. Donovan's Devils 940.54

UNITED STATES. OFFICE OF THE CHIEF OF NAVAL OPERATIONS -- HISTORY -- 20TH CENTURY

Berman, L. Zumwalt 92

UNITED STATES. PRESIDENT (1861-1865 : LINCOLN). EMANCIPATION PROCLAMATION

Brewster, T. Lincoln's Gamble 973.7

Oakes, J. Freedom national 973.7

Richards, L. L. Who freed the slaves? 342.73

Slotkin, R. Long Road to Antietam 973.7

UNITED STATES. SECRET SERVICE -- OFFICIALS AND EMPLOYEES -- BIOGRAPHY

Hill, C. Five days in November 973.922

Hill, C. Five presidents 363.28

Hill, C. Mrs. Kennedy and me 973.922

UNITED STATES. STRATEGIC COMMAND (2002-). CYBER COMMAND

Harris, S. @WAR 355.3

UNITED STATES. SUPREME COURT

Becker, J. Forcing the spring 346.73

Breyer, S. G. Making our democracy work 347

Breyer, S. G. Active liberty 342

Carpenter, D. Flagrant conduct 342.73

Cohen, A. Imbeciles 344

Coyle, M. The Roberts court 347.73

Faigman, D. L. Laboratory of justice 347

Feldman, N. Scorpions 920

Greenhouse, L. Becoming Justice Blackmun 92

Haygood, W. Showdown 347.73

Hirshman, L. Sisters in law 347.73

Lane, C. The day freedom died 976.3

Leiter, R. A. Landmark Supreme Court cases 347

Lewis, A. Gideon's trumpet 345

Marshall, T. Thurgood Marshall 347

Mersky, R. M. Landmark Supreme Court cases 347.73

Noonan, J. T. Narrowing the nation's power: the Supreme Court sides with the states 342

O'Brien, D. M. Storm center 347

O'Connor, S. D. Out of order 347.73

The Oxford companion to the Supreme Court of the United States 347

The Oxford guide to United States Supreme Court decisions 342

Rowan, C. T. Dream makers, dream breakers 92

Schultz, D. A. Encyclopedia of the United States Constitution 342

Shesol, J. Supreme power 347

Simon, J. F. What kind of nation 342

Smith, J. E. John Marshall 347

Toobin, J. R. The nine 347

Toobin, J. The oath 347.73

Tribe, L. H. Uncertain justice 342.73

Tushnet, M. In the balance 347.73

Urofsky, M. I. Dissent and the Supreme Court 342.73

Urofsky, M. I. Louis D. Brandeis 92

VanderVelde, L. Mrs. Dred Scott 92

Williams, J. Thurgood Marshall   **92**

UNITED STATES. SUPREME COURT
   See also Courts

**UNITED STATES. SUPREME COURT -- BIOG-
RAPHY**
   See also Biography

**UNITED STATES. SUPREME COURT -- ANEC-
DOTES**
O'Connor, S. D. Out of order   **347.73**

**UNITED STATES. SUPREME COURT -- BIOG-
RAPHY**
Jost, K. The Supreme Court A to Z   **347.73**
Justices of the United States Supreme Court **347.73**
Murphy, B. A. Scalia   **92**
Simon, J. F. FDR and Chief Justice Hughes **973.917**
Unger, H. G. John Marshall   **92**

**UNITED STATES. SUPREME COURT -- ENCY-
CLOPEDIAS**
Jost, K. The Supreme Court A to Z   **347.73**

**UNITED STATES. SUPREME COURT -- HIS-
TORY**
Gibson, L. S. Young Thurgood   **347.73**
Lombardo, P. A. Three generations, no imbe-
ciles   **344**
O'Connor, S. D. Out of order   **347.73**
Simon, J. F. What kind of nation   **342**
The Supreme Court justices   **347.73**

**UNITED STATES. SUPREME COURT -- HIS-
TORY -- 21ST CENTURY**
Coyle, M. The Roberts court   **347.73**
Toobin, J. The oath   **347.73**

**UNITED STATES. SUPREME COURT -- OFFI-
CIALS AND EMPLOYEES**
Gibson, L. S. Young Thurgood   **347.73**

**UNITED STATES. SUPREME COURT -- OFFI-
CIALS AND EMPLOYEES -- BIOGRAPHY**
Sotomayor, S. My beloved world   **92**
The Supreme Court justices   **347.73**

**UNITED STATES. SUPREME COURT -- OFFI-
CIALS AND EMPLOYEES -- SELECTION
AND APPOINTMENT -- HISTORY -- 20TH
CENTURY**
Haygood, W. Showdown   **347.73**

**UNITED STATES. SUPREME COURT -- PUB-
LIC OPINION**
Friedman, B. The will of the people   **347**

**UNITED STATES. VOTING RIGHTS ACT OF
1965**
Berman, A. Give us the ballot   **324.6**

**UNITED STATES. WAR DEPARTMENT -- BI-
OGRAPHY**
Marvel, W. Lincoln's autocrat   **92**

UNITED STATES. WARREN COMMISSION
Shenon, P. A cruel and shocking act   **973.922**

UNITED STATES. WHITE HOUSE OFFICE
Obama, M. American grown   **635**

United States/Government Printing Office
Style manual   **808**

UNITED STEELWORKERS OF AMERICA
   See also Labor unions

UNIVERSAL BIBLIOGRAPHY
Wright, A. Cataloging the world   **020.9**
The **universal** book of mathematics. Darling, D.
J.   **510**

UNIVERSAL DESIGN
Pierce, D. The accessible home   **728.087**
Universal design for the home. Jordan, W. A.   **728**
Universal Father: a life of John Paul II. O'Connor,
G.   **92**

UNIVERSAL HISTORY *See* World history
A **universal** history of the destruction of books.
Báez, F.   **900**

UNIVERSAL LANGUAGE
   See also Language and languages; Linguistics
Universal Man. Davenport-Hines, R. P. T.   **92**

UNIVERSAL MILITARY TRAINING *See* Draft
The **universal** tone. Santana, C.   **92**
Universe.   **523.1**
The **universe.**   **523.1**

UNIVERSE
Bell, J. The space book   **523.1**
Billings, L. Five billion years of solitude   **576.8**
Carroll, S. The Big Picture   **577**
Clark, S. The Unknown Universe   **523.1**
Goldberg, D. The Universe in the Rearview Mir-
ror   **539.7**
Goodstein, D. L. Feynman's lost lecture   **521**
Halpern, P. Edge of the universe   **523.1**
Hawking, S. The grand design   **530.1**
Krauss, L. M. A universe from nothing   **523.1**
Scharf, C. The Copernicus complex   **523.1**
Shubin, N. H. The universe within   **550**
Teilhard de Chardin, P. The phenomenon of
man   **113**
The universe   **523.1**
Weintraub, D. A. How old is the universe? **523.1**
A **universe** from nothing. Krauss, L. M.   **523.1**
The **universe** in a mirror. Zimmerman, R.   **629.43**
The **universe** in a nutshell. Hawking, S. W. **530.1**
The **Universe** in the Rearview Mirror. Goldberg,
D.   **539.7**
The **Universe** in Your Hand. Galfard, C.   **523.1**
The **universe** in zero words. Mackenzie, D. **512.9**
The **universe** within. Shubin, N. H.   **550**

UNIVERSITIES *See* Colleges and universities
UNIVERSITIES AND COLLEGES *See* Colleges
and universities

**UNIVERSITIES AND COLLEGES -- UNITED
STATES -- ADMISSION**
Jager-Hyman, J. B+ grades, A+ college applica-
tion   **378.1**

UNIVERSITIES AND COLLEGES -- UNITED

STATES -- DIRECTORIES
The Latino student's guide to college success **378.1**
UNIVERSITIES AND COLLEGES -- UNITED STATES -- FACULTY
Ecklund, E. H. Science vs. religion **215**
UNIVERSITIES AND COLLEGES -- UNITED STATES -- HISTORY
Wilder, C. S. Ebony and Ivy **379.26**
University Center for Human Values series
The lives of animals **179**
Pinsky, R. Democracy, culture, and the voice of poetry **811**
UNIVERSITY OF ALABAMA -- FOOTBALL -- HISTORY
Burke, M. Saban **796.332**
University of California (System)
Poems for the millennium **808.81**
University of California Press
Poems for the millennium **808.81**
UNIVERSITY OF CALIFORNIA, BERKELEY -- STUDENTS -- HISTORY
Rosenfeld, S. Subversives **378.1**
University of Chicago. Press
(comp) The Chicago manual of style **808**
UNIVERSITY OF NORTH CAROLINA AT CHAPEL HILL -- BASKETBALL -- HISTORY
Feinstein, J. The legends club **796.323**
UNIVERSITY OF OXFORD
Cartwright, J. Oxford revisited **942**
UNIVERSITY OF WASHINGTON -- ROWING -- HISTORY
Brown, D. J. The Boys in the Boat **797.12**
UNIVERSITY STUDENTS *See* College students
Unknown lands. Bellec, F. **910.4**
The **unknown** Matisse. Spurling, H. **92**
The **Unknown** Universe. Clark, S. **523.1**
Unlikely allies. Paul, J. R. **973.3**
Unlimited power. Robbins, T. **158**
UNMARRIED WOMEN *See* Single women
Unmastered. Angel, K. **828**
The **unnatural** history of the sea. Roberts, C. **909**
Unnatural selection. Monosson, E. **576.5**
Unorthodox. Feldman, D. **92**
Unplugged play. Conner, B. **790.1**
The **unquiet** ghost. Hochschild, A. **947.084**
The **unquiet** grave. Hendricks, S. **970.004**
The **Unraveling.** Sky, E. **956.7**
An **unreasonable** woman. Wilson, D. **92**
The **unredeemed** captive. Demos, J. **973.2**
Unseen hand. **891.8**
The **unseen** hand and other plays. Shepard, S. **812**
Unselfie. Borba, M. **649.7**
UNSELFISHNESS *See* Altruism
UNSKILLED LABOR
See also Labor
UNSKILLED LABOR -- SUPPLY AND DE-

MAND
See also Supply and demand
The **unspeakable.** Daum, M. **814**
Unspeakable acts, ordinary people. Conroy, J. **323.4**
Unstrange minds. Grinker, R. R. **616.85**
Unstuffed. Soukup, R. **646.7**
The **unsubscriber.** Knott, B. **811**
The **unsubstantial** air. Hynes, S. **940.4**
Untangled. Damour, L. **305.235**
The **unthinkable.** Ripley, A. **155.9**
Unthinkable. Pollack, K. M. **355.8**
Until Tuesday. Witter, B. **362.4**
Until We Are Free. Ebadi, S. **92**
Untouchables. Jadhav, N. **305.5**
UNTRUTH *See* Truthfulness and falsehood
The **unwanted** sound of everything we want. Keizer, G. **363.7**
Unweaving the rainbow. Dawkins, R. **501**
Unwin, Mike
The atlas of birds **598**
The **unwinding.** Packer, G. **973.924**
The **unwritten** rules of friendship. Elman, N. M. **649**
Up from history. Norrell, R. J. **92**
Up from slavery. Washington, B. T. **92**
Up, down, all-around stitch dictionary. Bernard, W. **746.43**
Updike. Pritchard, W. H. **813**
Updike. Begley, A. **92**
Updike, John, 1932-2009
Always looking **700**
Begley, A. Updike **92**
Collected poems, 1953-1993 **811**
Due considerations **814**
Higher gossip **818**
(ed) Selected poems **811**
About
Pritchard, W. H. Updike **813**
Upgraded to serious. McHugh, H. **811**
Upgrading and repairing PCs. **004.16**
UPHOLSTERY
Brown, A. Spruce **747**
Cone, S. Singer upholstery basics plus **684.1**
Dobson, C. The complete guide to upholstery **684.1**
UPHOLSTERY
See also Interior design
Upon the altar of the nation : a moral history of the American Civil War. Stout, H. S. **973.7**
UPPER ATMOSPHERE
See also Atmosphere
UPPER CLASS
Martin, W. Primates of Park Avenue **974.7**
Murray, C. Coming apart **305.8**
UPPER CLASS
See also Social classes
UPPER CLASS -- BIOGRAPHY

Bingham, E. Irrepressible   **306.76**

UPPER CLASS -- SOCIAL LIFE AND CUSTOMS -- 20TH CENTURY

Wilson, P. Lusitania   **910.4**

UPPER CLASS -- UNITED STATES -- BIOGRAPHY

Burns, J. M. The three Roosevelts   **973.91**

Wilson, P. Lusitania   **910.4**

UPPER CLASS -- WASHINGTON (D.C.) -- HISTORY -- 20TH CENTURY

Herken, G. The Georgetown set   **975.3**

UPPER CLASS WOMEN -- UNITED STATES -- BIOGRAPHY

Bingham, E. Irrepressible   **306.76**

UPPER CLASSES *See* Upper class

UPPER EAST SIDE (NEW YORK, N.Y.) -- BIOGRAPHY

Martin, W. Primates of Park Avenue   **974.7**

UPPER EAST SIDE (NEW YORK, N.Y.) -- SOCIAL LIFE AND CUSTOMS

Martin, W. Primates of Park Avenue   **974.7**

Uppity. White, B.   **92**

The **upright** thinkers. Mlodinow, L.   **509**

The **uprooted.** Handlin, O.   **325**

Upstyle your furniture. Jones, S.   **684.1**

Upton, Clive

Oxford rhyming dictionary   **423**

Upton, Eben

Upton, C. Oxford rhyming dictionary   **423**

URAL MOUNTAINS REGION (RUSSIA) -- HISTORY -- 20TH CENTURY

Eichar, D. Dead Mountain   **914.7**

Uranium. Zoellner, T.   **546**

URANIUM

Zoellner, T. Uranium   **546**

URANIUM

See also Chemical elements

URANIUM MINES AND MINING

Pasternak, J. Yellow dirt   **979.1**

URANUS (PLANET)

See also Planets

URBAN ANIMALS

DeStefano, S. Coyote at the kitchen door   **578.7**

Welcome to subirdia   **598**

URBAN AREAS *See* Cities and towns; Metropolitan areas

The **urban** cycling survival guide. Bambrick, Y.   **796.6**

URBAN DEVELOPMENT *See* Cities and towns -- Growth; City planning; Urbanization

URBAN ECOLOGY

See also Cities and towns; Ecology

URBAN ECOLOGY

Barilla, J. My Backyard Jungle   **577.5**

URBAN ECOLOGY -- SOCIAL ASPECTS

Owen, D. Green metropolis   **304.2**

URBAN FICTION

Honig, M. Urban grit   **016**

URBAN FICTION

See also Fiction

URBAN FICTION, AMERICAN -- BIBLIOGRAPHY

Honig, M. Urban grit   **016**

Morris, V. I. The readers' advisory guide to street literature   **016**

URBAN GEOLOGY

Williams, D. B. Stories in stone   **550**

Urban grit. Honig, M.   **016**

URBAN HOMESTEADING

See also Houses -- Buying and selling; Housing; Urban renewal

URBAN HOUSING *See* Housing

Urban Italian. Hyman, G.   **641.5**

URBAN LIFE *See* City and town life

URBAN PLANNERS

Caro, R. A. The power broker: Robert Moses and the fall of New York   **92**

Rybczynski, W. A clearing in the distance: Frederick Law Olmsted and America in the nineteenth century   **712**

URBAN PLANNING *See* City planning

URBAN POLICY

See also City and town life; Economic policy; Social policy; Urban sociology

URBAN POLICY -- UNITED STATES

Duany, A. Suburban nation   **307.76**

URBAN RENEWAL

Kanigel, R. Eyes on the street   **92**

URBAN RENEWAL

See also Metropolitan areas; Urban sociology

URBAN RENEWAL -- CANADA -- HISTORY -- 20TH CENTURY

Kanigel, R. Eyes on the street   **92**

URBAN RENEWAL -- UNITED STATES

Duany, A. Suburban nation   **307.76**

URBAN RENEWAL -- UNITED STATES -- HISTORY -- 20TH CENTURY

Kanigel, R. Eyes on the street   **92**

URBAN SCHOOLS

Falk, B. Teaching matters   **370.9**

URBAN SOCIOLOGY

Smith, P. D. City   **307.76**

URBAN SOCIOLOGY

See also Sociology

URBAN STREET LIFE *See* Street life

URBAN TRAFFIC *See* City traffic

URBAN TRANSPORTATION

Byrne, D. Bicycle diaries   **796.6**

Urban VIII, Pope, 1568-1644

         About

Hofstadter, D. The Earth moves   **509**

URBAN-RURAL MIGRATION *See* Internal migration

URBANIZATION

DeStefano, S. Coyote at the kitchen door **578.7**

Duany, A. Suburban nation **307.76**

Saunders, D. Arrival city **307.24**

URBANIZATION

   See also Cities and towns; Rural sociology; Social change; Social conditions; Urban sociology

URBANIZATION -- UNITED STATES

Duany, A. Suburban nation **307.76**

Urdang, Laurence

(ed) The timetables of American history **902**

Ureneck, Lou

The Great Fire **956.1**

Urofsky, Melvin I.

Dissent and the Supreme Court **342.73**

Finkelman, P. Landmark decisions of the United States Supreme Court **347**

Louis D. Brandeis **92**

Urrea, Luis Alberto

The devil's highway **325**

Urrutia, Matilde

My life with Pablo Neruda **92**

Urschel, Joe

The Year of Fear **364.152**

Urwand, Ben

The collaboration **791.43**

Ury, William

Getting past no **158**

US *See* United States

USA *See* United States

USA Today health reports: diseases and disorders [series]

Rodriguez, A. M. Autism spectrum disorders **616.85**

The **use** and abuse of literature. Garber, M. **801**

Use your head to get your foot in the door. Mackay, H. **650.14**

Useful Enemies. Rashke, R. **341.69**

USEFUL INSECTS *See* Beneficial insects

Useless landscape. Powell, D. A. **811**

A **user's** guide to the universe. Goldberg, D. **530**

USSR *See* Russia -- History -- 1917-1991, Soviet Union

USURY

Mayer, R. Quick cash **332**

UTILITARIANISM

   See also Ethics

UTILIZATION OF WASTE *See* Salvage

Utley, Robert Marshall

Sitting Bull: the life and times of an American patriot **92**

Utley, Robert Marshall, 1929-

Geronimo **92**

UTOPIA (TEX.)

Valby, K. Welcome to Utopia **976.4**

Utopia is creepy. Carr, N. G. **303.483**

UTOPIAN FICTION

   See also Fantasy fiction; Science fiction

UTOPIAN LITERATURE *See* Utopian fiction; Utopias

Utopianism and communitarianism [series]

Chevannes, B. Rastafari: roots and ideology **299.6**

UTOPIAS

Heilbroner, R. L. The worldly philosophers **330.1**

Plato The republic **888**

UTOPIAS

   See also Political science; Socialism

V

V Is for Vegetables. Anthony, M. **641.6**

V.S. Pritchett: a working life. Treglown, J. **92**

VACATION HOMES

   See also Houses

Vaccinated. Offit, P. A. **92**

VACCINATION

Allen, A. Vaccine **614.4**

Conis, E. Vaccine nation **614.4**

Offit, P. A. Deadly choices **614.4**

Offit, P. A. Vaccinated **92**

VACCINATION

   See also Immunization; Preventive medicine; Public health

VACCINATION -- UNITED STATES -- HISTORY -- 20TH CENTURY

Conis, E. Vaccine nation **614.4**

VACCINATION OF CHILDREN

Offit, P. A. Deadly choices **614.4**

Sears, R. W. The vaccine book **614.4**

Vaccine. Allen, A. **614.4**

The **vaccine** book. Sears, R. W. **614.4**

Vaccine nation. Conis, E. **614.4**

Vacher, Joseph, 1869-1898

      About

Starr, D. The killer of little shepherds **364.152**

VACUUM TUBES

   See also Electronic apparatus and appliances

Vaden, Rory

Procrastinate on purpose **650.1**

Vagina. Wolf, N. **305.42**

VAGINA

Wolf, N. Vagina **305.42**

Vaidhyanathan, Siva

The Googlization of everything **338.7**

Vaill, Amanda

Everybody was so young **759.13**

Somewhere **92**

Vaillancourt, Renee J.

Bare bones young adult services **027.62**

Vaillant, George E.

Triumphs of experience **305.31**

Vaillant, John
The tiger   **599.75**
Valby, Karen
Welcome to Utopia   **976.4**
Valenciana, Jesse
(jt. auth) Carruthers, J. Eat street   **641.76**
Valenti, Jessica, 1978-
Full Frontal Feminism   **305.42**
Sex object   **92**
(ed) Yes means yes!   **306.7**
Valentina, 1904-1989
        About
Fraser, K. Ornament and silence   **809**
VALENTINE'S DAY
     See also Holidays
Valentine, Amie
Kashuk, S. Real beauty   **646.7**
Valentine, Jean
Door in the mountain   **811**
Valery, Paul
Selected writings   **848**
Valiant Ambition. Philbrick, N.   **973.3**
Vallely, Paul
Pope Francis   **92**
Valley of death. Morgan, T.   **959.704**
Valley walls. Denny, G.   **796.52**
Valli, Clayton
(ed) The Gallaudet dictionary of American Sign
Language   **419**
Vallianatos, E. G.
(jt. auth) Jenkins, M. Poison spring   **363.73**
Vallone, Lynne
Becoming Victoria   **941.08**
VALOZHYN (BELARUS) -- BIOGRAPHY
Laskin, D. The Family   **92**
The **value** of a dollar.   **338.5**
The **value** of a dollar: colonial era to the Civil War,
1600-1865.   **338.5**
The **value** of nothing. Patel, R.   **330.1**
VALUES
Gentile, M. C. Giving voice to values   **174**
Kinsley, M. Old age   **814.54**
Peck, M. S. The road less traveled   **158**
Sandel, M. J. Justice   **172**
Shields, C. J. Aristotle   **185**
Wolfe, A. Moral freedom   **170**
VALUES
     See also Aesthetics; Ethics; Psychology
Valverde, Leonard A.
(ed) The Latino student's guide to college suc-
cess   **378.1**
Vamosi, Robert
When gadgets betray us   **004**
Vampira. Poole, W. S.   **92**
Vampira, 1921-2008
        About

Poole, W. S. Vampira   **92**
The **vampire** book. Melton, J. G.   **398**
VAMPIRE FILMS
     See also Horror films; Motion pictures
VAMPIRES
Guiley, R. E. The encyclopedia of vampires &
werewolves   **398**
VAMPIRES
     See also Folklore
VAMPIRES -- ENCYCLOPEDIAS
Bane, T. Encyclopedia of vampire mythology   **398**
Guiley, R. E. The encyclopedia of vampires &
werewolves   **398**
Melton, J. G. The vampire book   **398**
Van Aken, Janet
New World kitchen   **641.59**
Van Aken, Norman
New World kitchen   **641.59**
Van Allen, Jennifer
(jt. auth) Bede, P. N. The Runner's world big book
of marathon and half-marathon training   **796.425**
Van Beuren, Alexe
(jt. auth) Grimes, D. The B.T.C. old-fashioned gro-
cery cookbook   **641.59**
Van Buren, Martin, 1782-1862
        About
Widmer, E. L. Martin Van Buren   **92**
Van Buren, Peter
We meant well   **956**
Van den Hoven, Adrian
(ed) We Have Only This Life to Live   **848**
Van der Kolk, Bessel A., 1943-
The body keeps the score   **616.85**
Van der Leun, Gerard
Russell, E. A. Let it bleed   **781.66**
Van der Meer, Antonia
Coastal living beach house happy   **747**
Van Dokkum, Pieter, 1972-
Dragonflies   **595.7**
Van Doren, Adam, 1962-
        About
Van Doren, A. The house tells the story   **728**
Van Doren, Mark
(ed) Wordsworth, W. Selected poetry of William
Wordsworth   **821**
Van Duyn, Mona
Selected poems   **811**
Van Fleet, Connie
(ed) African American literature   **810.9**
Van Gogh. Bell, J.   **92**
Van Gogh. Naifeh, S.   **92**
Van Gogh paintings. Thomson, B.   **759.9**
Van Gogh, Vincent, 1853-1890
        About
Bell, J. Van Gogh   **92**
Van Heerden, Ivor Ll.

The storm 976.3
Van Leeuwen Artisan Ice Cream. 641
Van Leeuwen, Ben, 1984-
Van Leeuwen Artisan Ice Cream 641
Van Leeuwen, Peter
Van Leeuwen Artisan Ice Cream 641
Van Lew, Elizabeth L., 1818-1900
About
Abbott, K. Liar, Temptress, Soldier, Spy 973.7
Van Nieuwerburgh, Stijn
(jt. auth) Acharya, V. V. Guaranteed to fail 332.7
Van Nostrand's scientific encyclopedia. 503
Van Pelt, Robert Jan
(ed) At the edge of the abyss 940.53
Dwork, D. Holocaust: a history 940.53
Van Sciver, Noah
The Hypo 92
Van Sicklen, Margaret
The joy of origami 736
Van Tilburg, JoAnne
Among stone giants 92
Van Vechten, Carl, 1880-1964
About
Bernard, E. Carl Van Vechten and the Harlem Re-
naissance 92
White, E. The Tastemaker 92
Van Wyk, Ben-Erik
Food plants of the world 581.6
Van Zandt, Townes, 1944-1997
About
Kruth, J. To live's to fly 92
Van't Hul, Jean
The artful parent 745.5
The artful year 745.594
Vance, J. D.
About
Vance, J. D. Hillbilly elegy 92
Vancouver, George
About
Raban, J. Passage to Juneau 979.8
VanDeMark, Brian
McNamara, R. S. In retrospect 959.704
Vander Ark, Tom, 1959-
Getting smart 371.33
VANDERBILT COMMODORES (BASKET-
BALL TEAM) -- HISTORY
Maraniss, A. Strong inside 92
Vanderbilt, Cornelius, 1794-1877
About
Renehan, E. J. Commodore 92
Stiles, T. J. The first tycoon 92
Vanderbilt, Gloria, 1924-
About
Cooper, A. The rainbow comes and goes 92
Vanderbilt, Tom
Traffic 629.28

You may also like 153.8
VanderKam, James C.
(ed) The Encyclopedia of the Dead Sea scrolls 296.1
Vandermolen, Laurie Ann
(jt. auth) Acquista, A. The Mediterranean Family
Table 641.59
Vanderpoel, John H.
The human figure 743.4
VanderVelde, Lea
Mrs. Dred Scott 92
VanDuinkerken, Wyoma
(jt. auth) Mosley, P. A. The challenge of library
management 025.1
VanDyne, Stacia N.
(ed) Encyclopedia of American business 338
Vanhoenacker, Mark
Skyfaring 629.132
Vanished smile. Scotti, R. A. 759
A vanished world. Lowney, C. 946
Vanishing grace. Yancey, P. 277
The vanishing hitchhiker. Brunvand, J. H. 398.2
VANISHING SPECIES See Endangered species
The Vanishing Velazquez. Cumming, L. 759.6
Vanity Fair, the portraits. Carter, G. 779
Vann, John Paul
About
Sheehan, N. A bright shining lie: John Paul Vann
and America in Vietnam 959.704
Vanzetti, Bartolomeo, 1888-1927
About
Watson, B. Sacco and Vanzetti 345
Vardaman, Lisa
(ed) Our new public, a changing clientele 025.1
Vare, Ethlie Ann
Patently female 609.2
Vargas Llosa, Mario
The language of passion 864
Vargas Lopez, Wanda
About
Liebman, J. S. The wrong Carlos 364.152
VARIATION (BIOLOGY)
See also Biology; Genetics; Heredity
VARIATIONS (MUSIC)
See also Music
The varieties of religious experience. James, W. 210
VARIETY SHOWS (TELEVISION PROGRAMS)
See also Television programs
Varmus, Harold
About
Varmus, H. The art and politics of science 92
VARSITY SPORTS See College sports
Varty, Boyd
About
Varty, B. Cathedral of the wild 639.9
VASECTOMY
See also Sterilization (Birth control)

Vassallo, Marc
Inside the not so big house **728.37**
(jt. auth) Susanka, S. Not so big remodeling **643.7**
VASSALS See Feudalism
Vassiliev, Alexander
Haynes, J. E. Spies **327.12**
Weinstein, A. The haunted wood **327.12**
A **vast** conspiracy. Toobin, J. R. **973.929**
VATICAN -- CAPPELLA SISTINA
King, R. Michelangelo & the Pope's ceiling **759**
VATICAN CITY
Posner, G. God's Bankers **364.16**
VATICAN CITY -- FOREIGN RELATIONS See
Catholic Church -- Foreign relations
VAUDEVILLE
Trav S. D. No applause, just throw money; or, The
book that made vaudeville famous **792.7**
VAUDEVILLE
See also Amusements; Theater
Vaughan, Hal
Sleeping with the enemy **92**
Vaughan, William
(ed) Encyclopedia of artists **709**
Vavilov, N. I. (Nikolai Ivanovich), 1887-1943
About
Pringle, P. The murder of Nikolai Vavilov **92**
The **VB6** cookbook. **641.5**
Veblen, Sarah
The complete photo guide to perfect fitting **646.4**
Veblen, Thorstein, 1857-1929
The theory of the leisure class **305.5**
About
Commager, H. S. The American mind **973**
Heilbroner, R. L. The worldly philosophers **330.1**
Vecsey, George
Eight world cups **796.334**
VEDANTA
Goldberg, P. American Veda **294.5**
VEDANTA
See also Hinduism; Theosophy
Vedantam, Shankar
The hidden brain **154.2**
VEDAS
See also Hinduism; Sacred books
Vedge. Jacoby, K. **641.6**
**VEDGE (RESTAURANT : PHILADELPHIA,
PA.)**
Jacoby, K. Vedge **641.6**
Vega, Lope de
Three major plays **862**
VEGAN COOKING
Afro-vegan **641.59**
Atlas, N. Plant power **641.5**
But I could never go **641.5**
Jacoby, K. Vedge **641.6**
Liddon, A. The oh she glows cookbook **641.5**

Patalsky, K. Healthy happy vegan kitchen **641.5**
Raw, vegan, not gross **641.5**
Robertson, R. Vegan planet **641.5**
Romero, T. H. Salad samurai **641.83**
Ronnen, T. Crossroads **641.59**
Street vegan **641.5**
The VB6 cookbook **641.5**
Vegan holiday cooking from Candle Cafe **641.5**
Vegan holiday cooking from Candle Cafe. **641.5**
Vegan pie in the sky. Moskowitz, I. C. **641.5**
Vegan planet. Robertson, R. **641.5**
Vegan planet. Robertson, R. **641.5**
Vegan Soul kitchen. Terry, B. **641.5**
Vegan, vegetarian, omnivore. **641.5**
VEGANISM
Afro-vegan **641.59**
But I could never go **641.5**
Davis, B. Becoming vegan **613.2**
Gluten-free & vegan pie **641.3**
Hamshaw, G. Choosing raw **641.3**
Jacoby, K. Vedge **641.6**
Liddon, A. The oh she glows cookbook **641.5**
Moosewood restaurant favorites **641.5**
Patalsky, K. Healthy happy vegan kitchen **641.5**
Raw, vegan, not gross **641.5**
Robertson, R. Vegan planet **641.5**
Robin Robertson's vegan without borders **641.5**
Romero, T. H. Salad samurai **641.83**
Ronnen, T. Crossroads **641.59**
Street vegan **641.5**
The VB6 cookbook **641.5**
Vegan holiday cooking from Candle Cafe **641.5**
VEGANISM
See also Vegetarianism
VEGANISM -- HEALTH ASPECTS
Atlas, N. Plant power **641.5**
Davis, B. Becoming vegan **613.2**
**VEGANISM -- MORAL AND ETHICAL AS-
PECTS**
Atlas, N. Plant power **641.5**
The **Vegetable** Butcher. Mangini, C. **641.65**
The **vegetable** gardener's bible. Smith, E. C. **635**
The **vegetable** gardener's container bible. Smith, E.
C. **635**
VEGETABLE GARDENING
The backyard homestead **641**
Bartholomew, M. All new square foot garden-
ing **635**
Bellamy, A. Small-space vegetable gardens **635**
Bradley, F. M. Saving vegetable seeds **635**
Coleman, E. Winter harvest handbook **635**
Deardorff, D. What's wrong with my vegetable
garden? **635**
Deppe, C. The Tao of vegetable gardening **635**
Homegrown harvest **635**
Houbein, L. One Magic Square Vegetable Garden-

ing **635**

Jabbour, N. Groundbreaking food gardens **635**

Malone, H. The Power of Pulses **635.65**

McCrate, C. High-yield vegetable gardening **635**

Pleasant, B. Starter vegetable gardens **635**

Smith, E. C. The vegetable gardener's bible **635**

Smith, E. C. The vegetable gardener's container bible **635**

Vegetables from an Italian garden **641.6**

VEGETABLE GARDENING

  See also Gardening; Horticulture

VEGETABLE GARDENING -- ECONOMIC ASPECTS

Bartholomew, M. Square foot gardening high-value veggies **635**

VEGETABLE GARDENING -- UNITED STATES

Obama, M. American grown **635**

Vegetable harvest. Wells, P. **641.6**

VEGETABLE KINGDOM *See* Botany; Plants

Vegetable literacy. Madison, D. **641.6**

Vegetable love. Kafka, B. **641.6**

Vegetables. Culinary Institute of America **641.6**

VEGETABLES

  See also Food; Plants

VEGETABLES

Eatingwell Vegetables **641.65**

Jabbour, N. Groundbreaking food gardens **635**

Kafka, B. Vegetable love **641.6**

Kirk, M. The ultimate book of modern juicing **663**

VEGETABLES -- CANNING *See* Vegetables -- Preservation

VEGETABLES -- DISEASES AND PESTS -- CONTROL

Deardorff, D. What's wrong with my vegetable garden? **635**

What's wrong with my vegetable garden? **635**

VEGETABLES -- PRESERVATION

The all new ball book of canning and preserving **641.42**

Complete book of home preserving **641.4**

VEGETABLES -- PRESERVATION

  See also Canning and preserving

VEGETABLES -- SEEDS

Bradley, F. M. Saving vegetable seeds **635**

Vegetables from an Italian garden. **641.6**

VEGETARIAN COOKERY *See* Vegetarian cooking

VEGETARIAN COOKING

Bittman, M. How to cook everything vegetarian **641.5**

Bowl **641.81**

But I could never go **641.5**

The complete vegetarian cookbook **641.5**

Duclos, A. The plantiful table **641.5**

Dusoulier, C. The French market cookbook **641.5**

Fearnley-Whittingstall, H. River Cottage Veg **641.5**

Gentry, A. The Real Food Daily cookbook **641.5**

The heart of the plate **641.5**

Jacoby, K. Vedge **641.6**

Jaffrey, M. Madhur Jaffrey's world vegetarian **641.5**

Jones, A. A modern way to eat **641.5**

Katzen, M. The Moosewood Cookbook **641.5**

Liddon, A. The oh she glows cookbook **641.5**

Madison, D. The new vegetarian cooking for everyone **641.5**

Madison, D. Vegetarian cooking for everyone **641.5**

Madison, D. Vegetarian suppers from Deborah Madison's kitchen **641.5**

Moosewood Restaurant cooks at home **641.5**

Moosewood restaurant favorites **641.5**

Moskowitz, I. C. Vegan pie in the sky **641.5**

Natkin, M. Herbivoracious **641.5**

Ottolenghi, Y. Plenty more **641.6**

Raw, vegan, not gross **641.5**

Robertson, R. Vegan planet **641.5**

Ronnen, T. Crossroads **641.59**

Shaw, D. The essential vegetarian cookbook **641.5**

Shulman, M. R. Mediterranean harvest **641.5**

Shulman, M. R. The simple art of vegetarian cooking **641.5**

Thomas, A. Love soup **641.5**

Thug Kitchen **641.5**

Tourles, S. L. Raw energy **641.5**

The VB6 cookbook **641.5**

Vegan, vegetarian, omnivore **641.5**

Vegetarian dinner parties **641.5**

Waters, A. In the green kitchen **641.5**

Whole world vegetarian **641.5**

VEGETARIAN COOKING

  See also Cooking

Vegetarian cooking for everyone. Madison, D. **641.5**

Vegetarian dinner parties. **641.5**

Vegetarian India. Jaffrey, M. **641.595**

Vegetarian suppers from Deborah Madison's kitchen. Madison, D. **641.5**

VEGETARIANISM

Foer, J. S. Eating animals **641.3**

Hanoch, D. The yoga lifestyle **613.7**

Jaffrey, M. Vegetarian India **641.595**

VEGETARIANISM

  See also Diet

VEGETARIANS

Hanoch, D. The yoga lifestyle **613.7**

The **Vegiterranean** Diet. Hever, J. **613.2**

VEHICLES

  See also Transportation

Veit, Helen Zoe

  (ed) Food in the Civil War era **641.597**

Velázquez, Diego, 1599-1660

  About

Bailey, A. Velazquez: surrendering at Breda **759**

Cumming, L. The Vanishing Velazquez **759.6**

Velasco, Luis Alejandro, d. 2000
About
Garcia Marquez, G. The story of a shipwrecked sailor **910.4**

Velasquez-Manoff, Moises

An Epidemic of Absence **616.97**

Velazquez: surrendering at Breda. Bailey, A. **759**

Velie, Alan R.

(ed) Encyclopedia of American Indian literature **810**

VELIKAĬA SIBIRSKAĬA MAGISTRAL'

Greene, D. Midnight in Siberia **914.7**

Velikovsky, Immanuel, 1895-1979
About
Sagan, C. Broca's brain **500**

VELOCIRAPTORS

See also Dinosaurs

VELOCITY *See* Speed

Velshi, Ali

How to speak money **332.024**

Vendetta. Neff, J. **973.922**

Vendler, Helen Hennessy

Coming of age as a poet **820**

VENEERS AND VENEERING

See also Cabinetwork; Furniture

Venes, Donald, 1952-

(ed) Taber's cyclopedic medical dictionary **610.3**

Venezia, Ray

The everyday meat guide **641.36**

VENEZUELA -- HISTORY -- 1810-1830

Arana, M. Bolivar **92**

Venice. Madden, T. F. **945**

VENICE (ITALY)

Leon, D. My Venice and Other Essays **945**

VENICE (ITALY) -- HISTORY

Hale, S. Titian **92**

Madden, T. F. Venice **945**

VENICE (ITALY) -- SOCIAL LIFE AND CUSTOMS

Berendt, J. The city of falling angels **945**

Venis, Linda

(ed) Inside the room **808.2**

VENOM

Wilcox, C. Venomous **572**

Venomous. Wilcox, C. **572**

Venomous reptiles of the United States, Canada, and northern Mexico. Ernst, C. H. **597.9**

The venomous reptiles of the Western Hemisphere. Campbell, J. **597.96**

Venomous snakes of the world. O'Shea, M. **597.96**

Venona. Haynes, J. E. **327.12**

Venter, J. Craig, 1946-

Life at the Speed of Light **303.48**

VENTILATION

See also Air; Home economics; Household sanitation; Hygiene; Sanitation

VENTRILOQUISM

See also Amusements; Voice

VENTRILOQUISTS -- POETRY

Fay-LeBlanc, G. Death of a ventriloquist **811**

Ventrone, Jillian

From the Marine Corps to college **378.1**

VENTURE CAPITAL

See also Capital

VENUS (PLANET)

Wulf, A. Chasing Venus **523.9**

VENUS (PLANET)

See also Planets

VENUS (PLANET) -- EXPLORATION -- HISTORY -- 18TH CENTURY

Anderson, M. The day the world discovered the sun

VENUS (PLANET) -- TRANSIT

Wulf, A. Chasing Venus **523.9**

Venzon, Anne Cipriano

(ed) The United States in the First World War **940.3**

VERBAL LEARNING

See also Language and languages; Psychology of learning

Verdi with a vengeance. Berger, W. **782.1**

Verdi's Shakespeare. Wills, G. **822.3**

Verdi, Giuseppe, 1813-1901
About
Berger, W. Verdi with a vengeance **782.1**

Wills, G. Verdi's Shakespeare **822.3**

Verducci, Tom

Torre, J. The Yankee years **92**

Verdura. La Place, V. **641.6**

Veregin, Howard

(ed) Rand McNally Goodes World Atlas **912**

Verlaine, Paul

Selected poems **841**

Vermeer and the Delft school. Liedtke, W. A. **759.9**

Vermeer, Johannes, 1632-1675
About
Fraser, K. Ornament and silence **809**

Liedtke, W. A. Vermeer and the Delft school **759.9**

Snyder, L. J. Eye of the beholder **701**

White, M. Travels in Vermeer **92**

VERMIN *See* Household pests; Pests

VERMONT -- BIOGRAPHY

Axelrod, H. The point of vanishing **92**

Vernacchio, Al

For goodness sex **613.9**

Verner, Miroslav

The pyramids **932**

Verney family
About
Tinniswood, A. The Verneys **920**

The Verneys. Tinniswood, A. **920**

VERS LIBRE *See* Free verse

Versaci, Russell
Creating a new old house   **728**
VERSE SATIRE, ENGLISH.
Pope, A. Selected poetry   **821**
Versed. Armantrout, R.   **811**
VERSIFICATION
   See also Authorship; Poetics; Rhythm
VERTEBRATES
   See also Animals
VERTICAL GARDENING
Coronado, S. Grow a living wall   **635**
The **vertigo** years. Blom, P.   **940.2**
Verveer, Melanne
Fast forward   **650.1**
The **very** best of recipes for health.   **641.5**
A **very** brief history of eternity. Eire, C. M. N.   **236**
A **very** different age. Diner, S. J.   **973.8**
Very good lives.   **158**
Very short introductions [series]
Bushman, R. L. Mormonism   **289.3**
Catling, D. C. Astrobiology   **576.8**
Close, F. E. Nothing   **530**
Vespasian, Emperor of Rome, 9-79
      About
The twelve Caesars   **878**
Vespucci, Amerigo, 1451-1512
      About
Fernandez-Armesto, F. Amerigo   **92**
VESTA (ROMAN DEITY)
   See also Gods and goddesses
VESUVIUS (ITALY)
Scarth, A. Vesuvius: a biography   **551.2**
Vesuvius: a biography. Scarth, A.   **551.2**
VETERANS
Alexander, L. Biggest brother   **92**
Burgin, R. V. Islands of the damned   **940.54**
Cadillac Man Land of the lost souls   **92**
Cleland, M. Heart of a patriot   **92**
Dyer, G. The missing of the Somme   **940.4**
Guibert, E. Alan's war   **741.5**
Heard, A. The eyes of Willie McGee   **364.66**
Hillenbrand, L. Unbroken   **940.54**
Jordan, B. M. Marching Home   **973.7**
Kaplan, A. Y. The interpreter   **940.54**
Nelson, J. C. The remains of Company D   **920**
Voices of war   **355**
Witter, B. Until Tuesday   **362.4**
VETERANS
   See also Military art and science
VETERANS -- EDUCATION
Ventrone, J. From the Marine Corps to college   **378.1**
VETERANS -- EDUCATION
   See also Education
VETERANS -- HUNGARY -- BIOGRAPHY
The burning of the world   **92**

VETERANS -- MENTAL HEALTH -- UNITED STATES -- HANDBOOKS, MANUALS, ETC
Lawhorne-Scott, C. Military mental health care   **355.3**
VETERANS -- UNITED STATES
Bannerman, S. Homefront 911   **362.86**
Finkel, D. Thank You for Your Service   **362.86**
VETERANS DAY
   See also Holidays
VETERANS' FAMILIES -- UNITED STATES -- HANDBOOKS, MANUALS, ETC
Lawhorne-Scott, C. Military mental health care   **355.3**
VETERINARIANS
Boston, S. Lucky Dog   **636.089**
Herriot, J. All creatures great and small   **92**
Herriot, J. Every living thing   **636.089**
Herriot, J. James Herriot's dog stories   **636.7**
VETERINARY MEDICINE
Boston, S. Lucky Dog   **636.089**
Bowers, K. Zoobiquity   **636.089**
Goldstein, M. The nature of animal healing   **636.089**
Herriot, J. All creatures great and small   **92**
Herriot, J. James Herriot's animal stories   **636.089**
Kaplan, L. Help Your Dog Fight Cancer   **636.7**
The Merck veterinary manual   **636.089**
Schoen, A. M. Kindred spirits   **636.089**
VETERINARY MEDICINE
   See also Medicine
VETERINARY MEDICINE -- DICTIONARIES
Black's veterinary dictionary   **636.089**
Vetri, Marc
Mastering pasta   **641.82**
Rustic Italian food   **641.59**
Il viaggio di Vetri   **641.5**
VIADUCTS *See* Bridges
Vibrant food.   **641.5**
VIBRATION
   See also Mechanics; Sound
VICE
   See also Conduct of life; Ethics; Human behavior
The **vice** presidents. Waldrup, C. C.   **920.003**
VICE-PRESIDENTS
Abuse of power   **973.924**
Adams, J. My dearest friend   **92**
Becker, C. The Declaration of Independence **973.3**
Bernstein, R. B. Thomas Jefferson   **92**
Beschloss, M. R. The conquerors: Roosevelt, Truman, and the destruction of Hitler's Germany, 1941-1945   **940.53**
Black, C. M. Richard M. Nixon   **92**
Brookhiser, R. America's first dynasty   **973.4**
Burns, J. M. The three Roosevelts   **973.91**
Burstein, A. Madison and Jefferson   **973.4**
Busby, H. W. The thirty-first of March   **973.923**

Bush, G. All the best, George Bush   92
Caro, R. A. The path to power   92
Cerami, C. A. Jefferson's great gamble   973.4
Cohen, I. B. Science and the founding fathers 973.3
Cooper, J. M. The warrior and the priest: Woodrow Wilson and Theodore Roosevelt   92
Cordery, S. A. Alice   92
Crapol, E. P. John Tyler   92
Dallek, R. Harry S. Truman   92
Dallek, R. Nixon and Kissinger   92
Davis, W. C. An honorable defeat   973.7
DiSilvestro, R. L. Theodore Roosevelt in the Badlands   92
Egan, T. The big burn   973.91
Ellis, J. J. American sphinx: the character of Thomas Jefferson   92
Emery, F. Watergate   973.924
Finkelman, P. Millard Fillmore   92
Gordin, M. D. Red cloud at dawn   355
Gordon-Reed, A. Andrew Johnson   92
Gordon-Reed, A. The Hemingses of Monticello   920
Gordon-Reed, A. Thomas Jefferson and Sally Hemings   973.4
Grant, J. John Adams   92
Halberstam, D. The best and the brightest 973.922
Hitchens, C. Thomas Jefferson: author of America   92
Hofstadter, R. The American political tradition, and the men who made it   973
Holton, W. Abigail Adams   92
Kaiser, D. E. American tragedy   959.704
Karabell, Z. The last campaign   324.9
Kissinger, H. Diplomacy   327.2
Kotz, N. Judgment days   323
Kranish, M. Flight from Monticello   973.4
Larson, E. J. A magnificent catastrophe   324
Malone, J. W. It doesn't take a rocket scientist 920
Matthews, C. Kennedy & Nixon   973.922
May, G. John Tyler   92
McCullough, D. G. John Adams   92
McCullough, D. G. Mornings on horseback   92
McCullough, D. G. The path between the seas   972.87
McPherson, J. M. Drawn with the sword   973.7
Millard, C. The river of doubt   973.91
Miller, J. C. The Federalist era, 1789-1801   973.4
Morris, E. The rise of Theodore Roosevelt   92
Morris, E. Theodore Rex   92
Morrow, L. The best year of their lives   920
O'Toole, P. When trumpets call   92
Parmet, H. S. George Bush   92
Perlstein, R. Nixonland   973.924
Peters, C. Lyndon B. Johnson   92
Pietrusza, D. 1960: LBJ vs. JFK vs. Nixon 973.92
Pooley, E. The climate war   363.7

Rauchway, E. Murdering McKinley   973.8
Reeves, R. President Nixon   973.924
Remnick, D. Reporting   814
Reston, J. The conviction of Richard Nixon 973.924
Simon, J. F. What kind of nation   342
Staloff, D. Hamilton, Adams, Jefferson   973.4
Stewart, D. O. American emperor   973.4
Taking charge   973.923
Thomas, E. The war lovers   973.8
Unger, H. G. The last founding father   92
Vidal, G. Inventing a nation: Washington, Adams, Jefferson   973.4
Wheen, F. Strange days indeed   973.92
Widmer, E. L. Martin Van Buren   92
Wills, G. 'Negro president'   326
Woodward, B. The commanders   973.928
Woodward, B. The final days   973.924
Woodward, B. Shadow   973.92
Zacks, R. The pirate coast   973.4
Zelnick, B. Gore: a political life   92
Zimmermann, W. First great triumph   973

VICE-PRESIDENTS

See also Presidents

VICE-PRESIDENTS -- GHANA -- BIOGRAPHY

Mahama, J. D. My first coup d'etat and other true stories from the lost decades of Africa   966.705

VICE-PRESIDENTS -- UNITED STATES -- BIOGRAPHY

Waldrup, C. C. The vice presidents   920.003
Witcover, J. America's vice presidents   352.23

Vick, Liza

(ed) A basic music library   016

Vickers, Graham

Sandison, D. Neal Cassady   92

VICKSBURG (MISS.) -- SIEGE, 1863

Groom, W. Vicksburg, 1863   973.7
Vicksburg, 1863. Groom, W.   973.7

VICTIMS OF ATOMIC BOMBINGS *See* Atomic bomb victims

VICTIMS OF CRIME *See* Victims of crimes

VICTIMS OF CRIMES

Beloof, D. E. Victims' rights   345.73
Burns, S. The Central Park Five   364.1
Parry, R. L. People who eat darkness   364.152

VICTIMS OF CRIMES

See also Crime

VICTIMS OF CRIMES -- LEGAL STATUS, LAWS, ETC.

Beloof, D. E. Victims' rights   345.73

VICTIMS OF CRIMES -- UNITED STATES -- CASE STUDIES

McConnell, D. American honor killings   364.15

VICTIMS OF FAMINE -- KOREA (NORTH)

Kim, J. Under the same sky   92

VICTIMS OF TERRORISM -- INDIA -- MUMBAI

Levy, A. The siege   363.325

The **victims'** revolution. Bawer, B.   320

Victims' rights. Beloof, D. E.   345.73

Victor Fleming. Sragow, M.   92

Victor, Adam

   The Elvis encyclopedia   781.66

Victor, Terry

   (ed) The new Partridge dictionary of slang and unconventional English   427

Victoria. Wilson, A. N.   92

Victoria. Baird, J.   92

VICTORIA AMAZONICA

   Holway, T. The flower of empire   727

Victoria, Queen of Great Britain, 1819-1901

About

Baird, J. Victoria   92

Erickson, C. Her little majesty: the life of Queen Victoria   92

Hibbert, C. Queen Victoria   92

Vallone, L. Becoming Victoria   941.08

Williams, K. Becoming Queen Victoria   92

Wilson, A. N. Victoria   92

Victorian America. Schlereth, T. J.   973.8

VICTORIAN ARCHITECTURE

   Holway, T. The flower of empire   727

The **Victorian** city. Flanders, J.   942.1

Victorian house

   Inside the Victorian home   306

VICTORIANA

   See also Antiques; Collectibles

The **Victorians.** Wilson, A. N.   941.081

The **victors.** Ambrose, S. E.   940.54

Victory. Hirshman, L.   306.76

Victuals.   641.5

Vidal, Gore, 1925-2012

   The selected essays of Gore Vidal   814

   Inventing a nation: Washington, Adams, Jefferson   973.4

About

Parini, J. Empire of self   92

Vidal, G. Point to point navigation   92

VIDEO ART

   See also Art; Television; Video recording

VIDEO ARTISTS

   Bilal, W. Shoot an Iraqi   92

VIDEO DIRECTORS

   Waxman, S. Rebels on the backlot   920

VIDEO GAME DESIGN

   See also Video games

VIDEO GAMES

   Bissell, T. Extra lives   794.8

   Gallaway, B. Game on!   025.2

   McGonigal, J. Reality is broken   306.4

   Parkin, S. An illustrated history of 151 video games   794.8

VIDEO GAMES

   See also Electronic toys; Games

VIDEO GAMES -- HISTORY

   Harris, B. J. Console wars   338.7

VIDEO GAMES AND CHILDREN

   Gallaway, B. Game on!   025.2

VIDEO GAMES AND CHILDREN -- HEALTH ASPECTS

   Dunckley, V. L. Reset your child's brain   004.67

VIDEO TAPE ADVERTISING

   Miles, J. YouTube marketing power   658.8

VIDEO TELEPHONE

   See also Data transmission systems; Telephone; Television

VIENNA (AUSTRIA) -- HISTORY

   O'Connor The lady in gold   759.36

Vienna, 1814. King, D.   940.2

Vienne, Véronique

   (jt. auth) Heller, S. Becoming a graphic & digital designer   741.6

Viertel, Jack

   The secret life of the American musical   792.6

Vieth, David M.

   (ed) Dryden, J. All for love   822

Vietnam. Goscha, C.   959.7

Vietnam. Burrows, L.   770.92

Vietnam. Karnow, S.   959.704

VIETNAM (REPUBLIC) -- FOREIGN RELATIONS -- UNITED STATES

   Miller, E. Misalliance   959.704

VIETNAM -- COLONIZATION

   Goscha, C. Vietnam   959.7

VIETNAM -- DESCRIPTION AND TRAVEL

   Nguyen, L. The food of Vietnam   641.59

VIETNAM -- HISTORY

   Goscha, C. Vietnam   959.7

VIETNAM -- POLITICS AND GOVERNMENT

   FitzGerald, F. Fire in the lake   959.704

   Langguth, A. J. Our Vietnam   959.704

   Mann, R. A grand delusion   959.704

The **Vietnam** War.   959.704

VIETNAM WAR, 1961-1975

   Anderson, D. L. The Columbia guide to the Vietnam War   959.704

   Appy, C. G. American Reckoning   959.704

   Blehm, E. Legend   959.7

   Ellsberg, D. Secrets: a memoir of Vietnam and the Pentagon papers   959.704

   FitzGerald, F. Fire in the lake   959.704

   Freedman, L. Kennedy's wars   973.922

   Goldstein, D. M. The Vietnam War: the story and photographs   959.704

   Inside the Pentagon papers   959.704

   Kaiser, D. E. American tragedy   959.704

   Karnow, S. Vietnam   959.704

   Kissinger, H. Diplomacy   327.2

   Kissinger, H. Ending the Vietnam War   959.704

Langguth, A. J. Our Vietnam **959.704**

Lind, M. Vietnam, the necessary war **959.704**

Logevall, F. Embers of War **959.704**

Mann, R. A grand delusion **959.704**

Maraniss, D. They marched into sunlight **959.704**

McNamara, R. S. In retrospect **959.704**

Sallah, M. Tiger Force **959.704**

Sheehan, N. A bright shining lie: John Paul Vann and America in Vietnam **959.704**

Tuchman, B. W. The march of folly **909.08**

Tuchman, B. W. Practicing history **907**

The Vietnam War **959.704**

VIETNAM WAR, 1961-1975

    See also United States -- History -- 1961-1974

VIETNAM WAR, 1961-1975 -- AERIAL OPERA-TIONS

Hampton, D. The hunter killers **959.704**

VIETNAM WAR, 1961-1975 -- ART AND THE WAR

Nguyen, V. T. Nothing ever dies **959.704**

VIETNAM WAR, 1961-1975 -- ENCYCLOPE-DIAS

Tucker, S. C. The encyclopedia of the Vietnam War **959.704**

VIETNAM WAR, 1961-1975 -- GRAPHIC NOV-ELS

Tran, G. B. Vietnamerica **741.5**

VIETNAM WAR, 1961-1975 -- MEDICAL CARE

Glasser, R. J. 365 days **959.704**

VIETNAM WAR, 1961-1975 -- NAVAL OPERA-TIONS

Berman, L. Zumwalt **92**

VIETNAM WAR, 1961-1975 -- PERSONAL NAR-RATIVES, AMERICAN

Napoli, P. F. Bringing it all back home **959.704**

Ulander, P. A. Walking point **959.704**

Wolf, M. J. Abandoned in hell **959.704**

VIETNAM WAR, 1961-1975 -- PICTORIAL WORKS

Burrows, L. Vietnam **770.92**

VIETNAM WAR, 1961-1975 -- SECRET SER-VICE

Shultz, R. H. The secret war against Hanoi **959.704**

VIETNAM WAR, 1961-1975 -- SECRET SER-VICE -- UNITED STATES

Woods, R. B. Shadow warrior **92**

VIETNAM WAR, 1961-1975 -- UNITED STATES

Hendrickson, P. The living and the dead **959.704**

Patterson, J. T. The eve of destruction **973.923**

The **Vietnam** War: the story and photographs. Goldstein, D. M. **959.704**

Vietnam, the necessary war. Lind, M. **959.704**

Vietnamerica. Tran, G. B. **741.5**

VIETNAMESE AMERICANS

Pham, A. X. The eaves of heaven **92**

VIETNAMESE AMERICANS -- BIOGRAPHY

Tran, G. B. Vietnamerica **741.5**

VIETNAMESE CONFLICT, 1961-1975 *See* Vietnam War, 1961-1975

VIETNAMESE COOKING

Nguyen, L. The food of Vietnam **641.59**

Phan, C. The slanted door **641.59**

Phan, C. Vietnamese home cooking **641.59**

Vietnamese home cooking. Phan, C. **641.59**

VIETNAMESE REFUGEES

    See also Refugees

VIETNAMESE REFUGEES -- GRAPHIC NOV-ELS

Tran, G. B. Vietnamerica **741.5**

VIETNAMESE WAR, 1961-1975 *See* Vietnam War, 1961-1975

The **view** from Lazy Point. Safina, C. **508**

The **view** from the cheap seats. Gaiman, N. **824**

Viewpoints on American culture [series]

Sifters: Native American women's lives **920**

VIGILANTES

    See also Crime; Criminal law

VIKING ANTIQUITIES -- SCOTLAND -- LEW-IS WITH HARRIS ISLAND

Brown, N. M. Ivory Vikings **736**

VIKING CIVILIZATION

Brown, N. M. Ivory Vikings **736**

Viking knits and ancient ornaments. Lavold, E.

The **Vikings.** Roesdahl, E. **948**

VIKINGS

Ferguson, R. The Vikings **948**

The Oxford illustrated history of the Vikings **948**

Roesdahl, E. The Vikings **948**

Vikings: the North Atlantic saga **970.01**

The **Vikings.** Ferguson, R. **948**

Vikings: the North Atlantic saga. **970.01**

Vile, John R.

(ed) Encyclopedia of the First Amendment **342**

The Constitutional Convention of 1787 **342**

Encyclopedia of constitutional amendments, proposed amendments, and amending issues, 1789-2010 **342**

Villa, Pancho, 1878-1923

    About

Katz, F. The life and times of Pancho Villa **972.08**

The **Village.** Strausbaugh, J. **974.7**

A **village** life. Glück, L. **811**

Village of Secrets. Moorehead, C. **944**

VILLAGES

    See also Cities and towns

Villani, Cédric, 1973-

    About

Birth of a theorem **92**

Villiers, Elizabeth, Countess of Orkney, 1657?-1733

    About

Livingstone, N. The mistresses of Cliveden **942.009**

Villoro, Juan
God Is Round **796.334**

VILNIUS (LITHUANIA)
Milosz, C. To begin where I am **891.8**

Vincent, Isabel, 1965-
About
Vincent, I. Dinner with Edward **158.1**

Vincent, Leah
About
Vincent, L. Cut me loose **305.892**

Vincent, Peggy
Baby catcher **618.2**

Vincente Minnelli. Levy, E. **92**

Vindication. Gordon, L. **92**

VINES *See* Climbing plants

VINEYARDS
Cox, J. From vines to wines **634.8**
Olney, R. Lulu's Provencal table **641.59**

VINEYARDS
See also Farms

VINTAGE AUTOMOBILES *See* Antique and classic cars

The **Vintage** book of African American poetry. **811**

The **Vintage** book of contemporary world poetry. **808.81**

Vintage cakes. **641.86**

VINTAGE CARS *See* Antique and classic cars

Vintage original [series]
Mendelsund, P. What we see when we read **028**

Vintage spiritual classics [series]
The little flowers of St. Francis of Assisi **242**

Vinton, Nathaniel
The fall line **796.935**

Vinton, Sherri Brooks
Eat it up! **641.5**
Put 'em up! **641.6**

VIOLENCE
Bonair-Agard, R. Bury my clothes **811**
Canada, G. Fist, stick, knife, gun **305.23**
Fergusson, J. The world's most dangerous place **967.73**
Jones, G. Killing monsters **302.23**
McBee, T. P. Man alive **92**
Rhodes, R. Why they kill **364.3**
Sontag, S. Regarding the pain of others **303.6**

VIOLENCE
See also Aggressiveness (Psychology); Social psychology

VIOLENCE -- ENCYCLOPEDIAS
Guns in American society **363.33**

VIOLENCE -- HISTORY
Spierenburg, P. Violence and punishment **364.67**

VIOLENCE -- PHYSIOLOGICAL ASPECTS
Raine, A. The anatomy of violence **616.85**

VIOLENCE -- POETRY
Carr, J. 100 notes on violence **811**

VIOLENCE -- PSYCHOLOGICAL ASPECTS
Raine, A. The anatomy of violence **616.85**

VIOLENCE -- RELIGIOUS ASPECTS
Armstrong, K. Fields of Blood **201**

VIOLENCE -- UNITED STATES
Giffords, G. D. Enough **363.33**

VIOLENCE AGAINST WOMEN
Connors, J. I Will Find You **364.15**

VIOLENCE AGAINST WOMEN
See also Violence; Women

Violence and compassion. Bstan-'dzin-rgya-mtsho, D. L. X. **294.3**

Violence and punishment. Spierenburg, P. **364.67**

VIOLENCE IN MASS MEDIA
Jones, G. Killing monsters **302.23**

VIOLENT CRIME -- MEXICO -- CIUDAD JUÁREZ
Ainslie, R. C. The fight to save Juárez **363.45**

VIOLENT CRIMES -- UNITED STATES -- EN-CYCLOPEDIAS
Guns in American society **363.33**

VIOLET BAKERY (LONDON, ENGLAND)
Ptak, C. The Violet Bakery cookbook **641.86**

The **Violet** Bakery cookbook. Ptak, C. **641.86**

The **violinist's** thumb. Kean, S. **572.8**

VIOLINISTS
Lopez, S. The soloist **92**
Walker-Hill, H. From spirituals to symphonies **780**

VIOLINS
Grymes, J. A. Violins of hope **92**

Violins of hope. Grymes, J. A. **92**

VIOLISTS -- WEST BANK -- BIOGRAPHY
Tolan, S. Children of the stone **780**

Viorst, Judith
Imperfect control **158.1**

VIPERS *See* Snakes

Viral hate. Foxman, A. H. **364.15**

Virga, Vincent
(jt. auth) Katz, H. L. Civil War sketch book **973.7**
Eyes of the nation **973**

Virgil
The Aeneid **873**
The eclogues of Virgil **871**
The Georgics of Virgil **872**

VIRGINIA
Lebsock, S. A murder in Virginia **364.1**

VIRGINIA -- HISTORY
Geroux, W. The Mathews Men **940.54**
Taylor, A. The internal enemy **975.5**

VIRGINIA -- HISTORY -- REVOLUTION, 1775-1783
Kranish, M. Flight from Monticello **973.4**

VIRGINIA MUSEUM OF FINE ARTS -- CATA-LOGS
Von Habsburg, G. Faberge revealed **739.2**

Virginia Woolf. Lee, H. **823**

The **Virginia** Woolf reader. Woolf, V.   **828**
Virginia Woolf's nose. Lee, H.   **820**
Virginia Woolf: an inner life. Briggs, J.   **92**
Viroli, Maurizio
   Niccolo's smile: a biography of Machiavelli   **92**
**VIROLOGISTS -- UNITED STATES -- BIOGRA-
   PHY**
   Jacobs, C. D.   Jonas Salk   **92**
   Jonas Salk   **92**
VIROLOGY
   See also Microbiology
VIRTUAL LIBRARIES *See* Digital libraries
VIRTUAL REALITY
   Saler, M.   As if   **823**
Virtual reference best practices. Kern, M. K.   **025.5**
Virtual reference desk series
   Virtual reference service   **025.5**
Virtual reference service.   **025.5**
Virtual roots 2.0. Kemp, T. J.   **929**
Virtual unreality. Seife, C.   **025.04**
VIRTUE
   Shields, C. J.   Aristotle   **185**
VIRTUE
   See also Conduct of life; Ethics; Human be-
   havior
The **virtue** of selfishness. Rand, A.   **171**
VIRTUES *See* Virtue
The **virtues** of aging. Carter, J.   **305.26**
VIRUSES
   Collen, A.   10% human   **612.3**
   Garrett, L.   The coming plague   **614.4**
   Oldstone, M. B. A.   Viruses, plagues, and histo-
   ry   **614.4**
   Zimmer, C.   A planet of viruses   **362.196**
VIRUSES
   See also Microorganisms
Viruses, plagues, and history. Oldstone, M. B.
   A.   **614.4**
Viscott, David S.
   Emotional resilience   **158**
VISION
   Eckstut, A.   The Secret Language of Color   **535.6**
   Hoffman, D. D.   Visual intelligence   **152.14**
VISION
   See also Optics; Senses and sensation
VISION DISORDERS
   Axelrod, H.   The point of vanishing   **92**
   Sacks, O.   The mind's eye   **616.85**
VISION DISORDERS
   See also Vision
VISION IN ANIMALS
   See also Senses and sensation in animals
**VISION, MONOCULAR -- PSYCHOLOGICAL
   ASPECTS**
   Axelrod, H.   The point of vanishing   **92**
VISIONARIES

McCray, W. P.   The visioneers   **509**
The **visioneers.** McCray, W. P.   **509**
VISIONS
   See also Parapsychology; Religion; Spiritual
   gifts
Visions of God. Armstrong, K.   **248.2**
Visions of Infinity. Stewart, I.   **510**
Visions of jazz. Giddins, G.   **781.65**
The **visit.** Durrenmatt, F.   **832**
Visit sunny Chernobyl. Blackwell, A.   **363.73**
Visona, Monica Blackmun
   A history of art in Africa   **709**
Visser, Margaret
   The gift of thanks   **394**
The **visual** blues.   **704.03**
VISUAL COMMUNICATION
   Rendgen, S.   Understanding the world   **741.6**
VISUAL COMMUNICATION
   See also Communication
VISUAL COMMUNICATION -- HISTORY
   Lima, M.   The book of trees   **001.2**
The **visual** display of quantitative information.
   Tufte, E. R.   **001.4**
VISUAL HANDICAPS *See* Vision disorders
VISUAL IMPAIRMENTS *See* Vision disorders
Visual intelligence. Herman, A. E.   **152.14**
Visual intelligence. Hoffman, D. D.   **152.14**
Visual Judaism in late antiquity. Levine, L. I.   **704.9**
VISUAL LITERACY
   Herman, A. E.   Visual intelligence   **152.14**
   Mendelsund, P.   What we see when we read   **028**
VISUAL LITERACY
   See also Arts; Literacy; Semiotics
VISUAL MARKETING
   See also Marketing
VISUAL PERCEPTION
   Herman, A. E.   Visual intelligence   **152.14**
VISUAL PERCEPTION IN LITERATURE
   Mendelsund, P.   What we see when we read   **028**
Visual read less, learn more [series]
   Colgrove, D.   Teach yourself visually sewing **646.2**
   Keim, C.   Teach yourself visually crochet   **746.43**
   Michaels, C. F.   Teach yourself visually jewelry
   making & beading   **745.59**
   Ramsey, D.   Teach yourself visually car care &
   maintenance   **629.28**
   Turner, S.   Teach yourself visually knitting   **746.43**
VISUALIZATION OF INFORMATION *See* In-
   formation visualization
VITAL RECORDS *See* Registers of births, etc.
VITAL STATISTICS
   Vital Statistics of the United States 2014   **310**
VITAL STATISTICS
   See also Statistics
Vital Statistics of the United States 2014.   **310**
VITALITY

Roizen, M. F. This is your do-over   **613**

Vitamania. Price, C.   **612.3**

Vitamin N. Louv, R.   **155.9**

VITAMINS

Price, C. Vitamania   **612.3**

VITAMINS

See also Food; Nutrition

VITAMINS -- HISTORY

Price, C. Vitamania   **612.3**

Vitellius, Aulus, Emperor of Rome, 15-69

About

The twelve Caesars   **878**

VITICULTURE

Cox, J. From vines to wines   **634.8**

Robinson, J. Wine grapes   **664**

VITICULTURE *See* Grapes; Vineyards; Wine and wine making

VITICULTURE -- FRANCE -- BURGUNDY -- CASE STUDIES

Potter, M. Shadows in the vineyard   **364.16**

VITICULTURE -- UNITED STATES

Cox, J. From vines to wines   **634.8**

Vivaldo, Denise

Do it for le$$! weddings   **395**

VIVISECTION

See also Animal experimentation; Surgery

Vladimir Nabokov: the American years. Boyd, B.   **813**

Vladimir Nabokov: the Russian years. Boyd, B. **813**

Vlasic, Bill

Once upon a car   **338.4**

Vlastnik, Frank

Bloom, K. Broadway musicals   **792.6**

Vnuk, Rebecca

Read on-- women's fiction   **016**

The weeding handbook   **025.2**

Women's fiction   **016**

VOCABULARY

Blount, R. Alphabetter juice, or, The joy of text **818**

Crystal, D. The story of English in 100 words **422**

VOCABULARY

See also Language and languages

VOCAL MUSIC

See also Music

VOCATION

Rankin, L. The anatomy of a calling   **92**

VOCATION

See also Duty; Ethics; Occupations; Work

VOCATION -- CHRISTIANITY

Jakes, T. D. Destiny   **248.4**

VOCATION, CHOICE OF *See* Vocational guidance

VOCATIONAL EDUCATION

See also Education

VOCATIONAL GUIDANCE

101 careers in healthcare management   **362.106**

Bureau of Labor Statistics Occupational outlook handbook   **331.7**

Chideya, F. The episodic career   **650.1**

Citrin, J. M. The career playbook   **650.14**

Evans, D. Designing your life   **650.1**

Ferguson Publishing The top 100   **331.7**

Guillebeau, C. The $100 startup   **658.1**

Harris, C. A. Strategize to win   **650.1**

How to Be an Illustrator   **741.6**

Isay, D. Callings   **920.073**

Jerrard, J. Crisis in employment   **025.5**

Kay, A. This is how to get your next job   **650.14**

Kramer, A. S. Breaking through bias   **650.101**

Licht, A. Leave Your Mark   **650.1**

McKenna, A. Nontraditional careers for women and men   **331.702**

MFA vs NYC   **808.02**

Morgan, G. Undecided   **371.4**

Occupational outlook handbook 2013-2014 **331.12**

Parini, J. The art of teaching   **371.1**

Raskin, D. The dirty little secrets of getting your dream job   **650.14**

Shell, G. R. Springboard   **650.1**

Smith, L. R. No fears, no excuses   **650.1**

Tortorella, N. Starting your career as a freelance web designer   **006.7**

VOCATIONAL GUIDANCE

See also Counseling; Vocational education

VOCATIONAL GUIDANCE -- ENCYCLOPE-DIAS

J.G. Ferguson Publishing Company Encyclopedia of careers and vocational guidance   **331.7**

VOCATIONAL GUIDANCE -- INFORMATION SERVICES

Jerrard, J. Crisis in employment   **025.5**

VOCATIONAL GUIDANCE -- UNITED STATES -- HISTORY -- 21ST CENTURY

Chideya, F. The episodic career   **650.1**

VOCATIONAL GUIDANCE FOR PEOPLE WITH DISABILITIES

See also People with disabilities; Vocational guidance

VOCATIONAL GUIDANCE FOR WOMEN

Kramer, A. S. Breaking through bias   **650.101**

VOCATIONS *See* Occupations; Professions

VODUN *See* Voodooism

Vogel, Ezra F.

Deng Xiaoping and the transformation of China   **951.05**

Vogel, Kenneth P.

Big money   **324.7**

Vogel, Steve

The Pentagon   **355.6**

Through the perilous fight   **973.5**

Vogel, Steven, 1940-2015

The life of a leaf   **575.5**

Vogler, Amy

Lang, A. P. Serious barbecue   **641.5**

Vogue and the Metropolitan Museum of Art Costume Institute. Bowles, H.   **391**

Vogue knitting.   **746.43**

VOICE

Linklater, K. Freeing the natural voice   **808.5**

VOICE

See also Language and languages; Throat

VOICE -- POETRY

Fay-LeBlanc, G. Death of a ventriloquist   **811**

The **voice** at 3:00 a.m. Simic, C.   **811**

VOICE CULTURE

See also Public speaking; Singing; Speech

The **voice** is all. Johnson, J.   **818**

Voice of America. Heil, A. L.   **384.54**

VOICE OF AMERICA

Heil, A. L. Voice of America   **384.54**

The **voice** of reason; essays in objectivist thought. Rand, A.   **191**

Voices in our blood.   **323.1**

Voices in the Ocean. Casey, S.   **599.53**

Voices of an era [series]

Voices of early Christianity   **270.1**

Voices of early Christianity.   **270.1**

Voices of war.   **355**

Voices rising.   **976.3**

Voices that matter [series]

Reynolds, G. Presentation zen

Voigt, Emily

The dragon behind the glass   **597.176**

Volandes, Angelo E., 1971-

The conversation   **616.02**

VOLCANIC ERUPTIONS

McGuire, B. Waking the giant   **551.5**

Volcano cowboys. Thompson, D.   **551.21**

VOLCANOES

Calderazzo, J. Rising fire: volcanoes and our inner lives   **551.2**

Gates, A. E. Encyclopedia of earthquakes and volcanoes   **551.2**

Oppenheimer, C. Eruptions that shook the world   **551.2**

Scarth, A. Vesuvius: a biography   **551.2**

Thompson, D. Volcano cowboys   **551.21**

Winchester, S. Krakatoa: the day the world exploded, August 27, 1883   **551.2**

VOLCANOES

See also Geology; Mountains; Physical geography

VOLCANOES -- ENCYCLOPEDIAS

Gates, A. E. Encyclopedia of earthquakes and volcanoes   **551.2**

Volger, Lukas

Bowl   **641.81**

Volk, Audrey Morgen

About

Volk, P. Shocked   **92**

Volk, Patricia

About

Volk, P. Shocked   **92**

Volkogonov, Dmitrii Antonovich

Lenin   **947.084**

Volkov, Solomon

Romanov riches   **891.7**

St. Petersburg   **947**

Volland, Susan

Mastering Sauces   **641.81**

VOLLEYBALL

See also Ball games; Sports

Vollmann, William T., 1959-

(ed) The best American travel writing 2012   **808**

Poor people   **362.5**

Uncentering the Earth   **92**

Voloj, Julian

Ghetto Brother   **92**

Volpe, Joseph

About

Volpe, J. The toughest show on earth   **92**

Volpe, Lou

About

Sokolove, M. Drama high   **92**

Volpone and other plays. Jonson, B.   **822**

Voltaggio, Bryan

Home   **641.5**

Voltaire almighty. Pearson, R.   **92**

Voltaire, 1694-1778

The portable Voltaire   **848**

About

Durant, W. J. The story of philosophy   **109**

Pearson, R. Voltaire almighty   **92**

VOLUME (CUBIC CONTENT)

See also Geometry; Measurement; Weights and measures

VOLUNTARISM

Budd, K. The voluntourist   **361.7**

VOLUNTARISM *See* Volunteer work

VOLUNTARY ASSOCIATIONS *See* Associations

VOLUNTARY MILITARY SERVICE

Hornfischer, J. D. Service   **956.704**

VOLUNTARY ORGANIZATIONS *See* Associations

VOLUNTEER MILITARY SERVICE *See* Voluntary military service

VOLUNTEER WORK

Budd, K. The voluntourist   **361.7**

Posner, J. Find Me Unafraid   **92**

VOLUNTEER WORK -- DIRECTORIES

Green volunteers   **333.72**

The **voluntourist**. Budd, K.   **361.7**

Volvovski, Jenny

(jt. auth) Lamothe, M. The where, the why, and the

how 502
Von Braun. Neufeld, M. J. 92
Von Braun, Wernher, 1912-1977
About
Biddle, W. Dark side of the moon 92
Neufeld, M. J. Von Braun 92
Von Bremzen, Anya
About
Von Bremzen, A. Mastering the art of Soviet cooking 641.59
Von Drehle, Dave
Triangle: the fire that changed America 974.7
Von Furstenberg, Diane
About
Von Furstenberg, D. The woman I wanted to be 92
Von Habsburg, Geza
Faberge revealed 739.2
Von Kármán, Theodore, 1881-1963
About
Hargittai, I. The Martians of science 920
Von Mehren, Joan
Minerva and the muse: a life of Margaret Fuller 92
Von Neumann, John, 1903-1957
About
Dyson, G. Turing's cathedral 004
Hargittai, I. The Martians of science 920
Marton, K. The great escape 920
Von Oelhafen, Ingrid
(jt. auth) Tate, T. Hitler's forgotten children 940.53
Von Tunzelmann, Alex
Blood and Sand 973.92
Red heat 972.9
Von Ziegesar, Peter
The looking glass brother 92
Vongerichten, Jean-Georges, 1957-
(jt. auth) Ko, G. Home cooking with Jean-Georges 641.5
Vonn, Lindsey
Strong Is the New Beautiful 613.042
Vonnegut, Kurt
A man without a country 814
Vonnegut, Kurt, 1922-2007
About
Farrell, S. E. Critical companion to Kurt Vonnegut 813
Shields, C. J. And so it goes: Kurt Vonnegut: a life 92
Vonnegut, K. Kurt Vonnegut 813
VOODOO See Voodooism
Voodoo histories. Aaronovitch, D. 909.08
Voodoo queen. Ward, M. C. 92
Voodoo science. Park, R. L. 500
VOODOOISM
Ward, M. C. Voodoo queen 92
VOODOOISM
See also Religions

Vorgan, Gigi
(jt. auth) Small, G. 2 weeks to a younger brain 616.8
VOTER REGISTRATION
See also Elections; Suffrage
VOTING
Szpiro, G. G. Numbers rule 510
VOTING See Elections; Suffrage
VOTING RIGHTS ACT OF 1965
Kotz, N. Judgment days 323
Vouillamoz, José
(jt. auth) Robinson, J. Wine grapes 664
Vowell, Sarah
Assassination vacation 973
Vowell, Sarah, 1969-
Lafayette in the Somewhat United States 973.3
Unfamiliar fishes 996.9
The wordy shipmates 974
A **voyage** long and strange. Horwitz, T. 970.01
The **voyage** of Argo: the Argonautica. Apollonius 881
The **voyage** of the Beagle. Darwin, C. 508
Voyage of the Sable Venus and other poems. Lewis, R. C. 811
Voyage of the turtle. Safina, C. 597.92
Voyager. Pyne, S. J. 919
VOYAGER PROJECT
Bell, J. The interstellar age 919
VOYAGER PROJECT See Project Voyager
VOYAGERS See Explorers; Travelers
VOYAGES AND TRAVELS
Ananthaswamy, A. The edge of physics 530
Baggett, J. The lost girls 910.4
Bellec, F. Unknown lands 910.4
Bergreen, L. Marco Polo 92
Boissoneault, L. The Last Voyageurs 977
Conover, T. The routes of man 388.1
Cordingly, D. Women sailors and sailors' women 910.4
Dana, R. H. Two years before the mast 910.4
Green, B. Boltzmann's tomb 509
Henion, L. A. Phenomenal 910.4
Hoffman, C. The lunatic express 910.4
Literature of travel and exploration 910.4
McCarthy, A. Journeys home 929.1
Morris, J. Contact! 910.4
Mosler, L. Driving hungry 92
Nootebooms hotel./English Nomad's hotel 910.4
Points unknown 910
Sieberson, S. The naked mountaineer 92
Solnit, R. Wanderlust 796.51
Swift, V. Gardens of awe and folly 635
Travels with Herodotus 930
Ultimate travel 910.2
Waldman, C. Encyclopedia of exploration 910.3
World's best travel experiences 910.4
VOYAGES AND TRAVELS

See also Geography

VOYAGES AND TRAVELS -- ANECDOTES

McCarthy, A. Journeys home   **929.1**

VOYAGES AND TRAVELS -- HISTORY

Bellec, F. Unknown lands   **910.4**

Lester, T. The fourth part of the world   **912**

VOYAGES AROUND THE WORLD

Bergreen, L. Over the edge of the world   **910.4**

Blainey, G. Sea of dangers   **92**

Ridley, G. The discovery of Jeanne Baret   **92**

VOYAGES AROUND THE WORLD

See also Travel; Voyages and travels

VOYAGES AROUND THE WORLD -- HISTORY

Chaplin, J. E. Round about the earth   **910.4**

VOYAGES TO THE MOON *See* Imaginary voyages; Space flight to the moon

Vreeland, Diana

About

Stuart, A. M. Empress of Fashion   **92**

VUGHT (CONCENTRATION CAMP)

At the edge of the abyss   **940.53**

Vuillard, Édouard, 1868-1940

About

Edouard Vuillard   **759**

VULCAN (HYPOTHETICAL PLANET)

Levenson, T. The hunt for Vulcan   **523.4**

VULCAN (HYPOTHETICAL PLANET)

See also Planets

W

W.B. Yeats: a life. Foster, R. F.   **821**

W.C. Handy. Robertson, D.   **92**

W.E.B. Du Bois. Lewis, D. L.   **92**

The W.E.B. Du Bois lectures [series]

Fredrickson, G. M. Big enough to be inconsistent   **973.7**

Waal, F. B. M. de (Frans B. M.), 1948-

The age of empathy   **152.4**

Are We Smart Enough to Know How Smart Animals Are?   **591.5**

Bonobo   **599.88**

Our inner ape   **156**

Wachsmann, Nikolaus

Kl   **940.53**

Wachter, Robert

The digital doctor   **610.28**

Wacker, Grant

America's pastor   **92**

Wade, Becky

Run the World   **796.42**

Wade, Henry, 1914-2001

About

Hull, N. E. H. Roe v. Wade   **344**

Wade, Nicholas

Before the dawn   **599.93**

Wade, Stephen

The beautiful music all around us   **781.62**

Wadi, Sameh

The new mediterranean cookbook   **641.59**

Wadsworth, Kathryn

(jt. auth) Deardorff, D. What's wrong with my fruit garden?   **634**

(jt. auth) Deardorff, D. What's wrong with my houseplant?   **635.9**

(jt. auth) Deardorff, D. What's wrong with my vegetable garden?   **635**

Deardorff, D. C. What's wrong with my plant (and how do I fix it?)   **635**

WAFFEN-SS

Weale, A. Army of evil   **940.54**

WAFFEN-SS -- HISTORY

Weale, A. Army of evil   **940.54**

WAGE-PRICE POLICY

See also Inflation (Finance); Prices; Salaries, wages, etc.

WAGES *See* Salaries, wages, etc.

Wages of rebellion. Hedges, C.   **303.48**

Waging modern war. Clark, W. K.   **949.703**

The **Wagner** clan. Carr, J.   **920**

Wagner family

About

Carr, J. The Wagner clan   **920**

Wagner, Andreas

Arrival of the fittest   **572.8**

Wagner, E. J.

The science of Sherlock Holmes   **363.2**

Wagner, Jordan Lee

The synagogue survival kit   **296.4**

Wagner, Melissa

Friedman, V. M. Field guide to stains   **648**

Wagner, Richard, 1813-1883

About

Osborne, C. The complete operas of Richard Wagner   **792.5**

Wagner, Walter H.

Opening the Qur'an   **297.1**

Wagner-Martin, Linda

(ed) The Oxford book of women's writing in the United States   **810**

Wagons west. McLynn, F.   **978**

Wahab, Shaista

A brief history of Afghanistan   **958.1**

WAHHABIS

Lawrence, T. E. Seven pillars of wisdom   **940.4**

Wailer, Bunny

About

Grant, C. The natural mystics   **920**

WAILERS (MUSICAL GROUP)

Grant, C. The natural mystics   **920**

Wainaina, Binyavanga

About

Wainaina, B. One day I will write about this

place 823
Wait. Partnoy, F. 153.8
Wait till next year. Goodwin, D. K. 796.357
Waiting 'til the midnight hour. Joseph, P. E. 323.1
Waiting for snow in Havana. Eire, C. M. N. 92
Waiting for the barbarians. Mendelsohn, D. 801
Waiting on a train. McCommons, J. 385
Waits, Tom, 1949-
About
Hoskyns, B. Lowside of the road 92
Wakefield, Dan
(ed) Vonnegut, K. Kurt Vonnegut 813
Wakelyn, Jon L.
(ed) Leaders of the American Civil War 973.7
Wakeman, John
World authors, 1950-1970 920.003
World authors, 1970-1975 920.003
Waking giant. Reynolds, D. S. 973.5
Waking the giant. McGuire, B. 551.5
Wakoski, Diane
The diamond dog 811
Waksman, Steve
This ain't the summer of love 781.66
WAL-MART STORES, INC.
Featherstone, L. Selling women short 331.4
Walton, S. Sam Walton, made in America 92
Walcott, Derek, 1930-
Omeros 811
The Poetry of Derek Walcott 1948-2013 811
Wald, Elijah
Dylan Goes Electric! 781.66
Escaping the delta 92
How the Beatles destroyed rock 'n' roll 781.64
Waldbauer, Gilbert
What good are bugs? 595.7
Walden, or, Life in the woods. Thoreau, H. D. 818
Waldfogel, Joel
Scroogenomics 339.4
Waldin, Monty
Biodynamic gardening 635
Waldman, Anne
In the room of never grieve 811
Waldman, Carl
Atlas of the North American Indian 970.004
Encyclopedia of exploration 910.3
Encyclopedia of Native American tribes 970.004
Waldman, Jonathan
Rust 620.1
Waldman, Michael
The Fight to Vote 324.6
Waldman, Sarah
Little bites 641.5
Waldman, Steven
Founding faith 342
Waldmeir, Patti
Anatomy of a miracle 968.06

Waldron, Ann
Eudora 92
Waldrop, Keith
Transcendental studies 811
Waldrop, Rosmarie
Driven to abstraction 811
Waldrup, Carole Chandler
The vice presidents 920.003
Waldseemüller, Martin, 1470-1521?
About
Lester, T. The fourth part of the world 912
WALES
Morris, J. A writer's house in Wales 942.9
WALES -- HISTORY
Charles-Edwards, T. M. Wales and the Britons, 350-1064 942.901
Wales and the Britons, 350-1064. Charles-Edwards, T. M. 942.901
Waley, Arthur
(tr) Confucius The Analects 181
The No plays of Japan 895.6
A **walk** across America. Jenkins, P. 917
A **walk** in the woods. Bryson, B. 917
Walker's mammals of the world. Nowak, R. M. 599
Walker, Aidan
(ed) The Encyclopedia of wood 674
Walker, Alan
The wisdom of the bones 599.93
Walker, Alexander
Audrey 92
Walker, Alice, 1944-
The cushion in the road 814
Hard times require furious dancing 811
The same river twice 813
About
Alice Walker 813
Alice Walker's The color purple 813
Black women writers (1950-1980) 810
Gillespie, C. Critical companion to Alice Walker 813
Walker, A. The same river twice 813
Walker, Brian
(ed) Masters of American comics 741.5
Walker, Danielle
Danielle Walker's against all grain 641.563
Walker, Demetrius
About
Dohrmann, G. Play their hearts out 796.323
Walker, Gabrielle
The hot topic 363.7
Walker, Janice R.
The Columbia guide to online style 808
Walker, Jesse
The United States of paranoia 973
Walker, Margaret, 1915-1998
About

Black women writers (1950-1980)   **810**

Walker, Mary, d. 1872

About

Nathans, S. To free a family   **306.3**

Walker, Ronald W.

Massacre at Mountain Meadows   **979.2**

Walker, Thomas J.

Capinera, J. L. Field guide to grasshoppers, crickets, and katydids of the United States   **595.7**

Walker, William T.

Betrayal at Little Gibraltar   **940.436**

Walker-Hill, Helen

From spirituals to symphonies   **780**

WALKING

Baxter, J. The most beautiful walk in the world **914**

Solnit, R. Wanderlust   **796.51**

WALKING

See also Aerobics; Athletics; Human locomotion

WALKING -- FRANCE -- PARIS -- GUIDE-BOOKS

Baxter, J. Five nights in Paris   **914.4**

Walking point. Ulander, P. A.   **959.704**

Walking the Amazon. Stafford, E.   **918.1**

Walking the Bible. Feiler, B. S.   **915**

Walking the Nile. Wood, L.   **916.2**

Walking With Abel. Badkhen, A.   **305.896**

Walking with Jesus. Francis, P.   **282**

Walking with Ruskin. Cording, R.   **811**

Walking with the comrades. Roy, A.   **954**

Walking with the muses. Cleveland, P.   **92**

Walking zero. Raymo, C.   **526**

WALL DECORATION *See* Mural painting and decoration

WALL PAINTING *See* Mural painting and decoration

WALL STREET (NEW YORK, N.Y.)

Cramer, J. J. Confessions of a street addict   **332.6**

Ferguson, C. Predator nation   **330.973**

Fox, J. The myth of the rational market   **332.6**

Gage, B. The day Wall Street exploded   **974.7**

Gasparino, C. The sellout   **332**

Kelly, K. Street fighters   **332.6**

Lewis, M. Flash boys   **332.6**

Lowenstein, R. The end of Wall Street   **332.6**

Mahar, M. Bull!: a history of the boom, 1982-1999   **332.6**

Tett, G. Fool's gold   **332.6**

Where are the customers' yachts?   **332.64**

WALL STREET (NEW YORK, N.Y.)

See also Stock exchanges

Wall Street journal

The Wall Street Journal essential guide to management   **658**

WALL STREET JOURNAL

Tofel, R. J. Restless genius   **92**

Wolff, M. The man who owns the news   **92**

Wall Street journal book [series]

Noonan, P. A heart, a cross & a flag   **973.931**

Rabinowitz, D. No crueler tyrannies   **345**

The **Wall** Street Journal complete home owner's guidebook. Crook, D.   **643**

The **Wall** Street Journal essential guide to management. Wall Street journal   **658**

The **Wall** Street Journal: financial guidebook for new parents. Bradford, S. L.   **332.024**

Wall, Cheryl A.

(ed) Folklore, memoirs, and other writings   **398**

(ed) Hurston, Z. N. Novels and stories   **813**

Women of the Harlem Renaissance   **810**

Wall, Duncan

About

Wall, D. The ordinary acrobat   **796.47**

Wall, Joseph Frazier

Andrew Carnegie   **92**

Wallace, Alfred Russel, 1823-1913

About

McCalman, I. Darwin's armada   **576.8**

Slotten, R. A. The heretic in Darwin's court   **92**

Wallace, Anthony F. C.

The long bitter trail   **323.1**

Wallace, Benjamin

The billionaire's vinegar   **641.2**

Wallace, Carol, 1955-

(jt. auth) MacColl, G. To marry an English Lord   **974.7**

Wallace, Daniel

Beatty, S. The DC Comics encyclopedia   **741.5**

Edgerton, C. Papadaddy's book for new fathers **649**

Ultimate Star wars

Wallace, David Foster

Consider the lobster   **814**

The David Foster Wallace Reader   **813**

Franzen, J. Farther away   **814**

String theory   **796.342**

About

Max, D. T. c. Every love story is a ghost story **92**

Wallace, Michael

Burrows, E. G. Gotham   **974.7**

Wallace, Perry

About

Maraniss, A. Strong inside   **92**

Wallach, Eli, 1915-

About

Wallach, E. The good, the bad, and me   **92**

Wallach, Janet

Desert queen   **956**

Waller, Littleton Waller Tazewell, 1856-1926

About

Jones, G. Honor in the dust   **959.9**

Waller, Maureen

Sovereign ladies   **920**

Wallerstein, Judith S.
The unexpected legacy of divorce **306.89**
Wallis, Michael
Mankiller, W. Mankiller: a chief and her people **92**
Billy the Kid **92**
Route 66: the mother road **917**
Walliser, Jessica
Attracting beneficial bugs to your garden **628.9**
WALLPAPER
See also Interior design
WALLS
See also Buildings; Civil engineering
The **walls** came tumbling down. Stokes, G. **947.085**
Walls family
About
Sharfstein, D. J. The invisible line **305.8**
Walls, Jeannette
About
Walls, J. The glass castle **92**
Walsh, Adam
About
Matthews, J. Bringing Adam home **364.1**
Walsh, Bill, 1931-2007
The score takes care of itself **658.4**
About
Harris, D. The genius **92**
Walsh, Craig
Walsh, B. The score takes care of itself **658.4**
Walsh, Jim
The Replacements: all over but the shouting **920**
Walsh, John
The J. Paul Getty Museum and its collections **708.1**
Walsh, John Evangelist
Midnight dreary **818**
Moonlight **345**
Walsh, Judith E.
A brief history of India **954**
Walsh, Keri
(ed) The letters of Sylvia Beach **92**
Walsh, Maurice
Bitter freedom **941.508**
Walsh, Michael
(jt. auth) Jordan, D. The king's revenge **941.062**
Jordan, D. White cargo **326**
Walsh, Mikey
About
Walsh, M. Gypsy boy **92**
Walsh, Patrick C.
Dr. Patrick Walsh's guide to surviving prostate cancer **616.99**
Walsh, Peter
How to organize just about everything **640**
Lighten up **332.024**
Walsh, Stephen
Stravinsky: a creative spring **92**
Stravinsky: the second exile **92**

Walt Disney. Gabler, N. **92**
WALT DISNEY COMPANY
Gabler, N. Walt Disney **92**
WALT DISNEY PRODUCTIONS -- HISTORY -- 20TH CENTURY
Ghez, D. They drew as they pleased **741.58**
WALT DISNEY WORLD (FLA.)
See also Amusement parks
Walter Benjamin at the Dairy Queen. McMurtry, L. **818**
Walter de Gruyter GmbH & Co. KG
(comp) Museums of the World **069**
Walter, Carole
Great cookies **641.8**
Walter, Chip
Last ape standing **569.9**
Walters, Barbara, 1931-
About
Walters, B. Audition **92**
Walters, Kerry
The Underground Railroad **973.7**
Walton, Anthony
(ed) Every shut eye ain't asleep **811**
(ed) The Vintage book of African American poetry **811**
Walton, Bill, 1952-
About
Walton, B. Back from the dead **92**
Walton, Jo, 1964-
What Makes This Book So Great **813**
Walton, Sam
About
Walton, S. Sam Walton, made in America **92**
WALTZ
See also Dance
WALTZES (MUSIC)
See also Dance music
Wambach, Abby, 1980-
About
Wambach, A. Forward **92**
The **wandering** mind. Biever, J. A. **612.8**
Wanderlust. Solnit, R. **796.51**
Wanderlust. Krasno, J. **613.7**
Wandschneider, Rich
(ed) The longest trail **970.004**
Wanek, Catherine
(ed) The Art of natural building **690**
Wang, Pi
I ching The classic of changes **299.5**
Wann, David
The new normal **306**
Wansink, Brian
Mindless eating **616.85**
Slim by design **613.2**
Wanted women. Scroggins, D. **305.48**
Wanting in Arabic. Salah, T. **811**

Wanzer, Sidney H.
To die well   **179.7**

Wapner, Jessica
The Philadelphia chromosome   **616.99**

War. Junger, S.   **958.1**

WAR
Clausewitz, C. v. On war   **355**
Erlich, R. Inside Syria   **956.91**
Fiennes, R. Agincourt   **944**
Hanson, V. D. The father of us all   **355**
Harris, S. @WAR   **355.3**
Hastings, M. Warriors   **355**
Hedges, C. War is a force that gives us meaning   **355.02**
Hornfischer, J. D. Service   **956.704**
Junger, S. Fire   **909.82**
Morris, D. J. The evil hours   **616.85**
Morris, I. War! What is it good for?   **303.6**
Rehnquist, W. H. All the laws but one   **342**
Reporting America at war   **070.4**
Roach, M. Grunt   **355.07**
Rose, G. How wars end   **355**
Taylor, S. Commander   **92**
Witt, J. F. Lincoln's code   **343**

War & love, love & war. Poems./English./Selections   **892.4**

WAR (INTERNATIONAL LAW) -- HISTORY
Witt, J. F. Lincoln's code   **343**

WAR (PHILOSOPHY) -- HISTORY -- 20TH CENTURY
Preston, D. A higher form of killing   **940.4**

WAR -- DECISION MAKING
Hotta, E. Japan 1941   **940.54**

WAR -- ENCYCLOPEDIAS
War: from ancient Egypt to Iraq   **355**

WAR -- ETHICAL ASPECTS
Edmonds, B. R. God Is Not Here   **956.704**

WAR -- HISTORY
France, J. Perilous glory   **355**

WAR -- PSYCHOLOGICAL ASPECTS
Di Giovanni, J. Madness visible   **949.7**
Dreazen, Y. The invisible front   **92**

WAR -- PUBLIC OPINION
Doyle, D. H. The Cause of All Nations   **973.7**

WAR -- RELIGIOUS ASPECTS
Ronald, S. Heretic queen   **942.05**

WAR -- RELIGIOUS ASPECTS
See also Religion; War

WAR -- TERMINATION
Rose, G. How wars end   **355**

WAR -- UNITED STATES -- HISTORY
Witt, J. F. Lincoln's code   **343**

The **war** against the Jews, 1933-1945. Dawidowicz, L. S.   **940.53**

WAR AND CHILDREN *See* Children and war
WAR AND CIVILIZATION

Americans at war   **973**
Crane, D. Went the day well?   **940.2**
Dower, J. W. Cultures of war   **355**
Evans, M. Algeria   **965**
France, J. Perilous glory   **355**
Karnad, R. Farthest field   **940.54**
Morris, I. War! What is it good for?   **303.6**
Morrison, D. The black Nile   **962**
Stack, M. Every man in this village is a liar **956.05**

WAR AND CIVILIZATION
See also Civilization; War

WAR AND EMERGENCY LEGISLATION -- UNITED STATES -- HISTORY
Witt, J. F. Lincoln's code   **343**

WAR AND EMERGENCY POWERS -- UNITED STATES
Mayer, J. The dark side   **973.931**
Schlesinger, A. M. War and the American presidency   **327.1**

WAR AND RELIGION *See* War -- Religious aspects

WAR AND SOCIETY
Morris, I. War! What is it good for?   **303.6**
Nguyen, V. T. Nothing ever dies   **959.704**
Sontag, S. Regarding the pain of others   **303.6**

WAR AND SOCIETY -- ENGLAND -- HISTORY -- 19TH CENTURY -- SOURCES
Crane, D. Went the day well?   **940.2**

WAR AND SOCIETY -- HISTORY -- 20TH CENTURY
Collingham, L. The taste of war   **940.53**

WAR AND SOCIETY -- INDIA -- HISTORY -- 20TH CENTURY
Karnad, R. Farthest field   **940.54**

WAR AND SOCIETY -- UNITED STATES
Dower, J. W. Cultures of war   **355**

WAR AND SOCIETY -- UNITED STATES -- HISTORY
Anderson, F. The dominion of war   **973.2**
McPherson, J. M. The war that forged a nation   **973.7**

War and the American presidency. Schlesinger, A. M.   **327.1**
War as I knew it. Patton, G. S.   **940.54**
War at sea. Miller, N.   **940.54**
War at the end of the world. Duffy, J. P.   **940.54**
The **war** before independence, 1775-1776. Beck, D. W.   **973.3**

WAR BRIDES -- GREAT BRITAIN -- BIOGRAPHY
Barrett, D. GI brides   **940.53**

WAR CASUALTIES
See also War

WAR CORRESPONDENTS
Di Giovanni, J. The Morning They Came For Us   **956.91**

Kasinof, L. Don't be afraid of the bullets **953.305**

WAR CORRESPONDENTS -- UNITED STATES -- CORRESPONDENCE

Cronkite, W. Cronkite's war **070.4**

WAR CORRESPONDENTS -- YEMEN (REPUBLIC) -- BIOGRAPHY

Kasinof, L. Don't be afraid of the bullets **953.305**

WAR CRIME TRIALS

Lipstadt, D. E. The Eichmann trial **345**

WAR CRIME TRIALS

See also Trials

WAR CRIMES

Akcam, T. A shameful act **956.6**

Frederick, J. Black hearts **956.7**

Great lives from history: Notorious lives **920.003**

Sands, P. East West Street **345**

WAR CRIMES

See also Crimes against humanity; International law; War

WAR CRIMINALS

Bascomb, N. Hunting Eichmann **943.086**

Eichmann before Jerusalem **92**

Fest, J. C. Speer: the final verdict **92**

Great lives from history: Notorious lives **920.003**

Lifton, R. J. The Nazi doctors **940.53**

Lipstadt, D. E. The Eichmann trial **345**

My grandfather would have shot me **929.2**

Rashke, R. Useful Enemies **341.69**

Sereny, G. Albert Speer **92**

WAR CRIMINALS -- GERMANY -- HISTORY

Nagorski, A. The Nazi hunters **940.53**

WAR CRIMINALS -- UNITED STATES -- HISTORY -- 20TH CENTURY

Lichtblau, E. The Nazis next door **324.1**

WAR FILMS

See also Historical drama; Motion pictures

WAR GAMES

See also Military art and science; Military maneuvers; Simulation games; Tactics

WAR HORSES -- KOREA (SOUTH) -- HISTORY -- 20TH CENTURY

Hutton, R. Sgt. Reckless **951.904**

WAR HORSES -- UNITED STATES -- HISTORY -- 20TH CENTURY

Hutton, R. Sgt. Reckless **951.904**

WAR IN LITERATURE

Alexander, C. The war that killed Achilles **883**

The Norton book of modern war **808.8**

War is a force that gives us meaning. Hedges, C. **355.02**

The war lovers. Thomas, E. **973.8**

War made new. Boot, M. **355**

WAR OF 1812

Collins, G. William Henry Harrison **92**

Daughan, G. C. 1812: the Navy's war **973.5**

Smith, G. A. The slaves' gamble **973.5**

Snow, P. When Britain burned the White House **975.3**

Taylor, A. The civil war of 1812 **973.5**

Vogel, S. Through the perilous fight **973.5**

WAR OF 1812

See also Great Britain -- History -- 1714-1837; United States -- History -- 1783-1815

War of necessity: war of choice. Haass, R. **956.7**

War of nerves. Tucker, J. B. **358**

War of nerves. Tucker, J. B. **358**

WAR OF THE AMERICAN REVOLUTION *See* United States -- History -- 1775-1783, Revolution

War of the Whales. Horwitz, J. **333.95**

WAR OF THE WORLDS (RADIO PROGRAM)

Schwartz, A. B. Broadcast hysteria **791.44**

War of two. Sedgwick, J. **973.4**

The war on alcohol. McGirr, L. **363.4**

WAR ON TERRORISM

Bergen, P. L. The longest war **909.83**

Bergen, P. L. Manhunt **363.325**

Eichenwald, K. 500 days **973.931**

Elshtain, J. B. Just war against terror **363.32**

Filkins, D. The forever war **956.7**

Graff, G. M. The threat matrix **363.325**

Henican, E. Worth dying for **359.984**

Hersh, S. M. Chain of command **973.931**

Hickman, J. Murder at Camp Delta **355.1**

Johnsen, G. D. The last refuge **363.325**

Johnson, H. B. The age of anxiety **973.921**

Kaplan, R. D. Imperial grunts **973.931**

Kessler, R. The CIA at war **973.931**

Khan, M. R. My Guantanamo diary **909.83**

Kilcullen, D. The accidental guerrilla **355.4**

Mayer, J. The dark side **973.931**

Morell, M. J. The great war of our time **363.325**

National Commission on Terrorist Attacks Upon the United States The 9/11 Commission report **973.931**

Noonan, P. A heart, a cross & a flag **973.931**

Rice, C. No higher honor **327.73**

Schroen, G. C. First in **958.1**

Soufan, A. H. The black banners **973.931**

Stack, M. Every man in this village is a liar **956.05**

Suskind, R. The one percent doctrine **973.931**

The torture papers **973.931**

WAR ON TERRORISM *See* Terrorism -- Prevention

WAR ON TERRORISM, 2001-2009 -- BIOGRAPHY

Guantanamo diary **958.104**

WAR ON TERRORISM, 2001-2009 -- PERSONAL NARRATIVES, AMERICAN

Bolger, D. P. Why We Lost **956.704**

WAR PHOTOGRAPHERS -- UNITED STATES -- BIOGRAPHY

Addario, L. It's What I Do **92**

WAR PHOTOGRAPHY
Huffman, A. Here I Am 770.92
Sontag, S. Regarding the pain of others 303.6
WAR PHOTOGRAPHY
See also Photography; Photojournalism
WAR PHOTOGRAPHY -- 20TH CENTURY
Addario, L. It's What I Do 92
WAR POETRY
American war poetry 811
Komunyakaa, Y. Warhorses 811
The Oxford book of war poetry 808.81
Words for the hour 811
WAR POETRY
See also Poetry
WAR POETRY, ENGLISH -- HISTORY AND CRITICISM
Swift, D. Bomber County 821
WAR POETRY/COLLECTIONS
The Oxford book of war poetry 808.81
WAR POWERS *See* War and emergency powers
WAR PROTEST MOVEMENTS *See* Peace movements
WAR RELIEF
Bortolotti, D. Hope in hell 610
Orbinski, J. An imperfect offering 610
Rieff, D. A bed for the night 361.2
WAR SONGS
See also National songs; Songs
WAR STORIES
Democracy 741.5
The Norton book of modern war 808.8
Rhodes, R. Hell and Good Company 946.081
WAR STORIES
See also Fiction; Historical fiction
WAR TELEVISION PROGRAMS
See also Television programs
The **war** that forged a nation. McPherson, J. M. 973.7
The **war** that killed Achilles. Alexander, C. 883
WAR USE OF ANIMALS *See* Animals -- War use
WAR VETERANS *See* Veterans
War without end. La Guardia, A. 956.940
War! What is it good for? Morris, I. 303.6
War: from ancient Egypt to Iraq. 355
Warburg family
About
Chernow, R. The Warburgs 920
Warburg, Siegmund George Sir, 1902-1982
About
Ferguson, N. High financier 92
The **Warburgs**. Chernow, R. 920
Ward, Andrew
The slaves' war 973.7
Ward, Diane Raines
Water wars 333.91
Ward, Elisabeth I.

(ed) Vikings: the North Atlantic saga 970.01
Ward, F. De W. (Ferdinand De Wilton), 1812-1891
About
Ward, G. C. A disposition to be rich 974.7
Ward, Geoffrey C.
(jt. auth) Burns, K. The Roosevelts 920
The Civil War 973.7
Jazz 781.65
Unforgivable blackness 92
The West 978
Ward, Gerald W. R.
Chihuly 748.2
Ward, Jesmyn
(ed) The Fire This Time 305.896
About
Ward, J. Men We Reaped 92
Ward, Lester Frank, 1841-1913
About
Commager, H. S. The American mind 973
Ward, Martha Coonfield
Voodoo queen 92
Ward, Peter
(jt. auth) Kirschvink, J. A new history of life 576.8
Ward, Peter Douglas
Life as we do not know it 576.8
Ward, Rachel
Rich, C. Stained glass basics 748.5
Ward, Samuel, 1814-1884
About
Jacob, K. A. King of the lobby 92
Ward, Tess
The naked cookbook 641.302
Ward-Royster, Willa
How I got over 920
Ware, Charles Pickard
Slave songs of the United States 781.62
Ware, Susan
Letter to the world 920.72
Notable American women 920.003
Wareham, Dean
About
Wareham, D. Black postcards 92
Warhol, Andy, 1928-1987
About
Davis, D. The trip 700.92
Scherman, T. Pop 92
Warhorses. Komunyakaa, Y. 811
Wariner, Ruth
About
Wariner, R. The sound of gravel 92
Warlord. D'Este, C. 92
Warlords. Berthon, S. 940.53
The **warmth** of other suns. Wilkerson, I. 307
Warner, Deborah Jean
(ed) Instruments of science 502.8
Warner, Ezra J.

Generals in blue   920

Generals in gray   920

Warner, Judith

Perfect madness   306.8

Warner, Justin

The Laws of Cooking   641.502

Warner, Pat

The router book   684

Warner, Pop, 1871-1954

         About

Anderson, L. Carlisle vs. Army   796.332

Warner, Ralph E.

Stewart, M. Every landlord's legal guide   346.04

Everybody's guide to small claims court   347

Warner, Ty, 1944-

         About

Bissonnette, Z. The great Beanie Baby bubble   338.7

Warnes, David

Chronicle of the Russian tsars   947

Warnick, Melody

This Is Where You Belong   155.94

Warped passages. Randall, L.   530

Warren Bennis signature series

Conant, D. R. Touchpoints   658.4

Warren Buffett and the art of stock arbitrage. Buffett, M.   332.6

The **Warren** Buffett Way. Hagstrom, R. G.   332.6

Warren, Bill

Keep watching the skies!   791.43

Warren, Cat

What the dog knows   636.7

         About

Warren, C. What the dog knows   636.7

Warren, Earle, 1914-1994

         About

Dance, S. The world of Count Basie   920

Warren, Elizabeth

         About

Warren, E. A fighting chance   92

Warren, James A.

Haynes, F. The lions of Iwo Jima   940.54

Warren, Larkin

(jt. auth) Phelps, C. Runaway girl   362.74

Warren, Louis S.

Buffalo Bill's America   92

Warren, Rebecca

(ed) The politics book   320.01

Warren, Robert Penn, 1905-1989

The collected poems of Robert Penn Warren   811

         About

Blight, D. W. American oracle   973.7

Warren, Rosanna

(ed) The collected poems of Eugenio Montale 1925-1977   851

Warren, Wendy

New England Bound   306.362

Warrick, Joby, 1960-

Black flags   956.91

The **warrior** and the priest: Woodrow Wilson and Theodore Roosevelt. Cooper, J. M.   92

The **warrior** elite. Couch, D.   359.9

Warrior politics. Kaplan, R. D.   320

Warriors. Hastings, M.   355

WARS See Military history; Naval history; War

The **Wars** of the Roses. Weir, A.   942.04

The **Wars** of the Roses. Jones, D.   942.04

WARS OF THE ROSES, 1455-1485 See Great Britain -- History -- 1455-1485, Wars of the Roses

WARSHIPS

         See also Naval architecture; Naval art and science; Sea power; Ships

Wartzman, Rick

(ed) Drucker, P. F. The Drucker lectures   658

Washburn, Katharine

(ed) World poetry   808.81

WASHING See Laundry

Washington. Chernow, R.   92

WASHINGTON (D.C.)

Wilber, D. Q. A good month for murder   363.25

WASHINGTON (D.C.) -- BIOGRAPHY

Herken, G. The Georgetown set   975.3

WASHINGTON (D.C.) -- BUILDINGS, STRUCTURES, ETC

Gordon, J. S. Washington's monument   975.3

WASHINGTON (D.C.) -- BUILDINGS, STRUCTURES, ETC.

Gugliotta, G. Freedom's cap   975.3

The house that George built   975.3

WASHINGTON (D.C.) -- HISTORY

Roberts, C. Capital dames   793.7

WASHINGTON (D.C.) -- HISTORY -- 20TH CENTURY

Herken, G. The Georgetown set   975.3

WASHINGTON (D.C.) -- HISTORY -- CAPTURE BY THE BRITISH, 1814

Snow, P. When Britain burned the White House   975.3

Vogel, S. Through the perilous fight   973.5

WASHINGTON (D.C.) -- HISTORY -- CIVIL WAR, 1861-1865

Roberts, C. Capital dames   793.7

WASHINGTON (D.C.) -- SOCIAL LIFE AND CUSTOMS

The Scurlock Studio and Black Washington   779

WASHINGTON (D.C.) -- SOCIAL LIFE AND CUSTOMS -- ANECDOTES

Brower, K. A. The residence   975.3

WASHINGTON (STATE) -- HISTORY

Harmon, A. Indians in the making   970.004

WASHINGTON (STATE) -- RACE RELATIONS

Merlino, D. The hustle   796.323

Washington family

About

Baker, J. F. The Washingtons of Wessyngton Plantation 920

WASHINGTON MONUMENT (WASHINGTON, D.C.)

Gordon, J. S. Washington's monument 975.3

WASHINGTON MUTUAL, INC.

Grind, K. The lost bank 332.3

WASHINGTON POST

Bernstein, C. All the president's men 973.924

Washington rules. Bacevich, A. J. 355

Washington's crossing. Fischer, D. H. 973.3

Washington's Immortals. O'Donnell, P. K. 973.3

Washington's monument. Gordon, J. S. 975.3

Washington's secret war. Fleming, T. J. 973.3

Washington, Booker T., 1856-1915

Up from slavery 92

About

Davis, D. Guest of honor 973.91

Harlan, L. R. Booker T. Washington: the making of a black leader, 1856-1901 92

Harlan, L. R. Booker T. Washington: the wizard of Tuskegee, 1901-1915 92

Norrell, R. J. Up from history 92

Smock, R. W. Booker T. Washington 92

Uncle Tom or new Negro 370

Washington, B. T. Up from slavery 92

Washington, George, 1732-1799

Writings 973.4

About

Breen, T. H. George Washington's journey 92

Brookhiser, R. Founding father: rediscovering George Washington 92

Chernow, R. Washington 92

Ellis, J. J. Founding brothers 973.4

Ellis, J. J. His Excellency 92

Fischer, D. H. Washington's crossing 973.3

Fleming, T. J. Washington's secret war 973.3

Flexner, J. T. George Washington and the new nation, 1783-1793 92

Flexner, J. T. George Washington: anguish and farewell 1793-1799 92

Flexner, J. T. George Washington: the forge of experience, 1732-1775 92

Fowler, W. M. American crisis 973.3

Fraser, F. The Washingtons 92

Gaines, J. R. For liberty and glory 92

Gordon, J. S. Washington's monument 975.3

Johnson, P. George Washington: the Founding Father 92

Lockhart, P. D. The whites of their eyes 973.3

Nagy, J. A. George Washington's secret spy war 973.385

Randall, W. S. George Washington 92

Vidal, G. Inventing a nation: Washington, Adams, Jefferson 973.4

Wiencek, H. An imperfect god 973.4

Yaeger, D. George Washington's secret six 973.4

Washington, Harriet A.

Deadly monopolies 338.4

Infectious madness 616.89

Medical apartheid 174.2

Washington, James Melvin

(ed) A testament of hope 323.1

Washington, John, 1838-1918

About

Blight, D. W. A slave no more 326

Washington, Martha, 1731-1802

About

Brady, P. Martha Washington 92

Fraser, F. The Washingtons 92

Washington, Peter

(ed) Herbert, G. Herbert: poems 821

(comp) Keats, J. Poems 821

(ed) Persian poets 891

(comp) Rimbaud, A. Poems 841

Washington: the making of the American capital. Bordewich, F. M. 975.3

The **Washingtons.** Fraser, F. 92

The **Washingtons** of Wessyngton Plantation. Baker, J. F. 920

Wasik, Bill

(jt. auth) Murphy, M. Rabid 614.5

Wasiolek, Sue

(jt. auth) Crossman, A. Getting the best out of college 378.1

Wasmund, Shaa

Do less, get more 650.1

WASPS

See also Insects

Wassell, Gloria Russo

(jt. auth) Groza, V. Adopting older children 362.7

Wasserman, Dale

Cervantes Saavedra, M. d. Man of La Mancha 812

Wasserman, Fredda

Dresser, N. Saying goodbye to someone you love 155.9

Wasserman, Lew R., 1913-2002

About

Bruck, C. When Hollywood had a king 338.7

Wasserman, Noam

The founder's dilemmas 658.1

Wasserstein, Bernard

On the eve 305.892

Wasserstein, Wendy, 1950-2006

The Heidi chronicles and other plays 812

About

Playwrights at work 812

Salamon, J. Wendy and the lost boys

Wasson, Sam

Fifth Avenue, 5 AM 791.43

Fosse **92**

Waste. Stuart, T. **363.8**

WASTE (ECONOMICS)

Bloom, J. American wasteland **363.7**

WASTE (ECONOMICS)

See also Economics

WASTE DISPOSAL *See* Refuse and refuse disposal

WASTE MINIMIZATION

Stuart, T. Waste **363.8**

Wasted: a memoir of anorexia and bulimia. Hornbacher, M. **616.85**

WASTES, HAZARDOUS *See* Hazardous wastes

Watanabe, Judi

The Complete Photo Guide to Cardmaking **745.594**

Watch me. Huston, A. **92**

Watch my baby grow. **649.122**

Watch your back! Deyo, R. A. **617.5**

The **watchers.** Harris, S. **363.32**

WATCHES *See* Clocks and watches

Watching baseball smarter. Hample, Z. **796.357**

Watching giants. Kelsey, E. **599.5**

Watching the spring festival. Bidart, F. **811**

Watching the world change. Friend, D. **974.7**

The **watchman's** rattle. Costa, R. D. **501**

Water. Solomon, S. **553.7**

WATER

Kandel, R. S. Water from heaven **553.7**

Pielou, E. C. Fresh water **551.48**

Solomon, S. Water **553.7**

WATER

See also Earth sciences; Hydraulics

WATER AND CIVILIZATION

Solomon, S. Water **553.7**

WATER AND CIVILIZATION -- HISTORY

Fagan, B. Elixir **553.7**

WATER BIRDS

See also Birds

WATER CONSERVATION

Penick, P. The water-saving garden **635.9**

WATER CONSERVATION

See also Conservation of natural resources

WATER FLUORIDATION

See also Water supply

Water from heaven. Kandel, R. S. **553.7**

The **water** gardener's bible. Helm, B. **635.9**

WATER GARDENS

Helm, B. The water gardener's bible **635.9**

Speichert, C. G. Encyclopedia of water garden plants **635**

WATER GARDENS

See also Gardens; Landscape architecture

WATER LILIES IN ART

King, R. Mad enchantment **759.4**

WATER PLANTS *See* Freshwater plants; Marine plants

WATER POLLUTION

Mary, B. An American River

WATER POLLUTION

See also Environmental health; Pollution; Public health

WATER POWER

See also Energy resources; Hydraulics; Power (Mechanics); Renewable energy resources; Rivers; Water resources development

WATER PURIFICATION

See also Sanitation; Water supply

WATER QUALITY -- NEW JERSEY -- TOMS RIVER WATERSHED

Fagin, D. Toms River **363.72**

WATER RESOURCES DEVELOPMENT

Fishman, C. The big thirst **333.91**

Harden, B. A river lost **333.91**

WATER RESOURCES DEVELOPMENT

See also Energy development; Natural resources

WATER RIGHTS

Ward, D. R. Water wars **333.91**

WATER RIGHTS

See also Law

WATER SAFETY

Skolnick, A. One breath **797.2**

WATER SPORTS

See also Sports

WATER SPORTS -- SAFETY MEASURES *See* Water safety

WATER SUPPLY

DeBuys, W. E. A great aridness **551.6**

Fagan, B. Elixir **553.7**

Fishman, C. The big thirst **333.91**

Rothfeder, J. Every drop for sale **333.91**

Ward, D. R. Water wars **333.91**

WATER SUPPLY

See also Natural resources; Public utilities

WATER SUPPLY ENGINEERING

Matson, T. Earth ponds **627**

WATER SUPPLY ENGINEERING

See also Civil engineering; Engineering

WATER VALLEY, MISS. -- SOCIAL LIFE AND CUSTOMS

Grimes, D. The B.T.C. old-fashioned grocery cookbook **641.59**

Water wars. Ward, D. R. **333.91**

The **water-saving** garden. Penick, P. **635.9**

WATER-SUPPLY -- GOVERNMENT POLICY

Solomon, S. Water **553.7**

WATER-SUPPLY, RURAL -- MALAWI

Kamkwamba, W. The boy who harnessed the wind **92**

Watercolor essentials. O'Connor, B. **751.42**

WATERCOLOR PAINTING

Artist's painting techniques **751.4**

WATERCOLOR PAINTING

See also Painting

WATERCOLOR PAINTING -- TECHNIQUE

Robinson, M. A. Lessons in realistic watercolor   **751.422**

WATERFALLS

Spira, T. P. Waterfalls and wildflowers in the Southern Appalachians   **796.51**

Waterfalls and wildflowers in the Southern Appalachians. Spira, T. P.   **796.51**

Waterfield, Robin

Why Socrates died   **183**

Watergate. Emery, F.   **973.924**

Watergate. Olson, K. W.   **973.924**

WATERGATE AFFAIR, 1972-1974

Abuse of power   **973.924**

Bernstein, C. All the president's men   **973.924**

Dean, J. W. The Nixon Defense   **973.924**

Emery, F. Watergate   **973.924**

Hughes, K. Chasing shadows   **973.924**

Killen, A. 1973 nervous breakdown   **973.924**

Olson, K. W. Watergate   **973.924**

Reston, J. The conviction of Richard Nixon   **973.924**

Woodward, B. The final days   **973.924**

Woodward, B. Shadow   **973.92**

WATERGATE AFFAIR, 1972-1974

See also United States -- History -- 1961-1974

Waterloo. Cornwell, B.   **940.2**

Waterloo. Corrigan, G.   **940.2**

Waterloo. O'Keeffe, P.   **940.2**

WATERLOO, BATTLE OF, 1815

Barbero, A. The Battle   **940.2**

Cornwell, B. Waterloo   **940.2**

Corrigan, G. Waterloo   **940.2**

Crane, D. Went the day well?   **940.2**

O'Keeffe, P. Waterloo   **940.2**

Roberts, A. Waterloo: June 18, 1815   **940.2**

Schom, A. One hundred days   **944.05**

Simms, B. The longest afternoon   **940.2**

WATERLOO, BATTLE OF, WATERLOO, BELGIUM, 1815 -- PERSONAL NARRATIVES, BRITISH

Crane, D. Went the day well?   **940.2**

Waterloo: June 18, 1815. Roberts, A.   **940.2**

Waterman, Stephanie J.

(ed) Beyond the asterisk   **378.1**

Waters, Alice, 1944-

In the green kitchen   **641.5**

My pantry   **641.594**

Streiff, F. The art of simple food   **641.5**

Waters, Ethel, 1896-1977

About

Bogle, D. Heat wave   **92**

Waters, John, 1946-

About

Waters, J. Carsick   **92**

Waters, J. Role models   **92**

WATERWAYS

See also Transportation

WATERWISE GARDENING *See* Xeriscaping

WATERWORKS *See* Water supply

Wathey, John C.

The illusion of God's presence   **204**

Watkin, David, 1941-

A history of Western architecture   **720**

Watkins, Alexandra

Hello, my name is awesome   **658.8**

Watkins, Carleton Emmons

Carleton Watkins: the complete mammoth photographs   **778.9**

Watkins, D.

The Cook Up   **364.1**

Watkins, Mary, 1939-

About

Walker-Hill, H. From spirituals to symphonies   **780**

Watkins, S. Craig

Hip hop matters   **781.64**

Watman, Max

Chasing the white dog   **363.4**

WATSON (COMPUTER)

Baker, S. Final Jeopardy   **006.3**

Watson, Bruce

Freedom summer   **323.1**

Sacco and Vanzetti   **345**

Watson, Burton

(ed) The Columbia book of Chinese poetry   **895.1**

Watson, James D., 1928-

About

The annotated and illustrated double helix   **572.8**

Watson, J. D. Avoid boring people   **92**

Watson, J. D. Genes, girls, and Gamow   **92**

Watson, Lyall

Dark nature   **111**

Watson, Peter, 1943-

The German genius   **943**

The great divide   **909**

Ideas   **909**

Watson, Richard A.

Cogito ergo sum: the life of Rene Descartes   **92**

Watson, Sarah

Pen to thread   **746.44**

Watson, Victor

(ed) The Cambridge guide to children's books in English   **028.5**

Watstein, Sarah Barbara

(jt. auth) Stratton, S. E. The encyclopedia of HIV and AIDS   **362.196**

Watterson, Bill

The complete Calvin and Hobbes   **741.5**

Watts, Alan

The way of Zen   **294.3**

Watts, Duncan J.

Everything is obvious   **153.4**

Watts, Jill
  Hattie McDaniel   92
Watts, Jonathan
  When a billion Chinese jump   363.7
Watts, Steven
  Mr. Playboy   92
  The people's tycoon   92
  Self-help Messiah   92
Waugh family
            About
  Waugh, A. Fathers and sons   920
Waugh, Alexander
  Fathers and sons   920
  The House of Wittgenstein   920
Wave. Deraniyagala, S.   954.93
The **wave.** Casey, S.   551.46
WAVE MECHANICS
          See also Mechanics; Quantum theory; Waves
Wave of destruction. Krauss, E.   959.3
Wawro, Geoffrey
  A mad catastrophe   940.4
Wax, Ruby
  Sane new world   158.1
Waxman, Jamye
  How to break up with anyone   158.2
Waxman, Scott
  (jt. auth) Pennington, B. Billy Martin   92
Waxman, Sharon
  Rebels on the backlot   920
The **way** it is. Stafford, W. E.   811
Way more West. Dorn, E.   811
A **way** of being. Rogers, C. R.   150.19
The **way** of the knife. Mazzetti, M.   356
The **way** of the panda. Nicholls, H.   599.7
The **Way** of the Runner. Finn, A.   796.42
The **way** of Zen. Watts, A.   294.3
Way out there in the blue. FitzGerald, F.   973.927
The **way** the world works. Baker, N.   814
The **Way** Things Work Now. Macaulay, D.   600
The **way** to cook. Child, J.   641.5
The **Way** to the Spring. Ehrenreich, B.   956.95
The **way** to write for children. Aiken, J.   808.06
Way, Lawrence W.
  (ed) Current surgical diagnosis & treatment   617
Wayne, John, 1907-1979
            About
  Eliot, M. American titan   92
  Eyman, S. John Wayne: the life and legend   92
Wayne, Tiffany K.
  Critical companion to Ralph Waldo Emerson   818
Ways of curating. Obrist   707.5
Ways of forgetting, ways of remembering. Dower, J. W.   940.53
We are Americans. Perez, W.   371.82
We are Anonymous. Olson, P.   005.8
We are better than this. Kleinbard, E. D.   336.3

We are soldiers still. Moore, H. G.   959.704
We are still here. Iverson, P.   970.004
We care guides [series]
  Green volunteers   333.72
We could not fail. Paul, R.   920
We have met the enemy. Akst, D.   153.8
We Have Only This Life to Live.   848
We meant well. Van Buren, P.   920
We shall overcome. Boyd, H.   323.1
We Should All Be Feminists. Adichie, C. N.   305.42
We tell ourselves stories in order to live. Didion, J.   814
We were soldiers once--and young. Moore, H. G.   959.704
We wish to inform you that tomorrow we will be killed with our families. Gourevitch, P.   967.571
Weale, Adrian
  Army of evil   940.54
WEALTH
  Atwood, M. Payback   332.7
  Dedman, B. Empty mansions   92
  The great divergence   339.2
  Guest, R. Borderless economics   303.48
  Madrick, J. G. Age of greed   330.9
  Milanović, B. The haves and the have-nots   339.2
  Orman, S. The money class   332.024
  Ridley, M. The rational optimist   339.2
  Stiglitz, J. E. The price of inequality   305.5
WEALTH
          See also Economics; Finance
WEALTH -- HISTORY
  Milanović, B. The haves and the have-nots   339.2
WEALTH -- MORAL AND ETHICAL ASPECTS
  Madrick, J. G. Age of greed   330.9
WEALTH -- RELIGIOUS ASPECTS -- CHRISTIANITY
  Brown, P. Through the eye of a needle   270.2
  Lehmann, C. The money cult   261.8
WEALTH -- RELIGIOUS ASPECTS -- CHRISTIANITY -- HISTORY
  Brown, P. Through the eye of a needle   270.2
Wealth and power. Schell, O.   951
The **wealth** of nations. Smith, A.   330.1
WEALTHY PEOPLE *See* Rich
Weaner, Larry
  (jt. auth) Christopher, T. Garden revolution   577
WEAPONRY *See* Weapons
WEAPONS
  Emlen, D. J. Animal weapons   591.47
  Levy, J. Fifty Weapons That Changed the Course of History   355.8
Weapons & warfare.   623.4
WEAPONS -- HISTORY
  Stephenson, M. The last full measure   305.9
  World War I   940.3
WEAPONS INDUSTRY *See* Defense industry;

Firearms industry

Weapons of fitness. Zeisler, A.   **613.6**

Weapons of mass destruction.   **358**

**WEAPONS OF MASS DESTRUCTION -- GER-
MANY -- HISTORY -- 20TH CENTURY**

Preston, D. A higher form of killing   **940.4**

Weapons of math destruction. O'Neil, C.   **005.7**

WEAPONS, ATOMIC *See* Nuclear weapons

WEAPONS, NUCLEAR *See* Nuclear weapons

Wear and tear. Tynan, T.   **92**

Wearing God. Winner, L. F.   **231.7**

Weart, Spencer R.

The discovery of global warming   **551.6**

Weather. Lucas, D.   **811**

WEATHER

Allaby, M. The gardener's guide to weather and
climate   **635**

Barnett, C. Rain   **551.57**

Buckley, B. Weather: a visual guide   **551.5**

Linden, E. The winds of change   **551.6**

Redniss, L. Thunder & Lightning   **551.6**

Sobel, A. Storm surge   **551.55**

Williams, J. The AMS weather book   **551.5**

WEATHER -- ENCYCLOPEDIAS

Fry, J. L. The encyclopedia of weather and climate
change   **551.6**

WEATHER -- FOLKLORE

See also Folklore; Meteorology; Weather
forecasting

Weather bird. Giddins, G.   **781.65**

**WEATHER BROADCASTING -- UNITED
STATES**

Miles, K. Superstorm   **551.55**

WEATHER CONTROL

Fleming, J. R. Fixing the sky   **551.6**

WEATHER CONTROL

See also Meteorology; Weather

WEATHER FORECASTING

Cullen, H. The weather of the future   **551.63**

Ludlum, D. M. The Audubon Society field guide to
North American weather   **551.6**

Monmonier, M. S. Air apparent   **551.63**

WEATHER FORECASTING

See also Forecasting; Meteorology; Weather

The **weather** makers. Flannery, T. F.   **363.7**

WEATHER MODIFICATION *See* Weather control

The **weather** of the future. Cullen, H.   **551.63**

Weather's greatest mysteries solved! Cerveny, R.
S.   **304.2**

Weather: a visual guide. Buckley, B.   **551.5**

Weatherall, James Owen

The physics of Wall Street   **332.63**

Weatherford, J. McIver

Genghis Khan and the making of the modern
world   **92**

Native roots   **970.004**

Weatherford, Jack

Genghis Khan and the Quest for God   **950**

WEATHERMEN (ORGANIZATION)

Rudd, M. Underground   **92**

The **weaver's** idea book. Patrick, J.   **746.1**

Weaver-Zercher, David L.

(jt. auth) Kraybill, D. B. Amish grace   **364.152**

WEAVERS

Weber, N. F. The Bauhaus group   **920**

WEAVING

Corwin, L. Lena Corwin's made by hand   **746.6**

Dixon, A. The handweaver's pattern directory   **746.1**

Mitchell, S. Inventive weavng on a little loom **746.1**

Murphy, M. Woven to wear   **746.1**

Patrick, J. The weaver's idea book   **746.1**

WEAVING

See also Handicraft; Textile industry

WEAVING -- AFGHANISTAN

Badkhen, A. The world is a carpet   **958.1**

Web 2.0 for librarians and information professionals.
Kroski, E.   **020**

WEB SEARCH ENGINES

Auletta, K. Googled   **338.7**

Stross, R. Planet Google   **338.7**

WEB SEARCH ENGINES

See also Internet searching; World Wide Web

WEB SEARCHING *See* Internet searching; Web
search engines

WEB SERVERS

See also World Wide Web

WEB SERVICES

Arora, P. To the cloud   **004.67**

WEB SITE DEVELOPMENT

Krug, S. Don't make me think, revisited   **006.7**

WEB SITES

See also Internet resources; World Wide Web

WEB SITES -- DESIGN

Krug, S. Don't make me think, revisited   **006.7**

WEB SITES -- DESIGN

See also Design

WEB-BASED INSTRUCTION

See also Computer-assisted instruction

Webb, Caroline

How to have a good day   **650.1**

Webb, Jeremy

(ed) Nothing   **501**

Webb, Tim

(jt. auth) Beaumont, S. The world atlas of
beer   **641.2**

Weber, Eugen

Apocalypses   **200**

Weber, Kathleen

Della Fattoria bread   **641.81**

Weber, Nancy S.

Smith, A. H. The mushroom hunter's field guide **579.6**

Weber, Nicholas Fox, 1947-
The Bauhaus group **920**

Weber, Robert J.
The created self **155.2**

Weber, Thomas
Hitler's first war **940.4**

WEBLOGS
See also Diaries; Online journalism

Webster's New World Robert's rules of order. **060.4**

Webster, Camilla
(jt. auth) Pepper, C. The seven pearls of financial wisdom **332.024**

Webster, Charles
Paracelsus **92**

Webster, Daniel, 1782-1852
About
Kennedy, J. F. Profiles in courage **920**
Remini, R. V. Daniel Webster **328**

Webster, Jim
America--farm to table **641.597**

Webster, Noah, 1758-1843
About
Lepore, J. A is for American **306.44**

The **wedding** book. Weiss, M. **395**

WEDDING DECORATIONS
Style your perfect wedding **392.5**

WEDDING ETIQUETTE
Emily Post's wedding etiquette **395.2**

A **wedding** in Haiti. Alvarez, J. **818**

Wedding of the waters. Bernstein, P. L. **386**

WEDDINGS
Alvarez, J. A wedding in Haiti **818**
Emily Post's wedding etiquette **395.2**
Into the garden **808.8**
Mead, R. One perfect day **392**
Outcalt, T. Your beautiful wedding on any budget **395**
Style your perfect wedding **392.5**
Vivaldo, D. Do it for le$$! weddings **395**
Weiss, M. The wedding book **395**

WEDDINGS
See also Marriage

WEDDINGS -- PLANNING
Style your perfect wedding **392.5**

Wedge, Marilyn
A Disease Called Childhood **618.92**

Wednesday comics. **741.5**

The **weeding** handbook. Vnuk, R. **025.2**

Weeds. Mabey, R. **632**

WEEDS
Mabey, R. Weeds **632**

Weeds of North America. Dickinson, R. **632**

A **week** on the Concord and Merrimack rivers; Walden, or, Life in the woods; The Maine woods;

Cape Cod. Thoreau, H. D. **818**

The **weekend** that changed Wall Street. Bartiromo, M. **330.9**

Weidensaul, Scott
Living on the wind **598**
Of a feather **598**
Return to wild America **578**

Weierstrass, Karl, 1815-1897
About
Bell, E. T. Men of mathematics **920**

Weighing the world. Danson, E. **526**

WEIGHT LIFTING
Hesson, J. L. Weight training for life **613.7**
Pagano, J. Strength training exercises for women **613.7**
Pagano, J. Strength training for women **613.7**
Schuler, L. Strong **613.7**

WEIGHT LIFTING
See also Athletics; Exercise

WEIGHT LOSS
Ali, K. Fighting weight **92**
Baroni, B. Fat kid got fit **362.196**
Bittman, M. Food matters **613.2**
Brown, H. Body of truth **613.2**
Flippin, R. The diabetes reset **616.4**
Ludwig, D. Always hungry? **613.2**
Mann, T. Secrets from the eating lab **613.2**
Nesheim, M. Why calories count **613.2**
Roizen, M. F. This is your do-over **613**
Spiker, T. Down size **92**
Taubes, G. Why we get fat and what to do about it **613.7**
Weight Watchers 50th anniversary cookbook **641.5**

WEIGHT LOSS
See also Body weight

WEIGHT LOSS -- POPULAR WORKS
The whole30 **613.2**

WEIGHT LOSS -- PSYCHOLOGICAL ASPECTS
Brown, H. Body of truth **613.2**
Cruikshank, T. Meditate your weight **613.25**
Mann, T. Secrets from the eating lab **613.2**

WEIGHT TRAINING *See* Weight lifting

Weight training for life. Hesson, J. L. **613.7**

WEIGHT TRAINING FOR WOMEN
Pagano, J. Strength training exercises for women **613.7**
Schuler, L. Strong **613.7**

Weight Watchers 50th anniversary cookbook. **641.5**

Weight Watchers International Inc.
(comp) Weight Watchers 50th anniversary cookbook **641.5**

WEIGHTLESSNESS
See also Environmental influence on humans; Space medicine

WEIGHTLIFTING *See* Weight lifting

WEIGHTS AND MEASURES
Nicastro, N. Circumference   **526**
WEIGHTS AND MEASURES
See also Physics
Weigl, Rudolf, 1883-1957
             About
Allen, A. The fantastic laboratory of Dr. Weigl   **614.5**
Weil, Andrew
Eight weeks to optimum health   **613**
Fast Food, Good Food   **641.563**
Healthy aging   **612.6**
The healthy kitchen   **641.5**
             About
Lattin, D. The Harvard Psychedelic Club   **920**
Weil, Anne
Knitting without needles   **746.432**
Weil, Simone, 1909-1943
             About
Milosz, C. To begin where I am   **891.8**
Weiland, Matt
(ed) State by state   **973**
Weill, Kurt, 1900-1950
             About
Mordden, E. Love song   **920**
Schebera, J. Kurt Weill   **92**
Weinberg, Gerhard L.
A world at arms   **940.53**
Weinberg, Samantha
A fish caught in time   **597.3**
Weinberg, Steven, 1933-
To explain the world   **509**
Weinberger, David
Too big to know   **303.48**
Weinberger, Eliot
(ed) Borges, J. L. Selected non-fictions   **864**
(ed) The New Directions anthology of classical chinese poetry   **895.1**
(tr) Paz, O. The collected poems of Octavio Paz, 1957-1987   **861**
Weinberger, Sharon
Hodge, N. A nuclear family vacation   **623.4**
Weiner, Eva S.
(ed) The Oxford English dictionary   **423**
Weiner, Jennifer
             About
Weiner, J. Hungry heart   **92**
Weiner, Jonathan
Time, love, memory   **591.5**
Weiner, Mark Stuart
Black trials   **342**
Weiner, Stephen
101 outstanding graphic novels   **741.5**
Weiner, Tim
Enemies   **363.25**
Legacy of ashes   **327.12**

One man against the world   **973.924**
Weiner, William J.
Lang, A. E. Parkinson's disease   **616.8**
Weinfield, Henry
(comp) Bronk, W. Selected poems   **811**
Weinstein, Allen
The haunted wood   **327.12**
Weinstein, Arnold
A scream goes through the house   **801**
Weinstein, Bruce
Cooking know-how   **641.5**
The Great Big Pressure Cooker Book   **641.5**
A la mode   **641.865**
Vegetarian dinner parties   **641.5**
Weintraub, David A.
How old is the universe?   **523.1**
Is Pluto a planet?   **523.4**
Weintraub, Pamela
Cure unknown   **616.9**
Weintraub, Robert
No better friend   **304.2**
Weintraub, Stanley, 1929-
15 stars   **920**
Charlotte and Lionel   **92**
A Christmas far from home   **951.904**
Iron tears   **973.3**
Weir, Alison
The lost Tudor princess   **92**
Weir, Alison
Eleanor of Aquitaine   **92**
Henry VIII   **942.05**
The lady in the tower   **92**
The life of Elizabeth I   **942.05**
Mary, Queen of Scots, and the murder of Lord Darnley   **92**
The six wives of Henry VIII   **942.05**
The Wars of the Roses   **942.04**
Weir, Joanne
Sunset kitchen gypsy   **641.5**
Weir, Robert E.
(ed) Historical encyclopedia of American labor   **331.8**
Weir, Ryan O.
(ed) Managing Electronic Resources   **025.1**
Weird Life. Toomey, D.   **571**
Weisbrode, Kenneth
The Year of Indecision, 1946   **973.918**
Weise, Jillian
The book of goodbyes   **813**
Weisman, Alan
Countdown   **304.2**
The world without us   **304.2**
Weiss, Eben
The ultimate bicycle owner's manual   **796.6**
Weiss, Elaine
Family & friends' guide to domestic violence   **362.82**

Surviving domestic violence **362.82**

Weiss, Helga, 1929-
           About
  Helga's diary **940.53**

Weiss, Jeffrey
  Charcuteria **641.594**

Weiss, Lisa
  Hirigoyen, G. Pintxos **641.8**

Weiss, Michael
  Isis **956.05**

Weiss, Michael A.
  (jt. auth) Kolpan, S. Exploring wine **641.2**
  (jt. auth) Kolpan, S. Winewise **641.2**

Weiss, Mindy
  The wedding book **395**

Weiss, Mitch
  The Yankee comandante **92**
  Sallah, M. Tiger Force **959.704**

Weiss, Peter, 1916-1982
           About
  Sebald, W. G. On the natural history of destruction **833**

Weisskopf, Michael
           About
  Weisskopf, M. Blood brothers **92**

Weissova, Helga, 1929-
  Helga's diary **940.53**

Welch, Craig
  Shell games **364.1**

Welch, James
  Killing Custer **973.8**

Welch, Robert
  (ed) The Oxford companion to Irish literature **820**

Welcome to subirdia. **598**

Welcome to the Goddamn Ice Cube. Braverman, B. **974.81**

Welcome to the Orthodox Church. Mathewes-Green, F. **281.9**

Welcome to the universe. Gott, J. R. **523.1**

Welcome to Utopia. Valby, K. **976.4**

WELDING
  See also Blacksmithing; Forging; Ironwork; Manufacturing processes; Metalwork

Weldon, Fay
           About
  Weldon, F. Auto da Fay **823**

Weldon, Michele
  Escape Points **362.196**

Welky, David
  The thousand-year flood **363.34**

Well fed. **641.5**

Well, François
  Family trees **929.2**

Well-behaved women seldom make history. Ulrich, L. **305.4**

WELL-BEING

Langshur, E. Start here **158**

Lawson, N. Simply Nigella **641.5**

WELL-BEING -- ECONOMIC ASPECTS
  Davies, W. The happiness industry **304**

The **well-built** triathlete. Dixon, M. **796.42**

Well-designed. Kolko, J. **658.5**

A **well-ordered** thing: Dmitrii Mendeleev and the shadow of the periodic table. Gordin, M. D. **92**

The **well-tended** perennial garden. DiSabato-Aust, T. **635.9**

Welland, Michael
  Sand **553.6**

Weller's war. Weller, G. **940.53**

Weller, Anthony
  (ed) Weller, G. Weller's war **940.53**

Weller, George
  Weller's war **940.53**

Weller, Sam
  The Bradbury chronicles **92**

Weller, Sheila
  Girls like us **920**
  The News Sorority **070.1**

Welles, Gideon, 1802-1878
           About
  Symonds, C. L. Lincoln and his admirals **92**

Welles, Orson, 1915-1985
           About
  Callow, S. Orson Welles **92**
  My Lunches With Orson **791.43**
  Schwartz, A. B. Broadcast hysteria **791.44**

Welles, Sumner, 1892-1961
           About
  Fullilove, M. Rendezvous with destiny **973.917**

Wellings, Nigel
  Why can't I meditate? **158.12**

Wellington. Hibbert, C. **92**

Wellington, Arthur Wellesley, Duke of, 1769-1852
           About
  Hibbert, C. Wellington **92**

Wellman, Barry
  Networked **006.7**

WELLS
  See also Hydraulic engineering

Wells, C. M.
  Sailing from Byzantium **940.2**

Wells, Diana
  100 flowers and how they got their names **582.13**

Wells, Dicky, 1910-1985
           About
  Dance, S. The world of Count Basie **920**

Wells, H. G. (Herbert George), 1866-1946
           About
  McKillop, A. B. The spinster & the prophet **941.08**

Wells, Patricia
  The Food Lover's Guide to Paris **914.4**
  The French kitchen cookbook **641.594**

Patricia Wells at home in Provence   **641.59**
Patricia Wells' trattoria   **641.5**
The Provence cookbook   **641.5**
Salad as a meal   **641.8**
Vegetable harvest   **641.6**
Wells, Stanley W.
   The Oxford companion to Shakespeare   **822.3**
   (ed) Shakespeare, W. The complete works   **822.3**
   Shakespeare: for all time   **822.3**
Wells-Barnett, Ida B., 1862-1931
           About
   Cornel West on Black prophetic fire   **92**
   Giddings, P. Ida: a sword among lions   **92**
Weltman, Barbara
   J.K. Lasser's guide for tough times   **332.024**
Welty, Eudora, 1909-2001
   One time, one place   **976.2**
           About
   Marrs, S. Eudora Welty: a biography   **92**
   Meanwhile there are letters   **92**
   Pierpont, C. R. Passionate minds   **810**
   Waldron, A. Eudora   **92**
   Welty, E. One writer's beginnings   **92**
   What there is to say we have said   **92**
Welzer, Harald
   Soldaten   **940.54**
Wendy and the lost boys. Salamon, J.
Wengenmayr, Roland
   (ed) Renewable energy   **333**
Wenger, Debora Halpern
   Advancing the story   **070.1**
Wenger, J. Michael
   Goldstein, D. M. The Vietnam War: the story and
     photographs   **959.704**
Wenner, Jann S.
   (ed) Thompson, H.S. Fear and loathing at Rolling Stone
     Gonzo   **92**
Went the day well? Crane, D.   **940.2**
Weppelmann, Stefan
   (ed) The Renaissance portrait   **704.9**
WEREWOLVES
   See also Folklore
WEREWOLVES -- ENCYCLOPEDIAS
   Guiley, R. E. The encyclopedia of vampires &
     werewolves   **398**
Werker, Kim P.
   Keim, C. Teach yourself visually crochet   **746.43**
Werlock, Abby H. P.
   (ed) The Facts on File companion to the American
     novel   **813**
Werner, Eric
   Hartwood   **641.597**
Wert, Jeffry D.
   Cavalryman of the lost cause   **92**
   Custer   **92**
   Mosby's Rangers   **973.7**

Wertheim, L. Jon
   Blood in the cage   **92**
   This is your brain on sports   **796**
Wertheim, Margaret
   Physics on the fringe   **530.1**
Wertkin, Gerard C.
   (ed) Encyclopedia of American folk art   **745**
Weschler, Toni
   Taking charge of your fertility   **613.9**
Wesley, John, 1703-1791
           About
   Tomkins, S. John Wesley   **287**
Wesleyan poetry [series]
   Armantrout, R. Versed   **811**
   Brathwaite, E. K. Elegguas   **811**
   Guest, B. The collected poems of Barbara
     Guest   **811**
   Hillman, B. Cascadia   **811**
   Ignatow, D. I have a name   **811**
   Ignatow, D. Shadowing the ground   **811**
   Komunyakaa, Y. Thieves of paradise   **811**
   Shockley, E. The new black   **811**
   Tarn, N. Selected poems   **811**
   Valentine, J. Door in the mountain   **811**
Wesleyan poetry series
   Gizzi, P. In defense of nothing   **811**
   Hillman, B. Seasonal works with letters on fire **811**
WESLEYAN UNIVERSITY (MIDDLETOWN, CONN.)
   Steinberg, J. The gatekeepers   **378.1**
Wessel, David
   In Fed we trust   **332.1**
The **West**. Ward, G. C.   **978**
WEST (U.S.)
   Carter, R. A. Buffalo Bill Cody   **978**
   Gessner, D. All the Wild That Remains   **363.7**
   Martínez, R. Desert America   **330.9**
WEST (U.S.)
     See also United States
WEST (U.S.) -- BIOGRAPHY
   Hatch, T. The Last Outlaws   **364.15**
   Krakauer, J. Into the wild   **917**
   Morgan, R. Lions of the West   **920**
   Stiles, T. J. Jesse James   **364.15**
WEST (U.S.) -- COMMERCE -- HISTORY -- 19TH CENTURY
   Hyde, A. F. Empires, nations, and families   **978**
WEST (U.S.) -- DESCRIPTION
   Frazier, I. Great Plains   **917**
   Raban, J. Bad land   **978**
WEST (U.S.) -- DESCRIPTION AND TRAVEL
   Schmidt, T. The Lewis & Clark Trail   **978**
   Wallis, M. Route 66: the mother road   **917**
WEST (U.S.) -- EXPLORATION
   Black, G. Empire of shadows   **978.7**
WEST (U.S.) -- HISTORICAL GEOGRAPHY

Beck, W. A.   Historical atlas of the American West **911**

Hayes, D. Historical atlas of the American West **911**

WEST (U.S.) -- HISTORY

Ambrose, S. E. Nothing like it in the world   **385**

Bain, D. H. Empire express   **385**

Beck, W. A.   Historical atlas of the American West   **911**

Brown, D. A. The American West   **978**

Brown, D. A.   Bury my heart at Wounded Knee   **970.004**

Calloway, C. G. One vast winter count   **978**

Groom, W. Kearny's march   **979**

Gwynne, S. C. Empire of the summer moon   **92**

Morgan, R. Lions of the West   **920**

Raban, J. Bad land   **978**

Schwantes, C. A. The West the railroads made **338**

Sides, H. Blood and thunder   **978**

Ward, G. C. The West   **978**

WEST (U.S.) -- HISTORY

See also United States -- History

WEST (U.S.) -- IN ART

Dippie, B. W. The Frederic Remington Art Museum collection   **709**

Eisler, B. The Red Man's Bones   **92**

WEST (U.S.) -- IN ART -- CATALOGS

Hassrick, P. H. Art of the American West   **709**

WEST (U.S.) -- SOCIAL LIFE AND CUSTOMS

Frazier, I. Great Plains   **917**

WEST AFRICA

See also Africa

WEST BANK

Ehrenreich, B. The Way to the Spring   **956.95**

WEST BANK

See also Palestine

WEST BANK OF THE JORDAN RIVER See West Bank

WEST FLORIDA -- HISTORY, MILITARY -- 18TH CENTURY

DuVal, K. Independence Lost   **973.3**

WEST INDIAN LITERATURE (FRENCH)

See also Literature

WEST INDIES REGION See Caribbean Region

WEST INDIES, BRITISH -- COMMERCE -- GEORGIA -- HISTORY -- 18TH CENTURY

Pressly, P. M. On the rim of the Caribbean   **975.8**

WEST NICKEL MINES AMISH SCHOOL (PA.)

Kraybill, D. B. Amish grace   **364.152**

West of Eden. Stein, J.   **979.4**

West of Kabul, East of New York. Ansary, M. T.   **958.1**

The West Point History of the Civil War.   **973.7**

West Point History of World War II.   **940.53**

The West the railroads made. Schwantes, C. A. **338**

WEST VIRGINIA

Hickam, H. H. Rocket boys   **629.1**

West with the night. Markham, B.   **92**

West, Alan

(ed) Latino and Latina writers   **810**

West, Bing

The wrong war   **958.1**

West, Cornel, 1953-

Gates, H. L. The African-American century   **305**

Gates, H. L. The future of the race   **305.896**

About

Cornel West on Black prophetic fire   **92**

(ed) The radical King   **323**

West, Da-Hae

K-food   **641.595**

West, Diana

(jt. auth) Pitman, T. Sweet sleep   **649**

The womanly art of breastfeeding   **649**

West, Elliott

The last Indian war   **973.8**

West, Gareth

(jt. auth) West K-food   **641.595**

West, James L. W., 1946-

(ed) Styron, W. My generation   **814**

West, Jerry, 1938-

About

Lazenby, R. Jerry West   **92**

West, Kevin

Saving the season   **641.4**

West, Mae, 1892-1980

About

Pierpont, C. R. Passionate minds   **810**

West, Nathanael, 1903-1940

About

Meade, M. Lonelyhearts   **92**

West, Richard

Chaucer, 1340-1400   **821**

Tito   **949.7**

Westad, Odd Arne

Restless empire   **327**

Westerly. Schutt, W.   **811**

The Western canon. Bloom, H.   **809**

WESTERN CIVILIZATION

Aries, P. A History of private life   **909**

Barzun, J. From dawn to decadence   **940.2**

Cahill, T. How the Irish saved civilization **941.501**

Eire, C. M. N. A very brief history of eternity   **236**

Freeman, C. The closing of the Western mind **940.1**

Herman, A. The idea of decline in Western history   **909.08**

James, C. Cultural amnesia   **920**

Morris, I. Why the West rules--for now   **909**

WESTERN STATES -- HISTORY, MILITARY

Donovan, J. A terrible glory   **973.8**

WESTERN STORIES

See also Adventure fiction; Fiction; Historical fiction

WESTERN WORLD -- AFRICA

Halperin, D. Tinderbox **614.5**

WESTERN WRITERS

Anderson, W. T. Laura Ingalls Wilder country **92**

Lee, H. Willa Cather **92**

Pauly, T. H. Zane Grey **92**

Woodress, J. L. Willa Cather **92**

WESTERNS (TELEVISION PROGRAMS)

See also Television programs

Westfall, Richard S.

The life of Isaac Newton **92**

Westheimer, Ruth K.

The Doctor Is in

Westhoff, Ben

Dirty South **781.64**

WESTMINSTER ABBEY

See also Abbeys; Church buildings

Westmoreland, Susan

(ed) Good housekeeping (Periodical) The Good Housekeeping cookbook **641.5**

(ed) The Good Housekeeping step-by-step cookbook **641.4**

Westmoreland, William C.

About

Halberstam, D. The best and the brightest **973.922**

Westoll, Andrew

The chimps of Fauna Sanctuary **636.9**

WESTWARD MOVEMENT *See* Land settlement -- United States; United States -- Territorial expansion; West (U.S.) -- History

WETLAND ECOLOGY

See also Ecology

Wetzel, Dan

Haskins, D. Glory road **796**

Wex, Michael

Rhapsody in schmaltz **641.5**

Wexler, Alan

Waldman, C. Encyclopedia of exploration **910.3**

Wexler, Jay

Holy hullabaloos **342**

The **whale**. Hoare, P. **599.5**

The **whale** and the supercomputer. Wohlforth, C. **305.897**

The **Whalen** poem. Corbett, W. **811**

WHALES

Bortolotti, D. Wild blue **599.5**

Hargrove, J. Beneath the surface **599.53**

Hoare, P. The whale **599.5**

Horwitz, J. War of the Whales **333.95**

Kelsey, E. Watching giants **599.5**

Rothenberg, D. Thousand mile song **599.5**

WHALES

See also Mammals; Marine mammals

WHALES -- PSYCHOLOGY

Safina, C. Beyond words **591.56**

WHALING

Hoare, P. The whale **599.5**

WHALING

See also Commercial fishing; Hunting; Voyages and travels

WHALING -- FICTION

Philbrick, N. Why read Moby-Dick? **813**

WHALING -- HISTORY

Dolin, E. J. Leviathan **639.2**

Wharton, Edith, 1862-1937

Selected poems **811**

About

Adams, M. B. Shaggy muses **920**

Fraser, K. Ornament and silence **809**

Lee, H. Edith Wharton **92**

What a Fish Knows. Balcombe, J. **597.15**

What about this. Stanford, F. **811.54**

What Are You Looking at? Gompertz, W. **709**

What color is your parachute? 2017. **650.1**

What comes naturally. Pascoe, P. **346**

What Comes Next and How to Like It. Thomas, A. **92**

What Do I Read Next? **020**

What Do Women Want? Bergner, D. **305**

What doctors feel. Ofri, D. **610.69**

What everyone needs to know [series]

Ferguson, C. D. Nuclear energy **333.79**

Prud'homme, A. Hydrofracking **622**

What Everyone Needs to Know [series]

Allen, J. L. The Catholic church **282**

What everyone needs to know about Islam. Esposito, J. L. **297**

What evolution is. Mayr, E. **576.8**

What good are bugs? Waldbauer, G. **595.7**

What hath God wrought. Howe, D. W. **973.5**

What I talk about when I talk about running. **92**

What I Told My Daughter. Tassler, N. **155.433**

What if it's not Alzheimer's? **616.8**

What if?. Munroe, R. **500**

What is happening to news. Fuller, J. **070.4**

What is life worth? Feinberg, K. R. **362.88**

What is life? Margulis, L. **570.1**

What is philosophy? Ortega y Gasset, J. **196**

What it is. Barry, L. **741.5**

What it means to be 98[percent] chimpanzee. Marks, J. **599.93**

What Katie Ate. Davies, K. Q. **641.5**

What Katie Ate on the Weekend. Davies, K. Q.

What kind of nation. Simon, J. F. **342**

What Lincoln believed. Lind, M. **92**

What love comes to. Stone, R. **811**

What Makes This Book So Great. Walton, J. **813**

What money can't buy. Sandel, M. J. **330.1**

What narcissism means to me. Hoagland, T. **811**

What Nietzsche really said. Solomon, R. C. **193**

What philosophy can do. Gutting, G. **100**

What reptile? Mattison, C. **639.3**

What Stands in a Storm. Cross, K. **363.34**

What the best college students do. Bain, K. **378.1**

What the Bible really tells us. Wray, T. J. **220.6**

What the dog knows. Warren, C. **636.7**

What the dormouse said-- Markoff, J. **004**

What the eye hears. Seibert, B. **792.7**

What the fork are you eating? Sacks, S. **641.3**

What the robin knows. **598.8**

What there is to say we have said. **92**

What they don't teach you at Harvard Business School. McCormack, M. H. **650.1**

What to do when you can't get pregnant. Potter, D. A. **618.1**

What to do when you're new. Rollag, K. **158.2**

What to Expect the First Year. Murkoff, H. **649**

What to expect the first year. Murkoff, H. E. **649**

What to expect the second year. Murkoff, H. E. **649**

What to expect when you're expecting. Murkoff, H. **618.2**

What to feed your baby. Altmann, T. R. **649.3**

What to look for in winter. McWilliam, C. **92**

What to read when. Allyn, P. **028.5**

What we knew. Johnson, E. A. **943.086**

What we leave behind. Jensen, D. **304.2**

What we see when we read. Mendelsund, P. **028**

What will it take to make a woman president? Schnall, M. **305.4**

What work is. Levine, P. **811**

What works. Bohnet, I. **331.4**

What works for women at work. Williams, J. **650.1**

What would the Founders do? Brookhiser, R. **320**

What you must know about dialysis. Snyder, R. d. J. **617.4**

What your contractor can't tell you. Johnston, A. **690**

What's a disorganized person to do? Platt, S. **648**

What's going on in there? Eliot, L. **612.8**

What's the economy for, anyway? De Graaf, J. **330.9**

What's the matter with Kansas? Frank, T. **978.1**

What's wrong with my fruit garden? Deardorff, D. **634**

What's wrong with my houseplant? Deardorff, D. **635.9**

What's wrong with my plant (and how do I fix it?) Deardorff, D. C. **635**

What's wrong with my vegetable garden? Deardorff, D. **635**

What's wrong with my vegetable garden? **635**

Whatever it takes. Tough, P. **362.7**

WHEAT
Yafa, S. Grain of truth **633.1**

Wheat, Carolyn
How to write killer fiction **808.3**

WHEAT-FREE DIET
Yafa, S. Grain of truth **633.1**

Wheatley, Phillis

The poems of Phillis Wheatley **811**

The **wheel** of healing with ayurveda. Fondin, M. S. **615.5**

The **wheel** of life. Kubler-Ross, E. **150**

Wheelan, Charles
Naked statistics **519.5**

Wheelan, Joseph
Terrible swift sword **355.009**

WHEELCHAIR BASKETBALL
See also Basketball; Wheelchair sports

Wheeler, Brian K.
Clark, W. S. A field guide to hawks of North America **598**

Wheeler, Michael
The art of negotiation **658.4**

Wheeler, Sara
The magnetic north **910.4**

Wheelock, Katherine
(jt. auth) Parachini, C. Roberta's **641.82**

Wheels for the world. Brinkley, D. **338.7**

Wheen, Francis
Karl Marx **335.4**

Strange days indeed **973.92**

When a billion Chinese jump. Watts, J. **363.7**

When abortion was a crime. Reagan, L. J. **363.46**

When affirmative action was white. Katznelson, I. **323.1**

When America first met China. Dolin, E. J. **382**

When bad things happen to good people. Kushner, H. S. **296.3**

When Baghdad ruled the Muslim world. Kennedy, H. **956.7**

When breath becomes air. Kalanithi, P. **616.99**

When Britain burned the White House. Snow, P. **975.3**

When broken glass floats. Him, C. **959.604**

When China rules the world. Jacques, M. **327**

When elephants weep. Masson, J. M. **591.5**

When everything changed. Collins, G. **305.4**

When gadgets betray us. Vamosi, R. **004**

When Hollywood had a king. Bruck, C. **338.7**

When I am playing with my cat, how do I know she is not playing with me? Frampton, S. **844**

When I first held you. **306.874**

When I was a child I read books. Robinson, M. **814**

When in French. Collins, L. **92**

When lions roar. Maier, T. **941.084**

When March went mad. Davis, S. **796.323**

When memory speaks. Conway, J. K. **808**

When nobody was watching. Coffey, W. **796.334**

When pride still mattered: a life of Vince Lombardi. Maraniss, D. **92**

When religion becomes lethal. Kimball, C. **201**

When science meets religion. Barbour, I. G. **261.5**

When the Mississippi ran backwards. Feldman, J. **551.2**

When the Sun Bursts. Bollas, C. **616.89**

When trumpets call. O'Toole, P. **92**

When we were on fire. Zierman, A. **92**

When your adult child breaks your heart. Adamec, C. **616.89**

When Your Parent Moves in. Block, S. **306.874**

Where are the customers' yachts? **332.64**

Where China meets India. Thant Myint-U **959.1**

Where did the jobs go-- and how do we get them back? Johnson, J. **331.1**

Where divers dare. Peffer, R. **940.54**

Where do we go from here. King, M. L. **323.1**

Where I was from. Didion, J. **979.4**

Where nobody knows your name. Feinstein, J. **796.357**

Where shall I wander. Ashbery, J. **811**

Where stuff comes from. Molotch, H. L. **620**

Where the dark and the light folks meet. Sandke, R. **781.65**

Where the Dead Pause, and the Japanese Say Goodbye. Mockett, M. M. **952**

Where the heart beats. Larson, K. **700.1**

Where the Jews aren't. Gessen, M. **957.7**

Where the lightning strikes. Nabokov, P. **299.7**

Where You Go Is Not Who You'll Be. Bruni, F. **378.161**

The **where,** the why, and the how. Lamothe, M. **502**

Whewell, William, 1794-1866
About
Snyder, L. J. The philosophical breakfast club **509**

Which Lie Did I Tell? Goldman, W. **791.43**

WHICH-WAY STORIES *See* Plot-your-own stories

Whicher, Jonathan, 1814-1881
About
Summerscale, K. The suspicions of Mr. Whicher **364.152**

While America aged. Lowenstein, R. **331.2**

While America sleeps. Feingold, R. **327**

Whinney, Joe
Theo Chocolate **641.6**

Whipping Boy. Kurzweil, A. **92**

Whirlwind. Ferling, J. **973.3**

WHISKEY
Broom, D. The World Atlas of Whisky **641.2**

Bryson, L. Tasting whiskey **663**

Mitenbuler, R. Bourbon empire **663**

Risen, C. American Whiskey, Bourbon & Rye **641.2**

The **Whiskey** Rebellion. Hogeland, W. **973.4**

WHISKEY REBELLION, PA., 1794
Hogeland, W. The Whiskey Rebellion **973.4**

Whiskey tango foxtrot. Axelrod, A. **427**

Whisky, kilts, and the Loch Ness Monster. Starr, W. W. **914**

The **whisperers.** Figes, O. **947.084**

WHISTLE BLOWING

Bolkovac, K. The whistleblower **92**

Drabelle, D. The great American railroad war **385**

Greenwald, G. No place to hide **327.12**

WHISTLE BLOWING
See also Political corruption; Public interest

The **whistleblower.** Bolkovac, K. **92**

WHISTLEBLOWING *See* Whistle blowing

Whitaker, Jan
Service and style **381**

Whitaker, John O.
National Audubon Society field guide to North American mammals **599**

Whitaker, Richard
Buckley, B. Weather: a visual guide **551.5**

Whitaker, Robert
Anatomy of an epidemic **616.89**

The mapmaker's wife **981**

White apples and the taste of stone. Hall, D. **811**

WHITE ARYAN RESISTANCE
Ezekiel, R. S. The racist mind **320.5**

White cargo. Jordan, D. **326**

The **white** cascade. Krist, G. **979.7**

White coat, black hat. Elliott, C. **174.2**

WHITE COLLAR CRIMES
Niebuhr, G. W. Caught up in crime **016**

WHITE COLLAR CRIMES
See also Crime

White Girls. Als, H. **814**

The **White** House. Monkman, B. C. **975.3**

WHITE HOUSE (WASHINGTON, D.C.)
Brower, K. A. The residence **975.3**

The house that George built **975.3**

McDowell, M. All the presidents' gardens **635.09**

WHITE HOUSE (WASHINGTON, D.C.) -- HISTORY -- 20TH CENTURY -- ANECDOTES
Brower, K. A. The residence **975.3**

WHITE HOUSE (WASHINGTON, D.C.) -- HISTORY
The house that George built **975.3**

White House burning. Johnson, S. **336.3**

White House diary. Carter, J. **92**

WHITE HOUSE GARDENS (WASHINGTON, D.C.)
Obama, M. American grown **635**

WHITE HOUSE GARDENS (WASHINGTON, D.C.) -- HISTORY
McDowell, M. All the presidents' gardens **635.09**

White Mughals. Dalrymple, W. **954**

The **white** road. De Waal, E. **738.209**

The **white** rock. Thomson, H. **985**

WHITE SUPREMACIST MOVEMENTS *See* White supremacy movements

WHITE SUPREMACISTS
Meeink, F. Autobiography of a recovering skinhead **92**

Wilson, E. Patriotic gore **810**

WHITE SUPREMACY MOVEMENTS
Ezekiel, R. S. The racist mind   320.5
Meeink, F. Autobiography of a recovering skin-
head   92
Zeskind, L. Blood and politics   305.8
WHITE SUPREMACY MOVEMENTS
See also Race relations; Racism; Social
movements
The white war. Thompson, M.   940.4
White, Ana
The handbuilt home   684.1
White, Andrew C.
E-metrics for library and information profession-
als   025.2
White, April
(jt. auth) Wood, S. M. Apples to cider   663
White, Betz
Sewing green   646.4
White, Bill
About
White, B. Uppity   92
White, Burton L.
The new first three years of life   155.4
White, Charles
The life and times of Little Richard   92
White, Christine
Uniquely felt   746
White, Dan, 1967-
Under the stars   796.54
White, Dana Angelo
First bites   641.3
White, E. B. (Elwyn Brooks), 1899-1985
Essays of E.B. White   814
Strunk, W. The elements of style   808
About
Elledge, S. E. B. White   92
Garvey, M. Stylized   808
White, E.B. Letters of E.B. White   92
White, Edmund, 1940-
City boy   92
The flaneur   944.083
My lives   813
White, Edward
The Tastemaker   92
White, Graham J.
White, S. The sounds of slavery   326
White, Harry Dexter, 1892-1948
About
Steil, B. The battle of Bretton Woods   339.5
White, Katharine Sergeant Angell, 1892-1977
About
Life stories   920
White, Lawrence J.
(jt. auth) Acharya, V. V. Guaranteed to fail 332.7
White, Mark Andrew
(ed) The James T. Bialac Native American Art Col-

lection   704.03
White, Martha
(ed) White, E. B. Letters of E.B. White   92
White, Michael, 1956-
(jt. auth) Friedman, A. Classico e moderno 641.59
Leonardo   92
About
Travels in Vermeer   92
White, Richard
(ed) King Arthur in legend and history   942.01
Railroaded   385
White, Ron, 1944-
How Computers Work   004
White, Ronald C. (Ronald Cedric), 1939-
A. Lincoln   92
The eloquent president: a portrait of Lincoln
through his words   92
White, R. C. American Ulysses   92
White, Rowland
Into the Black   629.44
White, Shane
Prince of darkness   92
The sounds of slavery   326
White, Vivian
The Total Skywatcher's Manual   523.8
Whitefield-Madrano, Autumn
Face value   111.85
Whitehead, Lorne A.
(jt. auth) Kotter, J. P. Buy-in   650.1
Whitehouse, Beth
The match   92
Whitehouse, David
Into the Heart of Our World   551
Whitelaw, Ian
The history of fly fishing in fifty flies 799.124
Whiteman, David
Lobel, S. The meat bible   641.6
WHITES
Kaplan, C. Miss Anne in Harlem   700.92
Painter, N. I. The history of White people 305.8
**WHITES -- UNITED STATES -- ECONOMIC
CONDITIONS**
Murray, C. Coming apart   305.8
The whites of their eyes. Lockhart, P. D. 973.3
Whitesides, George M.
Frankel, F. On the surface of things   530.4
WHITEWATER INQUIRY, 1993-2000
Gormley, K. The death of American virtue 973.929
McDougal, S. The woman who wouldn't
talk   973.929
Whitey Bulger. Cullen, K.   364.1
Whitfield, Eileen
Pickford   92
Whitlatch, Jo Bell
(ed) Guide to reference   011
Whitlock, Dave

Talleur, R. W. L.L. Bean ultimate book of fly fishing **799.1**

Whitman, George W., 1829-1901
About
Roper, R. Now the drum of war **973.7**

Whitman, Walt
Selected poems **811**
Complete poetry and collected prose **811**
Leaves of grass **811**

Whitmer, Benjamin
(jt. auth) Louvin, C. Satan is real **920**

Whitney Museum of American Art
Livingston, J. The paintings of Joan Mitchell **759.13**

Whitney, Catherine
Bartiromo, M. The weekend that changed Wall Street **330.9**
(jt. auth) Sherrod, S. The courage to hope **975.8**

Whitney, Craig R.
All the stops **786.5**

Whitson, Signe
8 keys to end bullying **302.34**

Whittier, John Greenleaf
Selected poems **811**

Whittington, George P., 1913-1996
About
Kaplan, A. Y. The interpreter **940.54**

Whittle, Richard
Predator **623.74**

Who freed the slaves? Richards, L. L. **342.73**
Who gets what--and why. Roth, A. E. **330.01**
Who needs God. Kushner, H. S. **296.7**
Who shot rock & roll. Buckland, G. **781.66**
Who shot sports. Buckland, G. **779.97**
Who stole the American dream? Smith, H. **973.91**
Who the hell is Pansy O'Hara? Bond, J. **920**
Who was who in America. **920.003**
Who wrote the Dead Sea scrolls? Golb, N. **296.1**
Who's afraid of post-blackness? Touré
Who's afraid of Virginia Woolf? Albee, E. **812**
Who's who 2008. **920.003**
Who's who among African Americans. **920.003**
Who's who in America, 2008. **920.003**
Who's who in American art, 2008. **920.003**
Who's who in American politics 2007-2008. Jaques Cattell Press **920.003**
Who's who in British history. **920.003**
Who's who in finance and business 2008-2009. **920.003**
Who's who in the Jewish Bible. Mandel, D. **920.003**
Who's who of American women 2007. **920.003**
The **who,** what, and where of America. **317.3**
WHODUNITS See Mystery and detective plays; Mystery fiction; Mystery films; Mystery radio programs; Mystery television programs
The **whole** death catalog. Schechter, H. **306.9**

The **whole** equation. Thomson, D. **791.43**
The **whole** foods allergy cookbook. Pascal, C. **641.5**
The **whole** heart solution. Khan, J. **616.1**
WHOLE LANGUAGE
See also Education -- Experimental methods; Language arts
Whole world vegetarian. **641.5**
The **whole-brain** child. Siegel, D. J. **649**
The **whole30.** **613.2**
WHOLISTIC MEDICINE *See* Holistic medicine
Whooping crane. Nigge, K. **598**
Why "A" Students Work for "C" Students and Why "B" Students Work for the Government. Kiyosaki, R. T. **332.024**
Why be happy when you could be normal? Winterson, J. **823**
Why be Jewish? Bronfman, E. M. **296**
Why beauty is truth. Stewart, I. **539.7**
Why buildings fall down. Levy, M. **690**
Why calories count. Nesheim, M. **613.2**
Why can't I get better? Horowitz, R. I. **616.9**
Why can't I meditate? Wellings, N. **158.12**
Why cant U teach me 2 read? Fertig, S. **372.4**
Why cats land on their feet. Levi, M. **530**
Why courage matters. McCain, J. S. **179**
Why did the chicken cross the world? Lawler, A. **636.5**
Why does the world exist? Holt, J. **113**
Why don't jumbo jets flap their wings? Alexander, D. E. **629.13**
Why evolution is true. Coyne, J. A. **576.8**
Why football matters. Edmundson, M. **92**
Why Homer matters. Nicolson, A. **883**
Why I came West. Bass, R. **92**
Why jazz happened. Myers, M. **781.65**
Why Johnny can't read--and what you can do about it. Flesch, R. F. **372.4**
Why Mahler? Lebrecht, N. **92**
Why nations fail. Acemoglu, D. **330**
Why not me? Kaling, M. **92**
Why organizations struggle so hard to improve so little. Klubeck, M. **658.4**
Why people believe weird things. Shermer, M. **001.9**
Why read Moby-Dick? Philbrick, N. **813**
Why read the classics? Calvino, I. **809**
Why Socrates died. Waterfield, R. **183**
Why suicide? Marcus, E. **179.7**
Why terrorism works. Dershowitz, A. M. **303.6**
Why the Allies won. Overy, R. **940.53**
Why the Dalai Lama matters. Thurman, R. A. F. **294.3**
Why the West rules--for now. Morris, I. **909**
Why they kill. Rhodes, R. **364.3**
Why this world. Moser, B. **92**
Why translation matters. Grossman, E. **418**
Why we buy. Underhill, P. **658.8**

Why we can't wait. King, M. L.   **323.1**

Why we do it. Eldredge, N.   **155.3**

Why we get fat and what to do about it. Taubes, G.   **613.7**

Why We Lost. Bolger, D. P.   **956.704**

Why we love the dogs we do. Coren, S.   **636.7**

Why we make mistakes. Hallinan, J. T.   **153**

Why X matters [series]

   Grossman, E. Why translation matters   **418**

Whybrow, P. J.

   (ed) Travels with the fossil hunters   **560**

Whyte, Kenneth

   The uncrowned king   **92**

WICCA

   See also Paganism

WICCA -- UNITED STATES

   Mar, A. Witches of America   **299**

'wichcraft. Colicchio, T.   **641.8**

Wichman, Emily T.

   Librarian's guide to passive programming   **025.5**

Wick, Myra

   (ed) Mayo Clinic guide to a healthy pregnancy   **618.2**

Wicked bugs. Stewart, A.   **632**

WICKEDNESS *See* Good and evil

Wicker, Tom

   Dwight D. Eisenhower   **973.921**

   Shooting star: the brief arc of Joe McCarthy   **92**

Wickersham, Joan

   The suicide index   **155.9**

Wickham, Chris

   The inheritance of Rome   **940.1**

Wideman, John Edgar

     About

   Wideman, J. E. Hoop roots   **813**

Widmer, Edward L.

   Martin Van Buren   **92**

A **widow's** story. Oates, J. C.   **92**

WIDOWERS

   Vincent, I. Dinner with Edward   **158.1**

WIDOWHOOD

   Aikman, B. Saturday night widows   **306.88**

WIDOWS

   Aikman, B. Saturday night widows   **306.88**

   Leaming, B. Jacqueline Bouvier Kennedy Onassis   **92**

   Oates, J. C. A widow's story   **92**

   Roiphe, A. R. Epilogue   **92**

   Thomas, A. What Comes Next and How to Like It   **92**

WIDOWS

   See also Women

WIDOWS -- BIOGRAPHY

   Deraniyagala, S. Wave   **954.93**

WIDOWS -- GRAPHIC NOVELS

   Torres, A. American widow   **741.5**

Wiedemann, Julius

   (ed) Rendgen, S. Understanding the world   **741.6**

Wiederhorn, Jon

   (jt. auth) Turman, K. Louder Than Hell   **781.66**

Wiegand, Wayne A.

   (ed) Herald, D. T. Genreflecting   **016**

Wiegers, Michael

   (ed) Stanford, F. What about this   **811.54**

   (ed) Torre, M. d. l. Reversible monuments   **861**

Wieland, Karin

   Dietrich & Riefenstahl   **791.43**

Wiencek, Henry

   The Hairstons   **920**

   An imperfect god   **973.4**

   Master of the mountain   **973.4**

   National Geographic guide to America's great houses   **728.8**

Wiener, Roberta

   (ed) Cold War   **909.82**

Wiesel, Elie, 1928-2016

   All rivers run to the sea   **813**

   And the sea is never full   **813**

   Night   **92**

Wieseltier, Leon

   Kaddish   **296.4**

Wiesenthal, Simon

   The sunflower   **179.7**

     About

   Pick, H. Simon Wiesenthal   **940.53**

   Segev, T. Simon Wiesenthal   **92**

Wiessinger, Diane

   (jt. auth) Pitman, T. Sweet sleep   **649**

   The womanly art of breastfeeding   **649**

WIFE ABUSE

   See also Domestic violence

Wiffen, Charles

   (ed) The complete classical music guide   **780**

Wiggins, Arthur W.

   The five biggest unsolved problems in science   **500**

Wigner, Eugene P., 1902-1995

     About

   Hargittai, I. The Martians of science   **920**

   Marton, K. The great escape   **920**

Wigoder, Geoffrey

   (ed) Encyclopedia of Jewish life before and during the Holocaust   **940.53**

   (ed) The New encyclopedia of Judaism   **296**

WIGS

   See also Clothing and dress; Costume; Hair

WikiLeaks (Organization)

   (comp) The WikiLeaks files   **327.73**

WIKILEAKS (ORGANIZATION)

   The WikiLeaks files   **327.73**

The **WikiLeaks** files.   **327.73**

The **Wikipedia** revolution. Lih, A.   **031**

Wilber, Del Quentin

A good month for murder 363.25
Wilber, Tom
Under the surface 333.8
Wilberforce, William, 1759-1833
About
Hague, W. J. William Wilberforce 92
Wilbur, Richard, 1921-
Wilbur, R. Anterooms 811
Collected poems, 1943-2004 811
Wilcove, David S.
No way home 591.56
Wilcox, Christie
Venomous 572
Wild. Strayed, C. 92
WILD ANIMAL TRADE
Neme, L. A. Animal investigators 363.2
Smith, J. E. Stolen world 364.1
**WILD ANIMAL TRADE -- CORRUPT PRAC-
TICES**
Smith, J. E. Stolen world 364.1
WILD ANIMALS *See* Animals; Wildlife
The **wild** blue. Ambrose, S. E. 940.54
Wild blue. Bortolotti, D. 599.5
Wild by nature. Marquis, S. 613.6
The **wild** cat book. Sunquist, F. 599.75
WILD CATS
Sunquist, F. The wild cat book 599.75
Wild cats of the world 599.75
WILD CATS
See also Mammals
Wild cats of the world. 599.75
WILD CHILDREN
See also Exceptional children
Wild company. Ziegler, M. 381
WILD FLOWERS
Spellenberg, R. National Audubon Society field
guide to North American wildflowers, western re-
gion 582.13
Spira, T. P. Waterfalls and wildflowers in the South-
ern Appalachians 796.51
Thieret, J. W. National Audubon Society field
guide to North American wildflowers: eastern re-
gion 582.13
WILD FLOWERS
See also Flowers
**WILD FLOWERS -- APPALACHIAN REGION,
SOUTHERN -- GUIDEBOOKS**
Spira, T. P. Waterfalls and wildflowers in the South-
ern Appalachians 796.51
The **wild** frontier. Osborn, W. M. 970.004
Wild justice. Bekoff, M. 591.5
A **wild** justice. Mandery, E. J. 345.73
The **wild** life of our bodies. Dunn, R. 579
WILD OATS (MOTION PICTURE)
MacLaine, S. Above the line 92
Wild ones. Mooallem, J. 333.95

The **wild** places. Macfarlane, R. 914
Wild romance. Schama, C. 92
Wild Sex. Bondar, C. 591.562
Wild swans. Chang, J. 951.05
The **wild** trees. Preston, R. 577.3
WILDCATS *See* Wild cats
Wilde, Oscar, 1854-1900
The artist as critic 824
The importance of being earnest and other plays 822
About
Ellmann, R. Oscar Wilde 92
Wilder, Billy, 1906-2002
About
It's the pictures that got small 92
Sikov, E. On Sunset Boulevard: the life and times
of Billy Wilder 92
Wilder, Clint
(jt. auth) Pernick, R. Clean Tech Nation 333.794
Wilder, Craig Steven
Ebony and Ivy 379.26
Wilder, Laura Ingalls, 1867-1957
About
Anderson, W. T. Laura Ingalls Wilder country 92
Pioneer girl 92
Wilder, Shirley
About
Bernstein, N. The lost children of Wilder 362.73
Wilder, Thornton, 1897-1975
Collected plays & writings on theater 812
Our town 812
About
Playwrights at work 812
WILDERNESS AREAS
Macfarlane, R. The wild places 914
Stark, P. The last empty places 973
WILDERNESS AREAS -- UNITED STATES
Brinkley, D. The wilderness warrior 92
Wilderness at dawn. Morgan, T. 970
A **wilderness** of error. Morris, E. 364.152
A **wilderness** so immense. Kukla, J. 973.4
WILDERNESS SURVIVAL
Canterbury, D. Advanced bushcraft 613.69
Marquis, S. Wild by nature 613.6
Murphy, B. 81 days below zero 940.54
Roberts, D. Alone on the ice 919
Stilwell, A. The encyclopedia of survival tech-
niques 613.6
Wiseman, J. SAS survival handbook 613.6
WILDERNESS SURVIVAL
See also Camping; Outdoor life; Survival
skills
WILDERNESS SURVIVAL -- ALASKA
Murphy, B. 81 days below zero 940.54
**WILDERNESS SURVIVAL -- HANDBOOKS,
MANUALS, ETC**
Canterbury, D. Advanced bushcraft 613.69

Canterbury, D. Bushcraft 101 **613.6**

Canterbury, D. The Bushcraft field guide to trapping, gathering, and cooking in the wild **641.691**

The **wilderness** warrior. Brinkley, D. **92**

WILDFIRES

Dickman, K. On the burning edge **363.37**

Maclean, J. N. Fire and ashes **363.3**

Smith, J. Smokejumper **92**

Soles, C. The fire smart home handbook **643**

WILDFIRES

See also Fires

WILDFIRES -- UNITED STATES -- PREVENTION AND CONTROL

Soles, C. The fire smart home handbook **643**

WILDFLOWERS *See* Wild flowers

WILDGuides [series]

The world's rarest birds **598**

WILDLIFE

Shetterly, S. H. Settled in the wild **508**

WILDLIFE

See also Animals

WILDLIFE AND PESTICIDES *See* Pesticides and wildlife

WILDLIFE AS CARRIERS OF DISEASE *See* Animals as carriers of disease

WILDLIFE ATTRACTING

See also Animals

WILDLIFE CONSERVATION

Barilla, J. My Backyard Jungle **577.5**

Busch, A. The incidental steward **363.7**

Chadwick, D. H. The company we keep **333.95**

DeStefano, S. Coyote at the kitchen door **578.7**

Fraser, C. Rewilding the world **333.95**

Goodall, J. The ten trusts **333.95**

Lebbin, D. J. The American Bird Conservancy guide to bird conservation **333.95**

The monarch butterfly **595.7**

Neme, L. A. Animal investigators **363.2**

Nicholls, H. The way of the panda **599.7**

Owens, D. The eye of the elephant **333.95**

Owens, M. Secrets of the savanna **599**

Raffin, M. The birds of Pandemonium **639.97**

Sooyong Park Great Soul of Siberia **599.756**

World atlas of great apes and their conservation **599.8**

WILDLIFE CONSERVATION

See also Conservation of natural resources; Economic zoology; Endangered species; Environmental protection; Nature conservation

WILDLIFE CONSERVATION -- HAWAII

Williams, T. M. The odyssey of KP2 **599.79**

WILDLIFE CONSERVATION -- HUDSON RIVER VALLEY (N.Y. AND N.J.)

Busch, A. The incidental steward **363.7**

WILDLIFE CONSERVATION -- LAOS -- NAKAI-NAM THEUN NATIONAL BIODIVER-SITY CONSERVATION AREA

DeBuys, W. The last unicorn **591.68**

WILDLIFE CONSERVATION -- SOUTH AFRICA -- LONDOLOZI GAME RESERVE -- HISTORY

Varty, B. Cathedral of the wild **639.9**

WILDLIFE CONSERVATION -- UNITED STATES

Mooallem, J. Wild ones **333.95**

WILDLIFE CONSERVATION -- UNITED STATES -- HISTORY

Barrow, M. V. Nature's ghosts **333.95**

Wildlife of the world. **591**

Wildlife Photographer of the Year. **778.9**

WILDLIFE PHOTOGRAPHY

Wildlife Photographer of the Year **778.9**

WILDLIFE PHOTOGRAPHY

See also Nature photography; Photography

WILDLIFE REFUGES

Anthony, L. The elephant whisperer **599.67**

Westoll, A. The chimps of Fauna Sanctuary **636.9**

WILDLIFE REFUGES

See also Wildlife conservation

WILDLIFE REHABILITATION

Zickefoose, J. The bluebird effect **598**

WILDLIFE REHABILITATION -- HAWAII

Williams, T. M. The odyssey of KP2 **599.79**

WILDLIFE SANCTUARIES *See* Wildlife refuges

WILDLIFE SMUGGLING

Smith, J. E. Stolen world **364.1**

WILDLIFE WATCHING

The secret language of animals **591.5**

Wildsmith, Snow

Joining the United States Air Force **358.4**

Wilentz, Sean

Andrew Jackson **92**

(ed) Brinkley, A. John F. Kennedy **92**

The Politicians and the Egalitarians **306.2**

The rise of American democracy **973.5**

Wiles, Andrew

About

Singh, S. Fermat's enigma **512**

Wiley investment classics [series]

Allen, F. L. Only yesterday **973.91**

Wiley popular science [series]

Macdougall, J. D. A short history of planet earth **551.7**

Wiley, Bell Irvin

The life of Billy Yank **973.7**

The life of Johnny Reb **973.7**

Wiley, Keith

Designing and planting a woodland garden **635.9**

Wiley, Meredith S.

(jt. auth) Karr-Morse, R. Scared sick **155.9**

Wilhide, Elizabeth

Scandinavian Home **728**

Wilkerson, Isabel
The warmth of other suns   307
Wilkes, Lindsay
Sew classic clothes for girls
Wilkin, Karen
Ross, C. The world of Edward Gorey   **700.92**
Wilkins, Thurman
John Muir   **92**
Wilkinson, Alec
The ice balloon   **910.91**
The protest singer   **92**
Wilkinson, Frances C.
(jt. auth) Lewis, L. K. The complete guide to acquisitions management   **025.2**
Wilkinson, James, 1757-1825
            About
Linklater, A. An artist in treason   **92**
Wilkinson, Karen
The Art of tinkering   **500**
Wilkinson, Matt
Mr. Wilkinson's vegetables   **641.65**
Restless creatures   **591.47**
Wilkinson, Philip
The history of music in fifty instruments   **784.19**
Wilkinson, Richard
(jt. auth) Pickett, K. The spirit level   **306**
Wilkinson, Richard H.
The complete gods and goddesses of ancient Egypt   **299**
Wilkinson, Toby
The rise and fall of ancient Egypt   **932**
WILL *See* Brainwashing; Free will and determinism
Will Eisner. Schumacher, M.   **92**
The Will Eisner library [series]
Eisner, W. Comics and sequential art   **741.5**
Will Eisner: A Spirited Life. Andelman, B.   **741.5**
Will I ever be good enough? McBride, K.   **616.85**
Will I see my dog in heaven? Wintz, J.   **231.7**
Will in the world. Greenblatt, S. J.   **822.3**
Will my cancer come back?   **616.99**
The will of the people. Friedman, B.   **347**
WILL POWER *See* Self-control
Will the circle be unbroken? Terkel, S.   **128**
The will to power. Nietzsche, F. W.   **193**
Will write for food.   **808**
Will you miss me when I'm gone? Zwonitzer, M.   **781.642**
Willa Cather. Lee, H.   **92**
Willa Cather. Woodress, J. L.   **92**
Willan, Anne
(jt. auth) Cherniavsky, M. The cookbook library   **641.509**
The country cooking of France   **641.59**
Willenbrink, Mark
Drawing for the absolute beginner   **741.2**

Oil painting for the absolute beginner   **751.45**
Willenbrink, Mary
(jt. auth) Willenbrink, M. Drawing for the absolute beginner   **741.2**
Willenbrink, M. Oil painting for the absolute beginner   **751.45**
William E. Massey, Sr. lectures in the history of American civilization [series]
Welty, E. One writer's beginnings   **92**
William Eggleston's Guide. Szarkowski, J.   **779**
William Faulkner.   **813**
William Henry Harrison. Collins, G.   **92**
William II, German Emperor, 1859-1941
            About
Carter, M. George, Nicholas, and Wilhelm   **940.3**
Clay, C. King, Kaiser, Tsar   **920**
William James. Richardson, R. D.   **92**
William McKinley. Phillips, K. P.   **92**
William Wilberforce. Hague, W. J.   **92**
Williams family
            About
Demos, J. The unredeemed captive   **973.2**
Williams, Anthony D.
(jt. auth) Tapscott, D. Macrowikinomics   **303.4**
Williams, Art, Jr.
            About
Kersten, J. The art of making money   **92**
Williams, Bruce A.
(jt. auth) Carpini, M. X. D. After broadcast news   **071**
Williams, Bunny
Bunny Williams' on garden style
Williams, C. K.
Collected poems   **811**
Williams, Caroline Randall
Soul food love   **641.59**
Williams, Charles
The last great Frenchman   **944**
Williams, Chuck
(ed) Spieler, M. Paris   **641.5**
Williams, David
Bitterly divided   **973.7**
Williams, David B.
Stories in stone   **550**
Williams, Ernest
Stokes, D. W. The butterfly book   **595.7**
Williams, Eunice, 1696-1786
            About
Demos, J. The unredeemed captive   **973.2**
Williams, Florence
Breasts   **612.6**
Williams, Glyndwr
Arctic labyrinth   **910.4**
Williams, Hank, 1923-1953
            About
Escott, C. Hank Williams   **92**

Hemphill, P. Lovesick blues **92**

Williams, Heather Andrea
Help me to find my people **306.3**

Williams, Jack
The AMS weather book **551.5**

Williams, James D.
Gilbert, C. R. National Audubon Society field guide to fishes, North America **597**

Williams, Jay, 1981-
About
Williams, J. Life is not an accident **92**

Williams, Joan, 1952-
What works for women at work **650.1**

Williams, John, 1664-1729
About
Demos, J. The unredeemed captive **973.2**

Williams, Jonathan
Jubilant thicket **811**

Williams, Joseph M.
(ed) A manual for writers of research papers, theses, and dissertations **808.06**

Williams, Juan
Eyes on the prize: America's civil rights years, 1954-1965 **323.1**
I'll find a way or make one **378**
This far by faith **200**
Thurgood Marshall **92**

Williams, Kate
Ambition and desire **92**
Becoming Queen Victoria **92**

Williams, Katherine
Feldman, B. 112 Mercer Street **920**

Williams, Mary, 1967-
About
Williams, M. The lost daughter **979.4**

Williams, Richard, 1933-
The animator's survival kit **778.53**

Williams, Robert G.
Nichols, C. R. Encyclopedia of marine science **551.46**

Williams, Roger, 1604?-1683
About
Barry, J. M. Roger Williams and the creation of the American soul **974.5**
Gaustad, E. S. Roger Williams **92**

Williams, Susan
Spies in the congo **553.4**

Williams, Ted, 1918-2002
About
Bradlee, B. C. The kid **92**
Halberstam, D. The teammates **796**
Linn, E. Hitter: the life and turmoils of Ted Williams **92**

Williams, Tennessee, 1911-1983
Plays, 1937-1955 **812**
Plays, 1957-1980 **812**

A streetcar named desire **812**
About
Heintzelman, G. Critical companion to Tennessee Williams **812**
Lahr, J. Tennessee Williams **92**
Leverich, L. Tom **92**
Playwrights at work **812**
Spoto, D. The kindness of strangers: the life of Tennessee Williams **92**

Williams, Terrie M
About
Williams, T. M. The odyssey of KP2 **599.79**

Williams, Terry Tempest
Finding beauty in a broken world **814**

Williams, Wendy
The horse **636.1**
Kraken **594**

Williams, William Carlos, 1883-1963
The collected poems of William Carlos Williams **811**
Paterson **811**
About
Jarrell, R. No other book **809**
Leibowitz, H. A. Something urgent I have to say to you: the life and works of William Carlos Williams **92**

Williams-Sonoma foods of the world [series]
Spieler, M. Paris **641.5**

WILLIAMSBURG (NEW YORK, N.Y.) -- DESCRIPTION AND TRAVEL
Anasi, R. The last bohemia **974.7**

Williamson, Edwin
Borges, a life **92**
The Penguin history of Latin America **980**

Williamson, Marianne
Tears to triumph **299.93**

Williamson, Sheri L.
A field guide to hummingbirds of North America **598**

Willie Dixon. Inaba, M. **92**
Willie Mays. Hirsch, J. S. **92**
Willie Nelson. Patoski, J. N. **92**

Willingham, Emily
The informed parent **649.1**

Willis, Deborah, 1948-
Reflections in Black **770.92**
(jt. auth) Krauthamer, B. Envisioning emancipation **973.7**

Willkie, Wendell L. (Wendell Lewis), 1892-1944
About
Fullilove, M. Rendezvous with destiny **973.917**

Willman, David
The mirage man **363.325**

Willner, Nina
Forty Autumns

WILLPOWER See Self-control

WILLS

See also Genealogy; Registers of births, etc.

Wills, Christopher

Green Equilibrium   **577**

Wills, Garry, 1934-

Certain trumpets   **303.3**

The Future of the Catholic Church With Pope Francis   **282**

James Madison   **92**

Lincoln at Gettysburg   **973.7**

A necessary evil   **973**

'Negro president'   **326**

Outside looking in   **92**

Saint Augustine   **270.2**

Verdi's Shakespeare   **822.3**

About

Wills, G. Outside looking in   **92**

Wilmut, Ian

After Dolly   **176**

Wilsey, Sean

(ed) State by state   **973**

Wilson. Berg, A. S.   **92**

Wilson, A. N.

Betjeman   **92**

C.S. Lewis   **823**

Jesus   **232.9**

Victoria   **92**

The Victorians   **941.081**

Wilson, August

Fences   **812**

Jitney   **812**

Ma Rainey's black bottom   **812**

The piano lesson   **812**

Seven guitars   **812**

Two trains running   **812**

About

Playwrights at work   **812**

Wilson, Bee

Consider the fork   **643**

First bite   **641.01**

Swindled   **363.1**

Wilson, Brian, 1942-

About

Wilson, B. I am Brian Wilson   **92**

Wilson, David Sloan

Evolution for everyone   **576.8**

The neighborhood project   **307.7**

Wilson, Derek A.

Charlemagne   **92**

Out of the storm   **92**

Wilson, Diane

About

Wilson, D. An unreasonable woman   **92**

Wilson, Doug

Pudge   **92**

Wilson, Edmund, 1895-1972

Literary essays and reviews of the 1920s & 30s   **814**

Literary essays and reviews of the 1930s & 40s   **814**

Patriotic gore   **810**

About

Blight, D. W. American oracle   **973.7**

Wilson, Edward O.

Holldobler, B. The ants   **595.79**

Holldobler, B. Journey to the ants   **595.79**

Holldobler, B. The leafcutter ants   **595.7**

Holldobler, B. The superorganism   **595.7**

Consilience   **121**

The diversity of life   **333.95**

The future of life   **333.95**

In search of nature   **113**

About

Wilson, E. O. Letters to a Young Scientist   **570**

The Meaning of Human Existence   **128**

The social conquest of earth   **599.93**

A window on eternity   **333.95**

Wilson, Ellen Judy

Encyclopedia of the Enlightenment   **940.2**

Wilson, Frances

The ballad of Dorothy Wordsworth   **92**

Wilson, George

(ed) Literature and its times   **809**

Wilson, Harold Sir, 1916-1995

About

Wheen, F. Strange days indeed   **973.92**

Wilson, James

The earth shall weep   **970.004**

Wilson, Jason

(ed) The best American travel writing 2012   **808**

Wilson, Jeffrey

(ed) Gale encyclopedia of everyday law   **349**

Wilson, Jennifer

Running away to home   **305.8**

Wilson, Jose

Beard on food   **641.5**

Wilson, Katherine, 1974-

About

Wilson, K. Only in Naples   **945.731**

Wilson, Keith, 1927-

(ed) The Collected Letters of Thomas Hardy   **823**

Wilson, Lanford

21 short plays   **812**

The Talley trilogy   **812**

Wilson, Leigh Heather

(jt. auth) Kuhn, C. Buzzed   **615.7**

Wilson, Penny

Lusitania   **910.4**

Wilson, Peter H.

The Thirty Years War   **940.2**

Wilson, Ray W.

(jt. auth) Laughlin, S. The quality library   **025.1**

Wilson, Robert

Mathew Brady   **770.92**

Wilson, Robin J.
(ed) Sherlock Holmes in Babylon   **510**
Wilson, Ronaldo V.
Farther traveler   **818**
Wilson, Sondra K.
(ed) Johnson, J. W. Complete poems   **811**
Wilson, Ward
Five myths about nuclear weapons   **355.02**
Wilson, Wilkie
(jt. auth) Kuhn, C. Buzzed   **615.7**
Wilson, Woodrow, 1856-1924
About
Berg, A. S. Wilson   **92**
Brands, H. W. Woodrow Wilson   **92**
Cooper, J. M. The warrior and the priest: Woodrow
    Wilson and Theodore Roosevelt   **92**
Cooper, J. M. Woodrow Wilson   **92**
Hofstadter, R. The American political tradition, and
    the men who made it   **973**
Kissinger, H. Diplomacy   **327.2**
MacMillan, M. Paris 1919   **940.3**
Neu, C. E. Colonel House   **92**
Tooze, A. The deluge   **940.3**
Tuchman, B. W. Practicing history   **907**
Wilton, Andrew
American sublime   **759.13**
Wiltshire, Jo
(jt. auth) Cross, C. The baby book   **649.122**
Wimpenny, Jo
(jt. auth) Birkhead, T. Ten thousand birds   **598**
Winant, John Gilbert, 1889-1947
About
Olson, L. Citizens of London   **940.54**
Winchester, Simon
Atlantic   **551.46**
A crack in the edge of the world   **979.4**
Krakatoa: the day the world exploded, August 27,
    1883   **551.2**
The man who loved China   **92**
The map that changed the world   **526**
Pacific   **909**
The professor and the madman   **423**
The river at the center of the world   **915**
Skulls   **573.7**
WIND INSTRUMENTS
    See also Musical instruments
WIND INSTRUMENTS -- CONSTRUCTION
Pagliaro, M. The musical instrument desk refer-
    ence   **784.192**
WIND POWER
Ewing, R. A. Got sun? go solar   **697**
WIND POWER
    See also Energy resources; Power (Mechan-
    ics); Renewable energy resources
Wind, Herbert Warren
Five lessons   **796.352**

Winder, Elizabeth
Pain, Parties, Work   **811**
Windham, Ryder
(jt. auth) Wallace, D. Ultimate Star wars
WINDMILLS -- MALAWI
Kamkwamba, W. The boy who harnessed the
    wind   **92**
WINDOW GARDENING
    See also Gardening; Indoor gardening
A window on eternity.   **333.95**
WINDOWS
    See also Architecture -- Details; Buildings
Windows on the World complete wine course. Zraly,
    K.   **641.2**
Windows on the World Complete Wine Course. Zra-
    ly, K.   **641.2**
WINDOWS, STAINED GLASS *See* Glass paint-
    ing and staining
WINDS
    See also Meteorology; Navigation; Physical
    geography; Weather
The winds of change. Linden, E.   **551.6**
Windsor, Edie
About
Dickey, L. Then comes marriage   **346**
Windsor, House of
About
Andersen, C. Game of crowns   **941.085**
WINDSURFING
    See also Sailing
Wine. Old, M.   **641.2**
WINE AND WINE MAKING
    See also Alcoholic beverages
WINE AND WINE MAKING -- FRANCE
Potter, M. Shadows in the vineyard   **364.16**
Wine grapes. Robinson, J.   **664**
WINE TASTING
Old, M. Wine   **641.2**
Wineapple, Brenda
Ecstatic nation   **973.6**
Hawthorne: a life   **92**
(ed) Whittier, J. G. Selected poems   **811**
WINERIES -- FRANCE -- BURGUNDY -- CASE
    STUDIES
Potter, M. Shadows in the vineyard   **364.16**
Winewise. Kolpan, S.   **641.2**
Wing, Charlie
How your house works   **643**
Wingate, David, 1935-
About
Gehrman, E. Rare birds   **598**
Winik, Jay
1944   **940.53**
The great upheaval   **909.7**
Winik, Marion
The lunch-box chronicles   **306.85**

Winkfield, Jimmy, 1882-1974
  About
  Drape, J. Black maestro   **92**
Winkle, Kenneth J.
  Woodworth, S. E. Atlas of the Civil War   **973.7**
Winkless, Laurie
  Science and the City   **307.76**
Winks, Robin W.
  (ed) Mystery and suspense writers   **809**
Winner, Ellen
  Gifted children   **155.45**
Winner, Lauren F.
  Wearing God   **231.7**
Winning grants. Gerding, S. K.   **025.1**
Winship, Michael
  (ed) Madison, J. The Constitutional Conven-
  tion   **342**
Winslow Homer. Cikovsky, N.   **759.13**
Winslow, Kate
  (jt. auth) Tomlinson, S. Agricola cookbook **641.564**
Winslow, Valerie L.
  Classic human anatomy   **743.49**
Winston, Wayne L.
  Mathletics   **796**
WINTER
  See also Seasons
The **winter** fortress. Bascomb, N.   **940.54**
WINTER GARDENING
  See also Gardening
Winter harvest handbook. Coleman, E.   **635**
WINTER RESORTS
  See also Resorts
WINTER SPORTS
  See also Sports
WINTER SPORTS -- UNITED STATES
  Vinton, N. The fall line   **796.935**
The **Winter** War. Edwards, R.   **948.97**
Winter, Hannah
  (jt. auth) Meyer, J. Decision quality   **658.4**
Winter, J. M.
  (ed) Europe 1789 to 1914   **940.2**
Winter, Kathleen
  About
  Winter, K. Boundless   **910.9**
Winter, Ruth
  A consumer's dictionary of cosmetic ingredi-
  ents   **668**
  A consumer's dictionary of food additives **664**
Winterdance. Paulsen, G.   **798.8**
Winters, Kathleen C.
  Amelia Earhart   **92**
  Anne Morrow Lindbergh   **92**
Winters, Richard
  About
  Alexander, L. Biggest brother   **92**
Winterson, Jeanette, 1959-

  About
  Winterson, J. Why be happy when you could be
  normal?   **823**
Winthrop, John, 1588-1649
  About
  Bremer, F. J. John Winthrop   **974.4**
Wintle, Justin
  Perfect hostage   **92**
Wintz, Jack
  Will I see my dog in heaven?   **231.7**
WIRE CRAFT
  See also Handicraft; Metalwork
Wired for culture. Pagel, M.   **303.4**
Wired for war. Singer, P. W.   **355**
WIRELESS *See* Radio
WIRELESS COMMUNICATION SYSTEMS
  See also Telecommunication
WIRETAPPING
  Theoharis, A. G. Abuse of power   **363.325**
WIRETAPPING
  See also Criminal investigation; Right of pri-
  vacy
Wiring simplified. Richter, H. P.   **621.319**
WIRING, ELECTRIC *See* Electric wiring
Wirt, Mildred A. (Mildred Augustine), 1905-
  About
  Rehak, M. Girl sleuth   **813**
Wirths, Eduard, 1909-1945
  About
  Lifton, R. J. The Nazi doctors   **940.53**
Wirtz, James J.
  (ed) Weapons of mass destruction   **358**
Wisconsin studies in autobiography [series]
  Humez, J. M. Harriet Tubman   **92**
Wisdom. Hall, S. S.   **179**
Wisdom for a livable planet. McDaniel, C. N. **333.72**
The **wisdom** of crowds. Surowiecki, J.   **303.3**
The **wisdom** of the bones. Walker, A.   **599.93**
The **wisdom** of whores. Pisani, E.   **614.5**
Wise, Brownie
  About
  Kealing, B. Tupperware, unsealed   **338.7**
Wise, David
  Spy: the inside story of how the FBI's Robert Hans-
  sen betrayed America   **327.12**
Wise, Michael Owen
  Abegg, M. G. The Dead Sea scrolls   **296.1**
Wise, Steven M.
  Drawing the line   **179**
  Though the heavens may fall   **342**
Wiseman, Jillian
  Jill Wiseman's beautiful beaded ropes   **745.594**
Wiseman, John
  SAS survival handbook   **613.6**
Wiseman, Rosalind, 1969-
  Masterminds and wingmen   **649**

Wiseman, Shelley
   (jt. auth) Santibañez, R. Truly Mexican **641.59**
Wish I could be there. Shawn, A. **92**
WISHES
   See also Motivation (Psychology)
Wishful drinking. Fisher, C. **92**
Wit. Edson, M. **812**
WIT AND HUMOR
  Barry, D. You can date boys when you're forty **306.85**
  Blount, R. Save room for pie **641.3**
  Carlin, G. Napalm & silly putty **817**
  Diffee, M. Hand drawn jokes for smart attractive people **741.5**
  Munroe, R. What if? **500**
  Nawaz, Z. Laughing All the Way to the Mosque **92**
  Oxford dictionary of humorous quotations **808.88**
  Poehler, A. Yes please **92**
  Pratchett, T. A slip of the keyboard **824**
  Toasts **808.88**
WIT AND HUMOR
   See also Literature
The **wit** and wisdom of Mark Twain. Twain, M. **818**
The **witch** of lime street. Jaher, D. **92**
WITCHCRAFT
  Adler, M. Drawing down the moon **133.4**
  Carlson, L. M. A fever in Salem **133.4**
  Hoffer, P. C. The Salem witchcraft trials **345**
  Hutton, R. The triumph of the moon **133.4**
  Karlsen, C. F. The devil in the shape of a woman **133.4**
  The Penguin Book of Witches **133.4**
  Stark, R. For the glory of God **201**
WITCHCRAFT
   See also Folklore; Occultism
WITCHCRAFT -- ENCYCLOPEDIAS
  Guiley, R. E. The encyclopedia of witches, witchcraft, and Wicca **133.4**
WITCHCRAFT -- GERMANY -- HISTORY
  Robisheaux, T. The last witch of Langenburg **133.4**
The **Witches.** Schiff, S. **345**
WITCHES
   See also Witchcraft
WITCHES
  Guiley, R. E. The encyclopedia of witches, witchcraft, and Wicca **133.4**
  Ward, M. C. Voodoo queen **92**
Witches of America. Mar, A. **299**
Witcover, Jules
  America's vice presidents **352.23**
  The year the dream died **973.923**
With fire & sword. Nelson, J. L. **973.3**
With God on our side. Martin, W. C. **261.8**
With or without you. Ruta, D. **362.29**
With speed and violence. Pearce, F. **551.6**
With wings like eagles. Korda, M. **940.54**

Without end. Zagajewski, A. **891.8**
Without saying. Howard, R. **811**
Without title. Hill, G. **821**
Witkowski, Jan
  (ed) The annotated and illustrated double helix **572.8**
Witness. Chambers, W. **92**
WITNESS BEARING (CHRISTIANITY)
  Yancey, P. Vanishing grace **277**
WITNESSES
   See also Litigation; Trials
Witnesses of war. Stargardt, N. **940.53**
Witschey, Walter R. T.
  (ed) Encyclopedia of the ancient Maya **972.81**
Witt, John Fabian
  Lincoln's code **343**
Witter, Bret
  Edsel, R. M. The monuments men **940.53**
  Myron, V. Dewey **636.8**
  Stronger **92**
  Until Tuesday **362.4**
Wittgenstein family
        About
  Waugh, A. The House of Wittgenstein **920**
Wittgenstein's poker. Edmonds, D. **192**
Wittgenstein, Ludwig, 1889-1951
        About
  Edmonds, D. Wittgenstein's poker **192**
Wittman, Robert
  Priceless **364.1**
        About
  Kinney, D. The devil's diary **940.53**
The **wives.** Popoff, A. **891.7**
WIVES
   See also Family; Marriage; Married people; Women
WIVES
  Moore, W. How to create the perfect wife **823**
  Popoff, A. The wives **891.7**
  Ritz, D. After the Dance **782.42**
The **wives** of Henry VIII. Fraser, A. **920**
WIVES OF PRESIDENTS -- UNITED STATES
   See Presidents' spouses -- United States
The **wizards** of Langley. Richelson, J. **327.12**
Wizenberg, Molly
  A homemade life **92**
  Delancey **647.95**
Wizenberg, Molly
        About
  A homemade life **92**
  Wizenberg, M. Delancey **647.95**
Wodehouse. McCrum, R. **92**
Wodehouse, P. G. (Pelham Grenville), 1881-1975
        About
  McCrum, R. Wodehouse **92**
Woe is I. O'Conner, P. T. **428**

Wohlforth, Charles
Beyond Earth — **629.455**
The fate of nature — **304.2**
The whale and the supercomputer — **305.897**
Wohlleben, Peter
The Hidden Life of Trees — **582.16**
WOK COOKING
Richardson, A. The breath of a wok — **641.59**
WOK COOKING
See also Cooking
Wolbrink, Shelley
(ed) Great lives from history, the Middle Ages, 477-1453 — **920.003**
The **wolf** almanac. Busch, R. — **599.77**
Wolf Boys. Slater, D. — **364**
The **wolf** in the parlor. Franklin, J. — **636.7**
Wolf, Christopher
(jt. auth) Foxman, A. H. Viral hate — **364.15**
Wolf, Clark
(ed) 101 classic cookbooks — **641**
Wolf, Marvin J.
Abandoned in hell — **959.704**
Wolf, Naomi
The beauty myth — **305.4**
Promiscuities — **306.7**
Vagina — **305.42**
Wolf, Thomas
Bryan, P. L. Midnight assassin — **364.152**
Wolfe, Alan
Moral freedom — **170**
Wolfe, Charles K.
The life and legend of Leadbelly — **92**
Wolfe, David W.
Tales from the underground — **578.7**
Wolfe, Tom
From Bauhaus to our house — **720.9**
The right stuff — **629.45**
Wolfert, Paula
Couscous and other good food from Morocco — **641.59**
The food of Morocco — **641.59**
Mediterranean clay pot cooking — **641.59**
The slow Mediterranean kitchen — **641.5**
Wolff, Christoph
Johann Sebastian Bach — **92**
Wolff, Daniel
How Lincoln learned to read — **920**
Wolff, Michael
The man who owns the news — **92**
Wolff, Tobias, 1945-
About
Wolff, T. This boy's life: a memoir — **92**
Wolffe, Richard
Andres, J. Tapas — **641.8**
Wolfson, Elissa
Audubon birdhouse book — **728**

Wolfson, Richard
Simply Einstein — **530.1**
Wollstonecraft, Mary, 1759-1797
About
Gordon, C. Romantic outlaws — **92**
Gordon, L. Vindication — **92**
Wolmar, Christian
Blood, iron, & gold — **385**
Wolpert, Stanley A.
Gandhi's passion — **954.03**
A new history of India — **954**
WOLVES
Busch, R. The wolf almanac — **599.77**
Lopez, B. H. Of wolves and men — **599.77**
McAllister, I. The last wild wolves — **599.77**
McNamee, T. The return of the wolf to Yellowstone — **333.95**
Smith, D. W. Decade of the wolf — **599.77**
WOLVES -- PSYCHOLOGY
Safina, C. Beyond words — **591.56**
Womack, John
Zapata and the Mexican Revolution — **972.08**
Womack, Kenneth, 1966-
(jt. auth) Baker, W. The facts on file companion to Shakespeare — **822.3**
Woman. Angier, N. — **612.6**
WOMAN *See* Women
The **woman** behind the New Deal. Downey, K. — **92**
WOMAN CIRCUS PERFORMERS -- UNITED STATES -- BIOGRAPHY
Jensen, D. Queen of the air — **791.3**
The **woman** I kept to myself. Alvarez, J. — **811**
The **woman** I wanted to be. Von Furstenberg, D. — **92**
A **woman** in Berlin. — **940.53**
A **woman** in charge. Bernstein, C. — **92**
Woman of Rome: a life of Elsa Morante. Tuck, L. — **92**
The **woman** warrior. Kingston, M. H. — **92**
The **woman** who watches over the world. Hogan, L. — **818**
The **woman** who would be king. Cooney, K. — **92**
The **woman** who wouldn't talk. McDougal, S. — **973.929**
A **woman** without a country. Boland, E. — **821**
WOMAN-MAN RELATIONSHIP *See* Man-woman relationship
Woman-powered farm. Levatino, A. — **630**
The **womanly** art of breastfeeding. — **649**
The **Womanly** art of breastfeeding. — **649**
Women. Leibovitz, A. — **779**
WOMEN
Adichie, C. N. We Should All Be Feminists **305.42**
Beauvoir, S. d. The second sex — **305.4**
Cordingly, D. Women sailors and sailors' women — **910.4**
Ephron, N. I feel bad about my neck — **814**

Link, M. J. The Drummond Girls 92
Mildon, E. The soul searcher's handbook 131
Wolf, N. The beauty myth 305.4

WOMEN -- AFGHANISTAN
Nordberg, J. The underground girls of Kabul 305.42
Nordland, R. The Lovers 958.104

WOMEN -- AFGHANISTAN -- SOCIAL CONDITIONS -- 21ST CENTURY
Badkhen, A. The world is a carpet 958.1

WOMEN -- ALCOHOL USE
Glaser, G. Her best-kept secret 362.292
Johnston, A. D. Drink 362.292
Schaap, R. Drinking with men 92

WOMEN -- ALCOHOL USE -- UNITED STATES
Glaser, G. Her best-kept secret 362.292

WOMEN -- ATTITUDES
Annis, B. Work with me 306.3

WOMEN -- BIOGRAPHY
Brownstein, C. Hunger Makes Me a Modern Girl 92
Connors, J. I Will Find You 364.15
Frieda, L. The Deadly Sisterhood 945
James, E. Paris in love 92
Schatz, K. Rad women worldwide 920.72
Sherr, L. Sally Ride 92

WOMEN -- BIOGRAPHY
See also Biography

WOMEN -- BIOGRAPHY -- DICTIONARIES
Adamson, L. G. Notable women in American history 016
Adamson, L. G. Notable women in world history 016
Kuhlman, E. A. A to Z of women in world history 920.003

WOMEN -- BIOGRAPHY -- ENCYCLOPEDIAS
Encyclopedia of women's autobiography 920.003
Women in world history 920.003

WOMEN -- BIOGRAPHY -- JUVENILE LITERATURE
Schatz, K. Rad women worldwide 920.72

WOMEN -- BOOKS AND READING -- UNITED STATES
Vnuk, R. Women's fiction 016

WOMEN -- CANADA
Tye, D. Baking as biography 92

WOMEN -- CHINA
Chang, J. Wild swans 951.05
Chang, L. T. Factory girls 331.4

WOMEN -- CIVIL RIGHTS *See* Women's rights

WOMEN -- CLOTHING *See* Women's clothing

WOMEN -- COMMUNICATION
Kramer, A. S. Breaking through bias 650.101

WOMEN -- CONGO (REPUBLIC)
Shannon, L. A thousand sisters 305.9

WOMEN -- CRIMES AGAINST -- DEVELOPING COUNTRIES

Kristof, N. D. Half the sky 362.83

WOMEN -- ECONOMIC CONDITIONS -- 21ST CENTURY
Rosin, H. The end of men 305.42

WOMEN -- EDUCATION
See also Education

WOMEN -- EMANCIPATION *See* Women's rights

WOMEN -- EMPLOYMENT
Sandberg, S. Lean in 658.4
Williams, J. What works for women at work 650.1

WOMEN -- EMPLOYMENT
See also Employment

WOMEN -- EMPLOYMENT -- HISTORY
Kessler-Harris, A. Out to work 331.4

WOMEN -- EMPLOYMENT -- UNITED STATES -- HISTORY -- 20TH CENTURY
Berebitsky, J. Sex and the office 331.4

WOMEN -- EMPLOYMENT -- UNITED STATES -- JUVENILE LITERATURE
McKenna, A. Nontraditional careers for women and men 331.702

WOMEN -- ENGLAND
Livingstone, N. The mistresses of Cliveden 942.009

WOMEN -- EUROPE
Tuchman, B. W. A distant mirror 944

WOMEN -- FICTION
Vnuk, R. Read on-- women's fiction 016

WOMEN -- FRANCE
Guiliano, M. French women don't get facelifts 613

WOMEN -- FRANCE -- HISTORY
Bocquet Kiki de Montparnasse 759.4

WOMEN -- FRANCE -- PARIS -- BIOGRAPHY
Anselmo, L. My (part-time) Paris life 944.361

WOMEN -- GERMANY -- BIOGRAPHY
Gortemaker, H. B. Eva Braun 92

WOMEN -- GREAT BRITAIN
Dennison, M. Behind the Mask 92
Moran, C. How to be a woman 92

WOMEN -- GREAT BRITAIN -- SOCIAL CONDITIONS -- HUMOR
Moran, C. How to be a woman 92

WOMEN -- HEALTH AND HYGIENE
Contreras, B. Strong curves 613.7
Guiliano, M. French women don't get facelifts 613
The kind mama 618.1
Nagoski, E. Come as you are 613.9
Northrup, C. Goddesses never age 613
Pagano, J. Strength training exercises for women 613.7
Pregnancy day by day 618.2
Schuler, L. Strong 613.7
Sears, W. The healthy pregnancy book 618.2
Streicher, L. F. The essential guide to hysterectomy 618.1
Thomas, M. The French beauty solution 646.7

Vonn, L. Strong Is the New Beautiful **613.042**

WOMEN -- HEALTH AND HYGIENE
See also Health; Hygiene

WOMEN -- HISTORY
Rosin, H. The end of men **305.42**
Schatz, K. Rad women worldwide **920.72**

WOMEN -- HISTORY
See also Feminism; History

WOMEN -- HISTORY -- ENCYCLOPEDIAS
Women in world history **920.003**

WOMEN -- HYGIENE *See* Women -- Health and hygiene

WOMEN -- IDENTITY
Von Furstenberg, D. The woman I wanted to be **92**

WOMEN -- IDENTITY
See also Identity (Psychology)

WOMEN -- IDENTITY -- POETRY
Sinclair, S. Cannibal **811.6**

WOMEN -- INDIA
Faleiro, S. Beautiful thing **792.7**

WOMEN -- INDIANA -- BIOGRAPHY
Thorpe, H. Soldier girls **956.704**

WOMEN -- IRAN
Ebadi, S. Until We Are Free **92**

WOMEN -- IRAN -- GRAPHIC NOVELS
Satrapi, M. Embroideries **741**

WOMEN -- IRELAND
Moran, R. Paid for **306.74**

WOMEN -- KANSAS
Stratton, J. L. Pioneer women **978.1**

WOMEN -- LAW AND LEGISLATION
Green, L. On Your Case **344**

WOMEN -- LIFE SKILLS GUIDES
Matlen, T. The queen of distraction **616.85**

WOMEN -- MENTAL HEALTH
See also Mental health; Women -- Health and hygiene

WOMEN -- MENTAL HEALTH -- POPULAR WORKS
Matlen, T. The queen of distraction **616.85**

WOMEN -- NEW JERSEY -- BIOGRAPHY
Hernández, D. A cup of water under my bed **920.009**

WOMEN -- NEW YORK (STATE) -- NEW YORK -- BIOGRAPHY
Hauser, B. Enter Helen **92**

WOMEN -- ORDINATION *See* Ordination of women

WOMEN -- PAKISTAN
Holstein, K. A Different Kind of Daughter **92**
Lamb, C. I am Malala **92**

WOMEN -- PERSONAL FINANCE
Pepper, C. The seven pearls of financial wisdom **332.024**
Tengler, N. The women's guide to successful investing **332.6**

WOMEN -- PHYSICAL FITNESS

Zeisler, A. Weapons of fitness **613.6**

WOMEN -- PHYSICAL FITNESS
See also Physical fitness; Women -- Health and hygiene

WOMEN -- POETRY
Clifton, L. The collected poems of Lucille Clifton 1965-2010 **811**

WOMEN -- POLITICAL ACTIVITY
Encyclopedia of women and American politics **973**

WOMEN -- POLITICAL ACTIVITY -- UNITED STATES -- HISTORY -- 19TH CENTURY
Roberts, C. Capital dames **793.7**

WOMEN -- PORTRAITS
Leibovitz, A. Women **779**

WOMEN -- PSYCHOLOGY
Gottman, J. The man's guide to women **155.3**
Mohr, T. Playing big **650.1**
Whitefield-Madrano, A. Face value **111.85**

WOMEN -- RELIGIOUS LIFE -- SOUTHERN STATES
Circling faith **200.8**

WOMEN -- ROME
Freisenbruch, A. Caesars' wives **937**

WOMEN -- SELF-DEFENSE *See* Self-defense for women

WOMEN -- SEXUAL BEHAVIOR
Angel, K. Unmastered **828**
Bergner, D. What Do Women Want? **305**
Nagoski, E. Come as you are **613.9**
Wolf, N. Vagina **305.42**

WOMEN -- SEXUAL BEHAVIOR -- PSYCHO-LOGICAL ASPECTS
Borich, B. J. Body geographic **818**

WOMEN -- SOCIAL CONDITIONS
Armstrong, J. K. Sexy feminism **305.42**
Hauser, B. Enter Helen **92**
Hernández, D. A cup of water under my bed **920.009**
MacColl, G. To marry an English Lord **974.7**
Ryckman, P. Stiletto network **331.4**
Sered, S. S. Can't catch a break **362.83**
Spar, D. L. Wonder Women **305.42**

WOMEN -- SOCIAL CONDITIONS
See also Social conditions

WOMEN -- SOCIAL CONDITIONS -- 21ST CENTURY
Rosin, H. The end of men **305.42**

WOMEN -- SOUTH AFRICA
Burge, K. The born frees **305.242**

WOMEN -- SOUTHERN STATES
Faust, D. G. Mothers of invention **973.7**

WOMEN -- SPORTS *See* Sports for women

WOMEN -- SUFFRAGE
Dudden, F. E. Fighting chance **324.6**
Ginzberg, L. D. Elizabeth Cady Stanton **92**
Goldsmith, B. Other powers **92**

WOMEN -- SUFFRAGE

See also Suffrage; Women's rights

WOMEN -- SUFFRAGE -- HISTORY
Ginzberg, L. D. Elizabeth Cady Stanton   92

WOMEN -- TENNESSEE -- OAK RIDGE -- HISTORY
Kiernan, D. The girls of atomic city   976.8

WOMEN -- TEXAS -- HOUSTON -- SOCIAL LIFE AND CUSTOMS -- 20TH CENTURY
Koppel, L. The Astronaut Wives Club   629.45

WOMEN -- TRAVEL
Baggett, J. The lost girls   910.4
Howell, G. Gertrude Bell   92
Wallach, J. Desert queen   956

WOMEN -- UNITED STATES
Clancy, T. The Clancys of Queens   974.7
Kaplan, C. Miss Anne in Harlem   700.92

WOMEN -- UNITED STATES -- BIOGRAPHY
Brower, K. A. First women   973.099
Gubar, S. Memoir of a debulked woman   616.99
Holt, N. Rise of the Rocket Girls   629.4
Mackrell, J. Flappers   920
Smith, C. B. The rules of inheritance   616.99

WOMEN -- UNITED STATES -- HISTORY
Abbott, K. Liar, Temptress, Soldier, Spy   973.7
MacColl, G. To marry an English Lord   974.7

WOMEN -- UNITED STATES -- HISTORY -- 19TH CENTURY
Roberts, C. Capital dames   793.7

WOMEN -- UNITED STATES -- HISTORY -- SOURCES
Grunwald, L. Women's letters   305.4
Sigerman, H. The Columbia documentary history of American women since 1941   305.4

WOMEN -- UNITED STATES -- INTELLECTUAL LIFE
Kaplan, A. Dreaming in French   944

WOMEN -- UNITED STATES -- INTERVIEWS
Schnall, M. What will it take to make a woman president?   305.4

WOMEN -- UNITED STATES -- SOCIAL CONDITIONS -- 18TH CENTURY
Lepore, J. Book of ages   92

WOMEN -- UNITED STATES -- SOCIAL CONDITIONS -- 19TH CENTURY
Berkin, C. Civil War wives   920

WOMEN -- UNITED STATES -- SOCIAL CONDITIONS -- 20TH CENTURY
Coontz, S. A strange stirring   305.42
May, E. T. America and the pill   363.9

WOMEN -- VOCATIONAL GUIDANCE
Sandberg, S. Lean in   658.4

WOMEN -- WASHINGTON (D.C.)
Roberts, C. Capital dames   793.7

WOMEN -- WASHINGTON (D.C.) -- BIOGRAPHY
Roberts, C. Capital dames   793.7

WOMEN ACTORS *See* Actresses

WOMEN AIR PILOTS
Butler, S. East to the dawn   629.13
Haynsworth, L. Amelia Earhart's daughters   629.13
Markham, B. West with the night   92
Winters, K. C. Amelia Earhart   92

WOMEN AIR PILOTS
See also Air pilots; Women

WOMEN AIR PILOTS -- AFRICA -- BIOGRAPHY
Markham, B. West with the night   92

WOMEN AIR PILOTS -- GREAT BRITAIN -- BIOGRAPHY
Markham, B. West with the night   92

WOMEN ALCOHOLICS
Johnston, A. D. Drink   362.292

WOMEN ALCOHOLICS -- REHABILITATION -- UNITED STATES
Glaser, G. Her best-kept secret   362.292

WOMEN ALCOHOLICS -- UNITED STATES -- BIOGRAPHY
Bingham, E. Irrepressible   306.76

WOMEN AND LITERATURE -- ENGLAND -- HISTORY -- 19TH CENTURY
Montillo, R. The lady and her monsters   823

WOMEN AND LITERATURE -- GREAT BRITAIN -- HISTORY
The history of British women's writing   820

WOMEN AND LITERATURE -- UNITED STATES -- HISTORY
Showalter, E. A jury of her peers   810

WOMEN ANTHROPOLOGISTS -- UNITED STATES -- BIOGRAPHY
Ransby, B. Eslanda   92
Women artists. Heller, N.   920

WOMEN ARTISTS
See also Artists; Women

WOMEN ARTISTS
Albers, P. Joan Mitchell   92
Farrington, L. E. Creating their own image   709
The female gaze   704
Heller, N. Women artists   920
Hoban, P. Alice Neel   92
Holladay, W. C. A museum of their own   704
Levin, G. Lee Krasner   92
Peacock, M. The paper garden   92

WOMEN ARTISTS -- DICTIONARIES
Contemporary women artists   920.003

WOMEN ARTISTS -- EXHIBITIONS
The female gaze   704

WOMEN ASTRONAUTS
Ackmann, M. The Mercury 13: the untold story of thirteen American women and the dream of space flight   629.45
Haynsworth, L. Amelia Earhart's daughters   629.13
Sherr, L. Sally Ride   92

WOMEN ASTRONAUTS
See also Astronauts; Women

WOMEN ATHLETES
Colton, L. Counting coup   **796.323**
Cox, L. Swimming to Antarctica   **92**
Mortimer, G. The great swim   **920**
Wambach, A. Forward   **92**

WOMEN ATHLETES
See also Athletes; Women

WOMEN ATHLETES -- BIOGRAPHY
Rousey, R. My fight / your fight   **92**

WOMEN ATHLETES -- UNITED STATES
Wade, B. Run the World   **796.42**

WOMEN AUTHORS
Angelou, M. Letter to my daughter   **92**
Angelou, M. I know why the caged bird sings   **92**
Briggs, J. Virginia Woolf: an inner life   **92**
Cleage, P. Things I Should Have Told My Daughter   **92**
Danticat, E. Brother, I'm dying   **92**
Danticat, E. Create dangerously   **92**
Dinnage, R. Alone! alone!: lives of some outsider women   **920**
Ephron, N. The Most of Nora Ephron   **814**
Fraser, K. Ornament and silence   **809**
Gaskell, E. C. The life of Charlotte Bronte   **92**
Gillespie, M. A. Maya Angelou   **92**
Gooch, B. Flannery   **92**
Gordon, L. Charlotte Bronte   **92**
Harman, C. Jane's fame   **92**
Heller, A. C. Ayn Rand and the world she made   **92**
Hirshey, G. Not pretty enough   **92**
A homemade life   **92**
Hooks, B. Belonging   **92**
Janowitz, T. Scream   **92**
Kumin, M. The Pawnbroker's Daughter   **92**
Lee, H. Virginia Woolf   **823**
Matteson, J. The lives of Margaret Fuller   **920**
Melton, G. D. Love warrior   **92**
Memories   **92**
Moser, B. Why this world   **92**
Nokes, D. Jane Austen   **823**
Oates, J. C. The Lost Landscape   **92**
Oates, J. C. The journal of Joyce Carol Oates: 1973-1982   **92**
Patchett, A. Truth & beauty   **92**
Pierpont, C. R. Passionate minds   **810**
Proulx, A. Bird cloud   **92**
Rice, A. Called out of darkness   **92**
Roiphe, A. R. Art and madness   **92**
Roiphe, A. R. Epilogue   **92**
Roiphe, K. Uncommon arrangements   **920**
Seymour, M. Mary Shelley   **92**
Shields, C. Jane Austen   **823**
Smith, L. Dimestore   **92**
Smith, P. M train   **92**

Sontag, S. Reborn   **92**
Souder, W. On a farther shore   **92**
Stannard, M. Muriel Spark   **92**
A story larger than my own   **810.9**
Thompson, L. The six   **92**
Tomalin, C. Jane Austen   **823**
Tuck, L. Woman of Rome: a life of Elsa Morante   **92**
Woolf, V. Moments of being   **823**

WOMEN AUTHORS
See also Authors; Women

WOMEN AUTHORS -- BIOGRAPHY
Franklin, R. Shirley Jackson   **92**
Kanigel, R. Eyes on the street   **92**
O'Brien, E. Country Girl   **92**
Paterson, K. Stories of my life   **92**
Strayed, C. Wild   **92**

WOMEN AUTHORS -- RELIGIOUS LIFE
Circling faith   **200.8**

WOMEN AUTHORS, AMERICAN -- 19TH CENTURY -- BIOGRAPHY
Cohen, L. All we know   **920.72**
Matteson, J. The lives of Margaret Fuller   **920**

WOMEN AUTHORS, AMERICAN -- 20TH CENTURY -- BIOGRAPHY
Pioneer girl   **92**

WOMEN AUTHORS, AMERICAN -- 21ST CENTURY -- BIOGRAPHY
Christensen, K. Blue plate special   **92**

WOMEN AUTHORS, AMERICAN -- BIOGRAPHY
Adams, M. B. Shaggy muses   **920**
Cleage, P. Things I Should Have Told My Daughter   **92**
James, E. Paris in love   **92**
Pierpont, C. R. Passionate minds   **810**

WOMEN AUTHORS, AMERICAN -- LITERARY COLLECTIONS
A story larger than my own   **810.9**

WOMEN AUTHORS, AMERICAN -- NEW YORK (STATE) -- NEW YORK -- BIOGRAPHY
Vincent, I. Dinner with Edward   **158.1**

WOMEN AUTHORS, ENGLISH -- 20TH CENTURY -- BIOGRAPHY
Thompson, L. The six   **92**

WOMEN AUTHORS, IRISH -- 20TH CENTURY -- BIOGRAPHY
O'Brien, E. Country Girl   **92**

WOMEN AUTHORS, RUSSIAN -- 20TH CENTURY -- BIOGRAPHY
Memories   **92**

WOMEN BASKETBALL PLAYERS -- OKLAHOMA -- BIOGRAPHY
Reeder, L. Dust bowl girls   **796.323**

WOMEN BRIDGE PLAYERS -- UNITED

STATES
Lerner, B. The bridge ladies   **92**

WOMEN CABINET OFFICERS -- UNITED STATES -- BIOGRAPHY
Rice, C. No higher honor   **327.73**

WOMEN CARTOGRAPHERS
Felt, H. Soundings   **526**

WOMEN CARTOGRAPHERS -- UNITED STATES -- BIOGRAPHY
Felt, H. Soundings   **526**

WOMEN CHEMISTS -- BIOGRAPHY
Emling, S. Marie Curie and her daughters **920**

WOMEN CHEMISTS -- FRANCE
Dry, S. Curie   **92**

WOMEN COMEDIANS
Burnett, C. In such good company   **791.45**

WOMEN COMPOSERS
The Norton/Grove dictionary of women composers   **780.92**

WOMEN COMPOSERS -- BIOGRAPHY
Porter, C. H. Five lives in music   **780.92**

WOMEN COMPOSERS -- DICTIONARIES
The Norton/Grove dictionary of women composers   **780.92**

WOMEN COMPUTER SCIENTISTS -- UNITED STATES -- BIOGRAPHY
Ping Fu Bend, not break   **92**

WOMEN CONCENTRATION CAMP INMATES -- GERMANY -- RAVENSBRÜCK
Helm, S. Ravensbruck   **940.53**

WOMEN CONCENTRATION CAMP INMATES --POLAND --OŚWIĘCIM --BIOGRAPHY.
Moorehead, C. A train in winter

WOMEN COOKS
Pouillon, N. My organic life   **92**

WOMEN COOKS -- SOVIET UNION -- BIOGRAPHY
Von Bremzen, A. Mastering the art of Soviet cooking   **641.59**

WOMEN COOKS -- UNITED STATES -- BIOGRAPHY
Pouillon, N. My organic life   **92**

WOMEN DANCERS -- BIOGRAPHY
Duncan, I. My life   **92**

WOMEN DRUG ADDICTS -- MASSACHU-SETTS -- BOSTON -- SOCIAL CONDITIONS
Sered, S. S. Can't catch a break   **362.83**
Women during the Civil War. Harper, J. E. **973.7**

WOMEN EMPLOYEES -- UNITED STATES -- HISTORY
Berebitsky, J. Sex and the office   **331.4**

WOMEN ENTERTAINERS -- GERMANY -- BI-OGRAPHY
Dietrich & Riefenstahl   **791.43**

WOMEN EXECUTIVES
Ryckman, P. Stiletto network   **331.4**

Tarr-Whelan, L. Women lead the way   **658.4**

WOMEN EXECUTIVES -- ENCYCLOPEDIAS
Krismann, C. Encyclopedia of American women in
business   **920.003**

WOMEN FARMERS
Levatino, A. Woman-powered farm   **630**

WOMEN FASHION DESIGNERS -- ENGLAND -- BIOGRAPHY
Cohen, L. All we know   **920.72**

WOMEN FASHION DESIGNERS -- UNITED STATES -- BIOGRAPHY
Tynan, T. Wear and tear   **92**
Von Furstenberg, D. The woman I wanted to be **92**

WOMEN GARDENERS -- UNITED STATES -- ANECDOTES
Kassinger, R. A Garden of Marvels   **580**

WOMEN GYNECOLOGISTS -- SOMALIA -- BIOGRAPHY
Abdi, H. Keeping hope alive   **92**

WOMEN HEROES -- FRANCE -- BIOGRAPHY
Castor, H. Joan of Arc   **92**

WOMEN HUMAN RIGHTS WORKERS -- SO-MALIA -- BIOGRAPHY
Abdi, H. Keeping hope alive   **92**

WOMEN IMMIGRANTS -- UNITED STATES -- BIOGRAPHY
Barrett, D. GI brides   **940.53**

WOMEN IN ART
Hughes, R. Goya   **760**

WOMEN IN ASTRONOMY -- MASSACHU-SETTS -- HISTORY
Sobel, D. The glass universe   **522.197**

WOMEN IN BUSINESS *See* Businesswomen

WOMEN IN CHRISTIANITY
Chaves, M. Ordaining women   **262**
Voices of early Christianity   **270.1**

WOMEN IN CHRISTIANITY
   See also Christianity; Women

WOMEN IN ECONOMIC DEVELOPMENT
Verveer, M. Fast forward   **650.1**

WOMEN IN ISLAM
   See also Islam; Women

WOMEN IN LITERATURE
Benfey, C. E. G. A summer of hummingbirds **920**
Donoghue, E. Inseparable   **809**
Showalter, E. A jury of her peers   **810**
Ulrich, L. Well-behaved women seldom make his-
tory   **305.4**

WOMEN IN LITERATURE -- UNITED STATES
Showalter, E. A jury of her peers   **810**

WOMEN IN MEDICINE
   See also Medical personnel; Women

WOMEN IN MOTION PICTURES
Corliss, R. Mom in the movies   **791.43**

WOMEN IN MOTION PICTURES
   See also Motion pictures

WOMEN IN POLITICS -- UNITED STATES
Norgren, J. Belva Lockwood — 92
Traister, R. Big girls don't cry — 324

WOMEN IN POLITICS -- UNITED STATES -- ENCYCLOPEDIAS
Encyclopedia of women and American politics 973

WOMEN IN POLITICS -- UNITED STATES -- HISTORY -- 18TH CENTURY
Holton, W. Abigail Adams — 92

Women in science. Ignotofsky, R. — 509.252

WOMEN IN TELEVISION BROADCASTING
See also Television broadcasting

WOMEN IN THE ARMED FORCES See Women in the military

WOMEN IN THE BIBLE
Murphy, C. The Word according to Eve — 220.8

WOMEN IN THE MILITARY
Lemmon, G. T. Ashley's war — 92
Thorpe, H. Soldier girls — 956.704

WOMEN IN THE MILITARY
See also Military personnel; Women

WOMEN IN THE PROFESSIONS
Ryckman, P. Stiletto network — 331.4
Verveer, M. Fast forward — 650.1

WOMEN IN THE WORKPLACE
Kramer, A. S. Breaking through bias — 650.101
Sandberg, S. Lean in — 658.4

Women in world history. — 920.003

WOMEN INTELLECTUALS -- BIOGRAPHY
Cohen, L. All we know — 920.72

WOMEN INVENTORS
Vare, E. A. Patently female — 609.2

WOMEN JOURNALISTS
Ciezadlo, A. Day of honey — 92
Connors, J. I Will Find You — 364.15
Hernández, D. A cup of water under my bed 920.009
Hoffman, C. Greetings from Utopia Park — 92
Iversen, K. Full body burden — 363.17
Journalistas — 808.8
Moaveni, A. Honeymoon in Tehran — 92
Norris, M. The grace of silence — 92
Povich, L. The good girls revolt — 331.4
Ross, L. Reporting always — 070.4
Sheehy, G. Daring — 92
Walters, B. Audition — 92
Weldon, M. Escape Points — 362.196
Weller, S. The News Sorority — 070.1

WOMEN JOURNALISTS -- BIOGRAPHY
Kelly, M. Settle for More — 791.45

WOMEN JOURNALISTS -- ENGLAND -- BIOGRAPHY
Moran, C. How to be a woman — 92

WOMEN JOURNALISTS -- NEW YORK (STATE) -- NEW YORK -- BIOGRAPHY
Hernández, D. A cup of water under my bed 920.009

WOMEN JOURNALISTS -- UNITED STATES

Povich, L. The good girls revolt — 331.4

WOMEN JOURNALISTS -- UNITED STATES -- BIOGRAPHY
O'Neill, Z. All strangers are kin — 910.917

WOMEN JUDGES
Hirshman, L. Sisters in law — 347.73

WOMEN JUDGES
See also Judges; Women

WOMEN JUDGES -- UNITED STATES -- BIOGRAPHY
Hirshman, L. Sisters in law — 347.73

WOMEN LAWYERS
Ebadi, S. Until We Are Free — 92
Slevin, P. Michelle Obama — 92

Women lead the way. Tarr-Whelan, L. — 658.4

WOMEN LEGISLATORS -- UNITED STATES -- BIOGRAPHY
Clinton, H. R. Living history — 92
Warren, E. A fighting chance — 92

WOMEN LEGISLATORS -- UNITED STATES -- ENCYCLOPEDIAS
Encyclopedia of women and American politics 973

WOMEN MATHEMATICIANS
Holt, N. Rise of the Rocket Girls — 629.4
Lee Shetterly, M. Hidden Figures — 510.92

WOMEN MATHEMATICIANS -- GREAT BRITAIN -- BIOGRAPHY
Essinger, J. Ada's algorithm — 92

WOMEN MATHEMATICIANS -- MASSACHUSETTS -- HISTORY
Sobel, D. The glass universe — 522.197

WOMEN MEDIUMS -- UNITED STATES -- BIOGRAPHY
Jaher, D. The witch of lime street — 92

WOMEN MOTION PICTURE PRODUCERS AND DIRECTORS -- GERMANY -- BIOGRAPHY
Dietrich & Riefenstahl — 791.43

WOMEN MUSICIANS
Weller, S. Girls like us — 920

WOMEN MUSICIANS -- BIOGRAPHY
Porter, C. H. Five lives in music — 780.92

Women of letters [series]
Wall, C. A. Women of the Harlem Renaissance 810
Women of the Harlem Renaissance. Wall, C. A. 810
Women of the pleasure quarters. Downer, L. 792.7
Women of vision. — 770.82

WOMEN PHILANTHROPISTS -- BIOGRAPHY
Von Furstenberg, D. The woman I wanted to be 92

WOMEN PHOTOGRAPHERS
Gordon, L. Dorothea Lange — 92
Women of vision — 770.82

WOMEN PHOTOGRAPHERS -- BIOGRAPHY
Lubow, A. Diane Arbus — 92

WOMEN PHOTOGRAPHERS -- UNITED STATES

All about Eve **770**

WOMEN PHOTOGRAPHERS -- UNITED STATES -- BIOGRAPHY

Addario, L. It's What I Do **92**

WOMEN PHYSICIANS

See also Physicians; Women

WOMEN PIONEERS -- UNITED STATES -- BIOGRAPHY

Pioneer girl **92**

WOMEN POETS

Gordon, C. Mistress Bradstreet **92**

Leavell, L. Holding on upside down **92**

Smith, P. Shoulda been Jimi Savannah **811**

A story larger than my own **810.9**

WOMEN POETS, AMERICAN -- BIOGRAPHY

Alexander, E. The light of the world **92**

Santamaria, A. Joy **92**

WOMEN POLITICAL ACTIVISTS

Encyclopedia of women and American politics **973**

Giddings, P. Ida: a sword among lions **92**

Scroggins, D. Wanted women **305.48**

Wintle, J. Perfect hostage **92**

WOMEN POLITICAL ACTIVISTS -- UNITED STATES

Schnall, M. What will it take to make a woman president? **305.4**

WOMEN POLITICIANS

Clinton, H. R. Hard choices **92**

Pelosi, N. Know your power **92**

Schnall, M. What will it take to make a woman president? **305.4**

WOMEN POLITICIANS

See also Politicians; Women -- Political activity

WOMEN POLITICIANS -- GREAT BRITAIN -- BIOGRAPHY

Foreman, A. Georgiana, Duchess of Devonshire **941.07**

WOMEN PRESIDENTIAL CANDIDATES -- UNITED STATES

Schnall, M. What will it take to make a woman president? **305.4**

WOMEN PRISONERS -- GERMANY -- RAVENSBRÜCK

Helm, S. Ravensbruck **940.53**

WOMEN PRIVATE INVESTIGATORS -- PRESS COVERAGE -- CALIFORNIA

Crooks, P. The setup **363.28**

WOMEN PSYCHOTHERAPISTS -- UNITED STATES -- BIOGRAPHY

Smith, C. B. The rules of inheritance **616.99**

WOMEN ROCK MUSICIANS

Albertine, V. Clothes, Clothes, Clothes. Music, Music, Music. Boys, Boys, Boys **92**

Lauper, C. Cyndi Lauper **92**

WOMEN ROCK MUSICIANS -- UNITED

STATES -- BIOGRAPHY

Brownstein, C. Hunger Makes Me a Modern Girl **92**

Smith, P. M train **92**

WOMEN RUNNERS -- UNITED STATES -- BIOGRAPHY

Heminsley, A. Running like a girl **796.420**

Women sailors and sailors' women. Cordingly, D. **910.4**

WOMEN SCIENTISTS

Crane, K. Sea legs **92**

Dry, S. Curie **92**

Goodall, J. Beyond innocence **92**

Ignotofsky, R. Women in science **509.252**

Lowman, M. Life in the treetops **577.34**

Peterson, D. Jane Goodall: the woman who redefined man **92**

Reynolds, M. D. American women scientists **509**

Ridley, G. The discovery of Jeanne Baret **92**

WOMEN SCIENTISTS -- FAMILY RELATIONSHIPS

Emling, S. Marie Curie and her daughters **920**

WOMEN SHAMANS -- BIOGRAPHY

Henion, L. A. Phenomenal **910.4**

WOMEN SINGERS -- UNITED STATES -- BIOGRAPHY

Brownstein, C. Hunger Makes Me a Modern Girl **92**

Cole, N. Angel on my shoulder **92**

WOMEN SLAVES -- NORTH CAROLINA -- ORANGE COUNTY -- BIOGRAPHY

Nathans, S. To free a family **306.3**

WOMEN SOCCER PLAYERS -- UNITED STATES -- BIOGRAPHY

Coffey, W. When nobody was watching **796.334**

Wambach, A. Forward **92**

WOMEN SOCIAL REFORMERS -- UNITED STATES -- BIOGRAPHY

Bell-Scott, P. The firebrand and the First Lady **92**

WOMEN SOLDIERS

Blanton, D. They fought like demons **973.7**

De Pauw, L. G. Battle cries and lullabies **355**

Leonard, E. D. All the daring of the soldier **973.7**

Young, A. F. Masquerade: the life and times of Deborah Sampson, Continental soldier **92**

WOMEN SOLDIERS -- BIOGRAPHY -- DICTIONARIES

Amazons to fighter pilots **355**

WOMEN SOLDIERS -- FRANCE -- BIOGRAPHY

Castor, H. Joan of Arc **92**

WOMEN SOLDIERS -- UNITED STATES -- BIOGRAPHY

Thorpe, H. Soldier girls **956.704**

WOMEN SPIES

Blum, H. The Last Goodnight **940.54**

**WOMEN SPIES -- GREAT BRITAIN -- BIOG-
RAPHY**
Mulley, C. The Spy Who Loved   **940.54**
**WOMEN SPIES -- UNITED STATES -- BIOG-
RAPHY**
Blum, H. The Last Goodnight   **940.54**
Women still at work. Fideler, E. F.   **331.4**
**WOMEN SWIMMERS -- CANADA -- BIOGRA-
PHY**
Shapton, L. Swimming studies   **797.2**
**WOMEN SWIMMERS -- UNITED STATES --
BIOGRAPHY**
Beard, A. In the water they can't see you cry **797.2**
**WOMEN VETERANS -- UNITED STATES -- BI-
OGRAPHY**
Thorpe, H. Soldier girls   **956.704**
WOMEN WEAVERS -- AFGHANISTAN
Badkhen, A. The world is a carpet   **958.1**
WOMEN'S CLOTHING
Cheetham, K. Singer perfect plus   **646.2**
Hirsch, G. A modern guide to sportswear styles of
  the 1940s and 1950s   **646.4**
Ito, M. Simply sewn   **646.4**
Linett, A. The cool factor   **746.92**
Moses, S. The art of dressing curves **746.92**
Stevenson, N. J. Fashion   **391.009**
WOMEN'S CLOTHING
  See also Clothing and dress
Women's fiction. Vnuk, R.   **016**
WOMEN'S FRIENDSHIP *See* Female friendship
The **women's** guide to successful investing. Ten-
gler, N.   **332.6**
Women's letters. Grunwald, L.   **305.4**
WOMEN'S LIBERATION MOVEMENT *See*
  Women's movement
WOMEN'S MOVEMENT
Brownmiller, S. In our time   **305.42**
Mackrell, J. Flappers   **920**
Poems from the women's movement   **811**
The riot grrrl collection   **781.64**
Valenti, J. Full Frontal Feminism   **305.42**
WOMEN'S MOVEMENT
  See also Women -- Social conditions; Wom-
  en's rights
WOMEN'S RIGHTS
Adichie, C. N. We Should All Be Feminists **305.42**
American Civil Liberties Union The rights of
  women   **346.01**
Baker, J. H. Margaret Sanger   **92**
Sigerman, H. The Columbia documentary history
  of American women since 1941   **305.4**
Steinem, G. My life on the road   **92**
Strebeigh, F. Equal   **342**
The unfinished revolution   **305.42**
WOMEN'S RIGHTS
  See also Civil rights; Sex discrimination

**WOMEN'S RIGHTS -- DEVELOPING COUN-
TRIES**
Kristof, N. D. Half the sky   **362.83**
WOMEN'S SELF-DEFENSE *See* Self-defense for
women
WOMEN'S STUDIES
  See also Education
WOMEN, BLACK *See* Black women
WOMEN-MEN RELATIONSHIP *See* Man-wom-
an relationship
WOMEN-OWNED BUSINESS ENTERPRISES
Pimsleur, J. Million Dollar Women   **658.4**
WOMENS' CLOTHING
Linett, A. The cool factor   **746.92**
The **wonder** trail. Hely, S.   **917.28**
**WONDER WOMAN (FICTIONAL CHARAC-
TER)**
  See also Fictional characters; Superheroes
Wonder Woman (Fictional character)
                    About
Lepore, J. The Secret History of Wonder Wom-
an   **741.5**
**WONDER WOMAN (FICTITIOUS CHARAC-
TER)**
Lepore, J. The Secret History of Wonder Wom-
an   **741.5**
Wonder Women. Spar, D. L.   **305.42**
The **wonderful** future that never was. Popular me-
chanics magazine.   **609**
Wonderfully wordless. Martin, W. P. **011.62**
WONDERS *See* Curiosities and wonders
Wonders of the world [series]
Hill, R. Stonehenge   **936.2**
Wong, Kate
Johanson, D. C. Lucy's legacy   **569.9**
Wong, Lee Anne
Dumplings All Day Wong   **641.59**
Wong, Stephen
Smithsonian baseball   **796**
Woo, Ilyon
The great divorce   **92**
WOOD
The Encyclopedia of wood   **674**
Hoadley, R. B. Understanding wood   **684**
Norwegian wood   **634.9**
WOOD
  See also Building materials; Forest products;
  Fuel; Trees
WOOD -- ENCYCLOPEDIAS
The Encyclopedia of wood   **674**
WOOD BLOCK PRINTING *See* Wood engraving;
Woodcuts
WOOD CARVING
  See also Carving (Decorative arts); Decora-
  tion and ornament; Woodwork
WOOD ENGRAVING

See also Engraving

The **Wood** Fire Handbook. Thurkettle, V.   **697.1**

Wood, Allen W.
  (ed) Kant, I. Basic writings of Kant   **193**

Wood, Ghislaine
  (ed) Art deco 1910-1939   **709.04**

Wood, Gordon S., 1933-
  Empire of liberty   **973.4**
  The radicalism of the American Revolution   **973.3**

Wood, Grant, 1891-1942
         About
  Biel, S. American Gothic   **759.13**
  Evans, R. T. Grant Wood   **92**

Wood, Ira
  Piercy, M. So you want to write   **808.3**

Wood, James
  How fiction works   **808.3**

Wood, Jennifer
  Refined knits   **746.432**

Wood, Levison
  Walking the Nile   **916.2**

Wood, Michael
  In search of the Trojan War   **939**

Wood, Roger
  (jt. auth) Bradley, A. House of hits   **781.64**

Wood, Sherri Lynn
  Improv handbook for modern quilters   **746.46**

Wood, Stephen M.
  Apples to cider   **663**

Woodard, Colin
  American nations   **970.004**

WOODCUT ARTISTS
  Uglow, J. S. Nature's engraver   **92**
Wooden. Davis, S.   **92**

WOODEN TOY MAKING
  See also Toy making; Woodwork

Wooden, John, 1910-2010
         About
  Davis, S. Wooden   **92**

Woodford, Chris
  Atoms Under the Floorboards   **502**

Woodger, Elin
  Encyclopedia of the Lewis and Clark Expedition   **917**

Woodhouse, Violet
  Divorce & money   **346.01**

Woodhull, Victoria C., 1838-1927
         About
  Goldsmith, B. Other powers   **92**

WOODLAND GARDEN PLANTS
  Wiley, K. Designing and planting a woodland garden   **635.9**

Woodland knits. Dosen, S.   **746.43**

WOODPECKERS
  Gallagher, T. Imperial Dreams   **598.7**
  Gorman, G. Woodpeckers of the World   **598.7**

Shunk, S. A. Peterson Reference Guide to Woodpeckers of North America   **598.7**
Woodpeckers of the World. Gorman, G.   **598.7**

Woodress, James Leslie
  Willa Cather   **92**

Woodring, Carl
  (ed) The Columbia anthology of British poetry **821**

Woodrow Wilson. Brands, H. W.   **92**
Woodrow Wilson. Cooper, J. M.   **92**

WOODS *See* Forests and forestry; Lumber and lumbering; Wood

Woods, Randall B.
  Prisoners of hope   **973.923**
  Shadow warrior   **92**

Woods, Richard
  (ed) The Bloomsbury Guide to Christian Spirituality   **270**

Woods, Tiger, 1975-
         About
  Callahan, T. In search of Tiger   **92**
  Haney, H. The big miss   **796.352**

WOODSTOCK FESTIVAL, 1969
  Lang, M. The road to Woodstock   **781.66**

Woodstra, Chris
  (ed) All music guide to classical music   **016**

Woodward, Bill
  Prague winter   **943.71**

Woodward, Bob, 1943-
  All the president's men   **973.924**
  The commanders   **973.928**
  The final days   **973.924**
  Maestro: Greenspan's Fed and the American boom   **331.1**
  Plan of attack   **956.7**
  Shadow   **973.92**
  State of denial   **973.931**

Woodward, C. Vann
  The strange career of Jim Crow   **305.8**

Woodward, David R.
  World War I almanac   **940.3**

Woodward, Jeannette
  The transformed library   **020**

Woodward, Kenneth L.
  The book of miracles   **231.7**
  Making saints   **235**

WOODWORK
  Abram, N. Measure twice, cut once   **684**
  Hoadley, R. B. Understanding wood   **684**
  Huey, G. D. Shaker furniture projects   **684**
  Kelsey, J. Woodworking   **684**
  Warner, P. The router book   **684**
  Wolfson, E. Audubon birdhouse book   **728**

WOODWORK
  See also Architecture -- Details; Decorative arts; Wood

WOODWORK -- AMATEURS' MANUALS

The complete outdoor builder **690**
White, A. The handbuilt home **684.1**
Woodworking. Kelsey, J. **684**
WOODWORKING MACHINERY
    See also Machinery
Woodworth, Steven E.
Atlas of the Civil War **973.7**
Sherman **92**
Woody Allen on Woody Allen. Allen, W. **791.43**
Woody Guthrie. Klein, J. **92**
WOOL
Callahan, G. Hand dyeing yarn and fleece **746.6**
Ekarius, C. The field guide to fleece **677**
WOOL
    See also Animal products; Fabrics; Fibers
Wooldridge, Adrian
Masters of management **658**
Micklethwait, J. The company **338.7**
Woolf, Greg
(ed) The Cambridge illustrated history of the Roman world **937**
Woolf, Leonard, 1880-1969
    About
Glendinning, V. Leonard Woolf **92**
Woolf, Virginia, 1882-1941
A moment's liberty: the shorter diary **92**
Moments of being **823**
The Virginia Woolf reader **828**
    About
Adams, M. B. Shaggy muses **920**
Bloom, H. The Western canon **809**
Briggs, J. Virginia Woolf: an inner life **92**
Fraser, K. Ornament and silence **809**
Lee, H. Virginia Woolf **823**
Lee, H. Virginia Woolf's nose **820**
Ulrich, L. Well-behaved women seldom make history **305.4**
Woolf, V. A moment's liberty: the shorter diary **92**
Woolf, V. Moments of being **823**
Woolhouse, R. S.
(ed) Locke, J. An essay concerning human understanding **121**
Woolley, David
(ed) Swift, J. A tale of a tub, and other work **823**
Woolley, John T.
(ed) The presidency A to Z **973.09**
Woolman, John, 1720-1772
    About
Slaughter, T. P. The beautiful soul of John Woolman, apostle of abolition **92**
Wooster, Robert
(ed) Encyclopedia of Native American wars and warfare **970.004**
Wootton, David
The Invention of Science **509**
The **Word** according to Eve. Murphy, C. **220.8**

WORD BOOKS *See* Picture dictionaries
The **word** detective. Simpson, J. **423.092**
WORD GAMES
    See also Games; Literary recreations
Word histories and mysteries. **422**
WORD PROBLEMS (MATHEMATICS)
    See also Mathematics
WORD RECOGNITION
    See also Reading; Vocabulary
WORD SKILLS
    See also Reading
Worden, Alfred M., 1932-
    About
Worden, A. Falling to Earth **92**
Worden, Minky
(ed) The unfinished revolution **305.42**
The **words.** Sartre, J. P. **92**
WORDS *See* Vocabulary; Word skills
Words and rules. Pinker, S. **401**
Words for the hour. **811**
Words to rhyme with. Espy, W. R. **423**
Words Without Music. Glass, P. **92**
WORDS, NEW *See* New words
WORDS, OBSCENE
Nunberg, G. The ascent of the A-word **427**
Wordsworth, Dorothy, 1771-1855
    About
Wilson, F. The ballad of Dorothy Wordsworth **92**
Wordsworth, William
Selected poetry of William Wordsworth **821**
    About
Bloom, H. The Western canon **809**
Johnston, K. R. The hidden Wordsworth **821**
Wilson, F. The ballad of Dorothy Wordsworth **92**
The **wordy** shipmates. Vowell, S. **974**
The **work.** Moore, W. **92**
WORK
Crawford, M. B. Shop class as soulcraft **331**
De Botton, A. The pleasures and sorrows of work **331**
Shulman, B. The betrayal of work **331.2**
Terkel, S. Working **331.2**
WORK -- SOCIAL ASPECTS
De Botton, A. The pleasures and sorrows of work **331**
WORK AND FAMILY
    See also Family; Work
WORK ENVIRONMENT
Annis, B. Work with me **306.3**
Chapman, B. Everybody matters **658.4**
Williams, J. What works for women at work **650.1**
WORK ENVIRONMENT
    See also Environment; Work
WORK ETHIC
Manage your day-to-day **153.4**
WORK ETHIC

See also Ethics; Work

WORK GROUPS *See* Teams in the workplace

The **Work** of Charles and Ray Eames. Albrecht, D. **745.4**

WORK PLACES *See* Work environment

Work rules! **658.4**

Work rules! Bock, L. **658.4**

WORK SATISFACTION *See* Job satisfaction

Work songs. Gioia, T. **782.42**

WORK TEAMS *See* Teams in the workplace

Work with me. Annis, B. **306.3**

The **work-at-home** sourcebook. Arden, L. **338.7**

WORK-LIFE BALANCE

Manage your day-to-day **153.4**

Verveer, M. Fast forward **650.1**

Work. Pump. Repeat. Shortall, J. **649.33**

WORKAHOLISM

See also Compulsive behavior

The **workbench** guide to jewelry techniques. Young, A. **739.27**

WORKERS *See* Employees; Labor; Working class

WORKERS' COMPENSATION

See also Accident insurance; Health insurance; Social security

Working. Terkel, S. **331.2**

WORKING ANIMALS

See also Animals; Domestic animals; Economic zoology

WORKING ANIMALS -- HISTORY

Fagan, B. The intimate bond **591.5**

WORKING AT HOME *See* Home-based business; Telecommuting

WORKING CHILDREN *See* Child labor

WORKING CLASS

Clancy, T. The Clancys of Queens **974.7**

Dubofsky, M. Labor in America **331.8**

Labor rising **331.88**

Murolo, P. From the folks who brought you the weekend **331**

Murray, C. Coming apart **305.8**

Vance, J. D. Hillbilly elegy **92**

WORKING CLASS

See also Social classes

WORKING CLASS -- ECONOMIC ASPECTS -- UNITED STATES

Carbone, J. Marriage markets **306.85**

WORKING CLASS -- FRANCE -- PARIS -- HISTORY

Sante, L. The other Paris **944**

WORKING CLASS -- UNITED STATES -- BIOGRAPHY

Laskas, J. M. Hidden America **305.5**

WORKING CLASS -- UNITED STATES -- ECONOMIC CONDITIONS -- 21ST CENTURY

Barlett, D. L. The betrayal of the American dream **330.973**

WORKING CLASS -- UNITED STATES -- HISTORY

Labor rising **331.88**

Murolo, P. From the folks who brought you the weekend **331**

WORKING CLASS AFRICAN AMERICANS

Hobbs, J. The short and tragic life of Robert Peace **92**

WORKING CLASS FAMILIES -- RUSSIA (FEDERATION) -- OZËRSK (CHELIABINSKAIA OBLAST) -- HISTORY -- 20TH CENTURY

Brown, K. Plutopia **363.17**

WORKING DOGS

Orlean, S. Rin Tin Tin **636.7**

Warren, C. What the dog knows **636.7**

WORKING DOGS

See also Dogs; Working animals

WORKING ENVIRONMENT *See* Work environment

Working for yourself. Fishman, S. **343**

Working in America. Reef, C. **305**

WORKING MOTHERS

Shortall, J. Work. Pump. Repeat. **649.33**

Sweeney, J. If it's not one thing, it's your mother **362.734**

WORKING MOTHERS

See also Mothers; Women -- Employment

Working stiff. Mitchell, T. J. **614**

WORKING WOMEN *See* Women -- Employment

Workman, Katie

Dinner solved! **641.5**

The mom 100 cookbook **641.5**

WORKPLACE ENVIRONMENT *See* Work environment

WORKSITE ENVIRONMENT *See* Work environment

The **World.** **910.2**

WORLD *See* Earth

The **World** Almanac and Book of Facts 2015. **030**

A **world** at arms. Weinberg, G. L. **940.53**

The **world** atlas of beer. Beaumont, S. **641.2**

The **world** atlas of coffee. Hoffmann, J. **641.3**

World atlas of great apes and their conservation. **599.8**

The **World** Atlas of Whisky. Broom, D. **641.2**

The **World** Atlas of Whisky.

World authors, 1950-1970. Wakeman, J. **920.003**

World authors, 1970-1975. Wakeman, J. **920.003**

World authors, 1975-1980. Colby, V. **920.003**

World authors, 1980-1985. Colby, V. **809**

World authors, 1985-1990. Colby, V. **809**

World authors, 1990-1995. Thompson, C. **809**

World authors, 1995-2000. Thompson, C. **809**

World authors, 2000-2005. Rich, M. **920.003**

The **World** Beyond Your Head. Crawford, M. B. **155.2**

The **World** Book Encyclopedia.   **031**

World cheese book.   **641.3**

WORLD CUP (SOCCER)

God Is Round   **796.334**

Honigstein, R. Das Reboot   **796.334**

Vecsey, G. Eight world cups   **796.334**

WORLD CUP (SOCCER)

See also Soccer; Sports tournaments

WORLD ECONOMICS *See* Commercial geography; Commercial policy; Economic conditions; International competition

The **World** Encyclopedia of Flags. Znamierowski, A.   **929.9**

World energy crisis. Newton, D. E.   **333.79**

World explorers and discoverers.   **920.003**

World folklore for storytellers.   **398**

World Heritage sites.   **910.2**

WORLD HISTORY

Brown, C. S. A big history   **909**

Frankopan, P. The Silk Roads   **909**

Gibson, C. Empire's Crossroads   **972.9**

History   **909**

The history book   **909**

History of the world in 1,000 objects   **909**

Knauer, K. TIME History's Greatest Images **909.82**

MacGregor, N. A history of the world in 100 objects   **930.1**

McKillop, A. B. The spinster & the prophet **941.08**

National Geographic concise history of the world   **909**

National Geographic concise history of world religions   **200**

National Geographic Society (U.S.) National Geographic visual history of the world   **902.2**

The Oxford history of the twentieth century **909.82**

Pagden, A. Peoples and empires   **909**

Roberts, J. M. The new history of the world   **909**

Solomon, S. Water   **553.7**

Standage, T. A history of the world in 6 glasses   **394.1**

Watson, P. The great divide   **909**

WORLD HISTORY

See also History

WORLD HISTORY -- 14TH CENTURY

Tuchman, B. W. A distant mirror   **944**

WORLD HISTORY -- 14TH CENTURY

See also Middle Ages

WORLD HISTORY -- 15TH CENTURY

Cliff, N. Holy war   **909**

WORLD HISTORY -- 15TH CENTURY

See also Middle Ages

WORLD HISTORY -- 16TH CENTURY

Great events from history, The Renaissance & early modern era, 1454-1600   **909**

WORLD HISTORY -- 17TH CENTURY

Parker, G. Global crisis   **909**

WORLD HISTORY -- 18TH CENTURY

Craske, M. Art in Europe, 1700-1830   **709.03**

Great events from history, The 18th century, 1701-1800   **909.7**

Powell, J. Great lives from history, The 18th century, 1701-1800   **920.003**

WORLD HISTORY -- 1945-

Buruma, I. Year zero   **940.53**

WORLD HISTORY -- 19TH CENTURY

Emmerson, C. 1913   **909.82**

WORLD HISTORY -- 20TH CENTURY

Bohemians, bootleggers, flappers, and swells **810.8**

Laskin, D. The Family   **92**

Lukacs, J. A short history of the twentieth century   **909.82**

Sebestyen, V. 1946   **909.82**

WORLD HISTORY -- 20TH CENTURY -- PICTORIAL WORKS

Life: World War 2   **779**

WORLD HISTORY -- 21ST CENTURY

Gore, A. The future   **303.4**

WORLD HISTORY -- PICTORIAL WORKS

History   **909**

WORLD HISTORY -- SOURCES

History of the world in 1,000 objects   **909**

The **world** history of animation. Cavalier, S. **791.43**

The **world** in 2050. Smith, L. C.   **304.2**

The **world** is a carpet. Badkhen, A.   **958.1**

The **World** Is an Apple.   **759.4**

The **world** is blue. Earle, S. A.   **551.46**

The **World** Is Moving Around Me.   **972.94**

The **world** is on fire. Tevis, J.   **814**

The **world** is what it is. French, P.   **92**

A **world** lit only by fire. Manchester, W.   **940.2**

WORLD MAPS

Lester, T. The fourth part of the world   **912**

WORLD MUSIC

See also Folk music

The **world** must know. Berenbaum, M.   **940.53**

World ocean census. Crist, D. T.   **578.7**

World of art [series]

Boardman, J. Greek art   **709.3**

National Gallery of Art (U.S.) National Gallery of Art   **708**

Schoeser, M. World textiles: a concise history   **677**

Tregear, M. Chinese art   **709**

The **World** of Birds. Elphick, J.   **598**

The **world** of Count Basie. Dance, S.   **920**

The **world** of Edward Gorey. Ross, C.   **700.92**

The **world** of Jewish cooking. Marks, G.   **641.5**

World of made and unmade. Mead, J.   **811.54**

The **world** of Samuel Beckett, 1906-1946. Gordon, L. G.   **848**

World of sociology.   **301**

World of the sagas [series]

The Sagas of Icelanders   **839**

The **world** of trees. Johnson, H.   **582.16**

A **world** on fire. Foreman, A.   **973.7**

The **World** on Sunday. Baker, N.   **071**

World Order. Kissinger, H.   **327**

WORLD ORDER *See* International relations

World philosophers and their works.   **109**

World poetry.   **808.81**

WORLD POLITICS

  Kissinger, H. World Order   **327**

  Reynolds, D. Summits   **909.82**

  Von Tunzelmann, A. Blood and Sand   **973.92**

  Yergin, D. The prize   **338.2**

WORLD POLITICS

  See also Political science

WORLD POLITICS -- 1919-1932

  Tooze, A. The deluge   **940.3**

  Walsh, M. Bitter freedom   **941.508**

WORLD POLITICS -- 1945-

  Buruma, I. Year zero   **940.53**

WORLD POLITICS -- 1945- -- ENCYCLOPE-DIAS

  Encyclopedia of conflicts since World War II **909.82**

  Encyclopedia of the Cold War   **909.82**

WORLD POLITICS -- 1945-1955

  Dobbs, M. Six months in 1945   **940.53**

  Gordin, M. D. Red cloud at dawn   **355**

WORLD POLITICS -- 1945-1989

  Service, R. The End of the Cold War, 1985-1991   **909.82**

WORLD POLITICS -- 1945-1989

  Gaddis, J. L. George F. Kennan   **327**

WORLD POLITICS -- 1945-1991

  Costigliola, F. Roosevelt's lost alliances   **940.53**

  Ostrovsky, A. The Invention of Russia   **947.086**

  Sebestyen, V. 1946   **909.82**

WORLD POLITICS -- 1945-1991 -- ENCYCLO-PEDIAS

  Cold War   **909.82**

WORLD POLITICS -- 1965-

  Gorbachev, M. On my country and the world   **947.085**

  Huntington, S. P. The clash of civilizations and the remaking of world order   **909.82**

WORLD POLITICS -- 1989-

  Annan, K. A. Interventions   **341.23**

  Junger, S. Fire   **909.82**

WORLD POLITICS -- 1991-

  Brzezinski, Z. Strategic vision   **327.1**

WORLD POLITICS -- 20TH CENTURY

  Zinn, H. The historic unfullfilled promise **973.924**

WORLD POLITICS -- 21ST CENTURY

  Eichenwald, K. 500 days   **973.931**

  Elshtain, J. B. Just war against terror   **363.32**

  Kissinger, H. World Order   **327**

  Langewiesche, W. The atomic bazaar   **355**

  Ramo, J. C. The age of the unthinkable   **973.931**

WORLD POLITICS -- 21ST CENTURY -- FORE-CASTING

  Brzezinski, Z. Strategic vision   **327.1**

WORLD POLITICS, 1933-1945

  Katznelson, I. Fear itself   **973.917**

The **World** reacts to the Holocaust.   **940.53**

WORLD RECORDS

  Black Firsts: 4,000 Ground-breaking and Pioneer-ing Historical Events   **920**

  Terra Maxima   **902.2**

WORLD RECORDS

  See also Curiosities and wonders

WORLD RECORDS -- PERIODICALS

  Guinness world records 2015   **031**

WORLD RECORDS -- UNITED STATES -- MIS-CELLANEA

  Black firsts   **920**

World religions. Bowker, J.   **200**

WORLD SERIES (BASEBALL)

  See also Baseball; Sports tournaments

World spice at home. Bevill, A.   **641.6**

World textiles: a concise history. Schoeser, M.   **677**

The **world** that never was. Butterworth, A.   **335**

WORLD TRADE CENTER (NEW YORK, N.Y.)

  Dwyer, J. 102 minutes   **974.7**

  Friend, D. Watching the world change   **974.7**

  Langewiesche, W. American ground, unbuilding the World Trade Center   **974.7**

  Lutnick, H. On top of the world   **332.6**

  Smith, D. Report from ground zero   **363.34**

WORLD TRADE CENTER (NEW YORK, N.Y.) TERRORIST ATTACK, 2001 *See* September 11 terrorist attacks, 2001

WORLD TRADE CENTER TERRORIST AT-TACK, 2001

  Halberstam, D. Firehouse   **363.34**

  Magnum Photos, I. New York September 11   **770**

World War I.   **940.3**

WORLD WAR I *See* World War, 1914-1918

World War I almanac. Woodward, D. R.   **940.3**

World War I: the African Front. Paice, E.   **940.4**

World   War II.

WORLD WAR II *See* World War, 1939-1945

World War II.   **940.54**

World War II.   **940.53**

World War II writings. Liebling, A. J.   **940.54**

WORLD WAR III

  See also War; World politics

World War One. Stone, N.   **940.3**

WORLD WAR, 1914-1918

  Audoin-Rouzeau, S. 14-18, understanding the Great War   **940.3**

  Barr, J. A line in the sand   **956**

  Burg, D. F. Almanac of World War I   **940.3**

  Clay, C. King, Kaiser, Tsar   **920**

  Competing voices from the Russian Revolu-

tion   **947.084**
Downing, T. Secret Warriors   **940.4**
Dyer, G. The missing of the Somme   **940.4**
Gilbert, M. The First World War   **940.3**
Hughes-Wilson, J. The First World War in 100 objects   **940.3**
Jeffery, K. 1916   **909.82**
Kershaw, I. To Hell and Back   **940.5**
Kissinger, H. Diplomacy   **327.2**
McMeekin, S. The Berlin-Baghdad express   **940.3**
Neiberg, M. Fighting the Great War   **940.4**
Preston, D. A higher form of killing   **940.4**
Rehnquist, W. H. All the laws but one   **342**
Sacco, J. The Great War   **940.4**
Stone, N. World War One   **940.3**
Strachan, H. The First World War   **940.3**
Tuchman, B. W. The guns of August   **940.3**
The United States in the First World War   **940.3**
Walker, W. T. Betrayal at Little Gibraltar   **940.436**
Wawro, G. A mad catastrophe   **940.4**
Weber, T. Hitler's first war   **940.4**
Woodward, D. R. World War I almanac   **940.3**
World War I   **940.3**
WORLD WAR, 1914-1918
    See also Europe -- History -- 1871-1918; World history -- 20th century; World politics
WORLD WAR, 1914-1918 -- AERIAL OPERATIONS
Flood, C. B. First to Fly
Hamilton-Paterson, J. Marked for death   **940.44**
Hynes, S. The unsubstantial air   **940.4**
WORLD WAR, 1914-1918 -- ARMENIA
MacKeen, D. A. The hundred-year walk   **92**
WORLD WAR, 1914-1918 -- BIOGRAPHY
Hollis, M. Now all roads lead to France   **821**
WORLD WAR, 1914-1918 -- CAMPAIGNS
D'Este, C. Warlord   **92**
Eisenhower, J. S. D. Yanks: the epic story of the American Army in World War I   **940.4**
Mosier, J. The myth of the Great War   **940.4**
Ousby, I. The road to Verdun   **940.4**
Weber, T. Hitler's first war   **940.4**
WORLD WAR, 1914-1918 -- CAMPAIGNS -- ARAB COUNTRIES
Sattin, A. The Young T. E. Lawrence   **92**
WORLD WAR, 1914-1918 -- CAMPAIGNS -- BALKAN PENINSULA
Wawro, G. A mad catastrophe   **940.4**
WORLD WAR, 1914-1918 -- CAMPAIGNS -- EAST AFRICA
Paice, E. World War I: the African Front   **940.4**
WORLD WAR, 1914-1918 -- CAMPAIGNS -- FRANCE
Beevor, A. Ardennes 1944   **940.54**
Davenport, M. J. First over there   **940.4**
WORLD WAR, 1914-1918 -- CAMPAIGNS --

GALICIA (POLAND AND UKRAINE)
Wawro, G. A mad catastrophe   **940.4**
WORLD WAR, 1914-1918 -- CAMPAIGNS -- ITALY
A soldier on the southern front   **940.4**
WORLD WAR, 1914-1918 -- CAMPAIGNS -- MEUSE RIVER VALLEY
Walker, W. T. Betrayal at Little Gibraltar   **940.436**
WORLD WAR, 1914-1918 -- CAMPAIGNS -- MIDDLE EAST
Anderson, S. Lawrence in Arabia   **940.4**
Korda, M. Hero   **92**
WORLD WAR, 1914-1918 -- CAMPAIGNS -- WESTERN FRONT
Eisenhower, J. S. D. Yanks: the epic story of the American Army in World War I   **940.4**
Yockelson, M. A. Forty-seven days   **940.4**
WORLD WAR, 1914-1918 -- CASUALTIES
Hamilton-Paterson, J. Marked for death   **940.44**
WORLD WAR, 1914-1918 -- CASUALTIES -- GREAT BRITAIN
Scott, R. N. Many were held by the sea   **940.4**
WORLD WAR, 1914-1918 -- CAUSES
Clark, C. The sleepwalkers   **940.3**
Emmerson, C. 1913   **909.82**
Hastings, M. Catastrophe 1914   **940.3**
McMeekin, S. July 1914   **940.3**
WORLD WAR, 1914-1918 -- CONSCIENTIOUS OBJECTORS
Hochschild, A. To end all wars   **940.3**
WORLD WAR, 1914-1918 -- DIPLOMATIC HISTORY
Clark, C. The sleepwalkers   **940.3**
WORLD WAR, 1914-1918 -- ENCYCLOPEDIAS
The Encyclopedia of World War I   **940.3**
The United States in the First World War   **940.3**
WORLD WAR, 1914-1918 -- FRANCE
Kershaw, A. Avenue of spies   **940.53**
WORLD WAR, 1914-1918 -- GERMANY
Weber, T. Hitler's first war   **940.4**
WORLD WAR, 1914-1918 -- GREAT BRITAIN
Hochschild, A. To end all wars   **940.3**
WORLD WAR, 1914-1918 -- INFLUENCE
Tooze, A. The deluge   **940.3**
Walsh, M. Bitter freedom   **941.508**
WORLD WAR, 1914-1918 -- MIDDLE EAST
Korda, M. Hero   **92**
Lawrence, T. E. Seven pillars of wisdom   **940.4**
WORLD WAR, 1914-1918 -- NAVAL OPERATIONS
Larson, E. Dead wake   **940.4**
Scott, R. N. Many were held by the sea   **940.4**
WORLD WAR, 1914-1918 -- NAVAL OPERATIONS -- SUBMARINE
Preston, D. A higher form of killing   **940.4**
WORLD WAR, 1914-1918 -- NAVAL OPERA-

TIONS, BRITISH
Massie, R. K. Castles of steel | 940.4
Scott, R. N. Many were held by the sea | 940.4
WORLD WAR, 1914-1918 -- PARTICIPATION, AFRICAN AMERICAN
Slotkin, R. Lost battalions | 940.3
WORLD WAR, 1914-1918 -- PEACE
Hagedorn, A. Savage peace | 973.91
MacMillan, M. Paris 1919 | 940.3
Neu, C. E. Colonel House | 92
WORLD WAR, 1914-1918 -- PEACE
See also Peace
WORLD WAR, 1914-1918 -- PERSONAL NARRATIVES
The burning of the world | 92
A soldier on the southern front | 940.4
WORLD WAR, 1914-1918 -- PERSONAL NARRATIVES, AMERICAN
Hynes, S. The unsubstantial air | 940.4
Nelson, J. C. The remains of Company D | 920
WORLD WAR, 1914-1918 -- PERSONAL NARRATIVES, HUNGARIAN
The burning of the world | 92
WORLD WAR, 1914-1918 -- POLITICAL ASPECTS
Walsh, M. Bitter freedom | 941.508
WORLD WAR, 1914-1918 -- REGIMENTAL HISTORIES -- UNITED STATES
Nelson, J. C. The remains of Company D | 920
Slotkin, R. Lost battalions | 940.3
WORLD WAR, 1914-1918 -- SOCIAL ASPECTS
Hochschild, A. To end all wars | 940.3
WORLD WAR, 1914-1918 -- SOCIAL ASPECTS -- HUNGARY
The burning of the world | 92
WORLD WAR, 1914-1918 -- TERRITORIAL QUESTIONS
See also Boundaries
WORLD WAR, 1914-1918 -- TERRITORIAL QUESTIONS -- CROATIA -- RIJEKA
Hughes-Hallett, L. Gabriele d'Annunzio | 858
WORLD WAR, 1914-1918 -- TRANSPORTATION -- GREAT BRITAIN
Scott, R. N. Many were held by the sea | 940.4
WORLD WAR, 1914-1918 -- UNITED STATES
Davenport, M. J. First over there | 940.4
Yockelson, M. A. Forty-seven days | 940.4
WORLD WAR, 1939-1945
See also Europe -- History -- 1918-1945; World history -- 20th century; World politics
WORLD WAR, 1939-1945 -- AERIAL OPERATIONS
Groom, W. The aviators | 920
Henderson, B. B. Rescue at Los Banos | 940.53
Lewis, D. The Dog Who Could Fly | 940.54
WORLD WAR, 1939-1945 -- AERIAL OPERA-

TIONS -- JAPAN
Harding, S. Last to die | 940.54
Scott, J. M. Target Tokyo | 940.54
Wukovits, J. F. Hell from the heavens | 940.54
WORLD WAR, 1939-1945 -- AERIAL OPERATIONS, AMERICAN
Ambrose, S. E. The wild blue | 940.54
Cronkite, W. Cronkite's war | 070.4
Grayling, A. C. Among the dead cities | 940.54
Harding, S. Last to die | 940.54
Murphy, B. 81 days below zero | 940.54
Nelson, C. The first heroes | 940.54
Scott, J. M. Target Tokyo | 940.54
Zuckoff, M. Lost in Shangri-la | 940.54
WORLD WAR, 1939-1945 -- AERIAL OPERATIONS, AMERICAN -- PHILIPPINES
Henderson, B. B. Rescue at Los Banos | 940.53
WORLD WAR, 1939-1945 -- AERIAL OPERATIONS, JAPANESE
Wukovits, J. F. Hell from the heavens | 940.54
WORLD WAR, 1939-1945 -- AFRICAN AMERICANS
Kaplan, A. Y. The interpreter | 940.54
WORLD WAR, 1939-1945 -- AFRICAN AMERICANS
See also African Americans
WORLD WAR, 1939-1945 -- ALASKA
Murphy, B. 81 days below zero | 940.54
WORLD WAR, 1939-1945 -- AMPHIBIOUS OPERATIONS
Kennedy, P. M. Engineers of victory | 940.54
WORLD WAR, 1939-1945 -- AMPHIBIOUS OPERATIONS
See also World War, 1939-1945 -- Naval operations
WORLD WAR, 1939-1945 -- AMPHIBIOUS OPERATIONS, AMERICAN -- PHILIPPINES
Henderson, B. B. Rescue at Los Banos | 940.53
WORLD WAR, 1939-1945 -- ANECDOTES
Soldaten | 940.54
WORLD WAR, 1939-1945 -- ARMISTICES
Neiberg, M. Potsdam | 940.53
WORLD WAR, 1939-1945 -- ART AND THE WAR
See also Art
WORLD WAR, 1939-1945 -- ATLANTIC OCEAN
Blair, C. Hitler's U-boat war | 940.54
WORLD WAR, 1939-1945 -- ATROCITIES
Nagorski, A. The Nazi hunters | 940.53
WORLD WAR, 1939-1945 -- ATROCITIES
See also Atrocities
WORLD WAR, 1939-1945 -- ATROCITIES -- GERMANY
Wachsmann, N. Kl | 940.53
WORLD WAR, 1939-1945 -- AUSTRIA
Letts, E. The perfect horse | 940.54
WORLD WAR, 1939-1945 -- BALLOONS --

UNITED STATES
Hervieux, L. Forgotten **940.54**

WORLD WAR, 1939-1945 -- BATTLES, SIEGES, ETC. *See* World War, 1939-1945 -- Aerial operations; World War, 1939-1945 -- Campaigns; World War, 1939-1945 -- Naval operations

WORLD WAR, 1939-1945 -- BIOGRAPHY
Kaiser, C. The cost of courage **92**

WORLD WAR, 1939-1945 -- BIOGRAPHY
See also Biography

WORLD WAR, 1939-1945 -- BIOGRAPHY -- GRAPHIC NOVELS
Tyler, C. Soldier's heart **741.5**

WORLD WAR, 1939-1945 -- CAMPAIGNS
Dimbleby, J. The Battle of the Atlantic **940.54**
Jordan, J. W. American warlords **973.917**
Peffer, R. Where divers dare **940.54**

WORLD WAR, 1939-1945 -- CAMPAIGNS -- AFRICA, NORTH
Atkinson, R. An army at dawn **940.54**

WORLD WAR, 1939-1945 -- CAMPAIGNS -- ATLANTIC OCEAN
Blair, C. Hitler's U-boat war **940.54**
Dimbleby, J. The Battle of the Atlantic **940.54**

WORLD WAR, 1939-1945 -- CAMPAIGNS -- EUROPE
Ambrose, S. E. Citizen soldiers **940.54**
Ambrose, S. E. The victors **940.54**
Cronkite, W. Cronkite's war **070.4**

WORLD WAR, 1939-1945 -- CAMPAIGNS -- FRANCE
Hervieux, L. Forgotten **940.54**
Sacco, J. The Great War **940.4**

WORLD WAR, 1939-1945 -- CAMPAIGNS -- FRANCE -- NORMANDY
Hervieux, L. Forgotten **940.54**
Macintyre, B. Double cross **940.54**

WORLD WAR, 1939-1945 -- CAMPAIGNS -- FRANCE -- PARIS
Neiberg, M. The blood of free men **940.54**

WORLD WAR, 1939-1945 -- CAMPAIGNS -- ITALY
Atkinson, R. The day of battle **940.54**

WORLD WAR, 1939-1945 -- CAMPAIGNS -- JAPAN
Giangreco, D. M. Hell to pay **940.54**

WORLD WAR, 1939-1945 -- CAMPAIGNS -- JAPAN -- TOKYO
Harding, S. Last to die **940.54**

WORLD WAR, 1939-1945 -- CAMPAIGNS -- NEW GUINEA
Duffy, J. P. War at the end of the world **940.54**

WORLD WAR, 1939-1945 -- CAMPAIGNS -- NORTH AFRICA
Atkinson, R. An army at dawn **940.54**

WORLD WAR, 1939-1945 -- CAMPAIGNS --

NORTH ATLANTIC OCEAN
Peffer, R. Where divers dare **940.54**

WORLD WAR, 1939-1945 -- CAMPAIGNS -- OKINAWA ISLAND
Leckie, R. Okinawa **940.54**

WORLD WAR, 1939-1945 -- CAMPAIGNS -- PACIFIC AREA
Kennedy, P. M. Engineers of victory **940.54**
Wukovits, J. F. Hell from the heavens **940.54**

WORLD WAR, 1939-1945 -- CAMPAIGNS -- PACIFIC OCEAN
Toll, I. W. The conquering tide **940.54**

WORLD WAR, 1939-1945 -- CAMPAIGNS -- PHILIPPINES
Prados, J. Storm over Leyte **940.54**

WORLD WAR, 1939-1945 -- CAMPAIGNS -- PHILIPPINES -- LEYTE ISLAND
Prados, J. Storm over Leyte **940.54**

WORLD WAR, 1939-1945 -- CAMPAIGNS -- SOLOMON ISLANDS
Doyle, W. PT 109 **940.54**

WORLD WAR, 1939-1945 -- CAMPAIGNS -- SOUTH ASIA
Raghavan, S. India's war **940.53**

WORLD WAR, 1939-1945 -- CAMPAIGNS -- SOVIET UNION
Jones, M. K. The retreat **940.54**
Reid, A. Leningrad

WORLD WAR, 1939-1945 -- CAMPAIGNS -- WESTERN FRONT
Alexander, L. Biggest brother **92**
Ambrose, S. E. Band of brothers **940.54**
Atkinson, R. The guns at last light **940.54**
Hastings, M. Armageddon: the battle for Germany, 1944-45 **940.54**

WORLD WAR, 1939-1945 -- CARTOONS AND CARICATURES
See also Cartoons and caricatures

WORLD WAR, 1939-1945 -- CAUSES
Carley, M. J. 1939 **940.53**
Faber, D. Munich, 1938 **940.53**
Wasserstein, B. On the eve **305.892**

WORLD WAR, 1939-1945 -- CENSORSHIP
See also Censorship

WORLD WAR, 1939-1945 -- CHEMICAL WARFARE
See also Chemical warfare

WORLD WAR, 1939-1945 -- CHILDREN
Tate, T. Hitler's forgotten children **940.53**

WORLD WAR, 1939-1945 -- CHINA
Tuchman, B. W. Stilwell and the American experience in China, 1911-45 **327**

WORLD WAR, 1939-1945 -- CIVILIAN RELIEF
See also Charities; Food relief; Foreign aid; Reconstruction (1939-1951); World War, 1939-1945 -- War work

WORLD WAR, 1939-1945 -- COLLABORA-
TIONISTS

See also Collaborationists

WORLD WAR, 1939-1945 -- COLLABORA-
TIONISTS -- FRANCE

Kaplan, A. The collaborator: the trial & execution
of Robert Brasillach   848

WORLD WAR, 1939-1945 -- COMMANDO OP-
ERATIONS

Lulushi, A. Donovan's Devils   940.54

WORLD WAR, 1939-1945 -- COMMANDO
OPERATIONS -- CZECH REPUBLIC --
HOSTOUŇ

Letts, E. The perfect horse   940.54

WORLD WAR, 1939-1945 -- COMMANDO OP-
ERATIONS -- NORWAY

Bascomb, N. The winter fortress   940.54

WORLD WAR, 1939-1945 -- CONCENTRATION
CAMPS

Wachsmann, N. Kl   940.53
Wiesenthal, S. The sunflower   179.7

WORLD WAR, 1939-1945 -- CONCENTRA-
TION CAMPS -- WYOMING -- PICTORIAL
WORKS

Colors of confinement   940.53

WORLD WAR, 1939-1945 -- CRYPTOGRAPHY

McKay, S. The secret lives of codebreakers 940.54
Sebag-Montefiore, H. Enigma: the battle for the
code   940.54

WORLD WAR, 1939-1945 -- CZECH REPUBLIC
-- PRAGUE

Woodward, B. Prague winter   943.71

WORLD WAR, 1939-1945 -- DECEPTION

Macintyre, B. Double cross   940.54

WORLD WAR, 1939-1945 -- DESERTIONS

Glass, C. The deserters   940.54

WORLD WAR, 1939-1945 -- DESERTIONS

See also Military desertion

WORLD WAR, 1939-1945 -- DESTRUCTION
AND PILLAGE

Muller, M. Lost lives, lost art   709
Petropoulos, J. The Faustian bargain   709
Scott-Clark, C. The Amber Room   940.54

WORLD WAR, 1939-1945 -- DIPLOMATIC HIS-
TORY

Dobbs, M. Six months in 1945   940.54

WORLD WAR, 1939-1945 -- DISPLACED PER-
SONS See World War, 1939-1945 -- Refugees

WORLD WAR, 1939-1945 -- ECONOMIC AS-
PECTS -- UNITED STATES

Herman, A. Freedom's forge   940.53

WORLD WAR, 1939-1945 -- EDUCATION AND
THE WAR

See also Education

WORLD WAR, 1939-1945 -- ELECTRONIC IN-
TELLIGENCE -- GREAT BRITAIN

McKay, S. The secret lives of codebreakers 940.54

WORLD WAR, 1939-1945 -- ENCYCLOPEDIAS

Dunnigan, J. F. The Pacific War encyclopedia   940.54
Encyclopedia of World War II   940.53

WORLD WAR, 1939-1945 -- ENGLAND -- LON-
DON -- ANECDOTES

Cronkite, W. Cronkite's war   070.4

WORLD WAR, 1939-1945 -- EQUIPMENT AND
SUPPLIES

See also Military weapons

WORLD WAR, 1939-1945 -- ETHICAL AS-
PECTS

Burleigh, M. Moral combat   940.54
Grayling, A. C. Among the dead cities   940.54

WORLD WAR, 1939-1945 -- ETHICAL AS-
PECTS

See also Ethics

WORLD WAR, 1939-1945 -- EUROPE

Ambrose, S. E. Band of brothers   940.54
Pleshakov, K. Stalin's folly   940.54

WORLD WAR, 1939-1945 -- EUROPE -- END

Jones, M. After Hitler   940.53

WORLD WAR, 1939-1945 -- EVACUATION OF
CIVILIANS

See also Civil defense; World War, 1939-1945
-- Refugees

WORLD WAR, 1939-1945 -- FINLAND

Edwards, R. The Winter War   948.97

WORLD WAR, 1939-1945 -- FOOD SUPPLY

Collingham, L. The taste of war   940.53

WORLD WAR, 1939-1945 -- FOOD SUPPLY

See also Food relief

WORLD WAR, 1939-1945 -- FORCED REPA-
TRIATION

Shephard, B. The long road home   940.53

WORLD WAR, 1939-1945 -- FRANCE

Carroll, S. B. Brave genius   920
Moorehead, C. Village of Secrets   944

WORLD WAR, 1939-1945 -- FRANCE -- PARIS

Neiberg, M. The blood of free men   940.54

WORLD WAR, 1939-1945 -- GERMANY

Goebbels   92
Holland, J. The rise of Germany 1939-1941 940.54
Weale, A. Army of evil   940.54

WORLD WAR, 1939-1945 -- GERMANY -- PO-
ETRY

Across the land and the water   831

WORLD WAR, 1939-1945 -- GERMANY --
TECHNOLOGY

Bascomb, N. The winter fortress   940.54

WORLD WAR, 1939-1945 -- GERMANY -- WAR-
BURG

Felton, M. Zero Night   940.54

WORLD WAR, 1939-1945 -- GOVERNMENTS
IN EXILE

See also World War, 1939-1945 -- Diplomatic history

WORLD WAR, 1939-1945 -- GRAPHIC NOVELS
Guibert, E. Alan's war **741.5**

WORLD WAR, 1939-1945 -- GREAT BRITAIN
D'Este, C. Warlord **92**
Johnson, P. Churchill **92**
Lukacs, J. Five days in London, May 1940 **940.53**
Macintyre, B. Rogue Heroes **940.54**
Manchester, W. The last lion, Winston Spencer Churchill **92**
McKay, S. The secret lives of codebreakers **940.54**

WORLD WAR, 1939-1945 -- GREAT BRITAIN -- LITERATURE AND THE WAR
Swift, D. Bomber County **821**

WORLD WAR, 1939-1945 -- GREECE
McDougall, C. Natural Born Heroes **940.53**

WORLD WAR, 1939-1945 -- GUERRILLAS *See* World War, 1939-1945 -- Underground movements

WORLD WAR, 1939-1945 -- HISTORIOGRAPHY
Reynolds, D. In command of history **940.53**

WORLD WAR, 1939-1945 -- HUMOR
See also Wit and humor

WORLD WAR, 1939-1945 -- HUNGARY
Szegedy-Maszák, M. I kiss your hands many times **920**

WORLD WAR, 1939-1945 -- INDIA
Karnad, R. Farthest field **940.54**

WORLD WAR, 1939-1945 -- INFLUENCE
Ballard, J. G. Miracles of life **823**
Buruma, I. Year zero **940.53**

WORLD WAR, 1939-1945 -- ITALY
Katz, R. The battle for Rome **940.54**

WORLD WAR, 1939-1945 -- JAPAN
Hotta, E. Japan 1941 **940.54**
Sakamoto, P. R. Midnight in broad daylight **940.53**

WORLD WAR, 1939-1945 -- JAPAN -- HIROSHI-MA-SHI
Ham, P. Hiroshima Nagasaki **940.54**
Pellegrino, C. To hell and back **940.54**
Sakamoto, P. R. Midnight in broad daylight **940.53**

WORLD WAR, 1939-1945 -- JAPAN -- HISTORI-OGRAPHY
Dower, J. W. Ways of forgetting, ways of remembering **940.53**

WORLD WAR, 1939-1945 -- JAPAN -- NAGASA-KI-SHI
Ham, P. Hiroshima Nagasaki **940.54**

WORLD WAR, 1939-1945 -- JAPANESE AMERI-CANS
Reeves, R. Infamy **940.53**
Sakamoto, P. R. Midnight in broad daylight **940.53**

WORLD WAR, 1939-1945 -- JEWISH RESIS-TANCE

Goldberg, R. Motherland **940.531**

WORLD WAR, 1939-1945 -- JEWS
Maitland, L. Crossing the borders of time **940.53**

WORLD WAR, 1939-1945 -- JEWS
See also Jews

WORLD WAR, 1939-1945 -- JEWS -- DRAMA
Goodrich, F. The diary of Anne Frank **812**

WORLD WAR, 1939-1945 -- JEWS -- FRANCE -- BIOGRAPHY
Maitland, L. Crossing the borders of time **940.53**

WORLD WAR, 1939-1945 -- JEWS -- GRAPHIC NOVELS
Jacobson, S. Anne Frank **92**

WORLD WAR, 1939-1945 -- JEWS -- RESCUE
Joukowsky, A. Defying the Nazis **940.53**
Mazzeo, T. J. Irena's children **940.53**

WORLD WAR, 1939-1945 -- JEWS -- RESCUE -- FRANCE -- MARSEILLE
Zuccotti, S. Père Marie-Benoît and Jewish rescue **940.53**

WORLD WAR, 1939-1945 -- JEWS -- RESCUE -- POLAND
Ackerman, D. The zookeeper's wife **940.53**
Mazzeo, T. J. Irena's children **940.53**

WORLD WAR, 1939-1945 -- JOURNALISTS
Cronkite, W. Cronkite's war **070.4**
Lascher, B. Eve of a Hundred Midnights **070.449**

WORLD WAR, 1939-1945 -- JOURNALISTS
See also Journalists

WORLD WAR, 1939-1945 -- LITERATURE AND THE WAR
Poets of World War II **811**
Sebald, W. G. On the natural history of destruction **833**
Swift, D. Bomber County **821**

WORLD WAR, 1939-1945 -- MEDITERRANEAN SEA
Moses, S. At all costs **940.54**

WORLD WAR, 1939-1945 -- MILITARY INTEL-LIGENCE
Hastings, M. The secret war **940.54**
McKay, S. The secret lives of codebreakers **940.54**

WORLD WAR, 1939-1945 -- MILITARY INTEL-LIGENCE
See also Military intelligence

WORLD WAR, 1939-1945 -- MILITARY INTEL-LIGENCE -- GREAT BRITAIN
Soldaten **940.54**

WORLD WAR, 1939-1945 -- MISSING IN AC-TION
Zuckoff, M. Lost in Shangri-la **940.54**

WORLD WAR, 1939-1945 -- MISSING IN AC-TION
See also Missing in action; World War, 1939-1945 -- Prisoners and prisons

WORLD WAR, 1939-1945 -- MONUMENTS

See also Monuments
WORLD WAR, 1939-1945 -- MOTION PIC-
TURES AND THE WAR
Harris, M. Five Came Back   **791.43**
WORLD WAR, 1939-1945 -- MOTION PIC-
TURES AND THE WAR
See also Motion pictures; War films
WORLD WAR, 1939-1945 -- MUSEUMS
See also Museums
WORLD WAR, 1939-1945 -- NAVAL OPERA-
TIONS
Dimbleby, J. The Battle of the Atlantic   **940.54**
Toll, I. W. The conquering tide   **940.54**
Toll, I. W. Pacific crucible   **940.54**
Ujifusa, S. A man and his ship   **623.8**
Wukovits, J. F. Hell from the heavens   **940.54**
WORLD WAR, 1939-1945 -- NAVAL OPERA-
TIONS -- SUBMARINE
Blair, C. Hitler's U-boat war   **940.54**
Dimbleby, J. The Battle of the Atlantic   **940.54**
Peffer, R. Where divers dare   **940.54**
WORLD WAR, 1939-1945 -- NAVAL OPERA-
TIONS, AMERICAN
Ballard, R. D. Return to Midway   **940.54**
Borneman, W. R. The admirals   **920**
Doyle, W. PT 109   **940.54**
Thomas, E. Sea of thunder   **940.54**
WORLD WAR, 1939-1945 -- NAVAL OPERA-
TIONS, GERMAN
Peffer, R. Where divers dare   **940.54**
WORLD WAR, 1939-1945 -- NORTH AFRICA
Williams, S. Spies in the Congo   **553.4**
WORLD WAR, 1939-1945 -- OCCUPIED TER-
RITORIES
Lowe, K. Savage continent   **940.55**
WORLD WAR, 1939-1945 -- OCCUPIED TER-
RITORIES
See also Military occupation; World War,
1939-1945 -- Territorial questions
WORLD WAR, 1939-1945 -- PACIFIC OCEAN
Burgin, R. V. Islands of the damned   **940.54**
Costello, J. The Pacific War   **940.54**
Daws, G. Prisoners of the Japanese   **940.54**
Kershaw, A. Escape from the deep   **940.54**
Manchester, W. Goodbye, darkness   **940.54**
WORLD WAR, 1939-1945 -- PALESTINE
Hoffman, B. Anonymous soldiers   **956.94**
WORLD WAR, 1939-1945 -- PARTICIPATION,
AFRICAN AMERICAN
Hervieux, L. Forgotten   **940.54**
WORLD WAR, 1939-1945 -- PARTICIPATION,
JEWISH
Goldberg, R. Motherland   **940.531**
WORLD WAR, 1939-1945 -- PEACE
Dobbs, M. Six months in 1945   **940.53**
Jones, M. After Hitler   **940.53**

Morris, S. Supreme Commander   **327.73**
WORLD WAR, 1939-1945 -- PERSONAL NAR-
RATIVES
Brinkley-Rogers, P. Please Enjoy Your Happi-
ness   **070.92**
Karski, J. Story of a secret state   **940.53**
Woodward, B. Prague winter   **943.71**
WORLD WAR, 1939-1945 -- PERSONAL NAR-
RATIVES
See also Autobiographies; Biography
WORLD WAR, 1939-1945 -- PERSONAL NAR-
RATIVES, AMERICAN
Ambrose, S. E. Citizen soldiers   **940.54**
Roberts, A. Masters and commanders   **940.54**
WORLD WAR, 1939-1945 -- PERSONAL NAR-
RATIVES, BRITISH
Roberts, A. Masters and commanders   **940.54**
WORLD WAR, 1939-1945 -- PERSONAL NAR-
RATIVES, DUTCH
At the edge of the abyss   **940.53**
WORLD WAR, 1939-1945 -- PERSONAL NAR-
RATIVES, POLISH
Karski, J. Story of a secret state   **940.53**
WORLD WAR, 1939-1945 -- PERSONAL NAR-
RATIVES, YUGOSLAV
Tate, T. Hitler's forgotten children   **940.53**
WORLD WAR, 1939-1945 -- PHILIPPINES
Henderson, B. B. Rescue at Los Banos   **940.53**
WORLD WAR, 1939-1945 -- PICTORIAL
WORKS
Colors of confinement   **940.53**
WORLD WAR, 1939-1945 -- POETRY
Poets of World War II   **811**
Swift, D. Bomber County   **821**
WORLD WAR, 1939-1945 -- POETRY
See also Historical poetry; War poetry
WORLD WAR, 1939-1945 -- POLAND
Allen, A. The fantastic laboratory of Dr. Wei-
gl   **614.5**
Karski, J. Story of a secret state   **940.53**
WORLD WAR, 1939-1945 -- PRISONERS AND
PRISONS
At the edge of the abyss   **940.53**
Felton, M. Zero Night   **940.54**
Henderson, B. B. Rescue at Los Banos   **940.53**
Weintraub, R. No better friend   **304.2**
WORLD WAR, 1939-1945 -- PRISONERS AND
PRISONS
See also Concentration camps; Prisoners of
war; Prisons
WORLD WAR, 1939-1945 -- PRISONERS AND
PRISONS, AMERICAN
Colors of confinement   **940.53**
WORLD WAR, 1939-1945 -- PRISONERS AND
PRISONS, BRITISH
Soldaten   **940.54**

WORLD WAR, 1939-1945 -- PRISONERS AND PRISONS, JAPANESE

Henderson, B. B. Rescue at Los Banos **940.53**

Norman, E. M. Tears in the darkness **940.54**

WORLD WAR, 1939-1945 -- PROPAGANDA

See also Propaganda

WORLD WAR, 1939-1945 -- PROTEST MOVEMENTS

See also Protest movements

WORLD WAR, 1939-1945 -- PSYCHOLOGICAL ASPECTS

Glass, C. The deserters **940.54**

WORLD WAR, 1939-1945 -- PUBLIC OPINION

See also Public opinion

WORLD WAR, 1939-1945 -- RECONNAISSANCE OPERATIONS, AMERICAN

Harding, S. Last to die **940.54**

WORLD WAR, 1939-1945 -- RECONSTRUCTION *See* Reconstruction (1939-1951)

WORLD WAR, 1939-1945 -- REFUGEES

Richmond Mouillot, M. A fifty-year silence **940.53**

WORLD WAR, 1939-1945 -- REFUGEES

See also Political refugees

WORLD WAR, 1939-1945 -- REFUGEES -- FRANCE -- BIOGRAPHY

Maitland, L. Crossing the borders of time **940.53**

WORLD WAR, 1939-1945 -- REGIMENTAL HISTORIES

Weale, A. Army of evil **940.54**

WORLD WAR, 1939-1945 -- REGIMENTAL HISTORIES -- GERMANY

Weale, A. Army of evil **940.54**

WORLD WAR, 1939-1945 -- REGIMENTAL HISTORIES -- UNITED STATES

Alexander, L. Biggest brother **92**

Ambrose, S. E. Band of brothers **940.54**

Hervieux, L. Forgotten **940.54**

WORLD WAR, 1939-1945 -- REPARATIONS

Goodman, S. The Orpheus Clock **940.53**

WORLD WAR, 1939-1945 -- REPARATIONS

See also Reconstruction (1939-1951); World War, 1939-1945 -- Economic aspects

WORLD WAR, 1939-1945 -- RESISTANCE MOVEMENTS *See* World War, 1939-1945 -- Underground movements

WORLD WAR, 1939-1945 -- SCIENCE -- GERMANY

Biddle, W. Dark side of the moon **92**

Cassidy, D. C. Beyond uncertainty **92**

WORLD WAR, 1939-1945 -- SEARCH AND RESCUE OPERATIONS

Zuckoff, M. Lost in Shangri-la **940.54**

WORLD WAR, 1939-1945 -- SECRET SERVICE

Blum, H. The Last Goodnight **940.54**

Talty, S. Agent Garbo **940.5**

WORLD WAR, 1939-1945 -- SECRET SERVICE

See also Secret service

WORLD WAR, 1939-1945 -- SECRET SERVICE -- GREAT BRITAIN

Conant, J. The irregulars **940.54**

Mulley, C. The Spy Who Loved **940.54**

Sheinkin, S. Bomb **623.4**

Talty, S. Agent Garbo **940.5**

WORLD WAR, 1939-1945 -- SECRET SERVICE -- SOVIET UNION

Sheinkin, S. Bomb **623.4**

WORLD WAR, 1939-1945 -- SECRET SERVICE -- UNITED STATES

Lulushi, A. Donovan's Devils **940.54**

WORLD WAR, 1939-1945 -- SOCIAL ASPECTS -- JAPAN

Dower, J. W. Ways of forgetting, ways of remembering **940.53**

WORLD WAR, 1939-1945 -- SOVIET UNION

Moynahan, B. Leningrad **940.54**

Stalingrad **940.54**

WORLD WAR, 1939-1945 -- TENNESSEE -- OAK RIDGE

Kiernan, D. The girls of atomic city **976.8**

WORLD WAR, 1939-1945 -- TERRITORIAL QUESTIONS

See also Boundaries

WORLD WAR, 1939-1945 -- THEATER AND THE WAR

See also Theater

WORLD WAR, 1939-1945 -- TRANSPORTATION

See also Transportation

WORLD WAR, 1939-1945 -- TREATIES

Moorhouse, R. The Devils' Alliance **940.53**

Neiberg, M. Potsdam **940.53**

WORLD WAR, 1939-1945 -- TREATIES

See also Treaties

WORLD WAR, 1939-1945 -- UNDERGROUND MOVEMENTS

The lone assassin **943.086**

Moorehead, C. Village of Secrets **944**

Orbach, D. The plots against Hitler **940.53**

WORLD WAR, 1939-1945 -- UNDERGROUND MOVEMENTS -- FRANCE

Kaiser, C. The cost of courage **92**

WORLD WAR, 1939-1945 -- UNDERGROUND MOVEMENTS -- FRANCE -- PARIS

Kershaw, A. Avenue of spies **940.53**

WORLD WAR, 1939-1945 -- UNDERGROUND MOVEMENTS -- NORWAY

Bascomb, N. The winter fortress **940.54**

WORLD WAR, 1939-1945 -- UNDERGROUND MOVEMENTS -- POLAND

Allen, A. The fantastic laboratory of Dr. Weigl **614.5**

WORLD WAR, 1939-1945 -- UNITED STATES

Beyond Rosie 940

Curtis, B. Fields of Battle 940.54

Fullilove, M. Rendezvous with destiny 973.917

Geroux, W. The Mathews Men 940.54

Groom, W. The generals 940.54

Hamilton, N. The mantle of command 940.54

Moe, R. Roosevelt's second act 973.917

Olson, L. Those angry days 940.53

Russell, J. J. The Train to Crystal City 940.53

Slacks and calluses 940.53

Sone, M. Nisei daughter 979.7

Unger, I. George Marshall 92

Wortman, M. 1941 : Fighting the Shadow War 973.917

WORLD WAR, 1939-1945 -- UNITED STATES -- BIOGRAPHY

Groom, W. The generals 940.54

Hamilton, N. The mantle of command 940.54

WORLD WAR, 1939-1945 -- VETERANS

See also Veterans

WORLD WAR, 1939-1945 -- WAR CORRESPONDENTS See World War, 1939-1945 -- Journalists

WORLD WAR, 1939-1945 -- WOMEN

Beyond Rosie 940

Helm, S. Ravensbruck 940.53

Slacks and calluses 940.53

WORLD WAR, 1939-1945 -- WOMEN

See also Women

WORLD WAR, 1939-1945 -- WOMEN -- GREAT BRITAIN

Barrett, D. GI brides 940.53

WORLD WIDE WEB

Day, F. You're Never Weird on the Internet (Almost)

Kemp, T. J. Virtual roots 2.0 929

Pariser, E. The filter bubble 025.04

WORLD WIDE WEB

See also Internet

WORLD WIDE WEB (INFORMATION RETRIEVAL SYSTEM) See World Wide Web

WORLD WIDE WEB -- HISTORY

Wright, A. Cataloging the world 020.9

WORLD WIDE WEB SEARCHING See Internet searching; Web search engines

A **world** without ice. Pollack, H. N. 551.3

A **world** without Islam. Fuller, G. E. 297

The **world** without us. Weisman, A. 304.2

World's best travel experiences. 910.4

The **World's** classics [series]

Carlyle, T. Sartor resartus 824

Swift, J. A tale of a tub, and other work 823

WORLD'S COLUMBIAN EXPOSITION (1893: CHICAGO, ILL.)

Larson, E. The devil in the white city 364.15

WORLD'S FAIRS See Exhibitions; Fairs

The **World's** great speeches. 808.85

The **world's** most dangerous place. Fergusson, J. 967.73

The **world's** rarest birds. 598

WORLD'S RECORDS See World records

The **world's** strongest librarian. Hanagarne, J. 92

A **worldly** country. Ashbery, J. 811

The **worldly** philosophers. Heilbroner, R. L. 330.1

WORMS

Stewart, A. The earth moved 592

WORMS

See also Animals

Worrall, Simon

The poet and the murderer 364.15

Worrall-Thompson, Antony

The essential diabetes cookbook 641.5

WORRY

See also Emotions

Worse than slavery. Oshinsky, D. M. 365

Worse than the devil. Strang, D. A. 345

Worse than war. Goldhagen, D. J. 364.1

WORSHIP

See also Religion; Theology

The **worst** hard time. Egan, T. 978

Worster, Donald

A passion for nature 92

Shrinking the Earth 304.2

WORTH See Values

Worth dying for. Henican, E. 359.984

Worth, Robert F.

A rage for order 909

Worthen, John

D.H. Lawrence 92

D.H. Lawrence, the early years, 1885-1912 92

Worthington, Janet Farrar

(jt. auth) Walsh, P. C. Dr. Patrick Walsh's guide to surviving prostate cancer 616.99

Wortman, Marc

1941 : Fighting the Shadow War 973.917

Wouldn't take nothing for my journey now. Angelou, M. 814

WOUNDED, FIRST AID TO See First aid

WOUNDS AND INJURIES

Walton, B. Back from the dead 92

Wounds of passion. Hooks, B. 92

Woven to wear. Murphy, M. 746.1

WRANGEL ISLAND (RUSSIA) -- EXPLORATION

Niven, J. Ada Blackjack 92

Wrangham, Richard W.

Catching fire 641.3

Wranovics, John

Chaplin and Agee 92

Wrapped in rainbows. Boyd, V. 92

Wrapped in the flag. Conner, C. 322.4

WRATH See Anger

Wray, T. J.

The birth of Satan 235

What the Bible really tells us **220.6**

The **wreckers**. Bathurst, B. **910.4**

Wren, Christopher Sir, 1632-1723
About
Hollis, L. London rising **942**

WRESTLING
Patterson, P. Accepted **92**

WRESTLING
See also Athletics

The **Wright** brothers. McCullough, D. **92**

Wright, Alex
Cataloging the world **020.9**

Wright, C. D.
One with others **811**
Steal away **811**

Wright, Caroline
Mix + Match Cakes **641.86**

Wright, Charles
Negative blue **811**

Wright, Evan
Generation kill **956.7**

Wright, Frank Lloyd, 1867-1959
About
Howard, H. Architecture's odd couple **720.973**
Huxtable, A. L. Frank Lloyd Wright **92**
Secrest, M. Frank Lloyd Wright **92**
Storrer, W. A. The Frank Lloyd Wright companion **720.9**

Wright, Hillary
The prediabetes diet plan **616.4**

Wright, IO Tillett, 1985-
Darling Days **92**

Wright, James Arlington
Above the river **811**

Wright, Jay
Transfigurations **811**

Wright, Jennifer
It Ended Badly **302**

Wright, Julie
The happy sleeper **649**

Wright, Lawrence, 1947-
Going Clear **299**
The looming tower **973.931**
The terror years **363.325**
Thirteen Days in September **956.04**
Twins **155.44**

Wright, N. T.
Surprised by hope **236**

Wright, Orville, 1871-1948
About
Goldstone, L. Birdmen **629.13**
McCullough, D. The Wright brothers **92**
Wright, O. How we invented the airplane **92**

Wright, Richard, 1908-1960
About
Ellison, R. The collected essays of Ralph Ellison **814**
Ellison, R. Going to the territory **818**
Rowley, H. Richard Wright **813**
Wright, R. Black boy **92**

Wright, Robert A.
Our man in Tehran **955**

Wright, Robin
Dreams and shadows **956.05**

Wright, Sarah Bird
Critical companion to Nathaniel Hawthorne **813**

Wright, Wilbur, 1867-1912
About
Goldstone, L. Birdmen **629.13**
McCullough, D. The Wright brothers **92**
Wright, O. How we invented the airplane **92**

Wrinkles in time. Smoot, G. **523.1**

Write it down, make it happen. Klauser, H. A. **158**

The **Writer's** digest guide to good writing. **808**

A **writer's** house in Wales. Morris, J. **942.9**

Writer's Market. Brewer, R. L. **808**

WRITERS *See* Authors

Writers of the Black Chicago renaissance. **810.9**

WRITERS ON CRIME
Life stories **920**

WRITERS ON FILM
Ebert, R. Life itself **92**
Kellow, B. Pauline Kael **92**

WRITERS ON LAW
Blum, H. American lightning **364.152**
Bolt, R. A man for all seasons **822**
Boyle, K. Arc of justice **345**
Farrell, J. A. Clarence Darrow **92**
Feige, D. Indefensible **345**
Lepore, J. A is for American **306.44**
Russell, B. A history of Western philosophy **109**
Simon, J. F. What kind of nation **342**
Smith, J. E. John Marshall **347**

WRITERS ON MEDICINE
Bettelheim, B. Freud and man's soul **150.19**
Bloom, H. The Western canon **809**
Gawande, A. Better **616**
Gay, P. Freud **92**
Gay, P. A Godless Jew **150.19**
Hayman, R. A life of Jung **150.19**
Johnson, S. The ghost map **614.5**
Jung, C. G. Memories, dreams, reflections **150.19**
Kluger, J. Splendid solution: Jonas Salk and the conquest of polio **92**
Kubler-Ross, E. The wheel of life **150**
Lattin, D. The Harvard Psychedelic Club **920**
Macey, D. Frantz Fanon **92**
Motion, A. Keats **821**
Nuland, S. B. The doctors' plague **92**
Nuland, S. B. Lost in America **92**
Sacks, O. W. Uncle Tungsten **616.8**
Vendler, H. H. Coming of age as a poet **820**

WRITERS ON MUSIC
Avery, K. Everything is an afterthought   92
Szwed, J. F. Alan Lomax   92

WRITERS ON NATURE
Bass, R. Why I came West   92
Connors, P. Fire season   634.9
Davis, J. E. An Everglades providence   92
Dillard, A. The writing life   818
Dillard, A. An American childhood   92
Gioia, D. Can poetry matter?   809.1
Goodall, J. Beyond innocence   92
Gordon, L. Lives like loaded guns   92
Heat Moon, W. L. Roads to Quoz   917
Hollis, M. Now all roads lead to France   821
Kazin, A. An American procession   810
Lytle, M. H. The gentle subversive   92
Matthiessen, F. O. American renaissance   810
Montgomery, S. Birdology   598
Muir, J. Nature writings   508
Muir, J. The story of my boyhood and youth   92
Peterson, D. Jane Goodall: the woman who rede-
    fined man   92
Sullivan, R. The Thoreau you don't know   92
Weidensaul, S. Return to wild America   578
Wilkins, T. John Muir   92
Worster, D. A passion for nature   92

WRITERS ON POLITICS
Blight, D. W. American oracle   973.7
Camus, A. The rebel   303.6
Chadha, Y. Gandhi   954.03
Collins, P. The trouble with Tom: the strange after-
    life and times of Thomas Paine   92
Dallek, R. Nixon and Kissinger   92
DeGategno, P. J. Critical companion to Jonathan
    Swift   828
Epstein, J. Alexis De Tocqueville   92
Eteraz, A. Children of dust   92
Fraser, K. Ornament and silence   809
Gabriel, M. Love and capital   92
Gandhi, M. An autobiography   92
Glendinning, V. Leonard Woolf   92
Gordon, L. Vindication   92
Heilbroner, R. L. The worldly philosophers   330.1
Hitchens, C. Hitch-22   92
Kissinger, H. Years of renewal   973.924
Lelyveld, J. Great soul   92
McKillop, A. B. The spinster & the prophet   941.08
Mill, J. S. Autobiography   92
Mohandas Gandhi   92
Morris, S. J. Rage for fame: the ascent of Clare
    Boothe Luce   92
Pierpont, C. R. Passionate minds   810
Remnick, D. Reporting   814
Rudahl, S. A dangerous woman   335
Russell, B. A history of Western philosophy   109
Said, E. W. Out of place   92

Severin, T. In search of Robinson Crusoe   996
Steffens, L. The autobiography of Lincoln Stef-
    fens   92
Strathern, P. The artist, the philosopher, and the
    warrior   920
Tolstaia, T. Pushkin's children   891.7
Viroli, M. Niccolo's smile: a biography of Machia-
    velli   92
Wheen, F. Karl Marx   335.4
Wilson, E. Patriotic gore   810
Wolpert, S. A. Gandhi's passion   954.03

WRITERS ON RELIGION
Armstrong, K. Muhammad   297
Armstrong, K. Visions of God   248.2
Bainton, R. H. Here I stand: a life of Martin Lu-
    ther   92
Bartlett, R. Tolstoy   891.7
Bell, E. T. Men of mathematics   920
Bloom, H. The Western canon   809
Bolt, R. A man for all seasons   822
Borg, M. J. The first Paul   227
Butcher, C. A. Man of blessing   271
Collins, P. The trouble with Tom: the strange after-
    life and times of Thomas Paine   92
Connor, J. A. Pascal's wager   92
Damasio, A. R. Looking for Spinoza   152.4
Devlin, K. J. The unfinished game   519.2
Durant, W. J. The story of philosophy   109
Eire, C. M. N. Learning to die in Miami   92
Eire, C. M. N. Waiting for snow in Havana   92
Elie, P. The life you save may be your own   810
Erikson, E. H. Young man Luther   92
Eteraz, A. Children of dust   92
Existentialism from Dostoevsky to Sartre   142
Friedman, M. S. Encounter on the narrow ridge: a
    life of Martin Buber   92
Gaustad, E. S. Roger Williams   92
Hague, W. J. William Wilberforce   92
Hazleton, L. After the prophet   297
Kung, H. Great Christian thinkers   230
Lattin, D. The Harvard Psychedelic Club   920
The little flowers of St. Francis of Assisi   242
Marsden, G. M. Jonathan Edwards   92
Martin, J. The Jesuit guide to almost every-
    thing   248.4
Martin, V. Salvation: scenes from the life of St.
    Francis   92
Merton, T. The seven storey mountain   92
Merton, T. Intimate Merton   271
Metaxas, E. Bonhoeffer   92
Murphy-O'Connor, J. Paul   225.9
Nabokov, V. V. Lectures on Russian literature   891.7
Oberman, H. A. Luther: man between God and the
    Devil   92
Patel, E. Acts of faith   92
Ruden, S. Paul among the people   225.9

Russell, B. A history of Western philosophy **109**

Strathern, P. Death in Florence **945**

Taylor, B. B. An altar in the world **92**

Tomkins, S. John Wesley **287**

Wills, G. Saint Augustine **270.2**

Wilson, D. A. Out of the storm **92**

WRITERS ON THE SEA

King, D. Patrick O'Brian **823**

Writers on writers [series]

Dirda, M. On Conan Doyle; or, The whole art of storytelling **823**

The **writers'** and artists' yearbook guide to how to write. Bingham, H. **808.3**

WRITING

Brown, L. How to write anything **808**

The Chicago manual of style **808**

Kidder, T. Good prose **808.02**

Poe, M. Learning to communicate in science and engineering **501**

WRITING

See also Communication; Language and languages; Language arts

WRITING (AUTHORSHIP) See Authorship; Creative writing

WRITING -- HISTORY

Houston, K. Shady characters **411**

WRITING -- MATERIALS AND INSTRUMENTS

Modern calligraphy **745.6**

WRITING -- STUDY AND TEACHING See Handwriting

Writing Across the Landscape. **92**

Writing in time. Schell, J. **973.928**

The **writing** life. Dillard, A. **818**

WRITING OF NUMERALS

See also Handwriting; Numerals; Writing

Writing on the wall. Standage, T. **302.23**

Writing screenplays that sell. Hauge, M. **808.2**

Writing successful technology grant proposals. MacKellar, P. H. **025.1**

Writing the breakout novel. Maass, D. **808.3**

Writing to learn. Zinsser, W. K. **808**

Writing with intent. Atwood, M. **814**

Writing with pictures. Shulevitz, U. **808.06**

Writings. Washington, G. **973.4**

Writings. **818**

Writings. Hamilton, A. **973.4**

Writings. Du Bois, W. E. B. **814**

WRITINGS OF GAY MEN See Gay men's writings

WRITINGS OF LESBIANS See Lesbians' writings

Writings, 1903-1932. Stein, G. **818**

Writings, 1932-1946. Stein, G. **818**

Written in stone. Switek, B. **576.8**

Written in Stone. Stevens, C. **422**

Written into history. **071**

Wroe, Ann

Orpheus **398.2**

The **wrong** Carlos. Liebman, J. S. **364.152**

The **wrong** enemy. Gall, C. **958.104**

The **wrong** side of Murder Creek. Zellner, R. **92**

Wrong turn. Gentile, G. P. **355.02**

The **wrong** war. West, B. **958.1**

Wu, Tim, ca. 1973-

The master switch **384**

WuDunn, Sheryl

(jt. auth) Kristof, N. D. Half the sky **362.83**

Wukovits, John F., 1944-

Hell from the heavens **940.54**

Wulf, Andrea

The brother gardeners **635**

Chasing Venus **523.9**

Founding gardeners **712**

The invention of nature **92**

Wullschlager, Jackie

Chagall **92**

Hans Christian Andersen **839.8**

The **wurst** of Lucky peach. Ying, C. **641.3**

Wyatt Earp. Tefertiller, C. **92**

Wyatt, David K.

Thailand: a short history **959.3**

Wyatt, Neal

The readers' advisory guide to nonfiction **025.5**

Wyatt, Richard Jed, 1939-2002

About

Jamison, K. R. Nothing was the same **92**

Wyeth, Andrew, 1917-2009

About

Wyeth, A. Andrew Wyeth **92**

Wyeth, N. C. (Newell Convers), 1882-1945

About

Michaelis, D. N.C. Wyeth **92**

Wyman's gardening encyclopedia. Wyman, D. **635**

Wyman, David S.

(ed) The World reacts to the Holocaust **940.53**

Wyman, Donald

Wyman's gardening encyclopedia **635**

Wyn Jones, David

(ed) Haydn **92**

Wynbrandt, James

A brief history of Saudi Arabia **953.8**

The excruciating history of dentistry **617.6**

Wynette, Tammy, 1942-1998

About

McDonough, J. Tammy Wynette **92**

Wynn, Charles M.

Wiggins, A. W. The five biggest unsolved problems in science **500**

WYOMING

Bell, L. Claiming ground **92**

WYOMING -- BIOGRAPHY

Fuller, A. Leaving Before the Rains Come **305.409**

WYOMING -- DESCRIPTION AND TRAVEL

Proulx, A. Bird cloud **92**

Wyss, Roxanne

(jt. auth) Moore, K. Delicious dump cakes **641.86**

X

X-MEN (FICTIONAL CHARACTERS)

Lee, S. Stan Lee's How to draw comics **741.5**

X-RAYS

See also Electromagnetic waves; Radiation

XENOPHOBIA

See also Phobias

XERISCAPING

Bainbridge, D. A. Gardening with less water **635.9**

The bold dry garden **635.9**

Penick, P. The water-saving garden **635.9**

XERISCAPING

See also Landscape gardening; Water conservation

Xinran

China witness **920**

Message from an unknown Chinese mother **305.4**

Y

YA LITERATURE *See* Young adult literature

YACHTS AND YACHTING

See also Boatbuilding; Boats and boating; Ocean travel; Ships; Voyages and travels; Water sports

Yaeger, Don

Any given Monday **617.1**

George Washington's secret six **973.4**

Yafa, Stephen

Grain of truth **633.1**

Yagoda, Ben

Memoir **809**

Yaker, Rebecca

One-yard wonders **646.2**

Little one-yard wonders **646.2**

The **Yale** book of quotations. **082**

The **Yale** Child Study Center guide to understanding your child. Mayes, L. C. **649**

Yale language series

Zilkha, A. Modern English-Hebrew dictionary **492.4**

Yale library of military history [series]

Mansoor, P. R. Baghdad at sunrise **956.7**

Yale Nota bene [series]

Kiernan, B. The Pol Pot regime **959.6**

Tillich, P. The courage to be **179**

Yale series of younger poets [series]

Schutt, W. Westerly **811**

YALE UNIVERSITY -- ALUMNI AND ALUMNAE

Hobbs, J. The short and tragic life of Robert Peace **92**

Yalom, Marilyn

A history of the wife **306.872**

How the French invented love **944**

Yalta. Plokhy, S. M. **940.53**

YALTA CONFERENCE (1945)

Plokhy, S. M. Yalta **940.53**

The **Yamato** dynasty. Seagrave, S. **952.03**

YANA INDIANS

Kroeber, T. Ishi in two worlds **92**

Yanak, Ted

Cornelison, P. The great American history fact-finder **973**

Yancey, Philip

Vanishing grace **277**

Yang Lihui

Handbook of Chinese mythology **299.5**

Yang, Charles

The infinite gift **401**

Yang, Jeffrey

(tr) Liu, X. June fourth elegies **811**

YANGTZE RIVER VALLEY (CHINA)

Chetham, D. Before the deluge **951**

Shen, A. J. A tiger's heart **92**

Winchester, S. The river at the center of the world **915**

The **Yankee** comandante. Weiss, M. **92**

Yankee come home. Craig, W. **917.2**

The **Yankee** years. Torre, J. **92**

Yanks: the epic story of the American Army in World War I. Eisenhower, J. S. D. **940.4**

Yans-McLaughlin, Virginia

Ellis Island and the peopling of America **325**

YAQUI INDIANS -- RELIGION

Castaneda, C. The teachings of Don Juan **299.7**

Yardley, Jonathan

(ed) My life as author and editor **818**

Yarm, Mark

Everybody loves our town **781.66**

YARN

Anderson, S. The spinner's book of yarn designs **746.14**

Boggs, J. Spin art **746.12**

Callahan, G. Hand dyeing yarn and fleece **746.6**

Parkes, C. The knitter's book of yarn **677**

Yasso, Bart

(jt. auth) Bede, P. N. The Runner's world big book of marathon and half-marathon training **796.425**

Yate, Martin

Knock 'em dead cover letters **650.14**

Knock 'em dead 2015 **158**

Knock 'em dead cover letters **650.14**

Knock 'em dead resumes **650.14**

YAVAPAI INDIANS -- BIOGRAPHY

Burns, M. The only one living to tell **305.897**

Ybarra, Lea
  Monterrey, M. Americanos   **305.8**
Yeager, Jeff
  The cheapskate next door   **332.024**
Yeah! Yeah! Yeah! Stanley, B.   **781.64**
A **year** in Lapland. Beach, H.   **948.97**
A **year** in Provence.   **944.083**
A **year** in the life of William Shakespeare, 1599.
  Shapiro, J.   **822.3**
A **year** in the world. Mayes, F.   **914**
The **year** of cozy. Adarme, A.   **641.3**
The **Year** of Fear. Urschel, J.   **364.152**
A **year** of gingerbread houses. Samuell, K.   **745.5**
The **Year** of Indecision, 1946. Weisbrode,
  K.   **973.918**
The **year** of magical thinking. Didion, J.   **92**
Year of meteors. Egerton, D. R.   **973.7**
A **year** of reading. Ellington, E.   **011**
A **year** of Russian feasts. Jones, C. C.   **641.59**
The **year** the dream died. Witcover, J.   **973.923**
A **Year** Up. Chertavian, G.   **331.25**
YEAR UP (ORGANIZATION)
  Chertavian, G. A Year Up   **331.25**
The **year** Yellowstone burned. Henry, J.   **634.9**
Year zero. Buruma, I.   **940.53**
The **years** of extermination. Friedlander, S.   **940.53**
The years of Lyndon Johnson [series]
  Caro, R. A. The path to power   **92**
Years of renewal. Kissinger, H.   **973.924**
YEAST
  See also Fungi
Yeats, W. B. (William Butler), 1865-1939
  The collected poems of W.B. Yeats   **821**
    About
  Brown, T. The life of W.B. Yeats   **821**
  Foster, R. F. W.B. Yeats: a life   **821**
  Foster, R. F. W.B. Yeats: a life   **821**
  Heaney, S. Finders keepers   **821**
  Ross, D. A. Critical companion to William Butler
    Yeats   **821**
Yeh, Michelle Mi-Hsi
  (ed) Anthology of modern Chinese poetry   **895.1**
Yellin, Emily
  Our mothers' war   **940.53**
Yellin, Jean Fagan
  Harriet Jacobs: a life   **92**
Yellow dirt. Pasternak, J.   **979.1**
The **yellow** wind. Grossman, D.   **956.95**
The **yellow-lighted** bookshop. Buzbee, L.   **002**
YELLOWSTONE NATIONAL PARK
  Henry, J. The year Yellowstone burned   **634.9**
**YELLOWSTONE NATIONAL PARK -- ATLAS-
ES**
  Atlas of Yellowstone   **912.09**
**YELLOWSTONE NATIONAL PARK -- DIS-
COVERY AND EXPLORATION**

Black, G. Empire of shadows   **978.7**
Yeltsin, Boris
    About
  Tolstaia, T. Pushkin's children   **891.7**
**Yelverton, Thérèse, Viscountess Avonmore, 1832?-
1881**
    About
  Schama, C. Wild romance   **92**
YEMEN
  Johnsen, G. D. The last refuge   **363.325**
Yenne, Bill
  Sitting Bull   **92**
Yenser, Stephen
  (ed) Merrill, J. The collected poems of James Mer-
  rill   **811**
Yeoman, R. S.
  A guide book of United States coins   **737.4**
  Handbook of United States coins   **737.4**
Yergin, Daniel
  The prize   **338.2**
  The quest   **333.79**
Yes means yes!   **306.7**
Yes please. Poehler, A.   **92**
Yes, chef. Chambers, V.   **92**
YETI
  See also Monsters; Mythical animals
Yevtushenko, Yevgeny Aleksandrovich
  Selected poems   **891.7**
YEZIDI WOMEN -- IRAQ -- BIOGRAPHY
  The girl who escaped ISIS   **956.7**
YIDDISH LANGUAGE
  Lansky, A. Outwitting history   **002.07**
  Rosten, L. The new joys of Yiddish   **422**
YIDDISH LANGUAGE
  See also Language and languages
YIDDISH LANGUAGE -- DICTIONARIES
  Comprehensive Yiddish-English Dictionary   **439**
YIDDISH LITERATURE
  See also Jewish literature
Ying, Chris
  The Mission Chinese Food Cookbook   **641.595**
  The wurst of Lucky peach   **641.3**
Yockelson, Mitchell A., 1962-
  Forty-seven days   **940.4**
YOGA
  Budig, K. Aim true   **613.7**
  Goldberg, P. American Veda   **294.5**
  Grossman, G. B. Restorative yoga for life   **613.7**
  Iyengar, B. K. S. Light on life   **294**
  Krasno, J. Wanderlust   **613.7**
  Love, R. The Great Oom   **92**
  Pacheco, R. Do your om thing   **181**
YOGA
  See also Hindu philosophy; Hinduism; The-
  osophy
YOGA -- HISTORY

Broad, W. J. The science of yoga   **613.7**
YOGA EXERCISES *See* Hatha yoga
The **yoga** lifestyle. Hanoch, D.   **613.7**
YOGA, HATHA *See* Hatha yoga
Yogi Berra. Barra, A.   **92**
YOGIS
   Lattin, D. The Harvard Psychedelic Club   **920**
   Love, R. The Great Oom   **92**
Yogurt culture. Rule, C. S.   **641.6**
Yolen, Jane
   (ed) Favorite folktales from around the world **398.2**
YOM KIPPUR
     See also Jewish holidays
Yong, Ed
   I Contain Multitudes   **579**
Yoon, Carol Kaesuk
   Naming nature   **570.1**
York, ca. 1775-ca. 1815
     About
   Slaughter, T. P. Exploring Lewis and Clark   **978**
York, Cecily, Duchess of, 1415-1495
     About
   Gristwood, S. Blood sisters   **942.04**
YORUBA (AFRICAN PEOPLE)
     See also Africans; Indigenous peoples
The **Yosemite.** Muir, J.   **979.4**
YOSEMITE NATIONAL PARK (CALIF.)
   Denny, G. Valley walls   **796.52**
**YOSEMITE NATIONAL PARK (CALIF.) -- PIC-
   TORIAL WORKS**
   Ansel   Adams   in   Yosemite   Valley
Yoshino, Kenji
   Speak now   **346.73**
Yosipovitch, Gil
   Living with itch   **616.5**
You & yours: poems. Nye, N. S.   **811**
You are here. Ellard, C.   **153.7**
You are here. Bray, H.   **910.285**
You are not a gadget. Lanier, J.   **303.4**
You Are Not Special. McCullough, D. J.   **170**
You can adopt. Caughman, S.   **362.7**
You can date boys when you're forty. Barry,
D.   **306.85**
You can heal your life. Hay, L. L.   **158**
You can knit that. Herzog, A.   **746.432**
You can write a mystery. Roberts, G.   **808.3**
You can't always get what you want. Cutler,
S.   **781.66**
You can't make this stuff up. Gutkind, L.   **808**
You can't steal a gift. Lees, G.   **781.65**
You cannot be serious. McEnroe, J.   **796.342**
You feel so mortal. Shinner, P.   **814**
You have it made!   **641.5**
You just don't understand. Tannen, D.   **302.2**
You may also like. Vanderbilt, T.   **153.8**
You must set forth at dawn. Soyinka, W.   **92**

You're Never Weird on the Internet (Almost) Day, F.
Youn, Monica
   Blackacre   **811.6**
YOUNG ADULT AUTHORS
   Anderson, W. T. Laura Ingalls Wilder country   **92**
   Black women writers (1950-1980)   **810**
   Blight, D. W. American oracle   **973.7**
   Boylan, J. F. I'm looking through you   **92**
   Gates, H. L. Thirteen ways of looking at a black
   man   **920.71**
   Gunn, J. E. Isaac Asimov   **813**
   Hughes, L. I wonder as I wander   **818**
   Marshall, P. Triangular road   **92**
   Matteson, J. Eden's outcasts   **92**
   Paulsen, G. Winterdance   **798.8**
   Rampersad, A. The life of Langston Hughes Vol-
   ume I: 1902-1941   **92**
   Rampersad, A. The life of Langston Hughes Vol-
   ume II: 1941-1967   **818**
   Rehak, M. Girl sleuth   **813**
   Reisen, H. Louisa May Alcott   **92**
   Tirone Smith Girls of tender age   **92**
**YOUNG ADULT FICTION, AMERICAN -- BIB-
   LIOGRAPHY**
   Kallio, J. Read on ... speculative fiction for
   teens   **016**
   Morris, V. I. The readers' advisory guide to street
   literature   **016**
**YOUNG ADULT FICTION, ENGLISH -- BIBLI-
   OGRAPHY**
   Kallio, J. Read on ... speculative fiction for
   teens   **016**
Young Adult Library Services Association
   Vaillancourt, R. J. Bare bones young adult servic-
   es   **027.62**
YOUNG ADULT LITERATURE
   Schall, L. Teen talkback with interactive book-
   talks!   **021.7**
YOUNG ADULT LITERATURE
     See also Literature
**YOUNG ADULT LITERATURE -- BIBLIOGRA-
   PHY**
   Keane, N. J. 101 great, ready-to-use book lists for
   teens   **028.5**
**YOUNG ADULT LITERATURE -- BIO-BIBLI-
   OGRAPHY**
   Helbig, A. Dictionary of American young adult fic-
   tion, 1997-2001   **028.5**
**YOUNG ADULT SERVICES LIBRARIANS --
   UNITED STATES -- ATTITUDES**
   Eagle, M. Answering teens' tough questions **027.62**
YOUNG ADULTS *See* Teenagers; Youth
**YOUNG ADULTS -- CUBA -- HAVANA -- BIOG-
   RAPHY**
   Cooke, J. The other side of paradise   **972.91**
YOUNG ADULTS -- EMPLOYMENT -- UNITED

STATES

Chertavian, G. A Year Up **331.25**

YOUNG ADULTS -- FINANCE, PERSONAL

Kobliner, B. Get a financial life **332.024**

YOUNG ADULTS -- LIFE SKILLS GUIDES

Blake, J. Life after college **646.7**

YOUNG ADULTS -- VOCATIONAL EDUCATION -- UNITED STATES

Chertavian, G. A Year Up **331.25**

YOUNG ADULTS' LIBRARIES

Flowers, S. Evaluating teen services and programs **027.62**

Pattee, A. S. Developing library collections for today's young adults **027.62**

Schall, L. Teen talkback with interactive booktalks! **021.7**

Vaillancourt, R. J. Bare bones young adult services **027.62**

YOUNG ADULTS' LIBRARIES

See also Libraries

YOUNG ADULTS' LIBRARIES -- ACTIVITY PROGRAMS

Braafladt, K. Technology and literacy **027.62**

YOUNG ADULTS' LIBRARIES -- BOOK LISTS

Kallio, J. Read on ... speculative fiction for teens **016**

Keane, N. J. 101 great, ready-to-use book lists for teens **028.5**

YOUNG ADULTS' LIBRARIES -- EVALUATION -- UNITED STATES

Flowers, S. Evaluating teen services and programs **027.62**

YOUNG ADULTS' LIBRARIES -- UNITED STATES

Eagle, M. Answering teens' tough questions **027.62**

Young Al Capone. Balsamo, W. **92**

YOUNG CONSUMERS

See also Consumers

Young Eliot. Crawford, R. **92**

YOUNG GAY MEN -- ENGLAND -- BIOGRAPHY

Walsh, M. Gypsy boy **92**

Young house love. Petersik, S. **747**

Young man Luther. Erikson, E. H. **92**

Young Mandela. Smith, D. J. **92**

YOUNG MEN

See also Men; Youth

Young men & fire. MacLean, N. **634.9**

YOUNG MEN -- ARMENIA -- HISTORY -- BIOGRAPHY

MacKeen, D. A. The hundred-year walk **92**

YOUNG MEN -- LIFE SKILLS GUIDES

Blake, J. Life after college **646.7**

YOUNG MEN -- PSYCHOLOGY

Bayoumi, M. How does it feel to be a problem? **305.8**

YOUNG MEN -- UNITED STATES -- BIOGRAPHY

Axelrod, H. The point of vanishing **92**

Young Orson. McGilligan, P. **92**

YOUNG PEOPLE *See* Teenagers; Youth

YOUNG PERSONS *See* Teenagers; Youth

Young Stalin. Montefiore, S. **92**

The **Young** T. E. Lawrence. Sattin, A. **92**

Young Thurgood. Gibson, L. S. **347.73**

YOUNG WOMEN

Braverman, B. Welcome to the Goddamn Ice Cube **974.81**

Crabapple, M. Drawing Blood **92**

Kirsch, M. The girl's guide to absolutely everything **646.7**

Lamarche, U. Unabrow **92**

Orenstein, P. Girls and Sex **306.7**

YOUNG WOMEN

See also Women; Youth

YOUNG WOMEN -- CHINA -- BIOGRAPHY

Ping Fu Bend, not break **92**

YOUNG WOMEN -- CRIMES AGAINST -- JAPAN -- TOKYO

Parry, R. L. People who eat darkness **364.152**

YOUNG WOMEN -- FAMILY RELATIONSHIPS -- UNITED STATES

Hernández, D. A cup of water under my bed **920.009**

YOUNG WOMEN -- LIFE SKILLS GUIDES

Blake, J. Life after college **646.7**

Moffett, K. Not your mother's divorce **306.89**

YOUNG WOMEN -- SOUTH AFRICA -- SOCIAL CONDITIONS

Burge, K. The born frees **305.242**

YOUNG WOMEN -- UNITED STATES -- BIOGRAPHY

Lamarche, U. Unabrow **92**

Young, Alfred Fabian

Masquerade: the life and times of Deborah Sampson, Continental soldier **92**

Young, Anastasia

The workbench guide to jewelry techniques **739.27**

Young, Andrew, 1932-

About

Young, A. An easy burden **92**

Young, Brigham, 1801-1877

About

Turner, J. G. Brigham Young, pioneer prophet **289.3**

Young, Catherine

The Beetlebung Farm cookbook **641**

Young, Christian C.

Evolution and creationism **576.8**

Young, Glenn

(ed) The Best American short plays **812**

Young, Grace

(jt. auth) Richardson, A. The breath of a wok **641.59**

Young, Joel L.
(jt. auth) Adamec, C. When your adult child breaks your heart   **616.89**

Young, Jon, 1960-
About
What the robin knows   **598.8**

Young, Kevin
Ardency   **811**
Blue laws   **811.54**
(ed) Blues poems   **811**
(ed) Clifton, L. The collected poems of Lucille Clifton 1965-2010   **811**
(ed) The Hungry Ear   **811**
(ed) Jazz poems   **811**

Young, Lester
About
Dance, S. The world of Count Basie   **920**
Feather, L. From Satchmo to Miles   **920**

Young, Nancy Beck
(ed) Encyclopedia of the U.S. presidency   **352.23**

Young, Ralph
Dissent   **303.48**

Young, Rob
(jt. auth) Pilkey, O. H. The rising sea   **363.34**
Electric Eden   **781.62**

Young, Stephen
(ed) The Poetry anthology, 1912-2002   **811**

Young, Steve, 1961-
About
Benedict, J. QB   **92**

Young-Eisendrath, Polly
The self-esteem trap   **155.2**

Youngerman, Barry
Wahab, S. A brief history of Afghanistan   **958.1**

Youngstedt, Scott M.
Surviving with dignity   **362.84**

Yount, Lisa
Right to die and euthanasia   **179.7**

Your baby & child. Leach, P.   **649**

Your Baby and Child From Birth to Age Five. Leach, P.   **618.92**

Your beautiful wedding on any budget. Outcalt, T.   **395**

Your bones. Pizzorno, L.   **616.7**

Your Child in the Hospital. Keene, N.   **362.1**

Your child's teeth. Best-Boss, A.   **617.6**

Your eight-year-old. Ames, L. B.   **649**

Your five-year-old. Ames, L. B.   **649**

Your flying car awaits. Milo, P.   **909.82**

Your four-year-old. Ames, L. B.   **649**

Your guide to the Jewish holidays. Axelrod, M.   **296.4**

Your ideal cat. Hart, B. L.   **636.8**

Your immune system recovery plan. Blum, S. **616.97**

Your inner fish. Shubin, N.   **611**

Your kid's a brat and it's all your fault. Glickman, E.

R.   **649.1**

Your medical mind. Groopman, J. E.   **610**

Your one-year-old. Ames, L. B.   **649**

Your own terms. Davidds, Y.   **658.4**

Your pregnancy week by week.   **618.2**

Your seven-year-old. Ames, L. B.   **649**

Your six-year-old. Ames, L. B.   **649**

Your three-year-old. Ilg, F. L.   **649**

Your time to bake. Blakeslee, R. L.   **641.8**

Your two-year-old. Ames, L. B.   **649**

Your voice in my head. Forrest, E.   **362.196**

Yours ever. Mallon, T.   **808.86**

Yousafzai, Malala, 1997-
About
Lamb, C. I am Malala   **92**

YOUTH -- AFRICA
Posner, J. Find Me Unafraid   **92**

YOUTH -- BOOKS AND READING
Helbig, A. Dictionary of American young adult fiction, 1997-2001   **028.5**

YOUTH -- EDUCATION
Ray, B. E. Not quite adults   **306.8**

YOUTH -- EMPLOYMENT
Chertavian, G. A Year Up   **331.25**
Ray, B. E. Not quite adults   **306.8**

YOUTH -- EMPLOYMENT
See also Age and employment; Employment

YOUTH -- HEALTH AND HYGIENE
Columbia University/Health Service The Go ask Alice book of answers   **613**

YOUTH -- NEW YORK (N.Y.)
LeBlanc, A. N. Random family   **305.5**

YOUTH -- POETRY
Powell, D. A. Useless landscape   **811**

YOUTH -- POLITICAL ACTIVITY
Cole, J. The New Arabs   **909**

YOUTH -- RELIGIOUS LIFE
See also Religious life

YOUTH -- SEXUAL BEHAVIOR
Freitas, D. The end of sex   **176**

YOUTH -- SOUTH AFRICA
Burge, K. The born frees   **305.242**

YOUTH -- UNITED STATES
Klinenberg, E. Going solo   **306.81**
Ray, B. E. Not quite adults   **306.8**
Singular, S. The Spiral Notebook   **364.152**

YOUTH HOSTELS
See also Community centers; Hotels and motels

YOUTH LEADERS
Patel, E. Acts of faith   **92**
Rudd, M. Underground   **92**

YOUTH MOVEMENT
See also Social movements

The **youth** pill. Stipp, D.   **612.6**

YOUTUBE (ELECTRONIC RESOURCE)

Miles, J. YouTube marketing power **658.8**

YouTube marketing power. Miles, J. **658.8**

YPRES, 2ND BATTLE OF, IEPER, BELGIUM, 1915

Preston, D. A higher form of killing **940.4**

Yucatán. Sterling, D. **641.59**

YUCATÁN PENINSULA -- DESCRIPTION AND TRAVEL

Sterling, D. Yucatán **641.59**

YUCATAN (MEXICO)

Sterling, D. Yucatán **641.59**

Werner, E. Hartwood **641.597**

YUCCA MOUNTAIN REPOSITORY (NEV.)

D'Agata, J. About a mountain **979.3**

YUGOSLAV WAR, 1991-1995

Clark, W. K. Waging modern war **949.703**

Maass, P. Love thy neighbor **949.702**

Rieff, D. Slaughterhouse **949.7**

Rohde, D. Endgame **949.7**

YUGOSLAV WAR, 1991-1995 -- BOSNIA AND HERCEGOVINA -- PERSONAL NARRATIVES

Shapiro, S. The Bosnia list **92**

YUGOSLAVIA -- HISTORY

Razsa, M. Bastards of Utopia **303.48**

YUGOSLAVIA -- POLITICS AND GOVERNMENT

West, R. Tito **949.7**

Yung, Wing, 1828-1912

About

Leibovitz, L. Fortunate sons **951.05**

Yunte Huang

Charlie Chan **92**

Yves Saint Laurent. Lowit, R. **746.9**

Z

Zabar, Tracey

One sweet cookie **641.8**

Zabel, Diane

(ed) Reference reborn **025.5**

(ed) Rethinking collection development and management **025.2**

Zacharias, Karen Spears

A silence of mockingbirds **364.152**

Zacks, Richard

The pirate coast **973.4**

Zafar, Harris, 1979-

Demystifying Islam **297**

Zagajewski, Adam, 1945-

Eternal enemies **891.8**

Unseen hand **891.8**

Without end **891.8**

Zaharias, Babe Didrikson, 1911-1956

About

Ware, S. Letter to the world **920.72**

Zahav. Cook, S. **641.59**

ZAIRE *See* Congo (Democratic Republic)

Zakarian, Geoffrey, 1959-

My perfect pantry **641.5**

Zakarian, Margaret

My perfect pantry **641.5**

ZAMBIA -- BIOGRAPHY

Fuller, A. Leaving Before the Rains Come **305.409**

Zamoyski, Adam

Rites of peace **940.2**

Zamperini, Louis

About

Hillenbrand, L. Unbroken **940.54**

Zane Grey. Pauly, T. H. **92**

Zanini De Vita, Oretta

Pasta, a. d. p. t. Encyclopedia of pasta **641.8**

Zantovsky, Michael

Havel **943.704**

Zapata and the Mexican Revolution. Womack, J. **972.08**

Zapata, Emiliano, 1879-1919

About

Womack, J. Zapata and the Mexican Revolution **972.08**

Zappa, Frank

About

Zappa, F. The real Frank Zappa book **92**

Zapruder, Matthew

Come on all you ghosts **811**

Zaretsky, Robert

Boswell's enlightenment **92**

Zarkadakis, George

In Our Own Image **006.3**

Zebrowski, Ernest

Category 5 **363.34**

Zeilinga de Boer, Jelle

Earthquakes in human history **363.34**

Zeisler, Avital

Weapons of fitness **613.6**

Zeitlin, Maurice

Stepan-Norris, J. Left out **331.8**

Zeitoun. Eggers, D. **92**

Zeitoun, Abdulrahman

About

Eggers, D. Zeitoun **92**

Zeitz, Joshua

Flapper **305.4**

Zellner, Robert, 1939-

About

Zellner, R. The wrong side of Murder Creek **92**

Zelnick, Bob

Gore: a political life **92**

Zemurray, Samuel, 1877-1961

About

Cohen, R. The fish that ate the whale **338.7**

Zen and the art of motorcycle maintenance. Pirsig, R. M. **92**

Zen and the art of recording. **621.389**

ZEN BUDDHISM

Greenblat, M. R. A. Dharma Delight **294.3**

Suzuki, D. T. Manual of Zen Buddhism **294.3**

Watts, A. The way of Zen **294.3**

ZEN BUDDHISM

See also Buddhism

ZEN BUDDHISM -- INFLUENCE

Larson, K. Where the heart beats **700.1**

Zenger, John Peter, 1697-1746

About

Kluger, R. Indelible ink **686.209**

Zeno, of Elea, b. ca. 490 B.C.

About

Bell, E. T. Men of mathematics **920**

ZEPPELINS *See* Airships

Zeratsky, John

(jt. auth) Kowitz, B. Sprint **658.4**

ZERO (THE NUMBER)

Aczel, A. D. Finding zero **513.5**

Barrow, J. D. The book of nothing **111**

Zero Night. Felton, M. **940.54**

Zeskind, Leonard

Blood and politics **305.8**

ZEUS (GREEK DEITY)

See also Gods and goddesses

Zevon, Crystal

I'll sleep when I'm dead **92**

Zevon, Warren

About

Zevon, C. I'll sleep when I'm dead **92**

Zhao Ziyang, 1919-2005

About

Prisoner of the state **92**

Zheutlin, Peter

Rescue road **636.7**

The **Zhivago** affair. Finn, P. **891.73**

Zhukov, Georgiĭ Konstantinovich, 1896-1974

About

Roberts, G. Stalin's general **940.54**

Zickefoose, Julie

Baby Birds **598**

About

Zickefoose, J. The bluebird effect **598**

Ziegelman, Jane

(jt. auth) Coe, A. A square meal **641.5**

Zieger, Robert H.

American workers, American unions **331.8**

Ziegesar, Peter von

About

Von Ziegesar, P. The looking glass brother **92**

Ziegfeld. Mordden, E. **92**

Ziegfeld, Florenz, 1869-1932

About

Mordden, E. Ziegfeld **92**

Ziegler, Mel

About

Ziegler, M. Wild company **381**

Ziegler, Patricia

About

Ziegler, M. Wild company **381**

Zierman, Addie

About

Zierman, A. When we were on fire **92**

Zilkha, Avraham

Modern English-Hebrew dictionary **492.4**

ZIMBABWE

Fuller, A. Don't let's go to the dogs tonight **92**

Godwin, P. The fear

Rogers, D. The last resort **968.91**

ZIMBABWE -- BIOGRAPHY

Fuller, A. Leaving Before the Rains Come **305.409**

ZIMBABWE -- POLITICS AND GOVERN-MENT -- 1980-

Godwin, P. The fear

Lamb, C. House of stone **968.91**

Zimbardo, Philip G.

The time paradox **153.7**

Zimbardo, P. The Lucifer effect **155.9**

Zimmer, Carl

Microcosm **579.3**

A planet of viruses **362.196**

Soul made flesh **612.8**

Zimmerman, Robert

The universe in a mirror **629.43**

The **Zimmermann** telegram. Tuchman, B. W. **940.3**

Zimmermann, Elizabeth

Knitting without tears **746.4**

Zimmermann, Warren

First great triumph **973**

ZINC

See also Chemical elements; Metals

Zine, Edward E.

About

Murphy, T. W. Life in rewind **92**

ZINES

The riot grrrl collection **781.64**

ZINES *See* Fanzines

Zinman, Michael

About

Singer, M. Character studies **920**

Zinn & the art of road bike maintenance. **629.227**

Zinn, Howard, 1922-2010

The historic unfullfilled promise **973.924**

A people's history of the United States **973**

About

Duberman, M. Howard Zinn **92**

Zinn, Lennard

Zinn & the art of road bike maintenance **629.227**

Zinsser, William Knowlton

Writing to learn **808**

ZIONISM

Avineri, S. Herzl's vision **320.54**

Friedman, M. S. Encounter on the narrow ridge: a life of Martin Buber **92**

Hoffman, B. Anonymous soldiers **956.94**

La Guardia, A. War without end **956.940**

Laqueur, W. A history of Zionism **956.94**

Sachar, H. M. A history of Israel **956.94**

Shavit, A. My promised land **956.05**

ZIONISM -- PALESTINE -- HISTORY -- 20TH CENTURY

Hoffman, B. Anonymous soldiers **956.94**

ZIONIST MOVEMENT *See* Zionism

ZIP CODE

National five digit zip code and post office directory **383**

Zipes, Jack

(tr) The Original Folk and Fairy Tales of the Brothers Grimm **398.2**

The irresistible fairy tale **398.209**

Zizek, Slavoj

First as tragedy, then as farce **337**

Znamierowski, Alfred, 1940-

The World Encyclopedia of Flags **929.9**

ZODIAC

Goodman, L. Linda Goodman's sun signs **133.5**

Snodgrass, M. E. Signs of the zodiac **133.5**

ZODIAC

See also Astrology; Astronomy

Zoellner, Tom

The heartless stone **553.8**

Train **385**

Uranium **546**

Zoglin, Richard

Hope **92**

Zollman, Kevin

(jt. auth) Raeburn, P. The game theorist's guide to parenting **641.1**

ZOMBIES

Kaplan, M. Medusa's gaze and vampire's bite **001.944**

ZOMBIES

See also Dead; Folklore

Zombory-Moldován, Béla, 1885-1967

About

The burning of the world **92**

Zondervan classic reference series

Cruden, A. Cruden's Complete concordance **220.5**

Zondervan dictionary of Christian spirituality. **248**

Zondervan illustrated Bible dictionary. **220.3**

ZONING

See also City planning

ZOO ANIMALS -- BEHAVIOR

The secret language of animals **591.5**

ZOO KEEPERS

Halloran, A. R. The song of the ape **599.885**

Zoo story. French, T. **590.73**

Zoo: a history of zoological gardens in the West. Baratay, E. **590.73**

Zoobiquity. Bowers, K. **636.089**

ZOOGEOGRAPHY

Bambaradeniya, C. N. B. The illustrated atlas of wildlife **591.9**

The **zookeeper's** wife. Ackerman, D. **940.53**

ZOOLOGICAL GARDENS *See* Zoos

ZOOLOGICAL SPECIMENS -- COLLECTION AND PRESERVATION

See also Collectors and collecting

ZOOLOGISTS

Allen, A. The fantastic laboratory of Dr. Weigl **614.5**

Heinrich, B. Summer world **591.7**

ZOOLOGY

Fortey, R. Horseshoe crabs and velvet worms **595**

Heinrich, B. Life everlasting **591.7**

ZOOLOGY

See also Biology; Science

ZOOS

Ackerman, D. The zookeeper's wife **940.53**

Baratay, E. Zoo: a history of zoological gardens in the West **590.73**

French, T. Zoo story **590.73**

Robinson, P. T. Life at the zoo: behind the scenes with the animal doctors **590.73**

Zora Neale Hurston. **813**

Zora Neale Hurston: a life in letters. **92**

ZOROASTRIANISM

See also Religions

Zott, Lynn M.

(ed) The Beat generation **810**

Zoya

Zoya's story **958.1**

Zoya's story. Zoya **958.1**

Zraly, Kevin

Windows on the World complete wine course **641.2**

Zuba, Jesse

(ed) American religious poems **811**

Zuccotti, Susan

Père Marie-Benoît and Jewish rescue **940.53**

Under his very windows **940.53**

Zucker, Caren

(jt. auth) Donvan, J. In a different key **616.85**

Zuckerberg, Mark, 1984-

About

Kirkpatrick, D. The Facebook effect **338.7**

Russakoff, D. The prize **371.2**

Zuckerman, Ethan

Rewire **302.23**

Zuckerman, Gregory

The frackers **338.2**

Zuckerman, Peter

Buried in the sky **796.522**

Zuckerman, Phil

Living the Secular Life **211**

Zuckoff, Mitchell
 Frozen in Time **940.54**
 Lost in Shangri-la **940.54**
 Ponzi's scheme **364**
 Robert Altman **92**

Zuffi, Stefano
 Impelluso, L. Gods and heroes in art **700**

Zuk, M.
 Riddled with life **616.07**
 Sexual selections **591.56**
 Sex on six legs **595.7**

Zukofsky, Louis
 Selected poems **811**

ZULU (AFRICAN PEOPLE)
 See also Africans; Indigenous peoples

Zumwalt. Berman, L. **92**

Zumwalt, Elmo R., 1920-2000
 About
 Berman, L. Zumwalt **92**

Zunz, Olivier
 Philanthropy in America **361.7**

Zweig, Stefan, 1881-1942
 About
 Prochnik, G. The Impossible Exile **92**

Zwonitzer, Mark
 Will you miss me when I'm gone? **781.642**